# The Oxford–Duden G

# The Oxford–Duden German Dictionary

German–English/English-German

*Edited by*
the Dudenredaktion
and the German Section of
the Oxford University Press
Dictionary Department

*Chief Editors*
W. Scholze-Stubenrecht
J. B. Sykes

*Second Edition edited by*
M. Clark
O. Thyen

OXFORD
UNIVERSITY PRESS

OXFORD
UNIVERSITY PRESS

Great Clarendon Street, Oxford OX2 6DP

Oxford University Press is a department of the University of Oxford.
It furthers the University's objective of excellence in research, scholarship,
and education by publishing worldwide in

Oxford New York

Athens Auckland Bangkok Bogotá Buenos Aires Calcutta
Cape Town Chennai Dar es Salaam Delhi Florence Hong Kong Istanbul
Karachi Kuala Lumpur Madrid Melbourne Mexico City Mumbai
Nairobi Paris São Paulo Shanghai Singapore Taipei Tokyo Toronto Warsaw
with associated companies in Berlin Ibadan

Oxford is a registered trade mark of Oxford University Press
in the UK and in certain other countries

Published in the United States
by Oxford University Press Inc., New York



First published 1990
Reprinted in enlarged format 1994
Revised edition 1997
Second edition 1999
Reissue 2001



British Library Cataloguing in Publication Data
Data available

Library of Congress Cataloging in Publication Data
Data available

ISBN 0-19-860365-7

10 9 8 7 6 5 4 3 2 1

Typeset in Nimrod and Arial
by Latimer Trend & Co. Ltd., Plymouth
Printed in Italy

# Preface

The *Oxford-Duden German Dictionary* is produced jointly by two of the world's leading dictionary publishers, Oxford University Press and the Bibliographisches Institut, Mannheim. For this new edition the dictionary has been enlarged and updated to take account of new vocabulary and recent developments in English and German. Thousands of additional words and phrases, selected using the unparalleled databases maintained and continually expanded by the publishers for their celebrated native-speaker dictionaries such as the *Concise Oxford Dictionary* and *Das Große Wörterbuch der Deutschen Sprache*, reflect scientific and technological innovations as well as changes in politics, culture, and society. Reforms to the spelling of German ratified by the governments of Germany, Austria, and Switzerland in 1996 have been fully incorporated and are clearly signposted.

This new edition includes as a special feature detailed usage boxes to help with important areas of grammar and vocabulary. These boxes highlight differences between German and English which may create difficulty for the learner and translator, explaining them in detail and providing clear illustrative examples. Other boxes give the user key facts about sets of words that behave alike, for example, names of countries, languages, numbers, and days of the week. They also provide ways of discussing topics such as age, dates, time, and measurements and offer essential practical information on asking the way, formulating greetings, apologizing, and letter-writing. Cross-references to the boxes are given at all the relevant entries, making them easily accessible points of reference for students and valuable aids to teaching.

Also new to this edition is a special section in the centre of the dictionary containing a rich variety of sample letters designed to help the English user wishing to write a letter, fax, or CV in German, and vice versa. Panels at the front of the dictionary provide essential cultural information and explanations of political and legal institutions, including the European Union.

The editors believe that these new features and expanded, up-to-date coverage will enhance the reputation of the *Oxford-Duden German Dictionary* as the leading and most authoritative reference tool for school, college, and university students, business people, and all those who require the fullest possible information on German and English in a single volume.

MICHAEL CLARK

*Oxford University Press*

# Als Markenzeichen geschützte Wörter / Note on Proprietary Status

Die Zeichen ® oder Ⓦz machen als Markenzeichen geschützte Wörter (Bezeichnungen, Namen) kenntlich. Sollte eines dieser Zeichen einmal fehlen, so ist das keine Gewähr dafür, dass das betreffende Wort als Handelsname frei verwendet werden darf.

This dictionary includes some words which have, or are asserted to have, proprietary status as trade marks or otherwise. Their inclusion does not imply that they have acquired for legal purposes a non-proprietary or general significance, nor any other judgement concerning their legal status. In cases where the editorial staff have some evidence that a word has proprietary status, this is indicated in the entry for that word by the abbreviation ® or Ⓦz, but no judgement concerning the legal status of such words is made or implied thereby.

# Editors and Contributors

## Second Edition

**Oxford University Press**
Michael Clark
Bernadette Mohan
Robin Sawers
Gunhild Prowe
Neil Morris
Roswitha Morris

**Dudenverlag**
Olaf Thyen
Werner Scholze-Stubenrecht
Magdalena Seubel

**Data Input**
Muriel Ranivoalison
Susan Wilkin
Tabitha Tuckett
Anne McConnell

## First Edition

### Editors

**Oxford University Press**
John Sykes
Michael Clark
Robin Sawers
Vineeta Gupta
Bernadette Mohan
Colin Hope
Maurice Waite
John Pheby
Eva Vennebusch
Clare Rütsch
Judith Cunningham
Valerie Langrish
Christopher Burton
Timothy Connell

**Dudenverlag**
Werner Scholze-Stubenrecht
Roland Breitsprecher
Olaf Thyen
Brigitte Alsleben
Eckhard Böhle
Maria Dose
Gabriele Gassen
Wolfgang Eckey
Eva Krampe
Susanne Lücking
Marion Trunk-Nußbaumer

### Compilers

Christine Ayorinde
Cyprian Blamires
Ann Clark
John Craddock
Peter Dyer
Stuart Fortey
Susan Ghanouni
Lilian Hall
Fergus McGauran
Neil Morris
Ewald Osers
Ray Perkins
Gunhild Prowe
Eva Sawers
Amanda Thorndike
Richard Toms

**in the Institut für Anglistik und Amerikanistik der Universität Mainz in Germersheim**
Horst W. Drescher
Fee Engemann
Lothar Görke
Cosima Heise
Carola Jansen
Ferdinand Kiefer
Dagmar Steffen
Ulrike Kraus
Karina Nehl
Lotte Neiffer
Michael Petersen
Ulrike Röhrenbeck
Joachim Schwend
Magdalena Seubel
Annemarie Thiemann

# Inhalt / Contents

# Erläuterungen zum deutsch-englischen Text / Key to German-English Entries

## 1. Stichwort und Aussprache / Headword and pronunciation

**Stichwort. Alle Einträge sind streng alphabetisch angeordnet**
Headword. All entries are listed in strict alphabetical order

**bindend** *Adj.* binding (**für** on); definite ‹answer›
**Binder** *der;* **~s,** **~** Ⓐ (*Krawatte*) tie; Ⓑ (*Bindemittel*) binder; Ⓒ (*Landw.*) [reaper-]binder; Ⓓ (*Bauw.: Stein*) header; Ⓔ (*Bauw.: Dachbalken*) [roof] truss
**Binderei** *die;* **~, ~en** Ⓐ (*Blumen~*) wreath and bouquet department; Ⓑ (*Buch~*) bindery

**Binde-: ~strich** *der* hyphen; **~wort** *das; Pl.* **~wörter** (*Sprachw.*) conjunction
**Bind·faden** *der* string; **ein [Stück] ~:** a piece of string; **es regnet Bindfäden** (*ugs.*) it's raining cats and dogs (*coll.*)

**Kompositablock. Eine Tilde ersetzt jeweils den gemeinsamen ersten Bestandteil der Komposita**
Compound block with a swung dash representing the first element of each compound

**Die Ausspracheangaben (in IPA-Lautschrift) stehen unmittelbar hinter dem Stichwort (s.S. 17). Die Aussprache eines Kompositums ohne Ausspracheangabe lässt sich von derjenigen seiner Bestandteile herleiten**
Pronunciation is shown in IPA immediately after the headword (see p. 17).The pronunciation of a compound where none is given can be derived from the pronunciations of its elements

**Bischof** /ˈbɪʃɔf/ *der;* **~s, Bischöfe** /ˈbɪʃœfə/, **Bischöfin** *die;* **~, ~nen** bishop

**Bremse**[1] /ˈbrɛmzə/ *die;* **~, ~n** brake; **auf die ~ treten** put on the brakes
**Bremse**[2] *die;* **~, ~n** (*Insekt*) horsefly

**Mehrere gleich geschriebene, aber nicht bedeutungsgleiche Wörter erscheinen als separate Stichwörter und sind mit hochgestellten Ziffern nummeriert**
Headwords spelt the same but with different meanings are entered separately with a raised number

**Buxtehude** /bʊkstəˈhuːdə/ *in* **in/aus/nach ~** (*fig. ugs.*) at/from/to the back of beyond
**Buy-out** /ˈbajauːt/ *das;* **~s, ~s** (*Wirtsch.*) buyout
**BV** *Abk.* (*schweiz.*) **Bundesversammlung**
**BVG** *Abk.* Ⓐ **Bundesverwaltungsgericht;** Ⓑ **Bundesverfassungsgericht;** Ⓒ **Betriebsverfassungsgesetz**
**b.w.** *Abk.* **bitte wenden** p.t.o.
**Bypass** /ˈbaipɑs/ *der;* **~es, Bypässe** (*Med.*) bypass

**Auch Abkürzungen und Akronyme sind streng alphabetisch eingeordnet**
Abbreviations and acronyms follow the same strict alphabetical order as other headwords

**Ein senkrechter Strich nach dem ersten Bestandteil eines zusammengesetzten Verbs zeigt an, dass es sich um eine unfeste Zusammensetzung handelt**
A vertical bar indicates that a compound verb is separable

**dar|bieten** (*geh.*) ❶ *unr. tr. V.* Ⓐ (*anbieten*) offer; serve ‹drinks, food›; **die dargebotene Hand ausschlagen** (*fig.*) reject the proffered hand [of friendship] (*fig.*); Ⓑ (*aufführen, vortragen*) perform; **es wurden Gedichte und Lieder dargeboten** a recital of poems and songs was presented...

**dar|legen** *tr. V.* explain; set forth ‹reasons, facts›; expound ‹theory›; **jmdm. etw. ~:** explain sth. to sb.; **etw. schriftlich ~:** set sth. out in writing

**Ein unter einen Vokal gesetzter waagerechter Strich zeigt die Länge des Vokals und in mehrsilbigen Wörtern zugleich die Betonung der betreffenden Silbe an**
An underline indicates a long vowel, stressed in words of more than one syllable

**Ein hochgestellter Stern vor einem Stichwort zeigt an, dass es sich um eine alte, künftig nicht mehr gültige Schreibung handelt. (Siehe die Hinweise zur Rechtschreibreform des Deutschen auf S. 1707)**
Asterisk indicating old spelling. (See note on the reform of German spelling on p. 1707)

**dass, *daß** /das/ *Konj.* Ⓐ that; **entschuldigen Sie bitte, ~ ich mich verspätet habe** please forgive me for being late; please forgive my being late; **ich weiß, ~ du Recht hast** I know [that] you are right; **ich verstehe nicht, ~ sie ihn geheiratet hat** I don't understand why she married him...

**Ein in mittlerer Höhe auf der Zeile stehender Punkt im Stichwort markiert die Kompositionsfuge eines Kompositums**
A dot marks the juncture of the elements of a compound

**Degenerations·erscheinung** *die* sign of degeneration

**eggen** *tr. V.* (*Landw.*) harrow

**Ein unter einen Vokal gesetzter Punkt zeigt die Kürze des Vokals und in mehrsilbigen Wörtern zugleich die Betonung der betreffenden Silbe an**
An underdot indicates a short vowel, stressed in words of more than one syllable

## 2. Grammatische Angaben / Grammatical information

**Grammatische Gliederungspunkte und Wortartangaben**
Grammatical categories and parts of speech

**ehrenhaft** ❶ *Adj.* honourable ‹intentions, person›; **ein ~er Mann** an honourable man; a man of honour. ❷ *adv.* ‹act› honourably

**Die Formen des Genitivs und des Plurals eines Substantivs**
Genitive and plural forms of a noun

**Entwickler** *der;* **~s, ~** (*Fot.*) developer

**erröten** *itr. V.; mit sein* blush (**vor** with); **jmdn. zum Erröten bringen** make sb. blush

**Der Hinweis *mit sein* zeigt an, dass das betreffende Verb die Perfekttempora mit dem Hilfsverb *sein* bildet**
*mit sein* indicates that a verb is conjugated with the auxiliary verb *sein* in its perfect tenses

**Unregelmäßige Steigerungsformen eines Adjektivs**
Irregular comparative and superlative forms of an adjective

**fromm** /frɔm/; **frommer** *od.* **frömmer** /'frœmɐ/, **frommst...** *od.* **frömmst...** ❶ *Adj.* Ⓐ pious, devout ‹person›; devout ‹Christian›...

## 3. Semantische Gliederungspunkte und Angaben zu Stil, Sachbereich, räumlicher Zuordnung / Sense categories and labels

**Semantische Gliederungspunkte**
Sense categories

**Geheim·nummer** *die* Ⓐ (*Bankw.*) personal identification number; PIN; Ⓑ (*Telefonnummer*) ex-directory number; unlisted number (*Amer.*)

**gehören** ❶ *itr. V.* Ⓐ (*Eigentum sein*) **jmdm. ~:** belong to sb.; **das Haus gehört uns nicht** the house doesn't belong to us; we don't own the house; **der Jugend gehört die Zukunft** the future belongs to the young; **dir will ich ~** (*dichter.*) I want to be yours; **ihr Herz gehört einem anderen** (*geh.*) her heart belongs to another; Ⓑ (*Teil eines Ganzen sein*) **zu jmds. Freunden ~:** be one of sb.'s friends...

**Bedeutungsindikatoren**
Sense indicators

**Stilistische Kennzeichnungen**
Style labels

**Geier** /'gaiɐ/ *der;* **~s, ~:** vulture; **hol dich/hols der ~** (*ugs.*) to hell with you/it (*coll.*); **weiß der ~** (*salopp*) God only knows (*coll.*); Christ knows (*sl.*)

**Genom** /ge'no:m/ *das;* **~s, ~e** (*Biol.*) genome

**Gurtstraffer** *der;* **~s, ~** (*Kfz.-W.*) [seat-]belt tensioner

**Bereichsangaben**
Subject labels

**Angaben zur räumlichen Zuordnung**
Regional labels

**Holler** /'hɔlɐ/ *der;* **~s, ~** (**bes. südd., österr.**) ⇨ **Holunder**

**Karre** /'karə/ *die;* **~, ~n** (**bes. nordd.**) Ⓐ ⇨ **Karren**; Ⓑ (*abwertend: Fahrzeug*) [old] heap (*coll.*)

## 4. Übersetzungen / Translations

**Übersetzungen**
Translations

**Kle̱be·pflaster** *das* adhesive plaster; sticking plaster

**Durch Adjektive attribuierte Substantive**
Nouns modified by an adjective

**klein** /klai̯n/ ❶ *Adj.* A ▶ 411 little; small; small ‹format, letter›; little ‹finger, toe›: **das Kleid ist mir zu ~:**...

**Als Subjekte zu Verben auftretende Wörter**
Subjects of a verb

**klirren** /ˈklɪrən/ *itr. V.* ‹glasses, ice cubes› clink; ‹weapons in fight› clash; ‹window pane› rattle; ‹chains, spurs› clank, rattle; ‹harness› jingle; **mit der Kette/den Sporen ~:** clank *or* rattle the chain/one's spurs; **~der Frost** (*fig.*) sharp frost

**Kollokatoren (Wörter, mit denen zusammen das Stichwort häufig vorkommt) als Hilfe zur Auswahl der für den jeweiligen Kontext passenden Übersetzung**
Collocators—words often used with the headword, shown to help select the correct translation for each context

**kö̱niglich** ❶ *Adj.* A royal; B (*vornehm*) regal; C (*reichlich*) princely ‹gift, salary, wage›; lavish ‹hospitality›; D (*ugs.: außerordentlich*) tremendous (*coll.*) ‹fun›. ❷ *adv.* A (*reichlich*) ‹entertain› lavishly; ‹pay› handsomely; **~ beschenkt werden** be showered with lavish presents...

**Durch Adverbien attribuierte Verben oder Adjektive**
Verbs or adjectives modified by an adverb

**konzipieren** /kɔntsi̯ˈpi:rən/ ❶ *tr. V.* draft ‹speech, essay›; draw up, draft ‹plan, policy, etc.›; design ‹device, car, etc.›. ❷ *itr. V.* (*Med.*) conceive

**Als Objekte zu Verben auftretende Wörter**
Objects of a verb

**Das Zeichen ≈ signalisiert eine nur annähernde Entsprechung**
The sign ≈ is used to indicate approximate equivalence

**Malte̱ser-: ~hilfsdienst** *der* ≈ St John Ambulance Brigade; **~kreuz** *das* (*auch Technik*) Maltese cross; **~orden** *der* Order of the Knights of St John; **~ritter** *der* Knight of St John

## 5. Anwendungsbeispiele / Phrases

**Beispiele (jeweils mit einer Tilde an Stelle des Stichworts)**
Examples (with a swung dash representing the headword)

**ragen** /ˈra:gn̩/ *itr. V.* A (*vertikal*) rise [up]; ‹mountains› tower up; **aus dem Wasser ~:** stick *or* jut right out of the water; **in die Höhe** *od.* **in den Himmel ~:** tower *or* soar into the sky...

**Teile von Anwendungsbeispielen, zwischen denen ein kursiv gesetztes *od.* steht, sind synonym und gegeneinander austauschbar**
Parts of a phrase separated by *od.* are synonymous and interchangeable

**Regi̱erung** *die;* ~, **~en** A (*Herrschaft*) rule; (*eines Monarchen*) reign; **die ~ übernehmen** *od.* **antreten** take over; come to power; B (*eines Staates*) government

**Ruf** /ru:f/ *der;* **~[e]s, ~e** A call; (*Schrei*) shout; cry; (*Tierlaut*) call; B (*fig.: Aufforderung, Forderung*) call (**nach** for); **der ~ zu den Waffen** (*geh.*) the call to arms; **dem ~ des Herzens/Gewissens/der Natur folgen** *od.* **gehorchen** follow one's heart/listen to the voice of conscience/nature...

**Teile von Anwendungsbeispielen, zwischen denen ein Schrägstrich steht, sind syntaktisch gegeneinander austauschbar, aber nicht bedeutungsgleich**
Parts of a phrase separated by a slash are syntactically interchangeable but have different meanings

## 6. Verweise / Cross references

**Ein Pfeil verweist auf ein bedeutungsgleiches anderes Stichwort**
An arrow directs the user to another headword with the same meaning

**Stra̱mpler** *der;* **~s,** ~ ⇒ **Strampelhöschen**

**Mit ⇒ *auch* wird auf ein Stichwort verwiesen, unter dem noch zusätzliche Informationen zu finden sind**
⇒ *auch* directs the user to another headword where additional information can be found

**töten** /ˈtø:tn̩/ *tr., itr. V.* kill; deaden ‹nerve etc.›; **einen kranken Hund ~ lassen** have a sick dog put down; ⇒ *auch* **Blick** A; **Nerv** A

**tsche̱chisch** ▶ 553, ▶ 696 ❶ *Adj.* Czech. ❷ *adv.* **~ sprechend** Czech-speaking; ⇒ *auch* **deutsch**; **Deutsch**; **Deutsche**[2]

**Das Zeichen ▶ mit einer Zahl verweist auf eine Buchseite, auf der sich in einem Informationskasten zusätzliche Informationen finden**
An arrow ▶ and a page-number cross reference direct the user to a usage box containing additional information

# Key to English-German Entries / Erläuterungen zum englisch-deutschen Text

## 1. Headword and pronunciation / Stichwort und Aussprache

**Headword. All entries are listed in strict alphabetical order, except for *phrasal* verbs**
Stichwort. Alle Einträge – mit Ausnahme der *Phrasal Verbs* – sind streng alphabetisch angeordnet

**batch** /bætʃ/ *n.* Ⓐ (*of loaves*) Schub, *der;* Ⓑ (*of people*) Gruppe, *die;* Schwung, *der* (*ugs.*); (*of letters, books, files, papers*) Stapel, *der;* Schwung, *der* (*ugs.*); (*of rules, regulations*) Bündel, *das*
**batch: ~ file** *n.* (*Computing*) Stapeldatei, *die;* **~ 'processing** *n.* (*Computing*) Schub-, Stapelverarbeitung, *die;* **~ production** *n.* Stapelfertigung, *die*

**Compound block with a swung dash representing the first element of each compound**
Kompositablock. Eine Tilde ersetzt jeweils den gemeinsamen ersten Bestandteil der Komposita

**bate**[1] /beɪt/ *v.t.* **with ~d breath** mit angehaltenem *od.* (*geh.*) verhaltenem Atem; **~ one's breath** den Atem verhalten (*geh.*)
**bate**[2] *n.* (*Brit. coll.*) Rage, *die* (*ugs.*); **be in a [terrible] ~:** [schrecklich] in Rage sein; **get/fly into a ~:** in Rage geraten
**bath** /bɑːθ/ ❶ *n., pl.* **~s** /bɑːðz/ Ⓐ Bad, *das;* **have** *or* **take a ~:** ein Bad nehmen; Ⓑ (*vessel*) **~[tub]** Badewanne, *die;* **room with ~:** Zimmer mit Bad; ...

**Each phrasal verb is entered on a new line immediately following the entry for the first element**
Die *Phrasal Verbs* folgen, jedes auf einer neuen Zeile, direkt auf den Eintrag zu ihrem Grundverb

**bear**[2] ❶ *v.t.*, **bore** /bɔː(r)/, **borne** /bɔːn/...
**~ a'way** *v.t.* wegtragen; davontragen ‹Preis usw.›; **be borne away** fort- *od.* davongetragen werden
**~ 'down** ❶ *v.t.* niederdrücken; überwältigen ‹Feind›; **be borne down by the weight of ...:** von der Last (+ *Gen.*) gebeugt sein. ...
**~ 'off** ⇒ **~ away**
**~ on** ⇒ **~ upon**
**~ 'out** *v.t.* Ⓐ hinaustragen; Ⓑ (*fig.*) bestätigen ‹Bericht, Erklärung›; **~ sb. out** jmdm. Recht geben; **~ sb. out in sth.** jmdn. in etw. (*Dat.*) bestätigen

**beastly** /ˈbiːstlɪ/ *adj., adv.* (*coll.*) scheußlich

**Pronunciation is shown in IPA immediately after the headword (see p. 17).**
Die Ausspracheangaben (in IPA-Lautschrift) stehen unmittelbar hinter dem Stichwort (s. S. 17)

**Stress mark, showing stress on the following syllable. If no stress is shown in a compound block, it falls on the first element**
Betonungszeichen vor der betonten Silbe. Wo in Kompositablöcken keine Betonung angegeben ist, liegt der Ton auf dem ersten Bestandteil

**'beat-up** *adj.* (*coll.*) ramponiert (*ugs.*)

**bluff**[1] /blʌf/ ❶ *n.* (*act*) Täuschungsmanöver, *das;* Bluff, *der* (*ugs.*); **it's nothing but a ~:** das ist bloß [ein] Bluff; ⇒ *also* **call** 2 C. ❷ *v.i.* & *t.* bluffen (*ugs.*)
**bluff**[2] ❶ *n.* (*headland*) Kliff, *das;* Steilküste, *die;* (*inland*) Steilhang, *der.* ❷ *adj.* Ⓐ (*abrupt, blunt, frank, hearty*) raubeinig (*ugs.*); Ⓑ (*perpendicular*) steil; schroff ‹Felswand, Abhang, Küste›; breit ‹Schiffsbug›

**Headwords spelt the same but with different meanings are entered separately with a raised number**
Mehrere gleich geschriebene, aber nicht bedeutungsgleiche Wörter erscheinen als separate Stichwörter und sind mit hochgestellten Ziffern nummeriert.

**Abbreviations and acronyms follow the same strict alphabetical order as other headwords**
Auch Abkürzungen und Akronyme sind streng alphabetisch eingeordnet

**bryony** /ˈbraɪənɪ/ *n.* (*Bot.*) Zaunrübe, *die*
**BS** *abbr.* Ⓐ **British Standard** Britische Norm; Ⓑ **Bachelor of Surgery** „Bachelor" der Chirurgie; ⇒ *also* **B. Sc.**; Ⓒ (*Amer.*) **Bachelor of Science;** ⇒ *also* **B. Sc.**
**B. Sc.** /biːesˈsiː/ *abbr.* **Bachelor of Science** Bakkalaureus der Naturwissenschaften; **John Clarke ~** John Clarke, Bakkalaureus der Naturwissenschaften; **he is a** *or* **has a ~** ≈ er hat ein Diplom in Naturwissenschaften; ...
**BSE** *abbr.* **bovine spongiform encephalopathy** BSE
**BSI** *abbr.* **British Standards Institution** Britischer Normenausschuss
**BST** *abbr.* **British Summer Time** Britische Sommerzeit
**Bt.** *abbr.* **baronet**
**bubble** /ˈbʌbl/ ❶ *n.* Ⓐ Blase, *die;* (*small*)...

## 2. Grammatical information / Grammatische Angaben

**Grammatical categories and parts of speech**
Grammatische Gliederungspunkte und Wortartangaben

**capsize** /kæp'saɪz/ ❶ *v.t.* zum Kentern bringen. ❷ *v.i.* kentern

**catalysis** /kə'tælɪsɪs/ *n.*, *pl.* **catalyses** /kə'tælɪsi:z/ (*Chem.*) Katalyse, *die*

**Irregular plural of a noun**
Unregelmäßige Pluralform eines Substantivs

**Irregular tenses of a verb (see also table on pp. 1727–1728)**
Unregelmäßige Verbformen (siehe auch die Liste auf S. 1727–1728)

**choose** /tʃu:z/ ❶ *v.t.*, **chose** /tʃəʊz/...

**chug** /tʃʌg/ ❶ *v.i.*, **-gg-** ‹Motor:› tuckern. ❷ *n.* Tuckern, *das*

**Doubling of a final consonant of a verb before -ed *or* -ing**
Verdoppelung des Endkonsonanten eines Verbs vor -ed *oder* -ing

**Irregular comparative and superlative forms of an adjective**
Unregelmäßige Steigerungsformen eines Adjektivs

**dry** /draɪ/ ❶ *adj.*, **drier** /'draɪə(r)/, **driest** /'draɪɪst/ Ⓐ trocken; trocken, (*very dry*) herb ‹Wein›; ausgetrocknet ‹Fluss, Flussbett›...

## 3. Sense categories and labels / Semantische Gliederungspunkte und Angaben zu Stil, Sachbereich, räumlicher Zuordnung

**Sense categories**
Semantische Gliederungspunkte

**extremity** /ɪk'stremɪtɪ/ *n.* Ⓐ (*of branch, path, road*) äußerstes Ende; (*of region*) Rand, *der*; **the southernmost ~ of a continent** die Südspitze eines Kontinents; Ⓑ *in pl.* (*hands and feet*) Extremitäten *Pl.*;...

**facet** /'fæsɪt/ *n.* Ⓐ (*of many-sided body, esp. of cut stone*) Facette, *die*; Ⓑ (*aspect*) Seite, *die*; **every ~:** alle Seiten *od.* (*geh.*) Facetten

**Sense indicators**
Bedeutungsindikatoren

**Subject labels**
Bereichsangaben

**fax: ~ machine** *n.* Faxgerät, *das*; Fernkopierer, *der*; **~ modem** *n.* (*Computing*) Faxmodem, *das*; **~ number** *n.* Faxnummer, *die*
**genome** /'dʒi:nəʊm/ *n.* (*Biol.*) genome

**goalie** /'gəʊlɪ/ *n.* (*coll.*) Tormann, *der*; Schlussmann, *der* (*ugs.*)
**gob**[1] /gɒb/ *n.* (*sl.*) Gosche, *die* (*landsch. derb*); Schnauze, *die* (*derb abwertend*); Maul, *das* (*derb abwertend*); **shut your ~!** halts Maul! (*derb*); halt die Schnauze! (*derb*)
**gob**[2] *v.i.* (*sl.*: *spit*) rotzen (*derb*)

**Style labels**
Stilistische Kennzeichnungen

**Regional labels**
Angaben zur räumlichen Zuordnung

**hobo** /'həʊbəʊ/ *n.*, *pl.* **~es** (*Amer.*) Landstreicher, *der*/-streicherin, *die*
**Hogmanay** /'hɒgməneɪ/ *n.* (*Scot.*, *N. Engl.*) Silvester, *der od. das*

## 4. Translations / Übersetzungen

**Translations**
Übersetzungen

**ignore** /ɪg'nɔ:(r)/ *v.t.* ignorieren; nicht beachten; nicht befolgen ‹Befehl, Rat›; übergehen, überhören ‹Frage, Bemerkung›; **he ~d me in the street** er ist [auf der Straße] einfach an mir vorbeigegangen; **I shall ~ that remark!** ich habe das nicht gehört!

**insert** ❶ /ɪn'sɜːt/ *v.t.* Ⓐ einlegen ‹Film›; einwerfen ‹Münze›; einsetzen ‹Herzschrittmacher›; einstechen ‹Nadel›; ...

**Objects of a verb**
Als Objekte zu Verben auftretende Wörter

**intense** /ɪn'tens/ *adj.*, **~r** /ɪn'tensə(r)/, **~st** /ɪn'tensɪst/ Ⓐ intensiv; groß ‹Hitze, Belastung›; stark ‹Schmerzen›; kräftig, intensiv ‹Farbe›; äußerst groß ‹Aufregung›; ungeheuer ‹Kälte, Helligkeit›; **the day before the play opens is a period of ~ activity** am Tag vor der Premiere herrscht große Geschäftigkeit; Ⓑ (*eager, ardent*) eifrig, lebhaft ‹Diskussion›; stark, ausgeprägt ‹Interesse›...

**Nouns modified by an adjective**
Durch Adjektive attribuierte Substantive

**Collocators—words often used with the headword, shown to help select the correct translation for each context.**
Kollokatoren (Wörter, mit denen zusammen das Stichwort häufig vorkommt) als Hilfe zur Auswahl der für den jeweiligen Kontext passenden Übersetzung

**intensify** /ɪn'tensɪfaɪ/ ❶ *v.t.* intensivieren. ❷ *v.i.* zunehmen; ‹Hitze, Schmerzen:› stärker werden; ‹Kampf:› sich verschärfen

**Subjects of a verb**
Als Subjekte zu Verben auftretende Wörter

**keenly** /'kiːnlɪ/ *adv.* Ⓐ (*sharply*) scharf ‹geschliffen›; Ⓑ (*coldly*) scharf; Ⓒ (*eagerly*) eifrig ‹arbeiten›; brennend ‹interessiert sein›; **look forward ~ to sth.** auf etw. (*Akk.*) sehr gespannt sein; Ⓓ (*piercingly*) scharf ‹ansehen›...

**Verbs or adjectives modified by an adverb**
Durch Adverbien attribuierte Verben oder Adjektive

**The sign ≈ is used to indicate approximate equivalence**
Das Zeichen ≈ signalisiert eine nur annähernde Entsprechung

**keg** /keg/ *n.* Ⓐ (*barrel*) [kleines] Fass; Fässchen, *das;* Ⓑ *attrib.* **~ beer** *aus luftdichten Metallbehältern gezapftes, mit Kohlensäure versetztes Bier:* ≈ **Fassbier,** *das*

## 5. Phrases / Anwendungsbeispiele

**Examples (with a swung dash representing the headword)**
Beispiele (jeweils mit einer Tilde an Stelle des Stichworts)

**quandary** /'kwɒndərɪ/ *n.* Dilemma, *das;* **this demand put him in a ~:** diese Forderung brachte ihn in eine verzwickte Lage; **he was in a ~ about what to do next** er wusste nicht, was er als Nächstes tun sollte

**question** /'kwestʃn/ ❶ *n.* Ⓐ Frage, *die;* **ask sb. a ~:** jmdm. eine Frage stellen; **put a ~ to sb.** an jmdn. eine Frage richten; ... ...**beyond all** *or* **without~:** zweifellos; ohne Frage *od.* Zweifel; **be beyond all** *or* **be without ~:** außer allem Zweifel stehen; außer Frage sein *od.* stehen...

**Parts of a phrase separated by *or* are synonymous and interchangeable**
Teile von Anwendungsbeispielen, zwischen denen ein kursiv gesetztes *or* steht, sind synonym und gegeneinander austauschbar

**Parts of a phrase separated by a slash are syntactically interchangeable but have different meanings**
Teile von Anwendungsbeispielen, zwischen denen ein Schrägstrich steht, sind syntaktisch gegeneinander austauschbar, aber nicht bedeutungsgleich

**relapse** /rɪ'læps/ ❶ *v.i.* ‹Kranker:› einen Rückfall bekommen; **~ into** zurückfallen in (+ *Akk.*) ‹Götzendienst, Barbarei›; **~ into drug-taking/shoplifting** rückfällig werden [und wieder Drogen nehmen/Ladendiebstähle begehen]; **~ into silence/lethargy** wieder in Schweigen/Lethargie verfallen. ❷ *n.* Rückfall, *der* (**into** in + *Akk.*)

## 6. Cross references / Verweise

**An arrow directs the user to another headword with the same meaning**
Ein Pfeil verweist auf ein bedeutungsgleiches anderes Stichwort

**satiate** /'seɪʃɪeɪt/ ⇨ **sate**

**silver** /'sɪlvə(r)/ ❶ *n.* Ⓐ *no pl., no indef. art.* Silber, *das;* **the price of ~:** der Silberpreis; Ⓑ (*colour*) Silber, *das;* Ⓒ *no pl., no indef. art.* (*coins*) Silbermünzen *Pl.;* Silber, *das* (*ugs.*); **for thirty pieces** *or* **a handful of ~** (*fig.*) für einen Judaslohn; Ⓓ (*vessels, cutlery*) Silber, *das;* (*cutlery of other material*) Besteck, *das;* Ⓔ (*medal*) Silber, *das;* **win two ~s** zweimal Silber gewinnen. ❷ *attrib. adj.* silbern; Silber(pokal, -münze); **have a ~ tongue** zungenfertig sein; ⇨ *also* **spoon**[1] 1A...

**⇨ *also* directs the user to another headword where additional information can be found**
Mit ⇨ *also* wird auf ein Stichwort verwiesen, unter dem noch zusätzliche Informationen zu finden sind

**An arrow ▶ and a page-number cross reference direct the user to a usage box containing additional information**
Das Zeichen ▶ mit einer Zahl verweist auf eine Buchseite, auf der sich in einem Informationskasten zusätzliche Informationen finden

**solicitor** /sə'lɪsɪtə(r)/ *n.* ▶ **1261** Ⓐ (*Brit.: lawyer*) Rechtsanwalt, *der*/-anwältin, *die* (*der/dienicht vor höheren Gerichten auftritt*); Ⓑ (*Amer.: canvasser*) Werber, *der*

# Guide to the use of the Dictionary / Hinweise für die Benutzung des Wörterbuchs

## 1. Order of entries

### a) Headwords

Headwords (with the exception of phrasal verbs – see below) are entered in strict alphabetical order, ignoring hyphens, apostrophes, and spaces.

## 1. Anordnung der Artikel

### a) Alphabetische Ordnung der Stichwörter

Die Stichwörter sind (mit Ausnahme der *Phrasal verbs* im englisch-deutschen Teil; s. u.) streng alphabetisch angeordnet, wobei Bindestriche, Apostrophe und Wortzwischenräume keine Rolle spielen.

Examples/Beispiele: **liberal**
**liberal arts**
**liberalism**

**Pinte**
**Pin-up-Girl**
**Pinzette**

Abbreviations are also entered in alphabetical order in the main Dictionary.

Abkürzungen sind ebenfalls an ihrer entsprechenden Stelle im Alphabet zu finden.

Examples/Beispiele: **clutter**
**cm.** *abbr.*
**CND** *abbr.*

**Nockerl**
**NOK** ... *Abk.*
**nölen**

Headwords spelt the same but with unrelated meanings (homographs) are entered separately with a raised number following each.

Zwei oder mehr Stichwörter mit gleicher Schreibung (Homographe) werden mit hochgestellten Ziffern (jeweils hinter dem letzten Buchstaben) nummeriert und dieser Nummerierung entsprechend eingeordnet.

Examples/Beispiele: **dam**[1] ... [Stau]damm, *der*
**dam**[2] ... Muttertier, *das*

**Bank**[1] ... bench
**Bank**[2] ... bank

Each English phrasal verb is entered on a new line immediately following the entry for its first element, which is indicated by a swung dash.

Im englisch-deutschen Teil werden die *Phrasal verbs* auf einer neuen Zeile unmittelbar an das Grundwort angeschlossen, wobei dieses durch eine Tilde repräsentiert wird.

Examples/Beispiele: **track**
**~ 'down**
**'trackball**

**plump**[1]
**~ 'out**
**~ 'up**
**plump**[2]

### b) Compounds

Hyphenated English compounds and all German compounds are entered in their alphabetical place in the Dictionary, as are English compounds written as two or more words if they are regarded as having independent status in the language, e.g. **love affair**. Those not so regarded are given as phrases in the entry for their first word, so for example **love game** is given as **~game** under **love**.

### b) Einordnung von Komposita

Die im Englischen häufig getrennt geschriebenen Komposita werden als selbstständige Stichwörter behandelt, wenn sie als eigenständige Wörter gelten können; z. B. wird **love affair** als Stichwort an der entsprechenden Stelle im Alphabet aufgeführt. Wenn ein Kompositum als weniger eigenständig oder nur als Anwendungsbeispiel betrachtet wird, erscheint es unter dem Stichwort, das den ersten Bestandteil bildet, z. B. findet sich unter dem Stichwort **love** als Anwendungsbeispiel **love game**.

Where two or more compounds with the same first element occur consecutively, they are given in paragraph-like blocks. The first element is given only once at the beginning of the block and is thereafter represented by a swung dash (~).

In the English-German section, a compound in a block is spelt with the same initial letter—capital or small—as the first element at the beginning of the block, unless the opposite is shown.

Mehrere aufeinander folgende als Stichwörter aufgeführte Komposita mit gemeinsamem erstem Element sind im Wörterbuch zu Absätzen zusammengefasst. Dabei steht das erste Element nur am Anfang des Absatzes; es wird innerhalb des Absatzes durch eine Tilde repräsentiert.

Wenn im englisch-deutschen Teil in einem Kompositablock sowohl groß- als auch kleingeschriebene Stichwörter vorkommen, so erscheint das erste Element zu Beginn des Absatzes entweder in Groß- oder in Kleinschreibung. Bei davon abweichender Schreibung im selben Block steht dann vor der Tilde der zu verwendende Buchstabe.

Examples/Beispiele: **grand: ~niece** ... **G~ Prix**
**Great: ~ Bear** ... **g~coat**

In the German-English section, the first element of a block of compounds has a capital letter if the block contains only nouns, and a small letter if it contains no nouns. If the block contains nouns and other parts of speech, both forms of the first element are given.

Wenn im deutsch-englischen Teil das erste Element sowohl in Groß- als auch in Kleinschreibung gezeigt wird, gilt die Großschreibung für alle Substantive und die Kleinschreibung für die anderen Wortarten.

Examples/Beispiele: **Stech-: ~fliege** ... **~zirkel**
**kurz-: *~|treten** ... **~um**
**englisch-, Englisch-: ~horn** ... **~sprachig**

### c) Phrases

Idioms, fixed phrases, proverbs, and quotations are usually entered under only one word, and cross references, starting with ⇨ *also* or ⇨ *auch*, are given at other words under which the user might look. At **ask ❷**, for example, there is the cross reference ⇨ *also* trouble 1 A, because the expressions **you are asking for trouble** and **that's asking for trouble** are entered under **trouble**, and at **Stamm** 🄰 there is the cross reference ⇨ *auch* Apfel A, because the expression **der Apfel fällt nicht weit vom Stamm** is entered under **Apfel**.

### c) Einordnung von festen Wendungen

Aus mehreren Wörtern bestehende feste Wendungen, idiomatische Ausdrücke, Sprichwörter, Zitate und dergleichen sind gewöhnlich nur unter einem Stichwort verzeichnet. Das Wörterbuch gibt, wo es den Bearbeitern nützlich erschien, Verweise auf Fundstellen. Solche Verweise haben die Form ⇨ *also* ... bzw. ⇨ *auch* ... und stehen am Schluss eines Artikels bzw. eines Gliederungspunkts. So findet sich etwa unter **ask ❷** der Hinweis ⇨ *also* trouble 1 A, weil unter dem Stichwort **trouble** die Beispiele **you are asking for trouble** und **that's asking for trouble** zu finden sind, und unter **Stamm** 🄰 der Hinweis ⇨ *auch* Apfel A, weil unter **Apfel** die Redensart **der Apfel fällt nicht weit vom Stamm** behandelt ist.

## 2. Division of entries

### a) Numbered categories

When a word can be used as different parts of speech, these are numbered.

## 2. Untergliederung der Artikel

### a) Untergliederung durch Ziffern

Wenn ein Stichwort mehreren Wortarten angehören kann, steht vor jeder Wortartangabe eine Ziffer.

Examples/Beispiele: **blame** ... ❶ *v.t.* ... ❷ *n.*
**entgegen** ❶ *Adv.* ... ❷ *Präp. mit Dat.*

In verb entries, transitive, intransitive, and reflexive uses are also numbered.

Bei Verben unterscheiden die Ziffern außerdem den transitiven, intransitiven und reflexiven Gebrauch des Verbs.

Examples/Beispiele: **freeze** ... ❶ *v.i.* ... ❷ *v.t.*
**beschäftigen** ❶ *refl. V.* ... ❷ *tr. V.*

Entries for German prepositions are divided into numbered sections if they can take more than one case.

Bei deutschen Präpositionen dienen die Ziffern zur Untergliederung nach den Kasus, mit denen die Präposition stehen kann.

Example/Beispiel: **an** ... ❶ *Präp. mit Dat.* ... ❷ *Präp. mit Akk.*

### b) Letter categories

When a word has more than one sense (as a particular part of speech) the different senses are distinguished by letters.

### b) Untergliederung durch Buchstaben

Wenn ein Stichwort mehrere Bedeutungen haben kann, werden diese mit Buchstaben unterschieden.

Examples/Beispiele: **alien** ... ❶ *adj.* ... **A** *(strange)* ... **B** *(foreign)* ... **C** *(different)* ... **D** *(repugnant)* ... **E** *(contrary)* ...

**gemütlich** ❶ *Adj.* **A** *(behaglich)* ... **B** *(ungezwungen)* ... **C** *(umgänglich)* ... **D** *(gemächlich)* ...

## 3. The headword

### a) Form of the headword

The headword appears in bold type at the beginning of the entry.

Verbs are given as infinitives (without *to* in English).

Nouns are given in the nominative singular, but those which occur only in the plural are given in the nominative plural.

## 3. Das Stichwort

### a) Form des Stichworts

Das Stichwort erscheint fett gedruckt am Anfang des Artikels.

Verben erscheinen im Infinitiv. (Im Englischen ohne *to*.)

Substantive erscheinen im Nominativ Singular. Substantive, die nur als Plural vorkommen, erscheinen im Nominativ Plural.

Examples/Beispiele: **trousers** ... *n. pl.*

**Kosten** *Pl.*

German adjectives (and pronouns declined like adjectives) are given without endings, and adjectives which strictly speaking have no undeclined form are given with an ellipsis instead of any ending.

Deutsche Adjektive (und Pronomen, die wie Adjektive dekliniert werden) erscheinen in endungsloser Form. Auch Adjektive, die eigentlich keine endungslose Form haben, erscheinen ohne Endung, mit Auslassungspunkten.

Example/Beispiel: **äußer...**

Separate entries are given for all forms of the German definite article and of German pronouns which are not declined like adjectives. So, for example, **der**, **den**, **dem**, **die**, etc., **euch**, and **ihr** are all entered as headwords. In the same way, all forms of English pronouns are headwords – **her**, for example, as well as **she**.

German demonstrative pronouns are treated under the masculine nominative singular, e.g. **derjenige**. Inflected forms are entered as headwords with cross references to their root forms if these are not easily identifiable.

Deutsche Pronomen, die nicht wie Adjektive dekliniert werden, und die bestimmten Artikel erscheinen in allen Formen als selbstständige Stichwörter. Es erscheint also z. B. nicht nur **der**, sondern auch **des**, **dem**, **den** usw. als Stichwort, und die Form **euch** wird nicht unter **ihr** abgehandelt, sondern ist selbst Stichwort. Ebenso werden englische Pronomen in allen Formen als Stichwörter aufgeführt, also erscheint z. B. nicht nur **she**, sondern auch **her** als Stichwort.

Deutsche Demonstrativpronomen werden an der alphabetischen Stelle der maskulinen Form behandelt, also erscheinen z. B. **diejenige** und **dasjenige** unter dem Stichwort **derjenige**.

Als Stichwörter erscheinen auch bestimmte Flexionsformen, die sich nicht ohne weiteres auf ihre Grundform zurückführen lassen. Ein Verweis führt zur Grundform.

Examples/Beispiele: **did** ⇨ **do**[1]

**apices** *pl. of* **apex**

**höher** ... ⇨ **hoch**

**dasjenige** ⇨ **derjenige**

**zog** *1. u. 3. Pers. Sg. Prät. v.* **ziehen**

### b) Symbols used with headwords

With English headwords:

ˈ shows stress on the following syllable (for more information see 4).

### b) Zeichen am Stichwort

Am englischen Stichwort kann das folgende Zeichen auftreten:

ˈ Betonungszeichen vor der zu betonenden Silbe. (Näheres siehe unter 4.)

With German headwords:

_ indicates a long vowel or a diphthong, stressed in words of more than one syllable.

Am deutschen Stichwort können die folgenden Zeichen auftreten:

_ Betonungszeichen in Form eines Strichs unter betonten langen Vokalen.

Examples/Beispiele: **Hieb**, **Blau**, **Hörer**, **amtieren**

. indicates a short vowel, stressed in words of more than one syllable:

. Betonungszeichen in Form eines Punktes unter betonten kurzen Vokalen.

Examples/Beispiele: **Recht**, **bitter**

· shows the juncture of elements forming a word.

· Punkt, der bei zusammengesetzten Wörtern die Kompositionsfuge markiert.

Examples/Beispiele: **Kern·kraft**, **um·branden**

| shows the juncture of elements forming a compound verb and indicates that the verb is separable (for more information see Outline of German grammatical forms on pp. 1709–1711).

| senkrechter Strich, der bei zusammengesetzten Verben die Kompositionsfuge markiert und gleichzeitig anzeigt, dass das Verb unfest zusammengesetzt ist.

Examples/Beispiele: **vor|haben**, **um|werfen**

* preceding a German headword or compound indicates that the form is an 'old' spelling of the word, no longer valid according to the recently introduced reform of German spellings. See 'The revision of German spellings' on p. 1707

Das Zeichen * vor einem deutschen Stichwort kennzeichnet die betreffende Form als „alte" (d.h., aufgrund der Rechtschreibreform nicht mehr gültige) Schreibung. (Siehe „Die neue Regelung der deutschen Rechtschreibung" auf S. 1707)

Examples/Beispiele: **bewusstlos**, ***bewußtlos**
***einbleuen ⇨ einbläuen**

## 4. Pronunciation

The pronunciation of a headword is given in angle brackets immediately after it, in the International Phonetic Alphabet (IPA), which is explained on page 32. German pronunciations are based on the DUDEN-Aussprachewörterbuch, while English pronunciations are those common in educated Southern British English.

A *simple headword* without a pronunciation given is pronounced in the same way as the headword immediately before it.

The pronunciation of a *German derivative* with none given can be deduced from that of its root word. The stress, however, is always shown by _ or . (see 3b).

*Abbreviations* without pronunciations given are pronounced as their full forms, except for English ones consisting of two or more capital letters, which are pronounced as individual letters, with the stress on the last, e.g. **BBC** is pronounced /bi:bi:'si:/.

## 4. Angaben zur Aussprache

Die Aussprache des Stichworts ist in Lautschrift zwischen Schrägstrichen unmittelbar nach dem Stichwort angegeben. Die Ausspracheangaben für das Deutsche richten sich nach dem DUDEN-Aussprachewörterbuch, für das Englische nach der *Received Pronunciation* in Südengland. Die dabei verwendeten Zeichen der internationalen Lautschrift der *International Phonetic Association* (IPA) sind auf Seite 33 verzeichnet und erklärt.

Bei mehreren *gleich lautenden Stichwörtern* ist die Aussprache nur beim ersten Stichwort zu finden.

Bei deutschen *Ableitungen* ohne Ausspracheangabe kann die Aussprache vom Grundwort abgeleitet werden. Bei ihnen wird daher nur die Betonung angegeben, und zwar durch Zeichen am Stichwort selbst (s. 3b).

*Abkürzungen* ohne Ausspracheangabe werden wie ihre vollen Formen ausgesprochen. Dies gilt jedoch nicht für die aus mindestens zwei Großbuchstaben bestehenden englischen Abkürzungen, die wie die einzelnen Buchstaben mit Betonung des letzten gesprochen werden (**BBC** also z.B. wie /bi:bi:'si:/).

The pronunciation of a *compound* with none given can be derived from the pronunciations of its elements, and, unless the compound is in a block, the stress is always shown by the symbol ', _, or . (see 3b), e.g. '**doughnut** is pronounced as **dough** + **nut**, with the stress on **dough**, and **bau·sparen** is pronounced as **Bau** + **sparen**, with the stress on **bau**. With German compounds, juncture between elements is shown either by · in the headword (as in 3b) or, within a block of compounds, by the point where the compound is divided (as in 1b).

Bei *Komposita* ohne Ausspracheangabe ergibt sich die Aussprache aus der der einzelnen Bestandteile. Bei ihnen ist daher nur die Betonung angegeben, und zwar durch Zeichen am Stichwort selbst (s. 3b): '**doughnut** wird wie **dough** + **nut** ausgesprochen, die Betonung liegt auf **dough**, **bau·sparen** wird wie **Bau** + **sparen** ausgesprochen, die Betonung liegt auf **bau**. Bei deutschen Komposita wird die Kompositionsfuge entweder durch einen in das Stichwort gesetzten Punkt (siehe auch 3b) oder durch die Eingliederung des Stichworts in einen Block von Komposita (siehe auch 1b) deutlich.

If part of a German compound is not in the Dictionary as a headword, then just that part is given a pronunciation, with a hyphen standing for the rest.

Ist ein Bestandteil eines deutschen Kompositums nicht im Wörterbuch als Stichwort verzeichnet, wird die Aussprache nur für diesen Teil in Lautschrift angegeben, wobei für den anderen Teil ein Bindestrich steht.

Example/Beispiel: **Schausteller** /-ʃtɛlɐ/

If stress alone needs to be shown in angle brackets, each syllable is represented by a hyphen.

Wenn in einer Ausspracheklammer nur die Betonung angegeben werden soll, steht für jede Silbe ein waagerechter Strich.

Example/Beispiel: **come to** ❶ /'--/ *v.t.* ... ❷ /-'-/ *v.i.*

In blocks of compounds, stress is given as follows:

In Kompositablöcken ist die Betonung folgendermaßen angegeben:

In the English-German section:

Im englisch-deutschen Teil:

If no stress is shown (by the IPA stress mark), it falls on the first element.

Das erste Element ist normalerweise das betonte Element und nicht weiter gekennzeichnet. Ist ein anderes als das erste Element betont, so wird dies durch das IPA-Betonungszeichen gezeigt.

Example/Beispiel: **country: ~ folk** ... **~ 'gentleman**

In the German-English section:

Im deutsch-englischen Teil:

When the first element at the beginning of the block has a stress mark, this stress applies to all compounds in the block.

Wenn das erste Element zu Beginn des Blocks durch einen untergesetzten Punkt oder Strich als betont markiert ist, gilt dies für alle Komposita im Block.

Example/Beispiel: **Vanille-: ~eis** ... **~geschmack** ... **~pudding**

Exceptions are given in angle brackets, with a hyphen standing for each syllable.

Ausnahmen davon werden (zwischen Schrägstrichen) angegeben, wobei für jede Silbe ein waagerechter Strich steht.

Example/Beispiel: **drei-**, **Drei-:** ... **~käsehoch** /-'--/

When no stress is shown for the first element at the beginning of a block, the stress of each compound is given individually.

Wenn das erste Element zu Beginn des Blocks nicht als betont markiert ist, wird bei jedem Kompositum im Block die Betonung angegeben.

Example/Beispiel: **nord-**, **Nord-: ~seite** /'---/ ... **~stern** /'--/ ... **~-Süd-Dialog** ... **~-Süd-Gefälle** ... **~südlich**

## 5. Grammatical information

Grammatical information on a headword immediately follows the headword or its pronunciation. The part of speech comes first; if the word can be more than one part of speech, each is listed in a separate numbered section (see also 2a).

## 5. Grammatische Angaben

Unmittelbar nach dem Stichwort bzw. der Ausspracheangabe folgen die grammatischen Angaben zum Stichwort. Die Wortart wird an erster Stelle angegeben. Wenn das Stichwort mehreren Wortarten angehören kann, steht vor jeder Wortartangabe eine Ziffer (siehe auch 2a).

The following grammatical information is given:

Die folgenden grammatischen Angaben werden gemacht:

### a) Nouns

In the English-German section, nouns are labelled with the abbreviation *n.* and proper nouns with *pr. n.* Irregular plurals are always given.

### a) Bei Substantiven

Im englisch-deutschen Teil werden Substantive durch die Angabe *n.* gekennzeichnet. Eigennamen werden mit *pr. n.* gekennzeichnet; unregelmäßige Pluralformen werden angegeben.

Examples/Beispiele:
**boy** ... *n.*
**Australia** ... *pr. n.*
**bijou** ... *n., pl.* **~x**
**mouse** ... *n., pl.* **mice**
**haddock** ... *n., pl. same*

In the German-English section, nouns are denoted by the inclusion of a definite article.

Im deutsch-englischen Teil werden Substantive durch die Angabe des bestimmten Artikels gekennzeichnet.

Example/Beispiel: **Tante** ... *die*

If this article is in parentheses, the word is a proper noun and the article is used only in certain circumstances.

Steht der Artikel in runden Klammern, handelt es sich bei dem Substantiv um einen Eigennamen, der nur unter gewissen Umständen mit dem bestimmten Artikel gebraucht wird.

Examples/Beispiele:
**Belgien** ... *(das)*
**Karl** ... *(der)*

The definite article is followed by the genitive and plural endings for the noun with the headword represented by a swung dash.

Auf den Artikel folgen die Genitiv- und die Pluralendung des Substantivs. Dabei steht für das Stichwort die Tilde.

Example/Beispiel: **Tante** ... *die;* **~n, ~n**

If only one ending is given, it is the genitive, and the word has no plural.

Wird nur eine Endung angegeben, so handelt es sich um die Genitivendung, das Stichwort hat in diesem Fall keinen Plural.

Example/Beispiel: **Schlaf** ... *der;* **~[e]s**

The label *n. pl.* or *Pl.* indicates that the noun exists only in the plural.

Die Angabe *n. pl.* im Englischen bzw. *Pl.* im Deutschen weist darauf hin, daß das Wort nur im Plural vorkommt.

Examples/Beispiele:
**pants** ... *n. pl.*
**police** ... *n. pl.*
**Ferien** ... *Pl.*
**Niederlande** *Pl.*

### b) Verbs

Verbs are labelled as transitive, intransitive, or reflexive.

### b) Bei Verben

Verben werden als transitive, intransitive oder reflexive Verben gekennzeichnet.

Examples/Beispiele:
**engrave** ... *v. t.*
**creep** ... *v. i.*
**behave** ... *v. refl.*
**ehren** *tr. V.*
**leuchten** *itr. V.*
**freuen** ... *refl. V.*

In the English-German section the following additional information is given:

Im englisch-deutschen Teil werden folgende Angaben gemacht:

The entries for irregular verbs give their past tense, past participle, and any other forms necessary. Identical forms are given only once.

Bei unregelmäßigen Verben werden die Stammformen (Präteritum und 2. Partizip) angegeben, wobei gleich lautende Formen nur einmal genannt werden.

Examples/Beispiele: **hide**[1] ... **hid** ... **hidden**
**die**[2] ... **dying**
**make** ... **made**

The doubling of a final consonant before **-ed** or **-ing** is also shown.

Wenn der Endkonsonant eines Verbs bei der Bildung einer Form auf **-ed** oder **-ing** verdoppelt wird, wird das ebenfalls angegeben.

Example/Beispiel: **bat**[4] *v. t.*, **-tt-**

In the German-English section, the following additional information is given:

Im deutsch-englischen Teil werden darüber hinaus folgende Angaben gemacht:

Irregular verbs are labelled *unr.*, and their parts (present, preterite, and past participle) are given on pp. 1723–1726

Unregelmäßige Verben werden mit *unr.* bezeichnet, ihre Stammformen (Präsens, Präteritum und Partizip Perfekt) können auf S. 1723–1726 nachgeschlagen werden.

Examples/Beispiele: **klingen** *unr. itr. V.*
**leihen** ... *unr. tr. V.*

Verbs which are always or sometimes conjugated with *sein* rather than *haben* are labelled accordingly.

Verben, die nicht oder nicht immer mit *haben* konjugiert werden, sind mit einem entsprechenden Hinweis versehen.

Examples/Beispiele: **sterben** ... *mit sein*
**robben** ... *meist, mit Richtungsangabe nur, mit sein*

Separable compound verbs are indicated by a vertical line at the point where the word is split.

Bei unfest zusammengesetzten Verben zeigt ein ins Wort hineingesetzter senkrechter Strich, wo das Verb gegebenenfalls getrennt wird.

Example/Beispiel: **auf|stehen**

### c) Adjectives and adverbs

Irregular and, in the German-English section, umlauted comparative and superlative forms are given.

### c) Bei Adjektiven und Adverbien

Zu Adjektiven und Adverbien werden unregelmäßige und—im deutsch-englischen Teil—umlautende Steigerungsformen angegeben:

Examples/Beispiele: **bad** ... **worse** ... **worst**

**gut** ... **besser** ... **best** ...
**kalt** ... **kälter** ... **kältest** ...

### d) Prepositions

The entry for each German preposition indicates with which case or cases it is used.

### d) Bei Präpositionen

Für jede deutsche Präposition wird der Kasus angegeben, mit dem die Präposition steht.

Examples/Beispiele: **um** ... *Präp. mit Akk.*
**vor** ... ❶ *Präp. mit Dat.* ... ❷ *Präp. mit Akk.*

Contractions of a preposition and a definite article are shown thus:

Präpositionen, die mit dem bestimmten Artikel zusammengezogen sind, werden so gekennzeichnet:

Example/Beispiel: **vom** ... *Präp. + Art.*

**e) Compounds**

Compounds are always labelled with their part of speech or gender, but any further grammatical information is given at the entry for the second element.

**e) Bei Komposita**

Bei Komposita wird stets die Wortart angegeben. Wenn keine weiteren grammatischen Angaben gemacht werden, können diese dem Eintrag für das zweite Element des Kompositums entnommen werden.

Examples/Beispiele: **half:** ... **~-life** *n.*
**life** ... *n., pl.* **lives**
**Radau·bruder** *der*
**Bruder** ... *der;* **~s**, **Brüder**

## 6. Labels

After the grammatical information comes any necessary information on the style, usage, regional restrictions, or subject fields of a word, printed in italics within parentheses. Many labels are abbreviations, which are explained on pp. 34–37.

A label placed at the start of an entry or of a numbered or letter category applies to the whole of that entry or category.

**a) Style and usage labels**

Labels are used to mark all words and expressions which are not neutral in style. Both headwords and their translations are labelled to help the user to understand the headwords and to use the translations correctly in context.

The following style and usage labels are used to describe English:

## 6. Kennzeichnungen

Im Anschluss an die grammatischen Angaben wird der Benutzer auf die stilistische, zeitliche, regionale und fachliche Zuordnung des Stichworts hingewiesen. Diese Angaben stehen in Kursivschrift in runden Klammern. Sie sind häufig abgekürzt, eine Liste der verwendeten Abkürzungen befindet sich auf S. 34–37.

Wenn eine derartige Angabe am Anfang eines Artikels oder eines Gliederungspunktes steht, gilt sie für den ganzen Artikel oder Gliederungspunkt.

**a) Angaben zur stilistischen Bewertung**

Wörter und Wendungen, die nicht der normalsprachlichen Stilschicht angehören, werden sowohl in der Ausgangs- als auch in der Zielsprache mit Angaben zu ihrer stilistischen und zeitlichen Einordnung versehen. Der Benutzer kann somit die Stichwörter richtig verstehen und die Übersetzungen im korrekten Zusammenhang verwenden.

Für das Englische werden zur stilistischen Bewertung und zeitlichen Zuordnung die folgenden Angaben verwendet:

| | | |
|---|---|---|
| *(poet.)* | poetic (e.g. **beauteous**, **the deep**). | in dichterischer, poetischer Sprache verwendet (z.B. **beauteous**, **the deep**). |
| *(literary)* | literary or elevated (e.g. **bed of sickness**, **countenance**, **valorous**). | für einen gehobenen, literarischen Stil charakteristisch (z.B. **bed of sickness**, **countenance**, **valorous**). |
| *(rhet.)* | used for deliberate impressive or persuasive effect (e.g. **bounteous**, **plenteous**). | bewusst dazu eingesetzt, andere zu beeindrucken oder zu überzeugen (z.B. **bounteous**, **plenteous**). |
| *(formal)* | used only in formal speeches and writing (e.g. **hereafter**, **partake**). | bei offiziellen und formellen Gelegenheiten unter Menschen, die sich nicht gut kennen, verwendet (z.B. **hereafter**, **partake**). |
| *(coll.)* | everyday, conversational language; not generally written, but would not cause offence or ridicule (e.g. **Aussie**, **cropper**, **loo**). | gesprochene Alltagssprache, die in schriftlichen Texten im Allgemeinen nicht verwendet wird (z.B. **Aussie**, **cropper**, **loo**). |
| *(child lang.)* | used only by or to small children (e.g. **bow-wow**, **choo-choo**). | nur von kleinen Kindern oder im Umgang mit ihnen verwendet (z.B. **bow-wow**, **choo-choo**). |
| *(sl.)* | especially colloquial and expressive; often used only by particular groups (e.g. **crud**, **gob**, **shoot one's mouth off**). | besonders umgangssprachlich, oft nur von bestimmten Personengruppen verwendet (z.B. **crud**, **gob**, **shoot one's mouth off**). |
| *(coarse)* | coarse and offensive (e.g. **bollocks**, **fuck**, **piss**). | im Allgemeinen als anstößig empfunden (z.B. **bollocks**, **fuck**, **piss**). |

| | | |
|---|---|---|
| (*dated*) | somewhat old-fashioned; used particularly by older people (e.g. **by Jove**, **ripping**, **top-hole**). | zwar noch gelegentlich von älteren Leuten verwendet, aber altmodisch klingend (z.B. **by Jove**, **ripping**, **top-hole**). |
| (*arch.*) | found only in literature but still used jocularly, ironically, or for a deliberately old-fashioned effect (e.g. **forsooth**, **peradventure**). | heute nur noch gelegentlich in scherzhafter oder altertümelnder Weise verwendet (z.B. **forsooth**, **peradventure**). |
| (*Hist.*) | current term for an obsolete thing (e.g. **ducking stool**, **oubliette**). | bedeutet, dass die bezeichnete Sache, Einrichtung usw. heute nicht mehr existiert; das so gekennzeichnete Wort ist aber nicht veraltet (z.B. **ducking stool**, **oubliette**). |

The following style and usage labels are used to describe German:

Für das Deutsche werden zur stilistischen Bewertung und zeitlichen Zuordnung die folgenden Angaben verwendet:

| | | |
|---|---|---|
| (*dichter.*) | poetic (e.g. **Aar**, **Odem**). | in dichterischer, poetischer Sprache verwendet (z.B. **Aar**, **Odem**). |
| (*geh.*) | formal, cultivated, or elevated; sometimes considered solemn or affected (e.g. **Antlitz**, **signifikant**, **dergestalt**). | für einen feierlichen, gehobenen oder gewählten Stil charakteristisch (z.B. **Antlitz**, **signifikant**, **dergestalt**). |
| (*Papierdt.*) | formal and stilted; mainly written (e.g. **seitens**, **in Wegfall kommen**). | für einen unlebendigen, formellen und gespreizten Stil charakteristisch (z.B. **seitens**, **in Wegfall kommen**). |
| (*ugs.*) | everyday, conversational language; not generally written, but would not cause offence or ridicule (e.g. **Stunk**, **jmdm. über den Kopf wachsen**). | gesprochene Alltagssprache, die in schriftlichen Texten im Allgemeinen nicht verwendet wird (z.B. **Stunk**, **jmdm. über den Kopf wachsen**). |
| (*fam.*) | used only between people on very familiar terms; otherwise considered silly or ridiculous (e.g. **Popo**, **Beißerchen**). | nur unter miteinander sehr vertrauten Menschen gebräuchlich; kann sonst als albern empfunden werden (z.B. **Popo**, **Beißerchen**). |
| (*Kinderspr.*) | used only by and to small children (e.g. **Wauwau**, **heia**). | nur von kleinen Kindern oder im Umgang mit ihnen verwendet (z.B. **Wauwau**, **heia**). |
| (*salopp*) | especially colloquial and expressive; often used only by particular groups (e.g. **Sauferei**, **ins Gras beißen müssen**). | besonders umgangssprachlich, oft nur von bestimmten Personengruppen verwendet (z.B. **Sauferei**, **ins Gras beißen müssen**). |
| (*derb*) | coarse and offensive (e.g. **Fresse**, **abkratzen**). | im Allgemeinen als grob und anstößig empfunden (z.B. **Fresse**, **abkratzen**). |
| (*vulg.*) | especially coarse and offensive, mainly sexual terms (e.g. **ficken**, **Fotze**). | als besonders anstößig und vulgär empfunden; vor allem aus dem Bereich der Sexualität (z.B. **ficken**, **Fotze**). |
| (*volkst.*) | avoided by specialists as potentially misleading or insufficiently scientific; mainly names of plants, animals, and illnesses (e.g. **Karfunkel**, **Schusterpalme**). | von Fachleuten meist vermieden, weil missverständlich oder zu unspezifisch, vor allem Bezeichnungen für Pflanzen, Tiere und Krankheiten (z.B. **Karfunkel**, **Schusterpalme**). |
| (*veralt.*) | either dated or found only in literature but still used jocularly, ironically, or for a deliberately old-fashioned effect (e.g. **Schwindsucht**, **Spezerei**) | heute nicht mehr oder kaum noch gebraucht, aber in älterer Literatur zu finden oder heute noch in scherzhafter, ironischer oder altertümelnder Weise verwendet (z.B. **Schwindsucht**, **Spezerei**) |

**b) Regional labels**

Words and expressions restricted to particular areas of the English- and German-speaking worlds are labelled accordingly. For English, the most common labels are (*Brit.*), (*Amer.*), (*Austral.*), and (*Scot.*). German items may be labelled, (*österr.*), (*schweiz.*), (*nordd.*), (*südd.*), (*berlin.*), etc.

The label (*dial.*) or (*landsch.*) indicates that a word is used in a number of regions or dialects.

**b) Angaben zur regionalen Zuordnung**

Wörter und Wendungen, die nicht im gesamten englischen bzw. deutschen Sprachraum üblich sind, werden entsprechend gekennzeichnet. Für englische Stichwörter werden vor allem die Angaben (*Brit.*), (*Amer.*), (*Austral.*), (*Scot.*) usw. gemacht. Deutsche Stichwörter können mit, (*österr.*), (*schweiz.*), (*nordd.*), (*südd.*), (*berlin.*) usw. markiert sein.

Die Angabe (*dial.*) bzw. (*landsch.*) weist darauf hin, dass ein Wort in mehreren Regionen oder Mundarten gebräuchlich ist.

**c) Subject-field labels**

Terms used in specialist or technical fields are labelled accordingly.

**c) Bereichsangaben**

Wörter, die bestimmten Sachgebieten, Fachbereichen, Fach- oder Sondersprachen zuzuordnen sind, werden ebenfalls gekennzeichnet.

Examples/Beispiele: **colonnade** ... (*Archit.*)
**entr'acte** ... (*Theatre*)
**Gelbfieber** ... (*Med.*)
**Hirschfänger** ... (*Jägerspr.*)

German terms used in a number of fields but requiring only one translation are often simply labelled (*fachspr.*).

Deutsche Stichwörter, die mehreren Fachbereichen zugehören, aber nur eine Übersetzung haben, werden gelegentlich nur mit (*fachspr.*) gekennzeichnet.

Example/Beispiel: **binär** ... (*fachspr.*) binary

**d) Further usage labels**

Figurative, derogatory, euphemistic, etc. use is indicated with appropriate labels.

**d) Weitere Kennzeichnungen**

Bildlicher, abwertender, verhüllender usw. Gebrauch wird durch entsprechende Angaben markiert.

Examples/Beispiele: **assail** ... (*fig.*)
**intimate** ... (*euphem. ...*)
**hochkarätig** ... (*fig.*)
**Quatsch** ... (*abwertend*)

**e) Combinations of labels**

Labels combined within parentheses, with no separating punctuation, apply simultaneously: (*südd. ugs.*) means that the word is used in southern Germany and is colloquial; (*fig. coll.*) means that in the sense or context in question the word is used figuratively and is colloquial.

Labels separated by commas or slashes cannot apply simultaneously: (*Phys., Biol.*) means that the word occurs in the fields of both physics and biology; (*arch./joc.*) means that the word occurs either in older texts or in jocular use.

**e) Kombination von mehreren Kennzeichnungen**

Stehen in einer Klammer mehrere Kennzeichnungen nebeneinander, so gelten sie gleichermaßen: (*südd. ugs.*) bedeutet, dass das Wort in Süddeutschland gebräuchlich und umgangssprachlich ist; (*fig. coll.*) bedeutet, dass das Wort hier bildlich gebraucht wird und umgangssprachlich ist.

Werden die Kennzeichnungen durch Komma oder Schrägstrich getrennt, dann gelten sie unabhängig voneinander: (*Phys., Biol.*) bedeutet, dass das Wort zu den Fachbereichen Physik und Biologie gehört; (*arch./joc.*) bedeutet, dass das Wort entweder veraltet ist oder scherzhaft gebraucht wird.

## 7. Indicators

Indicators, printed in italics in parentheses before translations, distinguish between the various senses of a headword and, together with subject-field labels, tell the user which sense is being translated.

## 7. Indikatoren

Indikatoren sind kurze Hinweise, die angeben, zu welcher Bedeutung des Stichworts eine Übersetzung gehört. Sie stehen in Kursivschrift in runden Klammern vor der Übersetzung.

Examples/Beispiele: **flapjack** ... (*oatcake*) ... (*pancake*) ...
**below** ... (*position*) ... (*direction*) ... (*later in text*) ...
**Kanadier** ... (*Einwohner Kanadas*) ... (*Boot*) ...
**Luke** ... (*Dach~*) ... (*bei Schiffen*) ...

## 8. Translations and collocators

### a) Translations

Normally, one general translation is given for each word or sense of a word. If two or more are given, separated by semi-colons, they are synonymous and interchangeable.

## 8. Übersetzungen und Kollokatoren

### a) Die Übersetzung

Im Normalfall wird für jedes Stichwort bzw. jede Bedeutung eines Stichworts zuerst eine allgemeine Übersetzung gegeben; selten auch zwei oder mehrere gleichwertige und gegeneinander austauschbare Übersetzungen, die mit Semikolons aneinander gereiht sind.

Examples/Beispiele: **engrossing** ... fesselnd
**anchovy** ... An[s]chovis, *die;* Sardelle, *die*

**entzückt** ... delighted
**Elitedenken** ... élitist thinking; élitism

Unless qualified by labels, indicators, or collocators, a translation can be regarded as adequate in practically all contexts. Where necessary, a translation is labelled for style, region, etc. in a similar way to headwords.

Die angegebene Übersetzung, sofern sie nicht durch Zusätze (Kennzeichnungen, Indikatoren, Kollokatoren) eingeschränkt ist, kann als adäquate Übersetzung für nahezu alle Kontexte angesehen werden. Die Übersetzungen werden ähnlich wie die Stichwörter nötigenfalls mit Kennzeichnungen zur stilistischen Bewertung, zur regionalen Zuordnung usw. versehen.

Examples/Beispiele: **alongside** ... längsseits (*Seemannsspr.*)
**grub** ... Fressen, *das* (*salopp*)

**hoppnehmen** ... nab (*coll.*)
**Hornhautentzündung** ... keratitis (*Med.*)

Specialist terms are often given two translations: a general or popular one and a specialist one, which is labelled *(fachspr.)* or *(as tech. term)*.

Für Fachausdrücke werden oft zwei Übersetzungen gegeben, eine allgemeinsprachliche und eine fachsprachliche; die fachsprachliche Übersetzung ist dann mit *(fachspr.)* bzw. *(as tech. term)* gekennzeichnet.

Examples/Beispiele: **bilingual** ... zweisprachig; bilingual (*fachspr.*)

**Schote** ... pod; siliqua (*as tech. term*)

English nouns which can signify a person of either sex are generally given a translation for each.

Bei englischen Substantiven, die Menschen beiderlei Geschlechts bezeichnen können, wird als Übersetzung im Allgemeinen sowohl die männliche als auch die weibliche Form angegeben.

Examples/Beispiele: **European** ... Europäer, *der*/Europäerin, *die*
**buyer** ... Käufer, *der*/Käuferin, *die*
**client** ... Auftraggeber, *der*/-geberin, *die*

Words which are untranslatable because they have no equivalent in the other language (mainly the names of institutions, customs, foods, etc.) are given a short explanation (gloss) in italic type.

Stichwörter, die nicht übersetzt werden können, weil sie in der Zielsprache kein Äquivalent haben (meist Bezeichnungen für Institutionen, Bräuche, Esswaren u. a.), sind mit einer kurzen Erklärung (Glosse) in Kursivschrift versehen.

Examples/Beispiele: **gerrymander** ... *willkürlich in Wahlbezirke aufteilen, um einer politischen Partei Vorteile zu verschaffen*
**Christmas stocking** ... *von den Kindern am Heiligabend aufgehängter Strumpf, den der Weihnachtsmann mit Geschenken füllen soll*

**Einwohnermeldeamt** ... *local government office for registration of residents*
**Schützenfest** ... *shooting competition with fair*

A gloss is occasionally added to a translation to aid understanding of the headword.

Glossen dieser Art werden gelegentlich auch zusätzlich zu einer Übersetzung gegeben, um die Bedeutung des Stichworts zu erläutern.

Examples/Beispiele: **'clambake** *n.* (*Amer.*) Picknick, *das* (*bes. am Strand, bei dem Muscheln und Fisch auf heißen Steinen gebacken werden*)

**Bestarbeiter** *der,* **Bestarbeiterin**, *die* (*DDR*) best worker (*worker receiving an award as being the most efficient in the department, factory, etc.*)

The symbol ≈ indicates that the translation given is to be taken only as an approximate equivalent.

Das Symbol ≈ zeigt an, daß die vorgeschlagene Übersetzung nur als ungefähres Äquivalent des Stichworts zu verstehen ist.

Examples/Beispiele: **A level** ... ≈ Abitur, *das*

**Finanzamt** ... ≈ Inland Revenue

A cross reference of the form ⇒ indicates that a translation can be found under the entry referred to (see also 10).

Ein Verweis mit ⇒ auf ein anderes Stichwort zeigt, dass die Übersetzung dort nachgeschlagen werden kann (siehe auch 10).

**b) Collocators**

As the choice of the correct translation often depends on the context in which it is to be used, collocators (words with which a translation typically occurs) are frequently supplied for translations of verbs, adjectives, adverbs, and combining forms. They are printed in sanserif type in angle brackets.

**b) Kollokatoren**

Oft hängt die Wahl der richtigen Übersetzung davon ab, mit welchen anderen Wörtern die Übersetzung im Satz verbunden werden soll. Zu vielen Übersetzungen von Verben, Adjektiven, Adverbien und Wortbildungselementen sind deshalb einige typischerweise mit der Übersetzung verbundene Wörter, so genannte Kollokatoren, angegeben. Sie stehen in Groteskschrift in Winkelklammern.

Examples/Beispiele: **acquire** ... erwerben ‹Land, Besitz, Wohlstand, Kenntnisse›; sammeln ‹Erfahrungen›; ernten ‹Lob›

**flink** ... nimble ‹fingers›; sharp ‹eyes›; quick ‹hands›

If a collocator goes with more than one translation, the translations concerned are separated by commas instead of semi-colons.

Wenn Kollokatoren sich auf mehrere gleichwertige Übersetzungen beziehen, sind diese Übersetzungen mit Kommas statt mit Semikolons aneinander gereiht.

Examples/Beispiele: **achieve** ... herstellen, herbeiführen ‹Frieden, Harmonie›

**kürzen** ... shorten, take up ‹garment›; ... shorten, abridge ‹article, book›; ... reduce, cut ‹pension, budget, etc.›

With verbs, typical subjects and objects are given as collocators. Subjects are placed before the translation.

Kollokatoren zu Verben sind Substantive, die typischerweise entweder als Subjekte oder als Objekte des Verbs fungieren. Ist der Kollokator das Subjekt des Verbs, steht er vor der Übersetzung.

Examples/Beispiele: **hiss** ... ‹Katze, Lokomotive:› fauchen

**schwenken** ... ‹marching column› swing, wheel; ‹camera› pan; ‹path, road, car› swing

Objects are placed after the translation.

Ist der Kollokator das Objekt des Verbs, steht er hinter der Übersetzung.

Examples/Beispiele: **comb** ... kämmen ‹Haare, Flachs, Wolle› ... striegeln ‹Pferd› ... durchkämmen ‹Gelände, Wald›

**herunterreißen** ... pull off ‹plaster, wallpaper›; tear down ‹poster›

With English translations consisting of more than one word, collocators are placed at the appropriate point.

Bei mehrteiligen englischen Übersetzungen steht der Kollokator an der Stelle, wo er auch im Satz stehen müsste.

Example/Beispiel: **verheizen** ... use ‹troops› as cannon fodder; ... run ‹employee, subordinate, etc.› into the ground

With adjectives, collocators are nouns which the translations typically qualify. They are normally placed after the translation.

Kollokatoren zu Adjektiven sind Substantive, mit denen das Adjektiv typischerweise verwendet wird. Sie stehen normalerweise nach der Übersetzung.

Examples/Beispiele: **coated** ... gestrichen ‹Papier›; belegt ‹Zunge›; imprägniert ‹Stoff›; getönt ‹Glas, Linsen›

**grimmig** ... furious ‹person›; grim ‹face, expression›; fierce, ferocious ‹enemy, lion, etc.›

Where a collocator for an adjective is placed before the translation, the translation is postpositive—it must be used after the noun it qualifies.

Wenn ein Kollokator zu einem Adjektiv vor der Übersetzung steht, bedeutet dies, dass die Übersetzung nachgestellt werden muss.

Examples/Beispiele: **flowery** ... ‹Wiese› voller Blumen

**eisenhaltig** ... ‹food› containing iron

With a translation that is used in compounds, other elements with which it typically combines are given as collocators.

Bei Übersetzungen, die ein Wortbildungselement darstellen, werden als Kollokatoren solche Elemente angeführt, mit denen die Übersetzung typischerweise kombiniert wird.

Examples/Beispiele: **marine** ... See‹versicherung, -recht, -schifffahrt›

**-süchtig** ... ‹drug-, heroin-, morphine-, etc.›addicted

(Thus, **marine law** is translated as **Seerecht**, and **drogensüchtig** as **drug-addicted**. / Die Verbindung **marine law** wird also mit **Seerecht** übersetzt, **drogensüchtig** mit **drug-addicted**.)

With adverbs, collocators are verbs and adjectives which the translations typically qualify. Verbs are shown before the translation in the German-English section, but after it in the English-German, while adjectives and participles are always placed after, as in connected language.

Kollokatoren zu Adverbien sind Verben oder Adjektive oder adjektivisch gebrauchte Partizipien, mit denen das Adverb typischerweise verbunden wird. Dabei stehen im deutsch-englischen Teil Verben vor der Übersetzung, im englisch-deutschen Teil dahinter; Adjektive und Partizipien stehen immer hinter der Übersetzung, entsprechend ihrer Stellung im Satz.

Examples/Beispiele: **excessively** ... unmäßig ‹essen, trinken›

**flimsily** ... hastig ‹errichtet›; schlecht ‹gebunden, verpackt›

**probeweise** ... ‹employ› on a trial basis

**schwer** ... seriously ‹injured, wounded›; greatly, deeply ‹disappointed›; ‹punish› severely, heavily

### c) Translation of abbreviations

Abbreviations are normally translated by the corresponding abbreviation in the other language.

### c) Die Übersetzung von Abkürzungen

Abkürzungen erhalten normalerweise die entsprechende Abkürzung in der Zielsprache als Übersetzung.

Examples/Beispiele: **e.g.** ... z. B.

**GDR** ... DDR, *die*

**WEZ** ... GMT

**usw.** ... etc.

Where an abbreviation is best translated by one or more complete words, then they are given.

Wenn die gebräuchlichste zielsprachliche Entsprechung einer ausgangssprachlichen Abkürzung jedoch keine Abkürzung ist, wird als Übersetzung statt einer zielsprachlichen Abkürzung diese Entsprechung angegeben.

Examples/Beispiele: **s.a.e.** ... adressierter Freiumschlag

**GPO** ... Post, *die*

**Pkw** ... [private] car

**WC** ... toilet

If there is no corresponding abbreviation in the other language, the full form is translated or explained if not itself entered in the Dictionary.

Gibt es zu einer Abkürzung keine entsprechende Abkürzung in der Zielsprache, wird die volle Form angegeben und mit einer Übersetzung oder Erklärung versehen, sofern diese Vollform nicht selbst im Wörterverzeichnis zu finden ist.

Examples/Beispiele: **GCSE** ... **General Certificate of Secondary Education**

**FA** ... **Football Association** (*Britischer Fußballverband*)

**MA** ... **Mittelalter**

**ZDF** ... **Zweites Deutsches Fernsehen** Second German Television Channel

### d) Further information given with translations

Where necessary, translations are accompanied by information on usage, word order, etc.

The prepositions typically following verbs are given and translated.

### d) Zusätzliche Angaben bei Übersetzungen

Wo es nötig ist, sind die Übersetzungen mit Hinweisen zu ihrer Gebrauchsweise, ihrer Stellung im Satz usw. versehen.

Bei Verben wird der präpositionale Anschluss des Stichworts angegeben und übersetzt.

Examples/Beispiele: **conceal** ... verbergen (**from** vor + *Dat.*)

**sinnieren** ... ponder (**über** + *Akk.* over); muse (**über** + *Akk.* [up]on)

Where a German verb takes a case other than the accusative, this is shown, together with any English preposition used to 'translate' it.

Ebenso wird bei deutschen Verben der zum Anschluss an das Stichwort verwendete Kasus samt der entsprechenden englischen Präposition angegeben, sofern es sich nicht um den bei transitiven Verben stets erforderlichen Akkusativ handelt.

Example/Beispiel: **verdächtigen** ... suspect (*Gen.* of)

The indication *nachgestellt* or *postpos.* means that a translation of an adjective always follows its noun. (This is not shown when the fact is clear from the position of a collocator, as described in 8 b.)

Bei Übersetzungen von Adjektiven besagt der Hinweis *nachgestellt* bzw. *postpos.*, dass die angegebene Übersetzung dem Substantiv nachgestellt werden muss. (Dieser Hinweis entfällt, wenn die Stellung eines Kollokators dies schon, wie unter 8 b beschrieben, zeigt.)

Examples/Beispiele: **friendless** ... ohne Freund[e] *nachgestellt*

**stahlhart** ... as hard as steel *postpos.*

English translations marked *postpos.* can also be used predicatively, e.g. **she is as hard as steel**.

The indication *attr.* or *attrib.* means that a translation can be used attributively and not predicatively.

Mit *postpos.* markierte englische Übersetzungen können auch prädikativ gebraucht werden (also: **she is as hard as steel**).

Die Angabe *attr.* bzw. *attrib.* weist darauf hin, dass die angegebene Übersetzung nur als Attribut und nicht als Prädikatsteil verwendet werden darf.

Examples/Beispiele: **preferable** ... vorzuziehend *attr.*

**achtseitig** ... eight-page *attrib.*

The indication *präd.* or *pred.* means that a translation can be used predicatively and not attributively.

Die Angabe *präd.* bzw. *pred.* weist umgekehrt darauf hin, dass die angegebene Übersetzung nur als Prädikatsteil und nicht als Attribut verwendet werden darf.

Examples/Beispiele: **preferable** ... vorzuziehen *präd.*

**irreparabel** ... beyond repair *pred.*

The indication *Pl.* or *pl.* means that a translation of a noun exists only in the plural (in that sense).

Bei Übersetzungen von Substantiven bedeutet der Hinweis *Pl.* bzw. *pl.*, dass die angegebene Übersetzung ein Pluraletantum ist.

Examples/Beispiele: **measles** ... Masern *Pl.*
**cost** ... Kosten *Pl.*

**Brille** ... glasses *pl.*
**Polizei** ... police *pl.*

In the English-German section, German nouns are given the appropriate definite article. If this is in parentheses, the noun is a proper noun which is used with the article only in certain circumstances.

Im englisch-deutschen Teil erhalten als Übersetzungen angegebene deutsche Substantive den bestimmten Artikel. Steht der Artikel in runden Klammern, handelt es sich bei dem Substantiv um einen Eigennamen, der nur unter gewissen Umständen mit dem Artikel verbunden wird.

Examples/Beispiele: **cow**[1] ... Kuh, *die*
**table** ... Tisch, *der*

**Italy** ... Italien (*das*)
**Eve** ... Eva (*die*)

The indication *no art.* means that an English noun translation cannot be used with an article; *no def. art.* and *no indef. art.* mean that it cannot be used with a definite article and an indefinite article respectively.

Wenn Übersetzungen von deutschen Substantiven mit dem Hinweis *no art.* versehen sind, können sie nicht mit dem Artikel verbunden werden. Oft wird weiter differenziert zwischen *no def. art.* und *no indef. art.*

Example/Beispiel: **Ostermontag** ... Easter Monday *no def. art.*

Attributive use of an English noun is indicated by *attrib.* when it needs a separate translation.

Für den attributiven Gebrauch von englischen Substantiven wird oft eine eigene Übersetzung angegeben. Vor dieser Übersetzung steht dann der Hinweis *attrib.*

Examples/Beispiele: **marble** ... *attrib.* Marmor-
**mountain** ... *attrib.* Gebirgs-

## 9. Phrases

Following the general translation(s) of a headword are phrases in which the general translation(s) cannot be used. These include typical uses, fixed phrases, idioms, and proverbs. All are printed in bold serif type and are translated in their entirety. A swung dash is used to represent the headword.

## 9. Anwendungsbeispiele

Im Anschluss an die allgemeine[n] Übersetzung[en] des Stichworts werden Anwendungsbeispiele für Fälle gegeben, in denen die allgemeine Übersetzung nicht verwendbar ist. Außerdem werden typische Verwendungen des Stichworts, feste Wendungen, Redensarten und Sprichwörter gezeigt. Die Anwendungsbeispiele sind in halbfetter Times gedruckt und werden immer als Ganzes übersetzt. Innerhalb der Beispiele repräsentiert die Tilde das Stichwort.

Examples/Beispiele: **giggle** ... **have a ~ about sth.** ... **[a fit of] the ~s**

**knistern** ... **mit etw. ~** ... **eine ~de Atmosphäre**

In blocks of compounds, the swung dash in a phrase represents only the first element of the compound.

In Kompositablöcken steht auch in den Anwendungsbeispielen die Tilde immer nur für den ersten Bestandteil des Kompositums.

Examples/Beispiele: **apple:** ... **~ cart** ... **upset the ~ cart**

**selbst-**, **Selbst-:** ... **~bedienung** ... **hier ist ~bedienung**

Phrases and their translations can be given any of the labels mentioned in 6.

Die Anwendungsbeispiele und deren Übersetzungen werden gegebenenfalls mit den unter 6 erläuterten Kennzeichnungen versehen.

Examples/Beispiele: **corner** ... **cut ~s** (*fig.*)
**edge** ... **have/get the ~ [on sb./sth.]** (*coll.*)

**Strang** ... **über die Stränge schlagen** (*ugs.*)
**Kapitel** ... **das ist ein ~ für sich** (*fig.*)

In addition, any label attaching to a headword also applies to all phrases in that entry.

Außerdem gelten bereits für das Stichwort angegebene Kennzeichnungen auch für das Beispiel.

Examples/Beispiele: **beddy-byes** ... (*child lang.*) ... **off to ~**

**Schmäh** ... (*österr. ugs.*) ... **einen ~ führen**

To save space, phrases may be combined.

- Two complete phrases separated by a comma are synonymous and share a translation.

Aus Platzgründen werden oft mehrere Beispiele zusammengefasst.

- Wenn zwei vollständige Beispiele mit Komma aneinander gereiht sind, sind sie synonym und haben eine gemeinsame Übersetzung.

Examples/Beispiele: **cash** ... **pay [in] ~, pay ~ down** bar zahlen

**ausrasten** ... **er rastete aus, es rastete bei ihm aus** ... something snapped in him

– Where portions of a phrase or translation are separated by *or* or *od.*, they are synonymous and interchangeable.

– Wenn Teile eines Beispiels oder einer Übersetzung mit *or* bzw. *od.* aneinander gereiht sind, haben sie die gleiche Bedeutung und sind beliebig austauschbar.

Examples/Beispiele: **decision** ... **come to** *or* **arrive at** *or* **reach a ~:** zu einer Entscheidung kommen

**Bankrott** ... **seinen ~ anmelden** *od.* **ansagen** *od.* **erklären** declare oneself bankrupt

– Where portions of a phrase or translation are separated by a slash, they are syntactically interchangeable but have different meanings.

– Wenn Teile eines Beispiels bzw. seiner Übersetzung mit Schrägstrich aneinander gereiht sind, sind sie zwar syntaktisch austauschbar, haben aber nicht dieselbe Bedeutung.

Examples/Beispiele: **beginning** ... **at the ~ of February/the month** Anfang Februar/des Monats

**durchschaubar** ... **leicht/schwer ~ sein** be easy/difficult to see through

– Portions of a phrase and its translation in square brackets may be omitted, but always together, i.e. both phrase and translation are to be read either with or without the bracketed portions.

– Wenn Teile eines Beispiels und Teile seiner Übersetzung in eckigen Klammern stehen, stellen sie einen auslassbaren Zusatz zu dem Beispiel dar. Beispiel und Übersetzung müssen also beide entweder mit oder ohne den eingeklammerten Teil gelesen werden.

Examples/Beispiele: **clear** ... **make it ~ [to sb.] that** ...: [jmdm.] klar und deutlich sagen, dass ...

**verpflichten** ... **sich verpflichtet fühlen[, etw. zu tun]** feel obliged [to do sth.]

NB: Square brackets are also used generally to enclose optional elements of words and phrases, e.g. **choos[e]y**; **cost sb. dear[ly]**; **Wach[t]·turm**; **er vermochte [es] nicht, mich zu überzeugen**.

In phrases and their translations, *jmd., jmds., jmdm., jmdn., sb.* and *sb.'s* stand for any noun or pronoun indicating one or more persons, and *etw., einer Sache* (genitive or dative), *sth.*, or *sth.'s* stand for any noun or pronoun indicating one or more things.

NB: Eckige Klammern werden außerdem generell dazu verwendet, beliebig auslassbare Teile von Wörtern und Sätzen einzuklammern, z.B. **choos[e]y**; **cost sb. dear[ly]**; **Wach[t]·turm**; **er vermochte [es] nicht, mich zu überzeugen**.

In den Anwendungsbeispielen und ihren Übersetzungen werden Substantive und Pronomen, die Personen im weitesten Sinne bezeichnen, durch die Abkürzungen *jmd., jmds., jmdm., jmdn.* auf der deutschen und *sb., sb.'s* auf der englischen Seite vertreten. Substantive und Pronomen, die Sachen im weitesten Sinne bezeichnen, werden durch die Abkürzungen *etw.* (oder auch *einer Sache* im Genitiv und Dativ) auf der deutschen und *sth., sth.'s* auf der englischen Seite vertreten.

Example/Beispiel: **Ohr** ... **jmdm. etw. ins ~ flüstern** whisper sth. in sb.'s ear

In German phrases and translations, the reflexive pronoun *sich* is accusative unless it is marked (*Dat.*) ( = dative) or could only be dative, e.g. **etw. von sich geben; jmdm./sich Kühlung zufächeln**.

In phrases and their translations, stress which is unusual or affects meaning is shown using the symbols explained in 4.

In deutschen Anwendungsbeispielen und Übersetzungen ist das Wort *sich* ein Akkusativ, wenn es nicht mit (*Dat.*) gekennzeichnet ist oder aufgrund des Kontextes eindeutig Dativ ist (wie etwa in **etw. von sich geben; jmdm./sich Kühlung zufächeln**.).

Ungewöhnliche oder bedeutungsverändernde Betonungen werden bei Anwendungsbeispielen und deren Übersetzungen mithilfe der unter 4 erklärten Betonungszeichen angegeben.

Examples/Beispiele: **that** ... **he is 'like ~**

**somit** ... **und somit kommen wir zu Punkt 3**

In English phrases, *you, your, yourself*, etc. are generally translated as the 'familiar' *du, dich, dein*, etc. The more formal *Sie, Ihnen, Ihr*, etc. are used only when they are more appropriate for a given example. Similarly, the English colloquial contractions *can't, won't*, etc. are frequently used. In all cases it is up to the user to decide which forms are required by the context being translated.

Bei der Übersetzung von englischen Beispielsätzen ins Deutsche werden die Anrede *you* und ihre Formen im Allgemeinen durch das vertraulichere *du* und seine Formen wiedergegeben. Das förmlichere *Sie* wird nur verwendet, wenn das jeweilige Beispiel dies nahelegt. Ähnlich wird im Englischen häufig die umgangssprachliche Kurzform (z. B. *can't, won't, hasn't*) verwendet. Grundsätzlich bleibt es dem Benutzer überlassen, die Form dem Zweck und Kontext entsprechend zu wählen, für den die Übersetzung benötigt wird.

## 10. Cross references

Cross references beginning with ⇨ which take the place of a translation refer to a headword at which the translation is to be found. This kind of cross reference occurs mainly in the following circumstances:

– with synonyms

## 10. Verweise

Verweise mit ⇨ anstelle einer Übersetzung weisen auf ein anderes Stichwort, unter dem die Übersetzung zu finden ist. Diese Art von Verweis findet sich vor allem in den folgenden Fällen:

– bei Synonymen

Examples/Beispiele: **false move** ⇨ **false step**

**fortbringen** ... ⇨ **wegbringen**

– with variant spellings

– bei Wörtern mit mehreren Schreibweisen

Examples/Beispiele: **beduin** ⇨ **bedouin**

**winklig** ... ⇨ **winkelig**

– with masculine and feminine forms of a German noun which have the same translation.

– bei weiblichen und männlichen Formen eines deutschen Substantivs, die im Englischen die gleiche Übersetzung haben.

Example/Beispiel: **Primanerin** ... ⇨ **Primaner**

Cross references beginning with ⇨ which are followed by a colon and a list of translations occasionally occur at derivatives, such as nouns and adverbs derived from adjectives. They refer the user to the entry containing the indicators and collocators necessary for distinguishing the translations.

Verweise mit ⇨, die vor einer Reihe von Übersetzungen stehen, treten gelegentlich bei Ableitungen auf, z. B. bei Substantiven oder Adverbien, die von einem Adjektiv abgeleitet sind. Sie zeigen, wo die Indikatoren und Kollokatoren, die zur Unterscheidung der Übersetzungen nötig sind, zu finden sind.

Examples/Beispiele: **cogent** ... *adj.* (*convincing*) überzeugend ‹Argument, Grund›; zwingend ‹Grund›; (*valid*) stichhaltig ‹Kritik, Analyse›

**cogently** ... *adv.* ⇨ **cogent:** überzeugend; zwingend; stichhaltig

**verbreiten** ❶ *tr. V.* **A** (*bekannt machen*) spread ‹rumour, lies, etc.›; ... **B** (*weit ertragen*) spread ‹disease, illness, etc.›; disperse ‹seeds, spores, etc.›; **C** (*erwecken*) radiate ‹optimism, happiness, calm, etc.›; spread ‹fear›

**Verbreitung** *die;* ~, ~**en** **A** ⇨ **verbreiten 1 A, B, C:** spreading; ... dispersal; radiation

Cross references beginning with ⇨ *also* or ⇨ *auch* refer to headwords at which further information may be found. They either help the user to find a phrase or idiom (see also 1 c) or refer to an entry which serves as a model for a set of words because it is treated more comprehensively.

Verweise mit ⇨ *also* bzw. ⇨ *auch* weisen auf ein Stichwort hin, unter dem zusätzliche Informationen gefunden werden können. Diese Art von Verweis dient entweder zum Auffinden von festen Wendungen usw. (vgl. 1 c) oder weist auf ein Stichwort hin, das als Muster für einen bestimmten Typ besonders ausführlich behandelt wurde.

Examples/Beispiele: **Taurus** ... ⇨ *also* **Aries**

**Französisch** ... ⇨ *auch* **Deutsch**

Cross references consisting of ▶ and a page number direct the user to usage boxes which contain additional help and information, for example highlighting differences between German and English which may create difficulty for the learner and translator, or giving key facts about sets of words which behave alike, such as numbers or names of countries.

Verweise der Form ▶ + Seitenzahl weisen auf Info-Boxen hin, in denen weitere Informationen und Hilfen zu finden sind. Dort werden z. B. Fälle behandelt, in denen strukturelle Unterschiede zwischen dem Deutschen und dem Englischen Schwierigkeiten bereiten können, oder es finden sich grundlegende Informationen zum Gebrauch bestimmter Wortkategorien, deren Vertreter alle im Wesentlichen gleich „funktionieren", wie etwa die Zahlen oder die Ländernamen.

Examples/Beispiele: **French** ... ▶ 1275, ▶ 1340

**eins** ... ▶ 76, ▶ 752, ▶ 841

# Die für das Deutsche verwendeten Zeichen der Lautschrift / Phonetic symbols used in transcriptions of German words

| | | |
|---|---|---|
| a | hat | hat |
| a: | Bahn | ba:n |
| ɐ | Ober | 'o:bɐ |
| ɐ̯ | Uhr | u:ɐ̯ |
| ã | Grand Prix | grã'pri: |
| ã: | Abonnement | abɔnə'mã: |
| a͜i | weit | va͜it |
| a͜u | Haut | ha͜ut |
| b | Ball | bal |
| ç | ich | ɪç |
| d | dann | dan |
| d͜ʒ | Gin | d͜ʒɪn |
| e | Methan | me'ta:n |
| e: | Beet | be:t |
| ɛ | mästen | 'mɛstn̩ |
| ɛ: | wählen | 'vɛ:lən |
| ɛ̃ | Ragoût fin | ragu'fɛ̃ |
| ɛ̃: | Timbre | 'tɛ̃:br(ə) |
| ə | Nase | 'na:zə |
| f | Fass | fas |
| g | Gast | gast |
| h | hat | hat |
| i | vital | vi'ta:l |
| i: | viel | fi:l |
| i̯ | Studie | 'ʃtu:di̯ə |
| ɪ | Birke | 'bɪrkə |
| j | ja | ja: |
| k | kalt | kalt |
| l | Last | last |
| l̩ | Nabel | 'na:bl̩ |
| m̩ | Mast | mast |
| n | Naht | na:t |
| n̩ | baden | 'ba:dn̩ |
| ŋ | lang | laŋ |
| o | Moral | mo'ra:l |
| o: | Boot | bo:t |
| o̯ | loyal | lo̯a'ja:l |
| õ | Fondue | fõ'dy: |
| õ: | Fond | fõ: |
| ɔ | Post | pɔst |
| ø | Ökonom | øko'no:m |
| ø: | Öl | ø:l |
| œ | göttlich | 'gœtlɪç |
| œ̃: | Parfum | par'fœ̃: |
| ɔ͜y | Heu | hɔ͜y |
| p | Pakt | pakt |
| p͜f | Pfahl | p͜fa:l |
| r | Rast | rast |
| s | Hast | hast |
| ʃ | schal | ʃa:l |
| t | Tal | ta:l |
| t͜s | Zahl | t͜sa:l |
| t͜ʃ | Matsch | mat͜ʃ |
| u | kulant | ku'lant |
| u: | Hut | hu:t |
| u̯ | aktuell | ak'tu̯ɛl |
| ʊ | Pult | pʊlt |
| v | was | vas |
| x | Bach | bax |
| y | Physik | fy'zi:k |
| y: | Rübe | 'ry:bə |
| y̌ | Nuance | 'ny̌ã:sə |
| ʏ | Fülle | 'fʏlə |
| z | Hase | 'ha:zə |
| ʒ | Genie | ʒe'ni: |

| | | |
|---|---|---|
| \| | Glottal stop, e.g. Aa /a'\|a/. | Stimmritzenverschlusslaut („Knacklaut"), z. B. Aa /a'\|a/. |
| : | Length sign, indicating that the preceding vowel is long, e.g. Chrom /kro:m/. | Längezeichen, bezeichnet Länge des unmittelbar davor stehenden Vokals, z. B. Chrom /kro:m/. |
| ˜ | Indicates a nasal vowel, e.g. Fond /fõ:/. | Zeichen für nasale Vokale, z. B. Fond /fõ:/. |
| ' | Stress mark, immediately preceding a stressed syllable, e.g. Ballon /ba'lɔŋ/. | Betonung, steht unmittelbar vor einer betonten Silbe, z. B. Ballon /ba'lɔŋ/. |
| ˌ | Sign placed below a syllabic consonant, e.g. Büschel /'bʏʃl̩/. | Zeichen für silbischen Konsonanten, steht unmittelbar unter dem Konsonanten, z. B. Büschel /'bʏʃl̩/. |
| ˆ | Placed above or below a symbol indicates a non-syllabic vowel, e.g. Milieu /mi'li̯ø:/. | Halbkreis, untergesetzt oder übergesetzt, bezeichnet unsilbischen Vokal, z. B. Milieu /mi'li̯ø:/. |

# Die für das Englische verwendeten Zeichen der Lautschrift / Phonetic symbols used in transcriptions of English words

| | | | | | |
|---|---|---|---|---|---|
| ɑ: | bah | bɑ: | m | mat | mæt |
| ɑ̃ | ensemble | ɑ̃'sɑ̃mbl | n | not | nɒt |
| æ | fat | fæt | ŋ | sing | sɪŋ |
| æ̃ | lingerie | 'læ̃ʒərɪ | ɒ | got | gɒt |
| aɪ | fine | faɪn | ɔ: | paw | pɔ: |
| aʊ | now | naʊ | ɔ̃ | fait accompli | feɪt æ'kɔ̃pli: |
| b | bat | bæt | ɔɪ | boil | bɔɪl |
| d | dog | dɒg | p | pet | pet |
| dʒ | jam | dʒæm | r | rat | ræt |
| e | met | met | s | sip | sɪp |
| eɪ | fate | feɪt | ʃ | ship | ʃɪp |
| eə | fairy | 'feərɪ | t | tip | tɪp |
| əʊ | goat | gəʊt | tʃ | chin | tʃɪn |
| ə | ago | ə'gəʊ | θ | thin | θɪn |
| ɜ: | fur | fɜ:(r) | ð | the | ðə |
| f | fat | fæt | u: | boot | bu:t |
| g | good | gʊd | ʊ | book | bʊk |
| h | hat | hæt | ʊə | tourist | 'tʊərɪst |
| ɪ | bit, lately | bɪt, 'leɪtlɪ | ʌ | dug | dʌg |
| ɪə | nearly | 'nɪəlɪ | v | van | væn |
| i: | meet | mi:t | w | win | wɪn |
| j | yet | jet | x | loch | lɒx |
| k | kit | kɪt | z | zip | zɪp |
| l | lot | lɒt | ʒ | vision | 'vɪʒn |

| | | |
|---|---|---|
| : | Length sign, indicating that the preceding vowel is long, e.g. boot /bu:t/. | Längezeichen, bezeichnet Länge des unmittelbar davor stehenden Vokals, z. B. boot /bu:t/. |
| ' | Stress mark, immediately preceding a stressed syllable, e.g. ago /ə'gəʊ/. | Betonung, steht unmittelbar vor einer betonten Silbe, z. B. ago /ə'gəʊ/. |
| (r) | An 'r' in parentheses is pronounced only when immediately followed by a vowel sound, e.g. pare /peə(r)/; pare away /peər ə'weɪ/. | Ein „r" in runden Klammern wird nur gesprochen, wenn im Textzusammenhang ein Vokal unmittelbar folgt, z. B. pare /peə(r)/; pare away /peər ə'weɪ/. |

# Im Wörterverzeichnis verwendete deutsche Abkürzungen / German abbreviations used in this Dictionary

| | |
|---|---|
| **a.** | ander... |
| **ä.** | ähnlich... |
| **Abk.** | Abkürzung |
| **adj.** | adjektivisch |
| **Adj.** | Adjektiv |
| **adv.** | adverbial |
| **Adv.** | Adverb |
| **Akk.** | Akkusativ |
| **amerik.** | amerikanisch |
| **Amtsspr.** | Amtssprache |
| **Anat.** | Anatomie |
| **Anthrop.** | Anthropologie |
| **Archäol.** | Archäologie |
| **Archit.** | Architektur |
| **Art.** | Artikel |
| **Astrol.** | Astrologie |
| **Astron.** | Astronomie |
| **A.T.** | Altes Testament |
| **attr.** | attributiv |
| **Desspr.** | Aussprache |
| **Bauw.** | Bauwesen |
| **Bergmannsspr.** | Bergmannssprache |
| **berlin.** | berlinisch |
| **bes.** | besonders |
| **Bez.** | Bezeichnung |
| **bibl.** | biblisch |
| **bild. Kunst** | bildende Kunst |
| **Biol.** | Biologie |
| **Bodenk.** | Bodenkunde |
| **Börsenw.** | Börsenwesen |
| **Bot.** | Botanik |
| **BRD** | Bundesrepublik Deutschland |
| **brit.** | britisch |
| **Bruchz.** | Bruchzahl |
| **Buchf.** | Buchführung |
| **Buchw.** | Buchwesen |
| **Bürow.** | Bürowesen |
| **chem.** | chemisch |
| **christl.** | christlich |
| **Dat.** | Dativ |
| **DDR** | Deutsche Demokratische Republik |
| **Dekl.** | Deklination |
| **Demonstrativpron.** | Demonstrativpronomen |
| **d.h.** | das heißt |
| **dichter.** | dichterisch |
| **Druckerspr.** | Druckersprache |
| **Druckw.** | Druckwesen |
| **dt.** | deutsch |
| **DV** | Datenverarbeitung |
| **ehem.** | ehemals, ehemalig... |
| **Eisenb.** | Eisenbahn |
| **elektr.** | elektrisch |
| **Elektrot.** | Elektrotechnik |
| **Energievers.** | Energieversorgung |
| **Energiewirtsch.** | Energiewirtschaft |
| **engl.** | englisch |
| **etw.** | etwas |
| **ev.** | evangelisch |
| **fachspr.** | fachsprachlich |
| **fam.** | familiär |
| **Fem.** | Femininum |
| **Ferns.** | Fernsehen |
| **Fernspr.** | Fernsprechwesen |
| **fig.** | figurativ |
| **Finanzw.** | Finanzwesen |
| **Fischereiw.** | Fischereiwesen |
| **Fliegerspr.** | Fliegersprache |
| **Flugw.** | Flugwesen |
| **Forstw.** | Forstwesen |
| **Fot.** | Fotografie |
| **Frachtw.** | Frachtwesen |
| **Funkw.** | Funkwesen |
| **Gastr.** | Gastronomie |
| **Gattungsz.** | Gattungszahl |
| **Gaunerspr.** | Gaunersprache |
| **geh.** | gehoben |
| **Gen.** | Genitiv |
| **Geneal.** | Genealogie |
| **Geogr.** | Geographie |
| **Geol.** | Geologie |
| **Geom.** | Geometrie |
| **Handarb.** | Handarbeit |
| **Handw.** | Handwerk |
| **Hausw.** | Hauswirtschaft |
| **Her.** | Heraldik |
| **hess.** | hessisch |
| **Hilfsv.** | Hilfsverb |
| **hist.** | historisch |
| **Hochschulw.** | Hochschulwesen |
| **Holzverarb.** | Holzverarbeitung |
| **Indefinitpron.** | Indefinitpronomen |
| **indekl.** | indeklinabel |
| **Indik.** | Indikativ |
| **Inf.** | Infinitiv |
| **Informationst.** | Informationstechnik |
| **Interj.** | Interjektion |
| **iron.** | ironisch |
| **intr.** | intransitiv |
| **Jagdw.** | Jagdwesen |
| **Jägerspr.** | Jägersprache |
| **jmd.** | jemand |
| **jmdm.** | jemandem |
| **jmdn.** | jemanden |
| **jmds.** | jemandes |
| **Jugendspr.** | Jugendsprache |
| **jur.** | juristisch |
| **Kardinalz.** | Kardinalzahl |
| **kath.** | katholisch |
| **Kaufmannsspr.** | Kaufmannssprache |
| **Kfz.-W.** | Kraftfahrzeugwesen |
| **Kinderspr.** | Kindersprache |
| **Kochk.** | Kochkunst |
| **Konj.** | Konjunktion |
| **Kosew.** | Kosewort |
| **Kunstwiss.** | Kunstwissenschaft |
| **Kurzf.** | Kurzform |
| **Kurzw.** | Kurzwort |
| **landsch.** | landschaftlich |
| **Landw.** | Landwirtschaft |
| **Literaturw.** | Literaturwissenschaft |
| **Luftf.** | Luftfahrt |
| **ma.** | mittelalterlich |
| **MA.** | Mittelalter |
| **marx.** | marxistisch |
| **Mask.** | Maskulinum |
| **Math.** | Mathematik |
| **Mech.** | Mechanik |
| **Med.** | Medizin |
| **Meeresk.** | Meereskunde |
| **Met.** | Meteorologie |
| **Metall.** | Metallurgie |
| **Metallbearb.** | Metallbearbeitung |
| **Milit.** | Militär |
| **Mineral.** | Mineralogie |
| **mod.** | modifizierend |
| **Modalv.** | Modalverb |
| **Münzk.** | Münzkunde |
| **Mus.** | Musik |
| **Mythol.** | Mythologie |
| **Naturw.** | Naturwissenschaft |
| **Neutr.** | Neutrum |
| **niederdt.** | niederdeutsch |
| **Nom.** | Nominativ |
| **nordamerik.** | nordamerikanisch |
| **nordd.** | norddeutsch |
| **nordostd.** | nordostdeutsch |
| **nordwestd.** | nordwestdeutsch |

| | |
|---|---|
| **ns.** | nationalsozialistisch |
| **N.T.** | Neues Testament |
| **o.** | ohne; oben |
| **o. Ä.** | oder Ähnliches |
| **od.** | oder |
| **Ordinalz.** | Ordinalzahl |
| **orth.** | orthodox |
| **ostd.** | ostdeutsch |
| **österr.** | österreichisch |
| **Päd.** | Pädagogik |
| **Paläont.** | Paläontologie |
| **Papierdt.** | Papierdeutsch |
| **Parapsych.** | Parapsychologie |
| **Parl.** | Parlament |
| **Part.** | Partizip |
| **Perf.** | Perfekt |
| **Pers.** | Person |
| **pfälz.** | pfälzisch |
| **Pharm.** | Pharmazie |
| **Philat.** | Philatelie |
| **Philos.** | Philosophie |
| **Physiol.** | Physiologie |
| **Pl.** | Plural |
| **Plusq.** | Plusquamperfekt |
| **Polizeiw.** | Polizeiwesen |
| **Postw.** | Postwesen |
| **präd.** | prädikativ |
| **Prähist.** | Prähistorie |
| **Präp.** | Präposition |
| **Präs.** | Präsens |
| **Prät.** | Präteritum |
| **Pron.** | Pronomen |
| **Psych.** | Psychologie |
| **Raumf.** | Raumfahrt |
| **Rechtsspr.** | Rechtssprache |
| **Rechtsw.** | Rechtswesen |
| **refl.** | reflexiv |
| **regelm.** | regelmäßig |
| **Rel.** | Religion |
| **Relativpron.** | Relativpronomen |
| **rhein.** | rheinisch |
| **Rhet.** | Rhetorik |
| **röm.** | römisch |
| **röm.-kath.** | römisch-katholisch |
| **Rundf.** | Rundfunk |
| **s.** | siehe |
| **S.** | Seite |
| **scherzh.** | scherzhaft |
| **schles.** | schlesisch |
| **schott.** | schottisch |
| **Schülerspr.** | Schülersprache |
| **Schulw.** | Schulwesen |
| **schwäb.** | schwäbisch |
| **schweiz.** | schweizerisch |
| **Seemannsspr.** | Seemannssprache |
| **Seew.** | Seewesen |
| **Sexualk.** | Sexualkunde |
| **Sg.** | Singular |
| **s. o.** | siehe oben |
| **Soldatenspr.** | Soldatensprache |
| **Sozialpsych.** | Sozialpsychologie |
| **Sozialvers.** | Sozialversicherung |
| **Soziol.** | Soziologie |
| **spött.** | spöttisch |
| **Spr.** | Sprichwort |
| **Sprachw.** | Sprachwissenschaft |
| **Steuerw.** | Steuerwesen |
| **Stilk.** | Stilkunde |
| **Studentenspr.** | Studentensprache |
| **s.u.** | siehe unten |
| **Subj.** | Subjekt |
| **subst.** | substantivisch; substantiviert |
| **Subst.** | Substantiv |
| **südd.** | süddeutsch |
| **südwestd.** | südwestdeutsch |
| **Suff.** | Suffix |
| **Sup.** | Superlativ |
| **Textilw.** | Textilwesen |
| **Theol.** | Theologie |
| **thüring.** | thüringisch |
| **Tiermed.** | Tiermedizin |
| **tirol.** | tirolisch |
| **tr.** | transitiv |
| **Trenn.** | Trennung |
| **u.** | und |
| **u. a.** | und andere[s] |
| **u. Ä.** | und Ähnliches |
| **ugs.** | umgangssprachlich |
| **unbest.** | unbestimmt |
| **unpers.** | unpersönlich |
| **unr.** | unregelmäßig |
| **usw.** | und so weiter |
| **v.** | von |
| **V.** | Verb |
| **verächtl.** | verächtlich |
| **veralt.** | veraltet; veraltend |
| **Verhaltensf.** | Verhaltensforschung |
| **verhüll.** | verhüllend |
| **Verkehrsw.** | Verkehrswesen |
| **Vermessungsw.** | Vermessungswesen |
| **Versicherungsw.** | Versicherungs wesen |
| **vgl.** | vergleiche |
| **Vkl.** | Verkleinerungsform |
| **Völkerk.** | Völkerkunde |
| **Völkerr.** | Völkerrecht |
| **Volksk.** | Volkskunde |
| **volkst.** | volkstümlich |
| **vulg.** | vulgär |
| **Werbespr.** | Werbesprache |
| **westd.** | westdeutsch |
| **westfäl.** | westfälisch |
| **Wiederholungsz.** | Wiederholungszahlwort |
| **wiener.** | wienerisch |
| **Winzerspr.** | Winzersprache |
| **Wirtsch.** | Wirtschaft |
| **Wissensch.** | Wissenschaft |
| **Wz.** | Warenzeichen |
| **Zahnmed.** | Zahnmedizin |
| **z. B.** | zum Beispiel |
| **Zeitungsw.** | Zeitungswesen |
| **Zollw.** | Zollwesen |
| **Zool.** | Zoologie |
| **Zus.** | Zusammensetzung |
| **Zusschr.** | Zusammenschreibung |

# Im Wörterverzeichnis verwendete englische Abkürzungen / English abbreviations used in this Dictionary

| | |
|---|---|
| **abbr(s).** | abbreviation(s) |
| **abs.** | absolute |
| **adj(s).** | adjective(s) |
| **Admin.** | Administration, Administrative |
| **adv.** | adverb |
| **Aeronaut.** | Aeronautics |
| **Agric.** | Agriculture |
| **Alch.** | Alchemy |
| **Amer.** | American, America |
| **Anat.** | Anatomy |
| **Anglican Ch.** | Anglican Church |
| **Anglo-Ind.** | Anglo-Indian |
| **Ant.** | Antiquity |
| **Anthrop.** | Anthropology |
| **arch.** | archaic |
| **Archaeol.** | Archaeology |
| **Archit.** | Architecture |
| **art.** | article |
| **Astrol.** | Astrology |
| **Astron.** | Astronomy |
| **Astronaut.** | Astronautics |
| **attrib.** | attributive |
| **Austral.** | Australian, Australia |
| **Bacteriol.** | Bacteriology |
| **Bibl.** | Biblical |
| **Bibliog.** | Bibliography |
| **Biochem.** | Biochemistry |
| **Biol.** | Biology |
| **Bookk.** | Bookkeeping |
| **Bot.** | Botany |
| **Brit.** | British, Britain |
| **Can.** | Canadian, Canada |
| **Chem.** | Chemistry |
| **Cinemat.** | Cinematography |
| **coll.** | colloquial |
| **collect.** | collective |
| **comb.** | combination |
| **Commerc.** | Commerce, Commercial |
| **Communication Res.** | Communication Research |
| **compar.** | comparative |
| **condit.** | conditional |
| **conj.** | conjunction |
| **Constr.** | Construction |
| **constr.** | construed |
| **contr.** | contracted form |
| **def.** | definite |
| **Dent.** | Dentistry |
| **derog.** | derogatory |
| **dial.** | dialect |
| **Diplom.** | Diplomacy |
| **Dressm.** | Dressmaking |
| **Eccl.** | Ecclesiastical |
| **Ecol.** | Ecology |
| **Econ.** | Economics |
| **Educ.** | Education |
| **Electr.** | Electricity |
| **ellipt.** | elliptical |
| **emphat.** | emphatic |
| **esp.** | especially |
| **Ethnol.** | Ethnology |
| **Ethol.** | Ethology |
| **euphem.** | euphemistic |
| **excl.** | exclamation, exclamatory |
| **expr.** | expressing |
| **fem.** | feminine |
| **fig.** | figurative |
| **Footb.** | Football |
| **Gastr.** | Gastronomy |
| **Geneal.** | Genealogy |
| **Geog.** | Geography |
| **Geol.** | Geology |
| **Geom.** | Geometry |
| **Graph. Arts** | Graphic Arts |
| **Her.** | Heraldry |
| **Hist.** | History, Historical |
| **Horol.** | Horology |
| **Hort.** | Horticulture |
| **Hydraulic Engin.** | Hydraulic Engineering |
| **imper.** | imperative |
| **impers.** | impersonal |
| **incl.** | including |
| **Ind.** | Indian, India |
| **indef.** | indefinite |
| **Information Sci.** | Information Science |
| **int.** | interjection |
| **interrog.** | interrogative |
| **Int. Law** | International Law |
| **Ir.** | Irish, Ireland |
| **iron.** | ironical |
| **joc.** | jocular |
| **Journ.** | Journalism |
| **lang.** | language |
| **Ling.** | Linguistics |
| **Lit.** | Literature |
| **lit.** | literal |
| **Magn.** | Magnetism |
| **Managem.** | Management |
| **masc.** | masculine |
| **Math.** | Mathematics |
| **Mech.** | Mechanics |
| **Mech. Engin.** | Mechanical Engineering |
| **Med.** | Medicine |
| **Metalw.** | Metalwork |
| **Metaph.** | Metaphysics |
| **Meteorol.** | Meteorology |
| **Mil.** | Military |
| **Min.** | Mineralogy |
| **Motor Veh.** | Motor Vehicles |
| **Mount.** | Mountaineering |
| **Mus.** | Music |
| **Mythol.** | Mythology |
| **n.** | noun |
| **Nat. Sci.** | Natural Science |
| **Naut.** | Nautical |
| **neg.** | negative |
| **N. Engl.** | Northern English |
| **ns.** | nouns |
| **Nucl. Engin.** | Nuclear Engineering |
| **Nucl. Phys.** | Nuclear Physics |
| **Num.** | Numismatics |
| **N.Z.** | New Zealand |
| **obj.** | object |
| **Oceanog.** | Oceanography |
| **Ornith.** | Ornithology |
| **P** | Proprietary name |
| **Palaeont.** | Palaeontology |
| **Parapsych.** | Parapsychology |
| **Parl.** | Parliament |
| **pass.** | passive |
| **Pharm.** | Pharmacy |
| **Philat.** | Philately |
| **Philos.** | Philosophy |
| **Phonet.** | Phonetics |
| **Photog.** | Photography |
| **phr(s).** | phrase(s) |
| **Phys.** | Physics |
| **Physiol.** | Physiology |
| **pl.** | plural |
| **poet.** | poetical |
| **Polit.** | Politics |
| **poss.** | possessive |
| **postpos.** | postpositive |
| **p.p.** | past participle |
| **pred.** | predicative |
| **pref.** | prefix |
| **Prehist.** | Prehistory |

| | |
|---|---|
| **prep.** | preposition |
| **pres.** | present |
| **pres. p.** | present participle |
| **pr. n.** | proper noun |
| **pron.** | pronoun |
| **Pros.** | Prosody |
| **prov.** | proverbial |
| **Psych.** | Psychology |
| **p.t.** | past tense |
| **Railw.** | Railways |
| **RC Ch.** | Roman Catholic Church |
| **refl.** | reflexive |
| **rel.** | relative |
| **Relig.** | Religion |
| **Res.** | Research |
| **Rhet.** | Rhetoric |
| **rhet.** | rhetorical |
| **S. Afr.** | South African, South Africa |
| **sb.** | somebody |
| **Sch.** | School |
| **Sci.** | Science |
| **Scot.** | Scottish, Scotland |
| **Shipb.** | Shipbuilding |
| **sing.** | singular |
| **sl.** | slang |
| **Sociol.** | Sociology |
| **Soc. Serv.** | Social Services |
| **Soil Sci.** | Soil Science |
| **St. Exch.** | Stock Exchange |
| **sth.** | something |
| **subord.** | subordinate |
| **suf.** | suffix |
| **superl.** | superlative |
| **Surv.** | Surveying |
| **symb.** | symbol |
| **tech.** | technical |
| **Teleph.** | Telephony |
| **Telev.** | Television |
| **Theol.** | Theology |
| **Univ.** | University |
| **usu.** | usually |
| **v. aux.** | auxiliary verb |
| **Vet. Med.** | Veterinary Medicine |
| **v. i.** | intransitive verb |
| **voc.** | vocative |
| **v. refl.** | reflexive verb |
| **v. t.** | transitive verb |
| **v. t. & i.** | transitive and intransitive verb |
| **W. Ind.** | West Indian, West Indies |
| **Woodw.** | Woodwork |
| **Zool.** | Zoology |

# How do they work? Political systems and institutions / Wie funktionieren sie? Politische Systeme und Institutionen

A diagram can be worth a thousand words. One of the more difficult challenges facing the learner and the translator of German or English is to understand how the very different political institutions of each country work, in particular how the separate parts of each system fit together to form the whole. This kind of information, essential when reading, writing or talking about news and current affairs, is much more clearly represented in diagram form than by explanations or definitions. The following panels give a clear overview of the political systems of Germany, Austria, and Switzerland, the structure of the European Union, and the constitutions of the United Kingdom and the United States of America.

Ein Diagramm kann manchmal mehr als tausend Worte sagen. Ein nicht zu unterschätzendes Problem für jeden, der Englisch oder Deutsch lernt oder englische oder deutsche Texte zu übersetzen hat, besteht darin zu verstehen, wie die sehr unterschiedlichen politischen Institutionen in den betreffenden Ländern funktionieren, insbesondere wie die Teile des politischen Systems eines Landes zusammenhängen und ein Ganzes bilden. Solcherart Informationen, die man braucht, um über aktuelle politische Vorgänge lesen, schreiben oder sprechen zu können, lassen sich sehr viel klarer in einem Diagramm als durch Erklärungen oder Definitionen vermitteln.

Die folgenden Diagramme veranschaulichen das deutsche, das österreichische und das schweizerische politische System, den Aufbau der Europäischen Union und die Verfassungen des Vereinigten Königreichs und der Vereinigten Staaten von Amerika.

## Deutschland: Schematische Darstellung des politischen Systems

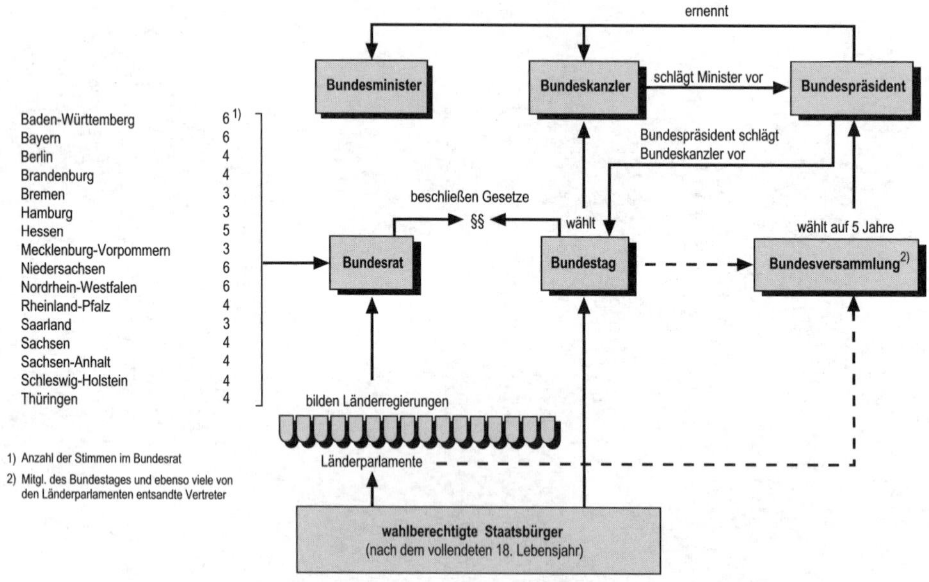

## Österreich: Politisches System

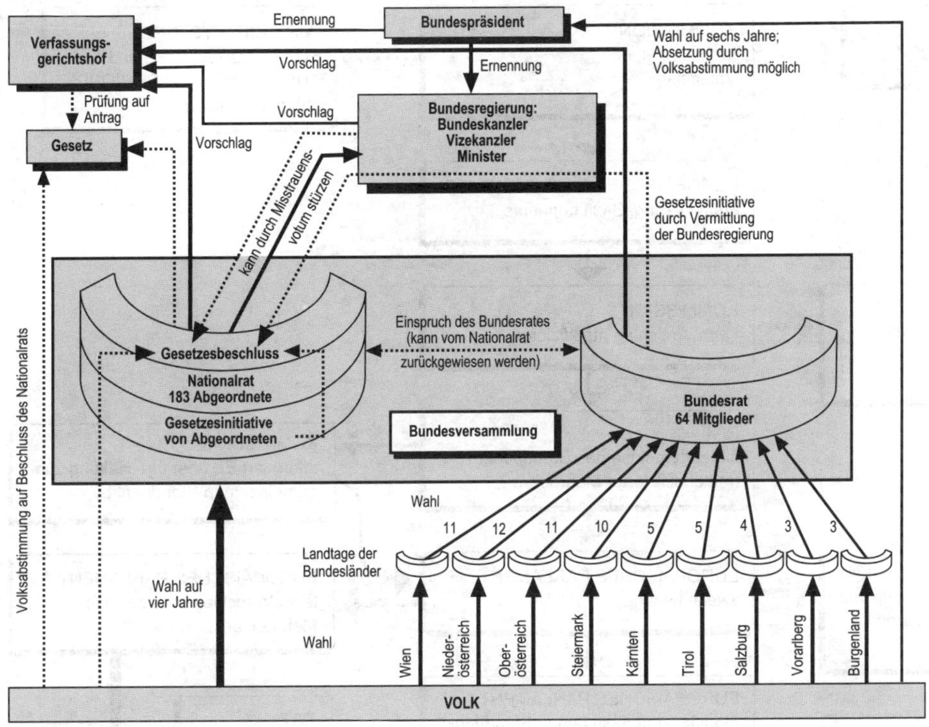


## Schweiz: Politisches System

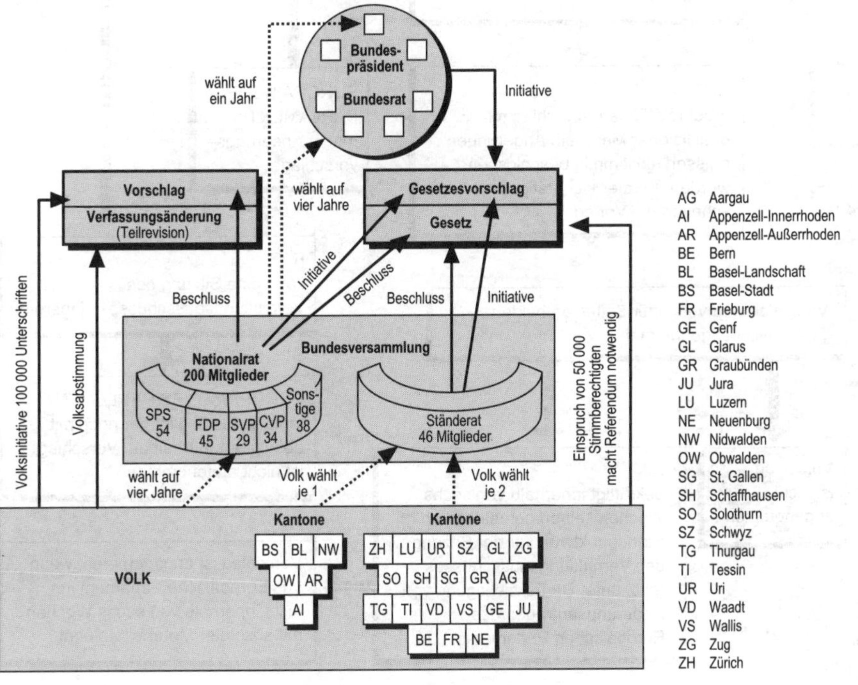


AG Aargau
AI Appenzell-Innerrhoden
AR Appenzell-Außerrhoden
BE Bern
BL Basel-Landschaft
BS Basel-Stadt
FR Frieburg
GE Genf
GL Glarus
GR Graubünden
JU Jura
LU Luzern
NE Neuenburg
NW Nidwalden
OW Obwalden
SG St. Gallen
SH Schaffhausen
SO Solothurn
SZ Schwyz
TG Thurgau
TI Tessin
UR Uri
VD Waadt
VS Wallis
ZG Zug
ZH Zürich

## Die Europäische Union: Gesetzgebungsverfahren

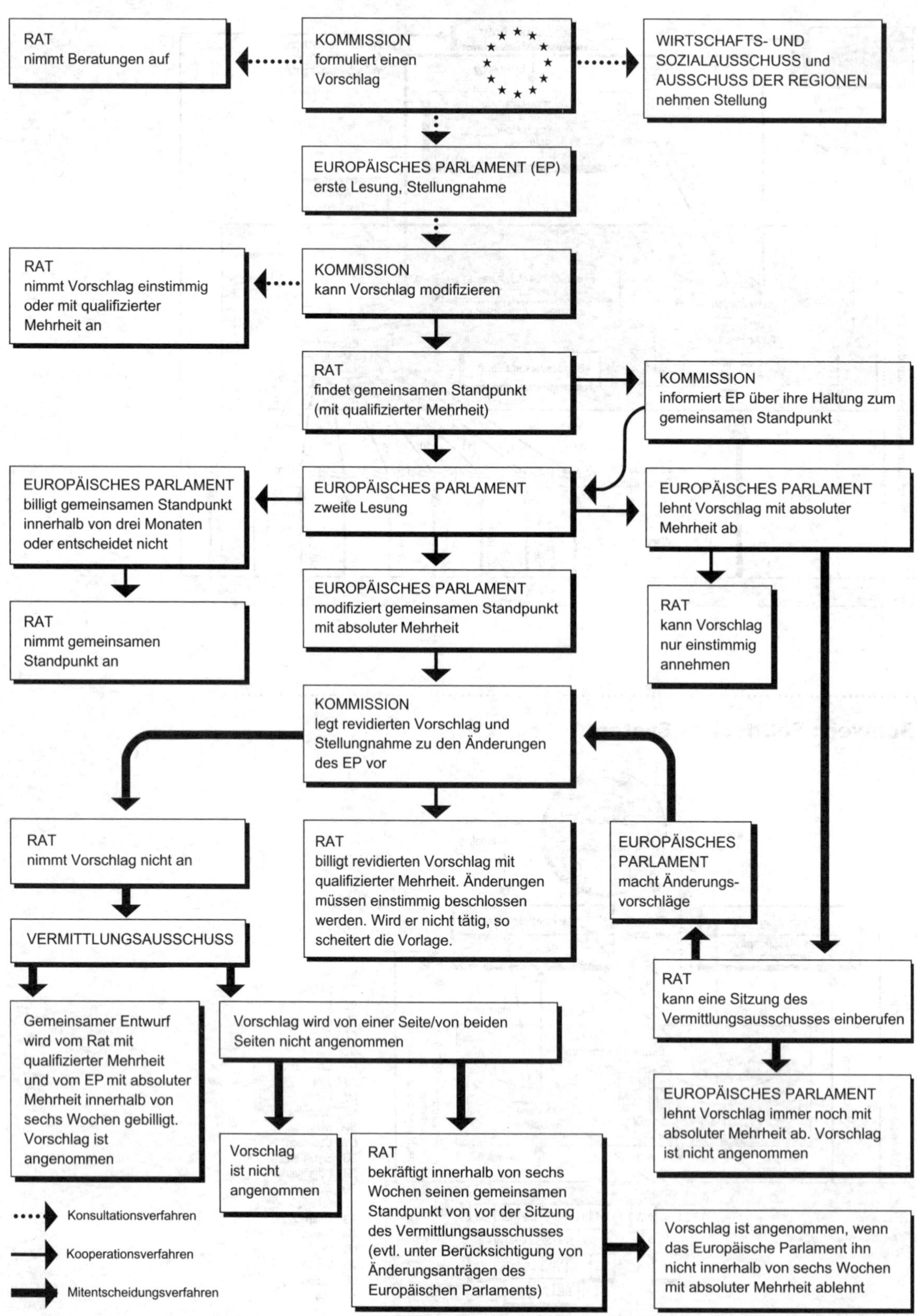
RAT
nimmt Beratungen auf
KOMMISSION
formuliert einen Vorschlag
WIRTSCHAFTS- UND SOZIALAUSSCHUSS und AUSSCHUSS DER REGIONEN nehmen Stellung
EUROPÄISCHES PARLAMENT (EP)
erste Lesung, Stellungnahme
RAT
nimmt Vorschlag einstimmig oder mit qualifizierter Mehrheit an
KOMMISSION
kann Vorschlag modifizieren
RAT
findet gemeinsamen Standpunkt (mit qualifizierter Mehrheit)
KOMMISSION
informiert EP über ihre Haltung zum gemeinsamen Standpunkt
EUROPÄISCHES PARLAMENT
billigt gemeinsamen Standpunkt innerhalb von drei Monaten oder entscheidet nicht
EUROPÄISCHES PARLAMENT
zweite Lesung
EUROPÄISCHES PARLAMENT
lehnt Vorschlag mit absoluter Mehrheit ab
RAT
nimmt gemeinsamen Standpunkt an
EUROPÄISCHES PARLAMENT
modifiziert gemeinsamen Standpunkt mit absoluter Mehrheit
RAT
kann Vorschlag nur einstimmig annehmen
KOMMISSION
legt revidierten Vorschlag und Stellungnahme zu den Änderungen des EP vor
RAT
nimmt Vorschlag nicht an
RAT
billigt revidierten Vorschlag mit qualifizierter Mehrheit. Änderungen müssen einstimmig beschlossen werden. Wird er nicht tätig, so scheitert die Vorlage.
EUROPÄISCHES PARLAMENT
macht Änderungsvorschläge
VERMITTLUNGSAUSSCHUSS
RAT
kann eine Sitzung des Vermittlungsausschusses einberufen
Gemeinsamer Entwurf wird vom Rat mit qualifizierter Mehrheit und vom EP mit absoluter Mehrheit innerhalb von sechs Wochen gebilligt. Vorschlag ist angenommen
Vorschlag wird von einer Seite/von beiden Seiten nicht angenommen
EUROPÄISCHES PARLAMENT
lehnt Vorschlag immer noch mit absoluter Mehrheit ab. Vorschlag ist nicht angenommen
Vorschlag ist nicht angenommen
RAT
bekräftigt innerhalb von sechs Wochen seinen gemeinsamen Standpunkt von vor der Sitzung des Vermittlungsausschusses (evtl. unter Berücksichtigung von Änderungsanträgen des Europäischen Parlaments)
Vorschlag ist angenommen, wenn das Europäische Parlament ihn nicht innerhalb von sechs Wochen mit absoluter Mehrheit ablehnt
Konsultationsverfahren
Kooperationsverfahren
Mitentscheidungsverfahren

## The European Union: Procedure for legislation

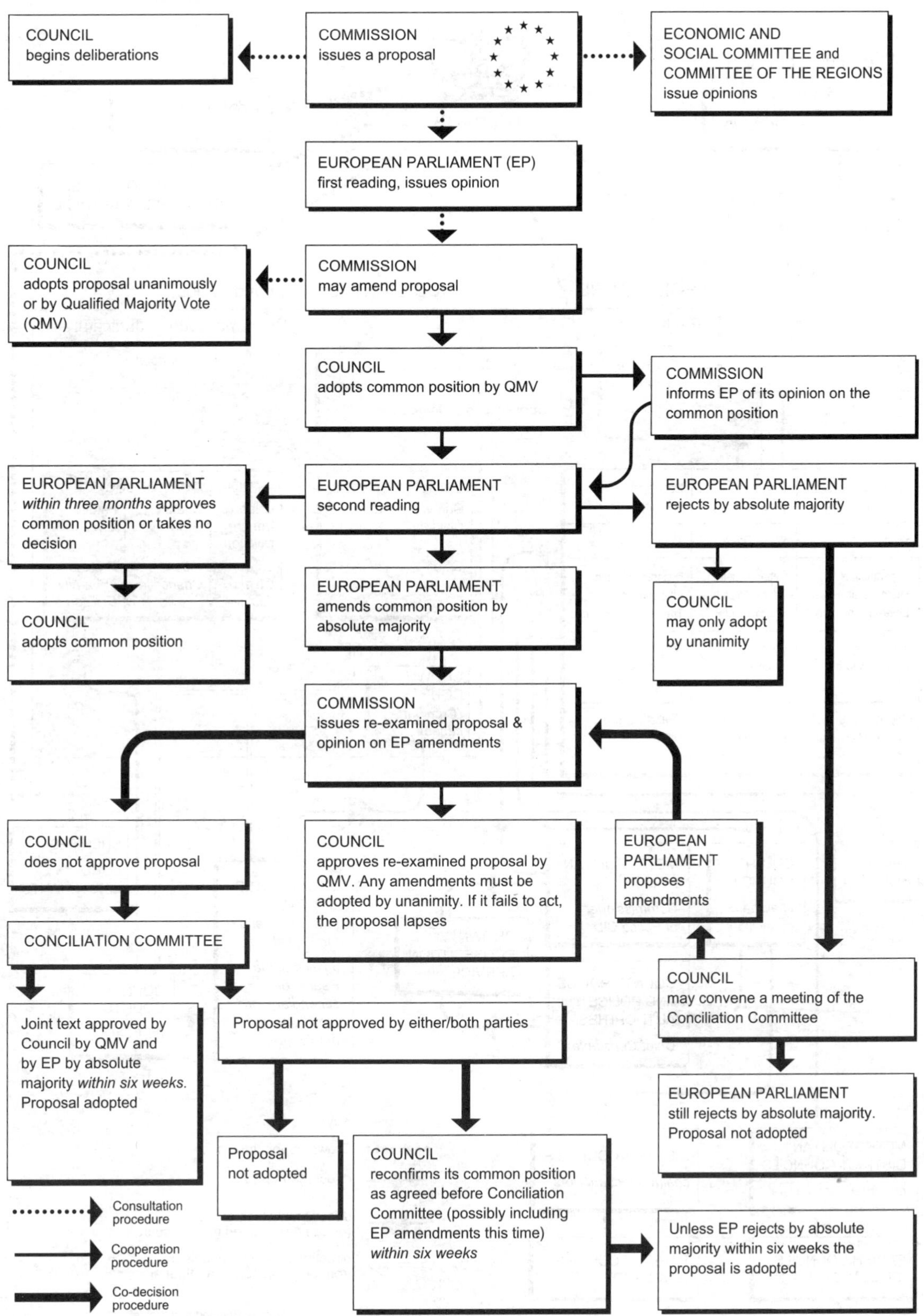

## The constitution of the United Kingdom

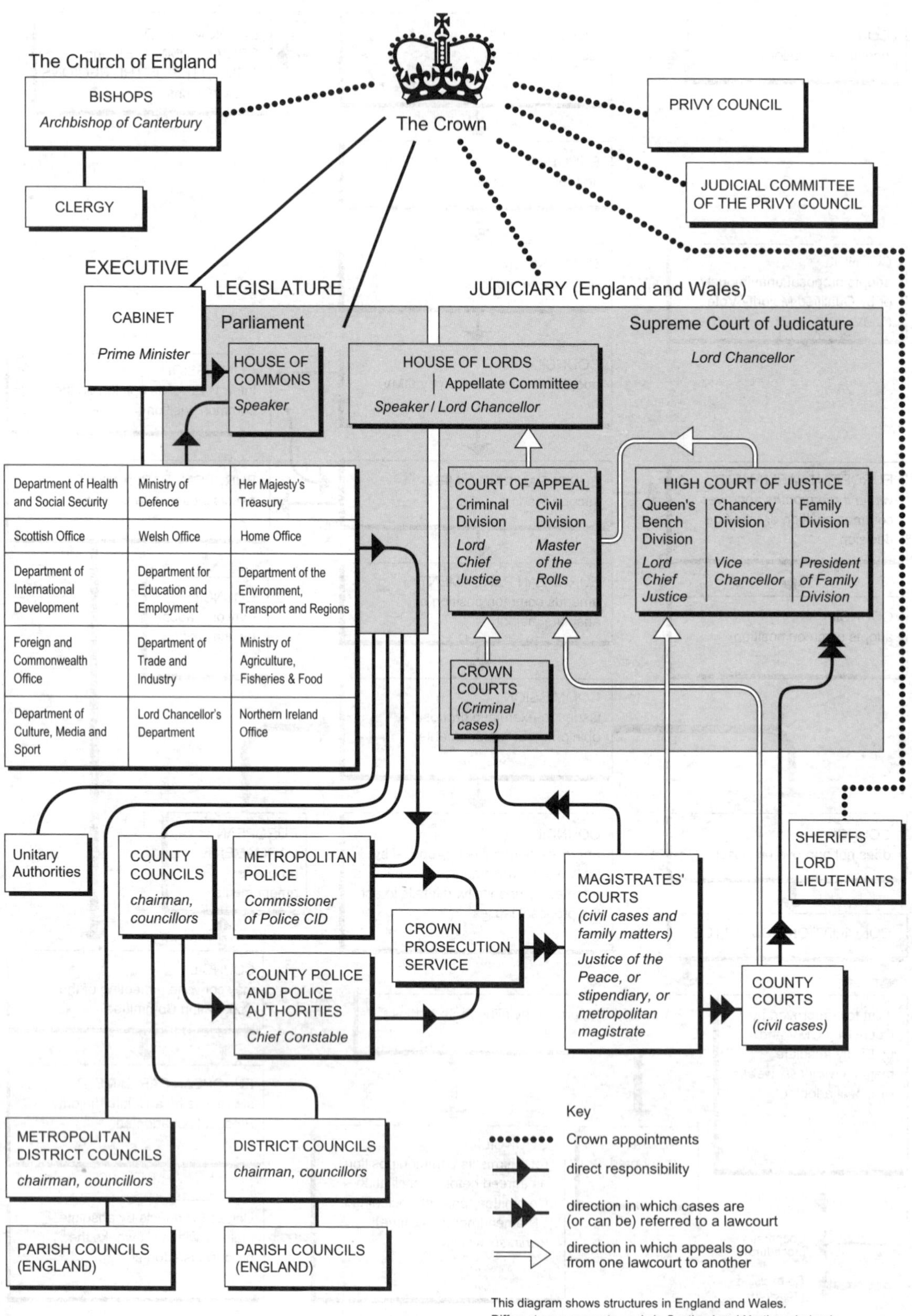


This diagram shows structures in England and Wales.
Different arrangements apply in Scotland and Northern Ireland.

## The US constitution

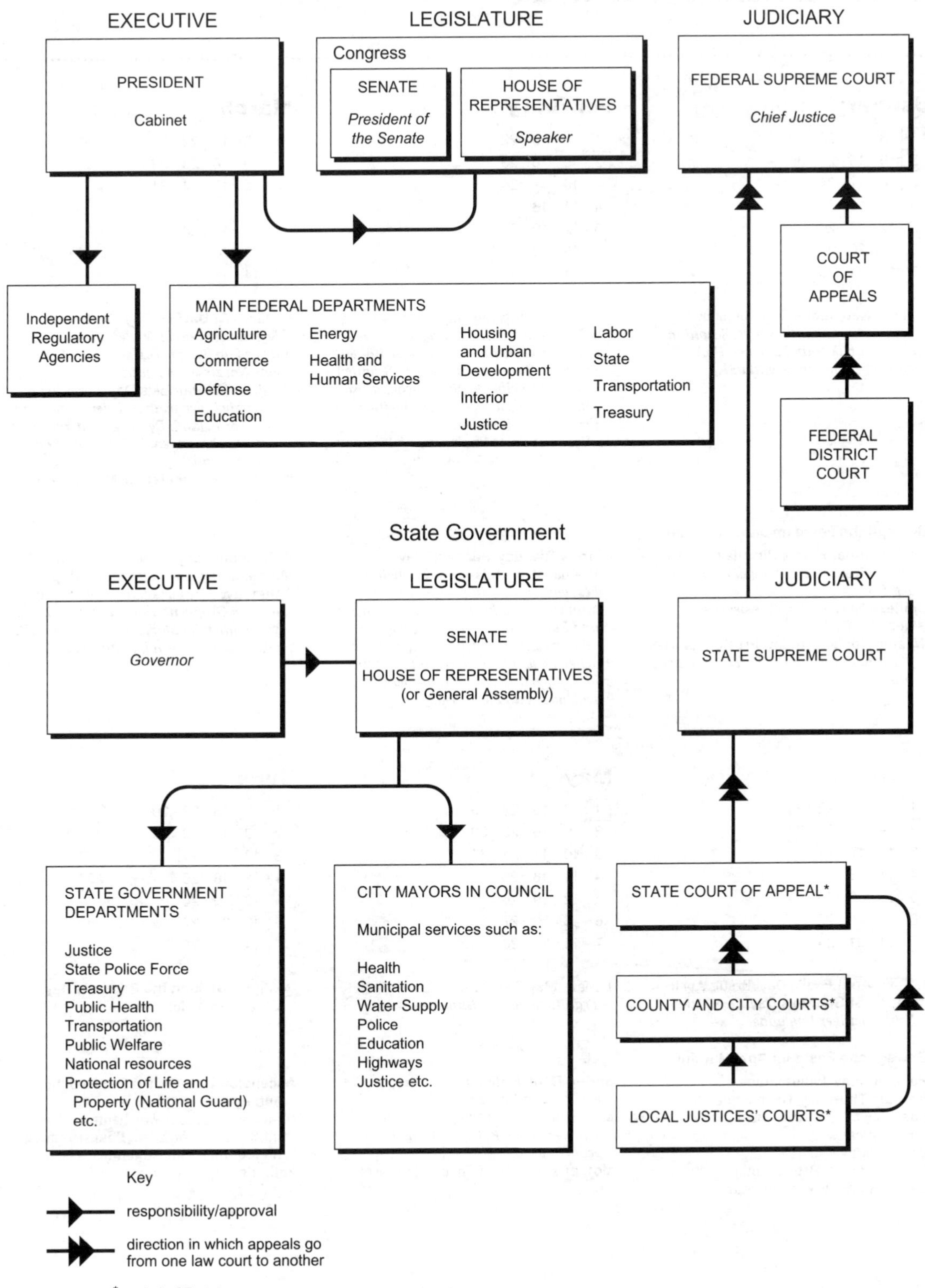

# Festtags-, Feiertags- und Brauchtumskalender

## January

1 8 15 22 29
2 9 16 23 30
3 10 17 24 31
4 11 18 25
5 12 19 26
6 13 20 27
7 14 21 28

1. Jan. – **New Year's Day** Neujahr. *Feiertag in England, Wales, Schottland, der Republik Irland und den USA.*
2. Jan. – *Feiertag in Schottland*

## February

1 8 15 22
2 9 16 23
3 10 17 24
4 11 18 25
5 12 19 26
6 13 20 27
7 14 21 28

2. Feb. – **Groundhog Day**. *An diesem Tag soll das Murmeltier aus dem Winterschlaf erwachen und aus seiner Höhle kommen. Wenn es dann seinen Schatten sieht – das heißt, die Sonne scheint – so soll dies sechs weitere Wochen winterliches Wetter bedeuten.*
14. Feb. – **St Valentine's Day** Valentinstag

## March

1 8 15 22 29
2 9 16 23 30
3 10 17 24 31
4 11 18 25
5 12 19 26
6 13 20 27
7 14 21 28

1. März – **St David's Day** Davidstag. *Schutzheiliger von Wales. Viele Waliser tragen an diesem Tag zu seinen Ehren eine Narzisse am Revers.*
17. März – **St Patrick's Day** Patrickstag. *Schutzheiliger Irlands. Feiertag in Irland und Nordirland. Der Tag wird auch in den USA begangen. In New York finden Umzüge statt.*
25. März – **Annunciation** Mariä Verkündigung

**Bewegliche Feste im Jan./Feb./März:**

**Martin Luther King's Birthday** Martin Luther Kings Geburtstag. *Feiertag in den USA.*
**Chinese New Year** Chinesisches Neujahrsfest
**Washington's Birthday/Presidents' Day** Washingtons Geburtstag. *Feiertag in den USA.*

**Shrove Tuesday/Pancake Day** Fastnachtsdienstag. *Traditionelles Fest vor dem Beginn der Fastenzeit. Man isst Pfannkuchen mit Zitronensaft und Zucker. Mancherorts werden "Pfannkuchenrennen" veranstaltet, bei denen es darum geht, einen Pfannkuchen im Laufen aus einer Pfanne herauszuschleudern und wieder aufzufangen.*

**Ash Wednesday** Aschermittwoch
**Mother's day** (UK – also **Mothering Sunday**) Muttertag. (*Der Muttertag wird in Großbritannien und Irland gewöhnlich im März, im deutschsprachigen Raum dagegen im Mai gefeiert.*)

## April

1 8 15 22 29
2 9 16 23 30
3 10 17 24
4 11 18 25
5 12 19 26
6 13 20 27
7 14 21 28

1. Apr. – **April Fool's Day** Erster April
23. Apr. – **St George's Day** Georgstag. *Schutzheiliger Englands.*

## May

1 8 15 22 29
2 9 16 23 30
3 10 17 24 31
4 11 18 25
5 12 19 26
6 13 20 27
7 14 21 28

1. Mai – **May Day** Erster Mai. *Traditionelles Frühlingsfest.*

## June

1 8 15 22 29
2 9 16 23 30
3 10 17 24
4 11 18 25
5 12 19 26
6 13 20 27
7 14 21 28

24. Juni – **St John the Baptist's Day** Johannistag, Johanni

**Bewegliche Feste im Apr./Mai/Juni:**

**Palm Sunday** Palmsonntag
**Maundy Thursday** Gründonnerstag
**First Day of Passover** Beginn des Passahfestes
**Good Friday** Karfreitag
**Easter** Ostern, Ostersonntag
**Easter Monday** Ostermontag

**Spring Bank Holiday*** *Feiertag in England und Wales.*
**Memorial Day** *Feiertag in den USA, an dem der in den Kriegen Gefallenen gedacht wird.*
**Mother's Day** (US, Canada) Muttertag

**Ascension Day** Christi Himmelfahrt, Auffahrt
**Shavuot** Schawout, Wochenfest
**Whit Sunday** Pfingsten, Pfingstsonntag
**Whit Monday** Pfingstmontag
**Father's Day** Vatertag

* **Bank Holiday:** Tag, an dem die Banken geschlossen sind (in England und Wales gewöhnlich gesetzlicher Feiertag).

## July

| | | | | |
|---|---|---|---|---|
| 1 | 8 | 15 | 22 | 29 |
| 2 | 9 | 16 | 23 | 30 |
| 3 | 10 | 17 | 24 | 31 |
| 4 | 11 | 18 | 25 | |
| 5 | 12 | 19 | 26 | |
| 6 | 13 | 20 | 27 | |
| 7 | 14 | 21 | 28 | |

4. Juli – **Independence Day** Unabhängigkeitstag. *Nationalfeiertag in den USA zur Feier der Unabhängigkeitserklärung des Jahres 1776. Traditionell mit Feuerwerken gefeiert.*

## August

| | | | | |
|---|---|---|---|---|
| 1 | 8 | 15 | 22 | 29 |
| 2 | 9 | 16 | 23 | 30 |
| 3 | 10 | 17 | 24 | 31 |
| 4 | 11 | 18 | 25 | |
| 5 | 12 | 19 | 26 | |
| 6 | 13 | 20 | 27 | |
| 7 | 14 | 21 | 28 | |

15. Aug. – **Assumption** Mariä Himmelfahrt

## September

| | | | | |
|---|---|---|---|---|
| 1 | 8 | 15 | 22 | 29 |
| 2 | 9 | 16 | 23 | 30 |
| 3 | 10 | 17 | 24 | |
| 4 | 11 | 18 | 25 | |
| 5 | 12 | 19 | 26 | |
| 6 | 13 | 20 | 27 | |
| 7 | 14 | 21 | 28 | |

**Bewegliche Feste im Juli/Aug./Sept.:**

**Summer Bank Holiday***. *Feiertag in England und Wales in Aug.*

**Labor Day** Tag der Arbeit. *Feiertag in den USA zu Ehren der arbeitenden Menschen.*

## October

| | | | | |
|---|---|---|---|---|
| 1 | 8 | 15 | 22 | 29 |
| 2 | 9 | 16 | 23 | 30 |
| 3 | 10 | 17 | 24 | 31 |
| 4 | 11 | 18 | 25 | |
| 5 | 12 | 19 | 26 | |
| 6 | 13 | 20 | 27 | |
| 7 | 14 | 21 | 28 | |

31. Okt. – **Halloween** Halloween. *Ursprünglich im Mittelalter ein religiöses Fest, das an Allerheiligen begangen wurde. Es wurden zur Vertreibung böser Geister und zum Geleit der Seelen der Toten, die an diesem Tag in ihre Häuser zurückkehren sollten, Feuer entzündet. Heute ein weltliches Fest, bei dem man sich – als Hexe, Geist usw. – verkleidet und maskiert. Aus ausgehöhlten Kürbissen, in die Löcher geschnitten sind, die Gesichtszüge andeuten sollen, stellt man Laternen her. Kinder spielen "Trick-or-Treat" – ein Brauch, bei dem Kinder an den Haustüren klingeln und böse Streiche androhen für den Fall, dass man ihnen nicht eine kleine Gabe mit auf den Weg gibt.*

## November

| | | | | |
|---|---|---|---|---|
| 1 | 8 | 15 | 22 | 29 |
| 2 | 9 | 16 | 23 | 30 |
| 3 | 10 | 17 | 24 | |
| 4 | 11 | 18 | 25 | |
| 5 | 12 | 19 | 26 | |
| 6 | 13 | 20 | 27 | |
| 7 | 14 | 21 | 28 | |

1. Nov. – **All Saints' Day** Allerheiligen
2. Nov. – **All Souls' Day** Allerseelen
5. Nov. – **Guy Fawkes/Bonfire Night** *Jahrestag des geplanten Sprengstoffanschlags auf das Parlament von 1605. Traditionell wird an diesem Tag ein Bildnis, nach Guy Fawkes, der damals festgenommen und aufgrund seiner Beteiligung an der Verschwörung hingerichtet wurde, "Guy" genannt, verbrannt. Es werden Feuerwerke abgebrannt und Freudenfeuer entzündet. Penny for the guy: Kinder stellen sich mit einem selbst gebastelten "Guy" auf und bitten Passanten um eine Geldgabe, indem sie rufen: "Penny for the guy!".*
11. Nov. – **Veteran's Day**. *Feiertag in den USA, der am Jahrestag des Endes des Ersten Weltkriegs zu Ehren der amerikanischen Veteranen und Opfer aller Kriege begangen wird.*
30. Nov. – **St Andrew's Day** Andreastag. *Schutzheiliger Schottlands.*

## December

| | | | | |
|---|---|---|---|---|
| 1 | 8 | 15 | 22 | 29 |
| 2 | 9 | 16 | 23 | 30 |
| 3 | 10 | 17 | 24 | 31 |
| 4 | 11 | 18 | 25 | |
| 5 | 12 | 19 | 26 | |
| 6 | 13 | 20 | 27 | |
| 7 | 14 | 21 | 28 | |

24. Dez. – **Christmas Eve** Heiligabend, Heiliger Abend
25. Dez. – **Christmas Day** Weihnachten, erster Weihnachtstag. *Feiertag in England, Wales, Schottland, Nordirland, der Republik Irland und den USA.*
26. Dez. – **Boxing Day** Zweiter Weihnachtstag. *Feiertag in England, Nordirland und Schottland. So genannt nach dem Brauch, an diesem Tage Lieferanten ein Weihnachtspäckchen zu schenken.*
– **St Stephen's Day** Stephanstag. *Feiertag in der Republik Irland zu Ehren des christlichen Märtyrers, der der Blasphemie beschuldigt und gesteinigt wurde.*
31. Dez. – **New Year's Eve** Silvester *In Schottland nennt man Silvester "Hogmanay". Nach der Hogmanay-Tradition bringt ein dunkelhaariger Mann, der um Mitternacht die Schwelle überschreitet, Glück.*

**Bewegliche Feste im Okt./Nov./Dez.:**

**Columbus Day** Kolumbustag. *Feiertag in den USA zur Erinnerung an die Entdeckung der Neuen Welt durch Christoph Kolumbus 1492.*

**Public Holiday in Republic of Ireland** Feiertag in der Republik Irland

**Remembrance Sunday** Remembrance Sunday. *Der dem 11. November (dem Jahrestag des Waffenstillstands vom 11. November 1918) am nächsten gelegene Sonntag, an dem der Toten beider Weltkriege und späterer Konflikte gedacht wird. Auch als* **Poppy Day** *bekannt, da man traditionell rote Mohnblumen trägt und mit roten Mohnblumen gewundene Kränze auf Grabmalen niedergelegt, um die Toten zu ehren.*

**Thanksgiving** Erntedankfest. *Ein jährlicher Nationalfeiertag in den USA. Kennzeichen sind religiöse Riten sowie ein traditionelles Truthahnessen. Der Feiertag erinnert an ein Erntefest, das die Pilgerväter 1621 gefeiert haben, und wird am vierten Donnerstag im November begangen.*

**First Sunday in Advent** Erster Advent

**Von den Mondphasen abhängige bewegliche Daten:**

**Eid-ul-Fitr** Id al-Fitr, Kleiner Bairam, "Zuckerfest"

**Eid-ul-Adha** Id al-Adha, Großer Bairam

**Islamic New Year** Islamisches Neujahrsfest

**Jewish New Year** (or **Rosh Hashanah**) Jüdisches Neujahrsfest (oder Rosch ha-Schana)

**Day of Atonement** (or **Yom Kippur**) Versöhnungstag (oder Jom Kippur)

**First Day of Tabernacles** (or **Succoth**) Erster Tag des Laubhüttenfestes (Sukkot)

**First Day of Ramadan** Erster Tag des Ramadan

# Calendar of traditions, festivals, and holidays

## Januar

| | | | | |
|---|---|---|---|---|
| 1 | 8 | 15 | 22 | 29 |
| 2 | 9 | 16 | 23 | 30 |
| 3 | 10 | 17 | 24 | 31 |
| 4 | 11 | 18 | 25 | |
| 5 | 12 | 19 | 26 | |
| 6 | 13 | 20 | 27 | |
| 7 | 14 | 21 | 28 | |

1 Jan – **Neujahr** New Year's Day
6 Jan – **Heilige Drei Könige, Epiphanias** Epiphany. *Public holiday in Austria and in parts of Germany.*

## Februar

| | | | |
|---|---|---|---|
| 1 | 8 | 15 | 22 |
| 2 | 9 | 16 | 23 |
| 3 | 10 | 17 | 24 |
| 4 | 11 | 18 | 25 |
| 5 | 12 | 19 | 26 |
| 6 | 13 | 20 | 27 |
| 7 | 14 | 21 | 28 |

2 Feb – **Mariä Lichtmess, Lichtmess** Candlemas. *In the Catholic Church, a festival marked by the blessing of candles and by candlelight processions. According to weather lore, if the bear sees its shadow when emerging from hibernation on this day – i.e. if the weather is sunny – it will creep back into its den, indicating six more weeks of wintry weather.*
14 Feb – **Valentinstag** St Valentine's Day

## März

| | | | | |
|---|---|---|---|---|
| 1 | 8 | 15 | 22 | 29 |
| 2 | 9 | 16 | 23 | 30 |
| 3 | 10 | 17 | 24 | 31 |
| 4 | 11 | 18 | 25 | |
| 5 | 12 | 19 | 26 | |
| 6 | 13 | 20 | 27 | |
| 7 | 14 | 21 | 28 | |

19 March – **Josephstag** St Joseph's Day. *Holiday in parts of Switzerland.*
25 March – **Mariä Verkündigung** Annunciation

**Movable dates in Jan/Feb/Mar:**

**Chinesisches Neujahrsfest** Chinese New Year
**Schmutziger Donnerstag, Weiberfastnacht** *Last Thursday of Carnival, when it is the custom in some areas for women to snip off men's ties.*
**Rosenmontag** *Day before Shrove Tuesday, when Carnival processions take place, particularly in the Rheinland.*
**Fastnachtsdienstag** Shrove Tuesday. *Traditional festival preceding Lent – the high point of the Carnival festivities, with parties, fancy-dress parades, masked balls, and processions.*
**Aschermittwoch** Ash Wednesday

## April

| | | | | |
|---|---|---|---|---|
| 1 | 8 | 15 | 22 | 29 |
| 2 | 9 | 16 | 23 | 30 |
| 3 | 10 | 17 | 24 | |
| 4 | 11 | 18 | 25 | |
| 5 | 12 | 19 | 26 | |
| 6 | 13 | 20 | 27 | |
| 7 | 14 | 21 | 28 | |

1 Apr – **Erster April** April Fool's Day

## Mai

| | | | | |
|---|---|---|---|---|
| 1 | 8 | 15 | 22 | 29 |
| 2 | 9 | 16 | 23 | 30 |
| 3 | 10 | 17 | 24 | 31 |
| 4 | 11 | 18 | 25 | |
| 5 | 12 | 19 | 26 | |
| 6 | 13 | 20 | 27 | |
| 7 | 14 | 21 | 28 | |

1 May – **Erster Mai** May Day. *Public holiday in Germany ("Maifeiertag"), Austria ("Staatsfeiertag"), and Switzerland ("Tag der Arbeit"); celebrated by trade unions as "Kampftag der Arbeit" ("worker's day of action") and marked by demonstrations and rallies.*

## Juni

| | | | | |
|---|---|---|---|---|
| 1 | 8 | 15 | 22 | 29 |
| 2 | 9 | 16 | 23 | 30 |
| 3 | 10 | 17 | 24 | |
| 4 | 11 | 18 | 25 | |
| 5 | 12 | 19 | 26 | |
| 6 | 13 | 20 | 27 | |
| 7 | 14 | 21 | 28 | |

24 June – **Johanisstag, Johanni** St John the Baptist's Day. *Feast of St John the Baptist, celebrated by some by the lighting of St John's fires in the evening.*
27 June – **Siebenschläfer**. *According to weather lore, if it rains on this day it will rain for the next seven weeks.*

**Movable dates in Apr/May/June:**

**Palmsonntag** Palm Sunday
**Beginn des Passahfestes** First Day of Passover
**Karfreitag** Good Friday
**Ostern, Ostersonntag** Easter Day, Easter Sunday. *At Easter, children traditionally hunt for Easter eggs which have supposedly been hidden by the Easter hare.*
**Ostermontag** Easter Monday
**Weißer Sonntag** Low Sunday. *The Sunday after Easter. In the Catholic Church, first communion is taken on this Sunday.*
**Muttertag** Mother's Day. *The second Sunday in May, on which mothers are particularly honoured by their children with gifts, visits, or written greetings. [Note that Mother's Day is usually in March in the UK and Republic of Ireland, and in May in the USA, Canada and German-speaking countries.]*
**Christi Himmelfahrt, Auffahrt** Ascension Day. *Public holiday in Germany, Austria, and Switzerland.*
**Vatertag** Father's Day. *On Ascension Day, groups of men, particularly fathers of families, often go off for the day on a walk or another excursion. A prominent feature of the day out is always a visit to one or more pubs, often resulting in excess alcohol consumption.*
**Schawout, Wochenfest** Shavuot
**Pfingsten, Pfingstsonntag** Whitsun, Whit Sunday
**Pfingstmontag** Whit Monday. *Public holiday in Germany, Austria, and Switzerland.*
**Fronleichnam** Corpus Christi. *Public holiday in Austria and in parts of Germany and Switzerland.*

## Juli

| | | | | |
|---|---|---|---|---|
| 1 | 8 | 15 | 22 | 29 |
| 2 | 9 | 16 | 23 | 30 |
| 3 | 10 | 17 | 24 | 31 |
| 4 | 11 | 18 | 25 | |
| 5 | 12 | 19 | 26 | |
| 6 | 13 | 20 | 27 | |
| 7 | 14 | 21 | 28 | |

## August

| | | | | |
|---|---|---|---|---|
| 1 | 8 | [15] | 22 | 29 |
| 2 | 9 | 16 | 23 | 30 |
| 3 | 10 | 17 | 24 | 31 |
| 4 | 11 | 18 | 25 | |
| 5 | 12 | 19 | 26 | |
| 6 | 13 | 20 | 27 | |
| 7 | 14 | 21 | 28 | |

15 Aug – **Mariä Himmelfahrt** Assumption

## September

| | | | | |
|---|---|---|---|---|
| 1 | 8 | 15 | 22 | 29 |
| 2 | 9 | 16 | 23 | 30 |
| 3 | 10 | 17 | 24 | |
| 4 | 11 | 18 | 25 | |
| 5 | 12 | 19 | 26 | |
| 6 | 13 | 20 | 27 | |
| 7 | 14 | 21 | 28 | |

## Oktober

| | | | | |
|---|---|---|---|---|
| 1 | 8 | 15 | 22 | 29 |
| 2 | 9 | 16 | 23 | 30 |
| [3] | 10 | 17 | 24 | [31] |
| 4 | 11 | 18 | 25 | |
| 5 | 12 | 19 | [26] | |
| 6 | 13 | 20 | 27 | |
| 7 | 14 | 21 | 28 | |

3 Oct – **Tag der deutschen Einheit** Day of German Unity. *Public holiday in Germany, commemorating the reunification of Germany on 3 October 1990.*
26 Oct – **Nationalfeiertag** *National holiday in Austria.*
31 Oct – **Reformationsfest** Reformation Day. *Public holiday in some parts of Germany, commemorating the Reformation.*

## November

| | | | | |
|---|---|---|---|---|
| [1] | 8 | 15 | 22 | 29 |
| [2] | 9 | 16 | 23 | 30 |
| 3 | 10 | 17 | 24 | |
| 4 | [11] | 18 | 25 | |
| 5 | 12 | 19 | 26 | |
| 6 | 13 | 20 | 27 | |
| 7 | 14 | 21 | 28 | |

1 Nov – **Allerheiligen** All Saints' Day
2 Nov – **Allerseelen** All Souls' Day
11 Nov – **Martinstag, Martini** St Martin's Day, Martinmas. *This day is often celebrated with a traditional meal of roast goose ('Martinsgans'). On the evening before, children take part in lantern-light processions.*
– **Beginn der Fastnachtszeit** Beginning of Carnival. *At 11 a.m., a toast of sparkling wine is drunk to mark the beginning of the so-called 'fifth season'.*

## Dezember

| | | | | |
|---|---|---|---|---|
| 1 | [8] | 15 | 22 | 29 |
| 2 | 9 | 16 | 23 | 30 |
| 3 | 10 | 17 | [24] | [31] |
| 4 | 11 | 18 | [25] | |
| 5 | 12 | 19 | [26] | |
| [6] | 13 | 20 | 27 | |
| 7 | 14 | 21 | 28 | |

6 Dec – **Nikolaustag** St Nicholas' Day. *Children are given presents to mark St Nicholas' Day. They put their shoes outside the door on the evening before for St Nicholas to leave their presents in.*
8 Dec – **Mariä Empfängnis** Feast of the Immaculate Conception
24 Dec – **Heiligabend, Heiliger Abend** Christmas Eve. *On Christmas Eve in the evening, children are given their Christmas presents, Christmas trees are put up and decorated, and candles are lit on the Christmas trees to burn during the giving of the presents. A crib is often placed under the tree.*
25 Dec – **Weihnachten, erster Weihnachtstag, Christtag** Christmas Day
26 Dec – (in Germany) **Zweiter Weihnachtstag**, (in Austria and Switzerland) **Stephanstag** St Stephen's Day. *Public holiday.*
31 Dec – **Silvester** New Year's Eve. *The turn of the year is usually celebrated with lively parties till late in the night. At midnight the New Year is greeted with a toast of sparkling wine and with fireworks.*

**Movable dates in Oct/Nov/Dec:**

**Volkstrauertag** *On the Sunday two weeks before the first Sunday in Advent, there is a national day of mourning in Germany to commemorate the dead of both World Wars and the victims of National Socialism.*
**Buß- und Bettag** Day of Prayer and Repentance. *The Wednesday eleven days before the first Sunday in Advent is a public holiday in some parts of Germany.*
**Erster Advent** First Sunday in Advent

**Movable dates related to lunar activity:**

**Id al-Fitr, Kleiner Bairam, "Zuckerfest"** Eid-ul-Fitr
**Id al-Adha, Großer Bairam** Eid-ul-Adha
**Islamisches Neujahrsfest** Islamic New Year
**Jüdisches Neujahrsfest, Rosch ha-Schana** Jewish New Year, Rosh Hashanah
**Versöhnungstag, Jom Kippur** Day of Atonement, Yom Kippur
**Erster Tag des Laubhüttenfestes (Sukkot)** First Day of Tabernacles (Succoth)
**Erster Tag des Ramadans** First Day of Ramadan

# Aa

**a, A** /a:/ *das;* ~, ~ Ⓐ (*Buchstabe*) a/A; **kleines a** a small a; **großes A** capital A; **das A und O** (*fig.*) the essential thing/things (*Gen.* for); **von A bis Z** (*fig. ugs.*) from beginning to end; **wer A sagt, muss auch B sagen** (*fig.*) if one starts a thing, one must go through with it; Ⓑ (*Musik*) [key of] A

**ä, Ä** /ɛ:/ *das;* ~, **~:** a umlaut

**a** *Abk.* **Ar, Are**

**à** /a/ *Präp. mit Nom., Akk.* (*Kaufmannsspr.*) **zehn Marken à 50 Pfennig** ten stamps at 50 pfennigs each; **zehn Kisten à zwölf Flaschen** ten cases of twelve bottles each

**A** *Abk.* Ⓐ **Autobahn** ≈ M; Ⓑ (*Phys.*) **Ampere** A

**Aa** /'a'|a/ *das;* ~ (*Kinderspr.*) poo[-poo] (*child lang.*); **Aa machen** do poo-poo *or* big jobs (*child lang.*); do a big job (*Amer. child lang.*)

**AA¹** *Abk.* **Anonyme Alkoholiker** AA

**AA²** *Abk.* **Auswärtiges Amt**

**Aachen** /'a:xn̩/ *(das);* **~s** Aix-la-Chapelle; Aachen

**Aal** /a:l/ *der;* **~[e]s, ~e** eel; **~ grün** (*Kochk.*) green eels; stewed eels; **~ blau** (*Kochk.*) blue eel; **glatt wie ein ~ sein** be as slippery as an eel; **sich [drehen und] winden** *od.* **krümmen wie ein ~:** twist and turn like an eel

**aalen** *refl. V.* (*ugs.*) stretch out; **sich in der Sonne/auf der Wiese** *usw.* **~:** lie stretched out in the sun/in the meadow *etc.*

**aal-, Aal-: ~glatt** (*abwertend*) ❶ *Adj.* slippery; **~glatt sein** be as slippery as an eel; ❷ *adv.* smoothly; **sich ~glatt herausreden** glibly talk one's way out; **~kasten** *der* eel trap; **~suppe** *die* eel soup

**a. a. O.** *Abk.* **am angegebenen Ort** loc. cit.

**Aar** /a:ɐ̯/ *der;* **~[e]s, ~e** (*dichter. veralt.*) eagle

**Aas** /a:s/ *das;* **~es, ~e** *od.* **Äser** /'ɛ:zɐ/ Ⓐ *Pl.* **~e** (*Kadaver*) carrion *no pl., no indef. art.;* rotten carcass; **~ fressen** eat carrion; Ⓑ *Pl.* **Äser** (*salopp*) (*abwertend*) swine; (*mit Anerkennung*) devil; **ein raffiniertes/kleines ~:** a cunning/little devil; **kein ~:** not one damned person

**Aas·blume** *die* (*Bot.*) carrion flower

**aasen** *itr. V.* (*ugs., bes. nordd.*) **mit etw. ~:** be wasteful with sth.; **mit dem Geld ~:** throw [one's] money around

**aas-, Aas-: ~fliege** *die* (*Zool.*) (*Calliphorinae*) blowfly; (*Sarcophaginae*) flesh fly; **~fresser** *der* (*Zool.*) carrion-eater; scavenger; **~geier** *der* vulture; **wie [die] ~geier** (*abwertend*) like vultures

**aasig** ❶ *Adv.* (*ugs.*) **~ frieren** be absolutely frozen; **~ kalt** damned cold; **es tut ~ weh** it hurts like mad (*coll.*). ❷ *Adj.* malicious; mean

**Aas-: ~käfer** *der* carrion beetle; **~seite** *die* (*Gerberei*) flesh side

**ab** /ap/ ❶ *Präp. mit Dat.* Ⓐ (*zeitlich*) from; **ab 1980** as from 1980; **Jugendliche ab 16 Jahren** young people over the age of 16; **ab [dem] 3. April** from the 3rd of April; **ab wann?** from when?; from what time?; Ⓑ (*bes. Kaufmannsspr.: räumlich*) ex; **ab Werk** ex works; **ab [unserem] Lager** ex store; ex warehouse (*Amer.*); **ab Frankfurt fliegen** fly from Frankfurt; **ab Köln führt der Zug einen Speisewagen** from Cologne onwards the train has a dining car; Ⓒ ([*Rang*]*folge*) from ... on[wards]; **ab der nächsten Ausgabe** from the next edition onwards; **ab zweitausend Stück aufwärts** from two thousand items onwards; **ab 20 DM** from 20 DM [upwards].
❷ *Adv.* Ⓐ (*weg*) off; away; **nicht weit ab vom Weg** not far [away] from the path; **an der Kreuzung links ab** turn off left at the junction; **[an etw.** (*Dat.*)**] ab sein** (*ugs.: sich [von etw.] gelöst haben*) have come off [sth.]; Ⓑ (*ugs.: Aufforderung*) off; away; **ab nach Hause** get off home; **ab die Post** (*fig.*) off you/we *etc.* go; **ab nach Kassel** (*fig.*) it's off and away; **X ab/X und Y ab** (*Theater*) exit X/exeunt X and Y; **Film/Ton ab!** (*Film*) camera!/sound!; **Film ab!** (*im Vorführraum*) film, please!; Ⓒ (*milit. Kommando*) **Gewehr ab!** order arms!; ⇒ *auch* **Helm¹** A; Ⓓ **ab und zu** *od.* (*norddt.*) **an** now and then; from time to time; ⇒ *auch* **auf** 3 E, F; **von** 1 A, B

**Abakus** /'a(:)bakʊs/ *der;* ~, **~:** abacus

**abänderbar, abänderlich** *Adj.* alterable

**ab|ändern** ❶ *tr. V.* alter; change; amend ‹text›. ❷ *itr. V.* (*Biol.*) mutate

**Ab·änderung** *die* alteration; (*eines Paragraphen*) amendment

**Abänderungs-: ~antrag** *der* ⇒ **Änderungsantrag; ~klage** *die* (*Rechtsw.*) application for a variation (*of periodical payments*)

**Abandon** /abã'dõ:/ *der;* **~s, ~s** (*Rechtsw.*) abandonment

**abandonnieren** /abãdɔ'ni:rən/ *tr., itr. V.* (*Rechtsw.*) abandon

**ab|arbeiten** ❶ *tr. V.* Ⓐ (*abgelten*) work for ‹meal›; work off ‹debt, amount›; **seine Überfahrt ~:** work one's passage; Ⓑ (*abnutzen*) wear out [with work]; **abgearbeitete Hände** work-worn hands; Ⓒ (*beseitigen*) remove; (*abfeilen*) file off. ❷ *refl. V.* slave [away]; work like a slave

**Ab·art** *die* variety

**ab·artig** *Adj.* deviant; abnormal

**Ab·artigkeit** *die* Ⓐ (*Eigenschaft*) abnormality; deviancy; Ⓑ (*Handlung*) abnormal act

**ab|äsen** *tr. V.* (*Jägerspr.*) crop

**ab|asten** *refl. V.* (*ugs.*) slave [away]; **sich mit etw. ~:** heave sth. around; **sich** (*Dat.*) **[mit etw.] einen ~** (*salopp*) slave away [heaving sth. around]

**ab|ätzen** *tr. V.* Ⓐ (*reinigen*) clean [with corrosive]; Ⓑ (*entfernen*) remove [with corrosive]; (*Med.*) cauterize

**Abb.** *Abk.* **Abbildung** Fig.

**ab|backen** *unr. itr. V.; mit sein* (*Kochk.*) ‹dough etc.› come away

**ab|baken** /'apba:kn̩/ *tr. V.* (*Seew.*) mark [with buoys]; buoy

**ab|balgen** *tr. V.* (*Jägerspr.*) skin ‹animal›

**Ab·bau** *der* Ⓐ (*Zerlegung*) dismantling; (*von Zelten, Lagern*) striking; Ⓑ (*Senkung*) reduction; Ⓒ ⇒ **abbauen** 1 D: cutback (*Gen.* in); pruning; **der ~ von Beamten** the cutback in civil service jobs; **der ~ von Vorurteilen** the breaking down of prejudices; Ⓓ (*Chemie, Biol.*) breakdown; Ⓔ (*Bergbau*) mining; (*im Steinbruch*) quarrying; (*von Flözen*) working

**ab|bauen** ❶ *tr. V.* Ⓐ (*zerlegen*) dismantle; strike ‹tent, camp›; dismantle, take down ‹scaffolding›; Ⓑ (*senken*) reduce ‹wages›; Ⓒ (*beseitigen*) gradually remove; break down ‹prejudices, inhibitions›; **etw. planmäßig ~:** phase sth. out; Ⓓ (*verringern*) cut back ‹staff›; prune ‹jobs›; Ⓔ (*Chemie, Biol.*) break down ‹carbohydrates, alcohol›; Ⓕ (*Bergbau*) mine ‹coal, gold›; quarry ‹stone›; work ‹seam›.
❷ *itr. V.* Ⓐ (*nachlassen*) fade; slow down; **kurz vor dem Ziel baute er stark ab** he faded badly just before the finish; **körperlich ~:** decay physically; Ⓑ (*Landw.*) ‹crop variety› decline in yield

**Abbau·produkt** *das* (*Chemie*) decomposition product; (*Biol.*) product of catabolism

**abbau·würdig** *Adj.* (*Bergbau*) workable

**ab|bedingen** *unr. tr. V.* (*Rechtsspr.*) waive

**ab|beißen** ❶ *unr. tr. V.* bite off; **eine Zigarre ~:** bite the end off a cigar. ❷ *unr. itr. V.* have a bite; **lass deinen Bruder [von der Banane] ~!** let your brother have a bite [of the banana]!

**ab|beizen** *tr. V.* (*Handw.*) strip ‹wooden object›; **die alte Farbe [von etw.] ~:** strip the old paint off [sth.]

**ab|bekommen** *unr. tr. V.* Ⓐ (*bekommen*) get; **sie hat keinen Mann ~** (*ugs.*) she didn't catch herself a husband; Ⓑ (*hinnehmen müssen*) **einen Schlag/ein paar Kratzer ~:** get hit/get a few scratches; **den ganzen Segen ~** (*ugs. iron.*) get the full benefit (*iron.*); **etwas ~** (*getroffen werden*) get *or* be hit; (*verletzt werden*) get *or* be hurt; **er hat im Krieg etwas ~** (*ugs.*) he was injured in the war; **der Wagen hat nichts ~:** the car wasn't damaged; Ⓒ (*entfernen können*) get ‹paint, lid, chain› off

**ab|berufen** *unr. tr. V.* recall ‹ambassador, envoy› **(aus, von** from); **Gott hat ihn aus diesem Leben ~** (*verhüll.*) God has taken him from us

**Ab·berufung** *die* recall

**ab|bestellen** *tr. V.* cancel ‹newspaper, hotel room, plumber, etc.›; ask to have ‹telephone› disconnected; **jmdn. ~:** cancel sb.'s appointment

**Ab·bestellung** *die* cancellation

**ab|betteln** *tr. V.* (*ugs.*) **jmdm. etw. ~:** beg sth. from sb.

**ab|bezahlen** *tr. V.* pay off ‹debts, television set, etc.›

**ab|biegen** ❶ *unr. itr. V.;* **▶818** *mit sein* turn off; **links/rechts/an der Kreuzung ~:** turn [off] left/right/at the junction. ❷ *unr. tr. V.* Ⓐ bend ‹rod, metal sheet, etc.›; Ⓑ (*ugs.: abwenden*) get out of (*coll.*) ‹obligation›; head off (*coll.*) ‹row›; **sie hat die Sache noch einmal abgebogen** she just managed to stop things going too far

**Abbieger** *der;* **~s, ~, Abbiegerin** *die;* **~, ~nen** (*Verkehrsw.*) motorist/cyclist/car *etc.* turning off

**Abbiege·spur** *die* the turning lane

**Ab·biegung** *die* the bend

**Ab·bild** *das* (*eines Menschen*) likeness; (*eines Gegenstandes*) copy; (*im Spiegel*) reflection; (*fig.*) portrayal

**ab|bilden** *tr. V.* copy; reproduce ‹object, picture›; portray, depict ‹person›; depict ‹landscape›; (*fig.*) portray; depict; **auf dem Foto ist ein Haus abgebildet** the photograph shows a house; **jmdn./einen Gegenstand/die Landschaft naturgetreu ~:** depict sb./copy *or* reproduce an object/depict the scenery faithfully

**Ab·bildung** *die* Ⓐ (*Bild*) illustration; (*Schaubild*) diagram; **die ~ einer unbekleideten Dame** a/the picture of a nude woman; Ⓑ (*das Abbilden*) reproduction; (*fig.*) portrayal

**Abbildungs·fehler** *der* (*Optik*) aberration; image defect

**ab|bimsen** *tr., itr. V.* (*ugs.*) crib ‹exercises›

**ab|binden** ❶ *unr. tr. V.* Ⓐ (*losbinden*) untie; undo; **die Schürze/Krawatte ~:** undo *or* untie one's apron/tie; **eine Schnur ~:** untie a piece of string; Ⓑ (*abschnüren*) put a tourniquet on ‹artery, arm, leg, etc.›; tie ‹umbilical cord›; Ⓒ (*Kochk.*) thicken ‹sauce, gravy›; bind ‹rissole etc.›; Ⓓ (*Zimmerei*) make trial assembly of; Ⓔ (*Landw.*) wean ‹calf›. ❷ *unr. itr. V.* (*Bauw.*) ‹concrete› set

**Ab·bitte** *die (geh.)* **jmdm. ~ leisten** *od.* **tun** ask sb.'s pardon

**ab|bitten** *unr. tr. V. (geh.)* **jmdm. etwas/vieles abzubitten haben** have something/a lot to apologize to sb. for

**ab|blasen** *unr. tr. V.* Ⓐ *(ugs.: absagen)* call off ‹enterprise, party›; Ⓑ *(Technik)* discharge ‹fumes›; Ⓒ *(Milit.)* **das Manöver/den Angriff/das Gefecht ~:** sound the retreat; Ⓓ *(Jägerspr.)* **die Jagd ~:** call off the hounds/beaters *etc.*

**ab|blassen** *itr. V.; mit sein* fade

**ab|blättern** *itr. V.; mit sein* flake off

**ab|bleiben** *unr. itr. V.; mit sein (ugs., bes. nordd.)* **wo ist er/es nur abgeblieben?** where has he/it got to *(Brit.)* *or* *(Amer.)* gone?; where can he/it be?

**abblendbar** *Adj.* **~er Innenspiegel** *od.* **Rückspiegel** anti-dazzle rear-view mirror

**Ab·blende** *die (Film)* fade[-out]

**ab|blenden** ❶ *tr., itr. V.* black out ‹window, lights›; dip *(Brit.)*, dim *(Amer.)* ‹headlights›; **bei Gegenverkehr frühzeitig ~:** dip *or* *(Amer.)* dim headlights promptly when there is oncoming traffic. ❷ *itr. V.* Ⓐ *(Film)* fade [out]; Ⓑ *(Fot.)* stop down

**Abblend-: ~licht** *das* dipped *(Brit.)* *or* *(Amer.)* dimmed beam; **mit ~licht fahren** drive on dipped *or* dimmed headlights; **~schalter** *der* dip switch *(Brit.)*; dimmer switch *(Amer.)*

**ab|blitzen** *itr. V.; mit sein (ugs.)* **sie ließ alle Verehrer ~:** she gave all her admirers the brush-off; **bei jmdm. [mit etw.] ~:** fail to get anywhere [with sth.] with sb. *(coll.)*

**ab|blocken** *tr. V. (Sport; auch fig.)* block

**ab|blühen** *itr. V.; mit haben od. sein (auch fig.)* fade

**ab|bohren** *tr. V. (Bergbau)* drill out

**Ab·brand** *der* Ⓐ *(Kerntechnik)* burn-up; Ⓑ *(Metall.)* melting loss

**ab|brausen** ❶ *tr. V.* ⇒ **abduschen.** ❷ *itr. V.; mit sein (ugs.)* roar off

**ab|brechen** ❶ *unr. tr. V.* Ⓐ *(abtrennen)* break off; break ‹needle, pencil›; **sich** *(Dat.)* **einen Fingernagel/Zahn ~:** break a fingernail/a tooth; Ⓑ *(zerlegen)* strike ‹tent, camp›; Ⓒ *(abreißen)* demolish, pull down ‹building, tower›; Ⓓ *(beenden)* break off ‹negotiations, [diplomatic] relations, discussion, conversation, connection, activity, training›; call off ‹strike›; *(vorzeitig, wider Erwarten)* cut short ‹conversation, studies, holiday, activity›; **den Kampf ~** *(Boxen)* stop the fight; **ein abgebrochenes Studium** an unfinished course of studies; **abgebrochene Sätze** fragmentary sentences; ⇒ *auch* **abgebrochen** 2.
❷ *unr. itr. V.* Ⓐ *mit sein (entzweigehen)* break [off]; **die Armlehne von dem Sessel ist mir abgebrochen, als ich ...** the arm broke off the armchair when I ...; Ⓑ *(aufhören)* break off; Ⓒ *mit sein (beendet werden)* **die Verbindung brach ab** the connection was cut off; Ⓓ *mit sein (steil abfallen)* fall away [steeply].
❸ *unr. refl. V.* **sich** *(Dat.)* **einen/keinen ~** *(salopp)* put/not put oneself out

**ab|bremsen** ❶ *tr. V.* Ⓐ brake; **vor der Kurve den Wagen ~:** slow the car down before the bend; Ⓑ retard ‹motion›; break ‹fall›; *(fig.)* curb ‹zeal›. ❷ *itr. V.* brake; apply the brakes; **stark/auf 40 ~:** brake hard/to 40

**ab|brennen** ❶ *unr. itr. V.; mit sein* Ⓐ *(zerstört werden)* be burned down; ‹farm› be burned out; **das Haus ist abgebrannt** the house has burned down; **wir sind schon zweimal abgebrannt** we've been burned out twice already; **dreimal umgezogen ist [so gut wie] einmal abgebrannt** *(Spr.)* you can lose just as much moving [house] three times as you can if your house burns down; ⇒ *auch* **abgebrannt** 2; **Grundmauer**; Ⓑ *(sich aufbrauchen)* ‹fuse› burn away; ‹candle› burn down; **abgebrannte Streichhölzer** used *or* burnt matches.
❷ *unr. tr. V.* Ⓐ let off ‹firework›; Ⓑ *(zerstören)* burn down ‹building›

**Abbreviatur** /abrevi̯a'tu:ɐ̯/ *die; ~, ~en* *(Druckw., Mus.)* abbreviation

**ab|bringen** *unr. tr. V.* Ⓐ **jmdn. von etw. ~:** make sb. give up sth.; **jmdn. vom Kurs ~:** make sb. change course; **jmdn. von der Fährte ~:** throw sb. off the scent; **jmdn. davon ~, etw. zu tun** stop sb. doing sth.; *(abraten)* dissuade sb. from doing sth.; **er lässt sich von seinem Plan nicht ~:** he can't be persuaded to give up *or* drop his plan; **jmdn. vom Thema ~:** get sb. away from the subject; Ⓑ *(ugs.: lösen)* **etw. [von etw.] ~:** get sth. off [sth.]

**ab|bröckeln** *itr. V.; mit sein (auch fig.)* crumble away; *(Börsenw.)* ‹price, exchange rate› decline gradually

**Ab·bruch** *der* Ⓐ demolition; pulling down; **etw. auf ~ verkaufen** sell sth. at demolition value; Ⓑ *(Beendigung)* breaking-off; *(Sport)* abandonment; *(Boxen)* stopping; **Sieger durch ~** *(Boxen)* winner when the fight was stopped; Ⓒ **einer Sache** *(Dat.)* **[keinen] ~ tun** do [no] harm to sth.; **das tut der Liebe keinen ~** *(ugs. scherzh.)* never mind *(coll.)*; Ⓓ *(eines Zelts, Lagers)* striking

**abbruch-, Abbruch-: ~arbeit** *die* demolition work; **~firma** *die* demolition firm; **~haus** *das* condemned house; **~reif** *Adj.* ripe for demolition *postpos.*; **~sieg** *der* *(Boxen)* win when the fight was stopped; **~unternehmen** *das* demolition firm

**ab|brühen** *tr. V. (Kochk.)* blanch; ⇒ *auch* **abgebrüht** 2

**ab|brummen** *tr. V. (ugs.)* do *(coll.)*; **er muss noch drei Jahre ~:** he has got another three years to do

**ab|buchen** *tr. V.* ‹bank› debit (**von** to); ‹creditor› claim by direct debit (**von** to); *(fig.: als verloren betrachten)* write off; **etw. ~ lassen** *(durch die Bank)* pay sth. by standing order; *(durch Gläubiger)* pay sth. by direct debit

**Ab·buchung** *die* debiting; **~ per Dauerauftrag** payment by standing order/direct debit

**ab|bügeln** *tr. V. (ugs.)* reject, brush aside ‹warning, question, criticism›; rebuff ‹person›

**ab|bummeln** *tr. V. (ugs.)* take time off in lieu for

**ab|bürsten** *tr. V.* Ⓐ brush off; **jmdm. den Schmutz ~:** brush the dirt off sb.; **den Schmutz von etw. ~:** brush the dirt off sth.; Ⓑ *(säubern)* brush ‹garment›; Ⓒ *(ugs.: zurechtweisen)* **jmdn. ~:** give sb. a dressing down

**ab|busseln** *tr. V. (österr.)* ⇒ **abküssen**

**ab|büßen** *tr. V.* Ⓐ serve [out] ‹prison sentence›; Ⓑ *(Rel.)* atone for; do penance for

**Abbüßung** *die; ~:* **nach ~ seiner Strafe** after serving [out] his sentence

**Abc** /a(:)be(:)'tse:/ *das; ~* Ⓐ ABC; **nach dem ~ ordnen** arrange alphabetically; Ⓑ *(fig.: Grundlagen)* ABC; fundamentals *pl.*

**Abc-Buch** *das (veralt.)* ⇒ **Fibel** A

**ab|checken** *tr. V.* check; check through ‹list›; check off ‹names etc.›

**Abc-Schütze** *der*, **Abc-Schützin** *die* child just starting school

**ABC-Staaten** *Pl.* **die ABC-Staaten** Argentina, Brazil, and Chile

**ab|dachen** /'apdaxn̩/ *refl. V. (Geogr.)* slope down

**Abdachung** *die; ~, ~en (Geogr.)* downward slope *or* incline

**ab|dämmen** *tr. V.* Ⓐ dam up ‹river, pond, lake›; dam off ‹meadow, land›; Ⓑ *(isolieren)* insulate

**Abdämmung** *die; ~, ~en* Ⓐ dam; *(am Ufer)* dyke; *(Verfahren)* damming; Ⓑ *(Isolierung)* insulation

**Ab·dampf** *der (Technik)* exhaust steam

**ab|dampfen** ❶ *itr. V.; mit sein* steam away; *(ugs.: abfahren)* set off. ❷ *tr. V. (Chemie)* evaporate

**ab|dämpfen** *tr. V.* muffle ‹sound›; dim ‹light›

**Abdampf-: ~heizung** *die* exhaust-steam heating; **~rück·stand** *der* residue from evaporation; **~turbine** *die* exhaust-steam turbine

**ab|danken** *itr. V.* ‹ruler› abdicate; ‹government, minister› resign; ⇒ *auch* **abgedankt** 2

**Abdankung** *die; ~, ~en* Ⓐ *(eines Herrschers)* abdication; *(eines Ministers, einer Regierung)* resignation; Ⓑ *(veralt.: Entlassung)* retirement; Ⓒ *(bes. schweiz.: Trauerfeier)* funeral service

**ab|darben** *refl. V.* **sich** *(Dat.)* **etw. [vom Munde] ~** *(geh.)* stint oneself to save sth.

**Abdeck·band** *das; Pl.* **~bänder** masking tape

**ab|decken** ❶ *tr. V.* Ⓐ open up; uncover ‹container›; **der Orkan hat viele Häuser abgedeckt** the hurricane blew the roofs off many houses; **das Bett ~:** pull back the bedspread/bedclothes; Ⓑ *(herunternehmen, -reißen)* take off; remove; **Bretter von einer Grube ~:** take planks off a trench; **der Sturm deckte das Dach ab** the storm blew the roof off; Ⓒ *(abräumen)* clear ‹table›; clear away ‹dishes›; Ⓓ *(zudecken)* cover [up] ‹trench, grave›; **etw. mit Plastikfolie ~:** cover sth. [up] with plastic film; Ⓔ *(schützen)* cover ‹person›; *(Schach)* defend; Ⓕ *(Sport)* mark ‹player›; Ⓖ *(bezahlen, ausgleichen, berücksichtigen)* cover; meet ‹need, demand›; deal with ‹problem›; Ⓗ *(veralt.: abhäuten)* skin; flay.
❷ *itr. V. (den Tisch ~)* clear the table

**Abdecker** *der; ~s, ~* ▶ 159 *(veralt.)* knacker *(Brit.)*; *(der Tiere abhäutet)* skinner

**Abdeckerei** *die; ~, ~en (veralt.)* knacker's yard; *(wo Tiere abgehäutet werden)* skinnery *(arch.)*

**Abdeck-: ~plane** *die* canvas; tarpaulin; **~platte** *die (Bauw.)* coping stone

**Ab·deckung** *die* Ⓐ *(Bedeckung)* covering; Ⓑ *(Ausgleich, Bezahlung, Berücksichtigung)* covering; *(von Bedürfnissen, Forderungen)* meeting; **zur ~ des Risikos** to cover the risk

**ab|dichten** *tr. V.* seal, stop up ‹hole, crack, gap›; seal ‹pipe, container›; plug ‹leak›; **das Fenster/die Tür ~:** draughtproof the window/the door

**Ab·dichtung** *die* Ⓐ seal; *(von Fenstern, Türen)* draughtproofing; Ⓑ *(Vorgang)* sealing/draughtproofing

**ab|dienen** *tr. V.* serve [out]

**abdingbar** *Adj. (Rechtsspr.)* alterable by mutual consent

**ab|dorren** *itr. V.; mit sein (geh.)* dry up and wither away

**ab|drängen** *tr. V.* push away; force away; drive ‹animal› away; **jmdn. von etw. ~:** push sb. away from sth.; **einen Spieler vom Ball ~** *(Fußball)* force a player off the ball; **das Auto wurde von der Straße abgedrängt** the car was forced off the road; **ein Schiff vom Kurs ~:** force a ship off course

**ab|drehen** ❶ *tr. V.* Ⓐ *(ausschalten)* turn off; turn *or* switch off ‹light, lamp, electricity, fire, radio›; **den Hahn ~** *(fig.)* turn off the supply; Ⓑ *(Film)* finish shooting ‹scene, film›; Ⓒ *(abtrennen)* twist off; **einem Huhn den Hals** *od.* **Kopf ~:** wring a chicken's neck; ⇒ *auch* **Gurgel**; Ⓓ *(abschrauben)* screw off ‹lid, top›.
❷ *itr. V.; meist mit sein (die Richtung ändern)* turn off; **nach Süden ~:** turn [off] southwards

**Ab·drift** *die (Seew.)* leeway

**ab|driften** *itr. V.; mit sein* Ⓐ *(Seew.)* be blown; make leeway *(Naut.)*; **nach rechts/links/ins Drogenmilieu ~** *(fig.)* drift to the Right/Left/into the world of drug addicts

**ab|drosseln** *tr. V. (Technik)* reduce ‹fuel or power supply›; throttle back ‹motor, engine›; *(stoppen)* cut ‹motor, engine›; *(fig.: verringern)* cut back; curb

**Ab·druck**[1] *der; Pl.* **Abdrücke** mark; imprint; *(Finger~)* fingermark; *(Fuß~)* footprint; footmark; *(Wachs~)* impression; *(Gips~)* cast; **einen ~ nehmen** *od.* **machen** make a cast/impression

**Ab·druck**[2] *der; Pl.* **~e** Ⓐ *(Vorgang)* printing; *(Wieder~)* reprinting; **vor dem ~:** before printing; Ⓑ *(Ergebnis)* *(einer Grafik)* print; *(eines Buchs, Artikels)* [printed] text

**ab|drucken** *tr. V.* print; *(veröffentlichen)* publish

**ab|drücken** ❶ *itr. V.* *(schießen)* pull the trigger; shoot; **auf jmdn./etw. ~:** shoot *or*

*old spelling (see note on page 1707)

fire at sb./sth. ❷ *tr. V.* Ⓐ (*abfeuern*) fire ‹revolver, gun›; Ⓑ (*zudrücken*) constrict; Ⓒ **jmdm. die Luft ~:** stop sb. breathing; Ⓓ **jmdm. das Herz ~:** burden sb.'s heart; Ⓔ (*ugs.: umarmen*) hug. ❸ *refl. V.* Ⓐ **sich [in etw.** (*Dat.*)**] ~:** make marks [in sth.]; ‹track› be imprinted [in sth.]; Ⓑ **sich [mit dem Fuß] ~:** push oneself away with one's foot

**ab|ducken** *tr., itr. V.* (*Boxen*) duck ‹punch›

**ab|dunkeln** *tr. V.* Ⓐ (*verdunkeln*) darken ‹room›; dim ‹light›; Ⓑ (*abtönen*) tone down

**ab|duschen** *tr. V.* Ⓐ **sich/jmdn. [kalt/warm] ~:** take/give sb. a [cold/hot] shower; **sich/jmdm. den Rücken ~:** shower one's/sb.'s back; Ⓑ (*entfernen*) shower off

**ab|ebben** *itr. V.; mit sein* recede; abate

***abend** ⇒ **Abend** A

**Abend** *der;* **~s, ~e** Ⓐ ▶ 369 evening; **es wird ~:** evening is drawing in; **als es ~ wurde** when evening came; **diesen ~:** that evening *or* night; (*heute*) this evening; tonight; **guten ~!** good evening; **des ~s** (*geh.*) of an evening; in the evenings; **eines [schönen] ~s** one evening; **am [frühen/späten] ~:** [early/late] in the evening; **am ~ vorher** *od.* **zuvor** the evening *or* (*coll.*) night before; the previous evening; **bis zum [späten] ~:** until [late in the] evening; (*als Frist*) by [late] evening; **am selben/nächsten ~:** the same/following evening *or* (*coll.*) night; **am ~ des 1. Mai** on the evening *or* (*coll.*) night of 1 May; **~ für ~, jeden ~:** every [single] evening *or* (*coll.*) night; **gegen ~:** towards evening; **während des ~s** during the evening; **während des ganzen ~s** throughout the [entire] evening; **zu ~ essen** have dinner; (*allgemeiner*) have one's evening meal; **was essen wir zu ~?** what are we having this evening?; what is there for dinner/supper?; **was machen wir jetzt mit dem angebrochenen ~?** (*ugs.*) what shall we do with the rest of the evening?; **je später der ~, desto schöner die Gäste** (*scherzh.*) we're the happier to see you now you 'have come; **du kannst mich [mal] am ~ besuchen** (*ugs. verhüll.*) you know what 'you can do (*coll.*); **heute/morgen/gestern ~:** this/tomorrow/yesterday evening; tonight/tomorrow night/last night (*coll.*); **was gibt es heute ~ [zu essen]?** what's for dinner/supper?; ⇒ *auch* **heilig** B; **Tag** A; Ⓑ (*Geselligkeit*) evening; (*Kultur~*) soirée; **ein bunter ~:** a social [evening] *or* (*coll.*) night; Ⓒ (*veralt.: Westen*) the Occident (*literary*); **gen ~:** to the west *or* (*literary*) Occident; Ⓓ (*geh.: Ende*) evening

**Abend-:** **~abitur** *das* 'Abitur' through evening classes; **~akademie** *die* evening school; **~andacht** *die* evening service; **~an·zug** *der* dinner dress; evening suit; **~aus·gabe** *die* evening edition; **~blatt** *das* evening [news]paper; **~brot** *das* evening meal; supper; **~brot essen** have one's evening meal; have supper; **wann gibt es ~brot?** when's supper?; **was gibt es zum ~brot?** what's for supper?; **~dämmerung** *die* [evening] twilight

**abende·lang** ❶ *Adj.* lasting whole evenings *postpos., not pred.* ❷ *adv.* for whole evenings

**abend-, Abend-:** **~essen** *das* dinner; **das ~essen einnehmen** (*geh.*) have dinner; **nach dem ~essen** after dinner; **was gibt es zum ~essen?** what's for dinner?; **~füllend** *Adj.* occupying a whole evening *postpos., not pred.*; **ein ~füllendes Programm** a full evening's programme; **~gage** *die* evening's fee; **~gebet** *das* evening prayers *pl.*; (*von Kindern*) bedtime prayers *pl.*; **das ~gebet sprechen** say one's evening/bedtime prayers; **~gottes·dienst** *der* evening service; (*kath. Rel.*) evening mass; **~gymnasium** *das* night school, evening classes *pl.* (*leading to the 'Abitur'*); **~himmel** *der* sunset sky; **~karte** *die* (*Gastron.*) evening menu; **~kasse** *die* box office (*open on the evening of the performance*); **~kleid** *das* evening dress *or* gown; **~kurs[us]** *der* evening class *or* course; **etw. in ~en lernen** learn sth. at night school

**Abendland** *das;* **~[e]s** West; Occident (*literary*)

**abendländisch** /-lɛndɪʃ/ *Adj.* Western; Occidental (*literary*)

**abendlich** ❶ *Adj.* evening ‹quiet, coolness› of the evening; **die ~en Straßen der Stadt** the streets of the town at evening. ❷ *adv.* **es war ~ still geworden** the stillness of evening had descended; **der Himmel ist ~ gerötet** the sky is showing the red colours of evening

**Abend·mahl** *das* Ⓐ (*im Gottesdienst*) Communion; **das ~ nehmen** receive Communion; Ⓑ (*N. T.*) Last Supper; Ⓒ (*bes. südd.*) ⇒ **Abendessen**

**Abendmahls-:** **~gottes·dienst** *der* Communion service; **~kelch** *der* Communion cup; **~wein** *der* Communion wine

**Abend-:** **~mahl·zeit** *die* dinner; evening meal; **die ~mahlzeit einnehmen** (*geh.*) have dinner *or* one's evening meal; **~messe** *die* (*kath. Rel.*) evening mass; **~nachrichten** *Pl.* evening news *sing.*; **~programm** *das* evening programmes *pl.*; **was gibts im ~programm?** what's on this evening?; **damit ist das heutige ~programm beendet** that is the end of our programmes for today; **~rot** *das:* **ein/das ~rot** the redness of the sunset sky; **gestern war ~rot** there was a red sunset last night; **~röte** *die* (*geh.*) ⇒ **Abendrot**

**abends** *Adv.* ▶ 752 in the evenings; **um sechs Uhr ~:** at six o'clock in the evening; **Montag** *od.* **montags ~:** [on] Monday evenings; **von morgens bis ~:** from morning to night

**Abend-:** **~schule** *die* night school; evening classes *pl.*; **~schüler** *der* student at evening classes; **~sonne** *die* evening sun; **~stern** *der* evening star; **~stille** *die* evening stillness; **die ländliche ~stille** the evening stillness of the countryside; **~studium** *das* (*DDR*) *course of evening classes leading to a degree or diploma;* **~stunde** *die* evening hour; **in den frühen/späten ~stunden** early/late in the evening; **bis in die späten ~stunden** till late in the evening; **~toilette** *die* evening dress; **in großer ~toilette** (*geh.*) in full evening dress; **~vorstellung** *die* evening performance; **~wind** *der* evening breeze; **~zeit** *die:* **zur ~zeit** in the evening; **~zeitung** *die* ⇒ **~blatt**; **~zug** *der* evening train

**Abenteuer** /ˈaːbn̩tɔyɐ/ *das;* **~s, ~** Ⓐ (*auch fig.*) adventure; **auf ~ ausgehen** go off in search of adventure; Ⓑ (*Unternehmen*) venture; Ⓒ (*Liebesaffäre*) affair

**Abenteuer-:** **~buch** *das* adventure book; **~geschichte** *die* adventure story

**abenteuerlich** ❶ *Adj.* Ⓐ (*riskant*) risky; hazardous; Ⓑ (*bizarr*) bizarre. ❷ *adv.* (*bizarr*) bizarrely; bizarrely, fantastically ‹dressed›

**Abenteuerlichkeit** *die;* **~** Ⓐ (*Gewagtheit*) riskiness; hazardousness; Ⓑ (*Bizarrheit*) bizarreness

**abenteuer-, Abenteuer-:** **~lust** *die* thirst for adventure; **~lustig** *Adj.* adventurous; **~lustig sein** have a thirst for adventure; **~roman** *der* adventure novel; **~spielplatz** *der* adventure playground; **~urlaub** *der* adventure holiday; **sie bieten ~urlaub an** they organize adventure holidays

**Abenteurer** /ˈaːbn̩tɔyrɐ/ *der;* **~s, ~:** adventurer

**Abenteurerin** *die;* **~, ~nen** adventuress

**Abenteurer-:** **~leben** *das* adventurer's life; **~natur** *die* Ⓐ (*Neigung*) adventurous nature; Ⓑ (*Mensch*) adventurous person

**aber** /ˈaːbɐ/ ❶ *Konj.* Ⓐ (*jedoch*) but; **wir ~ ...** we, however, ...; **~ trotzdem** but in spite of that; **da er das ~ nicht wusste** but *or* however, since he didn't know that; **oder ~ [auch]** or else; Ⓑ (*Einwand*) but; **~ warum denn?** but why?; **das stimmt ~ nicht** but that's not right; Ⓒ (*veralt.: Anknüpfung*) but; **als er ~ nicht kam ...** but when he didn't come ...

❷ *Adv.* (*veralt.: wieder*) **~ und abermals** again and again; time and again; ⇒ *auch* **aberhundert**; **abertausend**.

❸ *Partikel* **das ist ~ schön!** why, isn't that nice!; **~ ja/nein!** why, yes/no! **~ natürlich!** but *or* why of course!; **alles, ~ auch alles** everything, but everything; **~ immer!** (*ugs.*) why, certainly!; **das hat ~ geschmeckt** that really tasted good; **das ist ~ auch zu dumm** it's just 'too stupid *or* (*Amer.*) dumb; **das dauert ~** (*ugs.*) what a time it's taking!; **du bist ~ groß!** aren't you tall!; **hat der ~ eine große Nase!** hasn't he got a big nose!; **Sie kommen ~ spät heute** you 'are late today; **~, ~, meine Herrschaften!** now, now, [ladies and] gentlemen

**Aber** *das;* **~s, ~: ich dulde kein ~:** it's no use your objecting; ⇒ *auch* **Wenn**

**Aber·glaube[n]** *der* Ⓐ (*Irrglaube*) superstition; Ⓑ (*Vorurteil*) myth

**aber·gläubig** (*veralt.*), **aber·gläubisch** /-glɔybɪʃ/ *Adj.* superstitious

**aber·hundert** *unbest. Zahlw.* (*geh.*) hundreds [upon hundreds] of

**Aber·hunderte** *Pl.* (*geh.*) hundreds [upon hundreds]

**ab|erkennen** *unr. tr. V.* **jmdm. ein Recht ~:** revoke sb.'s right (**auf** + *Akk.* to); (*Sport*) **jmdm. den Sieg/Titel ~:** disallow sb.'s victory/strip sb. of his/her title

**Aberkennung** *die;* **~, ~en** revocation; (*Sport*) **die ~ ihres Sieges/Titels** disallowing her victory/stripping her of her title

**abermalig** *Adj.* (*wiederholt*) repeated; (*nochmalig*) renewed

**abermals** /ˈaːbɐmaːls/ *Adv.* once again; once more

**ab|ernten** *tr. V.* finish the harvesting of; finish harvesting *or* picking ‹fruit›; **das Getreide ist abgeerntet** the corn is all in; **die Apfelbäume waren fast abgeerntet** nearly all the fruit had been picked from the apple trees; **abgeerntete Felder** empty fields

**Aberration** /ap|ɛraˈtsi̯oːn/ *die;* **~, ~en** (*Astron., Optik*) aberration

**aber·tausend** *unbest. Zahlw.* (*geh.*) thousands [upon thousands] of

**Aber·tausende** *Pl.* (*geh.*) thousands [upon thousands]

**Aber·witz** *der* (*geh.*) lunacy; **ein ~:** a piece of lunacy

**aber·witzig** *Adj.* crazy

**ab|essen** *unr. tr. V.* Ⓐ (*wegessen*) **etw. [von etw.] ~:** eat sth. off [sth.]; Ⓑ (*leer essen*) clear ‹plate, table›; **abgegessene Teller** empty plates; **abgegessenes Geschirr** dirty dishes

**Abessinien** /abɛˈsiːni̯ən/ (*das*)*;* **~s** (*veralt.*) Ⓐ Abyssinia; Ⓑ (*scherzh.: FKK-Strand*) nudist beach

**Abessinier** *der;* **~s, ~, Abessinierin,** *die;* **~, ~nen** (*veralt.*) Abyssinian

**Abf.** *Abk.* **Abfahrt** dep.

**ab|fackeln** *tr. V.* (*Technik*) flare [off]

**abfahr·bereit** *Adj.* ready to go *or* leave *pred.*; **die ~en Fahrzeuge** the vehicles which are/were ready to leave

**ab|fahren** ❶ *unr. itr. V.; mit sein* Ⓐ (*wegfahren*) leave; depart; **wo fährt der Zug nach Paris ab?** where does the Paris train leave from?; Ⓑ (*hinunterfahren*) drive down; (*Skisport*) ski *or* go down; Ⓒ (*salopp: sich begeistern*) **auf jmdn./etw. [voll] ~:** be mad about sb./sth.; Ⓓ (*salopp: abgewiesen werden*) **jmdn. ~ lassen** tell sb. where he/she can go (*sl.*); **bei jmdm. ganz schön ~:** get absolutely nowhere with sb. (*coll.*).

❷ *unr. tr. V.* Ⓐ (*abtransportieren*) take away; Ⓑ (*abnutzen*) wear out; **abgefahrene Reifen** worn tyres; Ⓒ *auch mit sein* (*entlangfahren*) drive the whole length of ‹street, route›; drive through ‹district›; Ⓓ (*ugs.: abtrennen*) **jmdm. ein Bein ~:** run over sb. and sever his/her leg; Ⓔ (*Film, Ferns.*) start.

❸ *unr. refl. V.* (*sich abnutzen*) wear out

**Ab·fahrt** *die* Ⓐ departure; Ⓑ (*Skisport*) descent; (*Strecke*) run; ⇒ *auch* **Abfahrtslauf**; Ⓒ (*Autobahn~*) ⇒ **Ausfahrt** A

**abfahrt·bereit** ⇒ **abfahrbereit**

**Abfahrts-:** **~lauf** *der* (*Skisport*) downhill [racing]; **~läufer** *der*, **~läuferin** *die* (*Skisport*) downhill racer; **~rennen** *das* (*Skisport*) downhill [racing]

a

a

**Abfahrt[s]·zeit** *die* time of departure; departure time

**Ab·fall** *der* Ⓐ (*Küchen~ o. Ä.*) rubbish, (*Amer.*) garbage *or* trash *no indef. art., no pl.*; (*Fleisch~*) offal *no indef. art., no pl.*; (*Industrie~*) waste *no indef. art.*; (*auf der Straße*) litter *no indef. art., no pl.*; **den ~ runtertragen** (*ugs.*) empty the rubbish; Ⓑ (*Rückgang*) drop (*Gen.*, **in** + *Dat.* in); Ⓒ (*Abtrünnigkeit*) (*vom Glauben*) apostasy; (*eines Landes*) secession (**von** from)

**Abfall-:** **~beseitigung** *die* refuse disposal; (*industriell*) waste disposal; **~eimer** *der* rubbish *or* waste bin; trash *or* garbage can (*Amer.*); (*auf der Straße*) litter bin; trash *or* litter basket *or* can (*Amer.*)

**ab|fallen** *unr. itr. V.*; *mit sein* Ⓐ (*ugs.: herausspringen*) **wieviel fällt für jeden ab?** what will each person's share be?; **für dich wird auch eine Kleinigkeit ~:** you'll get something out of it too; **dabei fällt nicht viel ab** not much will come out of it; Ⓑ (*übrig bleiben*) be left [over]; Ⓒ (*herunterfallen*) fall off; Ⓓ (*verschwinden*) **von jmdm. ~:** leave sb.; **alle Unsicherheit fiel von ihm ab** he shed all his diffidence; Ⓔ (*sich lossagen*) ‹country› secede; **vom Glauben ~:** desert the faith; **seine Anhänger fielen von ihm ab** his followers deserted him; Ⓕ (*nachlassen*) drop; Ⓖ (*bes. Sport: zurückfallen*) drop *or* fall back; Ⓗ (*sich senken*) ‹land, hillside, road› drop away; slope; Ⓘ (*im Vergleich*) **gegenüber jmdm./etw.** *od.* **gegen jmdn./etw. stark ~:** be markedly inferior to sb./sth.; Ⓙ (*Seemannsspr.*) cast

**Abfall·haufen** *der* rubbish heap; (*in einer Werkstatt usw.*) waste pile

**ab·fällig** ❶ *Adj.* disparaging; derogatory. ❷ *adv.* **sich ~ über jmdn. äußern** make disparaging *or* derogatory remarks about sb.

**Abfall-:** **~produkt** *das* (*auch fig.*) by-product; (*Sekundärstoff*) secondary product; **~verwertung** *die* recycling of waste

**ab|fälschen** *tr. V.* (*Ballspiele*) deflect

**ab|fangen** *unr. tr. V.* Ⓐ intercept ‹agent, message, aircraft›; Ⓑ (*auf-, anhalten*) catch; Ⓒ (*Sport: einholen*) **jmdn. ~:** catch sb. up; catch up with sb.; Ⓓ (*abwehren*) repel ‹charge, assault›; ward off ‹blow, attack›; (*fig.*) stop ‹development›; cushion ‹impact›; Ⓔ (*Bauw.*) shore up; Ⓕ (*unter Kontrolle bringen*) get ‹vehicle, aircraft› under control

**Abfang·jäger** *der* (*Luftwaffe*) interceptor

**ab|färben** *itr. V.* Ⓐ ‹colour, garment, etc.› run; ‹wet paint etc.› leave marks; Ⓑ (*beeinflussen*) **auf jmdn./etw. ~:** rub off on sb./sth.

**ab|fasen** *tr. V.* (*Technik*) bevel ‹edge›

**ab|fassen** *tr. V.* write ‹report, letter, etc.›; draw up ‹will›

**Ab·fassung** *die* writing; (*eines Testaments*) drawing up

**ab|faulen** *itr. V.*; *mit sein* rot off

**ab|federn** ❶ *tr. V.* Ⓐ (*federnd abfangen*) absorb; Ⓑ (*Technik*) spring ‹axle etc.›. ❷ *itr. V.* bend at the knees on landing [to absorb the shock]; (*beim Absprung*) push off

**ab|fegen** *tr. V.* ⇒ **abkehren²**

**ab|feiern** *tr. V.* use up ‹excess hours worked› (*by taking time off*)

**ab|feilen** *tr. V.* Ⓐ (*entfernen*) file off; **etw. von etw. ~:** file sth. off sth.; Ⓑ (*verkürzen, glätten*) file down

**ab|fertigen** *tr. V.* Ⓐ handle, dispatch ‹mail›; deal with ‹applicant, application›; deal with, handle ‹passengers›; serve ‹customer›; clear ‹ship› for sailing; clear ‹aircraft› for take-off; clear ‹lorry› for departure; (*vorbereiten*) prepare ‹ship etc.› for departure; prepare ‹mail› for dispatch; (*kontrollieren*) clear; check; **der Zoll hat zügig abgefertigt** customs clearance was quick; Ⓑ (*ugs.: unfreundlich behandeln*) **jmdn. [grob/barsch] ~:** [roughly/rudely] turn sb. away; **er hat mich ganz kurz abgefertigt** he was very short with me; Ⓒ (*Sport*) trounce; **der Gegner wurde [mit] 5:1 abgefertigt** the opponent was trounced 5:1

**Ab·fertigung** *die* Ⓐ ⇒ **abfertigen** A: handling; dispatching; serving; clearing for sailing/take-off/departure; preparing for departure/dispatch; (*Kontrolle*) clearance; checking; **die unfreundliche ~ am Flughafen/im Laden** the unfriendly service at the airport/in the shop; Ⓑ (*Abteilung*) dispatch office; Ⓒ (*österr.*) ⇒ **Abfindung**

**Abfertigungs·schalter** *der* (*am Flughafen*) check-in desk; (*beim Zoll*) customs desk

**ab|feuern** *tr. V.* fire; **Schüsse/eine Kanone [auf jmdn./etw.] ~:** fire shots/a cannon [at sb./sth.]; **das ganze Magazin ~:** fire off the whole magazine

**ab|filtern, ab|filtrieren** *tr. V.* (*fachspr.*) filter out

**ab|finden** ❶ *unr. tr. V.* (*entschädigen*) **jmdn. mit etw. ~:** compensate sb. with sth.; **seine Gläubiger ~:** settle with one's creditors; **er wurde großzügig abgefunden** he received a generous settlement. ❷ *unr. refl. V.* **sich ~:** resign oneself; **sich ~ mit** come to terms with; learn to live with ‹noise, heat›; **sich damit ~, dass ...** come to terms with the fact that ...

**Abfindung** *die*; **~, ~en** Ⓐ (*Summe*) settlement; **eine ~ in Höhe von ... zahlen** make a settlement of ...; Ⓑ (*Vorgang*) (*Entschädigung*) compensation; (*von Gläubigern*) paying off

**Abfindungs·summe** *die* ⇒ **Abfindung** A

**ab|fischen** *tr. V.* fish out

**ab|flachen** /ˈapflaxn/ ❶ *tr. V.* (*flacher machen*) flatten [out]. ❷ *refl. V.* Ⓐ (*flacher werden*) flatten out; become flatter; Ⓑ (*nachlassen*) drop off

**Abflachung** *die*; **~, ~en** Ⓐ flattening; Ⓑ (*Nachlassen*) dropping off

**ab|flauen** *itr. V.*; *mit sein* die down; subside; ‹interest, conversation› flag; ‹business› become slack; ‹noise› abate; **die Konjunktur flaut ab** the economy is running down

**ab|fliegen** ❶ *unr. itr. V.*; *mit sein* ‹person› leave [by aeroplane]; ‹aircraft› take off; ‹bird› fly off *or* away; **die Maschine nach Brüssel fliegt um 13³⁰ Uhr ab** the plane for Brussels leaves at 13.30. ❷ *unr. tr. V.* Ⓐ (*wegbringen*) fly out (**aus** of); Ⓑ (*kontrollieren*) fly over ‹district›; fly along ‹road›

**ab|fließen** *unr. itr. V.*; *mit sein* Ⓐ flow off; (*wegfließen*) flow away; **aus etw. ~:** drain away from sth.; **von etw. ~:** run off sth.; **sämtliche Gewinne fließen ins Ausland ab** (*fig.*) all profits are siphoned off abroad; Ⓑ (*sich leeren*) **die Wanne fließt nicht ab** the bath won't empty

**Ab·flug** *der* departure

**Abflug-:** **~hafen** *der* (*Flugw.*) airport of departure; **die Maschine kehrte zum ~hafen zurück** the aircraft returned to the airport it had started from; **~zeit** *die* departure time

**Ab·fluss, *Ab·fluß** *der* Ⓐ drain; (*von Gewässern*) outlet; (*Rohr*) drainpipe; (*für Abwasser*) waste pipe; Ⓑ (*das Abfließen*) draining away; **der ~ von Kapital ins Ausland** (*fig.*) the flow of capital abroad

**Abfluss-, *Abfluß-:** **~graben** *der* drainage ditch; **~rohr** *das* outlet pipe

**Ab·folge** *die* sequence; **die ~ der Jahreszeiten** the cycle of the seasons

**ab|fordern** *tr. V.* **jmdm. etw. ~:** demand sth. of sb.

**ab|fotografieren** *tr. V.* take pictures of

**ab|fragen** *tr. V.* Ⓐ test; **jmdn.** *od.* **jmdm. die Vokabeln ~:** test sb. on his/her vocabulary; Ⓑ (*DV*) retrieve, read out ‹data›; interrogate ‹measuring instrument, store›

**ab|fressen** *unr. tr. V.* Ⓐ (*wegfressen*) **etw. [von etw.] ~:** eat sth. off [sth.]; Ⓑ (*leer fressen*) strip ‹tree, stem, etc.› bare

**ab|frieren** ❶ *unr. itr. V.*; *mit sein* **die Ohren froren ihm ab** he lost his ears through frostbite. ❷ *unr. refl. V.* **sich** (*Dat.*) **etw. ~:** lose sth. by frostbite; **sich** (*Dat.*) **einen ~** (*ugs.*) freeze to death (*coll.*)

**ab|frottieren** *tr. V.* rub down [thoroughly]

**ab|fühlen** *tr. V.* feel; palpate (*Med.*)

**Abfuhr** *die*; **~, ~en** Ⓐ (*Abtransport*) removal; Ⓑ (*Zurückweisung*) **jmdm. eine ~ erteilen** rebuff sb.; turn sb. down; **sich eine ~ holen** be rebuffed *or* turned down; **die Mannschaft holte sich eine deutliche ~:** the team was soundly trounced

**ab|führen** ❶ *tr. V.* Ⓐ (*nach Festnahme*) take away; Ⓑ (*zahlen*) pay out; **Steuern ans Finanzamt ~:** pay taxes to the Inland Revenue; Ⓒ *auch itr.* (*abbringen*) take away; **jmdn. vom Thema ~:** take sb. away from the subject. ❷ *itr. V.* Ⓐ (*für Stuhlgang sorgen*) be a laxative; have a laxative effect; **ein ~des Mittel** a laxative; **ein stark ~des Mittel** a purgative; Ⓑ (*den Darm leeren*) move one's bowels; Ⓒ (*abzweigen*) ‹road› branch off

**Abführ-:** **~mittel** *das* laxative; (*stärker*) purgative; **~pille** *die* laxative pill

**Abfüll-:** **~an·lage** *die* bottling/canning plant; **~datum** *das* bottling/canning date

**ab|füllen** *tr. V.* fill ‹sack, bottle, barrel›; **Wein in Flaschen ~:** bottle wine; **Bier in Dosen ~:** can beer

**ab|füttern¹** *tr., itr. V.* feed ‹animals›

**ab|füttern²** *tr. V.* line ‹coat, jacket›

**Ab·gabe** *die* Ⓐ handing in; (*eines Briefes, Pakets, Telegramms*) delivery; (*eines Gesuchs, Antrags*) submission; **gegen ~ des Coupons erhalten Sie ...** on handing in *or* producing the coupon you will receive ...; Ⓑ (*Steuer, Gebühr*) tax; (*auf Produkte*) duty; (*Gemeinde~*) rate; (*Beitrag*) contribution; Ⓒ (*Ausstrahlung*) release; emission; **eine ~ von 60 Watt** an output of 60 watts; Ⓓ (*Sport: Abspiel*) pass; Ⓔ (*das Abfeuern*) firing; Ⓕ (*das Äußern*) (*von Erklärungen*) giving; (*von Urteilen, Aussagen*) making; (*Stimm~*) casting; Ⓖ (*Verlust*) loss; (*Sport: von Punkten*) dropping; Ⓗ (*Verkauf*) selling; **„~ nur in Kisten"** 'sold only by the crate'

**abgaben·frei** ❶ *Adj.* ‹business, trade, product› free from tax; (*zollfrei*) duty-free. ❷ *adv.* without paying taxes

**Abgaben·ordnung** *die* (*Finanzw.*) tax law

**abgabe[n]·pflichtig** *Adj.* ‹person, business, trade› liable to tax; ‹product› subject to duty

**Abgabe·zug** *der* (*Schach*) sealed move

**Ab·gang** *der* Ⓐ (*das Weggehen*) leaving; departure; (*eines Zuges, Schiffes*) departure (*Theater*) exit; (*fig.*) departure; **sich einen guten ~ verschaffen** (*fig.*) make a good exit; Ⓑ (*jmd., der ausscheidet*) departure; (*Schule*) leaver; Ⓒ (*bes. Amtsspr.: Todesfall*) death; **den ~ machen** (*salopp*) kick the bucket (*sl.*); croak (*sl.*); Ⓓ (*Turnen*) dismount; Ⓔ (*Ausscheidung*) passing; (*von Eiter, Würmern*) discharge; **durch [einen] natürlichen ~:** by being passed naturally; Ⓕ ▶ 474 (*Med.: Fehlgeburt*) miscarriage; Ⓖ (*Absendung*) dispatch; **nach ~ des Briefes** after posting off *or* sending the letter; Ⓗ (*Kaufmannsspr.*) **die Ware findet reißenden ~:** the product is a best seller

**ab·gängig** *Adj.* (*bes. österr.*) missing

**Abgängigkeits·anzeige** *die* (*österr.*) ⇒ **Vermisstenanzeige**

**Abgangs·zeugnis** *das* (*Schulw.*) ≈ leaving certificate

**Ab·gas** *das* exhaust; (*in geschlossenem Raum*) exhaust fumes *pl.*; **~e** exhaust fumes; **industrielle ~e** waste gases

**abgas-, Abgas-:** **~entgiftung** *die* (*Kfz-W.*) emission control; **~frei** ❶ *Adj.* exhaust-free ‹engine›; ❷ *adv.* **das Auto fährt ~frei** the car produces no exhaust fumes; **~katalysator** *der* (*Kfz-W.*) catalytic converter; **~sonder·untersuchung** *die* (*Kfz-W.*) exhaust-emission check; **~turbine** *die* (*Technik*) exhaust-driven turbine; **~verwertung** *die* (*Technik*) utilization of exhaust-gas heat; **~wolke** *die* cloud of exhaust fumes

**ab|gaunern** *tr. V.* (*ugs.*) **jmdm. etw. ~:** con sb. out of sth. (*coll.*)

**abgearbeitet** ⇒ **abarbeiten** B

**ab|geben** ❶ *unr. tr. V.* Ⓐ (*aushändigen*) hand over; deliver ‹letter, parcel, telegram›; hand in, submit ‹application›; hand in ‹school work›; **etw. bei jmdm. ~:** deliver sth. *or* hand sth. over to sb.; **etw. für jmdn. ~:** leave sth. for sb.; **den Mantel in der Garderobe ~:**

*old spelling (see note on page 1707)

leave one's coat in the cloakroom; **B** (*abtreten*) **jmdm. [etwas] von etw. ~:** let sb. have some of sth.; **den Vorsitz/die Spitze ~:** give up the chair/the leadership; **einen Punkt/Satz/eine Runde ~** (*Sport*) drop a point/set/round; **C** (*abfeuern*) fire; **einen Schuss [auf jmdn./etw.] ~:** fire a shot [at sb./sth.]; **D** (*ausstrahlen*) emit ‹radiation›; radiate ‹heat›; give off ‹gas›; transmit ‹radio message›; **E** (*äußern*) make ‹judgement, statement›; cast ‹vote›; **seine Stimme für jmdn. ~:** cast one's vote in favour of sb.; vote for sb.; **F** (*fungieren als*) make; **eine traurige Figur ~:** cut a sorry figure; **G** (*verkaufen*) sell; (*zu niedrigem Preis*) sell off; **gebrauchte Skier billig abzugeben** second-hand skis for sale cheap; **H** *auch itr.* (*Sport: abspielen*) pass.

❷ *unr. refl. V.* (*sich befassen*) **sich mit jmdm./etw. ~:** spend time on sb./sth.; (*geringschätzig*) waste one's time on sb./sth

**ab·gebrannt** ❶ *2. Part. v.* **abbrennen**. ❷ *Adj.* (*ugs.*) broke (*coll.*)

**ab·gebrochen** ❶ *2. Part. v.* **abbrechen**. ❷ *Adj.* (*ugs. scherzh.*) **A** **ein ~er Mediziner** *usw.: a former medical etc. student who never completed his training;* **B** **ein ~er Riese** a midget

**abgebrüht** ❶ *2. Part. v.* **abbrühen**. ❷ *Adj.* (*ugs.*) hardened

**abgedankt** ❶ *2. Part. v.* **abdanken**. ❷ *Adj.* retired

**ab·gedroschen** *Adj.* (*ugs.*) hackneyed; well-worn; trite

**Abgedroschenheit** *die;* ~ (*ugs.*) triteness; hackneyedness

**abgefeimt** /ˈapgəfaimt/ *Adj.* infernally cunning ‹villain, rogue›; villainous ‹scheme›

**Abgefeimtheit** *die;* ~, **~en** (*Handlung*) piece of villainy; (*Charakter*) infernal cunning; **seine ~en** his villainy *sing.*

**ab·gegriffen** ❶ *2. Part. v.* **abgreifen**. ❷ *Adj.* **A** (*abgenutzt*) battered; **B** (*fig.: abgedroschen*) hackneyed; well-worn

**abgehackt** ❶ *2. Part. v.* **abhacken**. ❷ *Adj.* broken ‹voice›; clipped ‹speech›; fragmentary ‹sentence›. ❸ *adv.* in short bursts

**ab·gehangen** ❶ *2. Part. v.* **abhängen**[1]. ❷ *Adj.* hung; **ein gut ~es Steak** a well-hung steak

**abgehärmt** ❶ *2. Part. v.* **abhärmen**. ❷ *Adj.* careworn; haggard

**abgehärtet** ❶ *2. Part. v.* **abhärten**. ❷ *Adj.* (*körperlich*) tough; (*seelisch*) callous

**ab|gehen** ❶ *unr. itr. V.; mit sein* **A** (*sich entfernen*) leave; go away *or* off; (*Theater*) exit; go off; **von der Bühne ~:** leave the stage; **nach hinten ~:** go out at the back; **B** (*ausscheiden*) leave; **von der Schule ~:** leave school; **C** (*abfahren*) ‹train, ship, bus› leave, depart; **D** (*abgeschickt werden*) ‹message, letter› be sent [off]; **E** (*abzweigen*) branch off; (*in andere Richtung*) turn off; **F** (*sich lösen*) come off; ‹spot, stain› come out; ‹avalanche› come down; **G** (*Turnen*) dismount; **H** (*abgerechnet werden*) **von etw. [an jmdn.] ~:** have to be deducted from sth. [and paid to sb.]; **I** (*fehlen*) **jmdm. geht etw. [völlig] ab** sb. is [totally] lacking in sth.; **mir geht jedes Interesse daran ab** it does not interest me in the slightest; **sich** (*Dat.*) **nichts ~ lassen** never stint oneself; **J** (*ausgehen*) go off; **K** (*ausgeschieden werden*) ‹pus, worms› be discharged; (*mit normalen Ausscheidungen*) be passed; **jmdm. geht Kot ab** sb. has a motion *or* (*Amer.*) movement; **eine Blähung ~ lassen** break wind; **ihm ging einer ab** (*derb*) he shot his load (*coarse*); **L** (*aufgeben*) **~ von** abandon ‹demand, agreement, principle›; give up ‹habit›.

❷ *unr. tr. V.; auch mit sein* walk all along; go over ‹area› on foot

**abgehetzt** ❶ *2. Part. v.* **abhetzen**. ❷ *Adj.* exhausted; (*außer Atem*) breathless

**abgekämpft** *Adj.* worn out; exhausted; combat-weary ‹troops›

**abgekartet** *Adj.* (*ugs.*) pre-arranged; **von vornherein ~:** set up in advance; **eine ~e Sache, ein ~es Spiel sein** be rigged in advance

**abgeklappert** ❶ *2. Part. v.* **abklappern**. ❷ *Adj.* (*abwertend*) beat-up, (*Brit. sl.*) clapped-out ‹machine, bicycle, horse, etc.›; hackneyed, well-worn, trite ‹expression›

**abgeklärt** ❶ *2. Part. v.* **abklären**. ❷ *Adj.* serene

**Abgeklärtheit** *die;* ~: serenity

**abgelagert** ❶ *2. Part. v.* **ablagern**. ❷ *Adj.* mature ‹wine›; seasoned ‹timber, tobacco›; **gut ~es Holz** well-seasoned timber

**abgelebt** ❶ *2. Part. v.* **ableben**. ❷ *Adj.* [old and] weary ‹person›; worn ‹face›

**ab·gelegen** *Adj.* remote; (*einsam*) isolated; out-of-the-way ‹district›; (*abgeschieden*) secluded; (*fig.*) recondite

**Ab·gelegenheit** *die;* ~: remoteness; (*einsame Lage*) isolation

**ab|gelten** *unr. tr. V.* satisfy, settle ‹claim›; pay ‹overtime›; **die Mehrarbeit in Freizeit ~:** give time off in lieu of overtime pay; **diese Leistung war bereits mit der Jahresgebühr abgegolten** payment for this service was already covered in the annual fee; **jmdm. seine Treue gut ~:** reward sb. well for his/her loyalty; **eine Geldstrafe durch gemeinnützige Arbeit ~:** do community service in lieu of paying a fine; **die Gefängnisstrafe war bereits durch die Untersuchungshaft abgegolten** the prison sentence had already been served on remand

**Ab·geltung** *die;* ~, **~en** settlement

**abgemagert** ❶ *2. Part. v.* **abmagern**. ❷ *Adj.* emaciated; wasted

**ab·gemessen** ❶ *2. Part. v.* **abmessen**. ❷ *Adj.* (*geh.*) measured. ❸ *adv.* (*geh.*) in a measured fashion

**ab·geneigt** *Adj.* **einer Sache** (*Dat.*) **~ sein** be averse to sth.; **ein stiller, jeder Publicity ~er Mensch** a quiet person averse to public notice; **die jeder Reform ~en Politiker** the politicians opposed to any reform; **jmdm. ~ sein** be ill-disposed towards sb.; **[nicht] ~ sein, etw. zu tun** [not] be averse to doing sth.

**abgenutzt** ❶ *2. Part. v.* **abnutzen**. ❷ *Adj.* worn ‹tyre, chair, handle›; well-used ‹implement›; well-worn ‹phrase›

**Abgeordnete** *der/die; adj. Dekl.* member [of parliament]; (*in Berlin, Frankreich*) deputy; **Herr ~r [Schmidt]/Frau ~ [Müller]** (*im Parlament*) the honourable Member; **der [Herr] ~ Meier** Mr Meier

**Abgeordneten·haus** *das* parliament; (*in Berlin, Frankreich*) Chamber of Deputies

**ab|geraten** *unr. itr. V.; mit sein* (*veralt.*) **vom Weg ~:** lose one's way; stray from one's path

**ab·gerissen** ❶ *2. Part. v.* **abreißen**. ❷ *Adj.* **A** (*zerlumpt*) ragged; **B** (*zusammenhanglos*) disconnected; fragmentary

**Ab·gesandte** *der/die* (*veralt.*) ambassador; (*fig.*) emissary

**Ab·gesang** *der* **A** (*Abschied*) **ein ~ auf etw.** (*Akk.*) a farewell to sth.; **B** (*geh.: letztes Werk*) swan song; **C** (*Verslehre*) abgesang (*final part of Minnesang strophe*)

**abgeschabt** ❶ *2. Part. v.* **abschaben**. ❷ *Adj.* shabby; worn

**ab·geschieden** ❶ *2. Part. v.* **abscheiden**. ❷ *Adj.* **A** secluded; (*abgelegen*) isolated; **B** (*geh.: tot*) departed. ❸ *adv.* ‹live› in seclusion

**Abgeschiedenheit** *die;* ~: seclusion; (*Abgelegenheit*) isolation

**ab·geschlagen** ❶ *2. Part. v.* **abschlagen**. ❷ *Adj.* **A** (*Sport*) [well] beaten; **~ auf dem neunten Tabellenplatz** in lowly ninth place; **B** (*erschöpft*) exhausted; tired out

**ab·geschlossen** ❶ *2. Part. v.* **abschließen**. ❷ *Adj.* **A** (*abgesondert*) secluded; solitary; **B** (*in sich geschlossen*) enclosed; self-contained ‹flat›. ❸ *adv.* ‹live› in seclusion

**Ab·geschlossenheit** *die;* ~: seclusion; (*Abgelegenheit*) isolation

**abgeschmackt** /ˈapgəʃmakt/ *Adj.* tasteless

**ab·geschnitten** ❶ *2. Part. v.* **abschneiden**. ❷ *Adj.* isolated; **von der Außenwelt ~:** cut off from the outside world

**ab·gesehen** ❶ *2. Part. v.* **absehen**. ❷ *Adv.* **~ von jmdm./etw.** apart from sb./sth.; **~ davon, dass ...** apart from the fact that ...

**ab·gesessen** ❶ *2. Part. v.* **absitzen**. ❷ *Adj.* worn

**ab·gespannt** ❶ *2. Part. v.* **abspannen**. ❷ *Adj.* weary; exhausted

**Ab·gespanntheit** *die;* ~: weariness; exhaustion

**abgespielt** ❶ *2. Part. v.* **abspielen**. ❷ *Adj.* ‹record etc.› worn out with repeated playing

**ab·gestanden** ❶ *2. Part. v.* **abstehen**. ❷ *Adj.* **A** (*schal*) flat; (*fig.*) trite; **B** (*verbraucht*) stale

**ab·gestorben** ❶ *2. Part. v.* **absterben**. ❷ *Adj.* dead ‹branch, tree›; numb ‹fingers, legs, etc.›

**abgestumpft** ❶ *2. Part. v.* **abstumpfen**. ❷ *Adj.* apathetic and insensitive ‹person›; deadened ‹conscience, perception›; **gegenüber einer Sache ~ sein** be hardened to sth.

**Abgestumpftheit** *die;* ~: apathy and insensitivity

**abgetakelt** ❶ *2. Part. v.* **abtakeln**. ❷ *Adj.* (*salopp: heruntergekommen*) faded

**ab·getragen** ❶ *2. Part. v.* **abtragen**. ❷ *Adj.* well-worn

**ab·getreten** ❶ *2. Part. v.* **abtreten**. ❷ *Adj.* worn down

**abgewetzt** ❶ *2. Part. v.* **abwetzen**. ❷ *Adj.* well-worn; battered ‹case etc.›

**ab|gewinnen** *unr. tr. V.* **A** (*beim Spiel*) **jmdm. Geld ~:** win money from sb.; **B** (*erlangen von*) **jmdm. etw. ~:** get sth. out of sb.; win sth. from sb.; **einer Sache** (*Dat.*) **etw. ~:** win *or* gain sth. from sth.; **C** (*fig.*) **ich kann ihm/dem nichts ~:** he/it does not do anything for me (*coll.*); ⇒ *auch* **Geschmack A**

**abgewirtschaftet** ❶ *2. Part. v.* **abwirtschaften**. ❷ *Adj.* run down

**ab·gewogen** ❶ *2. Part. v.* **abwägen, abwiegen**. ❷ *Adj.* carefully weighed; balanced ‹judgement›; carefully considered ‹account›

**ab|gewöhnen** *tr. V.:* **jmdm. etw. ~:** make sb. give up *or* stop sth.; **sich** (*Dat.*) **etw. ~:** give up *or* stop sth.; **noch einen zum Abgewöhnen trinken/eine zum Abgewöhnen rauchen** (*ugs.*) have just one more (*coll.*); **zum Abgewöhnen [sein]** (*ugs.*) [be] awful

**abgewrackt** ❶ *2. Part. v.* **abwracken**. ❷ *Adj.* (*abwertend*) superannuated

**abgezehrt** *Adj.* emaciated

**abgezirkelt** ❶ *2. Part. v.* **abzirkeln**. ❷ *Adj.* measured out ‹flower beds›; carefully weighed ‹words›; **ein exakt ~er Pass** (*Sport*) a precisely calculated pass. ❸ *adv.* with calculated precision

**ab|gießen** *unr. tr. V.* **A** pour away ‹liquid›; drain ‹potatoes›; **den Eimer ~:** pour some water *etc.* out of the bucket; **B** (*bild. Kunst; Gießerei*) **etw. [in Bronze] ~:** cast sth. [in bronze]

**Ab·glanz** *der* **A** (*Reflex*) reflection; **B** (*Nachklang*) distant echo; pale reflection

**ab|gleichen** *unr. tr. V.* (*Funkw., Elektronik*) balance

**ab|gleiten** *unr. itr. V.; mit sein* (*geh.*) **A** (*abrutschen*) slide *or* slip off; **von/an etw.** (*Dat.*) **~:** slip *or* slide off sth.; **B** (*absinken*) **in etw.** (*Akk.*) **~:** slip down into sth.

**Ab·gott** *der* idol

**Abgötterei** /apgœtəˈrai/ *die;* ~: idolatry

**Ab·göttin** *die* idol

**abgöttisch** /ˈapgœtɪʃ/ ❶ *Adj.* idolatrous. ❷ *adv.* **jmdn. ~ verehren/lieben** idolize sb.

**ab|graben** *unr. tr. V.* dig out; ⇒ *auch* **Wasser A**

**ab|grasen** *tr. V.* **A** graze away ‹pasture›; **B** (*ugs.: absuchen*) **etw. nach etw. ~:** comb *or* scour sth. for sth.

**ab|greifen** *unr. tr. V.* **A** measure (*with one's hand*); **eine Strecke mit dem Zirkel ~:** measure a distance with compasses; ⇒ *auch* **abgegriffen 2**; **B** (*Elektrot.*) pick up

**ab|grenzen** *tr. V.* **A** bound; **etw. nach allen Seiten ~:** enclose sth.; **etw. gegen** *od.* **von etw. ~:** separate sth. from sth.; **B** (*unterscheiden*) differentiate; distinguish; (*festlegen*) demarcate; **zwei Theorien gegen-**

einander *od.* **voneinander ~:** differentiate between two theories; **sich von jmdm. ~:** differentiate oneself from sb.

**Abgrenzung** *die;* **~, ~en** Ⓐ boundary; **~ nach allen Seiten** enclosure; Ⓑ (*Unterscheidung*) differentiation; (*Festlegung*) demarcation; **Politik der ~:** policy of demarcation

**Ab·grund** *der* Ⓐ (*Schlucht*) abyss; chasm; (*Abhang*) precipice; Ⓑ (*fig. geh.*) dark abyss; **die Abgründe der menschlichen Seele** the depths of the human soul; **ein ~ von Verzweiflung** an abyss of despair

**abgründig** /ˈapgrʏndɪç/ (*geh.*) ❶ *Adj.* Ⓐ (*rätselhaft*) inscrutable ‹smile›; hidden ‹meaning›; dark ‹secret›; Ⓑ (*unermesslich*) unbounded. ❷ *adv.* Ⓐ (*rätselhaft*) ‹smile› inscrutably; Ⓑ (*sehr*) thoroughly

**abgrund·tief** *Adj.* out and out

**Ab·gruppierung** *die* salary downgrading

**ab|gucken** (*ugs.*) ❶ *tr. V.* Ⓐ **[bei** *od.* **von] jmdm. etw. ~:** learn sth. by watching sb.; Ⓑ **ich guck dir nichts ab!** (*fam.*) you needn't be self-conscious just because I'm watching you. ❷ *itr. V.* (*abschreiben*) **[bei jmdm.] ~:** copy [from sb.]; copy [sb. else's] work

**Ab·guss, *Ab·guß** *der* (*bild. Kunst, Gießerei*) (*Verfahren*) casting; (*Ergebnis*) cast; **ein ~ in Bronze** a bronze [cast]

**ab|haben** *unr. tr. V.* (*ugs.*) Ⓐ *auch itr.* (*erhalten*) **etwas/ein Stück** *usw.* **[von etw.] ~:** have some/a piece *etc.* [of sth.]. **du kannst gerne davon ~:** you're welcome to have some; Ⓑ (*abgenommen haben*) have off; **du hast die Mütze ja schon wieder ab!** why, you've got your cap off again!; Ⓒ (*entfernt haben*) have got off

**ab|hacken** *tr. V.* chop off; **jmdm. die Hand** *usw.* **~:** chop sb.'s hand *etc.* off; ⇒ *auch* **abgehackt** 2, 3

**ab|haken** *tr. V.* Ⓐ (*mit Haken versehen*) tick off; check off (*Amer.*); (*fig.: erledigen*) deal with; Ⓑ (*vom Haken abnehmen*) unclip

**ab|halftern** *tr. V.* Ⓐ (*ugs.: entlassen*) sack (*coll.*); Ⓑ (*das Halfter abnehmen von*) **ein Pferd ~:** take the halter off a horse

**ab|halten** *unr. tr. V.* Ⓐ (*fernhalten*) **[von jmdm./etw.] ~:** keep ‹person, wind, cold, flies, etc.› off [sb./sth.]; keep ‹trouble› away [from sb.]; Ⓑ (*hindern*) **jmdn. davon ~, etw. zu tun** stop sb. doing sth.; prevent sb. from doing sth.; Ⓒ (*durchführen*) hold ‹elections, meeting, referendum›; Ⓓ (*bei der Notdurft*) hold ‹child› out; Ⓔ (*weghalten*) hold away; **etw. ein Stück von sich ~:** hold sth. away from oneself

**Ab·haltung** *die* Ⓐ (*Verhinderung*) **eine [dringende] ~ haben** be [unavoidably] held up; Ⓑ (*Durchführung*) holding

**ab|handeln** *tr. V.* Ⓐ (*abkaufen*) **jmdm. etw. ~:** do a deal with sb. for sth.; Ⓑ (*herunterhandeln*) **jmdm. zehn Mark ~:** beat sb. down by ten marks; (*fig.*) **sich** (*Dat.*) **von etw. nichts ~ lassen** not be persuaded to part with any of sth.; Ⓒ (*darstellen*) treat; deal with

**abhanden** /apˈhandn̩/ *Adv.* **~ kommen** get lost; go astray; **etw. kommt jmdm. ~:** sb. mislays *or* loses sth.

**Ab·handlung** *die* Ⓐ (*Aufsatz*) treatise (**über** + *Akk.* on); Ⓑ (*das Abhandeln*) treatment

**Ab·hang** *der* slope; incline

**ab|hängen¹** *unr. itr. V.* Ⓐ (*abhängig sein*) **[ganz allein] von jmdm./etw. ~:** depend [entirely] on sb./sth.; **davon hängt sehr viel für mich ab** a lot depends on it for me; **von jmdm./etw. ~** (*angewiesen sein*) be dependent on sb./sth.; Ⓑ (*hängen*) hang; ⇒ *auch* **abgehangen** 2

**ab|hängen²** ❶ *tr. V.* Ⓐ (*abnehmen*) take down; **ein Bild von der Wand ~:** take a picture [down] off the wall; Ⓑ (*Eisenb.: abkuppeln*) uncouple; Ⓒ (*ugs.: abschütteln*) shake off ‹pursuer, competitor›. ❷ *itr. V.* (*den Hörer auflegen*) hang up

**abhängig** /ˈaphɛŋɪç/ *Adj.* Ⓐ **von jmdm./etw. ~ sein** (*bedingt*) depend on sb./sth.; (*angewiesen*) be dependent on sb./sth.; **von einer Droge ~ sein** be addicted to *or* dependent on a drug; **etw. von etw. ~ machen** make sth. conditional upon sth.; Ⓑ (*Sprachw.*) indirect *or* reported ‹speech›; subordinate ‹clause›; oblique ‹case›

**-abhängig** *Adj.* dependent on …

**Abhängige** *der/die; adj. Dekl.* (*Rechtsspr.*) dependant; (*Untergebene*) subordinate

**Abhängigkeit** *die;* **~, ~en** dependence; **~ von Drogen** addiction to *or* dependence on drugs; **in ~ von jmdm./etw. geraten** become dependent on sb./sth.

**-abhängigkeit** *die* dependence on …

**Abhängigkeits·verhältnis** *das* relationship of dependence (**zu** on)

**ab|härmen** *refl. V.* **sich [um jmdn.] ~:** pine away with grief [over sb.]; ⇒ *auch* **abgehärmt** 2

**ab|härten** *tr. V.* harden; **sich/seinen Körper durch Sport ~:** harden oneself/one's body with sporting activity; ⇒ *auch* **abgehärtet** 2

**Ab·härtung** *die;* **~:** hardening; **zur ~:** to harden oneself

**ab|haspeln** *tr. V.* Ⓐ (*abwickeln*) unwind; (*von einer Spule*) unreel; Ⓑ (*hastig vortragen*) reel off

**ab|hauen** ❶ *unr. tr. V.* Ⓐ (*abtrennen*) chop off; **jmdm. den Arm** *usw.* **~:** cut sb.'s arm *etc.* off. Ⓑ *Prät. nur* **haute ab** (*abschlagen*) knock off. ❷ *unr. itr. V.; mit sein; Prät. nur* **haute ab** (*salopp: verschwinden*) beat it (*coll.*); **hau ab!** get lost! (*coll.*)

**ab|häuten** *tr. V.* skin

**ab|heben** ❶ *unr. tr. V.* Ⓐ lift off ‹lid, cover, etc.›; **[den Hörer] ~:** answer [the telephone]; Ⓑ (*Kartenspiel*) (*in zwei Hälften teilen*) cut [the pack]; (*nehmen*) draw ‹card›; Ⓒ (*von einem Konto*) withdraw ‹money›; **ich möchte gern [Geld] ~:** I would like to make a withdrawal.
❷ *unr. itr. V.* Ⓐ (*in die Luft*) ‹balloon› rise; ‹aircraft, bird› take off; ‹rocket› lift off; **nachdem das Flugzeug abgehoben hatte** after takeoff; Ⓑ **auf etw.** (*Akk.*) **~:** lay emphasis on sth.; stress sth.; Ⓒ (*ugs.: unrealistisch werden*) lose touch with the real world; **der hat abgehoben** (*ist verrückt geworden*) he's cracked (*coll.*).
❸ *unr. refl. V.* (*sich abzeichnen*) stand out; contrast; **sich von** *od.* **gegen etw./von jmdm. ~:** stand out against *or* contrast with sth./sb.

**Ab·hebung** *die* withdrawal

**ab|heften** *tr. V.* file; **etw. in einem** *od.* **einen Ordner ~:** file sth.

**ab|heilen** *itr. V.; mit sein* heal up

**ab|helfen** *unr. itr. V.* **einem Bedürfnis ~:** meet a need; **einem Missstand ~:** put an end to an abuse; **einem Übelstand ~:** remedy an evil; **dem ist leicht abzuhelfen** that is easily remedied

**ab|hetzen** ❶ *tr. V.* ride ‹horse etc.› to exhaustion. ❷ *refl. V.* rush *or* dash [around]; **hetz dich doch nicht so ab!** don't rush around so much!; ⇒ *auch* **abgehetzt** 2

**ab|heuern** /ˈaphɔyɐn/ (*Seemannsspr.*) ❶ *tr. V.* pay off. ❷ *itr. V.* be paid off

**Ab·hilfe** *die* action to improve matters; **~ schaffen** find a remedy; put things right; **baldige/schnellste ~:** speedy/immediate action

**ab|hobeln** *tr. V.* Ⓐ plane down; Ⓑ (*entfernen*) plane off

**abhol·bereit** *Adj.* ready for collection *post-pos.*

**ab·hold** *Adj.* **einer Sache** (*Dat.*) **~ sein** (*geh.*) be averse to sth.

**ab|holen** *tr. V.* Ⓐ collect, pick up ‹parcel, book, tickets, etc.›; pick up, fetch ‹person›; **ein Paket auf der Post ~:** collect a parcel at the post office; **ich hole Sie am Bahnhof ab** I'll pick you up at the station; **jmdn. zum Essen ~:** call for sb. and go for a meal; Ⓑ (*ugs. verhüll.: verhaften*) take away

**Abholer** *der;* **~s, ~, Abholerin** *die;* **~, ~nen** (*Postw.*) *addressee who collects mail from the post office instead of having it delivered*

**Abhol·markt** *der* (*retail*) cash and carry [store]

**Abholung** *die;* **~, ~en** collection

**ab|holzen** *tr. V.* fell ‹trees›; clear ‹area› [of trees]

**Abhör·anlage** *die* listening *or* (*coll.*) bugging system

**ab|horchen** *tr. V.* listen to; **sich ~ lassen** (*beim Arzt*) have one's lungs/chest sounded

**ab|hören** *tr. V.* Ⓐ (*abfragen*) **jmdm.** *od.* **jmdn. Vokabeln ~:** test sb.'s vocabulary [orally]; **das Einmaleins ~:** ask questions on the multiplication table; Ⓑ (*anhören, heimlich hören*) listen to; Ⓒ (*überwachen*) tap ‹telephone, telephone conversation›; bug (*coll.*) ‹conversation, premises›; **jmdn. ~:** tap sb.'s telephone; Ⓓ ⇒ **abhorchen**

**Abhör·gerät** *das* listening device; bug (*coll.*)

**abhör·sicher** *Adj.* bug-proof (*coll.*); tap-proof ‹telephone›

**ab|hungern** *tr. V.* Ⓐ (*verlieren*) take off, lose ‹weight›; Ⓑ (*sparen*) **sich** (*Dat.*) **das Geld für die Reise ~:** go *or* (*Amer.*) do without to save the money for the trip

**Abi** /ˈabi/ *das;* **~s, ~s** (*Schülerspr.*) ⇒ **Abitur**

**ab|irren** *itr. V.; mit sein* (*geh.*) stray; **vom Weg ~:** stray from one's path; (*fig.*) stray; err

**ab|isolieren** *tr. V.* (*Elektrot.*) strip the insulation off

**Abisolier·zange** *die* wire strippers *pl.*

**Abitur** /abiˈtuːɐ̯/ *das;* **~s, ~e** ▶ **369** Abitur (*school-leaving examination at grammar school needed for entry to higher education*); ≈ A levels (*Brit.*); **sein** *od.* **das ~ machen** do *or* take one's Abitur; **haben Sie ~?** have you got your Abitur?

**Abiturient** /abituˈri̯ɛnt/ *der;* **~en, ~en** *sb. who is taking/has passed the 'Abitur'*

**Abiturienten·klasse** *die: class of pupils in last year at grammar school;* ≈ upper sixth *or* A-level class (*Brit.*)

**Abiturientin** *die;* **~, ~nen** ⇒ **Abiturient**

**Abitur·zeugnis** *das* Abitur certificate

**ab|jagen** ❶ *tr. V.* (*abnehmen*) **jmdm. etw. ~:** finally get sth. away from sb. ❷ *refl. V.* ⇒ **abhetzen** 2

**Abk.** *Abk.* **Abkürzung** abbr.

**ab|kämmen** *tr. V.* Ⓐ (*entfernen*) comb out; Ⓑ (*absuchen*) comb, scour (**nach** for)

**ab|kanten** *tr. V.* (*Technik*) fold (*near the edge*)

**ab|kanzeln** *tr. V.* (*ugs.*) **jmdn. ~:** give sb. a dressing down; reprimand sb.

**ab|kapiteln** *tr. V.* (*veralt.*) **jmdn. ~:** read sb. a lesson; chide sb. (*dated*)

**ab|kapseln** *tr. V.* encapsulate; **sich gegen die Umwelt ~** (*fig.*) isolate oneself from one's surroundings

**ab|karten** *tr. V.* ⇒ **abgekartet**

**ab|kassieren** ❶ *itr. V.* Ⓐ **bei jmdm. ~** (*im Restaurant*) give sb. his/her bill; (*ohne Rechnung*) settle up with sb.; Ⓑ (*ugs. abwertend*) rake it in (*coll.*); **bei jmdm. ~:** fleece sb.; Ⓒ (*ugs.*) ⇒ **kassieren** 2 B. ❷ Ⓐ **jmdn. ~** (*im Restaurant*) give sb. his/her bill; (*ohne Rechnung*) settle up with sb.; **die Fahrgäste ~:** take the fares; Ⓑ (*ugs. abwertend*) fleece ‹person›; rake in (*coll.*) ‹money›

**ab|kauen** *tr. V.* chew ‹pencil›; bite ‹fingernails›

**ab|kaufen** *tr. V.* Ⓐ **jmdm. etw. ~:** buy sth. from sb.; Ⓑ (*ugs.: glauben*) **das kaufe ich dir nicht ab** I'm not buying that story (*coll.*)

**Abkehr** *die;* **~: eine ~ von alten Traditionen** a rejection of *or* turning away from ancient traditions

**ab|kehren¹** *tr. V.* (*abwenden*) turn away; **sein Gesicht ~:** turn one's face away; **sich [von jmdm./etw.] ~:** turn away [from sb./sth.]; **sich von der Welt ~** (*fig.*) turn one's back on the world; **die uns abgekehrte Seite des Mondes/des Schiffes** the far side of the moon/the ship

**ab|kehren²** *tr. V.* Ⓐ (*entfernen*) brush off; **den Schmutz von etw. ~:** brush the dirt off sth.; Ⓑ (*säubern*) **etw. ~:** brush sth. clean

*old spelling (see note on page 1707)

a

**ab|ketteln, ab|ketten** *tr. (auch itr.) V. (Handarb.)* cast off

**ab|kippen** ❶ *tr. (auch itr.) V. (abladen)* tip out; dump ‹refuse›. ❷ *itr. V.; mit sein (herunterfallen)* tip over

**ab|klappern** *tr. V. (ugs.)* trudge round ‹town, district›; **alle Läden nach etw. ~:** do the rounds of all the shops looking for sth.; ⇨ *auch* **abgeklappert 2**

**ab|klären** *tr. V.* clear up; sort out *(coll.)*; ⇨ *auch* **abgeklärt 2**

**Ab·klatsch** *der (abwertend)* pale imitation; poor copy

**ab|klatschen** *tr. V.* Ⓐ *(beim Tanzen)* **jmdn. ~** *(clap one's hands and)* cut in to dance with sb.; **beim nächsten Tanz darf abgeklatscht werden** an excuse-me dance comes next; Ⓑ *(Ballspiele)* palm away ‹ball, shot›

**ab|klemmen** *tr. V.* Ⓐ *(zusammenpressen)* clamp; Ⓑ *(lösen)* disconnect; Ⓒ *(abtrennen)* sever

**ab|klingen** *unr. itr. V.; mit sein* Ⓐ *(leiser werden)* grow fainter; Ⓑ *(nachlassen)* subside; die away

**ab|klopfen** ❶ *tr. V.* Ⓐ *(entfernen)* knock *or* tap off; **jmdm. etw. [von der Jacke] ~:** tap sth. off sb.['s jacket]; Ⓑ *(säubern)* knock/tap the dirt/snow/crumbs *etc.* off; **sich** *(Dat.)* **die Hände ~:** clap one's hands together to knock the flour/powder *etc.* off; Ⓒ *(untersuchen)* tap; **etw. auf seine Zuverlässigkeit hin ~** *(fig.)* check the reliability of sth. ❷ *itr., tr. V. (Musik)* tap one's baton to stop

**ab|knabbern** *tr. V.* nibble off; gnaw off

**ab|knallen** *tr. V. (salopp)* shoot down; gun down

**ab|knapsen** *tr. V. (ugs.)* Ⓐ *(wegnehmen)* pinch *(coll.)*; **jmdm. etwas/ein Drittel von seinem Lohn ~:** take some/a third of sb.'s wages; Ⓑ ⇨ **abzwacken A**

**ab|kneifen** *unr. tr. V.* nip off; pinch off

**ab|knicken** ❶ *tr. V.* Ⓐ *(abbrechen)* snap *or* break off; Ⓑ *(knicken)* bend. ❷ *itr. V.; mit sein* Ⓐ *(abbrechen)* snap; break; Ⓑ *(einknicken)* bend over; **in der Hüfte ~:** bend at the hips; Ⓒ *(Verkehrsw.)* **~de Vorfahrt** priority for traffic turning right/left

**ab|knipsen** *tr. V. (ugs.)* snip off

**ab|knöpfen** *tr. V.* Ⓐ unbutton; Ⓑ *(salopp)* **jmdm. Geld ~:** get money out of sb.

**ab|knutschen** *tr. V. (ugs.)* Ⓐ kiss and fondle; Ⓑ *(sexuell)* **jmdn. ~/sich mit jmdm. ~:** smooch *(coll.)* or *(coll.)* neck with sb.; **sich ~:** smooch *(coll.)*; neck *(coll.)*

**ab|kochen** ❶ *tr. V.* Ⓐ *(keimfrei machen)* boil; Ⓑ *(salopp: schröpfen)* rip off *(coll.)*; fleece *(coll.)*. ❷ *itr. V. (im Freien kochen)* cook in the open air

**ab|kommandieren** *tr. V.* detail; *(fig.)* detail; send; **jmdn. zum Dienst/zu einer Einheit ~:** detail sb. for duty/to a unit; **jmdn. an die Front ~:** send sb. to the front

**Abkomme** *der;* **~n, ~n** *(geh.)* ⇨ **Nachkomme**

**ab|kommen** *unr. itr. V.; mit sein* Ⓐ *(abweichen)* **vom Weg ~:** lose one's way; **immer mehr vom Weg ~:** go further and further astray; **vom Kurs ~:** go off course; **von der Fahrbahn ~:** leave the road; **vom rechten Weg ~** *(fig. geh.)* stray from the straight and narrow; Ⓑ *(abschweifen)* digress; **vom Thema ~:** stray from the topic; digress; Ⓒ *(aufgeben)* **von einem Plan ~:** abandon *or* give up a plan; Ⓓ *(Sport)* **der Läufer ist gut/schlecht abgekommen** the runner got a good/bad start; **der Springer ist gut/schlecht abgekommen** the jumper made a good/bad take-off; Ⓔ *(Schießen)* aim

**Ab·kommen** *das;* **~s, ~:** agreement; **ein ~ [über etw.** *(Akk.)***] treffen** *od.* **schließen** come to an agreement [on sth.]

**abkömmlich** /ˈapkœmlɪç/ *Adj.* free; available

**Abkömmling** /ˈapkœmlɪŋ/ *der;* **~s, ~e** Ⓐ *(Nachkomme)* descendant; Ⓑ *(Chemie)* derivative

**ab|können** *unr. tr. V.* Ⓐ *(nordd.: mögen)* stand; *(vertragen)* take; Ⓑ *(ugs.: abgemacht werden dürfen)* **das Bild kann ab** that picture can go

**ab|konterfeien** *tr. V. (veralt.)* **jmdn. ~** *(zeichnen)* draw a good likeness of sb.; *(fotografieren)* take sb.'s photograph

**ab|koppeln** *tr. V.* uncouple; *(fig.)* separate; dissociate

**ab|kratzen** ❶ *tr. V.* Ⓐ *(entfernen) (mit den Fingern)* scratch off; *(mit einem Werkzeug)* scrape off; Ⓑ *(säubern)* scrape [clean]. ❷ *itr. V.; mit sein (derb)* croak *(sl.)*; snuff it *(sl.)*

**ab|kriegen** *tr. V. (ugs.)* ⇨ **abbekommen**

**ab|kucken** *tr., itr. V. (nordd.)* ⇨ **abgucken**

**ab|kühlen** ❶ *tr. V. (kühlen)* cool down; **jmds. Eifer ~** *(fig.)* dampen sb.'s ardour; **jmdn. ~** *(fig.)* cool sb. off. ❷ *itr. V.; meist mit sein (kühler werden)* cool down; get cooler; **es hat stark abgekühlt** it has become a lot cooler; **die Begeisterung kühlte ab** *(fig.)* enthusiasm waned. ❸ *refl. V. (kühler werden)* cool down; get cooler

**Ab·kühlung** *die* cooling; *(fig.)* cooling [off]

**Abkunft** /ˈapkʊnft/ *die;* **~** *(geh.)* descent; **ein Mädchen bürgerlicher ~:** a girl of bourgeois family

**ab|kupfern** *tr. V. (ugs.)* copy mechanically **(bei** from)

**ab|kuppeln** *tr. V.* ⇨ **abkoppeln**

**ab|kürzen** *tr., itr. V.* Ⓐ *(räumlich)*; **eine Strecke um 5 km ~:** shorten a distance by 5 km; **den Weg ~:** take a shorter route; **wir haben abgekürzt, indem wir durch die Gärten gegangen sind** we took a short cut through the gardens; Ⓑ *(zeitlich)* cut short; Ⓒ *(kürzer schreiben)* abbreviate **(mit** to); **sich [mit] H. S. ~:** have the initials H. S.

**Ab·kürzung** *die* Ⓐ *(Weg)* short cut; Ⓑ *(Wort)* abbreviation; Ⓒ *(das Abkürzen)* cutting short; **zur ~ des Verfahrens** to shorten the procedure

**Abkürzungs-: ~liste** *die* ⇨ **~verzeichnis; ~punkt** *der (Schriftw.)* full stop; **~verzeichnis** *das* list of abbreviations

**ab|küssen** *tr. V.* cover with kisses

**Abl.** *Abk.* **Ableitung**

**ab|lachen** *itr. V. (salopp)* laugh

**ab|laden** *unr. tr., itr. V.* Ⓐ unload, offload ‹case, sack, barrel, goods, vehicle›; dump, unload ‹gravel, sand, rubble›; **seine Sorgen bei jmdm. ~** *(fig.)* unburden oneself to sb.; Ⓑ *(Seew.: beladen)* load ‹ship›

**Ablader** *der;* **~s, ~, Abladerin** *die;* **~, ~nen** *(Seew.)* shipping agent

**Ab·lage** *die* Ⓐ *(Vorrichtung)* storage place; Ⓑ *(Raum)* storage room; Ⓒ *(Bürow.)* filing; Ⓓ *(von Eiern)* laying; Ⓔ *(schweiz.)* ⇨ **Annahmestelle, Zweigstelle**

**ab|lagern** ❶ *tr. V.* Ⓐ *(absetzen)* deposit; Ⓑ *(deponieren)* dump. ❷ *refl. V.* be deposited. ❸ *itr. V.; meist mit sein (reifen)* season; ⇨ *auch* **abgelagert 2**

**Ab·lagerung** *die* Ⓐ deposit; Ⓑ *(das Absetzen)* deposition; **bei der ~ von Mineralien** when minerals have been deposited; Ⓒ *(das Deponieren)* dumping; Ⓓ *(das Reifen)* seasoning

**ablandig** *Adj. (Seemannsspr.)* offshore

**Ablass, *Ablaß** /ˈaplas/ *der;* **Ablasses, Ablässe** *(kath. Rel.)* indulgence

**Ablass·brief, *Ablaß·brief** *der (hist.)* letter of indulgence

**ab|lassen** ❶ *unr. tr. V.* Ⓐ *(ablaufen lassen)* let out **(aus** of); **sein Wasser ~:** pass water; Ⓑ *(ausströmen lassen)* let off ‹steam›; let out ‹air›; **eine Blähung ~:** break wind; Ⓒ *(leeren)* empty; Ⓓ *(abgeben)* **jmdm. etw. ~:** let sb. have sth.; Ⓔ *(nachlassen)* **[jmdm.] vom Preis 20% ~:** give [sb.] a 20% discount; Ⓕ *(ugs.: nicht anziehen, befestigen)* leave ‹tie, hat, badge, etc.› off; Ⓖ *(salopp: äußern)* come out with.
❷ *unr. itr. V.* Ⓐ *(aufgeben)* **von etw. ~:** give sth. up; Ⓑ *(sich nicht mehr befassen)* **von jmdm./etw. ~:** leave sb./sth. alone

**Ablass-, *Ablaß-: ~prediger** *der (hist.)* pardoner; **~ventil** *das (Technik)* outlet valve

**Ablativ** /ˈablatiːf/ *der;* **~s, ~e** *(Sprachw.)* ablative

**Ab·lauf** *der* Ⓐ *(Verlauf)* course; **der ~ der Ereignisse** the course of events; **der ~ des Überfalls/des Programms/der Handlung** the sequence of events during the raid/the order of events on the programme/the development of the plot; Ⓑ *(das Stattfinden)* passing *or* going off; **für den reibungslosen ~ einer Veranstaltung sorgen** ensure that an event passes *or* goes off smoothly; Ⓒ *(Prozess)* process; Ⓓ *(Ende)* **nach ~ eines Jahres** after a year; **nach ~ einer Frist** at the end of a period of time; **mit ~ des Kalenderjahres** at the end of one calendar year; Ⓔ *(Abfluss)* outlet

**ab|laufen** ❶ *unr. itr. V.; mit sein* Ⓐ *(abfließen)* flow away; *(aus einem Behälter)* run *or* flow out; *(sich leeren)* empty; **das Badewasser ~ lassen** let the bathwater out; Ⓑ *(herabfließen)* run down; **von/an etw.** *(Dat.)* **~:** run off sth.; **an ihm läuft alles ab** *(fig.)* it's like water off a duck's back [with him]; **jmdn. ~ lassen** *(ugs.)* send sb. packing; **das Geschirr ~ lassen** let the dishes drain; Ⓒ *(verlaufen)* pass *or* go off; **gut/glimpflich abgelaufen sein** have gone *or* passed off well/smoothly; Ⓓ *(stehen geblieben sein)* ‹alarm clock› run down; ‹parking meter› expire; Ⓔ *(aufhören, ungültig werden)* ‹period, contract, passport› expire; Ⓕ *(abspulen)* **~ lassen** play ‹tape›; run ‹film› through; Ⓖ *(abrollen)* run out ‹rope etc.›; Ⓗ *(Seemannsspr.)* be launched.
❷ *unr. tr. V.* Ⓐ *auch mit sein (entlanglaufen)* walk all along; go over ‹area› on foot; *(schnell)* run all along; Ⓑ *(abnutzen)* wear down; ⇨ *auch* **Bein A; Fuß B; Schuhsohle**

**ab|lauschen** *tr. V. (geh.)* **jmdm. etw. ~:** learn sth. by listening to sb.

**Ab·laut** *der (Sprachw.)* ablaut

**ab|lauten** *itr. V. (Sprachw.)* undergo ablaut; **das sind ~de Verben** these verbs undergo ablaut

**ab|läuten** *itr. V.* Ⓐ ring the bell [to start]; Ⓑ *(veralt.: beim Telefon)* ring off

**ab|leben** *itr. V.; mit sein (geh.)* pass away; ⇨ *auch* **abgelebt 2**

**Ab·leben** *das (geh.)* decease; demise

**ab|lecken** *tr. V.* Ⓐ *(entfernen)* lick off; Ⓑ *(säubern)* lick clean; **sich** *(Dat.)* **die Finger ~:** lick one's fingers

**ab|ledern** *tr. V.* leather down

**ab|legen** ❶ *tr. V.* Ⓐ *(niederlegen)* lay *or* put down; lay ‹egg›; Ⓑ *(Bürow.)* file; Ⓒ *(nicht mehr tragen)* stop wearing; **abgelegte Kleidung** old clothes *pl.;* cast-offs *pl.;* Ⓓ *(aufgeben)* give up ‹habit›; lose ‹shyness›; put aside ‹arrogance›; Ⓔ *(machen, leisten)* swear ‹oath›; sit ‹examination›; give ‹account›; make ‹confession›; ⇨ *auch* **Bekenntnis A;** Ⓕ *(geh.: beabsichtigen)* **es auf etw.** *(Akk.)* **~:** want sth.
❷ *tr., itr. V.* Ⓐ *(ausziehen)* take off; **möchten Sie ~?** would you like to take your coat off?; Ⓑ *(Kartenspiel) (abwerfen)* discard; *(auflegen)* put down.
❸ *itr. V. (Seemannsspr.: losfahren)* **[vom Kai] ~:** cast off

**Ableger** *der;* **~s, ~** Ⓐ *(Bot.)* layer; Ⓑ *(Steckling)* cutting; *(fig. ugs.: Sohn)* offspring; *(fig.: Filiale)* offshoot

**ab|lehnen** ❶ *tr. V.* Ⓐ *(zurückweisen)* decline; decline, turn down ‹money, invitation, position›; reject ‹suggestion, applicant›; Ⓑ *(nicht genehmigen)* turn down; reject; reject, throw out ‹bill›; Ⓒ *(verweigern)* **es ~, etw. zu tun** refuse to do sth.; Ⓓ *(missbilligen)* disapprove of; reject. ❷ *itr. V.* decline; **sie haben ohne Begründung abgelehnt** *(nicht genehmigt)* they rejected it/them without giving any reason

**ablehnend** ❶ *Adj.* negative ‹reply, attitude›; **ein ~er Bescheid** a rejection. ❷ *adv.* **einer Sache** *(Dat.)* **~ gegenüberstehen** take a negative view of sth.; **sich ~ zu etw. äußern** voice one's opposition to sth.

**Ablehnung** *die;* **~, ~en** Ⓐ *(Zurückweisung)* rejection; **auf ~ stoßen** meet with opposition; Ⓑ *(Missbilligung)* disapproval; **auf ~ stoßen** meet with disapproval; Ⓒ *(Weigerung)* refusal

**ab|leisten** *tr. V.* serve out

**ab|leiten** ❶ *tr. V.* Ⓐ divert; Ⓑ *(herleiten; auch Sprachw., Math.)* **etw. aus/von etw.**

a

**~:** derive sth. from sth.; **das Wort ist aus dem Spanischen abgeleitet** the word is derived from Spanish; **C** (*Math.: differenzieren*) differentiate ‹function›. **2** *refl. V.* (*sich herleiten*) **sich aus/von etw. ~:** derive *or* be derived from sth.

**Ab·leitung** *die* **A** (*das Ableiten; auch Math., Sprachw.*) derivation; **B** (*Sprachw.: Wort; Math.: Ergebnis des Differenzierens*) derivative

**Ableitungs·silbe** *die* (*Sprachw.*) affix

**ab|lenken** **1** *tr. V.* **A** (*Richtung ändern*) deflect; **einen Verdacht von sich ~** (*fig.*) divert suspicion from oneself; **B** *auch itr.* (*abbringen*) **jmdn. von etw. ~:** distract sb. from sth.; **alles, was ablenkt** everything that is distracting; **C** *auch itr.* (*zerstreuen*) divert; **sich ~:** amuse *or* divert oneself; **das lenkt dich davon ab** that'll take your mind off it; **das lenkt ab** it's amusing *or* diverting. **2** *itr. V.* (*ausweichen*) **[vom Thema] ~:** change the subject

**Ab·lenkung** *die* **A** (*Richtungsänderung*) deflection; **B** (*Störung*) distraction; **C** (*Zerstreuung*) diversion

**Ablenkungs·manöver** *das* diversion[ary tactic]

**ablesbar** *Adj.* **~ sein** ‹scale, dial› be readable; **an etw.** (*Dat.*) **~ sein** (*fig.*) be detectable from sth.

**ab|lesen[1]** *unr. tr. V.* **A** (*wegnehmen*) pick off; **B** (*säubern*) pick clean; groom ‹coat›

**ab|lesen[2]** **1** *unr. tr., itr. V.* **A** read ‹speech, lecture›; **werden Sie frei sprechen oder ~?** will you be talking from notes or reading your speech?; **B** (*feststellen, prüfen*) check ‹time, speed, temperature›; **[das Gas/den Strom] ~:** read the gas/electricity meter; **die Temperatur auf dem** *od.* **am Thermometer ~:** read off the temperature on the thermometer; **das Thermometer/den Tacho ~:** read the thermometer/speedo. **2** *unr. tr. V.* (*erkennen*) see; gauge ‹significance›; **etw. an etw.** (*Dat.*) **~:** see sth. from sth.; **jmdm. jeden Wunsch von den Augen ~:** read sb.'s every wish in his/her eyes

**ab|leuchten** *tr. V.* shine a light all over

**ab|leugnen** *tr., itr. V.* deny ‹involvement, guilt›; deny any involvement in ‹crime›; **sie leugnet stur ab** she flatly denies it

**ab|lichten** *tr. V.* **A** (*fotokopieren*) photocopy; **B** (*fotografieren*) take a photograph of

**Ab·lichtung** *die* **A** (*das Fotografieren*) photographing; (*das Fotokopieren*) photocopying; **er ist mit der ~ der Beweisstücke fertig** he has finished photographing/photocopying the evidence; **B** (*Fotokopie*) photocopy

**ab|liefern** *tr., itr. V.* deliver ‹goods›; hand in ‹manuscript, examination paper, weapon, etc.›; (*fig. ugs.*) take/bring ‹person› **(in/auf** + *Dat.*, **bei** to); **er hat pünktlich abgeliefert** he delivered it/handed it in on time

**Ab·lieferung** *die* (*von Waren*) delivery; (*von Manuskripten usw.*) handing in

**ab|liegen** *unr. itr. V.* be out of the way; ⇒ *auch* **abgelegen**

**ab|listen** /ˈaplɪstn̩/ *tr. V.* **jmdm. etw. ~** (*durch Betrug*) swindle sb. out of sth.; (*durch Charme*) cajole sb. into giving sth.

**ab|locken** *tr. V.* **jmdm. etw. ~:** coax sth. out of sb.

**ablösbar** *Adj.* **A** removable; **B** (*Finanzw.*) redeemable

**ab|löschen** **1** *tr. V.* **A** (*trocknen*) blot ‹ink, letter, etc.›; **B** (*abwischen*) wipe ‹blackboard›; wipe out ‹writing›; **C** (*Kochk.*) **etw. mit Rotwein** *usw.* **~:** add red wine *etc.* to sth.; **D** (*löschen*) extinguish; put out. **2** *itr. V.* **A** (*trocknen*) blot it/them; **B** (*abwischen*) wipe [the blackboard]; **C** (*Kochk.*) **mit Rotwein** *usw.* **~:** add red wine *etc.*

**Ablöse** *die;* **~, ~n** **A** ⇒ **Ablösesumme**; **B** (*österr.*) *single payment made by tenant at start of tenancy*

**ab|lösen** **1** *tr. V.* **A** (*lösen*) **etw. [von etw.] ~:** get sth. off [sth.]; remove sth. [from sth.]; **B** (*abwechseln*) relieve; take over from; (*fig.: ersetzen*) replace; **sich** *od.* **einander ~:** take turns; **C** (*verhüll.: entlassen*) remove from office; **D** (*Finanzw.: tilgen*) redeem. **2** *refl. V.* (*sich lösen*) ‹retina› become detached; **sich von etw. ~:** come off sth.

**Ablöse·summe** *die* (*Sport*) transfer fee

**Ab·lösung** *die* **A** (*eines Postens*) changing; (*fig.: Verdrängung, Ersetzung*) replacement; **ich schicke Ihnen jemanden zur ~:** I'll send someone to relieve you; **B** (*Ersatz*) relief; **C** (*das Ablösen*) detaching; (*der Netzhaut*) detachment; **D** (*verhüll.: Entlassung*) removal; **E** (*Finanzw.: Tilgung*) redemption; **F** (*Psych.*) dissolution of an emotional tie/emotional ties; **die ~ von seinen Eltern** breaking away emotionally from his parents

**ab|luchsen** /ˈaplʊksn̩/ *tr. V.* (*salopp*) **jmdm. etw. ~:** get *or* (*sl.*) wangle sth. out of sb.

**Ab·luft** *die* (*Technik*) vitiated air

**ab|lutschen** *tr. V.* **A** suck off; (*säubern*) suck clean; **die Marmelade von den Fingern ~:** suck the jam off one's fingers; **ein abgelutschter Bonbon** a half-sucked sweet; **B** (*vulg.*) **jmdm. einen ~:** suck sb. off (*coarse*)

**ab|machen** *tr. V.* **A** (*ugs.: entfernen*) take off; take down ‹sign, rope›; **etw. von etw. ~:** take sth. off sth.; **B** (*vereinbaren*) agree; arrange; **abgemacht, wir kommen mit!** all right, we'll come; **C** (*klären*) sort out; **das muss er mit sich selbst ~:** that's something he'll have to sort out by himself

**Abmachung** *die;* **~, ~en** agreement; arrangement; **eine ~ [mit jmdm.] treffen** come to an agreement *or* arrangement [with sb.]

**ab|magern** **1** *itr. V.; mit sein* become thin; (*absichtlich*) slim; **bis auf die Knochen ~:** become a mere skeleton; ⇒ *auch* **abgemagert 2**. **2** *tr. V.* **A** (*Technik*) **das Gemisch ~:** make the mixture leaner; **B** (*verringern*) cut back on; (*leichter machen*) make lighter

**Abmagerung** *die;* **~, ~en** (*Vorgang*) weight loss; (*Zustand*) emaciation

**Abmagerungs·kur** *die* reducing diet; **eine ~ machen** go on a diet; **er macht gerade eine ~:** he's dieting at the moment

**ab|mähen** *tr. V.* mow

**ab|mahnen** *tr. V.* ⇒ **verwarnen**

**Ab·mahnung** *die* ⇒ **Verwarnung**

**ab|malen** *tr. V.* paint a picture of (**aus, von** from)

**Ab·marsch** *der* departure; **im ~ sein** be marching off; **~!** forward march!

**abmarsch·bereit** *Adj.* ready to depart; (*Milit.*) ready to march

**ab|marschieren** *itr. V.; mit sein* depart; (*Milit.*) march off

**ab|matten** /ˈapmatn̩/ *tr. V.* (*geh.*) fatigue

**ab|meißeln** *tr. V.* chisel *or* carve off

**Abmelde·bestätigung** *die: document confirming that one has notified the authorities of one's intention to move from an address*

**ab|melden** *tr. V.* **A** (*das Weggehen melden*) **sich/jmdn. ~:** report that one/sb. is leaving; **sich [bei jmdm.] vom Dienst ~:** report absent from duty [to sb.]; **B** (*Umzug melden*) *notify the authorities that one is moving from an address;* **abgemeldet sein** have given notice of moving away; **C** **ein Auto ~:** cancel a car's registration; **ein abgemeldetes Auto** a car of which the registration has been cancelled; **sein Telefon ~:** have one's phone disconnected; **seinen Fernseher ~:** cancel one's TV licence; **D** (*Sportjargon: beherrschen*) **jmdn. ~:** shut sb. out of the game/race *etc.*; **abgemeldet sein** be kept out of the game/race *etc.*; **E** (*ugs.*) **[bei jmdm.] abgemeldet sein** no longer be of interest [to sb.]; **er ist jetzt bei mir abgemeldet** I want nothing more to do with him

**Ab·meldung** *die* **A** (*beim Weggehen*) report that one is leaving; **B** (*beim Umzug*) *registration of a move with the authorities at one's old address;* **C** (*des Telefons*) disconnection; **D** **~ eines Autos/eines Fernsehers** cancellation of a car's registration/a television licence; **E** ⇒ **Abmeldebestätigung**

**ab|messen** *unr. tr. V.* **A** measure; (*fig.*) measure; assess; **B** (*abteilen*) measure off; ⇒ *auch* **abgemessen 2, 3**

**Ab·messung** *die* **A** (*Dimension*) dimension; measurement; **B** (*das Abmessen*) measuring

**ab|mildern** *tr. V.* **A** (*dämpfen*) break, cushion ‹fall, impact›; **B** (*abschwächen*) tone down; take the edge off

**Ab·moderation** *die* **A** (*das Abmoderieren*) signing-off; **sie ist gerade bei der ~:** she is just signing off; **B** (*Text, Wortlaut*) sign-off; **sie hat sich** (*Dat.*) **eine witzige ~ einfallen lassen** she found something witty to sign off with

**ab|moderieren** *tr. V.* sign off at the end of ‹programme, show›

**ab|montieren** **1** *tr. V.* (*entfernen*) take off, remove ‹part, wheel›; dismantle ‹machine, equipment›. **2** *itr. V.* (*Fliegerspr.: sich lösen*) come off

**ab|mühen** *refl. V.* **sich [mit jmdm./etw.] ~:** toil [for sb.'s benefit/with sth.]; **sie mühte sich mit dem schweren Koffer ab** she struggled with the heavy suitcase

**ab|murksen** *tr. V.* (*salopp*) do in (*sl.*)

**ab|müssen** *unr. itr. V.* (*ugs.*) **das muss ab** it will have to come off; **der Baum/das Plakat muss ab** the tree/poster will have to come down

**ab|mustern** (*Seemannsspr.*) **1** *tr. V.* (*entlassen*) discharge. **2** *itr. V.* sign off; **von einem Schiff ~:** leave a ship

**ab|nabeln** *tr. V.* **ein Kind ~:** cut a child's cord; **sich vom Elternhaus ~** (*fig.*) break away from the parental home

**ab|nagen** *tr. V.* gnaw off; **etw. von etw. ~:** gnaw sth. off sth.; **ein abgenagter Knochen** a gnawed bone

**ab|nähen** *tr. V.* take in ‹skirt, jacket, etc.›

**Abnäher** /ˈapnɛːɐ/ *der;* **~s, ~:** tuck

**Abnahme** /ˈapnaːmə/ *die;* **~, ~n** **A** (*das Entfernen*) removal; **vor/bei/nach der ~ des Verbandes** before/when/after the bandage was/is removed; **B** (*Verminderung*) decrease; decline; **C** (*Kauf*) purchasing; **bei ~ größerer Mengen** when large quantities are purchased; **D** (*Prüfung*) (*eines Gebäudes, einer Strecke*) inspection and approval; (*eines Fahrzeugs*) testing and passing; (*Freigabe*) passing; **E** (*Entgegennahme*) (*eines Eides*) administration; (*eines Versprechens*) extraction; (*einer Parade*) taking the salute (*Gen.* at)

**Abnahme·garantie** *die* guaranteed purchase; firm order

**abnehmbar** *Adj.* detachable; removable

**ab|nehmen** **1** *unr. tr. V.* **A** (*entfernen*) take off; remove; take down ‹picture, curtain, lamp›; **jmdm. das Bein ~:** take sb.'s leg off; **sich** (*Dat.*) **den Bart ~:** shave one's beard off; **B** (*übernehmen*) take; **jmdm. den Koffer ~:** take sb.'s suitcase [from him/her]; **kann/darf ich Ihnen etwas ~?** can/may I carry something for you?; **jmdm. einen Weg/eine Arbeit ~:** save sb. a journey/a job; **jmdm. seine Sorgen ~:** relieve sb. of his/her worries; **C** (*entgegennehmen*) **jmdm. ein Versprechen/einen Eid ~:** make sb. give a promise/swear an oath; **jmdm. die Beichte ~:** hear sb.'s confession; **eine Parade ~:** take the salute at a parade; **eine Prüfung ~:** conduct an examination; **D** (*prüfen*) inspect and approve; test and pass ‹vehicle›; **E** (*stehlen*) take; (*beschlagnahmen*) take away ‹driving licence, passport›; (*abgewinnen*) **jmdm. etw. ~:** take sth. off sb.; **jmdm. ein paar Meter ~:** gain a few metres over sb.; **F** (*abverlangen*) **jmdm. etw. ~:** charge sb. sth.; **G** (*abkaufen*) **jmdm. etw. ~:** buy sth. from sb.; **H** (*ugs.: glauben*) buy (*coll.*); **diese Geschichte nehme ich dir nicht ab** I'm not buying that story (*coll.*); **I** (*übertragen*) take ‹fingerprint›. **2** *unr. itr. V.* **A** *auch tr.* (*beim Telefon*) answer; **den Hörer ~:** pick up the receiver; **B** *auch tr.* (*Handarb.*) decrease; **C** ▶ 353 (*Gewicht verlieren*) lose weight; **sechs**

*old spelling (see note on page 1707)

**Kilo ~:** lose six kilos; **D** (*sich verringern*) decrease; drop; ‹attention, interest› flag; ‹brightness› diminish; **die Tage nehmen ab** the days are getting shorter; **wir haben ~den Mond** there is a waning moon

**Abnehmer** *der;* **~s, ~, Abnehmerin** *die;* **~, ~nen** buyer

**Ab·neigung** *die* dislike (**gegen** for); aversion (**gegen** to)

**ab|nicken** *tr. V.* (*ugs.*) **etw. ~:** nod sth. through; let sth. through on the nod

**abnorm** /ap'nɔrm/ **1** *Adj.* abnormal; (*ungewöhnlich*) exceptional. **2** *adv.* abnormally; (*ungewöhnlich*) unusually

**ab·normal** *Adj., adv.* (*bes. österr. u. schweiz.*) ⇒ **anormal**

**Abnormität** /apnɔrmi'tɛ:t/ *die;* **~, ~en A** (*Missbildung*) deformity; **B** (*Missgeburt*) freak

**ab|nötigen** *tr. V.* (*geh.*) **jmdm. Respekt ~:** compel sb.'s respect; **jmdm. ein Geständnis/die Zustimmung ~:** extract a confession/agreement from sb.

**ab|nutzen,** (*landsch.:*) **ab|nützen 1** *tr. V.* wear out. **2** *refl. V.* wear out; become worn; ‹expressions, arguments› become hackneyed; **das Material nutzt sich rasch ab** the material wears very quickly; ⇒ *auch* **abgenutzt** 2

**Ab·nutzung,** (*landsch.:*) **Ab·nützung** *die* wear [and tear] *no indef. art.*

**Abnutzungs·erscheinung** *die* sign of wear and tear; (*fig.*) sign of disenchantment

**Abonnement** /abɔnə'mã:/ *das;* **~s, ~s** subscription (+ *Gen.* to); (*Theater, Oper*) subscription ticket; **eine Zeitschrift im ~ beziehen** subscribe to *or* have a subscription to a magazine

**Abonnement[s]-: ~karte** *die* subscription ticket; **~konzert** *das* subscription concert

**Abonnent** /abɔ'nɛnt/ *der;* **~en, ~en, Abonnentin** *die;* **~, ~nen** subscriber (+ *Gen.* to); (*Theater, Oper*) season ticket holder

**abonnieren** /abɔ'ni:rən/ **1** *tr. V.* subscribe to; have a subscription to; (*Theater, Oper*) have a season ticket for. **2** *itr. V.* (*bes. schweiz.*) **abonniert sein auf** (+ *Akk.*) have a subscription to ‹newspaper, magazine, concerts›; (*Theater, Oper*) have a season ticket for; (*fig.*) get as a matter of course

**ab|ordnen** *tr. V.* send; **jmdn. als Delegierten ~:** delegate sb.; **jmdn. zu einer Konferenz ~:** delegate sb. to a conference; **jmdn. nach Wien ~:** send sb. to Vienna

**Ab·ordnung** *die* delegation

**Aboriginal** /ɛbə'rɪdʒinəl/ *der;* **~s, ~s** Aboriginal

**Aborigine** /ɛbə'rɪdʒini:/*der;* **~s, ~s** Aborigine

**Abort**[1] /a'bɔrt/ *der;* **~[e]s, ~e** (*veralt., noch fachspr.*) lavatory

**Abort**[2] *der;* **~s, ~e** (*Med.*) **A** ▸ **474** (*Fehlgeburt*) miscarriage; **B** (*Abtreibung*) abortion

**Abort·grube** *die* cesspool

**ab|packen** *tr. V.* pack; wrap ‹bread›; **abgepacktes Obst/abgepackte Fleischportionen** packaged fruit/pieces of meat

**ab|passen** *tr. V.* **A** (*abwarten*) wait for; **B** (*aufhalten*) catch

**ab|pausen** *tr., itr. V.* trace

**ab|pellen** *tr. V.* (*nordd.*) peel; peel the skin off ‹sausage›

**ab|perlen** *itr. V.; mit sein* **von etw. ~:** roll off sth.

**ab|pfeifen** (*Sport*) **1** *itr. V.* blow the whistle; **der Schiedsrichter hatte abgepfiffen** the whistle had gone. **2** *tr. V.* **A** (*unterbrechen*) [blow the whistle to] stop; **B** (*beenden*) blow the whistle for the end of ‹match, game, half›

**Ab·pfiff** *der* (*Sport*) final whistle; (*Halbzeit~*) half-time whistle

**ab|pflücken** *tr. V.* **A** pick; **sich** (*Dat.*) **etw. ~:** pick oneself sth.; **B** (*leer pflücken*) pick clean

**ab|placken** (*ugs.*), **ab|plagen** *refl. V.* slave away; flog oneself to death (*coll.*); **sich mit etw./jmdm. ~** *od.* **abplagen** slave away at sth./for sb.'s benefit; **sich mit einem Problem ~** *od.* **abplagen** wrestle with a problem

**ab|platten** /'applatn̩/ *tr. V.* flatten [out]

**ab|platzen** *itr. V.; mit sein* ‹lacquer, enamel, plaster› flake off; ‹button› fly off

**ab|prägen 1** *refl. V.* **sich in etw.** (*Dat.*) **~:** leave an impression in sth.; (*fig.*) leave its/their mark on sth. **2** *tr. V.* (*Technik*) take ‹cast›; make ‹mould›

**ab|prallen** *itr. V.; mit sein* rebound; bounce off; ‹missile› ricochet; **an** *od.* **von etw.** (*Dat.*) **~:** rebound/ricochet off sth.; **an jmdm. ~** (*fig.*) bounce off sb.

**Abpraller** *der;* **~s, ~** (*Sport*) rebound; (*ugs.: eines Geschosses*) ricochet

**ab|pressen** *tr. V.* **A** (*abnötigen*) **jmdm. etw. ~:** extort sth. from sb.; **B** (*abschnüren*) **das presste uns den Atem ab** it took our breath away

**Ab·produkt** *das* waste product

**ab|protzen 1** *tr. V.* (*Milit.*) unlimber. **2** *itr. V.* (*derb*) have *or* (*Amer.*) take a crap (*coarse*); crap (*coarse*)

**ab|pumpen** *tr. V.* pump out; extract ‹milk› by breast pump

**ab|putzen** *tr. V.* (*ugs.*) **A** wipe; **jmdm./sich das Gesicht** *usw.* **~:** clean sb.'s/one's face *etc.*; **B** (*entfernen*) **etw. von jmdm./etw. ~:** wipe sth. off sb./sth.

**ab|quälen** *refl. V.* **sich [mit etw.] ~:** struggle [with sth.]; **sich** (*Dat.*) **einen Brief ~:** force oneself to write a letter; **da hat er sich was abgequält** he must have had a struggle to get that out

**ab|qualifizieren** *tr. V.* denigrate; **jmdn./etw. als etw. ~:** dismiss sb./sth. as sth.; **sich selbst ~:** show oneself up

**ab|quetschen 1** *tr. V.* **jmdm. einen Arm/ein Bein ~:** crush sb.'s arm/leg. **2** *refl. V.* (*ugs.: hervorbringen*) **sich** (*Dat.*) **etw. ~:** force out ‹words, smile›; **sich** (*Dat.*) **ein paar Tränen ~:** squeeze out a few tears

**ab|rackern** *refl. V.* (*ugs.*) slave [away]; flog oneself to death (*coll.*); **sich mit etw. ~:** slave away at sth.

**Abraham** /'a:braham/ (*der*) **A** Abraham; **B** *in* **[sicher] wie in ~s Schoß** (*ugs.*) as safe as houses (*coll.*)

**Abrakadabra** /a:braka'da:bra/ *das;* **~s A** (*Zauberwort*) abracadabra; **B** (*unsinniges Gerede*) blitherings *pl.*

**ab|rasieren** *tr. V.* shave off; **jmdm./sich den Bart ~:** shave off sb.'s/one's beard

**ab|raten** *unr. itr., tr. V.* **jmdm. von etw. ~:** advise sb. against sth.; **jmdm. [davon] ~, etw. zu tun** advise sb. not to do sth. *or* against doing sth.; **da kann ich nur abraten** I can only advise you against it

**Ab·raum** *der* (*Bergbau*) overburden

**ab|räumen 1** *tr. V.* **A** clear away; **B** (*leer machen*) clear ‹table›; **C** (*Bergbau*) remove ‹overburden›. **2** *itr. V.* **A** clear away; **B** (*vom Tisch*) clear the table; **C** (*Bergbau*) remove the overburden

**ab|rauschen** *itr. V.; mit sein* (*ugs.*) (*schnell*) rush off; (*auffällig*) sweep off

**ab|reagieren 1** *tr. V.* work off; **seine Wut an jmdm. ~:** take one's anger out on sb. **2** *refl. V.* work off one's feelings

**ab|rechnen 1** *itr. V.* **A** cash up; **B** (*fig.*) **mit jmdm. ~:** call sb. to account. **2** *tr. V.* **A die Kasse ~:** reckon up the till; total the cash *or* register (*Amer.*); **seine Einnahmen ~:** agree one's takings; **seine Spesen ~:** claim one's expenses; **B** (*abziehen*) deduct

**Ab·rechnung** *die* **A** (*Schlussrechnung*) cashing up *no art.*; **die Kellnerin machte die ~:** the waitress was cashing up; **B** (*Aufstellung*) statement; (*Kaufmannsspr.: Bilanz*) balance; (*Dokument*) balance sheet; **der Tag der ~:** the day of reckoning; **C** (*Vergeltung*) reckoning; **D** (*Abzug*) deduction; **nach ~ der Unkosten** after deducting expenses; **etw. in ~ bringen** (*Amtsspr.*) deduct sth.; **in ~ kommen** (*Amtsspr.*) be deducted

**Abrechnungs-: ~stelle** *die* (*Finanzw.*) clearing house; **~verkehr** *der* (*Finanzw.*) clearing

**Ab·rede** *die* **A** arrangement; agreement; **B** **etw. in ~ stellen** deny sth.

**ab|regen** *refl. V.* (*ugs.*) calm down; **reg dich ab!** cool it! (*coll.*); calm down!

**ab|reiben** *unr. tr. V.* **A** (*entfernen*) rub off; (*Kochk.*) grate; **etw. von etw. ~:** rub/grate sth. off sth.; **abgeriebene Zitronenschale** grated lemon peel; **B** (*säubern*) rub; **[sich** (*Dat.*)**] die Hände an der Hose ~:** rub one's hands on one's trousers; **C** (*frottieren*) rub down; **jmds. Hände mit Schnee ~:** rub sb.'s hands with snow

**Ab·reibung** *die* **A** (*ugs.: Prügel*) hiding (*coll.*); licking (*Amer. coll.*); **jmdm. eine ~ verpassen** give sb. a good hiding; **B** (*Med.*) rubbing

**Ab·reise** *die* departure (**nach** for); **bei meiner ~:** when I left/leave

**ab|reisen** *itr. V.; mit sein* leave (**nach** for)

**Abreiß·block** *der; Pl.* **~s** *od.* **Abreißblöcke** tear-off notebook

**ab|reißen 1** *unr. tr. V.* **A** (*entfernen*) tear off; tear down ‹poster, notice›; pull off ‹button›; break off ‹thread›; ⇒ *auch* **Kopf A**; **B** (*niederreißen*) demolish, pull down ‹building›; demolish ‹area›; **C** (*salopp: ableisten*) get through; stick out (*coll.*); ⇒ *auch* **abgerissen** 2. **2** *unr. itr. V.; mit sein* **A** (*sich lösen*) fly off; ‹shoelace› break off; **B** (*aufhören*) come to an end; ‹connection, contact› be broken off; **in nicht ~der Folge** in a never-ending procession

**Abreiß·kalender** *der* tear-off calendar

**ab|reiten 1** *unr. itr. V.; mit sein* (*wegreiten*) ride off *or* away. **2** *unr. tr. V.* **A** *mit sein od. haben* (*entlangreiten*) ride the whole length of; ride over ‹district›; **B** (*Pferdesport: vorbereiten*) supple; **C** (*müde reiten*) ride to exhaustion; **D** (*Seemannsspr.*) ride out ‹storm›

**Abreite·platz, Abreit·platz** *der* (*Pferdesport*) warming-up arena

**ab|richten** *tr. V.* train

**Ab·richter** *der,* **Ab·richterin** *die* trainer

**Ab·richtung** *die;* **~:** training

**ab|riegeln** *tr., itr. V.* **A** (*zusperren*) **[die Tür] ~:** bolt the door; **B** (*absperren*) seal *or* cordon off ‹area›

**Abrieg[e]lung** *die;* **~, ~en** sealing *or* cordoning off

**ab|ringen** *unr. tr. V.* **A** (*abnötigen*) **jmdm. etw. ~:** extract sth. from sb.; **sich** (*Dat.*) **ein Lächeln ~:** force a smile; **B** (*entreißen*) **jmdm./einer Sache etw. ~:** wrest sth. from sb./sth.

**Ab·riss, *Ab·riß** *der* **A** ⇒ **abreißen 1 B**: demolition; pulling down; **auf ~ stehen** (*ugs.*) be scheduled for demolition; **B** (*von Eintrittskarten*) tear-off section; **C** (*knappe Darstellung*) outline

**Abriss-, *Abriss-: ~arbeiten** *Pl.* ⇒ **Abbrucharbeit**; **~birne** *die* demolition ball; wrecker's ball; **die ~birne kommt im Herbst** they're going to start demolition in autumn; **das Haus ist längst der ~birne zum Opfer gefallen** they pulled the building down ages ago

**ab|rollen 1** *tr. V.* unwind; **sich ~:** unwind [itself]. **2** *itr. V.; mit sein* **A** unwind [itself]; **B** (*vonstatten gehen*) go off; ‹events› unfold; **sein Leben rollte vor seinen Augen ab** his life passed before his eyes; **C** (*Sport*) roll over (**über** + *Akk.* on to)

**ab|rubbeln** *tr. V.* (*bes. nordd.*) **jmdn./sich ~:** dry sb./oneself by rubbing; rub sb./oneself down; **jmdm./sich den Rücken ~:** dry sb.'s/one's back by rubbing

**ab|rücken 1** *tr. V.* (*wegschicken*) move away. **2** *itr. V.; mit sein* **A** move away; **von jmdm./etw. ~:** move away from sb./sth.; **B** (*Milit.*) (*abmarschieren*) move out; (*zurückmarschieren*) march back; **C** (*ugs.: sich entfernen*) clear out (*coll.*)

**Ab·ruf** *der* **A** **auf ~:** on call; (*DV*) in retrievable form; **sich auf ~ bereithalten** be on call; **B** (*Kaufmannsspr.*) request for delivery; **etw. auf ~ kaufen** buy sth. on call purchase

**abrufbar** *Adj.* **A** (*DV*) retrievable; **B** (*Finanzw.*) withdrawable

a

**abruf·bereit** *Adj.* **A** on call *postpos.*; **B** (*Kaufmannsspr.*) ready for delivery on demand *postpos.*

**ab|rufen** *unr. tr. V.* **A** summon, call ‹person›; **er wurde ins Jenseits/aus diesem Leben abgerufen** (*geh. verhüll.*) he was taken from us; **B** (*DV*) retrieve; **C** (*Kaufmannsspr.*) **etw. ~:** ask for sth. to be delivered; **D** (*Finanzw.*) withdraw

**ab|runden** *tr. V.* **A** round off; **abgerundete Ecken** rounded corners; **B** (*auf eine runde Zahl bringen*) round up/down (**auf** + *Akk.* to); **etw. nach oben/unten ~:** round sth. up/down; **ein Betrag von abgerundet 27,50 Mark** a rounded [up/down] sum of 27.50 marks; **C** (*vervollkommnen*) round off; complete

**Ab·rundung** *die* **A** rounding off; **B** (*von Zahlen*) rounding up/down; **C** (*Vervollkommnung*) rounding off; **zur ~ des Geschmacks** to round off the taste

**ab|rupfen** *tr. V.* pull off

**abrupt** /ap'rʊpt/ **1** *Adj.* abrupt. **2** *adv.* abruptly

**ab|rüsten** *itr., tr. V.* disarm

**Ab·rüstung** *die; ~:* disarmament

**Abrüstungs-: ~konferenz** *die* disarmament conference; **~verhandlungen** *Pl.* disarmament negotiations

**ab|rutschen** *itr. V.; mit sein* **A** (*abgleiten*) slip; **von etw. ~:** slip off sth.; **das Pferd rutschte mit den Hinterbeinen ab** the horse's hind feet slipped; **sie ist mit dem Messer abgerutscht** her knife slipped; **B** (*nach unten rutschen*) slide down; ‹earth› subside; ‹snow› give way; ‹aircraft› side-slip; (*fig.*) ‹pupil, competitor, etc.› slip (**auf** + *Akk.* to); **C** (*moralisch absinken*) go downhill

**ABS** *Abk.* **Antiblockiersystem**

**Abs.** *Abk.* **A Absender; B Absatz**

**ab|säbeln** *tr. V.* (*ugs.*) hack off

**ab·sacken[1]** *itr. V.; mit sein* (*ugs.*) **A** (*nach unten sinken*) fall; ‹ground› subside; ‹aircraft› lose altitude; **B** (*moralisch absinken*) go downhill

**ab|sacken[2]** *tr. V.* sack ‹grain, sugar, etc.›

**Ab·sage** *die* **A** (*auf eine Einladung*) refusal; (*auf eine Bewerbung*) rejection; **jmdm. eine ~ erteilen** reject sb.; **eine ~ an jede Form totalitärer Politik** a rejection of all forms of totalitarian politics; **B** (*Rundf.*) closing announcement

**ab|sagen** **1** *tr. V.* cancel; withdraw ‹participation, cooperation›. **2** *itr. V.* **A** cry off; **jmdm. ~:** tell sb. one cannot come; put sb. off (*coll.*); **telefonisch ~:** ring to say one cannot come; **ich muss Ihnen für Donnerstag ~:** I must cancel our meeting/visit/appointment *etc.* on Thursday; **B dem Bewerber wurde abgesagt** the applicant was rejected; **C** (*Rundf.*) make the closing announcement

**ab|sägen** *tr. V.* **A** saw off; **B** (*ugs.*) **jmdn. ~:** get rid of sb.

**ab|sahnen** **1** *itr. V.* (*ugs.*) make a killing (*coll.*). **2** *tr. V.* **A** (*ugs.*) **100 000 Mark ~:** pocket 100,000 marks; **B** (*Rahm entfernen von*) cream ‹milk›

**ab|satteln** *tr., itr. V.* unsaddle

**Ab·satz** *der* **A** (*am Schuh*) heel; **auf dem ~ kehrtmachen, sich auf dem ~ herumdrehen** turn on one's heel; **B** (*Textunterbrechung*) break; **einen ~ machen** make a break; start a new line; **C** (*Abschnitt*) paragraph; **D** (*Kauf-mannsspr.*) sales *pl.*; **guten/keinen ~ finden** sell well/not sell at all; ⇒ *auch* **reißend**; **E** (*einer Innentreppe*) landing; (*zwischen Geschossen*) half landing; (*Mauer~*) ledge

**absatz-, Absatz-: ~chance** *die* (*Kaufmannsspr.*) sales prospect; **~flaute** *die* (*Kaufmannsspr.*) drop in sales; **~förderung** *die* (*Kaufmannsspr.*) sales promotion; **~gebiet** *das* (*Kaufmannsspr.*) sales territory; (*von Produkten*) market area; **~kick** *der* (*Fußball*) back-heel; **~markt** *der* (*Kaufmannsspr.*) market; **~schwierigkeiten** *Pl.* (*Kaufmannsspr.*) sales problems; (*beim Vertrieb*) marketing difficulties; **~steigerung** *die* (*Kaufmannsspr.*) increase in sales; **~trick** *der* (*Fußball*) clever back-heel; **~weise** *Adv.* paragraph by paragraph

**ab|saufen** *unr. itr. V.; mit sein* **A** (*salopp: untergehen*) go to the bottom; **B** (*derb: ertrinken*) drown; **C** (*ugs.*) ‹engine, car› flood; **D** (*salopp: sich mit Wasser füllen*) flood; **abgesoffen sein** be under water; be flooded

**ab|saugen** *tr. V.* **A** (*entfernen*) suck away; **etw. aus/von etw. ~:** suck sth. out of/off sth.; **B** (*säubern*) hoover (*Brit. coll.*); vacuum

**ab|schaben** *tr. V.* **A** (*entfernen*) scrape off; **sich** (*Dat.*) **den Bart ~** (*scherzh.*) have a shave; **B** (*säubern*) scrape [clean]; ⇒ *auch* **abgeschabt** 2

**ab|schaffen** **1** *tr. V.* **A** (*beseitigen*) abolish ‹capital punishment, regulation, customs duty, institution›; repeal ‹law›; put an end to ‹injustice, abuse›; **er möchte alle Flugzeuge ~:** he'd like to do away with aeroplanes completely; **B** (*aufgeben*) get rid of. **2** *refl. V.* (*südd., schweiz.*) (*sich abarbeiten*) slave away; work oneself hard; (*sich anstrengen*) go at it

**Ab·schaffung** *die* **A** abolition; (*von Gesetzen*) repeal; (*von Unrecht, Missstand*) ending; **B** (*Aufgabe*) **er sah sich zur ~ seines Autos/Hundes gezwungen** he was forced to get rid of *or* give up his car/dog

**ab|schälen** **1** *tr. V.* **A** (*lösen*) peel off; **etw. von etw. ~:** peel sth. off sth.; **B** (*befreien von*) bark ‹tree›. **2** *refl. V.* (*sich lösen*) peel off; **die Haut schält sich ab** the skin is peeling

**abschaltbar** *Adj.* which can be switched off *postpos., not pred.*; **das ist ~:** it can be switched off

**ab|schalten** **1** *tr., itr. V.* (*ausschalten*) switch off; turn off; shut down ‹power station›. **2** *itr. V.* (*ugs.: nicht zuhören; Abstand gewinnen*) switch off

**Ab·schaltung** *die* switching off; (*eines Kraftwerks*) shutdown

**Abschattung** /'ap-ʃatʊŋ/ *die; ~, ~en* shade; hue; (*fig.*) shade; nuance

**ab|schätzen** *tr. V.* estimate; size up ‹person, possibilities›; **jmdn. ~d betrachten** look at sb. appraisingly

**abschätzig** /'ap-ʃɛtsɪç/ **1** *Adj.* derogatory; disparaging. **2** *adv.* derogatorily; disparagingly

**Abschätzigkeit** *die* derogatoriness; disparagement

**ab|schauen** ⇒ **abgucken**

**Ab·schaum** *der* (*abwertend*) scum; dregs *pl.*

**ab|scheiden** *unr. tr. V.* **A** (*Chemie*) precipitate; (*Physiol.*) secrete; **B** (*geh.: abtrennen*) separate; (*fig.*) isolate; ⇒ *auch* **abgeschieden** 2

**Abscheider** *der; ~s, ~* (*Technik*) separator

**ab|scheren[1]** *unr. tr. V.* shear off ‹hair, wool›; shear ‹sheep, head›

**ab|scheren[2]** (*Technik*) **1** *tr. V.* (*abtrennen*) shear. **2** *itr. V.* (*sich lösen*) shear off

**Ab·scheu** *der; ~s,* (*selten:*) *die; ~:* detestation; abhorrence; **einen ~ vor jmdm./etw. haben** detest *or* abhor sb./sth.; **jmds. ~ erregen** arouse repugnance in sb.; repel sb.

**ab|scheuern** *tr. V.* **A** (*entfernen*) scrub off; **etw. von etw. ~:** scrub sth. off sth.; **B** (*säubern*) scrub; **C** (*beschädigen*) graze ‹skin›; wear away ‹cloth›; **ein abgescheuerter Kragen** a badly worn collar

**abscheu·erregend** *Adj.* ⇒ **abscheulich** 1 B

**abscheulich** /ap'ʃɔylɪç/ **1** *Adj.* **A** (*widerwärtig*) disgusting, awful ‹smell, taste›; repulsive, awful ‹sight›; **B** (*verwerflich, schändlich*) disgraceful ‹behaviour›; abominable ‹crime›. **2** *adv.* **A** disgracefully; abominably; **B** (*ugs.: sehr*) **~ frieren** freeze [half] to death (*coll.*); **das schmerzt ganz ~:** it hurts like hell (*coll.*); **~ kalt/scharf** terribly cold/sharp (*coll.*)

**Abscheulichkeit** *die; ~, ~en* ⇒ **abscheulich** 1: disgustingness; awfulness; repulsiveness; disgracefulness; abominableness

**ab|schicken** *tr. V.* send [off], post ‹letter, parcel›; dispatch, send [off], post ‹goods, money›; send ‹messenger›

**ab|schieben** **1** *unr. tr. V.* **A** push *or* shove away; **das Bett von der Wand ~:** push *or* shove the bed away from the wall; **B** (*abwälzen*) shift; **die Verantwortung/Schuld auf jmdn. ~:** shift [the] responsibility/the blame on to sb.; **C** (*Rechtsw.: ausweisen*) deport; **jmdn. über die Grenze ~:** put sb. over the border; **D** (*ugs.: entfernen*) get rid of; **jmdn. in ein Heim ~:** shove sb. into a home (*coll.*).
**2** *unr. itr. V.; mit sein* (*salopp: weggehen*) push off (*coll.*); shove off (*coll.*)

**Ab·schiebung** *die* (*Rechtsw.*) deportation

**Abschiebungs·haft** *die* (*Rechtsw.*) detention prior to deportation

**Abschied** /'ap-ʃi:t/ *der; ~[e]s, ~e* **A** (*Trennung*) parting (**von** from); farewell (**von** to); **[von jmdm./etw.] ~ nehmen** say goodbye [to sb./sth.]; take one's leave [of sb./sth.]; **von einer Gewohnheit ~ nehmen** give up a habit; **beim ~:** at parting; when saying goodbye; **sich zum ~ die Hände schütteln** shake hands on parting; **zum ~ Blumen schenken** give flowers as a parting gift; **jmdm. zum ~ zuwinken** wave goodbye to sb.; **B** (*geh.: Entlassung*) resignation; **seinen ~ nehmen** resign; ‹officer› resign one's commission; **den ~ erhalten** (*veralt.*) be discharged

**Abschieds-: ~besuch** *der* farewell visit; **~brief** *der* farewell letter; **~essen** *das* farewell dinner; **~feier** *die* (*Zeremonie*) farewell ceremony; (*Party*) farewell *or* leaving party; **~geschenk** *das* farewell *or* parting gift; (*einer Firma usw.*) leaving present; **~gesuch** *das* (*geh.*) letter of resignation; **sein ~gesuch einreichen** tender one's resignation; ‹officer› resign one's commission; **~gruß** *der* goodbye; farewell; **~kuss** *der* goodbye *or* parting kiss; **~rede** *die* farewell speech; **~schmerz** *der* sorrow at parting; **~spiel** *das* (*Fußball*) farewell appearance; **~szene** *die* scene of sentimental farewells; **~vorstellung** *die* farewell performance

**ab|schießen** *unr. tr. V.* **A** loose, fire ‹arrow›; fire ‹rifle, pistol, rocket, cannon›; launch ‹spacecraft›; **B** (*töten*) take; (*salopp*) shoot down ‹person›; **C** (*ugs.: entfernen*) kick *or* throw ‹person› out; **D** (*von sich geben*) fire off ‹question›; shoot ‹glance›; **E** (*zerstören*) shoot down ‹aeroplane›; put ‹tank› out of action; **F** (*wegreißen*) shoot off ‹arm, leg, etc.›

**ab|schilfern** *itr. V.; mit sein* peel

**ab|schinden** *unr. refl. V.* **sich ~:** work *or* (*Brit. coll.*) flog oneself to death; **sich mit etw. ~:** struggle along with sth.

**Abschirm·dienst** *der* (*Milit.*) counter-espionage service

**ab|schirmen** *tr. V.* **A** (*schützen*) shield; **jmdn./sich von der** *od.* **gegen die Umwelt ~:** screen sb./oneself off from the outside world; **B** (*abdecken*) cover ‹lamp›; screen off ‹light, radiation, radio station›

**Abschirmung** *die; ~, ~en* **A** (*Schutz*) shielding; (*von der Umwelt usw.*) screening off; **B** (*von Licht, Strahlung*) screening off

**ab|schirren** *tr. V.* unharness ‹horse›; unyoke ‹cattle›

**ab|schlachten** *tr. V.* slaughter

**ab|schlaffen** /'ap-ʃlafn̩/ (*ugs.*) **1** *tr., itr. V.* (*schlaff machen*) take it out of; **das schlafft ab** it takes it out of you; **ein abgeschlaffter Typ** a lackadaisical fellow; **er saß abgeschlafft im Sessel** he sat limply in his chair. **2** *itr. V.; mit sein* (*schlaff werden*) wilt; sag; **geistig ~:** lose one's intellectual vigour

**Ab·schlag** *der* **A** (*Kaufmannsspr.*) reduction; discount; **B** (*Teilzahlung*) interim payment; (*Vorschuss*) advance; **C** (*Fußball*) goalkeeper's kick out; **D** (*Hockey*) ⇒ **Bully**; **E** (*Golf*) tee; (*Schlag*) drive; **F** (*Finanzw.*) ⇒ **Disagio**

**ab|schlagen** **1** *unr. tr. V.* **A** knock off; (*mit dem Beil, Schwert usw.*) chop off; **jmdm. den Kopf ~:** chop off sb.'s head; **B** (*ablehnen*) refuse; **jmdm. etw. ~:** refuse *or* deny sb.

*old spelling (see note on page 1707)

sth.; Ⓒ (*abwehren*) beat *or* fend off; Ⓓ (*zerlegen*) dismantle; strike ‹tent›; Ⓔ (*Seemannsspr.*) unbend. ❷ *unr. itr. V.* Ⓐ *auch tr.* (*Fußball*) **[den Ball] ~:** kick the ball out; Ⓑ (*Hockey*) take a 15-metre hit. ❸ *unr. refl. V.* (*kondensieren*) **sich an etw.** (*Dat.*) **~:** condense on sth.; ⇒ *auch* **abgeschlagen** 2; **Wasser** E

**abschlägig** /ˈapʃlɛːgɪç/ (*Amtsspr.*) ❶ *Adj.* negative; **ein ~er Bescheid** a refusal *or* rejection. ❷ *adv.* **jmdn. ~ bescheiden** refuse sb.; **jmds. Gesuch** (*Akk.*) **~ bescheiden** reject sb.'s application

**Abschlag[s]·zahlung** *die* ⇒ **Abschlag** B

**ab|schlecken** *tr. V.* (*österr., südd.*) ⇒ **ablecken**

**ab|schleifen** ❶ *unr. tr. V.* Ⓐ (*entfernen*) (*von Holz*) sand off; (*von Metall, Glas usw.*) grind off; Ⓑ (*glätten*) sand down ‹wood›; grind down ‹metal, glass, etc.›; smooth down ‹broken tooth›. ❷ *unr. refl. V.* (*sich abnutzen*) wear away; **das schleift sich noch ab** (*fig.*) that will wear off in time

**Abschlepp·dienst** *der* (*Kfz-W.*) breakdown recovery service; tow[ing] service (*Amer.*)

**ab|schleppen** ❶ *tr. V.* Ⓐ tow away; take ‹ship› in tow; **ein Auto zur Werkstatt ~:** tow a car to the garage; Ⓑ (*salopp: mitnehmen*) **jmdn. ~:** drag sb. off. ❷ *refl. V.* (*ugs.: schwer tragen*) **sich mit/an etw.** (*Dat.*) **~:** break one's back carrying sth. (*fig.*)

**Abschlepp-: ~seil** *das* tow rope; (*aus Draht*) towing cable; **~stange** *die* tow bar; **~wagen** *der* breakdown vehicle; tow truck (*Amer.*); (*der Polizei*) tow-away vehicle

**abschließbar** *Adj.* lockable; **es ist nicht ~:** it cannot be locked

**ab|schließen** ❶ *unr. tr. V.* Ⓐ *auch itr.* (*zuschließen*) lock ‹door, gate, cupboard›; lock [up] ‹house, flat, room, park›; **vergiss nicht, abzuschließen!** don't forget to lock up!; Ⓑ (*absondern, trennen*) **etw. luftdicht ~:** seal sth. hermetically; **sich ganz [von der Welt] ~:** cut oneself off [from the world] completely; Ⓒ (*begrenzen*) border; Ⓓ (*zum Abschluss bringen*) bring to an end; conclude; **die Bücher ~:** balance the books; **sein Studium ~:** finish one's studies; **Bewerber mit abgeschlossenem Universitätsstudium** applicants with a degree; Ⓔ (*vereinbaren*) strike ‹bargain, deal›; make ‹purchase›; enter into ‹agreement›; **Geschäfte ~:** conclude deals; (*im Handel*) do business; ⇒ *auch* **abgeschlossen** 2; **Versicherung** B; **Wette**.
❷ *unr. itr. V.* Ⓐ (*begrenzt sein*) be bordered (**mit** by); Ⓑ (*aufhören, enden*) end; **~d sagte er ...** in conclusion he said ...; **seine ~den Worte waren ...** his concluding words were ...; **mit [einem] Gewinn/Verlust ~** (*Kaufmannsspr.*) show a profit/deficit; Ⓒ **mit jmdm./etw. abgeschlossen haben** have finished with sb./sth.; Ⓓ (*Kaufmannsspr.*) **die Vertragspartner wollen morgen ~:** the parties [to the contract] want to close tomorrow

**Ab·schluss**, ***Ab·schluß** *der* Ⓐ (*Verschluss*) seal; **ein luftdichter ~:** an airtight seal; Ⓑ (*abschließender Teil*) edge; Ⓒ (*Beendigung*) conclusion; end; **vor ~ der Arbeiten** before the completion of the work; **zum ~ noch eine Frage** one final question; **sich dem ~ nähern** be drawing to a conclusion; **kurz vor dem ~ stehen** be nearly finished *or* at an end; **etw. zum ~ bringen** finish sth.; bring sth. to an end *or* conclusion; **zum ~ kommen** *od.* **gelangen** be completed; **wir müssen mit unseren Verhandlungen zum ~ kommen** we must bring our negotiations to a close; **zum ~ unseres Programms** to end our programme; Ⓓ (*ugs.: ~zeugnis*) **einen/keinen ~ haben** (*Hochschulw.*) ≈ have a/have no degree *or* (*Amer.*) diploma; (*Schulw.*) ≈ have some/no GCSE passes (*Brit.*); (*Lehre*) have/not have finished one's apprenticeship; **ohne ~:** without gaining a degree *or* (*Amer.*) diploma/any GCSE passes (*Brit.*)/finishing one's apprenticeship; Ⓔ (*Kaufmannsspr.: Schlussrechnung*) balancing; Ⓕ (*Kaufmannsspr.: geschäftliche Vereinbarung*) business deal; **einen ~ über 2 Millionen Tonnen Getreide tätigen** make a deal for 2 million tons of grain; Ⓖ (*eines Geschäfts, Vertrags*) conclusion; **durch den ~ einer Versicherung** by taking out an insurance policy; Ⓗ (*Fußball*) finishing move

**Abschluss-**, ***Abschluß-: ~ball** *der* final dance; **~examen** *das* final examination; **~feier** *die* (*Schulw.*) leaving party; **~klasse** *die* (*Schulw.*) final year; **~kundgebung** *die* final rally; **~prüfung** *die* Ⓐ (*Schulw.*) leaving *or* (*Amer.*) final examination; (*Hochschulw.*) final examination; finals *pl.*; Ⓑ (*Wirtsch.*) audit; **~veranstaltung** *die* final event; **~zeugnis** *das* (*Schulw.*) ≈ leaving certificate (*Brit.*); ≈ diploma (*Amer.*)

**ab|schmatzen** *tr. V.* (*ugs.*) **jmdn. ~:** kiss sb. noisily

**ab|schmecken** *tr. V.* Ⓐ (*kosten*) taste; try; Ⓑ (*würzen*) season

**ab|schmeicheln** *tr. V.* **jmdm. etw. ~:** wheedle sth. out of sb.

**ab|schmelzen** ❶ *unr. itr. V.*; *mit sein* melt away. ❷ *unr. tr. V.* melt; (*fig.: verringern*) reduce [the size of] ‹assets, reserves›

**ab|schmettern** *tr. V.* (*ugs.*) throw out; **jmdn. ~:** turn a deaf ear to sb.

**ab|schmieren** ❶ *tr. V.* Ⓐ (*Technik*) grease; Ⓑ (*ugs.: abschreiben*) scribble down; (*unerlaubt*) copy; ‹child in school› crib (**von, bei** from). ❷ *itr. V.* Ⓐ (*ugs.*) crib (**von, bei** from); Ⓑ (*Fliegerspr.*) side-slip

**Abschmier·presse** *die* (*Kfz-W.*) grease gun

**ab|schminken** *tr. V.* Ⓐ **jmdn./sich ~:** remove sb.'s/one's make-up; **sich** (*Dat.*) **das Gesicht/die Augen ~:** remove the make-up from one's face/eyes; **als ich sie abgeschminkt sah** when I saw her without her make-up; Ⓑ (*salopp*) **sich** (*Dat.*) **etw. ~:** get sth. out of one's head

**ab|schmirgeln** *tr. V.*; Ⓐ (*polieren*) rub down with emery; (*mit Sandpapier*) sand down; Ⓑ (*entfernen*) rub off with emery; (*mit Sandpapier*) sand off

**ab|schmücken** *tr. V.* take the decorations off ‹Christmas tree›

**ab|schnacken** *tr. V.* (*nordd.*) ⇒ **abschwatzen**

**ab|schnallen** ❶ *tr. V.* Ⓐ (*abnehmen*) unfasten; **[sich** (*Dat.*)**] den Tornister/das Holzbein ~:** take off one's knapsack/wooden leg; Ⓑ (*losschnallen*) unfasten; **sich ~:** unfasten one's seat belt. ❷ *itr. V.* (*salopp*) Ⓐ (*nicht mehr folgen können*) switch off; Ⓑ (*fassungslos sein*) be flabbergasted; **da schnallst du [echt] ab** you'll be flabbergasted

**ab|schneiden** ❶ *unr. tr. V.* Ⓐ (*abtrennen*) cut off; cut down ‹sth. hanging›; **etw. von etw. ~:** cut sth. off sth.; **sich** (*Dat.*) **den Finger ~:** cut one's finger off; **sich** (*Dat.*) **eine Scheibe Brot/Fleisch ~:** cut oneself a slice of bread/meat; ⇒ *auch* **Scheibe** B; Ⓑ (*kürzer schneiden*) cut; **jmdm./sich die Haare/Fingernägel ~:** cut sb.'s/one's hair/fingernails; **ein Kleid/einen Rock [ein Stück] ~:** cut [a piece] off a dress/a skirt; **eine Zigarre ~:** cut the end off a cigar; Ⓒ **jmdm. den Weg ~:** take a short cut to get ahead of sb.; Ⓓ (*trennen, isolieren*) cut off; **die Truppen vom Nachschub ~:** cut off troops from reinforcements; ⇒ *auch* **abgeschnitten** 2; Ⓔ (*unterbinden*) **einen Einwurf/Einwand ~:** cut short an interjection/a protest.
❷ *unr. itr. V.* Ⓐ (*ver-, abkürzen*) ‹path, road› be a short cut; ‹pedestrian, driver› take a short cut; Ⓑ **bei etw. gut/schlecht ~:** do well/badly in sth.

**ab|schnellen** *refl. V.* **sich [vom Boden] ~:** take off

**ab|schnippeln** *tr. V.* (*ugs.*) **Stückchen von etw. ~:** cut little bits off sth.; (*mit der Schere*) snip bits off sth.

**Ab·schnitt** *der* Ⓐ (*Kapitel*) section; Ⓑ (*Milit.: Gebiet, Gelände*) sector; (*DDR: Wohnbereich*) district; (*DDR: Handelsbereich*) section (*comprising ten retail shops belonging to a manufacturing cooperative*); Ⓒ (*Zeitspanne*) phase; Ⓓ (*Kontroll~*) [detachable] portion; (*eines Schecks*) stub, counterfoil; **die Lebensmittelkarte hatte ~e für Butter, Brot, Zucker usw.** the ration card had coupons for butter, bread, sugar, etc.; Ⓔ (*Math.: eines Kreises*) segment

**Abschnitts·bevollmächtigte** *der* (*DDR*) ≈ community policeman

**abschnitt[s]·weise** ❶ *Adv.* in sections; **etw. ~ lesen** read sth. section by section. ❷ *adj.* sectionalized

**ab|schnüren** *tr. V.* Ⓐ apply a tourniquet to; **jmdm. die Luft/das Blut ~:** stop sb. from breathing/restrict sb.'s circulation; **einem Konkurrenten die Luft ~** (*fig.*) ruin a competitor; Ⓑ (*blockieren*) seal off

**ab|schöpfen** *tr. V.* skim off; (*fig.*) **den Rahm ~** (*am meisten bekommen*) take the lion's share; (*das Beste bekommen*) cream off the best; **den Gewinn** *od.* **Profit ~:** siphon off the profits; **überschüssige Kaufkraft ~:** absorb excess spending power

**ab|schotten** *tr. V.* Ⓐ (*Schiffbau*) separate by a bulkhead/bulkheads; Ⓑ (*fig.*) **etw. [von etw.] ~:** seal sth. off [from sth.]; **sich jmdm. gegenüber ~:** seal oneself off from sb.

**ab|schrägen** *tr. V.* **einen Balken/ein Brett ~:** bevel a beam/the edges of a plank

**ab|schrammen** ❶ *tr. V.* (*abschürfen*) graze; **sich** (*Dat.*) **das Knie/die Haut ~:** graze one's knee/one's skin. ❷ *itr. V.* Ⓐ (*nordd. salopp: weggehen*) push off (*coll.*); Ⓑ (*salopp: sterben*) croak (*sl.*); snuff it (*sl.*)

**abschraubbar** *Adj.* unscrewable

**ab|schrauben** *tr. V.* unscrew [and remove]; **etw. lässt sich ~:** sth. can be unscrewed

**ab|schrecken** ❶ *tr. V.* Ⓐ (*abhalten*) deter; **sein Aussehen schreckt viele ab** many people are put off by his appearance; Ⓑ (*fernhalten*) scare off; Ⓒ (*Metall.*) quench; Ⓓ (*Kochk.*) pour cold water over; put ‹boiled eggs› into cold water. ❷ *itr. V.* (*eine ~de Wirkung haben*) act as a deterrent; **das schreckt eher ab** it's more likely to put people off

**abschreckend** ❶ *Adj.* Ⓐ (*warnend*) deterrent; **ein ~es Beispiel für alle Raucher** a warning to all smokers; Ⓑ (*abstoßend*) repulsive. ❷ *adv.* **~ wirken** have a deterrent effect; **~ hässlich** repulsively ugly

**Abschreckung** *die*; **~, ~en** Ⓐ deterrence; **der ~** (*Dat.*) **dienen** serve as a deterrent; Ⓑ (*Mittel zur ~*) deterrent

**Abschreckungs-: ~politik** *die* policy of deterrence; **~potenzial** *das* deterrent potential; **~theorie** *die* (*Rechtsw.*) theory of the deterrent value of punishment; **~waffe** *die* deterrent [weapon]

**ab|schreiben** ❶ *unr. tr. V.* Ⓐ (*kopieren*) copy out; **sich** (*Dat.*) **etw. ~:** copy sth. down; (*aus einem Buch, einer Zeitung usw.*) copy sth. out; Ⓑ **etw. von jmdm. ~** (*in der Schule*) copy sth. from *or* off sb.; (*als Plagiator*) plagiarize sth. from sb.; Ⓒ (*Wirtsch.*) amortize, write down (**mit** by); Ⓓ (*ugs.: verlorengeben*) write off; **jmdn. abgeschrieben haben** have written sb. off; Ⓔ (*abnutzen*) use up ‹pencil, crayon, ballpoint or felt pen›; wear out ‹pen nib›.
❷ *unr. itr. V.* Ⓐ **bei** *od.* **von jmdm. ~** (*in der Schule*) copy off sb.; (*als Plagiator*) copy from sb.; Ⓑ (*brieflich absagen*) **jmdm. ~:** write to sb. and say one cannot come

**Ab·schreibung** *die* (*Wirtsch.*) Ⓐ (*das Abschreiben*) amortization; Ⓑ (*Betrag*) depreciation provision

**Abschreibungs-: ~gesellschaft** *die* (*Wirtsch.*) tax-loss company; **~möglichkeit** *die* (*Wirtsch.*) *possibility of setting off items against taxable income;* **~ruine** *die* (*salopp*) *building erected not for occupation, but for purposes of offsetting depreciation against tax*

a

a

**ab|schreiten** *unr. tr. V.* (*geh.*) Ⓐ *mit sein od. haben* (*entlanggehen an*) inspect ‹troops›; pace ‹distance›; Ⓑ (*schreitend abmessen*) pace out

**Ab·schrift** *die* copy

**ab|schrubben** *tr. V.* (*ugs.*) Ⓐ scrub; **sich/jmdn. den Rücken ~:** scrub one's/sb.'s back [down]; **sich/jmdn. ~:** scrub oneself/sb. [down]; Ⓑ (*schrubbend entfernen*) scrub away *or* off; **sich/jmdn. den Schmutz ~:** scrub the dirt off oneself/sb.

**ab|schuften** *refl. V.* (*ugs.*) work like a slave; **sosehr man sich auch abschuftet** however hard you slave *or* (*Brit. coll.*) graft

**ab|schuppen** ❶ *tr. V.* scale. ❷ *refl. V.* **die Haut schuppt sich ab** the skin flakes off

**ab|schürfen** *tr. V.* **sich** (*Dat.*) **die Knie/die Ellenbogen ~:** graze one's knees/one's elbows; **sich** (*Dat.*) **die Haut ~:** chafe the skin

**Ab·schürfung** *die* Ⓐ (*das Abschürfen*) grazing; Ⓑ (*Schürfwunde*) graze

**Ab·schuss, *Ab·schuß** *der* Ⓐ (*eines Flugzeugs*) shooting down; (*eines Panzers*) putting out of action; **der Pilot hatte 50 Abschüsse** the pilot had 50 kills; Ⓑ (*von Wild*) shooting; (*fig. salopp: Eroberung*) lay (*coll.*); **Tiere zum ~ freigeben** permit the shooting of animals; **jmdn. zum ~ freigeben** (*fig. ugs.*) throw sb. to the wolves (*fig.*); Ⓒ (*das Abfeuern*) (*von Geschossen, Torpedos*) firing; (*von Raketen in den Weltraum*) launching

**Abschuss·basis, *Abschuß·basis** *die* launch[ing] site

**abschüssig** /ˈapˈʃʏsɪç/ *Adj.* downward sloping ‹land›; **die Straße ist ~:** the road goes steeply downhill

**Abschuss-, *Abschuß-: ~liste** *die* (*fig. ugs.*) **er steht auf meiner ~liste** I've got it in for him (*coll.*); **auf der/jmds. ~liste stehen** be on the/sb.'s blacklist; **~prämie** *die* bounty (*for shot animals*); **~rampe** *die* launch[ing] pad

**ab|schütteln** *tr. V.* Ⓐ (*herunterschütteln*) shake down ‹fruit›; **[sich** (*Dat.*)**] den Staub/den Schnee [vom Mantel] ~:** shake off the dust/the snow [from one's coat]; ⇒ *auch* **Joch** A; Ⓑ **ein Tischtuch ~:** shake [out] a tablecloth; Ⓒ (*fig.: überwinden, loswerden*) shake off

**ab|schütten** *tr. V.* ⇒ **abgießen** A

**ab|schwächen** ❶ *tr. V.* Ⓐ (*mildern*) tone down, moderate ‹statement, criticism›; Ⓑ (*verringern*) lessen ‹effect, impression›; cushion ‹blow, impact›; Ⓒ (*Fot.*) reduce. ❷ *refl. V.* (*nachlassen*) ‹interest, demand› wane; ‹noise, storm› abate; **das Tief/Hoch schwächt sich ab** (*Met.*) the low/high-pressure area is weakening; **der Preisauftrieb schwächt sich ab** price increases are slowing down

**Ab·schwächung** *die*; **~, ~en** Ⓐ (*Milderung*) toning down, moderation; (*abgemilderte Form*) attenuation; Ⓑ (*eines Aufpralls, Stoßes usw.*) cushioning; Ⓒ (*Fot.*) reduction; Ⓓ (*das Nachlassen*) waning; (*eines Hochs, Tiefs*) weakening; (*zahlenmäßig*) drop (*Gen.* in)

**ab|schwatzen**, (*bes. südd.*) **ab|schwätzen** *tr. V.* **jmdm. etw. ~:** talk sb. into giving one sth.; **sich** (*Dat.*) **etw. von jmdm. ~ lassen** let oneself be talked into giving sb. sth.

**ab|schweifen** *itr. V.*; *mit sein*; Ⓐ digress; **ihr Blick schweifte ab** her gaze wandered; Ⓑ (*geh.: vom Weg abgehen*) stray

**Abschweifung** *die*; **~, ~en** digression

**ab|schwellen** *unr. itr. V.*; *mit sein* Ⓐ go down; Ⓑ (*geh.: zurückgehen*) ‹flood› subside; ‹noise› die away; ‹music› fade [away]

**ab|schwemmen** *tr. V.* Ⓐ wash away; Ⓑ (*durch Schwemmen reinigen*) wash down

**Abschwemmung** *die*; **~, ~en** washout

**ab|schwenken** ❶ *itr. V.*; *mit sein* turn aside; **links/rechts ~** (*abbiegen*) turn left/right; (*die Richtung allmählich ändern*) bear to the left/right. ❷ *tr. V.* **die Tropfen vom Glas ~:** shake the drops off the glass; **die Gläser ~:** rinse the glasses and shake the drops off them

*old spelling (see note on page 1707)

**ab|schwindeln** *tr. V.* **jmdm. etw. ~:** trick sb. out of sth.

**ab|schwirren** *itr. V.*; *mit sein* Ⓐ ‹bird, dragonfly› whirr away; ‹bee, beetle, fly, wasp› buzz away; Ⓑ (*ugs.: weggehen*) buzz off (*coll.*)

**ab|schwitzen** *tr. V.* sweat off

**ab|schwören** *unr. itr. V.* **dem Teufel/seinem Glauben ~:** renounce the Devil/one's faith; **dem Alkohol/Laster ~:** forswear *or* swear off alcohol/vice

**Ab·schwung** *der* Ⓐ (*Turnen*) dismount; **beim ~:** when dismounting; Ⓑ (*Wirtsch.: Rezession*) downward trend; **ein ~ der Konjunktur** a recession

**ab|segeln** ❶ *itr. V.* Ⓐ *mit sein* (*lossegeln*) sail away; **von Kiel ~:** sail from Kiel; Ⓑ (*die Saison beenden*) have the last sail of the season. ❷ *tr. V.* **die Küste ~:** sail along the coast

**ab|segnen** *tr. V.* (*ugs. scherzh.*) sanction

**absehbar** *Adj.* foreseeable; **in ~er Zeit** within the foreseeable future; **etw. ist noch gar nicht ~:** sth. cannot yet be predicted; **auf** *od.* **für ~e Zeit** for the foreseeable future; **nicht ~:** unforeseeable

**ab|sehen** ❶ *unr. tr. V.* Ⓐ (*voraussehen*) predict; foresee ‹event›; Ⓑ (*abzielen*) **er hat es darauf abgesehen, uns zu ärgern** he's out to annoy us; Ⓒ (*haben wollen*) **es auf etw.** (*Akk.*) **abgesehen haben** be after sth.; **sie hat es bloß auf sein Geld abgesehen** she's only after his money; **er hat es auf sie abgesehen** he's got his eye on her; Ⓓ (*schikanieren*) **der Chef hat es auf ihn abgesehen** the boss has got it in for him; Ⓔ ⇒ **abgucken** 1.
❷ *unr. itr. V.* Ⓐ (*nicht beachten*) **von etw. ~:** leave aside *or* ignore sth.; ⇒ *auch* **abgesehen** 2; Ⓑ (*verzichten*) **von etw. ~:** refrain from sth.; **von einer Anzeige/Klage ~:** not report sth./not press charges; Ⓒ ⇒ **abgucken** 2

**ab|seifen** *tr. V.* wash down [with soap]; **jmdn./sich ~:** soap sb./oneself down

**ab|seilen** ❶ *tr. V.* lower [with a rope]. ❷ *refl. V.* Ⓐ (*Bergsteigen*) abseil; Ⓑ (*salopp: sich davonmachen*) push *or* buzz off (*coll.*)

**Abseil·haken** *der* (*Bergsteigen*) abseil piton

***ab|sein** ⇒ **ab** 2A

**Ab·seite** *die* (*Textilw.*) wrong side

**abseitig** *Adj.* Ⓐ (*geh.: abseits gelegen*) remote; Ⓑ (*ausgefallen, abwegig*) esoteric; Ⓒ ⇒ **abartig**

**abseits** /ˈapzaiːts/ ❶ *Präp. mit Gen.* away from. ❷ *Adv.* Ⓐ (*entfernt*) far away; **etwas ~:** a little way away; Ⓑ (*Ballspiele*) **~ sein** *od.* **stehen** be offside

**Abseits** *das*; **~, ~** Ⓐ (*Sport*) **das war ein klares ~:** that was clearly offside; **im ~ stehen** be offside; **der Spieler lief ins ~:** the player put himself offside; Ⓑ (*fig.*) **im ~ stehen** have been pushed out into the cold; **ins ~ geraten** be pushed out into the cold

**abseits-, Abseits-: ~falle** *die* (*Sport*) offside trap; **~position** *die*, **~stellung** *die* (*Sport*) offside position; **sich in ~stellung befinden** be in an offside position; **~tor** (*Sport*) *das* offside goal; **~verdächtig** *Adj.* (*Sport*) which may have been offside *postpos.*; **[stark] ~verdächtig sein** look [very much] like offside

**ab|senden** *unr. od. regelm. tr. V.* dispatch

**Ab·sender** *der*, **Ab·senderin**, *die*; **~, ~nen** ▶ 187 sender; (**~angabe**) sender's address

**Ab·sendung** *die* dispatch

**ab|sengen** *tr. V.* singe off; singe ‹poultry›

**ab|senken** ❶ *refl. V.* **sich [zum See/Fluss hin] ~:** slope [down to the lake/river]. ❷ *tr. V.* Ⓐ (*Tiefbau*) lower; Ⓑ (*versenken*) sink; Ⓒ (*Gartenbau*) **Erdbeeren/Weinstöcke ~:** set strawberries/vines

**Absenker** *der*; **~s, ~** (*Gartenbau*) runner; set

**absentieren** /apzɛnˈtiːrən/ *refl. V.* (*geh., veralt.*) withdraw

**Absenz** /apˈtsɛnts/ *die*; **~, ~en** Ⓐ absence [of mind]; Ⓑ (*bes. österr., schweiz.*) absence (*from school*)

**ab|servieren** ❶ *itr. V.* clear away. ❷ *tr. V.* Ⓐ **ein Gedeck/den Tisch ~:** clear away a cover/clear the table; Ⓑ (*salopp: absetzen, kaltstellen*) throw out; Ⓒ (*salopp: töten*) **jmdn. ~:** bump sb. off (*coll.*)

**absetzbar** *Adj.* Ⓐ (*Steuerw.*) **[steuerlich] ~:** [tax-]deductible; Ⓑ (*verkäuflich*) saleable; Ⓒ ⇒ **absetzen** 1 D: **er ist nicht ~:** he cannot be dismissed/be removed from office

**ab|setzen** ❶ *tr. V.* Ⓐ (*abnehmen*) take off; Ⓑ (*hinstellen*) put down ‹glass, bag, suitcase›; Ⓒ (*aussteigen lassen*) **jmdn. ~** (*im öffentlichen Verkehr*) put sb. down; let sb. out (*Amer.*); (*im privaten Verkehr*) drop sb. [off]; Ⓓ (*entlassen*) dismiss ‹minister, official›; remove ‹chancellor, judge› from office; depose ‹king, emperor›; Ⓔ (*ablagern*) deposit; Ⓕ (*absagen*) drop; call off ‹strike, football match›; **einen Punkt von der Tagesordnung ~:** delete an item from the agenda; Ⓖ (*nicht mehr anwenden*) discontinue ‹treatment, therapy›; stop taking ‹medicine, drug›; Ⓗ (*von den Lippen nehmen*) take ‹glass, trumpet› from one's lips; (*nicht mehr schreiben mit*) lift ‹pen› from the paper; Ⓘ (*verkaufen*) sell; Ⓙ (*Steuerw.*) **etw. [von der Steuer] ~:** deduct sth. [from tax]; Ⓚ (*abwerfen*) throw ‹rider›; Ⓛ (*Druckw.: als neue Zeile beginnen*) start ‹section› on a new line; **die folgenden Zeilen ~:** treat the subsequent lines as a new paragraph; Ⓜ (*Druckw.: setzen*) compose; **einen Text/ein Manuskript ~:** set [up] a text/manuscript; Ⓝ (*Seemannsspr.*) **ein Boot [vom Ufer] ~:** push a boat off [from the shore]; Ⓞ (*hervorheben*) **farblich abgesetzt** of contrasting colour *postpos.*; **wir wollen den Saum farblich ~:** we want to use a contrasting colour for the hem; **den Saum mit Samt ~:** trim the hem with velvet.
❷ *refl. V.* Ⓐ (*sich ablagern*) be deposited ‹dust› settle; ‹particles in suspension› settle out; Ⓑ (*sich distanzieren*) **sich von etw. ~:** distance oneself from sth.; Ⓒ (*sich unterscheiden*) ⇒ **abheben** 4; Ⓓ (*ugs.: sich davonmachen*) get away; Ⓔ (*Milit.*) withdraw

**Absetzung** *die*; **~, ~en** Ⓐ ⇒ **absetzen** 1 D: dismissal; removal from office; deposition; Ⓑ (*Steuerw.*) deduction; Ⓒ (*Absage*) cancellation; (*eines Streiks, Fußballspiels usw.*) calling off; Ⓓ (*Abbruch*) discontinuation

**ab|sichern** ❶ *tr. V.* Ⓐ make safe; Ⓑ (*fig.*) substantiate ‹argument, conclusions›; validate ‹result›; **etw. rechtlich/vertraglich ~:** protect sth. legally/by contract; **tariflich abgesichert** protected by agreement *postpos.* ❷ *refl. V.* safeguard oneself; **sich vertraglich ~:** protect oneself by contract; **sich gegenseitig ~:** keep each other safe; **er will sich ~ für den Fall, dass …** he wants to cover himself against the possiblity that …; **sich nach allen Seiten ~:** guard against all eventualities; (*gegen Einwände*) forestall criticism

**Ab·sicherung** *die* Ⓐ (*das Sichermachen*) making safe; **die Polizei ist für die ~ des Geländes verantwortlich** the police are responsible for making the site safe; Ⓑ (*fig.*) substantiation; (*von Ergebnissen*) validation; **zur rechtlichen/vertraglichen ~ einer Sache** (*Gen.*) to protect sth. legally/by contract

**Ab·sicht** *die*; Ⓐ intention; **die ~ haben, etw. zu tun** plan *or* intend to do sth.; **etw. mit** *od.* **aus ~ tun** do sth. intentionally *or* deliberately; **etw. ohne** *od.* **nicht mit ~ tun** do sth. unintentionally; **das ist ~:** that's intentional; **in der besten ~:** with the best of intentions; **aus** *od.* **in politischer/therapeutischer ~:** with a political/therapeutic purpose; Ⓑ (*Rechtsw.*) intent; **in betrügerischer ~ handeln** act with intent to deceive

**ab·sichtlich** ❶ *Adj.* intentional; deliberate. ❷ *adv.* intentionally; deliberately

**Absichts·erklärung** *die* declaration of intent

**absichtslos** ❶ *Adj.* unintentional. ❷ *adv.* unintentionally

**Ab·siedlung** *die* (*Med.*) dissemination

**ab|singen** *unr. tr. V.* Ⓐ *auch itr.* **[etw.] vom Blatt ~:** sing [sth.] at sight; Ⓑ **unter Absingen der Nationalhymne/schmut-**

**ziger Lieder** singing the national anthem/ dirty songs

**ab|sinken** *unr. itr. V.; mit sein* [A] sink; (*fig.: im Niveau*) decline; [B] ‹temperature, blood pressure› drop; ‹interest, performance› decline; **in seinen Leistungen ~:** do *or* perform less well

**Absinth** /ap'zɪnt/ *der;* **~[e]s, ~e** absinth[e]

**ab|sitzen** ❶ *unr. tr. V.* [A] (*hinter sich bringen*) sit through; sit out ‹hours of duty etc.›; (*im Gefängnis*) serve; **zehn Jahre ~:** serve *or* (*coll.*) do ten years; **seine Jahre ~:** serve one's full sentence; [B] ⇒ **abgesessen** 2. ❷ *unr. itr. V. mit sein* **[vom Pferd] ~:** dismount [from one's horse]

**absolut** /apzo'lu:t/ ❶ *Adj.* (*auch Chemie, Physik*) absolute; pure ‹lyricism, art›; **der ~e Knüller** (*ugs.*) the high spot; **der ~e Nullpunkt** (*Physik*) absolute zero; **der ~e Ablativ** (*Sprachw.*) the ablative absolute; **die ~e Mehrheit** (*Pol.*) an absolute majority. ❷ *adv.* absolutely

**Absolutheit** *die;* **~, ~en** absoluteness

**Absolution** /apzolu'tsio:n/ *die;* **~, ~en** (*kath. Rel.*) absolution; **jmdm. die ~ erteilen** give sb. absolution

**Absolutismus** *der;* **~** (*hist.*) absolutism *no art.*

**absolutistisch** ❶ *Adj.* absolutist. ❷ *adv.* in an absolutist manner

**Absolvent** /apzɔl'vɛnt/ *der;* **~en, ~en, Absolventin** *die;* **~, ~nen** (*einer Schule*) one who has taken the leaving *or* (*Amer.*) final examination; (*einer Akademie*) graduate; **die ~en der Handelsschule/eines Lehrgangs** those who have/had attended a commercial college/completed a course of training; **er ist ~ einer Abendschule** he has attended an evening school; ⇒ *auch* **-in**

**absolvieren** /apzɔl'vi:rən/ *tr. V.* [A] complete; **das Gymnasium ~:** complete a grammar-school education; [B] (*erledigen, verrichten*) put in ‹hours›; do ‹performance, route, task›; make ‹visit›; do (*coll.*) ‹sights›; [C] (*kath. Rel.*) absolve

**Absolvierung** *die;* **~:** completion; **nach [der] ~ einiger Besuche/seines Studiums** having paid some visits/finished one's studies

**ab·sonderlich** *Adj.* strange; odd

**Absonderlichkeit** *die;* **~, ~en** strangeness; oddness

**ab|sondern** ❶ *tr. V.* [A] isolate ‹patient›; separate ‹prisoner›; [B] (*Biol., Physiol.*) secrete; exude ‹resin›; discharge ‹pus›; (*fig. abwertend*) emit. ❷ *refl. V.* **sich [von anderen] ~:** isolate oneself [from others]

**Absonderung** *die;* **~, ~en** [A] isolation; [B] (*Biol., Med.*) secretion; [C] (*österr.: Einzelhaft*) solitary confinement

**Absorbens** /ap'zɔrbɛns/ *das;* **~, Absorbenzien** *od.* **Absorbentia** (*Chemie, Physik*) absorbent

**Absorber** *der;* **~s, ~** [A] ⇒ **Absorbens**; [B] (*bei Kältemaschinen usw.*) absorber

**absorbieren** *tr. V.* [A] (*Chemie, Physik, Physiol.*) absorb; **~d** absorbent; [B] (*fig.*) absorb, engage ‹attention›

**Absorption** /apzɔrp'tsio:n/ *die;* **~** (*Chemie, Physik, Physiol.*) absorption

**Absorptions·vermögen** *das* (*Chemie, Physik, Physiol.*) absorbency

**ab|spalten** ❶ *unr. od. regelm. tr. V.* [A] (*abschlagen, fig.: trennen*) split off; [B] (*Chemie*) release. ❷ *unr. od. regelm. refl. V.* split off *or* away (**aus** from); **sich von jmdm./etw. ~:** split with sb./sth.

**Ab·spaltung** *die* [A] (*das Abschlagen, fig.: Trennung*) splitting-off; [B] (*Chemie*) separation

**Ab·spann** *der* (*Ferns.*) final credits

**ab|spannen** *tr. V.* [A] (*ausspannen*) unhitch ‹wagon›; unharness ‹horse›; unyoke ‹oxen›; [B] (*Technik: mit Seilen*) anchor ‹pole, mast›; ⇒ *auch* **abgespannt** 2

**Abspann·seil** *das* (*Brückenbau*) inclined tension cable

**Abspannung** *die;* **~, ~en** [A] (*Ermüdung*) weariness; fatigue; [B] (*Technik*) anchoring; (*Abspannseil*) anchoring cable

**ab|sparen** *refl. V.* **sich** (*Dat.*) **etw. von seinem Lohn/Taschengeld ~:** save for sth. out of one's wages/pocket money; **er hatte sich** (*Dat.*) **ein paar Mark abgespart** he had managed to save a few marks; ⇒ *auch* **Mund**

**ab|specken** (*salopp*) ❶ *tr. V.* shed. ❷ *itr. V.* [A] (*Gewicht verlieren*) lose weight; slim [down]; [B] (*fig.: schrumpfen*) slim down

**ab|speichern** *tr. V.* (*DV*) store

**ab|speisen** *tr. V.* [A] (*vertrösten*) **jmdn. mit etw. ~:** fob sb. off with sth.; [B] (*oft abwertend: beköstigen*) feed

**abspenstig** /'ap-ʃpɛnstɪç/ *Adj.* **jmdm. etw. ~ machen** get sb. to part with sth.; **jmdm. die Kunden/die Patienten/das Personal ~ machen** lure away sb.'s customers/ patients/staff; **jmdm. den Freund/die Freundin ~ machen** steal sb.'s boyfriend/ girlfriend

**ab|sperren** ❶ *tr. V.* [A] (*blockieren*) seal off; close off; [B] **jmdm. das Gas/das Wasser/ den Strom ~:** cut off sb.'s gas/water/electricity; [C] (*österr., südd.: abschließen*) lock ‹door›. ❷ *itr. V.* (*österr., südd.*) lock up

**Absperr-: ~gitter** *das* barrier; **~hahn** *der; Pl.* **~hähne,** (*fachspr.*) **~~en** (*Technik*) stopcock; **~kette** *die* cordon

**Ab·sperrung** *die* [A] (*Blockierung*) sealing off; closing off; [B] (*Sperre*) barrier

**Absperr·ventil** *das* (*Technik*) stop valve

**Ab·spiel** *das* (*Ballspiele*) [A] (*das Abspielen*) passing; [B] (*Schuss*) pass

**ab|spielen** ❶ *tr. V.* [A] (*ablaufen lassen*) **etw. ~:** play sth. through; [B] **die Nationalhymne/Internationale ~:** play the national anthem/Internationale; **ein Musikstück vom Blatt ~:** play a piece of music at sight; [C] (*Ballspiele*) pass; ⇒ *auch* **abgespielt** 2. ❷ *refl. V.* [A] (*stattfinden*) take place; [B] (*sich ereignen*) happen; take place; ‹course of events› proceed; ‹war› be waged; **da spielt sich [bei mir/ihm] nichts ab!** (*salopp*) nothing doing [as far as I'm/he's concerned] (*coll.*). ❸ *itr. V.* (*Ballspiele*) pass; **an jmdn. ~:** pass [the ball] to sb.

**ab|splittern** ❶ *itr. V.; mit sein* ‹wood› splinter off; ‹lacquer, paint› flake off. ❷ *refl. V.* (*fig.*) **sich von einer Gruppe/Partei ~:** split away from a group/party

**Ab·sprache** *die* agreement; arrangement; **eine ~ mit jmdm. treffen** come to an agreement *or* make an arrangement with sb.; **nach ~ mit** by arrangement with; **nach vorheriger/ohne vorherige ~:** after/ without prior consultation

**absprache·gemäß** *Adv.* as arranged *or* agreed

**ab|sprechen** ❶ *unr. tr. V.* [A] (*aberkennen*) **jmdm. etw. ~:** deprive sb. of sth.; [B] (*ableugnen*) **jmdm. etw. ~:** deny that sb. has sth.; **jmdm. das Recht auf etw.** (*Akk.*) **~:** deny sb.'s right to sth.; **jmdm. das Recht ~, etw. zu tun** deny sb. the right to do sth.; [C] (*vereinbaren*) arrange; **etw. miteinander ~:** arrange sth. together. ❷ *unr. refl. V.* (*sich einigen*) **sich [mit jmdm.] [über etw.** (*Akk.*)**] ~:** come to *or* reach an agreement [with sb.] [about sth.]

**ab|spreizen** *tr. V.* stretch out ‹arm, leg› sideways; splay out ‹fingers, toes›; spread out ‹hands›; extend ‹finger›

**ab|sprengen** *tr. V.* [A] (*lossprengen*) split off; (*Raumf.*) jettison ‹stage›; [B] (*fig.*) separate ‹troops›; **abgesprengte Truppenteile** isolated detachments of troops

**ab|springen** *unr. itr. V.; mit sein* [A] (*losspringen*) jump off; **[mit dem rechten/linken Bein] ~** ‹jumper› take off [on the right/left leg]; [B] (*herunterspringen*) jump down; **vom Fahrrad/Pferd ~:** jump off one's bicycle/ horse; **aus dem Flugzeug ~:** jump out of the aeroplane; **mit dem Fallschirm ~:** jump [with a parachute]; (*bei Gefahr*) bail out; **„Abspringen während der Fahrt verboten"** 'do not alight while the vehicle is in motion'; [C] (*abplatzen*) come off; ‹paint› flake off; ‹enamel› splinter off; [D] (*sich lösen*) fly off; ‹bicycle chain› jump off; [E] (*abprallen*) rebound; [F] (*ugs.: sich zurückziehen*) drop out; (*von einem Abkommen*) back out; **Kunden/Leser springen uns ab** we are losing customers/readers

**ab|spritzen** ❶ *tr. V.* [A] (*reinigen*) spray [down]; [B] (*entfernen*) spray off; **einer Kuh** (*Dat.*) **den Kot ~:** spray the muck off a cow; [C] (*ns. verhüll.: ermorden*) **jmdn. ~:** give sb. a lethal injection. ❷ *itr. V.* [A] (*vulgär: ejakulieren*) come (*coarse*); [B] *mit sein* (*veralt.: weggehen*) race off; [C] *mit sein* (*spritzend abprallen*) ‹liquid› splash off; ‹mud, mortar, etc.› splatter off

**Ab·sprung** *der* [A] (*das Losspringen*) take-off; [B] (*das Herunterspringen*) jump; [C] (*fig.*) break; **den ~ wagen** risk making the break; **den ~ schaffen** make the break; **den ~ verpassen** miss the boat

**Absprung·balken** *der* (*Leichtathletik*) take-off board

**ab|spulen** *tr. V.* [A] (*abwickeln*) unwind; **sich ~:** come unwound; [B] (*filmen*) shoot; [C] (*vorführen*) show; [D] (*salopp: herunterleiern*) reel off; [E] (*salopp: fahren*) cover

**ab|spülen** ❶ *tr. V.* [A] (*wegspülen*) wash off ‹dirt, dust›; [B] (*reinigen*) rinse off; **sich** (*Dat.*) **die Hände** *usw.* **~:** rinse one's hands *etc.*; [C] (*bes. südd.*) **das Geschirr ~:** wash the dishes. ❷ *itr. V.* (*bes. südd.*) wash up

**ab|stammen** *itr. V.* **von jmdm./vom Affen ~:** be descended from sb./the apes

**Abstammung** *die;* **~, ~en** ▶ **553** descent; **seiner ~ nach ist er Deutscher** he is German by descent

**Abstammungs·lehre** *die* theory of evolution

**Ab·stand** *der* [A] (*Zwischenraum*) distance; **in 20 Meter ~:** at a distance of 20 metres; **im ~ von 10 Metern** 10 metres apart; **~ halten** keep one's distance; [B] (*Punktunterschied*) gap; difference; (*Rangunterschied*) social distinction; **mit ~:** by far; far and away; [C] (*Zeitspanne*) interval; (*kürzer*) gap; **in Abständen von 20 Minuten** at 20-minute intervals; **[von etw.] ~ gewinnen** (*fig.*) have time to recover [from sth.]; **mir fehlt noch der innere ~ zu den Geschehnissen** these events are still too close to me; [D] (*Zurückhaltung, Distanz*) **~ halten** keep one's distance; **den [gebührenden/nötigen] ~ wahren** keep the proper/ necessary distance; [E] (*geh.: Verzicht*) **von etw. ~ nehmen** refrain from sth.; **von einer Intervention ~ nehmen** refrain from intervening; **davon ~ nehmen, etw. zu tun** refrain from doing sth.; **von einer Idee ~ nehmen** abandon an idea; [F] (*Entschädigung*) compensation; (*bei Übernahme einer Wohnung*) *payment for furniture and fittings left by previous tenant*

**Abstands·summe** *die* ⇒ **Abstand** F

**ab|statten** /'ap-ʃtatn̩/ *tr. V.* (*geh.*) **jmdm. einen Besuch ~:** pay sb. a visit; **jmdm. Bericht ~:** present one's *or* a report to sb.; **jmdm. seinen Dank ~:** convey one's thanks *or* express one's gratitude to sb.

**ab|stauben** *tr., itr. V.* [A] dust; [B] (*ugs.*) (*stehlen*) **etw. ~:** pinch (*coll.*) *or* nick (*Brit. coll.*) *or* (*Amer. coll.*) lift sth.; (*schnorren*) **etw. bei jmdm. ~:** sponge sth. from sb.; **sie haben ordentlich abgestaubt** they've been pinching things left, right, and centre (*coll.*)/sponging from all over the place; [C] (*Fußballjargon*) **ein Tor ~:** steal a goal

**Abstauber** *der;* **~s, ~** [A] ⇒ **Abstaubertor;** [B] (*Fußballjargon*) goal-hanger

**Abstauberin** *die;* **~, ~en** (*Fußballjargon*) goal-hanger

**Abstauber·tor** *das* (*Fußballjargon*) opportunist goal

**ab|stechen** ❶ *unr. tr. V.* [A] slaughter ‹animal› (*by cutting its throat*); **jmdn. ~** (*derb*) slit sb.'s throat; ⇒ *auch* **Kalb** A; [B] (*ab-, herauslösen*) slice off; cut edge of ‹lawn›; cut ‹peat›; **Teig/Klöße [mit dem Löffel] ~:** cut up dough/cut out dumplings [with a spoon]; [C] (*ablaufen lassen*) tap ‹beer, wine›; **einen Hochofen ~:** tap a blast furnace. ❷ *unr. itr.*

a

*V.* **von etw./jmdm. ~:** contrast with sth./sb.; **gegen etw. ~:** stand out against sth.

**Abstecher** *der;* **~s, ~:** side trip; (*fig.: Abschweifung*) digression

**ab|stecken** *tr. V.* **A** (*abgrenzen*) mark out; (*fig.*) define; **ein Gelände mit Pfählen/Pflöcken/Fähnchen ~:** mark out an area with stakes/pegs/flags; **B** (*Schneiderei*) pin up ‹hem›; **ein Kleid ~:** fit a dress [by pinning]

**ab|stehen** *unr. itr. V.* **A** (*nicht anliegen*) ‹hair› stand up, stick out; ‹pigtail[s]› stick out; ‹beard› grow out; **~de Ohren** protruding ears; **B** (*wegstehen*) **40 cm/zu weit von etw. ~:** be 40 cm. away/too far away from sth.; **C** (*geh.: Abstand nehmen*) **von einem Plan ~:** abandon a plan; **davon ~, etw. zu tun** refrain from doing sth.; **D** **Wasser ~ lassen** let water stand; ⇒ *auch* **abgestanden 2; Bein A**

**Ab·steige** *die;* **~, ~n** (*ugs. abwertend*) cheap and crummy hotel (*sl.*); (*Stundenhotel*) sleazy hotel

**ab|steigen** *unr. itr. V.; mit sein* **A** (*heruntersteigen*) **[vom Pferd/Fahrrad] ~:** get off [one's horse/bicycle]; **vom Karren ~:** get down from the cart; **„Radfahrer ~"** 'no cycling'; 'cycling prohibited'; **B** (*abwärts gehen*) go down; descend; **~d** descending ‹pipe, branch›; **vom Gipfel/ins Tal ~:** climb down *or* descend from the summit/into the valley; **gesellschaftlich ~** (*fig.*) decline in social status; **die ~de Linie** (*Geneal.*) the line of descent; ⇒ *auch* **Ast A**; **C** (*Sport*) be relegated; **D** (*übernachten, wohnen*) **in einem Hotel ~:** put up at a hotel

**Absteige·quartier** *das* **A** (*veralt.*) stopping place; **B** (*ugs. abwertend*) ⇒ **Absteige**

**Ab·steiger** *der* **A** **ein [gesellschaftlicher] ~:** one who has declined in social status; **B** (*Sport*) (*vor dem Abstieg stehend*) team threatened with *or* facing relegation; (*abgestiegen*) relegated team

**Ab·steigerin** *die* ⇒ **Absteiger A**

**Abstell·bahn·hof** *der* [rail] sidings *pl.*

**ab|stellen** ❶ *tr. V.* **A** (*absetzen*) put down; **B** (*unterbringen, hinstellen*) put; (*parken*) park; **C** (*ausschalten, abdrehen*); turn *or* switch off; turn off ‹gas, water›; **jmdm. das Gas/den Strom ~:** cut sb.'s gas/electricity off; **jmdm. das Telefon ~:** disconnect sb.'s telephone; **D** (*unterbinden*) put a stop to; **E** (*sein lassen*) stop; (*aufgeben*) give up; **F** (*beordern*) assign; detail [off] ‹soldiers›; **G** **etw. [weiter] von etw. ~** (*abrücken*) move sth. [further] away from sth.; (*entfernt stellen*) put sth. at a [greater] distance from sth.; **H** (*ausrichten*) **etw. auf etw.** (*Akk.*) **~:** gear sth. to sth.
❷ *itr. V.* **auf etw.** (*Akk.*) **~:** take account of sth.; take sth. into account; **darauf ~, dass ...** take account of *or* take into account the fact that ...

**Abstell-: ~gleis** *das* siding; **jmdn. aufs ~gleis schieben** (*fig. ugs.*) put sb. out of harm's way; **~kammer** *die* lumber room; **~raum** *der* storeroom

**ab|stemmen** ❶ *tr. V.* (*abmeißeln*) chisel off. ❷ *refl. V.* push with one's feet; **sich mit den Armen vom Boden ~:** push oneself up from the floor with one's arms

**ab|stempeln** *tr. V.* **A** frank ‹letter›; cancel ‹stamp›; **der Brief war in Hamburg abgestempelt** the letter had a Hamburg postmark; **B** (*fig.*) **jmdn. als** *od.* **zum Verbrecher/als geisteskrank ~:** label *or* brand sb. as a criminal/as insane

**ab|steppen** *tr. V.* backstitch

**ab|sterben** *unr. itr. V.; mit sein* **A** (*eingehen, verfallen*) [gradually] die; ⇒ *auch* **abgestorben 2**; **B** (*gefühllos werden*) go numb; **mir sind die Finger abgestorben** my fingers have gone numb; **C** (*verschwinden*) ‹custom, tradition› die out; ‹state, social order› wither away; **D** (*ugs.: ausgehen*) ‹engine› die

**Ab·stich** *der* **A** (*das Abstechen*) cutting; **B** (*Metall.*) tapping

**Abstich-: ~loch** *das* (*Metall.*) tapping hole; **~rinne** *die* (*Metall.*) tapping spout

**Ab·stieg** *der;* **~[e]s, ~e** **A** descent; **B** (*Niedergang*) decline; **[sozialer** *od.* **gesellschaftlicher] ~:** fall *or* drop in [social] status; **C** (*Sport*) relegation; **D** (*Weg abwärts*) way down

**abstiegs·gefährdet** *Adj.* (*Sport*) threatened with *or* facing relegation *postpos.*

**Abstiegs·kandidat** *der* (*Sportjargon*) candidate for relegation

**ab|stillen** ❶ *tr. V.* wean. ❷ *itr. V.* stop breastfeeding

**ab|stimmen** ❶ *itr. V.* vote; **es wird abgestimmt** a vote is taken; **geheim/namentlich/durch Handzeichen/durch Akklamation ~:** vote by secret ballot/by roll-call/by a show of hands/by acclamation; **über etw.** (*Akk.*) **~:** vote on sth.; **über etw.** (*Akk.*) **~ lassen** put sth. to the vote.
❷ *tr. V.* **A** (*vereinbaren*); **etw. [miteinander] ~:** discuss and agree on sth. [with each other]; **etw. mit jmdm. ~:** discuss and agree sth. with sb.; **B** (*harmonisieren*) **etw. auf etw.** (*Akk.*) **~:** suit sth. to sth.; (*Mode*) match sth. to sth.; **etw. auf jmdn. ~:** pitch sth. at sb.'s level; **eine fein abgestimmte Mischung** a finely balanced blend; **zwei/mehrere Dinge aufeinander ~:** make two/several things consistent with each other; **Zeitpläne/Programme aufeinander ~:** coordinate timetables/programmes; **C** (*Rundf., Ferns.: einstellen*) tune; **D** (*Kfz-W.*) tune [up]; adjust ‹carburettor›.
❸ *refl. V.* **sich über etw.** (*Akk.*) **~:** discuss and agree on sth.

**Ab·stimmung** *die* **A** (*Stimmabgabe*) vote; ballot; **eine geheime ~:** a secret ballot; **zur ~ schreiten** (*geh.*) *od.* **kommen** come to the vote; **eine ~ [über etw.** (*Akk.*)**] durchführen** take a vote [on sth.]; **bei der ~:** in the vote; (*während der ~*) during the voting; **B** (*Absprache*) agreement; **C** (*Harmonisierung*) coordination; **D** (*Rundf., Ferns.*) tuning

**Abstimmungs-: ~ergebnis** *das* result of a/the vote; **~nieder·lage** *die* defeat [in a/the vote]; **~sieg** *der* victory [in a/the vote]

**abstinent** /apsti'nɛnt/ *Adj.* **A** teetotal; **~ sein** be a non-drinker *or* teetotaller; **B** **sexuell ~:** sexually abstinent; continent; **politisch ~ sein** (*fig.*) abstain from politics

**Abstinenz** /apsti'nɛnts/ *die;* **~** **A** teetotalism; **~ üben** be teetotal; **B** **sexuelle ~:** sexual abstinence; continence; **politische ~** (*fig.*) political abstinence

**Abstinenzler** *der;* **~s, ~, Abstinenzlerin** *die;* **~, ~nen** teetotaller; non-drinker

**Abstinenzlertum** *das;* **~s** temperance

**ab|stoppen** ❶ *tr. V.* **A** (*zum Stillstand bringen*) halt; stop; check ‹advance›; stop ‹machine›; **B** (*mit der Stoppuhr*) **einen Läufer ~:** time a runner with a stopwatch; **die Zeit ~:** measure the time with a stopwatch. ❷ *itr. V.* come to a halt; ‹person› stop

**Ab·stoß** *der* **A** (*Fußball*) goal kick; **den ~ ausführen** take the goal kick; **B** (*Sport: beim Springen*) take-off

**ab|stoßen** ❶ *unr. tr. V.* **A** (*wegstoßen*) push off *or* away; **das Boot [vom Ufer] ~:** push the boat out [from the bank]; **B** (*beschädigen*) chip ‹crockery, paintwork, stucco, plaster›; batter ‹furniture›; scuff ‹shoes›; ⇒ *auch* **Horn**; **C** (*verkaufen*) sell off; **D** (*zurückweisen*) reject; **E** (*Physik*) repel; **F** (*anwidern*) repel; put off; **sich von jmdm./etw. abgestoßen fühlen** find sb./sth. repulsive.
❷ *unr. itr. V.* **A** *mit sein od. haben* (*sich entfernen*) be pushed off; **B** (*anwidern*) be repulsive.
❸ *refl. V.* **sich [vom Boden] ~:** push oneself off; (*beim Sprung*) take off

**abstoßend** *Adj.* repulsive

**Abstoßung** *die;* **~, ~en** **A** (*Physik, auch fig.*) repulsion; **B** (*Verkauf*) sale; **C** (*Med., Physiol.*) rejection

**ab|stottern** *tr. V.* (*ugs.*) pay for in instalments; pay off ‹debt› by instalments; **er muss jeden Monat 400 DM ~:** he has to pay out 400 DM in instalments every month

**ab|strafen** *tr. V.* punish

**Abstrafung** *die;* **~, ~en** punishment

**abstrahieren** /apstra'hi:rən/ ❶ *itr. V.* (*absehen*) **von etw. ~:** ignore sth.; leave sth. out of account. ❷ *tr., itr. V.* (*verallgemeinern*) abstract (**aus** from)

**ab|strahlen** ❶ *tr. V.* (*Physik*) radiate; (*Funkw., Elektrot.*) emit ‹wave, frequency›. ❷ *itr. V.* (*fig.*) **auf jmdn./etw. ~:** influence *or* affect sb./sth.

**Ab·strahlung** *die* (*Physik*) radiation; (*Funkw., Elektrot.*) emission

**abstrakt** /ap'strakt/ ❶ *Adj.* abstract. ❷ *adv.* abstractly; **~ denken** think in the abstract

**Abstraktheit** *die;* **~:** abstractness

**Abstraktion** /apstrak'tsjo:n/ *die;* **~, ~en** abstraction

**Abstraktions·vermögen** *das* capacity for abstraction

**Abstraktum** /ap'straktʊm/ *das;* **~s, Abstrakta** **A** (*Philos.*) abstract[ion]; **B** (*Sprachw.*) abstract noun

**ab|strampeln** *refl. V.* (*ugs.*) **A** (*beim Radfahren*) pedal; **sich** (*Dat.*) **einige Pfunde ~:** pedal off a few pounds; **B** ⇒ **abplacken**

**ab|streichen** ❶ *unr. tr. V.* **A** (*abstreifen*) wipe; (*durch Streichen entfernen*) wipe off; **B** (*ausstreichen*) cross off; **C** (*abziehen*) knock off; **davon muss man die Hälfte ~** (*fig.*) you have to take it with a pinch *or* grain of salt; **D** (*absuchen*) sweep ‹horizon›; comb ‹terrain›. ❷ *unr. itr. V.; mit sein* (*Jägerspr.*) fly away

**Ab·streicher** *der* ⇒ **Abtreter**

**ab|streifen** *tr. V.* **A** pull off; strip off ‹berries›; **sich** (*Dat.*) **die Handschuhe/den Ring ~:** take off *or* remove one's gloves/ring; **sich/jmdm. die Kleidung ~:** take off one's/sb.'s clothes; **die Asche [von der Zigarette/Zigarre] ~:** remove the ash [from one's cigarette/cigar]; **B** (*abwischen*) wipe; (*durch Streifen entfernen*) wipe off; **seine** *od.* **sich** (*Dat.*) **die Schuhe/Sohlen ~:** wipe one's feet; **C** (*absuchen*) comb (**nach** for)

**Abstreifer** *der;* **~s, ~** ⇒ **Abtreter**

**Abstreif·gitter** *das* grille (*for removing excess paint from paint roller*)

**ab|streiten** *unr. tr. V.* deny; **~, etw. getan zu haben** deny that one has done sth.; **das lässt sich nicht ~:** there's no denying that; that cannot be denied; **das kann ihm keiner ~:** you cannot deny him that

**Ab·strich** *der* **A** (*Med.*) taking of a swab; **einen ~ machen** take a swab; **B** (*Streichung, Kürzung*) cut; **~e [an etw.** (*Dat.*)**] machen** make cuts [in sth.]; (*Einschränkungen machen*) make concessions [as regards sth.]; **C** (*Musik*) downstroke

**ab|strömen** *itr. V.; mit sein* ‹water› flow away; ‹air mass› move away

**abstrus** /ap'stru:s/ *Adj.* (*geh.*) abstruse; (*absurd*) absurd

**ab|stufen** *tr. V.* **A** (*in Stufen anlegen*) terrace ‹slope, hill›; layer ‹hair›; **B** (*staffeln*) grade; **abgestufte Abschreckung** (*Milit.*) graduated deterrence; **C** (*nuancieren*) differentiate; (*Kunstwiss.*) nuance

**Ab·stufung** *die;* **~, ~en** **A** (*im Gelände*) terrace; **B** (*Staffelung*) gradation; **die soziale ~:** the social hierarchy; **C** (*Nuance*) shade; (*Nuancierung*) variety

**ab|stumpfen** ❶ *tr. V.* (*gefühllos machen*) deaden; ⇒ *auch* **abgestumpft 2**. ❷ *itr. V.; mit sein* (*gefühllos werden*) **man stumpft ab** one's mind becomes deadened; **gegen etw. ~:** become dead to sth.; **der Gerechtigkeitssinn stumpft ab** one's sense of justice becomes blunted

**Ab·sturz** *der* **A** fall; **B** (*eines Flugzeugs*) crash; **ein Flugzeug zum ~ bringen** cause a plane to crash; **C** (*Steilhang*) precipice

**ab|stürzen** *itr. V.; mit sein* **A** fall; ‹aircraft, pilot, passenger› crash; **tödlich ~:** fall/crash to one's death; **B** (*geh.: abfallen*) ‹cliff› plunge

**Absturz·stelle** *die* site of the [aircraft] crash

**Absturz·ursache** *die* cause of the crash

**ab|stützen** ❶ *refl. V.* support oneself (**mit** on, **an** + *Dat.* against); **sich von etw. ~:** push

*old spelling (see note on page 1707)

oneself away from sth. ❷ *tr. V.* support; (*Bauw.: gegen Einsturz*) shore up; (*fig.: untermauern*) support; back up

**Ab·stützung** *die* (*Bauw.*) shores *pl.*

**ab|suchen** *tr. V.* Ⓐ search (**nach** for); (*durchkämmen*) comb (**nach** for); drag ‹pond, river, etc.› (**nach** for); **den Himmel/Horizont ~:** scan the sky/horizon (**nach** for); Ⓑ (*absammeln*) **etw. von etw. ~:** pick sth. off sth.; **jmdm. die Läuse ~:** look for lice on sb.

**Ab·sud** /'apzu:t/ *der;* **~[e]s, ~e** (*veralt.*) decoction

**absurd** /ap'zʊrt/ *Adj.* absurd; **~es Theater** Theatre of the Absurd

**absurderweise** *Adv.* absurdly enough

**Absurdität** /apzʊrdi'tɛ:t/ *die;* **~, ~en** absurdity; (*Ungereimtheit*) inconsistency

**Abszess, *Abszeß** /aps'tsɛs/ *der* (*österr. auch: das*); **Abszesses, Abszesse ▶ 474** Ⓐ (*Med.*) abscess; Ⓑ (*Geschwür*) ulcer

**Abszisse** /aps'tsɪsə/ *die;* **~, ~en** (*Math.*) abscissa

**Abszissen·achse** *die* (*Math.*) axis of abscissae

**Abt** /apt/ *der;* **~[e]s, Äbte** /'ɛptə/ abbot

**Abt.** *Abk.* **Abteilung**

**ab|takeln** /'apta:kln/ *tr. V.* (*Seemannsspr.*) unrig ‹ship›; ⇒ *auch* **abgetakelt** 2

**ab|tanzen** *itr. V.* (*salopp*) dance

**ab|tasten** *tr. V.* **etw. ~:** feel sth. all over; **jmdn. auf Waffen** (*Akk.*) **~:** frisk sb. for weapons

**Abtast·nadel** *die*, **Abtast·stift** *der* stylus

**Abtau·automatik** *die* (*Elektrot.*) automatic defrost

**ab|tauchen** *itr. V.* Ⓐ (*Seemannsspr.*) submerge; Ⓑ (*ugs.*) **[in die Illegalität** *od.* **in den Untergrund] ~:** go underground

**ab|tauen** ❶ *itr. V.*; *mit sein* (*wegschmelzen*) melt away; (*eis-/schneefrei werden*) become clear of ice/snow; ‹refrigerator› defrost. ❷ *tr. V.* (*schnee-/eisfrei machen*) melt; thaw; de-ice ‹vehicle windows›; **den Schnee/das Eis von etw. ~:** melt the snow/ice off sth.; **einen Kühlschrank ~:** defrost a refrigerator

**Ab·tausch** *der* Ⓐ (*Schach*) exchange; Ⓑ ⇒ **Schlagabtausch**; Ⓒ (*schweiz.*) ⇒ **Tausch**

**ab|tauschen** *tr. V.* Ⓐ (*Schach*) exchange; Ⓑ **jmdm. etw. ~:** get sth. from sb. by swapping; Ⓒ (*schweiz.*) ⇒ **tauschen**

**Abtei** /ap'tai/ *die;* **~, ~en** abbey

**Abtei·kirche** *die* abbey [church]

**Abteil** *das;* **~[e]s, ~e** compartment; (*eines Regals*) shelf; **ein ~ erster/zweiter Klasse** a first-second-class compartment

**ab|teilen** *tr. V.* Ⓐ (*aufteilen*) divide [up]; Ⓑ (*abtrennen*) divide off

**Abteil-: ~fenster** *das* compartment window; **~tür** *die* compartment door

**Ab·teilung**[1] *die* dividing off

**Ab·teilung**[2] *die* Ⓐ department; (*einer Behörde*) department; section; **die ~ für Vor- und Frühgeschichte** the department of prehistory and early history; Ⓑ (*Zool.*) phylum; (*Bot.*) division; Ⓒ (*Milit.*) unit; Ⓓ (*veralt.: Teil*) part

**-abteilung** *die* ... department

**Abteilungs·leiter** *der*, **Abteilungs·leiterin** *die* head of department/section; departmental manager

**ab|telefonieren** *itr. V.* **[jmdm.] ~:** phone [sb.] to say one cannot come

**ab|telegrafieren** *itr. V.* **[jmdm.] ~:** send [sb.] a telegram to say one cannot come

**ab|teufen** *tr. V.* (*Bergbau*) sink

**ab|tippen** *tr. V.* (*ugs.*) type out

**Äbtissin** /ɛp'tɪsɪn/ *die;* **~, ~nen** abbess

**ab|tönen** *tr. V.* tint; (*Sprachw.*) shift

**Abtön·farbe** *die* tinting colour

**Ab·tönung** *die* Ⓐ (*das Abtönen*) tinting; (*Sprachw.*) vowel shift; Ⓑ (*Farbton*) tone; shade

**Abtönungs·partikel** *die* (*Sprachw.*) modal particle

**ab|töten** *tr. V.* destroy ‹parasites, germs›; deaden ‹nerve, feeling›; mortify ‹desire›

**Ab·tötung** *die;* **~** ⇒ **abtöten**: destruction; deadening; mortification

**ab|traben** *itr. V.*; *mit sein* trot off *or* away

**Abtrag** /'aptra:k/ *der;* **~[e]s** (*geh., veralt.*) **einer Sache** (*Dat.*) **~ tun** be detrimental to sth.

**ab|tragen** *unr. tr. V.* Ⓐ (*abnutzen*) wear out; ⇒ *auch* **abgetragen** 2; Ⓑ (*geh.: abräumen*) clear away; Ⓒ (*einebnen*) level; (*Geol.*) erode; Ⓓ (*abbauen*) demolish; (*zum Wiederaufbau*) take down; Ⓔ (*geh.: abbezahlen*) discharge ‹debt›; pay off ‹loan›; Ⓕ (*Med.*) (*entfernen*) remove; (*abbauen*) disperse

**abträgig** /'aptrɛ:gɪç/ (*schweiz.*), **abträglich** /'aptrɛ:klɪç/ *Adj.* (*geh.*) detrimental; harmful; (*nachteilig*) unfavourable; **einer Sache** (*Dat.*) **~ sein** be detrimental *or* harmful to sth.; **~e Kritik** unfavourable criticism

**Abtragung** *die;* **~, ~en** Ⓐ (*das Einebnen*) levelling; (*Geol.*) erosion; Ⓑ (*das Abbauen*) demolition; Ⓒ (*zum Wiederaufbau*) taking down; Ⓓ (*geh.: das Abbezahlen*) discharge; Ⓔ (*Med.: Entfernung*) removal; (*Abbau*) dispersal

**ab|trainieren** ❶ *itr. V.* gradually reduce one's training schedule. ❷ *tr. V.* **Fett/Pfunde ~:** get rid of fat/pounds

**Ab·transport** *der* ⇒ **abtransportieren**: taking away; removal; dispatch

**ab|transportieren** *tr. V.* take away; remove ‹dead, injured›; (*befördern*) dispatch ‹goods›

**ab|treiben** ❶ *unr. tr. V.* Ⓐ (*wegtreiben*) carry away; **jmdn./ein Schiff vom Kurs ~:** drive *or* carry sb./a ship off course; **der Wind hat den Ballon nach Westen abgetrieben** the wind carried the balloon westwards; Ⓑ abort ‹foetus›; **ein Kind ~ lassen** have an abortion; Ⓒ (*zu Tal treiben*) bring down; Ⓓ (*Med.: abgehen lassen*) expel; Ⓔ (*österr. Kochk.: rühren*) beat.
❷ *unr. itr. V.* Ⓐ *mit sein* (*weggetrieben werden*) be carried away; ‹ship› be carried off course; Ⓑ (*einen Abort vornehmen lassen*) have an abortion; (*Aborte vornehmen*) carry out *or* perform abortions

**Abtreibung** *die;* **~, ~en** abortion

**Abtreibungs-: ~paragraph** *der* abortion law (*Section 218 of the German criminal code*); ≈ Abortion Act; **~tourismus** *der: travelling to another country or state in order to obtain an abortion;* **~verbot** *das* ban on abortion; **~versuch** *der* attempted abortion

**ab|trennen** *tr. V.* Ⓐ detach; sever ‹arm, leg, etc.›; cut off ‹button, collar, etc.›; detach, tear off ‹paper, voucher›; Ⓑ (*abteilen, absondern*) divide off; Ⓒ (*Rechtsw.*) **ein Verfahren ~:** decide to handle a prosecution separately

**abtretbar** *Adj.* (*Rechtsw.*) transferable; cedable ‹territory›

**ab|treten** ❶ *unr. tr. V.* Ⓐ **sich** (*Dat.*) **die Füße/Schuhe ~:** wipe one's feet; **sich** (*Dat.*) **den Schnee/den Schmutz von den Schuhen ~:** wipe the snow/dirt off one's feet; Ⓑ (*überlassen*) **jmdm. etw. ~:** let sb. have sth.; Ⓒ (*Rechtsw.*) transfer; cede ‹territory›; Ⓓ (*abnutzen*) wear down.
❷ *unr. itr. V.*; *mit sein* Ⓐ (*Milit.*) dismiss; Ⓑ (*Theater, auch fig.*) exit; make one's exit; **XY tritt ab/die Arbeiter treten ab** exit XY/exeunt workers; **von der Bühne ~** (*fig.*) step down; leave the arena; Ⓒ (*zurücktreten*) step down; ‹monarch› abdicate; Ⓓ (*verhüll.: sterben*) make one's exit.
❸ *unr. refl. V.* (*sich abnutzen*) become worn; **sich leicht/schnell ~:** wear [out] easily/quickly

**Abtreter** *der;* **~s, ~:** doormat

**Abtretung** *die;* **~, ~en** (*Rechtsw.*) transfer; (*eines Staatsgebiets*) cession; **Deutschland wurde zur ~ Westpreußens gezwungen** Germany was forced to cede West Prussia

**Ab·trieb** *der* Ⓐ (*Vieh~*) bringing down of cattle; **beim ~:** when bringing the cattle down; Ⓑ (*österr. Kochk.*) mixture

**Ab·trift** *die;* **~, ~en** ⇒ **Abdrift**

**ab|trinken** ❶ *unr. tr. V.* drink off; **einen Schluck ~:** take a sip (*from a full glass*).
❷ *unr. itr. V.* take a sip (*from a full glass*)

**Ab·tritt** *der* Ⓐ (*Theater*) exit; Ⓑ (*Rücktritt*) resignation; Ⓒ (*veralt.: Toilette*) privy (*arch.*)

**Abtrocken·tuch** *das; Pl.* **Abtrockentücher** tea towel

**ab|trocknen** ❶ *tr. V.* dry; **das Geschirr ~:** dry the dishes; **sich** (*Dat.*) **die Hände/das Gesicht/die Tränen ~:** dry one's hands/face/tears; **ich muss noch [das Geschirr] ~:** I still have to dry the dishes. ❷ *itr. V.*; *mit sein* (*trocken werden*) dry off

**Abtropf·brett** *das* draining board (*Brit.*); drainboard (*Amer.*)

**ab|tropfen** *itr. V.*; *mit sein* drip off; ‹lettuce, dishes› drain; ‹clothing› drip-dry; **von etw. ~:** drip off sth.

**ab|trotzen** *tr. V.* **jmdm. etw. ~:** wrest sth. from sb.

**ab|trudeln** *itr. V.* Ⓐ (*Fliegerspr.*) go down in a spin; Ⓑ (*ugs.: weggehen*) push off *or* along (*coll.*)

**abtrünnig** *Adj.* (*einer Partei*) renegade; (*einer Religion, Sekte*) apostate; **ein ~er Vasall** a disloyal vassal; **der Kirche/dem Glauben ~ werden** desert the Church/the faith

**Abtrünnige** *der/die; adj. Dekl.* (*einer Partei*) renegade; deserter; (*einer Religion, Sekte*) apostate; turncoat

**Abtrünnigkeit** *die;* **~:** apostasy; (*Treulosigkeit*) disloyalty (**von** to)

**ab|tun** *unr. tr. V.* Ⓐ (*beiseite schieben*) dismiss; **etw. mit einer Handbewegung ~:** wave sth. aside; Ⓑ (*erledigen*) **damit ist die Sache abgetan** that's the end of the matter

**ab|tupfen** *tr. V.* dab away; **sich/jmdm. die Tränen ~:** dab away one's/sb.'s tears; **sich** (*Dat.*) **die Stirn/Mundwinkel ~:** dab one's brow/the corners of one's mouth

**ab|urteilen** *tr. V.* pass judgement on; (*fig.*) condemn

**Aburteilung** *die;* **~, ~en** passing of judgement (+ *Gen.* on); condemnation; (*fig.*) condemnation

**ABV** /a:be:'fau/ *der;* **~[s], ~[s]** (*DDR*) ⇒ **Abschnittsbevollmächtigte**

**Ab·verkauf** *der* (*österr., südd.*) sale

**ab|verkaufen** *tr. V.* (*österr., südd.*) sell off

**ab|verlangen** *tr. V.* **jmdm. etw. ~:** demand sth. of sb.; **jmdm. Geld ~:** demand money from sb.; **es wird Ihnen einige Mühe ~:** it will cost you some effort

**ab|wägen** *unr. od. regelm. tr., itr. V.* Ⓐ weigh up; **zwei Dinge gegeneinander ~:** weigh two things against each other; **die Vor- und Nachteile gegeneinander ~:** weigh the advantages and disadvantages; **lange ~:** weigh things/the problem *etc.* up for a long time; ⇒ *auch* **abgewogen** 2; Ⓑ (*veralt.*) ⇒ **abwiegen**

**abwägend** ❶ *Adj.* appraising. ❷ *adv.* appraisingly; **er sah mich kritisch-~ an** he looked at me, sizing me up critically

**Ab·wahl** *die* voting out; **seit seiner ~:** since he was voted out

**abwählbar** *Adj.* **er/dieses Fach ist [nicht] ~:** he can[not] be voted out/this subject can[not] be dropped

**ab|wählen** *tr. V.* vote out; drop ‹school subject›; **sechs Leute wurden aus dem Ausschuss abgewählt** six members of the committee were not re-elected

**ab|wälzen** *tr. V.* pass on (**auf** + *Akk.* to); shift ‹blame, responsibility› (**auf** + *Akk.* on to)

**abwandelbar** *Adj.* Ⓐ (*variierbar*) modifiable; **ein unendlich ~es Motiv/Thema** a motif/theme capable of infinite variation; Ⓑ (*Sprachw. veralt.*) ⇒ **flektierbar**

**ab|wandeln** *tr. V.* Ⓐ (*variieren*) adapt; modify; Ⓑ (*Sprachw. veralt.*) ⇒ **flektieren**

**ab|wandern** ❶ *itr. V.*; *mit sein* Ⓐ migrate (**aus** from, **in** + *Akk.* to); (*in ein anderes Land*) emigrate (**aus** from, **in** + *Akk.* to); Ⓑ (*fig.*) move over; ‹capital› be transferred; **in einen anderen Beruf ~:** move into a different job; **viele Spieler wandern aus der Liga ab** many players are leaving the league; Ⓒ (*Met.*) move away. ❷ *tr. V.*; *mit sein od. haben* (*wandernd zurücklegen*) walk *or* hike over; walk ‹route›

a

**Ab·wanderung** *die* [A] migration (**aus** from, **in** + *Akk.* to); (*in ein anderes Land*) emigration (**aus** from, **in** + *Akk.* to); [B] (*fig.*) moving over; **~ in einen anderen Beruf** movement into a different job; **~ des Kapitals** transfer of capital; **die ~ der Spieler aus der Liga** the departure of players from the league

**Abwanderungs·verlust** *der* (*Soziol.*) population drain

**Ab·wandlung** *die* adaptation; modification; (*Variante*) variation; **in ~ eines Wortes von Goethe** adapting a saying of Goethe's

**Ab·wärme** *die* (*Technik*) waste heat

**Ab·wart** *der;* **~s, ~e** (*schweiz.*) caretaker

**ab|warten** ❶ *itr. V.* wait; **sie warteten ab** they awaited events; **warte ab!** wait and see; (*als Drohung*) just you wait!; **warten wir [erst mal] ab** let's wait and see; **sich ~d verhalten** adopt an attitude of 'wait and see'; **eine ~de Haltung einnehmen** decide to await events; **~ und Tee trinken** (*ugs. scherzh.*) wait and see what happens. ❷ *tr. V.* [A] (*warten auf*) wait for; **wir müssen die Entwicklung der Dinge ~:** we must wait and see how things develop; **das bleibt [noch] abzuwarten** only time will tell; [B] (*warten auf das Ende von*) **etw. ~:** wait for sth. to end

**Abwartin** *die;* **~, ~nen** ⇒ **Abwart**

**abwärts** /'apvɛrts/ *Adv.* downwards; (*den Berg hinunter*) downhill; (*den Fluss hinunter*) downstream; **der Fahrstuhl fährt ~:** the lift is going down; **„~"** 'going down'; **vom Major [an] ~:** from the major down; **mit ihm/dem Land/ihrer Gesundheit geht es ~** (*fig.*) he/the country is going downhill/her health is deteriorating; **seit damals ging es eigentlich immer nur ~** (*fig.*) from that time on things really only got worse

**-abwärts** *Adv.* ▶306 **[weiter] rhein~/mosel~:** further down the Rhine/Mosel; **rhein~/mosel~ segeln** sail down the Rhine/Mosel

**abwärts-, Abwärts-: ~entwicklung** *die* deterioration; **die anhaltende ~entwicklung** the downward slide; ***~|gehen** ⇒ **abwärts**; **~trend** *der* downward trend

**Abwasch**[1] /'apvaʃ/ *der;* **~[e]s** [A] (*das Geschirrspülen*) washing-up (*Brit.*); washing dishes (*Amer.*); **den ~ machen** do the washing-up/wash the dishes; **wir erledigen das gleichzeitig, das ist dann <u>ein</u> ~** (*ugs.*) we'll deal with that at the same time, and so kill two birds with one stone; [B] (*schmutziges Geschirr*) dirty dishes *pl.*

**Abwasch**[2] *die;* **~, ~en** (*österr.*) sink

**abwaschbar** *Adj.* washable

**Abwasch·becken** *das* sink

**ab|waschen** ❶ *unr. tr. V.* wash off; wash [up] ‹dishes›; wash down ‹surface›; **etw. von etw. ~:** wash sth. off sth.; **sich** (*Dat.*) **den Schmutz/das Blut ~:** wash the dirt/blood off oneself; **sich** (*Dat.*) **die Hände/sein Gesicht ~:** wash one's hands/face; **eine Schmach ~** (*fig.*) wipe out a disgrace. ❷ *unr. itr. V.* wash up, do the washing-up (*Brit.*); wash the dishes (*Amer.*)

**Abwasch-: ~lappen** *der* dishcloth; **~mittel** *das* ⇒ **Spülmittel**; **~tuch** *das; Pl.* **~tücher** ⇒ **~lappen**; **~wasser** *das* ⇒ **Spülwasser** B

**Ab·wasser** *das; Pl.* **Abwässer** sewage; **industrielle Abwässer** industrial effluent

**Abwasser-: ~auf·bereitung** *die* sewage treatment; **~beseitigung** *die* disposal of sewage; **~kanal** *der* sewer; **~reinigung** *die* sewage purification

**ab|watschen** *tr. V.* (*ugs.*) lambaste (*coll.*)

**ab|wechseln** *refl., itr. V.* alternate; **die beiden wechselten sich ab** the two of them took turns; **ich wechsle mich mit ihr beim Geschirrspülen ab** she and I take it in turns to do the dishes; **Regen und Sonne wechselten miteinander ab** it rained and was sunny by turns

*old spelling (see note on page 1707)

**abwechselnd** *Adv.* alternately

**Abwechslung** *die;* **~, ~en** (*Wechsel*) change; (*Zerstreuung*) **etwas/wenig ~:** some/not much variety; **zur ~:** for a change; **die ~ lieben** (*verhüll.*) like a bit of variety

**abwechslungs-: ~arm** ❶ *Adj.* monotonous; ❷ *adv.* monotonously; **~halber** *Adv.* for a change; **~los** ❶ *Adj.* unvaried; **~los sein** lack variety; ❷ *adv.* monotonously; **~reich** ❶ *Adj.* varied; ❷ *adv.* **der Urlaub verlief sehr ~reich** the holiday *or* (*Amer.*) vacation was full of variety; **sich ~reich ernähren** eat a varied diet; **nicht sonderlich ~reich** without much variety; **~weise** *Adv.* ⇒ **abwechselnd**

**Ab·weg** *der* error; **auf ~e kommen** *od.* **geraten** go astray; **jmdn. auf ~e führen** lead sb. astray

**abwegig** *Adj.* (*irrig, unzutreffend*) erroneous; false ‹suspicion›; (*falsch, abzulehnen*) mistaken; wrong; (*ungewöhnlich*) outlandish; exceptional ‹case›

**Abwegigkeit** *die;* **~, ~en** ⇒ **abwegig**: erroneousness; falseness; mistakenness; wrongness; outlandishness; exceptionalness

**Ab·wehr** *die;* **~** [A] (*Ablehnung*) hostility; [B] (*Zurückweisung*) repulsion; (*von Schlägen*) fending off; [C] (*Widerstand*) resistance; [D] (*Milit.: Geheimdienst*) counter-intelligence; **er ist bei der ~:** he is in counter-intelligence; [E] (*Sport*) (*Hintermannschaft*) defence; (*~aktion*) clearance; clearing (*Amer.*)

**abwehr-, Abwehr-: ~bereit** *Adj.* ready to take defensive action *postpos.*; **~bereitschaft** *die* readiness to take defensive action; **~dienst** *der* counter-intelligence service

**ab|wehren** ❶ *tr. V.* [A] (*zurückschlagen*) repulse; fend off, parry ‹blow›; (*Sport*) clear ‹ball, shot›; save ‹match point›; [B] (*abwenden*) avert ‹danger, consequences›; [C] (*von sich weisen*) avert ‹suspicion›; deny ‹rumour›; decline ‹thanks›; [D] (*fernhalten*) deter; **um die Blicke Neugieriger abzuwehren** [in order] to give protection from the stares of inquisitive people.
❷ *itr. V.* [A] (*Sport*) clear; **zur Ecke ~:** clear the ball and give away *or* concede a corner; [B] (*ablehnend reagieren*) demur; **eine ~de Geste** *od.* **Handbewegung** a deprecatory gesture

**Abwehr-: ~kampf** *der* defensive action; (*über längere Zeit*) defence; **~kraft** *die* power of resistance; **~mechanismus** *der* (*Psychoanalyse, Physiol.*) defence mechanism; **~reaktion** *die* (*Physiol., fig.*) defensive reaction; **~spieler** *der,* **~spielerin** *die* (*Sport*) defender

**ab|weichen**[1] *unr. itr. V.; mit sein* [A] deviate; [B] (*sich unterscheiden*) differ; **voneinander ~:** differ from each other; **~des Verhalten** (*Soziol.*) deviant behaviour

**ab|weichen**[2] ❶ *itr. V.; mit sein* soften and come off. ❷ *tr. V.* soak off

**Abweichler** /'apvaiçlɐ/ *der;* **~s, ~, Abweichlerin** *die;* **~, ~nen** (*Politik*) deviationist

**abweichlerisch** *Adj.* (*Politik*) deviationist

**Abweichlertum** *das;* **~s** (*Politik*) deviationism *no art.*

**Abweichung** *die;* **~, ~en** [A] deviation; **~en von der Geschäftsordnung** departures from the standing orders; **in ~** (*Dat.*) **von** in contrast with; **die ~ der Magnetnadel** the variation of the compass needle; [B] (*Unterschied*) difference

**ab|weiden** *tr. V.* crop; browse ‹twigs, leaves›; (*abgrasen*) graze

**ab|weisen** *unr. tr. V.* [A] turn away; turn down ‹applicant, suitor›; [B] (*ablehnen*) reject; dismiss ‹action, case, complaint›; disallow ‹claim›

**abweisend** ❶ *Adj.* cold ‹look, tone of voice›; negative ‹reply›; **in ~em Ton** coldly. ❷ *adv.* coldly

**Ab·weisung** *die;* **~, ~en** ⇒ **abweisen**: turning away; turning down; rejection; dismissal; disallowance

**ab|wenden** ❶ *unr. od. regelm. tr. V.* [A] (*wegwenden*) turn away; **den Blick ~:** look away; avert one's gaze; **die Augen von etw. nicht ~ können** not be able to take one's eyes off sth.; **mit abgewendetem Kopf** with his/her head turned away; [B] *nur regelm.* (*verhindern*) avert; **etw. von jmdm. ~:** protect sb. from sth. ❷ *unr. od. regelm. refl. V.* [A] turn away; [B] (*fig.*) **sich von jmdm. ~:** turn one's back on sb.; (*sich jmdm. allmählich entfremden*) become estranged from sb.

**Ab·wendung** *die* [A] (*Abkehr*) **seit seiner ~ vom Sozialismus** since he turned away from socialism; **die ~ von der bisherigen Politik** turning away from previous policy; [B] (*Verhinderung*) **zur ~ einer Sache** (*Gen.*) in order to avert sth.

**ab|werben** *unr. tr. V.* lure away; entice away; **jmdn. jmdm. ~:** lure *or* entice sb. away from sb.

**Abwerber** *der;* **~s, ~, Abwerberin** *die;* **~, ~nen** recruiter (*enticing people away from their existing employment*)

**Ab·werbung** *die* enticement (**bei** from)

**ab|werfen** ❶ *unr. tr. V.* [A] (*herunterwerfen*) drop; ‹tree› shed ‹leaves, needles›; ‹stag› shed ‹antlers›; throw off ‹clothing›; jettison ‹ballast›; throw ‹rider›; (*Kartenspiel*) discard; **das Joch der Knechtschaft/Tyrannei** *usw.* **~** (*fig. geh.*) throw *or* cast off the yoke of bondage/tyranny *etc.*; ⇒ *auch* **Maske** A; [B] (*herunterstoßen*) knock down; [C] (*ins Spielfeld werfen*) throw out ‹ball›; [D] (*einbringen*) bring in; **Profit ~:** make a profit; **viel/wenig ~:** show a big/only a small profit. ❷ *unr. itr. V.* (*Sport*) throw the ball out

**ab|werten** ❶ *tr., itr. V.* devalue. ❷ *tr. V.* (*fig.: herabwürdigen*) run down; belittle

**abwertend** ❶ *Adj.* derogatory. ❷ *adv.* derogatorily; in a derogatory way

**Ab·wertung** *die* [A] devaluation; [B] (*fig.: Herabwürdigung*) reduction in status; (*eines Begriffs*) debasement; **eine ~ erfahren** lose status; **das soll keine ~ sein** that wasn't meant in any derogatory sense

**abwesend** ❶ *Adj.* [A] (*nicht zugegen*) absent; [B] (*zerstreut*) absent-minded. ❷ *adv.* absent-mindedly

**Abwesende** *der/die; adj. Dekl.* absentee

**Abwesenheit** *die;* **~** [A] (*Fehlen*) absence; **in ~** (*Rechtsw.*) in his/her/their absence; **durch ~ glänzen** (*iron.*) be conspicuous by one's absence; [B] (*fig.: Zerstreutheit*) absent-mindedness

**Ab·wetter** *Pl.* (*Bergbau*) foul air

**ab|wettern** *tr. V.* (*Seemannsspr., auch fig.*) weather

**ab|wetzen** ❶ *tr. V., refl. V.* wear away; ⇒ *auch* **abgewetzt** 2. ❷ *itr. V.; mit sein* (*ugs.: weglaufen*) bolt; scarper (*Brit. coll.*)

**ab|wichsen** *tr. V.* (*derb*) **sich** (*Dat.*) **einen ~:** wank (*Brit. coarse*); jerk [oneself] off (*coarse*); **jmdm. einen ~:** jerk sb. off (*coarse*); wank sb. (*Brit. coarse*)

**ab|wickeln** ❶ *tr. V.* [A] (*herunterwickeln*) unwind; [B] (*erledigen*) deal with ‹case›; do ‹business›; (*im Auftrag*) handle ‹correspondence›; conduct, handle ‹transaction, negotiations›; [C] (*organisieren*) stage; [D] (*Wirtsch.*) wind up. ❷ *refl. V.* [A] (*sich abspulen*) unwind [itself]; [B] (*durchgeführt werden*) take place; (*mit Erfolg*) go off

**Abwicklung** *die;* **~, ~en** [A] ⇒ **abwickeln** 1 B: dealing (*Gen.* with); doing; handling; conducting; [B] (*Organisation*) staging; **für eine reibungslose ~ der Veranstaltung sorgen** see to it that the function goes off smoothly; [C] (*Kaufmannsspr., Rechtsw.: Liquidation*) liquidation

**ab|wiegeln** ❶ *tr. V.* [A] pacify; calm down ‹crowd›; [B] (*abwertend*) appease. ❷ *itr. V.* [A] calm things down; [B] (*etw. herunterspielen*) play down the issue

**ab|wiegen** *unr. tr. V.* weigh out; weigh ‹single item›

**Abwiegler** *der;* **~s, ~, Abwieglerin** *die;* **~, ~nen** [A] peacemaker; [B] (*abwertend*) appeaser

**Abwieglung** *die;* **~, ~en** [A] conciliation; [B] (*abwertend*) appeasement

**ab|wimmeln** *tr. V.* (*ugs.*) get rid of ‹person›; get out of ‹duty, responsibility, etc.›

**Ab·wind** *der* Ⓐ (*Met.*) katabatic wind; Ⓑ (*Flugw.*) downwash

**ab|winkeln** *unr. tr. V.* bend; **mit abgewinkelten** (*in die Hüfte gestützten*) **Armen** with arms akimbo

**ab|winken** ❶ *itr. V.* (*2. Part. landsch. od. scherzh.: abgewunken*) **apathisch/uninteressiert ~:** wave it/them aside apathetically/uninterestedly; ❷ *tr. V.* (*Motorsport*) **ein Rennen ~:** wave the chequered flag; (*bei einer Unterbrechung*) stop a race; **einen Fahrer ~:** wave *or* flag down a driver

**ab|wirtschaften** *itr. V.* **endgültig abgewirtschaftet haben** have gone to the wall; be finished for good; ⇒ *auch* **abgewirtschaftet** 2

**ab|wischen** *tr. V.* Ⓐ (*wegwischen*) wipe away; **sich/jmdm. etw. ~:** wipe sth. off oneself/sb.; **sich/jmdm. den Schweiß von der Stirn ~:** wipe off the sweat from one's/sb.'s forehead; **Staub von den Regalen ~:** wipe off dust from the shelves; **sich/jmdm. die Tränen ~:** dry one's/sb.'s tears; Ⓑ (*säubern*) wipe; **sich/jmdm. die Nase/die Hände** *usw.* **~:** wipe one's/sb.'s nose/hands *etc.* (**an** + *Dat.* on); **damit können Sie sich den Hintern** *od.* **den Arsch ~** (*derb*) you know where you can stick that (*sl.*); (*es ist wertlos*) you might as well wipe your arse (*Brit.*) *or* (*Amer.*) ass with it (*coarse*)

**ab|wohnen** *tr. V.* Ⓐ wear out ‹furniture›; make ‹flat, house, room› shabby; **abgewohnt** shabby; Ⓑ use up ‹rent›

**ab|wracken** /ˈapvrakn̩/ *tr. V.* scrap; ⇒ *auch* **abgewrackt** 2

**Ab·wurf** *der* Ⓐ dropping; (*von Ballast*) jettisoning; **nach zwei Abwürfen wollte er nicht mehr reiten** after being thrown twice he didn't want to do any more riding; Ⓑ (*Fußball*) **beim ~ stolperte der Torwart** the goalkeeper stumbled as he threw the ball out; Ⓒ (*Handball, Wasserball*) goal throw; Ⓓ (*Speer-, Diskus-, Hammerwurf*) delivery; Ⓔ (*Hochsprung*) failure; Ⓕ (*Springreiten*) fault

**ab|würgen** *tr. V.* (*ugs.*) stifle; choke off; squash ‹proposal›; stall ‹car, engine›

**ab|zahlen** *tr. V.* pay off ‹debt, loan›; pay for ‹home, car, etc.›

**ab|zählen** ❶ *tr. V.* count; **„bitte das Fahrgeld abgezählt bereithalten!"** 'please tender exact fare'. ❷ *itr. V.* Ⓐ (*Sport, Milit.*) number off; **zu zweien/vieren ~:** number off in twos/fours; Ⓑ (*mit Abzählreim*) count out

**Abzähl·reim** *der* counting-out rhyme

**Ab·zahlung** *die;* **~, ~en** paying off; repayment; **etw. auf ~ kaufen/verkaufen** buy/sell sth. on easy terms *or* (*Brit.*) on HP

**Abzahlungs-: ~kauf** *der* credit *or* hire purchase; **~rate** *die* repayment; instalment

**Abzähl·vers** *der* ⇒ **Abzählreim**

**ab|zapfen** *tr. V.* tap ‹beer, wine›; let, draw off ‹blood›; draw off ‹petrol›; **Strom ~:** tap the electricity supply; **jmdm. Geld ~** (*ugs.*) touch sb. for some money (*coll.*)

**ab|zappeln** *refl. V.* (*fig. ugs.*) flog oneself; slave away

**ab|zäumen** *tr. V.* unbridle

**ab|zäunen** *tr. V.* fence off

**Abzäunung** *die;* **~, ~en** Ⓐ fencing off; Ⓑ (*Zaun*) fencing

**Abzehrung** *die;* **~, ~en** (*veralt.*) wasting away; cachexia (*Med.*); **er starb an ~:** he wasted away and died

**Ab·zeichen** *das* Ⓐ (*Kennzeichen*) emblem; (*fig.*) badge; **militärische ~:** military insignia; Ⓑ (*Ansecknadel, Plakette*) badge

**ab|zeichnen** ❶ *tr. V.* Ⓐ (*nachzeichnen, kopieren*) copy; Ⓑ (*signieren*) initial. ❷ *refl. V.* stand out; (*fig.*) begin to emerge; (*drohend*) loom

**Abzieh·bild** *das* transfer

**ab|ziehen** ❶ *unr. tr. V.* Ⓐ pull off; peel off ‹skin›; strip ‹bed›; **ein Laken/das Bettzeug ~:** pull off a sheet/the bedclothes; Ⓑ (*Fot.*) make a print/prints of; **zweimal ~:** make two prints of; Ⓒ (*Druckw.*) run off; **etw. 50-mal ~:** run off 50 copies of sth.; Ⓓ (*Milit., auch fig.*) withdraw; Ⓔ (*subtrahieren*) subtract; take away (*abrechnen*) deduct; (*kassieren*) charge for; **jmdm. zu viel ~:** overcharge sb.; **davon kannst du die Hälfte/das meiste ~** (*ugs.*) you have to take it with a pinch of salt; Ⓕ (*ugs.: abnehmen, ausziehen*) take off; Ⓖ (*schälen*) peel ‹peach, almond, tomato›; string ‹runner bean›; Ⓗ (*häuten*) skin; Ⓘ **eine Handgranate ~:** pull the pin of a hand grenade; Ⓙ (*herausziehen*) take out ‹key›; Ⓚ (*abfüllen*) **Wein auf Flaschen ~:** bottle wine; Ⓛ (*glätten*) **Parkett ~:** sand [down] parquet flooring; **ein Messer/Rasiermesser ~:** sharpen a knife/razor; Ⓜ (*Kochk.*) thicken; Ⓝ (*salopp: veranstalten*) throw ‹party›; crack ‹joke›; ⇒ *auch* **Schau** B.
❷ *unr. itr. V.* Ⓐ *mit sein* (*sich verflüchtigen*) escape; (*Met.*) move away; Ⓑ *mit sein* (*Milit.*) withdraw; Ⓒ *mit sein* (*ugs.: weggehen*) push off (*coll.*); go away; Ⓓ *mit sein* (*ugs.: beschleunigen*) **der Wagen zieht vielleicht ab!** the car really takes off; Ⓔ (*abdrücken*) fire

**Abzieher** *der;* **~s, ~, Abzieherin** *die;* **~, ~nen** (*Druckw.*) proof-puller

**Abzieh·presse** *die* (*Druckw.*) proof[ing] press

**ab|zielen** *itr. V.* **auf etw.** (*Akk.*) **~:** be aimed at *or* directed towards sth.

**ab|zirkeln** *tr. V.* measure off ‹area, section›; (*fig.*) delineate; measure ‹words›; ⇒ *auch* **abgezirkelt** 2, 3

**ab|zischen** *itr. V.; mit sein* (*salopp*) shoot off; **zisch ab!** (*verschwinde!*) beat it! (*coll.*); push off! (*coll.*)

**ab|zittern** *itr. V.; mit sein* (*salopp*) beat it (*coll.*); push off (*coll.*)

**ab|zocken** (*salopp abwertend*) ❶ *itr. V.* rake it in (*coll.*). ❷ *tr. V.* fleece ‹person›; rake in (*coll.*) ‹money›; **jmdm. 20 000 DM ~:** fleece sb. of 20,000 DM

**ab|zotteln** *itr. V.; mit sein* (*ugs.*) trot off *or* away

**Ab·zug** *der* Ⓐ (*an einer Schusswaffe*) trigger; **die Hand** *od.* **den Finger am ~ haben** (*auch fig.*) have one's finger on the trigger; Ⓑ (*Fot.*) print; Ⓒ (*Druckw.*) proof; Ⓓ (*Verminderung, Abgabe*) deduction; **etw. in ~ bringen** deduct sth.; Ⓔ (*Abmarsch, auch fig.*) withdrawal; **jmdm. freien ~ gewähren** give sb. free passage; Ⓕ (*Öffnung für Rauch usw.*) vent; Ⓖ (*von Rauch usw.*) escape

**abzüglich** /ˈaptsy:klɪç/ *Präp. mit Gen.* (*Kaufmannsspr.*) less; **~ 3% Rabatt** *od.* **Rabatt von 3%** less 3% discount

**abzugs-, Abzugs-: ~fähig** *Adj.* (*Steuerw.*) [tax-]deductible; **~frei** *Adj.* (*Steuerw.*) tax-free; **~graben** *der* drainage ditch; **~rohr** *das* flue; **~schach** *das* (*Schach*) discovered check

**ab|zupfen** *tr. V.* pluck off

**ab|zwacken** *tr. V.* (*ugs.*) Ⓐ **[sich** (*Dat.*)**] das Geld/die Zeit ~:** scrape the money together/spare the time; Ⓑ ⇒ **abzwicken**

**Ab·zweig** *der* (*Verkehrsw.*) turn-off

**Abzweig·dose** *die* (*Elektrot.*) junction box

**ab|zweigen** ❶ *itr. V.; mit sein* branch off. ❷ *tr. V.* Ⓐ (*bereitstellen*) set *or* put aside; **Geld für einen Plattenspieler ~:** put aside *or* put by money to buy a record player; Ⓑ (*verhüll.: sich heimlich aneignen*) appropriate

**Abzweigung** *die;* **~, ~en** Ⓐ turn-off; (*einer Pipeline*) branch; (*Gabelung*) fork; **die rechte ~ fahren** take the right fork; Ⓑ (*Nebenlinie*) branch line

**ab|zwicken** *tr. V.* pinch *or* nip off

**ab|zwingen** *unr. tr. V.* **jmdm. ein Geständnis ~:** force a confession out of sb.; **sich** (*Dat.*) **ein Lächeln ~:** force oneself to smile

**ab|zwitschern** *itr. V.; mit sein* (*ugs.*) clear off (*coll.*); push off (*coll.*)

**a cappella** /a kaˈpɛla/ *Adv.* a cappella

**Accent aigu** /aksãtɛˈgy/ *der;* **~ ~, ~s ~s** /aksãzɛˈgy/ acute [accent]

**Accent circonflexe** /aksãsirkõˈflɛks/ *der;* **~ ~, ~s ~s** circumflex [accent]

**Accent grave** /aksãˈgra:v/ *der;* **~ ~, ~s ~s** /aksãˈgra:v/ grave [accent]

**Accessoire** /aksɛˈso̯a:ɐ̯/ *das;* **~s, ~s** (*geh.*) accessory

**Acetat** /at͜seˈta:t/ *das;* **~s, ~e** (*Chemie*) acetate

**Aceton** *das;* **~s** (*Chemie*) acetone

**Acetylen** /at͜setyˈle:n/ *das;* **~s** (*Chemie*) acetylene

**Acetylen-: ~brenner** *der* oxyacetylene torch; **~gas** *das* acetylene

**ach** /ax/ ❶ *Interj.* Ⓐ (*betroffen, mitleidig*) oh [dear]; **~ Gott** o dear; Ⓑ (*bedauernd, unwirsch*) oh; Ⓒ (*klagend*) ah; alas (*dated*); **Ach und Weh schreien** scream blue *or* (*Amer.*) bloody murder; Ⓓ (*erstaunt*) oh; **~, wirklich?** no, really?; **~, der!** oh, him!; **~, ist das schön!** oh, how lovely!; Ⓔ **~ so!** oh, I see; **~ nein** no, no; **~ was** *od.* **wo!** of course not. ❷ *Adv.* (*meist iron.*) **unser ~ so edler Held** our oh-so-noble hero

**Ach** *das;* **~s** *in:* **mit ~ und Krach** (*ugs.*) by the skin of one's teeth; **mit ~ und Weh** with a lot of weeping and wailing

**Achat** /aˈxa:t/ *der;* **~[e]s, ~e** (*Min.*) agate

**achaten** *Adj.* agate

**Achill** /aˈxɪl/, **Achilles** /aˈxɪlɛs/ (*der*) Achilles

**Achilles-: ~ferse** *die* Achilles' heel; **~sehne** *die* ▶ 471 (*Anat.*) Achilles tendon

**Achilleus** /aˈxɪlo̯ys/ (*der*) ⇒ **Achill**

**Ach·laut, *Ach-Laut** *der* velar fricative; ach-laut

**achromatisch** *Adj.* (*Optik*) achromatic

**Achs-: ~abstand** *der* ⇒ **Radstand**; **~bruch** *der* ⇒ **Achsenbruch**

**Achse** /ˈaksə/ *die;* **~, ~n** Ⓐ (*Rad~*) axle; **auf [der] ~ sein** (*ugs.*) be on the road *or* move; Ⓑ (*Dreh~, Astron.*) axis; **sich um die** *od.* **um seine eigene ~ drehen** turn on one's/its own axis; Ⓒ (*Math.*) axis ; Ⓓ **die ~ Berlin-Rom** (*hist.*) the Berlin-Rome axis

**Achsel** /ˈaksl̩/ *die;* **~, ~n** (*Schulter*) shoulder; (*~höhle*) armpit; **jmdn. über die ~ ansehen** look down on sb.; look down one's nose at sb.; **die** *od.* **mit den ~n zucken** shrug one's shoulders; **jmdn. unter den ~ packen** seize sb. under the arms; **etw. unter die ~ klemmen** tuck sth. under one's arm

**achsel-, Achsel-: ~griff** *der* Ⓐ (*Rettungsgriff*) underarm grip; Ⓑ (*Ringen*) nelson; **~grube** *die* ⇒ **~höhle**; **~haare** *Pl.* hair *sing.* under one's arms; armpit hair *sing.*; **~höhle** *die* armpit; **~klappe** *die* epaulette; **~schnur** *die* (*Milit.*) aiguillette; **~schweiß** *der* underarm perspiration; **~stück** *das* (*Milit.*) ⇒ **~klappe**; **~zucken** *das;* **~~s** shrug [of the shoulders]; **sein dauerndes ~zucken** his continual shoulder-shrugging; **~zuckend** *Adj.* shrugging; **er ging ~zuckend hinaus** he went out with a shrug [of the shoulders]

**achsen-, Achsen-: ~ab·stand** *der* ⇒ **Radstand**; **~bruch** *der* broken axle; **~kreuz** *das* (*Math.*) axes *pl.* of coordinates; **~mächte** *Pl.* (*hist.*) Axis Powers; **~symmetrisch** *Adj.* (*Math.*) **~symmetrisch sein** have axial symmetry; **eine ~symmetrische Kurve** a curve with axial symmetry; an axially symmetric curve

**-achser** *der;* **~s, ~ ein Drei-/Sechs~:** a three-/six-axle vehicle *etc.*

**-achsig** *Adj.* **drei-/sechs~:** three-/six-axle

**Achs-: ~lager** *das* axle bearing; **~last** *die* (*Technik*) axle weight; **~schenkel** *der* (*Kfz-W.*) stub axle; **~stand** *der* ⇒ **Radstand**; **~welle** *die* (*Technik*) axle shaft

**acht**[1] /axt/ *Kardinalz.* ▶ 76, ▶ 752, ▶ 841 eight; **~ mal ~ ist 64** eight eights are *or* eight times eight makes 64; **wir waren ~** *od.* (*geh.*) **unser ~:** we were eight; **je ~ bilden eine Gruppe** they formed into groups of eight; **die ersten/letzten ~:** the first/last eight; **er ist ~ [Jahre]** he is eight [years old]; **mit ~ [Jahren]** as an eight-year-old; at eight years of age; **es ist ~ Uhr** it is eight o'clock; **um ~ Uhr zehn** at ten past eight; **um ~ [Uhr]** at eight [o'clock]; **um ~ herum, gegen ~:** [at] around *or* about eight [o'clock]; **um halb ~:** at half past seven; **~ Minuten vor/nach halb ~:** twenty-two minutes past seven/twenty-two minutes to eight; **dreiviertel ~** *od.* **Viertel vor ~:** [a] quarter to eight; **in ~ Tagen** in a week's time; a week from now; **Freitag/morgen in ~ Tagen** a week on Friday/a week tomorrow; **[heute] vor ~ Tagen** a week ago [today]; **gestern vor ~ Tagen** a week ago yesterday; **im Jahre ~ nach/vor Christi Geburt** in the year AD 8/8 BC; **die Linie ~ [des Busses/der Straßenbahn]** the number eight [bus/tram]; **es steht ~ zu ~/~ zu 2** (*Sport*) the score is eight all/eight to two; **ein Vater von ~ Kindern** a father of eight; ⇒ *auch* **Acht**[1]

**acht**[2] *in* **wir waren zu ~:** there were eight of us; **wir rückten ihm zu ~ auf die Bude** (*ugs.*) eight of us dropped in on him; **wir haben zu ~ ein Haus gemietet** the eight of us rented a house; **sie kamen zu ~:** eight of them came; **stellt euch zu ~ auf** make lines of eight

**acht...** *Ordinalz.* ▶207, ▶841 eighth; **der ~e** *od.* **8. September** the eighth of September; (*im Brief auch*) 8 September; **am ~en** *od.* **8. September** on the eighth of September; (*im Brief auch*) 8 September; **München, [den] 8. Mai 1984** Munich, 8 May 1984; **das ~e Kapitel/der ~e Abschnitt** chapter/section eight; **sie ging als Achte durchs Ziel** she came [in] *or* finished eighth; **jede ~e [Person/Kiste** *usw.*] one out of every eight [persons/crates *etc.*]; one [person/crate *etc.*] in eight; **jeder Achte** one out of every eight; one in eight

**Acht**[1] *die;* **~, ~en** A (*Zahl*) eight; **eine arabische/römische ~:** an arabic/Roman eight; **die ~ ist seine Glückszahl** eight is his lucky number; B (*Figur*) figure eight; C (*Verbiegung*) buckle; **mein Rad hat eine ~:** my wheel is buckled; D (*Spielkarte*) eight; E (*ugs.: Bus-, Bahnlinie*) [number] eight; F (*ugs.: Handschellen*) cuffs *pl.* (*coll.*); G (*auf der Speise-, Weinkarte*) **ich nehme die ~:** I'll have number eight

**Acht**[2] *die;* ~ (*hist.*) outlawry; **über jmdn. die ~ verhängen, jmdn. mit der ~ belegen** outlaw sb.; **jmdn. in ~ und Bann tun** (*kirchlich*) anathematize *or* put the ban on sb.; (*fig.*) ostracize sb.

**Acht**[3] *die;* ~ *in* **etw. außer [aller] ~ lassen** disregard *or* ignore sth.; **sich in ~ nehmen** take care; be careful; **sich vor jmdm./etw. in ~ nehmen** be wary of sb./sth.; **~ geben** *od.* (*veralt.*) **haben** be careful; watch out; **gib** *od.* (*veralt.*) **hab ~!** look out!; watch out!; **auf jmdn./etw. ~ geben** *od.* (*veralt.*) **haben** mind *or* take care of sb./sth.; **[auf jmds. Worte] ~ geben** *od.* (*veralt.*) **haben** pay attention [to what sb. says]; **~ geben** *od.* (*veralt.*) **haben müssen, dass ...** have to be careful that ...; **er gab** *od.* (*veralt.*) **hatte nicht sonderlich ~ darauf** he did not pay any particular attention to it; **in der Schule besser ~ geben** *od.* (*veralt.*) **haben** pay more attention at school; **auf sich** (*Akk.*) **~ geben** *od.* (*veralt.*) **haben** be careful

**-acht** *die* (*Kartenspiel*) eight of ...

**acht-, Acht-: ~ad[e]rig** *Adj.* (*Elektrot.*) eight-core; **~armig** *Adj.* eight-armed; **~armig sein** have eight arms; **~bänder** /-bɛndɐ/ *der;* **~~s, ~~** (*Verlagsw.*) eight-volume set; **~bändig** *Adj.* eight-volume; **~bändig sein/~bändig herausgebracht werden** be in/be published in eight volumes

**achtbar** *Adj.* (*geh.*) respectable; upright ‹principles›; **eine ~e Leistung** a creditable performance

**Achtbarkeit** *die;* ~ (*geh.*) respectability; (*einer Gesinnung*) uprightness

**acht·beinig** *Adj.* eight-legged; **~ sein** have eight legs

**Achte** *der/die; adj. Dekl.* eighth; **er war [in der Leistung] der ~:** he came eighth; **der ~ [des Monats]** the eighth [of the month]; **Heinrich der ~:** Henry the Eighth

*old spelling (see note on page 1707)

**acht-, Acht-: ~eck** *das* octagon; **~eckig** *Adj.* octagonal; **ein Würfel ist ~eckig** a cube has eight corners; **ein Gebäude ~eckig bauen** make a building octagonal; **ein ~eckiger Hut** an eight-sided hat; **~einhalb** *Bruchz.* ▶841 eight and a half

**achtel** /ˈaxtl̩/ *Bruchz.* ▶841 eighth; **ein ~ Kilo** an eighth of a kilo; **drei ~ Liter** three eighths of a litre

**Achtel**[1] *das* (*schweiz. meist der;* **~s, ~** ▶841 A eighth; B (*ugs.:* **~pfund**) eighth of a pound; ≈ two ounces; C (*ugs.:* **~liter**) eighth of a litre (*of wine*)

**Achtel**[2] *die;* **~, ~** (*Musik*) ⇒ **Achtelnote**

**Achtel-: ~finale** *das* (*Sport*) last sixteen; **~final·spiel** *das* (*Sport*) *match in the round before the quarter-finals;* **~liter** *der* eighth of a litre; **~los** *das* lottery ticket which has one eighth of the value of a whole ticket

**achteln** *tr. V.* **etw. ~:** divide/cut sth. up into eight pieces

**Achtel-: ~note** *die* (*Musik*) quaver; eighth note (*Amer.*); **~pause** *die* (*Musik*) quaver rest; eighth rest (*Amer.*); **~pfund** *das* eighth of a pound

***achte·mal** ⇒ **Mal**[1]

**achten** ❶ *tr. V.* respect; observe, respect ‹laws, commandments›; **jmdn./etw. hoch ~:** respect sb./sth. greatly; have a high regard for sb./sth. ❷ *itr. V.* A **auf etw.** (*Akk.*) **[nicht] ~** ([*nicht*] *auf etw. aufpassen*) [not] mind *or* look after sth.; (*von etw.* [*keine*] *Notiz nehmen*) pay [no] attention *or* heed to sth.; **es ist [besonders] darauf zu ~, dass ...** your attention is [particularly] drawn to the fact that ...; **auf jmdn. ~:** look out for sb.; (*aufpassen*) look after *or* keep an eye on sb.; B (*geh., veralt.*) ⇒ **erachten**

**ächten** /ˈɛxtn̩/ *tr. V.* A (*hist.: die Acht verhängen über*) outlaw; (*kirchlich*) anathematize; B (*gesellschaftlich*) ostracize; **sich geächtet fühlen** feel like an outcast; C (*verdammen*) ban ‹war, torture›

**Acht·ender** *der;* **~s, ~** (*Jägerspr.*) eight-pointer

***achten·mal** ⇒ **Mal**[1]

**achtens** /ˈaxtn̩s/ *Adv.* eighthly

**achtens·wert** *Adj.* respectable ‹person›; worthy, commendable ‹motive›

**Achter** /ˈaxtɐ/ *der;* **~s, ~** A (*Rudern*) eight; B ⇒ **Acht**[1] A, B, C; C (*ugs.: Autobus*) number eight; D (*ugs.: Schraube, Dübel usw.*) [number] eight

**achter-, Achter-: ~aus** *Adv.* (*Seemannsspr.*) astern; **~bahn** *die* roller coaster; **~bahn fahren** go *or* ride on the roller coaster; **~deck** *das* (*Seemannsspr.*) afterdeck; **~gruppe** *die* group of eight; **~lastig** /-lastɪç/ *Adj.* (*Seemannsspr.*) stern-heavy

**achterlei** *indekl. Gattungsz.* A *attr.* eight kinds *or* sorts of; eight different ‹sorts, kinds, sizes, possibilities›; B *subst.* eight [different] things

**achterlich** *Adj.* (*Seemannsspr.*) stern *attrib.*; **~ sein** be astern

**achtern** *Adv.* (*Seemannsspr.*) astern; aft; **nach ~ gehen** go astern; **nach ~ drehen** ‹wind› move astern; **von ~:** from astern

**Achter-: ~reihe** *die* row *or* line of eight; **~rennen** *das* (*Rudern*) eights race; **~schiff** *das* (*Seemannsspr.*) stern; **~steven** *der* (*Seemannsspr.*) sternpost

**acht-, Acht-: ~fach** *Vervielfältigungsz.* eightfold; **die ~fache Menge** eight times the quantity; **die ~- bis zehnfache Dosis** eight to ten times the [correct] dose; **etw. in ~facher Ausfertigung schicken** send eight copies of sth.; **~fach vergrößert/verkleinert, in ~facher Vergrößerung/Verkleinerung** magnified *or* enlarged/reduced eight times; **das Produkt ist ~fach geprüft worden** the product went through eight tests; **~fache** *das; adj. Dekl.* **das ~fache von 4 ist 32** eight fours are *or* eight times four makes 32; **er verdient das ~fache von mir** he earns eight times as much as I do; **um das ~fache steigen/steigern** increase ninefold *or* nine times; **~fältig** (*veralt.*) ⇒ **~fach**; **~flach** *das;* **~~s,** **~~e, ~flächner** /-flɛçnɐ/ *der;* **~~s, ~~:** octahedron; **~füßer** *der;* **~~s, ~~** (*Biol.*) octopod; **~füßig** *Adj.* eight-footed; (*Verslehre*) eight-foot, octonarian ‹line›; **~füßig sein** have eight feet

***acht|geben** ⇒ **Acht**[3]

**acht-, Acht-: ~geschossig** *Adj.* ⇒ **~stöckig**; **~gliedrig** *Adj.* eightmembered; **~groschen·junge** *der* (*abwertend*) A (*Denunziant, Spitzel*) informer; nark (*Brit. sl.*); B (*käufliches Subjekt*) hireling

***acht|haben** ⇒ **Acht**[3]

**acht-, Acht-: ~hebig** *Adj.* (*Verslehre*) ⇒ **~füßig**; **~hundert** *Kardinalz.* ▶841 eight hundred; **~hundertjahr·feier** *die* octocentenary [celebrations *pl.*]; **~hundertst...** *Ordinalz.* eight-hundredth; **~hunderttausend** *Kardinalz.* eight hundred thousand; **~jährig** *Adj.* (*8 Jahre alt*) eight-year-old *attrib.*; eight years old *pred.*; (*8 Jahre dauernd*) eight-year *attrib.*; **nach ~jährigem Studium** after eight years of study; **~jährig sterben** die at [the age of] eight; **seine ~jährige Tätigkeit an dem Institut** his eight years at the institute; **mit ~jähriger Verspätung** with a delay of eight years; eight years late; **~jährige** *der/die; adj. Dekl.* eight-year-old; **als ~jähriger** when one *etc.* is/was *etc.* eight years old; **~jährlich** ❶ *Adj.* eight-yearly; **in ~jährlichem Turnus** in an eight-year cycle; ❷ *adv.* every eight years; **~kampf** *der* (*Turnen*) eight-exercise gymnastic competition; **~kantig** ❶ *Adj.* (*Technik*) eight-sided; ❷ *adv.* (*salopp*) **~kantig rausfliegen** get kicked *or* (*sl.*) booted out; **jmdn. ~kantig rausschmeißen** throw sb. out on his/her ear (*coll.*); **~klassig** *Adj.* with eight classes; **~köpfig** *Adj.* eight-headed ‹monster›; ‹family, committee› of eight

**Achtling** /ˈaxtlɪŋ/ *der;* **~s, ~e** octuplet

**acht·los** ❶ *Adj.* heedless. ❷ *adv.* heedlessly

**Achtlosigkeit** *die;* **~:** heedlessness

**acht-, Acht-: ~mal** *Adv.* eight times; **~mal so groß/so viel/so viele** eight times as big/as much/as many; **~malig** *Adj.* **nach ~maliger Wiederholung bestand er die Prüfung** he passed the test at the ninth attempt; **nach ~maliger Aufforderung** at the eighth request; after being asked eight times; **trotz ~maligen Klingelns** in spite of ringing eight times; ***~millionen·mal** ⇒ **Mal**[1]; **~minuten·takt** /-'---/ *der* (*Fernspr.*): *system whereby telephone calls are charged at so much per eight minutes or part thereof;* **~minütig** *Adj.* eight-minute *attrib.*; lasting eight minutes *pred.*; **mit ~minütiger Verspätung** eight minutes late; **nach ~minütiger Sonnenbestrahlung** after eight minutes' exposure to the sun; **~monatig** *Adj.* (*8 Monate alt*) eight-month-old *attrib.*; eight months old *pred.*; (*8 Monate dauernd*) eight-month *attrib.*; lasting eight months *postpos.*; ⇒ *auch* **~jährig**; **~monatlich** ❶ *Adj.* eight-monthly; **im ~monatlichen Turnus** rotating every eight months; ❷ *adv.* every eight months; **~monats·kind** *das* child born a month prematurely; **~pfennig·marke** *die* eight-pfennig stamp; **~pfünder** /-pfʏndɐ/ *der;* **~~s, ~~:** eightpounder; **~pfündig** *Adj.* eight-pound; **~polig** *Adj.* (*Elektrot.*) eight-pin; eight-core ‹cable›; **~punkt·schrift** *die* (*Druckw.*) eight-point type; **~prozentig** *Adj.* eight per cent; **~räd[e]rig** *Adj.* eight-wheeled; **~räd[e]rig sein** have eight wheels

**achtsam** ❶ *Adj.* (*geh.*) attentive. ❷ *adv.* (*sorgsam*) carefully; with care; **mit etw. [äußerst] ~ umgehen** handle sth. with [extreme] care

**Achtsamkeit** *die;* **~:** attentiveness; (*Sorgsamkeit*) care

**acht-, Acht-: ~seitig** *Adj.* eight-page *attrib.* ‹letter, article›; **ein ~seitiges Vieleck** an eight-sided polygon; **~silber** *der;* **~~s, ~~** ⇒ **~silbler**; **~silbig** *Adj.* eight-syllable *attrib.*; octosyllabic; **~silbler** *der;* **~~s, ~~** (*Verslehre*) octosyllabic verse *or* line; **~sitzer** *der;* **~~s, ~~:** eight-seater; **~sitzig** *Adj.* eight-seater *attrib.*; **~sitzig sein** have eight seats; **~spaltig** (*Druckw.*) ❶ *Adj.* **~spaltiger Artikel** eight-column article; **~spaltig**

**sein** have eight columns; ❷ *adv.* **~spaltig setzen** print in eight columns; **~spänner** *der;* **~~s, ~~:** eight-in-hand; **~spännig** *Adj.* eight-horse; ⇒ *auch* **vierspännig**; **~sprachig** *Adj.* in eight languages *postpos.;* ⇒ *auch* **zweisprachig**; **~sprossig** *Adj.* ‹ladder› with eight rungs; **~sprossig sein** have eight rungs; **~spurig** *Adj.* eight-lane ‹road, motorway›; eight-track ‹cassette›; **~stellig** *Adj.* eight-figure *attrib.;* **~stellig sein** have eight figures *or* digits; **~stimmig** ❶ *Adj.* for eight-part; ❷ *adv.* in eight parts; **~stöckig** ❶ *Adj.* eight-storey *attrib.;* **~stöckig sein** have eight storeys *or* floors; be eight storeys high; ❷ *adv.* **~stöckig bauen** build to eight storeys; **~strophig** /-ʃtro:fɪç/ *Adj.* with eight verses *postpos., not pred.;* **~strophig sein** have eight verses; **~stufig** *Adj.* with eight steps *postpos., not pred.;* **~stufig sein** have eight steps; **~stunden·rhythmus** /-'---/ *der* eight-hour rhythm; **~stunden·tag** /-'--/ *der* eight-hour day; **~stündig** *Adj.* eight-hour *attrib.;* lasting eight hours *postpos., not pred.;* **mit ~stündiger Verspätung** eight hours late; **nach ~stündigem Warten** after waiting for eight hours; **~stündlich** ❶ *Adj.* eight-hourly; ❷ *adv.* every eight hours; **~tägig** *Adj.* (*8 Tage alt*) eight-day-old *attrib.;* (*8 Tage dauernd*) eight-day[-long] *attrib.;* **mit ~tägiger Verspätung** eight days late; **nach ~tägiger Dauer** after lasting for eight days; **sie sind meist ~tägig** they mostly last eight days; **~täglich** ❶ *Adj.* **in ~täglichem Wechsel** on an eight-day rota; ❷ *adv.* every eight days; **~tausend** *Kardinalz.* ▶**841** eight thousand; **~tausender** *der: mountain over eight thousand metres high;* **~teiler** *der* (*Rundf., Ferns.*) eight-part series/serial; **~teilig** *Adj.* eight-piece ‹tea service, tool set, etc.›; eight-part ‹series, serial›; **~teilig sein** have eight pieces; (*Rundf., Ferns.*) be in eight parts; **~tonner** *der;* **~~s, ~~:** eight-tonner

**Acht·uhr-:** eight o'clock ‹news, train, performance, etc.›

**acht-, Acht-:** **~und·ein·halb** *Bruchz.* eight and a half; **~und·vierziger** /--'--/ *der,* **~und·vierzigerin** /--'---/ *die* (*hist.*) forty-eighter (*one who took part in or sympathized with the 1848 revolution*); **~und·vierzig·stunden·woche** *die* forty-eight-hour week; **~und·zwanzig** *Kardinalz.* twenty-eight

**Achtung** *die;* ~ [A] (*Wertschätzung*) respect (**vor** + *Dat.* for); **gegenseitige ~:** mutual respect; **~ vor sich** (*Dat.*) **selbst** self respect; **alle ~!** well done!; [B] (*Respektierung*) respect (*Gen.* for); [C] (*Aufmerksamkeit*) attention; **~!** watch out!; **~! Stillgestanden!** (*Milit.*) attention!; **~, ~!** your attention, please!; „**~, Stufe!**" 'mind the step'; „**~, Hochspannung**" 'danger high voltage'; **~, fertig, los!** on your marks, get set, go!

**Ächtung** *die;* **~, ~en** [A] (*hist.*) outlawing; (*kirchlich*) anathematization; [B] (*gesellschaftliche* ~) ostracism; [C] (*Verdammung*) banning

**achtung·gebietend** *Adj.* (*geh.*) awe-inspiring

**achtungs-, Achtungs-:** **~applaus** *der* polite applause; **~erfolg** *der* reasonable success; **~voll** ❶ *Adj.* respectful; ❷ *adv.* respectfully

**acht-:** **~wöchentlich** ❶ *Adj.* eight-weekly; **im ~wöchentlichen Turnus/Wechsel** every eight weeks; ❷ *adv.* every eight weeks; **~wöchig** *Adj.* (*8 Wochen alt*) eight-week-old *attrib.;* (*8 Wochen dauernd*) eight-week[-long] *attrib.;* ⇒ *auch* **~jährig**; **~zackig** *Adj.* eight-pointed

**acht·zehn** *Kardinalz.* ▶**76**, ▶**752**, ▶**841** eighteen; **mit ~ [Jahren] wird man volljährig** one reaches the age of majority at eighteen; **18 Uhr** 6 p.m.; (*auf der 24-Stunden-Uhr*) eighteen hundred hours; 1800; **18 Uhr 33** 6.33 p.m.; (*auf der 24-Stunden-Uhr*) 1833

**achtzehn-, Achtzehn-:** **~ender** *der;* **~~s, ~~** (*Jägerspr.*) eighteen-pointer; **~hundert** *Kardinalz.* ▶**841** eighteen hundred; **das war [im Jahre] ~hundert** *od.* **1800** that was in [the year] eighteen hundred *or* 1800; **~hundert** *od.* **1800 DM pro Hektoliter** eighteen hundred *or* 1,800 DM per hectolitre; **~jährig** *Adj.* (*18 Jahre alt*) eighteen-year-old *attrib.;* eighteen years old *pred.;* (*18 Jahre dauernd*) eighteen-year *attrib.;* ⇒ *auch* **achtjährig**; **~jährige** *der/die; adj. Dekl.* eighteen-year-old; **als ~jähriger** when one *etc.* is/was *etc.* eighteen years old

**achtzehnt...** *Ordinalz.* ▶**207**, ▶**841** eighteenth; ⇒ *auch* **acht...**

**Acht·zehntel** *das* eighteenth

**acht·zeilig** *Adj.* eight-line *attrib.;* **~ sein** have eight lines

**achtzig** /'axtsɪç/ *Kardinalz.* ▶**76**, ▶**841** eighty; **[mit] ~ [km/h] fahren** drive at *or* (*coll.*) do eighty [k.p.h.]; **über/etwa ~ [Jahre alt] sein** be over/about eighty [years old]; **Mitte [der] ~ sein** be in one's mid-eighties; **in die ~ kommen** reach one's eighties; **mit ~ [Jahren]** at eighty [years of age]; **im Jahre ~ vor/nach Christi Geburt** in the year 80 BC/AD 80; **auf ~ sein** (*fig. ugs.*) be hopping mad (*coll.*)

**Achtzig** *die;* **~, ~en** eighty; ⇒ *auch* **Acht**[1] E

**achtziger** *indekl. Adj.* **ein ~ Jahrgang** an '80 vintage; **die ~ Jahre** the eighties

**Achtziger**[1] *der;* **~s, ~** [A] (*80-Jähriger*) eighty-year-old [man]; octogenarian; [B] (*ugs.: Autobus*) number eighty; [C] (*Wein*) '80 vintage

**Achtziger**[2] *die;* **~, ~** (*ugs.*) [A] (*Briefmarke*) eighty-pfennig/schilling *etc.* stamp; [B] (*Zigarre*) eighty-pfennig cigar

**Achtziger**[3] *Pl.* eighties; **in den ~n sein** be in one's eighties

**Achtzigerin** *die;* **~, ~nen** eighty-year-old [woman]; octogenarian

**Achtziger·jahre** *Pl.* ▶**76**, ▶**207** eighties *pl.*

**achtzig-, Achtzig-:** **~jährig** *Adj.* (*80 Jahre alt*) eighty-year-old *attrib.;* eighty years old *pred.;* (*80 Jahre dauernd*) eighty-year *attrib.;* ⇒ *auch* **achtjährig**; **~jährige** *der/die; adj. Dekl.* eighty-year-old; **~pfennig·marke** *die* eighty-pfennig stamp

**achtzigst...** /'axtsɪçst/ *Ordinalz.* ▶**841** eightieth; **zum Achtzigsten herzlichen Glückwunsch** best wishes on your eightieth birthday; ⇒ *auch* **acht...**

**Achtzigstel** *das;* **~s, ~** ▶**841** eightieth

**acht-, Acht-:** **~zimmer·wohnung** *die* eight-roomed flat; **~zöllig** *Adj.* eight-inch[-long] *attrib.;* eight-inch *attrib.* ‹pipe›; **~zöllig sein** be eight inches long; ‹pipe› be eight inches in diameter; **~zylinder** *der* (*ugs.*) eight-cylinder [engine/car]; **~zylinder·motor** *der* eight-cylinder engine; **~zylindrig** *Adj.* eight-cylinder *attrib.;* **~zylindrig sein** have eight cylinders

**ächzen** /'ɛçtsn̩/ *itr. V.* [A] (*schwer stöhnen*) groan; **~ und stöhnen** grunt and groan; [B] (*knarren*) creak

**Ächzer** *der;* **~s, ~** (*ugs.*) groan

**Acker** /'akɐ/ *der;* **~s, Äcker** /'ɛkɐ/ [A] field; **auf dem ~:** in the field; (*bei der Feldarbeit*) in the fields; **den ~ bestellen** till the field; [B] *Pl.* **~** (*altes Feldmaß*) ≈ half acre (*usually about 2,500 sq.m.*); **vier ~ Land/Wald** ≈ two acres of land/woodland

**acker-, Acker-:** **~bau** *der* agriculture *no indef. art.;* farming *no indef. art.;* **~bau treiben** farm; **~bau treibend** farming; **~bau und Viehzucht** farming and stockbreeding; **~bauer** *der;* **~~n, ~~n, ~bäuerin** *die* farmer; ***~bau·treibend** ⇒ **Ackerbau**; **~boden** *der* soil [for cultivation]; **~bürger** *der,* **~bürgerin** *die* (*hist.*) *citizen who farmed land within the city area;* **~furche** *die* furrow; **~gaul** *der* (*ugs. abwertend*) carthorse; old nag (*derog.*); **aus einem ~gaul kann man kein Rennpferd machen** (*Spr.*) you can't make a silk purse out of a sow's ear (*prov.*); **~gerät** *das* farm implement; **~krume** *die* topsoil; **~land** *das* farmland

**ackern** *itr. V.* (*salopp*) [A] (*schwer arbeiten*) slog one's guts out (*coll.*); [B] (*sich anstrengen*) put one's back into it (*coll.*); work like hell (*coll.*); [C] (*veralt.: pflügen*) plough

**Acker-:** **~schädling** *der* field pest; **~scholle** *die* clod [of earth]

**Acker·winde** *die* (*Bot.*) field bindweed

**a conto** /a 'kɔnto/ (*Bankw.*) on account

**Acryl-:** **~farbe** *die* acrylic paint; acrylic; **~faser** *die* acrylic fibre; acrylic; **~harz** *das* acrylic resin

**Action** /'ækʃən/ *die;* **~:** action

**a. D.** /a:'de:/ *Abk.* **außer Dienst** retd.

**A. D.** *Abk.* **Anno Domini** AD

**Adabei** *der;* **~s, ~s** (*österr. ugs.*) hanger-on

**ad absurdum** /at ap'zʊrdʊm/ *in* **etw. ~ ~ führen** demonstrate the absurdity of sth.

**ADAC** *Abk.* **Allgemeiner Deutscher Automobilclub** *German automobile association*

**ad acta** /at 'akta/ *in* **etw. ~ ~ legen** shelve sth.

**Adagio** /a'da:dʒo/ *das;* **~s, ~s** (*Musik*) adagio

**Adam**[1] /'a:dam/ (*der*) Adam; **seit ~s Zeiten** since the beginning of time; **bei ~ und Eva anfangen** (*ugs.*) begin from the beginning; **der alte ~:** the old Adam

**Adam**[2] *der;* **~s, ~s** (*ugs. scherzh.: Mann*) the male of the species

**Adam Riese** *in* **das macht nach ~ ~ 4,50 Mark** (*ugs. scherzh.*) my arithmetic makes it 4.50 marks (*coll. joc.*)

**Adams-:** **~apfel** *der* (*ugs. scherzh.*) Adam's apple; **~kostüm** *das* (*ugs. scherzh.*) **im ~kostüm** in one's birthday suit

**Adaptation** /adapta'tsi̯o:n/ *die;* **~, ~en** adaptation

**adaptieren** /adap'ti:rən/ *tr. V.* [A] adapt; **für den Bildschirm/Film ~:** adapt for television/the screen; [B] (*österr.: herrichten*) fit out

**Adaptierung** *die;* **~, ~en** [A] ⇒ **Adaptation**; [B] (*österr.: Herrichtung*) fitting-out

**Adaption** /adap'tsi̯o:n/ *die;* **~, ~en** ⇒ **Adaptation**

**adaptiv** /adap'ti:f/ *Adj.* adaptive

**adäquat** /at|ɛ'kva:t/ ❶ *Adj.* (*passend*) appropriate (*Dat.* to); suitable (*Dat.* for); (*angemessen*) adequate ‹reward, payment›; appropriate, suitable ‹measures, means›. ❷ *adv.* (*passend*) suitably; appropriately; (*angemessen*) adequately

**addieren** /a'di:rən/ ❶ *tr. V.* add [up]. ❷ *itr. V.* add. ❸ *refl. V.* add up

**Addier·maschine** *die* adding machine

**Addition** /adi'tsi̯o:n/ *die;* **~, ~en** addition

**additiv** /adi'ti:f/ *Adj.* additive

**Additiv** *das;* **~s, ~e** (*Chemie*) additive

**ade** /a'de:/ *Adv.* (*veralt.*) farewell; **jmdm. ~** *od.* **Ade sagen** bid farewell to sb.; take one's leave of sb.; **einer Sache** (*Dat.*) **~** *od.* **Ade sagen** (*fig.*) bid farewell to sth.

**Adebar** /'a:dəbar/ *der;* **~s, ~e** (*scherzh., bes. nordd.*) stork

**Adel** /'a:dl̩/ *der;* **~s** [A] nobility; **der niedere ~:** the lesser nobility *or* nobles; **der hohe ~:** the higher nobility; the aristocracy; **von ~ sein** be of noble blood; **~ verpflichtet** noblesse oblige; **er stammt aus altem ~:** he belongs to an old noble family; [B] (*Titel*) **der erbliche/persönliche ~:** a hereditary/non-hereditary title; (*hoher* ~) a hereditary/life peerage; [C] (*geh.: edle Gesinnung*) nobility

**adelig** ⇒ **adlig**

**Adelige** ⇒ **Adlige**

**adeln** ❶ *tr. V.* **jmdn. ~:** give sb. a title; (*in den hohen Adel erheben*) raise sb. to the peerage; (*fig.*) ennoble sb. ❷ *itr. V.* (*geh.*) ennoble

**Adels-:** **~brief** *der* patent of nobility; **~familie** *die,* **~geschlecht** *das* noble family; **~krone** *die: coronet of the untitled lowest rank of nobility;* **~prädikat** *das* title of nobility; **~stand** *der* nobility; (*hoher Adel*) nobility; peerage; **jmdn. in den ~stand erheben** give sb. a title/raise sb. to the peerage; **~titel** *der* title of nobility

**Adelung** *die;* **~, ~en** conferral of a title; (*in den hohen Adel*) ennoblement

**Adept** /a'dɛpt/ *der;* **~en, ~en, Adeptin** *die;* **~, ~nen** [A] (*hist.*) initiate; [B] (*scherzh.*) adherent; disciple

a

**Ader** /'a:dɐ/ *die;* ~, **~n** A ▶471 (*Anat., Zool.*) blood vessel; vein; (*Schlagader*) artery; **in seinen ~n fließt Bauernblut** there is peasant blood in his veins; **sich** (*Dat.*) **die ~n öffnen** (*geh.*) slash one's wrists; **jmdn. zur ~ lassen** (*veralt.*) bleed sb.; (*fig.*) milk sb.; ⇒ *auch* **Blut**; B (*Anlage, Begabung*) streak; C (*Bot., Geol.*) vein; D (*Elektrot.*) core

**Äderchen** /'ɛ:dɐçən/ *das;* **~s**, **~:** small blood vessel *or* vein; (*Bot.*) small vein

**Aderlass**, ***Aderlaß** /'a:dɐlas/ *der;* **Aderlasses**, **Aderlässe** /-lɛsə/ A (*Med.: Blutentnahme*) bleeding; B (*fig.*) drain; (*finanziell*) squeeze

**Aderung** /'a:dərʊŋ/ *die;* ~, **~en**, **Äderung** /'ɛ:dərʊŋ/ *die;* ~, **~en** veining

**Adhäsion** /athɛ'zi̯o:n/ *die;* ~, **~en** (*Phys., Med., Bot.*) adhesion

**Adhäsions-:** **~kraft** *die* (*Physik*) power of adhesion; **~verschluss**, ***~verschluß** *der* resealable closure

**ad hoc** /at 'hɔk/ *Adv.* A (*zu diesem Zweck*) ad hoc; B (*spontan*) on the spur of the moment

**Ad-hoc-:** **~-Bildung** *die* ⇒ **~-Prägung**; **~-Maßnahme** *die* ad hoc measure; **~-Prägung** *die* ad hoc coinage *or* formulation

**adieu** /a'di̯ø:/ *Adv.* (*veralt.*) adieu; farewell; **jmdm. ~** *od.* **Adieu sagen** bid sb. adieu *or* farewell

**Adieu** *das;* **~s**, **~s** (*veralt.*) adieu

**Adjektiv** /'atjɛkti:f/ *das;* **~s**, **~e** (*Sprachw.*) adjective

**adjektivisch** /'atjɛkti:vɪʃ/ (*Sprachw.*) ❶ *Adj.* adjectival. ❷ *Adv.* adjectivally

**Adjunkt** /at'jʊnkt/ *der;* **~en**, **~en**, **Adjunktin** *die;* ~, **~nen** (*veralt.*) low-grade civil servant

**adjustieren** /atjʊs'ti:rən/ *tr. V.* A (*Technik*) ⇒ **justieren** A; B (*österr. Amtsspr.*) provide with a uniform; kit out (*Brit.*)

**Adjustierung** *die;* ~, **~en** A ⇒ **Justierung** A; B (*österr. Amtsspr.*) uniform

**Adjutant** /atju'tant/ *der;* **~en**, **~en**, **Adjutantin** *die;* ~, **~nen** adjutant; aide-de-camp

**Adjutum** /at'ju:tʊm/ *das;* **~s**, **Adjuten** (*österr. Amtsspr.*) grant

**Adlatus** /at'la:tʊs/ *der;* ~, **Adlaten** *od.* **Adlati** (*scherzh.*) loyal assistant

**Adler** /'a:dlɐ/ *der;* **~s**, **~:** eagle; **der ~** (*Astron.*) Aquila; the Eagle

**adler-**, **Adler-:** **~auge** *das* (*fig.*) eagle eye; **~äugig** *Adj.* (*fig.*) eagle-eyed; **~blick** *der* eagle eye; **~farn** *der* (*Bot.*) eagle fern; bracken; **~horst** *der* eyrie; **~nase** *die* aquiline nose

**adlig** /'a:dlɪç/ *Adj.* noble; **~ sein** be a noble [man/woman]

**Adlige** *der/die; adj. Dekl.* noble [man/woman]

**Administration** /atminɪstra'tsi̯o:n/ *die;* ~, **~en** administration

**administrativ** /atminɪstra'ti:f/ ❶ *Adj.* administrative. ❷ *adv.* administratively

**Administrator** /atminɪs'tra:tɔr/ *der;* **~s**, **~en** /-tra'to:rən/, **Administratorin** *die;* ~, **~nen** ▶159 administrator

**administrieren** *itr. V.* administer

**Admiral** /atmi'ra:l/ *der;* **~s**, **~e** *od.* **Admiräle** /atmi'rɛ:lə/ A ▶91 admiral; B (*Schmetterling*) red admiral

**Admiralität** /atmirali'tɛ:t/ *die;* ~, **~en** admirals *pl.*; (*Marineführung*) admiralty

**Admiralsrang** *der* rank of admiral; **im ~ stehen** hold the rank of admiral

**ADN** *Abk.* (*DDR*) **Allgemeiner Deutscher Nachrichtendienst** *GDR press agency*

**Adoleszenz** /adolɛs'tsɛnts:/ *die;* ~ (*bes. Med., Psych.*) adolescence

**Adonis** /a'do:nɪs/ *der;* ~, **~se** Adonis

**Adonisröschen** *das* (*Bot.*) adonis; (*Adonis annua*) pheasant's eye

**adoptieren** /adɔp'ti:rən/ *tr. V.* adopt

**Adoption** /adɔp'tsi̯o:n/ *die;* ~, **~en** adoption

**Adoptiv-** /adɔp'ti:f-/: **~bruder** *der* adoptive brother; brother by adoption; **~eltern** *Pl.* adoptive parents; **~kind** *das* adoptive *or* adopted child; **~mutter** *die; Pl.* **~mütter** adoptive mother; **~schwester** *die* adoptive sister; sister by adoption; **~sohn** *der* adoptive *or* adopted son; **~tochter** *die* adoptive *or* adopted daughter; **~vater** *der* adoptive father

**Adrenalin** /adrena'li:n/ *das;* **~s** (*Physiol., Med.*) adrenalin

**Adressänderung**, ***Adreßänderung** *die* (*schweiz.*) change of address

**Adressat** /adrɛ'sa:t/ *der;* **~en**, **~en**, **Adressatin** *die;* ~, **~nen** addressee; (*einer Rede*) hearer; (*eines Buches*) reader; (*einer Sendung*) listener/viewer; (*nicht direkt angesprochen*) implied target

**Adressbuch**, ***Adreßbuch** *das:* **~ [der Stadt]** [town/city] directory

**Adresse** /a'drɛsə/ *die;* ~, **~n** A ▶187 (*auch DV*) address; (*fig.: Unternehmen*) establishment; **unter folgender ~:** at the following address; **eine Warnung an jmds. ~** (*Akk.*) **richten** (*fig.*) address a warning to sb.; **sich an die richtige ~ wenden** go to the right quarters (*fig.*); **bei jmdm. an die falsche ~ kommen** *od.* **geraten** (*ugs.*) come to the wrong address (*fig.*); **bei jmdm. an der falschen ~ sein** (*ugs.*) have come to the wrong place (*fig.*); B (*geh.: Botschaft*) message; (*Meinungsäußerung*) address

**Adressen-:** **~änderung** *die* change of address; **~büro** *das* mailing list broker; **~liste** *die* address list; **~verzeichnis** *das* directory of addresses

**adressieren** *tr. V.* address

**Adressiermaschine** *die* addressing machine; Addressograph ®

**adrett** /a'drɛt/ ❶ *Adj.* smart. ❷ *adv.* smartly

**Adria** /'a:dri̯a/ *die;* **~:** Adriatic

**adriatisch** /adri'a:tɪʃ/ *Adj.* **das Adriatische Meer** the Adriatic [Sea]

**adrig**, **ädrig** *Adj.* ⇒ **aderig**, **äderig**

**Adsorbens** /at'zɔrbɛns/ *das;* ~, **Adsorbenzien** *od.* **Adsorbentia** (*Chemie, Physik*) adsorbent

**adsorbieren** *tr. V.* (*Chemie, Physik*) adsorb

**Adsorption** /atzɔrp'tsi̯o:n/ *die;* ~, **~en** (*Chemie, Physik*) adsorption

**A-Dur** *das* (*Musik*) A major; **Sonate/Etüde in ~:** sonata/study in A major; **die ~-Etüde** the A major study

**Advent** /at'vɛnt/ *der;* **~s** A Advent; B (*Adventssonntag*) Sunday in Advent

**Adventist** *der;* **~en**, **~en** (*Rel.*) Adventist

**Advents-:** **~kalender** *der* Advent calendar; **~kranz** *der: garland of evergreens with four candles for the Sundays in Advent;* **~sonntag** *der* Sunday in Advent

**Adverb** /at'vɛrp/ *das;* **~s**, **~ien** (*Sprachw.*) adverb

**adverbial** /atvɛr'bi̯a:l/ (*Sprachw.*) ❶ *Adj.* adverbial; **~e Bestimmung** adverbial qualification. ❷ *adv.* adverbially; as an adverb

**Adverbialsatz** *der* adverbial clause

**adversativ** /atvɛrza'ti:f/ (*Sprachw.*) ❶ *Adj.* adversative. ❷ *adv.* adversatively

**Advocatus Diaboli** /atvo'ka:tʊs di'a:boli/ *der;* ~ ~, **Advocati** ~ (*kath. Kirche, fig.*) devil's advocate

**Advokat** /atvo'ka:t/ *der;* **~en**, **~en**, **Advokatin** *die;* ~, **~nen** ▶159 (*österr., schweiz., sonst veralt.*) lawyer; advocate (*arch.*); (*fig.: Fürsprecher*) advocate

**Advokatur** /atvoka'tu:ɐ̯/ *die;* ~, **~en** legal profession; (*Anwaltsbüro*) legal practice

**Advokaturbüro** *das* (*schweiz.*), **Advokaturskanzlei** *die* (*österr.*) legal practice

**aerob** /ae'ro:p/ *Adj.* (*Biol.*) aerobic

**Aerobic** /ɛ'ro:bɪk/ *das;* **~s** aerobics *sing.*

**aero-**, **Aero-** /aero- *od.* ɛ:ro-/: **~dynamik** *die* aerodynamics *sing.*; **~dynamisch** *Adj.* aerodynamic; **~gramm** *das* air[mail] letter; **~sol** /-'zo:l/ *das;* **~s**, **~e** aerosol

**Affaire** *die;* ~, **~n** (*veralt., österr.*), **Affäre** *die;* ~, **~n** affair; (*Angelegenheit*) affair; business; **die ~ Dreyfus** the Dreyfus affair; **sich aus der ~ ziehen** (*ugs.*) get out of it; **eine ~ von ein paar Stunden/Mark** (*ugs.*) a matter of a few hours/marks

**Äffchen** /'ɛfçən/ *das;* **~s**, **~:** little ape/monkey

**Affe** /'afə/ *der;* **~n**, **~n** A monkey; (*Menschen~*) ape; (*fig.*) **du bist wohl vom wilden ~n gebissen!** (*salopp*) you're off your head (*coll.*) *or* (*coll.*) rocker!; **seinem ~n Zucker geben** (*ugs.*) really let oneself go; **jmdn. zum ~n machen** (*ugs.*) make a monkey out of sb. (*coll.*); ⇒ *auch* **lausen**; **Schleifstein**; B (*derb: dummer Kerl*) oaf; clot (*Brit. coll.*); C (*derb: Geck*) dandy; **ein eingebildeter ~:** a conceited so-and-so (*coll.*); D (*Milit. ugs.*) knapsack; E (*salopp: Rausch*) **einen ~n [sitzen] haben** be plastered (*sl.*)

**Affekt** /a'fɛkt/ *der;* **~[e]s**, **~e** A (*Gemütsbewegung*) feeling; emotion; affect (*Psych.*); **im ~:** in the heat of the moment; B *Pl.* (*Leidenschaften*) passions

**affektgeladen** *Adj.* emotive

**Affekthandlung** *die* emotive act

**affektiert** /afɛk'ti:ɐ̯t/ (*abwertend*) ❶ *Adj.* affected. ❷ *adv.* affectedly

**Affektiertheit** *die;* ~, **~en** affectedness; affectation

**affektiv** /afɛk'ti:f/ (*Psych.*) ❶ *Adj.* affective. ❷ *adv.* affectively

**Affektstauung** *die* (*Psych.*) emotional block

**affen-**, **Affen-:** **~arsch** *der* (*derb*) stupid bugger (*coarse*); **das sind doch alles ~ärsche** they are a stupid lot of buggers (*coarse*); **~artig** *Adj.* (*wie Menschenaffen*) apelike; **mit ~artiger Geschwindigkeit** (*ugs.*) like a bat out of hell (*coll.*); **~brotbaum** *der* (*Bot.*) baobab *or* monkey-bread tree; **~haus** *das* monkey house; **~hitze** *die* (*salopp*) blazing heat; **es herrschte gestern eine ~hitze** yesterday was a real scorcher; **~jacke** *die*, **~jäckchen** *das* (*Soldatenspr. scherzh.*) monkey jacket; **~käfig** *der* monkey cage; **~liebe** *die* (*ugs.*) infatuation (**zu** with); **~mensch** *der* apeman; **~pinscher** *der* affenpinscher; **~schande** *die* (*salopp*) **es ist eine ~schande** it's monstrous; **~schaukel** *die* (*ugs. scherzh.*) A (*Milit.*) aiguillette; B (*Zopf*) looped plait; **~stall** *der* (*salopp*) dump (*coll.*); hole (*coll.*); **hier stinkt es wie in einem ~stall** (*derb*) this place smells like a pigsty (*sl.*); **~tanz** *der* (*salopp*) ⇒ **~theater**; **~tempo** *das* (*salopp*) **mit einem ~tempo** like mad (*coll.*); like the clappers (*Brit. coll.*); **ein ~tempo anschlagen** move like hell (*coll.*); **~theater** *das* (*salopp*) farce; **~weibchen** *das* female ape; **~zahn** *der* (*salopp*) ⇒ **~tempo**; **~zirkus** *der* (*salopp*) ⇒ **~theater**

**affig** (*ugs. abwertend*) ❶ *Adj.* dandyish; (*lächerlich*) ludicrous; (*affektiert*) affected. ❷ *adv.* **~ gekleidet** dressed in a dandyish/ludicrous/affected way

**Affigkeit** *die;* ~ (*ugs. abwertend*) ⇒ **affig**: dandyishness; ludicrousness; affectation

**Äffin** /'ɛfɪn/ *die;* ~, **~nen** female ape

**Affinität** /afini'tɛ:t/ *die;* ~, **~en** affinity (**zu** for)

**Affirmation** /afɪrma'tsi̯o:n/ *die;* ~, **~en** (*geh.*) affirmation

**affirmativ** /afɪrma'ti:f/ *Adj.* affirmative

**affizieren** /afi'tsi:rən/ *tr. V.* (*geh.*) influence; affect

**Affront** /a'frõ:/ *der;* **~s**, **~s** affront

**Afghane** /af'ga:nə/ *der;* **~n**, **~n** ▶553 A Afghan; B (*Hund*) Afghan hound

**Afghanin** *die;* ~, **~nen** ▶553 Afghan; ⇒ *auch* **-in**

**afghanisch** *Adj.* ▶553, ▶696 Afghan

**Afghanistan** /af'ga:nɪsta:n/ (*das*); **~s** Afghanistan

**Afrika** /'a:frika/ (*das*); **~s** Africa

**Afrikaans** /afri'ka:ns/ *das;* ~ ▶696 Afrikaans

**Afrikaforscher** *der*, **Afrikaforscherin** *die* African explorer

**Afrikaner** /afri'ka:nɐ/ *der;* **~s**, ~, **Afrikanerin** *die;* ~, **~nen** African; ⇒ *auch* **-in**

*old spelling (see note on page 1707)

**afrikanisch** *Adj.* African

**Afrikanistik** *die;* **~:** African studies *pl.*, *no art.*

**afro-, Afro-:** **~amerikaner** *der*, **~amerikanerin** *die* Afro-American; **~amerikanisch** *Adj.* Afro-American; **~asiatisch** *Adj.* Afro-Asian; **~kubanisch** *Adj.* Afro-Cuban; **~look** *der* Afro look

**After** /'aftɐ/ *der;* **~s, ~** ▶ 471 anus

**After-:** **~furche** *die* (*Anat.*) ▶ 471 anal cleft; **~mieter** *der*, **~mieterin** *die* (*veralt.*) subtenant; **~wissenschaft** *die* (*veralt. abwertend*) pseudoscience

**AG** *die Abk.* (A) **Aktiengesellschaft** PLC (*Brit.*); Ltd. (*private company*) (*Brit.*); Inc. (*Amer.*); (B) **Arbeitsgemeinschaft**

**Ägäis** /ɛ'gɛ:ɪs/ *die;* **~:** Aegean

**ägäisch** *Adj.* Aegean

**Agave** /a'ga:və/ *die;* **~, ~n** (*Bot.*) agave

**Agende** /a'gɛndə/ *die;* **~, ~n** (*ev. Kirche*) liturgy

**Agens** /'a:gɛns/ *das;* **~, Agenzien** /a'gɛntsi̯ən/ driving force; (*Philos., Sprachw.*) agent

**Agent** /a'gɛnt/ *der;* **~en, ~en** agent

**Agenten-:** **~aus·tausch** *der* exchange of [captured] agents; **~netz** *das* network of agents; **~ring** *der* spy ring; **~tätigkeit** *die* activity as a spy

**Agentin** *die;* **~, ~nen** [female] agent

**Agent provocateur** /a'ʒã: provoka'tø:ɐ̯/ *der;* **~ ~, ~s ~s** agent provocateur

**Agentur** /agɛn'tu:ɐ̯/ *die;* **~, ~en** agency

**Agentur·bericht** *der*, **Agentur·meldung** *die* agency report

**Agglomerat** /aglome'ra:t/ *das;* **~[e]s, ~e** (A) (*geh.: Anhäufung*) conglomeration; (B) (*Geol.*) agglomerate

**Agglomeration** /aglomera'tsi̯o:n/ *die;* **~, ~en** (*Soziol.*) agglomeration

**Agglutination** /aglutina'tsi̯o:n/ *die;* **~, ~en** (*Sprachw.*) agglutination

**agglutinierend** /agluti'ni:rənt/ *Adj.* (*Sprachw.*) agglutinative

**Aggregat** /agre'ga:t/ *das;* **~[e]s, ~e** (*Technik*) unit; (*Elektrot.*) set

**Aggregat·zustand** *der* (*Chemie*) state

**Aggression** /agrɛ'si̯o:n/ *die;* **~, ~en** aggression; **starke ~en haben** have strong feelings of aggression

**Aggressions-:** **~krieg** *der* war of aggression; **~politik** *die* policy of aggression; **~trieb** *der* aggressive drive

**aggressiv** /agrɛ'si:f/ ❶ *Adj.* aggressive. ❷ *adv.* aggressively

**Aggressivität** *die;* **~:** aggressiveness

**Aggressor** /a'grɛsɔr/ *der;* **~s, ~en** /-'so:rən/, **Aggressorin** *die;* **~, ~nen** aggressor

**Ägide** /ɛ'gi:də/ (*geh.*) *in* **unter jmds. ~** (*Dat.*) under sb.'s aegis

**agieren** /a'gi:rən/ *itr. V.* (*auch Theater, fig.*) act; **als jmd. ~:** play sb.

**agil** /a'gi:l/ *Adj.* (*beweglich*) agile; (*geistig rege*) mentally alert

**Agilität** /agili'tɛ:t/ *die;* **~:** agility; (*geistige Regsamkeit*) mental alertness

**Agitation** /agita'tsi̯o:n/ *die;* **~** (*Politik*) agitation; **~ betreiben** agitate

**Agitator** /agi'ta:tɔr/ *der;* **~s, ~en** /-ta'to:rən/, **Agitatorin** *die;* **~, ~nen** agitator

**agitatorisch** ❶ *Adj.* agitative; inflammatory ‹speech›. ❷ *adv.* for purposes of agitation

**agitieren** ❶ *itr. V.* agitate. ❷ *tr. V.* stir up

**Agitprop** /agɪt'prɔp/ *die;* **~** (*Politik*) agitprop

**Agnostiker** /a'gnɔstikɐ/ *der;* **~s, ~, Agnostikerin** *die;* **~, ~nen** (*Philos.*) agnostic

**Agnostizismus** /agnɔsti'tsɪsmʊs/ *der;* **~** (*Philos.*) agnosticism *no art.*

**Agonie** /ago'ni:/ *die;* **~, ~n: [die] ~:** the throes *pl.* of death; **in ~ liegen** be in the throes of death

**Agrar-** /a'gra:ɐ̯/**:** **~erzeugnis** *das* agricultural *or* farm product; **~erzeugnisse** agricultural *or* farm produce *or* products; **~gesellschaft** *die* agrarian society

**Agrarier** /a'gra:ri̯ɐ/ *der;* **~s, ~, Agrarierin** *die;* **~, ~nen** (*veralt.*) landowner

**agrarisch** *Adj.* agrarian; agricultural

**Agrar-:** **~land** *das* agrarian country; **~markt** *der* agrarian *or* agricultural products market; **~politik** *die* agricultural policy; **~produkt** *das* ⇒ **~erzeugnis**; **~wissenschaft** *die* ⇒ **Agronomie**; **~zoll** *der* import tariff (*on agricultural produce*)

**Agrément** /agre'mã:/ *das;* **~s, ~s** (*Diplomatie*) **jmdm. das ~ erteilen/verweigern** accord/refuse an agrément to sb.

**Agri·kultur** /agri-/ *die* (*geh.*) agriculture *no art.*

**Agrikultur·chemie** *die*, **Agro·chemie** /'a:gro-/ *die* (*DDR*) agricultural chemistry *no art.*

**Agronom** /agro'no:m/ *der;* **~en, ~en** agronomist

**Agronomie** /agrono'mi:/ *die;* **~:** agronomy *no art.*

**Agro·technik** *die* (*DDR*) agricultural technology *no art.*

**Ägypten** /ɛ'gʏptn̩/ (*das*); **~s** Egypt; **die Flucht nach ~:** the flight into Egypt

**Ägypter** *der;* **~s, ~, Ägypterin** *die;* **~, ~nen** ▶ 553 Egyptian

**ägyptisch** *Adj.* ▶ 553, ▶ 696 Egyptian; ⇒ *auch* **Finsternis** A

**Ägyptologe** /ɛgʏpto'lo:gə/ *der;* **~n, ~n** Egyptologist

**Ägyptologie** /ɛgʏptolo'gi:/ *die;* **~:** Egyptology *no art.*

**Ägyptologin** *die;* **~, ~nen** Egyptologist

**ah** /a:/ *Interj.* (*verwundert*) oh; (*freudig, genießerisch*) ah; (*verstehend*) oh; ah

**äh** /ɛ(:)/ *Interj.* (A) (*angeekelt*) ugh; (B) (*stotternd*) er; hum

**aha** /a'ha(:)/ *Interj.* (*verstehend*) oh[, I see]; (*triumphierend*) aha

**Aha-Erlebnis** *das* (*Psych.*) aha experience

**ahd.** *Abk.* **althochdeutsch** OHG

**ahistorisch** ❶ *Adj.* ahistorical. ❷ *adv.* ahistorically

**Ahle** /'a:lə/ *die;* **~, ~n** awl; (*des Schriftsetzers*) bodkin

**Ahn** /a:n/ *der;* **~[e]s,** *od.* **~en, ~en** (*geh.*) forebear; ancestor; (*fig.*) father

**ahnden** /'a:ndn̩/ *tr. V.* (*geh.*) punish

**Ahndung** *die;* **~:** punishment

**Ahne**[1] *der;* **~n, ~n** ⇒ **Ahn**

**Ahne**[2] *die;* **~, ~n** (*geh.*) ancestress; forebear; (*fig.*) spiritual forebear

**ähneln** /'ɛ:nl̩n/ *itr. V.* **jmdm. ~:** resemble *or* be like sb.; bear a resemblance to sb.; **jmdm. sehr/wenig ~:** strongly resemble *or* be very like sb./bear little resemblance to sb.; **das Mädchen ähnelt seiner Mutter** the girl takes after her mother; **jmdm. frappierend ~:** bear a striking resemblance to sb.; **einer Sache** (*Dat.*) **~:** be similar to sth.; be like sth.; **sich** *od.* (*geh.*) **einander ~:** resemble one another; be alike; **sich sehr/wenig ~:** resemble each other very strongly *or* be very much alike/bear little resemblance to each other

**ahnen** /'a:nən/ ❶ *tr. V.* (A) (*im Voraus fühlen*) have a presentiment *or* premonition of; **etw. dumpf** *od.* **dunkel ~:** have a vague presentiment *or* premonition of sth.; sense sth. dimly; (B) (*vermuten*) suspect; (*erraten*) guess; **wer soll denn ~, dass ...** who would know that ...; how are you supposed to know that ...; **das konnte ich doch nicht ~:** I had no way of knowing that; **du ahnst es nicht, wen/wo/wie ...** you'll never guess whom/where/how ...; **ach, du ahnst es nicht!** (*salopp*) oh heck (*coll.*); oh Lord (*coll.*); **davon haben wir überhaupt nichts geahnt** we didn't suspect it for one moment; **nichts Böses ~:** be unsuspecting; **ohne es zu ~:** without suspecting *or* realizing [it]; (C) (*vage erkennen*) just make out; **die Wagen waren in der Dunkelheit mehr zu ~ als zu sehen** one could sense the cars in the darkness, rather than see them.
❷ *itr. V.* (*geh.*) **mir ahnt nichts Gutes** I fear the worst; **es ahnte mir, dass ...** I suspected that ...; **ihm ahnte Schreckliches** he was filled with *or* had a dreadful [sense of] foreboding

**Ahnen-:** **~bild** *das* (A) (**~porträt**) ancestral portrait; (B) (*Völkerk.*) ⇒ **~figur**; **~figur** *die* (*Völkerk.*) figure *or* effigy of an ancestor; **~forschung** *die* genealogy; **~galerie** *die* gallery of ancestral portraits; **~kult** *der* ancestor worship; **ein javanischer ~kult** a Javanese ancestor cult; **~pass, *~paß** *der* (*ns.*) proof of ancestry (*proving Aryan descent*); **~tafel** *die* genealogical table; **~verehrung** *die* ancestor worship

**Ahn-:** **~frau** *die* (*geh. veralt.*) [first] ancestress; (*fig.*) spiritual forebear; **~herr** *der* (*geh. veralt.*) [first] ancestor; (*fig.*) father; **~herrin** *die* (*geh. veralt.*) [first] ancestor

**Ahnin** *die;* **~, ~nen** ⇒ **Ahne**[2]

**ähnlich** /'ɛ:nlɪç/ ❶ *Adj.* similar; **jmdm. ~ sein** be similar to *or* be like sb.; (**~** *aussehen*) resemble sb.; be like sb.; **das Kind ist seinem Vater ~:** the child takes after his father; **sich** (*Dat.*) *od.* (*geh.*) **einander ~ sein** be similar to one another; be alike; (**~** *aussehen*) resemble one another; be alike; **~ wie er/wir** like him/us; **~ wie etw. aussehen/klingen** look/sound like sth.; **ein einer Ratte ~es Tier** an animal similar to a rat; **das sieht dir/ihm ~!** (*ugs.*) that's you/him all over; that's just like you/him; **[etwas] Ähnliches** something similar.
❷ *adv.* similarly; ‹answer, react› in a similar way *or* manner; **~ dumm/naiv** *usw.* **argumentieren** argue in a similarly stupid/naïve *etc.* way *or* manner; **~ dumm/naiv sein** be similarly stupid/naïve; **uns geht es ~:** it is/will be much the same for us; (*wir denken, fühlen* **~**) we feel much the same.
❸ *Präp. mit Dat.* like

**Ähnlichkeit** *die;* **~, ~en** similarity; (*ähnliches Aussehen*) similarity; resemblance; **mit jmdm. ~ haben** be similar to *or* be like sb.; (*ähnlich aussehen*) bear a resemblance to *or* be like sb.; **mit etw. ~ haben** bear a similarity to sth.

**Ahnung** *die;* **~, ~en** (A) (*Vorgefühl*) presentiment; premonition; **eine ~ haben, dass ...** have a feeling *or* hunch that ...; (B) (*Befürchtung*) foreboding; (C) (*ugs.: Kenntnisse*) knowledge; **von etw. [viel] ~ haben** know [a lot] about sth.; **keine ~!** [I've] no idea; [I] haven't a clue; **du hast doch keine ~:** you don't know the first thing about it; **nicht die geringste** *od.* **keine blasse ~ [von etw.] haben** not have the faintest idea [about sth.]; **haben Sie eine ~, wer/wie ...?** have you any idea who/how ...?; **von Tuten und Blasen keine ~ haben, keine ~ von Ackerbau und Viehzucht haben** (*salopp*) not know the first thing about it; **hast du 'ne ~!** (*ugs.*) that's what you think!

**ahnungs·los** ❶ *Adj.* (*nichts ahnend*) unsuspecting; (*naiv, unschuldig*) naïve; innocent; (*unwissend*) naïve; **sich ~ stellen** play the innocent. ❷ *adv.* (*nichts ahnend*) unsuspectingly; all unawares; (*naiv, unschuldig*) naïvely; innocently; (*unwissend*) naïvely

**Ahnungslosigkeit** *die;* **~** (*Naivität, Unschuld*) naïvety; innocence; (*Unwissenheit*) naïvety

**ahnungs·voll** *Adj.* (*geh.*) full of presentiment *postpos.*; (*geheimnisvoll*) mysterious; (*Böses ahnend*) full of foreboding *postpos.*

**ahoi** /a'hɔy/ *Interj.* (A) (*Seemannsspr.*) **Boot/Schiff** *usw.* **~!** boat/ship *etc.* ahoy!; (B) ⇒ **helau**

**Ahorn** /'a:hɔrn/ *der;* **~s, ~e** maple

**Ahorn-:** **~blatt** *das* maple leaf; **~sirup** *der* maple syrup

**Ähre** /'ɛ:rə/ *die;* **~, ~n** (*von Getreide*) ear; head; (*von Gräsern*) head; (*Bot.: von Blüten*) spike; **~n lesen** glean

**Ähren-:** **~feld** *das* (*geh.*) field of [ripening/ripe] corn; **~kranz** *der* wreath of wheat ears; **~lese** *die* gleaning

**Aids** /e:ts/ *das;* **~** ▶ 474 AIDS

**Aids-:** **~kranke** *der/die* person suffering from AIDS; **~test** *der* AIDS test

**Air** /ɛ:ɐ̯/ *das;* **~s, ~s** (A) air; aura; (B) (*Musik*) air

**Airbag** /'ɛ:ɐ̯bɛk/ *der;* **~s, ~s** (*Kfz.-W.*) air bag

**Air·bus** /'ɛ:ɐ̯-/ *der* (*Flugw.*) airbus

**Airedale** /'ɛ:ɐ̯de:l/ *der;* **~s, ~s** Airedale

**Airedale·terrier** *der* Airedale terrier

**ais, Ais** /'a:ɪs/ *das;* ~, ~ (*Mus.*) A sharp

**Akademie** /akade'mi:/ *die;* ~, **~n** [A] academy; [B] (*Fachhochschule*) academy; (*Bergbau, Forst~, Bau~*) school; college; [C] (*österr.: künstlerische Veranstaltung*) cultural function

**Akademie·mitglied** *das* member of the/an academy; academician

**Akademiker** /aka'de:mikɐ/ *der;* **~s,** ~, **Akademikerin** *die;* ~, **~nen** [A] (*Hochschulabsolvent*) [university/college] graduate; [B] ⇒ **Akademiemitglied**

**akademisch** ❶ *Adj.* academic; **~er Rat** [university] lecturer; **~er Oberrat** senior [university] lecturer; **der ~e Mittelbau** *the non-professional teaching staff;* **das ~e Proletariat** *the mass of jobless graduates and graduates working in jobs for which they are overqualified;* **~er Lehrer** university teacher; **das ~e Viertel** *the 15 minutes' grace between the announced start and actual beginning of a lecture.* ❷ *adv.* academically; **~ [aus]gebildet sein** have [had] a university education; be university-educated; **dieses Problem stellt sich rein ~:** this problem is purely academic

**Akademisierung** *die;* **~: die ~ des Bundestages schreitet weiter fort** the Bundestag is becoming increasingly peopled with [university] graduates

**Akanthus** /a'kantʊs/ *der;* ~, ~ (*Bot., Kunstwiss.*) acanthus

**akausal** (*Philos.*) ❶ *Adj.* acausal. ❷ *adv.* acausally

**Akazie** /a'ka:tsi̯ə/ *die;* ~, **~n** (*auch volkst.: Robinie*) acacia

**Akelei** /akə'lai̯/ *die;* ~, **~en** aquilegia; columbine

**Akklamation** /aklama'tsi̯o:n/ *die;* ~, **~en** [A] (*Abstimmung durch Zuruf*) acclamation; **durch** *od.* **per ~:** by acclamation; [B] (*selten: Beifall*) acclamation *no pl.;* acclaim *no pl.*

**akklamieren** /akla'mi:rən/ (*geh.*) ❶ *itr. V.* (*zustimmen*) applaud. ❷ *tr. V.* (*durch Beifall*) acclaim

**Akklimatisation** /aklimatiza'tsi̯o:n/ *die;* ~, **~en** acclimatization

**akklimatisieren** *refl. V.* become *or* get acclimatized

**Akklimatisierung** *die;* ~, **~en** ⇒ **Akklimatisation**

**Akkolade** /ako'la:də/ *die;* ~, **~n** [A] (*Hist., Musik*) accolade; [B] (*Druckw.*) brace

**Akkord** /a'kɔrt/ *der;* **~[e]s, ~e** [A] (*Musik*) chord; [B] (*Wirtsch.*) (*~arbeit*) piecework; (*~lohn*) piecework pay *no indef. art., no pl.;* (*~satz*) piece rate; **im ~ sein** *od.* **arbeiten** be on piecework; **etw. im ~ tun** do sth. piecework; **im ~ hergestellt werden** be manufactured by pieceworkers; [C] (*geh.: Übereinstimmung*) accord; [D] (*Rechtsspr.: Einigung*) settlement

**Akkord-: ~arbeit** *die* piecework; **in ~arbeit hergestellt werden** be manufactured by pieceworkers; **~arbeiter** *der,* **~arbeiterin** *die* pieceworker

**Akkordeon** /a'kɔrdeɔn/ *das;* **~s, ~s** accordion

**Akkordeonist** *der;* **~en, ~en, Akkordeonistin** *die;* ~, **~nen, Akkordeon·spieler** *der,* **Akkordeon·spielerin** *die* accordionist

**Akkord-: ~lohn** *der* (*Wirtsch.*) piecework pay *no indef. art., no pl.;* **~satz** *der* (*Wirtsch.*) piece rate; **~zuschlag** *der* (*Wirtsch.*) piece-rate bonus

**akkreditieren** /akredi'ti:rən/ *tr. V.* [A] (*bes. Dipl.*) accredit (**bei** to); [B] (*Finanzw.*) **jmdn. ~:** grant sb. credit facilities; **akkreditiert sein** have credit facilities

**Akkreditierung** *die;* ~, **~en** [A] (*bes. Dipl.*) accreditation (**bei** to); [B] (*Finanzw.*) **meine ~ bei der Bank** my credit facilities *pl. or* credit arrangement at the bank; **eine ~ von DM 10 000** provision of 10,000 DM of credit

**Akkreditiv** /akredi'ti:f/ *das;* **~s, ~e** [A] (*Dipl.*) credentials *pl.;* [B] (*Finanzw.*) letter of credit

**Akku** /'aku/ *der;* **~s, ~s** (*ugs.*) ⇒ **Akkumulator** A

**Akkulturation** /akʊltura'tsi̯o:n/ *die;* ~, **~en** (*Völkerk., Sozialpsych.*) acculturation

**akkulturieren** *tr. V.* (*Völkerk., Sozialpsych.*) acculturate

**Akkumulation** /akumula'tsi̯o:n/ *die;* ~, **~en** (*geh., Wirtsch.*) accumulation

**Akkumulator** /akumu'la:tɔr/ *der;* **~s, ~en** /-la'to:rən/ (*Technik*) [A] (*Stromspeicher*) accumulator (*Brit.*); storage battery *or* cell; [B] (*Druckspeicher, DV*) accumulator

**akkumulieren** *tr., itr., refl. V.* (*geh., Wirtsch., Soziol.*) accumulate

**akkurat** /aku'ra:t/ ❶ *Adj.* [A] (*sorgfältig*) meticulous; (*sauber*) neat; [B] (*exakt, genau*) precise; exact. ❷ *adv.* [A] (*sorgfältig*) meticulously; (*sauber*) neatly; [B] (*exakt, genau*) precisely; exactly

**Akkuratesse** /akura'tɛsə/ *die;* ~ [A] (*Sorgfalt*) meticulousness; (*Sauberkeit*) neatness; [B] (*Exaktheit, Genauigkeit*) precision

**Akkusativ** /'akuzati:f/ *der;* **~s, ~e** (*Sprachw.*) accusative [case]; (*Wort im ~*) accusative [form]; **im/mit dem ~ stehen** be in/take the accusative [case]

**Akkusativ·objekt** *das* (*Sprachw.*) accusative *or* direct object

**Akne** /'aknə/ *die;* ~, **~n** ▶ 474 (*Med.*) acne

**Akonto** /a'kɔnto/ *das;* **~s, ~s** *od.* **Akonten** (*österr.*), **Akonto·zahlung** *die* ⇒ **Anzahlung**

**akquirieren** /akvi'ri:rən/ *itr. V.* (*Wirtsch.*) canvass [new] business

**Akquisiteur** /akvizi'tø:ɐ̯/ *der;* **~s, ~e, Akquisiteurin** *die;* ~, **~nen** (*Wirtsch.*) canvasser

**Akquisition** /akvizi'tsi̯o:n/ *die;* ~, **~en** (*Wirtsch.*) canvassing *no art.* for [new] business

**Akquisitor** /akvi'zi:tɔr/ *der;* **~s, ~en** /-zi'to:rən/, **Akquisitorin** *die;* ~, **~nen** (*österr.*) canvasser

**Akribie** /akri'bi:/ *die;* ~ (*geh.*) meticulousness; meticulous precision

**akribisch** /a'kri:bɪʃ/ ❶ *Adj.* meticulous; meticulously precise. ❷ *adv.* meticulously; with meticulous precision; **~ genau** meticulously accurate

**Akrobat** /akro'ba:t/ *der;* **~en, ~en** ▶ 159 acrobat

**Akrobaten·truppe** *die* troupe of acrobats

**Akrobatik** *die;* ~ [A] (*Körperbeherrschung*) acrobatic skill; [B] (*akrobatische Übungen*) acrobatics *pl.*

**Akrobatin** *die;* ~, **~nen** ▶ 159 acrobat

**akrobatisch** ❶ *Adj.* acrobatic. ❷ *adv.* acrobatically

**Akronym** /akro'ny:m/ *das;* **~s, ~e** (*Sprachw.*) acronym

**Akt**[1] /akt/ *der;* **~[e]s, ~e** [A] (*auch Theater, Zirkus~, Varietee~*) act; [B] (*Zeremonie*) ceremony; ceremonial act; [C] (*Geschlechts~*) sexual act; [D] (*~bild*) nude; [E] (*Amtshandlung*) action

**Akt**[2] *der;* **~[e]s, ~en** (*bes. südd., österr.*) ⇒ **Akte**

**Akt-: ~aufnahme** *die* nude photograph; **~bild** *das* nude [picture]

**Akte** *die;* ~, **~n** file; **die ~ Schulze** the Schulze file; **das kommt in die ~n** it goes on file; **~n über jmdn./etw. führen** keep a file on sb./sth.; **etw. zu den ~n legen** file sth. away; (*fig.*) lay sth. to rest; **über etw.** (*Akk.*) **die ~n schließen** close the file on sth.

**akten-, Akten-: ~berg** *der* (*ugs.*) mountain of files; **~deckel** *der* folder; **~einsicht** *die* (*Amtsspr.*) **~einsicht nehmen** examine the files; **jmdm. ~einsicht gewähren** allow sb. to examine the files; **~koffer** *der,* (*iron.*) **~köfferchen** *das* attaché case; **~kundig** *Adj.* on record; **~kundig werden** go on file; be recorded; **~mappe** *die* [A] (*~tasche*) briefcase; [B] (*~deckel*) folder; **~notiz** *die* [A] note [for the files]; **sich** (*Dat.*) **eine kurze ~notiz von etw. machen** make a brief note of sth. [for the files]; [B] (*längeres Schreiben*) memorandum; **~ordner** *der* file; **~schrank** *der* filing cabinet; **~stoß** *der* stack *or* pile of files; **~tasche** *die* briefcase; **~vermerk** *der* ⇒ **~notiz** A; **~wolf** *der* [paper] shredder; **~zeichen** *das* reference

**Akteur** /ak'tø:ɐ̯/ *der;* **~s, ~e, Akteurin** *die;* ~, **~nen** person involved; (*Theater*) member of the cast; (*Varietee*) performer; (*Sportjargon*) player; (*Boxen, Ringen*) contestant

**Akt-: ~foto** *das* nude photo; **~fotografie** *die* [A] nude photography *no art.;* [B] (*Bild*) nude photograph; **~gemälde** *das* nude [painting]

**Aktie** /'aktsi̯ə/ *die;* ~, **~n** (*Wirtsch.*) share; **~n** shares (*Brit.*); stock (*Amer.*); **sein Geld in ~n anlegen** invest one's money in shares (*Brit.*) *or* (*Amer.*) stocks; **die ~n fallen/steigen** share *or* stock prices are falling/rising; **junge ~n** new-issue shares *or* stocks; **wie stehen die ~n?** (*ugs. scherzh.*) (*wie gehts*) how are things?; (*wie sind die Chancen*) what are the prospects?; **seine/meine** *usw.* **~n steigen** (*fig. ugs.*) his/my *etc.* prospects are improving

**Aktien-: ~besitz** *der* shareholdings *pl.;* **~besitzer** *der,* **~besitzerin** *die* shareholder; **~gesellschaft** *die* joint-stock company; **~index** *der* share index; **~kapital** *das* share capital; **~kurs** *der* share price; **~markt** *der* stock market; **~mehrheit** *die* majority shareholding (*Gen.* in); **~paket** *das* block of shares; **~urkunde** *die* share certificate (*Brit.*); stock certificate (*Amer.*)

**Aktion** /ak'tsi̯o:n/ *die;* ~, **~en** [A] (*Unternehmung*) action *no indef. art.;* (*militärisch*) operation; **revolutionäre/politische ~en** revolutionary/political action *sing.;* [B] (*Kampagne*) campaign; **~ saubere Umwelt** campaign to clean up the environment; ⇒ *auch* **konzertiert**; [C] (*das Handeln*) action; **in ~ treten** go into action; ‹safety device› come into action; [D] (*Kaufmannsspr.: Verkauf zu Sonderpreisen*) sale

**Aktionär** /aktsi̯o'nɛ:ɐ̯/ *der;* **~s, ~e, Aktionärin** *die;* ~, **~nen** shareholder

**Aktionärs·versammlung** *die* shareholders' meeting

**Aktionismus** *der;* **~:** actionism *no art.*

**Aktionist** *der;* **~en, ~en, Aktionistin** *die;* ~, **~nen** actionist

**aktionistisch** ❶ *Adj.* actionist[ic]. ❷ *adv.* actionistically

**aktions-, Aktions-: ~art** *die* (*Sprachw.*) aspect; **~ausschuss,** ***~ausschuß** *der* action committee; **~bereich** *der* ⇒ **~radius**; **~einheit** *die* united action *no art.* (*Gen.* by); **~fähig** *Adj.* capable of action *postpos.;* **~fähigkeit** *die* ability to act; **~gemeinschaft** *die:* **eine ~gemeinschaft herstellen/fordern** bring about/demand united action (**von** by); **~gruppe** *die* action group; **~komitee** *das* action committee; **~preis** *der* (*Kaufmannsspr.*) sale price; **zum ~preis** at sale price; **~programm** *das* programme for action; **~radius** *der* [A] (*Luftwaffe, Seew.*) radius of action; [B] (*Wirkungsbereich*) range of activity; **~unfähig** *Adj.* incapable of action *postpos.;* **~zentrum** *das* [A] (*Mittelpunkt*) centre *or* focus for action; [B] (*Met.*) centre of action

**aktiv** /ak'ti:f/ ❶ *Adj.* [A] (*auch Chemie*) active; [B] (*Milit.*) serving *attrib.* ‹officer, soldier›; **er ist Soldat im ~en Dienst** he is a serving soldier; **er war in Vietnam ~:** he served in Vietnam; [C] **~e Bestechung** offering of a bribe/bribes to an official; **~e Handelsbilanz** favourable balance of trade; **~er Wortschatz** active vocabulary. ❷ *adv.* actively; **sich ~ verhalten** be active

**Aktiv**[1] /'akti:f/ *das;* **~s, ~e** (*Sprachw.*) active; **im ~ stehen** be in the active

**Aktiv**[2] /ak'ti:f/ *das;* **~s, ~e** *od.* **~s** (*bes. DDR*) committee

*old spelling (see note on page 1707)

**-aktiv**[1] *Adj.* (*Werbespr.*) **saug~:** extra-absorbent; **wasch~e Substanzen** substances with a strong cleansing action; **atmungs~s Gewebe** fabric which allows the skin to breathe

**-aktiv**[2] *das;* **~s, ~e** *od.* **~s** (*bes. DDR*) **Verkehrssicherheits~ / Bezirks~ / Eltern~** *usw.* traffic safety/district/parents *etc.* committee

**Aktiva** /ak'ti:va/ *Pl.* (*Wirtsch.*) assets

**Aktiv·bürger** *der*, **Aktiv·bürgerin** *die* (*schweiz.*) *citizen with full political and civil rights*

**Aktive**[1] /ak'ti:və/ *der/die; adj. Dekl.* (*Sport*) participant; (*eines Vereins, einer Gewerkschaft*) active member; (*der Feuerwehr*) regular

**Aktive**[2] *die;* **~n, ~n** (*salopp*) (*nicht selbst gedrehte Zigarette*) real fag (*Brit. sl.*); store-bought cigarette (*Amer.*); (*filterlose Zigarette*) plain fag (*sl.*); non-filter

**Aktiven** *Pl.:* ⇒ **Aktiva**

**Aktiv·geschäft** *das* (*Finanzw.*) lending and investment business

**aktivierbar** *Adj.* **er ist/sie sind** *usw.* **[politisch] ~:** he/they *etc.* can be [politically] mobilized

**aktivieren** *tr. V.* **A** mobilize ‹party members, group, class, etc.›; intensify, step up ‹work, campaign›; **den Kreislauf ~:** stimulate the circulation; **alte Freundschaften ~:** revive old friendships; **Beziehungen ~:** reactivate connections; **B** (*Chemie*) activate; **C** (*Finanzw.*) **etw. ~:** enter sth. on the assets side

**Aktivierung** *die;* **~, ~en A** (*von Parteimitgliedern, einer Gruppe, Klasse*) mobilization; (*einer Arbeit, Kampagne*) intensification; (*von Beziehungen*) reactivation; **die ~ des Kreislaufs/alter Freundschaften** stimulation of the circulation/reviving old friendships; **B** (*Chemie*) activation; **C** (*Finanzw.*) entry on the assets side; **die ~ von etw.** entering sth. on the assets side

**aktivisch** (*Sprachw.*) **1** *Adj.* active. **2** *adv.* actively; in the active form

**Aktivismus** *der;* **~** (*Politik*) activism *no art.*

**Aktivist** *der;* **~en, ~en, Aktivistin** *die;* **~, ~nen** activist

**aktivistisch** *Adj.* (*Politik*) activist

**Aktivität** /aktivi'tɛ:t/ *die;* **~, ~en** (*auch Chemie, Radio~*) activity

**Aktiv-: ~kohle** *die* activated carbon *or* charcoal; **~kohle·filter** *der,* (*fachspr. meist*) *das* activated-carbon *or* activated-charcoal filter; **~posten** *der* (*Kaufmannsspr., fig.*) asset; **~saldo** *der* (*Kaufmannsspr.*) credit balance; **~seite** *die* (*Kaufmannsspr.*) assets side; **~urlaub** *der* (*Werbespr.*) activity holiday; **~vermögen** *das* (*Kaufmannsspr.*) realizable assets *pl.;* **~zinsen** *Pl.* (*Kaufmannsspr.*) interest *sing.* receivable

**Akt-: ~malerei** *die* nude painting *no art.;* **~modell** *das* nude model

**Aktrice** /ak'tri:sə/ *die;* **~, ~n** actress

**Akt·studie** *die* nude study

**aktualisieren** /aktuali'zi:rən/ **1** *tr. V.* update. **2** *refl. V.* (*sich manifestieren*) be evident *or* clearly visible

**Aktualisierung** *die;* **~, ~en** updating; **er sorgte für die ~ des Themas** he ensured that the subject was made topical

**Aktualität** /aktuali'tɛ:t/ *die;* **~, ~en A** (*Gegenwartsbezug*) relevance [to the present]; **B** (*von Nachrichten usw.*) topicality; **C** (*Mode, Werbespr.*) up-to-the-minute style

**Aktuar** /ak'tua:ɐ̯/ *der;* **~s, ~e, Aktuarin** *die;* **~, ~nen ▶ 159 A** (*schweiz.: Schriftführer*) secretary; **B** (*veralt.*) ⇒ **Gerichtsschreiber**

**aktuell** /ak'tuɛl/ **1** *Adj.* **A** (*gegenwartsbezogen*) topical; (*gegenwärtig*) current; **von ~er Bedeutung** of relevance to the present *or* current situation; **dieses Problem ist nicht mehr ~:** this is no longer a problem; **B** (*neu*) up-to-the-minute; **das Aktuellste von den Olympischen Spielen** the latest from the Olympics; **eine ~e Sendung** (*Ferns., Rundf.*) a [news and] current affairs programme; **C** (*geh.: real*) real; **D** (*Mode, Werbespr.*) fashionable; **in den ~en Farben** in the latest colours. **2** *adv.* currently

**Akt-: ~zeichnen** *das* nude drawing *no art.;* **~zeichnung** *die* nude drawing

**Akupressur** /akuprɛ'su:ɐ̯/ *die;* **~, ~en** (*Med.*) acupressure

**Akupunkteur** /akupʊŋk'tø:ɐ̯/ *der;* **~s, ~e, Akupunkteurin** *die;* **~, ~nen** (*Med.*) acupuncturist

**akupunktieren** (*Med.*) **1** *tr. V.* perform acupuncture on; **sich ~ lassen** have acupuncture. **2** *itr. V.* perform acupuncture

**Akupunktur** /akupʊŋk'tu:ɐ̯/ *die;* **~, ~en** (*Med.*) acupuncture

**Akustik** /a'kʊstɪk/ *die;* **~ A** (*Lehre vom Schall*) acoustics *sing., no art.;* **B** (*Schallverhältnisse*) acoustics *pl.*

**akustisch 1** *Adj.* acoustic. **2** *adv.* acoustically; **ich habe Sie ~ nicht verstanden** I didn't hear *or* catch what you said

**akut** /a'ku:t/ **1** *Adj.* **A** (*vordringlich*) acute; pressing, urgent ‹question, issue›; **B** (*Med.*) acute. **2** *adv.* (*Med.*) in an acute form; **~ auftretende Asthmaanfälle** acute attacks of asthma

**Akut** *der;* **~[e]s, ~e** (*Schriftw.*) acute [accent]

**AKW** *Abk.* **Atomkraftwerk**

**Akzeleration** /aktselera'tsi̯o:n/ *die;* **~, ~en** (*Anthrop., Astron.*) acceleration

**Akzelerator** /aktsele'ra:tɔr/ *der;* **~s, ~en** /-ra'to:rən/ (*Kerntechnik*) accelerator

**Akzent** /ak'tsɛnt/ *der;* **~[e]s, ~e A** (*Sprachw.*) (*Betonung*) accent; stress; (*Betonungszeichen*) accent; **B ▶ 696** (*Sprachmelodie, Aussprache*) accent; **mit starkem koreanischem ~:** with a strong Korean accent; **C** (*Nachdruck, Gewicht*) emphasis; stress; (*in der Mode*) accent; **den ~ [besonders] auf etw.** (*Akk.*) **legen** lay *or* put [particular] emphasis *or* stress on sth.; **die ~e werden verschoben** the emphasis *or* stress is shifted; **neue ~e setzen** set new directions; **diesen Herbst liegen die [modischen] ~e bei ...** this autumn the accent is on ...; **1969 hat neue ~e gesetzt** 1969 saw the beginning of new trends

**akzent·frei 1** *Adj.* without an *or* any accent *postpos.* **2** *adv.* without an *or* any accent

**akzentuieren** /aktsɛntu'i:rən/ *tr. V.* **A** (*deutlich aussprechen*) enunciate; articulate; (*betonen*) accentuate; stress; **B** (*fig.: hervorheben, auch Mode*) accentuate

**Akzent·verschiebung** *die* **A** (*Sprachw.*) stress shift; **B** (*fig.*) shift of emphasis

**Akzept** /ak'tsɛpt/ *das;* **~[e]s, ~e** (*Finanzw.*) acceptance

**akzeptabel** /aktsɛp'ta:bl̩/ **1** *Adj.* acceptable. **2** *adv.* acceptably

**Akzeptanz** /aktsɛp'tants:/ *die* (*bes. Werbespr.*) acceptance

**akzeptieren** *tr. V.* accept

**Akzidens** /'aktsidɛns/ *das;* **~, Akzidenzien A** (*Philos.*) accident; accidental property; **B** (*Musik*) accidental

**akzidentell** /aktsidɛn'tɛl/, **akzidentiell** /-'tsi̯ɛl/ *Adj.* **A** (*Philos., geh.*) accidental (*Dat.* to); **B** (*Med.*) accidental

**Akzidenz** /aktsi'dɛnts:/ *die;* **~, ~en** (*Druckw.*) job; **~en** job-work *sing.;* job printing *sing.*

**à la** /a la/ (*Gastr., ugs.: im Stile von*) à la

**alaaf** /a'la:f/ *Interj.* (*rhein.*) hurrah; hurray; **Kölle ~!** hurrah, Cologne!

**Alabaster** /ala'bastɐ/ *der;* **~s, ~:** alabaster

**alabastern** *Adj.* (*geh.*) alabaster

**à la carte** /ala'kart/ (*Gastr.*) à la carte

**Alarm** /a'larm/ *der;* **~[e]s, ~e A** (*Warnung*) alarm; (*Flieger~*) air-raid warning; **~ geben** raise *or* sound *or* give the alarm; **blinder ~:** false alarm; **~ schlagen** (*ugs.*) raise *or* sound the alarm; **bei ~:** if there is an alarm; **B** (*~zustand*) alert; **da war ständig ~:** there was a permanent state of alert

**alarm-, Alarm-: ~anlage** *die* alarm system; **~bereit** *Adj.* on alert *postpos.;* ‹fire crew, police› on standby *postpos.*, standing by *pred.;* **~bereitschaft** *die* ⇒ **~bereit**: alert; **in [ständiger] ~bereitschaft** on [permanent] alert/standby; **jmdn./etw. in ~bereitschaft versetzen** place *or* put sb./sth. on alert/standby; **~fall** *der* alert; **im ~fall** in case of alert; in the event of an alert; **~glocke** *die* alarm bell

**alarmieren** *tr. V.* **A** (*zu Hilfe rufen*) call [out] ‹doctor, police, fire brigade, etc.›; **B** (*warnen*) alarm; **~d** alarming; **nichts Alarmierendes** nothing alarming

**Alarmierung** *die;* **~: bei rechtzeitiger ~ der Bergwacht** *usw.* if the mountain rescue service *etc.* is/had been called [out] in time; **eine sofortige ~ der Feuerwehr wäre geboten gewesen** the fire service *or* (*Amer.*) department should have been called [out] immediately; **zur ~ aller Demokraten führen** cause alarm on the part of all democrats

**Alarm-: ~klingel** *die* alarm bell; **~pikett** *das* (*schweiz.*) ⇒ **Überfallkommando**; **~ruf** *der* (*fig.*) warning cry; **~signal** *das* (*auch fig.*) warning signal; **~sirene** *die* alarm *or* warning siren; **~stufe** *die* alert stage; **höchste ~stufe** maximum alert; **~stufe eins/zwei/drei** stage one/two/three alert; **~übung** *die* practice drill; (*Milit.*) practice alert; **~vor·richtung** *die* alarm [device]; **~zeichen** *das* (*fig.*) warning signal; **~zustand** *der* state of alert; **sich im ~zustand befinden** ‹troops› be on alert; ‹fire service, police› be on standby; ‹country, province› be on a state of alert; **in den ~zustand versetzen** put ‹troops› on alert; place *or* put ‹fire service, police› on standby; place *or* put ‹country, province› on a state of alert

**Alaska** /a'laska/ (*das*)**;** **~s** Alaska

**Alaun** /a'laun/ *der;* **~s, ~e** alum

**Alaun·stift** *der* styptic pencil

**a-Laut** *der* A-sound

**Alb**[1] /alp/ *der;* **~[e]s, ~en** (*Myth.*) elf

**Alb**[2] *der;* **~[e]s, ~e** (*veralt.: Kobold*) *goblin believed to give sleeping people nightmares by sitting on their chests at night;* ≈ incubus; **wie ein ~ auf der Burst lasten** (*geh.*) lie *or* weigh heavily on sb.; **ein ~ plagte ihn** he had nightmares

**Albaner** /al'ba:nɐ/ *der;* **~s, ~, Albanerin** *die;* **~, ~nen ▶ 553** Albanian

**Albanien** /al'ba:ni̯ən/ (*das*)**;** **~s** Albania

**albanisch** *Adj.* **▶ 553** Albanian; ⇒ *auch* **deutsch**

**Albanisch** *das;* **~s** Albanian; ⇒ *auch* **Deutsch**

**Albatros** /'albatrɔs/ *der;* **~, ~se** (*Zool.*) albatross

**Alb-: ~druck** *der* nightmare; **~drücken** *das;* **~s** nightmares *pl*

**Albe** /'albə/ *die;* **~, ~n** (*christl. Kirchen*) alb

**Alben** ⇒ **Alb, Albe, Album**

**Alberei** *die;* **~, ~en** ⇒ **Albernheit B**

**albern**[1] *itr. V.* fool about *or* around

**albern**[2] *Adj.* **A** (*kindisch, töricht*) silly; foolish; **~es Zeug reden** talk silly *or* foolish nonsense; **stell dich nicht so ~ an** don't be so silly; **sich ~ benehmen** act silly; **sich** (*Dat.*) **~ vorkommen** feel silly; feel a fool; **B** (*ugs.: nebensächlich*) silly; stupid

**Albernheit** *die;* **~, ~en A** (*albernes Verhalten*) silliness; foolishness; **B** (*alberne Handlung*) silliness; (*alberne Bemerkung/alberner Witz*) silly remark/joke; **diese ~en** this silliness *sing.*

**Albinismus** /albi'nɪsmʊs/ *der;* **~:** albinism

**Albino** /al'bi:no/ *der;* **~s, ~s** albino

**Alb·traum** *der* nightmare

**Album** /'albʊm/ *das;* **~s, Alben** album

**Albumin** /albu'mi:n/ *das;* **~s, ~e** (*Biol.*) albumin

**Alchemie** /alçe'mi:/ *die;* **~** (*bes. österr.*), **Alchimie** /alçi'mi:/ *die;* **~:** alchemy *no art.*

**Alchemist** *der;* **~en, ~en** (*bes. österr.*), **Alchemistin** *die;* **~, ~nen** (*bes. österr.*), **Alchimist** *der;* **~en, ~en, Alchimistin** *die;* **~, ~nen** alchemist

**Alchimisten·küche** *die* alchemist's laboratory

**alchimistisch** ❶ *Adj.* alchemical; alchemistic. ❷ *adv.* alchemistically; ~ **beeinflusst** influenced by alchemy

**Aldehyd** /alde'hy:t/ *der;* ~**s**, ~**e** (*Chem.*) aldehyde

**Alemanne** /alə'manə/ *der;* ~**n**, ~**n**, **Alemannin** *die;* ~, ~**nen** Alemannian; **die** ~**n** Alemannians; (*Hist.*) the Alemanni

**alemannisch** *Adj.* Alemannic

**alert** /a'lɛrt/ *Adj.* (*ugs.*) dynamic

**Aleuten** /ale'u:tn̩/ *Pl.* **die** ~**:** the Aleutian Islands; the Aleutians

**Alexandriner** /alɛksan'dri:nɐ/ *der;* ~**s**, ~ (*Verslehre*) alexandrine

**Alfa·gras** /'alfa-/ *das* alfa grass

**Alge** /'algə/ *die;* ~, ~**n** alga

**Algebra** /'algebra, *österr.:* al'ge:bra/ *die;* ~, (*fachspr.*) **Algebren** algebra

**Algebraiker** *der;* ~**s**, ~, **Algebraikerin** *die;* ~, ~**nen** algebraist

**algebraisch** ❶ *Adj.* algebraic. ❷ *adv.* algebraically

**Algen-:** ~**pest** *die* seaweed plague; ~**pilz** *der* comycete

**Algerien** /al'ge:riən/ (*das*); ~**s** Algeria

**Algerier** *der;* ~**s**, ~, **Algerierin** *die;* ~, ~**nen** ▶ 553 Algerian

**algerisch** *Adj.* ▶ 553 Algerian

**Algier** /'alʒi:ɐ̯/ (*das*); ~**s** ▶ 700 Algiers

**Algorithmus** /algo'rɪtmus/ *der;* ~, **Algorithmen** (*Math.*, *DV*) algorithm

**alias** /'a:li̯as/ *Adv.* alias

**Alibi** /'a:libi/ *das;* ~**s**, ~**s** Ⓐ (*Rechtsw.*) alibi; Ⓑ (*Ausrede*) alibi (*coll.*); excuse

**Alibi-:** ~**frau** *die* token woman; ~**funktion** *die* use as an alibi (*coll.*) *or* excuse; ~**funktion haben** serve as an alibi (*coll.*) *or* excuse

**Alimente** /ali'mɛntə/ *Pl.* (*veralt.*, *noch ugs.*) maintenance *sing.* (*esp. for illegitimate child*); **jmdn. auf** ~ **verklagen** sue sb. for maintenance

**Alk**[1] /alk/ *der;* ~**[e]s**, ~**en** (*Zool.*) auk

**Alk**[2] *der;* ~**s** (*ugs.*) alcohol; booze (*coll.*); **hast du auch was ohne** ~**?** have you got anything non-alcoholic?

**alkäisch** /al'kɛ:ɪʃ/ *Adj.* (*Verslehre*) alcaic

**Alkali** /al'ka:li/ *das;* ~**s**, **Alkalien** alkali

**alkali·frei** *Adj.* (*Werbespr.*) non-alkaline

**alkalisch** *Adj.* (*Chemie*) alkaline

**Alkaloid** /alkalo'i:t/ *das;* ~**[e]s**, ~**e** (*Chemie*) alkaloid

**Alki** /'alki/ *der;* ~**s**, ~**s** (*salopp*) wino (*coll.*)

**Alkohol** /'alkoho:l/ *der;* ~**s**, ~**e** alcohol; **unter** ~ **stehen** (*ugs.*) be under the influence (*coll.*); **jmdn. unter** ~ **setzen** (*ugs.*) get sb. drunk; ⇒ *auch* **ertränken**

**alkohol-, Alkohol-:** ~**abhängig** *Adj.* dependent on alcohol *postpos.;* ~**abhängigkeit** *die* dependence on alcohol; alcohol dependence; ~**arm** *Adj.* low in alcohol *pred.;* ~**ausschank** *der* sale of alcohol[ic drinks]; **Kiosken ist der** ~**ausschank verboten** kiosks are forbidden to sell alcohol; **„kein** ~**ausschank an Jugendliche"** 'no alcohol may be sold to persons under 18'; ~**ein·fluss**, *~**ein·fluß** *der*, ~**ein·wirkung** *die* influence of alcohol *or* drink; **unter** ~**einfluss** *od.* ~**einwirkung [stehen]** [be] under the influence of alcohol *or* drink; ~**fahne** *die* smell of alcohol [on one's breath]; **eine** ~**fahne haben** smell of alcohol; **jmds.** ~**fahne riechen** smell the alcohol on sb.'s breath; ~**frei** *Adj.* Ⓐ (*ohne* ~*gehalt*) non-alcoholic; ~**freie Getränke** soft *or* non-alcoholic drinks; Ⓑ (*ohne* ~*ausschank*) dry ‹country, state, etc.›; Ⓒ (*ohne* ~*genuss*) ‹day, week, etc.› without alcohol; **einen** ~**freien Tag einlegen** spend a day without drinking alcohol; ~**gegner** *der*, ~**gegnerin** *die* opponent of alcohol; ~**gehalt** *der* alcohol content; ~**genuss**, *~**genuß** *der* consumption of alcohol; **infolge** ~**genusses** as a result of consuming alcohol; ~**haltig** *Adj.* containing alcohol *postpos.*, *not pred.;* ~**haltige Getränke** alcoholic drinks; **wenig/stark** ~**haltig sein** have a low/high alcohol content

**Alkoholika** /alko'ho:lika/ *Pl.* alcoholic drinks

**Alkoholiker** *der;* ~**s**, ~, **Alkoholikerin** *die;* ~, ~**nen** alcoholic

**alkoholisch** *Adj.* alcoholic

**alkoholisieren** *tr. V.* Ⓐ (*mit Alkohol versetzen*) alcoholize; Ⓑ (*scherzh.: betrunken machen*) **jmdn.** ~**:** get sb. drunk

**alkoholisiert** *Adj.* inebriated; **in** ~**em Zustand** in a state of inebriation

**Alkoholismus** *der;* ~**:** alcoholism *no art.*

**alkohol-, Alkohol-:** ~**konsum** *der* consumption of alcohol; **er hat in letzter Zeit einen beträchtlichen** ~**konsum** (*ugs.*) he has recently been hitting the bottle (*coll.*); ~**krank** *Adj.* (*Med.*) alcoholic; ~**missbrauch**, *~**mißbrauch** *der* alcohol abuse; ~**pegel** *der* (*scherzh.*) level of alcohol in one's blood; **sein** ~**pegel war schon ganz beträchtlich** he was already well primed (*coll.*); ~**reich** *Adj.* ‹drink, wine, etc.› with a high alcohol content; ~**reich sein** have a high alcohol content; ~**schmuggler** *der*, ~**schmugglerin** *die* bootlegger; ~**spiegel** *der* level of alcohol in one's blood; ~**steuer** *die* duty *or* tax on alcohol; ~**sucht** *die* alcohol addiction; alcoholism; ~**süchtig** *Adj.* addicted to alcohol *postpos.;* alcoholic; ~**süchtige** *der/die; adj. Dekl.* alcoholic; ~**sünder** *der*, ~**sünderin** *die* (*ugs.*) drunk[en] driver; ~**verbot** *das* ban on alcohol; **es herrschte** ~**verbot** alcohol was banned; ~**vergiftung** *die* alcohol[ic] poisoning

**Alkoven** /al'ko:vn̩/ *der;* ~**s**, ~**:** alcove; (*Bettnische*) bed recess

**all** /al/ *Indefinitpron. u. unbest. Zahlw.* ❶ *attr.* (*ganz, gesamt...*) all; **in** ~**er Deutlichkeit** in all clarity; ~**e Freude, die sie empfunden hat** all the joy she felt; ~**es Geld, das ich noch habe** all the money I have left; ~**er Eifer nützte ihm nichts** all his zeal was to no avail; **ich kann diese Leute** ~**e nicht leiden** I can't stand any of these people; **ich will euch** ~**e nicht mehr sehen** I don't want to see any of you again; **die Ärzte verdienen** ~**e sehr viel** doctors all earn a great deal; ~**es Geld spendete sie dem Roten Kreuz** she donated all her money to the Red Cross; ~**es Leid der Welt** all the suffering in the world; ~ **unser/mein** *usw.* **...** all our/my *etc.* ...; ~**es andere/Weitere/Übrige** everything else; ~**es Übrige hat sich nicht geändert** nothing else has changed; ~**es Schöne/Neue/Fremde** everything *or* all that is beautiful/new/strange; ~**es Gute!** all the best!; ~**e Fenster schließen** close all the windows; **sie gaben** ~**e Waffen ab** they handed in all their weapons; **wir/ihr/sie** ~**e** all of us/you/them; we/you/they all; **das sagen sie** ~**e** (*ugs.*) that's what they all say; ~**e Beteiligten/Anwesenden** all those involved/present; **trotz** ~**er Vorbehalte werde ich ...** in spite of all my reservations I shall ...; ~**e beide/**~**e zehn** both of them/all ten of them; ~**e Männer/Frauen/Kinder** all men/women/children; ~**e Mädchen über zwölf Jahre** all girls over twelve; ~**e Mädchen in der Schule** all the girls in the school; ~**e Bewohner der Stadt** all the inhabitants of the town; **ohne** ~**en Anlass** for no reason [at all]; without any reason [at all]; **gegen** ~**e Erwartungen** contrary to all expectations; ~**e Jahre wieder** every year; ~**e fünf Minuten/Meter** every five minutes/metres; **Bücher** ~**er Art** books of all kinds; all kinds of books; **in** ~**er Eile** with all haste; **in** ~**er Ruhe** in peace and quiet; **trotz** ~**er Versuche/Anstrengungen** despite all [his/her/their/*etc.*] attempts/efforts. ❷ *allein stehend* Ⓐ (*gesamt..., sämtlich*) everything; ~**es geht vorüber** everything passes [in time]; ~**es für die Braut/den Bastler** everything for the bride/handicraft enthusiast; **das** ~**es** all that; **ich weiß nicht, was das** ~**es soll** I don't know what all that is supposed to mean; **das ist** ~**es Unsinn** that is all nonsense; **von** ~**em etwas verstehen/wissen** understand/know a bit about everything; **wer** ~**es war** *od.* **wer war** ~**es dort** who was there?; **wen** ~**es habt ihr getroffen?** who did you meet?; **das sind** ~**es Gauner** they're all scoundrels; **was gab es dort** ~**es zu sehen?** what was there to see?; **was es nicht** ~**es gibt!** well, would you believe it!; well, I never!; ~**[es] und jedes** everything; (*wahllos*) anything and everything; **trotz** ~**em** in spite of *or* despite everything; **sie liebt ihren Hund über** ~**es** she loves her dog more than anything else; **zu** ~**em fähig sein** (*fig.*) be capable of anything; ~**es schon mal da gewesen** (*ugs.*) it's all happened before; **das kenne ich** ~**es schon** I've heard it all before; ~**es in** ~**em** all in all; **vor** ~**em** above all; ~**es klar** *od.* **in Ordnung** (*ugs.*) everything's fine *or* (*coll.*) OK; ~**es klar?** everything all right *or* (*coll.*) OK?; **dann treffen wir uns um 5**[00] **Uhr,** ~**es klar?** we'll meet at 5 o'clock then, all right *or* (*coll.*) OK?; **das ist** ~**es** that's all *or* (*coll.*) it; **ist das** ~**es?** is that all *or* (*coll.*) it?; **nach** ~**em, was man hört/weiß** to judge from everything *or* all one hears/knows; Ⓑ (*jeder einzelne*) everyone; ~**e miteinander** all together; **ihr seid/wir sind/sie sind ...,** ~**e miteinander** you/we/they are ..., all of you/us/them; ~**e auf einmal** all at once; **sprecht nicht** ~**e auf einmal!** don't all speak at once; **am besten, wir gehen** ~**e auf einmal zum Chef** the best thing would be for us all to go and see the boss together; ~**e, die ...** all those who ...; **der Kampf** ~**er gegen** ~**e** unfettered competition; **in** ~**em einverstanden sein** agree *or* be agreed on everything; **von** ~**em etwas nehmen** take a bit of everything; **er ist bei** ~**em, was er tut, sehr genau** he is very precise in everything he does; **sie ist in** ~**em sehr empfindlich** she is very sensitive about everything; Ⓒ (*Neutr. Sg.:* ~*e Beteiligten*) ~**es mal herhören!** (*ugs.*) listen everybody!; (*stärker befehlend*) everybody listen!; ~**es war nach Hause gegangen** (*ugs.*) everyone *or* everybody had gone home; ~**es aussteigen!** (*ugs.*) everyone *or* all out!; (*vom Schaffner gesagt*) all change!

**All** *das;* ~**s** space *no art.;* (*Universum*) universe

**all-:** ~**abendlich** ❶ *Adj.* regular evening; ❷ *adv.* every evening; ~**bekannt** *Adj.* (*geh.*) universally known; ~**da** *Adv.* (*veralt.*) there; ~**dem** ⇒ alledem; ~**dieweil[en]** ❶ *Konj.* (*veralt.*) since; because; ❷ *Adv.* all the while

**alle** *Adj.* Ⓐ (*ugs.: verbraucht, verkauft usw.*) ~ **sein** be all gone; ~ **werden** run out; **etw.** ~ **machen** finish sth. off; Ⓑ (*salopp: erschöpft*) all in *pred.;* Ⓒ **jmdn.** ~ **machen** (*salopp*) do sb. in (*sl.*)

**alle·dem** *Pron.: in* **trotz** ~**:** in spite of *or* despite all that; **von** ~ **wusste er nichts** he knew nothing about all that; **an** ~ **ist nichts wahr** there's no truth in any of it; **nichts von** ~**:** nothing of the sort *or* kind; **bei** ~**:** for all that; **zu** ~**:** in addition to *or* on top of all that

**Allee** /a'le:/ *die;* ~, ~**n** avenue

**Allee·baum** *der* avenue tree

**Allegorie** /alego'ri:/ *die;* ~, ~**n** allegory

**Allegorik** /ale'go:rɪk/ *die;* ~**:** allegory

**allegorisch** ❶ *Adj.* allegorical. ❷ *adv.* allegorically

**Allegretto** /ale'grɛto/ *das;* ~**s**, ~**s** *od.* **Allegretti** allegretto

**Allegro** /a'le:gro/ *das;* ~**s**, ~**s** *od.* **Allegri** allegro

**allein** /a'lai̯n/ ❶ *Adj.* Ⓐ (*ohne andere, für sich*) alone; on one's/its own; by oneself/itself; **sie waren** ~ **im Zimmer** they were alone in the room; **ganz** ~**:** all on one's/its own; **jmdn.** ~ **lassen** leave sb. alone *or* on his/her own; ~ **über den Atlantik segeln** sail alone across the Atlantic; Ⓑ (*einsam*) alone. ❷ *adv.* (*ohne Hilfe*) by oneself/itself; on one's/its own; **sie kann** ~ **schwimmen** she can swim by herself *or* on her own; **etw.** ~ **machen** (*herstellen*) make sth. oneself; (*tun*) do sth. oneself; **von** ~ (*ugs.*) by oneself/itself; **das müsstet ihr von** ~ **wissen** you shouldn't have to be told [that]. ❸ *Adv.* Ⓐ (*geh.: ausschließlich*) alone; **er** ~ **trägt die**

*old spelling (see note on page 1707)

**Verantwortung** he alone bears responsibility; it is his responsibility alone; **sie denkt ~ an sich** she thinks solely *or* only of herself; **~ durch den Glauben** by faith alone; only by faith; **nicht ~ ..., sondern auch ...** not only ..., but also ...; **B** (*von allem anderen abgesehen*) **[schon] ~ der Gedanke/[schon] der Gedanke ~:** the mere *or* very thought [of it]; **~ die Nebenkosten** the additional costs alone. **4** *Konj.* (*veralt.*) however; but; **~, es war zu spät** however, it was too late; it was too late, however

**Allein-: ~besitz** *der* sole *or* exclusive property; **im ~besitz von jmdm./in jmds. ~besitz sein** be sb.'s sole *or* exclusive property; **~besitzer** *der*, **~besitzerin** *die* sole owner

**alleine** (*ugs.*) ⇒ allein

**allein-, Allein-: ~erbe** *der*, **~erbin** *die* sole heir; ***~erziehend** *Adj.* single ‹mother, father, parent›; **~erziehende** *der/die; adj. Dekl.* single parent; **~flug** *der* (*Flugw.*) solo flight; **~gang** *der* **A** (*fig.: Tat*) independent initiative; **etw. im ~gang tun** do sth. off one's own bat; **B** (*Sport*) solo run; (*Radfahren*) solo ride; **die Etappe praktisch im ~gang fahren** be out on one's own for practically the whole stage; **ein Tor im ~gang erzielen** score a goal from a solo run; **C** (*Alpinistik*) solo ascent *or* climb; **~gesellschafter** *der*, **~gesellschafterin** *die* (*Rechtsw.*) sole proprietor; **~herrschaft** *die* autocratic rule; (*Diktatur*) dictatorship; **~herrscher** *der*, **~herrscherin** *die* (*auch fig.*) autocrat; (*Diktator, auch fig.*) dictator

**alleinig** *Adj.* sole; sole, exclusive ‹distribution rights›

**allein-, Allein-: ~inhaber** *der*, **~inhaberin** *die* (*Wirtsch.*) sole owner; **~reisende** *der/die* person travelling alone; **~schuld** *die* sole blame *or* responsibility *no indef. art.*; **~sein** *das* **A** (*das Verlassensein*) loneliness; **B** (*das Ungestörtsein*) privacy; ***~stehend** *Adj.* ‹person› living on his/her own *or* alone; (*ledig*) single ‹person›; **ich bin *~stehend** I live on my own *or* alone/am single; **~stehende** *der/die; adj. Dekl.* person living on his/her own *or* alone; (*Ledige[r]*) single person; **ich als ~stehender ...** living on my own I .../as a single person I ...; **~unter·halter** *der*, **~unter·halterin** *die* solo entertainer; **~verdiener** *der*, **~verdienerin** *die* sole earner; **~verschulden** *das* ⇒ **~schuld**; **~vertretung** *die* (*Wirtsch.*) sole agency; (*Politik*) sole representation; **~vertretungs·anspruch** *der* (*Politik*) claim to be the sole legitimate representative; **~vertrieb** *der*: **den ~vertrieb von etw. haben/übernehmen** be/become the sole *or* exclusive distributor of sth.; have acquired sole *or* exclusive distribution rights to sth.

**alle·mal** *Adv.* (*ugs.*) any time (*coll.*); **was der kann, das kann ich doch ~:** anything he can do, I can do too; ⇒ *auch* **ein**[1] 1

**allen·falls** *Adv.* **A** (*höchstens*) at [the] most; at the outside; **~ 40 Leute** 40 people at most *or* at the outside; at most 40 people; **B** (*nötigenfalls*) if need be; if necessary; **C** (*bestenfalls*) at best

**allenthalben** /ˈalənt'halbn̩/ *Adv.* (*geh.*) everywhere

**aller-: ~art** *indekl. unbest. Gattungsz.*; (*veralt.*) all kinds *or* sorts of; **~äußerst...** *Adj.* **A** (*entferntest*) farthest; **B** (*größt...*) extreme; utmost; **mit ~äußerster Vorsicht** with extreme *or* [the] utmost caution; **C** (*schlimmst...*) worst; **im ~äußersten Fall** if the worst comes/came to the worst; **~best...** **1** *Adj.* very best; **~besten Dank** thank you very much indeed; **der/die/das Allerbeste sein** be the best of all; **es wäre das Allerbeste, wenn du ihn selbst fragst** the best thing [of all] would be for you to ask him yourself; **das ist das Allerbeste, was du tun kannst** that's the best thing you can do; **jmdm. das Allerbeste wünschen** wish sb. all the [very] best; **du bist mein Allerbester** you are my darling; **2** *adv.* **am ~besten** best of all; **am ~besten wäre es, wenn ...** the best thing [of all] would be if ...; **~dings** **1** *Adv.* **A** (*einschränkend*) though; **es stimmt ~dings, dass ...** it's true though that ...; **B** (*zustimmend*) [yes,] certainly; **Habe ich dich geweckt? — Allerdings!** Did I wake you up? — You certainly did!; **2** *Partikel* (*Anteil nehmend*) to be sure; **das war ~dings Pech** that was bad luck, to be sure; **~erst...** *Adj.* **A** (*verstärkend: erst...*) very first; **der/die/das ~erste** the very first; **als ~erste[r] etw. tun** be the very first to do sth.; **das ~erste, was ich tun muss** the very first thing I must do; **B** (*best...*) very best; **~frühest...** **1** *Adj.* very earliest; **2** *adv.* **am ~frühesten** earliest of all; **~frühestens** *Adv.* at the very earliest

**Allergen** /alɛrˈge:n/ *das;* **~s**, **~e** (*Med.*) allergen

**Allergie** /alɛrˈgi:/ *die;* **~**, **~n** ▶ 474 (*Med.*) allergy

**Allergiker** /aˈlɛrgikɐ/ *der;* **~s**, **~**, **Allergikerin** *die;* **~**, **~nen** (*Med.*) allergy sufferer

**allergisch** **1** *Adj.* (*Med.*) allergic; **eine ~e Reaktion auf etw.** (*Akk.*) (*auch fig.*) an allergic reaction to sth.; **gegen etw. ~ sein** (*auch fig.*) be allergic to sth. **2** *adv.* **auf etw.** (*Akk.*) **~ reagieren** have an allergic reaction to sth.; **~ auf jmdn./etw. reagieren** (*fig.*) be allergic to sb./sth.

**aller-, Aller-: ~größt...** *Adj.* utmost ‹trouble, care, etc.›; biggest *or* largest ‹car, house, town, etc.› of all; tallest ‹person› of all; **am ~größten sein** be [the] biggest *or* largest/tallest of all; **~hand** *indekl. unbest. Gattungsz.* (*ugs.*) **A** *attr.* all kinds *or* sorts of; **B** *allein stehend* all kinds *or* sorts of things; **das ist ~hand!** (*viel*) that's a lot; (*sehr gut*) that's quite something; **das ist ja** *od.* **doch ~hand!** that's just not on (*Brit. coll.*); that really is the limit (*coll.*); **~heiligen** *das;* **~~s** (*bes. kath. Kirche*) All Saints' Day; All Hallows; **~heiligste** *das;* **~~n** **A** (*Tempelinneres*) inner sanctum; (*jüdisch, orth.*) holy of holies; (*fig.*) holy of holies; inner sanctum; **B** (*kath. Rel.*) Blessed Sacrament; **~herzlichst** **1** *Adj.* warmest ‹thanks, greetings, congratulations›; most cordial ‹reception, welcome, invitation›; **2** *adv.* ‹thank, greet, congratulate› most warmly; ‹welcome› most warmly *or* cordially; **Sie sind ~herzlichst eingeladen ...** you are most cordially invited ...; **~höchst...** **1** *Adj.* highest ... of all; **der ~höchste Gipfel** the highest peak of all; the topmost peak; **der ~höchste Berg der Welt** the highest mountain in the world; **es ist ~höchste Zeit, dass ...** it really is high time that ...; **am ~höchsten sein** be the highest of all; **die ~höchsten Kreise** the very highest circles; **auf ~höchste Anordnung** on orders from the very top; **der ~höchste** (*dichter.*) the Most High; **2** *adv.* **am ~höchsten** ‹fly, jump, etc.› the highest of all; **~höchstens** *Adv.* at the very most

**allerlei** *indekl. unbest. Gattungsz.* all kinds *or* sorts of; *allein stehend* all kinds *or* sorts of things

**Allerlei** *das;* **~s**, **~s** (*Gemisch*) potpourri; (*Durcheinander*) jumble; **Leipziger ~:** 'Leipzig-style' mixed vegetables (*carrots, green beans, peas, celery, kohlrabi, and asparagus*)

**aller-, Aller-: ~letzt...** *Adj.* **A** (*verstärkend*) very last; **der/die/das ~letzte** the very last [one]; **B** (*drückt Ablehnung aus*) most dreadful *or* awful (*coll.*); **das ist [ja** *od.* **wirklich] das Allerletzte** (*ugs.*) that [really] is the absolute limit; **C** (*~neuest...*) very latest; **~liebst** *Adj.* **A** (*verstärkend*) most favourite; **am ~liebsten besuchte er die Großmutter** best of all he liked to go and see his grandmother; **es wäre mir das Allerliebste** *od.* **am ~liebsten, wenn ...** I should like it best of all if ...; **das Allerliebste, was ich habe** my most favourite *or* treasured possession; **ihr Allerliebster/seine Allerliebste** her/his beloved; **B** (*reizend*) enchanting; delightful; **~meist** *Adv.* mostly; for the most part; **~meist...** **1** *Indefinitpron. u. unbest. Zahlw.* **A** (*die größte Menge*) by far the most *attrib.*; **das ~meiste/am ~meisten** most of all/by far the most; **B** (*der größte Teil*) **die ~meisten Gäste** the vast majority of the guests; **die ~meiste Zeit** by far the greatest part of the time; **die ~meisten [der Arbeiter** *usw.*] the vast majority [of the workers *etc.*]; **2** *Adv.* **am ~meisten** most of all; **die am ~meisten befahrene Straße** by far the most travelled road; **~mindest...** *Adj.* slightest; least; **das Allermindeste** the very least; **nicht das Allermindeste** absolutely nothing; **nicht im Allermindesten** not in the least *or* slightest; **zum Allermindesten** at the very least; **~nächst...** **1** *Adj.* very nearest *attrib.*; (*räumliche od. zeitliche Reihenfolge ausdrückend*) very next *attrib.*; very closest ‹relatives›; **in ~nächster Zeit** in the very near future; **am ~nächsten sein** be the nearest of all; **2** *adv.* **am ~nächsten** nearest of all; **~neu[e]st...** *Adj.* very latest *attrib.*; **das Allerneu[e]ste** the very latest; **~nötigst...**, **~notwendigst...** **1** *Adj.* absolutely necessary; **ich habe nur die ~nötigsten** *od.* **~notwendigsten Kleider gepackt** I only packed the clothes that are/were absolutely necessary; **am ~nötigsten** *od.* **~notwendigsten hätte ich ...** what I'm most badly in need of is/are ....; **es am ~nötigsten** *od.* **~notwendigsten haben, etw. zu tun** be most in need of doing sth.; **der hat es am ~nötigsten** *od.* **~notwendigsten!** (*ugs.*) he's a fine one to talk; **das Allernötigste** what is/was absolutely necessary; **2** *adv.* **am ~nötigsten** ‹need etc.› most badly; **~orts** (*veralt.*), **~orten** *Adv.* (*geh.*) everywhere; **~schlimmst...** **1** *Adj.* very worst *attrib.*; **der/die/das Allerschlimmste** *od.* **am ~schlimmsten sein** be the worst of all; **das Allerschlimmste** the worst of all; **sich auf das Allerschlimmste gefasst machen** prepare oneself for the very worst; **2** *adv.* **am ~schlimmsten** worst of all; **~schönst...** **1** *Adj.* most beautiful *attrib.*; loveliest *attrib.*; (*angenehmst...*) very nicest *attrib.*; **in ~schönster Harmonie** in perfect harmony; **das Allerschönste, was ich je gesehen habe** the loveliest thing I have ever seen; **das wäre ja noch das Allerschönste** that would beat everything; **2** *adv.* **am ~schönsten war, dass ...** the best thing of all was that ...; **da werden alle Vorurteile aufs Allerschönste bestärkt** (*iron.*) that's the best possible way of reinforcing everyone's prejudices; **~seelen** *das;* **~~s** (*kath. Kirche*) All Souls' Day; **~seits** *Adv.* **A** (*alle zusammen*) **guten Morgen ~seits!** good morning everyone *or* everybody; **B** (*überall*) on all sides; on every side; **~seits sehr geschätzt sein** be highly regarded by everyone; **~spätestens** *Adv.* at the very latest

**Allerwelts-: ~gesicht/~wort/~mittel** nondescript face/hackneyed word/cure-all

**Allerwelts·kerl** *der* Jack of all trades

**aller-, Aller-: ~wenigst...** **1** *Adj.* least ... of all; *Pl.* fewest ... of all; **er hat von allen das ~wenigste Geld** *od.* **am ~wenigsten Geld** he has the least money of all; **die ~wenigsten [Menschen] wissen das** very few [people] know that; **das Allerwenigste, was er hätte tun können** the very least he could have done; **2** *adv.* **am ~wenigsten abbekommen/arbeiten** get/work [the] least of all; **das hätte ich von ihm am ~wenigsten erwartet** he's the very last person I would have expected that of; **das am ~wenigsten!** anything but that!; **~wenigstens** *Adv.* at the very least; **~werteste** *der; adj. Dekl.* (*ugs. scherzh.*) posterior

**alles** ⇒ **all**

**alle·samt** *Indefinitpron. u. unbest. Zahlw.* (*ugs.*) all [of you/us/them]; **wir ~:** all of us; we all

**Alles-: ~brenner** *der* multi-fuel stove; **~fresser** *der* omnivore; **~kleber** *der* all-purpose adhesive *or* glue; **~könner** *der*, **~könnerin** *die* all-rounder; **~wisser** *der;* **~~s**, **~~**, **~wisserin** *die;* **~~**, **~~nen** (*abwertend*) know-all

**alle·zeit** *Adv.* (*veralt.*) ⇒ **allzeit**

**all-, All-: ~fällig** (*bes. österr., schweiz.*) **1** *Adj.* possible; **~fällige Verluste** any losses which may occur; **Allfälliges** miscellaneous; (*Tagesordnungspunkt*) any other business; ❷ *adv.* **~fällig anfallende Portokosten/~fällig vorkommende Ausnahmen** any postal charges/exceptions which may arise; **~gegenwart** *die (christl. Theol., fig.)* omnipresence; **~gegenwärtig** *Adj. (christl. Theol., fig.)* omnipresent

**all·gemein** ❶ *Adj.* general; universal ‹conscription, suffrage›; universally applicable ‹law, rule›; **auf ~en Wunsch** by popular *or* general request; **zur ~en Überraschung** to everyone's *or* everybody's surprise; **das ~e Wohl** the common good; **im ~en Interesse** in the common interest; in everybody's interest; **~e Redensarten** common expressions; **vom Allgemeinen auf das Besondere schließen** infer the particular from the general; **im Allgemeinen** in general; generally.
❷ *adv.* [A] *(überall, allerseits, von allen)* generally; *(generell, ausnahmslos)* universally; **es ist ~ üblich, das zu tun** it is [the] common practice to do it; **~ verbreitet** widespread; **es ist ~ bekannt, dass ...** it is common knowledge that ...; **~ gängig** common; **~ zugänglich** open to all *or* everybody; **~ gültige Regeln** universally *or* generally applicable rules; **eine ~ gültige Definition/These** a universally *or* generally valid definition/thesis; **etw. ~ gültig formulieren** formulate sth. in universally *or* generally applicable terms; **~ verbindlich** universally binding; **~ verständlich** comprehensible *or* intelligible to all *postpos.*; readily comprehensible *or* intelligible; **es wird ~ diskutiert** it is being discussed by people at large; **wird das ~ gewünscht?** is that the general wish?; [B] *(nicht speziell, oft abwertend: unverbindlich)* ‹write, talk, discuss, examine, be worded› in general terms; **eine ~ gehaltene Einführung** a general introduction; **das kann man nicht so ~ behaupten** one cannot generalize like that; [C] *(umfassend)*; **~ belesen/beschlagen sein** be well read/be knowledgeable about a wide range of subjects; **~ interessiert sein** have a wide range of interests

**allgemein-, Allgemein-: ~befinden** *das (Med.)* general state of health; general condition; **~begriff** *der (Philos., Sprachw.)* general concept; **~besitz** *der (auch fig.)* common property; ***~bildend** *Adj.* ‹school, course, etc.› providing a general *or* an all-round *or (Amer.)* all-around education; **das Zeitunglesen für *~bildend halten** hold that reading newspapers is of general educational value; **~bildung** *die* general *or* all-round *or (Amer.)* all-around education; ***~gültig** ⇒ **allgemein 2A**; **~gültigkeit** *die* universal *or* general applicability/validity; **~gut** *das (fig.)* common knowledge

**Allgemeinheit** *die;* ~, **~en** [A] *(Öffentlichkeit)* general public; public at large; [B] *(Unverbindlichkeit)* generality; [C] *Pl. (Äußerungen)* generalities

**allgemein-, Allgemein-: ~interesse** *das* public interest; **~medizin** *die* general medicine; **~mediziner** *der*, **~medizinerin** *die* general practitioner; GP; **~platz** *der* platitude; commonplace; ***~verbindlich, *~verständlich** ⇒ **allgemein 2A**; **~wissen** *das* general knowledge; **~wohl** *das* public welfare *or* good

**all-, All-: ~gewalt** *die (geh.)* omnipotence; **~gewaltig** *Adj. (geh.)* omnipotent; all-powerful; **der Allgewaltige** the Almighty; **~gütig** *Adj.* all-gracious; **~heil·mittel** *das (auch fig.)* cure-all; panacea; universal remedy

**Allianz** /a'li̯ants/ *die;* ~, **~en** alliance

**Alligator** /ali'ga:tɔr/ *der;* **~s, ~en** /...ga'to:rən/ alligator

**alliieren** /ali'i:rən/ *refl. V.* form an alliance; **sich mit jmdm. ~:** ally oneself with sb.

**alliiert** *Adj.* allied

**Alliierte** *der; adj. Dekl.* ally; **die ~n** the Allies

**Alliteration** /alıtera'tsi̯o:n/ *die;* ~, **~en** *(Verslehre)* alliteration

*old spelling (see note on page 1707)

**all-, All-: ~jährlich** ❶ *Adj.* annual; yearly; ❷ *adv.* annually; every year; **~macht** *die (geh.)* omnipotence; **~mächtig** *Adj.* omnipotent; all-powerful; **der ~mächtige Gott** Almighty God; **~mächtiger Gott!** *(ugs.)* good God!; heavens above!; **~mächtige** *der; adj. Dekl.* **der ~mächtige** Almighty God; the Almighty; **~mächtiger!** good God!; heavens above!

**all·mählich** ❶ *Adv.* gradually; **es wird ~ Zeit** it's about time; **ich werde ~ müde** I'm beginning to get tired; **wir sollten ~ gehen** it's time we got going. ❷ *adj.* gradual

**Allmende** /al'mɛndə/ *die;* ~, **~n** common land

**all-: ~monatlich** ❶ *Adj.* monthly; ❷ *adv.* monthly; every month; **~morgendlich** ❶ *Adj.* regular morning; ❷ *adv.* every morning; **~nächtlich** ❶ *Adj.* nightly; ❷ *adv.* nightly; every night

**Allonge·perücke** /a'lõ:ʒə-/ *die* full-bottomed wig

**allo-, Allo-: ~path** /-'pa:t/ *der;* **~~en, ~~en** allopath; **~pathie** /-pa'ti:/ *die;* **~~:** allopathy; **~pathin** *die;* **~~, ~~nen** allopath; **~pathisch** ❶ *Adj.* allopathic; ❷ *adv.* allopathically; **~phon** *das;* **~~s, ~~e** *(Sprachw.)* allophone

**Allotria** /a'lo:tria/ *das;* **~s** *od. Pl.* skylarking; **~ treiben** skylark; lark about *(coll.)*

**All-: ~parteien·regierung** *die* all-party government; **~rad·antrieb** *der (Kfz-W.)* all-wheel drive

**Allround-** /'ɔ:l'raʊnd-/ all-round; all-around *(Amer.)*

**Allround·man** /'ɔ:l'raʊndmən/ *der;* **~s, Allroundmen** /'ɔ:l'raʊndmən/ all-rounder

**all-, All-: ~seitig** ❶ *Adj.* [A] *(allgemein)* general; all-round, *(Amer.)* all-around *attrib.*; **zur ~seitigen Zufriedenheit** to the satisfaction of all *or* everyone; [B] *(umfassend)* comprehensive; **eine ~seitige Ausbildung** an all-round *or (Amer.)* all-around education; ❷ *adv.* [A] *(allgemein)* generally; **man war ~seitig einverstanden** there was agreement on all sides *or* general agreement; **~seitig geachtet** highly regarded by everyone; [B] *(umfassend)* comprehensively; **~seitig gebildet sein** have had an all-round *or (Amer.)* all-around education; **~seitig begabt/interessiert sein** have all-round *or (Amer.)* all-around talents/interests; **~seits** *Adv.* everywhere; on all sides; *(in jeder Hinsicht)* in all respects; in every respect; **~seits geschätzt** highly regarded by everyone; **~strom·gerät** *das (Elektrot.)* AC/DC appliance; **~stündlich** ❶ *Adj.* hourly; ❷ *adv.* hourly; every hour

**All·tag** *der* [A] *(Werktag)* weekday; **ein Mantel für den ~:** a coat for everyday wear; **zum ~ gehören** *(fig.)* be part of everyday life; [B] *(Einerlei)* daily routine; **der graue ~:** the dull routine of everyday life; **der ~ der Ehe** the day-to-day realities of married life; **morgen geht der graue ~ wieder los** it's back to the daily grind tomorrow

**all·täglich** ❶ *Adj.* [A] /'-'--/ *(gewöhnlich)* ordinary ‹face, person, appearance, etc.›; everyday ‹topic, event, sight›; commonplace ‹remark›; **ein nicht ~er Anblick** a sight one doesn't see every day; **etw. Alltägliches sein** be an everyday occurrence; **es ist nichts Alltägliches, wenn ...** it's not every day that ...; it doesn't happen every day that ...; [B] *(werktäglich)* everyday, workaday *attrib.* ‹clothes›; [C] /'-'--/ *(täglich)* daily.
❷ *adv.* [A] *(werktäglich)* [on] weekdays; [B] /'-'--/ *(täglich)* daily; every day

**Alltäglichkeit** *die;* ~, **~en** [A] *(das Alltäglichsein)* ordinariness; [B] *(Gewohnheit)* **eine ~ sein/zur ~ werden** be/become routine *or* commonplace; [C] *(alltäglicher Vorgang)* everyday occurrence

**all·tags** *Adv.* [on] weekdays

**Alltags-** everyday *attrib.*; of everyday life *postpos., not pred.*; **~pflicht** daily duty

**Alltags-: ~kleidung** *die* everyday *or* workaday clothes *pl.*; **~mensch** *der* ordinary person; **~sprache** *die (Sprachw.)* everyday language; **~trott** *der (abwertend)* daily round *or* grind; **jetzt geht der ~trott wieder los** now it's back to the daily grind

**all·um·fassend** ❶ *Adj.* all-embracing; encyclopaedic ‹knowledge›. ❷ *adv.* ‹plan, inform› in comprehensive detail; **~ gebildet sein** have had an all-round *or (Amer.)* all-around education

**Allüren** /a'ly:rən/ *Pl. (meist abwertend)* behaviour *sing.*; *(geziertes Benehmen)* affectations; airs and graces

**Alluvium** /a'lu:vi̯ʊm/ *das;* **~s** *(Geol.)* Holocene epoch

**all-, All-: ~wetter·straße** *die* all-weather road; **~wissend** *Adj.* omniscient; **er tut, als wäre er ~wissend** he acts as if he knew everything; **~wissenheit** *die;* **~~:** omniscience; **~wöchentlich** ❶ *Adj.* weekly; ❷ *adv.* weekly; every week; **~zeit** *Adv. (veralt.)* always; **~zeit bereit!** be prepared!

**all·zu** *Adv.* all too; **er war nicht ~ begeistert** he was not too *or* not all that enthusiastic; **nicht ~ viele** not all that many *(coll.)*; not too many; **kein ~ großes Gewicht** not too heavy a weight; **~ viele Fehler** far too many mistakes; **~ bald** all too soon; **~ früh** all too early; (~ *bald*) all too soon; **nicht ~ früh** not too early; **etw. ~ gern mögen** like sth. only too much; **etw. ~ gern tun** do sth. only too willingly; **ich möchte es doch ~ gern machen** I would be only too pleased *or* delighted to do it; **ich esse zwar Fisch, aber nicht ~ gern** I'll eat fish but I'm not all that fond *(coll.) or* not overfond of it; **~ lange** too long; **~ oft** too often; **nicht ~ oft** not too often; not all that often *(coll.)*; **~ sehr** too much; **~ sehr enttäuscht/begeistert** only too disappointed/enthusiastic; **nicht ~ sehr** not too much; not all that much *(coll.)*; **etw. ~ sehr/nicht ~ sehr mögen** like sth. all too much/not like sth. too much *or (coll.)* all that much; **nicht ~ sehr interessiert** not too *or (coll.)* not all that interested; **ich habe mich ~ sehr/nicht ~ sehr bemüht** I tried only too hard/did not try too hard; **~ viel** too much; **~ viel ist ungesund** one should never overdo things; you can have too much of a good thing

**All·zweck-** multi-purpose

**All·zweck-: ~halle** *die* multi-purpose hall; **~tuch** *das; Pl.* **~tücher** multi-purpose *or* all-purpose cloth

**Alm** /alm/ *die;* ~, **~en** mountain pasture; Alpine pasture

**Alm·ab·trieb** *der: driving of the cattle down from the mountain pastures in autumn*

**Almanach** /'almanax/ *der;* **~s, ~e** *(Buchw.)* *(hist.)* almanac; *(eines Verlages)* yearbook *(containing a selection from the firm's publications during the year)*

**Alm-: ~auf·trieb** *der: driving of the cattle up to the mountain pastures in spring;* **~hütte** *die* Alpine hut

**Almosen** /'almo:zn̩/ *das;* **~s, ~** [A] *(veralt.: Spende)* alms *pl.*; **von ~ leben** live on charity; [B] *(abwertend: dürftiges Entgelt)* pittance

**Alm-: ~rausch** *der (österr., südd.)* Alpine rose; alpenrose; **~wirtschaft** *die* Alpine farming *no art.*

**Aloe** /'a:loe/ *die;* ~, **~n** aloe

**Alp**[1] /alp/ *die;* ~, **~en** *(bes. schweiz.)* ⇒ **Alm**

***Alp**[2] ⇒ **Alb**[2]

**Alpaka**[1] /al'paka/ *das;* **~s, ~s** *(Lama, Wolle)* alpaca

**Alpaka**[2] *der;* **~s** *(Gewebe)* alpaca

**Alpaka**[3] *das;* **~s** *(veralt.: Neusilber)* German silver; nickel silver

**Alpaka·wolle** *die* alpaca wool

**Alp-: ~druck** ⇒ **Albdruck**; **~drücken** ⇒ **Albdrücken**

**Alpen** *Pl.* **die ~:** the Alps

**Alpen-** Alpine

**alpen-, Alpen-: ~dollar** *der (scherzh.)* [Austrian] schilling; **~glühen** *das;* **~~s** alpenglow; **~jäger** *Pl. (Milit.)* Alpine Troops; **~land** *das* Alpine country *or* region; **~ländisch** /-lɛndıʃ/ *Adj.* ‹music, customs, dances› of the Alpine region; ‹goods› from the Alpine region; **~pass**, ***~paß** *der* Alpine pass; **~republik** *die* (*ugs.*) Alpine Republic (*Austria or Switzerland*); **~rose** *die* rhododendron; Alpine rose; **~veilchen** *das* cyclamen; **~vorland** *das* foothills *pl.* of the Alps

**Alpha** /'alfa/ *das;* **~[s]**, **~[s]** alpha

**Alphabet** /alfa'be:t/ *das;* **~[e]s**, **~e** alphabet

**alphabetisch** ❶ *Adj.* alphabetical. ❷ *adv.* alphabetically; **etw. ~ ordnen** arrange sth. in alphabetical order *or* alphabetically

**alphabetisieren** *tr. V.* [A] (*ordnen*) arrange in alphabetical order *or* alphabetically; alphabetize; [B] (*lesen u. schreiben lehren*) **jmdn. ~:** teach sb. to read and write

**Alphabetisierung** *die;* ~ [A] (*das Ordnen*) alphabetization; [B] (*das Lehren*) teaching literacy skills; **eine Kampagne zur ~ der Bevölkerung** a campaign against illiteracy in the population

**alpha·numerisch** (*DV*) ❶ *Adj.* alphanumeric. ❷ *adv.* alphanumerically

**Alpha-: ~strahlen** *Pl.* (*Kernphysik*) alpha rays; **~teilchen** *das* (*Kernphysik*) alpha particle

**Alp·horn** *das* alpenhorn

**alpin** /al'pi:n/ *Adj.* [A] Alpine; **~e Kombination** (*Ski*) Alpine combined [event]; [B] (*Bergsteigen*) mountaineering

**Alpinismus** *der;* **~:** Alpinism *no art.*

**Alpinist** *der;* **~en**, **~en** Alpinist

**Alpinistik** *die;* **~:** Alpinism *no art.*

**Alpinistin** *die;* ~, **~nen** Alpinist

**alpinistisch** *Adj.* mountaineering *attrib.*

**Älpler** /'ɛlplɐ/ *der;* **~s**, ~, **Älplerin** *die;* ~, **~nen** inhabitant of the Alps

**Alp·traum** ⇒ **Albtraum**

**Alraune** /al'raune/ *die;* ~, **~n** mandrake

**als¹** *Konj.* [A] (*zeitlich*) when; (*während*) as; **~ wir zu Hause ankamen, [da] fing es an zu regnen** when *or* after we had arrived home, it started to rain; **gleich ~:** as soon as; **damals, ~:** [in the days] when; **gerade ~:** just as; **gerade ~ Tante Ida hier war** just when Aunt Ida was here; [B] (*nach Komp.*) than; **mehr/weniger ~:** more/less than; **mehr ~ arbeiten kann ich nicht** I can't do more than work; [C] (*bei Vergleichen*) **niemand/nirgends anders ~:** nobody/nowhere but; **mir fehlt nichts weiter, ~ dass ...** there is nothing wrong with me other than that ...; **sie arbeiten mit anderen Methoden ~ wir** they work with different methods from ours; **alles andere ~:** anything but; **kein anderer** *od.* **niemand anderes ~ Karl** none other than Karl; **anders ~ wir sein/leben** be different/live differently from us; **so viel/so weit ~ möglich** as much/as far as possible; **so bald/schnell ~ möglich** as soon/as quickly as possible; ⇒ *auch* **sowohl**; [D] (*bei Modalsätzen*) as if; as though; **~ ob** *od.* **wenn** as if; as though; **~ ob ich das nicht wüsste!** as if I didn't know; **~ ob das neu wäre!** as if that were something new; [E] (*in der Eigenschaft*) as; **~ Rentner/Arzt** as a pensioner/a doctor; **sich ~ Held fühlen** feel oneself [to be] a hero; **sich ~ wahr/falsch erweisen** prove [to be] true/false; **in seiner/ihrer Eigenschaft ~ ...** in his/her capacity as ...; [F] (*eine Folge ausdrückend*) **die Kinder sind zu klein, ~ dass sie das verstehen könnten** the children are too young to understand that; **die Zeit war zu kurz, ~ dass wir ...** time was too short for us to ...; [G] (*einen Grund ausdrückend*) **umso ..., ~ ...** all the more ... since *or* in that ...; [H] (*veralt.: vor Aufzählungen*) **~ [da sind]** to wit; namely; ⇒ *auch* **insofern**

**als²** *Adv.* (*westmd.*) [A] (*immer*) **~ etw. tun** keep on doing sth.; **gehen Sie ~ geradeaus** keep going straight on *or* ahead; [B] (*manchmal*) sometimes

**als-: ~bald** *Adv.* (*geh. veralt.*) (*sogleich*) immediately; at once; (*kurz danach*) soon; **~baldig** *Adj.* (*Papierdt.*) immediate; **„zum ~baldigen Verbrauch bestimmt"** 'for immediate consumption'; **~dann** *Adv.* (*geh. veralt.*) then

**also** /'alzo/ ❶ *Adv.* [A] (*folglich*) so; therefore; **~ kommst du mit?** so you're coming too?; you're coming too, then?; [B] (*veralt.: so*) thus. ❷ *Partikel* [A] (*das heißt*) that is; [B] (*nach Unterbrechung*) well [then]; **~, wie ich schon sagte** well [then], as I was saying; [C] (*verstärkend*); **~, kommst du jetzt oder nicht?** well, are you coming now or not?; **na ~!** there you are[, you see]; **~ schön** well all right then; **~ so was/nun!** well, I don't know; well, really; **~, so eine Frechheit** well, what a cheek; **~, gute Nacht** goodnight then; **~ dann** right then

**Als-ob** *das;* ~ (*Philos.*) **die Philosophie des ~:** the philosophy of 'as-if'

**alt** /alt/, **älter** /'ɛltɐ/, **ältest...** /'ɛltəst.../ *Adj.* [A] ▶ 76 old; **Alt und Jung** old and young; **seine ~en Eltern** his aged parents; **hier werde ich nicht ~** (*fig. ugs.*) I won't be staying here long; **das Alte Testament** the Old Testament; **die Alte Welt** the Old World; **~ aussehen** (*fig. salopp*) be in the cart (*sl.*); **eine drei Jahre ~e Tochter** a three-year-old daughter; **wie ~ bist du?** how old are you?; **man ist so ~, wie man sich fühlt** you're only as old as you feel; **aus Alt mach Neu** give your coat/furniture *etc.* a new lease of life; **immer die ~e Platte** *od.* **Leier** it's always the same old story; ⇒ *auch* **Dame**; **Eisen**; **Hase**; **Herr**; [B] (*nicht mehr frisch*) old; **~es Brot** stale bread; [C] (*vom letzten Jahr*) old; **~e Äpfel/Kartoffeln** last year's apples/potatoes; **im ~en Jahr** (*dieses Jahr*) this year; (*letztes Jahr*) last year; [D] (*seit langem bestehend*) ancient; old; **ein ~es Volk/ein ~er Brauch** an ancient people/an ancient *or* old custom; **eine ~e Freundschaft** a long-standing friendship; **in ~er Freundschaft, dein ...** yours, as ever, ...; [E] (*langjährig*) long-standing ‹acquaintance›; long-serving ‹employee›; [F] (*antik, klassisch*) ancient; [G] (*vertraut*) old familiar ‹streets, sights, etc.›; **ganz der/die Alte sein** be just the same; **es bleibt alles beim Alten** things will stay as they were; **das ist nicht das ~e Prag** it's not the old Prague I/we *etc.* knew; **alles geht seinen ~en Gang** everything goes on just as before; [H] (*ugs.*) (*vertraulich*) **~er Freund/~es Haus!** old friend/pal (*coll.*); (*bewundernd*) **ein ~er Fuchs/Gauner** an old fox/rascal; (*verstärkend*) **die ~e Hexe/der ~e Geizkragen** the old witch/skinflint

**Alt¹** *der;* **~s**, **~e** (*Musik*) [A] (*Stimmlage*) alto; (*Frauenstimme*) contralto; alto; [B] (*im Chor*) altos *pl.*; contraltos *pl.*; [C] (*Sängerin*) contralto; alto

**Alt²** *das;* **~[s]**, **~:** *top fermented, dark beer*

**Altan** /al'ta:n/ *der;* **~[e]s**, **~e** (*Archit.*) balcony

**Altar** /al'ta:ɐ̯/ *der;* **~[e]s**, **Altäre** /al'tɛ:rə/ altar; **eine Frau zum ~ führen** (*geh.*) lead a woman to the altar; **jmdn./etw. auf dem ~ des Vaterlands opfern** (*fig.*) sacrifice sb./sth. for one's country

**Altar-: ~bild** *das* altarpiece; **~gerät** *das* altar furniture; **~raum** *der* chancel

**alt-, Alt-: ~backen** *Adj.* [A] (*trocken*) stale ‹bread, roll, etc.›; [B] (*abwertend: altmodisch*) outdated ‹ideas, views, policies›; old-fashioned ‹clothes›; **~bau** *der; Pl.* **~~ten** old building; **~bauer** *der;* **~~n**, **~~n** old farmer; **~bäuerin** *die* old farmer's wife; **~bau·wohnung** *die* flat (*Brit.*) *or* (*Amer.*) apartment in an old building; old flat (*Brit.*) *or* (*Amer.*) apartment; **~bekannt** *Adj.* well-known; **~bewährt** *Adj.* well-tried; long-standing ‹tradition, acquaintanceship›; **~bier** *das: top fermented, dark beer;* **~bundes·kanzler** *der* former Federal Chancellor; **~bundes·präsident** *der* former Federal President; **~christlich** *Adj.* early Christian; **~deutsch** *Adj.* old German; German Renaissance ‹painting, art, etc.›

**Alte¹** *der; adj. Dekl.* [A] (*alter Mann*) old man; **komischer ~r** (*Theater*) comic old man; [B] (*salopp*) (*Vater, Ehemann*) old man (*coll.*); (*Chef*) governor (*coll.*); boss (*coll.*); [C] (*österr.: Wein*) *fully fermented wine*

**Alte²** *die; adj. Dekl.* [A] (*alte Frau*) old woman; **komische ~** (*Theater*) comic old woman; [B] (*salopp*) (*Mutter*) old woman (*coll.*); (*Ehefrau*) missis (*coll.*); old woman (*coll.*); (*Chefin*) boss (*coll.*)

**Alte³** *das; adj. Dekl.* **am ~n hängen** cling to the past; **~s und Neues** the old and the new; **er kann nichts ~s wegwerfen** he cannot throw anything old away

**Alte⁴** *Pl.; adj. Dekl.* [A] (*alte Menschen*) old people; [B] **die ~n** (*salopp: Eltern*) my/his *etc.* old man and old woman (*coll.*); (*Zool.: Tiereltern*) the parents; (*geh.: Menschen der Antike*) the ancients

**alt-, Alt-: ~ehrwürdig** *Adj.* (*geh.*) venerable; time-honoured ‹customs›; **~eingeführt** *Adj.* old-established; **~eingesessen** *Adj.* old-established; **~eingesessene** *der/die; adj. Dekl.* old-established inhabitant; **~eisen** *das* scrap iron; **~englisch** *Adj.* Old English

**Alten-: ~heim** *das* old people's home; old-age home (*Amer.*); **~pfleger** *der*, **~pflegerin** *die* geriatric nurse; **~tages·stätte** *die* old people's day centre; **~teil** *das: portion of farm property and certain rights retained by a farmer on handing over to his successor;* **sich aufs ~teil zurückziehen** (*fig.*) retire; **jmdn. aufs ~teil setzen** (*fig.*) send sb. into retirement; **~wohn·heim** *das* old people's home

**älter** /'ɛltɐ/ ❶ ⇒ **alt**. ❷ *Adj.* (*nicht mehr jung*) elderly; **eine Melodie für unsere ~en Hörer** a tune for our older listeners; ⇒ *auch* **Mitbürger**

**Alter** *das;* **~s**, ~ ▶ 76 [A] age; (*hohes ~*) old age; **im ~:** in one's old age; **mit dem ~:** with age; **er ist in meinem ~:** he is my age; **in meinem ~ wirst du sehen, dass ...** when you are my age you will see that ...; **im ~ von** at the age of; **eine Frau mittleren ~s** a middle-aged woman; **Kinder in diesem ~:** children of this age; **~ schützt vor Torheit nicht** (*Spr.*) there's no fool like an old fool (*prov.*); [B] (*alte Menschen*) old people *no art.*; [C] (*Menschen einer Altersstufe*) age group

**Alterchen** *das;* **~s**, ~ (*ugs.*) grandad (*coll.*)

**Ältere** *der/die; adj. Dekl.* [A] (*älterer Mensch*) older person/man/woman; **für uns ~:** for us older people; [B] (*bei Namen*) elder; **Hans Holbein der ~:** Hans Holbein the Elder

**Alter Ego** /'altɐ 'e:go/ *das;* ~ ~ (*Psych.; geh.: Freund*) alter ego

**altern** ❶ *itr. V.; mit sein* [A] (*älter werden*) age; [B] (*reifen*) mature. ❷ *tr. V.* (*alt machen*) age, mature ‹wine, spirits›

**alternativ** /altɛrna'ti:f/ ❶ *Adj.* (*auch: Industriekultur usw. ablehnend*) alternative. ❷ *adv.* [A] (*die Wahl lassend*) alternatively; [B] (*Industriekultur ablehnend*) ‹work, farm› using alternative methods; **~ leben/einkaufen** adopt an alternative life style/do one's shopping in alternative shops

**Alternativ·bewegung** *die* alternative movement

**Alternative¹** *die;* ~, **~n** alternative; **jmdn. vor die ~ stellen, mehr Miete zu zahlen oder auszuziehen** give sb. the alternative of either paying more rent or moving out

**Alternative²** *der/die; adj. Dekl.* supporter of the alternative society

**Alternativ-: ~energie** *die* alternative energy; **~kultur** *die* alternative culture

**alternieren** *itr. V.* alternate

**alt·erprobt** *Adj.* well-tried

**alters** *in* **seit ~, von ~ her** (*geh.*) from time immemorial

**alters-, Alters-: ~ab·stand** *der* age difference; **~an·gabe** *die* details *pl.* of one's age; **[nicht] zur ~angabe verpflichtet sein** [not] be obliged to give one's age; **~aufbau** *der* age structure; **~bedingt** ❶ *Adj.* occurring at a particular age *postpos.*, *not pred.*; (*im hohen Alter*) due to *or* caused by old age *postpos.*; ❷ *adv.* in relation to [one's/its] age; (*durch hohes Alter*) as a result of old age; **~beschwerden** *Pl.* complaints of old age; **~erscheinung** *die* sign of old age; **~fleck** *der* age spot; liver spot; **~gemäß** ❶ *Adj.* ‹behaviour, education, etc.› appropriate to one's/its age; ❷ *adv.* in a manner appropriate to one's/

a

# Altersangaben

## Wie alt?

***Wie alt ist sie?***
= How old is she?, What age is she?

***Sie ist vierzig [Jahre alt]***
= She is forty [years old] *od.* (*formeller*) forty years of age

***Er ist gerade sechzig geworden***
= He has just turned sixty

***im Alter von zwanzig Jahren, mit zwanzig***
= at the age of twenty, at twenty

***ein Fünfzigjähriger***
= a fifty-year-old [man], a man of fifty

***eine Fünfzigjährige***
= a fifty-year-old [woman], a woman of fifty

***ein zehnjähriges Mädchen***
= a ten-year-old girl

***ein achtzigjähriger Rentner***
= an eighty-year-old pensioner

## Älter oder jünger?

***Ich bin älter als du***
= I'm older than you [are]

***Sie ist viel jünger als er***
= She's much younger than him *od.* than he is

***Er ist vier Jahre älter als ich***
= He's four years older than me *od.* (*formeller*) four years my senior

***Du bist zwanzig Jahre jünger als sie***
= You're twenty years younger than her *od.* (*formeller*) twenty years her junior

***Sie sind gleich alt** od. **gleichaltrig***
= They are the same age

***Sie ist [genau]so alt wie Martin***
= She is [just] the same age as Martin

## Ungefähres Alter

***Er ist um die fünfzig***
= He's about fifty

***Sie ist etwas über sechzig***
= She's just over *od.* a little over sixty

***Er wird bald vierzig***
= He'll soon be forty, He's nearly forty

***Sie geht auf die siebzig zu***
= She's getting on for seventy

***Sie sind in den Sechzigern***
= They're in their sixties

***Er ist Ende/Anfang/Mitte dreißig***
= He's in his late thirties/early thirties/mid-thirties

***Er ist noch ein Teenager***
= He is still a teenager *od.* in his teens

***Er ist gerade zehn geworden***
= He's just ten

***Das Kind ist noch keine zehn Jahre alt***
= The child is barely ten years old

***für Kinder unter zwölf [Jahren]***
= for the under-twelves *od.* under-12s

***für alle über sechzig***
= for the over-sixties *od.* over-60s

***Sie fühlt sich/sieht aus wie zwanzig***
= She feels/looks like twenty

its age; **das Kind entwickelt sich/spielt ~gemäß** the child is developing/playing as it should at its age; **~genosse** *der*, **~genossin** *die* contemporary; person/child of the same age; **meine ~genossen** my contemporaries; people of my age; **er ist ein ~genosse von mir** he is the same age as I am; he is my age; **~grenze** *die* age limit; (*für Rente*) retirement age; **~gründe** *Pl.* reasons of age; **~gruppe** *die* age group; **~heim** *das* old people's home; old-age home (*Amer.*); **~herz** *das* ▶474| (*Med.*) *heart which has undergone physiological changes due to old age;* **~jahr** *das* (*schweiz.*) ⇒ **Lebensjahr**; **~klasse** *die* (*bes. Sport*) age group; **~leiden** *das* complaint of old age; **~los** *Adj.* ageless; **~mäßig** ❶ *Adj.* according to age *postpos., not pred.;* ❷ *adv.* (*dem Alter nach*) according to age; (*in Bezug auf das Alter*) as far as age is concerned; **~präsident** *der*, **~präsidentin** *die* president by seniority; **der ~präsident des Bundestages** the oldest member of the Bundestag, acting as president; **~rente** *die* old-age pension; **~ruhe·geld** *das* retirement pension; **~schwach** *Adj.* old and infirm ‹person›; old and weak ‹animal›; [old and] decrepit ‹object›; **~schwäche** *die* (*bei Menschen*) [old] age and infirmity; (*bei Tieren*) [old] age and weakness; (*von Dingen*) [age and] decrepitude; **~sicherung** *die* provision for one's old age; **~sichtig** *Adj.* presbyopic (*Med.*); **~sichtigkeit** *die* ▶474| presbyopia (*Med.*); **~sitz** *der* retirement home; **er wählte Genf als seinen ~sitz** he chose to spend his retirement in Geneva; **~starrsinn** *der* obstinacy of old age; **~stil** *der* later style; **~stufe** *die* age; **~unterschied** *der* age difference; **~versorgung** *die* provision for one's old age; **gibt es hier eine betriebliche ~versorgung?** do you have a pension scheme here?; **~werk** *das* later work; (*Gesamtheit*) later works *pl.*

**Altertum** *das;* **~s, Altertümer** /-ty:mɐ/ Ⓐ antiquity *no art.;* **das deutsche ~:** early German history; Ⓑ *Pl.* (*antike Kunstgegenstände*) antiquities

**Altertümelei** *die;* **~, ~en** archaism

**altertümeln** /ˈaltɐty:mln̩/ *itr. V.* archaize

**altertümlich** ❶ *Adj.* ancient ‹building, monument, etc.›; old-fashioned ‹dress, handwriting, etc.›; antiquated, old-fashioned ‹appliance, device, vehicle, etc.›. ❷ *adv.* ‹dress, furnish, decorate› in an old-fashioned style; ‹work, function, etc.› in an antiquated manner

**Altertümlichkeit** *die;* **~** ⇒ **altertümlich**: ancientness; old-fashionedness; antiquatedness

**Altertums-: ~forscher** *der*, **~forscherin** *die* archaeologist; **~forschung** *die*, **~kunde** *die* archaeology *no art.;* **~wert** *der: in* **~wert haben** have antique value

**Alterung** *die;* **~, ~en** Ⓐ (*das Altwerden*) ageing; Ⓑ (*von Werkstoffen*) ageing; (*von Legierungen*) ageing; age-hardening; Ⓒ (*von Wein usw.*) ageing; maturing

**Alterungs·prozess**, ***Alterungs·prozeß** *der* ageing process

**Älteste** /ˈɛltəstə/ *der/die; adj. Dekl.* Ⓐ (*Dorf~, Vereins~, Kirchen~ usw.*) elder; Ⓑ (*Sohn, Tochter*) eldest

**Ältesten·rat** *der* Ⓐ (*Bundesrepublik Deutschland*) *all-party parliamentary committee, which assists the Bundestag President in carrying out his duties and in regulating parliamentary business;* Ⓑ (*Völkerk.*) council of elders

**alt-, Alt-: ~flöte** *die* (*Querflöte*) alto *or* bass flute; (*Blockflöte*) alto *or* treble recorder; **~fränkisch** (*ugs. scherzh.*) ❶ *Adj.* old-fashioned; ❷ *adv.* in an old-fashioned way; **~französisch** *das* Old French; **~gedient** *Adj.* long-serving; **~glas·behälter** *der* bottle bank; **~gold** *das* old gold; **~griechisch** *Adj.* ancient Greek; (*Ling.*) classical *or* ancient Greek; ⇒ *auch* **deutsch, Deutsch, Deutsche**[2]; **~griechisch** *das* classical *or* ancient Greek; **~handel** *der* second-hand trade; **~her·gebracht** *Adj.* traditional; **~herren·mannschaft** *die* (*Sport*): *team of players over thirty-two;* ≈ over-thirties' team; **~hoch·deutsch** *Adj.* Old High German; **~hoch·deutsch** *das* Old High German

**Altist** *der;* **~en, ~en** (*Musik*) alto

**Altistin** *die;* **~, ~nen** (*Musik*) alto; contralto

**alt-, Alt-: ~jüngferlich** /-jʏŋfɐlɪç/ ❶ *Adj.* old-maidish; ❷ *adv.* like an old maid/old maids; **~kanzler** *der* former Chancellor; ex-Chancellor; **~katholik** *der*, **~katholikin** *die* Old Catholic; **~katholisch** *Adj.* Old Catholic; **~kleider·sammlung** *die* collection of old clothes; **~klug; ~kluger, ~klugst...** ❶ *Adj.* precocious; ❷ *adv.* precociously; **~klugheit** *die* precociousness; **~lage** *die* (*Musik*) alto range; **in der ~lage singen** be an alto; **~last** Ⓐ (*Ökologie*) old, improperly disposed of harmful waste *no indef. art.;* Ⓑ (*fig.*) inherited problem; **eine ~last aus den 60er-Jahren** a hangover from the sixties

**ältlich** /ˈɛltlɪç/ *Adj.* rather elderly; oldish

**alt-, Alt-: ~material** *das* scrap; **~meister** *der* Ⓐ (*Vorbild*) doyen; Ⓑ (*Sport*) ex-champion; former champion; **~meisterin** *die* Ⓐ (*Vorbild*) doyenne; Ⓑ (*Sport*) ex-champion; former champion; **~metall** *das* scrap metal; **~modisch** ❶ *Adj.* old-fashioned; ❷ *adv.* in an old-fashioned way; **~öl** *das* used oil; **~papier** *das* waste paper; **~partie** *die* (*Musik*) alto part; **~philologe** *der* classical scholar; **~philologie** *die* classical studies *pl., no art.;* **~philologin** *die* classical scholar; **~philologisch** *Adj.* classical; **~römisch** *Adj.* ancient Roman; **~rosa** *Adj.* old rose

**Altruismus** /altruˈɪsmus/ *der;* **~** (*geh.*) altruism

**Altruist** *der;* **~en, ~en, Altruistin** *die;* **~, ~nen** (*geh.*) altruist

**altruistisch** (*geh.*) ❶ *Adj.* altruistic. ❷ *adv.* altruistically

*old spelling (see note on page 1707)

**alt-, Alt-:** ~**sänger** *der* alto; ~**sängerin** *die* alto; contralto; ~**saxophon** *das* alto saxophone; ~**schlüssel** *der* (*Musik*) alto clef; ~**schnee** *der* old snow; ~**schneedecke** *die* layer *or* covering of old snow; ~**silber** *das* Ⓐ (*veralt.: bereits verarbeitet*) old silver; Ⓑ (*Silberart*) oxidized silver; ~**sprachler** /-ʃpra:xlɐ/ *der;* ~~**s**, ~~; ~**sprachlerin** *die;* ~~, ~~**nen** classicist; ~**sprachlich** *Adj.* classical; ~**sprachliches Gymnasium** *grammar school concentrating on classical rather than modern languages;* ~**stadt** *die* old [part of the] town; **die Düsseldorfer** ~**stadt** the old part of Düsseldorf; ~**stadt·sanierung** *die* renovation of the old part of a/the town; ~**stein·zeit** *die* Old Stone Age; Palaeolithic Age; ~**stein·zeitlich** *Adj.* Palaeolithic; ~**stimme** *die* alto voice; (*von Frau*) alto *or* contralto voice; ~**testamentarisch**, ~**testamentlich** *Adj.* Old Testament *attrib.;* ~**überliefert** *Adj.* traditional; ~**väterisch** /-fɛ:tərɪʃ/ ❶ *Adj.* old-fashioned; ❷ *adv.* in an old-fashioned way; ~**vertraut** *Adj.* old familiar *attrib.;* ~**vordern** /-fɔrdɐn/ *Pl.* (*veralt.*) forbears; forefathers; ancestors; ~**waren·händler** *der* second-hand dealer; ~**wasser** *das; Pl.* ~~: dead arm of a/the river; ~**weiber·geschwätz**, ~**weiber·gewäsch** *das* (*abwertend*) empty chatter; ~**weiber·sommer** *der* Ⓐ Indian summer; Ⓑ (*Spinnfäden*) gossamer

**Alu**[1] /'a:lu/ *das;* ~**s** (*ugs.*) aluminium (*Brit.*); aluminum (*Amer.*)

**Alu**[2] *die;* ~ *Abk.* (*ugs.*) **Arbeitslosenunterstützung** dole [money] (*Brit.*); unemployment pay

**Alu·folie** *die* aluminium (*Brit.*) *or* (*Amer.*) aluminum foil

**Aluminium** /alu'mi:ni̯um/ *das;* ~**s** aluminium (*Brit.*); aluminum (*Amer.*)

**Aluminium·folie** *die* aluminium foil

**Alumnat** /alʊm'na:t/ *das;* ~**[e]s**, ~**e** boarding school

**Alveolar** /alveo'la:ɐ̯/ *der;* ~**s**, ~**e** (*Sprachw.*) alveolar [consonant]

**Alweg·bahn** /'alve:k-/ *die: type of overhead, high-speed monorail system*

**Alzheimer·krankheit** *die* Alzheimer's disease

**am** /am/ *Präp. + Art.* Ⓐ = **an dem;** Ⓑ (*räumlich*) **am Boden** on the floor; **Frankfurt am Main** Frankfurt on [the] Main; **am Rande** on the edge; **am Institut für ...** at the Institute for ...; **am Marktplatz** on the market square *or* place; **am Baum lehnen** lean against the tree; **am Meer/Fluss** by the sea/on *or* by the river; **am Atlantik** on the Atlantic; **am Anfang/Ende** at the beginning/end; **es am Herzen haben** (*ugs.*) have heart trouble; **sich am Kopf stoßen** bang one's head; Ⓒ (*österr.: auf dem*) on the; Ⓓ ▶ **833** (*zeitlich*) on; **am Freitag** on Friday; **am 19. November** on 19 November; **am Anfang/Ende** at the beginning/end; **am letzten Freitag** last Friday; **am Morgen/Nachmittag** in the morning/afternoon; Ⓔ (*zur Bildung des Superlativs*) **das rote gefällt mir am besten** I like the red one [the] best; **am gescheitesten/schönsten sein** be the cleverest/most beautiful; **am schnellsten laufen** run [the] fastest; **das machen wir am besten nachher** it's best if we do it afterwards; Ⓕ (*nach bestimmten Verben*) **am Gelingen eines Planes** *usw.* **zweifeln** have doubts about *or* doubt the success of a plan *etc.;* **schuld am Scheitern eines Planes** *usw.* **sein** be to blame for the failure of a plan *etc.;* **am Wettbewerb teilnehmen** take part in the contest; Ⓖ (*zur Bildung der Verlaufsform*) **am Verwelken/Verfallen sein** be wilting/decaying; Ⓗ (*ugs.: bes. westf., rhein.*) **ich bin gerade am Kochen** I'm right in the middle of cooking; **er ist sein Auto am Putzen** he's cleaning his car

**Amalgam** /amal'ga:m/ *das;* ~**s**, ~**e** (*Chemie, auch fig.*) amalgam

**Amalgam·füllung** *die* (*Zahnmed.*) amalgam filling

**amalgamieren** *tr., refl. V.* (*Technik*) (*auch fig.*) amalgamate

**Amalgamierung** *die;* ~, ~**en** (*auch fig.*) amalgamation

**Amaryllis** /ama'rʏlɪs/ *die;* ~, **Amaryllen** amaryllis

**Amateur** /ama'tø:ɐ̯/ *der;* ~**s**, ~**e** (*auch abwertend*) amateur

**Amateur-** amateur

**-amateur** *der* amateur ...

**Amateur-:** ~**funk** *der* amateur radio operating; ~**funker** *der,* ~**funkerin** *die* amateur radio operator

**amateurhaft** ❶ *Adj.* amateurish. ❷ *adv.* amateurishly

**Amateurin** *die;* ~, ~**nen** ⇒ **Amateur**

**Amateur-:** ~**status** *der* (*Sport*) amateur status; ~**theater** *das* amateur theatre

**Amazonas** /ama'tso:nas/ *der;* ~ ▶ **306** Amazon

**Amazone** /ama'tso:nə/ *die;* ~, ~**n** Ⓐ (*Myth.*) Amazon; Ⓑ (*Reiterin*) woman rider; equestrienne; Ⓒ (*Fahrerin*) [woman] racing driver; Ⓓ (*veralt.: männlich wirkende Frau*) amazon

**Amazonen·springen** *das* (*Reiten*) women's showjumping; (*Veranstaltung*) women's showjumping competition

**Amazonien** /ama'tso:ni̯ən/ (*das*); ~**s** Amazonia

**Amber** /'ambɐ/ *der;* ~**s**, ~**[n]** ambergris

**Ambiente** /am'bi̯ɛntə/ *das;* ~**s** (*geh.*) ambience

**Ambition** /ambi'tsi̯o:n/ *die;* ~, ~**en** (*geh.*) ambition; ~**en auf etw.** (*Akk.*) **haben** have ambitions of getting sth.

**ambitioniert** /ambitsi̯o'ni:ɐ̯t/ *Adj.* (*geh.*) ambitious

**ambivalent** /ambiva'lɛnt/ (*geh.*) ❶ *Adj.* ambivalent. ❷ *adv.* ambivalently

**Ambivalenz** /ambiva'lɛnts/ (*geh.*) *die;* ~, ~**en** ambivalence

**Amboss**, ***Amboß** /'ambɔs/ *der;* **Ambosses, Ambosse** Ⓐ anvil; Ⓑ (*Anat.*) ▶ **471** anvil; incus

**Ambra** /'ambra/ *die;* ~, ~**s** ambergris

**Ambrosia** /am'bro:zi̯a/ *die;* ~ (*Myth.*) ambrosia

**ambrosisch** *Adj.* (*veralt., geh.*) ambrosial

**ambulant** /ambu'lant/ ❶ *Adj.* Ⓐ (*Med.*) outpatient *attrib.* ‹treatment, therapy, etc.›; **ein** ~**er Patient** an outpatient; Ⓑ (*umherziehend*) itinerant. ❷ *adv.* Ⓐ (*Med.*) **jmdn.** ~ **behandeln/versorgen** treat sb. as an outpatient *or* give sb. outpatient treatment/look after sb. as an outpatient; Ⓑ (*umherziehend*) ~ **mit etw. handeln** travel around selling sth.

**Ambulanz** /ambu'lants/ *die;* ~, ~**en** Ⓐ (*Feldlazarett*) field hospital; Ⓑ (*in Kliniken*) outpatient[s'] department; Ⓒ (*in Betrieben*) first-aid station; Ⓓ (*Krankenwagen*) ambulance

**Ambulatorium** /ambula'to:ri̯ʊm/ *das;* ~**s**, **Ambulatorien** (*bes. DDR*) outpatient[s'] department

**Ameise** /'a:maizə/ *die;* ~, ~**n** ant

**Ameisen·bär** *der* anteater

**Ameisen-:** ~**haufen** *der* anthill; ~**pfad** *der* (*Zool.*) ant run; ~**säure** *die* formic acid; ~**staat** *der* ant colony

**amen** /'a:mɛn/ *Adv.* (*christl. Rel.*) amen; **zu allem ja und Amen** *od.* ~ **sagen** (*ugs.*) agree to anything

**Amen** *das;* ~**s**, ~: Amen; **das ist so sicher wie das** ~ **in der Kirche** (*ugs.*) you can bet your bottom dollar on it (*coll.*); **sein** ~ **zu etw. geben** (*fig.*) give one's blessing to sth.

**Amerika** /a'me:rika/ (*das*); ~**s** America

**Amerikaner** /ameri'ka:nɐ/ *der;* ~**s**, ~ Ⓐ ▶ **553** American; Ⓑ (*Gebäck*) *small, flat iced cake*

**Amerikanerin** *die;* ~, ~**nen** ▶ **553** American

**amerikanisch** *Adj.* ▶ **553** American ⇒ *auch* **deutsch, Deutsch, Deutsche**[2]

**amerikanisieren** *tr. V.* Americanize

**Amerikanisierung** *die;* ~: Americanization

**Amerikanismus** *der;* ~, **Amerikanismen** Americanism

**Amerikanist** *der;* ~**en**, ~**en** specialist in American studies *pl.*

**Amerikanistik** *die;* ~: American studies *pl., no art.*

**Amerikanistin** *die;* ~, ~**nen** ⇒ **Amerikanist**

**amerikanistisch** *Adj.* American ‹studies›

**Amethyst** /ame'tʏst/ *der;* ~**[e]s**, ~**e** amethyst

**Ami** /'ami/ *der;* ~**[s]**, ~**[s]** (*ugs.*) Yank (*coll.*)

**Amigo** *der;* ~**s**, ~**s** (*Jargon*) buddy (*coll.*)

**Amino·säure** /a'mi:no-/ *die* (*Chemie*) amino acid

**Ammann** /'aman/ *der;* ~**[e]s**, **Ammänner** (*schweiz.*) (*Gemeinde~, Bezirks~*) ≈ mayor; (*Land~*) cantonal president

**Amme** /'amə/ *die;* ~, ~**n** (*Mensch*) wet nurse; (*Tier*) foster-mother

**Ammen·märchen** *das* fairy tale *or* story

**Ammer** /'amɐ/ *die;* ~, ~**n** bunting

**Ammoniak** /amo'ni̯ak/ *das;* ~**s** (*Chemie*) ammonia

**Ammonit** /amo'ni:t/ *der;* ~**en**, ~**en** (*Paläont.*) ammonite

**Amnesie** /amne'zi:/ *die;* ~, ~**n** ▶ **474** (*Med., Psych.*) amnesia

**Amnestie** /amnɛs'ti:/ *die;* ~, ~**n** amnesty

**amnestieren** *tr. V.* grant an amnesty to; amnesty

**Amnestierung** *die;* ~, ~**en**: **eine** ~ **politischer Gefangener** an amnesty for political prisoners

**Amöbe** /a'mø:bə/ *die;* ~, ~**n** (*Biol.*) amoeba

**Amöben·ruhr** *die* ▶ **474** (*Med.*) amoebic dysentery

**Amok** /'a:mɔk/ *der;* ~**s** *in* ~ **laufen** run amok; (*ugs.: wütend werden*) go wild (*coll.*); ~ **fahren** go berserk at the wheel

**Amok-:** ~**fahrer** *der,* ~**fahrerin** *die* berserk driver; ~**fahrt** *die* crazed drive; ~**lauf** *der* crazed rampage; ~**läufer** *der,* ~**läuferin** *die* madman; **der** ~**läufer, der mehrere Menschen erschossen hatte** the man who had gone berserk and shot several people; ~**schütze** *der,* ~**schützin** *die* crazed gunman/gunwoman

**a-Moll** *das* A minor; **Sonate/Etüde in** ~: sonata/étude in A minor

**a-Moll-:** ~**-Drei·klang** *der* A minor triad; ~**-Etüde** *die* study *or* étude in A minor; ~**-Sonate** *die* sonata in A minor; ~**-Tonleiter** *die* scale of A minor

**Amor** /'a:mɔr/ (*der*) Cupid; ~**s Pfeil** (*dichter.*) Cupid's arrow *or* dart

**amoralisch** (*geh.*) ❶ *Adj.* immoral. ❷ *adv.* immorally

**Amoralität** *die;* ~ (*geh.*) immorality

**Amorette** /amo'rɛtə/ *die;* ~, ~**n** (*Kunstwiss.*) amoretto; [little] cupid

**amorph** /a'mɔrf/ *Adj.* (*geh.*) amorphous

**Amortisation** /amɔrtiza'tsi̯o:n/ *die;* ~, ~**en** (*Wirtsch.*) Ⓐ (*Schuldentilgung*) amortization; Ⓑ (*Kostendeckung*) **die Berechnung der** ~ **der Maschine** calculating how long the machine will take to pay for itself

**amortisieren** (*Wirtsch.*) ❶ *tr. V.* Ⓐ (*tilgen*) amortize; pay off; Ⓑ (*einbringen*) repay ‹initial investment, acquisition costs›. ❷ *refl. V.* (*sich bezahlt machen*) pay for itself

**Amouren** /a'mu:rən/ *Pl.* (*veralt., noch scherzh.*) amours

**amourös** /amu'rø:s/ *Adj.* amorous

**Ampel** /'ampl̩/ *die;* ~, ~**n** ▶ **818** Ⓐ (*Verkehrs~*) traffic lights *pl.;* **die** ~ **sprang auf Rot** the traffic lights turned to red; **halten Sie an der nächsten** ~: stop at the next set of traffic lights; **eine** ~ **umfahren** knock over a traffic light; Ⓑ (*Hängelampe*) hanging lamp; Ⓒ (*für Pflanzen*) hanging flowerpot

**Ampel-:** ~**anlage** *die* set of traffic lights; ~**koalition** *die* (*ugs.*): *coalition between the SPD, FDP, and the Green Party*

**Ampere** /am'pɛ:ɐ̯/ *das;* **~[s]**, **~:** ampere; amp (*coll.*)

**Ampere-:** **~meter** *das* ammeter; **~stunde** *die* ampere-hour

**Ampfer** /'ampfɐ/ *der;* **~s**, **~** (*Bot.*) dock

**Amphibie** /am'fi:bjə/ *die;* **~**, **~n** (*Zool.*) amphibian

**Amphibien·fahrzeug** *das* amphibious vehicle

**amphibisch** (*Zool., Milit.*) ❶ *Adj.* amphibious. ❷ *adv.* amphibiously

**Amphi·theater** /am'fi:-/ *das* amphitheatre

**Amphore** /am'fo:rə/ *die;* **~**, **~n** amphora

**Amplitude** /ampli'tu:də/ *die;* **~**, **~n** (*Math., Physik*) amplitude

**Ampulle** /am'pʊlə/ *die;* **~**, **~n** (*Med.*) ampoule

**Amputation** /amputa'tsjo:n/ *die;* **~**, **~en** (*Med.*) amputation

**amputieren** *tr.* (*auch itr.*) *V.* amputate; **amputiert werden** ‹person› have an amputation; **jmdm. das Bein/den Arm ~:** amputate sb.'s leg/arm

**Amputierte** *der/die; adj. Dekl.* amputee

**Amsel** /'amzl̩/ *die;* **~**, **~n** blackbird

**Amt** /amt/ *das;* **~[e]s**, **Ämter** /'ɛmtɐ/ [A] (*Stellung*) post; position; (*hohes politisches od. kirchliches* **~**) office; **sein ~ antreten** take up one's post/take up office; **im ~ sein** be in office; **in ~ und Würden sein** be a man/woman of position and authority; **jmdn. aus dem ~ entfernen** remove sb. from his/her post/from office; **für ein ~ kandidieren** be a candidate for a post *or* position/an office; **von ~s wegen** because of one's profession *or* job; **kraft seines ~es** (*geh.*) by virtue of one's office; [B] (*Aufgabe*) task; job; (*Obliegenheit*) duty; **seines ~es walten** (*geh.*) discharge the duties of one's office; **Scharfrichter, walte deines ~es!** executioner, do your duty!; [C] (*Behörde*) (*Pass~, Finanz~, ~ für Statistik*) office; (*Sozial~, Fürsorge~, ~ für Denkmalpflege, Vermessungswesen*) department; **jmdn. dem zuständigen ~ melden** report sb. to the appropriate authorities; **von ~s wegen** by order of the authorities; ⇒ *auch* **auswärtig** C; [D] (*Gebäude usw.*) office; [E] (*Fernsprechvermittlung*) exchange; **das Fräulein vom ~** (*veralt.*) the operator; **vom ~ vermittelt werden** be put through by the operator; [F] (*kath. Rel.*) [sung] mass

**Ämtchen** /'ɛmtçən/ *das;* **~s**, **~** (*abwertend*) petty little job

**Ämter·patronage** *die* [political] patronage in the distribution of posts/offices

**Amt·frau** *die* ⇒ **Amtmann**

**amtieren** *itr. V.* [A] hold office; **der ~de Generalsekretär** the incumbent Secretary General; **der seit zwei Jahren ~de Generalsekretär** the Secretary-General who has been in *or* has held office for two years; **als Bürgermeister ~:** hold the office of mayor; [B] (*vorübergehend*) act (**als** as)

**amtlich** ❶ *Adj.* official; **~es Kennzeichen** registration number; (*ugs.: sicher*) definite; certain. ❷ *adv.* officially

**amtlicher·seits** *Adv.* officially

**Amt·mann** *der; Pl.* **Amtmänner** *od.* **Amtleute**, **Amt·männin** /-mɛnɪn/ *die;* **~**, **~nen** *senior civil servant*

**amts-**, **Amts-:** **~anmaßung** *die* (*Rechtsw.*) unauthorized assumption of authority; **~antritt** *der* assumption of office; **bei ~antritt** on assuming office; **~anwalt** *der: public prosecutor at a local court;* **~apparat** *der* machinery of officialdom; **~arzt** *der*, **~ärztin** *die* medical officer; **~ärztlich** ❶ *Adj.* **~ärztliche Gesundheits-/Impfbescheinigung** certificate of health/vaccination issued by the medical officer; **~ärztliche Untersuchung** examination by the medical officer; ❷ *adv.* ‹authorized, certified› by the medical officer; **sich ~ärztlich untersuchen lassen** have an official medical examination; **~blatt** *das* official gazette; **~bruder** *der* fellow clergyman; **~deutsch** *das* (*abwertend*) officialese; **~eid** *der* oath of office; **~einsetzung** *die* installation; **~enthebung** *die*, (*bes. österr. u. schweiz.*) **~entsetzung** *die* removal *or* dismissal from office; **~führung** *die* discharge of one's office; **~geheimnis** *das* [A] (*Schweigepflicht*) official secrecy *no art.;* **dem ~geheimnis unterliegen** be bound by official secrecy; [B] (*geheime Sache*) official secret; **~gericht** *das* [A] (*Instanz*) local *or* district court; [B] (*Gebäude*) local *or* district court building; **~geschäfte** *Pl.* official duties; **~handlung** *die* official act *or* duty; **~hilfe** *die* official assistance (*given by one authority to another*); **~kette** *die* chain of office; **~leitung** *die* exchange line; **~miene** *die* (*meist iron.*) official air; **~missbrauch**, ***~mißbrauch** *der* abuse of authority *or* one's position; **~müde** *Adj.* tired of office *postpos.;* **~nachfolger** *der*, **~nachfolgerin** *die* successor in office; **~person** *die* official; **~pflicht** *die* official duty; duty of one's office; **~richter** *der*, **~richterin** *die* (*veralt.*) local *or* district court judge; **~schimmel** *der* (*scherzh.*) officialism; bureaucracy; **der ~schimmel wiehert** that's bureaucracy for you; **~schwester** *die* fellow clergywoman; **~siegel** *das* official seal; (*Dienststempel*) official stamp; **~sitz** *der* [A] (*Ort*) [official] seat; [B] (*Gebäude*) official residence; **~sprache** *die* [A] (**~***deutsch*) official language; officialese (*derog.*); **in der ~sprache** in official language/officialese; [B] (*eines Landes, einer Organisation*) official language; **~stube** *die* (*veralt.*) office; **~stunden** *Pl.* office hours; **~tracht** *die* robes *pl.* of office; official dress; (*eines Geistlichen*) vestments *pl.;* **~verweser** *der;* **~~s**, **~~**, **~verweserin** *die;* **~~**, **~~nen** (*geh.*) deputy; (*eines Herrschers*) regent; **~vorsteher** *der*, **~vorsteherin** *die* head *or* chief [of a/the department]; **~vorsteher der Passstelle/des Zollamtes** head of the passport/customs office; **~zeit** *die* period *or* term of office; **~zimmer** *das* office

**Amulett** /amu'lɛt/ *das;* **~[e]s**, **~e** amulet; charm

**amüsant** /amy'zant/ ❶ *Adj.* amusing; entertaining. ❷ *adv.* in an amusing *or* entertaining way

**Amüsement** /amyzə'mã:/ *das;* **~s**, **~s** amusement

**Amüsier·betrieb** *der* (*oft abwertend*) nightclub; (*Spielhalle*) amusement arcade; arcade room (*Amer.*)

**amüsieren** ❶ *refl. V.* [A] (*sich vergnügen*) enjoy oneself; have a good time; **amüsier dich gut!** enjoy yourself!; have a good time!; **sich mit etw. ~** (*auch iron.*) have fun with sth.; **sich mit jmdm. ~:** have fun *or* a good time with sb.; [B] (*sich lustig machen*) be amused; **sich über jmdn./etw. ~:** find sb./sth. funny; (*über jmdn./etw. lachen*) laugh at sb./sth.; (*jmdn. verspotten*) make fun of sb./sth. ❷ *tr. V.* amuse; **amüsiert zusehen** look on with amusement; **was amüsiert dich denn so?** what do you find so amusing *or* funny?

**Amüsier·viertel** *das* nightclub district

**amusisch** *Adj.* (*geh.*) with no feeling for art *postpos., not pred.;* **[völlig] ~ sein** have no feeling [at all] for art.

**an** /an/ ❶ *Präp. mit Dat.* [A] (*räumlich*) at; (*auf*) on; **an einem Ort** at a place; **an der Tür/Wand** on the door/wall; **an der Wand stehen** stand by *or* against the wall; **eine Blase an der Ferse haben** have a blister on one's heel; **an der Mosel/Donau liegen** be [situated] on the Moselle/Danube; **Frankfurt an der Oder** Frankfurt on [the] Oder; **ein Lehrer an dieser Schule** a teacher at this school; **an etw. lehnen** lean against sth.; **nah an etw. stehen** stand close to sth.; **jmdn. an der Hand nehmen** take sb. by the hand; **Tür an Tür** next door to one another; **Laden an Laden** shop after shop; one shop after the other; **an jmdm. vorbeigehen/-sehen** go/look past sb.; **an etw. vorbeiplanen/vorbeibauen** plan/build without regard for sth.; ⇒ *auch* **Bord²**; **Land** A; [B] ▶ 207, ▶ 833 (*zeitlich*) on; **an jedem Sonntag** every Sunday; **an dem Abend, als er …** [on] the evening he …; **das war an dem Tag, als er …** that was the day he …; **an Ostern** (*bes. südd.*) at Easter; [C] (*nach bestimmten Substantiven, Adjektiven und Verben*) in; **acht an der Zahl** eight in number; **arm/reich an Vitaminen** low/rich in vitamins; **jung an Jahren** young in years; **jmdn. an etw. erkennen** recognize sb. by sth.; **das Beste an etw.** the best thing about sth.; **ein Mangel an etw.** a shortage of sth.; **an etw. arbeiten** be working on sth.; **an etw. leiden** suffer from sth.; **was haben Sie an Zeitungen?** what newspapers have you got?; **es an der Leber bekommen/haben** get/have liver trouble; **an einer Krankheit sterben** die of a disease; **was mir an der Sache nicht gefällt** what I don't like about it; **es ist an ihm, das zu tun** it is up to him to do it; **er/sie hat etwas an sich** there ist sth. about him/her; **was er an Rente bekam** what he received by way of a pension; **an [und für] sich** actually; **die Idee ist an [und für] sich ausgezeichnet** the idea is excellent in itself.
❷ *Präp. mit Akk.* [A] to; (*auf, gegen*) on; **etw. an jmdn. schicken** send sth. to sb.; **etw. an etw. hängen** hang sth. on sth.; **an die Tafel schreiben** write on the blackboard; **etw. an etw. lehnen** lean sth. against sth.; **[bis] an die Decke reichen** reach [up] to the ceiling; ⇒ *auch* **bis**; **Bord²**; **Land**; [B] (*nach bestimmten Substantiven, Adjektiven und Verben*) **an etw./jmdn. glauben** believe in sth./sb.; **an etw. denken** think of sth.; **sich an etw. erinnern** remember *or* recall sth.; **an die Arbeit gehen** get down to work; **eine Bitte/Frage an jmdn. haben** have a request to make of sb./a question to ask sb.; **an etw. appellieren** appeal to sth.; **einen Gruß an jmdn. ausrichten lassen** send greetings to sb.; **ich konnte kaum an mich halten vor Lachen/Ärger** I could hardly contain myself for laughing/hardly contain my anger.
❸ *Adv.* [A] (*Verkehrsw.*) **Köln an: 9.15** arriving Cologne 09.15; [B] (*ugs.: in Betrieb*) on; **die Waschmaschine/der Fernseher/das Licht/das Gas ist an** the washing machine/television/light/gas is on; **Scheinwerfer an!** spotlights on!; [C] (*ugs.: ungefähr*) around; about; **an [die] 20 000 DM** around *or* about 20,000 DM; [D] *in* **ohne [et]was an** (*ugs.*) with nothing on; without anything on; ⇒ *auch* **ab** 2 D; **von** 1 A, B

**Anabolikum** /ana'bo:likʊm/ *das;* **~s**, **Anabolika** (*Med.*) anabolic steroid

**Anachronismus** /anakro'nɪsmʊs/ *der;* **~**, **Anachronismen** anachronism

**anachronistisch** ❶ *Adj.* anachronistic. ❷ *adv.* anachronistically

**anaerob** /an|ae'ro:p/ *Adj.* (*Biol.*) anaerobic

**Anagramm** /ana'gram/ *das;* **~s**, **~e** anagram

**Anakoluth** /anako'lu:t/ *das od. der;* **~s**, **~e** (*Sprachw.*) anacoluthon

**Anakonda** /ana'kɔnda/ *die;* **~**, **~s** anaconda

**Anakreontik** /anakre'ɔntɪk/ *die;* **~** (*Literaturw.*) anacreontic verse

**anal** /a'na:l/ (*Anat., Psych.*) ❶ *Adj.* anal. ❷ *adv.* anally; **~ verkehren** have anal intercourse

**Analeptikum** /ana'lɛptɪkʊm/ *das;* **~s**, **Analeptika** (*Med.*) analeptic

**Anal·erotik** *die;* **~:** anal eroticism

**Analgetikum** /anal'ge:tikʊm/ *das;* **~s**, **Analgetika** (*Med.*) analgesic

**analog** /ana'lo:k/ ❶ *Adj.* [A] (*gleichartig*) analogous; **~ [zu] diesem Fall** analogous to this case; [B] (*Technik, DV*) analogue. ❷ *adv.* [A] (*gleichartig*) analogously; [B] (*Technik, DV*) ‹display, reproduce› in analogue form; **~ arbeitende Geräte** analogue devices

**Analogie** *die;* **~**, **~n** (*Entsprechung, auch Rechtsw., Biol., Sprachw.*) analogy; **in ~ zu etw.** in analogy to sth.

**Analog-:** **~rechner** *der* (*DV*) analogue computer; **~uhr** *die* analogue clock; (*Armbanduhr*) analogue watch

*old spelling (see note on page 1707)

# an

## Räumlich: Wo?

Zur Beschreibung der Lage verwendet man meist **on**:

***eine Verletzung am Knie***
= a wound on the knee

***die Bilder an der Wand***
= the pictures on the wall

***eine Stadt an der Mosel***
= a town on the Moselle

***ein Haus am Fluss***
= a house on *od.* by the river

Hier wird **by** verwendet, um die Nähe zum Fluss auszudrücken. Ebenso:

***Er stand am Fenster***
= He stood by *od.* at the window

Wenn es um die Lage an einem Ort oder Gebäude geht, heißt es **at**:

***am Tatort***
= at the scene of the crime

***am Haupteingang***
= at the main entrance

***an der Vorderseite***
= at the front

***am Ende der Straße***
= at the end of the road

***am Theater/Kino/Bahnhof***
= at the theatre/cinema/station

## Räumlich: Wohin?

Wenn *an* sich auf eine Bewegung in eine bestimmte Richtung bezieht, wird es meist mit **on** übersetzt:

***Lehne es an den Baum***
= Lean it on *od.* against the tree

***Hänge es an die Wand***
= Hang it on the wall

***Schreibe es an die Tafel***
= Write it on the blackboard

***Sie legte ihren Kopf an seine Schulter***
= She laid her head on his shoulder

Beim Wechsel von einer Person zur anderen bzw. von einem Ort zum anderen heißt es **to**:

***Schicke es an deinen Bruder***
= Send it to your brother

***die Übergabe an den neuen Besitzer***
= the transfer to the new owner

***Sie wurde an eine andere Schule versetzt***
= She was moved to another school

## Zeitlich: Wann?

In Verbindung mit einem bestimmten Tag, Datum oder Wochentag wird *an* bzw. *am* mit **on** (ohne **the**) übersetzt:

***am 6. Juli***
= on July 6th (*gesprochen*: on July the sixth, *in den USA auch*: July sixth)

***am Mittwoch***
= on Wednesday

***an seinem Geburtstag***
= on his birthday

***an einem schönen Frühlingstag***
= on a fine spring day

Ausnahmen (mit **the**) sind Daten ohne Angabe des Monats oder bestimmte Tage im Monat:

***am 6.***
= on the sixth

***am ersten/letzten Sonntag im Monat***
= on the first/last Sunday in the month

Bei vorangehenden oder folgenden Tagen steht meist nur **the**, d.h., *an* wird nicht übersetzt:

***Am Tag/Mittwoch davor waren wir in London gewesen***
= The day before/The previous Wednesday we had been in London

***Am nächsten Tag fuhr er zurück***
= The next day he went back

***Am übernächsten Dienstag sind wir in Rom***
= The Tuesday after next we'll be in Rome

In Verbindung mit Tageszeiten heißt es **in** oder, wenn sie näher beschrieben werden, **on**:

***am Morgen/Nachmittag/Abend***
= in the morning/afternoon/evening

***am ersten Morgen seines Besuchs***
= on the first morning of his visit

***an einem kalten Winterabend***
= on a cold winter evening

Eine Ausnahme ist wieder:

***am nächsten Morgen***
= the next morning

In Verbindung mit Festen (süddeutscher Wortgebrauch) heißt es **at**:

***an Ostern/Weihnachten***
= at Easter/Christmas

## Im Gegensatz zu aus

In der Bedeutung „in Betrieb" wird *an* mit **on** übersetzt:

***Das Licht/Die Spülmaschine ist an***
= The light/The dishwasher is on

## Im Gegensatz zu ab

Auf Fahrplänen (zur Angabe der Ankunftszeit) heißt es im Englischen **arriving** (Abkürzung **arr.**):

***Köln an 17.30***
= arriving *od.* arr. Cologne 17.30

***an 12.30 – ab 12.35***
= arr. 12.30 – dep. 1.35

**An·alphabet** *der;* **~en, ~en** Ⓐ illiterate [person]; **~ sein** be illiterate; Ⓑ (*fig. abwertend*) ignoramus; **ein politischer ~ sein** be politically illiterate

**Analphabetentum** *das;* **~s** illiteracy

**Analphabetin** *die;* **~, ~nen** ⇨ **Analphabet**

**Anal·verkehr** *der* anal intercourse

**Analysand** /analy'zant/ *der;* **~en, ~en, Analysandin** *die;* **~, ~nen** (*Psychoanalyse*) analysand

**Analyse** /ana'ly:zə/ *die;* **~, ~n** (*auch: Psycho~*) analysis

**analysieren** *tr. V.* analyse

**Analysis** /a'na:lyzɪs/ *die;* **~** (*Math.*) analysis

**Analyst** /ana'lʏst/ *der;* **~en, ~en, Analystin,** *die;* **~, ~nen** ▶ 159 (*Börsenw.*) analyst

**Analytiker** *der;* **~s, ~, Analytikerin** *die* analyst

**analytisch** ❶ *Adj.* analytical; **~e Geometrie** analytical geometry. ❷ *adv.* analytically

**Anämie** /anɛ'mi:/ *die;* **~, ~n** ▶ 474 (*Med.*) anaemia

**anämisch** /a'nɛ:mɪʃ/ *Adj.* (*Med., auch fig. abwertend*) anaemic

**Anamnese** /anam'ne:zə/ *die;* **~, ~n** (*Med.*) anamnesis

**Ananas** /'ananas/ *die;* **~, ~** *od.* **~se** pineapple

**Anapäst** /ana'pɛ:st/ *der;* **~[e]s, ~e** (*Verslehre*) anapaest

**Anapher** /a'nafɐ/ *die;* **~, ~n** (*Stilk.*) anaphora

**Anarchie** /anar'çi:/ *die;* **~, ~n** anarchy

**anarchisch** *Adj.* anarchic

**Anarchismus** *der;* **~:** anarchism

**Anarchist** *der;* **~en, ~en, Anarchistin** *die;* **~, ~nen** anarchist

**anarchistisch** *Adj.* anarchistic

**Anarcho·szene** *die* (*ugs.*) anarchist scene

**Anästhesie** /an|ɛste'zi:/ *die;* **~, ~n** (*Med.*) anaesthesia

**anästhesieren** *tr. V.* (*Med.*) anaesthetize

**Anästhesist** *der;* **~en, ~en, Anästhesistin** *die;* **~, ~nen** ▶ 159 (*Med.*) anaesthetist

**Anatolien** /ana'to:li̯ən/ *(das);* **~s** Anatolia

**Anatom** /ana'to:m/ *der;* **~en, ~en** (*Med.*) anatomist

a

**Anatomie** /anato'mi:/ *die;* ~, ~**n** (*Med.*) Ⓐ anatomy; Ⓑ (*Institut*) anatomical institute

**Anatomie·saal** *der* (*Med.*) anatomy lecture theatre

**anatomisch** /ana'to:mɪʃ/ (*Med.*) ❶ *Adj.* anatomical. ❷ *adv.* anatomically

**an|backen**[1] ❶ *unr. tr. V.* **etw. [kurz] ~:** bake sth. for a short time. ❷ *unr. itr. V.; mit sein* (*festbacken*) become baked on (**an** + *Dat.* to); stick (**an** + *Dat.* on to)

**an|backen**[2] *itr. V.; mit sein* (*nordd.: sich festsetzen*) stick (**an** + *Dat.* to)

**an|bahnen** ❶ *tr. V.* initiate ‹negotiations, talks, process, etc.›; develop ‹relationship, connection›. ❷ *refl. V.* ‹development› be in the offing; ‹friendship, relationship› start to develop; **zwischen den beiden bahnt sich etwas an** there is something going on between those two

**Anbahnung** *die;* ~, ~**en** ⇒ **anbahnen** 1: initiation; development

**an|bandeln** /'anbandl̩n/ (*südd., österr.*), **an|bändeln** /'anbɛndl̩n/ *itr. V.* (*ugs.*) **mit jmdm. ~** *od.* **anbändeln** (*flirten*) get off with sb. (*Brit. coll.*); pick sb. up; (*Streit anfangen*) pick a quarrel with sb.

**An·bau** *der; Pl.* ~**ten** Ⓐ building; **die Genehmigung für den ~ einer Garage an ein Haus bekommen** receive permission to build a garage on to a house; Ⓑ (*Gebäude*) extension; Ⓒ (*das Anpflanzen*) cultivation; growing

**-anbau** *der:* **Flachs~/Hopfen~/Futter~:** cultivation of flax/hop/fodder plants

**an|bauen** ❶ *tr. V.* Ⓐ build on; add; **eine Garage ans Haus ~:** build a garage on to the house; Ⓑ (*anpflanzen*) cultivate; grow. ❷ *itr. V.* (*das Haus vergrößern*) build an extension; (~ *lassen*) have an extension built

**Anbau-:** ~**fläche** *die* area of arable land; (*bebaute Fläche*) area under cultivation; ~**gebiet** *das:* **die besten ~gebiete für Getreide** the best cereal-growing *or* grain-growing areas; **die wichtigsten ~gebiete für Rotwein** the principal red-wine-growing areas *or* areas for red wine; ~**küche** *die* fitted kitchen; unit kitchen (*Amer.*); ~**möbel** *das* piece of unit furniture; **teure ~möbel** expensive unit furniture *sing.;* ~**schrank** *der* cupboard unit

**an|befehlen** *unr. tr. V.* (*geh.*) Ⓐ (*befehlen*) **jmdm. etw. ~:** urge sth. on sb.; Ⓑ (*anvertrauen*) **jmdm. etw. ~:** commend sth. to sb.; **jmdm. ein Kind ~:** commend a child to sb.'s care

**An·beginn** *der* (*geh.*) beginning; **von ~ [an]** right from the beginning

**an|behalten** *unr. tr. V.* (*ugs.*) **etw. ~:** keep sth. on

**an·bei** *Adv.* (*Amtsspr.*) herewith; **Rückporto ~:** return postage enclosed

**an|beißen** ❶ *unr. tr. V.* bite into; take a bite of; **er hat die Banane nur angebissen** he only took one bite of the banana; **zum Anbeißen sein** *od.* **aussehen** (*ugs.*) look good enough to eat. ❷ *unr. itr. V.* (*auch fig. ugs.*) bite; **bei ihr hat noch keiner angebissen** (*fig. ugs.*) she hasn't managed to hook anybody yet

**an|bekommen** *unr. tr. V.* (*ugs.*) Ⓐ (*anziehen können*) **etw. ~:** manage to get sth. on; Ⓑ (*anzünden od. starten können*) **ein Feuer/Streichholz ~:** manage to get a fire going/a match to light; **einen Motor ~:** manage to get an engine going *or* to start

**an|belangen** *tr. V.* **in was mich/diese Sache** *usw.* **anbelangt** as far as I am/this matter is *etc.* concerned

**an|bellen** *tr. V.* bark at

**an|bequemen** *refl. V.* (*geh.*) **sich einer Sache** (*Dat.*) **~:** adapt [oneself] to sth.

**an|beraumen** /'anbəraumən/ *tr. V.* (*Amtsspr.*) arrange, fix ‹meeting›; arrange, set, fix ‹date›

**Anberaumung** *die;* ~, ~**en** (*Amtsspr.*) ⇒ **anberaumen**: arrangement; fixing; setting; **wir bitten um ~ eines neuen Termins** we should like a new date to be arranged *or* set

*old spelling (see note on page 1707)

**an|beten** *tr. V.* (*auch fig.*) worship

**Anbeter** *der;* ~**s**, ~, **Anbeterin** *die;* ~, ~**nen** (*auch fig.*) worshipper; (*fig.: Verehrer*) admirer

**An·betracht** *der:* **in ~ einer Sache** (*Gen.*) in consideration *or* view of sth.; **in ~ dessen, dass ...** in view of the fact that ...

**an|betreffen** *unr. tr. V.* **in was mich/diese Sache** *usw.* **anbetrifft** as far as I am/this matter *etc.* is concerned

**an|betteln** *tr. V.* **jmdn. ~:** beg from sb.; **jmdn. um etw. ~:** beg sb. for sth.; **[auf der Straße] angebettelt werden** be stopped [in the street] by a beggar and asked for money

**Anbetung** *die;* ~, ~**en** (*auch fig.*) worship; (*fig.: Verehrung*) adoration

**anbetungs·würdig** *Adj.* adorable

**an|bezahlen** *tr. V.* make a down payment on; pay a deposit on

**an|biedern** /'anbi:dɐn/ *refl. V.* (*abwertend*) **sich [bei jmdm.] ~:** curry favour [with sb.]

**Anbiederung** *die;* ~, ~**en** (*abwertend*) currying favour (**an** + *Akk.* with)

**Anbiederungs·versuch** *der* (*abwertend*) attempt to curry favour

**an|bieten** ❶ *unr. tr. V.* offer; offer, tender ‹resignation›; **jmdm. etw. ~:** offer sb. sth.; **jmdm. seine Begleitung ~:** offer to accompany sb.; **jmdm. ~, etw. zu tun** offer to do sth. for sb.; **ich habe dir immer wieder angeboten, dir zu helfen** I offered time and again to help you; **Verhandlungen ~:** offer to negotiate; **ich habe nichts anzubieten** *od.* **zum Anbieten** I have nothing to offer you/them; **sich auf der Straße ~:** offer oneself on the streets; **jmdm. Schläge ~** (*iron.*) threaten to hit sb.
❷ *unr. refl. V.* Ⓐ offer one's services (**als** as); **sich ~, etw. zu tun** offer to do sth.; **sich fürs** *od.* **zum Geschirrspülen** *usw.* **~:** offer to do the dishes; Ⓑ (*nahe liegen*) ‹opportunity› present itself; ‹possibility, solution› suggest *or* present itself; **es bietet sich an, das zu tun** it would seem to be the thing to do; Ⓒ (*geeignet sein*) **sich für etw. ~:** be suitable for sth.; **dieses Tal bietet sich für die Einrichtung eines Sanatoriums geradezu an** this valley is an obvious place to build a sanatorium

**An·bieter** *der,* **An·bieterin** *die* (*Wirtsch.*) supplier

**an|binden** ❶ *unr. tr. V.* Ⓐ (*befestigen*) tie [up] (**an** + *Dat. od. Akk.* to); tie up, moor ‹boat› (**an** + *Dat. od. Akk.* to); tether ‹animal› (**an** + *Dat. od. Akk.* to); **er lässt sich nicht ~** (*fig.*) he won't be tied down; **man kann Kinder nicht ~** (*fig.*) you can't keep children on a lead; ⇒ *auch* **angebunden** 2; Ⓑ (*verbinden, anschließen*) link (**an** + *Akk.* to); Ⓒ (*Landw.*) rear. ❷ *unr. itr. V.* (*geh.*) **mit jmdm. ~** (*Streit anfangen*) pick a quarrel with sb.; (*flirten*) flirt with sb.

**An·bindung** *die* linking (**an** + *Akk.* to); (*psychische* ~) involvement (**an** + *Akk.* in)

**an|blaffen** *tr. V.* (*ugs., auch fig.*) bark at

**an|blasen** *unr. tr. V.* Ⓐ blow at; **jmdn. mit Rauch ~:** blow smoke at sb.; Ⓑ (*anfachen*) blow on; **einen Hochofen ~** (*Technik*) blow in a blast furnace; Ⓒ (*salopp: zurechtweisen*) **jmdn. ~:** bawl sb. out (*coll.*); Ⓓ **die Jagd ~:** sound the horn for the start of the hunt; Ⓔ (*Musik*) sound ‹note›; blow ‹instrument›

**an|blecken** *tr. V.* bare its/their teeth at; (*fig.*) bare his/her/their *etc.* teeth at

**an|bleiben** *unr. itr. V.; mit sein* (*ugs.*) stay on

**an|blenden** *tr. V.* flash [at]; **jmdn. mit einer Taschenlampe ~:** flash a torch at sb. (*Brit.*); shine a flashlight at sb. (*Amer.*)

**An·blick** *der* sight; **einen erfreulichen/traurigen ~ bieten** be a welcome/sad sight; **ihm wurde beim bloßen ~ schon schlecht** the mere sight of it made him sick; **beim ~ der Pyramiden** at the sight of the Pyramids; **es war ein ~ für Götter, als du ...** you looked a [real] sight when you ...

**an|blicken** *tr. V.* look at; **jmdn. mit großen Augen ~:** look at sb. wide-eyed; **jmdn. flüchtig/starr ~:** glance/stare at sb.

**an|blinken** *tr. V.* ⇒ **anblenden**

**an|blinzeln** *tr. V.* Ⓐ blink at; Ⓑ (*zuzwinkern*) wink at

**an|bohren** *tr. V.* Ⓐ bore into; (*mit der Bohrmaschine*) bore *or* drill into; **Saboteure hatten sämtliche Benzinfässer angebohrt** saboteurs had drilled holes in all the petrol drums; Ⓑ (*erschließen*) tap [by drilling]; (*fig. ugs.: befragen*) pump

**an|branden** *itr. V.; mit sein* (*auch fig.*) surge

**an|brassen** *tr. V.* (*Seemannsspr.*) brace up

**an|braten** *unr. tr. V.* (*Kochk.*) brown; **scharf ~:** sear

**an|brauchen** *tr. V.* (*ugs.*) start [using]; **eine angebrauchte Tube Senf** a half-used tube of mustard

**an|bräunen** ❶ *tr. V.* (*Kochk.*) brown [lightly]. ❷ *itr. V.; mit sein* (*ugs.: von der Sonne braun werden*) tan [lightly]

**an|brausen** *itr. V.; mit sein* roar up; **angebraust kommen** come roaring along; (*auf einen zu*) come roaring up

**an|brechen** ❶ *unr. tr. V.* Ⓐ crack; **sich** (*Dat.*) **einen Knochen ~:** crack a bone; Ⓑ (*öffnen*) open; start; **eine angebrochene Flasche** an opened bottle; Ⓒ (*zu verbrauchen beginnen*) break into ‹supplies, reserves›; **einen Hundertmarkschein ~:** break into *or* (*Amer.*) break a hundred mark note; **was machen wir mit dem angebrochenen Abend?** (*fig. ugs.*) what shall we do for the rest of the evening?
❷ *unr. itr. V.; mit sein* (*geh.: beginnen*) ‹dawn› break; ‹day› dawn, break; ‹darkness, night› come down, fall; ‹age, epoch› dawn; ‹autumn, winter› set in; ‹spring, summer› begin

**an|brennen** ❶ *unr. tr. V.* (*anzünden*) light. ❷ *unr. itr. V.; mit sein* Ⓐ burn; **jmdm. ist das Essen angebrannt** sb. has burnt the food; **nichts ~ lassen** (*fig. ugs.*) not miss out on anything; **der Torwart ließ nichts ~** (*Sportjargon*) the goalkeeper kept a clean sheet; Ⓑ (*zu brennen beginnen*) ‹wood, coal, etc.› catch

**an|bringen** *unr. tr. V.* Ⓐ (*befestigen*) put up ‹sign, aerial, curtain, plaque› (**an** + *Dat.* on); fix ‹lamp, camera› (**an** + *Dat.* [on] to); **an etw.** (*Dat.*) **angebracht sein** be fixed [on] to sth.; Ⓑ (*äußern*) make ‹request, complaint, comment, reference›; Ⓒ (*zeigen*) display, demonstrate ‹knowledge, experience›; Ⓓ (*ugs.: herbeibringen*) bring; (*nach Hause*) bring home; Ⓔ (*ugs.: verkaufen*) sell; move

**Anbringung** *die;* ~ ⇒ **anbringen** A: putting up; fixing

**An·bruch** *der* Ⓐ (*geh.: Beginn*) dawn[ing]; **der ~ des Tages** dawn; daybreak; **vor/nach/bei** *od.* **mit ~ der Nacht** before/after/at nightfall; **vor ~ der Dunkelheit** before darkness closes in; Ⓑ (*Bergbau*) lode; vein

**an·brüchig** *Adj.* (*Jägerspr.*) rotting

**an|brühen** *tr. V.* brew, make ‹tea, coffee›; blanch ‹tomatoes, almonds, etc.›

**an|brüllen** ❶ *tr. V.* Ⓐ ‹tiger, lion, etc.› roar at; ‹cow, bull, etc.› bellow at; Ⓑ (*ugs.: anschreien*) bellow *or* bawl at. ❷ *itr. V.* (*ugs.: zu übertönen versuchen*) **gegen etw. ~:** try to shout above [the noise of] sth.

**an|brummen** ❶ *tr. V.* (*auch ugs.: unfreundlich anreden*) growl at. ❷ *itr. V.; mit sein* **angebrummt kommen** come roaring along; (*auf einen zu*) come roaring up

**an|brüten** *tr. V.* begin to sit on ‹eggs›; **angebrütete Eier** eggs that have been sat on

**Anchovis** ⇒ **Anschovis**

**Anciennitäts·prinzip** /ãsjeni'tɛ:ts-/ *das* principle of seniority; **nach dem ~:** according to [the principle of] seniority

**Andacht** /'andaxt/ *die;* ~, ~**en** Ⓐ (*Sammlung im Gebet*) silent prayer *or* worship; **in tiefer ~:** in deep devotion; **in ~ versunken** sunk in silent prayer *or* worship *or* in one's devotions; Ⓑ (*innere Sammlung*) rapt attention; **mit großer ~:** with rapt attention; Ⓒ (*Gottesdienst*) prayers *pl.;* **eine ~**

**halten** hold a [short] service; **zur ~ gehen** go to prayers *or* to the service

**andächtig** /ˈandɛçtɪç/ ❶ *Adj.* Ⓐ (*ins Gebet versunken*) devout; reverent; Ⓑ (*innerlich gesammelt*) rapt; Ⓒ (*feierlich*) reverent. ❷ *adv.* Ⓐ (*ins Gebet versunken*) devoutly; reverently; Ⓑ (*innerlich gesammelt*) with rapt attention; raptly

**Andachts·bild** *das* (*Kunst, Rel.*) devotional picture

**andachts·voll** (*geh.*) ⇒ **andächtig**

**Andalusien** /andaˈluːzi̯ən/ (*das*); **~s** Andalusia

**an|dampfen** *itr. V.*; *mit sein* **angedampft kommen** (*ugs.*) come steaming along; (*auf einen zu*) come steaming up; (*fig. scherzh.*) come charging along, puffing and blowing; (*auf einen zu*) come charging up, puffing and blowing

**Andante** /anˈdantə/ *das;* **~s, ~s** (*Musik*) andante

**an|dauen** /ˈandau̯ən/ *tr. V.* (*Med.*) **angedaute Nahrung** partially digested food

**An·dauer** *die* continuance; **bei längerer ~ des Fiebers/des schlechten Wetters** if the fever continues *or* persists/the bad weather lasts for a long time

**an|dauern** *itr. V.* ‹negotiations› continue, go on; ‹weather, rain› last, continue

**andauernd** ❶ ⇒ **andauern**. ❷ *Adj.* continual; constant. ❸ *adv.* continually; constantly; **warum fragst du denn ~ dasselbe?** why do you keep on asking the same thing?

**Anden** /ˈandn̩/ *Pl.* **die ~:** the Andes

**an|denken** *unr. tr. V.* start thinking about

**An·denken** *das;* **~s, ~** Ⓐ memory; **jmds. ~ bewahren/in Ehren halten** keep/honour sb.'s memory; **jmdm. ein liebevolles ~ bewahren** keep fond memories of sb.; **zum ~ an jmdn./etw.** to remind you/us *etc.* of sb./sth.; **das schenke ich dir zum ~:** I'll give you that to remember me/us by; Ⓑ (*Erinnerungsstück*) memento, souvenir (**an** + *Akk.* of); (*Reise~*) souvenir (**an** + *Akk.* of)

**Andenken·jäger** *der,* **Andenken·jägerin** *die* souvenir hunter

**Anden·staat** *der* Andean country

**ander...** /ˈandɐ.../ *Indefinitpron.* ❶ *attr.* Ⓐ (*zweit..., weiter...*) other; **ein ~er Mann/eine ~e Frau/ein ~es Haus** another man/woman/house; **zum ~n Mal** (*veralt.*) [for] a second time; **eine ~e Frage** another *or* a further question; **~e Fragen** other *or* further questions; **das Kleid gefällt mir nicht, haben Sie noch ~e/ein ~es?** I don't like that dress, do you have any others/another?; Ⓑ **am/bis zum ~[e]n Tag** [on] the/by the next *or* following day; **von einem Tag zum ~n** from one day to the next; Ⓒ (*verschieden*) different; **wir ~n** the rest of us; **~er Meinung sein** be of a different opinion; take a different view; **das ~e Geschlecht** the opposite sex; **bei ~er Gelegenheit** another time; **statt dieses Wagens hätte ich gern einen ~en** instead of that car I would like a different one; ⇒ *auch* **Land**; **Städtchen**; Ⓓ (*neu*) **einen ~en Arbeitsplatz finden** find another job; **er ist ein ~er Mensch geworden** he is a changed man.

❷ *allein stehend* Ⓐ (*Person*) **ein ~er/eine ~e** another [one]; **die ~n** the others; **alle ~n** all the others; everyone else; **jeder/jede ~e** anyone *or* anybody else; **kein ~er/keine ~e** nobody *or* no one else; **was ist mit den ~n?** what about the others *or* the rest?; **ich will weder den einen noch den ~en heiraten** I don't want to marry either of them; **niemand ~er als ...** nobody *or* no one but ...; **da muss ein ~er kommen** (*fig.*) it will take more than you/him *etc.;* **einen ~[e]n/eine ~e haben** (*fig. ugs.*) have found somebody *or* someone else; **auf ~e hören** listen to others; **eine war schöner als die ~e** one was more beautiful than the other; **einer hinter dem ~[e]n** one after another *or* the other; **nicht drängeln, einer nach dem ~n** don't push, one after the other; **der eine oder [der] ~e** one or two *or* a few people; **wenn der eine oder [der] ~e von Ihnen etwas Genaueres wissen möchte** if any of you would like further details; ⇒ *auch* **recht** C; Ⓑ (*Sache*) **ein ~er/eine ~e/ein ~es** another [one]; **alles ~e** everything else; **ein[e]s nach dem ~[e]n** first things first; **das ~e schaffen wir schon allein** we can manage the rest on our own; **wir haben noch zwei ~e** we have two others; **es bleibt uns nichts ~es übrig** there's nothing else we can do; **sich eines ~n besinnen** change one's mind; **ich will weder das eine noch das ~e** I don't want either; (*will beides nicht tun*) I don't want to do either; **Möchtest du Tee oder Kaffee? — Weder das eine noch das ~e** Would you like tea or coffee? — Neither; **und ~es/vieles ~e mehr** and more/much more besides; **unter ~[e]m** among[st] other things; **so kam eins zum ~[e]n** what with one thing on top of the other; **das ist etwas [ganz] ~es** that's [something quite] different; **von etwas ~em sprechen** talk about something else; (*um das bisherige Thema zu vermeiden*) change the subject; **das bedeutet doch nichts ~es, als dass wir noch einmal ganz von vorn anfangen müssen** that means only one thing, that we must start all over again from the beginning; **ich habe nichts ~es erwartet** I didn't expect anything else; **dem hätte ich etwas ~es erzählt** (*fig. ugs.*) I would have given him a piece of my mind; **alles ~e als ...** anything but ...; **das ist alles ~e als das, was ich mir vorgestellt hatte** it's not at all what I had imagined; **~es zu tun haben** have other things to do

**änderbar** *Adj.* alterable

**anderen·falls** *Adv.* otherwise

**anderen·orts** *Adv.* (*geh.*) elsewhere

**anderen·tags** *Adv.* (*geh.*) [on] the next *or* following day

**anderen·teils** *Adv.* ⇒ **einesteils**

**anderer·seits** *Adv.* on the other hand

**Ander·konto** *das* (*Finanzw.*) trust account; client account

**ander·mal** *Adv.*: **ein ~:** another time

**andern-** ⇒ **anderen-**

**ändern** /ˈɛndɐn/ ❶ *tr. V.* change; alter; alter ‹garment›; change ‹person›; **etw. an etw.** (*Dat.*) **~:** change *or* alter sth. in sth.; **wenn ich an dem Kleid etwas ~ würde** if I was going to change anything about the dress; **daran kann man nichts ~:** nothing can be done *or* there's nothing you/we *etc.* can do about it; **das alles ändert nichts an der Tatsache, dass ...** none of that alters the fact that ... ❷ *refl. V.* change; alter; ‹person, weather› change; **daran hat sich nichts geändert** nothing about it has changed *or* altered

**ander·orts** ⇒ **anderenorts**

**anders** /ˈandɐs/ *Adv.* Ⓐ (*verschieden*) ‹think, act, feel, do› differently (**als** from *or esp. Brit.* to); ‹be, look, sound, taste› different (**als** from *or esp. Brit.* to); **es war alles ganz ~:** it was all quite different; **er ist irgendwie ~:** there is something different about him; he has changed somehow; **wie könnte es ~ sein!** (*iron.*) surprise, surprise! (*iron.*); **mir wird ganz ~** (*ugs.*) I feel weak at the knees; **es wäre alles ~ gekommen** it would all have been different *or* would have turned out differently; **es kommt immer ~, als man denkt** things never turn out the way you think they will; **es kam ~, als wir dachten** things didn't turn out the way we expected; **wir haben es uns ~ überlegt** we've changed our minds; **ich kann auch ~** (*ugs.*) you'd/he'd *etc.* better watch it (*coll.*); **das hört sich schon ~ an** (*ugs.*) that's more like it; **so und nicht ~:** this way and no other; exactly like that; **das kennt er nicht ~:** he's never known any different; **das kennen wir gar nicht ~ von ihm** we wouldn't expect anything else from him; **ich konnte nicht ~:** I couldn't help it; (*ich wurde gezwungen*) I had no choice; **das habe ich nicht ~ erwartet** I didn't expect anything else; that was just what I expected; **wie nicht ~ zu erwarten** as [was to be] expected; **wenn es nicht ~ geht** if there is no other way; **~ geartet** different; of a different nature *postpos;* **~ denkend** dissident; dissenting; **~ lautend** to the contrary *postpos.*; Ⓑ (*sonst*) else; **irgendwo/nirgendwo ~:** somewhere/nowhere else; **niemand ~:** nobody else; **jemand ~:** someone else; (*verneint, in Fragen*) anyone else; Ⓒ (*ugs.: andernfalls*) otherwise; or else

**anders-, Anders-: ~artig** *Adj.* different; **~artigkeit** *die* different nature; **das Bewusstsein seiner ~artigkeit** his consciousness that he was different; ***~denkend** ⇒ **anders** A; **~denkende** *der/die; adj. Dekl.* dissident; dissenter

**anderseits** ⇒ **andererseits**

**anders-, Anders-: ~farbig** ❶ *Adj.* different-coloured *attrib.;* of a different colour *postpos.;* ❷ *adv.* ‹decorated› in a different colour; **~farbig bezogen** covered in material of a different colour; **~farbige** *der/die* person of a different colour; ***~geartet** ⇒ **anders** A; **~geschlechtlich** *Adj.* of the opposite sex *postpos.;* **~gesinnte** /-gəˈzɪntə/ *der/die; adj. Dekl.* person of a different opinion; **die ~gesinnten** those with *or* of different opinions; **~gläubig** *Adj.* of a different faith *or* religion *postpos.;* **~gläubige** *der/die* person of a different faith *or* religion; **die ~gläubigen** those of different faiths *or* religions; **~herum** ❶ *Adv.* the other way round *or* (*Amer.*) around; **etw. ~herum drehen** turn sth. the other way; **~herum gehen/fahren** go/drive round *or* (*Amer.*) around the other way; ❷ *Adj.* ⇒ **~rum** 2; ***~lautend** ⇒ **anders** A; **~rum** (*ugs.*) ❶ *Adv.* ⇒ **~herum** 1; ❷ *Adj.* **~rum sein** be a poof (*Brit. coll.*) *or* a fairy (*sl. derog.*); be queer (*sl.*); **~sein** *das* (*geh.*) **sein ~sein akzeptieren** accept that one is different; **~wie** *Adv.* (*ugs.*) some other way; **~wo** *Adv.* (*ugs.*) elsewhere; **mach das doch ~wo** do it somewhere else *or* elsewhere; **weder dort noch ~wo** neither there nor anywhere else; **~woher** *Adv.* (*ugs.*) from elsewhere; from somewhere else; **kann man das ~woher beziehen?** can you get that [from] anywhere else?; **~wohin** *Adv.* (*ugs.*) elsewhere; somewhere else; **warum fahren wir nie ~wohin?** why do we never go somewhere else?; **wir fahren immer in die Berge, nie ~wohin** we always go up into the mountains, never anywhere else

**anderthalb** /ˈandɐtˈhalp/ *Bruchz.* ▶ 841 one and a half; **~ Pfund Mehl** a pound and a half of flour; **~ Stunden** an hour and a half; **~ Jahre [alt] sein** be eighteen months [old]

**anderthalb·fach** *Vervielfältigungsz.* one and a half times; **einen ~en Salto machen** do a one-and-a-half somersault; **den ~en Preis verlangen** demand half as much again

**anderthalb·mal** *Adv.* one and a half times; **~ so viel Geld** half as much money again; **~ so viele Besucher** half as many visitors again; **~ so groß wie ...** half as big again as ...

**Änderung** *die;* **~, ~en** change (+ *Gen.* in); alteration (+ *Gen.* to); (*an einem Kleidungsstück*) alteration (**an** + *Dat.* to); (*in einem Menschen*) change (**in** + *Dat.* in); **eine ~ vornehmen** make a change *or* an alteration; **eine ~ zum Besseren** a change for the better; **eine ~ des Programms** a change of programme; **das hat uns zu einer ~ des Programms veranlasst** it has caused us to change *or* alter the programme; **„~en vorbehalten"** 'subject to alteration'

**Änderungs-: ~antrag** *der* (*Politik*) amendment; **~kündigung** *die* (*Arbeitswelt*): *notice of intention to terminate agreement on terms and conditions of employment if changes to the agreement are not accepted;* **~schneiderei** *die* tailor's [that does alterations]; **~vorschlag** *der* suggested amendment *or* change; **~wunsch** *der* request for changes *or* alterations; **haben Sie irgendwelche ~wünsche?** are there any changes *or* alterations you would like to see?

**anderwärts** /-vɛrts/ *Adv.* (*geh.*) elsewhere

**anderweitig** /-vaitɪç/ ❶ *Adj.* (*sonstig*) other. ❷ *adv.* Ⓐ (*auf andere Weise*) in another way;

a

**~ beschäftigt sein** be otherwise engaged; B (*an jmd. anderen*) to somebody else

**an|deuten** 1 *tr. V.* A (*zu verstehen geben*) intimate; hint; **jmdm. etw. ~:** intimate *or* hint sth. to sb.; B (*nicht ausführen*) outline; (*kurz erwähnen*) indicate. 2 *refl. V.* (*sich abzeichnen*) be indicated; **sobald sich die ersten wärmeren Sommertage andeuteten** as soon as there was a suggestion of the first warm days of summer

**An·deutung** *die* A (*Anspielung*) hint; **eine ~ machen** give *or* drop a hint (**über** + *Akk.* about); **in ~en sprechen** talk in hints; B (*schwaches Anzeichen*) suggestion; hint

**andeutungs·weise** *Adv.* in the form of a hint *or* suggestion/hints *or* suggestions; **davon war nur ~ die Rede** it was only hinted at

**an|dichten** *tr. V.* **jmdm. etw. ~:** impute sth. to sb.; **man hatte ihm Wunderkräfte angedichtet** he had been credited with miraculous powers; **sie hatten ihm eine Affäre mit seiner Sekretärin angedichtet** they claimed that he'd had an affair with his secretary

**an|dicken** /'andɪkn̩/ *tr. V.* (*Kochk.*) thicken

**an|dienen** 1 *tr. V.* **jmdm. etw. ~:** offer sth. to sb.; (*aufdringlich*) press sth. on sb. 2 *refl. V.* **sich jmdm. ~:** offer oneself *or* one's services to sb.; (*aufdringlich*) press oneself *or* one's services on sb.

**an|diskutieren** *tr. V.* [begin to] discuss briefly

**an|docken** *tr., itr. V.* (*Raumf.*) **an etw.** (*Dat.*) **~:** dock with sth.

**an|donnern** *itr. V.* (*ugs.*) **angedonnert kommen** come roaring *or* thundering along; (*auf einen zu*) come roaring *or* thundering up

**An·drang** *der* A crowd; (*Gedränge*) crush; **es herrschte großer ~:** there was a large crowd/great crush; B (*von Blut, Milch*) rush; (*von Wasser*) surge

**an|drängen** *itr. V.; mit sein* surge (**gegen** against); ‹crowd› surge forward; ‹army› push forward; **gegen das Tor ~** (*Sport*) surge towards goal; **die ~de Flut/Menschenmenge** the surging tide/crowd

**andre...** ⇒ **ander...**

**Andreas** /an'dre:as/ (*der*) Andrew

**Andreas·kreuz** *das* A St Andrew's cross; B (*Verkehrsw.*) diagonal cross

**an|drehen** *tr. V.* A (*einschalten*) turn on; B (*ugs.: verkaufen*) **jmdm. etw. ~:** palm sb. off with sth.; palm sth. off on sb.; **lass dir bloß keinen von diesen Äpfeln ~:** don't let yourself be palmed off with any of those apples; C (*befestigen*) screw ‹nut› on; screw ‹screw› in; D (*salopp*) **jmdm. ein Kind ~:** knock sb. up (*sl.*); put sb. in the club (*Brit. sl.*)

**andrerseits** ⇒ **andererseits**

**an|dressieren** *tr. V.* A **einem Tier ein Kunststück/artfremdes Verhalten ~:** train an animal to perform a trick/to exhibit behaviour [patterns] foreign to the species; **andressiertes Verhalten** behaviour that is the result of training; B (*fig. abwertend*) train; drill

**an|dringen** *unr. itr. V.; mit sein* (*geh.*) surge (**gegen** against); **der ~de Feind** the enemy surging forward

**Androgen** /andro'ge:n/ *das;* **~s, ~e** (*Med.*) androgen

**androgyn** /andro'gy:n/ *Adj.* (*Psych., Bot.*) androgynous

**an|drohen** *tr. V.* **jmdm. etw. ~:** threaten sb. with sth.; **er hat mir Prügel angedroht** he threatened to beat me

**An·drohung** *die* threat; **unter ~ von Gewalt** with the *or* under threat of violence; **durch die ~ seines Rücktritts** by threatening to resign

**Android** /andro'i:t/ *der;* **~en, ~en, Androide** /andro'i:də/ *der;* **~n, ~n** android

**Androloge** /andro'lo:gə/ *der;* **~n, ~n, Andrologin** *die;* **~, ~nen** (*Med.*) andrologist

*old spelling (see note on page 1707)

**An·druck** *der;* **~[e]s, ~e** (*Druckw.*) A (*Probe*) proof; **bereit für den ~:** ready for proofing; B (*Beginn*) going to press; **lange vor dem ~:** long before going to press

**an|drucken** (*Druckw.*) 1 *tr. V.* A (*beginnen*) start printing; B (*zur Probe*) proof; pull proofs of. 2 *itr. V.* A (*beginnen*) start printing; go to press; **wir können ~ lassen** we can go to press; B (*zur Probe*) pull proofs

**an|drücken** *tr. V.* A press down; **den Bleistift leicht ~:** press lightly with the pencil; B (*einschalten*) switch on

**Andruck·exemplar** *das* (*Druckw.*) A printed copy; B (*Probe*) proof copy

**an|dudeln** *tr. V.* **in sich** (*Dat.*) **einen ~** (*salopp*) get plastered (*sl.*)

**an|dünsten** *tr. V.* (*Kochk.*) braise lightly

**Äneas** /ɛ'ne:as/ (*der*) Aeneas

**an|ecken** *itr. V.; mit sein* A (*anstoßen*) **an etw.** (*Dat.*) **~:** hit sth.; B (*ugs.: Ärger erregen*) **bei jmdm. ~:** rub sb. [up (*Brit.*)] the wrong way

**an|eifern** *tr. V.* (*südd., österr.*) spur on

**an|eignen** *refl. V.* A (*nehmen*) appropriate; **sich** (*Dat.*) **etw. widerrechtlich ~:** misappropriate sth.; B (*lernen*) acquire; learn; C (*angewöhnen*) acquire; pick up

**An·eignung** *die* A appropriation; **widerrechtliche ~:** misappropriation; B (*Lernen*) acquisition; learning; C (*Rechtsw.*) acquisition of title (*Gen.* to)

**an·einander** *Adv.* (*zusammen*) together; (*nebeneinander*) next to each other; next to one another; (*gegeneinander*) against each other; against one another; **Häuser ~ bauen** build houses on to each other; **dicht ~ gebaut** built very close together; **Raumschiffe ~ koppeln** link up spacecraft; **sich ~ klammern** cling together *or* to each other; **sich ~ kuscheln** snuggle *or* cuddle up [together *or* to each other *or* to one another]; **sie lagen ~ gekuschelt** they lay snuggled *or* cuddled up [together]; **Perlen auf einer Schnur ~ reihen** thread pearls/beads on a string; **~ grenzen** ‹properties, rooms, etc.› adjoin [each other *or* one another]; ‹countries› border on each other *or* one another; **~ liegen** lie next to each other; ‹properties› adjoin [each other *or* one another]; **~ prallen** collide; **~ rücken** move [up] closer together; **~ schlagen** strike each other *or* one another; **sich ~ schmiegen** snuggle *or* cuddle up [together *or* to each other *or* to one another]; **stellt euch mal mit dem Rücken ~:** stand back to back; **~ stoßen** strike each other; ‹heads, vehicles› collide; **sie stießen mit den Köpfen ~:** their heads collided; **mit jmdm. ~ geraten** (*sich prügeln*) come to blows with sb.; (*sich streifen*) quarrel with sb; **~ denken** think of each other *or* one another; **~ vorbeigehen** pass each other *or* one another; go past each other *or* one another; **sich ~ gewöhnen** get used to each other *or* one another; **~ vorbeireden** talk at cross purposes; **sich ~ festhalten** hold each other *or* one another

**aneinander-, Aneinander-:** ***~|bauen** *usw.* ⇒ **aneinander**; **~reihung** *die* stringing together; **eine bloße ~reihung von Tatsachen** a series of facts just strung together; ***~|rücken** *usw.* ⇒ **aneinander**

**Äneis** /ɛ'ne:ɪs/ *die;* **~:** Aeneid

**Anekdote** /anɛk'do:tə/ *die;* **~, ~n** anecdote

**anekdoten·haft** 1 *Adj.* anecdotal. 2 *adv.* ‹relate› in anecdotes

**anekdotisch** 1 *Adj.* anecdotal. 2 *adv.* **ein ~ gewürzter Vortrag** a lecture enlivened with anecdotes

**an|ekeln** *tr. V.* disgust; nauseate; **du ekelst mich an** you make me sick; **sich angeekelt abwenden** turn away in disgust

**Anemo·meter** /anemo-/ *das* (*Met.*) anemometer

**Anemone** /ane'mo:nə/ *die;* **~, ~n** anemone

**an|empfehlen** *unr. tr. V.* (*geh.*) recommend (*Dat.* to)

**an|erbieten** *unr. refl. V.* (*geh.*) offer one's services; **sich ~, etw. zu tun** offer to do sth.

**Anerbieten** *das;* **~s, ~** (*geh.*) offer

**anerkannt** *Adj.* recognized; recognized, acknowledged ‹authority, expert›; recognized, accepted, established ‹fact›

**anerkanntermaßen** *Adv.* **er gehört ~ zu den besten Spielern** he is generally recognized *or* acknowledged to be one of the best players

**anerkennen** *unr. tr. V.;* **ich erkenne an** (*od. seltener:* **anerkenne**), **anerkannt, anzuerkennen** A recognize ‹country, record, verdict, qualification, document›; acknowledge ‹debt›; accept ‹demand, bill, conditions, rules›; allow ‹claim, goal›; **ein Kind ~:** acknowledge a child as one's own; **jmdn. als gleichberechtigten Partner ~:** accept sb. as an equal partner; B (*nicht leugnen*) acknowledge; C (*würdigen*) acknowledge, appreciate ‹achievement, efforts›; appreciate ‹person›; respect ‹viewpoint, opinion›; **ein ~der Blick** an appreciative look; **~d nicken** nod appreciatively; **einige ~de Worte** a few words of appreciation

**anerkennens·wert** *Adj.* commendable

**anerkennenswerter·weise** *Adv.* commendably

**An·erkenntnis** *das;* **~ses, ~se** acknowledgement

**Anerkennung** *die;* **~, ~en** A ⇒ **anerkennen** A: recognition; acknowledgement; acceptance; allowance; B (*Zugeständnis*) acknowledgement; C (*Würdigung*) ⇒ **anerkennen** C: acknowledgement; appreciation; respect (*Gen.* for)

**an|erziehen** *unr. tr. V.* **jmdm. etw. ~:** instil sth. into sb.; **Kindern Pünktlichkeit ~:** bring children up to be punctual

**an|essen** *unr. refl. V.* **in sich** (*Dat.*) **einen Bauch ~:** develop a paunch

**an|fachen** *tr. V.* fan; (*fig.*) arouse ‹anger, curiosity, enthusiasm›; arouse, inflame ‹passion›; inspire, stir up ‹hatred›; inspire ‹hope›; ferment ‹discord, war›

**an|fahren** 1 *unr. tr. V.* A run into; hit; B (*herbeifahren*) deliver; C (*ansteuern*) stop *or* call at ‹village etc.›; ‹ship› put in at ‹port›; **das Schiff fährt die Insel einmal wöchentlich an** the boat calls at the island once a week; D (*zurechtweisen*) shout at; E (*in Betrieb nehmen*) commission ‹powerstation, blast furnace›. 2 *unr. itr. V.; mit sein* A (*starten*) start off; **das Anfahren am Berg** hill-starting; B (*heranfahren*) drive up; (*mit dem Fahrrad, Motorrad*) ride up; **angefahren kommen** come driving/riding up

**An·fahrt** *die* A (*das Anfahren*) journey; (*als Autofahrer*) drive; (*Ankunft*) arrival; B (*Weg*) approach; (*Einfahrt*) entrance

**Anfahrts-:** **~weg** *der* journey; (*als Autofahrer*) drive; **~zeit** *die* travelling time; **~zeiten als Arbeitszeit berechnen** count travelling time *sing.* as working time

**An·fall** *der* A (*Attacke*) attack; (*epileptischer ~, fig.*) fit; **einen ~ bekommen** *od.* (*ugs.*) **kriegen** have an attack/a fit; **in einem ~ von ...** (*fig.*) in a fit of ...; B (*Anfallendes*) amount (**an** + *Dat.* of); (*Ertrag*) yield (**an** + *Dat.* of)

**anfall·artig** 1 *Adj.* **~es Husten** fits *pl.* of coughing; coughing fits *pl.*; **~e Schmerzen** spasms *pl.* of pain. 2 *adv.* **plötzlich und ~ auftretende Zuckungen/Schmerzen** a sudden fit/sudden fits of twitching/a sudden spasm/sudden spasms of pain; **die Schmerzen kommen ~:** the pain comes in spasms

**an·fallen** 1 *unr. tr. V.* A (*angreifen*) attack; B (*geh.: befallen*) **Zweifel/Angst fiel mich an** I was assailed by doubt/fear; **Heimweh/Wut/Entsetzen fiel mich an** I was filled with homesickness/rage/horror; **Müdigkeit fiel mich an** I was overcome with tiredness. 2 *unr. itr. V.; mit sein* ‹costs› arise, be incurred; ‹interest› accrue; ‹work› come up; ‹parcels etc.› accumulate; **als Nebenprodukt/Nebenkosten ~:** be obtained as a by-product/be costs incurred; **alle ~den Reparaturen** any repairs that become necessary

**an·fällig** *Adj.* delicate ‹child›; temperamental ‹engine›; **gegen** *od.* **für etw. ~ sein** be susceptible to sth.; **für eine Krankheit ~ sein** be prone to an illness

**An·fälligkeit** *die;* ~, **~en** (*eines Kindes usw.*) delicateness; (*eines Motors usw.*) temperamental nature; **~ gegen** *od.* **für etw.** susceptibility to sth.; **~ für eine Krankheit** proneness to an illness

**anfalls·weise** *Adv.* **die Schmerzen kommen ~:** the pain comes in spasms

**An·fang** *der* ▶76, ▶207 beginning; start; (*erster Abschnitt*) beginning; **ohne ~ und Ende** without a beginning *or* an end; **[ganz] am ~ der Straße** [right] at the start of the street; **von den Anfängen** from the beginnings; **am** *od.* **zu ~:** at first; to begin with; **am ~ schuf Gott ...** in the beginning God created ...; **du hättest ihm gleich zu ~ sagen sollen, dass ...** you should have told him right at the beginning *or* outset that ...; **von ~ an** from the beginning *or* outset; **~ 1984/der Achtzigerjahre/Mai/der Woche** *usw.* at the beginning of 1984/the eighties/May/the week *etc.*; **von ~ bis Ende** from beginning to end *or* start to finish; **der ~ vom Ende** the beginning of the end; **im ~ war das Wort** (*bibl.*) in the beginning was the Word; **einen ~ machen** make a start; **ein ~ ist gemacht** it's a start; we've/they've *etc.* made a start; **den ~ machen** make a start; start; (*nach einem Zerwürfnis o. Ä.*) make the first move; **einen/keinen ~ finden** know/not know how to begin *or* start; **einen neuen ~ machen** make a new *or* fresh start; **aller ~ ist schwer** (*Spr.*) it's always difficult at the beginning; **seinen ~ nehmen** (*geh.*) begin; start; **in den** *od.* **seinen Anfängen stecken** be in its infancy; **wehret den Anfängen!** these things must be stopped at the outset; **aus bescheidenen Anfängen** from small *or* humble beginnings

**an·fangen** ❶ *unr. itr. V.* Ⓐ begin; start; **das fängt ja gut an!** (*ugs. iron.*) that's a good start! (*iron.*); **mit dreißig fängt das Leben erst an** life begins at thirty; **der Monat fing mit einem Donnerstag an** the first day of the month was a Thursday; **wer fängt an?** who is going to start?; **habt ihr schon angefangen?** have you already started?; **fangt doch bitte schon an** do please start; **er hat ganz klein/als ganz kleiner Angestellter angefangen** he started small/started [out] as a minor employee; **mit etw. ~:** start [on] sth.; **fang nicht wieder damit an!** don't start [all] that again!; **~, etw. zu tun** start to do sth.; **es fängt an zu schneien** *od.* **zu schneien an** it's starting *or* beginning to snow; **fang doch nicht gleich an zu weinen** don't start crying; **angefangen bei** *od.* **mit** *od.* **von ...** starting *or* beginning with ...; **Weiß fängt an** white starts; **er hat angefangen** (*mit dem Streit o. Ä.*) he started it; **[noch mal] von vorne ~:** start [again] from the beginning; start all over again; Ⓑ (*zu sprechen ~*) begin; **von etw. ~:** start on about sth.; Ⓒ (*eine Stelle antreten*) start; **bei einer Firma ~:** start working for a firm; start with a firm.
❷ *unr. tr. V.* Ⓐ begin; start; (*anbrechen*) start; **das Rauchen ~:** start smoking; **ich glaube, er will mit seiner Sekretärin was ~** (*ugs.*) I think he's trying to start something with his secretary; **auf seinem Schreibtisch lag ein angefangener Brief** on his desk lay a letter which he had started to write; Ⓑ (*machen*) do; **damit kann ich nichts/nicht viel ~:** that's no/not much good to me; (*das verstehe ich nicht/kaum*) that doesn't mean anything/much to me; **kannst du noch etwas damit ~?** is it any good *or* use to you?; **mit ihm ist heute nichts anzufangen** he is just not with it today; **mit ihm kann ich wenig ~:** he isn't my type of person; **er weiß nichts mit sich anzufangen** he doesn't know what to do with himself; **wie hast du das nun wieder angefangen?** how did you manage that?; **du musst etwas Solides ~:** you must get yourself a proper job/training *etc.*; **du hättest es ganz anders ~ müssen** you should have gone about it quite differently

**An·fänger** *der;* **~s, ~, An·fängerin** *die;* ~, **~nen** beginner; (*abwertend: Stümper*) amateur; (*am Heck eines Autos*) „~" 'learner'

**Anfänger·kurs** *der* beginners' course; course for beginners

**anfänglich** /'anfɛŋlɪç/ ❶ *Adj.* initial. ❷ *adv.* at first; initially

**anfangs** *Adv.* at first; initially; **gleich ~:** right at the beginning *or* outset

**Anfangs-: ~buchstabe** *der* initial [letter]; first letter; **~drittel** *das* (*Eishockey*) first period; **~erfolg** *der* initial success; **~gehalt** *das* starting salary; **~geschwindigkeit** *die* (*Physik*) initial velocity; **~gründe** *Pl.* rudiments; **~kapital** *das* starting capital; **~phase** *die* first *or* initial phase; **~reim** *der* initial *or* beginning rhyme; **~schwierigkeit** *die* initial difficulty; **~silbe** *die* first *or* initial syllable; **~stadium** *das* initial stage; **im ~stadium sein** be in its/their initial stages *pl.*; **~unterricht** *der* elementary instruction; **ein Englischbuch für den ~unterricht** an elementary-level English book; **~zeit** *die* starting time

**an|fassen** ❶ *tr. V.* Ⓐ (*fassen, halten*) take hold of; **die Kinder fassen jeden Dreck an** the children will pick up any bit of dirt; Ⓑ (*berühren*) touch; **fass mal meine Stirn an** feel my forehead; **nicht ~!** don't touch!; **Geschichte zum Anfassen** (*fig.*) history brought to life; **ich fasse nie wieder eine Spielkarte an** I'll never touch a pack of cards again; Ⓒ (*bei der Hand nehmen*) **jmdn. ~:** take sb.'s hand; **fasst euch an** take each other's hand; Ⓓ (*angehen*) approach, tackle ‹problem, task, etc.›; Ⓔ (*behandeln*) treat ‹person›; Ⓕ (*geh.: befallen*) **Ekel/Sehnsucht/Mitleid fasste mich an** I was seized with revulsion/filled with longing/pity.
❷ *itr. V.* (*mithelfen*) **[mit] ~:** lend a hand.
❸ *refl. V.* (*sich anfühlen*) feel; **das fasst sich wie Wolle an** it feels like wool

**an|fauchen** *tr. V.* Ⓐ ‹cat› spit at; Ⓑ (*fig.*) snap at

**an|faulen** *itr. V.; mit sein* ‹fruit› start to go bad; ‹wood› start to rot; **ein angefaulter Apfel/Balken** a bad apple/rotting beam

**anfechtbar** *Adj.* Ⓐ (*bes. Rechtsw.*) contestable; Ⓑ (*kritisierbar, bestreitbar*) disputable ‹statement, decision›; ‹book› open to criticism

**Anfechtbarkeit** *die;* ~ ⇒ **anfechtbar**: Ⓐ contestable nature; Ⓑ disputable nature

**an|fechten** *unr. tr. V.* Ⓐ (*bes. Rechtsw.*) challenge, dispute ‹validity, authenticity, statement›; contest ‹will›; contest, challenge ‹decision›; dispute ‹contract›; challenge ‹law, opinion›; Ⓑ (*beunruhigen*) trouble; bother; **was ficht dich an?** (*geh.*) what is wrong *or* the matter with you?

**Anfechtung** *die;* ~, **~en** Ⓐ (*bes. Rechtsw.*) ⇒ **anfechten** A: challenging; disputing; contesting; Ⓑ (*geh.: Versuchung*) temptation

**Anfechtungs·klage** *die* (*Rechtsw.*) action for nullification

**an|fegen** *itr. V.; mit sein* **angefegt kommen** (*ugs.*) come belting along (*coll.*); (*auf einen zu*) come belting up (*coll.*)

**an|feinden** *tr. V.* treat with hostility

**Anfeindung** *die;* ~, **~en** hostility; **trotz aller ~en** despite all the hostility *sing.* shown towards him/her *etc.*; **~en ausgesetzt sein** be exposed to hostility *sing.*

**an|fertigen** *tr. V.* make; do ‹homework, translation›; make up ‹medicament, preparation›; prepare, draw up ‹report›; cut, make ‹key›; **Kleider/einen Schlüssel ~ lassen** have clothes made/a key cut

**An·fertigung** *die* Ⓐ ⇒ **anfertigen**: making; doing; making up; preparing; drawing up; cutting; Ⓑ (*Erzeugnis*) **das Regal ist eine eigene ~ [von mir]** I made the shelves myself; **eine spezielle ~ sein** be specially made

**an|feuchten** *tr. V.* moisten ‹lips, stamp›; dampen, wet ‹ironing, cloth, etc.›

**an|feuern** *tr. V.* spur on; **~de Rufe/Gesten** shouts of encouragement/rousing gestures

**An·feuerung** *die* spurring on; **~ und Beifall** cheers and applause

**Anfeuerungs·ruf** *der* cheer

**an|finden** *unr. refl. V.* be found [again]; turn up

**an|flachsen** *tr. V.* (*ugs.*) tease; kid (*sl.*)

**an|flanschen** /'anflanʃn̩/ *tr. V.* (*Technik*) flange sth. on (**an** + *Dat. od. Akk.* to)

**an|flattern** *itr. V.; mit sein* **angeflattert kommen** come fluttering along; (*auf einen zu*) come fluttering up

**an|flehen** *tr. V.* beseech; implore; **jmdn. um etw. ~:** beg sb. for sth.

**an|fliegen** ❶ *unr. itr. V.; mit sein* fly in; (*beim Landen*) approach; come in to land; ‹bird etc.› fly in; **angeflogen kommen** come flying in; (*auf einen zu*) ‹bird› come flying up; **gegen den Wind ~:** fly into the wind.
❷ *unr. tr. V.* Ⓐ fly to ‹city, country, airport›; (*beim Landen*) approach ‹airport›; land on ‹runway etc.›; Ⓑ (*ansteuern*) ‹aircraft› approach; ‹bird› fly towards, approach

**an|flitzen** *itr. V.; mit sein* **angeflitzt kommen** (*ugs.*) come racing along; (*auf einen zu*) come racing up

**An·flug** *der* Ⓐ approach; **die Maschine befindet sich im ~ auf Berlin** the plane is now approaching Berlin; Ⓑ (*Hauch*) hint; trace; **ein humoristischer ~:** a hint *or* trace of humour; Ⓒ (*Anwandlung*) fit; **in einem ~ von Großzügigkeit** in a fit of generosity; Ⓓ (*Weg, Strecke*) flight

**an|flunkern** *tr. V.* (*ugs.*) tell fibs to

**an|fordern** *tr. V.* request, ask for ‹help›; ask for ‹catalogue›; order ‹goods, materials›; send for ‹ambulance›

**An·forderung** *die* Ⓐ (*das Anfordern*) request (*Gen.* for); **die ~ von Waren/Materialien** ordering goods/materials; Ⓑ (*Anspruch*) demand; **große/hohe ~en an jmdn./etw. stellen** make great demands on sb./sth.; **den ~en nicht gewachsen sein** not be up to the demands

**An·frage** *die* inquiry; (*Parl.*) question; **große/kleine ~** (*Parl.*) oral/written question

**an|fragen** ❶ *itr. V.* inquire; ask; **bei jmdm. um etw. ~:** ask sb. for sth. ❷ *tr. V.* (*schweiz.*) ask

**an|fressen** ❶ *unr. tr. V.* Ⓐ nibble [at]; ‹bird› peck [at]; Ⓑ (*zersetzen*) eat away [at]; **ein von Rost angefressenes altes Auto** a rusty old car. ❷ *unr. refl. V.* **sich** (*Dat.*) **einen Bauch ~** (*salopp*) develop a paunch; **die Tiere fressen sich einen Winterspeck an** the animals [eat to] put on winter fat

**an|freunden** *refl. V.* Ⓐ make *or* become friends; **sich mit jmdm./miteinander ~:** make *or* become friends with sb./become friends; Ⓑ (*fig.*) **sich mit einer Sache ~:** get to like sth.

**an|frieren** *unr. itr. V.; mit sein* **an etw.** (*Dat.*) **~:** freeze to sth.

**an|fügen** *tr. V.* add

**An·fügung** *die* addition

**an|fühlen** ❶ *refl. V.* feel; **sich hart/weich ~:** feel hard/soft; be hard/soft to the touch. ❷ *tr. V.* (*befühlen*) feel

**Anfuhr** *die;* ~, **~en** transport[ation]

**an|führen** *tr. V.* Ⓐ lead; lead, head ‹procession›; **unsere Mannschaft führt die Tabelle an** our team heads the table *or* is [at the] top of the table; Ⓑ (*zitieren*) quote; Ⓒ (*nennen*) quote, give, offer ‹example›; give, offer ‹reason, details, proof›; **zu meiner Entschuldigung möchte ich auch noch ~, dass ...** I should also like to mention in my defence that ...; Ⓓ (*benennen*) name; cite; Ⓔ (*ugs.: hereinlegen*) have on (*Brit. coll.*); dupe; **lass dich doch von ihm nicht ~:** don't be had on (*Brit.*) *or* taken in by him (*coll.*); Ⓕ (*Druckw.: mit Anführungszeichen versehen*) mark with opening quotation marks *or* (*Brit.*) inverted commas; **Buchtitel werden an- und abgeführt** book titles are put in quotation marks *or* (*Brit.*) inverted commas

**An·führer** *der,* **An·führerin** *die* Ⓐ (*Führer*) leader; Ⓑ (*Rädelsführer*) ringleader

**An·führung** *die* Ⓐ leadership; **unter [der] ~** (+ *Gen.*) under the leadership of; Ⓑ (*das Zitieren, Zitat*) quotation; Ⓒ (*Nennung*) ⇒ **anführen** C: quotation; giving; offering; **ich**

**beschränke mich auf die ~ einiger Beispiele** I will confine myself to quoting *or* giving *or* offering just a few examples; **D** *(Benennung)* naming; citing; **E** *(Druckw.: Anführungszeichen)* opening quotation mark

**Anführungs-: ~strich** *der*, **~zeichen** *das* quotation mark; inverted comma *(Brit.)*; **ein Wort mit ~strichen** *od.* **~zeichen versehen** put a word in quotation marks *or (Brit.)* inverted commas; **~striche** *od.* **~zeichen unten/oben** *(beim Diktieren o. Ä.)* quote/unquote; **halbe ~striche** *od.* **~zeichen** single quotation marks *or (coll.)* quotes

**an|füllen** ❶ *tr. V.* fill [up]; **mit etw. angefüllt sein** be filled *or* full with sth. ❷ *refl. V.* fill [up]

**an|funkeln** *tr. V.* flash one's eyes at

**an|futtern** *refl. V. in* **sich** *(Dat.)* **einen Bauch/ein Bäuchlein ~** *(ugs.)* develop a paunch/*(coll.)* a bit of a tummy

**An·gabe** *die* **A** *(das Mitteilen)* giving; **ohne ~ von Gründen** without giving [any] reasons; **zur ~ dieser Daten bist du verpflichtet** you are obliged to give this information; **B** *(Auskunft, Aussage)* **~n** information *sing.*; **jede einzelne ~ wurde überprüft** every piece of information has been checked; **C** *(Anweisung)* instruction; **D** *(Prahlerei)* boasting; bragging; *(angeberisches Benehmen)* showing-off; **das ist doch nur ~!** he is/they are *etc.* only boasting; **E** *(Ballspiele)* service; serve; **[eine] ~ machen** serve; **ich habe [die] ~:** it's my serve

**an|gaffen** *tr. V. (abwertend)* gape at

**an|gähnen** *tr. V.* yawn at

**an|galoppieren** *itr. V.; mit sein* **angaloppiert kommen** come galloping along; *(auf einen zu)* come galloping up

**an·gängig** *Adj.* permissible

**an|geben** ❶ *unr. tr. V.* **A** give ‹reason›; declare ‹income, dutiable goods›; name, cite ‹witness›; **welche Haarfarbe er hatte, kann ich nicht [genau] ~:** I cannot say *or* state [exactly] what colour hair he had; **zur angegebenen Zeit** at the appointed time; **wie oben angegeben** as stated *or* mentioned above; **der Zeuge gab an, er habe drei Schüsse gehört** the witness stated *or* maintained that he heard three shots; **B** *(bestimmen)* set ‹course, direction›; **den Takt ~:** keep time; **C** *(veralt.: anzeigen, melden)* report ‹theft etc.›; give away ‹accomplice etc.›; **jmdn./einen Diebstahl bei der Polizei ~:** report sb./a theft to the police; **das geb ich an!** I'm going to report that!
❷ *unr. itr. V.* **A** *(prahlen)* boast; brag; *(sich angeberisch benehmen)* show off; **er gibt vor den Mädchen damit an, dass ...** he boasts to all the girls that ...; **Väter geben mit ihren Kindern an** fathers boast *or* brag about their children; **~ wie eine Tüte [voll] Mücken** *(ugs.)* be just a big show-off *(coll.)*; **B** *(Ballspiele)* serve; **wer gibt an?** whose serve is it?; whose turn is it to serve?

**Angeber** *der;* **~s, ~, Angeberin** *die;* **~, ~nen** **A** *(Prahler)* boaster; braggart; *(sich angeberisch Benehmender)* show-off; **B** *(veralt.: Denunziant)* informer

**Angeberei** *die;* **~, ~en** **A** *(das Angeben)* boasting; bragging; *(angeberisches Benehmen)* showing-off; **das ist doch nichts als ~:** he's/they are *etc.* only boasting/showing off; **B** *(Handlung)* piece of showing-off; *(Äußerung)* boast; **mit seinen dummen ~en** with his stupid showing off/boasting

**angeberisch** *(ugs.)* ❶ *Adj.* boastful ‹person›; pretentious, showy ‹glasses, car, jacket›; *(im Benehmen)* ‹person› given to showing off; **~es Getue** *od.* **Verhalten** showing-off. ❷ *adv.* boastfully

**Angebetete** *der/die; adj. Dekl. (meist scherzh.)* beloved; *(Idol)* idol

**An·gebinde** *das (geh. veralt.)* gift; present

**angeblich** ❶ *Adj.* alleged. ❷ *adv.* supposedly; allegedly; **er ist ~ krank** he is supposed to be ill; *(er sagt, er sei krank)* he says he's ill

**an·geboren** *Adj.* innate ‹characteristic›; congenital ‹disease›; **die Schüchternheit ist ihm ~:** he is shy by nature *or* naturally shy

**An·gebot** *das* **A** offer; **B** *(Wirtsch.: Waren~)* range; **das ~ an** *od.* **von Gemüse ist immer saisonabhängig** the selection of vegetables available always depends on the season; **das Verhältnis von ~ und Nachfrage** the relationship between supply and demand; **C** *(Kaufmannsspr.: Sonder~)* [special] offer; **im ~:** on [special] offer; **~ der Woche** bargain of the week

**an·gebracht** ❶ *2. Part. v.* **anbringen.** ❷ *Adj.* appropriate

**an·gebunden** ❶ *2. Part. v.* **anbinden.** ❷ *Adj.* **A** tied down; **B** *in* **kurz ~** *(ugs.)* short; abrupt

**an·gedeihen** *unr. itr. V. in* **jmdm. etw. ~ lassen** *(geh.)* provide sb. with sth.; grant sb. sth.

**An·gedenken** *das* remembrance; **jmdm. ein treues ~ bewahren** keep sb. in fond remembrance; **mein Großvater seligen ~s** *(geh.)* my grandfather of blessed memory; **eine Zeit unseligen ~s** *(geh.)* a notorious period

**an·gegangen** ❶ *2. Part. v.* **angehen.** ❷ *Adj. (bes. ostmd.)* ‹food› that has gone off; **~ sein** have gone off

**angegilbt** /ˈangəgɪlpt/ *Adj.* yellowing; slightly yellowed

**an·gegossen** *Adj. in* **wie ~ sitzen/passen** *(ugs.)* fit like a glove

**angegraut** /ˈangəgraut/ *Adj.* greying

**an·gegriffen** ❶ *2. Part. v.* **angreifen.** ❷ *Adj.* weakened ‹health, stomach›; strained ‹nerves, voice›; *(erschöpft)* exhausted; *(nervlich)* strained

**angehaucht** ❶ *2. Part. v.* **anhauchen.** ❷ *Adj.* **links/rechts/sozialistisch** *usw.* **~ sein** have left-wing/right-wing/socialist *etc.* leanings

**an·geheiratet** *Adj.* **ein ~er Onkel/Vetter** *usw.* an uncle/a cousin *etc.* by marriage; **~ sein** be related by marriage

**angeheitert** /ˈangəhaitɐt/ *Adj.* tipsy; merry *(coll.)*

**an|gehen** ❶ *unr. itr. V.; mit sein* **A** *(sich einschalten, entzünden)* ‹radio, light, heating› come on; ‹fire› catch, start burning; **B** *(sich einschalten, entzünden lassen)* ‹radio, light› go on; ‹fire› light, catch; **C** *(ugs.: beginnen)* start; **D** *(anwachsen, wachsen)* ‹plant› take root; ‹vaccination› take; ‹bacteria› grow; **E** *(geschehen dürfen)* **es mag noch ~:** it's [just about] acceptable; **es geht nicht an, dass radikale Elemente die Partei unterwandern** radical elements must not be allowed to infiltrate the party; **F** *(bes. nordd.: wahr sein)* **das kann doch wohl nicht ~!** that can't be true!; **das kann [wohl] ~:** that could be true; **G** **gegen etw./jmdn. ~:** fight sth./sb.
❷ *unr. tr. V.* **A** *(angreifen)* attack; *(Sport)* tackle; challenge; **B** *(in Angriff nehmen)* tackle ‹problem, difficulty›; take ‹fence, bend›; **C** *(bitten)* ask; **jmdn. um etw. ~:** ask sb. for sth.; **D** *(betreffen)* concern; **was geht dich das an?** what's it got to do with you?; **das geht dich nichts an** it's none of your business; **was das/mich angeht, [so] ...** as far as that is/I am concerned ...

**angehend** *Adj.* budding ‹actor, artist, etc.›; prospective ‹teacher, husband, etc.›

**an|gehören** *itr. V.* **jmdm./einer Sache ~:** belong to sb./sth.; **der Regierung/einer Familie/Kommission ~:** be a member of the government/a family/committee; **einander ~** *(geh.)* belong to each other; **einer Nation ~:** be a national of a country

**an·gehörig** *Adj.* belonging *(Dat.* to); **dem Bündnis ~e Staaten** states belonging to the alliance

**Angehörige** *der/die; adj. Dekl.* **A** *(Verwandte)* relative; relation; **der nächste ~:** the next of kin; **B** *(Mitglied)* member

**Angeklagte** /ˈangəklaːktə/ *der/die; adj. Dekl.* accused; defendant

**angeknackst** *(ugs.)* ❶ *2. Part. v.* **anknacksen.** ❷ *Adj.* weakened ‹trust, confidence›; weakened ‹health›; **ihre Gesundheit ist ~:** she's not in the best of health *or (coll.)* not all that great

**angekränkelt** /ˈangəkrɛŋkl̩t/ *Adj.* sickly; **von Eitelkeit ~:** afflicted with vanity

**Angel** /ˈaŋl̩/ *die;* **~, ~n** **A** fishing rod; rod and line; **die ~ auswerfen/einziehen** cast/pull in the line; **B** *(Tür~, Fenster~ usw.)* hinge; **etw. aus den ~n heben** lift sth. off its hinges; *(fig.)* turn sth. upside down

**an·gelegen** ❶ *2. Part. v.* **anliegen.** ❷ *Adj. in* **sich** *(Dat.)* **etw. ~ sein lassen** concern oneself with sth.

**An·gelegenheit** *die* matter; *(Aufgabe, Problem)* affair; concern; **öffentliche/kulturelle ~en** public/cultural affairs; **das ist meine/nicht meine ~:** that is my affair *or* business/not my concern *or* business; **kümmere dich um deine eigenen ~en!** mind your own business; **sich in jmds. ~en mischen** meddle in sb.'s affairs; **in welcher ~?** in what connection?; **in eigener/in einer privaten ~:** on a personal/private matter

**an·gelegentlich** *(geh.)* ❶ *Adj.* pressing ‹question, request›; earnest ‹conversation, warning›. ❷ *adv.* ‹look› very closely, thoroughly; ‹ask, inquire› particularly; **sich mit einer Sache ~ beschäftigen** be intensively occupied with sth.; **jmdm. ~ empfehlen, nicht mehr zu rauchen** earnestly recommend sb. to give up smoking

**angelegt** ❶ *2. Part. v.* **anlegen.** ❷ *Adj.* **auf Verteidigung/Entspannung** *(Akk.)* **~ sein** be intended for defence/be intended to promote détente

**Angel-: ~gerät** *das* **A** fishing rod; rod and line; **B** fishing tackle; **~haken** *der* fish hook; **~leine** *die* fishing line

**angeln** ❶ *tr. V. (zu fangen suchen)* fish for; *(fangen)* catch; **er angelt sich immer die Fleischstücke aus der Suppe** *(fig.)* he always fishes the pieces of meat out of the soup; **sie hat sich einen reichen Mann geangelt** *(fig.)* she has hooked a rich husband. ❷ *itr. V.* angle; fish; **auf Hechte ~:** fish for pike; **nach etw. ~** *(fig.)* fish for sth.

**an|geloben** *tr. V. (österr.)* ⇨ **vereidigen**

**Angel-: ~punkt** *der* crucial point; *(eines Problems)* crux; *(zentrales Thema)* central issue; **~rute** *die* fishing rod; **~sachse** *der* **A** *(hist.)* Anglo-Saxon; **B** *(Engländer)* Englishman; **die ~sachsen** the English; *(Engländer u. Amerikaner)* the Anglo-Saxons; **~sächsin** *die* **A** *(hist.)* Anglo-Saxon; **B** *(Engländerin)* English woman/English girl; **~sächsisch** *Adj.* **A** *(hist.)* Anglo-Saxon; **B** *(englisch)* English; **die ~sächsischen Länder** the Anglo-Saxon countries; **~schein** *der* fishing permit *or* licence; **~schnur** *die* fishingline; **~sport** *der* angling *no art.*

**an·gemessen** ❶ *2. Part. v.* **anmessen.** ❷ *Adj.* appropriate; reasonable, fair ‹price, fee›; **den Umständen ~ sein** be appropriate to the circumstances. ❸ *adv.* ‹behave› appropriately; ‹reward› adequately; ‹recompense› reasonably, fairly

**an·genehm** ❶ *Adj.* pleasant; agreeable; **ist Ihnen die Temperatur/ist es so ~?** is the temperature all right for you/is it all right like that?; **es ist mir gar nicht ~, dass ...** I don't at all like it that ...; **wenn Ihnen das ~er ist** if you [would] prefer; **~e Reise/Ruhe!** [have a] pleasant journey/have a good rest; **[sehr] ~!** delighted to meet you; **das Angenehme mit dem Nützlichen verbinden** combine business with pleasure. ❷ *adv.* pleasantly; agreeably

**angepasst, *angepaßt** ❶ *2. Part. v.* **anpassen.** ❷ *Adj.* conformist

**Angepasstheit, *Angepaßtheit** *die;* **~:** conformism

**Anger** /ˈaŋɐ/ *der;* **~s, ~:** [village] green

**angeregt** ❶ *2. Part. v.* **anregen.** ❷ *Adj.* lively; animated. ❸ *adv.* **sich ~ unterhalten/~ diskutieren** have a lively *or* an animated conversation/discussion

*old spelling (see note on page 1707)

**angesäuselt** (*ugs.*) ❶ *2. Part. v.* **ansäuseln.** ❷ *Adj.* tipsy; merry (*coll.*)

**an·geschlagen** ❶ *2. Part. v.* **anschlagen.** ❷ *Adj.* groggy; poor, weakened ‹health›

**angeschmutzt** /'angəʃmʊtst/ *Adj.* slightly soiled

**Angeschuldigte** *der/die; adj. Dekl.* suspect

**angesehen** ❶ *2. Part. v.* **ansehen.** ❷ *Adj.* respected

**An·gesicht** *das;* **~[e]s, ~er,** *österr. auch* **~e** (*geh.*) Ⓐ (*Gesicht*) face; **von ~ zu ~:** face to face; **jmdm. von ~ zu ~ gegenüberstehen** stand facing sb. *or* face to face with sb.; **jmdn. von ~ kennen** know sb. by sight; Ⓑ *in* **im ~** (+ *Gen.*) ⇒ **angesichts** A

**angesichts** *Präp. mit Gen.* (*geh.*) Ⓐ **~ des Feindes/der Gefahr/des Todes/der Stadt/der Küste** in the face of the enemy/of danger/death/in sight of the town/coast; Ⓑ (*fig.: in Anbetracht*) in view of

**an·gespannt** ❶ *2. Part. v.* **anspannen.** ❷ *Adj.* Ⓐ (*angestrengt*) close ‹attention›; taut ‹nerves›; Ⓑ (*kritisch*) tense ‹situation›; tight ‹market, economic situation›. ❸ *adv.* ‹work› concentratedly; ‹listen› with concentrated attention

**Angespanntheit** *die;* **~** Ⓐ (*Angestrengtheit*) attentiveness; Ⓑ (*kritischer Zustand*) ⇒ **angespannt** B: tenseness; tightness

**angestammt** /'angəʃtamt/ *Adj.* hereditary ‹right›; inherited ‹property›; (*scherzh.: altgewohnt*) usual ‹seat, place›

**angestaubt** ❶ *2. Part. v.* **anstauben.** ❷ *Adj.* outdated

**angestellt** ❶ *2. Part. v.* **anstellen.** ❷ *Adj.* **bei jmdm. ~ sein** be employed by sb.; work for sb.; **fest ~ sein** have a permanent position

**Angestellte** *der/die; adj. Dekl.* ▶ 159 [salaried] employee; **die ~n des öffentlichen Dienstes** salaried public employees; **Arbeiter und ~:** workers and salaried staff; blue- and white-collar workers; **die leitenden ~n** the managerial staff; the managers; **sie ist ~ bei der Stadt** she works for the town council; (*im Gegensatz zur Beamtin/Arbeiterin*) she has a salaried position with the town council

**Angestellten-:** **~gewerkschaft** *die* white-collar union; **~verhältnis** *das* employment *no indef. art.* on a [monthly] salary; **im ~verhältnis stehen** be a salaried employee; (*kein Beamter sein*) not have guaranteed employment for life; **~versicherung** *die* [salaried] employees' insurance

**angestrengt** ❶ *2. Part. v.* **anstrengen.** ❷ *Adj.* close ‹attention›; concentrated ‹work, study, thought›; forced ‹joke›. ❸ *adv.* ‹work, think, search› concentratedly

**Angestrengtheit** *die;* **~** ⇒ **angestrengt** 2: closeness; concentratedness; forcedness

**an·getan** ❶ *2. Part. v.* **antun.** ❷ *Adj. in* **von jmdm./etw. ~ sein** be taken with sb./sth.; **dazu** *od.* **danach ~ sein, etw. zu tun** (*geh.*) be suitable for doing sth.

**Angetraute** /'angətrautə/ *der/die; adj. Dekl.* (*scherzh.*) better half (*joc.*)

**an·getrunken** ❶ *2. Part. v.* **antrinken.** ❷ *Adj.* [slightly] drunk

**an·gewandt** ❶ *2. Part. v.* **anwenden.** ❷ *Adj.* applied

**an·gewiesen** ❶ *2. Part. v.* **anweisen.** ❷ *Adj.: in* **auf etw.** (*Akk.*) **~ sein** have to rely on sth.; **auf jmdn./jmds. Unterstützung ~ sein** be dependent on *or* have to rely on sb./sb.'s support; **auf sich selbst ~ sein** be thrown back upon one's own resources; **ich war auf jeden Pfennig ~:** I needed every pfennig

**an|gewöhnen** *tr. V.* **jmdm. etw. ~:** get sb. used to sth.; accustom sb. to sth.; **jmdm. ~, etw. zu tun** get sb. used to *or* accustom sb. to doing sth.; **sich** (*Dat.*) **etw. ~:** get into the habit of sth.; **sich** (*Dat.*) **schlechte Manieren ~:** become ill-mannered; **[es] sich** (*Dat.*) **~, etw. zu tun** get into the habit of doing sth.; **sich** (*Dat.*) **das Rauchen ~:** take up smoking

**An·gewohnheit** *die* habit

**angezeigt** ❶ *2. Part. v.* **anzeigen.** ❷ *Adj.* (*geh.*) advisable

**an|giften** /'angɪftn̩/ *tr. V.* (*ugs.*) lay into (*coll.*); let fly at

**Angina** /aŋ'gi:na/ *die;* **~, Anginen** ▶ 474 angina

**Angina pectoris** /- 'pɛktorɪs/ *die;* **~ ~** ▶ 474 (*Med.*) angina [pectoris]

**an|gleichen** ❶ *unr. tr. V.* **etw. einer Sache** (*Dat.*) *od.* **an etw.** (*Akk.*) **~:** bring sth. into line with sth.; **Systeme einander ~:** bring systems into line with each other. ❷ *unr. refl. V.* **sich jmdm./etw. ~** *od.* **sich an jmdn./etw. ~:** become like sb./sth.; **sich [einander** *od.* **aneinander] ~:** become like each other *or* alike

**An·gleichung** *die:* **die ~ der Löhne an die Preise** bringing wages into line with prices

**Angler** *der;* **~s, ~, Anglerin** *die;* **~, ~nen** angler

**Anglikaner** /aŋgli'ka:nɐ/ *der;* **~s, ~, Anglikanerin** *die;* **~, ~nen** Anglican

**anglikanisch** ❶ *Adj.* Anglican. ❷ *adv.* **~ beeinflusst sein** be influenced by Anglicanism

**Anglikanismus** *der;* **~:** Anglicanism *no art.*

**anglisieren** *tr. V.* Anglicize

**Anglist** *der;* **~en, ~en** English specialist *or* scholar; Anglicist; (*Student*) English student

**Anglistik** *die;* **~:** Anglistics *sing.;* English [language and literature]; English studies *pl.*, *no art.*

**Anglistin** *die;* **~, ~nen** ⇒ **Anglist**

**anglistisch** *Adj.* Anglistics *attrib.*, English studies *attrib.* ‹seminar, journal›

**Anglizismus** *der;* **~, Anglizismen** Anglicism

**Anglo·amerikaner** /aŋglo|ameri'ka:nɐ/ *der*, **Anglo·amerikanerin** *die* Ⓐ Anglo-American; Ⓑ (*Angelsachse/Angelsächsin*) Anglo-Saxon; **die Angloamerikaner** the British and the Americans

**anglophil** /aŋglo'fi:l/ *Adj.* Anglophile

**an|glotzen** *tr. V.* (*ugs.*) gawp at (*coll.*)

**Angola** /aŋ'go:la/ (*das*); **~s** Angola

**Angolaner** *der;* **~s, ~, Angolanerin** *die;* **~, ~nen** Angolan

**Angora-** /aŋ'go:ra/: **~kaninchen** *das* angora rabbit; **~katze** *die* angora cat; **~wolle** *die* angora [wool]; **~ziege** *die* angora goat

**angreifbar** *Adj.* contestable

**an|greifen** ❶ *unr. tr. V.* Ⓐ (*attackieren; auch fig.*) attack; Ⓑ (*schwächen*) weaken, affect ‹health, heart›; affect ‹stomach, intestine, voice›; weaken ‹person›; **die Nerven ~:** be a strain on the nerves; **die Fahrt hat mich sehr angegriffen** I was exhausted by the journey; Ⓒ ([*be*]*schädigen*) attack ‹metal›; harm ‹hands›; Ⓓ (*anbrechen*) break into ‹supplies, savings, etc.›; Ⓔ (*ugs.: anfassen*) touch. ❷ *unr. itr. V.* (*einen Angriff machen; auch fig.*) attack

**An·greifer** *der*, **An·greiferin** *die* (*auch fig.*) attacker

**an|grenzen** *itr. V.* **an etw.** (*Akk.*) **~:** border on *or* adjoin sth.; **die ~den Grundstücke** the adjoining properties

**An·griff** *der* attack; **einen ~ fliegen** make *or* carry out an attack *or* an air raid; **zum ~ übergehen** go over to the attack; take the offensive; **zum ~ blasen** (*auch fig.*) sound the charge *or* attack; **etw. in ~ nehmen** set about *or* tackle sth.; **~ ist die beste Verteidigung** (*Spr.*) attack is the best form of defence

**angriffs-, Angriffs-:** **~drittel** *das* (*Eishockey*) attacking zone; **~fläche** *die:* **das Segel bot dem Wind eine große ~fläche** the sail presented a large area to the wind; **seinem Gegner eine ~fläche bieten** (*fig.*) leave oneself open to attack by one's opponent; **~fuß·ball** *der* attacking football; **~krieg** *der* war of aggression; **~lust** *die* aggression; aggressiveness; **~lustig** ❶ *Adj.* aggressive; ❷ *adv.* aggressively; **~punkt** *der* target; **~spieler** *der*, **~spielerin** *die* (*Sport*) Ⓐ (*offensiver Spieler*) attacking player; Ⓑ (*Stürmer*) forward; **~waffe** *die* offensive weapon

**an|grinsen** *tr. V.* grin at

**angst** /aŋst/ *Adj. in* **jmdm. ist/wird [es] ~ [und bange]** sb. is/becomes afraid *or* frightened; (*jmd. sorgt sich*) sb. is/becomes very worried *or* anxious

**Angst** *die;* **~, Ängste** /'ɛŋstə/ Ⓐ (*Furcht*) fear; (*Psych.*) anxiety; **~ bekommen** *od.* (*ugs.*) **kriegen** become *or* get frightened *or* scared; **~ [vor jmdm./etw.] haben** be afraid *or* frightened [of sb./sth.]; **eine existenzielle ~:** existential fear; angst; **jmdn. in ~ und Schrecken versetzen** worry and frighten sb.; **es mit der ~ [zu tun] bekommen** *od.* (*ugs.*) **kriegen** become *or* get frightened *or* scared; **jmdm. ~ einflößen/einjagen/machen** frighten *or* scare sb.; **jmdm. ~ [und Bange] machen** frighten *or* scare sb.; (*jmdn. unruhig machen*) make sb. very worried *or* anxious; **keine ~!** don't be afraid; **aus ~ [vor etw./jmdm.] sich verstecken** hide in fear [of sth./sb.]; **aus ~, sich zu verraten, sagte er kein einziges Wort** he didn't say a word for fear of betraying himself; **in ständiger ~ vor etw.** (*Dat.*) **leben** live in constant fear of sth.; **er hat mehr ~ als Vaterlandsliebe** (*ugs. scherzh.*) he's a scaredy-cat (*coll.*); he's chicken (*sl.*); **~ vor der eigenen Courage haben/bekommen** have got/get cold feet (*fig.*); Ⓑ (*Sorge*) worry; anxiety; **~ [um jmdn./etw.] haben** be worried *or* anxious [about sb./sth.]; **sie hat ~, ihn zu verletzen/enttäuschen** she is worried about hurting/disappointing him; **keine ~, ich vergesse es schon nicht!** don't worry, I won't forget [it]!; **keine ~, die Rechnung wird schon noch kommen!** the bill will come all right, don't [you] worry!; **in tausend Ängsten schweben** be terribly worried

**angst-, Angst-:** **~erfüllt** *Adj.* (*geh.*) frightened; terrified; **~frei** ❶ *Adj.* anxiety-free ‹atmosphere›; ‹school› with an anxiety-free atmosphere; ‹learning› without tears; ❷ *adv.* ‹live› without anxiety; ‹learn› without tears; **~gefühl** *das* feeling of anxiety; **~gegner** *der*, **~gegnerin** *die* (*Sport*) bogy opponent; (*Mannschaft*) bogy team; **~hase** *der* (*ugs. abwertend*) scaredy-cat (*coll.*)

**ängstigen** /'ɛŋstɪgn̩/ ❶ *tr. V.* frighten; scare; (*beunruhigen*) worry. ❷ *refl. V.* be frightened *or* afraid; (*sich sorgen*) worry; **sich vor etw.** (*Dat.*)**/um jmdn. ~:** be frightened *or* afraid of sth./worried about sb.

**ängstlich** /'ɛŋstlɪç/ ❶ *Adj.* Ⓐ (*verängstigt*) anxious; apprehensive; Ⓑ (*furchtsam, schüchtern*) timorous; timid; Ⓒ (*übertrieben*) **mit ~er Genauigkeit** with painful meticulousness; Ⓓ (*besorgt*) worried; anxious; **mit ~er Spannung** anxiously. ❷ *adv.* Ⓐ (*verängstigt*) anxiously; apprehensively; Ⓑ (*besorgt*) anxiously; **~ gespannt** anxiously; Ⓒ (*übermäßig genau*) meticulously; **~ bemüht** *od.* **darauf bedacht sein, etw. zu tun** be at great pains to do sth.

**Ängstlichkeit** *die;* **~** Ⓐ (*Furchtsamkeit*) timorousness; timidity; Ⓑ (*Schüchternheit*) timidity; Ⓒ (*übertriebene Genauigkeit*) **die ~, mit der er die Vorschriften befolgt** the painful meticulousness with which he follows regulations; Ⓓ (*Besorgnis*) anxiety

**Angst-:** **~neurose** *die* anxiety neurosis; **~psychose** *die* anxiety psychosis; **~röhre** *die* (*ugs. scherzh.*) topper (*coll.*); top hat

**angst-, Angst-:** **~schrei** *der* cry of fear; terrified cry; **~schweiß** *der* cold sweat; **der ~schweiß brach ihm aus** he broke out in a cold sweat; **~traum** *der* nightmare; **~verzerrt** *Adj.* ‹face› twisted in fear; **~voll** ❶ *Adj.* anxious; apprehensive; ❷ *adv.* anxiously; apprehensively; **~zustand** *der* [state of] panic; **~zustände haben/bekommen** *od.* (*ugs.*) **kriegen** be in a/get into a [state of] panic

**an|gucken** *tr. V.* (*ugs.*) look at; **sich** (*Dat.*) **etw./jmdn. ~:** look *or* have a look at sth./sb.; **guck dir das/den an!** [just] look at that/him!

**an|gurten** *tr. V.* strap in; **sich ~:** put on one's seat belt; (*im Flugzeug*) fasten one's seat belt

a

**Anh.** *Abk.* **Anhang** app.

**an|haben** *unr. tr. V.* Ⓐ (*ugs.: am Körper tragen*) have on; Ⓑ **jmdm./einer Sache etwas ~ können** be able to harm sb./harm *or* damage sth.; **er sorgte dafür, dass niemand ihm etwas ~ konnte** he made sure that no one could touch him; Ⓒ (*ugs.: in Betrieb haben*) have on

**an|haften** *itr. V.* (*geh.*) **ein Nachteil/Risiko haftet einer Sache** (*Dat.*) **an** there is a disadvantage/risk in *or* attached to sth.; **die Schmach haftet ihr noch heute an** the disgrace remains with her even today

**an|häkeln** *tr. V.* crochet on (**an** + *Akk.* to)

**An·halt** *der* clue (**für** to); (*für eine Vermutung*) grounds *pl.* (**für** for)

**an|halten** ❶ *unr. tr. V.* Ⓐ stop; **den Atem ~:** hold one's breath; Ⓑ (*auffordern*) urge; Ⓒ (*an etw. halten*) **etw. an etw.** (*Akk.*) **~:** hold sth. up against sth.; **jmdm./sich ein Kleidungsstück ~:** hold a garment up against sb./oneself. ❷ *unr. itr. V.* Ⓐ stop; Ⓑ (*andauern*) go on; last; Ⓒ **er hat [bei ihren Eltern] um sie** *od.* **um ihre Hand angehalten** he asked [her parents] for her hand [in marriage]

**anhaltend** ❶ *Adj.* constant; continuous. ❷ *adv.* constantly; continuously

**An·halter** *der* hitch-hiker; **per ~ fahren** hitch[-hike]

**An·halterin** *die* hitch-hiker

**Anhalte·weg** *der* (*Kfz-W.*) [overall] stopping distance

**Anhalts·punkt** *der* clue (**für** to); (*für eine Vermutung*) grounds *pl.* (**für** for)

**an·hand** ❶ *Präp. mit Gen.* with the help of; on the basis of ‹current developments›. ❷ *Adv.* **~ von** with the help of; on the basis of ‹current developments›

**An·hang** *der* Ⓐ (*eines Buches*) appendix; Ⓑ (*Anhängerschaft*) following; **der Minister und sein ~:** the minister and his followers; **hoffentlich bringt er nicht seinen ganzen ~ mit** let's hope he doesn't bring his whole gang along; Ⓒ (*Verwandtschaft*) family; (*in Heiratsanzeigen*) **Witwe ohne ~:** widow, no family *or* dependants

**an|hängen¹** *unr. itr. V.* (*geh.*) Ⓐ (*verbunden sein mit*) be attached to; Ⓑ (*glauben an*) subscribe to ‹belief, idea, theory, etc.›; **einer Sekte ~:** be an adherent *or* follower of a sect; Ⓒ (*verehren*) be devoted to

**an|hängen²** ❶ *tr. V.* Ⓐ hang up (**an** + *Akk.* on); Ⓑ (*ankuppeln*) couple on (**an** + *Akk.* to); hitch up ‹trailer› (**an** + *Akk.* to); Ⓒ (*anfügen*) add (**an** + *Akk.* to); Ⓓ (*ugs.: zuschreiben, anlasten*) **jmdm. etw. ~:** blame sb. for sth.; blame sth. on sb.; **er will mir nur was ~:** he just wants to pin something on me; Ⓔ (*ugs.: geben*) **jmdm. etw. ~:** give sb. sth.; **jmdm. einen Prozess ~:** bring an action against sb.; take sb. to court; **lass dir keine vergammelten Tomaten ~!** don't let yourself be palmed off with bad tomatoes. ❷ *refl. V.* Ⓐ hang on (**an** + *Akk.* to); Ⓑ (*ugs.: sich anschließen*) **sich [an jmdn.** *od.* **bei jmdm.] ~:** tag along [with sb.] (*coll.*)

**An·hänger** *der* Ⓐ (*Mensch*) supporter; (*einer Sekte*) adherent; follower; Ⓑ (*Wagen*) trailer; **eine Straßenbahn mit zwei ~n** a tram (*Brit.*) *or* (*Amer.*) trolley with two extra cars; Ⓒ (*Schmuckstück*) pendant; Ⓓ (*Schildchen*) label; tag

**Anhängerin** *die;* **~, ~nen** ⇒ **Anhänger** A

**Anhänger·kupplung** *die* tow bar

**Anhängerschaft** *die;* **~, ~en** supporters *pl.;* (*einer Sekte*) followers *pl.;* adherents *pl.;* **eine breite ~ gewinnen** gain a wide following

**anhängig** *Adj.* (*Rechtsw.*) pending ‹action›; **etw. ~ machen** start legal proceedings over sth.

**anhänglich** *Adj.* devoted ‹dog, friend›; devoted, affectionate ‹child›

**Anhänglichkeit** *die;* **~:** devotion (**an** + *Akk.* to); **aus alter ~** (*Nostalgie*) out of old affection

*old spelling (see note on page 1707)

**Anhängsel** /ˈanhɛŋzl̩/ *das;* **~s, ~** Ⓐ (*Überflüssiges*) appendage (*Gen.* to); Ⓑ (*veralt.: Anhänger*) pendant; (*am Armband*) charm

**An·hauch** *der* (*geh., auch fig.*) breath; (*Anflug*) trace; touch

**an|hauchen** *tr. V.* breathe on ‹mirror, glasses›; blow on ‹fingers, hands›

**an|hauen** *tr. V.* (*salopp*) accost; **jmdn. um 50 Mark ~:** touch (*coll.*) *or* tap sb. for 50 marks

**an|häufen** ❶ *tr. V.* accumulate; amass; (*hamstern*) hoard. ❷ *refl. V.* accumulate; pile up

**An·häufung** *die* Ⓐ (*das Anhäufen*) accumulation; amassing; (*das Hamstern*) hoarding; Ⓑ (*Haufen*) accumulation; (*von Hütten*) cluster

**an|heben¹** *unr. tr. V.* Ⓐ (*hochheben*) lift [up] ‹cupboard, carpet›; raise ‹glass›; Ⓑ (*erhöhen*) raise ‹prices, wages, etc.›

**an|heben²** *unr. itr. V.* (*geh.*) commence; begin; **zu weinen/sprechen ~:** start *or* begin to cry/speak; start *or* begin crying/speaking

**An·hebung** *die* increase (*Gen.* in); raising (*Gen.* of)

**an|heften** *tr. V.* tack [on] ‹hem, sleeve, etc.›; attach ‹label, list›; put up ‹sign, notice›; **etw. mit Büroklammern/Reißnägeln/Heftklammern ~:** [paper] clip/pin/staple sth. (**an** + *Akk.* to); **jmdm. einen Orden ~:** pin a medal on sb.

**anheim** (*geh.*) *in* **jmdm./dem Staate ~ fallen** ‹wealth, property› pass to sb./the state; **der Vergessenheit/der Zerstörung/einem Betrug ~ fallen** sink into oblivion/fall prey to destruction/fall victim to a fraud; (*geh.*) **etw. den Flammen/dem Feuer ~ geben** commit sth. to the flames/fire; **jmds. Obhut ~ gegeben werden** be entrusted to sb.'s care; **sich jmdm./einer Sache ~ geben** entrust oneself to sb./sth.; **sich Gott ~ geben** put one's trust in God; **[es] jmdm. ~ stellen, etw. zu tun** leave it to sb. to do sth.; **es bleibt/ist dir ~ gestellt, dich zu beschweren** it is up to you to complain

**anheimelnd** *Adj.* homely; cosy

**anheischig** /ˈanhai̯ʃɪç/ *Adj.* (*geh.*) *in* **sich ~ machen, etw. zu tun** undertake to do sth.; **jetzt macht er sich auch noch ~, mich über meine Pflichten zu belehren** now he even takes it upon himself to tell me what my duties are

**an|heizen** ❶ *tr. V.* Ⓐ fire up ‹stove, boiler, etc.›; Ⓑ (*fig. ugs.*) stimulate ‹interest›. ❷ *itr. V.* put the heating on; (*bei einer Lokomotive*) fire up

**an|herrschen** *tr. V.* (*geh.*) bark at

**an|hetzen** *itr. V.; mit sein* **angehetzt kommen** (*ugs.*) come rushing *or* tearing along; (*auf einen zu*) come rushing *or* tearing up

**an|heuern** /ˈanhɔy̯ɐn/ ❶ *tr. V.* Ⓐ (*Seemannsspr.*) sign on; Ⓑ (*fig. ugs.: einstellen*) sign on or up; (*um Hilfe bitten*) rope in. ❷ *itr. V.* (*Seemannsspr.*) sign on

**An·hieb** *der:* **auf [den ersten] ~** (*ugs.*) straight off; first go

**an|himmeln** *tr. V.* (*ugs.*) Ⓐ (*verehren*) idolize; worship; Ⓑ (*ansehen*) gaze adoringly at

**An·höhe** *die* rise; elevation; (*Hügel*) hill

**an|hören** ❶ *tr. V.* Ⓐ listen to; **etw. [zufällig] mit ~:** overhear sth.; **er wurde verurteilt, ohne vorher auch nur angehört worden zu sein** he was sentenced without even being given a hearing; **sich** (*Dat.*) **jmdn./etw. ~:** listen to sb./sth.; **ich kann das nicht länger** *od.* **mehr mit ~!** I can't listen to that any longer; Ⓑ (*anmerken*) **man hörte ihr die Verzweiflung an** one could hear the despair in her voice. ❷ *refl. V.* sound; **[das] hört sich nicht schlecht an** (*ugs.*) [that] doesn't sound bad

**Anhörung** *die;* **~, ~en** hearing

**Anhörungs·verfahren** *das* hearing

**an|hupen** *tr. V.* hoot at

**an|husten** *tr. V.* cough over; **jmdn. ~:** cough over sb. *or* in sb.'s face

**Anhydrid** /anhyˈdriːt/ *das;* **~s, ~e** (*Chemie*) anhydride

**Änigma** /ɛˈnɪgma/ *das;* **~s, ~ta** *u.* **Änigmen** (*geh.*) enigma

**änigmatisch** *Adj.* (*geh.*) enigmatic

**Anilin** /aniˈliːn/ *das;* **~s** (*Chemie*) aniline

**Anilin·leder** *das* aniline leather

**animalisch** /aniˈmaːlɪʃ/ *Adj.* Ⓐ animal; Ⓑ (*abwertend: triebhaft*) animal; bestial

**Animateur** /animaˈtøːɐ̯/ *der;* **~s, ~e** ▶ 159 host

**Animateurin** *die;* **~, ~nen** hostess

**Animation** /animaˈt̮si̯oːn/ *die;* **~, ~en** animation

**Animier·dame** *die* hostess

**animieren** /aniˈmiːrən/ *tr.* (*auch itr.*) *V.* Ⓐ encourage; **das soll zum Kaufen ~:** that's to encourage people to buy; **er fühlte sich [durch mein Beispiel] animiert** he felt prompted [by my example]; Ⓑ (*Film*) animate

**Animier-: ~lokal** *das* hostess bar; (*Nachtklub*) hostess nightclub; **~mädchen** *das* hostess

**Animosität** /animoziˈtɛːt/ *die;* **~, ~en** Ⓐ animosity; Ⓑ (*Äußerung*) hostile remark

**Animus** /ˈaːnimʊs/ *der;* **~** Ⓐ (*Psych.*) animus; Ⓑ (*ugs.: Ahnung*) **ich habe so einen ~, dass ...** I have a feeling *or* hunch that ...

**An·ion** *das* (*Chemie*) anion

**Anis** /aˈniːs/ *der;* **~[es], ~e** Ⓐ (*Pflanze*) anise; Ⓑ (*Gewürz*) aniseed; Ⓒ (*Branntwein*) aniseed brandy

**Anisette** /aniˈzɛt/ *der;* **~s, ~s** anisette

**Anis-: ~likör** *der* aniseed liqueur; **~plätzchen** *das* aniseed biscuit; **~schnaps** *der* aniseed brandy

**Ank.** *Abk.* **Ankunft** arr.

**an|kämpfen** *itr. V.* **gegen jmdn./etw. ~:** fight [against] sb./sth.; **gegen den Strom/Wind/die Elemente ~:** battle against the current/the wind/the elements

**an|karren** *tr. V.* (*ugs.*) cart along; bring along ‹supporters, followers›

**An·kathete** *die* (*Geom.*) adjacent side

**An·kauf** *der* purchase; **„Heinrich Meyer, An- und Verkauf"** 'Heinrich Meyer, second-hand dealer'; **„An- und Verkauf von ..."** 'we buy and sell ...'; **durch den ~ einer Sache** (*Gen.*) by purchasing *or* buying sth.; by the purchase of sth.

**an|kaufen** *tr. V.* purchase; buy

**an|keifen** *tr. V.* scream at

**Anker** /ˈaŋkɐ/ *der;* **~s, ~** Ⓐ (*eines Schiffs*) anchor; (*fig.*) support; **vor ~ gehen/liegen** *od.* **treiben** drop anchor/lie at anchor; **~ werfen** drop anchor; Ⓑ (*Elektrot.*) armature; Ⓒ (*Uhrmacherei*) anchor

**Anker-: ~boje** *die* anchor buoy; **~kette** *die* anchor cable; **~klüse** *die;* **~, ~n** hawse hole; (*Rohr*) hawsepipe

**ankern** *itr. V.* Ⓐ (*vor Anker gehen*) anchor; drop anchor; Ⓑ (*vor Anker liegen*) be anchored; lie at anchor

**Anker-: ~platz** *der* anchorage; **~wicklung** *die* (*Elektrot.*) armature winding; **~winde** *die* windlass

**an|ketten** *tr. V.* chain up (*Dat.*, **an** + *Akk.* to)

**an|kläffen** *tr. V.* yap at

**An·klage** *die* Ⓐ charge; **der Staatsanwalt hat ~ [wegen Mordes gegen ihn] erhoben** the public prosecutor brought a charge [of murder against him]; **unter ~ stehen** have been charged (**wegen** with); **jmdn. unter ~ stellen** charge sb. (**wegen** with); Ⓑ (*~vertretung*) prosecution; **der Vertreter der ~:** counsel for the prosecution; prosecuting counsel; Ⓒ (*geh.: Vorwurf*) accusation

**Anklage-: ~bank** *die; Pl.* **~bänke** dock; **auf der ~bank sitzen** (*auch fig.*) be in the dock; **~erhebung** *die* preferral of charges; **für eine ~erhebung hinreichend sein** be sufficient to justify preferring charges

**an|klagen** ❶ *tr. V.* Ⓐ (*Rechtsw.*) charge; accuse; **jmdn. einer Sache** (*Gen.*) *od.* **wegen etw. ~:** charge sb. with *or* accuse sb. of sth.; Ⓑ (*geh.: beschuldigen*) accuse; **jmdn./**

**sich einer Sache** (*Gen.*) **~:** accuse sb./oneself of sth.; **jmdn./sich ~, etw. zu tun** accuse sb./oneself of doing sth.; **sich als etw.** (*Nom. od. Akk.*) **~:** accuse oneself of being sth. ❷ *itr. V.* cry out in accusation; **ein ~des Buch** a book that cries out in accusation; **jmdn. ~d ansehen** look at sb. accusingly

**An·kläger** *der*, **An·klägerin** *die* prosecutor

**Anklage-: ~schrift** *die* indictment; **~vertreter** *der*, **~vertreterin** *die* prosecuting counsel; counsel for the prosecution; **~vertretung** *die* (*Vorgang, Partei*) prosecution

**an|klammern** ❶ *tr. V.* peg (*Brit.*), pin (*Amer.*) ‹clothes, washing› up (**an** + *Akk.* to); clip ‹copy, sheet, etc.› (**an** + *Akk.* to); (*mit Heftklammern*) staple ‹copy, sheet, etc.› (**an** + *Akk.* on). ❷ *refl. V.* **sich an jmdn./etw. ~:** cling to *or* hang on to sb./sth.

**An·klang** *der* (A) *in* **[bei jmdm.] ~ finden** meet with [sb.'s] approval; find favour [with sb.]; **mit dem Vorschlag wirst du keinen großen ~ finden** you won't find any great support for that proposal; **wenig/keinen/großen ~ finden** be poorly/badly/well received (**bei** by); (B) (*Ähnlichkeit*) echo (**an** + *Akk.* of); **Anklänge an etw.** (*Akk.*) **enthalten** be reminiscent of sth.

**an|klatschen** *tr. V.* (*ugs.*) slap ‹poster, wallpaper, etc.› up *or* on (**an** + *Akk.* to); plaster ‹hair› down

**an|kleben** ❶ *tr.* (*auch itr.*) *V.* stick up ‹poster, etc.› (**an** + *Akk.* on); **„Ankleben verboten"** 'stick (*Brit.*) *or* post no bills'; 'bill-posting prohibited'; **sich** (*Dat.*) **einen falschen Bart ~:** stick on a false beard. ❷ *itr. V.; mit sein* stick (**an** + *Dat.* to)

**an|kleckern** *itr. V.; mit sein* **angekleckert kommen** (*ugs.*) (*immer wieder kommen*) come trotting along (*coll.*); (*auf einen zu*) come trotting up (*coll.*); (*nach und nach eintreffen*) come drifting along *or* in

**Ankleide·kabine** *die* changing cubicle

**an|kleiden** *tr. V.* (*geh.*) dress; **sich ~:** get dressed; dress [oneself]

**Ankleide·raum** *der* dressing room

**an|klicken** *tr. V.* (*DV*) click on

**an|klingeln** *tr., itr. V.* (*ugs.*) **jmdn.** *od.* **bei jmdm. ~:** ring *or* call sb. [up]

**an|klingen** *unr. itr. V.* (A) (*erinnern*) be reminiscent (**an** + *Akk.* of); (B) *auch mit sein* (*wahrnehmbar sein*) be discernible; **ein Thema ~ lassen** touch on a theme

**an|klopfen** *itr. V.* knock (**an** + *Akk. od. Dat.* at *or* on); **bei jmdm. um etw. ~** (*ugs.*) try to touch (*coll.*) *or* tap sb. for sth.

**an|knabbern** *tr. V.* (*ugs.*) nibble [at]; **der Staat muss seine Goldreserven ~** (*fig.*) the state is having to dig into its gold reserves; **zum Anknabbern aussehen** (*fig.*) look good enough to eat

**an|knacksen** *tr. V.* (*ugs.*) crack ‹bone, rib›; (*fig.*) injure ‹pride›; badly affect ‹health›; ⇨ *auch* **angeknackst 2**

**an|knipsen** *tr. V.* (*ugs.*) switch *or* put on

**an|knüpfen** ❶ *tr. V.* (A) tie on (**an** + *Akk.* to); (B) (*beginnen*) start up ‹conversation›; open, start ‹negotiations›; establish ‹relations, business links›; form ‹relationship›; **eine Bekanntschaft mit jmdm. ~:** strike up an acquaintance with sb. ❷ *itr. V.* **an etw.** (*Akk.*) **~:** take sth. up; **ich knüpfe dort an, wo wir vorige Woche aufgehört haben** I'll pick up where we left off last week

**Anknüpfung** *die;* **~, ~en** (A) ⇨ **anknüpfen B**: starting up; opening; starting; establishment; forming; (B) **die ~ an etw.** (*Akk.*) taking sth. up; **unter [bewusster] ~ an etw.** (*Akk.*) with [conscious] reference to sth.

**Anknüpfungs·punkt** *der* starting point [for a/the conversation]

**an|knurren** *tr. V.* growl at; **sich [gegenseitig] ~** (*auch fig.*) growl at one another

**an|kohlen** *tr. V.* (*ugs.*) kid (*coll.*)

**an|kommen** ❶ *unr. itr. V.; mit sein* (A) (*eintreffen*) arrive; ‹letter, parcel› come, arrive; ‹bus, train, plane› arrive, get in; **seid ihr gut angekommen?** did you arrive safely *or* get there all right?; **ich bin beim 6. Kapitel angekommen** I have reached *or* got to the sixth chapter; **wann sollen die Zwillinge denn ~?** (*ugs.: geboren werden*) when are the twins due [to arrive]?; **bei ihr ist kürzlich das vierte Kind angekommen** (*ugs.: geboren worden*) she has just had her fourth child; (B) (*ugs.: Anklang finden*) **[bei jmdm.] [gut] ~:** go down [very] well [with sb.]; **damit kommt er bei mir nicht an** he won't get anywhere with me with that; **er ist ein Typ, der bei den Frauen ankommt** he is the sort who is a success with women; (C) **gegen jmdn./etw. ~:** be able to cope *or* deal with sb./fight sth.; (D) (*unpers.: abhängen*) **auf uns/auf das Wetter kommt es dabei nicht an** it doesn't depend on us/the weather; **es kommt [ganz] darauf an, ob …** it [all] depends whether …; **es kommt [ganz] darauf** *od.* **drauf an** (*ugs.*) it [all] depends; **es darauf** *od.* **drauf ~ lassen** (*ugs.*) take a chance; chance it; **es auf etw.** (*Akk.*) **~ lassen** [be prepared to] risk sth.; **man könnte es ja mal auf einen Versuch ~ lassen** one could at least give it a try; (E) (*unpers.: entscheidend, wichtig sein*) **es kommt auf etw.** (*Akk.*) **an** sth. matters; **auf die paar Mark/Minuten kommt es [mir] nicht an/soll es mir nicht ~:** a few marks/minutes don't matter [to me]; **es kommt auf jede Minute/jeden Pfennig an** every minute/pfennig counts; **es käme auf einen Versuch an** it's *or* it would be worth a try; **da kommt es auf drei Leute mehr auch nicht mehr an** three more people won't make any difference; **es kommt nicht darauf an, was er sagt** it's not what he says that matters; **darauf kommt es mir nicht so sehr an** that doesn't matter so much to me; (F) (*herankommen*) come along; **mit etw. ~** (*ugs.: etw. dauernd betonen*) harp on about sth.; (G) (*ugs.: Erfolg haben*) **er ist mit seinem Manuskript bisher noch bei keinem Verlag angekommen** up to now he hasn't had any success with publishers with his manuscript; **ohne Beziehungen kommt man heute nirgends mehr an** you won't *or* don't get anywhere these days without connections.
❷ *tr. V.* (*geh.*) (A) (*überkommen*) ‹fear, desire, etc.› come over; (B) **jmdn. hart/schwer** *usw.* **~:** be hard/difficult *etc.* for sb.

**Ankömmling** /ˈankœmlɪŋ/ *der;* **~s, ~e** newcomer; (*ugs.: Neugeborenes*) new arrival

**an|können** *unr. itr. V.* (A) **gegen jmdn./etw. ~:** be able to fight sb./sth.; (B) (*ugs.: an sein dürfen*) **das Licht/Radio/die Heizung kann jetzt wieder an** you/he *etc.* can put the light/radio/heating on again now

**an|koppeln** ❶ *tr. V.* couple ‹carriage› up (**an** + *Akk.* to); hitch ‹trailer› up (**an** + *Akk.* to); dock ‹spacecraft› (**an** + *Akk.* with). ❷ *itr. V.* ‹spacecraft› dock (**an** + *Akk.* with)

**an|kotzen** *tr. V.* (*salopp*) (A) throw up over; puke over (*coarse*); (B) (*fig.: anwidern*) **jmdn. ~:** make sb. sick

**an|krallen** *refl. V.* cling (**an** + *Akk. od. Dat.* at)

**an|kratzen** *tr. V.* scratch; (*fig. ugs.*) dent

**an|kreiden** *tr. V.* (*ugs.*) **jmdm. etw. ~:** hold sth. against sb.; **man kreidet ihm sein Verhalten als Schwäche an** his behaviour is seen *or* regarded as weakness; **das muss man ihm dick ~:** you've really got to hold that against him

**An·kreis** *der* (*Geom.*) escribed circle; excircle

**an|kreuzen** ❶ *tr. V.* mark with a cross; put a cross beside. ❷ *itr. V.; meist mit sein* **gegen den Wind ~** (*Segeln*) sail against *or* into the wind

**an|kriechen** *unr. itr. V.; mit sein* **angekrochen kommen** come creeping *or* crawling along; (*auf einen zu*) come creeping *or* crawling up

**an|kündigen** ❶ *tr. V.* announce; **kündige dich bitte vorher an** please let me/us *etc.* know in advance that you are coming *or* give me/us *etc.* advance notice; **ein Gewitter ~:** herald a storm; **eine angekündigte/nicht angekündigte Klassenarbeit** a class test announced in advance/a surprise test. ❷ *refl. V.* ‹spring, storm› announce itself; ‹illness› show itself

**An·kündigung** *die* announcement; **er besuchte uns ohne vorherige ~:** he visited us without letting us know in advance *or* with no advance notice

**Ankunft** /ˈankʊnft/ *die;* **~, Ankünfte** arrival; „**~**": 'arrivals'

**Ankunfts-: ~halle** *die* (*Flugw.*) arrival[s] hall; **~tafel** *die* arrivals board

**an|kuppeln** *tr. V.* ⇨ **ankoppeln 1**

**an|kurbeln** *tr. V.* (A) crank [up]; (B) (*fig.*) boost ‹economy, production, etc.›

**Ankurb[e]lung** *die;* **~, ~en** boosting; **Maßnahmen zur ~ der Wirtschaft** measures to boost the economy

**an|kuscheln** *refl. V.* **sich an jmdn.** *od.* **bei jmdm./an etw.** (*Akk.*) **~:** snuggle *or* cuddle up to sb./sth.

**Anl.** *Abk.* **Anlage** encl.

**an|lächeln** *tr. V.* smile at; **jmdn. freundlich ~:** give a friendly smile to sb.

**an|lachen** ❶ *tr. V.* smile at; **ich habe dich angelacht, nicht ausgelacht** I was laughing with you, not at you. ❷ *refl. V.* **sich** (*Dat.*) **jmdn. ~** (*ugs.*) get off with sb. (*Brit. coll.*); pick sb. up

**An·lage** *die* (A) (*das Anlegen*) (*einer Kartei*) establishment; (*eines Parks, Gartens usw.*) laying out; construction; (*eines Parkplatzes, Stausees*) construction; (B) (*Grün~*) park; (*um ein Schloss, einen Palast usw. herum*) grounds *pl.; die* **öffentlichen/städtischen ~n** public/municipal parks and gardens; (C) (*Angelegtes, Komplex*) complex; (D) (*Einrichtung*) facilities *pl.;* **sanitäre/militärische ~n** sanitary facilities/military installations; **die elektrische ~:** the electrical equipment; (E) (*Werk*) plant; (F) (*Musik~, Lautsprecher~ usw.*) equipment; system; (G) (*Geld~*) investment; (H) (*Konzeption*) conception; (*Struktur*) structure; (I) (*Veranlagung*) aptitude, gift, talent (**zu** for); (*Neigung*) tendency, predisposition (**zu** to); (J) ▶ 187 (*Beilage zu einem Brief*) enclosure; **als ~ sende ich Ihnen/erhalten Sie ein ärztliches Attest** please find enclosed *or* I enclose a medical certificate

**anlage-, Anlage-: ~bedingt** ❶ *Adj.* constitutional; ❷ *adv.* constitutionally; **~berater** *der*, **~beraterin** *die* ▶ 159 investment advisor; **~kapital** *das* investment capital

**an|lagern** (*Chemie*) ❶ *tr. V.* take up. ❷ *refl. V.* be taken up (**an** + *Akk.* by)

**Anlage·vermögen** *das* fixed assets *pl. or* capital

**an|landen** *tr. V.* land

**an|langen** ❶ *itr. V.; mit sein* arrive; **bei/auf/an etw.** (*Dat.*) **~:** arrive at *or* reach sth.; **bei Kapitel 3 ~:** reach *or* get to chapter 3. ❷ *tr. V.* (A) (*südd.: anfassen*) touch; (B) ⇨ **anbelangen**

**Anlass, *Anlaß** /ˈanlas/ *der;* **Anlasses, Anlässe** /ˈanlɛsə/ (A) (*Ausgangspunkt, Grund*) cause (**zu** for); **der ~ des Streites** the cause of the dispute; **etw. zum ~ nehmen, etw. zu tun** use *or* take sth. as an opportunity to do sth.; **ich möchte aus gegebenem ~ darauf hinweisen, dass …** I would like to take this opportunity to point out that …; **aus ~ seines Geburtstags** on the occasion of *or* to celebrate his birthday; **jmdm. ~ zu Beschwerden geben** give sb. cause for complaint; **~ zur Sorge/Beunruhigung/Klage geben** give cause for concern/unease/complaint; **beim geringsten/kleinsten ~:** for the slightest reason; **aus aktuellem ~:** because of current events; (B) (*Gelegenheit*) occasion; **bei festlichen Anlässen** on festive occasions

**an|lassen** ❶ *unr. tr. V.* (A) (*in Betrieb lassen*) leave ‹light, radio, heating, etc.› on; leave ‹engine, tap› on *or* running; leave ‹candle› burning; (B) (*anbehalten*) keep ‹coat, gloves, etc.› on; (C) (*in Gang setzen*) start [up]. ❷ *unr. refl. V.* **sich gut/schlecht ~:** make a *or* get off to a good/bad *or* poor start; **wie lässt sich der neue Mitarbeiter denn an?** how is your new colleague getting on?

**Anlasser** *der;* **~s, ~** (*Kfz-W.*) starter

**an·lässlich, *an·läßlich** *Präp. mit Gen.* on the occasion of

a

**an|lasten** *tr. V.* jmdm. ein Verbrechen ~: accuse sb. of a crime; jmdm. die Schuld an etw. (*Dat.*) ~: blame sb. for sth.; jmdm. etw. als Versagen ~: regard sth. as a failure on sb.'s part

**an|latschen** *itr. V.; mit sein* (*ugs.*) angelatscht kommen come trudging along; (*auf einen zu*) come trudging up; (*schlurfend*) come slouching along/up

**An·lauf** *der* [A] run-up; [mehr] ~ nehmen take [more of] a run-up; mit/ohne ~: with/without a run-up; er sprang mit/ohne ~: he did a running/standing jump; ein Sprung mit/ohne ~: a running/standing jump; [B] (*Versuch*) attempt; beim *od.* im ersten/dritten ~: at the first/third attempt *or* (*coll.*) go; einen [neuen] ~ nehmen make another attempt; have another go (*coll.*); [C] (*Sport*) (*Bahn*) runway; (*Strecke*) run-up

**Anlauf·adresse** *die* ⇒ **Anlaufstelle**

**an|laufen** ❶ *unr. itr. V.; mit sein* [A] angelaufen kommen come running along; (*auf einen zu*) come running up; [B] gegen jmdn./etw. ~: run at sb./sth.; gegen etw. ~ (*fig.*) fight against sth.; [C] (*Anlauf nehmen*) take a run-up; [D] (*zu laufen beginnen*) ‹engine› start [up]; (*fig.*) ‹film› open; ‹production, campaign, search› start; [E] (*sich färben*) turn; go; [F] (*beschlagen*) mist *or* steam up. ❷ *unr. tr. V.* put in at ‹port›

**Anlauf-:** ~**stelle** *die* [place of] refuge; place to go; ~stelle für solche Reiserufe the place to which to send such SOS messages; ~**zeit** *die* der Motor braucht einige Minuten ~zeit the engine needs a few minutes to warm up; morgens braucht sie immer eine gewisse ~zeit it always takes her a certain amount of time to get going in the mornings

**An·laut** *der* (*Sprachw.*) initial sound; der Konsonant wird im ~ stimmhaft gesprochen the consonant is voiced when in initial position

**an|lauten** *itr. V.* (*Sprachw.*) begin (mit with); der ~de Vokal the initial vowel

**an|läuten** *tr., itr. V.* (*bes. südd.*) ⇒ **anrufen** 1 C, 2 A

**an|legen** ❶ *tr. V.* [A] (*an etw. legen*) put *or* lay ‹domino, card› [down] (an + *Akk.* next to); place, position ‹ruler, protractor› (an + *Akk.* on); put ‹ladder› up (an + *Akk.* against); ein Gewehr auf jmdn./etw. ~: level a gun at sb./sth.; sie legte das Baby an she put the baby to her breast; einen strengen Maßstab [an etw. (*Akk.*)] ~: apply strict standards [to sth.]; [B] (*an den Körper legen*) die Flügel/Ohren ~: close its wings/lay its ears back; die Arme ~: put one's arms to one's sides; [C] (*geh.: anziehen, umlegen*) don; put on; [D] (*schaffen, erstellen*) lay out ‹town, garden, plantation, street›; start ‹file, album›; compile ‹statistics, index›; [E] (*gestalten, entwerfen*) structure ‹story, novel›; [F] (*investieren*) invest; [G] (*ausgeben*) spend (für on); [H] er legt es auf einen Streit an he is determined to have a fight; es darauf ~, etw. zu tun be determined to do sth.; [I] (*nachlegen*) put on. ❷ *itr. V.* [A] (*festmachen, landen*) moor; (*am Liegeplatz*) berth; [B] (*Kartenspiel*) lay a card/cards; bei jmdm. ~: lay a card/cards on sb.'s hand; ich kann nirgends/nicht ~: I can't go; [C] (*Domino*) play [a domino/dominoes]; [D] (*das Gewehr anlegen*) aim (auf + *Akk.* at). ❸ *refl. V.* sich mit jmdm. ~: pick an argument *or* a quarrel with sb.

**Anlege·platz** *der* berth

**Anleger** *der;* ~s, ~ [A] (*Schifffahrt*) jetty; landing pier; [B] (*Investor*) investor

**Anlegerin** *die;* ~, ~nen investor

**Anlege-:** ~**steg** *der* jetty; landing stage; ~**stelle** *die* mooring

**an|lehnen** ❶ *tr. V.* [A] (*an etw. lehnen*) lean (an + *Akk. od. Dat.* against); [B] leave ‹door› slightly open *or* ajar; leave ‹window› slightly open; die Tür war angelehnt the door was [left] slightly open *or* ajar. ❷ *refl. V.* sich [an jmdn. *od.* jmdm./etw.] ~: lean [on sb./against sth.]; er lehnte sich mit dem Rücken/der Schulter an die *od.* der Wand an he leaned back *or* leaned his back/leaned [with] his shoulder against the wall; sich an ein Vorbild ~ (*fig.*) follow an example

**Anlehnung** *die;* ~, ~en [A] dependence (an + *Akk.* on); (*Halt, Stütze*) support; ~ an jmdn./etw. suchen/finden look for/find support from sb./sth.; [B] (*Nachahmung*) in ~ an jmdn./etw. following *or* in imitation of sb./sth.

**Anlehnungs·bedürfnis** *das* need for love and affection

**anlehnungs·bedürftig** *Adj.* in need of love and affection *postpos.;* je mehr sie trank, desto ~er wurde sie (*scherzh.*) the more she drank, the more amorous and affectionate she became

**Anleihe** *die;* ~, ~n [A] (*Darlehen*) loan; [B] (*fig.*) borrowing; eine ~ bei Goethe/Picasso machen borrow from Goethe/Picasso

**an|leimen** *tr. V.* stick *or* glue on (an + *Akk. od. Dat.* to)

**an|leinen** *tr. V.* put ‹dog› on the lead; Hunde sind anzuleinen dogs must be kept on a lead; der Hund war nicht angeleint the dog was not on a lead

**an|leiten** *tr. V.* [A] (*unterweisen*) instruct; teach; jmdn. bei der Arbeit ~: instruct sb. in the work; teach sb. the work; [B] (*anhalten, erziehen*) teach; die Kinder zur Selbstständigkeit/Pünktlichkeit ~: teach the children to be independent/punctual

**An·leitung** *die* instructions *pl.*

**Anlern·beruf** *der* semi-skilled occupation *or* job

**an|lernen** ❶ *tr. V.* train; ein angelernter Arbeiter a semi-skilled worker. ❷ *refl. V.* sich (*Dat.*) etw. ~: learn sth. up; eine bloß angelernte Bildung a superficially acquired education

**Anlernling** /ˈanlɛrnlɪŋ/ *der;* ~s, ~e (*veralt.*) trainee; ~ sein be a trainee

**an|lesen** ❶ *unr. tr. V.* begin *or* start reading *or* to read. ❷ *unr. refl. V.* sich (*Dat.*) etw. ~: learn sth. by reading *or* from books; eine nur angelesene Kenntnis knowledge which comes straight out of books

**an|leuchten** *tr. V.* jmdn./etw. ~: shine a light on sb./light sth. up; den Dieb mit der Taschenlampe ~: shine a torch (*Brit.*) *or* (*Amer.*) flashlight on the thief

**an|liefern** *tr. V.* deliver

**An·lieferung** *die* delivery

**an|liegen** *unr. itr. V.* [A] (*an etw. liegen*) ‹pullover etc.› fit tightly *or* closely; ‹hair, ears› lie flat; ein eng ~der Pullover a tight- *or* close-fitting pullover; [B] (*ugs.: vorliegen*) be on; (*zu erledigen sein*) to be done; was liegt an? (*was kann ich für dich tun?*) what's up? (*coll.*)

**An·liegen** *das;* ~s, ~ (*Bitte*) request; (*Angelegenheit*) matter; etw. zu seinem persönlichen ~ machen take a personal interest in sth.

**anliegend** *Adj.* [A] (*angrenzend*) adjacent; [B] (*beiliegend*) enclosed

**Anlieger** *der;* ~s, ~, **Anliegerin** *die;* ~, ~nen resident; „Anlieger frei", „frei für Anlieger" 'access only'

**Anlieger-:** ~**staat** *der:* die ~staaten des Mittelmeers *usw.* the countries bordering the Mediterranean *etc.;* ~**verkehr** *der* residents' vehicles *pl.;* die Straße ist nur noch für den ~verkehr frei the street is only open to residents; „~verkehr frei" 'residents only'

**an|locken** *tr. V.* attract ‹customers, tourists, etc.›; lure ‹bird, animal›

**an|löten** *tr. V.* solder on (an + *Akk. od. Dat.* to)

**an|lügen** *tr. V.* lie to

**Anm.** *Abk.* **Anmerkung**

**an|machen** *tr. V.* [A] (*anschalten, -zünden usw.*) put *or* turn ‹light, radio, heating› on; light ‹fire›; [B] (*bereiten*) mix ‹cement, plaster, paint, etc.›; dress ‹salad›; [C] (*ugs.: anbringen*) put ‹curtain, sign› up; ein Schild an der Tür ~: put a sign up on the door; dem Hund das Halsband ~: put the collar on the dog; [D] (*ugs.: ansprechen*) ‹woman, girl› give ‹man, boy› the come-on (*coll.*); ‹man, boy› chat ‹woman, girl› up (*Brit. coll.*); [E] (*ugs.: begeistern, erregen*) get ‹audience etc.› going; das macht mich ungeheuer/nicht an it really turns me on (*coll.*)/does nothing for me (*coll.*); [F] (*provozieren*) mach mich nicht an! leave me alone!

**an|mahnen** *tr. V.* send a reminder about; er hat den angemahnten Betrag sofort überwiesen he paid the outstanding amount as soon as he received a reminder

**An·mahnung** *die* reminder; trotz mehrfacher ~: despite repeated reminders *pl.*

**an|malen** *tr. V.* [A] (*ugs.: bemalen*) paint; etw. rot ~: paint sth. red; [B] (*ugs.: schminken*) paint; sich ~: paint one's face; [C] (*auf etw. malen*) paint (an + *Akk.* on); (*auf etw. zeichnen*) draw (an + *Akk.* on); jmdm./sich einen Bart ~: paint *or* draw a beard on sb.'s/one's face *or* on sb./oneself

**An·marsch** *der* [A] (*das Anmarschieren*) advance; im ~ sein (*anrücken*) be advancing; (*ugs. scherzh.: unterwegs sein*) be on one's way; [B] (*ugs.: Weg*) walk

**an|marschieren** *itr. V.; mit sein* advance; anmarschiert kommen (*ugs.*) come marching along; (*auf einen zu*) come marching up

**Anmarsch·weg** *der* walk

**an|maßen** *refl. V.* sich (*Dat.*) etw. ~: claim sth. [for oneself]; arrogate sth. to oneself; was maßt du dir an? who do you think you are?; what do you think you are doing?; sich ~, etw. zu tun presume to do sth.; darüber kannst du dir gar kein Urteil ~: you have no right *or* it's not your place to pass judgement on that

**an·maßend** ❶ *Adj.* presumptuous; (*arrogant*) arrogant. ❷ *adv.* presumptuously; (*arrogant*) arrogantly

**Anmaßung** *die;* ~, ~en presumptuousness; presumption; (*Arroganz*) arrogance; so eine [freche] ~! what presumptuousness *or* presumption/arrogance!; es ist eine ~ zu behaupten, dass ... it is presumptuous to assert that ...

**an|meckern** *tr. V.* (*ugs.*) jmdn. ~: have a go at sb.

**Anmelde·formular** *das* [A] application form; [B] (*einer Meldebehörde*) registration form

**an|melden** *tr. V.* [A] (*als Teilnehmer*) enrol; jmdn./sich zu einem Kursus/in *od.* bei einer Schule ~: enrol sb./enrol for a course/at a school; sich schriftlich ~: register [in writing]; jmdn. zu einer Impfung ~: make an appointment for sb. to be vaccinated; [B] (*melden, anzeigen*) license, get a licence for ‹television, radio›; apply for ‹patent›; register ‹domicile, change of address, car, trade mark›; die Demonstration war nicht angemeldet no notification had been given of the demonstration; sich/seinen neuen Wohnsitz ~: register one's new address; jmdn./sich polizeilich *od.* bei der Polizei ~: register sb./register with the police; ⇒ *auch* **Konkurs**; [C] (*ankündigen*) announce; (*einen Termin vereinbaren*) sind Sie angemeldet? do you have an appointment?; sich beim Arzt ~: make an appointment to see the doctor; [D] (*geltend machen*) express, make known ‹reservation, doubt, wish›; put forward ‹demand›; assert ‹right›; [E] (*Kartenspiele: ansagen*) bid; [F] (*Fernspr.*) book; ein Gespräch nach Übersee ~: book an overseas call

**Anmelde·pflicht** *die* (*für den Wohnsitz*) obligation to register one's address; (*für Fernsehen, Radio*) obligation to obtain a licence; (*für das Auto*) obligation to register a/the vehicle; für Demonstrationen besteht ~: it is mandatory to notify the police in advance of demonstrations

**anmelde·pflichtig** *Adj.* ~ sein ‹television, radio› need a licence; ‹car› have to be registered; ‹demonstration› have to be notified; jeder Wohnungswechsel ist ~: every change of address must be registered

**An·meldung** *die* [A] (*zur Teilnahme*) enrolment; [B] ⇒ **anmelden** B: licensing; registration; notification; die ~ eines Patents

*old spelling (see note on page 1707)

the application for a patent; **C** (*Ankündigung*) announcement; (*beim Arzt, Rechtsanwalt usw.*) making an appointment; **D** ⇒ **anmelden** D: expression; putting forward; assertion; **E** (*Fernspr.*) booking; **die ~ eines Gesprächs** booking a call; **F** (*Formular, Schreiben*) registration [form]; **G** (*Büro, Schalter usw.*) reception; **sie müssen zuerst zur/in die ~ [gehen]** you must go to reception first

**an|merken** *tr. V.* **A** **jmdm. seinen Ärger/seine Verlegenheit** *usw.* **~:** notice that sb. is annoyed/embarrassed *etc.*; notice sb.'s annoyance/embarrassment *etc.*; **man merkt ihm [nicht] an, dass er krank ist** you can[not] tell that he is ill; **sich nichts ~ lassen** not let it show; **B** (*geh.: bemerken*) note; **C** (*geh.: anstreichen*) mark

**Anmerkung** *die;* **~, ~en** **A** (*Fußnote*) note; **B** (*geh.: Bemerkung*) comment; remark; **wenn ich dazu eine ~ machen darf** if I may comment on that

**an|mieten** *tr. V.* rent; hire, rent ‹car, van›

**an·mit** *Adv.* (*schweiz. Papierdt.*) herewith

**An·moderation** *die* **A** (*das Anmoderieren*) introducing; **sie ist noch bei der ~ der Sendung** she is still introducing the programme; **B** (*Text, Wortlaut*) introduction; **sie hat sich eine witzige ~ einfallen lassen** she thought of a witty way to introduce the programme

**an·moderieren** *tr. V.* introduce

**an|montieren** *tr. V.* fix on (**an** + *Akk. od. Dat.* to)

**an|motzen** *tr. V.* (*ugs.*) swear at

**an|müssen** *unr. itr. V.* have to be put on

**an|mustern** *tr., itr. V.* (*Seemannsspr.*) sign on

**An·mut** *die;* **~** (*geh.*) grace; (*Liebreiz, auch fig.: einer Landschaft usw.*) charm; (*fig.: eines Ausdrucks*) elegance; gracefulness; **mit ~:** gracefully

**an|muten** *tr.* (*auch itr.*) *V.* (*geh.*) **etw. mutet [jmdn.] fremd** *usw.* **an** sth. seems strange *etc.* [to sb.]; **alles mutete ihn wie ein Traum an** everything seemed like a dream to him; **ein seltsam ~der Anblick** a sight that seems strange to me/him *etc.*

**an·mutig** (*geh.*) ❶ *Adj.* graceful ‹girl, movement, dance›; charming, delightful ‹girl, smile, picture, landscape›. ❷ *adv.* ‹move, dance› gracefully; ‹smile, greet› charmingly, delightfully

**anmuts·voll** (*geh.*) ⇒ **anmutig**

**an|nageln** *tr. V.* nail on (**an** + *Akk. od. Dat.* to); nail up ‹notice, picture› (**an** + *Akk. od. Dat.* on); **wie angenagelt dastehen** (*ugs.*) stand [there] rooted to the spot

**an|nagen** *tr. V.* gnaw [at]; (*fig. geh.*) gnaw *or* nibble away at

**an|nähen** *tr. V.* sew on (**an** + *Akk.* to)

**an|nähern** ❶ *refl. V.* **A** approach; **die Straße nähert sich der Küste allmählich immer weiter an** the road gradually gets closer and closer to the coast; **sich einem Grenzwert ~** (*Math.*) converge towards a limit; **B** (*fig.: [menschlich] näher kommen*) **sich jmdm. ~:** come *or* get closer to sb.; **C** (*sich angleichen*) **sich einer Sache** (*Dat.*) **~:** come *or* get closer to sth. ❷ *tr. V.* (*angleichen*) bring closer (*Dat.* to); **verschiedene Standpunkte einander ~:** bring differing points of view closer together; **etw. einem Vorbild ~:** make sth. more like a model

**annähernd** ❶ *Adv.* (*ungefähr*) approximately; roughly; (*fast*) almost; nearly; **nicht ~ so teuer** not nearly as *or* nowhere near as expensive. ❷ *adj.* approximate; rough; **mit ~er Sicherheit** with a rough degree of certainty

**Annäherung** *die;* **~, ~en** **A** (*das Sichannähern*) approach (**an** + *Akk.* to); **bei ~ des Zuges** as the train approaches/approached; **B** (*fig.*) **es kam zu einer ~ der beiden Parteien** the two parties came *or* moved closer together; **eine ~ zwischen zwei Staaten herbeiführen** bring two states closer together; **C** (*Angleichung*) **eine ~ der gegenseitigen Standpunkte** bringing the points of view on each side closer together

**annäherungs-, Annäherungs-:** **~versuch** *der* advance; (*im politischen Bereich*) attempted rapprochement; **immer wieder plumpe ~versuche machen** keep making [very] obvious advances; **~weise** *Adv.* approximately; roughly; **~wert** *der* ⇒ **Näherungswert**

**Annahme** /ˈannaːmə/ *die;* **~, ~n** **A** (*das Annehmen*) acceptance; **die ~ eines Pakets verweigern** refuse to accept [delivery of] a parcel; **B** (*Vermutung*) assumption; **ich war der ~, dass ...** I assumed that ...; **in der ~, dass ...** on the assumption that ...; **gehe ich recht in der ~, dass ...?** am I right in assuming that ...?; **ich gehe einmal von der ~ aus, dass ...** I am working *or* going on the assumption that ...; **C** ⇒ **Annahmestelle**; **D** (*Billigung*) approval; (*einer Dissertation*) acceptance; **E** (*einer Gewohnheit*) adoption; (*eines Namens*) adoption; assumption; **F** (*Aufnahme*) taking on; **über jmds. ~ entscheiden** decide if sb. should be taken on; **~ an Kindes statt** (*veralt.*) adoption

**Annahme-:** **~schluss**, ***~schluß** *der* deadline [for acceptance]; **wann ist ~schluss?** when is the deadline [for acceptance]?; **freitags ist für Lottoscheine ~schluss** Friday is the last day of the week for lottery coupons; **~stelle** *die* (*für Lotto/Wetten usw.*) place where coupons/bets are accepted; (*einer Reinigung*) branch; (*für Reparaturen*) repairs counter/department; (*für Telegramme, Pakete usw.*) telegrams/parcels counter; (*für Lieferungen*) delivery point

**Annalen** /aˈnaːlən/ *Pl.* annals; **in die ~ der Firma eingehen** go down in the annals of the firm

**annehmbar** ❶ *Adj.* **A** (*akzeptabel*) acceptable; **B** (*recht gut*) reasonable. ❷ *adv.* reasonably [well]

**an|nehmen** ❶ *unr. tr. V.* **A** accept; take; accept ‹alms, invitation, condition, help›; take ‹food, telephone call›; accept, take [on] ‹task, job, repairs›; accept, take up ‹offer, invitation, challenge›; **die** *od.* **seine Wahl ~:** accept one's election; **B** (*Sport*) take; **er nahm den Ball mit dem Kopf an** he headed the ball down; **C** (*billigen*) approve; accept ‹dissertation›; pass ‹law›; approve, adopt ‹resolution›; **D** (*aufnehmen*) take on ‹worker, patient, pupil›; **E** (*hinnehmen*) accept ‹fate, verdict, punishment›; **F** (*adoptieren*) adopt; **jmdn. an Kindes statt ~** (*veralt.*) adopt sb.; **G** (*haften lassen*) take ‹dye, ink›; **kein Wasser ~:** repel water; be water-repellent; **Feuchtigkeit gut ~:** absorb moisture easily; **H** (*sich aneignen*) adopt ‹habit, mannerism›; adopt, assume ‹name, attitude›; put on ‹airs and graces›; **I** (*bekommen*) take on ‹look, appearance, form, tone, dimension›; **J** (*vermuten*) assume; presume; **ich nehme es an/nicht an** I assume *or* presume so/not; **das ist/ist nicht anzunehmen** that can/cannot be assumed; **K** (*voraussetzen*) assume; **etw. als gegeben** *od.* **Tatsache ~:** take sth. for granted *or* as read; **nehmen wir an, dass ...** let us assume that ...; **angenommen, [dass] ...** assuming [that] ...; **das kannst du ~!** (*ugs.*) you bet! (*coll.*); **L** (*Jägerspr.: angreifen*) attack; go for; **M** (*Jägerspr.: aufnehmen*) **eine/die Fährte ~:** take up a/the scent. ❷ *unr. refl. V.* (*geh.*) **sich jmds./einer Sache ~:** look after sb./sth.

**Annehmlichkeit** *die;* **~, ~en** comfort; (*Vorteil*) advantage

**annektieren** /anɛkˈtiːrən/ *tr. V.* annex

**Annektierung** *die;* **~, ~en, Annexion** /anɛˈksi̯oːn/ *die;* **~, ~en** annexation

**an|niesen** *tr. V.* sneeze over

**an|nieten** *tr. V.* rivet on (**an** + *Akk. od. Dat.* to)

**anno, *Anno** /ˈano/ *in* **~ 1910** *usw.* (*veralt.*) in [the year] 1910 *etc.*; **ein Auto von ~ 1932** (*veralt.*) a 1932 car; **~ dazumal** *od.* **dunnemals** *od.* **Tobak** (*ugs. scherzh.*) the year dot (*Brit. coll.*); long ago; **~ Domini 1656** (*veralt.*) in the year of our Lord 1656

**Annonce** /aˈnõːsə/ *die;* **~, ~n** advertisement; ad (*coll.*); advert (*Brit. coll.*)

**Annoncen·teil** *der* advertisement section

**annoncieren** ❶ *itr. V.* advertise. ❷ *tr. V.* (*ankündigen*) announce

**annullieren** /anʊˈliːrən/ *tr. V.* annul

**Annullierung** *die;* **~, ~en** annulment

**Anode** /aˈnoːdə/ *die;* **~, ~n** (*Physik*) anode

**an|öden** *tr. V.* (*ugs.*) bore stiff (*coll.*) *or* to death (*coll.*)

**anomal** /ˈanomaːl/ ❶ *Adj.* anomalous; abnormal. ❷ *adv.* anomalously; abnormally

**Anomalie** *die;* **~, ~n** ▶ **474** **A** anomaly; abnormality; **B** (*Med.: Missbildung*) abnormality

**anonym** /anoˈnyːm/ ❶ *Adj.* anonymous; **die Anonymen Alkoholiker** Alcoholics Anonymous. ❷ *adv.* anonymously

**Anonymität** /anonymiˈtɛːt/ *die;* **~:** anonymity

**Anonymus** /aˈnoːnymʊs/ *der;* **~, Anonymi** (*geh.*) anonymous writer/composer/artist *etc.*

**Anopheles** /aˈnoːfelɛs/ *die;* **~, ~** (*Zool.*) anopheles

**Anorak** /ˈanorak/ *der;* **~s, ~s** anorak

**an|ordnen** *tr. V.* **A** (*arrangieren*) arrange; **B** (*befehlen*) order

**An·ordnung** *die* **A** (*Ordnung, Aufstellung*) arrangement; **in alphabetischer ~:** in alphabetical order; **B** (*Weisung*) order; **haben Sie die nötigen ~en getroffen?** have you given all the necessary orders?; **auf meine ~/auf ~ des Arztes** on my/doctor's orders *pl.*

**an·organisch** *Adj.* inorganic

**anormal** ❶ *Adj.* abnormal. ❷ *adv.* abnormally

**an|packen** ❶ *tr. V.* **A** (*ugs.: greifen, anfassen*) grab hold of; **jmdn. am Arm ~:** grab [hold of] sb. by the arm; **musst du das Buch mit deinen Dreckpfoten ~?** must you touch the book with your dirty hands?; **B** (*beginnen, angehen*) tackle; **packen wir's an!** let's get down to it; **C** (*ugs.: behandeln*) treat. ❷ *itr. V.* (*ugs.: mithelfen*) **[mit] ~:** lend a hand

**an|pappen** (*ugs.*) ❶ *tr. V.* **etw. ~:** stick sth. on (**an** + *Dat.* to). ❷ *itr. V.; mit sein* stick (**an** + *Dat.* to)

**an|passen** ❶ *tr. V.* **A** (*passend machen*) fit; **jmdm. einen Anzug ~:** fit sb. for a suit; **Bauteile einander ~:** fit components together; **B** (*abstimmen*) suit (*Dat.* to); **die Renten wurden am 1. Januar angepasst** pensions were adjusted on 1 January. ❷ *refl. V.* adapt [oneself] (*Dat.* to); ‹animal› adapt; (*gesellschaftlich*) conform; **die am besten angepassten Arten** the species which have adapted best; ⇒ *auch* **angepasst 2**

**Anpassung** *die;* **~, ~en** adaptation (**an** + *Akk.* to); (*der Renten, Löhne usw.*) adjustment (**an** + *Akk.* to); (*an die Gesellschaft*) conformity

**anpassungs·fähig** *Adj.* adaptable

**Anpassungs-:** **~fähigkeit** *die* adaptability (**an** + *Akk.* to); **~schwierigkeiten** *Pl.* difficulties in adapting (**an** + *Akk.* to)

**an|peilen** *tr. V.* **A** (*Funkw.*) take a bearing on; **B** (*fig. ugs.: anstreben*) aim at; **C** (*anvisieren*) take a sight on

**an|peitschen** *tr. V.* drive on

**an|pesen** *itr. V.; mit sein* (*nordd. ugs.*) **angepest kommen** come tearing *or* (*coll.*) belting along; (*auf einen zu*) come tearing *or* (*coll.*) belting up

**an|pfeifen** ❶ *unr. tr. V.* **A** **das Spiel/die zweite Halbzeit ~:** blow the whistle to start the game/the second half; **B** (*salopp: zurechtweisen*) bawl out (*coll.*). ❷ *unr. itr. V.* blow the whistle

**An·pfiff** *der* **A** (*Sport*) whistle for the start of play; **der ~ zur zweiten Halbzeit** the whistle for the start of the second half; **B** (*salopp: Zurechtweisung*) bawling-out (*coll.*)

**an|pflanzen** *tr. V.* **A** (*pflanzen, bepflanzen*) plant; **B** (*anbauen*) grow; cultivate

**An·pflanzung** *die* **A** planting; **B** (*bepflanzte Fläche*) cultivated area; **eine ~ anlegen** lay out an area for cultivation

a

**an|pflaumen** *tr. V.* (*ugs.*) Ⓐ tease; take the mickey out of (*Brit. sl.*); Ⓑ ⇒ **anmeckern**

**Anpflaumerei** *die;* ~, ~**en** (*ugs.*) teasing; mickey-taking (*Brit. sl.*); **lass doch deine ~en** stop teasing *or* (*Brit. sl.*) taking the mickey

**an|pflocken** *tr. V.* tie ‹boat› up; tether ‹animal›

**an|picken**[1] *tr. V.* peck at

**an|picken**[2] (*österr. ugs.*) ❶ *tr. V.* stick on. ❷ *itr. V.; mit sein* be stuck on

**an|pinkeln** *tr. V.* (*ugs.*) pee on (*coll.*)

**an|pinnen** *tr. V.* (*nordd.*) pin up (**an** + *Akk.* on)

**an|pinseln** *tr. V.* (*ugs.*) Ⓐ (*anstreichen*) paint; Ⓑ (*an etw. pinseln*) paint (**an** + *Akk.* on)

**an|pirschen** *refl. V.* creep up (**an** + *Akk.* on)

**an|pissen** *tr. V.* (*derb*) piss on (*coarse*)

**An·pöbelei** *die* (*ugs.*) abuse; ~**en** abuse *sing.*

**an|pöbeln** *tr. V.* (*ugs.*) abuse

**an|pochen** *itr. V.* (*südd.*) ⇒ **anklopfen**

**An·prall** *der;* ~**[e]s** impact (**auf, an** + *Akk.* with, **gegen** against)

**an|prallen** *itr. V.; mit sein* crash; **gegen** *od.* **an etw. ~:** crash into sb./against sth.

**an|prangern** *tr. V.* denounce (**als** as)

**an|preisen** *unr. tr. V.* extol; **etw. als etw. ~:** extol sth. as being sth.; **jmdn./etw. jmdm. ~:** extol the virtues of sb./sth. to sb.; recommend sb./sth. highly to sb.

**an|preschen** *itr. V.; mit sein* **angeprescht kommen** (*ugs.*) come racing along; (*auf einen zu*) come racing up

**an|pressen** *tr. V.* press on (**an** + *Akk.* to)

**An·probe** *die* Ⓐ fitting; **zur ~ kommen** come for a fitting; Ⓑ (*Raum*) (*beim Schneider*) fitting room; (*im Kaufhaus*) changing room (*Brit.*); dressing room (*Amer.*)

**an|probieren** ❶ *tr. V.* try on; **jmdm. etw. ~:** try sth. on sb. ❷ *itr. V.* **~ kommen** (*ugs.*) come for a fitting

**an|pumpen** *tr. V.* (*ugs.*) borrow money from; **jmdn. um 20 Mark ~:** touch (*coll.*) *or* tap sb. for 20 marks

**an|pusten** *tr. V.* (*ugs.*) blow on

**an|quasseln** *tr. V.* (*salopp*), **an|quatschen** *tr. V.* (*salopp*) speak to

**Anrainer** /ˈanrainɐ/ *der;* ~**s**, ~ Ⓐ (*Nachbar*) neighbour; **als ~ des Sees habe ich ...** as I live on *or* by the lake, I have ...; Ⓑ (*bes. österr.: Anlieger*) resident; Ⓒ ⇒ **Anrainerstaat**

**Anrainer·grundstück** *das* neighbouring property; **die ~e des Sees** the properties on *or* by the lake

**Anrainerin** *die;* ~, ~**nen** ⇒ **Anrainer** A, B

**Anrainer·staat** *der* **die ~en des Bodensees** the countries bordering on Lake Constance

**an|ranzen** *tr. V.* (*salopp*) bawl out (*coll.*)

**Anranzer** *der;* ~**s**, ~ (*salopp*) bawling-out (*coll.*)

**an|rasen** *itr. V.; mit sein* (*ugs.*) race up; **gegen etw. ~:** crash into sth.; **angerast kommen** come racing along; (*auf einen zu*) come racing up

**an|raten** *unr. tr. V.* **jmdm. etw. ~:** recommend sth. to sb.; **jmdm. Vorsicht ~:** advise sb. to be careful; **auf Anraten des Arztes** on the *or* one's doctor's advice

**an|rattern** *itr. V.; mit sein* (*ugs.*) **angerattert kommen** come rattling along; (*auf einen zu*) come rattling up

**an|rauchen** *tr. V.* light up; **jmdm. eine Zigarette ~:** light up a cigarette for sb.; **eine angerauchte Zigarre** a partly smoked *or* half-smoked cigar

**an|räuchern** *tr. V.* lightly smoke

**an|rauen**, ***an|rauhen** *tr. V.* roughen

**an|raunzen** *tr. V.* (*salopp*) ⇒ **anranzen**

**Anraunzer** *der;* ~**s**, ~ (*salopp*) ⇒ **Anranzer**

**an|rauschen** *itr. V.; mit sein* (*ugs.*) **angerauscht kommen** come sweeping along; (*auf einen zu*) come sweeping up; ‹vehicle› come roaring along; (*auf einen zu*) come roaring up

**anrechenbar** *Adj.* [**auf etw.** (*Akk.*)] **~ sein** count [towards sth.]

**an|rechnen** *tr. V.* Ⓐ (*gutschreiben, verbuchen*) count; take into account; **jmdm. einen Betrag/seine Überstunden ~:** credit sb. with an amount/his/her overtime; **die Untersuchungshaft kann auf die Gefängnisstrafe angerechnet werden** time spent in custody can be counted as part of *or* taken into account in the prison sentence; **er bekam einen Pluspunkt angerechnet** he was given an extra mark; **jmdm. etw. als Verdienst/Fehler ~:** count sth. to sb.'s credit/as sb.'s mistake; **sich** (*Dat.*) **etw. zur Ehre ~** (*geh.*) consider sth. an honour; **jmdm. etw. hoch ~:** think highly of sb. for sth.; Ⓑ (*in Rechnung stellen*) **jmdm. etw. ~:** charge sb. for sth.; **das Porto wird dem Kunden angerechnet** postage is charged to the customer; **jmdm. zu viel ~:** overcharge sb.

**An·rechnung** *die* Ⓐ **unter ~ der Untersuchungshaft** counting *or* taking into account time spent in custody; **eine ~ der Untersuchungshaft/des Praktikums ist nicht möglich** it is not possible to take time spent in custody/practical work into account; Ⓑ (*Berechnung*) charge; **eine ~ der Transportkosten erfolgt nicht** transport costs (*Brit.*) *or* (*Amer.*) transportation costs are not charged; **etw. in ~ bringen** (*Papierdt.*) charge for sth.

**anrechnungs·fähig** *Adj.* (*Papierdt.*) ⇒ **anrechenbar**

**An·recht** *das* Ⓐ right; **ein ~ auf etw.** (*Akk.*) **haben** *od.* **besitzen** have a right to *or* be entitled to sth.; Ⓑ (*Abonnement*) subscription

**An·rede** *die* ▶ 91, ▶ 187 form of address; (*Brief~*) form of address; salutation; **wie ist die ~ eines Kardinals** *od.* **für einen Kardinal?** what is the correct form of address for a cardinal?

**Anrede-: ~fall** *der* ⇒ **~kasus**; **~für·wort** *das* ⇒ **~pronomen**; **~kasus** *der* vocative [case]

**an|reden** *tr. V.* Ⓐ address; **jmdn. mit „du" ~:** address sb. as 'du'; use 'du' to sb.; **jmdn. mit dem Vornamen ~:** address *or* call sb. by his/her Christian name; Ⓑ **gegen den Lärm ~:** talk above the noise; **gegen etw. ~** (*widersprechen*) argue [against sth.]

**Anrede·pronomen** *das* personal pronoun used as form of address

**an|regen** ❶ *tr. V.* Ⓐ (*ermuntern*) prompt; **jmdn. zum Nachdenken ~:** make sb. think; Ⓑ (*vorschlagen*) propose; suggest; raise ‹question›; **~, etw. zu tun** propose *or* suggest doing sth.; Ⓒ (*Physik*) excite. ❷ *tr.* (*auch itr.*) *V.* stimulate ‹imagination, digestion›; sharpen, whet, stimulate ‹appetite›; **Kaffee regt an** coffee acts as a stimulant; ⇒ *auch* **angeregt** 2

**anregend** *Adj.* stimulating; **ein ~es Mittel** a stimulant; **Kaffee wirkt/ist ~:** coffee acts as a stimulant

**An·regung** *die* Ⓐ (*das Anregen*) ⇒ **anregen** 2: stimulation; whetting; sharpening; **zur ~ der Verdauung/des Appetits** to stimulate the digestion/whet *etc.* the appetite; Ⓑ (*Denkanstoß, Idee*) stimulus; Ⓒ (*Vorschlag*) proposal; suggestion; Ⓓ (*Physik*) excitation

**Anregungs·mittel** *das* stimulant

**an|reichen** ⇒ **zureichen**

**an|reichern** /ˈanraiçɐn/ ❶ *tr. V.* Ⓐ (*gehaltvoller machen*) enrich; **Trinkwasser mit Fluor ~:** add fluoride to drinking water; Ⓑ (*akkumulieren*) accumulate; Ⓒ (*Kerntechnik*) enrich. ❷ *refl. V.* Ⓐ (*sich ansammeln*) accumulate; Ⓑ (*seinen Gehalt an etw. erhöhen*) be enriched

**Anreicherung** *die;* ~, ~**en** Ⓐ enrichment; **die ~ von Trinkwasser mit Fluor** the addition of fluoride to drinking water; Ⓑ (*Akkumulation*) accumulation; Ⓒ (*Kerntechnik*) enrichment

**an|reihen** ❶ *tr. V.* add (**an** + *Akk.* to). ❷ *refl. V.* **sich hinten [an die Schlange] ~:** join the end of the queue (*Brit.*); get on the end of the line (*Amer.*)

**An·reise** *die* Ⓐ journey [there/here]; **die ~ dauert 10 Stunden** the journey there/here takes ten hours; it takes 10 hours to get there/here; Ⓑ (*Ankunft*) arrival

**an|reisen** *itr. V.; mit sein* Ⓐ travel there/here; **mit der Bahn ~:** go/come by train; travel there/here by train; **die aus dem ganzen Land anreisenden Besucher** the visitors travelling there/here from all over the country; **angereist kommen** come; Ⓑ (*ankommen*) arrive

**Anreise·tag** *der* day of arrival; **für den An- und den Abreisetag bekommen Sie Spesen** your expenses will be paid for the days of the journey there and the journey back

**an|reißen** *unr. tr. V.* Ⓐ (*durchzureißen beginnen*) partly tear; Ⓑ (*in Gang setzen*) start [up]; Ⓒ (*anzünden*) strike ‹match›; Ⓓ (*Technik*) mark [out]; Ⓔ (*kurz ansprechen*) touch on; Ⓕ (*ugs.: anbrechen*) start; open; Ⓖ (*ugs. abwertend: anlocken*) lure

**An·reißer** *der* Ⓐ (*ugs. abwertend: Werber*) tout; Ⓑ (*ugs.: Ware*) big attraction; Ⓒ (*Berufsbez.*) marker-out

**Anreißerin** *die;* ~, ~**nen** ⇒ **Anreißer** A, C

**an·reißerisch** (*ugs. abwertend*) ❶ *Adj.* flashily commercial; gimmicky (*coll.*) ‹advertisement›. ❷ *adv.* **das Buch/die Reklame ist mir zu ~ aufgemacht** the book is too flashily commercial/the ad is too gimmicky for my liking (*coll.*)

**an|reiten** *unr. itr. V.; mit sein* Ⓐ **angeritten kommen** come riding along; (*auf einen zu*) come riding up; **gegen den Feind ~:** charge the enemy; Ⓑ (*ansteuern*) ride at ‹obstacle›; Ⓒ (*zureiten*) break in ‹horse›

**An·reiz** *der* incentive; **ein ~ zum Sparen** an incentive to save

**an|reizen** *tr.* (*auch itr.*) *V.* Ⓐ (*anspornen*) stimulate; encourage; **Steuerermäßigungen sollen zum Sparen ~:** tax reductions are supposed to stimulate *or* act as an incentive to saving; Ⓑ (*anregen, erregen*) stimulate

**an|rempeln** *tr. V.* barge into; (*absichtlich*) jostle

**an|rennen** ❶ *unr. itr. V.; mit sein* Ⓐ **angerannt kommen** come running along; (*auf einen zu*) come running up; **er kommt wegen jeder Kleinigkeit bei mir angerannt** he comes running to me about every little thing; Ⓑ **gegen den Sturm/feindliche Stellungen ~:** run into *or* against the storm/storm enemy positions; **gegen jmdn./etw. ~** (*fig.*) fight against sb./sth. ❷ *unr. refl. V.* (*ugs.*) **sich** (*Dat.*) **das Knie/den Kopf an etw.** (*Dat.*) **~:** bump one's knee/head on sth.

**Anrichte** *die;* ~, ~**n** Ⓐ (*Möbel*) sideboard; Ⓑ (*Raum*) pantry

**an|richten** *tr. V.* Ⓐ (*auch itr.*) arrange ‹food›; (*servieren*) serve; **es ist angerichtet** (*geh.*) dinner is served; Ⓑ cause ‹disaster, confusion, devastation, etc.›; **was hast du wieder alles angerichtet!** what have you gone and done now? (*coll.*)

**an|ritzen** *tr. V.* scratch

**an|rollen** ❶ *itr. V.; mit sein* Ⓐ (*zu rollen beginnen*) ‹vehicle, column, etc.› start moving; (*fig.*) ‹campaign, search operation› start; Ⓑ (*heranrollen*) roll up; ‹aircraft› taxi up; **angerollt kommen** come rolling along; (*auf einen zu*) come rolling up; Ⓒ **die Wellen rollten gegen den Deich an** the waves rolled in against the dike. ❷ *tr. V.* roll up ‹barrel›; (*auf einem Wagen o. Ä.*) wheel up

**an|rosten** *itr. V.; mit sein* start to rust; get [a bit] rusty; **ein angerostetes Messer** a rusting knife; a knife that has started to rust

**an|rösten** *tr. V.* roast lightly; toast ‹bread› lightly

**anrüchig** /ˈanrʏçɪç/ *Adj.* Ⓐ (*berüchtigt*) disreputable; Ⓑ (*unanständig*) indecent; (*obszön*) offensive

**Anrüchigkeit** *die;* ~ Ⓐ (*schlechter Ruf*) disreputableness; Ⓑ (*Unanständigkeit*) indecency; (*Obszönität*) offensiveness

*old spelling (see note on page 1707)

# Anreden und Titel

Die vier grundlegenden Anreden im Englischen sind:

***Mr*** (= Herr) für Männer

***Mrs*** (= Frau) für verheiratete Frauen

***Miss*** (= Fräulein bzw. Frau) für Mädchen und (auch ältere) unverheiratete Frauen

***Ms*** (= Frau) für (meist jüngere) Frauen

Im modernen Sprachgebrauch wird **Ms** oft statt **Miss** oder **Mrs** verwendet, es hat sich allerdings nicht so durchgesetzt wie im Deutschen die Anrede **Frau** für alle Frauen. Alle vier Anreden können entweder mit oder ohne den Vornamen stehen. Die nachgestellte Bezeichnung **Esq** (*Esquire* = Herr) wird meist in höheren britischen gesellschaftlichen Kreisen auf Briefen statt **Mr** verwendet, gilt aber heute als etwas altmodisch. Ebenfalls nachgestellt wird in den USA die Abkürzung **Jr** (= Junior) für den Sohn eines gleichnamigen Vaters.

····➤ **Briefeschreiben**

## Wie man jemanden anredet

Im Allgemeinen ist der Gebrauch im englischen Sprachraum weniger formell als in Deutschland, Österreich und der Schweiz. Für die Anrede mit „Sie" gibt es im Englischen keine Entsprechung, es wird immer **you** verwendet. Unter Kollegen, Nachbarn, in Gruppen und Vereinen spricht man sich generell mit Vornamen an. Vor allem in den USA redet man praktisch jeden, den man kennen lernt, sofort mit Vornamen an.

Beachten Sie, dass die Anreden **Mr**, **Mrs**, **Miss** und **Ms** nicht allein stehen dürfen (Ausnahme: Lehrerinnen werden noch von Schulkindern mit „miss" angeredet) und auch nicht in Kombination mit Titeln verwendet werden können:

***Guten Morgen, Herr Professor***
= Good morning, professor

***Guten Abend, Frau Doktor***
= Good evening, doctor

***Auf Wiedersehen, Herr Oberst***
= Goodbye, colonel

***Jawohl, Herr Minister***
= Yes, minister

In solchen Fällen wird oft der Name des bzw. der Angesprochenen hinzugefügt: „Good morning, Professor Evans" usw. Generell wird im englischen Sprachraum weniger Gebrauch von Titeln gemacht, sodass es etwa für „Herr Direktor" keine Entsprechung gibt. Man sagt also einfach **Mr** und den Namen.

Vorgesetzte beim Militär werden nicht mit dem Namen, sondern meist einfach mit **sir** oder der Rangbezeichnung angeredet, während in der Schule Lehrer und Lehrerinnen meist von den jüngeren Schülern mit **sir** bzw. **miss** angeredet werden.

Kunden in Geschäften, Restaurants usw. werden oft noch mit **sir** bzw. **madam** (im Plural **gentlemen** bzw. **ladies**) angeredet:

***Was darf es sein?***
= Can I help you, sir/madam?

***Was wünscht der Herr/die gnädige Frau zum Trinken?***
= What would you like to drink, sir/madam?

***Was wünschen die Damen/Herren?***
= What would you like, ladies/gentlemen?

## Anreden bei Würdenträgern und Adeligen

***Ihre Majestät***
= Your Majesty

***Eure Hoheit***
= Your Highness

***Euer Gnaden***
= Your Grace

***Eure Eminenz***
= Your Eminence

***Eure Heiligkeit***
= Your Holiness

## Wenn man von jemandem spricht

Beachten Sie auch hier, dass im englischen Sprachraum weniger Gebrauch von Titeln gemacht wird. Die Bezeichnung *Herr* bzw. *Frau* wird in Kombinationen wie „Herr Doktor Reiter", „Frau Professor Elisabeth Meinhardt" nicht übersetzt, da **Mr, Mrs, Ms** und **Miss** nicht mit Titeln kombiniert werden dürfen:

***Herr Doktor Dietrich Reiter***
= Dr Dietrich Reiter

***Frau Professor Elisabeth Meinhardt***
= Professor Elisabeth Meinhardt

***Herr Kapitän Richard Müller***
= Captain Richard Müller

***Herr Minister Baumann***
= [the minister] Mr Baumann

***Frau Direktorin Dr Stahlmeyer***
= [the director/head teacher] Dr Stahlmeyer

***Herr Kammersänger Eberhard Wächter***
= Kammersänger Eberhard Wächter

Im letzten Beispiel gibt es keine Übersetzung, am besten lässt man den Titel also in der deutschen Originalform.

Adelstitel und Kirchentitel werden im Englischen ähnlich wie im Deutschen behandelt:

***König Ludwig XIV. von Frankreich***
= King Louis XIV of France (*gesprochen* Louis the Fourteenth)

***Papst Johannes Paul II.***
= Pope John Paul II (*gesprochen* John Paul the Second)

***Prinzessin Ingeborg zu Schleswig-Holstein***
= Princess Ingeborg of Schleswig-Holstein

**an|rücken** ❶ *itr. V.; mit sein* ‹troops› advance; move forward; ‹firemen, police› move in; **morgen rücken meine Verwandten an** (*ugs. scherzh.*) my relatives are descending on me/us tomorrow. ❷ *tr. V.* push (**an** + *Akk.* against); (*ziehen*) pull (**an** + *Akk.* against)

**An·ruf** *der* [A] (*telefonischer* ~) call; **danke für den** ~**:** thanks for ringing (*Brit.*) *or* calling; [B] (*Zuruf*) call; (*eines Wachtpostens*) challenge; **auf** ~**:** when called/challenged; **ohne** ~ **schießen** shoot without warning

**Anruf·beantworter** *der;* ~**s,** ~**:** [telephone-]answering machine

**an|rufen** ❶ *unr. tr. V.* [A] call *or* shout to ‹friend, passer-by›; call ‹sleeping person›; hail ‹ship›; ‹sentry› challenge; [B] (*geh.: angehen, bitten*) appeal to ‹person, court› (**um** for); call upon ‹God›; **Gott um Gnade** ~**:** implore God's mercy; [C] (*telefonisch* ~) ring (*Brit.*); call; [D] (*geh.: begehren*) implore, beg ‹sb.'s mercy, help, protection, etc.›. ❷ *unr. itr. V.* [A] (*antelefonieren*) ring (*Brit.*); call; **bei jmdm.** ~**:** ring (*Brit.*) *or* call sb.; **ruf doch mal in Köln an** ring (*Brit.*) *or* call Cologne; **im Büro** ~**:** ring (*Brit.*) *or* call the office; [B] (*ugs., bes. südd.: telefonieren*) make a phone call; **ich muss nur mal kurz** ~**:** I must just make a quick phone call; **kann ich bei Ihnen/in Ihrem Büro mal** ~**?** can I just use your telephone *or* phone/telephone from your office *or* use your office telephone?

**Anrufer** *der;* ~**s,** ~, **Anruferin** *die;* ~, ~**nen** caller

**Anrufung** *die;* ~, ~**en** [A] (*einer Gottheit o. Ä.*) invocation; [B] (*eines Gerichts*) appeal (*Gen.* to)

**an|rühren** *tr. V.* [A] touch; **keine Zigaretten/kein Buch** ~**:** never touch cigarettes/never pick up a book; [B] (*bereiten*) mix; [C] (*geh.: beeindrucken*) move; touch

**ans** *Präp.* + *Art.* [A] = **an das;** [B] (*mit subst. Inf.*) **sich** ~ **Arbeiten machen** set to work; **wenn es** ~ **Bezahlen geht** when it comes to paying

**an|säen** *tr. V.* sow ‹grass, grain›

**An·sage** *die* [A] (*Ankündigung*) announcement; [B] (*Kartenspiel*) bid; **du hast die** ~**:** it's your bid

**an|sagen** ❶ *tr. V.* [A] (*ankündigen*) announce; ⇒ *auch* **Bankrott** A; **Kampf** D; [B] (*Kartenspiel*) bid; ⇒ *auch* **Schneider** C; [C] (*Büro.: diktieren*) dictate; [D] (*veralt.; mitteilen*) **sagt an, was ...** pray tell me/us what ... (*arch.*). ❷ *refl. V.* say that one is coming; **sich zum nächsten Wochenende/für Dienstagabend/bei jmdm.** ~**:** say that one is coming next weekend/Tuesday evening/to see sb.

**an|sägen** *tr. V.* make a saw cut in; start to saw through

**Ansager** *der;* ~**s,** ~, **Ansagerin** *die;* ~, ~**nen** ▶ 159 [A] (*Radio, Fernsehen*) announcer; [B] (*im Kabarett usw.*) master of ceremonies; (*Brit.*) compère

**an|sammeln** ❶ *tr. V.* (*anhäufen*) accumulate; amass ‹riches, treasure›. ❷ *refl. V.* [A] (*zusammenströmen*) gather; [B] (*sich anhäufen*) accumulate; (*fig.*) ‹anger, excitement› build up

**An·sammlung** *die* [A] (*von Gegenständen*) collection; (*Haufen*) pile, heap; (*von Wasser*) pool; [B] (*Auflauf*) crowd

**ansässig** /ˈanzɛsɪç/ *Adj.* resident; **eine in London ~e Firma** a firm with its registered office in London; **sich in Bayern ~ machen** settle in Bavaria

**An·satz** *der* **A** *(erstes Zeichen, Beginn)* beginnings *pl.;* **einen ~ zum Bauch haben** have the beginnings of a paunch; **Ansätze zur Besserung zeigen** show the first signs of improvement; **etw. im ~ unterdrücken** nip sth. in the bud; **die ersten Ansätze** the initial stages; **gute Ansätze zeigen** make a good start; **im ~** *(ansatzweise)* to some extent; **B** *(eines Körperteils)* base; **C** *(Musik)* *(Lippenstellung)* embouchure; *(Tonerzeugung)* attack; **D** *(Math.)* statement; **E** *(bes. Philos.: Lösungsversuch)* approach; **F** *(von Rost, Kalk usw.)* formation; *(Schicht)* coating; **G** *(Wirtsch.: Voranschlag)* estimate; *(im Staatsbudget)* amount budgeted; appropriation; **etw. für etw. in ~ bringen** *(Amtsspr.)* earmark sth. for sth.; **außer ~ bleiben** *(Amtsspr.)* be left out of account; be excluded; **H** *(Chemie: eines Versuchs)* setting up; **I** *(Technik)* *(Verlängerungsstück)* extension; *(Nahtstelle)* join

**ansatz-, Ansatz-: ~punkt** *der* starting point; point of departure; **~stück** *das* *(Technik)* extension; **~weise** *Adv.* to some extent

**an|saufen** *unr. refl. V.* *(salopp)* **sich** *(Dat.)* **einen [Rausch] ~:** get plastered *(sl.)*; **sich** *(Dat.)* **einen Bierbauch ~:** get a beer belly

**an|saugen** ❶ *tr. V.* *(geh. auch unr.)* suck in *or* up. ❷ *refl. V.* *(geh. auch unr.)* *(sich festsetzen)* ‹leech etc.› attach itself *(by suction)*

**Ansaug·rohr** *das* *(Kfz-W.)* intake manifold; *(beim Einzylindermotor)* inlet pipe

**an|säuseln** *refl. V.* **sich** *(Dat.)* **einen ~** *(ugs.)* get tipsy; ⇒ *auch* **angesäuselt** 2

**Anschaffe** /ˈanʃafə/ *die;* **~** *(salopp)* **auf [die] ~ gehen** *(sich prostituieren)* go on the game *(Brit. sl.)*; walk the streets *(Amer.)*; *(stehlen)* go out thieving

**an|schaffen** ❶ *tr. V.* **A** *(kaufen)* **[sich** *(Dat.)***] etw. ~** *(auch fig. ugs.)* get [oneself] sth.; **sich** *(Dat.)* **Kinder ~** *(fig. ugs.)* have children *or* *(coll.)* kids; **B** *(südd., österr.: befehlen)* **jmdm. ~, dass er etw. tut** order sb. to do sth.; **C** *(salopp: stehlen)* pinch *(coll)*. ❷ *itr. V.* **A** *(salopp: Prostitution betreiben)* **~ [gehen]** be on the game *(Brit. coll.)*; be walking the streets *(Amer.)*; **für jmdn. ~:** work as a prostitute for sb.; **B** *(südd., österr.: befehlen)* **[jmdm.] ~:** give [sb.] orders

**An·schaffung** *die* purchase; **~en machen** make purchases; **sich zur ~ eines Autos entschließen** decide to get *or* buy a car

**Anschaffungs-: ~kosten** *Pl.* original *or* initial cost *sing.;* acquisition cost *sing.;* **~wert** *der* value at the time of purchase

**an|schalten** *tr. V.* switch on

**an|schauen** *(bes. südd., österr., schweiz.)* ⇒ **ansehen**

**anschaulich** ❶ *Adj.* *(deutlich)* clear; *(bildhaft, lebendig)* vivid, graphic ‹style, description›; **etw. ~ machen** make sth. vivid; bring sth. to life; **etw. durch Beispiele ~ machen** illustrate sth. by examples; **ein ~er Unterricht** teaching that makes the subject come alive. ❷ *adv.* *(deutlich)* clearly; *(bildhaft, lebendig)* vividly; ‹describe› vividly, graphically

**Anschaulichkeit** *die;* **~** ⇒ **anschaulich**: clarity; vividness; graphicness

**Anschauung** *die;* **~, ~en A** *(Auffassung)* view; *(bestimmte Meinung)* opinion; **B** *(Eindruck, Erfahrung)* experience; **aus eigener ~:** from personal *or* one's own experience; **C** *(das Betrachten)* contemplation

**Anschauungs-: ~material** *das* illustrative material; *(für den Unterricht)* visual aids *pl.;* **~unterricht** *der* visual instruction; *(fig.)* object lesson; **~weise** *die* view

**An·schein** *der* appearance; **allem** *od.* **dem ~ nach** to all appearances; **es hat den ~, als ob ...** it appears *or* looks as if ...; **sich** *(Dat.)* **den ~ geben, als ob man etw. glaubt** pretend to believe sth.; **den ~ erwecken, etw. zu sein** give the impression of being sth.

**an·scheinend** *Adv.* apparently; seemingly

**an|scheißen** *(derb)* ❶ *unr. tr. V.* **A** *(betrügen)* con *(coll.)*; diddle *(coll.)*; **B** *(zurechtweisen)* **jmdn. ~:** give sb. a bollocking *(Brit. coarse)*; bawl sb. out *(coll.)*. ❷ *unr. itr. V.; mit sein* **da kommt er schon wieder angeschissen** there he is, come to make a bloody nuisance of himself again *(Brit. sl.)*

**an|schesen** *itr. V.; mit sein* *(nordd.)* **angeschest kommen** come rushing along; *(auf einen zu)* come rushing up

**an|schicken** *refl. V.* *(geh.)* **sich ~, etw. zu tun** *(sich bereit machen)* get ready *or* prepare to do sth.; *(anfangen, im Begriff sein)* be about to do sth.; be on the point of doing sth.

**an|schieben** *unr. tr. V.* push ‹vehicle›; **könnt ihr mich mal ~?** could you give me a push?

**an|schießen** ❶ *unr. tr. V.* **A** *(durch Schuss verletzen)* shoot and wound; **das Reh war nicht tot, nur angeschossen** the deer was not dead, only wounded; **B** *(bes. Fußball)* kick the ball against ‹player›; shoot straight at ‹goalkeeper›; **C** *(ugs.: kritisieren)*; **jmdn. ~:** give sb. some stick *(sl.)*; **D** *(Milit., Jagdw.: prüfen)* test. ❷ *unr. itr. V.; mit sein* **angeschossen kommen** come tearing *or* racing along; *(auf einen zu)* come tearing *or* racing up

**an|schimmeln** *itr. V.; mit sein* start to go mouldy; **angeschimmeltes Brot** bread that has started to go mouldy

**an|schirren** *tr. V.* harness ‹horse›

**An·schiss, *An·schiß** *der* *(salopp)* bollocking *(Brit. coarse)*; bawling-out *(coll.)*; **einen ~ kriegen** get a bollocking *(Brit. coarse)*; get bawled out *(coll.)*

**An·schlag** *der* **A** *(Bekanntmachung)* notice; *(Plakat)* poster; **einen ~ machen** put up a notice/poster; **B** *(Attentat)* assassination attempt; *(auf ein Gebäude, einen Zug o. Ä.)* attack; **einen ~ auf jmdn. verüben** make an attempt on sb.'s life; **einem ~ zum Opfer fallen** be assassinated; **C** *(Texterfassung)* keystroke; **200 Anschläge pro Minute [schreiben]** ≈ [have a typing speed of] 40 words a minute; **D** *(Musik)* touch; **E** *(Technik)* stop; **etw. bis zum ~ niederdrücken/aufdrehen** push sth. right down/turn sth. on as far as it will go; **F** *(Häkeln, Stricken)* first line of stitches; *(Vorgang)* casting on; **„~ 50 Maschen"** 'cast on 50 stitches'; **G** *(Milit., Jagdw.)* aiming position; **mit dem Gewehr im ~:** with rifle/rifles levelled; **in ~ bringen** level ‹gun›; **H** *(Kaufmannsspr.)* estimate; **etw. in ~ bringen** take sth. into account *or* consideration

**Anschlag·brett** *das* noticeboard *(Brit.)*; bulletin board *(Amer.)*

**an|schlagen** ❶ *unr. tr. V.* **A** *(aushängen)* put up, post ‹notice, announcement, message› **(an + Akk.** on); **B** *(Häkeln, Stricken)* cast on; **C** *(beim Versteckspiel)* tag; **D** *(beschädigen)* chip; **E** *(bei Musikinstrumenten)* strike ‹string, key, etc.›; strike, sound ‹gong›; **F** *(erklingen lassen)* play ‹note, melody, etc.›; **einen anderen/ernsthaften Ton ~** *(fig.)* adopt a different/serious tone; **G** *(beginnen)* **ein rascheres Tempo/eine schnellere Gangart ~:** increase one's pace; speed up; **H** *(befestigen)* fix on **(an + Akk.** to); *(mit Nägeln)* nail on **(an + Akk.** to); **I** *(beim Maschinenschreiben)* press, hit ‹key›; **J** *(Seemannsspr.: festbinden)* bend **(an + Dat.** to); **K** *(markieren)* **einen Baum ~:** mark a tree with a notch; **L** *(Milit., Jagdw. veralt.)* level ‹gun›; **M** *(österr.: anstechen)* tap ‹barrel›. ❷ *unr. itr. V.* **A** *mit sein* *(anstoßen)* **an etw.** *(Akk.)* **~:** knock against sth.; **mit dem Knie/Kopf an etw.** *(Akk.)* **~:** knock one's knee/head on sth.; **B** *(Schwimmen)* touch; **C** *(Tasten niederdrücken)* press *or* hit the keys; **D** *(wirken)* work; **E** *(ugs.: dick machen)* be fattening; **bei jmdm. ~:** make sb. put on weight; **F** *(bellen)* bark. ❸ *unr. refl. V.* *(stoßen)* **sich** *(Dat.)* **das Knie** *usw.* **~:** knock one's knee *etc.* **(an + Dat.** on)

**Anschlag·säule** *die* advertising column

**an|schleichen** ❶ *unr. itr. V.; mit sein* creep up; **angeschlichen kommen** come creeping along; *(auf einen zu)* come creeping up. ❷ *unr. refl. V.* **sich an jmdn./etw. ~:** creep up on sb./sth.

**an|schleifen**[1] *unr. tr. V.* grind; cut ‹precious stone›

**an|schleifen**[2] *tr. V.* *(ugs.)* drag along

**an|schlendern** *itr. V.; mit sein* **angeschlendert kommen** come strolling along; *(auf einen zu)* come strolling up

**an|schleppen** *tr. V.* **A** *(herbeibringen)* drag along; **B** *(zum Starten)* tow-start

**an|schließen** ❶ *unr. tr. V.* **A** *(befestigen)* lock, secure **(an + Akk.** *od.* **Dat.** to); **B** *(verbinden)* connect **(an + Akk.** *od.* **Dat.** to); connect up ‹electrical device›; *(mit Stecker und Steckdose)* plug in; **angeschlossene Sender** *(Rundf., Ferns.)* linked stations; **C** *(anfügen)* add. ❷ *unr. refl. V.* **A** *(sich beteiligen)*; **sich jmdm./einer Sache ~:** join sb./sth.; **B sich an etw.** *(Akk.)* *od.* **sich einer Sache** *(Dat.)* **~** *(zeitlich)* follow sth.; *(angrenzen an)* adjoin sth.; **an den Vortrag schloss sich eine Diskussion an** the lecture was followed by a discussion; **an das Haus schließen sich Stallungen an** stables adjoin the house; **C** *(beipflichten)* endorse; **ich schließe mich meinem Vorredner voll und ganz an** I endorse completely the remarks of the previous speaker; **D** *(sich zuwenden)* follow ‹example›; grow close to ‹person›; **sich leicht/schwer an andere ~:** make/not make friends easily. ❸ *unr. itr. V.* **an etw.** *(Akk.)* **~** ⇒ 2 B

**anschließend** ❶ *Adv.* afterwards; **~ an etw.** *(Akk.)* after sth. ❷ *adj.* subsequent; **ein Vortrag mit ~em Theaterbesuch** a lecture followed by a visit to the theatre

**An·schluss, *An·schluß** *der* **A** *(Netz~)* connection; *(Kabel)* cable; **~ an etw.** *(Akk.)* **erhalten/haben** be connected [up] to sth.; **elektrischen ~ erhalten/haben** be connected up to the mains; **B** *(telefonische Verbindung)* connection; **[keinen] ~ bekommen** [not] get through; **auf den ~ warten** wait to be connected; **C** *(Verkehrs~)* connection; *(Flugw.)* connecting flight; **Sie haben ~ nach ...** there is a connection to ...; **den ~ verpasst haben** have missed one's connection; *(fig. ugs.)* *(keinen Ehepartner gefunden haben)* have got left on the shelf; *(nicht Schritt gehalten haben)* have got left behind; **D** *(Telefon)* telephone; **kein ~ unter dieser Nummer** number unobtainable; **E** *(Kontakt)*; **~ finden** make friends; **~ suchen** want to meet and get to know people; **F** *(Verbindung nach vorn)* contact **(an + Akk.** with); **den ~ verlieren** lose contact **(an + Akk.** with); **im ~ an** following; after; **im ~ an unseren Brief vom ...** further to our letter of ...; **G** *(Sport)* ⇒ **~tor**; **H** *(Politik)* *(Vereinigung)* union **(an + Akk.** with); *(verhüll.: Annexion)* anschluss **(an + Akk.** with)

**Anschluss-, *Anschluß-: ~kabel** *das* connecting cable *or* *(esp. Brit.)* lead; *(zur Verlängerung)* extension cable *or* *(esp. Brit.)* lead; **~tor** *das,* **~treffer** *der* *(Sport)* goal which leaves/left the side only one down; **ihm gelang das ~tor** he pulled one back to leave the side only a goal down; **~zug** *der* connecting train; **den ~zug verpassen** miss one's connection

**an|schmieden** *tr. V.* forge on **(an + Akk.** to); **jmdn. an etw. ~** *(anketten)* chain sb. to sth.

**an|schmiegen** ❶ *tr. V.* nestle **(an + Akk.** against). ❷ *refl. V.* nestle up, snuggle up **(an + Akk.** to, against); **sich an den Körper ~** *(fig.)* ‹fabric, material› cling to the body

**an·schmiegsam** *Adj.* affectionate ‹child›; soft and smooth ‹material›

**an|schmieren** *tr. V.* **A** *(ugs.: täuschen)* con *(coll.)*; diddle *(coll.)*; **B** *(beschmutzen)* smear; **jmdn./sich/etw. mit etw. ~:** get *or* smear sth. all over sb./oneself/sth.

**an|schnallen** *tr. V.* strap on ‹rucksack›; put on ‹skis, skates›; **jmdn. ~** *(im Auto)* strap sb. in; **sich ~** *(im Auto)* put on one's seat belt; *(im*

*old spelling (see note on page 1707)

*Flugzeug*) fasten one's seat belt; **„bitte ~!"** 'fasten your seat belts, please'

**Anschnall-: ~gurt** *der* seat belt; **~pflicht** *die* compulsory wearing of seat belts

**an|schnauzen** *tr. V.* (*ugs.*) shout at

**An·schnauzer** *der* (*ugs.*) **einen ~ [ab]kriegen** get shouted at

**an|schneiden** *unr. tr. V.* Ⓐ cut [the first slice of]; **einen frischen Laib ~:** start a fresh loaf; Ⓑ (*ansprechen*) raise; broach; (*gesprächsweise berühren*) touch on; Ⓒ trim ‹flower›; Ⓓ (*Schneiderei*) **etw. an etw.** (*Akk.*) **~:** cut sth. in one piece with sth.; **angeschnittene Ärmel** sleeves cut in one piece with the garment; Ⓔ (*Verkehrsw.*, *Motorsport*) cut ‹corner›

**An·schnitt** *der* Ⓐ (*Schnittfläche*) cut end; Ⓑ (*erstes Stück*) first slice; end piece

**an|schnorren** *tr. V.* (*salopp*) **jmdn. [um etw.] ~:** tap sb. [for sth.] (*coll.*)

**Anschovis** /an'ʃo:vɪs/ *die;* **~, ~:** anchovy

**an|schrauben** *tr. V.* screw on (**an** + *Akk.* to)

**an|schreiben** ❶ *unr. tr. V.* Ⓐ (*hinschreiben*) write up (**an** + *Akk.* on); (*mit Kreide*) chalk up; **angeschrieben stehen** be written/chalked up; Ⓑ (*ugs.: stunden*) **[jmdm.] etw. ~:** chalk sth. up [to sb.'s account]; **bei jmdm. gut/schlecht angeschrieben sein** (*ugs.*) be in sb.'s good/bad books; be on sb.'s good/black list (*Amer.*); Ⓒ (*schriftlich benachrichtigen*) write to; **vierzig Prozent der angeschriebenen Studenten** forty per cent of the students written to. ❷ *unr. itr. V.* (*ugs.: Kredit geben*) give credit; **er lässt immer ~:** he always buys on tick (*coll.*)

**An·schreiben** *das* covering letter

**an|schreien** *unr. tr. V.* shout at

**An·schrift** *die* ▶ 187 address

**an|schuldigen** /'anʃʊldɪgn/ *tr. V.* (*geh.*) accuse (*Gen.*, **wegen** of); **der Angeschuldigte/die Angeschuldigten** the accused

**Anschuldigung** *die;* **~, ~en** accusation

**an|schwärmen** ❶ *itr. V.*; *mit sein* ‹bees› swarm in. ❷ *tr. V.* (*verehren*) idolize; adore

**an|schwärzen** *tr. V.* (*ugs.*) **jmdn. ~** (*in Misskredit bringen*) blacken sb.'s name; (*schlecht machen*) run sb. down (**bei** to); (*denunzieren*) inform *or* (*Brit. sl.*) grass on sb. (**bei** to)

**an|schweigen** *unr. tr. V.* **sich [gegenseitig]/jmdn. ~:** not speak *or* talk to each other/sb.

**an|schweißen** *tr. V.* (*Technik*) weld on (**an** + *Akk. od. Dat.* to)

**an|schwellen** *unr. itr. V.*; *mit sein* Ⓐ (*dicker werden*) swell [up]; **stark angeschwollen** very swollen; Ⓑ (*lauter werden*) grow louder; ‹noise› rise; Ⓒ (*zunehmen; auch fig.*) swell, grow; ‹water, river› rise

**An·schwellung** *die* swelling

**an|schwemmen** *tr. V.* wash up *or* ashore

**an|schwimmen** *unr. itr. V.*; *mit sein* **angeschwommen kommen** come swimming along; (*auf einen zu*) come swimming up; **gegen die Strömung/Flut ~:** swim against the current/tide

**an|schwindeln** *tr. V.* (*ugs.*) **jmdn. ~:** tell sb. fibs

**an|schwirren** *itr. V.*; *mit sein* (*heranfliegen*) **angeschwirrt kommen** come whirring *or* buzzing along; (*fig. ugs.*) come buzzing along; (*auf einen zu*) come buzzing up

**an|schwitzen** *tr. V.* (*Kochk.*) brown lightly (*in hot fat*)

**an|segeln** ❶ *itr. V.* Ⓐ *mit sein* **angesegelt kommen** come sailing along; (*auf einen zu*) come sailing up; Ⓑ (*Saison eröffnen*) open the sailing season. ❷ *tr. V.* make *or* head for

**an|sehen** ❶ *unr. tr. V.* Ⓐ (*anblicken*) look at; **jmdn. groß/böse ~:** stare at sb./give sb. an angry look; **hübsch** *usw.* **anzusehen sein** be pretty *etc.* to look at; Ⓑ (*betrachten*) look at; view, look at ‹flat, house›; watch ‹television programme›; see ‹play, film›; **sieh [mal] [einer] an!** (*ugs.*) well, I never! (*coll.*); Ⓒ (*erkennen*) **man sieht ihm sein Alter nicht an** he does not look his age; **man sieht ihr die Strapazen an** she's showing the strain; **man sieht ihr nicht an, dass sie krank ist** there is nothing to show that she is ill; **das sah man ihm nicht an** one would not have thought so to look at him; ⇒ *auch* **Nasenspitze**; Ⓓ (*zusehen*) **etw. [mit] ~:** watch sth.; **das kann man doch nicht [mit] ~:** I/you can't just stand by and watch that; **das habe ich lange genug angesehen** I've had *or* seen enough of that; **ich kann das nicht länger [mit] ~:** I can't stand this any longer; Ⓔ (*beurteilen*) see; Ⓕ (*auffassen*) regard; consider; **jmdn. als seinen Freund/als Betrüger ~:** regard sb. as a friend/a cheat; consider sb. [to be] a friend/a cheat; **etw. als/für seine Pflicht ~:** consider sth. one's duty. ❷ *unr. refl. V.* Ⓐ **sich** (*Dat.*) **etw. ~:** look at sth.; **sich** (*Dat.*) **ein Haus/Fernsehprogramm/Schauspiel/einen Film ~:** look at *or* view a house/watch a television programme/see a play/film; **das sehe sich einer an!** (*ugs.*) just look at that!; Ⓑ **das sieht sich hübsch/furchtbar** *usw.* **an** it looks pretty/terrible *etc.*

**Ansehen** *das;* **~s** Ⓐ (*Wertschätzung*) [high] standing *or* reputation; **hohes ~ genießen** enjoy high standing *or* a good reputation; **[bei jmdm.] in hohem ~ stehen** be held in high esteem *or* high regard [by sb.]; Ⓑ (*geh.: Aussehen*) appearance; **[nur] vom** *od.* **vom ~:** [only] by sight; **von** *od.* **vom ~ über jmdn. urteilen** judge sb. by appearances; **ohne ~ der Person** (*Rechtsw.*) without respect of persons

**an·sehnlich** *Adj.* Ⓐ (*beträchtlich*) considerable; Ⓑ (*gut aussehend, stattlich*) handsome; **er hat sich** (*Dat.*) **einen ~en Bauch angefuttert** he's developed quite a stomach

**an|seilen** *tr. V.* rope [up]; **sich ~:** rope up

***an|sein** ⇒ **an** 3 B

**an|sengen** *tr. V.* singe [slightly]; **es riecht angesengt** there's a smell of something singeing

**an|setzen** ❶ *tr. V.* Ⓐ (*in die richtige Stellung bringen*) position ‹ladder, jack, drill, saw›; **die Feder/das Glas ~:** put pen to paper/the glass to one's lips; **den Geigenbogen/die Trompete ~:** put *or* place the violin bow in the bowing position/put the trumpet to one's lips; ⇒ *auch* **Hebel**; Ⓑ (*anfügen*) attach, put on (**an** + *Akk. od. Dat.* to); fit (**an** + *Akk. od. Dat.* on to); Ⓒ (*festlegen*) fix ‹meeting etc.› (**für, auf** + *Akk.* for); fix, set ‹deadline, date, price›; Ⓓ (*veranschlagen*) estimate; **die Kosten mit drei Millionen ~:** estimate the cost at three million; **etw. zu niedrig/hoch ~:** underestimate/overestimate sth.; Ⓔ (*anrühren*) mix; prepare; Ⓕ (*ausbilden*) **Rost/Grünspan ~:** go rusty/become covered with verdigris; **Fett ~:** put on weight; **Knospen/Früchte ~:** form buds/set fruit; Ⓖ (*einsetzen*) **jmdn. auf einen Erpresser** *usw.*/**ein Projekt** *usw.* **~:** set *or* put sb. on to a blackmailer *etc.*/put sb. on [to] a project; **Hunde [auf eine Spur]/auf jmdn. ~:** set dogs on sb.'s/an animal's trail/on sb. ❷ *itr. V.* Ⓐ (*beginnen*) **zum Reden/Trinken ~:** open one's mouth to speak/raise the glass *etc.* to one's lips; **er setzte mehrmals [zum Sprechen] an, aber …** he kept opening his mouth to speak, but …; **zur Landung ~:** come in to land; **zum Sprung/Überholen ~:** get ready *or* prepare to jump/overtake; **hier muss die Diskussion/Kritik ~:** this is where the discussion/criticsm must start; Ⓑ ‹nose, tail, hair, etc.› start; Ⓒ (*sich festsetzen*) stick

**An·sicht** *die* Ⓐ (*Meinung*) opinion; view; **meiner ~ nach** in my opinion *or* view; **nach [der] ~ der Fachleute** in the opinion of the experts; **anderer/der gleichen ~ sein** be of a different/the same opinion; **der ~ sein, dass …** be of the opinion that …; **ich bin ganz Ihrer ~:** I entirely agree with you; **da bin ich anderer ~:** I disagree with you there; **die ~en sind geteilt** opinion is divided; Ⓑ (*Bild*) view; **Ludwigshafen in alten ~en** old views of Ludwigshafen; Ⓒ (*Kaufmannsspr.*) **zur ~:** on approval

**ansichtig** *Adj.* **jmds./einer Sache ~ werden** (*geh.*) catch sight of sb./sth.

**Ansichts-: ~karte** *die,* **~post·karte** *die* picture postcard; **~sache** *die: in* **~sache sein** be a matter of opinion; **~sendung** *die* article/articles [sent] on approval

**an|siedeln** ❶ *refl. V.* (*ansässig werden*) settle; ‹industry, bacteria› become established; **auf dieser Insel haben sich seltene Vogelarten angesiedelt** rare species of birds have colonized this island. ❷ *tr. V.* (*ansässig machen*) settle ‹immigrant, refugee, etc.›; establish ‹industry, species, variety, bacteria›; **die Attentäter sind rechts anzusiedeln** (*fig.*) it can be assumed that the assassins are rightists; **etw. in einem exotischen Milieu ~** (*fig.*) give sth. an exotic setting

**Ansiedelung** ⇒ **Ansiedlung**

**An·siedler** *der,* **An·siedlerin** *die* settler

**An·siedlung** *die* Ⓐ (*das Ansiedeln*) ⇒ **ansiedeln** 2: settlement; establishment; Ⓑ (*Ort*) settlement

**An·sinnen** *das;* **~s, ~:** [unreasonable] request; **ein freches/seltsames** *usw.* **~:** an impudent/a strange *etc.* request

**An·sitz** *der* Ⓐ (*Jägerspr.*) hide (*Brit.*); blind (*Amer.*); (*Hochsitz*) raised hide (*Brit.*) *or* (*Amer.*) blind; Ⓑ (*österr.: Haus*) residence

**an·sonst** *Konj.* (*österr.*, *schweiz.*) otherwise

**ansonsten** *Adv.* (*ugs.*) Ⓐ (*außerdem*) **der Verlag produziert … und ~ noch Kinderbücher** the publishing house produces … and, in addition, children's books; **aber ~ ist nichts Besonderes passiert** but apart from that *or* otherwise nothing particular has happened; Ⓑ (*andernfalls*) otherwise

**an|spannen** ❶ *tr. V.* Ⓐ (*einspannen*) harness, hitch up ‹horse etc.› (**an** + *Akk.* to); hitch up, yoke up ‹oxen› (**an** + *Akk.* to); hitch up ‹carriage, cart, etc.› (**an** + *Akk.* to); Ⓑ (*anstrengen*) strain; **seine ganze Kraft ~:** exert all one's energies. ❷ *itr. V.* hitch up; **~ lassen** have the carriage made ready

**An·spannung** *die* strain; **unter ~ aller seiner Kräfte/Gedanken** by exerting all one's energies/by intense mental effort

**an|spazieren** *itr. V.*; *mit sein* (*ugs.*) **anspaziert kommen** come strolling along; (*auf einen zu*) come strolling up

**An·spiel** *das* Ⓐ (*Sport: Zuspiel*) pass; Ⓑ (*Spielbeginn*) (*Schach*) **das ~ haben** make the first move; (*Kartenspiel*) **ich habe das ~:** it's my lead; (*Fußball*) ⇒ **Anstoß** C

**an|spielen** ❶ *itr. V.* Ⓐ (*hinweisen*) **auf jmdn./etw. ~:** allude to sb./sth.; **worauf wollen Sie ~?** what are you hinting at?; Ⓑ (*Spiel beginnen*) start; (*Fußball*) kick off; (*Kartenspiel*) lead; (*Schach*) make the first move. ❷ *tr. V.* Ⓐ (*Sport: zuspielen*) **jmdn. ~:** pass to sb.; Ⓑ (*Kartenspiel: ins Spiel bringen*) lead

**Anspielung** *die;* **~, ~en** allusion (**auf** + *Akk.* to); (*verächtlich, böse*) insinuation (**auf** + *Akk.* about)

**an|spinnen** ❶ *unr. tr. V.* (*beginnen*) [gradually] start ‹conversation›; start having ‹affair›; start hatching ‹intrigue, plot›. ❷ *unr. refl. V.* develop; **zwischen den beiden spinnt sich etwas an** there's something going on between those two

**an|spitzen** *tr. V.* Ⓐ (*spitz machen*) sharpen ‹pencil›; shape ‹stake, post› to a point; Ⓑ (*ugs.: antreiben*) **jmdn. ~:** give sb. a prod; **jmdn. ~, etw. zu tun** *od.* **dass er etw. tut** prod sb. into doing sth.

**An·sporn** *der* incentive

**an|spornen** *tr. V.* Ⓐ (*anfeuern*) spur on; encourage; Ⓑ (*die Sporen geben*) spur ‹horse›

**An·sprache** *die* Ⓐ (*Rede*) speech; address; **eine ~ halten** make a speech; give an address; Ⓑ (*Kontakt*) **~ suchen/haben** look for/have sb. to talk to

**ansprechbar** *Adj.* Ⓐ **ich bin jetzt beschäftigt und daher nicht ~:** you can't talk to me now, I'm too busy; **sie ist vor Müdigkeit nicht ~:** she's too tired to listen to anyone; Ⓑ (*zugänglich*) amenable; Ⓒ (*fähig zu reagieren*) responsive

a

**an|sprechen** ❶ *unr. tr. V.* Ⓐ speak to; (*zudringlich*) accost; **jmdn. mit „Herr Doktor" ~:** address sb. as 'doctor'; **jmdn. mit seinem Vornamen ~:** use sb.'s first name; **jmdn. auf etw./jmdn./um etw. ~:** speak to sb. about sth./sb./approach *or* ask sb. for sth.; Ⓑ (*gefallen*) appeal to; Ⓒ (*zur Sprache bringen*) mention; (*kurz, oberflächlich*) touch on; Ⓓ (*Jagdw., Milit.*) identify. ❷ *unr. itr. V.* Ⓐ (*gefallen*) **[gut] ~:** go down well (**bei** with); be well received (**bei** by); Ⓑ (*reagieren*) ‹patient, brake, clutch, etc.› respond (**auf** + *Akk.* to); Ⓒ (*wirken*) work; **bei jmdm. gut/nicht ~:** have/not have the desired effect on sb.; Ⓓ (*Musik*) **gut** *od.* **leicht ~** ‹instrument› be easy to play

**ansprechend** ❶ *Adj.* attractive; attractive, appealing ‹personality›. ❷ *adv.* attractively

**Ansprech·partner** *der*, **Ansprech·partnerin** *die* contact

**an|springen** ❶ *unr. itr. V.; mit sein* Ⓐ (*in Gang kommen*) start; Ⓑ (*sich nähern*) **angesprungen kommen** come bounding along; (*auf einen zu*) come bounding up; Ⓒ (*ugs.*) **auf ein Angebot/Geschäft ~:** take up an offer/agree to a deal; **sofort auf etw.** (*Akk.*) **~:** jump at sth. [straight away]. ❷ *unr. tr. V.* Ⓐ (*anfallen*) pounce on; Ⓑ (*an jmdm. hochspringen*) jump up at; Ⓒ (*Turnen*) mount ‹box, horse, beam› with a jump

**an|spritzen** ❶ *tr. V.* splash; (*mit Gartenschlauch, Zerstäuber, Wasserpistole*) spray. ❷ *itr. V.; mit sein* (*ugs.: sich nähern*) **angespritzt kommen** come rushing along; (*auf einen zu*) come rushing up

**An·spruch** *der* Ⓐ claim; (*Forderung*) demand; **hohe Ansprüche [an jmdn.] haben** *od.* **stellen** demand a great deal [of sb.]; **~ auf etw.** (*Akk.*) **erheben** lay claim to sth.; **[keine] Ansprüche stellen** make [no] demands; **in ~ nehmen** (*Gebrauch machen von*) take up, take advantage of ‹offer›; exercise ‹right›; (*beanspruchen*) take up ‹time›; **jmds. Zeit/Hilfe in ~ nehmen** make demands on sb.'s time/enlist sb.'s aid; **jmdn. [stark] in ~ nehmen** make [heavy] demands on sb.; **jmdn. völlig in ~ nehmen** take up all [of] sb.'s time; Ⓑ (*bes. Rechtsspr.: Anrecht*) claim; **[einen] ~/keinen ~ auf etw.** (*Akk.*) **haben** be/not be entitled to sth.; **auf etw.** (*Akk.*) **~ erheben** assert one's entitlement to sth.

**an·spruchs-, An·spruchs-: ~denken** *das* (*abwertend*): *attitude that everything one wants should be provided by the State;* **~los** ❶ *Adj.* Ⓐ (*genügsam*) undemanding; Ⓑ (*schlicht*) unpretentious; simple; ❷ *adv.* Ⓐ (*genügsam*) undemandingly; ‹live› modestly, simply; Ⓑ (*schlicht*) unpretentiously; simply; **~losigkeit** *die;* **~** ⇨ **~los** 1: undemanding nature; unpretentiousness; simplicity; **~voll** ❶ *Adj.* Ⓐ (*wählerisch*); demanding, discriminating ‹reader, audience, gourmet›; (*hohe Anforderungen stellend*) demanding; ambitious ‹subject›; Ⓑ (*Werbespr.*) exquisite; **eine ~volle Zigarette/ein ~voller Sekt** a cigarette for the discriminating smoker/champagne for the discriminating drinker; **die Cremeseife für Anspruchsvolle** the cream soap for people with discriminating taste; ❷ *adv.* (*Werbespr.*) exquisitely

**an|spucken** *tr. V.* spit at

**an|spülen** *tr. V.* wash up *or* ashore

**an|stacheln** *tr. V.* spur on (**zu** to); **jmds. Ehrgeiz/Eifer ~:** fire sb.'s ambition/enthusiasm

**Anstalt** /'anʃtalt/ *die;* **~, ~en** (*auch verhüll.*) institution; **eine ~ des öffentlichen Rechts** a public institution

**Anstalten** *Pl.* preparations; **[keine] ~ machen** *od.* (*geh.*) **treffen** make [no] preparations (**für** for); **~ machen/keine ~ machen, etw. zu tun** make a move/make no move to do sth.

**Anstalts-: ~geistliche** *der/die* [resident] chaplain; **~kleidung** *die* institutional clothing; **~leiter** *der*, **~leiterin** *die* (*einer Schule*) head; (*eines Erziehungsheims*) superintendent

*old spelling (see note on page 1707)

**An·stand¹** *der* (*Jägerspr.*) ⇨ **Ansitz** A

**An·stand²** *der* Ⓐ (*Schicklichkeit*) decency; **keinen ~ haben** have no sense of decency; **gegen jeden/den ~ verstoßen** offend against common decency; **sich mit ~ aus der Affäre ziehen** emerge from the affair with no damage to one's reputation; Ⓑ (*veralt.: Benehmen*) good manners *pl.;* **dir werde ich ~ beibringen** I'll give you a lesson in manners; Ⓒ (*südd., österr.: Ärger*) trouble; **[keinen] ~ an etw.** (*Dat.*) **nehmen** [not] object to sth.; **keinen ~ nehmen[, etw. zu tun]** (*nicht zögern*) not hesitate [to do sth.]

**an·ständig** ❶ *Adj.* Ⓐ (*sittlich einwandfrei, rücksichtsvoll*) decent; decent, clean ‹joke›; (*ehrbar*) respectable; (*gut angesehen*) decent, respectable ‹job›; **bleib ~!** (*auch scherzh.*) behave yourself!; be good!; Ⓑ (*ugs.: zufrieden stellend*) decent; respectable ‹result, marks›; Ⓒ (*ugs.: beträchtlich*) sizeable ‹sum, amount, debts›; **eine ~e Tracht Prügel** a good hiding (*coll.*); **ein ~es Stück gefahren sein** have come a tidy old (*coll.*) *or* pretty long way (*coll.*).
❷ *adv.* Ⓐ (*sittlich einwandfrei*) decently; (*ordentlich*) properly; Ⓑ (*ugs.: zufrieden stellend*) **jmdn. ~ bezahlen** pay sb. pretty well; **ganz ~ abschneiden** do quite well; **~ arbeiten** do good work; Ⓒ (*ugs.: ziemlich*) **~ ausschlafen** have a decent sleep; **es regnet ganz ~:** it's raining pretty hard; **jmdn. ~ eine knallen** really belt sb. one (*coll.*)

**anständigerweise** *Adv.* out of decency

**Anständigkeit** *die;* **~:** decency

**anstands-, Anstands-: ~besuch** *der* formal courtesy call (**bei** on); formal courtesy visit (**bei** to); **~dame** *die* (*veralt.*) chaperon; **~halber** *Adv.* out of politeness; for the sake of politeness; **~happen** *der* (*ugs.*) **einen ~happen übrig lassen** leave the last piece out of politeness; **~los** *Adv.* (*ohne Bedenken*) readily; without [any] hesitation; (*ohne Schwierigkeiten zu machen*) without [any] objection; **~unterricht** *der* lessons *pl.* in deportment *or* manners; **~wau·wau** *der* (*ugs. scherzh.*) chaperon

**an|stänkern** *tr. V.* (*salopp*) **jmdn. ~:** lay into sb. (*coll.*)

**an|starren** *tr. V.* stare at

**an·statt** ❶ *Konj.* **~ zu arbeiten/~ dass er arbeitet** instead of working. ❷ *Präp. mit Gen.* instead of

**an|stauben** *itr. V.; mit sein* get dusty; **leicht angestaubte Ware** slightly shopworn *or* (*Brit.*) shop-soiled goods *pl.*

**an|stauen** ❶ *tr. V.* dam up; (*fig.*) bottle up ‹feelings›. ❷ *refl. V.* ‹water› accumulate; (*fig.*) ‹feelings› build up

**an|staunen** *tr. V.* **jmdn./etw. ~:** gaze *or* stare in wonder at sb./sth.; **jmdn./etw. mit offenem Mund ~:** gape at sb./sth. in wonder

**an|stechen** ❶ *unr. tr. V.* Ⓐ prick; puncture ‹tyre›; **wie ein angestochenes Schwein, wie angestochen** (*derb*) like a wild thing; Ⓑ (*anzapfen*) tap ‹barrel›. ❷ *unr. itr. V.* (*anzapfen*) tap a/the barrel

**an|stecken** ❶ *tr. V.* Ⓐ (*feststecken*) pin on ‹badge, brooch›; (*am Finger*) put *or* slip ‹ring›; **jmdm. eine Brosche/einen Ring ~:** pin a brooch on sb./put *or* slip a ring on sb.'s finger; Ⓑ (*infizieren, auch fig.*) infect; **ich will dich nicht ~:** I don't want to give you my cold/germs *etc.;* Ⓒ (*bes. nordd., mitteld.: anzünden*) light; (*in Brand setzen*) set fire to. ❷ *itr. V.* (*sich übertragen*) be infectious *or* catching; (*durch Berührung*) be contagious; (*fig.*) be infectious *or* contagious

**ansteckend** *Adj.* infectious; (*durch Berührung*) contagious; (*fig.*) infectious; contagious

**Ansteck·nadel** *die* (*Brosche*) pin; (*Plakette*) badge

**Ansteckung** *die;* **~, ~en** infection; (*durch Berührung*) contagion

**Ansteckungs-: ~gefahr** *die* risk *or* danger of infection; **~herd** *der* source of [the/an] infection

**an|stehen** *unr. itr. V.* Ⓐ (*warten*) queue [up], (*Amer.*) stand in line (**nach** for); Ⓑ *südd. mit sein* (*geh.: sich ziemen*) **jmdm. [wohl/übel] ~:** [well/ill] become sb.; Ⓒ (*zu erledigen sein*) be waiting to be dealt with; (*zur Beratung ~*) be on the agenda; **die ~den Probleme** the problems to be dealt with; **etw. ~ lassen** defer sth.; Ⓓ (*Rechtsspr.: festgesetzt sein*) be fixed *or* set (**auf** + *Akk.* for); Ⓔ *in* **nicht ~, etw. zu tun** (*geh.*) have no hesitation in doing sth.; not hesitate to do sth.; Ⓕ (*Geol.*) outcrop; crop out

**an|steigen** *unr. itr. V.; mit sein* Ⓐ (*bergan führen*) ‹hill› rise; ‹person, road, path› climb, ascend; ‹garden, ground› slope up, rise; Ⓑ (*höher werden*) ‹water level, temperature, etc.› rise; (*fig.*) ‹price, cost, rent, etc.› rise, go up, increase

**an·stelle** ❶ *Präp. mit Gen.* instead of. ❷ *Adv.* **~ von** instead of; ⇨ *auch* **Stelle** A

**an|stellen** ❶ *refl. V.* Ⓐ (*warten*) queue [up], (*Amer.*) stand in line (**nach** for); Ⓑ (*ugs.: sich verhalten*) act; behave; **sich dumm/ungeschickt ~:** act *or* behave stupidly/be clumsy; **sich dumm/ungeschickt bei etw. ~:** go about sth. stupidly/clumsily; **sich geschickt ~:** go about it well; **stell dich nicht [so] an!** don't make [such] a fuss! ❷ *tr. V.* Ⓐ (*aufdrehen*) turn on; Ⓑ (*einschalten*) switch on; turn on, switch on ‹radio, television›; start ‹engine›; Ⓒ (*einstellen*) employ (**als** as); **bei jmdm. angestellt sein** be employed by sb.; Ⓓ (*ugs.: beschäftigen*) **jmdn. zum Kartoffelschälen** *usw.* **~:** get sb. to peel the potatoes *etc.;* Ⓔ (*anlehnen*) **etw. an etw.** (*Akk.*) **~:** put *or* place sth. against sth.; Ⓕ (*anrichten*) **etwas/Unfug ~:** get up to something/to mischief; **was hast du nun wieder angestellt?** what have you been up to this time?; **sieh, was du angestellt hast** see what you've done; Ⓖ (*ugs.: fertig bringen*) manage; **wie soll ich es ~, dass er nichts merkt/dass ich rechtzeitig hinkomme?** how do I stop him noticing anything?/make sure of getting there in time?; Ⓗ (*ugs.: versuchen*) try; Ⓘ (*vornehmen*) do ‹calculation›; draw, make ‹comparison›; carry out ‹experiment, investigation›; make ‹assumption›; **Überlegungen ~, wie ...** consider how ...

**anstellig** *Adj.* clever; skilful

**Anstelligkeit** *die;* **~:** ability; skill

**An·stellung** *die* Ⓐ (*das Einstellen*) employment; Ⓑ (*Stellung*) job; **ohne ~:** without a job; unemployed

**Anstellungs-: ~verhältnis** *das* employment *no indef. art.;* **~verhältnis auf Zeit** temporary employment; **~vertrag** *der* contract of employment

**an|steuern** *tr. V.* (*auch fig.*) head *or* make for; **ein Thema ~** (*fig.*) steer the conversation towards a subject

**An·stich** *der* Ⓐ (*das Anstechen*) tapping; broaching; **nach dem ~:** after tapping *or* broaching the barrel; Ⓑ (*Getränk*) **[frischer] ~:** newly tapped beer/wine

**an|stiefeln** *itr. V.; mit sein* **angestiefelt kommen** come marching along; (*auf einen zu*) come marching up

**Anstieg** *der;* **~[e]s, ~e** Ⓐ (*Zunahme, Erhöhung*) rise, increase (+ *Gen.* in); Ⓑ (*Steigung*) gradient; Ⓒ (*Aufstieg*) climb; ascent; (*Weg*) way up; (*für Bergsteiger*) ascent route

**an|stieren** *tr. V.* (*ugs.*) stare at

**an|stiften** *tr. V.* Ⓐ (*in Gang setzen*) instigate; (*verursachen*) cause, bring about ‹disaster, confusion›; Ⓑ (*verleiten*) **jmdn. [dazu] ~, etw. zu tun** incite sb. to do sth.; **jmdn. zum Betrug/Mord/zu einem Verbrechen ~:** incite sb. to deception/to murder/to commit a crime; **jmdn. zu dummen Streichen ~:** put sb. up to silly tricks

**An·stifter** *der*, **An·stifterin** *die* instigator

**An·stiftung** *die* incitement (**zu** to); **~ zu einer Straftat** incitement to commit a serious offence

**an|stimmen** *tr. V.* Ⓐ (*Musik*) start singing ‹song›; start playing ‹waltz, march, etc.›; play ‹note›; ‹band› strike up ‹waltz, march, etc.›; Ⓑ (*ausbrechen in*) **Proteste/ein Geschrei ~:** start protesting/shouting; **ein Freudengeheul ~:** burst into shouts of joy

**an|stinken** (*ugs.*) ❶ *unr. tr. V.* (*anwidern*) **jmdn. ~:** make sb. sick. ❷ *unr. itr. V.* *in*

**gegen jmdn./etw. nicht ~ können** be powerless against sb./sth.

**an|stolzieren** *itr. V.; mit sein* **anstolziert kommen** come strutting along; (*auf einen zu*) come strutting up

**An·stoß** *der* **A** (*Impuls*) stimulus (**zu** for); **den [ersten] ~ zu etw. geben** initiate sth.; **der ~ ging von ihr aus** she was the one who initiated things *or* [first] got things going; **es bedurfte eines neuen ~es** a fresh impetus was needed; **B ~ erregen** cause *or* give offence (**bei** to); **[keinen] ~ an etw.** (*Dat.*) **nehmen** [not] object to sth.; (*sich [nicht] beleidigt fühlen*) [not] take offence at sth.; ⇒ *auch* **Stein** B; **C** (*Fußball*) kick-off; **den ~ ausführen** kick off; **welche Mannschaft hat ~?** which side will kick off?; **D** (*Aufprall*) impact

**an|stoßen** ❶ *unr. itr. V.* **A** *mit sein* **an etw.** (*Akk.*) **~:** bump into sth.; **mit dem Kopf ~:** knock *or* bump one's head; **mit dem Koffer dauernd/überall ~:** keep bumping the case against things; **B** (*auf etw. trinken*) **[mit den Gläsern] ~:** clink glasses; **auf jmdn./etw. ~:** drink to sb./sth.; **C** (*Fußball*) kick off; **D** *auch mit sein* (*lispeln*) **[mit der Zunge] ~:** lisp; **E** *mit sein* (*Anstoß erregen*) give *or* cause offence (**bei** to); **man stößt leicht bei ihm an** he easily takes offence; **F** (*angrenzen*) **an etw.** (*Akk.*) **~:** adjoin sth.
❷ *unr. tr. V.* **A** (*einen Stoß geben*) **jmdn./etw. ~:** give sb./sth. a push; **jmdn. aus Versehen ~:** knock into sb. inadvertently; **jmdn. mit dem Ellenbogen/Fuß ~** (*als Zeichen*) nudge/kick sb.; **sich** (*Dat.*) **den Kopf/die Zehe ~:** knock *or* bang one's head/stub one's toe; **B eine Diskussion ~:** provoke a discussion

**anstößig** /ˈanʃtøːsɪç/ ❶ *Adj.* offensive; offensive, objectionable ‹behaviour›. ❷ *adv.* offensively; ‹behave› offensively, objectionably

**Anstößigkeit** *die;* **~, ~en** **A** offensiveness; (*einer Handlung*) offensiveness, objectionableness; **B** (*Handlung*) piece of offensive *or* objectionable behaviour; **~en** offensive *or* objectionable behaviour *sing.*

**an|strahlen** *tr. V.* **A** illuminate; (*mit Scheinwerfer*) floodlight; (*im Theater*) spotlight; **ein Gebäude rot ~:** illuminate a building with red light; **B** (*anblicken*) beam at; **ihre Augen strahlten ihn an** she beamed at him

**an|streben** *tr. V.* (*geh.*) aspire to; (*mit großer Anstrengung*) strive for

**anstrebens·wert** *Adj.* ⇒ **anstreben**: worth aspiring to/striving for *postpos.*

**an|streichen** *unr. tr. V.* **A** (*mit Farbe*) paint; (*mit Tünche*) whitewash; **B** (*hervorheben*) mark (**als** as); **etw. rot ~:** mark sth. in red; **C** (*anzünden*) strike, light ‹match›

**An·streicher** *der*, **An·streicherin** *die* (*ugs.*) [house] painter

**an|strengen** ❶ *refl. V.* (*sich einsetzen*) make an effort; exert oneself; (*körperlich*) exert oneself; **sich ~, etw. zu tun** make an effort to do sth.; **sich mehr/sehr ~:** make more of an effort/a great effort; **sich übermäßig** *od.* **zu sehr ~:** overexert oneself; **da hat er sich aber angestrengt** he has made a special effort *or* gone to a lot of trouble [there].
❷ *tr. V.* **A** (*anspannen*) strain ‹eyes, ears, voice›; **alle seine Kräfte ~:** make every effort; (*körperlich*) use all one's strength; **seinen Verstand ~:** think hard; **seine Fantasie ~:** exercise one's imagination; **B** (*strapazieren*) strain, put a strain on ‹eyes›; be a strain on ‹person›; **jmdn. zu sehr ~:** be too much of a strain on sb.; **C** (*Rechtsw.: einleiten*) **eine Klage/einen Prozess ~:** lay a charge/start proceedings (**gegen** against)

**anstrengend** *Adj.* (*körperlich*) strenuous; (*geistig*) demanding; **~ zu lesen/für die Augen sein** be a strain to read/on the eyes; **Nachtfahrten finde ich ~:** I find travelling at night a strain; **es war ~, dem Vortrag zu folgen** following the lecture was a strain

**Anstrengung** *die;* **~, ~en** **A** (*Einsatz*) effort; **~en machen** *od.* (*geh.*) **unternehmen** make an effort; **große ~en machen, etw. zu tun** make every effort to do sth.; **mit letzter/äußerster ~:** with one last/a supreme effort; **B** (*Strapaze*) strain

**An·strich** *der* **A** (*das Anstreichen*) painting; (*mit Tünche*) whitewashing; **B** (*Farbe*) paint; (*Tünche*) whitewash; **der erste/zweite ~:** the first/second coat; **C** (*Note*) touch; (*Aussehen*) air; **einer Sache** (*Dat.*) **einen bestimmten ~ geben** lend sth. a certain air; **D** (*beim Schreiben*) upstroke

**an|stricken** *tr. V.* **etw. an etw.** (*Akk.*) **~:** knit sth. on to sth.

**an|strömen** *itr. V.; mit sein* **A** (*heranfließen*) ‹water› flow in; ‹air› stream in; **von Westen ~de Kaltluft** a stream of cold air from the west; **B** (*herbeikommen*) pour *or* stream in; **angeströmt kommen** come pouring *or* streaming in

**an|stückeln**, **an|stücken** *tr. V.* add a piece to ‹carpet etc.›; **ein Kleid/Hemd ~:** lengthen a dress/shirt [by adding a piece on]; **etw. an etw.** (*Akk.*) **~:** attach sth. to sth.

**An·sturm** *der* **A** (*das Anstürmen*) onslaught; **B** (*Andrang*) (*auf Kaufhäuser, Schwimmbäder*) rush (**auf** + *Akk.* to); (*auf Banken, Waren*) run (**auf** + *Akk.* on)

**an|stürmen** *itr. V.; mit sein* **A** (*gegen etw. drängen*) **gegen etw. ~** ‹waves, wind› pound sth.; (*Milit.*) storm sth.; **B angestürmt kommen** come charging *or* rushing along; (*auf einen zu*) come charging *or* rushing up

**an|stürzen** *itr. V.; mit sein* **angestürzt kommen** come tearing *or* dashing along; (*auf einen zu*) come tearing *or* dashing up

**an|suchen** *itr. V.* (*österr., sonst veralt.*) **[bei jmdm.] um etw. ~** (*beantragen*) apply [to sb.] for sth.; (*bitten*) ask [sb.] for sth.

**Ansuchen** *das;* **~s, ~** (*österr., sonst veralt.*) (*Gesuch*) application (**auf** + *Akk.* for); (*Bitte*) request (**auf** + *Akk.* for); **auf jmds. ~** (*Akk.*) at sb.'s request

**an|sülzen** *tr. V.* (*salopp*) blether at

**Antagonismus** /antagoˈnɪsmʊs/ *der;* **~, Antagonismen** antagonism (*Gen.*, **zwischen** between)

**Antagonist** *der;* **~en, ~en**, **Antagonistin** *die;* **~, ~nen** antagonist

**antagonistisch** ❶ *Adj.* antagonistic. ❷ *adv.* antagonistically

**an|tanzen** *itr. V.; mit sein* (*ugs.*) show up (*coll.*); **angetanzt kommen** turn up

**Antarktis** /antˈ|arktɪs/ *die;* **~** (*Geogr.*) **die ~:** the Antarctic

**antarktisch** *Adj.* Antarctic

**an|tasten** *tr. V.* **A** (*verbrauchen*) break into ‹savings, provisions›; **das Geld taste ich nicht an** I shall not touch the money; **B** (*beeinträchtigen*) infringe, encroach on ‹right, freedom, privilege›; encroach on ‹property, private life›; **jmds. Ehre ~:** cast a slur on *or* impugn sb.'s honour; **C** (*berühren*) touch; (*fig.*) touch on ‹subject›

**an|tauchen** *itr. V.* (*österr.*) **A** (*anschieben*) push; **B** (*sich mehr anstrengen*) make more effort; try harder

**an|tauen** ❶ *itr. V.; mit sein* (*zu tauen beginnen*) ‹ice, snow› begin to melt *or* thaw; ‹foodstuff› begin to thaw. ❷ *tr. V.* (*tauen lassen*) **etw. ~:** allow sth. to thaw slightly

**an|täuschen** ❶ *tr. V.* (*Boxen*) **einen linken Haken ~ und mit der Rechten zuschlagen** feint with the left and throw a right. ❷ *itr. V.* (*Fußball, Rugby*) **[links/rechts] ~:** dummy (*Brit.*) *or* (*Amer.*) fake [to the left/right]

**An·teil** *der* **A** (*jmdm. zustehender Teil*) share (**an** + *Dat.* of); **~ an etw.** (*Dat.*) **haben** share in sth.; (*zu etw. beitragen*) play *or* have a part in sth.; **B** (*Wirtsch.*) share; **C** (*Interesse*) interest (**an** + *Dat.* in); **~ an jmdm./etw. nehmen** *od.* (*geh.*) **bekunden** take/show an interest in sb./sth.; **an jmds. Leid/Freude ~ nehmen** sympathize with sb. in his/her suffering/share in sb.'s joy; **viele Menschen nahmen ~ am Tod seiner Frau** many people felt for him when his wife died

**anteilig**, **anteil·mäßig** ❶ *Adj.* proportional; proportionate. ❷ *adv.* proportionally; proportionately

**Anteilnahme** *die;* **~** **A** (*Beteiligung*) participation; **unter reger ~ der Bevölkerung** with the active participation of the public; **B** (*Interesse*) interest (**an** + *Dat.* in); **C** (*Mitgefühl*) sympathy (**an** + *Dat.* with); **mit ~ zuhören** listen sympathetically

**Anteil·schein** *der* (*Wirtsch.*) share certificate

**Anteils·eigner** *der*, **Anteils·eignerin** *die* (*Wirtsch.*) shareholder

**an|telefonieren** *tr. V.* (*ugs.*) phone; call; ring (*Brit.*)

**Antenne** *die;* **~, ~n** **A** aerial; antenna (*Amer.*); **eine/keine ~ für etw. haben** (*fig. ugs.*) have a/no feeling for sth.; **B** (*Zool.*) antenna

**Anthologie** /antoloˈgiː/ *die;* **~, ~n** anthology

**anthrazit** /antraˈtsiːt/ *Adj.* anthracite[-grey]

**Anthrazit** *der;* **~s, ~e** anthracite

**anthrazit-: ~farben, ~farbig** *Adj.* anthracite[-coloured]; **~grau** *Adj.* anthracite-grey

**Anthropologe** /antropoˈloːgə/ *der;* **~n, ~n** ▶ **159** anthropologist

**Anthropologie** *die;* **~, ~n** anthropology *no art.*

**Anthropologin** *die;* **~, ~nen** ▶ **159** anthropologist; ⇒ *auch* **-in**

**anthropologisch** ❶ *Adj.* anthropological. ❷ *adv.* anthropologically

**anthropomorph** /antropoˈmɔrf/ *Adj.* anthropomorphic

**Anthropomorphismus** *der;* **~, Anthropomorphismen** **A** (*Übertragung*) anthropomorphism; **B** (*Eigenschaft*) anthropomorphic feature

**Anthroposoph** /antropoˈzoːf/ *der;* **~en, ~en** anthroposophist

**Anthroposophie** *die;* **~:** anthroposophy *no art.*

**Anthroposophin** *die;* **~, ~nen** anthroposophist; ⇒ *auch* **-in**

**anthroposophisch** *Adj.* anthroposophical

**anthropozentrisch** /antropoˈtsɛntrɪʃ/ ❶ *Adj.* anthropocentric. ❷ *adv.* anthropocentrically

**anti-, Anti-** /anti-/ anti-

**anti-, Anti-: ~alkoholiker** *der*, **~alkoholikerin** *die* teetotaller; **~autoritär** ❶ *Adj.* anti-authoritarian; ❷ *adv.* in an anti-authoritarian manner; **~autoritär eingestellt sein** take an anti-authoritarian view; **~baby·pille** *die* (*ugs.*) contraceptive pill; **~bakteriell** ❶ *Adj.* antibacterial; ❷ *adv.* **~bakteriell wirken** have an antibacterial action

**Antibiotikum** /antiˈbi̯oːtikʊm/ *das;* **~s, Antibiotika** (*Med.*) antibiotic

**anti-, Anti-: ~blockier·system** *das* (*Kfz-W.*) anti-lock braking system; **~christ**[1] /ˈ---/ *der;* **~[s]** Antichrist; **~christ**[2] /ˈ---/ *der;* **~en, ~en, ~christin** *die* antichristian; **~christlich** /ˈ----/ ❶ *Adj.* antichristian; ❷ *adv.* **~christlich eingestellt/gesinnt sein** be antichristian [in one's views]; **~demokratisch** ❶ *Adj.* anti-democratic; ❷ *adv.* **~demokratisch eingestellt/gesinnt sein** be anti-democratic [in one's views]; **~faschismus** *der* anti-fascism *no art.*; **~faschist** *der*, **~faschistin** *die* anti-fascist; **~faschistisch** ❶ *Adj.* anti-fascist; ❷ *adv.* **~faschistisch eingestellt/gesinnt sein** be anti-fascist [in one's views]; **~gen** *das* (*Med., Biol.*) antigen; **~haft·beschichtung** *die* non-stick coating; **~held** /ˈ---/ *der* anti-hero; **~heldin** /ˈ----/ *die* anti-heroine

**antichambrieren** /antiʃamˈbriːrən/ *itr. V.* **A** (*veralt.: warten*) wait in the antechamber; **B** (*geh. abwertend: dienern*) bow and scrape (**bei** to)

**antik** /anˈtiːk/ ❶ *Adj.* **A** (*des klassischen Altertums*) classical; **B** (*altertümelnd*) antique-style ‹furniture, fittings, etc.›; **C** (*aus vergangenen Zeiten*) antique. ❷ *adv.* (*altertümelnd*) ‹make, furnish, etc.› in antique style

**Antike** /anˈtiːkə/ *die;* **~, ~n** **A** (*Epoche*) classical antiquity *no art.*; **B** (*Kunstwerk*) classical work of art

a

**antikisieren** *itr. V.* imitate classical forms

**anti-, Anti-:** ~**klerikal** ❶ *Adj.* anticlerical; ❷ *adv.* ~**klerikal gesinnt/eingestellt sein** be anticlerical [in one's view]; ~**klerikal denken/handeln** think/act anticlerically; ~**klerikalismus** *der* anticlericalism; ~**klopf·mittel** *das* (*Kfz-W.*) antiknock [agent]; ~**kommunismus** *der* anticommunism; ~**kommunist** *der*, ~**kommunistin** *die* anticommunist; ~**kommunistisch** ❶ *Adj.* anticommunist; ❷ *adv.* ~**kommunistisch eingestellt/gesinnt sein** be anticommunist [in one's views]; ~**körper** /'----/ *der* (*Med.*) antibody

**Antillen** /an'tɪlən/ *Pl.*; **die [Großen/Kleinen]** ~: the [Greater/Lesser] Antilles

**Antilope** /anti'lo:pə/ *die*; ~, ~**n** antelope

**anti-, Anti-:** ~**militarismus** *der* antimilitarism; ~**militarist** *der*, ~**militaristin** *die* antimilitarist; ~**militaristisch** ❶ *Adj.* antimilitaristic; ❷ *adv.* ‹argue› along antimilitaristic lines; ~**militaristisch gesinnt/eingestellt sein** be antimilitaristic [in one's views]

**Antimon** /anti'mo:n/ *das*; ~**s** (*Chem.*) antimony

**Antinomie** /antino'mi:/ *die*; ~, ~**n** (*Philos.*, *Rechtsspr.*) antinomy

**Antipathie** /antipa'ti:/ *die*; ~, ~**n** antipathy; **eine ~ gegen jmdn./etw. haben** have an antipathy to sb./sth.

**Antipode** /anti'po:də/ *der*; ~**n**, ~**n**, **Antipodin** *die*; ~, ~**nen** Ⓐ (*Geogr.*) antipodean; Ⓑ (*geh.*) antipode; exact opposite

**an|tippen** *tr. V.* (*berühren*) give ‹person, thing› a [light] tap; touch ‹accelerator, brake, etc.›; (*fig.*) touch on ‹point, question›

**Antiqua** /an'ti:kva/ *die*; ~ (*Druckw.*) roman [type]

**Antiquar** /anti'kva:ɐ̯/ *der*; ~**s**, ~**e** ▶159 antiquarian bookseller; (*mit neueren gebrauchten Büchern*) second-hand bookseller

**Antiquariat** /antikva'ri̯a:t/ Ⓐ (*Handel*) antiquarian book trade; (*mit neueren gebrauchten Büchern*) second-hand book trade; Ⓑ (*Laden/Abteilung*) antiquarian bookshop/department; (*mit neueren gebrauchten Büchern*) second-hand bookshop/department; **modernes ~:** *shop/department selling remainders, defective copies, cheap editions, reprints, etc.*

**Antiquarin** *die*; ~, ~**nen** ⇒ **Antiquar**

**antiquarisch** ❶ *Adj.* antique; (*Buchw.*) antiquarian; (*von neueren gebrauchten Büchern*) second-hand. ❷ *adv.* **ein Buch ~ kaufen** buy a book second-hand

**antiquiert** /anti'kvi:ɐ̯t/ (*abwertend*) ❶ *Adj.* antiquated. ❷ *adv.* in an antiquated way

**Antiquität** *die*; ~, ~**en** antique

**Antiquitäten-:** ~**händler** *der*, ~**händlerin** *die* ▶159 antique dealer; ~**laden** *der*; *Pl.* ~**läden** antique shop; ~**sammler** *der*, ~**sammlerin** *die* collector of antiques; ~**sammlung** *die* collection of antiques

**anti-, Anti-:** ~**rakete** /'----/, ~**raketen·rakete** *die* anti-missile missile; ~**semit** *der*, ~**semitin** *die* anti-Semite; ~**semitisch** ❶ *Adj.* anti-Semitic; anti-Semite; ❷ *adv.* anti-Semitically; ~**semitisch eingestellt/gesinnt sein** be anti-Semitic [in one's views]; ~**semitismus** *der*; ~~, ~**semitismen** anti-Semitism; ~**septisch** *Adj.* (*Med.*) antiseptic; ~**statisch** ❶ *Adj.* (*Physik*) antistatic; ❷ *adv.* ~**statisch wirken** have an antistatic action; ~**teilchen** /'----/ *das* (*Kernphysik*) antiparticle; ~**these** /'----/ *die* antithesis

**antithetisch** ❶ *Adj.* antithetical. ❷ *adv.* antithetically

**Antizipation** /antitsipa'tsi̯o:n/ *die*; ~, ~**en** (*geh.*) anticipation

**antizipieren** *tr. V.* (*geh.*) anticipate

**anti·zyklisch** ❶ *Adj.* Ⓐ (*in unregelmäßiger Folge*) irregular; Ⓑ (*Wirtsch.*) counter-cyclical. ❷ *adv.* Ⓐ (*unregelmäßig*) irregularly; at irregular intervals; Ⓑ (*Wirtsch.*) in a counter-cyclical way

*old spelling (see note on page 1707)

**Antlitz** /'antlɪts/ *das*; ~**es**, ~**e** (*dichter.*, *geh.*) countenance (*literary*); face

**Antonym** /anto'ny:m/ *das*; ~**s**, ~**e** (*Sprachw.*) antonym

**an|törnen** /'antœrnən/ ⇒ **anturnen**[1]

**an|traben** *itr. V.* Ⓐ *mit sein* (*sich nähern*) come trotting along; **angetrabt kommen** come trotting along; (*auf einen zu*) come trotting up; **jmdn. ~ lassen** (*ugs.: kommen lassen*) get sb. to come along promptly; Ⓑ start trotting; break into a trot; (*aus dem Stillstand*) set off at a trot

**Antrag** /'antra:k/ *der*; ~**[e]s**, **Anträge** Ⓐ (*Gesuch*) application, request (**auf** + *Akk.* for); (*Rechtsw.: schriftlich*) petition; **einen ~ auf etw.** (*Akk.*) **stellen** make an application for sth.; apply for sth.; (*Rechtsw.: schriftlich*) enter a petition for sth.; **einem ~ stattgeben** grant an application/a petition; **auf jmds. ~:** at sb.'s request; (*Rechtsw.: schriftlich*) in response to sb.'s petition; Ⓑ (*Formular*) application form; Ⓒ (*Heirats~*) proposal of marriage; **jmdm. einen ~ machen** propose to sb.; Ⓓ (*Parl.*) motion; **einen ~ auf etw.** (*Akk.*) **stellen** *od.* **einbringen** table *or* put forward a motion for sth.; Ⓔ **jmdm. unzüchtige Anträge machen** make improper suggestions to sb.

**an|tragen** *unr. tr. V.* (*geh.*) offer; **jmdm. ~, etw. zu tun** put it to sb. that he/she should do sth.

**Antrags·formular** *das* application form

**antrags·gemäß** *adv.* in accordance with the/your/his *etc.* request

**Antrag·steller** *der*; ~**s**, ~, **Antrag·stellerin** *die*; ~, ~**nen** applicant

**an|trainieren** *tr. V.* **jmdm./sich Muskeln ~:** develop sb.'s/one's muscles; **Pünktlichkeit lässt sich ~:** you can train yourself to be punctual

**an|trauen** *tr. V.* (*veralt.*) **jmdn. jmdm. ~:** marry sb. to sb.; **meine [mir] angetraute Gattin** my wedded wife

**an|treffen** *unr. tr. V.* find; (*zufällig*) come across; **er trifft mich nie zu Hause an** he never catches me in

**an|treiben** ❶ *unr. tr. V.* Ⓐ (*vorwärts treiben*) drive ‹animals, column of prisoners› on *or* along; (*fig.*) urge; **jmdn. zur Eile/zu immer besseren Leistungen ~** (*fig.*) urge sb. to hurry up/urge *or* drive sb. on to better and better performances; Ⓑ (*in Bewegung setzen*) drive; power ‹ship, aircraft›; Ⓒ (*veranlassen*) drive; **jmdn. [dazu] ~, etw. zu tun** drive sb. to do sth.; Ⓓ (*anschwemmen*) **etw. ~:** wash sth. up (**an** + *Akk.* on to); **etw. an den Strand ~:** wash sth. ashore *or* up; Ⓔ (*Gartenbau*) force.
❷ *unr. itr. V.*; *mit sein* (*herantreiben*) drift *or* float ashore

**An·treiber** *der*, **An·treiberin** *die* (*abwertend*) slave driver

**an|treten** ❶ *unr. itr. V.*; *mit sein* Ⓐ (*sich aufstellen*) form up; (*in Linie*) line up; (*Milit.*) fall in; **in Reih und Glied ~:** form up in rank and file; fall in; Ⓑ (*sich stellen*) meet one's opponent; (*als Mannschaft*) line up; **~ gegen** meet; (*als Mannschaft*) line up against; **zum Rückspiel ~:** line up for the return match; Ⓒ (*sich einfinden*) report (**bei** to); **zum Dienst/zur Arbeit ~:** report for duty/work.
❷ *unr. tr. V.* Ⓐ start ‹job, apprenticeship›; take up ‹position, appointment›; start, set out on ‹journey›; begin ‹prison sentence›; come into ‹inheritance›; **jmds. Nachfolge ~:** succeed sb.; **den Urlaub ~:** go on holiday; Ⓑ (*festtreten*) tread down ‹soil›

**An·trieb** *der* Ⓐ (*Triebkraft*) drive; **ein Fahrzeug mit elektrischem ~:** an electrically powered *or* driven vehicle; Ⓑ (*Anreiz*) impulse; (*Psych.*) drive; impulse; **jmdm. neuen ~ geben** give sb. fresh impetus; **aus eigenem** *od.* **freiem** *od.* **persönlichem ~:** of one's own accord; on one's own initiative

**Antriebs-:** ~**achse** *die* (*Technik*) driving axle; ~**kraft** *die* (*Technik*) motive *or* driving power; ~**rad** *das* (*Technik*) drive wheel; ~**welle** *die* (*Technik*) drive shaft

**an|trinken** ❶ *unr. refl. V.* **sich** (*Dat.*) **einen Rausch/Schwips ~:** get drunk/tipsy; **sich** (*Dat.*) **einen ~** (*ugs.*) get sloshed (*coll.*); **sich** (*Dat.*) **Mut ~:** give oneself Dutch courage. ❷ *unr. tr. V.* start drinking ‹wine, coffee, etc.›; start drinking from ‹glass›; start drinking out of ‹bottle›; **eine schon angetrunkene Flasche Wein** a bottle of wine that has/had already been started

**An·tritt** *der* Ⓐ beginning; **bei ~ seiner Stellung** on taking up his post; **vor ~ Ihres Urlaubs** before you go *or* before going on holiday (*Brit.*) *or* (*Amer.*) vacation; **vor ~ der Reise** before setting out on the journey; **bei ~ des Erbes/Amtes** on coming into the inheritance/taking up office; Ⓑ (*Sport*) acceleration *no indef. art.*

**Antritts-:** ~**besuch** *der* [formal] first visit; **seinen ~besuch bei jmdm. machen** pay one's [formal] first visit to sb.; ~**rede** *die* inaugural speech; ~**vor·lesung** *die* inaugural lecture

**an|trocknen** *itr. V.*; *mit sein* Ⓐ (*festkleben*) **an etw.** (*Dat.*) **~:** dry and stick to sth.; Ⓑ (*ein wenig trocknen*) start *or* begin to dry

**an|tuckern** *itr. V.*; *mit sein* (*ugs.*) **angetuckert kommen** come chugging along; (*auf einen zu*) come chugging up

**an|tun** *unr. tr. V.* Ⓐ **sich** (*Dat.*) **etw. Gutes ~:** give oneself a treat; treat oneself; **jmdm. ein Leid ~:** hurt sb.; **jmdm. etwas Böses/ein Unrecht ~:** do sb. harm/an injustice; **tu mir das nicht an!** don't do that to me!; **tu dir keinen Zwang an!** (*ugs.*) don't stand on ceremony!; **sich** (*Dat.*) **etw. ~** (*ugs. verhüll.*) do away with oneself; Ⓑ **das/er** *usw.* **hat es ihr angetan** she was taken with it/him *etc.*; ⇒ *auch* **angetan** 2; Ⓒ (*geh.: anziehen*) **[sich** (*Dat.*)**] etw. ~:** put sth. on; don sth.

**an|turnen**[1] /'antœrnən/ (*ugs.*) ❶ *tr. V.* **jmdn. ~** ‹drugs, music, etc.› turn sb. on (*coll.*). ❷ *itr. V.* turn people on (*coll.*)

**an|turnen**[2] *itr. V.*; *mit sein* (*ugs.*) **angeturnt kommen** come romping along; (*auf einen zu*) come romping up

**Antwerpen** /ant'vɛrpn̩/ (*das*); ~**s** ▶700 Antwerp

**Antwort** /'antvɔrt/ *die*; ~, ~**en** Ⓐ (*Erwiderung*) answer; reply; (*bei Examen usw.*) answer; **er gab mir keine ~:** he didn't answer [me] *or* reply; he made no answer *or* reply; **er gab mir keine ~ auf meine Frage** he did not reply to *or* answer my question; **wer viel fragt, bekommt viel Antwort[en]** (*Spr.*) you'll have to make up your own mind; **keine ~ ist auch eine ~:** your/her *etc.* silence speaks for itself; **in ~ auf etw.** (*Akk.*) (*Amtsspr.*) in reply to sth.; **um ~ wird gebeten** (*auf Einladungskarten*) RSVP; Ⓑ (*Reaktion*) response; **als ~ auf etw.** (*Akk.*) in response to sth.

**antworten** *itr. V.* Ⓐ (*erwidern*) answer; reply; **auf etw.** (*Akk.*) **~:** answer sth.; reply to sth.; **jmdm. ~:** answer sb.; reply to sb.; **jmdm. auf seine Frage ~:** reply to *or* answer sb.'s question; **wie/was soll ich ihm ~?** what answer shall I give him?/what shall I tell him?; **mit Ja/Nein ~:** answer yes/no; Ⓑ (*reagieren*) respond (**auf** + *Akk.* to)

**Antwort-:** ~**post·karte** *die* (*Postw.*) reply card; ~**schein** *der*: **internationaler ~schein** (*Postw.*) international reply coupon; ~**schreiben** *das* reply (**auf** + *Akk.* to)

**an|vertrauen** ❶ *tr. V.* Ⓐ (*übergeben*) **jmdm. etw. ~:** entrust sth. to sb.; entrust sb. with sth.; **sein Kind jmdm. ~:** entrust one's child to sb.'s care; Ⓑ (*mitteilen*) **jmdm./seinem Tagebuch etw. ~:** confide sth. to sb./one's diary. ❷ *refl. V.* Ⓐ (*sich mitteilen*) **sich jmdm. ~:** confide in sb.; Ⓑ (*sich schützen lassen*) **sich jmdm./einer Sache ~:** put one's trust in sb./sth.

**an·verwandt** *Adj.* (*geh.*) related

**An·verwandte** *der/die* (*geh.*) relation

**an|visieren** *tr. V.* Ⓐ (*Milit.*) align the *or* one's sights on; Ⓑ (*anstreben*) aim at

**an|wachsen** *unr. itr. V.*; *mit sein* Ⓐ (*festwachsen*) grow on; **wieder ~** ‹finger, toe› grow back on; **die transplantierte Haut ist angewachsen** the skin graft has/skin grafts have taken; **angewachsene Ohrläppchen** earlobes attached to the sides of one's head; B (*Wurzeln schlagen*) take root; **steh nicht da wie angewachsen** (*ugs.*) don't just stand there like a stuffed dummy; C (*zunehmen*) increase; grow

**an|wackeln** *itr. V.; mit sein* (*ugs.*) **angewackelt kommen** come waddling along; (*auf einen zu*) come waddling up

**an|wählen** *tr. V.* dial; **jmdn. ~:** dial sb.'s number

**Anwalt** /ˈanvalt/ *der; ~[e]s,* **Anwälte** /ˈanvɛltə/, **Anwältin** *die; ~, ~nen* ▶ 159 A (*Rechts~*) lawyer; solicitor (*Brit.*); attorney (*Amer.*); (*vor Gericht*) barrister (*Brit.*); attorney[-at-law] (*Amer.*); advocate (*Scot.*); **einen ~ nehmen** get a lawyer *or* (*Amer.*) an attorney; B (*Fürsprecher*) advocate; champion

**Anwalts·büro** *das* A (*Räume*) lawyer's office; solicitor's office (*Brit.*); B (*Sozietät*) firm of solicitors (*Brit.*); law firm (*Amer.*)

**Anwaltschaft** *die; ~, ~en* A (*Gesamtheit der Anwälte*) legal profession; B (*Amt*) ⇒ **Anwalt** A: profession of lawyer/solicitor/attorney/barrister/advocate; C (*Vertretung*) **die ~ in einer Sache übernehmen/ablehnen** take on/refuse to take on a case

**Anwalts-: ~kammer** *die* (*Rechtsw.*) *professional association of lawyers;* **~kanzlei** *die* ⇒ **~büro**

**an|wandeln** *tr. V.* (*geh.*) come over

**An·wandelung, An·wandlung** *die* (*Laune*) mood; (*leichter Anfall*) fit; **in einer ~ von Großzügigkeit** *usw.* in a fit of generosity *etc.;* **dann bekommt er wieder seine ~en** then he gets one of his moods again; **eine ~ von Furcht/Schwermütigkeit** a sudden feeling of fear/a fit of melancholy

**an|wärmen** *tr. V.* warm up; warm ‹hands, feet›

**An·wärter** *der* A candidate (**auf** + *Akk.* for); (*Sport*) contender (**auf** + *Akk.* for); B (*auf den Thron*) claimant; (*Thronerbe*) heir (**auf** + *Akk.* to)

**An·wärterin** *die* A ⇒ **Anwärter** A; B (*auf den Thron*) claimant; (*Thronerbin*) heiress (**auf** + *Akk.* to)

**Anwartschaft** *die; ~, ~en* candidacy, candidature (**auf** + *Akk.* for); (*Sport*) being in contention (**auf** + *Akk.* for); (*auf den Thron, einen Titel*) claim (**auf** + *Akk.* to)

**an|watscheln** *itr. V.; mit sein* (*ugs.*) **angewatschelt kommen** come waddling along; (*auf einen zu*) come waddling up

**an|wehen** ❶ *tr. V.* A (*geh.: gegen jmdn. wehen*) ‹wind, breeze› blow [up]on; B (*anhäufen*) drift ‹snow, sand, etc.›. ❷ *itr. V.; mit sein* (*sich anhäufen*) drift

**an|weisen** *unr. tr. V.* A (*beauftragen*) **jmdn. ~:** give sb. instructions; **jmdn. ~, etw. zu tun** instruct *or* direct sb. to do sth.; B (*zuweisen*) **jmdm. etw. ~:** allocate sth. to sb.; C (*anleiten*) instruct; D (*überweisen*) remit; (*die Auszahlung veranlassen*) order the payment of; ⇒ *auch* **angewiesen** 2

**An·weisung** *die* A (*Anordnung*) instruction; **~ haben, etw. zu tun** have instructions to do sth.; **auf ~ der Behörde** by order of *or* on instructions *pl.* from the authorities; B (*das Zuteilen*) allocation; C (*Gebrauchs~*) instructions *pl.;* D (*Überweisung*) remittance; (*Anordnung zur Auszahlung*) **die ~ erfolgt demnächst** payment will be ordered shortly; E (*Bankw.: Formular*) payment order

**anwendbar** *Adj.* applicable (**auf** + *Akk.* to); **schwer ~:** difficult to apply; **die Regel ist hier nicht ~:** the rule doesn't apply here

**Anwendbarkeit** *die; ~:* applicability (**auf** + *Akk.* to)

**an|wenden** *unr.* (*auch regelm.*) *tr. V.* use, employ ‹process, trick, method, violence, force›; use ‹medicine, money, time›; take ‹care, trouble› (**auf** + *Akk.* over); apply ‹rule, paragraph, proverb, etc.› (**auf** + *Akk.* to); **sich auf etw.** (*Akk.*) **~ lassen** be applicable to sth.; apply to sth.

**Anwender** *der; ~s, ~,* **Anwenderin** *die; ~, ~nen* (*DV*) user

**An·wendung** *die* A ⇒ **anwenden**: use; employment; taking; application; **etw. in ~** (*Akk.*) *od.* **zur ~ bringen** (*Amtsspr.*) apply sth.; **zur ~ kommen** *od.* **gelangen, ~ finden** (*Amtsspr.*) ‹rule, paragraph, etc.› apply, be applicable; B (*DV, Med.*) application

**Anwendungs-: ~bereich** *der,* **~gebiet** *das* range of application; (*eines Gesetzes, einer Regel*) scope; **~möglichkeit** *die* possible use *or* application

**an|werben** *unr. tr. V.* recruit (**für** to); (*Milit.*) enlist, recruit; **sich ~ lassen** be recruited; (*Milit.*) enlist (**für** in)

**An·werbung** *die* ⇒ **anwerben**: recruitment (**für** to); enrolment (**für** in)

**an|werfen** *unr. tr. V.* A (*ugs.: in Gang bringen*) start [up] ‹machine, engine, vehicle›; swing ‹propeller›; put *or* switch on ‹electrical device›; B (*an etw. werfen*) **Kalk/Mörtel** *usw.* **an eine Wand ~:** rough-cast a wall [with lime/plaster *etc.*]

**An·wesen** *das* property

**anwesend** *Adj.* present; **die nicht ~en Mitglieder** the members [who are/were] not present; **bei etw. ~ sein** be present at sth.; **ich war nicht ganz ~** (*fig. ugs. scherzh.*) I wasn't quite with it (*coll.*)

**Anwesende** *der/die; adj. Dekl.* **die ~n** those present; **jeder ~/einige ~/alle ~n** everyone/some of those/all those present; **~ natürlich ausgenommen** present company excepted, of course

**Anwesenheit** *die; ~:* presence; **in ~:** in the presence (*Gen. od.* **von** of)

**Anwesenheits·liste** *die* attendance list

**an|wetzen** *itr. V.; mit sein* (*ugs.*) **angewetzt kommen** come rushing *or* tearing along; (*auf einen zu*) come rushing *or* tearing up

**an|widern** /ˈanviːdɐn/ *tr. V.* nauseate

**an|winkeln** *tr. V.* bend ‹knee, arm, etc.›

**an|winseln** *tr. V.* whimper at; **jmdn. um Hilfe ~:** come whining to sb. for help

**Anwohner** /ˈanvoːnɐ/ *der; ~s, ~,* **Anwohnerin** *die; ~, ~nen* resident; **Parken nur für ~:** residents-only parking

**Anwohnerschaft** *die* residents *pl.*

**An·wurf** *der* A (*Vorwurf*) (*esp. unjustified*) reproach; (*Beschuldigung*) (*esp. false*) accusation; B (*Handball*) throw-off; (*Korbball*) centre pass

**an|wurzeln** *itr. V.; mit sein* take root; **wie angewurzelt [da] stehen/stehen bleiben** stand rooted to the spot

**An·zahl** *die* number; **eine ganze ~:** a whole lot

**an|zahlen** *tr. V.* put down *or* pay a deposit on; (*bei Ratenzahlung*) make a down payment on; **50 DM ~:** put down 50 marks as a deposit/make a down payment of 50 marks

**an|zählen** *tr. V.* (*Boxen*) **jmdn. ~:** start to give sb. the count

**An·zahlung** *die* deposit; (*bei Ratenzahlung*) down payment; **eine ~ auf etw.** (*Akk.*) **machen** *od.* **leisten** put down *or* pay a deposit on sth./make a down payment on sth.

**an|zapfen** ❶ *tr. V.* A tap ‹barrel, tree›; B (*ugs.: zum Abhören*) tap ‹telephone line, wire›; C (*ugs.*) ⇒ **anpumpen**. ❷ *itr. V.* tap a/the barrel; **frisch ~:** tap a/the new barrel

**An·zeichen** *das* sign; indication; (*Med.*) symptom; **alle ~ deuten darauf hin, dass ...** all the signs *or* indications are that ...

**an|zeichnen** *tr. V.* A (*an etw. zeichnen*) draw (**an** + *Akk.* on); B (*markieren*) mark

**Anzeige** /ˈantsaiːgə/ *die; ~, ~n* A (*Straf~*) report; **gegen jmdn. [eine] ~ [wegen etw.] erstatten** report sb. to the police/the authorities [for sth.]; **jmdn./etw. zur ~ bringen** (*Amtsspr.*) report sb./sth. to the police/the authorities; B (*Inserat*) advertisement; **eine ~ in einer Zeitung aufgeben** place an advertisement in a newspaper; C (*Bekanntmachung*) announcement; D (*ablesbarer Stand*) display; (*eines Messinstruments*) reading; E (*Gerät*) display unit

**an|zeigen** *tr. V.* A (*Strafanzeige erstatten*) **jmdn./etw. ~:** report sb./sth. to the police/the authorities; **sich selbst ~:** voluntarily admit an/the offence; B (*zeigen*) show; indicate; show ‹time, date›; C (*bekannt geben*) announce; D (*wissen lassen, geh.: ankündigen*) **jmdm. etw. ~:** inform *or* notify sb. of sth.; **jmdm. ~, dass ...** inform *or* notify sb. [of the fact] that ...

**Anzeigen-: ~blatt** *das* advertiser; **~teil** *der* advertisement section *or* pages *pl.;* **~werbung** *die* newspaper and magazine advertising

**Anzeige·pflicht** *die* A statutory obligation to report a/the birth/death/[criminal] offence *etc.;* B ⇒ **Meldepflicht** A

**An·zeiger** *der* A indicator; B (*Zeitung*) advertiser

**Anzeige·tafel** *die* (*Sport*) scoreboard

**an|zetteln** *tr. V.* (*abwertend*) hatch ‹plot, intrigue›; instigate ‹revolt›; foment ‹war›

**an|ziehen** ❶ *unr. tr. V.* A (*an sich ziehen*) draw up ‹knees, feet, etc.›; B (*anlocken*) attract; draw; (*durch Schönheit, freundliches Betragen usw.*) attract; **sich von jmdm. angezogen fühlen** feel attracted to sb.; C (*anspannen*) tighten, pull tight ‹rope, wire, chain›; tighten ‹guitar string›; D (*festziehen*) tighten ‹screw, knot, belt, etc.›; put on, pull on ‹handbrake›; E (*Kleidung anlegen*) dress; **sich ~:** get dressed; F put on ‹clothes›; **sich** (*Dat.*) **etw. ~:** put sth. on; **jmdm. etw. ~:** put sth. on sb.; (*als Hilfeleistung*) put sth. on for sb.; G (*aufnehmen*) absorb ‹moisture›; take on ‹taste, smell›; H (*Physik*) ‹magnet, body, etc.› attract.
❷ *unr. itr. V.* A (*Tempo beschleunigen*) accelerate; B (*sich in Bewegung setzen*) ‹car, train› pull away, move off; ‹horse› move off; C (*Brettspiel*) make the first move; move *or* go first; D (*Börsenw., Kaufmannsspr.*) ‹prices, costs› rise, increase; ‹shares, securities, commodities› advance, move ahead

**anziehend** *Adj.* attractive; engaging ‹manner, smile›

**An·ziehung** *die* attraction

**Anziehungs·kraft** *die* A (*Physik*) attractive force; force of attraction; B (*Reiz*) attraction

**an|zischen** ❶ *tr. V.* A hiss at; B (*ugs.: anfahren*) snarl at. ❷ *itr. V.; mit sein* (*ugs.: sich nähern*) **angezischt kommen** come whizzing along; (*auf einen zu*) come whizzing up

**an|zockeln** *itr. V.; mit sein* (*ugs.*) **angezockelt kommen** come jogging along; (*auf einen zu*) come jogging up; ‹cart› come trundling along/up

**An·zug** *der* A (*Herren~*) suit; **jmdn. aus dem ~ stoßen** *od.* **boxen** (*salopp*) beat *or* knock the living daylights (*coll.*) *or* the hell (*coll.*) out of sb.; B **im ~ sein** ‹danger› be imminent; ‹storm› be approaching; ‹fever, illness› be coming on; ‹enemy› be advancing; C (*Beschleunigung*) acceleration; D (*Brettspiele*) first move; **~ haben** have the first move

**anzüglich** /ˈantsyːklɪç/ ❶ *Adj.* A insinuating ‹remark, question›; **werde bloß nicht ~!** just don't start making insinuating remarks; B (*anstößig*) offensive ‹joke, remark›. ❷ *adv.* A in an insinuating way; B (*anstößig*) offensively

**Anzüglichkeit** *die* ⇒ **anzüglich** A, B: A (*Art*) insinuating nature; offensiveness; B (*Bemerkung*) insinuating remark; offensive remark/joke

**Anzug·stoff** *der* suiting

**Anzugs·vermögen** *das* acceleration

**an|zünden** *tr. V.* light; **ein Gebäude** *usw.* **~:** set fire to a building *etc.;* set a building *etc.* on fire

**An·zünder** *der* (*Gas~*) gas lighter; (*Feuer~*) firelighter (*Brit.*)

**an|zweifeln** *tr. V.* doubt; question

**an|zwinkern** *tr. V.* wink at

**an|zwitschern** *refl. V.* (*ugs.*) *in* **sich** (*Dat.*) **einen ~:** get sloshed (*coll.*)

**AOK** *Abk.* **Allgemeine Ortskrankenkasse**

**Äols·harfe** /ˈɛːɔls-/ *die* aeolian harp

**Äon** /ɛˈoːn/ *der; ~s, ~en* (*geh.*) aeon

**Aorta** /aˈɔrta/ *die; ~,* **Aorten** ▶ 471 (*Med.*) aorta

**Apanage** /apa'na:ʒə/ *die;* ~, ~**n** apanage; (*fig.*) subsidy

**apart** /a'part/ ❶ *Adj.* individual *attrib.*; ~ **sein** be individual in style. ❷ *adv.* [A] in an individual style; [B] (*Buchhandel: einzeln*) individually

**Apartheid** /a'pa:ɐthait/ *die;* ~: apartheid *no art.*

**Apartheid·politik** *die* policy of apartheid

**Apartheit** *die;* ~: individuality

**Apartment** /a'partmənt/ *das;* ~**s**, ~**s** studio flat (*Brit.*); flatlet (*Brit.*); small flat (*Brit.*); studio apartment (*Amer.*)

**Apartment·haus** *das* block of studio flats (*Brit.*) *or* (*Amer.*) studio apartments

**Apathie** /apa'ti:/ *die;* ~, ~**n** apathy

**apathisch** /a'pa:tɪʃ/ ❶ *Adj.* apathetic. ❷ *adv.* apathetically

**Apenninen** /apɛ'ni:nən/ *Pl.* **die** ~: the Apennines

**Apennin[en]·halbinsel** *die* Apennine peninsula

**aper** /'a:pɐ/ *Adj.* (*südd., österr., schweiz.*) snowless; bare of snow *pred.*; ‹street› clear of snow *pred.*

**Aperçu** /apɛr'sy:/ *das;* ~**s**, ~**s** (*geh.*) bon mot

**Aperitif** /aperi'ti:f/ *der;* ~**s**, ~**s** aperitif

**apern** /'a:pɐn/ *itr. V.* (*südd., österr., schweiz.*) **es apert** the snow is going; **die Hänge/Straßen** ~: the snow on the slopes is going/the streets are becoming clear of snow

**Apex** /'a:pɛks/ *der;* ~, **Apizes** /'a:pitse:s/ [A] (*Astron.*) apex; [B] (*Sprachw.*) (*Längezeichen*) length mark; (*Betonungszeichen*) stress mark

**Apfel** /'apfl/ *der;* ~**s**, **Äpfel** /'ɛpfl/ [A] apple; **der ~ fällt nicht weit vom Stamm** *od.* (*ugs. scherzh.*) **Pferd** (*Spr.*) it's in the blood; **~ im Schlafrock** (*Kochk.*) apple dumpling; **Äpfel und Birnen zusammenzählen, Äpfel mit Birnen addieren** (*ugs.*) lump together totally different things; **[etw.] für einen ~ und ein Ei [kaufen]** [buy sth.] for a song; **in den sauren ~ beißen [und etw. tun]** (*ugs.*) grasp the nettle [and do sth.]; [B] (~*baum*) apple tree

**Apfel-:** ~**baum** *der* apple tree; ~**blüte** *die* [A] apple blossom; [B] (*das Blühen*) blossoming of the apple trees; **während der ~blüte** while the apple trees are/were in blossom

**Äpfelchen** *das;* ~**s**, ~: little apple

**apfel-, Apfel-:** ~**grün** apple-green; ~**korn** *der* apple-flavoured schnapps; ~**kuchen** *der* apple cake; (*mit Äpfeln belegt*) apple flan; **gedeckter ~kuchen** apple pie; ~**most** *der* [A] (~*saft*) apple juice; [B] (*südd.: gegorener ~saft*) cider; ~**mus** *das* apple purée; (*zu Fleisch*) apple sauce; ~**saft** *der* apple juice; ~**schimmel** *der* dapple-grey [horse]

**Apfelsine** /apfl'zi:nə/ *die;* ~, ~**n** [A] orange; [B] (*Baum*) orange tree

**Apfel-:** ~**strudel** *der* apfelstrudel; ~**tasche** *die* apple turnover *or* puff; ~**wein** *der* cider; ~**wickler** *der* (*Zool.*) codling moth

**Aphorismus** /afo'rɪsmʊs/ *der;* ~, **Aphorismen** (*geh.*) aphorism

**aphoristisch** (*geh.*) ❶ *Adj.* aphoristic. ❷ *adv.* aphoristically

**Aphrodisiakum** /afrodi'zi:akʊm/ *das;* ~**s**, **Aphrodisiaka** (*Med.*) aphrodisiac

**Aplomb** /a'plõ:/ *der;* ~**s** (*geh.*) aplomb

**APO, Apo** /'a:po/ *die;* ~: *Abk.* **außerparlamentarische Opposition**

**apodiktisch** /apo'dɪktɪʃ/ *Adj.* (*Philos., geh.*) apodictic

**Apokalypse** /apoka'lʏpsə/ *die;* ~, ~**n** apocalypse

**apokalyptisch** /apoka'lʏptɪʃ/ (*Rel., fig.*) ❶ *Adj.* apocalyptic; **die Apokalyptischen Reiter** the Four Horsemen of the Apocalypse. ❷ *adv.* apocalyptically

**apokryph** /apo'kry:f/ *Adj.* (*Rel., fig.*) apocryphal; **die Apokryphen** the Apocrypha *sing.*

**apolitisch** ❶ *Adj.* apolitical. ❷ *adv.* apolitically

*old spelling (see note on page 1707)

**Apoll** /a'pɔl/ *der;* ~**s**, ~**s** (*geh.*) Apollo

**apollinisch** /apɔ'li:nɪʃ/ *Adj.* (*bes. Philos.*) apollonian

**Apollo** /a'pɔlo/ *der;* ~**s**, ~**s** (*Myth., geh.*) Apollo

**Apologet** /apolo'ge:t/ *der;* ~**en**, ~**en** apologist

**Apologetik** /apolo'ge:tɪk/ *die;* ~, ~**en** [A] (*geh.: Rechtfertigung*) apologia (*Gen.* for); [B] (*Theol.*) apologetics *sing.*

**Apologetin** *die;* ~, ~**nen** apologist

**Apologie** /apolo'gi:/ *die;* ~, ~**n** (*geh.*) apologia (*Gen.* for)

**Aporie** /apo'ri:/ *die;* ~, ~**n** (*Philos., geh.*) aporia

**Apostel** /a'pɔstl/ *der;* ~**s**, ~: apostle; **die zwölf ~**: the twelve Apostles

**-apostel** *der* (*meist iron.*) apostle of ‹economic growth, world peace, etc.›; **ein Frischluft~/Gesundheits~**: a fresh air/health fanatic; **ein Spar~/Abnehm~**: an enthusiastic advocate of saving/slimming

**Apostel-:** ~**brief** *der* epistle; ~**geschichte** *die* [A] (*apokryphe Geschichte*) Apocryphal New Testament story; [B] (*Buch des N. T.*) Acts of the Apostles *constr. as sing.*

**a posteriori** /a: pɔste'rio:ri/ (*Philos.*) a posteriori

**aposteriorisch** *Adj., adv.* (*Philos.*) a posteriori

**apostolisch** /apɔs'to:lɪʃ/ *Adj.* (*Theol.*) [A] apostolic; **das Apostolische Glaubensbekenntnis** the Apostles' Creed; [B] (*päpstlich*) apostolic; **~er Segen** apostolic blessing; **Apostolischer Nuntius** Apostolic Nuncio; **Apostolischer Stuhl** Holy See

**Apostroph** /apo'stro:f/ *der;* ~**s**, ~**e** (*Sprachw.*) apostrophe

**apostrophieren** *tr. V.* [A] (*Sprachw.: mit Apostroph versehen*) apostrophize; [B] **jmdn./etw. als etw. ~**: refer to sb./sth. as sth.; describe sb./sth. as sth.

**Apotheke** /apo'te:kə/ *die;* ~, ~**n** [A] chemist's [shop] (*Brit.*); drugstore (*Amer.*); (*im Krankenhaus*) dispensary; [B] (*Haus~*) medicine cabinet; (*Reise~, Bord~*) first-aid kit; [C] (*ugs. abwertend: teures Geschäft*) expensive shop; **das ist eine richtige ~**: they charge an arm and a leg there (*coll.*)

**apotheken·pflichtig** *Adj.* obtainable only at a chemist's [shop] (*Brit.*) *or* (*Amer.*) drugstore *postpos.*

**Apotheker** *der;* ~**s**, ~, **Apothekerin** *die;* ~, ~**nen** ▶ 159 [dispensing] chemist (*Brit.*); druggist

**Apotheker·preise** *Pl.* (*fig. ugs.*) fancy prices (*coll.*)

**Apotheose** /apote'o:zə/ *die;* ~, ~**n** (*geh.*) apotheosis

**App.** *Abk.* [A] **Apparat** ext.; [B] **Appartement** Apt.

**Apparat** /apa'ra:t/ *der;* ~**[e]s**, ~**e** [A] (*Technik*) apparatus *no pl.*; (*Haushaltsgerät*) appliance; (*kleiner*) gadget; [B] (*Radio~*) radio; (*Fernseh~*) television; (*Rasier~*) razor; (*elektrisch*) shaver; (*Foto~*) camera; **wir haben einen neuen Fernseher gekauft, der alte ~ war 15 Jahre alt** we've bought a new television — our old set was fifteen years old; [C] (*Telefon*) telephone; (*Nebenstelle*) extension; **am ~ verlangt werden** be wanted on the telephone; **am ~!** speaking!; **bleiben Sie am ~!** hold the line; **wer war am ~?** who answered?; who did you speak to?; [D] (*Personen und Hilfsmittel*) organization; (*Verwaltungs~*) system; [E] (*ugs.: etwas Ausgefallenes, Riesiges*) whopper (*coll.*); (*dicker Mensch*) heavyweight; [F] (*Hochschulw.: Bücher*) *reference collection of books for a particular course;* [G] (*Lesarten*) apparatus; **[text]kritischer ~**: apparatus criticus; critical apparatus

**Apparate·bau** *der* (*Technik*) design and manufacture of apparatus

**Apparate·medizin** *die* (*oft abwertend*) high-technology medicine

**apparativ** /apara'ti:f/ ❶ *Adj.* [A] (*Technik*) **~e Einrichtungen** technical equipment *sing.*; **~e Lehrmittel** machine aids in the classroom; **~e Diagnostik** machine-aided diagnosis; [B] (*Verwaltung*) **der ~e Ausbau der Organisation** the expansion of the organization's administrative system. ❷ *adv.* [A] (*Technik*) with the aid of machines *or* technical equipment; **~ am Leben erhalten werden** be kept alive by life support systems; [B] (*Verwaltung*) organizationally

**Apparatschik** /apa'ratʃɪk/ *der;* ~**s**, ~**s** (*abwertend*) apparatchik

**Apparatur** /apara'tu:ɐ/ *die;* ~, ~**en** apparatus *no pl.*; equipment *no indef. art., no pl.*; (*fig.*) apparatus *no pl*; ~**en** (*Kontrollinstrumente usw.*) instruments and controls

**Apparillo** /apa'rɪlo/ *der;* ~**s**, ~**s** (*ugs. scherzh.*) contraption (*coll.*); **Der Karpfen wiegt 6 Kilo. — Mann, ist das ein ~!** The carp weighs 6 kilos — That's 'some 'fish!

**Appartement** /apartə'mã:, *schweiz. auch:* -'mɛnt/ *das;* ~**s**, ~**s** (*schweiz. auch:* ~**e**) [A] ⇨ **Apartment**; [B] (*Hotelsuite*) suite

**Appeal** /ə'pi:l/ *der;* ~**s** appeal

**Appeasement** /ə'pi:zmənt/ *das;* ~**s** (*Politik, meist abwertend*) appeasement

**Appell** /a'pɛl/ *der;* ~**s**, ~**e** [A] (*Mahnung*) appeal (**zu** for, **an** + *Akk.* to); **einen ~ an jmdn. richten** make an appeal to sb.; appeal to sb.; [B] (*Milit.*) muster; (*Anwesenheits~*) roll-call; (*Besichtigung*) inspection; **zum ~ antreten** fall in for roll-call inspection; [C] (*Jagdw.*) obedience; **~/keinen ~ haben** be/not be obedient

**Appellation** /apɛla'tsio:n/ *die;* ~, ~**en** (*Rechtsw., schweiz. sonst veralt.*) appeal

**Appellativ** /apɛla'ti:f/ *das;* ~**s**, ~**e**, **Appellativum** /apɛla'ti:vʊm/ *das;* ~**s**, **Appellativa** (*Sprachw.*) appellative; common noun

**appellieren** *itr. V.* appeal (**an** + *Akk.* to)

**Appendix**[1] /a'pɛndɪks/ *der;* ~, **Appendizes** /-dɪtse:s/ *od.* ~**es**, ~**e** [A] (*geh.: Anhängsel*) appendage; [B] (*Buchw.*) appendix

**Appendix**[2] *der od.* (*fachspr.:*) *die;* ~, **Appendizes** ▶ 471 (*Anat.*) appendix

**Apperzeption** /apɛrtsɛp'tsio:n/ *die;* ~, ~**en** (*Philos., Psych.*) apperception

**Appetit** /ape'ti:t/ *der;* ~**[e]s**, ~**e** (*auch fig.*) appetite (**auf** + *Akk.* for); **~ auf etw. haben/bekommen** fancy sth.; **ich hätte so richtig ~ auf ...** I could just fancy *or* eat ...; I could really go for ... (*Amer.*); **guten ~!** enjoy your meal!; **jmdm. den ~ verderben** spoil sb.'s appetite; **das verschlug uns/ihnen** *usw.* **den ~**: that took away our/their *etc.* appetite; **mit ~ essen** enjoy one's food; **der ~ kommt beim** *od.* **mit dem Essen** appetite comes with eating (*prov.*)

**appetit·anregend** *Adj.* [A] (*appetitlich*) appetizing; [B] (*den Appetit fördernd*) ‹medicine etc.› that stimulates the appetite; **~ wirken** stimulate the appetite; **ein ~es Mittel** an appetite stimulant

**Appetit-:** ~**happen** *der* canapé; ~**hemmer** *der;* ~**s**, ~ ⇨ ~**zügler**

**appetitlich** ❶ *Adj.* [A] (*appetitanregend*) appetizing; [B] (*sauber, ansprechend*) attractive and hygienic; [C] (*adrett*) attractive. ❷ *adv.* [A] (*appetitanregend*) appetizingly; [B] (*sauber, ansprechend*) attractively and hygienically ‹packed›; **ein ~ gedeckter Tisch** an attractively laid table

**appetit-, Appetit-:** ~**los** ❶ *Adj.* without any appetite *postpos.*; **~los sein** have lost one's appetite; **immer noch ~los sein** still have no appetite; ❷ *adv.* without any appetite; ~**losigkeit** *die;* ~: lack of appetite; ~**zügler** *der* appetite suppressant

**Appetizer** /'æpɪtaɪzə/ *der;* ~**s**, ~ (*Pharm.*) appetite stimulant

**applanieren** *tr. V.* (*österr.*) smooth over; settle

**applaudieren** /aplau'di:rən/ *itr.* (*veralt. auch tr.*) *V.* applaud; **jmdm./einer Sache ~**: applaud sb./sth.

**Applaus** /a'plaus/ *der;* ~**es**, ~**e** applause

**applikabel** /apli'ka:bl/ *Adj.* (*geh.*) applicable

**Applikation** /aplika'tsio:n/ *die;* ~, ~**en** [A] (*DV*) application; [B] (*Med.: Verabreichung*) administration; (*äußerlich*) application; Ⓒ (*Textilw.*) appliqué

**applizieren** /apli'tsi:rən/ *tr. V.* Ⓐ (*Med.*) administer; (*äußerlich*) apply; Ⓑ (*Textilw.*) appliqué

**apportieren** /apɔr'ti:rən/ *tr.* (*auch itr.*) *V.* (*Jägerspr.*) retrieve; fetch

**Apportier·hund** *der* retriever

**Apposition** *die* (*Sprachw.*) apposition

**appretieren** /apre'ti:rən/ *tr. V.* (*bes. Textilind.*) dress, finish ‹fabric, linen›

**Appretur** /apre'tu:ɐ̯/ *die;* ~, ~**en** (*bes. Textilind.*) dressing; finishing

**Approbation** /aproba'tsi̯o:n/ *die;* ~, ~**en** licence to practise (*as a doctor, dentist, chemist*)

**approbieren** /apro'bi:rən/ *tr. V.* (*österr., sonst veralt.*) approve

**approbiert** *Adj.* registered ‹doctor, dentist, chemist›

**Apr.** *Abk.* **April** Apr.

**Après-Ski** /aprɛ'ʃi:/ *das;* ~**s** Ⓐ (*Kleidung*) après-ski outfit; Ⓑ (*Unterhaltung*) après-ski [entertainment]

**Aprikose** /apri'ko:zə/ *die;* ~, ~**n** Ⓐ (*Frucht*) apricot; Ⓑ (*Baum*) apricot tree

**Aprikosen·marmelade** *die* apricot jam

**April** /a'prɪl/ *der;* ~[**s**], ~**e** ▶ 207 April; **der** ~: April; ~, ~! April fool!; **der 1.** ~: the first of April; (*in Bezug auf Aprilscherze*) April Fool's *or* All Fools' Day; **jmdn. in den** ~ **schicken** make an April fool of sb.

**April-:** ~**scherz** *der* April-fool trick; **das ist doch wohl ein** ~**scherz!** (*fig.*) you/they *etc.* can't be serious!; you/they *etc.* must be joking!; ~**wetter** *das* April weather

**a priori** /a:pri'o:ri/ (*Philos.*) a priori

**apriorisch** *Adj., adv.* (*Philos.*) a priori

**apropos** /apro'po:/ *Adv.* apropos; by the way; incidentally

**Aquädukt** /akvɛ'dʊkt/ *der od. das;* ~[**e**]**s**, ~**e** aqueduct

**aquamarin** /akvama'ri:n/ ⇒ ~**blau**

**Aquamarin** *der;* ~**s**, ~**e** aquamarine

**aquamarin·blau** *Adj.* aquamarine

**Aquanaut** /akva'naut/ *der;* ~**en**, ~**en**, **Aquanautin** *die;* ~, ~**nen** aquanaut

**Aquaplaning** /akva'pla:nɪŋ/ *das;* ~**s** aquaplaning

**Aquarell** /akva'rɛl/ *das;* ~**s**, ~**e** (*Malerei*) watercolour [painting]

**Aquarell·farbe** *die* watercolour

**aquarellieren** *itr. V.* paint in watercolours

**Aquarell-:** ~**maler** *der*, ~**malerin** *die;* watercolour painter; watercolourist; ~**malerei** *die* Ⓐ (*Maltechnik*) watercolour painting; **in** ~**malerei** in watercolour; Ⓑ (*Bild*) watercolour

**Aquarien** /a'kva:ri̯ən/ ⇒ **Aquarium**

**Aquarien-:** ~**fisch** *der* aquarium fish; ~**haus** *das* aquarium

**Aquarium** /a'kva:ri̯ʊm/ *das;* ~**s**, **Aquarien** aquarium

**Aquatinta** /akva'tɪnta/ *die;* ~, **Aquatinten** (*bild. Kunst*) aquatint

**Äquator** /ɛ'kva:tɔr/ *der;* ~**s;** ~**en** /-'to:rən/ (*Erd*~, *Math.*) equator

**äquatorial** /ɛkvato'ri̯a:l/ *Adj.* equatorial

**Äquator·taufe** *die* crossing-the-line ceremony

**Aquavit** /akva'vi:t/ *der;* ~**s**, ~**e** aquavit

**Äquilibrist** /ɛkvili'brɪst/ *der;* ~**en**, ~**en**, **Äquilibristin** *die;* ~, ~**nen** equilibrist

**Äquinoktium** /ɛkvi'nɔktsi̯ʊm/ *das;* ~**s**, **Äquinoktien** (*Geogr.*) equinox

**äquivalent** /ɛkviva'lɛnt/ *Adj.* equivalent

**Äquivalent** *das;* ~[**e**]**s**, ~**e** equivalent; (*Ersatz*) appropriate replacement; (*Entschädigung*) appropriate compensation

**Äquivalenz** /ɛkviva'lɛnts/ *die;* ~, ~**en** (*auch Math., Logik*) equivalence

**Ar** /a:ɐ̯/ *das od. der;* ~**s**, ~**e** ▶ 301 are

**Ära** /'ɛ:ra/ *die;* ~, **Ären** era; **die** ~ **Kreisky** the Kreisky era

**Araber** /'a:rabɐ/ *der;* ~**s**, ~ ▶ 553 (*auch Pferd*) Arab; Arabian

**Araberin** *die;* ~, ~**nen** ▶ 553 Arab; Arabian

**Arabeske** /ara'bɛskə/ *die;* ~, ~**n** (*bild. Kunst, Musik*) arabesque

**Arabien** /a'ra:bi̯ən/ (*das*); ~**s** Arabia

**arabisch** *Adj.* ▶ 553, ▶ 696 Arabian; Arab; Arabic ‹language, numeral, dialect, alphabet, literature›; **die Arabische Halbinsel** the Arabian Peninsula; **das Arabische** Arabic; ⇒ *auch* **deutsch, Deutsche**[2]

**Arabisch** *das;* ~[**s**] ▶ 696 Arabic ⇒ *auch* **Deutsch**

**Arabistik** /ara'bɪstɪk/ *die;* ~: Arabic studies *pl., no art.*

**Aralie** /a'ra:li̯ə/ *die;* ~, ~**n** (*Bot.*) aralia

**aramäisch** /ara'mɛ:ɪʃ/ *Adj.* Aramaic; **das Aramäische** Aramaic; ⇒ *auch* **deutsch, Deutsch, Deutsche**[2]

**Arancini** /aran'tʃi:ni/, **Aranzini** /aran'tsi:ni/ *Pl.* (*bes. österr.*) *sugar- or chocolate-coated candied orange peel*

**Aräo·meter** /arɛo-/ *das* (*Physik*) hydrometer

**Arbeit** /'arbait/ *die;* ~, ~**en** Ⓐ (*auch Sport, Jagdw., Physik*) work *no indef. art.;* (*Politik, Soziol.: Arbeitskraft*) labour *no indef. art.;* **die** ~[**en**] **am Staudamm** [the] work on the dam; **an die** ~ **gehen, sich an die** ~ **machen** get down to work; **die** ~ **mit Asbest ist gesundheitsschädigend** working with asbestos is injurious to health; **eine widerliche** ~ **sein** be a revolting job *or* task; **die** ~ **läuft uns nicht davon** (*scherzh.*) the work can wait; **ganze** *od.* **gründliche** ~ **leisten** *od.* **tun** *od.* **machen** (*auch fig. iron.*) make a good job of it; **nur halbe** ~ **machen** leave the job half-done; only half do the job; **Tag der** ~: Labour Day; **an** *od.* **bei der** ~ **sein** be at work; **jmdm. bei der** ~ **zusehen** watch sb. working *or* at work; **mit der** ~ **beginnen** start work; **bei der** ~ **mit Chemikalien** when working with chemicals; **viel** ~ **haben** have a lot of work [to do]; **seine** ~ **tun** *od.* **machen** do one's job; **gute** ~ **leisten** do good work; work well; [**wieder**] **an die** ~! [back] to work!; **die** ~ **niederlegen** stop work; (*bei manueller* ~) down tools; **der/die hat die** ~ **nicht erfunden** (*scherzh.*) he/she is not the world's hardest worker; **etw. in** ~ **geben** have sth. made; **jmdm. etw. in** ~ **geben** get sb. to make sth.; **etw. in** ~ **haben** be working on sth.; ~ **schändet nicht** work's no disgrace; **erst die** ~, **dann das Vergnügen** business before pleasure; Ⓑ (*Mühe*) trouble; ~ **machen** cause bother *or* trouble; **jmdm.** ~ **machen** make work for sb.; **machen Sie sich keine** ~! don't go to *or* put yourself to any trouble; **sich** (*Dat.*) ~ [**mit etw.**] **machen** take trouble [over sth.]; **viel** ~ **machen** *od.* **kosten** cost a lot of effort *or* hard work; **das war eine** ~! what a job that was!; Ⓒ (~*splatz*, ~*sstätte*) work *no indef. art.;* (*Stellung*) job; **eine** ~ **suchen/finden** look for/find work *or* a job; **die** ~ **Suchenden** those looking for work; **eine** ~ **als ...** work *or* a job as ...; **zur** *od.* (*ugs.*) **auf** ~ **gehen** go to work; **auf** ~ **sein** (*ugs.*) be at work; **auf** ~ **gehen** (*ugs.: berufstätig sein*) work; have a job; **ohne** ~ **sein** be out of work; be unemployed; **bei jmdm. in** ~ **stehen** *od.* **sein** work for sb.; be employed by sb.; **vor/nach der** ~ (*ugs.*) before/after work; Ⓓ (*Aufträge*) work *no indef. art.;* Ⓔ (*Produkt, Ausführung*) work; (*handwerkliche* ~) piece of work; (*kurze schriftliche* ~) article; (*Dissertation*) dissertation; Ⓕ (*Klassen*~) test; **eine** ~ **schreiben/schreiben lassen** do/set a test

**arbeiten** ❶ *itr. V.* Ⓐ (*Arbeit leisten*) work; **zu** ~ **haben** have work to do; ~ **wie ein Pferd/**(*ugs.*) **ein Wilder** work like a slave *or* a Trojan/(*coll.*) like mad; **er arbeitet für zwei** he does the work of two; **an etw.** (*Dat.*) ~: work on sth.; **an sich** (*Dat.*) ~: work to improve one's abilities; **mit Silber/Akrylfarben** ~: work in silver/acrylic paints; **mit Behinderten/Taubstummen** ~: work with the disabled/the deaf and dumb; **sein Geld** ~ **lassen** (*fig.*) make one's money work for one; Ⓑ (*beruflich tätig sein*) work; **seine Frau arbeitet** his wife has a job *or* works; **40 Stunden in der Woche** ~: work 40 hours a week *or* a 40-hour week; **das Büro arbeitet freitags nur bis** $14^{00}$ (*fig.*) the office closes at 2 p.m. on Fridays; **bei der Bahn/einer Firma** ~: work on the railways (*Brit.*) *or* (*Amer.*) at the railroad/for a firm; Ⓒ **über jmdn./etw.** ~ (*sich befassen mit*) work on sb./sth.; Ⓓ (*wirksam sein*) **für/gegen jmdn./etw.** ~: work for/against sb./sth.; **die Zeit arbeitet für/gegen uns** time is on our side/against us; **an jmds. Untergang** (*Dat.*) ~: work to bring about sb.'s downfall; Ⓔ (*funktionieren*) ‹heart, lungs, etc.› work, function; ‹machine› work, operate; **mit Gas/Sonnenenergie** ~: run on gas/solar energy; **automatisch** ~: be automatic; **in meinem Magen arbeitet es** (*fig.*) my stomach is grumbling; Ⓕ (*ankämpfen*) work hard (**gegen** against); Ⓖ (*sich verändern*) ‹wood› warp; ‹must› ferment; ‹dough› rise; Ⓗ (*Sport*) work (**mit** with); Ⓘ (*schneidern*) **wo/bei wem lassen Sie** ~? where do you have *or* get your clothes made?; who makes your clothes?

❷ *tr. V.* Ⓐ (*herstellen*) make; (*in Ton, Silber, usw.*) work; make; fashion; Ⓑ (*tun*) do; **was** ~ **Sie?** what are you doing?; (*beruflich*) what do you do for a living?; what's your job?

❸ *refl. V.* Ⓐ **sich müde/krank** ~: tire oneself out/make oneself ill with work; **sich zu Tode** ~: work oneself to death; Ⓑ (*Strecke zurücklegen*); **sich durch etw./in etw.** (*Akk.*) ~: work one's way through/into sth.; **sich nach oben** ~ (*fig.*) work one's way up; Ⓒ **sich** (*Dat.*) **die Hände wund** ~: work one's fingers to the bone; Ⓓ *unpers.* **hier arbeitet es sich gut** this is a good place to work; **mit dieser Maschine arbeitet es sich gut/schneller** this machine is easy to work with/the work goes faster with this machine; **mit ihm arbeitet es sich angenehm** it's nice working with him; he's pleasant to work with

**Arbeiter** *der;* ~**s**, ~ ▶ 159 worker; (*Bau*~, *Land*~) labourer; (*beim Straßenbau*) workman; **der** ~ **Karl Müller** the factory worker/labourer/workman Karl Müller; **wir suchen** ~ **und Arbeiterinnen für folgende Bereiche** we are looking for men and women to work in the following areas; ~ **und Arbeiterinnen werden oft ...** male and female workers are often ...; **die** ~ (*als Klasse*) the workers

**arbeiter-, Arbeiter-:** ~**auf·stand** *der* workers' rebellion *or* revolt; ~**bewegung** *die* (*Politik*) labour movement; ~**biene** *die* (*Zool.*) worker [bee]; ~**denkmal** *das* Ⓐ workers' monument; monument to the working classes; Ⓑ (*ugs. scherzh.*) monument to inactivity (*joc.*); ~**dichter** *der*, ~**dichterin** *die* poet of the working class; ~**familie** *die* working-class family; ~**feindlich** *Adj.* anti-working-class; ~**freundlich** *Adj.* favouring the workers *postpos.;* ~**führer** *der*, ~**führerin** *die* workers' leader; ~**gewerkschaft** *die* trade union (*Brit.*); labor union (*Amer.*)

**Arbeiterin** *die;* ~, ~**nen** ▶ 159 (*auch Zool.*) worker; ⇒ *auch* **Arbeiter**

**Arbeiter-:** ~**jugend** *die* young working people; (*Organisation*) labour youth movement *or* organization; ~**kampf·lied** *das* workers' [rallying] song; ~**kind** *das* working-class child; ~**klasse** *die* working class[es *pl.*]; ~**kontrolle** *die* (*bes. DDR*) worker control; ~**lied** *das* workers' song; ~**massen** *Pl.* working masses; ~**milieu** *das* working-class environment; **aus dem** ~**milieu stammen** come from a working-class environment *or* background; ~**organisation** *die* labour organization; ~**partei** *die* workers' party; ~**priester** *der*, ~**priesterin** *die* worker-priest; ~**rat** *der* workers' council

**Arbeiterschaft** *die;* ~: workers *pl.;* **aus der** ~: from among the workers

**Arbeiter-:** ~**schriftsteller** *der*, ~**schriftstellerin** *die* worker-writer; working-class writer; ~**selbstverwaltung** *die* workers' control *no indef. art.;* (*Gremium*) workers' management committee; **in** ~**selbstverwaltung arbeiten** be under workers' control;

**~siedlung** *die* workers' housing estate (*Brit.*) *or* (*Amer.*) housing development; **~stadt** *die* workers' town; (*ugs.: Industriestadt, in der viele Arbeiter leben*) working-class town; **~student** *der* (*DDR*) worker-student; **~-und-Bauern-Fakultät** *die* (*DDR*) workers and farmers' faculty (*preparing young workers for university study*); **~-und-Bauern-Inspektion** *die* (*DDR*) *body charged with monitoring the implementation of party and Government policy in economic and social affairs;* **~-und-Bauern-Staat** *der* (*DDR*) workers' and farmers' state; **~-und-Soldaten-Rat** *der* (*hist.*) workers' and soldiers' council; **~unruhen** *Pl.* unrest *sing.* among the workers; **~verein** *der* workers' association; **~verräter** *der*, **~verräterin** *die* (*Politik abwertend*) traitor to the working class; **~viertel** *das* working-class district *or* area; **~wohl·fahrt** *die* workers' welfare association

**Arbeit·geber** *der* employer

**Arbeitgeber·anteil** *der* employer's contribution

**Arbeitgeberin** *die;* ~, **~nen** [female] employer; ⇒ *auch* **-in**

**Arbeitgeber-: ~seite** *die* employers' side; **~verband** *der* employers' association *or* organization

**Arbeitnehmer** *der;* **~s, ~:** employee

**Arbeitnehmer·anteil** *der* employee's contribution

**Arbeitnehmerin** *die;* ~, **~nen** [female] employee; ⇒ *auch* **-in**

**Arbeitnehmer-: ~organisation** *die* workers' organization; **~seite** *die* employees' side

**Arbeits·ab·lauf** *der* programme of work

**arbeitsam** *Adj.* (*geh. veralt.*) Ⓐ (*fleißig*) industrious; hard-working; Ⓑ (*von Arbeit erfüllt*) **ein ~es Leben** a life of hard work; **ein paar ~e Monate vor sich haben** have a few months of hard work ahead of one

**arbeits-, Arbeits-: ~amt** *das* job centre (*Brit.*); employment exchange; labour exchange (*Brit. dated*); **~an·fall** *der* volume of work; **~an·fang** *der* starting time [at work]; **~anfang ist um 6 Uhr** work starts at 6 a.m.; **~an·leitung** *die* instructions *pl.*; **~an·tritt** *die* **vor ~antritt** before starting work *or* the/a job; **bei ~antritt** when you start/he starts *etc.* work; **~an·zug** *der* working clothes *pl.*; **blauer ~anzug** blue overalls *pl.*; **~atmosphäre** *die* working atmosphere; **~auf·fassung** *die* attitude to one's work; **~aufwand** *der:* **mit großem ~aufwand** with a great deal of work; **das wäre mir zu viel ~aufwand** it would be *or* involve too much work [for me]; **~auf·wendig** ❶ *Adj.* requiring a great deal of work *postpos.*, *not pred.*; **[sehr] ~aufwendig sein** require a great deal of work; ❷ *adv.* in a way that requires/required a great deal of work; **~aus·fall** *der* loss of working hours; **ein ~ausfall von einigen Wochen** a loss of several working weeks; **~bedingungen** *Pl.* working conditions; **~beginn** *der* ⇒ **~anfang**; **~belastung** *die* workload; **~bereich** *der* Ⓐ (*Tätigkeit*) area of work; (**~gebiet**) field of work; **das gehört nicht in meinen ~bereich** that's not part of my job; Ⓑ (*im Raum*) working area; Ⓒ (*eines Krans*) working radius; **~beschaffung** *die* job creation; creation of employment; **~beschaffungs·maßnahme** *die* job-creation measure; **~beschaffungs·programm** *das* job-creation programme; **~bescheinigung** *die* certificate of employment (*issued to employee on leaving job, and listing responsibilities, length of service, etc.*); **~biene** *die* Ⓐ (*Zool.*) worker bee; Ⓑ (*ugs.: emsige Frau*) busy bee; **~dienst** *der* Ⓐ (*Arbeit*) (*low-paid*) community-service work; Ⓑ (*Organisation*) community service agency; Ⓒ ⇒ **Reichsarbeitsdienst**; **~direktor** *der*, **~direktorin** *die* personnel director (*with special responsibility for safeguarding the interests of the employees within the framework of co-determination*); **~disziplin** *die* discipline in one's approach to work; **~eifer** *der* enthusiasm for one's work; **~ende** *das* finishing time [at work]; **nach/bei ~ende** after work/when it's time to go; **um fünf Uhr haben wir** *od.* **ist bei uns ~ende** we finish work at five o'clock; **~erlaubnis** *die* work permit; **~erleichternd** ❶ *Adj.* labour-saving; ❷ *adv.* in a labour-saving way; **~erleichterung** *die* saving of labour; **eine große ~erleichterung für jmdn. sein** make sb.'s work a great deal easier; save sb. a great deal of work; **~essen** *das* (*bes. Politik*) working lunch/dinner; **~ethos** *das* work ethic; **~fähig** *Adj.* fit for work *postpos.*; (*grundsätzlich*) able to work *postpos.*; viable ‹government›; **~fähigkeit** *die* fitness for work; (*grundsätzlich*) ability to work; **~feld** *das* (*geh.*) field of work; **~frei** *Adj.* **ein paar Tage/eine Woche ~frei** a few days/a week off; **Montag ist/haben wir ~frei** we've got Monday off; **~freude** *die* enthusiasm for one's work; **~friede** (*geh.*), **~frieden** *der* industrial peace; peaceful labour *or* industrial relations *pl.*; **~früh·stück** *das* working breakfast; **~gang** *der* Ⓐ (*einzelne Operation*) operation; Ⓑ (*Ablauf*) process; **~gebiet** *das* field of work; **~gemeinschaft** *die* team; (*Hochschulw.*) study group; **~genehmigung** *die* work permit; **~gerät** *das* Ⓐ (*Gegenstand*) tool; Ⓑ (*Gesamtheit*) tools *pl.*; equipment *no indef. art.*, *no pl.*; **~gericht** *das* industrial tribunal; **~gruppe** *die* study group; **~haus** *das* (*hist.*) *correctional institution for minor offenders where prisoners are required to work;* workhouse (*Amer.*); **~hypothese** *die* working hypothesis; **~intensiv** (*Wirtsch.*) ❶ *Adj.* labour-intensive; ❷ *adv.* labour-intensively; **~kampf** *der* industrial action; **~kampfmaßnahme** *die* form of industrial action; **~kleidung** *die* work clothes *pl.*; **~klima** *das* working atmosphere; **~kollege** *der*, **~kollegin** *die* (*bei Arbeitern*) workmate (*Brit.*); fellow worker; (*bei Angestellten, Beamten*) colleague; **~kraft** *die* Ⓐ (*Vermögen zu arbeiten*) capacity for work; **seine ~kraft verkaufen** sell one's labour; **die menschliche ~kraft wird durch Roboter ersetzt** human labour is being replaced by robots; Ⓑ (*Mensch*) worker; **~kreis** *der* study group; **~lager** *das* labour camp; **~last** *die* burden of work; **~leben** *das* Ⓐ (*Berufstätigkeit*) working life; Ⓑ (*Arbeitswelt*) world of work; working life *no art.*; **~leistung** *die* rate of output; **~lohn** *der* wage; wages *pl.*; (*auf einer Rechnung*) labour [costs *pl.*]; **~los** *Adj.* Ⓐ unemployed; out of work *postpos.*; Ⓑ *in* **~loses Einkommen** unearned income

**Arbeitslose** *der/die; adj. Dekl.* unemployed person/man/woman *etc.*; **die ~n** the unemployed *or* jobless; **es gab 2 Mio. ~:** there were 2 million [people] unemployed *or* out of work; **viele ~:** many unemployed people; many people who are/were unemployed *or* out of work

**Arbeitslosen-: ~geld** *das* (*full-rate*) earnings-related unemployment benefit; **~heer** *das* army of unemployed; **~hilfe** *die* Ⓐ (*Geld*) reduced-rate unemployment benefit; Ⓑ (*Institution*) reduced-rate unemployment benefit system; **~unterstützung** *die* (*volkst.*) unemployment benefit *or* pay; **~versicherung** *die* unemployment insurance; **~ziffer** *die* unemployment figures *pl.*

**arbeits-, Arbeits-: ~losigkeit** *die;* **~~:** unemployment *no indef. art.*; **eine ~losigkeit von 0,5%** a level of unemployment of 0.5%; **~mangel** *der* lack of work; **~markt** *der* labour market; **~material** *das* materials *pl.*; (*einschließlich Werkzeugen*) materials [and equipment *or* tools]; (*für den Unterricht*) teaching aids *pl.*; **~medizin** *die* occupational medicine and health care; **~methode** *die* working method; method of working; **~minister** *der*, **~ministerin** *die* minister for employment; Secretary for Employment (*Brit.*); Secretary of Labor (*Amer.*); **~ministerium** *das* ministry for employment; Department of Employment (*Brit.*); Department of Labor (*Amer.*); **~mittel** *das* material; (*Werkzeug, Wörterbuch usw.*) tool; **~mittel** *Pl.* materials/tools; (*Schreibzeug*) materials; **~moral** *die* morale of the workers/staff; **~nachweis** *der* Ⓐ (*das Nachweisen*) information *no indef. art.* about situations vacant; Ⓑ (*Stelle*) employment office; **~niederlegung** *die* walkout; **mit ~niederlegungen drohen** threaten walkouts; **~ordnung** *die* Ⓐ (*Einteilung*) organization of the work; Ⓑ (*Regelung des Betriebsablaufs*) [office/factory/shop] regulations *pl.*; **~organisation** *die* organization of the/one's work; **~ort** *der* place of work; **~papier** *das* Ⓐ (*Thesenblatt*) working paper; Ⓑ *Pl.* (*das Arbeitsverhältnis betreffende Papiere*) employment papers

**arbeit·sparend** ❶ *Adj.* labour-saving. ❷ in a labour-saving way

**Arbeits-: ~pause** *die* break; **eine ~pause machen** take a break; **~pensum** *das* work quota; **~pferd** *das* (*auch fig.*) workhorse; **~plan** *der* work plan *or* schedule; **~platz** *der* Ⓐ (*Platz im Betrieb*) workplace; **am ~platz** at one's workplace; Ⓑ (**~stätte**) place of work; **den ~platz wechseln** change one's place of work; Ⓒ (**~verhältnis**) job; **~platz·sicherung** *die* safeguarding of jobs; **zur ~platzsicherung** to safeguard jobs; **~platz·studie** *die* job study; **~platz·wechsel** *der* change of job; **~probe** *die* sample of one's work; **~prozess**, ***~prozeß** *der* Ⓐ (*Berufstätigkeit*) **im ~prozess stehen** be in employment; have a job; **jmdn. wieder in den ~prozess eingliedern** get sb. back to work; Ⓑ (**~ablauf**) work process; **~raum** *der* Ⓐ workroom; (*Büroraum*) office; Ⓑ ⇒ **Arbeitszimmer**; **~recht** *das* labour law; **~rechtlich** *Adj.* **~rechtliche Fragen/Literatur** issues relating to/literature on labour law; **ein ~rechtlicher Streitfall** a dispute concerning labour law; **~reich** *Adj.* ‹life, week, etc.› full of hard work; **~richter** *der*, **~richterin** *die: judge on an industrial tribunal;* **~ruhe** *die* break [from work]; **gestern herrschte in ganz Italien ~ruhe** commerce and industry was at a standstill throughout Italy yesterday; **~sache** *die* Ⓐ *Pl.* work things; Ⓑ *Pl.* (*Kleidung*) work[ing] things *or* clothes; Ⓒ (*Rechtsw.*) labour law dispute; **~scheu** *Adj.* work-shy; **~schluss**, ***~schluß** *der* ⇒ **~ende**; **~schutz** *der* protection of health and safety standards at work; **~schutz·bestimmung** *die* regulation concerning [the protection of] health and safety at work; **~sitzung** *die* working session; **~sklave** *der* slave labourer; **als ~sklaven verkauft werden** be sold as slave labour; **~soziologie** *die* occupational sociology; **~speicher** *der* (*DV*) main memory; **~stätte** *die* Ⓐ (*geh.*) **das war Beethovens/Schillers ~stätte** this is [the place] where Beethoven/Schiller worked *or* did his work; Ⓑ (*Stätte beruflicher Tätigkeit*) place of work; **~stelle** *die* Ⓐ ⇒ **Arbeitsstätte** B; Ⓑ (*Job*) ⇒ **Stelle** G; Ⓒ (*Abteilung*) department; **~stil** *der* style of working; **~studie** *die* work study; **~stunde** *die* hour of work; **2 ~stunden** (*bei Reparaturen usw.*) two hours' labour; **die Herstellung erfordert 2 000 ~stunden** manufacture takes 2, 000 man-hours; **~suche** *die* search for a job *or* for work; **auf ~suche sein** be looking for a job; **~süchtig** *Adj.* **~süchtig sein** be a compulsive worker *or* (*coll.*) a workaholic; **~tag** *der* working day; **mein erster ~tag nach dem Urlaub** my first day back at work after the holiday (*Brit.*) *or* (*Amer.*) vacation; **das war ein harter ~tag** that was a hard day's work; **~tagung** *die* conference; **~takt** *der* (*Technik*) power stroke; **~team** *das* team; **~technik** *die* work[ing] technique; **~teilig** ❶ *Adj.* ‹society, mode of production, etc.› based on the division of labour; ❷ *adv.* **die Produktion ~teilig gestalten** base production on the principle of the division of labour; **~teilung** *die* division of labour; **~tempo** *das* rate of work; work rate; **~therapie** *die* occupational therapy; **~tier** *das* Ⓐ work animal; Ⓑ (*Arbeitssüchtiger*) compulsive worker; workaholic (*coll.*); **~tisch** *der* work table; (*für Schreibarbeiten*) desk; (*für technische Arbeiten*) [work]bench; **~titel** *der* working title; **~überlastung** *die*

*old spelling (see note on page 1707)

overwork; **er klagt über ~überlastung** he complains that he's overworked

**Arbeit-: ~suche** *die* ⇒ **Arbeitssuche; ~suchende** *der/die; adj. Dekl.* person/man/woman looking for work; **die ~suchenden** those looking for work

**arbeits-, Arbeits-: ~unfähig** *Adj.* unable to work *postpos.;* (*krankheitsbedingt*) unfit for work *postpos.;* **die Arbeitsunfähigen** those unable to work/unfit for work; **~unfähigkeit** *die* ⇒ **~unfähig**: inability to work; unfitness for work; **~un·fall** *der* industrial accident; **er hatte einen ~unfall** he had an accident at work; **~un·lust** *die* disinclination to work; **~unter·lage** *die* work paper; **das benutzt er als ~unterlage** he works from that; **~un·willig** *Adj.* unwilling to work *postpos.;* **~verfahren** *das* work process; **~verhältnis** *das* [A] *contractual relationship between employer and employee;* **ein ~verhältnis eingehen** enter employment; **in einem ~verhältnis stehen** be in employment; [B] *Pl.* working conditions; conditions of work; **~vermittlung** *die* [A] (*Tätigkeit*) arranging employment; [B] (*Stelle*) employment exchange; job centre (*Brit.*); (*Firma*) employment agency; **~verteilung** *die* allocation of [the] work; **~vertrag** *der* contract of employment; **~verweigerung** *die* refusal to work; **~vor·gang** *der* work process; **~vor·lage** *die:* **eine Skizze als ~vorlage benutzen** work from a sketch; **dieses Buch hat ihm als ~vorlage gedient** he worked from that book; **~weise** *die* [A] way *or* method of working; [B] (*Funktionsweise*) mode of operation; **~welt** *die* world of work; **~willig** *Adj.* **~willig sein** be willing to work; **~willige Kollegen** fellow employees who are willing to work; **~wissenschaft** *die* ergonomics *sing.;* **~woche** *die* [A] week's work; **während seiner ersten ~woche** during his first week at work; [B] (*wöchentliche ~zeit*) working week; **~wut** *die* fit of work-mania; **~wütig** *Adj.* **~wütig sein** suffer from work-mania; **~zeit** *die* [A] working hours *pl.;* **während der ~zeit** during working hours; **die ~zeit beginnt um 8 Uhr** work starts at 8 o'clock; [B] working time; **die tägliche/wöchentliche ~zeit** the working day/week; [C] (*als Ware*) labour time; **2 Stunden ~zeit** two hours' labour; **wir berechnen keine ~zeit** we don't charge for labour; **ich lasse mir die ~zeit bezahlen** I charge for my time; **~zeit·verkürzung** *die* reduction in working hours; **~zeug** *das* [A] work things *pl.;* [B] (*Kleidung*) work[ing] things *pl. or* clothes *pl.;* **~zeugnis** *das* reference [from one's employer]; **~zimmer** *das* study

**arbiträr** /arbi'trɛ:ɐ̯/ (*geh.*) ❶ *Adj.* arbitrary. ❷ *adv.* in an arbitrary way; arbitrarily

**archaisch** /ar'ça:ɪʃ/ ❶ *Adj.* archaic. ❷ *adv.* in an archaic way; archaically

**archaisieren** *itr. V.* (*geh.*) archaize; **eine ~de Sprache verwenden** use *or* employ an archaistic *or* a deliberately archaic style

**Archaismus** *der;* ~, **Archaismen** (*Sprachw., Stilk., Kunstw.*) archaism

**Archäologe** /arçɛo'lo:gə/ *der;* **~n, ~n** ▶ 159 archaeologist

**Archäologie** *die;* **~:** archaeology *no art.*

**Archäologin** *die;* ~, **~nen** ▶ 159 archaeologist

**archäologisch** ❶ *Adj.* archaeological. ❷ *adv.* archaeologically

**Arche** /'arçə/ *die;* ~, **~n** ark; **die ~ Noah** Noah's Ark

**Arche·typ** *der* (*Psych., Philos.*) archetype

**arche·typisch** (*Psych., Philos.*) ❶ *Adj.* archetypal. ❷ *adv.* archetypally

**Arche·typus** *der* ⇒ **Archetyp**

**Archimedes** /arçi'me:dɛs/ (*der*) Archimedes

**archimedisch** *Adj.* Archimedean; **das ~e Prinzip** Archimedes' Principle

**Archipel** /arçi'pe:l/ *der;* **~s, ~e** archipelago; **„der ~ Gulag"** 'the Gulag archipelago'

**Architekt** /arçi'tɛkt/ *der;* **~en, ~en** ▶ 159 architect

**Architekten·büro** *das* [A] architect's office; [B] (*Firma*) firm of architects

**Architektin** *die;* ~, **~nen** ▶ 159 architect

**Architektonik** /arçitɛk'to:nɪk/ *die;* ~, **~en** architectonics *sing., no art.*

**architektonisch** ❶ *Adj.* architectonic. ❷ *adv.* architectonically

**Architektur** /arçitɛk'tu:ɐ̯/ *die;* ~, **~en** [A] architecture; [B] (*Bauwerk*) edifice

**Archiv** /ar'çi:f/ *das;* **~s, ~e** archives *pl.;* archive

**Archivalien** /arçi'va:li̯ən/ *Pl.* papers and documents in/from the archives

**Archivar** /arçi'va:ɐ̯/ *der;* **~s, ~e, Archivarin** *die;* ~, **~nen** ▶ 159 archivist

**Archiv·bild** *das* archive picture *or* photograph

**archivieren** *tr. V.* **etw. ~:** archive sth.; put sth. in the archives

**Archivierung** *die;* ~, **~en** archiving

**ARD** *Abk.* **Arbeitsgemeinschaft der öffentlich-rechtlichen Rundfunkanstalten der Bundesrepublik Deutschland** *national radio and television network in Germany*

**Ardennen** /ar'dɛnən/ *Pl.* **die ~:** the Ardennes

**Ardennen·offensive** *die* (*hist.*) Ardennes offensive

**Are** /'a:rə/ *die;* ~, **~n** (*schweiz.*) ⇒ **Ar**

**Areal** /are'a:l/ *das;* **~s, ~e** [A] area; [B] (*Grundstück*) grounds *pl.;* [C] (*Biol.*) range

**areligiös** *Adj.* areligious

**Ären** ⇒ **Ära**

**Arena** /a're:na/ *die;* ~, **Arenen** [A] (*hist., Sport, fig.*) arena; [B] (*Stierkampf~*) bullring; [C] (*Manege*) [circus] ring

**Areopag** /areo'pa:k/ *der;* **~s** (*hist.*) Areopagus

**arg** /ark/, **ärger** /'ɛrgɐ /,/ **ärgst...** /'ɛrgst.../ ❶ *Adj.* [A] (*geh., landsch.: schlimm*) bad ‹weather, condition, state›; serious ‹situation, wound›; hard ‹times›; extremely hackneyed ‹cliché›; **etw. noch ärger machen** make sth. worse; **an nichts Arges denken** be completely unsuspecting; **das Ärgste befürchten** fear the worst; **wenn es zum Ärgsten kommt** if the worst comes to the worst; **im ~en liegen** be in a sorry state; [B] (*geh. veralt.: böse*) wicked; evil; **es ist nichts Arges an ihm** there is no malice in him; [C] (*geh., landsch.: unangenehm groß, stark*) severe ‹pain, hunger, shock›; severe, bitter ‹disappointment›; serious ‹dilemma, error›; extreme, (*coll.*) terrible ‹embarrassment›; gross ‹exaggeration, injustice›; heavy ‹drinker›; **in ~er Bedrängnis/Not sein** be in desperate straits; **mein ärgster Feind** my worst enemy *or* arch-enemy; **unser ärgster Konkurrent** our most dangerous competitor; **es herrschte ein ~es Gedränge** there was a dreadful crush (*coll.*).
❷ *adv.* (*geh., landsch.*) extremely, (*coll.*) awfully, (*coll.*) terribly ‹painful, cold, steep, expensive, heavy, etc.›; severely, bitterly ‹disappointed›; extremely, (*coll.*) terribly ‹embarassed›; ‹suffer, weaken› severely; ‹offend› deeply; ‹deceive› badly; ‹rain, pull, punch› hard; ‹hurt› a great deal; **der Garten ist ~ verwahrlost** the garden is badly neglected; **sich ~ blamieren** make a complete fool of oneself; **ihr treibt es gar zu ~!** you're going too far!; **etwas ~ laut** a bit too loud; **ich hab ihn ~ gern** I like him very much *or* (*coll.*) an awful lot; **hast du es ~ eilig?** are you in a great *or* (*coll.*) terrible hurry?; **es geht ihm ~ schlecht/gut** things are going really badly/well for him; **Schmeckt dir das Bier? — Nicht so ~:** Do you like the beer? — Not that much

**Arg** *das;* **~s** (*geh. veralt.*) malice; **kein ~ an der Sache finden** see no harm in it

**Argentinien** /argɛn'ti:ni̯ən/ (*das*); **~s** Argentina; the Argentine

**Argentinier** *der;* **~s, ~, Argentinierin** *die;* ~, **~nen** ▶ 553 Argentinian; Argentine; ⇒ *auch* **-in**

**argentinisch** *Adj.* ▶ 553 Argentinian; Argentine

**ärger** ⇒ **arg**

**Ärger** /'ɛrgɐ/ *der;* **~s** [A] annoyance; (*Zorn*) anger; **etw. erregt jmds. ~:** sth. annoys sb.; **seinem ~ Luft machen** vent one's anger; **seinen ~ an jmdm. auslassen** vent one's anger on sb.; [B] (*Unannehmlichkeiten*) trouble; **häuslicher/beruflicher ~:** domestic problems *pl.*/problems *pl.* at work; **[jmdm.] ~ machen** cause [sb.] trouble; make trouble [for sb.]; **so ein ~!** how annoying!; **~ bekommen** get into trouble; **sonst gibt es ~:** otherwise there'll be trouble!

**ärgerlich** ❶ *Adj.* [A] annoyed; (*zornig*) angry; **ein ~es Gesicht machen** look annoyed/angry; **~ über jmdn. sein** be annoyed at/angry with sb.; **~ über etw.** (*Akk.*) **sein** be annoyed/angry about sth.; **~ über sich selbst** annoyed/angry at oneself; **~ werden** get angry/annoyed; [B] (*Ärger erregend*) annoying; irritating; **wie ~!** how annoying! ❷ *adv.* [A] with annoyance; (*zornig*) angrily; [B] (*Ärger erregend*) annoyingly; irritatingly

**Ärgerlichkeit** *die;* ~ [A] annoyance; (*Zorn*) anger; [B] (*einer Sache*) troublesomeness; **bei aller ~ war es doch von Vorteil** even though it was annoying, it was still an advantage

**ärgern** ❶ *tr. V.* [A] **jmdn. ~:** annoy sb.; (*zornig machen*) make sb. angry; **so was ärgert einen natürlich** that sort of thing is annoying, of course; [B] (*reizen, necken*) tease. ❷ *refl. V.* get annoyed; (*zornig werden*) get angry; (*verärgert sein*) be annoyed/angry; **sich über jmdn. ~:** get annoyed/angry at sb.; **sich zu Tode ~** (*fig.*) be annoyed/angry to the point of distraction; **sich schwarz** *od.* **grün und blau ~:** fret and fume; **nicht ~, nur wundern!** (*ugs.*) there's no point in getting worked *or* (*coll.*) het up about it

**Ärgernis** *das;* **~ses, ~se** [A] offence; **Erregung öffentlichen ~ses** (*Rechtsspr.*) creating a public nuisance; [B] (*etw. Ärgerliches*) annoyance; irritation; **häusliche/berufliche ~se** minor domestic troubles/irritations and annoyances at work; [C] (*etw. Anstößiges*) nuisance; (*etw. Skandalöses*) scandal; outrage

**arg-, Arg-: ~list** *die* (*geh.*) (*Hinterlist*) guile; deceit; (*Heimtücke, Rechtsw.*) malice; **~listig** ❶ *Adj.* (*hinterlistig*) guileful; deceitful; deceitful ‹plan›; (*heimtückisch*) malicious; crafty ‹smile›; **~listige Täuschung** (*Rechtsspr.*) malicious deception; ❷ *adv.* (*hinterlistig*) guilefully; deceitfully; (*heimtückisch*) maliciously; ‹smile› craftily; **~listigkeit** *die;* **~~, ~~en** [A] (*Hinterlistigkeit*) guilefulness; deceitfulness; (*eines Plans, einer Absicht*) deceitfulness; (*Heimtücke*) malice; [B] (*arglistige Handlung*) ⇒ **arglistig** A: guileful *or* deceitful/malicious act; **~los** ❶ *Adj.* [A] guileless ‹person›; guileless, innocent ‹question, remark›; [B] (*ohne Argwohn*) unsuspecting; **~los, wie ich war ...** all unsuspecting as I was ...; **wie kannst du nur so ~los sein?** how can you be so naïve?; ❷ *adv.* [A] guilelessly; innocently; [B] (*ohne Argwohn*) unsuspectingly; **~losigkeit** *die;* ~ [A] (*eines Menschen*) guilelessness; (*einer Äußerung, Absicht*) innocence; **ich bin von seiner ~losigkeit überzeugt** I'm convinced he is not being deceitful/malicious; [B] (*Vertrauensseligkeit*) unsuspecting nature

**Argon** /'argɔn/ *das;* **~s** (*Chemie*) argon

**ärgst...** ⇒ **arg**

**Argument** /argu'mɛnt/ *das;* **~[e]s, ~e** (*auch Math.*) argument

**Argumentation** /argumɛnta'tsi̯o:n/ *die;* ~, **~en** argumentation

**argumentativ** /argumɛnta'ti:f/ ❶ *Adj.* **ein ~er Wahlkampf** an election campaign marked by reasoned argument; **eine rein ~e Auseinandersetzung** a conflict based solely on reasoned argument. ❷ *adv.* by [reasoned] argument; **er ist ihr ~ überlegen** he is superior to her in argument

**argumentieren** *itr. V.* argue; **damit kannst du nicht ~!** you can't use that as an argument

**Argus·augen** /'argʊs-/ *Pl.* (*geh.*) eagle eye *sing.;* **jmdn. mit ~ beobachten** watch sb. like a hawk

**Argwohn** /'arkwo:n/ *der;* **~[e]s** suspicion; **jmds. ~ erregen/zerstreuen** arouse/allay sb.'s suspicions *pl.*; ~ **gegen jmdn. hegen** be suspicious of sb.; ⇒ *auch* **schöpfen** 1 C

**argwöhnen** /'arkwø:nən/ *tr. V.* (*geh.*) suspect; **sie argwöhnten einen Verräter in ihm** they suspected him of being a traitor

**argwöhnisch** (*geh.*) ❶ *Adj.* suspicious. ❷ *adv.* suspiciously

**Aridität** /aridi'tɛ:t/ *die;* ~ (*Geogr.*) aridity

**Arie** /'a:ri̯ə/ *die;* ~, ~**n** aria

**Arier** /'a:ri̯ɐ/ *der;* ~**s**, ~, **Arierin** *die;* ~, ~**nen** (*Völkerk., Sprachw., ns.*) Aryan

**arisch** *Adj.* (*Völkerk., Sprachw., ns.*) Aryan

**arisieren** *tr. V.* (*ns.*) Aryanize

**Aristokrat** /arɪsto'kra:t/ *der;* ~**en**, ~**en** aristocrat

**Aristokratie** /arɪstokra'ti:/ *die;* ~, ~**n** aristocracy

**Aristokratin** *die;* ~, ~**nen** aristocrat

**aristokratisch** ❶ *Adj.* aristocratic. ❷ *adv.* aristocratically

**Aristoteles** /arɪs'to:telɛs/ (*der*) Aristotle

**Aristoteliker** /arɪsto'te:likɐ/ *der;* ~**s**, ~, **Aristotelikerin** *die;* ~, ~**nen** Aristotelian

**aristotelisch** *Adj.* Aristotelian

**Arithmetik** /arɪt'me:tɪk/ *die;* ~, ~**en** Ⓐ arithmetic *no art.*; Ⓑ (*Buch*) textbook on arithmetic

**arithmetisch** ❶ *Adj.* arithmetical. ❷ *adv.* arithmetically

**Arkade** /ar'ka:də/ *die;* ~, ~**n** Ⓐ arch; **in** *od.* **unter den** ~**n** under the arcade; Ⓑ (*Bogenreihe, Gang*) arcade

**arkadisch** *Adj.* (*dichter.*) Arcadian

**Arktis** /'arktɪs/ *die;* ~ (*Geogr.*) **die** ~: the Arctic

**arktisch** ❶ *Adj.* (*auch fig.*) arctic. ❷ *adv.* **das Klima ist** ~ **beeinflusst** the climate is influenced by the Arctic

**Arkus** /'arkʊs/ *der;* ~, ~ /'arku:s/ (*Geom.*) arc

**arm** /arm/, **ärmer** /'ɛrmɐ/, **ärmst...** /'ɛrmst.../ *Adj.* (*auch fig.*) poor; **wir sind um 100 Mark ärmer** we are 100 marks worse off *or* [the] poorer; **Arm und Reich** (*veralt.*) rich and poor [alike]; **die Gegensätze zwischen Arm und Reich** the differences between rich and poor; **selig sind, die da geistlich** ~ **sind** (*bibl.*) blessed are the poor in spirit; **um etw. ärmer sein/werden** have lost/lose sth.; ~ **an Bodenschätzen/Nährstoffen** poor in mineral resources/nutrients; **das Gebiet ist** ~ **an Wasser** the area is short of water; ~ **an Vitaminen sein** ‹food› be lacking in *or* low in vitamins; **der/die Ärmste** *od.* **Arme** the poor man/boy/woman/girl; **ach, du Armer** *od.* **Ärmster!** (*meist iron.*) oh, you poor thing!; **ich Armer!** (*dichter. veralt.*) woe is me!; ⇒ *auch* **dran** B

**Arm** *der;* ~[**e**]**s**, ~**e** Ⓐ ▸ 471 arm; **jmdn. am** ~ **führen** lead sb. by the arm; **er nahm** *od.* (*geh.*) **schloss sie in die** ~**e** he took her in his arms; **jmdm. in die** ~**e fallen** *od.* (*geh.*) **sinken** fall *or* sink into sb.'s arms; **nimm mich auf den** ~**!** carry me!; **etw. unter den** ~ **nehmen** put sth. under one's arm; **einen Mantel über dem** ~ **tragen** carry a coat over one's arm; **jmds.** ~ **nehmen** take sb.'s arm; take sb. by the arm; **jmdm. den** ~ **bieten** (*geh.*) offer sb. one's arm; **jmdn. im** ~ **halten** embrace sb.; **sich** (*Dat.*) **in den** ~**en liegen** lie in each other's *or* one another's arms; **sich aus jmds.** ~**en lösen** (*geh.*) free oneself from sb.'s embrace; **er hat einen langen** ~ (*fig.*) his power and influence extend a long way; **den längeren** ~ **haben** (*fig. ugs.*) have more clout (*coll.*); **jmds. verlängerter** ~ **sein** (*fig.*) be sb.'s tool *or* instrument; **jmdn. auf den** ~ **nehmen** (*fig. ugs.*) have sb. on (*Brit. coll.*); pull sb.'s leg; **jmdm. in den** ~ **fallen** (*fig.*) stay sb.'s hand; **jmdm. in die** ~**e laufen** bump *or* run into sb.; **er ist mir in die** ~**e gelaufen** I bumped *or* ran into him; **jmdn. jmdm. in die** ~**e treiben** drive sb. into sb.'s arms; **jmdn. dem Alkoholismus/Terrorismus in die** ~**e treiben** drive sb. to alcoholism/to adopt terrorist tactics; **sich jmdm. in die** ~**e werfen** throw oneself into sb.'s arms; **jmdn. mit offenen** ~**en aufnehmen** *od.* **empfangen** welcome sb. with open arms; **jmdm. [mit etw.] unter die** ~**e greifen** help sb. out [with sth.]; **jmdn. am steifen** ~ **verhungern lassen** (*salopp*) put the screws (*coll.*) *or* (*coll.*) squeeze on sb.; **ein** ~/**zwei** ~**e voll Reisig** an armful/two armfuls of brushwood; ⇒ *auch* **Bein** A; Ⓑ (*armartiger Teil*) arm; (*einer Waage*) beam; Ⓒ (*Ärmel*) arm; sleeve; **ein Hemd/eine Bluse mit halbem** ~: a short-sleeved shirt/blouse

**Armada** /ar'ma:da/ *die;* ~, **Armaden** *u.* ~**s** (*auch fig.*) armada

**arm·amputiert** *Adj.* ‹person› with an *or* one arm/both [his/her] arms amputated; **er ist** ~: he has had an arm/both [his] arms amputated

**Armatur** /arma'tu:ɐ̯/ *die;* ~, ~**en** (*Technik*) Ⓐ fitting; Ⓑ (*im Kfz*) instrument

**Armaturen·brett** *das* instrument panel; (*im Kfz*) dashboard

**Arm-:** ~**band** *das; Pl.* ~**bänder** bracelet; (*Uhr*~) strap; ~**band·uhr** *die* wristwatch; ~**beuge** *die* ▸ 471 Ⓐ inside of the/one's elbow; crook of the/one's arm; Ⓑ (*Turnen*) press-up (*Brit.*); push-up; ~**bewegung** *die* arm movement; ~**binde** *die* Ⓐ armband; Ⓑ (*Med.*) sling; ~**bruch** *der* fracture of the arm; **er wurde mit einem** ~**bruch ins Krankenhaus gebracht** he was taken to hospital with a fractured arm; ~**brust** *die* crossbow

**Ärmchen** /'ɛrmçən/ *das;* ~**s**, ~: [little] arm

**Arme** *der/die; adj. Dekl.* poor man/woman; pauper; **die** ~**n** the poor *pl*; ⇒ *auch* **arm**

**Armee** /ar'me:/ *die;* ~, ~**n** Ⓐ (*Streitkräfte*) armed forces *pl.*; Ⓑ (*Landstreitkräfte, Verband, fig.*) army

**Armee-:** ~**fahrzeug** *das* army vehicle; ~**korps** *das* army corps

**Ärmel** /'ɛrməl/ *der;* ~**s**, ~: sleeve; **die** ~ **hochkrempeln** (*fig. ugs.*) roll up one's sleeves; **[sich** (*Dat.*)**] etw. aus dem** ~ **schütteln** (*ugs.*) produce sth. just like that; **leck mich am** ~**!** (*salopp verhüll.*) get stuffed (*Brit. sl.*)

**Ärmel·auf·schlag** *der* cuff

**Armeleute-:** ~**essen** *das* poor man's food; ~**geruch** *der* smell of poverty; ~**viertel** *das* poor district

**Ärmel·halter** *der* sleeve band

**Ärmel·kanal** *der* (*Geogr.*) **der** ~: the [English] Channel

**Ärmel·schoner** *der;* ~**s**, ~, **Ärmelschützer** *der;* ~**s**, ~: oversleeve

**Armen-:** ~**haus** *das* (*hist., fig.*) poorhouse; **Irland war das** ~**haus Europas** (*fig.*) Ireland was the poor man of Europe; ~**häusler** *der;* ~~**s**, ~~, ~**häuslerin** *die;* ~~, ~~**nen** (*hist.*) inmate of the poorhouse

**Armenien** /ar'me:ni̯ən/ (*das*); ~**s** Armenia

**Armenier** *der;* ~**s**, ~, **Armenierin** *die;* ~, ~**nen** ▸ 553 Armenian

**armenisch** *Adj.* ▸ 553, ▸ 696 Armenian; ⇒ *auch* **deutsch, Deutsch**

**Armen-:** ~**kasse** *die* poor-relief fund; ~**recht** *das* (*Rechtsw.*) right to legal aid; ~**viertel** *das* poor district

**Armensünder-** (*österr.*) ⇒ **Armsünder-**

**ärmer** ⇒ **arm**

***Arme·sünder, Arme·sünderin** ⇒ **Sünder**

**Armesünder·glocke** *die* ⇒ **Armsünderglocke**

**armieren** *tr. V.* Ⓐ (*Milit. veralt.*) arm; Ⓑ (*Technik*) reinforce ‹concrete›; armour, sheathe ‹cable›

**-armig** *adj.* -armed; **sieben**~: seven-armed ‹candelabrum›; **dick**~ ‹person› with fat arms

**Arm-:** ~**länge** *die* arm length; (*Abstand*) arm's length; **ein Stück von** ~**länge** a piece the length of an *or* one's arm; ~**lehne** *die* armrest; ~**leuchter** *der* Ⓐ candelabra; Ⓑ (*ugs. verhüll.*) berk (*Brit. coll.*); jerk (*coll.*)

**ärmlich** /'ɛrmlɪç/ ❶ *Adj.* cheap ‹clothing›; shabby ‹flat, office›; meagre ‹meal›; **in** ~**en Verhältnissen leben** live in impoverished circumstances; **aus** ~**en Verhältnissen** from a poor family. ❷ *adv.* cheaply ‹dressed, furnished›; ~ **leben/wohnen** live in impoverished circumstances

**Ärmlichkeit** *die;* ~ Ⓐ ⇒ **ärmlich** A: cheapness; shabbiness; meagreness; Ⓑ (*Armut*) poverty

**Ärmling** /'ɛrmlɪŋ/ *der;* ~**s**, ~**e** oversleeve

**Arm-:** ~**loch** *das* Ⓐ armhole; Ⓑ (*salopp verhüll.*) berk (*Brit. coll.*); jerk (*coll.*); ~**muskel** *der* ▸ 471 arm muscle; ~**prothese** *die* artificial arm; arm prosthesis (*Med.*); ~**reif** *der* armlet; ~**schiene** *die* Ⓐ (*hist.*) (*für den Oberarm*) brassard; (*für den Unterarm*) vambrace; Ⓑ (*Med.*) arm splint

**arm·selig** ❶ *Adj.* Ⓐ (*sehr arm, dürftig, unbefriedigend*) miserable; miserable, wretched ‹dwelling›; pathetic ‹result, figure›; meagre ‹meal, food›; paltry ‹return, salary, sum, fee›; ~**e 10 Mark** a paltry 10 marks; Ⓑ (*abwertend: erbärmlich*) miserable, wretched ‹swindler, quack›; pathetic, miserable, wretched ‹coward›; pathetic, miserable ‹amateur, bungler›. ❷ *adv.* ~ **leben** lead *or* live a miserable life; ~ **eingerichtet** miserably *or* wretchedly furnished

**Armseligkeit** *die;* ~ ⇒ **armselig** 1: miserableness; wretchedness; patheticness; meagreness; paltriness

**Arm·sessel** *der* armchair

**ärmst...** ⇒ **arm**

**Arm-:** ~**stuhl** *der* armchair; ~**stumpf** *der* stump of the/one's arm

**Armsünder-:** ~**glocke** *die* (*hist.*) *bell tolled during an execution;* ~**miene** *die* (*scherzh.*) expression of misery and remorse

**Armut** /'armu:t/ *die;* ~ (*auch fig.*) poverty; **die** ~ **des Landes an Rohstoffen** (*fig.*) the country's lack of raw materials; **geistige** ~ (*fig.*) lack of culture; cultural poverty

**Armuts·zeugnis** *das: in* **ein** ~ **sein** be a sign of inadequacy; **jmdm. ein** ~ **ausstellen** expose sb.'s inadequacy

***Armvoll** *der;* ~, ~: armful; **zwei** ~ **Reisig** two armfuls of brushwood

**Arnika** /'arnika/ *die;* ~, ~**s** arnica

**Arom** /a'ro:m/ *das;* ~**s**, ~**e** (*dichter.*) ⇒ **Aroma** A

**Aroma** /a'ro:ma/ *das;* ~**s**, **Aromen** *od.* (*veralt.*) **Aromata** Ⓐ (*Duft*) aroma; (*Geschmack*) flavour; taste; Ⓑ (*Substanz, Essenz*) flavouring

**aromatisch** /aro'ma:tɪʃ/ *Adj.* Ⓐ (*duftend*) aromatic; ~ **duften** give off an aromatic fragrance; Ⓑ (*wohlschmeckend*) distinctive ‹taste›; **sehr** ~ **schmecken** have a very distinctive taste

**aromatisieren** *tr. V.* (*wohlriechend machen*) aromatize; (*wohlschmeckend machen*) flavour ‹tea, ice cream, chewing gum, etc.›

**Aron[s]·stab** /'a:rɔn(s)-/ *der* arum; **Gefleckter** ~: cuckoo-pint; lords-and-ladies

**Arrak** /'arak/ *der;* ~**s**, ~**e** *od.* ~**s** arrack

**Arrangement** /arɑ̃ʒə'mɑ̃:/ *das;* ~**s**, ~**s** (*geh., Mus.*) arrangement; **ein** ~ **treffen** come to an arrangement; ~: **Gil Evans** arranger: Gil Evans

**Arrangeur** /arɑ̃'ʒø:ɐ̯/ *der;* ~**s**, ~**e**, **Arrangeurin** *die;* ~, ~**nen** (*Musik*) arranger

**arrangieren** /arɑ̃'ʒi:rən/ ❶ *tr. V.* (*geh., Musik*) arrange. ❷ *itr. V.* (*Musik*) **er kann gut** ~: he's a good arranger. ❸ *refl. V.* **sich** ~: adapt, adjust; **sich mit jmdm.** ~: come to an accommodation with sb.; **sich mit etw.** ~: come to terms with sth.

**Arrest** /a'rɛst/ *der;* ~[**e**]**s**, ~**e** Ⓐ (*Milit., Rechtsw., Schule*) detention; **einen Schüler mit** ~ **bestrafen** (*veralt.*) punish a pupil by putting him in detention; Ⓑ (*Zivilrecht*) **persönlicher** ~: attachment; **dinglicher** ~: attachment; distraint; **etw. unter** ~ **stellen** *od.* **mit** ~ **belegen** attach sth.

**Arrestant** /arɛs'tant/ *der;* ~**en**, ~**en**, **Arrestantin** *die* ~, ~**nen** detainee

**Arrest·zelle** *die* detention cell

**arretieren** /are'ti:rən/ *tr. V.* Ⓐ *auch itr.* lock; Ⓑ (*veralt.: festnehmen*) detain; arrest

**Arretierung** *die;* ~, ~**en** Ⓐ locking; Ⓑ (*Vorrichtung*) latch; Ⓒ (*veralt.: Festnahme*) detention; arrest

*old spelling (see note on page 1707)

**Arrhythmie** /aryt'mi:/ *die;* ~, ~**n** ▶ 474 (*Med.*) arrhythmia

**arrivieren** /ari'vi:rən/ *itr. V.; mit sein* (*geh.*) arrive; **zum Superstar/zum Staatsfeind Nummer eins** ~: achieve superstar status/ become public enemy number one; **ein arrivierter Schriftsteller** a successful writer; (*abwertend*) a parvenu writer

**Arrivierte** *der/die; adj. Dekl.* (*geh.*) man/ woman who has/had arrived; (*abwertend: Emporkömmling*) parvenu

**arrogant** /aro'gant/ (*abwertend*) ❶ *Adj.* arrogant. ❷ *adv.* arrogantly

**Arroganz** /aro'gants/ *die;* ~ (*abwertend*) arrogance

**arrondieren** /arɔn'di:rən/ *tr. V.* (*geh.*) round off ‹property, territory, etc.›

**Arsch** /arʃ/ *der;* ~**[e]s, Ärsche** /'ɛrʃə/ (*derb*) Ⓐ arse (*Brit. coarse*); bum (*Brit. coll.*); ass (*Amer. coarse*); **den** ~ **voll kriegen** get a bloody good hiding (*Brit. sl.*); **der** ~ **der Welt** (*fig.*) the back of beyond; **ihm geht der** ~ **mit Grundeis** (*fig.*) he is scared shitless (*coarse*); he is shitting himself (*coarse*); **den** ~ **offen haben** (*fig.*) be round the bloody twist (*Brit. sl.*); be crazy; **den** ~ **zukneifen** (*fig.*) kick the bucket (*sl.*); croak (*sl.*); **jmdm. den** ~ **aufreißen** (*fig.*) make sb. sweat blood; **jmdn. am** ~ **haben** (*fig.*) have sb. by the short and curlies (*Brit. sl.*); have sb. by the balls (*coarse*); **leck mich am** ~**!** (*fig.*) piss off (*sl.*); get stuffed (*Brit. sl.*); (*verflucht noch mal!; na, so was!*) bugger me! (*coarse*); **er kann mich [mal] am** ~ **lecken** (*fig.*) he can piss off (*sl.*); he can kiss my arse (*Brit. coarse*) *or* ass (*Amer. sl.*); **auf den** ~ **fallen** (*fig.*) come unstuck (*coll.*); **sich auf den** ~ **setzen** (*fig.*) (*fleißig arbeiten*) get *or* pull one's finger out (*coll.*); (*perplex sein*) freak (*coll.*); **jmdm. in den** ~ **kriechen** (*fig.*) kiss sb.'s arse (*Brit. coarse*) *or* ass (*Amer. sl.*); **das kannst du dir in den** ~ **stecken** (*fig.*) you can shove it up your arse (*Brit. coarse*) *or* ass (*Amer. sl.*); **ich könnte mir in den** ~ **beißen** I could kick myself; **jmdm. in den** ~ **treten** kick sb. *or* give sb. a kick up the arse (*Brit. coarse*) *or* kick in the ass (*Amer. sl.*); (*fig.*) give sb. a kick up the backside; **im** ~ **sein** (*fig.*) be buggered (*coarse*); **ein [ganzer]** ~ **voll** (*fig.*) a hell of a lot; Ⓑ (*widerlicher Mensch*) arsehole (*Brit. coarse*); asshole (*Amer. sl.*); ~ **mit Ohren** arsehole (*Brit. coarse*); asshole (*Amer. sl.*); Ⓒ (*nichts geltender Mensch*) piece of dirt; **wir sind die Ärsche hier** we are just so much dirt here

**arsch-, Arsch-:** ~**backe** *die* (*derb*) cheek (*coll.*) [of the/one's arse (*Brit. coarse*) *or* bum (*Brit. coll.*) *or* ass (*Amer. sl.*)]; ~**ficker** *der;* ~~**s**, ~~ (*vulg.*) arse-fucker (*Brit. coarse*); bum-fucker (*Brit. coarse*); butt-fucker (*Amer. coarse*); ~**geige** *die* (*derb abwertend*) arsehole (*Brit. coarse*); ~**klar** *Adj.* (*derb*) bloody (*Brit. sl.*) *or* damned obvious; **Ich mache mit. Ist doch** ~**klar** I'm game. 'Course I bloody am (*Brit. sl.*); ~**kriecher** *der*, ~**kriecherin** *die* (*derb abwertend*) arse-licker (*Brit. coarse*); ass-licker (*Amer. sl.*); ~**kriecherei** *die* (*derb abwertend*) arse-licking (*Brit. coarse*); ass-licking (*Amer. sl.*); ~**loch** *das* (*derb*) Ⓐ (*widerlicher Mensch*) arsehole (*Brit. coarse*); asshole (*Amer. sl.*); **Mensch, ich bin doch ein** ~**loch** what a stupid arse (*Brit. coarse*) *or* (*Amer. sl.*) ass I am; Ⓑ (*bedauernswerter Mensch*) poor bloody sod (*Brit. sl.*); poor bastard; ~**-und-Titten-Presse** *die* (*salopp*) tit-and-bum press (*Brit. sl.*); tit-and-ass press (*Amer. sl.*); ~**wisch** *der* (*derb abwertend*) useless piece of paper

**Arsen** /ar'ze:n/ *das;* ~**s** arsenic

**Arsenal** /arze'na:l/ *das;* ~**s**, ~**e** arsenal

**arsen·haltig** *Adj.* containing arsenic *postpos., not pred.*; arsenical; ~**/stark** ~ **sein** contain arsenic/have a high arsenic content

**Arsenik** /ar'ze:nɪk/ *das;* ~**s** arsenic; arsenic trioxide

**Art** /a:ɐ̯t/ *die;* ~, ~**en** Ⓐ (*Sorte*) kind; sort; (*Biol.: Spezies*) species; **Tische/Bücher aller** ~: tables/books of all kinds *or* sorts; all kinds *or* sorts of tables/books; **einzig in seiner** ~: unique of its kind; **ein Verbrecher übelster** ~: the worst sort *or* kind of criminal; **jede** ~ **von Gewalt ablehnen** reject all forms of violence; **diese** ~ **[von] Menschen** that kind *or* sort of person; people like that; **[so] eine** ~ **...** a sort *or* kind of ...; **aus der** ~ **schlagen** not be true to type; (*in einer Familie*) be different from all the rest of the family; **in der** ~ **eines Gorillas** like a gorilla; Ⓑ (*Wesen*) nature; (*Verhaltensweise*) manner; way; **es liegt nicht in ihrer** ~ *od.* **ist nicht ihre** ~, **das zu tun** it's not [in] her nature to do that; **das entspricht nicht seiner** ~: it's not [in] his nature; that's not his way; Ⓒ (*gutes Benehmen*) behaviour; **das ist doch keine** ~**!** that's no way to behave!; **was ist denn das für eine** ~**?** what sort of behaviour is that?; **die feine englische** ~ (*ugs.*) the proper way to behave; Ⓓ (*Weise*) way; **auf diese** ~: in this way; **auf verschiedene** ~**en** in various ways; **auf welche** ~**?** in what way?; **auf grausamste** ~: in the cruellest way; **in einer** ~: in a way; **die richtige** ~, **darauf zu reagieren** the right way to react to it; **auf die eine oder andere** ~: in one way or another; ~ **und Weise** way; **seine** ~ **und Weise zu arbeiten** his way of working; **Schweinesteak nach** ~ **des Hauses** (*Kochk.*) pork steak à la maison; **nach Schweizer** *od.* **auf schweizerische** ~ (*Kochk.*) Swiss style; **dass es eine** ~ **hat/hatte** (*veralt.*) with a vengeance

**Art·angabe** *die* (*Sprachw.*) adverb of manner; (*Phrase*) adverbial phrase of manner

**Artefakt** /arte'fakt/ *das;* ~**[e]s**, ~**e** (*geh.*) artefact

**art·eigen** *Adj.* (*Biol.*) species-specific

**arten-, Arten-:** ~**reich** *Adj.* (*Biol.*) species-rich; ~**reichtum** *der* (*Biol.*) species-richness; ~**schutz** *der* protection of species; species protection

**art·erhaltend** *Adj.* (*Biol.*, *Verhaltensf.*) species-preserving

**Art·erhaltung** *die* (*Biol.*, *Verhaltensf.*) preservation of the species

**Arterie** /ar'te:ri̯ə/ *die;* ~, ~**n** ▶ 471 artery

**arteriell** /arte'ri̯ɛl/ *Adj.* (*Anat.*) arterial

**Arterien·verkalkung** *die* ▶ 474 hardening of the arteries; arteriosclerosis (*Med.*)

**Arterio·sklerose** /arteri̯o-/ *die* ▶ 474 (*Med.*) arteriosclerosis

**artesisch** /ar'te:zɪʃ/ *Adj.* **in** ~**er Brunnen** artesian well

**art-, Art-:** ~**fremd** *Adj.* (*Biol.*) foreign [to a/ the species]; ~**genosse** *der*, ~**genossin** *die* conspecific; creature of the same species; ~**gerecht** ❶ *Adj.* appropriate for *or* to the species *postpos.*; ❷ *adv.* in a way appropriate for *or* to the species ~**gleich** *Adj.* (*Biol.*) ‹animal, individual› of the same species

**Arthritis** /ar'tri:tɪs/ *die;* ~, **Arthritiden** ▶ 474 (*Med.*) arthritis

**arthritisch** *Adj.* (*Med.*) arthritic

**Arthrose** /ar'tro:zə/ *die;* ~, ~**n** ▶ 474 (*Med.*) arthrosis

**artifiziell** /artifi'tsi̯ɛl/ (*geh.*) ❶ *Adj.* artificial. ❷ *adv.* artificially

**artig** ❶ *Adj.* Ⓐ well-behaved; good; **sei** ~: be good; be a good boy/girl/dog *etc.*; Ⓑ (*geh. veralt.: höflich*) courteous; Ⓒ (*veralt.: nett*) charming. ❷ *adv.* Ⓐ **sich** ~ **benehmen** be good; behave well; Ⓑ (*geh. veralt.: höflich*) courteously; Ⓒ (*veralt.: nett*) charmingly

**-artig** ❶ *Adj.* **marmor**~**/gold**~: marble-like/gold-like. ❷ *adv.* **sich explosions**~ **vermehren** increase explosively; **sich kegel**~ **verjüngen** taper like a cone

**Artigkeit** *die;* ~, ~**en** Ⓐ (*geh. veralt.*) courteousness; Ⓑ (*Redensart*) pleasantry; (*Kompliment*) compliment; **jmdm.** ~**en sagen** say nice things to sb./pay sb. compliments

**Artikel** /ar'ti:kl̩/ *der;* ~**s**, ~ Ⓐ article; Ⓑ (*Ware*) article; item

**Artikulation** /artikula'tsi̯o:n/ *die;* ~, ~**en** articulation

**artikulieren** ❶ *tr., itr. V.* articulate; enunciate; (*Sprachw., geh.: zum Ausdruck bringen*) articulate. ❷ *refl. V.* Ⓐ (*sich ausdrücken*) express oneself; Ⓑ (*zum Ausdruck kommen*) express itself; be expressed

**Artillerie** /artɪlə'ri:/ *die;* ~, ~**n** artillery

**Artillerie·beschuss**, ***Artillerie·beschuß** *der* artillery fire

**Artillerist** *der;* ~**en**, ~**en** artilleryman

**artilleristisch** (*Milit.*) ❶ *Adj.* ~**e Unterstützung** artillery support. ❷ *adv.* ~ **unterstützt werden** have artillery support

**Artischocke** /arti'ʃɔkə/ *die;* ~, ~**n** artichoke

**Artischocken·boden** *der* artichoke bottom

**Artist** /ar'tɪst/ *der;* ~**en**, ~**en** ▶ 159 Ⓐ [variety/circus] artiste *or* performer; Ⓑ (*geh.: Virtuose*) artist

**Artistik** *die;* ~ Ⓐ circus/variety performance *no art.*; Ⓑ (*Geschicklichkeit*) skill; Ⓒ (*geh.: formale Könnerschaft*) artistry

**Artistin** *die;* ~, ~**nen** ▶ 159 ⇒ **Artist**

**artistisch** ❶ *Adj.* Ⓐ **eine** ~**e Glanzleistung** a superb circus/variety performance; **sein** ~**es Können** his skill as a [circus/variety] artiste; Ⓑ (*geschickt*) masterly; Ⓒ (*geh.: technisch perfekt*) virtuoso *attrib.* ❷ *adv.* Ⓐ **eine** ~ **anspruchsvolle Nummer** a circus/variety act of great virtuosity; Ⓑ (*geschickt*) in a masterly way *or* fashion; Ⓒ (*geh.: technisch perfekt*) with great artistry *or* virtuosity

**Artothek** /arto'te:k/ *die;* ~, ~**en** art lending library

**Artus** /'artʊs/ (*der*) [King] Arthur

**art·verwandt** *Adj.* related

**Arznei** /a:ɐ̯ts'nai:/ *die;* ~, ~**en** (*veralt.*) medicine; medicament; (*zur äußeren Anwendung*) medicament; **eine bittere/heilsame** ~ **für jmdn. sein** (*fig. ugs.*) be a painful/salutary lesson for sb.

**Arznei-:** ~**buch** *das* pharmacopoeia; ~**kunde**, ~**lehre** *die* pharmacology; ~**mittel** *das* medicine; medicament; (*zur äußeren Anwendung*) medicament; ~**mittel·gesetz** *das: law relating to the manufacture and distribution of medicines;* ~**mittel·missbrauch**, *~**mittel·mißbrauch** *der* abuse of medicines; ~**mittel·sucht** *die* addiction to medicines; pharmacomania (*Med.*); ~**schränkchen** *das* medicine cabinet

**Arzt** /a:ɐ̯tst/ *der;* ~**es, Ärzte** ▶ 159 /'ɛ:ɐ̯tstə/ doctor; physician (*arch./formal*); **zum** ~ **gehen** go to the doctor['s]; **Sie sollten mal zum** ~ **gehen** you ought to see a/the doctor; **praktischer** ~, (*fachspr.*) ~ **für Allgemeinmedizin** general practitioner; GP; **..., wie vom** ~ **verordnet** ... as directed by a physician; **ein** ~ **für Kinder-/Frauenkrankheiten** a paediatrician/gynaecologist

**Arzt·beruf** *der* job of doctor; **in den** ~ **drängen** crowd into the medical profession; **den** ~ **ergreifen** become a doctor

**Ärzte-:** ~**kammer** *die: professional body of doctors;* ≈ General Medical Council (*Brit.*); ~**muster** *das* medical sample

**Ärzteschaft** *die;* ~: medical profession

**Arzt-:** ~**frau** *die* doctor's wife; ~**helferin** *die* ▶ 159 doctor's receptionist

**Ärztin** /'ɛ:ɐ̯tstɪn/ *die;* ~, ~**nen** ▶ 159 doctor; physician (*formal*); ⇒ *auch* **Arzt**; **-in**

**ärztlich** /'ɛ:ɐ̯tstlɪç/ ❶ *Adj.* medical; **auf** ~**e Verordnung** on doctor's orders; **alle** ~**e Kunst** all the doctor's/doctors' skill. ❷ *adv.* **sich** ~ **behandeln lassen** have medical treatment; „~ **empfohlen**" 'recommended by doctors'

**Arzt-:** ~**praxis** *die* doctor's surgery (*Brit.*) *or* practice; ~**rechnung** *die* doctor's bill; ~**wahl** *die:* **das Recht der freien** ~**wahl** the right to choose one's doctor

**as, As**[1] /as/ *das;* ~, ~ (*Musik*) [key of] A flat

***As**[2] ⇒ **Ass**[1]

**A-Saite** *die* (*Musik*) A-string

**Asbest** /as'bɛst/ *der;* ~**[e]s**, ~**e** asbestos

**Asbest-:** ~**anzug** *der* asbestos suit; ~**platte** *die* (*für Töpfe*) asbestos mat; (*für Bügeleisen*) asbestos stand

**Asch·becher** *der* ⇒ **Aschenbecher**
**asch·blond** *Adj.* ash blond
**Asche** /'aʃə/ *die;* ~, ~**n** ash[es *pl.*]; (*sterbliche Reste*) ashes *pl.*; **in ~ liegen/legen** (*fig. geh.*) lie/lay in ashes; **sich** (*Dat.*) **~ aufs Haupt streuen** (*fig. geh.*) wear sackcloth and ashes
**Asch·eimer** *der* (*nordd.*) rubbish *or* waste bin
**Aschen-:** ~**bahn** *die* (*Sport*) cinder track; ~**becher** *der* ashtray
**Aschen·brödel** /-brø:dl/ *das;* ~**s**, ~ (*auch fig.*) Cinderella
**Aschen-:** ~**eimer** *der* (*nordd.*) ⇒ **Mülleimer**; ~**platz** *der* (*Tennis*) cinder-court
**Aschen·puttel** /-pʊtl/ *das;* ~**s**, ~ ⇒ **Aschenbrödel**
**Aschen·regen** *der* rain of ash
**Ascher** *der;* ~**s**, ~ (*ugs.*) ashtray
**Ascher·mittwoch** *der* Ash Wednesday
**asch-:** ~**fahl** *Adj.* ashen; ~**grau** *Adj.* ash-grey; (~*fahl*) ashen
**Ascorbin·säure** /askɔr'bi:n-/ *die* ascorbic acid
**As-Dur** *das* (*Musik*) A flat major; ⇒ *auch* **A-Dur**
**Ase** /'a:zə/ *der;* ~**n**, ~**n** (*germ. Myth.*) one of the Aesir; **die ~n** the Aesir
**äsen** /ɛ:zn̩/ *itr. V.* (*Jägerspr.*) browse; (*weiden*) graze
**aseptisch** (*Med.*) ❶ *Adj.* aseptic. ❷ *adv.* aseptically
**Äser** ⇒ **Aas**
**asexuell** ❶ *Adj.* asexual. ❷ *adv.* asexually
**Asiat** /a'zi̯a:t/ *der;* ~**en**, ~**en**, **Asiatin** *die;* ~, ~**nen** Asian
**asiatisch** *Adj.* Asian; (*ost*~) Asian; oriental; **~ aussehen** have an Asiatic look about one
**Asien** /'a:zi̯ən/ (*das*); ~**s** Asia
**Askese** /as'ke:zə/ *die;* ~: asceticism
**Asket** /as'ke:t/ *der;* ~**en**, ~**en**, **Asketin** *die;* ~, ~**nen** ascetic
**asketisch** ❶ *Adj.* ascetic. ❷ *adv.* ascetically
**Äskulap·stab** /ɛsku'la:p-/ *der* staff of Aesculapius
**as-Moll** *das* (*Musik*) A flat minor
**Äsop** /ɛ'zo:p/ (*der*) Aesop
**asozial** ❶ *Adj.* asocial; (*gegen die Gesellschaft gerichtet*) antisocial; **ein ~er Mensch** a social misfit. ❷ *adv.* asocially; antisocially
**Asoziale** *der/die; adj. Dekl.* social misfit
**Asparagus** /as'pa:ragʊs/ *der;* ~ [A] (*Bot.*) asparagus; [B] (*Grün*) asparagus fern
**Aspekt** /as'pɛkt/ *der;* ~**[e]s**, ~**e** aspect
**Asphalt** /as'falt/ *der;* ~**[e]s**, ~**e** asphalt
**Asphalt·decke** *die* (*Straßenbau*) asphalt surface
**asphaltieren** *tr. V.* asphalt
**Asphalt-:** ~**literat** *der* (*ns. abwertend*): *writer associated with urban rootlessness and decadence;* ~**straße** *die* asphalt road
**Aspik** /as'pi:k/ *der* (*österr. auch* **das**); ~**s**, ~**e** aspic
**Aspirant** /aspi'rant/ *der;* ~**en**, ~**en**, **Aspirantin** *die;* ~, ~**nen** [A] (*Anwärter*) candidate; [B] (*DDR: Wissenschaftler*) research student (*with some teaching responsibilities*)
**Aspiration** /aspira'tsi̯o:n/ *die;* ~, ~**en** (*Sprachw.*) aspiration
**aspirieren** ❶ *tr. V.* (*Sprachw.*) aspirate. ❷ *itr. V.* (*österr. geh.*) **auf etw.** (*Akk.*) **~:** be a candidate for sth.
**aß** /a:s/ *1. u. 3. Pers. Sg. Prät. v.* **essen**
**Ass**[1], ***Aß** /as/ *das;* **Asses, Asse** ace
**Ass**[2], ***Aß** *das;* **Asses, Asse** (*österr. ugs.: Abszess*) boil
**assanieren** /asa'ni:rən/ *tr. V.* (*österr.*) clean up
**äße** /'ɛ:sə/ *1. u. 3. Pers. Sg. Konjunktiv II v.* **essen**
**Assekuranz** /aseku'rants/ *die;* ~, ~**en** (*Wirtsch.*) assurance (*Brit.*); insurance
**Assel** /'asl̩/ *die;* ~, ~**n** [A] (*Zool.*) isopod; [B] (*Keller*~, *Mauer*~) woodlouse

*old spelling (see note on page 1707)

**Asservat** /asɛr'va:t/ *das;* ~**[e]s**, ~**e** (*Rechtw.*) exhibit
**Assessor** /a'sɛsɔr/ *der;* ~**s**, ~**en** /asɛ'so:rən/, **Assessorin** *die;* ~, ~**nen** ▶ 159 *holder of a higher civil service post, e.g. teacher or lawyer, who has passed the necessary examinations but has not yet completed his/her probationary period;* ⇒ *auch* **-in**
**Assimilation** /asimila'tsi̯o:n/ *die;* ~, ~**en** (*auch fachspr.*) assimilation (**an** + *Akk.* to)
**assimilieren** (*auch fachspr.*) ❶ *tr. V.* assimilate. ❷ *refl. V.* assimilate (**an** + *Akk.* to)
**Assistent** /asɪs'tɛnt/ *der;* ~**en**, ~**en**, **Assistentin** *die;* ~, ~**nen** ▶ 159 assistant; ⇒ *auch* **wissenschaftlich; -in**
**Assistenz** /asɪs'tɛnts/ *die;* ~, ~**en** assistance
**Assistenz-:** ~**arzt** *der*, ~**ärztin** *die* junior doctor; ~**professor** *der*, ~**professorin** *die* assistant professor; reader (*Brit.*)
**assistieren** *itr. V.* **[jmdm.] ~:** assist [sb.] (**bei** at)
**Assonanz** /aso'nants/ *die;* ~, ~**en** (*Verslehre*) assonance
**Assoziation** /asotsi̯a'tsi̯o:n/ *die;* ~, ~**en** association
**Assoziations·freiheit** *die* (*Rechtsw.*) freedom of association
**assoziativ** /asotsi̯a'ti:f/ ❶ *Adj.* associative. ❷ *adv.* associatively
**assoziieren** ❶ *tr. V.* (*bes. Psych., geh.*) associate; **bei einem Namen** *usw.* **etw. ~:** associate sth. with a name *etc.* ❷ *itr. V.* make associations; **frei ~:** free-associate. ❸ *refl. V.* (*sich an-, zusammenschließen*) form an association; **der Sudan ist der EG assoziiert** the Sudan is associated with the EC
**Ast** /ast/ *der;* ~**[e]s**, **Äste** /'ɛstə/ [A] branch; bough; **den ~ absägen, auf dem man sitzt** (*fig. ugs.*) saw off the branch one is sitting on; **auf dem absteigenden ~ sein** (*fig. ugs.*) be going downhill; [B] (*in Holz*) knot; [C] (*landsch.*) (*Rücken*) back; (*Buckel*) hunchback; humpback; **sich** (*Dat.*) **einen ~ lachen** (*ugs.*) split one's sides [with laughter]
**AStA** /'asta/ *der;* ~**[s]**, ~**[s]** *od.* **Asten** *Abk.* **Allgemeiner Studentenausschuss** ≈ Students' Union
**Ästchen** /'ɛstçən/ *das;* ~**s**, ~: [small] branch
**Aster** /'astɐ/ *die;* ~, ~**n** aster; (*Herbst*~) Michaelmas daisy
**Ast·gabel** *die* (*zwischen Stamm und Ast*) fork of a/the tree; (*zwischen Ast und Zweig*) fork of a/the branch
**Ästhet** /ɛs'te:t/ *der;* ~**en**, ~**en**, **Ästhetin** *die;* ~, ~**nen** aesthete
**Ästhetik** /ɛs'te:tɪk/ *die;* ~, ~**en** [A] aesthetics *sing.*; [B] (*Buch*) [book on] aesthetics; [C] (*das Ästhetische*) aesthetics *pl*; (*Schönheitssinn*) aesthetic sense; **er hat keinen Sinn für ~:** he has no aesthetic sense
**ästhetisch** ❶ *Adj.* aesthetic. ❷ *adv.* aesthetically
**ästhetisieren** *tr.* (*auch itr.*) *V.* (*geh.*) aestheticize
**Ästhetizismus** *der;* ~ (*geh.*) aestheticism
**ästhetizistisch** *Adj.* (*geh.*) aestheticist; aestheticizing *attrib.*
**Asthma** /'astma/ *das;* ~**s** ▶ 474 asthma
**Asthmatiker** /ast'ma:tikɐ/ *der;* ~**s**, ~, **Asthmatikerin** *die;* ~, ~**nen** asthmatic
**asthmatisch** ❶ *Adj.* asthmatic. ❷ *adv.* asthmatically; **~ bedingte Beschwerden** complaints linked to asthma
**astig** *Adj.* knotty
**Ast·loch** *das* knothole
**astral** /as'tra:l/ *Adj.* astral
**Astral·leib** *der* astral body
**ast·rein** ❶ *Adj.* (*ugs.*) (*in Ordnung*) on the level (*coll.*); (*echt*) genuine; (*salopp: prima, toll*) fantastic (*coll.*); great (*coll.*). ❷ *adv.* (*salopp: prima*) fantastically (*coll.*)
**Astrologe** /astro'lo:gə/ *der;* ~**n**, ~**n** ▶ 159 astrologer; (*fig.*) forecaster; pundit; **Kreml-~** (*fig.*) Kremlin-watcher *or* Kremlinologist

**Astrologie** *die;* ~: astrology *no art.*
**Astrologin** *die;* ~, ~**nen** ▶ 159 ⇒ **Astrologe**
**astrologisch** ❶ *Adj.* astrological. ❷ *adv.* astrologically; **sich ~ beraten lassen** consult an astrologer
**Astronaut** /astro'nau̯t/ *der;* ~**en**, ~**en** ▶ 159 astronaut
**Astronautik** /astro'nau̯tɪk/ *die;* ~: astronautics *sing., no art.*
**Astronautin** *die;* ~, ~**nen** astronaut; ⇒ *auch* **-in**
**astronautisch** ❶ *Adj.* astronautical. ❷ *adv.* astronautically; **~ interessiert** interested in astronautics; **jmdn. ~ ausbilden** train sb. in astronautics
**Astronom** /astro'no:m/ *der;* ~**en**, ~**en** ▶ 159 astronomer
**Astronomie** *die;* ~: astronomy *no art.*
**Astronomin** *die;* ~, ~**nen** ▶ 159 astronomer
**astronomisch** *Adj.* astronomical
**astro-, Astro-** /astro-/: ~**physik** *die* astrophysics *sing., no art.*; ~**physikalisch** ❶ *Adj.* astrophysical; ❷ *adv.* astrophysically; ~**physiker** *der*, ~**physikerin** *die* ▶ 159 astrophysicist
**Ast·werk** *das;* ~**[e]s** branches *pl.*
**Äsung** *die;* ~, ~**en** (*Jägerspr.*) grazing
**Asyl** /a'zy:l/ *das;* ~**s**, ~**e** [A] [political] asylum; **jmdm. ~ gewähren** grant sb. asylum; [B] (*Obdachlosen*~) hostel [for the homeless]
**Asylant** /azy'lant/ *der;* ~**en**, ~**en**, **Asylantin** *die;* ~, ~**nen** person granted [political] asylum; (*Asylbewerber*) person seeking [political] asylum
**Asylanten·heim** *das* asylum seekers' hostel
**Asyl-:** ~**bewerber** *der*, ~**bewerberin** *die* person seeking [political] asylum; ~**recht** *das* (*Rechtsw.*) [A] right of [political] asylum; [B] (*eines Staates*) right to grant [political] asylum; ~**werber** *der;* ~~**s**, ~~, ~**werberin** *die;* ~~, ~~**nen** (*österr.*) ⇒ ~**bewerber**
**Asymmetrie** *die;* ~, ~**n** asymmetry
**asymmetrisch** ❶ *Adj.* asymmetrical. ❷ *adv.* asymmetrically
**asynchron** ❶ *Adj.* asynchronous; **Bild und Ton sind ~:** sound and picture are out of synchronization. ❷ *adv.* asynchronously
**Aszendent** /astsɛn'dɛnt/ *der;* ~**en**, ~**en** (*Astron., Astrol., Genealogie*) ascendant
**A. T.** *Abk.* **Altes Testament** OT
**ata** /'ata/ *in* **~ [~] gehen** (*Kinderspr.*) go walkies (*child lang., coll.*)
**Atavismus** /ata'vɪsmʊs/ *der;* ~, **Atavismen** (*Biol., Psych.*) atavism
**atavistisch** (*Biol., Psych.*) ❶ *Adj.* atavistic. ❷ *adv.* atavistically
**Atelier** /atə'li̯e:/ *das;* ~**s**, ~**s** studio
**Atelier-:** ~**aufnahme** *die* (*Film, Fot.*) studio shot; ~**fest** *das* studio party; ~**wohnung** *die* studio flat (*Brit.*) *or* (*Amer.*) apartment
**Atem** /'a:təm/ *der;* ~**s** breath; **sein ~ wurde schneller** his breathing became faster; **einen kurzen ~ haben** be short of breath; (*fig.*) not have much staying power; **einen langen ~ haben** (*fig.*) have great staying power; **jmdn. in ~ halten** (*in Spannung halten*) keep sb. in suspense; (*pausenlos beschäftigen*) keep sb. busy *or* at it; **den ~ anhalten** hold one's breath; **jmdm. den ~ verschlagen** take sb.'s breath away; **~ holen** *od.* (*geh.*) **schöpfen** (*auch fig.*) get one's breath back; **außer ~ sein/geraten** *od.* **kommen** be/get out of breath; **[wieder] zu ~ kommen** get one's breath back; **nach ~ ringen** (*geh.*) gasp for air
**atem-, Atem-:** ~**beklemmung** *die* shortness of breath; ~**beraubend** ❶ *Adj.* breathtaking; ❷ *adv.* breathtakingly; ~**beschwerden** *Pl.* trouble *sing.* with one's breathing; ~**holen** *das;* ~~**s** breathing; **der Taucher kam zum ~holen an die Oberfläche** the diver came up to the surface for air; ~**los** ❶ *Adj.* breathless; ❷ *adv.* breathlessly; ~**losigkeit** *die;* ~~:

breathlessness; **~luft** *die* the air one breathes; **~maske** *die* (*Med.*) breathing mask; **~not** *die* difficulty in breathing; **~pause** *die* breathing space; **~technik** *die* breathing technique; **~übung** *die* breathing exercise; **~wege** *Pl.* respiratory tract *sing. or* passages; **~zug** *der* breath; **bis zum letzten ~zug** (*geh.*) to the last breath; **in einem** *od.* **im selben ~zug** in the same breath

**Atheismus** /ate'ɪsmʊs/ *der;* **~:** atheism *no art.*

**Atheist** *der;* **~en, ~en, Atheistin** *die;* **~, ~nen** atheist

**atheistisch** ❶ *Adj.* atheistic. ❷ *adv.* atheistically; **er ist ~ erzogen worden** he had an atheistic upbringing

**Athen** /a'te:n/ *(das);* **~s** ▶ 700 Athens

**Athener** ▶ 700 ❶ *indekl. Adj.* Athens *attrib.;* of Athens *postpos.* ❷ *der;* **~s, ~:** Athenian; ⇒ *auch* **Kölner**

**Athenerin** *die;* **~, ~nen** Athenian

**athenisch** *Adj.* Athenian

**Äther** /'ɛ:tɐ/ *der;* **~s, ~** (*Chemie, Physik, geh.*) ether

**ätherisch** /ɛ'te:rɪʃ/ *Adj.* (*Chemie, dichter.*) ethereal

**Äther-: ~narkose** *die* (*Med.*) ether anaesthesia; **~wellen** *Pl.* (*veralt.*) waves in the ether

**Äthiopien** /ɛ'ti̯o:pi̯ən/ *(das);* **~s** Ethiopia

**Äthiopier** *der;* **~s, ~, Äthiopierin** *die;* **~, ~nen** Ethiopian; ⇒ *auch* **-in**

**Athlet** /at'le:t/ *der;* **~en, ~en** Ⓐ (*Sportler*) athlete; Ⓑ (*ugs.*) muscleman

**Athletik** /at'le:tɪk/ *die;* **~:** athletics *sing., no art.*

**Athletin** *die;* **~, ~nen** athlete; ⇒ *auch* **-in**

**athletisch** *Adj.* athletic

**Äthyl·alkohol** *der* (*Chemie*) ethyl alcohol; ethanol

**Äthylen** /ɛty'le:n/ *das;* **~s** (*Chemie*) ethylene

**Atlant** /at'lant/ *der;* **~en, ~en** (*Archit.*) telamon; atlas

**Atlanten** ⇒ **Atlas[1], Atlant**

**Atlantik** /at'lantɪk/ *der;* **~s** Atlantic

**atlantisch** *Adj.* (*Geogr.*) Atlantic; **der Atlantische Ozean** the Atlantic Ocean

**Atlas[1]** /'atlas/ *der;* **~** *od.* **~ses, Atlanten** *od.* **~se** atlas

**Atlas[2]** *der;* **~** *od.* **~ses, ~se** (*Textilw.*) atlas

**atmen** /'a:tmən/ ❶ *itr. V.* breathe; (*Physiol., Bot.*) respire. ❷ *tr. V.* (*geh., auch fig.: erfüllt sein von*) breathe

**Atmosphäre** /atmo'sfɛ:rə/ *die;* **~, ~n** (*auch fig.*) atmosphere

**atmosphärisch** ❶ *Adj.* atmospheric; ⇒ *auch* **Störung B.** ❷ *adv.* atmospherically

**Atmung** *die;* **~:** breathing; (*Physiol., Bot.*) respiration

**Atmungs-: ~apparat** *der* (*Med.*) respirator; **~organ** *das* respiratory organ

**Ätna** /'ɛ:tna/ *der;* **~[s]** Mount Etna

**Atoll** /a'tɔl/ *das;* **~s, ~e** atoll

**Atom** /a'to:m/ *das;* **~s, ~e** atom

**atomar** /ato'ma:ɐ̯/ ❶ *Adj.* atomic; (*Atomwaffen betreffend*) nuclear; nuclear, atomic ‹age, weapons›. ❷ *adv.* **~ angetrieben** nuclear-powered; atomic-powered; **~ aufrüsten** build up nuclear arms

**Atom-, atom-: ~ausstieg** *der* abandonment of nuclear power; **~bombe** *die* nuclear bomb; atom bomb; **~bomben·sicher** *Adj.* nuclear-bomb-proof; **~bombenversuch** *der* nuclear [weapons] test; **~bunker** *der* fallout shelter; **~energie** *die* nuclear *or* atomic energy *no indef. art.;* **~explosion** *die* nuclear *or* atomic explosion; **~gewicht** *das* atomic weight

**atomisieren** *tr. V.* Ⓐ (*vernichten*) **etw. ~:** smash sth. to atoms; Ⓑ (*zerstäuben*) atomize ‹liquid›; Ⓒ (*abwertend: zerstückelnd behandeln*) atomize

**Atomismus** *der;* **~** (*Philos.*) atomism *no art.*

**atom-, Atom-: ~kern** *der* atomic nucleus; **~klub** *der* (*Politik ugs.*) nuclear club; **~kraft** *die* nuclear *or* atomic power *no indef. art.;* **~kraft·werk** *das* nuclear *or* atomic power station; **~krieg** *der* nuclear war; **~macht** *die* nuclear power; **~meiler** *der* atomic pile; **~modell** *das* (*Physik*) model of the/an atom; **~müll** *der* nuclear *or* atomic waste; **~physik** *die* nuclear *or* atomic physics *sing., no art.;* **~physiker** *der,* **~physikerin** *die* nuclear *or* atomic physicist; **~pilz** *der* mushroom cloud; **~rakete** *die* nuclear *or* atomic missile; **~reaktor** *der* nuclear reactor; **~spreng·kopf** *der* nuclear warhead; **~stopp** *der* nuclear freeze; **~streit·macht** *die* nuclear force; **~strom** *der* (*ugs.*) electricity generated by nuclear power; **~test·stopp·abkommen** *das* (*Politik*) nuclear test ban treaty; **~tod** *der* death in a nuclear war/accident; **„Kampf dem ~tod!"** 'ban the bomb'; **~-U-Boot** *das* nuclear[-powered] submarine; **~uhr** *die* atomic clock; **~unterseeboot** *das* ⇒ **~-U-Boot**; **~waffe** *die* nuclear *or* atomic weapon; **~waffen·frei** *Adj.* nuclear-free; **~waffensperr·vertrag** *der* (*Politik*) Nuclear Non-proliferation Treaty; **~zeichen** *das* (*Chemie*) [chemical] symbol; **~zeit·alter** *das* nuclear *or* atomic age; **~zerfall** *der* (*Physik*) radioactive decay; **~zertrümmerung** *die* (*Physik*) splitting of the atom

**atonal** *Adj.* (*Musik*) atonal

**Atonalität** *die;* **~** (*Musik*) atonality

**atoxisch** *Adj.* (*bes. Biol., Med.*) non-toxic

**Atrium** /'a:triʊm/ *das;* **~s, Atrien** atrium

**Atrium·haus** *das* (*Archit.*) house with an atrium

**ätsch** /ɛ:tʃ/ *Interj.* (*Kinderspr.*) ha ha

**Attaché** /ata'ʃe:/ *der;* **~s, ~s** attaché

**Attacke** /a'takə/ *die;* **~, ~n** Ⓐ ▶ 474 (*auch Med.*) attack (**auf** + *Akk.* on); Ⓑ (*Reiter~*) [cavalry] charge; **eine ~ [gegen jmdn./etw.] reiten** charge [sb./sth.]; (*fig.*) make an attack [on sb./sth.]

**attackieren** *tr. V.* Ⓐ attack; Ⓑ (*Milit.: zu Pferde*) charge

**Attentat** /'atn̩ta:t/ *das;* **~[e]s, ~e** assassination attempt; (*erfolgreiches*) assassination; **ein ~ auf jmdn. verüben** make an attempt on sb.'s life/assassinate sb.; **ein ~ [auf jmdn.] vorhaben** (*fig. ugs. scherzh.*) want to ask a favour [of sb.]

**Attentäter** /'atn̩tɛ:tɐ/ *der;* **~s, ~, Attentäterin** *die;* **~, ~nen** would-be assassin; (*bei erfolgreichem Attentat*) assassin

**Attest** /a'tɛst/ *das;* **~[e]s, ~e** medical certificate; doctor's certificate

**attestieren** *tr. V.* certify; **jmdm. seine Unzurechnungsfähigkeit ~:** certify sb. as not responsible for his/her own actions

**Attika** /'atika/ *(das);* **~s** Attica

**attisch** /'atɪʃ/ *Adj.* Attic

**Attitüde** /ati'ty:də/ *die;* **~, ~n** (*geh.*) posture

**Attraktion** /atrak'tsi̯o:n/ *die;* **~, ~en** attraction

**attraktiv** /atrak'ti:f/ ❶ *Adj.* attractive. ❷ *adv.* attractively

**Attraktivität** /atraktivi'tɛ:t/ *die;* **~:** attractiveness

**Attrappe** /a'trapə/ *die;* **~, ~n** dummy; **die ~ eines Fernsehgeräts/einer Flasche** a dummy television set/bottle

**Attribut** /atri'bu:t/ *das;* **~[e]s, ~e** attribute

**attributiv** /atribu'ti:f/ (*Sprachw.*) ❶ *Adj.* attributive. ❷ *adv.* attributively

**Attribut·satz** *der* (*Sprachw.*) attributive clause

**atü** /a'ty:/ *Abk.* (*veralt.*) **Atmosphärenüberdruck; 1 ~:** 2 atm.; **3 ~:** 4 atm.

**atypisch** (*geh.*) ❶ *Adj.* atypical. ❷ *adv.* atypically

**atzen** /'atsn̩/ *tr. V.* (*Jägerspr.*) feed

**ätzen** /'ɛtsn̩/ ❶ *tr. V.* Ⓐ etch; Ⓑ (*Med.*) cauterize ‹wound›. ❷ *itr. V.* corrode

**ätzend** ❶ *Adj.* Ⓐ corrosive; (*fig.*) caustic ‹wit, remark, criticism›; pungent ‹smell›; acrid ‹smoke›; Ⓑ (*Jugendspr.*) (*gut*) great (*coll.*); ace (*sl.*); (*schlecht*) grotty (*Brit. coll.*); grot (*Brit. coll.*). ❷ *adv.* caustically ‹ironic, critical›

**Ätz·natron** *das* (*Chemie*) caustic soda

**Atzung** *die;* **~, ~en** (*Jägerspr.*) Ⓐ (*Fütterung*) feeding; Ⓑ (*Nahrung*) food; (*fig. scherzh.*) fodder

**Ätzung** *die;* **~, ~en** Ⓐ etching; Ⓑ (*Med.*) cauterization

**au** /au̯/ *Interj.* Ⓐ (*bei Schmerz*) ow; ouch; Ⓑ (*bei Überraschung, Begeisterung*) oh

**Au** *die;* **~, ~en** (*südd., österr.*) ⇒ **Aue A**

**aua** /'au̯a/ *Interj.* (*ugs.; Kinderspr.*) ow; ouch

**Aubergine** /obɛr'ʒi:nə/ *die;* **~, ~n** aubergine (*Brit.*); eggplant

**auch** /au̯x/ ❶ *Adv.* Ⓐ (*ebenso, ebenfalls*) as well; too; also; **Klaus war ~ dabei** Klaus was there as well *or* too; Klaus was also there; **Ich gehe jetzt. — Ich ~:** I'm going now — So am I; **Mir ist warm. — Mir ~:** I feel warm — So do I; **... — Ja, das ~:** ... — Yes, that too; **~ gut!** that's all right too; **das kann ich ~!** I can do that too; **was er verspricht, tut er ~:** what he promises to do, he does; **wenn er sagt, er kommt, dann kommt er ~:** if he says he's going to come, then he'll come; **nicht nur ..., sondern ~ ...** not only ..., but also ...; **grüß deine Frau und ~ die Kinder** give my regards to your wife and the children too; **sehr gut, aber ~ teuer** very good but expensive too; **~ das noch!** that's all I/we *etc.* need!; **oder ~:** or; **oder ~ nicht** or not, as the case may be; **das weiß ich ~ nicht** I don't know either; **ich weiß ~ das nicht** I don't know that either; **ich habe ~ keine Lust/kein Geld** I don't feel like it either/don't have any money either; **das hat ~ nichts genützt** that did not help either; **wir waren unter anderem ~ in Florenz** we were in Florence, among other places; ⇒ *auch* **sowohl**; Ⓑ (*sogar, selbst*) even; **~ wenn** even if; **wenn ~:** even if *or* though; **ohne ~ nur zu fragen/eine Sekunde zu zögern** without even asking/hesitating for a second; Ⓒ (*außerdem, im Übrigen*) besides; **und ich sehe ~ gar nicht ein, warum ...** nor do I see why ...; and besides, I don't see why ...

❷ *Partikel* Ⓐ *not translated* **etwas anderes habe ich ~ nicht erwartet** I never expected anything else; **du bist aber ~ ein Trottel** (*ugs.*) you're a real idiot[, you are] (*coll.*); **so schlimm ist es ~ [wieder] nicht** it's not as bad as all that; **den Teufel ~:** damn it [all]!; **nun hör aber ~ zu!** now listen!; **wozu [denn] ~?** what's the point? why should I/you *etc.?*; Ⓑ (*zweifelnd*) **bist du dir ~ im Klaren, was das bedeutet?** are you sure you unterstand what that means?; **bist du ~ glücklich?** are you truly happy?; **lügst du ~ nicht?** you're not lying, are you?; Ⓒ (*mit Interrogativpron.*) **wo .../wer .../wann .../was ...** *usw.* **~:** wherever/whoever/whenever/whatever *etc.* ...; **wie dem ~ sei** however that may be; Ⓓ (*konzessiv*) **mag er ~ noch so klug sein** however clever he may be; no matter how clever he is; **so oft ich ~ anrief** however often I rang; no matter how often I rang; **so gern ich es ~ täte, ...** much as I should like to [do it]; **so sehr er sich ~ bemühte** much as he tried; **wenn ~!** never mind

**Audienz** /au̯'di̯ɛnts/ *die;* **~, ~en** audience

**Audimax** /au̯di'maks/ *das;* **~** (*Studentenspr.*) main lecture hall

**audiovisuell** /au̯di̯ovi'zu̯ɛl/ ❶ *Adj.* audio-visual. ❷ *adv.* audio-visually

**auditiv** /au̯di'ti:f/ ❶ *Adj.* auditory. ❷ *adv.* auditorily

**Auditorium** /au̯di'to:ri̯ʊm/ *das;* **~s, Auditorien** Ⓐ (*Hörsaal*) auditorium; **~ maximum** (*Hochschulw.*) main lecture hall; Ⓑ (*Zuhörerschaft*) audience

**Aue** /'au̯ə/ *die;* **~, ~n** Ⓐ (*dichter.*) mead (*poet.*); meadow; Ⓑ (*Geogr.*) water meadow

**Auen·wald** *der* riverside forest

**Auer-** /'au̯ɐ-/**: ~hahn** *der; Pl.* **~hähne** [cock] capercaillie; **~henne** *die* [female *or* hen] capercaillie; **~huhn** *das* capercaillie; **~ochse** *der* aurochs

**auf** /au̯f/ ❶ *Präp. mit Dat.* Ⓐ on; **~ See** at sea; **~ dem Baum** in the tree; **~ der Erde** on earth; **~ der Welt** in the world; **~ der Straße** in the street; **~ dem Platz** in the square; **~ meinem Konto** in my account; **~ den Hebriden/Skye** in the Hebrides/on

Skye; **~ Meereshöhe** at sea level; **~ beiden Augen blind** blind in both eyes; **das Thermometer steht ~ 15°** the thermometer stands at *or* says *or* reads 15°; **B** (*bei Räumen, Gebäuden, Institutionen*) at ‹post office, town, hall, police station›; **~ seinem Zimmer** (*ugs.*) in his room; **Geld ~ der Bank haben** have money in the bank; **~ der Polizei** (*ugs.*) at the police station; **~ der Schule/Uni** at school/university; **C** (*bei Veranstaltungen usw.*) at ‹party, wedding›; on ‹course, trip, walk, holiday, tour›; **D was hat es damit ~ sich?** what's it all about?; **damit hat es nichts/etwas ~ sich** there is nothing/something in it.
❷ *Präp. mit Akk.* **A** on; on to; **sich ~ einen Stuhl setzen** sit down on a chair; **sich ~ das Bett legen** lie down on the bed; **er nahm den Rucksack ~ den Rücken** he lifted the rucksack up on to his back; **~ einen Berg steigen** climb up a mountain; **sich** (*Dat.*) **einen Hut ~ den Kopf setzen** put a hat on [one's head]; **~ den Mond fliegen** fly to the moon; **~ die See hinausfahren** go out to sea; **jmdm. ~ den Fuß treten** step on sb.'s foot; **~ die Straße gehen** go [out] into the street; **~ den Grund des Meeres sinken** sink to the bottom of the sea; **jmdn. ~ den Rücken legen** lay sb. on his/her back; **jmdn. ~ den Rücken drehen** turn sb. on to his/her back; **~ die Hebriden** to the Hebrides; **~ die andere Seite der Schranke gehen** go over to the other side of the barrier; **etw. ~ ein Konto überweisen** transfer sth. to an account; **das Thermometer ist ~ 0° gefallen** the thermometer has fallen to 0°; **~ ihn!** (*ugs.*) get him!; **B** (*bei Institutionen, Veranstaltungen*) to; **~ die Schule/Uni gehen** go to school/university; **~ einen Lehrgang gehen** go on a course; **~ Reisen/Urlaub/Tournee gehen** go travelling/on holiday/on tour; **C** (*bei Entfernungen*) **~ 10 km [Entfernung]** for [a distance of] 10 km; **wir näherten uns der Hütte [bis] ~ 30 m** we approached to within 30 m of the hut; **D** (*zeitlich*) for; **~ Jahre [hinaus]** for years [to come]; **etw. ~ nächsten Mittwoch festlegen/verschieben** arrange sth. for/postpone sth. until next Wednesday; **die Nacht von Sonntag ~ Montag** Sunday night; **das fällt ~ einen Montag** it falls on a Monday; **wir verschieben es ~ den 3. Mai** we'll postpone it to the 3 May; **sich ~ morgen vertagen** adjourn until tomorrow; **komm doch mal ~ eine Tasse Tee herüber** come round for a cup of tea some time; **E** (*zur Angabe der Art und Weise*) **~ diese Art und Weise** in this way; **~ die Tour erreichst du bei mir nichts** (*ugs.*) you won't get anywhere with me like that; **komm mir bloß nicht ~ die Sentimentale!** (*salopp*) don't try *or* come the old sentimental bit with me! (*coll.*); **auf die Billige** (*salopp*) on the cheap; **~ Deutsch** in German; **~ das Sorgfältigste/Herzlichste** (*geh.*) most carefully/warmly; **~ a enden** end in a; **Wörter ~ a** words ending in a; **F** (*aufgrund*) **~ Wunsch** on request; **~ vielfachen Wunsch/wiederholte Aufforderung [hin]** in response to numerous requests/repeated demands; **~ meine Bitte** at my request; **~ seine Initiative** on his initiative; **~ Befehl** on command; **~ meinen Vorschlag [hin]** at my suggestion; **erst ~ meinen Brief [hin]** only as a result of my letter; **G** (*sonstige Verwendungen*) **ein Teelöffel ~ einen Liter Wasser** one teaspoon to one litre of water; **das Bier geht ~ mich** (*ugs.*) the beer's on 'me (*coll.*); **~ wen geht die Cola?** who's paying for the Coke?; **Welle ~ Welle brandete ans Ufer** wave upon wave broke on the shore; **einen Text ~ orthographische Fehler [hin] durchsehen** examine a text for orthographical errors; **jmdn. ~ Tb untersuchen** examine sb. for TB; **jmdn. ~ seine Eignung prüfen** test sb.'s suitability; **~ die Sekunde/den Millimeter [genau]** [precise] to the second/millimetre; **ein Kabel ~ 1,50 m kürzen/abschneiden** shorten a cable to 1.50 m; **~ ein gutes Gelingen** to our/your success; **~ deine Gesundheit** your health; **~ bald/morgen!** (*bes. südd.*) see you soon/tomorrow; **~ 10 zählen** (*bes. südd.*) count [up] to 10; ⇒ *auch* **einmal** 1 A; **machen** 3 F.
❸ *Adv.* **A** (*aufgerichtet, aufgestanden*) up; **~!** up you get!; (*zu einem Hund*) up!; **Sprung ~! Marsch, marsch!** (*Milit.*) Up! At the double!; **B sie waren längst ~ und davon** they had made off long before; **jetzt heißts ~ und davon** it's time to be off; ⇒ *auch* **aufmachen, davonmachen**; **C** (*bes. südd.: los*) come on; **~ gehts** off we go; let's go; **D** (*Aufforderung, sich aufzumachen*) **~ ins Schwimmbad!/nach Schifferstadt!** come on, off to the swimming pool!/to Schifferstadt!; **E ~ und ab** *od.* (*geh.*) **nieder** up and down; **das Auf und Ab** the up-and-down movement; **das Auf und Ab des Lebens** (*fig.*) the ups and downs of life; **F ~ und ab** (*hin und her*) up and down; to and fro; **G** (*Aufforderung, sich etw. aufzusetzen*) **Helm/Hut/Brille ~!** helmet/hat/glasses on!; **H** (*ugs.: geöffnet, offen*) open; **Fenster/Türen/Mund ~!** open the window/doors/your mouth!
❹ **~ dass** *Konj.* (*veralt.*) so that; **~ dass er sich nicht erkälte[te]** lest he should catch [a] cold

**auf|arbeiten** *tr. V.* **A** (*erledigen*) catch up with ‹correspondence etc.›; **B** (*studieren, analysieren*) review ‹literature, material›; look back on and reappraise ‹one's past, childhood›; **C** (*restaurieren, überholen*) refurbish

**Aufarbeitung** *die*; **~, ~en A** (*Erledigung*) **die ~ der Post** catching up with the post (*Brit.*) *or* mail; **B** (*das Studieren, Analysieren*) **die ~ der Literatur/Kindheit** reviewing the literature/looking back on and reappraising one's childhood; **C** (*Restaurierung*) refurbishing

**auf|atmen** *itr. V.* **A** (*fig.: erleichtert sein*) breathe a sigh of relief; **ein Aufatmen** a sigh of relief; **B** (*tief atmen*) breathe deeply

**auf|backen** *regelm.* (*auch unr.*) *tr. V.* crisp up ‹bread, rolls, etc.›

**auf|bahren** *tr. V.* lay out ‹body, corpse›; **jmdn./einen Toten ~:** lay out sb.'s body; **aufgebahrt sein** ‹king, president, etc.› lie in state

**Auf·bau** *der*; **~[e]s, ~ten A** (*das Aufbauen*) construction; building; (*das Wiederaufbauen*) reconstruction; rebuilding; **B** (*von Staat, Ökonomie, gesellschaftlicher Ordnung*) building; **den wirtschaftlichen ~ beschleunigen** speed up economic development; **C** (*Biol.*) synthesis; **D** (*Struktur*) structure; **E** *Pl.* (*Schiffbau*) superstructure *sing.*; **F** (*Bauw.*) superstructure; **einen zweistöckigen ~ genehmigen** approve the addition of two extra storeys; **G** (*Kfz-W.*) body

**Aufbau·arbeit** *die* construction work; (*bei Wiederaufbau*) reconstruction work

**auf|bauen** ❶ *tr. V.* **A** *auch itr.* (*errichten, aufstellen*) erect ‹hut, kiosk, podium›; set up ‹equipment, train set›; build ‹house, bridge›; put up ‹tent›; (*wieder aufbauen*) rebuild ‹house, bridge›; **ein Haus neu ~:** rebuild a house; **B** (*hinstellen, arrangieren*) lay *or* set out ‹food, presents, etc.›; **C** (*fig.: schaffen*) build ‹state, economy, social order, life, political party, etc.›; build up ‹business, organization, army, spy network›; **sich** (*Dat.*) **ein neues Leben ~:** build a new life [for oneself]; **D** (*fig.: strukturieren*) structure; **E** (*fig.: fördern*) **jmdn./etw. zu etw. ~:** build sb./sth. up into sth.; **jmdn. als etw. ~:** build sb. up as sth.; **F** (*gründen*) **etw. auf etw.** (*Dat.*) **~:** base sth. upon sth.; **G** (*Biol.*) synthesize.
❷ *itr. V.* **auf etw.** (*Dat.*) **~:** be based on sth.
❸ *refl. V.* **A** (*ugs.: sich hinstellen*) plant oneself (**vor** + *Dat.* in front of); **B** (*sich zusammensetzen*) be composed (**aus** of); **C** (*sich auftürmen, sich bilden*) ‹clouds, pressure, tension, etc.› build up

**aufbauend** *Adj.* constructive ‹criticism, geological process›; restorative ‹medicine›; nutrient ‹substance›

**auf|bäumen** /ˈaufbɔymən/ *refl. V.* rear up; **sich gegen jmdn./etw. ~** (*fig.*) rise up against sb./sth.

**Aufbau·prinzip** *das* structural principle

**auf|bauschen** ❶ *tr. V.* **A** (*aufblähen*) billow; billow, belly [out] ‹sail›; **B** (*fig.: hochspielen*) blow up (*coll.*); exaggerate. ❷ *refl. V.* (*fig.: sich auswachsen*) **sich [zu etw.] ~:** blow up [into sth.] (*coll.*)

**Aufbauten** ⇒ **Aufbau**

**auf|begehren** *itr. V.* (*geh.*) rebel

**auf|behalten** *unr. tr. V.* **etw. ~:** keep sth. on

**auf|beißen** *unr. tr. V.* **etw. ~:** bite sth. open; **sich** (*Dat.*) **die Lippe ~:** bite one's lip [and make it bleed]

**auf|bekommen** *unr. tr. V.* **A** (*öffnen können*) **etw. ~:** get sth. open; **B** (*aufessen können*) manage to eat; **C** (*aufsetzen können*) **etw. ~:** get sth. on; **D** (*aufgegeben bekommen*) be given

**auf|bereiten** *tr. V.* **A** (*Hüttenw., Bergbau*) dress, prepare ‹ore, coal›; **Erz magnetisch ~:** separate ore magnetically; **B** (*Wasserwirtsch.*) purify; treat; **C** (*Kerntechnik*) reprocess; **D** (*Statistik*) process; **E** (*geh.*) (*bearbeiten*) adapt; (*erschließen*) reconstruct; **etw. literarisch/dramatisch ~:** put sth. into literary/dramatic form

**Auf·bereitung** *die* ⇒ **aufbereiten** A-E: dressing; preparation; purification; treatment; reprocessing; processing; adaptation; reconstruction

**Aufbereitungs·anlage** *die* (*Hüttenw.*) preparation plant; (*Wasserwirtsch.*) purification works *sing.*; treatment plant; (*Kerntechnik*) reprocessing plant

**auf|bessern** *tr. V.* improve; increase ‹pension, wages, etc.›

**Auf·besserung** *die* improvement (*Gen.* in); (*bei Renten, Löhnen, Gehältern*) increase (*Gen.* in); **zur ~ seines Taschengeldes/seiner Sprachkenntnisse** to increase his pocket money/to improve his linguistic proficiency

**auf|bewahren** *tr. V.* keep; store, keep ‹medicines, food, provisions›; (*fig.: bewahren, erhalten*) preserve ‹memory, name, writings›; **die Fahrkarte/das Testament musst du gut ~:** you must keep your ticket safe/keep the will in a safe place; **etw. kühl ~:** store sth. in a cool place

**Auf·bewahrung** *die* **A** ⇒ **aufbewahren**: keeping; storage; **jmdm. etw. zur ~ geben/anvertrauen** give sth. to sb. for safe keeping/entrust sb. with the care of sth.; **bei ~ im Kühlschrank** if kept in a refrigerator; **B** (*Verkehrsw.*) left-luggage office (*Brit.*); baggage check room (*Amer.*)

**Aufbewahrungs-: ~ort** *der*: **das ist kein geeigneter ~ort für Dokumente/Lebensmittel** that is not a suitable place to keep documents/keep *or* store food; **~schein** *der* (*Verkehrsw.*) left-luggage ticket (*Brit.*); baggage check *or* ticket (*Amer.*)

**auf|biegen** ❶ *unr. tr. V.* **A etw. ~:** bend sth. open; **B** (*hochbiegen*) bend up[wards]. ❷ *unr. refl. V.* **A** bend open; **B** (*sich hochbiegen*) bend up[wards]

**auf|bieten** *unr. tr. V.* **A** (*aufwenden*) exert ‹strength, energy, will power, influence, authority›; call on ‹skill, wit, powers of persuasion or eloquence›; **B** (*einsetzen*) call in ‹police, troops›; **C** (*Milit. veralt.: ausheben*) call up ‹troops›; raise ‹army›; **D** (*zur Eheschließung*) **ein Brautpaar ~:** read *or* call the banns of a couple to be married; **E** (*bei Versteigerung*) **etw. [mit 400 Mark] ~:** put sth. up for auction [at a starting price of 400 marks]

**Aufbietung** *die*; **~ A unter ~ aller Kräfte/seiner ganzen Überredungskunst** summoning up all one's strength/calling on all one's persuasive skills; **B** (*Milit. veralt.*) calling up; (*einer Armee*) raising

*old spelling (see note on page 1707)

**auf|binden** *unr. tr. V.* **A** *(öffnen, lösen)* untie; undo; **sich/jmdm. die Schuhe ~:** undo one's/sb.'s shoes; **B** *(hochbinden)* tie *or* put up ‹hair›; tie ‹plant› up straight; **jmdm./sich die Haare ~:** tie *or* put up sb.'s/one's hair; **C** *(auf den Rücken binden)* **jmdm./einem Tier eine Last ~:** tie a burden on to sb.'s/an animal's back; **D** *(ugs.: weismachen)* **wer hat dir das aufgebunden?** who spun you that yarn?; **jmdm. ein Märchen/eine Fabel ~:** spin sb. a yarn; ⇒ *auch* **Bär**; **E** *(binden auf)* **etw. auf etw.** *(Akk.)* **~:** tie sth. on to sth.; **F** *(Buchw.: binden)* bind

**auf|blähen** **1** *tr. V.* distend ‹body, stomach›; puff out ‹cheeks, feathers›; flare ‹nostrils›; billow, fill, belly [out] ‹sail›; billow ‹washing, clothing›; *(fig.: vergrößern)* over-inflate; **ein aufgeblähter Beamtenapparat** *(fig.)* an overblown bureaucracy. **2** *refl. V.* **A** ‹sail› billow *or* belly out; ‹balloon, lungs, chest› expand; ‹stomach› swell up, become swollen *or* distended; **B** *(abwertend: sich aufspielen)* puff oneself up

**Auf·blähung** *die (fig.)* overexpansion

**aufblasbar** *Adj.* inflatable

**auf|blasen** **1** *unr. tr. V.* blow up; inflate; **die Backen ~:** puff out one's cheeks; **etw. zu etw. ~** *(fig.)* blow sth. up into sth. **2** *unr. refl. V. (ugs. abwertend: sich aufspielen)*; **sich ~ [wie ein Frosch]** puff oneself up **(mit** about); ⇒ *auch* **aufgeblasen 2**

**auf|bleiben** *unr. itr. V.; mit sein* **A** *(geöffnet bleiben)* stay open; **B** *(nicht zu Bett gehen)* stay up

**auf|blenden** **1** *tr. V. (Kfz-W.)* **die Scheinwerfer ~:** switch one's headlights to full beam; **mit aufgeblendeten Scheinwerfern fahren** drive with headlights on full beam. **2** *itr. V.* **A** *(Kfz-W.)* switch to full beam; **B** *(Fot., Film)* open up the lens; increase the [lens] aperture

**auf|blicken** *itr. V.* **A** look up; *(kurz)* glance up; **von etw. ~:** look/glance up from sth.; **B** *(verehrend)* **zu jmdm. ~:** look up to sb.

**auf|blinken** *itr. V.* **A** ‹light› flash; ‹metal› glint; ‹star› blink; **B** *(ugs.: kurz aufblenden)* flash one's headlights

**auf|blitzen** *itr. V.* flash; ‹wave, white caps› sparkle

**auf|blühen** *itr. V.; mit sein* **A** bloom; come into bloom; ‹bud› open; **eine halb/voll aufgeblühte Tulpe** a half-open tulip/a tulip in full bloom; **B** *(fig.: aufleben)* blossom [out]; **C** *(fig.: einen Aufschwung nehmen)* ‹trade, business, town, industry› flourish and expand; ‹cultural life, science› blossom and flourish

**auf|bocken** *tr. V.* **etw. ~:** jack sth. up

**auf|bohren** *tr. V.* **etw. ~:** drill a hole in sth.; drill ‹tooth›; bore out ‹cylinder, engine›

**auf|branden** *itr. V.; mit sein (geh.)* **die Wellen brandeten an den Felsen auf** the waves broke against the rock with a roar; **Beifall/Jubel brandete auf** *(fig.)* thunderous applause/cheering burst out

**auf|braten** *unr. tr. V.* **etw. ~:** fry sth. up [again]

**auf|brauchen** *tr. V.* use up

**auf|brausen** *itr. V.; mit sein* **A** *(zornig werden)* flare up; **schnell/leicht ~:** be quick-tempered *or* hot-tempered; have a quick temper; **B** *(zu brausen beginnen)* ‹sea, surf, wave› surge [up]; ‹liquid› seethe, boil up; ‹wind› rise to a roar; **Beifall/Jubel brauste auf** there was a sudden roar of applause/a thunderous cheer went up

**aufbrausend** *Adj.* quick-tempered; hot-tempered; **ein ~es Temperament haben** be quick-tempered *or* hot-tempered; have a quick temper

**auf|brechen** **1** *unr. tr. V.* **A** *(öffnen)* break open ‹lock, safe, box, crate, etc.›; break into ‹car›; force [open] ‹door›; break up ‹ground, surface›; *(geh.: aufreißen)* tear open ‹letter, telegram›; *(fig.)* break down ‹[social] structures›; break ‹system›; **B** *(Jägerspr.: ausnehmen)* gut. **2** *unr. itr. V.; mit sein* **A** *(sich öffnen)* ‹bud› open [up], burst [open]; ‹ice [sheet], surface, ground› break up; ‹wound› open; **alte Wunden brechen auf** *(fig.)* old wounds are opening [again]; **B** *(sich auf den Weg machen)* set off, start out **(zu** on); **C** *(geh.: spürbar werden)* become evident; emerge

**auf|brennen** *unr. tr. V.* **einem Tier ein Zeichen/ein Mal ~:** brand an animal; **jmdm. eins ~** *(salopp: auf jmdn. schießen)* let sb. have it

**auf|bringen** *unr. tr. V.* **A** *(beschaffen)* find; raise, find ‹money›; *(fig.)* find, summon [up] ‹strength, energy, courage›; find ‹patience›; **B** *(kreieren)* introduce, start ‹fashion, custom›; introduce ‹slogan, theory›; start, put about ‹rumour›; **C** *(in Wut bringen)* **jmdn. ~:** make sb. angry; infuriate sb.; **D** *(aufwiegeln)* **jmdn. gegen jmdn./etw. ~:** set sb. against sb./sth.; **E** *(auftragen)* put on, apply ‹paint, ointment, varnish, etc.›; **F** *(Seew.)* seize; *(in den Hafen bringen)* bring in; **G** *(bes. südd.)* ⇒ **aufbekommen A, B, C**

**Auf·bruch** *der* **A** departure; *(fig. geh.)* awakening; **im ~ begriffen sein** be on the point of departure *or* of setting off; *(fig. geh.)* experience an awakening; **das Zeichen zum ~ geben** give the signal to set off *or* leave; **zum ~ rüsten** get ready to set off *or* leave; **B** *(aufgebrochene Stelle)* crack

**Aufbruchs·stimmung** *die:* **es herrschte allgemeine ~:** everybody was getting ready to go; **bist du schon in ~?** are you all ready to go?

**auf|brühen** *tr. V.* brew [up]

**auf|brüllen** *itr. V.* let out *or* give a roar; ‹animal› bellow

**auf|brummen** *tr. V. (ugs.)* **jmdm. etw. ~:** slap sth. on sb. *(coll.)*; **einem Schüler viele Hausaufgaben ~:** lumber *(Brit.) or* burden a pupil with a lot of homework; **jmdm. die Kosten für etw. ~:** land sb. with the costs for sth.

**auf|bügeln** *tr. V.* iron; **etw. [auf etw.** *(Akk.)***] ~:** iron sth. on [to sth.]; **Flicken zum Aufbügeln** iron-on patches

**auf|bürden** *tr. V. (geh.)* **jmdm./einem Tier etw. ~:** load sth. on to sb./an animal; **jmdm./sich etw. ~** *(fig.)* burden sb./oneself with sth.; **jmdm. die Schuld ~:** put the blame on sb.

**auf|bürsten** *tr. V.* **etw. ~:** brush sth. up; give sth. a brush-up

**auf|decken** **1** *tr. V.* **A** uncover; **das Bett ~:** pull back the covers; **sich im Schlaf ~:** throw off one's covers; **B** *(Kartenspiele)* show; **die** *od.* **seine Karten ~** *(fig.)* lay one's cards on the table *(fig.)*; **C** *(enthüllen)* expose ‹corruption, error, weakness, misdeeds, crime, plot, abuse, etc.›; *(erkennen und bewusst machen)* reveal, uncover ‹connections, motive, processes, cause, error, weakness, contradiction, etc.›; **D** *(für eine Mahlzeit)* **etw. ~:** put sth. on the table. **2** *itr. V.* lay the table

**Auf·deckung** *die* ⇒ **aufdecken 1 C**: exposure; revelation; uncovering

**auf|donnern** *refl. V. (ugs. abwertend)* tart *(Brit.) or* doll oneself up *(coll.)*; get tarted *(Brit.) or* dolled up *(coll.)*

**auf|drängen** **1** *tr. V.* **jmdm. etw. ~:** force sth. on sb.; **jmdm. seine Ansichten ~:** force *or* impose one's views on sb. **2** *refl. V.* **A** **sich jmdm. ~:** force one's company *or* oneself on sb.; **ich will mich aber nicht ~:** I don't want to impose; **B** *(fig.: in den Sinn kommen)* **mir drängte sich der Verdacht auf, dass ...** I couldn't help suspecting that ...; **dieser Gedanke drängt sich [einem] förmlich auf** one simply can't help but think so; the thought is unavoidable

**auf|drehen** **1** *tr. V.* **A** *(öffnen)* unscrew ‹bottle cap, nut›; undo ‹screw›; turn on ‹tap, gas, water›; open ‹valve, bottle, vice›; **B** *(ugs.: laut stellen)* turn up ‹radio, record player, etc.›; **C** *(ugs.: aufziehen)* wind up ‹musical box, watch, toy, etc.›; **D** *(zu Locken drehen)* turn up, twist up ‹moustache›; **sich/jmdm. die Haare ~:** put one's/sb.'s hair in curlers. **2** *itr. V. (ugs.)* **A** *(das Tempo steigern)* **[voll] ~:** put one's foot [right] down *(coll.)*; step on the gas *(Amer.)*; *(fig.)* step the pace [right] up; **B** *(in Schwung kommen)* get into the mood; get going

**auf·dringlich** **1** *Adj.* importunate, *(coll.)* pushy ‹person›; insistent ‹music, advertisement, questioning›; pestering *attrib.* ‹journalist›; pungent ‹perfume, smell›; loud, gaudy ‹colour, wallpaper›; **~e Vertraulichkeit** overfamiliarity; **~e Freundlichkeit** overfriendliness; **sei nicht so ~!** don't pester so!; **~ riechen** have a pungent smell; be pungent. **2** *adv.* ‹behave› importunately, *(coll.)* pushily; ‹ask› insistently

**Aufdringlichkeit** *die;* **~, ~en** **A** ⇒ **aufdringlich**: insistent manner; insistence; importunity; pushiness *(coll.)*; pungency; **B** *(Äußerung, Handlung)* piece of overfamiliarity; **die ~en der Männer** the overfamiliarity *sing.* of the men

**auf|dröseln** /ˈaufdrøːzl̩n/ *tr. V. (ugs., auch fig.)* unravel; unpick ‹piece of knitting›

**Auf·druck** *der;* **~[e]s, ~e** **A** imprint; **B** *(Philat.)* ⇒ **Überdruck²**

**auf|drucken** *tr. V.* **etw. auf etw.** *(Akk.)* **~:** print sth. on sth.; **Briefumschläge mit aufgedruckter Adresse** envelopes with the address printed on them

**auf|drücken** *tr. V.* **A** *(öffnen)* push open; **B** *(aufplatzen lassen)* squeeze ‹pimple, boil›; **C** *(aufstempeln, aufprägen)* **etw. auf etw.** *(Akk.)* **~:** stamp sth. on sth.; **jmdm. einen Kuss ~:** plant a kiss on sb.; **einer Sache** *(Dat.)* **sein Gepräge ~** *(fig.)* leave one's mark *or* stamp on sth.; ⇒ *auch* **Stempel A**; **D** *(auf etw. drücken)* **etw. auf etw.** *(Akk.)* **~:** press sth. on to sth.; **drück den Bleistift nicht so fest auf** don't press so hard with your pencil

**auf·einander** *Adv.* on top of one another *or* each other; *(zusammen)* together; *(gegeneinander)* against each other; against one another; **die Bücher sollen ~ liegen** the books should lie one on top of the other; **zwei Autos waren ~ gefahren** two cars had collided with each other *or* one another; **~ warten** wait for each other *or* one another; **~ zugehen** walk towards *or* approach one another *or* each other; **die Zähne ~ beißen** clench one's teeth; **~ folgen** follow each other *or* one another; **~ folgend** successive; **an mehreren ~ folgenden Tagen** several days running; on several successive days; **wenn es regnet, hängt man den ganzen Tag im Hotel ~** *(ugs.)* when it rains, people hang around on top of each other all day in the hotel; **die Hunde ~ hetzen** set the dogs on each other *or* one another; **~ prallen** crash into each other *or* one another; collide; ‹armies› clash; *(fig.)* ‹opinions› clash; **etw. ~ schichten** stack sth. up; **Kisten ~ türmen** stack crates [up] one on top of the other; **wo die Linien ~ stoßen** where the lines meet; **~ treffen** ‹teams, enemies, opponents, streets› meet; ‹missiles› collide, hit each other; hit one another

***aufeinander|beißen** *usw.* ⇒ **aufeinander**

**Aufeinander·folge** *die;* **~:** sequence; **in rascher ~:** in rapid *or* quick succession

***aufeinander|folgen** *usw.* ⇒ **aufeinander**

**Aufenthalt** /ˈauf|ɛnthalt/ *der;* **~[e]s, ~e** **A** stay; **der ~ im Depot ist verboten** personnel/the public *etc.* are not permitted to remain within the depot; **~ nehmen** *(geh.)* reside; **B** *(Fahrtunterbrechung)* stop; **der Zug hatte dort [10 Minuten] ~:** the train stopped there [for 10 minutes]; **ohne ~ durchfahren** travel through non-stop *or* without stopping; **C** *(geh.: Ort)* residence

**-aufenthalt** *der:* **Frankreich~/Italien~:** stay in France/Italy

**Aufenthalts-: ~bewilligung** *die* ⇒ **~erlaubnis**; **~dauer** *die* length of stay; **bei einer ~dauer von weniger als sechs Monaten** for a stay of less than six months; **~erlaubnis** *die* residence permit; **~genehmigung** *die* ⇒ **~erlaubnis**; **~ort** *der* [place of] residence; **jmds. ~ort ermitteln** establish sb.'s whereabouts *pl.*; **~raum** *der* (*in einer Schule o. Ä.*) common room (*Brit.*); (*in einer Jugendherberge*) day room; (*in einem Betrieb o. Ä.*) recreation room; (*in einem Hotel o. Ä.*) lounge

**auf|erlegen, auf·erlegen** *tr. V.* (*geh.*) **jmdm. etw. ~:** impose sth. on sb.; **du solltest dir etwas Zurückhaltung ~:** you should exercise some restraint; **die Kosten wurden dem Kläger auferlegt** costs were awarded against the plaintiff; **jmdm. eine schwere Prüfung ~:** subject sb. to *or* put sb. through a severe test

**auf|erstehen** *unr. itr. V.; mit sein* rise [again]; **von den Toten ~:** rise from the dead; **Christus ist auferstanden** Christ is risen

**Auferstehung** *die;* ~, **~en** resurrection

**auf·erwecken** *tr. V.* **jmdn. ~:** bring sb. back to life; raise sb. from the dead; **jmdn. von den Toten ~:** raise sb. from the dead; **der Lärm hätte einen Toten ~ können** (*fig.*) the noise was enough to waken the dead

**Auf·erweckung** *die:* **die ~ eines Toten** raising someone from the dead

**auf|essen** *unr. tr.* (*auch itr.*) *V.* eat up

**auf|fächern** ❶ *tr. V.* fan [out]; (*fig.*) set out. ❷ *refl. V.* fan out; **sich in Einzeldisziplinen ~:** develop into seperate disciplines

**auf|fädeln** *tr. V.* **etw. [auf etw.** (*Akk.*)**] ~:** thread sth. on to sth.

**auf|fahren** ❶ *unr. itr. V.; mit sein* Ⓐ (*aufprallen*) **auf ein anderes Fahrzeug ~:** drive *or* run into the back of another vehicle; **auf etw./jmdn. ~:** drive *or* run into sth./sb.; **das Schiff ist auf ein Riff aufgefahren** the ship has run aground on a reef; Ⓑ (*aufschließen*) **auf den Vordermann zu dicht ~:** drive too close to the car in front; tailgate; **fahr doch nicht so dicht** *od.* **nah auf!** don't drive so close!; **zu dichtes Auffahren** driving too close to the vehicle in front; tailgating; Ⓒ (*vorfahren*) drive up; Ⓓ (*in Stellung gehen*) move up [into position]; Ⓔ (*Bergmannsspr.*) go/come up; **aufgefahren kommen** come up; Ⓕ (*gen Himmel fahren*) ascend; Ⓖ (*aufschrecken*) start; **aus dem Schlaf ~:** awake with a start; Ⓗ (*aufbrausen*) flare up.
❷ *unr. tr. V.* Ⓐ (*in Stellung bringen*) bring *or* move up; Ⓑ (*ugs.: auftischen*) serve up

**auf·fahrend** *Adj.* quick-tempered; hot-tempered

**Auf·fahrt** *die* Ⓐ (*das Hinauffahren*) climb; drive up; **die ~ zum Gipfel** the drive up to the summit; Ⓑ (*zu Gebäuden*) drive; Ⓒ (*zur Autobahn*) slip road (*Brit.*); access road (*Amer.*); Ⓓ (*schweiz.*) (*Himmelfahrt*) Ascension; (*Himmelfahrtstag*) Ascension [Day]

**Auffahrts·fest** *das* (*schweiz.*) feast of the Ascension

**Auffahr·unfall** *der* rear-end collision

**auf|fallen** *unr. itr. V.; mit sein* Ⓐ (*auffällig sein*) stand out; **diese Fettflecken/Druckfehler fallen kaum auf** these grease marks/printing errors are hardly noticeable; **tu das so, dass es nicht auffällt** do it so that it doesn't attract attention *or* so that nobody notices; **er fällt durch seine abstehenden Ohren auf** the fact that his ears stick out makes him conspicuous; **seine Abwesenheit fiel nicht auf** his absence was not noticed; **um nicht aufzufallen** so as not to attract attention; **sie will nur ~:** she just wants to attract attention; **jmdm. fällt etw. auf** sb. notices sth.; sth. strikes sb.; **fällt dir an diesem Satz etwas auf?** does anything strike you about that sentence?; **er ist mir angenehm/unangenehm aufgefallen** he made a good/bad impression on me; **ist Ihnen nichts aufgefallen?** did you not notice anything?; did nothing strike you?; **so etwas fällt sofort/nie auf** that sort of thing will be noticed right away/will never be noticed; **es fiel allgemein auf, dass ...** it was generally noticed that ...; Ⓑ (*auftreffen*) fall (**auf** + *Akk.* on [to]); strike (**auf** + *Akk.* sth.); **das ~de Licht** the light falling on [to] *or* striking the surface *etc.*; (*Optik*) the incident light

**auffallend** ❶ *Adj.* (*auffällig*) conspicuous; (*eindrucksvoll, bemerkenswert*) striking ‹contrast, figure, appearance, beauty, similarity›; **das Auffallendste an ihr** the most striking thing about her. ❷ *adv.* (*auffällig*) conspicuously; (*eindrucksvoll, bemerkenswert*) ‹contrast, differ› strikingly; **stimmt ~!** (*scherzh.*) you're so right!

**auf·fällig** ❶ *Adj.* conspicuous; garish, loud ‹colour›; **eine recht ~e Erscheinung sein** have a most striking appearance. ❷ *adv.* conspicuously; **sich ~ kleiden** dress showily; **~er hätte er es nicht machen können** he couldn't have made it more obvious [if he had tried]

**Auf·fälligkeit** *die* Ⓐ conspicuousness; (*Grellheit*) garishness; loudness; Ⓑ (*etw. Auffälliges*) distinctive feature

**auf|falten** ❶ *tr. V.* fold open; unfold. ❷ *refl. V.* (*Geol.*) fold upward

**auf|fangen** *unr. tr. V.* Ⓐ (*fangen*) catch; (*fig.*) regain control of ‹aircraft›; Ⓑ (*aufnehmen, sammeln*) collect; collect, catch ‹liquid›; (*fig.*) receive ‹refugees›; Ⓒ (*wahrnehmen*) catch ‹words, conversation›; (*Funkw.: empfangen*) pick up; Ⓓ (*absorbieren*) absorb; Ⓔ (*Milit.: aufhalten*) hold ‹attack, advance›; Ⓕ (*Handarb.*) pick up ‹stitch›; Ⓖ (*ausgleichen*) offset ‹price increase etc.›

**Auffang·lager** *das* reception camp

**auf|fassen** *tr. V.* Ⓐ (*ansehen als*) **etw. als etw. ~:** see *or* regard sth. as sth.; **etw. als Scherz/Kompliment/Beleidigung/Kritik ~:** take sth. as a joke/compliment/insult/criticism; **etw. persönlich/falsch ~:** take sth. personally/misunderstand sth.; Ⓑ (*begreifen*) grasp; comprehend

**Auf·fassung** *die* Ⓐ (*Meinung, Ansicht*) view; (*Begriff*) conception; **nach meiner ~:** in my view; **der ~ sein, dass ...** take the view that ...; be of the opinion that ...; **eine andere ~ von etw. haben** take a different view of sth.; Ⓑ ⇒ **Auffassungsgabe**

**Auffassungs-: ~gabe** *die* powers *pl.* of comprehension; **eine leichte/schnelle ~gabe haben** be quick on the uptake; **~sache** *die: in* **~sache sein** depend on one's point of view; **~vermögen** *das* ⇒ **~gabe**

**auf|fegen** *tr.* (*auch itr.*) *V.* (*bes. nordd.*) sweep up

**auffindbar** *Adj.* findable; **der Schlüssel muss doch ~ sein!** we must be able to find the key somewhere!; **es ist nirgends/nicht ~:** it's nowhere to be found/it can't be *or* isn't to be found; **schwer/leicht ~ sein** be hard/easy to find

**auf|finden** *unr. tr. V.* find

**auf|fischen** *tr. V.* (*ugs.*) fish out (*coll.*)

**auf|flackern** *itr. V.; mit sein* flicker up; (*fig.*) ‹hope› flicker up; ‹revolt, unrest, passion, anger› flare up

**auf|flammen** *itr. V.; mit sein* (*auch fig.*) flare up; **in seinen Augen flammte Zorn auf** (*fig.*) his eyes flashed with anger

**auf|fliegen** *unr. itr. V.; mit sein* Ⓐ (*hochfliegen*) fly up; Ⓑ (*sich öffnen*) fly open; Ⓒ (*ugs.: scheitern*) ‹illegal organization, drug ring› be *or* get busted (*coll.*); **den Parteitag/einen Schmugglerring ~ lassen** ruin *or* (*Brit. sl.*) scupper the party conference/bust a smuggling ring (*coll.*)

**auf|fordern** *tr. V.* Ⓐ *auch itr.* **jmdn. ~, etw. zu tun** call upon *or* ask sb. to do sth.; **jmdn. zur Teilnahme/Zahlung ~:** call upon *or* ask sb. to take part/ask sb. for payment; **ich fordere Sie zum letzten Mal auf, ...** I am asking you for the last time ...; **jmdn. dringend ~, etw. zu tun** urgently request sb. to do sth.; Ⓑ (*einladen, ermuntern*) **jmdn. ~, etw. zu tun** invite *or* ask sb. to do sth.; **jmdn. zu einem Spaziergang/zum Mitspielen/Sitzen ~:** invite sb. for a walk/invite *or* ask sb. to join in/sit down; **jmdn. [zum Tanz] ~:** ask sb. to dance

**auffordernd** ❶ *Adj.* **mit einer ~en Geste** with a gesture of invitation; **mit ~em Blick** with a look of encouragement. ❷ *adv.* encouragingly

**Auf·forderung** *die* Ⓐ request; (*nachdrücklicher*) demand; **nach dreimaliger/mehrmaliger ~:** after three/repeated requests; Ⓑ (*Einladung, Ermunterung*) invitation

**Aufforderungs·satz** *der* (*Sprachw.*) clause/*sentence expressing a wish, desire, or command*

**auf|forsten** ❶ *tr. V.* afforest; (*wieder ~*) reforest; **einen Wald ~:** restock a forest. ❷ *itr. V.* establish woods; (*wieder ~*) re-establish the woods

**Aufforstung** *die;* ~, **~en** afforestation; (*Wieder~*) reforestation; **die ~ der Wälder** restocking the forests

**auf|fressen** ❶ *unr. tr. V.* Ⓐ eat up; (*fig.*) swallow up ‹small business›; eat up ‹savings, money, etc.›; **er wird dich [deswegen] nicht [gleich] ~** (*ugs.*) he won't *or* isn't going to bite your head off [for that]; Ⓑ (*fig. ugs.: krank machen*) **jmdn. ~:** eat sb. up; Ⓒ (*fig.: auflösen*) **etw. ~** ‹acid etc.› eat sth. ❷ *unr. itr. V.* ‹animal› eat [all] its food up; (*salopp*) ‹person› eat [everything] up

**auf|frischen** ❶ *tr. V.* Ⓐ (*wieder frisch machen*) freshen up; brighten up ‹colour, paintwork›; renovate ‹polish, furniture›; (*restaurieren*) restore ‹tapestry, fresco, etc.›; (*fig.*) revive ‹old memories›; renew ‹acquaintance, friendship›; **seine Englischkenntnisse ~:** brush up one's [knowledge of] English; Ⓑ (*auffüllen*) stock up on ‹supplies›. ❷ *itr. V.; auch mit sein* ‹wind› freshen

**Auffrischung** *die;* ~, **~en** ⇒ **auffrischen:** Ⓐ freshening up; brightening up; renovation; restoration; renewal; **zur ~ meiner Englischkenntnisse** to brush up my [knowledge of] English; Ⓑ **die ~ der Biervorräte** *usw.* stocking up on beer [supplies] *etc.*

**aufführbar** *Adj.* stageable ‹play, ballet, opera›; performable ‹piece of music›

**auf|führen** ❶ *tr. V.* Ⓐ put on, stage ‹play, ballet, opera›; screen, put on ‹film›; perform ‹piece of music›; put on ‹concert›; **führ doch nicht so ein Theater auf!** don't make such a fuss!; Ⓑ (*nennen*) cite, quote, adduce ‹example, reason, fact›; cite ‹witness›; **Waren/Preise in einem Verzeichnis ~:** list goods/prices. ❷ *refl. V.* behave; **er hat sich wieder einmal aufgeführt** he made another fuss

**Auf·führung** *die* Ⓐ performance; **zur ~ bringen** (*Papierdt.*) put on, stage ‹play, ballet, opera›; screen, put on ‹film›; perform ‹piece of music›; put on ‹concert›; **zur ~ gelangen** *od.* **kommen** (*Papierdt.*) ‹play, ballet, opera› be staged; ‹film› be screened; ‹piece of music, composer› be performed; ‹concert› be put on; Ⓑ (*Nennung*) ⇒ **aufführen** 1 B: citation; quotation; listing

**Aufführungs·recht** *das* performing rights *pl.*

**auf|füllen** ❶ *tr. V.* Ⓐ (*voll füllen, füllen*) fill up; fill in ‹hole, gap, crack›; Ⓑ (*fig.: ergänzen*) replenish ‹stocks›; bring ‹team, battalion, etc.› up to full strength; Ⓒ (*ugs.: nachfüllen*) **Wasser/Öl/Benzin ~:** top up (*Brit.*) *or* (*Amer.*) fill up with water/oil/fill up with petrol (*Brit.*) *or* (*Amer.*) gasoline. ❷ *refl. V.* (*Met.*) ‹low-pressure area› fill

**auf|futtern** *tr.* (*auch itr.*) *V.* (*fam.*) eat up

**auf|füttern** *tr. V.* rear ‹animal› (**mit** on)

**Auf·gabe** *die* Ⓐ (*zu Bewältigendes*) task; **sich** (*Dat.*) **zur ~ machen, etw. zu tun** make it one's task *or* job to do sth.; **sich** (*Dat.*) **etw. zur ~ machen** make sth. one's task *or* job; Ⓑ (*Pflicht*) task; responsibility; duty; Ⓒ (*fig.: Zweck, Funktion*) function; Ⓓ (*Schulw.*) (*Übung*) exercise; (*Prüfungs~*) question; Ⓔ (*Schulw.: Haus~*) piece of homework; **~n** homework *sing.*; **ich muss noch ~n machen** I still have homework to do; Ⓕ (*Rechen~, Mathematik~*) problem; Ⓖ (*Beendigung*) abandonment; Ⓗ (*Kapitulation*) retirement; (*im Schach*) resignation; **jmdn. zur ~ zwingen** force sb. to retire/resign; Ⓘ (*Verzicht*) giving up; (*eines Plans, einer Forderung*) giving up; abandonment; dropping; (*eines Berufs, Versuchs*) giving up; abandonment; Ⓙ (*einer Postsendung*) posting (*Brit.*); mailing (*Amer.*); (*eines Telegramms*) handing in; (*einer Bestellung, einer*

*old spelling (see note on page 1707)

*Annonce*) placing; **K** (*von Gepäck*) depositing; (*am Flughafen*) checking in; **L** (*bes. Volleyball*) service

**auf|gabeln** *tr. V.* (*salopp*) pick up; **wo hat die Firma bloß diesen Analphabeten aufgegabelt?** where on earth did the firm get hold of this illiterate?

**Aufgaben-: ~bereich** *der*, **~gebiet** *das* area of responsibility; **~stellung** *die* nature of the task; **sich mit der neuen ~stellung vertraut machen** (*bei Ressortwechsel*) familiarize oneself with one's new duties *or* responsibilities; **~verteilung** *die* **A** (*das Verteilen*) allocation of duties *or* responsibilities; **B** (*das Verteiltsein*) distribution of responsibilities

**Aufgabe-: ~ort** *der* (*Postw.*) place of posting (*Brit.*) *or* (*Amer.*) mailing; **~stempel** *der* (*Postw.*) postmark [showing time and place of posting (*Brit.*) *or* (*Amer.*) mailing]

**Auf·gang** *der* **A** (*Sonnen~, Mond~ usw.*) rising; **B** (*Treppe*) stairs *pl.*; staircase; stairway; (*in einem Bahnhof, zu einer Galerie, einer Tribüne*) steps *pl.*; **C** (*Weg*) **der ~ zur Burgruine** the path up to the ruined castle; **D** (*Turnen*) mount (**auf** + *Akk.* on to)

**auf|geben** ❶ *unr. tr. V.* **A** (*beenden*) give up; **gibs auf!** (*ugs.*) you might as well give up!; why don't you give up!; **B** (*sich trennen von*) give up ‹habit, job, flat, business, practice, etc.›; give up, abandon, drop ‹plans, demand›; give up, abandon ‹profession, attempt›; give up, stop ‹smoking, drinking›; **C** (*verloren geben*) give up ‹patient›; give up hope on *or* with ‹wayward son, daughter, etc.›; give up, abandon ‹chessman›; **sich selbst ~:** give oneself up for lost; **D** (*nicht länger zu gewinnen versuchen*) give up ‹struggle›; retire from ‹race, competition›; **eine Partie ~:** concede a game; **E** (*übergeben, übermitteln*) post (*Brit.*), mail ‹letter, parcel›; hand in, (*telefonisch*) phone in ‹telegram›; place ‹advertisement, order›; check ‹luggage› in; (*am Flughafen*) check ‹baggage› in; (*zur Aufbewahrung im Bahnhof*) deposit ‹luggage›; **F** (*Schulw.: als Hausaufgabe*) set (*Brit.*); assign (*Amer.*); **viel/nichts ~:** set (*Brit.*) *or* (*Amer.*) assign a lot of/no homework; **G** (*zur Lösung vorlegen*) **jmdm. ein Rätsel/eine Frage ~:** set (*Brit.*) *or* (*Amer.*) assign sb. a puzzle/pose sb. a question; **H** (*geh. veralt.: auftragen, auferlegen*) **jmdm. ~, etw. zu tun** charge sb. with doing sth.; **es war ihr aufgegeben, schweigend zu dulden** it was her lot to suffer in silence; **I** (*landsch.: auf den Teller geben*) serve [up]; **jmdm. etw. ~:** serve sb. [up] sth.

❷ *unr. itr. V.* **A** give up; (*im Sport*) retire; (*Schach*) resign; **B** ⇒ **aufschlagen** 1 D; **C** (*landsch.: Essen auf den Teller geben*) dish up; **jmdm. ~:** serve sb.; **jmdm. zum zweiten Mal ~:** give sb. a second helping

**auf·geblasen** ❶ *2. Part. v.* **aufblasen.** ❷ *Adj.* puffed up

**Aufgeblasenheit** *die*; **~:** self-importance

**Auf·gebot** *das* **A** (*aufgebotene Menge*) contingent; (*Sport: Mannschaft*) contingent; squad; (*an Arbeitern*) squad; **ein gewaltiges ~ an Polizisten/Fahrzeugen/Material** a huge force of police/array of vehicles/materials; **B** (*zur Heirat*) notice of an/the intended marriage; (*kirchlich*) banns *pl.*; **das ~ bestellen** give notice of an/the intended marriage; (*kirchlich*) put up the banns

**auf·gedreht** ❶ *2. Part. v.* **aufdrehen.** ❷ *Adj.* (*ugs.*) in high spirits *pred.*; **er war unheimlich ~:** he was in tremendously high spirits

**auf·gedunsen** *Adj.* bloated

**auf|gehen** *unr. itr. V.*; *mit sein* **A** (*am Horizont erscheinen*) rise; **B** (*sich öffnen* [*lassen*]) ‹door, parachute, wound› open; ‹stage curtain› go up, rise; ‹knot, button, zip, bandage, shoelace, stitching› come undone; ‹boil, pimple, blister› burst; ‹flower, bud› open [up]; **das Weckglas ist wieder aufgegangen** the top has come off the preserving jar; **C** (*keimen*) come up; **D** (*aufgetrieben werden*) ‹dough, cake› rise; **E** (*Math.*) ‹calculation› work out, come out; ‹equation› come out; **3 geht in 12 auf** 3 goes into 12; 12 is divisible by 3; **12 durch 3 geht glatt** *od.* **genau auf** 3 goes into 12 without a remainder; **7 durch 3 geht nicht auf** threes into seven won't go; **seine Rechnung ging nicht auf** (*fig.*) he had miscalculated; **die Patience geht auf** (*fig.*) the game of patience comes out; **F** (*klar werden*) **etw. geht jmdm. auf** sb. realizes sth.; **der Sinn dieses Satzes ist mir noch nicht ganz aufgegangen** I don't quite grasp the meaning of this sentence; **G** (*einbezogen werden*) **in etw.** (*Dat.*) **~:** become absorbed into sth.; ⇒ *auch* **Flamme**; **H** (*Erfüllung finden*) **in etw.** (*Dat.*) **~:** be completely absorbed in sth.; **er geht ganz in seiner Familie auf** his whole life revolves around his family; **I** (*Jagdw.: beginnen*) **die Jagd geht im August auf** the hunting season *or* open season starts in August

**auf|geilen** *tr. V.* (*salopp*) **jmdn. [mit/durch etw.] ~:** get sb. randy [with sth.]; **sich [an etw.** (*Dat.*)**] ~:** get randy [with sth.]; (*fig.*) get worked up [about sth.]

**aufgeklärt** ❶ *2. Part. v.* **aufklären.** ❷ *Adj.* enlightened; (*sexualkundlich*) **~ sein/werden** know/be taught the facts of life; ⇒ *auch* **Absolutismus**

**Aufgeklärtheit** *die*; **~:** enlightened views *pl.*; **bei aller ~:** although he is/they are *etc.* so enlightened

**aufgekratzt** ❶ *2. Part. v.* **aufkratzen.** ❷ *Adj.* (*ugs.*) in high spirits *pred.*; **in ~er Stimmung** in high spirits

**Auf·geld** *das* (*landsch.*) ⇒ **Aufschlag** B

**auf·gelegt** ❶ *2. Part. v.* **auflegen.** ❷ *Adj.* **A** (*gelaunt*) **gut/schlecht/heiter** *usw.* **~ sein** be in a good/bad/cheerful *etc.* mood; **zu etw. ~ sein** be in the mood for sth.; **dazu ~ sein, etw. zu tun** be in the mood to do sth.; **B** (*offensichtlich*) **ein ~er Schwindel** a blatant swindle

**auf·gelöst** ❶ *2. Part. v.* **auflösen.** ❷ *Adj.* distraught; **vor Schmerz/Trauer/Freude ~ sein** be beside oneself with pain/grief/joy; ⇒ *auch* **Träne**

**aufgeräumt** ❶ *2. Part. v.* **aufräumen.** ❷ *Adj.* jovial

**aufgeregt** ❶ *2. Part. v.* **aufregen.** ❷ *Adj.* (*erregt*) excited; (*nervös, beunruhigt*) agitated. ❸ *adv.* (*erregt*) excitedly; (*nervös, beunruhigt*) agitatedly

**Aufgeregtheit** *die*; **~:** excitement; agitation; (*Nervosität*) agitation

**auf·geschlossen** ❶ *2. Part. v.* **aufschließen.** ❷ *Adj.* open-minded (**gegenüber** as regards, about); (*interessiert, empfänglich*) receptive, open (+ *Dat.*, **für** to); (*mitteilsam*) communicative; (*zugänglich*) approachable; **einer Sache** (*Dat.*) **~ gegenüberstehen** be open-minded about sth.

**Auf·geschlossenheit** *die* ⇒ **aufschließen** 2: open-mindedness; receptiveness; openness; communicativeness; approachableness

**auf·geschmissen** *Adj.* (*ugs.*) *in* **[ganz] [schön] ~ sein** be [right] up the creek (*sl.*); be in a [real] fix

**auf·geschossen** *2. Part. v.* **aufschießen**

**aufgesetzt** ❶ *2. Part. v.* **aufsetzen.** ❷ *Adj.* put on

**aufgestellt** ❶ *2. Part. v.* **aufstellen.** ❷ *Adj.* (*schweiz.*) ⇒ **aufgeschlossen**

**aufgeweckt** ❶ *2. Part. v.* **aufwecken.** ❷ *Adj.* bright; sharp

**Aufgewecktheit** *die*; **~:** brightness; sharpness

**auf|gießen** *unr. tr. V.* **A** (*aufbrühen*) make, brew [up] ‹tea›; make ‹coffee›; **B** (*gießen auf, darauf gießen*) **etw. [auf etw.** (*Akk.*)**] ~:** pour sth. on [to sth.]; **C** (*übergießen*) **etw. mit Milch/Wasser** *usw.* **~:** pour milk/water *etc.* on [to] sth.

**auf|gliedern** *tr. V.* subdivide, break down, split up (**in** + *Akk.* into); structure ‹essay›; (*nach Kategorien*) categorize; **aufgegliedert nach Berufen/Einkommen** broken down by occupation/income

**Auf·gliederung** *die* ⇒ **aufgliedern**: subdivision; breakdown; structuring; categorization

**auf|glimmen** *unr.* (*auch regelm.*) *itr. V.*; *mit sein* [begin to] glimmer; (*fig.*) ‹hope, suspicion› flicker up

**auf|glühen** *itr. V.*; *mit sein* [begin to] glow; (*fig.*) ‹passion› begin to burn; **eine Hoffnung glühte in ihm auf** he felt a gleam of hope

**auf|graben** *unr. tr. V.* (*umgraben*) dig over; (*freilegen*) dig up

**auf|greifen** *unr. tr. V.* **A** (*festnehmen*) pick up; **B** (*sich befassen mit*) take *or* pick up ‹subject, suggestion›; **C** (*fortsetzen*) take up again; continue

**auf Grund, aufgrund** ⇒ **Grund** C

**Auf·guss, *Auf·guß** *der* infusion; (*fig.*) rehash

**Aufguss·beutel, *Aufguß·beutel** *der*; (*Teebeutel*) tea bag; (*für Kräutertee*) herb sachet

**auf|haben** (*ugs.*) ❶ *unr. tr. V.* **A** (*aufgesetzt haben*) have on; wear; **sie hat ihre Brille nicht aufgehabt** she didn't have her glasses on; she wasn't wearing her glasses; **B** (*geöffnet haben*) have ‹zip› undone; have ‹door, window, jacket, blouse› open; **die Augen ~:** have one's eyes open; **seinen Laden/sein Büro ~:** have one's shop/office open; be open; **C** (*aufbekommen haben*) have got ‹cupboard, case, safe, etc.› open; have got ‹knot, zip› undone; **D** (*für die Schule*) **etw. ~:** have sth. as homework; **viel/wenig ~:** have a lot of/not have much homework; **haben wir etwas in** *od.* **für Englisch auf?** have we got any English homework?; **E** (*aufgegessen haben*) have eaten up *or* finished.

❷ *unr. itr. V.* ‹shop, office› be open; **wir haben bis 17.30 auf** we are open until 5.30 p.m.

**auf|hacken** *tr. V.* (*mit einer Hacke*) break up; (*mit dem Schnabel*) peck *or* break open

**auf|halsen** /ˈaufhalzn̩/ *tr. V.* (*ugs.*) **jmdm./sich etw. ~:** saddle sb./oneself with sth.; **sich** (*Dat.*) **etw. ~ lassen** get oneself saddled with sth.

**auf|halten** ❶ *unr. tr. V.* **A** (*anhalten*) halt; halt, check ‹inflation, advance, rise in unemployment›; **jmdn. an der Grenze ~:** hold sb. up at the border; **B** (*stören*) hold up; **C** (*ugs.: geöffnet halten*) hold ‹sack, door, etc.› open; **die Augen [und Ohren] ~:** keep one's eyes [and ears] open; **die Hand ~** (*auch fig.*) hold out one's hand.

❷ *unr. refl. V.* **A** (*sich befassen*) **sich mit jmdm./etw. ~:** spend [a long] time on sb./sth.; **sich zu lange mit jmdm./etw. ~:** spend too long on sb./sth.; **sich bei etw. ~:** linger over sth.; **B** (*verweilen*) stay; **tagsüber hielt er sich im Museum auf** he spent the day in the museum; **sich im Winter in der Küche ~:** live in the kitchen in the winter; **der Gesuchte soll sich in Frankreich ~:** the wanted man is thought to be in France

**auf|hängen** ❶ *tr. V.* **A** (*auf etw. hängen*) hang up; hang ‹picture, curtains›; **die Wäsche ~:** hang up the washing *or* (*Amer.*) wash; (*draußen*) hang out the washing; **den Hörer ~:** hang up; **B** (*erhängen*) hang; **jmdn. an etw.** (*Dat.*) **~:** hang sb. from sth.; **C** (*ugs.*) **jmdm. etw. ~** (*andrehen*) palm sth. off on sb.; (*glauben machen*) talk sb. into believing sth.; (*aufbürden*) saddle sb. with sth.; **D** **etw. an einer Frage/einem bestimmten Fall** *usw.* **~:** use a question/a specific case *etc.* as a peg to hang sth. on.

❷ *refl. V.* (*sich erhängen*) hang oneself; **wo kann ich mich ~?** (*ugs. scherzh.*) where can I hang up my things?

**Aufhänger** *der*; **~s, ~** **A** (*Schlaufe*) loop; **B** (*fig.: aktuelles Ereignis*) peg; **ein guter ~ für etw.** a good peg to hang sth. on

**Aufhängung** *die*; **~** (*Technik*) suspension

**auf|hauen** *unr.* (*ugs. auch regelm.*) *tr. V.* **A** (*öffnen*) knock a hole in ‹ice, wall›; crack open ‹nut, coconut›; **B** (*ugs.: verletzen*) **sich** (*Dat.*) **das Knie/die Stirn usw. ~:** gash one's knee/forehead *etc.*

**auf|häufen** ❶ *tr. V.* pile up; (*fig.*) amass ‹treasure, riches›. ❷ *refl. V.* (*auch fig.*) pile up; accumulate

**auf|heben** *unr. tr. V.* **A** (*hochheben*) pick up; pick *or* lift up ‹heavy object, burden›; lift [off] ‹lid, cover›; **B** (*aufbewahren*) keep; preserve; **gut/schlecht aufgehoben sein** be/not be in good hands (**bei** with); **dein Geheimnis ist bei mir sicher aufgehoben** your secret is

a

quite safe with me; **C** (*abschaffen*) abolish; repeal ‹law›; rescind, revoke ‹order, instruction›; cancel ‹contract›; lift ‹ban, prohibition›; **das neue Gesetz hebt die alte Regelung auf** the new law supersedes the old regulation; ⇒ *auch* **aufschieben** A; **D** (*ausgleichen*) cancel out; neutralize, cancel ‹effect›; **sich [gegenseitig] ~:** cancel each other out; **E** (*beenden*) close ‹meeting›; lift ‹blockade, siege, martial law›; **die Tafel ~** (*geh.*) bring the meal to a close; **F** (*erheben*) **die Hand/den Kopf ~:** raise one's hand/head

**Aufheben** *das;* **~s** *in* **viel ~[s]/kein ~ von jmdm./etw. machen** make a great fuss/not make any fuss about sb./sth.; **ohne jedes/großes ~:** without any/a great deal of *or* much fuss

**Auf·hebung** *die* **A** (*Abschaffung*) ⇒ **aufheben** C: abolition; repeal; rescindment; revocation; cancellation; lifting; **B** (*Beendigung*) ⇒ **aufheben** E: closure; lifting

**Aufhebungs·vertrag** *der* agreement to terminate a/the contract

**auf|heitern** ❶ *tr. V.* (*heiterer stimmen*) cheer up; brighten up ‹life›. ❷ *refl. V.* **A** (*froher werden*) ‹mood, face, expression› brighten; **B** (*heller werden*) ‹weather› clear *or* brighten up; ‹sky› brighten. ❸ *itr. V.* **es heitert auf** it is clearing up; **zeitweilig ~d** [some] bright periods

**Aufheiterung** *die;* **~, ~en A** (*des Wetters*) bright period; **B** (*Erheiterung*) cheering up; **zur allgemeinen ~:** to cheer everyone up

**auf|heizen** (*bes. Physik, Technik*) ❶ *tr. V.* heat [up]; (*fig.*) inflame ‹tensions, conflict›; fuel ‹mistrust›. ❷ *refl. V.* heat up

**auf|helfen** *unr. itr. V.* **A** (*beim Aufstehen helfen*) **jmdm. ~:** help sb. up; (*fig.*) help sb. [to get] back on his/her feet again; **B** (*aufbessern*) boost ‹self-confidence, income›

**auf|hellen** ❶ *tr. V.* **A** (*heller machen*) brighten; lighten ‹hair, shadow, darkness›; (*fig.*) brighten [up] ‹mood, life›; **B** (*klären*) shed *or* cast *or* throw light on. ❷ *refl. V.* **A** (*hell werden*) ‹sky› brighten; ‹hair› turn *or* go lighter; ‹day, weather› brighten [up]; **sein Gesicht/seine Miene hellte sich auf** his face/expression brightened; **es hat sich aufgehellt** it's brightened up; **B** (*durchschaubar werden*) ‹sense, meaning› become clear

**Aufheller** *der;* **~s, ~ A** (*Fot.*) fill-in photoflood; **B** (*in Waschmitteln*) colour-intensifier; brightener; **C** (*ugs.: Medikament*) pep pill (*coll.*)

**auf|hetzen** *tr. V.* incite; **jmdn. zur Meuterei/zu Gewalttaten ~:** incite sb. to mutiny/violence

**Aufhetzung** *die;* **~, ~en** incitement

**auf|heulen** *itr. V.* **A** (*heulen*) ‹siren› wail; ‹animal› howl; ‹engine, crowd› give a roar; **B** (*ugs.: weinen*) howl

**auf|holen** ❶ *tr. V.* make up ‹time, delay›; make up, pull back ‹lead›; catch up on ‹studies, neglected work›; **ein paar Sekunden/Meter ~:** make up *or* pull back a few seconds/metres. ❷ *itr. V.* **A** catch up; ‹train› make up time; ‹athlete, competitor› make up ground; (*Zeit ~*) make up time; **B** (*Börsenw.*) ‹shares› rise

**auf|horchen** *itr. V.* prick up one's ears; **die Öffentlichkeit ~ lassen** (*fig.*) make the public [sit up and] take notice

**auf|hören** *itr. V.* stop; ‹friendship› end; (*ugs.: das Arbeitsverhältnis aufgeben*) finish; **das muss ~!** this has got to stop!; **da hört [sich] doch alles auf!** (*ugs.*) that really is the limit! (*coll.*); **die Musik hörte auf** the music ended *or* came to an end; (*wurde abgebrochen*) the music stopped; **es hat aufgehört zu schneien** it's stopped snowing; **[damit] ~, etw. zu tun** stop doing sth.; **nicht [damit] ~, etw. zu tun** keep on doing sth.; **hört mit dem Lärm/Unsinn auf** stop that noise/nonsense; **ich habe mit dem Buch aufgehört und ein anderes angefangen** I've stopped reading that book and started another; **mit dem Fußboden kannst du jetzt aufhören, der ist sauber genug** you can leave the floor now, it's clean enough; **ich höre hier bald auf** I'm just about to finish; (*kündige bald*) I'm giving up this job soon; **ohne aufzuhören** without stopping; ⇒ *auch* **Spaß** B

**auf|jagen** *tr. V.* start ‹game, animals› from cover; put up ‹birds›; **jmdn. aus dem Schlaf ~** (*fig.*) rouse sb. [violently] from his/her sleep

**auf|jauchzen** *itr. V.;* **[vor Freude/Entzücken** *usw.*] **~:** shout for joy/with delight *etc.*

**auf|jaulen** *itr. V.* howl; give a howl

**Auf·kauf** *der* buying up; **durch Aufkäufe kleiner Firmen** by buying up smaller firms

**auf|kaufen** *tr. V.* buy up

**Auf·käufer** *der,* **Auf·käuferin** *die* buyer

**auf|kehren** *tr.* (*auch itr.*) *V.* (*bes. südd.*) sweep up

**auf|keimen** *itr. V.; mit sein* sprout; (*fig.*) ‹suspicion, doubt, fear, longing, reluctance› begin to grow; ‹hope, passion, love, sympathy› burgeon

**aufklappbar** *Adj.* ‹chair, table› which folds open; folding *attrib.* ‹chair, table›; fold-back ‹car hood›; opening *attrib.* ‹window›; hinged ‹flap, lid›; **eine zu einem Doppelbett ~e Couch** a settee which converts into a double bed

**auf|klappen** ❶ *tr. V.* open, fold open ‹chair, table›; open [up] ‹suitcase, trunk›; fold back ‹car hood›; open ‹window, door, book, knife›. ❷ *itr. V.; mit sein* ‹shutters, door› open, swing open

**auf|klaren** *itr. V.* (*Met.*) ‹sky› clear; ‹weather› clear up; **örtlich ~d** clearing locally

**auf|klären** ❶ *tr. V.* **A** (*klären*) clear up ‹matter, mystery, question, misunderstanding, error, confusion›; solve ‹crime, problem›; elucidate, explain ‹event, incident, cause›; resolve ‹contradiction, disagreement›; **B** (*unterrichten*) enlighten; (*informieren*) inform; **jmdn. über jmdn./etw. ~:** enlighten/inform sb. about sb./sth.; **jmdn. [darüber] ~, wie .../was ...** enlighten/inform sb. how .../what ...; **C** (*sexualkundlich*) **ein Kind ~:** tell a child the facts of life; educate a child in sexual matters; **D** (*Milit.*) reconnoitre.
❷ *refl. V.* **A** (*sich klären*) ‹misunderstanding, mystery› be cleared up; **B** (*sich aufhellen*) ‹weather› clear up; brighten [up]; ‹sky› clear, brighten

**Aufklärer** *der;* **~s, ~ A** (*hist.*) philosopher of the Enlightenment; **B** (*Luftwaffe: Flugzeug*) reconnaissance plane *or* aircraft; **C** (*Milit.: Soldat, Spion*) scout

**Aufklärerin** *die;* **~, ~nen** ⇒ **Aufklärer** A, C

**aufklärerisch** ❶ *Adj.* ‹mission, intention› to instruct and inform, to combat ignorance. ❷ *adv.* **~ wirken** instruct and inform; combat ignorance

**Auf·klärung** *die* **A** ⇒ **aufklären** 1 A: clearing up; solution; elucidation; explanation; resolution; **ihm gelang die ~ des Verbrechens** he succeeded in solving the crime; **B** (*Information*) information; **jmdm. einige ~en geben** give sb. some information *sing.;* **C** (*Belehrung*) enlightenment; (*von offizieller Stelle*) informing; **um ~ darüber bitten, was vorgefallen ist** ask to be told what has happened; **D** (*über Sexualität*) education in sexual matters; **die ~ der Kinder** telling the children the facts of life; **E** (*hist.*) **die ~:** the Enlightenment; **F** (*Milit.*) reconnaissance

**Aufklärungs-: ~arbeit** *die* educational work; **politische ~arbeit** political education; **~buch** *das* sex education book; **~film** *der* sex education film; **~flug** *der* (*Luftwaffe*) reconnaissance flight *or* mission; **~flugzeug** *das* (*Luftwaffe*) reconnaissance plane *or* aircraft; **~kampagne** *die* information campaign; **~schrift** *die* information pamphlet; **~ziel** *das* (*Milit.*) reconnaissance objective

**auf|klauben** *tr. V.* (*landsch., auch fig.*) pick up

**auf|kleben** *tr. V.* stick on; (*mit Kleister*) paste on; (*mit Klebstoff, Leim*) stick *or* glue on

**Auf·kleber** *der* sticker; adhesive label

**auf|klinken** *tr. V.* open ‹door› by the handle

**auf|klopfen** *tr. V.* **A** (*öffnen*) crack open; **B** (*aufschütteln*) plump up ‹cushion etc.›

**auf|knacken** *tr. V.* **A** crack [open] ‹nut, cherry stone, etc.›; **B** (*ugs.: aufbrechen*) break into ‹car, desk, drawer›; break down ‹door›; crack ‹safe›

**auf|knien** ❶ *itr. V.; auch mit sein* (*Turnen*) kneel (**auf** + *Akk. od. Dat.* on). ❷ *refl. V.* kneel (**auf** + *Akk./Dat.* on)

**auf|knöpfen** *tr. V.* **A** unbutton; undo; **B etw. auf etw.** (*Akk.*) **~:** button sth. on to sth.

**auf|knoten** *tr. V.* untie, undo ‹parcel, bundle, etc.›; unknot ‹string, rope›

**auf|knüpfen** (*ugs.*) ❶ *tr. V.* **A** (*erhängen*) string up (*coll.*), hang (**an** + *Dat.* from); **B** (*aufknoten*) undo, untie ‹knot, parcel, bundle›; unknot ‹string, rope›. ❷ *refl. V.* hang oneself

**auf|kochen** ❶ *tr. V.* **A** (*zum Kochen bringen*) bring to the boil; **B** (*noch einmal kochen*) reboil. ❷ *itr. V.* **A** *mit sein* (*zu kochen beginnen*) come to the boil; **etw. ~ lassen** bring sth. to the boil; **B** (*südd., österr.: üppig kochen*) prepare a magnificent spread

**auf|kommen** *unr. itr. V.; mit sein* **A** (*entstehen*) ‹wind› spring up; ‹storm, gale› blow up; ‹fog› come down; ‹rumour› start; ‹suspicion, doubt, feeling› arise; ‹fashion, style, invention› come in; ‹boredom› set in; ‹mood, atmosphere› develop; **etw. ~ lassen** give rise to sth.; **B ~ für** (*bezahlen*) bear, pay ‹costs›; pay for ‹damage›; pay, defray ‹expenses›; be liable for ‹debts›; stand ‹loss›; **für jmdn. ~:** pay for sb.'s upkeep; **C ~ für** (*Verantwortung tragen für*) be responsible for; **D er lässt niemanden neben sich** (*Dat.*) **~:** he won't let anybody become a rival; he brooks no rivals (*literary*); **E** (*auftreffen*) land (**auf** + *Akk.* on); **F** (*Sport: aufholen*) (*beim Wettlauf*) close the gap; (*Fußball, Boxen*) come back; **G** (*sich behaupten*) **gegen jmdn./etw. ~:** prevail against sb./sth.; **H** (*bes. südd.: entdeckt werden*) be discovered; **wenn das aufkommt, ...** if it comes out, ...; **I** (*Seemannsspr.: in Sicht kommen*) approach

**Aufkommen** *das;* **~s, ~** (*Wirtsch.*) revenue (**aus** from)

**auf|kratzen** *tr. V.* **A** (*öffnen*) scratch open ‹wound, sore›; **B** (*verletzen*) scratch

**auf|kreischen** *itr. V.* ‹person› shriek, give a shriek; ‹brake, saw› screech

**auf|krempeln** *tr. V.* roll up ‹sleeves, trousers›; **jmdm./sich die Ärmel ~:** roll up sb.'s/one's sleeves

**auf|kreuzen** *itr. V.* **A** *mit sein* (*ugs.: erscheinen*) turn up; **B** *auch mit sein* (*Seemannsspr.*) **gegen den Wind ~:** beat to windward

**auf|kriegen** (*ugs.*) ⇒ **aufbekommen**

**auf|künden** (*geh., schweiz.*), **auf|kündigen** *tr. V.* terminate ‹lease, contract›; cancel ‹subscription, membership›; foreclose ‹mortgage›; **seinen Dienst ~:** hand in one's notice; **jmdm. die Freundschaft/den Gehorsam ~** (*geh.*) break off one's friendship with sb./refuse sb. further obedience

**Auf·kündigung** *die* ⇒ **aufkündigen**: termination; cancellation; foreclosure; breaking off

**Aufl.** *Abk.* **Auflage** ed.

**auf|lachen** *itr. V.* give a laugh; laugh; (*schallend*) burst out laughing

**auf|laden** ❶ *unr. tr.* (*auch itr.*) *V.* **A** load (**auf** + *Akk.* on [to]); **B** (*ugs.: tragen lassen*) **jmdm. etw. ~:** load sb. with sth.; (*fig.*) saddle *or* load sb. with sth.; **C** (*Physik: elektrisch laden*) charge [up] ‹battery›; put ‹battery› on charge; (*nach Entladung auch*) recharge; **emotional aufgeladen** (*fig.*) emotionally charged; **D** (*Kfz-W.*) supercharge ‹engine›. ❷ *unr. refl. V.* (*Physik*) ‹battery› charge, become charged; (*nach Entladung*) recharge; become recharged; **sich elektrostatisch ~:** become electrostatically charged

**Auf·ladung** *die* **A** (*Kfz-W.*) supercharging; **B** (*Physik*) (*das Aufladen*) charging [up]; (*nach Entladung*) recharging

**Auf·lage** *die* **A** (*Buchw.*) edition; (*gedruckte ~ einer Zeitung*) print run; (*verkaufte ~ einer Zeitung*) circulation; **dieses Buch/diese Zeitung hat hohe ~n erreicht** large numbers of copies of this book have been sold/this newspaper has reached high circulation figures; **sieben ~n erleben** go through seven editions; **B** (*bes. Rechtsw.: Verpflichtung*) condition; **mit der ~, etw. zu tun** with the

*old spelling (see note on page 1707)

condition that *or* on condition that one does sth.; **[es] jmdm. zur ~ machen, dass ...** impose on sb. the condition that ...; **C** (*DDR Wirtsch.*) target; **D** (*auf Sitzmöbeln*) cushion; **E** (*Metallüberzug*) plating; **eine ~ aus Silber haben** be silver-plated; **F** (*Stütze*) rest; support

**Auflage·fläche** *die* supporting surface

**Auflagen·höhe** *die* (*Buchw.*) number of copies printed; (*einer Zeitung*) circulation

**auflagen·stark** *Adj.* high-circulation ‹newspaper, magazine›; **~ sein** have a high *or* large circulation

**Auf·lager** *das* (*Bauw.*) support; bearer; (*beweglich*) bearing

**auflandig** (*Seemannsspr.*) onshore

**auf|lassen** *unr. tr. V.* **A** (*ugs.: offen lassen*) leave open; **B** (*ugs.: aufbehalten*) keep on; **C** (*ugs.: aufbleiben lassen*) let ‹child› stay up; **D** (*aufsteigen lassen*) send up ‹balloon, rocket, satellite›; release ‹carrier pigeon›; **E** (*bes. südd., österr.: schließen; Bergbau: stilllegen*) close *or* shut down; **eine aufgelassene Grube** a closed-down pit

**Auflassung** *die; ~, ~en* (*bes. südd., österr.: Schließung; Bergbau: Stilllegung*) closing *or* shutting down

**auf|lauern** *itr. V.* **jmdm. ~:** lie in wait for sb.; (*~ und angreifen*) waylay sb.

**Auf·lauf** *der* **A** (*Menschen~*) crowd; **B** (*Speise*) soufflé

**auf|laufen** *unr. itr. V.; mit sein* **A** (*Seemannsspr.*) run aground (**auf** + *Akk. od. Dat.* on); **B** (*Sport*) **zur Spitze/zu den Führenden ~:** move to the front/catch up with the leaders; **C** (*aufprallen*) **auf jmdn./etw. ~:** run into sb./sth.; **jmdn. ~ lassen** (*Fußball*) body-check sb.; **D** (*sich ansammeln*) accumulate; mount up

**Auflauf·form** *die* baking dish; (*für Eierspeisen*) soufflé dish

**auf|leben** *itr. V.; mit sein* revive; (*fig.: wieder munter werden*) come to life; liven up; **etw. ~ lassen** revive sth.

**auf|lecken** *tr. V.* lap up

**auf|legen** ❶ *tr. V.* **A** (*auf etw. legen*) put on ‹record, coal, logs, tablecloth, adhesive plaster, saddle›; **noch ein Gedeck ~:** set another place; **das Silber ~:** put out the silverware; **jmdm. das Fleisch ~:** serve sb. his/her meat; **jmdm. die Hand ~** ‹faith healer› lay one's hands on sb.; **den Hörer ~:** put down the receiver; **B** (*Buchw.*) publish; **ein Buch neu** *od.* **wieder ~:** bring out a new edition of a book; (*nachdrucken*) reprint a book; **C** (*Finanzw.*) issue, float ‹shares›; **D** (*Seemannsspr.*) lay up ‹ship›.
❷ **A** *itr. V.* (*den Hörer ~*) hang up; ring off (*Brit.*) **B** (*salopp*) deejay (*coll.*)

**auf|lehnen** ❶ *refl. V.* **sich gegen jmdn./etw. ~:** rebel *or* revolt against sb./sth. ❷ *tr. V.* (*landsch.: aufstützen*) **sich/die Arme auf etw.** (*Akk. od. Dat.*) **~:** lean on sth./lean *or* rest one's arms on sth.

**Auflehnung** *die; ~, ~en* rebellion; revolt

**auf|leimen** *tr. V.* glue on (**auf** + *Akk.* to)

**auf|lesen** *unr. tr. V.* **A** (*aufsammeln*) pick up; gather [up]; (*fig. ugs.: sich holen*) pick up, catch ‹germ, disease, illness›; **B** (*ugs.: mitnehmen*) pick up; **jmdn. von der Straße ~:** pick sb. up off the street

**auf|leuchten** *itr. V.; auch mit sein* light up; (*für kurze Zeit*) flash; ‹brake light› come on; ‹star› shine out; (*fig.*) ‹eyes, face› light up

**auf|liegen** ❶ *unr. itr. V.* **A** (*auf etw. liegen*) lie, rest (**auf** + *Dat.* on); **B** (*Seemannsspr.*) be laid up. ❷ *unr. refl. V.* (*ugs.: sich wundliegen*) get bedsores

**Auflieger** *der; ~s, ~:* trailer

**auf|listen** *tr. V.* list

**Auflistung** *die; ~, ~en* **A** (*das Auflisten*) listing; **B** (*Liste*) list

**auf|lockern** ❶ *tr. V.* **A** (*locker machen*) break up, loosen ‹soil›; loosen ‹stuffing, hair›; **die Muskeln ~:** loosen up one's muscles; **aufgelockerte Bewölkung** broken cloud; **B** (*abwechslungsreicher machen*) introduce some variety into ‹landscape, lesson, lecture›; relieve, break up ‹pattern, façade›; **C** (*unbeschwerter machen*) make ‹mood, atmosphere, evening› more relaxed. ❷ *refl. V.* (*seine Muskeln lockern*) loosen up

**Auf·lockerung** *die* **A** (*des Bodens*) breaking up; loosening; (*einer Füllung, des Haars*) loosening; (*der Muskeln*) loosening up; **B** (*einer Fassade, eines Musters*) relieving; breaking up; **zur ~ des Unterrichts/Vortrags** to introduce some variety into the lesson/lecture; **C** **zur ~ der Stimmung/Atmosphäre/des Abends** to make the mood/atmosphere/evening more relaxed

**auf|lodern** *itr. V.; mit sein* (*geh.*) ‹fire› blaze *or* flare up; ‹flames› leap up; (*fig.*) ‹jealousy, hatred, anger, passion› flare up; **wie eine Fackel ~:** go up like a torch

**auflösbar** *Adj.* soluble; soluble, solvable ‹equation, problem›; dissoluble ‹marriage›

**Auf·lösbarkeit** *die; ~* ⇒ **auflösbar**: solubility; solvability; dissolubility

**auf|lösen** ❶ *tr. V.* **A** dissolve; resolve ‹difficulty, contradiction›; solve ‹puzzle, equation›; break off ‹engagement›; terminate, cancel ‹arrangement, contract, agreement›; dissolve, disband ‹organization›; remove ‹brackets›; **etw. in seine Bestandteile ~:** resolve sth. into its constituent parts; ⇒ *auch* **Haushalt**; **B** (*geh.: aufbinden*) undo, untie ‹knot, shoelace, plait›; let down ‹hair›; (*fig.*) disentangle; **C** (*Musik*) cancel ‹accidental›; resolve ‹discord›; **D** (*Optik, Fot.*) resolve.
❷ *refl. V.* **A** dissolve; ‹parliament› dissolve itself; ‹crowd, demonstration› break up; ‹fog, mist› disperse, lift; ‹cloud› break up; (*fig.*) ‹resistance, vision› dissolve; ‹empire, kingdom, social order› disintegrate; **sich in etw.** (*Akk.*)**/in nichts ~** (*auch fig.*) dissolve into sth./into nothing; **B** (*geh.: aufgehen*) ‹shoelace, hair, bow› come undone; **C** (*sich aufklären*) ‹misunderstanding, difficulty, contradiction› be resolved; ‹puzzle, equation› be solved; ⇒ *auch* **aufgelöst** 2

**Auf·lösung** *die* **A** ⇒ **auflösen** 1 A-D: dissolving; resolution; solution; breaking off; termination; cancellation; dissolution; disbandment; removal; undoing; untying; disentanglement; **B** ⇒ **auflösen** 2 A: dissolving; dispersing; lifting; breaking up; (*fig.*) dissolving; disintegration; **C** (*Verstörtheit*) distraction

**Auflösungs-: ~erscheinung** *die* sign of disintegration; **~zeichen** *das* (*Musik*) natural

**auflüpfisch** /ˈauflʏpfɪʃ/ *Adj., adv.* (*schweiz.*) ⇒ **aufmüpfig**

**aufm** /ˈaufm̩/ (*ugs.*) = **auf dem**

**auf|machen** ❶ *tr. V.* **A** (*öffnen*) open; undo ‹button, knot›; open, undo ‹parcel, packet›; **B** (*ugs.: eröffnen*) open [up] ‹shop, theatre, business, etc.›; **C** (*gestalten*) get up; present; **das wurde von der Presse groß aufgemacht** the press gave it headline treatment. ❷ *itr. V.* **A** (*geöffnet werden*) ‹shop, office, etc.› open; **B** (*ugs.: die Tür öffnen*) open up; open the door; **jmdm. ~:** open the door to sb.; **mach auf!** open up!; **C** (*ugs.: eröffnet werden*) ‹shop, business› open [up]. ❸ *refl. V.* (*aufbrechen*) set out; start [out]

**Auf·macher** *der* (*Zeitungsw.*) (*Schlagzeile*) lead headline; (*Bild*) main front-page photograph

**Aufmachung** *die; ~, ~en* **A** (*Gestaltung*) presentation; (*Kleidung*) get-up; **ein Buch in ansprechender ~:** an attractively presented book; **B** (*Zeitungsw.*) **die Zeitungen haben darüber in großer ~ berichtet** it was splashed across the pages of the newspapers; **C** ⇒ **Aufmacher**

**auf|malen** *tr. V.* paint on

**Auf·marsch** *der* **A** (*Milit.: zum Kampf*) deployment; **B** (*Parade*) march past; parade; **C** (*schweiz.: Zulauf*) attendance

**Aufmarsch·gebiet** *das* (*Milit.*) deployment area

**auf|marschieren** *itr. V.; mit sein* draw up; assemble; (*heranmarschieren*) march up; (*vorbeimarschieren*) march past; parade; ‹demonstrators, delegations› parade; **die Zeugen zur Vernehmung ~ lassen** (*salopp*) march the witnesses in for examination; **Truppen sind an der Grenze aufmarschiert** troops were deployed along the border

**auf|meißeln** *tr. V.* chisel open

**auf|merken** *itr. V.* **A** (*aufhorchen*) [sit up and] take notice; **B** (*geh.: aufpassen*) pay attention (**auf** + *Akk.* to)

**aufmerksam** ❶ *Adj.* **A** (*konzentriert*) attentive ‹pupil, reader, observer›; keen, sharp ‹eyes›; **~e Nachbarn hatten bemerkt, dass ...** observant neighbours had noticed that ...; **jmdn. auf jmdn./etw. ~ machen** draw sb.'s attention to sb./sth.; bring sb./sth. to sb.'s notice; **jmdn. darauf ~ machen, dass ...** draw sb.'s attention to *or* bring to sb.'s notice the fact that ...; **auf jmdn./etw. ~ werden** become aware of *or* notice sb./sth.; **~ werden** notice; **B** (*höflich*) attentive; **danke, sehr ~:** thank you, that's very *or* most kind of you.
❷ *adv.* attentively

**Aufmerksamkeit** *die; ~, ~en* **A** (*Konzentration*) attention; **jmds. ~** (*Dat.*) **entgehen** escape sb.'s attention; **B** (*Höflichkeit*) attentiveness; **C** (*Geschenk*) **eine [kleine] ~:** a small gift

**aufmischen** *tr. V.* **A** liven up ‹disco, meeting, city etc.›; shake up ‹organization, political party, etc.›; **etw. richtig ~:** give sth. a good shake-up; **B** (*ugs.: verprügeln*) beat up

**auf|möbeln** *tr. V.* (*ugs.*) **A** (*verbessern*) do up; **seinen Ruf/seine Deutschkenntnisse ~:** polish up one's reputation/knowledge of German; **B** (*beleben*) pep *or* buck up (*coll.*); (*aufmuntern*) buck (*coll.*) *or* cheer up

**auf|montieren** *tr. V.* mount; fit [on]

**auf|motzen** *tr. V.* (*ugs.*) tart up (*Brit. coll.*); doll up (*coll.*); repackage ‹edition, novel, record›; (*schneller machen*) soup up (*coll.*) ‹car, engine›

**auf|mucken, auf|mucksen** *itr. V.* (*ugs.*) kick up *or* make a fuss; **gegen etw. ~:** balk at sth.

**auf|muntern** *tr. V.* **A** (*aufheitern*) cheer up; **B** (*beleben*) liven up; pep up (*coll.*); **C** (*ermutigen*) encourage; **jmdn. zum Weitermachen/Widerstand/Kampf** *usw.* **~:** encourage sb. to carry on/resist/ fight *etc.*

**Aufmunterung** *die; ~, ~en* **A** (*Aufheiterung*) cheering up; **B** (*Belebung*) livening up; pepping up (*coll.*); **eine Tasse Kaffee zur ~:** a cup of coffee to liven *or* (*coll.*) pep me/you *etc.* up; **C** (*Ermutigung*) encouragement

**aufmüpfig** /ˈaufmʏpfɪç/ (*ugs.*) ❶ *Adj.* rebellious. ❷ *adv.* rebelliously

**Aufmüpfigkeit** *die; ~:* rebelliousness

**aufn** /ˈaufn̩/ (*ugs.*) = **auf den**

**auf|nähen** *tr. V.* sew on; **etw. auf etw.** (*Akk.*) **~:** sew sth. on [to] sth.

**Aufnahme** *die; ~, ~n* **A** (*Beginn*) (*von Verhandlungen, Gesprächen*) opening; starting; (*der Arbeit, einer Ermittlung, der Produktion*) start; (*von Beziehungen, Verbindungen*) establishment; (*von Studien, einer Tätigkeit*) taking up; **vor ~ der Arbeit** before starting work; **B** (*Empfang*) reception; (*Beherbergung*) accommodation; **jmds. ~ in ein Krankenhaus** sb.'s admission to hospital; **jmdm. eine herzliche ~ bereiten** give sb. a warm reception; **sie fanden ~ bei einer Familie** they were taken in [and looked after] by a family; **C** (*in einen Verein, eine Schule, Organisation*) admission (**in** + *Akk.* into); **D** (*von Hypotheken, Geld, Anleihen*) raising; **E** (*Aufzeichnung*) taking down; (*von Personalien, eines Diktats*) taking [down]; **die ~ des Protokolls der Sitzung** taking the minutes of the meeting; **F** (*das Fotografieren*) photographing; (*eines Bildes*) taking; (*das Filmen*) shooting; filming; **bei der ~:** while taking the photograph/while shooting *or* filming; **G** (*Bild*) picture; shot; photo[graph]; **eine ~ machen** take a picture *or* shot *or* photo[graph]; **H** (*das Aufnehmen auf Tonträger, das Aufgenommene*) recording; **I** (*Anklang*) reception; response (*Gen.* to); **J** (*Einverleibung, Absorption*) absorption; **K** (*das Einschließen, Verzeichnen*) inclusion; **die ~ eines Wortes in den Wortschatz** the adoption of a word into the

a

language; [L] (~*raum*) reception (*Brit.*); reception office (*Amer.*); **in der ~ warten** wait in reception (*Brit.*) *or* (*Amer.*) the reception office

**aufnahme-, Aufnahme-: ~antrag** *der* application for membership; **~bedingung** *die* [A] condition of admission; **~bedingungen** conditions *or* terms of admission; [B] *Pl.* (*bei Tonaufnahme*) recording conditions; (*Fot., Film*) shooting conditions; **~fähig** *Adj.* [A] (*konzentriert*) receptive (**für** to); **ich bin nicht mehr ~fähig** I can't take any more in; [B] (*Wirtsch.*) receptive ‹market›; **~fähigkeit** *die* [A] (*Konzentration*) receptivity (**für** to); ability to take things in; [B] (*Wirtsch.*) receptivity (**für** to); **~gebühr** *die* enrolment fee; **~land** *das* host country; **~leiter** *der*, **~leiterin** *die* (*Film, Rundf., Ferns.*) production manager; **~prüfung** *die* entrance examination; **~studio** *das* (*Tonstudio*) recording studio; (*Filmstudio*) film studio; **~wagen** *der* recording van

**aufnahms-, Aufnahms-** (*österr.*) ⇒ aufnahme-, Aufnahme-

**auf|nehmen** *unr. tr. V.* [A] (*hochheben*) pick up; lift up; (*aufsammeln*) pick up; (*fig.*) **es mit jmdm./etw. ~/nicht ~ können** be a/no match for sb./sth.; **an Intelligenz kann es keiner mit ihm ~:** nobody can compare with him for intelligence; [B] (*beginnen mit*) open, start ‹negotiations, talks›; establish ‹relations, contacts›; take up ‹studies, activity, occupation›; start ‹production, investigation›; (*fortsetzen*) take up ‹idea, theme›; **den Kampf gegen etw. ~** (*fig.*) take up the fight against sth.; **etw. wieder ~:** resume sth.; **um ein Wort des Kanzlers aufzunehmen** to borrow an expression used by the chancellor; [C] (*empfangen*) receive; (*beherbergen*) take in; (*fig.: umhüllen*) ‹night, darkness, mist› envelop; **in ein** *od.* **einem Krankenhaus aufgenommen werden** be admitted to hospital; [D] (*beitreten lassen*) admit (**in** + *Akk.* to); **jmdn. als Mitglied in einen Verein** *usw.* **~:** admit sb. as a member of a club *etc.;* admit sb. to membership of a club *etc.;* **jmdn. als Teilhaber in sein Geschäft ~:** bring sb. into one's business as a partner; [E] (*einschließen, verzeichnen*) include; [F] (*fassen*) take; hold; absorb ‹immigrants, goods, workers›; [G] (*erfassen*) take in, absorb ‹impressions, information, etc.›; **etw. ganz in sich ~:** take sth. in *or* absorb sth. completely; [H] (*absorbieren*) absorb; **wieder Nahrung ~** ‹patient› take food again; [I] (*leihen*) raise ‹mortgage, money, loan›; [J] (*reagieren auf*) receive; **etw. positiv/mit Begeisterung ~:** give sth. a positive/an enthusiastic reception; [K] (*aufschreiben*) take down; take [down] ‹dictation, particulars›; (*Kartographie*) survey and record ‹area, district›; [L] (*fotografieren*) take ‹picture›; take a photograph of, photograph ‹scene, subject›; (*filmen*) film; [M] (*auf Tonträger*) record; [N] (*Handarbeit*) increase ‹stitch›; [O] (*bes. Fußball*) take ‹ball›; ‹goalkeeper› take, gather ‹ball›; [P] (*nordd.: aufwischen*) mop *or* wipe up; [Q] (*österr.: einstellen*) take on ‹staff, workers›

**Aufnehmer** *der;* **~s, ~** (*nordd.*) cloth

**äufnen** /ˈɔyfnən/ *tr. V.* (*schweiz.*) accumulate ‹money, fortune›

**auf|nesteln** *tr. V.* undo

**auf|norden** *tr. V.* (*ns.*) nordicize

**auf|nötigen** *tr. V.* **jmdm. etw. ~:** force sth. on sb.; **die Lage nötigt uns Zurückhaltung auf** the situation forces us to be cautious

**auf|oktroyieren** /ˈaufǀɔktroaji:rən/ *tr. V.* **jmdm. etw. ~:** impose *or* force sth. on sb.

**auf|opfern** ❶ *tr. V.* (*geh.: opfern*) sacrifice (*Dat.* to). ❷ *refl. V.* (*sich einsetzen*) devote oneself sacrificingly (**für** to)

**aufopfernd** ❶ *Adj.* self-sacrificing ‹person, love, work›. ❷ *adv.* self-sacrificingly

**Auf·opferung** *die* [A] (*das Opfern*) sacrifice; [B] (*das Sicheinsetzen*) self-sacrifice

**aufopferungs·voll** ⇒ **aufopfernd**

**auf|packen** *tr. V.* **etw. ~:** load sth. on; **jmdm./einem Tier etw. ~:** load sth. on to sb./an animal; **sich** (*Dat.*) **etw. ~:** load oneself with sth.; **jmdm./sich etw. ~** (*fig.*) burden sb./oneself with sth.

**auf|päppeln** *tr. V.* feed up; (*fig.*) pep up

**auf|passen** *itr. V.* [A] look *or* watch out; (*konzentriert sein*) pay attention; **pass mal auf!** (*ugs.*) (*du wirst sehen*) you just watch!; (*hör mal zu!*) now listen; (*sei aufmerksam!*) pay attention!; **aufgepasst!** (*ugs.*) look *or* watch out!; **kannst du denn nicht ~?** can't you be more careful?; **wir haben immer aufgepasst, aber jetzt ist meine Frau doch schwanger** (*ugs.*) we've always been careful, but my wife's got pregnant all the same (*coll.*); [B] (*beaufsichtigen*) **auf jmdn./etw. ~:** keep an eye on sb./sth.

**Aufpasser** *der;* **~s, ~** [A] (*abwertend*) spy; [B] (*Wärter, Bewacher*) guard; (*aus Gründen des Anstands*) chaperon

**Aufpasserin** *die;* **~, ~nen** [A] (*abwertend*) spy; [B] (*Wärterin*) guard; (*Anstandsdame*) protector; chaperon

**auf|peitschen** *tr. V.* [A] (*bewegen*) whip up ‹sea, waves›; [B] (*erregen*) inflame ‹passions, emotions, senses›; inflame, stir up ‹populace, crowd›

**auf|peppen** /ˈaufpɛpn̩/ *tr. V.* (*salopp*) pep up (*coll.*)

**auf|pflanzen** ❶ *tr. V.* [A] (*aufstellen*) set up; [B] fix ‹bayonet›. ❷ *refl. V.* **sich vor jmdm./etw. ~** (*ugs.*) plant oneself in front of sb./sth.

**auf|pfropfen** *tr. V.* (*auch fig.*) graft on (**auf** + *Akk.* to)

**auf|picken** *tr. V.* [A] (*aufnehmen*) ‹bird› peck up; (*fig. ugs.*) pick up ‹expression, idea, piece of information›; [B] (*öffnen*) peck open; [C] (*österr.: aufkleben*) stick on (**auf** + *Akk.* to)

**auf|platzen** *itr. V.; mit sein* burst open; ‹seam, cushion› split open; ‹wound› open up

**auf|plustern** ❶ *tr. V.* ruffle [up] ‹feathers›; puff up ‹cheeks›; (*fig. ugs.: aufbauschen*) blow up (**zu** into). ❷ *refl. V.* [A] ‹bird› ruffle [up] its feathers; [B] (*ugs. abwertend: sich wichtig tun*) puff oneself up

**auf|polieren** *tr. V.* (*auch fig.*) polish up

**auf|polstern** *tr. V.* reupholster

**auf|prägen** *tr. V.* emboss; stamp; **jmdm./einer Sache einen Stempel ~** (*fig.*) leave one's/its mark on sb./sth.

**Auf·prall** *der;* **~[e]s, ~e** impact

**auf|prallen** *itr. V.; mit sein* **auf etw.** (*Akk.*, *seltener Dat.*) **~:** strike *or* hit sth.; (*auf etw. auffahren*) collide with *or* run into sth.

**Auf·preis** *der* extra *or* additional charge; **gegen ~:** for an extra *or* additional charge

**auf|probieren** *tr. V.* try on ‹hat, cap, spectacles›

**auf|pulvern** *tr.* (*auch itr.*) *V.* (*ugs.*) pep up (*coll.*); boost, lift ‹morale›; **Kaffee pulvert [einen] auf** coffee peps you up (*coll.*)

**auf|pumpen** ❶ *tr. V.* pump up, inflate ‹tyre›; inflate ‹air mattress, rubber boat›; pump up *or* inflate the tyres of *or* on ‹bicycle›. ❷ *refl. V.* (*ugs.*) ‹bird› ruffle [up] its feathers

**auf|putschen** *tr. V.* (*abwertend*) [A] (*stimulieren*) stimulate; arouse ‹passions, urge›; **~de Mittel** stimulants; **jmdn./sich mit Kaffee ~:** give sb. coffee/drink coffee as a stimulant; [B] (*aufhetzen*) incite; stir up (**gegen** against)

**Aufputsch·mittel** *das* stimulant

**Auf·putz** *der* get-up; **die Häuser standen in festlichem ~:** the houses were festively decorated

**auf|putzen** *tr. V.* [A] decorate ‹Christmas tree, building, etc.›; [B] (*fig. ugs.*) **mit bürgerlichen Ideen aufgeputzter Sozialismus** socialism dressed up in bourgeois ideas

**auf|quellen** *unr. itr. V.; mit sein* [A] (*größer werden*) swell up; ‹dough› rise; **aufgequollene Augen/Wangen** swollen eyes/cheeks; [B] (*geh.: emporsteigen, auch fig.*) well *or* rise up; ‹smoke› rise [up]

**auf|raffen** ❶ *tr. V.* (*hochnehmen*) gather up. ❷ *refl. V.* [A] (*sich erheben*) pull oneself up [on to one's feet]; struggle to one's feet; [B] (*sich überwinden*) pull oneself together; **sich dazu ~, etw. zu tun** bring oneself to do sth.; **sich zu einer Arbeit/Entscheidung ~:** bring oneself to do a piece of work/come to a decision

**auf|ragen** *itr. V.* tower [up]; ‹tower, mountain range› rise up

**auf|rappeln** *refl. V.* (*ugs.*) [A] ⇒ **aufraffen** 2 A, B; [B] (*Schwäche überwinden*) recover

**auf|rauchen** *tr. V.* finish [smoking] ‹cigarette, pipe, etc.›; **die ganze Schachtel/alle Zigaretten ~:** get through *or* smoke the whole packet/all the cigarettes

**auf|rauen, *auf|rauhen** *tr. V.* roughen [up]; nap ‹cloth›

**auf|räumen** ❶ *tr. V.* [A] (*in Ordnung bringen*) tidy *or* clear up; (*fig.*) sort out; [B] (*wegräumen*) clear *or* put away. ❷ *itr. V.* [A] (*Ordnung machen*) tidy *or* clear up; (*fig.*) sort things out; [B] (*beseitigen*) **mit jmdm./etw. ~:** eliminate sb./sth.

**Aufräumungs·arbeiten** *Pl.* clearance work *sing.*

**auf|rechnen** *tr. V.* [A] (*berechnen*) charge for; [B] (*verrechnen*) **etw. gegen etw. ~:** set sth. off against sth.

**auf·recht** ❶ *Adj.* [A] (*aufgerichtet*) upright ‹position›; upright, erect ‹posture, bearing›; **der ~e Gang ist für den Menschen charakteristisch** human beings characteristically walk upright; **etw. ~ hinstellen** place sth. upright *or* in an upright position; [B] (*redlich*) upright. ❷ *adv.* (*aufgerichtet*) ‹walk, sit, hold oneself› straight, erect; **die Aussicht/Hoffnung hält ihn ~** (*fig.*) the prospect/hope keeps him going; **sich kaum noch ~ halten können** be hardly able to stand

**aufrecht|erhalten** *unr. tr. V.* maintain; maintain, keep up ‹deception, fiction, contact, custom›; keep to ‹decision›; **nur der Gedanke an ein kühles Bier erhielt ihn aufrecht** (*fig.*) it was only the thought of a cool beer that kept him going

**Aufrecht·erhaltung** *die* ⇒ **aufrechterhalten**: maintenance; keeping up; **zur ~ des Kontakts** in order to maintain contact

**auf|regen** ❶ *tr. V.* (*erregen*) excite; (*ärgerlich machen*) annoy; irritate; (*beunruhigen*) agitate; (*ugs.: entrüsten*) upset; **du regst mich auf** you're getting on my nerves. ❷ *refl. V.* get worked up (**über** + *Akk.* about)

**Auf·regung** *die* (*Erregung*) excitement *no pl.;* (*Beunruhigung*) agitation *no pl.;* **jmdn. in ~ versetzen** make sb. excited/agitated; **nur keine ~!** don't get excited!; **alles war in heller ~:** everything was in utter confusion; **der Vorfall hat das ganze Land in ~ versetzt** the whole country is in an uproar over the case

**auf|reiben** ❶ *unr. tr. V.* [A] (*zermürben*) wear down; [B] (*vernichten*) wipe out; [C] (*wund reiben*) **sich** (*Dat.*) **die Hände/Fersen** *usw.* **~:** rub one's hands/heels *etc.* sore; **das Seil hatte ihm die Hände aufgerieben** the rope had chafed his hands. ❷ *unr. refl. V.* wear oneself out

**aufreibend** ❶ *Adj.* wearing; trying ‹day, time›; (*stärker*) gruelling. ❷ *adv.* tryingly, exasperatingly

**auf|reihen** ❶ *tr. V.* [A] thread ‹beads, pearls›; [B] (*aufstellen*) line up; put in a row/rows. ❷ *refl. V.* (*sich aufstellen*) line up

**auf|reißen** ❶ *unr. tr. V.* [A] (*öffnen*) tear *or* rip open; tear open ‹collar, shirt, etc.›; wrench open ‹drawer›; fling open ‹door, window›; **die Augen/den Mund ~:** open one's eyes/mouth wide; [B] (*beschädigen*) tear *or* rip open; rip, tear ‹clothes›; break up ‹road, soil›; **sich** (*Dat.*) **die Haut/den Ellbogen/Ärmel ~:** gash one's skin/elbow/rip *or* tear one's sleeve; [C] (*bes. Fußballjargon*) open up ‹defence›; [D] (*aufbrechen*) tear up ‹road surface, pavement›; [E] (*Bautechnik*) make a drawing of; [F] (*salopp: Kontakt finden mit*) pick up (*coll.*); [G] (*salopp: sich verschaffen*) get hold of; get, land oneself ‹job›.
❷ *itr. V.; mit sein* (*auseinander reißen*) ‹clothes› tear, rip; ‹seam› split; ‹wound› open; ‹clouds› break up

**auf|reizen** *tr. V.* [A] (*erregen*) excite ‹senses, imagination›; rouse ‹passions›; (*wütend machen*) provoke; [B] (*aufwiegeln*) incite; **jmdn. zum Widerstand ~:** incite sb. to resist

*old spelling (see note on page 1707)

**auf·reizend** ❶ *Adj.* provocative. ❷ *adv.* provocatively

**auf|ribbeln** *tr. V.* (*ugs.*) unpick

**Aufrichte** *die;* ~, ~n (*schweiz.*) topping-out ceremony

**auf|richten** ❶ *tr. V.* A (*hochrichten*) **den Kopf/Oberkörper ~:** raise one's head/upper body; **jmdn. ~** (*auf die Beine stellen*) help sb. up; **jmdn. im Bett ~:** sit sb. up in bed; **sich ~:** stand up [straight]; (*aus gebückter Haltung*) straighten up; (*nach einem Sturz*) get to one's feet; **sich im Bett ~:** sit up in bed; **sich zur vollen Länge ~:** draw oneself up to one's full height; B (*errichten*) erect; put up; (*fig.*) build up ‹business, empire›; C (*trösten*) **jmdn. [wieder] ~:** give fresh heart to sb.; D (*beleben*) restore ‹pride, self-confidence›; **jmds. Mut ~:** give sb. new courage. ❷ *refl. V.* (*Mut schöpfen*) take heart; **sich an jmdm./etw. [wieder] ~:** take heart from sb./sth.

**auf·richtig** ❶ *Adj.* honest, sincere ‹person, efforts›; sincere ‹regret, sympathy, affection›; genuine ‹pleasure, admiration›; **~ zu jmdm.** *od.* **gegen jmdn. sein** be honest *or* straightforward with sb.; **wenn ich ~ sein soll** to be honest *or* frank. ❷ *adv.* sincerely; ‹speak› honestly, frankly

**Auf·richtigkeit** *die* sincerity; (*eines Menschen*) honesty; sincerity

**Auf·riss, *Auf·riß** *der* A (*Bautechnik*) elevation; **etw. im ~ darstellen** draw sth. in elevation; B (*Darstellung*) outline

**Aufriss·zeichnung, *Aufriß·zeichnung** *die* (*Bautechnik*) elevation

**auf|ritzen** *tr. V.* A (*öffnen*) slit [open]; B (*verletzen*) scratch; **sich** (*Dat.*) **die Haut/den Arm ~:** scratch oneself/one's arm

**auf|rollen** *tr. V.* A (*zusammenrollen*) roll up; coil *or* roll up ‹hose, cable›; (*auf eine Rolle*) roll up ‹hose, cable›; **sich** (*Dat.*) **die Haare ~** (*ugs.*) put one's hair up in rollers *or* curlers; B (*auseinander rollen*) unroll; unfurl ‹flag›; C (*aufkrempeln*) roll up ‹sleeve, trouser leg›; D (*erörtern*) go into ‹subject, question›; **der Prozess musste noch einmal aufgerollt werden** the case had to be retried; E (*Milit.*) **den Feind ~:** turn ‹enemy, enemy position›

**auf|rücken** *itr. V.; mit sein* A (*aufschließen*) move up; **dicht aufgerückt stehen** stand close [up] together; B (*befördert werden*) move up; be promoted; **zum Major ~:** be promoted to major; **in eine leitende Stellung ~:** rise to a managerial position

**Auf·ruf** *der* A (*das Aufrufen*) call; **„Eintritt nur nach ~"** 'do not enter until called'; B (*Appell*) appeal (**an** + *Akk.* to); **einen ~ an jmdn. richten** appeal to sb.; C (*DV*) call; D (*Bankw.*) calling-in

**auf|rufen** *unr. tr. V.* A *auch itr.* (*auffordern*) **jmdn. ~, etw. zu tun** call upon sb. to do sth.; **jmdn. zum Widerstand/zu Spenden ~:** call on sb. to resist/for donations; **zum [General]streik ~:** call a [general] strike; B (*namentlich*) call ‹name›; **jmdn. ~:** call sb.; call sb.'s name; **einen Schüler ~:** call upon a pupil to answer; C (*Rechtsw.*) appeal for ‹witnesses› [to come forward]; **etwaige Erben ~:** call on possible heirs to make themselves known; D (*DV*) call

**Aufruhr** *der;* ~s, ~e A (*Widerstand*) revolt; rebellion; **in ~ sein** be in revolt; B (*Erregung*) turmoil; **jmdn./etw. in ~ versetzen** plunge *or* throw sb./sth. into [a state of] turmoil

**auf|rühren** *tr. V.* A stir up; B (*geh.: hervorrufen*) stir up, rouse ‹feelings›; C (*in Erinnerung rufen*) stir up ‹memory›; rake up ‹scandal, story›; D (*geh.: erregen*) upset; disturb

**Aufrührer** *der;* ~s, ~, **Aufrührerin** *die;* ~, ~nen rabble-rouser

**aufrührerisch** ❶ *Adj.* A (*aufwiegelnd*) seditious; inflammatory; B (*in Aufruhr befindlich*) rebellious. ❷ *adv.* (*aufwiegelnd*) seditiously

**auf|runden** *tr. V.* round off (**auf** + *Akk.* to)

**auf|rüsten** *tr., itr. V.* arm; **wieder ~:** rearm

**Auf·rüstung** *die* armament

**auf|rütteln** *tr. V.* **jmdn. [aus dem Schlaf] ~:** shake sb. out of his/her sleep; **jmds. Gewissen ~** (*fig.*) stir sb.'s conscience; **jmdn. aus seiner Apathie/Lethargie** *usw.* **~** (*fig.*) shake sb. out of his/her apathy/lethargy *etc.*

**aufs** *Präp.* + *Art.* A = **auf das;** B **~ Klo gehen** (*ugs.*) go to the loo (*Brit. coll.*) *or* (*Amer. coll.*) john; **sich ~ Bitten verlegen** resort to appeals

**auf|sagen** *tr. V.* A (*sagen*) recite; B (*geh.: aufkündigen*) **[jmdm.] seinen Dienst ~:** give in one's notice [to sb.] (*Brit.*); give [one's] notice [to sb.] (*Amer.*); **jmdm. die Freundschaft ~:** break with sb.

**auf|sammeln** *tr. V.* A (*aufheben*) pick *or* gather up; B (*ugs.: aufgreifen*) pick up

**aufsässig** /ˈaufzɛsɪç/ ❶ *Adj.* A (*trotzig*) recalcitrant; B (*veralt.: rebellisch*) rebellious. ❷ *adv.* A (*trotzig*) recalcitrantly; B (*veralt.: rebellisch*) rebelliously

**Aufsässigkeit** *die;* ~, ~en A (*Trotz*) recalcitrance; (*Rebellion*) rebelliousness; B (*Handlung*) piece of recalcitrance/rebelliousness

**auf|satteln** *tr. V.* saddle ‹horse›; hitch up ‹trailer, sled›

**Auf·satz** *der* A (*Schul~, Abhandlung*) essay; (*in einer Zeitschrift*) article; B (*Aufbau*) top *or* upper part; C (*Orgelbau*) resonator; D (*Tafel~*) epergne

**Aufsatz-: ~heft** *das* essay book; **~thema** *das* essay subject

**auf|saugen** *unr.* (*auch regelm.*) *tr. V.* soak up; (*fig.*) absorb; (*verschlucken*) absorb; swallow up

**auf|schauen** (*südd., österr., schweiz.*) ⇒ **aufblicken**

**auf|schaukeln** *refl. V.* A (*Tech.*) ‹vehicle› start rocking more and more violently; B (*ugs.: sich steigern*) ‹excitement etc.› build up

**auf|schäumen** ❶ *itr. V.; meist mit sein* ‹champagne, beer, etc.› foam up; ‹sea› foam. ❷ *tr. V.* (*Technik*) **etw. auf die Wand ~:** apply sth. to *or* spray sth. on to the wall as a foam

**auf|scheinen** *unr. itr. V.; mit sein* (*auch fig., auch österr. Amtsspr.*) appear

**auf|scheuchen** *tr. V.* A (*aufjagen*) put up ‹birds, animals›; B (*ugs.: in Unruhe versetzen*) startle; **jmdn. aus seiner Gleichgültigkeit/Lethargie** *usw.* **~:** shake *or* jolt sb. out of his/her apathy/lethargy

**auf|scheuern** ❶ *tr. V.* (*verletzen*) chafe; **sich** (*Dat.*) **die Haut/die Fersen ~:** chafe one's skin/heels. ❷ *refl. V.* (*verletzt werden*) become chafed *or* sore

**auf|schichten** *tr. V.* stack up; build [up] ‹wall, mound, stack, pile›; pile up ‹straw› [in layers]

**auf|schieben** *unr. tr. V.* A (*verschieben*) postpone; put off; **aufgeschoben ist nicht aufgehoben** there'll be another opportunity; there is always another time; B slide open ‹door, window›; slide *or* draw back ‹bolt›

**auf|schießen** ❶ *unr. itr. V.; mit sein* A (*nach oben schießen*) shoot up; ‹flames› shoot *or* leap up; B (*schnell wachsen*) shoot up; **ein lang aufgeschossener Junge** a tall gangling *or* gangly youth. ❷ *unr. tr. V.* (*Seemannsspr.*) coil [up]

**Auf·schlag** *der* A (*das Aufprallen*) impact; B (*Preis~*) extra charge; surcharge; C (*Ärmel~*) cuff; (*Hosen~*) turn-up; (*Revers*) lapel; D (*Tennis usw.*) serve; service; **jetzt habe ich ~:** now it's my serve

**auf|schlagen** ❶ *unr. itr. V.* A *mit sein* (*aufprallen*) **auf etw.** (*Dat. od. Akk.*) **~:** hit *or* strike sth.; **mit der Stirn/dem Kopf ~:** hit one's forehead/head on sth.; B *auch mit sein* (*teurer werden*) ‹price, rent, costs› go up; C (*Tennis usw.*) serve; **Sie schlagen auf!** it's your serve *or* service; D (*auflodern*) ‹flames› leap up; ‹fire› leap *or* blaze up. ❷ *unr. tr. V.* A (*öffnen*) crack ‹nut, egg› [open]; knock a hole in ‹ice›; **sich** (*Dat.*) **das Knie/den Kopf ~:** fall and cut one's knee/head; B (*aufblättern*) open ‹book, newspaper›; (*zurückschlagen*) turn back ‹bedclothes, blanket›; **schlagt S. 15 auf!** turn to page 15; C **die Augen ~:** open one's eyes; D (*hoch-, umschlagen*) turn up ‹collar, sleeve, trouser leg›; E (*aufbauen*) set up ‹camp›; pitch, put up ‹tent›; put up ‹bed, hut, scaffolding›; F (*erhöhen*) put up, raise, increase ‹prices›; **5% auf etw.** (*Akk.*) **~:** put 5% on sth.; G (*sich niederlassen*) **seinen Wohnsitz in der Hauptstadt/einem Bauernhaus ~:** take up residence in the capital/a farmhouse; H (*Stricken*) cast on

**Auf·schläger** *der,* **Auf·schlägerin** *die* (*Tennis usw.*) server

**Aufschlag-: ~fehler** *der* (*Tennis usw.*) [service] fault; **~zünder** *der* percussion fuse

**auf|schlecken** *tr. V.* lap up

**auf|schließen** ❶ *unr. tr. V.* A unlock; **jmdm. die Tür ~:** unlock the door for sb.; B (*Bergbau*) develop; C (*Chemie, Biol.*) break down; D (*Amtsspr.: erschließen*) develop. ❷ *unr. itr. V.* A **[jmdm.] ~:** unlock the door/gate *etc.* [for sb.]; B (*aufrücken*) close up; (*Milit.*) close ranks; **die Autos fuhren dicht aufgeschlossen** the cars were bumper to bumper; C (*Sport*) catch up (**zu** with)

**auf|schlitzen** *tr. V.* slit open; slash open ‹stomach, dress›

**auf|schluchzen** *tr. V.* give a sob; (*stoßweise schluchzen*) sob convulsively

**Auf·schluss, *Auf·schluß** *der* A (*Auskunft*) information *no pl.*; **über etw.** (*Akk.*) **~ geben** give *or* provide information about sth.; **jmdm. über etw.** (*Akk.*) **~ geben** inform sb. about sth.; **über etw.** (*Akk.*) **~ verlangen** demand an explanation of sth.; B (*Bergbau*) development; C (*Chemie, Biol.*) breaking up; D (*im Gefängnis*) **um 7 Uhr ist ~:** the cells are unlocked at 7 o'clock

**auf|schlüsseln** *tr. V.* break down (**nach** according to)

**Aufschlüsselung, Aufschlüsslung** *die;* ~, ~en breakdown

**aufschluss·reich, *aufschluß·reich** *Adj.* informative; (*enthüllend*) revealing

**auf|schnallen** *tr. V.* A (*öffnen*) unbuckle; unstrap; unbuckle, unfasten ‹belt›; B (*befestigen*) strap on; **sich** (*Dat.*) **den Rucksack ~:** strap one's rucksack on [to] one's back

**auf|schnappen** ❶ *tr. V.* A (*ugs.: hören*) pick up; B (*auffangen*) snap up. ❷ *itr. V.; mit sein* (*sich öffnen*) snap *or* spring open

**auf|schneiden** ❶ *unr. tr. V.* A (*öffnen*) cut open; cut ‹knot›; lance ‹abscess, boil›; **sich** (*Dat.*) **den Finger ~:** cut one's finger [open]; **ein neues Buch ~:** cut the pages of a new book; B (*zerteilen*) cut, slice ‹bread, cake, cheese›; carve, slice ‹meat, poultry›. ❷ *unr. itr. V.* (*ugs. abwertend: prahlen*) boast, brag (**mit** about)

**Auf·schneider** *der,* **Auf·schneiderin** *die* (*ugs. abwertend*) boaster; braggart

**Auf·schneiderei** *die* (*ugs. abwertend*) boasting; bragging

**auf|schnellen** *itr. V.; mit sein* leap up

**Auf·schnitt** *der* [assorted] cold meats *pl.*/cheeses *pl.*; **kalter ~:** cold cuts *pl.*

**auf|schnüren** *tr. V.* undo, untie ‹knot, parcel, string›; unlace, undo ‹shoe, boot, corset›

**auf|schrauben** *tr. V.* A (*öffnen, lösen*) unscrew; unscrew the top of ‹bottle, jar, etc.›; B (*auf etw. schrauben, mit Schrauben befestigen*) screw on (**auf** + *Akk.* to)

**auf|schrecken** ❶ *tr. V.* (*erschrecken*) startle; make ‹person› jump; **jmdn. aus dem Schlaf ~:** startle sb. from his/her sleep. ❷ *itr. V.; im Präsens und Prät. auch unr.; mit sein* start [up]; **aus dem Schlaf ~:** awake with a start; start from one's sleep; **aus einem Traum/seinen Gedanken ~:** start from a dream/one's reflections

**Auf·schrei** *der* cry; (*stärker*) yell; (*schriller*) scream; **ein ~ der Empörung** *od.* **Entrüstung** (*fig.*) an outcry

**auf|schreiben** ❶ *unr. tr. V.* A write down; **[sich** (*Dat.*)**] etw. ~:** make a note of sth.; **er wurde von einem Polizisten aufgeschrieben** the policeman took his name and particulars; **B** (*ugs.: verordnen*) prescribe ‹medicine›. ❷ *unr. itr. V.* (*bes. südd., österr.: anschreiben*) give credit; **bei jmdm. ~ lassen** get credit from sb.

**auf|schreien** *unr. itr. V.* cry out; (*stärker*) yell out; (*schrill*) scream

**Auf·schrift** *die* **A** (*Beschriftung*) inscription; (*Etikett*) label; **B** (*Anschrift*) address

**Auf·schub** *der* delay; (*absichtliche Verschiebung*) postponement; **die Sache duldet keinen ~:** the matter brooks no delay; **jmdm. ~ gewähren** (*Zahlungs~*) allow *or* grant sb. a period of grace; **ein ~ der Hinrichtung** a reprieve

**auf|schürfen** *tr. V.* **sich** (*Dat.*) **das Knie/die Haut ~:** graze one's knee/oneself

**auf|schütteln** *tr. V.* shake *or* plump up ‹pillow, cushion›

**auf|schütten** *tr. V.* **A** (*auf etw. schütten*) pour on ‹liquid›; **etw. auf etw.** (*Akk.*) **~:** pour sth. on *or* over sth.; **noch etwas Kohle [auf die Glut] ~:** put some more coal on [the fire]; **B** (*aufhäufen*) pile up; pile *or* heap up ‹sand, earth, straw›; **C** (*errichten*) build ‹dam, embankment, pile›; (*erhöhen*) raise ‹road›; (*verbreitern*) widen ‹road›; **D** (*Geol.*) deposit

**Aufschüttung** *die;* **~, ~en** **A** (*Erhöhung*) earth bank; **B** (*Geol.*) deposit

**auf|schwatzen,** (*bes. südd.*) **auf|schwätzen** *tr. V.* **jmdm. etw. ~:** talk sb. into having sth.; **sich** (*Dat.*) **etw. ~ lassen** be talked into having sth.

**auf|schwellen** ❶ *unr. itr. V.; mit sein* **A** (*dick werden*) swell up; **aufgeschwollene Leiber/Wangen** swollen bodies/cheeks; **B** (*laut werden*) swell. ❷ *tr. V.* (*auch fig.*) swell

**auf|schwemmen** *tr. V.* **jmdn./jmds. Gesicht ~:** make sb./sb.'s face bloated

**auf|schwingen** ❶ *unr. refl. V.* **A** (*emporfliegen*) ‹bird› soar up; **B** (*sich aufraffen*) **sich ~, etw. zu tun** bring oneself to do sth.; **sich zum Arbeiten/zu einem Entschluss/Brief ~:** bring oneself to get down to work/bring oneself to make a decision/write a letter; **C** **sich zum Sittenrichter/Diktator** *usw.* **~:** set oneself up as a judge of morals/as a dictator *etc.* ❷ *unr. itr. V.* (*Turnen*) swing [oneself] up

**Auf·schwung** *der* **A** (*Auftrieb*) uplift; **das gab mir neuen ~:** that gave me a lift; **B** (*gute Entwicklung*) upswing; upturn (*Gen.* in); **einen ~ erleben** experience an upswing *or* upturn; **C** (*Turnen*) swing up

**auf|sehen** *unr. itr. V.* **A** look up; **B** (*bewundern*) **zu jmdm. ~:** look up to sb.

**Aufsehen** *das;* **~s** stir; sensation; **[großes] ~ erregen** cause *or* create a [great] stir *or* sensation; **sich ohne großes ~ davonmachen** make off without causing a lot of fuss; **um jedes ~ zu vermeiden, reiste er inkognito** to avoid causing *or* creating a stir, he travelled incognito

**aufsehen·erregend** *Adj.* sensational

**Auf·seher** *der* (*im Gefängnis*) warder (*Brit.*); [prison] guard (*Amer.*); (*im Park*) park-keeper; (*im Museum, auf dem Parkplatz*) attendant; (*bei Prüfungen*) invigilator (*Brit.*); proctor (*Amer.*); (*auf einem Gut, Sklaven~*) overseer; (*im Warenhaus*) shopwalker (*Brit.*); floorwalker (*Amer.*)

**Aufseherin** *die;* **~, ~nen** (*im Gefängnis*) warder (*Brit.*); [prison] guard (*Amer.*); (*im Museum*) attendant; (*bei Prüfungen*) invigilator (*Brit.*); proctor (*Amer.*); (*im Warenhaus*) shopwalker (*Brit.*); floorwalker (*Amer.*)

***auf|sein** ⇒ **auf** 3 A, H

**aufseiten** *Präp.* + *Gen.* **~ der Direktion** on the management side

**auf|setzen** ❶ *tr. V.* **A** put on ‹hat, glasses, mask›; **eine Miene/ein Lächeln ~** (*fig.*) put on an expression/a smile; **sich** (*Dat.*) **etw. ~:** put sth. on; **B** (*aufs Feuer setzen*) put on; **Wasser [zum Kochen] ~:** put water on [to boil]; **C** (*entwerfen*) draft; (*verfassen*) draw up ‹minutes, contract, will›; **D** (*aufrecht hinsetzen*) **jmdn. ~:** sit sb. up; **sich ~:** sit up; **E** (*auf eine Unterlage*) set down; lower ‹record player arm›; **den Fuß ~:** put one's foot on the ground *or* down; **F** (*aufschichten*) stack [up]; **G** (*aufrecht hinstellen*) set up ‹skittles›; **H** (*Seemannsspr.*) beach; **I** (*Flugw.*) land ‹aircraft›; set ‹aircraft› down. ❷ *itr. V.* ‹aircraft› touch down, land; ⇒ *auch* **aufgesetzt** 2; **Horn** A; **Dämpfer** B

**Auf·setzer** *der* (*Fußball, Handball*) bouncer; bouncing ball

**auf|seufzen** *itr. V.* **[laut/tief] ~:** heave a [loud/deep] sigh

**Auf·sicht** *die* **A** (*Überwachung*) supervision; (*bei Prüfungen*) invigilation (*Brit.*); proctoring (*Amer.*); **[die] ~ haben** *od.* **führen** be in charge (**über** + *Akk.* of); (*bei Prüfungen*) invigilate (*Brit.*); proctor (*Amer.*); **eine ~ führende Person** a person in charge; **die ~ führende Behörde** the supervising authority; **der ~ führende Lehrer** the teacher in charge *or* on duty; **ohne ~:** unsupervised; without supervision; **unter [jmds.] ~** (*Dat.*) under [sb.'s] supervision; **unter ärztlicher/polizeilicher ~:** under medical/police supervision; **während der Pause auf dem Schulhof ~ haben** ‹teacher› be on duty during break; **B** (*Person*) person in charge; (*Lehrer*) teacher in charge *or* on duty; (*im Museum*) attendant

***aufsicht·führend** ⇒ **Aufsicht** A

**Aufsicht·führende** *der/die; adj. Dekl.:* ⇒ **Aufsicht** B

**Aufsichts-:** **~beamte** *der,* **~beamtin** *die* attendant; (*im Bahnhof*) supervisor; **~pflicht** *die* (*Rechtsw.*) legal responsibility *or* obligation to exercise proper supervision; **die elterliche ~pflicht** legal parental responsibility to keep children under proper supervision; **~rat** *der* (*Wirtsch.*) **A** (*Gremium*) board of directors; supervisory board; **B** (*Mitglied*) member of the board [of directors] *or* supervisory board; **~rätin** *die* ⇒ **~rat** B

**auf|sitzen** *unr. itr. V.* **A** *mit sein* (*auf ein Reittier*) mount; (*auf ein Fahrzeug*) get on; **auf ein Pferd ~:** mount a horse; **aufgesessen!** (*Milit.*) mount!; **B** *mit sein* (*Turnen*) come to a sitting position; **C** *mit sein* (*hereinfallen*) **jmdm./einer Sache ~:** be taken in by sb./sth.; **D** (*ugs.: aufrecht sitzen*) sit up; **E** (*aufliegen*) **auf etw.** (*Dat.*) **~** ‹machine part, beam, etc.› sit on sth.; **F** (*Seemannsspr.*) be grounded *or* aground

**Aufsitzer** *der;* **~s, ~** (*österr.*) flop (*coll.*)

**auf|spalten** ❶ *unr.* (*auch regelm.*) *tr. V.* split; (*fig.*) split [up]. ❷ *unr. refl. V.* split

**Auf·spaltung** *die* splitting; (*fig.*) splitting [up]

**auf|spannen** *tr. V.* **A** (*öffnen*) open, put up ‹umbrella, parasol›; stretch out ‹net, jumping-sheet›; put up ‹tennis net, badminton net, etc.›; **B** (*spannen*) stretch, mount ‹canvas› (**auf** + *Akk.* on)

**auf|sparen** *tr. V.* (*auch fig.*) save [up]; keep

**auf|speichern** ❶ *tr. V.* (*auch fig.*) store up; **seine aufgespeicherte Wut/Energie** (*fig.*) his pent-up rage/energy. ❷ *refl. V.* (*auch fig.*) build up

**auf|sperren** *tr. V.* **A** (*ugs.: öffnen*) **[weit] ~:** open wide; **B** (*bes. südd., österr.: aufschließen*) unlock

**auf|spielen** ❶ *refl. V.* **A** (*ugs. abwertend: angeben*) put on airs; **sich vor jmdm. ~:** show off in front of sb.; **B** (*als etw. hinstellen*) **sich als Held/Märtyrer ~:** act the hero/martyr; **sich als Kenner/als jmds. Anwalt ~:** set oneself up as an expert/as sb.'s lawyer. ❷ *itr. V.* **A** (*musizieren*) play; **zum Tanz ~:** play dance music; **B** (*Sport*) **groß/eindrucksvoll ~:** give a fine/impressive display

**auf|spießen** *tr. V.* **A** run ‹animal, person› through; skewer ‹piece of meat›; (*mit der Gabel*) take ‹piece of meat› on one's fork; (*auf die Hörner nehmen*) gore; **jmdn. mit seinen Blicken ~** (*fig.*) look daggers at sb.; **B** (*befestigen*) pin ‹butterfly, insect›

**auf|splittern** ❶ *itr. V.; mit sein* ‹wood› splinter. ❷ *tr. V.* (*in Teile auflösen*) split up ‹party, group, country, etc.›. ❸ *refl. V.* ‹party, group, country, etc.› split up

**Aufsplitterung** *die;* **~, ~en** ⇒ **aufsplittern:** splintering; splitting up

**auf|sprengen** *tr. V.* force [open]; break open; (*mit Sprengstoff*) blow open

**auf|springen** *unr. itr. V.; mit sein* **A** (*hochspringen*) jump *or* leap up; **B** (*auf ein Fahrzeug*) jump on; **auf etw.** (*Akk.*) **~:** jump on [to] sth.; **C** (*rissig werden*) crack; ‹skin, lips› crack, chap; **D** (*sich öffnen*) ‹door, window› fly *or* burst open; ‹bud, seed pod› burst open; **E** (*auftreffen*) bounce

**auf|spriten** /ˈaufʃprɪtn/ *tr. V.* fortify ‹wine›

**auf|spritzen** ❶ *itr. V.; mit sein* **A** (*hochspritzen*) ‹blood› spurt [up]; ‹mud, spray, waves, sea, surf› spray up; **B** (*ugs.: aufspringen*) leap up; leap to one's feet. ❷ *tr. V.* spray on; **etw. auf etw.** (*Akk.*) **~:** spray sth. on [to] sth.

**auf|sprudeln** *itr. V.; mit sein* ‹spring, water› bubble up

**auf|sprühen** ❶ *tr. V.* spray on; **etw. auf etw.** (*Akk.*) **~:** spray sth. on [to] sth. ❷ *itr. V.; mit sein* ‹flames› shoot up; ‹sparks, spray› fly up; ‹water› spray up

**Auf·sprung** *der* landing; (*eines Balls*) bounce

**auf|spulen** *tr. V.* wind ‹cotton, ribbon, fishing line› on to a/the reel *or* spool

**auf|spüren** *tr. V.* (*auch fig.*) track down

**auf|stacheln** *tr. V.* **A** (*aufhetzen*) incite; **jmdn. zur Revolte/zum Widerstand** *usw.* **~:** incite sb. to revolt/offer resistance *etc.*; **B** (*anspornen*) spur on ‹person, team›; fire ‹passion, jealousy, imagination, etc.›

**auf|stampfen** *itr. V.* stamp; **mit dem Fuß ~:** stamp one's foot

**Auf·stand** *der* rebellion; revolt; **im ~:** in rebellion *or* revolt

**auf·ständisch** *Adj.* rebellious; rebel *attrib.*, insurgent ‹army unit›

**Aufständische** *der/die; adj. Dekl.* rebel; insurgent

**auf|stapeln** *tr. V.* stack up

**auf|stauen** ❶ *refl. V.* ‹water› pile up; (*fig.*) ‹anger, aggression, bitterness, etc.› build up; **aufgestaute Wut/Erbitterung** *usw.* (*fig.*) pent-up rage/bitterness *etc.* ❷ *tr. V.* dam [up]; **etw. in sich** (*Dat.*) **~** (*fig.*) bottle sth. up inside [one]

**auf|stechen** *unr. tr. V.* **A** lance, prick ‹boil›; prick ‹blister›; lance ‹abscess›; **jmdm./sich eine Blase ~:** prick sb.'s/one's blister; **B** (*ugs.: aufdecken*) uncover; bring to light

**auf|stecken** ❶ *tr. V.* **A** put up ‹curtains›; turn up ‹hem, dress, trousers›; **sich** (*Dat.*) **das Haar/die Zöpfe ~:** pin *or* put one's hair/plaits up; **sie trug das Haar aufgesteckt** she wore her hair up; **Kerzen auf den Leuchter ~:** put candles on the candelabrum; **B** (*ugs.: aufgeben*) **etw. ~:** give sth. up; pack sth. in (*coll.*); **einen Plan ~:** give up a plan. ❷ *itr. V.* (*bes. Sport: aufgeben*) retire

**auf|stehen** *unr. itr. V.* **A** *mit sein* (*vom Sitzplatz*) stand up; (*aus dem Liegen*) get up; get to one's feet; (*aus dem Bett*) get up; (*als Kranker*) get up; get out of bed; **aus seinem Sessel ~:** get up from one's chair; **vom Tisch ~:** rise from the table; **für jmdn. im Bus ~:** get up for sb. in the bus; **da musst du früher** *od.* **eher ~!** (*ugs.*) you'll have to be a lot sharper than that!; ⇒ *auch* **Huhn** A; **B** (*offen stehen*) ‹door, window, etc.› be open; **C** *mit sein* (*geh. veralt.: sich auflehnen*) rise in revolt; **gegen jmdn./etw. ~:** rise [up] against sb./sth.

**auf|steigen** *unr. itr. V.; mit sein* **A** (*auf ein Fahrrad, einen Wagen usw.*) get *or* climb on; **auf etw.** (*Akk.*) **~:** get *or* climb on [to] sth.; **auf ein Pferd ~:** get on [to] *or* mount a horse; **B** (*bergan steigen*) climb; **zum Gipfel ~:** climb [up] to the top *or* summit; **C** (*hochsteigen*) ‹smoke, mist, sap, air, moon, sun› rise; ‹storm› gather; **eine ~de Linie** (*fig.*) an ascending line; **D** (*beruflich, gesellschaftlich*) rise (**zu** to); **zum Direktor ~:** rise to the post of *or* to be manager; **zu Macht und Einfluss ~:** rise to power and influence; **E** (*hochfliegen*) go up; ‹bird› soar up; **in** *od.* **mit einem Ballon ~:** go up in a balloon; **F** **an die Oberfläche ~:** rise to the surface; **G** (*geh.: entstehen*) **in jmdm. ~** ‹hatred, revulsion, fear, etc.› rise [up] in sb.; ‹memory, thought› come into sb.'s mind; ‹doubt› arise in sb.'s mind; ‹tears› well up inside sb.; **H** (*Sport*) be

*old spelling (see note on page 1707)

promoted, go up (**in** + *Akk.* to); **I** (*geh.: aufragen*) rise up; tower

**Auf·steiger** *der* **A** **ein [sozialer] ~:** a social climber; **B** (*Sport*) (*aufsteigende Mannschaft*) promotion team *or* side; (*aufgestiegene Mannschaft*) newly promoted side

**Auf·steigerin** *die* ⇒ **Aufsteiger** A

**auf|stellen** ❶ *tr. V.* **A** (*hinstellen*) put up (**auf** + *Akk.* on); set up ‹skittles›; (*aufrecht hinstellen*) stand up; **B** (*postieren*) post; station; **C** (*auswählen*) select, pick ‹team, player›; put together ‹team of experts›; raise ‹army›; **jmdn. für ein Spiel ~** (*Sport*) play sb. in a match; pick *or* select sb. for a match; **D** (*nominieren*) nominate; put up; **jmdn. als Kandidaten ~:** nominate sb. *or* put sb. up as a candidate; **E** (*errichten*) put up; put up, erect ‹scaffolding, monument›; put in, install ‹machine›; **F** (*hochstellen*) erect ‹spines›; turn up ‹collar›; **die Ohren ~** ‹animal› prick up its ears; **G** (*ausarbeiten*) work out ‹programme, budget, plan›; draw up ‹contract, statute, balance sheet›; make [out], draw up ‹list›; set up ‹hypothesis›; establish ‹norm›; prepare ‹statistics›; **eine Formel für etw. ~:** devise a formula for sth.; **H** (*erzielen*) set up, establish ‹record›; **I** (*formulieren*) put forward ‹theory, conjecture, demand›; **J** (*bes. südd.: aufsetzen*) put on ‹soup, potatoes, etc.›; **K** (*nordd.*) ⇒ **anstellen** F.
❷ *refl. V.* **A** (*postieren*) position *or* place oneself; take up position; (*in einer Reihe, zum Tanz*) line up; **sich im Kreis ~:** form a circle; **sich in Reih und Glied ~** (*Milit.*) fall in; **B** ‹hairs, bristles› rise

**Auf·stellung** *die* **A** ⇒ **aufstellen** 1 A: putting up; setting up; standing up; **B** ⇒ **aufstellen** E: putting up; erection; installation; **C** (*einer Mannschaft, eines Spielers*) selection; picking; (*einer Spezialeinheit*) putting together; (*eines Heeres*) raising; (*aufgestellte Mannschaft*) [team] line-up; **D** (*Nominierung*) nomination; **E** (*Milit.*) **~ nehmen** *od.* **beziehen** line up; **das Bataillon hatte vor dem Palast ~ genommen** *od.* **bezogen** the battalion was drawn up in front of the palace; **F** ⇒ **aufstellen** G: working out; drawing up; making out; setting up; establishment; preparation; **G** (*das Erzielen*) setting up; establishment; **H** (*das Formulieren*) putting forward; **I** (*Liste*) list; (*Tabelle*) table

**auf|stemmen** *tr. V.* **A** (*öffnen*) force ‹door› open [with a crowbar]; force *or* prise ‹box› open [with a crowbar]; **B** (*aufstützen*) **seinen Fuß/Arm ~:** brace one's foot/arm (**auf** + *Akk.* on)

**auf|stieben** *unr. itr. V.; mit sein* fly up

**Aufstieg** *der;* **~[e]s, ~e** **A** (*das Hinaufsteigen*) climb; ascent; **B** (*Aufwärtsentwicklung*) rise; **den ~ zum Geschäftsleiter/in den Vorstand schaffen** succeed in rising to the position of manager/rising to become a member of the board of directors; **ein wirtschaftlicher/sozialer ~:** economic/social advancement; **C** (*Sport*) promotion (**in** + *Akk.* to); **D** (*Weg*) way up; **ein gefährlicher ~ zum Gipfel** a dangerous route up *or* ascent to the summit

**Aufstiegs-: ~chance** *die* prospect of promotion; **~spiel** *das* (*Sport*) promotion decider

**auf|stöbern** *tr. V.* **A** (*aufjagen*) put up ‹birds, animals›; **B** (*entdecken*) track down; run to earth

**auf|stocken** *tr.* (*auch itr.*) *V.* **A** **ein Gebäude ~:** add a storey to a building; **wir haben aufgestockt** we've added another storey; **B** (*vermehren, erweitern*) increase ‹capital, budget, funds, pensions›; build up ‹supplies›; **die Gesellschaft stockt auf** the company is increasing its capital

**auf|stöhnen** *itr. V.* groan; **laut/erleichtert ~:** give *or* utter a loud groan/a sigh of relief

**auf|stören** *tr. V.* **A** (*aufschrecken*) put up ‹bird, animal›; disturb ‹wasps' nest, anthill›; **B** (*stören*) disturb

**auf|stoßen** ❶ *unr. tr. V.* **A** (*öffnen*) push open; (*mit einem Fußtritt*) kick open; **B** (*heftig aufsetzen*) **etw. auf etw.** (*Akk.*) **~:** bang sth. down on sth.; **den Stock auf den Boden ~:** thump one's stick on the ground; **C** (*verletzen*) **sich** (*Dat.*) **den Ellbogen** *usw.* **~:** graze one's elbow *etc.* ❷ *unr. itr. V.* **A** (*rülpsen*) belch; burp (*coll.*); ‹baby› bring up wind, (*coll.*) burp; **B** *auch mit sein* (*Aufstoßen verursachen*) **[jmdm.] ~:** repeat [on sb.]; **das könnte Ihnen übel ~** (*fig.*) you might have to pay dearly for that (*fig.*); you could live to regret that; **C** *mit sein* (*ugs.: auffallen*) **jmdm. ~:** strike sb.

**auf|streben** *itr. V.* (*geh.*) tower [up]; **steil ~de Felswände** towering rock walls

**aufstrebend** *Adj.* rising ‹talent, bourgeoisie, industry›; ‹nation, people› striving for progress; **ein ~er junger Mann** an ambitious and up-and-coming young man

**auf|streichen** *unr. tr. V.* spread ‹butter, jam, etc.› (**auf** + *Akk.* on); put on, apply ‹ointment, paint› (**auf** + *Akk.* to)

**auf|streuen** *tr. V.* sprinkle on; **etw. auf etw.** (*Akk.*) **~:** sprinkle sth. on sth.; **den Tieren Stroh ~:** put down straw for the animals

**Auf·strich** *der* **A** (*Brot~*) spread; **B** (*Schriftw.*) upstroke; **C** (*Musik*) up-bow

**auf|stülpen** *tr. V.* **A** (*stülpen auf*) **etw. auf etw.** (*Akk.*) **~:** plonk sth. on sth.; **B** (*hochschlagen*) turn *or* roll up ‹sleeves, trousers›; turn up ‹collar›; **die Lippen ~** (*fig.*) purse one's lips; (*verführerisch*) pout

**auf|stützen** ❶ *tr. V.* **A** (*auf etw. stützen*) **die Ellbogen/Arme auf etw.** (*Akk. od. Dat.*) **~:** rest one's elbows/arms on sth.; **mit aufgestütztem Kopf** with one's head resting on one's hands; **B** (*aufrichten*) **jmdn./sich [im Bett] ~:** prop sb./oneself up [in bed]. ❷ *refl. V.* support oneself

**auf|suchen** *tr. V.* **A** (*hingehen zu*) call on, go and see ‹friends, relatives›; visit ‹museum, grave, monument›; **den Arzt ~:** go to the doctor; go and see the doctor; **die Toilette ~:** go to the toilet *or* lavatory; **B** (*in einem Buch usw.*) look up

**auf|summen, auf|summieren** ❶ *tr. V.* (*DV*) sum. ❷ *refl. V.* add *or* mount up

**auf|takeln** /ˈaufta:kl̩n/ *refl. V.* (*ugs. abwertend*) tart (*Brit.*) *or* doll oneself up (*coll.*); **aufgetakelt** tarted (*Brit.*) *or* dolled up (*coll.*)

**Auf·takt** *der* **A** prelude; (*Beginn*) start; **den ~ zu etw. bilden** form the prelude to sth./be the start of sth.; **B** (*Musik*) upbeat; anacrusis; **C** (*Verslehre*) anacrusis

**auf|tanken** ❶ *tr. V.* fill up; refuel ‹aircraft›; **2 000 Liter ~** ‹aircraft› take on 2,000 litres; **neue Kräfte ~** (*fig.*) recharge one's batteries (*fig.*). ❷ *itr. V.* fill up; ‹aircraft› refuel

**auf|tauchen** *itr. V.; mit sein* **A** (*aus dem Wasser*) surface; ‹frogman, diver› surface, come up; **B** (*sichtbar werden*) appear; (*aus dem Dunkel, dem Nebel*) emerge; appear; **C** (*erscheinen, gefunden werden*) turn up; (*fig.*) ‹problem, question, difficulties› crop up, arise

**auf|tauen** ❶ *tr. V.* thaw ‹ice, frozen food›; thaw [out] ‹earth, ground›; defrost ‹windscreen›; ‹sun› thaw the ice on ‹windscreen›. ❷ *itr. V.; mit sein* (*auch fig.*) thaw; ‹earth, ground› thaw [out]; **der See ist wieder aufgetaut** the ice on the lake has melted

**auf|teilen** *tr. V.* **A** (*verteilen*) share out (**unter** + *Akk. od. Dat.* among); **B** (*aufgliedern*) divide [up] (**in** + *Akk.* into)

**Auf·teilung** *die* ⇒ **aufteilen** A, B: sharing out (**unter** + *Akk. od. Dat.* among); dividing [up] (**in** + *Akk.* into)

**auf|tischen** ❶ *tr. V.* **A** (*servieren*) serve [up]; **jmdm. etw. ~:** serve sb. with sth.; **B** (*ugs. abwertend: erzählen*) serve up ‹excuses, lies, etc.›; **jmdm. etw. ~:** serve sb. up with sth. ❷ *itr. V.* **jmdm. reichlich ~:** serve sb. up a substantial meal

**Auftrag** *der;* **~[e]s, Aufträge** **A** (*Anweisung*) instructions *pl.;* (*Aufgabe*) task; job; **in jmds. ~** (*Dat.*) on sb.'s instructions; **Luigi, ich habe einen ~ für dich** I've got a job for you, Luigi; **im ~ des/der ...** (*für jmdn.*) on behalf of the ...; (*auf jmds. Anweisung*) on the instructions of the ...; **jmdm. den ~ geben** *od.* **erteilen, etw. zu tun** instruct sb. to do sth.; give sb. the job of doing sth.; **einen ~ ausführen** carry out an instruction *or* order; **den ~ haben, etw. zu tun** have been instructed to do sth.; **B** (*Bestellung*) order; (*bei Künstlern, Architekten usw.*) commission; **ein ~ über** *od.* **auf etw.** (*Akk.*) an order/a commission for sth.; **etw. in ~ geben** (*Kaufmannsspr.*) order/commission sth. (**bei** from); **C** (*Mission*) task; mission; **D** (*das Auftragen [von Farbe]*) application

**auf|tragen** ❶ *unr. tr. V.* **A** **jmdm. ~, etw. zu tun** instruct sb. to do sth.; **jmdm. eine Besorgung/eine Botschaft ~:** instruct sb. to get sth./to deliver a message; **er hat mir aufgetragen, dich zu grüßen** he asked me to pass on his regards; **B** (*aufstreichen*) apply, put on ‹paint, make-up, ointment, etc.›; **etw. auf etw.** (*Akk. od. Dat.*) **~:** apply sth. to sth.; put sth. on sth.; **C** (*verschleißen*) wear out ‹clothes›; **D** (*geh.: servieren*) serve [up]. ❷ *unr. itr. V.* **A** ‹clothes› be too bulky; **B** (*ugs.: übertreiben*) **dick** *od.* **stark ~:** lay it on thick (*coll.*)

**Auftrag-: ~geber** *der,* **~geberin** *die* client; customer; (*eines Künstlers, Architekten, Schriftstellers usw.*) client; **~nehmer** *der;* **~~s, ~~, ~nehmerin** *die;* **~~, ~~nen** contractor

**auftrags-, Auftrags-: ~buch** *das* (*Kaufmannsspr.*) order book; **~gemäß** ❶ *Adj.* in accordance with instructions *postpos.;* ❷ *adv.* as instructed; as ordered; as per instructions; **~lage** *die* (*Kaufmannsspr.*) situation as regards orders; **~rückgang** *der* (*Kaufmannsspr.*) falling-off of orders; **~werk** *das* commissioned work

**auf|treffen** *unr. itr. V.; mit sein* **auf etw.** (*Akk.*) **~:** strike *or* hit sth.; **mit der Stirn auf etw.** (*Akk.*) **~:** hit one's forehead on sth.

**auf|treiben** ❶ *unr. tr. V.* **A** (*aufwirbeln*) raise ‹dust›; blow up ‹dry leaves, sand›; **B** (*aufblähen*) bloat; swell; make ‹dough› rise; **C** (*ugs.: ausfindig machen*) get hold of; **ein Quartier ~:** find somewhere to stay; **D** (*auf den Markt*) drive ‹livestock› to market; (*auf die Almen*) drive ‹cattle, livestock› up to [the] high pastures. ❷ *unr. itr. V.; mit sein* ‹body, corpse, face› become bloated *or* swollen; ‹dough› rise

**auf|trennen** *tr. V.* unpick; undo; unpick ‹garment›

**auf|treten** ❶ *unr. itr. V.; mit sein* **A** tread; **er kann mit dem verletzten Bein nicht ~:** he can't walk on *or* put his weight on his injured leg; **B** (*sich benehmen*) behave; **forsch/schüchtern ~:** have a forceful/shy manner; **mit Entschlossenheit ~:** act with firmness; **C** (*fungieren*) appear; **als Zeuge/Kläger ~:** appear as a witness/a plaintiff; **als Vermittler/Sachverständiger ~:** act as mediator/be called in as an expert; **gegen jmdn./etw. ~:** speak out against sb./sth.; **D** (*als Künstler, Sänger usw.*) appear; **sie ist seit Jahren nicht mehr aufgetreten** she hasn't given any public performances for years; **zum ersten Mal ~:** make one's first appearance; **E** (*die Bühne betreten*) enter; **F** (*auftauchen*) ‹problem, question, difficulty› crop up, arise; ‹difference of opinion› arise; (*vorkommen*) occur; ‹pest, symptom, danger› appear.
❷ *unr. tr. V.* kick open ‹door, gate›

**Auftreten** *das;* **~s** **A** (*Benehmen*) manner; **B** (*das Fungieren*) appearance; **C** (*das Vorkommen*) occurrence; (*von Schädlingen, Gefahren*) appearance; **seit dem ~ von Aids** since the appearance of AIDS

**Auf·trieb** *der* **A** (*Physik*) buoyancy; (*in der Luft*) lift; **B** (*Elan, Aufschwung*) impetus; **das hat ihm ~/neuen ~ gegeben** that has given him a lift/given him new impetus; **neuen ~ erhalten** ‹industry, economy› receive a boost; **C** (*von Vieh zum Markt*) **der ~ an** *od.* **von Ferkeln** *usw.* the number of piglets *etc.* [brought] for sale; **D** (*auf Almen*) **der ~ des Viehs** the driving of cattle up to [the] high pastures

**Auftriebs·kraft** *die* (*Physik*) buoyancy; (*in der Luft*) lift

**Auf·tritt** *der* **A** (*als Künstler, Sänger usw.*) appearance; **B** (*Theater: das Auftreten*) entrance; (*Szene*) scene; **er hat erst im 3. Akt seinen ~:** he doesn't make his entrance until the third act; Ⓒ (*Streit*) row; **jmdm. einen ~ machen** go off the deep end at sb. (*coll.*)

**auf|trumpfen** *itr. V.* show one's superiority; show how good one is; **„Na siehst du", trumpfte sie auf** 'there you are', she crowed; **mit seinem Wissen/seinen Leistungen ~:** show off with one's knowledge/achievements

**auf|tun** ❶ *unr. refl. V.* (*geh.: sich öffnen*) open; (*fig.*) ‹abyss, plain, street, new world, new horizons› open up; **sich jmdm. ~:** open up before sb. ❷ *unr. tr. V.* Ⓐ (*ugs.: entdecken*) find; Ⓑ (*ugs.: servieren*) **jmdm./sich etw. ~:** help sb./oneself to sth.; Ⓒ (*geh.: öffnen*) open ‹door, window›; **den Mund/die Augen ~:** open one's mouth/eyes; Ⓓ (*landsch.: aufsetzen*) put on ‹hat, spectacles, etc.›. ❸ *unr. itr. V.* **jmdm./sich ~:** help sb./oneself (**von** to)

**auf|türmen** ❶ *tr. V.* pile up (**zu** into). ❷ *refl. V.* ‹mountain range› tower up; (*fig.*) ‹work, problems, difficulties› pile up

**auf|wachen** *itr. V.; mit sein* (*auch fig.*) wake up, awaken (**aus** from); **aus der Narkose/Ohnmacht ~:** come round from the anaesthetic/faint

**auf|wachsen** *unr. itr. V.; mit sein* grow up

**auf|wallen** *itr. V.; mit sein* boil up; **etw. ~ lassen** bring sth. to the boil; **in jmdm. ~** (*fig. geh.*) ‹joy, tenderness, hatred, passion, etc.› surge [up] within sb.

**Auf·wallung** *die; ~, ~en* (*geh.*) surge

**Auf·wand** *der; ~[e]s* Ⓐ expenditure (**an** + *Dat.* of); (*das Aufgewendete*) cost; expense; **mit einem ~ von 1,5 Mio. Mark** at a cost of 1.5 million marks; **ein unnützer ~ an Zeit** a waste of time; **der dazu nötige ~ an Zeit/Kraft** the time/energy needed; Ⓑ (*Luxus*) extravagance; **~ [mit etw.] treiben** be extravagant [with sth.]

**aufwändig** ⇨ **aufwendig**

**Aufwands·entschädigung** *die* expense allowance

**auf|wärmen** ❶ *tr. V.* heat *or* warm up ‹food›; (*fig. ugs.: wieder erwähnen*) rake *or* drag up. ❷ *refl. V.* Ⓐ (*sich wärmen*) warm oneself up; Ⓑ (*Sport*) warm up

**Aufwarte·frau** *die* (*bes. md.*) cleaning woman; domestic help

**auf|warten** *itr. V.* Ⓐ (*geh.*) **jmdm. mit etw. ~** (*anbieten*) offer sb. sth.; (*vorsetzen*) serve sb. [with] sth.; Ⓑ (*zu bieten haben*) **mit etw. ~:** come up with sth.; Ⓒ (*veralt.: bedienen*) **jmdm. ~:** wait *or* attend on sb.; **bei Tisch ~:** wait *or* serve at table

**aufwärts** *Adv.* upwards; (*bergauf*) upwards; uphill; **den Fluss ~:** upstream; **~!** (*beim Fahrstuhl*) going up!; **vom Major [an] ~:** from major up; **~ führen** (*fig.*) lead towards prosperity; **mit seiner Gesundheit/dem Land/Geschäft geht es ~:** his health is improving/the country/firm is doing better; **mit ihm geht es ~** (*gesundheitlich*) he's getting better; (*finanziell, geschäftlich, beruflich, in der Schule*) he's doing better

**-aufwärts** *Adv.* ▶306 **[weiter] rhein~/mosel~:** further up the Rhine/Mosel; **rhein~/mosel~ segeln** sail up the Rhine/Mosel

**Aufwärts-: ~entwicklung** *die* upward trend; **~haken** *der* (*Boxen*) uppercut; **~trend** *der* upward trend

**Auf·wartung** *die: in* **jmdm. seine ~ machen** (*geh.*) make *or* pay a courtesy call on sb.; pay sb. a courtesy visit

**Aufwasch** *der; ~[e]s* (*bes. md.*) ⇨ **Abwasch**[1]

**auf|waschen** *unr. tr., itr. V.* (*bes. md.*) wash up; **das ist ein/geht in einem Aufwaschen** (*ugs.*) it can all be done in one go

**auf|wecken** *tr. V.* wake [up]; waken; (*fig.*) waken; ⇨ *auch* **aufgeweckt**

**auf|wehen** ❶ *tr. V.* Ⓐ (*hochwehen*) blow up; raise, blow up ‹dust›; Ⓑ (*aufhäufen*) pile up ‹snow, leaves, etc.›; Ⓒ (*öffnen*) blow open. ❷ *itr. V.; mit sein* (*emporwirbeln*) blow up

**auf|weichen** ❶ *tr. V.* soften; (*fig.*) weaken ‹system›; **den Boden ~:** make the ground soft *or* sodden. ❷ *itr. V.; mit sein* become soft; soften up; (*fig.*) weaken

**auf|weisen** *unr. tr. V.* Ⓐ (*zeigen*) demonstrate; show; Ⓑ (*erkennen lassen*) show; exhibit; **der Ort hat viele Sehenswürdigkeiten aufzuweisen** the town has many sights to offer

**auf|wenden** *unr.* (*auch regelm.*) *tr. V.* use ‹skill, influence›; expend ‹energy, resources›; spend ‹money, time›; **viel Geld/seine ganze Freizeit für etw. ~:** spend a great deal of money/all one's spare time on sth.

**auf·wendig** ❶ *Adj.* lavish; (*kostspielig*) costly; expensive. ❷ *adv.* lavishly; (*kostspielig*) expensively

**Auf·wendung** *die* Ⓐ ⇨ **aufwenden**: using; expenditure; spending; **unter ~ von etw.** by using/expending/spending sth.; Ⓑ *Pl.* (*Kosten*) expenditure *sing.*

**auf|werfen** ❶ *unr. tr. V.* Ⓐ (*aufhäufen*) pile *or* heap up ‹earth, snow, etc.›; build, raise ‹embankment, dam, etc.›; Ⓑ (*öffnen*) fling open ‹door, window›; Ⓒ (*ansprechen*) raise ‹problem, question›; Ⓓ (*hochwerfen*) throw up; **den Kopf ~:** toss one's head; Ⓔ (*schürzen*) **die Lippen ~:** purse one's lips; **aufgeworfene Lippen** pursed lips. ❷ *unr. refl. V.* (*abwertend: sich aufspielen*) **sich zu etw. ~:** set oneself up as sth.; **sich zum Richter ~:** set oneself up as judge

**auf|werten** *tr. V.* Ⓐ *auch itr.* revalue; Ⓑ (*fig.*) enhance the status of; enhance ‹standing, reputation, status›

**Auf·wertung** *die* revaluation; **dieses Amt hat durch ihn eine ~ erfahren** he has enhanced the status of this office

**auf|wickeln** *tr. V.* Ⓐ wind up; (*ohne Rolle, Spule*) roll *or* coil up; Ⓑ (*auf Lockenwickler*) **jmdm./sich die Haare ~:** put sb.'s/one's hair in curlers; **sich** (*Dat.*) **die Haare ~ lassen** have one's hair curled; Ⓒ (*öffnen*) unwrap, undo ‹parcel, bundle›

**Aufwiegelei** *die; ~, ~en* (*abwertend*) incitement [to revolt]

**auf|wiegeln** /ˈaufviːgl̩n/ *tr. V.* (*abwertend*) incite; stir up (**gegen** against); **jmdn. zum Aufstand/Streik ~:** incite sb. to rebel/strike

**Aufwiegelung** *die; ~, ~en* (*abwertend*) incitement; **die ~ der Massen zum Widerstand** inciting the masses to resist

**auf|wiegen** *unr. tr. V.* make up for; **die Vorteile wiegen die Nachteile auf** the advantages offset the disadvantages; ⇨ *auch* **Gold**

**Aufwiegler** *der; ~s, ~,* **Aufwieglerin** *die; ~, ~nen* (*abwertend*) agitator

**aufwieglerisch** (*abwertend*) ❶ *Adj.* seditious; inflammatory, seditious ‹speech, pamphlet›. ❷ *adv.* seditiously

**Aufwieglung** ⇨ **Aufwiegelung**

**Auf·wind** *der* (*Met.*) anabatic wind; (*Flugw.*) up-current; **wieder ~ bekommen** (*fig.*) get new impetus (**durch** from)

**auf|wirbeln** ❶ *tr. V.* swirl up; swirl up, raise ‹dust›; ⇨ *auch* **Staub**. ❷ *itr. V.; mit sein* swirl up

**auf|wischen** *tr. V.* Ⓐ (*entfernen*) wipe *or* mop up; Ⓑ (*säubern*) wipe ‹floor›; (*mit Wasser*) wash; **die Küche/das Badezimmer ~:** wipe/wash the kitchen/bathroom floor

**auf|wogen** *itr. V.; mit sein* (*dichter.*) ‹sea› surge

**auf|wühlen** *tr. V.* churn up ‹water, sea, mud, soil›; (*fig.*) stir ‹person, emotions, passions› deeply; (*auf schmerzhafte Weise*) upset ‹person› deeply; **ein ~des Erlebnis** (*fig.*) a deeply moving experience; **jmdn. bis ins Innerste ~:** move sb. to the depths of his/her soul

**auf|zahlen** (*südd., österr.*) ❶ *tr. V.* **20 Mark ~:** pay 20 marks on top; pay an extra 20 marks. ❷ *itr. V.* pay extra; make an additional payment

**auf|zählen** *tr. V.* enumerate; list; enumerate, give ‹dates, names, facts›

**Auf·zahlung** *die* (*südd., österr.*) additional payment

**Auf·zählung** *die* Ⓐ (*das Aufzählen*) enumeration; listing; Ⓑ (*Liste*) list

**auf|zäumen** *tr. V.* bridle ‹horse›; **etw. verkehrt ~** (*fig.*) go about sth. the wrong way; ⇨ *auch* **Pferd** A

**auf|zehren** (*geh.*) ❶ *tr. V.* exhaust ‹food, supplies, savings›; (*fig.*) consume, sap ‹energy, strength›. ❷ *refl. V.* wear oneself out; ‹energy, supplies, money, etc.› give out

**auf|zeichnen** *tr. V.* Ⓐ (*notieren*) record; Ⓑ (*zeichnen*) draw

**Auf·zeichnung** *die* Ⓐ (*das Notieren*) recording; Ⓑ (*das Aufgezeichnete*) record; (*Film~, Magnetband~*) recording; **~en** (*Notizen*) notes; Ⓒ (*das Zeichnen*) drawing

**auf|zeigen** *tr. V.* (*nachweisen*) demonstrate; show; (*darlegen*) expound; (*hinweisen auf*) point out; highlight

**auf|ziehen** ❶ *unr. tr. V.* Ⓐ (*öffnen*) pull open ‹drawer›; open, draw [back] ‹curtains›; undo ‹zip›; undo, untie ‹bow›; Ⓑ (*die Feder spannen von*) wind up ‹clock, watch, toy, etc.›; Ⓒ (*spannen, aufkleben*) mount ‹photograph, print, etc.› (**auf** + *Akk.* on); stretch ‹canvas›; **Saiten/neue Saiten auf ein Instrument ~:** string/restring an instrument; **neue Saiten ~:** put new strings on; ⇨ *auch* **Saite**; Ⓓ (*großziehen*) bring up, raise ‹children›; raise, rear ‹animals›; raise ‹plants, vegetables›; Ⓔ (*ugs.: gründen*) set up ‹company, department, business, political party, organization, system›; Ⓕ (*ugs.: durchführen*) organize, stage ‹festival, event, campaign, rally›; **wir haben das Ganze völlig falsch aufgezogen** we've gone about it completely the wrong way; Ⓖ (*ugs.: verspotten*) rib (*coll.*), tease (**mit, wegen** about); **sie hat ihn damit aufgezogen, dass er so große Ohren hat** she ribbed him (*coll.*) *or* poked fun at him because of his big ears; Ⓗ (*nach oben ziehen*) pull *or* draw up; haul up ‹fishing nets, heavy load›; hoist, run up ‹flag›; hoist ‹sail›; raise ‹barrier, curtain, sluice gate, signal, drawbridge, etc.›; Ⓘ (*auftrennen*) undo; unpick; unpick ‹garment›; Ⓙ (*auf eine Spritze*) draw up ‹vaccine etc.›; Ⓚ (*füllen*) fill ‹hypodermic syringe›. ❷ *unr. itr. V.; mit sein* Ⓐ (*näher kommen*) ‹storm› gather, come up; ‹clouds› gather; ‹star, mist, haze› come up; Ⓑ (*sich aufstellen*) take up position; (*aufmarschieren*) march up

**Auf·zucht** *die* raising; rearing

**Auf·zug** *der* Ⓐ (*Lift*) lift (*Brit.*); elevator (*Amer.*); (*Lasten~, Bau~*) hoist; Ⓑ (*abwertend: Aufmachung*) get-up; Ⓒ (*Theater: Akt*) act; Ⓓ (*Aufmarsch*) parade; (*feierlicher Zug*) procession; **der ~ der Garde** the mounting of the guard

**Aufzugs·schacht** *der* lift (*Brit.*) *or* (*Amer.*) elevator shaft

**auf|zwingen** ❶ *unr. tr. V.* **jmdm. etw. ~:** force sth. [up]on sb.; **jmdm. seinen Willen ~:** impose one's will [up]on sb. ❷ *unr. refl. V.* **sich jmdm. ~:** impose oneself *or* force one's company [up]on sb.; **der Gedanke zwingt sich [einem] ja förmlich auf** the idea positively forces itself upon you

**Aug·apfel** *der* eyeball; **er hütet das wie seinen ~:** it's his most treasured possession; **sie ist der ~ ihrer Großmutter** (*fig.*) she is the apple of her grandmother's eye

**Auge** /ˈaugə/ *das; ~s, ~n* Ⓐ ▶471 eye; **gute/schlechte ~n haben** have good/poor eyesight; **er hat so gute ~n, dass ...** his eyesight is so good that ...; **meine ~n sind schlechter geworden** my eyesight has deteriorated; **auf einem ~ blind sein** be blind in one eye; (*fig.*) have two different sets of standards; **ich konnte ihm nicht in die ~n sehen** (*fig.*) I could not look him in the eye; **etw. mit eigenen ~n gesehen haben** have seen sth. with one's own eyes; **die ~n schließen** *od.* **zumachen** close *or* shut one's eyes; **mit bloßem ~:** with the naked eye; **ihm fallen die ~n zu** his eyelids are drooping; **ganz kleine ~n haben** (*fig.*) be all sleepy; **~n links/rechts/geradeaus!** (*Milit.*) eyes left/right/front!; **mit verbundenen ~n** blindfold[ed]; **jmdn. aus großen ~n unschuldig ansehen** look at sb. all wide-eyed and innocent; **hast du keine ~n im Kopf?** haven't you got eyes in your head?; are you blind?; **etw. im ~ haben** have sth. in one's eye; (*fig.: haben wollen*) have one's eye on sth.; **das ~ des Gesetzes**

*old spelling (see note on page 1707)

(*fig.: Polizist*) the law (*coll.*); **so weit das ~ reicht** as far as the eye can see; **die ~n sind größer als der Magen** *od.* **Bauch** (*fig. ugs.*) your *etc.* eyes are bigger than your *etc.* belly; **ihr/ihm** *usw.* **gingen die ~n auf** (*fig.*) the scales fell from her/his *etc.* eyes; **ihm/ihr** *usw.* **werden die ~n noch aufgehen** (*fig.*) he/she *etc.* is in for a rude awakening; **da wird er ~n machen** (*fig. ugs.*) his eyes will pop out of his head; **ihnen fielen fast die ~n aus dem Kopf** their eyes nearly popped out of their heads; **ein ~ voll Schlaf nehmen** (*fig. ugs.*) have forty winks *or* a short nap; **da blieb kein ~ trocken** (*fig. ugs.*) everyone laughed till they cried *or* till the tears ran down their faces; (*es blieb niemand verschont*) no one was safe; **ich traute meinen [eigenen] ~n nicht** (*ugs.*) I couldn't believe my eyes; **~n wie ein Luchs haben** have eyes like a lynx; **ich habe doch hinten keine ~n** (*ugs.*) I haven't got eyes in the back of my head; **nur ~n für jmdn. haben** (*fig.*) have eyes only for sb.; **ich kann doch meine ~n nicht überall haben!** I can't be looking everywhere at once; **sie hat ihre ~n überall** she doesn't miss a thing; **[große] ~n machen** (*fig. ugs.*) be wide-eyed; **jmdm. [schöne] ~n machen** (*fig. veralt.*) make eyes at sb.; **die ~n offen haben** *od.* **offen halten [ob, ...]** (*fig.*) keep one's eyes open [and see whether ...]; **die ~n vor etw.** (*Dat.*) **verschließen** (*fig.*) shut *or* close one's eyes to sth.; **sich** (*Dat.*) **nach jmdm./etw. die ~n ausgucken** *od.* **aus dem Kopf sehen** (*fig. ugs.*) look out eagerly *or* expectantly for sb./sth.; **ein ~** *od.* **beide ~n zudrücken** (*fig.*) turn a blind eye; **ein ~ auf jmdn./etw. geworfen haben** (*fig.*) have taken a liking to sb./have one's eye on sth.; **ein ~ auf jmdn./etw. haben** (*Acht geben*) keep an eye on sb./sth.; (*Gefallen finden*) have taken a fancy to sb./have one's eye on sth.; **ein ~/ein sicheres ~ für etw. haben** have an eye/a sure eye for sth.; **kein ~ von jmdm. lassen** (*fig.*) not take one's eyes off sb.; **ich habe ja schließlich ~n im Kopf** (*ugs.*) I'm not blind, you know; **jmdm. die ~n öffnen** (*fig.*) open sb.'s eyes; **sich** (*Dat.*) **die ~n ausweinen** *od.* **aus dem Kopf weinen** (*fig.*) cry one's eyes out; **jmdn./etw. nicht aus den ~n lassen** not take one's eyes off sb./sth.; not let sb./sth. out of one's sight; **jmdn./etw. aus dem ~** *od.* **den ~n verlieren** lose sight of sb./sth.; (*fig.*) lose contact *or* touch with sb./lose touch with sth.; **ich kann vor Arbeit/Müdigkeit nicht mehr aus den ~n gucken** (*ugs.*) I've got so much work I don't know whether I'm coming or going/I'm so tired I can't see straight; **aus den ~n, aus dem Sinn!** (*Spr.*) out of sight, out of mind; **geh mir aus den ~n!** get out of my sight!; **ein solches Ereignis muss auch etwas fürs ~ sein** such an event must also have visual appeal; **das ist mehr fürs ~:** it's only [there] for decoration; **jmdm./einander ~ in ~ gegenüberstehen** face sb./one another; **Aug in Aug** (*veralt.*) face to face; **jmdn./etw. im ~ behalten** (*fig.*) keep an eye on sb./bear *or* keep sth. in mind; **in jmds. ~n** (*Dat.*) (*fig.*) to sb.'s mind; in sb.'s opinion; **jmdm. ins ~** *od.* **in die ~n fallen** *od.* **springen** (*fig.*) hit sb. in the eye; **etw. ins ~ fassen** (*fig.*) consider sth.; think about sth.; **ins ~ fassen, etw. zu tun** (*fig.*) have it in mind to do sth.; contemplate doing sth.; **einer Sache** (*Dat.*) **ins ~ sehen** (*fig.*) face sth.; **der Wahrheit/Gefahr ins ~ sehen** (*fig.*) face up to the truth/danger; **ins ~ gehen** (*fig. ugs.*) (*schlimm ausgehen*) end in disaster; (*erfolglos ausgehen*) end in failure; **mit einem lachenden und einem weinenden ~** (*fig.*) with mixed feelings; **mit offenen ~n schlafen** (*ugs.*) be daydreaming; **mit offenen ~n durch die Welt gehen** (*fig.*) walk about with one's eyes open; **jmdn./etw. mit anderen** *od.* **neuen ~n betrachten** *od.* **ansehen** (*fig.*) see sb./sth. in a different *or* new light; **~ um ~, Zahn um Zahn** an eye for an eye, a tooth for a tooth; **unter vier ~n** (*fig.*) in private; **unter jmds. ~n** (*Dat.*) right in front of sb.; right under sb.'s nose; **komm mir nicht mehr unter die ~n!** never let me set eyes on you again!; **jmdm. jeden Wunsch von den ~n ablesen** (*fig.*) anticipate sb.'s every wish; **vor aller ~n** in front of everybody; **jmdm. etw. vor ~n führen** *od.* **halten** *od.* **stellen** (*fig.*) bring sth. home to sb.; **wenn man sich** (*Dat.*) **das mal vor ~n führt** (*fig.*) when you stop and think about it; **jmdn./etw. vor ~n haben** (*fig.*) see sb./sth. in one's mind's eye; ⇒ *auch* **auskratzen** 1 A; **beleidigen**; **blau**; **Null[1]** B; **schließen** 1 A; **schwarz** 1 A; **schweben** A; **zutun**; Ⓑ (*auf Würfeln, Spielkarten, Dominosteinen*) pip; **drei ~n werfen** throw a three; **wie viele ~n hat er geworfen?** how many has he thrown?; Ⓒ (*Keim*) eye; bud; (*bei Kartoffeln*) eye; Ⓓ ⇒ **Fettauge**

**äugeln** /'ɔyɡl̩n/ ❶ *itr. V.* (*hinsehen*) **nach jmdm./etw. ~:** cast secret glances at sb./sth. ❷ *tr. V.* (*Gartenbau*) bud

**äugen** /'ɔyɡn̩/ *itr. V.* peer

**Augen-:** **~abstand** *der* (*Med.*) interocular distance; **~arzt** *der*, **~ärztin** *die* ▶ 159 eye specialist; **~aufschlag** *der* [upward] glance; **mit unschuldigem ~aufschlag** with wide-eyed innocence; **~binde** *die* blindfold; (*Verband*) eye bandage

**Augen·blick** /*auch:* --'-/ *der* moment; **alle ~e** (*ugs.*) all the time; ⇒ *auch* **Moment[1]**

**augenblicklich** /*auch:* --'--/ ❶ *Adj.* Ⓐ (*unverzüglich*) immediate; Ⓑ (*gegenwärtig*) present; (*vorübergehend*) temporary; (*einen Augenblick dauernd*) momentary. ❷ *adv.* Ⓐ (*sofort*) immediately; at once; Ⓑ (*zur Zeit*) at the moment

**augen·blicks** *Adv.* immediately; at once

**Augenblicks-:** **~erfolg** *der* short-lived success; **~sache** *die* matter of a moment

**augen-, Augen-:** **~braue** *die* ▶ 471 eyebrow; **~brauen·stift** *der* eyebrow pencil; **~deckel** *der* (*ugs.*) eyelid; **~fällig** ❶ *Adj.* striking; (*offensichtlich*) obvious; ❷ *adv.* strikingly; (*offensichtlich*) obviously; **~farbe** *die* colour of one's eyes; **~fehler** *der* eye defect; **~fleck** *der* (*Biol.*) eyespot; ocellus; **~glas** *das; Pl.* **~gläser** (*österr., sonst Amtsspr.*) (*Monokel*) monocle; (*Zwicker*) pince-nez; **~gläser** (*Brille*) spectacles; **~heil·kunde** *die* ophthalmology; **~höhe** *die* eye level; **in/auf ~höhe** at/to eye level; **~höhle** *die* eye socket; **~klappe** *die* eye-patch; **~klinik** *die* eye hospital; **~krankheit** *die* eye disease; disease of the eye; **~lid** *das* ▶ 471 eyelid; **~-Make-up** *das* eye make-up; **~maß** *das:* **ein gutes/schlechtes ~maß haben** have a good eye/no eye for distances; **jegliches ~maß verlieren** (*fig.*) lose all sense of proportion; **~mensch** *der* (*ugs.*) visual type *or* person; **~merk** *das:* **sein ~merk auf jmdn./etw. richten** *od.* **lenken** give one's attention to sb./sth.; **~optiker** *der*, **~optikerin** *die* ▶ 159 ophthalmic optician; **~paar** *das* (*geh.*) pair of eyes; **~ränder** *Pl.* rims of one's/the eyes; **sie hatte gerötete ~ränder** the rims of her eyes were red; **~ringe** *Pl.* rings under the eyes; **~schatten** *Pl.* shadows under the eyes

**Augen·schein** *der* (*geh.*) Ⓐ (*Eindruck*) appearance; **dem ~ nach** by all appearances; **dem ersten ~ nach** at first sight; **allem ~ zum Trotz** despite all appearances; Ⓑ (*Betrachtung*) inspection; **jmdn./etw. in ~ nehmen** have a close look at sb./sth.; give sb./sth. a close inspection

**augen·scheinlich** (*geh.*) ❶ *Adj.* (*scheinbar*) apparent; evident; (*sichtbar*) obvious; evident. ❷ *adv.* (*scheinbar*) apparently; evidently; (*sichtbar*) obviously; evidently

**augen-, Augen-:** **~schmaus** *der* (*scherzh.*) feast for the eyes; **~spiegel** *der* (*Med.*) ophthalmoscope; **~spiegelung** *die* (*Med.*) ophthalmoscopy; **~stern** *der* Ⓐ (*dichter.: Pupille*) pupil; Ⓑ (*veralt.: Liebstes*) apple of one's eye; **~trost** *der* (*Bot.*) eyebright; **~weide** *die* feast for the eyes; **~wimper** *die* eyelash; **~winkel** *der* corner of one's eye; **~wischerei** *die* eyewash; **~zahn** *der* eye tooth; **~zeuge** *der* eyewitness; **~zeuge sein** be an eyewitness; **~zeugen·bericht** *der* eyewitness report; **~zeugin** *die* ⇒ **~zeuge**; **~zwinkern** *das;* **~s:** **mit einem ~zwinkern** with a wink; **durch ~zwinkern** by winking; **~zwinkernd** ❶ *Adj.* tacit ‹agreement›; ❷ *adv.* with a wink

**Augias·stall** /au'gi:as-/ *der* (*geh.*) Augean stables; **den ~ ausmisten** *od.* **reinigen** create order out of chaos

**-äugig** /-|ɔyɡɪç/ *Adj.* ▶ 471 -eyed; **ein~/blau~/groß~/hell~:** one-eyed/blue-eyed/big-eyed/bright-eyed

**Augur** /'augʊr/ *der;* **~s** *od.* **~en** /-'gu:rən/, **~en** (*geh., spött.*) pundit

**Auguren·lächeln** *das* (*geh.*) knowing smile

**August[1]** /au'gʊst/ *der;* **~[e]s** *od.* **~, ~e** ▶ 207 August; ⇒ *auch* **April**

**August[2]** /'augʊst/ *in* **dummer ~:** clown

**augusteisch** /augʊs'te:ɪʃ/ *Adj. in* **~es Zeitalter** (*geh.*) Augustan age

**Augustiner** /augʊs'ti:nɐ/ *der;* **~s, ~:** Augustinian monk

**Augustinerin** *die;* **~, ~nen** Augustinian nun

**Augustinus** /augʊs'ti:nʊs/ (*der*) St Augustine

**Auktion** /auk'tsio:n/ *die;* **~, ~en** auction

**Auktionator** /auktsio'na:tɔr/ *der;* **~s, ~en** /-na'to:rən/, **Auktionatorin** *die;* **~, ~nen** ▶ 159 auctioneer

**Aula** /'aula/ *die;* **~, Aulen** *od.* **~s** (*einer Universität*) [great] hall; (*einer Schule*) [assembly] hall

**Aupair·mädchen**, **Au-pair-Mädchen** /o'pɛ:r-/ *das* au pair [girl]

**Aura** /'aura/ *die;* **~, Auren** (*geh.*) aura

**Aureole** /aure'o:lə/ *die;* **~, ~n** Ⓐ (*Heiligenschein*) aureole; halo; Ⓑ (*Met.*) aureole

**aus** /aus/ ❶ *Präp. mit Dat.* Ⓐ (*räumlich:* ~ *dem Inneren von*) out of; **~ dem Bett steigen** get out of bed; **~ der Flasche trinken** drink out of the bottle *or* from the bottle; Ⓑ (*Herkunft, Quelle, Ausgangspunkt angebend, auch zeitlich*) from; **~ Spanien/Griechenland** *usw.* from Spain/Greece *etc.*; **er kommt** *od.* **stammt ~** *od.* **ist gebürtig ~ Hamburg** he comes from Hamburg; **~ der Ferne** from a distance; (*von weitem*) from far away; **jmdm. etw. ~ dem Urlaub mitbringen** bring sth. back from holiday *or* (*Amer.*) one's vacation for sb.; **~ guter Familie stammen** come from a good family; **~ dem Deutschen ins Englische** from German into English; **etw. ~ dem Zusammenhang reißen** take sth. out of [its] context; Ⓒ (*Veränderung eines Zustandes angebend*) **~ der Mode/Übung sein** be out of fashion/training; **~ dem Gleichgewicht** out of balance; **~ tiefem Schlaf erwachen** awake from a deep sleep; Ⓓ (*Grund, Ursache angebend*) out of; **etw. ~ Erfahrung wissen** know sth. from experience; **~ folgendem Grund** for the following reason; **~ Versehen** inadvertently; by mistake; **~ einer Laune heraus** on impulse; **~ Furcht vor** for fear of; **~ Spaß/Jux** (*ugs.*) for fun/a laugh; **ein Verbrechen ~ Leidenschaft** a crime of passion; **~ sich heraus** on one's own initiative; of one's own accord; Ⓔ (*hergestellt ~*) made of; **eine Bank ~ Holz/Stein** a bench made of wood/stone; a wooden/stone bench; **etw. ~ Fertigteilen bauen** build sth. out of prefabricated components; **eine Figur ~ Holz schnitzen** carve a figure in wood; **~ etw. bestehen** consist of sth.; Ⓕ (*Entwicklung angebend*) **~ ihm ist ein guter Arzt geworden** he made a good doctor; **~ der Sache wird nichts** nothing will come of it; **~ den Raupen entwickeln sich Schmetterlinge** caterpillars develop into butterflies; **einen Soldaten ~ jmdm. machen** make a soldier out of sb.; **etwas ~ sich machen** make something of oneself; **~ ihm ist nichts geworden** he never made anything of his life; Ⓖ (*österr.: in*) in; **eine Prüfung ~ Biologie** an examination in biology.

❷ *Adv.* Ⓐ (*vorbei, vorüber, zu Ende*) **~ sein** ‹play, film, war› be over, have ended; **wann ist die Vorstellung ~?** what time does the performance end?; **die Schule ist ~:** school is out *or* has finished; **mit ihm ist es ~:** he's had it (*coll.*); he's finished; **es ist ~ mit dem schönen Leben/der Faulenzerei** the good life is over/[there'll be] no more lazing around; **zwischen uns ist es ~:** it's [all] over between us; **~ jetzt!** that's enough; **~, habe ich gesagt** that's enough, I said; **~ und vorbei** over and done with; ⇒ *auch* **aushaben**; Ⓑ (*ausgeschaltet*) off; „~" (*an Lichtschaltern*) 'out'; (*an Geräten*) 'off'; **Licht/Radio ~!** lights *pl.* out!/turn the radio off; Ⓒ (*erloschen*) out; Ⓓ (*Sport: im Aus*) out; Ⓔ (*außer Haus, ausgegangen*) out; Ⓕ (*bes. Kinderspr.: ausgeschieden*) out; Ⓖ **vom Flugplatz/Fenster/obersten Stockwerk ~:** from the airport/window/top storey; **von hier/München ~:** from here/Munich; **von seinem Standpunkt ~:** from his point of view; **von mir ~** (*ugs.*) if you like *or* want; **von sich** (*Dat.*) **~:** of one's own accord; Ⓗ **auf etw.** (*Akk.*) **~ sein** after *or* interested in sth.; ⇒ *auch* **ein²**

**Aus** *das;* ~ Ⓐ **der Ball ging ins ~** (*Tennis*) the ball was out; (*Fußball*) the ball went out of play; **den Ball ins ~ schlagen** hit the ball out; Ⓑ (*Sport: das Ausscheiden*) exit; (*fig.*) end

**aus|arbeiten** ❶ *tr. V.* Ⓐ (*erstellen*) work out, develop ‹guidelines, system, method›; prepare, draw up ‹agenda, draft, regulations, contract›; prepare ‹leaflet›; Ⓑ (*vollenden*) work out the details of ‹plan, proposal, list, lecture, etc.›; elaborate the details of ‹picture, drawing›. ❷ *refl. V.* (*durch Sport, körperliche Anstrengung*) work out; have a workout

**Ausarbeitung** *die;* ~, **~en** Ⓐ ⇒ **ausarbeiten** 1 A: working out; developing; preparation; drawing up; Ⓑ ⇒ **ausarbeiten** 1 B: working out the details; elaboration of the details

**aus|arten** *itr. V.; mit sein* Ⓐ degenerate (**in** + *Akk.*, **zu** into); Ⓑ (*sich schlecht benehmen*) become unruly

**aus|atmen** *itr., tr. V.* breathe out; exhale

**aus|backen** *regelm.* (*auch unr.*) *tr. V.* (*Kochk.*) Ⓐ (*in Fett*) fry; Ⓑ (*fertigbacken*) **etw. ~:** bake sth. until it is done

**aus|baden** *tr. V.* (*ugs.*) carry *or* take the can for (*Brit. coll.*); take the rap for (*coll.*)

**aus|baggern** *tr. V.* Ⓐ excavate ‹hole, basement, ditch, etc.›; Ⓑ (*säubern*) dredge ‹channel, river bed, etc.›; Ⓒ (*herausholen*) dredge up ‹mud, detritus, etc.›

**aus|balancieren** ❶ *tr. V.* (*auch fig.*) balance. ❷ *refl. V.* balance; (*fig.*) balance out

**aus|baldowern** *tr. V.* (*ugs.*) spy out

**Aus·ball** *der* (*Ballspiele*) **auf ~ entscheiden** decide that the ball was out; **bei ~:** when the ball goes out of play

**Aus·bau** *der* Ⓐ (*Erweiterung*) extension; (*einer Straße*) improvement; **ein ~ des Hauses** an extension to the house; **der ~ der Beziehungen zwischen zwei Staaten/Organisationen** the building of closer relations between two states/organizations; Ⓑ (*Ausgestaltung*) conversion (**zu** into); Ⓒ (*Entfernung*) removal (**aus** from)

**aus|bauen** *tr. V.* Ⓐ (*entfernen*) remove (**aus** from); Ⓑ (*erweitern*) extend; (*fig.*) build up, cultivate ‹friendship, relationship›; expand ‹theory, knowledge, market›; **eine Fachhochschule zu einer Universität ~:** expand *or* enlarge a college into a university; **eine Straße ~:** improve a road; **seinen Vorsprung weiter ~** (*fig.*) extend one's lead; **seine Position ~** (*fig.*) consolidate *or* strengthen one's position; **ein Gebäude zu einem** *od.* **als Theater ~:** convert a building into a theatre *or* for use as a theatre

**ausbau·fähig** *Adj.* ‹building etc.› suitable for extension; ‹market› that can be expanded; ‹position, job› with [good] prospects; **er hat ~e Englischkenntnisse** he has a good grounding in English

**aus|bedingen** *unr. refl. V.* **sich** (*Dat.*) **etw. ~** (*etw. verlangen*) insist on sth.; (*etw. zur Bedingung machen*) make sth. a condition; **sich** (*Dat.*) **das Recht/die Freiheit ~, etw. zu tun** reserve the right/freedom to do sth.

**aus|beißen** *unr. refl. V.* **sich** (*Dat.*) **einen Zahn ~:** break a tooth (**an** + *Dat.* on); **sich** (*Dat.*) **an einem Problem die Zähne ~** (*fig.*) sweat over a problem

**aus|bekommen** *unr. tr. V.* (*ugs.*) get off

**aus|bessern** *tr. V.* Ⓐ (*reparieren*) repair; fix (*Amer.*); mend ‹clothes›; touch up ‹paintwork›; Ⓑ (*beseitigen*) mend; **einen Schaden an etw.** (*Dat.*) **~:** repair damage to sth.

**Aus·besserung** *die* repair

**ausbesserungs-, Ausbesserungs-: ~arbeiten** *Pl.* repairs; repair work *sing.*; **~bedürftig** *Adj.* in need of repair *postpos.*; **~werk** *das* (*Eisenb.*) repair shed

**aus|beulen** ❶ *tr. V.* Ⓐ remove a/the dent/the dents in; (*mit einem Hammer*) beat out; Ⓑ (*dehnen*) make baggy; **ausgebeulte Knie** baggy knees. ❷ *refl. V.* ‹trousers› go baggy; ‹pocket› bulge

**Aus·beute** *die* yield; (*einer Untersuchung*) results *pl.*; (*eines Einkaufsbummels*) spoils *pl.*; **unsere ganze ~ betrug drei Pilze** we ended up with only three mushrooms between us

**aus|beuteln** *tr. V.* (*bes. österr.*) shake out

**aus|beuten** *tr. V.* (*auch abwertend*) exploit

**Ausbeuter** *der;* ~s, ~, **Ausbeuterin** *die;* ~, ~nen (*abwertend*) exploiter

**ausbeuterisch** (*abwertend*) ❶ *Adj.* exploitative. ❷ *adv.* exploitatively

**Ausbeuter·klasse** *die;* ~ (*abwertend*) exploiting class

**Ausbeutung** *die;* ~, ~en exploitation

**aus|bezahlen** *tr. V.* Ⓐ (*auszahlen*) pay [out]; **er bekommt 2 000 DM ausbezahlt** his take-home pay is 2,000 marks; Ⓑ (*entlohnen*) pay; (*~ und entlassen*) pay off; Ⓒ (*abfinden*) buy out ‹shareholder, joint heir, etc.›

**Aus·bezahlung** *die* ⇒ **ausbezahlen**: payment; paying; paying off; buying out

**aus|bilden** ❶ *tr. V.* Ⓐ (*schulen, unterrichten*) train; **sich in etw.** (*Dat.*) **~ lassen** take a training in sth.; (*studieren*) study sth.; **sich als** *od.* **zu etw. ~ lassen** train to be sth.; (*studieren*) study to be sth.; **sich im Gesang/Zeichnen ~ lassen** take singing lessons/study drawing; **jmdn. an einem Instrument/einer Maschine ~:** teach sb. to play an instrument/train sb. on a machine *or* to use a machine; Ⓑ (*fördern*) cultivate, develop ‹talent, skill, feeling, etc.›; Ⓒ (*entwickeln*) develop; (*gestalten*) design; (*formen*) shape; form.
❷ *refl. V.* Ⓐ (*sich schulen*) **sich in etw.** (*Dat.*) **~:** take a training in sth.; (*studieren*) study sth.; Ⓑ (*sich entwickeln*) develop

**Ausbilder** *der;* ~s, ~, **Ausbilderin** *die;* ~, ~nen instructor

**Ausbildner** *der;* ~s, ~, **Ausbildnerin** *die;* ~, ~nen (*österr.*) instructor

**Aus·bildung** *die* Ⓐ (*Schulung*) training; **sich noch in der ~ befinden** still be training; (*an einer Lehranstalt*) still be at college; Ⓑ (*Entwicklung*) development

**Ausbildungs-: ~bei·hilfe** *die* [education] grant; (*für Berufsschüler, Lehrlinge*) training grant; **~beruf** *der* trade requiring an apprenticeship; **~förderung** *die* provision of [education] grants; (*für Berufsschüler, Lehrlinge*) provision of training grants; **~gang** *der* training syllabus; **~platz** *der* trainee post; (*für Lehrlinge*) apprenticeship; **~stätte** *die* place of training; **~vertrag** *der* articles of apprenticeship

**aus|bitten** *unr. refl. V.* Ⓐ (*geh.: erbitten*) **sich** (*Dat.*) **von jmdm. etw. ~:** request sth. from sb.; ask sb. for sth.; Ⓑ (*verlangen*) **sich** (*Dat.*) **etw. ~:** demand sth.; **ich bitte mir Ruhe/mehr Sorgfalt aus** I must insist on silence/that you take more care

**aus|blasen** *unr. tr. V.* Ⓐ (*löschen, ausatmen*) blow out; Ⓑ (*leer blasen*) blow ‹egg›

**aus|blassen** *itr. V.; mit sein* (*geh.*) fade

**aus|bleiben** *unr. itr. V.; mit sein* Ⓐ (*nicht eintreten*) ‹effect, disaster, success, reward› fail to materialize; ‹symptom› be absent, not appear; **es konnte nicht ~, dass ...** it was inevitable that ...; **das Ausbleiben einer Nachricht** the absence *or* lack of any news; **beim Ausbleiben der Regelblutung** if a period is missed; Ⓑ (*fernbleiben*) ‹guests, visitors, customers› stay away, fail to appear; ‹order, commission, help, offer, support, rain› fail to arrive; **wenn jahrelang der Regen ausbleibt** if the rains fail year after year; **sein Ausbleiben** his absence; Ⓒ (*nicht heimkommen*) stay out; Ⓓ (*ugs.: ausgeschaltet bleiben*) stay off; Ⓔ (*stocken*) ‹pulse, breathing› stop

**aus|bleichen** ❶ *unr. itr. V.; mit sein* fade; **ausgebleichte Gebeine/Haare** bleached bones/hair. ❷ *tr. V.* bleach; ‹light, sun› fade ‹material, curtains, etc.›

**aus|blenden** ❶ *tr. V.* (*Rundf., Ferns., Film*) fade out; (*fig.: nicht berücksichtigen*) take no account of, leave out of account ‹facts, information›. ❷ *refl. V.* (*Rundf., Ferns.*) **sich [aus einer Übertragung] ~:** fade oneself out of a transmission

**Aus·blendung** *die* (*Film, Rundf., Ferns.*) fade-out; **nach unserer ~ aus der Übertragung** after we leave this transmission

**Aus·blick** *der* Ⓐ view (**auf** + *Akk.* of); **jmdm. den ~ versperren** block *or* obstruct sb.'s view; **ein Zimmer mit ~ aufs Meer/auf die Berge** a room overlooking the sea/with a view of the mountains; Ⓑ (*Vorausschau*) **jmdm. einen ~ auf etw.** (*Akk.*) **geben** give sb. a preview of sth.; **einen optimistischen ~ in die Zukunft gestatten** permit an optimistic view of the prospects for the future

**aus|blicken** *itr. V.* (*geh.*) **nach jmdm./etw. ~:** look out for sb./sth.

**aus|bluten** *itr. V.; mit sein* bleed to death; (*fig.*) bleed dry; **~ lassen** bleed ‹animal›

**aus|bohren** *tr. V.* Ⓐ (*bohren*) bore; (*mit Bohrgerät*) drill; (*erweitern*) drill out; Ⓑ (*entfernen*) bore out; (*mit Bohrgerät*) drill out

**aus|bomben** *tr. V.* bomb out; ⇒ *auch* **Ausgebombte**

**aus|booten** *tr. V.* Ⓐ (*ugs.: verdrängen*) get rid of (**aus** from); Ⓑ (*Seew.: an Land bringen*) disembark ‹passengers› by boat

**aus|borgen** *tr. V.* (*ugs.*) Ⓐ (*sich ausleihen*) **[sich** (*Dat.*)**] etw. ~:** borrow sth. (**von, bei** from); Ⓑ (*überlassen*) **jmdm. etw. ~:** lend sb. sth.; lend sth. to sb.

**aus|braten** ❶ *unr. itr. V.; mit sein* ‹fat› run out (**aus** of). ❷ *unr. tr. V.* (*auslassen*) fry the fat out of ‹bacon›

**aus|brechen** ❶ *unr. itr. V.; mit sein* Ⓐ (*entkommen, auch Milit.*) break out (**aus** of); (*fig.*) break free (**aus** from); Ⓑ (*austreten*) **jmdm. bricht der [kalte] Schweiß aus** sb. breaks into a [cold] sweat; Ⓒ ‹volcano› erupt; Ⓓ (*beginnen*) break out; ‹crisis› break; ‹misery, despair› set in; ⇒ *auch* **Wohlstand**; Ⓔ **in Gelächter/Weinen ~:** burst out laughing/crying; **in Beifall/Tränen ~:** burst into applause/tears; **in den Ruf ~ „...“** break into the cry, '...'; **in Schweiß ~:** break out into a sweat; **in Zorn/Wut ~:** explode with anger/rage; Ⓕ (*sich lösen*) ‹hook, dowel, etc.› come out; **ihm waren zwei Zähne ausgebrochen** he had broken two teeth; Ⓖ (*Richtung ändern*) ‹car, horse› swerve.
❷ *unr. tr. V.* Ⓐ take *or* knock down ‹wall›; **Steine aus einer Wand ~:** knock stones out of a wall; **sich** (*Dat.*) **einen Zahn ~:** break a tooth; **eine Tür/ein Fenster [in einer Mauer] ~:** put a doorway/window [in a wall]; Ⓑ (*erbrechen*) bring up; vomit [up]

**Aus·brecher** *der,* **Aus·brecherin** *die;* ~, ~nen (*ugs.*) escaped prisoner *or* convict; (*gewohnheitsmäßiger*) jail-breaker

**aus|breiten** ❶ *tr. V.* Ⓐ (*entfalten*) spread [out] ‹map, cloth, sheet, etc.›; open out ‹fan, newspaper›; (*nebeneinander legen*) spread out; **ein Tuch über etw.** (*Akk. od. Dat.*) **~:** spread *or* put a cloth over sth.; **seine Wünsche/Pläne/Ansichten/sein Leben vor jmdm. ~** (*fig.*) unfold one's desires/plans/views/life story to sb.; Ⓑ (*ausstrecken*) **die Arme/Flügel ~:** spread one's arms/its wings; **die Arme nach jmdm. ~:** stretch out one's arms to sb.
❷ *refl. V.* Ⓐ (*sich verbreiten*) spread; Ⓑ (*ugs.: sich breit machen*) spread oneself out; Ⓒ (*sich erstrecken*) extend; stretch [out];

*old spelling (see note on page 1707)

**D** (*abwertend: erörtern*) **sich über etw.** (*Akk.*) **~:** go on [at great length] about sth.

**aus|brennen** ❶ *unr. itr. V.; mit sein* **A** (*zu Ende brennen*) burn out; **ausgebrannte Kernbrennstäbe** (*fig.*) spent nuclear fuel rods; **B** (*zerstört werden*) ‹building, room› be gutted, be burnt out; ‹ship, aircraft, vehicle› be burnt out; **ausgebrannt sein** be burnt out; **C** (*ugs.: seine Habe verlieren*) be burnt out. ❷ *unr. tr. V.* **A** (*reinigen*) cauterize ‹wound›; **B** (*entfernen*) burn out; burn off ‹weeds›; ⇒ *auch* **ausgebrannt** 2

**aus|bringen** *unr. tr. V.* **A** (*sprechen*) propose; **einen Trinkspruch** *od.* **Toast auf jmdn./etw. ~:** propose a toast to sb./sth.; **B** (*Seemannsspr.*) lower ‹boat, anchor›; lay, lower ‹net›; lay *or* run out ‹mooring line›

**Aus·bruch** *der* **A** (*Flucht*) escape; (*lit. or fig.*), breakout (*also Mil.*) (**aus** from); **an ~ denken** think of escape; **B** (*Beginn*) outbreak; **vor/nach ~ des Krieges** before/after the outbreak of war; **zum ~ kommen** break out; ‹crisis, storm› break; **C** (*Gefühls~*) outburst; (*stärker*) explosion; (*von Wut, Zorn*) eruption; explosion; **zum ~ kommen** explode; erupt; **D** (*eines Vulkans*) eruption

**Ausbruchs·versuch** *der* attempted breakout *or* escape; (*fig.*) attempt to break free; (*Milit.*) attempted breakout

**aus|brüten** *tr. V.* **A** hatch out; (*im Brutkasten*) incubate; **B** (*ugs.: sich ausdenken*) hatch [up] ‹plot, scheme›; **C** **etwas/einen Infekt ~** (*ugs.: krank werden*) be going down with something/an infection

**aus|buchen** *tr. V.* (*Kaufmannsspr., Bankw.*) **etw. ~** (*streichen*) delete sth. from the accounts; (*abschreiben*) write sth. off; ⇒ *auch* **ausgebucht** 2

**aus|buchten** *tr. V.* bulge; widen ‹road› (*to form a parking area, passing point, etc.*)

**Ausbuchtung** *die; ~, ~en* bulge

**aus|buddeln** *tr. V.* (*ugs., auch fig.*) dig up

**aus|bügeln** *tr. V.* **A** (*ugs.: bereinigen*) iron out ‹differences, problem, misunderstanding, defect›; make good ‹loss, mistake›; **B** iron ‹shirt, dress, etc.›; press ‹seam, suit, trousers›; iron out ‹crease, fold›

**aus|buhen** *tr. V.* (*ugs.*) boo

**Aus·bund** *der* (*oft iron.*) **ein ~ an** *od.* **von Tugend** a paragon *or* model of virtue; **ein ~ an** *od.* **von Bosheit/Frechheit** malice/impudence itself *or* personified

**aus|bürgern** *tr. V.* **jmdn. ~:** deprive sb. of citizenship

**Ausbürgerung** *die; ~, ~en* deprivation of citizenship

**aus|bürsten** *tr. V.* brush out ‹dust, dirt› (**aus** of); brush ‹clothes, upholstery, etc.›

**aus|büxen** /ˈausbʏksn̩/ *itr. V.; mit sein* (*ugs.*) skedaddle (*coll.*); scarper (*Brit. coll.*); **jmdm. ~:** run away from sb.; **vor jmdm./etw. ~:** run away from sb./sth.

**aus|checken** *tr. V.* check out

**Aus·dauer** *die* staying power; stamina; (*Beharrlichkeit*) perseverance; (*Hartnäckigkeit*) persistence; **[beim Lernen, Lesen] ~/keine ~ haben** have/lack perseverance [when it comes to learning, reading]

**aus·dauernd** ❶ *Adj.* **A** ‹runner, swimmer, etc.› with stamina *or* staying power; (*beharrlich*) persevering; tenacious; (*hartnäckig*) persistent; unflagging ‹diligence, enthusiasm, efforts›; enduring ‹love, sympathy›; **B** (*Bot.*) perennial. ❷ *adv.* perseveringly; tenaciously; (*hartnäckig*) persistently

**Ausdauer·training** *das* stamina training

**aus·dehnbar** *Adj.* ‹company, market› capable of expansion; ‹norm, application, etc.› capable of extension *or* of being extended (**auf** + *Akk.* to); elastic ‹material›

**aus|dehnen** ❶ *tr. V.* **A** (*räumlich*) stretch ‹clothes, piece of elastic›; expand ‹rail›; (*fig.*) extend ‹power, borders, trading links›; expand, increase ‹capacity›; **B** (*einbeziehen*) **etw. auf etw.** (*Akk.*) **~:** extend sth. to sth.; **C** (*zeitlich*) prolong; **ein ausgedehntes Frühstück** a leisurely breakfast; **ausgedehnte Ausflüge/Spaziergänge** extended trips/walks. ❷ *refl. V.* **A** (*räumlich*) ‹metal, water, gas, etc.› expand; ‹fog, mist, fire, epidemic› spread; (*fig.*) ‹business, firm, trade› expand; **B** (*zeitlich*) go on (**bis** until); **C** (*sich erstrecken*) extend; **ein ausgedehnter Park** an extensive park; **sich bis zum Meer ~:** extend *or* stretch to the sea

**Aus·dehnung** *die* **A** (*Zunahme an Volumen, Vergrößerung*) expansion; (*fig.: der Macht, von Beziehungen, Grenzen*) extension; **B** (*zeitlich*) prolongation; (*von Öffnungszeiten*) extension; **C** (*Ausmaß, Größe*) extent

**ausdehnungs-, Ausdehnungs-: ~fähig** *Adj.* (*bes. Physik*) expansible; capable of expansion *postpos.*; **~fähigkeit** *die* (*bes. Physik*) expansibility; **~koeffizient** *der* (*Physik*) coefficient of expansion

**aus|denken** ❶ *unr. refl. V.* **sich** (*Dat.*) **etw. ~:** think of sth.; (*erfinden*) think sth. up; (*sich vorstellen*) imagine sth.; **sich** (*Dat.*) **etw. in allen Einzelheiten ~:** think sth. out in every detail; **da musst du dir schon etwas anderes ~!** you'll have to come up with *or* think of something better than that! ❷ *unr. tr. V.* (*zu Ende denken*) **etw. ~:** think sth. out *or* through [completely]; **[das ist] nicht auszudenken** it's impossible to imagine; (*zu schrecklich*) it does not bear thinking about

**aus|deuten** *tr. V.* interpret; **etw. falsch ~:** misinterpret sth.; **etw. dahin ~, dass ...** interpret sth. to mean that ...

**aus|deutschen** *tr. V.* (*österr.*) **jmdm. etw. ~:** explain sth. to sb. in words of one syllable

**Aus·deutung** *die* interpretation

**aus|dienen** *itr. V.* (*Milit. veralt.*) **ausgedient haben** have finished *or* completed one's military service; (*fig. ugs.*) have had it (*coll.*); ⇒ *auch* **ausgedient** 2

**aus|diskutieren** *tr. V.* **etw. ~:** discuss sth. fully *or* thoroughly

**aus|dorren** ⇒ **ausdörren** 2

**aus|dörren** ❶ *tr. V.* dry up; dry up, parch ‹land, soil›; parch ‹throat, lips›. ❷ *itr. V.; mit sein* dry up; ‹land, soil› dry up, become parched; ‹plant› wither

**aus|drehen** *tr. V.* **A** (*ausschalten*) switch *or* turn off ‹radio, light, engine›; turn off ‹gas›; **B** (*Technik*) drill [out] ‹hole›

**Aus·druck**[1] *der; ~[e]s,* **Ausdrücke** **A** (*Wort*) expression; (*Terminus*) term; **du sollst nicht solche Ausdrücke gebrauchen** you mustn't use language like that; **Sie haben sich im ~ vergriffen** your choice of words is most unfortunate; **dumm/ärgerlich** *usw.* **ist gar kein ~:** stupid/angry *etc.* isn't the word for it; **B** (*Ausdrucksweise, Gesichts~*) expression; **etw. zum ~ bringen** express sth.; give expression to sth.; **einer Sache** (*Dat.*) **~ geben** *od.* **verleihen** (*geh.*) express sth.; **mit dem ~ der Entrüstung/des Dankes** with an expression of indignation/thanks; **in etw.** (*Dat.*) **zum ~ kommen** be expressed *or* find expression in sth.

**Aus·druck**[2] *der; ~[e]s, ~e* (*Nachrichtenw., DV*) printout

**aus|drucken** ❶ *tr. V.* **A** (*Druckerspr.: fertig drucken*) finish printing ‹book etc.›; **B** (*Nachrichtenw., DV*) print out; **C** (*angeben, aufführen*) **im Katalog [mit 400 DM] ausgedruckt** listed in the catalogue [at 400 marks]; **in Abänderung unseres ausgedruckten Programms** in a change to our advertised programme. ❷ *itr. V.* (*Druckerspr.*) **gut/schlecht ~:** print well/badly

**aus|drücken** ❶ *tr. V.* **A** (*auspressen*) squeeze ‹juice› out; squeeze [out] ‹lemon, orange, grape, etc.›; squeeze out ‹sponge›; squeeze ‹boil, pimple›; **den Saft aus einer Zitrone ~:** squeeze *or* press the juice out of *or* from a lemon; **B** (*auslöschen*) stub out ‹cigarette›; pinch out ‹candle›; **C** (*formulieren, widerspiegeln*) express; **anders ausgedrückt** to put it another way; **... und das ist noch milde ausgedrückt** ..., and that's putting it mildly; **jmdm. seinen Dank ~:** express one's thanks to sb.; **etw. in** *od.* **mit Worten ~:** express sth. in *or* put sth. into words; **seine Miene drückte Zufriedenheit aus** his expression was one of contentment. ❷ *refl. V.* **A** (*sich äußern*) express oneself; **um mich gelinde/höflich auszudrücken** to put it mildly/politely; **B** (*offenbar werden*) be expressed

**ausdrücklich** /*od.* -ˈ--/ ❶ *Adj.* express *attrib.* ‹command, wish, etc.›; explicit ‹reservation›; **gegen jmds. ~es Verbot** although sb. has/had expressly forbidden it. ❷ *adv.* expressly; ‹mention› explicitly; **etw. ~ betonen** give sth. particular emphasis

**ausdrucks-, Ausdrucks-: ~fähigkeit** *die* expressiveness; (*sprachliche Gewandtheit*) articulateness; **~kraft** *die* expressive power; expressiveness; **~los** ❶ *Adj.* **A** expressionless; **B** (*ohne Ausdruckskraft*) unexpressive ‹style, delivery, etc.›; ❷ *adv.* **A** expressionlessly; **B** (*ohne Ausdruckskraft*) unexpressively; **~losigkeit** *die* **A** expressionlessness; **B** (*Fehlen von Ausdruckskraft*) lack of expressiveness; **~mittel** *das* means of expression; **~schwach** ❶ *Adj.* unexpressive; **~schwach sein** be lacking in expression; ❷ *adv.* unexpressively; **~stark** ❶ *Adj.* expressive; forceful ‹language›; bold ‹pattern, colour›; ❷ *adv.* expressively; **~tanz** *der* expressive dance; **~voll** ❶ *Adj.* expressive; ❷ *adv.* expressively; **~weise** *die* way of expressing oneself

**aus|dünnen** *tr. V.* thin out

**aus|dünsten** ❶ *tr. V.* (*ausströmen*) give off; ‹factory› emit ‹fumes etc.›. ❷ *itr. V.* (*Feuchtigkeit abgeben*) transpire

**Aus·dünstung** *die* **A** (*das Ausdünsten*) transpiration; **B** (*Dampf*) vapour; (*Geruch*) odour

**aus·einander** *Adv.* **A** (*voneinander getrennt*) apart; **etw. ~ schreiben** write sth. as separate words; **zwei Schüler ~ setzen** seat two pupils apart; **weit ~ stehen** be far apart; ‹teeth› be widely spaced; ‹eyes, legs› be wide apart; **weit ~ stehende Zähne** widely spaced teeth; **etw. ~ bekommen** *od.* (*ugs.*) **kriegen [können]** be able to get sth. apart; **~ brechen** break up; **etw. ~ brechen** break sth. up; **etw. ~ breiten** spread sth. out; **das hat die beiden ~ gebracht** this led to the two of them parting company; **nichts kann sie ~ bringen** nothing can part them; **sich ~ entwickeln** develop away; ‹friends etc.› grow apart [from each other *or* one another]; **~ falten** +*Akk.* unfold; open ‹newspaper›; **~ gehen** part; ‹crowd› disperse; ‹views› differ, diverge; ‹streets› diverge; ‹relationship› break up; (*ugs.*) ‹person› get round and podgy; **zwei Verbündete ~ zu dividieren suchen** seek to drive a wedge between two allies; **zwei Dinge ~ halten** distinguish between two things; **zwei Menschen ~ halten** tell two people apart; **~ klaffen** ‹hole, wound› gape; (*fig.*) ‹views› be poles apart; **etw. ~ klamüsern** (*nordd. ugs.*) unravel sth.; sort sth. out; **~ laufen** run off in different directions; ‹crowd› scatter; ‹roads etc.› diverge; ‹paint etc.› run; **sich ~ leben** grow apart (**mit** from); **etw. ~ nehmen** take sth. apart; **jmdn. ~ nehmen** (*salopp.*) take sb. apart (*coll.*); **etw. ~ reißen** tear sth. up; **eine Familie ~ reißen** tear a family apart; **Dinge ~ rücken** move things apart; **~ rücken** move apart; **etw. ~ schrauben** unscrew sth. and take it apart; **jmdm. etw. ~ setzen** explain sth. to sb.; **er hat sich mit diesem Problem seit Jahren ~ gesetzt** he's concerned himself with this problem for years; **sich mit den Dingen [ernsthaft] ~ setzen** give things serious thoughts; **sich mit jmdm. ~ setzen** have it out with sb.; argue the/a matter out with sb.; **sich mit seinen Gläubigern ~ setzen** battle with one's creditors; **etw. ~ sprengen** burst sth. [apart *or* open]; **~ stieben** scatter; **~ treiben** +*Akk.* scatter ‹birds, animals›; disperse ‹crowd, clouds›; **~ treiben** drift apart; **den Tisch ~ ziehen** pull out the table leaf; **sich ~ ziehen** ‹column, competitors in race› string *or* spread out; **sie sind [im Alter] ein Jahr ~:** they are a year apart in age; **~!** get away from each other!; break it up!; **~ sein** (*ugs.*) (*sich getrennt haben*) have separated; have split up; (*aufgelöst sein*) ‹engagement› have been broken off; be off; ‹marriage, relationship, friendship› have broken up; **B** (*eines aus dem *anderen*) **Behauptungen/Formeln** *usw.* **~ ableiten** deduce propositions/formulae *etc.* one from another

***auseinander|bekommen** *usw.* ⇒ **auseinander** A

**Auseinandersetzung** *die;* ~, **~en** **A** (*eingehende Beschäftigung*) examination (**mit** of); **B** (*Diskussion*) debate, discussion (**über** + *Akk.* about, on); **C** (*Streit*) argument; (*zwischen Arbeitgeber und Arbeitnehmer*) dispute; **es kam wegen etw. zu einer ~:** an argument/a dispute developed over sth.; **D** (*Kampfhandlung*) clash; **es kam zu ~en zwischen Polizisten und Demonstranten** there were clashes between police and demonstrators; **E** (*Rechtsw.*) partition

***auseinander|sprengen** *usw.* ⇒ **auseinander** A

**aus|erkiesen** *unr. tr. V.* (*geh.*, *Präsensformen dicht. veralt.*) choose; **zu etw. auserkoren sein** be chosen for sth.

**Aus·erkorene** *der/die; adj. Dekl.* (*scherzh.*) intended (*coll.*)

**aus·erlesen** ❶ *Adj.* (*geh.*) select ‹company, audience›; choice ‹fruits, wines, etc.›; exquisite ‹taste›; **von ~er Eleganz** of exquisite elegance. ❷ *adv.* (*überaus*) exquisitely ‹beautiful, fine, charming›

**aus|ersehen** *unr. tr. V.* (*geh.*) choose

**aus|erwählen** *tr. V.* (*geh.*) choose; **zu etw. auserwählt sein** be chosen for sth.; **das auserwählte Volk** (*jüd. Rel.*) the chosen people

**Aus·erwählte** *der/die; adj. Dekl.* **A** (*geh.*) chosen one; **die ~n** the chosen; **B** (*scherzh.*) (*Freund[in]*) beloved (*joc.*); (*Verlobte[r]*) intended (*coll.*)

**aus·fahrbar** *Adj.* telescopic ‹aerial›; retractable, pop-up ‹headlights›

**aus|fahren** ❶ *unr. tr. V.* **A** **jmdn. ~** (*im Kinderwagen, Rollstuhl*) take sb. out for a walk; (*im Auto o. Ä.*) take sb. out for a drive *or* ride; **B** (*ausliefern*) deliver ‹newspapers, parcels, laundry›; **C** (*Technik: nach außen bringen*) extend ‹aerial, crane, landing flaps, telescope, etc.›; lower ‹undercarriage›; raise ‹periscope›; **D** (*abnutzen*) damage; **ausgefahrene Straßen** rutted and damaged roads; ⇒ *auch* **Gleis** B; **E** *mit sein* **eine Kurve ~:** take a bend wide; **F** (*maximal beschleunigen*) drive ‹car› flat out; run ‹engine› at full power; **G** (*die Kapazität ausnutzen*) **etw. voll/zu 40% ~:** operate *or* run sth. at full capacity/40% of capacity; **H** (*Seemannsspr.: ausbringen*) lay out, run out ‹warp, cable›; run out ‹anchor›; rig out, set ‹boom›.
❷ *unr. itr. V.; mit sein* **A** (*spazieren fahren*) go out for a drive; **B** (*hinausfahren*) ‹boat, ship› put to sea; ‹train› leave, pull out; ‹car, lorry› leave; **aus dem Hafen ~:** leave harbour; **der Zug fuhr aus dem Bahnhof aus** the train pulled out of *or* left the station; **C** (*Bergmannsspr.: aus dem Schacht fahren*) come up; **D** (*Technik: hervorkommen*) extend; **E** (*den Körper verlassen*) **[von jmdm.] ~** ‹evil spirit etc.› leave sb.

**Aus·fahrt** *die* **A** (*Stelle zum Hinausfahren, Autobahn~*) exit (*Gen.* from); **die ~ Bremen-Ost** the Bremen-East exit; the exit for Bremen East; **B** (*das Hinausfahren*) departure; (*Bergmannsspr.: aus dem Schacht*) ascent; **bei der ~ aus dem Bahnhof sahen wir ...** as the train pulled out of *or* left the station, we saw ...; **bei der ~ aus dem Hafen tutete das Schiff** as it left [the] harbour, the ship hooted; **der Zug hat keine ~:** the train has not been given the signal for departure; **C** (*Spazierfahrt*) (*mit dem Auto*) drive; (*mit dem Fahrrad, Motorrad*) ride; **eine ~ machen** go for a drive/ride

**Ausfahrt·signal** *das* (*Eisenb.*) starting signal

**Ausfahrts-: ~schild** *das; Pl.* **~ ~er** exit sign; **~signal** *das* (*Eisenb.*) ⇒ **Ausfahrtsignal**; **~straße** *die* exit [road]

**Aus·fall** *der* **A** (*das Nichtstattfinden*) cancellation; **ein hoher ~ an Unterrichtsstunden** a large number of cancelled lessons; **B** (*Einbuße, Verlust*) loss; (*an Einnahmen, Lohn*) drop (*Gen.* in); **C** (*Technik*) (*eines Motors*) failure; (*einer Maschine, eines Autos*) breakdown; (*fig.: eines Organs*) failure; loss of function; **D** (*das Ausscheiden*) retirement; (*vor einem Rennen*) withdrawal; (*Abwesenheit*) absence; **nach [dem] ~ von vier Läufern** after four runners had retired *or* dropped out; **E** (*das Herausfallen*) **zum ~ der Haare/Zähne führen** cause hair loss/cause teeth to fall out; **F** (*Ergebnis*) outcome; result; **G** (*beleidigende Äußerungen*) attack (**gegen** on); **H** (*Fechten*) lunge; **im ~:** in the lunge position; **I** (*Gewichtheben*) split; **in den ~ springen** split the legs; **J** (*Turnen*) splits *pl.*; **K** (*Milit.: Ausbruch*) rally; sortie

**aus|fallen** *unr. itr. V.; mit sein* **A** (*herausfallen*) fall out; **mir fallen die Haare aus** my hair is falling out; **B** (*nicht stattfinden*) be cancelled; **etw. ~ lassen** cancel sth.; **der Unterricht/die Schule fällt morgen aus** lessons are cancelled/there is no school tomorrow; **C** (*ausscheiden*) drop out; (*während eines Rennens*) retire; drop out; (*fehlen*) be absent; **wenn der Pilot ausfällt, muss der Kopilot das Steuer übernehmen** if the pilot becomes unable to fly the plane, the co-pilot must take over the controls; **D** (*nicht mehr funktionieren*) ‹engine, brakes, signal› fail; ‹machine, car› break down; **der Strom fiel aus** there was a power failure; **E** (*ein bestimmtes Ergebnis zeigen*) turn out; **gut/schlecht** *usw.* **~:** turn out well/badly *etc.*; **wie ist die Prüfung ausgefallen?** (*für dich*) how did you do in the examination?; (*insgesamt*) what were the examination results like?; **die Niederlage fiel sehr deutlich aus** the defeat turned out to be *or* was most decisive; **F** (*Milit.: einen Ausfall machen*) make a sortie; **G** (*Chemie: sich abscheiden*) be precipitated; **H** (*Sprachw.: wegfallen*) be dropped; ⇒ *auch* **ausgefallen** 2

**aus|fällen** *tr. V.* (*Chemie*) precipitate

**ausfallend** *Adj.* **[gegen jmdn.] ~ sein/werden** be/become abusive [towards sb.]

**aus·fällig** *Adj.* ⇒ **ausfallend**

**Ausfalls·erscheinung** *die* (*Med.*) deficiency symptom

**Ausfall·straße** *die* (*Verkehrsw.*) main road [leading] out of the/a town/city

**Ausfall[s]·winkel** *der* (*Physik*) angle of reflection

**Ausfall·zeit** *die* (*Versicherungsw.*) credited service period

**aus|fasern** *itr. V.; meist mit sein* fray

**aus|fechten** *unr. tr. V.* fight out

**aus|fegen** *tr.* (*auch itr.*) *V.* (*bes. nordd.*) sweep up ‹dirt›; sweep out ‹room etc.›; ⇒ *auch* **eisern** C

**aus|feilen** *tr. V.* file down ‹key, cogwheel, etc.›; file [out] ‹hole›; (*fig.*) polish ‹speech, essay, poem, etc.›

**aus|fertigen** *tr. V.* (*Amtsspr.*) **A** (*ausstellen*) draw up ‹document, agreement, will, etc.›; issue ‹passport, certificate›; make out ‹bill, receipt›; **B** (*unterzeichnen*) sign

**Aus·fertigung** *die* (*Amtsspr.*) **A** ⇒ **ausfertigen** A: drawing up; issuing; making out; **B** (*Exemplar*) copy; **in doppelter/dreifacher ~:** in duplicate/triplicate; **etw. in vier ~en einreichen** submit four copies of sth.

**aus·findig** *Adv.* **in jmdn./etw. ~ machen** find sb./sth.

**aus|flicken** *tr. V.* (*ugs.*) patch up

**aus|fliegen** ❶ *unr. itr. V.; mit sein* **A** (*hinausfliegen*) fly out; **die ganze Familie ist ausgeflogen** (*ugs. fig.*) the whole family has gone out [for a walk/drive *etc.*]; **B** (*flügge werden*) leave the nest. ❷ *unr. tr. V.* **jmdn./etw. ~:** fly sb./sth. out; (*per Luftbrücke*) airlift sb./sth.

**aus|fließen** *unr. itr. V.; mit sein* (*herausfließen*) flow *or* run out (**aus** of)

**aus|flippen** *itr. V.; mit sein* (*salopp*) **A** freak out (*coll.*); **ausgeflippt** (*im Drogenrausch*) freaked *or* spaced out (*coll.*); **eine ausgeflippte Idee** a freaky idea (*coll.*); **B** (*überschnappen*) flip one's lid *or* one's top (*coll.*)

**Aus·flucht** *die;* ~, **Ausflüchte** /-flʏçtə/ excuse; **Ausflüchte machen** make excuses

**Aus·flug** *der* **A** outing; (*vom Reisebüro o. Ä. organisiert*) excursion; (*Wanderung*) ramble; walk; (*fig.*) excursion; **einen ~ machen** go on an outing/excursion; go for a ramble *or* walk; **B** (*das Ausschwärmen*) flight [from the nest/hive]; **C** (*Imkerei: Flugloch*) [hive] entrance

**Ausflügler** /ˈausfly:klɐ/ *der;* **~s**, ~, **Ausflüglerin** *die;* ~, **~nen** tripper (*Brit.*); day tripper; excursionist (*Amer.*)

**Ausflugs-: ~dampfer** *der* pleasure steamer; (*allgemeiner*) excursion boat; **~lokal** *das* restaurant/café catering for [day] trippers; **~ort** *der* resort for [day] trippers; **~verkehr** *der* (*am Wochenende*) weekend holiday traffic; (*an Feiertagen*) holiday traffic; **~ziel** *das* destination for [day] trippers; **unser ~ziel war ...** the destination of our excursion *or* outing was ...

**Aus·fluss**, ***Aus·fluß** *der* **A** (*das Ausfließen*) outflow; (*von Gas*) escape; **B** ▸ **474** (*Med.: Absonderung*) discharge; **C** (*geh.: Auswirkung*) product; **D** (*Abfluss*) outlet; **E** (*Technik: ausfließende Menge*) outflow

**aus|folgen** *tr. V.* (*österr.*) issue; release ‹body›

**aus|formen** *tr. V.* **A** (*formen*) shape (**zu** into); **B** (*endgültig gestalten*) give final shape to ‹text, work of art›

**aus|formulieren** *tr. V.* formulate ‹ideas, questions›; flesh out ‹paper› [from notes]

**Aus·formung** *die* **A** (*das Ausformen*) shaping; **B** (*Gestalt*) form

**aus|forschen** *tr. V.* **A** (*ausfragen*) question (**nach** about); **B** (*herausfinden*) find out; (*erforschen*) investigate; (*zu Spionagezwecken*) gather information on; **C** (*österr. Amtsspr.: ausfindig machen*) find

**Aus·forschung** *die* **A** (*Befragung*) questioning; **B** (*das Herausfinden*) finding out; (*das Erforschen*) investigation; **zur ~ von militärischen Betrieben** to gather information about military establishments; **C** (*österr. Amtsspr.: Ermittlung*) finding

**aus|fragen** *tr. V.* **jmdn. ~:** question sb., ask sb. questions (**nach, über** + *Akk.* about); (*verhören*) interrogate sb. (**nach, über** + *Akk.* about); **so fragt man die Leute aus** that would be telling

**aus|fransen** ❶ *itr. V.; mit sein* fray. ❷ *tr. V.* fringe

**aus|fressen** *unr. tr. V.* **etw. ausgefressen haben** (*ugs.*) have been up to sth. (*coll.*)

**Aus·fuhr** *die;* ~, **~en** **A** (*das Exportieren*) export; **B** (*Export*) exports *pl.*

**ausführbar** *Adj.* **A** (*durchführbar*) practicable; workable ‹plan›; **B** (*für die Ausfuhr geeignet*) exportable

**aus|führen** *tr. V.* **A** (*ausgehen mit*) **jmdn. ~:** take sb. out; **B** (*spazieren führen*) take ‹person, animal› for a walk; take *or* lead ‹prisoners› out for their exercise; **C** (*exportieren*) export; **D** (*durchführen*) carry out ‹work, repairs, plan, threat›; execute, carry out ‹command, order, commission›; execute, perform ‹movement, dance step›; put ‹idea, suggestion› into practice; perform ‹operation›; perform, carry out ‹experiment, analysis›; **die ~de Gewalt** (*Politik*) the executive power; **E** (*Fußball, Eishockey usw.*) take ‹penalty, free kick, corner›; **F** (*ausarbeiten*) **etw. ~:** work sth. out in detail *or* fully; **etw. näher ~:** work sth. out in more detail; **G** (*erläutern, darlegen*) explain

**Ausfuhr-: ~gut** *das* article for export; **~güter** goods for export; **~hafen** *der* port of exportation; **~land** *das* (*Wirtsch.*) **A** (*Land, das ausführt*) exporting country; **B** (*Land, in das ausgeführt wird*) export market

**ausführlich** /*auch:* ˈ-ˈ-/ ❶ *Adj.* detailed, full ‹account, description, report, discussion›; thorough, detailed, full ‹investigation, debate›; detailed ‹introduction, instruction, letter›; **~ werden** go into detail. ❷ *adv.* in detail; ‹investigate› thoroughly, fully; **etw. ~er/sehr ~ beschreiben** describe sth. in more *or* greater/in great detail

**Ausführlichkeit** /*auch:* ˈ-ˈ--/ *die;* ~ ⇒ **ausführlich** 1: fullness; thoroughness; **mit großer ~:** in great detail; (*umständlich*) at great length

*old spelling (see note on page 1707)

**Ausfuhr-: ~prämie** *die* (*Wirtsch.*) export premium; **~sperre** *die* (*Wirtsch.*) ⇒ **~verbot**

**Aus·führung** *die* **A** (*das Durchführen*) ⇒ **ausführen** D: carrying out; execution; performing; implementation; playing; giving; **zur ~ gelangen** *od.* **kommen** (*Papierdt.*) ‹plan› be carried out *or* put into effect; **B** (*Fußball, Eishockey*) taking; **nach der ~ des Freistoßes** after the free kick has/had been taken; **C** (*Art der Herstellung*) (*Version*) version; (*äußere* ~) finish; (*Modell*) model; (*Stil*) style; **in der gleichen ~:** of the same design; **D** (*Darlegung*) explanation; (*Bemerkung*) remark; observation; **E** (*Ausarbeitung*) **der Entwurf war fertig, jetzt ging es an die ~ des Romans/der Einzelheiten** the draft was ready, and the next task was to work the novel out in detail/ to work out the details

**Ausfuhr·verbot** *das* (*Wirtsch.*) export embargo

**aus|füllen** *tr. V.* **A** (*füllen*) fill in ‹trench, excavation, gravel pit›; (*zustopfen*) fill ‹hole, joint›; **B** (*beanspruchen, einnehmen*) take up ‹space›; ‹person› fill ‹chair, doorway, etc.›; **ihr Leben ist ganz mit Arbeit ausgefüllt** her life is completely taken up by work; **C** (*die erforderlichen Angaben eintragen in*) fill in ‹form, crossword puzzle›; write *or* make out ‹prescription, cheque›; **D** (*verbringen*) fill ‹pause›; **seine freie Zeit mit etw. ~:** fill [up] one's free time with sth.; **er füllte die Wartezeit mit Lesen aus** he filled in the time [he had to wait] with reading; **E** (*in Anspruch nehmen*) take up; **F** (*bekleiden, versehen*) **seinen Posten gut/nicht ~:** do one's job well/not do one's job; **G** (*innerlich befriedigen*) **jmdn. ~:** fulfil sb.; give sb. fulfilment; **ihr Beruf füllt sie ganz aus** she finds complete fulfilment in her work; **er lebt ein ausgefülltes Leben** he lives a full life

**aus|füttern** *tr. V.* line

**Aus·gabe** *die* **A** (*das Austeilen*) distribution; giving out; (*von Essen*) serving; **die ~ des Essens erfolgt ab ...** lunch/dinner *etc.* is [served] from ...; **B** (*das Aushändigen*) issuing; (*von Meldungen, Nachrichten*) release; **nach ~ des Befehls** after the order was/ had been issued; **C** (*Geld~*) item of expenditure; expense; **~n** expenditure *sing.* (**für** on); **seine ~n überstiegen seine Einnahmen** his outgoings exceeded his income; **D** (*Edition, Auflage*) edition; (*Nummer einer Zeitschrift; Finanzw., Postw.*) issue; **~ erster/letzter Hand** *first/last edition personally supervised by the author;* **die letzte ~ der Tagesschau** (*fig.*) the late news bulletin; **E** ⇒ **Ausgabestelle**; **F** (*Ausführung, auch fig.*) version; **G** (*DV*) output

**Ausgabe-: ~gerät** *das* (*DV*) output device; **~kurs** *der* (*Finanzw.*) issue price

**Ausgaben-: ~buch** *das* petty-cash book; **~politik** *die* expenditure policy

**Ausgabe·stelle** *die* (*Schalter*) issuing counter; (*Büro*) issuing office

**Aus·gang** *der* **A** (*Erlaubnis zum Ausgehen*) time off; (*von Soldaten*) leave; **zwei Tage ~ haben** ‹servant› have two days off; ‹soldier› have a two-day pass; **bis sechs Uhr ~ haben** ‹servant› be free till six; ‹soldier› have a pass until six; **B** (*Tür ins Freie*) exit (*Gen.* from); **C** (*Endpunkt, Grenze*) **am ~ des Dorfes/der Allee/des Waldes** at the end of the village/avenue/on the edge of the forest; **D** (*Anat.: Öffnung eines Organs*) outlet; **E** (*Ende*) end; (*eines Romans, Films usw.*) ending; **F** (*Ergebnis*) outcome; (*eines Wettbewerbs*) result; **ein Unfall mit tödlichem ~:** an accident with fatal consequences; a fatal accident; **G** (*Ausgangspunkt*) starting point; **seinen ~ von etw. nehmen** take sth. as one's starting point; ‹style, plan, suggestion› originate with sth.; **H** (*Bürow.: Postversand*) posting (*Brit.*); mailing; **I** (*Bürow.: abgehende Post*) outgoing mail; **J** (*Spaziergang*) walk; **das war der erste ~ des Rekonvaleszenten** that was the convalescent's first time out **K** (*Elektrot.*) output

**ausgangs** ❶ *Adv.* **~ von** on the outskirts of. ❷ *Präp. mit Gen.* **A** (*räumlich*) coming out of; **B** (*zeitlich*) at the end of; **ein Mann ~ der Fünfziger** a man in his late fifties

**Ausgangs-: ~basis** *die* starting point; **~lage** *die* initial position *or* situation; **~position** *die* initial position; starting position; (*bei einem Rennen*) starting position; **~punkt** *der* starting point; **~sperre** *die* (*bes. Milit.*) (*für Zivilisten*) curfew; (*für Soldaten*) confinement to barracks; **[eine] ~sperre verhängen** impose a curfew/confine the soldiers/regiment *etc.* to barracks; **~sperre haben** be confined to barracks; **~sprache** *die* (*Sprachw.*) source language; **~stellung** *die* **A** (*Sport*) starting position; **B** (*Milit.*) initial position; **~zeile** *die* (*Druckw.*) break line

**aus|geben** ❶ *unr. tr. V.* **A** (*austeilen*) distribute; give out; serve ‹food, drinks›; **B** (*aushändigen, erteilen; Finanzw., Postw.: herausgeben*) issue; (*fig.*) put about ‹story, rumour›; **C** (*verbrauchen*) spend ‹money› (**für** on); **D** (*ugs.: spendieren*) **einen ~:** treat everybody; (*eine Runde geben*) stand a round of drinks (*coll.*); **ich gebe [dir] einen aus** I'll treat you; **E** (*fälschlich bezeichnen*) **jmdn./etw. als** *od.* **für jmdn./etw. ~:** pretend sb./sth. is sb./sth.; **sich als jmd./etw.** *od.* **für jmdn./etw. ~:** pretend to be sb./ sth.; **F** (*DV*) output.
❷ *unr. refl. V.* **sich [völlig** *od.* **vollständig] ~:** push oneself right to the limit

**ausgebeult** *2. Part. v.* **ausbeulen**

**ausgebombt** *2. Part. v.* **ausbomben**

**Ausgebombte** *der/die; adj. Dekl.* person who has/had been bombed out; **die ~n** those who have/had been bombed out

**aus·gebrannt** ❶ *2. Part. v.* **ausbrennen.** ❷ *Adj.* (*fig.*) burnt out

**ausgebucht** ❶ *2. Part. v.* **ausbuchen.** ❷ *Adj.* (*ausverkauft, belegt, auch fig. ugs.*) booked up

**ausgebufft** /'ausgəbʊft/ *Adj.* (*salopp*) (*clever*) canny; (*durchtrieben*) crafty

**Aus·geburt** *die* (*geh. abwertend*) **A** (*übles Erzeugnis*) evil product; **eine ~ der Hölle** the spawn of hell; **B** (*Inbegriff*) epitome

**aus·gedient** ❶ *2. Part. v.* **ausdienen.** ❷ *Adj.* (*ugs.: unbrauchbar*) worn out, (*Brit. coll.*) clapped out, (*Amer. coll.*) beat up ‹vehicle, engine, etc.›

**ausgedörrt** *2. Part. v.* **ausdörren**

**aus·gefallen** ❶ *2. Part. v.* **ausfallen.** ❷ *Adj.* unusual

**Ausgeflippte** *der/die; adj. Dekl.* (*salopp*) dropout (*coll.*)

**ausgefranst** *2. Part. v.* **ausfransen**

**ausgefuchst** *Adj.* (*ugs.*) wily; crafty; **~e Spezialisten** experienced specialists

**ausgeglichen** ❶ *2. Part. v.* **ausgleichen.** ❷ *Adj.* **A** (*harmonisch*) balanced, harmonious ‹structure, façade, etc.›; well-balanced ‹person›; **ein ~es Wesen haben** have an even *or* well-balanced temperament; **B** (*stabil*) stable; equable ‹climate›; **C** (*Sport*) even

**Ausgeglichenheit** *die;* ~ (*einer Struktur, Fassade usw.*) balance; harmony; **die ~ ihres Wesens/ihre ~:** the evenness of her temperament

**aus·gegoren** *Adj.* **[voll] ~:** fully fermented; (*fig.*) fully worked out ‹plan, idea›

**Ausgeh·anzug** *der* best suit; (*Milit.*) walking-out uniform (*Brit.*)

**aus|gehen** ❶ *unr. itr. V.; mit sein* **A** (*irgendwohin gehen*) go out; **er geht selten aus** he doesn't go out much; **B** (*fast aufgebraucht sein; auch fig.*) run out; **jmdm. geht etw. aus** sb. is running out of sth.; **ihr ging die Geduld/der Gesprächsstoff aus** (*fig.*) she ran out of patience/conversation; **ihm geht der Atem** *od.* **die Luft** *od.* (*ugs.*) **die Puste aus** (*er gerät außer Atem*) he is getting short *or* out of breath; he is running out of puff (*Brit. coll.*); (*er verliert seine Kraft, Energie*) he is running out of steam (*fig.*); (*er ist finanziell am Ende*) he is going broke (*coll.*); **C** (*ausfallen*) fall out; **mir gehen die Haare aus** I'm losing my hair; my hair is falling out; **D** (*aufhören zu brennen*) go out; **E** (*enden*) end; **unentschieden ~:** end in a draw; **gut/schlecht ~:** turn out well/ badly; ‹story, film› end happily/unhappily; ⇒ *auch* **leer** A; **straffrei**; **F** (*herrühren*) **von jmdm./etw. ~:** come from sb./sth.; **G** **von etw. ~** (*etw. zugrunde legen*) take sth. as one's starting point; **gehen wir davon aus, dass ...** let us assume that ...; let us start from the assumption that ...; **du gehst von falschen Voraussetzungen aus** you're starting from false assumptions; **H** **auf Abenteuer ~:** look for adventure; **auf Entdeckungen ~:** be bent on making discoveries; **auf Eroberungen ~** (*scherzh.*) set out *or* be aiming to make a few conquests; **I** (*seinen Ausgang nehmen*) **vom Hauptplatz** *usw.* ~ ‹road› lead off from the main square *etc.;* (*strahlenförmig*) radiate from the main square *etc.;* **J** (*ausgestrahlt werden*) radiate; **von jmdm./etw. geht Ruhe/Sicherheit aus** sb./sth. radiates calm/confidence; **K** (*abgeschickt werden*) be sent off; **die ~de Post** the outgoing mail; **L** (*blasser werden*) ‹colour› run; ‹fabric› fade.
❷ *unr. refl. V.* (*österr.: ausreichen*) be enough; ‹equation, calculation› come out; **es geht sich aus** there's enough; (*zeitlich*) there's enough time

**ausgehend** *Adj.* **im ~en Mittelalter** towards the end of the Middle Ages; **das ~e 19. Jahrhundert** the end of *or* closing years of the 19th century

**ausgehungert** ❶ *2. Part. v.* **aushungern.** ❷ *Adj.* **A** (*sehr hungrig*) starving; **nach etw. ~ sein** (*fig.*) be starved of sth.; **B** (*abgezehrt*) emaciated

**Ausgeh-: ~uniform** *die* (*Milit.*) walking-out uniform (*Brit.*); **~verbot** *das* curfew; (*Milit.*) confinement to barracks

**ausgeklügelt** *2. Part. v.* **ausklügeln**

**ausgekocht** ❶ *2. Part. v.* **auskochen.** ❷ *Adj.* (*ugs. abwertend: durchtrieben*) crafty

**aus·gelassen** ❶ *2. Part. v.* **auslassen.** ❷ *Adj.* exuberant ‹mood, person›; lively ‹party, celebration›; (*wild*) boisterous. ❸ *adv.* exuberantly; (*wild*) boisterously; **nebenan wurde ~ gefeiert** there was a lively party going on next door

**Aus·gelassenheit** *die* exuberance; (*Wildheit*) boisterousness

**Ausgeliefertsein** *das;* **~s** helplessness

**aus·gelitten** *Adj.* in **er hat ~** (*geh.*) he has been released from his suffering

**aus·gemacht** ❶ *2. Part. v.* **ausmachen.** ❷ *Adj.* **A** (*beschlossen*) agreed; **es ist [eine] ~e Sache, dass ...** it is an accepted fact that ...; **B** (*vollkommen*) complete; complete, utter ‹nonsense›; **eine ~e Dummheit** downright stupidity. ❸ *adv.* (*überaus*) extremely; (*ausgesprochen*) decidedly

**aus·genommen** ❶ *2. Part. v.* **ausnehmen.** ❷ *Konj.* (*außer*) except; apart from; **alle sind anwesend, ~ er** *od.* **er ~:** everyone is present apart from *or* except him; **er kommt bestimmt, ~ es regnet** he's sure to come, unless it rains

**ausgepicht** /'ausgəpɪçt/ *Adj.* (*ugs.*) crafty; **ein ~er Bursche** a wily customer (*coll.*)

**ausgeprägt** ❶ *2. Part. v.* **ausprägen.** ❷ *Adj.* (*ausgesprochen, stark entwickelt*) distinctive ‹personality, character›; marked ‹inclination, tendency, disinclination›; pronounced ‹feature, tendency›; **einen ~en Sinn für etw. haben** have a highly developed sense of sth.

**ausgepumpt** ❶ *2. Part. v.* **auspumpen.** ❷ *Adj.* (*salopp: erschöpft*) knackered (*Brit. coll.*); shattered (*Brit. coll.*); tuckered out (*Amer. coll.*)

**ausgerechnet** ❶ *2. Part. v.* **ausrechnen.** ❷ *Adv.* (*ugs.: gerade*) **~ heute/morgen** today/tomorrow of all days; **~ hier** here of all places; **~ Sie** you of all people; **~ jetzt kommt er/muss er kommen** he would have to come [just] now [of all times]; **~ ihm muss das passieren** it would have to happen to him of all people; **~ das** that of all things

**aus·geschlafen** ❶ *2. Part. v.* **ausschlafen.** ❷ *Adj.* (*ugs.: gewitzt*) wide awake

**aus·geschlossen** ❶ *2. Part. v.* ausschließen. ❷ *Adj.* **das ist ~:** that is out of the question; **es ist nicht ~, dass ...** one cannot rule out the possibility that ...; it is not impossible that ...; **jeder Irrtum ist ~:** there can be no possibility of a mistake

**aus·geschnitten** ❶ *2. Part. v.* ausschneiden. ❷ *Adj.* low-cut ‹dress, blouse, etc.›; **ein tief/weit ~es Kleid** a dress with a plunging neckline; a very low-cut dress

**ausgesorgt** *Adj.* (*ugs.*) **[finanziell] ~ haben** be comfortably off

**ausgespielt** ❶ *2. Part. v.* **ausspielen.** ❷ *Adj. in* **~ haben** be finished; **bei mir hat er ~** (*ugs.*) he's had it as far as I'm concerned (*coll.*)

**aus·gesprochen** ❶ *2. Part. v.* **aussprechen.** ❷ *Adj.* definite, marked ‹preference, inclination, resemblance›; pronounced ‹dislike›; marked ‹contrast›; **~es Pech/Glück haben** be decidedly unlucky/lucky; **ein ~es Talent für etw.** a definite talent for sth.; **ein ~er Gegner von etw. sein** be a strong opponent of sth. ❸ *adv.* (*besonders*) decidedly; downright ‹stupid, ridiculous, ugly›

**aus|gestalten** *tr. V.* A (*in bestimmter Weise gestalten*) arrange; (*formulieren*) formulate; B (*ausbauen*) develop (**zu** into)

**Aus·gestaltung** *die* A ⇒ **ausgestalten** A, B: arrangement; development; formulation; B (*Form*) form

**ausgestellt** ❶ *2. Part. v.* **ausstellen.** ❷ *Adj.* flared ‹skirts, trousers, etc.›

**aus·gestorben** ❶ *2. Part. v.* **aussterben.** ❷ *Adj.* **[wie] ~:** deserted; **die Stadt ist wie ~:** this is like a ghost town

**Ausgestoßene** *der/die; adj. Dekl.* outcast

**aus·gesucht** ❶ *2. Part. v.* **aussuchen.** ❷ *Adj.* A (*erlesen*) choice; exquisite ‹jewellery, clothes, furniture›; select ‹company›; B (*besonders groß*) exceptional; extreme; C (*wenig Auswahl bietend*) **diese Sachen sind ziemlich ~:** there aren't many good things left. ❸ *adv.* exceptionally; extremely

**aus·gewachsen** ❶ *2. Part. v.* **auswachsen.** ❷ *Adj.* A fully-grown; adult ‹man, woman›; B (*fig. ugs.*) (*richtig*) real ‹storm, gale›; (*groß*) full-blown ‹scandal›; utter, complete ‹nonsense, fool, idiot›

**aus·gewogen** ❶ *2. Part. v.* **auswiegen.** ❷ *Adj.* (*ausgeglichen*) balanced; [well-]balanced ‹personality›. ❸ *adv.* in a balanced way

**Aus·gewogenheit** *die;* **~:** balance

**ausgezeichnet** /*od.* ˈ-ˈ--/ ❶ *2. Part. v.* **auszeichnen.** ❷ *Adj.* excellent; outstanding ‹expert›. ❸ *adv.* excellently; **~ Tennis spielen können** be an excellent tennis player; **sie passt ~ zu ihm** she suits him very well indeed

**ausgiebig** /ˈausgi:bɪç/ ❶ *Adj.* A substantial, large ‹meal›; good long ‹walk, sleep, rest, drive›; extensive ‹study›; abundant ‹credit›; **ein ~er Regen** continuous heavy rain; **~en Gebrauch von etw. machen** make full use of sth.; B (*veralt.*) ⇒ **ergiebig.** ❷ *adv.* ‹profit› handsomely; ‹read› extensively; **von etw. ~ Gebrauch machen** make full use of sth.; **~ frühstücken** eat a substantial breakfast; **~ wandern** walk extensively; **etw. ~ betrachten** have a long close look at sth.; **sich ~ strecken** have a good stretch; **~ gähnen** have a good yawn

**aus|gießen** *unr. tr. V.* A (*aus einem Gefäß gießen*) pour out (**aus** of); B (*leeren*) empty; C (*geh.: über jmdn./etw. gießen*) pour (**über** + *Akk.* over); **seinen Spott/seine Verachtung/seinen Zorn über jmdn. ~:** pour scorn/contempt on sb./vent one's rage on sb.; D (*Technik: ausfüllen*) fill (**mit** with)

**Ausgießung** *die;* **~** *in* **die ~ des Heiligen Geistes** (*christl. Rel.*) the effusion of the Holy Spirit

**Ausgleich** *der;* **~[e]s, ~e** A (*von Unregelmäßigkeiten*) evening out; (*von Spannungen*) easing; (*von Differenzen, Gegensätzen*) reconciliation; (*eines Konflikts*) settlement; (*Schadensersatz*) compensation; (*einer Rechnung, Schuld*) settlement; (*eines Kontos*) balancing; **einen ~ der verschiedenen Interessen anstreben** strive to reconcile differing interests; **um ~ bemüht sein** be at pains to promote compromise; **als** *od.* **zum ~ für etw.** to make up *or* compensate for sth.; **im Büro hat er wenig Bewegung, deshalb spielt er Tennis zum ~:** he doesn't get much exercise in the office, so, to compensate, he plays tennis; **eine auf ~ und Zusammenarbeit gerichtete Politik** policies aimed at conciliation and cooperation; **zum ~ Ihrer Rechnung/Ihres Kontos** in settlement of your invoice/to balance your account; **einen ~ in etw.** (*Dat.*) **finden** be made up *or* compensated for by sth.; B (*Gleichgewicht*) balance; C (*Sport*) equalizer; **den ~ erzielen, zum ~ kommen** equalize; score the equalizer

**aus|gleichen** ❶ *unr. tr. V.* even out ‹irregularities, differences in height›; ease ‹tensions›; reconcile ‹differences of opinions, contradictions›; settle ‹conflict›; redress ‹injustice›; compensate for ‹damage›; equalize, balance ‹forces, values›; make up for, compensate for ‹misfortune, lack›; (*Kaufmannsspr.*) settle ‹bill, debt›; discharge ‹obligation›; make up ‹loss›; (*Bankw.*) balance ‹account, budget›; **etw. durch etw. ~:** compensate for sth. by sth.; make up for sth. with sth.; **~de Gerechtigkeit** poetic justice; ⇒ *auch* **ausgeglichen** 2. ❷ *unr. refl. V.* A (*sich nivellieren*) balance out; (*sich ganz aufheben*) cancel each other out; **das gleicht sich wieder aus** one thing makes up for the other; B (*Kaufmannsspr., Bankw.*) ‹account, budget› balance. ❸ *unr. itr. V.* (*Sport*) equalize; **zum 3:3 ~:** level the scores at three all

**Ausgleichs-: ~amt** *das:* *authority which administers system of compensation paid to individuals for damage and losses during and immediately after the Second World War;* **~getriebe** *das* (*Technik*) differential gear; **~sport** *der* sport for fitness; **~tor** *das,* **~treffer** *der* (*Ballspiele*) equalizer; **~zahlung** *die* compensation payment

**aus|gleiten** *unr. itr. V.; mit sein* (*geh.*) ⇒ **ausrutschen**

**aus|gliedern** *tr. V.* hive off; (*fig.: ausklammern*) exclude

**aus|glühen** *tr. V.* A (*Med.*) sterilize by heating; B (*Technik*) anneal

**aus|graben** *unr. tr. V.* dig up; dig [out] ‹trench, hole›; dig out ‹trapped person, avalanche victim, etc.›; dig up, excavate ‹archaeological object›; excavate ‹temple, settlement, etc.›; dig, lift ‹potatoes›; (*aus dem Grab*) disinter, exhume ‹body, corpse›; (*fig. ugs.*) dig up; dig up, unearth ‹old manuscripts, maps, etc.›; **eine alte Geschichte wieder ~** (*fig.*) dig *or* rake up an old story; ⇒ *auch* **Kriegsbeil**

**Aus·grabung** *die* (*Archäol.*) A excavation; B (*Fund*) find

**Ausgrabungs-: ~arbeit** *die* excavation work *no pl.;* **~arbeiten** excavation work *sing.;* **~stätte** *die* excavation site

**aus|greifen** *unr. itr. V.* step out; **~d** extended ‹gallop›; striding ‹movement›; long ‹stride›; **weit ~d** widely spreading ‹branches›; (*fig.*) wide-ranging ‹speech›; large-scale ‹plans, objectives›

**aus|grenzen** *tr. V.* mark off (**aus** from); mark out ‹area›; (*ausklammern, isolieren*) exclude (**aus** from)

**Ausgrenzung** *die;* **~:** marking off; (*einer Fläche*) marking out; (*Ausklammerung, Isolierung*) exclusion

**aus|gründen** *tr. V.* (*Wirtsch.*) hive off (**aus** from)

**Ausguck** *der;* **~[e]s, ~e** A (*ugs., auch Seemannsspr.*) lookout post; **~ halten** keep a lookout (**nach** for); B (*Seemannsspr.: Matrose*) lookout

**aus|gucken** *itr. V.* (*ugs.*) keep a lookout (**nach** for); ⇒ *auch* **Auge** A

**Aus·guss**, ***Aus·guß** *der* A (*Becken*) sink; B (*Abfluss*) wastepipe; C (*landsch.: Tülle*) spout

**aus|haben** (*ugs.*) ❶ *unr. tr. V.* A (*ausgelesen haben*) have finished; B (*ausgezogen haben*) have taken off. ❷ *unr. itr. V.* (*Schule, Unterricht beendet haben*) finish school

**aus|hacken** *tr. V.* A hoe ‹weeds›; lift ‹potatoes, turnips, etc.› using a hoe; B (*auspicken*) **jmdm. die Augen ~:** peck out sb.'s eyes; ⇒ *auch* **Krähe**; C (*österr.: zerlegen*) cut up

**aus|haken** ❶ *tr. V.* unhook. ❷ *refl. V.* come unhooked; ‹zip fastener› come undone. ❸ *itr. V.* (*unpers.*) **es hakte bei ihr aus** (*ugs.*) (*sie begriff es nicht*) she just didn't get it; (*ihre Geduld war zu Ende*) she lost her patience

**aus|halten** ❶ *unr. tr. V.* A (*ertragen*) stand, bear, endure ‹pain, suffering, hunger, blow, noise, misery, heat, etc.›; withstand ‹attack, pressure, load, test, wear and tear›; stand up to ‹strain, operation›; **er konnte es zu Hause nicht mehr ~:** he couldn't stand it at home any more; **er hält es nirgends lange aus** he never stays in one place for long; (*wechselt häufig die Stellung*) he never stays in one job for long; **den Vergleich mit jmdm./etw. ~:** stand comparison with sb./sth.; **es lässt sich ~:** it's bearable; I can put up with it; **hier lässt es sich ~:** I could get to like this place; **er konnte es im Bett nicht ~:** he couldn't stand being in bed; **es ist nicht/nicht mehr zum Aushalten** it is/has become unbearable *or* more than anyone can bear; **es ist nicht mehr zum Aushalten mit dir** you've become unbearable; **das Material muss viel ~:** the material has to take a lot of wear [and tear]; B (*ugs. abwertend: jmds. Unterhalt bezahlen*) keep; **er lässt sich von seiner Freundin ~:** he gets his girlfriend to keep him; C (*Musik: anhalten*) hold. ❷ *unr. itr. V.* (*durchhalten*) hold out

**aus|handeln** *tr. V.* negotiate

**aus|händigen** *tr. V.* hand over; issue ‹passport, document, etc.›; **jmdm. etw. ~:** hand sth. over to sb./issue sb. with sth.

**Aushändigung** *die;* **~:** handing over; (*eines Passes, Dokuments usw.*) issue

**Aus·hang** *der* notice; **einen ~ machen** put up a notice

**Aushänge·bogen** *der* (*Druckw.*) advance sheet

**aus|hängen**[1] *unr. itr. V.* ‹notice, timetable, etc.› have been put up; **am schwarzen Brett ~:** be up on the noticeboard (*Brit.*) *or* (*Amer.*) bulletin board

**aus|hängen**[2] ❶ *tr. V.* A (*öffentlich anschlagen*) put up ‹notice, timetable, etc.›; B (*herausheben*) take ‹door› off its hinges; take ‹window› out; unhitch ‹coupling›. ❷ *refl. V.* A (*sich lösen*) ‹chain› come undone *or* unfastened; ‹shutter, door, etc.› come off its hinges; B (*sich glätten*) ‹crease› drop out

**Aus·hänger** *der* (*Druckw.*) ⇒ **Aushängebogen**

**Aushänge·schild** *das; Pl.* **~er** [advertising] sign; advertisement (*lit. or fig.*)

**aus|harren** *itr. V.* (*geh.*) hold out; **an jmds. Seite** (*Dat.*) **~:** remain at sb.'s side; **auf seinem Posten ~:** remain *or* wait at one's post

**aus|härten** *tr., itr. V.* (*Technik*) cure

**aus|hauchen** *tr. V.* (*geh.*) give off ‹smell, fumes›; exhale, give off ‹perfume, scent›; **seinen Geist** *od.* **sein Leben** *od.* **seine Seele ~** (*geh. verhüll.*) breathe one's last (*literary*)

**aus|hauen** *unr. tr. V.* A (*hineinschlagen*) hew out; B (*ausmeißeln*) carve ‹statue, inscription, etc.›; C (*fällen*) thin out ‹trees›; D (*roden*) clear ‹forest, vineyard, etc.›; E (*auslichten*) prune ‹trees, bushes, etc.›

**aushäusig** /ˈaushɔyzɪç/ *Adj.* out-of-house, (*Amer.*) independent ‹worker, contractor›; **[viel] ~ sein** be away from home [a great deal]

**aus|heben** *unr. tr. V.* A (*ausschaufeln*) dig out ‹earth, sand, etc.›; dig ‹trench, grave›; B ⇒ **aushängen**[2] 1 B; C (*aus dem Nest nehmen*) steal ‹eggs, birds›; (*leeren*) rob ‹nest›; (*fig.: unschädlich machen*) break up ‹gang, ring, etc.›; raid ‹club, casino, hiding place, outpost›; pick up, catch ‹criminal, terrorist›; D (*österr.*) empty ‹postbox›; E (*veralt.: einziehen*) levy, recruit ‹troops, army›; F (*Ringen*) **jmdn. ~:** execute a pick-up on sb.

**aus|hebern** *tr. V.* (*Med.*) **jmdm. den Magen ~:** pump out sb.'s stomach

*old spelling (see note on page 1707)

**aus|hecken** *tr. V.* (*ugs.*) hatch ‹plan, intrigue›; plan ‹attack›; **immer neue Streiche ~:** keep on thinking up new tricks

**aus|heilen** ❶ *itr. V.; mit sein* ‹injury, organ› heal [up]; ‹patient, illness› be cured. ❷ *tr. V.* **bis er seine Verletzung ausgeheilt hatte** until his injury had healed

**aus|helfen** *unr. itr. V.* help out; **jmdm. [mit** *od.* **bei etw.] ~:** help sb. out [with sth.]

**aus|heulen** *refl. V.* (*ugs.*) **sich bei jmdm. ~:** cry one's heart out on sb.'s shoulder

**Aus·hilfe** *die* Ⓐ (*das Aushelfen*) help; **sie arbeitet in der Kantine zur ~:** she helps out in the canteen; Ⓑ (*Aushilfskraft*) temporary worker; (*in Läden, Gaststätten*) temporary helper *or* assistant; (*Sekretärin*) temporary secretary; temp (*coll.*); **als ~ arbeiten** help out on a temporary basis

**Aushilfs-, aushilfs-: ~arbeit** *die* temporary work *no pl.*; **~arbeiten** temporary work *sing.*; temporary jobs; **~kraft** *die* temporary worker; (*in Läden, Gaststätten*) temporary helper *or* assistant; (*Sekretärin*) temporary secretary; temp (*coll.*); **~weise** *adv.* on a temporary basis

**aus|höhlen** *tr. V.* hollow out; erode ‹rock, cliff, etc.›; (*fig.: untergraben*) undermine; **ausgehöhlte Wangen** (*fig.*) hollow cheeks; **einen Begriff ~** (*fig.*) render a concept meaningless

**Aushöhlung** *die;* ~, **~en** Ⓐ ⇒ **aushöhlen**: hollowing out; erosion; undermining; Ⓑ (*ausgehöhlte Stelle*) hollow

**aus|holen** ❶ *itr. V.* Ⓐ (*zu einer Bewegung ansetzen*) **[mit dem Arm] ~:** draw back one's arm; (*zum Schlag*) raise one's arm; **er holte zum Schlag aus** he raised his fist/sword *etc.* to strike; **er holte zum Wurf aus** he drew back his arm ready to throw; **zum Gegenschlag ~** (*fig.*) prepare to counterattack; **zu einem Coup ~** (*fig.*) prepare a coup; Ⓑ (*ausgreifen*) step out; **[weit] ~de Schritte** long strides; Ⓒ (*weitschweifig sein*) range far afield; (*weit zurückgehen*) go back a long way.
❷ *tr. V.* (*landsch.: ausfragen*) **jmdn. über etw.** (*Akk.*) *od.* **nach etw. ~:** question *or* (*coll.*) quiz sb. about sth.

**aus|holzen** *tr. V.* Ⓐ (*lichten*) thin out; Ⓑ (*abholzen*) clear

**aus|horchen** *tr. V.* **jmdn. über etw.** (*Akk.*) *od.* **nach etw. ~:** sound sb. out about sth.

**Aus·hub** *der* (*Tiefbau*) Ⓐ excavation; Ⓑ (*ausgehobene Erde*) excavated material

**aus|hungern** *tr. V.* starve out ‹city, fortress, garrison, etc.›; ⇒ *auch* **ausgehungert 2**

**aus|husten** ❶ *tr. V.* cough up. ❷ *itr.*, *auch refl. V.* (*zu Ende husten*) finish coughing

**aus|ixen** *tr. V.* (*ugs.*) x out

**aus|jäten** *tr. V.* weed ‹garden, flower bed›; weed out ‹dandelions etc.›; **Unkraut ~:** weed

**aus|kämmen** *tr. V.* Ⓐ (*entfernen*) comb out ‹dust, dirt›; **jmdm./sich etw. aus dem Haar ~:** comb sth. out of sb.'s/one's hair; Ⓑ (*glätten, ordnen*) comb out ‹hair›

**aus|kegeln** *tr. V.* Ⓐ **einen Pokal** *usw.* **~:** bowl for a cup *etc.*; Ⓑ (*südd., österr.: ausrenken*) **sich/jmdm. den Arm ~:** put one's/sb.'s arm out [of joint]

**aus|kehren** *tr.* (*auch itr.*) *V.* (*bes. südd.*) ⇒ **ausfegen**

**aus|keimen** *itr. V.; auch mit sein* germinate; ‹potatoes› sprout

**aus|kennen** *unr. refl. V.* (*in einer Stadt, an einem Ort usw.*) know one's way around *or* about; (*in einem Fach, einer Angelegenheit usw.*) know what's what; **sie kennt sich in dieser Stadt aus** she knows her way around the town; **man kennt sich bei ihm nicht aus** you don't know where you are with him; **sich [gut] mit/in etw.** (*Dat.*) **~:** know [a lot] about sth.; **sich mit den Klassikern/jmds. Jargon ~:** be familiar with the classics/sb.'s jargon; **sich bei den Frauen ~:** know a lot about women

**aus|kernen** *tr. V.* stone

**aus|kippen** *tr. V.* Ⓐ (*entfernen aus*) tip out; Ⓑ (*leeren*) empty

**aus|klammern** *tr. V.* Ⓐ (*Math.*) place outside the brackets; Ⓑ (*beiseite lassen*) leave aside; (*nicht zulassen*) exclude

**aus|klamüsern** *tr. V.* (*ugs.*) figure *or* work out

**Aus·klang** *der* Ⓐ (*geh.; Abschluss*) end; **zum ~ der Saison/des Festes** to end *or* close the season/festival; Ⓑ (*Musik: Ende*) final notes/chord/chorus *etc.*; **einen heiteren ~ haben** end brightly

**ausklappbar** /ˈau̯sklapba:ɐ̯/ *Adj.* fold-out; **die Couch ist ~:** the couch folds out

**aus|klarieren** *tr. V.* (*Zollw., Seew.*) clear

**aus|klauben** *tr. V.* (*südd., österr., schweiz.*) pick out

**aus|kleiden** ❶ *tr. V.* Ⓐ (*geh.: entkleiden*) undress; Ⓑ (*überziehen mit*) line. ❷ *refl. V.* (*geh.*) undress; disrobe (*formal*)

**Aus·kleidung** *die* lining; (*eines Schwimmbeckens, Gartenteichs*) liner

**aus|klingen** *unr. itr. V.* Ⓐ *mit sein* (*ausgehen*) end; Ⓑ *mit sein* (*verklingen*) ‹song› finish; ‹music, final notes› die away; Ⓒ ‹bell› cease *or* stop ringing

**aus|klinken** ❶ *tr.* (*auch itr.*) *V.* release. ❷ *refl. V.* release itself/themselves; (*fig.*) opt out

**aus|klopfen** *tr. V.* Ⓐ (*entfernen*) (*mit einem Stock, Schläger*) beat out (**aus** + *Dat.* of); (*durch Anklopfen*) knock *or* tap out (**aus** + *Dat.* of); Ⓑ (*säubern*) beat ‹carpet›; knock *or* tap ‹pipe› out

**Aus·klopfer** *der;* **~s, ~:** carpet beater

**aus|klügeln** *tr. V.* think out; work out; **ein ausgeklügeltes System** a cleverly devised system

**aus|kneifen** *unr. itr. V.; mit sein* (*ugs.*) run away (**vor, aus** from)

**aus|knipsen** *tr. V.* (*ugs.*) switch *or* turn off

**aus|knobeln** *tr. V.* (*ugs.*) Ⓐ (*durch Knobeln entscheiden*) **sie knobelten aus, wer anfangen sollte** they threw dice to decide who would start; **die nächste Runde Bier ~:** throw dice to decide who will stand the next round of beer; Ⓑ (*austüfteln*) work out

**ausknöpfbar** /ˈau̯sknœpfba:ɐ̯/ *Adj.* removable, detachable ‹lining›

**aus|kochen** *tr. V.* Ⓐ (*kochen, säubern*) boil; Ⓑ (*keimfrei machen*) sterilize ‹instruments etc.› [in boiling water]; Ⓒ (*salopp abwertend: sich ausdenken*) concoct; ⇒ *auch* **ausgekocht 2**

**aus|kommen** *unr. itr. V.; mit sein* Ⓐ (*ausreichend haben, zurechtkommen*) **mit etw. ~:** manage on *or* (*coll.*) get by on sth.; **ohne jmdn./etw. ~:** manage without *or* (*coll.*) get by without sb./sth.; **der Motor kommt mit sechs Litern aus** the engine can run for a hundred kilometres on six litres; Ⓑ (*sich verstehen*) **mit jmdm. [gut] ~:** get along *or* on [well] with sb.; **mit ihm ist einfach nicht auszukommen** he's just impossible to get on with; Ⓒ (*südd., österr.: entkommen*) escape (**aus** + *Dat.* from); Ⓓ (*bes. schweiz.: bekannt werden*) get out

**Auskommen** *das;* **~s** Ⓐ (*Lebensunterhalt*) livelihood; **sein ~ haben** make a living; Ⓑ **mit ihm/ihr ist kein ~:** he/she is quite impossible [to get on with]

**auskömmlich** /ˈau̯skœmlɪç/ ❶ *Adj.* adequate; **ein ~es Gehalt haben** earn enough to live on. ❷ *adv.* adequately

**aus|kosten** *tr. V.* (*geh.*) Ⓐ (*genießen*) **etw. ~:** enjoy sth. to the full; Ⓑ (*erleiden*) suffer

**aus|kotzen** (*derb*) ❶ *tr. V.* puke up (*coarse*). ❷ *refl. V.* puke (*coarse*); **sich bei jmdm. ~** (*fig.*) have a bloody good moan to sb. (*Brit. sl.*)

**aus|kramen** *tr. V.* (*ugs.*) dig out; (*fig.*) dig up ‹memories, knowledge, story›

**aus|kratzen** ❶ *tr. V.* Ⓐ (*entfernen*) scrape out ‹dirt, remains, deposit, etc.› (**aus** from); scratch ‹words, writing, inscription› out; (*reinigen*) scrape [out] ‹bowl, pan, etc.›; **jmdm. am liebsten die Augen ~ mögen** (*ugs.*) want to scratch sb.'s eyes out; Ⓑ (*Med.*) ⇒ **ausschaben B**. ❷ *itr. V.; mit sein* (*salopp*) do a bunk (*Brit. coll.*); beat it (*coll.*); **vor jmdm. ~:** beat it to avoid sb.

**Auskratzung** *die;* ~, **~en** (*Med.*) ⇒ **Ausschabung**

**aus|kriechen** *unr. itr. V.; mit sein* hatch [out]

**aus|kriegen** *tr. V.* (*ugs.*) ⇒ **ausbekommen**

**aus|kristallisieren** ❶ *tr. V.* crystallize out. ❷ *itr. V.; mit sein* crystallize out

**aus|kugeln** *tr. V.* **sich** (*Dat.*) **den Arm/die Schulter** *usw.* **~:** put one's arm/shoulder *etc.* out [of joint]; dislocate one's arm/shoulder *etc.*; **jmdm. den Arm/die Schulter ~:** dislocate sb.'s arm/shoulder *etc.*

**aus|kühlen** ❶ *tr. V.* chill ‹person, body› through. ❷ *itr. V.; mit sein* cool down

**Aus·kühlung** *die* loss of body heat; exposure

**auskultieren** /au̯skʊlˈti:rən/ *tr. V.* (*Med.*) auscultate

**aus|kundschaften** *tr. V.* find out; trace ‹arrival, relative›; find ‹opportunity›; track down ‹refugee, criminal, enemy, etc.›; sound out ‹mood, attitude›; spy out ‹place›

**Auskunft** *die;* ~, **Auskünfte** Ⓐ (*Information*) piece of information; **Auskünfte** information *sing.*; **[jmdm. über etw.** (*Akk.*)**] ~ geben** *od.* **erteilen** give [sb.] information [about sth.]; **sie gab auf alle Fragen ~:** she answered all the questions; **können Sie mir bitte ~ geben, wann ...?** (*geh.*) can you please tell me when ...?; **~/Auskünfte über jmdn./etw. einholen** *od.* **einziehen** obtain information about sb./sth.; ⇒ *auch* **näher B**; Ⓑ (*Stelle*) information desk/counter/office/centre *etc.*; (*Fernspr.*) directory enquiries *no art.* (*Brit.*); directory information *no art.* (*Amer.*); „~" 'Information'; 'Enquiries' (*Brit.*)

**Auskunftei** *die;* ~, **~en** private detective agency; (*Kredit~*) credit reference agency

**Auskunfts-: ~beamte** *der*, **~beamtin** *die* enquiry office clerk (*Brit.*); information office clerk (*Amer.*); **~büro** *das* information office; enquiry office (*Brit.*); **~dienst** *der* (*Fernspr.*) directory enquiries *no art.* (*Brit.*); directory information *no art.* (*Amer.*); **~pflicht** *die* (*Rechtsw.*) obligation to provide information; **~schalter** *der* information counter; **~stelle** *die* information office

**aus|kuppeln** *itr. V.* disengage the clutch; declutch

**aus|kurieren** *tr. V.* heal ‹wound› [completely]; **jmdn. ~:** cure sb. [completely]; **der Spieler, der seit Wochen eine Oberschenkelzerrung auskuriert** the player, who has been recovering from a thigh strain for weeks

**aus|lachen** *tr. V.* **jmdn. ~:** laugh at sb.; **lass dich nicht ~:** don't be ridiculous

**aus|laden**[1] *unr. tr. V.* unload (**aus** from)

**aus|laden**[2] *unr. tr. V.* **jmdn. ~:** cancel one's invitation to sb.

**ausladend** *Adj.* prominent ‹forehead›; jutting ‹chin›; broad ‹shoulders›; extensive ‹roots›; widely spreading ‹branches›; (*fig.*) sweeping ‹gestures, movements›

**Aus·lage** *die* Ⓐ *Pl.* (*Unkosten*) expenses; **unsere ~n für Strom/Heizung/Wasser** *usw.* our outlay *sing.* on electricity/heating/water *etc.*; Ⓑ (*ausgestellte Ware*) item *or* article on display; **~n** goods on display; Ⓒ (*Schaufenster*) shop window; window display; (*Vitrine*) display cabinet; Ⓓ (*Boxen*) stance; **in der linken/rechten ~ boxen** use the orthodox stance/be a southpaw (*coll.*) *or* left-hander; Ⓔ (*Fechten*) on-guard position; Ⓕ (*Rudern*) recovery; **in die ~ gehen** recover

**Aus·land** *das* foreign countries *pl.*; **im/ins ~:** abroad; **aus dem ~:** from abroad; **aus dem sozialistischen und dem kapitalistischen ~:** from other countries, both socialist and capitalist; **die Literatur/Intervention/Hilfe des ~s** foreign literature/intervention/aid; **die Meinung des ~s** opinion abroad; **das ~ hat zurückhaltend reagiert** foreign reaction *or* the reaction of other countries *pl.* was guarded

**Ausländer** *der;* **~s, ~:** foreigner; alien (*Admin. lang., Law*); **~ sein** be a foreigner

**ausländer·feindlich** *Adj.* hostile to foreigners *postpos.*

**Ausländerin** *die;* ~, **~nen** ⇒ **Ausländer**; ⇒ *auch* **-in**

a

a

**ausländisch** *Adj.* foreign; exotic ‹plant, animal›

**Auslands-: ~anleihe** *die* (*Bankw.*) foreign loan; **~aufenthalt** *der* stay abroad; **~beziehungen** *Pl.* foreign relations; **~deutsche** *der/die* expatriate German; German national living abroad; **~gespräch** *das* (*Fernspr.*) international call; **~korrespondent** *der* foreign correspondent; **~reise** *die* trip abroad; **~schule** *die: school run by one country on another's territory;* **~schutzbrief** *der* (*Versicherungsw.*) international travel cover documents *pl.;* **~tournee** *die* foreign tour; **~vertretung** *die* [A] (*von Firmen usw.*) foreign agency; [B] (*diplomatische Vertretung*) foreign mission

**aus|langen** *itr. V.* (*landsch.*) [A] (*ausholen*) **[mit dem Arm] ~:** draw back one's arm; (*zum Schlag*) raise one's hand; **nach jmdm. ~:** raise one's arm to hit sb.; [B] (*ausreichen*) be enough

**Auslass, *Auslaß** *der;* **Auslasses, Auslässe** (*Technik*) outlet

**aus|lassen** ❶ *unr. tr. V.* [A] (*weglassen*) leave out; leave out, omit ‹detail, passage, word, etc.›; [B] (*versäumen*) miss ‹chance, opportunity, etc.›; [C] (*abreagieren*) vent (**an** + *Dat.* on); release ‹tension›; **seinen Ärger/Zorn/seine Wut an jmdm. ~:** vent one's anger on sb.; take one's anger out on sb.; [D] (*ugs.: nicht tragen, nicht einschalten*) **etw. ~:** leave sth. off; [E] (*zerlassen*) melt ‹bacon fat› down; melt ‹butter›; [F] (*länger machen*) let down; (*weiter machen*) let out.
❷ *unr. refl. V.* (*abwertend: sich äußern*) talk, speak (**über** + *Akk.* about); (*schriftlich*) write (**über** + *Akk.* about); (*sich verbreiten*) hold forth (**über** + *Akk.* about); **sich im Detail/näher ~:** go into detail/more detail; ⇒ *auch* **ausgelassen** 2, 3

**Auslassung** *die;* **~, ~en** [A] (*Weglassung*) omission; [B] (*oft abwertend: Äußerung*) remark

**Auslassungs-: ~punkte** *Pl.* omission marks; ellipsis *sing.;* **~zeichen** *das* (*Sprachw.*) apostrophe

**aus|lasten** *tr. V.* [A] (*voll laden*) fully load; [B] (*voll ausnutzen*) **etw. ~:** use sth. to full capacity; **seine/ihre** *usw.* **Kapazität ~** ‹mine, factory, etc.› be working to full capacity; **ausgelastet sein** ‹mine, factory, etc.› be working to full capacity; [C] (*voll beanspruchen*) fully occupy; (*befriedigen*) fulfil

**aus|latschen** *tr. V.* (*ugs.*) wear ‹shoes etc.› out of shape

**Auslauf** *der* [A] **keinen/zu wenig ~ haben** have no/too little chance to run around outside; **der Hund braucht viel ~:** the dog needs plenty of exercise; [B] (*Raum*) space to run around in; (*für Hühner, Enten usw.*) run; (*für Pferde*) paddock; [C] (*Fechten*) run-back; (*Ski*) outrun; run-out; [D] (*Abfluss*) outlet

**aus|laufen** ❶ *unr. itr. V.; mit sein* [A] (*herausfließen*) run out (**aus** of); ‹pus› drain; [B] (*leer laufen*) empty; ‹eye› drain; ‹egg› run out; (*undicht sein*) leak; [C] (*in See stechen*) sail, set sail (**nach** for); [D] (*erlöschen*) ‹contract, agreement, etc.› run out; [E] (*nicht fortgesetzt werden*) ‹model, line› be dropped *or* discontinued; **etw. ~ lassen** drop *or* discontinue sth.; [F] (*zum Stillstand kommen*) come *or* roll to a stop; [G] (*auseinander laufen*) ‹colour, ink, etc.› run; [H] (*Sport: abbremsen*) slow down; [I] (*enden*) ‹path, road, etc.› end, (*allmählich*) peter out; [J] (*übergehen*) run (**in** + *Akk.* into); **spitz ~de Türme** towers tapering to a point; [K] (*einen bestimmten Ausgang nehmen*) end.
❷ *unr. refl. V.* **die Kinder konnten sich mal richtig ~:** the children could run about to their heart's content

**Aus·läufer** *der* [A] (*Geogr.*) foothill *usu. in pl.;* [B] (*Met.*) (*eines Hochs*) ridge; (*eines Tiefs*) trough; [C] (*Bot.*) runner; [D] (*schweiz.: Bote*) delivery man/boy

**Aus·läuferin** *die* (*schweiz.*) delivery woman/girl

**aus|laugen** *tr. V.* leach ‹soil›; leach [out] ‹salts etc.› (**aus** from); (*fig.*) drain, exhaust, wear out ‹person›; exhaust ‹economy›

*old spelling (see note on page 1707)

**Aus·laut** *der* (*Sprachw.*) final sound; auslaut; **im ~:** in final position

**aus|lauten** *itr. V.* (*Sprachw.*) **auf „d" ~:** have 'd' in final position; **ein ~der Konsonant** a final consonant

**aus|läuten** *tr. V.* [A] **das alte Jahr ~:** ring out the old year; [B] (*veralt.: bekannt machen*) ring out; proclaim

**aus|leben** ❶ *refl. V.* [A] (*das Leben genießen*) live life to the full; **sich in seiner Arbeit ~:** find complete fulfilment in one's work; [B] (*sich entfalten*) find *or* be given complete expression. ❷ *tr. V.* (*geh.: verwirklichen*) give full expression to; realize ‹talent›

**aus|lecken** *tr.* (*auch itr.*) *V.* lick out (**aus** of)

**aus|leeren** *tr. V.* empty [out]; empty ‹ashtray, dustbin, etc.›; (*austrinken*) drain

**aus|legen** *tr. V.* [A] (*zur Ansicht, Einsicht hinlegen*) lay out; display ‹goods, exhibits›; [B] (*bedecken mit*) **etw. mit Fliesen/Teppichboden ~:** tile/carpet sth.; **einen Schrank [mit Papier] ~:** line a cupboard [with paper]; [C] (*leihen*) lend; **jmdm. etw.** *od.* **etw. für jmdn. ~:** lend sb. sth.; lend sth. to sb.; **ich habe das Porto für dich ausgelegt** I paid the postage for you; [D] (*interpretieren*) interpret; **etw. falsch ~:** misinterpret sth.; **etw. als Furcht ~:** take sth. to be fear; [E] (*für Tiere*) lay ‹bait›; put down ‹poison›; set ‹trap, net›; [F] (*Technik: verlegen*) lay ‹mine, cable, fuse, etc.›; [G] (*Landw.*) plant; [H] (*Technik: auf eine bestimmte Leistung hin*) **etw. auf** *od.* **für etw. ~:** design sth. for sth.

**Ausleger** *der;* **~s, ~** [A] (*eines Krans*) jib; boom; [B] (*Bootsbau*) outrigger

**Auslege·ware** *die* carpeting

**Auslegung** *die;* **~, ~en** interpretation

**aus|leiern** (*ugs.*) ❶ *itr. V.; mit sein* wear out; ‹clothes› go baggy; **ausgeleiert** worn out; baggy ‹pullover, trousers, etc.›. ❷ *refl. V.* wear out; ‹pullover, trousers› go baggy; ‹elastic band, material› lose its stretch. ❸ *tr. V.* wear out; make ‹pullover, trousers, etc.› go baggy; make ‹rubber band› lose its stretch

**Ausleihe** *die;* **~, ~n** [A] (*das Ausleihen*) lending; [B] (*Stelle*) issue desk

**aus|leihen** *unr. tr. V.* [A] (*leihen*) borrow; **[sich (*Dat.*)] etw. von jmdm. ~:** borrow sth. from sb.; [B] (*verleihen*) lend; **jmdm.** *od.* **an jmdn. etw. ~:** lend sb. sth.; lend sth. to sb.

**aus|lernen** *itr. V.* finish one's apprenticeship; **ein ausgelernter Schreiner** a trained carpenter; **man lernt nie aus** (*Spr.*) you learn something new every day

**Aus·lese** *die* [A] (*Auswahl*) selection; **eine ~ treffen** make a selection; [B] (*geh.: Elite*) elite; cream; [C] (*Wein*) *fine wine made with selected bunches of fully ripe grapes*

**aus|lesen**[1] *unr. tr. V.* [A] (*aussondern*) pick out (**aus** from); [B] (*von Minderwertigem befreien*) sort ‹peas, lentils, etc.›

**aus|lesen**[2] *unr. tr. V.* (*ugs.*) **etw. ~:** finish [reading] sth.; **etw. in einem Zug ~:** read sth. [from beginning to end] at one sitting

**Auslese·verfahren** *das* selection process

**aus|leuchten** *tr. V.* illuminate; (*fig.*) throw light on; (*untersuchen*) probe; **die Bühne ~:** floodlight the stage

**aus|lichten** *tr.* (*auch itr.*) *V.* prune ‹bush, tree, etc.›; thin ‹wood, area, etc.›

**aus|liefern** *tr. V.* [A] (*übergeben*) **jmdm. etw.** *od.* **etw. an jmdn. ~:** hand sth. over to sb.; **jmdn. an ein Land ~:** extradite sb. to a country; **jmdm./einer Sache ausgeliefert sein** (*fig.*) be at the mercy of sb./sth.; [B] *auch itr.* (*Kaufmannsspr.: liefern*) deliver

**Aus·lieferung** *die* [A] (*Übergabe*) handing over; (*an ein Land*) extradition; **jmds. ~ fordern** demand that sb. be handed over/extradited; [B] (*Kaufmannsspr.: Lieferung*) delivery

**Auslieferungs-: ~abkommen** *das* ⇒ **~vertrag**; **~antrag** *der* application for extradition; **~lager** *das* (*Wirtsch.*) distribution centre; **~vertrag** *der* extradition treaty

**aus|liegen** *unr. itr. V.* [A] (*zur Ansicht, Einsicht*) be displayed; ‹newspapers, plans, etc.› be laid out, be available; [B] (*zum Fang*) ‹trap› be set

**Aus·linie** *die* (*Ballspiele*) touchline

**aus|loben** *tr. V.* **10 000 DM ~:** offer a reward of 10,000 marks; (*bei einem Wettbewerb*) offer a prize of 10,000 marks

**aus|löffeln** *tr. V.* [A] (*aufessen*) **etw. ~:** spoon up [all of] sth.; **jetzt muss** *od.* **kann er die Suppe ~[, die er sich eingebrockt hat]** (*fig.*) he's made his [own] bed and now he must lie in it; [B] (*leer essen*) spoon up everything out of ‹plate, bowl, etc.›

**aus|loggen** *refl. V.* (*DV*) log off *or* out

**aus|löschen** *tr. V.* [A] (*löschen*) extinguish, put out ‹fire, lamp›; snuff, put out, extinguish ‹candle›; (*geh.*) extinguish ‹light›; [B] (*beseitigen*) rub out, erase ‹drawing, writing›; ‹wind, rain› obliterate ‹tracks, writing›; (*fig.*) obliterate, wipe out ‹memory›; extinguish ‹life›; wipe out ‹people, population›

**aus|losen** *tr. V.* **etw. ~:** draw lots for sth.; **es wurde ausgelost, wer beginnt** lots were drawn to decide who would start; **den Gewinner ~:** draw lots to decide the winner

**aus|lösen** ❶ *tr. V.* [A] (*in Gang setzen*) trigger ‹mechanism, device, etc.›; set off, trigger ‹alarm›; release ‹camera shutter›; [B] (*hervorrufen, herbeiführen*) provoke ‹discussion, anger, laughter, reaction, outrage, heart attack, sympathy›; cause ‹sorrow, horror, surprise, disappointment, panic, war›; excite, arouse ‹interest, enthusiasm›; evoke ‹memories›; draw ‹applause›; trigger [off] ‹crisis, chain of events, rebellion, strike›; [C] (*veralt.: einlösen, freikaufen*) redeem; [D] (*südd., österr.: lösen aus, von*) remove, take out (**aus** from); shell ‹peas, beans›. ❷ *refl. V.* ‹alarm› go off

**Auslöser** *der;* **~s, ~** (*Fot.*) shutter release; (*fig., Psych., Verhaltensf.*) trigger

**Aus·losung** *die* draw

**Aus·lösung** *die* [A] (*Betätigung*) (*eines Mechanismus*) triggering; (*eines Alarms*) setting off; triggering; [B] (*Hervorrufung, Herbeiführung*) ⇒ **auslösen** B: provocation; causing; exciting; arousal; evocation; drawing; triggering [off]; [C] (*veralt.: Einlösung, Freikauf*) redemption

**aus|loten** *tr. V.* [A] (*Seew.*) sound the depth of; sound, plumb ‹depth›; (*fig.*) sound out ‹intentions›; **ein Problem ~** (*fig.*) try to get to the bottom of a problem; [B] (*Bauw.*) plumb ‹wall›

**aus|lüften** ❶ *tr., itr. V.* air. ❷ *refl. V.* (*ugs. scherzh.*) get some fresh air

**aus|lutschen** *tr. V.* (*ugs.*) suck out ‹juice›; suck the juice from ‹orange, lemon, etc.›

**ausm** /'ausm̩/ (*ugs.*) = **aus dem**

**aus|machen** *tr. V.* [A] (*ugs.: ausschalten, auslöschen*) put out ‹light, fire, cigarette, candle›; turn *or* switch off ‹television, radio, hi-fi›; turn off ‹gas›; [B] (*vereinbaren*) agree; **einen Termin/ein Honorar ~:** agree [on] a deadline/fee; **etw. mit jmdm. ~:** agree sth. with sb.; [C] (*auszeichnen, kennzeichnen*) make up; constitute; **was einen großen Künstler ausmacht** what goes to make a great artist; **die Farben machen den Reiz seiner Bilder aus** it is the colours which make his pictures attractive; [D] (*ins Gewicht fallen*) make a difference; **wenig/nichts/viel ~:** make little/no/a great *or* big difference; [E] (*stören*) **das macht mir nichts aus** I don't mind [that]; **macht es Ihnen etwas aus, wenn …?** would you mind if …?; **würde es Ihnen etwas ~, den Platz zu wechseln?** would you mind swapping places?; [F] (*klären*) settle; **etw. mit sich allein/mit seinem Gewissen ~:** sort sth. out for oneself/with one's conscience; [G] (*erkennen*) make out; **es lässt sich nicht mit Sicherheit ~, ob …** it cannot be determined with certainty whether …; [H] (*betragen*) come to; **der Zeitunterschied/die Entfernung macht … aus** the time difference/distance is …; ⇒ *auch* **ausgemacht**

**aus|malen** ❶ *tr. V.* [A] (*mit Farbe ausfüllen*) colour in; [B] (*mit Malereien ausschmücken*) **das Innere einer Kirche ~:** decorate the interior of a church with murals/frescoes etc.; **C** (*schildern*) describe. ❷ *refl. V.* **sich** (*Dat.*) **etw. ~:** picture sth. to oneself; imagine sth.; **das hatte ich mir so schön ausgemalt** I had pictured it as being so beautiful

**aus|manövrieren** *tr. V.* outmanœuvre

**aus|marschieren** *itr. V.; mit sein* march out (**aus** of)

**Aus·maß** *das* **A** (*Größe, Ausdehnung*) size; dimensions *pl.*; **die ~e des Rumpfs/Kraters** *usw.* the size *sing. or* dimensions of the fuselage/crater *etc.*; **gewaltige ~e haben** be of huge *or* vast dimensions; **B** (*Umfang, Grad*) extent; **bis zu einem gewissen ~:** to a certain extent; **erschreckende ~e annehmen** assume horrifying dimensions; **eine Katastrophe unvorstellbaren ~es** a disaster on an unimaginable scale

**aus|mergeln** /'ausmɛrgl̩n/ *tr. V.* emaciate; **ausgemergelt** gaunt, emaciated ‹face, body›

**aus|merzen** /'ausmɛrtsn̩/ *tr. V.* **A** (*ausrotten*) eradicate ‹pests, insects, weeds, etc.›; **B** (*beseitigen*) eliminate ‹errors, slips, etc.›; eliminate, cut out ‹offensive passages›; **C** (*aussondern*) cull ‹animal›

**aus|messen** *unr. tr. V.* measure up

**aus|misten** *tr.* (*auch itr.*) *V.* **A** (*von Mist säubern*) muck out; **B** (*ugs.: von Unbrauchbarem leeren, aussortieren*) clear out

**aus|mustern** *tr. V.* **A** (*Milit.: als untauglich erklären*) **jmdn. ~:** reject sb. as unfit [for service]; **B** (*als unbrauchbar ausscheiden*) take ‹vehicle, machine› out of service

**Aus·nahme** *die;* **~, ~n** exception; **mit ~ von Peter/des Pfarrers** with the exception of Peter/of the priest; **ohne ~:** without exception; **mit** *od.* **bei jmdm. eine ~ machen** make an exception in sb.'s case; **~n bestätigen die Regel, keine Regel ohne ~:** the exception proves the rule

**Ausnahme-: ~erscheinung** *die* exceptional phenomenon; **~fall** *der* exceptional case; **im ~fall** in exceptional cases; **~situation** *die* exceptional situation; **~zustand** *der* state of emergency

**ausnahms-: ~los** ❶ *Adj.* unanimous ‹approval, agreement›; ❷ *adv.* without exception; **~weise** *Adv.* by way of *or* as an exception; **Dürfen wir mitkommen? — Ausnahmsweise ja** May we come too? — Yes, just this once; **er hat es mir ~weise erlaubt** he gave me permission by way of an exception; **kann ich heute ~weise früher weg?** can I go earlier today, just as a special exception?; **wenn ich ~weise keinen Schirm bei mir habe** when, just for once, I don't have my umbrella with me

**aus|nehmen** ❶ *unr. tr. V.* **A** gut ‹fish, rabbit, chicken›; **B** (*ausschließen von*) exclude; (*gesondert behandeln*) make an exception of; **jeder irrt sich einmal, ich nehme mich nicht aus** everyone makes mistakes once in a while, and I'm no exception; ⇒ *auch* **ausgenommen** 2; **C** (*die Eier herausnehmen aus*) rob ‹nest›; **D** (*ugs. abwertend: neppen*) **jmdn. ~:** fleece sb. ❷ *unr. refl. V.* (*geh.: wirken*) look; (*sich anhören*) sound

**ausnehmend** (*geh.*) ❶ *Adj.* exceptional. ❷ *adv.* exceptionally

**aus|nüchtern** *tr., itr., refl. V.* sober up

**Ausnüchterung** *die;* **~, ~en** sobering up; **jmdn. zur ~ auf die Wache bringen** take sb. to the [police] station to sober up

**Ausnüchterungs·zelle** *die* drying-out cell

**aus|nutzen,** (*bes. südd., österr.*) **aus|nützen** *tr. V.* **A** (*nutzen*) **etw. [voll] ~:** take [full] advantage of sth.; make [full] use of sth.; **den Raum/seine Zeit für etw. ~:** use the space/one's time for sth.; **B** (*Vorteil ziehen aus*) take advantage of; (*ausbeuten*) exploit

**Aus·nutzung** *die,* (*bes. südd., österr.*) **Aus·nützung** *die;* **~:** use; (*Ausbeutung*) exploitation; **unter voller ~ einer Sache** (*Gen.*) making full use of sth.

**aus|packen** ❶ *tr., itr. V.* unpack (**aus** from); unwrap ‹present›; (*fig. ugs.: erzählen*) come out with. ❷ *itr. V.* (*ugs.*) **A** (*Geheimnisse verraten*) talk (*coll.*); squeal (*sl.*); **B** (*seine Meinung sagen*) sound off

**aus|peitschen** *tr. V.* whip; (*aufgrund eines Gerichtsurteils*) flog

**Auspeitschung** *die;* **~, ~en** whipping; (*aufgrund eines Gerichtsurteils*) flogging

**aus|pendeln** *itr. V.; mit sein* commute; **die über die Grenze ~den Arbeitnehmer** those commuting to work over the border

**Aus|pendler** *der* commuter; **die Stadt hat mehr Einpendler als ~:** more people commute to the city than from it

**aus|pennen** (*salopp*) ❶ *itr., refl. V.* have a decent *or* good kip (*Brit. coll.*) *or* sleep-in. ❷ *tr. V.* **seinen Rausch ~:** sleep it off

**aus|pfeifen** *unr. tr. V.* **jmdn./etw. ~:** give sb./sth. the bird

**aus|pflanzen** *tr. V.* plant out

**Auspizium** /aus'pi:tsi̯ʊm/ *das;* **~s, Auspizien;** (*geh.*) auspice; **unter jmds. Auspizien** (*Dat.*) under sb.'s auspices

**aus|plaudern** *tr. V.* let out; blab

**aus|plündern** *tr. V.* **A** (*ausrauben*) **jmdn./etw. ~:** rob sb./sth. [of everything]; **B** (*völlig plündern, auch fig.*) plunder

**aus|polstern** *tr. V.* pad; pad ‹jacket, coat, etc.› [out]; **gut ausgepolstert sein** (*fig. scherzh.*) be well upholstered (*joc.*)

**aus|posaunen** *tr. V.* (*ugs. abwertend*) tell the whole world about (*fig.*)

**aus|powern** /-po:vɐn/ *tr. V.* (*ugs. abwertend*) bleed ‹organization, country, nation› dry *or* white; exploit ‹workers, masses›; (*fig.*) impoverish ‹soil, fields, market›

**aus|prägen** ❶ *refl. V.* **A** (*offenbar werden*) show itself; ‹contradiction› manifest itself; **B** (*sich herausbilden*) develop; ‹peculiarity› become more pronounced; ⇒ *auch* **ausgeprägt** 2. ❷ *tr. V.* (*prägen*) mint (**zu** into)

**Aus·prägung** *die* **A** (*das Prägen*) minting; **B** (*charakteristische Form*) form; **C** (*das Sichherausbilden*) development [in a more pronounced form]; (*der Persönlichkeit*) moulding

**aus|pressen** *tr. V.* press *or* squeeze out ‹juice›; squeeze ‹orange, lemon›; (*mit einer Presse*) press the juice from ‹grapes etc.›; press out ‹juice, oil›; (*fig.: ausbeuten*) squeeze ‹country, population, etc.› [dry]; (*fig.: ausfragen*) grill; (*aus Neugier*) pump; ⇒ *auch* **Zitrone**

**aus|probieren** *tr. V.* try out

**Aus·puff** *der* exhaust

**Auspuff-: ~gase** *Pl.* exhaust fumes *pl.*; **~rohr** *das* exhaust pipe; **~topf** *der* silencer (*Brit.*); muffler (*Amer.*)

**aus|pumpen** *tr. V.* pump out; ⇒ *auch* **ausgepumpt** 2

**aus|punkten** *tr. V.* (*Boxen*) outpoint; beat on points; (*fig.*) outdo

**aus|pusten** *tr. V.* (*ugs.*) blow out; blow ‹egg›

**aus|putzen** ❶ *tr. V.* **A** (*auslichten, beschneiden*) prune; **B** (*bes. südd.: reinigen*) clean out; **C** (*veralt.: schmücken*) deck out. ❷ *itr. V.* (*Fußball*) play as sweeper

**Aus·putzer** *der;* **~s, ~, Aus·putzerin** *die;* **~, ~nen** (*Fußball*) sweeper

**aus|quartieren** *tr. V.* move out; billet out ‹troops›

**aus|quatschen** (*salopp*) ❶ *tr. V.* let out; blab; **alles ~:** spill the beans (*coll.*). ❷ *refl. V.* **sich mit jmdm. ~:** have a really *or* (*Amer.*) real good chat with sb.; (*sich aussprechen*) have a heart-to-heart with sb. (*coll.*)

**aus|quetschen** *tr. V.* **A** squeeze out; squeeze ‹orange, lemon, etc.›; **B** (*ugs.: ausfragen*) grill; (*aus Neugier*) pump; ⇒ *auch* **Zitrone**

**aus|radieren** *tr. V.* rub out; erase; (*fig.*) annihilate, wipe out ‹village, city, etc.›; liquidate ‹person›

**aus|rangieren** *tr. V.* (*ugs.*) throw out; discard; scrap ‹vehicle, machine›; **ausrangierte Fahrzeuge** scrap vehicles

**aus|rasieren** *tr. V.* shave ‹neck, leg, etc.›; shave off ‹hair›; **jmdm./sich die Haare im Nacken/den Nacken ~:** shave sb.'s/one's neck

**aus|rasten**[1] *itr. V.; mit sein* (*Technik*) disengage; **er rastete aus, es rastete bei ihm aus** (*fig. salopp*) something snapped in him

**aus|rasten**[2] *itr., refl. V.* (*südd., österr.*) have a decent *or* good rest

**aus|rauben** *tr. V.* rob

**aus|räubern** *tr. V.* raid; rob; (*scherzh.: plündern*) raid; **jmdn. ~:** rob sb. [of everything]; (*fig.*) clean sb. out

**aus|räuchern** *tr. V.* (*auch fig.*) smoke out; fumigate ‹room›

**aus|raufen** *tr. V.* pull *or* tear out; **ich könnte mir die Haare ~** (*fig.*) I could kick myself

**aus|räumen** ❶ *tr. V.* **A** (*herausnehmen*) clear out (**aus** of); clear *or* move out ‹furniture› (**aus** of); **B** (*leer räumen*) clear out; **C** (*beseitigen*) clear up; dispel ‹prejudice, suspicion, misgivings›; **D** (*ugs.: ausrauben*) clear out (*coll.*); **E** (*Med.*) remove; (*mit der Kürette*) curette. ❷ *itr. V.* clear everything out

**aus|rechnen** ❶ *tr. V.* **A** (*lösen*) work out; **B** (*errechnen*) work out; calculate. ❷ *refl. V.* **das kannst du dir leicht ~** (*ugs.*) you can easily work that out [for yourself]; **sich** (*Dat.*) **Vorteile/gute Chancen ~:** reckon that one has advantages/good prospects; ⇒ *auch* **ausgerechnet** 2

**Aus·rede** *die* excuse

**aus|reden** ❶ *itr. V.* (*zu Ende reden*) finish [speaking]. ❷ *tr. V.* **jmdm. etw. ~:** talk sb. out of sth.; **sie versuchten, ihm das Mädchen auszureden** (*ugs.*) they tried to persuade him to give up the girl. ❸ *refl. V.* (*südd., österr.*) ⇒ **aussprechen** 2 C

**aus|regnen** *itr., refl. V.* (*unpers.*) stop raining

**aus|reiben** *unr. tr. V.* **A** (*entfernen aus*) rub out ‹stain etc.›; **B** (*reinigen*) rub ‹pot, pan, etc.› clean; wipe out ‹glasses›; **sich** (*Dat.*) **die Augen ~:** rub one's eyes; **C** (*österr.: scheuern*) scrub

**aus|reichen** *itr. V.* **A** (*genügen*) be enough *or* sufficient (**zu** for); **die Zeit/der Platz reicht [nicht] aus** there's [not] enough *or* sufficient time/space; **B** (*ugs.: auskommen*) get by (*coll.*), manage (**mit** on)

**ausreichend** ❶ *Adj.* sufficient; enough; (*als Note*) fair. ❷ *adv.* sufficiently; **etw. ~ begründen/erklären** give an adequate justification for/explanation of sth.

**aus|reifen** *itr. V.; mit sein* ‹fruit, cereal, etc.› ripen fully; ‹cheese, wine, etc.› mature fully; (*fig.*) mature [fully]

**Aus·reise** *die:* **jmdm. die ~ verweigern** refuse sb. permission to leave [the/a country]; **vor/bei der ~:** before/when leaving the country

**Ausreise-: ~erlaubnis** *die,* **~genehmigung** *die* exit permit

**aus|reisen** *itr. V.; mit sein* leave [the country]; **aus einem Land/nach Österreich** *usw.* **~:** leave a country/go to Austria *etc.*

**ausreise·willig** *Adj.* wanting to leave the country *postpos.*

**aus|reißen** ❶ *unr. tr. V.* tear out; pull out ‹plants, weeds›; **jmdm. die Haare ~:** tear sb.'s hair out; **einer Fliege** (*Dat.*) **die Beine/Flügel ~:** pull a fly's legs/wings off. ❷ *unr. itr. V.; mit sein* **A** (*sich lösen*) ‹sleeve› come off *or* away; ‹button, handle› come off; (*einreißen*) ‹buttonhole› tear; ‹seam› split, pull apart; **B** (*ugs.: weglaufen*) run away (*Dat.* from); **von zu Hause ~:** run away from home; **C** (*Sport: Vorsprung gewinnen*) break away (*Dat.* from)

**Aus·reißer** *der* **A** (*ugs.*) runaway; **B** (*Statistik*) outlier; **C** (*Sport: Läufer/Radfahrer*) runner/rider breaking away from the field; **D** (*Schießsport*) stray bullet

**Ausreißerin** *die;* **~, ~nen** ⇒ **Ausreißer** A, C

**aus|reiten** ❶ *unr. itr. V.; mit sein* **A** (*wegreiten*) ride out (**aus** of); **B** (*einen Ausritt machen*) go for a ride; go riding. ❷ *unr. tr. V.* (*Reitsport*) **A** (*bewegen*) exercise; **B** (*die Höchstleistung abfordern*) **ein Pferd ~:** ride a horse to its limit

**aus|reizen** *tr. V.* (*Kartenspiel*) **seine Karten ~:** bid the full value of one's cards

**aus|renken** *tr. V.* dislocate; **jmdm./sich den Arm ~:** dislocate sb.'s/one's arm; **sich [nach jmdm.] den Hals ~** (*ugs.*) crane one's neck [to look for sb.]

a

**aus|richten** ❶ *tr. V.* Ⓐ (*übermitteln*) **jmdm. etw. ~:** tell sb. sth.; **ich werde es ~:** I'll pass the message on; **kann ich ihm etwas ~?** can I give him a message?; **richte ihr einen Gruß [von mir] aus** give her my regards; **jmdm. ~, dass ...** tell sb. that ...; Ⓑ (*einheitlich anordnen*) line up; **etw./sich in einer Linie ~:** line sth. up/line up; Ⓒ (*Technik: in eine bestimmte Lage bringen*) align, line up (**auf** + *Akk.* with); Ⓓ (*fig.*) **etw. auf jmdn./etw. ~:** orientate sth. towards sb./sth.; **sein ganzes Denken und Handeln auf etw.** (*Akk.*) **~:** direct all one's thoughts and energies towards sth.; **etw. nach** *od.* **an jmdm./etw. ~:** gear sth. to sb./sth.; **seine Entscheidung an den Bedürfnissen der Menschen ~:** make one's decision to fit in with people's needs; **reformerisch/kommunistisch ausgerichtet sein** be oriented towards reform/be communist in one's/its orientations; Ⓔ (*erwirken*) accomplish; achieve; **bei jmdm. wenig/nichts ~ können** not be able to get very far/anywhere with sb.; **gegen jmdn./etw. etwas ~ können** be able to do something against sb./sth.; **gegen ihn wirst du nichts ~ können** you won't be able to do anything about him; Ⓕ (*veranstalten*) organize; **jmdm. die Hochzeit ~:** make the arrangements for sb.'s wedding; Ⓖ (*schweiz.: zahlen*) pay (**an** + *Akk.* to); make ‹payment›. ❷ *refl. V.* Ⓐ (*Milit.*) dress ranks; **sich nach seinem Vorder-/Hinter-/Nebenmann ~:** line [oneself] up with the person in front/behind/next to one; Ⓑ **sich an einem Vorbild ~:** follow an example

**Aus·richtung** *die* Ⓐ (*Technik: das Ausrichten*) alignment; Ⓑ (*Orientierung*) orientation (**auf** + *Akk.* towards); (*an Bedürfnissen, Interessen*) gearing (**an** + *Dat.*, **nach** to); Ⓒ (*Veranstaltung*) organization; **die ~ einer Hochzeit** making the arrangements for a wedding; Ⓓ (*schweiz.: Zahlung*) payment

**aus|ringen** *unr. tr. V.* (*bes. ostmitteld.*) ⇒ **auswringen**

**aus|rinnen** *unr. itr. V.; mit sein* (*bes. südd., österr.*) Ⓐ (*herausfließen*) run out; Ⓑ (*leer werden*) empty

**Aus·ritt** *der* Ⓐ (*das Ausreiten*) riding out; Ⓑ (*Spazierritt*) ride [out]

**aus|roden** *tr. V.* root *or* grub up ‹tree, bush›; clear ‹forest›

**aus|rollen** ❶ *tr. V.* roll out. ❷ *itr. V.; mit sein* roll to a stop

**aus|rotten** *tr. V.* eradicate ‹weeds, vermin, etc.›; (*fig.*) wipe out ‹family, enemy, etc.›; eradicate, stamp out ‹superstition, idea, evil, etc.›; eliminate ‹error›

**aus|rücken** ❶ *itr. V.; mit sein* Ⓐ (*bes. Milit.: in den Einsatz gehen*) move out; ‹fire brigade, police› turn out; Ⓑ (*ugs.: weglaufen*) make off; **seinen Bewachern ~:** give one's guards the slip; **von zu Hause ~:** run away from home. ❷ *tr. V.* Ⓐ (*Druckw.*) **etw. [nach links/rechts] ~:** set sth. out to the left/right; Ⓑ (*Technik: auskuppeln*) disengage

**Aus·ruf** *der* cry

**aus|rufen** *unr. tr. V.* Ⓐ (*äußern*) call out; **„Schön!", rief er aus** 'Lovely', he exclaimed; **jmdn.** *od.* **jmds. Namen ~ lassen** have a call put out for sb.; (*im Hotel*) have sb. paged; **die Haltestellen ~:** call out [the names of] the stops; Ⓑ (*offiziell verkünden*) proclaim; declare ‹state of emergency›; call ‹strike›; **jmdn. zum König/als Präsidenten ~:** proclaim sb. king/president; Ⓒ (*zum Kauf anbieten*) **seine Waren ~:** cry one's wares

**Ausrufe-: ~satz** *der* (*Sprachw.*) exclamation; exclamatory clause; **~wort** *das; Pl.* **~wörter** (*Sprachw.*) interjection; **~zeichen** *das* exclamation mark

**Ausrufung** *die; ~, ~en* ⇒ **ausrufen** B: proclamation; declaration; calling; **nach seiner ~ zum König/Präsidenten** after he had been proclaimed king/president

**Ausrufungs·zeichen** *das* (*österr., schweiz.*) exclamation mark

**aus|ruhen** ❶ *refl., itr. V.* (*sich erholen*) have a rest; **[sich] ein wenig/richtig ~:** rest a little/have a proper *or* good rest; **ausgeruht sein** be rested; ⇒ *auch* **Lorbeer** C. ❷ *tr. V.* (*ruhen lassen*) rest

**aus|rupfen** *tr. V.* pluck out ‹feathers, hair›; pull up ‹grass, weeds, flowers›

**aus|rüsten** *tr. V.* Ⓐ equip; equip, fit out ‹ship›; **ein Auto mit Sicherheitsgurten ~:** fit safety belts to a car; fit a car with safety belts; Ⓑ (*Textilw.: veredeln*) finish

**Aus·rüstung** *die* Ⓐ (*das Ausrüsten*) equipping; (*von Schiffen*) equipping; fitting out; **die ~ des Autos mit Gurten** *usw.* the fitting of belts *etc.* to the car; Ⓑ (*Ausrüstungsgegenstände, technische Einrichtung*) equipment *no pl.*; **eine neue ~:** a new set of equipment; **technische ~en** technical equipment *sing.*; Ⓒ (*Textilw.*) finishing

**Ausrüstungs·gegenstand** *der* item of equipment

**aus|rutschen** *itr. V.; mit sein* slip; (*fig.*) put one's foot in it; **jmdm. rutscht das Beil/die Feder aus** sb.'s axe/pen slips

**Ausrutscher** *der; ~s, ~* Ⓐ (*ugs., auch fig.*) slip; Ⓑ (*Sport: Niederlage*) surprise defeat

**Aus·saat** *die* Ⓐ sowing; **mit der ~ beginnen** begin sowing; Ⓑ (*Saatgut*) seed

**aus|säen** *tr.* (*auch itr.*) *V.* (*auch fig.*) sow

**Aus·sage** *die* Ⓐ (*Feststellung*) statement; stated view; **nach ~ von Experten** according to what the experts say; Ⓑ (*vor Gericht, bei der Polizei*) statement; **eine ~ machen** make a statement; give evidence; **die ~ verweigern** refuse to make a statement; (*vor Gericht*) refuse to give evidence; **~ steht gegen ~:** it's one person's word against another's; Ⓒ (*geistiger Gehalt*) message; **dem Gemälde fehlt jede ~:** the painting conveys nothing

**Aussage·kraft** *die* meaningfulness; (*Ausdruckskraft*) expressiveness

**aussage·kräftig** *Adj.* meaningful; (*ausdruckskräftig*) expressive

**aus|sagen** ❶ *tr. V.* Ⓐ (*zum Ausdruck bringen*) say; **damit wird ausgesagt, dass ...** this expresses the idea that ...; Ⓑ (*eine bestimmte Aussagekraft haben*) ‹picture, novel, etc.› express; Ⓒ (*vor Gericht, vor der Polizei*) **~, dass ...** state that ...; (*unter Eid*) testify that ... ❷ *itr. V.* make a statement; (*unter Eid*) testify

**aus|sägen** *tr. V.* saw out

**Aussage-: ~satz** *der* (*Sprachw.*) affirmative clause; **~verweigerung** *die* (*Rechtsw.*) refusal to give evidence

**Aus·satz** *der* ▶474 (*Med. veralt., fig.*) leprosy

**aussätzig** *Adj.* (*Med. veralt., fig.*) leprous

**Aussätzige** *der/die; adj. Dekl.* (*Med. veralt., fig.*) leper

**aus|saufen** *unr. tr.* (*auch itr.*) *V.* Ⓐ ‹animal› drink [up] ‹water etc.› (**aus** out of); empty ‹trough etc.›; Ⓑ (*derb*) **den ganzen Schnaps/eine halbe Flasche [Schnaps] ~:** drink all the schnapps/half a bottle [of schnapps]; **ein Glas Bier in einem Zuge ~:** down a glass of beer in one (*sl.*)

**aus|saugen** *regelm.* (*geh. auch unr.*) *tr. V.* Ⓐ suck out (**aus** of); (*leer saugen*) suck dry; **eine Wunde/Apfelsine ~:** suck the poison out of a wound/suck the juice from an orange; Ⓑ (*fig.: ausbeuten*) **jmdn./etw. ~:** bleed sb./sth. [white]; **jmdn. bis aufs Blut** *od.* **Mark ~:** bleed sb. white

**aus|schaben** *tr. V.* Ⓐ scrape out; Ⓑ (*Med.*) remove; (*mit der Kürette*) curette

**Ausschabung** *die; ~, ~en* ⇒ **Kürettage**

**aus|schachten** *tr. V.* excavate; sink ‹well, shaft›

**Ausschachtung** *die; ~, ~en* Ⓐ (*das Ausschachten*) excavation; (*eines Brunnens, Schachtes*) sinking; Ⓑ (*Grube, Schacht usw.*) excavation

**aus|schälen** *tr. V.* (*auch Med.*) remove (**aus** from)

**aus|schalten** *tr. V.* Ⓐ (*abstellen*) switch *or* turn off; Ⓑ (*ausschließen*) eliminate; exclude ‹emotion, influence›; dismiss ‹doubt, objection›; shut out ‹feeling, thought›

**Aus·schaltung** *die* Ⓐ (*das Abstellen*) switching *or* turning off; **bei ~ des Geräts** when switching *or* turning off the apparatus; Ⓑ (*Eliminierung*) ⇒ **ausschalten** B: elimination; exclusion; dismissal

**Aus·schank** *der; ~[e]s,* **Ausschänke** /ˈausʃɛŋkə/ Ⓐ serving; **„Heute kein ~"** 'closed today'; **„Kein ~ an Jugendliche unter 16 Jahren"** 'persons under sixteen will not be served with alcoholic drinks'; Ⓑ (*Schanktisch*) bar; counter; Ⓒ (*Gaststätte*) bar; pub (*Brit.*); bar (*Amer.*)

**Aus·schau** *in* **nach jmdm./etw. ~ halten** look out for *or* keep a lookout for sb./sth.

**aus|schauen** *itr. V.* Ⓐ (*Ausschau halten*) **nach jmdm./etw. ~** (*auch fig.*) look out for *or* keep a lookout for sb./sth.; Ⓑ (*südd., österr.*) ⇒ **aussehen**

**aus|schaufeln** *tr. V.* dig out ‹earth, rubble, buried person›; dig ‹trench, grave, hole, etc.›

**Ausscheid** *der; ~[e]s, ~e* (*bes. DDR Sport*) qualifier

**aus|scheiden** ❶ *unr. itr. V.; mit sein* Ⓐ (*eine Gemeinschaft verlassen*) **aus etw. ~:** leave sth.; **aus dem Amt ~:** leave office; Ⓑ (*Sport*) be eliminated; (*wegen Defekt, Verletzung*) retire; Ⓒ (*nicht in Betracht kommen*) **diese Möglichkeit/dieser Kandidat scheidet aus** this possibility/candidate has to be ruled out. ❷ *unr. tr. V.* Ⓐ (*absondern*) (*Physiol.*) excrete ‹waste›; eliminate, expel ‹poison›; exude ‹sweat›; (*Chem.*) precipitate; Ⓑ (*aussondern*) eliminate; rule out ‹proposal, possibility›

**Aus·scheidung** *die* Ⓐ ⇒ **ausscheiden** 2 A: excretion; elimination; expulsion; exudation; precipitation; Ⓑ *Pl.* (*Physiol.*) excreta; Ⓒ (*Sport*) qualifier

**Ausscheidungs-: ~kampf** *der* (*Sport*) qualifier; **~organ** *das* (*Physiol.*) excretory organ; **~runde** *die* (*Sport*) qualifying round; **~spiel** *das* (*Sport*) qualifying game *or* match

**aus|schelten** *unr. tr. V.* scold

**aus|schenken** ❶ *tr. V.* Ⓐ (*servieren*) serve ‹alcohol, drink›; Ⓑ (*eingießen*) pour out; (*verteilen*) serve. ❷ *itr. V.* serve drinks

**aus|scheren** *itr. V.; mit sein* Ⓐ (*eine Gruppe, Reihe usw. verlassen*) ‹car, driver› pull out; ‹ship› break out of [the] line; ‹aircraft› peel off, break formation; (*fig.*) (*aus einer Organisation*) pull out (**aus** of); Ⓑ (*aus der Spur geraten*) skid

**aus|schicken** *tr. V.* send out

**aus|schießen** *unr. tr. V.* Ⓐ **jmdm. ein Auge ~:** shoot sb.'s eye out; Ⓑ (*Druckw.*) impose; Ⓒ (*Schießsport*) hold ‹competition›; shoot for ‹prize›; **den besten Schützen ~:** hold a competition to find the best marksman; **die Sache ~** (*salopp*) ‹cowboys etc.› shoot it out (*coll.*)

**aus|schiffen** *tr. V.* disembark ‹passengers›; unload ‹cargo›

**aus|schildern** *tr. V.* signpost

**aus|schimpfen** *tr. V.* **jmdn. ~:** give sb. a telling-off; tell sb. off

**aus|schlachten** *tr. V.* Ⓐ (*ugs.: brauchbare Teile ausbauen aus*) cannibalize ‹machine, vehicle›; break ‹vehicle› for spares; Ⓑ (*ugs. abwertend: ausnutzen*) exploit; **etw. politisch ~:** make political capital out of sth.; Ⓒ eviscerate ‹animal›

**aus|schlafen** ❶ *unr. itr., refl. V.* have a good *or* proper sleep; **[hast du jetzt] ausgeschlafen?** have you had a long enough sleep?; **ich hatte** *od.* **war nicht ausgeschlafen** I hadn't had enough sleep. ❷ *unr. tr. V.* **seinen Rausch ~:** sleep off the effects of alcohol

**Aus·schlag** *der* Ⓐ (*Haut~*) rash; **[einen] ~ bekommen** break out *or* come out in a rash; Ⓑ (*Abweichung*) (*einer Magnetnadel, Waage*) deflection; (*eines Pendels*) swing; **den ~ geben** (*fig.*) turn *or* tip the scales (*fig.*); **das gab den ~ für seine Entscheidung** that was the crucial factor in his decision; that decided him

**aus|schlagen** ❶ *unr. tr. V.* Ⓐ (*herausschlagen*) knock out; **jmdm. einen Zahn ~:**

*old spelling (see note on page 1707)

knock one of sb.'s teeth out; **B** *(ablehnen)* turn down; reject; refuse ‹inheritance›; **C** *(löschen)* beat out ‹fire›; **D** *(auskleiden)* line ‹room, walls›; **E** *(Handw.: breit schlagen)* beat out.
❷ *unr. itr. V.* **A** *(stoßen)* ‹horse› kick; **B** *auch mit sein (schwingen)* ‹needle, pointer› be deflected, swing; ‹divining rod› dip; ‹scales› turn; ‹pendulum› swing; **C** *auch mit sein (sprießen)* come out [in bud]; **D** *(zu Ende schlagen)* **ausgeschlagen haben** ‹clock› have stopped striking; *(fig. geh.)* ‹heart› have stopped [beating]; **E** *mit sein (sich entwickeln)* turn out; **zu jmds. Nachteil ~:** turn out to sb.'s disadvantage

**ausschlag·gebend** *Adj.* decisive; **das war ~ für seine Entscheidung** that was the crucial factor in his decision; that decided him

**aus|schlecken** ⇒ **auslecken**

**aus|schließen** *unr. tr. V.* **A** *(aus einer Gemeinschaft entfernen)* expel **(aus** from); **B** *(nicht teilnehmen lassen)* exclude **(aus** from); **er schließt sich von allem aus** he won't join in anything; **C** *(ausnehmen)* exclude; exclude, rule out ‹possibility›; **die zwei Behauptungen schließen einander aus** the two statements are mutually exclusive; **D** *(unmöglich machen)* **jedes Missverständnis/jeden Irrtum** *usw.* **~:** rule out all possibility of misunderstanding/error *etc.*; **es ist nicht auszuschließen, dass ...** one cannot rule out the possibility that ...; **E** *(aussperren)* lock out; **F** *(Druckw.)* justify; ⇒ *auch* **ausgeschlossen 2**

**aus·schließlich** /*od.* '-'--, -'--/ ❶ *Adj.* *(alleinig)* exclusive; exclusive, sole ‹concern, right›. ❷ *Adv.* *(nur)* exclusively; **das ist ~ sein Verdienst** the credit is his alone. ❸ *Präp. mit Gen.* *(ohne, außer)* excluding; exclusive of; **der Preis versteht sich ~ Porto** the price does not include postage

**Ausschließlichkeit** /*od.* '-'---/ *die;* **~:** exclusiveness; **er widmet sich seinem Beruf mit einer ~, die ...** he devotes himself to his job with a single-mindedness which ...

**Aus·schlupf** *der* way out; *(Möglichkeit zum Entkommen)* means of escape

**aus|schlüpfen** *itr. V.; mit sein* hatch [out]; ‹butterfly› emerge

**aus|schlürfen** *tr. V.* sip ‹drink› noisily; suck ‹oyster, egg›; **sein Glas/seine Tasse ~:** empty one's glass/cup noisily

**Aus·schluss, *Aus·schluß** *der* **A** *(das Ausschließen)* exclusion **(von** from); *(aus einer Gemeinschaft)* expulsion **(aus** from); *(aus einem Wettbewerb)* disqualification **(aus** from); **unter ~ der Öffentlichkeit** with the public excluded; *(Rechtsw.)* in camera; **B** *(Druckw.)* spaces *pl.*; spacing material

**aus|schmücken** *tr. V.* decorate; deck out; *(fig.)* embellish ‹story, incident, report, etc.›

**Ausschmückung** *die;* **~, ~en** **A** ⇒ **ausschmücken:** decoration; decking out; embellishment; **B** *(etw. Ausschmückendes)* decoration; *(erfundene Einzelheit)* embellishment

**aus|schnaufen** *(österr., südd. ugs.)* ⇒ **verschnaufen**

**aus|schneiden** *unr. tr. V.* **A** *(herausschneiden)* cut out; **B** prune ‹tree›; **einen Apfel ~:** cut the rotten parts out of an apple; ⇒ *auch* **ausgeschnitten 2**

**Aus·schnitt** *der* **A** *(Zeitungs~)* cutting; clipping; **B** *(Hals~)* neck; **ein tiefer ~:** a plunging neckline; **er versuchte, ihr in den ~ zu gucken** he tried to look down the front of her dress; **C** *(Teil, Auszug)* part; *(eines Textes)* excerpt; *(eines Films)* clip; excerpt; *(Bild~)* detail; **etw. in ~en lesen/kennen lernen** read/show/get to know parts of sth.; **D** *(Kreis~)* sector; **E** *(Loch)* [cut-out] opening

**ausschnitt·weise** ❶ *Adj.* **die ~ Lektüre ist unbefriedigend** reading extracts is unsatisfactory; **die ~ Wiedergabe einer Rede/Vorführung eines Films** the reporting of parts of a speech/showing clips from a film. ❷ *adv.* **etw. ~ zitieren/abdrucken** quote/print extracts from sth.; **einen Film ~ zeigen** show clips from a film

**aus|schnitzen** *tr. V.* **etw. ~:** carve sth. out

**aus|schöpfen** *tr. V.* **A** *(herausschöpfen)* scoop out **(aus** from); *(mit dem Schöpflöffel)* ladle out **(aus** of); **Wasser aus einem Boot ~:** bale water out of a boat; **B** *(leeren)* bale ‹boat› out; **C** *(voll ausnutzen)* exhaust; **alle Lebensgenüsse voll ~:** enjoy to the full all the pleasures life has to offer

**aus|schrauben** *tr. V.* screw out **(aus** of)

**aus|schreiben** *unr. tr. V.* **A** *(nicht abgekürzt schreiben)* **etw. ~:** write sth. out in full; **einen Betrag ~:** write an amount out in words; **B** *(ausstellen)* write *or* make out ‹cheque, invoice, receipt›; **C** *(bekannt geben)* announce, call ‹election, meeting›; impose ‹tax›; advertise ‹flat, job›; put ‹supply order etc.› out to tender

**Aus·schreibung** *die* **A** ⇒ **ausschreiben C:** announcement; calling; imposition; advertisement; **die ~ von Lieferungen** the invitation of tenders for supplies; **B** *(Text)* announcement; *(bei Wahlen)* election notice; *(Steuerw.)* schedule; *(Anzeige, Inserat)* advertisement; *(Angebotseinholung)* invitation to tender

**aus|schreien** ❶ *unr. tr. V.:* ⇒ **ausrufen C.** ❷ *unr. refl. V.* **sich** *(Dat.)* **die Kehle** *od.* **die Lunge ~:** shout *or* yell one's head off

**aus|schreiten** *(geh.)* ❶ *unr. itr. V.; mit sein* step out. ❷ *unr. tr. V.* **eine Strecke ~:** pace out a distance

**Ausschreitung** *die;* **~, ~en** **A** *(Gewalttätigkeit)* act of violence; **es kam zu ~en** violence broke out; **B** *(veralt.: Ausschweifung)* excess

**aus|schulen** *tr. V.* **ausgeschult werden** leave school

**Aus·schulung** *die:* **nach der ~:** after leaving school

**Aus·schuss, *Aus·schuß** *der* **A** *(Kommission)* committee; **B** *(Waren)* rejects *pl.*

**Ausschuss-, *Ausschuß-:** **~mitglied** *das* committee member; **~quote** *die* reject rate; **~sitzung** *die* committee meeting; **~ware** *die* rejects *pl.*

**aus|schütteln** *tr. V.* shake ‹dust, tablecloth, etc.› out

**aus|schütten** *tr. V.* **A** tip out ‹water, sand, coal, etc.›; *(ausleeren)* empty ‹bucket, bowl, container›; *(verschütten)* spill; **jmdm. seinen Kummer ~** *(fig.)* recount one's woes *pl.* to sb.; **sich vor Lachen ~ [wollen]** *(ugs.)* split one's sides laughing; die laughing *(coll.)*; ⇒ *auch* **Herz B**; **B** *(auszahlen)* distribute ‹dividends, prizes, etc.›

**Ausschüttung** *die;* **~, ~en** **A** distribution; **B** *(Börsenw.)* dividend [paid]

**aus|schwärmen** *itr. V.; mit sein (auch fig.)* swarm out; ‹soldiers› deploy; *(fächerartig)* fan out

**aus|schwefeln** *tr. V.* **A** *(desinfizieren)* sulphur; fumigate with sulphur; **B** *(entfernen)* smoke out ‹insects, vermin› with sulphur

**aus|schweifen** *itr. V.; mit sein* **A** ‹imagination› run riot; **B** *(in seiner Lebensweise)* indulge in excess

**ausschweifend** ❶ *Adj.* wild ‹imagination, emotion, hope, desire, orgy›; extravagant ‹idea›; exaggerated ‹account, portrayal›; riotous, wild ‹enjoyment›; dissolute, dissipated ‹life›; dissolute ‹person›. ❷ *adv.* **~ leben** lead a dissolute life

**Ausschweifung** *die;* **~, ~en** *(im Genießen)* dissolution; dissipation; **nächtliche ~en** nightly excesses; *(stärker)* nightly orgies

**aus|schweigen** *unr. refl. V.* remain silent

**aus|schwemmen** *tr. V.* **A** wash out; wash *or* flush out ‹impurities, poisons›; **B** *(aushöhlen)* erode ‹rock›; erode, wash away ‹beach, river bank›

**aus|schwenken** ❶ *tr. V.* **A** *(nach außen schwenken)* swing out; **B** *(reinigen)* rinse out. ❷ *itr. V.; mit sein* ‹lorry, tram› swing out; *(Milit.)* ‹rearguard etc.› wheel; **nach rechts/links ~!** left-wheel/right-wheel!

**aus|schwitzen** *tr. V.* **A** *(ausscheiden)* sweat out; **eine Erkältung ~** *(fig.)* sweat out a cold; **B** *(aussondern)* ‹wall, stone, etc.› sweat ‹moisture etc.›; ‹tree, plant› exude ‹sap etc.›; **C** *(Kochk.)* sweat ‹onion, flour›

**aus|segnen** *tr. V.* *(christl. Kirchen)* give the last blessing to ‹dead person›

**aus|sehen** *unr. itr. V.* look **(wie** like); **gut ~:** look good; *(gesund)* look well; *(schön)* be good-looking; **gut ~d** good-looking; **zum Fürchten ~:** look terrifying; **es sieht nach Regen aus** it looks like rain; **nach etwas/nichts ~** *(ugs.)* look something special/not look anything special; **wie sieht ein Okapi aus?** what does an okapi look like?; **wie siehts aus, kannst du mitkommen?** *(ugs.)* how are you fixed, can you come with us? *(coll.)*; **na, wie siehts aus, wie weit seid ihr?** *(ugs.)* how is it going, how far have you got *(Brit.) or (Amer.)* are you?; **wie sieht der denn aus?!** what does he look like!; just look at him!; **ich habe [vielleicht] ausgesehen!** I looked a real sight!; **es sieht danach** *od.* **so aus, als ob ...** it looks as if ...; **Erfolgreicher junger Unternehmer! Der sieht [mir] gerade danach aus!** *(iron.)* A successful young executive! I bet!; **sehe ich so** *od.* **danach aus?** *(ugs.)* what do you take me for?; **so siehst du aus!** *(ugs.)* you've got another think coming *(coll.)*; that's what you think!; **es sieht [nicht] gut mit ihm/damit aus** things [don't] look good for him/on that front; ⇒ *auch* **danach D**

**Aussehen** *das;* **~s** appearance; **dem ~ nach** going *or* judging by appearances; **etw. nach dem ~ beurteilen** judge sth. by appearances

***aus|sein** ⇒ **aus 2**

**außen** /'ausn/ *Adv.* **A** outside; **die Vase ist ~ bemalt** the vase is painted on the outside; **~ an der Windschutzscheibe** on the outside of the windscreen; **nach ~ hin** on the outside; outwardly; **das Fenster geht nach ~ auf** the window opens outwards; **von dem Skandal darf nichts nach ~ dringen** *(fig.)* nothing must get out about the scandal; **er ist nur auf Wirkung nach ~ [hin] bedacht** *(fig.)* he is only concerned with [outward] effect; **von ~:** from the outside; **Hilfe von ~ nötig haben** *(fig.)* need outside help; **er läuft/spielt ~** *(Sport)* he's running in the outside lane/playing on the wing; **~ vor bleiben** *(ugs.)* be ignored; **jmdn./etw. ~ vor lassen** *(ugs.)* ignore sb./sth.; **~ vor lassen, dass ...** *(ugs.)* ignore the fact that ...; **B** *(österr.: [hier] draußen)* outside; out here; **hier ~:** out here

**Außen** *der;* **~, ~** *(Sport)* wing; winger

**Außen-:** **~ansicht** *die* exterior view; **~antenne** *die* outdoor aerial; **~arbeiten** *Pl.* outside work; **~aufnahme** *die (Film)* exterior [shot]; location shot; **~bahn** *die (Sport)* outside lane; **~bezirk** *der* outlying district

**Außenborder** /-bɔrdɐ/ *der;* **~s, ~** *(ugs.: Motor, Boot)* outboard

**Außenbord·motor** *der* outboard motor

**außenbords** *Adv.* *(Seemannsspr.)* outboard; **das Schiff muss ~ gestrichen werden** the hull of the ship must be painted

**aus|senden** *unr. (auch regelm.) tr. V.* **A** *(wegschicken)* send out; **B** *(ausstrahlen)* send out, emit ‹rays, light, etc.›; transmit ‹news, radio programme, etc.›

**außen-, Außen-:** **~dienst** *der:* **im ~dienst sein** *od.* **arbeiten, ~dienst machen** *od.* **haben** be working out of the office; ‹salesman› be on the road; **~durchmesser** *der* external diameter; **~fläche** *die* outer surface; *(der Hand)* back [of the hand]; **~geleitet** *Adj.* *(Soziol.)* other-directed; **~handel** *der* foreign trade *no art.*; **~handels·bilanz** *die* balance of trade; **~haut** *die* [outer] skin; *(aus Metallplatten)* shell plating; **~kurve** *die* outside bend; **~läufer** *der*, **~läuferin** *die (Ballspiele)* wing half; **~linie** *die (Ballspiele)* touchline; **~minister** *der*, **~ministerin** *die* ▶ **159** Foreign Minister; Foreign Secretary *(Brit.)*; Secretary of State *(Amer.)*; **~ministerium** *das* Foreign Ministry; Foreign and Commonwealth Office *(Brit.)*; Foreign Office *(Brit. coll.)*; State Department *(Amer.)*; **~netz** *das (Ballspiele)* outside of the net; **~pfosten** *der (Ballspiele)* outside of the

a

post; ~**politik** *die* foreign politics *sing.; (bestimmte)* foreign policy/policies *pl.;* ~**politiker** *der,* ~**politikerin** *die* politician concerned with foreign affairs; ~**politisch** ❶ *Adj.* foreign-policy *attrib.* ‹debate›; ‹question› relating to foreign policy; ‹mistake› in foreign policy; ‹reporting› of foreign affairs; ‹experience› in foreign affairs; ‹speaker, expert› on foreign affairs; **auf ~politischem Gebiet** in foreign affairs; ❷ *adv.* as regards foreign policy; **~politisch gesehen** from the point of view of foreign policy; **~politisch unter Druck geraten** come under foreign pressure; ~**posten** *der* outpost; ~**rist** *der (bes. Fußball)* outside of the *or* one's foot; ~**rolle** *die* flick-up; ~**seite** *die* outside; *(eines Stoffes)* right side; *(fig.: eines Menschen)* exterior

**Außenseiter** *der;* ~**s**, ~, **Außenseiterin** *die;* ~, ~**nen** *(Sport, fig.)* outsider

**Außen-:** ~**spiegel** *der* exterior mirror; ~**stände** *Pl.* outstanding debts *or* accounts

**Außenstehende** *der/die; adj. Dekl.* outsider

**Außen-:** ~**stelle** *die* branch; ~**stürmer** *der,* ~**stürmerin** *die (Ballspiele)* winger; outside forward; ~**tasche** *die* outside pocket; ~**temperatur** *die* outside temperature; *(im Freien herrschende Temperatur)* outdoor temperature; **bei 15° ~temperatur** when the temperature outdoors is 15°; ~**wand** *die* external *or* outside wall; ~**welt** *die* outside world; ~**winkel** *der* exterior angle; ~**wirtschaft** *die* foreign trade and investment

**außer** /ˈausɐ/ ❶ *Präp. mit Dat.* Ⓐ *(abgesehen von)* apart from; aside from *(Amer.)*; *(ausgenommen auch)* except [for]; **alle ~ mir** all except [for] me; Ⓑ *(außerhalb von)* out of; **~ Atem** out of breath; **~ Haus[es]/Land[es] sein** be out of the house/country; **~ Landes gehen** leave the country; **~ Zweifel stehen** be beyond doubt; **~ sich sein** be beside oneself (**vor** with); Ⓒ *(zusätzlich zu)* in addition to.

❷ *Präp. mit Akk.* **etw. ~ jeden Zweifel stellen** make sth. very clear *or* clear beyond all doubt; **vor Wut/Dankbarkeit/Erleichterung ~ sich geraten** become beside oneself with rage/be overcome with gratitude/relief; ⇒ *auch* **Acht**[3]; **Betrieb** B; **Dienst** B; **Frage** C; **Gefecht** A; **Kraft** G; **Kurs** B; **Zeit** B; **Zweifel**.

❸ *Konj. (es sei denn)* except; **ich komme, ~ es regnet** I'll come unless it rains; **~ dass ...** except that ...; **~ wenn ...** except when ...; **niemand ~ ich selbst** nobody but me

**äußer...** /ˈɔysɐ.../ *Adj.* Ⓐ *(sich außen befindend)* outer ‹layer, courtyard, ring road›; outer, outside ‹wall, door›; external ‹diameter›; outside ‹pocket›; outlying ‹district, area›; external ‹injury›; **die ~e Seite** the outside; Ⓑ *(von außen kommend)* external ‹cause, force, etc.›; Ⓒ *(von außen wahrnehmbar)* outward ‹appearance, similarity, effect, etc.›; external ‹form, circumstances›; Ⓓ *(auswärtig)* foreign ; **Minister des Äußeren** ⇒ **Außenminister**

**außer-, Außer-:** ~**acht·lassung** /--ˈ---/ *die;* ~~**:** disregard; **unter ~achtlassen** *od.* **~achtlassung der Vorschriften** disregarding *or* ignoring the regulations; ~**beruflich** *Adj.* ‹interests, pressures, etc.› outside one's job; ~**dem** /*auch:* --ˈ-/ *Adv. (dazu)* as well; besides; *(überdies)* besides; anyway; **sie ist Ärztin, Politikerin und ~dem noch Mutter von drei Kindern** she is a doctor, a politician, and a mother of three children as well; ~**dienstlich** ❶ *Adj.* private; social, unofficial ‹event›; unofficial ‹commitment, activity›; ❷ *adv.* out of working hours; **mit jmdm. ~dienstlich verkehren** meet with sb. on a social basis

**Äußere** *das;* ~**n** [outward] appearance; **das ~ täuscht oft** appearances are often deceptive; **dem ~n nach zu urteilen** to judge by appearances; judging by appearances

**außer-, Außer-:** ~**ehelich** ❶ *Adj.* extramarital ‹relationship›; illegitimate ‹child, birth›; ❷ *adv.* outside marriage; **ein ~ehelich geborenes Kind** a child born out of wedlock; ~**europäisch** *Adj.* non-European; **Reisen ins ~europäische Ausland** journeys to countries outside Europe; ~**fahrplan·mäßig** /-ˈ---ˈ-/ ❶ *Adj.* unscheduled ‹train, bus›; ❷ *adv.* **dieser Zug verkehrt ~fahrplanmäßig** this train is not a scheduled one; ~**gerichtlich** *(Rechtsw.)* ❶ *Adj.* out of court *attrib.* ‹settlement, arrangement›; ‹settlement, arrangement› arrived at *or* reached out of court; ❷ *adv.* **sich ~gerichtlich einigen** arrive at *or* reach a settlement out of court; ~**gewöhnlich** ❶ *Adj.* Ⓐ *(vom Üblichen abweichend)* unusual; **dies ist ein ganz ~gewöhnlicher Fall** this case is quite out of the ordinary; this is a most unusual case; Ⓑ *(das Gewohnte übertreffend)* exceptional; ❷ *adv.* Ⓐ *(unüblich)* unusually; Ⓑ *(sehr)* exceptionally; ~**halb** ❶ *Präp. mit Gen.* outside; **~halb der Legalität** *(fig.)* outside the law; **~halb der Sprechstunde/Dienstzeit** out of *or* outside consulting hours/working hours *or* office hours; ❷ *Adv.* out of town; **~halb von Bremen wohnen** live outside Bremen; **nach/von ~halb** out of/from out of town; ~**irdisch** ❶ *Adj.* Ⓐ *(nicht auf der Erde)* ‹phenomenon, object› in space; Ⓑ *(von einem anderen Planeten)* extraterrestrial; *(fig. dichter.)* heavenly ‹beauty etc.›; ❷ *adv.* Ⓐ *(nicht auf der Erde)* ‹stationed etc.› in space; Ⓑ *(fig. dichter.: überirdisch)* **~irdisch anmutende Musik** heavenly-sounding music; ~**kirchlich** ❶ *Adj.* civil ‹wedding›; non-ecclesiastical ‹organization›; ❷ *adv.* **sie sind ~kirchlich getraut** they had a civil wedding; they had a registry-office wedding *(Brit.)*; ~**kraft·setzung** /-ˈ---/ *die* repeal; *(des Kriegsrechts)* lifting

**äußerlich** ❶ *Adj.* Ⓐ *(an der Außenseite)* external ‹use, injury›; **zur ~en Anwendung** for external use; Ⓑ *(nach außen hin)* outward ‹appearance, calm, similarity, etc.›; Ⓒ *(oberflächlich)* superficial; **einer Sache** *(Dat.)* **~ sein** *(geh.)* be extrinsic to sth. ❷ *adv.* Ⓐ *(an der Außenseite)* externally; Ⓑ *(nach außen hin)* outwardly; **~ gesehen** on the face of it

**Äußerlichkeit** *die;* ~, ~**en** Ⓐ *(äußere Form)* formality; Ⓑ *(Unwesentliches)* minor point; Ⓒ *Pl. (Aussehen)* appearances; Ⓓ *Pl. (Philos., Rel.)* externals

**äußern** ❶ *tr. V.* express, voice ‹opinion, view, criticism, reservations, disapproval, doubt›; express ‹joy, happiness, wish›; voice ‹suspicion›. ❷ *refl. V.* Ⓐ *(Stellung nehmen)* **sich über etw.** *(Akk.)* **~:** give one's view on sth.; **ich möchte mich dazu jetzt nicht ~:** I don't want to comment on that at present; **sich abfällig/begeistert über etw.** *(Akk.)* **~:** make disparaging remarks about sth./speak enthusiastically about sth.; **sich dahin gehend ~, dass ...** make a comment to the effect that ...; Ⓑ *(in Erscheinung treten)* ‹illness› manifest itself (**in** + *Dat.*, **durch** in); ‹emotion› show itself, be expressed (**in** + *Dat.* in, **durch** through)

**außer-:** ~**ordentlich** ❶ *Adj.* Ⓐ *(ungewöhnlich)* extraordinary; Ⓑ *(zusätzlich)* extraordinary ‹meeting›; special ‹court, conference›; ⇒ *auch* **Professor** A; Ⓒ *(das Gewohnte übertreffend)* exceptional; ❷ *adv. (sehr)* exceptionally; ‹value› highly; extremely ‹pleased, relieved›; **~ordentlich viel Mühe** an enormous *or* exceptional amount of trouble; ~**orts** *Adv. (schweizer., österr.)* out of town; ~**parlamentarisch** ❶ *Adj.* extra-parliamentary ‹opposition, organization, etc.›; ❷ *adv.* outside parliament; ~**plan·mäßig** *Adj.* Ⓐ unscheduled; unbudgeted ‹expenditure›; ⇒ *auch* **Professor** A; Ⓑ ⇒ **~fahrplanmäßig**; ~**schulisch** ❶ *Adj.* ‹topics, problems› unconnected with school; out-of-school *attrib.* ‹activities›; ‹interests› outside school; ❷ *adv.* outside school; ~**sprachlich** *Adj.* extra-linguistic

**äußerst** *Adv.* extremely; extremely, exceedingly ‹important›; **~ knapp gewinnen/entkommen** *usw.* only just win/escape *etc.*

**äußerst...** *Adj.* Ⓐ extreme; **mit ~er Umsicht/Behutsamkeit/Missbilligung** with extreme *or* the utmost circumspection/care/disapproval; **mit ~er Willenskraft** using all one's will power; **aufs Äußerste erschrocken/angestrengt/verwirrt** frightened in the extreme/strained to the utmost/utterly confused; **von ~er Wichtigkeit sein** be of extreme *or* the utmost importance; **im ~en Norden/Süden der Stadt/des Landes** in the northernmost/southernmost part of the town/in the far north/south of the country; Ⓑ *(letztmöglich)* latest possible, last possible ‹date, deadline›; *(höchst...)* highest ‹price›; *(niedrigst...)* lowest ‹price›; **das Äußerste wagen/versuchen** risk/try everything; **bis zum Äußersten gehen** go to the last extreme; Ⓒ *(schlimmst...)* worst; **im ~en Fall** if the worst comes/came to the worst; **auf das Äußerste gefasst sein** be prepared for the worst; ⇒ *auch* **äußer...** A

**außer·stand** /*auch:* ˈ---/, **außerstande** *Adv.* **~e sein, etw. zu tun** *(nicht befähigt)* be unable to do sth.; *(nicht in der Lage)* not be in a position to *or* not be able to do sth.; **jmdn. außerstand setzen, etw. zu tun** make it impossible for sb. to do sth.

**äußersten·falls** *Adv.* Ⓐ at most; **~ bis 19 Uhr** until 7 p.m. at the outside; Ⓑ ⇒ **schlimmstenfalls**

**außertourlich** /-tuːɐ̯lɪç/ *(österr.)* ❶ *Adj.* additional ‹bus, train›; additional, special ‹concert›. ❷ *adv.* in addition; **~ befördert werden** be promoted ahead of turn

**Äußerung** *die;* ~, ~**en** Ⓐ *(Bemerkung)* comment; remark; **eine amtliche ~:** an official comment *or* statement; Ⓑ *(Ausdruck)* expression

**aus|setzen** ❶ *tr. V.* Ⓐ *(verlassen)* abandon ‹baby, animal›; *(auf einer einsamen Insel)* maroon; *(ansiedeln)* release ‹animal› [into the wild]; *(ins Freiland bringen)* plant out ‹plants, seedlings›; Ⓑ *(auf See)* launch, lower ‹boat›; get ‹passengers› into the boats; *(an Land bringen)* put ‹passengers› ashore; Ⓒ *(der Einwirkung von etw. überlassen)* expose *(Dat.* to); **jmdm. ausgesetzt sein** be at sb.'s mercy; **dem Spott/der Kritik/einer Gefahr** *usw.* **ausgesetzt sein** be exposed to ridicule/criticism/a danger *etc.;* **Belastungen/Missdeutungen ausgesetzt werden** be subject to strains/misinterpretations; Ⓓ *in* **an jmdm./etw./allem etwas auszusetzen haben** find fault with sb./sth./everything; **was hast du an ihm/daran auszusetzen?** what don't you like about him/it?; **daran war nichts auszusetzen** there was nothing wrong with that; **ich habe nur eines daran auszusetzen** I've only one objection to make about it; Ⓔ *(zur Verfügung stellen)* offer ‹reward, prize, salary›; bequeath, leave ‹inheritance›; **eine große Summe für etw. ~:** provide a large sum for sth.; **jmdm.** *od.* **für jmdn. eine Rente ~:** provide sb. with a pension; settle an annuity on sb.; Ⓕ *(Kaufmannsspr.)* prepare ‹consignment› [for packing]; Ⓖ *(unterbrechen)* interrupt; Ⓗ *(Rechtsw.)* suspend ‹proceedings›; defer ‹judgement, imprisonment›; ⇒ *auch* **Bewährung** A.

❷ *itr. V.* Ⓐ *(aufhören)* stop; ‹engine, machine› cut out, stop; ‹heart› stop [beating]; Ⓑ *(eine Pause machen)* ‹player› miss a turn; **mit etw. ~:** stop sth.; **mit der Arbeit/dem Training [ein paar Wochen] ~:** stop work/training [for a few weeks]; **mit seinem Studium ~:** interrupt one's studies; **mit den Tabletten ~:** stop taking the tablets

**Aus·setzer** *der,* **Aus·setzerin** *die (Kaufmannsspr.) employee who prepares consignments etc. for packing*

**Aussetzung** *die;* ~, ~**en** Ⓐ ⇒ **aussetzen** 1 A: abandonment; marooning; release [into the wild]; planting out; Ⓑ ⇒ **aussetzen** 1 B: launching; lowering; Ⓒ ⇒ **aussetzen** 1 E: offering; bequesting; leaving; Ⓓ ⇒ **aussetzen** 1 H: suspension; deferment

**Aus·sicht** *die* Ⓐ *(Blick)* view (**auf** + *Akk.* of); **ein Zimmer mit ~ aufs Meer** a room overlooking the sea; **jmdm. die ~ nehmen/versperren** block *or* obstruct sb.'s view; Ⓑ *(Perspektive)* prospect (**auf** + *Akk.* of); **das sind ja vielleicht [heitere] ~en!** *(iron.)* that's a fine prospect! *(iron.)*; **~ auf etw.** *(Akk.)* **haben** have the prospect of sth.; **sie hat nicht die geringste ~ auf Erfolg** she hasn't the slightest chance *or* prospect of success; **er hat gute ~en, gewählt zu werden** he stands a good chance of being elected; **etw. in ~ haben** have the prospect of sth.;

*old spelling (see note on page 1707)

have sth. in prospect; **jmdn./etw. für etw. in ~ nehmen** consider sb./sth. for sth.; **in ~ stehen** be in prospect; **jmdm. etw. in ~ stellen** hold out the prospect of sth. to sb.; **weitere ~en** (*Met.*) further outlook *sing.*

**aussichts·los** ❶ *Adj.* hopeless. ❷ *adv.* hopelessly

**Aussichtslosigkeit** *die;* **~:** hopelessness

**aussichts-, Aussichts-: ~punkt** *der* vantage point; **~reich** *Adj.* Ⓐ promising; Ⓑ (*österr.: mit schöner Aussicht*) **in ~reicher Wohnlage** offering attractive views *postpos.*; **~turm** *der* lookout *or* observation tower; **~voll** *Adj.* promising; **~wagen** *der* observation car

**aus|sieben** *tr. V.* sift out; screen ‹coal›; filter out ‹frequencies›; (*fig.*) select; pick out ‹candidates etc.›; weed out ‹weak candidates etc.›

**aus|siedeln** *tr. V.* move out and resettle; (*evakuieren*) evacuate

**Aussiedelung** *die;* **~, ~en** ⇒ **Aussiedlung**

**Aus·siedler** *der,* **Aus·siedlerin** *die* (*Auswanderer*) emigrant; (*Evakuierter*) evacuee; (*Umsiedler*) resettled person

**Aussiedler·hof** *der: farm, formerly part of a strip-farming system and with its buildings in the village, now resited away from the village on a single area of land*

**Aus·siedlung** *die* (*Evakuierung*) evacuation; (*Umsiedlung*) resettlement

**aus|sinnen** *unr. tr. V.* (*geh.*) think up; devise ‹plan›

**aus|sitzen** *unr. tr. V.* **etw. ~:** sit sth. out

**aus|söhnen** ❶ *refl. V.* **sich mit jmdm./** (*fig.*) **etw. ~:** become reconciled with sb./to sth.; **sie haben sich ausgesöhnt** they have become reconciled; they have made it up. ❷ *tr.* (*auch itr.*) *V.* reconcile; **jmdn. mit jmdm./** (*fig.*) **etw. ~:** reconcile sb. with sb./to sth.

**Aussöhnung** *die;* **~, ~en** reconciliation

**aus|sondern** *tr. V.* Ⓐ (*ausscheiden*) weed out; **ausgesonderte Ware** reject goods *pl.*; Ⓑ (*auswählen*) sort *or* pick out; select

**Aussonderung** *die;* **~, ~en** Ⓐ weeding out; Ⓑ (*das Auswählen*) selection

**aus|sortieren** *tr. V.* sort out

**aus|spähen** ❶ *itr. V.* (*ausschauen*) keep a lookout (**nach** for). ❷ *tr. V.* (*auskundschaften*) spy out; spy on ‹organization›

**aus|spannen** ❶ *tr. V.* Ⓐ unharness, unhitch ‹horse, mule›; unyoke ‹oxen›; Ⓑ (*salopp: wegnehmen*) **jmdm. etw. ~:** get sb. to part with sth.; **jmdm. den Freund/die Freundin ~:** pinch sb.'s boyfriend/girlfriend (*coll.*); Ⓒ (*lösen*) unhitch ‹cart, plough, etc.›; take out ‹sheet of paper› (**aus** of); Ⓓ (*ausbreiten*) spread out ‹cloth, net›; stretch ‹rope, cable, line›; **die Flügel ~:** spread its/their wings. ❷ *itr. V.* Ⓐ (*ausruhen*) take *or* have a break; Ⓑ (*Pferde ~*) unharness *or* unhitch the horses; (*Ochsen ~*) unyoke the oxen

**Aus·spannung** *die* relaxation

**aus|sparen** *tr. V.* leave ‹line etc.› blank; (*fig.*) leave out; omit; **eine ausgesparte Lücke** a gap left free

**Aussparung** *die;* **~, ~en** Ⓐ (*das Aussparen*) leaving blank; Ⓑ (*Stelle*) gap; (*im Text*) blank space

**aus|speien** (*geh.*) ❶ *unr. tr. V.* Ⓐ (*ausspucken*) spit out; Ⓑ (*erbrechen*) bring up; vomit [up]. ❷ *unr. itr. V.* spit; **vor jmdm. ~:** spit at sb.'s feet

**aus|sperren** ❶ *tr. V.* Ⓐ (*ausschließen*) lock out; shut ‹animal› out; Ⓑ (*im Streik*) lock out. ❷ *itr. V.* organize a lockout; lock the workforce out

**Aus·sperrung** *die* lockout

**aus|spielen** ❶ *tr. V.* Ⓐ (*Kartenspiel*) lead; **sein ganzes Wissen ~** (*fig.*) make use of all one's knowledge; bring all one's knowledge to bear; **einen/seinen letzten Trumpf ~** (*fig.*) play one's last trump card; Ⓑ (*manipulieren*) **jmdn./etw. gegen jmdn./etw. ~:** play sb./sth. off against sb./sth.; Ⓒ (*Sport: spielen um*) play for ‹cup, title, etc.›; Ⓓ (*als Preis aussetzen*) put up as ‹prize money›; Ⓔ (*Sport*) (*deklassieren*) outplay; (*umspielen*) beat; go round; Ⓕ (*Theater*) act out; ⇒ *auch* **ausgespielt** 2. ❷ *itr. V.* (*Kartenspiel*) lead; **wer spielt aus?** whose lead is it?

**aus|spinnen** *unr. tr. V.* elaborate ‹story, idea›; develop, pursue ‹train of thought›

**aus|spionieren** *tr. V.* Ⓐ (*entdecken, herausbekommen*) spy out; **die Zahlenkombination des Safes ~:** discover the combination of the safe by spying; Ⓑ (*ugs.: aushorchen*) pump

**aus|spotten** *tr. V.* (*bes. österr., schweiz.*) ⇒ **verspotten**

**Aus·sprache** *die* Ⓐ (*von Wörtern*) pronunciation; (*Art des Artikulierens*) articulation; (*Akzent*) accent; ⇒ *auch* **feucht**; Ⓑ (*Gespräch*) discussion; (*zwangloseres*) talk; **eine offene ~ herbeiführen** bring things out into the open

**Aussprache-: ~angabe** *die,* **~bezeichnung** *die* phonetic transcription; **~angaben haben** show pronunciation; **~wörterbuch** *das* pronouncing dictionary; dictionary of pronunciation

**aussprechbar** *Adj.* pronounceable; **nicht ~:** unpronounceable; impossible to pronounce *postpos.*; unrepeatable ‹thought, idea, wish›

**aus|sprechen** ❶ *unr. tr. V.* Ⓐ pronounce; Ⓑ (*ausdrücken*) express; voice ‹suspicion, request›; (*verkünden*) pronounce ‹judgement, sentence, etc.›; grant ‹divorce›; **~, dass ...** state that ...; **der Regierung sein Vertrauen ~:** pass a vote of confidence in the government. ❷ *unr. refl. V.* Ⓐ (*sich sprechen lassen*) be pronounced; **ihr Name spricht sich schwer aus** her name is difficult to pronounce; Ⓑ (*äußern*) speak; **sich lobend/missbilligend über jmdn./etw. ~:** speak highly/disapprovingly of sb./sth.; **er hat sich nicht näher darüber ausgesprochen** he did not say anything further about it; **sich für jmdn./etw. ~:** declare *or* pronounce oneself in favour of sb./sth.; **sich gegen jmdn./etw. ~:** declare *or* pronounce oneself against sb./sth.; Ⓒ (*offen sprechen*) say what's on one's mind; **sich über etw.** (*Akk.*) **mit** *od.* **bei jmdm. ~:** have a heart-to-heart talk with sb. about sth.; **na los, sprich dich aus!** (*ugs.*) come on, get it off your chest!; Ⓓ (*Strittiges klären*) have it out, talk things out (**mit** with); **wir haben uns über alles ausgesprochen** we had everything out. ❸ *unr. itr. V.* (*zu Ende sprechen*) finish [speaking]; ⇒ *auch* **ausgesprochen** 2, 3

**aus|spritzen** *tr. V.* Ⓐ squirt out ‹liquid, contents›; **sein Gift gegen jmdn. ~** (*fig.*) spit venom at sb.; Ⓑ (*reinigen*) flush out; rinse out ‹tooth›; syringe ‹ear›; Ⓒ (*löschen*) put out ‹fire› [with a hose/hoses]

**Aus·spruch** *der* remark; (*Sinnspruch*) saying

**aus|spucken** ❶ *itr. V.* spit; **vor jmdm. ~:** spit at sb.'s feet. ❷ *tr. V.* Ⓐ spit out; (*fig. ugs.*) ‹machine, factory, computer› spew out; cough up (*coll.*) ‹money›; regurgitate ‹facts, information, etc.›; **nun los, spucks aus, sei nicht so schüchtern!** (*ugs. fig.*) come on, spit it out and don't be so shy!; Ⓑ (*ugs.: erbrechen*) sick up (*Brit. coll.*); throw up

**aus|spülen** *tr. V.* Ⓐ (*reinigen*) rinse out; (*Med.*) irrigate; wash out; **sich** (*Dat.*) **den Mund ~:** rinse one's mouth out; Ⓑ (*entfernen*) flush *or* wash out; ‹river, sea› wash away, erode ‹soil, rock›

**Aus·spülung** *die* ⇒ **ausspülen** A, B: rinsing out; irrigation; washing out; flushing *or* washing out; washing away; erosion

**aus|staffieren** /ˈausʃtafiːrən/ *tr. V.* kit *or* rig out; fit out, furnish ‹room etc.›; (*verkleiden*) dress up; **sie hat ihre Tochter sonntäglich ausstaffiert** she dressed her daughter up in her Sunday best

**Aus·staffierung** *die* outfit; get-up (*coll.*)

**Aus·stand** *der* strike; **im ~ sein** be on strike; **in den ~ treten** go on strike

**aus·ständig** *Adj.* (*südd., österr.: ausstehend*) outstanding

**aus|stanzen** *tr. V.* punch out

**aus|statten** /ˈausʃtatn̩/ *tr. V.* provide (**mit** with); (*mit Kleidung*) provide; fit out; (*mit Gerät*) equip ‹office, kitchen, hospital, school, etc.›; (*mit Möbeln, Teppichen, Gardinen usw.*) furnish ‹room, flat, office, etc.›; **mit Rechten/Befugnissen ausgestattet sein** be vested with powers/authority *sing.*; have powers/authority *no pl.* vested in one; **mit Talent ausgestattet sein** be endowed with talent; **ein prächtig ausgestatteter Band** a splendidly produced volume

**Ausstattung** *die;* **~, ~en** Ⓐ (*das Ausstatten*) ⇒ **ausstatten**: provision; fitting out; equipping; furnishing; vesting; production; Ⓑ (*Ausrüstung*) equipment; (*Innen~ eines Autos*) trim; Ⓒ (*Einrichtung*) furnishings *pl.*; Ⓓ (*Aufmachung*) (*eines Films, Theaterstücks*) décor and costumes; (*Verpackung*) packaging; (*eines Buchs*) design and layout; (*typographisch*) design

**Ausstattungs-: ~film** *der* period film; **~stück** *das* spectacular [opera/play *etc.*]

**aus|stechen** *unr. tr. V.* Ⓐ **jmdm. die Augen ~:** put *or* gouge sb.'s eyes out; Ⓑ (*entfernen*) dig up ‹plants›; cut ‹turf›; Ⓒ (*herstellen*) dig [out] ‹trench, hole, etc.›; (*Kochk.*) press *or* cut out ‹biscuits›; Ⓓ (*übertreffen*) outdo; **jmdn. bei jmdm. ~:** oust sb. in sb.'s affections/esteem/favour; **jmdn. in etw.** (*Dat.*) **~:** outshine sb. *or* put sb. in the shade in sth.

**aus|stehen** ❶ *unr. itr. V.* **noch ~** ‹debt› be outstanding; ‹decision› be still to be taken, have not yet been taken; ‹book› be still to appear; ‹solution› be still to be found; **ihre Entscheidung/Antwort steht noch aus** I am/we are *etc.* still awaiting their decision/reply; **eine offizielle Bestätigung steht noch aus** there has as yet been no official confirmation; **~de Forderungen** outstanding demands; **Geld ~ haben** (*ugs.*) have money owing [one]; **euer Besuch bei mir steht noch aus** you still owe me a visit.
❷ *unr. tr. V.* (*ertragen*) endure ‹pain, suffering›; suffer ‹worry, anxiety›; (*erdulden*) put up with; **ausgestanden sein** be all over; **ich kann ihn/das nicht ~:** I can't stand *or* bear him/it

**aus|steigen** *unr. itr. V.*; *mit sein;* Ⓐ (*aus einem Auto, Boot*) get out (**aus** of); (*aus einem Zug, Bus*) get off; alight (*formal*); (*Fliegerspr.: abspringen*) bale out; **aus einem Zug/Bus ~:** get off a train/bus; alight from a train/bus (*formal*); **alles ~!** all change!; Ⓑ (*ugs.: sich nicht mehr beteiligen*) **~ aus** opt out of; give up ‹show business, job›; leave ‹project›; Ⓒ (*Sport: aus einem Rennen o. Ä.*) drop out (**aus** of); retire (**aus** from); Ⓓ (*ugs.: der Gesellschaft den Rücken kehren*) drop out

**Aussteiger** *der;* **~s, ~, Aussteigerin** *die;* **~, ~nen** (*ugs.*) dropout (*coll.*)

**aus|stellen** *tr. V.* Ⓐ *auch itr.* (*im Schaufenster*) put on display; display; (*im Museum, auf einer Messe*) exhibit; **ausgestellt sein** ‹goods› be on display/be exhibited; ‹painting› be exhibited; **die Galerie wird Hans Meyer ~:** the gallery is going to put on a Hans Meyer exhibition; **bekannte Künstler/viele Betriebe stellen hier aus** famous artists/many firms exhibit here; Ⓑ (*ausfertigen*) make out, write [out] ‹cheque, prescription, receipt›; make out ‹bill›; issue ‹visa, passport, certificate›; **einen Scheck auf jmdn. ~:** make out a cheque to sb.; Ⓒ (*ugs.: ausschalten*) turn *or* switch off ‹cooker, radio, heating, engine›; Ⓓ (*nach außen stellen*) open out ‹window›; roll out ‹blind›; pull out ‹aerial›; Ⓔ (*aufstellen*) put up ‹poster, sign›; post ‹sentry›; set ‹trap›; ⇒ *auch* **ausgestellt** 2

**Aussteller** *der;* **~s, ~, Ausstellerin** *die;* **~, ~nen** Ⓐ (*auf Messen*) exhibitor; Ⓑ (*eines Dokuments*) issuer; (*Behörde*) issuing authority; (*eines Schecks*) drawer

**Aus·stellung** *die* Ⓐ (*das Präsentieren*) exhibiting; Ⓑ (*das Ausfertigen*) ⇒ **ausstellen** B: making out; writing [out]; issuing; **Datum und Ort der ~:** date and place of issue; Ⓒ (*Veranstaltung*) exhibition; Ⓓ (*das Aufstellen*) ⇒ **ausstellen** E: putting up; posting; setting

**Ausstellungs-: ~datum** *das* date of issue; **~fläche** *die* exhibition area; **~gelände** *das* exhibition site; **~halle** *die* exhibition hall; **~katalog** *der* exhibition catalogue; **~ort**

a

*der* place of issue; **~raum** *der* (A) exhibition space; (B) (*Zimmer*) exhibition room; **~stand** *der* exhibition stand; **~stück** *das* (*in Schaufenstern usw.*) display item; (*in Museen usw.*) exhibit; (*auf Messen*) **dieses Fahrzeug ist ein ~stück** this vehicle is for display purposes only; **dein Auto ist ja nicht gerade ein ~stück!** (*iron.*) your car isn't exactly much to look at!

**Aussterbe·etat** *der* (*ugs.*) *in* **auf dem ~ sein** *od.* **stehen, sich auf dem ~ befinden** be on its last legs

**aus|sterben** *unr. itr. V.; mit sein* (*auch fig.*) die out; ‹species› die out, become extinct; **ein ~des Handwerk** (*fig.*) a dying craft; **die Dummen sterben nicht** *od.* **nie aus** there's one born every minute

**Aus·steuer** *die* trousseau (*consisting mainly of household linen*)

**aus|steuern** *tr. V.* (A) (*Elektronik*) modulate ‹signal, wave›; (*bei der Aufnahme*) control the recording level of; control the power level of ‹amplifier›; (B) **ein Auto ~:** [use the steering wheel to] bring a car under control; (C) (*Versicherungsw.*) **jmdn. ~:** end sb.'s entitlement to benefits

**Ausstieg** *der:* **~[e]s, ~e** (A) (*Ausgang*) exit; (*Tür*) door[s]; (*~luke*) hatch; (B) (*das Aussteigen*) climbing out (**aus** of); **„kein ~"** 'no exit'; **der ~ aus dem Bus/Zug** getting off the bus/train; alighting from the bus/train (*formal*); **der ~ aus der Höhle** the way up out of the cave; (C) (*fig.*) **ein ~ aus dem heiklen Thema** a way of getting off the awkward subject

**aus|stopfen** *tr. V.* stuff ‹cushion, animal, doll, etc.›; fill ‹crack›

**Aus·stoß** *der* (*Wirtsch.*) output

**aus|stoßen** *unr. tr. V.* (A) (*nach außen pressen*) expel; give off, emit ‹gas, fumes, smoke›; fire ‹torpedo›; (B) give ‹cry, whistle, laugh, etc.›; let out ‹cry, scream, yell›; heave, give ‹sigh›; utter ‹curse, threat, accusation, etc.›; (C) **jmdm. ein Auge ~:** put sb.'s eye out; **sich** (*Dat.*) **einen Zahn ~:** knock a tooth out; (D) (*ausschließen*) (*aus einem Verein, einer Gesellschaft*) expel (**aus** from); (*aus der Armee*) drum out (**aus** of); **sich ausgestoßen fühlen** feel an outcast; ⇒ *auch* **Ausgestoßene**; (E) (*Wirtsch.*) turn out; produce

**aus|strahlen** ❶ *tr. V.* (A) (*verbreiten, auch fig.*) radiate; radiate, give off ‹heat›; ‹lamp› give out ‹light›; (B) (*Rundf., Ferns.*) broadcast; transmit; (C) (*ausleuchten*) floodlight. ❷ *itr. V.* (A) (*ausgehen*) radiate; ‹heat› radiate, be given off; ‹light› be given out; (*fig.*) ‹pain› spread, extend; (B) (*wirken*) **auf jmdn./etw. ~:** communicate itself to sb./influence sth.

**Aus·strahlung** *die* (A) (*Wirkung*) radiation; (*eines Menschen*) charisma; **~ haben** ‹person› have charisma; (B) (*Rundf., Ferns.*) transmission

**aus|strecken** ❶ *tr. V.* extend, stretch out ‹arms, legs›; stretch out ‹hand›; put out ‹feelers›; stick *or* put out ‹tongue›; **mit ausgestreckten Armen** with arms extended; with outstretched arms. ❷ *refl. V.* stretch [oneself] out; **ausgestreckt am Boden liegen** lie stretched out on the floor

**aus|streichen** *unr. tr. V.* (A) (*durchstreichen*) cross *or* strike out; delete; (*fig.*) obliterate; **jmds. Namen auf einer Liste ~:** cross sb.'s name off a list; (B) (*verteilen*) spread; (C) (*Kochk.*) grease ‹tin, pan, etc.›; (D) (*füllen*) fill, smooth over ‹cracks›

**aus|streuen** *tr. V.* (A) (*verstreuen*) scatter; distribute ‹gifts, leaflets, money›; spread, put about ‹rumour, story, lies, etc.›; **er ließ ~, dass ...** he caused the rumour to be spread about that ...; (B) (*bestreuen*) **etw. mit etw. ~:** sprinkle sth. with sth.

**Aus·strich** *der* (*Med., Biol.*) smear

**aus|strömen** ❶ *tr. V.* radiate ‹warmth›; give off ‹scent›; (*fig.*) radiate ‹optimism, confidence, etc.›. ❷ *itr. V.; mit sein* stream *or* pour out; ‹gas, steam› escape; **etw. strömt von jmdm./etw. aus** (*fig.*) sb./sth. radiates sth.

*old spelling (see note on page 1707)

**aus|suchen** *tr. V.* choose; pick; **such dir was aus!** choose what you want; take your pick; **man kann es sich nicht immer ~:** there isn't always any choice in the matter; ⇒ *auch* **ausgesucht** 2, 3

**aus|sülzen** *refl. V.* (*salopp*) (*lange reden*) go on [and on]; (*zu Ende reden*) finish spouting

**aus|täfeln** *tr. V.* panel

**aus|tapezieren** *tr. V.* paper

**aus|tarieren** *tr. V.* (A) (*ins Gleichgewicht bringen*) balance ‹scales›; (B) (*österr.: Tara feststellen von*) determine the tare of

**Aus·tausch** *der* (A) exchange; **im ~ für** *od.* **gegen** in exchange for; (B) (*das Ersetzen*) replacement (**gegen** with); (*Sport*) substitution (**gegen** by)

**austauschbar** *Adj.* interchangeable; (*ersetzbar*) replaceable ‹parts etc.›

**aus|tauschen** ❶ *tr. V.* (A) exchange (**gegen** for); (B) (*ersetzen*) replace (**gegen** with); (*Sport*) substitute (**gegen** by). ❷ *refl. V.* (*über etw. sprechen*) exchange views/experiences [with each other]

**Austausch-:** **~motor** *der* (*Kfz-W.*) replacement engine; **~schüler** *der,* **~schülerin** *die* exchange pupil *or* student

**aus|teilen** *tr. V.* distribute (**unter** + *Dat.* among, **an** + *Akk.* to); (*aushändigen*) hand *or* give out ‹books, post, etc.› (**an** + *Akk.* to); issue, give ‹orders›; deal [out] ‹cards›; give out ‹marks, grades›; administer ‹sacrament›; (*servieren*) serve ‹food etc.›; (*fig.*) give ‹blessing›; **Prügel ~** (*fig.*) hand out beatings

**Aus·teilung** *die* ⇒ **austeilen**: distribution; handing *or* giving out; issuing; giving; dealing [out]; administering; serving

**Auster** /ˈaustɐ/ *die;* **~, ~n** oyster

**Austern-:** **~bank** *die; Pl.* **~bänke** oyster bed; oyster bank; **~fischer** *der* oystercatcher; **~park** *der* oyster farm; **~zucht** *die* oyster farming

**aus|tilgen** *tr. V.* (A) (*vernichten*) exterminate ‹pests, race›; eradicate ‹weeds›; wipe out, eradicate ‹disease›; (B) (*streichen, auch fig.*) obliterate

**aus|toben** ❶ *refl. V.* (A) (*spielen*) romp about; have a good romp; (B) (*sich amüsieren*) indulge oneself; **die Jugend will sich ~:** youth must have its fling. ❷ *tr. V.* (*abreagieren*) work off ‹anger etc.› (**an** + *Dat.* on)

**aus|tollen** *refl. V.* (*ugs.*) romp about; have a good romp

**Austrag** *der;* **~[e]s** (A) (*das Austragen*) settlement; resolution; (B) (*Sport*) holding; (C) (*österr.*) ⇒ **Altenteil**

**aus|tragen** *unr. tr. V.* (A) (*zustellen*) deliver ‹newspapers, post›; (B) (*im Mutterleib*) carry ‹child› to full term; (*nicht abtreiben*) have ‹child›; (C) (*ausfechten*) settle; (*bis zum Ende*) carry on ‹quarrel, hostilities›; settle, resolve ‹conflict, differences›; fight out ‹battle›; **etw. vor Gericht ~:** take sth. to court; **einen Streit mit jmdm. ~:** have it out with sb.; (D) (*Sport*) hold ‹race, competition, etc.›; (E) (*löschen*) delete, take out ‹data, figures›; (*aus einer Liste*) cross ‹person, name› off

**Aus·träger** *der* delivery boy/man; (*Zeitungsjunge*) newspaper boy

**Aus·trägerin** *die* delivery woman/girl; (*Zeitungsmädchen*) newspaper girl

**Austragung** *die;* **~, ~en** (A) carrying on; (*bis zum Ende*) (*eines Streits*) settlement; (B) (*Sport*) holding

**Austragungs-:** **~modus** *der* (*bes. Sport*) procedure; **~ort** *der* (*Sport*) venue

**Australide** /austraˈliːdə/ *der/die; adj. Dekl.* Australoid

**Australien** /ausˈtraːli̯ən/ *(das);* **~s** Australia; **~ und Ozeanien** Australasia

**Australier** *der;* **~s, ~, Australierin** *die;* **~, ~nen** ▶553 Australian; **er ist Australier/sie ist Australierin** he/she is [an] Australian

**australisch** *Adj.* ▶553 Australian

**aus|träumen** *itr.* (*auch tr.*) *V.* finish dreaming; **der Traum [vom Glück] ist ausgeträumt** the dream [of happiness] is over

**aus|treiben** ❶ *unr. tr. V.* (A) (*verbannen*) exorcize, cast out ‹evil spirit, demon›; (B) (*abgewöhnen*) **jmdm. etw. ~:** cure sb. of sth.; (C) (*geh.: vertreiben, auch fig.*) drive out (**aus** from); (D) (*auf die Weide*) drive ‹cattle, sheep› out to pasture; (E) (*hervorbringen*) put forth ‹leaves, buds›; produce ‹blossom›. ❷ *unr. itr. V.* (A) (*ausschlagen*) sprout; (B) (*hervorkommen*) ‹shoot, bud› appear

**Austreibung** *die;* **~, ~en** expulsion (**aus** from); (*von Dämonen*) exorcism; casting out

**aus|treten** ❶ *unr. tr. V.* (A) tread out ‹spark, cigarette end›; trample out ‹fire›; (B) (*bahnen*) tread out ‹path›; **ausgetretene Pfade** (*fig.*) well-trodden paths; (C) (*abnutzen*) wear down; **eine ausgetretene Steintreppe** a stone staircase with worn-down steps; (D) (*weiten*) wear out ‹old shoes›; break in ‹new shoes›.
❷ *unr. itr. V.; mit sein* (A) (*ugs.: zur Toilette gehen*) pay a call (*coll.*); **der Schüler fragte, ob er ~ dürfe** the pupil asked to be excused; (B) (*ausscheiden*) **aus etw. ~:** leave sth.; **aus einer Vereinigung ~:** resign from a society; (C) (*Jägerspr.*) come out into the open; **aus der Deckung ~:** break cover; (D) (*nach außen gelangen*) come out; (*entweichen*) escape; ‹blood› issue; ‹pus› be discharged

**Austriazismus** /au̯striaˈtsɪsmʊs/ *der;* **~, Austriazismen** Austrianism

**aus|tricksen** *tr. V.* (*ugs.*) trick

**aus|trinken** ❶ *tr. V.* finish, drink up ‹wine, beer, coffee, etc.›; finish, drain ‹glass, bottle, etc.›. ❷ *itr. V.* drink up

**Aus·tritt** *der* (A) (*das Ausscheiden*) leaving; (*aus einem Verband, einer Vereinigung*) resignation (**aus** from); **seinen ~ aus der Partei/Kirche erklären** announce that one is leaving the party/church; **die Partei hatte viele ~e zu verzeichnen** the party recorded a large drop in membership; (B) (*das Hervorquellen*) outflow; (*das Entweichen*) escape; (*von Blut*) issue; (*von Eiter*) discharge

**Austritts·erklärung** *die* [notice of] resignation

**aus|trocknen** ❶ *tr. V.* (A) (*ausdörren*) dry out; dry up ‹river bed, marsh›; parch ‹throat›; (B) (*trockenlegen*) drain ‹marsh, swamp›. ❷ *itr. V.; mit sein* dry out; ‹river bed, pond, etc.› dry up; ‹skin, hair› become dry; ‹throat› become parched

**Austro·marxismus** /au̯stro-/ *der* Austro-Marxism

**aus|trompeten** *tr. V.* (*ugs.*) ⇒ **ausposaunen**

**aus|trudeln** ❶ *itr. V.* (*ugs.*) **etw. ~ lassen** let sth. fizzle out. ❷ *tr. V.* (*ugs.*) ⇒ **auswürfeln**

**aus|tüfteln** *tr. V.* (*ugs.*) (*ausarbeiten*) work out; (*ersinnen*) think up

**aus|üben** *tr. V.* (A) (*nachgehen*) practise ‹art, craft›; follow ‹profession›; carry on ‹trade›; do ‹job›; **welche Tätigkeit üben Sie aus?** what is your occupation?; (B) (*innehaben*) hold ‹office›; wield, exercise ‹power›; exercise ‹control›; (*wahrnehmen*) exercise ‹right›; (*wirksam werden lassen*) exert

**Aus·übung** *die* ⇒ **ausüben**: practising; following; carrying on; doing; holding; wielding; exercising

**aus|ufern** *itr. V.; mit sein* (A) (*überhand nehmen*) get out of hand; (B) (*selten: über die Ufer treten*) burst *or* break its banks

**Aus·verkauf** *der* [clearance] sale; (*wegen Geschäftsaufgabe*) closing-down (*Brit.*) *or* (*Amer.*) liquidation sale; (*fig.: Verrat*) sell-out; **etw. im ~ kaufen** buy sth. at the sale[s]

**aus|verkaufen** *tr. V.* (A) (*verkaufen*) sell out of; **Mineralwasser ist ausverkauft** there is no mineral water left [in stock]; (B) (*räumen*) sell off, clear ‹stock›; clear ‹warehouse, shop›

**ausverkauft** *Adj.* sold out; **vor ~em Haus spielen** play to a full house; **~e Ränge** (*Sport*) packed stands

**aus|wachsen** ❶ *unr. refl. V.* (A) (*sich normalisieren*) right *or* correct itself; (B) (*sich entwickeln*) grow (**zu** into). ❷ *unr. itr. V.; mit sein* (A) (*ugs.: verzweifeln*) go round the bend (*coll.*); **zum Auswachsen sein** be enough to drive you up the wall (*coll.*); (B) (*keimen*) sprout prematurely

**Aus·wahl** *die* **A** *(das Auswählen)* choice; selection; **Sie haben die [freie] ~:** the choice is yours; you can choose whichever you like; **drei Sorten/Tee und Kaffee stehen zur Wahl** there are three kinds to choose from/one can choose between tea and coffee; **bei uns stehen Ihnen mehr als 600 Wagen zur ~:** we offer you a choice of over 600 cars; **eine ~ treffen** make a selection; **B** *(Auslese)* selection; *(von Gedichten, Erzählungen)* anthology; selection; **C** *(Sortiment)* range; **viel/wenig ~ haben** have a wide/limited selection **(an** + *Dat.*, **von** of); **hier hat man keine ~:** there is no choice here; **Backwaren in reicher ~:** a wide selection of bread, cakes, and pastries; **D** *(Sport: Mannschaft)* [selected] team

**Auswahl·band** *der* anthology

**aus|wählen** *tr. V.* choose, select **(aus** from, **unter** + *Dat.* from among); **sich** *(Dat.)* **etw. ~:** choose *or* select sth. [for oneself]

**Auswahl-: ~mannschaft** *die (Sport)* [selected] team; **~möglichkeit** *die* choice; **~prinzip** *das* method of selection; **~spieler** *der*, **~spielerin** *die (Sport)* [selected] player

**aus|walzen** *tr. V.* roll out ‹metal›; *(fig. ugs.)* drag out ‹subject›; **eine Geschichte zu einem Roman ~:** spin a story out into a novel

**Aus·wanderer** *der*, **Aus·wanderin** *die* emigrant

**aus|wandern** *itr. V.; mit sein* emigrate **(nach, in** + *Akk.* to); ‹tribe› migrate

**Aus·wanderung** *die* emigration

**auswärtig** /ˈausvɛrtɪç/ *Adj.* **A** *(woanders befindlich)* non-local; **eine ~e Filiale/Bank** a branch/bank in another area/town; **B** *(von woanders stammend)* ‹student, guest, etc.› from out of town; **C** *(das Ausland betreffend)* foreign; **der Minister des Auswärtigen** the Foreign Minister; the Foreign Secretary *(Brit.)*; the Secretary of State *(Amer.)*; **das Auswärtige Amt** the Foreign Ministry; the Foreign and Commonwealth Office *(Brit.)*; the Foreign Office *(Brit. coll.)*; the State Department *(Amer.)*; **der ~e Dienst** the foreign service

**auswärts** *Adv.* **A** *(nach außen)* outwards; **B** *(nicht zu Hause)* ‹sleep, live› away from home; **~ essen** eat out; **C** *(nicht am Ort)* in another town; *(Sport)* away; **ich habe ~ zu tun** I have to do a few things out of town; **~ sprechen** *(ugs. scherzh.)* talk foreign *(coll.)*

**Auswärts-: ~sieg** *der (Sport)* away win; **~spiel** *das (Sport)* away match *or* game

**aus|waschen** *unr. tr. V.* **A** wash out; *(ausspülen)* rinse out; **B** *(Geol.)* erode

**auswechselbar** *Adj.* changeable; exchangeable; *(untereinander)* interchangeable; *(ersetzbar)* replaceable

**aus|wechseln** **1** *tr. V.* **A** change **(gegen** + *Akk.* for); **B** *(ersetzen)* replace **(gegen** with); *(Sport)* substitute ‹player›; **A gegen B ~:** replace A by B; **sie war wie ausgewechselt** she was a different person. **2** *itr. V. (Sport)* bring on a substitute; make a substitution

**Auswechsel·spieler** *der*, **Auswechsel·spielerin** *die (Sport)* substitute

**Auswechselung**, **Auswechslung** *die; ~, ~en* change; *(Ersatz)* replacement; *(Sport)* substitution; **die ~ von A gegen B** the replacement of A by B

**Aus·weg** *der* way out **(aus** of); **der letzte ~ für jmdn. sein** be a last resort for sb.

**ausweg·los** **1** *Adj.* hopeless. **2** *adv.* hopelessly

**Ausweglosigkeit** *die; ~:* hopelessness

**aus|weichen** *unr. itr. V.; mit sein* **A** *(Platz machen)* make way *(Dat.* for); *(wegen Gefahren, Hindernissen)* get out of the way *(Dat.* of); **[nach] rechts/nach der Seite ~:** move to the right/move aside to make way/get out of the way; **B** *(entgehen wollen)* get out of the way *(Dat.* of); **einem Schlag/Angriff ~:** dodge a blow/evade an attack; **C** *(meiden)* **dem Feind ~:** avoid [contact with] the enemy; **jmdm./einem Kampf/Hindernis ~** *(auch fig.)* avoid sb./a fight/an obstacle; **einer Frage/Entscheidung/einem Zwang/Verbot ~:** evade a question/decision/obligation/ban; **~de Antworten** evasive answers; **der Beantwortung weiterer Fragen ~:** avoid answering any more questions; **D** *(zurückgreifen)* **auf etw.** *(Akk.)* **~:** switch [over] to sth.

**Ausweich·manöver** *das* evasive manœuvre; **~** *Pl.* evasive action *sing.*; **das sind doch nur ~** *(fig.)* these are just evasions

**aus|weinen** **1** *refl. V.* have a good cry; **sie hat sich bei mir darüber ausgeweint** *(ugs.)* she had a cry on my shoulder about it. **2** *tr. V. (geh.)* **seinen Kummer/sein Elend ~:** find relief for one's sorrow/misery in tears; ⇒ *auch* **Auge** A. **3** *itr. V.* finish crying

**Ausweis** /ˈauswais/ *der; ~es, ~e* **A** card; *(Personal~, Kennkarte)* identity card; *(Mitglieds~)* membership card; **B** *(österr. veralt.: Zeugnis)* certificate; *(Schulzeugnis)* report; **C** *in* **nach ~** *(Papierdt.)* ⇒ **ausweislich**

**aus|weisen** **1** *unr. tr. V.* **A** *(aus dem Land)* expel **(aus** from); **B** *(erkennen lassen)* **jmdn. als etw. ~:** show that sb. is/was sth.; **seine Papiere wiesen ihn als ... aus** his papers proved *or* established his identity as ...; **C** *(angeben)* reveal; **D** *(zeigen)* demonstrate ‹ability, skill, etc.›. **2** *unr. refl. V.* **A** *(seinen Ausweis zeigen)* prove *or* establish one's identity [by showing one's papers]; **können Sie sich ~?** do you have any means of identification?; **B** *(sich erweisen)* **sich als etw. ~:** prove oneself to be sth.

**ausweislich** *Präp. mit Gen. (Papierdt.)* according to

**Ausweis·papiere** *Pl.* identity papers

**Aus·weisung** *die* expulsion **(aus** from)

**aus|weiten** **1** *tr. V. (dehnen)* stretch; *(fig.: erweitern)* expand **(zu** into); extend ‹jurisdiction, study›. **2** *refl. V.* **A** *(zu weit werden)* stretch; **B** *(sich erweitern)* expand; **sich zur Krise ~:** develop *or* grow into a crisis

**Ausweitung** *die; ~, ~en* expansion; *(des Studiums, der Gerichtsbarkeit)* extension

**aus·wendig** *Adv.* **etw. ~ können/lernen** know/learn sth. [off] by heart; **etw. ~ spielen/aufsagen** play/recite sth. from memory; **das kenne ich ja schon ~** *(ugs. abwertend fig.)* I know it backwards; ⇒ *auch* **inwendig**

**Auswendig·lernen** *das* learning by heart

**aus|werfen** *unr. tr. V.* **A** cast ‹net, anchor, rope, line, etc.›; **B** *(herausschleudern)* throw out ‹sparks›; ‹volcano› eject, spew out ‹lava, ash, etc.›; eject ‹cartridge case›; **C** *(geh.: ausspucken)* cough up ‹blood, phlegm, etc.›; **D** *(ausschaufeln)* throw up ‹earth, sand, etc.›; **E** *(anlegen)* dig [out] ‹trench, pit, ditch, etc.›; **F** *(zur Ausgabe bestimmen)* allocate ‹sum›; pay [out] ‹dividend, premium, etc.›; **G** *(produzieren)* produce; turn out; **H** **jmdm. ein Auge ~:** put sb.'s eye out *(by throwing sth.)*

**auswertbar** *Adj.* **A** **leicht/schwer ~ sein** be easy/difficult to analyse and evaluate; **maschinell ~:** machine-analysable; **B** *(nutzbar)* utilizable

**aus|werten** *tr. V.* **A** analyse and evaluate; **B** *(nutzbar machen)* utilize

**Aus·wertung** *die* **A** analysis and evaluation; *(das Nutzbarmachen)* utilization; **B** *(Ergebnis)* analysis

**aus|wetzen** *tr. V.:* ⇒ **Scharte** A

**aus|wickeln** *tr. V.* **A** *(Verpackung entfernen)* unwrap **(aus** from); **B** unwind ‹person› **(aus** from)

**aus|wiegen** *unr. tr. V.* **A** *(das Gewicht feststellen)* weigh; **B** *(portionsweise)* weigh out; ⇒ *auch* **ausgewogen** 2, 3

**aus|winden** *unr. tr. V. (südd., schweiz.)* wring out

**aus|wirken** *refl. V.* have an effect **(auf** + *Akk.* on); **sich in etw.** *(Dat.)* **~:** result in sth.; **sich günstig/negativ** *usw.* **~:** have a favourable/an unfavourable *etc.* effect **(auf** + *Akk.* on); **sich zu jmds. Vorteil ~:** work to sb.'s advantage

**Aus·wirkung** *die (Wirkung)* effect **(auf** + *Akk.* on); *(Folge)* consequence **(auf** + *Akk.* for); *(Rückwirkung)* repercussion **(auf** + *Akk.* on)

**aus|wischen** **1** *tr. V.* **A** *(entfernen)* wipe ‹dirt etc.› out **(aus** of); **B** *(säubern)* wipe [clean]; **sich** *(Dat.)* **die Augen ~:** wipe one's eyes; **C** *in* **jmdm. eins ~** *(ugs.)* get one's own back on sb. *(coll.)*. **2** *itr. V.; mit sein (ugs.)* get away, escape *(Dat.* from)

**aus|wringen** *unr. tr. V. (bes. nordd.)* wring out

**Aus·wuchs** *der* **A** ▸ 474 *(Wucherung)* growth; excrescence *(Med., Bot.)*; *(Missbildung)* deformity; **B** *(fig.)* unhealthy product; *(Folge)* harmful consequence; *(Übersteigerung, Missstand)* excess; **C** *(Landw.)* premature sprouting of the kernel

**aus|wuchten** *tr. V. (Technik)* **die Räder ~:** balance the wheels

**Aus·wurf** *der* **A** *(Med.)* sputum; **~/blutigen ~ haben** be bringing up phlegm/coughing up blood; **B** *(das Auswerfen)* ejection; **C** *(Lava, Geröll usw.)* ejected material; ejecta *pl.*; **D** *(abwertend: Abschaum)* scum

**aus|würfeln** *tr. V.* **eine Runde Bier** *usw.* **~:** throw dice to decide who will pay for a round of beer *etc.*

**aus|zacken** *tr. V.* serrate; *(mit der Zickzackschere)* pink ‹fabric›

**aus|zahlen** **1** *tr. V.* **A** *(aushändigen)* pay out; **sich** *(Dat.)* **einen Scheck ~ lassen** cash a cheque; **ausgezahlt bekommt er 1 650 Mark** his net pay is 1,650 marks; **B** *(entlohnen)* pay off; buy out ‹business partner, shareholder, etc.›. **2** *refl. V. (sich lohnen)* pay off; *(einbringen)* pay; **Verbrechen zahlen sich nicht aus** crime doesn't pay

**aus|zählen** *tr. V.* **A** *(zählen)* count [up] ‹votes etc.›; **B** *(Boxen)* count out; **C** *auch itr. (aussondern)* choose by counting; *(bei Kinderspielen)* count out

**Aus·zahlung** *die* **A** *(das Aushändigen)* paying out; **B** *(das Entlohnen)* paying off; *(eines Geschäftspartners)* buying out

**Aus·zählung** *die* counting [up]; **mit der ~ wurde bereits begonnen** the count had already started

**aus|zanken** *tr. V. (bes. ostmd.)* **jmdn. ~:** give sb. a scolding *or* a telling off

**aus|zehren** *tr. V. (geh.)* exhaust ‹person, soil›; ‹disease› debilitate ‹person›; *(abzehren)* emaciate ‹person›

**Auszehrung** *die; ~* **A** *(Kräfteverfall)* emaciation; **B** *(veralt.: Schwindsucht)* consumption

**aus|zeichnen** **1** *tr. V.* **A** *(mit einem Preisschild)* mark, price **(mit** at); **etw. mit einem Preisschild ~:** put a price tag on sth.; **B** *(ehren)* honour; **jmdn. mit einem Orden ~:** decorate sb. [with a medal]; **jmdn./etw. mit einem Preis/Titel ~:** award a prize/title to sb./sth.; **C** *(Druckw.: hervorheben)* display; **wichtige Stellen sind durch Kursivschrift ausgezeichnet** important sections are displayed in italics; **D** *(Druckw.: zum Satz fertig machen)* mark up; **E** *(bevorzugt behandeln)* single out for special favour; *(ehren)* single out for special honour; **jmdn. mit** *od.* **durch etw. ~** *(bevorzugt behandeln)* favour sb. with sth.; *(ehren)* honour sb. with sth.; **F** *(kennzeichnen)* distinguish **(gegenüber, vor** + *Dat.* from); **Klugheit und Fleiß zeichneten ihn aus** he was distinguished by his intelligence and industriousness.

**2** *refl. V. (sich hervortun) (durch eine Eigenschaft)* stand out **(durch** for); *(durch Leistung)* ‹person› distinguish oneself **(durch** by); **sich als Politiker/im Sport ~:** distinguish oneself as a politician/at sport; **der Stoff zeichnet sich durch seine Haltbarkeit aus** the outstanding feature of the material is its durability; ⇒ *auch* **ausgezeichnet** 2, 3

**Aus·zeichnung** *die* **A** *(von Waren)* marking; **B** *(Schildchen)* [price] ticket *or* tag; **C** *(Ehrung)* honouring; *(mit Orden)* decoration; *(Gunstbeweis)* mark of favour; **die ~ mit dem „Oscar" war sein größter Erfolg** the award of the Oscar was his greatest success; **die ~ der Preisträger** the presentation of awards to the winners; **D** *(Orden)* decoration; *(Preis)* award; prize; **E**

a

(*Druckw.: das Hervorheben*) displaying; **F** (*Druckw.: das Satzfertigmachen*) marking up; **G** (*Druckw.: Zeichen im Manuskript*) mark; **H** *in* **mit ~:** with distinction

**Aus·zeit** *die* (*Basketball, Volleyball, Schach*) timeout

**ausziehbar** *Adj.* extendible; telescopic ‹aerial›; extending *attrib.* ‹ladder›; sliding-leaf *attrib.* ‹table›

**aus|ziehen** ❶ *unr. tr. V.* **A** (*vergrößern*) pull out ‹couch›; extend ‹table, tripod, etc.›; **B** (*ablegen*) take off, remove ‹clothes›; **C** (*entkleiden*) undress; **sich ~:** undress; get undressed; **sich ganz/nackt ~:** strip off *or* undress completely; **jmdn. mit den Augen ~** (*ugs.*) undress sb. with one's eyes; **D** (*auszupfen*) pull out ‹hair etc.›; **E** (*herausschreiben*) extract ‹words, passages, etc.›; **F** (*nachzeichnen*) draw in; **mit Tusche ~:** ink in; **ausgezogene und punktierte Linien** continuous and dotted lines.
❷ *unr. itr. V.; mit sein* **A** (*aus einer Wohnung usw.*) move out (**aus** of); **B** (*losgehen*) set off; **auf Abenteuer/zur Jagd ~:** set off *or* out in search of adventure/for the hunt

**Auszieh·tisch** *der* extending table; sliding-leaf table

**aus|zischen** *tr. V.* hiss ‹speaker, play, etc.›

**Auszubildende** *der/die; adj. Dekl.* ▶ **159** (*bes. Amtsspr.*) trainee; (*im Handwerk*) apprentice

**Aus·zug** *der* **A** (*das Ausziehen*) move; **B** (*Abschrift*) extract; (*Bankw.*) statement; **C** (*Textstelle*) extract; excerpt; **D** (*das Hinausgehen*) departure; (*feierlich*) procession (**aus** out of); (*als Protest*) walk out; **der ~ der Kinder Israel** (*bibl.*) the Exodus; **E** (*Extrakt*) extract; **F** (*schweiz.*) *first age group of men liable for military service*

**auszugs·weise** *Adv.* in extracts *or* excerpts; **etw. ~ lesen** read extracts from sth.

**aus|zupfen** *tr. V.* pluck out; pull out ‹weeds›

**autark** /au̯'tark/ *Adj.* **A** (*Wirtsch.*) self-sufficient; autarkic *as tech. term;* **B** (*geh.: eigenständig, selbstgenügsam*) independent; self-sufficient

**Autarkie** /au̯tar'ki:/ *die;* **~, ~n** **A** (*Wirtsch.*) self-sufficiency; autarky *as tech. term;* **B** (*geh.: Selbstgenügsamkeit*) self-sufficiency; independence

**authentisch** /au̯'tɛntɪʃ/ ❶ *Adj.* (*echt*) authentic; (*zuverlässig*) reliable ‹report›. ❷ *adv.* authentically; ‹prove› reliably

**Authentizität** /au̯tɛntitsi'tɛ:t/ *die;* **~** (*geh.*) authenticity

**Autismus** /au̯'tɪsmʊs/ *der;* **~** ▶ **474** (*Med.*) autism

**Autist** *der;* **~en, ~en, Autistin** *die;* **~, ~nen** autistic

**autistisch** (*Med.*) ❶ *Adj.* autistic. ❷ *adv.* autistically

**Auto** /'au̯to/ *das;* **~s, ~s** car; automobile (*Amer.*); **~ fahren** drive [a car]; (*mitfahren*) go in the car; **mit dem ~ fahren** go by car; **er hat wie ein Auto geguckt** (*ugs.*) his eyes popped out of his head

**Auto·atlas** *der* road atlas

**Auto·bahn** *die* motorway (*Brit.*); expressway (*Amer.*); (*mit Gebühren*) turnpike (*Amer.*); (*in Germany, Austria, Switzerland also*) autobahn

**Autobahn-** motorway (*Brit.*), expressway (*Amer.*) ‹exit, intersection, junction, service area, etc.›

**Autobahn-: ~auf·fahrt** *die* motorway access road (*Brit.*); expressway entrance [ramp] (*Amer.*); **~aus·fahrt** *die* motorway (*Brit.*) *or* (*Amer.*) expressway exit; **~dreieck** *das* motorway (*Brit.*) *or* (*Amer.*) expressway junction *or* merging point; **~gebühr** *die* motorway (*Brit.*) *or* (*Amer.*) expressway toll; **~kreuz** *das* motorway (*Brit.*) *or* (*Amer.*) expressway interchange; **~rast·stätte** *die* motorway (*Brit.*) *or* (*Amer.*) expressway service area; **~vignette** *die* ⇒ **Gebührenvignette**; **~zubringer** *der* motorway (*Brit.*) *or* (*Amer.*) expressway approach road *or* feeder [road]

*old spelling (see note on page 1707)

**auto-, Auto-: ~biographie** /-----'-/ *die* autobiography; **~biographisch** /----'--/ ❶ *Adj.* autobiographical; ❷ *adv.* autobiographically; **~bus** *der* bus; (*Reisebus*) coach; **~car** *der* (*schweiz.*) coach

**Autodafé** /au̯toda'fe:/ *das;* **~s, ~s** **A** (*hist.: Ketzerverbrennung*) auto-da-fé; **B** (*Bücherverbrennung*) book-burning

**Auto·didakt** /-di'dakt/ *der;* **~en, ~en, Autodidaktin** *die;* **~, ~nen** autodidact; **~ sein** be an autodidact; be self-taught

**auto·didaktisch** ❶ *Adj.* self-study *attrib.*, self-teaching *attrib.* ‹aids, materials›; **~es Studium** self-study; self-instruction. ❷ *adv.* **sich ~ weiterbilden** continue one's education by self-study

**Autodrom** *das;* **~s, ~e** **A** ⇒ **Motodrom**; **B** (*österr.: für Skooter*) dodgems *pl.;* bumper cars *pl.*

**auto-, Auto-: ~elektrik** *die* automotive electrics *pl.;* (*Anlage*) [car] electrical system; **~erotik** *die* auto-eroticism *no art.;* **~fähre** *die* car ferry; **~fahren** *das;* **~~s** driving; motoring; **~fahrer** *der* [car] driver; **~fahrer·gruß** *der* (*ugs.*) *driver's tapping of the forehead in response to stupid action by other driver, cyclist, pedestrian, etc.;* **~fahrerin** *die* [car] driver; **~fahrt** *die* ▶ **265** drive; **~fokus** *der* autofocus; **~frei** *Adj.* ‹day, time› when no cars are/were allowed on the road; ‹place› where no cars are/were allowed; **X ist ~frei** no cars are allowed in X; **~fried·hof** *der* (*ugs.*) car dump; **~gen** /-'ge:n/ ❶ *Adj.* **A** (*Technik*) **~genes Schneiden/Schweißen** gas *or* oxyacetylene cutting/welding; **B** (*Psych.*) **~genes Training** autogenic training; autogenics; ❷ *adv.* (*Technik*) **~gen schweißen/schneiden** weld/cut using an oxyacetylene flame; **~gramm** /--'-/ *das;* **~~s, ~~e** autograph; **~gramm·jäger** /--'---/ *der,* **~gramm·jägerin** *die* autograph hunter; **~hypnose** /---'--/ *die* (*Psych.*) autohypnosis; **~karte** *die* road map; **~kino** *das* drive-in cinema; **~knacker** *der,* **~knackerin** *die;* **~~, ~~nen** (*ugs.*) car burglar; **~kolonne** *die* line of cars; **~krat** /au̯to'kra:t/ *der;* **~en, ~~en** autocrat; **~kratie** /---'-/ *die;* **~~, ~~n** autocracy; **~kratin** *die;* **~~, ~~nen** ⇒ **Autokrat**; **~kratisch** /-'--/ ❶ *Adj.* autocratic; ❷ *adv.* autocratically; **~marder** *der* car burglar; **~marke** *die* make of car

**Automat** /au̯to'ma:t/ *der;* **~en, ~en** **A** (*Verkaufs~*) [slot] machine; vending machine; (*Spiel~*) slot machine; fruit machine; (*Musik~*) jukebox; **B** (*in der Produktion, auch fig.: Mensch*) robot; automaton; **ich bin doch kein ~:** I'm not a machine; **C** (*Math., DV*) automaton

**Automaten-: ~knacker** *der,* **~knackerin** *die;* **~~, ~~nen** (*ugs.*) thief who breaks into slot machines; **~restaurant** *das* vending machine restaurant; automat (*Amer.*)

**Automatik** *die;* **~, ~en** (*Technik*) **A** (*Vorrichtung*) automatic control mechanism; (*Getriebe~*) automatic transmission; **eine ~ haben** ‹car› have automatic transmission; ‹camera› have automatic exposure control; **B** (*Vorgang*) automatic process

**Automatik·gurt** *der* (*Kfz-W.*) inertia-reel belt

**Automation** *die;* **~:** automation

**automatisch** (*auch fig.*) ❶ *Adj.* automatic. ❷ *adv.* automatically

**automatisieren** *tr. V.* automate

**Automatisierung** *die;* **~, ~en** automation

**Automatismus** *der;* **~, Automatismen** **A** (*Technik, fig.*) automatic mechanism; **B** (*Med., Biol., Psych.*) automatism *no art.*

**Auto-: ~mechaniker** *der,* **~mechanikerin** *die* motor mechanic; **~minute** *die:* ▶ **265** **zehn ~minuten entfernt sein** be ten minutes [away] by car; be ten minutes' drive [away]; **~mobil** /--'-/ *das;* **~~s, ~~e** (*geh.*) motor car; automobile (*Amer.*)

**Automobil-: ~aus·stellung** *die* motor show (*Brit.*); automobile show (*Amer.*); **~bau** *der* car manufacture; **~industrie** *die* motor industry

**auto-, Auto-: ~mobilist** /----'-/ *der;* **~~en, ~~en, ~mobilistin** *die;* **~~, ~~nen** (*bes. schweiz.*) motorist; car driver; **~mobil·klub** /---'--/ *der* motoring organization; **~nom** /--'-/ ❶ *Adj.* autonomous; autonomic ‹nervous system›; ❷ *adv.* autonomously; **~nomie** /---'-/ *die;* **~~, ~~n** autonomy; **~nummer** *die* [car] registration number; **~papiere** *Pl.* car documents; **~pilot** *der* (*Flugw.*) autopilot

**Autopsie** /au̯tɔ'psi:/ *die;* **~, ~n** (*Med.*) autopsy; postmortem [examination]

**Autor** /'au̯tɔr/ *der;* **~s, ~en** ▶ **159** /-'to:rən/ author

**Auto-: ~radio** *das* car radio; **~reifen** *der* car tyre; **~reise·zug** *der* Motorail train (*Brit.*); auto train (*Amer.*)

**Autoren·kollektiv** *das* authors' collective

**Auto-: ~rennen** *das* (*Sportart*) motor (*Brit.*) *or* (*Amer.*) auto racing; (*Veranstaltung*) motor (*Brit.*) *or* (*Amer.*) auto race; **~reparatur** *die* car repair; repair to the/a car

**Autorin** *die;* **~, ~nen** authoress; author

**Autorisation** /au̯toriza'tsi̯o:n/ *die;* **~, ~en** authorization

**autorisieren** *tr. V.* authorize

**autoritär** /au̯tori'tɛ:ɐ̯/ ❶ *Adj.* authoritarian. ❷ *adv.* in an authoritarian manner

**Autorität** /au̯tori'tɛ:t/ *die;* **~, ~en** authority; **als ~ auf einem Gebiet gelten** be regarded as an authority in a field

**autoritativ** /au̯torita'ti:f/ ❶ *Adj.* (*geh.*) authoritative. ❷ *adv.* authoritatively

**autoritäts·gläubig** *Adj.* trusting in authority *pred.*

**Autoritäts·gläubigkeit** *die* trust in authority

**Autor·korrektur** *die* (*Buchw.*) author's correction; (*Fahne*) author's proof; (*Korrekturlesen*) author's reading of the proofs

**Autorschaft** *die;* **~:** authorship

**auto-, Auto-: ~schalter** *der* drive-in counter; **~schlange** *die* queue *or* line of cars; **~schlosser** *der,* **~schlosserin** *die* ⇒ **~mechaniker**; **~schlüssel** *der* car key; **~skooter** *der* dodgem; bumper car; **~stopp** *der* hitch-hiking; hitching (*coll.*); **per** *od.* **mit ~stopp fahren, ~stopp machen** hitch-hike; hitch (*coll.*); **~strich** *der* (*ugs.*) *area where prostitutes wait to be picked up by kerb-crawlers;* **~stunde** *die:* **zwei ~stunden entfernt sein** be two hours [away] by car; be two hours' drive [away]; **~suggestion** /----'-/ *die* (*Psych.*) autosuggestion; **~telefon** *das* car telephone; **~test** *der* car test; **~tür** *die* car door; **~typie** /---'-/ *die;* **~~, ~~n** (*Druckw.*) half-tone photoengraving; **~unfall** *der* car accident; **~verkehr** *der* [motor] traffic; **~verleih** *der,* **~vermietung** *die* car hire (*Brit.*) *or* rental firm *or* service; **~werkstatt** *die* garage; car repair shop; **~zubehör** *das* car accessories *pl.*

**autsch** /au̯tʃ/ *Interj.* ouch; ow

**Au·wald** *der* ⇒ **Auenwald**

**auweh** /au̯'ve:/ *Interj.* oh dear; (*Ausruf des Schmerzes*) ouch

**auwei[a]** /au̯'vai̯(a)/ *Interj.* (*ugs.*) oh dear

**Avance** /a'vã:sə/ *die;* **~, ~n** *in* **jmdm. ~n machen** make approaches to sb.; (*geh.: einen Flirt beginnen*) make advances to sb.

**avancieren** /avã'si:rən/ *itr. V.; mit sein* (*geh.*) **zu etw. ~:** be promoted to sth. (*also iron.*); rise to sth.; **zum Bestseller ~** (*fig.*) become a best seller

**Avantgarde** /avã'gardə/ *die;* **~, ~n** avant-garde; (*Politik*) vanguard (*fig.*)

**Avantgardismus** *der;* **~:** avant-gardism

**Avantgardist** *der;* **~en, ~en, Avantgardistin** *die;* **~, ~nen** member of the avant-garde; avant-gardist

**avantgardistisch** ❶ *Adj.* avant-garde. ❷ *adv.* ‹paint etc.› in an avant-garde style

**AvD** *Abk.* **Automobilclub von Deutschland** Automobile Club of Germany

**Ave-Maria** /'a:vema'ri:a/ *das;* **~s, ~s** (*kath. Kirche*) Ave Maria; Hail Mary

**Avers** /a'vɛrs/ *der;* **~es, ~e** (*Münzk.*) obverse

**Aversion** /avɛrˈzi̯o:n/ *die;* ~, ~**en** aversion; **eine ~** *od.* **~en gegen jmdn./etw. haben** have an aversion to sb./sth.

**Avis** /aˈvi:/ *der od. das;* ~ (*Kaufmannsspr., Bankw.*) advice; (*schriftlich*) advice note

**avisieren** /aviˈzi:rən/ *tr. V.* (*bes. Wirtsch.*) send notification of; advise *or* notify of

**Aviso** /aˈvi:zo/ *das;* ~**s**, ~**s** (*österr.*) ⇒ **Avis**

**Avocado** /avoˈka:do/ *die;* ~, ~**s** avocado [pear]

**Axel** /ˈaksl̩/ *der;* ~**s**, ~ (*Eis-, Rollkunstlauf*) axel

**axial** /aˈksi̯a:l/ *Adj.* (*Technik*) axial

**Axiom** /aˈksi̯o:m/ *das;* ~**s**, ~**e** axiom

**Axiomatik** /aksi̯oˈma:tɪk/ *die;* ~ Ⓐ (*Lehre*) axiomatics *sing.; no art.;* study of axioms; Ⓑ (*Verfahren*) axiomatization

**axiomatisch** ❶ *Adj.* axiomatic. ❷ *adv.* axiomatically

**Axt** /akst/ *die;* ~, **Äxte** /ˈɛkstə/ axe; **die ~ im Haus erspart den Zimmermann** (*Spr.*) it saves trouble if you don't have to get someone in; **sich benehmen wie die ~ im Walde** behave like a boor

**Axt·hieb** *der* blow of the/an axe

**Azalee** /at̮saˈle:ə/ *die;* ~, ~**n**, **Azalie** /aˈt̮sa:li̯ə/ *die;* ~, ~**n** azalea

**Azetat** ⇒ **Acetat**

**Azimut** /at̮siˈmu:t/ *das od. der;* ~**s** (*Astron.*) azimuth

**Azoren** /aˈt̮so:rən/ *Pl.* **die ~:** the Azores

**Azteke** /at̮sˈte:kə/ *der;* ~**n**, ~**n**, **Aztekin** *die;* ~, ~**nen** Aztec

**Azteken·reich** *das* Aztec empire

**Azubi** /ˈa:t̮subi/ *der;* ~**s**, ~**s**/*die;* ~, ~**s** (*ugs.*) ⇒ **Auszubildende**

**Azur** /aˈt̮su:ɐ̯/ *der;* ~**s** (*dichter.*) Ⓐ (*Farbe*) azure; Ⓑ (*Himmel*) azure (*literary*)

**azur·blau, azurn** *Adj.* (*geh.*) azure[-blue]

**azyklisch** /ˈat̮sy:klɪʃ/ *Adj.* Ⓐ (*unregelmäßig*) irregular; Ⓑ (*Bot., Chemie*) acyclic

# B b

b, B /beː/ *das;* ~, ~ **A** (*Buchstabe*) b/B; **B** (*Musik*) [key of] B flat; ⇨ *auch* **a**, **A**

**B** *Abk.* **Bundesstraße** ≈ A (*Brit.*)

**BA** *Abk.* **Bundesanstalt für Arbeit**

**BAB** *Abk.* **Bundesautobahn** ≈ M (*Brit.*)

**babbeln** /'babl̩n/ *itr., tr. V.* (*landsch. ugs.*) (*auch abwertend*) babble

**Babel** /'baːbl̩/ **1** (*das*); ~s Babel; **der Turm zu** ~**:** the Tower of Babel. **2** *das;* ~s, ~ **A** (*Sünden*~) hotbed of vice; sink of iniquity; **B** (*vielsprachiger Ort*) babel

**Baby** /'beːbi/ *das;* ~s, ~s baby

**Baby-:** ~**artikel** *Pl.* baby goods; ~**ausstattung** *die* layette

**Babylon** /'baːbylɔn/ **1** (*das*); ~s Babylon. **2** *das;* ~s, ~s ⇨ **Babel 2**

**Babylonien** /baby'loːni̯ən/ (*das*); ~s Babylonia

**Babylonier** *der;* ~s, ~, **Babylonierin** *die;* ~, ~nen Babylonian

**babylonisch** *Adj.* Babylonian; **ein** ~**es Sprachgewirr** a babel of languages; **der Babylonische Turm** the Tower of Babel

**baby-, Baby-:** ~**sitten** /-sɪtn̩/ *itr. V.; nur im Inf.* (*ugs.*) babysit; ~**sitter** /-sɪtɐ/ *der;* ~~s, ~~, ~**sitterin** *die;* ~~, ~~nen babysitter; ~**sitting** /-sɪtɪŋ/ *das;* ~s babysitting; ~**speck** *der* (*ugs.*) puppy fat (*Brit.*); baby fat (*Amer.*); ~**strich** *der* (*ugs.*) child prostitution; ~**waage** *die* baby scales; ~**wäsche** *die* baby clothes

**bacchantisch** /ba'xantɪʃ/ (*geh.*) **1** *Adj.* Bacchanalian. **2** *adv.* in a Bacchanalian manner *or* fashion

**Bach** /bax/ *der;* ~[e]s, **Bäche** /'bɛçə/ **A** stream; brook; **den** ~ **runtergehen** (*ugs.*) ‹company› go downhill; **B** (*Rinnsal*) stream [of water]; ⇨ *auch* **Bächlein**

**bach·ab** *Adv.* downstream

**Bache** /'baxə/ (*Jägerspr.*) *die;* ~, ~n wild sow

**Bächelchen** /'bɛçl̩çən/ *das;* ~s, ~**:** rivulet

**Bach·forelle** *die* brown trout

**Bächlein** /'bɛçlai̯n/ *das;* ~s, ~**:** rivulet; **ein** ~ **machen** (*Kinderspr.*) do a wee-wee (*child lang.*)

**Bach·stelze** *die* (*Motacilla alba alba*) white wagtail; (*M.a. yarrellii*) pied wagtail

**Back** /bak/ *die;* ~, ~en (*Seemannsspr.*) **A** (*Decksaufbau*) forecastle; fo'c's'le; **B** (*Schüssel*) wooden serving bowl (*in which sailors' food is served*); **C** (*Tisch*) mess table; **D** (*Tischgemeinschaft*) mess

**Back·blech** *das* baking sheet

**Back·bord** *das* (*Seew., Luftf.*) port [side]; **über** ~**:** over the port side

**backbord[s]** /'bakbɔrt(s)/ *Adv.* (*Seew., Luftf.*) on the port side

**Bäckchen** /'bɛkçən/ *das;* ~s, ~**:** [little] cheek

**Backe** /'bakə/ *die;* ~, ~n **A** ▶ 471 (*Wange*) cheek; **au** ~**!** (*ugs.*) oh heck (*coll.*); ⇨ *auch* **voll** 1 A; **B** ▶ 471 (*ugs.: Gesäß*~) buttock; cheek (*sl.*); ⇨ *auch* **abreißen** C; **C** (*Seitenteil*) (*eines Schraubstocks*) jaw; cheek; (*eines Gewehrs*) cheekpiece; (*Brems*~) (*eines Autos*) shoe; (*eines Fahrrads*) block

**backen**[1] /'bakn̩/ **1** *unr. itr. V.* **A** bake; do the baking; **ich backe immer selbst** I do all my own baking; **B** (*garen*) ‹cake etc.› bake; **der Kuchen muss noch 10 Minuten** ~**:** the cake has to stay in the oven for another 10 minutes; **C** ‹oven› bake. **2** *unr. tr. V.* **A** bake ‹cakes, bread, etc.›; **ich backe vieles selbst** I do a lot of my own baking; (*fig.*) **das frisch gebackene Ehepaar** (*ugs.*) the newly-weds *pl.* (*coll.*); **eine frisch gebackene Ärztin** (*ugs.*) a newly-fledged doctor; **B** (*bes. südd.: braten*) roast; (*in der Bratpfanne*) fry; **C** (*trocknen*) dry ‹fruit, mushrooms, etc.›; bake ‹brick›

**backen**[2] (*bes. nordd.*) **1** *itr. V.* ‹snow, earth› stick (**an** + *Dat.* to). **2** *tr. V.* stick (**an** + *Akk.* on to)

**Backen-:** ~**bart** *der* side whiskers *pl.*; sideboards *pl.* (*sl.*); ~**bremse** *die* (*Technik*) (*eines Autos*) shoe brake; (*eines Fahrrads*) block brake; ~**knochen** *der* ▶ 471 cheekbone; ~**streich** *der* (*veralt.*) slap in the face; ~**tasche** *die* [cheek] pouch; ~**zahn** *der* ▶ 471 molar; **kleiner** *od.* **vorderer/großer** *od.* **hinterer** ~**zahn** premolar/back molar

**Bäcker** /'bɛkɐ/ *der;* ~s, ~ ▶ 159 **A** baker; ~ **lernen** learn the baker's trade; learn to be a baker; **er will** ~ **werden/ist** ~**:** he wants to be/is a baker; **B** (*Geschäft*) baker's [shop]; **zum** ~ **gehen** go to the baker's; **beim** ~**:** at the baker's

**Back·erbsen** *Pl.* (*Kochk.*) *small crisp round noodles added to soup*

**Bäckerei** *die;* ~, ~en **A** (*Bäckerladen*) baker's [shop]; (*Backstube*) bakery; **B** (*das Backen*) baking; **C** (*Handwerk*) bakery trade; **D** (*südd., österr.*) ⇨ **Backwerk**

**Bäcker-:** ~**geselle** *der,* ~**gesellin** *die* journeyman baker; ~**hand·werk** *das* bakery trade

**Bäckerin** *die;* ~, ~nen ▶ 159 baker

**Bäcker-:** ~**innung** *die* bakers' guild; ~**junge** *der* (*Gehilfe*) baker's boy *or* lad; (*Lehrling*) baker's apprentice; ~**laden** *der; Pl.* ~**läden** baker's shop; ~**lehre** *die* baker's apprenticeship; ~**lehrling** *der* baker's apprentice; ~**meister** *der,* ~**meisterin** *die* master baker

**Bäckers·frau** *die* baker's wife

**back-, Back-:** ~**fertig** *Adj.* oven-ready; ~**fisch** *der* **A** (*Kochk.*) fried fish (*in breadcrumbs*); **B** (*veralt.: Mädchen*) teenager; teenage girl; ~**form** *die* baking tin (*Brit.*); baking pan (*Amer.*); (*für Kuchen*) cake tin (*Brit.*); cake pan (*Amer.*); (*aus Ton*) earthenware baking mould

**Background** /'bɛkgraunt/ *der;* ~s, ~s background

**Backhähnchen** *das* fried chicken (*in breadcrumbs*)

**Back-:** ~**hendl** *das* (*österr.*), ~**huhn** *das* fried chicken (*in breadcrumbs*); ~**mulde** *die* ⇨ ~**trog**; ~**obst** *das* dried fruit; ~**ofen** *der* oven; (*beim Bäcker*) [baker's] oven; ~**pfeife** *die* (*bes. nordd.*) slap in the face; ~**pfeifen·gesicht** *das* (*salopp abwertend*) ⇨ **Ohrfeigengesicht**; ~**pflaume** *die* prune; ~**pulver** *das* baking powder; ~**rohr** *das* (*südd., österr.*), ~**röhre** *die* oven; ~**stein** *der* brick; ~**stein·bau** *der; Pl.* ~~**ten** brick building; ~**stein·gotik** *die* (*Kunstwiss.*) brick Gothic [architecture]; ~**stube** *die* bakery; bakehouse; ~**trog** *der* kneading trough; dough tray *or* trough; ~**waren** *Pl.* bread, cakes, and pastries; ~**werk** *das* biscuits *or* (*Amer.*) cookies and pastries

**Bad** /baːt/ *das;* ~[e]s, **Bäder** /'bɛːdɐ/ **A** (*Wasser*) bath; **[sich** (*Dat.*)**] ein** ~ **einlaufen lassen** run [oneself] a bath; **B** (*das Baden*) bath; (*das Schwimmen*) swim; (*im Meer o. Ä.*) bathe; **ein** ~ **nehmen** (*geh.*) have *or* take a bath; (*schwimmen*) go for a swim; (*im Meer o. Ä.*) bathe; **nach dem** ~**:** after bathing; **beim** ~ **im Meer/** (*fig.*) **in der Sonne** when bathing in the sea/when sunbathing; **jmdm. Bäder verordnen** (*Med.*) prescribe a course of baths for sb.; **C** (*Badezimmer*) bathroom; **ein Zimmer mit** ~**:** a room with [private] bath; **D** (*Schwimm*~) [swimming] pool; swimming bath; **E** (*Heil*~) spa; (*Seebad*) [seaside] resort; **F** (*Technik, Chemie*) bath

**Bade-:** ~**anstalt** *die* swimming baths *pl.* (*Brit.*); public pool (*Amer.*); ~**an·zug** *der* swimming *or* bathing costume; swimsuit; ~**arzt** *der* spa doctor; ~**gast** *der* **A** (*im Schwimmbad*) bather; swimmer; **B** (*im Kurort*) visitor to a/the spa; ~**hose** *die* swimming *or* bathing trunks *pl;* ~**kabine** *die* changing cubicle (*Brit.*); locker (*Amer.*); ~**kappe** *die* swimming *or* bathing cap; ~**kur** *die* course of treatment at a spa; ~**mantel** *der* dressing gown; bathrobe; (*Strandkleidung*) beach robe; ~**matte** *die* bath mat; ~**meister** *der,* ~**meisterin** *die* swimming pool attendant; ~**mütze** *die* swimming *or* bathing cap

**baden** **1** *itr. V.* **A** (*in der Wanne*) have *or* take a bath; bath; **warm/kalt** ~**:** have *or* take a hot/cold bath; **B** (*schwimmen*) bathe; swim; ~ **gehen** go for a bathe *or* a swim; go bathing *or* swimming; **[bei** *od.* **mit etw.]** ~ **gehen** (*ugs.*) come a cropper (*coll.*) [over sth.]. **2** *tr. V.* bath ‹child, patient, etc.›; bathe ‹wound, face, eye, etc.›; **in Schweiß gebadet** (*fig.*) bathed in sweat; **du bist wohl als Kind zu heiß gebadet worden!** (*ugs. scherzh.*) you must have been dropped on your head as a baby

**Baden** /'baːdn̩/ (*das*); ~s Baden

**Badener** /'baːdənɐ/ *der;* ~s, ~, **Badenerin** *die;* ~, ~nen, (*ugs.*) **Badenser** /ba'dɛnzɐ/ *der;* ~s, ~, **Badenserin** *die;* ~, ~nen inhabitant of Baden; (*von Geburt*) native of Baden; ⇨ *auch* **Kölner**

**Baden-Württemberger** **1** *indekl. Adj.* Baden-Württemberg *attrib.* **2** *der;* ~s, ~**:** native of Baden-Württemberg; (*Einwohner*) inhabitant of Baden-Württemberg

**Bade-:** ~**ofen** *der* bathwater heater; ~**ort** *der* **A** (*Seebad*) [seaside] resort; **B** (*Kurort*) spa; ~**platz** *der* bathing place

**Bäder** ⇨ **Bad**

**Bade-:** ~**sachen** *Pl.* bathing *or* swimming things; ~**saison** *die* bathing *or* swimming season; (*im Kurort*) spa season; ~**salz** *das* bath salts *pl.;* ~**schwamm** *der* [bath] sponge; ~**strand** *der* bathing beach; ~**tuch** *das; Pl.* ~**tücher** bath towel; ~**wanne** *die* bath[tub]; ~**wasser** *das* bath water; ~**wetter** *das* bathing weather; weather warm enough *or* suitable for bathing *or* swimming; ~**zeit** *die* **A** (*bei Heilbehandlungen*) immersion time; **B** (*in* ~*anstalten*) swimming time; **die** ~**zeit ist beendet** the pool is now closing; **C** ⇨ ~**saison**; ~**zeug** *das* (*ugs.*) bathing *or* swimming things *pl.;* ~**zimmer** *das* bathroom; ~**zusatz** *der* (~*salz*) bath salts; (*Schaumbad*) bubble bath

**badisch** *Adj.* of Baden *postpos.;* ‹wine, produce, etc.› from Baden; **die** ~**e Mundart** the Baden dialect; **das Badische** (*Sprachw.*) the Baden dialect; (*Region*) Baden

**Badminton** /'bɛtmɪntən/ *das;* ~s badminton

**baff** /baf/ *in* ~ **sein** (*ugs.*) be flabbergasted

**Bafög** /'baːfœk/ *das;* ~s (*ugs.*) [state] grant; **[800 Mark]** ~ **kriegen** get a [state] grant [of 800 Marks]; ⇨ *auch* **BAföG**

**BAföG** *Abk.* **Bundesausbildungsförderungsgesetz**

**Bagage** /ba'gaːʒə/ *die;* ~, ~n (*abwertend*) (*Familie*) tribe (*derog.*); (*Gesindel*) rabble;

*old spelling (see note on page 1707)

crowd (*coll.*); **die ganze ∼:** the whole lot of them

**Bagatell-: ∼betrag** *der* trifling amount; **∼delikt** *das* (*Rechtsw.*) petty *or* minor offence

**Bagatelle** /baga'tɛlə/ *die;* ∼, **∼n** Ⓐ (*Kleinigkeit*) trifle; bagatelle; **das ist keine ∼:** it's no mere trifle; Ⓑ (*Musik*) bagatelle

**bagatellisieren** ❶ *tr. V.* trivialize; minimize. ❷ *itr. V.* trivialize matters

**Bagatell-: ∼sache** *die* petty *or* minor case; **∼schaden** *der* minor damage *no indef. art.*; **∼schäden** minor damage *sing.*

**Bagger** /'bagɐ/ *der;* **∼s, ∼:** excavator; digger; (*Schwimmbagger*) dredger

**Bagger·führer** *der,* **Bagger·führerin** *die* excavator driver; (*eines Schwimmbaggers*) dredger master

**baggern** ❶ *itr. V.* Ⓐ excavate; (*mit dem Schwimmbagger*) dredge; Ⓑ (*Volleyball*) dig the ball. ❷ *tr. V.* Ⓐ excavate; (*mit dem Schwimmbagger*) dredge; Ⓑ (*Volleyball*) dig ‹ball›

**Bagger·see** *der* flooded gravel pit

**Baguette** /ba'gɛt/ *die;* ∼, **∼n** baguette

**bah** /ba:/ *Interj.* ugh

**bäh** /bɛ:/ *Interj.* Ⓐ (*bei Ekel*) ugh; (*schadenfroh*) hee-hee; tee-hee; Ⓑ (*von Schafen*) baa

**Bahama·inseln** /ba'ha:ma-/, **Bahamas** *Pl.* **die ∼:** the Bahamas

**bähen** /'bɛ:ən/ *tr. V.* (*südd., österr., schweiz.*) toast ‹bread, roll, etc.›

**Bahn** /ba:n/ *die;* ∼, **∼en** Ⓐ (*Weg*) path; way; (*von Wasser*) course; **sich** (*Dat.*) **∼ brechen** ‹invention, idea› establish itself; **einer Sache ∼ brechen** pave *or* prepare the way for sth.; **jmdn. aus der ∼ werfen** *od.* **bringen** *od.* **schleudern** (*fig.*) knock sb. sideways (*fig.*); **auf die schiefe ∼ geraten** (*fig.*) go astray; ⇒ *auch* **ebnen**; **tüchtig** 1 A; Ⓑ (*Strecke*) path; (*Umlauf∼*) orbit; (*einer Rakete*) [flight] path; (*eines Geschosses*) trajectory; **sich in neuen ∼en bewegen** (*fig.*) break new *or* fresh ground (*fig.*); **etw. [wieder] in die richtige ∼ lenken** (*fig.*) get sth. [back] on the right track (*fig.*); Ⓒ (*Sport*) track; (*für Pferderennen*) course (*Brit.*); track (*Amer.*); (*für einzelne Teilnehmer*) lane; (*Kegel∼*) alley; (*Schlitten∼, Bob∼*) run; (*Bowling∼*) lane; **∼ frei!** make way!; get out of the way!; Ⓓ (*Fahr∼*) lane; Ⓔ (*Eisen∼*) train; (*Bahnnetz*) railways *pl.*; railroad *pl.* (*Amer.*); **jmdn. zur ∼ bringen/an der ∼ abholen** take sb. to/pick sb. up from the station; **mit der** *od.* **per ∼:** by train; **∼ fahren** go by train; Ⓕ (*Straßen∼*) tram; streetcar (*Amer.*); Ⓖ (*Schienenweg*) railway [track]; Ⓗ (*Streifen*) (*Stoff∼*) length; (*Tapeten∼*) strip; length; (*eines Rocks*) panel

**bahn-, Bahn-: ∼amtlich** *Adj.* (*Amtsspr.*) official railway; **∼arbeiter** *der,* **∼arbeiterin** *die* railway *or* (*Amer.*) railroad worker; **∼beamte** *der,* **∼beamtin** *die* railway *or* (*Amer.*) railroad official; **∼brechend** *Adj.* pioneering; **∼brechend für etw. sein** pave *or* prepare the way for sth.; **∼brechendes geleistet haben** have done pioneering work; **∼brecher** *der,* **∼brecherin** *die;* **∼∼, ∼∼nen** pioneer; **∼bus** *der* railway bus

**Bähnchen** /'bɛ:nçən/ *das;* **∼s, ∼:** narrow-gauge railway; (*in Vergnügungsparks usw.*) miniature railway

**Bahn·damm** *der* railway *or* (*Amer.*) railroad embankment

**bahnen** *tr. V.* clear ‹way, path›; ‹river etc.› carve out ‹channel, bed›; **jmdm./einer Sache einen Weg ∼:** clear the *or* a way for sb./sth.; (*fig.*) pave *or* prepare the way for sb./sth.; **sich** (*Dat.*) **einen Weg durch etw. ∼:** force a *or* one's way through sth.

**bahnen·weise** *Adv.* in lengths; (*bei Tapeten*) in strips *or* lengths

**bahn-, Bahn-: ∼fahrt** *die* train *or* rail journey; **∼frei** *Adj., adv.* (*Kaufmannsspr.*) free on rail; **∼gleis** *das* railway *or* (*Amer.*) railroad track *or* line

**Bahn·hof** *der* [railway *or* (*Amer.*) railroad] station; **∼ Käfertal** Käfertal station; **sich im/am ∼ treffen** meet at the station; **ich verstehe nur ∼** (*ugs.*) it's [all] double Dutch to me; **[ein] großer ∼** (*ugs.*) the red-carpet treatment; **jmdm. einen großen ∼ bereiten** (*ugs.*) roll *or* put out the red carpet for sb.

**Bahnhofs-: ∼buch·handlung** *die* station bookshop; (*Bücherstand*) station bookstall; **∼gast·stätte** *die* station restaurant; **∼halle** *die* station concourse; **∼hotel** *das* station hotel; **∼mission** *die* ≈ Travellers' Aid (*charitable organization for helping rail travellers in need of care or assistance*); **∼platz** *der* square in front of the station; **∼restaurant** *das* station restaurant; **∼vor·platz** *der* station forecourt; **∼vorstand** *der,* **∼vorsteher** *der,* **∼vorsteherin** *die* station manager; **∼wirtschaft** *die* station buffet

**bahn-, Bahn-: ∼körper** *der* permanent way; **∼lagernd** ❶ *Adj.* to be collected from the station *postpos.*; ❷ *adv.* **Waren ∼lagernd schicken** send goods to await collection at the station; **∼linie** *die* railway *or* (*Amer.*) railroad line; **∼meisterei** *die;* **∼∼, ∼∼en** permanent way (*Brit.*) *or* (*Amer.*) railroad maintenance department; **∼polizei** *die* railway *or* (*Amer.*) railroad police; **∼post** *die* travelling *or* railway post office (*Brit.*); **∼reise** *die* train *or* rail journey; (*Pauschalreise*) package holiday (*Brit.*) *or* (*Amer.*) vacation trip by train; **∼reisende** *der/die* [rail] passenger; **∼schranke** *die* level crossing (*Brit.*) *or* (*Amer.*) grade crossing barrier/gate; **∼station** *die* [railway *or* (*Amer.*) railroad] halt (*Brit.*) *or* (*Amer.*) stop; **∼steig** /-ʃtaik/ *der;* **∼[e]s, ∼e** [station] platform; **∼steig·karte** *die* platform ticket; **∼überführung** *die* Ⓐ underbridge; underline bridge; Ⓑ (*ugs.: Brücke über die Bahnlinie*) bridge over the/a railway *or* (*Amer.*) railroad; **∼über·gang** *der* level crossing (*Brit.*); grade *or* railroad crossing (*Amer.*); **∼unterführung** *die* Ⓐ overbridge; overline bridge; Ⓑ (*ugs.: Brücke für die Eisen∼*) railway *or* (*Amer.*) railroad bridge; **∼verbindung** *die* rail (*Brit.*) *or* train connection; **∼wärter** *der* level-crossing (*Brit.*) *or* (*Amer.*) grade-crossing attendant; crossing keeper; (*Streckenwärter*) linesman (*Brit.*); trackman (*Amer.*); **∼wärter·häuschen** *das* crossing keeper's hut

**Bahre** /'ba:rə/ *die;* ∼, **∼n** Ⓐ (*Kranken∼*) stretcher; Ⓑ (*Toten∼*) bier

**Bahr·tuch** *das; Pl.* **Bahrtücher** pall

**Bai** /bai/ *die;* ∼, **∼en** bay

**bairisch** /'bairɪʃ/ *Adj.* Bavarian

**Baiser** /bɛ'ze:/ *das;* **∼s, ∼s** meringue

**Baisse** /'bɛ:sə/ *die;* ∼, **∼n** (*Börsenw.*) fall; **auf ∼ spekulieren** speculate for a fall; bear

**Baisse·spekulant** *der;* **∼en, ∼en, Baissier** /bɛ'sie:/ *der;* **∼s, ∼s** (*Börsenw.*) bear

**Bajonett** /bajo'nɛt/ *das;* **∼[e]s, ∼e** bayonet

**Bajonett-: ∼fassung** *die* (*Elektrot.*) bayonet socket; **∼verschluss, *∼verschluß** *der* bayonet connection

**Bajuware** /baju'va:rə/ *der;* **∼n, ∼n, Bajuwarin** *die;* ∼, **∼nen** (*scherzh.*) Bavarian

**bajuwarisch** *Adj.* (*scherzh.*) Bavarian

**Bake** /'ba:kə/ *die;* ∼, **∼n** Ⓐ (*vor Eisenbahnübergängen, an Autobahnen*) countdown marker; Ⓑ (*zur Absperrung*) [movable] barrier; Ⓒ (*für Schiffe, Flugzeuge*) beacon; Ⓓ (*Vermessungsw.*) ranging pole; range pole

**Bakelit** Ⓦⓩ /bakə'li:t/ *das;* **∼s** bakelite ®

**Baken·tonne** *die* (*Seew.*) marker buoy

**Bakkarat** /'bakara(t)/ *das;* **∼s** baccarat

**Bakken** /'bakn̩/ *der;* **∼s,** ∼ (*Skispringen*) [jumping] hill

**Bakschisch** /'bakʃɪʃ/ *das;* **∼[e]s, ∼e** baksheesh

**Bakterie** /bak'te:ri̯ə/ *die;* ∼, **∼n** bacterium; **voller ∼n** full of germs

**bakteriell** /bakte'ri̯ɛl/ (*Med., Biol.*) ❶ *Adj.* bacterial. ❷ *adv.* **∼ verursacht** caused by bacteria

**Bakterien-: ∼kultur** *die* bacterial culture; **∼träger** *der,* **∼trägerin** *die* carrier

**Bakteriologe** /bakteri̯o'lo:gə/ *der;* **∼n, ∼n** bacteriologist

**Bakteriologie** *die;* **∼:** bacteriology *no art.*

**Bakteriologin** *die;* ∼, **∼nen** bacteriologist

**bakteriologisch** ❶ *Adj.* bacteriological. ❷ *adv.* ‹investigate, detect› using bacteriological methods

**bakterizid** /bakteri'tsi:t/ (*Med.*) ❶ *Adj.* bactericidal. ❷ *adv.* **∼ wirken** act as a bactericide; have a bactericidal effect

**Bakterizid** *das;* **∼s, ∼e** bactericide

**Balalaika** /bala'laika/ *die;* ∼, **∼s** *od.* **Balalaiken** balalaika

**Balance** /ba'laŋsə/ *die;* ∼, **∼n** balance; **die ∼ halten/verlieren** keep/lose one's balance; **die ∼ zwischen ... und ... halten** (*fig.*) keep a balance between ... and ...

**Balance·akt** *der* (*auch fig.*) balancing act

**balancieren** /balaŋ'si:rən/ ❶ *itr. V.*; *mit sein* (*auch fig.*) balance; **über etw.** (*Akk.*) **∼:** pick one's way precariously across sth. ❷ *tr. V.* balance

**Balancier·stange** *die* balancing pole

**balbieren** /bal'bi:rən/ *tr. V.* ⇒ **Löffel** A

**bald** /balt/ *Adv.* Ⓐ **eher** /'e:ɐ̯/, **am ehesten** /-'e:əstn̩/ (*in kurzer Zeit*) soon; (*leicht, rasch*) quickly; easily; **∼ danach** *od.* **darauf** soon afterwards; **so ∼ als** *od.* **wie möglich** as soon as possible; **möglichst ∼:** as soon as possible; **so etwas kommt so ∼ nicht wieder vor** something like that won't happen again in a long while *or* (*coll.*) in a hurry; **bist du ∼ still?** will you just be quiet; **wirds ∼?** how much longer are you going to be?; get a move on, will you; **bis** *od.* **auf ∼:** see you soon; **seit ∼ zwei Jahren** for nearly two years; Ⓑ (*ugs.: fast*) almost; nearly; **das ist ∼ nicht mehr schön** that's getting beyond a joke (*Brit.*); that's not funny any more (*Amer.*); Ⓒ (*veralt.*) *in* **∼ ..., ∼ ...** now ..., now ...; **∼ so, ∼ so** now this way, now that

**Baldachin** /'baldaxi:n/ *der;* **∼s, ∼e** baldachin; (*über dem Bett*) canopy

**Bälde** /'bɛldə/ *in* **in ∼** (*Papierdt.*) in the near future

**baldig** *Adj.* speedy; quick; **auf ∼es Wiedersehen** (*geh.*) see you again soon

**baldigst** *Adv.* as soon as possible

**bald·möglichst** *adv.* (*Papierdt.*) as soon as possible

**baldowern** /bal'do:vɐn/ (*ugs.*) ❶ *tr. V.* check out. ❷ *itr. V.* check everything out

**Baldrian** /'baldria:n/ *der;* **∼s, ∼e** valerian

**Baldrian·tropfen** *Pl.* valerian drops

**Balearen** /bale'a:rən/ *Pl.* **die ∼:** the Balearic Islands

**Balg**[1] /balk/ *der;* **∼[e]s, Bälge** /'bɛlgə/ Ⓐ (*von Tieren*) pelt; skin; (*eines Vogels*) skin; **einem Tier den ∼ abziehen** skin an animal; Ⓑ (*salopp*) (*Bauch*) belly; (*Leib*) body; ⇒ *auch* **rücken** 2 A; Ⓒ (*Bot. od. südd.*) (*Haut*) skin; (*Hülle, Schote*) pod; Ⓓ (*Blase∼; bei einer Kamera*) bellows *pl.*

**Balg**[2] *das;* **∼[e]s, Bälger** /'bɛlgɐ/ *od.* **Bälge** /'bɛlgə/ (*ugs., oft abwertend*) kid (*sl.*); brat (*derog.*)

**balgen** *refl. V.* (*ugs.*) scrap (*coll.*); **sich um etw. ∼:** scrap (*coll.*) over sth.; (*fig.*) fight over sth.

**Balgen** *der;* **∼s,** ∼ (*Fot.*) bellows *pl.*

**Balgerei** *die;* ∼, **∼en** (*ugs.*) scrap (*coll.*)

**Balg·geschwulst** *die* sebaceous cyst

**Balkan** /'balka:n/ *der;* **∼s** Ⓐ (*Halbinsel*) **der ∼:** the Balkans; **auf dem ∼:** in the Balkans; Ⓑ (*Gebirge*) Balkan Mountains

**Balkan·halbinsel** *die* Balkan Peninsula

**balkanisieren** *tr. V.* (*auch fig.*) Balkanize

**Balkanisierung** *die;* ∼, **∼en** (*auch fig.*) Balkanization

**Balkan·staat** *der* Balkan State

**Balken** /'balkn̩/ *der;* **∼s,** ∼ Ⓐ (*Holz∼*) beam; (*aus Stahl*) beam; girder; (*Stütz∼*) prop; shore; **lügen, dass sich die ∼ biegen** tell a [complete] pack of lies; ⇒ *auch* **Splitter, Wasser** A; Ⓑ (*Her.*) fess; Ⓒ (*Schwebe∼*) beam; Ⓓ (*Musik*) cross-stroke; Ⓔ (*Waage∼*) beam; Ⓕ (*Leichtathletik*) (*beim Weitsprung*) take-off board; (*beim Kugelstoßen*) stop board; toe board; Ⓖ (*dicker Strich*) thick stroke; (*fette Linie*) thick line

b

**Balken-: ~decke** *die* ceiling with wooden beams; **~konstruktion** *die* timber-frame structure; **~über·schrift** *die* (*Zeitungsw.*) banner headline; **~waage** *die* beam-balance

**Balkon** /bal'kɔŋ, bal'ko:n/ *der;* **~s, ~s** /bal'kɔŋs/ *od.* **~e** /bal'ko:nə/ **A** balcony; **B** (*Theater*) [dress] circle; (*im Kino*) circle; **~ sitzen** sit in the [dress] circle; **C** (*ugs.: Busen*) big boobs *pl.* (*coll.*); big bust

**Balkonien** /bal'ko:ni̯ən/ (*das*); **~s** (*ugs. scherzh.*) **nach ~ fahren** stay at home and relax on one's own balcony

**Balkon-: ~pflanze** *die* balcony plant; **~tür** *die* balcony door; **~zimmer** *das* room with a balcony

**Ball** /bal/ *der;* **~[e]s, Bälle** /'bɛlə/ **A** ball; **~ spielen** play ball; **am ~ sein** have the ball; (*fig. ugs.*) be in touch; be on the ball (*coll.*); **am ~ bleiben** keep [possession of] the ball; (*fig.*) stick (*coll.*) *or* keep at it; **hart am ~ bleiben** (*fig. ugs.*) stay right with it (*coll.*); **jmdm./einander/sich [gegenseitig] die Bälle zuspielen** *od.* **zuwerfen** (*fig.*) feed sb./each other lines; **B** (*Sportjargon: Schuss, Wurf*) ball; (*aufs Tor*) shot; **C** (*Fest*) ball; **D** (*Punkt*) (*Tennis*) point; (*Baseball*) ball; **E** (*fig.: Kugel*) ball; **der glühende ~ der Sonne** (*geh.*) the fiery orb of the sun

**ballaballa** /bala'bala/ *Adj.* (*salopp*) crackers (*sl.*); daft

**Ballade** /ba'la:də/ *die;* **~, ~n** ballad

**balladenhaft, balladesk** /bala'dɛsk/ *Adj.* ballad-like

**Ballast** /ba'last/ *der;* **~[e]s, ~e** ballast; (*fig.: in Buch, Artikel usw.*) padding; **~ abwerfen** *od.* **über Bord werfen** shed *or* jettison ballast; (*fig.*) rid oneself of unnecessary burdens; **jmdn./etw. als ~ empfinden** (*fig.*) find sb./sth. a burden *or* an encumbrance

**Ballast·stoffe** *Pl.* (*Med.*) roughage *sing.*

**Bällchen** /'bɛlçən/ *das;* **~s, ~:** [little] ball

**ballen** **1** *tr. V.* clench ‹fist›; crumple ‹paper› into a ball; press ‹snow etc.› into a ball; ⇒ *auch* **Faust**; **geballt** 2. **2** *refl. V.* ‹clouds› gather, build up; ‹crowd› gather; ‹traffic› build up; ‹fist› clench; (*fig.*) ‹problems, difficulties, etc.› accumulate, mount up

**Ballen** *der;* **~s, ~** **A** (*Packen*) bale; **ein ~ Stroh/Stoff** a bale of straw/cloth; **B** (*Hand~, Fuß~*) ball; (*bei Tieren*) pad; **C** (*Med.*) bunion; **D** (*Wurzel~*) [root] ball

**ballen·weise** *Adv.* by the bale

**Ballerei** *die;* **~, ~en** (*ugs.*) shoot-out

**Ballerina** /balə'ri:na/ *die;* **~, Ballerinen** ▶ 159 ballerina; ballet dancer

**Baller·mann** *der* (*ugs.*) shooting iron (*coll.*); shooter (*coll.*)

**ballern** (*ugs.*) **1** *itr. V.* **A** (*schießen*) fire [away]; bang away; **B** (*schlagen*) bang, hammer (**gegen** on). **2** *tr. V.* **A** (*werfen*) hurl; **B** **jmdm. eine ~:** sock sb. one (*sl.*); **C** (*Sportjargon*) fire ‹ball›

**Ballett** /ba'lɛt/ *das;* **~[e]s, ~e** ballet; **beim ~ sein** (*ugs.*) be a dancer with the ballet; be a ballet dancer

**Ballett·abend** *der* evening ballet programme *or* performance

***Ballettänzer** *der,* ***Ballettänzerin** *die* ballet dancer

**Balletteuse** /balɛ'tø:zə/ *die;* **~, ~n** dancer

**Ballett-: ~meister** *der* ballet master; **~meisterin** *die* ballet mistress; **~musik** *die* ballet music; **~ratte** *die* (*ugs. scherzh.*) ballet pupil; **~röckchen** *das* tutu; **~schuh** *der* ballet shoe; **~schule** *die* ballet school; **~tänzer** *der,* **~tänzerin** *die* ballet dancer; **~truppe** *die* ballet company; (*im Gegensatz zu den Solotänzern*) corps de ballet

**Ball-: ~führung** *die* (*Ballspiele*) ball control; **~haus** *das* real-tennis court; (*hist.*) tennis court

**Ballistik** *die;* **~:** ballistics *sing., no art.*

**Ballistiker** *der;* **~s, ~, Ballistikerin** *die;* **~, ~nen** ballistics expert

**ballistisch** **1** *Adj.* ballistic. **2** *adv.* ballistically

*old spelling (see note on page 1707)

**Ball-: ~junge** *der* ballboy; **~kleid** *das* ball dress *or* gown; **~königin** *die* belle of the ball; **~künstler** *der,* **~künstlerin** *die* (*Fußballjargon*) artist with the ball

**Ballon** /ba'lɔŋ/ *der;* **~s, ~s** **A** balloon; **B** (*salopp: Kopf*) nut (*coll.*); **eins auf** *od.* **an den ~ kriegen** get hit on the nut (*coll.*); **[so] einen ~ kriegen** *od.* **bekommen** go as red as a beetroot; **C** (*Flasche*) demijohn; **D** (*Chemie*) carboy

**Ballon-: ~mütze** *die* Mao cap; **~reifen** *der* balloon tyre

**Ball-: ~saal** *der* ballroom; **~spiel** *das* ball game; **~spielen** *das;* **~~s** playing ball *no art.;* **~spielen verboten** no ball games; **~technik** *die* ball control

**Ballung** /'balʊŋ/ *die;* **~, ~en** build-up; concentration; (*fig.: von Problemen, Schwierigkeiten*) accumulation

**Ballungs-: ~gebiet** *das,* **~raum** *der* conurbation; **~zentrum** *das* centre of population; **ein ~zentrum der chemischen Industrie** a centre of the chemical industry

**Ball·wechsel** *der* (*Tennis, Tischtennis, Badminton*) rally

**Balsam** /'balza:m/ *der;* **~s, ~e** balsam; balm; (*fig.*) balm; **~ auf jmds. Wunden gießen** (*fig.*) pour balm on sb.'s wounds

**Balsam·essig** *der* balsamic vinegar

**balsamieren** ⇒ **einbalsamieren**

**balsamisch** **1** *Adj.* **A** (*wohlriechend*) balmy; fragrant; (*lindernd*) soothing ‹cream, ointment, etc.›; **B** (*Balsam enthaltend*) balsamic. **2** *adv.* fragrantly ‹scented›; soothingly ‹cooling›

**Balte** /'baltə/ *der;* **~n, ~n, Baltin** *die;* **~, ~nen** person *or* man/woman from the Baltic; Balt; **er ist Balte** he comes from the Baltic

**Baltikum** /'baltikʊm/ *das;* **~s** Baltic States *pl.*

**baltisch** *Adj.* Baltic

**Balustrade** /balʊs'tra:də/ *die;* **~, ~n** balustrade

**Balz** /balts/ *die;* **~, ~en** **A** (*Liebesspiel*) courtship display; **B** (*Zeit*) mating season

**balzen** *itr. V.* perform its/their courtship display

**Balz·zeit** *die* mating season

**Bambi** /'bambi/ *das;* **~s, ~s** (*Kinderspr.*) little deer

**Bambule** /bam'bu:lə/ *die;* **~, ~n** (*salopp*) shindy; **~ machen** go on the rampage

**Bambus** /'bambʊs/ *der;* **~** *od.* **~ses, ~se** bamboo

**Bambus-: ~rohr** *das* bamboo [cane]; **~sprossen** *Pl.* bamboo shoots; **~vorhang** *der* (*Politik*) bamboo curtain

**Bammel** /'baml̩/ *der;* **~s** (*ugs.*) **~ vor jmdm./etw. haben** be scared stiff of sb./sth. (*coll.*)

**bammeln** (*bes. nordd.*) ⇒ **baumeln**

**banal** /ba'na:l/ **1** *Adj.* **A** (*abwertend: platt*) banal; trite, banal ‹speech, reply, response, excuse›; **B** (*gewöhnlich*) commonplace; ordinary. **2** *adv.* **A** (*abwertend: platt*) banally; tritely; **B** (*gewöhnlich*) **~ gesagt** to put it plainly and simply

**banalisieren** *tr. V.* make ‹idea› seem trite; trivialize ‹idea, feeling›

**Banalität** *die;* **~, ~en** **A** (*das Banalsein*) ⇒ **banal** 1 A, B: banality; triteness; commonplaceness; ordinariness; **B** (*Äußerung*) banality

**Banane** /ba'na:nə/ *die;* **~, ~n** banana

**Bananen-: ~dampfer** *der* banana boat; **~flanke** *die* (*Fußballjargon*) curving cross; **~republik** *die* (*abwertend*) banana republic; **~schale** *die* banana skin; **~split** *das;* **~~s, ~~s** banana split; **~stecker** *der* (*Elektrot.*) banana plug

**Banause** /ba'nauzə/ *der;* **~n, ~n** (*abwertend*) philistine

**banausenhaft** (*abwertend*) **1** *Adj.* philistine. **2** *adv.* in a philistine way

**Banausentum** *das;* **~s** (*abwertend*) philistinism *no indef. art.*

**Banausin** *die;* **~, ~nen** ⇒ **Banause**

**banausisch** ⇒ **banausenhaft**

**band** /bant/ *1. u. 3. Pers. Sg. Prät. v.* **binden**

**Band**[1] *das;* **~[e]s, Bänder** /'bɛndɐ/ **A** (*Schmuck~; auch fig.*) ribbon; (*Haar~, Hut~*) band; (*Schürzen~*) string; (*zum Zusammenhalten, Kleben*) tape; (*für Sicherheitsgurte usw.*) webbing; **das Blaue ~:** the Blue Riband *or* Ribbon; **das Bundesverdienstkreuz am ~e** the Federal Service Cross on a ribbon; **B** (*Mess~*) tape measure; measuring tape; (*Farb~*) ribbon; (*Ziel~, Isolier~*) tape; **C** (*Ton~*) [magnetic] tape; **etw. auf ~ (*Akk.*) aufnehmen** tape[-record] sth.; **etw. auf ~ (*Akk.*) sprechen/diktieren** record/dictate sth. on to tape; **D** (*Förder~*) conveyor belt; (*Fließ~*) production line; **am ~ stehen** work on the production line; **vom ~ laufen** come off the production line; **etw. auf ~ (*Akk.*) legen** put sth. into production; **am laufenden ~** (*ugs.*) nonstop; continuously; **E** (*Anat.*) ligament; **F** (*Säge~*) band; **G** (*Beschlag*) hinge; **H** (*Metall~ um Ballen usw.*) band; (*Fass~*) hoop; **I** (*Nachrichtenw.*) [frequency] band

**Band**[2] *der;* **~[e]s, Bände** /'bɛndə/ volume; **etw. spricht Bände** (*ugs.*) sth. speaks volumes

**Band**[3] /bɛnt/ *die;* **~, ~s** band; (*Beat~, Rock~ usw.*) band; group

**Band**[4] *das;* **~[e]s, ~e** **A** (*dichter. veralt.: Fessel*) bond; fetter; shackle; **jmdn. in ~e schlagen** clap sb. in irons; **in ~en liegen** lie in chains; **B** (*fig.: Unfreiheit*) **~e** shackles; **frei von allen ~en** free from all ties; **C** (*fig.: Bindung*) **ein ~ der Liebe/Freundschaft** a bond of love/friendship; **die ~e des Bluts** the ties of blood; **verwandtschaftliche ~e** family ties; **zarte ~e knüpfen** (*geh., scherzh.*) start a romance

**Bandage** /ban'da:ʒə/ *die;* **~, ~n** bandage; **mit harten ~n kämpfen** (*fig.*) fight with the gloves off (*fig.*)

**bandagieren** /banda'ʒi:rən/ *tr. V.* bandage

**Band-: ~aufnahme** *die* tape recording; **~breite** *die* **A** (*Nachrichtenw.*) bandwidth; **B** (*fig.: Bereich, Umfang*) range

**Bändchen**[1] /'bɛntçən/ *das;* **~s, ~:** little ribbon

**Bändchen**[2] *das;* **~s, ~** (*kleines Buch*) little volume

**Bande**[1] /'bandə/ *die;* **~, ~n** **A** (*Verbrecher~*) gang; **B** (*ugs.: Gruppe*) mob (*coll.*); crew

**Bande**[2] *die;* **~, ~n** **A** (*Sport*) [perimeter] barrier; (*mit Reklame*) billboards *pl.;* (*Billard*) cushion; (*der Reitbahn*) rail; (*der Kegelbahn*) side; edge; (*im Zirkus*) ring fence; (*der Eisbahn*) boards *pl.;* **B** (*Physik*) band

**Band·eisen** *das* strip iron

**Bandel** /'bandl̩/ *das;* **~s, ~** (*bayr., österr. ugs.*), **Bändel** /'bɛndl̩/ *der od. das;* **~s, ~** (*landsch.*) ribbon; (*Schuhband*) shoelace; **jmdn. am ~ haben** (*ugs.*) have got sb. on a string

**Banden-: ~bildung** *die* formation of an armed gang; **~chef** *der,* **~chefin** *die* (*ugs.*), **~führer** *der,* **~führerin** *die* gang leader; **~krieg** *der* gang war; **~spektrum** *das* (*Physik*) band spectrum; **~unwesen** *das* ⇒ **~wesen**; **~werbung** *die: advertising on hoardings around the perimeter of a football pitch etc.;* **~wesen** *das* gangsterism; activities of the criminal gangs

**Bänder** ⇒ **Band**[1]

**Banderole** /bandə'ro:lə/ *die;* **~, ~n** **A** (*Steuer~*) revenue stamp *or* seal; **B** (*Kunstwiss.*) banderole

**Bänder-: ~riss,** ***~riß** *der* ▶ 474 (*Med.*) torn ligament; **~zerrung** *die* ▶ 474 (*Med.*) pulled ligament

**Band-: ~förderer** *der* (*Technik*) conveyor belt; **~geschwindigkeit** *die* tape speed

**-bändig** /-bɛndɪç/ *adj.* (*Buchw.*) -volume; **viel~/acht~:** multi-volume/eight-volume ‹encyclopaedia etc.›; ‹encyclopaedia etc.› in many/eight volumes

**bändigen** /'bɛndɪgn̩/ *tr. V.* tame ‹animal›; control ‹person, anger, child, thoughts, voice›; (*fig.*) control, master, overcome ‹desire, urge, etc.›; bring ‹fire› under control; keep ‹floods, river, natural forces› in check; overcome ‹tiredness›

**Bändigung** *die;* ~ ⇒ **bändigen**: taming; controlling; mastering; overcoming; **die ~ von Naturgewalten** keeping natural forces in check

**Bandit** /ban'di:t/ *der;* **~en, ~en** bandit; brigand; (*fam. scherzh.*) rascal; (*fig. abwertend*) robber; **einarmiger ~** (*ugs.*) one-armed bandit (*coll.*)

**Band·keramik** *die* (*Archäol.*) (A) Bandkeramik; band ceramics; **~en** Bandkeramik pieces; (B) (*Epoche*) Danubian I stage

**Bandleader** /'bɛntli:dɐ/ *der;* **~s, ~:** bandleader

**Band-: ~maß** *das* tape measure; measuring tape; **~nudeln** *Pl.* tagliatelle *sing.*; **~säge** *die* bandsaw; **~scheibe** *die* ▶ 471 [intervertebral] disc; **~scheiben·schaden** *der* slipped disc; **~scheiben·vorfall** *der* ▶ 474 (*Med.*) prolapsed intervertebral disc (*Med.*); slipped disc; **~stahl** *der* strip steel; steel strip; **~wurm** *der* tapeworm; **~wurm·satz** *der* (*ugs.*) interminable sentence

**bang** /baŋ/ ⇒ **bange**

**Bang·büx[e]** *die* (*nordd. ugs.*) scaredy-cat (*coll.*); chicken (*coll.*)

**bange; banger, bangst...** *od.* **bänger** /bɛŋɐ/, **bängst...** /bɛŋst.../ **1** *Adj.* afraid; scared; (*besorgt*) anxious; worried; **mir ist/wurde ~ [zumute]** I am *or* feel/became scared *or* frightened; **das wirst du schon schaffen, da ist mir gar nicht ~:** you'll manage that all right, I'm sure of it; **jmdn. ~ machen** scare *or* frighten sb.; **ihm wurde ~ und bänger** he became more and more afraid *or* scared; **mir ist ~ vor ihm/davor** I'm afraid *or* frightened *or* scared of him/it; **Bangemachen gilt nicht** (*ugs.*); (*gekniffen wird nicht*) you can't chicken out now (*coll.*); (*ich lasse mich nicht ängstigen*) you can't put the wind up (*coll.*) *or* scare me. **2** *adv.* anxiously

**Bange** *die;* ~ (*bes. nordd.*) fear; **[nur] keine ~!** don't be afraid; (*sei nicht besorgt*) don't worry; **da habe ich keine ~:** I've no fears about that; **[große] ~ vor jmdm./etw. haben** be [very] scared *or* frightened of sb./sth; **jmdm. ~ machen** scare *or* frighten sb.; ⇒ *auch* **bange 1**

**bangen** *itr. V.* be anxious *or* worried; **um jmdn./etw. ~:** be anxious *or* worried about sb./sth.; worry about sb./sth.; **ihm bangt [es] vor dir/der Operation** he's afraid *or* frightened of you/the operation

**Bangigkeit** *die;* ~ (*Furcht*) fear; (*Beklemmung*) apprehension; (*Besorgnis*) anxiety

**Bangladesch** /baŋgla'dɛʃ/ *(das);* **~s** Bangladesh

**bänglich** /'bɛŋlɪç/ **1** *Adj.* nervous; timid. **2** *adv.* nervously; timidly

**Bangnis** *die;* **~, ~se** (*geh.*) (*Furcht*) fear; (*Besorgnis*) anxiety; (*Beklommenheit*) trepidation

**Banjo** /'banjo/ *das;* **~s, ~s** banjo

**Bank**[1] /baŋk/ *die;* **~, Bänke** /'bɛŋkə/ (A) (*Sitz~, Parlaments~, Schul~; Sport: Ersatz~, Turngerät*) bench; (*mit Lehne*) bench seat; (*Kirchen~*) pew; (*Anklage~*) dock; **setz dich in deine ~!** (*Schul~*) sit at your desk; **etw. auf die lange ~ schieben** (*ugs.*) put sth. off; **vor leeren Bänken spielen** play to an empty house; **durch die ~** (*ugs.*) every single one; the whole lot of them; (B) (*Werk~*) workbench; (*Dreh~*) lathe; (C) (*Sand~*) sandbank; (D) (*Austern~*) bed; (*Korallen~*) [coral] reef; (E) (*Nebel~, Wolken~*) bank; (F) (*Geol.*) layer; bed; (G) (*Ringen*) crouch [position]

**Bank**[2] *die;* **~, ~en** (A) bank; **Geld auf der ~ [liegen] haben** have money in the bank; **ein Konto bei einer ~ eröffnen** open an account with a bank; **bei einer ~ arbeiten** *od.* **sein** work in a bank; **Geld bei der ~ abheben** withdraw money from the bank; (B) (*Glücksspiel*) bank; **die ~ sprengen** break the bank; **die ~ halten** be [the] banker; have the bank

**Bank-: ~angestellte** *der/die; adj. Dekl.*, (*veralt.*) **~beamte** *der,* **~beamtin** *die* ▶ 159 bank employee

**Bänkchen** /'bɛŋkçən/ *das;* **~s, ~:** little *or* small bench; (*mit Lehne*) little *or* small seat

**Bank-: ~direktor** *der,* **~direktorin** *die* director of a/the bank; **~ein·bruch** *der* bank raid

**Bänkel-** /'bɛŋkl̩-/: **~lied** *das* street ballad; **~sang** *der* performance of street ballads; **~sänger** *der,* **~sängerin** *die* singer of street ballads

**Banker** *der;* **~s, ~, Bankerin** *die;* **~, ~nen** (*ugs.*) banker

**bankerott** /baŋkə'rɔt/ ⇒ **bankrott**

**Bankert** /'baŋkɐt/ *der;* **~s, ~e** (*veralt. abwertend*) bastard

**Bankett**[1] /baŋ'kɛt/ *das;* **~[e]s, ~e** banquet

**Bankett**[2] *das;* **~[e]s, ~e, Bankette** *die;* **~, ~n** (A) (*an Straßen*) shoulder; (*unbefestigt*) verge; **„~ nicht befahrbar"** 'soft verges'; (B) (*an Häusern*) footing

**Bank-: ~fach** *das* (A) (*Berufsgebiet*) banking *no art.*; banking profession; (B) (*Schließfach*) safe-deposit box; **~filiale** *die* branch of a/the bank; **~gebäude** *das* bank; **~geheimnis** *das* (*Wirtsch.*) bankers' duty to maintain confidentiality; **~gut·haben** *das* bank balance; **~halter** *der,* **~halterin** *die* (*Glücksspiel*) banker; **~haus** *das* banking house

**Bankier** /baŋ'ki̯e:/ *der;* **~s, ~s** banker

**Bank-: ~kauffrau** *die,* **~kaufmann** *der* [qualified] bank/building society/stock market clerk; **~konto** *das* bank account; **~kredit** *der* bank loan; **~lehre** *die* training as a bank clerk; **~leit·zahl** *die* sort code; **~nachbar** *der,* **~nachbarin** *die* (*Schulw.*) **er war mein ~nachbar** he sat next to me [at school]; **~note** *die* ▶ 337 banknote; bill (*Amer.*); **~raub** *der* bank robbery; **~räuber** *der,* **~räuberin** *die* bank robber

**bankrott** /baŋ'krɔt/ *Adj.* (A) bankrupt; **jmdn./etw. ~ machen** bankrupt sb./sth.; **Bankrott** *od.* ***bankrott gehen** go bankrupt; (B) (*fig.*) (*moralisch*) bankrupt; (*politisch*) discredited

**Bankrott** *der;* **~[e]s, ~e** (A) bankruptcy; **seinen ~ anmelden** *od.* **ansagen** *od.* **erklären** declare oneself bankrupt; **~ machen** go bankrupt; ⇒ *auch* **bankrott**; (B) (*fig.*) downfall; (*moralisch*) bankruptcy

**Bankrott·erklärung** *die* declaration of bankruptcy; (*fig.*) declaration of [one's own] failure

**Bankrotteur** /baŋkrɔ'tø:ɐ̯/ *der;* **~s, ~e, Bankrotteurin** *die;* **~, ~nen** bankrupt

**Bank-: ~überfall** *der* bank raid; **~üblich** *Adj.* **das ist ~üblich** that is normal banking practice; **~übliche Zinssätze** normal bank interest rates; **~verbindung** *die* particulars of one's bank account; **~verkehr** *der* bank transactions *pl.*; **~vollmacht** *die* third-party mandate; (*given by firm*) signing powers *pl.*; **~wesen** *das* banking system

**Bann** /ban/ *der;* **~[e]s** (A) (*hist.*) excommunication; **den ~ über jmdn. aussprechen** *od.* **verhängen, jmdn. mit dem ~ belegen, jmdn. in den ~ tun** excommunicate sb.; (B) (*geh.: Wirkung*) spell; **in jmds. ~/im ~e einer Sache stehen** be under sb.'s spell/under the spell of sth.; **jmdn. in seinen ~ schlagen** *od.* **ziehen** cast one's/its spell over sb.

**Bann·bulle** *die* (*hist.*) bull of excommunication

**bannen** *tr. V.* (A) (*festhalten*) entrance; captivate; **[wie] gebannt** ‹watch, listen, etc.› spellbound; **ein Geschehen auf die Leinwand/auf Zelluloid ~** (*fig.*) capture an event on canvas/film; ⇒ *auch* **Platte** A; (B) (*vertreiben*) exorcize ‹spirit›; avert, ward off ‹danger›; banish ‹worries, poverty›; (*geh.*) banish ‹disease›; (C) (*hist.: exkommunizieren*) excommunicate

**Banner** *das;* **~s, ~:** banner; **das ~ der Freiheit/des Fortschritts hochhalten** (*fig.*) hold high the banner of freedom/progress

**Banner·träger** *der,* **~trägerin** *die* (*auch fig.*) standard-bearer

**Bann·fluch** *der* (*hist.*) excommunication; anathema; **den ~ gegen jmdn. schleudern** excommunicate *or* anathematize sb.

**bannig** *Adv.* (*nordd. ugs.*) extremely; terribly (*coll.*)

**Bann-: ~kreis** *der* (*geh.*) influence; **in jmds. ~kreis/in den ~kreis einer Sache geraten** fall under sb.'s influence/the influence of sth.; **~meile** *die: restricted area surrounding government buildings, where no public meetings or marches may be held;* **~spruch** *der* (*hist.*) excommunication; anathema

**Bantam-** /'bantam-/: **~gewicht** *das* (*Schwerathletik*) (A) bantamweight; ⇒ *auch* **Fliegengewicht**; (B) (*Sportler*) ⇒ **~gewichtler**; **~gewichtler** /-gə'vɪçtlɐ/ *der;* **~~s, ~~:** bantamweight; **~huhn** *das* bantam

**Bantu** /'bantu/ *der;* **~s, ~[s]** Bantu

**Bantu-: ~frau** *die* Bantu woman; **~sprache** *die* Bantu language

**Baptismus** /bap'tɪsmʊs/ *der;* **~:** Baptist faith

**Baptist** *der;* **~en, ~en** Baptist

**Baptisterium** /baptɪs'te:ri̯ʊm/ *das;* **~s, Baptisterien** (*christl. Rel., Kunstwiss.*) (A) (*Gebäude*) baptistery; (B) (*Taufbecken*) [baptismal] font; (*in einer Baptistenkapelle*) baptistery

**Baptistin** *die;* **~, ~nen** Baptist

**baptistisch** *Adj.* Baptist

**bar** /ba:ɐ̯/ **1** *Adj.* (A) ▶ 337 cash; **~es Geld** cash; **in ~:** in cash; **etw. [in] ~ bezahlen** pay for sth. in cash; pay cash for sth.; **Verkauf/Reparaturen nur gegen ~:** cash sales only/repairs must be prepaid in cash; **gegen ~ verkauft/gekauft** sold/bought for cash; ⇒ *auch* **Münze** A; (B) (*pur*) pure; sheer; utter, pure, sheer ‹nonsense›; absolute ‹reality›; (C) (*veralt.: nackt*) bare; **~en Hauptes** bareheaded; **einer Sache** (*Gen.*) **~ [sein]** (*geh.*) [be] devoid of *or* without sth. **2** *adv.* ▶ 337 in cash; **~ auf die Hand** (*ugs.*) *od.* (*salopp*) **Kralle** cash on the nail

**Bar**[1] *die;* **~, ~s** (A) (*Nachtlokal*) nightclub; bar; (B) (*Theke*) bar

**Bar**[2] *das;* **~s, ~s** (*Physik, Met.*) bar; **2,5 ~:** 2.5 bar[s]

**Bär**[1] /bɛ:ɐ̯/ *der;* **~en, ~en** bear; **ein richtiger ~** (*ugs.*) a hulking great brute of a man (*fig. coll.*); **ich bin hungrig wie ein ~** (*ugs.*) I'm so hungry I could eat a horse (*coll.*); **er ist stark/schläft wie ein ~** (*ugs.*) he is as strong as an ox/sleeps like a log; **der Große/Kleine ~** (*Astron.*) the Great/Little Bear; Ursa Major/Minor; **jmdm. einen ~en aufbinden** have sb. on (*coll.*); pull sb.'s leg

**Bär**[2] *der;* **~s, ~en** (*Technik*) ram

**Baracke** /ba'rakə/ *die;* **~, ~n** hut; **eine elende ~:** a miserable shack

**Baracken-: ~lager** *das* hutted camp; **~siedlung** *die* shanty town

**Barbar** /bar'ba:ɐ̯/ *der;* **~en, ~en** (*auch hist.*) barbarian

**Barbarei** *die;* **~, ~en** (A) (*Rohheit*) barbarity; (B) (*Kulturlosigkeit*) barbarism *no indef. art.*

**Barbarin** *die;* **~, ~nen** (*auch hist.*) barbarian

**barbarisch** **1** *Adj.* (A) (*roh*) barbarous; savage; barbarous, brutal ‹torture›; (B) (*unzivilisiert*) barbaric; barbaric, uncivilized ‹person›; (C) (*furchtbar*) dreadful (*coll.*), terrible (*coll.*) ‹noise, cold, etc.›; (D) (*hist.*) barbarian. **2** *adv.* (A) (*roh*) barbarously; ‹torture› barbarously, brutally; (B) (*unzivilisiert*) barbarically; in an uncivilized manner; (C) (*sehr*) dreadfully (*coll.*); terribly (*coll.*)

**Barbarismus** *der;* **~, Barbarismen** (*Sprachw.*) barbarism

**Barbe** /'barbə/ *die;* **~, ~n** (*Zool.*) barbel

**bärbeißig** /-bai̯sɪç/ **1** *Adj.* gruff. **2** *adv.* gruffly

**Bar-: ~bestand** *der* (*Buchf.*) cash in hand; (*Finanzw.*) cash reserve; **~betrag** *der* cash sum; **ein ~betrag von 800 DM** a sum of 800 marks in cash

**Barbier** /bar'bi:ɐ̯/ *der;* **~s, ~e, Barbierin** *die;* **~, ~nen** (*veralt., noch scherzh.*) barber

**barbieren** *tr. V.* (*veralt.*) **jmdn. ~:** shave sb.; (*den Bart beschneiden*) trim sb.'s beard

**Barbiturat** /barbitu'ra:t/ *das;* **~s, ~e** (*Pharm.*) barbiturate

**Barbitur·säure** /barbi'tu:ɐ̯-/ *die* (*Chemie*) barbituric acid

**bar-: ~brüstig** /-brʏstɪç/ *Adj.;* bare-breasted; **~busig** /-bu:zɪç/ *Adj.* topless ‹pin-up, waitress, etc.›

**Barchent** /'barçn̩t/ *der;* **~[e]s, ~e** barchent

**Bar·dame** *die* barmaid; (*verhüll.: Prostituierte*) hostess

**Barde** /'bardə/ *der;* **~n, ~n** bard

**bären-, Bären-: ~dienst** *der: in* **jmdm. einen ~dienst erweisen** do sb. a disservice; **~dreck** *der* (*südd., österr.*) liquorice; **~fell** *das* bearskin; **~fell·mütze** *die* bearskin; **~führer** *der,* **~führerin** *die* **A** (*veralt.*) bear trainer; **B** (*ugs. scherzh.: Fremdenführer*) guide; **für jmdn. den ~führer abgeben/spielen** show *or* shepherd sb. around; **~haut** *die: in* **auf der ~haut liegen** (*ugs.*) lounge *or* laze about; **~hunger** *der* (*ugs.*) **einen ~hunger haben/kriegen** be famished (*coll.*) *or* starving (*coll.*)/get famished (*coll.*) *or* ravenous (*coll.*); **~kräfte** *Pl.* (*ugs.*) the strength *sing.* of an ox; **~kräfte haben** be as strong as an ox; **~natur** *die* (*ugs.*) very tough constitution; **eine ~natur haben** be very tough; **~ruhe** *die* (*ugs.*) complete unflappability (*coll.*); **eine ~ruhe haben** be completely unflappable (*coll.*); **~stark** *Adj.* as strong as an ox *postpos.*

**Barett** /ba'rɛt/ *das;* **~[e]s, ~e** (*eines Geistlichen*) biretta; (*eines Richters, Professors*) cap; (*Baskenmütze*) beret

**Bar·frau** *die* ▶ 159 barmaid

**bar-, Bar-: ~fuß** *indekl. Adj.* barefooted; **~fuß herumlaufen/gehen** run about/go barefoot; **~fuß·arzt** *der* barefoot doctor; **~füßer** *der;* **~~s, ~~:** discalced *or* barefoot monk; **~füßerin** *die;* **~~, ~~nen** discalced nun; **~füßig** /-fy:sɪç/ *Adj.* (*geh.*) barefooted

**barg** /bark/ *1. u. 3. Pers. Sg. Prät. v.* **bergen**

**bar-, Bar-: ~geld** *das* ▶ 337 cash; **~geld·los** **1** *Adj.* ▶ 337 cashless; **2** *adv.* without using cash; **~geschäft** *das* (*Kaufmannsspr.*) cash transaction; **~häuptig** /-hɔyptɪç/ *Adj.* (*geh.*) bareheaded; **~hocker** *der* bar stool

**Bärin** /'bɛ:rɪn/ *die;* **~, ~nen** she-bear

**Bariton** /'ba(:)ritɔn/ *der;* **~s, ~e** **A** baritone [voice]; **B** (*im Chor*) baritones *pl.;* **C** (*Partie*) baritone part; **D** (*Sänger*) baritone

**Bariton·schlüssel** *der* (*Musik*) baritone clef

**Barium** /'ba:ri̯ʊm/ *das;* **~s** (*Chemie*) barium

**Bark** /bark/ *die;* **~, ~en** barque

**Barkarole** /barka'ro:lə/ *die;* **~, ~n** (*Musik*) barcarole

**Barkasse** /bar'kasə/ *die;* **~, ~n** launch

**Bar·kauf** *der* (*Kaufmannsspr.*) cash purchase; **3% Skonto bei ~ geben** give a 3% discount on cash purchases

**Barke** /'barkə/ *die;* **~, ~n** [small] rowing boat

**Bar·keeper** /'ba:ɐ̯ki:pɐ/ *der;* **~s, ~** ▶ 159 barman; barkeeper (*Amer.*)

**Bärlapp** /'bɛ:ɐ̯lap/ *der;* **~s, ~e** (*Bot.*) lycopod

**Bar-: ~mädchen** *das* bar hostess; **~mann** *der* ▶ 159 barman; barkeeper (*Amer.*)

**barmen** /'barmən/ *itr. V.* (*nordd.*) lament (*literary*)

**barmherzig** /barm'hɛrtsɪç/ (*geh.*) **1** *Adj.* merciful; compassionate; (*mildtätig*) charitable; **selig sind die Barmherzigen** (*bibl.*) blessed are the merciful; **~er Gott/Himmel!** merciful God/Heaven!; **die Barmherzigen Brüder/Schwestern** the hospitallers/the Sisters of Mercy; ⇒ *auch* **Samariter. 2** *adv.* mercifully; compassionately; (*mildtätig*) charitably

**Barmherzigkeit** *die;* **~** (*geh.*) mercy; compassion; (*Mildtätigkeit*) charity; **gegen** jmdn. **~ üben** show compassion/charity towards sb.

**Bar·mittel** *Pl.* cash resources

**Bar-: ~mixer** *der* barman; barkeeper (*Amer.*); **~mixerin** *die;* **~, ~nen** barmaid

**barock** /ba'rɔk/ **1** *Adj.* **A** baroque; **B** (*schwülstig*) baroque, florid ‹style etc.›; (*üppig*) voluptuous ‹figure›. **2** *adv.* **A** ‹conceived, designed, etc.› in the baroque style; **B** (*schwülstig*) floridly

**Barock** *das od. der;* **~[s]** **A** (*Stil*) baroque; **das Zeitalter des ~:** the baroque period *or* age; **B** (*Zeit*) baroque period *or* age

**Barock-: ~dichtung** *die* baroque poetry; **~engel** *der* baroque angel; **~kirche** *die* baroque church; **~musik** *die* baroque music; **~zeit** *die* baroque period *or* age

**Barometer** /baro'me:tɐ/ *das* barometer; **das ~ steht auf Sturm** the barometer is pointing to 'Storm'; (*fig.*) the atmosphere is very strained

**Barometer·stand** *der* barometer reading

**baro·metrisch** *Adj.* barometric

**Baron** /ba'ro:n/ *der;* **~s, ~e** ▶ 91 baron; (*als Anrede*) **[Herr] ~:** ≈ my lord

**Baroness, *Baroneß, Baronesse** /baro'nɛs(ə)/ *die;* **~, Baronessen** baroness (*baron's daughter*); (*als Anrede*) **[verehrte] ~:** ≈ my lady

**Baronin** *die;* **~, ~nen** ▶ 91 baroness (*baron's wife*); (*als Anrede*) **[Frau] ~:** ≈ my lady

**Barrakuda** /bara'ku:da/ *der;* **~s, ~s** (*Zool.*) barracuda

**Barras** /'baras/ *der;* **~** (*Soldatenspr.*) army; **beim ~:** in the army; **zum ~ müssen** have to go into the army

**Barrel** /'bɛrəl/ *das;* **~s, ~s** barrel; **10 ~[s] Öl** ten barrels of oil

**Barren** /'barən/ *der;* **~s, ~** **A** (*Gold~, Silber~ usw.*) bar; **B** (*Sport*) parallel bars *pl.;* **C** (*südd., österr.: Trog*) trough

**Barriere** /ba'ri̯e:rə/ *die;* **~, ~n** (*auch fig.*) barrier

**Barrikade** /bari'ka:də/ *die;* **~, ~n** barricade; **auf die ~n gehen** *od.* **steigen** (*ugs.*) go on the warpath

**Barrikaden·kampf** *der* fight on the barricades; **Barrikadenkämpfe** fighting *sing.* on the barricades

**barsch** /barʃ/ **1** *Adj.* curt. **2** *adv.* curtly; **jmdn. ~ anfahren** snap at sb.

**Barsch** *der;* **~[e]s, ~e** (*Zool.*) perch

**Barschaft** *die;* **~, ~en** [ready] cash; **seine ganze ~ bestand aus 20 Mark** all he had was 20 marks

**Bar·scheck** *der* open *or* uncrossed cheque

**Barschheit** *die;* **~:** curtness

**Barsoi** /bar'zɔy/ *der;* **~s, ~s** borzoi

**Bar·sortiment** *das* (*Buchhandel*) book wholesaler's; book distribution centre

**barst** /barst/ *1. u. 3. Pers. Sg. Prät. v.* **bersten**

**Bart** /ba:ɐ̯t/ *der;* **~[e]s, Bärte** /'bɛ:ɐ̯tə/ **A** (*Kinn~*) beard; (*Oberlippen~, Schnurr~*) moustache; **er bekommt jetzt einen ~:** his beard is starting to grow; **sich** (*Dat.*) **einen ~ wachsen** *od.* **stehen lassen** grow a beard; **einen acht Tage alten ~ haben** have a week's growth on one's chin; (*fig.*) **der ~ ist ab** (*ugs.*) that's quite enough; **wenn er das noch mal macht, dann ist der ~ aber ab** if he does it once more, that'll be it (*coll.*); **der Witz hat [so] einen ~** (*ugs.*) that joke is as old as the hills; **beim ~e des Propheten** (*scherzh.*) cross my heart; **etw. in seinen ~ brummen** *od.* **murmeln** mumble sth.; **jmdm. um den ~ gehen** (*abwertend*) butter sb. up; **B** (*von Ziegen, Vögeln, Getreide, Muscheln*) beard; (*von Katzen, Mäusen, Robben*) whiskers *pl.;* **C** (*am Schlüssel*) bit

**Bart·binde** *die* moustache-trainer

**Bärtchen** /'bɛ:ɐ̯tçən/ *das;* **~s, ~:** [small] beard; (*Schnurr~*) [thin] moustache

**Barteln** /'bartl̩n/ *Pl.* (*Zool.*) barbels

**Barten·wal** *der* (*Zool.*) whalebone whale

**Bart-: ~faden** *der* (*Zool.*) barbel; **~flaum** *der* down; **~flechte** *die* **A** (*an Bäumen*) lichen of the family Usneaceae; (*Usnea*) old man's beard; **B** (*beim Menschen*) sycosis; **~geier** *der* (*Zool.*) bearded vulture; **~haar** *das* beard; (*von Robben*) whiskers *pl.*

**Bar·theke** *die* bar

**Barthel** /'bartl̩/ *in* **wissen, wo ~ [den] Most holt** (*ugs.*) know every trick in the book

**bärtig** /'bɛ:ɐ̯tɪç/ *Adj.* bearded; **Bärtige** men with beards

**bart-, Bart-: ~los** *Adj.* beardless; **~nelke** *die* sweet william; **~stoppel** *die* piece of stubble; **~stoppeln** stubble *sing.;* **~tracht** *die* style of beard; **~träger** *der* man with a beard; **~wuchs** *der* growth of beard; **starken ~wuchs haben** have a strong growth of beard; **~wuchs bei Frauen** women's facial hair

**Bar·vermögen** *das* cash resources *pl.*

**Baryt** /ba'ry:t/ *der;* **~[e]s, ~e** (*Mineral.*) barytes

**Bar-: ~zahlung** *die* cash payment; **bei ~zahlung** for cash payment; if payment is made in cash; **~zahlungs·rabatt** *der* cash discount

**Basalt** /ba'zalt/ *der;* **~[e]s, ~e** basalt

**Basal·temperatur** /ba'za:l-/ *die* (*Med.*) basal body temperature

**Basar** /ba'za:ɐ̯/ *der;* **~s, ~e** **A** (*im Orient, Wohltätigkeits~*) bazaar; **B** (*DDR*) (*Warenhaus*) department store; (*Ladenstraße*) shopping precinct *or* (*Amer.*) mall

**Base**[1] /'ba:zə/ *die;* **~, ~n** **A** (*veralt.: Cousine*) cousin; **B** (*schweiz.: Tante*) aunt

**Base**[2] *die;* **~, ~n** (*Chemie*) base

**Baseball** /'beɪsbɔ:l/ *der;* **~s** baseball

**Basedow·krankheit** /'ba:zədo-/ *die* ▶ 474 (*Med.*) exophthalmic goitre; Graves' disease

**Basel** /'ba:zl̩/ (*das*)*;* **~s** ▶ 700 Basle

**Basen** ⇒ **Basis, Base**

**basieren** *itr. V.* **auf etw.** (*Dat.*) **~:** be based on sth.

**Basilika** /ba'zi:lika/ *die;* **~, Basiliken** (*Kunstwiss.*) basilica

**Basilikum** /ba'zi:likʊm/ *das;* **~s** basil

**Basilisk** /bazi'lɪsk/ *der;* **~en, ~en** (*Fabeltier, Leguan*) basilisk

**Basilisken·blick** *der* basilisk stare

**Basis** /'ba:zɪs/ *die;* **~, Basen** **A** (*Grundlage*) basis; **auf einer festen ~ ruhen** have a firm basis; **etw. auf eine feste ~ stellen** put sth. on a firm foundation (*fig.*); **B** (*Math., Archit., Fläche, Zahl, Milit.*) base; **C** (*marx.*) base; **~ und Überbau** base and superstructure; **D** (*Politik*) grass roots *pl.;* **an der ~ arbeiten** work at grass-roots level

**Basis·arbeit** *die* (*Politik*) work at grass-roots level

**basisch** (*Chemie*) **1** *Adj.* basic. **2** *adv.* ‹react› as a base

**Basis-: ~demokratie** *die* (*Politik*) grass-roots democracy; **~gruppe** *die* (*Politik*) action group (*usually left-wing*); **~lager** *das* base camp

**Baske** /'baskə/ *der;* **~n, ~n** ▶ 553 Basque

**Baskenland** *das;* **~[e]s** Basque region

**Baskenmütze** *die* beret

**Basket·ball** /'ba(:)skətbal/ *der* basketball

**Baskin** *die;* **~, ~nen** Basque

**baskisch** *Adj.* ▶ 553, ▶ 696 Basque

**Basler** /'ba:zlɐ/ **1** *indekl. Adj.* of Basle *postpos.* **2** *der;* **~s, ~:** native of Basle; (*Einwohner*) inhabitant of Basle; ⇒ *auch* **Kölner**

**Baslerin** *die;* **~, ~nen** ⇒ **Basler**[2]

**Bas·relief** /'ba-/ *das* (*Kunstwiss.*) bas-relief

**bass, *baß** /bas/ *Adv. in* **~ erstaunt sein** (*veralt.*) be quite taken aback

**Bass, *Baß** *der;* **Basses, Bässe** /'bɛsə/ (*Musik*) **A** (*Stimmlage*) bass [voice]; **B** (*im Chor*) basses *pl.;* bass section; **C** (*Partie*) bass part; **D** (*Sänger*) bass; **E** (*Instrument*) double bass; bass (*coll.*); **F** (*Lautsprecher*) bass speaker; woofer

**Bass·bariton, *Baß·bariton** *der* bass-baritone

*old spelling (see note on page 1707)

**Basset** /'bæsɪt/ *der;* ~**s**, ~**s** basset [hound]
**Bassett·horn** /ba'sɛt-/ *das* basset horn
**Bass·geige**, ***Baß·geige** *die (volkst.)* double bass
**Bassin** /ba'sɛ̃:/ *das;* ~**s**, ~**s** *(Schwimm~)* pool; *(im Garten)* pond
**Bassist** *der;* ~**en**, ~**en** *(Musik)* Ⓐ *(Sänger)* bass; Ⓑ *(Instrumentalist)* double bass player; bassist; *(in einer Rockband)* bass guitarist
**Bassistin** *die;* ~, ~**nen** ⇨ **Bassist** B
**Bass-**, ***Baß-:** ~**klarinette** *die* bass clarinet; ~**lautsprecher** *der* bass loudspeaker; woofer; ~**saite** *die* bass string; ~**schlüssel** *der (Musik)* bass clef; ~**stimme** *die* bass voice
**Bast** /bast/ *der;* ~**[e]s**, ~**e** Ⓐ bast; *(Raffia~)* raffia; Ⓑ *(Jägerspr.)* velvet
**basta** /'basta/ *Interj. (ugs.)* that's enough; **und damit ~!** and that's that
**Bastard** /'bastart/ *der;* ~**s**, ~**e** Ⓐ *(veralt.: uneheliches Kind)* bastard; Ⓑ *(Biol.)* hybrid; Ⓒ *(salopp)* bastard
**Bastard·schrift** *die (Druckw.)* bastard type
**Bastel-:** ~**arbeit** *die* Ⓐ *(Gegenstand)* piece of handicraft work; ~**arbeiten** handicraft work *sing.;* Ⓑ handicraft work; ~**ecke** *die (in einer Zeitung, Zeitschrift)* handicraft corner *or* column
**Bastelei** *die;* ~, ~**en** Ⓐ *(Gegenstand)* piece of handicraft work; ~**en** handicraft work *sing.;* Ⓑ *(ugs.: das Basteln)* handicraft work
**basteln** /'bastl̩n/ ❶ *tr. V.* make; make, build ‹model, device›. ❷ *itr. V. (Bastelarbeiten herstellen)* make things [with one's hands]; do handicraft work; **an etw.** *(Dat.)* ~: be working on sth.; *(etw. herstellen)* be making sth.; *(etw. laienhaft bearbeiten)* tinker with sth.; **sein Hobby ist Basteln:** his hobby is making things [with his hands]; his hobby is handicraft work
**Bast·faser** *die* bast fibre
**Bastille** /bas'ti:jə/ *die;* ~: Bastille
**Bastion** /bas'ti̯o:n/ *die;* ~, ~**en** bastion
**Bastler** /'bastlɐ/ *der;* ~**s**, ~, **Bastlerin** *die;* ~, ~**nen** handicraft enthusiast; **ein guter/leidenschaftlicher ~ sein** be good *or* clever with one's hands/love making [and repairing] things
**Bastonade** /basto'na:də/ *die;* ~, ~**n** bastinado
**Bast·rock** *der* bast skirt; *(aus Raffia)* raffia skirt
**bat** /ba:t/ *1. u. 3. Pers. Sg. Prät. v.* **bitten**
**BAT** *Abk.* **Bundesangestelltentarif**
**Bataille** /ba'taljə/ *die;* ~, ~**n** *(veralt.)* battle
**Bataillon** /batal'jo:n/ *das;* ~**s**, ~**e** *(Milit.)* battalion
**Bataillons-:** ~**führer** *der*, ~**kommandeur** *der (Milit.)* battalion commander
**Bathy·sphäre** /baty-/ *die (Meereskunde)* abyssal zone
**Batik** /'ba:tɪk/ *der;* ~**s**, ~**en** *od. die;* ~, ~**en** batik
**batiken** ❶ *tr. V.* **etw. ~:** decorate sth. with batik work. ❷ *itr. V.* do batik work
**Batist** /ba'tɪst/ *der;* ~**[e]s**, ~**e** batiste
**batisten** *Adj.* batiste
**Batterie** /batə'ri:/ *die;* ~, ~**n** Ⓐ *(Milit., Elektrot., Technik)* battery; Ⓑ *(ugs.: große Anzahl)* battery; *(von Flaschen)* rows *pl.*
**batterie-, Batterie-:** ~**betrieb** *der* battery operation; **auf ~betrieb laufen** run on batteries; ~**betrieben** *Adj.* battery-operated; ~**gerät** *das* battery[-operated] device; *(Radio)* battery set; ~**huhn** *das* battery chicken; *(Henne)* battery hen
**Batzen** /'batsn̩/ *der;* ~**s**, ~ Ⓐ *(ugs.: Klumpen)* lump; Ⓑ *(ugs.: Menge)* pile *(coll.)*; **ein [schöner** *od.* **ganzer] ~ Geld** a pile *(coll.)* [of money]; Ⓒ *(MA.: Münze)* batz
**Bau¹** /bau̯/ *der;* ~**[e]s**, ~**ten** Ⓐ *(Errichtung)* building; construction; **im ~ sein, sich im ~ befinden** be under construction; **mit dem ~ [von etw.] beginnen** start construction [of sth.]; start building [sth.]; Ⓑ *(Gebäude)* building; Ⓒ *(Baustelle)* building site; **auf dem ~ arbeiten** *(Bauarbeiter sein)* be in the building trade; **auf den** *od.* **zum ~ gehen** *(Bauarbeiter werden)* go into the building trade; **vom ~ sein** *(fig. ugs.)* be an expert; Ⓓ *(Struktur)* structure; Ⓔ *(Körperbau)* build; **von schmalem ~ sein** be slenderly built; have a slender physique; Ⓕ *(Landw.: Anbau)* growing
**Bau²** /bau̯/ *der;* ~**[e]s**, ~**e** Ⓐ *(Höhle) (Kaninchen~)* burrow; hole; *(Fuchs~)* earth; *(Wolfs~)* lair; *(Dachs~)* sett; earth; *(Biber~)* lodge; Ⓑ *(ugs.: Wohnung)* **nicht aus dem ~ gehen/kommen** not stick *or* put one's nose outside the door *(coll.)*; Ⓒ *(Soldatenspr.: Strafe)* glasshouse *(Mil. sl.)*; **er bekam sieben Tage ~:** he got seven days in the glasshouse; Ⓓ *(Bergmannsspr.: Stollen)* workings *pl.*
**-bau** *der;* -~**s** *(Landw.)* -growing
**Bau-:** ~**abschnitt** *der* phase *or* stage of building; ~**amt** *das* department of planning and building inspection; ~**arbeiten** *Pl.* building *or* construction work *sing.; (Straßenarbeiten)* roadworks; ~**arbeiter** *der*, ~**arbeiterin** *die* ▶ 159 building *or* construction worker; ~**art** *die* type of construction; **ein Haus in italienischer ~art** a house built in the Italian style; ~**aufsicht** *die* supervision of building *or* construction [work]; ~**beginn** *der* start of building *or* construction; ~**boom** *der* building boom; ~**bude** *die* site hut; ~**büro** *das* site office
**Bauch** /baux/ *der;* ~**[e]s**, **Bäuche** /'bɔyçə/ Ⓐ ▶ 471 stomach; belly; abdomen *(Anat.)*; tummy *(coll.)*; *(fig.: von Schiffen, Flugzeugen)* belly; **mir tut der ~ weh** I have [a] stomach ache *or (coll.)* tummy ache; **sich** *(Dat.)* **den ~ voll schlagen** *(ugs.)* stuff oneself *(coll.)*; **jmdm. den ~ aufschneiden** *(salopp)* cut sb. open; **ein Kind im ~ haben** *(ugs.)* have a baby on the way; **er hat ihr einen dicken ~ gemacht** *(salopp)* he put her in the club *(sl.)*; **ein voller ~ studiert nicht gern** *(Spr.)* you can't work hard on a full stomach; **ich habe nichts im ~** *(ugs.)* I haven't had anything to eat; **sich** *(Dat.)* **[vor Lachen] den ~ halten** *(ugs.)* split one's sides [with laughing]; *(fig.)* **auf den ~ fallen** *(ugs.)* come a cropper *(sl.)* **(mit** with); **vor jmdm. auf dem ~ liegen** *od.* **kriechen** *(ugs. abwertend)* crawl *or* grovel to sb.; **aus dem hohlen ~** *(salopp)* off the top of one's head *(sl.)*; Ⓑ *(Wölbung)* paunch; corporation *(coll.)*; *(fig.: eines Kruges usw.)* belly; Ⓒ *(Kochk.) (beim Schwein)* belly; *(beim Kalb)* flank
**Bauch-:** ~**an·satz** *der* beginnings *pl.* of a paunch; ~**atmung** *die* abdominal respiration; ~**binde** *die* Ⓐ woollen body belt; Ⓑ *(ugs.: bei Zigarren, Büchern)* band; ~**decke** *die* ▶ 471 *(Med.)* abdominal wall; ~**fell** *das* ▶ 471 *(Anat.)* peritoneum; ~**fleisch** *das (Kochk.) (vom Schwein)* belly pork; *(vom Rind)* flank; ~**flosse** *die (Zool.)* ventral fin; ~**gegend** *die* stomach region; region of the stomach; ~**grimmen** *das (veralt.)* stomach ache *or* pains *pl.;* ~**höhle** *die (Anat.)* ▶ 471 abdominal cavity; ~**höhlen·schwangerschaft** *die (Med.)* abdominal pregnancy
**bauchig** *Adj.* bulbous
**Bauch-:** ~**klatscher** /-klat͡ʃɐ/ *der;* ~~**s**, ~~ *(ugs.)* bellyflop *(coll.)*; ~**kneifen** *das;* ~~**s** stomach ache *or* pains *pl.;* ~**laden** *der; Pl.* ~**läden** vendor's tray; ~**lage** *die* prone position; **in der ~lage schlafen** sleep on one's front; ~**landung** *die (ugs.)* belly landing
**Bäuchlein** /'bɔyçlai̯n/ *das;* ~**s**, ~: stomach; tummy *(coll.)*
**bäuchlings** /'bɔyçlɪŋs/ *Adv.* on one's stomach
**bauch-, Bauch-:** ~**muskel** *der* ▶ 471 stomach muscle; ~**nabel** *der* ▶ 471 *(ugs.)* belly button *(coll.)*; tummy button *(coll.)*; ~**pinseln** *tr. V.:* ⇨ **gebauchpinselt**; ~**reden** *itr. V.; nur Inf. gebr.* ventriloquize; ~**redner** *der*, ~**rednerin** *die* ventriloquist; ~**schmerz** *der* stomach pain; ~**schmerzen** stomach ache *sing.;* stomach pains; ~**schuss**, *~**schuß** *der* shot in the stomach; *(Verwundung)* stomach wound; ~**speck** *der* Ⓐ *(Kochk.)* belly of pork; Ⓑ *(ugs.: Fettansatz)* spare tyre *(coll.)*; ~**speichel·drüse** *die* ▶ 471 pancreas; ~**tanz** *der* belly dance; ~**tanzen** *itr. V.; nur Inf. gebr.* belly dance; ~**tänzerin** *die* belly dancer
**Bauchung** *die;* ~, ~**en** bulge
**Bauch-:** ~**weh** *das (ugs.)* tummy ache *(coll.)*; stomach ache; ~**welle** *die (Turnen)* hip-circle
**Baude** /'bau̯də/ *die;* ~, ~**n** *(ostmd.)* mountain hut; *(Berggasthof)* mountain inn
**Bau-:** ~**denkmal** *das* architectural monument; ~**element** *das* component
**bauen** ❶ *tr. V.* Ⓐ build, construct ‹house, road, bridge, etc.›; build ‹nest, lair›; make ‹burrow›; **sich** *(Dat.)* **ein Haus ~:** have a house built; **sich** *(Dat.)* **sein Haus selbst ~:** build one's own house; ⇨ *auch* **Bett** A; Ⓑ *(entwickeln, herstellen)* build ‹model, vehicle, aircraft, organ›; make ‹violin, piano›; **sich** *(Dat.)* **einen Anzug ~ lassen** *(ugs. scherzh.)* have a suit made; **einen Satz ~** *(Sprachw.)* construct a sentence; Ⓒ *(ugs.)* **das Abitur/seinen Doktor ~:** do one's Abitur/Ph.D.; Ⓓ *(ugs.: verursachen)* **einen Unfall ~:** have an accident; Ⓔ *(Landw.: an~)* grow; Ⓕ *(veralt.: bestellen)* cultivate.
❷ *itr. V.* Ⓐ build; **wir wollen ~:** we want to build a house; *(~ lassen)* we want to have a house built; **zurzeit wird nicht viel gebaut** there's not much building going on at the moment; **solide/großzügig ~:** build solidly/on a lavish scale; **modern ~:** build in a modern style; **hoch ~:** put up high-rise buildings; **an etw.** *(Dat.)* **~:** do building work on sth.; Ⓑ *(vertrauen)* **auf jmdn./etw. ~:** rely on sb./sth.
**Bauer¹** /'bau̯ɐ/ *der;* ~**n**, ~**n** Ⓐ *(Landwirt)* farmer; *(als Vertreter einer ärmlichen Klasse)* peasant; *(ugs. abwertend)* peasant; **die dümmsten ~n haben die dicksten Kartoffeln** *(abwertend)* fortune favours fools *(prov.)*; **was der ~ nicht kennt, das frisst er nicht** *(abwertend)* some people won't eat anything they've never seen before; Ⓑ *(beim Schach)* pawn; Ⓒ *(in Kartenspielen)* jack; Ⓓ *(beim Kegeln)* corner; copper
**Bauer²** *das od. der;* ~**s**, ~: [bird]cage
**-bauer** *der;* -~**s**, -~ *(Bauw.)* -constructor
**Bäuerchen** /'bɔyɐçən/ *das;* ~**s**, ~ Ⓐ **[ein] ~ machen** *(Kinderspr.)* burp; Ⓑ ⇨ **Bäuerlein**
**Bäuerin** /'bɔyərɪn/ *die;* ~, ~**nen** *(Landwirtin)* [lady] farmer; *(Frau eines Landwirts)* farmer's wife; *(als Vertreterin einer ärmlichen Klasse)* peasant [woman]
**Bäuerlein** /'bɔyɐlai̯n/ *das;* ~**s**, ~: [simple] peasant
**bäuerlich** /'bɔyɐlɪç/ ❶ *Adj. (landwirtschaftlich)* farming *attrib.; (ländlich)* rural; **kleine ~e Betriebe** small farms. ❷ *adv.* rurally
**Bauern-:** ~**aufstand** *der* peasants' revolt; ~**brot** *das* ⇨ **Landbrot**; ~**bub** *der (südd., österr., schweiz.)* ⇨ ~**junge**; ~**bursche** *der* ⇨ ~**junge**; ~**dorf** *das* farming village; ~**fang** *der: in* **auf ~fang ausgehen** *(ugs. abwertend)* set out to con people out of their money *(coll.)*; ~**fänger** *der (ugs. abwertend)* con man *(coll.)*; con artist *(coll.)*; ~**fängerei** *die;* ~~ *(ugs. abwertend)* con tricks *pl. (coll.)*; **das ist ~fängerei** it's a con *(coll.)*; ~**fängerin** *die (ugs. abwertend)* con artist *(coll.)*; ~**frühstück** *das: fried potatoes mixed with scrambled egg and bacon;* ~**gut** *das* farm; ~**haus** *das* farmhouse; ~**hoch·zeit** *die* country wedding; ~**hof** *der* farm; ~**junge** *der* country lad; *(~sohn)* farmer's son; ~**kalender** *der* farming calendar; ~**krieg** *der (hist.)* peasants' revolt; **der Große ~krieg, die ~kriege** the Peasant[s'] War; ~**legen** *das;* ~~**s** driving out small farmers; ~**lümmel** *der (abwertend)* loutish yokel; ~**mädchen** *das* country girl; *(~tochter)* farmer's daughter; ~**möbel** *das* piece of rustic-style furniture; **teure ~möbel** expensive rustic-style furniture *sing.;* ~**partei** *die* Ⓐ Agrarian Party; Ⓑ *(DDR)* Peasants' Party; ~**regel** *die* country saying
**Bauernschaft** *die;* ~: farmers *pl.;* farming community; *(als ärmliche Klasse)* peasantry; peasants *pl.*

b

**bauern-, Bauern-: ~schlau** ❶ *Adj.* cunning; sly; crafty; ❷ *adv.* cunningly; slyly; craftily; **~schläue** *die* peasant cunning *or* slyness *or* craftiness; **~sohn** *der* farmer's son; **~stand** *der* farming community; **~stube** *die* room furnished in rustic style; **~tochter** *die* farmer's daughter; **~tölpel** *der (abwertend)* yokel; country bumpkin

**Bauerntum** *das;* **~s** *(Bauernstand)* farming community; *(bäuerliches Wesen)* character of the farming community

**Bauers-: ~frau** *die* farmer's wife; *(Landwirtin)* [lady] farmer; *(Frau vom Lande)* countrywoman; **~leute** *Pl.* Ⓐ *(veralt.)* country folk; Ⓑ *(Bauer und Bäuerin)* **die [beiden] ~leute** the farmer and his wife; **~mann** *der; Pl.* **~leute** *(veralt.)* countryman

**bau-, Bau-: ~erwartungs·land** *das* land shortly to be made available for building; **~fach** *das* building trade; **~fällig** *Adj.* ramshackle; badly dilapidated; unsafe ‹roof, ceiling›; **~fälligkeit** *die* bad state of dilapidation; badly dilapidated state; **~firma** *die* building *or* construction firm; **~flucht** *die,* **~flucht·linie** *die* building line; **~gelände** *das* (*~stelle*) building site; (*~land*) building land; **~genehmigung** *die* planning permission and building regulations clearance; **~genossenschaft** *die: cooperative housing association which builds and maintains houses or flats for its members;* **~gerüst** *das* scaffolding; **~gewerbe** *das* building trade; **~grube** *die* excavation; **~handwerk** *das* building trade; **~handwerker** *der,* **~handwerkerin** *die* skilled building worker; building craftsman/craftswoman; **~helfer** *der,* **~helferin** *die* builder's labourer; **~herr** *der,* **~herrin** *die* client *(for whom a house etc. is being built);* **„~herr: Stadt Mannheim"** 'under construction for the city of Mannheim'; **er ist ~herr** he is having a house built; **~holz** *das* building timber; **~hütte** *die* Ⓐ site hut; Ⓑ *(MA.)* stonemasons' lodge; **~ingenieur** *der,* **~ingenieurin** *die* ▶159 building engineer; **~jahr** *das* year of construction; *(bei Autos)* year of manufacture; **für Modelle dieses ~jahres** for models manufactured in that year; **das ~jahr des Hauses** the year in which the house was built; **welches ~jahr ist dein Wagen?** what year is your car?; **mein Auto ist ~jahr 75** my car is a 1975 model; **~kasten** *der* construction set *or* kit; *(mit Holzklötzen)* box of bricks; **~kasten·system** *das* unit construction system; **~klotz** *der; Pl. ugs. auch* **~klötzer** building brick; **~klötze[r] staunen** *(salopp)* be staggered *(coll.) or* flabbergasted; **~klötzchen** *das* building brick; **~kolonne** *die* construction gang; **~kosten** *Pl.* building *or* construction costs; **~kosten·zuschuss,** ***~kosten·zuschuß** *der: contribution to cost of building, rebuilding, or renovation paid by tenant to landlord;* **~kran** *der* construction crane; **~kunst** *die (geh.)* architecture; **~land** *das* building land; **~leiter** *der,* **~leiterin** *die* clerk of the works; **~leitung** *die* engineers supervising the building *or* construction work; (*~büro*) site office

**baulich** ❶ *Adj.;* structural ‹alteration, condition, defect, etc.›; architectural ‹character, value›; **~e Anlagen** buildings. ❷ *adv.* **ein Gebäude ~ verbessern/verändern** carry out structural improvements/alterations to a building; **den Stadtkern ~ neu gestalten** redevelop the town centre

**Baulichkeit** *die;* **~, ~en** building

**Bau-: ~los** *das* section; **~löwe** *der (ugs. abwertend)* building speculator; **~lücke** *die* vacant lot

**Baum** /baum/ *der;* **~[e]s, Bäume** /'bɔymə/ Ⓐ tree; **auf einen ~ klettern** climb up [into] a tree; **er ist stark wie ein ~:** he's as strong as an ox; *(fig.)* **es ist dafür gesorgt, dass die Bäume nicht in den Himmel wachsen** nobody has everything his own way all of the time; **alte Bäume soll man nicht verpflanzen** old people are happiest left in their familiar surroundings; **Bäume ausreißen können** *(ugs.)* be *or* feel ready to tackle anything; **der ~ der Erkenntnis** *(bibl.)* the Tree of Knowledge; **vom ~ der Erkenntnis essen** learn by experience; find out for oneself; **zwischen ~ und Borke sitzen** *od.* **stecken** be on the horns of a dilemma; ⇒ *auch* **Wald;** Ⓑ *(ugs.: Weihnachtsbaum)* [Christmas] tree; **den ~ anzünden** light the candles on the tree; Ⓒ *(Seemannsspr.)* boom

**Bau·markt** *der* Ⓐ building *or* construction market; Ⓑ *(Kaufhaus)* DIY hypermarket

**baum·arm** *Adj.* very thinly wooded; **relativ ~:** relatively thinly wooded

**Bau-: ~maschine** *die* piece of construction plant *or* machinery; **~maschinen** construction plant *sing. or* machinery; **~maßnahme** *die (Amtsspr.)* building project; **~material** *das* building material; (*~materialien*) building materials *pl.*

**Baum-: ~bestand** *der* tree stock; **~blüte** *die* Ⓐ blossoming of the trees; Ⓑ *(Zeitraum)* **zur ~blüte/während der ~blüte** when/while the trees are in blossom

**Bäumchen** /'bɔymçən/ *das;* **~s, ~:** small tree; *(junger Baum)* sapling; young tree; **~, wechsle dich** *(Kinderspiel)* puss in the corner; *(ugs. scherzh.: Partnerwechsel)* partner-swapping

**Bau·meister** *der,* **Bau·meisterin** *die* Ⓐ *(hist.)* [architect and] master builder; Ⓑ *(Bautechniker, Bauhandwerker)* master builder; *(Bauunternehmer)* building contractor *(with professional qualifications)*

**baumeln** /'baumln/ *itr. V.* Ⓐ *(ugs.)* dangle **(an** + *Dat.* from); **die Beine ~ lassen** dangle one's legs; Ⓑ *(derb: gehängt werden)* swing *(sl.)*

**bäumen** /'bɔymən/ *refl. V.:* ⇒ **aufbäumen**

**baum-, Baum-: ~farn** *der* tree fern; **~frevel** *der* unlawful and malicious damaging of trees; **~grenze** *die* ▶411 treeline; timberline; **~gruppe** *die* clump of trees; **~krone** *die* treetop; crown [of the/a tree]; **~kuchen** *der: tall cylindrical cake, hollow in the centre;* **~lang** *Adj. (ugs.)* tremendously tall *(coll.);* **~läufer** *der (Zool.)* treecreeper; **~los** *Adj.* treeless; **~reich** *Adj.* wooded; **~riese** *der (geh.)* giant tree; **~rinde** *die* bark [of trees]; **~schere** *die* tree pruner; **~schule** *die* tree nursery; **~stamm** *der* tree trunk; **~stark** *Adj.* as strong as an ox *postpos.;* **~sterben** *das;* **~~s, ~~:** dying-off of trees; **~strunk** *der* dead tree stump; **~stumpf** *der* tree stump; **~wachs** *das* grafting wax

**Baum·wolle** *die* cotton

**baum·wollen** *Adj.* cotton

**Baum-: ~wollernte** *die* cotton harvest; **~wollpflücker** *der,* **~wollpflückerin** *die* cotton picker; **~wollplantage** *die* cotton plantation; **~wollspinnerei** *die* Ⓐ cotton spinning; Ⓑ *(Betrieb)* cotton mill

**Baum·wurzel** *die* tree root

**bau-, Bau-: ~ordnung** *die* building regulations *pl.;* **~plan** *der (Entwurf, Zeichnung)* building plans *pl.; (für eine Maschine)* designs *pl.; (fig.)* structure; **~planung** *die* building design; **~platz** *der* site for building *or* construction; **~polizei** *die* building inspectorate; **~polizeilich** ❶ *Adj.* building ‹regulations›; **eine ~polizeiliche Kontrolle** a visit from the building inspector/inspectors; ❷ *adv.* ‹detected, approved, etc.› by the building inspectorate; **~preis** *der* building costs *pl.;* **~rat** *der* chief architect; **~recht** *das* planning laws and building regulations *pl.;* **~reif** *Adj.* **ein ~reifes Grundstück** a cleared building plot; **~reihe** *die* series; *(bei Lokomotiven)* class

**Bäurin** ⇒ **Bäuerin**

**bäurisch** /'bɔyrɪʃ/ *(abwertend)* ❶ *Adj.* boorish; oafish. ❷ *adv.* boorishly; oafishly

**Bau-: ~ruine** *die (ugs.)* building abandoned only half-finished; **~satz** *der* kit

**Bausch** /bauʃ/ *der;* **~[e]s, ~e** *od.* **Bäusche** /'bɔyʃə/ Ⓐ *(am Kleid, Ärmel)* puff; **einen ~ machen** *(ugs.)* ‹dress› bulge; Ⓑ **ein ~ Watte** a wad of cotton wool; Ⓒ **etw. in ~ und Bogen verwerfen/verdammen** reject/condemn sth. wholesale

**Bau·schaffende** /-ʃafn̩də/ *der/die; adj. Dekl. (DDR)* building *or* construction worker

**Bäuschchen** /'bɔyʃçən/ *das;* **~s, ~:** [small] wad

**bauschen** ❶ *tr. V.* billow, fill ‹sail, curtains, etc.›; **gebauschte Ärmel** puffed *or* puff sleeves. ❷ *refl. V.* ‹dress, sleeve› puff out; *(ungewollt)* bunch up; become bunched up; *(im Wind)* ‹curtain, flag, etc.› billow [out]

**bauschig** ❶ *Adj.* puffed ‹dress›; baggy ‹trousers›. ❷ *adv.* **~ fallen** ‹skirt› be full

**Bau-: ~schlosser** *der,* **~schlosserin** *die* fitter [in the building trade]; **~schutt** *der* building rubble; **~soldat** *der,* **~soldatin** *die (DDR): conscript allowed to do non-military (esp. building) work*

**bau·sparen** *itr. V.; nur Inf. gebr.* save with a building society

**Bau·sparer** *der,* **Bau·sparerin** *die* building-society investor

**Bauspar-: ~kasse** *die* ≈ building society; **~vertrag** *der* savings contract with a building society *(to save a specified sum which earns interest and is later used to pay for the building of a house)*

**Bau-: ~stahl** *der* structural steel; **~stein** *der* Ⓐ building stone; Ⓑ *(Bestandteil)* element; component; *(Elektronik, DV)* module; **die ~steine der Materie** the constituents of matter; Ⓒ (*~klötzchen*) building brick; **~stelle** *die* building site; *(beim Straßenbau)* roadworks *pl.; (bei der Eisenbahn)* site of engineering works; **„Betreten der ~stelle verboten"** 'no entry *or* access for unauthorized persons'; **die Strecke war wegen einer ~stelle gesperrt** the road was closed because of roadworks/the line was closed because of engineering works; **~stil** *der* architectural style; **im italienischen ~stil** in the Italian style; **~stoff** *der* Ⓐ building material; Ⓑ *(Biol.)* nutrient; **~stopp** *der* suspension of building work **(für** on); **~substanz** *die* fabric [of the building/buildings]; *(Bestand an Gebäuden)* building stock; **~summe** *die* building costs *pl.;* **~tätigkeit** *die* building activity; **~teil** *das* component

**Bauten** *Pl.:* ⇒ **Bau**

**Bau-: ~tischler** *der,* **~tischlerin** *die* [building] joiner; **~unternehmen** *das* building firm; **~unternehmer** *der,* **~unternehmerin** *die* ▶159 building contractor; builder; **~vorhaben** *das* building project; **~weise** *die* Ⓐ method of building *or* construction; Ⓑ (*~art*) type of construction; **in geschlossener/offener ~weise errichtet** built as terrace houses/detached houses; **~werk** *das* building; *(Brücke, Staudamm)* structure; **~wirtschaft** *die* building *or* construction industry

**Bauxit** /bau'ksi:t/ *der;* **~s, ~e** bauxite

**bauz** /bauts/ *Interj.* flop

**Bau-: ~zaun** *der* site fence; **~zeichnung** *die* construction drawing; **~zeit** *die* construction time

**Bayer** /'baie/ *der;* **~n, ~n, Bayerin** *die;* **~, ~nen** ▶553 Bavarian

**bay[e]risch** ▶553, ▶696 ❶ *Adj.* Bavarian; **der Bayerische Wald** the Bayerischer Wald; the Bavarian Forest. ❷ *adv.* **~ sprechen** speak Bavarian dialect; *(mit bayerischem Akzent)* speak with a Bavarian accent; **~ gekleidet** dressed in Bavarian costume; ⇒ *auch* **deutsch, badisch**

**Bayern** /'baiɐn/ *(das);* **~s** Bavaria

**Bazi** /'ba:tsi/ *der;* **~s, ~s** *(südd., österr. abwertend)* Ⓐ *(Faulpelz)* lazy good-for-nothing; Ⓑ *(Wichtigtuer)* big-head *(coll.)*

**Bazille** /ba'tsɪlə/ *die;* **~, ~n** *(ugs.)* ⇒ **Bazillus**

**Bazillen·träger** *der,* **Bazillen·trägerin** *die* carrier

**Bazillus** /ba'tsɪlʊs/ *der;* **~, Bazillen** Ⓐ bacillus; Ⓑ *(fig.)* cancer; **der ~ der Korruption** the cancer of corruption

*old spelling (see note on page 1707)

**Bazooka** /ba'zu:ka/ *die;* ~, ~**s** bazooka

**Bd.** *Abk.* **Band** Vol.

**Bde.** *Abk.* **Bände** Vols.

**BDM** *Abk.* **Bund Deutscher Mädel** (*ns.*) *National Socialist organization for girls*

**B-Dur** /'be:-/ *das* (*Musik*) B flat major; ⇒ *auch* **A-Dur**

**BE** *Abk.* **Broteinheit**

**beabsichtigen** /bə'|apzıçtıgn̩/ *tr. V.* intend; ~, **etw. zu tun** intend *or* mean to do sth.; **das war nicht beabsichtigt** it wasn't intentional *or* deliberate; **was hast du mit dieser Frage beabsichtigt?** what did you mean by your question?; **die beabsichtigte Wirkung** the intended *or* desired effect

**beachten** *tr. V.* (A) observe, follow ‹rule, regulations›; follow ‹instruction›; heed, follow ‹advice›; obey ‹traffic signs›; observe ‹formalities›; (B) (*berücksichtigen*) **etw.** ~: take account of sth.; (*Aufmerksamkeit schenken*) pay attention to *or* take notice of sth.; **es ist zu** ~, **dass ...** please note that ...; (C) (*beobachten*) notice; **jmdn. nicht** ~: ignore sb.

**beachtens·wert** *Adj.* remarkable; (*erwähnenswert*) noteworthy

**beachtlich** ❶ *Adj.* (A) (*erheblich*) considerable; marked, considerable ‹improvement, increase, change, etc.›; notable, considerable ‹success›; **er verdient jetzt** ~**e zehntausend Mark im Monat** he is now earning as much as ten thousand marks a month; (B) (*anerkennenswert*) important ‹job, post›; **Beachtliches leisten** make one's mark; (C) (*Amtsspr.: zu berücksichtigen*) ~ **sein** have to be given due consideration.
❷ *adv.* considerably; ‹improve, increase, change› markedly, considerably

**Beachtung** *die* (A) (*Einhaltung*) ⇒ **beachten A**: observance; following; heeding; obeying; **bei** ~ **der Regeln** if one observes *or* follows the rules; (B) (*Berücksichtigung*) consideration; **unter** ~ **aller Umstände** taking all the circumstances into account; (C) (*Aufmerksamkeit*) attention; ~/**keinerlei** ~ **finden** receive attention/be ignored completely; **jmdm./einer Sache** ~/**keine** ~ **schenken** pay attention/no attention to sb./sth.; take notice/no notice of sb./sth.

**beackern** *tr. V.* (A) (*ugs.: bearbeiten*) go over ‹subject›; plough through ‹literature, regulations›; (B) (*ugs.: überreden*) **jmdn.** ~: work on sb. (*coll.*); (C) (*bebauen*) cultivate

**Beamte** /bə'|amtə/ *der; adj. Dekl.* ▶ **159** official; (*Staats*~) [permanent] civil servant; (*Kommunal*~) [established] local government officer *or* official; (*Polizei*~) [police] officer; (*Zoll*~) [customs] officer *or* official; **ein typischer** ~**r** a typical civil servant; **ein kleiner** ~**r** (*meist abwertend*) a minor *or* (*derog.*) petty official

**Beamten-:** ~**apparat** *der* bureaucracy; ~**beleidigung** *die* insulting a public servant; ~**bestechung** *die* bribery of a public servant/public servants; ~**deutsch** *das* (*abwertend*) officialese (*derog.*); ~**laufbahn** *die* career in the civil service *or* as a civil servant; **die** ~**laufbahn einschlagen** join *or* enter the civil service; become a civil servant; ~**recht** *das* administrative law; ~**seele** *die* (*abwertend*) petty official *or* bureaucrat; ~**silo** *der* (*ugs. scherzh.*) huge impersonal office block full of bureaucrats

**Beamtentum** *das;* ~**s** (A) civil service mentality; (B) (*Beamtenschaft*) civil servants *pl.*; civil service; (*in den Gemeinden*) local government officers *or* officials *pl.*

**Beamten·verhältnis** *das:* **im** ~ **stehen** be a [permanent] civil servant; **ins** ~ **übernommen werden** attain permanent status

**beamtet** *Adj.* ~ **sein** have permanent civil servant status; **ein** ~**er Lehrer** a teacher with permanent civil servant status

**Beamtete** *der/die; adj. Dekl.* (*Amtsspr.*) ⇒ **Beamte, Beamtin**

**Beamtin** *die;* ~, ~**nen** ▶ **159** ⇒ **Beamte**; (*Polizei*~) [woman] police officer

**beängstigen** *tr. V.* (*veralt.*) alarm

**beängstigend** ❶ *Adj.* worrying ‹feeling›; unsettling ‹sign›; eerie ‹silence›; alarming ‹speed›; **ein** ~**es Gedränge** a frightening crush of people; **sein Zustand ist** ~: his condition is giving cause for anxiety. ❷ *adv.* alarmingly; ~ **schnell** at an alarming speed

**beanspruchen** *tr. V.* (A) claim; **etw.** ~ **können** be entitled to expect sth.; (B) (*ausnutzen*) make use of ‹person, equipment›; take advantage of ‹hospitality, offer of help, services›; **jmds. Geduld übermäßig** ~: try *or* strain sb.'s patience; (C) (*abverlangen*) demand ‹energy, attention, stamina›; **das beansprucht ihn sehr/wenig** that demands a lot/doesn't demand much of him; **sein Beruf beansprucht ihn sehr/völlig** his job is very demanding/takes up all his time and energy; (D) (*benötigen*) take up ‹time, space, etc.›

**Beanspruchung** *die;* ~, ~**en** (A) demands *pl.* (*Gen.* on); (B) (*Inanspruchnahme*) **die** ~ **durch den Beruf** the demands of his/her job; ~**en** (*Dat.*) **ausgesetzt werden** ‹material, machine› be subjected to stresses *or* strains

**beanstanden**, (*österr. auch*) **beanständen** *tr. V.* object to; take exception to; (*sich beklagen über*) complain about; **an der Arbeit ist nichts/allerlei zu** ~: there is nothing/there are all sorts of things wrong with the work; **die Waren wurden beanstandet** there were complaints about the goods; ~, **dass ...** complain that ...

**Beanstandung** *die;* ~, ~**en** complaint; **Anlass zu** ~**en geben** give cause for complaint *sing.*

**beantragen** *tr. V.* (A) apply for; ~, **versetzt zu werden** apply to be transferred; apply for a transfer; **etw. bei den Behörden** ~: apply to the authorities for sth.; (B) (*fordern*) call for; demand; (C) (*vorschlagen*) propose; ~, **etw. zu tun** propose doing sth.; **Schluss der Debatte** ~: move the closure

**beantworten** *tr. V.* answer; reply to, answer ‹letter›; respond to ‹insult›; return ‹greeting›; **jmdm. eine Frage** ~: answer a question for sb.; **bitte** ~ **Sie meine Frage mit Ja oder Nein** please answer yes or no to my question

**Beantwortung** *die;* ~, ~**en** (A) **die** ~ **einer Frage/eines Briefes** an answer to a question/a reply *or* an answer to a letter; **in** ~ (*Amtsspr.*) in reply (*Gen.* to); **zur** ~ **Ihrer Frage** in order to answer your question; (B) (*Reaktion*) response; **die** ~ **seiner Beleidigung** the response to his insult

**bearbeiten** *tr. V.* (A) deal with; work on, handle ‹case›; (B) (*adaptieren*) adapt (**für** for); **ein Buch völlig neu** ~: revise a book completely; **ein Stück für Klavier** ~: arrange a piece for the piano; (C) (*behandeln*) treat (**mit** with); work ‹wood, metal, leather, etc.›; **etw. mit Politur/einem Hammer/einer Feile** *usw.* ~: polish/hammer/file *etc.* sth.; **etw. mit einer Drahtbürste** ~: work on sth. with a wire brush; (D) cultivate ‹field, land›; (*fig. ugs.*) hammer away on ‹piano, organ›; **den Boden** ~: work the soil; (E) (*ugs.: schlagen*) beat [repeatedly]; **jmdn. mit den Fäusten** ~: pummel sb.; (F) (*untersuchen*) treat, examine ‹subject, aspect›; (G) (*ugs.: überreden*) work on; **jmdn.** ~, **dass er etw. macht** work on sb. to get him to do sth.

**Bearbeiter** *der,* **Bearbeiterin** *die* (A) **der zuständige Bearbeiter:** the person who is dealing/who dealt with the matter; **sie war nicht die Bearbeiterin des Antrags** she did not deal with the application; (B) (*eines Romans, Schauspiels*) adapter; (*eines Textes*) reviser; (*Herausgeber*) editor; (*eines Musikstücks*) arranger

**Bearbeitung** *die;* ~, ~**en** (A) **die** ~ **eines Antrags/eines Falles** *usw.* dealing with an application/working on *or* handling a case *etc.*; **die** ~ **der Post ist ...** dealing with the mail is...; (B) (*Fassung, Veränderung*) adaptation; (*eines Musikstücks*) arrangement; **die englische** ~: the English version; (C) (*Behandlung*) treatment; (*von Holz, Metall, Leder usw.*) working; **die** ~ **des Metalls ist schwer** it is difficult to work the metal; **zur weiteren** ~: in order to be worked further/for further treatment; (D) (*Untersuchung*) examination; (*eines Themas*) treatment

**Bearbeitungs-:** ~**gebühr** *die* administrative charge; (*Bankw.*) handling charge; ~**methode** *die:* ~**methoden für Stahl** *usw.* methods of working steel *etc.*; ~**zeit** *die:* **die** ~**zeit für etw.** the time required to deal with sth.

**beargwöhnen** *tr. V.* **jmdn./etw.** ~: be suspicious of sb./sth.; regard sb./sth. with suspicion; **beargwöhnt werden** be regarded with suspicion

**Beat** /bi:t/ *der;* ~**s**, ~**s** (A) beat; (B) (*Musikrichtung*) beat [music]

**Beat-:** ~**band** *die* beat group; ~**club** *der:* ⇒ ~**lokal**; ~**fan** *der* beat fan; ~**lokal** *das* beat club

**beatmen** *tr. V.* (*Med.*) **jmdn. [künstlich]** ~: administer artificial respiration to sb.; (*während einer Operation*) ventilate sb.

**Beatmung** *die;* ~, ~**en: [künstliche]** ~: artificial respiration; (*während einer Operation*) ventilation

**Beatmungs·gerät** *das* respirator

**Beat·musik** *die* beat music

**Beatnik** /'bi:tnık/ *der;* ~**s**, ~**s** beatnik

**Beat·schuppen** *der* (*ugs.*) beat club

**Beau** /bo:/ *der;* ~**s**, ~**s** dandy

**Beaufort·skala** /'bo:fɐt-/ *die* (*Met.*) Beaufort scale

**beaufsichtigen** *tr. V.* supervise; mind, look after ‹child›; **jmdn. bei der Arbeit** ~: supervise sb. while he/she is working

**Beaufsichtigung** *die;* ~, ~**en** supervision; **unter** ~ **stehen** be kept under supervision

**beauftragen** *tr. V.* (A) **jmdn./einen Ausschuss** *usw.* **mit etw.** ~: entrust *or* charge sb./a committee *etc.* with sth.; **jmdn./einen Ausschuss** *usw.* ~, **etw. zu tun** give sb./a committee *etc.* the job *or* task of doing sth.; **jmdn.** ~, **die Urkunden zu unterschreiben** authorize sb. to sign the documents; **man hat mich beauftragt, Sie darüber zu informieren** I have been asked to tell you about this; **einen Künstler/Architekten** ~, **etw. zu tun** commission an artist/architect to do sth.; (B) (*beordern*) **jmdn.** ~, **etw. zu tun** order sb. to do sth.

**Beauftragte** *der/die; adj. Dekl.* representative; **der** ~ **der DDR für Kirchenfragen** the GDR official responsible for church affairs

**beaugapfeln** *tr. V.* (*scherzh.*) **jmdn./etw.** ~: give sb./sth. the once-over (*coll.*)

**beäugen** *tr. V.* eye ‹person›; inspect ‹thing›

**beaugenscheinigen** /bə'|augn̩ʃainıgn̩/ *tr. V.* (*Amtsspr., scherzh.*) inspect

**Beauté** /bo'te:/ *die;* ~, ~**s** (*geh.*) beauty

**bebändert** /bə'bɛndɐt/ *Adj.* decorated with ribbons; beribboned

**bebauen** *tr. V.* (A) build on; develop; **ein Gelände mit Häusern** ~: build houses on a site; **mit etw. bebaut werden** have sth. built on it; (B) cultivate ‹land›; **einen Acker mit Kartoffeln** ~: grow potatoes in a field

**bebaut** *Adj.* **ein [dicht]** ~**es Gebiet** a densely built-up area; **ein** ~**es Gelände** a developed site

**Bebauung** *die;* ~, ~**en** (A) (*mit Gebäuden*) development; (B) (*Gebäude*) buildings *pl.*; **das Gebiet hat eine völlig uneinheitliche** ~: the buildings in this area lack any unity of style; (C) (*eines Ackers*) cultivation

**Bebauungs·plan** *der* development plan

**Bébé** /be'be:/ *das;* ~**s**, ~**s** (*schweiz.*) baby

**beben** /'be:bn̩/ *itr. V.* (A) shake; tremble; (B) (*geh.: zittern*) tremble, shake (**vor** + *Dat.* with); ‹lips› tremble; ‹knees› shake

**Beben** *das;* ~**s**, ~ (A) shaking; trembling; (B) (*Erd*~) quake (*coll.*); earthquake; (C) (*geh.: Zittern*) shaking; trembling; **das** ~ **seiner Stimme** the tremble in his voice

**bebildern** *tr. V.* illustrate

**Bebilderung** *die;* ~, ~**en** illustrations *pl.*

**bebrillt** /bə'brılt/ *Adj.* bespectacled

**bebrüten** *tr. V.* (A) brood; incubate; (B) (*Biol.*) incubate

**Becher** /'bɛçɐ/ *der;* ~**s**, ~ (A) (*Glas*~, *Porzellan*~) glass; tumbler; (*Plastik*~) beaker;

cup; (*Eis*~) (*aus Glas, Metall*) sundae dish; (*aus Pappe*) tub; (*Joghurt*~) carton; **ein ~ Eis** a tub of ice cream; **B** (*bei Pflanzen*) cupule; cup

**Becher·glas** *das* (*Chemie*) beaker

**bechern** *tr., itr. V.* (*ugs. scherzh.*) **[einen] ~:** have a few (*coll.*); **bis zum frühen Morgen ~:** booze into the small hours

**Becher·werk** *das* (*Technik*) bucket elevator

**becircen** /bəˈtsɪrtsn̩/ *tr. V.* (*ugs.*) **A** bewitch ‹man›; **B** (*überreden*) **jmdn. ~[, dass er etw. tut]** wrap sb. round one's little finger [and get him to do sth.]

**Becken** /ˈbɛkn̩/ *das;* **~s, ~** **A** (*Wasch*~) basin; (*Abwasch*~) sink; (*Toiletten*~) pan; bowl; **B** (*Anat.*) ▶ 471 pelvis; **C** *Pl.* (*Musik*) cymbals; **D** (*Schwimm*~) pool; (*Plansch*~) paddling pool; (*eines Brunnens, einer Schleuse*) basin; (*Fisch*~) pond; **E** (*Geol.*) basin

**Becken-: ~bruch** *der* ▶ 474 (*Med.*) pelvic fracture; fractured pelvis; **~end·lage** *die* (*Med.*) breech position; **~knochen** *der* ▶ 471 hip bone; pelvic bone

**Beckmesser** /ˈbɛkmɛsɐ/ *der;* **~s, ~** (*abwertend*) caviller; carper

**Beckmesserei** *die;* **~, ~en** (*abwertend*) cavilling; carping

**Beckmesserin** *die;* **~, ~nen** ⇒ **Beckmesser**

**beckmessern** *itr. V.* (*abwertend*) cavil; carp

**bedachen** /bəˈdaxn̩/ *tr. V.* put the roof on ‹house›; **bedacht** roofed; covered ‹bridge›

**bedacht** ❶ *2. Part. v.* **bedenken; bedachen.** ❷ *Adj.* **A** carefully considered; (*umsichtig*) circumspect; **B** **auf etw.** (*Akk.*) **~ sein** be intent on sth.; **auf seinen eigenen Vorteil ~ sein** have an eye to one's own advantage; **darauf ~/sehr ~ sein, etw. zu tun** be intent on doing sth./be [most] anxious to do sth.; **[ängstlich] darauf ~ sein, dass etw. nicht geschieht** be [extremely] anxious to prevent sth. from happening; **er ist stets auf korrekte Kleidung ~:** he makes a point of being correctly dressed. ❸ *adv.* in a carefully considered way; (*umsichtig*) circumspectly

**Bedacht** *der: in* **ohne ~:** rashly; without thinking *or* forethought; **mit ~:** in a carefully considered way; (*umsichtig*) circumspectly; **voll ~:** very carefully; **auf etw.** (*Akk.*) **~ nehmen** (*geh.*) pay regard to sth.

**Bedachte** *der/die; adj. Dekl.* (*Rechtsw.*) beneficiary; (*eines Legats*) legatee

**bedächtig** /bəˈdɛçtɪç/ ❶ *Adj.* **A** deliberate; measured ‹steps, stride, speech›; **B** (*besonnen*) thoughtful; well-considered ‹words›; (*vorsichtig*) careful. ❷ *adv.* **A** deliberately; **~ reden** speak in measured tones; **B** (*besonnen*) thoughtfully; (*vorsichtig*) carefully

**Bedächtigkeit** *die;* **~** **A** deliberateness; **B** (*Besonnenheit*) thoughtfulness; (*Vorsichtigkeit*) carefulness

**bedachtsam** (*geh.*) ❶ *Adj.* thoughtful; (*vorsichtig*) careful. ❷ *adv.* thoughtfully; (*vorsichtig*) carefully

**Bedachung** *die;* **~, ~en** **A** roofing; **B** (*Dach*) roof

**bedang** /bəˈdaŋ/ *1. u. 3. Pers. Sg. Prät. v.* **bedingen**[2]

**bedanken** ❶ *refl. V.* say thank you; express one's thanks; **ich bedanke mich** thank you; (*ugs. iron.: nein danke!*) thank you 'very much; **sich bei jmdm. [für etw.] ~:** thank sb. *or* say thank you to sb. [for sth.]; **sich bei jmdm. ~, dass er/sie etw. getan hat** thank sb. for doing sth.; **dafür kannst du dich bei ihm ~** (*ugs. iron.*) you've got him to thank for that (*iron.*). ❷ *tr. V.* (*geh.*) **etw. ~:** express one's thanks for sth.; **Seien Sie herzlich bedankt** please accept my/our warmest thanks

**Bedarf** /bəˈdarf/ *der;* **~[e]s** **A** need (**an** + *Dat.* of); requirement (**an** + *Dat.* for); (*Bedarfsmenge*) needs *pl.;* requirements *pl.;* **Dinge des täglichen ~s** everyday necessities; **der persönliche ~:** one's personal needs *pl.;* **bei ~:** if and when the need arises; if required; **bei dringendem ~:** in cases of urgent need; **~ an etw.** (*Dat.*) **haben** (*Kaufmannsspr.*) require sth.; **je nach ~:** as required; **kein ~!** (*salopp*) I don't feel like it; **B** (*Nachfrage*) demand (**an** + *Dat.* for); **dafür besteht kein ~:** there is no demand for it/them; **mein ~ an Überraschungen ist für heute gedeckt** (*fig.*) I've had enough surprises for 'one day

**-bedarf** *der;* **-~[e]s** ... requirement

**bedarfs-, Bedarfs-: ~ampel** *die* (*Verkehrsw.*) pedestrian-controlled *or* -operated lights; **~deckung** *die* satisfaction of its/one's needs *or* requirements; **~fall** *der: in* **im ~fall[e]** if required; if the need arises/arose; **~gerecht** ❶ *Adj.* designed to meet requirements; tailor-made; **eine ~gerechte Versorgung der Bevölkerung** a supply system tailored to the needs of the people; ❷ *adv.* in line with demand; **~güter** *Pl.* consumer goods; **~halte·stelle** *die* request stop; **~weckung** *die;* **~~:** stimulation of demand

**bedauerlich** *Adj.* regrettable; unfortunate

**bedauerlicher·weise** *Adv.* regrettably; unfortunately

**bedauern** *tr., itr. V.* **A** feel sorry for; **sie hat es gern, bedauert zu werden** she likes people to feel sorry for her; **sie lässt sich gerne ~:** she likes being pitied; **B** ▶ 268 (*schade finden*) regret; **ich bedaure sehr, dass ...** I am very sorry that ...; **wir ~, Ihnen mitteilen zu müssen** we regret to [have to] inform you; **bedaure!** sorry!

**Bedauern** *das;* **~s** **A** sympathy; **jmdm. sein ~ ausdrücken** offer one's sympathy to sb.; **B** ▶ 268 (*Betrübnis*) regret; **zu meinem ~:** to my regret; **ich habe zu meinem ~ gehört, dass ...** I was sorry to hear that ...; **zu unserem ~ müssen wir Ihnen mitteilen, dass ...** we regret to [have to] inform you that ...; it is with regret that we must inform you that ...; **mit ~:** with regret; **mit ~ habe ich festgestellt, dass ...** I have discovered to my regret that ...

**bedauerns-: ~wert** (*geh.*), **~würdig** *Adj.* unfortunate ‹person, coincidence›; regrettable, unfortunate ‹incident›

**bedecken** ❶ *tr. V.* **A** cover (**mit** with); **mit etw. bedeckt sein** be covered with sth.; **von Schlamm/Schmutz bedeckt sein** be covered in mud/dirt; **B** (*österr.: ausgleichen*) meet ‹costs›. ❷ *refl. V.* cover oneself up

**bedeckt** *Adj.* overcast ‹sky›; **bei ~em Himmel** when the sky is overcast; **sich ~ halten** (*fig.*) keep a low profile

**Bedecktsamer** /-zaːmɐ/ *der;* **~s, ~** (*Bot.*) angiosperm

**bedecktsamig** /-zaːmɪç/ *Adj.* (*Bot.*) angiospermous

**Bedeckung** *die* **A** covering; **B** (*Schutz*) guard; **zehn Mann ~:** a ten-man bodyguard *sing.;* **C** (*das Bedeckende*) covering; **D** (*österr.: Deckung*) meeting

**bedenken** ❶ *unr. tr. V.* **A** consider; think about; **wenn ich es recht bedenke/wenn man es recht bedenkt** when I/you stop and think about it; **~, dass ...** consider *or* think that ...; **B** (*beachten*) take into consideration; **du musst ~, dass ...** you should bear in mind that *or* take into consideration the fact that ...; **ich gebe [dir]/er gab [uns] zu ~, dass ...** I would ask you/he asked us to bear in mind that *or* take into consideration the fact that ...; **C** (*geh.: beschenken*) **jmdn. reich ~:** shower sb. with gifts; **jmdn. mit etw. ~:** present sb. with sth.; **jmdn. großzügig mit Lob ~:** lavish praise on sb. ❷ *refl. V.* reflect; think; **ohne sich lange zu ~:** without stopping to reflect

**Bedenken** *das;* **~s, ~** **A** reflection; **nach kurzem/langem ~:** after a moment's/after much reflection *or* consideration; **ohne ~:** without hesitation; **B** (*Zweifel*) doubt; reservation; **~ haben** *od.* **hegen** *od.* (*geh.*) **tragen** have doubts *or* reservations (**gegen** about); **aber jetzt kommen mir ~:** but now I'm having second thoughts

**bedenken·los** ❶ *Adj.* unconsidered; (*ohne Zögern*) unhesitating; prompt ‹intervention›; (*skrupellos*) unscrupulous. ❷ *adv.* without a moment's hesitation; without stopping to think; (*ohne Zögern*) without hesitation; ‹intervene› promptly; (*skrupellos*) unscrupulously

**Bedenkenlosigkeit** *die;* **~:** lack of consideration; (*mangelndes Zögern*) absence of any hesitation; (*Skrupellosigkeit*) unscrupulousness; lack of scruples

**bedenkens·wert** *Adj.* ‹argument, suggestion› worthy of consideration; **~ sein** be worth considering *or* worthy of consideration

**bedenklich** ❶ *Adj.* **A** dubious, questionable ‹methods, transactions, etc.›; **B** (*bedrohlich*) alarming; disturbing; **~ sein/werden** be giving/be starting to give cause for concern; **C** (*besorgt*) concerned; apprehensive; anxious; **ein ~es Gesicht machen** look concerned *etc.;* **das machte** *od.* **stimmte mich ~** (*ließ mich nachdenken*) that gave me food for thought; (*machte mich ängstlich*) that gave me cause for concern. ❷ *adv.* **A** alarmingly; disturbingly; **B** (*besorgt*) apprehensively; anxiously

**Bedenklichkeit** *die;* **~** **A** dubiousness; questionableness; **B** (*Bedrohlichkeit*) alarming *or* disturbing nature

**Bedenk·zeit** *die* time for reflection; **um ~/einige Tage ~ bitten** ask for some time/a few days to think about it; **nach einer kurzen ~:** after a pause for thought; **ich gebe Ihnen vierundzwanzig Stunden ~:** I'll give you twenty-four hours to think about it

**bedeppert** /bəˈdɛpɐt/ *Adj.* (*salopp*) (*ratlos*) confused and embarrassed; (*töricht, dümmlich*) gormless (*coll.*); (*niedergeschlagen*) crestfallen

**bedeuten** *tr. V.* **A** (*bezeichnen, heißen*) mean; **was bedeutet dieses Wort?** what does that word mean?; what is the meaning of that word?; **was soll das ~?** what does that mean?; **er weiß, was es bedeutet, krank zu sein** he knows what it means to be ill; **„Ph. D." bedeutet Doktor der Philosophie** 'Ph.D.' stands for Doctor of Philosophy; **was bedeutet diese Zeremonie?** what's the significance of this ceremony?; **B** (*sein*) represent; **das bedeutet ein Wagnis** that is being really daring; **einen Eingriff in die Pressefreiheit ~:** amount to *or* represent an attack on press freedom; **C** (*hindeuten auf*) mean; **das bedeutet nichts Gutes** that bodes ill; that's a bad sign; **schönes Wetter ~:** mean good weather; be a sign of good weather to come; **D** (*wichtig sein*) mean; **Geld bedeutet ihm nichts** money means nothing to him; **das hat nichts zu ~:** that doesn't mean anything; **E** (*geh.: anraten*) **jmdm. ~, etw. zu tun** intimate *or* indicate to sb. that he/she should do sth.; **F** (*veralt.: belehren*) inform

**bedeutend** ❶ *Adj.* **A** (*wichtig*) significant, important ‹step, event, role, measure, etc.›; important ‹city, port, artist, writer, etc.›; **B** (*groß*) considerable; substantial; considerable ‹success›; substantial ‹pension›. ❷ *adv.* considerably

**bedeutsam** ❶ *Adj.* **A** ⇒ **bedeutend; B** (*viel sagend*) meaningful; significant. ❷ *adv.* meaningfully; significantly

**Bedeutung** *die;* **~, ~en** **A** meaning; significance; **einer Sache** (*Dat.*) **zu große ~ beimessen** attach too much significance to sth.; **B** (*Wort*~) meaning; **C** (*Tragweite*) significance; importance; **[an] ~ gewinnen** become more significant; **nichts von ~:** nothing important *or* significant; nothing of [any] importance *or* significance; **D** (*Berühmtheit*) importance; **ein Mann von ~:** an important figure

**bedeutungs-, Bedeutungs-: ~erweiterung** *die* (*Sprachw.*) extension of meaning; **~gehalt** *der* semantic content (*Ling.*); meaning; **~lehre** *die* (*Sprachw.*) semantics; **~los** *Adj.* insignificant; unimportant; **~losigkeit** *die;* **~~:** insignificance; unimportance; **~schwer** *Adj.* (*geh.*) loaded with meaning; (*folgenschwer*) critical; momentous; **~unterschied** *der* (*Sprachw.*) difference in meaning; **~verengung** *die* (*Sprachw.*) restriction of meaning; **~voll** ❶ *Adj.* **A** significant; **B** (*viel sagend*)

*old spelling (see note on page 1707)

meaningful; meaning ‹look›; ❷ *adv.* meaningfully; significantly; **∼wandel** *der* (*Sprachw.*) change in *or* of meaning; semantic change (*Ling.*); **∼wörter·buch** *das* defining dictionary

**bedienen** ❶ *tr. V.* Ⓐ wait on; ‹waiter, waitress› wait on, serve; ‹sales assistant› serve; (*salopp: sexuell*) satisfy; **jmdn. vorn und hinten ∼** (*ugs.*) wait on sb. hand and foot; **werden Sie schon bedient?** are you being served?; **aufmerksam bedient werden** receive attentive service; Ⓑ (*handhaben*) operate ‹machine›; Ⓒ *in* **[mit etw.] gut/schlecht bedient sein** (*ugs.*) be well-served/ill-served [by sth.]; **mit diesem Artikel sind Sie gut bedient** this article will give you good value for money; **bedient sein** (*salopp*) have had enough; have had all one can take; Ⓓ (*Kartenspiel*) play; **Kreuz/Trumpf ∼:** play a club/trump; **eine Farbe ∼:** follow suit; Ⓔ (*Fußball*) **jmdn. ∼:** pass to sb.; **die Stürmer mit hervorragenden Pässen ∼:** provide the forwards with excellent service; Ⓕ ‹means of transport› serve; operate on ‹route›; maintain ‹network of routes›.
❷ *itr. V.* Ⓐ (*im Restaurant, Geschäft*) serve; **wer bedient hier?** who is serving here?; Ⓑ (*Kartenspiel*) follow suit; **falsch ∼:** revoke.
❸ *refl. V.* Ⓐ help oneself; **sich selbst ∼** (*im Geschäft, Restaurant usw.*) serve oneself; Ⓑ (*geh.*) **sich einer Sache** (*Gen.*) **∼:** make use of *or* use sth.

**Bedienerin** *die;* **∼, ∼nen** (*österr.*) cleaning woman

**bedienstet** /bəˈdi:nstət/ *Adj. in* **∼ sein** (*österr.*) be employed (**bei** by)

**Bedienstete** *der/die; adj. Dekl.* Ⓐ (*Amtsspr.*) employee; Ⓑ (*veralt.: Diener*) servant

**Bediente** /bəˈdi:ntə/ *der/die; adj. Dekl.* (*veralt.*) servant

**Bedienung** *die;* **∼, ∼en** Ⓐ (*das Bedienen*) service; **∼ inbegriffen** service included; Ⓑ (*das Handhaben*) operation; **für die ∼ dieser Maschine bekommt er ...** for operating this machine he receives ...; Ⓒ (*Person*) (*in einem Lokal*) waiter/waitress; (*in einem Geschäft*) [sales] assistant; (*gesamtes Personal*) staff; **hallo, ∼!** waiter/waitress!; Ⓓ (*österr.*) cleaning woman

**Bedienungs-: ∼an·leitung** *die* operating instructions *pl.;* (*Heft*) instruction book; **∼auf·schlag** *der,* **∼geld** *das:* ⇒ **Bedienungszuschlag;** **∼fehler** *der* operator's error; **∼mannschaft** *die* operating crew; (*am Geschütz*) gun crew; **∼zu·schlag** *der* service charge

**bedingen**[1] /bəˈdɪŋən/ *tr. V.* Ⓐ cause; Ⓑ (*erfordern*) require; demand; (*voraussetzen*) presuppose; Ⓒ (*abhängig sein von*) **einander ∼:** be interdependent *or* mutually dependent

**bedingen**[2] *unr. refl. V.* (*veralt.*) **sich** (*Dat.*) **etw. ∼:** stipulate sth.; make sth. a condition

**bedingt** /bəˈdɪŋt/ ❶ *Adj.* Ⓐ qualified ‹praise, acceptance, approval›; Ⓑ (*von etw. abhängig*) conditional; **∼er Reflex** (*Physiol.*) conditioned reflex; **psychologisch ∼ sein** have psychological causes. ❷ *adv.* **∼ richtig/gelten** partly/be partly true; **nur ∼ tauglich** fit for certain duties only

**-bedingt** *Adj.* associated with *postpos.;* due to *postpos.;* **alters∼:** associated with old age *postpos.;* **berufsbedingte Krankheiten** occupational illnesses; **witterungsbedingte Schäden** damage caused by the weather

**Bedingtheit** *die;* **∼, ∼en** Ⓐ (*Abhängigkeit*) relative nature; (*Begrenztheit*) limited *or* restricted nature; Ⓑ (*Bestimmtheit*) **wechselseitige ∼:** interdependence; mutual dependence

**Bedingung** *die;* **∼, ∼en** condition; **etw. zur ∼ machen** make sth. a condition; **zu annehmbaren ∼en** on acceptable terms; **unter diesen ∼en** on these conditions; **unter keiner ∼:** under no circumstances; **unter der ∼, dass ...** on condition that ...; **∼ ist, dass ...** it is a condition that ...

**bedingungs-, Bedingungs-: ∼form** *die* (*Sprachw.*) conditional; **∼los** ❶ *Adj.* unconditional ‹surrender, acceptance, etc.›; absolute, unquestioning ‹obedience, loyalty, devotion›; ❷ *adv.* ‹surrender, accept, etc.› unconditionally; ‹subordinate oneself› unquestioningly; **sich ∼los für jmdn. einsetzen** give sb. one's unqualified support; **∼satz** *der* (*Sprachw.*) conditional clause

**bedrängen** *tr. V.* Ⓐ besiege ‹town, fortress, person›; put ‹opposing player› under pressure; **vom Feind bedrängt sein** be hard pressed by the enemy; **mit Fragen bedrängt werden** be assailed with questions; Ⓑ (*belästigen*) pester; Ⓒ (*belasten*) distress; **von Zweifeln bedrängt** beset with doubts; **in einer bedrängten/sehr bedrängten Lage sein** be hard-pressed/be in a difficult/desperate situation *or* in dire straits *pl.*

**Bedrängnis** *die;* **∼, ∼se** (*geh.*) (*innere Not*) distress; (*wirtschaftliche Not*) [great] difficulties *pl.;* **in ∼ geraten/sein** get into/be in great difficulties *pl.;* **in arger ∼:** in dire straits *pl.;* **jmdn. in ∼ bringen** cause sb. great difficulties/distress

**bedripst** /bəˈdrɪpst/ *Adj.* (*nordd. ugs.*) (*ratlos*) confused and embarrassed; (*niedergeschlagen*) crestfallen

**bedrohen** *tr. V.* Ⓐ threaten; Ⓑ (*gefährden*) threaten; endanger; **den Frieden ∼:** be a threat *or* danger to peace; **vom Feuer bedroht sein** be in danger of catching fire; **vom Aussterben bedroht sein** be threatened with extinction

**bedrohlich** ❶ *Adj.* (*drohend*) threatening, menacing ‹gesture›; (*Unheil verkündend*) ominous; (*gefährlich*) dangerous. ❷ *adv.* (*drohend*) threateningly; menacingly; (*Unheil verkündend*) ominously; (*gefährlich*) dangerously; **∼ nahe kommen** come ominously/dangerously near

**Bedrohlichkeit** *die;* **∼:** dangerousness; (*einer Krankheit usw.*) dangerous nature

**Bedrohung** *die* threat (*Gen.* to); **in ständiger ∼:** under a constant threat

**bedrucken** *tr. V.* print; **etw. mit einer Adresse ∼:** print an address on sth.; **ein mit Blumen bedrucktes Kleid** a flower-print dress

**bedrücken** *tr. V.* Ⓐ depress; **es bedrückt mich, dass ...** I feel depressed that ...; **bedrückt dich was?** is something weighing on your mind?; Ⓑ (*veralt.: unterdrücken*) oppress

**bedrückend** *Adj.* oppressive; depressing ‹sight, thought, news›

**bedruckt** *Adj.* printed; print *attrib.* ‹dress etc.›

**bedrückt** *Adj.* depressed; oppressed ‹people›

**Bedrückung** *die;* **∼, ∼en** depression; (*eines Volkes*) oppression

**Beduine** /beduˈi:nə/ *der;* **∼n, ∼n,** **Beduinin** *die;* **∼, ∼nen** Bed[o]uin

**bedungen** /bəˈdʊŋən/ *2. Part. v.* **bedingen**[2]

**bedürfen** *unr. itr. V.* (*geh.*) **jmds./einer Sache ∼:** require *or* need sb./sth.; **es bedarf einer Sache** there is need for sth.; **es bedarf nur eines Wortes von Ihnen** you need only say so; **es bedarf keines weiteren Wortes** no more need be said; **es bedarf einiger Mühe** (*geh.*) some effort is needed *or* required

**Bedürfnis** *das;* **∼ses, ∼se** need (**nach** for); **dafür besteht kein ∼:** there is no necessity for that; **das ∼ haben, etw. zu tun** feel a need to do sth.; **ein ∼ nach etw. haben** be in need of sth.; **es war mir ein ∼, das zu tun** I felt the need to do it

**bedürfnis-, Bedürfnis-: ∼anstalt** *die* (*Amtsspr.*) public convenience; **∼befriedigung** *die* satisfaction of one's needs; (*polit. Ökonomie*) satisfaction of needs; **∼los** ❶ *Adj.* ‹person› with few [material] needs; modest, simple ‹life›; **∼los sein** have few [material] needs; ❷ *adv.* **∼los leben** have a [very] modest lifestyle; **∼losigkeit** *die;* **∼:** lack of [material] needs

**bedürftig** *Adj.* Ⓐ needy; **die Bedürftigen** the needy; those in need; Ⓑ *in* **jmds./einer Sache ∼ sein** (*geh.*) be in need of sb./sth.

**Bedürftigkeit** *die;* **∼:** neediness; **die ∼ einer Familie feststellen** means-test a family

**beduseln** *refl. V.* (*ugs.*) get merry (*coll.*); **ich war beduselt** (*fig.*) my head was spinning

**Beef·steak** /ˈbi:fste:k/ *das* [beef]steak; **deutsches ∼:** ≈ beefburger

**beehren** (*geh.*) ❶ *tr. V.* Ⓐ **jmdn. mit seinem Besuch/seiner Anwesenheit ∼** (*auch iron.*) honour sb. with a visit/one's presence; Ⓑ (*gespreizt: besuchen*) **∼ Sie uns bald wieder** (*im Geschäft/privat*) we hope to have the pleasure of your custom/company again. ❷ *refl. V.* **sich ∼, etw. zu tun** have the honour to do sth.

**beeiden** /bəˈ|aidn̩/ *tr. V.* **∼, dass ...** swear [on oath] that ...; **eine Aussage ∼:** swear to the truth of a statement

**beeidigen** /bəˈ|aidɪgn̩/ Ⓐ (*geh.*) ⇒ **beeiden;** Ⓑ (*veralt.: vereidigen*) swear in; **ein beeidigter Zeuge** a sworn witness

**beeilen** *refl. V.* Ⓐ hurry [up (*coll.*)]; **beeil dich!** hurry [up]; **sich bei einer Arbeit ∼:** hurry over a task; **du musst dich aber mächtig beeilt haben** (*ugs.*) you must have really got a move on (*coll.*); Ⓑ (*nicht zögern*) **sich ∼, etw. zu tun** hasten to do sth.

**Beeilung** *Interj.* **[los], ∼!** (*ugs.*), **∼ bitte!** (*ugs.*) get a move on! (*coll.*); hurry up!

**beeindrucken** *tr. V.* impress; **sich von etw. ∼ lassen** be impressed by sth.; **∼d** impressive

**beeinflussbar, *beeinflußbar** *Adj.* **leicht/schwer ∼ sein** ‹person› be easily influenced/hard *or* difficult to influence; **das ist nicht ∼:** it cannot be influenced

**beeinflussen** /bəˈ|ainflʊsn̩/ *tr. V.* influence; influence, affect ‹result, process, etc.›; **jmdn./etw. positiv/nachhaltig ∼:** have a positive/lasting influence on sb./sth.; **sich leicht ∼ lassen** be easily influenced

**Beeinflussung** *die;* **∼, ∼en** Ⓐ (*das Einflussnehmen*) influencing; **seine ∼ durch die Schule** the influence of the school on him; Ⓑ (*Einfluss*) influence

**beeinträchtigen** /bəˈ|aintrɛçtɪgn̩/ *tr. V.* restrict ‹sights, freedom›; detract from, spoil ‹pleasure, enjoyment›; spoil ‹appetite, good humour›; detract from, diminish ‹value›; diminish, impair ‹quality›; impair ‹reactions, efficiency, vision, hearing›; damage, harm ‹sales, reputation›; reduce ‹production›; **jmdn. in seiner Freiheit ∼:** restrict sb.'s freedom; **sich beeinträchtigt fühlen** feel hampered

**Beeinträchtigung** *die;* **∼, ∼en** ⇒ **beeinträchtigen:** restriction; detracting (+ *Gen.* from); spoiling; diminution; impairment; damage (*Gen.* to); harm (*Gen.* to); reduction; **eine ∼ der Freiheit** a restriction on one's freedom

**beelenden** *tr. V.* (*schweiz.*) sadden

**Beelzebub** /ˈbe:ltsə-/ (*der*) Beelzebub; **den Teufel mit** *od.* **durch ∼ austreiben** (*fig.*) replace one evil by *or* with another

**beenden, beendigen** *tr. V.* end; finish ‹piece of work, dissertation, etc.›; end, conclude ‹negotiations, letter, lecture›; complete, finish ‹studies›; end, bring to an end ‹meeting, relationship, dispute, strike›; **das Fest wurde mit einem Feuerwerk beendet** the celebration ended with a firework display; **damit ∼ wir unser heutiges Programm** that brings to an end our programmes for today

**Beendigung** *die;* **∼,** **Beendung** *die;* **∼** (*Ende*) end; (*Fertigstellung*) completion; **nach/vor ∼ des Unterrichts** after/before school is/was over

**beengen** *tr. V.* hinder, restrict ‹movements›; (*fig.*) restrict ‹freedom [of action]›; **das Kleid/dieses Zimmer beengt mich** the dress hinders *or* restricts my movements/this room is too cramped for me; **beengt wohnen** live in cramped surroundings *or* conditions; **sich beengt fühlen** feel cramped; (*fig.: durch Regeln usw.*) feel constricted; **diese kleinbürgerliche Atmosphäre beengte ihn** (*fig.*) he found this petit bourgeois atmosphere stifling *or* restricting

**Beengtheit** *die;* **∼** (*von Räumen*) crampedness; **ein Gefühl der ∼:** a feeling of being cramped

**beerben** *tr. V.* **jmdn. ∼:** inherit sb's estate

**beerdigen** /bəˈ|e:ɐ̯dɪgn̩/ *tr. V.* bury; **jmdn. kirchlich ∼:** give sb. a Christian burial

b

**Beerdigung** *die;* ~, ~**en** (*Bestattung*) burial; (*Trauerfeier*) funeral; **auf der falschen ~ sein** (*salopp, scherzh.*) have come to the wrong place
**Beerdigungs·institut** *das* [firm *sing.* of] undertakers *pl. or* funeral directors *pl.*
**Beere** /ˈbeːrə/ *die;* ~, ~**n** berry
**Beeren-:** ~**auslese** *die: wine made from selected overripe grapes;* ~**obst** *das* soft fruit
**Beet** /beːt/ *das;* ~**[e]s**, ~**e** (*Blumen~*) bed; (*Gemüse~*) plot
**Beete** ⇨ **Bete**
**befähigen** /bəˈfɛːɪɡn̩/ *tr. V.* **jmdn. ~, etw. zu tun** enable sb. to do sth.; ‹qualifications, training, etc.› qualify sb. to do sth.
**befähigt** ❶ *2. Part. v.* **befähigen.** ❷ *Adj.* Ⓐ (*qualifiziert*) qualified; Ⓑ (*begabt*) gifted
**Befähigung** *die;* ~ Ⓐ (*Qualifikation*) qualification; **die ~ zum Internisten/Hochschulstudium/Richteramt** the qualifications *pl.* for becoming an internist/studying at university/being a judge; Ⓑ (*Können*) ability; (*Talent*) talent; **seine ~ zum Schriftsteller** his talent as a writer *or* for writing
**Befähigungs·nachweis** *der* (*Amtsspr.*) proof of one's qualifications
**befahl** /bəˈfaːl/ *1. u. 3. Pers. Sg. Prät. v.* **befehlen**
**befahrbar** *Adj.* passable; navigable ‹canal, river›; **nicht ~:** impassable/unnavigable
**befahren**[1] *unr. tr. V.* Ⓐ drive on, use ‹road›; drive across, use ‹bridge, pass›; use ‹railway line›; **die Straße kann nur im Sommer ~ werden** this road is passable only in summer; **die Straße ist nur in einer Richtung zu ~:** traffic can only use the road in one direction; **„Seitenstreifen nicht ~!"** 'keep off verges'; **die Straße ist stark/wenig ~:** the road is heavily/little used; **eine stark ~e Straße** a busy road; Ⓑ sail ‹sea›; navigate, sail up/down ‹river, canal›; **eine stark ~e Wasserstraße** a busy waterway; **die Weltmeere ~:** sail the oceans; Ⓒ (*Bergmannsspr.*) **eine Grube ~:** go down a mine
**befahren**[2] *Adj.* Ⓐ (*Seemannsspr.*) seasoned; experienced; Ⓑ (*Jägerspr.*) inhabited ‹earth etc.›
**Befall** *der;* ~**[e]s** ~ (*Landw.*) attack (*Gen.* on; **durch, von** by)
**befallen** *unr. tr. V.* Ⓐ (*überkommen*) overcome; ‹misfortune› befall; **Fieber/eine Grippe befiel ihn** (*geh.*) he was stricken by fever/influenza; **von Panik/Angst/Heimweh** *usw.* **~ werden** be seized *or* overcome with *or* by panic/fear/homesickness *etc.*; **von einer Ohnmacht/Schwäche/von Resignation ~ werden** faint/feel faint/be overcome with a feeling of resignation; Ⓑ ‹pests› attack
**befangen** ❶ *Adj.* Ⓐ (*gehemmt*) self-conscious, awkward ‹person›; **jmdn. ~ machen** make sb. self-conscious *or* awkward; Ⓑ (*bes. Rechtsw.: voreingenommen*) biased; **einen Richter als ~ ablehnen** challenge a judge on grounds of bias; Ⓒ **in einem Glauben/Irrtum ~ sein** (*geh.*) labour under a belief/misapprehension; **in Vorurteilen ~ sein** be prejudiced. ❷ *adv.* self-consciously; awkwardly
**Befangenheit** *die;* ~ Ⓐ self-consciousness; awkwardness; Ⓑ (*bes. Rechtsw.: Voreingenommenheit*) bias
**Befangenheits·antrag** *der* (*Rechtsw.*) challenge on grounds of bias
**befassen** ❶ *refl. V.* **sich mit etw. ~:** occupy oneself with sth.; (*studieren*) study sth.; ‹article, book› deal with sth.; **sich nicht mit Kleinigkeiten ~:** not concern *or* bother oneself with trivial details; **mit diesem Thema haben wir uns lange genug befasst** we've spent enough time on this subject; **sich mit jmdm./einem Fall/einer Angelegenheit ~:** deal with *or* attend to sb./a case/matter; **ich habe mich schon mit dieser Sache befasst** I've already been into this matter; **sich viel mit jmdm. ~:** give sb. a great deal of attention; spend a great deal of time with sb.; **sich mit jedem Kind einzeln ~** ‹teacher› give each child individual attention.
❷ *tr. V.* (*bes. Amtsspr.*) **jmdn. mit etw. ~:** get *or* instruct sb. to deal with sth.; **die mit diesem Fall befasste Behörde** the authorities dealing *or* involved with this case
**befehden** /bəˈfeːdn̩/ *tr. V.* Ⓐ (*hist.*) feud with; Ⓑ (*geh.*) attack ‹plan, proposal, etc.›; **sich/einander ~:** feud [with each other]; attack each other
**Befehl** /bəˈfeːl/ *der;* ~**[e]s**, ~**e** Ⓐ order; command; **jmdm. den ~ geben, etw. zu tun** order *or* command sb. to do sth.; **den ~ haben, etw. zu tun** be under orders *or* have been ordered to do sth.; **auf jmds. ~** (*Akk.*) on sb.'s orders; **auf ~ handeln** act under orders; **~ ist ~:** orders are orders; **zu ~ [Herr Leutnant/Oberst/General/Kapitän]!** yes, sir!; aye, aye, sir! (*Navy*); **dein Wunsch ist** *od.* **sei mir ~** (*ugs. scherzh.*) your wish is my command; Ⓑ (*Befehlsgewalt*) command; **den ~ über jmdn./etw. haben** have command of *or* be in command of sb./sth.; **unter jmds. ~** (*Dat.*) **stehen** be under sb.'s command; **den ~ übernehmen** take command; Ⓒ (*DV*) instruction; command
**befehlen** ❶ *unr. tr., itr. V.* Ⓐ order; (*Milit.*) order; command; (*heißen*) tell; **jmdm. Stillschweigen ~:** order sb. to keep silent; **man befahl ihm zu warten** he was told to wait; **er befahl die Räumung des Dorfes** he ordered the village to be cleared; **er befiehlt gern** he likes to order people about; **von Ihnen lasse ich mir nichts ~:** I don't take orders from you; **[ganz] wie Sie ~** (*veralt.*) [just] as you wish; **~ gnädige Frau sonst noch etwas?** (*veralt.*) is there anything else, ma'am?; Ⓑ (*beordern*) order; (*zu sich*) summon; **jmdn. zum Rapport ~:** order/summon sb. to report; Ⓒ (*geh. veralt.*) commend; **seine Seele Gott/in Gottes Hände ~** (*bibl.*) commend one's soul to God; **befiehl dem Herrn deine Wege!** (*bibl.*) commit thy ways unto the Lord.
❷ *unr. itr. V.* have command; be in command; **über eine Armee ~:** have command of *or* be in command of an army
**befehligen** *tr. V.* have command of; be in command of; **von ... befehligt werden** be commanded by ...; be under the command of ...
**befehls-, Befehls-:** ~**aus·gabe** *die* (*Milit.*) issuing of orders; briefing; ~**bereich** *der* [area of] command; ~**empfänger** *der*, ~**empfängerin** *die* recipient of an order/orders; **bloße ~empfänger [der Zentrale] sein** just follow *or* take orders [from headquarters]; ~**form** *die* (*Sprachw.*) imperative [form]; ~**gemäß** ❶ *Adj.* **die ~gemäße Durchführung des Plans** *usw.* carrying out the plan *etc.* in accordance with orders *or* as ordered; ❷ *adv.* in accordance with orders; as ordered; ~**gewalt** *die* command (**über** + *Akk.* of); **jmds. ~gewalt** (*Dat.*) **unterstehen** be under sb.'s command; ~**haber** /-haːbɐ/ *der;* ~~**s**, ~~ (*Milit.*) commander; ~**notstand** *der* (*Rechtsw.*) **unter ~notstand handeln** be acting under orders; **in einem ~notstand sein/sich in einem ~notstand befinden** have to obey orders; ~**satz** *der* (*Sprachw.*) imperative sentence; ~**stab** *der* (*Eisenb.*) station official's rod and signalling disc; ≈ guard's flag; ~**ton** *der* peremptory tone; ~**verweigerung** *die* refusal to obey an order/orders; ~**widrig** ❶ *Adj.* contrary to orders *postpos.*; ❷ *adv.* contrary to orders
**befeinden** *tr. V.* be hostile to; **die Juden wurden dort befeindet** there was hostility to the Jews there
**befestigen** *tr. V.* Ⓐ fix (**mit** with); **etw. mit Stecknadeln/Bindfaden ~:** fasten sth. with pins/string; **etw. mit Schrauben/Leim ~:** fasten *or* fix sth. with screws/fix *or* stick sth. with glue; **etw. an der Wand ~:** fix sth. to the wall; **einen Anhänger an einem Koffer ~:** attach *or* fasten a label to a case; **ein Boot an einem Pfosten ~:** tie up *or* moor a boat to a post; Ⓑ (*haltbar machen*) stabilize ‹bank, embankment›; make up ‹road, path, etc.›; Ⓒ (*sichern*) fortify ‹town etc.›; strengthen ‹border›; Ⓓ (*festigen*) consolidate ‹reputation, authority›; enhance ‹standing›; strengthen ‹friendship, confidence›
**Befestigung** *die;* ~, ~**en** Ⓐ (*Milit.*) fortification; Ⓑ ⇨ **befestigen** A: fixing; fastening; attachment; tying up; mooring; Ⓒ (*Haltbarmachung*) (*eines Ufers*) stabilization; (*eines Weges*) making up; Ⓓ (*Stärkung*) ⇨ **befestigen** D: consolidation; enhancement; strengthening
**Befestigungs-:** ~**an·lage** *die* fortifications *pl.*; ~**linie** *die* line of fortifications
**befeuchten** /bəˈfɔyçtn̩/ *tr. V.* moisten; damp ‹hair, cloth›; **von Tränen/Tau befeuchtet** moist *or* wet with tears/dew
**befeuern** *tr. V.* Ⓐ (*beheizen*) fuel; Ⓑ (*beschießen*) shoot at; fire on; Ⓒ (*ugs.: bewerfen*) pelt (**mit** with); Ⓓ (*geh.: anfeuern*) inspire; Ⓔ (*Schifffahrt, Flugw.*) mark ‹coastline, runway, etc.› with lights *or* beacons
**Befeuerung** *die* lights *pl.*; beacons *pl.*
**Beffchen** /ˈbɛfçən/ *das;* ~**s**, ~: [collar *sing.* with] bands *pl.* (*worn esp. by Protestant clergymen*)
**befiehlst** /bəˈfiːlst/, **befiehlt** /bəˈfiːlt/ *2., 3. Pers. Sg. Präsens v.* **befehlen**
**befinden** ❶ *unr. refl. V.* be; **sich im Urlaub/auf Reisen ~:** be on holiday/be away on a trip; **unter ihnen befand sich jemand, der ...** among them there was somebody who ...; **sich wohl ~** (*geh.*) be well. ❷ *unr. tr. V.* (*geh.*) Ⓐ **etw. für gut/richtig ~:** find *or* consider sth. [to be] good/right; **jmdn. für tauglich ~:** declare sb. [to be] fit; **jmdn. für** *od.* **als schuldig ~:** find sb. guilty; Ⓑ (*äußern*) declare; assert. ❸ *unr. itr. V.* **über etw.** (*Akk.*) **~:** decide [on] sth.; make a decision on sth.; **darüber habe ich nicht zu ~:** that's not for me to decide
**Befinden** *das;* ~**s** Ⓐ health; (*eines Patienten*) condition; **sich nach jmds. ~ erkundigen** enquire after *or* about sb.'s health; **wie ist Ihr ~ heute?** (*geh.*) how are you today?; Ⓑ (*geh.: Urteil*) judgement; **etw. nach eigenem ~ entscheiden** use one's own judgement in deciding sth.; **nach seinem/ihrem [eigenen] ~:** in his/her [own] judgement *or* estimation
**befindlich** *Adj.* Ⓐ (*liegend*) to be found *postpos.*; **das in der Kasse ~e Geld** the money in the till; **eine am Stadtrand ~e Siedlung** an estate [situated] on the edge of town; Ⓑ (*in einem Zustand*) **die im Bau ~en Häuser** the houses [which are/were] under construction
**Befindlichkeit** *die;* ~, ~**en** (*geh.*) state
**befingern** *tr. V.* (*salopp*) finger
**beflaggen** *tr. V.* **etw. ~:** decorate *or* [be]deck sth. with flags; **ein Schiff ~:** dress a ship
**Beflaggung** *die;* ~: decoration with flags; (*eines Schiffes*) dressing
**beflecken** *tr. V.* Ⓐ stain; **sich mit Blut ~** (*verhüll. geh.*) stain one's hand with blood; Ⓑ (*fig.*) besmirch; stain; defile ‹sanctity›
**Befleckung** *die;* ~ (*fig.*) besmirching; staining; (*eines Heiligtums*) defilement
**befleißigen** *refl. V.* (*geh.*) **sich eines klaren Stils/höflicheren Tons** *usw.* **~:** make a great effort to cultivate a clear style/to adopt a more polite tone of voice *etc.*; **sich größter Zurückhaltung ~:** endeavour to exercise the greatest restraint
**befliegen** *unr. tr. V.* fly ‹route›; **eine stark beflogene Route** a route with heavy [air] traffic
**beflissen** /bəˈflɪsn̩/ (*geh.*) ❶ *Adj.* keen; eager; (*emsig*) assiduous; zealous; **~ sein/ängstlich ~ sein, etw. zu tun** be keen *or* eager/anxious to do sth. ❷ *adv.* keenly; eagerly; (*emsig*) assiduously; zealously
**Beflissenheit** *die;* ~: keenness; eagerness; (*Emsigkeit*) assiduousness; zeal
**beflissentlich** *Adj.:* ⇨ **geflissentlich**
**beflügeln** *tr. V.* (*geh.*) Ⓐ **jmdn. ~:** inspire sb.; ‹success, praise› spur sb. on, inspire sb.; Ⓑ (*schneller machen*) **jmds. Schritte/Gang**

*old spelling (see note on page 1707)

~ ‹fear, joy› wing sb.'s steps; **jmdn. ~:** spur sb. on

**befohlen** /bəˈfoːlən/ *2. Part. v.* **befehlen**

**befolgen** *tr. V.* follow, obey ‹instruction, grammatical rule›; obey, comply with ‹law, regulation›; follow, take ‹advice›; follow ‹suggestion›

**Befolgung** *die;* ~ ⇒ **befolgen**: following; obedience (*Gen.* to); compliance (*Gen.* with); **die ~ des Gesetzes** obedience to *or* compliance with the law

**Beförderer** *der,* **Beförderin** *die* carrier

**befördern** *tr. V.* [A] carry; transport; convey; **etw. mit der Post/per Schiff/Luftfracht ~** (*schicken*) send sth. by post/sea/air; **jmdn. ins Freie** *od.* **an die Luft ~** (*ugs.*) chuck (*coll.*) *or* throw sb. out; ⇒ *auch* **Jenseits**; [B] (*aufrücken lassen*) promote; **zum Direktor befördert werden** be promoted to director

**Beförderung** *die* [A] (*Waren~*) carriage; transport; conveyance; (*Personen~*) transport; conveyance; **Schäden, die bei der ~ entstehen** damage in transit; **die ~ per Luft/zu Lande** carriage *or* transport by air/road; **Züge zur ~ der Urlaubsreisenden** trains to carry the holiday passengers; [B] (*das Aufrücken*) promotion (**zu** to)

**Beförderungs-: ~bedingungen** *Pl.* conditions of carriage; **~kosten** *Pl.* cost *sing.* of transport *or* transportation; transport *or* transportation costs; **~mittel** *das* means of transport; **~pflicht** *die: obligation on bus companies, airlines, etc. to accept and convey passengers and goods*

**Befördrerin** *die* carrier

**befrachten** *tr. V.* load (**mit** with); **mit Emotionen befrachtet** (*fig.*) ‹discussion etc.› charged with emotion; **mit Geschichte befrachtet** (*fig.*) ‹castle, church, etc.› steeped in history

**Befrachter** *der,* **Befrachterin** *die;* ~, **~nen** freighter

**befrackt** *Adj.* **ein ~er Herr** a gentleman wearing *or* in tails

**befragen** *tr. V.* [A] (*ausfragen*) question (**über** + *Akk.* about); **einen Zeugen ~:** question *or* examine a witness; **auf Befragen:** when questioned; [B] (*fragen*) ask; consult; **jmdn. nach seiner Meinung ~:** ask sb. for his/her opinion; **ein Orakel/die Karten ~:** consult an oracle/the cards

**Befragte** *der/die; adj. Dekl.* man/woman/person questioned; **20% der ~n** 20% of those questioned

**Befragung** *die;* ~, **~en** [A] questioning; (*vor Gericht*) questioning; examination; **eine ~ aller Schüler vornehmen** question all the pupils; [B] (*Konsultation*) consultation; **nach ~ des Arztes** after consulting the doctor; [C] (*Umfrage*) opinion poll

**befreien** ❶ *tr. V.* [A] free ‹prisoner›; set ‹animal› free; **jmdn. aus den Händen seiner Entführer ~:** rescue sb. from the hands of his/her abductors; [B] (*frei machen*) liberate ‹country, people› (**von** from); [C] (*freistellen*) exempt (**von** from); **jmdn. vom Turnunterricht/Wehrdienst/von einer Pflicht ~:** excuse sb. [from] physical education/exempt sb. from military service/release sb. from an obligation; **jmdn. von einer Aufgabe ~:** excuse sb. from *or* let sb. off a task; [D] (*erlösen*) **jmdn. von Schmerzen ~:** free sb. of pain; **von seinen Leiden befreit werden** (*durch den Tod*) be released from one's sufferings; **jmdn. von Angst/einer Sorge ~:** remove sb.'s fear/free sb. of a worry; **ein ~des Lachen** a laugh which breaks/broke the tension; [E] (*reinigen*) **die Straße von Schnee/Eis ~:** clear the road of snow/ice; **etw. von Läusen ~:** rid sth. of lice. ❷ *refl. V.* free oneself (**von** from); **sich von Vorurteilen/traditionellen Denkweisen ~:** rid oneself of prejudice *sing.*/break away from traditional ways of thinking

**Befreier** *der,* **Befreierin** *die;* ~, **~nen** liberator

**befreit** ❶ *Adj.* relieved; **sich ~ fühlen** feel relieved. ❷ *adv.* with relief; **~ aufatmen** heave a sigh of relief

**Befreiung** *die;* ~ [A] freeing; **eine ~ des Kindes aus den Händen der Entführer** ... rescuing the child from the hands of its abductors ...; [B] (*das Freiwerden*) liberation; **die ~ der Frau** the emancipation of women; [C] (*Erlösung*) **die ~ von Schmerzen** release from pain; [D] (*Erleichterung*) relief; [E] (*Freistellung*) exemption; **um ~ vom Sportunterricht/von einer Pflicht bitten** ask to be excused [from] sport/released from an obligation

**Befreiungs-: ~armee** *die* army of liberation; **~bewegung** *die* liberation movement; **~front** *die* liberation front; **~kampf** *der* liberation struggle; **~krieg** *der* [A] war of liberation; [B] *Pl.* (*hist.*) Wars of Liberation (*1813-1815*); **~versuch** *der* rescue bid *or* attempt; (*Ausbruchsversuch*) escape bid *or* attempt

**befremden** /bəˈfrɛmdn̩/ ❶ *tr. V.* **jmdn. ~:** put sb. off; (*erstaunen*) take sb. aback; **es befremdete ihn, dass ...** he was taken aback [to find] that ... ❷ *itr. V.* be disturbing

**Befremden** *das;* **~s** surprise and displeasure

**befremdlich** (*geh.*) ❶ *Adj.* strange; odd. ❷ *adv.* strangely

**Befremdung** *die;* ~ ⇒ **Befremden**

**befreunden** /bəˈfrɔyndn̩/ *refl. V.* [A] make *or* become friends (**mit** with); **sich miteinander ~:** make *or* become friends; [B] (*gewöhnen*) **sich mit etw. ~:** get used to sth.

**befreundet** *Adj.* **[gut** *od.* **eng] ~ sein** be [good *or* close] friends (**mit** with); **ein uns** (*Dat.*) **~es Ehepaar/~er Schauspieler** a couple with whom we are friends/an actor who is a friend of ours; **~e Familien/Kinder** families which are friendly with each other/children who are friends; **das ~e Ausland** friendly [foreign] countries

**befrieden** *tr. V.* (*geh.*) bring peace to ‹country›; **das Land ist jetzt befriedet** (*oft verhüll.*) the country is now at peace

**befriedigen** /bəˈfriːdɪgn̩/ *tr.* (*auch itr.*) *V.* [A] satisfy; satisfy, meet ‹demand, need›; satisfy, fulfil ‹wish›; satisfy, gratify ‹lust›; **seine Gläubiger ~:** satisfy one's creditors; **das Ergebnis befriedigte mich** the result satisfied me *or* was satisfactory to me; **seine Leistung befriedigte [nicht]** his performance was [un]satisfactory; **leicht/schwer zu ~ sein** be easy/hard to satisfy; be easily/not easily satisfied; [B] (*ausfüllen*) ‹job, occupation, etc.› fulfil; [C] (*sexuell*) satisfy; **sich [selbst] ~:** masturbate

**befriedigend** ❶ *Adj.* [A] satisfactory; satisfactory, adequate ‹reply, performance›; **nicht ~ sein** be unsatisfactory/inadequate; **in Latein hat er „~" bekommen** ≈ he got a C in Latin; [B] (*erfüllend*) ‹job, occupation, etc.› fulfilling. ❷ *adv.* satisfactorily; ‹answer› satisfactorily, adequately

**befriedigt** ❶ *Adj.* satisfied. ❷ *adv.* with satisfaction

**Befriedigung** *die;* ~ [A] ⇒ **befriedigen** A: satisfaction; meeting; fulfilment; gratification; **sexuelle ~:** sexual satisfaction; **zur ~ deiner Neugier** to satisfy your curiosity; [B] (*Genugtuung*) satisfaction; **~ darin finden, etw. zu tun** get satisfaction from doing sth.

**Befriedung** *die;* **~: ein Plan zur ~ des Landes** a plan to bring peace to the country

**befristen** *tr. V.* **etw. ~:** limit the duration of sth. (**auf** + *Akk.* to)

**befristet** *Adj.* temporary ‹visa›; fixed-term ‹ban, contract›; **ein auf zwei Jahre ~er Vertrag** a two-year fixed-term contract; **~ sein** ‹visa, permit› be valid for a limited period [only]; **auf ein Jahr ~ sein** ‹visa, permit› be valid for one year; **ein auf zwei Jahre ~es Abkommen** an agreement running for *or* lasting two years

**Befristung** *die;* ~, **~en** setting of a time limit/time limits; **mit einer ~ auf fünf Jahre gelten** have a time limit of five years

**befruchten** *tr. V.* [A] fertilize ‹egg›; pollinate ‹flower›; impregnate ‹female›; (*fig. geh.*) make ‹fields, land› fertile; **ein Tier künstlich ~:** artificially inseminate an animal; [B] (*geh.*) **jmdn./etw. ~, einen ~den Einfluss auf jmdn./etw. haben** have *or* be a stimulating *or* inspiring influence [up]on sb./sth.

**Befruchtung** *die;* ~, **~en** [A] ⇒ **befruchten** A: fertilization; pollination; impregnation; **künstliche ~:** artificial insemination; [B] (*geh.: Anregung*) stimulation; inspiration

**befugen** *tr. V.* authorize; **dazu befugt sein, etw. zu tun** be authorized to do sth.; **befugte/nicht befugte Personen** authorized/unauthorized persons

**Befugnis** *die;* ~, **~se** authority; **seine ~se überschreiten** exceed one's authority *sing.*; **die ~ haben, etw. zu tun** have the authority to do sth.; be authorized to do sth.

**befühlen** *tr. V.* feel; (*streicheln*) run one's fingers over; fondle

**befummeln** *tr. V.* (*ugs.*) [A] paw (*coll.*); [B] (*sexuell berühren*) grope (*coll.*); feel up (*coll.*); [C] (*regeln, erledigen*) fix; take care of

**Befund** *der* (*bes. Med.*) result[s *pl.*]; **ohne ~:** negative

**befürchten** *tr. V.* fear; **ich befürchte, dass ...** I am afraid that ...; **das Schlimmste ~:** fear the worst; **das ist nicht zu ~:** there is no fear of that; **eine militärische Auseinandersetzung ~:** fear that there may be a military conflict

**Befürchtung** *die;* ~, **~en** fear; **die ~ haben** *od.* (*geh.*) **hegen, dass ...** be afraid that ...

**befürworten** /bəˈfyːɐ̯vɔrtn̩/ *tr. V.* support; (*genehmigen*) approve

**Befürworter** *der;* **~s,** ~, **Befürworterin** *die;* ~, **~nen** supporter

**Befürwortung** *die;* ~, **~en** support; (*Genehmigung*) approval

**begaben** *tr. V.* (*geh.*) endow

**begabt** /bəˈgaːpt/ *Adj.* talented; gifted; **hoch ~:** highly gifted *or* talented; **vielseitig ~ sein** be many-talented; have many talents; **für etw. ~ sein** have a gift *or* talent for sth.

**Begabte** *der/die; adj. Dekl.* gifted *or* talented person/man/woman *etc.*

**Begabten·förderung** *die* assistance to gifted pupils/students

**Begabung** *die;* ~, **~en** [A] (*Talent*) talent; gift; **eine ~ [für etw.] haben** have a gift *or* talent [for sth.]; **die ~ haben, etw. zu tun** (*iron.*) have a talent for *or* the knack of doing sth. (*iron.*); [B] (*begabter Mensch*) talented person/man/woman *etc.*; talent; **er war eine musikalische ~:** he had a talent for music

**begaffen** *tr. V.* (*ugs. abwertend*) gawp at (*coll.*); stare at

**begann** /bəˈgan/ *1. u. 3. Pers. Sg. Prät. v.* **beginnen**

**begasen** /bəˈgaːzn̩/ *tr. V.* (*Landw.*) gas

**begatten** /bəˈgatn̩/ ❶ *tr. V.* mate with; ‹man, husband› copulate with; ‹stallion, bull› cover. ❷ *refl. V.* mate; ‹persons› copulate

**Begattung** *die* mating; (*bei Menschen*) copulation

**Begattungs·organe** *Pl.* reproductive organs

**begaunern** *tr. V.* (*ugs. abwertend*) **jmdn. ~:** rip sb. off (*coll.*); swindle sb.

**begeben** *unr. refl. V.* (*geh.*) [A] proceed; make one's way; go; **sich nach Hause/ins Hotel ~:** proceed *or* make one's way *or* go home/into the hotel; **sich auf den Heimweg ~:** start for home; **sich zu Bett ~:** retire to bed; **sich in ärztliche Behandlung ~:** get medical treatment; go to a doctor for treatment; ⇒ *auch* **Gefahr**; [B] (*beginnen*) commence; **sich daran ~, etw. zu tun** commence doing sth.; **sich an die Arbeit ~:** commence work; [C] (*unpers.: geschehen*) happen; occur; **es begab sich aber zu der Zeit, dass ...** (*bibl.*) and it came to pass in those days that ...; [D] (*verzichten auf*) **sich einer Möglichkeit/eines Rechts** *usw.* **~:** forgo an opportunity/a right *etc.*

**Begebenheit** *die;* ~, **~en** (*geh.*) event; occurrence

**begegnen** /bəˈgeːgnən/ *itr. V.; mit sein* [A] **jmdm. ~:** meet sb.; **sich** (*Dat.*) *od.* **einander ~:** meet [each other]; **ihre Blicke begegneten sich** (*Dat.*) (*geh.*) their eyes met; [B] (*antreffen*) **einer Sache** (*Dat.*) **~:** encounter sth.; come across sth.; **solche Ausdrücke ~ einem** one encounters such

b

b

expressions; **C** (*geh.: widerfahren*) **etw. begegnet jmdm.** sth. happens to sb.; **D** (*geh.: behandeln*) **jmdm. freundlich/höflich** *usw.* **~:** behave in a friendly/polite *etc.* way towards sb.; treat sb. in a friendly/polite *etc.* way; **einem Vorschlag kühl ~:** treat a suggestion with coolness; **E** (*geh.: entgegentreten*) counter ‹accusation, attack›; combat ‹illness, disease, misuse of drugs, alcohol, etc.›; meet ‹difficulty, danger›; deal with ‹emergency›

**Begegnung** *die;* **~, ~en** **A** meeting; (*das Antreffen*) encounter; **eine Stätte internationaler ~en** an international meeting place; **B** (*Sport*) match; **die ~ Schweden gegen Italien** the match between Sweden and Italy

**Begegnungs·stätte** *die* (*Amtsspr.*) community centre

**begehbar** *Adj.* **der Weg ist nicht ~:** the path cannot be used *or* is impassable; **ein ~es Dach** a roof that is safe to walk on; **etw. besser ~ machen** make sth. easier to walk along

**begehen** *unr. tr. V.* **A** commit ‹crime, adultery, indiscretion, sin, suicide, faux-pas, etc.›; make ‹mistake›; **eine [furchtbare] Dummheit/Taktlosigkeit ~:** do something [really] stupid/tactless; **einen Mord an jmdm. ~:** murder sb.; **ein oft begangener Fehler** a frequent *or* common mistake; ⇒ *auch* **Verrat**; **B** (*geh.: feiern*) celebrate; **ein Fest würdig ~:** celebrate an occasion fittingly; **C** (*abgehen*) inspect [on foot]; **D** (*gehen*) walk along ‹path›; walk across ‹bridge›; (*benutzen*) use

**Begehr** /bəˈɡeːɐ̯/ *der od. das;* **~s** (*veralt.*) wish; desire; **was ist euer ~?** what is it that you require?

**begehren** *tr. V.* **A** (*haben wollen*) desire; wish for; desire ‹woman›; **ein Mädchen zur Frau ~** (*veralt.*) ask for a girl's hand in marriage; **du sollst nicht ~ ...** (*bibl.*) thou shalt not covet ...; ⇒ *auch* **Herz B**; **B** (*veralt.: wollen*) desire; **C** (*bitten um*) ask for

**Begehren** *das;* **~s** (*geh.*) desire, wish (**nach** for); **jmdn. nach seinem ~ fragen** inquire *or* ask what sb. desires; **einem ~ entsprechen** grant sb.'s request

**begehrens·wert** *Adj.* desirable

**begehrlich** **1** *Adj.* (*gierig*) greedy; (*verlangend*) longing. **2** *adv.* (*gierig*) greedily; (*verlangend*) longingly

**Begehrlichkeit** *die;* **~, ~en** (*Gier*) greed; (*Verlangen*) desire

**begehrt** *Adj.* much sought-after; **~ bei den Damen sein** be much in demand with the ladies

**Begehung** *die;* **~, ~en** **A** (*Ausführung*) **die ~ eines Verbrechens/eines Fehlers** committing a crime/making a mistake; **B** (*Feier*) celebration; **C** (*das Abgehen*) inspection [on foot]

**begeifern** *tr. V.* (*abwertend: schmähen*) run down; vilify

**begeistern** **1** *tr. V.* **jmdn. [für etw.] ~:** fill *or* fire sb. with enthusiasm [for sth.]; **das Publikum ~:** fire the audience; **das kann mich nicht ~:** that leaves me cold. **2** *refl. V.* get *or* be enthusiastic (**für** about); **sich an der schönen Landschaft/für die Oper ~:** be very fond of the beautiful scenery/be keen on opera

**begeisternd** *Adj.* rousing

**begeistert** **1** *Adj.* enthusiastic; **von jmdm./etw. ~ sein** be taken by *or* with sb./be enthusiastic about sth. **2** *adv.* enthusiastically

**Begeisterung** *die;* **~:** enthusiasm; **etw. aus ~ tun** do sth. out of enthusiasm; **in ~ geraten** become *or* get enthusiastic

**begeisterungs-, Begeisterungs-: ~fähig** *Adj.* ‹children, people, etc.› who are able to get enthusiastic *or* are capable of enthusiasm; **~fähig sein** be able to get enthusiastic; **er ist sehr ~fähig** his enthusiasm is easily aroused; **~fähigkeit** *die* capacity for enthusiasm; **~sturm** *der* storm of enthusiastic applause

*old spelling (see note on page 1707)

**Begier** *die;* **~** (*geh.*), **Begierde** /bəˈɡiːɐ̯də/ *die;* **~de, ~den** desire (**nach** for); **fleischliche ~den** (*veralt.*) desires of the flesh; carnal desires

**begierig** **1** *Adj.* eager; (*gierig*) greedy; hungry; **ganz ~ auf jmds. Besuch** (*Akk.*) **sein** be eagerly looking forward to sb.'s visit; **~ sein, etw. zu tun** be [desperately] eager to do sth.; **mit ~en Blicken** with hungry *or* greedy glances. **2** *adv.* eagerly; (*gierig*) greedily; hungrily

**begießen** *unr. tr. V.* **A** water ‹plants›; baste ‹meat›; **jmdn./etw. mit Wasser ~:** pour water over sb./sth.; **B** (*ugs.*) **etw. ~:** celebrate sth. with a drink; **das muss begossen werden** that calls for a drink; ⇒ *auch* **Nase**

**Beginn** /bəˈɡɪn/ *der;* **~[e]s** start; beginning; **[gleich] zu** *od.* **am ~:** [right] at the start *or* beginning; **mit ~ des Semesters** at the start of the semester

**beginnen** **1** *unr. itr. V.* start; begin; **mit einer Arbeit/dem Studium ~:** start *or* begin a piece of work/one's studies; **mit dem Bau ~:** start *or* begin building; **dort beginnt der Wald** the forest starts there. **2** *unr. tr. V.* **A** start; begin; start ‹argument›; **B** (*unternehmen*) go *or* set about; **~, etw. zu tun** go *or* set about doing sth.; **was hättet ihr nur ohne mich begonnen?** what would you have done without me?; **nichts mit sich zu ~ wissen** not know what to do with oneself

**Beginnen** *das;* **~s** (*geh.*) enterprise

**beginnend** *Adj.* incipient; **mit der ~en Morgendämmerung** as dawn begins/began to break; **im ~en 19. Jahrhundert** at the beginning of the 19th century

**beglaubigen** /bəˈɡlaubɪɡn̩/ *tr. V.* **A** certify; authenticate ‹account, report, etc.›; **eine beglaubigte Kopie** a certified copy; ⇒ *auch* **notariell**; **B** (*akkreditieren*) accredit (*Dat.*, **bei** to)

**Beglaubigung** *die;* **~, ~en** **A** certification; (*eines Berichts*) authentication; **zur ~:** for certification; to be certified; **B** (*Akkreditierung*) accreditation

**Beglaubigungs·schreiben** *das* letter of accreditation

**begleichen** *unr. tr. V.* settle, pay ‹bill, debt›; pay ‹sum›; **mit jmdm. eine Rechnung zu ~ haben** (*fig.*) have a score to settle with sb.

**Begleichung** *die;* **~** (*einer Rechnung, einer Schuld*) settlement; payment; (*einer Summe*) payment; **ein Scheck zur ~ meiner Schulden** a cheque in payment of my debts

**Begleit·brief** *der* covering *or* accompanying letter

**begleiten** *tr. V.* **A** accompany; escort ‹ship›; **jmdn. zur Tür ~:** show sb. to the door; **jmdn. nach Hause ~:** see sb. home; **B** (*Musik*) accompany (**an, auf** + *Dat.* on); **C** (*fig.*) accompany; **von Erfolg begleitet werden** be attended by success; **etw. mit einem Kommentar ~:** add a commentary to sth.

**Begleiter** *der;* **~s, ~, Begleiterin** *die;* **~, ~nen** **A** companion; (*zum Schutz*) escort; (*Führer[in]*) guide; **ihr ständiger ~/seine ständige ~in** (*verhüll.*) his/her constant companion; **B** (*Musik*) accompanist

**Begleit-: ~erscheinung** *die* concomitant; (*einer Krankheit*) accompanying symptom; **das Alter und seine unangenehmen ~erscheinungen** old age and its attendant ills; **~instrument** *das* accompanying instrument; **~musik** *die* background music; (*fig.*) accompaniment; **~papiere** *Pl.* accompanying documents; **~person** *die* escort; **Kinder haben nur mit einer ~person Zutritt** children must be accompanied by an adult; **~schein** *der* (*Zollw.*) [customs] bond note; **~schiff** *das* escort [vessel]; **~schreiben** *das* ⇒ **~brief**; **~text** *der* accompanying text; **~um·stand** *der* attendant circumstance

**Begleitung** *die;* **~, ~en** **A** **er bot uns seine ~ an** he offered to accompany us; **in ~ einer Frau/eines Erwachsenen** in the company of *or* accompanied by a woman/an adult; **er ist in ~ hier** he's here with someone; **B** (*Musik*) accompaniment; **ohne ~** **singen/spielen** sing/play unaccompanied *or* without accompaniment; **die ~ übernehmen** take over as accompanist; **C** (*Person[en]*) companion[s]; (*zum Schutz*) escort

**beglotzen** *tr. V.* (*ugs.*) gawp at (*coll.*)

**beglücken** *tr. V.* (*geh.*) **jmdn. ~:** make sb. happy; delight sb.; **jmdn. mit etw. ~** (*oft iron.*) favour sb. with sth.; **die Frauen/Männer ~:** gratify women/men; **ein ~des Erlebnis** a gladdening experience

**Beglücker** *der;* **~s, ~, Beglückerin** *die;* **~, ~nen** bringer of happiness (*Gen.* to)

**beglückt** **1** *Adj.* happy; delighted. **2** *adv.* happily; delightedly

**Beglückung** *die;* **~, ~en** **A** **zur ~ der Menschheit beitragen** contribute to the sum of human happiness; **die ~ des Volkes** bringing Utopia to the people; **B** (*Glück*) happiness; delight

**beglück·wünschen** *tr. V.* congratulate (**zu** on); **sich zu etw. ~:** congratulate oneself on sth.

**begnaden** /bəˈɡnaːdn̩/ *tr. V.* (*geh.*) bless

**begnadet** *Adj.* (*geh.*) divinely gifted

**begnadigen** *tr. V.* pardon; reprieve; **einen zum Tode Verurteilten zu „lebenslänglich" ~:** commute the convicted prisoner's death sentence to life imprisonment

**Begnadigung** *die;* **~, ~en** reprieving; (*Straferlass*) pardon; reprieve

**Begnadigungs-: ~gesuch** *das* application for reprieve; **~recht** *das* right to grant reprieve

**begnügen** /bəˈɡnyːɡn̩/ *refl. V.* **sich mit etw. ~:** content oneself *or* make do with sth.; **sich damit ~, etw. zu tun** content oneself with doing sth.

**Begonie** /beˈɡoːni̯ə/ *die;* **~, ~n** begonia

**begonnen** /bəˈɡɔnən/ *2. Part. v.* **beginnen**

**begraben** *unr. tr. V.* **A** bury; **dort möchte ich nicht ~ sein** (*ugs.*) I wouldn't live there if you paid me (*coll.*); **B** (*fig.: aufgeben*) abandon ‹hope, plan, etc.›; **du kannst dich ~ lassen** (*ugs.*) you may as well give up; **du kannst dich mit diesem Plan ~ lassen** (*ugs.*) that plan won't get you anywhere

**Begräbnis** /bəˈɡrɛːpnɪs/ *das;* **~ses, ~se** burial; (*~feier*) funeral

**Begräbnis-: ~feier** *die* funeral; **~kosten** *Pl.* funeral expenses; **~stätte** *die* (*geh.*) burial place

**begradigen** /bəˈɡraːdɪɡn̩/ *tr. V.* straighten

**Begradigung** *die;* **~, ~en** straightening

**begrast** /bəˈɡraːst/ *Adj.* grass-covered

**begreifbar** *Adj.* comprehensible; understandable; **schwer ~ sein** be difficult to comprehend *or* understand

**begreifen** **1** *unr. tr. V.* **A** understand; understand, grasp, comprehend ‹connection, problem, meaning, necessity of sth., concept›; **er konnte nicht ~, was geschehen war** he could not grasp what had happened; **kaum zu ~ sein** be almost incomprehensible; **hast du mich begriffen?** you understand?; **B** (*Verständnis zeigen für*) understand; **das begreife, wer will** it's beyond me; **C** (*geh.: betrachten*) regard, see (**als** as); **D** **etw. in sich ~** (*veralt.*) include sth.; **E** (*ugs.: befühlen*) feel; (*betasten*) touch. **2** *itr. V.* understand; **schnell** *od.* **leicht/langsam** *od.* **schwer ~:** be quick/slow on the uptake; be quick/slow to grasp things

**begreiflich** *Adj.* understandable; **das ist mir nicht ~:** I can't understand it; **jmdm. etw. ~ machen** make sb. understand sth.

**begreiflicher·weise** *Adv.* understandably; **~ hat er das abgelehnt** understandably enough, he refused

**begrenzen** *tr. V.* **A** limit, restrict (**auf** + *Akk.* to); **B** (*die Grenze bilden von*) mark the boundary of; **durch etw. begrenzt sein** be bounded by sth.

**begrenzt** *Adj.* limited; restricted

**Begrenztheit** *die;* **~:** limitedness

**Begrenzung** *die;* **~, ~en** **A** (*Grenze*) boundary; (*Zaun*) boundary fence; **B** (*das Begrenzen*) limiting; restriction; (*der Geschwindigkeit*) restriction

**Begriff** *der* (A) concept; (*Terminus*) term; **in ~en denken** think abstractly; (B) (*Auffassung*) idea; **einen/keinen ~ von etw. haben** have an idea/no idea of sth.; **keinen ~ davon haben, wie ...** have no idea how ...; **sich** (*Dat.*) **keinen ~ von etw. machen können** not be able to imagine sth.; **nach menschlichen ~en** in human terms; **für meine ~e** in my estimation; **ein/kein ~ sein** be/not be well known; **jmdm. ein/kein ~ sein** mean something/nothing to sb.; **der ganzen Welt ein ~ sein** be known all over the world; (C) **im ~ sein** *od.* **stehen, etw. zu tun** be about to do sth.; (D) (*Begreifen*) **schwer** *od.* **langsam von ~ sein** (*ugs. abwertend*) be slow on the uptake

**begriffen** /bəˈɡrɪfn̩/ ❶ *2. Part. v.* **begreifen.** ❷ *Adj. in* **im Aufbruch/Fallen ~ sein** be leaving/falling; **in der Entwicklung/im Bau ~ sein** be in [the] process of development/construction

**begrifflich** ❶ *Adj.* conceptual. ❷ *adv.* conceptually; **~ denken** think abstractly

**begriffs-, Begriffs-: ~bestimmung** *die* definition [of the/a concept]; **~mäßig** *Adj., adv.:* ⇒ **begrifflich; ~stutzig,** (*österr.:*) **~stützig** (*abwertend*) ❶ *Adj.* obtuse; slow-witted; gormless (*coll.*); ❷ *adv.* obtusely; slow-wittedly; gormlessly (*coll.*); **~stutzigkeit** *die;* **~~,** (*österr.:*) **~stützigkeit** *die;* **~~** (*abwertend*) obtuseness; slow-wittedness; gormlessness (*coll.*); **~vermögen** *das* comprehension; **über jmds. ~vermögen** (*Akk.*) **hinausgehen** be beyond sb.'s comprehension *or* grasp; **~verwirrung** *die* conceptual confusion

**begründen** ❶ *tr. V.* (A) substantiate ‹statement, charge, claim›; give reasons for ‹decision, refusal, opinion›; **womit** *od.* **wie begründet sie ihren Entschluss/ihr Verhalten?** what reasons does she give for her decision?/how does she account for her behaviour?; **etw. sachlich ~:** give objective reasons for sth.; **~, warum man etw. tut** give one's reason[s] for doing sth.; **er begründete seinen Meinungswechsel damit, dass ...** he gave as the reason for his change of opinion the fact that ...; **ein Urteil ~:** give the grounds for a judgement; ⇒ *auch* **begründet;** (B) (*gründen*) found; establish ‹fame, reputation›; start ‹family›; **einen Hausstand ~:** set up house. ❷ *refl. V.* be based; **wie begründet sich das?** what is that based on?

**Begründer** *der,* **Begründerin** *die* founder

**begründet** *Adj.* well-founded; reasonable ‹demand, objection, complaint›; **sachlich ~:** objectively based; **nicht ~:** unfounded; **in etw.** (*Dat.*) **~ sein** be the result of sth.

**Begründung** *die;* **~, ~en** (A) reason[s]; **mit der ~, dass ...** on the grounds that ...; **seine ~ war ...** the reason/reasons he gave was/were ...; **für diese These fehlt eine ~:** there is no evidence to support this thesis; **etw. zur ~ einer Sache** (*Gen.*) **sagen** give sth. as the reason for sth.; **ohne jede ~:** without giving any reasons; (B) (*Gründung*) founding; establishment; (*eines Hausstands*) setting up; (*einer Familie*) starting

**begrünen** *tr. V.* **etw. ~:** plant greenery in/on sth.; (*mit Rasen*) grass sth.; **etw. [mit Rasen/Bäumen/Sträuchern** *usw.*] **~:** plant sth. with grass/trees/shrubs *etc.*

**begrüßen** *tr. V.* (A) greet; ‹host, hostess› greet, welcome; **ich freue mich, Sie in meinem Hause ~ zu dürfen** (*geh.*) it's a pleasure to welcome you into my home; **ich begrüße Sie** how do you do?; **es würde uns freuen, wenn wir Sie Freitagabend bei uns ~ dürften** (*geh.*) we should be delighted to have the pleasure of your company on Friday evening; (B) (*gutheißen*) welcome ‹suggestion, proposal›; **ich begrüße es, dass ...** I am glad that ...; **es wäre zu ~, wenn ...** it would be a welcome development if ...; (C) (*schweiz.*) consult

**begrüßens·wert** *Adj.* welcome

**Begrüßung** *die;* **~, ~en** greeting; (*von Gästen*) welcoming; (*Zeremonie*) welcome (*Gen.* for); **jmdm. zur ~ einen Strauß Blumen überreichen** welcome sb. with a bouquet of flowers; **sich** *od.* (*geh.*) **einander zur ~ die Hand schütteln** shake hands by way of greeting

**Begrüßungs-: ~an·sprache** *die* speech of welcome; welcoming speech; **~kuss, *~kuß** *der* welcoming kiss; **~rede** *die* ⇒ **~ansprache; ~wort** *das; Pl.* **~~e** word of welcome

**begucken** *tr. V.* (*ugs.*) look at; have *or* take a look at; **lass dich mal ~:** let's have *or* take a look at you

**begünstigen** /bəˈɡʏnstɪɡn̩/ *tr. V.* (A) favour; encourage ‹exports, trade, growth›; further ‹plan›; **vom Rückenwind begünstigt** assisted *or* helped by a following wind; **vom Schicksal begünstigt werden** be blessed by fate; (B) (*bevorzugen*) favour; show favour to; (C) (*Rechtsw.*) **jmdn. ~:** be an accessory of sb. after the fact

**Begünstigung** *die;* **~, ~en** (A) ⇒ **begünstigen** A: favouring; encouragement; furthering; (B) (*Bevorzugung*) preferential treatment; (C) (*Rechtsw.*) being an accessory after the fact

**begutachten** *tr. V.* (A) examine and report on; **ein Gemälde/das Flugzeugwrack ~, um etw. festzustellen** examine a painting/the [aircraft] wreckage in order to establish sth.; **ein Gebäude ~:** carry out a survey of a building; (B) (*ugs.*) look at; have *or* take a look at; **lass dich mal ~!** let's have *or* take a look at you

**Begutachter** *der;* **~s, ~, Begutachterin** *die;* **~, ~nen** ⇒ **Gutachter**

**Begutachtung** *die;* **~, ~en** examination; (*von Gebäuden*) survey; **eine schriftliche ~:** a written report

**begütert** /bəˈɡyːtɐt/ *Adj.* (A) wealthy; affluent; (B) (*veralt.*) landed *attrib.* ‹gentry, nobility, etc.›; **~ sein** own land

**begütigen** /bəˈɡyːtɪɡn̩/ *tr. V.* placate; mollify; pacify; **~d auf jmdn. einreden** speak soothingly to sb.

**Begütigung** *die;* **~, ~en** placating; mollifying; pacifying

**behaart** /bəˈhaːɐ̯t/ *Adj.* hairy; **grau/schwarz/stark ~ sein** be covered with grey/black hair/covered with hair; **stark ~e Beine** very hairy legs

**Behaarung** *die;* **~, ~en** covering of hair; (*Haar*) hair *no indef. art.;* **seine starke ~ auf dem Rücken** the thick hair on his back

**behäbig** /bəˈhɛːbɪç/ ❶ *Adj.* (A) stolid and portly; (B) (*langsam und schwerfällig*) slow and ponderous; (C) (*geruhsam und gemütlich*) placid and easygoing; (D) (*ausladend*) large and solid ‹furniture, house›. ❷ *adv.* slowly and ponderously

**Behäbigkeit** *die;* **~** (A) portliness; stoutness; (B) (*Langsamkeit*) slowness and ponderousness; (C) (*ausladende Form*) size and solidity

**behacken** *tr. V.* (A) hoe ‹plants›; (B) (*hacken an*) hack at

**behaftet** *Adj.* (*geh.*) **mit einem Makel/einer Krankheit ~ sein** be marked with a blemish/afflicted with a disease; **mit einem schlechten Ruf/einem Fehler/Laster ~ sein** have a bad name/a defect/be tainted with a vice; **mit Fehlern ~ sein** contain defects

**behagen** /bəˈhaːɡn̩/ *itr. V.* please; **das behagt mir/behagt mir nicht** that pleases/does not please me; I like/do not like that; **er behagt mir gar nicht** I don't like him at all

**Behagen** *das;* **~s** (*Zufriedenheit*) contentment; (*Vergnügen*) pleasure; **mit [sichtlichem] ~:** with [obvious] contentment/pleasure; **etw. mit ~ essen** eat sth. with relish

**behaglich** ❶ *Adj.* (A) comfortable; comfortable, cosy ‹atmosphere, room, home, etc.›; **es jmdm./sich ~ machen** make sb./oneself comfortable; (B) (*genießerisch, zufrieden*) contented. ❷ *adv.* (A) comfortably, cosily ‹warm, furnished›; (B) (*genießerisch, zufrieden*) contentedly

**Behaglichkeit** *die;* **~** ⇒ **behaglich** 1: (A) comfortableness; cosiness; (B) contentment

**behalten** *unr. tr. V.* (A) keep; keep on ‹workers, employees›; keep, retain ‹value, expressive power, etc.›; **den Hut auf dem Kopf ~:** keep one's hat on; **Nahrung bei sich ~:** keep food down; **jmdn. als Gast bei sich ~:** have sb. stay on as one's guest; **etw. für sich ~:** keep sth. to oneself; **die Nerven/die Ruhe ~:** keep one's nerve/keep calm; **ob wir das gute Wetter ~?** will the good weather hold?; (B) (*zurück~*) be left with; **einen Herzschaden** *usw.* **~:** be left with a weak heart *etc.;* **sie behielt von dem Unfall ein steifes Knie** the accident left her with a stiff knee; (C) (*sich merken*) remember ‹number, date›; **ich habe die Adresse nicht ~:** I've forgotten the address; **er kann Geschichtszahlen schlecht ~:** he has no memory for historical dates; **jmdn. in freundlicher Erinnerung ~:** have fond memories of sb.; ⇒ *auch* **Recht** D

**Behälter** /bəˈhɛltɐ/ *der;* **~s, ~** (A) container; (*für Abfälle*) receptacle; (B) (*Container*) container

**Behälter-: ~schiff** *das* container ship; **~verkehr** *der* container traffic

**Behältnis** *das;* **~ses, ~se** (*geh.*) container

**behämmern** *tr. V.* hammer

**behämmert** *Adj.* (*salopp*) ⇒ **bekloppt**

**behänd** /bəˈhɛnt/, **behände** ❶ *Adj.* (*geschickt*) deft; adroit; (*flink*) nimble; agile. ❷ *adv.;* s. *Adj.:* deftly; adroitly; nimbly; agilely

**behandeln** *tr. V.* (A) (*umgehen mit*) treat ‹person›; handle ‹matter, machine, device›; **jmdn. freundlich/herablassend/schlecht ~:** treat sb. in a friendly way/condescendingly/badly; **eine Maschine sachgemäß ~:** handle *or* use a machine correctly; **sie weiß, wie man Kinder/den Chef ~ muss** she knows how to handle children/the manager; (B) (*bearbeiten*) treat (**mit** with); (C) (*darstellen, analysieren*) deal with, treat ‹subject, question, theme›; (D) ▶ 474 (*ärztlich*) treat ‹patient, illness, symptom› (**mit** with; **auf** + *Akk.,* **wegen** for); **jmdn. ambulant/stationär ~:** give sb. treatment as an outpatient/inpatient; **der ~de Arzt** the doctor treating the patient

**Behändigkeit** *die;* **~** ⇒ **behänd** 1: deftness; adroitness; nimbleness; agility

**Behandlung** *die;* **~, ~en** ▶ 474 (A) treatment; **eine solche ~ lasse ich mir nicht gefallen** I won't stand for being treated like that; **bessere ~ verdienen** deserve better treatment *or* to be treated better; **bei einem/diesem Arzt in ~ sein** be under medical treatment/this doctor; (B) (*Besprechung*) discussion; (*Analyse*) treatment

**behandlungs-, Behandlungs-: ~bedürftig** *Adj.* **~bedürftig sein** require treatment; **~kosten** *Pl.* cost *sing.* of treatment; **~methode** *die* method of treatment; **~pflicht** *die: obligation on a doctor to respond to a call for medical assistance;* **~raum** *der* treatment room; **~stuhl** *der* chair for the patient; (*beim Zahnarzt*) [dentist's] chair; **~weise** *die* ⇒ **~methode**

**behandschuht** *Adj.* gloved

**Behang** *der;* **~[e]s, Behänge** (A) (*Wand~*) hanging; (B) (*am Baum*) decoration; (*Ertrag*) crop; (C) (*Jägerspr.*) (*Ohr*) lop-ear; (*Ohren*) lop ears *pl.*

**behangen** *Adj.* **ein mit Äpfeln ~er Baum** a tree laden with apples; **mit Schmuck ~:** festooned with jewellery

**behängen** *tr. V.* (A) **etw. mit etw. ~:** hang *or* decorate sth. with sth.; (B) (*ugs. abwertend*) **jmdn./sich mit etw. ~:** festoon sb./oneself with sth.

**beharken** *tr. V.* (A) (*Soldatenspr.*) rake with gunfire; (B) (*salopp*) pitch into (*coll.*); set about (*coll.*)

**beharren** *itr. V.* (A) **auf etw.** (*Dat.*) **~** (*etw. nicht aufgeben*) persist in sth.; (*auf etw. bestehen*) insist on sth.; **darauf ~, etw. zu tun** insist on doing sth.; (B) (*beharrlich behaupten*) insist; (C) (*geh.: bleiben*) (*an einem Ort*) remain; (*in einem Zustand*) persist

**Beharren** *das;* **~s** insistence

**beharrlich** ❶ *Adj.* dogged; persistent. ❷ *adv.* doggedly; persistently; **~ bei seiner Meinung bleiben** stick doggedly to one's opinion

**Beharrlichkeit** *die;* ~: doggedness; persistence

**Beharrung** *die;* ~: persistence

**Beharrungs·vermögen** *das* (*Physik*) inertia

**behauchen** *tr. V.* Ⓐ breathe on; Ⓑ (*Phon.*) aspirate; **behauchte Konsonanten** aspirates

**behauen** *unr. tr. V.* hew; **roh ~e Steine** rough-hewn stone blocks

**behaupten** /bəˈhaʊptn̩/ ❶ *tr. V.* Ⓐ maintain; assert; ~, **jmd. zu sein/etw. zu wissen** claim to be sb./know sth.; **das kann man nicht** ~: you cannot say that; **man behauptet** *od.* **es wird behauptet, dass ...** it is said *or* claimed that ...; ⇒ *auch* **steif** 2 C; Ⓑ (*verteidigen*) maintain ‹position›; retain ‹record›; ⇒ *auch* **Feld** F. ❷ *refl. V.* Ⓐ assert oneself; (*nicht untergehen*) hold one's ground; (*dableiben*) survive; **die Kirche/der Dollar konnte sich** ~: the church/the dollar was able to maintain its position; Ⓑ (*Sport*) win through

**Behauptung** *die;* ~, ~**en** Ⓐ claim; assertion; Ⓑ (*Verteidigung*) **für die ~ seiner Stellung kämpfen** fight to maintain one's position; Ⓒ (*Durchsetzung*) assertion

**behausen** *tr. V.* (*geh.*) house; accommodate, put up ‹guest›

**Behausung** *die;* ~, ~**en** Ⓐ (*geh.: das Behausen*) housing; accommodation; Ⓑ (*oft abwertend: Wohnung*) dwelling

**Behaviorismus** /bihevjəˈrɪsmʊs/ *der;* ~ (*Verhaltensf.*) behaviourism *no art.*

**behavioristisch** (*Biol., Psych.*) ❶ *Adj.* behaviourist. ❷ *adv.* behaviouristically

**beheben** *unr. tr. V.* Ⓐ remove ‹doubt, danger, difficulty›; repair ‹damage›; remedy ‹abuse, defect›; clear ‹disturbance›; Ⓑ (*österr.: abheben*) withdraw ‹money›

**Behebung** *die;* ~, ~**en** Ⓐ ⇒ **beheben** A: removal; repair; remedying; clearing; Ⓑ (*österr.: Abhebung*) withdrawal

**beheimaten** *tr. V.* provide a home for ‹person›; **Tiere/Pflanzen in einer Gegend** ~: introduce animals/plants into an area

**beheimatet** *Adj.* Ⓐ (*heimisch*) **an einem Ort/in einem Land ~ sein** ‹plant, animal, tribe, race› be native *or* indigenous to a place/country; ‹person› come from a place/country; **wo ist er ~?** where does he come from?; Ⓑ (*ansässig*) resident (**in** + *Dat.* in)

**beheizbar** *Adj.* heatable; **eine ~e Heckscheibe** a heated rear window

**beheizen** *tr. V.* heat

**Beheizung** *die;* ~: heating

**Behelf** /bəˈhɛlf/ *der;* ~**[e]s**, ~**e** (*Notlösung*) stopgap; makeshift; (*Ersatz*) substitute

**behelfen** *unr. refl. V.* Ⓐ **sich mit etw.** ~: make do *or* manage with sth.; Ⓑ (*zurechtkommen*) get by; manage; **sich allein** ~: get by *or* manage on one's own

**behelfs-, Behelfs-:** ~**aus·fahrt** *die* (*Verkehrsw.*) temporary exit (*from a motorway*); ~**heim** *das* makeshift *or* temporary home; ~**mäßig** ❶ *Adj.* makeshift; temporary; ❷ *adv.* in a makeshift way *or* fashion; ~**unterkunft** *die* temporary dwelling; ~**weise** *Adv.* (*vorübergehend*) temporarily; (*ersatzweise*) as a substitute

**behelligen** /bəˈhɛlɪgn̩/ *tr. V.* (*lästig werden für*) bother; (*zudringlich werden gegenüber*) pester

**Behelligung** *die;* ~, ~**en ich verbitte mir solche ~en** stop bothering *or* pestering me

**behelmt** /bəˈhɛlmt/ *Adj.* helmeted

***behend, *behende** ⇒ **behänd**

**beherbergen** *tr. V.* Ⓐ accommodate, put up ‹guest›; Ⓑ (*Raum bieten für*) accommodate; Ⓒ (*enthalten*) contain

**Beherbergung** *die;* ~: accommodation

**Beherbergungs·gewerbe** *das* hotel trade

**beherrschen** ❶ *tr. V.* Ⓐ rule; **den Markt** ~: dominate *or* control the market; **von Hassgefühlen/Leidenschaften beherrscht sein** (*geh.*) be ruled by feelings of hatred/by passions; Ⓑ (*meistern*) control ‹vehicle, animal›; be in control of ‹situation›; Ⓒ (*bestimmen, dominieren*) dominate ‹townscape, landscape, discussions, relationship›; Ⓓ (*zügeln*) control ‹feelings›; control, curb ‹impatience›; **seine Zunge** ~ (*geh.*) curb one's tongue; Ⓔ (*gut können*) have mastered ‹instrument, trade›; have a good command of ‹language›; **es kostet viele Jahre ständiger Übung, ein Instrument zu** ~: it takes many years of constant practice to master an instrument; **Englisch fast so gut wie Deutsch** ~: speak English almost as well as German. ❷ *refl. V.* control oneself; **ich kann mich** ~ (*iron.*) I can resist the temptation (*iron.*); **kannst du dich so wenig ~, dass ...?** have you got so little self-control that ...?

**Beherrscher** *der;* ~**s**, ~, **Beherrscherin** *die;* ~, ~**nen** ruler

**beherrscht** ❶ *Adj.* self-controlled. ❷ with self-control; **völlig** ~: with complete self-control

**Beherrschtheit** *die;* ~: self-control

**Beherrschung** *die;* ~ Ⓐ control; (*Verwaltung*) rule; (*eines Markts*) domination; control; Ⓑ (*das Meistern*) control; Ⓒ (*Beherrschtheit*) self-control; **seine** *od.* **die ~ verlieren** lose one's self-control; Ⓓ (*das Können*) mastery

**beherzigen** /bəˈhɛrt͜sɪgn̩/ *tr. V.* **etw.** ~: take sth. to heart; heed sth.

**beherzigens·wert** *Adj.* worth taking to heart *or* heeding *postpos.*

**Beherzigung** *die;* ~: heeding; **dies zur ~!** I want you to heed *or* take good heed of this

**beherzt** ❶ *Adj.* spirited; **einige Beherzte** a few brave souls. ❷ *adv.* spiritedly

**Beherztheit** *die;* ~: spirit

**behexen** *tr. V.* bewitch

**behilflich** /bəˈhɪlflɪç/ *Adj.* **jmdm. [beim Aufräumen** *usw.*] **~ sein** help sb. [clear up *or* with the clearing-up *etc.*]; **kann ich [Ihnen] ~ sein?** can I help [you]?

**behindern** *tr. V.* Ⓐ hinder; hamper, impede ‹movement›; hold up ‹traffic›; impede ‹view›; **jmdn. in etw.** (*Dat.*) ~: hinder sb. in sth.; **ein behindertes Kind** a handicapped child; Ⓑ (*Sport, Verkehrsw.*) obstruct

**Behinderte** *der/die; adj. Dekl.* handicapped person; **die ~n** the handicapped; **WC für** ~: toilet for disabled persons

**behinderten·gerecht** ❶ *Adj.* ‹accommodation, toilet, bus, lift, etc.› which caters for the needs of people with disabilities. ❷ *adv.* **das Hotel ist ~ ausgestattet** the hotel is equipped to cater for [the needs of] people with disabilities

**Behinderung** *die;* ~, ~**en** Ⓐ **um ~en bei der Zollabfertigung zu vermeiden** to avoid hold-ups at customs; **zur ~ des Flugverkehrs beitragen** help to cause delays to air traffic; **~ der Sicht** obstruction to the view; Ⓑ (*Sport, Verkehrsw.*) obstruction; **Falschparken mit** ~: parking illegally and causing an obstruction; Ⓒ (*Hindernis*) hindrance; Ⓓ (*Gebrechen*) handicap

**behobeln** *tr. V.* plane

**behorchen** *tr. V.* Ⓐ (*ugs.*) listen to; Ⓑ (*belauschen*) eavesdrop on

**Behörde** /bəˈhøːɐ̯də/ *die;* ~, ~**n** Ⓐ authority; (*Amt, Abteilung*) department; **die ~n** the authorities; Ⓑ (*Gebäude*) government offices *pl.*/[local] council offices *pl.*

**Behörden-:** ~**apparat** *der* administrative apparatus; (*abwertend: Bürokratie*) bureaucracy; ~**deutsch** *das* (*abwertend*) officialese

**behördlich** ❶ *Adj.* official; **~e Genehmigung** permission from the authorities; official permission; **auf ~e Anordnung** by order of the authorities. ❷ *adv.* officially; **das ist ~ genehmigt worden** it has been approved by the authorities

**behördlicher·seits** *Adv.* (*durch die Behörde*) by the authorities; (*seitens der Behörde*) on the part of the authorities

**behost** /bəˈhoːst/ *Adj.* (*ugs.*) in trousers *postpos.*

**Behuf** *der;* ~**[e]s**, ~**e** *in* **zu diesem ~[e]** (*veralt.*) to this end

**behufs** *Präp. mit Gen.* (*veralt.*) with a view to

**behuft** /bəˈhuːft/ *Adj.* hooved

**behum[p]sen** /bəˈhʊmpsn̩, bəˈhʊmzn̩/ *tr. V.* (*ugs., bes. ostmd.*) diddle (*coll.*)

**behüten** *tr. V.* (*bewahren, beschützen*) protect (**vor** + *Dat.* from); (*sorgen für*) take care of; (*bewachen*) guard; **ein Geheimnis** ~: keep a secret; **jmdn. vor einer Gefahr** ~: keep *or* safeguard sb. from a danger; **[Gott] behüte!** God *or* Heaven forbid!

**Behüter** *der;* ~**s**, ~, **Behüterin** *die;* ~, ~**nen** (*geh.*) protector

**behütet** *Adj.* sheltered ‹upbringing, life›

**behutsam** /bəˈhuːtzaːm/ ❶ *Adj.* careful; cautious; cautious, discreet ‹question›; (*zartfühlend*) gentle. ❷ *adv.* carefully; cautiously; (*zartfühlend*) gently

**Behutsamkeit** *die;* ~: care; caution; (*Zartgefühl*) gentleness

**bei** /bai̯/ *Präp. mit Dat.* Ⓐ (*nahe*) near; (*dicht an, neben*) by; **die Schlacht ~ Leipzig** the battle of Leipzig; **irgendwo ~ Stuttgart** somewhere near Stuttgart; **nahe ~m Bahnhof** near the station; **~m Gepäck/Auto** *usw.* **bleiben** stay with the luggage/car; **wer steht da ~ ihm?** who is standing there with him?; **sich ~ jmdm. entschuldigen/beklagen/erkundigen** apologize/complain to sb./ask sb.; **wir haben Physik ~ Herrn Meyer** we do physics with Mr Meyer; **der Wert liegt ~ 10 000 Mark** the value is around *or* about ten thousand marks; **~m Fenster herausschauen** (*österr.*) look out of the window; Ⓑ (*unter*) among; **war heute ein Brief für mich ~ der Post?** was there a letter for me in the post today?; Ⓒ (*an*) by; **jmdn. ~ der Hand nehmen** take sb. by the hand; **jmdn. ~ der Schulter packen** seize sb. by the shoulder; ⇒ *auch* **beim** B; Ⓓ (*im Wohnbereich*) (*längerfristig*) with; (*kurzfristig*) at; **~ uns tut man das nicht** we don't do that; **~ mir [zu Hause]** at my house; **~ uns um die Ecke/gegenüber** round the corner from us/opposite us; **~ seinen Eltern leben** live with one's parents; **wir sind ~ ihr eingeladen** we have been invited to her house; **wir treffen uns ~ uns/Peter** we'll meet at our/Peter's place; **morgen schlafe ich ~ meinen Großeltern** I'm sleeping at my grandparents' tomorrow; **~ uns in Österreich** in Austria [where I/we come from/live]; **[hier/damals] ~ uns in Österreich** here in Austria/in Austria in those days; **wir haben ~ [den] Clarks gefeiert** we went to a party at the Clarks'; (*im Geschäft*) **~m Bäcker/Fleischer** *usw.* at the baker's/butcher's *etc.*; **~ uns in der Firma** in our company; **~ Schmidt** (*auf Briefen*) c/o Schmidt; Ⓔ (*im geistigen Bereich*) with; **~ jmdm. Verständnis finden** get sympathy and understanding from sb.; **die Verantwortung liegt ~ Ihnen** responsibility lies with you; Ⓕ (*im Arbeitsbereich*) **~ einer Firma sein** be with a company; **~ jmdm./einem Verlag arbeiten** work for sb./a publishing house; **~ der Bundeswehr/Luftwaffe sein** be in the forces/air force; ⇒ *auch* ~ A; Ⓖ (*im Bereich eines Vorgangs*) at; **~ einer Hochzeit/einem Empfang** *usw.* **sein** be at a wedding/reception *etc.*; **~ der Organisation von etw./~ einer Aufführung mitwirken** be involved in the organization of sth./appear in a production; Ⓗ (*im Werk von*) **~ Goethe** in Goethe; **~ Schiller heißt es ...** Schiller says *or* writes that ...; Ⓘ (*im Falle von*) in the case of; **wie ~ den Römern** as with the Romans; **hoffentlich geht es nicht wie ~ mir** I hope the same thing doesn't happen as happened in my case; Ⓙ (*im eigenen Bereich*) with; **etw. ~ sich haben** have sth. with *or* on one; **~ sich [selbst] anfangen** start with oneself; **nicht [ganz] ~ sich sein** be not quite with it; **~ mir ist es zehn Uhr** I make it ten o'clock; Ⓚ (*Zeitpunkt*) at ‹beginning, end›; **~ seiner Ankunft/seinem Eintritt** on his arrival/entry; **~ diesen Worten errötete er** at this he blushed; Ⓛ (*Zeitspanne*) **~ Tag/Nacht** by day/night; **~ Sonnenaufgang/-untergang** at sunrise/sunset; **~ unserer Begegnung** at our meeting; **~ einem**

*old spelling (see note on page 1707)

**Unfall** in an accident; ~ **einer Schlägerei** in a brawl; ~ **Tisch sein** be at table; ~ **der Arbeit** at work; ⇒ *auch* ~**m** B; [M] (*gleichzeitig mit*) with; ~ **zunehmendem Alter** with advancing age; [N] (*modal*) ~ **Tag und Nacht** day and night; ~ **Tageslicht** by daylight; ~ **Nebel** in fog; ~ **Kälte** when it's cold; ~ **einem Glas Wein** over a glass of wine; ~ **offenem Fenster schlafen** sleep with the window open; [O] (*betreffs*) with; **das gilt auch** ~ **...** this applies to ... also; ~ **so etwas ist er geschickt** he is skilled at things like that; [P] (*im Falle von*) „~ **Feuer Scheibe einschlagen**" 'in case of fire, break glass'; „~ **Regen Schleudergefahr**" 'slippery when wet'; ~ **hohem Fieber** when sb. has a high temperature; [Q] (*aufgrund von*) with; ~ **dieser Hitze** in this heat; ~ **diesem Sturm/Lärm** with this storm blowing/noise going on; ~ **deinen guten Augen/ihrem Talent** with your good eyesight/her talent; **er erblasste** ~ **der Nachricht** he turned pale at the news; [R] (*trotz*) ~ **all seinem Engagement/seinen Bemühungen** in spite of *or* despite *or* for all his commitment/efforts; ~ **allem Verständnis, aber ich kann das nicht** much as I sympathize, I cannot do that; [S] (*in Beteuerungsformeln*) by; ~ **Gott!** by God!; ~ **meiner Ehre!** (*veralt.*) upon my honour!

**bei|behalten** *unr. tr. V.* keep, retain ‹distinction, wording, penalty, measure, practice, laws›; keep up ‹custom, habit›; continue, maintain ‹way of life›; keep to ‹course, method›; preserve, maintain ‹attitude›

**Beibehaltung** *die;* ~ ⇒ **beibehalten**: keeping; retention; keeping up; continuance; maintenance; preservation

**bei|biegen** *unr. tr. V.* (*ugs.*) **jmdm. etw.** ~: get sb. to understand sth.

**Bei·blatt** *das* insert

**Bei·boot** *das* ship's boat

**bei|bringen** *unr. tr. V.* [A] **jmdm. etw.** ~: teach sb. sth.; **jmdm. Gehorsam** ~: teach sb. obedience; **ich werde dir** ~, **mich zu betrügen!** (*ugs.*) I'll teach you to cheat me! (*coll.*); [B] (*ugs.: mitteilen*) **jmdm.** ~, **dass ...** break it to sb. that ...; [C] (*zufügen*) **jmdm./sich etw.** ~: inflict sth. on sb./oneself; [D] (*beschaffen*) produce ‹witness, evidence›; provide, supply ‹reference, proof›; produce, furnish ‹money›

**Beichte** /ˈbaiçtə/ *die;* ~, ~**n** confession *no def. art.;* **zur** ~ **gehen** go to confession; **jmdm. die** ~ **abnehmen** hear sb.'s confession

**beichten** ❶ *itr. V.* go to confession; ~ **gehen** go to confession. ❷ *tr. V.* (*fig.*) confess

**Beicht-:** ~**formel** *die* form of confession; ~**geheimnis** *das* seal of confession; ~**gespräch** *das* (*kath. Rel.*) talk with the priest before confession; ~**stuhl** *der* confessional; ~**vater** *der* father confessor

**beid-:** ~**armig** ❶ *Adj.* two-handed; (*mit* ~*en Armen gleich geschickt*) ambidextrous; ❷ *adv.* with both hands; ~**beinig** ❶ *Adj.* two-legged; ❷ *adv.* with both feet

**beide** /ˈbaidə/ *Indefinitpron. u. Zahlw.* [A] *mit Art. od. Pron.* **die/seine** ~**n Brüder** the/his two brothers; (*mit Nachdruck*) both the/his brothers; **die** ~**n ersten Strophen** the first two verses; **kennst du die** ~**n?** do you know those two?; **alle** ~: both of us/you/them; **sie sind alle** ~ **sehr schön** they're both very nice; both of them are very nice; **sie sind** ~ **nicht hübsch** neither of them is pretty; **ihr/euch** ~: you two; **ihr/euch** ~ **nicht** neither of you; **wir/uns** ~: the two of us/both of us; [B] *o. Art.* both; **er hat** ~ **Eltern verloren** he has lost both [his] parents; **mit** ~**n Händen** with both hands; ~ **Male** both times; **ich habe** ~ **gekannt** I knew both of them; ~ **haben hier gearbeitet** both [of them] worked here; **einer/eins von** ~**n** one of the two; **keiner/keins von** ~**n** neither [of them]; [C] *Neutr. Sg.* both *pl.;* ~**s ist möglich** either is possible; **ich glaube** ~**s/**~**s nicht** I believe both things/neither thing; **das ist** ~**s nicht richtig** neither of those is correct; **er hat sich in** ~**m geirrt** he was wrong on both counts; **er hatte von** ~**m wenig Ahnung** he had little idea of either

***beide·mal** ⇒ **Mal**[1]

**beiderlei** /ˈbaidɐˈlai/ *Gattungsz., indekl.* ~ **Geschlechts** of both sexes; **von** ~ **Art** of both kinds; **das Abendmahl in** *od.* **unter** ~ **Gestalt** (*ev. Rel.*) communion in both kinds

**beider·seitig** ❶ *Adj.* mutual ‹decision, agreement›; ~**e Freude** joy on both sides; **zur** ~**en Überraschung** to the surprise of both of us/them; **in** ~**em Einverständnis** by mutual agreement. ❷ *adv.* by both sides; **eine** ~ **interessierende Frage** a question of interest to both sides. ❸ *Adv.* on both sides

**beider·seits** ❶ *Präp. mit Gen.* on both sides of. ❷ *Adv.* on both sides

**beid-:** ~**füßig** *Adj., adv.* with both feet; ~**händig** ❶ *Adj.* [A] (*mit* ~*en Händen gleich geschickt*) ambidextrous; [B] (*mit* ~*en Händen*) two-handed; ❷ *adv.* with two hands; **eine** ~**händig geschlagene Rückhand** a two-handed backhand

**bei|drehen** *itr. V.* (*Seemannsspr.*) heave to

**beid·seitig** ❶ *Adj.* mutual. ❷ *adv.* [A] (*auf beiden Seiten*) ‹be printed etc.› on both sides; ~ **gelähmt sein** be paralysed down both sides; [B] (*gegenseitig*) ⇒ **beiderseitig** 2

**beidseits** (*bes. schweiz.*) ⇒ **beiderseits**

**bei·einander** *Adv.* together; **etw.** ~ **haben** have got sth. together; **er hat sie nicht alle** ~ (*ugs.*) he's not all there (*coll.*); ~ **sein** (*ordentlich sein*) be neat and tidy; **gut/schlecht** ~ **sein** (*ugs.*) be in good/bad shape; **nicht ganz** ~ **sein** (*ugs.*) be not quite all there (*coll.*) ~ **Trost suchen** seek comfort from each other

***beieinander|haben** *usw.* ⇒ **beieinander**

**Beieinander·sein** *das* get-together

***beieinander|sitzen** *usw.* ⇒ **beieinander**

**Bei·fahrer** *der,* **Bei·fahrerin** *die* [A] (*im Kfz*) [front-seat] passenger; (*auf dem Motorrad*) pillion passenger; (*im Beiwagen*) sidecar passenger; [B] (*berufsmäßig*) co-driver; (*auf einem LKW*) driver's mate

**Beifahrer·sitz** *der* (*im Kfz*) passenger seat; (*eines Motorrads*) pillion

**Bei·fall** *der* [A] applause; (*Zurufe*) cheers *pl.;* cheering; (*Händeklatschen*) applause; clapping; **stürmischer** *od.* **tosender** ~: a storm of applause; ~ **klatschen/spenden** applaud; **jmdn.** ~ **heischend ansehen** look at sb. in the hope of getting applause; [B] (*Zustimmung*) approval; ~ **finden** meet with approval; **jmdn.** ~ **heischend ansehen** look at sb. in the hope of getting approval;

***beifall·heischend** ⇒ **Beifall**

**bei·fällig** ❶ *Adj.* approving; favourable ‹judgement›; ~**es Gemurmel** murmurs *pl.* of approval. ❷ *adv.* approvingly; ~ **nicken** nod approvingly *or* in approval; ~ **aufgenommen werden** be received favourably *or* with approval

**Beifall·klatschen** *das* clapping; applause

**Beifalls-:** ~**äußerung** *die* expression of approval; ~**bekundung** *die,* ~**bezeigung** *die;* demonstration of approval; ~**kundgebung** *die* ovation; ~**kundgebungen** ovation *sing.;* ~**ruf** *der* shout of approval; cheer; ~**sturm** *der* storm of applause

**bei|fügen** *tr. V.* [A] (*dazulegen*) **einer Bewerbung etw.** ~: enclose sth. with an application; **einem Paket eine Zollerklärung** ~: attach a customs declaration to a parcel; **einem Blumenstrauß eine Grußkarte** ~: put a greetings card in with a bouquet; [B] (*hinzufügen*) add; **dem Teig Zucker/Mehl** ~: add sugar/flour to the mixture

**Bei·fügung** *die* [A] (*Sprachw.*) attribute; [B] (*Amtsspr.: das Beifügen*) **unter** ~ **eines Lebenslaufs/Schecks** enclosing a curriculum vitae/cheque

**Bei·fuß** *der* (*Bot.*) artemisia; (*Artemisia vulgaris*) mugwort

**Bei·gabe** *die* [A] (*das Beigeben*) **unter** ~ (*Dat.*) **von etw.** adding sth.; [B] (*Hinzugefügtes*) addition; (*Beilage*) side dish

**beige** /beːʃ/ *Adj.* beige; **ein** ~ *od.* (*ugs.*) ~**s Kleid** a beige dress

**Beige** *das;* ~, ~ *od.* (*ugs.*) ~**s** beige

**bei|geben** ❶ *unr. tr. V.* [A] (*hinzufügen*) add (*Dat.* to); [B] (*mitgeben*) assign (*Dat.* to). ❷ *unr. itr. V.* **in klein** ~ (*ugs.*) give in

**beige·farben** *Adj.* beige[-coloured]

**bei|gehen** *unr. itr. V.; mit sein* (*nordd.*) ⇒ **darangehen**

**Beigeordnete** *der/die; adj. Dekl.* ≈ town council official

**Bei·geschmack** *der* **einen bitteren** *usw.* ~ **haben** have a slightly bitter *etc.* taste [to it]; taste slightly bitter *etc.;* **dieses Wort hat einen negativen** ~ (*fig.*) this word has slightly negative overtones *pl.;* **einen** ~ **von Petroleum haben** have a slight taste of paraffin (*Brit.*) *or* (*Amer.*) kerosene; taste slightly of petrol

**bei|gesellen** (*geh.*) ❶ *tr. V.* **jmdm. jmdn.** ~: put sb. with sb. ❷ *refl. V.* **sich jmdm.** ~: attach oneself to sb.

**Bei·heft** *das* (*zum Lehrbuch*) supplement; (*einer Zeitschrift*) supplementary number

**bei|heften** *tr. V.* **einer Sache** (*Dat.*) **etw.** ~: attach sth. to sth.

**Bei·hilfe** *die* [A] (*materielle Hilfe*) aid; assistance; (*Geldunterstützung*) [financial] aid *or* assistance; (*Zuschuss für Kleidung, Heizung, Miete, Kinderreiche, Studenten usw.*) allowance; (*Subvention*) subsidy; [B] (*Rechtsw.: Mithilfe*) aiding and abetting; **jmdn. wegen** ~ **zum Mord anklagen** charge sb. with aiding and abetting a murder *or* with acting as accessory to a murder

**Bei·klang** *der* (*geh.*) [accompanying] sound; (*fig.*) overtone[s *pl.*]; underlying note

**Bei·koch** *der,* **Bei·köchin** *die* assistant chef

**bei|kommen** *unr. itr. V.; mit sein* [A] (*gewachsen sein*) **jmdm.** ~: get the better of sb.; [B] (*bewältigen*) **den Schwierigkeiten/der Unruhe/jmds. Sturheit** ~: overcome the difficulties/deal with the unrest/cope with sb.'s obstinacy; [C] (*ugs.: herbeikommen*) come; [D] (*ugs.: heranreichen*) reach; [E] *unpers.* (*geh.*) **es kommt jmdm. bei, etw. zu tun** sb. has the idea of doing sth.

**Bei·kost** *die* diet supplement; **vitaminreiche/nahrhafte** ~ **bekommen** have a vitamin-rich/nutritious supplementary diet

**Beil** /bail/ *das;* ~**[e]s,** ~**e** [A] axe; (*kleiner*) hatchet; (*Fleischer*~) cleaver; [B] (*Fall*~) guillotine

**bei|laden** *unr. tr. V.* [A] (*zuladen*) add; [B] (*Rechtsw.*) summon ‹third party interested in the outcome of a case›

**Bei·ladung** *die* additional load

**Bei·lage** *die* [A] (*Zeitungs*~) supplement; [B] (*zu Speisen*) side dish; (*Gemüse*~) vegetables *pl.;* (*Salat*~) side salad; **ein Fleischgericht mit diversen** ~**n** a meat dish with a selection of trimmings; [C] (*das Beilegen*) enclosure; **unter** ~ **von ...** enclosing ...; **gegen** ~ **von Rückporto** if return postage is enclosed; [D] (*österr.: Anlage*) enclosure (**zu** with)

**Bei·lager** *das* [A] (*geh. veralt.: Beischlaf*) sexual intercourse; [B] (*hist.: Akt der Eheschließung*) consummation of the marriage

**bei·läufig** ❶ *Adj.* [A] (*nebensächlich*) casual; casual, passing ‹remark, mention›; [B] (*österr.: ungefähr*) approximate; rough. ❷ *adv.* [A] (*nebenbei*) casually; **etw.** ~ **erwähnen** *od.* **bemerken** mention sth. casually *or* in passing; ~ **bemerkt, ...** incidentally, ...; **etw.** ~ **erfahren** learn sth. by chance; **jmdn.** ~ **ausfragen** get information unobtrusively from sb.; [B] (*österr.: ungefähr*) approximately; roughly

**Beiläufigkeit** *die;* ~, ~**en** [A] (*Nonchalance*) casualness; [B] (*Nebensächlichkeit*) triviality; ~**en** trivia

**bei|legen** *tr. V.* [A] (*dazulegen*) enclose; (*einem Buch, einer Zeitschrift*) insert (*Dat.* in); **einem Brief** *usw.* **etw.** ~: enclose sth. with a letter *etc.;* [B] (*schlichten*) settle ‹dispute, controversy, etc.›; [C] (*beimessen*) attach; **einer Sache** (*Dat.*) **Gewicht/Bedeutung** *usw.* ~: attach weight/importance *etc.* to sth.; [D]

b

(*geben, verleihen*) **jmdm. einen Titel/Namen ~:** bestow *or* confer a title/bestow a name on sb.; **sich** (*Dat.*) **einen Titel/Namen ~:** assume *or* adopt a title/name

**Beilegung** *die;* ~, ~**en** settlement

**beileibe** /bai̯'laibə/ *Adv.* ~ **nicht** certainly not; **er ist ~ kein Genie** he is by no means a genius

**Bei·leid** *das* sympathy; **[mein] herzliches** *od.* **aufrichtiges ~!** please accept my sincere condolences; **jmdm. sein [aufrichtiges] ~ [zu etw.] aussprechen** offer one's [sincere] condolences *pl.* to sb. [on sth.]

**Beileids-:** ~**besuch** *der* visit of condolence; visit to offer one's condolences; ~**bezeigung** *die;* ~~, ~~**en**, ~**bezeugung** *die* expression of sympathy; ~**karte** *die* condolence *or* sympathy card

**Beil·hieb** *der* blow with an/the axe

**bei|liegen** *unr. itr. V.* **A** (*beigefügt sein*) **einem Brief ~:** be enclosed with a letter; **dem Buch liegt ein Prospekt bei** the book contains a catalogue as an insert; **B** (*geh. veralt.: Geschlechtsverkehr haben mit*) **jmdm. ~:** lie with sb. (*arch.*); **C** (*Seemannsspr.*) lie to

**bei·liegend** *Adj.* (*Amtsspr.*) enclosed; ~ **senden wir ...** please find enclosed ...

**beim** /baim/ *Präp.* + *Art.* **A** = **bei dem; B jmdn. ~ Ärmel zupfen** tug at sb.'s sleeve; ~ **Film sein** be in films; **C** (*zeitlich*) **er will ~ Arbeiten nicht gestört werden** he doesn't want to be disturbed when *or* while [he's] working; ~ **Essen spricht man nicht** you shouldn't talk while [you're] eating; **den Hund darf man ~ Fressen nicht stören** you mustn't disturb the dog while it's eating; ~ **Verlassen des Gebäudes** when *or* on leaving the building; ~ **Fasching** at carnival time; ~ **Lesen/Essen/Duschen sein** be reading/be having breakfast/dinner *etc.*/be taking a shower

**bei|mengen** *tr. V.* add (*Dat.* to)

**Beimengung** *die;* ~, ~**en A** (*das Beimengen*) addition; **B** (*Zusatz*) admixture

**bei|messen** *unr. tr. V.* attach; **jmdm./einer Sache Bedeutung/Wert** *usw.* **~:** attach importance/value *etc.* to sb./sth.

**bei|mischen** *tr. V.* (*geh.*) add (*Dat.* to); **meiner Bewunderung war Grauen beigemischt** (*fig.*) my admiration was tinged with horror

**Bei·mischung** *die* **A** (*das Beimischen*) addition; **B** (*Zusatz*) admixture

**Bein** /bain/ *das;* ~**[e]s**, ~**e A** ▶ 471 leg; **jmdm. ~e machen** (*ugs.*) make sb. get a move on (*coll.*); **du hast jüngere ~e** (*ugs.*) your legs are younger than mine; **ein langes ~ machen** (*Fußballjargon*) make a sliding tackle; **ein ~ stehen lassen** (*Fußballjargon*) put *or* (*coll.*) stick one's foot out; **sich** (*Dat.*) **die ~e nach etw. ablaufen** (*fig.*) chase round everywhere for sth.; **er hat sich** (*Dat.*) **kein ~ ausgerissen** (*ugs.*) he didn't overexert himself; **jmdm. ein ~ stellen** (*zum Stolpern bringen*) trip sb.; (*fig.: hereinlegen*) put *or* throw a spanner *or* (*Amer.*) a monkey wrench in sb.'s works; **jmdm. [einen] Knüppel** *od.* **Prügel zwischen die ~e werfen** (*fig.*) put *or* throw a spanner *or* (*Amer.*) a monkey wrench in sb.'s works; **das hat ~e gekriegt** (*fig. ugs.*) it seems to have [grown legs and] walked (*coll.*); **die ~e in die Hand** *od.* **unter die Arme nehmen** (*fig. ugs.*) (*sich beeilen*) step on it (*coll.*); (*weglaufen*) take to one's heels; **die ~e unter jmds. Tisch strecken** (*fig. ugs.*) live at sb.'s expense; **sich** (*Dat.*) **die ~e in den Bauch stehen** (*fig. ugs.*) cool one's heels; **alles, was ~e hat** (*fig. ugs.*) everyone who possibly can; **wieder auf den ~en sein** be back on one's feet again; **[wieder] auf die ~e kommen** (*ugs.*) get back on one's/its feet [again]; **jmdn./etw. [wieder] auf die ~e bringen** (*ugs.*) put sb./sth. back on his/her/its feet again; **eine Firma/Expedition/ein Programm auf die ~e stellen** (*ugs.*) start a business/mount an expedition/put together a programme; **jmdm. auf die ~e helfen** help sb. to his/her feet; (*fig. ugs.*) help to get *or* put sb. back on his/her feet again; **ich kann mich nicht mehr/kaum noch auf den ~en halten** I can't/can hardly stand up; **auf eigenen ~en stehen** (*fig.*) stand on one's own two feet; support oneself; **auf schwachen ~en stehen** (*fig.*) ‹argument› rest on shaky foundations; ‹firm› be in a precarious position; **das geht in die ~e** (*Alkohol*) it makes you unsteady on your feet; (*Musik*) it makes you want to get up and dance; **mit beiden ~en im Leben** *od.* **[fest] auf der Erde stehen** have both feet [firmly] on the ground; **mit dem linken ~ zuerst aufgestanden sein** (*ugs.*) have got out of bed on the wrong side; **mit einem ~ im Gefängnis/Grab[e] stehen** (*fig.*) stand a good chance of ending up in prison/have one foot in the grave; **von einem ~ aufs andere treten** (*ugs.*) shift from one foot to the other; **auf einem ~ kann man nicht stehen** (*scherzh.*) one drink isn't enough to wet one's whistle; ⇒ *auch* **Klotz** A; **Kopf** E; **vertreten** 2; **B** (*Hosenbein, Teil eines Möbelstückes, Stativ*) leg; **C** (*nordd.: Fuß*) foot; **D** (*südd., österr., schweiz.: Knochen*) bone; **jmdm. in die ~e fahren** go right through sb.; ⇒ *auch* **Mark**[2] A

**bei·nah[e]** /'baina:(ə)/ *Adv.* almost; nearly; **wir wären ~ zu spät gekommen** we were nearly too late; **ich möchte ~ sagen, dass ...** I would almost say that ...

**Beinahe·zusammenstoß** *der* (*Flugw.*) airmiss

**Bei·name** *der* epithet

**bein-, Bein-:** ~**amputation** *die* leg amputation; ~**amputiert** *Adj.* ‹person› with a *or* one leg/both [his/her] legs amputated; **sie ist ~amputiert** she has had a leg/both [her] legs amputated; ~**arbeit** *die* (*beim Boxen, Ringen, Tanzen*) footwork; (*beim Schwimmen*) leg action; ~**bruch** *der* broken leg; **das ist [doch] kein ~bruch!** (*ugs.*) it's not the end of the world (*coll.*)

**beinern** /'bainɐn/ *Adj.* **A** (*knöchern*) bone *attrib.*; made of bone *postpos.*; **B** (*aus Elfenbein*) ivory *attrib.*; made of ivory *postpos.*

**Bein-:** ~**fleisch** *das* (*österr.*) beef cooked and served on the bone; ~**freiheit** *die* legroom

**beinhalten** /bə'|ɪnhaltn̩/ *tr. V.* (*Papierdt.*) involve

**bein·hart** (*österr., südd.*) **1** *Adj.* rock-hard; tough ‹movie›; ‹person› as hard as nails. **2** *adv.* ~ **gefroren** frozen hard; ~ **spielen** (*Sportjargon*) be hard and physical

**Bein·haus** *das* (*hist.*) charnel house

**-beinig** *Adj.* ▶ 471 -legged; **drei~/lang~:** three-legged/long-legged; **ein zwölf~es Insekt** an insect with twelve legs

**Bein-:** ~**kleid** *das* (*veralt.*) trousers *pl.*; ~**leiden** *das* ▶ 474 (*Med.*) leg condition

**Beinling** /'bainlɪŋ/ *der;* ~**s**, ~**e** (*veralt.*) leg

**Bein-:** ~**prothese** *die* artificial leg; ~**schere** *die* (*Ringen*) leg scissors *sing.*; ~**schiene** *die* **A** (*Sport*) [long] shin pad; (*Cricket, Hockey*) pad; **B** (*Teil der Rüstung*) greave *usu. in pl.*; ~**stumpf** *der* stump [of the leg]

**bei|ordnen** *tr. V.* **A jmdm. jmdn. ~:** assign sb. to assist sb.; **B** (*Rechtsw.*) **als Pflichtverteidiger beigeordnet werden** be called in as duty solicitor (*Brit.*) *or* (*Amer.*) court-appointed lawyer; **C** (*Sprachw.*) ⇒ **nebenordnen**

**Bei·ordnung** *die* **A** (*Sprachw.*) coordination; **B** (*Rechtsw.*) assignment

**Bei·pack** *der* extra item [ordered]

**bei|packen** *tr. V.* **einer Warensendung etw. ~:** pack sth. in with a consignment of goods

**Beipack·zettel** *der* instruction leaflet

**bei|pflichten** /'baipflɪçtn̩/ *itr. V.* **jmdm. [in einer Sache] ~:** agree with sb. [on sth.]; **einem Vorschlag** *usw.* **~:** agree with a proposal *etc.*; **Sie werden mir darin ~, dass ...** you will agree with me that ...

**Bei·programm** *das* supporting programme

**Bei·rat** *der* advisory committee *or* board

**beirren** *tr. V.* **sich durch nichts/von niemandem ~ lassen** not be put off *or* deterred by anything/anybody; not let anything/anybody put one off *or* deter one; **nichts konnte ihn in seinen Ansichten ~:** nothing could shake him in his views

**Beirut** /bai̯'ru:t/ (*das*); ~**s** Beirut

**beisammen** /bai̯'tsamən/ *Adv.* together; **[gut] ~ sein** (*ugs.*) be in good health *or* shape

**beisammen-, Beisammen-:** ~**|haben** *unr. tr. V.* **A** (*gesammelt haben*) have got together; **B er hat nicht alle ~** (*ugs.*) he's not all there (*coll.*); he's a bit soft in the head (*coll.*); ~**|halten** *unr. tr. V.* keep together; hold on to ‹money›; *~**|sein** ⇒ **beisammen**; ~**sein** *das* get-together; ~**|sitzen** *unr. itr. V.* sit together

**Bei·satz** *der* (*Sprachw.*) appositive

**Bei·schlaf** *der* (*geh., Rechtsw.*) sexual intercourse

**bei|schließen** *unr. tr. V.* (*österr.*) **einem Brief** *usw.* **etw. ~:** enclose sth. with a letter *etc.*

**Bei·schluss, *Bei·schluß** *der* (*österr.: Anlage*) enclosure

**Bei·segel** *das* (*Segeln*) additional sail

**Bei·sein** *das: in* **im ~ von jmdm., in jmds. ~:** in the presence of sb. *or* in sb.'s presence; **ohne ~ von jmdm., ohne jmds. ~:** in the absence of sb. *or* in sb.'s absence

**bei·seite** *Adv.* **A** (*auf die Seite*) aside; **jmdn. ~ ziehen/schieben** draw/push sb. to one side *or* aside; **etw. ~ bringen** get sth. hidden away; hide sth. away; **etw. ~ lassen** (*fig.*) leave sth. aside; **etw. ~ legen** (*sparen*) put sth. by *or* aside; (*Angefangenes weglegen*) put *or* lay sth. aside; **jmdn./die Leiche ~ schaffen** (*ugs.*) get rid of sb./the body; **die Beute/das Geld ~ schaffen** (*ugs.*) stash (*coll.*) *or* hide the loot/money away; **jmdn./etw. ~ schieben** (*fig.*) push sb./sth. aside; **B** (*auf der Seite*) on *or* to one side; ~ **stehen** (*fig.*) take second place

**Beis[e]l** /'baizl̩/ *das;* ~**s**, ~ *od.* ~**n** (*österr.*) pub (*Brit.*); bar (*Amer.*)

**bei|setzen** *tr. V.* **A** (*geh.: beerdigen*) bury; inter; lay to rest; inter ‹ashes›; **B** (*Seemannsspr.*) set, hoist ‹sail›

**Bei·setzung** *die;* ~, ~**en** (*geh.*) funeral; burial

**Beisetzungs·feierlichkeiten** *Pl.* funeral [ceremony] *sing.*

**Bei·sitz** *der* assessorship; **den ~ haben** act as assessor

**Bei·sitzer** *der;* ~**s**, ~, **Bei·sitzerin** *die;* ~, ~**nen** assessor; (*bei Ausschüssen*) committee member

**Bei·spiel** *das* **A** example (**für** of); **zum ~:** for example *or* instance; **wie zum ~:** as for example; such as; **ohne ~ sein** be without parallel *or* unparalleled; (*unerhört sein*) be outrageous; **B** (*Vorbild*) example; **ein warnendes ~:** a warning; **jmdm. ein ~ geben** set an example to sb.; **sich** (*Dat.*) **an jmdm./etw. ein ~ nehmen** follow sb.'s example/take sth. as one's example; **mit gutem ~ vorangehen** set a good example

**beispiel·gebend** *Adj.* exemplary; ~ **für jmdn. sein** be an example to sb.

**beispielhaft 1** *Adj.* exemplary. **2** *adv.* in an exemplary fashion

**beispiel-, Beispiel-:** ~**halber** *Adv.* ⇒ **beispielshalber**; ~**los 1** *Adj.* unparalleled; (*unerhört*) outrageous; **2** *adv.* incomparably ‹well, badly, etc.›; ~**los erfolgreich/grausam** with unparalleled success/cruelty; ~**satz** *der* (*Sprachw.*) example sentence; illustrative sentence

**beispiels-:** ~**halber** *Adv.* for example *or* instance; **etw. ~halber anführen** offer *or* give sth. by way of example; ~**weise** *Adv.* for example *or* instance

**bei|springen** *unr. itr. V.; mit sein* **jmdm. [in der Not] ~:** leap *or* rush to sb.'s aid *or* assistance [in an emergency]; **jmdm. mit Geld ~:** help sb. out with money

---

*old spelling (see note on page 1707)

**beißen** /'baisn/ ❶ *unr. tr., itr. V.* Ⓐ bite; **in etw.** (*Akk.*) **~:** bite into sth.; **auf etw.** (*Akk.*) **~:** bite on sth.; **an den Nägeln ~:** bite one's nails; **sich** (*Dat.*) **die Lippen wund ~:** bite one's lips till they bleed; **ich habe mich** *od.* **mir auf die Zunge/in die Lippe gebissen** I've bitten my tongue/lip; **der Hund hat mir** *od.* **mich ins Bein gebissen** the dog bit me in the leg; **nach jmdm./etw. ~:** snap at sb./sth.; **der Hund biss [wild] um sich** the dog snapped [wildly] in all directions; Ⓑ (*bissig sein; auch fig.*) bite; Ⓒ (*ätzen*) sting; **in die** *od.* **in den Augen ~:** sting one's eyes; make one's eyes sting; **auf der Zunge ~:** burn the tongue; Ⓓ (*Angelsport: an~*) bite; Ⓔ (*kauen*) **nicht mehr [richtig] ~ können** no longer be able to chew things [properly]; **nichts/nicht viel zu ~ haben** (*fig.*) have nothing/not have much to eat; **sich in den Arsch** (*derb*) *od.* **Hintern** (*salopp*) **~** (*fig.*) kick oneself.
❷ *unr. refl. V.* (*ugs.*) ‹colours, clothes› clash

**beißend** *Adj.* biting ‹cold›; acrid ‹smoke, fumes›; sharp ‹frost›; biting, cutting ‹wind›; pungent, sharp ‹smell, taste›; (*fig.*) biting ‹ridicule›; cutting ‹irony›

**Beißerchen** *das;* **~s, ~** (*fam.*) toothy-peg (*child lang.*)

**Beißerei** *die;* **~, ~en** fight

**Beiß-:** **~ring** *der* teething ring; **~zange** *die* ⇨ **Kneifzange**

**Bei·stand** *der* Ⓐ (*geh.: Hilfe*) aid; assistance; help; **jmdm. ~ leisten** give sb. aid *or* assistance; come to sb.'s aid *or* assistance; Ⓑ (*Rechtsw.: Rechtshelfer*) *lay person acting in support of a defendant*

**Beistands-:** **~abkommen** *das* (*Politik*) treaty of mutual assistance; **~pakt** *der* (*Politik*) mutual assistance pact; **~vertrag** *der* (*Politik*) treaty of mutual assistance

**bei|stehen** *unr. itr. V.* **jmdm. ~:** aid *or* assist *or* help sb.; (*zur Seite stehen*) stand by sb.

**bei|stellen** *itr. V.* (*österr.: bereitstellen*) make available; provide

**Beistell-:** **~möbel** *das* piece of occasional furniture; **teure ~möbel** expensive occasional furniture *sing.*; **~tisch** *der,* **~tischchen** *das* occasional table; (*im Restaurant*) side table

**Bei·steuer** *die* (*südd.*) contribution

**bei|steuern** *tr. V.* contribute; make ‹contribution›

**bei|stimmen** *itr. V.:* ⇨ **zustimmen**

**Bei·strich** *der* (*veralt.*) comma

**Beitel** /'baitl/ *der;* **~s, ~:** chisel

**Beitrag** /'baitra:k/ *der;* **~[e]s, Beiträge** /'baitrɛ:gə/ Ⓐ (*Zahlung, Mitwirkung*) contribution; (*Versicherungs~*) premium; (*Mitglieds~*) subscription; **einen ~ zu etw. leisten** make a contribution to sth.; Ⓑ (*Aufsatz, Kommentar*) article (**zu** on); (*in einer Zeitschrift, einem Sammelband*) article, contribution (**zu** on)

**bei|tragen** *unr. tr., itr. V.* contribute (**zu** to); **das Seine/viel zu etw. ~:** contribute one's share/a great deal to sth.

**beitrags-, Beitrags-:** **~frei** *Adj.* non-contributory; ‹person› not liable to pay contributions; **~gruppe, ~klasse** *die* (*Sozialw.*) contribution class (*Brit.*); insurance group (*Amer.*); **~marke** *die* stamp; **~pflicht** *die* (*Sozialw.*) liability to pay contributions; **~pflichtig** *Adj.* (*Sozialw.*) ‹employee› liable to pay contributions; ‹earnings› on which contributions are payable; **~satz** *der* contribution rate; **~zahlung** *die* contribution

**bei|treiben** *unr. tr. V.* (*Rechtsw.*) enforce payment of

**Beitreibung** *die;* **~, ~en** (*Rechtsw.*) enforcement of payment

**bei|treten** *unr. itr. V.;* *mit sein* Ⓐ (*Mitglied werden bei*) join; **einem Verein** *usw.* **~:** join a club *etc.*; Ⓑ (*sich anschließen an*) **einem Abkommen/Pakt ~:** accede to an agreement/a pact; Ⓒ (*Rechtsw.*) **einem Verfahren/einer Verhandlung ~:** attend proceedings *pl.*/a hearing

**Bei·tritt** *der* Ⓐ (*Eintritt*) joining; **seinen ~ erklären** affirm one's wish to become a member; Ⓑ (*Rechtsw.*) **jmds. ~ anordnen** *od.* **verfügen** order sb. to attend [the proceedings]

**Beitritts·erklärung** *die* declaration (*affirming one's wish to become a member*)

**Bei·wagen** *der* Ⓐ (*Seitenwagen*) sidecar; Ⓑ (*veralt.: Anhänger*) (*einer U-Bahn*) car; (*einer Straßenbahn*) trailer

**Beiwagen-:** **~fahrer** *der,* **~fahrerin** *die* sidecar passenger; **~maschine** *die* motorcycle combination (*Brit.*); sidecar motorcycle (*Amer.*)

**Bei·werk** *das* accessories *pl.*; **in Opern ist die Handlung oft nur ~:** in opera the plot is often of only secondary importance

**bei|willigen** *itr. V.* (*schweiz.*) ⇨ **zustimmen**

**bei|wohnen** *itr. V.* Ⓐ (*geh.: anwesend sein*) **einer Sache** (*Dat.*) **~:** be present at *or* attend sth.; Ⓑ (*veralt. verhüll.*) **jmdm. ~:** lie with sb. (*arch.*)

**Bei·wort** *das;* **~[e]s, Beiwörter** Ⓐ ⇨ **Adjektiv**; Ⓑ (*Epitheton*) epithet

**Beiz** /baits/ *die;* **~, ~en** (*schweiz.*) ⇨ **Beize³**

**Beize¹** /'baitsə/ *die;* **~, ~n** Ⓐ (*Holzbearb.*) [wood] stain; Ⓑ (*Gerberei*) bate; Ⓒ (*Textilbearb.*) mordant; Ⓓ (*Metallbearb.*) pickle; Ⓔ (*Landw.*) disinfectant; seed dressing; Ⓕ (*Tabakind.*) sauce; Ⓖ (*Kochk.*) marinade; Ⓗ (*das Beizen*) ⇨ **~n**: staining; bating; mordanting; pickling; disinfecting; sauce casing; marinading

**Beize²** *die;* **~, ~n** (*Jagdw.*) hawking

**Beize³** *die;* **~, ~n** (*schweiz.*) pub (*Brit.*); bar (*Amer.*)

**beizeiten** /bai'tsaitn/ *Adv.* in good time

**beizen¹** /'baitsn/ *tr. V.* (*mit Beize behandeln*) Ⓐ (*Holzbearb.*) stain; Ⓑ (*Gerberei*) bate; Ⓒ (*Textilbearb.*) mordant; Ⓓ (*Landw.*) disinfect, dress ‹seed›; Ⓔ (*Metallbearb., Tabakind.*) pickle; Ⓕ (*Kochk.*) marinate

**beizen²** *tr., itr. V.* (*Jägerspr.*) hawk

**Beizer** *der;* **~s, ~, Beizerin** *die* stainer

**bei|ziehen** *unr. tr. V.* (*südd., österr., schweiz.*) call in ‹lawyer, psychologist, expert, etc.›; bring in, enlist ‹helpers›; consult, make use of ‹reference book etc.›

**Bei·ziehung** *die* (*südd., österr., schweiz.*) calling in

**Beiz-:** **~jagd** *die* ⇨ **Beize²**; **~vogel** *der* falcon; hawk

**bejahen** /bə'ja:ən/ ❶ *tr. V.* Ⓐ (*mit Ja beantworten*) **etw. ~:** give an affirmative answer to sth.; answer sth. in the affirmative; Ⓑ (*gutheißen, befürworten*) approve of; **das Leben ~:** have a positive *or* an affirmative attitude to life. ❷ *itr. V.* answer in the affirmative; give an affirmative answer; **sie bejahte lebhaft** she replied with an animated 'yes'

**bejahend** ❶ *Adj.* affirmative; affirmative, positive ‹attitude›. ❷ *adv.* ‹answer› in the affirmative; ‹nod› affirmatively

**bejahrt** /bə'ja:ɐt/ *Adj.* (*geh.*) advanced in years

**Bejahrtheit** *die;* **~:** advanced age

**Bejahung** *die;* **~, ~en** Ⓐ affirmative answer *or* reply; **ein Zeichen/eine Geste der ~:** an affirmative sign/gesture; Ⓑ (*das Gutheißen*) approval

**bejammern** *tr. V.* lament; **die Toten ~:** lament for the dead; **dazu neigen, sich selbst zu ~:** tend towards self-pity

**bejammerns·wert** *Adj.* pitiable ‹person›; wretched ‹situation›; lamentable, pitiable ‹condition, state›; pitiful ‹sight›

**bejubeln** *tr. V.* cheer; acclaim; **jmdn. als Helden** *usw.* **~:** acclaim sb. as a hero *etc.*

**bekacken** (*vulg.*) ❶ *tr. V.* shit (*coarse*) in ‹nappy etc.›; **bekackte Windeln** shitty nappies (*Brit.*) *or* (*Amer.*) diapers (*coarse*). ❷ *refl. V.* shit oneself (*coarse*)

**bekakeln** *tr. V.* (*ugs.*) talk over; discuss

**bekämpfen** *tr. V.* Ⓐ fight against; **sich [gegenseitig] ~:** fight [one another *or* each other]; Ⓑ (*einzudämmen versuchen*) combat, fight ‹disease, epidemic, pest›; combat ‹unemployment, crime, alcoholism›; curb ‹curiosity, prejudice›

**Bekämpfung** *die;* **~** Ⓐ fight (+ *Gen.* against); **zur ~ des Feindes aufrufen** call for battle against the enemy; Ⓑ ⇨ **bekämpfen** B: combating; fighting; curbing; **zur ~ einer Krankheit beitragen** contribute to combating *or* fighting a disease; **unsere Aufgabe ist die ~ der Kriminalität/Arbeitslosigkeit** our task is to combat crime/unemployment

**bekannt** /bə'kant/ ❶ *2. Part. v.* **bekennen.** ❷ *Adj.* Ⓐ (*von vielen gewusst*) well-known; **es wurde ~, dass ...** it became known *or* public knowledge that ...; **für etw. ~ sein** be well known for sth.; **es ist nichts davon ~:** nothing is known concerning it; **wegen etw. ~ sein** be well-known on account of sth.; **etw. ~ machen** announce sth.; (*der Öffentlichkeit*) make sth. public; (*veröffentlichen*) publish sth.; **etw. ~ geben** announce sth.; Ⓑ (*berühmt*) well-known; famous; **~er sein** be better known; **international ~ sein** be internationally known *or* famous; Ⓒ (*vertraut, bewusst*) **die Aufgaben sind ihm ~:** he knows what his duties are; **sie ist mir ~:** I know her; **davon ist mir nichts ~:** I know nothing about that; **mit jmdm. ~ sein/werden** know *or* be acquainted with sb./get to know *or* become acquainted with sb.; **mit etw. ~ sein/werden** be/become familiar *or* acquainted with sth.; **jmdn./sich mit jmdm. ~ machen** introduce sb./oneself to sb.; **Darf ich ~ machen? Meine Eltern** may I introduce my parents?; **jmdn./sich mit etw. ~ machen** acquaint sb./oneself with sth.; **jmdm. ~ vorkommen** seem familiar to sb.; **der Witz kommt mir ~ vor** I think I've heard that joke somewhere before

**Bekannte** *der/die adj. Dekl.* Ⓐ acquaintance; Ⓑ (*verhüll.: Freund/Freundin*) boyfriend/girl[friend]

**Bekannten·kreis** *der* circle of acquaintances; **jmds. engerer** *od.* **näherer ~:** sb.'s circle of close acquaintances

**bekannter·maßen** *Adv.* (*Papierdt.*) ⇨ **bekanntlich**

**Bekannt·gabe** *die;* **~:** announcement

***bekannt|geben** ⇨ **bekannt** 2 A

**Bekanntheit** *die;* **~** Ⓐ (*Kenntnis*) acquaintance, familiarity (*Gen.* with); Ⓑ (*Berühmtheit*) fame

**Bekanntheits·grad** *der;* **~es einen großen ~ haben** be very well known

**bekanntlich** *Adv.* as is well known; **etw. ist ~ der Fall** it is known that sth. is the case; sth. is known to be the case; **der Walfisch ist ~ ein Säugetier** it is well known that the whale is a mammal; **~ sind Steuererhöhungen sehr unbeliebt** we all know that tax increases are highly unpopular

***bekannt|machen** ⇨ **bekannt** 2 A

**Bekannt·machung** *die;* **~, ~en** Ⓐ (*das ~machen*) announcement; (*das Veröffentlichen*) publication; Ⓑ (*Mitteilung*) announcement; notice

**Bekanntschaft** *die;* **~, ~en** Ⓐ (*Bekanntsein*) acquaintance; **bei näherer ~:** on closer acquaintance; **jmds. ~ machen** make sb.'s acquaintance; **du wirst bald mit der Polizei ~ machen** (*ugs.*) you're going to get into trouble with the police soon; **dein Hosenboden wird gleich mit meiner Hand ~ machen** (*ugs.*) you'll feel my hand across your backside any minute; Ⓑ (*Mensch, den man kennt*) acquaintance; (*Bekanntenkreis*) circle of acquaintances

***bekannt|werden** ⇨ **bekannt** 2 A

**bekaufen** *refl. V.* make a bad buy

**bekehren** ❶ *tr. V.* convert (**zu** to); **jmdn. zum Anhänger des Buddhismus/Nacktbadens/Monetarismus ~:** convert sb. to Buddhism/nude bathing/monetarism; **vom Alkohol bekehrt sein** have turned one's back on alcohol. ❷ *refl. V.* become converted (**zu** to)

**Bekehrer** *der;* **~s, ~, Bekehrerin** *die;* **~, ~nen** converter; (*Missionar*) missionary

**Bekehrte** *der/die; adj. Dekl.* convert

**Bekehrung** *die;* **~, ~en** (*auch fig.*) conversion (**zu** to)

**bekennen** ❶ *unr. tr. V.* Ⓐ (*eingestehen*) admit ‹mistake, defeat›; confess ‹sin›; admit, confess ‹guilt, truth›; Ⓑ (*Rel.*) profess; **die Bekennende Kirche** (*hist.*) the Confessional Church. ❷ *refl. V.* **sich zu Buddha/Mohammed ~:** profess *or* declare one's faith in Buddha/Muhammad; **nur wenige seiner früheren Freunde bekannten sich zu ihm** only a few of his former friends stood by him; **sich zu seiner Vergangenheit ~:** acknowledge one's past; **sich zu seiner Schuld ~:** admit *or* confess one's guilt; **sich zum Sozialismus ~:** declare one's belief in socialism; **sich schuldig/nicht schuldig ~:** admit *or* confess/not admit *or* not confess one's guilt; (*vor Gericht*) plead guilty/not guilty; **sich zu einem Bombenanschlag ~:** claim responsibility for a bomb attack; **sich als jmd[n]. ~:** admit *or* confess that one is sb.; admit *or* confess to being sb.

**Bekenner** *der;* **~s, ~, Bekennerin** *die;* **~, ~nen** confessor

**Bekenner-: ~brief,** *der* letter (*Gen.* from) claiming responsibility; **~geist** *der,* **~mut** *der;* courage of one's convictions

**Bekenntnis** *das;* **~ses, ~se** Ⓐ (*Eingeständnis*) confession; **ein ~ ablegen** make a confession; Ⓑ (*Eintreten*) **ein ~ für die Sache des Friedens/zum Frieden** a declaration of belief in the cause of peace/a declaration for peace; **ein ~ zum Christentum/zur Demokratie ablegen** profess one's faith in Christianity/declare one's belief in democracy; Ⓒ (*Konfession*) denomination; Ⓓ (*formulierter Inhalt*) confession; **das Augsburger ~:** the Confession of Augsburg

**bekenntnis-, Bekenntnis-: ~freiheit** *die* religious freedom; freedom of worship; **~kirche** *die* Confessional Church; **~los** *Adj.* not belonging to any denomination *postpos., not pred.;* **~los sein** not belong to any denomination; **~schule** *die* denominational school

**bekieken** *tr. V.* (*nordd. ugs.*) look at; have a look at

**bekiffen** *refl. V.* get stoned (*sl.*)

**bekifft** /bəˈkɪft/ *Adj.* (*ugs.*) stoned (*sl.*)

**beklagen** ❶ *tr. V.* (*geh.*) Ⓐ (*betrauern*) mourn; **Menschenleben waren nicht zu ~:** there were no fatalities; there was no loss of life; Ⓑ (*bedauern*) lament; **sein/jmds. Los ~:** lament *or* bewail one's fate/deplore sb.'s fate; **wir haben einen großen Umsatzrückgang zu ~:** we have to note with regret a large drop in sales. ❷ *refl. V.* complain; **sich über jmdn./etw. ~:** complain about sb./sth.; **ich kann mich nicht ~:** I can't complain; **du kannst dich nicht ~:** you've got nothing to complain about *or* no reason to complain

**beklagens-: ~wert, ~würdig** (*geh.*) ❶ *Adj.* pitiful ‹sight, impression›; pitiable ‹person›; lamentable, pitiable, deplorable ‹condition, state›; wretched ‹situation›; ❷ *adv.* lamentably; deplorably

**beklagt** /bəˈklaːkt/ *Adj.* **die ~e Partei** the defendant; (*bei Ehescheidungen*) the respondent; **die ~en Personen** the defendants

**Beklagte** *der/die; adj. Dekl.* defendant; (*bei Ehescheidungen*) respondent

**beklatschen** *tr. V.* Ⓐ clap; applaud; Ⓑ (*ugs.: klatschen über*) gossip about

**beklauen** *tr. V.* (*salopp*) rob; do (*coll.*)

**bekleben** *tr. V.* **eine Wand** *usw.* **mit etw. ~:** stick sth. all over a wall *etc.;* **mit etw. beklebt sein** have sth. stuck all over it

**bekleckern** (*ugs.*) ❶ *tr. V.* **seinen Schlips** *usw.* **mit Soße** *usw.* **~:** drop *or* spill sauce *etc.* down one's tie *etc.;* **mit Senf bekleckerte Teller** plates smeared with mustard. ❷ *refl. V.* **ich habe mich bekleckert** I've dropped *or* spilled sth. down myself; **sich mit Soße** *usw.* **~:** drop *or* spill sauce *etc.* down oneself; ⇒ *auch* **Ruhm**

**beklecksen** *tr. V.* spatter; **etw. mit Tinte** *usw.* **~:** spatter ink *etc.* on sth.

**bekleiden** *tr. V.* Ⓐ clothe; **mit etw. bekleidet sein** be dressed in *or* be wearing sth.; Ⓑ (*geh.: innehaben*) occupy, hold ‹office, position›; Ⓒ (*geh. veralt.: versehen*) **jmdn. mit etw. ~:** bestow sth. on sb.

**Bekleidung** *die* clothing; clothes *pl.;* garments *pl.;* (*Aufmachung*) dress; attire

**Bekleidungs-: ~gewerbe** *das,* **~handwerk** *das* clothing trade; **~industrie** *die* clothing industry; **~stück** *das* ⇒ **Kleidungsstück**; **~vorschriften** *Pl.* dress regulations; regulations governing dress

**bekleistern** *tr. V.* (*ugs.*) Ⓐ (*mit Kleister bestreichen*) apply paste to; Ⓑ (*bekleben*) **etw. mit Aufklebern** *usw.* **~:** plaster stickers *etc.* all over sth.

**beklemmen** *tr. V.* oppress; **jmdm. das Herz** *od.* **jmds. Herz ~** (*geh.*) weigh upon sb.'s heart

**beklemmend** ❶ *Adj.* oppressive. ❷ *adv.* oppressively

**Beklemmung** *die;* **~, ~en** oppressive feeling; (*Angst*) [feeling of] unease; (*stärker*) [feeling of] apprehension; **ich bekomme** *od.* **kriege ~en** I feel as if I'm being stifled

**beklommen** /bəˈklɔmən/ ❶ *Adj.* uneasy; shaky ‹voice›; (*stärker*) apprehensive. ❷ *adv.* uneasily; (*stärker*) apprehensively

**Beklommenheit** *die;* **~:** uneasiness; (*stärker*) apprehensiveness

**beklönen** *tr. V.* (*nordd. ugs.*) talk over

**beklopfen** *tr. V.* tap

**bekloppt** /bəˈklɔpt/ *Adj.* (*salopp*) barmy (*Brit. coll.*); loony (*coll.*); **dieser ~e Fahrer** this nutcase of a driver (*Brit. coll.*); this nutty driver (*coll.*); **ein Bekloppter** a nutcase (*Brit. coll.*); a nut (*coll.*)

**beknackt** *Adj.* (*salopp*) lousy (*coll.*); **ein ~er Typ** a berk (*Brit. coll.*); a jerk (*coll.*); **so was Beknacktes** what a load of rubbish! (*coll.*)

**beknien** *tr. V.* (*ugs.*) beg

**bekochen** *tr. V.* (*ugs.*) cook for

**beködern** *tr. V.* (*Angeln*) bait ‹hook›

**bekommen** ❶ *unr. tr. V.* Ⓐ (*erhalten*) get; get, receive ‹money, letter, reply, news, orders›; **ich habe seit Monaten keinen Brief mehr von ihm ~:** I haven't had a letter from him for months; **Anschluss/eine Verbindung [zu einem Ort] ~:** get through [to a place]; **fünf Tage Urlaub ~:** get five days' holiday (*Brit.*) *or* (*Amer.*) vacation; **drei Monate Gefängnis ~:** get *or* receive three months in prison; **eine Flasche** *usw.* **an den Kopf ~:** get hit on the head with a bottle *etc.;* **was ~ Sie?** (*im Geschäft*) can I help you?; (*im Lokal, Restaurant*) what would you like?; (*wie viel Geld?*) how much is that?; (*bei mehreren Sachen*) how much does that come to?; **wir ~ Regen/besseres Wetter** we're going to get some rain/some better weather; there's rain/better weather on the way; **sie bekommt ein Kind** she's expecting a baby; **wann bekommt sie ihr Kind?** when is the baby due?; Ⓑ (*finden, erlangen*) get; obtain; catch ‹train, bus, flight›; **eine Vorstellung/einen Eindruck von etw. ~:** get some *or* an idea/impression of sth.; **seinen Willen ~:** get one's way; Ⓒ (*ein bestimmtes Ziel erreichen*) get; **etw. durch die Tür/in den Kofferraum ~:** get sth. through the door/into the boot (*Brit.*) *or* (*Amer.*) trunk; **etw. zu Papier ~:** get sth. down on paper; **jmdn. nicht aus dem Bett ~:** be unable to get sb. out of bed *or* up; **jmdn. zum Reden ~:** get sb. to talk; **jmdn. dazu ~, die Wahrheit zu sagen** get sb. to tell the truth; **etw. sauber/wohnlich ~:** get sth. clean/make sth. homely *or* comfortable; Ⓓ (*entwickeln, erleiden*) get ‹goose pimples, measles, spots, diarrhoea, practice, experience, etc.›; **Hunger/Durst ~:** get hungry/thirsty; **einen roten Kopf/eine Glatze ~:** go red/bald; **Mut/Angst ~:** take heart/become frightened; **Gestalt/Form ~:** take shape; **er bekommt einen Bart** he's growing a beard; **sie bekommt eine Brust** her breasts are developing; **Zähne ~** ‹baby› teethe; **er bekommt seine Weisheitszähne** his wisdom teeth are coming through; Ⓔ (+ *Inf.*) **etw. zu essen/trinken ~:** have sth. to eat/drink; **wo bekomme ich etwas zu essen/trinken?** where can I get something to eat/drink?; **etw./jmdn. zu fassen ~:** get hold of sth./lay one's hands on sb.; ⇒ *auch* **hören, spüren**; Ⓕ + *2. Part.* get; **etw. geschenkt ~:** get [given] sth. *or* be given sth. as a present; **etw. direkt vom Verlag geschickt ~:** get sth. direct from the publisher; **seine Arbeit von anderen gemacht ~:** get one's work done by other people; Ⓖ **in es nicht über sich** (*Akk.*) **~, etw. zu tun** be unable to bring oneself to do sth.
❷ *unr. itr. V.;* mit *sein* **jmdm. gut ~:** do sb. good; be good for sb.; **jmdm. [gut] ~** ‹food, medicine› agree with sb.; **jmdm. schlecht** *od.* **nicht ~:** not be good for sb.; not do sb. any good; ‹food, medicine› not agree with sb.; **wohl bekomms!** your [very good] health!

**bekömmlich** /bəˈkœmlɪç/ *Adj.* easily digestible; **leicht/schwer ~ sein** be easily digestible/difficult to digest

**Bekömmlichkeit** *die;* **~:** easy digestibility

**beköstigen** /bəˈkœstɪɡn̩/ *tr. V.* cater for; **er wird von seiner Tante beköstigt** he gets his meals provided by his aunt

**Beköstigung** *die;* **~** Ⓐ catering *no indef. art.;* Ⓑ (*Kost*) food *no indef. art.*

**bekotzen** *tr. V.* (*derb*) puke over (*coarse*)

**bekräftigen** *tr. V.* reinforce ‹statement›; reaffirm ‹promise›; confirm, strengthen ‹suspicion, conviction›; **eine Vereinbarung durch Handschlag ~:** seal an agreement with a handshake

**Bekräftigung** *die* confirmation

**bekränzen** /bəˈkrɛntsn̩/ *tr. V.* **jmdn./etw. ~:** crown sb. with a wreath/garland sth.

**bekreuzen** ❶ *tr. V.* (*kath. Kirche*) make the sign of the cross over. ❷ *refl. V.* ⇒ **bekreuzigen**

**bekreuzigen** *refl. V.* (*kath. Kirche*) cross oneself

**bekriegen** *tr. V.* wage war on; (*fig.*) fight; **bekriegt werden** be attacked; **sich ~:** be at war; (*fig.*) fight [each other *or* one another]

**bekritteln** *tr. V.* (*abwertend*) find fault with (*in a petty way*)

**bekritzeln** *tr. V.* scribble on; **die Wände waren von oben bis unten bekritzelt** the walls were covered with graffiti; **die Buchränder mit Anmerkungen ~:** scribble comments in the margins of the book

**bekrönen** *tr. V.* (*auch fig., Archit.*) crown

**bekucken** (*nordd.*) ⇒ **begucken**

**bekümmern** *tr. V.* **jmdn. ~:** cause sb. worry; **das braucht dich nicht zu ~:** you needn't worry about that

**Bekümmernis** *die* (*geh.*) worry; trouble; (*stärker*) distress

**bekümmert** /bəˈkʏmɐt/ ❶ *Adj.* worried; troubled; (*stärker*) distressed. ❷ *adv.* **~ schweigen** maintain a worried silence

**bekunden** /bəˈkʊndn̩/ ❶ *tr. V.* Ⓐ (*geh.: zeigen*) express; Ⓑ (*Rechtsw.: bezeugen*) make ‹statement›; **er bekundete, dass ...** he testified that ... ❷ *refl. V.* (*geh.: sich zeigen*) manifest itself

**Bekunden** *das: in* **nach seinem/ihrem** *usw.* **eigenen ~:** according to his/her *etc.* own statement[s]

**Bekundung** *die;* **~, ~en** expression; (*Aussage*) statement

**belabern** *tr. V.* (*salopp abwertend*) keep on [and on] at

**belächeln** *tr. V.* smile [pityingly/tolerantly *etc.*] at; **belächelt werden** meet with a pitying smile

**belachen¹** *tr. V.* laugh at

**beladen¹** *unr. tr. V.* Ⓐ (*mit einer Ladung versehen*) load ‹ship›; load [up] ‹car, wagon›; **Be- und Entladen gestattet/verboten** loading and unloading permitted/no loading or unloading; Ⓑ (*zu tragen geben*) load up ‹horse, donkey›; Ⓒ (*reich bedecken*) load ‹table›

**beladen²** *Adj.* loaded, laden (**mit** with); **hoch ~:** heavily laden; **mit etw. ~ sein** be laden with sth.; **sie war schwer mit Paketen ~:** she was loaded *or* laden down with parcels; **mit Sorgen/Schuld ~ sein** (*fig.*) ‹person› be burdened with cares/guilt; **mit einem Fluch ~ sein** be under a curse

**Belag** /bəˈlaːk/ *der;* **~[e]s, Beläge** /bəˈlɛːgə/ **A** (*Schicht*) coating; film; (*Zungen~*) fur *no indef. art.;* coating; (*Zahn~*) film; **Sie haben einen ~ auf der Zunge** your tongue is coated; **B** (*Fußboden~*) covering; (*Straßen~*) surface; (*Brems~*) lining; **C** (*von Kuchen, Pizza, halben Brötchen*) topping; (*von Sandwiches*) filling

**Belagerer** /bəˈlaːgərɐ/ *der;* **~s, ~:** besieger

**belagern** *tr. V.* **A** (*Milit.*) besiege; lay siege to; **B** (*fig.: bedrängen*) besiege

**Belagerung** *die;* **~, ~en A** (*Milit.*) siege; **B** (*fig.: Bedrängung*) besieging

**Belagerungs-: ~maschine** *die* siege machine; **~zu·stand** *der* state of siege; (*Ausnahmezustand*) state of emergency; **den ~zustand ausrufen** declare a state of siege/emergency; **über die Stadt wurde der ~zustand verhängt** the town was declared under siege/a state of emergency was declared in the town

**belämmern** /bəˈlɛmɐn/ *tr. V.* (*nordd. ugs.*) bother; (*sehr aufdringlich*) pester

**belämmert** *Adj.* (*ugs.*) **A** (*niedergedrückt*) miserable; **er stand [wie] ~ da** he stood there miserably; **B** (*scheußlich*) awful (*coll.*); terrible (*coll.*); dreadful (*coll.*)

**Belang** /bəˈlaŋ/ *der;* **~[e]s, ~e A** (*Bedeutung*) **[für etw.] von/ohne ~ sein** be of importance/of no importance [for sth.]; **für jmdn. von/ohne ~ sein** be important/not be important to sb.; **B** *Pl.* (*Interessen*) interests; **jmds. ~e wahrnehmen/vertreten** look after/represent sb.'s interests

**belangen** *tr. V.* **A** (*Rechtsw.*) sue; (*strafrechtlich*) prosecute; **jmdn. wegen etw. ~:** sue/prosecute sb. for sth.; **B** (*veralt. unpers.: betreffen*) **was mich/ihn** *usw.* **belangt, so …** as far as I am/he *etc.* is concerned, …

**belang-, Belang-: ~los** *Adj.* (*trivial*) trivial; (*unerheblich*) of no importance (**für** for); **~losigkeit** *die;* **~~, ~~en A** (*Trivialität*) triviality; (*Unerheblichkeit*) unimportance; **B** (*triviale Äußerung*) triviality; **~voll** *Adj.* (*geh.*) important (**für** for)

**belassen** *unr. tr. V.* **A** (*unverändert lassen*) leave; **jmdn. in seinem Amt ~:** keep sb. in his/her post; **~ wir es dabei** let's leave it at that; **B** (*überlassen*) **jmdm. etw. ~:** let sb. keep sth.

**belastbar** *Adj.* **A** (*mit Last, Gewicht*) tough, resilient ‹material›; ‹material› able to withstand stress *pred.;* **[nur] mit 3,5 t ~ sein** be able to take a load of [only] 3.5 t; **B** (*beanspruchbar*) tough, resilient ‹person›; **seelisch/körperlich ~ sein** be emotionally/physically tough *or* resilient; be able to stand emotional/physical stress; **ein ~er Mitarbeiter** an employee who can work under pressure; **die Umwelt ist nicht weiter ~:** the pressures on the environment have become intolerable

**Belastbarkeit** *die;* **~, ~n A** (*von Material*) ability to withstand stress; (*von Konstruktionen*) load-bearing capacity; **B** (*von Menschen*) toughness; resilience; (*von Mitarbeitern*) ability to work under pressure

**belasten** *tr. V.* **A** (*beschweren*) load ‹vehicle etc.›; put weight on ‹ski›; **der Fahrstuhl darf nur mit vier Personen belastet werden** the lift (*Brit.*) *or* (*Amer.*) elevator must not carry more than four persons; **B** (*beeinträchtigen*) pollute ‹atmosphere›; put pressure on ‹environment›; **C** (*in Anspruch nehmen*) burden (**mit** with); **D** (*zu schaffen machen*) **jmdn. ~** ‹responsibility, guilt› weigh upon sb.; ‹thought› weigh upon sb.'s mind; **Fett belastet den Magen** fat puts a strain on the stomach; **es belastet ihn seelisch schwer, dass ihn seine Frau verlassen hat** the fact that his wife has left him is causing him great emotional strain and distress; **E** (*Rechtsw.: schuldig erscheinen lassen*) incriminate; **~des Material** incriminating evidence; **F** (*Geldw.*) **jmds. Konto mit 100 DM ~:** debit sb.'s account with 100 DM; **jmdn. mit zusätzlichen Steuern ~:** increase the tax burden on sb.; **den Staatshaushalt ~:** place a burden on the national budget; **das Haus ist mit einer Hypothek belastet** the house is encumbered with a mortgage

**belästigen** /bəˈlɛstɪgn̩/ *tr. V.* bother; (*sehr aufdringlich*) pester; (*sexuell*) molest; **sich von etw. belästigt fühlen** regard sth. as a nuisance

**Belästigung** *die;* **~, ~en am schlimmsten empfanden wir die ~ durch die Reporter/Insekten** we found the worst thing was being pestered by reporters/bothered by insects; **etw. als ~ empfinden** regard sth. as a nuisance

**Belastung** /bəˈlastʊŋ/ *die;* **~, ~en A die ~ der Atmosphäre/Umwelt durch Schadstoffe** the pollution of the atmosphere by harmful substances/the pressure on the environment caused by harmful substances; **B** (*Inanspruchnahme*) strain; **für jmdn. eine ~ sein** put a strain on sb.; **C** (*Bürde, Sorge*) burden; **das stellte eine schwere seelische ~ für sie dar** it was causing her great strain and distress; **D** (*Rechtsw.: Beschuldigung*) incrimination; **E** (*Geldw.*) charge; (*steuerlich*) burden; **außergewöhnliche ~en** extraordinary expenses (*partly deductible as a charge on one's income*); **eine weitere ~ meines Kontos kann ich mir nicht erlauben** I can't afford to draw any more money from my account; **F** (*Beschwerung*) loading; **die maximale ~ der Brückenpfeiler** the safe maximum load for the bridge piers

**belastungs-, Belastungs-: ~-EKG** *das* (*Med.*) electrocardiogram after effort; **~fähig** *Adj.* ⇒ **belastbar**; **~grenze** *die* limit; (*der Atmosphäre, des Wasserhaushalts*) maximum tolerable level of pollution; **~material** *das* (*Rechtsw.*) incriminating evidence; **~probe** *die* (*bei Menschen*) endurance test; (*bei Materialien*) stress test; (*bei Konstruktionen*) load test; **~spitze** *die* (*Elektrot.*) peak load; **~zeuge** *der* (*Rechtsw.*) witness for the prosecution

**belatschern** /bəˈlaːtʃɐn/ *tr. V.* (*berlin. salopp*) **A jmdn. ~, dass er etw. macht** talk sb. into doing sth.; **er hat mich belatschert** he talked me into it; **B** (*ansprechen*) accost

**belauben** *refl. V.* come into leaf; **belaubte Pappeln** poplars in leaf

**Belaubung** *die;* **~ A** coming into leaf; **B** (*Laubwerk*) foliage; leaves *pl.*

**belauern** *tr. V.* **jmdn. ~** (*versteckt beobachten*) watch sb. from hiding; (*mit lauerndem Blick beobachten*) keep *or* watch sb. carefully; keep a watchful eye on sb.

**belaufen** *unr. refl. V.* **sich auf … (*Akk.*) ~:** amount *or* come to …; ‹rent, price› come to …, be …

**belauschen** *tr. V.* **A** eavesdrop on; **B** (*geh.: beobachten*) observe

**Belcanto** /belˈkanto/ *der;* **~s** (*Musik*) bel canto

**beleben ❶** *tr. V.* **A** (*in Schwung bringen*) enliven; liven up (*coll.*); (*wieder ~*) put new life into; stimulate ‹demand›; **B** (*lebendig gestalten*) enliven; brighten up; **C** (*lebendig machen*) give life to; **D** (*bevölkern*) inhabit; populate. **❷** *refl. V.* **A** (*lebhafter werden*) ‹eyes› light up; ‹face› brighten [up]; ‹market, economic activity› revive, pick up; **B** (*lebendig, bevölkert werden*) come to life; **sich neu belebt fühlen** feel revived

**belebend ❶** *Adj.* stimulating; invigorating. **❷** *adv.* **~ wirken** have a stimulating *or* invigorating effect

**belebt** *Adj.* **A** (*lebhaft, bevölkert*) busy ‹street, crossing, town, etc.›; **B** (*lebendig, auch fig.*) living; **die ~e Natur** the living world of nature

**Belebtheit** *die;* **~:** bustle; bustling activity

**Belebung** *die;* **~, ~en** revival; **eine ~ der Wirtschaft** a revival in the economy; **eine ~ des Absatzes** a stimulation of demand; **ein Getränk** *usw.* **zur ~:** a drink *etc.* to revive oneself

**belecken** *tr. V.* lick; **von Kultur/Geschichte nicht/wenig beleckt sein** (*fig. ugs.*) have no/not much trace of culture/knowledge of history

**Beleg** /bəˈleːk/ *der;* **~[e]s, ~e A** (*Beweisstück*) piece of [supporting] documentary evidence; (*Quittung*) receipt; **~e** [supporting] documentary proof *sing. or* evidence *sing. no indef. art.*/receipts; **B** (*Beispiel*) instance, example (**für** of); (*Quellennachweis*) reference; **als ~ für etw.** as evidence for sth.; **ein ~ für ein Wort** an example of the use of a word; **C** (*Archäol.: Fundstück*) find

**Beleg·arzt** *der* doctor on duty (*who shares responsibility for hospital inpatients*)

**belegbar** *Adj.* verifiable

**belegen ❶** *tr. V.* **A** (*Milit.: beschießen*) bombard; (*mit Bomben*) attack; **B** (*mit Belag versehen*) cover ‹floor› (**mit** with); fill ‹flan base, sandwich›; top ‹open sandwich›; **eine Scheibe Brot mit Schinken/Käse ~:** put some ham/cheese on a slice of bread; **C** (*reservieren*) reserve, book ‹seat, table, room›; (*nutzen*) occupy ‹seat, room, etc.›; (*Hochschulw.*) enrol for, register for ‹seminar, lecture course›; **D** (*Sport*) **den ersten/letzten Platz ~:** come first *or* take first place/come last; **E** (*nachweisen*) prove; give a reference for ‹quotation›; (*fig.*) substantiate ‹demand›; **etw. mit** *od.* **durch Quittungen ~:** support sth. with receipts; **F** (*versehen*) **jmdn./etw. mit etw. ~:** impose sth. on sb./sth.; **jmdn. mit einem Spitznamen ~:** give sb. a nickname; **G eine Schule mit Flüchtlingen ~:** accommodate refugees in a school. **❷** *itr. V.* (*Hochschulw.*) enrol *or* register [for seminars/lectures] for the coming semester

**Beleg-: ~exemplar** *das* voucher copy; (*für Autoren*) author's copy; **~frist** *die* (*Hochschulw.*) enrolment period; **~leser** *der* (*DV*) document reader; **~material** *das* documentary evidence

**Belegschaft** *die;* **~, ~en** staff; employees *pl.*

**Belegschafts-: ~aktie** *die* employees' share; **~mitglied** *das* employee; **~versammlung** *die* meeting of the staff

**Beleg-: ~stelle** *die* reference; **~stück** *das* ⇒ **~exemplar**

**belegt ❶** *2. Part. v.* **belegen. ❷** *Adj.* **A ein ~es Brot** (*offen*) an open *or* (*Amer.*) open-face sandwich; (*zugeklappt*) a sandwich; **ein ~es Brötchen** (*offen*) a roll with topping; an open-face roll (*Amer.*); (*zugeklappt*) a filled roll; a sandwich roll (*Amer.*); **B** (*mit Belag bedeckt*) coated, furred ‹tongue, tonsils›; **C** (*heiser*) husky ‹voice›; **eine ~e Stimme haben** be hoarse; **D** (*nicht mehr frei*) ‹room, flat› occupied; ‹hotel, hospital› full

**Belegung** *die;* **~, ~en** (*Reservierung*) reservation; booking; (*Nutzung*) occupying

**belehnen** *tr. V.* **A** (*hist.*) **jmdn. mit Land/einem Amt ~:** enfeoff sb. with land/in an office; **B** (*schweiz.*) ⇒ **beleihen**

**belehrbar** *Adj.* teachable

**belehren** *tr. V.* **A** (*lehren*) teach; instruct; (*aufklären*) enlighten; (*informieren*) inform; advise; **jmdn. über etw.** (*Akk.*) **~:** inform sb. about sth.; **jmdn. über seine Rechte ~/die Bedeutung des Eides ~** (*Rechtsw.*) inform *or* advise sb. of his/her rights/caution *or* warn sb. about the meaning of the oath; **B** (*von einer irrigen Meinung abbringen*) **sich ~ lassen** [be willing to] listen *or* take advice *or* be told; **ich bin belehrt** I've learnt something; **sich eines anderen ~ lassen müssen** learn otherwise; ⇒ *auch* **besser**

**belehrend** *Adj.* didactic

**Belehrung** *die;* **~, ~en A** (*das Belehrtwerden*) instruction; **B** (*Zurechtweisung*) lecture; **C** (*Rechtsw.*) caution; warning

**beleibt** /bəˈlaipt/ *Adj.* (*geh.*) stout; portly; corpulent

**Beleibtheit** *die;* **~** (*geh.*) stoutness; portliness; corpulence

**beleidigen** /bəˈlaidɪgn̩/ *tr. V.* insult; offend; **jmds. Ehre ~:** offend sb.'s honour; **~d** offensive; **~de Äußerungen** (*Rechtsw.*) (*schriftlich*) libellous statements; (*mündlich*) slanderous statements; **das beleidigt mein Ohr/mein Auge** (*fig.*) it offends my ear/eye

**beleidigt** *Adj.* insulted; offended; (*gekränkt*) offended; **ein ~es Gesicht machen** put on

b

a hurt expression; **er ist schnell ~:** he easily takes offence; **jmdn. ~ ansehen** give sb. an offended look

**Beleidigung** *die;* ~, **~en** insult; (*Rechtsw.*) (*schriftlich*) libel; (*mündlich*) slander; **etw. als ~ empfinden** regard sth. as an insult; **eine ~ für das Auge/Ohr** (*fig.*) an offence to the eye/ear

**Beleidigungs-: ~klage** *die* (*Rechtsw.*) (*wegen schriftlicher Beleidigung*) action for libel; libel action; (*wegen mündlicher Beleidigung*) action for slander; slander action; **eine ~klage gegen jmdn. erheben** sue sb. for libel/slander; bring an action for libel/slander against sb.; **~prozess**, ***~prozeß** *der* (*Rechtsw.*) (*wegen schriftlicher Beleidigung*) libel suit; (*wegen mündlicher Beleidigung*) slander suit

**beleihen** *unr. tr. V.* Ⓐ (*als Pfand nehmen*) grant a loan on the security of; grant a mortgage on ‹home, property›; raise money on ‹insurance, policy›; **etw. ~ lassen** raise a loan/mortgage on sth.; **ihr Schmuck wurde mit 15 000 DM beliehen** she raised a loan of 15,000 DM on her jewellery; Ⓑ (*hist.*) ⇒ **belehnen** A

**Beleihung** *die;* ~, **~en die ~ von etw.** raising a loan on sth.

***belemmern** ⇒ **belämmern**

***belemmert** ⇒ **belämmert**

**belesen** *Adj.* well-read

**Belesenheit** *die;* ~ **[große] ~:** [very] wide reading

**Beletage** /bɛle'ta:ʒə/ *die;* ~, **~n** (*veralt.*) first floor (*Brit.*); second floor (*Amer.*)

**beleuchten** *tr. V.* Ⓐ illuminate; light up; light ‹stairs, room, street, etc.›; **festlich beleuchtet** festively lit; Ⓑ (*fig.: untersuchen*) examine ‹topic, problem›

**Beleuchter** *der;* **~s**, ~ (*Theater, Film*) lighting technician

**Beleuchter·brücke** *die* (*Theater, Film*) lighting bridge

**Beleuchterin** *die;* ~, **~nen** (*Theater, Film*) lighting technician

**Beleuchtung** *die;* ~, **~en** Ⓐ (*Licht*) light; **die ~ in der Stadt fiel aus** all the lights *pl.* of the town went out; Ⓑ (*das Beleuchten*) lighting; (*Anstrahlung*) illumination; Ⓒ (*fig.: Untersuchung*) examination

**Beleuchtungs-: ~an·lage** *die* lighting installation; **~effekt** *der* lighting effect; **~technik** *die* lighting engineering

**beleumdet** /bə'lɔymdət/, **beleumundet** /bə'lɔymʊndət/ *Adj.* **übel/gut ~ sein** have a bad/good reputation

**belfern** /'bɛlfɐn/ ❶ *itr. V.* (*ugs.*) bark; (*fig.*) ‹cannon› boom; ‹rifle› crack. ❷ *tr. V.* bark; bark [out] ‹order›

**Belgien** /'bɛlgi̯ən/ (*das*); **~s** Belgium

**Belgier** /'bɛlgi̯ɐ/ *der;* **~s**, ~, **Belgierin** *die;* ~, **~nen** ▶ 553 Belgian; ⇒ *auch* **-in**

**belgisch** *Adj.* ▶ 553 Belgian; ⇒ *auch* **deutsch; Deutsche**[2]

**Belgrad** /'bɛlgra:t/ (*das*); **~s** ▶ 700 Belgrade

**belichten** ❶ *tr. V.* Ⓐ (*Fot.*) expose; **eine Aufnahme richtig/falsch ~:** give a shot the right/wrong exposure; Ⓑ (*fachspr.: beleuchten*) light. ❷ *itr. V.* (*Fot.*) **richtig/falsch/kurz ~:** use the right/wrong exposure/a short exposure time

**Belichtung** *die* Ⓐ (*Fot.*) exposure; Ⓑ (*fachspr.: Licht*) light

**Belichtungs-: ~automatik** *die* (*Fot.*) automatic exposure control; **~dauer** *die* (*Fot.*) ⇒ **~zeit**; **~messer** *der;* **~~s**, **~~** (*Fot.*) exposure meter; **~tabelle** *die* (*Fot.*) exposure table; **~zeit** *die* (*Fot.*) exposure time

**belieben** *itr. V.* (*unpers.*) (*geh.*) **[ganz] wie es dir beliebt** [just] as you like; **was beliebt?** (*veralt.*) what can I do for you?; **wie beliebt?** (*veralt.*) I beg your pardon?; ~, **etw. zu tun** like doing sth.; **Sie ~ zu scherzen** (*iron.*) you are joking, of course; **ihr könnt tun, was euch** (*Dat.*) **beliebt** you can do what you like

**Belieben** *das;* **~s es steht in deinem ~/es bleibt Ihrem ~ überlassen** it is up to you; **nach ~:** just as you/they *etc.* like

**beliebig** ❶ *Adj.* any; **du kannst ein ~es Beispiel/einen ~en Tag wählen** you can choose any example/day you like; **fünf ~e Personen** any five people; **in ~er Reihenfolge** in any order; **eine ~e Reihe von Beispielen** an arbitrary series of examples; **die Reihenfolge/Farbe ist ~:** any order/colour will do.
❷ *adv.* as you like/he likes *etc.;* **~ lange/viele** as long/many as you like/he likes *etc.;* **wähle eine ~ große Zahl** choose any number[, as high as] you like; **wir konnten ~ lange wegbleiben** we could stay out [for] as long as we liked; **diese beiden Begriffe sind nicht ~ austauschbar** these two terms are not interchangeable at will

**beliebt** *Adj.* popular; favourite *attrib.;* **sich [bei jmdm.] ~ machen** make oneself popular [with sb.]

**Beliebtheit** *die;* **~:** popularity; **sich großer ~** (*Gen.*) **erfreuen** (*geh.*) enjoy great popularity

**beliefern** *tr. V.* supply; **jmdn. mit etw. ~:** supply sb. with sth.

**Belieferung** *die* supply; **die ~ von jmdm. mit etw.** supplying sb. with sth.

**Belladonna** /bɛla'dɔna/ *die;* ~, **Belladonnen** (*Bot., Pharm.*) belladonna

**bellen** /'bɛlən/ ❶ *itr. V.* Ⓐ ‹dog, fox› bark; ‹hound› bay; (*fig.*) ‹cannon› boom; Ⓑ (*laut husten*) have a hacking cough; **ein ~der Husten** a hacking cough. ❷ *tr. V.* (*abwertend*) bark out ‹orders›

**Belletristik** /bɛle'trɪstɪk/ *die;* **~:** belles-lettres *pl.*

**belletristisch** ❶ *Adj.* belletristic ‹literature›; **ein ~er Verlag** a publishing house specializing in belletristic literature. ❷ *adv.* **er hat seine Darstellung ~ aufgelockert** he made his account lighter and more entertaining

**belobigen** /bə'lo:bɪgn̩/ *tr. V.* commend

**Belobigung** *die;* ~, **~en** commendation; **jmdm. eine ~ aussprechen** commend sb.

**Belobigungs·schreiben** *das* letter of commendation

**belohnen** *tr. V.* Ⓐ (*beschenken*) reward; **jmdn. mit/für etw. ~:** reward sb. with/for sth.; Ⓑ (*vergelten*) repay, reward ‹patience, loyalty, trust›

**Belohnung** *die;* ~, **~en** Ⓐ (*Lohn*) reward; **eine ~ für etw. aussetzen** offer a reward for sth.; Ⓑ (*das Belohnen*) rewarding

**Belt** /bɛlt/ *der;* **~s** (*Geogr.*) **der Kleine/Große ~:** The Little/Great Belt

**belüften** *tr. V.* ventilate; (*auslüften*) air; **das Zimmer wurde nur durch eine kleine Luke in der Decke belüftet** the only means of ventilation in the room was a small skylight

**Belüftung** *die* ventilation

**Belüftungs·anlage** *die* ventilation system

**Beluga**[1] /be'lu:ga/ *die;* ~, **~s** (*Zool.*) beluga [sturgeon]; (*Wal*) white whale

**Beluga**[2] *der;* **~s** beluga caviare

**belügen** *unr. tr. V.* **jmdn. ~:** lie to *or* tell lies to sb.; **sich selbst ~:** deceive oneself; ⇒ *auch* **Strich**

**belustigen** ❶ *tr. V.* **jmdn. ~:** amuse sb.; (*zum Lachen bringen*) make sb. laugh. ❷ *refl. V.* Ⓐ (*geh.*) **sich über jmdn./etw. ~:** make fun of *or* laugh at sb./sth.; Ⓑ (*veralt.: sich vergnügen*) amuse oneself

**belustigt** ❶ *Adj.* amused. ❷ *adv.* in amusement

**Belustigung** *die;* ~, **~en** Ⓐ (*Fest, Vergnügen*) entertainment; Ⓑ (*Belustigtsein, Belustigtwerden*) amusement; **der allgemeinen ~ dienen** serve to amuse everybody

**bemächtigen** /bə'mɛçtɪgn̩/ *refl. V.* (*geh.*) Ⓐ (*in seine Gewalt bringen*) **sich einer Sache/eines Menschen ~:** seize sth./a person; **sich der Regierungsgewalt/des Thrones ~:** seize power/the throne; Ⓑ (*überkommen*) **Angst bemächtigte sich seiner** he was seized by fear; **Unruhe/Unsicherheit bemächtigte sich seiner** a feeling of unease/uncertainty came over him; **Entsetzen bemächtigte sich eines jeden** everyone was horrified

**bemäkeln** *tr. V.* (*ugs.*) find fault with

**bemalen** ❶ *tr. V.* Ⓐ (*bunt streichen*) paint; (*verzieren*) decorate ‹porcelain etc.›; **mit etw. bemalt sein** be painted/decorated with sth.; Ⓑ (*ugs.: stark schminken*) paint. ❷ *refl. V.* (*ugs.*) paint one's face; put on one's warpaint (*coll.*); **warum hast du dich so bemalt?** why have you put so much warpaint on? (*coll.*)

**Bemalung** *die;* ~, **~en** Ⓐ (*Bemalen*) painting; (*Verzierung*) decorating; Ⓑ (*Farbschicht*) painting

**bemängeln** /bə'mɛŋl̩n/ *tr. V.* find fault with; **Bremsen/Reifen ~:** find the brakes/tyres to be faulty; **etw. an jmdm./etw. ~:** criticize sth. about sb./sth.

**Bemäng[e]lung** *die;* ~, **~en** criticism; **die häufige ~ von Fabrikationsfehlern** the frequent complaints about *or* of manufacturing defects

**bemannen** *tr. V.* man

**Bemannung** *die;* ~, **~en** Ⓐ (*das Bemannen*) manning; Ⓑ (*Mannschaft*) crew

**bemänteln** /bə'mɛntl̩n/ *tr. V.* cover up

**Bemänt[e]lung** *die;* ~, **~en** covering up

**Bembel** /'bɛmbl̩/ *der;* **~s**, ~ (*hess.: Krug*) mug; (*zum Servieren*) jug; pitcher

**bemeistern** (*geh. veralt.*) ❶ *tr. V.* master; control ‹rage, excitement, etc.›. ❷ *refl. V.* control oneself

**bemerkbar** *Adj.* noticeable; perceptible; **sich ~ machen** (*auf sich aufmerksam machen*) attract attention [to oneself]; (*eine Wirkung ausüben, sich zeigen*) ‹disadvantage› become apparent; ‹tiredness› make itself felt; **mach dich ~, wenn du etwas brauchst** if you need anything, let me know

**bemerken** *tr. V.* Ⓐ (*wahrnehmen*) notice; **ich wurde nicht bemerkt** I was unobserved; **sie bemerkte zu spät, dass ...** she realized too late that ...; Ⓑ (*äußern*) remark; **nebenbei bemerkt** by the way; incidentally

**Bemerken** *das;* **~s** (*Amtsspr.*) *in* **mit dem ~ ...** with the comment ...

**bemerkenswert** ❶ *Adj.* (*beachtlich, bedeutend*) remarkable; notable; (*Aufmerksamkeit verdienend, auffallend*) remarkable. ❷ *adv.* remarkably

**Bemerkung** *die;* ~, **~en** Ⓐ (*Äußerung*) remark; comment; Ⓑ (*Notiz*) note; (*Anmerkung*) comment

**bemessen** ❶ *unr. tr. V.* **etw. nach etw. ~:** measure sth. according to sth.; **die Zeit ist kurz/sehr knapp ~:** time is short *or* limited/very limited; **das Trinkgeld war reichlich ~:** the tips were generous. ❷ *unr. refl. V.* (*Amtsspr.*) **sich ~ nach** be measured on the basis of; **die Vergütung bemisst sich nach ...** payment is calculated on the basis of ...

**Bemessung** *die* calculation; **die ~ der Strafe richtet sich nach der Schwere des Deliktes** the penalty is fixed in accordance with the seriousness of the offence

**Bemessungs·grundlage** *die* (*Amtsspr.*) basis for assessment

**bemitleiden** *tr. V.* pity; feel sorry for; **er ist zu ~:** he is to be pitied; **sich selbst ~:** feel sorry for oneself

**bemitleidens·wert** *Adj.* pitiable

**Bemitleidung** *die;* **~:** pity *no indef. art.* (+ *Gen.* for)

**bemittelt** *Adj.* (*veralt.*) well-to-do; well off

**Bemme** /'bɛmə/ *die;* ~, **~n** (*ostmd.*) open *or* (*Amer.*) open-face sandwich; (*mit Butter bestrichen*) slice of bread and butter; (*zusammengeklappt*) sandwich

**bemogeln** *tr. V.* (*ugs.*) cheat; diddle (*coll.*); con (*sl.*)

**bemoost** *Adj.* mossy; covered in moss *postpos.;* **ein ~es Haupt** (*ugs., bes. Studentenspr.*) a perpetual student

**bemühen** ❶ *refl. V.* Ⓐ (*sich anstrengen*) try; make an effort; **sich sehr ~:** try hard; make

*old spelling (see note on page 1707)

a great effort; **sich ~, etw. zu tun** try *or* endeavour to do sth.; **bemüht sein, etw. zu tun** endeavour to do sth.; **bitte, ~ Sie sich nicht [weiter]!** please do not trouble yourself [any further]; **B** (*sich kümmern*) **sich um jmdn./etw. ~:** seek to help sb./endeavour *or* strive to achieve sth.; **um das Wohl der Hotelgäste bemüht sein** make every effort to ensure the comfort and enjoyment of the hotel patrons; **C** (*zu erlangen suchen*) **sich um etw. ~:** try *or* endeavour to obtain sth.; **sich um eine Stelle/Wohnung ~:** try to get a job/a flat (*Brit.*) *or* (*Amer.*) apartment; **sich um eine Dame ~:** pay every attention to a lady; **sich um einen Regisseur/Trainer/Wissenschaftler ~:** try *or* endeavour to obtain the services of a director/manager/scientist; **D** (*geh.: sich begeben*) proceed (*formal*); **er hat sich sogar in meine Wohnung bemüht** he even took the trouble to go/come to my flat. **2** *tr. V.* (*geh.*) **A** (*in Anspruch nehmen*) trouble; call in, call upon the services of ‹lawyer, architect, etc.›; (*als Beweis heranziehen*) bring in a quotation/quotations from ‹author, philosopher, etc.›; **B** (*bitten, zu kommen*) trouble sb. to come; **jmdn. ins oberste Stockwerk ~:** trouble sb. to come/go up to the top floor

**Bemühen** *das;* **~s** (*geh.*) effort; endeavour; **unser ~ um eine Sanierung dieses Stadtteils** our efforts *pl. or* endeavours *pl.* to redevelop this part of the town; **trotz jahrelangen ~s** despite years of effort

**bemühend** *Adj.* (*schweiz.*) [painfully] embarrassing; (*unerfreulich*) unpleasant

**bemüht 1** *2. Part. v.* **bemühen. 2** *Adj.* forced; forced, constrained ‹cheerfulness›; constrained ‹person›

**Bemühung** *die;* **~, ~en A** (*Anstrengung*) effort; endeavour; **alle ~en waren vergeblich** all efforts were in vain; **trotz aller ~en, allen ~en zum Trotz** in spite of *or* despite all our/his *etc.* efforts; **vielen Dank für Ihre ~en** thank you very much for your efforts *or* trouble; **niemand wollte ihn in seinen ~en unterstützen** no one wanted to support him in his endeavours; **B** *Pl.* (*Dienstleistung*) services

**bemüßigen** *refl. V.* (*geh.*) **sich einer Sache** (*Gen.*) **~:** make use of sth.

**bemüßigt** /bəˈmy:sɪçt/ (*geh. iron.*) *in* **sich ~ sehen** *od.* **fühlen** *od.* **finden, etw. zu tun** feel obliged to do sth.; feel it incumbent on oneself to do sth.

**bemuttern** *tr. V.* mother

**Bemutterung** *die;* **~, ~en** mothering

**benachbart** *Adj.* neighbouring *attrib.;* **~e Fachgebiete** related fields of study; **ihre Häuser sind ~:** their houses are next door to each other

**benachrichtigen** /bəˈna:xrɪçtɪgn̩/ *tr. V.* inform; notify; **jmdn. von etw. ~:** inform *or* notify sb. of *or* about sth.

**Benachrichtigung** *die;* **~, ~en** notification; **ich bitte um sofortige ~:** I wish to be informed *or* notified immediately; **warum habt ihr uns denn keine ~ geschickt?** why didn't you contact us *or* let us know?

**benachteiligen** *tr. V.* put at a disadvantage; ‹disability› handicap; (*diskriminieren*) discriminate against; **sich benachteiligt fühlen** feel at a disadvantage/feel discriminated against; **er fühlte sich von seinen Lehrern benachteiligt** he felt unfairly treated by his teachers; **ein wirtschaftlich benachteiligtes Gebiet** an economically deprived area; **die sozial benachteiligten Schichten** the underprivileged classes

**Benachteiligte** *der/die; adj. Dekl.* disadvantaged person; **die ~n** the disadvantaged; those at a disadvantage; **die sozial ~n** the underprivileged; the socially deprived

**Benachteiligung** *die;* **~, ~en** (*Vorgang*) discrimination (*Gen.* against); (*Zustand*) disadvantage (*Gen.* to); **der Firma wurde eine ~ der Frauen vorgeworfen** the firm was accused of discriminating against women

**benagen** *tr. V.* gnaw *or* nibble [at] ‹bread, cheese, etc.›; gnaw [at] ‹tree, bark, etc.›

**benähen** *tr. V.* **einen Rock** *usw.* **mit etw. ~:** sew sth. on to a skirt *etc.*

**benässen** *tr. V.* (*geh.*) wet

***Bendel ⇒ Bändel**

**benebeln** *tr. V.* befuddle; **mit benebeltem Kopf aufwachen** wake up with a muzzy head

**Benediktiner** /benedɪkˈti:nɐ/ *der;* **~s, ~ A** (*Mönch*) Benedictine [monk]; **B** (*Kräuterlikör*) benedictine

**Benediktinerin** *die;* **~, ~nen** Benedictine [nun]

**Benediktiner·orden** *der* Benedictine order; order of St. Benedict

**Benefiz** /beneˈfi:ts/ *das;* **~es, ~e A** (*veralt.: Vorstellung*) benefit performance; **B** (*Wohltätigkeitsveranstaltung*) charity performance/match, *etc.*

**Benefizkonzert** *das* charity concert

**Benefiz·spiel** *das* charity game *or* match

**benehmen 1** *unr. refl. V.* behave (**wie** like); (*in Bezug auf Umgangsformen*) behave [oneself]; **sich schlecht ~:** behave badly; misbehave; **sie kann sich einfach nicht ~:** she simply does not know how to behave; **wenn du dich nicht ~ kannst, ...** if you can't behave yourself, ... **2** *unr. tr. V.* (*geh.: wegnehmen*) **es benahm mir den Atem** it took my breath away

**Benehmen** *das;* **~s A** behaviour; **kein ~ haben** have no manners *pl.;* **B** (*Amtsspr.*) **in sich mit jmdm. ins ~ setzen** make contact with sb.

**beneiden** *tr. V.* envy; be envious of; **jmdn. um etw. ~:** envy sb. sth.; **du bist [nicht] zu ~:** I [don't] envy you

**beneidens·wert 1** *Adj.* enviable. **2** *adv.* enviably

**Benelux** /ˈbe:nelʊks/ *Abk.* Benelux

**Benelux·staaten** *Pl.* Benelux countries

**benennen** *unr. tr. V.* **A** (*mit einem Namen versehen*) name; **etw./jmdn. nach jmdm. ~:** name sth./name *or* call sb. after *or* (*Amer.*) for sb.; **B** (*namhaft machen*) call ‹witness›; **jmdn. als Kandidaten ~:** nominate sb. as a candidate; **jmdn. als** *od.* **zum Zeugen ~:** call sb. as a witness

**Benennung** *die* **A** (*Namengebung*) naming; **B** (*das Namhaftmachen*) **durch ~ zweier weiterer Zeugen** by calling two more witnesses; **C** (*Name*) name; (*Bezeichnung*) designation

**benetzen** *tr. V.* (*geh.*) moisten; ‹dew› cover; **mit Tau/von Schweiß benetzt** covered *or* wet with dew/damp with perspiration

**Bengale** /bɛŋˈga:lə/ *der;* **~n, ~n,** Bengali; Bengalese

**Bengalen** (*das*)*;* **~s** Bengal

**Bengali** /bɛŋˈga:li/ *das;* **~[s]** Bengali

**Bengalin** *die;* **~, ~nen ⇒ Bengale**

**bengalisch** *Adj.* ▶ 696 Bengalese; Bengali, Bengalese ‹people, language›; **~e Beleuchtung, ~es Feuer** Bengal light *or* fire

**Bengel** /ˈbɛŋl̩/ *der;* **~s, ~** *od.* (*nordd.*) **~s A** (*abwertend: junger Bursche*) young rascal; **B** (*fam.: kleiner Junge*) little lad *or* boy; **ein süßer ~:** a dear little lad *or* boy; **C** (*veralt.: Knüppel*) stick

**Benimm** /bəˈnɪm/ *der;* **~s** (*ugs.*) manners *pl.;* **jmdm. ~ beibringen** teach sb. some manners

**Benjamin** /ˈbɛnjami:n/ *der;* **~s, ~e** (*scherzh.*) youngest boy; **er ist der ~ der Familie** he's the baby of the family

**benommen** /beˈnɔmən/ **1** *2. Part. v.* **benehmen. 2** *Adj.* bemused; dazed; (*durch Fieber, Medikamente, Alkohol*) muzzy (**von** from)

**Benommenheit** *die;* **~:** bemused *or* dazed state; (*durch Fieber, Medikamente, Alkohol*) muzziness

**benoten** *tr. V.* mark (*Brit.*); grade (*Amer.*); **einen Test mit „gut" ~:** mark a test 'good' (*Brit.*); assign a grade of 'good' to a test (*Amer.*)

**benötigen** *tr. V.* need; require; **das benötigte Geld** the necessary money

**Benotung** *die;* **~, ~en A** (*das Benoten*) marking (*Brit.*); grading (*Amer.*); **sich um eine gerechte ~ bemühen** try *or* endeavour to mark (*Brit.*) *or* (*Amer.*) grade fairly; **B** (*Note*) mark (*Brit.*); grade (*Amer.*)

**benutzbar** *Adj.* usable; **„Aufzug vorübergehend nicht ~"** 'lift temporarily out of service'; **schwer ~:** difficult to use

**benutzen,** (*bes. südd.*) **benützen** *tr. V.* use (**für** for); take, use ‹car, lift›; take ‹train, taxi›; use, consult ‹reference book›; **das benutzte Geschirr** the dirty dishes; **etw. als Vorwand/Alibi ~:** use sth. as an excuse/alibi; **wir benutzten den freien Tag zu einem Ausflug** we made use of *or* took advantage of the free day to go on an excursion

**Benutzer,** (*bes. südd.*) **Benützer** *der;* **~s, ~:** user; (*eines entliehenen Buchs*) borrower

**benutzer·freundlich** *Adj.* user-friendly

**Benutzerin,** (*bes. südd.*) **Benützerin** *die;* **~, ~nen ⇒ Benutzer**

**Benutzer·kreis** *der* users *pl.;* (*von Büchereien*) borrowers *pl.;* **ein großer ~:** a large number of users/borrowers

**Benutzung** *die;* **~,** (*bes. südd.*) **Benützung** *die;* **Benützung** use; **jmdm. etw. zur ~ überlassen** give sb. the use of sth.; allow sb. to use sth.; **in ~** (*Dat.*) **sein** be in use; **etw. in ~** (*Akk.*) **nehmen** bring sth. into use; **etw. zur ~ freigeben** open sth.; **unter ~ einer Sache** (*Gen.*) making use of sth.

**Benutzungs-: ~gebühr** *die* charge; (*in Büchereien*) borrowing charge; **die ~gebühr für etw.** the charge for using/borrowing sth.; **~ordnung** *die:* **die ~ordnung der Badeanstalt/Bibliothek** *usw.* the rules and conditions *pl.* for the use of the pool/library *etc.*

**Benzin** /bɛnˈtsi:n/ *das;* **~s** petrol (*Brit.*); gasoline (*Amer.*); gas (*Amer. coll.*); (*Wasch~*) benzine; (*Feuerzeug~*) petrol (*Brit.*); gasoline (*Amer.*); *lighter fuel*

**Benzin-: ~dunst** *der* petrol (*Brit.*) *or* (*Amer.*) gasoline fumes *pl.;* **~einspritzung** *die;* **~** (*Kfz-W.*) fuel injection

**Benziner** *der;* **~s, ~** (*ugs.*) car that runs on petrol (*Brit.*) *or* (*Amer.*) gasoline; car with a petrol (*Brit.*) *or* (*Amer.*) gasoline engine; petrol-driven (*Brit.*) *or* (*Amer.*) gasoline-powered car

**Benzin-: ~feuerzeug** *das* petrol (*Brit.*) *or* (*Amer.*) gasoline lighter; **~gut·schein** *der* petrol (*Brit.*) *or* (*Amer.*) gasoline coupon; **~kanister** *der* petrol (*Brit.*) *or* (*Amer.*) gasoline can; **~leitung** *die* fuel pipe; **~motor** *der* petrol (*Brit.*) *or* (*Amer.*) gasoline engine; **~preis** *der* price of petrol (*Brit.*) *or* (*Amer.*) gasoline; **~pumpe** *die* petrol (*Brit.*) *or* (*Amer.*) gasoline pump; **~tank** *der* petrol (*Brit.*) *or* (*Amer.*) gasoline tank; **~uhr** *die* (*Kfz-W.*) fuel gauge; **~verbrauch** *der* fuel consumption

**Benzoe** /ˈbɛntsoe/ *die;* **~** (*Chemie*) [gum] benzoin

**Benzoe·säure** *die* (*Chemie*) benzoic acid

**Benzol** /bɛnˈtso:l/ *das;* **~s, ~e** (*Chemie*) benzene

**beobachtbar** *Adj.* observable

**beobachten** /bəˈ|o:baxtn̩/ *tr. V.* **A** observe; watch; (*als Zeuge*) see; **er hat beobachtet, wie sie das Radio stahl** he watched her steal the radio; **jmdn. ~ lassen** put sb. under surveillance; have sb. watched; **B** (*bemerken*) notice; observe; **etw. an jmdm. ~:** notice sth. about sb.; **eine Veränderung an jmdm. ~:** notice a change in sb.; **C** (*geh.: beachten*) observe

**Beobachter** *der;* **~s, ~, Beobachterin** *die* observer

**Beobachtung** *die;* **~, ~en A** (*das Beobachten, die Feststellung*) observation; **~en anstellen** keep a watch; **zur ~:** for observation; **unter ~ stehen** be kept under surveillance; **B** (*geh.: Beachtung*) observation

**Beobachtungs-: ~ballon** *der* observation balloon; **~gabe** *die* powers *pl.* of observation; **~posten** *der* observation post; **auf ~posten stehen** be on lookout duty; **~station** *die* **A** (*im Krankenhaus*) observation ward; **B ⇒ Wetterstation**

b

**beölen** *refl. V.* (*Jugendspr.*) kill *or* (*coarse*) piss oneself laughing

**beordern** *tr. V.* order; **jmdn. nach Hause/ins Ausland ~:** order *or* summon sb. home/order sb. [to go] abroad

**bepacken** *tr. V.* load; **etw./jmdn./sich mit etw. ~:** load sth. up with/load sb./oneself with sth.

**bepflanzen** *tr. V.* plant (**mit** with)

**Bepflanzung** *die* [A] (*das Bepflanzen*) planting (**mit** with); [B] (*Pflanzen*) plants *pl.* (*Gen.* in)

**bepflastern** *tr. V.* [A] (*ugs.*) put a plaster on ‹wound etc.›; [B] (*mit Pflasterung versehen*) pave; (*fig.: mit Orden, Aufklebern usw.*) plaster; [C] (*Soldatenspr.: bombardieren*) plaster (*coll.*); bombard

**bepinkeln** (*ugs.*) ❶ *tr. V.* pee on (*coll.*). ❷ *refl. V.* wet oneself

**bepinseln** *tr. V.* [A] (*ugs.: einpinseln*) paint ‹gums›; brush ‹dough, cake mixture›; [B] (*ugs. abwertend: anstreichen*) paint; **etw. mit Farbe ~:** paint sth.

**bepissen** *tr. V.* (*derb*) piss on (*coarse*)

**Beplankung** /bəˈplaŋkʊŋ/ *die;* ~, ~**en** (*Boots~*) planking; (*Flugzeug~*) skin

**bepudern** *tr. V.* powder

**bequasseln** *tr. V.* (*salopp*) ⇒ **bequatschen** A

**bequatschen** *tr. V.* (*salopp*) [A] (*bereden*) **etw. [ausführlich] ~:** have a [long] jaw about sth. (*coll.*); [B] (*überreden*) persuade; **jmdn. ~, dass er mitkommt** talk sb. into coming along

**bequem** /bəˈkveːm/ ❶ *Adj.* [A] (*angenehm*) comfortable; **es sich** (*Dat.*) **~ machen** make oneself comfortable; **machen Sie es sich ~:** make yourself at home; [B] (*mühelos*) easy; **ein ~es Leben führen** have an easy *or* comfortable life; [C] (*abwertend: träge*) lazy; idle. ❷ *adv.* [A] (*angenehm*) comfortably; **liegen/sitzen Sie ~ so?** are you comfortable like that?; [B] (*leicht*) easily; comfortably

**bequemen** *refl. V.* (*geh.*) [A] (*abwertend*) **sich dazu ~, etw. zu tun** (*sich herablassen*) condescend *or* deign to do sth.; (*sich endlich entschließen*) bring oneself to do sth; [B] (*veralt.: sich fügen*) become adapted (*Dat.* to)

**bequemlich** *Adj.* (*veralt.*) ⇒ **bequem**

**Bequemlichkeit** *die;* ~, ~**en** [A] (*Annehmlichkeit, Komfort*) comfort; [B] (*Trägheit*) laziness; idleness; **aus [reiner] ~:** out of [sheer] laziness *or* idleness

**berappen** /bəˈrapn̩/ *tr., itr. V.* (*ugs.*) cough up (*coll.*), shell out (*coll.*), fork over (*sl.*) ‹money›

**beraten** ❶ *unr. tr. V.* [A] advise; **jmdn. gut/schlecht ~:** give sb. good/bad advice; **sich ~ lassen** take *or* get advice (**von** from); **du bist gut ~, wenn du ...** you'd be well advised to ...; [B] (*besprechen*) discuss ‹plan, matter›. ❷ *unr. itr. V.* **über etw.** (*Akk.*) **~:** discuss sth.; **sie berieten lange** they were a long time in discussion. ❸ *unr. refl. V.* **sich mit jmdm. ~, ob ...** discuss with sb. whether ...; **sich mit seinem Anwalt ~:** consult one's lawyer

**beratend** *Adj.* advisory, consultative ‹function, role, etc.›

**Berater** *der;* ~**s**, ~, **Beraterin** *die;* ~, ~**nen** adviser

**Berater-:** ~**stab** *der* team of advisers; ~**vertrag** *der* consultancy contract

**beratschlagen** /bəˈraːtʃlaːgn̩/ ❶ *tr. V.* discuss. ❷ *itr. V.* **über etw.** (*Akk.*) **~:** discuss sth.

**Beratschlagung** *die;* ~, ~**en** discussion

**Beratung** *die;* ~, ~**en** [A] advice *no indef. art.;* (*durch Arzt, Rechtsanwalt*) consultation; **ohne juristische ~:** without [taking] legal advice; [B] (*Besprechung*) discussion; **Gegenstand der ~ war ...** the subject under discussion was ...; **sich zur ~ zurückziehen** withdraw for discussions *pl.;* [C] ⇒ **Beratungsstelle**

**Beratungs-:** ~**kosten** *Pl.* consultation fees; ~**stelle** *die* advice centre (*Brit.*); counseling center (*Amer.*); ~**zimmer** *das* conference room

**berauben** *tr. V.* (*auch fig.*) rob; **jmdn. einer Sache** (*Gen.*) **~** (*geh.*) rob sb. of sth.; **jmdn. seiner Freiheit/Hoffnungen ~** (*fig.*) deprive sb. of his/her freedom/hopes

**Beraubung** *die;* ~, ~**en** robbing *no indef. art.*

**berauschen** (*geh.*) ❶ *tr. V.* (*auch fig.*) intoxicate; ‹alcohol› intoxicate, inebriate; ‹drug› make euphoric; ‹speed› exhilarate; **der Erfolg/die Macht berauschte ihn** he was intoxicated *or* drunk with success/drunk with power. ❷ *refl. V.* become intoxicated; **sich an etw.** (*Dat.*) **~:** become intoxicated with sth.; **sich an seinen eigenen Worten ~:** become carried away by one's own words

**berauschend** ❶ *Adj.* intoxicating; **~ auf jmdn. wirken** have an intoxicating effect on sb.; heady, intoxicating ‹perfume, scent›; **das ist nicht ~** (*ugs.*) it's nothing very special *or* (*coll.*) nothing to write home about. ❷ *adv.* **~ schön** enchantingly beautiful; **der Abend war ~ schön** (*iron.*) the evening was just great (*iron.*)

**Berber** /ˈbɛrbɐ/ *der;* ~**s**, ~ [A] Berber; [B] (*Teppich*) Berber carpet/rug; [C] (*Pferderasse*) Barbary horse; [D] (*Nichtsesshafter*) tramp

**Berberin** *die;* ~, ~**nen** ⇒ **Berber** A, D

**Berberitze** /bɛrbəˈrɪtsə/ *die;* ~, ~**n** (*Bot.*) common barberry

**Berber·teppich** *der* Berber carpet/rug

**berechenbar** /bəˈrɛçn̩baːɐ̯/ *Adj.* calculable; predictable ‹behaviour›

**Berechenbarkeit** *die;* ~: calculability; (*des Verhaltens*) predictability

**berechnen** *tr. V.* [A] (*ermitteln*) calculate ‹quantity, cost, price, risk, etc.›; predict ‹behaviour, consequences›; (*fig.*) calculate ‹effect›; [B] (*anrechnen*) charge; **jmdm. etw. mit 10 Mark ~:** charge sb. 10 marks for sth.; **jmdm. etw. nicht ~:** not charge sb. for sth.; **für etw. nichts ~:** not charge for sth.; make no charge for sth.; **jmdn. zu viel ~:** overcharge sb.; charge sb. too much; [C] (*kalkulieren*) calculate; (*vorsehen*) intend; **der Architekt berechnete die Bauzeit auf sieben Monate** the architect estimated that the construction time would be seven months; **für sechs Personen berechnet sein** ‹recipe, buffet› be for six people

**berechnend** *Adj.* calculating

**Berechnung** *die* [A] (*das Berechnen*) calculation; **nach meiner ~, meiner ~ nach** according to my calculations *pl.;* [B] (*abwertend: Eigennutz*) [calculating] self-interest; **etw. aus ~ tun** do sth. from motives of self-interest; [C] (*Überlegung*) deliberation; calculation; **mit kühler ~ vorgehen** act with cool deliberation

**berechtigen** /bəˈrɛçtɪgn̩/ ❶ *tr. V.* entitle; **jmdn. ~, etw. zu tun** entitle sb. *or* give sb. the right to do sth.; **das berechtigt ihn zu dieser Kritik** it entitles him *or* gives him the right to criticize [in this way]. ❷ *itr. V.* **die Karte berechtigt zum Eintritt** the ticket entitles the bearer to admission; **sein Talent berechtigt zu den schönsten Hoffnungen** his talent gives grounds for very great hopes indeed; **das berechtigt zu der Annahme, dass ...** it justifies the assumption that ...

**berechtigt** *Adj.* justified, legitimate ‹demand, criticism, objection, doubt, complaint, hope›; just ‹accusation›; **jmd. ist ~, etw. zu tun** sb. is authorized to do sth.

**berechtigterweise** *Adv.* (*Papierdt.*) legitimately; with justification

**Berechtigung** *die;* ~, ~**en** [A] (*Befugnis*) entitlement; (*Recht*) right; **mit welcher ~ kritisiert er mich?** what right has he to criticize me?; [B] (*Rechtmäßigkeit*) legitimacy; **seine/ihre ~ haben** be justified *or* legitimate

**Berechtigungs·schein** *der* authorization; (*zum Zutritt, Einlass usw.*) pass

**bereden** ❶ *tr. V.* [A] (*besprechen*) talk over; discuss; [B] (*überreden*) **jmdn. ~, etw. zu tun** talk sb. into doing sth.; **sich ~ lassen, etw. zu tun** let oneself be talked into doing sth. ❷ *refl. V.* **sich [mit jmdm.] über etw.** (*Akk.*) **~:** talk sth. over *or* discuss sth. [with sb.]

**beredsam** /bəˈreːtzaːm/ ❶ *Adj.* (*beredt*) eloquent; (*iron.: redefreudig*) **~ sein** have the gift of the gab (*coll.*). ❷ *adv.* (*beredt*) eloquently; (*iron.: redefreudig*) **~ für etw. werben** use one's gift of the gab to promote sth. (*coll.*)

**Beredsamkeit** *die;* ~ ⇒ **beredsam:** eloquence; gift of the gab (*coll.*)

**beredt** /bəˈreːt/ ❶ *Adj.* (*auch fig.*) eloquent; **~es Zeugnis von etw. ablegen** bear eloquent witness to sth.; **es herrschte ein ~es Schweigen** there was a meaningful silence. ❷ *adv.* eloquently

**beregnen** *tr. V.* water ‹field› using an overhead sprinkling system; water ‹lawn› using a sprinkler

**Beregnung** *die;* ~ ⇒ **beregnen:** watering using an overhead sprinkling system/a sprinkler

**Beregnungs·anlage** *die* overhead sprinkling system

**Bereich** *der;* ~[e]s, ~e [A] (*Gebiet*) area; **im ~/außerhalb des ~s der Stadt** within/outside the town; **im nördlichen ~:** in northern areas *pl.;* [B] (*Sphäre*) sphere; area; (*Fachgebiet*) field; area; **in jmds. ~** (*Akk.*) **fallen** be [within] sb.'s province; **im ~ des Möglichen liegen** be within the bounds *pl.* of possibility; **aus dem ~ der Kunst/Politik** from the sphere of art/politics; [C] (*Wirkungsfeld*) **im privaten/staatlichen ~:** in the private/public sector; **sich im ~ eines Tiefs befinden** be under the influence of a low-pressure area

**bereichern** /bəˈraiçɐn/ ❶ *refl. V.* get rich; **sich an jmdm./etw. ~:** make a great deal of money at sb.'s expense/out of sth. ❷ *tr. V.* enrich; enlarge, increase ‹collection, knowledge›; **diese Erfahrung hat mich bereichert** I gained a lot from the experience

**Bereicherung** *die;* ~, ~**en** [A] (*das Sichbereichern*) moneymaking; [B] (*Nutzen*) valuable acquisition; **eine wertvolle ~ der koreanischen Literatur** a valuable addition to Korean literature

**bereifen**[1] *tr. V.* put tyres on ‹car›; put a tyre on ‹wheel›; **neu ~:** put a new tyre/new tyres on; **gut bereift sein** ‹car› have good tyres

**bereifen**[2] ❶ *tr. V.* cover with hoar frost *or* rime. ❷ *itr. V.* become covered with hoar frost *or* rime

**Bereifung** *die;* ~, ~**en** [set *sing.* of] tyres *pl.*

**bereinigen** ❶ *tr. V.* [A] (*klären*) clear up ‹misunderstanding›; settle, resolve ‹dispute›; **mit jmdm. etw. zu ~ haben** have sth. to sort out with sb.; [B] (*verbessern*) correct ‹text›; adjust, correct ‹statistics› (**um** for). ❷ *refl. V.* resolve itself; sort itself out

**Bereinigung** *die* (*eines Missverständnisses*) clearing up; (*eines Streites*) settlement; resolution; (*eines Textes*) correction; (*einer Statistik*) adjustment; correction

**bereisen** *tr. V.* travel around *or* about; travel through ‹towns›; (*beruflich*) ‹representative etc.› cover ‹area›; **fremde Länder ~:** travel in foreign countries; **ganz Afrika ~:** travel throughout Africa

**bereit** /bəˈrait/ *Adj.* [A] (*fertig, gerüstet*) ready; ⇒ *auch* **bereithaben, bereithalten;** [B] (*gewillt*) **~ sein, etw. zu tun** be willing *or* ready *or* prepared to do sth.; **sich ~ zeigen/finden, etw. zu tun** show oneself/be willing *or* ready *or* prepared to do sth.; **sich ~ erklären, etw. zu tun** declare oneself willing *or* ready to do sth.

**bereiten** ❶ *tr. V.* [A] (*zu~*) prepare; make ‹tea, coffee›; run ‹bath›; **jmdm. *od.* für jmdn. etw. ~:** prepare/make/run sth. for sb.; [B] (*zufügen*) cause ‹trouble, sorrow, frustration, difficulty, etc.›; **jmdm. Freude/einen begeisterten Empfang ~:** give sb. great pleasure/an enthusiastic reception; **einer Sache** (*Dat.*) **ein Ende ~:** put an end to sth. ❷ *refl. V.* (*geh.: sich vor~*) prepare oneself; **sich zum Sterben ~:** prepare to die

*old spelling (see note on page 1707)

**bereit-**: ~|**haben** *unr. tr. V.* have ready; ~|**halten** ❶ *unr. tr. V.* have ready; (*für Notfälle*) keep ready. ❷ *unr. refl. V.* be ready; **der Arzt musste sich auf Abruf ~halten** the doctor was on call; ~|**legen** *tr. V.* lay out ready; **jmdm.** *od.* **für jmdn. etw. ~legen** lay sth. out ready for sb.; ~|**liegen** *unr. itr. V.* be ready; ‹surgical instruments, tools, papers› be laid out ready; ~|**machen** ❶ *tr. V.* get ready; make up ‹bed›. ❷ *refl. V.* get ready

**bereits** *Adv.* already; **sie sind ~ gestern angekommen** they [in fact] arrived yesterday; **~ seit fünf Jahren** for [as long as] five years; **~ vor drei Stunden** three 'hours ago; **~ damals** even then *or* at that time; **~ im 17. Jh.** as early as the 17th century; **~ am nächsten Tag** by the very next day; **~ in zwei Wochen** in only two weeks' time

**Bereitschaft** *die;* ~; **~en** Ⓐ willingness; readiness; preparedness; **etw. in ~ haben** have sth. ready; Ⓑ (*ugs.: ~sdienst*) **~ haben** ‹doctor, nurse› be on call; ‹policeman, fireman› be on standby duty; ‹chemist's› be on rota duty (*for dispensing outside normal hours*); Ⓒ (*Einheit*) unit

**Bereitschafts-**: **~arzt** *der* doctor on call; **~dienst** *der:* **~dienst haben** ‹doctor, nurse› be on call; ‹policeman, fireman› be on standby duty; ‹chemist's› be on rota duty (*for dispensing outside normal hours*); **~polizei** *die* police; (*bei Demonstrationen usw.*) riot police

**bereit-**: ~|**stehen** *unr. itr. V.* be ready; ‹car, train, aircraft› be waiting; ‹troops› be standing by; **für uns steht ein Auto ~:** a car is/will be waiting for us; **etw. ~stehen haben** have sth. ready; ~|**stellen** *tr. V.* place ready; get ready ‹food, drinks›; provide, make available ‹money, funds›; **die Getränke sind nebenan ~gestellt** the drinks are ready next door

**Bereitung** *die;* ~ (*Papierdt.*) preparation; (*von Tee, Kaffee*) making

**bereit·willig** ❶ *Adj.* willing. ❷ *adv.* readily

**Bereitwilligkeit** *die;* ~: willingness

**berennen** *unr. tr. V.* storm, attack ‹castle, fortress›; (*Sport*) storm, (*Amer.*) rush ‹goal›

**berenten** *tr. V.* (*Amtsspr.*) **jmdn. ~:** retire sb. on a pension; **sich ~ lassen** retire on a pension

**bereuen** ❶ *tr. V.* regret; **seine Sünden ~:** repent [of] one's sins; **ich bereue, dass ...** I'm sorry *or* I regret that ...; **nichts zu ~ haben** have no regrets. ❷ *itr. V.* be sorry; (*Rel.*) repent

**Berg** /bɛrk/ *der;* ~[e]s, ~e Ⓐ ▶411 hill; (*im Hochgebirge*) mountain; **über ~ und Tal** up hill and down dale; **~ Heil!** *greeting between mountaineers;* **wenn der ~ nicht zum Propheten kommt, muss der Prophet zum ~e kommen** (*Spr.*) if the mountain won't come to Muhammad, then Muhammad must go to the mountain (*prov.*); **jmdm. goldene ~e versprechen** (*fig.*) promise sb. the moon; **mit etw. hinter dem** *od.* **hinterm ~ halten** (*fig.*) keep sth. to oneself; keep quiet about sth.; **mit seiner Meinung nicht hinter dem** *od.* **hinterm ~ halten** (*fig.*) not keep one's views *pl.* to oneself; not hesitate to speak one's mind; **~e versetzen [können]** (*fig.*) [be able to] move mountains (*fig.*); **über den ~ sein** (*ugs.*) be out of the wood (*Brit.*) *or* (*Amer.*) woods; ‹patient› be on the mend, have turned the corner; **[längst] über alle ~e sein** (*ugs.*) be miles away; Ⓑ *Pl.* (*Gebirge*) mountains; **in die ~e fahren** go up into the mountains; Ⓒ (*Haufen*) enormous *or* huge pile; (*von Akten, Abfall auch*) mountain

**berg-, Berg-**: **~ab** /-'-/ *Adv.* downhill; **einen steilen Weg ~ab fahren** go down a steep path; **mit dem Patienten/der Firma geht es ~ab** (*fig. ugs*) the patient's getting worse/ the firm's going downhill; **~abwärts** /-'--/ *Adv.* downhill; **~ahorn** *der* sycamore [maple]; **~akademie** *die* school of mining

**Bergamotte** /bɛrga'mɔtə/ *die;* ~, **~n** Ⓐ (*Pomeranze*) bergamot [orange]; Ⓑ (*Birne*) bergamot [pear]

**berg-, Berg-**: **~amt** *das* [local] mining authority; **~an** /-'-/ ⇒ **~auf**; **~arbeiter** *der,* **~arbeiterin** *die* miner; mineworker; **~auf** /-'-/ *Adv.* uphill; **es geht ~auf mit der Firma** (*fig. ugs.*) things are looking up for the firm; **mit dem Patienten gehts ~auf** the patient's on the mend; **~aufwärts** /-'--/ *Adv.* uphill; **~bahn** *die* mountain railway; (*Seilbahn*) mountain cableway; **~bau** *der* mining; **~bauer** *der;* **~~n, ~~n, ~bäuerin** *die* mountain farmer; **~dorf** *das* mountain village

**berge·hoch** ⇒ **berghoch**

**Berge·lohn** *der* salvage payment

**bergen** *unr. tr. V.* Ⓐ (*retten*) rescue, save ‹person›; salvage ‹ship›; salvage, recover ‹cargo, belongings›; (*einbringen*) gather *or* get in ‹harvest›; **jmdn. tot/lebend ~:** recover sb.'s body/ rescue sb. alive; **sich geborgen fühlen** feel safe; **die Segel ~** (*Seemannsspr.*) take in *or* furl the sails; Ⓑ (*geh.: enthalten*) hold; **Gefahren/Vorteile in sich** (*Dat.*) **~** (*fig.*) hold dangers/have advantages; Ⓒ (*geh.: ver~*) hide; (*vor Regen*) shelter; (*vor Sonne*) protect; **den Kopf in den Händen ~:** bury one's head in one's hands

**berg-, Berg-**: **~fach** *das* mining *no art.;* **~fahrt** *die* Ⓐ (*Schifffahrt*) passage upstream; Ⓑ (*Hochgebirgstour*) mountaineering expedition; **auf ~fahrt gehen** go mountaineering; **~fest** *das* (*ugs.*) party to celebrate reaching the halfway stage; **~fex** /-fɛks/ *der;* **~~es, ~~e** (*ugs.*) enthusiastic climber; mountaineering freak (*coll.*); **~fried** /-fri:t/ *der;* **~~[e]s, ~~e** keep; **~führer** *der,* **~führerin** *die* ▶159 mountain guide; **~geist** *der: legendary sorcerer, kobold, gnome, or giant living inside a mountain;* **~gipfel** der mountain peak *or* top; summit; **~grat** *der* mountain ridge; **~hoch** ❶ *Adj.* as high as a mountain/as mountains; mountainous ‹waves, seas›; ❷ *adv.* **~hoch aufsteigende Wellen** mountainous waves *or* seas; **~hütte** *die* mountain hut

**bergig** *Adj.* hilly; (*mit hohen Bergen*) mountainous

**Berg-**: **~ingenieur** *der,* **~ingenieurin** *die* [qualified] mining engineer; **~kessel** *der* corrie; cirque; **~kette** *die* range *or* chain of mountains; mountain range *or* chain; **~krankheit** *die* mountain sickness; **~kristall** *der* rock crystal; **~kuppe** *die* [rounded] peak *or* mountain top; **~land** *das* hilly country *no indef. art;* (*mit hohen ~en*) mountainous country *no indef. art.;* **das spanische ~land** the hill country of Spain; **das Schottische ~land** the Highlands of Scotland

**Bergler** /'bɛrklɐ/ *der;* **~s, ~, Berglerin** *die;* **~, ~nen** mountain-dweller

**Berg·mann** *der; Pl.* **Bergleute** ▶159 miner; mineworker

**berg·männisch** /-mɛnɪʃ/ ❶ *Adj.* miner's *attrib.* ❷ *adv.* by miners

**Bergmanns-**: **~gruß** *der* miner's greeting; **~sprache** *die* mining terminology

**berg-, Berg-**: **~massiv** *das* massif; **~not** *die:* **in ~not sein/geraten** ‹climber› be/get into difficulties while climbing [in the mountains]; **jmdn. aus ~not retten** rescue sb. who has got into difficulties while climbing [in the mountains]; **~predigt** *die* Sermon on the Mount; **~recht** *das* laws relating to mining; **~rennen** *das* (*Motorsport*) hill climbing; **ein ~rennen** a hill climb; **~rettungs·dienst** *der* ⇒ **~wacht**; **~riese** *der* giant of a mountain; **~rücken** *der* mountain ridge; **~rutsch** *der* landslide; landslip; **~sattel** *der* saddle; col; **~schuh** *der* mountaineering boot; **~see** *der* mountain lake; **~spitze** *die* [mountain] peak; mountain top; **~sport** *der* mountaineering; mountain climbing; **~station** *die* top station; **~steigen** *unr. itr. V.; mit haben od. sein; nur im Inf. und Part.* go mountaineering *or* mountain climbing; **~steigen** *das;* **~~s** mountaineering *no art.;* mountain climbing *no art.;* **~steiger** *der,* **~steigerin** *die;* **~~, ~~nen** ▶159 mountaineer; mountain climber; **~steigerisch** ❶ *Adj.* mountaineering; ❷ *adv.* **~steigerisch [gesehen]** from a mountaineering point of view; **~stock** *der* Ⓐ (*Spazierstock*) alpenstock; Ⓑ ⇒ **Gebirgsstock**; **~straße** *die* Ⓐ mountain road; Ⓑ (*Geogr.*) **die ~straße** the Bergstraße (*hilly wine-growing and orchard district between Darmstadt and Heidel~*); **~sturz** *der* rock fall; **~tour** *die* trip up into the mountains; (*zu Fuß*) mountain climb; (*Wanderung*) hike in the mountains; **~-und-Tal-Bahn** *die* roller coaster; switch back (*Brit.*); big dipper (*Brit.*); **~-und-Tal-Fahrt** *die* journey full of steep climbs and descents; **das war die reinste ~-und-Tal-Fahrt** it was just like going up and down on a roller coaster *or* (*Brit.*) switchback

**Bergung** *die;* **~, ~en** Ⓐ (*erste Hilfe*) rescue; saving; Ⓑ (*von Schiffen, Gut*) salvaging; salvage; Ⓒ (*der Ernte*) gathering in

**Bergungs-**: **~arbeiten** *Pl.* rescue work *sing.;* **~kommando** *das* rescue team; **~schiff** *das* salvage vessel; **~versuch** *der* rescue attempt; (*Versuch, ein Schiff zu bergen*) salvage attempt

**Berg-**: **~volk** *das* mountain people; **~vorsprung** *der* spur; (*Absatz*) ledge; **~wacht** *die* mountain rescue service; **~wand** *die* mountain face; **~wanderung** *die* hike in the mountains; **~welt** *die* (*geh.*) mountain landscape

**Berg·werk** *das* mine; **im ~ arbeiten** work down the mine

**Bergwerks·gesellschaft** *die* mining company

**Berg-**: **~wesen** *das* (*Bergbau*) mining *no art.;* **~wiese** *die* mountain pasture

**Beriberi** /beri'be:ri/ *die;* ~ ▶474 (*Med.*) beriberi

**Bericht** /bə'rɪçt/ *der;* **~[e]s, ~e** report; **einen ~ von etw.** *od.* **über etw.** (*Akk.*) **geben** give a report on sth.; **[jmdm.] [von etw.] ~ erstatten** report *or* give a report [to sb.] [on sth.]

**berichten** *tr., itr. V.* report; **jmdm. etw. ~:** report sth. to sb.; **über etw.** (*Akk.*) *od.* **von etw. ~:** report on sth.; **es wird berichtet, dass ...** it is reported that ...; **es wird soeben berichtet, dass ...** reports are coming in that ...; **mir ist berichtet worden, dass ...** I have heard a report/reports that ...; **wie uns berichtet wurde** according to reports reaching us

**Bericht-**: **~erstatter** /-ɛɐ̯ʃtatɐ/ *der;* **~~s, ~~, ~erstatterin** *die;* **~~, ~~nen** reporter; (*Referent*) rapporteur; **unser ~erstatter aus Paris** our Paris correspondent; **~erstattung** *die* reporting *no indef. art.;* **zur ~erstattung zurückgerufen werden** ‹ambassador etc.› be recalled to make a report; **die ~erstattung durch Presse und Rundfunk über diese Ereignisse** press and radio coverage of these events; **~haus** *das* (*schweiz.*) information centre

**berichtigen** *tr. V.* correct

**Berichtigung** *die;* **~, ~en** correction; (*berichtigte Fassung*) corrected version; **der Lehrer gab uns die Arbeiten zur ~ zurück** the teacher gave the work back to us for the corrections to be done

**Berichts-**: **~heft** *das* (*Schulw.*) (*apprentice's/ trainee's*) record book; **~jahr** *das* (*bes. Wirtsch.*) year [covered by the report]

**beriechen** *unr. tr. V.* Ⓐ (*riechen an*) smell; sniff [at]; Ⓑ (*ugs.: vorsichtig Kontakt aufnehmen mit*) **sich [gegenseitig] ~:** size each other *or* one another up

**berieseln** *tr. V.* Ⓐ (*besprühen*) water ‹field› using an overhead sprinkling system; water ‹lawn› using a sprinkler; Ⓑ (*ugs. abwertend*) **mit Werbung/Musik berieselt werden** be subjected to a constant [unobtrusive] stream of advertisements/to constant background music

**Berieselung** *die* Ⓐ ⇒ **berieseln**: watering using an overhead sprinkling system/a sprinkler; Ⓑ (*ugs. abwertend*) **die ständige ~ mit Musik** subjection to constant background music

**Berieselungs·anlage** *die* sprinkler system

**beringen** *tr. V.* put a ring on; ring ‹bird›

**Bering·straße** /'be:rɪŋ-/ *die* (*Geogr.*) Bering Strait

b

**beringt** *Adj.* beringed ‹finger, hand›; ‹hand› covered with rings

**beritten** Ⓐ(*reitend*) mounted; on horseback *postpos.*; Ⓑ(*mit Pferden ausgerüstet*) mounted; **gut ~ sein** have good mounts *or* horses

**Berittene** *der/die; adj. Dekl.* rider; horseman/horsewoman

**Berlin** /bɛr'li:n/ *(das)*; **~s ▶ 700** Berlin

**Berliner**[1] **▶ 700** ❶ *indekl. Adj.* Berlin; **~ Weiße [mit Schuss]** *light, very fizzy beer flavoured with a dash of raspberry juice or woodruff.* ❷ *der;* **~s, ~:** Berliner; ⇒ *auch* **Kölner**

**Berliner**[2] *der;* **~s, ~** (**~** *Pfannkuchen*) [jam (*Brit.*) *or* (*Amer.*) jelly] doughnut

**Berlinerin** *die;* **~, ~nen** Berliner; ⇒ *auch* **-in**

**berlinerisch** *Adj.* (*ugs.*) ⇒ **berlinisch**

**berlinern** *itr. V.* (*ugs.*) speak [in] Berlin dialect

**berlinisch** *Adj.* **▶ 700** Berlin *attrib.*; **im Berlinischen** (*Sprachw.*) in Berlin dialect; **„Schrippe" ist ~:** 'Schrippe' is Berlin dialect

**Bermuda·inseln** /bɛr'mu:da-/ *Pl.* Bermuda *sing., no art.*; Bermudas

**Bermudas** *Pl.* Ⓐ Bermudas; Bermuda *sing., no art.*; Ⓑ ⇒ **Bermudashorts**

**Bermuda·shorts** *Pl.* Bermuda shorts

**Bern** /bɛrn/ *(das)*; **~s ▶ 700** Bern[e]

**Berner** *indekl.* **▶ 700** ❶ *Adj.* Bernese; **eine ~ Zeitung** a Bern[e] newspaper; **die ~ Konvention** the Berne Convention; **das ~ Oberland** the Bernese Oberland. ❷ *der;* **~s, ~:** Bernese

**Bernerin** *die;* **~, ~nen** Bernese

**Bernhardiner** /bɛrnhar'di:nɐ/ *der;* **~s, ~:** St. Bernard [dog]

**Bern·stein** /'bɛrn-/ *der* amber

**bernstein·farben** *Adj.* amber[-coloured]

**Berserker** /bɛr'zɛrkɐ/ *der;* **~s, ~** Ⓐ(*hist.*) berserker; berserk; Ⓑ **wie ein ~ arbeiten** work like mad (*coll.*); **wie ein ~ auf jmdn. einschlagen** go berserk and attack sb.

**bersten** /'bɛrstn̩/ *unr. itr. V.; mit sein* (*geh.*) ‹ice› break *or* crack up; ‹glass› shatter [into pieces]; ‹wall› crack up; **[bis] zum B~ voll** *od.* **gefüllt sein** be full to bursting point; **vor Neugier/Ungeduld/Freude/Zorn ~** (*fig.*) be bursting with curiosity/impatience/joy/rage

**berüchtigt** /bə'rʏçtɪçt/ *Adj.* notorious (**wegen** for); (*verrufen*) disreputable; **als Raufbold ~ sein** be a notorious ruffian

**berücken** *tr. V.* (*geh.*) captivate; charm; enchant; **ein ~der Anblick** an enchanting *or* a bewitching sight

**berücksichtigen** /bə'rʏkzɪçtɪgn̩/ *tr. V.* Ⓐ(*einbeziehen*) take into account *or* consideration; **jmds. Alter ~:** make allowances for sb.'s age; **wir müssen auch ~, dass etwa 7% der Arbeitszeit durch Krankheit entfallen** we also have to allow for the fact that about 7% of working time is lost through illness; Ⓑ(*beachten*) consider ‹applicant, application, suggestion›

**Berücksichtigung** *die;* **~** Ⓐ(*das Einbeziehen*) **bei ~ aller Umstände** taking all the circumstances into account; **in** *od.* **unter ~ der Vor- und Nachteile** taking account of all the advantages and disadvantages; Ⓑ(*Beachtung*) consideration; **eine ~ Ihres Auftrags ist nicht möglich** we cannot consider your application

**Beruf** *der;* **~[e]s, ~e ▶ 159** Ⓐ occupation; (*akademischer, wissenschaftlicher, medizinischer* **~**) profession; (*handwerklicher* **~**) trade; (*Stellung*) job; (*Laufbahn*) career; **was sind Sie von ~?** what do you do for a living?; what is your occupation?; **er ist von ~ Bäcker/Lehrer** *od.* **Bäcker/Lehrer von ~:** he's a baker by trade/a teacher by profession; **20 Jahre im ~ stehen** have been in the profession/trade for 20 years; **von ~s wegen** because of one's job; **den ~ verfehlt haben** (*scherzh.*) have missed one's vocation; ⇒ *auch* **ergreifen, frei**; Ⓑ(*geh. veralt.*) ⇒ **Berufung B**

**berufen**[1] ❶ *unr. tr. V.* Ⓐ(*einsetzen*) appoint; **jmdn. auf einen Lehrstuhl/in ein Amt ~:** appoint sb. to a chair/an office; Ⓑ(*ugs.: beschreien*) **berufe es nicht!** don't speak too soon!; **ich will es nicht ~, aber bisher hat die Sache immer geklappt** I don't want to tempt fate *or* providence, but until now it's worked every time; Ⓒ(*veralt.: zusammenrufen*) call, summon ‹person› (**zu** to); call a meeting of ‹council, cabinet, etc.›.
❷ *unr. refl. V.* **sich auf etw.** (*Akk.*) **~:** refer to sth.; quote *or* cite sth.; **sich auf jmdn. als Zeugen ~:** appeal to sb. as a witness; **wenn Sie sich vorstellen, können Sie sich auf mich ~:** when you introduce yourself, you can mention my name

**berufen**[2] *Adj.* Ⓐ competent; **aus ~em Munde** from somebody *or* one competent *or* qualified to speak; Ⓑ(*prädestiniert*) **sich dazu ~ fühlen, etw. zu tun** feel called to do sth.; feel one has a mission to do sth.; **sich zu großen Taten ~ fühlen** feel called to great things; **zum Dichter/zu Höherem ~ sein** have a vocation as a poet/be destined for greater things

**beruflich** ❶ *Adj.* occupational, vocational ‹training etc.›; (*bei akademischen Berufen*) professional ‹training etc.›; **seine ~e Tätigkeit** his occupation; **er hat ~e Probleme** he has problems at work *or* in his job; **aus ~en Gründen** because of one's job; (*bei akademischen Berufen*) for professional reasons. ❷ *adv.* **meine Reise war ~ bedingt** my trip was business-related; **~ erfolgreich sein** be successful in one's career; **~ viel unterwegs sein** be away a lot on business; **sich ~ weiterbilden** undertake further job training; **~ verhindert sein** be detained by one's work

**berufs-, Berufs-: ~armee** *die* ⇒ **~heer**; **~aus·bildung** *die* occupational *or* vocational training; (*als Lehrer, Wissenschaftler, Arzt*) professional training; **eine [solide] ~ausbildung [als etw.] bekommen** receive [a thorough] training [as sth.]; **~aussichten** *Pl.* job prospects (*in a particular profession etc.*); **~beamte** *der* ≈ established civil servant; ⇒ *auch* **Beamte**; **~beamtentum** *das* civil service with life-long job security; **~beamtin** *die* ⇒ **~beamte**; **~bedingt** *Adj.* occupational ‹disease›; ‹expenses, difficulties› connected with one's job; **~berater** *der,* **~beraterin** *die* **▶ 159** vocational adviser; **~beratung** *die* vocational guidance; **~bezeichnung** *die* job title; **~bezogen** *Adj.* vocationally orientated; **~bild** *das* outline of a/the profession/trade as a career; **~bildend** *Adj.* **~bildende Schule** vocational training school; **~boxer** *der,* **~boxerin** *die* **▶ 159** professional boxer; **~erfahren** *Adj.* [professionally] experienced; with considerable [professional] experience *postpos., not pred.*; **~erfahrung** *die* [professional] experience; **~ethos** *das* (*geh.*) professional code of ethics; **~fach·schule** *die* vocational college (*providing full-time vocational training*); **~fahrer** *der,* **~fahrerin** *die* [professional] driver; **~feuerwehr** *die* [professional] fire service; **~fremd** *Adj.* ‹task, work, job› unconnected with the profession/trade for which one has been trained; **„~fremde werden eingearbeitet"** '[on-the-job] training will be given where necessary'; **~geheimnis** *das* professional secret; (*Schweigepflicht*) professional secrecy; **~genossenschaft** *die: professional/trade association having liability for industrial safety and insurance;* **~gruppe** *die* occupational group; **~heer** *das* regular *or* professional army; **~kleidung** *die* [prescribed] work[ing] clothes *pl.*; **~krankheit** *die* occupational disease; **~leben** *das* working life; **im ~leben stehen** be working; **ins ~leben treten** start one's working life; start in one's first job; **~mäßig** ❶ *Adj.* professional; ❷ *adv.* professionally; **~offizier** *der,* **~offizierin** *die* regular officer; **~politiker** *der,* **~politikerin** *die* **▶ 159** professional politician; **~richter** *der,* **~richterin** *die* **▶ 159** full-time salaried judge; **~risiko** *das* occupational risk; **~schule** *die* vocational school; **~schüler** *der,* **~schülerin** *die* student at a vocational school; **~soldat** *der,* **~soldatin** *die* **▶ 159** regular *or* professional soldier; **~sportler** *der,* **~sportlerin** *die* professional sportsman; **~stand** *der* profession; (*Gewerbe*) trade; **~ständisch** *Adj.* professional; **~tätig** *Adj.* working *attrib.*; **es gibt mehr ~tätige Männer als Frauen** more men than women have a job *or* are in paid employment; **[halbtags] ~tätig sein** work [part-time]; **~tätige** *der/die; adj. Dekl.* working person; **~tätige** *Pl.* working people; **~unfähigkeit** *die* incapacity (*to follow one's profession/trade*); **~verband** *der* professional/trade association; **~verbot** *das: debarment from practising a particular profession or trade;* (*für den öffentlichen Dienst*) *official debarment, on political grounds, from all civil service professions;* **~verbrecher** *der,* **~verbrecherin** *die* professional criminal; **~verkehr** *der* rush hour traffic; **~wahl** *die* choice of career; **~wechsel** *der* change of career; **~wunsch** *der* preferred choice of career; **~zweig** *der* branch of the profession/trade

**Berufung** *die;* **~, ~en** Ⓐ(*für ein Amt*) offer of an appointment (**auf, in, an** + *Akk.* to); **seit seiner ~ nach ...** since he took up the appointment in ...; Ⓑ(*innerer Auftrag*) vocation; **die ~ zum Künstler in sich** (*Dat.*) **verspüren** feel one has a vocation as an artist; Ⓒ(*das Sichberufen*) **unter ~** (*Dat.*) **auf jmdn./etw.** referring *or* with reference to sb./sth.; Ⓓ(*Rechtsw.: Einspruch*) appeal; **~ einlegen** lodge an appeal; appeal; **in die ~ gehen** appeal; Ⓔ(*veralt.: Einberufung*) summoning

**Berufungs-: ~frist** *die* (*Rechtsw.*) period within which an appeal must be lodged; period allowed for an appeal; **~instanz** *die* (*Rechtsw.*) court of appeal; **~verfahren** *das* (*Rechtsw.*) appeal proceedings *pl.*

**beruhen** *itr. V.* **auf etw.** (*Dat.*) **~:** be based on sth.; **etw. auf sich** (*Dat.*) **~ lassen** let sth. rest; ⇒ *auch* **Gegenseitigkeit**

**beruhigen** /bə'ru:ɪgn̩/ ❶ *tr. V.* calm [down]; quieten, pacify ‹child, baby›; (*trösten*) soothe; (*die Befürchtung nehmen*) reassure; salve, soothe ‹conscience›; **die Nerven/den Magen ~:** calm one's nerves/settle the stomach; **beruhigt schlafen/nach Hause gehen können** be able to sleep/go home with one's mind set at ease.
❷ *refl. V.* ‹person› calm down; ‹wind› drop, die down; ‹sea› become calm; ‹storm› abate, die down; ‹struggle, traffic› lessen; ‹rush of people› subside; ‹prices, stock exchange, stomach› settle down; **die Lage beruhigt sich** the situation is becoming more stable; **meine Nerven haben sich beruhigt** my nerves have steadied

**Beruhigung** *die;* **~** Ⓐ ⇒ **beruhigen 1**: calming [down]; quietening; pacifying; soothing; salving; reassurance; **jmdm. etw. zur ~ geben** give sb. sth. to calm him/her [down]; Ⓑ(*das Ruhigwerden*); **eine ~ des Wetters ist vorauszusehen** the weather can be expected to become more settled; **zu Ihrer ~ kann ich sagen, ...** you'll be reassured to know that ...; **jmdm. ein Gefühl der ~ geben** reassure sb.; **eine ~ der politischen Lage ist nicht zu erwarten** we should not expect that the political situation will become more stable

**Beruhigungs-: ~mittel** *das* sedative; tranquillizer; **~pille** *die* sedative [pill]; tranquillizer; (*fig.*) sop; **~spritze** *die* sedative injection; **~zelle** *die* cooling-off cell; holding cell; **~zigarette** *die* calming cigarette; cigarette to calm one's nerves

**berühmt** /bə'ry:mt/ *Adj.* famous; **durch diesen Roman wurde er ~:** the novel made him famous; **wegen** *od.* **für etw. ~ sein** be famous for sth.; **das ist nicht gerade ~** (*ugs. iron.*) it's nothing to write home about (*coll.*) *or* no big deal (*coll.*)

**berühmt-berüchtigt** *Adj.* notorious

**Berühmtheit** *die;* **~, ~en** Ⓐ(*Ruhm*) fame; **~ erlangen/gewinnen** become famous/win fame; **zu trauriger ~ gelangen** become notorious; Ⓑ(*Mensch*) celebrity

*old spelling (see note on page 1707)

b

## Berufe

***Was machen Sie beruflich?, Was sind Sie von Beruf?***
= What's your job?, What do you do for a living?

***In welcher Branche sind Sie tätig?***
= What's your field [of work]?, What's your line of business?

***Ich arbeite bei einer Bank/in einer Buchhandlung/bei einem Verlag***
= I work in *od.* for a bank/in a bookshop/at a publisher's *od.* for a publisher

***Er ist in der Textilindustrie/Versicherungsbranche tätig***
= He is in textiles/insurance

***Ich arbeite bei einem kleinen Unternehmen/einem großen Konzern***
= I am with *od.* work for a small company *od.* firm/a large combine *od.* group

***Sie besitzt/leitet einen kleinen Betrieb***
= She owns/runs a small business

***Mein Mann ist bei der gleichen Firma angestellt***
= My husband works for *od.* is employed by the same firm

***Sie arbeitet ganztags*** od. ***hat eine Ganztagsstelle***
= She works full time *od.* has a full-time job

***Er arbeitet halbtags*** od. ***hat eine Halbtagsstelle/Teilzeitstelle***
= He works part time *od.* has a part-time job

***Ich arbeite freiberuflich/bin selbstständig***
= I work freelance/am self-employed

Beachten Sie, dass bei der Angabe des Berufs im Englischen der unbestimmte Artikel **a/an** verwendet wird. Auch wird mit der Berufsbezeichnung keine Aussage über das Geschlecht gemacht; es gibt zwar ein paar Ausnahmen (**authoress, manageress**), diese Formen werden aber meist als sexistisch vermieden:

***Er ist [von Beruf] Bäcker***
= He's a baker [by trade]

***Sie ist Lehrerin [von Beruf]***
= She's a teacher [by profession]

***Michael will Systemanalytiker werden***
= Michael wants to be a systems analyst

***Bettina ist als Journalistin tätig***
= Bettina works as a journalist

Wenn man ausdrücklich von einer Frau in einem bestimmten Beruf spricht, stellt man der Berufsbezeichnung das Wort **woman** oder **female** voran:

***Sie möchte lieber von einer Ärztin behandelt werden***
= She prefers to be treated by a woman doctor

***Es gibt mehr und mehr Anwältinnen***
= There are more and more women *od.* female lawyers

Aber:

***Sie ist Ärztin/Anwältin***
= She's a doctor/lawyer

### Stellensuche

***Ich suche eine Stelle als Sekretärin***
= I am looking for a job as a secretary

***Bei den Stellenanzeigen habe ich nichts Geeignetes gefunden***
= I didn't find anything suitable in the situations vacant

***Ich will mich um diese Stelle bewerben***
= I want to apply for this job

***Der Bewerbung sind ein Lebenslauf und ein Foto beizulegen***
= A CV and a photograph should be sent with the application

***Können Sie am 24. März zu einem Vorstellungsgespräch kommen?***
= Could you come for an interview on March 24th?

***Wann wäre Ihr frühestmöglicher Einstellungstermin?***
= What is the earliest [date] you could start?

**berühren** *tr. V.* Ⓐ (*anrühren*) touch; **sich** *od.* (*geh.*) **einander ~:** touch; **„Bitte Waren nicht ~!"** 'please do not touch the merchandise'; Ⓑ (*kurz erwähnen*) touch on ‹topic, issue, question›; Ⓒ (*beeindrucken*) affect; **das berührte ihn seltsam/schmerzlich** he was strangely affected/painfully moved by it; **wir fühlten uns davon unangenehm/peinlich berührt** it made an unpleasant impression on us/made us feel embarrassed; **das berührt mich [überhaupt] nicht** it's a matter of [complete] indifference to me

**Berührung** *die;* **~, ~en** Ⓐ (*das Berühren*) touch; **mit etw. in ~** (*Akk.*) **kommen** come into contact with sth.; **jede ~ mit jmdm. vermeiden** avoid all physical contact with sb.; **bei der geringsten ~:** at the slightest touch; Ⓑ (*Kontakt*) contact; **mit jmdm./etw. in ~** (*Akk.*) **kommen** come into contact with sb./sth.; **jmdn. in ~** (*Akk.*) **mit jmdm./etw. bringen** bring sb. into contact with sb./sth.; Ⓒ (*Erwähnung*) mention

**berührungs-, Berührungs-: ~angst** *die* (*Psych.*) fear of contact; haptephobia (*Psych.*); **~los** (*Physik, Technik*) ❶ *Adj.* contactless; non-contact; ❷ *adv.* without direct contact; **~punkt** *der* Ⓐ (*Math.*) point of contact *or* tangency; Ⓑ (*Gemeinsamkeit*) point of contact; **politische ~punkte mit jmdm. besitzen** have the same views as sb. on a number of political issues

**Beryll** /be'rʏl/ *der;* **~s, ~e** (*Mineral.*) beryl

**Beryllium** /be'rʏli̯ʊm/ *das;* **~s** (*Chemie*) beryllium

**besabbern** *tr. V.* (*salopp*) slobber [on *or* over]

**besäen** *tr. V.* sow

**besagen** *tr. V.* say; (*bedeuten*) mean; **das besagt noch gar nichts/sehr viel** that doesn't mean anything/means a great deal

**besagt** *Adj.* (*Amtsspr.*) aforementioned

**besamen** /bə'za:mən/ *tr. V.* fertilize; (*künstlich*) inseminate

**besammeln** *refl. V.* (*schweiz.*) ⇒ **versammeln**

**Besammlung** *die;* **~, ~en** (*schweiz.*) ⇒ **Versammlung**

**Besamung** *die;* **~, ~en** fertilization; (*künstlich*) insemination

**Besan** /be'za:n/ *der;* **~s, ~e** Ⓐ (*Segel*) mizzen[sail]; Ⓑ (*~mast*) mizzenmast

**besänftigen** /bə'zɛnftɪgn̩/ ❶ *tr. V.* calm [down]; pacify; calm, soothe ‹temper›. ❷ *refl. V.* calm down; ‹sea› become calm

**Besänftigung** *die;* **~:** calming [down]; pacifying; (*von jmds. Zorn*) calming; soothing

**Besan·mast** *der* mizzenmast

**besät** /bə'zɛ:t/ *Adj.* sown (**mit** with); (*fig.*) covered (**mit, von** with); **mit Blütenblättern/Sternen ~:** strewn with petals/studded with stars

**Besatz** *der* Ⓐ (*Mode: Borte*) trimming *no indef. art.*; Ⓑ (*Jagdw., Landw., Fischereiw.*) stock

**Besatzer** /bə'zatsɐ/ *der;* **~s, ~, Besatzerin** *die;* **~, ~nen** member of the occupying forces; **die Besatzer** the occupying forces

**Besatzung** *die* Ⓐ (*Mannschaft*) crew; Ⓑ (*Milit.: Verteidigungstruppe*) garrison; Ⓒ (*Milit.: Okkupationstruppen*) occupying troops *pl. or* forces *pl.*

**Besatzungs-: ~armee** *die* occupying army; army of occupation; **~kind** *das: child of a [coloured] member of the occupying forces and a local woman;* **~macht** *die* occupying power; **~truppen** *Pl.* occupying troops *or* forces; **~zone** *die* occupied zone

**besaufen** *unr. refl. V.* (*salopp*) get boozed up (*Brit. sl.*) *or* canned (*Brit. sl.*) *or* bombed (*Amer. sl.*); ⇒ *auch* **sinnlos** 2 C

**Besäufnis** /bə'zɔyfnɪs/ *die;* **~, ~se** *od. das;* **~ses, ~se** (*salopp*) booze-up (*Brit. sl.*); blast (*Amer. sl.*)

**besäuseln** *refl. V.* (*ugs.*) get merry (*Brit. coll.*) *or* tipsy; **besäuselt** merry (*coll.*); tipsy

**beschädigen** *tr. V.* damage

**Beschädigte** *der/die; adj. Dekl.* (*veralt.*) disabled person

**Beschädigung** *die* Ⓐ (*das Beschädigen*) damaging; Ⓑ (*Schaden*) damage; **zahlreiche/mehrere ~en** a lot of/quite a lot of damage *sing.*

**beschaffbar** *Adj.* obtainable; **schwer/leicht ~:** difficult/easy to obtain

**beschaffen**[1] *tr. V.* obtain; get; get ‹job›; **ein Quartier ~:** find accommodation; **jmdm. etw. ~:** obtain/get sb. sth. *or* sth. for sb.; **sich** (*Dat.*) **Geld/die Genehmigung ~:** get [hold of] money/get *or* obtain the permit/licence

**beschaffen**[2] *Adj.* **so ~ sein, dass ...** ‹goods, materials› be made in such a way that ...; ‹substance› be such that ...

**Beschaffenheit** *die;* **~:** composition; (*von Menschen*) make-up; **raue/glatte ~:** roughness/smoothness

**Beschaffung** *die* ⇒ **beschaffen**[1]: obtaining; getting; finding

**Beschaffungs-: ~amt** *das* (*Milit.*) ≈ Procurement Executive (*Brit.*) *or* (*Amer.*) Office; **~kosten** *Pl.* procurement cost *sing.; cost sing.* of acquisition; **~kriminalität** *die* crime in the pursuit of drug acquisition

**beschäftigen** /bə'ʃɛftɪgn̩/ ❶ *refl. V.* **sich mit etw. ~:** occupy *or* busy oneself with sth.; **sich viel mit Musik/den Kindern ~:** devote a great deal of one's time to music/the children; **sich mit den Schriften Hegels ~:** be engaged in a study of the writings of

Hegel; **sich mit einem Fall ~:** deal with a case; **mit etw. beschäftigt sein** be [busy] working on sth.; **sehr beschäftigt sein** be very busy.
❷ *tr. V.* Ⓐ (*geistig in Anspruch nehmen*) **jmdn. ~:** be on sb.'s mind; preoccupy sb.; **was beschäftigt dich so?** what's on your mind?; **Märchen ~ die Fantasie der Kinder** fairy stories engage children's imaginations; Ⓑ (*angestellt haben*) employ ‹workers, staff›; **bei einer Firma beschäftigt sein** work for a firm; Ⓒ (*zu tun geben*) occupy; **jmdn. mit etw. ~:** give sb. sth. to occupy him/her; **du musst die Kinder ~:** you must keep the children occupied

**Beschäftigte** *der/die; adj. Dekl.* employee; **die Fabrik/das Kaufhaus hat 500 ~:** the factory has a workforce/the department store has a staff of 500

**Beschäftigung** *die; ~, ~en* Ⓐ (*Tätigkeit*) activity; occupation; **bei dieser ~ solltest du ihn nicht stören** you shouldn't disturb him while he's occupied with that; **einer ~ nachgehen** pursue an activity; Ⓑ (*berufliche Tätigkeit*) job; **seiner ~ nachgehen** go about one's business; **er geht wieder seiner ~ nach** he's now back at work; **ohne ~ sein** not be working; (*unfreiwillig*) be unemployed; Ⓒ (*mit einer Frage, einem Problem*) consideration (**mit** of); (*Untersuchung, Studium*) study (**mit** of); Ⓓ (*das Angestelltwerden*) employment; Ⓔ (*das Beschäftigtsein*) **die ~ in diesem Betrieb/im Staatsdienst** working for this firm/in the Civil Service

**beschäftigungs-, Beschäftigungs-:** **~grad** *der* (*Wirtsch.*) level of employment; **~los** *Adj.* Ⓐ (*untätig*) **~los sein** have nothing to do; Ⓑ (*ohne Arbeit*) **~los sein** not be working; (*unfreiwillig*) be unemployed; **~therapie** *die* (*Med.*) occupational therapy

**beschälen** *tr. V.* cover, serve ‹mare›

**Beschäler** *der; ~s, ~:* breeding stallion; stud horse

**beschallen** *tr. V.* Ⓐ fill with sound; Ⓑ (*Med.*) treat with ultrasonic waves *or* ultrasound

**beschämen** *tr. V.* shame; **jmdn. durch seine Großmütigkeit ~:** make sb. ashamed by one's generosity

**beschämend** ❶ *Adj.* Ⓐ (*schändlich*) shameful; Ⓑ (*demütigend*) humiliating; **für jmdn. ~ sein** be humiliating for sb.; bring humiliation upon sb. ❷ *adv.* shamefully

**beschämt** *Adj.* ashamed; abashed; **ein ~es Gesicht** a shamefaced expression; **sich ~ fühlen** be ashamed *or* abashed

**Beschämung** *die; ~:* shame; **zu meiner ~ muss ich gestehen, dass ...** to my shame I must confess that ...

**beschatten** *tr. V.* Ⓐ (*geh.*) shade; (*fig.*) overshadow, cast a cloud over ‹event›; cloud ‹face›; Ⓑ (*heimlich überwachen*) shadow; **jmdn. ~ lassen** have sb. shadowed; Ⓒ (*Fußball, Hockey*) mark closely

**Beschatter** *der; ~s, ~,* **Beschatterin** *die; ~, ~nen* shadow

**Beschattung** *die; ~* (*eines Verdächtigen*) shadowing

**Beschau** *die* inspection

**beschauen** *tr. V.* (*bes. md.*) ⇒ **betrachten**

**Beschauer** *der; ~s, ~,* **Beschauerin** *die; ~, ~nen* viewer

**beschaulich** /bəˈʃaulɪç/ ❶ *Adj.* Ⓐ (*behaglich*) peaceful, tranquil ‹life, manner, etc.›; meditative, contemplative ‹person, character›; Ⓑ (*kath. Rel.*) **~e Orden** contemplative orders. ❷ *adv.* peacefully; tranquilly

**Beschaulichkeit** *die; ~:* peacefulness; tranquillity

**Bescheid** /bəˈʃait/ *der; ~[e]s, ~e* Ⓐ (*Auskunft*) information; (*Antwort*) answer; reply; **jmdm. ~ geben** *od.* **sagen[, ob ...]** let sb. know or tell sb. [whether ...]; **sage bitte im Restaurant ~, dass ...** please let the restaurant know *or* let them know in the restaurant that ...; **jmdm. ~ sagen** (*ugs.: sich beschweren*) give sb. a piece of one's mind (*coll.*); **[über etw.** (*Akk.*)**] ~ wissen** know [about sth.]; **in einer Stadt/mit Autos ~ wissen** know one's way around a town/know about cars; **jmdm. ~ stoßen** (*ugs.*) give sb. a dressing-down (*coll.*); **Entschuldigung, wissen Sie hier ~?** excuse me, do you know your way around here?; Ⓑ (*Entscheidung*) decision; **ein abschlägiger/günstiger ~:** a refusal/a positive reply

**bescheiden**[1] ❶ *unr. tr. V.* Ⓐ (*Amtsspr.: Mitteilung machen an*) **jmdn./etw. abschlägig ~:** turn sb./sth. down; refuse sb./sth.; **jmdn. ~[, dass ...]** inform *or* notify sb. [that ...]; Ⓑ (*geh.: zuteil werden lassen*) **jmdm. etw. ~:** grant sb. sth.; **es war ihm nicht beschieden, den Erfolg seines Romans zu erleben** it was not granted to him to live to see the success of his novel. ❷ *unr. refl. V.* (*geh.*) be content; **man muss sich ~ können** one has to be able to make do with less *or* moderate one's needs

**bescheiden**[2] ❶ *Adj.* Ⓐ (*unaufdringlich*) modest; modest, unassuming ‹person, behaviour›; Ⓑ (*einfach*) modest; simple ‹meal›; **darf ich die ~e Frage stellen, wie ...?** (*auch iron.*) may I venture to ask how ...?; **aus ~en Anfängen** from modest *or* humble beginnings; **in ~en Verhältnissen aufwachsen** grow up in humble circumstances; Ⓒ (*dürftig*) modest ‹salary, results, pension, etc.›; Ⓓ (*ugs. verhüll.: sehr schlecht*) lousy (*coll.*); bloody awful (*Brit. coll.*).
❷ *adv.* modestly; **darf ich mal ganz ~ anfragen, wie ...?** (*auch iron.*) may I venture to ask how ...?

**Bescheidenheit** *die; ~:* modesty; **keine falsche ~!** don't be shy!; **~ ist eine Zier, doch weiter kommt man ohne ihr** (*scherzh.*) modesty is a virtue, but it doesn't get you very far; **aus falscher ~:** out of false modesty

**Bescheidung** *die* (*geh.*) moderation in one's needs

**bescheinen** *unr. tr. V.* shine [up]on; **vom Mond/von der Sonne beschienen** moonlit/sunlit

**bescheinigen** /bəˈʃainɪɡn̩/ *tr. V.* **etw. ~:** confirm sth. in writing; **den Tod [auf dem Totenschein] ~:** sign the death certificate; **jmdm. den Empfang des Geldes ~:** acknowledge receipt of the money; (*durch Quittung*) give sb. a receipt for the money; **sich** (*Dat.*) **~ lassen, dass man arbeitsunfähig ist/die Rechnung bezahlt hat** get oneself certified as unfit for work/get a receipt for the bill; **du wirst deinen Fehler noch bereuen, das kann ich dir ~** (*fig.*) you'll regret your mistake, I can guarantee you that

**Bescheinigung** *die; ~, ~en* Ⓐ (*Schriftstück*) written confirmation *no indef. art.*; (*Schein*) certificate; (*Quittung*) receipt; **eine ~ des Arztes** a doctor's certificate; a certificate from the doctor; a medical certificate; Ⓑ (*das Bescheinigen*) confirmation in writing

**bescheißen** *unr. tr. V.* (*derb*) **jmdn. ~:** rip sb. off (*coll.*); screw sb. (*coarse*); **jmdn. um etw. ~:** do sb. out of sth. (*coll.*)

**beschenken** *tr. V.* **jmdn. ~:** give sb. a present/presents; **jmdn. reich ~:** shower sb. with presents; **jmdn. mit etw. ~:** give sb. sth. as a present; **sich [gegenseitig] ~:** give each other presents

**bescheren** ❶ *tr. V.* Ⓐ (*schenken*) **jmdn. [mit etw.] ~:** give sb. [sth. as] a Christmas present/Christmas presents; **jmdm. etw. ~:** give sb. sth. for Christmas; Ⓑ (*zuteil werden lassen*) **ihnen waren keine Kinder beschert** they were not blessed with children; **ich bin gespannt, was uns dieser Tag ~ wird** I wonder what today will bring; **ihm waren noch viele Jahre des Glücks beschert** he was granted many more happy years. ❷ *itr. V.* **nach dem Abendessen wird beschert** the presents are given out after supper

**Bescherung** *die; ~, ~en* Ⓐ (*zu Weihnachten*) giving out of the Christmas presents; **die Kinder konnten die ~ kaum erwarten** the children could hardly wait for the presents to be given out; Ⓑ (*ugs. iron.: unangenehme Überraschung*) **das ist ja eine schöne ~:** this is a pretty kettle of fish; **jetzt haben wir die ~:** that's done it, I told you so; **nun guck dir die ~ an** just look at this mess

**bescheuert** *Adj.* (*salopp*) Ⓐ (*verrückt*) barmy (*Brit. coll.*); nuts (*coll.*); Ⓑ (*unangenehm*) stupid ‹task, party, etc.›; **jmdn./etw. ~ finden** find sb./sth. a real pain [in the neck] (*coll.*)

**beschichten** *tr. V.* (*Technik*) coat; **mit Kunststoff beschichtet** plastic-coated

**Beschichtung** *die; ~, ~en* (*Technik*) coating

**beschicken** *tr. V.* Ⓐ supply ‹market, shop›; send representatives to ‹meeting, congress, etc.›; send exhibits to ‹art exhibition›; Ⓑ (*Technik: füllen*) charge ‹furnace›

**beschickert** /bəˈʃɪkɐt/ *Adj.* (*ugs.: angetrunken*) tipsy; merry (*Brit. coll.*)

**Beschickung** *die; ~, ~en* (*Technik: eines Hochofens*) (*das Beschicken*) charging; (*Füllung*) charge

**beschießen** *unr. tr. V.* Ⓐ fire *or* shoot at; (*mit Artillerie*) bombard; Ⓑ (*Kernphysik*) bombard

**Beschießung** *die; ~, ~en* ⇒ **beschießen**: Ⓐ **die ~ der feindlichen Flugzeuge** firing *or* shooting at the enemy aircraft; **hält diese ~ weiter an, ...** if this firing *or* shooting/bombardment continues ...; Ⓑ **die ~ mit Neutronen/Alphateilchen** bombardment with neutrons/alpha particles

**beschildern** *tr. V.* label ‹jar etc.›; put up direction signs along ‹road, path›

**Beschilderung** *die* Ⓐ labelling; **die ~ der Straße/des Wanderwegs** putting up direction signs along the road/footpath; Ⓑ (*Schilder*) direction signs

**beschimpfen** *tr. V.* abuse; swear at; **ich lasse mich von Ihnen nicht ~!** I won't stand for being sworn at *or* abused by you

**Beschimpfung** *die; ~, ~en* Ⓐ (*das Beschimpfen*) abuse *no indef. art.*; **die öffentliche ~ des Staatsoberhaupts** publicly insulting the head of state; Ⓑ (*Äußerung*) insult; **~en** abuse *sing.*; insults

**beschirmen** *tr. V.* (*geh.*) Ⓐ (*beschützen*) protect (**vor** + *Dat.* from); Ⓑ (*vor Licht*) shade

**beschirmt** *Adj.* (*scherzh.*) **~ sein** have an *or* one's umbrella [with one]

**Beschiss, *Beschiß** *der;* **Beschisses** (*derb*) rip-off (*coll.*); **das ist doch alles ~!** it's a rip-off (*coll.*) *or* swindle

**beschissen** /bəˈʃɪsn̩/ (*derb*) ❶ *Adj.* lousy (*coll.*); shitty (*coarse*). ❷ *adv.* ‹behave› in a bloody awful manner (*Brit. coll.*), shittily (*coarse*); **ihm geht es ~:** he's having a lousy *or* (*Brit.*) bloody awful time of it (*sl.*)

**beschlafen** *unr. tr. V.* (*ugs.*) Ⓐ (*den Beischlaf ausüben mit*) lay (*sl.*); sleep with; Ⓑ (*überdenken*) sleep on

**Beschlag** *der* Ⓐ (*an Truhen*) metal fitting; (*an Fenstern, Türen, Möbelstücken, Sätteln*) metal mount; (*Scharnier*) hinge; (*Schließe*) clasp; Ⓑ *in* **jmdn./etw. mit ~ belegen** *od.* **in ~ nehmen, jmdn./etw. in ~ halten** monopolize sb./sth.; Ⓒ (*Hufeisen*) horseshoe

**beschlagen**[1] ❶ *unr. tr. V.* shoe ‹horse›; **ein Fass mit Reifen ~:** hoop a barrel; **Schuhsohlen mit Nägeln ~:** stud the soles of shoes with [hob]nails. ❷ *unr. itr. V.*; *mit sein* ‹window› mist up (*Brit.*), fog up (*Amer.*); (*durch Dampf*) steam up; **~e Scheiben** misted-up/fogged-up/steamed-up windows. ❸ *unr. refl. V.* mist up (*Brit.*); fog up (*Amer.*); (*durch Dampf*) steam up

**beschlagen**[2] *Adj.* knowledgeable; **in etw.** (*Dat.*) **[gut] ~ sein** be knowledgeable about sth.; **auf einem Gebiet ~ sein** be knowledgeable about *or* well-versed in a subject

**Beschlagenheit** *die; ~:* thorough *or* sound knowledge (**auf** + *Dat.* of)

*old spelling (see note on page 1707)

**Beschlag·nahme** /-na:mə/ *die;* ~, ~**n** seizure; confiscation

**beschlagnahmen** *tr. V.* A (*konfiszieren*) seize; confiscate; B (*scherzh.: in Anspruch nehmen*) **jmdn.** ~: monopolize sb.

**Beschlagnahmung** *die;* ~, ~**en** ⇒ **Beschlagnahme**

**beschleichen** *unr. tr. V.* A (*heranschleichen an*) creep up on *or* to; steal up to; ‹hunter› stalk ‹game, prey›; B (*geh.: überkommen*) creep over

**beschleunigen** /bəˈʃlɔynɪgn̩/ ❶ *tr. V.* speed up; increase ‹speed›; quicken ‹pace, step[s], pulse›; accelerate ‹atomic particle›; speed up, expedite ‹work, delivery›; hasten ‹departure, collapse›; accelerate, speed up, expedite ‹process›; **etw. beschleunigt erledigen** deal with sth. as a matter of priority. ❷ *refl. V.* ‹speed, heart rate› increase; ‹pulse› quicken. ❸ *itr. V.* ‹car› accelerate; ‹engine› speed up

**Beschleuniger** *der;* ~**s**, ~ (*Kernphysik*) accelerator

**Beschleunigung** *die;* ~, ~**en** A ⇒ **beschleunigen 1**: speeding up; increasing; quickening; acceleration; expedition; hastening; **eine ~ der Arbeit erreichen** speed up the work; **eine weitere ~ des Tempos** a further increase in speed; B (*ugs.: ~svermögen*) acceleration; **eine gute ~ haben** have good acceleration; C (*Physik*) acceleration

**Beschleunigungs-:** ~**anlage** *die* ⇒ **Beschleuniger**; ~**vermögen** *das* (*Technik*) (*eines Kfz*) acceleration; (*eines Motors*) throttle response; ~**wert** *der* (*Technik*) acceleration figure

**beschließen** ❶ *unr. tr. V.* A (*entscheiden*) ~, **etw. zu tun** decide *or* resolve to do sth.; **das ist beschlossene Sache** it's settled; B (*einen Mehrheitsbeschluss fassen über*) pass ‹law›; ~, **etw. zu tun** resolve to do sth.; C (*beenden*) end; end, conclude ‹lecture›; end, close ‹letter›; **seine Tage ~** (*geh.*) end one's days. ❷ *unr. itr. V.* **über etw.** (*Akk.*) ~: decide concerning sth.

**beschlossen** /bəˈʃlɔsn̩/ ❶ *2. Part. v.* **beschließen.** ❷ *in* **in etw.** (*Dat.*) ~ **sein** *od.* **liegen** (*geh.*) be summed up in sth.

**Beschluss**, ***Beschluß** *der* A (*Entscheidung*) decision; (*gemeinsam festgelegt*) resolution; **einen ~ fassen** come to a decision/pass a resolution; **laut ~ des Gerichtes/der Direktion** in accordance with the decision of the court/management; B (*veralt.: Ende*) end; **zum ~:** to end *or* conclude

**beschluss-**, ***beschluß-**, **Beschluss-**, ***Beschluß-:** ~**fähig** *Adj.* quorate; ~**fähig sein** have a quorum; be quorate; ~**fähigkeit** *die* presence of a quorum; **die ~fähigkeit herstellen** make a quorum; ~**fassung** *die* (*Amtsspr.*) **einen Entwurf zur ~fassung vorlegen** submit a draft resolution; ~**organ** *das* decision-making body; ~**unfähig** *Adj.* inquorate; ~**unfähig sein** not have a quorum; be inquorate

**beschmeißen** *unr. tr. V.* (*salopp*) **jmdn./sich [gegenseitig] mit etw.** ~: pelt sb./each other with sth.; **jmdn./etw. mit Schmutz** *od.* **Dreck ~** (*fig.*) fling mud at sb./sth.

**beschmieren** *tr. V.* A **etw./sich ~:** get sth./oneself in a mess; **sich** (*Dat.*) **die Kleidung/Hände mit etw. ~:** smear *or* get sth. [smeared] all over one's clothes/hands; B (*abwertend*) (*bemalen*) daub paint all over; (*bekritzeln*) scrawl *or* scribble all over; C (*bestreichen*) **sein Brot mit etw. ~:** spread sth. on one's bread; **das Brot mit Butter ~:** butter the bread; **etw. mit Fett/Salbe ~:** grease sth./smear ointment on sth.; D (*abwertend: voll schreiben*) cover ‹paper›

**beschmunzeln** *tr. V.* smile at

**beschmutzen** *tr. V.* **etw. ~:** make sth. dirty; **ganz beschmutzt sein** be covered in dirt; **jmds. Namen/Gedenken ~** (*fig.*) besmirch sb.'s name/memory; **sich ~** (*verhüll.*) dirty oneself

**beschneiden** *unr. tr. V.* A (*stutzen*) cut, trim, clip ‹hedge›; prune, cut back ‹bush›; cut back ‹tree›; trim ‹book block›; **einem Vogel die Flügel ~:** clip a bird's wings; B (*Med., Rel.*) circumcise; **ein Beschnittener** a circumcised boy/man; C (*einschränken*) cut ‹salary, income, wages›; restrict ‹rights›; **jmdn. in seinen Rechten ~:** restrict sb.'s rights

**Beschneidung** *die;* ~, ~**en** A (*das Stutzen*) ⇒ **beschneiden** A: trimming; cutting; clipping; pruning; cutting back; B (*Einschränkung*) ⇒ **beschneiden** C: cutting; restriction; **die ~ seines Einkommens in Kauf nehmen** accept a cut in [one's] income; C (*Med., Rel.*) circumcision

**beschneit** *Adj.* snow-covered

**beschnüffeln** *tr. V.* A (*beriechen*) sniff at; B (*ugs.: prüfen*) **jmdn./sich ~:** size sb./each other up; C (*ugs. abwertend: bespitzeln*) spy on

**beschnuppern** *tr. V.:* ⇒ **beschnüffeln** A, B

**beschönigen** /bəˈʃø:nɪgn̩/ *tr. V.* gloss over

**Beschönigung** *die;* ~, ~**en** glossing over; **das wäre eine ~:** that would be to gloss over the true situation

**beschränken** /bəˈʃrɛŋkn̩/ ❶ *tr. V.* restrict; limit; **etw. auf etw.** (*Akk.*) ~: restrict *or* limit sth. to sth.; **jmdn. in seinen Rechten ~:** restrict sb.'s rights; **die Mittel sind beschränkt** my/our *etc.* resources are limited; **beschränkte Verhältnisse** straitened circumstances. ❷ *refl. V.* tighten one's belt (*fig.*); **sich auf etw.** (*Akk.*) ~: restrict *or* confine oneself to sth.

**beschrankt** *Adj.* ‹level crossing› with barriers; ~ **sein** have barriers

**beschränkt** ❶ *Adj.* A (*abwertend: dumm*) dull-witted; B (*engstirnig*) ‹person› of restricted *or* limited outlook; narrow-minded ‹person›; narrow[-minded] ‹views, outlook›; ~ **sein** have a restricted *or* limited outlook; be narrow-minded; **einen ~en Horizont haben** have limited horizons *pl.* ❷ *adv.* narrow-mindedly; in a narrow-minded way

**Beschränktheit** *die;* ~ A (*Dummheit*) lack of intelligence; **in ihrer ~:** with her limited intelligence; B (*das Begrenztsein*) limitedness; restrictedness

**Beschränkung** *die;* ~, ~**en** A (*das Beschränken*) limitation; restriction; B (*das, was beschränkt*) restriction; **jmdm./einer Sache ~en auferlegen** impose restrictions on sb./sth.

**beschreiben** *unr. tr. V.* A write on; (*voll schreiben*) write ‹page, side, etc.›; **eng beschriebene Seiten** closely written pages; B (*darstellen*) describe; **ich kann dir [gar] nicht ~, wie ..., es ist [gar] nicht zu ~, wie ...** I [simply] can't tell you how ...; **ihre Leiden waren nicht zu ~:** her sufferings were indescribable *or* beyond description; **wer beschreibt seine Freude, als ...** who could describe his joy when ...; C (*durch Kreisbewegung herstellen*) describe ‹circle, orbit, curve, etc.›

**Beschreibung** *die;* ~, ~**en** A description; **jeder ~ spotten** defy *or* be beyond description; B (*Gebrauchsanweisung*) instructions *pl.*

**beschreien** *unr. tr. V.:* ⇒ **berufen**[1] 1 B

**beschreiten** *unr. tr. V.* (*geh.*) walk along ‹path etc.›; **neue Wege ~** (*fig.*) tread new paths; ‹medicine, technology, etc.› pursue new methods; **den Rechtsweg ~:** have recourse to litigation

**Beschrieb** *der* (*schweiz.*) description

**beschriften** /bəˈʃrɪftn̩/ *tr. V.* label; address ‹envelope, letter›; inscribe ‹stone›; letter ‹sign›

**Beschriftung** *die;* ~, ~**en** A labelling; (*eines Briefes*) addressing; (*eines Steines*) inscribing; (*eines Schildes*) lettering; B (*Aufschrift*) label; (*eines Briefes*) address; (*eines Steines*) inscription; (*eines Schildes*) lettering

**beschuhen** /bəˈʃu:ən/ *tr. V.* (*Technik*) shoe; tip [with metal]

**beschuht** *Adj.* shod; **ein weiß ~er Fuß** a foot [shod] in a white shoe

**beschuldigen** /bəˈʃʊldɪgn̩/ *tr. V.* accuse (+ *Gen.* of); **jmdn. des Mordes/des Mordes an seiner Frau ~:** accuse sb. of murder/of the murder of his wife; **jmdn. ~, etw. getan zu haben/etw. zu sein** accuse sb. of doing/being sth.

**Beschuldigte** *der/die; adj. Dekl.* accused

**Beschuldigung** *die;* ~, ~**en** accusation; ~**en gegen jmdn. erheben** make accusations against sb.

**beschummeln** *tr. V.* (*ugs.*), **beschupsen** *tr. V.* (*salopp*) cheat; diddle (*coll.*); burn (*Amer. sl.*); **jmdn. um etw. ~** *od.* **beschupsen** diddle *or* do sb. out of sth. (*coll.*)

**Beschuss**, ***Beschuß** *der* A fire; (*aus Kanonen*) shelling; (*mit Pfeilen*) shooting; **unter ~ nehmen** fire at/shell/shoot at; (*fig.: kritisieren*) attack; **[heftig** *od.* **stark] unter ~ geraten/stehen** *od.* **liegen** (*auch fig.*) come/be under [heavy] fire; B (*Physik*) ~ **mit Neutronen** *usw.* bombardment with neutrons *etc.*

**beschützen** *tr. V.* protect (**vor** + *Dat.* from); ~**d den Arm um jmdn. legen** put a protective arm around sb.; ~**de Werkstätte** sheltered workshop

**Beschützer** *der;* ~**s**, ~, **Beschützerin** *die;* ~, ~**nen** protector (**vor** from)

**beschwatzen**, (*bes. südd.*) **beschwätzen** *tr. V.* (*ugs.*) A **jmdn. ~:** talk sb. round; **jmdn. zu etw. ~:** talk sb. into sth.; **jmdn. ~, etw. zu tun** talk sb. into doing sth.; B (*bereden*) chat about *or* over

**Beschwerde** /bəˈʃve:ɐ̯də/ *die;* ~, ~**n** A complaint (**gegen, über** + *Akk.* about); ~ **führen** (*Amtsspr.*) *od.* **einlegen** (*Rechtsw.*) lodge a complaint; (*gegen einen Entscheid*) lodge an appeal; B ▸ 474 *Pl.* (*Schmerz*) pain *sing.;* (*Leiden*) trouble *sing.;* **er fragte mich nach meinen ~n** he asked me what the trouble was; **jmdm. [ziemliche/große] ~n machen** give sb. [quite a lot of/considerable] pain; ~**n [mit der Verdauung** *usw.***] haben** have trouble [with one's digestion *etc.*]; **die ~n des Alters** the aches and pains *or* infirmities of old age

**beschwerde-**, **Beschwerde-:** ~**aus·schuss**, *~**aus·schuß** *der* (*DDR*) appeal tribunal (*against actions of official bodies*); ~**buch** *das* complaints book; ~**frei** ❶ *Adj.* trouble-free; (*ohne Schmerzen*) free from pain *postpos.;* ❷ *adv.* without pain; **relativ ~frei leben** live a life relatively free from pain; ~**frist** *die* (*Rechtsw.*) time limit for lodging an appeal; ~**führer** *der*, ~**führerin** *die* complainant; (*gegen einen Entscheid*) appellant; ~**weg** *der:* **in auf dem ~weg** by appealing; by means of an appeal

**beschweren** /bəˈʃve:rən/ ❶ *refl. V.* complain (**über** + *Akk.*, **wegen** about); **sich bei jmdm. ~:** complain to sb. ❷ *tr. V.* weight; (*etw. Schweres auflegen*) weight down; (*fig.: belasten*) burden ‹person, memory›

**beschwerlich** ❶ *Adj.* arduous; (*ermüdend*) exhausting; **jmdm. ~ fallen** (*veralt., geh.*) ‹person, children› be a burden to sb.; **jmdm. fällt etw. ~** (*veralt. geh.*) sb. finds sth. troublesome. ❷ *adv.* laboriously; with an effort

**Beschwerlichkeit** *die;* ~, ~**en** A arduousness; B *Pl.* (*Anstrengungen*) tribulations

**Beschwernis** *die;* ~, ~**se** (*geh.*) tribulation

**Beschwerung** *die;* ~, ~**en** A weighting; **zur ~:** in order to weight it [down]; B (*Gegenstand*) weight; **etw. als ~ benutzen** use sth. as ballast

**beschwichtigen** /bəˈʃvɪçtɪgn̩/ *tr. V.* pacify; calm ‹excitement›; placate, mollify ‹anger etc.›; **sein Gewissen ~:** ease one's conscience; **er versucht [uns] zu ~, wenn wir in Streit geraten** he tries to conciliate *or* placate us when we quarrel; ~**de Worte** soothing words

**Beschwichtigung** *die;* ~, ~**en** pacification; (*des Zorns, Hasses*) mollification

**Beschwichtigungs·politik** *die* policy of appeasement

**beschwindeln** *tr. V.* (*ugs.*) **jmdn. ~:** tell sb. a fib/fibs; (*betrügen*) hoodwink sb.

**beschwingt** /bəˈʃvɪŋt/ ❶ *Adj.* elated, lively ‹mood›; lively, lilting ‹tune, melody›; ~ **sein/sich ~ fühlen** ‹person› be/feel elated; ~**en Schrittes/Fußes** (*geh.*) with a spring in one's step. ❷ *adv.* ~ **gehen** walk with a spring in one's step; ~ **tanzen** dance with great élan

b

**Beschwingtheit** *die;* **~:** elation; (*einer Melodie*) liveliness; (*des Ganges*) springiness

**beschwipst** /bəˈʃvɪpst/ *Adj.* tipsy

**beschwören** *unr. tr. V.* **A** **~, dass ...** swear that ...; **etw. ~:** swear to sth.; **eine Aussage ~:** swear a statement on *or* under oath; **B** charm ‹snake›; **C** (*erscheinen lassen*) invoke, conjure up ‹spirit›; (*fig.*) evoke, conjure up ‹pictures, memories, etc.›; **ein Unheil ~:** make a disaster happen (*by thinking/talking about it*); **die Vergangenheit ~:** revive memories of the past; **D** (*bitten*) beg; implore; **in ~dem Ton** in a beseeching *or* imploring tone; **mit ~dem Blick** with an imploring glance; **sie sah ihn ~d an** she looked at him imploringly; **E** (*veralt.: bannen*) exorcize ‹evil spirit›

**Beschwörung** *die;* **~, ~en** **A** (*Zauberspruch*) spell; incantation; **B** (*Bitte*) entreaty; **C** (*das Erscheinenlassen*) invoking; conjuring up

**Beschwörungs·formel** *die* incantation

**beseelen** /bəˈzeːlən/ *tr. V.* animate; **ein fester Glaube beseelte ihn** a steadfast faith was his inspiration

**besehen** *unr. tr. V.* have a look at; **sich (*Dat.*) etw. [genau] ~:** have a [close] look at sth.; inspect sth. [closely]; **er besah sich im Spiegel** he looked at himself in the mirror

**beseitigen** /bəˈzaitɪgn̩/ *tr. V.* **A** (*entfernen*) remove; get rid of; eliminate ‹error, difficulty›; dispose of ‹rubbish›; clear ‹snow›; eradicate ‹injustice, abuse›; **B** (*verhüll.: ermorden*) dispose of; eliminate

**Beseitigung** *die;* **~** **A** removal; (*eines Fehlers, einer Schwierigkeit*) elimination; (*des Mülls*) disposal; (*eines Missstands*) eradication; **B** (*verhüll.: Ermordung*) elimination

**beseligen** /bəˈzeːlɪgn̩/ *tr. V.* fill with delight *or* joy; **ein ~des Gefühl/ein ~der Gedanke** a delightful *or* blissful feeling/thought

**Besen** /ˈbeːzn̩/ *der;* **~s, ~** **A** broom; (*Reisig~*) besom; (*Hand~*) brush; **~ und Schaufel** dustpan and brush; **die Hexe auf ihrem ~:** the witch on her broomstick; **ich fress einen ~, wenn das stimmt** (*salopp*) I'll eat my hat if that's right (*coll.*); **neue ~ kehren gut** (*Spr.*) a new broom sweeps clean (*prov.*); **mit eisernem ~ [aus]kehren** (*fig.*) apply drastic remedies; **B** (*salopp abwertend: Frau*) battleaxe (*coll.*)

**besen-, Besen-:** **~binder** *der,* **~binderin** *die;* **~~, ~~nen** broom-maker; (*von Reisigbesenbinder*) besom-maker; **~ginster** *der* (*Bot.*) broom; **~kammer** *die* broom cupboard; broom closet (*Amer.*); **~macher** *der,* **~macherin** *die* broom-maker; **~rein** *Adj.* swept clean *postpos.;* **~schrank** *der* ⇒ **~kammer**; **~stiel** *der* broom handle; (*eines Reisigbesens*) broomstick; **er läuft herum, als habe er einen ~stiel verschluckt** (*ugs.*) he runs around as stiff as a ramrod

**besessen** /bəˈzɛsn̩/ **1** *2. Part. v.* **besitzen**. **2** *Adj.* **A** possessed; **vom Teufel ~ sein** be possessed by *or* (*dated*) of the Devil; **wie ~:** like one possessed; **B** (*heftig ergriffen*) obsessive ‹gambler›; fanatical ‹racing driver, footballer, etc.›; **von einer Idee** *usw.* **~ sein** be obsessed with an idea *etc.*

**Besessene** *der/die; adj. Dekl.* **ein ~r/eine ~:** one possessed; **zum/zur ~n werden** become like one possessed; become fanatical

**Besessenheit** *die;* **~** **A** (*durch einen Dämon, Teufel*) possession; **B** (*Ergriffenheit*) obsessiveness; **mit wahrer ~:** in a truly obsessive manner; **zur ~ werden** become obsessive *or* an obsession

**besetzen** *tr. V.* **A** (*mit Pelz, Spitzen*) edge; trim; **mit Perlen/Edelsteinen besetzt** set with pearls/precious stones; **B** (*belegen; auch Milit.: erobern*) occupy; (*füllen*) fill (**mit** with); (*Jagdw., Fischereiw.*) stock ‹shoot, pond, etc.›; (*reservieren*) keep, reserve ‹seat, table, etc.›; **der Bus kann mit 50 Personen besetzt werden** the bus can carry 50 people; **C** (*vergeben*) fill ‹post, position, role, etc.›; cast ‹role, play, etc.›; **einen Ausschuss ~:** fill [the places on] a committee; **die frei werdenden Stellungen werden nicht mehr neu besetzt** no new appointments are being made to positions which become vacant

**besetzt** *Adj.* occupied; ‹table, seat› taken *pred.;* ‹washing machine, drier, etc.› in use *pred.;* (*gefüllt*) full; filled to capacity; **es** *od.* **die Leitung/die Nummer ist ~:** the line/number is engaged *or* (*Amer.*) busy; **er ist im Moment ~:** he is occupied *or* busy at the moment; **die amerikanisch ~e Zone** the American zone of occupation

**Besetzt·zeichen** *das* (*Fernspr.*) engaged tone (*Brit.*); busy signal (*Amer.*)

**Besetzung** *die;* **~, ~en** **A** (*einer Stellung*) filling; (*einer Rolle*) casting; (*eines Ausschusses*) composition; (*Jagdw., Fischereiw.*) stocking *no indef. art.;* **B** (*Mitwirkende*) (*Film, Theater usw.*) cast; (*einer Popgruppe*) line-up; **das Stück in hervorragender ~ sehen** see the play with an outstanding cast; **in der besten/der neuen ~ antreten** (*Sport*) ‹team› field its best side/new line-up; **die erste/zweite ~** (*Theater*) the first/second cast; **C** (*Eroberung*) occupation; **die ~ des Brückenkopfes** the taking of the bridgehead

**besichtigen** /bəˈzɪçtɪgn̩/ *tr. V.* see ‹sights›; see the sights of ‹town›; look round ‹building›; view ‹house, flat›; (*prüfend*) inspect ‹troops, joc.: baby, girlfriend›

**Besichtigung** *die;* **~, ~en** viewing; (*Führung*) tour; (*Prüfung von Truppen*) inspection; **etw. zur ~ freigeben** open sth. to visitors *or* to the public; **die ~ der Kirche ist zwischen 10 und 16 Uhr möglich** the church is open to visitors between 10 a.m. and 4 p.m.

**Besichtigungs-:** **~reise** *die* sightseeing trip; **~zeit** *die* opening time

**besiedeln** *tr. V.* **A** settle (**mit** with); **neu ~:** resettle; **ein dicht/dünn besiedeltes Land** a densely/thinly populated country; **B** (*heimisch sein in*) ‹animal, plant› inhabit, be found in

**Besiedlung** *die* settlement

**Besiedlungs·dichte** *die* population density

**besiegeln** *tr. V.* set the seal on; **sein Schicksal ist besiegelt** his fate is sealed

**Besieg[e]lung** *die;* **~, ~en** sealing; **die ~ von etw. sein** seal sth.; **zur ~ des Geschäftes/unserer Freundschaft** to seal the transaction/our friendship

**besiegen** *tr. V.* **A** defeat; **sich besiegt geben** admit defeat; **B** (*überwinden*) overcome ‹doubts, difficulties, curiosity, etc.›

**Besiegte** *der/die; adj. Dekl.* loser

**besingen** *unr. tr. V.* **A** (*geh.*) celebrate in verse; (*durch ein Lied*) celebrate in song; **B** **eine Platte ~:** make a record [of songs]

**besinnen** **1** *unr. refl. V.* **A** think it *or* things over; **sich anders/eines Besseren ~:** change one's mind/think better of it; **B** (*sich erinnern*) **sich [auf jmdn./etw.] ~:** remember *or* recall [sb./sth.]; **sich darauf ~, wann ...** recall when ...; **wenn ich mich recht besinne** if I remember correctly; **C** (*sich bewusst werden*) **sich auf die Bedeutung von etw. ~:** become aware of the significance of sth. **2** *unr. tr. V.* reflect on

**besinnlich** *Adj.* contemplative; thoughtful ‹person›; reflective ‹story›; **in einer ~en Stunde** in a quiet moment; when one has time to think; **ein ~er Abend** an evening of reflection

**Besinnlichkeit** *die;* **~:** contemplation; **Stunden der ~:** moments of reflection

**Besinnung** *die;* **~** **A** consciousness; **die ~ verlieren** (*das Bewusstsein verlieren*) lose consciousness; (*ohnmächtig werden*) faint; **ohne** *od.* **nicht bei ~:** unconscious; **[wieder] zur ~ kommen** come to; regain consciousness; **B** (*Nachdenken*) reflection; **zur ~ kommen** stop and think things over; **ehe ich recht zur ~ kommen konnte** before I had time to think; **jmdn. zur ~ bringen** bring sb. to his/her senses

**Besinnungs·aufsatz** *der* reflective essay

**besinnungs·los** **1** *Adj.* **A** (*bewusstlos*) unconscious; **B** (*fig.*) mindless, blind ‹rage, hatred›; **~ vor Angst** out of one's mind with fear. **2** *adv.* mindlessly; **~ auf jmdn. einschlagen** hit out at sb. in a blind *or* uncontrollable rage

**Besinnungslosigkeit** *die;* **~:** unconsciousness *no art.;* **er betrank sich bis zur ~:** he drank himself into oblivion

**Besitz** *der* **A** property; **nur wenig ~ haben** have only a few possessions *pl.;* **jmdm. den rechtmäßigen ~ [einer Sache (*Gen.*)] streitig machen** dispute sb.'s legal title to his/her property [in sth.]; **B** (*das ~en*) possession; **sich in jmds. ~ (*Dat.*) befinden, in jmds. ~ (*Dat.*) sein** be in sb.'s possession; **es befindet sich seit mehreren Generationen im ~ unserer Familie** it has been in our family for several generations; **sich in privatem ~ befinden** be privately owned; be in private ownership *or* hands; **in amerikanischem ~:** in American ownership; **in jmds. ~ (*Akk.*) übergehen** *od.* **kommen** pass *or* come into sb.'s possession; **in den ~ eines Hauses** *usw.* **kommen** become the owner of a house *etc.;* (*durch eigene Bemühungen*) gain possession of a house *etc.;* **im ~ einer Sache (*Gen.*)/von etw. sein, etw. in ~ haben** be in possession of sth.; possess sth.; **im vollen ~ seiner geistigen Kräfte sein** be in full possession of one's faculties; **etw. in [seinen] ~ nehmen, von etw. ~ ergreifen** take possession of sth.; **von jmdm. ~ ergreifen** (*geh.*) take hold of sb.; **C** (*Landbesitz*) estate

**besitz-, Besitz-:** **~anspruch** *der* claim to ownership; **einen ~anspruch auf etw. (*Akk.*) anmelden** file a claim to ownership of sth.; **~anzeigend** *Adj.* (*Sprachw.*) possessive; **~bürgertum** *das* property-owning bourgeoisie

**besitzen** *unr. tr. V.* **A** own; have ‹quality, talent, etc.›; (*nachdrücklicher*) possess; **seit wann besitzt er ein Auto?** since when does he own a car?; how long has he had a car?; **alles, was er besaß** all he possessed; **keinen Pfennig ~** (*ugs.*) not have a penny to one's name; **er besaß die Frechheit/Unverschämtheit, zu ...** he had the cheek *or* nerve/impertinence to ...; **die ~de Klasse** the propertied class; **das Recht ~, zu ...** have the right to ...; **B** (*geh. verhüll.*) **eine Frau ~:** possess a woman

**Besitzer** *der;* **~s, ~** **A** owner; (*eines Betriebs usw.*) proprietor (*formal*); **den ~ wechseln** change hands *pl.;* **B** (*österr.*) property owner

**besitz·ergreifend** *Adj.* ‹troops etc.› taking possession

**Besitz·ergreifung** *die* seizure

**Besitzerin** *die;* **~, ~nen** ⇒ **Besitzer**

**Besitzer-:** **~stolz** *der* pride of ownership; **voller ~stolz** very much the proud owner; **~wechsel** *der* change of ownership

**besitz-, Besitz-:** **~gier** *die* cupidity; acquisitiveness; **~los** *Adj.* destitute; **die ~lose Klasse** the propertyless class; **~nahme** *die;* **~~, ~~n** appropriation; (*mit Gewalt*) seizure; **~stand** *der* standard of living; **den ~stand wahren** maintain living standards

**Besitztum** *das;* **~s, Besitztümer** /-tyːmɐ/ **A** possession; **B** (*Gut*) estate

**Besitzung** *die;* **~, ~en** (*geh.*) estate

**Besitz·verhältnisse** *Pl.* matters relating to ownership; (*marxistische Theorie*) conditions of ownership

**besoffen** /bəˈzɔfn̩/ **1** *2. Part. v.* **besaufen**. **2** *Adj.* (*salopp*) boozed [up] (*sl.*); plastered (*sl.*); pissed *pred.* (*sl.*); **völlig ~:** completely stoned (*sl.*); blind drunk

**Besoffene** *der/die; adj. Dekl.* (*salopp*) drunk

**besohlen** *tr. V.* sole; **neu ~:** resole

**Besohlung** *die;* **~** **A** soling; **eine neue ~ der Schuhe** resoling the shoes; **B** (*Sohle*) sole

**besolden** *tr. V.* pay ‹soldier›; pay ‹civil servant› his/her salary; **eine gut besoldete Stelle** a well-paid job

**Besoldung** /bəˈzɔldʊŋ/ *die;* **~, ~en** pay; (*Gehalt*) salary

*old spelling (see note on page 1707)

**Besoldungs-: ~gruppe** *die* salary bracket; **~ordnung** *die* [tables of] pay scales *pl.* (*for civil servants*)

**besonder...** /bəˈzɔndɐ.../ *Adj.* special; (*mehr als gewohnt*) particular ‹pleasure, enthusiasm, effort, etc.›; (*hervorragend*) exceptional ‹quality, beauty, etc.›; **im Besonderen** in particular; **im Allgemeinen und im Besonderen** in general and in particular; **ein ~es Ereignis** an unusual *or* a special event; **keine ~en Vorkommnisse wurden gemeldet** no incidents of any particular note were reported; **~e Merkmale** (*im Pass usw.*) distinguishing marks; **~en Wert auf etw.** (*Akk.*) **legen** lay particular emphasis on sth.; **keine ~e Leistung** no great achievement; **einen ~en Geschmack haben** ‹person› have exceptional taste; ‹dish› have an unusual taste; **es ist mir eine [ganz] ~e Freude/Ehre** it is a particular pleasure/honour for me

**Besondere** *das; adj. Dekl.* **A etwas [ganz] ~s** something [really] special; **nichts ~s** nothing special; (*nichts Interessantes*) nothing of note *or* worth mentioning; **das ist doch nichts ~s** there's nothing special *or* unusual about that; **das ~ daran** the special thing about it; **B** (*Einzelerscheinung*) **vom ~n zum Allgemeinen kommen** proceed from the particular to the general

**Besonderheit** *die; ~, ~en* special *or* distinctive feature; (*Eigenart*) peculiarity; **dieser Fall stellt eine ~ dar** this is a special case

**besonders** *Adv.* **A** particularly; **~ du solltest das wissen** you of all people should know that; **~ bei schönem Wetter** especially in fine weather; **das hat ihn ~ gefreut** that gave him particular pleasure; **das braucht man wohl nicht ~ zu erwähnen** presumably one does not have to mention this specifically; **nicht ~ viel Geld haben** not be particularly well off; **B nicht ~ sein** be nothing special; be nothing to write home about; **ich fand den Film nicht ~:** I didn't think the film was anything special *or* was up to much; **es geht ihm nicht ~:** he doesn't feel too well; **C** (*getrennt*) separately

**besonnen** /bəˈzɔnən/ **1** *2. Part. v.* **besinnen**. **2** *Adj.* prudent; (*umsichtig*) circumspect; **ruhig und ~:** calm and collected; **~es Urteil** considered judgement. **3** *adv.* prudently; (*umsichtig*) circumspectly

**Besonnenheit** *die; ~* ⇒ **besonnen** 2: prudence; circumspection

**besonnt** /bəˈzɔnt/ *Adj.* sunlit

**besorgen** *tr. V.* **A** get; (*kaufen*) buy; **jmdm. etw. ~:** get/buy sb. sth. *or* sth. for sb.; **ich will mir das Buch ~:** I want to get the book [for myself]; **B** (*ugs. verhüll.: stehlen*) **sich** (*Dat.*) **etw. ~:** help oneself to sth.; **C** (*erledigen*) take care of; deal with; prepare ‹edition›; **einen Brief ~:** post a letter; **er besorgte die Auswahl der Gedichte** he was responsible for the selection of poems; **was du heute kannst ~, das verschiebe nicht auf morgen** (*Spr.*) never put off to tomorrow what you can do today (*prov.*); **D** (*betreuen*) look after ‹children, flowers, etc.›; **jmdm. den Haushalt/die Wäsche ~:** keep house/do the washing for sb.; **E es jmdm. ~** (*ugs.: heimzahlen*) get back at sb. (*coll.*); get one's own back on sb. (*Brit. coll.*); (*derb: geschlechtlich befriedigen*) give it to sb. (*sl.*)

**Besorgnis** *die; ~, ~se* concern; **echte ~ [um jmdn./über etw.** (*Akk.*)**] empfinden** be genuinely concerned [about sb./sth.]; **jmds. ~ erregen** cause sb. concern; **jmds. ~se zerstreuen** put an end to sb.'s worries

**besorgnis·erregend** *Adj.* serious; **~ sein** give cause for concern

**besorgt** **1** *Adj.* worried (**über** + *Akk.*, **um** about); concerned *usu. pred.* (**über** + *Akk.*, **um** about); **er macht einen sehr ~en Eindruck** he appears to be very concerned; **sie war rührend um das Wohl ihrer Gäste ~:** she showed a touching concern for the well-being of her guests; **er war ~, es könnte etwas passieren** he was concerned lest something should happen *or* worried that something might happen. **2** *adv.* with concern; (*ängstlich*) anxiously; **sich sehr ~ äußern** express one's great concern

**Besorgtheit** *die; ~:* concern

**Besorgung** *die; ~, ~en* **A** purchase; **[einige] ~en machen** do some shopping; **kleinere ~en machen** do odd bits of shopping; **B** (*das Beschaffen*) getting; (*das Kaufen*) buying; **C** (*das Betreuen*) **die ~ des Haushalts** *usw.* looking after the household *etc.*

**bespannen** *tr. V.* **A** cover ‹wall, chair, car, etc.›; string ‹racket, instrument›; **B** (*mit Zugtieren*) **einen Wagen mit einem Pferd ~:** harness a horse to a cart; **mit zwei Schimmeln bespannt** harnessed to *or* pulled by two white horses

**Bespannung** *die; ~, ~en* covering; (*eines Schlägers, eines Instruments*) stringing

**bespeien** *unr. tr. V.* (*geh.*) spit at

**bespiegeln** *tr. V.* **A sein eigenes Ich** *od.* **sich selbst ~:** contemplate one's own ego; **B** (*darstellen*) mirror; portray

**bespielbar** *Adj.* **A das Band ist nicht mehr ~:** one can no longer record on this tape; **B** (*Sport*) playable ‹ground, tennis court›

**bespielen** *tr. V.* **A** make a recording on ‹tape, cassette›; **ein Band mit Liedern ~:** record songs on a tape; **die Kassette ist schon bespielt** the cassette already has a recording on it; **B** (*Theaterw.*) **eine Bühne ~:** play a theatre

**bespitzeln** *tr. V.* spy on

**Bespitz[e]lung** *die; ~, ~en* spying

**bespötteln** *tr. V.* mock; make fun of

**besprechen** **1** *unr. tr. V.* **A** discuss; talk over; (*rezensieren*) review; **gut/schlecht besprochen werden** get a good/bad review; (*mehrfach*) get good/bad reviews; **B** (*aufnehmen*) **eine Kassette ~:** make a [voice] recording on a cassette; (*statt eines Briefes*) record a message on a cassette; **eine Platte mit Gedichten ~:** make a record of poems; **C** (*beschwören*) **etw. ~:** utter a magic incantation *or* spell over sth. **2** *unr. refl. V.* confer (**über** + *Akk.* about); **sich [ausführlich] über etw.** (*Akk.*) **~:** discuss sth. [in detail]; **sich mit jmdm. ~:** have a talk with sb.; confer with sb. (*formal*)

**Besprechung** *die; ~, ~en* **A** discussion; (*Konferenz*) meeting; **in einer ~ sein, [gerade] eine ~ haben** be in a meeting; **B** (*Rezension*) review (*Gen.*, **von** of); **C** (*das Beschwören*) incantation

**Besprechungs·exemplar** *das* (*Buchw.*) review copy

**besprengen** *tr. V.* sprinkle

**besprenkeln** *tr. V.* spatter

**bespringen** *unr. tr. V.* ‹stallion, bull, etc.› cover, mount ‹mare, cow, etc.›

**bespritzen** *tr. V.* **A** splash; (*mit einem Wasserstrahl*) spray; **B** (*beschmutzen*) bespatter

**besprühen** *tr. V.* spray

**bespucken** *tr. V.* **jmdn. [mit etw.] ~:** spit [sth.] at sb.

**Bessemer·birne** /ˈbɛsəmɐ-/ *die* (*Metallbearb.*) Bessemer converter

**besser** /ˈbɛsɐ/ **1** ⇒ **gut**.
**2** *Adj.* **A** better; **~ dran sein** be better off; **[auch] schon [mal] ~e Zeiten gesehen haben** (*ugs.*) have seen better days; **es wäre ~, du hieltest deinen Mund** it would be better if you kept your mouth shut; **~ werden** get better; ‹work etc.› improve; **umso ~:** so much the better; all the better; **es wurde noch ~** (*iron.*) there was more *or* better to come (*iron.*); that wasn't the best of it (*iron.*); **das wäre ja noch ~!** (*iron.*) that really is the limit!; **ich habe Besseres zu tun** I've got better things to do; **~ ist ~:** better safe than sorry; just to be on the safe side; **jmdn. eines Besseren belehren** (*geh.*) put sb. right; **schließlich hat er sich doch eines Besseren belehren lassen** in the end he accepted that he was wrong; ⇒ *auch* **besinnen**; **B** (*sozial höher gestellt*) superior; upper-class; **~e** *od.* **die ~en Kreise** more elevated circles; **es verkehren hier die ~en Leute** you get a better *or* superior class of people here; **eine ~e Gegend/Adresse** a smart[er] *or* [more] respectable area/address; **jmdn. [finanziell] ~ stellen** improve sb.'s [financial] position; **C** (*abwertend*) glorified; **wir arbeiten in einer ~en Baracke** we work in a glorified hut.
**3** *adv.* **A [immer] alles ~ wissen** always know better; **es ~ haben** be better off; (*es leichter haben*) have an easier time of it; **es kommt noch ~** (*iron.*) it gets even better (*iron.*); **~ gesagt** to be [more] precise; **sie war nicht ganz offen, oder ~ gesagt, sie hat uns belogen** she was not quite frank, or to put it bluntly, she lied to us; **es geht ihm ~:** he feels better; **kurze Zeit später ging es ihr schon wieder ~:** a short time later, she had already recovered; **B** (*lieber*) **das lässt du ~ sein** *od.* (*ugs.*) **bleiben** you'd better not do that; **er ließe es ~ bleiben, sich einzumischen** he would be better advised not to interfere; **er täte ~ daran, zu ...** he would do better to ...; **geh ~ zum Arzt** you'd better go to the doctor

***besser|gehen** ⇒ **besser** 3 A

**Bessergestellte** /-gəʃtɛltə/ *Pl.; adj. Dekl.* **die ~n** the better off; the well-to-do

**bessern** **1** *refl. V.* improve; ‹person› mend one's ways. **2** *tr. V.* improve; reform ‹criminal›

***besser|stellen** ⇒ **besser** 3 A

**Besserung** *die; ~* **A** (*Genesung*) recovery; **[ich wünsche dir] gute ~:** [I hope you] get well soon; **sich auf dem Wege der ~ befinden** be on the road to recovery *or* on the mend; **B** (*Verbesserung*) improvement (+ *Gen.* in); (*eines Kriminellen*) reform; **~ geloben** promise to mend one's ways

**Besserungs·anstalt** *die* (*ugs. veralt.*) reform school; reformatory (*esp. Amer.*)

**besser-, Besser-: ~wissen** *das* ⇒ **~wisserei**; **~wisser** *der; ~~s, ~~* (*abwertend*) know-all; smart aleck; **~wisserei** /----'-/ *die; ~~* (*abwertend*) superior attitude; **~wisserin** *die; ~~, ~~nen* ⇒ **~wisser**; **~wisserisch** *Adj.* (*abwertend*) superior; know-all; **sei nicht so ~wisserisch!** don't always pretend you know better

**best...** /ˈbɛst.../ **1** ⇒ **gut**.
**2** *Adj.* **A** *attr.* best; **aus ~em Hause sein** *od.* **stammen** come from one of the very best families; **bei ~er Gesundheit/Laune sein** be in the best of health/spirits *pl.*; **im ~en Falle** at best; **er wird im ~en Falle mit einer Geldstrafe davonkommen** the best he can hope for is to get off with a fine; **in den ~en Jahren, im ~en Alter** in one's prime; **~e** *od.* **die ~en Grüße an ...** (*Akk.*) best wishes to ...; **mit den ~en Grüßen** *od.* **Wünschen** with best wishes; (*als Briefschluss*) ≈ yours sincerely; **~en Dank** many thanks *pl.*; ⇒ *auch* **Dank, Familie, Weg, Wille**; **B es ist** *od.* **wäre das Beste, wenn ...** it would be best if ...; **es wäre das Beste, zu ...** it would be best to ...; **er hielt es für das Beste, sofort abzureisen** he thought it best to leave immediately; **am ~en** best; **am ~en fährst du mit dem Zug** it would be best for you to go by train; **du bleibst am ~en zu Hause** you had best stay at home; **alles aufs Beste regeln** *od.* **richten** arrange everything in the best way possible; **es steht nicht zum Besten mit etw.** things are not going too well for sth.; **mit seiner Gesundheit steht es nicht zum Besten** his health is none too good; **der/die/das nächste ~e ...** the first ... one comes across; **sie hat den ersten ~en Mann geheiratet, der ihr über den Weg lief** she married the first man who happened to cross her path; **eine Geschichte/einen Witz zum Besten geben** entertain [those present] with a story/a joke; **jmdn. zum Besten halten** *od.* **haben** pull sb.'s leg; **C** *subst.* best; **der Beste in unserer Gruppe** the best person in our group; **der/die Beste der Klasse** the best [pupil/student] in the class; **das Beste vom Besten** the very best; **das Beste ist gerade gut genug** only the best is good enough; **sein Bestes tun** do one's best; **das Beste aus etw./daraus machen** make the best of sth./of it; **aufs** *od.* **auf das Beste hoffen** hope for the best; **ich will nur dein**

**Bestes** I am doing this for your own good; **zu deinem Besten** for your benefit; in your best interests *pl.*

**bestallen** /bəˈʃtalən/ *tr. V.* (*Amtsspr.*) appoint (**zu, als** as)

**Bestallung** *die* (*Amtsspr.*) appointment (**zu, als** as)

**Bestallungs·urkunde** *die* (*Amtsspr.*) certificate of appointment

**Bestand** *der* **A** continued existence; survival; **keinen ~ haben, nicht von ~ sein** not last; not last long; **B** (*Vorrat*) stock (**an** + *Dat.* of); ⇒ *auch* **eisern** 1 D; **C** (*Forstw.*) **~ von Eichen und Buchen** [mixed] stand of oaks and beeches; **Bestände durchforsten** thin out standing timber; **D** (*österr.*: *Dauer des Bestehens*) **nach 15 jährigem ~:** after 15 years of existence; after existing for 15 years; **E** (*südd., österr.*: *Pacht*) **etw. in ~ haben/geben** lease sth./lease sth. [out]

**bestanden** /bəˈʃtandn̩/ ❶ *2. Part. v.* **bestehen.** ❷ *Adj.* **A von** *od.* **mit etw. ~ sein** have sth. growing on it; **mit Blumen ~e Wiesen** flower-covered meadows; meadows full of flowers; **mit Tannen ~e Hügel** fir-covered hills; **B nach ~er Prüfung** after passing one's examination; **C** (*schweiz.*: *alt*) elderly

**beständig** ❶ *Adj.* **A** (*dauernd*) constant; **B** (*gleich bleibend*) constant; steadfast ‹person›; (*zuverlässig*) reliable; settled ‹weather›; (*Chemie*) stable ‹compound›; **seine Leistungen sind ~:** his work is consistent; **C** (*widerstandsfähig*) resistant (**gegen, gegenüber** to). ❷ *adv.* **A** constantly; **sie klagt ~:** she is constantly *or* for ever complaining; **B** (*gleich bleibend*) consistently

**-beständig** *adj.* **hitze~/wetter~/säure~:** heat-/weather-/acid-resistant

**Beständigkeit** *die;* **~ A** constancy; steadfastness; (*bei der Arbeit*) consistency; (*Zuverlässigkeit*) reliability; **B** (*Widerstandsfähigkeit*) resistance (**gegen, gegenüber** to)

**Bestands·aufnahme** *die* stocktaking; **[eine] ~ machen** do a stocktaking; take inventory (*Amer.*); (*fig.*) take stock

**Bestand·teil** *der* component; **ein notwendiger ~ unserer Nahrung** an essential part *or* element of our diet; **sich in seine ~e auflösen** fall apart; fall to pieces; **etw. in seine [sämtlichen] ~e zerlegen** dismantle sth. [completely]

**Best·arbeiter** *der,* **Best·arbeiterin** *die* (*DDR*) best worker (*worker receiving an award as being the most efficient in the department, factory, etc.*)

**bestärken** ❶ *tr. V.* confirm; **jmdn. in seinem Plan** *od.* **Vorsatz** *od.* **darin ~, etw. zu tun** strengthen sb.'s resolve *or* confirm sb. in his/her resolve to do sth. ❷ *refl. V.* grow

**Bestärkung** *die* confirmation

**bestätigen** /bəˈʃtɛːtɪgn̩/ ❶ *tr. V.* confirm; endorse ‹document›; acknowledge ‹receipt›; **ein Urteil ~** (*Rechtsw.*) uphold a judgement; **jmdn. [in seinem Amt] als Schulleiter** *usw.* **~:** confirm sb.'s appointment as headmaster (*Brit.*) *or* (*Amer.*) principal *etc.*; **hiermit wird bestätigt, dass ...** (*in Urkunden*) this is to confirm *or* certify that ...; **jmdm. [schriftlich] ~, dass er ...** give sb. [written] confirmation that he ...; certify that sb. ...; **sich in seiner Meinung/in seinen Vorurteilen bestätigt fühlen** have one's opinion/prejudices reinforced; **einen Brief/eine Bestellung ~** (*Kaufmannsspr.*) acknowledge [receipt of] a letter/an order. ❷ *refl. V.* be confirmed; ‹rumour› prove to be true; **damit hat sich meine Vermutung bestätigt** this confirmed my supposition

**Bestätigung** *die;* **~, ~en** confirmation; (*des Empfangs*) acknowledgement; (*schriftlich*) letter of confirmation; **zur ~ seiner Aussage erbrachte er Beweise** he produced evidence to support *or* back up his statement; **die ~ [in seinem Amt] als ...** the confirmation of his appointment as ...

**bestatten** /bəˈʃtatn̩/ *tr. V.* (*geh.*) inter (*formal*); bury; **bestattet werden** be laid to rest

**Bestatter** *der;* **~s, ~, Bestatterin** *die;* **~, ~nen** ▶ 159 undertaker; mortician (*Amer.*); (*bei Firmennamen*) funeral director

**Bestattung** *die;* **~, ~en** (*geh.*) interment (*formal*); burial; (*Feierlichkeit*) funeral; **„Meier und Schulze, ~en"** 'Meier and Schulze, Funeral Directors *or* (*Amer.*) Morticians'

**Bestattungs-: ~institut** *das,* **~unternehmen** *das* [firm of] undertakers *pl. or* funeral directors *pl.*; funeral parlor (*Amer.*)

**bestäuben** /bəˈʃtɔybn̩/ *tr. V.* **A** dust; **B** (*Biol.*) pollinate

**Bestäubung** *die;* **~, ~en** (*Biol.*) pollination

**bestaunen** *tr. V.* marvel at; (*bewundernd anstarren*) gaze in wonder at; (*bewundernd anerkennen*) be lost in admiration for

**best·bezahlt** *Adj.* best-paid

**beste** ⇒ **best...**

**Beste** *das;* **~n** ⇒ **best...** 2 C

**bestechen** ❶ *unr. tr. V.* **A** bribe; **B** (*für sich einnehmen*) win over, captivate ‹audience etc.›. ❷ *unr. itr. V.* win people over

**bestechend** *Adj.* attractive; captivating, winning ‹smile, charm›; persuasive ‹argument, logic›; tempting ‹offer›; **von ~er Logik** irresistibly logical; **in ~er Form** (*Sport*) in irresistible form

**bestechlich** *Adj.* corruptible; open to bribery *postpos.*

**Bestechlichkeit** *die;* **~:** corruptibility

**Bestechung** *die;* **~, ~en** bribery *no indef. art.*; **eine ~:** a case of bribery; **der ~ eines Beamten/der ~ schuldig sein** be guilty of bribing of an official/of bribery; **aktive ~** (*Rechtsw.*) giving bribes; **passive ~** (*Rechtsw.*) accepting bribes

**Bestechungs-: ~geld** *das* bribe; **~skandal** *der* bribery scandal; **~summe** *die* bribe; **~versuch** *der* attempted bribery

**Besteck** /bəˈʃtɛk/ *das;* **~[e]s, ~e A** cutlery setting; **noch ein ~ auflegen** lay another place; **~e putzen** polish cutlery; **B** (*ugs.*: *Gesamtheit der ~e*) cutlery; **C** (*Med.*) [set *sing.* of] instruments *pl.*; **D** (*Seemannsspr.*) fix; (*aus Kurs und Geschwindigkeit bestimmt*) dead reckoning [position]

**bestecken** *tr. V.* **A mit B ~:** stick B in/on A; **der Adventskranz war mit Tannenzapfen besteckt** the Advent wreath had fir cones stuck in it

**Besteck-: ~kasten** *der* cutlery box; (*größer*) canteen; **~schublade** *die* cutlery drawer

**bestehen** ❶ *unr. itr. V.* **A** exist; **die Schule besteht noch nicht sehr lange** the school has not been in existence *or* has not been going for very long; **es besteht [die] Aussicht/Gefahr, dass ...** there is a prospect/danger that ...; **darüber bestand noch immer keine Klarheit** it was still unclear; **es besteht noch** *od.* **noch besteht die Hoffnung, dass ...** there is still hope that ...; **~ bleiben** remain; ‹doubt› persist; ‹regulation› remain in force; **etw. ~ lassen** retain sth.; **einen Einwand ~ lassen** allow an objection to stand; **B** (*fortdauern*) survive; last; (*standhalten*) hold one's own; **gegen diese Konkurrenz werden wir kaum ~ können** we shall hardly be able to survive *or* keep going in the face of this competition; **seine Arbeit kann vor jeder Kritik ~:** his work can stand up to any criticism; **in einer Gefahr** *usw.* **~:** prove oneself in a dangerous situation *etc.*; **C** (*zusammengesetzt sein*) **aus etw. ~:** consist of sth.; (*aus einem Material*) be made of sth.; **in etw.** (*Dat.*) **~:** consist of *or* in sth.; **ihre Aufgabe besteht in der Aufstellung der Liste** her task is to draw up the list; **der Unterschied besteht darin, dass ...** the difference is that ...; **eine Möglichkeit besteht darin, zu beweisen ...** one possibility would be to prove ...; **D** (*beharren*) **auf etw.** (*Dat.*) **~:** insist on sth.; **er bestand darauf, den Chef zu sprechen** he insisted on seeing the boss; **ich bestehe darauf, dass man mich darüber informiert** I insist that I be *or* on being informed about it; **E** (*die Prüfung ~*) pass [the examination].

❷ *unr. tr. V.* **A** pass ‹test, examination›; **B** (*ertragen*) withstand ‹blows of fate›; face up to ‹difficulties›

**Bestehen** *das;* **~s A** existence; **die Firma feiert ihr 10-jähriges ~:** the firm is celebrating its tenth anniversary; **seit ~ der Bundesrepublik** since the Federal Republic came into existence; since the founding of the Federal Republic; **B** (*einer Prüfung*) passing; **mit ~ der Prüfung** on passing the examination; **C** (*Beharren*) insistence (**auf** + *Dat.* on)

***bestehen|bleiben** ⇒ **bestehen** 1 A

**bestehend** *Adj.* existing; current ‹conditions›; **das seit 5 Jahren ~e Gesetz** the law which has been in existence for five years

***bestehen|lassen** ⇒ **bestehen** 1 A

**bestehlen** *unr. tr. V.* **jmdn. [um etw.] ~:** rob sb. [of sth.]

**besteigen** *unr. tr. V.* **A** climb; mount ‹horse, bicycle›; climb into ‹pulpit›; ascend ‹throne›; **B** (*betreten*) board ‹ship, aircraft›; get on ‹bus, train›; **C** ⇒ **bespringen**

**Besteigung** *die* ascent

**Bestell·buch** *das* order book

**bestellen** ❶ *tr. V.* **A** order (**bei** from); **sich** (*Dat.*) **etw. ~:** order sth. [for oneself]; **würden Sie mir bitte ein Taxi ~?** would you order me a taxi?; **B** (*reservieren lassen*) reserve ‹table, tickets›; **C** (*kommen lassen*) **jmdn. [für 10 Uhr] zu sich ~:** ask sb. to go/come to see one [at 10 o'clock]; **jmdn. in ein Café ~:** ask sb. to meet one in a café; **beim** *od.* **zum Arzt bestellt sein** have an appointment with the doctor; **dastehen wie bestellt und nicht abgeholt** (*ugs. scherzh.*) stand there like a little boy/girl lost; **D** (*ausrichten*) **jmdm. etw. ~:** pass on sth. to sb.; tell sb. sth.; **bestell deinem Mann schöne Grüße von mir** give your husband my regards; **würden Sie Ihrer Kollegin etwas von mir ~?** would you give your colleague a message from me?; **er lässt dir ~, dass ...** he left a message [for you] that ...; **nichts/nicht viel zu ~ haben** have no say/little *or* not much say; **E** (*ernennen*) appoint (**zu, als** as); **F** (*bearbeiten*) cultivate, till ‹field›; keep, look after ‹garden›; **G es ist um jmdn./etw.** *od.* **mit jmdm./etw. schlecht bestellt** sb./sth. is in a bad way; **mit seiner Gesundheit ist es schlecht bestellt** he is in poor health. ❷ *itr. V.* order

**Besteller** *der;* **~s, ~, Bestellerin** *die;* **~, ~nen** customer (*who has ordered sth.*)

***Bestelliste** ⇒ **Bestellliste**

**Bestell-: ~liste** *die* checklist (*of goods for ordering*); **~nummer** *die* order number; **~schein** *der* order form

**Bestellung** *die* **A** order (**über, auf** + *Akk.* for); (*das Bestellen*) ordering *no indef. art.*; **bei ~ von/bei ~en über mehr als 1 000 Stück** if more than 1,000 are ordered/for orders of more than 1,000; **auf ~:** to order; (*im Lokal*) **eine ~ aufgeben** give one's order; **jmds. ~/die ~en aufnehmen** take sb.'s/the orders; **B** (*Reservierung*) reservation; **C** (*Nachricht*) **eine ~ übermitteln** *od.* **ausrichten** pass on a message; **D** (*das Ernennen*) appointment; (*Wahl*) selection; **E** (*das Bearbeiten*) cultivation; tilling; **~ des Gartens** gardening; work on the garden

**Bestell·zettel** *der* order form

**besten·falls** *Adv.* at best

**Besten·liste** *die* (*Sport*) list of top athletes/sportsmen

**bestens** *Adv.* **A** excellently; extremely well; **sich ~ verstehen** get on splendidly; **sich ~ unterhalten** have a splendid time; **B** (*vielmals*) **jmdn. ~ grüßen** give sb. one's best wishes; **wir danken Ihnen/bedanken uns ~:** we thank you very much

**besteuern** *tr. V.* tax; **besteuert sein** be subject to tax; **höher besteuert werden** be more heavily taxed; **etw. höher ~:** increase the tax on sth.

**Besteuerung** *die* taxation; **bei einer ~ des Einkommens von 45%** where income is taxed at [a rate of] 45%

*old spelling (see note on page 1707)

**best-, Best-: ~form** *die* (*Sport*) best form; **in ~form** in top form; **~gehasst, *~gehaßt** *Adj.* (*ugs. iron.*) most heartily disliked; **~gekleidet** *Adj.* best-dressed

**bestialisch** /bɛs'ti̯a:lɪʃ/ ❶ *Adj.* Ⓐ (*abwertend*) bestial; Ⓑ (*ugs.: schrecklich*) ghastly (*coll.*); awful (*coll.*). ❷ *adv.* Ⓐ (*abwertend*) in a bestial manner; **~ schreien** scream like a wild beast; Ⓑ (*ugs.: schrecklich*) awfully (*coll.*); unbearably; **~ kalt** beastly cold

**Bestialität** /bɛsti̯ali'tɛ:t/ *die;* **~, ~en** Ⓐ bestiality; **ein Verbrechen von solcher ~:** a crime of such a bestial nature *or* of such brutality; Ⓑ (*Tat*) brutality; atrocity

**Bestiarium** /bɛs'ti̯a:ri̯ʊm/ *das;* **~s, Bestiarien** bestiary

**besticken** *tr. V.* embroider; **ein mit Perlen besticktes Kleid** a dress sewn with pearls

**Bestie** /'bɛsti̯ə/ *die;* **~, ~n** (*auch fig. abwertend*) beast

**bestimmbar** *Adj.* ascertainable; (*identifizierbar*) identifiable; **nicht [genau] ~ sein** be impossible to ascertain/identify [precisely]

**bestimmen** ❶ *tr. V.* Ⓐ (*festsetzen*) decide on; fix ‹price, time, etc.›; **das Gesetz bestimmt, dass ...** the law provides that ...; **nichts zu ~ haben** have no say; **jmdn. zum** *od.* **als Nachfolger ~:** decide on sb. as one's successor; (*nennen*) name sb. as one's successor; Ⓑ (*vorsehen*) destine; intend; set aside ‹money›; **das ist für dich bestimmt** that is meant for you; **er ist zu Höherem bestimmt** he is destined for higher things; **füreinander bestimmt sein** be meant for each other; Ⓒ (*ermitteln, definieren*) identify ‹part of speech, find, plant, etc.›; determine ‹age, position›; define ‹meaning›; Ⓓ (*prägen*) determine the character of; give ‹landscape, townscape› its character; **unser Leben ~:** play a dominant *or* decisive role in our lives; Ⓔ (*veranlassen*) **jmdn. zum Nachgeben/Bleiben ~:** induce sb. to give in/stay; **sich von jmdm. zu etw. ~ lassen** allow sb. to talk one into sth. ❷ *itr. V.* Ⓐ make the decisions; **hier bestimme ich** I'm in charge *or* the boss here; my word goes around here; Ⓑ (*verfügen*) **über jmdn. ~:** tell sb. what to do; **[frei] über etw.** (*Akk.*) **~:** do as one wishes with sth.

**bestimmend** ❶ *Adj.* decisive; determining. ❷ *adv.* decisively

**bestimmt** ❶ *Adj.* Ⓐ (*speziell*) particular; (*gewiss*) certain; (*genau*) definite; **soll es ein ~es Buch sein?** have you a particular book in mind?; **es sind immer ganz ~e Leute, die so was tun** it is always a particular type of person who does something like that; **ich habe schon eine ~e Vorstellung davon, wie ...** I already have a clear *or* definite idea of how ...; **ich kann noch nichts Bestimmtes sagen** I can say nothing definite *or* I cannot say anything definite yet; **ich habe nichts Bestimmtes vor** I am not doing anything in particular; Ⓑ (*festgelegt*) fixed; given ‹quantity›; Ⓒ (*Sprachw.*) definite ‹article etc.›; Ⓓ (*entschieden*) firm; **in sehr ~em Ton** very firmly; in a very firm voice; **~es Auftreten** resolute manner.
❷ *adv.* Ⓐ (*deutlich*) clearly; (*genau*) precisely; Ⓑ (*entschieden*) firmly; **sich ~ gegen etw. aussprechen** express one's firm opposition to sth.
❸ *Adv.* for certain; **du weißt es doch [ganz] ~ noch** I'm sure you must remember it; **ganz ~, ich komme** I'll definitely come; yes, certainly, I'll come; **Vergiss sie nicht wieder. — Nein, ~ nicht** Don't forget them again — Don't worry, I won't; **sie wird das ~ schaffen** she is certain *or* bound to manage it; **er hat es ~ vergessen** he is bound to have forgotten; **ich habe das ~ liegen gelassen** I must have left it behind; **das ist ~ nicht richtig** that can't be right

**Bestimmtheit** *die;* **~** Ⓐ firmness; (*im Auftreten*) decisiveness; **etw. mit aller ~ sagen/ablehnen** say sth. very firmly/reject sth. categorically; Ⓑ (*Gewissheit*) **mit ~:** for certain

**Bestimmung** *die* Ⓐ (*das Festsetzen*) fixing; Ⓑ (*Vorschrift*) regulation; **gesetzliche ~en** legal requirements; Ⓒ (*Zweck*) purpose; **eine Brücke** *usw.* **ihrer ~ übergeben** [officially] open a bridge *etc.*; Ⓓ (*das Ermitteln*) identification; (*eines Begriffs*) definition; (*des Alters, der Position*) determination; (*der Bedeutung*) definition; **~ der Satzteile** distinguishing the parts of a sentence; parsing; Ⓔ (*Sprachw.*) modifier; **adverbiale ~:** adverbial qualification; Ⓕ (*Schicksal*) **das ist ~:** that is destiny *or* fate; **göttliche ~:** Divine Providence; **es war höhere ~, dass wir uns begegneten** it was ordained [by fate] that we should meet; Ⓖ (*veralt.: ~sort*) destination

**bestimmungs-, Bestimmungs-: ~bahnhof** *der* (*Eisenb.*) destination; **~gemäß** *Adv.* in accordance with the regulations *or* requirements [of the law]; **~hafen** *der* [port of] destination; **~ort** *der; Pl.* **~e** destination; **~wort** *das; Pl.* **~wörter** (*Sprachw.*) qualifying element (*of a compound*); modifier

**best-, Best-: ~leistung** *die* best performance; (*absolute ~leistung*) record; **persönliche ~leistung** personal best; **~mann** *der* (*Seew.*) mate (*of a coaster*); **~marke** *die* (*Sport*) record; **~möglich** ❶ *Adj.* best possible; **das ~mögliche tun/getan haben** do the best one can/have done the best one could; ❷ *adv.* as well as possible *or* as one possibly can

**Best.-Nr.** *Abk.* **Bestellnummer** order no.

**bestochen** /bə'ʃtɔxn̩/ *2. Part. v.* **bestechen**

**bestrafen** *tr. V.* punish (**für, wegen** for); **es wird mit Gefängnis bestraft** it is punishable by imprisonment

**Bestrafung** *die;* **~, ~en** punishment; (*Rechtsw.*) penalty; (*Geldstrafe*) fine

**bestrahlen** *tr. V.* Ⓐ (*beleuchten*) illuminate; floodlight ‹building›; (*scheinen auf*) ‹sun etc.› shine on; (*erhellen*) light up; Ⓑ (*Med.*) treat ‹tumour, part of body› using radiotherapy; (*mit Höhensonne*) use sunray *or* sunlamp treatment on ‹part of body›

**Bestrahlung** *die;* **~, ~en** Ⓐ (*Med.*) radiation [treatment] *no indef. art.*; (*bes. mit Röntgenstrahlen*) radiotherapy *no art.*; (*mit Höhensonne*) sunray *or* sunlamp treatment; Ⓑ (*das Beleuchten*) illumination; (*eines Gebäudes*) floodlighting; (*der Bühne*) lighting; **eine intensive ~ durch die Sonne** concentrated exposure to the sun's rays

**Bestrahlungs·lampe** *die* radiation lamp; (*Höhensonne*) sun[ray] lamp

**Bestreben** *das* endeavour[s *pl.*]; **in seinem** *od.* **im ~, keine Schwächen zu zeigen** in his efforts *or* endeavours to show no weakness

**bestrebt** *Adj.* **~/sehr ~ sein, etw. zu tun** endeavour/take great pains *or* go to great trouble to do sth.

**Bestrebung** *die;* **~, ~en** effort; (*Versuch*) attempt

**bestreichen** *unr. tr. V.* **A mit B ~:** spread B on A; **sein Brot mit Butter ~:** spread butter on one's bread; butter one's bread; **den Braten/das Hähnchen mit Öl** *usw.* **~:** baste the roast/chicken with oil *etc.*; **die Plätzchen mit Eigelb ~:** brush *or* coat the biscuits (*Brit.*) *or* (*Amer.*) cookies with egg yolk

**bestreiken** *tr. V.* take strike action against; **diese Firma wird bestreikt** there is a strike [on] at this firm

**bestreitbar** *Adj.* disputable; questionable, dubious ‹argument›; **es ist nicht ~[, dass ...]** it is indisputable *or* cannot be denied [that ...]

**bestreiten** *unr. tr. V.* Ⓐ dispute; contest; (*leugnen*) deny; **er bestreitet, dass ...** he denies that ...; **es lässt sich nicht/wohl kaum ~, dass ...** it cannot/can hardly be denied that ...; there is no disputing/it can hardly be disputed that ...; **jmdm. ein Recht auf etw.** (*Akk.*) **~:** dispute *or* challenge sb.'s right to sth.; Ⓑ (*finanzieren*) finance ‹studies›; pay for ‹studies, sb.'s keep, etc.›; meet ‹costs, expenses›; Ⓒ (*gestalten*) carry ‹programme, conversation, etc.›; Ⓓ (*Sport*) take part in ‹game›

**Bestreitung** *die;* **~** Ⓐ financing; Ⓑ **eine ~ seiner Aussage liegt mir fern** I have no intention of disputing *or* challenging his statement

**bestreuen** *tr. V.* **etw. mit Zucker ~:** sprinkle sth. with sugar; **einen Weg mit Sand/Salz ~:** scatter sand on a path/salt a path

**bestricken** *tr. V.* Ⓐ ensnare; captivate; Ⓑ (*für andere stricken*) knit things for

**bestrumpft** /bə'ʃtrʊmpft/ *Adj.* stockinged; **lila ~:** in mauve stockings

**Bestseller** /'bɛstzɛlɐ/ *der;* **~s, ~:** best seller

**Bestseller-: ~autor** *der,* **~autorin** *die* best-selling author; **~liste** *die* best-seller list

**bestücken** *tr. V.* fit; equip; (*mit Waffen*) arm; (*mit Waren*) stock [up]

**Bestückung** *die;* **~, ~en** equipment; (*mit Waffen*) armament; (*mit Waren*) stocking; **eine ordnungsgemäße ~ des Lagers garantieren** ensure that the correct stock level is maintained at the warehouse

**bestuhlen** /bə'ʃtu:lən/ *tr. V.* provide with seats

**Bestuhlung** *die;* **~, ~en** Ⓐ fitting of [the] seats (*Gen.* in); Ⓑ (*Stühle*) seating

**bestürmen** *tr. V.* Ⓐ storm; (*Fußball*) besiege ‹goal›; Ⓑ (*bedrängen*) besiege (**mit** with)

**Bestürmung** *die* storming; (*Angriff*) assault

**bestürzen** *tr. V.* dismay; (*erschüttern*) shake; (*erschrecken*) alarm; **es hat ihn sehr bestürzt zu hören, dass ...** he was deeply dismayed to hear that ...

**bestürzend** *Adj.* disturbing; (*erschreckend*) alarming

**bestürzt** ❶ *Adj.* dismayed (**über** + *Akk.* about); (*erschrocken*) alarmed (**über** + *Akk.* about); **sie machte ein [sehr] ~es Gesicht** her face fell [a mile (*coll.*)]; she looked [deeply] dismayed. ❷ *adv.* with dismay *or* consternation; **jmdn. [ganz** *od.* **sehr] ~ ansehen** look at sb. in *or* with [great] consternation

**Bestürzung** *die;* **~:** dismay; consternation; **mit ~ feststellen, dass ...** find to one's consternation that ...

**bestusst, *bestußt** /bə'ʃtʊst/ *Adj.* (*salopp*) barmy (*Brit. coll.*); loopy (*coll.*)

**Best-: ~wert** *der* optimum result; (*~leistung*) maximum performance figure; (*beim Wettbewerb*) maximum mark; **~zeit** *die* (*Sport*) best time; **[persönliche] ~zeit** personal best [time]; **~zeit laufen/schwimmen** run/swim a best time/one's personal best *or* one's best time

**Besuch** /bə'zu:x/ *der;* **~[e]s, ~e** Ⓐ visit; **ein ~ bei jmdm.** a visit to sb.; (*kurz*) a call on sb.; **~ eines Museums** *usw.* visit to a museum *etc.*; **bei seinem letzten ~:** on his last visit; **wir erwarten den ~ alter Freunde** we are expecting a visit from some old friends; **~ von jmdm. bekommen** receive a visit from sb.; **auf** *od.* **zu ~ kommen** come for a visit; (*auf länger*) come to stay; **er ist bei uns auf ~:** he is staying with us; **jmdm. einen ~ abstatten** pay sb. a visit; Ⓑ (*das ~en*) visiting; (*Teilnahme*) attendance; **der ~ der Schule/Vorlesungen/Gottesdienste** attendance at school/lectures/services; **die Konzerte erfreuen sich eines regen ~s** the concerts are well attended; Ⓒ (*Gast*) visitor; (*Gäste*) visitors *pl.*; **~ bekommen/erwarten** have/expect visitors/a visitor; **ich bekomme gleich ~:** I've got visitors/a visitor coming any minute

**-besuch** *der:* **Deutschland~/England~/USA-Besuch:** visit to Germany/England/the USA; **Messe~:** visit to the/a fair

**besuchen** *tr. V.* Ⓐ visit ‹person›; (*weniger formell*) go to see ‹person›; **gestern hat mich ein alter Bekannter besucht** yesterday an old friend came to see me *or* called on me; Ⓑ visit ‹place›; go to ‹exhibition, theatre, museum, etc.›; (*zur Besichtigung*) go to see ‹church, exhibition, etc.›; **die Schule/Universität ~:** go to *or* (*formal*) attend school/university; **hast du diese Ausstellung schon besucht?** have you been to [see] this exhibition yet?; **er hat sämtliche Lokale der Umgebung besucht** he patronized all the pubs (*Brit.*) *or* (*Amer.*) bars in the neighbourhood; ⇒ *auch* **besucht**

b

b

**Besucher** *der* visitor; ~ **eines Museums** *usw.* visitor to a museum *etc.*; **die ~ des Theaters** the theatre audience; the theatre goers; **er ist ständiger ~ der Oper/von Konzerten** he is a regular opera-goer/concert-goer; **alle ~ des Kurses/der Vorstellung/des Vortrags** all those attending the course/performance/lecture

**-besucher** *der*: **Berlin~**: visitor to Berlin; **Messe~**: visitor to the/a fair

**Besucherin** *die*; ~, ~**nen** ⇒ **Besucher**

**Besucher-**: ~**strom** *der* stream of visitors; ~**zahl** *die* number of visitors

**Besuchs-**: ~**erlaubnis** *die* visiting permit; ~**ritze** *die* (*ugs. scherzh.*) join between the [twin] beds; ~**tag** *der* visiting day; ~**zeit** *die* visiting time *or* hours *pl.*; **es ist keine ~zeit** it is not visiting time

**besucht** *Adj.* **gut/schlecht ~**: well/poorly attended ‹lecture, performance, etc.›; much/little frequented ‹restaurant etc.›

**besudeln** *tr. V.* (*geh. abwertend*) besmirch; **jmds. Andenken/Namen ~** (*fig.*) cast a slur on sb.'s memory/name

**Beta** /'be:ta/ *das*; ~**[s]**, ~**s** beta

**Beta·blocker** /-blɔkɐ/ *der*; ~**s**, ~ (*Med.*) betablocker

**betagt** /bə'ta:kt/ *Adj.* (*geh.*) elderly; (*scherzh.*) ancient ‹car etc.›; **noch als ~er Mann** even in his old age

**Betagtheit** *die*; ~ (*geh.*) old age

**betanken** *tr. V.* refuel

**betasten** *tr. V.* feel [with one's fingers]

**Beta-**: ~**strahlen** *Pl.* (*Physik*) beta rays; ~**teilchen** *das* (*Physik*) beta particle

**betätigen** ❶ *refl. V.* busy *or* occupy oneself; **sich politisch/literarisch/körperlich ~**: engage in political/literary/physical activity; **sich als etw. ~**: act as sth.; **wenn du dich ~ willst, kannst du mir beim Spülen helfen** if you want to do something [useful], you can help me with the washing-up. ❷ *tr. V.* operate ‹lever, switch, flush, etc.›; press ‹button›; apply ‹brake›

**Betätigung** *die*; ~, ~**en** Ⓐ activity; **ich werde schon eine ~ für dich finden** I'll find you something to do; Ⓑ (*das Bedienen*) operation; (*einer Bremse*) application; (*eines Knopfes*) pressing

**Betätigungs-**: ~**drang** *der* [compulsive] urge to be up and doing [something]; ~**feld** *das* sphere of activity

**betatschen** *tr. V.* (*salopp abwertend*) finger; (*sexuell*) paw (*coll.*)

**betäuben** /bə'tɔybn̩/ *tr. V.* Ⓐ (*Med.*) anaesthetize; make numb, deaden ‹nerve›; **einen Patienten örtlich ~**: give a patient a local anaesthetic; Ⓑ (*unterdrücken*) ease, deaden ‹pain›; quell, still ‹unease, fear›; **seinen Kummer mit Alkohol ~** (*fig.*) drown one's sorrows [in drink]; Ⓒ (*benommen machen*) daze; (*mit einem Schlag*) stun; **ein ~der Duft** a heady *or* intoxicating scent; **ein ~der Lärm** a deafening noise

**Betäubung** *die*; ~, ~**en** Ⓐ (*Med.*) anaesthetization; (*Narkose*) anaesthesia; **eine örtliche ~ vornehmen** administer a local anaesthetic; **zur ~ der Schmerzen** to deaden the pain; Ⓑ (*Benommenheit*) daze

**Betäubungs·mittel** *das* narcotic; (*Med.*) anaesthetic

**Betäubungsmittel·gesetz** *das* narcotics law (*regulating the use of cocaine, morphine, cannabis, etc.*)

**betaut** /bə'taut/ *Adj.* (*geh.*) covered in dew *postpos.*; bedewed (*literary*)

**Bet·bruder** /'be:t-/ *der* (*abwertend*) overpious type (*coll.*)

**Bete** /'be:tə/ *die*; ~, ~**n** *in* **Rote ~**: beetroot (*Brit.*); [red] beet (*Amer.*)

**beteilen** *tr. V.* (*österr.*) provide (**mit** with)

**beteiligen** ❶ *refl. V.* **sich an etw.** (*Dat.*) ~: participate *or* take part in sth.; **er hat sich kaum an der Diskussion beteiligt** he took hardly any part in the discussion; **sich an einem Geschäft ~**: take a share in *or* come in on a deal; **sich an etw. mit einer Million ~**: contribute a million to sth. ❷ *tr. V.* **jmdn. [mit 10%] an etw.** (*Dat.*) ~: give sb. a [10%] share of sth.

**beteiligt** *Adj.* Ⓐ involved (**an** + *Dat.* in); Ⓑ (*finanziell*) **an einem Unternehmen/am Gewinn ~ sein** have a share in a business/in the profit; **er ist mit 20 000 DM ~**: he has a 20,000 mark share

**Beteiligte** *der/die*; *adj. Dekl.* person involved (**an** + *Dat.* in); (*an einem Spiel, einer Sitzung usw.*) participant (**an** + *Dat.* in); **die [meisten] an dem Unfall/der Affäre ~n** [most of] those involved in the accident/affair

**Beteiligung** *die*; ~, ~**en** Ⓐ (*Teilnahme*) participation (**an** + *Dat.* in); (*Zahl der Beteiligten*) number of participants (**an** + *Dat.* in); (*an einem Verbrechen*) involvement (**an** + *Dat.* in); **unter ~ von** with the participation of; Ⓑ (*Anteil*) share (**an** + *Dat.* in); **eine ~ am Gewinn/Umsatz** a share in the profits/turnover

**Betel** /'be:tl̩/ *der*; ~**s** betel

**Betel·nuss**, ***Betel·nuß** *die* betel nut

**beten** /'be:tn̩/ ❶ *itr. V.* pray (**für, um** for); **zu Gott ~, dass etw. geschehen möge** pray to God that sth. should happen; **es wird gebetet** prayers are said. ❷ *tr. V.* say ‹prayer›

**Beter** *der*; ~**s**, ~, **Beterin** *die*; ~, ~**nen** prayer (= *one who prays*)

**beteuern** /bə'tɔyɐn/ *tr. V.* affirm; assert, protest ‹one's innocence›; **jmdm. seine Liebe ~**: avow one's love to sb.; **sie beteuerte, dass sie mit dieser Sache nichts zu tun habe** she protested that she had nothing to do with this business

**Beteuerung** *die*; ~, ~**en** ⇒ **beteuern**: affirmation; assertion; protestation

**Bet·haus** *das* synagogue

**betiteln** /bə'ti:tl̩n/ *tr. V.* Ⓐ (*ugs. abwertend*) **jmdn. [mit] X/mit einem Schimpfnamen ~**: call sb. X/a rude name; Ⓑ (*mit Titel anreden*) **jmdn. [mit] Doktor/Professor ~**: address sb. as *or* call sb. 'Doctor'/'Professor'; Ⓒ (*mit Titel versehen*) give ‹book etc.› a title

**Beton** /be'tɔŋ, *bes. österr.*: be'to:n/ *der*; ~**s**, ~**s** /-ɔŋs/ *od.* ~**e** /-o:nə/ concrete

**Beton-**: ~**bau** *der*; *Pl.* ~~**ten** Ⓐ concrete building; Ⓑ (*Bauweise*) concrete construction *no art.*; ~**bunker** *der* Ⓐ concrete bunker; (*Luftschutzbunker*) concrete shelter; Ⓑ (*abwertend*: ~**bau**) concrete box

**betonen** /bə'to:nən/ *tr. V.* Ⓐ stress ‹word, syllable›; accent ‹syllable, beat›; **ein Wort falsch ~**: put the wrong stress on a word; Ⓑ (*hervorheben*) emphasize; **ich möchte ~, dass ...** I should like to emphasize *or* stress that ...; **warum betont er seine Herkunft so?** why does he lay such stress on his origins?; **die Taille ~**: accentuate the waist

**betonieren** /beto'ni:rən/ *tr. V.* Ⓐ concrete; surface ‹road etc.› with concrete; lay a concrete floor in ‹cellar etc.›; **frisch betonierte Fläche** recently laid concrete; Ⓑ (*festlegen*) harden ‹attitude›; reinforce ‹prejudice›

**Betonierung** *die*; ~, ~**en** Ⓐ concreting; Ⓑ (*Betondecke*) concrete surface

**Beton-**: ~**klotz** *der* Ⓐ concrete block; Ⓑ (*abwertend*: *massiver* ~**bau**) concrete monolith; ~**kopf** *der* (*abwertend*) hardliner; ~**mischer** *der*, ~**misch·maschine** *die* concrete mixer

**betont** /bə'to:nt/ ❶ *Adj.* Ⓐ stressed; accented; Ⓑ (*bewusst*) pointed, studied; deliberate, studied ‹simplicity, elegance›. ❷ *adv.* pointedly; deliberately; **sich ~ sportlich kleiden** wear clothes with a strong *or* pronounced sporting character; **sich ~ zurückhaltend verhalten** behave with studied reserve

**Beton·träger** *der* concrete beam

**Betonung** *die*; ~, ~**en** Ⓐ stressing; accenting; Ⓑ (*Akzent*) stress; accent (*esp. Mus.*); (*Intonation*) intonation; Ⓒ (*das Hervorheben*) emphasis (*Gen.* on); (*von Formen, Farben*) accentuation; **ein Lernprogramm mit ~ des Musisch-Kreativen** a syllabus with the emphasis on artistic creativity

**Betonungs·zeichen** *das* stress mark

**Beton·wüste** *die* (*ugs. abwertend*) concrete desert

**betören** /bə'tø:rən/ *tr. V.* (*geh.*) Ⓐ captivate; bewitch; Ⓑ (*verblenden*) beguile, entice ‹purchaser, consumer›

**Betörung** *die*; ~, ~**en** (*geh.*) captivation; bewitching

**betr.** *Abk.* **betreffs, betrifft** re

**Betr.** *Abk.* **Betreff** re

**Betracht** /bə'traxt/ *in* **jmdn./etw. in ~ ziehen** consider sb./sth.; **jmdn./etw. außer ~ lassen** discount *or* disregard sb./sth.; **eine Frage außer ~ lassen** pass over a question; (*zeitweilig*) leave a question on one side; **er/sie kommt/kommt nicht in ~**: he/she can/cannot be considered; **das kommt nicht in ~**: that is not worth considering; that is out of the question; **außer ~ bleiben** be passed over; (*zeitweilig*) be left on one side

**betrachten** *tr. V.* Ⓐ look at; (*bei einer Tätigkeit*) watch; observe; (*fig.*: *studieren*) observe, study ‹history, development, etc.›; **sich** (*Dat.*) **etw. [genau] ~**: take a [close] look at sth.; watch *or* observe sth. [closely]; **sich im Spiegel ~**: look at oneself in the mirror; (*längere Zeit*) contemplate oneself in the mirror; **jmdn. von oben bis unten ~**: look sb. up and down; **genau/bei Licht betrachtet** (*fig.*) upon closer consideration/seen in the light of day; Ⓑ (*für etw. halten*) **jmdn./etw. als ... ~**: regard sb./sth. as ...; **sich als jmds. Freund ~**: regard oneself as *or* consider oneself sb.'s friend; Ⓒ (*beurteilen*) consider; view; **objektiv betrachtet** viewed objectively; from an objective point of view; **so betrachtet** seen in this light *or* from this point of view

**Betrachter** *der*; ~**s**, ~, **Betrachterin** *die*; ~, ~**nen** observer

**beträchtlich** /bə'trɛçtlɪç/ ❶ *Adj.* considerable; **um ein Beträchtliches** to a considerable degree. ❷ *adv.* considerably

**Betrachtung** *die*; ~, ~**en** Ⓐ contemplation; (*Untersuchung*) examination; **bei genauer[er] ~**: upon close[r] examination; (*fig.*) upon close[r] consideration; **bei nachträglicher ~**: [viewed] in retrospect; Ⓑ (*Überlegung*) observation; ~**en über etw.** (*Akk.*) **anstellen** make observations *or* comments about sth.

**Betrachtungs·weise** *die* way of looking at things; (*Standpunkt*) point of view

**Betrag** /bə'tra:k/ *der*; ~**[e]s, Beträge** /bə'trɛ:gə/ sum; amount; **ein Scheck über einen ~ von 1 000 DM** a cheque for 1,000 marks; **~ dankend erhalten** (*auf Quittungen*) received *or* paid with thanks

**betragen** ❶ *unr. itr. V.* be; (*bei Geldsummen*) come to; amount to; **die Zeitdifferenz beträgt 3 Stunden** the time difference is three hours. ❷ *unr. refl. V.* behave (**gegenüber, gegen** towards)

**Betragen** *das*; ~**s** behaviour; (*in der Schule*) conduct; **in ~ eine gute Note bekommen** get a good mark for conduct

**Betragens·note** *die* mark for conduct

**betrauen** *tr. V.* **jmdn. mit etw. ~**: entrust sb. with sth.; **jmdn. damit ~, etw. zu tun** entrust sb. with the task of doing sth.

**betrauern** *tr. V.* mourn ‹death, loss›; **jmdn. ~**: mourn for sb.

**beträufeln** *tr. V.* sprinkle (**mit** with drops of)

**Betrauung** *die*; ~: entrusting

**Betreff** /bə'trɛf/ *der*; ~**[e]s**, ~**e** (*Amtsspr.*, *Kaufmannsspr.*) subject; matter; (~**zeile**) heading; reference line; **den ~ angeben** state the subject [of the letter]; (*im Brief*) ~: **Ihr Schreiben vom 26. d. M.** re: your letter of the 26th inst.

**betreffen** *unr. tr. V.* Ⓐ concern; ‹new rule, change, etc.› affect; **was mich betrifft, ...** as far as I'm concerned ...; **was mich betrifft, bin ich** *od.* **ich bin einverstanden** for my part I am in agreement; **was das betrifft, ...** as regards that; as far as that goes; Ⓑ (*geh.*: *widerfahren*) befall; Ⓒ (*geh. veralt.*: *bestürzt machen*) hurt; **es hat mich schmerzhaft betroffen zu hören, dass ...** it saddened

*old spelling (see note on page 1707)

b

me to hear that ...; Ⓓ(*geh. veralt.: ertappen*) apprehend

**betreffend** *Adj.* concerning; **der ~e Sachbearbeiter** the person concerned with *or* dealing with this matter; **in dem ~en Fall** in the case concerned *or* in question

**Betreffende** *der/die; adj. Dekl.* person concerned; **die ~n** the people concerned

**betreffs** *Präp. mit Gen.* (*Amtsspr., Kaufmannsspr.*) concerning

**betreiben** *unr. tr. V.* Ⓐ tackle ‹task›; proceed with, (*energisch*) press ahead with ‹task, case, etc.›; pursue ‹policy, studies›; carry on ‹trade›; **auf jmds./sein B~ (*Akk.*) [hin]** at the instigation of sb./at his instigation; **das Tischlerhandwerk ~:** ply the carpenter's trade; Ⓑ(*führen*) run ‹business, shop›; **Radsport ~:** go in for cycling as a sport; Ⓒ(*antreiben*) drive (**mit** by); **etw. elektrisch ~:** drive sth. by electricity *or* electrically; **ein atomar/mit Dampf betriebenes Schiff** a nuclear-powered/steam-powered ship; Ⓓ(*schweiz.: Rechtsw.*) sue (*for payment of a debt*)

**Betreibung** *die; ~,* **~en die ~ eines Geschäfts/einer Anlage** running a business/driving a plant

**betresst, *betreßt** /bəˈtrɛst/ *Adj.* braided

**betreten**[1] *unr. tr. V.* (*hineintreten in*) enter; (*treten auf*) walk *or* step on to; (*begehen*) walk on ‹carpet, grass, etc.›; **er hat das Haus nicht mehr** *od.* **nie wieder ~:** he never set foot in the house again; **„B~ verboten"** 'Keep off'; (*kein Eintritt*) 'Keep out'; **„B~ der Baustelle verboten"** 'Building site. No entry *or* Keep out'; **den Rasen nicht ~:** keep off the grass; ⇒ *auch* **Neuland**

**betreten**[2] ❶ *Adj.* embarrassed; **ein ~es Gesicht machen** look embarrassed. ❷ *adv.* with embarrassment; **man schwieg ~:** there was an embarrassed silence

**Betretenheit** *die; ~:* embarrassment

**betreuen** /bəˈtrɔyən/ *tr. V.* look after; care for ‹invalid›; supervise ‹youth group›; see to the needs of ‹tourists, sportsmen›; look after, be in charge of ‹department etc.›

**Betreuer** *der; ~s, ~* (*für Alte, Kranke, Behinderte*) social worker; (*für Kinder*) minder; (*für Entlassene aus Krankenhaus/Gefängnis*) aftercare worker; (*für Sportler, Künstler*) manager; (*für Touristen*) courier; travel guide; (*einer Delegation*) secretary

**Betreuerin** *die; ~,* **~nen** Ⓐ(*Kinder~*) childminder; (*ganztägig*) nanny (*Brit.*); nursemaid (*Amer.*); (*Krankenpflegerin*) nurse; Ⓑ ⇒ **Betreuer**

**Betreuung** *die; ~* Ⓐ care *no indef. art.;* **die ~ der Gäste** taking care of the guests; **jmdn. zur ~ des Großvaters einstellen** take on sb. to look after *or* care for grandfather; **zwei Reiseleiter waren zu unserer ~ vorhanden** there were two couriers *or* travel guides to see to our needs; Ⓑ(*Person*) minder; (*Krankenpfleger*) nurse

**Betrieb** *der; ~[e]s, ~e* Ⓐ business; (*Firma*) firm; **ein staatlicher ~:** a state-owned *or* nationalized concern; **ein landwirtschaftlicher ~:** an agricultural holding; **im ~ sein/bleiben/essen** be/stay/eat at work; ⇒ *auch* **volkseigen**; Ⓑ(*das In-Funktion-Sein*) operation; (*Arbeitsprozess*) working process; operations *pl., no art.;* **in ~ sein** be running; be in operation; **außer ~ sein** be out of order; **in/außer ~ setzen** start up/stop ‹machine etc.›; (*ein-/ausschalten*) switch on/off; **in ~ nehmen** put into operation; put ‹bus, train› into service; **ein Kraftwerk wird in ~ genommen** a power plant is commissioned; **den ~ einstellen** close down *or* cease operations; (*in einer Fabrik*) stop work; (*einer Buslinie o. Ä.*) withdraw the service; **den [ganzen] ~ aufhalten** (*ugs.*) hold everybody up; Ⓒ(*ugs.: Treiben*) bustle; commotion; (*Verkehr*) traffic; **es herrscht großer ~, es ist viel ~:** it's very busy; **bei dem ~ kann man nicht arbeiten** one cannot work with all that [commotion] going on

**betrieblich** *Adj.* firm's; company; (*inner~*) internal; within the company *postpos.;* **aus ~en Gründen** for reasons to do with the state of the company

**betriebsam** ❶ *Adj.* busy; (*ständig ~*) constantly on the go *postpos.;* **~e Naturen** hyperactive types; eager beavers (*coll.*); (*Frauen*) busy bees (*coll.*). ❷ *adv.* busily

**Betriebsamkeit** *die; ~:* [bustling] activity; **eine hektische ~ an den Tag legen** become frantically busy

**betriebs-, Betriebs-: ~angehörige** *der/die* employee; *Pl.* company staff; **~an·leitung** *die,* **~an·weisung** *die* operating instructions *pl.;* (*Heft*) instruction manual; **~arzt** *der,* **~ärztin** *die* company doctor; **~aus·flug** *der* staff outing; **~begehung** *die* factory *etc.* inspection tour; **~bereit** *Adj.* ready to be put into operation *postpos.;* **~bereit sein** be operational; **~besichtigung** *die* visit to a firm; (*Fabrikbesichtigung*) factory visit; (*eines landwirtschaftlichen Betriebs*) farm visit; **~blind** *Adj.* inured to the shortcomings of working methods *postpos.;* professionally blinkered; **~blind werden** get into a rut *or* become blinkered in one's work; **~blindheit** *die* blinkered attitude to one's work; **~eigen** *Adj.* company-owned; **~erlaubnis** *die* operating permit; **~ferien** *Pl.* firm's annual close-down *sing.;* **das Geschäft hat ~ferien** the shop is closed for its annual holidays; **„Wegen ~ferien geschlossen"** 'closed for annual holidays'; **~fertig** *Adj.:* ⇒ **~bereit**; **~fest** *das* firm's party; **~fremd** *Adj.* who are not company employees *postpos., not pred.;* outside; **„Zutritt ~fremden nicht gestattet"** 'Staff Only'; **~frieden** *der* harmonious relationship between employer and employed (*which all parties are obliged to uphold*); industrial peace; **~führer** *der,* **~führerin** *die* ⇒ **~leiter**; **~führung** *die* ⇒ **~leitung**; **~geheimnis** *das* company secret; trade secret (*also fig.*); **das ~geheimnis verletzen** infringe the confidentiality of company matters; **~gruppe** *die* trade union membership (*within one company*); **~intern** ❶ *Adj.* internal; internal company *attrib.;* ❷ *adv.* internally; within the company; **~kapital** *das* Ⓐ working capital; Ⓑ(*Anfangskapital*) initial capital; **~kinder·garten** *der* play school for employees' children; **~klima** *das* working atmosphere; **~kosten** *Pl.* running costs; (*einer Firma*) operating costs; **~kranken·kasse** *die* company sickness insurance scheme; **~leiter** *der,* **~leiterin** *die* manager; (*einer Fabrik*) works manager; **~leitung** *die* management [of the firm]; **~nudel** *die* (*ugs.*) Ⓐ live wire in the office; (*Komiker*) office comedian; Ⓑ(*übergeschäftige Person*) eager beaver (*coll.*); (*Frau*) busy bee (*coll.*); **~obfrau** *die,* **~obmann** *der,* **~obmännin** *die; ~~,* **~~nen** workers' representative (*in a small firm*); **~prüfung** *die* audit of a/the firm's accounts (*by the taxation authorities*); **~rat** *der; Pl.:* **~räte** Ⓐ works committee; Ⓑ(*Person*) member of a/the works committee; **~rätin** *die* ⇒ **~rat** B; **~rats·mitglied** *das* member of a/the works committee; **~rats·vorsitzende** *der/die* chairman of a/the works committee; **~rente** *die* company pension; **~ruhe** *die:* **~ruhe haben** ‹business, factory› be closed; **~schließung** *die* closure [of a/the firm]; **~schluss, *~schluß** *der* (*im Geschäft*) end of business hours; (*in der Fabrik*) end of working hours; **kurz vor ~schluss** shortly before it was time to go home *or* (*coll.*) knocking-off time; **nach ~schluss geht er gleich nach Hause** after work he goes straight home; **~sicher** *Adj.* [operationally] safe; **~sicher sein** be safe to operate *or* run; **~sicherheit** *die* [operational] safety; (*in der Fabrik*) safety at work; **~stilllegung** *die* closure [of a/the firm]; (*eines Werks*) works closure; **~störung** *die* malfunction; **~system** *das* (*DV*) operating system; **~treue** *die* loyalty to a/the company; **10-jährige ~treue** 10 years' service with a/the company; **~unfall** *der* Ⓐ(*veralt.*) industrial accident; Ⓑ(*ugs.: Ungeschicklichkeit*) slip-up; little mishap; **~vereinbarung** *die: agreement between 'Betriebsrat' and management;* **~verfassung** *die* code of industrial relations (*covering worker participation and representation*); **~verfassungs·gesetz** *das* industrial relations law (*for the private sector*); **~versammlung** *die* meeting of the workforce; **~wirt** *der,* **~wirtin** *die* graduate in business management; **~wirtschaft** *die* business management; **~wirtschaftlich** ❶ *Adj.* business management *attrib.;* ❷ *adv.* from the business management standpoint; **~wirtschafts·lehre** *die* [theory of] business management; (*Fach*) management studies *sing., no art.;* **~wissenschaft** *die* ⇒ **~wirtschaftslehre**; **~zeitung** *die* company newspaper

**betrinken** *unr. refl. V.* get drunk; **sich fürchterlich/sinnlos ~:** get terribly/blind drunk

**betroffen** /bəˈtrɔfn̩/ ❶ *2. Part. v.* **betreffen.** ❷ *Adj.* upset; (*bestürzt*) dismayed; **zutiefst** *od.* **im Innersten ~:** extremely upset; (*gekränkt*) deeply hurt. ❸ *adv.* in dismay *or* consternation; **~ schweigen** be too upset/dismayed to say anything

**Betroffene** *der/die; adj. Dekl.* person affected; **die von ... ~n** those affected by ...

**Betroffenheit** *die; ~:* dismay; consternation

**betrog** /bəˈtroːk/ *1. u. 3. Pers. Sg. Prät. v.* **betrügen**

**betrogen** *2. Part. v.* **betrügen**

**betrüben** ❶ *tr. V.* sadden; **seine Eltern durch sein Verhalten ~:** cause one's parents distress through one's behaviour. ❷ *refl. V.* (*geh. veralt.*) **sich über etw. (*Akk.*) ~:** become dejected *or* depressed about sth.

**betrüblich** *Adj.* gloomy; (*deprimierend*) depressing; **ich muss Ihnen die ~e Mitteilung machen, dass ...** unfortunately I have to inform you that ...

**betrüblicher·weise** *Adv.* unfortunately; (*traurigerweise*) sadly

**Betrübnis** /bəˈtryːpnɪs/ *die; ~,* **~se** (*geh.*) sadness

**betrübt** /bəˈtryːpt/ ❶ *Adj.* (*traurig*) sad (**über** + *Akk.* about); (*deprimiert*) dismayed, depressed (**über** + *Akk.* about); gloomy ‹face etc.›; **~ aussehen** look gloomy; ⇒ *auch* **Tod.** ❷ *adv.* sadly; (*schwermütig*) gloomily

**betrug** /bəˈtruːk/ *1. u. 3. Pers. Sg. Prät. v.* **betragen**

**Betrug** *der; ~[e]s; Pl. schweiz.:* **Betrüge** deception; (*Mogelei*) cheating *no indef. art.;* (*Delikt*) fraud; **das ist [glatter] ~:** that's [plain] fraud/cheating; **mehrfacher** *od.* (*Rechtsw.*) **fortgesetzter ~:** repeated fraud; **ein frommer ~:** a well-meaning deception; (*Selbsttäuschung*) [a case of] self-deception

**betrügen** ❶ *unr. tr. V.* Ⓐ deceive; be unfaithful to ‹husband, wife›; (*Rechtsw.*) defraud ‹firm, customer, etc.›; (*beim Spielen*) cheat; **sich [in etw. (*Dat.*)] betrogen sehen** be deceived [in sth.]; (*in seinem Vertrauen*) be betrayed [in sth.]; (*enttäuscht*) be let down [in sth.]; **er sah sich in all seinen Hoffnungen betrogen** all his hopes were dashed; he was disappointed in all his hopes; **sich selbst ~:** deceive oneself; Ⓑ(*um etw. bringen*) **jmdn. um 100 DM ~:** cheat *or* (*coll.*) do sb. out of 100 marks; (*arglistig*) swindle sb. out of 100 marks; **um sein Recht betrogen werden** be cheated of one's rights.
❷ *unr. itr. V.* cheat; (*bei Geschäften*) swindle people

**Betrüger** *der; ~s, ~:* swindler; (*Hochstapler*) con man (*coll.*); (*beim Spielen*) cheat; (*der Ehefrau*) deceiver

**Betrügerei** *die; ~,* **~en** deception; (*beim Spielen usw.*) cheating; (*bei Geschäften*) swindling; **eine kleine ~:** a bit of a swindle *or* of swindling; a bit of cheating; **deine ~en** your swindling *sing.*/cheating *sing.*

**Betrügerin** *die; ~,* **~nen** swindler; (*beim Spielen*) cheat; (*des Ehemanns*) deceiver

**betrügerisch** *Adj.* deceitful; (*Rechtsw.*) fraudulent; **in ~er Absicht** with intent to deceive

**betrunken** /bəˈtrʊŋkn̩/ ❶ *2. Part. v.* **betrinken.** ❷ *Adj.* drunken *attrib.;* drunk *pred.;* **ein total ~er Fahrer** a completely drunk and incapable driver. ❸ *adv.* drunkenly

**Betrunkene** *der/die; adj. Dekl.* drunk; **eine ~:** a drunken woman

**Bet-:** ~**saal** *der* meeting hall; [primitive] chapel; ~**schwester** *die* (*abwertend*) over-pious type (*coll.*); ~**stuhl** *der* prayer stool

**Bett** /bɛt/ *das;* ~[e]s, ~en Ⓐ bed; **das ~ machen** make the bed; **die ~en bauen** (*ugs. scherzh.*) make the beds; **jmdm. das Frühstück ans ~ bringen** bring sb. breakfast in bed; **sie ging an sein ~/saß an seinem ~:** she went to/sat at his bedside; **jmdn. aus dem ~ holen** (*ugs.*) get sb. out of bed; **er kommt nur schwer aus dem ~:** he doesn't like getting up; **im ~:** in bed; **[mit Fieber] im ~ liegen** be in bed [with a temperature]; **ins** *od.* **zu ~ gehen, sich ins** *od.* **zu ~ legen** go to bed; **ins ~ fallen** (*ugs.*) fall into bed; **die Kinder ins ~ bringen** put the children to bed; **das ~ hüten [müssen]** (*fig.*) [have to] stay in bed; **er hütet seit einer Woche das ~** (*fig.*) he has been in bed for a week; **das ~ mit jmdm. teilen** (*fig. geh.*) share bed and board with sb.; live together with sb.; **mit jmdm. ins ~ gehen** *od.* **steigen** (*fig. ugs.*) go to bed with sb.; **sich ins gemachte ~ legen** (*fig.*) have everything handed to one on a plate (*fig.*); ⇒ *auch* **fesseln, klingeln;** Ⓑ (*Feder~*) duvet; Ⓒ (*Fluss~*) bed; **der Fluss hat sich ein neues ~ gesucht** the river has formed a new bed; Ⓓ (*Technik*) bed

**Bet·tag** *der* ⇒ **Buß- und Bettag**

**Bett-:** ~**an·zug** *der* (*schweiz.*), ~**bezug** *der* duvet cover; ~**couch** *die* bed settee; studio couch; ~**decke** *die* Ⓐ blanket; (*gesteppt*) quilt; Ⓑ (*Tagesdecke*) bedspread

**Bettel** /ˈbɛtl̩/ *der;* ~s Ⓐ (*ugs.*) junk (*coll.*); Ⓑ (*veralt.:* ~n) begging *no art.*

**bettel-, Bettel-:** ~**arm** *Adj.* destitute; penniless; ~**brief** *der* begging letter

**Bettelei** *die;* ~, ~en begging *no art.*

**Bettel-:** ~**mann** *der; Pl.:* ~**leute** (*veralt.*) beggar; ~**mönch** *der* mendicant friar

**betteln** /ˈbɛtl̩n/ *itr. V.* beg (**um** for); **~ gehen** go begging; **„B~ verboten!"** 'No begging'; **bei jmdm. um etw. ~:** beg sb. for sth.; **darum ~, aufbleiben zu dürfen** beg to be allowed to stay up

**Bettel-:** ~**orden** *der* mendicant order; ~**stab** *der: in* **jmdn. an den ~stab bringen** reduce sb. to penury; ~**weib** *das* (*veralt.*) beggar woman

**betten** (*geh.*) ❶ *tr. V.* Ⓐ lay; **jmdn. flach ~:** lay sb. [down] flat; **jmdn. weich ~:** make a soft bed for sb. to lie on; **weich gebettet sein** (*fig.*) have an easy time of it; be featherbedded; Ⓑ (*ein~*) **etw. in etw.** (*Akk.*) **~:** embed sth. in sth. ❷ *refl. V.* (*fig.*) **wie man sich bettet, so liegt man** as you make your bed, so you must lie on it; **sich weich ~:** feather one's nest

**Betten-:** ~**burg** *die* Ⓐ (*Hotel*) giant hotel; Ⓑ (*Urlaubsort*) overdeveloped resort; ~**machen** *das;* ~~s making the beds *no art.;* (*allgemein*) making beds *no art.;* **das tägliche ~machen** the daily making of beds; ~**mangel** *der* shortage of beds

**bett-, Bett-:** ~**feder** *die* Ⓐ bedspring; Ⓑ *Pl.* (*Füllung*) [pillow/bed] feathers; ~**flasche** *die* hot-water bottle; ~**genosse** *der,* ~**genossin** *die* bedfellow; ~**geschichte** *die* (*abwertend*) Ⓐ (*Verhältnis*) purely physical relationship; **seine ~geschichten schildern** describe one's bedroom experiences; Ⓑ (*Klatschgeschichte*) bedroom saga; **~geschichten der Filmstars** gossip about film stars' love lives; ~**gestell** *das* bedstead; ~**häschen** *das,* ~**hase** *der* (*ugs. scherzh.*) sex kitten; ~**himmel** *der* bed canopy; ~**hupferl** /-hʊpfɐl/ *das;* ~s, ~~: bedtime treat; ~**jäckchen** *das,* ~**jacke** *die* bedjacket; ~**kante** *die* edge of the bed; ~**kasten** *der* bedding box (*under a bed*); ~**lade** *die* (*südd., österr.*) ⇒ ~**gestell;** ~**lägerig** /-lɛːɡərɪç/ *Adj.* bedridden; ~**laken** *das* sheet; ~**lektüre** *die* bedtime reading *no indef. art.*

**Bettler** /ˈbɛtlɐ/ *der;* ~s, ~: beggar

**Bettlerin** *die;* ~, ~nen beggar [woman]

**bett-, Bett-:** ~**nässen** *das;* ~~s bed-wetting *no art.;* ~**nässer** *der;* ~~s, ~~, ~**nässerin** *die;* ~~, ~~nen bed-wetter; ~**pfanne** *die* bedpan; ~**reif** *Adj.* (*ugs.*) ready for bed *pred.;* ~**ruhe** *die* bed rest; **zwei Wochen [absolute] ~ruhe** two weeks of [complete] bed rest; ~**schwere** *die* **die nötige** *od.* **notwendige ~schwere haben** (*ugs.*) be ready for one's bed; ~**statt** *die;* ~, ~**stätten** /-ʃtɛtn̩/ (*südd., österr.*), ~**stelle** *die* ⇒ **Bettgestell;** ~**szene** *die* (*Film*) bedroom scene; ~**tuch** *das; Pl.* ~**tücher** sheet; ~**über·zug** *der* duvet cover

***Bettuch** ⇒ **Betttuch**

**Bett·umrandung** *die* bedside carpeting (*on three sides of the bed*)

**Bettung** *die;* ~, ~en (*Eisenb., Straßenbau*) roadbed

**Bett-:** ~**vorlage** *die,* ~**vorleger** *der* bedside rug; ~**wäsche** *die* bedlinen; ~**zeug** *das* (*ugs.*) bedclothes *pl.*

**betucht** /bəˈtuːxt/ *Adj.* (*ugs.*) **[gut] ~:** well-heeled (*coll.*); well-off

**betulich** /bəˈtuːlɪç/ ❶ *Adj.* Ⓐ fussy; (*besorgt*) worried; agitated; Ⓑ (*gemächlich*) leisurely; unhurried. ❷ *adv.* Ⓐ fussily; Ⓑ (*gemächlich*) in a calm unhurried way

**Betulichkeit** *die;* ~ Ⓐ fussiness; (*Besorgtheit*) agitation; Ⓑ (*Gemächlichkeit*) calm unhurried manner

**betun** *unr. refl. V.* (*ugs.*) fuss around

**betupfen** *tr. V.* dab

**betuppen** /bəˈtʊpn̩/ *tr. V.* (*nordwestd. ugs.*) diddle (*coll.*); do (*coll.*)

**betütern** /bəˈtyːtɐn/ (*nordd. ugs.*) ❶ *tr. V.* mollycoddle. ❷ *refl. V.* get merry *or* tipsy

**betütert** *Adj.* (*nordd. ugs.*) Ⓐ (*beschwipst*) merry; tipsy; Ⓑ (*verwirrt*) not quite with it *pred.* (*coll.*)

**beugbar** *Adj.* (*Sprachw.*) declinable ‹noun, adjective›; conjugable ‹verb›

**Beuge** /ˈbɔyɡə/ *die;* ~, ~n Ⓐ (*Turnen*) bend; **eine ~ machen** bend over; (*Knie~*) **in die ~ gehen** do a knees-bend; Ⓑ (*Biegung*) bend; Ⓒ (*Arm~/Bein~*) crook of one's arm *or* elbow/knee

**Beuge·haft** *die* (*Rechtsw.*) coercive detention

**Beugel** /ˈbɔyɡl̩/ *das;* ~s, ~ (*österr.*) filled croissant

**Beuge·muskel** *der* ▶ 471 (*Anat.*) flexor

**beugen** ❶ *tr. V.* Ⓐ bend; bow ‹head›; **den Rumpf ~:** bend from the waist; **gebeugt gehen** walk with a stoop; **vom Alter/vom Kummer gebeugt** (*geh.*) bent *or* bowed with age *postpos.*/bowed down with grief *postpos.;* Ⓑ (*geh.: brechen*) **jmdn. ~:** break sb.'s resistance; **jmds. Starrsinn/Stolz ~:** break sb.'s stubborn/proud nature; Ⓒ (*Sprachw.: flektieren*) inflect ‹word›; decline ‹noun, adjective›; conjugate ‹verb›; **stark/schwach gebeugt werden** be strong/weak; have strong/weak endings; **ein stark/schwach gebeugtes Adjektiv** an adjective with strong/weak endings; Ⓓ (*Rechtsw.*) bend ‹law›; **das Recht ~:** pervert the course of justice; Ⓔ (*Physik*) diffract ‹light ray etc.›. ❷ *refl. V.* Ⓐ bend over; (*sich bücken*) stoop; **sich nach vorn/hinten ~:** bend forwards/bend over backwards; **sich aus dem Fenster ~:** lean out of the window; **sich über den Tisch/das Geländer** *usw.* **~:** lean over the table/the banisters *etc.;* **er beugte sich über ihre Hand** he bowed his head over her hand; Ⓑ (*sich fügen*) give way; give in; **sich dem Druck ~:** yield *or* give way to pressure; **sich der Mehrheit ~:** bow to the will of the majority

**Beugung** *die;* ~, ~en Ⓐ (*das Biegen*) bending; (*Biegung*) bend; Ⓑ (*Sprachw.*) inflexion; (*eines Substantivs*) declension; (*eines Verbs*) conjugation; **ein Adjektiv mit starker/schwacher ~:** an adjective with strong/weak endings *or* inflexion; Ⓒ (*Rechtsw.: des Gesetzes*) bending; **~ des Rechts** perversion of justice; Ⓓ (*Physik*) diffraction

**Beugungs·endung** *die* ⇒ **Flexionsendung**

**Beule** /ˈbɔylə/ *die;* ~, ~n Ⓐ bump; swelling; (*Furunkel*) boil; Ⓑ (*Vertiefung*) dent (**an** + *Dat.* in); (*Vorwölbung*) bump; bulge

**beulen** *itr. V.* bulge; ‹trousers› be baggy

**Beulen·pest** *die* bubonic plague

**beunruhigen** /bəˈ|ʊnruːɪɡn̩/ ❶ *tr. V.* worry; **es beunruhigte ihn sehr** it made him very worried; **über etw.** (*Akk.*) **beunruhigt sein** be worried about sth.; **bist du nicht beunruhigt darüber, dass ...?** aren't you worried that ...? ❷ *refl. V.* worry **(um, wegen** about)

**Beunruhigung** *die;* ~, ~en worry; concern; **eine deutliche ~:** an obvious sense of concern

**beurkunden** /bəˈ|uːɐ̯kʊndn̩/ *tr. V.* record; (*belegen*) document, provide a record of

**beurlauben** /bəˈ|uːɐ̯laubn̩/ ❶ *tr. V.* Ⓐ **jmdn. [für zwei Tage] ~:** give sb. [two days'] leave of absence; **sich ~ lassen** obtain leave of absence; **beurlaubt sein** be on leave [of absence]; **Professor X ist in diesem Semester beurlaubt** Professor X is on sabbatical leave this term; Ⓑ (*suspendieren*) suspend. ❷ *refl. V.* (*veralt.*) take one's leave

**Beurlaubung** *die;* ~, ~en Ⓐ leave of absence *no indef. art.;* **eine [einjährige] ~ beantragen** apply for [one year's] leave of absence; ‹professor› apply for a [one-year] sabbatical; Ⓑ (*Suspendierung*) suspension

**beurteilen** *tr. V.* judge; assess; **etw. falsch ~:** misjudge sth.; assess sth. wrongly; **sie ~ die Lage als kritisch** they judge the situation to be critical *or* see the situation as critical; **er kann doch nicht ~, was wirklich passiert ist** he cannot possibly tell *or* is in no position to say what really happened

**Beurteilung** *die;* ~, ~en Ⓐ judgement; (*einer Lage usw.*) assessment; **bei nüchterner ~ der Ereignisse muss man ...** if one views the events dispassionately, one has to ...; Ⓑ (*Gutachten*) assessment; (*für eine Bewerbung*) reference

**Beurteilungs·maßstab** *der* criterion of judgement/assessment

**Beuschel** /ˈbɔyʃl̩/ *das;* ~s, ~ Ⓐ (*österr., bayr.*) *dish made of finely chopped lights usu. with heart and other offal;* Ⓑ (*österr. salopp: Lunge*) lung; Ⓒ (*österr. salopp: Eingeweide*) guts *pl.* (*coll.*)

**Beute**[1] /ˈbɔytə/ *die;* ~, ~n Ⓐ (*Gestohlenes*) haul; loot *no indef. art.;* (*Kriegs~*) booty; spoils *pl.;* **eine ~ in Millionenhöhe machen** make a haul worth millions; **fette ~ machen** get rich pickings *pl.;* Ⓑ (*von Raubtieren*) prey; (*eines Jägers*) bag; **[seine] ~ schlagen** catch one's prey; **leichte ~:** easy prey; Ⓒ (*geh.: Opfer*) prey (+ *Gen.* to); **eine ~ der Flammen werden** be consumed by the flames

**Beute**[2] *die;* ~, ~n (*Imkerspr.*) hive

**beute·gierig** *Adj.* Ⓐ rapacious; on the prowl *postpos.;* ravening ‹wolf›; Ⓑ (*auf Raub aus*) greedy for loot *postpos.*

**Beutel** /ˈbɔytl̩/ *der;* ~s, ~ Ⓐ bag; (*kleiner, für Tabak usw.*) pouch; Ⓑ (*ugs.: Geld~*) purse; **jmds. ~ ist leer** sb. is broke (*coll.*); **tief in den ~ greifen müssen** have to dig deep into one's pocket; **etw. reißt ein großes Loch in jmds. ~:** sth. makes a big hole in sb.'s pocket; Ⓒ (*Zool.*) pouch

**beuteln** ❶ *tr. V.* Ⓐ (*südd., österr.: schütteln*) shake; Ⓑ (*fig.: hart bedrängen*) batter; **das Leben hat ihn gebeutelt** life has given him some hard knocks; Ⓒ (*übervorteilen*) **jmdn. ~:** take sb. for a ride (*coll.*). ❷ *itr. V.* bulge; ‹trousers› be baggy

**Beutel-:** ~**ratte** *die* opossum; ~**schneider** *der,* ~**schneiderin** *die* (*veralt.*) Ⓐ cutpurse (*arch.*); (*Gauner*) crook; Ⓑ (*geh.: Nepper*) shark; racketeer; ~**tier** *das* marsupial

**Beute·zug** *der* thieving spree; raid

**Beutler** /ˈbɔytlɐ/ *der;* ~s, ~ (*Zool.*) marsupial

**bevölkern** /bəˈfœlkɐn/ ❶ *tr. V.* populate; inhabit; (*besiedeln*) settle; (*fig.*) fill; invade; **ein stark/dünn** *od.* **wenig bevölkertes Land** a densely/thinly *or* sparsely populated country; **von Touristen bevölkert** (*fig.*) full of tourists. ❷ *refl. V.* become populated; ‹bar, restaurant, etc.› fill up

**Bevölkerung** *die;* ~, ~en Ⓐ population; (*Volk*) people; Ⓑ (*Besiedlung*) settling

*old spelling (see note on page 1707)

**Bevölkerungs-: ~abnahme** *die* decline in population; **~dichte** *die* population density; **~explosion** *die* population explosion; **~gruppe** *die* section of the population; **~schicht** *die* section *or* stratum of society; **~schwund** *der* ⇒ **~abnahme**; **~statistik** *die* demography *no art.*; **~zahl** *die* population; **~zunahme** *die*, **~zuwachs** *der* increase in population

**bevollmächtigen** /bəˈfɔlmɛçtɪgn̩/ *tr. V.* **jmdn. [dazu] ~, etw. zu tun** authorize sb. to do sth.; (*in Rechtshandlungen*) give sb. power of attorney to do sth.

**Bevollmächtigte** *der/die; adj. Dekl.* authorized representative

**Bevollmächtigung** *die;* ~, **~en** authorization; (*Rechtsw.*) power of attorney

**bevor** /bəˈfoːɐ̯/ *Konj.* before; **noch ~ ich antworten konnte** before I could [even] reply; **~ du nicht unterschreibst/unterschrieben hast** until you sign/have signed

**bevor·munden** *tr. V.* **jmdn. ~:** impose one's will on sb.; **sie wollen sich nicht länger ~ lassen** they do not want to be dictated to any longer

**Bevormundung** *die;* ~, **~en** imposing one's will (+ *Gen.* on); **wie kann sie sich diese ~ durch ihre Eltern gefallen lassen?** how can she put up with her parents telling her what to do?

**bevor·raten** *tr. V.* (*Amtsspr.*) lay in stocks of ‹goods, materials›; **gut bevorratet werden/sein** be kept/be well stocked *or* supplied

**bevor|stehen** *unr. itr. V.* be near; be about to happen; **[unmittelbar] ~:** be imminent; **jmdm. steht etw. bevor** sth. is in store for sb.; **mir steht etwas Schlimmes bevor** there's something unpleasant in store for me; **die schwerste Prüfung steht ihm noch bevor** he has still to face his severest test; his severest test is still to come

**bevorstehend** *Adj.* forthcoming; coming ‹winter›; **[unmittelbar] ~:** imminent; **die [dir/uns] ~en Probleme** the problems facing you/us

**bevorzugen** /bəˈfoːɐ̯tsuːgn̩/ *tr. V.* **A** prefer (**vor** + *Dat.* to); **B** (*begünstigen*) favour; give preference *or* preferential treatment to (**vor** + *Dat.* over)

**bevorzugt** **1** *Adj.* favoured; (*privilegiert*) privileged; preferential ‹treatment›. **2** *adv.* **jmdn. ~ behandeln** give sb. preferential treatment; **jmdn. ~ abfertigen/bedienen** give sb. priority *or* precedence/serve sb. first; **etw. ~ erledigen/bearbeiten** give sth. priority

**Bevorzugung** *die;* ~, **~en** preferential treatment; preference (*Gen.*, **von** for)

**bewachen** *tr. V.* guard; (*Ballspiele*) mark; **die Gefangenen werden streng bewacht** a close watch is kept on the prisoners; the prisoners are closely guarded; **ihr Mann bewacht sie wie ein Schießhund** her husband watches over her like a guard dog; **bewachter Parkplatz** car park with an attendant

**Bewacher** *der;* **~s**, ~, **Bewacherin** *die;* ~, **~nen** guard; (*Ballspiele*) marker

**bewachsen** *unr. tr. V.* grow over; cover; **eine mit Efeu ~e Laube** a summerhouse overgrown with ivy; an ivy-covered summerhouse; **ein dicht ~es Tal/Blumenbeet** a valley full of dense vegetation/a border packed with flowers

**Bewachung** *die;* ~, **~en** **A** guarding; (*Ballspiele*) marking; **zur ~ des Geländes** to guard the site; **unter scharfer ~:** closely guarded; **jmdn. unter ~ stellen** put sb. under guard; **sich der ~ entziehen** (*Ballspiele*) escape one's marker/markers; **B** (*Wachmannschaft*) guard

**bewaffnen** /bəˈvafnən/ **1** *tr. V.* arm; **ein Heer [neu] ~:** supply an army with [new] weapons. **2** *refl. V.* (*auch fig.*) arm oneself (**mit** with)

**bewaffnet** *Adj.* armed; **bis an die Zähne ~:** armed to the teeth; **~er Raubüberfall/Widerstand** armed robbery/resistance; **mit Fotoapparaten ~** (*fig.*) armed with cameras

**Bewaffnete** *der/die; adj. Dekl.* armed man/woman/person; **~:** people bearing arms; armed men/women

**Bewaffnung** *die;* ~, **~en** **A** arming; **B** (*Waffen*) weapons *pl.*

**bewahren** *tr. V.* **A** **jmdn. vor etw.** (*Dat.*) **~:** protect *or* preserve sb. from sth.; **vor einer Enttäuschung bewahrt bleiben** be saved *or* spared a disappointment; **[Gott** *od.* **i] bewahre!** good Lord, no!; (*Gott behüte*) God forbid!; **B** (*erhalten*) **seine Fassung** *od.* **Haltung ~:** keep *or* retain one's composure; **Stillschweigen/Treue ~:** remain silent/faithful; **sich** (*Dat.*) **etw. ~:** retain *or* preserve sth.; **C** (*geh.: auf~*) keep; **etw. im Gedächtnis ~** (*fig.*) preserve the memory of sth.; **etw. im Herzen ~** (*fig.*) treasure sth. in one's heart

**bewähren** **1** *refl. V.* prove oneself/itself; prove one's/its worth; **sich als [guter] Freund ~:** prove to be a [good] friend; **sich im Leben ~:** prove oneself in life; make something of one's life; **das Gerät hat sich doch noch bewährt** this apparatus has turned out to be useful after all; **sich gut/schlecht ~:** prove/not prove to be worth while *or* a success; **sich am besten ~:** prove to be best; **unsere Freundschaft hat sich über all die Jahre bewährt** our friendship has stood the test of time over all these years.
**2** *tr. V.* (*veralt.*) prove

**bewahrheiten** /bəˈvaːɐ̯haitn̩/ *refl. V.* prove to be true; **an ihm bewahrheitet sich der Spruch, dass ...** he demonstrates the truth of the saying that ...

**bewährt** *Adj.* proven ‹method, design, etc.›; well-tried, tried and tested ‹recipe, cure›; reliable ‹worker›

**Bewahrung** *die;* ~ **A** protection *no indef. art.* (**vor** + *Dat.* from); **B** (*geh.: Auf~*) keeping; **C** (*Beibehaltung*) **zur ~ seines Andenkens** to preserve his memory

**Bewährung** *die;* ~, **~en** **A** (*Rechtsw.*) probation; **3 Monate Gefängnis mit ~:** three months suspended sentence [with probation]; **eine Strafe zur ~ aussetzen** [conditionally] suspend a sentence on probation; **B** (*das Sichbewähren*) proving; (*das Testen*) testing

**Bewährungs-: ~auf·lage** *die* (*Rechtsw.*): *obligation imposed as a condition of sentence being suspended;* **~frist** *die* (*Rechtsw.*) period of probation; **~helfer** *der*, **~helferin** *die* probation officer; **~hilfe** *die* (*Rechtsw.*) probation supervision; (*Dienst*) probation service; **~probe** *die* [crucial] test; trial [of one's/its worth]; **jmdn./jmds. Nerven auf eine [harte] ~probe stellen** subject sb. to a [severe] test/be a severe test of sb.'s nerves; **~zeit** *die* (*Rechtsw.*) probation period

**bewaldet** /bəˈvaldət/ *Adj.* wooded

**Bewaldung** *die;* ~, **~en** **A** tree cover; (*Wälder*) woodlands *pl.*; **eine spärliche ~:** a few trees *pl.*; **B** (*Aufforstung*) afforestation *no indef. art.*

**bewältigen** /bəˈvɛltɪgn̩/ *tr. V.* deal with; cope with; overcome ‹difficulty, problem›; cover ‹distance›; (*innerlich verarbeiten*) get over ‹experience›; **die Vergangenheit ~:** come to terms with the past

**Bewältigung** *die;* ~, **~en** ⇒ **bewältigen**: coping with; overcoming; covering; getting over, coming to terms with; **zur ~ der Arbeit** *usw.* to deal *or* cope with the work *etc.*

**bewandert** /bəˈvandɐt/ *Adj.* well-versed; knowledgeable; **auf einem Gebiet/in etw.** (*Dat.*) **~ sein** be well-versed *or* well up in a subject/in sth.

**Bewandtnis** /bəˈvantnɪs/ *die;* ~, **~se** **mit etw. hat es [s]eine eigene/besondere ~:** there's a particular explanation for sth. *or* a [special] story behind sth.; **mit jmdm. hat es seine eigene/besondere ~:** there's a special story about sb.; sb. is a special case; **damit hat es folgende ~:** the story behind *or* reason for it is this

**bewässern** *tr. V.* irrigate; (*begießen*) water

**Bewässerung** *die;* ~, **~en** irrigation; (*das Begießen*) watering

**Bewässerungs-: ~an·lage** *die* irrigation system; (*für Grünflächen usw.*) watering system; **~graben** *der* irrigation ditch; **~kanal** *der* irrigation channel; **~system** *das* irrigation system

**bewegbar** *Adj.* movable

**bewegen**[1] /bəˈveːgn̩/ **1** *tr. V.* **A** move; **den Koffer von der Stelle ~:** move *or* shift the suitcase [from the spot]; **die Pferde/den Hund ~:** exercise the horses/the dog; **Erde ~:** shift *or* remove earth; **B** (*ergreifen*) move; **eine ~de Rede** a moving speech; **niemand wusste, was ihn so bewegte** nobody knew what was affecting him so deeply; **C** (*innerlich beschäftigen*) preoccupy; **das bewegt mich schon lange** I have been preoccupied with this *or* this has exercised my mind for a long time.
**2** *refl. V.* **A** move; **die Blätter bewegten sich sanft** the leaves stirred gently; **der Hund bewegte sich nicht** the dog did not stir *or* was quite still; **B** (*ugs.: sich Bewegung verschaffen*) **ich muss mich ein bisschen ~:** I must get some exercise; **du solltest/musst dich mehr ~:** you ought to/must take more exercise; **C** (*fig.*) **seine Ausführungen ~ sich in der gleichen Richtung** his comments have the same drift *or* are on the same lines; **D** (*schwanken*) vary; fluctuate; **der Preis bewegt sich zwischen 10 DM und 20 DM** the price varies *or* fluctuates between 10 and 20 marks; **E** (*sich verhalten*) behave; **sich mit großer Sicherheit ~:** bear oneself with great confidence

**bewegen**[2] *unr. tr. V.* **jmdn. dazu ~, etw. zu tun** ‹thing› make sb. do sth., induce sb. to do sth.; (*überreden*) ‹person› prevail upon *or* persuade sb. to do sth.; **jmdn. zu etw. ~:** talk sb. into sth.; **jmdn. zum Einlenken ~:** persuade sb. to give way

**Beweg·grund** *der* motive

**beweglich** **1** *Adj.* **A** movable; mobile ‹troops etc.›; moving ‹target›; **die ~en Teile einer Maschine** the moving parts of a machine; **seine ~e Habe** one's goods and chattels *pl.*; one's personal effects *pl.*; **~e Feste** movable feasts; **etw. ist leicht/schwer ~:** sth. is easy/difficult to move; **B** (*rege*) agile, active ‹mind›; (*wendig*) flexible ‹policy›; **geistig ~ sein** be nimble-minded; have an agile mind; **C** (*veralt.: rührend*) moving. **2** *adv.* (*veralt.*) movingly

**Beweglichkeit** *die;* ~ **A** mobility; **B** (*Wendigkeit*) agility; **taktische ~:** tactical flexibility

**bewegt** /bəˈveːkt/ **1** *2. Part. v.* **bewegen**[1]. **2** *Adj.* **A** eventful; (*unruhig*) turbulent; **ein ~es Leben** an eventful/turbulent life; **sie hat eine ~e Vergangenheit** she has a colourful past; **B** (*gerührt*) moved *pred.*; emotional ‹words, voice›; **mit tief ~en Worten/~er Stimme** in words/a voice heavy with emotion; **C** (*unruhig*) **leicht/stark ~** ‹sea› slightly choppy/very rough

**Bewegung** *die;* ~, **~en** **A** movement; (*bes. Technik, Physik*) motion; (*von Erdmassen*) moving; **in ~ sein** ‹person› be on the move; ‹thing› be in motion; **sie ist immer in ~:** she is never still; **jmdn. in ~ bringen/halten** get sb. moving *or* going/keep sb. on the go; **eine Maschine** *usw.* **in ~ setzen** start [up] a machine *etc.*; **sich in ~ setzen** ‹train etc.› start to move; ‹procession› move off; ‹person› get moving; ⇒ *auch* **Hebel**; **B** (*körperliche ~*) exercise; **C** (*Ergriffenheit*) emotion; **große ~ auslösen** arouse strong emotions *pl. or* feelings *pl.*; **D** (*Bestreben, Gruppe*) movement

**bewegungs-, Bewegungs-: ~ab·lauf** *der* sequence of movements; **~drang** *der* urge to be on the move; **~energie** *die* (*Physik*) kinetic energy; **~freiheit** *die* freedom of movement; **~krieg** *der* mobile warfare; **~los** **1** *Adj.* motionless; **vor Schreck ~los** paralysed with fright; **2** *adv.* without moving; **~los liegen/sitzen/stehen** lie/sit/stand motionless; **~losigkeit** *die;* **~~:** motionlessness; immobility; **~studie** *die* time and motion study; **~therapie** *die* physical *or* exercise therapy; **~unfähig** *Adj.* unable

b

to move *postpos.; (gelähmt)* paralysed; ‹vehicle› immobilized

**bewehren** *tr. V. (veralt.)* arm ‹person›; fortify ‹castle›

**beweih·räuchern** /bəˈvaiṛɔyçan/ *tr. V.* surround with incense; *(fig. abwertend)* idolize; **sich selbst ~:** sing one's own praises; blow one's own trumpet

**Beweih·räucherung** *die (fig. abwertend)* idolization; adulation

**beweinen** *tr. V.* lament; *(weinend)* weep over; **jmdn./jmds. Tod ~:** mourn sb./sb.'s passing

**Beweinung** *die;* **~: die ~ Christi** the mourning of Christ

**Beweis** /bəˈvais/ *der;* **~es, ~e** proof *(Gen.,* **für** of); *(Zeugnis)* evidence; **belastende ~e** incriminating evidence; **einen ~/~e für etw. haben** have proof/evidence of sth.; **haben Sie einen ~ dafür, dass ...?** have you any proof/evidence that ...?; **als** *od.* **zum ~ seiner Aussage/Theorie** to substantiate *or* in support of his statement/theory; **bis zum ~ des Gegenteils** until there is proof/evidence to the contrary; **den ~ für etw. antreten** *od.* **erbringen** produce proof [in support] of sth.; **aus Mangel an ~en** owing to lack of evidence; **etw. unter ~ stellen** *(Amtsspr.)* provide proof of sth.; **sie lassen sich kaum unter ~ stellen** they are hardly susceptible of proof; **jmdm. einen ~ seines Vertrauens/seiner Hochachtung geben** give sb. a token of one's trust/esteem; **zahlreiche ~e der Anteilnahme** numerous expressions of sympathy

**Beweis-: ~antrag** *der (Rechtsw.)* application to produce evidence; **~aufnahme** *die (Rechtsw.)* hearing of [the] evidence

**beweisbar** *Adj.* provable; susceptible of proof *postpos.;* **das ist nicht ~:** it cannot be proved

**beweisen** ❶ *unr. tr. V.* Ⓐ prove; **jmdm. seine Beteiligung an etw.** *(Dat.)* **~:** prove sb.'s participation in sth.; **dem Angeklagten konnte die Tat nicht bewiesen werden** it could not be proved that the accused committed the deed; **was [noch] zu ~ wäre** which has yet to be proved; **was zu ~ war** which was the point at issue *or* which needed clarifying; Ⓑ *(zeigen)* show; **damit beweist er seine mangelnde Einsicht** that shows his lack of understanding. ❷ *unr. refl. V.* prove oneself *or* one's worth **(vor** + *Dat.* to)

**beweis-, Beweis-: ~erhebung** *die* ⇒ **~aufnahme; ~führung** *die* Ⓐ *(Rechtsw.)* presentation of the evidence *or* case; Ⓑ *(Argumentation)* reasoning; argumentation; **~gegen·stand** *der (Rechtsw.)* issue; **~kraft** *die* value as evidence; *(einer Argumentation)* cogency; **~kräftig** *Adj.* of value as evidence *postpos.; (Rechtsw.)* of probative value *postpos.;* cogent ‹reasoning›; conclusive ‹test result›; **~last** *die (Rechtsw.)* Ⓐ *(~pflicht)* burden of proof; Ⓑ *(Nachteil) disadvantage due to one's inability to prove a fact material to one's case;* **~material** *das* evidence; *(~stück)* piece of evidence; **~mittel** *das (Rechtsw.)* form of evidence; **~not** *die* want of proof; lack of evidence; **sich in ~not befinden** lack evidence; be short of evidence; **~pflichtig** *Adj. (Rechtsw.)* **für etw. ~pflichtig sein** be obliged to furnish proof of sth.; **~stück** *das* piece of evidence; **~stücke [für etw.]** evidence *sing.* [of sth.]

**bewenden** *unr. V.: in* **es bei** *od.* **mit etw. ~ lassen** [have to] content oneself with sth.

**Bewenden** *das;* **~s damit hat es sein ~:** that is the end of the matter; **damit, dass sie entlassen wird, wird es keineswegs sein ~ haben** even if she is dismissed, the matter won't end there

**bewerben** ❶ *unr. refl. V.* apply **(um** for); **sich bei einer Firma** *usw.* **~:** apply to a company *etc.* [for a job]; **sich als Buchhalter** *usw.* **~:** apply for a job as a bookkeeper *etc.;* **die Firma bewarb sich um den Auftrag** the firm competed for the contract. ❷ *unr. tr. V.* advertise; promote

*old spelling (see note on page 1707)

**Bewerber** *der;* **~s, ~, Bewerberin** *die;* **~, ~nen** Ⓐ applicant; *(Sport: Titel~)* contender; Ⓑ *(veralt.: Freier)* suitor; ⇒ *auch* **-in**

**Bewerbung** *die* application **(um** for)

**Bewerbungs-: ~bogen** *der* application form; **~schreiben** *das* letter of application; **~unterlagen** *Pl.* documents in support of an/the application

**bewerfen** *unr. tr. V.* Ⓐ **jmdn./etw. mit etw. ~:** throw sth. at sb./sth.; **jmdn. mit [faulen] Eiern ~:** pelt sb. with [rotten] eggs; **jmds. Namen mit Schmutz ~** *(fig.)* sling mud at sb. *(fig.)*; drag sb.'s good name through the mud; Ⓑ *(Bauw.)* render ‹wall›; **mit Lehm beworfen** covered *or* faced with clay

**bewerkstelligen** /bəˈvɛrkʃtɛlɪgn̩/ *tr. V.* pull off, manage ‹deal, sale, etc.›; **es ~, etw. zu tun** contrive *or* manage to do sth.

**Bewerkstelligung** *die* managing

**bewertbar** *Adj.* assessable

**bewerten** *tr. V.* assess; rate; *(dem Geldwert nach)* value **(mit** at); *(beurteilen)* judge ‹person›; *(Schulw., Sport)* mark; grade *(Amer.)*; **etw. als Heldentat ~:** rate sth. as a heroic deed; **etw. zu hoch/niedrig ~:** overrate/underrate sth.; *(dem Geldwert nach)* overvalue/undervalue sth.; **Arbeiten schlecht ~** *(Schulw.)* give work low marks *or (Amer.)* grades; **einen Aufsatz mit [der Note] „gut" ~:** mark *or (Amer.)* grade an essay 'good'; **eine Kür mit Noten zwischen 5,6 und 5,9 ~** *(Eiskunstlauf, Turnen)* give a programme marks between 5.6 and 5.9

**Bewertung** *die* Ⓐ *(das Bewerten)* assessment; *(des Geldwerts)* valuation; *(eines Menschen)* judgement; *(das Benoten einer Schularbeit)* marking; grading *(Amer.)*; Ⓑ *(Äußerung)* assessment; *(Note)* mark; grade *(Amer.)*

**Bewertungs·maß·stab** *der* criterion of assessment

**bewies** /bəˈviːs/ *1. u. 3. Pers. Sg. Prät. v.* **beweisen**

**bewiesen** /bəˈviːzn̩/ *1. u. 3. Pers. Pl. Prät. u. 2. Part. v.* **beweisen**

**bewiesenermaßen** *Adv.* demonstrably; as can be proved

**bewilligen** /bəˈvɪlɪgn̩/ *tr. V.* grant; award ‹salary, grant›; *(im Parlament usw.)* approve ‹sum, tax increase, etc.›; **jmdm. eine Stundung/zwei Mitarbeiter** *usw.* **~:** allow sb. deferment/two assistants *etc.*

**Bewilligung** *die;* **~, ~en** granting; *(Zustimmung)* approval; *(eines Gehalts, Stipendiums)* award

**bewimpert** /bəˈvɪmpɐt/ *Adj.* lashed; *(Zool.)* ciliate

**bewirken** *tr. V.* bring about; cause; **~, dass etw. geschieht** cause sth. to happen; **damit/dadurch hast du nur bewirkt, dass ...** all you have achieved by this *or* the only effect of this is that ...; **nichts/das Gegenteil bei jmdm. ~:** have *or* produce no effect/the opposite effect on sb.; **durch gutes Zureden bewirkt man bei ihm nichts** you don't get anywhere with him by talking to him nicely

**bewirten** /bəˈvɪrtn̩/ *tr. V.* feed; **jmdn. mit etw. ~:** serve sth. to sb.; serve sb. sth.

**bewirtschaften** *tr. V.* Ⓐ run, manage ‹estate, farm, restaurant, business, etc.›; Ⓑ *(bestellen)* farm ‹fields, land›; cultivate ‹field›; Ⓒ *(staatlich lenken)* ration; **den Wohnraum ~:** make living accommodation subject to government control; **Devisen ~:** operate currency controls

**Bewirtschaftung** *die;* **~, ~en** Ⓐ running; management; Ⓑ *(Bestellung)* farming; cultivation; Ⓒ *(staatliche Lenkung)* government control

**Bewirtung** *die;* **~, ~en** provision of food and drink; *(Gastfreundschaft)* hospitality; **die ~ der Gäste** catering for the guests

**bewitzeln** *tr. V.* joke about; poke fun at

**bewog** /bəˈvoːk/ *1. u. 3. Pers. Sg. Prät. v.* **bewegen²**

**bewogen** *2. Part. v.* **bewegen²**

**bewohnbar** *Adj.* habitable

**Bewohnbarkeit** *die;* **~:** suitability *or* fitness for habitation

**bewohnen** *tr. V.* inhabit, live in ‹house, area›; live in ‹room, flat›; live on ‹4th storey etc.›; ‹animal, plant› be found in

**Bewohner** *der;* **~s, ~, Bewohnerin** *die;* **~, ~nen** *(eines Hauses, einer Wohnung)* occupant; *(einer Stadt, eines Gebietes)* inhabitant; **ein ~ der Steppe** *(Mensch)* a steppe-dweller; *(Tier, Pflanze)* a native of the steppes; **ein ~ des Waldes** a forest-dweller; *(Tier)* a woodland creature

**Bewohnerschaft** *die;* **~, ~en** inhabitants *pl.; (eines Wohnblocks)* occupants *pl.*

**bewohnt** *Adj.* occupied ‹house etc.›; inhabited ‹area›; **ist das Haus noch ~?** is the house still lived in *or* occupied?

**bewölken** /bəˈvœlkn̩/ *refl. V.* cloud over; become overcast; **seine Stirn bewölkte sich** *(fig.)* his face darkened

**bewölkt** *Adj.* cloudy; overcast; **dicht** *od.* **stark ~:** heavily overcast; **der Himmel ist nur leicht ~:** there is only a light cloud cover

**Bewölkung** *die;* **~, ~en** Ⓐ clouding over; Ⓑ *(Wolkendecke)* cloud [cover]; **wechselnde ~:** variable amounts *pl.* of cloud

**Bewölkungs-: ~auf·lockerung** *die* breaking up of the cloud cover; **~zunahme** *die* increase in the cloud cover

**Bewuchs** *der* plant cover; vegetation *no indef. art.*

**Bewunderer** *der;* **~s, ~, Bewunderin** *die;* **~, ~nen** admirer

**bewundern** *tr. V.* admire **(wegen, für** for); **ich kann sie nur ~:** I really admire her

**bewunderns-: ~wert, ~würdig** ❶ *Adj.* admirable; worthy of admiration *postpos.;* ❷ *adv.* admirably; in an admirable fashion

**Bewunderung** *die;* **~, ~en** admiration

**bewunderungs·würdig** ⇒ **bewundernswert**

**Bewurf** *der (Bauw.)* rendering

**bewusst, *bewußt** /bəˈvʊst/ ❶ *Adj.* Ⓐ *(im Bewusstsein vorhanden)* conscious ‹reaction, behaviour, etc.›; *(absichtlich)* deliberate ‹lie, deception, attack, etc.›; **~e Ablehnung** conscious *or* deliberate rejection; **ein ~er Sozialist** a convinced socialist; **etw. ist/wird jmdm. ~:** sb. is/becomes aware of sth.; sb. realizes sth.; **mir war nicht recht ~, was ich tat** I was not really conscious of what I was doing; **jmdm. etw. ~ machen** make sb. realize sth.; **sich** *(Dat.)* **etw. ~ machen** realize sth.; Ⓑ *(klar erkennend)* **ein ~er Mensch** a thinking person; **sich** *(Dat.)* **einer Sache** *(Gen.)* **~ sein/werden** be/become aware *or* conscious of something; Ⓒ *(bekannt)* particular; *(fraglich)* in question *postpos.* ❷ *adv.* Ⓐ *(absichtlich)* deliberately; Ⓑ *(klar erkennend)* consciously; **~er leben** live with greater awareness

**Bewusstheit, *Bewußtheit** *die;* **~:** deliberateness

**bewusst·los, *bewußt·los** *Adj.* unconscious; **~ zusammenbrechen** collapse unconscious; **der/die Bewusstlose** the unconscious man/woman

**Bewusstlosigkeit, *Bewußtlosigkeit** *die;* **~:** unconsciousness; **aus der ~ erwachen** regain consciousness; **bis zur ~** *(ugs.)* ad nauseam

***bewußt|machen** ⇒ **bewusst** 1 A

**Bewusst·sein, *Bewußt·sein** *das* Ⓐ *(deutliches Wissen)* awareness; **im ~ seiner Kraft** [secure] in the knowledge *or* awareness of one's strength; **im ~, seine Pflicht getan zu haben** conscious of having done one's duty; **sich** *(Dat.)* **etw. ins ~ rufen** remember *or* recall sth.; **jmdm. etw. ins ~ bringen** remind sb. of sth.; **gewisse Themen in das allgemeine ~ bringen** make the general public aware of certain issues; bring certain issues to the notice of the general public; **etw. mit ~ erleben** be fully aware of sth. [one is experiencing]; **jmdm. zu[m] ~ kommen** become clear to sb.; **jetzt erst kam ihr zu ~, dass ...** only now did she realize that ...; Ⓑ *(Psych., Politik, Philos. usw.)* consciousness; **ein historisches ~:** a consciousness *or* awareness of history; Ⓒ (*geistige Klarheit*) consciousness; **das ~ verlieren** lose consciousness; **wieder zu ~ kommen, das ~ wieder erlangen** regain consciousness; **bei vollem ~ sein** be fully conscious; **bei vollem ~ operiert werden** be operated on while fully conscious

**bewusstseins-, *bewußtseins-, Bewusstseins-, *Bewußtseins-: ~bildung** *die* creation of [greater] awareness; **eine politische ~bildung** the creation of political consciousness *or* awareness; **~erweiternd** ❶ *Adj.* mind-expanding; psychedelic; ❷ *adv.* **~erweiternd wirken** have a mind-expanding effect; **~erweiterung** *die* expansion of consciousness; **~spaltung** *die* (*Med.*, *Psych.*) split consciousness; schizophrenia; **~störung** *die* disturbance of consciousness; **~trübung** *die* clouding *or* dimming of consciousness; **~verändernd** ❶ *Adj.* mind-bending ‹drug›; **dieses Erlebnis war ~verändernd** this experience changed sb.'s outlook; ❷ *adv.* **auf jmdn. ~verändernd wirken** change sb.'s awareness; **~veränderung** *die* change of awareness *or* outlook

**Bewusstwerdung, *Bewußtwerdung** *die;* **~:** development of awareness

**bez.** *Abk.* **bezahlt** pd.

**bezahlbar** *Adj.* affordable; (*wirtschaftlich vernünftig*) economic; **diese Miete ist für ihn kaum ~:** he can hardly afford this rent

**bezahlen** ▶ 337 ❶ *tr. V.* pay ‹person, bill, taxes, rent, amount›; pay for ‹goods etc.›; **etw. [in] bar ~:** pay [in] cash for sth.; **etw. mit [einem] Scheck ~:** pay for sth. by cheque; **jmdm. etw. ~:** pay for sth. for sb.; **bekommst du das Essen bezahlt?** do you get your meals paid for?; **[jmdm.] für etw. 10 DM ~:** pay [sb.] 10 marks for sth.; **bezahlter Urlaub** paid leave; holiday[s] with pay; **er musste seinen Leichtsinn teuer ~** (*fig.*) he had to pay dearly for his carelessness; **das macht sich bezahlt** it pays off; **als ob ers bezahlt bekäme** *od.* **kriegte** (*ugs.*) for all he's worth (*coll.*); like a mad thing; **gut/schlecht bezahlt** well-paid/badly *or* poorly paid; **hoch ~:** highly paid.
❷ *itr. V.* pay; **Herr Ober, ich möchte ~** *od.* **bitte ~:** waiter, the bill *or* (*Amer.*) check please; **heute bezahle ich** it's on me today (*coll.*)

**Bezahlung** *die* payment; (*Lohn, Gehalt*) pay; **die ~ der Waren** the payment for the goods; **gegen ~ arbeiten** work for payment *or* money

**bezähmen** ❶ *tr. V.* Ⓐ contain, control ‹wrath, curiosity, impatience›; restrain ‹desire›; Ⓑ (*veralt.: zähmen*) tame. ❷ *refl. V.* restrain oneself

**bezaubern** ❶ *tr. V.* enchant; **von etw. bezaubert** enchanted with *or* by sth. ❷ *itr. V.* enchant; be enchanting

**bezaubernd** ❶ *Adj.* enchanting; **es war ~ von euch, das Fest zu geben** it was wonderfully kind of you to give the party. ❷ *adv.* enchantingly

**bezecht** /bəˈt͜sɛçt/ *Adj.* drunken *attrib.;* drunk *pred.*

**bezeichnen** *tr. V.* Ⓐ **jmdn./sich/etw. als etw. ~:** call sb./oneself/sth. sth.; describe sb./oneself/sth. as sth.; **das muss man schon als anmaßend ~:** that can only be described as arrogant; **wie bezeichnet man das?** what is it called?; **mit dem Wort bezeichnet man eine Art Jacke** this word is used to denote *or* describe a kind of jacket; **jmdn. als Halunken** *od.* **mit dem Wort Halunke ~:** describe sb. as a scoundrel; call sb. a scoundrel; **jmdn. als Feigling ~:** call sb. a coward; **etw. als Verrat ~:** call sth. treachery; **so kann man das auch ~:** that's one way of describing it; Ⓑ (*Name sein für*) denote; Ⓒ (*markieren*) mark; (*durch Zeichen angeben*) indicate

**bezeichnend** *Adj.* characteristic, typical (*für* of); (*bedeutsam*) significant; **das ist ~ für ihn** that is typical *or* characteristic of him

**bezeichnender·weise** *Adv.* characteristically; typically; (*als Zeichen dafür*) significantly

**Bezeichnung** *die* Ⓐ marking; (*Angabe durch Zeichen*) indication; Ⓑ (*Name*) name; **mir fällt die richtige ~ dafür nicht ein** I can't think of the right word for it/them

**bezeigen** (*geh.*) ❶ *tr. V.* show; give proof of ‹courage›; **jmdm. Ehrfurcht** *od.* **Respekt ~:** show sb. respect. ❷ *refl. V.* **sich dankbar/erkenntlich ~:** show one's gratitude/appreciation

**bezeugen** *tr. V.* Ⓐ testify to; **er/sie bezeugte, dass …** he/she testified that …; **der Ort ist schon im 8. Jh. [dokumentarisch] bezeugt** [the existence of] this place is documented as early as the 8th century; Ⓑ (*bezeigen*) show; **jmdm. sein Wohlwollen ~:** give sb. proof of one's goodwill

**Bezeugung** *die* Ⓐ attestation; (*das Bezeugen*) testifying (*Gen.* to); Ⓑ (*das Bezeigen*) showing; demonstration

**bezichtigen** /bəˈt͜sɪçtɪɡn̩/ *tr. V.* accuse; **jmdn. des Verrats ~:** accuse sb. of treachery; **jmdn. ~, etw. getan zu haben** *od.* **er/sie habe etw. getan** accuse sb. of having done sth.

**Bezichtigung** *die;* **~, ~en** accusation

**beziehbar** *Adj.* Ⓐ ready for occupation *postpos.;* Ⓑ (*anwendbar*) applicable (**auf** + *Akk.* to)

**beziehen** ❶ *unr. tr. V.* Ⓐ cover, put a cover/covers on ‹seat, cushion, umbrella, etc.›; **die Betten frisch ~:** put clean sheets on the beds; **einen Schirm neu ~:** re-cover an umbrella; **das Sofa ist mit Leder bezogen** the sofa is upholstered in leather; Ⓑ (*einziehen in*) move into ‹house, office›; Ⓒ (*Milit.*) take up ‹position, post›; **einen klaren Standpunkt ~** (*fig.*) adopt a clear position; take a definite stand; ⇒ *auch* **Stellung**; Ⓓ (*regelmäßig erhalten*) receive, obtain [one's supply of] ‹goods›; take ‹newspaper›; draw, receive ‹pension, salary›; **Prügel ~** (*ugs.*) get a hiding (*coll.*); Ⓔ (*in Beziehung setzen*) apply (**auf** + *Akk.* to); **etw. auf sich ~:** take sth. personally; **seine Kritik auf etw.** (*Akk.*) **~:** direct one's criticism at sth.
❷ *unr. refl. V.* Ⓐ **es/der Himmel bezieht sich** it/the sky is clouding over *or* becoming overcast; Ⓑ **sich auf jmdn./etw. ~** (*sich berufen auf*) ‹person, letter, etc.› refer to sb./sth.; (*betreffen*) ‹question, statement, etc.› relate to sb./sth.; **wir ~ uns auf Ihr Schreiben vom 28. 8./unser Telefongespräch** with reference to your letter of 28 August/our telephone conversation; **diese Kritik bezieht sich nicht auf dich** this criticism is not aimed at you

**Bezieher** *der;* **~s, ~, Bezieherin** *die;* **~, ~nen** (*einer Zeitung*) reader; subscriber (*Gen.*, **von** to); (*einer Rente, eines Gehalts*) recipient; ⇒ *auch* **-in**

**Beziehung** *die* Ⓐ (*Verbindung*) relations *pl.* (**zu** with); **gute ~en** *od.* **eine gute ~ zu jmdm./einer Firma haben** have good relations with sb./a firm; be on good terms with sb./a firm; **intime ~en zu jmdm. haben** have intimate relations with sb.; **diplomatische ~en aufnehmen/unterhalten/abbrechen** establish/maintain/break off diplomatic relations; Ⓑ *Pl.* (*Verbindungen, die Vorteile verschaffen*) connections (**zu** with); **etw. durch ~en bekommen** get sth. through connections; **seine ~en spielen lassen** pull some strings; Ⓒ (*Verhältnis*) relationship (**zwischen** between, **zu** with); (*Verständnis*) affinity (**zu** for); **zu jmdm. keine ~ haben** be unable to relate to sb.; **er hat keine ~ zur Kunst** he has a blind spot where the arts are concerned; the arts are a closed book to him; Ⓓ (*Zusammenhang*) connection (**zu** with); **zwischen A und B besteht keine/eine ~:** there is no/a connection between A and B; **A zu B in ~ setzen** relate A to B; see A in relation to B; **A und B in ~ zueinander setzen** relate A and B to each other; connect *or* link A and B; **das steht in keiner ~ dazu** that is not connected with *or* related to it; **in dieser/jeder ~:** in this/every respect; **in mancher ~:** in many respects; **mit ~ auf etw.** (*Akk.*) with reference to sth.

**beziehungs-, Beziehungs-: ~kiste** *die* (*ugs.*) relationship; **~los** ❶ *Adj.* unconnected; unrelated; ❷ *adv.* without any connection; **~reich** *Adj.* evocative; rich in associations *postpos.;* (*vielseitig*) many-faceted; **~weise** *Konj.* Ⓐ (*oder vielmehr*) that is; or to be precise; Ⓑ (*und im anderen Fall*) and … respectively; (*oder*) or; **die beiden Münzen waren aus Kupfer ~weise aus Nickel** the two coins were made of copper and of nickel respectively; **sie sind in Schwarz ~weise in Weiß lieferbar** they are available in black or in white

**beziffern** /bəˈt͜sɪfɐn/ ❶ *tr. V.* Ⓐ (*nummerieren*) number; **bezifferter Bass** (*Musik*) figured bass; Ⓑ (*angeben*) estimate (**auf** + *Akk.* at); **den Schaden auf 3 000 DM ~:** estimate the damage at 3,000 marks. ❷ *refl. V.* **sich auf 10 Millionen** (*Akk.*) **DM ~:** come *or* amount to 10 million marks

**Bezifferung** *die;* **~, ~en** Ⓐ numbering; Ⓑ (*Zahlen*) numbers *pl.*

**Bezirk** /bəˈt͜sɪrk/ *der;* **~[e]s, ~e** Ⓐ district; **Vertreter für den ~ Südhessen** representative for the South Hessen area; Ⓑ (*Verwaltungs~*) [administrative] district; (*DDR*) [administrative] area; (*in West-Berlin*) borough; Ⓒ (*DDR: Behörde*) local *or* area authority; **auf dem ~:** at the local *or* area authority offices *pl.*

**bezirklich** *Adj.* district *attrib.;* (*DDR*) area *attrib.*

**Bezirks-: ~amt** *das* district *or* (*DDR*) area authority; **~bürger·meister** *der,* **~bürger·meisterin** *die* Borough Mayor (*in Berlin*); **~gericht** *das* district *or* (*DDR*) area court; **~hauptfrau** *die,* **~hauptmann** *der; Pl.* **~hauptleute** (*österr.*) *chief officer of an administrative district;* **~haupt·mannschaft** *die* (*österr.*) district authority; **auf der ~hauptmannschaft** at the district authority offices; **~klasse** *die* (*Sport*) district *or* (*DDR*) area league; **~leiter** *der,* **~leiterin** *die* Ⓐ (*DDR*) head of the area administration; Ⓑ (*Kaufmannsspr.*) area manager; **~regierung** *die* (*BRD*) district authority; **~stadt** *die* (*DDR*) chief town of the area; area capital; **~tag** *der* (*DDR*) area assembly; **~verordneten·versammlung** *die* borough assembly (*in Berlin*)

**bezirzen** /bəˈt͜sɪrt͜sn̩/ ⇒ **becircen**

**bezog** /bəˈt͜soːk/ *1. u. 3. Pers. Sg. Prät. v.* **beziehen**

**bezogen** ❶ *2. Part. v.* **beziehen.** ❷ *Adj.* **~ auf jmdn./etw.** [seen] in relation to sb./sth.

**-bezogen** *Adj.* -related

**Bezogene** *der/die; adj. Dekl.* drawee (*of cheque*)

***bezug** ⇒ **Bezug** D

**Bezug** *der* Ⓐ (*für Kissen usw.*) cover; (*für Polstermöbel*) loose cover; slip cover (*Amer.*); (*für Betten*) duvet cover; (*für Kopfkissen*) pillowcase; Ⓑ (*Erwerb*) obtaining; (*Kauf*) purchase; **~ einer Zeitung** taking a newspaper; **bei ~ von mehr als 100 Stück** if more than 100 are ordered; Ⓒ *Pl.* (*österr. auch Sg.*) (*Gehalt*) salary *sing.;* **die Bezüge der Beamten** the salaries of the civil servants; Ⓓ (*Verbindung*) connection, link (**zu** with); **der Film vermeidet jeden ~ zur Gegenwart** this film avoids all allusion to the present; **mit** *od.* **unter ~ auf etw.** (*Akk.*) (*Amtsspr.*, *Kaufmannsspr.*) with reference to sth.; **in ~ auf jmdn./etw.** concerning *or* regarding sb./sth.; **auf etw.** (*Akk.*) **~ nehmen** (*Amtsspr.*, *Kaufmannspr.*) refer to sth.; **~ nehmend auf unser Telex** with reference to our telex

**Bezüger** /bəˈt͜syːɡɐ/ *der;* **~s, ~, Bezügerin** *die;* **~, ~nen** (*schweiz.*) Ⓐ ⇒ **Bezieher**; Ⓑ (*von Steuern*) collector

**bezüglich** /bəˈt͜syːklɪç/ ❶ *Präp. mit Gen.* concerning; regarding. ❷ *Adj.* **auf etw.** (*Akk.*) **~:** relating to sth.; **die darauf ~en Paragraphen** the relevant paragraphs; **~es Fürwort** (*Sprachw.*) relative pronoun

**Bezugnahme** /bəˈt͜suːknaːmə/ *die;* **~, ~n** (*Amtsspr.*) reference; **unter ~ auf etw.** (*Akk.*) with reference to sth.

b

b

**bezugs-, Bezugs-: ~aktie** *die* (*Wirtsch.*) new share; **~berechtigt** *Adj.* entitled to receive goods/payment *postpos.*; **~berechtigt sind folgende** the following are entitled to benefit; **~fertig** *Adj.* ready to move into *pred.*; **eine ~fertige Wohnung** a flat (*Brit.*) *or* (*Amer.*) apartment that is ready to move into; **~person** *die* (*Psych., Soziol.*) **jedes Kind braucht eine ~person** every child needs someone it can relate to and take as an example; **~preis** *der* [subscription] price; **~punkt** *der* point of reference; **~quelle** *die* source of supply; (*Firma*) supplier; **~recht** *das* (*Wirtsch.*) preemptive *or* subscription right; **~satz** *der* (*Sprachw.*) relative clause; **~schein** *der* [ration] coupon; **auf ~schein** on coupons *pl.*; **~system** *das* **A** (*Koordinatensystem*) reference frame; **B** (*System des Denkens usw.*) terms *pl.* of reference

**bezuschussen** /bəˈtsu:ʃʊsn̩/ *tr. V.* (*Amtsspr.*) subsidize

**Bezuschussung** *die;* ~, **~en** **A** subsidization; **B** (*Betrag*) subsidy

**bezwecken** /bəˈtsvɛkn̩/ *tr. V.* aim to achieve; aim at; **was willst du damit ~?** what do you expect to achieve by [doing] that?; **was soll das ~?** what is the point of that?; what is that supposed to achieve?

**bezweifeln** *tr. V.* doubt; question; **sie bezweifelt, dass** *od.* **ob ...** she doubts whether ...; **ich bezweifle nicht, dass ...** I do not doubt that ...; **das ist nicht zu ~:** there is no doubt about that; **das möchte ich doch ~:** I have my doubts about that

**bezwingbar** *Adj.* **A** (*zu besiegen*) conquerable; (*fig.*) controllable; **er/sie/es ist ~:** he/she/it can be beaten *or* overcome; **B** (*zu bewältigen*) manageable; negotiable ‹course, slope›

**bezwingen** **1** *unr. tr. V.* conquer ‹enemy, mountain, pain, etc.›; defeat ‹opponent›; take, capture ‹fortress›; master ‹pain, hunger›; **seinen Zorn/seine Neugier ~:** keep one's anger/curiosity under control; **er konnte diese Piste/diesen Pass nicht ~:** he was unable to negotiate this course/pass. **2** *unr. refl. V.* control *or* restrain oneself

**bezwingend** *Adj.* compelling; irresistible ‹smile›

**Bezwinger** *der,* **Bezwingerin** *die;* ~, **~nen** conqueror

**Bezwingung** *die;* ~, **~en** **A** defeat; (*Sieg*) victory (+ *Gen.* over); (*fig.*) control; **B** (*Bewältigung*) conquest

**BfA** *Abk.* **Bundesversicherungsanstalt für Angestellte**

**BGB** *Abk.* **Bürgerliches Gesetzbuch**

**BGH** *Abk.* **Bundesgerichtshof**

**BGS** *Abk.* **Bundesgrenzschutz**

**BH** /be:ˈha:/ *der;* **~[s], ~[s]** *Abk.* **Büstenhalter** bra

**bi** /bi:/ *indekl. Adj.* (*salopp*) bi (*sl.*)

**Biathlon** /ˈbi:atlɔn/ *das;* **~s, ~s** (*Sport*) biathlon

**bibbern** /ˈbɪbɐn/ *itr. V.* (*ugs.*) (*vor Kälte*) shiver (**vor** with); (*vor Angst*) shake, tremble (**vor** with); **um jmdn./etw. ~:** fear *or* tremble for sb./sth.

**Bibel** /ˈbi:bl̩/ *die;* ~, **~n** (*auch fig.*) Bible

**bibel-, Bibel-: ~fest** *Adj.* well versed in the Bible *postpos.*; who knows his/her *etc.* Bible *postpos., not pred.*; **du bist ziemlich ~fest** you know your Bible pretty well; **~forscher** *der,* **~forscherin** *die* (*veralt.*) Jehovah's Witness; **~spruch** *der* biblical saying; **~stunde** *die: Bible reading with discussion and prayer;* **~vers** *der* verse from the Bible; **~wort** *das; Pl.* **~~e** biblical saying

**Biber**[1] /ˈbi:bɐ/ *der;* **~s, ~:** beaver; **Mantel aus ~:** beaver coat

**Biber**[2] *der od. das;* **~s** (*Stoff*) flannelette

**Biber-: ~geil** *das;* **~[e]s** castor; **~pelz** *der* beaver [fur]; (*einzelner Pelz*) beaver pelt; **ein Mantel** *usw.* **aus ~pelz** a beaver coat *etc.*; **~schwanz** **A** beaver's tail; **B** (*Ziegel*) plain *or* plane tile (*with curved lower edge*)

*old spelling (see note on page 1707)

**Bibliograph** /biblioˈgra:f/ *der;* **~en, ~en** ▶ 159 bibliographer

**Bibliographie** *die;* ~, **~n** bibliography

**bibliographieren** *tr. V.* **A** **Bücher/Titel ~:** list books/titles in a bibliography; **B** (*Daten feststellen*) establish the bibliographical details of ‹book, essay›; identify ‹book›; identify the source of ‹essay etc.›

**Bibliographin** *die;* ~, **~nen** ▶ 159 ⇒ **Bibliograph**

**bibliographisch** **1** *Adj.* bibliographical. **2** *adv.* bibliographically; as a bibliography

**Bibliomane** /biblioˈma:nə/ *der;* **~n, ~n** bibliomaniac

**Bibliomanie** *die;* **~:** bibliomania

**Bibliomanin** *die;* ~, **~nen** ⇒ **Bibliomane**

**bibliophil** /biblioˈfi:l/ *Adj.* **A** bibliophilic ‹interests etc.›; bibliophile ‹collector›; **B** (*wertvoll*) for the bibliophile *postpos.*; **~e Ausgabe** collector's edition

**Bibliophile** *der/die; adj. Dekl.* bibliophile; book lover

**Bibliophilie** *die;* **~:** bibliophily (*formal*); love of books

**Bibliothek** /biblioˈte:k/ *die;* ~, **~en** library; **bei** *od.* **an einer ~ angestellt sein** have a job in a library

**Bibliothekar** /bibliote'ka:ɐ̯/ *der;* **~s, ~e, Bibliothekarin** *die;* ~, **~nen** ▶ 159 librarian

**Bibliotheks-: ~benutzer** *der,* **~benutzerin** *die* library user; **„die ~benutzer werden gebeten, ...“** 'readers are requested ...'; **~katalog** *der* library catalogue; **~wesen** *das* library system

**biblisch** /ˈbi:blɪʃ/ *Adj.* biblical; **ein ~es Alter** a grand old age

**Bick·beere** /ˈbɪk-/ *die* (*nordd.*) ⇒ **Heidelbeere**

**Bidet** /biˈde:/ *das;* **~s, ~s** bidet

**bieder** /ˈbi:dɐ/ **1** *Adj.* **A** unsophisticated; (*langweilig*) stolid; (*treuherzig*) trusting; **B** (*veralt.: rechtschaffen*) upright. **2** *adv.* in an unsophisticated manner; **etw. brav und ~ ausführen** carry sth. out faithfully and unquestioningly

**Biederkeit** *die;* ~ **A** (*Rechtschaffenheit*) [bourgeois] probity; [stolid] uprightness; **B** (*Rückständigkeit*) conventional attitudes *pl.*; (*Einfältigkeit*) lack of sophistication

**Bieder·mann** *der* **A** (*veralt.*) man of integrity *or* probity; **B** (*Spießer*) petty bourgeois

**biedermännisch** /ˈbi:dɐmɛnɪʃ/ *Adj.* **A** (*veralt.*) stolidly upright; **B** (*spießig*) stuffily correct; petty bourgeois

**Biedermeier** *das;* **~s** Biedermeier [period/style]

**Biedermeier-: ~stil** *der* Biedermeier style; **~sträußchen** *das: small bouquet wrapped in white lace-paper;* **~zeit** *die* Biedermeier period

**Bieder·sinn** *der* (*geh.*) [stolid] uprightness; moral rectitude

**biegbar** *Adj.* flexible; pliable ‹material›; **leicht ~:** easily bent

**Biege** /ˈbi:gə/ *die;* ~, **~n** bend; **eine ~ drehen** (*salopp*) stretch one's legs; **eine ~ fahren/fliegen** (*salopp*) go for a spin [in the car/aircraft]

**biegen** /ˈbi:gn̩/ **1** *unr. tr. V.* **A** bend; incline ‹head›; **das Recht ~** (*fig. veralt.*) bend the law; **mit gebogenem Rücken sitzen** sit with one's back hunched; **B** (*österr., Sprachw.*) ⇒ **beugen** 1 C. **2** *unr. refl. V.* bend; (*nachgeben*) give; sag; **der Tisch bog sich unter der Last der Speisen** the table sagged *or* groaned under the weight of the food; **sich vor Lachen ~** (*ugs.*) double up with laughter; **ihre Augenbrauen ~/ihre Nase biegt sich nach oben** her eyebrows curve upward/her nose is turned up. **3** *unr. itr. V.; mit sein* **A** turn; **um die Ecke ~:** turn the corner; ‹car› take the corner; **B** **auf Biegen oder** *od.* **und Brechen** (*ugs.*) at all costs; by hook or by crook; **es geht auf Biegen oder** *od.* **und Brechen** (*ugs.*) it has come to the crunch *or* (*Amer.*) showdown

**biegsam** *Adj.* flexible; pliable ‹material›; supple ‹joints, person›; **ein ~er Charakter** (*fig.*) a malleable personality

**Biegsamkeit** *die;* ~ ⇒ **biegsam**: flexibility; pliability; suppleness; (*fig.*) malleability

**Biegung** *die;* ~, **~en** **A** bend; **eine [enge] ~ nach rechts machen** bend [sharply] to the right; **B** (*österr. Sprachw.*) ⇒ **Beugung** B

**Biene** /ˈbi:nə/ *die;* ~, **~n** **A** bee; **B** (*ugs. veralt.: Mädchen*) bird (*Brit. sl.*); dame (*Amer. sl.*); **eine flotte ~:** a smashing bird (*Brit. sl.*); a luscious piece (*sl.*)

**Bienen-: ~fleiß** *der* unflagging industry; **mit wahrem ~fleiß ging er daran** he set about it industriously; **~haus** *das* apiary; **~honig** *der* bees' honey; **~kasten** *der* beehive; (*as tech. term*) frame hive; **~königin** *die* queen bee; **~korb** *der* straw hive; **~schwarm** *der* swarm of bees; **~sprache** *die* language of bees; **~staat** *der* bee colony; **~stich** *der* **A** bee sting; **B** (*Kuchen*) *cake with a topping of sugar and almonds (and sometimes a cream filling)*; **~stock** *der* beehive; **~wachs** *das* beeswax; **~zucht** *die* beekeeping; **~züchter** *der,* **~züchterin** *die* beekeeper

**Biennale** /biɛˈna:lə/ *die;* ~, **~n** biennial

**Bier** /bi:ɐ̯/ *das;* **~[e]s,** (*Sorten:*) **~e** beer; **ein kleines/großes ~:** a small/large [glass of] beer; **zwei ~:** two beers; two glasses of beer; **10 verschiedene ~e** ten different beers *or* types of beer; **das ist [nicht] mein ~** (*ugs.*) that is [not] my affair *or* business; **etw. wie sauer** *od.* **saures ~ anpreisen** praise sth. to the skies in an effort to get rid of it/them

**Bier-: ~bar** *die* beer bar; **~bauch** *der* (*ugs. spött.*) beer belly; **~brauer** *der* [beer] brewer; **~brauerei** *die* **A** **die ~brauerei** the brewing of beer; brewing beer; **B** (*Betrieb*) brewery; **~brauerin** *die* ⇒ **~brauer**

**Bierchen** *das;* **~s,** ~ (*ugs.*) **A** (*gute Sorte*) **so ein ~:** such a beer; a beer like that; **das ist ein ~!** that's quite some beer! (*Brit.*); great beer! (*Amer.*); **B** (*Glas Bier*) little [glass of] beer

**bier-, Bier-: ~deckel** *der* beer mat; **~dose** *die* beer can; **~durst** *der:* **[schrecklichen] ~durst haben** be [badly] in need of a beer; **~ernst** (*ugs.*) **1** *Adj.* deadly serious; solemn; **2** *adv.* solemnly; **so ~ernst** with such deadly seriousness; **~ernst** *der* deadly seriousness; **~fass,** ***~faß** *das* beer barrel; **~filz** *der* beer mat; **~flasche** *die* beer bottle; (*voll*) bottle of beer; **~garten** *der* beer garden; **~glas** *das* beer glass; **~kasten** *der* beer crate; **~keller** *der* beer cellar; **~kneipe** *die* ≈ pub (*Brit.*); beerhouse (*Amer.*); **~krug** *der* beer mug; (*aus Glas, Zinn*) tankard; **~kutscher** *der,* **~kutscherin** *die* (*ugs.*) brewery delivery driver; **~laune** *die* (*ugs.*) **in einer ~laune, aus einer ~laune heraus** in an exuberant mood; **~leiche** *die* (*ugs. scherzh.*) drunk lying dead to the world; **~lokal** *das* pub (*Brit.*); beerhouse (*Amer.*); **~ruhe** *die* (*ugs.*) unruffled calm; unflappability (*coll.*); **~schinken** *der: slicing sausage containing pieces of ham;* **~schwemme** *die* beer hall; **~seidel** *das* beer mug; (*aus Glas, Zinn*) tankard; **~selig** (*scherzh.*) **1** *Adj.* beery ‹mood›; **~selig, wie er war** in his beerily happy state; **2** *adv.* in a beerily happy state; ‹laugh› in beery merriment; **~stube** *die* ≈ small pub (*Brit.*); beer bar (*Amer.*); **~suppe** *die: soup containing beer, sugar, and eggs or rye bread;* **~tisch** *der:* **am ~tisch** over a glass of beer; in the pub (*Brit.*) *or* (*Amer.*) bar; **~trinker** *der,* **~trinkerin** *die* beerdrinker; **~verlag** *der,* **~vertrieb** *der* beer wholesaler's; **~wärmer** *der;* **~~s, ~~:** beer-warmer; **~wurst** *die: smoked slicing sausage containing beef, pork, bacon, and spices;* **~zeitung** *die* joke newspaper (*made up for a closed group*); **~zelt** *das* beer tent; **~zipfel** *der: tag worn by member of a student corporation, bearing its colours*

**Biese** /ˈbi:zə/ *die;* ~, **~n** **A** (*bes. Milit.*) trouser stripe; (*Paspel*) piping; **B** (*Fältchen*) tuck

**Biest** /biːst/ *das;* ~**[e]s,** ~**er** (*ugs. abwertend*) Ⓐ (*Tier, Gegenstand*) wretched thing; (*Bestie*) creature; **ein riesiges ~ von einem Elefanten** a huge elephant; Ⓑ (*Mensch*) beast (*derog.*); wretch; **das freche ~:** the cheeky devil (*coll.*)

**Biesterei** *die;* ~, ~**en** (*ugs. abwertend*) (*Gemeinheit*) beastly trick (*coll.*); (*etw. Ärgerliches*) blasted nuisance (*coll.*)

**biestig** (*ugs. abwertend*) ❶ *Adj.* Ⓐ beastly (*coll.*) (**zu** to); **ganz schön ~ werden** turn really nasty; Ⓑ (*unangenehm*) filthy, beastly (*coll.*) ‹weather›; frightful (*coll.*) ‹cold›. ❷ *adv.* Ⓐ (*gemein*) nastily; in a beastly way (*coll.*); Ⓑ (*sehr*) horribly (*coll.*)

**Biet** /biːt/ *das;* ~**[e]s,** ~**e** (*schweiz.*) area

**bieten** /ˈbiːtn̩/ ❶ *unr. tr. V.* Ⓐ offer; put on ‹programme etc.›; provide ‹shelter, guarantee, etc.›; (*bei Auktionen, Kartenspielen*) bid (**für, auf** + *Akk.* for); **jmdm. Geld/eine Chance ~:** offer sb. money/a chance; **wir ~ beim Pokern bis zu 5 DM** we play poker for stakes of up to five marks; **was** *od.* **wie viel bietest du mir dafür?** what will you give me for it?; **jmdm. den Arm ~** (*geh.*) offer sb. one's arm; **jmdm. die Hand zur Versöhnung ~** (*fig. geh.*) hold out the olive branch to sb.; **für Jugendliche wird nichts geboten** there is nothing for young people to do; **eine hervorragende Leistung ~:** put up an outstanding performance; **das bietet keine Schwierigkeiten** that presents no difficulties; **das Stadion bietet Platz für 40 000 Personen** the stadium has room for *or* can hold 40,000 people; Ⓑ **ein schreckliches/gespenstisches** *usw.* **Bild ~:** present a terrible/eerie *etc.* picture; be a terrible/eerie *etc.* sight; **einen prächtigen Anblick ~:** look splendid; be a splendid sight; Ⓒ (*zumuten*) **das lasse ich mir nicht ~:** I won't put up with *or* stand for that.
❷ *unr. refl. V.* **sich jmdm. ~:** present itself to sb.; **es bietet sich ...** there is ...; **hier bietet sich dir eine Chance** this is an opportunity for you; this offers you an opportunity; **ihnen bot sich ein Bild des Grauens** a horrific sight confronted them.
❸ *unr. itr. V.* bid (**auf** + *Akk.* for); **jeder kann auf einer Auktion ~:** anyone can make a bid at an auction

**Bieter** *der;* ~**s,** ~, **Bieterin** *die;* ~, ~**nen** bidder

**Bifokal·brille** /bifoˈkaːl-/ *die* bifocal spectacles *pl.*; bifocals *pl.*

**Bigamie** /bigaˈmiː/ *die;* ~, ~**n** bigamy *no def. art.*

**Bigamist** *der;* ~**en,** ~**en, Bigamistin** *die;* ~, ~**nen** bigamist

**Bigband** /ˈbɪg ˈbænd/ *die;* ~, ~**s** big band

**Bigbusiness** /ˈbɪg ˈbɪznɪs/ *das;* ~**:** big business *no art.*; **zum ~ gehören** belong to the world of big business

**bigott** /biˈgɔt/ (*abwertend*) ❶ *Adj.* Ⓐ religiose; over-devout; Ⓑ (*scheinheilig*) sanctimonious; holier-than-thou; (*heuchlerisch*) hypocritical; ~**e Heuchler** sanctimonious hypocrites. ❷ *adv.* sanctimoniously; (*heuchlerisch*) hypocritically

**Bigotterie** /bigɔtəˈriː/ *die;* ~ (*abwertend*) religious bigotry; religiosity; (*Scheinheiligkeit*) sanctimoniousness

**Bijou** /biˈʒuː/ *das;* ~**s,** ~**s** (*veralt., schweiz.*) piece of jewellery; ~**s** jewellery *sing.*

**Bijouterie** /biʒutəˈriː/ *die;* ~, ~**n** (*veralt., schweiz.*) jeweller's shop

**Bike** /baik/ *das;* ~**s,** ~**s** (*Jargon*) bike

**Biker** /ˈbaikɐ/ *der;* ~**s,** ~**s** (*Jargon*) biker

**Bikini** /biˈkiːni/ *der;* ~**s,** ~**s** bikini; **im ~:** in a bikini/in bikinis

**bi·konkav** *Adj.* (*Optik*) biconcave

**bi·konvex** *Adj.* (*Optik*) biconvex

**bi·labial** *Adj.* (*Phon.*) bilabial

**Bilanz** /biˈlants/ *die;* ~, ~**en** Ⓐ (*Kaufmannsspr., Wirtsch.*) balance sheet; **die ~ des Jahres** the year's results *pl.*; **eine ~ aufstellen** make up the accounts *pl.*; draw up a balance sheet; Ⓑ (*Ergebnis*) outcome; (*Endeffekt*) net result; **erfreuliche ~:** happy outcome; **~ ziehen** take stock; sum things up; **[die] ~ aus etw. ziehen** draw conclusions *pl.* about sth.; (*rückblickend*) take stock of sth.

**Bilanz-:** ~**analyse** *die* (*Wirtsch., Kaufmannsspr.*) balance sheet analysis; ~**buchhalter** *der,* ~**buchhalterin** *die* (*Wirtsch., Kaufmannsspr.*) [stewardship] accountant

**bilanzieren** (*Wirtsch., Kaufmannsspr.*) ❶ *itr. V.* balance; **mit ... DM ~:** show a balance of ... marks. ❷ *tr. V.* balance ‹account›; show ‹turnover› in the balance sheet; (*fig.*) sum up

**Bilanz-:** ~**prüfer** *der,* ~**prüferin** *die* (*Wirtsch., Kaufmannsspr.*) auditor; ~**summe** *die* (*Wirtsch., Kaufmannsspr.*) balance sheet total

**bi·lateral** (*Politik*) ❶ *Adj.* bilateral. ❷ *adv.* bilaterally

**Bild** /bɪlt/ *das;* ~**[e]s,** ~**er** Ⓐ picture; (*in einem Buch usw.*) illustration; (*Spielkarte*) picture *or* court card; **ein ~ [von jmdm./etw.] machen** take a picture [of sb./sth.]; **wie viele ~er hast du noch auf dem Film?** how many photos *or* exposures have you left on the film?; **ein ~ von einem Mann/einer Frau sein** be a fine specimen of a man/woman; be a fine-looking man/woman; **ein lebendes ~:** a tableau vivant; Ⓑ (*Aussehen*) appearance; (*Anblick*) sight; **das ~ der Stadt** the appearance of the town; the townscape; **ein ~ des Jammers sein** *od.* **bieten** be a pathetic sight; **ein ~ für [die] Götter [sein]** (*scherzh.*) [be] a sight for sore eyes; Ⓒ (*Metapher*) image; metaphor; **im ~ bleiben** extend *or* continue the metaphor; Ⓓ (*Abbild*) image; (*Spiegel~*) reflection; **er ist [ganz] das ~ seines Vaters** he is the [very] image of his father; Ⓔ (*Vorstellung*) image; **ein falsches/merkwürdiges ~ von etw. haben** have a wrong impression/curious idea of sth.; **sich** (*Dat.*) **ein ~ von jmdm./etw. machen** form an impression of sb./sth.; **jmdn. [über etw.** (*Akk.*)**] ins ~ setzen** put sb. in the picture [about sth.]; **[über etw.** (*Akk.*)**] im ~e sein** be in the picture [about sth.]; **ich bin im ~e** (*als Reaktion: ich verstehe*) I'm with you; Ⓕ (*Theater*) scene

**Bild-:** ~**archiv** *das* picture library; ~**aus·fall** *der* loss of picture *or* vision; ~**aus·schnitt** *der* section of a/the picture; (*bes. Kunst*) detail; ~**autor** *der,* ~**autorin** *die* photographer (*who takes the photographs for a book*); ~**band** *der* copiously illustrated book

**bildbar** *Adj.* formable (**aus** from); malleable ‹personality, mind›; **schwer ~e Laute** sounds which are difficult to form

**Bild-:** ~**bei·lage** *die* pictorial *or* illustrated supplement; ~**bericht** *der* photo-reportage; ~**beschreibung** *die* picture description; ~**dokument** *das* pictorial document; (*Film*) pictorial record

**bilden** ❶ *tr. V.* Ⓐ form (**aus** from); (*modellieren*) mould (**aus** from); **den Charakter ~:** form *or* mould sb.'s personality; **eine Gasse ~:** make a path *or* passage; **sich** (*Dat.*) **ein Urteil [über jmdn./etw.] ~:** form an opinion [of sb./sth.]; Ⓑ (*ansammeln*) build up ‹fund, capital›; Ⓒ (*darstellen*) be, represent ‹exception etc.›; constitute ‹rule etc.›; **den Höhepunkt des Abends bildete sein Auftritt** his appearance was the high spot of the evening; Ⓓ (*erziehen*) educate; **Reisen bildet den Geist** travel broadens the mind.
❷ *refl. V.* Ⓐ (*entstehen*) form; **eine starke Opposition bildete sich** a strong opposition developed *or* came into being; Ⓑ (*lernen*) educate oneself.
❸ *itr. V.* **Lesen bildet** reading educates *or* cultivates the mind; **Reisen bildet** travel broadens the mind

**bildend** *Adj.* Ⓐ **die ~e Kunst, die ~en Künste** the plastic arts *pl.* (*including painting and architecture*); Ⓑ (*belehrend*) educational

**Bilder·bogen** *der* pictorial broadsheet

**Bilder·buch** *das* picture book (*for children*); **aussehen wie im** *od.* **aus dem ~:** look a picture

**Bilderbuch-:** perfect ‹landing, weather›; picture book ‹weather, village›; story book ‹marriage, career›; archetypal ‹Catholic, proletarian, capitalist›

**Bilder-:** ~**geschichte** *die* picture story; (*Comic*) strip cartoon; ~**kult** *der* idolatry; ~**rahmen** *der* picture frame; ~**rätsel** *das* picture puzzle; (*Rebus*) rebus; ~**schrift** *die* pictographic [system of] writing; (*Hieroglyphen*) hieroglyphics *pl.*; ~**sturm** *der* (*hist.*) iconoclasm; ~**stürmer** *der,* ~**stürmerin** *die* (*hist.; auch fig.*) iconoclast

**bild-, Bild-:** ~**fläche** *die*: **auf der ~fläche erscheinen** (*ugs.*) appear on the scene; (*auftauchen*) turn up; **von der ~fläche verschwinden** (*ugs.*) (*rasch weggehen*) make oneself scarce (*coll.*); (*aus der Öffentlichkeit verschwinden*) disappear from the scene; ~**folge** *die* Ⓐ (*im Film*) sequence of shots; Ⓑ [picture] sequence; ~**frequenz** *die* (*Film, Ferns.*) picture frequency; ~**geschichte** *die* ⇒ **Bildergeschichte**; ~**haft** ❶ *Adj.* graphic; pictorial, illustrative ‹language, sense, etc.›; vivid ‹imagination, clarity, etc.›; ❷ *adv.* graphically; (*lebhaft*) vividly; ~**haftigkeit** *die;* ~~**:** vividness; graphic quality; (*der Sprache*) pictorial *or* illustrative quality; ~**hauer** *der* ▶159 sculptor; ~**hauerei** /---ˈ-/ *die;* ~~**:** sculpture *no def. art.*; ~**hauerin** *die;* ~~, ~~**nen** ▶159 sculptress; ~**hauerisch** /-hauərɪʃ/ *Adj.* sculptural; ~**hauer·kunst** *die* ⇒ **Bildhauerei**; ~**hübsch** *Adj.* really lovely; stunningly beautiful ‹girl›

**bildlich** ❶ *Adj.* pictorial; (*übertragen*) figurative; ~**er Ausdruck,** ~**e Wendung** figure of speech; image. ❷ *adv.* Ⓐ pictorially; **sich etw. ~ vorstellen** picture sth. to oneself; Ⓑ figuratively; **~ gesprochen** metaphorically speaking

**Bild-:** ~**material** *das* pictures *pl.* (**über** + *Akk.* of); (*Fotos/Film*) photographic/film material (**über** + *Akk.* of); ~**mischer** *der,* ~**mischerin** *die;* ~~, ~~**nen** (*Ferns.*) vision mixer

**bildnerisch** ❶ *Adj.* artistic; creative ‹abilities›. ❷ *adv.* artistically

**Bildnis** /ˈbɪltnɪs/ *das;* ~**ses,** ~**se** portrait; (*Plastik*) sculpture

**Bild-:** ~**platte** *die* video disc; ~**platten·spieler** *der* video disc player; ~**qualität** *die* picture quality; ~**reportage** *die* photo-reportage; ~**reporter** *der,* ~**reporterin** *die* photojournalist; ~**röhre** *die* (*Ferns.*) picture tube

**bildsam** *Adj.* (*geh.*) malleable; impressionable

**Bild·schärfe** *die* (*Fot., Ferns.*) definition

**Bild·schirm** *der* (*Ferns., Informationst.*) screen; **am ~ arbeiten** work at *or* with a VDU; **einen Text am ~ korrigieren** correct a text on screen

**bildschirm-, Bildschirm-:** ~**arbeit** *die* VDU work *no art., no pl.*; ~**gerät** *das* VDU; visual display unit; ~**gerecht** *Adj.* in screen format *postpos.*; ~**schoner** *der;* ~~**s,** ~~ (*DV*) screen saver; ~**text** *der* viewdata; ~**zeitung** *die* teletext

**bild-, Bild-:** ~**schnitzer** *der,* ~**schnitzerin** *die* wood carver; wood sculptor; ~**schön** *Adj.* really lovely; stunningly beautiful ‹girl, woman›; ~**seite** *die* Ⓐ (*einer Münze*) obverse; (*beim Werfen*) **die ~seite ist oben** it's heads; Ⓑ (*bei Büchern, Zeitungen*) picture page; **zwei ~seiten** two pages of pictures; ~**serie** *die* series *or* sequence of pictures; ~**stelle** *die* picture and film library; ~**stock** *der* wayside shrine; ~**störung** *die* interference *no def. art.* on vision; ~**synchron** *Adj.* (*Film, Ferns.*) synchronized [with the picture]; ~**telefon** *das* video telephone; ~**teppich** *der* tapestry

**Bildung** *die;* ~, ~**en** Ⓐ (*Erziehung*) education; (*Kultur*) culture; **eine umfassende ~:** a broad educational and cultural background; **das gehört zur allgemeinen ~:** that is something every educated person should know; **[keine] ~ haben** be [un]educated; ([*un*]*kultiviert sein*) be [un]cultivated *or* [un]cultured; Ⓑ (*das Formen, Schaffung*) formation; **die ~ einer Untersuchungskommission** setting up a committee of investigation; **C** (*Form, Gestalt*) form; shape; **die seltsamen ~en der Wolken/Eiskristalle** the strange formations of the clouds/ice crystals

**bildungs-, Bildungs-: ~anstalt** *die* (*Amtsspr.*) educational establishment; **~arbeit** *die* educational work *no art.*; **~beflissen** *Adj.* keen on education *postpos.*; (*sich bilden wollend*) keen on self-improvement *postpos.*; **~bürger** *der*, **~bürgerin** *die* [traditionally educated] middle-class intellectual; **~chancen** *Pl.* educational opportunities; **~dünkel** *der* intellectual arrogance *or* snobbery; **~einrichtung** *die* ⇒ **~anstalt**; **~erlebnis** *das* formative experience; **~fähig** *Adj.* fast-learning; receptive to teaching *postpos.*; **~feindlich** *Adj.* hostile to education *postpos.*; anti-education; **~gang** *der* educational career; **~grad** *der* level of education; **~gut** *das* material for one's general education; (*Kulturgut*) cultural heritage; **~hunger** *der* thirst for education; **~hungrig** *Adj.* eager to be educated *postpos.*; **~ideal** *das* educational ideal; **~lücke** *die* gap in one's education; **das ist eine ~lücke!** that's culpable ignorance!; **~monopol** *das* monopoly of education; **~not·stand** *der* state of emergency in education; **~politik** *die* educational policy; **~politisch** *Adj.* educational-policy *attrib.* ‹measure, strategy›; ‹discussion› concerning educational policy; **~reform** *die* educational reform; **~reise** *die* educational tour; **~roman** *der* (*Literaturw.*) novel of character development; Bildungsroman; **~stätte** *die* (*geh.*) educational establishment; (*Universität*) seat of learning; **~urlaub** *der* educational leave; **~weg** *der* educational course; **der zweite ~weg** the second chance to study; the alternative way of studying (*in adult classes*); **auf dem zweiten ~weg** using the second chance to study (*in adult classes*); **~wesen** *das* education system; **das ~wesen** education

**Bild-: ~unter·schrift** *die* caption; **~wand** *die* [projection] screen; **~werfer** *der* epidiascope; **~werk** *das* (*geh.*) sculpture; **~wörter·buch** *das* pictorial dictionary; (*für Kinder*) picture dictionary; **~zuschrift** *die* reply enclosing a photograph

**Bilge** /'bɪlgə/ *die*; **~, ~n** (*Seemannsspr.*) bilge

**bilingual** /bilɪŋ'gu̯a:l/ **1** *Adj.* bilingual. **2** *adv.* bilingually

**Billard** /'bɪljart, *österr.*: bi'ja:ɐ̯/ *das*; **~s, ~e,** *österr.*: **~s** billiards

**Billard-: ~kugel** *die* billiard ball; **~stock** *der* billiard cue; **~tisch** *der* billiard table

**Billet** /bɪl'e:/ *das* **~s, ~s** (*schweiz.*), **Billett** /bɪl'jɛt/ *das*; **~[e]s, ~e** *od.* **~s** **A** (*schweiz., sonst veralt.*) [entrance] ticket; **B** (*schweiz., sonst veralt.*) [train/tram/bus] ticket; **C** (*österr., sonst veralt.*) note; **D** (*österr.: Glückwunschkarte*) greetings card (*Brit.*); greeting card (*Amer.*)

**Billiarde** /bɪ'li̯ardə/ *die*; **~, ~n** thousand million million; quadrillion (*Amer.*)

**billig** /'bɪlɪç/ **1** *Adj.* **A** cheap; **ein ~er Preis** (*ugs.*) a low price; **B** (*abwertend: primitiv*) shabby, cheap ‹trick›; feeble ‹excuse›; **ist dir das nicht zu ~?** isn't that beneath you?; **ein ~er Trost** cold comfort; **C** (*veralt.: angemessen*) reasonable; proper. **2** *adv.* **A** cheaply; **~ einkaufen** shop cheaply; **~ abzugeben** (*in Anzeigen*) for sale cheap; **~ davonkommen** (*fig. ugs.*) get off lightly; **B** (*veralt.: angemessen*) **nicht mehr als ~:** no more than is reasonable *or* proper; **jeder ~ denkende Mensch** any fair-minded person; ⇒ *auch* **recht**

**Billig·angebot** *das* special *or* cut-price offer

**billigen** *tr. V.* approve; **~, dass jmd. etw. tut** approve of sb.'s doing sth.; **ich kann nicht ~, dass du dich daran beteiligst** I cannot approve of *or* condone your taking part; **etw. stillschweigend ~:** give sth. one's tacit approval

**billigermaßen, billigerweise** *Adv.* rightly; justifiably

**Billig-: ~flagge** *die* flag of convenience; **~flug** *der* cheap flight

**Billigkeit** *die*; **~ A** cheapness; low cost; **B** (*Rechtsw. od. geh.*) fairness; equitableness

**Billig-: ~laden** *der*; *Pl.* **~läden** cut-price shop; **~lohn** *der* low wages *pl.*; **~lohn·land** *das* lowwage country; **~preis** *der* low price; (*verbilligter Preis*) cut price

**Billigung** *die*; **~:** approval; **jmds. ~ finden** meet with *or* receive sb.'s approval

**Billig·ware** *die* cheap goods; **~n** cheap goods

**Billion** /bɪ'li̯o:n/ *die*; **~, ~en ▶841** trillion; million million

**Bilsen·kraut** /'bɪlzn̩-/ *das* henbane

**Bilux·lampe** /'bi:lʊks-/ *die* twin-filament bulb

**bim** /bɪm/ *Interj.* ding; **~, bam** ding dong

**Bimbam** *in* **[ach du] heiliger ~!** (*ugs.*) [oh] my sainted aunt! (*sl.*); glory be! (*coll.*)

**Bi·metall** *das* (*Technik*) bimetallic strip; **aus ~:** bimetallic

**Bimmel** /'bɪml̩/ *die*; **~, ~n** (*ugs.*) [ting-a-ling] bell

**Bimmel·bahn** *die* (*ugs. scherzh.*) narrow-gauge railway (*with a warning bell*)

**Bimmelei** *die*; **~** (*ugs. abwertend*) constant ringing; (*lautmalend*) ting-a-ling-a-ling

**bimmeln** *itr. V.* (*ugs.*) ring

**Bimse** /'bɪmzə/ *Pl.* (*ugs.*) **~ kriegen** get a walloping (*coll.*) *or* thrashing

**bimsen** *tr. V.* (*ugs.*) **A** (*drillen*) drill; **B** (*einexerzieren*) practise; **C** (*Schülerspr.: pauken*) mug up (*sl.*)

**Bims·stein** /'bɪms-/ *der* **A** pumice stone; **B** (*Gestein*) pumice; **C** (*Baustein*) pumice block

**bin** /bɪn/ *1. Pers. Sg. Präsens v.* **sein**[1]

**binar** /bi'na:ɐ̯/, **binär** /bi'nɛ:ɐ̯/, **binarisch** /bi'na:rɪʃ/ *Adj.* (*fachspr.*) binary

**binaural** /binau̯'ra:l/ *Adj.* (*Med., Technik*) binaural

**Binde** /'bɪndə/ *die*; **~, ~n** **A** (*Verband*) bandage; (*Augen~*) blindfold; **B** (*Arm~*) armband; **C** (*ugs.: Damen~*) [sanitary] towel (*Brit.*) *or* (*Amer.*) napkin; **D** (*veralt.: Krawatte*) tie; **sich** (*Dat.*) **einen hinter die ~ gießen** *od.* **kippen** (*ugs.*) have a drink or two

**Binde-: ~gewebe** *das* (*Anat.*) **▶471** connective tissue; **~glied** *das* [connecting] link; **~haut** *die* (*Anat.*) **▶471** conjunctiva; **~haut·entzündung** *die* **▶474** (*Med.*) conjunctivitis *no art.*; **~mittel** *das* binder

**binden 1** *unr. tr. V.* **A** (*bündeln*) tie; **etw. zu etw. ~:** tie sth. into sth.; **B** (*herstellen*) make up ‹wreath, bouquet›; make ‹broom›; **C** (*fesseln*) bind; **jmdn. an Händen und Füßen ~:** bind sb. hand and foot; ⇒ *auch* **gebunden, Hand**; **D** (*verpflichten*) bind; **ich bin zu jung, um mich schon zu ~:** I am too young to be tied down; **nicht mehr gebunden sein** be free of any ties; **E** (*befestigen, auch fig.*) tie (**an** + *Dat.* to); **nicht an einen Ort gebunden sein** (*fig.*) not be tied to one place; **jmdn. an sich** (*Akk.*) **~** (*fig.*) make sb. dependent on one; **F** (*knüpfen*) tie ‹knot, bow, etc.›; knot ‹tie›; **G** (*festhalten*) bind ‹soil, mixture, etc.›; thicken ‹sauce›; **der Regen bindet den Staub** the rain lays the dust; **H** (*Buchw.*) bind; **I** (*Musik*) slur; **J** (*Verslehre*) **Wörter durch Reime ~:** link words in rhyme; **in gebundener Rede/Sprache** in verse. **2** *unr. itr. V.* (*fest machen*) bind

**bindend** *Adj.* binding (**für** on); definite ‹answer›

**Binder** *der*; **~s, ~** **A** (*Krawatte*) tie; **B** (*Bindemittel*) binder; **C** (*Landw.*) [reaper-]binder; **D** (*Bauw.: Stein*) header; **E** (*Bauw.: Dachbalken*) [roof] truss

**Binderei** *die*; **~, ~en** **A** (*Blumen~*) wreath and bouquet department; **B** (*Buch~*) bindery

**Binde-: ~strich** *der* hyphen; **~wort** *das*; *Pl.* **~wörter** (*Sprachw.*) conjunction

**Bind·faden** *der* string; **ein [Stück] ~:** a piece of string; **es regnet Bindfäden** (*ugs.*) it's raining cats and dogs (*coll.*)

**Bindung** *die*; **~, ~en** **A** (*Beziehung*) relationship (**an** + *Akk.* to); **seine politische ~ an die Sozialdemokraten** his political commitment to *or* ties with the Social Democrats; **B** (*Verbundenheit*) attachment (**an** + *Akk.* to); **C** (*Ski~*) binding; **D** (*Chemie*) bond; **E** (*Weberei*) weave

**Bingo** /'bɪŋgo/ *das*; **~[s]** bingo

**binnen** /'bɪnən/ *Präp. mit Dat. od.* (*geh.*) *Gen.* within; **~ Jahresfrist** within a year; **~ kurzem** soon

**binnen-, Binnen-: ~bords** *Adv.* (*Seemannsspr.*) inboard; **~deich** *der* inner dike; **~deutsch 1** *Adj.* ‹dialect› spoken in Germany; ‹word, expression, etc.› used in Germany; **2** *adv.* in Germany; **~fischerei** *die* freshwater fishing; **~gewässer** *das* inland water; **~hafen** *der* inland port; **~handel** *der* domestic *or* home trade; **~land** *das* interior; **im ~land** inland; **~ländisch** *Adj.* inland; **~markt** *der* (*Wirtsch.*) domestic *or* home market; **europäischer ~markt** internal European market; **~meer** *das* inland sea; **~reim** *der* (*Literaturw.*) internal rhyme; **~schifffahrt** *die* inland navigation; **~schiffer** *der*, **~schifferin** *die* member of an inland ship's crew; (*auf Schlepp-, Schubkahn*) bargee (*Brit.*); bargeman/bargewoman (*Amer.*); **~see** *der* lake; **~staat** *der* land locked country *or* state; **~zoll** *der* internal duty *or* tariff

**binokular** /binoku'la:ɐ̯/ *Adj.* binocular

**Binom** /bi'no:m/ *das*; **~s, ~e** (*Math.*) binomial

**binomisch** *Adj.* (*Math.*) binomial

**Binse** /'bɪnzə/ *die*; **~, ~n** (*Bot.*) rush; **in die ~n gehen** (*ugs.*) (*misslingen*) fall through; (*verloren gehen, entzweigehen*) go for a burton (*Brit. coll.*); come to grief (*Amer.*); ‹money› go down the drain (*coll.*); ‹vehicle, machine› pack up (*sl.*); **die Prüfung ist in die ~n gegangen** the exam was a disaster

**Binsen·weisheit** *die* truism

**Bio** /'bi:o/ (*Schülerspr.*) biol (*school sl.*); biology

**Bio-** (*ugs.*) organic ‹farmer, garden, vegetables, etc.›

**bio-, Bio-: ~aktiv 1** *Adj.* biological ‹washing powder›; **2** *adv.* biologically; **~chemie** *die* biochemistry; **~chemiker** *der*, **~chemikerin** *die* **▶159** biochemist; **~chemisch** *Adj.* biochemical; **~dynamisch 1** *Adj.* organic; **2** *adv.* organically; **~ethik** *die* bioethics *sing.*; **~gas** /'---/ *das* (*Ökologie*) biogas; **~genese** *die* biogenesis; **~genetisch** *Adj.* biogenetic; **~graph** *der* biographer; **~graphie** *die* **A** (*Beschreibung*) biography; **B** (*Lebenslauf*) life [history]; **~graphin** *die*; **~, ~nen** biographer; **~graphisch** *Adj.* biographical; **~laden** /'----/ *der*; *Pl.* **~läden** (*ugs.*) health food shop; **~loge** *der*; **~n, ~n ▶159** biologist; **~logie** *die*; **~:** biology *no art.*; **~login** *die*; **~, ~nen ▶159** biologist; ⇒ *auch* **-in**; **~logisch 1** *Adj.* **A** biological; **ein ~logisches Standardwerk** a standard work of biology; **B** (*natürlich*) natural ‹medicine, cosmetic, etc.›; **2** *adv.* **A** biologically; **B** (*natürlich*) naturally; **~masse** *die* biomass

**Bionik** /bi'o:nɪk/ *die*; **~:** bionics *sing.*, *no art.*

**Bio·physik** *die* biophysics *sing.*, *no art.*

**bio·physikalisch** *Adj.* biophysical

**Biopsie** /bio̯'psi:/ *die*; **~, ~n** (*Med.*) biopsy

**Bio-: ~rhythmus** *der* biorhythm; **~sphäre** /-'--/ *die* biosphere; **~tonne** *die* biobin; green bin

**Biotop** /bio'to:p/ *der od. das*; **~s, ~e** (*Biol.*) biotope

**Bio·wissenschaften** *Pl.* life sciences

**bi·polar** *Adj.* (*bes. Math., Physik*) bipolar

**bi·quadratisch** *Adj.* (*Math.*) biquadratic

**Bircher·mü[e]sli** /'bɪrçɐmy:(ə)sli/ *das* muesli (*made with fresh fruit*)

**Birke** /'bɪrkə/ *die*; **~, ~n** **A** (*Baum*) birch [tree]; **B** (*Holz*) birch[wood]

**Birken-: ~holz** *das* birch[wood]; **~wald** *der* birchwood; (*größer*) birch forest; **~wasser** *das*; *Pl.* **~wässer** hair lotion made from birch sap

*old spelling (see note on page 1707)

**Birk-:** **~hahn** *der; Pl.* **~hähne** blackcock; **~huhn** *das* black grouse

**Birma** /'bɪrma/ *(das);* **~s** Burma

**Birmane** /bɪr'ma:nə/ *der;* **~n,** **~n, Birmanin** *die;* **~,** **~nen** Burmese; ⇒ *auch* **-in**

**Birn·baum** *der* **A** pear tree; **B** *(Holz)* pearwood

**Birne** /'bɪrnə/ *die;* **~,** **~n** **A** pear; **B** *(Glüh~)* [light]bulb; **C** *(salopp: Kopf)* nut *(coll.)*; **eine weiche ~ haben** *(salopp)* be soft in the head

**Birnen·geist** *der* pear brandy

**bis** /bɪs/ ▸**207** ❶ *Präp. mit Akk.* **A** *(zeitlich)* until; till; *(die ganze Zeit über und ~ zu einem bestimmten Zeitpunkt)* up to; up until; up till; *(nicht später als)* by; **ich muss ~ fünf Uhr warten** I have to wait until *or* till five o'clock; **~ [einschließlich] Freitag** by Friday; **von Dienstag ~ Donnerstag** from Tuesday to Thursday; Tuesday through Thursday *(Amer.)*; **von sechs ~ sieben [Uhr]** from six until *or* till seven [o'clock]; **~ Ende März ist er zurück/verreist** he'll be back by/away until the end of March; **~ dann** *od.* **dahin will ich Ergebnisse sehen/muss ich mich noch gedulden** I want to see results by then/I must be patient until then; **~ wann dauert das Konzert?** till *or* until when does the concert go on?; how long does the concert last?; **~ jetzt ist nichts geschehen** up to now *or* so far nothing has happened; **~ dann/gleich/später/morgen/nachher!** see you then/in a while/later/tomorrow/later!; **~ spätestens Montag** *od.* **Montag spätestens** by Monday at the latest; **er ist [nur] ~ 17 Uhr hier** he is [only] here until *or* till 5 o'clock; **er ist [spätestens] ~ 17 Uhr hier** he will be here by 5 o'clock [at the latest]; ⇒ *auch* **dato**; **B** *(räumlich)* to; **dieser Zug fährt nur ~ Offenburg** this train only goes to *or* as far as Offenburg; **~ wohin fährt der Bus?** how far does the bus go?; **nur ~ Seite 100** only up to *or* as far as page 100; **~ 5 000 Mark** up to 5,000 marks; **von Anfang ~ Ende** from beginning to end; **~ dahin sind es 2 km** it's 2 km to there; **C** *in* **~ auf** *(einschließlich)* down to; *(mit Ausnahme von)* except for; **~ auf weiteres** for the time being; **D** *in* **~ zu** up to; **Städte ~ zu 50 000 Einwohnern** towns of up to 50,000 inhabitants.
❷ *Adv.* **~ zu 6 Personen** up to six people; **Kinder ~ 6 Jahre** children up to the age of six *or* up to six years of age; **die Feier dauerte ~ gegen 10 Uhr** the party went on until *or* till about 10 o'clock; **~ gegen 10 Uhr ist es fertig** it will be ready by about 10 o'clock; **~ nach Köln** to Cologne; **~ an die Decke** up to the ceiling; **~ ins Kleinste** *od.* **Letzte** down to the smallest *or* last detail.
❸ *Konj.* **A** *(nebenordnend)* to; **vier ~ fünf** four to five; **heiter ~ wolkig** fair or cloudy; **B** *(bevor nicht)* until; till; **~ dass der Tod euch scheidet** *(geh.)* until *or* till death do you part; **C** *(österr.: sobald)* when; **gleich ~ er aufgewacht ist** as soon as he's woken up

**Bisam** /'bi:zam/ *der;* **~s,** **~e** *od.* **~s** **A** ⇒ **Moschus**; **B** *(Pelz)* musquash

**Bisam·ratte** *die* muskrat

**Bischof** /'bɪʃɔf/ *der;* **~s, Bischöfe** /'bɪʃœfə/, **Bischöfin** *die;* **~,** **~nen** bishop

**bischöflich** *Adj.* episcopal

**Bischofs-:** **~amt** *das* episcopate; office of bishop; **~hut** *der* bishop's hat; **~konferenz** *die* conference of bishops; **~mütze** *die* [bishop's] mitre; **~sitz** *der* seat of a/the bishopric; **~stab** *der* [bishop's] crosier *or* crook; **~stadt** *die* ⇒ **~sitz**

**Bise** /'bi:zə/ *die;* **~,** **~n** *(schweiz.): north[-east] wind to the north of the Alps;* bise

**Bi·sexualität** *die* bisexuality

**bi·sexuell** ❶ *Adj.* bisexual. ❷ *adv.* bisexually

**bis·her** *Adv.* up to now; *(aber jetzt nicht mehr)* until now; till now; **~ war alles in Ordnung** everything has been all right up to now/everything was all right until *or* till now; **er hat sich ~ nicht gemeldet** he hasn't been in touch up to now *or* as yet; **das wusste ich ~ nicht** I didn't know that till now *or* before; **ein ~ unbekanntes Buch** a hitherto *or* previously unknown book

**bisherig** *Adj.* *(vorherig)* previous; *(momentan)* present; **sie ziehen um, ihre ~e Wohnung wird zu klein** they are moving — their present flat is getting too small; **sie sind umgezogen, ihre ~e Wohnung wurde zu klein** they have moved — their previous flat became too small

**Biskaya** /bɪs'ka:ja/ *die;* **~: die ~/der Golf von ~:** the Bay of Biscay

**Biskuit** /bɪs'kvi:t/ *das od. der;* **~[e]s,** **~s** *od.* **~e** **A** sponge biscuit; **B** *(~teig)* sponge

**Biskuit-:** **~rolle** *die* Swiss roll; **~teig** *der* sponge mixture

**bis·lang** *Adv.:* ⇒ **bisher**

**Bismarck·hering** /'bɪsmark-/ *der* Bismarck herring

**Bison** /'bi:zɔn/ *der;* **~s,** **~s** bison

**Biss, *Biß** /bɪs/ *der;* **Bisses, Bisse;** **A** bite; **B** *(ugs.: Engagement)* punch

**bisschen, *bißchen** *indekl. Indefinitpron.* **A** *(in der Funktion eines Adjektivs)* **ein ~ Geld/Brot/Milch/Wasser** a bit of *or* a little money/bread/a drop of *or* a little milk/water; **ich würde ihm kein ~ Geld mehr leihen** I wouldn't lend him any more money at all; **das ~ Geld/Farbe** that [little] bit of money/[little] drop of paint; **ein/kein ~ Angst haben** be a bit/not a bit frightened; **B** *(in der Funktion eines Adverbs)* **ein/kein ~:** a bit *or* a little/not a *or* one bit; **ich werde mich ein ~ aufs Ohr legen** I'm going to lie down for a bit; **er hat mir kein ~ geholfen** he didn't help me one [little] bit; **ein klein ~:** a little bit; **ein ~ zu viel/mehr** a bit too much/a bit more; **ein ~ sehr teuer sein** be getting rather expensive; **C** *(in der Funktion eines Substantivs)* **ein ~:** a bit; a little; *(bei Flüssigkeiten)* a drop; a little; **von dem ~ werde ich nicht satt** that little bit/drop won't fill me up; **das/kein ~:** the little [bit]/not a *or* one bit; ⇒ *auch* **lieb** 1 D

**bissel** /'bɪsl/ *(südd., österr. ugs.)* ⇒ **bisschen**

**Bissen** *der;* **~s,** **~:** mouthful; **lass mich mal einen kleinen ~ davon probieren** let me try a small piece *or* a little bit; **sie brachte keinen ~ herunter** she couldn't eat a thing; **ich muss erst mal einen ~ essen** I must have a bite to eat first; **ein fetter ~** *(fig.)* a really good deal; **jmdm. die ~ in den Mund zählen** *(fig.)* watch how much sb. eats; **ihm blieb der ~ im Hals[e] stecken** *(ugs.)* the food stuck in his throat; **sich** *(Dat.)* **jeden** *od.* **den letzten ~ vom Munde absparen** scrimp [and save]

**bisserl** /'bɪsɐl/ ⇒ **bissel**

**bissig** ❶ *Adj.* **A** **~ sein** ‹dog› bite; **ein ~er Hund** a dog that bites; **„Vorsicht, ~er Hund"** 'beware of the dog'; **B** cutting, caustic ‹remark, tone, etc.›; **du brauchst doch nicht gleich so ~ zu werden** there's no need to bite my/his *etc.* head off; **C** *(Sportjargon)* **ein ~er Spieler** a sharp, attacking player. ❷ *adv.* *(boshaft)* ‹say› cuttingly, caustically; ‹grin› maliciously

**Bissigkeit** *die;* **~,** **~en** **A** *(von Hunden)*; **Kettenhunde neigen zur ~:** dogs that are chained up tend to bite; **B** *(Schärfe)* **die ~ seiner Antwort zeigte nur, wie wütend er war** his cutting *or* caustic answer just showed how angry he was; **C** *(Bemerkung)* cutting *or* caustic remark

**Biss·wunde, *Biß·wunde** *die* bite

**bist** /bɪst/ *2. Pers. Sg. Präsens v.* **sein**

**biste** *(ugs.)* = **bist du;** ⇒ *auch* **haste**

**Bistro** /'bɪstro/ *das;* **~s,** **~s** bistro

**Bistum** /'bɪstu:m/ *das;* **~s, Bistümer** /'bɪsty:mɐ/ bishopric; diocese; **das ~ Limburg** the diocese of Limburg

**bis·weilen** *Adv.* *(geh.)* from time to time; now and then

**Bit** /bɪt/ *das;* **~s,** **~[s]** *(DV)* bit

**Bitt·brief** *der* letter of request; *(Bittgesuch)* petition

**bitte** /'bɪtə/ *Höflichkeitsformel* **A** *(bittend)* please; **können Sie mir ~ sagen ...?** could you please tell me ...?; **~ nicht!** no, please don't!; *(ich möchte nicht)* I'd rather not; **~ nach Ihnen** after you; **~, ~ machen** *(Kindersp r.)* clap hands [to mean 'please']; **B** *(auffordernd)* please; **der Nächste ~!** next please!; **ja, ~?** *(am Telefon)* hello?; yes?; **nehmen Sie ~ Platz** please sit down; **~[, treten Sie ein]!** *(geh.)* come in!; **~ hier, hier ~!** over here, please!; **~ [schön]?** *(im Laden)* can I help you?; *(im Lokal)* what would you like?; **Hast du mal ein Tempotuch für mich? — Bitte [schön** *od.* **sehr]!** Could you let me have a tissue? — There you are; **~, gern/selbstverständlich** certainly/of course; **Entschuldigung! — Bitte!** I'm sorry — That's all right; **~, nur zu** [go on,] help yourself; **C** *(bejahend)* please; **aber ~!** yes, do; **~ ja!, ja ~!** yes please!; **D** *(Dank erwidernd)* **~ [schön** *od.* **sehr]** not at all; you're welcome; **E** *(nachfragend)* **[wie] ~?** sorry?; *(iron.)* what?; **F** *(missbilligend)* all right; **aber ~, macht, was ihr wollt** just [go ahead and] do what you want; **na ~!** there you are!

**Bitte** *die;* **~,** **~n** request; *(inständig)* plea; **eine große ~ [an jmdn.]/nur die eine ~ haben** have a [great] favour to ask [of sb.]/have [just] one request *or* just one thing to ask; **auf seine ~ hin** at his request; **jmdm. keine ~ abschlagen** *od.* **ausschlagen können** not be able to refuse sb. anything

**bitten** ❶ *unr. itr. V.* **A** **um etw. ~:** ask for *or* request sth.; *(inständig)* beg for sth.; **der Blinde bat um eine milde Gabe** the blind man begged for alms; **ich bitte einen Moment um Geduld/Ihre Aufmerksamkeit** I must ask you to be patient for a moment/may I ask for your attention for a moment; **darf ich [um den nächsten Tanz] ~?** may I have the pleasure [of the next dance]?; **[ich] bitte gehorsamst, gehen zu dürfen** *(veralt., scherzh.)* [I] respectfully beg permission to leave; **es half ihm kein Bitten:** pleading was *or* pleas were of no avail; **~ und betteln** beg and plead; **B** *(einladen)* ask; **ich lasse ~:** [please] ask him/her/them to come in; **der Herr Konsul lässt ~:** the consul will see you now; **darf ich zu Tisch ~?** may I ask you to come and sit down at the table?; **C** *(geh.: Fürsprache einlegen)* plead; **bei jmdm. für jmdn. ~:** plead with sb. on sb.'s behalf.
❷ *unr. tr. V.* **A** *(sich höflich wenden an)* **jmdn. um etw. ~:** ask sb. for sth.; **darf ich Sie um Feuer/ein Glas Wasser ~?** could I ask you for a light/a glass of water, please?; **darf ich die Herrschaften um Geduld/Ruhe ~?** could I ask you to be patient/silent?; **es wird gebeten, die Tiere nicht zu füttern** please do not feed the animals; **allmächtiger Gott, wir ~ dich, erhöre uns!** almighty God, we beseech Thee to hear us; **ich bitte dich um alles in der Welt** I beg [of] you; **[aber] ich bitte dich/Sie!** [please] don't mention it; **so, jetzt geht ihr ins Bett, aber ein bisschen plötzlich, wenn ich ~ darf** into bed with you, at once if you please; **darum möchte ich doch sehr gebeten haben!** *(ugs.)* I should hope so *(coll.)*; **ich muss doch [sehr] ~!** really!; **er ließ sich nicht lange** *od.* **erst ~:** he didn't have to be asked twice; **er lässt sich gern ~:** he likes to be asked; **jmdn. zu sich ~:** ask sb. to come and see one; **B** *(einladen)* ask, invite; **jmdn. zum Tee [zu sich] ~:** ask *or* invite sb. to tea; **jmdn. ins Haus/Zimmer ~:** ask *or* invite sb. [to come] in; **jmdn. zum Tanz ~:** ask sb. to dance; **er wurde für neun Uhr zur Direktion gebeten** he was asked to be at the manager's office at 9 o'clock; **jmdn. zu Tisch ~:** ask sb. to come and sit down at the table

**bitter** ❶ *Adj.* **A** bitter; plain ‹chocolate›; **B** *(schmerzlich)* bitter ‹experience, irony, contempt, disappointment, etc.›; painful, hard ‹loss›; painful, bitter, hard ‹truth›; hard ‹time, fate, etc.›; **eine ~e Lehre** a hard lesson; **bis zum ~en Ende** to the bitter end; **das ist mein ~ster Ernst** I am deadly serious; **eine solche Erfahrung ist ~:** an experience like that is a bitter one; **C** *(verbittert)* bitter; **ein ~es Gefühl** a feeling of bitterness; **er hatte einen ~en Zug um den Mund** he had a look of bitterness on his face; **jmdn. ~ machen** embitter sb.; make sb. bitter; Ⓓ (*groß, schwer*) bitter ‹cold, tears, grief, remorse, regret›; dire ‹need›; desperate ‹poverty›; grievous ‹injustice, harm›; **es herrschte [eine] ~e Kälte** it was bitterly cold; Ⓔ (*verbittert*) bitter ‹enemy›. ❷ *adv.* Ⓐ (*verbittert*) bitterly; Ⓑ (*sehr stark*) desperately; ‹regret› bitterly; **etw. ~ nötig haben** be in dire need of sth.; **das wird sich ~ rächen** you'll/he'll *etc.* pay dearly for that

**bitter-: ~arm** *Adj.* wretchedly poor; **~böse** ❶ *Adj.* furious; ❷ *adv.* furiously; **~ernst** ❶ *Adj.* deadly serious; **damit ist es mir ~ernst!** I am deadly serious; ❷ *adv.* **ich meine das ~ernst** I mean it deadly seriously; **~kalt** *Adj.* bitterly cold

**Bitterkeit** *die;* **~** Ⓐ (*auch fig.*) bitterness; Ⓑ (*Verbitterung*) bitterness

**bitterlich** ❶ *Adj.* slightly bitter ‹taste›; **etwas ~:** slightly bitter. ❷ *adv.* (*heftig*) ‹cry, complain, etc.› bitterly

**Bitter-: ~mandel** *die* bitter almond; **~mandel·öl** *das* bitter almond oil; oil of bitter almonds

**Bitternis** *die;* **~, ~se** (*geh.*) Ⓐ (*Geschmack*) bitterness; Ⓑ (*Gefühl*) bitterness; (*Leiden*) suffering

**Bitter·salz** *das* Epsom salts *pl.*

**bitter·süß, bitter-süß** *Adj.* (*auch fig.*) bittersweet

**Bitte·schön** *das;* **~s mit einem höflichen ~ überreichte er das Geschenk** he said politely 'this is for you' as he presented the gift

**Bitt-: ~gang** *der* Ⓐ (*zu jmdm.*) **ein ~gang [nach einem Ort]** going [to a place] with a request; **einen ~gang zu jmdm. machen** go to sb. with a request; Ⓑ (*kath. Rel.: ~prozession*) Rogation procession; **~gebet** *das* (*Rel.*) prayer of supplication; **~gesuch** *das* petition; **~gottes·dienst** *der* (*Rel.*) Rogation service; **~prozession** *die* (*kath. Rel.*) Rogation procession

**bitt·schön** (*ugs. Höflichkeitsformel*) **~, der Herr** there we are, sir; **Vielen Dank. — Bittschön, gern geschehen** Thank you very much — My pleasure; ⇒ *auch* **bitte** B

**Bitt-: ~schreiben** *das* petition; **~schrift** *die* petition; **~steller** /-ʃtɛlɐ/ *der;* **~~s, ~~, ~stellerin** *die;* **~~, ~~nen** petitioner

**Bitumen** /biˈtuːmən/ *das;* **~s, ~** (*auch:*) **Bitumina** /-mina/ (*Chemie*) bitumen

**bitzeln** /ˈbɪtsl̩n/ *itr. V.* (*südd., westd.*) tingle; ‹fabric, itching-powder, etc.› prickle

**bivalent** /bivɐˈlɛnt/ *Adj.* (*Chemie, Sprachw.*) bivalent

**Biwak** /ˈbiːvak/ *das;* **~s, ~s** (*bes. Milit., Bergsteigen*) bivouac

**biwakieren** *itr. V.* (*bes. Milit., Bergsteigen*) bivouac

**bizarr** /biˈtsar/ ❶ *Adj.* bizarre; fantastic, grotesque ‹coral reef, tree, formation, etc.›. ❷ *adv.* bizarrely

**Bizarrerie** /bitsarəˈriː/ *die;* **~, ~n** bizarreness; (*Handlung*) bizarre action

**Bizeps** /ˈbiːtsɛps/ *der;* **~[es], ~e** biceps

**BKA** *Abk.* **Bundeskriminalamt**

**B-Klarinette** /ˈbeː-/ *die* B-flat clarinet

**Blabla** /blaˈblaː/ *das;* **~[s]** (*ugs.*) blah[-blah] (*coll.*)

**Blach·feld** /ˈblax-/ *das* (*dichter. veralt.*) plain; champaign (*literary*)

**Blackbox·methode** /ˈblɛkbɔks-/ *die* (*Kybernetik*) black-box method

**Black-out** /ˈblɛkaʊt/ *das od. der;* **~s, ~s** blackout

**blaffen** /ˈblafn̩/, **bläffen** /ˈblɛfn̩/ *itr. V.* Ⓐ bark; give a short bark; (*kläffen*) yap; Ⓑ (*schimpfen*) snap

**Bläh·bauch** *der* (*ugs.*) bloated belly; **einen ~ kriegen/haben** get/be bloated

**blähen** /ˈblɛːən/ ❶ *tr. V.* Ⓐ swell, distend ‹stomach›; billow, fill, belly [out] ‹sail›; billow ‹sheet, curtain, clothing›; Ⓑ (*aufblasen*) flare ‹nostrils›; **mit vor Stolz geblähter Brust schritt er ...** his chest swollen with pride, he strode ... ❷ *refl. V.* Ⓐ (*rund werden*) ‹sail› billow *or* belly out; ‹nostrils› dilate; Ⓑ (*angeben*) puff oneself up. ❸ *itr. V.* (*Blähungen verursachen*) cause flatulence *or* wind; **~de Speisen** flatulent foods; **das bläht fürchterlich** it causes terrible flatulence

**Blähung** *die;* **~, ~en** flatulence *no art., no pl.;* wind *no art., no pl.;* **~en** flatulence *sing.;* wind *sing.;* **eine ~ abgehen lassen** break wind

**blaken** /ˈblaːkn̩/ *itr. V.* (*nordd.*) smoke

**bläken** /ˈblɛːkn̩/ *itr. V.* (*ugs. abwertend*) ‹child› yell; bawl; ‹animal› bellow

**blakig** *Adj.* (*nordd.*) smoky *pred.*

**blamabel** /blaˈmaːbl/ ❶ *Adj.* shameful, disgraceful ‹behaviour etc.›; embarrassing ‹situation›. ❷ *adv.* shamefully; disgracefully

**Blamage** /blaˈmaːʒə/ *die;* **~, ~n** disgrace

**blamieren** /blaˈmiːrən/ ❶ *tr. V.* (*bloßstellen*) disgrace; (*in Verlegenheit bringen*) embarrass. ❷ *refl. V.* (*sich bloßstellen*) disgrace oneself; (*sich lächerlich machen*) make a fool of oneself

**blanchieren** /blãˈʃiːrən/ *tr. V.* (*Kochk.*) blanch

**blank** /blaŋk/ *Adj.* Ⓐ (*glänzend*) shiny; **etw. ~ reiben/polieren** rub/polish sth. till it shines; **die Gläser werden nicht ~:** the glasses won't polish to a shine; Ⓑ (*ugs.: abgewetzt*) shiny; **~ polierte Schuhe** brightly polished shoes; Ⓒ (*unbekleidet*) bare; naked; **mit ~en Beinen kannst du nicht gehen** you can't go without any tights/stockings/socks on; Ⓓ (*ugs.: mittellos*) **~ sein** be broke (*coll.*); Ⓔ (*bloß*) bare ‹wood, plaster, earth, etc.›; **er ist mit dem ~en Messer auf mich losgegangen** he came at me with his knife drawn; Ⓕ (*rein*) pure; sheer; utter ‹mockery›; Ⓖ (*dichter.: hell*) bright; **der Blanke Hans** (*dichter. nordd.*) the stormy North Sea; Ⓗ (*österr.: ohne Mantel*) coatless; without a coat

**Blankett** /blaŋˈkɛt/ *das;* **~s, ~e** Ⓐ (*Wirtsch.*) blank [form]; (*mit Blankounterschrift*) signed blank [form]; Ⓑ (*Technik*) blank

**blanko** /ˈblaŋko/ *Adv.* Ⓐ (*bei Schriftstücken*) blank; **ich schreibe dir mal ~ einen Scheck aus** I'll write you a blank cheque; Ⓑ (*bei Papier*) plain

**Blanko-: ~scheck** *der* (*Wirtsch., fig.*) blank cheque; **~unter·schrift** *die* blank signature; **~voll·macht** *die* (*Wirtsch., fig.*) carte blanche

***blank·poliert** ⇒ **blank** A

**Blank·vers** *der* blank verse

**Bläschen** /ˈblɛːsçən/ *das;* **~s, ~** Ⓐ [small] bubble; Ⓑ (*in der Haut*) [small] blister

**Bläschen·aus·schlag** *der* ▶474 (*Med.*) herpes simplex

**Blase** /ˈblaːzə/ *die;* **~, ~n** Ⓐ bubble; (*im Farbenanstrich*) blister; **~n werfen** *od.* **ziehen** ‹paint› blister; ‹wallpaper› bubble; **es regnet ~n** it's pelting [down]; Ⓑ (*in der Haut*) blister; **sich** (*Dat.*) **~n laufen** get blisters [from walking/running]; Ⓒ ▶471 (*Harn~*) bladder; **eine erkältete ~ haben/sich** (*Dat.*) **die ~ erkälten** have/get a chill in the bladder; **eine schwache ~ haben** (*ugs.*) have a weak bladder; Ⓓ (*salopp abwertend: Leute*) mob (*coll.*)

**Blase·balg** *der; Pl.* **Blase·bälge** bellows *pl.;* pair of bellows

**blasen** ❶ *unr. itr. V.* Ⓐ blow; Ⓑ (*ein Blasinstrument spielen*) play; **auf dem Kamm ~:** play the comb; Ⓒ **zum Angriff/Rückzug/Aufbruch ~:** sound the charge/retreat/departure; Ⓓ (*wehen*) ‹wind› blow; Ⓔ (*bes. südd., österr.: kühlen*) **in die Suppe/auf eine Brandwunde ~:** blow on one's soup/a burn. ❷ *unr. tr. V.* Ⓐ blow; Ⓑ (*spielen*) play ‹musical instrument, tune, melody, etc.›; Ⓒ (*wehen*) ‹wind› blow; Ⓓ (*formen*) blow ‹bottle, glass, etc.›; Ⓔ (*derb*) suck off (*coarse*); **jmdm. einen ~:** suck sb. off (*coarse*); give sb. a blow job (*coarse*). ❸ *unr. unpers. V.* **es bläst** it's windy *or* blowy

**Blasen-: ~bildung** *die* blistering; **sonst kommt es zur ~bildung** or blisters will form; **~katarrh** *der* ▶474 (*Med.*) cystitis *no indef. art.;* **~leiden** *das* bladder complaint; **ein ~leiden haben** have bladder trouble *or* a bladder complaint; **~stein** *der* (*Med.*) bladder stone; vesical calculus (*Med.*); **~tee** *der:* *herbal tea taken for bladder complaints*

**Bläser** /ˈblɛːzɐ/ *der;* **~s, ~** Ⓐ (*Musik*) wind player; **die ~:** the wind section *sing.;* Ⓑ (*Bergmannsspr.*) blower

**Bläser·ensemble** *das* wind ensemble

**Bläserin** *die;* **~, ~nen** (*Musik*) wind player

**Bläser·quartett** *das* wind quartet

**blasiert** /blaˈziːɐ̯t/ (*abwertend*) ❶ *Adj.* blasé. ❷ *adv.* in a blasé way

**Blasiertheit** *die;* **~:** blasé attitude

**blasig** *Adj.* blistered ‹paint, skin›; bubbly ‹liquid›; [light and] frothy ‹dough›

**Blas-: ~instrument** *das* wind instrument; **~kapelle** *die* brass band; **~musik** *die* brass band music; (**~kapelle**) brass band; **~orchester** *das* brass band

**Blasphemie** /blasfeˈmiː/ *die;* **~, ~n** blasphemy

**blasphemisch** ❶ *Adj.* blasphemous. ❷ *adv.* blasphemously

**Blas·rohr** *das* Ⓐ (*Waffe*) blowpipe; Ⓑ (*Technik*) blast pipe

**blass, *blaß** /blas/ ❶ *Adj.* Ⓐ pale ‹face, skin, colour, complexion›; pale, wan ‹light, glow›; faint ‹writing›; (*fig.*) colourless ‹account, portrayal, etc.›; **~ werden** turn *or* go pale; (*vor Angst, Schreck*) pale; turn *or* go pale; **Rot macht dich ~:** red makes you look pale [in the face]; **~ wie eine Wand/wie der Tod** white as a sheet/deathly pale; **~ vor Neid sein/werden** (*fig.*) be/turn *or* go green with envy; Ⓑ (*schwach*) faint, dim ‹recollection, suspicion›; faint ‹hope, similarity›; only slight ‹effect›; Ⓒ **der ~e Neid** sheer *or* pure envy. ❷ *adv.* (*matt*) palely

**blass·blau, *blaß·blau** *Adj.* pale blue

**Blässe** /ˈblɛsə/ *die;* **~** (*der Haut*) paleness; pallor; (*der Farbe*) paleness; (*des Lichts*) paleness; wanness

**Bläss·huhn, *Bläß·huhn** /ˈblɛs-/ *das* coot

**blässlich, *bläßlich** ❶ *Adj.* Ⓐ rather pale; palish; Ⓑ (*unscheinbar, nichts sagend*) colourless ‹person, account, portrayal, etc.›. ❷ *adv.* (*nichts sagend*) colourlessly

**blass·rosa, *blaß·rosa** *indekl. Adj.* pale pink

**Blatt** /blat/ *das;* **~[e]s, Blätter** /ˈblɛtɐ/ Ⓐ (*von Pflanzen*) leaf; **kein ~ vor den Mund nehmen** not mince one's words; Ⓑ (*Papier*) sheet; **ein ~ Papier** a sheet of paper; **fliegende Blätter** loose leaves *or* sheets; **[noch] ein unbeschriebenes ~ sein** (*ugs.*) (*unerfahren sein*) be inexperienced; (*unbekannt sein*) be an unknown quantity; Ⓒ (*Buchseite usw.*) page; leaf; **etw. vom ~ spielen** sight-read sth.; **auf einem anderen ~ stehen** (*fig.*) be [quite] another *or* a different matter; Ⓓ (*Zeitung*) paper; Ⓔ (*Spielkarten*) hand; **das ~ hat sich gewendet** (*ugs.*) things have changed; Ⓕ (*am Werkzeug, Ruder*) blade; Ⓖ (*Grafik*) print; Ⓗ (*Jägerspr.*) shoulder

**Blatt·ader** *die* leaf vein

**Blättchen** /ˈblɛtçən/ *das;* **~s, ~** Ⓐ (*von Pflanzen*) [small] leaf; Ⓑ (*Papier*) [small] sheet; Ⓒ (*abwertend: Zeitung*) rag (*derog.*)

**Blätter·dach** *das* leafy canopy

**blatterig** ⇒ **blattrig**

**blätterig** ⇒ **blättrig**

**-blätterig** ⇒ **-blättrig**

**blättern** /ˈblɛtɐn/ ❶ *itr. V.* Ⓐ **in einem Buch ~:** leaf through a book; Ⓑ *mit sein* (*zerfallen*) flake; Ⓒ *mit sein* (*sich ablösen*) ‹paint, plaster, etc.› flake off. ❷ *tr. V.* put down [one by one]; **er blätterte mir 50 Mark auf den Tisch** he counted me out fifty marks in notes on the table

**Blattern** *Pl.* ▶474 smallpox *sing.*

**Blatter·narbe** *die* pockmark

**blatternarbig** *Adj.* pockmarked

**Blätter-: ~pilz** *der* agaric; **~schmuck** *der* (*geh.*) foliage; **~teig** *der* puff pastry; **~teig·gebäck** *das* puff pastries *pl.;* **~wald** *der*

*old spelling (see note on page 1707)

(*scherzh.*) press; **es rauscht im ~wald** there are murmurings *or* rumblings in the press; **~werk** *das* foliage

**blatt-, Blatt-: ~feder** *die* (*Technik*) leaf spring; **~gewächs** *das* (*Bot.*) foliage plant; **~gold** *das;* gold leaf; **~grün** *das* chlorophyll; **~knospe** *die* leaf bud; **~laus** *die* aphid; greenfly; **~los** *Adj.* leafless; **~metall** *das* foil; **~pflanze** *die* foliage plant

**blattrig** *Adj.* pockmarked

**blättrig** *Adj.* **A** (*von Pflanzen*) leafy; **B** (*abblätternd*) flaky

**-blättrig** *adj.* -leaved

**blatt-, Blatt-: ~säge** *die* wide-bladed [hand-]saw; **~salat** *der* green salad; **~silber** *das* silver leaf; **~wanze** *die* lygus bug; **~weise** *Adv.* **A** (*bei Pflanzen*) leaf by leaf; **B** (*bei Papier*) sheet by sheet; **~werk** *das* (*geh.*) foliage

**blau** /blau/ *Adj.* blue; **ein ~es Auge [haben/ (ugs.) kriegen]** [have/get] a black eye; **mit einem ~en Auge davonkommen** (*fig. ugs.*) get off fairly lightly; **jmdm. ein ~es Auge hauen** *od.* **schlagen** give sb. a black eye; **etw. nicht nur wegen jmds. schöner ~er Augen tun** not do sth. just out of the goodness of one's heart; **ein ~er Fleck** a bruise; **die ~en Jungs** (*ugs.: die Marine*) the boys in blue; **der Blaue Planet** Earth; **die ~e Stunde** (*dichter.*) the twilight hour; **die ~e Blume [der Romantik]** the Blue Flower [of the Romantics]; **ein ~er Brief** (*ugs.*) (*Kündigung*) one's cards *pl.;* (*Schulw.*) *letter informing parents that their child is in danger of having to repeat a year;* **Forelle ~** (*Kochk.*) blue trout; **einen ~en Montag einlegen** *od.* **machen** (*ugs.*) skip work on Monday; **sein ~es Wunder erleben** (*ugs.*) get a nasty surprise; **jmdm. ~en Dunst vormachen** (*ugs.*) pull the wool over sb.'s eyes; **~ sein** (*fig. ugs.*) be tight (*coll.*) *or* canned (*sl.*); **~ sein wie ein Veilchen** *od.* **wie eine [Strand]haubitze** *od.* **wie [zehn]tausend Mann** (*salopp*) be [completely] canned (*sl.*)

**Blau** *das;* **~s, ~** *od.* (*ugs.:*) **~s** blue

**blau-, Blau-: ~alge** *die* blue-green alga; **~äugig** *Adj.* **A** blue-eyed; **B** (*naiv*) naive; **~äugigkeit** /-|ɔygɪçkait/ *die;* **~** (*fig.*) naïvety; **~bart** *der* Bluebeard; **~beere** *die* bilberry; whortleberry; **~blütig** *Adj.* (*meist iron.*) blue-blooded

**Blaue**[1] /'blauə/ *das;* **~n** blue; **das ~ vom Himmel [herunter]lügen** (*ugs.*) lie like anything; tell a pack of lies; **jmdm. das ~ vom Himmel [herunter] versprechen** (*ugs.*) promise sb. the earth *or* the moon; **wir wollen einfach ins ~ fahren** we'll just set off and see where we end up; ⇒ *auch* **Fahrt** C

**Blaue**[2] *der;* **~n, ~n** (*ugs.*) **A** (*Hundertmarkschein*) hundred-mark note; **acht ~ kosten** cost eight hundred marks; **B** (*veralt.: Polizist*) cop (*coll.*); copper (*coll.*)

**Bläue** /'blɔyə/ *die;* **~** (*geh.*) blue; blueness; (*des Himmels*) blue

**bläuen** *tr. V.* **A** (*färben*) dye ‹material, clothes, etc.› blue; turn ‹litmus paper› blue; **B** (*aufhellen*) blue

**blau-, Blau-: ~färbung** *die* blue colour; blueness; **~felchen** *das* Blaufelchen; whitefish; **~filter** *der od. das* (*Fot.*) blue filter; **~fuchs** *der* **A** (*Tier*) Arctic fox; blue fox; **B** (*Fell*) blue fox [fur]; **~grau** *Adj.* blue-grey; bluish grey; **~grün** *Adj.* blue-green; bluish green; **~hemd** *das* (*DDR*) **A** (*Hemd*) blue shirt [of the Free German Youth]; **B** (*ugs.: Mitglied*) member of the Free German Youth; **~holz** *das* logwood; **~kabis** *der* (*schweiz.*), **~kohl** *der* (*bes. nordd.*), **~kraut** *das* (*südd., österr.*) ⇒ **Rotkohl**

**bläulich** *Adj.* bluish

**Blau·licht** *das; Pl.* **~er** flashing blue light; **ein Krankenwagen raste mit ~ vorbei** an ambulance raced past with [its] blue light flashing

**blau-, Blau-: ~|machen** (*ugs.*) ❶ *itr. V.* skip work; ❷ *tr. V.* **den Freitag ~machen** skip work on Friday; **~mann** *der* (*ugs.*) boiler suit; **~meise** *die* blue tit; **~papier** *das* [blue] carbon paper; **~pause** *die* blueprint; **~rot** *Adj.* purple; **~säure** *die* (*Chemie*) prussic acid; hydrocyanic acid; **~schimmel** *der* blue mould; **~schwarz** *Adj.* blue-black; **~stichig** /-ʃtɪçɪç/ *Adj.* (*Fot.*) with a blue cast *postpos., not pred.;* **~stichig sein** have a blue cast; **~stift** *der* blue pencil; **~strumpf** *der* (*abwertend*) bluestocking; **~tanne** *die* blue spruce; Colorado spruce; **~wal** *der* blue whale

**Blazer** /'ble:zɐ/ *der;* **~s, ~:** blazer

**Blech** /blɛç/ *das;* **~[e]s, ~e** **A** (*Metall*) sheet metal; **B** (*Platte*) metal sheet; (*Grob~*) metal plate; **C** (*Back~*) [baking] tray; **D** (*ugs.: Unsinn*) rubbish; nonsense; tripe (*coll.*); **E** (*ugs. abwertend: Orden*) medals *pl.;* gongs *pl.* (*coll.*); **F** (*Musik: ~bläser*) brass

**Blech-: ~bläser** *der,* **~bläserin** *die* brass player; **die ~bläser** (*im Orchester*) the brass [section] *sing;* **~blas·instrument** *das* brass instrument; **~büchse** *die,* **~dose** *die* tin; **~eimer** *der* metal bucket

**blechen** *tr., itr. V.* (*ugs.*) cough up (*coll.*); fork out (*coll.*)

**blechern** /'blɛçɐn/ ❶ *Adj.* **A** (*aus Blech*) metal; **B** (*metallisch klingend*) tinny ‹sound, voice›. ❷ *adv.* (*metallisch*) tinnily

**Blech-: ~instrument** *das* brass instrument; **~kiste** *die* (*ugs. abwertend*) crate (*sl.*); **~lawine** *die* (*ugs. scherzh.*) solid line of cars; **~musik** *die* (*abwertend*) brass band music; **~napf** *der* metal bowl

**Blechner** *der;* **~s, ~, Blechnerin** *die;* **~, ~nen** (*südd.*) ⇒ **Klempner**

**Blech-: ~schaden** *der* (*Kfz-W.*) damage *no indef. art.* to the bodywork; **~schere** *die* metal shears *pl.;* **~schmied** *der,* **~schmiedin** *die* (*nordwestd.*) ⇒ **Klempner**; **~trommel** *die* tin drum

**blecken** /'blɛkn̩/ *tr. V.* **die Zähne ~:** bare one's/its teeth

**Blei**[1] /blai/ *das;* **~[e]s, ~e** **A** lead; **~ gießen** *pour lead into cold water to tell one's fortune for the coming year;* **jmdm. wie ~ in den Gliedern** *od.* **Knochen liegen** ‹tiredness, exhaustion, shock, etc.› make sb.'s limbs feel like lead; **jmdm. wie ~ im Magen liegen** (*schwer verdaulich sein*) weigh heavily on sb.'s stomach; (*jmdn. bedrücken*) prey on sb.'s mind; **B** (*Lot*) plumb [bob]; **C** (*veralt.*) (*Gewehrkugeln*) lead

**Blei**[2] *der od. das;* **~[e]s, ~e** (**~stift**) pencil

**Bleibe** *die;* **~, ~n** place to stay; **keine ~ haben** have nowhere to stay

**bleiben** /'blaibn̩/ *unr. itr. V.; mit sein* **A** (*an einem Ort*) stay; remain; **~ Sie bitte am Apparat** hold the line please; **wo bleibt er so lange?** where has he got to?; **wo bleibst du denn so lange?** where have you been *or* what's been keeping you all this time?; **wo bleibt der Kaffee?** where has the coffee got to?; what has happened to the coffee?; **wo sind die Blumen geblieben?** what's happened to the flowers?; **wo ~ nur die Jahre?** how the years have flown!; **zum Abendessen ~:** stay for supper; **auf dem Weg ~:** keep to *or* stay on the path; **da ~ wir ganz unter** (*Dat.*) *od.* **für uns** there will just be us; **jmdm. in Erinnerung** *od.* **im Gedächtnis ~:** stay in sb.'s mind *or* memory; **von etw. ~** (*ugs.*) stay *or* keep away from sth.; **das bleibt unter uns** (*Dat.*) that's [just] between ourselves; **zusehen, wo man bleibt** (*ugs.*) have to fend for oneself; **ich kann sehen, wo ich bleibe** I'm left to shift for myself; **jmdn. zum Bleiben auffordern** ask sb. to stay; **hier ist meines Bleibens nicht länger** (*veralt., scherzh.*) I shall not stay here any longer; **bleibe im Lande und nähre dich redlich** there's a good living to be had in your own country; ⇒ *auch* **Rahmen** B; **Sache** B; **B** (*Zustand, Eigenschaft beibehalten*) stay; remain; **der Kuchen bleibt mehrere Tage frisch** the cake will keep for several days; **bleib ruhig!** keep calm!; **das Geschäft bleibt heute geschlossen** the shop is closed today; **der Brief blieb unbeantwortet** the letter went *or* remained unanswered; **unbestraft/unbeachtet ~:** go unpunished/go unnoticed *or* escape notice; **dieser Tag wird uns** (*Dat.*) **immer unvergessen ~:** we shall always remember this day; **sitzen ~:** stay *or* remain sitting down *or* seated; **~ Sie doch bitte sitzen** please don't get up; **ich bleibe lieber stehen** I would rather stand; **Freunde ~:** remain friends; go on being friends; **C** (*übrig ~*) be left; remain; **uns** (*Dat.*) **bleibt noch Zeit** we still have time; **bis zur Abreise bleibt uns weniger als eine Stunde** there is less than an hour before we leave; **es blieb ihm keine Hoffnung mehr** he had no hope left; **was bleibt mir dann noch?** what shall I have left?; ⇒ *auch* **Wahl**; **D** (*für die Zukunft*); **es bleibt abzuwarten, ob ...** it remains to be seen whether ...; **es bleibt zu hoffen, dass ...** we can only hope that ...; **bei dem Wein ~ wir** we'll stick to *or* with *or* keep to this wine; **E** (*nicht ändern*) **bei etw. ~:** keep *or* stick to sth.; **ich bleibe dabei, dass ...** I still say that ...; **dabei bleibt es!** that's that; that's the end of it; **F** (*verhüll.: sterben*) **im Feld/im Krieg/auf See ~:** die *or* fall in action/die in the war/at sea; **G etw. ~ lassen** give sth. a miss; forget sth.; **das wirst du mal schön ~ lassen** you can forget about that; **das Rauchen ~ lassen** give up *or* stop smoking

**bleibend** *Adj.* lasting; permanent ‹damage›

***bleiben|lassen** ⇒ **bleiben** G

**Bleibe·recht** *das* right of abode

**bleich** /blaiç/ *Adj.* **A** pale; **~ vor Angst/Wut sein** be white with fear/rage; **~ wie eine Wand/wie der Tod** white as a sheet/deathly pale; **~ werden** turn *or* go pale; (*vor Angst, Schreck*) pale; turn *or* go pale; **B** (*geh.: fahl*) pale ‹light, gleam›

**Bleiche** *die;* **~, ~n** **A** (*veralt.: für Wäsche*) bleaching field; bleaching ground; **B** (*geh.: Blässe*) paleness; (*des Gesichts, der Haut*) pallor; paleness

**bleichen**[1] *tr. V.* bleach

**bleichen**[2] *regelm.* (*veralt. auch unr.*) *itr. V.* become bleached; bleach; **in der Sonne ~:** be bleached by the sun

**bleich-, Bleich-: ~gesicht** *das; Pl.* **~er** **A** pale face; (*ugs.: blasser Mensch*) pale-faced *or* pasty-faced type (*coll.*); **B** (*scherzh.: Weißer*) paleface; **~gesichtig** *Adj.* (*ugs.*) pale-faced; pasty-faced; **~mittel** *das* bleach; bleaching agent; **~sucht** *die* (*veralt.*) chlorosis; greensickness

**bleiern** /'blaiɐn/ ❶ *Adj.* **A** (*aus Blei*) lead; **er schwimmt wie eine ~e Ente** (*ugs. scherzh.*) he can't swim for toffee (*Brit. coll.*) *or* swim a stroke; **B** (*geh.: bleifarben*) leaden ‹sky, grey›; **C** (*schwer*) heavy ‹sleep, tiredness, etc.›; leaden ‹heaviness›; **seine Füße waren ~:** his feet were like lead. ❷ *adv.* (*fig.: schwer*) heavily; **es lag ihr ~ in den Gliedern** her limbs felt like lead *or* as heavy as lead

**blei-, Blei-: ~erz** *das* lead ore; **~farben, ~farbig** *Adj.* lead-coloured; lead-grey; leaden ‹sky›; **~frei** ❶ *Adj.* unleaded ‹fuel›; ❷ *adv.* **~frei fahren/tanken** drive on/use unleaded fuel; **~fuß** *der:* *in* **mit ~fuß fahren** (*ugs. scherzh.*) drive with one's foot down to the floor; **~gehalt** *der* lead content; **~gewicht** *das* (*auch fig.*) lead weight; **~gießen** *das: pouring lead into cold water to tell one's fortune for the coming year;* **~glanz** *der* (*Mineral.*) galena; **~glas** *das* lead glass; **~haltig** *Adj.* ‹petrol, paint, etc.› containing lead; plumbiferous, lead-bearing ‹ore›; **~haltig sein** ‹petrol, paint, etc.› contain lead; **die Luft hier ist ziemlich ~haltig** (*salopp scherzh.*) there's plenty of lead flying around; **~hütte** *die* lead works *sing.;* **~kristall** *das* lead crystal; **~kugel** *die* **A** (*Geschoss*) lead bullet; **B** (*Kugel*) lead ball; **~oxid, ~oxyd** *das* (*Chemie*) lead oxide; **~satz** *der* (*Druckw.*) hot-metal composition; **~schürze** *die* lead apron; **~schwer** ❶ *Adj.* heavy as lead *postpos.;* ❷ *adv.* heavily; like a heavy *or* lead weight; **~soldat** *der* lead soldier

**Blei·stift** *der* pencil; **mit ~:** in pencil

**Bleistift-: ~absatz** *der* stiletto heel; **~mine** *die* [pencil] lead; **~spitzer** *der* pencil sharpener; **~zeichnung** *die* pencil drawing

b

**Blei·vergiftung** *die* lead poisoning

**Blende** *die;* ~, ~n A *(Lichtschutz)* shade; *(am Fenster)* blind; *(im Auto)* [sun] visor; B *(Optik, Film, Fot.: Vorrichtung)* diaphragm; **die ~ öffnen/schließen** open up the aperture/stop down; C *(Film, Fot.:* ~*nzahl)* aperture setting; f-number; **mit** *od.* **bei ~ 8** at [an aperture setting of] f/8; **~ 11 einstellen** set the aperture to *or* at f/11; D *(Film: Einstellung)* fade; **einen Film mit einer ~ anfangen/enden lassen** start a film with a fade-in/end a film with a fade-out; E *(Stoffstreifen)* trimming; F *(Archit.)* blind window/arch/niche *etc.;* G *(Chemie)* blende

**blenden** ❶ *tr. V.* A *(auch beeindrucken, täuschen)* dazzle; B *(blind machen)* blind; C *(Kürschnerei)* blend. ❷ *itr. V.* A ‹light› be dazzling; B *(täuschen)* dazzle people

**Blenden·automatik** *die (Fot.)* automatic aperture control

**blendend** ❶ *Adj.* splendid; brilliant ‹musician, dancer, speech, achievement, etc.›; **es geht mir ~:** I feel wonderfully well *or* wonderful. ❷ *adv.* **wir haben uns ~ amüsiert** we had a wonderful *or* marvellous time

**Blender** *der;* ~s, ~, **Blenderin** *die;* ~, ~nen *(ugs.)* fraud; phoney *(sl.)*

**blend·frei** *Adj.* A *(nicht blendend)* non-dazzle; B *(nicht spiegelnd)* non-dazzle; non-reflective

**Blend·laterne** *die* dark lantern

**Blendung** *die;* ~, ~en A dazzling; B *(Täuschung)* deception; C *(Strafe)* blinding; D *(Kürschnerei)* blending

**Blend·werk** *das (geh. abwertend)* deception; **ein ~ des Teufels** a trap set by the devil

**Blesse** /ˈblɛsə/ *die;* ~, ~n A *(Fleck)* blaze; B *(Tier)* horse/cow *etc.* with a/the blaze

**Bless·huhn**, ***Bleß·huhn** *das* ⇨ **Blässhuhn**

**blessiert** /blɛˈsiːɐ̯t/ *Adj. (geh., scherzh.) (verletzt)* injured; *(verwundet)* wounded

**Blessur** /blɛˈsuːɐ̯/ *die;* ~, ~en *(veralt., scherzh.) (Verletzung)* injury; *(Wunde)* wound

**bleu** /bløː/ *indekl. Adj.* light *or* pale blue

**Bleu** *das;* ~s, ~ *od. (ugs.)* ~s light *or* pale blue

**blich** /blɪç/ *1. u. 3. Pers. Sg. Prät. v.* **bleichen²**

**Blick** /blɪk/ *der;* ~[e]s, ~e A *(das Anschauen)* look; *(flüchtig)* glance; **jmdm. einen ~/sich ~e zuwerfen** give sb. a look/exchange glances; **einen kurzen ~ auf etw.** *(Akk.)* **werfen** take a quick look at *or* glance [briefly] at sth.; **einen ~ riskieren** *(ugs.)* venture a glance; **jmds. ~** *(Dat.)* **ausweichen** avoid sb.'s glance *or* eye; **jmds. ~** *(Akk.)* **erwidern** return sb.'s look *or* gaze; **ein ~ in die Vergangenheit/Zukunft** a look back [into the past]/a look into the future; **auf den ersten ~:** at first glance; **auf den zweiten ~:** looking at it again *or* a second time; **etw. mit einem ~ sehen** see sth. at a glance; **keinen ~ für jmdn./etw. haben** take no notice of sb./sth.; **jmdn./etw. im ~ haben** be looking at sb./sth.; **wenn ~e töten könnten!** if looks could kill; **einen ~ hinter die Kulissen werfen** *od.* **tun** take a look behind the scenes; **den ~ heben** *(geh.)* raise one's eyes; look up; **den ~ senken** *(geh.)* lower one's eyes; look down; **mein ~ fiel auf den Brief** my eye fell on the letter; the letter caught my eye; **er wendete keinen ~ von der attraktiven Frau** his eyes never left the attractive woman; **jmdn. mit seinen ~en verschlingen** devour sb. with one's eyes; **jmdn. mit ~en durchbohren** look piercingly at sb.; ⇨ *auch* **Liebe** A; **würdigen** B; B *(Ausdruck)* look in one's eyes; **mit misstrauischem ~:** with a suspicious look in one's eye; **mit zärtlichem ~:** with a tender look in one's eyes; ⇨ *auch* **böse**; C *(Aussicht)* view; **ein Zimmer mit ~ aufs Meer** a room with a sea view; **jmdn./etw. aus dem ~ verlieren** lose sight of sb./sth.; **etw. im ~ haben** be able to see sth.; D *(Urteil[skraft])* eye; **einen sicheren/geschulten ~ für etw. haben** have a sure/trained eye for sth.; **keinen ~ für etw. haben** have no eye for sth.; **seinen ~ für etw. schärfen** sharpen one's awareness of sth.

**blicken** ❶ *itr. V.* look; *(flüchtig)* glance; **jmdm. gerade in die Augen ~:** look sb. straight in the eye; **zur Seite ~:** look away; **auf das vergangene Jahr ~** *(fig.)* look back on the past year; **das lässt tief ~** *(ugs.)* that's very revealing. ❷ *tr. V.* **sich ~ lassen** put in an appearance; **lass dich mal wieder ~:** come again some time; **er hat sich lange nicht mehr ~ lassen** he hasn't been seen for a long time; **sie wagt es nicht, sich ~ zu lassen** she dare not show her face; **er lässt sich ja nie ~:** he's never around *(coll.)*

**Blick-:** ~**fang** *der* eye-catcher; **als ~fang dienen** serve to catch the eye; ~**feld** *das* field of vision *or* view; **er hat ein recht enges ~feld** *(fig.)* he has really narrow horizons *pl.;* **jmdn./etw. ins ~feld der Öffentlichkeit rücken** make sb./sth. the focus of public attention; ~**kontakt** *der* eye contact; ~**punkt** *der* view; field of vision; **im ~punkt der Öffentlichkeit stehen** *(fig.)* be in the public eye; **jmdn. in den ~punkt rücken** *(fig.)* single sb. out; **in den ~punkt treten** *(fig.)* become the focus of attention; enter the limelight; ~**richtung** *die* A line of sight *or* vision; **in ~richtung [nach] rechts** to the *or* on your right; looking to your right; B *(fig.)* perspective; ~**winkel** *der* A angle of vision; B *(fig.)* point of view; viewpoint; perspective

**blieb** /bliːp/ *1. u. 3. Pers. Sg. Prät. v.* **bleiben**

**blies** /bliːs/ *1. u. 3. Pers. Sg. Prät. v.* **blasen**

**blind** /blɪnt/ ❶ *Adj.* A blind; **~ werden** go blind; **auf einem Auge ~ sein** be blind in one eye; **auf dem Auge ist sie ~** *(fig. ugs.)* she refuses to see that; **~ für etw. sein** be blind to sth.; **~ vor Tränen** *(geh.)* blinded by tears; ⇨ *auch* **Huhn**; B *(maßlos)* blind ‹rage, hatred, fear, etc.›; indiscriminate ‹violence›; **~ fliegen** fly blind; **~ schreiben** touch-type; C *(kritiklos)* blind ‹obedience, enthusiasm, belief, etc.›; **~er Eifer schadet nur** *(Spr.)* haste makes waste *(prov.)*; D *(trübe)* clouded ‹glass›; dull, tarnished ‹metal›; E *(verdeckt)* concealed; invisible ‹seam›; **ein ~er Passagier** a stowaway; F **~er Alarm** a false alarm; G *(undurchschaubar)* **der ~e Zufall** pure *or* sheer chance; **das ~e Walten des Schicksals** *(geh.)* the unfathomable workings *pl.* of fate; H *(vorgetäuscht)* false ‹pocket, buttonhole, etc.›; blind ‹window, arch, etc.›. ❷ *adv.* A *(ohne hinzusehen)* without looking; *(wahllos)* blindly; wildly; B *(unkritisch)* ‹trust› implicitly; ‹obey› blindly; C *(verdeckt)* **der Mantel wird ~ geknöpft** the coat has concealed buttons

**Blind·band** *der; Pl.* ~**bände** *(Buchw.)* dummy

**Blind·darm** *der* A ▶ 471 *(Anat.: Teil des Dickdarms)* caecum; B *(volkst.: Wurmfortsatz)* appendix

**Blind·darm-:** ~**entzündung** *die* ▶ 474 *(volkst.)* appendicitis; ~**operation** *die (volkst.)* appendix operation; ~**reizung** *die (volkst.)* grumbling appendix

**Blinde** *der/die; adj. Dekl.* blind person; blind man/woman; **die ~n** the blind; **das sieht doch ein ~r [mit dem Krückstock]** *(ugs.)* anyone *or* any fool can see that; ⇨ *auch* **einäugig**

**Blinde·kuh** *in* **~ spielen** play blind man's buff

**Blinden-:** ~**anstalt** *die* ⇨ ~**heim**; ~**führer** *der,* ~**führerin** *die* blind person's guide; ~**heim** *das* home for the blind; ~**hund** *der* guide dog; ~**schrift** *die* Braille; ~**stock** *der* white stick

**blind-, Blind-:** ~**fenster** *das (Bauw.)* blind window; *~|**fliegen** ⇨ **blind** 1A; ~**flug** *der* blind flight; *(das ~fliegen)* blind flying; **im ~flug** ‹land, take off, etc.› blind; ~**gänger** *der;* ~~s, ~~ A *(Geschoss)* unexploded shell; dud *(sl.)*; B *(salopp: Versager)* dead loss *(coll.)*

**Blindheit** *die;* ~ *(auch fig.)* blindness; **[wie] mit ~ geschlagen sein** be [as if struck] blind

**Blind·landung** *die (Flugw.)* blind landing

**blindlings** /ˈblɪntlɪŋs/ *Adv.* blindly; ‹trust› implicitly

**blind-, Blind-:** ~**material** *das (Druckw.)* spacing material; ~**schleiche** /-ʃlaiçə/ *die;* ~~, ~~n slowworm; blindworm; *~|**schreiben** ⇨ **blind** 1A; ~**spiel** *das (Schach)* blindfold game; ~**wütig** ❶ *Adj.* raging ‹anger, hatred, fury, etc.›; wild ‹rage›; ~**wütige Schläge** furious blows; ❷ *adv.* in a blind rage *or* fury; ~**wütigkeit** *die;* ~~: blind rage *or* fury

**blinken** /ˈblɪŋkn̩/ ❶ *itr. V.* A *(Verkehrsw.)* indicate; B *(Signal geben)* **mit Lampen ~:** flash lamps; C *(leuchten)* ‹light, glass, crystal› flash; ‹star› twinkle; ‹metal, fish› gleam; ‹water, wine› sparkle; **das ganze Haus blinkte vor Sauberkeit** the whole house was sparkling clean. ❷ *tr. V. (Signal geben)* flash; **SOS ~:** flash an SOS [signal]

**Blinker** *der;* ~s, ~ A *(am Auto)* indicator [light]; winker; B *(Angeln)* spoon[-bait]

**Blink-:** ~**feuer** *das (Seew.)* flashing light; ~**gerät** *das (Milit.)* signalling apparatus; signal lamp; ~**leuchte** *die (Kfz-W.)* indicator [light]; winker; ~**licht** *das; Pl.* ~~**er** *(Verkehrsw.)* flashing light; ~**licht·anlage** *die (Verkehrsw.)* flashing lights *pl.;* ~**signal** *das,* ~**zeichen** *das* flashlight signal

**blinzeln** /ˈblɪntsl̩n/ *itr. V.* blink; *(mit einem Auge, um ein Zeichen zu geben)* wink

**Blitz** /blɪts/ *der;* ~es, ~e A *(bei Gewitter)* lightning *no indef. art.;* **ein ~:** a flash of lightning; **der ~ hat eingeschlagen** lightning has struck; **war das ein ~?** was that [a flash of] lightning?; **seine Augen schossen ~e** *(fig.)* his eyes flashed; **potz ~!** *(veralt.)* upon my soul!; good heavens!; **[schnell] wie der ~:** like lightning; as fast as lightning; **wie ein geölter ~** *(ugs.)* like greased lightning; **wie ein ~ aus heiterem Himmel** like a bolt from the blue; **wie ein ~ einschlagen** be a bombshell; **wie vom ~ getroffen** thunderstruck; B *(~licht)* flash

**blitz-, Blitz-:** ~**ab·leiter** *der* lightning conductor; ~**aktion** *die* lightning operation; ~**angriff** *der (Milit.)* lightning attack; ~**artig** ❶ *Adj.* lightning; ❷ *adv.* like lightning; ‹disappear› in a flash; ~**blank** *Adj. (ugs.)* ~**blank [geputzt]** sparkling clean; brightly polished ‹shoes›

**blitzeblank** ⇨ **blitzblank**

**blitzen** ❶ *itr. V.* A *unpers. (bei Gewitter)* **es blitzte** *(einmal)* there was a flash of lightning; *(mehrmals)* there was lightning; there were flashes of lightning; **bei dir blitzt es** *(ugs. scherzh.)* your slip is showing; Charlie's dead *(Brit. coll.)*; it's snowing down south *(Brit. coll.)*; B *(glänzen)* ‹light, glass, crystal› flash; ‹metal› gleam; **sie hatte weiße, ~de Zähne** she had sparkling white teeth; **das Haus blitzte vor Sauberkeit** the house was sparkling clean; **Zorn blitzte aus ihren Augen** *(fig.)* her eyes flashed with anger; C *(nackt laufen)* streak *(coll.)*; D *(ugs.: mit Blitzlicht)* use [a] flash; **er fing wie wild an zu ~:** he started to flash away like mad *(coll.)*.
❷ *tr. V. (ugs.: mit Blitzlicht)* take a flash photo of

**Blitzer** *der;* ~s, ~, **Blitzerin** *die;* ~, ~nen *(ugs.)* streaker *(coll.)*

**Blitzes·schnelle** *die: in* **in** *od.* **mit ~:** at lightning speed; ‹disappear› in a flash

**blitz-, Blitz-:** ~**gerät** *das (Fot.)* flash [unit]; flashgun; ~**gescheit** *Adj.* very bright; ~**gespräch** *das* priority call *(with tenfold call charge)*; ~**krieg** *der (Milit.)* blitzkrieg; ~**licht** *das; Pl.* ~**er** flash[light]; **mit ~licht** by flash[light]; ~**licht·aufnahme** *die* flash[light] photograph; ~**licht·foto** *das* flash photo[graph]; ~**reise** *die* flying visit; ~**sauber** *Adj.* ~**sauber [geputzt]** sparkling clean; ~**schlag** *der* flash of lightning; **von einem ~schlag getroffen werden** be struck *or* hit by lightning; ~**schnell** ❶ *Adj.* lightning *attrib.;* **~schnell sein** be like lightning; ❷ *adv.* like lightning; ‹disappear› in a flash; **das alles geschah so ~schnell, dass …** it all happened so quickly that …;

*old spelling (see note on page 1707)

**~sieg** *der (Milit.)* lightning victory; **~start** *der* lightning start; **~telegramm** *das* priority telegram (*with tenfold charge*); **~umfrage** *die* light-ning poll; **~würfel** *der (Fot.)* flashcube

**Blizzard** /ˈblɪzɐt/ *der;* **~s, ~s** blizzard

**blochen** /ˈblɔxn̩/ *tr., itr. V. (bes. schweiz.)* polish

**Blocher** *der;* **~s, ~** *(schweiz.)* floor polisher

**Block** /blɔk/ *der;* **~[e]s, Blöcke** /ˈblœkə/ *od.* **~s** Ⓐ *Pl. nur* **Blöcke** *(Brocken)* block; *(Fels~)* boulder; Ⓑ *(Wohn~)* block; Ⓒ *Pl. nur* **Blöcke** *(Gruppierung von politischen Kräften, Staaten)* bloc; Ⓓ *(Schreib~)* pad; Ⓔ *(Basketball)* screen; *(Volleyball)* block; Ⓕ *Pl. nur* **~s** *(Eisenb.)* block; Ⓖ *(Philat.)* block; Ⓗ *(ns.: Organisationseinheit)* block [of houses]

**Blockade** /blɔˈka:də/ *die;* **~, ~n** Ⓐ *(Absperrung)* blockade; **eine ~ brechen** run a blockade; Ⓑ *(Druckw.)* [space marked by] turned letter[s] *(indicating missing or illegible material)*

**Blockade·brecher** *der,* **Blockade·brecherin** *die;* **~, ~nen** blockade-runner

**Block-:** **~bildung** *die* formation *or* creation of a bloc/blocs; **~buchstabe** *der* block capital *or* letter

**blocken** ❶ *tr. V.* Ⓐ *(südd.: bohnern)* polish; Ⓑ *(bes. Boxen: abfangen; Ballspiele: sperren)* block. ❷ *itr. V.* Ⓐ *(südd.: bohnern)* polish; Ⓑ *(bes. Boxen: abfangen; Ballspiele: sperren)* block; Ⓒ *(Jägerspr.)* perch

**block-, Block-:** **~flöte** *die* recorder; **~frei** *Adj.* non-aligned ‹country, state›; **~freie** *der; adj. Dekl.* non-aligned country *or* state; **~haus** *das,* **~hütte** *die* log cabin

**blockieren** ❶ *tr. V.* Ⓐ *(sperren)* blockade ‹country, port›; block ‹access road, border crossing point, etc.›; Ⓑ *(verstopfen)* block; jam ‹telephone line›; Ⓒ *(unterbrechen)* block ‹supply›; stop, halt ‹traffic›; Ⓓ *(anhalten)* lock ‹wheel, machine, etc.›; Ⓔ *(unterbinden)* block ‹negotiations, proposal, etc.›; Ⓕ *(Druckw.)* mark with turned letter[s] *etc. (to indicate missing or illegible material).* ❷ *itr. V. (stehen bleiben)* ‹wheels› lock; ‹gears› jam

**Blockierung** *die;* **~, ~en** ⇒ **blockieren**: blockade; blocking; locking; jamming; stopping; halting

**Block-:** **~partei** *die (bes. DDR)* bloc party; **~politik** *die (bes. DDR)* bloc policy; **~schokolade** *die* cooking chocolate; **~schrift** *die* block capitals *pl. or* letters *pl.;* **~staaten** *Pl.* aligned countries *or* states; **die ~staaten des Westens und des Ostens** the countries of the Western and Eastern blocs; **~stunde** *die (Schulw.)* double period; **~unterricht** *der* theme-work teaching *no art.;* teaching using the theme method *or* approach *no art.;* **~wart** *der (ns.)* block warden

**blöd[e]** /ˈblø:t, ˈblø:də/ ❶ *Adj.* Ⓐ *(schwachsinnig)* mentally deficient; imbecilic; Ⓑ *(unsinnig, ugs.: dumm)* stupid; idiotic *(coll.)*; Ⓒ *(ugs.: unangenehm)* stupid; **das Blöde ist nur, dass ...** the stupid thing is that ... ❷ *adv.* Ⓐ *(schwachsinnig)* imbecilically; Ⓑ *(unsinnig, ugs.: dumm)* stupidly; idiotically *(coll.)*; **er hat vielleicht ~ geguckt** a really stupid look came across his face; **frag doch nicht so ~:** don't ask such stupid *or (coll.)* idiotic questions; Ⓒ *(ärgerlich)* stupidly

**Blödel** /ˈblø:dl/ *der;* **~s, ~** ⇒ **Blödian**

**Blödelei** *die;* **~, ~en** Ⓐ messing *or* fooling about *no indef. art.;* Ⓑ *(Äußerung)* silly joke

**blödeln** *itr. V.* Ⓐ mess *or* fool about; Ⓑ *(sich äußern)* make silly jokes

**blöder·weise** *Adv. (ugs.)* stupidly

**Blöd·hammel** *der (salopp abwertend)* stupid fool *or (coll.)* idiot *or (Brit. coll.)* twit *or (Amer. coll.)* jerk

**Blödheit** *die;* **~, ~en** Ⓐ *(Dummsein)* stupidity; Ⓑ *(dumme Äußerung)* stupid remark; *(dumme Tat)* stupidity; Ⓒ *(Schwachsinnigkeit)* mental deficiency; imbecility

**Blödian** /ˈblø:dia:n/ *der;* **~s, ~e** *(ugs. abwertend)* idiot *(coll.)*; fool

**Blödler** *der;* **~s, ~, Blödlerin** *die (ugs.)* silly joker

**Blödling** *der;* **~s, ~e** ⇒ **Blödian**

**blöd-, Blöd-:** **~mann** *der (salopp)* stupid idiot *(coll.) or* fool; **~sinn** *der (ugs. abwertend)* nonsense; **jetzt habe ich ~sinn gemacht** now I've [gone and] messed it up; **mach doch keinen ~sinn!** don't be stupid; **was machst du denn da für einen ~sinn?** what are you messing about at?; **hör jetzt auf mit dem ~sinn** stop that nonsense; stop fooling *or* messing around; **höherer ~sinn** *(iron.)* high-flown nonsense; **~sinnig** ❶ *Adj.* Ⓐ *(ugs.: unsinnig)* stupid; idiotic *(coll.)*; Ⓑ *(schwachsinnig)* mentally deficient; imbecilic; ❷ *adv. (ugs.)* stupidly; idiotically *(coll.)*; **frag doch nicht so ~sinnig** don't ask such stupid *or (coll.)* idiotic questions; **~sinnigkeit** *die;* **~~** *(ugs.)* stupidity; idiocy *(coll.)*

**blöken** /ˈblø:kn̩/ *itr. V.* ‹sheep› bleat; ‹cattle› low

**blond** /blɔnt/ *Adj.* fair-haired, blond ‹man, race›; blonde, fair-haired ‹woman›; blond/blonde, fair ‹hair›; **ein ~es Gift** *(ugs. scherzh.)* a blonde bombshell; **~ gefärbt** dyed blond/blonde; **~ gelocktes Haar** fair curly hair; **ein ~ gelocktes Kind** a child with fair curly hair

**Blond** *das;* **~s** blond; *(von Frauenhaar)* blonde; **ihr ~ ist aus der Tube** her blonde hair comes from a bottle

**Blonde**[1] *der/die; adj. Dekl. (blonder Mann)* fair-haired *or* blond man; *(blonde Frau)* blonde

**Blonde**[2] *das od. die; adj. Dekl. (ugs.: Bier)* light beer; ≈ lager

***blond·gefärbt, *blond·gelockt** ⇒ **blond**

**blondieren** *tr. V.* bleach; *(mit Färbemittel)* dye blond/blonde; **sich ~ lassen** have one's hair bleached/dyed blond/blonde

**Blondierung** *die;* **~, ~en** Ⓐ ⇒ **blondieren**: bleaching; dyeing blond/blonde; Ⓑ *(blonde Farbe)* blond colour

**Blondine** /blɔnˈdi:nə/ *die;* **~, ~n** blonde

**Blond·kopf** *der* Ⓐ *(Kopf)* blond/blonde hair; fair hair; Ⓑ *(Kind)* blond/blonde child; fair-haired child

**bloß** /blo:s/ ❶ *Adj.* Ⓐ *(nackt)* bare; naked; **du kannst nicht mit ~en Beinen gehen** you can't go without tights/stockings/socks; **mit ~em Oberkörper** stripped to the waist; **den Pullover kann man nicht auf der ~en Haut tragen** you can't wear this pullover next to the skin *or* with nothing on underneath; **mit ~em Kopf** bare-headed; **mit ~en Füßen** barefoot; **mit ~en Händen** with one's bare hands; **auf der ~en Erde** on the ground; Ⓑ *(nichts als)* mere ‹words, promises, triviality, suspicion, etc.›; **der ~e Gedanke daran** the mere *or* very thought of it; **er kam mit dem ~en Schrecken davon** he escaped with no more than a fright; **nach dem ~en Augenschein beurteilen** judge simply by appearances; **ein ~er Zufall** mere *or* pure chance; **~es Gerede** mere gossip.

❷ *Adv. (ugs.: nur)* only; **ich habe ~ noch zehn Mark** I only have ten marks left; **das ist alles ~ deine Schuld** it's all your fault; **ich habe das Buch, ~ weiß ich nicht mehr, wo ich es hingelegt habe** I've got the book, but *or* only I don't know where I've put it.

❸ *in* **nicht ~ ..., sondern auch ...** not only ..., but also ...; **er sagt das nicht ~, er glaubt es auch** he doesn't just say it, he believes it as well.

❹ *Partikel (verstärkend)* **was hast du dir ~ dabei gedacht?** what on earth *or* whatever were you thinking of?; **sieh ~ zu, dass ...** just make sure that ...; **wie konnte das ~ geschehen?** how on earth did it happen?

**Blöße** /ˈblø:sə/ *die;* **~, ~n** Ⓐ *(geh.: Nacktheit)* nakedness; Ⓑ **sich** *(Dat.)* **eine/keine ~ geben** show a/not show any weakness; **er wollte sich** *(Dat.)* **nicht die ~ geben, das einzugestehen** he didn't want to show a weakness by admitting it; **jmdm. eine ~ bieten** reveal a weakness to sb.; Ⓒ *(Gerberei)* skin prepared for tanning; Ⓓ *(im Wald)* clearing; Ⓔ *(Fechten)* target; **eine ~ freigeben** *od.* **öffnen** present a target

**bloß-, Bloß-:** **~|legen** *tr. V.* uncover; expose; *(fig.) (herausfinden)* uncover; reveal ‹error, defect, etc.›; *(enthüllen)* expose; reveal ‹error, defect, etc.›; **~|liegen** *unr. itr. V.; mit sein* be uncovered *or* exposed; **~|stellen** *tr. V.* show up; unmask, expose ‹swindler, criminal, etc.›; **sich ~stellen** show oneself up; **~stellung** *die* ⇒ **~stellen**: showing up; unmasking; exposure; **~|strampeln** *refl. V.* kick the *or* one's covers off

**Blouson** /bluˈzõ:/ *das od. der;* **~s, ~s** blouson; bomber jacket

**blubbern** /ˈblʊbɐn/ *itr. V. (ugs.)* Ⓐ *(Blasen bilden)* bubble; Ⓑ *(undeutlich reden)* mutter; mumble

**Blücher** /ˈblʏçɐ/ *in* **er/sie geht ran wie ~** *(ugs.)* he/she really goes hard at it

**Bluejeans** /ˈblu:dʒi:ns/ *Pl. od. die;* **~, ~:** [blue] jeans *pl.;* denims *pl.;* **er trug ~ eine ~:** he wore [a pair of] jeans *or* denims

**Blues** /blu:s/ *der;* **~, ~** *(Musik, Tanz)* blues *pl.*

**Bluff** /blʊf/ *der;* **~s, ~s** bluff

**bluffen** *tr., itr. V.* bluff

**blühen** /ˈbly:ən/ *itr. V.* Ⓐ ‹plant› flower, bloom, be in flower *or* bloom; ‹flower› bloom, be in bloom, be out; ‹tree› be in blossom; **~de Gärten/Wiesen** gardens/meadows full of flowers; **es blüht** there are flowers in bloom; **diese Rosensorte blüht rot** this type of rose has red flowers; **Azaleen zum Blühen bringen** get azaleas to flower; Ⓑ *(florieren)* flourish; thrive; Ⓒ *(ugs.: bevorstehen)* **jmdm. ~:** be in store for sb.; **das Gleiche blüht mir nächste Woche** I've got the same thing coming [to me] next week; **da blüht dir ja was Nettes** *(iron.)* that'll be nice for you *(iron.)*; **das kann dir auch noch ~:** the same may *or* could happen to you; **sonst blüht dir was!** otherwise you'll catch it!

**blühend** *Adj.* Ⓐ *(frisch, gesund)* glowing ‹colour, complexion, etc.›; radiant ‹health›; **ein ~es Geschäft** a flourishing trade; **er sieht ~ aus** he looks marvellous *or* the picture of health; **aussehen wie das ~e Leben** look the very picture of health; **sie starb im ~en Alter von 20 Jahren** she died at 20, in the full bloom of youth; Ⓑ *(übertrieben)* vivid, lively ‹imagination›; absolute, utter ‹nonsense›

**Blühet** *die;* **~** *(schweiz.)* blossom

**Blümchen** /ˈbly:mçən/ *das;* **~s, ~:** [little] flower

**Blümchen·kaffee** *der (ugs. scherzh.)* Ⓐ weak coffee; Ⓑ *(Kaffee-Ersatz)* coffee substitute

**Blume** /ˈblu:mə/ *die;* **~, ~n** Ⓐ *(auch fig. dichter.)* flower; **vielen Dank für die ~n** *(iron.)* thank you very much *(iron.)*; thanks for nothing; **etw. durch die ~ sagen** say sth. in a roundabout way; **jmdm. etw. durch die ~ sagen** *od.* **zu verstehen geben** tell sb. sth. in a roundabout way; Ⓑ *(des Weines)* bouquet; Ⓒ *(des Biers)* head; Ⓓ *(Jägerspr.: des Hasen, Kaninchens)* tail; scut

**blumen-, Blumen-:** **~beet** *das* flower bed; **~bukett** *das (geh.)* bouquet [of flowers]; **~draht** *der* florist's wire; **~erde** *die* potting compost; **~fenster** *das* window full of flowers; *(spezielles Fenster)* flower window; **~flor** *der (geh.)* abundance of flowers; **~frau** *die* flower woman; **~fülle** *die* abundance of flowers; **~garten** *der* flower garden; **~geschäft** *das* florist's; flower shop; **~geschmückt** *Adj.* flower bedecked; adorned with flowers *postpos.;* **~gruß** *der* bouquet of flowers; **~händler** *der,* **~händlerin** *die* florist; **~kasten** *der* flower box; *(vor einem Fenster)* window box; **~kind** *das* flower child; **~kohl** *der* cauliflower; **~korb** *der (für ~)* flower basket; *(mit ~)* basket of flowers; **~kranz** *der* floral wreath; garland of flowers; **~laden** *der; Pl.* **~läden** ⇒ **~geschäft**; **~mädchen** *das* flower girl; **~markt** *der* flower market; **~muster** *das* floral pattern; **~pracht** *die* magnificent display of flowers; **~rabatte** *die* flower border; herbaceous border; **~reich** ❶ *Adj.* Ⓐ *(voller ~)* full of flowers *postpos.;* flowery; Ⓑ flowery ‹language, style, etc.›; ❷ *adv.* ‹speak› in a flowery way; ‹write› in a flowery style; **~schale** *die* (*Schale für* ~) plant bowl; (*Schale mit* ~) bowl of plants; **~schmuck** *der* floral decoration; **~stand** *der* flower stall; **~stock** *der* [flowering] pot plant; **~strauß** *der; Pl.* **~sträuße** bunch of flowers; (*Bukett*) bouquet of flowers; **~teppich** *der* carpet of flowers; **~topf** *der* Ⓐ (*Topf für Pflanzen*) flowerpot; Ⓑ (*ugs.: Topfpflanze*) [flowering] pot plant; **damit kannst du keinen ~topf gewinnen** (*ugs.*) that won't get you anywhere; **~uhr** *die* floral clock; **~vase** *die* (*Vase für* ~) [flower] vase; (*Vase mit* ~) vase of flowers; **~zwiebel** *die* bulb

**blümerant** /blymaˈrant/ *Adj.* queasy; **mir ist ~:** I feel queasy

**blumig** ❶ *Adj.* flowery ‹language, style, perfume, wine, etc.›. ❷ *adv.* ‹speak› in a flowery way; ‹write› in a flowery style

**Blunze** /ˈbluntsə/ *die;* ~, **~n**, **Blunzen** *die;* **~n**, **~n** (*bayr., österr.*) Ⓐ black pudding; Ⓑ (*ugs. abwertend: Frau*) fat cow (*sl. derog.*)

**Bluse** /ˈbluːzə/ *die;* ~, **~n** blouse; **ganz schön etwas in** *od.* **unter der ~ haben** (*salopp*) be well stacked (*coll. joc.*) *or* well endowed (*joc.*); **jmdm. an die ~ gehen** (*salopp*) try to grope sb.'s boobs *pl.* (*coll.*)

**Blüse** /ˈblyːzə/ *die;* ~, **~n** (*Seemannsspr.*) light

**blusig** ❶ *Adj.* bloused. ❷ *adv.* **~ geschnitten/fallend** bloused

**Blust** /bluːst/ *der od. das* (*veralt., schweiz.*) blossom

**Blut** /bluːt/ *das;* **~[e]s** ▶ 471 blood; **deine Stirn ist ja voller ~:** your forehead is covered in blood; **~ abgenommen bekommen** have a blood sample taken; **gleich ins ~ gehen** pass straight into the bloodstream; **jmdm. steigt das ~ in den Kopf** the blood rushes to sb.'s head; **es wurde viel ~ vergossen** there was a great deal of bloodshed; **er kann kein ~ sehen** he can't stand the sight of blood; **er lag in seinem ~:** he lay in a pool of blood; **~ und Boden** (*ns.*) blood and soil; **wenn sie so was sieht, kocht ihr das ~ in den Adern** (*fig.*) when she sees something like that, it makes her blood boil; **den Zuschauern gefror** *od.* **stockte** *od.* **gerann das ~ in den Adern** (*fig.*) the spectators' blood ran cold; **heißes/feuriges ~ haben** (*fig.*) be hot-blooded; **französisches/russisches ~ in den Adern haben** (*fig.*) have French/Russian blood in one *or* in one's veins (*fig.*); **~ ist dicker als Wasser** (*fig.*) blood is thicker than water (*fig.*); **ein junges ~** (*fig. dichter.*) a young thing (*fig.*); **an jmds. Händen klebt ~** (*fig. geh.*) there is blood on sb.'s hands (*fig.*); **blaues ~ in den Adern haben** (*fig.*) have blue blood in one's veins (*fig.*); **kaltes ~ bewahren** (*fig.*) remain cold and unmoved; **böses ~ machen** *od.* **schaffen** (*fig.*) cause *or* create bad blood; **~ und Wasser schwitzen** (*fig. ugs.*) sweat blood (*fig. coll.*); **~ geleckt haben** (*fig. ugs.*) have got a taste for it; **[nur/immer] ruhig ~!** (*ugs.*) keep your hair on! (*Brit. coll.*); keep your cool! (*coll.*); **jmdn. bis aufs ~ quälen** *od.* **peinigen** (*fig.*) torment sb. mercilessly; **jmdm. im ~ liegen** (*fig.*) be in sb.'s blood (*fig.*); **ins ~ gehen** get into one's blood; really get one going; **etw. mit seinem ~ besiegeln** (*dichter.*) lay down one's life for sth.; **nach [jmds.] ~ lechzen** *od.* **dürsten** (*geh.*) thirst for [sb.'s] blood (*fig.*)

**blut-, Blut-: ~ader** *die* ▶ 471 (*Anat.*) vein; **~alkohol** *der* blood alcohol level; **~andrang** *der* ▶ 474 (*Med.*) congestion; hyperaemia (*Med.*); **~apfelsine** *die* ⇨ **~orange**; **~arm** *Adj.* (*Med.*) anaemic; **~armut** *die* ▶ 474 (*Med.*) anaemia; **~auffrischung** *die* (*fig.*) **die Firma braucht eine ~auffrischung** the company needs some new blood; **~aus·strich** *der* (*Med.*) blood smear; **~aus·tausch** *der* (*Med.*) exchange transfusion; **~bad** *das* bloodbath; **~bahn** *die* bloodstream; **~bank** *die; Pl.* **~~en** (*Med.*) blood bank; **~befleckt** *Adj.* bloodstained; **seine Hände sind ~befleckt** (*fig.*) he has blood on his hands (*fig.*); **~beschmiert** *Adj.* smeared with blood *postpos.*; **~bild** *das* (*Med.*) blood picture; **~bildung** *die* (*Med.*) blood formation; **~blase** *die* blood blister; **~buche** *die* copper beech; **~druck** *der; Pl.* **~drücke** blood pressure; **~druck·messung** *die* blood-pressure test; **~drucksenkend** *Adj.* (*Med.*) anti-hypertensive; **~dürstig** *Adj.* (*geh.*) bloodthirsty

**Blüte** /ˈblyːtə/ *die;* ~, **~n** Ⓐ flower; bloom; (*eines Baums*) blossom; **die ~ der Jugend** (*dichter.*) the flower of the young men; **~n treiben** flower; bloom; ‹tree› blossom; **seltsame** *od.* **wunderliche ~n treiben** (*fig.*) produce strange effects; ‹custom, fashion› take strange forms; **seine Fantasie trieb üppige/die seltsamsten ~n** (*fig.*) his imagination produced extravagant/the strangest fancies; Ⓑ (*das Blühen*) flowering; blooming; (*Baum~*) blossoming; **die ~ der Tulpen/Obstbäume hat schon begonnen** the tulips have started to flower *or* bloom/the fruit trees have started to blossom; **in [voller] ~ stehen** be in [full] flower *or* bloom/blossom; **in der ~ seiner Jahre** (*fig. geh.*) in his prime; in the prime of his life; Ⓒ (*geh.: Entwicklungsstand*) **seine/ihre ~ erreichen** ‹culture› reach its full flowering; **die Renaissance war für die Kunst eine Zeit der ~:** art flourished during the Renaissance; Ⓓ (*ugs.: falsche Banknote*) dud note (*sl.*); Ⓔ (*ugs. abwertend: unfähiger Mensch*) duffer

**Blut·egel** *der* leech

**bluten** *itr. V.* Ⓐ (*Blut verlieren*) bleed (**aus** from); **mir blutet das Herz** (*iron.*) it makes my heart bleed (*iron.*); **~den Herzens, mit ~dem Herzen** with a heavy heart; **wie ein Schwein ~** (*derb*) bleed like a stuck pig; Ⓑ (*ugs.: viel bezahlen*) **[ganz schön] ~:** cough up (*sl.*) *or* fork out (*coll.*) a[n awful] lot of money (**für** for)

**Blüten-: ~blatt** *das* petal; **~flor** *der* (*dichter.*) abundance of flowers; **~honig** *der* blossom honey; **~hülle** *die* (*Bot.*) perianth; **~kelch** *der* (*Bot.*) calyx; **~knospe** *die* flower bud; **~lese** *die* (*veralt.*) florilegium (*arch.*); **~meer** *das* (*geh.*) sea of flowers; **~pflanze** *die* (*Bot.*) flowering plant; **~stand** *der* (*Bot.*) inflorescence; **~staub** *der* (*Bot.*) pollen

**Blut·entnahme** *die* taking of a blood sample; **zur ~entnahme zum Arzt gehen** go to the doctor to have a blood sample taken

**blüten·weiß** *Adj.* sparkling white

**Blüten·zweig** *der* flowering branch; (*kleiner*) flowering twig

**Bluter** /ˈbluːtɐ/ *der;* **~s**, ~ ▶ 474 (*Med.*) haemophiliac

**Blut·erguss**, ***Blut·erguß** *der* ▶ 474 haematoma; (*blauer Fleck*) bruise

**Bluterin** *die;* ~, **~nen** ⇨ **Bluter**

**Bluter·krankheit** *die* ▶ 474 haemophilia *no art.*

**Blüte·zeit** *die* Ⓐ **die ~ der Geranien ist von Mai bis Oktober** geraniums flower *or* are in flower from May to October; **während der ~ der Obstbäume** when the fruit trees are/were in blossom; Ⓑ (*fig.*) heyday; **seine ~ erleben** ‹culture, empire› be in its heyday; **das frühe 17. Jahrhundert war eine ~ des Dramas** drama flourished in the early 17th century

**blut-, Blut-: ~farb·stoff** *der* (*Physiol.*) haemoglobin; **~fleck[en]** *der* bloodstain; **~flüssigkeit** *die* ⇨ **~plasma**; **~gefäß** *das* ▶ 471 (*Anat.*) blood vessel; **~geld** *das* (*veralt.*) blood money; **~gerinnsel** *das* blood clot; **~gerinnung** *die* (*Physiol.*) clotting of the blood; **~gerüst** *das* (*geh.*) scaffold; **~getränkt** *Adj.* blood-soaked; **~gier** *die* (*auch fig.*) bloodlust; **~gierig** *Adj.* (*auch fig.*) bloodthirsty; **~gruppe** *die* (*Med.*) blood group; blood type; **jmds. ~gruppe bestimmen** *od.* **feststellen** blood type sb.; type sb.'s blood; **er hatte ~gruppe 0** he was blood group 0; **~gruppen·bestimmung** *die* (*Med.*) blood-typing; **~gruppen·untersuchung** *die* (*Med.*) blood test; **~hund** *der* bloodhound; (*fig.*) bloodthirsty murderer

**blutig** ❶ *Adj.* Ⓐ bloody; **jmdn. ~ schlagen** beat sb. to a pulp; **~ geschlagen werden** be left battered and bleeding; Ⓑ (*fig. ugs.: total, völlig*) absolute, complete ‹beginner, layman, etc.›; **das ist mein ~er Ernst!** I am deadly serious. ❷ *adv.* bloodily; **sich ~ rächen** take bloody revenge

**blut-, Blut-: ~jung** *Adj.* very young; **~konserve** *die* (*Med.*) container of stored blood; **~konserven** stored blood; **~körperchen** *das;* **~~s**, **~~** ▶ 471 (*Anat.*) blood corpuscle; **rote/weiße ~körperchen** red/white corpuscles; **~krebs** *der* ▶ 474 (*Med.*) leukaemia; **~kreis·lauf** *der* (*Physiol.*) blood circulation; **~kuchen** *der* (*Med.*) blood clot; clot of blood; **~lache** *die* pool of blood; **~leer** *Adj.* bloodless; **ihr Gesicht wurde ganz ~leer** the blood drained from her face; **~leere** *die* restricted blood supply; ischaemia (*Med.*); **~mangel** *der* Ⓐ lack of blood; Ⓑ (*Anämie*) anaemia; **~orange** *die* blood orange; **~pfropf** *der* (*Physiol.*) blood clot; clot of blood; **~plasma** *das* (*Physiol.*) blood plasma; **~plättchen** *das* (*Physiol.*) blood platelet; **~probe** *die* (*Med.*) Ⓐ (*~entnahme, ~untersuchung*) blood test; Ⓑ (*kleine ~menge*) blood sample; **~rache** *die* blood revenge; blood vengeance; **~rausch** *der* (*geh.*) murderous frenzy; **~reinigend** blood-cleansing; **~reinigung** *die* purification of the blood; **~reinigungs·tee** *der* blood-cleansing tea; **~rot** *Adj.* blood-red; **~rünstig** /-rʏnstɪç/ ❶ *Adj.* bloodthirsty; ❷ *adv.* bloodthirstily; **~sauger** *der*, **~saugerin** *die;* **~~**, **~~nen** Ⓐ (*Insekt, abwertend: Ausbeuter*) bloodsucker; Ⓑ (*Vampir*) vampire

**Bluts-: ~bande** *Pl.* blood ties; **~brüderschaft** *die* blood brotherhood; **~brüderschaft schließen** become blood brothers

**blut-, Blut-: ~schande** *die* incest; **~schänder** *der;* **~~s**, **~~**, **~schänderin** *die;* **~~**, **~~nen** incestuous person; **~schänderisch** *Adj.* incestuous; **~schuld** *die* (*geh.*) blood guilt; **~schwamm** *der* ▶ 474 (*Med.*) strawberry mark; **~senkung** *die* (*Med.*) erythrocyte sedimentation test; **zur ~senkung gehen** (*ugs.*) go to have a sedimentation test; **~serum** *das* (*Physiol.*) blood serum; **~spende** *die* (*das Spenden*) giving *no indef. art.* of blood; donation of blood; (*~menge*) blood donation; **~spender** *der*, **~spenderin** *die* blood donor; **~spende·zentrale** *die* blood donor centre; **~spucken** *das;* **~~s** ▶ 474 spitting of blood; haemoptysis (*Med.*); **~spur** *die* Ⓐ trail of blood; Ⓑ *Pl.* (*auf Kleidung o. Ä.*) traces of blood; **~stillend** *Adj.* styptic; **~stillende Mittel** styptics; **~strom** *der* bloodstream

**Bluts·tropfen** *der* drop of blood

**Blut·sturz** *der* Ⓐ (*ugs.: aus Mund und Nase*) **er erlitt einen ~sturz** he was bleeding from [his] nose and mouth; Ⓑ (*Med.*) haemorrhage

**bluts-, Bluts-: ~verwandt** *Adj.* related by blood *postpos.*; **sie ist nicht ~verwandt mit ihm** she is not related to him by blood; **sie sind nicht ~verwandt** they are not blood relations; **~verwandte** *der/die* blood relation; **~verwandtschaft** *die* blood relationship

**blut-, Blut-: ~tat** *die* (*geh.*) bloody deed; **~transfusion** *die* blood transfusion; **~triefend** *Adj.* dripping with blood *pred.*; **~überströmt** *Adj.* streaming with blood *pred.*; covered in blood *pred.*; **~übertragung** *die* blood transfusion

**Blut-und-Boden-Dichtung** *die;* ~ (*abwertend*) blood-and-soil literature

**Blutung** *die;* ~, **~en** Ⓐ bleeding *no indef. art., no pl.*; haemorrhage; **innere/äußere ~en** internal/external bleeding *sing.*; **eine ~ im Gehirn** a brain haemorrhage; Ⓑ (*Regel~*) period

*old spelling (see note on page 1707)

**blut-**, **Blut-:** **~unterlaufen** *Adj.* suffused with blood *postpos.;* bloodshot ‹eyes›; **~untersuchung** *die (Med.)* blood test; **~vergießen** *das;* **~~s** bloodshed; **~vergiftung** *die* ▶ 474 blood poisoning *no indef. art., no pl.;* **~verlust** *der* loss of blood; **~verschmiert** *Adj.* bloodstained, smeared with blood *pred.;* **~wäsche** *die (Med.)* purification of the blood; **~wurst** *die* black pudding; **~zirkulation** *die* blood circulation; **~zoll** *der (geh.)* toll of lives; **~zucker** *der (Physiol.)* blood sugar; **~zucker·spiegel** *der (Physiol.)* blood-sugar level; **~zufuhr** *die* blood supply

**b-Moll** /'be:mɔl/ *das* B flat minor; ⇒ *auch* **a-Moll**

**BMX-Fahrrad**, **BMX-Rad** /beɛm'ɪks:.../ *das* BMX [bike]

**BND** *Abk.* **Bundesnachrichtendienst**

**Bö** /bø:/ *die;* **~**, **~en** gust [of wind]; *(mit Niederschlag)* squall; **in ~en orkanartig** gusting to hurricane force

**Boa** /'bo:a/ *die;* **~**, **~s** *(Schlange, Feder~)* boa

**Bob** /bɔp/ *der;* **~**, **~s** bob[sleigh]

**Bob-:** **~bahn** *die* bob[sleigh] run; **~fahrer** *der,* **~fahrerin** *die* bobber; **~mannschaft** *die* bob[sleigh] team; **~rennen** *das* bob[sleigh] racing; *(einzelne Veranstaltung)* bob[sleigh] race; **~sport** *der* bobsleighing; **~tail** /-teɪl/ *der;* **~~s**, **~~s** [Old English] sheepdog

**Boccia** /'bɔtʃa/ *das;* **~s** boccie; boccia

**Bock**[1] /bɔk/ *der;* **~[e]s**, **Böcke** /'bœkə/ **A** *(Reh~, Kaninchen~)* buck; *(Ziegen~)* billy goat; he-goat; *(Schafs~)* ram; **ein steifer ~** *od.* **steif wie ein ~ sein** *(ugs.)* be as stiff as a board; **stur wie ein ~ sein** *(ugs.)* be as stubborn as a mule; **stinken wie ein ~** *(salopp)* stink to high heaven *(coll.)*; **jmdn. stößt der ~** *(ugs.)* sb. is being contrary *(coll.)*; **etw. aus ~ tun** *(ugs.)* do sth. just for the fun of it; **einen ~ schießen** *(fig. ugs.)* boob *(Brit. coll.)*; make a boo-boo *(Amer. coll.)*; *(einen Fauxpas begehen)* drop a clanger *(coll.)*; **den ~ zum Gärtner machen** *(ugs.)* be asking for trouble; **die Böcke von den Schafen trennen** *(fig.)* separate the sheep from the goats; **einen/keinen ~ auf etw.** *(Akk.)* **haben** *(ugs.)* fancy/not fancy sth.; **einen/keinen ~ haben, etw. zu tun** *(ugs.)* fancy/not fancy doing sth.; **B** *(ugs.: Schimpfwort)* **der geile alte ~:** the randy old goat; **sturer ~!** you stubborn git *(sl. derog.)*; **C** *(Gestell)* trestle; **D** *(Turnen)* buck; **E** *(Kutsch~)* box

**Bock**[2] *das;* **~s** *(Bier)* bock [beer]

**bock-**, **Bock-:** **~beinig** *(ugs.)* **1** *Adj.* contrary *(coll.)*; stubborn and awkward; **2** *adv.* contrarily *(coll.)*; **~bier** *das* bock [beer]

**bocken** *itr. V.* **A** *(nicht weitergehen)* refuse to go on; *(vor einer Hürde)* refuse; *(sich aufbäumen)* buck; rear; **die alte Karre bockt mal wieder** *(salopp)* the old heap is playing up again; **B** *(fam.: trotzig sein)* be stubborn and awkward; play up; **C** *(Landw.: brünstig sein)* be on heat; **D** *(derb: koitieren)* have it away *or* off *(sl.)*; have a screw *(coarse)*

**bockig** **1** *Adj.* stubborn and awkward; contrary *(coll.)*. **2** *adv.* stubbornly [and awkwardly]; contrarily *(coll.)*

**Bock-:** **~kitz** *das (Jägerspr.)* young buck; **~mist** *der (salopp)* bilge *no indef. art. (sl.)*; bullshit *no indef. art. (coarse)*; **einen ziemlichen ~mist verzapfen** come out with a load of bilge; **einen schönen ~mist machen** make a real cock-up *(Brit. sl.) or* a holy mess

**Bocks-:** **~bart** *der* **A** *(bei der Ziege)* [goat's] beard; *(beim Mann)* goatee [beard]; **B** *(Bot.)* goat's-beard; **~beutel** *der* **A** *(Flasche)* bocksbeutel; *wide, bulbous bottle for fine Franconian wines;* **B** *(Wein)* bocksbeutel wine; *Franconian wine sold in a bocksbeutel*

**Bock·schein** *der (salopp) (prostitute's)* certificate of health

**Bocks-:** **~fuß** *der* goat's foot; **~horn** *das* **sich [nicht] [von jmdm.] ins ~horn jagen lassen** *(ugs.) (sich [nicht] einschüchtern lassen)* [not] let oneself be browbeaten [by sb.]; *(sich [nicht] erschrecken und verwirren lassen)* [not] let oneself get worked up into a state [by sb.]

**Bock-:** **~springen** *das (Turnen)* vaulting [over the buck]; *(ohne Gerät)* leapfrog; **~sprung** *der* **A** *(Turnen) (Disziplin)* vaulting [over the buck]; *(einzelner Sprung)* vault [over the buck]; **B** *(ungelenker Sprung)* [ungainly] jump *or* leap; **~sprünge machen** jump *or* leap about; **vor Freude ~sprünge machen** jump for joy; **~wurst** *die* bockwurst

**Boden** /'bo:dn̩/ *der;* **~s**, **Böden** /'bø:dn̩/ **A** *(Erde)* ground; soil; **er wäre am liebsten im ~ versunken** he wished the ground would open and swallow him up; **den ~ für jmdn./etw. [vor]bereiten** prepare the ground for sb./sth.; **[bei jmdm.] auf fruchtbaren ~ fallen** ‹advice, warning› have some effect [on sb.]; **etw. [nicht] aus dem ~ stampfen können** [not] be able to conjure sth. up [out of thin air]; **wie aus dem ~ gestampft** *od.* **gewachsen** as if by magic; **B** *(Fuß~)* floor; **bei ihr kann man vom ~ essen** her floors are so clean that you could eat off them; **zu ~ fallen/sich zu ~ fallen lassen** fall/drop to the ground; **der Boxer ging zu ~:** the boxer went down; **die Augen zu ~ schlagen** look down; **jmdn. zu ~ schlagen** *od. (geh.)* **strecken** knock sb. down; floor sb.; *(fig.)* **sich auf unsicherem ~ bewegen** be on shaky ground *(fig.)*; **sich auf schwankenden ~ begeben** get into a risky area *(fig.)*; **jmdm. wird der ~ unter den Füßen zu heiß** *od.* **brennt der ~ unter den Füßen** *(ugs.)* things are getting too hot for sb. *(fig.)*; **festen ~ unter den Füßen haben** be back on terra firma; *(Tatsachen behaupten)* be on firm ground; *(wirtschaftlich gesichert sein)* be firmly on one's feet; **jmdm. den ~ unter den Füßen wegziehen** cut the ground from under sb.'s feet; **einem Gerücht/einer Theorie den ~ entziehen** scotch a rumour/explode a theory; **sie hatte das Gefühl, den ~ unter den Füßen zu verlieren** she felt the ground fall from beneath her feet; **er scheint völlig den ~ unter den Füßen verloren zu haben** the bottom seems to have dropped out of his world; **am ~ liegen** be bankrupt; **am ~ zerstört [sein]** *(ugs.)* [be] shattered *(coll.)*; **jmdn. zu ~ drücken** ‹cares, worries› get on top of sb.; **C** *(Grundlage)* **bleiben wir doch auf dem ~ der Tatsachen** let's stick to the facts; **hart auf den ~ der Wirklichkeit zurückgeholt werden** be brought back down to earth with a bump *(fig.)*; **auf dem ~ der Verfassung/des Gesetzes stehen** ‹person› be within the constitution/law; **D** *(Terrain)* **heiliger ~:** holy ground; **feindlicher ~:** enemy territory; **auf französischem ~:** on French soil; **~ gutmachen** *od.* **wettmachen** *(ugs.)* make up ground; **[an] ~ gewinnen/verlieren** gain/lose ground; **E** *(unterste Fläche)* bottom; *(Hosen~)* seat; *(Torten~)* base; **auf dem ~ des Meeres** at the bottom of the sea; on the seabed; ⇒ *auch* **doppelt**; **F** *(Dach~, Heu~)* loft; *(Wäsche~)* drying room; **auf dem ~:** in the loft/drying room

**boden-**, **Boden-:** **~abwehr** *die (Milit.)* ground defence; **~bearbeitung** *die* cultivation of the land; tillage; **~belag** *der (Teppich, Linoleum)* floor covering; *(Fliesen, Parkett)* flooring; **~beschaffenheit** *die* **A** *(der Erde)* condition of the soil; **B** *(des Fußbodens)* condition of the ground; conditions *pl.* underfoot; **~biologie** *die* soil biology; **~-~-Rakete** *die (Milit.)* surface-to-surface missile; **~erosion** *die* soil erosion; **~ertrag** *der* crop yield; **~feuchtigkeit** *die* soil moisture; **~fräse** *die (Landw.)* rotary cultivator; **~freiheit** *die (Technik)* ground clearance; **~frost** *der* ground frost; **~gefecht** *das (Milit.)* ground battle; **~haftung** *die (Kfz-W.)* roadholding *no indef. art.;* **~haltung** *die (Landw.)* deep-litter system *(of poultry farming)*; **~heizung** *die* underfloor heating; **~kammer** *die* attic; **~kampf** *der* **A** *(Judo, Ringen)* groundwork; **B** *(Milit.)* ground battle; **~kunde** *die* soil science; **~lang** *Adj.* full-length ‹skirt, dress, etc.›; **~los** *Adj.* **A** *(tief)* bottomless; **ins ~lose fallen** fall into a bottomless abyss; **B** *(ugs.: unerhört)* incredible, unbelievable ‹foolishness, meanness, etc.›; **~-Luft-Rakete** *die (Milit.)* surface-to-air missile; **~nähe** *die (Flugw.)* **in ~nähe** at a low level; **~nebel** *der* ground mist; *(dichter)* ground fog; **~nutzung** *die* agricultural land use; **~personal** *das (Flugw.)* ground staff; **~raum** *der* loft; **~recht** *das (Rechtsw.)* land law; **~reform** *die* land reform; **~rente** *die* ground rent; **~satz** *der* sediment; *(von Kaffee)* grounds *pl.; (fig.) (Rest)* residue; *(Grundbestandteil)* basic component *or* ingredient; **~schätze** *Pl.* mineral resources

**Bodensee** *der;* **~s** Lake Constance

**boden-**, **Boden-:** **~sicht** *die (Flugw.)* ground visibility; **~spekulation** *die* land speculation; **~ständig** *Adj.* indigenous, native ‹culture, population, etc.›; local ‹custom, craft, cuisine, tradition›; ‹novel› rooted in the soil; **~ständigkeit** *die;* **~~** **die ~ständigkeit des echten Kölners geht so weit, dass ...** the roots of the genuine native of Cologne go so deep that ...; **die Schwarzwaldbauern verlieren ihre ~ständigkeit** the farmers of the Black Forest are losing the close links with their native soil; **~station** *die (Raumf.)* ground station; **~streitkräfte** *Pl.:* ⇒ **~truppen**; **~treppe** *die* attic stairs *pl.;* **~truppen** *Pl.* ground forces *or* troops; **~turnen** *das* floor exercises *pl.;* **~vase** *die* large vase *(standing on the floor)*; **~verhältnisse** *Pl.* ground conditions; **~welle** *die* **A** *(Unebenheit)* bump; **B** *(Funkw.)* ground wave; **~wichse** *die (schweiz.)* floor polish

**bodigen** /'bo:dɪgn̩/ *tr. V. (schweiz.: besiegen)* beat; defeat

**Bodmerei** /bo:dmə'rai̯/ *die;* **~**, **~en** *(Seew.)* bottomry

**Bodybuilder** /'bɔdibɪldɐ/ *der;* **~s**, **~**, **Body·builderin** *die;* **~**, **~nen** bodybuilder

**Bodybuilding** /bɔdibɪldɪŋ/ *das;* **~s** body-building *no art.;* **~ betreiben** do bodybuilding exercises

**Bodycheck** /'bɔditʃɛk/ *der;* **~s**, **~s** *(Eishockey)* body-check

**Böe** /'bø:ə/ *die;* **~**, **~n** ⇒ **Bö**

**Bofist** /'bo:fɪst/ *der;* **~[e]s**, **~e** puffball

**bog** /bo:k/ *1. u. 3. Pers. Sg. Prät. v.* **biegen**

**Bogen** /'bo:gn̩/ *der;* **~s**, **~**, *(südd., österr.:)* **Bögen** /'bø:gn̩/ **A** *(gebogene Linie)* curve; *(Math.)* arc; *(Skifahren)* turn; *(Schlittschuhlaufen)* curve; **einen ~ schlagen** move in a curve; **der Weg macht/beschreibt einen ~:** the path bends/the path describes a curve; **immer, wenn ich sie auf der Straße sehe, mache ich einen großen ~** *(fig. ugs.)* whenever I see her in the street I make a detour [round her]; **einen großen ~ um jmdn./etw. machen** *(fig. ugs.)* give sb./sth. a wide berth; **das Wasser spritzte in hohem ~ heraus** the water spurted out in a great arc; **in hohem ~ hinausfliegen** *(fig. ugs.)* be chucked out *(sl.)*; **große ~ spucken** *(ugs.)* talk big; ⇒ *auch* **heraushaben**; **B** *(Archit.)* arch; **C** *(Waffe)* bow; **den ~ überspannen** *(fig.)* go too far; **D** *(Musik: Geigen~ usw.)* bow; **E** *(Papier~)* sheet; **ein ~ Schreibpapier/Packpapier** a sheet of writing paper/wrapping paper; **ein A4-~:** a sheet of A4 paper; **F** *(Musik: Zeichen)* slur; *(bei gleicher Notenhöhe)* tie

**bogen-**, **Bogen-:** **~brücke** *die* arch bridge; **~fenster** *das* arched window; **~förmig** *Adj.* arched; **~führung** *die (Musik)* bowing *no indef. art.;* **~gang** *der* **A** *(Arkaden)* arcade; **B** *(Anat.)* semicircular canal; **~lampe** *die (Elektrot.)* arc lamp; **~pfeiler** *der* pillar *or* column of the/an arch; **~säge** *die* coping saw; **~schießen** *das (Sport)* archery *no art.;* **~schütze** *der,* **~schützin** *die (Sport)* archer

**Boheme** /bo'e:m/ *die;* **~:** bohemian world *or* society

**Bohemien** /boe'mi̯ɛ̃:/ *der;* **~s**, **~s** bohemian

**Bohle** /'bo:lə/ *die;* **~**, **~n** [thick] plank

**Bohlen·belag** *der* planking *no indef. art.*

**böhmakeln** /'bø:makl̩n/ *itr. V. (österr. ugs. abwertend)* speak with a dreadful Czech accent

**Böhme** /ˈbøːmə/ *der;* **~n, ~n** Bohemian

**Böhmen** /ˈbøːmən/ *(das);* **~s** Bohemia

**Böhmer·wald** *der* Bohemian Forest

**Böhmin** *die;* **~, ~nen** Bohemian; ⇒ *auch* **-in**

**böhmisch** *Adj.* Bohemian

**Böhnchen** /ˈbøːnçən/ *das;* **~s, ~:** [small] bean

**Bohne** /ˈboːnə/ *die;* **~, ~n** bean; **grüne ~n** green beans; French beans *(Brit.)*; **dicke/weiße ~n** broad/haricot beans; **gebackene ~n** casserole *sing.* of beans with pork; **blaue ~n** *(Soldatenspr. veralt., noch scherzh.)* bullets; **nicht die ~** *(ugs.)* not one little bit

**Bohnen-: ~ein·topf** *der* bean stew; **~kaffee** *der* A *(~)* real coffee; **gemahlener ~kaffee** ground coffee; B *(Getränk)* real coffee; **~kraut** *das* savory; **~salat** *der* bean salad; **~stange** *die* *(auch ugs.: Mensch)* beanpole; **~stroh** *das* **dumm wie ~stroh** *(ugs.)* as thick as two short planks *(coll.)*; **~suppe** *die* bean soup

**Bohner** *der;* **~s, ~** ⇒ **Bohnerbesen**

**Bohner-: ~besen** *der* floor polisher; floor-polishing brush; **~maschine** *die* floor polisher; floor-polishing machine

**bohnern** *tr., itr. V.* polish; **hier ist frisch gebohnert** this floor has/these stairs have *etc.* been freshly polished; **„Vorsicht, frisch gebohnert!"** 'freshly polished floor/stairs *etc.*'

**Bohner·wachs** *das* floor polish

**bohren** /ˈboːrən/ ❶ *tr. V.* A bore; *(mit Bohrer, Bohrmaschine)* drill, bore ‹hole›; sink ‹well, shaft›; bore, drive ‹tunnel›; sink ‹pole, post etc.› **(in** + *Akk.* into); B *(bearbeiten)* drill ‹wood, concrete, etc.›; C *(drücken in)* poke **(in** + *Akk.* in[to]). ❷ *itr. V.* A *(eine Bohrung vornehmen)* drill; **in einem Zahn ~:** drill a tooth; **in der Nase ~:** pick one's nose; **nach Öl/Wasser** *usw.* **~:** drill for oil/water *etc.*; B *(fig.: nagen)* gnaw; **Zweifel bohrten in ihm** he had nagging doubts; C *(ugs.: drängen, fragen)* keep on; **jetzt hört auf zu ~:** now, don't keep on; **ich habe so lange gebohrt, bis ...** I kept on and on until ... ❸ *refl. V.* *(eindringen)* bore its way; **das Flugzeug hatte sich tief in die Erde gebohrt** the aircraft had buried itself deep in the ground

**bohrend** *Adj.* A gnawing ‹pain, hunger, remorse›; B *(hartnäckig)* piercing ‹look etc.›; probing ‹question›

**Bohrer** *der;* **~s, ~** A *(Gerät)* drill; *(zum Vorbohren)* gimlet; B *(Arbeiter)* driller

**Bohrerin** *die;* **~, ~nen** ⇒ **Bohrer B**

**Bohr-: ~insel** *die* drilling rig; *(für Öl)* drilling rig; oil rig; **~kern** *der (Technik)* drill core; **~loch** *das* borehole; *(in Metall, Holz)* drill hole; *(einer Ölquelle)* well; **~maschine** *die* drill; **~meißel** *der* bit; **~probe** *die* core [sample]; **~schrauber** *der* power drill/screwdriver; **~turm** *der* derrick

**Bohrung** *die;* **~, ~en** A ⇒ **bohren 1 A:** drilling; boring; sinking; driving; B *(Bohrloch)* borehole; *(in Holz, Metall)* drill hole; C *(lichte Weite)* **die ~ des Zylinders** the bore of the cylinder

**böig** *Adj.* gusty; *(mit Niederschlag)* squally; **~ auffrischend** freshening in gusts/squalls

**Boiler** /ˈbɔylɐ/ *der;* **~s, ~:** boiler; *(im Haushalt)* water heater

**Boje** /ˈboːjə/ *die;* **~, ~n** buoy

**Bolero** /boˈleːro/ *der;* **~s, ~s** A *(Tanz, Jacke)* bolero; B *(Hut)* bolero hat

**Bolid** /boˈliːt/ *der;* **~s** *od.* **~en, ~e** *od.* **~en** *(Astron.)* bolide

**Bolivianer** /boliˈvi̯aːnɐ/ *der;* **~s, ~, Bolivianerin** *die;* **~, ~nen** Bolivian; ⇒ *auch* **-in**

**bolivianisch** *Adj.* Bolivian

**Bolivien** /boˈliːvi̯ən/ *(das);* **~s** Bolivia

**bölken** /ˈbœlkn̩/ *itr. V.* *(nordd., westd.)* ‹cow› moo; ‹sheep› bleat; ‹person› bawl, shout

**Bolle**[1] /ˈbɔlə/ *die;* **~, ~n** *(berlin.)* A *(Zwiebel)* onion; B *(Loch in der Socke)* hole

**Bolle**[2] *(der)* *in* **sich wie ~ [auf dem Milchwagen] amüsieren** *(berlin.)* have a marvellous *or* *(coll.)* great time

*old spelling (see note on page 1707)

**Böller** /ˈbœlɐ/ *der;* **~s, ~** A *(Geschütz)* [small] cannon *(used on ceremonial occasions)*; B *(Feuerwerkskörper)* banger

**bollern** /ˈbɔlɐn/ *itr. V.; mit sein (bes. nordd.)* thud; **die Kinder bollerten die Treppe hinunter** the children clattered down the stairs

**böllern** *itr. V.* **es wurde 21-mal geböllert** there was a 21-gun salute

**Böller·schuss, *Böller·schuß** *der* gun salute; **der Admiral wurde mit fünf Böllerschüssen begrüßt** the admiral was greeted with a five-gun salute

**Boller·wagen** *der (nordd.)* handcart

**Bollette** /bɔˈlɛtə/ *die;* **~, ~n** *(österr. Amtsspr.)* customs declaration

**Boll·werk** *das* A *(Befestigung)* bulwark; *(fig.)* bulwark; bastion; stronghold; B *(Kai)* quay

**Bolschewik** /bɔlʃeˈvɪk/ *der;* **~en, ~i,** *(abwertend:)* **~en, Bolschewikin** *die;* **~, ~nen** A *(hist.)* Bolshevik; B *(abwertend: Kommunist)* Bolshevik; Commie *(coll. derog.)*

**bolschewisieren** /bɔlʃeviˈziːrən/ *tr. V.* Bolshevize

**Bolschewismus** /bɔlʃeˈvɪsmʊs/ *der;* **~:** Bolshevism *no art.*

**Bolschewist** *der;* **~en, ~en, Bolschewistin** *die;* **~, ~nen** Bolshevist

**bolschewistisch** ❶ *Adj.* A Bolshevik; Bolshevist; B *(abwertend)* Bolshevik; bolshy *(sl.)*. ❷ *adv.* A **~ geführt** Bolshevik-led; led by the Bolsheviks; B *(abwertend)* **~ unterwandert sein** be Bolshevik-infiltrated; be infiltrated by the Bolsheviks

**bolzen** /ˈbɔltsn̩/ *(ugs.)* ❶ *itr. V.* *(Fußball spielen)* kick the ball about. ❷ *tr. V.* *(treten)* slam, *(coll.)* belt ‹ball›; kick ‹stone›

**Bolzen** *der;* **~s, ~** A *(Stift)* pin; bolt; *(mit Gewinde)* bolt; B *(Geschoss)* bolt

**bolzen·gerade** ❶ *Adj.* perfectly *or* absolutely straight ‹back›. ❷ *adv.* ‹sit, stand› bolt upright

**Bolzen·schneider** *der* bolt cutters *pl.*

**Bolzerei** *die;* **~, ~en** *(ugs.)* [aimless] kick-about

**Bolz·platz** *der* [children's] football area; **hier war in meiner Jugend der ~:** this is where we used to have kick-abouts *(Brit.)* when I was young

**bömakeln** ⇒ **böhmakeln**

**Bombardement** /bɔmbardəˈmãː/ *das;* **~s, ~s** A *(Milit. veralt.: Artilleriebeschuss)* bombardment; B *(Milit.: Bombenabwurf)* bombing; C *(ugs.: Überhäufung)* **ein ~ mit Briefen/von Fragen** a flood of letters/deluge of questions

**bombardieren** /bɔmbarˈdiːrən/ *tr. V.* A *(Milit. veralt.: beschießen)* bombard; B *(Milit.: Bomben abwerfen auf)* bomb; C *(ugs.: bewerfen, überhäufen)* bombard

**Bombardierung** *die;* **~, ~en** A *(Milit. veralt.: Beschuss)* bombardment; B *(Milit.: Bombenabwurf)* bombing; C *(ugs.: das Bewerfen)* bombardment; D *(ugs.: Überhäufung)* **die ~ mit Fragen/Bitten** the rush of questions/requests

**Bombast** /bɔmˈbast/ *der;* **~[e]s** *(abwertend)* bombast *no indef. art.*

**bombastisch** *(abwertend)* ❶ *Adj.* bombastic ‹speech, language, style, etc.›; ostentatious ‹architecture, production›. ❷ *adv.* ‹speak, write› bombastically; ostentatiously ‹dressed›

**Bombe** /ˈbɔmbə/ *die;* **~, ~n** A *(Sprengkörper)* bomb; **die Nachricht schlug ein wie eine ~:** the news came as a bombshell; **die ~ ist geplatzt** *(fig. ugs.)* the balloon has gone up *(fig.)*; B *(ugs.: Atom~)* **die ~:** the bomb *(coll.)*; C *(Sportjargon: Schuss)* thunderbolt; tremendous shot *(coll.)*; D *(Geol.)* bomb; E *(ugs.: Hut)* bowler [hat]

**bomben** ❶ *tr. V.* *(ugs.: bombardieren)* bomb. ❷ *itr. V.* *(Sportjargon: schießen)* slam; blast *(coll.)*

**bomben-, Bomben-: ~angriff** *der* bomb attack; bombing raid; **einen ~angriff fliegen** fly a bombing raid; **~an·schlag** *der* bomb attack; **~attentat** *das* bomb attack; **~drohung** *die* bomb threat; **~erfolg** *der* *(ugs.)* smash hit *(sl.)*; **~fest** *Adj.* A *(unzerstörbar)* bombproof; B /ˈ-ˈ-/ *(ugs.: unveränderbar)* dead certain; **~fest stehen** be dead certain; be a dead cert *(Brit. sl.)*; **mein Entschluss steht ~fest** my mind is completely made up; **~flug·zeug** *das* bomber; **~form** *die* *(ugs.)* top form; **~gehalt** *das* *(ugs.)* tremendous salary *(coll.)*; **er kriegt doch sicher ein ~gehalt** he must earn a fortune *or* *(coll.)* bomb; **~geschäft** *das* *(ugs.)* **ein ~geschäft machen** do a roaring trade; **ein/kein ~geschäft sein** be/not be a gold mine *(fig.)*; **~geschwader** *das* bomber wing; bomber group *(Amer.)*; **~krater** *der* bomb crater; **~nacht** *die* night of bombing; **~rolle** *die* *(ugs.)* tremendous *or* terrific part *(coll.)*; **~schaden** *der* bomb damage *no indef. art.*; **~schuss, *~schuß** *der* *(Sportjargon)* thunderbolt; tremendous shot *(coll.)*; **~sicher** ❶ *Adj.* A *(unzerstörbar)* bombproof; B /ˈ-ˈ-/ *(ugs.: gewiss)* dead certain; **das ist eine ~sichere Sache** that's dead certain; that's a dead cert *(Brit. sl.)* *or* a sure thing *(Amer.)*; **ein ~sicherer Tipp** a dead cert [tip] *(Brit. sl.)*; a sure thing *(Amer.)*; ❷ *adv.* *(ugs.: gewiss)* as sure as eggs are eggs *(coll.)*; **~splitter** *der* bomb fragment *or* splinter; **~stimmung** *die* *(ugs.)* tremendous *or* fantastic atmosphere *(coll.)*; **~teppich** *der:* **das Gebiet wurde mit einem ~teppich belegt** the area was carpet-bombed; **~terror** *der* terrorist bombing; **~trichter** *der* bomb crater

**Bomber** *der;* **~s, ~** A *(ugs.: Flugzeug)* bomber; B *(Sportjargon)* **der ~ der Nation** the player with the fiercest shot in the country

**Bomber·verband** *der* bomber wing; bomber group *(Amer.)*

**bombig** *(ugs.)* ❶ *Adj.* super *(coll.)*; smashing *(coll.)*; terrific *(coll.)*; fantastic *(coll.)*. ❷ *adv.* **sich ~ schlagen** make a terrific *or* fantastic showing *(coll.)*

**Bommel** /ˈbɔml̩/ *die;* **~, ~n** *od. der;* **~s, ~** *(bes. nordd.)* bobble; pompom

**Bon** /bɔŋ/ *der;* **~s, ~s** A voucher; coupon; B *(Kassenzettel)* receipt; sales slip

**Bonbon** /bɔŋˈbɔŋ/ *der od. (österr. nur) das;* **~s, ~s** A sweet; candy *(Amer.)*; *(fig.)* treat; B *(ugs. scherzh.; bes. ns.: Parteiabzeichen)* [party] badge

**bonbon·farben, bonbon·farbig** *Adj.* *(abwertend)* candy-coloured

**Bonbonniere** /bɔŋbɔˈni̯eːrə/ *die;* **~, ~n** A *(Behälter)* sweet jar *(Brit.)*; candy jar *(Amer.)*; B *(Schachtel)* box of chocolates

**bonbon-, Bonbon-: ~papier** *das* sweet wrapper; sweet paper; **~rosa** *indekl. Adj.* candy pink; bright pink

**bongen** /ˈbɔŋən/ *(ugs.)* ❶ *tr. V.* ring up; **gebongt sein** *(ugs.)* be fine; **ist gebongt!** *(ugs.)* fine! ❷ *itr. V.* **ich habe falsch gebongt** I've rung up the wrong amount

**Bongo** /ˈbɔŋgo/ *das;* **~s, ~s** *od. die;* **~, ~s** bongo [drum]

**Bonhomie** /bɔnoˈmiː/ *die;* **~, ~n** *(geh.)* bonhomie

**Bonifatius** /boniˈfaːtsi̯ʊs/, **Bonifaz** /boniˈfaːts/ *(der)* Boniface

**Bonität** /boniˈtɛːt/ *die;* **~** *(Kaufmannsspr.)* creditworthiness; [good] credit rating

**Bonmot** /bõˈmoː/ *das;* **~s, ~s** bon mot

**Bonn** *(das);* **~s** ▶ 700| Bonn

**Bonner** ▶ 700| ❶ *indekl. Adj.* Bonn; **die ~ Regierung** the FRG Government. ❷ *der;* **~s, ~:** inhabitant of Bonn; *(von Geburt)* native of Bonn; ⇒ *auch* **Kölner**

**Bonnerin** *die;* **~, ~nen** ⇒ **Bonner 2**

**Bonsai** *der;* **~s, ~s** bonsai [tree]

**Bonus** /ˈboːnʊs/ *der;* **~** *od.* **~ses, ~** *od.* **~se,** *(auch:)* **Boni** /ˈboːni/ A *(Kaufmannsspr.)* *(Rabatt)* discount; *(Dividende)* extra dividend; *(Versicherungsw.)* bonus; B *(Schadenfreiheitsrabatt)* [no-claims] bonus; C *(Punktvorteil)* bonus points *pl.*

**Bon·vivant** /bõviˈvãː/ *der;* **~s, ~s** *(geh.)* bon vivant

**Bonze** /'bɔntsə/ *der;* ~**n**, ~**n** Ⓐ *(abwertend: Funktionär)* bigwig *(coll.)*; big noise *(coll.)*; big wheel *(Amer. coll.)*; Ⓑ *(Mönch)* bonze

**Boogie-Woogie** /'bʊgi'vʊgi/ *der;* ~**s**, ~**s** boogie-woogie

**Boom** /bu:m/ *der;* ~**s**, ~**s** boom

**Boot** /bo:t/ *das;* ~**[e]s**, ~**e** boat; **wir sitzen alle in einem** *od.* **im selben** ~ *(fig. ugs.)* we're all in the same boat

**booten** /'bu:tn̩/ *tr. V. (DV)* boot [up]; **neu** ~: reboot

**Boots-:** ~**bau** *der* boatbuilding *no art.;* ~**fahrt** *die* boat trip; ~**haken** *der* boathook; ~**haus** *das* boathouse; ~**länge** *die* [boat's] length; ~**mann** *der Pl.* ~**leute** Ⓐ *(Handelsmarine)* ≈ boatswain, bosun; Ⓑ *(Bundesmarine)* ≈ petty officer; ~**steg** *der* landing stage; ~**verleih** *der* Ⓐ *(das Verleihen)* boat hire; hiring of boats; Ⓑ *(Unternehmen)* boat hire [business]

**Bor** /bo:ɐ̯/ *das;* ~**s** *(Chemie)* boron

**Borax** /'bo:raks/ *der;* ~**[es]** *(Chemie)* borax

**Bord**[1] /bɔrt/ *das;* ~**[e]s**, ~**e** Ⓐ *(Wandbrett)* shelf; Ⓑ *(veralt., noch schweiz.: Abhang)* bank

**Bord**[2] *der;* ~**[e]s**, ~**e** *(eines Schiffes)* side; **an** ~: on board; **an** ~ **eines Schiffes/der „Baltic"** on board *or* aboard a ship/the 'Baltic'; **alle Mann an** ~**!** all aboard!; **über** ~: overboard; **über** ~ **gehen** go overboard; **Mann über** ~**!** man overboard!; **etw. über** ~ **werfen** *(auch fig.)* throw sth. overboard; **von** ~ **gehen** leave the ship; ‹passengers at destination› disembark, leave the ship; *(aus dem Flugzeug)* leave the aircraft

**Bord-:** ~**buch** *das* log[book]; ~**computer** *der* on-board computer

**bordeaux** *indekl. Adj.* ⇒ **bordeauxrot**

**Bordeaux** /bɔr'do:/ *der;* ~, ~ /bɔr'do:s/ ⇒ **Bordeauxwein**

**bordeaux·rot** *Adj.* bordeaux-red; claret

**Bordeaux·wein** *der* Bordeaux [wine]; **roter** ~: claret

**bord·eigen** *Adj.* ships/plane's [own] *attrib.*

**Bordell** /bɔr'dɛl/ *das;* ~**s**, ~**e** brothel; **in ein** ~ **gehen** visit a brothel

**Bordell-:** ~**besucher** *der* patron of a/the brothel; ~**gegend** *die* red-light district

**Bord-:** ~**flugzeug** *das* ship's aircraft; ~**funk** *der* [ship's/aircraft] radio; ~**funker** *der*, ~**funkerin** *die* radio operator; ~**kamera** *die* on-board camera; ~**personal** *das (Flugw.)* cabin crew; ~**rechner** *der* ⇒ ~**computer**; ~**stein** *der* kerb; ~**stein·kante** *die* [edge of the] kerb

**Bordüre** /bɔr'dy:rə/ *die;* ~, ~**n** edging

**Bord-:** ~**waffen** *Pl.* armament *sing.;* ~**wand** *die* /ship's/ side/side [of the/an aircraft]

**Boreas** /'bo:reas/ *der;* ~: north wind

**Borg** /bɔrk/ *in* **auf** ~ *(veralt.)* on credit; on tick *(Brit. coll.)*; on the cuff *(Amer. coll.)*

**borgen** /'bɔrgn̩/ *tr., itr. V.* Ⓐ *(geben)* lend; **jmdm. etw.** ~: lend sb. sth.; lend sth. to sb.; Ⓑ *(erhalten)* borrow; **[sich** *(Dat.)***] etw. von jmdm.** ~: borrow sth. from sb.

**Borgis** /'bɔrgɪs/ *die;* ~ *(Druckw.)* 9-point type; bourgeois *(Hist.)*

**Borke** /'bɔrkə/ *die;* ~, ~**n** Ⓐ *(Rinde)* bark; Ⓑ *(ugs.: auf Wunden)* scab

**Borken-:** ~**flechte** *die* ▶ 474 *([Tier]med.)* ringworm; ~**käfer** *der* bark beetle; ~**krepp** *der* bark crêpe; crépon; ~**schokolade** *die: thin-sheet chocolate made into rough-surfaced rolls;* chocolate bark

**borkig** *Adj.* Ⓐ *(rissig)* cracked ‹earth›; chapped, cracked ‹skin›; Ⓑ *(ugs.)* ‹knee, arm, etc.› covered in scabs

**Born** /bɔrn/ *der;* ~**[e]s**, ~**e** *(dichter.)* spring; fount *(poet./rhet.)*

**borniert** /bɔr'ni:ɐ̯t/ *(abwertend)* ❶ *Adj.* narrow-minded; bigoted. ❷ *adv.* in a narrow-minded *or* bigoted way

**Borniertheit** *die;* ~, ~**en** Ⓐ *(Eigenschaft)* narrow-mindedness; bigotry; Ⓑ *(Äußerung, Handlung)* piece of narrow-mindedness *or* bigotry

**Borretsch** /'bɔrɛtʃ/ *der;* ~**[e]s** borage

**Bor-:** ~**salbe** *die* boric acid ointment; ~**säure** *die (Chemie)* boric acid *(Chem.)*; boracic acid

**Börse** /'bœrzə/ *die;* ~, ~**n** Ⓐ *(Aktienbörse)* stock market; **an der** ~: on the stock market; Ⓑ *(Gebäude)* stock exchange; Ⓒ *(geh. veralt.: Geld~)* purse; Ⓓ *(Boxen)* purse

**börsen-, Börsen-:** ~**beginn** *der* opening of the [stock] market; **bei** ~**beginn** when the [stock] market opens/opened; ~**bericht** *der* stock market report; ~**fähig**, ~**gängig** *Adj. (Wirtsch.)* ‹commodity, security, etc.› negotiable on the stock market; ~**gang** *der (Wirtsch.)* [stock market] flotation; ~**geschäft** *das* stock market transaction; ~**krach** *der* stock market crash; collapse of the [stock] market; ~**kurs** *der* [stock] market price; ~**makler** *der*, ~**maklerin** *die* ▶ 159 stockbroker; ~**notierung** *die* [stock exchange] quotation; ~**schluss**, *~**schluß** *der* close of the [stock] market; **bei** ~**schluss** when the [stock] market closes/closed; ~**spekulation** *die* speculation on the stock market; ~**sturz** *der* ⇒ ~**krach**; ~**tendenz** *die* [stock] market trend; ~**tipp**, *~**tip** *der* market tip

**Börsianer** *der;* ~**s**, ~, **Börsianerin** *die;* ~, ~**nen** *(ugs.)* Ⓐ *(Makler[in])* stockbroker; Ⓑ *(Spekulant[in])* stock market speculator

**Borste** /'bɔrstə/ *die;* ~, ~**n** Ⓐ bristle; Ⓑ *Pl. (ugs.: beim Menschen)* hair *sing.;* **seine** ~**n aufstellen** *(fig.)* bristle

**Borsten·vieh** *das (ugs.) (Schwein)* pig; *(Schweine)* pigs *pl.*

**borstig** ❶ *Adj.* Ⓐ *(struppig)* bristly; Ⓑ *(grob)* crusty ‹person, manner, etc.›. ❷ *adv. (grob)* crustily

**Borte** /'bɔrtə/ *die;* ~, ~**n** braiding *no indef. art.;* trimming *no indef. art.;* edging *no indef. art.*

**Bor·wasser** *das* boric acid [eye] lotion

**bös** /bø:s/ ⇒ **böse** 1 C, D, 2

**bös·artig** ❶ *Adj.* Ⓐ *(heimtückisch)* malicious ‹person, remark, etc.›; vicious ‹animal›; Ⓑ *(Med.)* malignant; ❷ *adv. (heimtückisch)* maliciously

**Bös·artigkeit** *die* Ⓐ maliciousness; *(von Tieren)* viciousness; Ⓑ *(Med.)* malignancy

**Böschung** /'bœʃʊŋ/ *die;* ~, ~**en** *(an der Straße)* bank; embankment; *(am Bahndamm)* embankment; *(am Fluss)* bank

**Böschungs·winkel** *der* gradient

**böse** /'bø:zə/ ❶ *Adj.* Ⓐ *(verwerflich)* wicked; evil; **eine** ~ **Zunge haben** have a wicked *or* malicious tongue; **Schneewittchen hatte eine** ~ **Stiefmutter** Snow White had a wicked stepmother; **etw. aus** ~**r Absicht/** ~**m Willen tun** do sth. with evil intent; **Böses mit Gutem vergelten** repay evil with good; **jmdm. Böses tun** *(geh.)* do sb. harm; **ich will dir doch nichts Böses** I don't mean you any harm; *(bei Rat, Bemerkung)* I don't mean it nastily; Ⓑ *(übel)* bad ‹times, illness, dream, etc.›; nasty ‹experience, affair, situation, trick, surprise, etc.›; **ein** ~**s Ende nehmen** end in disaster; **eine** ~ **Geschichte** a bad *or* nasty business; **nichts Böses ahnen** be unsuspecting; **nichts Böses ahnend** unsuspectingly; not suspecting anything is/was wrong; **den** ~**n Blick haben** have the evil eye; **die** ~ **Sieben** *(fig.)* the unlucky seven; Ⓒ ▶ 268 *(ugs.) (wütend)* mad *(coll.)*; *(verärgert)* cross; ~ **mit jmdm.** *od.* **auf jmdn. werden** get mad at *(coll.)*/cross with sb.; ~ **auf jmdn.** *od.* **mit jmdm. sein** be mad at *(coll.)*/cross with sb.; ~ **über etw.** *(Akk.)* **sein** be mad at *(coll.)*/cross about sth.; **im Bösen auseinander gehen** part on bad terms; ⇒ *auch* **Blut**; Ⓓ *(fam.: ungezogen)* naughty; Ⓔ *(ugs.: entzündet)* bad, sore ‹knee, finger, etc.›; Ⓕ *(ugs.: arg)* terrible *(coll.)* ‹pain, fall, shock, disappointment, storm, etc.›.
❷ *adv.* Ⓐ *(übel)* ‹end› badly; **mit ihm wird es noch** ~ **enden** he'll come to a bad end; **das wird** ~ **enden** it is bound to end in disaster; **es war doch nicht** ~ **gemeint** I didn't mean it nastily; Ⓑ *(ugs.) (wütend)* angrily; *(verärgert)* crossly Ⓒ *(ugs.: arg)* terribly *(coll.)*; ‹hurt› badly; **er hat sich** ~ **geirrt** he was badly wrong; **er ist** ~ **gefallen** he had a nasty fall *(coll.)*

**Böse**[1] *der/die; adj. Dekl.* evil *or* wicked person; **er spielt den** ~**n** he plays the villain *or (coll.)* baddy; **die** ~**n kommen in die Hölle** the wicked go to hell

**Böse**[2] *der; adj. Dekl. (veralt.: Teufel)* the Evil One; the Devil

**Böse·wicht** *der; Pl.* ~**er** Ⓐ *(ugs. scherzh.: Schlingel)* rascal; Ⓑ *(veralt., noch fig.: Schuft)* villain; **jedes Mal bin ich der** ~ *(fig.)* I'm always the villain of the piece

**boshaft** /'bo:shaft/ ❶ *Adj.* malicious. ❷ *adv.* maliciously

**Boshaftigkeit** *die;* ~, ~**en** Ⓐ maliciousness; Ⓑ *(Bemerkung)* malicious remark; *(Handlung)* piece of maliciousness

**Bosheit** *die;* ~, ~**en** Ⓐ *(Art)* malice; **mit konstanter** ~: out of sheer spite; Ⓑ *(Bemerkung)* malicious remark; *(Handlung)* piece of maliciousness

**Boskop** /'bɔskɔp/ *der;* ~**s**, ~, **Boskoop** /'bɔsko:p/ *der;* ~**s**, ~ russet

**Bosnien** /'bɔsniən/ *(das);* ~**s** Bosnia

**Bosnien und Herzegowina** /--hertse'go:vina/ *(das);* ~**s** Bosnia-Herzegovina

**Bosporus** /'bɔspɔrʊs/ *der;* ~: Bosporus

**Boss**, ***Boß** /bɔs/ *der;* **Bosses**, **Bosse** *(ugs.)* boss *(coll.)*

**Bossa Nova** /'bɔsa'no:va/ *der;* ~, ~**s** bossa nova

**bosseln** /'bɔsl̩n/ *tr., itr. V. (ugs.)* **etw./an etw.** *(Dat.)* ~: beaver away *(Brit.) or* slave away making sth.; **er braucht immer was zu** ~: he always needs to be working on *or* making something

**bös-, Bös-:** ~**willig** ❶ *Adj.* malicious; wilful ‹desertion›; ❷ *adv.* maliciously; wilfully ‹desert›; ~**willigkeit** *die;* ~~: malice; maliciousness

**bot** /bo:t/ *1. u. 3. Pers. Sg. Prät. v.* **bieten**

**Botanik** /bo'ta:nɪk/ *die;* ~ Ⓐ botany *no art.;* Ⓑ *(ugs.: Natur)* nature

**Botaniker** *der;* ~**s**, ~, **Botanikerin** *die;* ~, ~**nen** ▶ 159 botanist; ⇒ *auch* **-in**

**botanisch** ❶ *Adj.* botanical. ❷ *adv.* botanically

**botanisieren** *itr. V.* botanize

**Botanisier·trommel** *die (veralt.)* [botanist's] vasculum

**Bötchen** /'bø:tçən/ *das;* ~**s**, ~: little boat

**Bote** /'bo:tə/ *der;* ~**n**, ~**n** Ⓐ *(Überbringer)* messenger; *(fig.)* herald; harbinger; Ⓑ *(Laufbursche)* errand boy; messenger [boy]

**Boten-:** ~**dienst** *der* job as a messenger/errand boy; **sie verdient sich ein Taschengeld durch** ~**dienste** she earns pocket money as a messenger *or* by carrying messages/running errands; ~**gang** *der* errand; ~**gänge erledigen** run errands; ~**lohn** der [messenger's/errand boy's] payment *or* tip

**Botin** *die;* ~, ~**nen** ⇒ **Bote** A, B: messenger; errand girl

**bot·mäßig** *(geh. veralt.)* ❶ *Adj. (gehorsam)* obedient; *(untertänig)* submissive. ❷ *adv. (gehorsam)* obediently; *(untertänig)* submissively

**Botmäßigkeit** *die;* ~ *(geh. veralt.)* Ⓐ *(Herrschaft)* dominion; sway; Ⓑ *(Gehorsam)* obedience; *(Untertänigkeit)* submissiveness

**Botschaft** *die;* ~, ~**en** Ⓐ *(geh.: Nachricht)* message; **die freudige** ~: the good *or* happy news; **die Frohe** ~ *(christl. Rel.)* the Gospel; Ⓑ *(Verlautbarung)* message; Ⓒ *(diplomatische Vertretung, auch Gebäude)* embassy

**-botschaft** *die:* **Friedens-/Kriegs-/Sieges**~: news of peace/war/victory

**Botschafter** *der;* ~**s**, ~, **Botschafterin** *die;* ~, ~**nen** ▶ 159 ambassador

**Botschafts-:** ~**rat** *der* counsellor; ~**sekretär** *der* [embassy] secretary

**Böttcher** /'bœtçɐ/ *der;* ~**s**, ~ ▶ 159 cooper

**Böttcherei** *die;* ~, ~**en** Ⓐ *(Handwerk)* cooper's trade; cooperage *no art.;* Ⓑ *(Werkstatt)* cooper's workshop; cooperage

**Böttcherin** *die;* ~, ~**nen** ▶ 159 ⇒ **Böttcher**

**Bottich** /ˈbɔtɪç/ *der;* ~**s,** ~**e** tub

**Bottnische Meer·busen** /ˈbɔtnɪʃə/ *der* Gulf of Bothnia

**Bouclé¹, Buklee** /buˈkleː/ *das;* ~**s,** ~**s** bouclé [yarn]

**Bouclé², Buklee** *der;* ~**s,** ~**s** **A** (*Stoff*) bouclé; **B** (*Teppich*) bouclé carpet

**Boudoir** /buˈdo̯aːɐ̯/ *das;* ~**s,** ~**s** (*veralt.*) boudoir

**Bouillabaisse** /bujaˈbɛːs/ *die;* ~, ~**s** /-ˈbɛːs/ (*Kochk.*) bouillabaisse

**Bouillon** /bulˈjɔŋ/ *die;* ~, ~**s** **A** (*Brühe*) bouillon; consommé; **B** (*Med.*) bouillon; broth

**Bouillon·würfel** *der* bouillon cube

**Boule** /buːl/ *das;* ~**s** boule[s *pl.*]

**Boulette** ⇒ **Bulette**

**Boulevard** /buləˈvaːɐ̯/ *der;* ~**s,** ~**s** boulevard

**Boulevard-:** ~**blatt** *das* ⇒ ~**zeitung;** ~**presse** *die* (*abwertend*) popular press; ~**stück** *das* (*Theater*) boulevard drama; ~**theater** *das* light theatre; ~**zeitung** *die* (*abwertend*) popular rag (*derog.*); tabloid

**Bouquet** /buˈkeː/ *das;* ~**s,** ~**s** ⇒ **Bukett**

**Bourbone** /bʊrˈboːnə/ *der;* ~**n,** ~**n, Bourbonin** *die;* ~, ~**nen** (*hist.*) Bourbon

**bourgeois** /bʊrˈʒo̯a/ *Adj.* (*abwertend, auch Soziol.*) bourgeois

**Bourgeois** *der;* ~, ~ (*abwertend, auch Soziol.*) bourgeois

**Bourgeoisie** /bʊrʒo̯aˈziː/ *die;* ~, ~**n** (*abwertend, auch Soziol.*) bourgeoisie

**Boutique** /buˈtiːk/ *die;* ~, ~**s** *od.* ~**n** boutique

**Bovist** ⇒ **Bofist**

**Bowden·zug** /ˈbaudn̩-/ *der* (*Technik*) Bowden cable

**Bowle** /ˈboːlə/ *die;* ~, ~**n** **A** punch (*made of wine, champagne, sugar, and fruit or spices*); **B** (*Gefäß*) punchbowl

**bowlen** /ˈboʊlən/ *itr. V.* (*Sport*) (*auf der Bahn*) bowl; (*auf dem Rasen*) play bowls

**Bowlen·glas** *das; Pl.* **Bowlengläser** punch glass

**Bowler** /ˈboulɐ/ *der;* ~**s,** ~**:** bowler [hat]

**Bowling** /ˈboulɪŋ/ *das;* ~**s,** ~**s** (*auf der Bahn*) [tenpin] bowling; (*auf dem Rasen*) bowls; ~ **spielen gehen** go [tenpin] bowling/go to play bowls

**Bowling·bahn** *die* [tenpin] bowling alley

**Box** /bɔks/ *die;* ~, ~**en** **A** (*Lautsprecher*) speaker; **B** (*Pferde-*) [loose] box; **C** (*für Autos*) [partitioned off] [parking] space; **D** (*Kamera*) box camera; **E** (*Behälter*) box; **F** (*Montageplatz*) pit; **an den** ~**en** in the pits

**Boxcalf** ⇒ **Boxkalf**

**boxen** ❶ *itr. V.* box; **gegen jmdn.** ~**:** fight sb.; box [against] sb.; **um die Weltmeisterschaft** *usw.* ~**:** fight for the world championship *etc.*; **jmdm. in den Magen** ~**:** punch sb. in the stomach. ❷ *tr. V.* **A** (*schlagen*) punch; **B** (*Sportjargon: kämpfen gegen*) fight. ❸ *refl. V.* **A** (*ugs.: Weg bahnen*) fight one's way; **B** (*ugs.: sich prügeln*) have a punch-up (*coll.*) *or* fight; **hört auf, euch zu** ~**:** stop fighting

**Boxer** *der;* ~**s,** ~ ▶ 159 **A** (*Sportler, Hund*) boxer; **B** (*ugs.: Schlag*) punch

**Boxer·aufstand** *der* (*hist.*) Boxer Rebellion

**Boxerin** *die;* ~, ~**nen** ▶ 159 boxer

**boxerisch** *Adj.* boxing ‹skill, know-how, etc.›

**Boxer-:** ~**motor** *der* (*Technik*) horizontally opposed engine; ~**nase** *die* boxer's nose

**Box·hand·schuh** *der* boxing glove

**Box·kalf** /-kalf/ *das;* ~**s,** ~**s** boxcalf

**Box-:** ~**kampf** *der* **A** (*Kampf*) boxing match; (*im Streit*) fist fight; **er hat 200** ~**kämpfe ausgetragen** he's had 200 fights *or* bouts; **B** (*Disziplin*) boxing *no art.*; ~**ring** *der* boxing ring; ~**sport** *der* boxing *no art.*; ~**staffel** *die* boxing team

**Boy** /bɔy/ *der;* ~**s,** ~**s** **A** (*Diener*) servant; (*im Hotel*) pageboy; **B** (*Jugendspr.*) (*junger Mann*) boy; (*Freund*) boyfriend

**Boykott** /bɔyˈkɔt/ *der;* ~**[e]s,** ~**s** boycott; **einem Land den** ~ **erklären** declare a boycott of a country

**Boykott·hetze** *die* (*DDR Amtspr., Rechtsw.*) anti-state agitation

**boykottieren** *tr. V.* boycott

**Boykott·maßnahme** *die* boycott [action]; **sich zu weiteren** ~**n gegen ein Land entschließen** decide to tighten the boycott of a country

**Bozen** /ˈboːtsn̩/ (*das*); ~**s** Bolzano

**BR** *Abk.* **Bayrischer Rundfunk** Bavarian Radio

**brabbeln** /ˈbrabl̩n/ *tr., itr. V.* (*ugs.*) mutter; mumble; ‹baby› babble

**Brabbel·wasser** *das* (*ugs. scherzh.*) **A** schnapps; **B** ~ **getrunken haben** (*ugs. scherzh.*) have verbal diarrhoea (*sl.*)

**brach¹** /braːx/ *1. u. 3. Pers. Sg. Prät. v.* **brechen**

**brach²** *Adj.* (*veralt.*) fallow; (*auf Dauer*) uncultivated; waste

**Brache** *die;* ~, ~**n** **A** (*Feld*) [piece of] fallow land; (*auf Dauer*) [piece of] uncultivated *or* waste land; **B** (*Zeit*) fallow period

**brachial** /braˈxi̯aːl/ *Adj.* **A** violent; ~**e Gewalt** brute force; **B** (*Med.*) brachial

**Brachial·gewalt** *die* brute force

**Brachiosaurus** /braxi̯oˈzaurʊs/ *der;* ~, **Brachiosaurier** /...zauri̯ɐ/ brachiosaurus

**Brach·land** *das* fallow [land]; (*auf Dauer*) uncultivated *or* waste land

**brach|liegen** *unr. itr. V.* (*auch fig.*) lie fallow; (*auf Dauer*) lie waste

**brachte** /ˈbraxtə/ *1. u. 3. Pers. Sg. Prät. v.* **bringen**

**Brach·vogel** *der* curlew

**brackig** *Adj.* (*niederd.*) brackish

**Brack·wasser** *das* brackish water

**Brahmane** /braˈmaːnə/ *der;* ~**n,** ~**n, Brahmanin** *die;* ~, ~**nen** Brahmin

**brahmanisch** *Adj.* Brahminical

**Brainstorming** /ˈbreɪnstɔːmɪŋ/ *das;* ~**s** brainstorming; **ein** ~**:** a brainstorming session

**bramarbasieren** /bramarbaˈziːrən/ *itr. V.* (*geh. abwertend*) brag, boast (**von** about)

**Bram·segel** /ˈbraːm-/ *das* topgallant sail

**Branche** /ˈbrãːʃə/ *die;* ~, ~**n** **A** [branch of] industry; **alle** ~**n der Bekleidungsindustrie** all branches of the clothing industry; **er kennt sich in der** ~ **am besten aus** he has the most knowledge of the industry; **B** (*Fachgebiet*) field; **die** ~ **wechseln** move into a different field

**branche[n]-, Branche[n]-:** ~**fremd** *Adj.* new to the industry *postpos.*; ‹person› who knows nothing of the industry *postpos., not pred.*; ~**kenntnisse** *Pl.* knowledge *sing.* of the industry; ~**kundig** *Adj.* experienced in the industry *postpos.*; with knowledge of the industry *postpos., not pred.*; ~**üblich** *Adj.* usual in the industry *postpos.*; **im Baugewerbe** ~**üblich** usual in the building industry

**Branchen·verzeichnis** *das* classified directory; (*Telefonbuch*) yellow pages *pl.*

**Brand** /brant/ *der;* ~**[e]s, Brände** ▶ 474 /ˈbrɛndə/ **A** fire; **B** (*Brennen*) **beim** ~ **der Scheune** when the barn caught fire; **in** ~ **geraten** catch fire; **etw. in** ~ **setzen** *od.* **stecken** set fire to sth.; set sth. on fire; **C** (*ugs.: Durst*) raging thirst; **einen fürchterlichen** ~ **haben** have a terrible thirst; **D** (*Med.*) **[trockener/feuchter]** ~**:** [dry/moist] gangrene; **E** (*Bot.*) blight

**brand-, Brand-:** ~**aktuell** *Adj.* very latest ‹news›; up-to-the-minute ‹report›; red-hot ‹news item, issue›; highly topical ‹book›; ~**an·schlag** *der* arson attack (**auf** + *Akk.* on); ~**bekämpfung** *die* firefighting *no art.*; ~**binde** *die* dressing [for burns]; ~**blase** *die* [burn] blister; ~**bombe** *die* fire bomb; incendiary bomb; ~**direktor** *der* chief fire officer; fire chief (*Amer.*); ~**eilig** *Adj.* (*ugs.*) extremely urgent

**branden** *itr. V.* (*geh.*) break; ~**der Beifall** (*fig.*) thunderous applause

**Branden·burg** (*das*); ~**s** Brandenburg

**Brandenburger** ❶ *indekl. Adj.* Brandenburg *attrib.*; **das** ~ **Tor** the Brandenburg Gate. ❷ *der;* ~**s,** ~**:** native of Brandenburg; (*Einwohner*) inhabitant of Brandenburg; **die** ~**:** the people of Brandenburg

**brandenburgisch** *Adj.* Brandenburg *attrib.*

**brand-, Brand-:** ~**fackel** *die* firebrand; flaming torch; ~**fleck** *der* burn mark; ~**gefahr** *die* danger of fire; **bei** ~**gefahr** when there is danger of fire; ~**gefährlich** *Adj.* perilous; highly dangerous; ~**geruch** *der* smell of burning; ~**herd** *der* source of the fire

**brandig** *Adj.* **A** ‹smell› of burning; burnt ‹taste›; **es riecht** ~**:** there is a smell of burning; **B** (*Med.*) gangrenous; **C** (*Bot.*) suffering from blight *postpos.*

**brand-, Brand-:** ~**kasse** *die* fire insurance company; ~**katastrophe** *die* disastrous fire; ~**leger** /-leːgɐ/ *der;* ~**s,** ~~, ~**legerin** *die;* ~~, ~~**nen** (*österr.*) ⇒ ~**stifter;** ~**legung** *die;* ~~, ~~**en** (*österr.*) ⇒ ~**stiftung;** ~**mal** *das* (*geh.*) burn mark; (*fig.: Stigma*) stigma; ~**marken** *tr. V.* brand ‹person›; denounce ‹thing›; **jmdn. [als Verräter]** ~**marken** brand sb. [as a traitor]; ~**mauer** *die* fire wall; ~**meister** *der* chief fire officer; fire chief (*Amer.*); ~**neu** *Adj.* (*ugs.*) brand-new; ~**opfer** *das* **A** (*Rel.*) burnt offering; **B** (*Opfer eines* ~*es*) fire victim; victim of the/a fire; ~**rede** *die* fiery tirade; ~**salbe** *die* ointment for burns; ~**satz** *der* incendiary mixture; ~**schaden** *der* fire damage *no pl., no indef. art.*; **die** ~**schäden in den Wäldern** the damage to forests caused by fire; ~**schatzen** *tr. V.* (*hist.*) pillage and threaten to burn; ~**schatzung** *die;* ~~, ~~**en** (*hist.*) pillaging and threat of burning; ~**schutz** *der* fire safety *no art.*; ~**sohle** *die* insole; ~**stelle** *die* **A** scene of the fire; **B** (*verbrannte Stelle*) burn; (*größer*) burnt patch; ~**stifter** *der,* ~**stifterin** *die* arsonist; ~**stiftung** *die* arson; **eine** ~**stiftung** a case of arson; ~**teig** *der* (*Kochk.*) choux pastry

**Brandung** *die;* ~, ~**en** surf; breakers *pl.*; **die** ~ **donnerte gegen die Felsen** the breakers crashed against the rocks; **bei starker** ~**:** when the surf is high

**Brandungs-:** ~**boot** *das* surfboat; ~**welle** *die* breaker

**Brand-:** ~**versicherung** *die* fire insurance; (*Gesellschaft*) fire-insurance company; ~**wache** *die* **A** fire-watcher; (*Mannschaft*) fire-watchers *pl.*; **B** (*Dienst*) fire-watch; ~**wunde** *die* burn; (*Verbrühung*) scald; ~**zeichen** *das* brand

**brannte** /ˈbrantə/ *1. u. 3. Pers. Sg. Prät. v.* **brennen**

**Brannt·wein** *der* spirits *pl.*; **Wodka ist ein** ~**:** vodka is a type of spirit

**Branntwein-:** ~**brenner** *der,* ~**brennerin** *die;* ~~, ~~**nen** distiller; ~**monopol** *das* monopoly of spirits; liquor monopoly (*Amer.*); ~**steuer** *die* tax on spirits; liquor tax (*Amer.*)

**Brasil¹** /braˈziːl/ *der;* ~**s,** ~**e** *od.* ~**s** Brazil[ian] tobacco

**Brasil²** *die;* ~, ~**[s]** Brazil cigar

**Brasil·holz** *das* brazilwood

**Brasilianer** /braziˈli̯aːnɐ/ *der;* ~**s,** ~, **Brasilianerin** *die;* ~, ~**nen** ▶ 553 Brazilian; ⇒ *auch* **-in**

**brasilianisch** *Adj.* ▶ 553 Brazilian

**Brasilien** /braˈziːli̯ən/ (*das*); ~**s** Brazil

**Brasil-:** ~**tabak** *der* Brazil[ian] tobacco; ~**zigarre** *die* Brazil cigar

***Brass, Braß** *der;* **Brasses** (*ugs.*) ~ **haben, in** ~ **sein** be mad (*coll.*) *or* angry; **in** ~ **kommen** get mad (*coll.*) *or* angry; **jmdn. in** ~ **bringen** make sb. mad (*coll.*) *or* angry

**Brasse** /ˈbrasə/ *die;* ~, ~**n** (*Seemannsspr.*) brace

**brät** /brɛːt/ *3. Pers. Sg. Präsens v.* **braten**

**Brät** *das;* ~**s** *lean minced pork used esp. as filling for sausages*

---

*old spelling (see note on page 1707)

**Brat·apfel** *der* baked apple

**braten** /'bra:tn̩/ ❶ *unr. tr. V.* (*auf dem Herd*) fry; (*im Backofen*) (*mit Fett, im eigenen Saft*) roast; (*ohne Fett*) bake; **etw. braun ~:** fry sth. until it is brown; **etw. am Spieß ~:** roast sth. on a spit. ❷ *unr. itr. V.* (*auf dem Herd*) fry; (*im Backofen*) (*mit Fett, im eigenen Saft*) roast; (*ohne Fett*) bake; **in der Sonne ~** (*fig.*) roast in the sun

**Braten** *der;* **~s, ~:** joint; (*gebratene Portion*) roast [meat] *no indef. art.;* **sonntags gab es bei uns immer ~:** we always had a roast *or* a joint on Sundays; **kalter ~:** cold meat; **den fetten ~ konnte er sich nicht entgehen lassen** (*fig. ugs.*) he couldn't miss the chance of making such a big killing (*coll.*); **den ~ riechen** (*fig. ugs.*) smell a rat

**Braten-: ~fett** *das* [meat] fat; [meat] juices *pl.;* **~rock** *der* (*veralt. scherzh.*) frock coat; **~saft** *der* meat juice[s *pl.*]; **~soße** *die* gravy; **~wender** *der* slice; turner

**Brat-: ~fett** *das* [cooking] fat; **~fisch** *der* fried fish; **~hähnchen** *das,* (*südd., österr.*) **~hendl** *das* Ⓐ roast chicken; (*gegrillt*) broiled chicken; Ⓑ (*Hähnchen zum ~en*) roasting chicken; (*zum Grillen*) broiling chicken; **~hering** *der* fried herring; **~huhn** *das,* **~hühnchen** *das* ⇒ **~hähnchen; ~kartoffeln** *Pl.* fried potatoes; home fries (*Amer.*); ⇒ *auch* **daher** B; **~kartoffel·verhältnis** *das* (*ugs. veralt.*) **er hat ein ~kartoffelverhältnis mit ihr** he treats her as his meal ticket; **~ofen** *der* oven; **~pfanne** *die* frying pan; **~röhre** *die* ⇒ **~ofen; ~rost** *der* grill

**Bratsche** /'bra:tʃə/ *die;* **~, ~n** (*Musik*) viola

**Bratschen·schlüssel** *der* (*Musik*) ⇒ **Altschlüssel**

**Bratschist** *der;* **~en, ~en, Bratschistin** *die;* **~, ~nen** violist; viola player

**Brat-: ~spieß** *der* Ⓐ spit; Ⓑ (*Gericht*) kebab; **~wurst** *die* Ⓐ [fried/grilled] sausage; Ⓑ (*Wurst zum ~en*) sausage [for frying/grilling]

**Brauch** /braux/ *der;* **~[e]s, Bräuche** /'brɔyçə/ custom; **so ist es ~, so will es der ~:** that's the custom; **das ist bei ihnen so ~:** that's their custom; **nach altem ~:** in accordance with an old custom

**brauchbar** ❶ *Adj.* useful; (*benutzbar*) usable; wearable ‹clothes›; (*ordentlich*) decent ‹worker, pupil›; **er ist ganz ~:** he is a decent worker/pupil *etc.* ❷ *adv.* **er schreibt/arbeitet ganz ~:** he's a useful writer/he does useful work

**Brauchbarkeit** *die;* **~:** usefulness; (*Benutzbarkeit*) usability

**brauchen** ❶ *tr. V.* Ⓐ (*benötigen*) need; **alles, was man zum Leben braucht** everything one needs in order to live reasonably; **ich kann dich jetzt nicht ~** (*fam.*) I don't want you around just now; **deine guten Ratschläge kann ich nicht ~:** I can well do without your advice; Ⓑ (*aufwenden müssen*) **mit dem Fahrrad/Auto braucht er nur zehn Minuten** it only takes him ten minutes on his bicycle/by car; **er hat für die Arbeit Jahre gebraucht** the work took him years; **wie lange brauchst du dafür?** how long will it take you?; (*im Allgemeinen*) how long does it take you?; Ⓒ (*benutzen, verwenden, ver~*) use; **ich könnte es gut ~:** I could do with it.
❷ *itr. V.* (*geh. veralt.: bedürfen*) **es braucht keines weiteren Beweises** no further proof is needed *or* necessary.
❸ *mit Inf. mit „zu", verneintes od. eingeschränktes Modalverb* need; **du brauchst nicht zu helfen** there is no need [for you] to help; you don't need to help; **du brauchst doch nicht gleich zu weinen** there's no need to start crying; **das hättest du nicht zu tun ~:** there was no need to do it; you needn't have done that; **das hätte nicht zu sein ~:** that needn't have happened; **es braucht nicht sofort zu sein** it doesn't need *or* have to be done immediately; **du brauchst es [mir] nur zu sagen** you only have to tell me; **du brauchst es nur zu sagen** you only have to say so

**Brauchtum** *das;* **~s, Brauchtümer** /-ty:mɐ/ custom; **zum ~ dieser Region gehört ...** one of the customs in this area is ...

**Braue** /'brauə/ *die;* **~, ~n** ▶ **471** [eye]brow

**brauen** ❶ *tr. V.* Ⓐ brew; Ⓑ (*ugs.: aufbrühen, zubereiten*) brew [up] ‹tea, coffee›; concoct ‹potion etc.›; mix ‹cocktail›. ❷ *itr. V.* Ⓐ (*Bier ~*) brew [beer]; Ⓑ (*dichter.: wallen*) ‹mist, fog› gather

**Brauer** *der;* **~s, ~:** brewer

**Brauerei** *die;* **~, ~en** Ⓐ brewing; Ⓑ (*Betrieb*) brewery

**Brauerin** *die;* **~, ~nen** brewer

**Brau-: ~haus** *das* brewery; **~meister** *der,* **~meisterin** *die* master brewer

**braun** /braun/ *Adj.* Ⓐ brown; **~ werden** (*sonnengebräunt*) get brown; get a tan; **sich von der Sonne ~ brennen lassen** sit/lie in the sun and get a tan; **~ gebrannt** [sun]-tanned; Ⓑ (*abwertend: nationalsozialistisch*) Nazi; **er war ~:** he was a Nazi

**Braun** *das;* **~s, ~,** (*ugs.*) **~s** brown

**braun·äugig** *Adj.* brown-eyed; **~ sein** have brown eyes

**Braun·bär** *der* brown bear

**Braune** *der; adj. Dekl.* Ⓐ bay [horse]; Ⓑ (*österr.: Kaffee*) [cup of] white coffee (*Brit.*); [cup of] coffee with milk/cream

**Bräune** /'brɔynə/ *die;* **~:** [sun]tan

**bräunen** ❶ *tr. V.* Ⓐ tan; **die Sonne hat sein Gesicht stark gebräunt** the sun has tanned his face a deep brown; Ⓑ (*Kochk.*) brown. ❷ *itr. V.* Ⓐ **die südliche Sonne bräunt stark** the Southern sun gives you a good tan; Ⓑ (*Kochk.*) ‹meat› brown; ‹cake› go golden brown; ‹butter› go brown

**braun-, Braun-:** ***~gebrannt** ⇒ **braun** A; **~hemd** *das* (*ns.*) Ⓐ brown shirt; Ⓑ (*Träger des ~hemds*) Brownshirt; **~kohl** *der* ⇒ **Grünkohl; ~kohle** *die* brown coal; lignite

**bräunlich** *Adj.* brownish

**Braunschweig** /'braunʃvaik/ (*das*); **~s** ▶ **700** Braunschweig; Brunswick (*Hist.*)

**braunschweigisch** *Adj.* Braunschweig *attrib.;* ⇒ *auch* **hannoversch**

**Bräunung** *die;* **~, ~en** browning; (*durch die Sonne*) [sun]tan

**Bräunungs·studio** *das* solarium

**Braus** /braus/ ⇒ **Saus**

**Brause** /'brauzə/ *die;* **~, ~n** Ⓐ fizzy drink; (*~pulver*) sherbet; Ⓑ (*veralt.: Dusche*) shower; **sich unter die ~ stellen** take *or* have a shower; Ⓒ (*Sprühteil*) (*einer Gießkanne*) rose; (*einer Dusche*) shower head

**Brause-: ~bad** *das* (*veralt.*) Ⓐ shower [bath]; Ⓑ (*Duschbad*) shower; **ein ~bad nehmen** take *or* have a shower; **~kopf** *der* (*veralt.*) hothead; **~limonade** *die* fizzy lemonade

**brausen** ❶ *itr. V.* Ⓐ ‹wind, water, etc.› roar; (*fig.*) ‹organ, applause, etc.› thunder; **hier braust der Verkehr bei Tag und Nacht** there is a constant roar of traffic here day and night; Ⓑ (*duschen*) [take *or* have a] shower; Ⓒ (*sich schnell bewegen*) race. ❷ *tr. V.* put ‹children etc.› under the shower. ❸ *refl. V.* [take *or* have a] shower

**Brausen** *das;* **~s** roar; **das ~ in meinen Ohren** the ringing *or* buzzing in my ears

**Brause-: ~pulver** *das* sherbet; **~tablette** *die* effervescent tablet

**Braut** /braut/ *die;* **~, Bräute** /'brɔytə/ Ⓐ bride; Ⓑ (*Verlobte*) fiancée; bride-to-be; Ⓒ (*ugs.: Freundin*) girl[friend]

**-braut** *die* (*ugs.*) **Fußball~:** football player's/fan's girlfriend/wife; **Rocker~:** rocker's girl; (*Mitglied der Bande*) girl rocker

**Braut-: ~bett** *das* (*hist.*) bridal bed; **~eltern** *Pl.* bride's parents

**Bräutigam** /'brɔytɪgam/ *der;* **~s, ~e** Ⓐ [bride]groom; Ⓑ (*veralt.: Verlobter*) fiancé; husband-to-be

**Braut-: ~jungfer** *die* bridesmaid; **~kleid** *das* wedding dress; **~kranz** *der* bridal wreath; **~leute** *Pl.:* ⇒ **~paar; ~mutter** *die; Pl.* **~mütter** bride's mother; **~nacht** *die* wedding night; **~paar** *das* bridal couple; bride and groom; **~schau** *die:* **in auf ~schau gehen, ~schau halten** (*ugs. scherzh.*) go *or* be looking for a wife; **~schleier** *der* bridal veil; **~vater** *der* bride's father

**brav** /bra:f/ ❶ *Adj.* Ⓐ (*artig*) good; **sei [schön] ~:** be good; **sei ein ~es Kind** be a good boy/girl; Ⓑ (*redlich*) honest; upright; **er soll ein ~es Mädchen heiraten** he should marry a good honest girl; Ⓒ (*hausbacken*) plain and conservative ‹clothes›; Ⓓ (*veralt.: tapfer*) brave. ❷ *adv.* Ⓐ **nun iss schön ~ deine Suppe** be a good boy/girl and eat up your soup; eat up your soup like a good boy/girl; **die Kinder spielten ~ in ihrem Zimmer** the children were being good and playing quietly in their room; Ⓑ (*redlich*) honestly; Ⓒ (*bieder*) **[recht] ~ spielen/schreiben** play/write quite nicely; Ⓓ (*veralt.: tapfer*) bravely

**bravo** /'bra:vo/ *Interj.* bravo

**Bravo** *das;* **~s, ~s** cheer; **das laute ~ der Zuschauer** the loud cheers *or* cheering of the audience; **ein ~ für ...** three cheers for ...

**Bravo·ruf** *der* cheer

**Bravour** /bra'vu:ɐ̯/ *die;* **~** Ⓐ stylishness; **mit ~:** with style and élan; Ⓑ (*Tapferkeit*) daring and bravery

**Bravour·leistung** *die* brilliant performance

**bravourös** /bravu'rø:s/ ❶ *Adj.* Ⓐ (*rasant*) **mit ~em Tempo** at magnificent speed; Ⓑ (*meisterhaft*) brilliant. ❷ *adv.* Ⓐ (*rasant*) with great dash; Ⓑ (*meisterhaft*) brilliantly

**Bravour·stück** *das* piece of bravura; brilliant performance

**BRD** *Abk.* **Bundesrepublik Deutschland** FRG

**Break** /breɪk/ *das;* **~s, ~s** (*Sport, Musik*) break

**Breakdance** /breɪkdæns/ *der;* **~[s]** breakdancing

**brechbar** *Adj.* Ⓐ breakable; **nicht ~:** unbreakable; Ⓑ (*ablenkbar*) refrangible

**Brech-: ~bohne** *die* French bean (*Brit.*); green bean; **~durch·fall** *der* diarrhoea and vomiting *no indef. art.;* **~eisen** *das* ⇒ **~stange**

**brechen** /'brɛçn̩/ ▶ **474** ❶ *unr. tr. V.* Ⓐ break; cut ‹marble, slate, etc.›; **Blumen ~** (*dichter.*) pluck flowers; **sich** (*Dat.*) **den Arm/das Genick ~:** break one's arm/neck; **nichts zu ~ und zu beißen haben** (*geh.*) not have anything at all to eat; Ⓑ (*ablenken*) break ‹water etc.›; refract ‹light›; Ⓒ (*bezwingen*) overcome ‹resistance›; break ‹will, silence, record, blockade, etc.›; Ⓓ (*nicht einhalten*) break ‹agreement, contract, promise, the law, etc.›; Ⓔ (*ugs.: er~*) bring up.
❷ *unr. itr. V.* Ⓐ *mit sein* break; ‹leather› crack; **mir bricht das Herz** (*fig.*) it breaks my heart; **~d voll sein** be full to bursting; Ⓑ (*Beziehungen aufgeben*) break; **er brach mit der Familientradition** he broke [away from] the family tradition; **mit einer Gewohnheit ~:** break a habit; Ⓒ *mit sein* (*hervorkommen*) break (**durch** through); Ⓓ (*ugs.: sich er~*) throw up.
❸ *unr. refl. V.* ‹waves etc.› break (**an** + *Dat.* on); ‹rays etc.› be refracted

**Brecher** *der;* **~s, ~** Ⓐ (*Welle*) breaker; Ⓑ (*Maschine*) crusher

**Brech-: ~mittel** *das* emetic; **der Mann ist ein echtes ~mittel** (*fig. ugs. abwertend*) that man makes me sick (*coll.*) *or* (*coarse*) want to puke; **~reiz** *der* nausea; **~stange** *die* crowbar; **mit der ~stange vorgehen** (*fig.*) go about it with a sledgehammer; **ein Sieg mit der ~stange** (*Sport*) a victory by sheer force

**brecht[i]sch** /'brɛçt(ɪ)ʃ/ *Adj.* Brechtian

**Brechung** *die;* **~, ~en** Ⓐ (*Physik*) refraction; Ⓑ (*Sprachw.*) breaking

**Brechungs·winkel** *der* (*Physik*) angle of refraction

**Bredouille** /bre'dʊljə/ *die;* **~, ~n** (*ugs.*) **in der ~ sein** *od.* **sitzen** be in real trouble; **in die ~ kommen** get into real trouble

**Bregen** /'bre:gn̩/ *der;* **~s, ~** (*nordd.*) brains *pl.*

b

b

**Brei** /brai̯/ *der;* ~**[e]s**, ~**e** (*Hafer*~) porridge (*Brit.*), oatmeal (*Amer.*) *no indef. art.;* (*Reis*~) rice pudding; (*Grieß*~) semolina *no indef. art.;* **etw. zu einem ~ verrühren** make sth. into a mash *or* purée; **um den [heißen] ~ herumreden** (*ugs.*) beat about the bush

**breiig** *Adj.* mushy; **eine ~e Masse** a thick paste

**breit** /brai̯t/ **1** *Adj.* **A** ▸ **489** wide ‹street, river, bridge, window, margin, etc.›; broad, wide ‹hips, face, shoulders, forehead, etc.›; **etw. ~er machen** widen sth.; **einen ~en Buckel** *od.* **Rücken haben** (*fig. ugs.*) have broad shoulders (*fig.*); **die Beine ~ machen** (*auch fig.*) open one's legs; **die Schuhe ~ treten** stretch one's shoes out of shape; **ein ~es Lachen** a guffaw; **eine ~e Aussprache** a broad accent; **B** (*bei Maßangaben*) wide; **ein 5 cm ~er Saum** a hem 5 cm wide; **einen Finger ~ sein** be the width of a finger *or* a finger's breadth; **C** (*groß*) **die ~e Masse** the general public; most people *pl.;* **die ~e Öffentlichkeit** the general public; **~e Bevölkerungsschichten** large sections of the population; **ein ~es Interesse finden** arouse a great deal of interest; **D** (*ugs.: im Rausch*) high (*coll.*); stoned (*sl.*); **E sich ~ machen** take up room; (*sich ausbreiten*) be spreading; (*sich niederlassen*) make oneself at home; **mach dich nicht so ~:** don't take up so much room.

**2** *adv.* **A ~ gebaut** sturdily *or* well built; **~ lachen** guffaw; **etw. ~ darstellen** (*fig.*) describe sth. in great detail; **B der Stoff liegt doppelt ~:** the material is double width; **C ~ gefächert** wide ‹range, choice›

**breit·beinig** **1** *Adj.* rolling ‹gait›. **2** *adv.* with one's legs apart; **er stand ~ vor uns** he stood squarely in front of us

**Breite** *die;* ~, ~**n** **A** ▸ **489** width; breadth; (*bei Maßangaben*) width; **etw. der ~ nach durchsägen** saw through sth. widthways *or* widthwise; **etw. in epischer ~ schildern** (*fig.*) describe sth. in great detail *or* down to the last detail; **in die ~ gehen** (*ugs.*) put on weight; **B** (*Geogr.*) latitude; **auf/unter 50° nördlicher ~:** at/below latitude 50° north; **C** *Pl.* (*Gebiet*) **in diesen ~n** in these latitudes

**breiten** *tr., refl. V.* (*geh.*) spread

**Breiten-:** ~**grad** *der* degree of latitude; **New York und Mailand liegen auf demselben ~grad** New York and Milan have the same latitude; **der 30. ~grad** the 30th parallel; ~**kreis** *der* [line of] latitude; parallel; ~**sport** *der* popular sport; ~**wirkung** *die* widespread effect

**breit-, Breit-:** ~**flächig** *Adj.* wide; **~flächig gebaut** built over a wide area *postpos.;* *~**gefächert** ⇒ **breit** 2C; ~**krempig** *Adj.* broad-brimmed; *~|**machen** ⇒ **breit** 1E; ~**randig** *Adj.* broad-brimmed; ~|**schlagen** *unr. tr. V.* (*ugs.*) **sich zu etw. ~schlagen lassen** let oneself be talked into sth.; **er ließ sich ~schlagen** he let himself be persuaded; ~**schult[e]rig** *Adj.* broad-shouldered; ~**schwanz** *der* caracul; broadtail; ~**seite** *die* **A** (*eines Tisches, Gebäudes, Zimmers usw.*) long side; (*eines Schiffes*) side; **B** ([*Abfeuern der*] *Geschütze*) broadside; ~**spur** *die* (*Eisenb.*) broad gauge; ~**spurig** *Adj.* broad-gauge ‹railway etc.›; ‹car etc.› with a wide track; ~|**treten** *unr. tr. V.* (*ugs. abwertend*) go on about; **das Thema ist ~getreten** this subject has been flogged to death; ~**wand** *die* (*Kino*) wide *or* big screen; ~**wand·film** *der* widescreen *or* big-screen film

**Bremen** (*das*); ~**s** ▸ **700** Bremen

**Bremer** ▸ **700** **1** *indekl. Adj.* Bremen; **der ~ Hafen** the Port of Bremen. **2** *der;* ~**s**, ~**:** native/inhabitant of Bremen; ⇒ *auch* **Kölner**

**Bremerin** *die;* ~, ~**nen** ⇒ **Bremer** 2

**bremisch** *Adj.* Bremen *attrib.*

**Brems-:** ~**backe** *die* (*Kfz-W.*) brake shoe; ~**belag** *der* (*Kfz-W.*) brake lining

**Bremse**[1] /ˈbrɛmzə/ *die;* ~, ~**n** brake; **auf die ~ treten** put on the brakes

*old spelling (see note on page 1707)

**Bremse**[2] *die;* ~, ~**n** (*Insekt*) horsefly

**bremsen** **1** *itr. V.* brake; **der Dynamo bremst ganz erheblich** the dynamo has quite a considerable braking effect. **2** *tr. V.* **A** brake; (*um zu halten*) stop; **B** (*fig.*) slow down ‹rate, development, production, etc.›; restrict ‹imports etc.›; **jmdn. ~** (*ugs.*) stop sb.; **er ist nicht [mehr] zu ~** (*ugs.*) there's no stopping him. **3** *refl. V.* (*ugs.*) stop oneself; hold oneself back

**Bremser** *der;* ~**s**, ~, **Bremserin** *die;* ~, ~**nen** (*Eisenb., Bobsport*) brakeman

**Brems-:** ~**flüssigkeit** *die* (*Kfz-W.*) brake fluid; ~**hebel** *der* brake arm; ~**klotz** *der* **A** (*am Fahrrad*) brake block; (*am Wagen*) brake pad; **B** (*Klotz, der vor das Rad geschoben wird*) [wheel] chock; **C** (*fig.*) obstacle to progress; ~**kraft·verstärker** *der* (*Kfz-W.*) brake servo; ~**leitung** *die* (*Kfz-W.*) brake pipe; ~**leuchte** *die*, ~**licht** *das; Pl.* ~~**er** brake light; ~**pedal** *das* brake pedal; ~**probe** *die* brake test; ~**scheibe** *die* (*Kfz-W.*) brake disc; ~**spur** *die* skid mark; ~**trommel** *die* (*Kfz-W.*) brake drum

**Bremsung** *die;* ~, ~**en** braking

**Brems-:** ~**weg** *der* braking distance; ~**zug** *der* brake cable; ~**zylinder** *der* (*Kfz-W.*) brake cylinder

**brenn-, Brenn-:** ~**bar** *Adj.* [in]flammable; combustible; **leicht ~bar** highly [in]flammable *or* combustible; ~**dauer** *die* **A** (*einer Glühlampe*) life; **B** (*im ~ofen*) firing time; ~**eisen** *das* **A** ⇒ ~**schere**; **B** (*für Brandzeichen*) branding iron

**brennen** /ˈbrɛnən/ **1** *unr. itr. V.* **A** ‹wood etc.› burn; ‹house etc.› burn, be on fire; **schnell/leicht ~:** catch fire quickly/easily; **es brennt!** fire!; **in der Hotelbar hat es gebrannt** there was a fire in the hotel bar; **wo brennt's denn?** (*fig. ugs.*) what's the panic?; **B** (*glühen*) be alight; **C** (*leuchten*) be on; **in ihrem Zimmer brennt Licht** there is a light on in her room; **das Licht ~ lassen** leave the light on; **die Birne/Kerze brennt ganz schwach** the bulb is glowing very dimly/the candle is burning very low; **D** (*scheinen*) **die Sonne brannte so stark** the sun was so strong; **die Sonne brannte** the sun was burning down; **E** (*schmerzen*) ‹wound etc.› burn, sting; ‹feet etc.› hurt, be sore; **mir ~ die Augen** my eyes are stinging *or* smarting; **Pfeffer brennt auf der Zunge** pepper burns the tongue; **F** (*trachten*) **darauf ~, etw. zu tun** be dying *or* longing to do sth.; **auf Rache ~:** be bent on *or* dying for revenge; **G** (*ungeduldig sein*) **vor Neugier ~:** be dying to know; **er brannte vor Ehrgeiz** he was burning with ambition. **2** *unr. tr. V.* **A** burn ‹hole, pattern, etc.›; **einem Tier ein Zeichen ins Fell ~:** brand an animal; **gebranntes Kind scheut das Feuer** (*Spr.*) once bitten, twice shy (*prov.*); **B** (*mit Hitze behandeln*) fire ‹porcelain etc.›; distil ‹spirits›; **gebrannter Kalk** quicklime; **C** (*rösten*) roast ‹coffee beans, almonds, etc.›; brown ‹flour, sugar, etc.›

**brennend** **1** *Adj.* (*auch fig.*) burning; urgent ‹topic, subject›; lighted ‹cigarette›; raging ‹thirst›; violent ‹homesickness›. **2** *adv.* **ich würde ~ gern mal ein Wochenende dort verbringen** I should absolutely love to spend a weekend there; **ich wüsste ~ gern, ob ...** I'm dying to know whether ...; **es scheint dich ja ~ zu interessieren, was besprochen wurde** you seem to be dying to know what was discussed

**Brenner** *der;* ~**s**, ~**:** burner

**Brennerei** *die;* ~, ~**en** **A** distilling; **B** (*Betrieb*) distillery

***Brennessel** ⇒ **Brennnessel**

**Brenn-:** ~**glas** *das* burning glass; ~**holz** *das* firewood; ~**material** *das* fuel; **wir benutzen alte Zeitungen als ~material** we use old newspapers to burn on the fire; ~**nessel** *die* stinging nettle; ~**ofen** *der* kiln; ~**punkt** *der* (*auch Mathematik, Optik*) focus; **im ~punkt des Interesses stehen** be the focus of attention *or* interest; **in den ~punkt der Diskussion rücken** become the focal point of discussion; ~**schere** *die* curling tongs *pl.* (*Brit.*); curling iron (*Amer.*); ~**spiegel** *der* (*Optik*) burning mirror; ~**spiritus** *der* methylated spirits; ~**stab** *der* (*Kerntechnik*) fuel rod; ~**stoff** *der* fuel; ~**weite** *die* (*Optik*) focal length

**brenzlig** /ˈbrɛntslɪç/ *Adj.* **A** ‹smell, taste, etc.› of burning *not pred.;* **~ riechen/schmecken** smell of burning/taste burnt; **B** (*ugs.: bedenklich*) dicey (*coll.*); **mir wird die Sache zu ~:** things are getting too hot for me

**Bresche** /ˈbrɛʃə/ *die;* ~, ~**n** gap; breach; **[für jmdn.] in die ~ springen** stand in [for sb.]; **für jmdn./etw. eine ~ schlagen** give one's backing to sb./sth.

**Bretagne** /breˈtanjə/ *die;* ~**:** Brittany

**Bretone** /breˈtoːnə/ *der;* ~**n**, ~**n**, **Bretonin** *die;* ~, ~**nen** Breton

**Brett** /brɛt/ *das;* ~**[e]s**, ~**er** **A** board; (*lang und dick*) plank; (*Diele*) floorboard; **hier ist die Welt [wie] mit ~ern vernagelt** (*ugs.*) this place is like the end of the earth; **das schwarze ~:** the noticeboard; **ein ~ vor dem Kopf haben** (*fig. ugs.*) be thick; **ich habe heute einfach ein ~ vor dem Kopf** (*fig. ugs.*) I just can't think straight today; **das ~ bohren, wo es am dünnsten ist** (*fig. ugs.*) take the easy way out; **B** (*für Spiele*) board; **C** *Pl.* (*Skisport*) skis; **D** *Pl.* (*Bühne*) stage *sing.;* boards; **auf den ~ern stehen** be on [the] stage *or* on the boards; **die ~er, die die Welt bedeuten** (*geh.*) the stage *sing.;* the boards; **E** *Pl.* (*Boxen*) floor *sing.;* canvas *sing.;* **er schickte seinen Gegner auf die ~er** he put his opponent on the canvas; he floored his opponent

**Brettchen** *das;* ~**s**, ~ **A** *wooden board used for breakfast;* **B** (*zum Schneiden*) board

**Brettel** /ˈbrɛtl̩/ *das;* ~**s**, ~**[n]** (*südd., österr.*) **A** board; **B** *Pl.* (*Skisport*) skis

**Bretter-:** ~**boden** *der* wooden floor; ~**bude** *die* [wooden] hut, shack; ~**verschlag** *der* [wooden] shed; ~**wand** *die* wooden wall *or* partition; ~**zaun** *der* wooden fence

**Brett·spiel** *das* board game

**Brevier** /breˈviːɐ̯/ *das;* ~**s**, ~**e** **A** (*kath. Rel.*) breviary; **B** (*Leitfaden*) guide (**für** to)

**Brezel** /ˈbreːtsl̩/ *die;* ~, ~**n**, **Brezen** /ˈbreːtsn̩/ *der;* ~**s**, ~ *od. die;* ~, ~ (*österr.*) pretzel

**Bridge** /brɪtʃ/ *das;* ~**:** bridge

**Brief** /briːf/ *der;* ~**[e]s**, ~**e** ▸ **187** **A** letter; **blauer ~** (*ugs.*) warning letter; **offener ~** (*fig.*) open letter; **jmdm. ~ und Siegel [auf etw.** (*Akk.*)**] geben** (*fig.*) promise sb. faithfully *or* give sb. one's word [on sth.]; **B** (*Rauschgiftpäckchen*) deck

**Brief-:** ~**beschwerer** *der;* ~**s**, ~**:** paperweight; ~**block** *der; Pl.* ~~**s** *od.* ~**blöcke** writing pad; letter pad; ~**bogen** *der* sheet of writing paper *or* notepaper; ~**bögen mit Kopf** letter-headed writing paper *sing. or* notepaper *sing.;* ~**bombe** *die* letter bomb

**Briefchen** *das;* ~**s**, ~ **A ein ~ Nähnadeln/Streichhölzer** a packet of needles/book of matches; **B** (*kurzer Brief*) note

**Brief-:** ~**druck·sache** *die* (*Postw.*) printed paper (*sent as a letter*); **eine ~drucksache** a piece of printed matter; **die Gebühren für ~drucksachen** the rates for printed matter *sing.;* ~**freund** *der*, ~**freundin** *die* penfriend; pen pal (*coll.*); ~**geheimnis** *das* privacy of the post; secrecy of correspondence; ~**karte** *die* correspondence card; ~**kasten** *der* **A** postbox; pillar box (*Brit.*); **B** (*privat*) letter box; **lebender/toter ~kasten** (*Geheimdienstjargon*) [live] letter box/letter box; **C** (*in der Zeitung*) agony column (*coll.*)

**Briefkasten-:** ~**firma** *die* accommodation address; ~**tante** *die* (*ugs. scherzh.*) agony aunt (*coll.*)

**Brief-:** ~**kopf** *der* **A** letter-heading; **B** (*aufgedruckt*) letterhead; ~**kuvert** *das* (*veralt.*) ⇒ ~**umschlag**

**brieflich** **1** *Adj.* written. **2** *adv.* by letter

**Brief·marke** *die* [postage] stamp

**Briefmarken-:** ~**album** *das* stamp album; ~**sammler** *der*, ~**sammlerin** *die* stamp collector; philatelist; ~**sammlung** *die* stamp collection; **wollen Sie sich meine ~sammlung ansehen?** (*fig. verhüll.*) come up and see my etchings (*joc.*)

# Briefeschreiben

## Der Umschlag

Im Gegensatz zu deutschen Anschriften steht der Titel des Adressaten zusammen mit dem Namen auf der ersten Zeile. Vor allem in Großbritannien haben Häuser oft einen Namen anstelle einer oder zusätzlich zur (vor dem Straßennamen stehenden!) Hausnummer. In GB folgt dann die Stadt, aber bei einer kleineren Ortschaft oder einem Stadtteil steht diese(r) davor auf einer eigenen Zeile; nach der Stadt folgt meist die Grafschaft, es sei denn, es handelt sich um eine 'county town', die der Grafschaft ihren Namen gibt, oder eine Großstadt mit eigener Postleitzahl (**postcode**). Letztere steht dann allein auf der letzten Zeile. Britische Adressen können also leicht sieben oder sogar acht Zeilen einnehmen. In den USA dagegen werden die Adressen einfacher gehalten; hier steht auch die Postleitzahl (**Zip code**) an letzter Stelle, davor aber der Staat, auf zwei Buchstaben abgekürzt (CA = California, NJ = New Jersey usw.).

■ **GB:**

Mr James Bainbridge
od: James Bainbridge Esq.
5 Avon Crescent
Kenilworth
Warwickshire
CV8 2PQ

Ms B. Gordon
Kirkbrae
10 Strathmore Road
Cults
Aberdeen
AB1 9TJ

Sir Alan and Lady Weston
Aberdare House
Llanyre
Llandrindod Wells
Powys
LD1 6DX

■ **USA:**

Robert J. Hale Jr.
1496 Pacific Boulevard
Monterey
CA 93940

Mrs Nancy Bright
PO Box 731
Milville
NJ 08332

Miss Abigail Schott
c/o Floyd
1100 North Street
Harrisburg
PA 17105

**PO Box** = *Postfach*, **c/o** (für **care of**) = bei. Zu den verschiedenen Anreden (Mr, Mrs, Miss, Ms usw.)

••••➤ Anreden und Titel

Bei Geschäftsbriefen kann der Name des Adressaten entweder vor- oder nach der Firma bzw. Organisation stehen, im letzteren Fall oft mit **FAO** (**for the attention of**) oder **Attn.** (**attention**) davor. In den USA ist es üblich, nach dem Namen des Inhabers einer leitenden Position diese anzugeben. Partnerschaften und Firmen mit dem Zusatz "& Co." kann **Messrs.** = *Herren* vorangestellt werden.

Messrs. Gibbons & Prestwick
FAO Anita Dobby
45 Albright Way
London
W11 2BJ

John C. Wagner
President
Bix Corporation
222 Madison Avenue
New York
NY 10016

Der Absender steht, wenn überhaupt, links oben oder auf der Rückseite.

## Der Brief selbst

Die Adresse des Absenders steht oben entweder rechts oder in der Mitte, darunter das Datum:

10 Copthall Avenue
West Drayton
Middlesex
UB7 2FL

24th September 1997

## Anrede

Es gibt fast nur die eine Möglichkeit – **Dear** und der Name des Adressaten, bloß der Vorname bei Freunden und Verwandten oder wenn man weniger formell erscheinen will, sonst Titel und Familienname:

Dear Charles/Mary/Mr Churchill/Dr Watson/Professor Andrews

Bei Geschäftsbriefen schreibt man, wenn man den Namen des Adressaten nicht kennt, **Dear Sir or Madam**, und wenn man eine Firma oder andere Organisation anschreibt, **Dear Sirs.**

## Schlussformel

| | | | |
|---|---|---|---|
| ***Informell:*** | Yours<br>Charles | Love<br>Mary | All our love<br>Brian and Wendy |
| ***Etwas formeller:*** | With best wishes | Kind regards | |
| ***Formell:*** | Yours sincerely (*brit.*)<br>Yours truly (*amerik.*) | | |
| ***Sehr formell:*** | Yours faithfully (*brit.*)<br>Yours very truly (*amerik.*) | | |

**Brief-: ~öffner** *der* letter-opener; **~papier** *das* writing paper; notepaper; **~partner** *der*, **~partnerin** *die* penfriend; **~porto** *das* [letter] rate; **~post** *die* letter post; **~roman** *der* epistolary novel; **~schreiber** *der*, **~schreiberin** *die* [letter-]writer; **~sendung** *die* item sent by letter post; **~tasche** *die* wallet; **~taube** *die* carrier pigeon; **~träger** *der* ▶ 159 postman; letter-carrier (*Amer.*); **~trägerin** *die* ▶ 159 postwoman; female letter-carrier (*Amer.*); **~umschlag** *der* envelope; **~waage** *die* letter scales *pl.*; **~wahl** *die* postal vote; **~wechsel** *der* Ⓐ correspondence; **einen ~wechsel führen** have a *or* be in correspondence; **mit jmdm. in ~wechsel stehen** be in correspondence *or* correspond with sb.; Ⓑ (*gesammelte ~e*) correspondence

**Brie·käse** /'bri:-/ *der* Brie

**Bries** /bri:s/ *das;* **~es, ~e** thymus [gland] (*esp. of calf*); (*Kochk.*) sweetbreads *pl.*

**briet** /bri:t/ *1. u. 3. Pers. Sg. Prät. v.* **braten**

**Brigade** /bri'ga:də/ *die;* **~, ~n** Ⓐ (*Milit.*) brigade; Ⓑ (*DDR*) work team; [work] brigade

**Brigade·general** *der* (*Milit.*) brigadier

**Brigadier** Ⓐ /briga'dje:/ *der;* **~s, ~s** (*Milit.*) brigadier; Ⓑ /briga'dje: *od.* briga'di:ɐ/ *der;* **~s, ~s** *od.* **~e** (*DDR*) [work] team leader; brigade leader

**Brigadierin** *die;* **~, ~nen** (*DDR*) [work] team leader; brigade leader; ⇒ *auch* **-in**

**Brigg** /brɪk/ *die;* **~, ~s** (*Seew.*) brig

**Brikett** /bri'kɛt/ *das;* **~s, ~s** briquette

**brillant** /brɪl'jant/ ❶ *Adj.* brilliant. ❷ *adv.* brilliantly

**Brillant**[1] /brɪl'jant/ *der;* **~en, ~en** brilliant

**Brillant**[2] *die;* **~** (*Druckw.*) 3-point type

**Brillantine** /brɪljan'ti:nə/ *die;* **~, ~n** (*veralt.*) brilliantine

**Brillant-: ~kollier** *das* (*brilliant-cut*) diamond necklace; **~ring** *der* (*brilliant-cut*) diamond ring; **~schliff** *der* brilliant cut; **~schmuck** *der* (*brilliant-cut*) diamond jewellery

**Brillanz** /brɪl'jants/ *die;* **~** Ⓐ brilliance; Ⓑ (*Akustik*) clarity; sound quality

**Brille** /'brɪlə/ *die;* **~, ~n** Ⓐ glasses *pl.*; spectacles *pl.*; specs (*coll.*) *pl.*; **eine ~:** a pair of glasses *or* spectacles; **eine ~ tragen** wear glasses *or* spectacles; **etw. durch eine gefärbte ~ sehen** (*fig.*) look at sth. subjectively *or* from one's own point of view; **etw. durch eine rosa[rote] ~ sehen** *od.* **betrachten** (*fig.*) see sth. through rose-coloured *or* rose-tinted spectacles; Ⓑ (*ugs.: Klosett~*) [lavatory *or* toilet] seat

**Brillen-: ~etui** *das*, **~futteral** *das* glasses case; spectacle case; **~gestell** *das* spectacle frame; [glasses] frame; **~glas** *das* [spectacle] lens; **~schlange** *die* Ⓐ (*Zool.*) spectacled cobra; Ⓑ (*ugs. scherzh.*) **in der Schule wurde ich oft ~schlange genannt** I was often called 'four-eyes' at school; **~träger** *der*, **~trägerin** *die* person who wears glasses; person with glasses

**brillieren** /brɪl'ji:rən/ *itr. V.* (*geh.*) be brilliant

**Brimborium** /brɪm'bo:ri̯ʊm/ *das;* **~s** (*ugs. abwertend*) hoo-ha (*coll.*)

**bringen** /'brɪŋən/ *unr. tr. V.* Ⓐ (*her~*) bring; (*hin~*) take; **sie brachte mir/ich brachte ihr ein Geschenk** she brought me/I took her a present; **Unglück/Unheil [über jmdn.] ~:** bring misfortune/disaster [upon sb.]; **jmdm. Glück/Unglück ~:** bring sb. [good] luck/bad luck; **jmdm. eine Nachricht ~:** bring sb. news; **der letzte Winter brachte uns viel Schnee** (*fig.*) we had a lot of snow last winter; Ⓑ (*begleiten*) take; **jmdn. nach Hause/zum Bahnhof ~:** take sb. home/to the station; **das Auto in die Garage ~:** put the car in the garage; **die Kinder ins Bett** *od.* **zu Bett ~:** put the children to bed; C **es zu etwas/nichts ~:** get somewhere/get nowhere *or* not get anywhere; **er hat es zu nichts weiter gebracht als zum Redaktionsassistenten** he didn't get further than assistant editor; **es bis zum Direktor ~:** make it to director; **es zu hohem Ansehen ~:** acquire standing *or* a high reputation; **es weit ~:** get on *or* do very well; **es im Leben weit ~:** go far in life; D **jmdn. ins Gefängnis ~** ‹crime, misdeed› land sb. in prison *or* gaol; **eine Sache vor Gericht ~:** take a matter to court; **das Gespräch auf etw./ein anderes Thema ~:** bring the conversation round to sth./change the topic of conversation; **jmdn. wieder auf den rechten Weg ~** (*fig.*) get sb. back on the straight and narrow; **jmdn. zum Lachen/zur Verzweiflung ~:** make sb. laugh/drive sb. to despair; **jmdn. dazu ~, etw. zu tun** get sb. to do sth.; **du hast mich auf eine gute Idee gebracht** you have given me a good idea; **etw. hinter sich ~** (*ugs.*) get sth. over and done with; **es nicht über sich** (*Akk.*) **~ [können], etw. zu tun** not be able to bring oneself to do sth.; **etw. an sich** (*Akk.*) **~** (*ugs.*) collar sth. (*sl.*); E (*mit Präp.* **um**) **jmdn. um seinen Besitz ~:** do sb. out of his property (*coll.*); **jmdn. um den Schlaf/Verstand ~:** rob sb. of his/her sleep/drive sb. mad; F (*veröffentlichen*) publish; **die Zeitschrift bringt jetzt eine Artikelserie über ...** the magazine is running a series of articles about ...; **was bringt denn die Zeitung heute darüber?** what does it say about it in today's paper?; **alle Zeitungen brachten Berichte über das Massaker** all the papers carried reports of the massacre; G (*senden*) broadcast; **um 23.00 Uhr ~ wir die letzten Nachrichten** the late-night news will be at 11 o'clock; **das Fernsehen bringt eine Sondersendung** there is a special programme on television; **einen Film im Fernsehen ~:** show a film on television; **das Fernsehen hat nichts darüber gebracht** there was nothing about it on television; H (*dar~*) **das/ein Opfer ~:** make the/a sacrifice; **eine Nummer/ein Ständchen ~:** perform a number/a serenade; I (*er~*) **einen großen Gewinn/hohe Zinsen ~:** make a large profit/earn high interest; **das Gemälde brachte 50 000 DM** the painting fetched 50,000 marks; **das bringt nichts** (*ugs.*) it's pointless; J **das bringt es mit sich, dass ...** that means that ...; **seine Krankheit bringt es mit sich, dass ...** it's because of *or* to do with his illness that ...; K (*verursachen*) cause ‹trouble, confusion›; **es kann dir doch nur Vorteile ~:** it can only be to your advantage; L (*salopp: schaffen, erreichen*) **das bringst du doch nicht** you'll never do it; **der Wagen/diese Kneipe bringts doch nicht** the car/this pub is no good; **der Wagen bringt 210 km/h** the car can *or* will do 210 km/h; M (*hinein~, heraus~, bewegen*) get (**in** + *Akk.* into, **aus** out of); **der Schrank ist viel zu groß, als dass ich ihn allein von der Stelle ~ könnte** the cupboard is far too big for me to shift on my own; **den Wagen zum Laufen ~:** get the car to go; **ich bringe den Schlüssel nicht ins Schloss** (*bes. südd.*) I can't get the key into the lock

**Bring·schuld** *die* (*Rechtsw.*): *debt to be paid at the creditor's domicile*

**brisant** /bri'zant/ *Adj.* explosive; **ein recht ~es Unternehmen** a highly risky undertaking; **~e Sprengstoffe** highly explosive materials

**Brisanz** /bri'zants/ *die;* ~, **~en** A explosiveness; explosive nature; **ein Thema von hoher politischer ~:** a highly explosive political subject; B (*Waffenkunde*) explosive force

**Brise** /'bri:zə/ *die;* ~, **~n** breeze

**Britannien** /bri'tanjən/ (*das*); **~s** Britain; (*hist.*) Britannia

**Brite** /'brɪtə/ *der;* **~n, ~n** ▶ 553 Briton; **die ~n** the British; **er ist [kein] ~:** he is [not] British; **der ~ gewann eine Medaille** the British athlete/scholar *etc.* won a medal

**Britin** *die;* ~, **~nen** ▶ 553 Briton; British girl/woman; **die ~nen** the British [girls/women]; **sie ist [keine] ~:** she is [not] British; ⇒ *auch* **-in**

**britisch** *Adj.* ▶ 553 British; **die Britischen Inseln** the British Isles

**Bröckchen** /'brœkçən/ *das;* **~s,** ~: bit; small piece

**bröckchen·weise** *Adv.* ⇒ **brockenweise**

**bröckelig** *Adj.* crumbly

**bröckeln** /'brœkl̩n/ *tr., itr. V.* A crumble; B *mit sein* **von der Decke/Wand ~:** crumble away from the ceiling/wall

**Brocken** /'brɔkn̩/ *der;* **~s,** ~ A (*von Brot*) hunk, chunk; (*von Fleisch*) chunk; (*von Lehm, Kohle, Erde*) lump; B (*fig.*) **ein paar ~ Englisch** a smattering of English; **ein paar ~ eines Gesprächs auffangen** catch a few snatches of a conversation; **jmdm. einen fetten ~ wegschnappen** (*ugs.*) snap up a real opportunity from under sb.'s nose; **das war ein harter ~** (*ugs.*) that was a tough *or* a hard nut to crack; C (*ugs.: dicke Person*) lump; **ist das ein ~!** what a big fat lump he/she is!

**brocken·weise** *Adv.* (*auch fig.*) bit by bit

**bröcklig** ⇒ **bröckelig**

**brodeln** /'bro:dl̩n/ *itr. V.* bubble; **es brodelt in der Masse/Bevölkerung** (*fig.*) there is seething unrest among the masses/in the population

**Brodem** /'bro:dəm/ (*geh.*) vapour (*literary*)

**Broiler** /'brɔylɐ/ *der;* **~s,** ~ (*DDR*) ⇒ **Brathähnchen**

**Brokat** /bro'ka:t/ *der;* **~[e]s, ~e** brocade

**Brokat·kleid** *das* brocade dress

**Brokkoli** /'brɔkoli/ *der;* **~s, ~[s]** broccoli

**Brom** /bro:m/ *das;* **~s** (*Chemie*) bromine

**Brom·beere** /'brɔm-/ *die* A bramble; blackberry bush; B (*Frucht*) blackberry; **~n pflücken gehen** go blackberrying

**Brombeer-: ~konfitüre** *die,* **~marmelade** *die* blackberry jam; **~strauch** *der* bramble; blackberry bush

**Bronchial-: ~asthma** *das* ▶ 474 (*Med.*) bronchial asthma; **~katarrh** *der* ▶ 474 (*Med.*) ⇒ **Bronchitis**; **~tee** *der* bronchial tea

**Bronchie** /'brɔnçi̯ə/ *die;* ~, **~n** ▶ 471 (*Med.*) bronchial tube; bronchus

**Bronchitis** /brɔn'çi:tɪs/ *die;* ~, **Bronchitiden** ▶ 474 (*Med.*) bronchitis

**Bronze** /'brõ:sə/ *die;* ~: bronze; **diese Leistung reichte gerade noch für ~** (*Sportjargon*) this performance was just enough to get a bronze; ⇒ *auch* **Gold**

**Bronze·medaille** *die* bronze medal

**bronzen** /'brõ:sn̩/ *Adj.* bronze ‹object›; bronzed ‹skin›; **~ schimmern** glint like bronze

**Bronze·zeit** *die* Bronze Age

**Brosame** /'bro:za:mə/ *die;* ~, **~n** (*geh. veralt., auch fig.*) crumb

**Brosche** /'brɔʃə/ *die;* ~, **~n** brooch

**broschiert** /brɔ'ʃi:rt/ *Adj.* paperback; **eine ~e Ausgabe** a paperback *or* soft-cover edition; **~e Heftchen** booklets

**Broschüre** /brɔ'ʃy:rə/ *die;* ~, **~n** booklet; pamphlet; (*Reiseprospekt*) brochure

**Brösel** /'brø:zl̩/ *der;* **~s,** ~, (*österr.*) *das;* **~s,** ~: breadcrumb

**bröselig** *Adj.* crumbly

**bröseln** 1 *itr. V.* crumble. 2 *tr. V.* crumble

**Brot** /bro:t/ *das;* **~[e]s, ~e** A bread *no pl.,* *no indef. art.;* (*Laib ~*) loaf [of bread]; **wes ~ ich ess, des Lied ich sing** (*Spr.*) he/she is not going to bite the hand that feeds him/her; **Bier ist flüssiges ~** (*scherzh.*) beer is full of nourishment; **der Mensch lebt nicht vom ~ allein** (*Spr.*) man shall not live by bread alone (*bibl.*); **~ und Arbeit finden** find a paid job; B (*Scheibe ~*) slice [of bread]; C ⇒ **Butter~**; D (*Lebensunterhalt*) daily bread (*fig.*); **das ist ein hartes ~:** it's a hard way to earn a *or* your living

**Brot-: ~aufstrich** *der* spread; **~belag** *der* topping; (*im zusammengeklappten ~*) filling; **~beruf** *der* occupation that enables one to make a living; **~beutel** *der* satchel

**Brötchen** /'brø:tçən/ *das;* **~s,** ~: roll; **kleinere ~ backen [müssen]** (*fig. ugs.*) [have to] lower one's sights; **seine/die ~ verdienen** (*ugs.*) earn one's/the daily bread

**Brötchen·geber** *der;* **~s,** ~, **Brötchengeberin** *die;* ~, **~nen** (*scherzh.*) employer

**brot-, Brot-: ~einheit** *die* carbohydrate unit; **~erwerb** *der* way to earn a living; **~fabrik** *die* bakery (*producing bread on a large scale*); **~frucht·baum** *der* breadfruit tree; **~kanten** *der* [bread] crust; **~kasten** *der* bread bin; **~korb** *der* bread basket; **jmdm. den ~korb höher hängen** (*ugs.*) put sb. on short rations; (*fig.*) put the squeeze on sb. (*coll.*); **~krume** *die,* **~krümel** *der* breadcrumb; **~kruste** *die* [bread] crust; **~laib** *der* loaf [of bread]; **~los** *Adj.* unemployed; **jmdn. ~los machen** put sb. out of work; **das ist eine ~lose Kunst** there's no money in that; **~maschine** *die* bread slicer; **~messer** *das* bread knife; **~neid** *der* jealousy of sb.'s position/salary; **~rinde** *die* [bread] crust; **~scheibe** *die* slice of bread; **~schneide·maschine** *die* ⇒ **~maschine**; **~studium** *das:* **für einen großen Teil der Studenten heute ist die Medizin ein reines ~studium** a lot of today's students choose medicine because it will get them a well-paid job; **~teig** *der* bread dough; **~zeit** *die* (*südd.*) A (*Pause*) [tea/coffee/lunch] break; B (*Vesper*) snack; (*Vesper~*) sandwiches *pl.*

**Browser** /'braʊzɐ/ *der;* **~s,** ~ (*DV*) browser

**brr** /br̩/ *Interj.* A (*bei Kälte*) brr; (*vor Ekel*) ugh; B (*Zuruf an Zugtier*) whoa

**BRT** *Abk.* **Bruttoregistertonne** grt

**Bruch**[1] /brʊx/ *der;* **~[e]s, Brüche** /'brʏçə/ ▶ 474 A (*das Brechen*) break; **der ~ des Deiches/Dammes** the breaching (*Brit.*) *or* (*Amer.*) breaking of the dike/dam; **das hätte ~ geben können** (*ugs.*) there could have been a crash; **~ machen** (*ugs.*) break things; (*Fliegerspr.*) crash; **in die Brüche gehen** (*zerbrechen*) break; get broken; (*enden*) break up; **zu ~ gehen** break; get broken; **etw. zu ~ fahren** smash sth. up; B (*~stelle*) break; **die Brüche im Deich** the breaches (*Brit.*) *or* (*Amer.*) breaks in the dike; C (*Med.: Knochen~*) fracture; break; D (*Med.: Eingeweide~*) hernia; rupture; **sich** (*Dat.*) **einen ~ heben** rupture oneself *or* give oneself a hernia [by lifting sth.]; E (*fig.*) (*eines Versprechens*) breaking; (*eines Abkommens, Gesetzes, einer Verfassung*) break; violation; (*mit der Vergangenheit, Tradition, Partei*) break (**mit** with); (*einer Freundschaft*) break; (*einer Ehe*) break-up; **ein ~ des Waffenstillstandes** a violation of the ceasefire; **der ~ mit dem Elternhaus** the break with home; **es kam zum ~ zwischen ihnen** they broke up; F ▶ 841 (*Math.*) fraction; G (*Kaufmannsspr.: beschädigte Ware*) **diese Schokolade ist ~:** this chocolate is broken; H (*Falte*) crease; **nach dem ~ falten** fold along the crease/creases; I (*salopp: Einbruch*) break-in; **einen ~ machen** do a break-in

**Bruch**[2] *der od. das;* **~[e]s, Brüche** (*Sumpfland*) marsh

**bruch-, Bruch-: ~band** *das; Pl.* **~bänder** (*Med.*) truss; **~bude** *die* (*ugs. abwertend*) hovel; dump (*coll.*); **~fest** *Adj.* unbreakable

**brüchig** /'brʏçɪç/ *Adj.* A brittle, crumbly ‹rock, brickwork›; **das Leder mit Creme einreiben, damit es nicht ~ wird** rub cream into the leather to keep it from cracking; **der Stoff ist ziemlich ~:** the material is splitting quite a bit; B (*fig.*) crumbling ‹relationship, marriage, etc.›; C (*rau*) rough; cracked

**Brüchigkeit** *die;* ~ A brittleness; crumbliness; B **die ~ ihrer Beziehung/Ehe ist für alle offenbar** it is obvious to everyone that their relationship/marriage is breaking up; C (*Rauheit*) roughness

**bruch-, Bruch-: ~|landen** *itr. V.; mit sein; nur im Inf. u. 2. Part.* crash-land; make a crash-landing; **~landung** *die* crash-landing; **~los** *Adj.* without a break *postpos.*; **~operation** *die* hernia operation; **~pilot** *der*

*old spelling (see note on page 1707)

(*ugs.*) crash-happy pilot; **~rechnen** *itr. V.; nur im Inf.* do fractions; **~rechnen** *das* fractions *pl.*; **jmdm. [das] ~rechnen beibringen** teach sb. how to do fractions; **beim ~rechnen ...** when doing fractions ...; **~rechnung** *die* fractions *pl.*; **~schaden** *der* breakage; **~schokolade** *die* broken chocolate; **~sicher** *Adj.* unbreakable; **~stein** *der* undressed stone; **~stelle** *die* break; (*von Knochen auch*) fracture; **die ~stelle mit Klebstoff bestreichen** apply adhesive to the broken area; **~strich** *der* fraction line; **~stück** *das* fragment; (*großes Stück*) piece; (*fig.*) snatch; **~stückhaft** ❶ *Adj.* fragmentary; ❷ *adv.* in a fragmentary way; **~teil** *der* fraction; **im ~teil einer Sekunde** in a fraction of a second; in a split second; **er kam um den ~teil einer Sekunde zu spät** he came a split second too late; **~zahl** *die* ▶ 841 fraction

**Brücke** /ˈbrʏkə/ *die;* ~, **~n** **A** (*auch: Schiffs~, Zahnmed., Bodenturnen, Ringen*) bridge; **die** *od.* **alle ~n hinter sich** (*Dat.*) **abbrechen** (*fig.*) burn one's bridges (*fig.*); **jmdm. eine [goldene] ~** *od.* **[goldene] ~n bauen** (*fig.*) make things easier for sb.; **B** (*Landungs~*) landing stage; **C** (*Teppich*) rug; **D** (*Anat.*) pons [Varolii]

**Brücken-: ~bau** *der; Pl.* **~~ten** **A** building *or* construction of a/the bridge; (*allgemein*) bridge-building; bridge construction; **B** (*Brücke*) bridge [structure]; **~bogen** *der* arch [of a/the bridge]; **~geländer** *das* parapet; railing; **~heilige** *der/die* sculptured saint [on a/the bridge]; **~kopf** *der* (*Milit., auch fig.*) bridgehead; **~pfeiler** *der* pier [of a/the bridge]; **~waage** *die* weighbridge; **~zoll** *der* [bridge] toll; **~zoll bezahlen** pay a [bridge] toll

**Bruder** /ˈbruːdɐ/ *der;* **~s, Brüder** /ˈbryːdɐ/ **A** (*auch: Mitmensch, Mönch*) brother; **die Brüder Müller** the Müller brothers; the brothers Müller; **~ Peter** Brother Peter; **und willst du nicht mein ~ sein, so schlag ich dir den Schädel ein** if you're not my friend, then I'll treat you as an enemy; **der große ~** (*fig.*) Big Brother; **der große/kleine ~** (*fig. scherzh.*) the larger/smaller edition; **unter Brüdern** (*fig. ugs. scherzh.*) between *or* amongst friends; **B** (*ugs. abwertend: Mann*) guy (*coll.*); **ein ziemlich windiger ~:** a bit of a dodgy (*Brit.*) *or* shady character (*coll.*); **~ Lustig** *od.* **Leichtfuß** (*veralt. scherzh.*) light-hearted fellow; ⇒ *auch* **warm 1 C**

**Bruder·bund** *der* (*geh., bes. DDR*) comradeship; fraternal links *pl.*

**Brüderchen** /ˈbryːdɐçən/ *das;* **~s, ~:** little brother; **ein kleines ~:** a little brother

**Bruder-: ~herz** *das* (*veralt., noch scherzh.*) dear brother; **hör mal, ~herz** listen, brother dear; **~krieg** *der* fratricidal war; **~kuss, *~kuß** *der* brotherly kiss; **~land** *das* (*geh., bes. DDR*) fraternal country

**brüderlich** ❶ *Adj.* brotherly; (*im politischen Bereich*) fraternal. ❷ *adv.* in a brotherly way; (*im politischen Bereich*) fraternally; **etw. ~ [mit jmdm.] teilen** share sth. [with sb.] in a fair and generous way

**Brüderlichkeit** *die;* **~:** brotherliness; (*im politischen Bereich*) fraternity

**Bruder-: ~liebe** *die* brotherly love; **~mord** *der* fratricide; **~mörder** *der,* **~mörderin** *die* fratricide

**Bruder·partei** *die* (*bes. DDR*) fraternal party

**Bruderschaft** *die;* ~, **~en** (*Rel.*) brotherhood

**Brüderschaft** *die: in* **[mit jmdm.] Brüderschaft trinken** drink to close friendship [with sb.] (*agreeing to use the familiar 'du' form*)

**Bruder-: ~volk** *das* **A** (*bes. DDR*) sister people; **B** (*veralt. geh.*) kindred people; **~zwist** *der* feud between brothers; (*im politischen Bereich*) fraternal feud

**Brühe** /ˈbryːə/ *die;* ~, **~n** **A** stock; (*als Suppe*) clear soup; broth; **B** (*ugs. abwertend: Getränk*) muck; **eine abscheuliche ~** (*fig.*) a revolting concoction; **C** (*abwertend: verschmutztes Wasser*) dirty *or* filthy water; **D** (*Kochk.: Kochwasser*) water; **E** (*ugs.: Schweiß*) sweat

**brühen** *tr. V.* **A** blanch; **B** (*auf~*) brew, make ‹tea›; make ‹coffee, soup›

**brüh-, Brüh-: ~warm** (*ugs.*) ❶ *Adj.* hot ‹news›; very latest ‹gossip etc.›; ❷ *adv.* **etw. ~warm weitererzählen** pass sth. on *or* spread sth. around straight away; **~würfel** *der* stock cube; **~wurst** *die* sausage (*which is heated in boiling water*)

**Brüll·affe** *der* (*Zool.*) howler [monkey]; howling monkey

**brüllen** /ˈbrʏlən/ ❶ *itr. V.* **A** ‹bull, cow, etc.› bellow; ‹lion, tiger, etc.› roar; ‹elephant› trumpet; **B** (*ugs.: schreien*) roar; shout; **vor Schmerzen/Lachen ~:** roar with pain/laughter; **brüll nicht so!** there's no need to shout like that; **nach jmdm. ~:** shout to *or* for sb.; **~des Gelächter** roars *pl.* of laughter; **das ist [ja] zum Brüllen** (*ugs.*) it's a [real] scream; what a scream; **C** (*ugs.: weinen*) howl; bawl; **er brüllte wie am Spieß** he bawled his head off. ❷ *tr. V.* yell; shout

**Brumm-: ~bär** *der* (*ugs.*) grouch (*coll.*); **~bass, *~baß** *der* **A** (*ugs.*) deep *or* bass voice; **B** ⇒ **Kontrabass**

**brummeln** /ˈbrʊml̩n/ *tr., itr. V.* (*ugs.*) mumble; mutter

**brummen** /ˈbrʊmən/ *tr., itr. V.* **A** ‹insect› buzz; ‹bear› growl; ‹engine etc.› drone; **mir brummt der Schädel** *od.* **Kopf** (*ugs.*) my head is buzzing; **B** (*sich ~d bewegen*) ‹fly etc.› buzz; ‹lorry etc.› thunder; ‹moped› buzz; **C** (*unmelodisch singen*) drone; **D** (*mürrisch sprechen*) mumble; mutter; **E** (*ugs. veralt.: in Haft sein*) do time (*coll.*); **zwei Jahre ~:** do two years; **F** (*ugs.: nachsitzen*) stay behind

**Brummer** *der;* **~s, ~** (*ugs.*) **A** (*Fliege*) bluebottle; **B** (*Lkw*) heavy lorry (*Brit.*) *or* truck

**Brummi** *der;* **~s, ~s** (*ugs.*) lorry (*Brit.*); truck

**brummig** (*ugs.*) ❶ *Adj.* grumpy. ❷ *adv.* grumpily

**Brumm-: ~kreisel** *der* humming top; **~schädel** *der* (*ugs.*) thick head; **~ton** *der; Pl.* **~töne** humming noise

**brünett** /bryˈnɛt/ *Adj.* dark-haired ‹person›; dark ‹hair›; **sie ist ~:** she's [a] brunette

**Brünette** *die;* ~, **~n** brunette

**Brunft** /brʊnft/ *die;* ~, **Brünfte** /ˈbrʏnftə/ (*Jägerspr.*) ⇒ **Brunst**

**brunften** *itr. V.* (*Jägerspr.*) ⇒ **brunsten**

**Brunft·hirsch** *der* (*Jägerspr.*) rutting stag

**brunftig** *Adj.* (*Jägerspr.*) rutting ‹male animal›; ‹female animal› in *or* on heat

**Brunft-: ~schrei** *der* (*Jägerspr.*) bell; **~zeit** (*Jägerspr.*) ⇒ **Brunstzeit**

**Brunnen** /ˈbrʊnən/ *der;* **~s, ~** **A** well; (*fig. geh.*) fountain (*literary*); **den ~ [erst] zudecken, wenn das Kind hineingefallen ist** lock the stable door after the horse has bolted (*fig.*); **B** (*Spring~*) fountain; **C** (*Wasser einer Heilquelle*) spring water; **~ trinken** take the waters *pl.*

**Brunnen-: ~becken** *das* basin [of a/the fountain]; **~figur** *die* figure on a/the fountain; **~haus** *das* pump room; **~kresse** *die* watercress; **~kur** *die* [spa] cure; **eine ~kur machen** take a cure/a course of treatment at a spa; **~putzer** *der: in* **schaffen wie ein ~putzer** (*ugs., bes. südwestd.*) slave away; work like a horse; **~vergifter** *der;* **~~s, ~~, ~vergifterin** *die;* **~~nen** water poisoner; (*fig. abwertend*) troublemaker; **~vergiftung** *die* water poisoning; (*fig. abwertend*) troublemaking

**Brünnlein** /ˈbrʏnlain/ *das;* **~s, ~** **A** [little] well; **B** (*Springbrunnen*) [little] fountain

**Brunst** /brʊnst/ *die;* ~, **Brünste** /ˈbrʏnstə/ (*von männlichen Tieren*) rut; (*von weiblichen Tieren*) heat; **Männchen/Weibchen in der ~:** rutting males/females in *or* on heat

**brunsten** *itr. V.* ‹male animal› rut; ‹female animal› be in *or* on heat

**brünstig** /ˈbrʏnstɪç/ ❶ *Adj.* rutting ‹male animal›; ‹female animal› in *or* on heat. ❷ *adv.* **~ röhren** bell

**Brunst-: ~schrei** *der* bell; **~zeit** *die* (*bei männlichen Tieren*) rut; rutting season; (*bei weiblichen Tieren*) [season of] heat

**brunzen** /ˈbrʊntsn̩/ *itr. V.* (*landsch. derb*) [have a] piss (*coarse*); take a leak (*sl.*)

**brüsk** /brʏsk/ ❶ *Adj.* brusque; abrupt. ❷ *adv.* brusquely; abruptly

**brüskieren** *tr. V.* offend; (*stärker*) insult; (*schneiden*) snub

**Brüskierung** *die;* ~, **~en** ⇒ **brüskieren**: piece of offensive behaviour; insult; snub

**Brüssel** /ˈbrʏsl̩/ (*das*); **~s** ▶ 700 Brussels

**Brüsseler** ▶ 700 ❶ *indekl. Adj.* Brussels; **~ Spitzen** Brussels lace *sing.* ❷ *der;* **~s, ~:** inhabitant of Brussels; (*von Geburt*) native of Brussels; ⇒ *auch* **Kölner**

**Brüsselerin** *die;* ~, **~nen** ⇒ **Brüsseler 2**

**Brust** /brʊst/ *die;* ~, **Brüste** /ˈbrʏstə/ **A** ▶ 471 chest; (*fig. geh.*) breast; heart; **~ an ~:** face to face; **sich in die ~ werfen** puff oneself up; **mit geschwellter ~:** proudly; as proud as a peacock; **er sang aus voller ~:** he sang lustily; **einen zur ~ nehmen** (*ugs.*) have a drink or two; **schwach auf der ~ sein** (*ugs.: anfällig sein*) have a weak chest; (*ugs.: wenig Geld haben*) be short [of money]; **B** ▶ 471 (*der Frau*) breast; **einem Kind die ~ geben** breastfeed a baby; **C** (*Hähnchen~*) breast; (*Rinder~*) brisket; **D** (*Sport*) breaststroke

**Brust-: ~bein** *das* ▶ 471 breastbone; **~beutel** *der* purse (*worn around the neck*); **~drüse** *die* ▶ 471 (*Anat.*) mammary gland

**brüsten** /ˈbrʏstn̩/ *refl. V.* (*abwertend*) **sich mit etw. ~:** boast *or* brag about sth.

**brust-, Brust-: ~fell·entzündung** *die* ▶ 474 (*Med.*) pleurisy; **~flosse** *die* (*Zool.*) (*bei Fischen*) pectoral fin; (*beim Wal*) flipper; **~haar** *das* hair on the chest; chest hair; **~harnisch** *der* (*hist.*) breastplate; **~hoch** *Adj.* chest-high; **~höhe** *die:* **in ~höhe** at chest height; **~höhle** *die* ▶ 471 (*Anat.*) thoracic cavity; **~kasten** (*ugs.*) ▶ 471 chest; **~kind** *das* (*ugs.*) breastfed baby; **~korb** *der* ▶ 471 (*Anat.*) thorax (*Anat.*); **~krebs** *der* breast cancer; cancer of the breast; **~schutz** *der* (*Fechten*) plastron; **~schwimmen** *itr. unr. V.; nur im Inf.* do [the] breaststroke; **~schwimmen** *das* breaststroke; **~stimme** *die* (*Musik*) chest-voice; **~stück** *das* (*Kochk.*) breast; (*vom Rind*) brisket; **~tasche** *die* breast pocket; (*Innentasche*) inside breast pocket; (*an der Latzhose*) front pocket; **~tee** *der* pectoral tea; **~ton** *der; Pl.* **~töne** (*Musik*) chest tone; **im ~ton der Überzeugung** (*fig.*) with utter conviction; **~tuch** *das; Pl.* **~tücher** neckerchief (*worn with traditional costume*); **~umfang** *der* chest measurement; (*bei Frauen*) bust measurement

**Brüstung** *die;* ~, **~en** **A** parapet; (*Balkon~*) balustrade; (*Logen~*) ledge; **B** (*Fenster~*) breast

**Brust-: ~warze** *die* ▶ 471 nipple; **~wickel** *der* (*Med.*) chest compress; **~wirbel** *der* ▶ 471 (*Anat.*) thoracic vertebra

**Brut** /bruːt/ *die;* ~, **~en** **A** (*das Brüten*) brooding; **B** (*Jungtiere, auch fig. scherzh.: Kinder*) brood; **C** (*abwertend: Gesindel*) mob

**brutal** /bruˈtaːl/ ❶ *Adj.* brutal; violent ‹attack, programme, etc.›; brute ‹force, strength›. ❷ *adv.* brutally

**brutalisieren** *tr. V.* brutalize

**Brutalisierung** *die;* **~:** brutalization

**Brutalität** /brutaliˈtɛːt/ *die;* ~, **~en** **A** brutality; **B** (*Handlung*) act of brutality *or* violence

**Brut·apparat** *der* incubator

**brüten** /ˈbryːtn̩/ ❶ *itr. V.* **A** brood; **B** (*geh.: lasten*) hang heavily; **~de Hitze** stifling heat; **~d heiß** (*ugs.*) boiling *or* stifling hot; **C** (*grübeln*) ponder (**über** + *Dat.* over); **über einem Plan ~:** work on a plan; **in dumpfes Brüten versinken** *od.* **verfallen** fall to brooding. ❷ *tr. V.* (*Kernphysik*) breed

***brütend·heiß** ⇒ **brüten 1B**

**Brüter** *der;* **~s, ~** (*Kernphysik*) breeder; **schneller ~:** fast breeder

**Brut-: ~henne** *die* sitting hen; **~hitze** *die* (*ugs.*) stifling *or* sweltering heat; **~kasten** *der* incubator; **in ihrem Haus ist eine Hitze wie in einem ~kasten** it's like an oven in her house; **~pflege** *die* (*Zool.*) care of the brood; **~reaktor** *der* (*Kernphysik*) breeder reactor; **~stätte** *die* breeding ground; (*fig.*) breeding ground (*Gen.*, **für** for); hotbed (*Gen.*, **für** for)

**brutto** /'brʊto/ *Adv.* ▶353 gross; **~ 4 000 DM, 4 000 DM ~:** 4,000 marks gross; **~ 800 kg** 800 kilos gross

**Brutto-: ~einkommen** *das* gross income; **~ertrag** *der* gross return; **~gehalt** *das* gross salary; **~gewicht** *das* gross weight; **~inlands·produkt** *das* (*Wirtsch.*) gross domestic product; **~preis** *der* full price; **~raum·zahl** *die* gross register tonnage; **~register·tonne** *die* (*Seew.*) gross register[ed] ton; **~sozial·produkt** *das* (*Wirtsch.*) gross national product

**brutzeln** /'brʊtsl̩n/ ❶ *itr. V.* sizzle; **die Kartoffeln müssen noch 10 Minuten ~:** the potatoes have to fry [gently] for another ten minutes. ❷ *tr. V.* (*ugs.*) fry [up]; **sich** (*Dat.*) **etw. ~:** fry oneself sth.

**Bruyère·holz** /bry'jɛ:r-/ *das* brierwood

**BSE** /beɛs'e:/ *die* ▶474 BSE

**Btx** /be:te:'ɪks/ *Abk.* **Bildschirmtext**

**Bub** /bu:p/ *der;* **~en, ~en** (*südd., österr., schweiz.*) boy; lad

**Bübchen** /'by:pçən/ *das;* **~s, ~** (*südd., österr., schweiz.*) [little] boy; [little] lad

**Bube** /'bu:bə/ *der;* **~n, ~n** Ⓐ (*Kartenspiele*) jack; knave; Ⓑ (*veralt. abwertend*) scoundrel; rogue; knave; **der böse ~:** the bad boy

**Buben-: ~streich** *der* Ⓐ childish prank; Ⓑ (*veralt.: Übeltat*) knavish trick; **~stück** *das* (*veralt.*) knavish trick

**Bubi** /'bu:bi/ *der;* **~s, ~s** Ⓐ [little] boy *or* lad *or* fellow; Ⓑ (*salopp abwertend: Schnösel*) young lad

**Bubi-: ~kopf** *der* bobbed hair[cut]; bob; **sie hat sich** (*Dat.*) **einen ~kopf schneiden lassen** she had her hair bobbed; **~kragen** *der* (*veralt.*) Peter Pan collar

**Bübin** *die;* **~, ~nen** scoundrel

**bübisch** /'by:bɪʃ/ ❶ *Adj.* Ⓐ mischievous; Ⓑ (*veralt. abwertend: schurkisch*) villainous. ❷ *adv.;* ⇒ 1: mischievously; villainously

**Buch** /bu:x/ *das;* **~[e]s, Bücher** /'by:çɐ/ Ⓐ book; **über seinen Büchern sitzen** pore over one's books; **das Goldene ~ der Stadt** the visitors' book of the town; **sie ist ein aufgeschlagenes** *od.* **offenes ~ für mich** I can read her like an open book; **das ~ der Bücher** the Book of Books; **wie ein ~ reden** (*ugs.*) talk nineteen to the dozen; **ein Detektiv/ein Faulpelz, wie er im ~e steht** a classic [example of a] detective/a complete lazybones; **ein ~ mit sieben Siegeln** a closed book; a complete mystery; **sich [mit etw.] ins ~ der Geschichte eintragen** (*geh.*) go down in the annals *pl.* of history [for sth.]; **ein schlaues ~** (*ugs.*) a reference book/textbook; **die fünf Bücher Mose** the Pentateuch; **das erste/zweite/dritte/vierte/fünfte ~ Mose** Genesis/Exodus/Leviticus/Numbers/Deuteronomy; Ⓑ (*Dreh~*) script; Ⓒ (*Geschäfts~*) book; **er führt selbst die Bücher** he keeps his own books *or* accounts; **über etw.** (*Akk.*) **~ führen/genau ~ führen** keep a record of sth./keep an exact record of sth.; **zu ~[e] schlagen** (*den Etat beeinflussen*) be reflected in the budget; (*ins Gewicht fallen*) have a big influence; **es schlägt mit ca. 200 DM zu ~[e]** it makes a difference of about 200 marks; Ⓓ (*Wettliste*) book; **~ machen** make a book

**Buch-: ~besprechung** *die* book review; **~binder** *der* ▶159 bookbinder; **~binderei** *die* Ⓐ bookbinding; Ⓑ (*Betrieb*) bindery; **~binderin** *die;* **~~, ~~nen** ▶159 bookbinder; **~block** *der; Pl.* **~blöcke** *od.* **~~s** book block; **~deckel** *der* [book] cover (*front or back*); **~druck** *der* letterpress printing; **im ~druck** in letterpress; **~drucker** *der* ▶159 printer; **~druckerei** *die* Ⓐ letterpress printing; Ⓑ (*Betrieb*) printing works; **~druckerin** *die* ▶159 printer; **~drucker·kunst** *die* art of printing

**Buche** *die;* **~, ~n** Ⓐ beech [tree]; Ⓑ (*Holz*) beech[wood]

**Buch-: ~ecker** *die* beech nut; **~einband** *der* binding; [book] cover

**buchen**[1] *tr. V.* Ⓐ enter; **etw. auf ein Konto ~:** enter sth. into an account; **etw. als Erfolg ~** (*fig.*) count sth. as a success; **einen Sieg für sich ~** (*fig.*) chalk up a victory; Ⓑ (*vorbestellen*) book ‹holiday, trip, flight›; book, reserve ‹seat, berth, room›

**buchen**[2] *Adj.* beech; of beech[wood] *postpos.*

**Buchen-: ~hain** *der* beech grove; **~holz** *das* beechwood; **~wald** *der* beech wood

**Bücher-: ~bord** *das* Ⓐ ⇒ **~brett**; Ⓑ ⇒ **~regal**; **~brett** *das* bookshelf

**Bücherei** *die;* **~, ~en** library

**Bücher-: ~freund** *der,* **~freundin** *die* book lover; **~gestell** *das* bookshelves *pl.;* **~kiste** *die* book crate; (*Kiste mit ~n*) crate of books; **~narr** *der,* **~närrin** *die* book fiend; **sie ist eine wahre ~närrin** she's really mad on books; **~regal** *das* bookshelves *pl.;* **~schrank** *der* bookcase; **~sendung** *die:* **etw. als ~sendung aufgeben/schicken** send sth. at printed paper rate; **das ist eine ~sendung** this can be/has been sent at printed paper rate; **~stube** *die* bookshop; **~stütze** *die* bookend; **~verbot** *das* (*kath. Kirche*) ban on books; **~verbrennung** *die* burning of books; **~wand** *die* Ⓐ bookshelf unit; Ⓑ (*Wand mit ~regal*) wall of bookshelves; **~weisheit** *die* (*abwertend*) book learning; **~wurm** *der* (*scherzh.*) bookworm

**Buch-: ~fink** *der* chaffinch; **~form** *die: in* **in ~form** in book form; **~führung** *die* bookkeeping; **einfache/doppelte ~führung** single/double-entry bookkeeping; **~gemeinschaft** *die* book club; **~halter** *der,* **~halterin** *die* ▶159 bookkeeper

**buchhalterisch** ❶ *Adj.* bookkeeping *attrib.* ❷ *adv.* **~ gesehen** from a bookkeeping point of view

**Buch-: ~haltung** *die* Ⓐ accountancy; Ⓑ (*Abteilung*) accounts department; **~handel** *der* book trade; **im ~handel erhältlich** available from bookshops; **~händler** *der,* **~händlerin** *die* ▶159 bookseller; **~handlung** *die* bookshop; **„~handlung Franz Maier“** 'Franz Maier's Bookshop'; **~hülle** *die* [book] cover; **~illustration** *die* book illustration; **~klub** *der* book club; **~kritik** *die* book review; **~laden** *der; Pl.* **~läden** ⇒ **~handlung**

**Büchlein** *das;* **~s, ~:** little book

**Buch-: ~macher** *der,* **~macherin** *die* ▶159 bookmaker; bookie (*coll.*); **~malerei** *die* illumination; **~messe** *die* book fair; **~prüfer** *der,* **~prüferin** *die* auditor; **~rücken** *der* spine

**Buchs·baum** /'bʊks-/ *der* box [tree]

**Buchse** /'bʊksə/ *die;* **~, ~n** Ⓐ (*Elektrot.*) socket; Ⓑ (*Technik*) bush; liner

**Büchse** /'bʏksə/ *die;* **~, ~n** Ⓐ tin; **die ~ der Pandora** Pandora's box; Ⓑ (*ugs.: Sammel~*) [collecting] box; Ⓒ (*Gewehr*) rifle; (*Schrot~*) shotgun; **jmdm. vor die ~ kommen** come into sb.'s sights *pl.*

**Büchsen-: ~fleisch** *das* tinned (*Brit.*) *or* (*Amer.*) canned meat; **~gemüse** *das* tinned (*Brit.*) *or* (*Amer.*) canned vegetables *pl.;* **~macher** *der,* **~macherin** *die* ▶159 gunsmith; **~milch** *die* tinned (*Brit.*) *or* (*Amer.*) canned milk; **~öffner** *der* tin-opener (*Brit.*); can opener (*Amer.*)

**Buchstabe** /'bu:xʃta:bə/ *der;* **~ns, ~n** letter; (*Druckw.*) character; **ein großer/kleiner ~:** a capital [letter]/small letter; **nach dem ~n des Gesetzes** (*fig.*) according to the letter of the law; **sich auf seine vier ~n setzen** (*ugs. scherzh.*) sit [oneself] down

**buchstaben-, Buchstaben-: ~getreu** ❶ *Adj.* literal; ❷ *adv.* to the letter; **~rätsel** *das* word puzzle; **~rechnung** *die* simple algebra; **~schloss, *~schloß** *das* letter-lock; **~schrift** *die* alphabetic script; **~wort** *das; Pl.* **~wörter** acronym

**buchstabieren** *tr. V.* Ⓐ spell; Ⓑ (*mühsam lesen*) spell out

**buchstäblich** /'bu:xʃtɛ:plɪç/ ❶ *Adv.* literally. ❷ *Adj.* literal

**Buch·stütze** *die* ⇒ **Bücherstütze**

**Bucht** /bʊxt/ *die;* **~, ~en** Ⓐ bay; Ⓑ (*für Schweine*) sty; (*für Pferde*) stall

**Buchtel** /'bʊxtl̩/ *die;* **~, ~n** (*österr.*) yeast pastry with jam or poppy-seed filling

**Buch·titel** *der* title

**Buchung** *die;* **~, ~en** Ⓐ entry; Ⓑ ⇒ **buchen**[1] B: booking; reservation

**Buchungs·maschine** *die* accounting machine

**Buch-: ~weizen** *der* buckwheat; **~wesen** *das* book trade; (*Studienfach*) the book trade; **~wissen** *das* (*abwertend*) book learning; **das ist nur ~wissen** that is only knowledge gained from books; **~zeichen** *das* bookmark[er]

**Bücke** /'bʏkə/ *die;* **~, ~n** (*Turnen*) stoop vault

**Buckel** /'bʊkl/ *der;* **~s, ~** Ⓐ (*ugs.: Rücken*) back; **den ~ voll kriegen** get a good hiding (*coll.*); **einen ~ machen** ‹cat› arch its back; ‹person› hunch one's shoulders; **rutsch mir den ~ runter!** (*salopp*) get lost! (*coll.*); **der kann** *od.* **soll mir mal den ~ runterrutschen** (*salopp*) he can get lost *or* take a running jump (*coll.*); **den ~ voll Schulden haben** be up to one's neck *or* ears in debt; **den ~ hinhalten** (*fig.*) take the blame; carry the can (*Brit. coll.*); **einen krummen ~ machen, den ~ krumm machen** (*fig.*) bow and scrape; kowtow; **genug/viel auf dem ~ haben** (*fig.*) have enough/a lot on one's plate (*fig.*); **schon 40 Jahre** *od.* **Jährchen auf dem ~ haben** be 40 already; **wenn du so viele Jahre auf dem ~ hast wie ich** when you are as old as I am; ⇒ *auch* **breit** 1 A; Ⓑ (*Rückenverkrümmung*) hunchback; hump; Ⓒ (*ugs.: Hügel*) hillock; Ⓓ (*ugs.: gewölbte Stelle*) bump

**buckelig** ⇒ **bucklig**

**buckeln** *itr. V.* (*ugs.*) Ⓐ (*abwertend*) bow and scrape; kowtow; **vor jmdm. ~:** kowtow to sb.; **nach oben ~ und nach unten treten** bow to superiors and kick underlings; Ⓑ ‹cat› arch its back

**Buckel·rind** *das* zebu

**bücken** /'bʏkn̩/ *refl. V.* bend down; **sich nach etw. ~:** bend down to pick sth. up

**bucklig** *Adj.* Ⓐ hunchbacked; humpbacked; Ⓑ (*ugs.: uneben*) bumpy

**Bucklige** *der/die; adj. Dekl.* hunchback; humpback

**Bückling**[1] /'bʏklɪŋ/ *der;* **~s, ~e** (*ugs. scherzh.: Verbeugung*) bow

**Bückling**[2] *der;* **~s, ~e** (*Hering*) smoked herring; bloater

**Büdchen** /'by:tçən/ *das;* **~s, ~:** little hut

**Buddel** /'bʊdl/ *die;* **~, ~n** (*nordd.*) bottle

**Buddelei** /'bʊdə'lai/ *die;* **~, ~en** (*ugs. abwertend*) digging *no pl.;* **eine ~:** a piece of digging

**Buddel·kasten** *der* sandpit

**buddeln** (*ugs.*) ❶ *itr. V.* dig; **die Kinder ~ im Garten/im Sand** the children are digging about in the garden/sand. ❷ *tr. V.* Ⓐ dig ‹hole, tunnel›; Ⓑ (*ausgraben*) dig up; **etw. aus der Erde ~:** dig sth. up out of the ground

**Buddha** /'bʊda/ *der;* **~s, ~s** Buddha

**Buddhismus** *der;* **~:** Buddhism *no art.*

**Buddhist** *der;* **~en, ~en, Buddhistin** *die;* **~, ~nen** Buddhist

**buddhistisch** ❶ *Adj.* Buddhist *attrib.* ❷ *adv.* **~ beeinflusst** influenced by Buddhism

**Bude** /'bu:də/ *die;* **~, ~n** Ⓐ kiosk; (*Markt~*) stall; (*Jahrmarkts~*) booth; Ⓑ (*Bau~*) hut; Ⓒ (*ugs.: Haus*) dump (*coll.*); Ⓓ (*ugs.: Zimmer*) room; digs *pl.* (*Brit. coll.*); **Leben in die ~ bringen** liven the place up; **mir fällt die ~ auf den Kopf** I'm feeling *or* getting claustrophobic; **[jmdm.] die ~ auf den Kopf stellen** turn the *or* sb.'s place upside down; **jmdm. die ~ einrennen** pester *or*

*old spelling (see note on page 1707)

badger sb.; **jmdm. auf die ~ rücken** (*mit einem Anliegen*) go/come round to sb.'s place; (*als Besuch*) drop in on sb.; **E** (*ugs. abwertend: Laden, Lokal*) outfit (*coll.*)

**Budel** /'bu:dl̩/ *die;* ~, **~n** (*bayr., österr.*) counter

**Buden-:** **~besitzer** *der*, **~besitzerin** *die* stallholder; stallkeeper; **~zauber** *der* (*ugs. veralt.*) **~zauber machen** have a rave-up (*coll.*)

**Budget** /bʏ'd͜ʒe:/ *das;* **~s, ~s** budget

**budgetär** /bʏd͜ʒe'tɛ:ɐ̯/ *Adj.* budgetary

**Budget-:** **~beratung** *die* budget discussion; **~entwurf** *der* draft budget

**Budike** /bu'di:kə/ *die;* ~, **~n** (*berl.*) **A** little shop; **B** (*Lokal*) pub (*Brit.*); bar

**Budiker** *der;* **~s,** ~ (*berl.*) landlord

**Budikerin** *die;* ~, **~nen** landlady

**Budo** /'bu:do/ *das;* **~s** budo

**Büfett** /by'fɛt/ *das;* **~[e]s, ~s** *od.* **~e** **A** sideboard; **B** (*Schanktisch*) bar; **C** (*Verkaufstisch*) counter; **D** **kaltes ~:** cold buffet; **E** (*schweiz.: Bahnhofsrestaurant*) station restaurant

**Büfett·fräulein** *das* barmaid (*Brit.*)

**Büfettier** /byfɛ'tie:/ *der;* **~s, ~s** barman

**Büffel** /'bʏfl̩/ *der;* **~s, ~:** buffalo

**Büffelei** *die* (*ugs.*) swotting *no pl.* (*Brit. sl.*)

**Büffel-:** **~herde** *die* herd of buffalo; **~leder** *das* buffalo hide

**büffeln** (*ugs.*) **1** *itr. V.* swot (*Brit. sl.*); cram. **2** *tr. V.* swot up (*Brit. sl.*); cram

**Buffet** /by'fe:/ *das;* **~s, ~s,** (*österr. auch:*) **Büffet** /by'fɛt/ *das;* **Büffets, Büffets** ⇒ **Büfett**

**Buffo** /'bʊfo/ *der;* **~s, ~s** *od.* **Buffi** buffo

**Bug** /bu:k/ *der;* **~[e]s, ~e** *u.* **Büge** /'by:gə/ **A** *Pl.:* **~e** (*Schiffs~*) bow; (*Flugzeug~*) nose; **jmdm. eine vor den ~ knallen** (*salopp*) (*einen Schlag versetzen*) sock (*coll.*) *or* give sb. one; (*einschüchtern*) sock (*coll.*) *or* give it to sb.; ⇒ *auch* **Schuss** A; **B** (*Schulterstück*) shoulder; **C** *Pl.:* **Büge** (*Technik*) brace; strut

**Bügel** /'by:gl̩/ *der;* **~s,** ~ **A** hanger; **über einen/einem ~:** on a hanger; **B** (*Steig~*) stirrup; **C** (*Brillen~*) earpiece; **D** (*an einer Tasche, Geldbörse*) frame; **E** (*Griff einer Handtasche*) handle; **F** (*Stromabnehmer*) bow; pantograph; **G** (*Säge~*) frame; **H** (*Gewehr~*) trigger guard

**bügel-, Bügel-:** **~automat** *der* ⇒ **~maschine**; **~brett** *das* ironing board; **~eisen** *das* iron; **~falte** *die* [trouser] crease; **~frei** *Adj.* non-iron; **~maschine** *die* ironing machine

**bügeln** *tr., itr. V.* iron ‹clothes›; ⇒ *auch* **gebügelt**

**Bügel·säge** *die* hacksaw

**Buggy** /'bagi/ *der;* **~s, ~s** buggy

**Bügler** *der;* **~s,** ~, **Büglerin** *die;* ~, **~nen** ironer

**Bug-:** **~rad** *das* (*Flugw.*) nose wheel; **~see** *die* (*Seemannsspr.*) ⇒ **~welle**

**Bugsier·dampfer** *der* (*Seemannsspr.*) tug [boat]

**bugsieren** /bʊ'ksi:rən/ *tr. V.* **A** (*ugs.*) shift; manœuvre; steer ‹person›; **B** (*Seemannsspr.*) tow

**Bug-:** **~spriet** *das od. der* (*Seemannsspr.*) bowsprit; **~welle** *die* (*Seemannsspr.*) bow wave

**buh** /bu:/ *Interj.* boo; **~ rufen** boo

**Buh** *das;* **~s, ~s** (*ugs.*) boo; **die ~s** the boos *or* booing *sing.*

**Buhei** /bu'hai̯/ *das;* **~s** (*bes. westd.*) fuss

**buhen** *itr. V.* (*ugs.*) boo

**Bühl** /by:l/ *der;* **~[e]s, ~e** (*südd., schweiz., österr.*) hill

**Buhle**[1] /'bu:lə/ *der;* **~n, ~n** (*dichter. veralt.*) paramour

**Buhle**[2] *die;* ~, **~n** (*dichter. veralt.*) paramour; mistress

**buhlen** /'bu:lən/ *itr. V.* **A** (*abwertend*) **um jmds. Gunst ~:** court sb.'s favour; **um jmds. Anerkennung ~:** strive for recognition by sb.; **um jmdn. ~** (*veralt.*) court *or* woo sb.; **B** (*veralt.: eine Liebschaft haben*) **mit jmdm. ~:** have a liaison with sb.

**Buhler** *der;* **~s,** ~ **A** ⇒ **Buhle**[1]; **B** (*geh. abwertend: Werber*) wooer

**Buhlerin** *die;* ~, **~nen** ⇒ **Buhle**[2]

**buhlerisch** (*veralt. abwertend*) **1** *Adj.* **A** amorous; **B** (*werbend*) ingratiating. **2** *adv.* **A** amorously; **B** (*werbend*) ingratiatingly

**Buh·mann** *der* (*ugs.*) **A** whipping boy; scapegoat; **B** (*Schreckgestalt*) bogyman

**Buhne** /'bu:nə/ *die;* ~, **~n** groyne

**Bühne** /'by:nə/ *die;* ~, **~n** **A** stage; **es gab mehrmals Beifall auf offener ~:** there were several rounds of applause during the play; **ein Stück auf die ~ bringen** put on *or* stage a play; **seit Monaten steht er jeden Abend als Faust auf der ~:** he has been playing Faust [on the stage] every evening for months; **auf der politischen ~** (*fig.*) on the political scene; **über die ~ bringen** (*ugs.*) finish ‹process›; get ‹event› over; **über die ~ gehen** (*ugs.*) go off; **von der ~ des Lebens abtreten** (*geh. verhüll.*) depart this life; **von der ~ abtreten** disappear from *or* leave the scene; **B** (*Theater*) theatre; **die Städtischen ~n Köln** the Cologne municipal theatres; **das Stück ging über alle ~n** the play was put on *or* staged in all the theatres; **an** *od.* **bei der ~ sein** be on the stage *or* in the theatre; **zur ~ gehen** go on the stage *or* into the theatre; **C** (*landsch.: Dachboden*) attic; loft; **D** (*landsch.: Heuboden*) [hay] loft; **E** (*Hebe~*) lift; ramp

**bühnen-, Bühnen-:** **~anweisung** *die* stage direction; **~arbeiter** *der*, **~arbeiterin** *die* ▶ 159 stagehand; **~aus·sprache** *die* standard *or* received pronunciation; **~ausstattung** *die* stage set; **~autor** *der*, **~autorin** *die* playwright; **~bearbeitung** *die* stage adaptation; **~beleuchtung** *die* stage lighting; **~bild** *das* [stage] set; **~bildner** *der;* **~~s, ~~, ~bildnerin** *die;* **~~, ~~nen** stage *or* set designer; **~dekoration** *die* [stage] setting; stage decoration; **~dichtung** *die* drama; theatre; **~effekt** *der* stage effect; **~eingang** *der* stage door; **~erfahrung** *die* stage experience; **~erfolg** *der* **A** stage success; **das Stück hatte einen großen ~erfolg** the play was a big success; **B** (*Theaterstück*) stage hit; **ein großer ~erfolg am Broadway** a big Broadway hit; **~fassung** *die* ⇒ **~bearbeitung**; **~gerecht** *Adj.* suitable for the stage; stage ‹adaptation›; **etw. ~gerecht bearbeiten** adapt sth. for the stage; **~himmel** *der* cyclorama; **~kunst** *die* ⇒ **Schauspielkunst**; **~maler** *der*, **~malerin** *die* scene-painter; **~manuskript** *das* script; **~musik** *die* incidental music; **~raum** *der* stage [and backstage]; **~reif** *Adj.* ‹play etc.› ready for the stage; ‹imitation etc.› worthy of the stage; dramatic ‹entrance etc.›; **~schaffende** *der/die; adj. Dekl.* dramatic artist; **~stück** *das* stage play; **~technik** *die* stage equipment *or* machinery; **~werk** *das* work for the stage; (*im engeren Sinne: dramatisches Werk*) dramatic work; **~wirksam** *Adj.* effective on the stage *pred.*; **~wirkung** *die* dramatic effectiveness

**Buh·ruf** *der* boo

**buk** /bu:k/ *1. u. 3. Pers. Sg. Prät. v.* **backen**

**Bukarest** /'bu:karɛst/ (*das*); **~s** ▶ 700 Bucharest

**Bukett** /bu'kɛt/ *das;* **~s, ~s** *od.* **~e** **A** (*geh.*) bouquet; **ein ~ Rosen** a bouquet of roses; **B** (*bei Wein*) bouquet

**Bukolik** /bu'ko:lɪk/ *die;* ~ (*Literaturw.*) bucolic *or* pastoral poetry

**bukolisch** *Adj.* **A** (*Literaturw.*) bucolic; pastoral; **b** (*geh.: idyllisch*) idyllic

**Bulette** /bu'lɛtə/ *die;* ~, **~n** (*bes. berl.*) rissole; **ran an die ~n!** (*ugs.*) go to it! (*coll.*)

**Bulgare** /bʊl'ga:rə/ *der;* **~n, ~n** Bulgarian

**Bulgarien** /bʊl'ga:ri̯ən/ (*das*); **~s** Bulgaria

**Bulgarin** *die;* ~, **~nen** Bulgarian; ⇒ *auch* **-in**

**bulgarisch** *Adj.* ▶ 696 Bulgarian; ⇒ *auch* **deutsch, Deutsch**

**Bulk·ladung** /'bʌlk-/ *die* (*Seemannsspr.*) bulk cargo

**Bull-** /bʊl-/: **~auge** *das* circular porthole; **~dogge** *die* bulldog

**Bulldozer** /'bʊldo:zɐ/ *der;* **~s, ~:** bulldozer

**Bulle**[1] /'bʊlə/ *der;* **~n, ~n** **A** bull; **B** (*ugs. abwertend: Mann*) great ox; big bull; **C** (*salopp abwertend: Polizist*) cop (*coll.*); **die ~n kommen!** here come the fuzz (*sl.*) *or* the cops (*coll.*)!

**Bulle**[2] *die;* ~, **~n** **A** (*päpstlicher Erlass*) bull; ⇒ *auch* **golden**; **B** (*Urkundensiegel*) bulla

**bullen-, Bullen-:** **~beißer** *der;* **~~s, ~~** **A** ⇒ **Bulldogge**; **B** (*ugs. abwertend: Mensch*) aggressive fellow; **~hitze** *die* (*ugs.*) sweltering *or* boiling heat; **~kalb** *das* bull calf; **~stark** *Adj.* (*ugs.*) as strong as an ox *pred.*

**bullern** /'bʊlɐn/ *itr. V.* (*ugs.*) ‹water› bubble [away]; ‹fire etc.› roar [away]

**Bulletin** /bʏl'tɛ̃:/ *das;* **~s, ~s** bulletin

**bullig** **1** *Adj.* **A** beefy, stocky ‹person, appearance, etc.›; chunky, hefty ‹car›; **B** (*drückend*) sweltering, boiling ‹heat›. **2** *adv.* swelteringly; **~ heiß** boiling hot

**Bull·terrier** *der* bull terrier

**Bully** /'bʊli/ *das;* **~s, ~s** (*Sport*) bully; **das ~ ausführen** take a bully

**bum** /bʊm/ *Interj.* bang

**Bumerang** /'bu:məraŋ/ *der;* **~s, ~e** *od.* **~s** boomerang; **es erwies sich als ~** (*fig.*) it boomeranged [on him/her/them]

**Bumerang·effekt** *der* boomerang effect

**Bummel** /'bʊml̩/ *der;* **~s,** ~ **A** stroll (**durch** around); **einen ~ [durch den Park] machen** go for *or* take a stroll [in the park]; **B** (*durch Lokale*) pub crawl (*coll.*)

**Bummelant** /bʊmə'lant/ *der;* **~en, ~en**, **Bummelantin** *die;* ~, **~nen** (*ugs. abwertend*) **A** slowcoach (*Brit.*); slowpoke (*Amer.*); dawdler; **B** (*Faulenzer*) idler; loafer

**Bummelei** *die;* ~, **~en** (*ugs. abwertend*) **A** dawdling; **B** (*Faulenzerei*) idling *or* loafing about

**bummelig** (*ugs. abwertend*) **1** *Adj.* **A** slow; **B** (*nachlässig*) slovenly; slipshod. **2** *adv.* **A** slowly; **B** (*nachlässig*) in a slovenly *or* slipshod way

**Bummel·liese** *die* (*ugs. abwertend*) slowcoach; dawdler

**bummeln** *itr. V.* **A** *mit sein* (*ugs.*) stroll (**durch** around); **[im Park] ~ gehen** go for *or* take a stroll [in the park]; **B** *mit sein* (*ugs.: durch Lokale*) go round the pubs (*Brit. coll.*); go on a pub crawl (*Brit. coll.*); **C** (*ugs. abwertend: trödeln*) dawdle; **bei den Schulaufgaben ~:** dawdle over one's homework; **D** (*ugs. abwertend: faulenzen*) laze about; do nothing

**Bummel-:** **~streik** *der* go-slow; (*bei Beamten usw.*) work to rule; **in einen ~streik treten** go on a go-slow; **~zug** *der* (*ugs.*) slow *or* stopping train

**bummern** /'bʊmɐn/ *itr. V.* (*landsch.*) bang; **gegen die Tür ~:** bang on the door

**Bummler** *der;* **~s,** ~, **Bummlerin** *die;* ~, **~nen** (*ugs.*) **A** (*Spaziergänger*) stroller; **B** ⇒ **Bummelant**

**bummlig** ⇒ **bummelig**

**bums** /bʊms/ *Interj.* bang!; **es machte laut ~:** there was a loud bang *or* thud

**Bums** *der;* **~es, ~e** **A** (*ugs.*) bang; (*dumpfer*) thud; thump; **B** (*salopp abwertend: Lokal*) dive (*coll.*); **C** (*salopp abwertend: Tanzvergnügen*) hop (*coll.*); **D** (*Fußballjargon*) **einen unerhörten ~ haben** have a tremendous shot

**bumsen** **1** *itr. V.* (*ugs.*) **A** *unpers.* **es bumste ganz furchtbar** there was a terrible bang/thud *or* thump; **es bumste an der Tür** there was a bang/thump on the door; **an dieser Kreuzung bumst es mindestens einmal am Tag** (*fig.*) there's at least one smash *or* crash a day at this junction; **hör auf, oder es bumst [gleich]!** (*fig.*) stop it, or you'll catch it [in a minute]! (*coll.*); **B** (*schlagen*) bang; (*dumpfer*) thump; **gegen die Tür ~:** bang/thump on the door; **C** *mit sein* (*stoßen*) bang; bash; **er ist mit dem Kopf gegen die Wand gebumst**

he banged *or* bashed his head on the wall; D (*salopp: koitieren*) have it off (*sl.*); screw (*coarse*).
2 *tr. V.* A (*Fußballjargon*) thump; B (*salopp: koitieren mit*) have it off with (*sl.*); screw (*coarse*); **gebumst werden** get laid (*sl.*); be screwed (*coarse*)

**bums-, Bums-: ~lokal** *das* (*ugs. abwertend*) dive (*coll.*); **~musik** *die* (*ugs. abwertend*) oompah music (*coll.*); **~voll** *Adj.* (*salopp*) full to bursting *pred.*

**Bund**[1] /bʊnt/ *der;* **~[e]s, Bünde** /'bʏndə/ A (*Verband, Vereinigung*) association; society; (*Bündnis, Pakt*) alliance; **der Dritte im ~e** (*fig.*) the third in the trio; **der Alte ~/der Neue ~** (*Rel.*) the Old/New Testament; **den ~ der Ehe eingehen, den ~ fürs Leben schließen** (*geh.*) enter into the bond of marriage; **mit jmdm. im ~e sein** *od.* **stehen** be in league with sb.; B (*föderativer Staat*) federation; **der ~ und die Länder** the Federation *or* Federal Government and the Länder *or* States; (*in Austria*) the Federation *or* Federal Government and the provinces; C (*ugs.: ~eswehr*) forces *pl; **beim ~:*** in the forces *pl.;* **zum ~ gehen** do one's military service; **er hat sich freiwillig zum ~ gemeldet** he joined up voluntarily; D (*an Röcken od. Hosen*) waistband; E (*an Instrumenten*) fret

**Bund**[2] *das;* **~[e]s, ~e** bunch; **ein ~ Petersilie/Mohrrüben/Spargel** a bunch of parsley/carrots/asparagus

**Bündchen** /'bʏntçən/ *das;* **~s, ~** (*am Hals*) [neck]band; (*am Ärmel*) [sleeve] band; (*an der Taille*) [waist]band; (*am Knöchel*) [ankle] band

**Bündel** /'bʏndl/ *das;* **~s, ~** A bundle; **ein ~ von Fragen** (*fig.*) a set *or* cluster of questions; **ein hilfloses/schreiendes ~** (*ugs.*) a helpless/howling little bundle; **jeder hat sein ~ zu tragen** (*fig.*) everybody has his cross to bear; **sein ~ packen** *od.* **schnüren** pack one's bags *pl.;* B (*Zusammengebundenes*) bundle; sheaf; C (*Geom.*) sheaf

**bündeln** *tr. V.* bundle up ‹newspapers, old clothes, rags, etc.›; tie ‹banknotes etc.› into bundles/a bundle; tie ‹flowers, radishes, carrots, etc.› into bunches/a bunch; sheave ‹straw, hay, etc.›

**bündel·weise** *Adv.* by the bundle; in bundles; (*bei Blumen, Möhren, Radieschen usw.*) by the bunch; in bunches

**bundes-, Bundes-: ~amt** *das* federal department (**für** of); (*schweiz.*) federal office (**für** of); **~angestellten·tarif** *der* [civil servants'] statutory salary scale; **~anleihe** *die* government bond; **~anstalt** *die* federal institute (**für** of); **~anwalt** *der* A Federal Prosecutor; B (*beim ~verwaltungsgericht*) prosecutor in the Supreme Administrative Court; C (*schweiz.*) public prosecutor; **~anwältin** *die* ⇨ **~anwalt**; **~anwaltschaft** *die* A Federal Supreme Court prosecutors *pl.;* B (*beim ~verwaltungsgericht*) Supreme Administrative Court prosecutors *pl.;* **~anzeiger** *der* federal gazette; **~arbeitsgericht** *das* Federal Labour Court; **~ausbildungs·förderungsgesetz** *das* Federal Education and Training Assistance Act; **~autobahn** *die* federal motorway; **~bahn** *die* Federal Railway; **~bank** *die* federal bank; **die Deutsche ~bank** the German Federal Bank; **~beamte** *der,* **~beamtin** *die* federal civil servant; **~behörde** *die* federal authority; **~bruder** *der* fellow member [of a/the students' association]; **~bürger** *der,* **~bürgerin** *die* German citizen; **~deutsch** *Adj.* West German; **der ~deutsche Alltag** everyday life in West Germany; **~deutsche** *der/die; adj. Dekl.* West German; **~ebene** *die:* **auf ~ebene** at federal *or* national level; **~eigen** *Adj.* federal-owned; nationalized; **~gebiet** *das* federal territory; **das ~gebiet** (*Deutschland*) Germany; **~genosse** *der,* **~genossin** *die* ally; **~gericht** *das* Federal Court; **~gerichts·hof** *der* Federal Supreme Court; **~gesetzblatt** *das* Federal Law Gazette; **~grenzschutz** *der* Federal Border Police; **~haupt·stadt** *die* federal capital; **~haus** *das* Federal Parliament; (*Gebäude*) federal parliament [building]; **~haushalt** *der* federal *or* national budget; **~heer** *das* (*österr., schweiz.*) [federal] armed forces *pl.;* **~kabinett** *das* Federal Cabinet; **~kanzlei** *die* Federal Chancellery; **~kanzler** *der* A Federal Chancellor; B (*schweiz.*) Chancellor of the Confederation; **~kanzler·amt** *das* Federal Chancellery; **~kanzlerin** *die* ⇨ **~kanzler**; **~kriminal·amt** *das* Federal Criminal Investigation Agency; **~lade** *die* (*jüd. Rel.*) Ark of the Covenant; **~land** *das* [federal] state; (*österr.*) province; **~liga** *die* national *or* federal division; **~ligist** /-lɪgɪst/ *der* **~~en, ~~en** team in the national *or* federal division; **~marine** *die* Federal Navy; West German Navy; **~minister** *der,* **~ministerin** *die* Federal Minister; **~ministerium** *das* Federal Ministry; **~mittel** *Pl.* federal funds; **~nachrichten·dienst** *der* Federal Intelligence Agency; **~post** *die* Federal Post Office; **~präsident** *der,* **~präsidentin** *die* A [Federal] President; B (*schweiz.*) President of the Confederation; **~rat** *der* A [Federal] Upper House of Parliament; Bundesrat; B (*österr., schweiz.*) Federal Council; **~rechnungs·hof** *der* Federal Audit Office; **~recht** *das* federal law; **~regierung** *die* Federal Government; **~republik** *die* federal republic; **die ~republik Deutschland** The Federal Republic of Germany; **~republikanisch** *Adj.* West German; **~richter** *der,* **~richterin** *die* federal judge; **~sieger** *der,* **~siegerin** *die* national winner; **~staat** *der* federal state; **~straße** *die* federal highway; ≈ A road (*Brit.*)

**Bundes·tag** *der* [Federal] Lower House of Parliament; Bundestag

**Bundestags-: ~abgeordnete** *der/die* member of parliament; member of the Bundestag; **~fraktion** *die* parliamentary group; group in the Bundestag; **~präsident** *der,* **~präsidentin** *die* President of the Bundestag; **~wahl** *die* parliamentary *or* general election

**bundes-, Bundes-: ~trainer** *der,* **~trainerin** *die* national team manager; national coach; **~treue** *die* federal allegiance; **~verband** *der* federal association; **~verband der Deutschen Industrie** Federation of German Industries; **~verdienst·kreuz** *das* Order of Merit of the Federal Republic; **~verfassung** *die* federal constitution; **~verfassungs·gericht** *das* Federal Constitutional Court; **~versammlung** *die* Federal Assembly; **~versicherungs·anstalt** *die* federal insurance institution; **die ~versicherungsanstalt für Angestellte** the Federal Insurance Institution [for salaried employees]; **~verwaltungs·gericht** *das* Supreme Administrative Court; **~wehr** *die* [Federal] Armed Forces *pl.;* **~weit** 1 *Adj.* nationwide; national; 2 *adv.* nationwide; nationally; **~zwang** *der* federal obligation

**Bund-: ~falten** *Pl.* pleats; **~falten·hose** *die* pleat[ed]-front trousers *pl.;* **~hose** *die* knee breeches

**bündig** /'bʏndɪç/ 1 *Adj.* A concise; succinct; B (*schlüssig*) conclusive; ⇨ *auch* **kurz** 1 B; C (*Bauw.*) flush; level. 2 *adv.* A concisely; succinctly; ⇨ *auch* **kurz** 2 B; B (*schlüssig*) conclusively; C (*Bauw.*) flush

**Bündigkeit** *die;* **~** A conciseness; succinctness; B (*Schlüssigkeit*) conclusiveness

**Bündnis** /'bʏntnɪs/ *das;* **~ses, ~se** alliance

**bündnis-, Bündnis-: ~frei** *Adj.* nonaligned; **~grüne** *der/die* (*Politik*) ⇨ **Grüne**[2]; **~partner** *der,* **~partnerin** *die* ally; **~politik** *die* A alliance policy; B (*um ~se zu schließen*) policy of alliance; **~system** *das* system of alliance; **das atlantische ~system** the Atlantic alliances *pl.;* **~treue** *die* loyalty to the alliance

**Bund·weite** *die* waist; (*Maß*) waist measurement

**Bungalow** /'bʊŋgalo/ *der;* **~s, ~s** bungalow

**Bunker** /'bʊŋkɐ/ *der;* **~s, ~** A (*auch Behälter*) bunker; (*für Getreide*) silo; (*für Raketen*) silo; bunker; B (*Luftschutz~*) air-raid shelter; C (*salopp: Gefängnis*) clink (*sl.*)

**bunkern** 1 *tr. V.* A bunker ‹coal›; store ‹grain etc.›; B (*salopp: verstecken*) stash away (*coll.*). 2 *itr. V.* (*Seemannsspr.*) refuel

**Bunsen·brenner** /'bʊnzn̩-/ *der* Bunsen burner

**bunt** /bʊnt/ 1 *Adj.* A (*farbig*) coloured; (*vielfarbig*) colourful; **~e Farben/Kleidung** bright colours/brightly coloured *or* colourful clothes; **~e Luftballons** different coloured balloons; **zu ~e Kleidung** garish clothing; B (*fig.*) colourful ‹sight›; varied ‹programme etc.›; **ein ~er Abend** a social [evening]; **ein ~er Teller [mit Äpfeln, Nüssen und Süßigkeiten]** a plate of assorted fruit, nuts, and sweets (*Brit.*) *or* (*Amer.*) candy; **Männer und Frauen bilden eine ~e Reihe** men and women alternate; **Buntes** (*DDR ugs.*) West German currency; ⇨ *auch* **Hund** A; C (*ungeordnet*) confused ‹muddle etc.›; **ein ~es Treiben** a real hustle and bustle; **jetzt wird es mir zu ~** (*ugs.*) that's *or* it's too much.
2 *adv.* A colourfully; **die Vorhänge waren ~ geblümt** the curtains had a colourful floral pattern; **etw. ~ bemalen/streichen** paint sth. a bright colour/in bright colours; **~ schillernd** iridescent; **~ bemalte Eier** brightly *or* colourfully painted eggs; **~ gefärbte Federn** multicoloured feathers; **~ gefiederte Vögel** birds with colourful *or* brightly coloured feathers; **~ gekleidet sein** be colourfully dressed; have colourful clothes; B (*fig.*) **ein ~ gemischtes Programm** a varied programme; **ein ~ gemischtes Publikum** a very mixed audience/(*im Restaurant*) clientele; C (*ungeordnet*) **~ durcheinander liegen** be in a complete muddle; **es zu ~ treiben** (*ugs.*) go too far; overdo it

**bunt-, Bunt-: *~bemalt** ⇨ **bunt** 2A; **~druck** *der; Pl.* **~~e** A (*Verfahren*) colour printing; B (*Gedrucktes*) colour print; **~film** *der* ⇨ **Farbfilm**; ***~geblümt** ⇨ **bunt** 2 A; ***~gefärbt** ⇨ **bunt** 2 A; ***~gefiedert** ⇨ **bunt** 2 A; **~metall** *das* non-ferrous metal; **~papier** *das* coloured paper; **~sand·stein** *der* A red sandstone; B (*Geol.*) Bunter; **~scheckig** *Adj.* spotted; ***~schillernd** ⇨ **bunt** 2 A; **~specht** *der* spotted woodpecker; **~stift** *der* coloured pencil/crayon; **~wäsche** *die* coloureds *pl.*

**Bürde** /'bʏrdə/ *die;* **~, ~n** (*geh.*) weight; load; (*fig.*) burden; **jmdm. zur ~ werden** (*fig.*) become a burden to sb.

**bürden** *tr. V.* (*geh. veralt.*) **die Verantwortung für etw. auf jmds. Schultern** (*Akk.*) **~:** burden sb. with the responsibility for sth.

**Bure** /'bu:rə/ *der;* **~n, ~n** Boer

**Buren·krieg** *der* Boer War

**Bürette** /bʏ'rɛtə/ *die;* **~, ~n** (*Chemie*) burette

**Burg** *die;* **~, ~en** A castle; B (*Strand~*) wall of sand; C (*Sand~*) [sand]castle; D (*Jägerspr.*) lodge

**Burg-: ~anlage** *die* castle buildings *pl.;* castle complex; **~berg** *der* castle hill; (*aufgeschüttet*) castle mound; **~bewohner** *der,* **~bewohnerin** *die* inhabitant of a/the castle; **die ~bewohner** those living in the castle

**Bürge** /'bʏrgə/ *der;* **~n, ~n** A guarantor; **einen ~n stellen** offer surety *or* a guarantor; **er muss zwei ~n stellen** he has to give the names of two guarantors; B (*fig.*) guarantee

**bürgen** *itr. V.* A **für jmdn./etw. ~:** vouch for *or* act as guarantor for sb./vouch for or guarantee sth.; **wer bürgt mir dafür, dass ich das Geld zurückbekomme?** who can guarantee *or* what guarantee do I have that I'll get the money back?; B (*fig.*) guarantee; **der Name bürgt für Qualität** the name is a guarantee of quality

**Bürger** *der;* **~s, ~** A (*Staats~*) citizen; **akademischer ~** (*veralt.*) [university] student; ⇨ *auch* **Uniform**; B (*einer Gemeinde*) citizen; resident; **die Bremer ~:** the citizens *or* people of Bremen; **die ~ von Calais** the burghers of Calais; C (*Bourgeois*) bourgeois

*old spelling (see note on page 1707)

**Bürger-:** **~aktion** *die* public campaign; **~beauftragte** *der/die* ombudsman; **~begehren** *das* public petition; **~beteiligung** *die* public participation *or* involvement; **~entscheid** *der* local referendum; **~forum** *das* open forum; public debate; **~haus** *das* [bourgeois] town house

**Bürgerin** *die;* ~, **~nen** Ⓐ (*Staats~*) citizen; Ⓑ (*einer Gemeinde*) citizen; resident; Ⓒ (*zur Bourgeoisie gehörend*) bourgeois[e]

**Bürger-:** **~initiative** *die* citizens' action group; **~krieg** *der* civil war; **der Spanische ~krieg** the Spanish Civil War

**bürgerlich** ❶ *Adj.* Ⓐ (*staats~*) civil ‹rights, marriage, etc.›; civic ‹duties›; **das Bürgerliche Gesetzbuch** the [German] Civil Code; **sein ~er Name** his real name; Ⓑ (*dem Bürgertum zugehörig*) middle class; **die ~e Küche** good plain cooking; good home cooking; **das ~e Trauerspiel** domestic tragedy; Ⓒ (*Polit.*) non-socialist; (*nicht marxistisch*) non-Marxist; Ⓓ (*abwertend: spießerhaft*) bourgeois.
❷ *adv.* Ⓐ ‹think, etc.› in a middle-class way; **~ leben** live a middle-class life; **gut ~ essen** have a good plain meal; (*gewohnheitsmäßig*) eat good plain food; Ⓑ (*abwertend: spießerhaft*) in a bourgeois way; **dieses ~ engstirnige Denken** this bourgeois, narrow-minded way of thinking

**Bürgerliche** *der/die; adj. Dekl.* Ⓐ (*Nichtadlige*) commoner; Ⓑ (*Polit.*) non-socialist

**Bürgerlichkeit** *die;* **~:** middle-class *or* bourgeois way of life; **eine erdrückende Atmosphäre der ~:** a stifling middle-class *or* bourgeois atmosphere

**bürger-, Bürger-:** **~meister** *der* ▶ 91, ▶ 159 mayor; **~meister·amt** *das* Ⓐ (*Gemeindeverwaltung*) local authority; Ⓑ (*Amt des ~meisters*) office of mayor; Ⓒ (*Gebäude*) local council offices *pl.;* **~meisterin** *die* ▶ 91, ▶ 159 mayor; **~mut** *der* ⇒ **Zivilcourage**; **~nah** *Adj.* which/who reflects the general public's interests *postpos., not pred.;* **~nahe Politik** politics for the people; **~nähe** *die:* **~nähe in der Politik** politics for the people; **~nähe bewahren** keep a close relationship with the people; **~pflicht** *die* civic duty; duty as a citizen; ⇒ *auch* **Ruhe** F; **~recht** *das* one of the civil rights; **~rechte** civil rights; **~rechtler** *der;* **~~s,** ~~, **~rechtlerin** *die;* ~~, **~~nen** civil-rights campaigner; **~rechts·bewegung** *die* civil-rights movement; **~rechts·kämpfer** *der,* **~rechts·kämpferin** *die* ⇒ **~rechtler**

**Bürgerschaft** *die;* ~, **~en** Ⓐ citizens *pl.;* **die ganze ~:** all the citizens; Ⓑ (*in Hamburg u. Bremen*) city parliament

**Bürger·schreck** *der* bogey of the middle classes

**Bürgers-:** **~frau** *die* (*veralt.*) Ⓐ middle-class woman; Ⓑ (*zur Bourgeoisie gehörend*) bourgeoise; **~mann** *der; Pl.* **~leute** (*veralt.*) Ⓐ middle-class man; Ⓑ (*zur Bourgeoisie gehörend*) bourgeois

**Bürger-:** **~sohn** *der* Ⓐ son of a middle-class family; Ⓑ (*zur Bourgeoisie gehörend*) son of a bourgeois family; **~stand** *der* (*veralt.*) Ⓐ middle class; Ⓑ (*Großbürgertum*) bourgeoisie; **~steig** *der* pavement (*Brit.*); sidewalk (*Amer.*); **~tochter** *die* Ⓐ daughter of a middle-class family; Ⓑ (*zur Bourgeoisie gehörend*) daughter of a bourgeois family

**Bürgertum** *das;* **~s** Ⓐ middle class; Ⓑ (*wohlhabender Bürgerstand*) bourgeoisie

**Bürger·wehr** *die* vigilante group

**Burg-:** **~fräulein** *das* (*hist.*) daughter of the lord of the/a castle; **~fried** *der;* **~~[e]s, ~~e** ⇒ **Bergfried**; **~friede** *der* Ⓐ truce; Ⓑ (*hist.: Schutz*) castle precincts *pl.;* **~graben** *der* [castle] moat; **~graf** *der* (*hist.*) burgrave; **~gräfin** *die* (*hist.*) chatelaine; **~herr** *der* (*hist.*) lord of the/a castle; **~herrin** *die* (*hist.*) lady of the/a castle

**Bürgin** /ˈbʏrgɪn/ *die;* ~, **~nen** ⇒ **Bürge**

**Burg·ruine** *die* castle ruins *pl.;* ruined castle

**Bürgschaft** *die;* ~, **~en** Ⓐ (*Rechtsw.*) guarantee; security; **die ~ für jmdn./etw. übernehmen** agree to act as sb.'s guarantor/to guarantee sth.; Ⓑ (*Garantie*) guarantee; **~ für etw. leisten** vouch for *or* guarantee sth.; Ⓒ (*Betrag*) penalty

**Bürgschafts-:** **~erklärung** *die* guarantee; **~nehmer** *der;* **~~s,** ~~, **~nehmerin** *die;* ~~, **~~nen** creditor

**Burgund** /burˈgʊnt/ (*das*)*;* **~s** Burgundy

**Burgunder** *der;* **~s,** ~ Ⓐ (*Einwohner, auch hist.*) Burgundian; Ⓑ (*Wein*) burgundy

**Burgunderin** *die;* ~, **~nen** ⇒ **Burgunder** A

**Burgunder·wein** *der* burgundy

**Burg-:** **~verlies** *das* [castle] dungeon; **~vogt** *der* ⇒ **~graf**

**Burin** *die;* ~, **~nen** Boer; ⇒ *auch* **-in**

**Burkina Faso** /burˈkiːna ˈfaːzo/ (*das*) Burkina

**Burkiner** *der;* **~s,** ~, **Burkinerin** *die;* ~, **~nen** Burkinan; ⇒ *auch* **-in**

**burkinisch** *Adj.* Burkinan

**burlesk** /burˈlɛsk/ *Adj.* burlesque

**Burleske** *die;* ~, **~n** (*Theater, Musik*) burlesque

**Burma** /ˈburma/ ⇒ **Birma**

**Burnus** /ˈburnʊs/ *der;* **~ses, ~se** burnous

**Büro** /byˈroː/ *das;* **~s, ~s** office

**Büro-:** **~angestellte** *der/die* ▶ 159 office worker; **~arbeit** *die* office work *no pl.;* **alle ~arbeiten** all types of office work; **~artikel** *der* item of office equipment; **~artikel** *Pl.* office supplies *or* equipment; **~bedarf** *der* office supplies *pl.;* **~gehilfe** *der* office boy; **~gehilfin** *die* office girl; **~haus** *das* office block; **~hengst** *der* (*ugs. abwertend*) office clerk; pen-pusher (*coll.*); **~kauffrau** *die,* **~kaufmann** *der* [qualified] office executive; **~klammer** *die* paper clip; **~kraft** *die* clerical worker

**Bürokrat** /byroˈkraːt/ *der;* **~en, ~en** (*abwertend*) bureaucrat

**Bürokratie** /byrokraˈtiː/ *die;* ~, **~n** bureaucracy

**Bürokratin** *die;* ~, **~nen** bureaucrat

**bürokratisch** ❶ *Adj.* bureaucratic. ❷ *adv.* bureaucratically

**bürokratisieren** *tr. V.* bureaucratize

**Bürokratismus** *der;* ~ (*abwertend*) bureaucracy

**Büro-:** **~maschine** *die* office machine; **~material** *das* ⇒ **~bedarf**; **~mensch** *der* (*ugs.*) office clerk; **~schluss,** ***~schluß** *der* [office] closing time; **bei uns ist um 17 h ~schluss** our office closes at 5 o'clock; **nach ~schluss** after the office closes/the offices close; after office hours; **~tätigkeit** *die* office work; an office job; **Mädchen für leichte ~tätigkeit gesucht** girl required to carry out basic clerical duties; **~zeit** *die* office hours *pl.;* **während der ~zeit** during office hours

**Bursch** /burʃ/ *der;* **~en, ~en** Ⓐ *member of a student fraternity;* Ⓑ ⇒ **Bursche**

**Bürschchen** /ˈbʏrʃçən/ *das;* ~, **~:** little fellow; little chap; **ein freches ~:** a cheeky little devil; **sei vorsichtig, mein ~:** be careful, sonny *or* laddie

**Bursche** /ˈburʃə/ *der;* **~n, ~n** Ⓐ boy; lad; Ⓑ (*junger Mann*) young man; **die jungen ~n aus dem Dorf** the village youths; **er hält sich für einen ganz tollen ~n** (*ugs.*) he thinks he's really something; **er ist ein toller ~** (*ugs.*) he's a reckless devil; Ⓒ (*abwertend: Kerl*) guy (*coll.*); character; **ein übler ~:** a nasty piece of work (*coll.*); Ⓓ (*ugs.: Prachtexemplar*) specimen; **der Hecht, den er gefangen hat, ist ein prächtiger ~:** the pike he caught is a real whopper (*coll.*); Ⓔ (*Milit. hist.*) batman; orderly; Ⓕ ⇒ **Bursch** A

**Burschenschaft** *die;* ~, **~en** students' duelling society

**Burschenschafter** *der;* **~s, ~:** member of a/the students' duelling society

**burschikos** /burʃiˈkoːs/ ❶ *Adj.* Ⓐ sporty ‹clothes, look›; [tom]boyish ‹behaviour, girl, haircut›; Ⓑ (*ungezwungen*) casual ‹comment, behaviour, etc.›. ❷ *adv.* Ⓐ [tom]boyishly; **sich ~ benehmen** behave like a [tom]boy; Ⓑ (*ungezwungen*) in a colloquial way

**Burschikosität** /burʃikoziˈtɛːt/ *die;* ~, **~en** ⇒ **burschikos** 1: sportiness; [tom]boyishness; casualness

**Burse** /ˈburzə/ *die;* ~, **~n** (*hist.*) hostel (*for students and journeymen*)

**Bürste** /ˈbʏrstə/ *die;* ~, **~n** Ⓐ brush; Ⓑ (*Haarschnitt*) crew cut; Ⓒ (*Elektrot.*) brush

**bürsten** *tr. V.* Ⓐ brush; Ⓑ (*vulg.: koitieren*) screw (*coarse*)

**Bürsten-:** **~abzug** *der* (*Druckw.*) brush proof; **~binder** *der:* in **trinken** (*ugs.*) *od.* (*salopp*) **saufen wie ein ~binder** drink like a fish; **~macher** *der,* **~macherin** *die* broom- and brushmaker; **~schnitt** *der* crew cut

**Bürzel** /ˈbʏrtsl̩/ *der;* **~s,** ~ Ⓐ (*Zool.*) rump; Ⓑ (*Jägerspr.*) tail

**Bus** /bʊs/ *der;* **~ses, ~se** bus; (*Privat- und Reisebus auch*) coach

**Bus·bahn·hof** *der* bus station; (*für Reisebusse auch*) coach station

**Busch** /bʊʃ/ *der;* **~[e]s, Büsche** /ˈbʏʃə/ Ⓐ bush; (*fig.*) **auf den ~ klopfen** (*ugs.*) sound things out; **bei jmdm. auf den ~ klopfen** (*ugs.*) sound sb. out; **mit etw. hinterm ~ halten** (*ugs.*) keep sth. to oneself; **es ist etw. im ~** (*ugs.*) something's up; **sich [seitwärts] in die Büsche schlagen** (*ugs.*) slip away; Ⓑ (*Geogr.*) bush; Ⓒ (*ugs.: Urwald*) jungle; **aus dem ~ kommen** have come from the backwoods *pl.;* Ⓓ (*Strauß*) bunch; Ⓔ (*Büschel*) tuft; **ein ~ Haare/Federn** a tuft of hair/feathers

**Busch·bohne** *die* dwarf bean

**Büschel** /ˈbʏʃl̩/ *das;* **~s,** ~ (*von Haaren, Federn, Gras usw.*) tuft; (*von Heu, Stroh*) handful; **ein ~ Federn** a tuft of feathers

**büschel·weise** *Adv.* ⇒ **Büschel**: in tufts/in handfuls; **~ Unkraut** whole clumps of weeds

**Buschen** *der;* **~s,** ~ (*südd., österr. ugs.*) **ein ~ [Blumen/Zweige]** a bunch [of flowers]/bundle [of twigs]; **einen ~ über die Tür hängen** hang a bundle of twigs above the door

**Buschen·schenke** *die* (*österr.*) ⇒ **Strauß·wirtschaft**

**buschig** *Adj.* bushy; **~e Rosen** rose bushes

**Busch-:** **~mann** *der* Bushman; **~mann·frau** *die* Bushman woman; **~messer** *das* machete; **~werk** *das* bushes *pl.;* **~wind·röschen** *das* wood anemone

**Busen** /ˈbuːzn̩/ *der;* **~s,** ~ Ⓐ bust; **sie hat wenig ~** (*ugs.*) she has very little bosom; **in dem Film wurde viel ~ gezeigt** (*ugs.*) in this film there was plenty of bosom on display; **eine Schlange** *od.* **Natter an seinem ~ nähren** (*veralt.*) nourish a viper in one's bosom (*literary*); Ⓑ (*dichter. veralt.: Brust*) bosom; breast; **am ~ der Natur** (*fig. scherzh.*) in the bosom of nature; Ⓒ (*dichter. veralt.: Inneres*) bosom; heart; Ⓓ (*dichter. veralt.: Mieder*) bodice; bosom

**busen-, Busen-:** **~frei** *Adj.* topless; **~freund** *der,* **~freundin** *die* (*oft iron.*) bosom friend; **~star** *der* (*ugs.*) sex symbol

**Bus-:** **~fahrer** *der,* **~fahrerin** *die* ▶ 159 bus driver; (*von Reisebussen auch*) coach driver; **~halte·stelle** *die* bus stop; (*von Reisebussen auch*) coach stop; **~linie** *die* bus route; **mein Haus liegt an der ~linie 7** my house is on the number 7 bus route

**Bussard** /ˈbʊsart/ *der;* **~s, ~e** (*Zool.*) buzzard

**Buße** /ˈbuːsə/ *die;* ~, **~n** Ⓐ (*Rel.*) penance *no art.;* **~ tun** (*veralt.*) do penance; Ⓑ (*Reue*) repentance; Ⓒ (*Rechtsw.*) damages *pl.;* Ⓓ (*schweiz. Rechtsspr.: Geldstrafe*) fine

**Bussel** /ˈbʊsl̩/ *das;* **~s, ~[n]** ⇒ **Busserl**

**busseln** ⇒ **busserln**

**büßen** /ˈbyːsn̩/ ❶ *tr. V.* Ⓐ (*Rel.: sühnen*) atone for; expiate; Ⓑ (*bestraft werden für*) atone for; **das sollst du mir ~:** you'll pay for that; Ⓒ (*fig.: bezahlen*) pay for. ❷ *itr. V.* Ⓐ (*Rel.*) **für etw. ~:** atone for *or* expiate sth.; Ⓑ (*bestraft werden*) suffer; Ⓒ (*fig.: bezahlen*) pay

b

**Büßer** *der;* **~s,** ~ (*Rel.*) penitent

**Büßer-:** **~gewand** *das,* **~hemd** *das* penitential robe; **sich im ~hemd zeigen, im ~hemd erscheinen** (*fig.*) show repentance

**Büßerin** *die;* ~, **~nen** (*Rel.*) penitent

**Busserl** /'bʊsɐl/ *das;* **~s,** **~[n]** (*südd., österr. ugs.*) kiss

**busserln** *tr., itr. V.* (*südd., österr. ugs.*) kiss

**buß-, Buß-:** **~feier** *die* (*kath. Rel.*) ⇨ **~gottesdienst**; **~fertig** (*Rel.*) ❶ *Adj.* penitent; (*fig.*) repentant; ❷ *adv.* penitently; **~fertigkeit** *die* (*Rel.*) penitence; (*fig.*) repentance; **~gang** *der* (*geh.*) **einen ~gang antreten** *od.* **machen** go to beg for forgiveness; **~gebet** *das* (*Rel.*) prayer of repentance *or* penitence; **~geld** *das* (*Rechtsw.*) fine; **~geld·bescheid** *der* official demand for payment of a fine; **einen ~geldbescheid bekommen** be fined (**von** by); **~gesang** *der* (*Rel.*) hymn of repentance; **~gottes·dienst** *der* (*kath. Rel.*) service of confession and general absolution

**Bussi** /'bʊsi/ *das;* **~s, ~s** (*ugs.*) kiss

**Bussole** /bʊ'so:lə/ *die;* ~, **~n** compass; (*Elektrot.*) galvanometer

**Buß-:** **~prediger** *der,* **~predigerin** *die* repentance preacher; **~predigt** *die* sermon calling to repentance; **~sakrament** *das* (*Rel.*) sacrament of penance; **~tag** *der* Ⓐ (*kath. Rel.*) day of repentance; Ⓑ ⇨ **~- und Bettag**; **~- und Bettag** *der* (*ev. Kirche*) Wednesday eleven days before Advent (*as day of penance*)

**Büsten·halter** *der* bra; brassière (*formal*)

**Bus-:** **~verbindung** *die* Ⓐ (*Linie*) bus service; Ⓑ (*Anschluss*) bus connection; (*für Reisebusse auch*) coach connection; **~verkehr** *der* bus service; (*von Fernreisebussen auch*) coach service

**Butan** /bu'ta:n/ *das;* **~s, ~e** (*Chemie*) butane

**Butan·gas** *das* butane gas

**Butt** /bʊt/ *der;* **~[e]s, ~e** flounder; butt

**Bütt** /bʏt/ *die;* ~, **~en** speaker's platform; [carnival] soapbox; **in der ~ stehen** stand on the platform *or* soapbox; **in die ~ steigen** take the platform; get up on the soapbox

**Butte** *die;* ~, **~n** Ⓐ (*südd., österr., schweiz.*) ⇨ **Bütte**; Ⓑ (*Winzerspr.*) dosser; pannier

**Bütte** *die;* ~, **~n** Ⓐ tub; Ⓑ (*Papierherstellung*) vat

**Büttel** /'bʏtl/ *der;* **~s,** ~ Ⓐ (*abwertend*) lackey; Ⓑ (*veralt.: Häscher*) bailiff; Ⓒ (*geh. abwertend: Polizist*) minion of the law

**Bütten** *das;* **~s** ⇨ **~papier**

**Bütten-:** **~papier** *das* handmade paper (*with deckle edge*); **~rand** *der* deckle edge; **~rede** *die* carnival speech; **~redner** *der,* **~rednerin** *die* carnival speaker

**Butter** /'bʊtɐ/ *die;* **~:** butter; **gute ~** (*veralt.*) butter; **[es ist] alles in ~** (*ugs.*) everything's fine; **sie lässt sich** (*Dat.*) **nicht die ~ vom Brot nehmen** (*ugs.*) she doesn't let anyone put one over on her; **jmdm. die ~ aufs** *od.* **auf dem Brot nicht gönnen** (*ugs.*) begrudge sb. everything

**Butter-:** **~bemme** *die* (*ostmd.*) ⇨ **~brot**; **~berg** *der* (*ugs.*) butter mountain; **~blume** *die* (*Löwenzahn*) dandelion; (*Sumpfdotterblume*) marsh marigold; (*Hahnenfuß*) buttercup; **~brot** *das* piece *or* slice of bread and butter; (*zugeklappt*) sandwich; **ein ~brot mit Schinken** a slice of bread and butter with ham on it/a ham sandwich; **für ein ~brot** (*ugs.*) for next to nothing; ‹buy, sell› for a song; **musst du mir ständig aufs ~brot streichen** *od.* **schmieren, dass ...?** (*ugs.*) do you have to keep rubbing it in that ...?; **~brot·papier** *das* greaseproof paper; **~creme** *die* buttercream; **~creme·torte** *die* buttercream cake; **~dose** *die* butter dish; **~fahrt** *die* (*ugs.*) sea trip to buy duty-free goods; **~fass, *~faß** *das* [butter] churn; **~fett** *das* butterfat; **~flöckchen** *das* flake of butter

**Butterfly** /'bʌtəflai/ *der;* **~s** Ⓐ (*Schwimmen*) butterfly [stroke]; Ⓑ (*Eiskunstlauf*) split jump

**butter·gelb** *Adj.* butter yellow

**butterig** *Adj.* buttery

**Butter-:** **~käse** *der* rich creamy cheese; **~keks** *der* butter biscuit; **~krem** *die* (*ugs. auch:*) *der* ⇨ **~creme**; **~messer** *das* butter knife; **~milch** *die* buttermilk

**buttern** ❶ *itr. V.* make butter. ❷ *tr. V.* Ⓐ butter; grease ‹baking tray› with butter; Ⓑ (*ugs.: aufwenden*) put (**in** + *Akk.* into)

**butter-, Butter-:** **~pilz** *der* boletus lutens; **~säure** *die* (*Chemie*) butyric acid; **~schmalz** *das* clarified butter; **~stulle** *die* (*nordd., bes. berlin.*) ⇨ **~brot**; **~teig** *der* short pastry [made with butter]; **~weich** ❶ *Adj.* Ⓐ beautifully soft; **eine ~weiche Landung** (*fig.*) a [really] soft landing; Ⓑ (*ohne Festigkeit*) vague ‹agreement, promise›; **wenn man ihm schmeichelt, wird er ~weich** if you flatter him, he's like putty in your hands; Ⓒ (*Sportjargon*) gentle ‹shot, pass›; ❷ *adv.* Ⓐ gently; **die Maschine landete ~weich** the machine landed gently; Ⓑ (*Sportjargon*) gently

**Buttje** /'bʊtjə/ *der;* **~s, ~s, Buttjer** /'bʊtjɐ/ *der;* **~rs, ~rs** (*nordd.*) kid (*coll.*)

**Büttner** /'bʏtnɐ/ *der;* **~s,** ~, **Büttnerin** *die;* ~, **~nen** ⇨ **Böttcher**

**Button** /bʌtn/ *der;* **~s, ~s** badge

**buttrig** ⇨ **butterig**

**Butze·mann** *der* (*fam.*) bogyman

**bützen** /'bʏtsn̩/ *tr., itr. V.* (*rhein.*) kiss

**Butzen·scheibe** *die* bullseye pane

**Büx** /bʏks/ *die;* ~, **~en, Buxe** /'bʊksə/ *die;* **~e, ~en** (*nordd.*) trousers *pl.*; pants *pl.* (*Amer.*); **zwei ~en** *od.* **Buxen** two pairs of trousers *or* (*Amer.*) pants

**Buxtehude** /bʊkstə'hu:də/ *in* **in/aus/nach ~** (*fig. ugs.*) at/from/to the back of beyond

**Buy-out** /'baiaut/ *das;* **~s, ~s** (*Wirtsch.*) buyout

**BV** *Abk.* (*schweiz.*) **Bundesversammlung**

**BVG** *Abk.* Ⓐ **Bundesverwaltungsgericht;** Ⓑ **Bundesverfassungsgericht;** Ⓒ **Betriebsverfassungsgesetz**

**b.w.** *Abk.* **bitte wenden** p.t.o.

**Bypass** /'baipas/ *der;* **~es, Bypässe** (*Med.*) bypass

**Byte** /bait/ *das;* **~s, ~[s]** (*DV*) byte

**Byzantiner** /bʏtsan'ti:nɐ/ *der;* **~s,** ~, **Byzantinerin** *die;* ~, **~nen** Byzantine

**byzantinisch** *Adj.* Byzantine; **das Byzantinische Reich** the Byzantine Empire

**Byzantinismus** *der;* ~ (*geh. abwertend*) obsequiousness; sycophancy

**Byzantinistik** *die;* **~:** Byzantine studies *pl.*, *no art.*

**Byzanz** /bʏ'tsants/ (*das*); **~':** Byzantium

**bzgl.** *Abk.* **bezüglich**

**bzw.** *Abk.* **beziehungsweise**

**c, C** /tse:/ *das;* ~, ~ Ⓐ (*Buchstabe*) c/C; Ⓑ (*Musik*) [key of] C; ⇒ *auch* **a, A**
**C** *Abk.* **Celsius** C
**ca.** *Abk.* **cirka** c.
**Cabaret** /kaba're:/ ⇒ **Kabarett**
**Cabrio** ⇒ **Kabrio**
**Cabriolet** /kabrio'le:/ ⇒ **Kabriolett**
**cachieren** ⇒ **kaschieren**
**Café** /ka'fe:/ *das;* **~s,** **~s** café; **ins ~ gehen** go to a/the café
**Cafeteria** /kafetə'ri:a/ *die;* ~, **~s** cafeteria
**cal** *Abk.* **[Gramm]kalorie** cal.
**Calcium** ⇒ **Kalzium**
**Call·boy** /'kɔ:l.../ *der;* **~s,** **~s** call boy
**Callgirl** /'kɔ:lgə:l/ *das;* **~s,** **~s** call girl
**Callgirl·ring** *der* call-girl ring
**Calvados** /kalva'do:s/ *der;* ~, **~:** calvados
**calvinistisch** ⇒ **kalvinistisch**
**Calypso** /ka'lɪpso/ *der;* **~s,** **~s** calypso
**Camcorder** /'kamkɔrdɐ/ *der;* **~s,** ~ ⇒ **Kamerarecorder**
**Camembert** /'kaməmbe:ɐ̯/ *der;* **~s,** **~s** Camembert
**Camion** /'kami̯õ/ *der;* **~s,** **~s** (*schweiz.*) lorry (*Brit.*); truck (*Amer.*)
**Camouflage** /kamu'fla:ʒə/ *die;* ~, **~n** (*bes. Milit.; veralt.*) camouflage
**camouflieren** *tr. V.* (*veralt.*) camouflage
**Camp** /kɛmp/ *das;* **~s,** **~s** camp
**campen** /'kɛmpn̩/ *itr. V.* camp
**Camper** *der;* **~s,** ~, **Camperin** *die;* ~, **~nen** camper
**Camping** /'kɛmpɪŋ/ *das;* **~s** camping; **zum ~ [nach X] fahren** go camping [in X]
**Camping-:** **~aus·rüstung** *die* camping equipment; **~beutel** *der* duffle bag; **~bus** *der* motor caravan; camper; **~führer** *der* camping guide[book]; **~platz** *der* campsite; campground (*Amer.*); **~stuhl** *der* [folding] camp chair; **~tisch** *der* [folding] camp table
**Campus** /'kampʊs/ *der;* ~ (*Hochschulw.*) campus
**Canaille** ⇒ **Kanaille**
**Canasta** /ka'nasta/ *das;* **~s** canasta
**Cancan** /kã'kã:/ *der;* **~s,** **~s** cancan
**Candela** /kan'de:la/ *die;* ~, ~ (*Physik*) candela
**Cannabis** /'kanabɪs/ *der;* **~:** cannabis
**Cannelloni** /kanɛ'lo:ni/ *Pl.* cannelloni
**Cañon** /'kanjɔn/ *der;* **~s,** **~s** canyon
**Canossa** ⇒ **Kanossa**
**Cantilever·bremse** /'kæntɪli:vɐ/ *die* cantilever brake
**Canto** /'kanto/ *der;* **~s,** **~s** (*Literaturw.*) canto
**Cantus** /'kantʊs/ *der;* ~, ~ (*Musik*) cantus; principal *or* melody voice
**Cape** /ke:p/ *das;* **~s,** **~s** cape
**Cappuccino** /kapʊ'tʃi:no/ *der;* **~s,** **~[s]** cappuccino
**Capriccio** /ka'prɪtʃo/ *das;* **~s,** **~s** (*Musik*) capriccio
**Car** /ka:ɐ̯/ *der;* **~s,** **~s** (*schweiz.*) coach
**Caravan** /'ka(:)ravan/ *der;* **~s,** **~s** Ⓐ (*Kombi*) estate car; station wagon (*Amer.*); Ⓑ (*Wohnwagen*) caravan; trailer (*Amer.*)
**Carbid** ⇒ **Karbid**
**Cargo** ⇒ **Kargo**
**Caritas** /'ka:ritas/ *die;* **~:** Caritas (*Catholic welfare organization*); **ich bin doch nicht von der ~!** (*ugs.*) I'm not a charitable institution!
**Carnet [de Passages]** /kar'nɛ (də pa'sa:ʒə)/ *das;* ~ [~], **~s** [~] /kar'nɛ (də pa'sa:ʒə)/ (*Verkehrsw.*) carnet
**cartesianisch** /karte'zi̯a:nɪʃ/ *Adj.* Cartesian
**Cartoon** /kar'tu:n/ *der od. das;* **~s,** **~s** cartoon
**Casanova** /kaza'no:va/ *der;* **~s,** **~s** Casanova
**Cäsar** /'tsɛ:zar/ (*der*) Caesar
**Cäsaren-** /tsɛ'za:rən-/**:** **~herrschaft** *die* dictatorship; **~wahn·sinn** *der* [dictatorial] megalomania
**Cäsarismus** /tsɛza'rɪsmʊs/ *der;* **~:** Caesarism; absolutism
**Cäsaropapismus** /tsɛzaropa'pɪsmʊs/ *der;* **~:** Caesaropapism *no art.*
**Cashew·nuss, *Cashew·nuß** /'kɛʃu-/ *die* cashew nut
**Cashflow** /kæʃ'floʊ/ *der;* **~s** (*Wirtsch.*) [gross] cash flow
**Casino** ⇒ **Kasino**
**Cassata** /ka'sa:ta/ *die od. das;* ~, **~s** cassata
**Cassette** ⇒ **Kassette**
**Catch-as-catch-can** /'kætʃəz'kætʃ'kæn/ *das;* **~:** catch-as-catch-can; all-in wrestling
**catchen** /'kɛtʃn̩/ *itr. V.* do all-in wrestling; **das Catchen** all-in wrestling
**Catcher** /'kɛtʃɐ/ *der;* **~s,** ~, **Catcherin** *die;* ~, **~nen** all-in wrestler
**Cayenne·pfeffer** /ka'jɛn-/ *der* cayenne [pepper]
**CB-Funk** /tse:'be:-/ *der;* **~s** (*Nachrichtent.*) CB radio
**CD** /tse:'de:/ *die;* ~, **~s** CD
**CD-Brenner** *der* CD burner; CD writer
**CD-ROM** /tsede'rɔm/ *die;* ~, **~[s]** (*DV*) CD-ROM
**CD-ROM-Lauf·werk** *das* (*DV*) CD-ROM drive
**CD-Spieler** /tse:'de:-/ *der* compact disc player
**CDU** *Abk.* **Christlich-Demokratische Union [Deutschlands]** [German] Christian Democratic Party
**C-Dur** /'tse:-/ *das* C major; ⇒ *auch* **A-Dur**
**C-Dur-Dreiklang** *der* C major triad
**Cedille** /se'di:j(ə)/ *die;* ~, **~n** (*Sprachw.*) cedilla
**Cellist** /tʃɛ'lɪst/ *der;* **~en,** **~en,** **Cellistin** *die;* ~, **~nen** ▶ **159** cellist; ⇒ *auch* **-in**
**Cello** /'tʃɛlo/ *das;* **~s,** **~s** *od.* **Celli** cello
**Cello·konzert** *das* cello concerto
**Cellophan** Ⓦ *das;* **~s,** **Cellophane** Ⓦ /tsɛlo'fa:n(ə)/ *die;* **~:** Cellophane ®
**Celsius** /'tsɛlzi̯ʊs/ ▶ **728** centigrade; Celsius (*Phys.*)
**Celsius·skala** *die* Celsius *or* centigrade scale
**Cembalo** /'tʃɛmbalo/ *das;* **~s,** **~s** *od.* **Cembali** harpsichord
**Cent** /tsɛnt/ *der;* **~s,** **~[s]** ▶ **337** cent
**Center** /'sɛntɐ/ *das;* **~s,** ~ Ⓐ (*Großmarkt*) centre; Ⓑ (*Einkaufszentrum*) shopping centre *or* (*Amer.*) mall
**Centime** /sã'ti:m/ *der;* **~s,** **~s** ▶ **337** centime
**Cercle** /'sɛrkl̩/ *der;* **~s,** **~s** Ⓐ **~ halten** (*veralt.*) hold court; Ⓑ (*österr.: im Theater*) front stalls *pl.*
**Cervelat** /'sɛrvəla/ *der;* **~s,** **~s** (*schweiz.*) cervelat [sausage]
**ces, Ces** /tsɛs/ *das;* ~ (*Musik*) C flat
**Ces-Dur** *das* C flat major; ⇒ *auch* **A-Dur**
**Ceylon** /'tsailɔn/ (*das*); **~s** (*hist.*) Ceylon (*Hist.*)
**Ceylonese** *der;* **~n,** **~n,** **Ceylonesin** *die;* ~, **~nen** (*hist.*) Ceylonese
**cf.** *Abk.* **conferatur** cf.
**C-Flöte** /'tse:-/ *die* soprano recorder
**Cha-Cha-Cha** /'tʃa 'tʃa 'tʃa/ *der;* **~s,** **~s** cha-cha-cha
**Chaise** /'ʃɛ:zə/ *die;* ~, **~n** Ⓐ (*veralt.: Kutsche*) [closed] chaise; Ⓑ (*ugs. abwertend: Auto*) jalopy; banger (*Brit. sl.*)
**Chaiselongue** /ʃɛzə'lõ:k/ *die;* ~, **~n** *od.* **~s** chaise longue
**Chalet** /ʃa'le:/ *das;* **~s,** **~s** Ⓐ Alpine [cowherd's] hut; Ⓑ (*Landhaus*) [Swiss] chalet
**Chamäleon** /ka'mɛ:leɔn/ *das;* **~s,** **~s** (*auch fig.*) chameleon
**Chamois** /ʃa'mo̯a/ *das;* ~ Ⓐ (*Farbe*) chamois; parchment [colour]; Ⓑ ⇒ **~leder**
**Chamois·leder** *das* chamois [leather]
**Champagner** /ʃam'panjɐ/ *der;* **~s,** **~:** champagne (*from Champagne*)
**champagner·farben** *Adj.* champagne-coloured
**Champignon** /'ʃampɪnjɔn/ *der;* **~s,** **~s** mushroom
**Champion** /'tʃɛmpi̯ən/ *der;* **~s,** **~s** (*Sport*) champion; (*Mannschaft*) champions *pl.*
**Chance** /'ʃã:sə/ *die;* ~, **~n** Ⓐ (*Gelegenheit*) chance; **eine ~/keine ~/mehr ~n haben, etw. zu tun** have a chance/no chance/more chance of doing sth.; **die ~n [zu gewinnen] stehen eins zu hundert** the chances [of winning] are one in a hundred; (*bes. beim Wetten*) the odds [against winning] are 100:1 *or* a hundred to one; **ich gebe dir eine letzte ~:** I'll give you one last chance; **eine/keine ~ sehen, zu ...** see a/no chance *or* hope of ...; **sie rechnen sich** (*Dat.*) **eine ~ aus, 2 Punkte zu machen** they reckon they have a chance of scoring 2 points; **~n/eine ~ vergeben** (*Sport*) give away chances/a chance; Ⓑ *Pl.* (*Aussichten*) prospects; **seine ~n stehen gut/schlecht** his prospects are good/poor; **[bei jmdm] ~n haben** stand a chance [with sb.]
**Chancen·gleichheit** *die* (*Päd., Soziol.*) equality of opportunity *no art.*
**changieren** /ʃã'ʒi:rən/ *itr. V.* shimmer (*in different colours*); iridesce; **~d** iridescent; **~de Seide** shot silk
**Chanson** /ʃã'sõ:/ *das;* **~s,** **~s** chanson; cabaret-style song
**Chansonette, Chansonnette** /ʃãsɔ'nɛtə/ *die;* ~, **~n** chanteuse; (*im Kabarett*) cabaret singer
**Chansonnier** /ʃãsɔ'ni̯e:/ *der;* **~s,** **~s** singer/composer of chansons; chansonnier
**Chansonniere** /ʃãsɔ'ni̯e:rə/ *die;* ~, **~n** singer/composer of chansons; chansonnière
**Chaos** /'ka:ɔs/ *das;* **~:** chaos *no art.*; **in der Wohnung herrschte ein einziges ~:** the flat (*Brit.*) *or* (*Amer.*) apartment was in total chaos
**Chaos·theorie** *die* (*Physik*) chaos theory
**Chaot** /ka'o:t/ *der;* **~en,** **~en,** **Chaotin** *die;* ~, **~nen** Ⓐ (*Politik*) anarchist (*trying to undermine society*); (*bei Demonstrationen*) violent demonstrator; Ⓑ (*salopp: unordentlicher Mensch*) **ein [furchtbarer] Chaot sein** be [terribly] disorganized
**chaotisch** ❶ *Adj.* chaotic. ❷ *adv.* chaotically; **es geht ~ zu** there is chaos
**Chapeau claque** /ʃapo'klak/ *der;* ~ ~, **~x ~s** /ʃapo'klak/ opera hat
**Charade** ⇒ **Scharade**
**Charakter** /ka'raktɐ/ *der;* **~s,** **~e** /-'te:rə/ Ⓐ character; personality; **etw. prägt** *od.*

**formt den ~:** sth. moulds one's character *or* is character-forming; **die seinen ~ prägenden** *od.* **formenden Jahre** his formative years; **Geld verdirbt den ~:** money spoils people; **sie hat einen schwierigen/ist ein schwieriger ~:** she has/is a complex personality; **gegensätzliche ~e haben/sein** have entirely different personalities/be quite different in personality *or* character; **er ist ein mieser ~** (*ugs.*) he's a lousy so-and-so (*coll.*); Ⓑ (*~stärke*) [strength of] character; **keinen ~ haben** lack [strength of] character; be spineless; Ⓒ (*Eigenart*) character; **die Mitteilung hat vertraulichen ~:** the communication is of a confidential nature

**charakter-, Charakter-: ~an·lage** *die* trait; **gute/schlechte ~anlagen haben** have good/bad qualities *or* a good/bad disposition; **~bild** *das* profile; **~bildend** *Adj.* character-forming; **~bildung** *die* formation of character; **jmds. ~bildung** the formation of sb.'s character; **~darsteller** *der* actor of complex parts; **~darstellerin** *die* actress of complex parts; **~eigenschaft** *die* characteristic; trait; **~fehler** *der* fault [of character]; **~fest** *Adj.* steadfast; **~festigkeit** *die* firmness *or* strength of character

**charakterisieren** *tr. V.* characterize

**Charakterisierung** *die; ~, ~en* characterization; (*Schilderung*) portrayal

**Charakteristik** *die; ~, ~en* characterization

**Charakteristikum** *das; ~s,* **Charakteristika** (*geh.*) characteristic (+ *Gen. od.* **für** of)

**charakteristisch** ❶ *Adj.* characteristic, typical (**für** of). ❷ *adv.* characteristically; in a typical manner

**charakteristischerweise** *Adv.* characteristically [for him/her]

**Charakter·kopf** *der* striking head; **ein ~ sein** have a magnificent *or* striking head

**charakterlich** ❶ *Adj.* character *attrib.* ‹defect, development, training›; personal ‹qualities›; **~e Veränderungen** personality changes. ❷ *adv.* in [respect of] character; **jmdn. ~ formen** mould sb.'s character; (*schulen*) give sb. character-training

**charakter·los** ❶ *Adj.* unprincipled; characterless, colourless ‹style, playing, townscape›; (*niederträchtig*) despicable; (*labil*) spineless. ❷ *adv.* in an unprincipled fashion; (*ohne Ausdruck*) colourlessly; drearily; (*niederträchtig*) despicably; (*labil*) spinelessly

**Charakterlosigkeit** *die; ~, ~en* Ⓐ lack of principle; (*Niederträchtigkeit*) despicableness; (*Labilität*) weakness of character; spinelessness; Ⓑ (*Handlung*) unprincipled/despicable action; (*Äußerung*) unprincipled/despicable remark

**Charakterologie** /karakterolo'gi:/ *die; ~:* characterology *no art.*

**charakter-, Charakter-: ~rolle** *die* (*Theater*) complex part *or* character; **~schwach** *Adj.* of weak character *postpos.*; spineless; **~schwäche** *die* weakness of character; spinelessness *no pl.*; **~schwein** *das* (*ugs. abwertend*) unprincipled bastard (*coll.*); **~stärke** *die* strength of character; (*Entschlossenheit*) strength of mind; **~studie** *die* character study; **~voll** *Adj.* Ⓐ (*~fest*) steadfast; showing strength of character *postpos.*, *not pred.*; Ⓑ (*ausdrucksvoll*) distinctive; ‹house etc.› of character; strongly characterized, individual ‹features›; **~zug** *der* characteristic

**Charge** /'ʃarʒə/ *die; ~, ~n* Ⓐ (*bes. Milit.: Dienstgrad, Person*) rank; **die unteren ~n** the lower ranks (*Mil.*)/orders; **die oberen ~n** the upper ranks (*Mil.*)/echelons; Ⓑ (*Theater: Nebenrolle*) small character part

**Charisma** /'ça:rɪsma/ *das; ~s,* **Charismen** charisma

**charismatisch** /çarɪs'ma:tɪʃ/ *Adj.* charismatic

**Charleston** /'tʃarlstn̩/ *der; ~, ~s* Charleston

**charmant** /ʃar'mant/ ❶ *Adj.* charming; **sich von seiner ~esten Seite zeigen** show one's most attractive side. ❷ *adv.* charmingly; with much charm

**Charme** /ʃarm/ *der; ~s* charm; **seinen ganzen ~ spielen lassen** *od.* **aufbieten** turn on all one's charm

**Charmeur** /ʃar'mø:ɐ̯/ *der; ~s, ~s od. ~e* charmer

**Charmeuse** /ʃar'mø:z/ *die; ~* (*Textilw.*) charmeuse

**Charta** /'karta/ *die; ~, ~s* (*Politik*) charter

**Charter** /'tʃartɐ/ *der; ~s, ~s* charter agreement

**Charter-: ~flug** *der* charter flight; **~maschine** *die* chartered aircraft

**chartern** *tr. V.* charter ‹aircraft, boat›; hire [the services of] ‹guide, firm›

**Charts** /tʃarts/ *Pl.* charts

**chassidisch** /xa'si:dɪʃ/ *Adj.* (*jüd. Rel.*) Hasidic

**Chassidismus** *der; ~* (*jüd. Rel.*) Hasidism *no art.*

**Chassis** /ʃa'si:/ *das; ~* /ʃa'si:(s)/, *~* /ʃa'si:s/ (*Kfz-W., Elektrot.*) chassis

**Chateaubriand** /ʃatobri'ã:/ *das; ~s, ~s* (*Kochk.*) Chateaubriand [steak]

**chatten** /'tʃɛtn̩/ *itr. V.* (*DV Jargon*) chat

**Chauffeur** /ʃɔ'fø:ɐ̯/ *der; ~s, ~e* ▶ 159 driver; (*privat angestellt*) chauffeur

**Chauffeuse** /ʃɔ'fø:zə/ *die; ~n, ~n,* ▶ 159 (*bes. schweiz.*) driver; (*privat angestellt*) chauffeur; chauffeuse (*dated*)

**chauffieren** *tr., itr. V.* (*veralt.*) drive

**Chaussee** /ʃo'se:/ *die; ~, ~n* (*veralt.*) (*surfaced*) [high] road; highway (*Amer.*)

**Chauvi** /'ʃo:vi/ *der; ~s, ~s* (*ugs. abwertend*) male chauvinist (*coll. derog.*)

**Chauvinismus** /ʃovi'nɪsmʊs/ *der; ~:* chauvinism; **männlicher ~:** male chauvinism

**Chauvinist** *der; ~en, ~en* (*abwertend*) chauvinist; (*männlicher ~*) male chauvinist

**Chauvinistin** *die; ~, ~nen* chauvinist

**chauvinistisch** (*abwertend*) ❶ *Adj.* chauvinistic; (*männlich-~*) male chauvinist. ❷ *adv.* chauvinistically; (*männlich-~*) in a male chauvinist way

**Check** (*schweiz.*) ⇒ **Scheck**

**checken** /'tʃɛkn̩/ *tr. V.* Ⓐ (*bes. Technik: kontrollieren*) check; examine; **sich [vom Arzt] ~ lassen** (*ugs.*) have a check-up [from the doctor]; Ⓑ (*salopp: begreifen*) twig (*coll.*); (*bemerken*) spot; **ich habe das noch nicht gecheckt** I haven't got it yet; Ⓒ (*Eishockey: stoppen*) check ‹player›

**Check·liste** *die* checklist; (*Passagierliste*) passenger list

**Chef** /ʃɛf/ *der; ~s, ~s* Ⓐ (*Leiter*) (*einer Firma, Abteilung, Regierung*) head; (*der Polizei, des Generalstabs*) chief; (*einer Partei, Bande*) leader; (*Vorgesetzter*) superior; boss (*coll.*); **wer ist denn hier der ~?** who's in charge here?; Ⓑ (*salopp: Anrede*) **hallo, ~:** hey, chief *or* squire (*Brit. coll.*); hey mister (*Amer. coll.*)

**Chef-** *in Zus.* chief

**Chef-: ~arzt** *der,* **~ärztin** *die: head of one or more specialist departments in a hospital;* (*Direktor[in]*) superintendent (*of small hospital*); **~dramaturg** *der,* **~dramaturgin** *die* (*Theater*) [chief] literary adviser; **~etage** *die* management floor; **Unruhe in den ~etagen auslösen** cause a flutter in the boardrooms; **~ideologe** *der,* **~ideologin** *die* leading ideologist

**Chefin** *die; ~, ~nen* Ⓐ (*Leiterin*) (*einer Firma, Abteilung, Regierung*) head; (*einer Partei, Bande*) leader; (*Vorgesetzte*) superior; boss (*coll.*); Ⓑ (*ugs.: Frau des Chefs*) boss's wife (*coll.*); Ⓒ (*salopp: Anrede*) missis (*coll.*); ma'am (*Amer.*)

**Chef-: ~koch** *der,* **~köchin** *die* ▶ 159 chef; head cook; **~redakteur** *der,* **~redakteurin** *die,* chief editor; (*Verlagsw. auch*) managing editor; **~sekretärin** *die* director's secretary; **~visite** *die* senior consultant's round (*in the wards*)

**Chemie** /çe'mi:/ *die; ~* Ⓐ (*Wissenschaft*) chemistry *no art.*; Ⓑ (*ugs.: Chemikalien*) chemicals *pl.*; **der Pudding ist reine ~:** the pudding is nothing but chemicals *or* is purely synthetic

**Chemie-: ~arbeiter** *der,* **~arbeiterin** *die,* chemical worker; **~betrieb** *der* chemical firm; **~faser** *die* synthetic *or* man-made fibre; **~ingenieur** *der,* **~ingenieurin** *die,* chemical engineer; **~laborant** *der,* **~laborantin** *die* chemical laboratory assistant; **~werker** *der,* **~werkerin** *die,* (*ugs.*) chemical worker

**Chemikalie** /çemi'ka:li̯ə/ *die; ~, ~n* chemical

**Chemiker** /'çe:mikɐ/ *der; ~s, ~,* **Chemikerin** *die; ~, ~nen* ▶ 159 (*graduate*) chemist; ⇒ *auch* **-in**

**Cheminée** /'ʃmɪne/ *das; ~s, ~s* (*schweiz.*) open fireplace

**chemisch** ❶ *Adj.* chemical; **~er Versuch** chemistry experiment; **eine/die ~e Reinigung** a/the dry-cleaner's; (*Vorgang*) dry-cleaning; **die ~e Keule** Chemical Mace ®. ❷ *adv.* chemically; **~ bleichen** bleach with chemicals

**chemisieren** *tr. V.* (*DDR*) chemicalize; make increased use of chemicals in ‹agriculture›

**chemo-, Chemo-: ~techniker** *der,* **~technikerin** *die,* industrial chemist; (*Chemieingenieur*) chemical engineer; **~therapeutisch** *Adj.* (*Med.*) chemotherapeutic; **~therapie** *die* (*Med.*) chemotherapy; **mit einer ~therapie beginnen** start a course of chemotherapy

**Chenille** /ʃə'nɪljə/ *die; ~, ~n* chenille

**Cheque** /ʃɛk/ ⇒ **Scheck**

**Cherrybrandy** /'tʃɛri 'brɛndi/ *der; ~s, ~s* cherry brandy

**Cherub** /'çe:rʊp/ *der; ~s,* **Cherubim** /'çe:rubi:m/ *od.* **Cherubinen** /çe:ru'bi:nən/ (*Rel.*) cherub

**cherubinisch** *Adj.* cherubic

**Chester·käse** /'tʃɛstɐ-/ *der* (*usu. processed*) Cheddar cheese

**chevaleresk** /ʃəvalə'rɛsk/ (*geh.*) ❶ *Adj.* chivalrous; gentlemanly. ❷ *adv.* chivalrously

**Chevreau·leder** /ʃə'vro:-/ *das* kid

**Chianti** /'ki̯anti/ *der; ~s, ~s* Chianti

**Chiasmus** /'çi̯asmʊs/ *der; ~* (*Rhet.*) chiasmus *no art.*

**chic** *usw.* ⇒ **schick** *usw.*

**Chicorée** /'ʃikore/ *der; ~s od. die; ~:* chicory

**Chiffon** /'ʃɪfõ/ *der; ~s, ~s* chiffon

**Chiffre** /'ʃɪfrə/ *die; ~, ~n* Ⓐ (*Zeichen*) symbol; Ⓑ (*Geheimzeichen*) cipher; **~n** cipher *sing.*; **in ~n (*Dat.*) schreiben** write in code; Ⓒ (*in Annoncen*) box number; **Zuschriften unter ~ ...** reply quoting box no. ...; Ⓓ (*Rhet.*) cipher

**Chiffre·schrift** *die* code

**chiffrieren** *tr. V.* [en]code; **chiffriert** coded; in [a secret] code *postpos.*

**Chignon** /ʃɪn'jõ:/ *der; ~s, ~s* chignon

**Chihuahua** /tʃi'u̯au̯a/ *der; ~s, ~s* chihuahua

**Chile** /'tʃi:le, 'çi:lə/ *(das); ~s* Chile

**Chilene** /tʃi'le:nə, çi'le:nə/ *der; ~n, ~n,* **Chilenin** *die; ~, ~nen* ▶ 553 Chilean; ⇒ *auch* **-in**

**chilenisch** *Adj.* ▶ 553 Chilean

**Chile·salpeter** *der* Chile salpeter *or* nitre

**Chili** /'tʃi:li/ *der; ~s, ~es* Ⓐ *Pl.* (*Schoten*) chillies; Ⓑ (*Gewürz*) chilli [powder]; Ⓒ ⇒ **Chilisoße**

**Chiliasmus** /çi'li̯asmʊs/ *der; ~* (*christl. Rel.*) chiliasm *no art.*

**Chili·soße** *die* chilli sauce

**Chimäre** /çi:mɛ:rə/ *die; ~, ~n* Ⓐ ⇒ **Schimäre**; Ⓑ (*Biol.*) chimera

**China** /'çi:na/ *(das); ~s* China

**China-: ~kohl** *der* Chinese cabbage; (*im Handel*) Chinese leaves *pl.*; **~kracher** *der* Chinese cracker; **~papier** *das* rice paper

**Chinchilla**[1] /tʃɪn'tʃɪla/ *das; ~s, ~s* Ⓐ (*Pelz*) chinchilla; Ⓑ (*Kaninchen*) chinchilla [rabbit]

*old spelling (see note on page 1707)

**Chinchilla**[2] *die;* ~, ~**s** (*Zool.*) chinchilla

**Chinese** /çi'ne:zə/ *der;* ~**n**, ~**n** ▶553 Chinese; **zum** ~**n essen gehen** (*ugs.*) eat Chinese (*coll.*)

**Chinesin** *die;* ~, ~**nen** ▶553 Chinese; ⇒ *auch* **-in**

**chinesisch** ▶553, ▶696 ❶ *Adj.* Chinese; ~**er Tee** China tea; **die Chinesische Mauer** the Great Wall of China. ❷ *adv.* in the Chinese manner *or* style; ~ **essen** have a Chinese meal; eat Chinese (*coll.*)

**-chinesisch** *das;* -~[**s**] ... jargon

**Chinin** /çi'ni:n/ *das;* ~**s** quinine

**chinin·haltig** *Adj.* containing quinine *postpos., not pred.;* ~ **sein** contain quinine

**Chintz** /tʃɪnts/ *der;* ~**:** chintz

**Chip** /tʃɪp/ *der;* ~**s**, ~**s** Ⓐ (*Spielmarke*) chip; Ⓑ (*Kartoffel*~) [potato] crisp (*Brit.*) *or* (*Amer.*) chip; Ⓒ (*Elektronik*) [micro]chip

**Chip·karte** *die* smart card

**Chippendale** /'tʃɪpəndeɪl/ *das;* ~[**s**] Chippendale

**Chiromant** /çiro'mant/ *der;* ~**en**, ~**en** palmist

**Chiromantie** *die;* ~**:** chiromancy *no art.;* palmistry *no art.*

**Chiromantin** *die;* ~, ~**nen** ⇒ **Chiromant**

**Chiropraktik** *die;* ~ (*Med.*) chiropractic *no art.*

**Chiropraktiker** *der;* ~**s**, ~, **Chiropraktikerin** *die;* ~, ~**nen** ▶159 (*Med.*) chiropractor

**Chirurg** /çi'rʊrk/ *der;* ~**en**, ~**en** ▶159 surgeon

**Chirurgie** /çirʊr'gi/ *die;* ~, ~**n** Ⓐ (*Disziplin*) surgery *no art.;* Ⓑ (*Abteilung*) surgical department; (*Station*) surgical ward; **auf der** ~ **liegen** be in the surgical ward

**Chirurgin** *die;* ~, ~**nen** surgeon; ⇒ *auch* **-in**

**chirurgisch** ❶ *Adj.* surgical. ❷ *adv.* (*operativ*) surgically; by surgery

**Chitin** /çi'ti:n/ *das;* ~**s** chitin

**Chitin·panzer** *der* (*Zool.*) chitinous exoskeleton

**Chlor** /klo:ɐ̯/ *das;* ~**s** chlorine

**Chloral** /klo'ra:l/ *das;* ~**s** (*Chemie*) chloral

**Chlorat** /klo'ra:t/ *das;* ~**s**, ~**e** (*Chemie*) chlorate

**chloren** *tr. V.* chlorinate

**chlor·haltig** *Adj.* containing chlorine *postpos., not pred.;* ~/**stark** ~ **sein** contain chlorine/have a high chlorine content

**Chlorid** /klo'ri:t/ *das;* ~**s**, ~**e** (*Chemie*) chloride

**chlorieren** *tr. V.* (*Chemie*) chlorinate

**chlorig** *Adj.* ~**e Säure** (*Chemie*) chlorous acid

**Chloroform** /kloro'fɔrm/ *das;* ~**s** chloroform

**chloroformieren** *tr. V.* chloroform

**Chlorophyll** /kloro'fʏl/ *das;* ~**s** (*Bot.*) chlorophyll

**Chlor-:** ~**säure** *die* (*Chemie*) chloric acid; ~**wasser** *das* Ⓐ (*ugs.: gechlortes Wasser*) chlorinated water; Ⓑ (*Chemie*) chlorine water; ~**wasser·stoff** *der* (*Chemie*) hydrogen chloride

**Choke** /tʃoʊk/ *der;* ~**s**, ~**s**, **Choker** /tʃoʊkɐ/ *der;* ~**s**, ~ (*Kfz-W.*) [manual] choke

**Cholera** /'ko:lera/ *die;* ~ ▶474 (*Med.*) cholera

**Choleriker** /ko'le:rikɐ/ *der;* ~**s**, ~, **Cholerikerin** *die;* ~, ~**nen** Ⓐ choleric type *or* (*Psych.*) subject; **ein klassischer Choleriker:** a textbook example of the choleric temperament; Ⓑ (*ugs.: jähzorniger Mensch*) irascible person; **ein Choleriker sein** have a short fuse

**cholerisch** ❶ *Adj.* irascible; choleric ‹temperament›. ❷ *adv.* irascibly

**Cholesterin** /çolɛste'ri:n/ *das;* ~**s** (*Med.*) cholesterol

**Cholesterin·spiegel** *der* (*Physiol.*) cholesterol level

**Chor**[1] /ko:ɐ̯/ *der;* ~[**e**]**s**, **Chöre** /'kø:rə/ Ⓐ choir; (*in Oper, Sinfonie*) chorus; **im** ~ **rufen/brüllen** shout/roar in chorus; Ⓑ (*Komposition; im Theater*) chorus

**Chor**[2] *der od.* (*selten:*) *das;* ~[**e**]**s**, ~**e** *od.* **Chöre** Ⓐ (*Altarraum*) choir; Ⓑ (*Empore*) choir loft; (*mit der Orgel*) organ loft

**Choral** /ko'ra:l/ *der;* ~**s**, **Choräle** /ko'rɛ:lə/ Ⓐ (*Kirchenlied*) chorale; Ⓑ (*gregorianischer* ~) [Gregorian] chant

**Choral-:** ~**bearbeitung** *die* (*Musik*) arrangement of a chorale; ~**vor·spiel** *das* (*Musik*) chorale prelude

**Choreograph** /koreo'gra:f/ *der;* ~**en**, ~**en** ▶159 choreographer

**Choreographie** *die;* ~, ~**n** choreography

**choreographieren** *tr., itr. V.* choreograph

**Choreographin** *die;* ~, ~**nen** choreographer; ⇒ *auch* **-in**

**choreographisch** *Adj.* choreographic

**Chor-:** ~**frau** *die* (*kath. Rel.*) canoness; ~**führer** *der*, ~**führerin** *die* (*Theater*) leader of the chorus; ~**gebet** *das* (*kath. Rel.*) canonical hour (*as part of divine office*); ~**gestühl** *das* choir stalls *pl.;* ~**herr** *der* (*kath. Rel.*) canon [regular]

**Chorist** *der;* ~**en**, ~**en** ⇒ **Chorsänger**

**Choristin** *die;* ~, ~**nen** ⇒ **Chorsängerin**

**Chor-:** ~**knabe** *der* choirboy; chorister; ~**konzert** *das* choral concert; ~**leiter** *der*, chorus master; (*des Kirchenchors*) choirmaster; ~**leiterin** *die* chorus mistress; (*eines Kirchenchors*) choir mistress; ~**musik** *die* choral music; ~**rock** *der* surplice; ~**sänger** *der*, ~**sängerin** *die* member of the chorus

**Chorus** /'ko:rʊs/ *der;* ~, ~**se** (*Jazz*) theme

**Chose** /'ʃo:zə/ *die;* ~, ~**n** (*ugs.*) Ⓐ (*Angelegenheit*) business (*derog.*); Ⓑ (*Gegenstände*) stuff; **die ganze** ~**:** the whole lot (*coll.*) *or* (*coll.*) shoot *or* (*coll.*) caboodle

**Chow-Chow** /tʃau 'tʃau/ *der;* ~**s**, ~**s** chow

**Christ**[1] /krɪst/ *der;* ~**en**, ~**en** Christian

**Christ**[2] (*der*) (*Christus*) Christ

**christ-, Christ-:** ~**baum** *der* Ⓐ (*bes. südd.*) Christmas tree; **nicht alle auf dem** ~**baum haben** (*ugs.*) be dotty (*Brit. coll.*); be not quite all there (*Brit. coll.*); be missing some marbles (*coll.*); Ⓑ (*milit. Jargon: Leuchtsignale*) target marker [flare]; ~**baum-** ⇒ **Weihnachtsbaum-;** ~**demokrat** *der*, ~**demokratin** *die* (*Politik*) Christian Democrat; ~**demokratisch** (*Politik*) ❶ *Adj.* Christian Democrat; ❷ *adv.* in a Christian Democrat manner *or* spirit; ~**demokratisch regiert** governed by Christian Democrats

**Christen-:** ~**gemeinde** *die* Christian community; ~**glaube[n]** *der* Christian faith

**Christenheit** *die;* ~**:** Christendom *no art.;* **die ganze** ~**:** the whole Christian community; all Christians *pl.*

**Christen·lehre** *die* Ⓐ (*christl. Kirchen*) [Church] teaching of Christian doctrine; Ⓑ (*DDR Schulw.*) Christian religious instruction

**Christentum** *das;* ~**s** Christianity *no art.;* (*Glaube*) Christian faith; **sich zum** ~ **bekennen** profess the Christian faith; declare oneself a Christian

**Christen·verfolgung** *die* persecution of Christians

**Christ·fest** *das* (*veralt., noch südd., österr.*) ⇒ **Weihnachtsfest**

**christianisieren** /krɪstjani'zi:rən/ ❶ *tr. V.* Christianize; convert to Christianity. ❷ *itr. V.* make conversions to Christianity

**Christianisierung** *die;* ~**:** Christianization

**Christin** *die;* ~, ~**nen** Christian; ⇒ *auch* **-in**

**christ-, Christ-:** ~**katholisch** *Adj.* (*schweiz.*) ⇒ **altkatholisch;** ~**kind** *das* Ⓐ (*Jesus*) infant Jesus; Christ-child; Ⓑ (*weihnachtliche Gestalt*) Christ-child (*as bringer of Christmas gifts*); **er glaubt noch ans** ~**kind** (*fig. iron.*) he still believes in Father Christmas; Ⓒ (*bes. südd., österr.: Geschenk*) Christmas present; ~**kindchen** *das* ⇒ ~**kind** A, B; ~**kindl** *das;* ~~**s** (*südd., österr.*) ⇒ ~**kind** A, B, C; ~**königs·fest** *das* (*kath. Rel.*) feast of Christ the King

**christlich** ❶ *Adj.* Christian; **die** ~**e Seefahrt** (*scherzh.*) seafaring; **wir stehen um halb neun auf — eine halbwegs** ~**e Zeit** (*ugs. scherzh.*) we get up at half-past eight — a more or less civilized time. ❷ *adv.* in a [truly] Christian spirit; ~ **leben** live a Christian life; **Kinder** ~ **erziehen** give children a Christian upbringing; ~ **geprägt** imbued with Christian principles

**Christlichkeit** *die;* ~**:** Christian spirit

**Christ-:** ~**messe** *die* (*kath. Rel.*) Christmas Mass; ~**mette** *die* (*kath. Rel.*) Christmas Mass; (*ev. Rel.*) midnight service [on Christmas Eve]; ~**nacht** *die* Christmas night

**Christoph** /'krɪstɔf/ (*der*) Christopher

**Christophorus** /krɪs'to:forʊs/ (*der*)**: der heilige** ~**:** St Christopher

**Christ-:** ~**rose** *die* Christmas rose; ~**stollen** *der* [German] Christmas loaf (*with candied fruit, almonds, etc.*)

**Christus** /'krɪstʊs/ (*der*)*;* ~ *od.* **Christi** Christ; **1000 vor/nach Christi Geburt** 1000 BC/AD 1000

**Christus-:** ~**dorn** *der; Pl.* ~~**e** (*Bot.*) crown of thorns; ~**kopf** *der* (*Kunst*) head of Christ; ~**monogramm** *das* Christogram; chi-rho

**Christ·vesper** *die* (*kath. u. ev. Rel.*) Christmas Eve vespers (*with music*)

**Chrom** /kro:m/ *das;* ~**s** chromium

**Chromatik** /kro'ma:tɪk/ *die;* ~ Ⓐ (*Musik*) chromaticism; Ⓑ (*Physik*) chromatics *pl.*

**chromatisch** *Adj.* chromatic

**chrom-, Chrom-:** ~**blitzend** *Adj.* gleaming with chrome *postpos.;* ~**dioxid·kassette** *die* chrome[-dioxide] cassette; ~**gelb** *das* chrome yellow; ~**leder** *das* chrome leather; ~**nickel·stahl** *der* chrome-nickel steel

**Chromosom** /kromo'zo:m/ *das;* ~**s**, ~**en** (*Biol.*) chromosome

**Chromosomen·satz** *der* (*Biol.*) chromosome set

**Chromosphäre** /kromo'sfɛ:rə/ *die* (*Astron.*) chromosphere

**Chrom·stahl** *der* chrome steel

**Chronik** /'kro:nɪk/ *die;* ~, ~**en** chronicle

**chronisch** ❶ *Adj.* (*Med., auch ugs.*) chronic; **an** ~**em Geldmangel leiden** (*ugs.*) suffer from a chronic shortage of money. ❷ *adv.* (*Med., auch ugs.*) chronically

**Chronist** /kro'nɪst/ *der;* ~**en**, ~**en** ▶159 chronicler

**Chronistik** *die;* ~**:** historiography *no art.*

**Chronistin** *die;* ~, ~**nen** ⇒ **Chronist**

**Chronologie** *die;* ~**:** chronology; **die** ~ **der Ereignisse** *od.* **des Geschehens** the sequence of events; **[nach] unserer/jüdischer** ~**:** according to our/the Jewish calendar

**chronologisch** ❶ *Adj.* chronological; ~**er Fehler** mistake regarding the date. ❷ *adv.* chronologically; in chronological order

**Chronometer** /krono'me:tɐ/ *das;* ~**s**, ~**:** chronometer

**chronometrisch** ❶ *Adj.* chronometric. ❷ *adv.* chronometrically

**Chrysantheme** /kryzan'te:mə/ *die;* ~, ~**n** chrysanthemum

**Chuzpe** /'xʊtspə/ *die;* ~ (*salopp abwertend*) chutzpah; **die** ~ **haben, etw. zu tun** have the nerve to do sth. (*coll.*)

**CIA** /si:aɪ'eɪ/ *der od. die;* ~**:** CIA

**Cicero** *die od.* (*schweiz.*) *der;* ~, ~ (*Druckw.*) pica; 12-point type

**Cidre** /si:dɐ/ *der;* ~**s** [Normandy/Brittany] cider

**Cimbal** ⇒ **Zimbal**

**Cineast** /sine'ast/ *der;* ~**en**, ~**en**, **Cineastin** *die;* ~, ~**nen** Ⓐ (*Filmschaffende[r]*) film-maker; Ⓑ (*Kenner[in]*) film expert; (*Filmfan*) film fan

**circa** ⇒ **zirka**

**Circe** /'tsɪrtsə/ *die;* ~, ~**n** Circe; enchantress

**Circulus vitiosus** /'tsɪrkulʊs vi'tsio:zʊs/ *der;* ~ ~, **Circuli vitiosi** (*geh.*) vicious circle

**Circus** ⇒ **Zirkus**

**cis, Cis** /tsɪs/ *das;* ~ (*Musik*) C sharp

**Cis-Dur** *das* (*Musik*) C sharp major; ⇒ *auch* **A-Dur**

C

C

**cis-Moll** *das* (*Musik*) C sharp minor; ⇒ *auch* **a-Moll**

**Citoyen** /sitoa'jɛ̃:/ *der;* **~s, ~s** (*politically aware*) citizen

**City** /'sɪti/ *die;* **~, ~s** city centre

**City·ruf** *der* area paging service

**Clair-obscur** /klɛrɔps'ky:ɐ̯/ *das;* **~[s]** (*Kunst*) chiaroscuro

**Clan** /kla:n/ *der;* **~s, ~e** *od.* **~s** Ⓐ (*salopp: Interessengemeinschaft*) clique; Ⓑ (*in Schottland; auch salopp: Familie*) clan

**Claque** /'klakə/ *die;* **~:** claque; hired applauders *pl.*

**Claqueur** /kla'kø:ɐ̯/ *der;* **~s, ~e** claqueur; hired applauder

**Clavicembalo** /klavi'tʃɛmbalo/ *das;* **~s, ~s** (*Musik*) harpsichord

**clean** /kli:n/ *Adj.* (*ugs.*) clean (*coll.*); **~ werden** come off drugs

**Clearing** /'kli:rɪŋ/ *das;* **~s, ~s** (*Wirtsch.*) clearing

**clever** /'klɛvɐ/ ❶ *Adj.* (*raffiniert*) shrewd; (*intelligent, geschickt*) clever; smart. ❷ *adv.; s. Adj.:* shrewdly; cleverly; smartly

**Cleverness**, ***Cleverneß** /'klɛvɐnɛs/ *die;* **~** ⇒ **clever** 1: shrewdness; cleverness; smartness (*Amer.*)

**Cliché** ⇒ **Klischee**

**Clinch** /klɪntʃ/ *der;* **~[e]s** Ⓐ (*Boxen*) clinch; **in den ~ gehen** go into a clinch; Ⓑ (*ugs.: Auseinandersetzung*) conflict; **mit jmdm. im ~ liegen** be locked in dispute with sb.; **[mit jmdm.] in den ~ gehen** start quarrelling *or* wrangling [with sb.]

**clinchen** *itr. V.* (*Boxen*) go into a clinch

**Clip** /klɪp/ *der;* **~s, ~s** Ⓐ ⇒ **Ohrklipp;** Ⓑ (*Video~*) video

**Clipper** Ⓦⓩ /'klɪpɐ/ *der;* **~s, ~** (*veralt.*) [long-haul] airliner (*on overseas routes*)

**Clique** /'klɪkə/ *die;* **~, ~n** Ⓐ (*abwertend: Interessengemeinschaft*) clique; Ⓑ (*Freundeskreis*) set; lot (*coll.*); (*größere Gruppe*) crowd (*coll.*); (*Jugendliche*) gang (*coll.*); **er gehört mit zur unserer ~:** he's one of our crowd (*coll.*) *or* lot (*coll.*)

**Cliquen-: ~[un]wesen** *das,* **~wirtschaft** *die* (*ugs. abwertend*) clique system

**Clivia** /'kli:vi̯a/ *die;* **~, Clivien** (*Bot.*) clivia

**Clochard** /klɔ'ʃa:r/ *der;* **~s, ~s** down-and-out; tramp

**Clog** /klɔk/ *der;* **~s, ~s** clog

**Clou** /klu:/ *der;* **~s, ~s** (*ugs.*) main point; (*Glanzpunkt*) highlight; **der besondere ~:** the really special thing [about it]; **das ist doch gerade der ~:** but that's the great thing about it

**Clown** /klaun/ *der;* **~s, ~s** clown; **sich zum ~ machen** make oneself look a fool *or* look ridiculous; **jmdn. zum ~ machen** make a clown of sb.; treat sb. as a clown

**Clownerie** /klaunə'ri:/ *die;* **~, ~n: ~[n]** clowning *no pl.*

**Clownin** /'klaunɪn/ *die;* **~, ~nen** clown; ⇒ *auch* **Clown**

**Club** ⇒ **Klub**

**Cluster** /'klastɐ/ *der;* **~s, ~[s]** (*Kernphysik, Musik, Sprachw.*) cluster

**cm** *Abk.* ▶ 489 **Zentimeter** cm.

**c-Moll** /tse:-/ *das* C minor; ⇒ *auch* **a-Moll**

**Co.** *Abk.* **Compagnie** Co.

**Coach** /koutʃ/ *der;* **~s, ~s** ▶ 159 (*Sport*) coach; (*bes. Fußball: Trainer*) manager

**coachen** /'koutʃn̩/ *tr., itr. V.* (*Sport*) coach; (*Trainer sein*) manage

**Coaching** /'ko:tʃɪŋ/ *das;* **~s** coaching

**Coca** /'ko:ka/ *das;* **~s, ~s** *od. die;* **~, ~s** (*ugs.*) Coke ®

**Cockerspaniel** /'kɔkɐ-/ *der;* **~s, ~s** cocker spaniel

**Cockpit** /'kɔkpɪt/ *das;* **~s, ~s** cockpit; (*bei großen Linienflugzeugen*) flight deck

**Cocktail** /'kɔkteɪl/ *der;* **~s, ~s** Ⓐ (*Getränk; auch Salat usw.*) cocktail; Ⓑ (*Party*) cocktail party; (*DDR: Empfang*) reception

**Cocktail-: ~empfang** *der* [cocktail] reception; **~kleid** *das* cocktail dress; **~party** *die* cocktail party; **~schürze** *die* hostess apron

**Code** ⇒ **Kode**

**Codein** ⇒ **Kodein**

**Codex** ⇒ **Kodex**

**Cœur** /kø:ɐ̯/ *das;* **~[s], ~[s]** (*Kartenspiel*) hearts *pl.*; (*einzelne Karte*) heart; ⇒ *auch* **Pik²**

**cognac** /'kɔnjak/ *indekl. Adj.* cognac[-coloured]

**Cognac** Ⓦⓩ *der;* **~s, ~s** Cognac

**cognac·farben** *Adj.* cognac[-coloured]

**Coiffeur** /koa'fø:ɐ̯/ *der;* **~s, ~e, Coiffeuse** /koa'fø:zə/ *die;* **~, ~n** (*schweiz., sonst geh.: Friseur/Friseuse*) hairdresser; (*Schöpfer/Schöpferin von Haarmoden*) hairstylist

**Coiffure** /koa'fy:ɐ̯/ *die;* **~, ~n** Ⓐ (*geh.: Frisierkunst*) hairdressing; (*Schöpfung von Haarmoden*) hairstyling; Ⓑ (*schweiz.: Frisiersalon*) hairdresser's [salon]

**Cola** /'ko:la/ *das;* **~s, ~s** *od. die;* **~, ~s** (*ugs.*) Coke ®

**Collage** /kɔ'la:ʒə/ *die;* **~, ~n** collage; (*als Form/Technik*) **die ~:** collage

**Collie** /'kɔli/ *der;* **~s, ~s** collie

**Colloquium** ⇒ **Kolloquium**

**Colonia·kübel** /ko'lo:ni̯a-/ *der* (*österr.*) dustbin; garbage *or* trash can (*Amer.*)

**Color-** /'ko'lɔ:ɐ̯-/ (*Fot.*) **~film/~dia/~negativ** colour film/slide/negative

**Colt** Ⓦⓩ /kɔlt/ *der;* **~s, ~s** Colt ® [revolver]

**Combo** /'kɔmbo/ *die;* **~, ~s** small (jazz *or* dance) band; combo (*sl.*)

**Come-back** /kam'bɛk/ *das;* **~s, ~s** comeback; **ein ~ feiern** stage a comeback

**COMECON, Comecon** /'kɔmekɔn/ *der od. das;* **~:** Comecon

**Comic** /'kɔmɪk/ *der;* **~s, ~s** Ⓐ comic strip; (*Heft*) comic; Ⓑ (*Film*) cartoon film

**Comic-: ~heft** *das* comic; **~held** *der* comic-strip hero

**Comicstrip** /'kɔmɪk 'strɪp/ *der;* **~[s], ~s** comic strip

***Comic strip** /'kɔmɪk 'strɪp/ *der;* **~ ~[s], ~ ~s** comic strip

**Composer** /kɔm'po:zɐ/ *der;* **~s, ~** (*Druckw.*) composer

**Computer** /kɔm'pju:tɐ/ *der;* **~s, ~:** computer; **über ~** (*Akk.*) **gehen** *od.* **laufen** be computerized; be done by computer; **auf ~** (*Akk.*) **umstellen** computerize

**computer-, Computer-: ~animation** *die* (*DV*) computer animation; **~an·lage** *die* computer system; **~ausdruck** *der; Pl.* **~~s, ~~e** computer printout; **~blitz** *der* (*Fot.*) computerized [electronic] flash; **~diagnostik** *die* (*Med.*) computer[-aided] diagnosis; **~gerecht** ❶ *Adj.* computer-compatible; ❷ *adv.* in computer-compatible form; **~gesteuert** *Adj.* computer-controlled; **~gestützt** *Adj.* computer-assisted

**computerisieren** *tr. V.* computerize ‹data, system›; (*aufbereiten*) make ‹data› computer-compatible

**Computer-: ~kriminalität** *die* computer crime; **~kunst** *die* computerized art; **~satz** *der* (*Druckw.*) computer setting **~spiel** *das* computer game; **~tomographie** *die* (*Med.*) Ⓐ (*Methode*) computer tomography; computed tomography; Ⓑ (*Bild*) computed tomogram

**Comte** /kõ:t/ *der;* **~, ~s** (*French*) count

**Comtesse** /kõ'tɛs/ *die;* **~, ~n** ⇒ **Komtess**

**Conceptart** /'kɔnsɛpt|a:ɐ̯t/ *die;* **~** (*Kunstwiss.*) concept[ual] art

**Concerto grosso** /kɔn'tʃɛrto 'grɔso/ *das;* **~ ~, Concerti grossi** (*Musik*) concerto grosso

**Concierge** /kõ'si̯ɛrʃ/ *der/die;* **~, ~s** concierge

**Conditio sine qua non** /kɔn'di:tsi̯o 'zi:nə 'kva: 'no:n/ *die;* **~ ~ ~ ~** (*Philos.*) sine qua non

**Conférencier** /kõferã'si̯e:/ *der;* **~s, ~s** compère (*Brit.*); master of ceremonies

**Confiserie** ⇒ **Konfiserie**

**Confiteor** /kɔn'fi:teɔr/ *das;* **~** (*kath. Rel.*) Confiteor; general confession

**Connaisseur** /kɔnɛ'sø:ɐ̯/ *der;* **~s, ~s** (*geh.*) connoisseur

**Consommé** /kõsɔ'me:/ *die;* **~, ~s** *od. das;* **~s, ~s** (*Kochk.*) consommé

**Container** /kɔn'te:nɐ/ *der;* **~s, ~:** container; (*für Müll*) [refuse] skip; (*für Altglas*) bottle bank

**Container-: ~bahn·hof** *der* container station; **~hafen** *der* container port *or* terminal; **~schiff** *das* container ship; **~verkehr** *der* container traffic *no art.*

**Contenance** /kõtə'nã:s(ə)/ *die;* **~** (*geh.*) composure; **die ~ [be]wahren/verlieren** keep/lose one's composure *or* countenance

**Contergan** Ⓦⓩ /kɔntɛr'ga:n/ *das;* **~s** thalidomide

**Contergan·kind** *das* thalidomide child

**cool** /ku:l/ (*ugs.*) ❶ *Adj.* Ⓐ (*gelassen*) cool; **~ bleiben** keep one's cool (*sl.*); Ⓑ (*gut*) fabulous (*coll.*); Ⓒ (*reell*) reliable; (*anständig*) decent; reasonable. ❷ *adv.* Ⓐ (*gelassen*) coolly; Ⓑ (*gut*) fabulously (*coll.*); Ⓒ (*anständig*) decently; reasonably

**Cool·jazz** /'ku:l 'dʒæz/ *der;* **~:** cool jazz

**Copilot, Copilotin** ⇒ **Kopilot**

**Copyright** /'kɔpirait/ *das;* **~s, ~s** copyright

**Copyshop** /'kɔpiʃɔp/ *der* photocopy[ing] shop; copyshop

**coram publico** /'ko:ram/ (*geh.*) in public

**Cord** /kɔrt/ *der;* **~[e]s, ~e** *od.* **~s** cord; (**~samt**) corduroy

**Cord-: ~an·zug** *der* cord/corduroy suit; **~hose** *die* [pair *sing.* of] corduroy trousers *pl. or* cords *pl.*; **~jeans** *Pl.* corduroy jeans; cords

**Cordon bleu** /kɔrdõ'blø/ *das;* **~ ~, ~s ~s** /kɔrdõ'blø/ (*Kochk.*) veal escalope cordon bleu

**Cord-: ~rock** *der* corduroy skirt; **~samt** *der* corduroy

**Core** /kɔ:/ *das;* **~[s], ~s** (*Kernphysik*) core

**Cornedbeef** /'kɔ:nd 'bi:f/ *das;* **~s** corned beef

**Corner** /'kɔ:nə/ *der;* **~s, ~** (*österr. Fußball*) corner [kick]

**Cornflakes** /'kɔ:nfleɪks/ *Pl.* cornflakes

**Cornichon** /kɔrni'ʃõ:/ *das;* **~s, ~s** [fine-quality] gherkin

**Corona** ⇒ **Korona**

**Corps** ⇒ **Korps**

**Corpus** ⇒ **Korpus**

**Corpus Delicti** /'kɔrpus de'lɪkti/ *das;* **~ ~, Corpora** /'kɔrpora/ **Delicti** Ⓐ (*Rechtsspr.*) weapon [used]; Ⓑ (*meist scherzh.: Beweisstück*) piece of incriminating evidence

**Corso** ⇒ **Korso**

**Cortison** ⇒ **Kortison**

**Costa Rica** /'kɔsta 'ri:ka/ (*das*); **~s** Costa Rica

**Costa-Ricaner** *der;* **~s, ~, Costa-Ricanerin** *die;* **~, ~nen** Costa Rican

**costa-ricanisch** *Adj.* Costa Rican

**CO-Test** /tse'|o:-/ *der* (*Kfz-W.*) exhaust emission test (*for carbon monoxide content*)

**Couch** /kautʃ/ *die;* **~, ~s;** (*schweiz. auch:*) *der;* **~s, ~[e]s** sofa; **auf die ~ müssen** (*fig.*) need to see a psychiatrist

**Couch-: ~garnitur** *die* three-piece suite; **~tisch** *der* coffee table

**Couleur** /ku'lø:ɐ̯/ *die;* **~, ~s** Ⓐ (*Richtung*) shade [of opinion]; persuasion; **Politiker jeglicher ~:** politicians of every shade of opinion *or* of every hue; Ⓑ (*Studentenspr.: Band u. Mütze*) fraternity colours *pl.*; **~ tragen** wear one's fraternity's colours

**Coulomb** /ku'lõ:/ *das;* **~s, ~** (*Physik*) coulomb

**Count-down, Countdown** /'kaunt'daun/ *der od. das;* **~s, ~s** (*Raumf., auch fig.*) countdown

**Countrymusic** /'kʌntrɪmju:zɪk/ *die;* **~:** country music

**Coup** /ku:/ *der;* **~s, ~s** coup; **einen ~ landen** (*ugs.*) pull off a coup

**Coupé** /ku'pe:/ *das;* **~s, ~s** Ⓐ coupé; Ⓑ (*österr., sonst veralt.: Abteil*) compartment

**Couplet** /ku'ple:/ *das;* **~s, ~s** satirical song (*with refrain*)

---

*old spelling (see note on page 1707)

**Coupon** /ku'põ:/ *der;* **~s, ~s** Ⓐ (*Gutschein*) coupon; voucher; (*im Café*) ticket; (*zum Abreißen*) counterfoil; **auf** *od.* **für** *od.* **gegen diesen ~ bekommen Sie ...** for this voucher you will receive ...; Ⓑ (*Finanzw.*) [interest] coupon; Ⓒ (*Stoff*) piece; length

**Cour** /ku:ɐ̯/ *in* **einer Frau/Dame die ~ machen** *od.* **schneiden** (*veralt.*) pay court to a woman/lady

**Courage** /ku'ra:ʒə/ *die;* ~ (*ugs.*) courage; **im letzten Moment verließ sie die ~:** at the last moment she lost her nerve; ⇒ *auch* **Angst**

**couragiert** /kura'ʒi:ɐ̯t/ ❶ *Adj.* (*mutig*) courageous; (*beherzt*) spirited. ❷ *adv.* ⇒ **1:** courageously; spiritedly

**Courtage** /kʊr'ta:ʒə/ *die;* **~, ~n** brokerage; broker's commission

**Courtoisie** /kʊrto̯a'zi:/ *die;* **~, ~n** (*veralt.*) courtesy

**Cousin** /ku'zɛ̃:/ *der;* **~s, ~s** (*male*) cousin; ⇒ *auch* **Grad** A

**Cousine** /ku'zi:nə/ *die;* **~, ~n** (*female*) cousin

**Couturier** /kutʏ'ri̯e:/ *der;* **~s, ~s** couturier

**Couvert** /ku've:ɐ̯/ *das;* **~s, ~s** Ⓐ ⇒ **Kuvert**; Ⓑ (*für Bettdecken*) [quilt] cover

**Cover** /'kavɐ/ *das;* **~s, ~s** Ⓐ (*von Illustrierten*) cover; Ⓑ (*von Schallplatten*) sleeve

**Cover·girl** *das* cover girl

**covern** /'kavɐn/ *tr. V.* cover ‹song, record›

**Cover·version** /'kavə.../ *die* cover [version]

**Cowboy** /'kau̯bɔy/ *der;* **~s, ~s** cowboy

**Cowboy-: ~hut** *der* cowboy hat; stetson; **~stiefel** *der* cowboy boot

**Cox Orange** /'kɔks|orã:ʒə/ *der;* **~ ~, ~ ~:** Cox's orange pippin

**Crack** /krɛk/ *der;* **~s, ~s** ace; crack player; (*Athlet*) crack athlete; **ein ~ im Schwimmen/Radfahren** a crack swimmer/cyclist

**Cracker** /'krɛkɐ/ *der;* **~s, ~[s]** cracker

**Crash·kurs** /'krɛʃ.../ *der* crash course

**Credo** ⇒ **Kredo**

**creme** /kre:m/ *indekl. Adj.* cream

**Creme** /kre:m/ *die;* **~, ~s,** (*schweiz.:*) **~n** Ⓐ (*Kosmetik, Kochk.*) cream; Ⓑ (*oft iron.: Oberschicht*) cream; top people; **die ~ der Gesellschaft** the cream of society

**creme·farben** *Adj.* cream[-coloured]

**cremen** *tr. V.* ⇒ **eincremen**

**Creme-: ~schnitte** *die* cream slice; **~törtchen** *das* cream tart[let]; **~torte** *die* cream cake *or* gateau

**cremig** ❶ *Adj.* creamy; **etw. ~ schlagen** beat sth. into a cream. ❷ *adv.* like cream

**Crêpe**[1] /krɛp/ *die;* **~, ~s** (*Kochk.*) crêpe

**Crêpe**[2] *der;* **~, ~s** ⇒ **Krepp**

**Crescendo** /krɛ'ʃɛndo/ *das;* **~s, ~s** (*Musik*) crescendo

**Creutzfeldt-Jakob-Krankheit** /'krɔyt͡sfɛlt 'ja:kɔp.../ *die* ▶474 (*Med.*) Creutzfeldt-Jakob disease

**Crew** /kru:/ *die;* **~, ~s** Ⓐ (*eines Schiffs/Flugzeugs*) crew; Ⓑ (*Gruppe*) team; Ⓒ (*Marine: Kadetten*) group of cadets (*in the same year*); class

**Croissant** /kro̯a'sã:/ *das;* **~s, ~s** croissant

**Cromargan** Ⓦⓩ /kromar'ga:n/ *das;* **~s** stainless [chrome-nickel] steel

**Croquette** ⇒ **Krokette**

**Crosscountry** /krɔs'kantri/ *das;* **~[s], ~s** (*Sport*) cross-country [race]

**Croupier** /kru'pi̯e:/ *der;* **~s, ~s** ▶159 croupier

**Crux** /krʊks/ *die;* ~ Ⓐ (*Schwierigkeit*) trouble (+ *Gen.*, **bei** with); Ⓑ (*Sorgen*) **man hat seine ~ mit ihnen** they are a real trial; (*sie sind eine Last*) they are a real burden

**C-Schlüssel** /'t͡se:-/ *der* (*Musik*) C clef

**ČSFR** /t͡ʃɛs|ɛf|'ɛr/ *Abk.* **Tschechoslowakei**

**ČSSR** /t͡ʃe|ɛs|ɛs'|ɛr/ (*hist.*) ⇒ **ČSFR**

**CSU** *Abk.* **Christlich-Soziale Union** CSU

**c.t.** *Abk.* **cum tempore; Beginn: 20 Uhr ~:** 8.15 p.m. start

**CT** (*Med.*) *Abk.* **Computertomographie** CT

**cum grano salis** /kʊm 'gra:no 'za:lɪs/ (*geh.*) taken with a pinch of salt

**cum laude** /kʊm 'lau̯də/ (*Hochschulw.*) with distinction; *third of four grades of successful doctoral examination*

**cum tempore** /kʊm 'tɛmpore/ (*Hochschulw.*) 15 minutes after the time indicated

**Cunnilingus** /kʊni'lɪŋgʊs/ *der;* **~, Cunnilingi** (*Sexualk.*) cunnilingus

**Cup** /kap/ *der;* **~s, ~s** cup

**Cup·finale** *das* (*Fußball*) Cup Final; (*andere Sportarten*) final of the Cup

**Cupido** /ku'pi:do/ (*der*); **~s** (*Myth.*) Cupid

**Curettage** ⇒ **Kürettage**

**Curie** /kʏ'ri:/ *das;* **~[s], ~[s]** (*Physik*) curie

**Curling** /'kə:lɪŋ/ *das;* **~s** (*Sport*) curling

**curricular** /kʊriku'la:ɐ̯/ *Adj.* (*Päd.*) curricular

**Curriculum** /kʊ'ri:kulʊm/ *das;* **~s, Curricula** (*Päd.*) curriculum; (*genauer festgelegt*) syllabus

**Curriculum·forschung** *die* curricular research

**Curry** /'kœri/ *das;* **~s, ~s** Ⓐ (*auch: der*) curry powder; Ⓑ (*Gericht*) curry

**Curry-: ~sauce, ~soße** *die* curry sauce; **~wurst** *die: sliced fried sausage sprinkled with curry powder and served with ketchup*

**Cut** /kœt, kat/ *der;* **~s, ~s** Ⓐ (*Sakko*) morning coat; Ⓑ (*Boxen*) cut (*esp. above the eye*)

**Cutaway** /'kœtəve/ *der;* **~s, ~s** ⇒ **Cut** A

**cutten** /'katn̩/ *tr., itr. V.* (*Film, Rundf., Ferns.*) cut; edit

**Cutter** /'katɐ/ *der;* **~s, ~, Cutterin** *die;* **~, ~nen** ▶159 (*Film, Ferns., Rundf.*) editor

**cuttern** ⇒ **cutten**

**CVJM** *Abk.* Ⓐ **Christlicher Verein Junger Männer** YMCA; Ⓑ **Christlicher Verein Junger Menschen;** *combined form of YMCA and YWCA*

**CVP** *Abk.* (*schweiz.*) **Christlich-demokratische Volkspartei** Christian Democratic People's Party

**Cw-Wert** /t͡se:'ve:-/ *der* (*Technik*) $c_d$ [value]

**Cyan** /t͡sʏa:n/ *das;* **~s** (*Chem.*) cyanogen

**Cyanid** /t͡sʏa'ni:t/ *das;* **~s, ~e** (*Chemie*) cyanide

**Cyber·sex** /'sai̯bɐ/ *der* cybersex

**Cyberspace** /'sai̯bɐspeɪs/ *der;* ~ (*DV*) cyberspace

**Cymbal** ⇒ **Zimbal**

# Dd

**d, D** /deː/ *das;* ~, ~ Ⓐ (*Buchstabe*) d/D; Ⓑ (*Musik*) [key of] D; ⇒ *auch* **a**, A

**D** *Abk.* **Damen**

**da** /daː/*Adv.* Ⓐ (*dort*) there; **da draußen/drinnen/drüben/unten** out/in/over/down there; **da hinten/vorn[e]** [there] at the back/front; **da hinab/hinauf/hinüber** down/up/over that way; **geh da herum** go round that way; **he, Sie da!** hey, you there!; **der Kerl da** that fellow [over there]; **ich möchte von dem da** I'd like some of that one; **halt, wer da?** (*Milit.*) halt, who goes there?; **hallo, wer ist denn da?** (*am Telefon*) hello, who's that [speaking]?; **gleich sind wir da** we're almost there; we'll be there in a minute; **ach, da ist meine Brille!** so 'that's where my glasses are!; oh, 'there are my glasses!; **da bist du ja!** there you are [at last]!; **da, ein Reh!** look, [there's] a deer!; **da, wo die Straße nach X abzweigt** where the road to X turns off; at the turning for X; **da und da** at such-and-such a place; **da und dort** here and there; (*manchmal*) now and again *or* then; Ⓑ (*hier*) here; **da bin ich** here I am; **da hast du das Buch** here's the book; **da, nimm schon!** here [you are], take it!; ⇒ *auch* **da sein, dahaben**; Ⓒ (*zeitlich*) then; (*in dem Augenblick*) at that moment; **ich hatte mich gerade ins Bett gelegt, da klingelte das Telefon** I had just got into bed when the telephone rang; **von da an** from then on; **in meiner Jugend, da war alles besser** back in my young days, everything was better [then]; Ⓓ (*deshalb*) **der Zug war schon weg, da habe ich den Bus genommen** the train had already gone, so I took the bus; Ⓔ (*ugs.: in diesem Fall*) **da kann man nichts machen** there's nothing one can do about it *or* that; **was gibts denn da zu lachen?** what's there to laugh about [there]?; what's funny about that?; **da kann ich [ja] nur lachen!** that's plain ridiculous!; that just makes me laugh!; **was tut man da?** what does one do in a case like this?; Ⓕ (*altertümelnd: nach Relativpronomen; wird nicht übersetzt*) **..., der da sagt ...**, who says; Ⓖ (*hervorhebend; wird meist nicht übersetzt*) **ich habe da einen Kollegen, der ...** I have a colleague who ...; **da fällt mir noch was ein** [oh yes] another thought strikes me; Ⓗ **da sein** be there; (*hier sein*) be here; (*übrig sein*) be left; **ist Herr X da?** is Mr X about *or* available?; **er ist schon da** he has already arrived; **der neue Katalog ist da** the new catalogue is in; **ist ein Brief für mich da?** is there a letter for me?; **es ist niemand da** there is nobody there/here; **es muss noch Brot da sein:** there must be some bread left; **du musst essen, was da ist** you must eat what there is; **der Schlüssel ist wieder da** the key is back again; (*ist gefunden worden*) the key has turned up [again]; **ich bin gleich wieder da** I'll be right *or* straight back; **ich melde mich, wenn ich wieder da bin** I'll get in touch when I get back; **es/sie sind nur dazu da, zu ...** it only exists/they only exist to ...; its/their only purpose is to ...; **dafür** *od.* **dazu ist es ja da!** that's what it's [there] for!; Ⓘ **da sein** (*sich ereignen*) occur; ‹moment› have arrived; ‹situation› have arisen; **ein solcher Fall ist noch nie da gewesen** such a case has never occurred before *or* is unprecedented; **er überbot alles bisher Dagewesene** he surpassed all previous achievements; Ⓙ **da sein** (*existieren, leben*) be left; be still alive; **da warst du noch gar nicht da** (*ugs.*) you weren't around then; that was before your time; **sie war nur noch für ihn da** he had her to himself; Ⓚ **da sein** (*ugs.: klar bei Bewusstsein sein*) **ganz** *od.* **voll da sein:** be completely with it (*coll.*); **ich bin noch nicht ganz da** I'm not quite with it yet (*coll.*); I haven't quite come round yet; **er ist [geistig] wieder voll da** he is in full possession of his faculties again Ⓛ (*Note: in North German colloquial usage pronominal adverbs are often divided so that* **da** *appears on its own with the remainder of the adverb at the end of the clause; see footnotes under* **dabei, dafür, dagegen, daher, damit, danach, davon, davor, dazu, dazwischen**).

❷ *Konj.* Ⓐ (*weil*) as; since; **da ich ein Feigling bin, wagte ich es nicht** being a coward *or* since I'm a coward I didn't dare to; **da es [gerade] regnet** as *or* seeing that it's raining; Ⓑ (*geh.: als*) when; **jetzt, da es feststand, dass ...** now that it was definite that ...

**da-:** ❶ *Bei den aus* **da-** *od.* **dar-** *und einer Präposition gebildeten Adverbien* (**dabei, dafür, damit, daran** *usw.*) *wird* **da[r]-** *im Allgemeinen durch* it *oder, wenn es sich auf einen Plural bezieht, durch* them *übersetzt; z. B.* **es gibt nur eine Tür, jeder muss dadurch** there is only one door and everyone has to pass through it; **die Tulpen sind schön; wieviel verlangen Sie dafür?** the tulips are nice; how much are you asking for them? *Wenn jedoch der Bestandteil* **da[r]-** *besonders betont ist, dann ist* that *bzw.* those *die angemessenere Übersetzung:* **also darauf willst du hinaus!** so that's what you're getting at! **Haben die Spritzen nicht geholfen? — Nein, dadurch ist ihm nur noch schlechter geworden** Didn't the injections help? — No, those only made him worse. *Wenn auf das Adverb ein* **dass** *mit Nebensatz folgt, bietet sich häufig die Formulierung* the fact that *an:* **dadurch gekennzeichnet, dass ...** characterized by the fact that ... *Wenn Haupt- u. Nebensatz dasselbe Subjekt haben oder wenn ein Infinitivsatz angeschlossen ist, kommt man durch die Verbindung von Präposition und Verbalsubstantiv zu einer eleganten Übersetzung:* **wir sind dafür, dass wir weitermachen** *od.* **weiterzumachen** we are in favour of continuing. *Das ist manchmal sogar bei verschiedenen Subjekten möglich, wenn man ein Possessivpronomen* (his, our *usw.*) *hinzusetzt:* **er ist dafür, dass wir weitermachen** he is in favour of our continuing.

❷ *Die Einträge für diese Adverbien berücksichtigen nur einen Teil der möglichen Kontextbeispiele mit Verben oder Substantiven. Es empfiehlt sich deshalb, auch unter den jeweiligen Verben oder Substantiven nachzuschlagen; so kann man z. B. die Übersetzung für* **danach fragen** (ask about it/them) *über* **nach etw. fragen** *unter dem Stichwort* **fragen** *erschließen*

**d. Ä.** *Abk.* **der Ältere**

**da|behalten** *unr. tr. V.* keep [there]; (*hier behalten*) keep here; **sie hat die Kinder gleich ~:** she simply kept the children at her place; **kann ich das Buch ~?** can I keep the book [here]?

**da·bei** *Adv.* Ⓐ (*bei etw.*) with it/them; (*bei jmdm.*) with him/her/them; (*beigeschlossen*) enclosed; **eine Tankstelle mit einer Werkstatt ~:** a filling station with its own workshop [attached]; **nahe ~** (*in der Nähe*) near it; close by; **wir wollen es ~ lassen** (*fig.*) we'll leave it at that; Ⓑ (*währenddessen*) at the same time; (*bei diesem Anlass*) then; on that occasion; **er aß weiter und redete ~:** he went on eating and talked as he did so; **die ~ entstehenden Kosten** the expense involved; **er ist ~ gesehen worden, wie er das Geld nahm** he was seen [in the act of] taking the money; **eine unangenehme Reparatur — man muss ~ unterm Auto liegen** an unpleasant job — you have to lie under the car to do it; **ich hoffe, Sie haben alle ~ etwas gelernt** I hope you have all learned something from it *or* in the process; **eine Massenkarambolage — ~ gab es zwei Tote** a big pile-up — two people were killed [in it]; **~ kam es zu erbitterten Kämpfen** this gave rise to bitter fighting; Ⓒ (*außerdem*) **~ [auch]** what is more; **es war eiskalt und [auch] nass ~:** it was freezing cold and damp into the bargain; **er ist sehr beschäftigt, aber ~ immer freundlich** he is very busy but even so always friendly; Ⓓ (*hinsichtlich des Erwähnten*) about it/them; **was hast du dir denn ~ gedacht?** what were you thinking of?; what came over you?; **er hat sich nichts ~ gedacht** he saw no harm in it; **ich fühle mich ganz und gar nicht wohl ~:** I am not at all happy about it; **da ist doch nichts ~!** there's really no harm in it!; (*es ist nicht schwierig*) there's nothing to it!; ⇒ *auch* **bleiben** E; **da-**; Ⓔ (*obwohl*) but; **er suchte nach dem Brief, ~ hatte er ihn in der Hand** he was looking for the letter and all the time he had it in his hand; Ⓕ **~ sein** (*anwesend sein*) be there; be present (**bei** at); (*teilnehmen*) take part (**bei** in); **bei der Sitzung ~ sein** be at *or* attend the meeting; **~ sein ist alles!** it's taking part that counts; **Wer kommt mit? — Ich bin ~!** Who's coming? — Count me in!; **ein wenig Angst ist immer ~:** there is always an element of fear; Ⓖ **[gerade] ~ sein, etw. zu tun** be just doing sth.; **Spülst du das Geschirr? — Ich bin schon ~:** Will you wash up? — I'm already in the middle of it; *NB In senses* a, b, *and* d *the word can occur in two parts in North German coll. usage, e.g.* **da ist eine Karte bei** there is a card with it

**dabei-: ~|bleiben** *unr. itr. V.; mit sein* (*dort*) stay there; be there; (*bei einer Tätigkeit*) stick to it; (*bei einer Firma, der Armee*) stay on; **~|haben** *unr. tr. V.* have with one; **ich habe kein Geld ~:** I haven't got any money with me *or* on me; **sie wollte die Kinder nicht ~haben** (*ugs.*) she didn't want to have the children there *or* around; ***~|sein** ⇒ **dabei** F, G; **~|sitzen** *unr. itr. V.* sit there; **~|stehen** *unr. itr. V.* stand by; stand there

**da|bleiben** *unr. itr. V.; mit sein* stay there; (*hier bleiben*) stay here; **[noch] ~:** stay on

**da capo** /daˈkaːpo/ Ⓐ (*Musik*) da capo; Ⓑ (*Beifallsruf*) **~!** encore!

**d'accord** /daˈkoːɐ̯/ (*bes. österr.*) **mit jmdm. ~ gehen** *od.* **sein** agree with sb.

**Dach** /dax/ *das;* **~[e]s, Dächer** /ˈdɛçɐ/ Ⓐ roof; **[ganz oben] unterm ~** *od.* (*ugs. scherzh.*) **unterm ~ juchhe** [right up] in the attic; **ein/kein ~ über dem Kopf haben** (*ugs.*) have a/no roof over one's head; **[mit jmdm.] unter einem ~ leben** live under the same roof [with *or* as sb.]; **etw. unter ~ und Fach bringen** get sth. [safely] under cover; bring in sth.; (*fig.: erfolgreich beenden*) get sth. all wrapped up; **unter ~ und Fach sein** be under cover; ‹harvest› be safely [gathered] in; (*fig.: erfolgreich beendet*) wrapped up; ‹contract etc.› be signed and sealed; **das ~ der Welt** (*fig.*) the roof of the world; Ⓑ (*fig. ugs.*) **jmdm. aufs ~ steigen** give sb. a piece of one's mind; ‹superior officer etc.› haul sb. over the coals;

*old spelling (see note on page 1707)

**jmdm. eins aufs ~ geben** bash sb. over the head; (*tadeln*) give sb. a dressing down; tear a strip off sb. (*coll.*); **eins aufs ~ bekommen** *od.* **kriegen** get a bash on the head; (*eine Rüge erhalten*) get it in the neck (*coll.*)

**dach-, Dach-: ~antenne** *die* roof aerial; roof antenna (*Amer.*); **~balken** *der* roof beam; **~boden** *der* loft; **auf dem ~boden** in the loft; **~decker** /-dɛkɐ/ *der;* **~~s, ~~, ~deckerin** *die;* **~~, ~~nen** ▶ 159 roofer; (*für Reetdächer*) thatcher; **das kannst du halten wie ein ~decker** (*ugs.*) it's all the same to me; **~decker·arbeiten** *Pl.* roofing work *sing.;* (*mit Reet*) thatching work *sing.;* **~fenster** *das* skylight; (*~gaube*) dormer window; **~first** *der* [roof] ridge; **~förmig** *Adj.* roof-shaped; **~förmiger Vorsprung** rooflike projection; **~garten** *der* A roof garden; B ⇒ **~terrasse**; **~gaube** *die* (*bes. Bauw.*) dormer window; **~gebälk** *das* roof timbers *pl.;* **~gepäck·träger** *der* (*Kfz-W.*) roof rack; **~geschoss**, ***~geschoß** *das* attic [storey]; **~gesellschaft** *die* (*Wirtsch.*) holding company; **~gesims** *das* eaves *pl.;* **~gestühl** *das* ⇒ **~stuhl**; **~giebel** *der* gable; **~gleiche** /-glaiçə/ *die;* **~~, ~~n** (*österr.*) ⇒ **Richtfest**; **~hase** *der* (*scherzh.*) cat; moggie (*coll.*); **~kammer** *die* attic [room]; (*ärmlich*) garret; **~konstruktion** *die* A roof structure; (*Entwurf*) roof design; B (*das Konstruieren*) construction of the roof; **~lawine** *die: mass of snow sliding from a roof*

**Dächlein** /ˈdɛçlain/ *das;* **~s, ~:** little roof

**Dach-: ~luke** *die* skylight; **~organisation** *die* umbrella organization; **~pappe** *die* roofing felt; **~pfanne** *die* pantile; **~platte** *die* flat tile; (*Schindel*) shingle; (*aus Schiefer*) slate; **~reiter** *der* ridge turret; **~rinne** *die* gutter

**Dachs** /daks/ *der;* **~es, ~e** A (*Tier*) badger; B (*ugs.: unerfahrener Bursche*) greenhorn; **er ist noch ein ganz junger ~:** he's still wet behind the ears; C (*ugs.: Kind*) **vorlauter** *od.* **frecher kleiner ~:** little rascal; young whippersnapper

**Dachs-: ~bär** *der* (*Jägerspr.*) [male] badger; **~bau** *der; Pl.* **~~e** badger's earth *or* set

**Dach-: ~schaden** *der* A (*ugs.*) **einen ~schaden haben** be not quite right in the head; be slightly screwy (*coll.*); B (*Schaden am ~*) roof damage; **~schiefer** *der* roofing slate; **~schindel** *die* [roof] shingle; **~schräge** *die* roof angle; pitch of the roof

**Dachs·hund** *der* (*fachspr.*) ⇒ **Dackel** A

**Dächsin** /ˈdɛksɪn/ *die;* **~, ~nen** [female] badger; badger sow

**Dach-: ~sparren** *der* rafter; **~stroh** *das* straw thatch; **~stübchen** *das* (*veralt.*) little attic room; (*ärmlich*) garret; **~stube** *die* (*veralt.*) ⇒ **~kammer**; **~stuhl** *der* roof truss

**dachte** /ˈdaxtə/ *1. u. 3. Pers. Sg. Prät. v.* **denken**

**Dach-: ~terrasse** *die* roof terrace; **~traufe** *die* eaves *pl.;* **~verband** *der* ⇒ **~organisation**; **~wohnung** *die* attic flat (*Brit.*) *or* (*Amer.*) apartment; **~ziegel** *der* roof tile; **~ziegel·verband** *der* (*Med.*) [rib] strapping; **~zimmer** *das* attic room

**Dackel** /ˈdakl̩/ *der;* **~s, ~** A (*Hund*) dachshund; B (*Schimpfwort*) clot (*Brit. coll.*)

**Dackel·beine** *Pl.* (*ugs. scherzh.*) [stumpy] bow legs

**Dada** /ˈdada/ *der;* **~[s]** A Dada; B (*Gruppe*) Dada[ist group]

**Dada-Bewegung** *die* Dadaist movement; Dadaism

**Dadaismus** *der;* **~:** Dadaism *no art.*

**Dadaist** *der;* **~en, ~en, Dadaistin** *die;* **~, ~nen** Dadaist

**dadaistisch** *Adj.* Dadaist

**da·dran** (*ugs.*) ⇒ **daran**

**da·drauf** (*ugs.*) ⇒ **darauf**

**da·draus** (*ugs.*) ⇒ **daraus**

**da·drin** (*ugs.*) ⇒ **darin**

**da·drinnen** (*ugs.*) ⇒ **darinnen**

**da·drüber** (*ugs.*) ⇒ **darüber**

**da·drum** (*ugs.*) ⇒ **darum**

**da·drunter** (*ugs.*) ⇒ **darunter**

**da·durch** *Adv.* A (*durch diese Öffnung hindurch*) through it/them; (*geh.: wodurch*) through which; **soll ich dadurch gehen oder dadurch?** should I go through this one or that one *or* through here or through there?; B (*durch diesen Umstand*) as a result; (*durch dieses Mittel*) in this way; by this [means]; **ich nehme den D-Zug, ~ bin ich zwanzig Minuten eher da** I'll take the express, that way I'll get there twenty minutes earlier; **er hat sich ~ selbst geschadet** by doing this he has damaged his own interests; C **~, dass er es [nicht] tat, konnte er ...** as a result of [not] doing it *or* by [not] doing it he was able to ...; **~, dass er älter ist, hat er einige Vorteile** he has several advantages by virtue of being older *or* because he is older; ⇒ *auch* **da-**

**da·für** *Adv.* A (*für diese Sache, diesen Zweck*) for it/them; **~ gebe ich gern etwas [Geld]** I'll gladly give some money for that; **~ haben wir Sie schließlich eingestellt!** after all, that's what we took you on for!; **Magenschmerzen? Pfefferminztee ist sehr gut ~** (*ugs.*) Stomach ache? Peppermint tea is very good for that; **~, dass ...** considering that ...; (*damit*) so that ...; **~ sorgen[, dass ...]** see to it [that ...]; **der Grund ~, dass ...** the reason why ...; B (*zugunsten dieser Sache*) for it; **~ sein** be in favour [of it]; **ich bin ganz ~:** I'm all for it; **er ist nicht ~, dass sie allein fährt** he's against her going alone; **das ist ein/kein Beweis ~, dass ...** this is proof/no proof that ... *or* proves/does not prove that ...; **ein Beispiel ~ ist ...** an example of this is ...; **alles spricht ~, dass ...** all the evidence *or* everything suggests that ...; C (*als Gegenleistung*) in return [for it]; (*beim Tausch*) in exchange; (*stattdessen*) instead; **heute hat er keine Zeit, ~ will er morgen kommen** he has no time today, so he wants to come tomorrow instead; **in Mathematik ist er zwar eine Niete, aber ~ kann er sehr gut zeichnen** he is useless at maths, but then *or* on the other hand he can draw very well; D (*als etw. [geltend]*) **der Stein ist kein Rubin, aber man könnte ihn ~ halten** the stone is not a ruby, but one might think it was *or* take it for one; **er ist schon 60, aber ~ hält ihn niemand** he is 60 but nobody would think so; **sie ist ihre Mutter, nicht ihre Schwester, aber sie könnte ~ gelten** she is her mother, not her sister, though she could pass for it; E **etwas/nichts ~ können** be/not be responsible; **~ kann er nichts[, dass ...]** it's not his fault [that ...]; he can't help it [that ...]; **die können sehr wohl etwas ~, dass es so ist** they are very much responsible for things being the way they are; ⇒ *auch* **da-**; NB *In senses* A, B, *and* D *the word can occur in two parts in North German coll. usage, e.g.* **da kriege ich nichts für** I'm getting nothing for it

**dafür-: ~|halten** *unr. itr. V.* (*geh.*) consider; be of the opinion; **nach meinem Dafürhalten** in my opinion; ***~|können** ⇒ **dafür** E; **~|stehen** *unr. itr. V.* A (*veralt.: bürgen*) **~stehen, dass ...** guarantee that ...; **~stehen, wie sich die Kinder benehmen** be responsible for the way the children behave; B (*österr.: sich lohnen*) **das** *od.* **es steht [nicht] ~:** it is [not] worth it

**DAG** *Abk.* **Deutsche Angestellten-Gewerkschaft** German Employees' Union

**dagegen** *Adv.* A (*gegen das Genannte*) against it/them; **der Wagen raste auf den Pfeiler zu und prallte ~:** the car careered towards the pillar and crashed into it; **er stieß aus Versehen ~:** he knocked into it by mistake; **ich protestiere energisch ~, dass Sie mich verleumden** I must protest strongly against this slander; **etwas ~ haben** have sth. against it; object [to it]; **ich habe nichts ~:** I've no objection; I don't mind; **haben Sie etwas** *od.* (*ugs.*) **was ~, wenn ...?** do you mind if ...?; **was hat er ~, dass wir Freunde sind?** why does he object to our being friends?; **~ sein** be opposed to it *or* against it; **die Mehrheit war ~, das Angebot anzunehmen** the majority was against *or* opposed to accepting the offer; **wir kennen kein Mittel ~:** we know of no cure for it; **~ kann man nichts machen** there is nothing one can do about it; B *konjunktional* (*im Vergleich dazu*) by *or* in comparison; compared with that; (*jedoch*) on the other hand; **sein Sohn ist dunkelhaarig, seine Tochter ~ blond** his son has dark hair, but his daughter on the other hand is blonde; C (*als Gegenwert*) in exchange; **er hat ein anderes Gerät ~ eingetauscht** he got another machine in exchange [for it]; ⇒ *auch* **da-**; NB *In senses* a, c *the word can occur in two parts in North German coll. usage, e.g.* **da kann niemand gegen sein** nobody can have any objection [to that]

**dagegen-: ~|halten** *unr. tr. V.* A (*entgegnen*) counter; (*einwenden*) object; **er hielt ~, dass ...** his rejoinder *or* answer was that ...; B (*ugs.: vergleichen*) hold it/them against; compare it/them with; **halte das Original ~:** compare it with the original; **~|setzen** *tr. V.* put forward [in opposition]; **„Das stimmt doch gar nicht", setzte er ~:** 'That's quite untrue,' he objected; **nichts ~zusetzen haben** offer no counter-argument; (*nichts einwenden*) make no objection; (*es nicht leugnen*) not deny it; **~|sprechen** *unr. itr. V.* be against it/them; **zahlreiche Gründe sprechen/nichts spricht ~, dass du ein paar Tage freinimmst** there are numerous reasons/there is no reason why you should not take a couple of days off; **was spricht ~?** what is the objection?; **~|stellen** *refl. V.* oppose it; **~|stemmen** *refl. V.* oppose it vigorously; fight it

**da|haben** *unr. tr. V.* (*Zusschr. nur im Inf. u. 2. Part.*) (*ugs.*) have [here]; (*im Hause*) have in the house; **mal sehen, ob ich noch eins da habe** I'll see whether I've got one left

**da·heim** *Adv.* (*bes. südd., österr., schweiz.*) A (*zu Hause*) at home; (*nach Präp.*) home; **ich bin für niemanden ~:** I'm not at home to anybody; **~ anrufen** phone *or* ring home; **wie geht es ~?** how are things at home?; **sind Sie hier ~?** do you live here?; **bei mir ~:** at my place; **~ ist ~!** there's no place like home! (*prov.*); east, west, home's best (*prov.*); B (*in der Heimat*) [back] home; **bei uns ~:** back home where I/we come from; **nach ~ schreiben** write home; **wo bist du ~?** where do you come from?

**Daheim** *das;* **~s** (*bes. südd., österr., schweiz.*) home

**Daheim·gebliebene** *der/die; adj. Dekl.* one who stayed at home; **die ~gebliebenen** those who stayed at home; those back home

**da·her** *Adv.* A (*von dort*) from there; **~ habe ich meine neuen Stiefel** that's where I got my new boots from; **von ~ droht keine Gefahr** there is no danger from 'that quarter; **~ weht also der Wind!** (*ugs.*) so 'that's the way the wind blows! (*fig.*); B (*durch diesen Umstand*) hence; **~ kommt seine gute Laune** that's why he's in a good mood; that's the reason for his good mood; **das/die Krankheit kommt ~, dass ...** the reason for this/the illness is that ...; **~ der Name Bratkartoffel!** (*scherzh.*) that explains it; so that's why!; **~ wusste er das** *od.* **hat er das** that's how he knew; that's where he got it from; C *konjunktional* (*deshalb*) therefore; so; D (*bes. südd.: hierhin*) here; NB *In senses* a, b, *and* d *the word can occur in two parts in coll. usage, e.g.* **da hast du die Klamotten her** that's where you got those clothes from

**daher-, Daher-: ~|bringen** *unr. tr. V.* (*südd., österr.*) A (*mitbringen*) bring [with one]; (*nach Hause*) bring home; B (*abwertend: sagen*) come out with (*coll.*); **~|fliegen** *unr. itr. V.;* *mit sein* A (*umherfliegen*) fly around; B (*heranfliegen*) fly up; **~geflogen kommen** come flying along; (*auf jmdn. zu*) come flying up; **~gelaufen** *Adj.* (*abwertend*) that nobody's heard of *postpos.;* **jeder ~gelaufene Kerl** any guy who comes along; any Tom, Dick, or Harry; **~gelaufene** *der/die; adj. Dekl.* (*abwertend*) nonentity; **jeder ~gelaufene** absolutely anybody [who comes along]; **~|kommen** *unr. itr. V.* come along; (*gemütlich*) stroll along; (*auf jmdn. zu*) come/stroll up; (*auftreten*) turn up; **wie kann man nur in so einem Aufzug ~kommen?**

d

how can one go around dressed like that?; **~reden** (*abwertend*) ❶ *itr. V.* Ⓐ talk off the cuff; Ⓑ (*viel reden*) blather on; **[so] dumm ~reden** talk [such] rubbish; ❷ *tr. V.* Ⓐ say off the cuff; Ⓑ (*wortreich sagen*) prattle; **was er so ~redet** his blathering on; the things he comes out with

**da·hier** *Adv.* (*österr., schweiz., sonst veralt.*) here

**da|hin** Ⓐ (*nach dort*) there; **~ und dorthin** this way and that; Ⓑ (*fig.*) **~ musste es kommen** it had to come to that; **~ hat ihn seine Wettleidenschaft gebracht** that's where his betting mania has got him; **du wirst es ~ bringen, dass ...** you'll carry things *or* matters so far that ...; Ⓒ **bis ~:** to there; (*zeitlich*) until then; **bis ~ sind es 75 km** it's 75 km from here; **bis ~ sind es noch zehn Minuten** there are another ten minutes to go until then; **es steht mir bis ~** (*ugs.*) I am sick and tired of it *or* fed up to the back teeth with it (*coll.*); Ⓓ /-'-/ (*verloren, vorbei*) **~ sein** be *or* have gone; **mein neuer Mantel ist ~:** my new coat is ruined *or* (*coll.*) has had it; Ⓔ (*in diesem Sinne*) **~ [gehend], dass ...** to the effect that ...; **man kann dieses Schreiben auch ~ [gehend] auslegen/verstehen, dass ...** one can also interpret/take this letter as meaning that ...

**da·hinab** *Adv.* down there; down that way

**da·hinauf** *Adv.* up there; up that way

**da·hinaus** *Adv.* out there; (*in die Richtung*) out that way

**dahin-:** **~|bewegen** *refl. V.* move on one's way; **~|dämmern** *itr. V.; mit sein* be semi-conscious; **~|eilen** *itr. V.; mit sein* (*geh.*) hurry along *or* on one's way; ‹time› fly [past]

**da·hinein** *Adv.* in there; (*hier hinein*) in here

**dahin-:** **~|fahren** *unr. itr. V.; mit sein* Ⓐ (*dichter.: wegfahren*) depart; Ⓑ (*dichter.: vorbeifahren*) go *or* pass on one's/its way; Ⓒ (*veralt.: sterben*) pass away; depart this life (*literary*); **~|fliegen** *unr. itr. V.; mit sein* (*dichter.*) Ⓐ (*wegfliegen*) fly on its way; ‹person› fly away; Ⓑ (*vergehen*) fly past; **~|fließen** *unr. itr. V.; mit sein* (*geh.*) flow along *or* on its way

**da·hingegen** *Adv.* on the other hand

**dahin-:** **~|gehen** *unr. itr. V.; mit sein* Ⓐ (*geh.: vergehen*) pass; ‹years› go by; Ⓑ (*geh.: vorbeigehen*) go *or* pass on one's way; Ⓒ (*verhüll.: sterben*) pass away; **~gestellt** *in* **es ist** *od.* **bleibt ~gestellt** it remains to be seen; **ob etwas Vernünftiges dabei herauskommt, sei ~gestellt** we must wait and see whether this produces any useful result; **etw. ~gestellt sein lassen** leave sth. open [for the moment]; **~|jagen** *itr. V.; mit sein* (*geh.*) tear *or* race along; **~|kümmern** *itr. V.; mit sein* (*geh.*) fade away; (*im Gefängnis usw.*) languish; **~|leben** *itr. V.* live one's life; **~|plätschern** *itr. V.; mit sein* **das Gespräch plätscherte an der Oberfläche ~:** the conversation was very superficial *or* remained at the level of small talk; **~|raffen** *tr. V.* (*geh. verhüll.*) carry off; **~|sagen** *tr. V.* say without thinking; **das war nur so ~gesagt** that was just a casual *or* off-the-cuff remark; **~|scheiden** *unr. itr. V.; mit sein* (*geh. verhüll.*) pass away; depart this life (*literary*); **~|schwinden** *unr. itr. V.; mit sein* (*geh.*) Ⓐ (*abnehmen*) dwindle; ‹courage, interest, hope› fade; Ⓑ (*vergehen*) pass; **~|siechen** *itr. V.; mit sein* (*geh.*) waste away; **~|stehen** *unr. itr. V.* **[es] steht [noch] ~:** [it] remains to be seen

**da·hinten** *Adv.* over there

**da·hinter** *Adv.* behind it/them; (*folgend*) after it/them; **ein Haus mit einem Garten ~:** a house with a garden behind *or* at the back; **was sich wohl ~ verbirgt?** (*fig.*) what can be behind it?; **sich ~ klemmen** *od.* **setzen** *od.* **knien** (*fig. ugs.*) buckle down to it; pull one's finger out (*coll.*); **~ kommen** (*fig. ugs.*) find out; **sich ~ machen** (*fig. ugs.*) get down to it; **mach dich ~!** get on with it!; **~ stecken** (*fig. ugs.: Grund, Ursache, Urheber sein*) be behind it/them; **es steckt nichts/nicht viel ~** (*fig. ugs.*) there is nothing/not much to it/them; **~ stehen** (*fig.: dafür eintreten*) be behind it/them; [fully] support it/them; (*fig.: dazu stehen*) stand by it/them; (*fig.: dem zugrunde liegen*) be behind it; be at the root of it; ⇒ *auch* **da-**

***dahinter·her** *Adj.* (*ugs.*) **~ sein** make a big effort; put oneself out; **nie macht ihr eure Aufgaben von euch aus, ich muss immer ~ sein** you never do your homework without being reminded, I've always got to keep on at you

***dahinter|klemmen** *usw.* ⇒ **dahinter**

**da|hinüber** *Adv.* over/across there

**da|hinunter** *Adv.* down there; (*in diese Richtung*) down that way

**dahin-:** **~|vegetieren** *itr. V.* **[elend] ~vegetieren** drag out a miserable existence; **~|ziehen** ❶ *unr. itr. V.; mit sein* go *or* move on one's/its way; ‹clouds› drift by; ❷ *unr. refl. V.* ‹path› pass along

**Dahlie** /'da:li̯ə/ *die;* ~, **~n** dahlia

**Dakapo** /da'ka:po/ *das;* **~s**, **~s** (*Musik*) encore

**daktylisch** /dak'ty:lɪʃ/ *Adj.* (*Verslehre*) dactylic

**Daktylo-** /'daktylo/: **~graphin** /-'gra:fɪn/ *die;* ~, **~nen** (*schweiz.*) typist; **~skopie** /-sko'pi:/ *die;* ~, **~n** dactyloscopy *no art.;* fingerprint identification *no art.*

**Daktylus** /'daktylʊs/ *der;* ~, **Daktylen** (*Verslehre*) dactyl

**da-:** **~|lassen** *unr. tr. V.* (*ugs.*) leave [here]; (*dort lassen*) leave there; **[jmdm.] keine Nachricht ~lassen** leave [sb.] no message; **~|liegen** *unr. itr. V.* lie there; ‹building etc.› stand there

**Dalk** /dalk/ *der;* **~[e]s**, **~e** (*südd., österr. ugs.*) [clumsy] clot (*Brit. coll.*); jerk (*coll.*)

**Dalken** *Pl.* (*österr.*) [yeast-dough] fritters

**dalkert** /'dalkɐt/ (*südd., österr. ugs.*) ❶ *Adj.* daft; **~e Kuh** silly woman (*derog.*). ❷ *adv.* stupidly

**Dalle** /'dalə/ *die;* ~, **~n** (*bes. südd.*) dent

**Dalles** /'daləs/ *der;* ~ (*ugs.*) **im ~ sein** be broke (*coll.*)

**dalli** /'dali/ *Adv.* (*ugs.*) **aber [ein bisschen] ~!** and make it snappy (*coll.*); **[~] ~!** get a move on!; (*beim Laufen*) come on, at the double!

**Dalmatien** /dal'ma:tsi̯ən/ (*das*); **~s** Dalmatia

**Dalmatiner** /dalma'ti:nɐ/ *der;* **~s**, ~, **Dalmatinerin** *die;* ~, **~nen** Dalmatian

**dalmatinisch** *Adj.* Dalmatian

**damalig** /'da:ma:lɪç/ *Adj.* at that *or* the time *postpos.;* **der ~e Bundeskanzler** the then Federal Chancellor; the Federal Chancellor at that *or* the time; **das ~e Leben** life in those days; **die ~e Regierung** the government of the day; **unter den ~en Umständen** in the circumstances obtaining at the time; **im ~en Gallien** in what was then Gaul

**damals** /'da:ma:ls/ *Adv.* then; at that time; **~, als ...** at the time *or* in the days when ...; **von ~:** of that time *or* those days; (*aus dieser Zeit*) from that time *or* those days; **seit ~:** since then; **wie es ~ war** what it was like in those days

**Damast** /da'mast/ *der;* **~[e]s**, **~e** damask

**damasten** *Adj.* (*geh.*) damask

**Damaszener·klinge** /damas'tse:nɐ-/ *die* Damascus blade

**damaszieren** /damas'tsi:rən/ *tr. V.* damascene ‹blade, sword›

**Dämchen** /'dɛ:mçən/ *das;* **~s**, ~ Ⓐ little lady; Ⓑ (*Kind*) [proper] little lady; little madam; Ⓒ (*abwertend: Prostituierte*) lady of the night

**Dame** /'da:mə/ *die;* ~, **~n** Ⓐ ▶ **91**, ▶ **187** (*Frau*) lady; **sehr verehrte** *od.* **meine ~n und Herren!** ladies and gentlemen; **was wünschen Sie, meine ~?** may I help you, madam?; **ein Abend mit ~n** a ladies' night; **die Abfahrt/die 200 Meter der ~n** (*Sport*) the women's downhill/200 metres; **bei den ~n siegte die deutsche Staffel** (*Sport*) the German team won in the women's event; **die ~ des Hauses** the lady of the house; **meine Alte ~** (*veralt. scherzh.*) my mater (*dated sl.*); **ganz ~ sein** be the complete lady; ⇒ *auch* **Welt F**; Ⓑ (*Schach, Kartenspiele*) queen; Ⓒ (*Spiel*) draughts (*Brit.*); checkers (*Amer.*); Ⓓ (*Doppelstein*) king

**Dame·brett** *das* draughtboard (*Brit.*); checkerboard (*Amer.*)

**Dämel** /'dɛ:ml̩/ *der;* **~s**, ~ (*salopp*) fool; **du ~!** you clot! (*Brit. sl.*); you jerk! (*coll.*)

**Damen-:** **~bart** *der* [unwanted] facial hair; **~begleitung** *die:* **in/ohne ~begleitung** in the company of a lady/unaccompanied; with/without a female companion; **~bekanntschaft** *die* lady friend; **eine ~bekanntschaft machen** (*ugs.*) meet *or* get to know someone of the opposite sex; **~besuch** *der* lady visitor/visitors; **~besuch ist ab 20⁰⁰ untersagt** no female visitors after 8 p.m.; **~binde** *die* sanitary towel (*Brit.*) *or* (*Amer.*) napkin; **~doppel** *das* (*Sport*) women's doubles *pl.;* **~einzel** *das* (*Sport*) women's singles *pl.;* **~fahr·rad** *das* lady's bicycle; **~friseur** *der* ladies' hairdresser; **~fußball** *der* women's football; **~garnitur** *die* set of women's underwear; **~gesellschaft** *die* Ⓐ ladies' party; Ⓑ (*Begleitung von ~*) female company; **in ~gesellschaft** in the company of a lady/of ladies

**damenhaft** ❶ *Adj.* ladylike; **~e Kleidung** clothes fit for a lady. ❷ *adv.* like a lady; in a ladylike manner

**Damen-:** **~kapelle** *die* women's band; **~konfektion** *die* ladies' wear; **~kränzchen** *das* (*veralt.*) ladies' circle; **~mannschaft** *die* women's team; **~rad** *das* lady's bicycle; **~salon** *der* ladies' hairdressing salon (*Brit.*); beauty salon (*Amer.*); **~sattel** *der* Ⓐ side-saddle; **im ~sattel reiten** ride side-saddle; Ⓑ (*Fahrradsattel*) ladies' saddle; **~schneider** *der*, **~schneiderin** *die* ▶ **159** dressmaker; **~schuh** *der* lady's shoe; **~schuhe** ladies' shoes; **~sitz** *der* (*Reiten*) **im ~sitz reiten** ride side-saddle; **~stift** *das* (*veralt.*) home for elderly gentlewomen (*esp. members of the aristocracy*); **~toilette** *die* Ⓐ (*WC*) ladies' toilet; ladies' restroom (*Amer.*); Ⓑ (*Kleidung*) ladies' [formal] wear; **~unter·wäsche** *die* ladies' underwear; **~wahl** *die* ladies' choice; **jetzt ist ~wahl** now it's the ladies' turn to choose their partners; **~welt** *die* (*scherzh.*) **die ~welt** the ladies *pl.;* the fair sex

**Dame-:** **~spiel** *das* Ⓐ **das ~spiel** draughts (*Brit.*); checkers (*Amer.*); Ⓑ (*Partie*) game of draught *or* (*Amer.*) checkers; **~stein** *der* draughtsman (*Brit.*); checker (*Amer.*)

**Dam·hirsch** /'dam-/ *der* fallow deer; (*männliches Tier*) fallow buck

**damisch** /'da:mɪʃ/ (*südd., österr. ugs.*) ❶ *Adj.* Ⓐ (*dumm*) stupid; Ⓑ (*schwindlig*) dizzy. ❷ *adv.* (*dumm*) stupidly

**da·mit** ❶ *Adv.* Ⓐ (*mit dieser Sache*) with it/them; **was will er ~ [machen]?** what's he going to do with it/them?; **meint er mich ~?** does he mean me?; **ich bin gleich ~ fertig** I'll be finished in a moment; **du hast recht ~ gehabt** you were right there *or* about that; **er hatte nicht ~ gerechnet** he had not expected that *or* reckoned with that; **~ habe ich nichts zu tun** I have nothing to do with it/them; **er kommt immer wieder ~ an** he's for ever harping on it; **was ist denn ~?** what's the matter with it/them?; what about it/them?; **wie wäre es ~?** how about it?; **~ hat es noch Zeit** there's no hurry about that/those; **Schluss** *od.* **genug ~!** that's enough [of that]; **hör auf ~!** stop it!; **her ~!** let's have it/them!; hand it/them over!; Ⓑ (*gleichzeitig*) with that; thereupon; Ⓒ (*daher*) thus; as a result; **er hatte kein Alibi, und gehörte ~ zu den Verdächtigen** he had no alibi and was therefore one of the suspects; ⇒ *auch* **da-**; *NB In sense* a *the word can occur in two parts in North German coll. usage, e.g.* **da habe ich nicht mit gerechnet** I didn't expect that.
❷ *Konj.* so that; **er kam früher, ~ sie mehr Zeit hatten** *od.* (*geh.*) **hätten** he came earlier so that they would have more time

*old spelling (see note on page 1707)

**Dämlack** /ˈdɛːmlak/ *der;* **~s, ~e** *od.* **~s** (*salopp*) clot (*Brit. coll.*); twerp (*coll.*); jerk (*coll.*)

**dämlich** /ˈdɛːmlɪç/ (*ugs. abwertend*) ❶ *Adj.* stupid. ❷ *adv.* stupidly; **~ fragen** ask stupid questions

**Dämlichkeit** *die;* **~, ~en** (*ugs. abwertend*) Ⓐ (*Art*) stupidity; Ⓑ (*Handlung*) piece of stupidity

**Damm** /dam/ *der;* **~[e]s, Dämme** /ˈdɛmə/ Ⓐ (*Schutzwall*) embankment; levee (*Amer.*); (*Deich*) dike; (*Stau~*) dam; (*durch Wasser, Watt, Sumpf*) causeway; (*fig.*) bulwark (**gegen** against); **einen ~ gegen etw. errichten** (*fig.*) form a barrier *or* defence against sth.; Ⓑ (*Straßen~, Bahn~*) embankment; Ⓒ (*nord[ost]d.: Straße*) road[way]; Ⓓ (*fig.*) **wieder/nicht auf dem ~ sein** (*ugs.*) be fit *or* in good shape again/not be fit *or* in good shape; **jmdn. wieder auf den ~ bringen** (*ugs.*) put sb. back on his/her feet; Ⓔ (*Anat.*) ▶ **471** perineum

**Dämm-** insulating

**Dammbruch** *der* ⇒ **Damm:** breach in a dam/dike; collapse of an embankment/a causeway

**dämmen** /ˈdɛmən/ *tr. V.* Ⓐ (*geh.: aufhalten*) hold back; dam ‹river, stream›; stem ‹flood›; Ⓑ (*Technik: nicht durchlassen*) retain, keep in ‹heat›; (*ausschließen*) keep out ‹noise, heat›

**Dämmer** *der;* **~s** (*dichter.*) twilight; (*Halbdunkel*) half-light; **der ~ des Halbschlafs** (*fig.*) stupefied half-sleep

**dämmerig** ⇒ **dämmrig**

**Dämmer·licht** *das* twilight; (*trübes Licht*) dim light

**dämmern** /ˈdɛmɐn/ *itr. V.* Ⓐ **es dämmert** (*morgens*) it is getting light; (*abends*) it is getting dark; (*mit Zeitangabe*) it gets light/dark; **der Morgen dämmert** the day is dawning *or* breaking; **der Abend dämmert** dusk is falling; Ⓑ (*ugs.: klar werden*) **jmdm. ~:** dawn upon sb.; **mir dämmert da etwas** the penny is beginning to drop; (*ich habe einen Verdacht*) I am beginning to smell a rat; **jetzt dämmerts [bei] mir** now I'm beginning to understand; Ⓒ (*im Halbschlaf*) doze; **vor sich hin ~:** doze; (*nicht klar bei Bewusstsein*) be semi-conscious

**Dämmer-: ~schlaf** *der* Ⓐ (*Halbschlaf*) half-sleep; doze; Ⓑ (*Med.*) twilight sleep; **~schoppen** *der* [early] evening drink; **~stündchen** *das* early evening get-together; **~stunde** *die* (*geh.*) twilight hour; **in der ~stunde** at twilight *or* dusk

**Dämmerung** *die;* **~, ~en** Ⓐ (*Abend~*) twilight; dusk; **in der [abendlichen] ~:** in the twilight *or* gloaming; **bei** *od.* **mit/vor Einbruch der ~:** at/before dusk *or* nightfall; **die Stunden der ~:** the twilight hours; Ⓑ (*Morgen~*) dawn; daybreak; **die ~ bricht an** dawn *or* day is breaking; **bei** *od.* **mit/vor Anbruch der ~:** at/before dawn *or* daybreak; Ⓒ (*Halbdunkel*) semi-darkness; half-light; **der Raum lag in tiefer ~:** the room was in deep shadow *or* gloom

**Dämmer·zustand** *der* Ⓐ (*Halbschlaf*) half-sleep; doze; Ⓑ (*Bewusstseinstrübung*) semi-conscious state; coma

**dämmrig** *Adj.* Ⓐ **es ist** *od.* **wird schon ~** (*morgens*) it is beginning to get light; day is breaking; (*abends*) it is beginning to get dark; night is falling; **draußen ist es noch ~:** it is still quite dark outside; Ⓑ (*halbdunkel*) gloomy; dim ‹light›

**Damm-: ~riss,** ***~riß** *der* (*Med.*) perineal tear; **~schnitt** *der* (*Med.*) episiotomy

**Dämmung** *die;* **~, ~en** (*Technik*) insulation

**Damm·weg** *der* embankment/dike path; (*Verbindung durch Wasser, Watt, Sumpf*) causeway

**Damokles·schwert** /ˈdaːmoklɛs-/ *das* (*geh.*) sword of Damocles

**Dämon** /ˈdɛːmɔn/ *der;* **~s, ~en** /dɛˈmoːnən/ Ⓐ (*böser Geist*) demon; **gute und böse ~en** good and evil spirits; Ⓑ (*geh.: im Menschen*) daemon; daemonic inner force

**dämonenhaft** *Adj.* demoniac

**Dämonie** /dɛmoˈniː/ *die;* **~, ~n** (*geh.*) daemonic power; (*eines Künstlers*) daemonic genius; **eine** *od.* **die ~ des Schicksals** a cruel stroke of fate

**dämonisch** ❶ *Adj.* daemonic; (*teuflisch*) diabolical. ❷ *adv.* daemonically; **~ grinsen** grin like a demon

**dämonisieren** *tr. V.* demonize; portray as a demon/demons

**Dämonisierung** *die;* **~, ~en** demonization; portrayal as a demon/demons

**Dämonismus** *der;* **~:** demonism *no art.*

**Dampf** /dampf/ *der;* **~[e]s, Dämpfe** /ˈdɛmpfə/ Ⓐ steam *no pl., no indef. art.;* (*Rauch*) smoke *no pl., no indef. art.;* (*Physik*) [water] vapour *as tech. term, no pl., no indef. art.;* **wallende Dämpfe** clouds of steam; **giftige Dämpfe einatmen** breathe in toxic vapour *or* fumes; **etw. mit ~ behandeln** steam sth.; **mit ~ betrieben [werden]** [be] steam-powered *or* steam-driven; **unter ~** (*Dat.*) **stehen** *od.* **sein** have steam up; **~ aufmachen** (*veralt.: stärker feuern*) get up [more] steam; (*ugs.: energischer spielen*) put on an effort; **da ist/aus etw. ist der ~ raus** (*ugs.*) it/sth. has lost its momentum; **~ ablassen** (*auch ugs.: Ärger abreagieren*) let off steam; **jmdm. ~ [unterm Hintern] machen** (*ugs.*) make sb. get on with it; put pressure on sb.; **~ drauf haben** (*ugs.*) be really shifting (*coll.*) *or* moving; (*vital sein*) be full of beans; **~ dahinter/hinter etw.** (*Akk.*) **machen** *od.* **setzen** (*ugs.*) (*sich beeilen*) get a move on/get a move on with sth.; (*andere zur Eile treiben*) get things *pl.*/sth. moving; **dieser Boxer hat ~ in den Fäusten** this boxer packs quite a punch; Ⓑ (*ugs.: Angst*) **vor jmdm./etw. [mächtigen** *od.* **unheimlichen] ~ haben** be [absolutely] terrified of sb./in a [blue] funk about sth. (*coll.*); Ⓒ (*bayr.: Alkoholrausch*) **einen ~ haben** be drunk

**Dampf-: ~antrieb** *der* steam drive; (*Eisenb.*) steam traction; **mit ~antrieb** steam-driven; **~bad** *das* steam *or* Turkish bath; (*Raum*) steam *or* Turkish baths *pl.;* **~boot** *das* steamboat; **~bügel·eisen** *das* steam iron; **~druck** *der; Pl.* **~drücke** steam pressure

**dampfen** *itr. V.* Ⓐ (*Dampf abgeben*) steam (**vor** + *Dat.* with, due to); Ⓑ *mit sein* (*fahren*) steam; Ⓒ *mit sein* (*ugs.: mit Zug, Schiff reisen*) chug; (*wegfahren*) chug off

**dämpfen** /ˈdɛmpfn̩/ *tr. V.* Ⓐ (*mit Dampf garen*) steam ‹fish, vegetables, potatoes›; Ⓑ (*glätten*) press with a damp cloth; (*mit Dampfbügeleisen*) steam iron; Ⓒ (*mildern*) muffle, deaden ‹sound›; attenuate ‹high notes›; dim, turn down ‹lights›; **die** *od.* **seine Stimme ~:** lower one's voice; **den Ton einer Trompete ~:** mute a trumpet; ⇒ *auch* **gedämpft**; Ⓓ (*abschwächen*) cushion, absorb ‹blow, impact, shock›; damp ‹vibrations›; (*fig.*) temper, diminish ‹joy›; dampen ‹enthusiasm›; assuage ‹sb.'s wrath›; calm ‹anger, excitement›; (*Wirtsch.*) curb ‹price rises›; slow down ‹inflation›

**Dampfer** *der;* **~s, ~:** steamer; **mit dem ~ fahren** go by steamer; **auf dem falschen ~ sein** *od.* **sitzen** (*fig. ugs.*) be barking up the wrong tree; have got it wrong

**Dämpfer** *der;* **~s, ~** Ⓐ (*beim Klavier*) damper; (*bei Streich- u. Blasinstrumenten*) mute; Ⓑ (*fig.*) **einen ~ bekommen** (*ugs.*) have one's enthusiasm dampened; (*gerügt werden*) be taken down a peg or two; **jmdm. einen ~ aufsetzen** dampen sb.'s enthusiasm; Ⓒ (*Technik*) damper; (*Stoß~*) shock absorber

**Dampfer·linie** *die* steamer service; (*Gesellschaft*) steamship line

**dampf-, Dampf-: ~förmig** *Adj.* vaporous; vapour *attrib.* ‹state›; **~hammer** *der* steam hammer; **~heizung** *die* steam heating

**dampfig** *Adj.* steamy; (*dunstig*) misty

**Dampf-: ~kessel** *der* boiler; **~kochtopf** *der* pressure cooker; **~kraft** *die* steam power; **~kraft·werk** *das* steam[-driven] power station; **~lok[omotive]** *die* steam locomotive *or* engine; **~maschine** *die* steam engine; **~nudel** *die* (*südd., Kochk.*) steamed yeast dumpling; **aufgehen wie eine ~nudel** (*ugs.*) fill out like a balloon; **~pfeife** *die* steam whistle; (*mit Druckluft betrieben*) compressed-air whistle; **~schiff** *das* steamer; (*bes. hist.*) steamship; ***~schiffahrt, ~schiff·fahrt** *die* steam navigation; **~turbine** *die* steam turbine

**Dämpfung** *die;* **~, ~en** Ⓐ (*der Stimme*) lowering; (*von hohen Tönen*) attenuation; (*von Licht*) dimming; **~ des Schalls/der Töne** deadening of sound/sounds; Ⓑ (*Stoß~*) cushioning; absorption; (*von Schwingungen*) damping; (*fig.*) (*von Freude, Leidenschaft*) tempering; diminishing; (*von Begeisterung*) dampening; (*von Wut, Aufregung*) calming; (*Wirtsch.: des Preisauftriebs*) curbing; (*der Konjunktur*) slowing down

**Dampf·walze** *die* Ⓐ steamroller; Ⓑ (*ugs. scherzh.: Frau*) mountain of flesh

**Dam·wild** *das* fallow deer *pl.*

**da·nach** *Adv.* Ⓐ (*zeitlich*) after it/that; then; **noch tagelang ~:** for days after[wards]; **eine Stunde ~:** an hour later; **ich dusche gern kalt, ~ fühlt man sich gleich viel frischer** I like a cold shower, you feel really refreshed afterwards; Ⓑ (*räumlich: dahinter*) after it/them; **voran gingen die Eltern, ~ kamen die Kinder** the parents went in front, the children following after *or* behind; **Kommt Mainz vor oder nach Wiesbaden? — Danach** Is Mainz before or after Wiesbaden? — After; Ⓒ (*ein Ziel angebend*) towards it/them; **er sprang/griff ~:** he jumped/made a grab for it/them; **~ lasst uns alle streben** let us all strive for that; Ⓓ (*entsprechend*) in accordance with it/them; **ein Brief ist gekommen; ~ ist sie schon unterwegs** a letter has arrived, according to which she is already on her way; **~ zu urteilen** to judge by that; **ihr kennt die Regeln, nun richtet euch ~!** you know the rules, so stick to *or* abide by them; **~ steht mir nicht der Sinn,** (*ugs.*) **mir ist nicht ~:** I'm not in the mood; I don't feel like it; **es sieht ~ aus/~ aus, als ob ...** it looks like it/looks as though ...; **~ siehst du [gerade] aus!** (*ugs. iron.*) tell that to the Marines!; **es ist billig, aber es ist auch ~** (*ugs.*) it's cheap and looks it; **es ist nur ein kleiner Schnellimbiss, und das Essen ist auch ~:** it's only a small snack bar and the food's what you might expect; ⇒ *auch* **da-**; NB *In sense* **D** *the word can occur in two parts in North German coll. usage, e.g.* **es ist billig, da ist es aber auch nach** it's cheap and looks it

**Danaer·geschenk** /ˈdaːnaɐ-/ *das* (*geh.*) Greek gift

**Dancing** /ˈdaːnsɪŋ/ *das;* **~s, ~s** (*bes. österr.*) Ⓐ (*Lokal*) dance hall; Ⓑ (*Veranstaltung*) dance

**Dandy** /ˈdɛndi/ *der;* **~s, ~s** dandy

**dandyhaft** ❶ *Adj.* dandyish; foppish ‹manner›. ❷ *adv.* like a dandy/dandies

**Dandytum** *das;* **~s** Ⓐ (*Art*) dandyish nature; Ⓑ (*Schicht*) **das ~:** the dandies *pl.* (*as a group*)

**Däne** /ˈdɛːnə/ *der;* **~n, ~n** ▶ **553** Dane; **er ist ~:** he is Danish *or* a Dane

**da·neben** *Adv.* Ⓐ (*an der/die Seite davon*) next to *or* beside him/her/it/them *etc.;* Ⓑ (*im Vergleich dazu*) in comparison; Ⓒ (*außerdem*) in addition [to that]; besides [that]; **man muss ~ auch berücksichtigen, wie schwer es ist** one must consider at the same time *or* as well how difficult it is; Ⓓ **~ sein** (*ugs.*) ‹reaction, remark› be out of order (*coll.*); ‹person› (*verwirrt sein*) be in a complete daze; (*sich unwohl fühlen*) not be oneself; be under the weather (*coll.*); **die Entscheidung war total ~:** the decision was all wrong; **er sah völlig ~ aus** he looked a real freak (*coll.*)

**daneben-: ~|benehmen** *unr. refl. V.* (*ugs.*) blot one's copybook (*coll.*); spoil one's record; (*sich aufführen*) make an exhibition of oneself; **~|fallen** *unr. itr. V.; mit sein* miss; **~|gehen** *unr. itr. V.; mit sein* Ⓐ (*das Ziel verfehlen*) miss [the target]; Ⓑ (*ugs.: fehlschlagen*) misfire; be a flop (*sl.*); **das geht sowieso ~:** it won't be any good; **~|geraten** *unr. itr. V.; mit sein* (*ugs.*) **[jmdm.] ~geraten** go wrong [on sb.]; **~|greifen** *unr. itr. V.* Ⓐ (*vorbeigreifen*) miss [one's aim] (*when reaching for sth.*);

d

**beim Klavierspielen ~greifen** play a wrong note/some wrong notes on the piano; **B** (*ugs.*) **im Ausdruck ~greifen** (*aus Unkenntnis*) say the wrong thing; (*aus Taktlosigkeit*) put one's foot in it; **mit seiner Prognose ~greifen** be wide of the mark with one's prognosis; **~|halten** *unr. tr. V.* (*ugs.: vergleichen*) **wenn man X ~hält** when compared with X; **~|hauen** *unr. tr. V.*; **A** (*nicht treffen*) miss; **B** (*ugs.: sich irren*) be wide of the mark; **mit der Antwort hat er ziemlich ~gehauen** his answer was well wide of the mark *or* (*coll.*) way out; **~|liegen** *unr. itr. V.* (*ugs.*) be wide of the mark; **mit dieser Meinung liegst du aber sehr ~:** your estimation is quite wrong *or* (*coll.*) way out; **~|schießen** *unr. itr. V.* **A** (*Ziel verfehlen*) miss [the target]; **mit Absicht ~schießen** shoot to miss; **B** ⇒ **~hauen** B; ***~|sein** ⇒ **daneben** D; **~|tippen** *itr. V.* (*ugs.*) guess wrong; **~getippt!** wrong!; **~|treffen** *unr. itr. V.* miss [the target]; **~getroffen!** missed!

**Dänemark** /'dɛ:nəmark/ (*das*); **~s** Denmark

**dang** /daŋ/ *1. u. 3. Pers. Sg. Prät. v.* **dingen**

**da·nieden** *Adv.* (*dichter. veralt.*) here below [on earth]

**danieder|liegen** *unr. itr. V.* (*geh.*) **A** (*krank sein*) be laid low; **schwer [krank]/sterbend ~:** lie seriously ill/dying; **B** (*Wirtsch.*) ‹trade, economy› be depressed

**Dänin** *die;* **~, ~nen** ▶ **553** Dane; Danish woman/girl; ⇒ *auch* **-in**

**dänisch** /'dɛ:nɪʃ/ *Adj.* ▶ **553**, ▶ **696** Danish; ⇒ *auch* **deutsch**, **Deutsch**

**dank** /daŋk/ *Präp. mit Dat. u. Gen. im Sg. u. meist mit Gen. im Pl.* thanks to; **~ einem Zufall** *od.* **eines Zufalls** by chance; owing to a coincidence

**Dank** *der;* **~[e]s** **A** thanks *pl.*; **jmdm. seinen ~ abstatten** offer one's thanks to sb.; **jmdm. seinen [herzlichen/allerherzlichsten] ~ aussprechen** express one's/sincere/most sincere/thanks *or* gratitude to sb.; **jmdm. ~ sagen** thank sb.; offer one's thanks to sb.; **jmdm. [großen] ~ schulden** *od.* **schuldig sein** (*geh.*), **jmdm. zu [großem] ~ verpflichtet sein** owe sb. a [great] debt of gratitude; **kein Wort des ~es sagen** not say *or* offer a word of thanks; **als** *od.* **zum ~ dafür, dass ich seinen Hund in Pflege genommen hatte** as a way of saying 'thank you' to me for looking after his dog; **zum ~ dafür hat sie mir noch ins Gesicht gespuckt** (*iron.*) all the thanks I got was that she spat in my face; **und das ist nun der ~ dafür** (*iron.*) so that's all the thanks I get!; **zum ~ für seine Verdienste** in grateful recognition of his services; **mit vielem** *od.* **bestem ~ zurück** thanks for the loan; (*bes. geschrieben*) returned with thanks!; **etw. mit ~ annehmen** accept sth. with thanks; **von [tiefem] ~ erfüllt sein** (*geh.*) be filled with a [deep] sense of gratitude; **damit wird er [bei mir] wenig/keinen ~ ernten** he won't get much/any thanks [from me] for that; **B** (*in ~esformeln*) **haben Sie ~!** please accept my thanks; **vielen/besten/herzlichen ~!** thank you very much; many thanks; **vielen ~, dass du mir beim Umzug geholfen hast** thank you very much for helping me with the move; **[nein,] vielen ~!** (*iron.*) no, thank you!; **tausend ~!** (*ugs.*) very many thanks [indeed]; ⇒ *auch* **heiß**

**Dank·adresse** *die* [official] letter of thanks

**dankbar** **1** *Adj.* **A** (*voller Dank*) grateful; (*anerkennend*) appreciative ‹child, audience, etc.›; **in ~er Anerkennung** (+ *Gen.*)/**Erinnerung an** (+ *Akk.*) in grateful recognition/memory of; **[jmdm.] für etw. ~ sein** be grateful [to sb.] for sth.; **sich ~ zeigen** show one's gratitude *or* appreciation; **sie sind für jede Abwechslung ~:** they are thankful for any diversion; **für eine baldige Antwort wären wir ~:** we should be grateful for an early reply; **ich wäre Ihnen sehr ~, wenn Sie ... könnten** I should be very grateful if you could ...; **B** (*lohnend*) rewarding ‹job, part, task, etc.›; **C** (*ugs.: haltbar*) hard-wearing ‹material, clothes›; (*unempfindlich*) easy-care ‹garment, plant, etc.›.
**2** *adv.* gratefully; **etw. ~ annehmen** *od.* **entgegennehmen** accept sth. gratefully *or* with thanks; **jmdn. ~ anblicken** give sb. a look of gratitude

**Dankbarkeit** *die;* **~:** gratitude; **etw. aus ~ tun** do sth. out of gratitude; **in/mit [aufrichtiger/tiefer] ~:** in/with [sincere/deep] gratitude

**Dank·brief** *der* letter of thanks; thank-you letter

**danke** /'daŋkə/ *Höflichkeitsformel* thank you; (*ablehnend*) no, thank you; **Darf ich Ihnen noch Tee nachgießen? — Ja ~[, gern]** May I pour you some more tea? — Yes, please[, I'd like some]; **Gefällt es Ihnen hier bei uns? — Ja ~, sehr sogar** Do you like it here? — Yes, thank you, very much; **nein ~, ~ nein** no, thank you; **Soll ich Ihnen helfen? — Danke, es geht schon** Shall I help you? — No thank you *or* No thanks, it's all right; **~ schön/sehr/vielmals** thank you very much; **~ schön sagen** say 'thank you'; **Wie gehts? — Mir gehts ~** (*ugs.*) How are you? — I'm OK [thanks] (*coll.*); **sonst gehts dir [wohl] ~!** (*ugs.*) what do you think you're doing?; have you taken leave of your senses?

**danken** **1** *itr. V.* (*Dank aussprechen*) thank; **jmdm. für etw. [vielmals] ~:** thank sb. [very much] for sth.; **ich danke Ihnen vielmals** thank you very much; **er dankte kurz und verließ das Zimmer** he said a quick 'thank you' and left the room; **danke der [gütigen] Nachfrage!** (*meist scherzh. od. iron.*) thanks for asking; kind of you to ask; **Betrag ~d erhalten** [payment] received with thanks; **~d ablehnen** decline with thanks; **dafür danke ich bestens** (*iron.*) thanks a lot (*coll.*); **na, ich danke!** (*ugs.*) no, 'thank you!; **ich danke für Obst und Südfrüchte** (*ugs.*) no, thanks; ⇒ *auch* **Knie**.
**2** *tr. V.* **A** **[aber bitte,] nichts zu ~:** don't mention it; not at all; **es wird einem noch nicht einmal gedankt** you don't even get any thanks [for it]; **sie hat ihm seine Hilfe schlecht gedankt** she gave him a poor reward for his help; **er dankte ihnen ihre Güte mit Ungehorsam** (*iron.*) the only reward they got [from him] for their kindness was disobedience; **B** (*geh.: ver~*) **jmdm. etw. ~:** owe sb. sth.; owe sth. to sb.; **nur diesem Umstand ist es zu ~, dass ...** it was only thanks to this that ...

**dankens·wert** *Adj.* commendable ‹effort etc.›; **es ist ~, dass er uns hilft** it is kind *or* very good of him to help [us]

**dankenswerter·weise** *Adv.* kindly; generously; **~ haben sich viele freiwillig gemeldet** commendably many have volunteered

**Danke·schön** *das;* **~s** thank you; **ein [herzliches] ~ sagen** express one's [sincere] thanks; **nicht einmal ein ~ bekommen** not get so much as a thank you

**Dankes·wort** *das; Pl.* **~e** word of thanks

**Dank-:** **~gebet** *das* prayer of thanksgiving; **~gottes·dienst** *der* thanksgiving service; **~sagung** *die;* **~, ~en** (*Text*) expression of thanks; (*Karte*) note of thanks; (*Brief*) letter of thanks; **~schreiben** *das* letter of thanks

**dann** /dan/ *Adv.* **A** then; **was machen wir ~?** what shall we do then *or* after that?; **was ~?** what happens then?; **noch drei Tage, ~ ist Ostern** another three days and it will be Easter; **was soll ~ werden?** what will happen then?; **bis ~:** see you then; **~ und ~:** at such and such a time; (*an dem und dem Tag*) on such and such a date; **von ~ bis ~:** from such and such a date/time to such and such a date/time; **~ und wann** now and then; **B** (*räumlich: dahinter*) **zuerst kam die Kapelle, ~ folgten die Pfadfinder** first came the band, then *or* followed by the Scouts; **an die Gärten schließt sich ~ Ödland an** then at the end of the gardens there is a piece of wasteland; **C** (*rangmäßig danach*) **er ist der Klassenbeste, ~ kommt sein Bruder** he is top of the class, followed by his brother *or* then comes his brother; **D** (*unter diesen Umständen*) **~ will ich nicht weiter stören** then *or* in that case I won't disturb you any further; **na ~!** well, that's different!; **[na,] ~ eben nicht!** in that case, forget it!; **~ bis morgen** see you tomorrow, then; **wenn er selbst nicht hinfahren kann, wer ~?** if he can't go there himself, who can?; **nur ~, wenn ...** only if ...; **lehnt er ab, ~ werden wir klagen** if he refuses, [then] we shall complain; **E** (*außerdem*) **~ noch ...** then ... as well; **und ~ kommt noch die Mehrwertsteuer hinzu** and then there's VAT (*Brit.*) *or* (*Amer.*) tax to add on top of that; **zuletzt fiel ~ noch der Strom aus** finally to top it all there was a power failure; **F** (*demnach*) **~ hast du also die ganze Zeit mit zugehört** so you've been listening the whole time; **G** (*schließlich*) **es hat ~ doch noch geklappt** it was all right in the end

**dannen** /'danən/ *Adv.* in **von ~** (*veralt.*) from thence (*arch./literary*); **von ~ eilen/gehen** hasten away/depart

**dantesk** /dan'tɛsk/ *Adj.* (*geh.*) Dantesque

**dantisch** /'dantɪʃ/ *Adj.* Dantean

**Danzig** /'dantsɪç/ (*das*); **~s** Gdansk; (*vor 1945*) Danzig

**daran** /da'ran/ *Adv.* **A** (*an dieser/diese Stelle, an diesem/diesen Gegenstand*) on it/them; **es klebt etwas ~:** something is sticking to it/them; **es hängt etwas ~:** something is hanging from it/them; **er klammert sich ~** (*auch fig.*) he clings to it; **~ riechen** take a sniff at it/them; **~ vorbei** past it/them; **kommen wir noch einmal ~ vorbei?** shall we be passing it/them again?; **dicht ~:** close to it/them; **nahe ~ sein, etw. zu tun** be on the point of doing sth.; **B** (*hinsichtlich dieser Sache*) about it/them; **denken Sie ~:** think about it/them; **das Beste/Schlimmste ~:** the best/worst part of *or* about it/them; **~ ist nichts zu machen** there's nothing one can do about it; **~ wird sich nichts ändern** nothing will alter this fact; **kein Wort ~ ist wahr** not a word of it is true; **er arbeitet schon lange ~:** he has been working on it/them for a long time; **wir haben keinen Bedarf mehr ~:** we no longer have any need of it/them; **mir liegt viel ~:** it means a lot to me; **mir liegt ~, zu erfahren, wie er zu der Sache steht** I'd really like *or* I'd be interested to know his view of this matter; **Sie werden viel Freude ~ haben** you will get a lot of pleasure from it; **C** (*aufgrund dieser Sache*) **ich wäre beinahe ~ erstickt** I almost choked on it; it almost made me choke; **er ist ~ gestorben** he died of it; **D** (*an diesen Vorgang*) **~ anschließend** *od.* **im Anschluss ~ fand eine Diskussion statt** after that there was a discussion; ⇒ *auch* **da-**; **dran**

**daran-** (⇒ *auch* **dran-**): **~|geben** *unr. tr. V.* (*geh.*) sacrifice; **~|gehen** *unr. itr. V.; mit sein* set about it; **~gehen, etw. zu tun** set about doing sth.; **~|machen** *refl. V.* (*ugs.*) set about it; (*ernstlich*) get down to it; **sich ~machen, etw. zu tun** get down to/set about doing sth.; **~|setzen** **1** *tr. V.* devote ‹energy etc.› to it; summon up ‹ambition› for it; (*aufs Spiel setzen*) risk ‹one's life, one's honour› for it; **er hat alles** *od.* **alle seine Kräfte ~gesetzt, um dieses Ziel zu erreichen** he spared no effort to achieve *or* devoted all his energy to achieving this aim; **2** *refl. V.* (*ugs.: in Angriff nehmen*) get down to it; **sich ~setzen, etw. zu tun** get down to doing sth.; **~|wenden** *unr. od. regelm. tr. V.* (*geh.*) devote ‹time, effort› to it

**darauf** /da'rauf/ *Adv.* **A** (*auf dieser/diese Stelle*) on it/them; (*oben ~*) on top of it/them; **er isst gern Frikadellen mit Senf ~:** he likes eating rissoles with mustard on top; **er goss Wasser ~:** he poured water on [to] it/them; **B** (*auf ein Ziel hin*) **er hat ~ geschossen** he shot at it/them ; **~ müsst ihr zugehen** that's what you must head towards *or* make for; **ich muss ~ dringen** I must insist on it; **er ist ganz versessen ~:** he is mad [keen] on it (*coll.*); **also darauf willst**

*old spelling (see note on page 1707)

**du hinaus** so 'that's what you're getting at; **~ wollen wir anstoßen!** let's drink to that!; **C** (*auf diese Angelegenheit*) about it; **wir kamen nur kurz ~ zu sprechen** we only talked about it briefly *or* touched on it; **wie kommt du nur ~?** what makes you think that?; **wie kommst du ~, so etwas anzunehmen?** how do you come to assume such a thing?; **D** (*danach*) after that; **erst ein Blitz, unmittelbar ~ ein Donnerschlag** first there was lightning, immediately followed by a clap of thunder; **ein Jahr ~/kurz ~ starb er** he died a year later/shortly afterwards; **zuerst kamen die Kinder, ~ folgten die Festwagen** first came the children, then followed *or* followed by the floats; **dieser und der ~ folgende Wagen** this car and the one behind *or* following it; **am ~ folgenden Tag** the following day; next day; **E** (*infolgedessen, ~hin*) because of that; as a result; **F der Gutschein ist verfallen, ~ bekommen Sie nichts mehr** the voucher is out of date, you won't get anything on *or* for that; **~ fußen alle unsere Überlegungen** all our deliberations are based on it *or* this; ⇒ *auch* **da-**; **drauf**; **tags**

**darauf-** (⇒ *auch* **drauf-**): ***~folgend** ⇒ **darauf D**; **~hin** /--'-/ *Adv.* **A** (*infolgedessen*) as a result [of this/that]; consequently; (*zeitlich*) thereupon; **B** (*unter diesem Gesichtspunkt*) with a view to this/that; **etw. ~hin prüfen, ob es geeignet ist** examine sth. to see whether it is suitable

**daraus** /da'raus/ *Adv.* **A** (*aus diesem Raum, Behälter o. Ä. heraus*) from it/them; out of it/them; **er holte eine Flasche und goss ~ ein** he fetched a bottle and poured out drinks from it; **sie öffnete den Koffer und holte ein Kleid ~ hervor** she opened the suitcase and took out a dress *or* took a dress out of it; **B** (*aus dieser Angelegenheit, Sache*) from it/them; out of it/them; **wir alle wissen das und sollten ~ lernen** we all know that and should learn from it; **sie hat ihm nie einen Vorwurf ~ gemacht** she never reproached him for it *or* made an issue out of it; **mach dir nichts ~:** don't worry about it; **dieser Stoff ist hübsch, ~ nähe ich mir ein Kleid** this material is pretty, I'm going to make myself a dress out of it; **Kartoffeln sind nicht nur zum Essen da, viele machen Schnaps ~:** potatoes are not only for eating — a lot of people make schnapps from them; **~ ist eine große Firma geworden** it has become *or* turned into a large business; **was ist ~ geworden?** what has become of it?; **~ wird nichts** nothing will come of it; **C** (*aus dieser Quelle, Unterlage*) from it/them; **~ geht eindeutig hervor, dass ...** from this it is clear that ...

**darben** /'darbn̩/ *itr. V.* (*geh.*) **A** (*in Not leben*) live in want; (*sich sehr einschränken*) go short; pinch and scrape; **die ~den Massen** the indigent *or* destitute masses; **wir haben sehr gedarbt** we suffered great want; **B** (*Hunger leiden*) go hungry

**dar|bieten** (*geh.*) **1** *unr. tr. V.* **A** (*anbieten*) offer; serve ‹drinks, food›; **die dargebotene Hand ausschlagen** (*fig.*) reject the proffered hand [of friendship] (*fig.*); **B** (*aufführen, vortragen*) perform; **es wurden Gedichte und Lieder dargeboten** a recital of poems and songs was presented. **2** *unr. refl. V.* **sich jmds. Blicken ~:** expose oneself to sb.'s gaze; **eine herrliche Aussicht bot sich uns dar** a marvellous view met our eyes

**Darbietung** *die;* ~, **~en** (*geh.*) **A** presentation; **B** (*Aufführung*) performance; (*beim Varietee usw.*) act

**dar|bringen** *unr. tr. V.* offer; **jmdm. ein Ständchen ~:** serenade sb.

**darein** /da'rain/ *Adv.* (*geh.*) in it/them; ⇒ *auch* **da-**

**darein-:** **~|finden** *unr. refl. V.* (*geh.*) come to terms with it; (*sich daran gewöhnen*) become accustomed to it; **~|fügen** *refl. V.* (*geh.*) resign oneself to it; **~|reden** *itr. V.* **jmdm. ~reden** meddle *or* interfere in sb.'s affairs/decisions *etc.*; (*unterbrechen*) interrupt sb.; **niemand hat ihm ~zureden** nobody has any right to [try to] tell him what to do; **~|setzen** *tr. V.* devote to it; **alles** *od.* **seine ganze Energie ~setzen, etw. zu tun** concentrate all one's efforts on doing sth.; **er setzt seinen ganzen Ehrgeiz ~, als erster fertig zu sein** he has made it his great ambition to finish first

**darf** /darf/ *1. u. 3. Pers. Sg. Präsens v.* **dürfen**

**darfst** /darfst/ *2. Pers. Sg. Präsens v.* **dürfen**

**darin** /da'rɪn/ *Adv.* **A** (*in dieser Sache o. Ä.*) in it/them; (*drinnen*) inside [it/them]; **die ~ enthaltenen Briefe** the letters contained in it/them *or* (*formal*) therein; **B** (*in dieser Hinsicht*) in that respect; **~ stimme ich völlig mit Ihnen überein** I entirely agree with you there; ⇒ *auch* **da-**

**darinnen** /da'rɪnən/ *Adv.* (*geh.*) in it/them; therein (*formal*)

**dar|legen** *tr. V.* explain; set forth ‹reasons, facts›; expound ‹theory›; **jmdm. etw. ~:** explain sth. to sb.; **etw. schriftlich ~:** set sth. out in writing

**Darlegung** *die;* ~, **~en** explanation

**Darlehen** /'da:ɐ̯le:ən/ *das;* **~s, ~:** loan; **ein ~ aufnehmen** get *or* raise a loan; **jmdm. ein ~ gewähren** give *or* grant sb. a loan

**Darlehens-:** **~kasse** *die* credit bank; **~nehmer** *der;* **~~s, ~~, ~nehmerin** *die;* **~~, ~~nen** (*Bankw.*) borrower; **~summe** *die* amount of the loan; **eine ~summe von ...** a loan amounting to ...; **~vertrag** *der* loan agreement

**Darm** /darm/ *der;* **~[e]s, Därme** /'dɛrmə/ **A ▶ 471** intestines *pl.*; bowels *pl.*; **[jmdm.] auf den ~ schlagen** give sb. diarrhoea; **den ~ entleeren** evacuate *or* empty one's bowels; **Erkrankungen des ~es** intestinal diseases; **B** (*als Saiten*) gut; **C** (*als Wursthaut*) skin

**Darm-:** **~aus·gang** *der* **▶ 471** (*Anat.*) anus; **~blutung** *die* **▶ 474** (*Med.*) intestinal haemorrhage; **~bruch** *der* (*Med.*) enterocele; **~entleerung** *die* evacuation of the bowels; **~grippe** *die* **▶ 474** gastric influenza; **~katarrh** *der* **▶ 474** (*Med.*) enteritis; **~krebs** *der* cancer of the intestine *or* bowel; **~saite** *die* gut string; **~spülung** *die* (*Med.*) enema; **~tätigkeit** *die* (*Med.*) functioning of the bowels; **~trägheit** *die* **▶ 474** (*Med.*) constipation; **~trakt** *der* **▶ 471** (*Anat.*) intestinal tract; **~verschlingung** *die* **▶ 474** (*Med.*) volvulus; **~verschluss**, ***~verschluß** *der* **▶ 474** (*Med.*) intestinal obstruction

**darnach** (*veralt.*) ⇒ **danach**

**darneben** (*veralt.*) ⇒ **daneben**

**darnieder-** ⇒ **danieder-**

**darob** /da'rɔp/ *Adv.* (*veralt.*) **A** (*darüber*) about it/them; **er wunderte sich ~, dass ...** he was surprised that ...; **B** (*deswegen*) because of it; ⇒ *auch* **da-**

**Darre** /'darə/ *die;* ~, **~n** **A** (*Vorrichtung*) [drying] kiln; **B** (*das ~n*) drying

**dar|reichen** *tr. V.* (*geh.*) **A** (*anbieten*) proffer; **B** (*überreichen*) **jmdm. ein Geschenk usw. ~:** present sb. with a gift *etc.*

**darren** *tr. V.* dry

**Darr-:** **~gewicht** *das* [kiln-]dry weight (*of wood*); **~malz** *das* [kiln-]dried malt

**darstellbar** *Adj.* **A** (*abbildbar*) depictable; portrayable; **ist das grafisch ~?** can that be represented graphically?; **grafisch ~e Entwicklungen** developments which can be shown on a graph *or* diagram; **B** (*spielbar*) playable ‹part›; **C** (*Chemie*) **ein leicht ~er Stoff** a material which can easily be produced

**dar|stellen** **1** *tr. V.* **A** (*abbilden*) depict; portray; **etw. grafisch ~:** present sth. graphically; (*als Graph*) show sth. on a graph; **wen/was stellt dieses Bild dar?** whom does this picture portray/what does this picture represent?; **die ~de Geometrie** descriptive geometry; **die ~de Kunst** the performing arts *pl.*; **ein ~der Künstler** a performer; **B** (*verkörpern*) play; act; **den Othello ~:** play *or* act [the part of] Othello; **etwas/mehr/nichts ~:** make [a bit of] an impression/more of an impression/not make any sort of an impression; ‹gift etc.› look good/look better/not look anything special; **C** (*schildern*) describe ‹person, incident, etc.›; present ‹matter, argument›; **falsch/verzerrt ~:** misrepresent/distort ‹facts›; **es wurde dann so dargestellt, als sei das unser Wunsch gewesen** it was then put in such a way as to suggest that we had wanted it; **so schlimm, wie du ihn darstellst, ist er auch nicht** he is not as bad as you make him out to be; **D** (*sein, bedeuten*) represent; constitute; **das zweite Kind stellt eine große Belastung für sie dar** the second child means a heavy load for her; **E** (*Chemie*) produce. **2** *refl. V.* **A** (*sich erweisen, sich zeigen*) prove [to be]; turn out to be; **sich jmdm. als ... ~:** appear to sb. as ...; **nach dem Bericht stellt sich die Sache ungefähr so dar** according to the report the situation appears to be roughly this; **B** (*sich selbst schildern*) portray oneself (**als** + *Akk.* as); **sie lieben es, sich als Wohltäter darzustellen** they like to present themselves in the role of benefactors

**Darsteller** *der;* **~s, ~:** actor; **der ~ des Hamlet** the actor playing Hamlet; **berühmt als ~ des Hamlet** famous for his portrayal of Hamlet *or* as an interpreter of Hamlet

**Darstellerin** *die;* ~, **~nen** actress; ⇒ *auch* **Darsteller**

**darstellerisch** **1** *Adj.* acting *attrib.*; **das Darstellerische** the interpretative aspect; **eine einmalige ~e Leistung** a marvellow piece of acting; **ihre ~en Fähigkeiten** her abilities as an actress. **2** *adv.* from an acting point of view

**Darstellung** *die* **A** representation; (*Schilderung*) portrayal; (*Bild*) picture; **grafische/schematische ~:** diagram; (*Graph*) graph; **B** (*Beschreibung, Bericht*) description; account; **bei seiner ~ der geschichtlichen Tatsachen** in his account *or* rendering of the historical facts; **C** (*einer Theaterrolle*) interpretation; performance; (*einer Szene usw.*) performance; **seine ~ des Mephisto** his portrayal *or* interpretation of Mephisto; **etw. zur ~ bringen** portray sth.; (*aufführen*) perform sth.; **D** (*Chemie*) production

**Darstellungs-:** **~form** *die* form of representation; **~mittel** *das* representational technique; (*eines Schauspielers*) acting technique

**dar|tun** *unr. tr. V.* (*geh.*) (*darlegen*) state ‹fact, one's reasons›; (*erklären*) explain; (*demonstrieren*) demonstrate; **er hat zur Genüge dargetan, wie ...** he gave a sufficient account of how ...

**darüber** *Adv.* **A** (*über dem Genannten*) over *or* above it/them; **~ liegen** be higher; **wir wohnen im zweiten Stock und er ~:** we live on the second floor and he lives above us; **sie liegen mit ihrem Angebot weit ~:** their offer is much higher; **~ stehen** (*fig.*) be above such things; **B** (*über es [hinweg]*) over it/them; **~ führen zu wenige Brücken** too few bridges go across it/them; **~ hinaus** in addition [to that]; (*noch obendrein*) what is more; **~ hinaus sein** (*zu alt dafür sein*) be beyond that stage [now]; (*es überwunden haben*) have got over it; **~ fahren/steigen** run/climb over it/them; **sie fuhr rasch mit der Hand/mit einem Tuch ~:** she quickly ran her hand over it/wiped it with a cloth; **sich ~ machen** (*fig. ugs.*) get down to it/them; (*zu essen beginnen*) get stuck into it (*coll.*); (*zu trinken beginnen*) get to work on it; **C** (*über dieser/diese Angelegenheit*) about it/them; **~ kann kein Zweifel bestehen** there can be no doubt about it; **ich habe fast den ganzen Tag ~ gesessen** I spent almost the whole day over *or* on it; **~ wollen wir hinwegsehen** we will overlook it; **D** (*über diese Grenze, dieses Maß hinaus*) above [that]; over [that]; **Kinder im Alter von 5 Jahren und ~:** children of 5 and over; **der Preis beträgt 50 Mark oder etwas ~:** the price is 50 marks or a bit more; **Ist es schon 12 Uhr? — Aber ja, es ist schon 10 Minuten ~:** Is it twelve o'clock yet? — Oh yes, it's already ten past; **man braucht 4 Wochen,**

manchmal auch etwas ~: it takes four weeks, sometimes rather longer *or* more; **E** (*währenddessen*) in the process; **es war ~ Abend geworden** meanwhile it had become evening; **F** (*währenddessen und deshalb*) because of it/them; as a result; **der Film war so spannend, dass er ~ seine Sorgen vergaß** the film was so exciting that it made him forget his worries; ⇨ *auch* **da-**

***darüber|fahren** *usw.* ⇨ **darüber** A, B

**darum** /daˈrʊm/ *Adv.* **A** (*um diese Stelle herum*) [a]round it/them; **ein Häuschen mit einem Garten ~ [herum]** a little house surrounded by a garden; **B** (*hinsichtlich dieser Angelegenheit*) **ich werde mich ~ bemühen** I will try to deal with it; (*versuchen, es zu bekommen*) I'll try to get it; **sie wird nicht ~ herumkommen, es zu tun** she won't get out of *or* avoid doing it; **~ ist es mir nicht zu tun, ~ geht es mir nicht** that's not the point as far as I'm concerned; that's not what I'm after; **es geht mir ~, eine Einigung zu erzielen** my concern *or* aim is to reach an agreement; **C** /ˈ--/ (*deswegen*) because of that; for that reason; **ach, ~ ist er so schlecht gelaunt!** so that's why he's in such a bad mood!; **er ist zwar klein, aber ~ nicht schwach** he is small but that doesn't mean that he's weak; **Warum weinst du? — Darum!** Why are you crying? — Because!; ⇨ *auch* **da-**

**darum-: ~|binden** *unr. tr. V.* tie [a]round it/them; **~|kommen** *unr. itr. V.*; *mit sein* lose it/them; **~kommen, etw. zu tun** miss the opportunity of doing sth.; miss out on [doing] sth. (*coll.*); **~|legen** *tr. V.* put around it/them

**darunter** /daˈrʊntɐ/ *Adv.* **A** (*unter dem Genannten/das Genannte*) under *or* beneath it/them; **wir wohnen im 2. Stock und er ~:** we live on the second floor and he lives under us *or* on the floor below; **sie hatte nichts ~ an** she was wearing nothing underneath; **etw. ~ schreiben** write/type sth. underneath *or* at the bottom; (*ab Unterschrift*) sign sth. underneath *or* at the bottom; **seinen Namen/seine Unterschrift ~ setzen** put one's name/one's signature to it; **~ gehen** (*ugs.: darunter passen*) fit *or* go underneath; **B** (*unter dieser Grenze, diesem Maß*) less; **10° oder etwas ~:** 10° or a bit less; **~ kann ich die Vase nicht verkaufen** I can't sell the vase for less; **Bewerber im Alter von 40 Jahren und ~:** applicants aged 40 and under; **~ tut er es nicht** (*ugs.*) he's not satisfied with anything less; **~ bleiben** remain lower; (*niedriger sein*) be lower; **viele forderten 20%, wir bleiben aber ~:** many demanded 20%, but we kept below this; **~ gehen** go below that; **~ liegen** be lower; (*weniger bekommen*) get less; **die Parallelklasse liegt mit ihren Leistungen ~:** the parallel class's performance is not as good; **C** (*unter dieser Sache*) **was verstehen Sie ~?** what do you understand by that?; **was hat man ~ zu verstehen?** what is one to make of it/that?; what is it/that supposed to mean?; **sie hat sehr ~ gelitten** she suffered a great deal from *or* because of it/that; **D** (*unter dieser/diese Menge, dazwischen*) amongst them; **in vielen Ländern, ~ der Schweiz** in many countries, including Switzerland; **~ fallen** be included; be amongst them; (*in diese Kategorie fallen*) come under it; **etw. ~ mischen** mix sth. in; mix sth. with it; **sich ~ mischen** mingle with it/them; ⇨ *auch* **da-**

***darunter|bleiben** *usw.* ⇨ **darunter**

**Darwinismus** /darviˈnɪsmʊs/ *der;* **~:** Darwinism *no art.*

**darwinistisch** **1** *Adj.* Darwinian; Darwinist. **2** *adv.* in Darwinian terms

**das** /das/ **1** *best. Art.* the; **~ Leben im Dschungel** life in the jungle; **~ Weihnachtsfest** Christmas; **~ Frankreich/London des 19. Jahrhunderts** nineteenth-century France/London; **~ Laufen/Sprechen fällt ihm schwer** walking/talking is difficult for him; **~ Gute/Schöne** what is good/beautiful.

**2** *Demonstrativpron.* **A** *attr.* **das Kind/Buch/Auto war es** it was 'that child/book/car; **B** *selbstständig* **das [da]** that one; **das [hier]** this one [here]; **~ mit dem blonden Haar/roten Umschlag** the one with the fair hair/red cover; **~ Schwein, ~!** the dirty pig!; **mein Auto, ~ ist kaputt** (*ugs.*) oh, my car — it's conked out (*coll.*).

**3** *Relativpron.* (*Mensch*) who; that; (*Sache, Tier*) which; that; **~ Mädchen, ~ da drüben entlanggeht** the girl walking along over there; **ich sah ein Mädchen/Hündchen, ~ aus dem Fenster schaute** I saw a girl/little dog looking out of the window

***da|sein** ⇨ **da** 1 H-K

**Da·sein** *das* **A** (*Vorhandensein*) existence; **etw. ins ~ rufen** create sth.; (*gründen*) found sth.; **B** (*menschliche Existenz*) life; **sich/jmdm. das ~ erleichtern** make life easier for oneself/sb.; **ein trauriges ~ führen** lead a miserable existence; ⇨ *auch* **Fristen, Kampf**; **C** (*Zugegensein*) presence

**Daseins-: ~berechtigung** *die* right to exist; **das findet darin** *od.* **dadurch seine ~berechtigung** this justifies its existence; **~form** *die* form *or* mode of existence; **~freude** *die* ⇨ **Lebensfreude**; **~kampf** *der* struggle for existence

**da·selbst** *Adv.* (*geh. veralt.*) there

**da|sitzen** *unr. itr. V.* **A** sit there; **B** (*ugs.: ohne etw. auskommen müssen*) be left [there]; **ich saß ohne Geld da** I was stuck there without any money; **jetzt sitzen wir da!** now we're stuck!

**dasjenige** ⇨ **derjenige**

**dass, *daß** /das/ *Konj.* **A** that; **entschuldigen Sie bitte, ~ ich mich verspätet habe** please forgive me for being late; please forgive my being late; **ich weiß, ~ du Recht hast** I know [that] you are right; **ich verstehe nicht, ~ sie ihn geheiratet hat** I don't understand why she married him; **es ist schon 3 Jahre her, ~ wir zum letzten Mal im Theater waren** it is three years since *or* it was three years ago when we last went to the theatre; **B** (*nach Pronominaladverbien o. Ä.*) [the fact] that; (*bei gleichen Subjekten*) **er leidet darunter, ~ er kleiner ist** he suffers from the fact that he is smaller *or* from being smaller; **Wissen erwirbt man dadurch, ~ man viel liest** one acquires knowledge by reading a great deal; (*bei verschiedenen Subjekten*) **das liegt daran, ~ du nicht aufgepasst hast** that is due to the fact that you did not pay attention; that comes from your not paying attention; **ich bin dagegen, ~ er geht** I am against his going; **C** (*mit Konsekutivsatz*) that; **[so]~:** so that; in such a way that; **ich bin so müde, ~ ich kaum gehen kann** I am so tired [that] I can hardly walk; **er lachte so [sehr], ~ ihm die Tränen in die Augen traten** he laughed so much that he almost cried; **D** (*mit Finalsatz*) so that; **hilf ihm doch, ~ er endlich fertig wird** do help him so that he'll finally be ready/finished; **E** (*mit Wunschsatz*) if only; **~ er doch käme!** if only he would come!; **~ ihn doch der Teufel hole!** to hell with him!; **~ mir das nicht noch einmal passiert!** see that it doesn't happen again!; **o ~ ich dich bald wieder sehe!** (*poet.*) oh that I may see you again soon!; **F** (*bedauernder Ausruf*) **~ er so jung sterben musste!** how terrible *or* it's so sad that he had to die so young!; **~ mir das passieren musste!** why did it have to [go and] happen to me!; ⇨ *auch* **als, [an]statt, auf, außer, nur, ohne, kaum**

**dasselbe** ⇨ **derselbe**

**dasselbige** ⇨ **derselbige**

**Dassel·fliege** *die* botfly

**da|stehen** *unr. itr. V.* **A** (*[untätig] stehen*) [just] stand there; **wie stehst du denn da!** what a way to stand!; **krumm ~:** slouch; **~ wie die Kuh** *od.* **der Ochs vorm neuen Tor** *od.* **Scheunentor** *od.* **vorm Berg** (*salopp*) be completely baffled; **B** (*in einer bestimmten Lage sein*) find oneself; **gut/schlecht/[ganz] anders ~:** be in a good/bad/[quite] different position; **[ganz] allein ~:** be [all] alone in the world; **nun, wie stehe ich jetzt da?** (*ugs.*) just look at me now!; (*bei einer bestimmten Leistung*) how about that?; (*verzweifelt*) now I'm sunk! (*coll.*); **wie stehen wir denn jetzt vor den Nachbarn da?** what will the neighbours think of us now?; **mit leeren Händen/als Lügner** *usw.* **~:** be left empty-handed/looking like a liar *etc.*

**Datei** /daˈtai/ *die;* **~, ~en** data file

**Datei-: ~manager** *der* (*DV*) file manager; **~name** *der* (*DV*) file name; **~verwaltung** *die* (*DV*) file management

**Daten** /ˈdaːtn̩/ *Pl.* (*Angaben*) data; (*persönliche ~*) particulars; **die technischen ~ eines Typs** the technical specification *sing.* of a model; ⇨ *auch* **Datum** A, C

**Daten-: ~autobahn** *die* (*DV*) data highway; **~bank** *die; Pl.* **~~en** data bank; **~bestand** *der* database; **~erfassung** *die* data collection *or* capture; **~handschuh** *der* dataglove; **~helm** *der* data helmet; virtual reality helmet; **~highway** /...haiweɪ/ *der;* **~~s, ~~s** ⇨ **~autobahn**; **~schutz** *der* data protection; **~schutzbeauftragte** *der/die* data protection officer; **~technik** *die* data systems [engineering]; **~träger** *der* data carrier; **~typist** *der;* **~~en, ~~en, ~typistin** *die;* **~~, ~~nen** data processing keyboarder; **~verarbeitung** *die* data processing *no def. art.*; **~verarbeitungsanlage** *die* data processor; (*größeres System*) data processing system

**datieren** /daˈtiːrən/ **1** *tr. V.* date; **vom 1. Mai datiert** dated 1 May; **archäologische Funde [ins 3. Jh.] ~:** date archaeological finds [to the third century AD]. **2** *itr. V.* (*stammen*) date (**aus** from); **der Brief datierte vom 4. Mai** the letter was dated 4 May

**Dativ** /ˈdaːtiːf/ *der;* **~s, ~e** (*Sprachw.*) dative [case]; (*Wort im ~*) dative [form]; **im/mit dem ~ stehen** be in/take the dative [case]

**Dativ·objekt** *das* (*Sprachw.*) indirect object

**dato** /ˈdaːto/ *in* **bis ~** (*Kaufmannsspr., sonst ugs.*) to date

**Dato·wechsel** *der* (*Bankw.*) time bill

**Datscha** /ˈdatʃa/ *die;* **~, ~s** *od.* **Datschen, Datsche** /ˈdatʃə/ *die;* **Datsche, Datschen** (*DDR*) dacha

**Dattel** /ˈdatl̩/ *die;* **~, ~n** date

**Dattel-: ~palme** *die* date palm; **~traube** *die: popular name for various large, elongated black grapes*

**Datterich** /ˈdatərɪç/ ⇨ **Tatterich**

**Datum** /ˈdaːtʊm/ *das;* **~s, Daten** /ˈdaːtn̩/ **A** **▶ 187|, ▶ 207|** (*Zeitangabe, Zeitpunkt*) date; **das heutige ~:** the date today; today's date; **was für ein/welches ~ haben wir heute?** what is the date today?; **der Brief trägt das ~ vom 6. Mai** the letter is dated 6 May; **unter dem heutigen/gestrigen ~ übersandten wir Ihnen ...** in today's/yesterday's mail we sent you ...; **ein Schriftstück mit dem ~ versehen** date a document; **eine Entdeckung neueren ~s** a recent discovery; **B** (*Faktum*) fact

**Datums-: ~grenze** *die* date line; **~stempel** *der* date stamp

**Daube** /ˈdaubə/ *die;* **~, ~n** **A** (*am Fass*) stave; **B** (*beim Eisschießen*) tee

**Dauer** /ˈdauɐ/ *die;* **~, ~n** **A** (*Zeitraum*) length; duration; **die ~ eines Vertrags** the term of a contract; **die ~ des Besuchs** the length of the visit; **von kurzer** *od.* **nicht von [langer] ~ sein** not last long; be short-lived; **für die ~ eines Jahres** *od.* **von einem Jahr** for a period of one year; **während der ~ unseres Aufenthalts** for the duration of our stay; (*die ganze Zeit*) throughout our whole stay; **B** (*Fortbestehen*) **von ~ sein** last [long]; **ihr Glück hatte keine ~** *od.* **war nicht von ~:** her happiness was short-lived *or* did not last [long]; **auf die ~:** in the long run; **der Lärm ist auf die ~ nicht zu ertragen** the noise is not tolerable for any length of time; **auf die ~ möchte ich hier nicht wohnen** I wouldn't want to live here permanently *or* indefinitely; **auf ~:** permanently; for good; **er hat die Stelle**

*old spelling (see note on page 1707)

# Datum

Im Englischen gibt es mehrere Möglichkeiten, das Datum zu schreiben oder zu sagen:

***der 10. Mai***
= (*geschrieben*) May 10, 10 May, May 10th, 10th May
= (*gesprochen*) May the tenth, the tenth of May *od.* (*amerik.*) May tenth

Die folgenden Beispiele beziehen sich auf die häufigsten Versionen, die überall in der englischsprachigen Welt verwendet werden: **May 10** bzw. **May 10th** für die schriftliche Form, die auch so im Briefkopf erscheint, und **May the tenth** für die gesprochene Form.

Selbstverständlich werden Daten auch nur mit Ziffern angegeben, vor allem in Geschäftsbriefen. Hier ist zu beachten, dass in den USA die Reihenfolge Monat, Tag, Jahr (mit Bindestrich) ist. Der Monat erscheint also an erster Stelle (May 10th 1995 = 5-10-1995). Im britischen Gebrauch hingegen ist die Reihenfolge wie auch im deutschen Tag, Monat, Jahr (10.5.1995, oft auch mit Schrägstrich: 10/5/1995).

## Der Wievielte?

***Der Wievielte ist heute?***
= What's the date [today]?

***Heute ist der zehnte Mai***
= Today is *od.* It's May the tenth

***Am Wievielten ist die Hochzeit?***
= What date is the wedding?

***Die Hochzeit ist am 22.***
= The wedding is on the 22nd (*gesprochen*: twenty-second)

| | GESCHRIEBEN | GESPROCHEN |
|---|---|---|
| ***der 1. Mai*** | May 1st, May 1 | May the first |
| ***der 21. Mai*** | May 21st, May 21 | May the twenty-first |
| ***der 30. Mai 1994*** | May 30th *od.* May 30 1994 *od.* (*amerik.*) May 30, 1994 | May the thirtieth nineteen ninety-four |
| ***Montag, der 3. Mai*** | Monday May 3rd *od.* May 3 | Monday May the third |
| ***21.5.1966*** | 21.5.66 *od.* (*amerik.*) 5-21-66 | twenty-one five *od.* (*amerik.*) five twenty-one sixty-six |

## In welchem Jahr?

| | | |
|---|---|---|
| ***1900*** | 1900 | nineteen hundred |
| ***1905*** | 1905 | nineteen [oh] five, nineteen hundred and five |
| ***1920*** | 1920 | nineteen twenty[1] |
| ***das Jahr 2000*** | the year 2000 | the year two thousand |
| ***im Jahr 2000*** | in the year 2000 | in the year two thousand |
| ***2001*** | 2001 | two thousand and one |
| ***230 n.Chr.*** | 230 AD[2] | two hundred and thirty AD [ei'di:] |
| ***55 v.Chr.*** | 55 BC[3] | fifty-five BC [bi'si:] |
| ***das 16. Jahrhundert*** | the 16th century | the sixteenth century |

[1] Meist wird das **hundred and** bei der Jahresangabe weggelassen; es wird aber manchmal doch hinzugefügt, vor allem bei den Jahren 01 bis 09 des Jahrhunderts.

[2] = anno domini

[3] = before Christ

## Wann?

***am Freitag***
= on Friday

***am 6. März***
= on March 6th (*gesprochen*: on March the sixth)

***am Freitag, dem 6. März***
= on Friday March 6th (*gesprochen*: on Friday March the sixth)

Beachten Sie, dass **the** nicht geschrieben und nur vor der Ordinalzahl für das Datum gesprochen wird.

Ausnahme: Wenn nur die Zahl (ohne Angabe des Monats) genannt wird, wird **the** auch geschrieben:

***Wir treffen uns am 6.***
= We're meeting on the 6th

***Der Termin ist am Ersten***
= The deadline is on the first

***Sie kommen am nächsten Ersten***
= They are coming on the first of next month

Auch bei der Angabe des Monats wird **the** nicht verwendet:

***im Juni***
= in June

***letztes Jahr im Juni***
= last June

***im Juni nächsten Jahres***
= next June

***Mitte Juni***
= in the middle of June

***Ende/Anfang Juni***
= at the end/beginning of June

Vor Jahresangaben steht immer **in**:

***1945 kam er aus dem Krieg zurück***
= In 1945 he came back from the war

Für „im Jahr[e]" sagt man meist einfach **in**; **in the year ...** ist stilistisch etwas gehoben und bezieht sich meist auf geschichtliche Daten:

***im Jahr[e] 55 v.Chr.***
= in [the year] 55 BC

***im Jahr[e] 27 n.Chr.***
= in [the year] 27 AD

## Sonstige Ausdrücke

***vom 5. November an***
= from November 5th [onwards]

***ab kommendem Dienstag***
= from next Tuesday

***vom 21. bis zum 30.***
= from the 21st to the 30th

***Es wird bis Freitag/bis zum 14. fertig***
= It will be ready by Friday/by the 14th

***Es wird erst am Freitag fertig***
= It won't be ready until Friday

***um den 16. Mai [herum]***
= around May 16th

***in den Sechzigerjahren***
= in the sixties *od.* 60s

***in den Achtzigerjahren des 19. Jahrhunderts***
= in the 1880s

***der Roman des 19. Jahrhunderts***
= the 19th century novel

***ein Komponist des 17. Jahrhunderts***
= a 17th century composer

***ein Gebäude aus dem 14. Jahrhundert***
= a 14th century building

***Das Auto ist ein 1990er Modell/ist Baujahr 1990***
= The car's a 1990 model

***der Aufstand von 1912***
= the 1912 uprising

**jetzt auf ~:** his job is now permanent; he now has tenure (*Amer. Sch./Univ.*)

**dauer-, Dauer-: ~arbeitslose** *der/die* long-term unemployed person; **~auftrag** *der* (*Finanzw.*) standing order; **per** *od.* **durch ~auftrag** by standing order; **~ausweis** *der* long-term pass; **~belastung** *die* continual *or* constant strain; (*Technik*) permanent load; **~beschäftigung** *die* permanent job *or* (*formal*) position; **~brenner** *der* **A** (*Ofen*) slow-burning stove; **B** (*ugs.: Theaterstück usw.*) long-running success; (*Schlager*) evergreen; **~einrichtung** *die* permanent institution; **~erfolg** *der* long-running success; **~erscheinung** *die* permanent feature (**bei, in** of); **~frost** *der* long period of frost; **es herrschte ~frost** there was a long period of frost; **~gast** *der* **A** (*im Hotel usw.*) long-stay guest *or* resident; (*scherzh.: Besucher*) long-term visitor (*who outstays his/her welcome*); **B** (*im Lokal*) regular; **~geschwindigkeit** *die* cruising speed; **~haft** **1** *Adj.* **A** (*von langer ~*) [long-]lasting, enduring ‹peace, friendship, etc.›; **B** (*haltbar*) durable; hard-wearing; **2** *adv.* lastingly; with long-lasting effect; **~karte** *die* season ticket; **~lauf** *der* jogging *no art.*; **ein ~lauf** a jog; **einen ~lauf machen** go for a jog; go jogging; **im ~lauf** at a jog; **~lösung** *die* permanent solution; **~lutscher** *der* large lollipop; all-day sucker (*Amer.*); **~mieter** *der*, **~mieterin** *die* long-term tenant

**dauern**[1] *itr. V.* last; ‹job etc.› take; **der Film dauert zwei Stunden** the film lasts [for] *or* goes on for two hours; **bei ihm dauert alles furchtbar lange** everything takes him a terribly long time; **einen Moment, es dauert nicht lange** just a minute, it won't take long; **etw. dauert seine Zeit** sth. takes time; **ein Weilchen wird es schon noch ~:** it will be *or* take a little while longer; **es dauert mir zu lange** it takes too long for me; **das dauert** (*ugs.*) that will take [some] time; **diese Freundschaft wird ~** (*geh.*) this friendship will last *or* endure

**dauern**[2] *tr. V.* (*geh.*) **die Waisen dauerten ihn** he felt sorry for the orphans; **es dauert mich, dass ...** I regret *or* I am sorry that ...

**dauernd** **1** *Adj.* constant, perpetual ‹noise, interruptions, etc.›; permanent ‹institution›; **~er Wohnsitz** permanent residence. **2** *adv.* constantly; (*immer*) always; the whole time; **er kommt ~ zu spät** he is for ever *or* keeps on arriving late

**Dauer-: ~obst** *das* fruit which keeps well; **~parker** *der*; **~~s, ~~, ~parkerin** *die*; **~~, ~~nen** resident with a parking permit; (*im Parkhaus*) holder of a reserved parking space; **~redner** *der*, **~rednerin** *die* (*abwertend*) voluble speaker; **~regelung** *die* permanent arrangement; **~regen** *der* continuous rain; **~schach** *das* perpetual check; **~schaden** *der* (*Med.*) **ein ~schaden/ ~schäden** permanent damage *no indef. art.*; (*Verletzung*) permanent injury; **~stellung** *die* permanent position; **~strom** *der* (*Elektrot.*) constant current; **~test** *der* long-term test; **~ton** *der*; *Pl.* **~töne** continuous tone; **~welle** *die* perm; permanent wave; **sie will sich** (*Dat.*) **~wellen legen lassen** *od.* (*ugs.*) **machen lassen** she wants to have her hair permed; **~wurst** *die* smoked sausage (*with good keeping properties, esp. salami*); **~zustand** *der* permanent state [of affairs]; **zum ~zustand werden** become permanent *or* a permanent state

**Däumchen** /ˈdɔymçən/ *das*; **~s, ~:** little thumb; **~ drehen** (*ugs.*) twiddle one's thumbs

**Daumen** /ˈdaumən/ *der*; **~s, ~** ▶ 471 thumb; **am ~ lutschen** suck one's thumb; (*fig. ugs.*) [sit there and] starve; **jmdm.** *od.* **für jmdn. den** *od.* **die ~ drücken** *od.* **halten** keep one's fingers crossed for sb.; **auf etw.** (*Dat.*) **den ~ haben, auf etw.** (*Akk.*) **den ~ halten** (*ugs.*) keep a careful eye *or* check on sth.; **jmdm. den ~ aufs Auge drücken** (*ugs.*) put the screws *pl.* on sb.; **[etw.] über den ~ peilen** (*ugs.*) make a guesstimate [of sth.] (*coll.*); **über den ~ gepeilt** at a rough estimate

**daumen-, Daumen-: ~abdruck** *der*; *Pl.* **~abdrücke** thumbprint; **~breit** *Adj.* as wide as your thumb *postpos.*; ≈ an inch across *postpos.*; **~lutscher** *der*, **~lutscherin** *die*; **~~, ~~nen** (*oft abwertend*) thumbsucker; **~nagel** *der* ▶ 471 thumbnail; **~register** *das* thumb index; **~schrauben** *Pl.* (*hist.*) thumbscrews; **jmdm. die ~schrauben anlegen** (*fig.*) put the screws on sb.

**Däumling** /ˈdɔymlɪŋ/ *der*; **~s, ~e** **A** (*Märchengestalt*) Tom Thumb; **B** (*Schutzkappe*) thumbstall

**Daune** /ˈdaunə/ *die*; **~, ~n** down [feather]; **~n** down *sing.*; **man geht weich wie auf ~n** it's like walking on thistledown

**daunen-, Daunen-: ~bett** *das* down-filled quilt; **~kissen** *das* down[-filled] cushion; (*für das Bett*) down[-filled] pillow; **~weich** *Adj.* downy soft; as soft as down *postpos.*

**Daus** /daus/ (*veralt.*) *in* **ei der ~!, was der ~!** what the deuce *or* dickens! (*coll.*)

**David** /ˈdaːfɪt/ (*der*) David

**David[s]·stern** *der* star of David

**davon** /daˈfɔn/ *Adv.* **A** (*von dieser Stelle entfernt*) from it/them; (*von dort*) from there; (*mit Entfernungsangabe*) away [from it/them]; **nur einige Meter ~ [entfernt] ist eine Mauer** there is a wall only a few metres away [from it]; **wir sind noch weit ~ entfernt** (*fig.*) we are still a long way from that; we still have a long way to go; **B** (*von dieser Stelle weg*) from it/them; **sie konnte die Augen nicht ~ abwenden** she could not take her eyes off it *or* away from it; **dies ist die Hauptstraße und ~ zweigen einige Nebenstraßen ab** this is the main road and a few side roads branch off it; **C** (*hinsichtlich dieser Sache, darüber*) about it/them; **er redet nur davon** he talks only of this; he talks of *or* about nothing else; **D** (*durch diese Angelegenheit verursacht, dadurch*) by it/them; thereby; **~ betroffen sein** be affected by it/them; **~ wirst du krank** it will make you ill; **~ kriegt man Durchfall** you get diarrhoea from [eating] that/those; that gives/those give you diarrhoea; **das kommt ~!** (*ugs.*) [there you are,] that's what happens; (*es geschieht dir usw. recht*) it serves you/him/her/them right; **das kommt ~, dass du nicht genug schläfst** that's the result of [your] not getting enough sleep; **das hast du nun ~!** that's what comes of it!; **~ hast du doch nichts** you won't *or* don't get anything out of it; there's nothing in it for you; **E** (*als Teil eines Ganzen; dessen, deren*) of it/them; **das Gegenteil ~ ist wahr** the opposite [of this] is true; **ich hätte gern ein halbes Pfund ~:** I would like half a pound of that/those; **geben Sie mir vier ~:** give me four of them; **hast du schon ~ gegessen/genommen?** have you had/taken some of that/those?; **F** (*aus diesem Material, auf dieser Grundlage*) from *or* out of it/them; **hier ist Wolle, du kannst dir einen Schal ~ stricken** here is some wool, you can knit yourself a scarf with it; **~ kann man nicht leben** you can't live on that; ⇒ *auch* **da-**; *NB The word can occur in two parts in North German coll. usage, e.g.* **da weiß ich nichts von** I don't know anything about it

**davon-: ~|bleiben** *unr. itr. V.*; *mit sein* keep away; **du sollst ~bleiben!** don't touch it/them!; leave it/them alone!; **~|fahren** *unr. itr. V.*; *mit sein* leave; (*mit dem Auto*) drive away *or* off; (*mit dem Fahrrad, Motorrad*) ride away *or* off; **dem ~fahrenden Zug nachschauen** look after the departing train; (*aus dem Bahnhof*) watch the train as it pulls out; **jmdm. ~fahren** leave sb. behind; **ich muss mich beeilen, sonst fährt mir der Bus ~:** I must hurry or the bus will leave without me *or* I'll miss the bus; **er fährt allen ~** (*ist schneller als alle*) he leaves the rest standing; **~|fliegen** *unr. itr. V.*; *mit sein* fly away *or* off; **~|gehen** *unr. itr. V.*; *mit sein* walk away *or* off; **~|kommen** *unr. itr. V.*; *mit sein* get away; escape; **mit dem Leben ~kommen** escape with one's life; **mit dem Schrecken/einer Geldstrafe ~kommen** get off with a fright/a fine; **~|lassen** *unr. tr. V.* *in* **die Finger ~lassen** ⇒ **Finger** A; **~|laufen** *unr. itr. V.*; *mit sein* **A** (*weglaufen*) run away; **er ist mir ~gelaufen** he's made off; **es ist zum Davonlaufen** (*ugs.*) it really turns you off (*coll.*); it makes you want to run a mile; **B** (*ugs.: überraschend verlassen*) **jmdm. ~laufen** walk out on sb.; **dieser Partei laufen die Wähler ~:** the voters are deserting this party; **C** (*unkontrollierbar steigen*) spiral; **die Kosten des Projekts sind uns ~gelaufen** the costs of the project have got out of control; **die Preise laufen den Einkommen ~:** prices are outstripping incomes; **~|machen** *refl. V.* make off (**mit** with); **~|schleichen** *unr. itr. V.* *mit sein*; *auch refl. V.* slink off *or* away; **~|stehlen** *unr. refl. V.* (*geh.*) steal away; **~|tragen** *unr. tr. V.* **A** (*wegtragen*) carry away; take away ‹rubbish›; **B** (*geh.: erringen*) win, gain ‹a victory, fame›; **den Sieg ~tragen** win; be victorious; (*Sport*) be the winner/winners; **C** (*geh.: sich zuziehen*) receive, suffer ‹injuries›; **~|ziehen** *unr. itr. V.*; *mit sein* **A** (*Sport*) pull away; **B** (*weggehen*) go on one's way

**davor** /daˈfoːɐ̯/ *Adv.* **A** (*vor dieser/diese Stelle*) in front of it/them; **etw. ~ legen/stellen** put sth. in front of it/them; **sich ~ schieben** move in front of it/them; (*es/sie bedecken*) cover it/them; **sich ~ stellen** plant oneself in front of it/them; **ein Haus mit einem Garten ~:** a house with a garden at the front *or* in front; **Kommt Mainz vor oder nach Wiesbaden? — Davor** Is Mainz before or after Wiesbaden? — Before; **B** (*zeitlich*) before [it/them]; **~ macht er einen Dauerlauf von 30 Minuten** he goes jogging for 30 minutes beforehand *or* first; **kurz ~ stehen** be close to it; (*vor einer Tat*) be about to do it; **C** (*in Verbindung mit bestimmten Verben und Substantiven*) **wir haben ihn ~ gewarnt** we warned him of *or* about it/them; **er hat Angst ~, erwischt zu werden** he is afraid of being caught; **wir sind ~ geschützt** we are protected from it/them; ⇒ *auch* **da-**; *NB In some uses under* A *and* C *the word occurs in North German colloquial usage in two parts, e.g.* **da habe ich keine Angst vor** I'm not afraid of it/them

***davor|legen** *usw.* ⇒ **davor** A, B

**dazu** /daˈtsuː/ *Adv.* **A** (*zusätzlich zu dieser Sache*) with it/them; (*gleichzeitig*) at the same time; (*außerdem*) what is more; **~ reicht man am besten Salat** it's/they're best served with lettuce/salad; **er ist dumm und ~ auch noch frech** he is stupid and insolent into the bargain; **B** (*darüber*) about *or* on it/them; **was meinen Sie ~?** what do you think about it?; what is your opinion on this?; **C** (*zu diesem Zweck*) for it; (*es zu tun*) to do it; **D** (*zu diesem Ergebnis*) to it; **ich kann nichts ~ tun** I can't do anything to help; **er ist zu alt ~:** he is too old for it; **~ reicht das Geld nicht** we haven't enough money for that; **~ sind sie ja da!** that's what they are there for!; **~ kann ich dir nur raten** I would strongly advise you to do it; **im Widerspruch** *od.* **Gegensatz ~:** contrary to this/that; **~ war sie nicht in der Lage** she was not in a position to do it *or* do so; **er hatte ~ keine Lust** he didn't want to *or* didn't feel like it; **ich komme nie ~/nie ~, es zu tun** I never get round to it/to doing it; **wie komme ich ~?** (*ugs.*) it would never occur to me; why on earth should I?; ⇒ *auch* **da-**; *NB In senses* B *and* D *the word occurs in North German colloquial usage in two parts, e.g.* **da habe ich keine Lust zu** I don't feel like it

**dazu-: ~|geben** *unr. tr. V.* **A** (*beisteuern*) give towards it; **B** (*zusätzlich geben*) add; give as well; **C** (*Kochk.*) add; ⇒ *auch* **Senf**; **~|gehören** *tr. V.* **A** (*zu dieser Sache, Kategorie gehören*) belong to it/them; (*als Zusatz*) go with it/them; **der Wein gehört ~** (*ist nicht wegzudenken*) the wine belongs with it; you have to have wine, it's all part of it; (*ist im Preis inbegriffen*) the wine is included [in the price]; **das gehört [mit] ~:** it's all part of it; (*es ist Sitte*) it's the done thing (*coll.*); **alles, was ~gehört** everything that goes with it/them; **B** (*erforderlich sein*) **sie hat**

---

*old spelling (see note on page 1707)

**alles, was ~gehört, um Karriere zu machen** she has what it takes to make a successful career; **es gehört Mut/schon einiges ~:** it takes courage/quite something; **~gehörig** *Adj.* Ⓐ appropriate; which goes/go with it/them *postpos.*; (*farblich usw. passend*) matching; **ein Schloss und die ~gehörigen Schlüssel** a lock and the keys that fit it; Ⓑ (*erforderlich*) necessary; **~|gesellen** *refl. V.* join in; (*als Zuschauer*) gather round; **~|kommen** *unr. itr. V.; mit sein* Ⓐ (*hinkommen*) arrive [on the scene]; turn up; Ⓑ (*außerdem kommen*) **es kommen noch einige Gäste ~:** there are still some guests to come; **kommt noch etwas ~?** (*fig.*) is there anything else [you would like]?; **~ kommt, dass ...** (*fig.*) what's more, ...; on top of that, ...; ⇒ *auch* **kommen** M; **~|lernen** *tr., itr. V.* [etwas] **~lernen** learn [something new]; **man kann immer noch [etwas] ~lernen** there's always something [new] to learn

**da·zu·mal** *Adv.* (*veralt., noch scherzh. altertümelnd*) in those days; ⇒ *auch* **Anno**

**dazu-:** **~|rechnen** *tr. V.* add on; **wenn man noch ~rechnet ...** (*fig.*) when you also consider ...; **~|setzen** *refl. V.* sit down next to him/her/you/them; **darf ich mich ~setzen?** may I join you *or* sit here?; **~|tun** *unr. tr. V.* (*ugs.*) add; **das Seine ~tun** do one's bit; (*mit Geld*) chip in (*coll.*); **ohne jmds. Dazutun** without sb.'s help; (*ohne jmds. Beteiligung*) without involving sb.; **~|verdienen** *tr., itr. V.* earn ‹sth.› extra; (*als Nebenbeschäftigung*) earn ‹sth.› on the side; **seine Frau verdient noch [etwas] ~:** his wife earns something as well

**dazwischen** /da'tsvɪʃn̩/ *Adv.* Ⓐ in between; between them; (*darunter*) among them; Ⓑ (*unterwegs*) on the way; (*währenddessen*) during this

**dazwischen-:** **~|fahren** *unr. itr. V.; mit sein* Ⓐ (*eingreifen*) step in [and sort things out]; Ⓑ (*unterbrechen*) break in; **~|funken** *itr. V.* (*ugs.*) put a spanner in the works; (*sich einmischen*) put one's oar in; **jmdm. ~funken** put a spoke in sb.'s wheel; mess it up for sb.; **~|kommen** *unr. itr. V.; mit sein* Ⓐ (*zwischen diese Dinge kommen*) **mit dem Hemd/Finger ~kommen** get one's shirt/finger caught [in it]; Ⓑ (*als Störung auftreten*) **[jmdm.] ~kommen** complicate matters [for sb.]; (*es verhindern*) prevent it; **mir ist etwas ~gekommen** I had problems; (*immer noch*) I've got problems; **wenn nur nichts ~kommt** as long as there are no hitches *or* complications; Ⓒ (*~ an der Reihe sein*) **[noch] ~kommen** come in between; **~|liegen** *unr. itr. V.* lie in between; **Jahre lagen ~:** years had passed; **da liegen doch schon Tage ~:** that was days ago; **die ~liegende Zeit/Strecke** the intervening period/distance; **die ~liegenden Ereignisse** the events which have/had occurred in the mean while; **~|reden** *itr. V.* Ⓐ (*unterbrechen*) interrupt; Ⓑ (*umzustimmen versuchen*) **jmdm. ~reden** try to make sb. change his/her mind; **~|rufen** ❶ *unr. itr. V.* interrupt [by shouting]; ❷ *unr. tr. V.* interrupt [loudly] with; interject; **~|schalten** *tr. V.* Ⓐ (*Elektrot.*) insert; Ⓑ (*fig.*) interpose; (*vorteilhaft*) use as an intermediary; **~|stehen** *unr. itr. V.* Ⓐ (*Einigung verhindern*) be obstructive; stand in the way; Ⓑ (*zwischen diesen Gegensätzen stehen*) be [somewhere] in the middle; Ⓒ (*zwischen den Erwähnten stehen*) stand amongst them; **~|treten** *unr. itr. V.; mit sein* Ⓐ (*eingreifen*) intervene; **sein Dazwischentreten** his intervention; Ⓑ (*Uneinigkeit verursachen*) come between them

**DB** *Abk.* **Deutsche Bundesbahn** German Federal Railways

**DBP** *Abk.* (*hist.*) **Deutsche Bundespost** German Federal Post Office

**DDR** *Abk.* (*hist.*) **Deutsche Demokratische Republik** GDR

**DDR-Bürger** *der,* **DDR-Bürgerin** *die* (*hist.*) GDR citizen

**D-Dur** /'de:-/ *das* D major; ⇒ *auch* **C-Dur**

**Deal** /di:l/ *der od. das;* **~s, ~s** (*salopp*) deal

**dealen** /'di:lən/ *itr. V.* (*ugs.*) push drugs; **mit LSD ~:** push LSD

**Dealer** *der;* **~s, ~, Dealerin** *die;* **~, ~nen** (*ugs.*) pusher

**Debakel** /de'ba:kl̩/ *das;* **~s, ~:** debacle; fiasco; (*schwere Niederlage*) rout

**Debatte** /de'batə/ *die;* **~, ~n** debate (**über** + *Akk.* on); (*Streit*) argument (**über** + *Akk.* about); **etw. in die ~ werfen** introduce *or* bring sth. into the debate; **[nicht] zur ~ stehen** [not] be under discussion; (*auf der Tagesordnung*) [not] be on the agenda; **etw. zur ~ stellen** put sth. up for discussion

**debattieren** *tr., itr. V.* debate; (*weniger formell*) discuss; **[mit jmdm.] über etw. ~:** discuss sth. [with sb.]

**Debattier·klub** *der* debating society

**Debet** /'de:bɛt/ *das;* **~s, ~s** (*Finanzw.*) debit [side]

**debil** /de'bi:l/ *Adj.* Ⓐ (*Med.*) mentally subnormal; Ⓑ (*abwertend*) feeble-minded

**Debilität** /debili'tɛ:t/ *die;* **~** Ⓐ (*Med.*) mental subnormality; Ⓑ (*abwertend*) feeble-mindedness

**Debitor** /'de:bitɔr/ *der;* **~s, ~en** /debi'to:rən/, **Debitorin** *die;* **~, ~nen** (*Finanzw.*) debtor

**Debüt** /de'by:/ *das;* **~s, ~s** debut; **sein ~ [als Autor** *usw.***] geben** make one's debut [as an author *etc.*]

**Debütant** /deby'tant/ *der;* **~en, ~en** newcomer [making his debut]; (*in einer Mannschaft, Truppe, usw.*) new face

**Debütantin** *die;* **~, ~nen** Ⓐ ⇒ **Debütant**; Ⓑ (*in der Gesellschaft*) debutante

**Debütantinnen·ball** *der* debutantes' ball

**debütieren** /deby'ti:rən/ *itr. V.* make one's debut

**Dechant** /dɛ'çant/ *der;* **~en, ~en** (*kath. Kirche*) dean

**dechiffrieren** *tr. V.* decipher ‹code, message›; decode ‹message, (fig.) conventions›

**Deck** /dɛk/ *das;* **~[e]s, ~s** Ⓐ (*eines Schiffes*) deck; **alle Mann an ~!** all hands on deck!; **auf ~ sein** be on deck; **unter ~ gehen** go below [decks]; **auf dem obersten/im mittleren/unteren ~:** on the top/middle/lower deck; Ⓑ (*Park~*) storey; level; **auf ~ 6 fahren** drive up to level 6; Ⓒ (*im Autobus*) deck

**Deck-:** **~adresse** *die* accommodation *or* (*Amer.*) cover address; **~an·strich** *der* top coat; **~auf·bauten** *Pl.* superstructure *sing.*; **~bett** *das* ⇒ **Oberbett**; **~blatt** *das* Ⓐ (*Bot.*) bract; Ⓑ (*von Zigarre*) wrapper; Ⓒ (*Titelblatt*) title page

**Deckchen** *das;* **~s, ~** Ⓐ small tablecloth; Ⓑ (*Zier~, Häkel~*) [small] crocheted mat *or* cover

**Decke** /'dɛkə/ *die;* **~, ~n** Ⓐ (*Tisch~*) tablecloth; **eine neue ~ auflegen** put a clean cloth on [the table]; Ⓑ (*Woll~, Pferde~, auch fig.*) blanket; (*Reise~*) rug; (*Deckbett, Stepp~*) quilt; (*Tages~*) bedspread; **sich** (*Dat.*) **die ~ über den Kopf ziehen** pull the covers *pl.* over one's head; **unter die ~ kriechen** slip under the covers; **sich nach der ~ strecken [müssen]** (*ugs.*) [have to] cut one's coat according to one's cloth; **mit jmdm. unter einer ~ stecken** (*ugs.*) be hand in glove with sb.; be in cahoots with sb. (*coll.*); Ⓒ (*Zimmer~*) ceiling; **mir fällt die ~ auf den Kopf** (*ugs.*) (*ich bekomme Platzangst*) I feel claustrophobic *or* shut in; (*ich langweile mich*) I get sick of [the sight of] these four walls; **an die ~ gehen** (*ugs.*) hit the roof (*coll.*); **[vor Freude] [bis] an die ~ springen** jump for joy; Ⓓ (*Radmantel*) [outer] cover; Ⓔ (*Fahrbahn~*) surface; Ⓕ (*Buchw.: Bucheinband*) cover; Ⓖ (*Jägerspr.: Haut, Fell*) skin

**Deckel** /'dɛkl̩/ *der;* **~s, ~** Ⓐ lid; (*auf Flaschen, Gläsern usw.*) top; (*Schacht~, Uhr~, Buch~ usw.*) cover; Ⓑ (*Bier~*) beer mat; Ⓒ (*salopp: Kopfbedeckung*) headgear *no pl.*; **jmdm. eins auf den ~ geben** (*ugs.*) haul sb. over the coals; take sb. to task

**Deckel·krug** *der* tankard (*with a lid*)

**deckeln** *tr. V.* (*ugs.*) take to task; tell off

**decken** ❶ *tr. V.* Ⓐ (*breiten, legen*) spread; Ⓑ (*mit einem Dach o. Ä. versehen*) roof ‹house›; cover ‹roof›; **ein Dach/Haus mit Ziegeln/Stroh ~:** tile/thatch a roof/house; Ⓒ **den Tisch ~:** lay *or* set the table; **es ist [für fünf Personen] gedeckt** the table is set [for five]; Ⓓ (*schützen*) cover; (*bes. Fußball: abschirmen*) mark ‹player›; (*vor Gericht usw.*) cover up for ‹accomplice, crime, etc.›; Ⓔ (*befriedigen*) satisfy, meet ‹need, demand›; **mein Bedarf ist gedeckt** (*ugs.*) I've had enough; Ⓕ (*Finanzw., Versicherungsw.*) cover; Ⓖ (*genau beschreiben*) describe accurately; cover; Ⓗ (*begatten*) cover; ‹stallion› serve ‹mare›.
❷ *itr. V.* Ⓐ (*Fußball*) mark; (*Boxen*) keep up one's guard; **besser ~:** improve one's marking/guard; Ⓑ (*den Tisch ~*) lay *or* set the table; Ⓒ ‹colour› cover.
❸ *refl. V.* Ⓐ (*Geom.*) be congruent; Ⓑ (*gleich sein*) coincide; tally; **ihre Aussage deckt sich nicht mit seiner** her statement does not agree with his

**Decken-:** **~balken** *der* ceiling beam; **~beleuchtung** *die* ceiling light; **~fluter** *der;* **~~s, ~~:** uplighter; **~gemälde** *das* ceiling painting; **~malerei** *die* ceiling painting; **~träger** *der* [iron] ceiling joist

**Deck-:** **~farbe** *die* paint (*which covers well*); body colour; (*für Gouachen*) gouache colour; **~feder** *die* cover; tectrix (*Ornith.*); **~flügel** *der* elytron; **~haar** *das* Ⓐ (*bei Tieren*) guard hair; Ⓑ (*bei Menschen*) top hair; **~hengst** *der* stud horse; breeding stallion; **~mantel** *der,* **~mäntelchen** *das* (*abwertend*) cover; **unter dem ~mantel der Entwicklungshilfe** *usw.* using development aid *etc.* as a blind *or* cover; under the guise of development aid *etc.*; **~name** *der* alias; assumed name; (*eines Spions, milit. Programms*) code name; (*einer Organisation*) cover name; **~plane** *die* waterproof cover; (*bes. geteert*) tarpaulin; **~platte** *die* cover; **~station** *die* stud

**Deckung** *die;* **~, ~en** Ⓐ (*das Schützen*) covering (*esp. Mil.*); (*Feuerschutz*) covering fire; (*Boxen, Fechten*) guard; (*bes. Fußball*) marking; (*Schach*) protection; Ⓑ (*Schutz; auch fig.*) cover (*esp. Mil.*); (*Schach*) defence; (*Boxen*) guard; (*bes. Fußball: die deckenden Spieler*) defence; **~ nehmen, in ~ gehen** take cover; **~ suchen/in ~ bleiben** look for/stay under cover; **[volle] ~!** take cover!; Ⓒ (*Finanzw.: das Begleichen*) meeting; **zur ~ seiner Schulden** to meet his debts; Ⓓ (*Finanzw.: Sicherheit*) cover [ing]; **der Scheck ist ohne ~:** the cheque is not covered; **als ~ für seine Schulden** as security for his debts; Ⓔ (*Befriedigung*) satisfaction; Ⓕ (*Übereinstimmung*) **Pläne** *usw.* **zur ~ bringen** make plans *etc.* agree; bring plans *etc.* into line; Ⓖ (*von Tieren: Begatten*) covering; (*einer Stute*) service

**deckungs-, Deckungs-:** **~auf·lage** *die* (*Verlagsw.*) break-even quantity; **~fehler** *der* (*bes. Fußball*) marking error; **~gleich** *Adj.* (*Geom.*) congruent; **unsere Meinungen sind ~gleich** (*fig.*) our opinions coincide *or* are the same

**Deck-:** **~weiß** *das* opaque white; **~wort** *das; Pl.* **~wörter** code word

**Decoder** /de'ko:dɐ/ *der;* **~s, ~** (*Elektronik*) decoder

**decodieren** ⇒ **dekodieren**

**Decrescendo** /dekrɛ'ʃɛndo/ *das;* **~s, ~s** *od.* **Decrescendi** (*Musik*) decrescendo

**Dedikation** /dedika'tsio:n/ *die;* **~, ~en** dedication

**Dedikations·exemplar** *das* presentation copy (*containing dedication*)

**dedizieren** /dedi'tsi:rən/ *tr. V.* dedicate; **jmdm. ein Exemplar ~:** inscribe a copy to sb.

**Deduktion** /deduk'tsio:n/ *die;* **~, ~en** (*Philos., Kybernetik*) deduction

**deduktiv** /deduk'ti:f/ (*Philos.*) ❶ *Adj.* deductive. ❷ *adv.* deductively; **~ folgern** conclude by deduction

**deduzieren** /dedu'tsi:rən/ *tr. V.* (*bes. Philos.*) deduce

d

**Deern** /de:ɐ̯n/ *die;* ~, **~s** (*nordd.*) lass

**Deez** ⇒ **Dez**

**DEFA** /'de:fa/*die;* ~ *Abk.* **Deutsche Film-Aktiengesellschaft** (*German film company*)

**de facto** /de: 'fakto/ *Adv.* de facto (*esp. Polit., Law*); in reality

**De-facto-Anerkennung** *die* de facto recognition

**Defaitismus** *usw.* (*schweiz.*) ⇒ **Defätismus** *usw.*

**Defäkation** /defɛka'tsi̯o:n/ *die;* ~, **~en** (*Med.*) defecation

**Defätismus** /defɛ'tɪsmʊs/ *der;* ~ (*oft abwertend*) defeatism

**Defätist** *der;* **~en, ~en, Defätistin** *die;* ~, **~nen** (*abwertend*) defeatist

**defätistisch** (*oft abwertend*) ❶ *Adj.* defeatist. ❷ *adv.* in a defeatist manner

**defekt** /de'fɛkt/ *Adj.* Ⓐ defective; faulty; **~ sein** have a defect; be faulty; (*nicht funktionieren*) not be working; Ⓑ (*fig.*) deficient ‹mind, understanding›

**Defekt** *der;* **~[e]s, ~e** Ⓐ defect, fault (**an** + *Dat.* in); Ⓑ ▶ 474 (*Psych., Med.*) defect (**an** + *Dat.* in); **Heilung mit bleibendem ~:** cure leaving a permanent handicap

**defektiv** /defɛk'ti:f/ *Adj.* (*Sprachw.*) defective

**Defektivum** /defɛk'ti:vʊm/ *das;* **~s, Defektiva** (*Sprachw.*) defective

**defensiv** /defɛn'zi:f/ ❶ *Adj.* Ⓐ (*verteidigend; auch Sport*) defensive; Ⓑ (*sicherheitsbewusst*) safety-conscious. ❷ *adv.* Ⓐ (*verteidigend; auch Sport*) defensively; Ⓑ (*sicherheitsbewusst*) in a safety-conscious manner

**Defensive** *die;* ~, **~n** Ⓐ defensive; **in der ~:** on the defensive; **jmdn. in die ~ drängen** force sb. on [to] the defensive; **in die ~ geraten** go on [to] the defensive; Ⓑ (*Sport*) **die ~:** defensive play; **aus der ~ heraus** from defensive positions *pl.*

**Defensiv-:** **~krieg** *der* defensive war; **~spiel** *das* (*Sport*) defensive play

**Defilee** /defi'le:/ *das;* **~s, ~s,** (*auch:*) **~n** parade; march past

**defilieren** /defi'li:rən/ *itr. V.; mit haben od. sein* **vor jmdm./etw. ~:** parade before *or* march past sb./sth.

**definierbar** *Adj.* definable; (*identifizierbar*) identifiable; **nicht [näher] ~:** indefinable; (*nicht zu identifizieren*) unidentifiable

**definieren** /defi'ni:rən/ ❶ *tr. V.* define; (*identifizieren*) identify. ❷ *refl. V.* (*sich als etw. verstehen*) describe oneself (**durch** in terms of)

**Definition** /defini'tsi̯o:n/ *die;* ~, **~en** definition

**definitiv** /defini'ti:f/ ❶ *Adj.* definitive; final ‹answer, decision›; (*sicher*) definite. ❷ *adv.* finally; (*sicher*) definitely

**definitorisch** /defini'to:rɪʃ/ ❶ *Adj.* ‹problem› of definition; ‹skill› at defining. ❷ *adv.* with regard to definition

**defizient** /defi'tsi̯ɛnt/ *Adj.* deficient

**Defizit** /'de:fitsɪt/ *das;* **~s, ~e** Ⓐ (*Fehlbetrag*) deficit; Ⓑ (*Mangel*) deficiency; **~ an etw.** (*Dat.*) lack of sth.

**defizitär** /defitsi'tɛ:ɐ̯/ ❶ *Adj.* Ⓐ (*Defizit aufweisend*) ‹trade etc.› which shows/showed a deficit *not pred.*; ‹firm etc.› which runs/ran at a loss *not pred.*; Ⓑ (*Defizit verursachend*) which leads/led to a deficit *postpos., not pred.* ❷ *adv.* **~[er] arbeiten** *od.* **wirtschaften** show a [bigger] deficit; run at a [bigger] loss

**Deflation** /defla'tsi̯o:n/ *die;* ~, **~en** (*Wirtsch.*) deflation

**deflationär** /deflatsi̯o'nɛ:ɐ̯/, **deflationistisch** *Adj.* (*Wirtsch.*) deflationary

**Deflations·politik** *die* (*Wirtsch.*) deflationary policy

**Deflektor** /de'flɛktɔr/ *der;* **~s, ~en** /-'to:rən/ (*Technik*) deflector

**Defloration** /deflora'tsi̯o:n/ *die;* ~, **~en** (*Med.*) defloration

*old spelling (see note on page 1707)

**deflorieren** /deflo'ri:rən/ *tr. V.* deflower

**Deformation** *die* Ⓐ (*Physik*) deformation; Ⓑ ▶ 474 (*Med.*) deformation; (*Missbildung*) deformity

**deformieren** *tr. V.* Ⓐ (*verformen*) distort; put out of shape; **deformiert** out of shape *pred.*; distorted; Ⓑ (*entstellen*) deform (*also fig.*); (*verunstalten*) disfigure ‹face etc.›; (*verstümmeln*) mutilate

**Deformierung** *die* Ⓐ (*Verformung*) deformation; distortion; Ⓑ (*Entstellung*) deformation; (*Verunstaltung*) disfigurement; (*Verstümmelung*) mutilation; (*Missbildung*) deformity

**Deformität** /defɔrmi'tɛ:t/ *die;* ~, **~en** ▶ 474 (*Med.*) deformity

**Defraudant** /defrau̯'dant/ *der;* **~en, ~en** (*veralt.*) defrauder; swindler; (*bei Unterschlagung*) embezzler

**Defroster** /de'frɔstɐ/ *der;* **~s,** ~ Ⓐ (*Gerät*) defroster; Ⓑ (*Spray*) de-icer

**deftig** /'dɛftɪç/ (*ugs.*) ❶ *Adj.* Ⓐ [good] solid *attrib.*, good and solid *pred.* ‹meal etc.›; [nice] big, [nice] fat ‹sausage etc.›; (*tüchtig*) [really] big ‹surprise›; sound ‹hiding›; (*hoch*) tremendous, (*coll.*) terrific ‹price, bill, etc.›; Ⓑ (*derb*) crude, coarse ‹joke, speech, etc.›. ❷ *adv.* good and proper (*coll.*)

**Degen**[1] *der;* **~s,** ~ (*hist.*) [doughty] warrior

**Degen**[2] /'de:gn̩/ *der;* **~s,** ~ Ⓐ (*Waffe*) [light] sword (*esp. for duelling*); (*Rapier*) rapier; Ⓑ (*Sportgerät*) épée

**Degeneration** /degenera'tsi̯o:n/ *die;* ~, **~en** degeneration (**zu** into)

**Degenerations·erscheinung** *die* sign of degeneration

**degenerativ** /degenera'ti:f/ ❶ *Adj.* degenerative. ❷ *adv.* **es ist ~ verändert** it has degenerated

**degenerieren** /degene'ri:rən/ *itr. V.; mit sein* degenerate (**zu** into)

**degeneriert** *Adj.* degenerate; (*überzüchtet*) overbred

**Degen-:** **~fechten** *das* épée [fencing] *no art.*; **~klinge** *die* sword blade; **~korb** *der* [sword] guard; **~scheide** *die* scabbard

**degoutant** /degu'tant/ (*geh.*) ❶ *Adj.* disgusting. ❷ *adv.* in a disgusting manner

**degoutieren** /degu'ti:rən/ *tr. V.* (*geh.*) disgust

**degradieren** /degra'di:rən/ *tr. V.* Ⓐ (*im Rang o. Ä.*) demote; **vom Feldwebel zum einfachen Schützen degradiert werden** be demoted from [the rank of] sergeant to [a] mere private; Ⓑ (*herabwürdigen*) **jmdn./etw. zu etw. ~:** reduce sb./sth. to [the level of] sth.

**Degradierung** *die;* ~, **~en** Ⓐ (*im Rang*) demotion; Ⓑ (*Herabwürdigung*) degradation; reduction (**zu** to the level of)

**Degression** /degrɛ'si̯o:n/ *die;* ~, **~en** Ⓐ (*Wirtsch.*) progressive reduction [of unit cost]; Ⓑ (*Steuerw.*) degression

**degressiv** /degrɛ'si:f/ *Adj.* (*Wirtsch., Steuerw.*) degressive

**degustieren** /degʊs'ti:rən/ *tr. V.* (*bes. schweiz.*) taste; sample

**dehnbar** *Adj.* Ⓐ (*elastisch*) ‹material etc.› that stretches *not pred.*; elastic ‹waistband etc.›; stretch ‹fabric›; **etw. ist ~:** sth. can be stretched; Ⓑ (*fig.: vage*) elastic; **das ist ein ~er Begriff** it's a loose concept; that can mean what you want it to mean

**Dehnbarkeit** *die;* ~ (*auch fig.*) elasticity

**dehnen** /'de:nən/ ❶ *tr. V.* Ⓐ stretch; Ⓑ (*lang aussprechen*) lengthen, draw out ‹vowel, word›; **etw. gedehnt sagen/aussprechen** say/pronounce sth. slowly; (*lässig*) drawl sth. ❷ *refl. V.* Ⓐ stretch; **er dehnte sich wohlig** he stretched [himself] luxuriantly; Ⓑ (*lange dauern*) **sich endlos ~:** go on for ever (*coll.*); go on and on; **die Minuten ~ sich zu Stunden** the minutes seem like hours

**Dehnung** *die;* ~, **~en** Ⓐ (*das Dehnen*) stretching; (*eines Vokals*) lengthening; Ⓑ (*Dehnbarkeit*) elasticity

**Dehnungs-:** **~fuge** *die* (*Bauw.*) expansion joint; **~-h** *das* (*Phon.*) 'h' lengthening the preceding vowel; **~zeichen** *das* (*Phon.*) length mark

**dehydrieren** *tr. V.* (*Chemie*) dehydrogenate

**Deibel** /'dai̯bl̩/ ⇒ **Deiwel**

**Deich** /dai̯ç/ *der;* **~[e]s, ~e** dike; **mit etw. über den ~ gehen** (*nordd.*) make off with sth.

**Deich-:** **~bau** *der* building of a/the dike; (*allgemein*) dike-building; **~bruch** *der* breach (*Brit.*) *or* (*Amer.*) break in the dike; (*Brechen des Deichs*) breaching (*Brit.*) *or* (*Amer.*) breaking of the dike; **~genossenschaft** *die* ⇒ **~verband**; **~graf** *der* (*veralt.*) ⇒ **~vorsteher**; **~krone** *die* top of the dike

**Deichsel** /'dai̯ksl̩/ *die;* ~, **~n** shaft; (*in der Mitte*) pole; (*aus zwei Stangen*) shafts *pl.*

**Deichsel·kreuz** *das* Ⓐ (*Griff*) shaft handle; Ⓑ (*Symbol*) Y[-shaped] cross

**deichseln** *tr. V.* (*ugs.*) fix; (*durch eine List*) wangle (*sl.*)

**Deich-:** **~verband** *der* association of owners of diked land; **~vorland** *das: land above mean high water mark on the seaward side of a dike;* **~vorsteher** *der,* **~vorsteherin** *die* chairman of a 'Deichverband'

**deifizieren** /deifi'tsi:rən/ *tr. V.* (*geh.*) deify

**dein**[1] /dai̯n/ *Possessivpron.* your; (*Rel., auch altertümelnd*) thy; **viele Grüße von deinem Emil/deiner Karin/deinen Müllers** with best wishes, yours Emil/Karin/the Müllers; **~ Wille geschehe** (*Rel.: im Vaterunser*) Thy will be done; **heute Abend kannst du ~en Humphrey Bogart im Fernsehen sehen** you can watch your beloved Humphrey Bogart *or* that Humphrey Bogart of yours on television tonight; **das Buch dort, ist das ~[e]s?** that book over there, is it yours?; **sind das ihre Schuhe oder ~e?** are those her shoes or yours?; **das war nicht mein Wunsch, sondern ~er** *od.* (*geh.*) **der ~e** it was not my wish but yours; **ewig/stets der deine** (*geh.*) yours ever; **du und die ~en** *od.* **Deinen** (*geh.*) you and yours *or* your family; **der/die deine** (*geh.*) your husband/wife; **das ~e** *od.* **Deine** (*geh.*) your possessions *pl. or* property; **du musst das ~e** *od.* **Deine tun** (*was du kannst*) you must do what you can; (*~en Teil*) you must do your bit *or* share; ⇒ *auch* **mein**[1]

**dein**[2] (*geh. veralt.*), **deiner** *Gen. des Personalpronomens* **du** (*geh.*) of you; **ich gedenke ~(er)** *od.* (*geh.*) **~ auf ewig** I will always remember you; **man lachte ~er** they laughed at you

**deiner·seits** /'dai̯nɐ'zai̯ts/ *Adv.* (*von deiner Seite*) on your part; (*auf deiner Seite*) for your part

**deines·gleichen** *indekl. Pron.* people *pl.* like you; (*abwertend*) the likes *pl.* of you; your sort *or* kind; **unter ~:** amongst your own sort *or* kind; **für dich und ~** (*abwertend*) for your sort; for the likes of you

**deines·teils** *Adv.* for your part

**deinet·halben** (*veralt.*) ⇒ **deinetwegen** A

**deinet·wegen** *Adv.* Ⓐ because of you; on your account; (*für dich*) on your behalf; (*dir zuliebe*) for your sake; **ich habe mir ~ große Sorgen gemacht** I have been very worried about you *or* on your account; Ⓑ (*du hast nichts dagegen*) **du hast gesagt, ~ könnten wir gehen** you said we could go as far as you were concerned

**deinet·willen** *Adv. in* **um ~:** for your sake

**deinige** /'dai̯nɪgə/ *Possessivpron.* (*geh. veralt.*) **der/die/das ~:** yours; **die ~n** *od.* **Deinigen** your family *sing.*; **das ~** *od.* **Deinige:** what is yours; your property; **du musst das ~** *od.* **Deinige tun** (*was du kannst*) you must do what you can; (*deinen Teil*) you must do your bit *or* share

**Deismus** /de'ɪsmʊs/ *der;* **~:** deism *no art.*

**deistisch** *Adj.* deistic

**Deiwel** /'dai̯vl̩/ *der;* **~s** (*nordd.*), **Deixel** /'dai̯ksl̩/ *der;* (*südd.*) **Deixels** devil; ⇒ *auch* **Teufel**

**de jure** /de: 'ju:rə/ *Adv.* de jure; legally

**De-jure-Anerkennung** *die* de jure recognition

**Deka** /ˈdɛka/ *das;* **~s, ~s** (*österr.*) decagram; **12 ~:** 12 decagrams

**Dekade** /deˈka:də/ *die;* **~, ~n** Ⓐ (*zehn Tage*) ten days *pl.;* Ⓑ (*zehn Jahre*) decade

**dekadent** /dekaˈdɛnt/ *Adj.* decadent

**Dekadenz** /dekaˈdɛnts/ *die;* **~:** decadence

**dekadisch** *Adj.* **~es Zahlensystem** decimal system; **~er Logarithmus** (*Math.*) common logarithm

**Deka-: ~eder** *das* (*Geom.*) decahedron; **~gramm** *das* decagram; **~liter** *der* decalitre

**Dekalog** /dekaˈlo:k/ *der;* **~[e]s** (*Rel.*) decalogue

**Dekan** /deˈka:n/ *der;* **~s, ~e** Ⓐ (*Universität*) dean; Ⓑ (*kath. Kirche*) dean; Ⓒ (*ev. Kirche*) superintendent

**Dekanat** /dekaˈna:t/ *das;* **~s, ~e** Ⓐ (*Universität*) dean's office; Ⓑ (*kath. Kirche*) deanery; Ⓒ (*Amt eines Dekans*) office of dean

**Dekanin** *die;* **~, ~nen** ⇒ **Dekan**

**dekartellisieren** /dekartɛliˈzi:rən/ *tr. V.* (*Wirtsch.*) decartelize

**dekatieren** /dekaˈti:rən/ *tr. V.* (*Textilw.*) decatise

**Deklamation** /deklamaˈtsi̯o:n/ *die;* **~, ~en** Ⓐ (*Vortrag*) recitation; Ⓑ (*abwertend: hohles Gerede*) [empty] rhetoric *no pl.*

**deklamatorisch** /deklamaˈto:rɪʃ/ ❶ *Adj.* Ⓐ (*ausdrucksvoll*) declamatory; Ⓑ (*abwertend: hohl*) rhetorical. ❷ *adv.* Ⓐ (*ausdrucksvoll*) expressively; Ⓑ (*abwertend: hohl klingend*) rhetorically; in expansive terms

**deklamieren** /deklaˈmi:rən/ *tr., itr. V.* recite

**Deklaration** /deklaraˈtsi̯o:n/ *die;* **~, ~en** (*Politik, Zoll-, Steuer-, Postwesen*) declaration

**deklarieren** /deklaˈri:rən/ *tr. V.* declare; **etw. als etw. ~:** declare sth. to be sth.; **zur atomwaffenfreien Zone deklariert werden** be declared a nuclear-free zone

**deklassieren** *tr. V.* Ⓐ (*Soziol.*) disadvantage; Ⓑ (*herabsetzen*) reduce; downgrade; Ⓒ (*Sport*) outclass; (*beim Rennen*) leave standing

**Deklassierung** *die;* **~, ~en** Ⓐ (*Soziol.*) disadvantaging; reduction in circumstances; Ⓑ (*Herabsetzung*) downgrading; Ⓒ (*Sport*) outclassing

**deklinabel** /dekliˈna:bl̩/ *Adj.* (*Sprachw.*) declinable

**Deklination** /deklinaˈtsi̯o:n/ *die;* **~, ~en** Ⓐ (*Sprachw.*) declension; **die starke/schwache ~:** the strong/weak declension; Ⓑ (*Astron., Physik*) declination

**deklinierbar** *Adj.* (*Sprachw.*) declinable

**deklinieren** /dekliˈni:rən/ *tr. V.* (*Sprachw.*) decline; **ein Wort schwach/stark ~:** decline a word as weak/strong

**dekodieren** *tr. V.* (*fachspr.*) decode

**Dekolleté, Dekolletee** /dekɔlˈte:/ *das;* **~s, ~s** low[-cut] neckline; décolletage; **Kleid mit tiefem ~:** very low-cut dress; dress with a plunging neckline

**dekolletieren** /dekɔlˈti:rən/ *tr. V.* make *or* cut with a low neckline

**dekolletiert** *Adj.* Ⓐ (*ausgeschnitten*) décolleté; low-cut ‹back, neckline›; Ⓑ (*Dekolleté tragend*) **~e Damen** ladies in low-cut dresses; **[tief] ~ sein** *od.* **gehen** wear a [very] low-cut dress/[very] low-cut dresses

**Dekolonisation** *die* decolonization

**dekolonisieren** *tr. V.* decolonize

**Dekompression** *die* decompression

**Dekompressions·kammer** *die* decompression chamber

**Dekontamination** *die* decontamination

**Dekonzentration** *die* (*der Verwaltung*) decentralization; (*der Industrie usw.*) deconcentration

**Dekor** /deˈko:ɐ̯/ *das;* **~s, ~s** *od.* **~e** Ⓐ (*Verzierung*) decoration; (*Muster*) pattern; **ein Zimmer im ~ der Dreißigerjahre** a room in the 1930s style; Ⓑ (*Theater, Film*) décor; setting

**Dekorateur** /dekoraˈtø:ɐ̯/ *der;* **~s, ~e, Dekorateurin** *die;* **~, ~nen** ▶ 159 (*Schaufenster~*) window dresser; (*von Innenräumen*) interior decorator *or* designer; (*Dekorationsmaler*) scene-painter

**Dekoration** /dekoraˈtsi̯o:n/ *die;* **~, ~en** Ⓐ (*das Dekorieren*) decoration; (*von Schaufenstern*) window dressing; **zur ~:** for decoration; Ⓑ (*Schmuck, Ausstattung*) decorations *pl.;* (*Schaufenster~*) window display; (*Theater, Film*) set; scenery *no pl.;* **bloße ~ sein** be purely for decoration purposes; Ⓒ (*Orden[verleihung]*) decoration

**Dekorations-: ~maler** *der,* **~malerin** *die* interior decorator; (*Theater*) [stage] decorator; scene-painter; **~stoff** *der* furnishing fabric; **~stück** *das* part of the décor; (*Theater*) piece of scenery

**dekorativ** /dekoraˈti:f/ ❶ *Adj.* decorative. ❷ *adv.* decoratively

**dekorieren** /dekoˈri:rən/ *tr. V.* Ⓐ (*ausschmücken*) decorate ‹room etc.›; dress ‹shop window›; Ⓑ (*mit Orden auszeichnen*) decorate (**mit** with); **hoch dekoriert** much decorated

**Dekorierung** *die;* **~, ~en** ⇒ **Dekoration A, C**

**Dekorum** /deˈko:rʊm/ *das;* **~s** (*veralt.*) decorum *no art.;* **das ~ verletzen/wahren** offend against/observe the proprieties *pl.*

**Dekostoff** /ˈde:ko-/ *der* furnishing fabric

**Dekrescendo** ⇒ **Decrescendo**

**Dekret** /deˈkre:t/ *das;* **~[e]s, ~e** decree

**dekretieren** *tr. V.* decree

**dekuvrieren** /dekuˈvri:rən/ ❶ *tr. V.* (*entlarven*) expose. ❷ *refl. V.* (*schlechte Züge zeigen*) reveal oneself; **sich als etw. ~:** reveal oneself to be sth.

**Deleatur** /deleˈa:tʊr/ *das;* **~s, ~, Deleatur·zeichen** *das* (*Druckw.*) deletion mark

**Delegation** /delegaˈtsi̯o:n/ *die;* **~, ~en** delegation (**an** + *Akk.* to; **bei** at)

**Delegations·chef** *der,* **Delegations·chefin** *die* head of a/the delegation

**delegieren** /deleˈgi:rən/ *tr. V.* Ⓐ (*abordnen*) send as a delegate/as delegates (**zu** to); **jmdn. ins Komitee ~:** select sb. as one's representative on the committee; Ⓑ (*übertragen*) delegate ‹task etc.› (**an** + *Akk.* to)

**Delegierte** *der/die; adj. Dekl.* delegate; (*Sport*) representative (**bei** at)

**Delegierten-: ~konferenz** *die* delegates' *or* delegate conference; **~versammlung** *die* delegates' *or* delegate assembly

**delektieren** /delɛkˈti:rən/ ❶ *tr. V.* **jmdn. mit etw. ~:** entertain *or* regale sb. with sth. ❷ *refl. V.* **sich an etw.** (*Dat.*) **~:** regale oneself with sth.; (*fig.*) take delight in sth.

**Delfin** *usw.* ⇒ **Delphin** *usw.*

**delikat** /deliˈka:t/ ❶ *Adj.* Ⓐ (*wohlschmeckend*) delicious; (*fein*) subtle, delicate ‹bouquet, aroma›; **~ riechen** have a delicate bouquet/aroma; Ⓑ (*Diskretion erfordernd, heikel*) delicate; (*geh.: empfindlich*) **in so persönlichen Dingen ist sie sehr ~:** she is very sensitive about such personal matters; Ⓒ (*geh.: behutsam*) discreet; (*taktvoll*) tactful; **~e Andeutung** subtle *or* discreet reference. ❷ *adv.* Ⓐ (*lecker*) deliciously; Ⓑ (*geh.: behutsam*) delicately; **etw. ~ behandeln** handle sth. tactfully *or* discreetly

**Delikatesse** /delikaˈtɛsə/ *die;* **~, ~n** Ⓐ (*Leckerbissen*) delicacy; (*fig.*) treat; **als besondere ~:** as a special delicacy/treat; Ⓑ (*geh.: Feingefühl*) delicacy; (*Takt*) tact; discretion; **eine Angelegenheit mit ~ behandeln** handle a matter discreetly

**Delikatessen·geschäft, Delikatess·geschäft, *Delikateßgeschäft** *das* delicatessen

**Delikatess·gurke, *Delikateß·gurke** *die* [fine-quality] gherkin

**Delikt** /deˈlɪkt/ *das;* **~[e]s, ~e** offence

**delinquent** /delɪŋˈkvɛnt/ *Adj.* (*bes. Rechtsw.*) delinquent; criminal ‹conduct›

**Delinquent** *der;* **~en, ~en, Delinquentin** *die;* **~, ~nen** offender

**Delinquenz** *die;* **~** (*bes. Rechtsw.*) delinquency

**delirieren** /deliˈri:rən/ *itr. V.* be delirious

**Delirium** /deˈli:ri̯ʊm/ *das;* **~s, Delirien** delirium; **im ~ liegen/sein** lie/be in a delirium; **im ~ reden** speak in one's delirium

**Delirium tremens** /-ˈtre:mɛns/ *das;* **~** ▶ 474 (*Med.*) delirium tremens; **im ~ sterben** die in a state of delirium [tremens]

**deliziös** /deliˈtsi̯ø:s/ (*geh.*) ❶ *Adj.* delicious; delectable; **~ schmecken** taste delicious. ❷ *adv.* deliciously

**Delle** /ˈdɛlə/ *die;* **~, ~n** Ⓐ (*ugs.*) dent; **eine ~ in die Stoßstange fahren** drive into something and dent one's bumper; Ⓑ (*Geogr.*) hollow

**delogieren** *tr. V.* (*bes. österr.*) evict

**Delphin**[1] /dɛlˈfi:n/ *der;* **~s, ~e** dolphin

**Delphin**[2] *das;* **~s** (*Schwimmen*) butterfly [stroke]

**Delphinarium** /dɛlfiˈna:ri̯ʊm/ *das;* **~s, Delphinarien** dolphinarium

**Delphin·schwimmen** *das* butterfly

**delphisch** /ˈdɛlfɪʃ/ ❶ *Adj.* Delphic ‹oracle›; enigmatic ‹remark etc.›. ❷ *adv.* enigmatically

**Delta**[1] /ˈdɛlta/ *das;* **~[s], ~[s]** (*Buchstabe*) delta

**Delta**[2] *das;* **~s, ~s** *od.* **Delten** ▶ 306 (*Fluss~*) delta

**delta-, Delta-: ~förmig** *Adj.* delta-shaped; triangular; deltaic ‹estuary›; **~mündung** *die* delta [estuary]; **~strahlen** *Pl.* (*Kernphysik*) delta rays

**De-Luxe-Ausstattung** /dəˈlyks-/ *die:* **eine ~ haben** be fitted with de luxe equipment; ‹car etc.› be a de luxe model; ‹room› have de luxe fittings

**dem** /de:m/ ❶ *best. Art., Dat. Sg. v.* **der**[1] 1 *u.* **das** 1: **ich gab ~ Mann/~ Kind das Buch** I gave the man/the child the book; I gave the book to the man/to the child; **hast du ~ Peter das Geld gegeben?** (*ugs.*) have you given Peter the money?; **ich half ~ Mann/~ Kind** I helped the man/the child; **er hat sich ~ Okkultismus zugewandt** he turned to occultism; **aus ~ Libanon/Baltikum kommen** come from Lebanon/the Baltic area; **~ Theater/Kino seinen Ruhm verdanken** owe one's fame to the stage/films. ❷ *Demonstrativpron., Dat. Sg. v.* **der**[1] 2 *u.* **das** 2 Ⓐ *attr.* **gib es dem Mann/Kind** give it to 'that man/child; **mit dem Messer kann man fast alles schneiden** you can cut almost anything with 'that knife; Ⓑ *selbstständig* **gib es nicht dem, sondern dem da!** don't give it to him, give it to that man/child *etc.;* **Zwiebeln schneide ich nicht mit dem [hier], sondern mit dem da** I chop onions with 'that knife, not with this one.
❸ *Relativpron., Dat. Sg. v.* **der**[1] 3 *u.* **das** 3 (*Mensch*) **der Mann/das Kind, ~ ich das Geld gab** the man/the child to whom I gave the money *or* (*coll.*) [that] I gave the money to; **der Mann, ~ ich geholfen habe** the man whom *or* that I helped; (*Sache*) **das Messer, mit ~ ich Zwiebeln schneide** the knife with which I chop onions *or* (*coll.*) that I chop onions with

**Demagoge** /demaˈgo:gə/ *der;* **~n, ~n** (*abwertend*) demagogue

**Demagogie** /demagoˈgi:/ *die;* **~, ~n** (*abwertend*) demagogy

**Demagogin** *die;* **~, ~nen** (*abwertend*) demagogue

**demagogisch** (*abwertend*) ❶ *Adj.* demagogic. ❷ *adv.* by demagogic means; (*zu ~en Zwecken*) for demagogic purposes; **~ reden** talk like a demagogue

**Demarche** /deˈmarʃ(ə)/ *die;* **~, ~n** (*Dipl.*) diplomatic move

**Demarkation** /demarkaˈtsi̯o:n/ *die;* **~, ~en** demarcation; (*Staatsgrenze*) frontier

**Demarkations·linie** *die* demarcation line

**demarkieren** *tr. V.* demarcate

**demaskieren** ❶ *refl. V.* Ⓐ (*Maske ablegen*) unmask; take one's mask off; Ⓑ (*sich offenbaren*) reveal oneself [as what one is]; appear in one's true colours; **sich als etw. ~:** reveal *or* show oneself to be sth. ❷ *tr. V.* (*entlarven*) unmask; expose; **jmdn. als etw. ~:** reveal sb. as sth.

d

d

**Dementi** /de'mɛnti/ *das;* **~s, ~s** denial
**dementieren** ❶ *tr. V.* deny. ❷ *itr. V.* deny it
**Dementierung** *die;* **~, ~en** denial
**dem·entsprechend** ❶ *Adj.* appropriate; **das Wetter war schlecht und die Stimmung ~:** the weather was bad and the general mood was correspondingly bad *or* bad too; **Er hat eine Villa in Cannes und eine Luxusjacht. Sein Einkommen ist auch ~:** He has a villa in Cannes and a luxury yacht. And he has an income to match *or* to go with it. ❷ *adv.* accordingly; (*vor Adjektiven*) correspondingly; **~ wird er bezahlt** he is paid accordingly
**dem-: ~gegenüber** *Adv.* in contrast; (*jedoch*) on the other hand; **~gemäß** ❶ *adv.* Ⓐ (*infolgedessen*) consequently; Ⓑ (*entsprechend*) accordingly; ❷ *Adj.* in accordance with it/them *postpos.;* (*angemessen*) appropriate; **ein Zimmer mit Vollpension kostet nur 18 Mark — das Essen ist ~gemäß** a room with full board only costs 18 marks — the food is what you'd expect [at that price]
**Demimonde** /dəmi'mõ:d/ *die;* **~** (*abwertend*) demi-monde
**Demission** *die;* **~, ~en** (*Politik*) resignation; **jmdn. zur ~ zwingen** force sb. to resign; **um seine ~ bitten** ask to be relieved of one's duties
**demissionieren** *itr. V.* Ⓐ (*Politik: zurücktreten*) resign; Ⓑ (*schweiz.: kündigen*) hand in one's notice (**auf** + *Akk.* for)
**dem-: ~jenigen** ⇒ **derjenige**; **~nach** *Adv.* therefore; (*laut dessen*) according to that; **~nächst** *Adv.* in the near future; shortly; **~nächst in diesem Theater** coming soon [to this theatre]; (*ugs. scherzh.*) some time soon
**Demo** /'dɛmo/ *die;* **~, ~s** (*ugs.*) demo; **auf der ~:** at the demo
**demobilisieren** *tr. V.* Ⓐ demobilize ‹army, industry›; Ⓑ (*veralt.: entlassen*) discharge ‹soldier›
**Demobilisierung** *die;* **~, ~en** demobilization
**Demodulation** *die;* **~, ~en** (*Nachrichtent.*) demodulation
**Demo·graphie** *die* demography *no art.*
**demo·graphisch** ❶ *Adj.* demographic. ❷ *adv.* demographically
**Demokrat** /demo'kra:t/ *der;* **~en, ~en** Ⓐ democrat; Ⓑ (*Parteimitglied*) Democrat
**Demokratie** /demokra'ti:/ *die;* **~, ~n** Ⓐ (*Prinzip*) democracy *no art.;* **zur ~ zurückkehren** return to democracy *or* democratic government; Ⓑ (*Staat*) democracy
**Demokratie·verständnis** *das* understanding *or* conception of democracy
**Demokratin** *die;* **~, ~nen** ⇒ **Demokrat**
**demokratisch** ❶ *Adj.* Ⓐ democratic ‹principle, process, etc.›; Ⓑ (*zur Demokratischen Partei gehörend*) Democratic. ❷ *adv.* democratically; **es wurde ~ gewählt** democratic elections were held; **bei uns geht es ~ zu** we run things on democratic lines; **~ eingestellt sein** have democratic attitudes
**demokratisieren** *tr. V.* Ⓐ democratize; make democratic; Ⓑ (*allgemein zugänglich machen*) make generally available; make ‹art› generally accessible; bring ‹art, fashion› to the people
**Demokratisierung** *die;* **~** Ⓐ (*eines Staates, einer Institution*) democratization; Ⓑ (*das Zugänglichmachen*); **die ~ der Mode/des Reisens** making fashion/travel generally available *or* accessible
**demolieren** /demo'li:rən/ *tr. V.* Ⓐ (*zerstören*) wreck; smash up ‹furniture›; Ⓑ (*österr.: abreißen*) demolish
**Demolierung** *die;* **~, ~en** Ⓐ (*Zerstörung*) wrecking; (*von Möbeln*) smashing up; Ⓑ (*österr.: Abriss*) demolition
**Demonstrant** /demɔn'strant/ *der;* **~en, ~en** demonstrator
**Demonstrantin** *die;* **~, ~nen** demonstrator; ⇒ *auch* **-in**

*old spelling (see note on page 1707)

**Demonstration** /demɔnstra'tsi̯o:n/ *die;* **~, ~en** Ⓐ (*Protestkundgebung*) demonstration (**für** in support of, **gegen** against); Ⓑ (*Bekundung, Veranschaulichung*) demonstration; **zur ~ seines guten Willens** as a demonstration of *or* to demonstrate his good will
**Demonstrations-: ~marsch** *der* demonstration; (*gegen etw.*) protest march; **~objekt** *das* exhibit (*used to demonstrate a point*); **~recht** *das* right to demonstrate; **~verbot** *das* ban on demonstrations; **~zug** *der* column *or* procession of demonstrators
**demonstrativ** /demɔnstra'ti:f/ ❶ *Adj.* Ⓐ (*betont*) demonstrative; pointed; **ein ~es Nein** an emphatic no; Ⓑ (*Sprachw.*) demonstrative; Ⓒ (*anschaulich*) graphic ‹example etc.›. ❷ *adv.* pointedly; (*aus Protest*) in protest; **ich sah ~ weg** I intentionally looked the other way; **sie blieben ~ sitzen** they remained seated in protest *or* to make their point
**Demonstrativ·pronomen** *das* (*Sprachwissenschaft*) demonstrative pronoun
**demonstrieren** /demɔn'stri:rən/ ❶ *itr. V.* demonstrate (**für** in support of, **gegen** against). ❷ *tr. V.* demonstrate; **jmdm. etw. ~:** demonstrate sth. to sb.
**Demontage** /demɔn'ta:ʒə/ *die;* **~, ~n** (*auch fig.*) dismantling; (*eines Schiffes*) breaking-up; **soziale ~** (*Politik*) dismantling of the welfare state
**demontieren** *tr. V.* Ⓐ (*abbrechen*) dismantle; (*zerlegen*) break up ‹ship, aircraft›; Ⓑ (*abmontieren*) take off; Ⓒ (*fig.*) eradicate ‹prejudices›; damage ‹reputation›
**Demontierung** *die;* **~, ~en** ⇒ **Demontage**
**Demoralisation** /demoraliza'tsi̯o:n/ *die;* **~, ~en** ⇒ **Demoralisierung**
**demoralisieren** *tr. V.* Ⓐ (*Moral untergraben*) corrupt; Ⓑ (*entmutigen*) demoralize
**Demoralisierung** *die;* **~, ~en** demoralization; (*Sittenverfall*) moral decline
**Demoskop** /demo'sko:p/ *der;* **~en, ~en** opinion pollster
**Demoskopie** /demosko'pi:/ *die;* **~, ~n** Ⓐ (*Meinungsforschung*) [public] opinion research *no art.;* Ⓑ (*Umfrage*) opinion poll
**Demoskopin** *die;* **~, ~nen** opinion pollster
**demoskopisch** ❶ *Adj.* opinion research ‹institute, methods, data, etc.›; ‹data etc.› from opinion polls *or* opinion research; **das ~e Ergebnis** the result of the opinion poll; **~e Umfrage** [public] opinion poll. ❷ *adv.* through opinion polls *or* research; **etw. ~ untersuchen** conduct an opinion poll on sth.
**dem·selben** ⇒ **derselbe**
**Demut** /'de:mu:t/ *die;* **~:** humility; **in** *od.* **mit ~:** with humility
**demütig** /'de:my:tɪç/ ❶ *Adj.* humble; (*respektvoll*) respectful. ❷ *adv.* humbly; (*respektvoll*) respectfully
**demütigen** ❶ *tr. V.* humiliate; humble ‹sb.'s pride›. ❷ *refl. V.* humble oneself; **sich vor jmdm. ~:** humble oneself before sb.
**Demütigung** *die;* **~, ~en** humiliation
**Demuts·gebärde** *die* (*Verhaltensf.*) attitude of submission
**dem·zufolge** *Adv.* consequently; therefore
**den¹** /de:n/ ❶ *best. Art., Akk. Sg. v.* **der¹** 1: **ich sah ~ Mann/~ Hund/~ Stein** I saw the man/the dog/the stone; **wir haben ~ „Faust" gelesen** we read 'Faust'; **hast du ~ Peter gesehen?** (*ugs.*) have you seen Peter?; **in ~ Libanon reisen** travel to Lebanon; **~ Sozialismus/Kapitalismus ablehnen** reject socialism/capitalism.
❷ *Demonstrativpron., Akk. Sg. v.* **der¹** 2: Ⓐ *attr.* **ich meine den Mann/den Hund/den Stein, nicht ~ anderen** I mean 'that man/'that dog/'that stone, not the other; Ⓑ *selbstständig* **ich meine den [da]** I mean 'that one.
❸ *Relativpron., Akk. Sg. v.* **der¹** 3: **der Mann/Hund/Stein, ~ ich gesehen habe** the man/dog/stone that I saw
**den²** ❶ *best. Art., Dat. Pl. v.* **der¹** 1, **die¹** 1, **das** 1: **ich gab es ~ Männern/Frauen/Kindern** I gave it to the men/women/children; **ich habe mich mit ~ Berichten/Theorien/Büchern befasst** I dealt with the reports/theories/books; **er war bei ~ Müllers zu Besuch** (*ugs.*) he visited the Müllers. ❷ *Demonstrativpron., Dat. Pl. v.* **der¹** 2 A, **die¹** 2 A, **das** 2 A: **ich gab es den Männern/den Frauen/den Kindern** I gave it to 'those men/'those women/'those children
**Denaturalisation** *die;* **~, ~en** denaturalization
**denaturalisieren** *tr. V.* denaturalize
**denaturieren** /denatu'ri:rən/ ❶ *tr. V.* Ⓐ (*geh.: verändern*) warp the personality of; (*entmenschen*) dehumanize; Ⓑ (*bes. Chemie*) denature ‹alcohol, foodstuffs, protein, fissile material, etc.›. ❷ *itr. V.; mit sein* (*geh.*) **zu etw. ~:** degenerate into sth.
**Dendrit** /dɛn'dri:t/ *der;* **~en, ~en** ▶ 471 (*Geol., Anat.*) dendrite
**denen** /'de:nən/ ❶ *Demonstrativpron., Dat. Pl. v.* **der¹** 2 B, **die¹** 2 B, **das** 2 B: **gib es ~, nicht den anderen** give it to 'them, not to the others; **~ gehört das Buch** the book belongs to 'them; **~, die uns geholfen haben, helfen wir auch** we help those who have helped us. ❷ *Relativpron., Dat. Pl. v.* **der¹** 3, **die¹** 3 **das** 3: **die Menschen, ~ wir Geld gegeben haben** the people to whom we gave money; **die Tiere, ~ er geholfen hat** the animals that he helped; **die Bücher, mit ~ sie aufgewachsen ist** the books she grew up with
**dengeln** /'dɛŋl̩n/ *tr. V.* (*Landw.*) sharpen (*by hammering out irregularities*)
**Den Haag** /de:n 'ha:k/ (*das*); **~s** ▶ 700 The Hague
**denjenigen** ⇒ **derjenige**
**Denk-: ~an·satz** *der* intellectual approach; **~an·stoß** *der* something to think about; **jmdm. einen ~anstoß geben** give sb. food for thought; **~art** *die* way of thinking; **~auf·gabe** *die* brain-teaser
**denkbar** ❶ *Adj.* conceivable; **in einem Zustand, wie er schlimmer nicht ~ ist** in the worst state imaginable. ❷ *adv.* (*sehr, äußerst*) extremely; **die Lösung ist ~ leicht** the solution could not be easier *or* is as easy as could be; **die ~ beste Methode** the best method imaginable
**denken** /'dɛŋkn̩/ ❶ *unr. itr. V.* think (**an** *od.* [*südd., österr.*] **auf** + *Akk.* of, **über** + *Akk.* about); **kleinlich/liberal/edel ~:** be pettyminded/liberal-minded/noble-minded; **spießig/reaktionär ~:** have a bourgeois/reactionary mind *or* bourgeois/reactionary views; **wie denkst du darüber?** what do you think about it?; what's your opinion of it?; **ich weiß nicht, wie ich darüber ~ soll** I don't know what to think *or* make of it; **erst ~, dann handeln** think before you act; **der Mensch denkt, [und] Gott lenkt** (*Spr.*) man proposes, God disposes; **Denken ist Glückssache** you/he/she *etc.* thought wrong; **~de Menschen** thinking people; **so darfst du nicht ~:** you mustn't think that; **schlecht von jmdm. ~:** think badly of sb.; **jmdm. zu ~ geben** make sb. think; (*stutzig machen*) make sb. suspicious; **denk mal, Eva hat sich verlobt!** just think, Eva has got engaged!; **denk mal an!** (*spött.*) just imagine!; imagine that!; **denk daran, dass …/zu …** don't forget that …/to …; **ich darf gar nicht an die Kosten ~:** I daren't think of the cost; the cost doesn't bear thinking about; **der wird noch an mich ~:** I'll give him something to remember; **das geschieht schon, solange ich ~ kann** this has been going on as long as I can remember; **ich muss an meine Familie ~:** I have to think of *or* consider my family; **an was für einen Schuh haben Sie denn gedacht?** what sort of shoe did you have in mind?; **ich komme nach Hause, denke an nichts Böses** I came home, quite unsuspecting; **ich denke nicht daran!** no way!; not on your life!; **ich denke nicht daran, das zu tun** I've no intention *or* I wouldn't dream of doing that.
❷ *unr. tr. V.* think; **was sollen bloß die Nachbarn ~?** what will the neighbours

think?; **einen Gedanken zu Ende ~:** think an idea through; **er dachte den gleichen Gedanken** the same thought occurred to him; **ich habe nichts Böses dabei gedacht** I didn't mean any harm [by it]; **das denke ich auch** I think so too; **ich denke schon** I think so; **was** *od.* **wie viel haben Sie denn gedacht?** how much did you have in mind?; **wer hätte das gedacht?** who would have thought it?; **[typischer Fall von] denkste!** (*ugs.*) how wrong can one be!; (*da irrst du dich*) that's what 'you think!; **da weiß man nicht, was man ~ soll** one doesn't know what to think; **das hätte ich nie von dir gedacht** I would never have thought it of you; **eine gedachte Linie** an imaginary line; **ein gedachter Punkt** an imaginary point.
❸ *unr. refl. V.* Ⓐ (*sich vorstellen*) think; imagine; **ich habe mir gedacht, dass wir ein paar Tage in Urlaub fahren** I was thinking *or* thought that we could go on holiday for a few days; **du kannst dir ~, dass ...** you can imagine that ...; as you can imagine, ...; **das kann ich mir ~/nicht ~:** I can well believe/cannot believe that; **das habe ich mir so gedacht** I imagined it like this; this is what I had in mind; **das hast du dir so gedacht!** that's what you thought; **das hättest du dir doch ~ können, dass ...** you should have realized that ...; **das habe ich mir [gleich] gedacht** that's [just] what I thought; (*bei Verdacht*) I thought *or* suspected as much; **das hätte ich mir ~ können!** I might have known it!; **ich denke mir mein[en] Teil** I can put two and two together *or* work things out for myself; Ⓑ **sich** (*Dat.*) **etw. bei etw. ~** (*beabsichtigen*) mean sth. by sth.; **ich habe mir nichts [Böses] dabei gedacht** I didn't mean any harm [by it]; **er denkt sich nichts dabei** he doesn't think anything of it; ⇒ *auch* **gedacht**

**Denken** *das;* **~s** thinking; (*Denkweise*) thought; **logisches/abstraktes ~:** logical/abstract thought

**Denker** *der;* **~s, ~, Denkerin** *die;* **~, ~nen** thinker

**denkerisch** ❶ *Adj.* intellectual. ❷ *adv.* intellectually

**Denker·stirn** *die* (*oft scherzh.*) intellectual's high brow

**denk-, Denk-: ~fähig** *Adj.* capable of thinking *postpos.*; intellectually able; **~fähigkeit** *die;* ability to think; intellectual capacity; **~faul** *Adj.* mentally lazy; **sei nicht so ~faul** use your brains; **~fehler** *der* flaw in one's reasoning; **das war ein ~fehler** that was poor thinking

**Denk·mal** *das;* **~s, Denkmäler** *od.* (*geh.*) **Denkmale** Ⓐ (*Monument*) monument; memorial; **jmdm. ein ~ errichten** *od.* **setzen** erect *or* put up a memorial to sb.; **mit der Klinik hat er sich ein ~ gesetzt** (*fig.*) by building the clinic he has ensured that his name will live on; Ⓑ (*Zeugnis*) monument

**Denkmal[s]-: ~pflege** *die* preservation of historic monuments; **~schutz** *der* protection of historic monuments; **unter ~schutz stehen/stellen** be/put under a preservation order

**Denk-: ~modell** *das* hypothesis; **~pause** *die* pause for thought; **eine ~pause machen** *od.* **einlegen** pause for thought; (*bei Verhandlungen usw.*) have a break [to think things over]; **~schrift** *die* memorandum; **~sport·auf·gabe** *die* brain-teaser; **~spruch** *der* maxim; motto; **~übung** *die* intellectual exercise

**Denkungs·art** *die* way of thinking

**denk-, Denk-: ~vermögen** *das:* **[kreatives] ~vermögen** ability to think [creatively]; **~weise** *die* way of thinking; [mental] attitude; **eine solch niedrige ~weise** such low-mindedness; **~würdig** *Adj.* memorable; **~würdigkeit** *die* Ⓐ memorable nature; **der ~würdigkeit eines Ereignisses bewusst** aware how memorable an event is; Ⓑ (*Ereignis*) memorable event; **~zettel** *der* warning; lesson; **jmdm. einen ~zettel verpassen** teach sb. a lesson

**denn** /dɛn/ ❶ *Konj.* Ⓐ (*kausal*) for; because; Ⓑ (*geh.: als*) than; **schöner/besser/größer ~ je [zuvor]** more beautiful/better/greater than ever; Ⓒ (*konzessiv*) **es sei ~, ...** unless ...; **ich spreche nicht mehr mit ihm, er müsste sich ~ geändert haben** (*veralt.*) I'm not speaking to him again unless he changes his ways; ⇒ *auch* **geschweige**.
❷ *Partikel* Ⓐ (*in Fragesätzen: oft nicht übersetzt*) **Die Kirschen sind wahnsinnig teuer! — Wie viel kosten sie ~?** The cherries are frightfully expensive! — How much are they then?; **was ist ~ da los?** what 'is going on there?; **ist er ~ krank gewesen?** has he been ill, then?; **wie geht es dir ~?** tell me, how are you?; **wer will ~ aufgeben?** who is talking of giving up?; **ist das ~ so wichtig?** is that really so important?; **was muss ich ~ machen?** what am I to do, then?; **wie hieß sie ~ noch?** now what was her name?; **wie heißt du ~?** tell me your name; **wieso ~?** why is that?; (*stärker*) what ever for?; **warum ~ nicht?** why ever not?; **was soll das ~?** what's all this about?; (*wozu ist das gut?*) what's this in aid of?; **was ~ [sonst]?** well, what [else] then?; **wohin [fahrt ihr] ~?** where [are you going] then?; Ⓑ (*in Aussagesätzen verstärkend, oft folgernd*) **so wollen wir ~ zur Abstimmung kommen** let's get on with the voting now; **das ist ~ doch die Höhe!** that really is the limit!; **er starb ~ auch bald** and so he soon died.
❸ *Adv.* (*nordd.: dann*) then **na, ~ man los!** right then, let's get going!

**dennoch** /ˈdɛnɔx/ *Adv.* nevertheless; even so; **ein höfliches und ~ eisiges Lächeln** a polite yet frosty smile

**Denotat** /denoˈtaːt/ *das;* **~s, ~e** (*Sprachw.*) denotation

**Denotation** /denotaˈtsi̯oːn/ *die;* **~, ~en** (*Logik, Sprachw.*) denotation

**denselben** ⇒ **derselbe**

**dental** /dɛnˈtaːl/ ❶ *Adj.* (*Anat., Med., Sprachw.*) dental; **~e Laute** dentals. ❷ *adv.* (*Sprachw.*) dentally

**Dental** *der;* **~s, ~e** (*Sprachw.*) dental

**Dentist** /dɛnˈtɪst/ *der;* **~en, ~en, Dentistin** *die;* **~, ~nen** (*veralt.*) dentist

**Denunziant** /denʊnˈtsi̯ant/ *der;* **~en, ~en, Denunziantin** *die;* **~, ~nen** (*abwertend*) informer; grass (*sl.*)

**Denunziation** /denʊntsi̯aˈtsi̯oːn/ *die;* **~, ~en** (*abwertend*) denunciation (*by an informer*)

**denunziatorisch** /denʊntsi̯aˈtoːrɪʃ/ *Adj.* (*abwertend*) Ⓐ (*denunzierend*) **ein ~es Klima** a climate which favours informing; **~e Äußerungen seines eigenen Vaters** statements informing against him made by his own father; Ⓑ (*öffentlich verurteilend*) denunciatory; condemnatory

**denunzieren** /denʊnˈtsiːrən/ *tr. V.* (*abwertend*) Ⓐ (*anzeigen*) denounce; (*bei der Polizei*) inform against; grass on (*sl.*) (**bei** to); Ⓑ (*als negativ hinstellen*) denounce

**Deo** /ˈdeːo/ *das;* **~s, ~s, Deodorant** /de|odoˈrant/ *das;* **~s, ~s** (*auch:*) **~e** deodorant

**deodorierend** /de|odoˈriːrənt/ *Adj.* deodorant

**Deo·spray** *das* deodorant spray

**Departement** /departəˈmãː, *schweiz.:* departəˈmɛnt/ *das;* **~s, ~s** *od.* (*schweiz.:*) **~e** department

**Dependance** /depãˈdãːs/ *die;* **~, ~n** Ⓐ (*Hotelw.*) annexe; Ⓑ (*Zweigstelle*) branch

**Dependenz** /depɛnˈdɛnts/ *die;* **~, ~en** Ⓐ (*Philos.*) dependence (**von** on); Ⓑ (*Sprachw.*) dependency

**Dependenz·grammatik** *die* (*Sprachw.*) dependency grammar

**Depesche** /deˈpɛʃə/ *die;* **~, ~n** (*veralt.*) telegram (**an** + *Akk.* to)

**depeschieren** (*veralt.*) ❶ *tr. V.* send a telegram giving ‹time of arrival etc.›; **~, dass ...** wire that ... (*coll.*). ❷ *itr. V.* send a telegram (**an** + *Akk.* to)

**deplaciert, deplatziert, *deplaziert** /deplaˈtsiːɐ̯t/ *Adj.* out of place *pred.*; misplaced ‹remark etc.›

**Depolarisation** *die* (*Physik*) depolarization

**Deponie** /depoˈniː/ *die;* **~, ~n** tip (*Brit.*); dump; **geordnete ~:** controlled tip (*Brit.*), sanitary landfill (*Amer.*) (*subsequently covered and planted with trees etc.*)

**deponieren** *tr. V.* Ⓐ (*im Safe o. Ä.*) deposit (**bei** with); Ⓑ (*an einem bestimmten Platz*) put

**Deponierung** *die;* **~:** depositing

**Deportation** /depɔrtaˈtsi̯oːn/ *die;* **~, ~en** transportation (**in** + *Akk.*, **nach** to); (*ins Ausland*) deportation (**in** + *Akk.*, **nach** to)

**deportieren** /depɔrˈtiːrən/ *tr. V.* transport (**in** + *Akk.*, **nach** to); (*ins Ausland*) deport (**in** + *Akk.*, **nach** to)

**Deportierte** *der/die; adj. Dekl.* transportee; (*ins Ausland*) deportee

**Depositar** /depoziˈtaːɐ̯/ *der;* **~s, ~e, Depositär** /depoziˈtɛːɐ̯/ *der;* **~s, ~e** (*Finanzw.*) depositary

**Depositen** /depoˈziːtn̩/ *Pl.* (*Finanzw.*) deposits

**Depot** /deˈpoː/ *das;* **~s, ~s** Ⓐ (*Aufbewahrungsort*) depot; (*Lagerhaus*) warehouse; (*für Möbel usw.*) depository; (*im Freien, für Munition o. Ä.*) dump; (*für Straßenbahnen, Omnibusse*) depot; garage; (*in einer Bank*) strongroom; safe deposit; Ⓑ (*hinterlegte Wertgegenstände*) deposits *pl.*; Ⓒ (*Med.*) deposit

**Depot-: ~fett** *das* (*Biol., Med.*) adipose; **~fund** *der* (*Archäol.*) cache [find]; **~geschäft** *das* (*Finanzw.*) safe-deposit business; **~präparat** *das* (*Med.*) depot preparation

**Depp** /dɛp/ *der;* **~en** (*auch:*) **~s, ~en** (*auch:*) **~e** (*bes. südd., österr., schweiz. abwertend*) Ⓐ (*Dummkopf*) twit (*coll.*); nitwit (*coll.*); **und ich ~ bin darauf reingefallen** and like a fool I fell for it; Ⓑ (*Schwachsinniger*) cretin

**deppert** /ˈdɛpɐt/ (*südd., österr. abwertend*) ❶ *Adj.* stupid; (*begriffsstutzig*) thick. ❷ *adv.* **stell dich doch nicht so ~ an** don't act so stupid

**Depression** /deprɛˈsi̯oːn/ *die;* **~, ~en** (*Wirtsch., Psych., Met.*) depression; **an ~en leiden** suffer from [fits *pl.* of] depression *sing.*

**depressiv** /deprɛˈsiːf/ ❶ *Adj.* Ⓐ depressive; Ⓑ (*Wirtsch.*) depressive ‹effect›; depressed ‹phase›. ❷ *adv.* Ⓐ **~ veranlagt sein** have a tendency towards depression; Ⓑ (*Wirtsch.*) **den Markt ~ beeinflussen** have a depressive influence on *or* depress the market

**Depressivität** /deprɛsiviˈtɛːt/ *die;* **~** (*Psych.*) depression

**deprimieren** /depriˈmiːrən/ *tr. V.* depress

**deprimierend** *Adj.* depressing

**deprimiert** ❶ *Adj.* depressed. ❷ *adv.* dejectedly

**Deputat** /depuˈtaːt/ *das;* **~[e]s, ~e** Ⓐ (*Schulw.*) teaching load; **mit einem halben ~ unterrichten** have half the normal teaching load; Ⓑ (*Sachleistung*) payment in kind; **ein ~ Kohlen/Milch** *usw.* **erhalten** receive free coal/milk *etc.*

**Deputation** /deputaˈtsi̯oːn/ *die;* **~, ~en** deputation; (*bei Konferenzen*) delegation

**deputieren** /depuˈtiːrən/ *tr. V.* depute; delegate; **jmdn. zu einer Konferenz ~:** depute *or* delegate sb. to attend a conference

**Deputierte** *der/die; adj. Dekl.* (*Mitglied einer Deputation*) delegate; (*Abgeordnete[r]*) deputy

**der**[1] /deːɐ̯/ ❶ *best. Art. Nom.* the; **~ Kleine** the little boy; **~ Tod** death; **~ Montag/April/Winter** Monday/April/winter; **~ „Faust"/** (*ugs.*) **~ Dieter** 'Faust'/Dieter; **~ Kapitalismus/Sozialismus/Buddhismus/Islam** capitalism/socialism/Buddhism/Islam; **~ 1. FC Köln** Cologne FC; **er ist der Fußballer/Komponist** he's 'the footballer/composer; **~ Washingtonplatz** Washington Square; **~ Bodensee/Mount Everest** Lake Constance/Mount Everest; **~ Iran/Sudan** Iran/the Sudan; **~ Mensch/Mann ist ...**

d

man is .../men are ...
❷ *Demonstrativpron.* [A] *attr.* **der Mann war es** it was 'that man; [B] *selbstständig* he; **der war es** it was 'him; **der und arbeiten!** (*ugs.*) [what,] him work! (*coll.*); **~ mit der Glatze** (*ugs.*) him with the bald head (*coll.*); **der [da]** (*Mann/Junge*) that man/boy; (*Gegenstand, Tier*) that one; **der [hier]** (*Mann/Junge*) this man/boy; (*Gegenstand, Tier*) this one; **der Idiot, ~!** (*salopp*) what an idiot!.
❸ *Relativpron.* (*Mensch*) who; that; (*Sache, Tier*) which; that; **der Mann, ~ da drüben entlanggeht** the man walking along over there; **ich sah einen Mann/Hund, ~ aus dem Fenster schaute** I saw a man/dog looking out of the window.
❹ *Relativ- u. Demonstrativpron.* the one who; **~ das getan hat** the man *etc.* who did it

**der**[2] ❶ *best. Art.* [A] *Gen. Sg. v.* **die**[1] 1: **der Hut ~ Frau** the woman's hat; **der Henkel ~ Tasse** the handle of the cup; **das Wiehern ~ Stute** the neighing of the mare; the mare's neighing; **die Freuden ~ Liebe** the joys of love; **der Untergang ~ „Titanic"** the sinking of the Titanic; **am Ende ~ Hauptstraße** at the end of the High Street; **der Einfluss ~ NATO/UNO** the influence of NATO/the UN; [B] *Dat. Sg. v.* **die**[1] 1: **sein schwarzes Haar hat er von ~ Mutter** he got his black hair from his mother; **der Henkel an ~ Tasse** the handle of the cup; **sein Buch ist ~ Callas gewidmet** his book is dedicated to Callas; **in ~ Türkei** in Turkey; **seit ~ Aufklärung** since the Enlightenment; [C] *Gen. Pl. v.* **der**[1] 1, **die**[1] 1, **das** 1: **das Haus ~ Freunde** our/their *etc.* friends' house; **das Zimmer ~ Schwestern** our/their *etc.* sisters' room; **das Bellen ~ Hunde** the barking of the dogs.
❷ *Demonstrativpron.* [A] *Gen. Sg. v.* **die**[1] 2: **es ist das Kind der Frau, die gestern hier war** he's/she's the child of the woman who was here yesterday; [B] *Dat. Sg. v.* **die**[1] 2 *attr.* **der Frau [da/hier] gehört es** it belongs to that woman there/this woman here; *selbstständig* **gib es der da!** (*ugs.*) give it to 'her; **alles nur wegen der** (*ugs.*) all because of her; [C] *Gen. Pl. v.* **die**[1] 2: **die Ansichten der Leute lehne ich ab** I reject the views of those people.
❸ *Relativpron.*; *Dat. Sg. v.* **die**[1] 3 (*Mensch*) **die Frau, ~ ich es gegeben habe** the woman to whom I gave it; the woman I gave it to; (*Tier, Sache*) **die Katze, ~ er einen Tritt gab** the cat [that] he kicked; **die Lawine, unter ~ er begraben wurde** the avalanche under which he was buried

**derangiert** /derã'ʒiːɐt/ *Adj.* dishevelled

**der·art** *Adv.* **jmdn. ~ schlecht/unfreundlich behandeln, dass ...;** treat sb. so badly/ in such an unfriendly way that ...; **~ gute Vorbereitungen** such good preparations; **eine ~ schöne Frau** such a beautiful woman; **es hat lange nicht mehr ~ geregnet** it hasn't rained as hard as that for a long time; **sie hat ~ geschrien, dass ...** she screamed so much that ...

**der·artig** ❶ *Adj.* such; **ein ~er Wutausbruch** such a fit of fury; **Derartiges** things *pl.* like that; **etwas Derartiges** a thing like that; such a thing. ❷ *adv.* ⇒ **derart**

**derb** /dɛrp/ ❶ *Adj.* [A] strong, tough ‹material›; stout, strong, sturdy ‹shoes›; [B] (*kräftig*) solid, substantial ‹food›; [C] (*kraftvoll, deftig*) earthy ‹scenes, humour›; [D] (*unverblümt*) crude, coarse ‹expression, language›; [E] (*unfreundlich*) gruff. ❷ *adv.* [A] strongly ‹made, woven, etc.›; [B] (*heftig*) roughly; [C] (*kraftvoll, deftig*) earthily; **um es einmal ~ zu sagen** to put it crudely; [D] (*unverblümt*) crudely; coarsely; [E] (*unfreundlich*) gruffly

**Derbheit** *die;* **~, ~en** [A] ⇒ **derb** C, D: earthiness; crudity; coarseness; [B] (*Äußerung*) crudity

**derb·knochig** *Adj.* big-boned

**Derby** /'dɛrbi/ *das;* **~s, ~s** [A] (*Pferdesport*) Derby; [B] (*Fußball*) derby; **das ~ der beiden Lokalrivalen** the local derby

*old spelling (see note on page 1707)

**Deregulierung** *die;* **~, ~en** deregulation

**der·einst** *Adv.* [A] (*geh.*) one *or* some day; [B] (*veralt.*) once; at one time

**der·einstig** *Adj.* (*geh.*) future

**deren** /'deːrən/ ❶ *Relativpron.* [A] *Gen. Sg. v.* **die**[1] 3 *attr.* (*Menschen*) whose; (*Sachen, Tiere*) of which; **die Katastrophe, ~ Folgen furchtbar waren** the disaster, the consequences of which were frightful; *selbstständig* **die Großmutter, ~ wir uns gerne erinnern** our grandmother, of whom we have fond memories; **eine Anrede, ~ er sich gern bediente** a form of address which *or* that he liked to use; [B] *Gen., Pl. v.* **der**[1] 3, **die**[1] 3, **das** 3 *attr.* (*Menschen*) whose; (*Sachen, Tiere*) **Maßnahmen, ~ Folgen wir noch nicht absehen können** measures, the consequences of which we cannot yet foresee.
❷ *Demonstrativpron.* [A] *Gen. Sg. v.* **die**[1] 2 *attr.* **meine Tante, ihre Freundin und ~ Hund** my aunt, her friend and 'her dog; **die Universität und ~ Abteilungen** the university and its departments; *selbstständig* **Tante Frieda? Deren erinnere ich mich nicht mehr** Aunt Frieda? I don't remember 'her; [B] *Gen. Pl. v.* **der**[1] 2, **die**[1] 2, **das** 2 *attr.* **meine Verwandten und ~ Kinder** my relatives and their children; **die Schulen und ~ Lehrpersonal** the schools and their teaching staff; *selbstständig* **Bücher/Kinder? Deren hat er genug** (*geh.*) Books/ Children? He's got enough of those

**derent-: ~halben** *Adv.* (*veralt.*), **~wegen** *Adv.* ❶ *relativ* on whose account; on account of whom; because of whom; (*von Sachen*) on account of which; because of which; **die Frau, ~wegen er seine Familie verlassen hat** the woman on whose account *or* for whom he left his family; **die Tasche, ~wegen du das ganze Haus abgesucht hast** the purse for which you searched the entire house; ❷ *demonstrativ* because of them; **~willen** *Adv.* ❶ *relativ* **um ~willen** for whose sake; for the sake of whom; (*von Sachen*) for the sake of which; **die Erbstücke, um ~willen sich die Kinder zerstritten** the heirlooms over which the children fell out; **die Parkplätze, um ~willen es so heiße Diskussionen gab** the car parks about which there were such impassioned debates; ❷ *demonstrativ* **um ~willen** for her/ their sake

**derer** /'deːrɐ/ *Demonstrativpron.*; *Gen. Pl. v.* **der**[1] 2, **die**[1] 2, **das** 2; *vorausweisend* **das Schicksal ~, die verschollen sind** the fate of those who are missing; **die Zahl ~, die das glauben, nimmt ab** the number of people who believe that is declining; **das Schloss ~ von Fleckenstein** (*geh.*) the castle of the family Fleckenstein

**deret-:** ⇒ **derent-**

**der·gestalt** *Adv.* (*geh.*) **~, dass ...** in such a way that ...; **Widrigkeiten, die uns ~ belasten[, dass ...]** adversities which weigh so heavily upon us [that ...]; **~ ausgerüstet/ vorbereitet** thus equipped/prepared

**der·gleichen** *indekl. Demonstrativpron.* [A] *attr.* such; like that *postpos.*, *not pred.*; [B] *allein stehend* that sort of thing; such things *pl.*; things *pl.* like that; **nichts ~:** nothing of the sort; **es gibt ~ mehr** there's more of that sort of thing; **und ~ [mehr]** and suchlike; **nichts ~ tun** do nothing of the sort

**Derivat** /deri'vaːt/ *das;* **~[e]s, ~e** (*Chemie, Sprachw., Biol., Bankw.*) derivative

**Derivativ** /deriva'tiːf/ *das;* **~s, ~e** (*Sprachw.*) derivative

**der·jenige** /-jeːnɪɡə/, **die·jenige, das·jenige** *Pl.* **die·jenigen** *Demonstrativpron.* [A] *mit Relativsatz* **~, der ...** (*Mensch*) the one who ...; (*Sache*) the one which ...; **die Kinder ~n, die ...** the children of those who ...; **er ist immer ~, welcher** (*ugs.*) it's always him (*coll.*); **ach, du bist diejenige, welche** (*ugs.*) oh, so you're the one; [B] *mit nachfolgendem Gen.* that; **diejenigen** those; **seine Frau ist charmanter als diejenige seines Bruders** (*geh.*) his wife is more charming than his brother's

**derlei** /'deːɐ̯lai/ *indekl. Demonstrativpron.* [A] *attr.* such; like that *postpos.*, *not pred.*; [B] *selbstständig* that sort of thing; such things *pl.*; things *pl.* like that

**der·maßen** *Adv.* **~ schön** *usw.*, **dass ...** so beautiful *etc.* that ...; **ein ~ intelligenter Mensch** such an intelligent person; **er hat mich ~ belogen, dass ...** he has lied to me so much that ...

**Dermatologe** /dɛrmato'loːɡə/ *der;* **~n, ~n** dermatologist

**Dermatologie** /dɛrmatolo'ɡiː/ *die;* **~:** dermatology *no art.*

**Dermatologin** *die;* **~, ~nen** dermatologist

**Dermato·plastik** *die* (*Med.*) dermatoplasty (*Med.*); plastic surgery

**Dero** /'deːro/ *indekl. Pron.* (*veralt.*) Your

**ders.** *Abk.* **derselbe**

**derselbe** /deːɐ̯'zɛlbə/, **dieselbe, dasselbe,** *Pl.* **dieselben** *Demonstrativpron.* [A] *attr.* the same; **~ Mann/dieselbe Frau/dasselbe Dorf** the same man/woman/village; [B] *selbstständig* the same one; **er sagt immer dasselbe** he always says the same thing; **sie ist immer noch [ganz] dieselbe** she is still [exactly] the same; **es sind immer dieselben, die ...** it's always the same people *or* ones who ...; **noch einmal dasselbe, bitte** (*ugs.*) [the] same again please; [C] *selbstständig* (*Amtsspr. veralt.*) the same; **~n/desselben** of same; **... des Angeklagten. Derselbe hatte ...:** ... of the defendant. He had ...

**derselbige** /deːɐ̯'zɛlbɪɡə/, **dieselbige, dasselbige,** *Pl.* **dieselbigen** (*veralt.*) ⇒ **derselbe**

**der·weil[en]** ❶ *Adv.* meanwhile; in the meantime. ❷ *Konj.* while

**Derwisch** /'dɛrvɪʃ/ *der;* **~[e]s, ~e** dervish

**der·zeit** *Adv.* [A] (*zurzeit*) at present; at the moment; [B] (*veralt.: damals*) at that time; then

**der·zeitig** *Adj.* [A] (*jetzig*) present; current; [B] (*veralt.: damalig*) at that time *postpos.*

**des**[1] /dɛs/ ❶ *best. Art.*; *Gen. Sg. v.* **der**[1] 1, **das** 1: **die Mütze ~ Jungen** the boy's cap; **das Wiehern ~ Pferdes:** the neighing of the horse; the horse's neighing; **das Klingeln ~ Telefons** the ringing of the telephone; **er hat das schwarze Haar ~ Vaters** he has his father's black hair; **nördlich ~ Schillerplatzes** to the north of Schiller Square. ❷ *Demonstrativpron.*; *Gen. Sg. v.* **der**[1] 2, **das** 2: **er ist der Sohn des Mannes, der gestern hier war** he's the son of the man who was here yesterday

**des**[2] (*veralt.*) [A] ⇒ **dessen**; [B] ⇒ **wes**

**des**[3], **Des** *das;* **~, ~** (*Musik*) D flat

**Desaster** /de'zastɐ/ *das;* **~s, ~:** disaster

**desavouieren** /dɛs|avu'iːrən/ *tr. V.* (*geh.*) [A] (*bloßstellen*) expose; [B] (*nicht anerkennen*) repudiate

**Desavouierung** *die;* **~, ~en** ⇒ **desavouieren**: exposure; repudiation

**Des-Dur** *das* D flat major; ⇒ *auch* **C-Dur**

**desensibilisieren** *tr. V.* (*Fot., Med., fig.*) desensitize

**Deserteur** /dezɛr'tøːɐ̯/ *der;* **~s, ~e** (*Milit.*) deserter

**desertieren** *itr. V.*; *mit sein* (*Milit., fig.*) desert

**Desertion** /dezɛr'tsi̯oːn/ *die;* **~, ~en** (*Milit.*) desertion

**des·gleichen** *Adv.* likewise; **er ist Antialkoholiker, ~ seine Frau** he is a teetotaller, as is *or* and so is his wife; **es fehlt an Papier, ~ an Schreibmaschinen** there's a shortage of paper and also [of] typewriters

**des·halb** *Adv.* for that reason; because of that; **~ bin ich zu dir gekommen** that is why I came to you; **aber ~ ist sie nicht dumm** but that doesn't mean she is stupid; **~ also!** so that's why *or* the reason!; **er war krank, [und] ~ konnte er nicht kommen** he was ill, [and] so he couldn't come; **..., aber ~ könnt ihr gerne noch bleiben** ..., but you're still welcome so stay

**Desiderat** /dezide'raːt/ *das;* **~[e]s, ~e, Desideratum** /dezide'raːtʊm/ *das;* **~s, Desiderata** [A] (*Buchw.*) suggestion; **dieses**

**Buch ist schon seit langem ein ~ in unserer Bibliothek** it was suggested a long time ago that our library should acquire this book; **B** (*geh.: Erwünschtes*) desideratum

**Design** /di'zain/ *das;* **~s, ~s** design

**Designat** /dezɪ'gna:t/ *das;* **~[e]s, ~e** (*Sprachw., Logik*) designatum

**Designation** /dezɪgna'tsi̯o:n/ *die;* **~, ~en** designation

**Designer** /di'zainɐ/ *der;* **~s, ~, Designerin** *die;* **~, ~nen** ▸ 159 designer

**Designer·droge** /-'--/ *die;* **~, ~n** designer drug

**designieren** /dezɪ'gni:rən/ *tr. V.* (*geh.*) designate (**zu** as)

**desillusionieren** /dɛs|iluzi̯o'ni:rən/ *tr. V.* disillusion

**Desillusionierung** *die;* **~, ~en** disillusionment

**Des·infektion** /dɛs|-/ *die* disinfection; **zur ~:** to disinfect it/them

**Desinfektions·mittel** *das* disinfectant

**des·infizieren** *tr. V.* disinfect

**Des·infizierung** *die* disinfection

**Des·information** *die* disinformation *no indef. art.;* **~en** disinformation *sing.*

**Des·integration** *die* (*Soziol., Psych.*) disintegration

**Des·interesse** *das* lack of interest (**an** + *Dat.* in)

**des·interessiert** ❶ *Adj.* uninterested. ❷ *adv.* uninterestedly

**Deskription** /deskrɪp'tsi̯o:n/ *die;* **~, ~en** (*geh.*) description

**deskriptiv** /deskrɪp'ti:f/ ❶ *Adj.* descriptive. ❷ *adv.* descriptively

**Desktoppublishing** /'dɛsktɔp'pʌblɪʃɪŋ/ *das;* **~s** (*DV*) desktop publishing

**Desodorant** /dɛs|odo'rant/ ⇒ **Deodorant**

**desolat** /dezo'la:t/ *Adj.* (*geh.*) wretched

**Des·organisation** *die* (*geh.*) **A** disintegration; **B** (*fehlende Planung*) disorganization *no indef. art.;* lack of organization

**des·orientieren** *tr. V.* disorientate

**Des·orientiertheit, Des·orientierung** *die;* **~:** confusion

**Des·oxidation, Des·oxydation** *die* (*Chemie*) deoxidation

**Desoxiribo[se]nuklein·säure** /dɛs|ɔksyri'bo(:zə)nukle'i:n-/, **Desoxyribo[se]nuklein·säure** /dɛs|ɔksyri'bo(:zə)nukle'i:n-/ *die* (*Biochemie*) deoxyribonucleic acid

**despektierlich** /despɛk'ti:ɐ̯lɪç/ (*geh.*) ❶ *Adj.* (*abfällig, geringschätzig*) disparaging; (*respektlos*) disrespectful. ❷ *adv.;* ⇒ **1:** disparagingly; disrespectfully

**Desperado** /dɛspe'ra:do/ *der;* **~s, ~s** desperado

**desperat** /dɛspe'ra:t/ *Adj.* (*geh.*) desperate; **eine ~e Stimmung** a mood of desperation

**Despot** /dɛs'po:t/ *der;* **~en, ~en** despot; (*fig. abwertend*) tyrant

**Despotie** /dɛspo'ti:/ *die;* **~, ~n** despotism

**Despotin** *die;* **~, ~nen** ⇒ **Despot**

**despotisch** ❶ *Adj.* despotic. ❷ *adv.* despotically

**Despotismus** *der;* **~:** despotism

**des·selben** ⇒ **derselbe**

**dessen** /'dɛsn̩/ ❶ *Relativpron.; Gen. Sg. v.* **der**[1] 3, **das** 3 *attr.* (*Mensch*) whose; **der Onkel, ~ Besuch wir erwarten** the uncle from whom we are expecting a visit; (*Sache, Tier*) **der Garten, ~ Fläche 2 000 m² beträgt** the garden, the area of which is 2,000 m²; *selbstständig* **der Großvater, ~ wir uns gern erinnern** our grandfather, of whom we have fond memories; **ein Sprichwort, ~ er sich gern bedient** a proverb which *or* that he likes to use.
❷ *Demonstrativpron.; Gen. Sg. v.* **der**[1] 2, **das** 2 *attr.* **mein Onkel, sein Sohn und ~ Hund** my uncle, his son, and 'his dog; **das Waldsterben und ~ Folgen** the death of the forests and its consequences; *selbstständig* **Onkel August? Dessen erinnere ich mich noch sehr gut** Uncle August? I remember 'him well

**dessent-: ~halben** (*veralt.*), **~wegen** *Adv.* ❶ *relativ* on whose account; on account of whom; because of whom; (*von Sachen*) on account of which; because of which; **das Verbrechen, ~wegen er verurteilt wurde** the crime of which he was convicted; ❷ *demonstrativ* because of him; (*von Sachen*) because of this; **~willen** *Adv.* ❶ *relativ* **um ~willen** for whose sake; for the sake of whom; (*von Sachen*) for the sake of which; **das Treffen, um ~willen wir dorthin reisten** the meeting for which we travelled there; ❷ *demonstrativ* **um ~willen** for his sake

***dessen·ungeachtet** ⇒ **ungeachtet**

**Dessert** /dɛ'se:ɐ̯/ *das;* **~s, ~s** dessert

**Dessert-: ~teller** *der* dessert plate; **~wein** *der* dessert wine

**Dessin** /dɛ'sɛ̃:/ *das;* **~s, ~s** **A** design; pattern; **B** (*Entwurf*) design; **C** (*Billard*) path [of the ball]

**Dessous** /dɛ'su:/ *das;* **~** /dɛ'su:(s)/, **~** /dɛ'su:s/ (*geh.*) (*ladies'*) underwear *no indef. art.*

**destabilisieren** *tr. V.* (*Politik*) destabilize

**Destabilisierung** *die;* **~, ~en** (*Politik*) destabilization

**Destillat** /dɛstɪ'la:t/ *das;* **~[e]s, ~e** distillate

**Destillateur** /dɛstɪla'tø:ɐ̯/ *der;* **~s, ~e, Destillateurin** *die;* **~, ~nen** distiller

**Destillation** /dɛstɪla'tsi̯o:n/ *die;* **~, ~en** **A** (*Chemie*) distillation; **B** (*von Weinbrand*) distilling; (*Anlage*) distillery

**Destillator** /dɛstɪ'la:tɔr/ *der;* **~s, ~en** /-la'to:rən/ still

**Destille** /dɛs'tɪlə/ *die;* **~, ~n** **A** bar; **B** (*Branntweinbrennerei*) distillery

**destillieren** *tr. V.* **A** (*Chemie*) distil; **destilliertes Wasser** distilled water; **B** (*fig.*) condense (**zu** into); **aus einer Dokumentation eine Reportage ~:** condense records into a report

**Destillier·kolben** *der* distillation flask

**desto** *Konj., nur vor Komp.* **je eher, ~ besser** the sooner the better; **~ ängstlicher** the more anxious/anxiously; **ich schätzte ihn ~ mehr** I appreciated him all the more; **~ schlimmer für ihn** so much the worse for him; **~ besser für uns** all the better for us

**Destruktion** /destrʊk'tsi̯o:n/ *die;* **~, ~en** destruction

**Destruktions·trieb** *der* (*Psych.*) destructive urge

**destruktiv** /destrʊk'ti:f/ ❶ *Adj.* destructive. ❷ *adv.* destructively; **~ auf etw.** (*Akk.*) **wirken** have a destructive effect on sth.

**Destruktivität** /destrʊktivi'tɛ:t/ *die;* **~:** destructiveness

**des·wegen** *Adv.* ⇒ **deshalb**

**Deszendent** /dɛstsɛn'dɛnt/ *der;* **~en, ~en** (*Genealogie, Astrol.*) descendant

**Deszendenz·theorie** *die* theory of evolution

**Detail** /de'tai/ *das;* **~s, ~s** detail; **ins ~ gehen** go into detail; **in allen ~s** in the fullest detail; **bis ins [kleinste] ~:** down to the smallest detail

**detail-, Detail-: ~frage** *die* question of detail; **~getreu** ❶ *Adj.* accurate in every detail *postpos.;* ❷ *adv.* accurately in every detail; **~kenntnisse** *Pl.* detailed knowledge *sing.*

**detaillieren** /deta'ji:rən/ *tr. V.* explain ‹plan, suggestion, etc.› in detail; **etw. genauer ~:** explain sth. in more *or* greater detail

**detailliert** ❶ *Adj.* detailed. ❷ *adv.* in detail; **sehr ~:** in great detail

**Detail·schilderung** *die* detailed account; (*Beschreibung*) detailed description

**Detektei** /detɛk'tai/ *die;* **~, ~en** [private] detective agency

**Detektiv** /detɛk'ti:f/ *der;* **~s, ~e** ▸ 159 [private] detective; **die ~e von Scotland Yard** the detectives from Scotland Yard

**Detektiv-: ~büro** *das* ⇒ **Detektei**; **~geschichte** *die* detective story

**Detektivin** *die;* **~, ~nen** ▸ 159 [private] detective

**detektivisch** ❶ *Adj.* **mit ~em Scharfsinn** with the keen perception of a detective; **in ~er Kleinarbeit** by detailed detective work. ❷ *adv.* like a detective

**Detektiv·roman** *der* detective novel

**Detektor** /de'tɛktɔr/ *der;* **~s, ~en** /-'to:rən/ (*Technik, Funkw.*) detector

**Detergens** /de'tɛrgɛns/ *das;* **~, Detergenzien** (*Chemie*) detergent

**Determinante** /detɛrmi'nantə/ *die;* **~, ~n** (*Math., Biol.*) determinant

**Determination** /detɛrmina'tsi̯o:n/ *die;* **~, ~en** (*Philos., Biol., Psych.*) determination

**determinieren** *tr. V.* determine

**Determiniertheit** *die;* **~** (*Philos.*) determined nature; **die gesellschaftliche ~ der Sprache** the socially determined nature of language

**Determinismus** *der;* **~** (*Philos.*) determinism *no art.*

**deterministisch** ❶ *Adj.* deterministic. ❷ *adv.* deterministically

**Detonation** /detona'tsi̯o:n/ *die;* **~, ~en** detonation; explosion; **eine Bombe zur ~ bringen** detonate a bomb

**detonieren** /deto'ni:rən/ *itr. V.; mit sein* detonate; explode

**Deubel** /'dɔy̆bl̩/ *der;* **~s, ~** (*nordd.*) ⇒ **Teufel**

**deucht** /'dɔy̆çt/ *3. Pers. Sg. Präsens v.* **dünken**

**deuchte** *3. Pers. Sg. Prät. v.* **dünken**

**Deut** /dɔy̆t/ **keinen ~:** not one bit; **du bist keinen ~ besser als er** you're not one bit *or* whit better than he is

**deutbar** *Adj.* interpretable

**Deutelei** *die;* **~, ~en** (*abwertend*) speculation

**deuteln** /'dɔy̆tl̩n/ *itr. V.* quibble (**an** + *Dat.* about); **daran gibt es nichts zu ~:** there are no ifs and buts about it

**deuten** /'dɔy̆tn̩/ ❶ *itr. V.* **A** point; **[mit dem Finger] auf jmdn./etw. ~:** point [one's finger] at sb./sth.; **B** (*hinweisen*) **auf etw.** (*Akk.*) **~:** point to *or* indicate sth.; **sein Verhalten deutet darauf hin, dass ...** his behaviour indicates that .... ❷ *tr. V.* interpret; **die Zukunft ~:** read the future; **etw. falsch ~:** misinterpret sth.

**Deuter** *der;* **~s, ~** **A** interpreter; **B** (*österr.: Tipp*) hint; clue

**Deuterin** *die;* **~, ~nen** interpreter

**deutlich** ❶ *Adj.* **A** clear; **daraus wird ~, dass/wie ...** this makes it clear that/how ...; **B** (*eindeutig*) clear; plain; clear, distinct ‹recollection, feeling›; clear ‹victory›; **das ist ~:** that is [quite] plain *or* clear; **das war ~ [genug]** that was clear *or* plain enough; **~ werden** make oneself plain *or* clear; **muss ich noch ~er werden?** do I have to speak more plainly?.
❷ *adv.* **A** clearly; **~ sichtbar/erkennbar/hörbar sein** be clearly *or* plainly visible/recognizable/audible; **B** (*eindeutig*) clearly; plainly; **[klar und] ~ sagen, dass ...** make it [perfectly *or* quite] clear that ...; **jmdm. etw. ~ zu verstehen geben** make sth. clear *or* plain to sb.

**Deutlichkeit** *die;* **~, ~en** **A** clarity; **B** (*Eindeutigkeit*) clearness; plainness; (*von Erinnerungen*) clearness; distinctness; **in** *od.* **mit aller ~ sagen, dass ...** make it perfectly clear *or* plain that ...; **seine Antwort ließ an ~ nichts zu wünschen übrig** his answer could not have been clearer; **C** *Pl.* (*Grobheiten*) rude remarks

**deutlichkeits·halber** *Adv.* for the sake of clarity

**deutsch** /dɔy̆tʃ/ ▸ 553, ▸ 696 ❶ *Adj.* **A** German; **die ~e Schrift** German script; **Deutscher Schäferhund** Alsatian; German shepherd [dog]; **mit typisch ~er Gründlichkeit** with typical Teutonic *or* German thoroughness; **Deutsche Mark** Deutschmark; German mark; **der Deutsche Orden** the Teutonic Order; **Deutsche Bundesbahn** German Federal Railway; **Deutsche Bundespost** German Federal Post Office; **Deutsche Demokratische Republik** German Democratic Republic; **Deutscher Fußball-Bund** German Football Association; **Deutscher Gewerkschaftsbund** German Trade Union Federation; **das**

**Deutsche Reich** the German Reich *or* Empire; **Deutsche Presse-Agentur** German Press Agency; **Deutsches Rotes Kreuz** German Red Cross; **B** (*die Sprache betreffend*) German; **die ~e Schweiz** German-speaking Switzerland; ⇒ *auch* **Deutsch** A. **2** *adv.* **~ sprechen/schreiben** speak/write German; **~ geschrieben sein** be written in German; **~ fühlen** feel German; **etw. ~ aussprechen** pronounce sth. in a German way; **mit jmdm. ~ reden** *od.* **sprechen** (*fig. ugs.*) be blunt with *or* speak bluntly to sb.; **dieses Gebiet war damals ~ besetzt/verwaltet** this area was under German occupation/administration at that time

**Deutsch** *das;* **~[s]** ▶ **696** **A** German; **gutes/fließend ~ sprechen** speak good/fluent German; **ein perfektes ~:** faultless *or* perfect German; **kein ~ [mehr] verstehen** (*ugs.*) not understand plain English; **auf/in ~:** in German; **was heißt das Wort auf ~?** what is the word in German?; what is the German for that word?; **auf [gut] ~** (*fig. ugs.*) in plain English; **~ sprechend** German-speaking; **B** (*Unterrichtsfach*) German *no art.*; **er ist gut in ~:** he's good at German; **wen habt ihr in ~?** who do you have for German?

**Deutsch·amerikaner** *der,* **Deutsch·amerikanerin** *die* German-American

**deutsch·amerikanisch** *Adj.* German-American

**Deutsch·arbeit** *die* (*Schulw.*) German test

**deutsch-deutsch** *Adj.* intra-German

**Deutsche**[1] /ˈdɔytʃə/ *der/die; adj. Dekl.* ▶ **553** German; **~[r] sein** be German; **er ist kein ~r** he's not German; **als ~r** as a German; **er hat eine ~ geheiratet** he married a German girl/woman

**Deutsche**[2] *das; adj. Dekl.* ▶ **696** **A** German; **das ~ ist …** German is …; **aus dem ~n/ins ~ übersetzen** translate from/into German; **B** (*deutsche Eigenart*) **alles ~:** all things *pl. or* everything German; **das typisch ~ daran** what is/was typically German about it

**Deutschen·feind** *der,* **Deutschen·feindin** *die* anti-German; Germanophobe

**deutsch·englisch** *Adj.* Anglo-German ‹relations, cooperation, etc.›; German-English ‹dictionary, anthology, etc.›

**Deutschen·hass,** ***Deutschen·haß** *der* hatred of the Germans; Germanophobia *no indef. art.*

**deutsch-, Deutsch-: ~feindlich** *Adj.* anti-German; Germanophobe; **~feindlichkeit** *die* Germanophobia *no indef. art.;* anti-German feeling; **~französisch** *Adj.* Franco-German ‹relations, border, etc.›; German-French ‹dictionary, anthology, etc.›; **der ~-Französische Krieg** the Franco-Prussian War; **~freundlich** *Adj.* pro-German; Germanophile; **~herren** *Pl.* (*hist.*) Teutonic Knights; **~herrenorden** *der* (*hist.*) Teutonic Order of Knights; **~kanadier** *der,* **~kanadierin** *die* German-Canadian

**Deutschland** (*das*)*;* **~s** Germany; **die beiden ~:** the two Germanies

**Deutschland-: ~fahrt** *die* trip through Germany; **~frage** *die* (*Politik*) German question; **~lied** *das* the song 'Deutschland, Deutschland über alles'; **~politik** *die* (*innerdeutsche Politik*) intra-German policy; (*gegenüber Deutschlandpolitik*) policy towards Germany; **~politisch 1** *Adj.* ‹speaker› for intra-German affairs; ‹committee› on intra-German affairs; **2** *adv.* ‹interested› in intra-German affairs; **~politisch gesehen** from the point of view of intra-German affairs; **~reise** *die* trip to Germany; (*Rundreise*) tour of Germany

**deutsch-, Deutsch-: ~lehrer** *der,* **~lehrerin** *die* German teacher; **~schweiz** *die* (*schweiz.*) German-speaking Switzerland; **~schweizer** *der,* **~schweizerin** *die* German-Swiss; **~schweizerisch** *Adj.* German-Swiss; **~sowjetisch** *Adj.* German-Soviet; **~sprachig** *Adj.* **A** German-speaking; **~sprachige** *Pl.* German speakers; **B** (*in ~er Sprache*) German-language *attrib.* ‹newspaper, edition, broadcast›; ‹teaching› in German; German ‹literature›; **~sprachlich** *Adj.* German[-language *attrib.*]; ***~sprechend** ⇒ **Deutsch** A; **~stämmig** *Adj.* of German origin *postpos.;* **~stämmige** *Pl.* ethnic Germans; **~stunde** *die* German lesson

**Deutschtum** *das;* **~s A** (*deutsche Wesensart*) Germanness; **B** (*Volkszugehörigkeit*) German nationality; **C** (*die Deutschen*) Germans *pl.*

**Deutschtümelei** /-ty:məˈlai/ *die;* **~, ~en** (*abwertend*) jingoistic emphasis on things German

**Deutsch·unterricht** *der* German teaching; (*Unterrichtsstunde*) German lesson; **~ erteilen** *or* **geben** teach German; ⇒ *auch* **Englischunterricht**; **Unterricht**

**Deutung** *die;* **~, ~en** interpretation

**Deutungs·versuch** *der* attempt at interpretation; **ein ~ dieser Parabel** an attempt to interpret this parable

**Devalvation** /devalvaˈtsio:n/ *die;* **~, ~en** (*Finanzw.*) devaluation

**Devise** /deˈvi:zə/ *die;* **~, ~n** motto; **sich** (*Dat.*) **etw. zur ~ machen** make sth. one's motto

**Devisen** *Pl.* foreign exchange *sing.;* (*Sorten*) foreign currency *sing. or* exchange *sing.*

**Devisen-: ~abkommen** *das* (*Politik*) foreign exchange agreement; **~bewirtschaftung** *die* foreign exchange control; **~börse** *die* foreign exchange market; **~bringer** *der* foreign exchange earner; **~geschäft** *das* foreign exchange business *or* dealings *pl.;* (*einzelne Transaktion*) foreign exchange transaction; **~kurs** *der* exchange rate; rate of exchange; **~markt** *der* foreign exchange market; **~schmuggel** *der* [foreign] currency smuggling; **~sperre** *die* exchange embargo; **~vergehen** *das* currency offence; breach of exchange control regulations

**devot** /deˈvo:t/ (*geh.*) **1** *Adj.* **A** (*abwertend*) obsequious; **B** (*veralt.: demütig*) humble. **2** *adv.* **A** (*abwertend*) obsequiously; **B** (*veralt.: demütig*) humbly

**Devotionalien** /devotsioˈna:liən/ *Pl.* (*Rel.*) devotional objects

**Dextrose** /dɛksˈtro:zə/ *die;* **~:** dextrose

**Dez** /de:ts/ *der;* **~es, ~e** (*salopp*) nut (*coll.*); bonce (*sl.*)

**Dez.** *Abk.* **Dezember** Dec.

**Dezember** /deˈtsɛmbɐ/ *der;* **~s, ~** ▶ **207** December; ⇒ *auch* **April**

**Dezennium** /deˈtsɛnium/ *das;* **~s, Dezennien** (*geh.*) decennium; decade

**dezent** /deˈtsɛnt/ **1** *Adj.* quiet ‹colour, pattern, suit›; subdued ‹lighting, music›; discreet ‹smile, behaviour›; gentle ‹irony›. **2** *adv.* discreetly; ‹dress› unostentatiously

**dezentral** **1** *Adj.* **A** non-central ‹location›; **B** (*von verschiedenen Stellen ausgehend*) decentralized. **2** *adv.* **A** outside the centre; **B** ⇒ **1** B: decentrally

**Dezentralisation** *die;* **~, ~en** decentralization

**dezentralisieren** *tr. V.* decentralize

**Dezentralisierung** *die;* **~, ~en** decentralization

**Dezenz** /deˈtsɛnts/ *die;* **~ A** discreetness; **B** (*Eleganz*) unostentatious elegance

**Dezernat** /detsɛrˈna:t/ *das;* **~[e]s, ~e** department

**Dezernent** /detsɛrˈnɛnt/ *der;* **~en, ~en, Dezernentin** *die;* **~, ~nen** head of department

**dezi-, Dezi-** /ˈde:tsi-/ deci

**Dezibel** /detsiˈbɛl/ *das;* **~s, ~:** decibel

**dezidiert** /detsiˈdi:ɐt/ (*geh.*) **1** *Adj.* firm ‹demand, view›; **mit einigen ~en Fragen** with some determined questioning. **2** *adv.* ‹support, demand› firmly; ‹question› determinedly

**Dezi-: ~gramm** *das* decigram; **~liter** *der od. das* decilitre

**dezimal** /detsiˈma:l/ *Adj.* decimal

**Dezimal-: ~bruch** *der* ▶ **841** decimal [fraction]; **~klassifikation** *die* decimal *or* Dewey classification; **~rechnung** *die* decimal arithmetic *no art.;* **~stelle** *die* decimal place; **~system** *das* decimal system; **~waage** *die* decimal balance; **~zahl** *die* ▶ **841** decimal [number]

**Dezime** /ˈde:tsimə/ *die;* **~, ~n** (*Musik*) tenth

**Dezi·meter** *der od. das* decimetre

**dezimieren** /detsiˈmi:rən/ **1** *tr. V.* decimate. **2** *refl. V.* be drastically reduced

**Dezimierung** *die;* **~, ~en A** decimation; **B** (*starker Rückgang*) drastic reduction (*Gen.* in)

**DFB** *Abk.* **Deutscher Fußball-Bund**

**DGB** *Abk.* **Deutscher Gewerkschaftsbund** German Trade Union Federation

**dgl.** *Abk.* **dergleichen, desgleichen**

**d. Gr.** *Abk.* **der/die Große**

**d. h.** *Abk.* **das heißt** i. e.

**Di.** *Abk.* **Dienstag** Tue[s].

**Dia** /ˈdi:a/ *das;* **~s, ~s** slide; transparency

**Diabetes** /diaˈbe:tɛs/ *der;* **~** ▶ **474** diabetes

**Diabetiker** /diaˈbe:tikɐ/ *der;* **~s, ~, Diabetikerin,** *die;* **~, ~nen** diabetic

**diabetisch** *Adj.* diabetic

**Dia·betrachter** *der* [slide] viewer

**Diabolik** /diaˈbo:lɪk/ *die;* **~** (*geh.*) diabolic malevolence

**diabolisch** (*geh.*) **1** *Adj.* diabolic; diabolically malevolent. **2** *adv.* with diabolic malevolence

**diachron** /diaˈkro:n/ **1** *Adj.* diachronic. **2** *adv.* diachronically

**Diachronie** /diakroˈni:/ *die;* **~** (*Sprachw.*) diachrony *no art.*

**diachronisch** *Adj.* ⇒ **diachron**

**Diadem** /diaˈde:m/ *das;* **~s, ~e** diadem

**Diadochen** /diaˈdɔxn̩/ *Pl.* (*geh.*) rivals for the succession

**Diadochen·kämpfe** *Pl.* (*geh.*) power struggle *sing.*

**Diagnose** /diaˈgno:zə/ *die;* **~, ~n** diagnosis; **eine ~ stellen** make a diagnosis

**Diagnose·zentrum** *das* diagnostic clinic

**Diagnostik** /diaˈgnɔstɪk/ *die;* **~** (*Med., Psych.*) diagnostics *sing., no art.*

**Diagnostiker** *der;* **~s, ~, Diagnostikerin** *die;* **~, ~nen** (*Med., Psych.*) diagnostician

**diagnostisch** **1** *Adj.* diagnostic. **2** *adv.* diagnostically

**diagnostizieren** /diagnɔstiˈtsi:rən/ **1** *tr. V.* diagnose. **2** *itr. V.* **auf etw.** (*Akk.*) **~:** diagnose sth.

**diagonal** /diagoˈna:l/ **1** *Adj.* diagonal. **2** *adv.* diagonally; **etw. ~ lesen** (*ugs.*) skim through sth.

**Diagonale** *die;* **~, ~n** diagonal

**Diagramm** *das* graph; (*von Gegenständen*) diagram

**Diakon** /diaˈko:n/ *der;* **~s** *od.* **~en, ~e[n]** deacon

**Diakonie** /diakoˈni:/ *die;* **~** (*ev. Kirche*) welfare and social work

**Diakonin** *die;* **~, ~nen** deaconess

**diakonisch** *Adj.* welfare and social ‹work, facilities, etc.›

**Diakonisse** /diakoˈnɪsə/ *die;* **~, ~n, Diakonissin** *die;* **~, ~nen** deaconess

**dia·kritisch** *Adj.* **in ~es Zeichen** (*Sprachw.*) diacritical mark *or* sign; diacritic

**Dialekt** /diaˈlɛkt/ *der;* **~[e]s, ~e** dialect; **~ sprechen** speak in dialect

**dialektal** /dialɛkˈta:l/ *Adj.* dialectal

**dialekt-, Dialekt-: ~ausdruck** *der; Pl.* **~ausdrücke** dialect expression; **~forschung** *die* dialect research; **~frei 1** *Adj.* **~freies Deutsch sprechen** speak German without a trace of [any] dialect; **2** *adv.* **~frei sprechen** speak without a trace of [any] dialect

**Dialektik** /diaˈlɛktɪk/ *die;* **~ A** (*Philos.*) dialectics *pl.;* (*Diamat*) dialectic; **B** (*Gegensätzlichkeit*) conflicting nature

**Dialektiker** *der;* **~s, ~, Dialektikerin** *die;* **~, ~nen** (*Philos.*) dialectician

**dialektisch** **1** *Adj.* **A** (*Philos.*) dialectical; **B** ⇒ **dialektal**. **2** *adv.* dialectically

---

*old spelling (see note on page 1707)

**Dialog** /dia'lo:k/ *der;* **~[e]s, ~e** dialogue
**dialogisch** *Adj.* dialogic; ‹story› in dialogue form
**Dialyse** /dia'ly:zə/ *die;* **~, ~n** (*Physik, Chemie, Med.*) dialysis
**Dialyse·zentrum** *das* dialysis centre
**Diamant¹** /dia'mant/ *der;* **~en, ~en** diamond
**Diamant²** *die;* **~** (*Druckw.*) diamond ($4\frac{1}{2}$ *points Pica*); brilliant (*4 points Pica*)
**diamanten** *Adj.* diamond
**Diamant[en]-: ~schleifer** *der*, **~schleiferin** *die* diamond cutter; **~schmuck** *der* diamond jewellery; diamonds *pl.*; **~staub** *der* diamond dust
**Diamat, DIAMAT** /dia'ma(:)t/ *der;* **~** *Abk.* **dialektischer Materialismus**
**diametral** /diame'tra:l/ **1** *Adj.* **A** (*Geom.*) diametral; **B** (*fig. geh.*); diametrical ‹opposition›; diametrically opposed ‹views›; **im ~en Gegensatz zu etw. stehen** be diametrically opposed to sth. **2** *adv.* (*geh.*) diametrically; **~ entgegengesetzt sein** be diametrically opposed
**Dia-: ~positiv** *das* slide; transparency; **~projektor** *der* slide projector; **~rahmen** *der* slide mount
**Diärese** /diɛ're:zə/ *die;* **~, ~n** (*Sprachw., Metrik, Rhet., Philos.*) diaeresis
**Diarrhö, Diarrhöe** /dia'rø:/ *die;* **~, Diarrhöen ▶ 474** (*Med.*) diarrhoea
**Diaspora** /di'aspora/ *die;* **~:** Diaspora
**Diastole** /di'astole/ *die;* **~, ~n** /dia'sto:lən/ (*Med.*) diastole
**Diät** /di'ɛ:t/ *die;* **~, ~en** diet; **eine ~ einhalten** keep to a diet; **nach einer ~ leben** live on a diet; **jmdn. auf ~ setzen** put sb. on a diet; **~ kochen** cook according to a/one's diet; **~ essen** be on a diet; **[strikt] ~ leben** keep to a [strict] diet
**Diät-: ~assistent** *der*, **~assistentin** *die* **▶ 159** dietician; **~bier** *das* diabetic beer
**Diäten** *Pl.* [parliamentary] allowance *sing.*
**Diätetik** /diɛ'te:tɪk/ *die;* **~, ~en** dietetics *sing., no art.*
**diätetisch** *Adj.* dietetic; dietary; **eine ~e Lebensweise** living on a diet
**Diät·fahrplan** *der* (*ugs.*) diet
**Diätist** *der;* **~en, ~en, Diätistin** *die;* **~, ~nen** dietician
**Diät-: ~koch** *der*, **~köchin** *die* dietary cook; **~kost** *die* dietary food; **~küche** *die* **A** dietary kitchen; **B** (*Schonkost*) dietary food; **~kur** *die* diet cure
**Diatonik** /dia'to:nɪk/ *die;* **~** (*Musik*) diatonicism; diatonic system
**diatonisch** *Adj.* (*Musik*) diatonic
**Diät·plan** *der* dietary plan; diet plan; diet
**dich** /dɪç/ **1** *Akk. des Personalpron.* **du** you. **2** *Akk. des Reflexivpron. der 2. Pers. Sg.* yourself; **wäschst du ~?** are you washing [yourself]?; **entschuldige ~!** apologize!
**Dichotomie** /dɪçoto'mi:/ *die;* **~, ~n** (*Bot., Philos., Sprachw.*) dichotomy
**dicht** /dɪçt/ **1** *Adj.* **A** thick ‹hair, fur, plumage, moss›; thick, dense ‹foliage, fog, cloud›; dense ‹forest, thicket, hedge, crowd›; heavy, dense ‹traffic›; densely ranked, close-ranked ‹rows of houses›; heavy ‹snowstorm›; (*fig.*) dense ‹prose, dialogue, etc.›; full, packed ‹programme›; **in ~er Folge** in rapid *or* quick succession; **B** (*undurchlässig*) (*für Luft*) airtight; (*für Wasser*) watertight ‹shoes›; (*für Licht*) heavy ‹curtains, shutters›; **~ machen** seal ‹crack›; make airtight/watertight; seal the crack[s]/leak[s] in ‹roof, window, etc.›; waterproof ‹material, umbrella, etc.›; **nicht ganz ~ sein** (*salopp*) have a screw loose (*coll.*); **C** (*ugs.: geschlossen*) shut; closed.
**2** *adv.* **A** densely ‹populated, foliated›; thickly, densely ‹wooded›; tightly, closely ‹packed›; **~ bebaut** heavily built up; **~ verschneit** thick with snow; **~ besetzt** full; packed; **~ behaart** [very] hairy; **~ an ~** *od.* **~ gedrängt stehen/sitzen** stand/sit close together; **das Dorf war ~ verschneit** the village was covered in a thick blanket of snow *or* was deep in snow; **~ bewachsene Hügel** hills covered with dense vegetation; **B** (*undurchlässig*) tightly; **C** *mit Präp.* (*nahe*) **~ neben** right next to; **sich ~ bei jmdn. halten** keep close to sb.; **~ daran** hard by; **~ nebeneinander** close together; **~ vor/hinter ihm** right *or* just in front of/behind him; **die Polizei ist ihm ~ auf den Fersen** the police are hard *or* close on his heels; **D** (*zeitlich: unmittelbar*) **ich war ~ daran, es zu tun** I was just about to do it; **~ bevorstehen** be imminent; **das Fest steht ~ bevor** the party is almost upon us/them *etc.*
**dicht·auf** *Adv.* close behind
***dichtbebaut** *usw.* ⇒ **dicht** 2 A
**Dichte** /'dɪçtə/ *die;* **~** **A** (*Physik, fig.*) density; **B** (*Undurchdringlichkeit*) **ein Nebel von solcher ~:** such [a] dense *or* thick fog
**dichten¹** /'dɪçtn̩/ **1** *itr. V.* **[gut] ~:** make a good seal. **2** *tr. V.* make airtight/watertight; seal ‹joint etc.›; seal the crack[s]/leak[s] in ‹window, roof, etc.›
**dichten²** **1** *itr. V.* **A** write poetry; **B** **sein ganzes Dichten und Trachten** all his thoughts and endeavours. **2** *tr. V.* (*verfassen*) write; compose
**Dichter** *der;* **~s, ~ ▶ 159** poet; (*Schriftsteller*) writer; author
**Dichter·fürst** *der* (*veralt.*) prince among poets; (*Schriftsteller*) prince among writers
**Dichterin** *die;* **~, ~nen ▶ 159** poet[ess]; (*Schriftstellerin*) writer; author[ess]
**dichterisch** **1** *Adj.* poetic; (*schriftstellerisch*) literary. **2** *adv.;* ⇒ **1**: poetically; literarily
**Dichter-: ~komponist** *der*, **~komponistin** *die* poet/writer and composer; **~kreis** *der* circle of poets; (*von Schriftstellern*) circle of writers; **~lesung** *die* reading (*by a poet or writer from his own works*)
**Dichterling** *der;* **~s, ~e** (*abwertend*) poetaster (*derog.*); rhymester (*derog.*)
**Dichter-: ~schule** *die* school of poets; (*von Schriftstellern*) school of writers; **~sprache** *die* poetic language
**dicht-: *~gedrängt** ⇒ **dicht** 2 A; **~|halten** *unr. itr. V.* (*ugs.*) keep one's mouth shut (*coll.*)
**Dicht·kunst** *die* **A** art of poetry; **B** (*Fähigkeit, Talent*) poetic talent; **C** (*Poesie*) poetry *no art.*
**dicht|machen** (*ugs.*) **1** *tr. V.* shut; close; (*endgültig*) shut *or* close down; **die Polizei hat ihm die Bar dichtgemacht** the police shut *or* closed down his bar. **2** *itr. V.* **A** shut; close; (*endgültig*) shut *or* close down; **B** (*Sportjargon*) **hinten ~:** close the game down at the back
**Dichtung¹** *die;* **~, ~en** **A** sealing; **zur ~ der Fugen** to seal the joints; **B** (*Vorrichtung*) seal; (*am Hahn usw.*) washer; (*am Vergaser, Zylinder usw.*) gasket
**Dichtung²** *die;* **~, ~en** **A** literary work; work of literature; (*in Versform*) poetic work; poem; (*fig. ugs.*) fiction; **~ und Wahrheit** fact and fiction; truth and fantasy; **Goethes „~ und Wahrheit"** Goethe's 'Poetry and Truth'; **B** (*Dichtkunst*) literature; (*in Versform*) poetry
**Dichtungs-: ~masse** *die* sealing compound; sealant; **~mittel** *das* integral waterproofing agent *or* waterproofer; **~ring** *der*, **~scheibe** *die* sealing ring; (*am Hahn*) washer
**dick** /dɪk/ **1** *Adj.* **A** thick; thick, chunky ‹pullover›; stout ‹tree›; fat ‹person, arms, legs, behind, etc.›; big ‹bust›; **~ und rund** *od.* **fett sein** (*ugs.*) be round and fat; **~ werden** get fat; **das Kleid macht ~:** the dress makes you look fat; **Kuchen macht ~:** cakes are fattening *or* make you fat; **ein ~es Auto fahren** (*fig. ugs.*) drive a great big car (*coll.*); **ein Mädchen ~ machen** (*salopp*) put a girl in the club (*sl.*); **B** (*mit Maßangaben*) thick; **5 cm ~ sein** be 5 cm thick; **5 cm ~e Bretter** planks 5 cm thick; 5 cm thick planks; **C** (*stark*) *thick* ‹carpet, wall, layer›; **mit jmdm. durch ~ und dünn gehen** stay *or* stick with sb. through thick and thin; **es nicht so ~ haben** (*ugs.*) not be very well off; **D** (*ugs.: angeschwollen*) swollen ‹cheek, ankle, tonsils, etc.›; **E** (*dicht*, **~flüssig**) thick ‹hair, fog, soup, sauce, etc.›; **im ~sten Verkehr** (*fig. ugs.*) in the heaviest traffic; **mitten in der ~sten Arbeit** (*fig. ugs.*) just when we're/they're *etc.* right up to our/their *etc.* necks in work (*coll.*); **F** (*ugs.: außergewöhnlich groß*) big ‹mistake, order›; hefty, (*coll.*) fat ‹fee, premium, salary›; **einen ~en Tadel verdienen** deserve heavy criticism; **jmdm. ein ~es Lob aussprechen** give sb. a great deal of prise *or* high praise; **das ~e Ende kommt noch** (*ugs.*) the worst is yet to come; **G** (*ugs.: eng*) close ‹friends, friendship, etc.›.
**2** *adv.* **A** **etw. ~ unterstreichen** underline sth. heavily; **sich ~ anziehen** wrap up warm[ly]; **B** (*mit Maßangabe*) **etw. 5 cm ~ schneiden/auftragen** *usw.* cut/apply sth. 5 cm. thick; **C** (*stark*) thickly; **~ geschminkt/bemalt** heavily made up; **~ auftragen** (*ugs. abwertend*) lay it on thick (*sl.*); **D** **~ geschwollen** (*ugs.*) badly swollen; **E** **~ befreundet sein** (*ugs.*) be close friends
**dick-, Dick-: ~bauch** *der* (*scherzh.*) fatty; (*mit Spitzbauch*) potbelly; **~bauchig** *Adj.* large-bellied, big-bellied ‹vase, pot, etc.›; **~bäuchig** *Adj.* corpulent; portly; (*mit Spitzbauch*) pot-bellied ‹person›; **~darm** *der* **▶ 471** (*Anat.*) large intestine
**dicke** *Adv.* (*ugs.*) easily; **wir haben noch ~ Zeit** we've got plenty of time; **von etw. ~ genug haben** have had quite enough of sth.; **jmdn./etw. ~ haben** (*salopp*) have had a bellyful of sb./sth.
**Dicke¹** *die;* **~:** thickness; (*von Menschen, Körperteilen*) fatness
**Dicke²** *der/die; adj. Dekl.* **A** (*ugs.*) fatty (*coll.*); fat man/woman; **die ~n** (*im Allgemeinen*) fatties (*coll.*); fat people; **B** (*Kosename*) podge (*coll.*)
**dicken** **1** *tr. V.* thicken. **2** *itr. V.; auch mit sein* thicken
**Dickerchen** *das;* **~s, ~** (*ugs. scherzh.*) podge (*coll.*)
**dicke|tun** *unr. refl. V.* (*ugs. abwertend*) show off; (*durch Reden*) boast; brag; **sich mit etw. ~:** boast *or* brag about sth.; **sich mit seiner Kraft ~:** show off one's strength
**dick-, Dick-: ~fellig** (*ugs. abwertend*) **1** *Adj.* thick-skinned; **~fellig sein** have a thick skin; be thick-skinned; **2** *adv.* in a thick-skinned way; **~felligkeit** *die;* **~** (*ugs. abwertend*) insensitivity; **~flüssig** *Adj.* thick; viscous (*as tech. term*); **~flüssigkeit** *die* thickness; viscosity (*as tech. term*); **~häuter** *der;* **~s, ~:** pachyderm; (*fig.*) thick-skinned person
**Dickicht** /'dɪkɪçt/ *das;* **~[e]s, ~e** thicket; (*im Wald*) dense undergrowth *no indef. art.;* (*fig.*) jungle
**dick-, Dick-: ~kopf** *der* (*ugs.*) mule (*coll.*); **du bist ein ~kopf** you're as stubborn as a mule; **einen ~kopf haben** be stubborn *or* pigheaded; **~köpfig** (*ugs.*) **1** *Adj.* stubborn; pigheaded; **2** *adv.* stubbornly; pigheadedly; **~leibig** *Adj.* (*geh.*) corpulent; fat; (*fig.*) thick, fat ‹document, book›; **~leibigkeit** *die;* **~** (*geh.*) corpulence; fatness
**dicklich** *Adj.* **A** plumpish; chubby; **B** (*dickflüssig*) thick
**dick-, Dick-: ~macher** *der* (*ugs.*) fattening food; **~milch** *die* sour milk; **~schädel** *der* ⇒ **~kopf**; **~schalig** *Adj.* thick-skinned ‹orange, tomato, etc.›; **~|tun** *unr. refl. V.* ⇒ **dicketun**; **~wandig** *Adj.* thick-walled, thick-sided ‹vessel, container›; **~wanst** *der* (*salopp abwertend*) fatso (*sl.*)
**Didaktik** /di'daktɪk/ *die;* **~, ~en** **A** didactics *sing., no art.;* theory of teaching and methodology; **B** (*Unterrichtsmethode*) teaching method
**Didaktiker** *der;* **~s, ~, Didaktikerin** *die;* **~, ~nen** **A** educationalist; **B** (*jmd. mit didaktischen Fähigkeiten*) teacher
**didaktisch** **1** *Adj.* didactic. **2** *adv.* didactically
**die¹** **1** *best. Art. Nom.* the; **~ Kleine** the little girl; **~ Liebe/Freundschaft** love/friendship; **~ „Iphigenie"**/(*ugs.*) **Helga** 'Iphigenia'/Helga; **~ Demokratie/Diktatur/Monarchie** democracy/dictatorship/

d

monarchy; ~ **Bardot** (*ugs.*) Bardot; ~ **[Frankfurter] Eintracht** (*ugs.*) Eintracht Frankfurt; **sie ist die Sängerin/Schauspielerin** she's 'the singer/actress; ~ **Marktstraße** Market Street; ~ **Schweiz/Türkei** Switzerland/Turkey; ~ **Frau/Menschheit** women *pl.*/mankind; ~ **„Concorde“/„Klaus Störtebeker“** 'Concorde'/the 'Klaus Störtebeker'; ~ **Kunst/Oper** art/opera.
❷ *Demonstrativpron.* Ⓐ *attr.* **die Frau war es** it was 'that woman; Ⓑ *selbstständig* she; **die war es** it was 'her; **die und arbeiten!** (*ugs.*) [what,] her work!; ~ **mit dem Hund/den lila Haaren** (*ugs.*) her with the dog/purple hair; **die [da]** (*Frau, Mädchen*) that woman/girl; (*Gegenstand, Tier*) that one; ~ **blöde Kuh**, ~**!** (*fig. salopp*) what a silly cow! (*sl.*).
❸ *Relativpron. Nom.* (*Mensch*) who; that; (*Sache, Tier*) which; that; **die Frau, ~ da drüben entlanggeht** the woman walking along over there; **ich sah eine Frau/Katze, ~ aus dem Fenster schaute** I saw a women/cat looking out of the window.
❹ *Relativ- u. Demonstrativpron.* the one who; ~ **das getan hat** the woman *etc.* who did it

**die²** ❶ *best. Art.* Ⓐ *Akk. Sg. v.* **die¹** 1: **ich sah ~ Frau/Ratte** I saw the women/rat; **wir sahen ~ „Zauberflöte“** we saw the 'Magic Flute'; **hast du ~ Ute gesehen?** (*ugs.*) have you seen Ute?; **er hat ~ Callas geheiratet** (*ugs.*) he married Callas; **ich fuhr durch ~ Marktstraße** I drove through Market Street; Ⓑ *Nom. u. Akk. Pl. v.* **der 1¹, die¹ 1, das 1:¹ [er fragte] ~ Männer/Frauen/Kinder** [he asked] the men/women/children. ❷ *Demonstrativpron. Nom. u. Akk. Pl. v.* **der¹ 1, die¹ 1, das 1:** *attr.* **ich meine die Männer/Frauen/Kinder, die gestern hier waren** I mean those men/women/children who were here yesterday; *selbstständig* **ich meine die [da]** I mean 'them. ❸ *Relativpron.* Ⓐ *Akk. Sg. v.* **die¹** 3: (*bei Menschen*) **die Frau, ~ ich gesehen habe** the woman who *or* that I saw; (*bei Sachen, Tieren*) **die Straße, ~ ich entlangging** the street [that *or* which] I walked along; ~ **Maus, ~ ~ Katze fing** the mouse which *or* that the cat caught; Ⓑ *Nom. u. Akk. Pl. v.* **der¹ 3, die¹ 3, das 3:** (*bei Menschen*) **die Männer/Frauen/Kinder, ~ ich gesehen habe/~ dort gehen** the men/women/children I saw/walking along over there; (*bei Sachen, Tieren*) **die Nägel/Birnen/Bücher, ~ da liegen/~ jemand da hingelegt hat** the nails/pears/books lying there/which somebody put there

**Dieb** /di:p/ *der;* **~[e]s, ~e** thief; **haltet den ~!** stop thief!

**Dieberei** *die;* **~, ~en** Ⓐ (*das Stehlen*) thieving; Ⓑ (*Diebstahl*) theft

**Diebes-: ~bande** *die* (*abwertend*) gang of thieves; **~beute** *die* stolen goods *pl. or* property; **~gut** *das* stolen goods *pl.* or property; **~nest** *das* thieves' hideout; **~tour** *die* **auf ~tour gehen/sein** go/have gone [out] thieving *or* stealing; **auf ~touren sein** have been [out] thieving *or* stealing on a number of occasions

**Diebin** *die;* **~, ~nen** [woman] thief; ⇨ *auch* **-in**

**diebisch** ❶ *Adj.* Ⓐ thieving; Ⓑ (*verstohlen*) mischievous. ❷ *adv.* mischievously; **sich ~ über etw.** (*Akk.*) **freuen** take a mischievous pleasure in sth.

**Diebstahl** /'di:p-ʃta:l/ *der;* **~[e]s, Diebstähle** /'di:p-ʃtɛ:lə/ theft; **einfacher ~:** theft; **schwerer ~:** burglary and theft; **räuberischer ~:** *robbery accompanied by use of violence to keep possession of the stolen property;* **[ein] geistiger ~:** plagiarism *no indef. art*

**Diebstahl·versicherung** *die* insurance against theft

**die·jenige, diejenigen** ⇨ **derjenige**

**Diele** /'di:lə/ *die;* **~, ~n** Ⓐ hall[way]; Ⓑ (*Fußbodenbrett*) floorboard

*old spelling (see note on page 1707)

**dielektrisch** /die'lɛktrɪʃ/ *Adj.* (*Physik, Elektrot.*) dielectric

**dielen** *tr. V.* lay floorboards in ‹room›; board ‹floor›

**Dielen·brett** *das* floorboard

**dienen** /'di:nən/ *itr. V.* Ⓐ be in service; **jmdm. ~:** serve sb.; **als Magd ~:** serve as a maid; **der Gerechtigkeit ~** (*geh.*) serve the cause of justice; **bei Hof ~:** wait *or* serve at court; ⇨ *auch* **Herr**; Ⓑ (*veralt.: Militärdienst tun*) do military service; **beim Heer ~:** serve in the army; **acht Jahre ~:** do eight years' military service; ⇨ *auch* **gedient** 2; Ⓒ (*nützlich sein*) serve; **das dient einer guten Sache** it is in a good cause; **diese Maßnahmen ~ der Sicherheit am Arbeitsplatz** these measures help towards safety at work; Ⓓ (*helfen*) help (**in** + *Dat.* in); **womit kann ich ~?** what can I do for you?; can I help you?; **mit 20 DM wäre mir schon gedient** 20 marks would do; **damit ist mir wenig gedient** it's not much help *or* use to me; **damit kann ich leider nicht ~:** I'm afraid I can't help you there; Ⓔ (*verwendet werden*) serve; **als Museum ~:** serve *or* be used as a museum; **als Ersatz/Vorwand ~:** serve as a substitute/pretext; **das soll dir als Warnung ~:** let that serve as *or* be a warning to you; **zur Unterstützung einer Theorie ~:** serve to support a theory

**Diener** *der;* **~s, ~:** servant; **einen ~ machen** (*ugs.*); bow; make a bow; ⇨ *auch* **stumm**

**Dienerin** /'di:nərɪn/ *die;* **~, ~nen** maid; servant

**dienern** *itr. V.* (*abwertend*) bow; (*fig.*) bow and scrape

**Dienerschaft** *die;* **~:** servants *pl.;* domestic staff

**dienlich** *Adj.* helpful; useful; **jmdm./einer Sache ~ sein** be helpful *or* of help to sb./sth.; **kann ich Ihnen mit etwas ~ sein?** (*geh.*) can I be of any assistance to you?

**Dienst** /di:nst/ *der;* **~[e]s, ~e** Ⓐ (*Tätigkeit*) work; (*von Soldaten, Polizeibeamten, Krankenhauspersonal usw.*) duty; **seinen ~ antreten** start work/go on duty; **zum ~ gehen** go to work/go on duty; **~ haben** be at work/on duty; ‹doctor› be on call; ‹chemist› be open; **~ habend** *od.* **tuend** duty ‹officer›; ‹official, doctor› on duty; **außerhalb des ~es** outside work/when off duty; **im ~ sein** be at work/on duty; **nicht im ~ sein** not be at work/be off duty; **der Unteroffizier vom ~** (*Milit.*) the duty NCO; **der Chef vom ~** (*Zeitungsw.*) the duty editor; **~ ist ~ und Schnaps ist Schnaps** (*ugs.*) you shouldn't mix business and pleasure; Ⓑ (*Arbeitsverhältnis*) post; **den** *od.* **seinen ~ quittieren** resign one's post; (*Milit.*) leave the service; ‹officer› resign one's commission; **jmdn. aus dem ~/seinen ~en entlassen** dismiss sb.; **jmdn. in ~ nehmen** (*veralt.*) employ *or* engage sb.; **in jmds. ~[en] sein** *od.* **stehen** (*veralt.*) be in sb.'s employ; **Major** *usw.* **außer ~ [sein]** [be a] retired major *etc.;* **im ~ einer guten Sache** (*Gen.*) **stehen** be in a good cause; **sich in den ~ einer guten Sache** (*Gen.*) **stellen** devote oneself to a good cause; **etw. in ~ stellen** put sth. into service *or* commission; Ⓒ (*Tätigkeitsbereich*) service; **der höhere ~ der Beamtenlaufbahn** the senior civil service; ⇨ *auch* **öffentlich**; Ⓓ (*Hilfe*) **seine ~e [anbieten]** [offer] one's services; **jmdm. einen ~ tun** help sb.; **~ am Kunden** (*ugs.*) customer service; **seinen ~ tun** ‹machine, appliance› serve its purpose; **jmdm. gute ~e tun** serve sb. well; give sb. good service; **jmdm. mit etw. einen schlechten ~ erweisen** do sb. a disservice *or* a bad turn with sth.; **zu jmds. ~en** *od.* **jmdm. zu ~en sein** *od.* **stehen** (*geh.*) be at sb.'s disposal *or* service; **jmdm. den ~ versagen** fail sb.; Ⓔ (*Hilfs~, Spionage~*) [intelligence] service; (*Nachrichten~,*) service; Ⓕ (*Kunstwiss.*) respond

**-dienst** *der* service; **Schicht~:** shift work

**Dienst-: ~abteil** *das* (*Eisenb.*) guard's compartment; **~adel** *der* (*hist.*) *nobility whose titles derive from being in the king's service* **~ältest...** *Adj.* longest-serving

**Diens·tag** /di:ns-/ *der* ▶ 207, ▶ 833 Tuesday; **am ~:** on Tuesday; (*jeden ~*) on Tuesday; **~, der 1. Juni** Tuesday the first of June; Tuesday, 1 June; **am ~, dem 1. Juni** *od.* **den 1. Juni** on Tuesday 1 June *or* June 1st; **er kommt ~:** he is coming on Tuesday; **die letzten ~e** the last few Tuesdays; **eines ~s** one Tuesday; **den ganzen ~ über** all day Tuesday; the whole of Tuesday; **ab nächsten** *od.* **nächstem ~:** from next Tuesday [onwards]; **die Nacht von ~ auf** *od.* **zum Mittwoch** Tuesday night; **~ in einer Woche** *od.* **in acht Tagen** Tuesday week; a week on Tuesday; **~ vor einer Woche** a week last Tuesday; **~ früh** Tuesday morning; ⇨ *auch* **Dienstagabend, dienstagabends** *usw.*

**Dienstag·abend** *der* ▶ 833 Tuesday evening; Tuesday night (*coll.*); **[am] ~:** [on] Tuesday evening/night

**dienstag·abends** *Adv.* ▶ 833 [on] Tuesday evenings

**dienstägig** /'di:nstɛ:gɪç/ *Adj.* **die/unsere ~e Sendung** *usw.* Tuesday's programme *etc.;* the/our programme *etc.* on Tuesday

**dienstäglich** ▶ 833 ❶ *Adj.* [regular] Tuesday. ❷ *adv.* on Tuesday

**dienstag-, Dienstag-: ~mittag** *der* ▶ 833 Tuesday lunchtime; **~mittags** *Adv.* ▶ 833 Tuesday lunchtimes; **~morgen** *der* ▶ 833 Tuesday morning; **~morgens** *Adv.* ▶ 833 [on] Tuesday mornings; **~nachmittag** *der* ▶ 833 Tuesday afternoon; **~nachmittags** *Adv.* ▶ 833 [on] Tuesday afternoons; **~nacht** *die* ▶ 833 Tuesday night; **~nachts** *Adv.* ▶ 833 [on] Tuesday nights

**diens·tags** *Adv.* ▶ 833 on Tuesday[s]; **~abends/morgens** on Tuesday evening[s]/morning[s]; on a Tuesday evening/morning

**Dienstag·vormittag** *der* ▶ 833 Tuesday morning

**dienstag·vormittags** *Adv.* ▶ 833 [on] Tuesday mornings

**dienst-, Dienst-: ~alter** *das* length of service; **er hat ein ~alter von 6 Jahren** he has 6 years of service; **~älteste** *der/die* longest-serving person; **~an·tritt** *der* commencement of one's duties; **~an·weisung** *die* instruction; **laut ~anweisung** according to instructions *pl.;* **~auf·fassung** *die* conception of duty; **~auf·sicht** *die* supervision; **die ~aufsicht liegt bei ...** ... has supervisory responsibility; **~aufsichts·beschwerde** *die* complaint to the supervising authority (*about a public servant or government department*); **~ausweis** *der* [official] identity card; **~bar** *Adj.* **sich jmdm. ~bar erzeigen** (*veralt.*) show one's willingness to serve sb.; **ein ~barer Geist** (*ugs. scherzh.*) a ministering angel; **sich** (*Dat.*) **jmdn./etw. ~bar machen** get good service from sb./utilize sth.; **einer Sache** (*Dat.*) **jmdn./etw. ~bar machen** make sb./sth. serve sth.; **sich** (*Dat.*) **die Kräfte der Natur/die Atomenergie ~bar machen** harness the power of nature/atomic energy; **~barkeit** *die;* **~, ~en** Ⓐ (*geh.*) **jmdn. in seine ~barkeit bringen** bring sb. under one's power; **in jmds. ~barkeit geraten** come under sb.'s power; Ⓑ (*hist.*) bondage; servitude; Ⓒ (*jur.*) easement; **~beflissen** ❶ *Adj.* zealous; eager; ❷ *adv.* zealously; eagerly; **~beflissenheit** *die* zeal; eagerness; **~beginn** *der* start of work; **vor/nach/bei ~beginn** before/after/at the start of work; **~bereich** *der* area of responsibility; **~bereit** *Adj.* ‹chemist› open *pred.;* ‹doctor› on call *or* duty; ‹dentist› on duty; **die nächste ~bereite Apotheke** the nearest chemist that is/was open; **~bereitschaft** *die:* **~bereitschaft haben** ‹chemist› be open; ‹doctor› be on call *or* duty; ‹dentist› be on duty; **~bezüge** *Pl.* salary *sing.;* **~bote** *der* servant; **~boten·eingang** *der* tradesmen's entrance; **~bezeichnung** *die* title; **~eid** *der* official oath; **~eifer** *der* zeal; eagerness; **~eifrig** ❶ *Adj.* zealous; eager; ❷ *adv.* zealously; eagerly; **~enthebung** *die* suspension from duty; **~fähig** *Adj.* fit for work *postpos.;* (*Milit.*) fit for service *postpos.;* **~fahrt** *die* ⇨ **~reise**; **~frei** *Adj.* free ‹time›; **an ~freien Tagen** on days off; **~frei**

**haben/bekommen** have/get time off; **am Montag ~frei haben** have Monday off; **Heiligabend ist ~frei** Christmas Eve is a holiday; **~gebrauch** *der:* **nur für den ~gebrauch bestimmt** for official use only; **~geheimnis** *das* Ⓐ professional secret; (*im Staats~*) official secret; Ⓑ professional secrecy; (*im Staats~*) official secrecy; **unter das ~geheimnis fallen** be a professional/official secret; **~geschäfte** *Pl.* business *sing.;* **in ~geschäften** on business; (*von Beamten*) on official business; **~gespräch** *das* Ⓐ business meeting; (*von Beamten*) official meeting; Ⓑ (*Telefongespräch*) business call; (*von Beamten*) official call; **~grad** *der* (*Milit.*) rank; **~gradabzeichen** *das* (*Milit.*) insignia [of rank]; ***~habend** ⇒ **Dienst** A; **~habende** *der/die; adj. Dekl.* (*Offizier*) duty officer; (*Beamter/Arzt*) official/doctor on duty; **~herr** *der,* **~herrin** *die* employer; **~hund** *der* dog used for police/security work; **ein Polizist mit seinem ~hund** a policeman with his dog; **~jahr** *das* year of service; **~jubiläum** *das* anniversary; **anlässlich seines 25-jährigen ~jubiläums** to mark his completion of 25 years' service; **~kleidung** *die* uniform; **~kleidung tragen** wear a uniform; **~leister** *der;* **~~s, ~~, ~leisterin** *die;* **~~, ~~nen** Ⓐ (*Firma, auch DV*) service provider; Ⓑ (*Person*) worker in the service sector; **~leistung** *die* (*auch Wirtsch.*) service

**Dienstleistungs-: ~abend** *der* late opening evening; **~bereich** *der* (*Wirtsch.*) ⇒ **~sektor**; **~beruf** *der* (*Wirtsch.*) service[-sector] occupation; **~betrieb** *der* (*Wirtsch.*) business in the service sector; **~branche** *die* (*Wirtsch.*) Ⓐ service industry; Ⓑ ⇒ **~sektor**; **~gesellschaft** *die* (*Soziol.*) service economy; **~gewerbe** *das* (*Wirtsch.*) service industries *pl.;* **~job** *der* (*Wirtsch.*) service[-sector] job; **~sektor** *der* (*Wirtsch.*) service sector **~unternehmen** *das* (*Wirtsch.*) service enterprise; service business; **~zentrum** *das* (*Wirtsch.*) service centre

**dienstlich** ❶ *Adj.* Ⓐ business ‹call›; (*im Staatsdienst*) official ‹letter, call, etc.›; Ⓑ (*offiziell*) official; **~ werden** (*ugs.*) get businesslike and formal. ❷ *adv.* on business; (*im Staatsdienst*) on official business

**dienst-, Dienst-: ~mädchen** *das* (*veralt.*) maid; **~magd** *die* (*veralt.*) maid; **~mann** *der; Pl.:* **~männer** *od.* **~leute** (*veralt.*) porter; **~marke** *die* [police] identification badge; ≈ warrant card (*Brit.*) *or* (*Amer.*) ID card; **~mütze** *die* regulation cap; **~nehmer** *der;* **~~s, ~~, ~nehmerin** *die;* **~~, ~~nen** (*österr.*) ⇒ **Arbeitnehmer, Arbeitnehmerin**; **~ordnung** *die* official regulations *pl.;* **~personal** *das* servants *pl.;* (*in einem Hotel*) domestic staff; **~pflicht** *die* Ⓐ compulsory service; Ⓑ (*bei Beamten*) duty; **~pflichtig** *Adj.* liable for compulsory service *postpos.;* **~pistole** *die* service pistol; **~plan** *der* duty roster; **~rang** *der* (*Milit.*) rank; **~recht** *das* ≈ civil service law; **~rechtlich** ❶ *Adj.* ≈ under civil service law *postpos.;* ❷ *adv.* ≈ under civil service law; ≈ ‹regulated› by civil service law; **~reise** *die* business trip; **auf ~reise sein** be on a business trip *or* away on business; **~sache** *die* Ⓐ official matter; Ⓑ (*Schreiben*) official letter; Ⓒ (*Postw.*) item of official mail; (*Brief*) official letter; **~schluss, *~schluß** *der;* end of work; **um 17 Uhr ist ~schluss** work finishes at 5 o'clock; **nach ~schluss** after work; **~schluss haben** finish work/have finished work; **~schreiben** *das* official letter; **~stelle** *die* office; (*Abteilung*) department; **~stellen·leiter** *der,* **~stellen·leiterin** *die* office head; (*einer Abteilung*) department head; **~stempel** *der* official stamp; **~stunden** *Pl.* Ⓐ working hours; **während der ~stunden** during working hours; Ⓑ (*Öffnungszeiten*) **~stunden haben** be open; **~tauglich** *Adj.* (*Milit.*) fit for service *postpos.;* ***~tuend** ⇒ **Dienst** A; **~tuende** *der/die; adj. Dekl.* ⇒ **~habende**; **~unfähig** *Adj.* unfit for work *postpos.;* (*Milit.*) unfit for service *postpos.;* **~untauglich** *Adj.* (*Milit.*) unfit for service *postpos.;* **~vergehen** *das* offence against [official] regulations; **~verhältnis** *das: contractual relationship between employee and employer in the public service;* **ein ~verhältnis eingehen** become a public employee; **~verpflichten** *tr. V.* (*nur im Inf. u. 2. Part.*) conscript; **~vertrag** *der* contract of employment; **~vorschrift** *die* regulations *pl.;* (*Milit.*) service regulations; **~wagen** *der* official car; (*Geschäftswagen*) company car; **~weg** *der* proper *or* official channels *pl.;* **den ~weg gehen** *od.* **einhalten** go through the proper *or* official channels; **auf dem ~weg** through the proper *or* official channels; **~wohnung** *die* (*von Firmen*) company flat (*Brit.*) *or* (*Amer.*) apartment; (*von staatlichen Stellen*) government flat (*Brit.*) *or* (*Amer.*) apartment; (*vom Militär*) army/navy/air force flat (*Brit.*) *or* (*Amer.*) apartment; **~zeit** *die* Ⓐ period of service; **eine ~zeit von 40 Jahren** 40 years' service; Ⓑ (*tägliche Arbeitszeit*) working hours *pl.;* **außerhalb der ~zeit** outside working hours; **~zeugnis** *das* testimonial; **~zimmer** *das* office

**dies** /di:s/ ⇒ **dieser**

**dies·bezüglich** ❶ *Adj.* relating to *or* regarding this *postpos., not pred.* ❷ *adv.* regarding this; on this matter

**diese** /'di:zə/ ⇒ **dieser**

**Diesel** /'di:zl̩/ *der;* **~s, ~:** diesel

**die·selbe** ⇒ **derselbe**

**die·selbige** ⇒ **derselbige**

**Diesel-: ~kraft·stoff** *der* diesel fuel; **~lokomotive** *die* diesel locomotive; **~motor** *der* diesel engine; **~öl** *das* diesel oil

**dieser** /'di:zɐ/, **diese, dieses, dies** *Demonstrativpron.* Ⓐ *attr.* this; *Pl.* these; **dieses Buch/diese Bücher [da]** that book/those books [there]; **diesen Sommer/diese Weihnachten** this summer/this Christmas; **[zu] Anfang dieses Jahres/~ Woche** at the beginning of this year/this week; **in ~ Nacht wird es noch schneien/begann es zu schneien** it will snow tonight/it started to snow that night; **er hat ~ Tage Geburtstag** it's his birthday within the next few days; **ich habe ihn ~ Tage noch gesehen** I saw him the other day; **diese Inge ist doch ein Goldschatz/Idiot** that Inge is a treasure/an idiot, isn't she?; **wer ist denn diese Inge?** who is this Inge?; **diese Russen** these *or* those Russians; Ⓑ *selbstständig* **diese[r] [hier/da]** this one [here]/that one [there]; **diese** *Pl.* **[hier/da]** these [here]/those [there]; **dies alles** all this; **diese ..., jene ...** (*geh.*) the latter ..., the former ...; **dies und das,** (*geh.*) **dieses und jenes** this and that; **~ und jener** (*geh.*) (*einige*) some [people] *pl.;* (*ein paar*) a few [people] *pl.;* **~ oder jener** (*geh.*) (*der eine oder andere*) someone or other; (*mancher*) some people *pl.*

**dieser·art** (*geh.*) ❶ *indekl. Demonstrativpron.* of this/that kind *postpos..* ❷ *Adv.* in this/that way

**dieses** ⇒ **dieser**

**diesig** *Adj.* hazy

**dies-: ~jährig** *Adj.* this year's; **unser ~jähriges Treffen** our meeting this year; **~mal** *Adv.* this time; **~seitig** *Adj.* Ⓐ **das ~seitige Rheinufer** this side of the Rhine; **die ~seitigen Grenzdörfer** the villages on this side of the border; Ⓑ (*geh.*) worldly; secular ‹world›; **~seits** ❶ *Präp. mit Gen.* on this side of; ❷ *Adv.* **~seits von** on this side of

**Diesseits** *das;* **~: im ~:** in this world; **das ~:** this world

**Dietrich** /'di:trɪç/ *der;* **~s, ~e** picklock; (*Nachschlüssel*) skeleton key

**die·weil** (*veralt.*) ❶ *Konj.* Ⓐ (*zeitl.*) while; Ⓑ (*kausal*) because. ❷ *adv.* in the mean time *or* the mean while

**diffamatorisch** /dɪfama'to:rɪʃ/ *Adj.* (*geh.*) defamatory

**diffamieren** /dɪfa'mi:rən/ *tr. V.* defame; **~de Äußerungen** defamatory utterances

**Diffamierung** *die;* **~, ~en** defamation; (*Bemerkung*) defamatory statement; **eine ~ des Gegners** defamation of one's opponent's character

**Differential** *usw.* ⇒ **Differenzial** *usw.*

**Differenz** /dɪfə'rɛnt͜s/ *die;* **~, ~en** Ⓐ (*auch Math.*) difference; Ⓑ (*Meinungsverschiedenheit*) difference [of opinion]

**Differenz·betrag** *der* difference

**Differenzial** /dɪfərɛn't͜si̯a:l/ *das;* **~s, ~e** Ⓐ (*Math.*) differential; Ⓑ (*Technik*) differential [gear]

**Differenzial-: ~getriebe** *das* (*Technik*) differential [gear]; **~gleichung** *die* (*Math.*) differential equation; **~rechnung** *die* (*Math.*) differential calculus

**differenzier·bar** *Adj.* Ⓐ distinguishable; Ⓑ (*Math.*) differentiable

**differenzieren** ❶ *tr. V.* Ⓐ be discriminating in ‹judgement, opinion›; (*unterscheiden*) differentiate; Ⓑ (*Math.*) differentiate; Ⓒ (*DDR Landw.*) grade. ❷ *itr. V.* differentiate; make a distinction/distinctions (**zwischen** between); (*bei einem Urteil, einer Behauptung*) be discriminating; **genau ~:** make a precise distinction/precise distinctions. ❸ *refl. V.* ‹methods› become more subtly differentiated; ‹life, language› become more complex; ‹taste› become more sophisticated

**differenziert** ❶ *Adj.* subtly differentiated ‹methods, colours›; complex ‹life, language, person, emotional life›; sophisticated ‹taste›; diverse ‹range›; **ein sehr ~er Bericht** a precise and subtle analysis. ❷ *adv.* **~ urteilen** be discriminating in one's judgement; **etw. ~ darlegen** give a precise and subtle analysis of sth.

**Differenziertheit** *die;* **~** ⇒ **differenziert** 1: differentiation; complexity; sophistication; diversity

**Differenzierung** *die;* **~, ~en** (*von Methoden*) greater differentiation; (*des Lebens, der Sprache*) greater complexity; (*des Geschmacks*) greater sophistication

**Differenz·menge** *die* (*Math.*) **die ~ A\B** the complement of the set B relative to A

**differieren** /dɪfə'ri:rən/ *itr. V.* (*geh.*) differ (**um** by)

**diffizil** /dɪfi't͜si:l/ *Adj.* (*geh.*) difficult; (*kompliziert*) complex; (*peinlich genau*) meticulous

**diffus** /dɪ'fu:s/ ❶ *Adj.* Ⓐ (*Physik, Chemie*) diffuse; Ⓑ (*geh.*) vague; vague and confused ‹idea, statement, etc.›. ❷ *adv.* in a vague and confused way

**Diffusion** /dɪfu'zi̯o:n/ *die;* **~, ~en** (*Physik, Chemie*) diffusion

**Digestivum** /digɛs'ti:vʊm/ *das;* **~s, Digestiva** Ⓐ digestive; digestant; Ⓑ (*Chemie*) digestive

**digital** /digi'ta:l/ (*DV*) ❶ *Adj.* digital. ❷ *adv.* digitally

**Digital·anzeige** *die* digital display

**digitalisieren** *tr. V.* (*DV*) digitalize

**Digital-: ~rechner** *der* (*DV*) digital computer; (*Taschenrechner*) digital calculator; **~uhr** *die* digital clock; (*Armbanduhr*) digital watch

**Dikta** ⇒ **Diktum**

**Diktaphon** /dɪkta'fo:n/ *das;* **~s, ~e** Dictaphone ®

**Diktat** /dɪk'ta:t/ *das;* **~[e]s, ~e** Ⓐ dictation; **nach ~ schreiben** take dictation; **etw. nach ~ schreiben** write/type sth. from dictation; Ⓑ (*das Diktierte*) dictation; **ein ~ aufnehmen** take dictation; Ⓒ (*Schulw.*) dictation; Ⓓ (*geh.: Befehl*) dictate; (*Politik*) diktat; **das ~ der Mode** the dictates *pl.* of fashion

**Diktator** /dɪk'ta:tɔr/ *der;* **~s, ~en** /-'to:rən/, **Diktatorin** *die;* **~, ~nen** (*auch fig.*) dictator

**diktatorisch** ❶ *Adj.* (*auch fig.*) dictatorial. ❷ *adv.* (*auch fig.*) dictatorially

**Diktatur** /dɪkta'tu:ɐ̯/ *die;* **~, ~en** (*auch fig.*) dictatorship

**diktieren** /dɪk'tieren/ *tr. V.* dictate

**Diktier·gerät** *das* dictating machine

**Diktion** /dɪk't͜si̯o:n/ *die;* **~, ~en** (*geh.*) style and diction

**Diktionär** /dɪkt͜si̯o'nɛ:ɐ̯/ *das od. der;* **~s, ~e** (*veralt.*) dictionary

d

**Diktum** /ˈdɪktʊm/ *das;* **~s, Dịkta** (*geh.*) Ⓐ dictum; Ⓑ (*veralt.: Entscheid*) dictum; pronouncement

**dilatorisch** /dilaˈto:rɪʃ/ (*geh.*) ❶ *Adj.* dilatory. ❷ *adv.* dilatorily; in a dilatory manner

**Dilemma** /diˈlɛma/ *das;* **~s, ~s** *od.* **Dilemmata** dilemma

**Dilettant** /dilɛˈtant/ *der;* **~en, ~en, Dilettạntin** *die;* **~, ~nen** (*auch abwertend*) dilettante

**dilettạntisch** (*abwertend*) ❶ *Adj.* dilettante; amateurish. ❷ *adv.* amateurishly

**Dilettantịsmus** *der;* **~** (*meist abwertend*) dilettantism; amateurism

**dilettieren** /dilɛˈti:rən/ *itr. V.* (*geh.*) dabble

**Dill** /dɪl/ *der;* **~[e]s, ~e,** *österr. auch:* **Dịlle** *die;* **~, ~n** (*Gattung*) Anethum; **Echter ~:** dill

**Diluvium** /diˈlu:vi̯ʊm/ *das;* **~s** (*Geol. veralt.*) **das ~:** the Pleistocene

**Dimension** /dimɛnˈzi̯o:n/ *die;* **~, ~en** (*Physik, fig.*) dimension

**-dimensional** /dimɛnzi̯oˈna:l/ *Adj.* -dimensional; **mehr~/drei~:** multi-/three-dimensional

**dimensionịeren** *tr. V.* (*Technik*) dimension

**Diminuendo** /dimiˈnu̯ɛndo/ *das;* **~s, ~s** *od.* **Diminuẹndi** (*Musik*) diminuendo

**diminutiv** /diminuˈti:f/ *Adj.* (*Sprachw.*) diminutive

**Diminutịv** *das;* **~s, ~e** (*Sprachw.*) diminutive

**Dimmer** /ˈdɪmɐ/ *der;* **~s, ~** (*Elektrot.*) dimmer

**DIN** /di:n/ *Abk.* **Deutsche Industrie-Norm[en]** *German Industrial Standard[s];* DIN; **DIN-Format** DIN size; **DIN-A4-Format** A4

**dinarisch** /diˈna:rɪʃ/ *Adj.* Dinaric

**Diner** /diˈne:/ *das;* **~s, ~s** Ⓐ (*geh.*) [formal] dinner; Ⓑ (*Abendessen*) dinner

**Ding**[1] /dɪŋ/ *das;* **~[e]s, ~e** Ⓐ (*Gegenstand, Objekt*) thing; **das ~ an sich** (*Philos.*) the thing-in-itself; **die Welt der ~e** (*Philos.*) the world of material objects; **jedes ~ hat zwei Seiten** there are two sides to everything; ⇒ *auch* **Namen**; Ⓑ *Pl.* (*Ereignisse*) things; **nach Lage der ~e** the way things are; **wie die ~ stehen** as things stand; **über den ~en stehen** be above such things; ⇒ *auch* **harren**; Ⓒ *Pl.* (*Angelegenheiten*) matters; **persönliche/private ~e** personal/private matters; **in ~en des Geschmacks** in matters of taste; **wie ich die ~e sehe** as I see things *or* matters; **reden wir von anderen ~en** let's talk about something else; **gut ~ will Weile haben** it takes time to do a thing well; **die letzten ~e** the last things; **ein ~ der Unmöglichkeit sein** be quite impossible; **das geht nicht mit rechten ~en zu** there's something funny about it; **vor allen ~en** above all; Ⓓ **guter ~e sein** (*geh.*) be in good spirits; Ⓔ (*Hist.*) ⇒ **Thing**

**Ding**[2] *das;* **~[e]s, ~er** Ⓐ (*ugs.: Gegenstand, Sache*) thing; **das ist ja ein ~!** that's really something; **ein ~ drehen** ‹criminal› pull a job (*sl.*); **jmdm. ein ~ verpassen** (*salopp*) clout sb. one (*coll.*); **mach keine ~er!** stop having me on (*Brit. coll.*); stop putting me on (*Amer. coll.*); Ⓑ (*ugs.: Mädchen*) thing; creature; Ⓒ (*salopp: Penis*) thing (*coll.*); tool (*sl.*)

**dịngen** *unr. tr. V.* Ⓐ (*geh.*) hire; **ein gedungener Schreiberling** a mercenary hack; **ein gedungener Mörder** a hired killer; Ⓑ (*veralt.: anstellen*) hire; take on

**dịng·fest** *in* **jmdn. ~ machen** arrest *or* apprehend sb.

**Dinghi, Dingi** /ˈdɪŋgi/ *das;* **~s, ~s** dinghy

**dịnglich** *Adj.* Ⓐ real; **die ~e Welt** the material world; the world of objects; Ⓑ (*Rechtsspr.*) real ‹right, security, etc.›

**Dings**[1] /dɪŋs/ *der/die;* **~** (*ugs.: Mensch*) thingamy (*coll.*); thingumajig (*coll.*); what's-his-name/-her-name

**Dịngs**[2] *das;* **~** (*ugs.*) Ⓐ (*Gegenstand*) thingamy (*coll.*); thingumajig (*coll.*) what-d'you-call-it; Ⓑ (*Ort*) what's-its-name; what's-it-called

**Dịngs·bums** /-bʊms/ *der/die/das* ⇒ **Dings**[1], **Dings**[2]

**Dịng·wort** *das; Pl.* **Dingwörter** naming word

**dinieren** /diˈni:rən/ *itr. V.* (*geh.*) dine

**Dinkel** /ˈdɪŋkl/ *der;* **~s, ~** (*Landw.*) spelt

**Dinner** /ˈdɪnɐ/ *das;* **~s, ~[s]** dinner

**Dịno** *der;* **~s, ~s** (*ugs.*) dinosaur

**Dinosaurier** /dinoˈzau̯ri̯ɐ/ *der;* **~s, ~** dinosaur

**Diode** /diˈo:də/ *die;* **~, ~n** (*Elektrot.*) diode

**Diọden·rücklicht** *das* LED rear light

**Diolen** Ⓦⓩ /di̯oˈle:n/ *das;* **~s** (*Textilind.*) Terylene ®

**dionysisch** /di̯oˈny:zɪʃ/ ❶ *Adj.* Dionysiac; Dionysian. ❷ *adv.* Dionysiacally

**Diopter** /diˈɔptɐ/ *das;* **~s, ~** (*am Gewehr*) [optical] sight; (*an einer Kamera*) [direct-vision] frame finder

**Dioptrie** /diɔpˈtri:/ *die;* **~, ~n** (*Optik*) dioptre

**Dioskuren** /di̯ɔsˈku:rən/ *Pl.* (*geh.*) heavenly twins; inseparable friends

**Dioxid** /ˈdi:|ɔksi:t/ *das;* **~s, ~e, Dioxyd** /ˈdi:|ɔksy:t/ *das;* **~s, ~e** (*Chemie*) dioxide

**Dioxin** /ˈdi:|ɔksi:n/ *das;* **~s** (*Chemie*) dioxin

**Diözesạn** *der;* **~en, ~en** member of the/a diocese

**Diözese** /diøˈtse:zə/ *die;* **~, ~n** diocese

**Diphtherie** /dɪfteˈri:/ *die;* **~, ~n** ▶ 474 (*Med.*) diphtheria

**diphthẹrisch** *Adj.* (*Med.*) diphtherial

**Diphthong** /dɪfˈtɔŋ/ *der;* **~s, ~e** (*Sprachw.*) diphthong

**diphthongieren** /dɪftɔŋˈgi:rən/ *tr. V.* (*Sprachw.*) diphthongize

**Diphthongịerung** *die;* **~, ~en** (*Sprachw.*) diphthongization

**diphthọngisch** (*Sprachw.*) ❶ *Adj.* diphthongal. ❷ *adv.* **etw. ~ aussprechen** pronounce sth. as a diphthong

**Dipl.-Ing.** *Abk.* **Diplomingenieur** *academically qualified engineer*

**Dipl.-Kfm.** *Abk.* **Diplomkaufmann** *holder of a diploma in commerce*

**Dipl.-Landw.** *Abk.* **Diplomlandwirt** *holder of a diploma in agriculture*

**diploid** /diploˈi:t/ *Adj.* (*Biol.*) diploid

**Diplom** /diˈplo:m/ *das;* **~s, ~e** Ⓐ ≈ [first] degree (*in a scientific or technical subject*); (*für einen Handwerksberuf*) diploma; **sein ~ machen** do one's *or* a degree/diploma; Ⓑ (*Urkunde*) ≈ degree certificate (*in a scientific or technical subject*); (*für einen Handwerksberuf*) diploma

**Diplom-:** qualified

**Diplọm·arbeit** *die* ≈ degree dissertation (*for a first degree in a scientific or technical subject*); (*für einen Handwerksberuf*) dissertation [submitted for a/the diploma]

**Diplomat** /diploˈma:t/ *der;* **~en, ~en** ▶ 159 (*auch fig.*) diplomat

**Diplomạten-:** **~gepäck** *das* diplomatic bags *pl.*; **~koffer** *der* attaché case; executive case; **~pass,** ***~paß** *der* diplomatic passport; **~viertel** *das* embassy district

**Diplomatie** /diplomaˈti:/ *die;* **~** Ⓐ diplomacy; Ⓑ (*die Diplomaten*) diplomatic corps

**Diplomạtin** *die;* **~, ~nen** ▶ 159 (*auch fig.*) diplomat

**diplomạtisch** (*auch fig.*) ❶ *Adj.* diplomatic. ❷ *adv.* diplomatically

**diplomịeren** *tr. V.* (*Hochschulw.*) **jmdn. ~:** award sb. a degree/diploma

**diplomịert** *Adj.* qualified

**Diplọm-:** **~ingenieur** *der,* **~ingenieurin** *die* ▶ 91, ▶ 159 (*academically*) qualified engineer; **~prüfung** *die* ≈ degree examination (*in a scientific or technical subject*); (*für einen Handwerksberuf*) diploma examination

**Dipol** /ˈdi:po:l/ *der;* **~s, ~e** (*Physik, Antenne*) dipole

**Dịpol·antenne** *die* dipole antenna

**dippen** /ˈdɪpn̩/ *tr. V.* (*Seemannsspr.*) dip ‹flag›

**dir** /di:ɐ̯/ ❶ *Dat. des Personalpron.* **du** to you; (*nach Präpositionen*) you; **ich gab es ~:** I gave it to you; **ich gab ~ das Buch** I gave you the book; **Freunde von ~:** friends of yours; **gehen wir zu ~:** let's go to your place; ⇒ *auch* **mir** 1 A, B. ❷ *Dat. des Reflexivpron. der 2. Pers. Sg.* yourself; **hast du ~ seine Vorschläge genau überlegt?** have you given careful thought to his suggestions?; **hast du ~ gedacht, dass ...** did you think that ...; **du willst ~ ein neues Kleid kaufen** you want to buy yourself a new dress; **nimm ~ noch von dem Braten** help yourself to some more roast

**direkt** /diˈrɛkt/ ❶ *Adj.* direct. ❷ *adv.* Ⓐ (*geradewegs*) straight; directly; Ⓑ (*sofort*) directly; straight; **etw. ~ übertragen** broadcast sth. live; Ⓒ (*nahe*) directly; **~ am Marktplatz** right by the market square; Ⓓ (*unmittelbar*) direct; **sich ~ mit jmdm. verbinden lassen** get a direct line to sb.; Ⓔ (*unverblümt*) directly; Ⓕ (*ugs.: geradezu*) really; really, positively ‹dangerous, witty›

**Dirẹkt·flug** *der* direct flight

**Dirẹktheit** *die;* **~:** directness

**Direktion** /dirɛkˈtsi̯o:n/ *die;* **~, ~en** Ⓐ management; (*von gemeinnützigen, staatlichen Einrichtungen*) administration; Ⓑ (*die Geschäftsleiter*) management; Ⓒ (*Büroräume*) managers' offices *pl.*

**Direktiọns-:** **~assistent** *der,* **~assistentin** *die* management trainee; **~sekretärin** *die* manager's secretary

**Direktive** /dirɛkˈti:və/ *die;* **~, ~n** (*geh.*) directive

**Dirẹkt·mandat** *das* (*Politik*) **[über] ~:** [by] direct mandate

**Direktor** /diˈrɛktɔr/ *der;* **~s, ~en** ▶ 91, ▶ 159 /...ˈto:rən/ Ⓐ (*einer Schule*) headmaster; (*eines Hochschulinstituts*) director; (*einer Fachschule o. dergl.*) principal; Ⓑ (*einer gemeinnützigen Einrichtung*) director; (*einer Strafanstalt*) governor; Ⓒ (*Wirtsch.*) director; manager; (*einer bestimmten Abteilung*) manager

**Direktorat** /dirɛktoˈra:t/ *das;* **~[e]s, ~e** Ⓐ (*Amt, Amtszeit*) (*einer Schule*) headship; (*gemeinnütziger Einrichtungen*) directorship; Ⓑ (*Dienstzimmer*) headmaster's/headmistress's office

**Direktọren·sessel** *der* (*ugs.*) directorship; managership

**direktorial** /dirɛktoˈri̯a:l/ *Adj.* directorial

**Direktorin** /dirɛkˈto:rɪn/ *die;* **~, ~nen** ▶ 91, ▶ 159 Ⓐ (*einer Schule*) headmistress; (*eines Hochschulinstituts*) director; (*einer Fachschule o. dergl.*) principal; Ⓑ ⇒ **Direktor** B, C; ⇒ *auch* **-in**

**Direktorium** /dirɛkˈto:ri̯ʊm/ *das;* **~s, Direktọrien** board of directors

**Direktrice** /dirɛkˈtri:sə/ *die;* **~, ~n** head designer; (*in einem Einzelhandelsgeschäft*) manageress

**Dirẹkt-:** **~saft** *der* juice direct from the fruit; **~sendung** *die* ⇒ **~übertragung**; **~student** *der,* **~studentin** *die* (*DDR*) campus student; **~studium** *das* (*DDR*) campus course; **~übertragung** *die* live transmission *or* broadcast; **~verbindung** *die* Ⓐ (*Eisenb.*) direct connection; through train; (*Flugw.*) direct flight; Ⓑ (*Fernspr.*) direct [telephone] connection; **~wahl** *die* Ⓐ **in** *od.* **durch ~wahl** by direct election; Ⓑ (*Fernspr.*) direct dialling

**Direx**[1] /ˈdi:rɛks/ *der;* **~, ~e, Dịrex**[2] *die;* **~, ~en** (*Schülerspr.*) head

**Dirigent** /diriˈgɛnt/ *der;* **~en, ~en** ▶ 159 conductor

**Dirigẹnten-:** **~pult** *das* conductor's rostrum; **~stab** *der,* **~stock** *der* [conductor's] baton

**Dirigẹntin** *die;* **~, ~nen** ▶ 159 conductor

**dirigieren** /diriˈgi:rən/ *tr. V.* Ⓐ *auch itr.* conduct; Ⓑ (*führen*) steer ‹person›; **jmdn. an einen Ort ~:** send sb. to a place; Ⓒ run ‹business, company›; Ⓓ (*lenken*) steer ‹vehicle›; (*fahren*) drive

**Dirigismus** /diriˈgɪsmʊs/ *der;* **~** (*Wirtsch.*) dirigisme

**dirigịstisch** *Adj.* (*Wirtsch.*) dirigiste

**Dirn** /dɪrn/ *die;* **~, ~en** Ⓐ (*bayr., österr.*) maid; Ⓑ (*nordd.*) girl; lass (*esp. Scot.*)

---

*old spelling (see note on page 1707)

**Dirndl** /ˈdɪrndl̩/ *das;* ~s, ~: dirndl

**Dirndl·kleid** *das* dirndl

**Dirne** /ˈdɪrnə/ *die;* ~, ~n **A** prostitute; **B** (*veralt.: Mädchen*) girl; lass (*esp. Scot.*)

**Dirnen·viertel** *das* red-light district

**Dis** /dɪs/ *das;* ~, ~ (*Musik*) D sharp

**Disagio** /dɪsˈ|a:dʒo/ *das;* ~s (*Finanzw.*) disagio

**Discjockey** /ˈdɪskdʒɔke/ *der* ⇒ **Diskjockey**

**Disco** /ˈdɪsko:/ *die;* ~, ~s disco

**Discount-:** /dɪsˈkaunt/ discount; **~geschäft/~preis** discount shop/price

**Dis-Dur** *das* (*Musik*) D sharp major; ⇒ *auch* **A-Dur**

**Disengagement** /dɪsɪnˈgeɪdʒmənt/ *das;* ~s (*Politik*) disengagement

**Disharmonie** /*auch:* ˈ----/ *die* **A** (*Musik*) disharmony; discord; dissonance; **B** (*von Farben*) clash; **C** (*geh.: Uneinigkeit*) disagreement; disharmony *no indef. art.;* **solche ~n** such disharmony *sing. or* disagreements

**disharmonieren** *itr. V.* **A** (*Musik*) be discordant *or* dissonant; **B** ‹colours› clash; **C** (*geh.: uneinig sein*) disagree

**disharmonisch** *Adj.* **A** (*Musik*) disharmonious; discordant; dissonant; **B** (*nicht zusammenstimmend*) clashing ‹colours›; **C** (*geh.: uneinig*) disharmonious

**Disjunktion** /dɪsjʊŋkˈtsi̯o:n/ *die;* ~, ~en (*Logik*) disjunction

**disjunktiv** /dɪsjʊŋkˈti:f/ *Adj.* (*Sprachw.*) disjunctive

**Diskant** /dɪsˈkant/ *der;* ~s, ~e **A in einen schneidenden ~ umschlagen** ‹voice› become gratingly shrill; **B** (*einer Singstimme, beim Klavier*) treble; **C** (*beim Cantus firmus*) descant

**Diskette** /dɪsˈkɛtə/ *die;* ~, ~n (*DV*) floppy disc

**Disketten·lauf·werk** *das* (*DV*) [floppy-]disc drive

**Disk·jockey** /ˈdɪskdʒɔke/ *der* disc jockey

**Disko** ⇒ **Disco**

**Diskont** /dɪsˈkɔnt/ *der;* ~s, ~e (*Finanzw.*) **A** discount; **B** discount rate

**Diskonten** *Pl.* (*Finanzw.*) inland *or* domestic bills of exchange

**Diskont·erhöhung** *die* (*Finanzw.*) raising of the discount rate

**diskontieren** *tr. V.* (*Finanzw.*) discount

**Diskontinuität** *die;* ~, ~en **A** discontinuity; **B** (*Politik*) *principle that bills not passed before the end of a legislative period must be reintroduced in the next parliament*

**Diskont·satz** *der* (*Finanzw.*) discount rate

**Diskothek** /dɪskoˈte:k/ *die;* ~, ~en **A** (*Tanzlokal*) discothèque; **B** (*Schallplatten*) record collection; **C** (*Raum für Schallplatten*) record library

**diskreditieren** /dɪskrediˈti:rən/ *tr. V.* discredit

**Diskrepanz** /dɪskreˈpants/ *die;* ~, ~en discrepancy (**zwischen** between)

**diskret** /dɪsˈkre:t/ **1** *Adj.* **A** (*vertraulich*) confidential ‹discussion, report›; (*unauffällig*) discreet ‹action›; **B** (*taktvoll*) tactful ‹behaviour, reserve›; **sie ist sehr ~:** she is very discreet; **C** (*dezent*) quiet ‹colour, elegance›; subtle ‹perfume›; **D** (*Technik, Physik, Math.*) discrete. **2** *adv.* **A** (*vertraulich*) confidentially; **etw. ~ behandeln** treat sth. in confidence; **B** (*taktvoll*) tactfully; **sich ~ zurückziehen** retire discreetly; **C** (*dezent*) discreetly; **~ gemustert sein** have a subdued pattern

**Diskretion** /dɪskreˈtsi̯o:n/ *die;* ~ **A** (*Verschwiegenheit, Takt*) discretion; **in einer Angelegenheit äußerste/strengste ~ wahren** treat a matter in the strictest confidence; **~ [ist] Ehrensache** you can rely on my discretion; **B** (*Unaufdringlichkeit*) discreetness

**diskriminieren** /dɪskrimiˈni:rən/ *tr. V.* **A** (*herabwürdigen*) disparage; **B** (*benachteiligen*) discriminate against

**Diskriminierung** *die;* ~, ~en **A** discrimination (**von** against); **B** (*Handlung*) act of discrimination; (*Äußerung*) discriminatory remark

**Diskurs** /dɪsˈkʊrs/ *der;* ~es, ~e **A** (*Abhandlung*) discourse; **B** (*geh.: Unterhaltung*) discourse *no indef. art.* (*literary*); conversation; **einen ~ [mit jmdm.] haben/führen** have *or* hold a conversation [with sb.]; **C** (*Wortwechsel*) exchange [of words]; altercation; **D** (*Sprachw.*) discourse

**diskursiv** /dɪskʊrˈzi:f/ (*Philos.*) **1** *Adj.* discursive. **2** *adv.* discursively

**Diskus** /ˈdɪskʊs/ *der;* ~ *od.* ~ses, **Disken** *od.* ~se (*Leichtathletik*) discus

**Diskussion** /dɪskʊˈsi̯o:n/ *die;* ~, ~en discussion; (*Gesprächsrunde, Tagesgespräch*) discussion; debate; **etw. zur ~ stellen** put sth. up for discussion; **[nicht] zur ~ stehen** [not] be under discussion

**Diskussions-:** **~abend** *der* discussion [evening]; **~beitrag** *der* contribution to a/the discussion; **~grund·lage** *die* basis of a/the discussion; **als ~grundlage dienen** serve as a basis for [a/the] discussion; **~leiter** *der,* **~leiterin** *die* chairman [of the discussion]; **~teilnehmer** *der,* **~teilnehmerin** *die* participant [in a/the discussion]

**Diskus-:** **~werfen** *das;* ~~s (*Leichtathletik*) [throwing the] discus; **das ~werfen ist ...** [throwing] the discus is ...; **die Meisterschaften im ~werfen** the discus championships; **~werfer** *der,* **~werferin** *die* discus-thrower; **~wurf** *der* (*Leichtathletik*) **A** (*Disziplin*) throwing the discus; **beim ~wurf** in the discus; **B** (*einzelner Wurf*) [discus] throw

**diskutabel** /dɪskuˈta:bl̩/ *Adj.,* **diskutierbar** *Adj.* **[äußerst] ~:** [very well] worth considering *or* discussing *postpos.*

**diskutieren** /dɪskuˈti:rən/ **1** *itr. V.* **über etw.** (*Akk.*) **~:** discuss sth.; **darüber wird viel zu viel diskutiert** there's much too much discussion about that; **darüber lässt sich ~:** that's debatable; **wir haben stundenlang diskutiert** our discussion went on for hours. **2** *tr. V.* discuss

**dis-Moll** *das* (*Musik*) D sharp minor; ⇒ *auch* **a-Moll**

**disparat** *Adj.* disparate

**Dispatcher** /dɪsˈpɛtʃɐ/ *der;* ~s, ~, **Dispatcherin** *die;* ~, ~nen (*DDR Technik*) controller

**Dispens** /dɪsˈpɛns/ *der;* ~es, ~e (*österr. u. kath. Kirche nur:*) *die;* ~, ~en (*bes. kath. Kirche*) dispensation (**von** from)

**dispensieren** *tr. V.* (*auch fig.*) dispense (*form., Eccl.*), excuse (**von** from)

**Dispensierung** *die;* ~, ~en **A** (*Befreiung*) dispensation (*form., Eccl.*), exemption (**von** from); **B** (*Pharm.*) dispensing; **Wartezeit bei ~en** waiting period for dispensed *or* made-up prescriptions

**Dispersion** /dɪspɛrˈzi̯o:n/ *die;* ~, ~en (*Physik, Chemie*) dispersion

**Dispersions·farbe** *die* emulsion paint

**Disponent** /dɪspoˈnɛnt/ *der;* ~en, ~en **A** (*Wirtsch.*) junior departmental manager; **B** (*am Theater*) manager

**Disponentin** *die;* ~, ~nen **A** (*Wirtsch.*) junior departmental manager; **B** (*am Theater*) manageress

**disponibel** /dɪspoˈni:bl/ *Adj.* (*verfügbar*) available; (*vielseitig einsetzbar*) versatile

**disponieren** *itr. V.* **A** (*verfügen*) **über jmdn./etw. ~** (*zur Verfügung haben*) have sb./sth. at one's disposal; **nach Belieben über jmdn./etw. ~:** do just as one wishes *or* likes with sb./sth.; **B** (*vorausplanen*) plan ahead

**disponiert** *Adj.* **A gut/schlecht ~ sein** be in good form *or* on form/be in bad form *or* off form; **B** (*Med.*) **für** *od.* **zu etw. ~ sein** be disposed to sth.

**Disposition** /dɪspoziˈtsi̯o:n/ *die;* ~, ~en **A** (*Verfügungsgewalt*) right of disposal; **jmdm. zur** *od.* **zu jmds. ~ stehen** be at sb.'s disposal; **jmdm. etw. zur ~ stellen** place sth. at sb.'s disposal; **jmdn. zur ~ stellen** (*Amtsspr.*) suspend sb.; **B** (*Planung*) arrangement; **~en treffen** make arrangements; **C** (*Gliederung*) plan; **D** (*Med.: Anlage*) disposition (**zu, für** to)

**Dispositions·kredit** *der* (*Finanzw.*) overdraft facility

**Disput** /dɪsˈpu:t/ *der;* ~[e]s, ~e (*geh.*) dispute, argument (**über** + *Akk.* about)

**disputabel** /dɪspuˈta:bl̩/ *Adj.* (*geh.*) disputable

**Disputation** /dɪsputaˈtsi̯o:n/ *die;* ~, ~en (*Hochschulw., geh.: Streit*) disputation

**disputieren** *itr. V.* (*geh.*) discuss; (*streiten*) dispute; **über etw.** (*Akk.*) **~:** discuss/dispute sth.

**Disqualifikation** *die* (*auch Sport*) disqualification

**disqualifizieren** *tr. V.* (*auch Sport*) disqualify

**Disqualifizierung** *die;* ~, ~en (*auch Sport*) disqualification

**Diss.** *Abk.* **Dissertation** diss.

**Dissens** /dɪˈsɛns/ *der;* ~es, ~e (*geh.*) dissent *no indef. art.;* disagreement (**über** + *Akk.* over)

**Dissertation** /dɪsɛrtaˈtsi̯o:n/ *die;* ~, ~en [doctoral] dissertation *or* thesis

**Dissident** /dɪsiˈdɛnt/ *der;* ~en, ~en, **Dissidentin,** *die;* ~, ~nen dissident; (*Rel.*) nonbeliever

**Dissimilation** /dɪsimilaˈtsi̯o:n/ *die;* ~, ~en (*Sprachw., Biol.*) dissimilation

**dissimilieren** *tr. V.* (*Sprachw., Biol.*) dissimilate

**dissonant** /dɪsoˈnant/ *Adj.* (*Musik*) dissonant

**Dissonanz** /dɪsoˈnants/ *die;* ~, ~en (*Musik*) dissonance

**Distanz** /dɪsˈtants/ *die;* ~, ~en **A** (*Abstand*) distance; **in einiger ~:** some distance away; **~ zu etw. gewinnen** (*fig.*) distance oneself from sth.; **B** (*Rangunterschied, Zurückhaltung*) **~ wahren** *od.* **halten** keep one's distance; **die soziale ~:** the social gap; **auf ~ bleiben** *od.* **gehen** keep one's distance; **C** (*Leichtathletik, Rennsport*) distance; **gegen Ende der ~:** towards the end of the race; **D** (*Boxen: Abstand, Rundenzahl*) distance; **jmdn. auf ~ halten** keep sb. at long range

**distanzieren** **1** *refl. V.* **sich von jmdm./etw. ~:** dissociate oneself from sb./sth. **2** *tr. V.* (*Sport: überrunden*) outdistance, outpace (**um** by); (*schlagen*) beat (**um** by)

**distanziert** **1** *Adj.* distant; reserved; reserved ‹politeness›. **2** *adv.* in a distant *or* reserved manner; with reserve

**Distel** /ˈdɪstl̩/ *die;* ~, ~n thistle

**Distel·fink** *der* goldfinch

**Distichon** /ˈdɪstɪçɔn/ *das;* ~s, **Distichen** (*Verslehre*) distich

**distinguiert** /dɪstɪŋˈgi:ɐ̯t/ (*geh.*) **1** *Adj.* distinguished. **2** *adv.* in a distinguished manner

**Distribution** /dɪstribuˈtsi̯o:n/ *die;* ~, ~en (*auch Wirtsch., Math., Sprachw.*) distribution

**distributiv** /dɪstribuˈti:f/ *Adj.* (*Sprachw., Math.*) distributive

**Distrikt** /dɪsˈtrɪkt/ *der;* ~[e]s, ~e district; area; (*Bezirk*) district

**Disziplin** /dɪstsiˈpli:n/ *die;* ~, ~en **A** (*Ordnung*) discipline; **~ halten** keep discipline; (*sich diszipliniert verhalten*) behave in a disciplined way; **B** (*Selbstbeherrschung*) [self-]discipline; **C** (*Wissenschaftszweig, Sport*) discipline

**disziplinär** /dɪstsipliˈnɛ:ɐ̯/ (*bes. österr.*) **1** *Adj.* disciplinary. **2** *adv.* disciplinarily. **gegen jmdn. ~ vorgehen** take disciplinary action against sb.

**disziplinarisch** **1** *Adj.* **A** disciplinary; **B** (*streng*) severe. **2** *adv.* **A gegen jmdn. ~ vorgehen** take disciplinary action against sb.; **jmdm. ~ unterstellt sein** be answerable to sb. in matters of discipline; **B** (*streng*) **jmdn. ~ bestrafen** punish sb. severely

**Disziplinar-:** **~maßnahme** *die* disciplinary measure; **~strafe** *die* **A** (*Sport*) disciplinary penalty; **mit einer ~strafe rechnen**

**müssen** have to expect disciplinary action; **eine hohe ~strafe** a heavy fine; **er erhielt eine ~strafe von 100 DM** he was fined 100 marks; (B) *(Eishockey)* misconduct penalty; (C) *(veralt.)* disciplinary measure; **~verfahren** *das* disciplinary proceedings *pl.*

**disziplinieren** ❶ *tr. V.* discipline. ❷ *refl. V.* discipline oneself

**diszipliniert** ❶ *Adj.* (A) *(geordnet)* well-disciplined; (B) *(beherrscht)* disciplined. ❷ *adv.* (A) *(geordnet)* in a well-disciplined way; (B) *(beherrscht)* in a disciplined way

**Disziplinierung** *die;* ~, ~**en** disciplining *no indef. art.*

**disziplin-, Disziplin-:** ~**los** ❶ *Adj.* undisciplined; ❷ *adv.* in an undisciplined way; ~**losigkeit** *die;* ~ ~: lack of discipline; ~**schwierigkeiten** *Pl.* discipline problems; problems in maintaining discipline

**dithyrambisch** *Adj.* *(Literaturw.)* dithyrambic

**Dithyrambus** /dity'rambʊs/ *der;* ~, **Dithyramben** (A) *(Literaturw.)* dithyramb

**dito** /'di:to/ *Adv.* *(Kaufmannsspr., auch ugs.)* ditto

**Diuretikum** /diu're:tikʊm/ *das;* ~**s, Diuretika** *(Med.)* diuretic

**diuretisch** *Adj.* *(Med.)* diuretic

**Diva** /'di:va/ *die;* ~, ~**s** *u.* **Diven** (A) *(Künstlerin)* prima donna; diva; *(Film~)* great [film] star; (B) *(eingebildeter Mensch)* prima donna

**divergent** /divɛr'gɛnt/ ❶ *Adj.* *(auch fig., Math.)* divergent. ❷ *adv.* *(auch fig., Math.)* divergently; ~ **verlaufen** diverge

**Divergenz** /divɛr'gɛnts/ *die;* ~, ~**en** *(auch Math.)* divergence; *(Meinungsverschiedenheit)* divergence of opinion

**divergieren** *itr. V.* *(auch Math.)* diverge

**divers...** /di'vɛrs.../ *Adj.* various; *(von derselben Sorte)* several; **die ~esten ...** the most diverse ...

**Diversifikation** /divɛrzifika'tsio:n/ *die;* ~, ~**en** *(Wirtsch.)* diversification

**diversifizieren** /divɛrzifi'tsi:rən/ *tr., itr. V.* *(Wirtsch.)* diversify

**Diversion** /divɛr'zio:n/ *die;* ~, ~**en** *(bes. DDR)* subversion

**Divertimento** /divɛrti'mɛnto/ *das;* ~**s,** ~**s** *u.* **Divertimenti** *(Musik)* divertimento

**Divertissement** /divɛrtɪsə'mã:/ *das;* ~**s,** ~**s** *(Musik)* divertissement

**Dividend** /divi'dɛnt/ *der;* ~**en,** ~**en** *(Math.)* dividend

**Dividende** /divi'dɛndə/ *die;* ~, ~**n** *(Börsenw., Wirtsch.)* dividend

**Dividenden·ausschüttung** *die* *(Börsenw., Wirtsch.)* payment of the dividend/of dividends

**dividieren** /divi'di:rən/ *tr. V.* *(Math.)* divide

**Divis** /di'vi:s/ *das;* ~**es,** ~**e** *(Druckw.)* hyphen

**Division** /divi'zio:n/ *die;* ~, ~**en** *(Math., Milit.)* division

**Divisions·kommandeur** *der* *(Milit.)* divisional commander

**Divisor** /di'vi:zɔr/ *der;* ~**s,** ~**en** /-vi'zo:rən/ *(Math.)* divisor

**Diwan** /'di:va:n/ *der;* ~**s,** ~**e** *(veralt.: Sofa, Literaturw.: Gedichte)* divan

**Dixieland** /'dɪksɪlænd/ *der;* ~**[s]** Dixieland

**d. J.** *Abk.* (A) **dieses Jahres;** (B) **der/die Jüngere**

**DJH** *Abk.* **Deutscher Jugendherbergsverband** German Youth Hostel Association

**DKP** *Abk.* **Deutsche Kommunistische Partei** Communist Party of Germany

**DLRG** *Abk.* **Deutsche Lebens-Rettungs-Gesellschaft** German Life Saving Society

**dm** *Abk.* **Dezimeter** dm

**DM** *Abk.* **D-Mark, Deutsche Mark** DM

**D-Mark** /'de:-/ *die* Deutschmark

**d. M.** *Abk.* **dieses Monats** inst.; **am 13. ~:** on the thirteenth inst.

**d-Moll** /'de:-/~ *das* *(Musik)* D minor; ⇒ *auch* **a-Moll**

**DNS** *Abk.* *(Chemie)* **Desoxyribonukleinsäure** DNA

**do.** *Abk.* **dito** do.

**Do.** *Abk.* **Donnerstag** Thur[s].

**Dobermann** /'do:bɐman/ *der;* ~**s, Dobermänner** Dobermann [pinscher]

**doch** /dɔx/ ❶ *Konj.* but. ❷ *Adv.* (A) *(je~)* but; (B) *(dennoch)* all the same; still; *(trotzdem)* nevertheless; all the same; *(wider Erwarten)* after all; **aber ich habe ihn ~ erkannt** but I recognized him all the same; but I still recognized him; **und ~:** and yet; **aber die Ausstellung war ~ ganz interessant** but the exhibition was actually quite interesting; (C) *(geh.: weil)* **wusste er ~, dass ...** because he knew that ...; (D) *(als Antwort)* **Das kannst du nicht! — Doch!** You can't do that! — [Oh] yes I can!; **Das stimmt nicht! — Doch!** That's not right! — [Oh] yes it is!; **Hast du keinen Hunger? — Doch!** Aren't you hungry? — Yes [I am]!; **~ schon, aber ...** yes, I do/he does *etc.*, but ...; (E) *(Angezweifeltes richtig stellend: tatsächlich)* **er war also ~ der Mörder!** so he 'was the murderer!; **sie hat es also ~ gesagt** so she 'did say it; (F) *(etw. für unnütz erklärend)* in any case; **du kannst mir ~ nicht helfen** there's nothing you can do to help me. ❸ *Partikel* (A) *(auffordernd, Ungeduld, Empörung ausdrückend) oft nicht übersetzt* **das hättest du ~ wissen müssen** you [really] should have known that; **du hast ~ selbst gesagt, dass ...** *(rechtfertigend)* you did say yourself that ...; **gib mir ~ bitte mal die Zeitung** pass me the paper, please; **Kinder, seid ~ nicht so laut!** don't make so much noise, children!; **reg dich ~ nicht so auf!** don't get so worked up!; **paß ~ auf!** [oh,] do be careful!; **das ist ~ nicht zu glauben** that's just incredible; (B) *(Zweifel ausdrückend)* **du hast ~ meinen Brief erhalten?** you did get my letter, didn't you?; **es wird ihm ~ nichts passiert sein?** you don't think something has happened to him[, do you]?; (C) *(Bestätigung erwartend)* **Sie kommen ~ morgen?** you will be coming tomorrow, won't you?; (D) *(Überraschung ausdrückend) nicht übersetzt;* **das ist ~ Karl!** there's Karl!; (E) *(an Bekanntes erinnernd)* **er ist ~ nicht mehr der Jüngste** he's not as young as he used to be[, you know]; **ich bin ~ deine Schwester** I 'am your sister[, you know]; (F) *(nach Vergessenem fragend)* **wie war ~ sein Name?** now what was his name?; (G) *(verstärkt Bejahung/Verneinung ausdrückend)* **gewiss/sicher ~:** [why] certainly; of course; **ja ~:** [yes,] all right *or (coll.)* OK; **nein ~:** [no,] of course not; **nicht ~!** *(abwehrend)* [no,] don't!; **sollen sie ~!** let them, then!; well, let them!; (H) *(Wunsch verstärkend)* **wäre es ~ ...** if only it were ...

**Docht** /dɔxt/ *der;* ~**[e]s,** ~**:** wick

**Docht·schere** *die* snuffers *pl.*

**Dock** /dɔk/ *das;* ~**s,** ~**s** dock

**Dock·arbeiter** *der* dock worker; docker

**Docke** *die;* ~, ~**n** (A) *(Garnbündel)* skein; (B) *(Getreidebündel)* shock; stook; (C) *(südd.: Puppe)* doll

**docken**[1] *tr. V.* shock, stook ‹corn›; wind ‹thread› into a skein/skeins

**docken**[2] ❶ *itr. V.* *(Seew., Raumf.)* dock. ❷ *tr. V.* *(Seew.)* dock ‹ship›; put ‹ship› in dock

**Docker** *der;* ~**s,** ~**:** docker

**Dock·hafen** *der* dock

**Dodekaeder** /dodeka'|e:dɐ/ *das;* ~**s,** ~ *(Geom.)* dodecahedron

**Dodekaphonie** /dodekafo'ni:/ *die;* ~ *(Musik)* twelve-tone technique

**Doge** /'do:ʒə/ *der;* ~**n,** ~**n** doge

**Dogge** /'dɔgə/ *die;* ~, ~**n** (A) **Deutsche ~:** Great Dane; (B) **Englische ~:** mastiff

**Dogma** /'dɔgma/ *das;* ~**s, Dogmen** *(bes. kath. Kirche, auch fig.)* dogma

**Dogmatik** /dɔ'gma:tik/ *die;* ~, ~**en** (A) *(Theol.)* dogmatics *sing., no art.;* (B) *(fig. abwertend)* dogmatism

**Dogmatiker** *der;* ~**s,** ~, **Dogmatikerin** *die;* ~, ~**nen** *(Theol., auch fig.)* dogmatist

**dogmatisch** *(Theol., auch fig.)* ❶ *Adj.* dogmatic. ❷ *adv.* dogmatically

**dogmatisieren** *tr. V.* *(Theol., auch fig.)* dogmatize

**Dogmatismus** *der;* ~ *(oft abwertend)* dogmatism

**Dogmen·geschichte** *die* *(Theol.)* history of dogma

**Dohle** /'do:lə/ *die;* ~, ~**n** jackdaw

**Dohne** /'do:nə/ *die;* ~, ~**n** springe

**Döhnkes** /'dø:nkəs/ *Pl.* *(nordd.)* stories; yarns

**Doktor** /'dɔktɔr/ *der;* ~**s,** ~**en** /-'to:rən/ (A) *(Titel)* doctorate; doctor's degree; **den/seinen ~ machen** do a/one's doctorate; **den ~ haben** have a doctorate *or* doctor's degree; **zum ~ promoviert werden** be awarded one's doctorate *or* doctor's degree; (B) ▸ 91 *(Träger)* doctor; **er ist ~ der Philosophie** he is a doctor of philosophy; **guten Tag, Frau ~!** hello, Doctor; *(Frau eines ~s)* hello, Mrs X; **Herr ~ Krause** Doctor Krause; (C) *(ugs.: Arzt)* doctor; **der Onkel ~** *(Kinderspr.)* the nice doctor; **~ spielen** play doctors and nurses

**Doktorand** /dɔkto'rant/ *der;* ~**en,** ~**en** student taking his/her doctorate; **er ist ~ bei Professor Meier** he is studying for his doctorate under Professor Meier

**Doktoranden·kolloquium** *das* research students' colloquium

**Doktorandin** *die;* ~, ~**nen** ⇒ **Doktorand**

**Doktor·arbeit** *die* doctoral thesis *or* dissertation (**über** + *Akk.* on)

**Doktorat** /dɔkto'ra:t/ *das;* ~**[e]s,** ~**e** (A) *(veralt.: Doktorwürde)* doctorate; (B) *(österr.)* ⇒ **Doktorprüfung**

**Doktor-:** ~**diplom** *das* Ph. D. certificate; doctoral diploma *(Amer.)*; ~**examen** *das* ⇒ ~**prüfung**; ~**grad** *der* doctorate; doctor's degree; **den ~grad erwerben** gain *or* get one's doctorate *or* doctor's degree; ~**hut** *der* (A) *(Hut)* doctor's cap; (B) *(ugs.)* ⇒ ~**grad**

**Doktorin** *die;* ~, ~**nen** doctor; ⇒ *auch* **-in**

**Doktor-:** ~**ingenieur** *der* doctor of engineering science; ~**mutter** *die* *(ugs.)* [thesis] supervisor; ~**prüfung** *die* examination for a/one's doctorate; ~**titel** *der* title of doctor; **den ~titel führen** *(sich ~titel nennen)* call oneself doctor; *(den ~grad haben)* have a doctorate *or* doctor's degree; ~**vater** *der* *(ugs.)* [thesis] supervisor; ~**würde** *die* doctorate; doctor's degree

**Doktrin** /dɔk'tri:n/ *die;* ~, ~**en** doctrine

**doktrinär** /dɔktri'nɛ:ɐ̯/ ❶ *Adj.* doctrinal; *(abwertend: starr, einseitig)* doctrinaire. ❷ *adv.* doctrinally; *(abwertend: starr, einseitig)* in a doctrinaire way

**Doktrinär** *der;* ~, ~**e** (A) *(Verfechter einer Doktrin)* advocate of a/the doctrine; (B) *(abwertend)* doctrinaire

**Dokument** /doku'mɛnt/ *das;* ~**[e]s,** ~**e** (A) *(Urkunde)* document; (B) *(Zeugnis)* document; record; (C) *(DDR: Parteibuch)* party membership book

**Dokumentalist** /dɔkumɛnta'lɪst/ *der;* ~**en,** ~**en, Dokumentalistin** *die;* ~, ~**nen** *(DDR),* **Dokumentar** /dɔkumɛn'ta:r/ *der;* **Dokumentars, Dokumentare, Dokumentarin** *die;* ~, ~**nen** documentalist

**Dokumentar-:** ~**bericht** *der* documentary report; ~**film** *der* documentary [film]

**dokumentarisch** ❶ *Adj.* documentary. ❷ *adv.* **etw. ~ belegen** provide documentary evidence of *or* for sth.; **etw. ~ festhalten** make a documentary record of sth.

**Dokumentar-:** ~**literatur** *die* documentary literature; ~**theater** *das* documentary drama

**Dokumentation** /dɔkumɛnta'tsio:n/ *die;* ~, ~**en** (A) *(das Dokumentieren)* documentation; (B) *(Material)* documentary account; *(Bericht)* documentary report; (C) *(das Beweisen)* demonstration; (D) *(Beweis, Ausdruck)* evidence

**dokumentieren** ❶ *tr. V.* (A) *(bekunden)* demonstrate ‹readiness, cast of mind, sympathy, interest›; express, register ‹protest›; (B) *(belegen)* document; (C) *(darstellen)* record ‹behaviour, event›. ❷ *refl. V.* *(offenbar werden)* **sich in** *od.* **an etw.** *(Dat.)* **~:** be demonstrated by sth.

*old spelling (see note on page 1707)

**Dolby** (Wz) /'dɔlbi/ *das;* **~s** Dolby system ®

**Dolce Vita** /'dɔltʃə 'vi:ta/ *das od. die;* **~:** dolce vita; **~ machen** (*ugs.*) live a life of luxury and pleasure

**Dolch** /dɔlç/ *der;* **~[e]s, ~e** dagger

**Dolch-: ~stich** *der* stab [with a dagger]; **~stoß** *der* (A) (*Stoß*) dagger thrust; (B) (*fig.: Hinterhalt*) stab in the back; **~stoß·legende** *die* myth of the stab in the back

**Dolde** /'dɔldə/ *die;* **~, ~n** (*Bot.*) umbel

**Dolden-: ~blütler** *der* (*Bot.*) (A) (*aus der Ordnung ~blütler) plant of the order Umbelliflorae;* (B) ⇒ **~gewächs**; **~gewächs** *das* (*Bot.*) umbellifer

**Dole** /'do:lə/ *die;* **~, ~n** (*südd.*) drain

**doll** /dɔl/ (*bes. nordd., salopp*) ❶ *Adj.* (A) (*ungewöhnlich*) incredible; amazing; (B) (*verrückt*) batty (*coll.*); ⇒ *auch* **oll**; (C) (*großartig*) fantastic (*coll.*); great (*coll.*); (*iron.*) great (*coll.*); (D) (*schlimm*) dreadful (*coll.*). ❷ *adv.* (A) (*verrückt*) like a madman; (B) (*großartig*) fantastically [well] (*coll.*); (C) (*sehr*) ‹hurt› dreadfully (*coll.*), like mad; ‹shake, rain› good and hard (*coll.*); **es regnet immer ~er** it's chucking it down harder than ever (*coll.*); **sich ~ freuen** be terribly pleased (*coll.*)

**Dollar** /'dɔla:ɐ̯/ *der;* **~s, ~s** ▶ 337 dollar; **zwei ~:** two dollars

**Dollar-: ~kurs** *der* dollar rate; **~zeichen** *das* dollar sign

**Dolle** *die;* **~, ~n** rowlock

**Doll·punkt** *der* (*ugs.*) bone of contention

**Dolly** /'dɔli/ *der;* **~s, ~s** (*Film*) dolly

**Dolmetsch** /'dɔlmɛtʃ/ *der;* **~[e]s, ~e** (A) (*bes. österr.: ~er*) interpreter; (B) (*geh.: Fürsprecher, Verkünder*) spokesman (*Gen.* for)

**dolmetschen** ❶ *itr. V.* (*übersetzen*) act as interpreter (**bei** at); (*als Dolmetscher arbeiten*) work as *or* be an interpreter. ❷ *tr. V.* act as interpreter at ‹discussion etc.›

**Dolmetscher** *der;* **~s, ~** ▶ 159 interpreter; **sich über einen** *od.* **mithilfe eines ~ unterhalten** talk through an interpreter

**Dolmetscherin** *die;* **~, ~nen** ▶ 159 ⇒ **Dolmetscher**; ⇒ *auch* **-in**

**Dolmetscher-: ~institut** *das,* **~schule** *die* institute *or* school of interpreting

**Dolomit** /dolo'mi:t/ *der;* **~s, ~e** (*Geol.*) dolomite

**Dolomiten** *Pl.* **die ~:** the Dolomites

**Dom** /do:m/ *der;* **~[e]s, ~e** (A) cathedral; (*fig.*) dome; **der Kölner ~, der ~ zu Köln** Cologne Cathedral; (B) (*Geol.*) dome

**Domäne** /do'mɛ:nə/ *die;* **~, ~n** (A) (*Spezialgebiet*) domain; (B) (*Staatsgut*) demesne

**Domestik** /domɛs'ti:k/ *der;* **~en, ~en** (*veralt. abwertend*) domestic

**Domestikation** /domɛstika'tsi̯o:n/ *die;* **~, ~en** domestication

**Domestike** *der;* **~n, ~n** ⇒ **Domestik**

**Domestikin** *die;* **~, ~nen** (*verhüll.*) sub girl (*coll.*)

**domestizieren** /domɛsti'tsi:rən/ *tr. V.* domesticate; (*fig.*) tame; subdue

**Dom-: ~freiheit** *die* (*hist.*): *area of a city, usually around the cathedral, under the jurisdiction of the Church;* **~herr** *der* (*kath. Rel.*) canon

**Domina**[1] /'do:mina/ *die;* **~, Dominä** abbess; mother superior

**Domina**[2] *die;* **~, ~s** (*verhüll.*) mistress; dominatrix

**dominant** /domi'nant/ ❶ *Adj.* (*auch Biol.*) dominant. ❷ *adv.* dominantly

**Dominant·akkord** *der* (*Musik*) dominant chord

**Dominante** *die;* **~, ~n** (A) (*Hauptmerkmal*) dominant feature; (B) (*Musik*) (*Quint*) dominant; (*Dreiklang*) ⇒ **Dominantakkord**

**Dominant·sept·akkord** *der* (*Musik*) dominant seventh chord

**Dominanz** /domi'nants/ *die;* **~, ~en** (*auch Biol.*) dominance

**dominieren** /domi'ni:rən/ ❶ *itr. V.* dominate; ‹aspect› predominate, dominate; **~d** dominant. ❷ *tr. V.* dominate

**Dominikaner** /domini'ka:nɐ/ *der;* **~s, ~, Dominikanerin** *die;* **~, ~nen** (A) (*Mönch/Nonne*) Dominican; (B) (*Einwohner/Einwohnerin der Dominikanischen Republik*) Dominican

**Dominikaner·orden** *der* Dominican order

**dominikanisch** *Adj.* Dominican; **die Dominikanische Republik** the Dominican Republic

**Domino**[1] /'do:mino/ *der;* **~s, ~s** (*Mantel, Person*) domino

**Domino**[2] *das;* **~s, ~s** (*Spiel*) dominoes *sing.*

**Domino**[3] *der;* **~s, ~s** (*österr.: ~stein*) domino

**Domino-: ~spiel** *das* (A) dominoes *sing.;* (B) (*~steine*) [set *sing.* of] dominoes *pl.;* (C) (*~partie*) game of dominoes; **~stein** *der* (A) (*Spielstein*) domino; (B) (*Gebäck*) *small chocolate-covered cake with layers of marzipan, jam, and gingerbread*

**Domizil** /domi'tsi:l/ *das;* **~s, ~e** (A) (*geh.*) domicile; residence; **bei jmdm./in einer Stadt** *usw.* **~ nehmen** take up residence with sb./in a town *etc.;* (B) (*Finanzw.*) place of payment

**domizilieren** *tr. V.* (*Finanzw.*) domicile

**Dom-: ~kapitel** *das* (*kath. Kirche*) cathedral chapter; **~kapitular** *der* (*kath. Kirche*) canon; **~pfaff** *der;* **~~en** *od.* **~~s, ~~e[n]** (*Zool.*) bullfinch; **~prediger** *der* (*ev. Kirche*) cathedral preacher; **~propst** *der* (*kath. Kirche*) dean; provost

**Dompteur** /dɔmp'tø:ɐ/ *der;* **~s, ~e, Dompteurin** *die;* **~, ~nen, Dompteuse** /dɔmp'tø:zə/ *die;* **~, ~n** tamer

**Donau** /'do:nau̯/ *die;* **~** ▶ 306 Danube

**Donau-: ~monarchie** *die;* **~** (*hist.*) Austro-Hungarian Empire; **~schwaben** *Pl.: German settlers on the middle Danube*

**Dönkes** /'dœnkəs/ *Pl.* (*nordd.*) ⇒ **Döhnkes**

**Donner** /'dɔnɐ/ *der;* **~s, ~** (*auch fig.*) thunder; **der erste ~:** the first clap *or* peal of thunder; **wie vom ~ gerührt dastehen** *od.* **sein** be thunderstruck; **~ und Blitz** *od.* **Doria!** (*veralt.*) by Jove! (*dated coll.*)

**Donner-: ~balken** *der* (*salopp*) bog (*Brit. sl.*); latrine; (*Sitzstange*) latrine seat; **~getöse** *das* thunderous din; **~gott** *der* god of thunder; **~keil** *der* (A) (*ugs.: Ausruf des Erstaunens*) my word; (B) (*Werkzeug, Belemnit*) thunderstone; **~littchen** /-'lɪtçən/, **~lüttchen** /'-lʏtçən/ (*nordd.: Ausruf des Erstaunens*) my word; wow

**donnern** ❶ *itr. V.* (A) (*unpers.*) thunder; **es hat gedonnert und geblitzt** there was thunder and lightning; (B) (*fig.*) ‹gun› thunder, boom [out]; ‹engine› roar; ‹hooves› thunder; **~der Applaus** thunderous applause; (C) *mit sein* (*sich laut fortbewegen*) ‹train, avalanche, etc.› thunder; (D) (*ugs.: schlagen*) thump, hammer (**an** + *Akk.*, **gegen** on); (E) *mit sein* (*ugs.: prallen*) **gegen etw. ~:** smash into sth.; **der Ball donnerte an die Latte** the ball slammed against the bar; (F) (*ugs.: schimpfen*) **gegen etw. ~:** rage against sth. ❷ *tr. V.* (A) (*ugs.: schleudern*) sling (*coll.*); hurl; (B) (*ugs.: schlagen*) slam; **jmdm. eine** *od.* **ein paar ~:** thump sb.; give sb. a good thumping; (C) (*ugs.: schimpfen*) thunder

**Donner·schlag** *der* clap *or* peal of thunder; **die Nachricht traf uns wie ein ~:** the news completely stunned us

**Donners·tag** *der* ▶ 207, ▶ 833 Thursday; ⇒ *auch* **Dienstag**

**donnerstags** *Adv.* ▶ 833 on Thursday[s]; ⇒ *auch* **dienstags**

**Donner-: ~stimme** *die* thundering voice; **~wetter** *das* (A) (*ugs.: Krach*) row; **das wird ein [schönes] ~wetter geben** *od.* **setzen** that will cause a hell of a row (*coll.*); **ein ~wetter über sich ergehen lassen müssen** be given what for (*coll.*); (B) /'--'--/ (*ugs.: Ausruf der Verärgerung*) **zum ~wetter [noch einmal]!** damn it!; **warum, zum ~wetter, ...?** why, for Heaven's sake, ...?; (C) /'--'--/ (*ugs.: Ausruf der Bewunderung*) my word; wow

**Don Quichotte** /dɔnki'ʃɔt/ (*der*) Don Quixote

**Donquichotterie** /dɔnkiʃɔtə'ri:/ *die;* **~, ~n** quixotism; quixotry

**doof** /do:f/ (*ugs. abwertend*) ❶ *Adj.* (A) (*einfältig*) stupid; dumb (*coll.*); dopey (*coll.*); **~ bleibt ~[, da helfen keine Pillen]** once a fool, always a fool; (B) (*langweilig*) boring; (C) (*ärgerlich*) stupid. ❷ *adv.* (*beschränkt*) stupidly; **da hat er vielleicht ~ geguckt** he didn't half make (*Brit.*) *or* really made a stupid face

**Doofheit** *die;* **~, ~en** (*ugs. abwertend*) (A) stupidity; dumbness (*coll.*); (B) (*Äußerung*) stupid *or* (*coll.*) dumb remark

**Doofi** /'do:fi/ *der;* **~s, ~s** (*ugs.*) dope (*coll.*); dummy; [stupid] twit (*coll.*); **steh nicht da wie Klein ~ mit Plüschohren!** stop looking so stupid!

**Doofkopp** /-kɔp/ *der;* **~s, Doofköppe** /-kœpə/, **Doofmann** *der;* **Doofmann[e]s, Doofmänner** (*ugs. abwertend*) dope (*coll.*); dummy; [stupid] twit (*coll.*)

**dopen** /'dɔpn̩/ *tr. V.* dope ‹horse etc.›; **jmdn. ~:** give sb. drugs; **gedopt sein** ‹athlete› have taken drugs; **sich ~:** take drugs

**Doping** /'dɔpɪŋ/ *das;* **~s, ~s** (A) (*bei Sportlern*) taking drugs; (*das Verabreichen von Drogen*) administering drugs; (B) (*von Pferden usw.*) doping

**Doping·kontrolle** *die* (*Sport*) drug[s] test

**Doppel** /'dɔpl̩/ *das;* **~s, ~** (A) (*Kopie*) duplicate; copy; (B) (*Sport*) doubles *sing. or pl.*; **im gemischten/das gemischte ~ gewinnen** win the mixed doubles; **ein ~:** a game of doubles; (*im Turnier*) a doubles match

**doppel-, Doppel-: ~adler** *der* double eagle; **~agent** *der,* **~agentin** *die* double agent; **~album** *das* double album *or* LP; **~-b** *das* (*Musik*) double flat; **~band** *der* double[-sized] volume; **~belastung** *die* double burden *or* load; **~belichtung** *die* (*Fot.*) double exposure; **~beschluss, *~beschluß** *der* (*Politik*) twin-track decision; **~besteuerung** *die* double taxation; **~bett** *das* double bed; **~bock** *das* extra-strong bock beer; **~bödig** /-bø:dɪç/ ❶ *Adj.* ambiguous; ❷ *adv.* ambiguously; **~bödigkeit** *die;* **~, ~~en** ambiguity; **~bogen** *der* double sheet; **~bruch** *der* (*Math.*) compound *or* complex fraction; **~decker** *der;* **~~s, ~~** (A) (*Flugzeug*) biplane; (B) (*Omnibus*) double-decker [bus]; **~deutig** /-dɔytɪç/ ❶ *Adj.* (A) ambiguous; (B) (*anzüglich*) suggestive; **eine ~deutige Bemerkung** a double entendre; ❷ *adv.* (A) ambiguously; (B) (*anzüglich*) suggestively; **~deutigkeit** *die;* **~, ~~en** (A) ambiguity; (B) (*Anzüglichkeit*) suggestiveness; (*anzügliche Äußerung*) double entendre; **~fenster** *das* double-glazed window; **~fenster haben** have double glazing; **~flinte** *die* double-barrelled shotgun; **~gänger** *der;* **~~s, ~~, ~gängerin** *die;* **~, ~~nen** double; **~gleisig** ❶ *Adj.* (A) (*mit zwei Gleisen*) double-tracked; (B) (*zwielichtig*) dubious; ❷ *adv.* (A) (*mit zwei Gleisen*) **diese Strecke ist ~gleisig ausgebaut** this section is double-tracked *or* has two tracks; **~gleisig fahren** (*fig.*) adopt a two-pronged strategy; (B) (*zwielichtig*) dubiously; **~griff** *der* (*Musik*) double-stop; **~haus** *das* pair of semi-detached houses; **~haus·hälfte** *die* semi[-detached house]; **~heft** *das* double issue; **~hoch·zeit** *die* double wedding; **~kinn** *das* double chin; **~klick** *der;* **~~s, ~~s** (*DV*) double click; **~knoten** *der* double knot; **~konsonant** *der* (*Sprachw.*) double consonant; **~konzert** *das* double concerto; **~kopf** *der* (*Kartenspiel*) Doppelkopf; **~lauf** *der* double barrel; **~laut** *der* (*Sprachw.*) (A) (*Diphthong*) diphthong; (B) (*~konsonant*) double consonant; (C) (*~vokal*) double vowel; **~leben** *das* double life; **~moral** *die* double standards *pl.;* **~mord** *der* double murder

**doppeln** *tr. V.* (A) (*südd., österr.*) resole; (B) (*DV*) reproduce

**doppel-, Doppel-: ~naht** *die* French seam; **~name** *der* double-barrelled name (*Brit.*); hyphenated name; **~pass, *~paß** *der* (*Fußball*) one-two; **~punkt** *der* colon; **~reihig** *Adj.* ⇒ **zweireihig**; **~rolle** *die* dual role; **~schicht** *die* double shift; **eine ~schicht fahren** work a double shift; **~schlag** *der* (A) (*Musik*) turn; (B) (*Tennis, Tischtennis,*

d

*Badminton*) double hit; **~seite** *die* (*Zeitungsw.*) double page; **~seitig** ❶ *Adj.* Ⓐ (*Zeitungsw.*) two-page *attrib.*; double-page *attrib.*; Ⓑ (*Med.*) double ‹pleurisy, pneumonia›; bilateral ‹paralysis›; ❷ *adv.* Ⓐ (*Zeitungsw.*) **~seitig gedruckt** printed across two pages *or* a double page; Ⓑ (*Med.*) **~seitig gelähmt** paralysed on both sides; **~sieg** *der* first and second place; **einen ~sieg feiern** celebrate taking first and second place; **~sinnig** ❶ *Adj.* ambiguous; ❷ *adv.* ambiguously; **~spiel** *das* Ⓐ (*Sport*) doubles *sing.* or *pl.*; Ⓑ (*abwertend: Unehrlichkeit*) double game; **~steck·dose** *die* (*Elektrot.*) double socket; **~stecker** *der* (*Elektrot.*) two-way plug *or* adapter; **~stöckig** *Adj.* two-storey ‹house›; double-decker *attrib.* ‹bus›; (*fig.*) double ‹whisky etc.›; **ein ~stöckiges Bett** a bunk bed; **~stunde** *die* double period

**doppelt** ❶ *Adj.* Ⓐ (*zweifach*) double; dual ‹nationality›; **die ~e Länge/Breite/Menge** double *or* twice the length/breadth/quantity; **~e Buchführung** (*Kaufmannsspr.*) double-entry bookkeeping; **ein ~er Klarer** (*ugs.*) a double schnapps; **ein ~er Boden** a false bottom; Ⓑ (*besonders groß, stark*) redoubled ‹enthusiasm, attention›; **mit ~er Kraft arbeiten** work with twice as much energy; ❷ *adv.* Ⓐ (*zweimal*) **~ konzentriert** double concentrated; **der Stoff liegt ~:** the material is double-width; **~ genäht hält besser** (*Spr.*) it's better to be on the safe side; better safe than sorry; **das ist ~ gemoppelt** (*ugs.*) that's just saying the same thing twice over; **~ so groß/alt wie ...** twice as large/old as ...; **~ so viel** twice as much; **das/diese Platte habe ich ~:** I have two of them/two copies of this record; **etw. ~ nehmen** double sth. up; **~ sehen** see double; **etw. ~ und dreifach bereuen/prüfen** regret sth. deeply/test and retest sth.; Ⓑ (*ganz besonders, noch mehr*) **~ einsam** twice as lonely; **sich ~ anstrengen** try twice as hard; **es ~ bereuen, dass ...** be even more sorry that ...

**Doppelte**[1] *das; adj. Dekl.* **das ~ bezahlen** pay twice as much; pay double; **um/auf das ~ steigen** triple/double; **etw. um das ~ erhöhen** triple sth.; **um das ~ größer** three times as large; **das ~ leisten** do double the work *or* twice as much work

**Doppelte**[2] *der; adj. Dekl.* (*ugs.*) double

**doppelt·kohlen·sauer** *Adj.* (*Chemie*) **...saures Natron** sodium bicarbonate; bicarbonate of soda; **...saurer Kalk** calcium bicarbonate

**Doppelt·sehen** *das;* **~s** (*Med.*) double vision; diplopia (*Med.*)

**Doppel·tür** *die* double door

**Doppelung** *die;* **~, ~en** doubling

**doppel-, Doppel-:** **~verdiener** *der* Ⓐ *Pl.* (*Eheleute*) married couple who are both earning; Ⓑ (*mit zwei Einkommen*) person with an income from two jobs; **~verdiener sein** have an income from two jobs; **~verdienerin** *die* ⇒ **~verdiener** B; **~vokal** *der* (*Sprachw.*) double vowel; **~zentner** *der* ▶ **353** 100 kilograms; quintal; **~zimmer** *das* double room; **~züngig** /-tsʏŋɪç/ (*abwertend*) ❶ *Adj.* two-faced; ❷ *adv.* **~züngig reden** be two-faced; **~züngigkeit** *die;* **~~** (*abwertend*) ⇒ **~züngig**: double-facedness; two-facedness

**Doppler·effekt** *der;* **~[e]s** (*Physik*) Doppler effect

**Dorado** /do'ra:do/ ⇒ **Eldorado**

**Dorf** /dɔrf/ *das;* **~[e]s, Dörfer** /'dœrfɐ/ (*auch ugs.: die Einwohner*) village; **auf dem ~:** in the country; **vom ~ kommen** *od.* **stammen** come from the country; **aufs ~ ziehen** move to the country; **über die Dörfer** from village to village; **über die Dörfer fahren** drive on country roads; **das olympische ~:** the Olympic village; **das sind mir/für mich böhmische Dörfer** (*ugs.*) it's all Greek to me; **auf/über die Dörfer gehen** (*Skat*) lead the side suits; **aus** *od.* **in jedem ~ einen Hund haben** (*Skat*) have a more or less even distribution; ⇒ *auch* **potemkinsch**

**Dorf-:** **~akademie** *die* (*DDR*) village adult education centre; **~älteste** *der* village elder; **~anger** *der* village green; **~bewohner** *der,* **~bewohnerin** *die* villager

**Dörfchen** /'dœrfçən/ *das;* **~s, ~:** small village; hamlet

**Dorf·depp** *der* (*bes. südd., österr.*) village idiot

**dörfisch** ❶ *Adj.* rustic. ❷ *adv.* rustically

**Dorf-:** **~jugend** *die* young people *pl.* of the village; village youth; **~krug** *der* (*nordd.*) village inn *or* (*Brit.*) pub

**Dörfler** /'dœrflɐ/ *der;* **~s, ~, Dörflerin** *die;* **~, ~nen** villager

**dörflich** *Adj.* village *attrib.* ‹life, traditions, etc.›; (*ländlich*) rural ‹character›

**Dorf-:** **~polizist** *der* village policeman; **~schenke** *die* village inn *or* (*Brit.*) pub; **~schönheit** *die* village beauty; **~schulze** *der* (*veralt.*) mayor of the/a village; **~trottel** *der* village idiot

**dorisch** /'do:rɪʃ/ *Adj.* Ⓐ (*Archit.*) Doric; Ⓑ (*Musik*) Dorian ‹mode›

**Dorn**[1] /dɔrn/ *der;* **~[e]s, ~en** (*ugs. auch:*) **Dörner** /'dœrnɐ/ Ⓐ (*an Rosen o. Ä.*) thorn; **jmdm. ein ~ im Auge sein** annoy sb. intensely; **sein Weg war voller ~en** (*fig. geh.*) his life was no bed of roses; Ⓑ (*Bot.*) thorn; spine; Ⓒ (*dichter.: ~busch*) thorn bush

**Dorn**[2] *der;* **~[e]s, ~e** Ⓐ (*Metallstift*) spike; (*an der Gürtelschnalle*) tongue; Ⓑ (*Technik*) (*zum Weiten von Löchern o. Ä.*) punch; (*zum Biegen von Blechen o. Ä.*) mandrel

**Dorn·busch** *der* thorn bush; **der brennende ~** (*bibl.*) the burning bush

**dornen-, Dornen-:** **~gestrüpp** *das* tangle of thorn bushes; **~krone** *die* crown of thorns; **~reich** *Adj.* (*fig. geh.*) hard ‹life, fate›; thorny ‹path›; **~strauch** *der* thorn bush; **~voll** *Adj.* (*fig. geh.*) ⇒ **~reich**

**Dorn·fort·satz** *der* ▶ **471** (*Anat.*) spinous process

**dornig** *Adj.* Ⓐ (*mit Dornen*) thorny; Ⓑ (*geh.: schwierig*) hard ‹life, fate›; thorny ‹path, subject, question›

**Dorn-:** **~röschen** (*das*) the Sleeping Beauty; **~röschen·schlaf** *der* (*iron.*) long sleep

**dorren** /'dɔrən/ *itr. V.; mit sein* (*geh.*) dry up

**dörren** /'dœrən/ ❶ *tr. V.* (*trocken machen*) dry. ❷ *itr. V.; mit sein* dry

**Dörr-:** **~fleisch** *das* (*südd.*) lean bacon; **~obst** *das* dried fruit; **~pflaume** *die* prune

**dorsal** /dɔr'za:l/ *Adj.* Ⓐ (*Med.*) dorsal ‹artery, nerve›; spinal ‹curvature›; Ⓑ (*Phon.*) dorsal

**Dorsch** /dɔrʃ/ *der;* **~[e]s, ~e** cod; (*junger Kabeljau*) codling

**dort** /dɔrt/ *Adv.* there; **jmdn./etw. ~ behalten** keep sb./sth. there; **~ bleiben** stay there; ⇒ *auch* **da** 1 A

**dort-:** ***~|behalten** *usw.* ⇒ **dort**; **~her** *Adv.* **[von] ~her** from there; **~hin** *Adv.* there; **bis ~hin** as far as there; **ich ging ~hin, wo der Wagen wartete** I went to where the car was waiting; **~hinab** *Adv.* down there; down that way; **~hinauf** *Adv.* up there; up that way; **bis ~hinauf** up to there; **~hinaus** *Adv.* out there; (*in diese Richtung*) out that way; **frech bis ~hinaus** (*ugs.*) [as] cheeky as anything; **das ärgert mich bis ~hinaus** (*ugs.*) that really gets me *or* my goat (*coll.*); **~hinein** *Adv.* in there; **~hinunter** *Adv.* down there

**dortig** *Adj.* there *postpos.*

**dort·zu·lande** *Adv.* (*geh.*) in that country; there

**Döschen** /'dø:sçən/ *das;* **~s, ~** ⇒ **Dose** A: small tin/box

**Dose** /'do:zə/ *die;* **~, ~n** Ⓐ (*Blech~*) tin; (*Pillen~*) box; (*Zucker~*) bowl; Ⓑ (*Konserven~*) can; tin (*Brit.*); (*Bier~*) can; **Bier aus der ~:** canned beer; beer in cans; Ⓒ (*Steck~*) socket

**dösen** /'dø:zn̩/ *itr. V.* (*ugs.*) doze; **vor sich hin ~:** doze

**dosen-, Dosen-:** **~bier** *das* canned beer; **~fertig** *Adj.* ready in the can *or* (*Brit.*) tin *postpos.*; **~fleisch** *das* canned *or* (*Brit.*) tinned meat; **~milch** *die* canned *or* (*Brit.*) tinned milk; **~öffner** *der* can-opener; tin-opener (*Brit.*)

**dosierbar** *Adj.* **etw. ist genau** *od.* **exakt ~:** sth. can be measured out in precise *or* exact doses

**dosieren** *tr. V.* **etw. ~:** measure out the required dose of sth.; (*zuführen*) administer the required dose of sth.; **ein Medikament genau/niedriger ~:** measure out/administer an exact/a smaller dose of a medicine; **sorgfältig dosierte Mengen** carefully measured doses; **seine Zuneigung sehr dosiert verteilen** (*fig.*) dispense one's affection in very small doses

**Dosierung** *die;* **~, ~en** Ⓐ measuring out; (*das Zuführen*) administering; (*fig.*) dispensing; Ⓑ ⇒ **Dosis**

**dösig** /'dø:zɪç/ (*ugs.*) ❶ *Adj.* Ⓐ (*schläfrig*) drowsy; dozy; Ⓑ (*benommen*) dopey (*coll.*); **ich habe einen ganz ~en Kopf** my head is all muzzy; Ⓒ (*unaufmerksam*) dozy (*coll.*). ❷ *adv.* Ⓐ (*schläfrig*) drowsily; Ⓑ (*benommen*) dopily (*sl.*); Ⓒ (*unaufmerksam*) dozily (*coll.*)

**Dosimeter** /dozi'me:tɐ/ *das;* **~s, ~** (*Physik*) dosimeter

**Dosis** /'do:zɪs/ *die;* **~, Dosen** (*auch fig.*) dose; **die tägliche ~:** the daily dosage

**Döskopp** /'dø:skɔp/ *der;* **~s, Dösköppe** /'dø:skœpə/ (*salopp*) dozy twit (*Brit. coll.*); dimwit

**Dossier** /dɔ'sie:/ *das,* (*veraltet:*) *der;* **~s, ~s** dossier

**Dotation** /dota'tsio:n/ *die;* **~, ~en** endowment

**dotieren** /do'ti:rən/ *tr. V.* Ⓐ **eine Position gut/mit 5 000 DM ~:** offer a good salary/a salary of 5,000 marks with a position; Ⓑ (*Physik*) dope

**dotiert** ❶ *2. Part. v.* **dotieren.** ❷ *Adj.* **hoch ~:** highly paid; **eine gut/mit 5 000 DM im Monat ~e Stellung** a well-paid position/a position with a monthly salary of 5,000 marks; **das Rennen ist gut ~:** good prize money is being put up for the race

**Dotierung** *die;* **~, ~en** Ⓐ (*das Dotieren*) **die ~ des Wettbewerbs/Rennens** putting up the prize money for the competition/race; Ⓑ (*Entgelt*) remuneration; salary; (*Preis, Gewinn*) prize

**Dotter** /'dɔtɐ/ *der od. das;* **~s, ~** Ⓐ (*Eigelb*) yolk; Ⓑ (*Zool.: Nährsubstanz*) vitellus; yolk

**dotter-, Dotter-:** **~blume** *die* marsh marigold; **~gelb** *Adj.* bright yellow; **~sack** *der* (*Zool.*) yolk sac

**doubeln** /'du:bl̩n/ ❶ *tr. V.* stand in for ‹actor›; use a stand-in for ‹scene›; **sich ~ lassen** use *or* have a stand-in. ❷ *itr. V.* **für jmdn. ~:** stand in for sb.

**Double** /'du:bl̩/ *das;* **~s, ~s** Ⓐ (*Ersatzdarsteller[in]*) stand-in; Ⓑ (*Doppelgänger, Sport: doppelter Gewinn*) double; Ⓒ (*Musik: Variation*) double

**Doublé** /du'ble:/ *das;* **~s, ~s** Ⓐ (*Schmuck*) rolled gold; Ⓑ (*Fechten*) double hit

**doublieren** ⇒ **dublieren**

**Douglasie** /du'gla:ziə/ *die;* **~, ~n, Douglas·fichte** /'du:glas-/, **Douglas·tanne** *die* Douglas fir *or* spruce

**down** /daʊn/ *Adj.* (*salopp*) down

**Doyen** /dọa'jɛ̃:/ *der;* **~s, ~s** doyen

**Doyenne** /dọa'jɛn/ *die;* **~, ~n** doyenne

**Dozent** /do'tsɛnt/ *der;* **~en, ~en, Dozentin** *die;* **~, ~nen** ▶ **159** lecturer (**für** in); ⇒ *auch* **-in**

**Dozentur** /dotsɛn'tu:ɐ̯/ *die;* **~, ~en** lectureship (**für** in)

**dozieren** /do'tsi:rən/ ❶ *itr. V.* Ⓐ (*lehren*) lecture (**über** + *Akk.* on, **an** + *Dat.* at); Ⓑ (*belehrend reden*) lecture. ❷ *tr. V.* „...“, **dozierte sie** '...,' she said in a lecturing tone

**dpa** /de:pe:'|a:/ *die;* **~** *Abk.* **Deutsche Presse-Agentur** German Press Agency

*old spelling (see note on page 1707)

**Dr.** *Abk.* ▶ 91 | **Doktor** Dr; ⇒ *auch* **Dr. phil.**

**Drache** /ˈdraxə/ *der;* ~**n**, ~**n** (*Myth.*) dragon

**Drachen** *der;* ~**s**, ~ A (*Papier*~) kite; **einen ~ steigen lassen** fly a kite; B (*salopp: zänkische Frau*) dragon; C (*Fluggerät*) hang-glider; D (*Segelboot*) dragon

**Drachen-:** ~**blut** *das* (*Myth.; Chemie*) dragon's blood; ~**fliegen** *das* (*Sport*) hang-gliding; ~**saat** *die* (*geh.*) seeds *pl.* of discord

**Dragée**, **Dragee** /draˈʒe:/ *das;* ~**s**, ~**s** dragée

**Dragoner** /dragoˈne/ *der;* ~**s**, ~ A (*salopp: resolute Frau*) battleaxe (*coll.*); B (*hist.: Soldat*) dragoon

**Draht** /dra:t/ *der;* ~**[e]s**, **Drähte** /ˈdrɛ:tə/ A (*dünnes Metall*) wire; B (*Leitung*) wire; cable; (*Telefonleitung*) line; wire; C (*Telefonverbindung*) line; **per** *od.* **über** ~: by wire *or* cable; **hast du einen ~ zur Polizei?** (*fig.*) have you got a direct line to the police?; **heißer** ~: hot line; **auf ~ sein** (*ugs.*) be on the ball (*coll.*); **jmdn. auf ~ bringen** (*ugs.*) make sb. get a move on

**Draht-:** ~**aus·löser** *der* (*Fot.*) cable release; ~**bürste** *die* wire brush

**Drähtchen** /ˈdrɛ:tçən/ *das;* ~**s**, ~: little wire

**drahten** *tr. V.* (*veralt.*) wire (*coll.*); (*ins Ausland*) cable; **an jmdn./nach Paris ~, dass ...** wire/cable sb./Paris to say that ...

**Draht-:** ~**esel** *der* (*ugs. scherzh.*) bike (*coll.*); ~**funk** *der* wired radio; ~**geflecht** *das* wire mesh; ~**gitter** *das* wire netting *no indef. art.;* ~**glas** *das* wire glass

**drahtig** *Adj.* wiry ‹person, hair›

**draht-**, **Draht-:** ~**los** (*Nachrichtenw.*) ❶ *Adj.* wireless; ❷ *adv.* **etw. ~los telegrafieren/übermitteln** radio sth.; ~**schere** *die* wire cutters *pl.;* ~**seil** *das* [steel] cable; ~**seil·bahn** *die* cable railway; ~**seil·künstler** *der*, ~**seil·künstlerin** *die* tightrope walker; ~**verhau** *der od. das* (*Barriere*) wire entanglement; (*Käfig*) wire enclosure; ~**zange** *die* cutting pliers *pl.;* ~**zaun** *der* wire fence; ~**zieher** /-tsi:ɐ/ *der* A (*Beruf*) wire-drawer; B (*Hintermann*) wire puller; ~**ziehere̲i** *die;* ~~, ~~**en** wire works; ~**zieherin** *die* ⇒ ~**zieher**

**Drainage** /drɛˈna:ʒə/ *die;* ~, ~**n** (*Med., Landw., Kfz-W.*) drainage

**drainieren** /drɛˈni:rən/ *tr. V.* (*Med., Landw.*) drain

**Draisine** /draiˈzi:nə/ *die;* ~, ~**n** A (*Laufrad*) dandy-horse; B (*Schienenfahrzeug*) trolley

**drakonisch** /draˈko:nɪʃ/ ❶ *Adj.* Draconian. ❷ *adv.* in a Draconian way

**drall** /dral/ *Adj.* strapping ‹girl›; full, rounded ‹cheeks, face, bottom›

**Drall** *der;* ~**[e]s**, ~**e** A (*bei Feuerwaffen*) rifling; B (*eines Geschosses, Balls*) spin; **er hat einen ~ nach rechts** (*fig.*) he leans to the right *or* has right-wing tendencies; C (*Physik*) (*Verdrehung*) torsion; (*Rotation*) rotation; (*Drehimpuls*) angular momentum

**Dralon** Ⓦ /ˈdra:lɔn/ *das;* ~**s** Dralon ®

**Drama** /ˈdra:ma/ *das;* ~**s**, **Dramen** drama; **ein einziges/furchtbares ~** (*fig.*) an absolute/a terrible disaster; **das ~ um die Entführung** (*fig.*) the drama of *or* surrounding the hijack

**Dramatik** /draˈma:tɪk/ *die;* ~: drama

**Dramatiker** *der;* ~**s**, ~, **Dramatikerin** *die;* ~, ~**nen** dramatist

**dramatisch** ❶ *Adj.* dramatic. ❷ *adv.* dramatically; **der Autor hat den Stoff ~ bearbeitet** the author adapted the material as a drama *or* for the stage

**dramatisieren** *tr. V.* dramatize

**Dramaturg** /dramaˈtʊrk/ *der;* ~**en**, ~**en** (*Theater*) literary and artistic director (*who also plans the programme of performances and advises on choice of costumes, scenery, etc.*); (*Rundf., Ferns.*) script editor

**Dramaturgie** /dramatʊrˈgi:/ *die;* ~, ~**n** A (*Dramenlehre*) dramaturgy; B (*Gestaltung*) dramatization; C (*Abteilung*) (*Theater*) literary and artistic director's department; (*Rundf., Ferns.*) script department

**Dramaturgin** *die;* ~, ~**nen** ⇒ **Dramaturg**

**dramaturgisch** ❶ *Adj.* dramaturgical; (*gestalterisch*) dramaturgical; dramatic; **die ~e Abteilung** (*Theater*) the literary and artistic director's department; (*Rundfunk, Fernsehen*) the script department. ❷ *adv.* **~ wirkungsvoll in Szene gesetzt** staged effectively; **~ gerechtfertigt** justified on dramaturgical grounds

**dran** /dran/ *Adv.* (*ugs.*) A (*an einer/eine Sache*) **das Schild bleibt ~:** the sign stays up; **gib noch etwas Mehl ~:** add some more flour; **halt deine Hand mal hier ~:** put your hand on this; **häng das Schild ~!** put the sign up!; **ich komme/kann nicht ~:** I can't reach; **mach doch ein Schild ~:** put a sign up; B **arm ~ sein** be in a bad way; **gut/schlecht ~ sein** be well off/badly off; (*sich gut/schlecht fühlen*) be well/not very well; **früh/spät ~ sein** be early/late; **an dem Gerücht ist was ~:** there is something in the rumour; **an ihm ist doch nichts ~:** he's got nothing going for him (*coll.*); (*er ist sehr mager*) there's nothing of him; **ich bin ~** *od.* (*scherzh.*) **am ~sten** (*ich bin an der Reihe*) it's my turn; I'm next; (*ich werde zur Verantwortung gezogen*) I'll be for the high jump *or* (*sl.*) for it (*Brit.*); I'll be under the gun (*Amer.*); **nicht wissen wie** *od.* **wo man ~ ist** not know where one stands; **nicht wissen wie** *od.* **wo man mit jmdm. ~ ist** not know where one is with sb.; ⇒ *auch:* **daran; ~bleiben; ~geben; ~hängen** *usw.;* **glauben**

**Dränage** /drɛˈna:ʒə/ *die;* ~, ~**n** (*auch Med.*) drainage

**dran|bleiben** *unr. itr. V.; mit sein* (*ugs.*) (*am Telefon*) hold *or* (*coll.*) hang on; (*das Programm weiter verfolgen*) stay tuned; (*an der Arbeit*) stick at it (*coll.*); **am Gegner/an der Arbeit ~:** stick to one's opponent (*coll.*)/stick at one's work (*coll.*); ⇒ *auch* **dran** A

**drang** /draŋ/ *1. u. 3. Pers. Sg. Prät. v.* **dringen**

**Drang** *der;* ~**[e]s**, **Dränge** /ˈdrɛŋə/ A (*Antrieb*) urge; **ein ~ nach Bewegung/Freiheit** an urge to move/be free; B (*Bedrängnis*) pressure

**dränge** /ˈdrɛŋə/ *1. u. 3. Pers. Sg. Konjunktiv II v.* **dringen**

**dran-:** ~**|geben** *unr. tr. V.* give up ‹time›; give, sacrifice ‹one's life›; ⇒ *auch* **dran** A; ~**|gehen** *unr. itr. V.; mit sein* (*ugs.*) A (*berühren*) touch; B (*in Angriff nehmen*) **~gehen, etw. zu tun** get down to doing sth.

**Drängelei** *die;* ~, ~**en** (*abwertend*) A pushing [and shoving]; **hören Sie doch mit Ihrer ~ auf** stop pushing [and shoving]; B (*mit Wünschen, Bitten*) pestering

**drängeln** /ˈdrɛŋl̩n/ (*ugs.*) ❶ *itr. V.* A (*schieben*) push [and shove]; B (*auf jmdn. einreden*) go on (*coll.*); **zum Aufbruch ~:** go on about it being time to leave (*coll.*). ❷ *tr. V.* A (*schieben*) push; shove; B (*einreden auf*) pester; go on at (*coll.*). ❸ *refl. V.* **sich nach vorn/durch die Menge** *usw.* **~:** push one's way to the front/through the crowd *etc.;* **sich danach ~, etw. zu tun** (*fig.*) fall over oneself to do sth. (*coll.*)

**drängen** /ˈdrɛŋən/ ❶ *itr. V.* A (*schieben*) push; **die Menge drängte zum Ausgang** the crowd pressed towards the exit; B (*fordern*) demand; **auf etw.** (*Akk.*) **~:** press for sth.; **zum Aufbruch ~:** insist that it is/was time to leave; **zur Eile ~:** hurry us/them *etc.* up; **darauf ~, dass ...** insist that ...; C **die Zeit drängt** time is pressing; **~de Fragen/Probleme** pressing *or* urgent questions/problems; D (*Sport*) press *or* push forward. ❷ *tr. V.* A (*schieben*) push; B (*antreiben*) press; urge; **jmdn. zur Bezahlung ~:** press sb. to pay; **es drängt mich, Ihnen zu sagen, dass ...** I feel I have to *or* must tell you that ...
❸ *refl. V.* ‹visitors, spectators, etc.› crowd, throng; ‹crowd› throng; **sich nach vorn/durch die Menge ~:** push one's way to the front/through the crowd; **sich in den Vordergrund ~** (*fig.*) make oneself the centre of attention

**Dränger** *der;* ~**s**, ~ ⇒ **Stürmer** B

**Drängerei** *die;* ~, ~**en** (*abwertend*) pushing [and shoving]

**Drangsal** /ˈdraŋza:l/ *die;* ~, ~**e** (*geh.*) (*Not*) hardship; (*Qual*) suffering

**drangsalieren** *tr. V.* (*abwertend*) (*quälen*) torment; (*plagen*) plague

**dran-:** ~**|halten** *unr. refl. V.* (*ugs.*) get a move on (*coll.*); ⇒ *auch* ~ A; ~**|hängen¹** (*ugs.*) ❶ *tr. V.* A (*aufwenden*) **viel Zeit/Geld ~hängen** put a lot of time/money into it; B (*anschließen*) **ein paar Tage an seinen Urlaub ~hängen** add a few days on to one's holiday (*Brit.*) *or* (*Amer.*) vacation; ❷ *refl. V.* (*verfolgen*) stay *or* (*coll.*) stick close behind; ⇒ *auch* **dran** A; ~**|hängen²** *unr. itr. V.* **da hängt noch viel Arbeit ~:** it still needs a lot of work

**dränieren** /drɛˈni:rən/ *tr. V.* (*auch Med.*) drain

**dran-:** ~**|kommen** *unr. itr. V.; mit sein* (*ugs.*) have one's turn; (*beim Spielen*) have one's turn *or* go; **ich kam als erste/erster ~:** it was my turn first; (*beim Arzt, Zahnarzt usw.*) I was the first one; **wer kommt jetzt ~?** who's next?; **jeder von uns kommt mal ~** (*verhüll.*) we've all got to go some time; **ich bin heute in Latein ~gekommen** (*aufgerufen worden*) I got picked on to answer in Latin today (*coll.*); ⇒ *auch* **dran** A; ~**|kriegen** *tr. V.* (*ugs.*) **jmdn. ~kriegen** get sb.; (*zum Arbeiten bringen*) get sb. at it (*coll.*); ~**|machen** *refl. V.* (*ugs.*) **sich ~machen, etw. zu tun** get down to doing sth.; **wenn sich die Kinder ~machen, ist der Kuchen gleich weg** once the children get started on it the cake won't last long; ⇒ *auch* **dran** A; ~**|nehmen** *unr. tr. V.* (*ugs.*) (*beim Friseur usw.*) see to; (*beim Arzt*) see; **jmdn. ~nehmen** (*in der Schule*) pick on sb. [to answer]; ~**|setzen** (*ugs.*) ❶ *tr. V.* (*einsetzen*) **seine ganze Kraft ~setzen, etw. zu erreichen** put all one's energy into achieving sth.; **alles ~setzen** put everything into it; make every effort; ❷ *refl. V.* (*beginnen*) get down to it

**dransten** /ˈdranstn̩/ ⇒ **dran** B

**dran|wollen** *unr. itr. V.* (*ugs.*) want [to have] a turn; (*beim Spielen*) want [to have] a turn *or* go

**Draperie** /drapəˈri:/ *die;* ~, ~**n** (*veralt.*) drapery

**drapieren** /draˈpi:rən/ *tr. V.* drape

**Dräsine** ⇒ **Draisine**

**Drastik** /ˈdrastɪk/ *die;* ~ (*eines Witzes, Schwanks*) crude explicitness; (*eines Berichts usw.*) graphicness

**drastisch** ❶ *Adj.* A crudely explicit ‹joke, story, etc.›; graphic ‹report, account›; B (*empfindlich spürbar*) drastic ‹measure, means›. ❷ *adv.* A (*grob*) with crude explicitness; (*deutlich*) graphically; B (*einschneidend*) drastically; ‹punish› severely

**drauf** /drauf/ *Adv.* (*ugs.*) on it; **da wäre ich nie ~ gekommen** I would never have thought of that; **da lege ich keinen Wert ~:** it's not important to me; **da zeigt sich, wer was ~ hat** that'll show who can and who can't; **da kannst du mal zeigen, was du ~ hast** here's your chance to show what you can do; **die Rolle/die dollsten Sprüche/90 Sachen ~ haben** have *or* know the part off pat (*Brit.*) *or* (*Amer.*) have the part down pat/have the most amazing patter/be doing 90; **~ und dran sein, etw. zu tun** be just about to do *or* be on the verge of doing sth.; **halt mal den Finger hier ~:** put your finger on here; **ich kriege den Deckel nicht ~:** I can't get the lid on; **der Deckel geht nicht ~:** the lid won't go on; **mach einen neuen Deckel ~:** put a new lid on [it]; **gut/schlecht** *usw.* **~ sein** (*fig. ugs.*) be in a good/bad *etc.* mood; ⇒ *auch* **darauf** A–E; **draufgehen; draufhalten** *usw.;* **scheißen**

**drauf-**, **Drauf-:** ~**|bekommen** *unr. tr. V.* (*ugs.*) **in eins ~bekommen** (*gescholten werden*) get it in the neck (*coll.*); (*geschlagen werden*) get a smack; ~**gänger** *der;* ~~**s**, ~~: daredevil; (*veralt.: Frauenheld*) ladykiller; ~**gängerin** *die;* ~~, ~~**nen** daredevil;

**~gängerisch** *Adj.* daring; audacious; **~gängertum** *das;* **~~s** daredevilry; **~|geben** *unr. tr. V.* (*ugs.*) **A** (*dazugeben*) **etw./was ~geben** add sth./add a bit on; **B** *in* **jmdm. eins ~geben** (*schlagen*) give sb. a smack; (*zurechtweisen*) put sb. in his/her place; **C** (*österr.: als Zugabe*) **etw. ~geben** play/sing/dance *etc.* sth. as an encore; **~|gehen** *unr. itr. V.; mit sein* (*ugs.*) **A** (*umkommen*) kick the bucket (*sl.*); **B** (*verbraucht werden*) go; **für etw. ~gehen** ‹money› go on sth.; **für diese Sitzungen geht immer viel Zeit ~:** these meetings always take up a lot of time; **C** (*entzweigehen*) get busted (*coll.*) *or* broken; **~|halten** *unr. itr. V.* (*ugs.*) shoot; **~halten und abdrücken** aim and fire; **~|hauen** *unr. itr. V.* (*ugs.*) **mein Arm tut noch weh, da darfst du nicht ~hauen** my arm still hurts, you're not to bash it; **einen ~hauen** have a booze-up (*Brit. coll.*); go on a binge (*coll.*); **~|kommen** *unr. itr. V.; mit sein* (*ugs.*) **jmdm. ~kommen** get on to sb.; **jmdm. ~kommen, dass er etw. tut** catch sb. doing sth.; ⇒ *auch* **drauf**; **~kriegen** *tr. V.* (*ugs.*) **eins ~kriegen** (*von einem Kind: geschlagen werden*) get smacked; (*besiegt werden*) get a thrashing; **~|legen** (*ugs.*) **1** *tr. V.* **150 DM/noch etwas ~legen** fork out (*coll.*) an extra 150 marks/a bit more; **2** *itr. V.* lay out (*sl.*); **ich lege dabei noch ~:** it's costing me money; ⇒ *auch* **drauf**

**drauf·los** *Adv.* **nichts wie ~!** go on!

**drauflos-: ~|arbeiten** *itr. V.* work away; (*anfangen zu arbeiten*) get straight down to work; **~|gehen** *unr. itr. V.; mit sein* (*ugs.*) get going; **~|reden** *itr. V.* talk away; (*anfangen zu reden*) start talking away; **~|schimpfen** *itr. V.* (*ugs.*) curse away; (*anfangen zu schimpfen*) start cursing away; **~|wirtschaften** *itr. V.* (*ugs. abwertend*) splash out money right, left, and centre (*Brit. coll.*); throw one's money around

**drauf-: ~|machen** *tr. V.* **einen ~machen** (*ugs.*) paint the town red; **~|stehen** *unr. itr. V.* (*ugs.*) be on it; **~|zahlen** (*ugs.*) **1** *tr. V.* **noch etwas/1250 DM ~zahlen** fork out (*coll.*) *or* pay a bit more/an extra 1,250 marks; **2** *itr. V.* (*Unkosten haben*) **ich zahle dabei noch ~:** it's costing me money; **diejenige sein, die immer nur ~zahlt** (*fig.*) be the one who makes all the sacrifices

**draus** /draus/ *Adv.* (*ugs.*) ⇒ **daraus**

**draußen** /'drausn̩/ *Adv.* **A** (*außerhalb*) outside; **hier/da ~:** out here/there; **~ vor der Tür** at the door; **nach/von ~:** outside/from outside; **„Hunde müssen ~ bleiben"** 'no dogs[, please]'; **bleib ~:** stay outside; **~ auf dem Land** (*fig.*) out in the country; **B** (*irgendwo*) out there; **da/hier ~:** out there/here; **weit/weiter ~:** far/further out; **~ in der Welt** (*fig.*) in the world outside

**drechseln** /'drɛksl̩n/ *tr. V.* turn; (*fig. iron.*) compose ‹statement›; turn ‹phrase, verse›

**Drechsler** *der;* **~s, ~:** turner

**Drechsler-: ~arbeit** *die* piece of turned work; **~arbeiten** [pieces *pl.* of] turned work *sing.*; **~bank** *die; Pl.* **~bänke** lathe

**Drechslerei** *die;* **~, ~en** turner's workshop; turnery

**Drechslerin** *die;* **~, ~nen** ⇒ **Drechsler**

**Dreck** /drɛk/ *der;* **~[e]s A** (*ugs.*) dirt; (*sehr viel, Ekel erregend*) filth; (*Schlamm*) mud; (*Kot*) mess; muck; **in den ~ fallen** fall in the dirt/mud/muck; **deine Hände sind schwarz vor ~:** your hands are filthy [dirty]; **vor ~ starren** be covered in dirt; be filthy [dirty]; **~ machen** make a mess; **~ am Stecken haben** have a skeleton in the cupboard (*Brit.*) *or* (*Amer.*) closet; **aus dem [gröbsten] ~ [heraus] sein** (*ugs.*) be over the worst; **jmdn. aus dem ~ ziehen** (*ugs.*) take sb. out of the gutter; **etw. in den ~ ziehen** *od.* **treten** drag sth. through the mud *or* mire; **im ~ stecken/sitzen** (*ugs.*) be in a [real] mess *or* in the mire; **mit ~ und Speck** (*ugs.*) unwashed; **jmdn./etw. mit ~ bewerfen** throw *or* (*coll.*) sling mud at sb./sth.; **B** (*salopp abwertend: Angelegenheit*) **bei/wegen jedem ~ regt er sich auf** he gets worked up about every piddling little thing (*coll.*); **mach deinen ~ allein** do it yourself; **kümmere dich um deinen eigenen ~:** mind your own damn business; **ein ~** *od.* **der letzte ~ sein** (*salopp abwertend*) be the lowest of the low; **das geht dich einen ~ an** (*salopp*) none of your damned business (*sl.*); **er kümmert sich einen ~ darum** (*salopp*) he doesn't give a damn about it; **er hat uns einen ~ zu befehlen** (*salopp*) he's got no damn right to order us around; **jmdn. wie [den letzten] ~ behandeln** (*ugs.*) treat sb. like dirt; **C** (*salopp abwertend: Zeug*) rubbish *no indef. art.*; junk *no indef. art.*; (*Nahrungsmittel*) junk *no indef. art.*

**Dreck-: ~arbeit** *die* (*salopp*) **A** (*schmutzige Arbeit*) dirty *or* messy work *no indef. art., no pl.*; dirty *or* messy job; **B** (*minderwertige Arbeit*) dirty *or* menial work *no indef. art., no pl.*; dirty *or* menial job; **~ding** *das; Pl.* **~~er** (*salopp*) **A** (*schmutziges Ding*) dirty *or* filthy thing; **B** (*minderwertiges Ding*) damn thing (*coll.*); **~eimer** *der* (*südd. ugs.*) rubbish bin; **~fink** *der* (*salopp*) filthy pig (*coll.*); (*Kind, das etw. schmutzig macht*) mucky pup (*Brit. coll.*); **~fleck** *der* (*ugs.*) stain; dirty mark

**dreckig 1** *Adj.* **A** (*ugs.: schmutzig, ungepflegt, auch fig.*) dirty; (*sehr, Ekel erregend schmutzig, auch fig.*) filthy; **mach dich nicht ~:** don't get yourself dirty; **B** (*salopp abwertend: unverschämt*) cheeky; **C** (*salopp abwertend: gemein*) dirty, filthy ‹swine etc.›; foul ‹crime›. **2** *adv.* **A es geht ihm ~** (*ugs.*) he's in a bad way; **B** (*salopp abwertend: unverschämt*) cheekily; **~ grinsen** have a cheeky grin on one's face

**Dreck-: ~loch** (*salopp abwertend*) (*Zimmer*) dump (*coll.*); (*Wohnung*) dump (*coll.*); hole (*coll.*); **~nest** *das* (*salopp abwertend*) hole (*coll.*); dump (*coll.*); **~sack** *der* (*derb*) bastard (*coll.*); **der ~sack von Torhüter** that dirty bastard of a goalkeeper; **~sau** *die* (*derb*) dirty *or* filthy swine; **~schaufel** *die* (*ugs.*) dustpan; **~schleuder** *die* (*derb abwertend*) **A** (*Mundwerk*) foul mouth; **halt deine ~schleuder!** keep your filthy trap shut (*sl.*); **B** (*Person*) foul mouth; **~schwein** *das* (*derb*) dirty *or* filthy swine

**Drecks·kerl** *der* (*derb*) dirty *or* filthy swine

**Dreck-: ~spatz** *der* **A** (*fam.: Kind*) grubby little so-and-so (*coll.*); (*Kind, das etw. schmutzig macht*) mucky pup (*Brit. coll.*); **B** (*ugs.: Ärger erregender Mensch*) filthy so-and-so (*coll.*); **~wetter** *das* (*ugs. abwertend*) lousy (*coll.*) *or* filthy weather; **~zeug** *das* (*ugs. abwertend*) rubbish *no indef. art.*; junk *no indef. art.*; (*Nahrungsmittel*) junk *no indef. art.*

**Dreh** /dre:/ *der;* **~s, ~s** (*ugs.*) **A** (*Einfall, Kunstgriff*) **den ~ heraushaben[, wie man es macht]** have [got] the knack [of doing it]; **auf/hinter den richtigen ~ kommen** get the knack *or* the hang of it (*coll.*); **B** *in* **um den ~:** about that

**Dreh-: ~achse** *die* axis [of rotation]; **~arbeiten** *Pl.* (*Film*) shooting *sing.* (**zu** of); **die ~arbeiten fanden in ... statt** the film was shot in ...; **~bank** *die; Pl.* **~bänke** lathe

**drehbar 1** *Adj.* revolving *attrib.* ‹stand, stage›; swivel *attrib.* ‹chair›; **~ sein** revolve/swivel. **2** *adv.* **~ gelagert** pivoted

**Dreh-: ~bewegung** *die* rotary motion; rotation; **sie machte eine rasche ~bewegung** she turned *or* spun round quickly; **~bleistift** *der* propelling pencil (*Brit.*); mechanical pencil (*Amer.*); **~brücke** *die* swing bridge; **~buch** *das* screenplay; [film] script; **~buch·autor** *der*, **~buch·autorin** *die* scriptwriter; (*als Berufsbez.*) screenwriter; scriptwriter; **~bühne** *die* revolving stage

**drehen 1** *tr. V.* **A** turn; **du kannst es ~ und wenden, wie du willst** (*fig.*) whichever way you look at it; **B** (*ugs.: einstellen*) **das Radio laut/leise ~:** turn the radio up/down; **die Flamme klein/die Heizung auf klein ~:** turn the heat/heating down; **C** (*formen*) twist ‹rope, thread›; roll ‹cigarette›; make ‹pill› by rolling; **sich** (*Dat.*) **eine [Zigarette] ~:** roll a cigarette; **D** (*Film*) shoot ‹scene›; film ‹report›; make, shoot ‹film›; ‹star› make ‹film›; **E** (*ugs. abwertend: beeinflussen*) **es so ~, dass ...** work it so that ... (*coll.*); **daran ist nichts zu ~ und zu deuteln** there are no two ways about it; **F** (*ugs. abwertend: anstellen*) **etwas ~:** get up to sth.; ⇒ *auch* **Ding² A, krumm, Mangel, Nase, Runde, Strick, Wolf.**
**2** *itr. V.* **A** (*Richtung ändern*) ‹car› turn; ‹wind› change, shift; **B an etw.** (*Dat.*) **~:** turn sth.; (*spielend, aus Langeweile*) twiddle sth.; **am Radio ~:** turn/twiddle a knob/knobs on the radio; **da muss einer dran gedreht haben** (*salopp*) somebody must have fiddled about *or* messed around with it; **C** (*Film*) shoot [a/the film]; film.
**3** *refl. V.* **A** turn; ‹wind› change, shift; (*um eine Achse*) turn; rotate; revolve; (*um einen Mittelpunkt*) revolve (**um** around); (*sehr schnell*) spin; **sie drehten sich im Tanz** they spun around; **mir dreht sich alles** (*ugs.*) everything's going round and round; **sich auf den Bauch ~:** turn over on to one's stomach; **B** (*ugs.: zum Gegenstand haben*) **sich um etw. ~:** be about sth.; **es dreht sich darum, dass ...** it's about the fact that ...; **alles dreht sich um ihn** everything revolves around him; (*er steht im Mittelpunkt des Interesses*) he is the centre of attention; **C** (*österr. ugs.: aufbrechen*) push off (*coll.*)

**Dreher** *der;* **~s, ~ A** ▶ 159 (*Beruf*) lathe operator; **B** (*Tanz*) *Austrian folk dance, similar to the Ländler*

**Dreherin** *die;* **~, ~nen** ▶ 159 ⇒ **Dreher A**

**Dreh-: ~feld** *das* (*Elektrot.*) rotating field; **~impuls** *der* (*Physik*) angular momentum; **~kolben·motor** *der* rotary engine; **~kran** *der* revolving *or* slewing crane; **~kreuz** *das* turnstile; **~maschine** *die* lathe; **~moment** *das* (*Physik*) torque; **~orgel** *die* barrel organ; **~ort** *der* (*Film*) location; **~pause** *die* (*Film*) break in shooting; **~punkt** *der* pivot; (*eines Sturms*) centre; **der ~- und Angelpunkt einer Sache** (*fig.*) the key element in sth.; **~restaurant** *das* revolving restaurant; **~schalter** *der* rotary switch; **~scheibe** *die* (*Eisenb.*) turntable; (*fig.*) hub; **~strom** *der* (*Elektrot.*) three-phase current; **~stuhl** *der* swivel chair; **~tag** *der* (*Film*) day of shooting; **~tür** *die* revolving door

**Drehung** *die;* **~, ~en A** turn; (*um eine Achse*) turn; rotation; revolution; (*um einen Mittelpunkt*) revolution; (*sehr schnell*) spin; (*beim Motor*) revolution; **eine halbe/ganze ~:** a half/complete turn; **eine ~ um 180° [machen]** [do] a 180° turn; (*fig.*) [do] a complete about-face; **B** (*das Drehen*) turning; (*sehr schnell*) spinning

**Dreh-: ~wurm** *der* **A** *in* **einen** *od.* **den ~wurm kriegen/haben** (*salopp*) get/feel giddy; **B** (*Finne*) coenurus; **~zahl** *die* revolutions *or* (*coll.*) revs (*esp. per minute*); **bei einer bestimmten ~zahl** at a particular number of revolutions *or* (*coll.*) revs per minute; **~zahl·bereich** *der:* **im unteren/oberen ~zahlbereich** at lower/higher revs (*coll.*); **~zahl·messer** *der;* **~~s, ~~:** revolution counter; rev counter (*coll.*); tachometer

**drei** *Kardinalz.* ▶ 76, ▶ 752, ▶ 841 three; **er isst/arbeitet für ~:** he eats enough for three/does the work of three people; **aller guten Dinge sind ~!** all good things come in threes; (*nach zwei missglückten Versuchen*) third time lucky!; **nicht bis ~ zählen können** (*ugs.*) be as thick as two [short] planks (*Brit. coll.*); be dead from the neck up (*coll.*); ⇒ *auch* **acht¹**; **heilig A**

**Drei** *die;* **~, ~en** three; **eine ~ schreiben/bekommen** (*Schulw.*) get a C; ⇒ *auch* **Acht¹ A, B, D, E; Zwei B**

**drei-, Drei-: ~achser** *der;* **~~s, ~~** (*ugs.*) three-axled vehicle; **~achtel·takt** *der* (*Musik*) three-eight time; **~ad[e]rig** *Adj.* (*Elektrot.*) three-core; **~akter** *der;* **~~s, ~~:** three-act play; **~bändig** *Adj.* three-volume; **~bein** *das* (*ugs.*) three-legged stool;

*old spelling (see note on page 1707)

**~beinig** *Adj.* three-legged; **~bett·zimmer** *das* room with three beds; **~blättrig** *Adj.* (*Bot.*) three-leaved; trifoliate (*Bot.*)

**3-D-Brille** /draiˈdeː-/ *die* 3-D glasses *pl.*

**3-D-Effekt** *der* 3-D effect

**drei-, Drei-: ~dimensional** ❶ *Adj.* three-dimensional; ❷ *adv.* three-dimensionally; in three dimensions; **einen Film ~dimensional sehen** watch a film in 3-D; **~eck** *das* Ⓐ (*Geom.*) triangle; **das Goldene ~eck** the Golden Triangle; Ⓑ (*bes. Fußball*) top corner; **~eckig** *Adj.* triangular; three-cornered; **~ecks·verhältnis** *das* eternal triangle; **~ein·halb** *Bruchz.* ▸841 three and a half; **~einig** *Adj. in* **der ~einige Gott** (*christl. Rel.*) the triune God[head]; **~einigkeit** *die* (*christl. Rel.*) trinity; **die Heilige ~einigkeit** the [Holy] Trinity

**Dreier** *der;* **~s, ~** Ⓐ (*ugs.*) ⇒ **Drei**; Ⓑ (*ugs.: im Lotto*) three winning numbers; Ⓒ (*hist.: Münze*) three-pfennig piece; Ⓓ (*Golf*) threesome; Ⓔ (*ugs.: Sprungbrett*) three-metre board; ⇒ *auch* **Achter** C, D

**Dreier-: ~kombination** *die* (*Ski*) Alpine combined event; **~reihe** *die* row of three; **~takt** *der* (*Musik*) triple time

**dreierlei** *indekl. Gattungsz.* Ⓐ *attr.* three kinds *or* sorts of; three different ‹sorts, kinds, sizes, possibilities›; Ⓑ *subst.* three [different] things

**drei-, Drei-: ~fach** *Vervielfältigungsz.* triple; **die ~fache Menge** three times *or* triple the amount; three times as much; **ein ~fach [es] Hoch!** three cheers!; **ein ~fach verschnürtes Paket** a parcel tied three times; **~fach verstärkt** triple reinforced; ⇒ *auch* **achtfach**; **~fache** *das; adj. Dekl.* **das ~fache essen/kosten** eat/cost three times as much; **das ~fache von 3 ist 9** three times three is nine; **auf ein ~faches** *od.* **auf das ~fache steigen** treble; triple; ⇒ *auch* **Achtfache**; **~faltigkeit** /-ˈ--/ *die;* **~~** (*christl. Rel.*) Trinity; **~farben·druck** /-ˈ--/ *der; Pl.* **~~e** Ⓐ (*Verfahren*) three-colour process; **im ~farbendruck [gedruckt]** printed by the three-colour process; Ⓑ (*einzelner Druck*) three-colour print; **~felder·wirtschaft** /-ˈ---/ *die* three-field *or* three-course system; **~fuß** *der* Ⓐ (*für Kessel usw.*) trivet; tripod; Ⓑ (*Schemel*) three-legged stool; Ⓒ (*zum Besohlen*) three-way last; **~gang·schaltung** *die* three-speed gearbox *or* gears *pl. or* (*Amer.*) gear shift; **~gespann** *das* team of three horses; (*fig.: von Direktoren o. Ä.*) triumvirate; **eine Kutsche mit ~gespann** a three-horse carriage; **das unzertrennliche ~gespann** (*fig.*) the inseparable trio *or* threesome; **~gestrichen** *Adj.* (*Musik*) **das ~gestrichene C** the C two octaves above middle C; **~gestrichene Oktave** three-line octave; **~groschen·heft** /-ˈ---/ *das* (*abwertend*) cheap novelette; dime novel (*Amer.*)

**Dreiheit** *die;* **~:** trinity

**drei-, Drei-: ~hundert** *Kardinalz.* ▸841 three hundred; **~jährig** *Adj.* (*3 Jahre alt*) three-year-old *attrib.;* (*3 Jahre dauernd*) three-year *attrib.;* ⇒ *auch* **achtjährig**; **~jährlich** ❶ *Adj.* three-yearly; triennial; ❷ *adv.* every three years; triennially; ⇒ *auch* **achtjährlich**; **~kampf** *der* (*Sport*) triathlon; **~kantig** *Adj.* three-sided; triangular; **~kantstahl** *der* (*Technik*) triangular section steel [rod]; **~käse·hoch** /-ˈ--/ *der;* **~~s, ~~s** (*ugs. scherzh.*) [little] nipper (*Brit. sl.*); little kid (*sl.*); **~klang** *der* triad; **~klassen·wahlrecht** /-ˈ---/ *das* (*hist.*) three-class franchise; **~könige** /-ˈ--/ (*das*); **~~:** Epiphany *sing.*; **an** *od.* **zu/nach ~könige** at/after Epiphany; **~köpfig** *Adj.* ‹family, crew› of three; three-headed ‹monster›; **~ländereck** /-ˈ---/ *das: region where three countries meet;* **~mal** *Adv.* three times; ⇒ *auch* **achtmal**; **~malig** *Adj.* **eine ~malige Warnung/Wiederholung** three warnings/repeats; ⇒ *auch* **achtmalig**; **~meilen·zone** /-ˈ---/ *die* three-mile zone; **~meter·brett** /-ˈ--/ *das* three-metre board

**drein** (*ugs.*) ⇒ **darein**

**drein-: ~|blicken** *itr. V.* **mürrisch** *usw.* **~blicken** look morose *etc.*; **~|finden** *unr. refl. V.* (*ugs.*) get used to things; **~|reden** *itr. V.* (*ugs.*) **jmdm. ~reden** (*sich einmischen*) interfere in sb.'s affairs; (*jmdm. Vorschriften machen*) tell sb. what to do; **~|schauen** *itr. V.* ⇒ **~blicken**; **~|schlagen** *unr. itr. V.* (*ugs.*) lay into him/her/them *etc.* (*coll.*)

**drei-, Drei-: ~phasen·strom** /-ˈ--/ *der* (*Elektrot.*) three-phase current; **~polig** *Adj.* (*Elektrot.*) three-core ‹cable›; three-pin ‹adapter›; **~punkt·gurt** *der* lap and diagonal belt; **~rad** *das* Ⓐ (*Kinderfahrrad*) tricycle; Ⓑ (*Kleintransporter*) three-wheeled van; **~räd[e]rig** *Adj.* three-wheeled; **~satz** *der,* **~satz·rechnung** *die* rule of three; **~schiffig** *Adj.* (*Archit.*) with a nave and two aisles *postpos.;* **~seitig** *Adj.* three-sided ‹figure›; three-page ‹letter, leaflet, etc.›; **~sekunden·regel** /-ˈ---/ *die* (*Sport*) three-second rule; **~silbig** *Adj.* trisyllabic; three-syllable *attrib.;* **~spaltig** (*Druckw.*) ❶ *Adj.* three-column; ⇒ *auch* **achtspaltig**; ❷ *adv.* ‹printed, set› in three columns; **~spänner** *der;* **~~s, ~~:** three-horse carriage; **~spitz** *der* (*hist.*) tricorn; three-cornered hat; **~sprachig** ❶ *Adj.* trilingual; ❷ *adv.* Ⓐ **~sprachig erzogen werden** be brought up speaking three languages; Ⓑ ‹written› in three languages; ⇒ *auch* **zweisprachig**; **~sprung** *der* triple jump

**dreißig** /ˈdraisɪç/ *Kardinalz.* ▸76, ▸841 thirty; ⇒ *auch* **achtzig**

**Dreißig** *die;* **~:** thirty

**dreißiger** *indekl. Adj.* **ein ~ Jahrgang** a '30 vintage; **die ~ Jahre** the thirties

**Dreißiger**[1] *der;* **~s, ~** (*30-jähriger*) thirty-year-old; ⇒ *auch* **Achtziger**[1] B, C

**Dreißiger**[2] *die;* **~, ~** (*ugs.*) Ⓐ (*Briefmarke*) thirty-pfennig/schilling *etc.* stamp; Ⓑ (*Zigarre*) thirty-pfennig cigar

**Dreißiger**[3] *Pl.* thirties; **eine Frau in den ~n** a woman in her thirties

**Dreißigerin** *die;* **~, ~nen** ⇒ **Dreißiger**[1]

**Dreißiger·jahre** *Pl.* ▸76, ▸207 thirties *pl.*

**dreißig-, Dreißig-: ~jährig** *Adj.* (*30 Jahre alt*) thirty-year-old *attrib.;* (*30 Jahre dauernd*) thirty-year *attrib.;* **der ~jährige Krieg** the Thirty Years' War; ⇒ *auch* **achtjährig**; **~jährige** *der/die; adj. Dekl.* thirty-year-old; **~pfennig·marke** /--ˈ---/ *die* thirty-pfennig stamp

**dreißigst...** /ˈdraisɪçst.../ *Ordinalz.* ▸207, ▸841 thirtieth; ⇒ *auch* **acht...**; **achtzigst...**

**Dreißigstel** *das;* **~s, ~** ▸841 thirtieth

**dreist** /draist/ ❶ *Adj.* brazen; barefaced ‹lie›. ❷ *adv.* brazenly

**drei·stellig** *Adj.* three-figure *attrib.* ‹number, sum›; ⇒ *auch* **achtstellig**

**Dreistigkeit** *die;* **~, ~en** Ⓐ (*Art*) brazenness; **er besaß die ~, zu ...** he had the audacity *or* cheek to ...; Ⓑ (*Handlung*) brazen act; (*Bemerkung*) brazen remark

**drei-, Drei-: ~stimmig** ❶ *Adj.* ‹song› for three voices; three-voice ‹choir›; three-part ‹singing›; ❷ *adv.* ‹sing› in three voices; ‹play› in three parts; **~stöckig** ❶ *Adj.* three-storey *attrib.;* ⇒ *auch* **achtstöckig**; ❷ *adv.* ‹build› three storeys high; **~stufen·rakete** /-ˈ---/ *die* three-stage rocket; **~stündig** *Adj.* three-hour *attrib.;* ⇒ *auch* **achtstündig**; **~stündlich** ❶ *Adj.* three-hourly; ❷ *adv.* every three hours; **~tägig** *Adj.* (*3 Tage alt*) three-day-old *attrib.;* (*3 Tage dauernd*) three-day *attrib.;* ⇒ *auch* **achttägig**; **~täglich** ❶ *Adj.* **in ~täglichem Wechsel** on a three-day rota; ❷ *adv.* every three days; **~tausend** *Kardinalz.* ▸841 three thousand; **~tausender** *der* mountain more than three thousand metres high; **~teilig** *Adj.* three-part *attrib.* ‹documentary, novel, etc.›; three-piece *attrib.* ‹suit›; **~teilig sein** be in three parts/consist of three pieces; ***~viertel** ⇒ **viertel**; **~viertel·lang** /-ˈ--/ *Adj.* three-quarter-length; **~viertel·liter·flasche** /---ˈ---/ *die* three-quarter-litre bottle; **~viertel·mehrheit** /-ˈ---/ *die* three-quarters majority; **~viertel·stunde** /--ˈ--/ *die* three-quarters of an hour; **~viertel·takt** /-ˈ--/ *der* three-four time; **im ~vierteltakt** in three-four time; **~wege·katalysator** *der* (*Kfz-W.*) three-way catalytic converter; **~wertig** *Adj.* Ⓐ (*Chemie*) trivalent; Ⓑ (*Sprachw.*) three-place *attrib.;* **~wöchentlich** ❶ *Adj.* three-weekly; ❷ *adv.* every three weeks; ⇒ *auch* **achtwöchentlich**; **~wöchig** *Adj.* (*3 Wochen alt*) three-week-old *attrib.;* (*3 Wochen dauernd*) three-week *attrib.;* **~zack** *der;* **~~s, ~~e** trident; **~zackig** *Adj.* three-pointed; **~zehn** *Kardinalz.* ▸76, ▸752, ▸841 thirteen; **jetzt schlägts aber ~zehn!** (*ugs.*) that's going too far; ⇒ *auch* **achtzehn**; **~zehnhundert** ▸841 *Kardinalz.* one thousand three hundred; thirteen hundred; **~zehnt...** *Ordinalz.* thirteenth; ⇒ *auch* **acht**; **~zehntel** *das* thirteenth; **~zeilig** *Adj.* three-line *attrib.;* **~zeilig sein** have three lines; **~zimmer·wohnung** *die* three-room flat (*Brit.*) *or* (*Amer.*) apartment

**Dresche** /ˈdrɛʃə/ *die;* **~** (*salopp*) walloping (*coll.*); thrashing; **~ kriegen** get a walloping (*coll.*) *or* thrashing

**dreschen** ❶ *unr. tr. V.* Ⓐ thresh; Ⓑ (*salopp: prügeln*) wallop (*coll.*); thrash; Ⓒ (*salopp: schießen*) wallop (*coll.*) ‹ball›; **den Ball ins Netz ~:** slam the ball into the net (*coll.*); ⇒ *auch* **Skat**. ❷ *unr. itr. V.* Ⓐ thresh; Ⓑ (*salopp: schlagen*) thump; bang; **mit der Faust auf den Tisch ~:** bang one's fist on the table; pound *or* bang the table with one's fist

**Drescher** *der;* **~s, ~, Drescherin** *die;* **~, ~nen** thresher

**Dresch-: ~flegel** *der* flail; **~maschine** *die* threshing machine

**Dresden** /ˈdreːsdn̩/ (*das*); **~s** ▸700 Dresden

**Dresd[e]ner** /ˈdreːsd(ə)nɐ/ ▸700 ❶ *indekl. Adj.* Dresden. ❷ *der;* **~s, ~:** native of Dresden; (*Einwohner*) inhabitant of Dresden; ⇒ *auch* **Kölner**

**Dresd[e]nerin** *die;* **~, ~nen** ⇒ **Dresd[e]ner** 2

**Dress, *Dreß** /drɛs/ *der;* **~** *od.* **Dresses, Dresse;** (*österr. auch die;* **~, Dressen**) Ⓐ (*Sportkleidung*) kit (*Brit.*); (*Fußball, Hockey usw.*) kit (*Brit.*); strip (*Brit. coll.*); Ⓑ (*ugs.: Kleidung*) outfit

**Dresseur** /drɛˈsøːɐ̯/ *der;* **~s, ~e, Dresseurin** *die;* **~, ~nen** [animal] trainer

**dressierbar** *Adj.* trainable; **nicht/gut ~:** untrainable/easy to train

**dressieren** *tr. V.* Ⓐ train ‹animal›; **darauf dressiert sein, etw. zu tun** be trained to do sth.; **der Hund ist auf den Mann dressiert** the dog is trained to attack people; Ⓑ (*Kochk.*) dress ‹poultry, fish, game›; decorate ‹cake etc.›; pipe ‹icing, marzipan, etc.›

**Dressing** /ˈdrɛsɪŋ/ *das;* **~s, ~s** dressing

**Dressman** /ˈdrɛsmən/ *der;* **~s, Dressmen** male model

**Dressur** /drɛˈsuːɐ̯/ *die;* **~, ~en** Ⓐ training; (*fig. abwertend*) conditioning; Ⓑ (*Kunststück*) trick; Ⓒ (*~reiten*) dressage

**Dressur-: ~pferd** *das* dressage horse; **~prüfung** *die* (*Reiten*) dressage [test]; **~reiten** *das* dressage

**dribbeln** /ˈdrɪbl̩n/ *itr. V.* (*Ballspiele*) dribble [the ball]

**Dribbling** /ˈdrɪblɪŋ/ *das;* **~s, ~s** (*Ballspiele*) piece of dribbling; **seine Stärken sind Kopfball und ~:** his strengths are heading and dribbling

**Drift** /drɪft/ ⇒ **Trift** A

**driften** *itr. V.; mit sein* (*auch fig.*) drift

**Drill**[1] /drɪl/ *der;* **~[e]s** drilling; (*Milit.*) drill

**Drill**[2] *der;* **~s, ~e** ⇒ **Drillich**

**Drill·bohrer** *der* drill

**drillen** *tr. V.* Ⓐ (*auch Milit.*) drill; **auf etw.** (*Akk.*) **gedrillt sein** be well-drilled in sth.; **jmdn. auf Angriff ~:** train sb. to attack; Ⓑ (*Landw.*) drill; Ⓒ (*bohren*) drill ‹hole›

**Drillich** /ˈdrɪlɪç/ *der;* **~s, ~e** drill

**Drillich·zeug** *das* [heavy cotton twill] overalls *pl.*

**Drilling** /ˈdrɪlɪŋ/ *der;* **~s, ~e** Ⓐ (*Geschwister*) triplet; Ⓑ (*Gewehr*) triple-barrelled shotgun

d

**Drill·maschine** *die* (*Landw.*) drill

**drin** /drɪn/ *Adv.* Ⓐ (*ugs.: darin*) in it; **da könnte für mich was ~ sein** something might come out of it [for me]; **das ist/mehr als 2 000 DM sind nicht ~:** that/any more than 2,000 marks is not on (*Brit. coll.*) *or* (*Amer. coll.*) is no go; **es ist noch alles ~** (*bei einem Fußballspiel usw.*) there's still everything to play for; **nach drei Tagen ist man wieder ~** (*wieder eingearbeitet*) after three days you're back in the swing of things; ⇒ *auch* **darin**; Ⓑ (*ugs.: ~nen*) inside; **hier/da ~:** in here/there; ⇒ *auch* **~nen**

**dringen** /ˈdrɪŋən/ *unr. itr. V.* Ⓐ *mit sein* (*gelangen*) ‹water, smell, etc.› penetrate, come through; ‹news› get through; **in etw.** (*Akk.*) **~:** get into *or* penetrate sth.; **durch etw. ~:** come through *or* penetrate sth.; ‹person› push one's way through sth.; **die Nachricht ist nicht bis zu mir gedrungen** the news did not get through to me; **in** *od.* **an die Öffentlichkeit ~:** get out; become public knowledge; Ⓑ *mit sein* (*geh.: einwirken*) **in jmdn. ~:** press *or* urge sb.; **mit Fragen/Ermahnungen in jmdn. ~:** ply sb. with questions/press warnings on sb.; **sich gedrungen fühlen, etw. zu tun** (*veralt.*) feel obliged *or* compelled to do sth.; Ⓒ (*fordern*) **auf etw.** (*Akk.*) **~:** insist upon sth.

**dringend** ❶ *Adj.* Ⓐ (*eilig*) urgent; Ⓑ (*eindringlich, stark*) urgent ‹appeal›; strong ‹suspicion, advice›; compelling ‹need›. ❷ *adv.* Ⓐ (*sofort*) urgently; Ⓑ (*zwingend*) ‹recommend, advise, suspect› strongly; **jmdn. ~ bitten, etw. zu tun** insist that sb. does sth.; **~ erforderlich sein** be imperative *or* essential

**dringlich** /ˈdrɪŋlɪç/ ❶ *Adj.* urgent. ❷ *adv.* urgently; **jmdn. ~ bitten, etw. zu tun** plead hard with sb. to do sth.

**Dringlichkeit** *die;* **~:** urgency

**Dringlichkeits·antrag** *der* (*Parl.*) emergency motion

**Drink** /drɪŋk/ *der;* **~s, ~s** drink

**drinnen** /ˈdrɪnən/ *Adv.* inside; (*im Haus*) indoors; inside; **von ~:** from inside/indoors; **nach ~ gehen** go in[side]/indoors; **~ im Haus** indoors; **hier/da ~:** in here/there

**drin-: ~|sitzen** *unr. itr. V.* (*ugs.*) be right in it (*coll.*); **~|stecken** *itr. V.* (*ugs.*) Ⓐ (*beschäftigt sein*) **[bis über beide Ohren] in etw.** (*Dat.*) **~stecken** be up to one's ears in sth. (*coll.*); Ⓑ (*vorhanden sein*) **ich bin überzeugt, dass viel in ihm ~steckt** I am convinced he has a lot in him; **da steckt nichts für dich ~:** there's nothing in it for you; **da steckt viel Arbeit ~:** there's a lot of work in that; Ⓒ (*voraussehen können*) **da steckt man nicht ~:** there's no [way of] telling; **~|stehen** *unr. itr. V.; südd. auch mit sein* **in etw.** (*Dat.*) **~stehen** be in sth.

**dritt** /drɪt/ *in* **wir waren zu ~:** there were three of us; **eine Ehe zu ~:** a ménage à trois; ⇒ *auch* **acht**[2]

**dritt...** *Ordinalz.* ▶ 207, ▶ 841 third; **wer ist der Dritte im Bunde?** who is the third person?; **in Gegenwart Dritter** in the presence of other people; **ein Drittes wäre noch zu erwägen** there is a third point that ought to be considered; **wenn zwei sich streiten, freut sich der Dritte** (*Spr.*) when two people argue, somebody else benefits; **der lachende Dritte** the one to benefit (*from a dispute between two others*); ⇒ *auch* **acht...**

**dritt·best...** *Adj.* third-best

***Dritteil** *das;* **~s, ~e** (*veralt.*), **Drittel** *das,* (*schweiz. meist* **der**); **~s, ~** ▶ 841 third

**dritteln** *tr. V.* split *or* divide ‹cost, profit› three ways; divide ‹number› by three

***dritte·mal, *dritten·mal** ⇒ **Mal**[1]

**drittens** *Adv.* thirdly

**dritt-, Dritt-: ~größt...** *Adj.* third-largest; **~höchst...** *Adj.* third-highest; **~klassig** *Adj.* (*meist abwertend*) third-class ‹hotel, railway carriage›; third-rate ‹actor, novel, artist›; **~klässler, *~kläßler** *der;* **~~s, ~~, ~klässlerin, *~kläßlerin** *die;* **~~, ~~nen** third-former; **~letzt...** *Adj.* antepenultimate; **~schuldner** *der,* **~schuldnerin** *die* (*Rechtsw.*) garnishee

**Drive** /draif/ *der;* **~s, ~s** (*auch Jazz, Golf, Tennis*) drive

**Dr. jur.** *Abk.* **doctor juris** LL D; ⇒ *auch* **Dr. phil.**

**DRK** *Abk.* **Deutsches Rotes Kreuz** German Red Cross

**Dr. med.** *Abk.* **doctor medicinae** MD; ⇒ *auch* **Dr. phil.**

**Dr. med. dent.** *Abk.* **doctor medicinae dentoriae** DMD; ⇒ *auch* **Dr. phil.**

**drob** /drɔp/ ⇒ **darob**

**droben** /ˈdroːbn̩/ *Adv.* (*südd., österr., sonst geh.*) up there; **da/hier ~:** up there/here

**dröge** /ˈdrøːɡə/ (*nordd.*) ❶ *Adj.* (*auch fig.*) dry. ❷ *adv.* drily

**Droge** /ˈdroːɡə/ *die;* **~, ~n** drug; **unter ~n stehen** be on drugs

**drogen-, Drogen-: ~abhängig** *Adj.* addicted to drugs *postpos.;* **~abhängig sein/werden** be/become a drug addict; **~abhängige** *der/die; adj. Dekl.* drug addict; **~abhängigkeit** *die* drug addiction; **~handel** *der* drug trafficking; **~missbrauch, *~mißbrauch** *der* drug abuse; **~süchtig** *Adj.* ⇒ **~abhängig**; **~szene** *die* drug scene; **~tote** *der/die* drug-related death

**Drogerie** /drogəˈriː/ *die;* **~, ~n** chemist's [shop] (*Brit.*); drugstore (*Amer.*)

**Drogist** *der;* **~en, ~en, Drogistin** *die;* **~, ~nen** ▶ 159 chemist (*Brit.*); druggist (*Amer.*)

**Droh·brief** *der* threatening letter

**drohen** /ˈdroːən/ *itr. V.* threaten; **er drohte ihm mit erhobenem Zeigefinger** he raised a warning finger to him; **jmdm. mit etw. ~:** threaten sb. with sth.; **die Regierung hat mit dem Abbruch der diplomatischen Beziehungen gedroht** the government threatened to break off diplomatic relations; **den Angeklagten droht die Todesstrafe** the accused are threatened with the death penalty; **ein Gewitter drohte** a storm was threatening

**drohend** ❶ *Adj.* impending ‹danger, strike, disaster›; threatening ‹gesture, clouds›. ❷ *adv.* threateningly

**Droh·gebärde** *die* threatening gesture

**Drohn** /droːn/ *der;* **~en, ~en, Drohne** *die;* **~e, ~en** drone

**dröhnen** /ˈdrøːnən/ *itr. V.* Ⓐ ‹voice, music› boom; ‹machine› roar; ‹room etc.› resound (**von** with); **~der Applaus** thunderous applause; **er brach in ~des Gelächter aus** he roared with laughter; **mir dröhnt der Schädel** (*ugs.*) my head's ringing; Ⓑ (*Drogenjargon: Rausch verursachen*) **das dröhnt** it gives you a high (*coll.*)

**Dröhnung** *die;* **~, ~en** (*Drogenjargon*) Ⓐ (*Dosis*) fix (*sl.*); Ⓑ (*Rausch*) high (*coll.*)

**Drohung** *die;* **~, ~en** threat; **eine ~ wahr machen** carry out a threat

**drollig** /ˈdrɔlɪç/ ❶ *Adj.* Ⓐ (*spaßig*) funny; comical; (*niedlich*) sweet; cute (*Amer.*); Ⓑ (*seltsam*) odd; peculiar; **werde nicht ~:** don't get funny. ❷ *adv.* Ⓐ (*spaßig*) comically; (*niedlich*) sweetly; cutely (*Amer.*); Ⓑ (*seltsam*) oddly; peculiarly

**Dromedar** /ˈdroːmedaːɐ̯/ *das;* **~s, ~e** dromedary

**Drops** /drɔps/ *der od. das;* **~, ~:** fruit *or* (*Brit.*) acid drop; **saurer** *od.* **saures ~:** acid drop (*Brit.*); sour ball (*Amer.*)

**drosch** /drɔʃ/ *1. u. 3. Pers. Sg. Prät. v.* **dreschen**

**Droschke** /ˈdrɔʃkə/ *die;* **~, ~n** Ⓐ hackney carriage; Ⓑ (*veralt.: Taxi*) [taxi] cab

**Droschken-: ~kutscher** *der* hackney coachman; **~platz** *der* (*Amtsspr.*) taxi rank

**Drossel**[1] /ˈdrɔsl/ *die;* **~, ~n** thrush

**Drossel**[2] *die;* **~, ~n** (*Technik*) ⇒ **~spule, ~ventil**

**Drossel·klappe** *die* (*Technik*) throttle *or* butterfly valve

**drosseln** *tr. V.* Ⓐ turn down ‹heating, air conditioning›; throttle back ‹engine›; reduce *or* restrict the flow of ‹steam, air›; check ‹flow›; Ⓑ (*herabsetzen*) reduce; cut back *or* down; reduce ‹speed›

**Drossel·spule** *die* (*Elektrot.*) choking coil

**Drosselung** *die;* **~, ~en** ⇒ **drosseln**: turning down; throttling back; reduction *or* restriction of the flow; checking; reduction; cutback

**Drossel·ventil** *das* (*Technik*) throttle valve

**Dr. phil.** *Abk.* **doctor philosophiae** Dr; **~ Hans Schulz** Dr Hans Schulz; Hans Schulz, Ph. D.; **sie ist ~, nicht Dr. med.** she is a Ph. D. *or* a Doctor of Philosophy, not a Doctor of Medicine

**Dr. rer. nat.** *Abk.* **doctor rerum naturalium** Doctor of Natural Science

**Dr. rer. pol.** *Abk.* **doctor rerum politicarum** Doctor of Political Science

**Dr. theol.** *Abk.* **doctor theologiae** DD

**drüben** /ˈdryːbn̩/ *Adv.* Ⓐ **dort** *od.* **da ~:** over there; **~ auf der anderen Seite** over on the other side; Ⓑ (*in der DDR*) in the East; (*in der Bundesrepublik, in West-Berlin*) in the West; **von ~ kommen** come from across the border/sea *etc.*

**drüber** /ˈdryːbɐ/ (*ugs.*) ⇒ **darüber**

**drüber-** (*ugs.*) ⇒ **darüber**

**Druck**[1] /drʊk/ *der;* **~[e]s, Drücke** /ˈdrʏkə/ Ⓐ (*Physik*) pressure; **einen ~ im Kopf/Magen haben** (*fig.*) have a feeling of pressure in one's head/stomach; Ⓑ (*das Drücken*) **ein ~ auf den Knopf** a touch of *or* on the button; Ⓒ (*Zwang*) pressure; **auf jmdn. ~ ausüben** put pressure on sb.; **unter ~ stehen/handeln** be/act under pressure; **jmdn. unter ~ setzen** put pressure on sb.; **~ dahinter machen** (*ugs.*) put some pressure on; **in** *od.* **im ~ sein** (*ugs.*) be under pressure of time; Ⓓ *Pl.* **~s** (*Drogenjargon: Injektion*) fix (*sl.*); **sich** (*Dat.*) **einen ~ setzen** give oneself a fix (*sl.*)

**Druck**[2] *der;* **~[e]s, ~e** Ⓐ (*das ~en*) printing; (*Art des Druckens*) print; **in ~ gehen** go to press; **etw. in ~ geben** send sth. to press; **~ und Verlag Meier & Sohn** printed and published by Meier and Son; **im ~ erscheinen** appear in print; **im ~ sein** be being printed; Ⓑ (*Bild, Grafik usw.*) print; Ⓒ *Pl.* (*fachspr.*) **~s** (*Textilw.*) print; Ⓓ (*~schrift*) printed work; **frühe persische ~e** early printed works from Persia

**Druck-: ~ab·fall** *der* (*Physik*) drop *or* fall in pressure; **~an·zug** *der* pressure suit; **~anstieg** *der* (*Physik*) rise *or* increase in pressure; **~ausgleich** *der* (*Physik, Med.*) (*Vorgang*) equalization of pressure; (*Zustand*) balance of pressure; **~blei·stift** *der* propelling pencil; **~bogen** *der* printed sheet; **~buchstabe** *der* block letter *or* capital

**Drückeberger** /ˈdrʏkəbɛrɡɐ/ *der;* **~s, ~** (*ugs. abwertend*) shirker

**Drückebergerei** *die;* **~** (*ugs. abwertend*) shirking

**Drückebergerin** *die;* **~, ~nen** ⇒ **Drückeberger**

**druck·empfindlich** *Adj.* pressure-sensitive ‹material›; easily bruised ‹fruit›; ‹area of the body› sensitive to pressure

**drucken** *tr., itr. V.* print

**drücken** /ˈdrʏkn̩/ ❶ *tr. V.* Ⓐ (*pressen*) press; press, push ‹button›; **jmdm. die Hand ~:** squeeze sb.'s hand; **jmdn. zur Seite/an die Wand ~:** push sb. aside/against the wall; **jmdn. ans Herz** *od.* **an sich** (*Akk.*) **~:** clasp sb. to one's breast; **jmdm. etw. in die Hand ~:** press sth. into sb.'s hand; Ⓑ (*heraus~*) squeeze ‹juice, pus› (**aus** out of); Ⓒ (*liebkosen*) **jmdn. ~:** hug [and squeeze] sb.; Ⓓ (*Druck verursachen, quetschen*) ‹shoe, corset, bandage, etc.› pinch; Ⓔ (*geh.: be~*) ‹conscience› weigh heavily [up]on sb.; **jmds. Stimmung ~:** depress sb.'s spirits; Ⓕ (*herabsetzen*) push *or* force down ‹price, rate›; depress ‹sales›; bring down ‹standard›; **den Rekord ~:** beat *or* break the record; **den Rekord um zwei Sekunden ~:** take two seconds off the record; Ⓖ (*Kartenspiel*) discard; Ⓗ (*Gewichtheben*)

*old spelling (see note on page 1707)

press; **I** (*Drogenjargon: injizieren*) **sich** (*Dat.*) **einen Schuss ~:** give oneself a fix (*sl.*).
**2** *itr. V.* **A** press; **auf den Knopf ~:** press *or* push the button; **„bitte ~"** 'push'; **die Hitze drückt** *od.* **ist ~d** (*fig.*) the heat is oppressive; **das drückte auf die Stimmung/unsere gute Laune** (*fig.*) it spoilt the atmosphere/dampened our spirits; ⇨ *auch* **Tränendrüse**; **B** (*Druck verursachen*) ‹shoe, corset, bandage› pinch; **der Rucksack drückt** the rucksack is pressing *or* digging into me; **C** (*herabsetzen*) **auf etw.** (*Akk.*) **~:** push *or* force sth. down; **D** (*Drogenjargon*) fix (*sl.*).
**3** *refl. V.* **A** **sich in die Ecke ~:** squeeze [oneself] into the corner; **die Kinder drückten sich ängstlich in die Ecke** the children huddled frightened in the corner; **sich aus dem Saal ~:** slip out of the hall; **B** (*ugs.*) shirk; **sich vor etw.** (*Dat.*) **~:** get out of *or* dodge sth.; **sich vor einer Pflicht/Verantwortung/Aussprache ~:** shirk a duty/responsibility/avoid a frank discussion; **sich vor der Arbeit/ums Bezahlen ~:** get out of *or* avoid doing any work/paying

**drückend** *Adj.* **A** burdensome ‹responsibility›; grinding ‹poverty›; heavy ‹debt, taxes›; serious ‹worries›; **B** (*schwül*) oppressive

**Drucker** *der;* **~s, ~** ▶ 159 printer

**Drücker** *der;* **~s, ~** **A** (*Tür~*) handle; (*eines Schnappschlosses*) latch; (*Abzug am Gewehr*) trigger; **auf den letzten ~** (*ugs.*) at the very last minute; **B** (*Knopf*) [push-]button; (*Klingelknopf*) [bell] push; **am ~ sitzen** *od.* **sein** (*fig. ugs.*) be in charge; **C** (*ugs.: Werber*) hawker of magazine subscriptions; **D** (*ugs.: Unterton, Nuance*) touch

**Druckerei** *die;* **~, ~en** printing works; (*Firma*) printing house; printer's

**Druckerei·arbeiter** *der,* **Druckerei·arbeiterin** *die* print worker

**Drucker·farbe** *die* ⇨ **Druckfarbe**

**Druckerin** *die;* **~, ~nen** ▶ 159 printer

**Drückerin** *die;* **~, ~nen** ⇨ **Drücker** C

**Druck·erlaubnis** *die* permission to print; **die ~ verweigern** refuse to allow the book/article *etc.* to be printed

**Drucker-:** **~presse** *die* ⇨ **Druckmaschine**; **~schwärze** *die* printer's *or* printing ink; **~sprache** *die* printers' terminology; **~zeichen** *das* printer's mark

**druck-, Druck-:** **~erzeugnis** *das* piece of printed matter; **~erzeugnisse** printed matter *sing.*; **~fahne** *die* galley proof; **~farbe** *die* printer's *or* printing ink; **~fehler** *der* misprint; printer's error; **~fehler·teufel** *der* (*scherzh.*) misprint gremlin; **~fertig** *Adj.* ready for press *pred.*; **~fest** *Adj.* pressure-resistant; **~form** *die* [type] forme; **~frisch** *Adj.* hot off the press *postpos.*; **~grafik**, **~graphik** *die* (*Kunstwiss.*) graphic reproduction; **~kabine** *die* pressurized cabin; **~knopf** *der* **A** press stud (*Brit.*); snap fastener; **B** (*an Geräten*) push-button; **~kosten** *Pl.* printing costs

**Drucklegung** *die;* **~, ~en** printing; **die ~** *od.* **mit der ~ beginnen** go to press

**druck-, Druck-:** **~luft** *die* (*Physik*) compressed air; **~luft·bremse** *die* air brake; **~maschine** *die* printing press; **~messer** *der;* **~~s, ~~:** pressure gauge; **~mittel** *das* means of bringing pressure to bear (**gegenüber** on); **~papier** *das* printing paper; **~platte** *die* [printing] plate; **~posten** *der* (*ugs.*) cushy job (*coll.*); **~pumpe** *die* (*Technik*) pressure pump; **~punkt** *der* **A** (*bei Waffen*) first trigger pressure; **B** (*bei Flugzeugen*) centre of pressure; **~reif** **1** *Adj.* ready for publication; (*~fertig*) ready for press; (*fig.*) polished, perfectly formulated ‹phrase, reply›; **2** *adv.* ‹speak› in a polished manner; **~sache** *die* **A** (*Postw.*) printed matter; **B** (*Druckw.*) printed stationery; **~schrift** *die* **A** block letters *pl.*; **B** (*Schriftart*) type[face]; **C** (*Schriftwerk*) pamphlet

**drucksen** /ˈdrʊksn̩/ *itr. V.* (*ugs.*) hum and haw (*coll.*)

**druck-, Druck-:** **~stelle** *die* mark (*where pressure has been applied*); (*an Obst*) bruise; **die ~stelle von der Zahnklammer** the tender spot where the brace has/had been pressing; **~stock** *der* block; **~taste** *die* push-button; **~technisch** **1** *Adj.* printing *attrib.* ‹process›; **ein ~technisches Problem** a problem from the point of view of printing. **2** *adv.* from the point of view of printing; **~type** *die* type; **~verband** *der* pressure bandage; **~verfahren** *das* printing process; **~vorlage** *die* printer's copy; **~wasser·reaktor** *der* pressurized-water reactor; **~welle** *die* (*Physik*) shock wave; **~werk** *das* publication; printed work; **~wesen** *das* printing; **~zylinder** *der* (*Fotoreproduktion*) printing cylinder; (*Offset~*) impression cylinder

**Drude** /ˈdruːdə/ *die;* **~, ~n** (*Myth.*): *nocturnal female spirit that causes nightmares*

**Druden·fuß** *der* pentagram

**druff** /drʊf/ (*ugs. landsch.*) ⇨ **drauf**

**Druide** /druˈiːdə/ *der;* **~n, ~n** (*hist.*) Druid

**drum** /drʊm/ *Adv.* (*ugs.*) **A** ⇨ **darum**; **B** [a]round; **um etw. ~ herum** [all] [a]round sth.; **ein Haus mit einem Garten ~:** a house with a garden [a]round it; **~ rumreden** beat about *or* (*Amer.*) around the bush; **eben ~:** that's precisely why; **seis ~:** never mind; [that's] too bad; **alles, was ~ und dran ist** *od.* **hängt** all the things that go with it; (*bei einer Sachlage*) all the circumstances; **alles** *od.* **das [ganze] Drum und Dran** (*bei einer Mahlzeit*) all the trimmings; (*bei einer Feierlichkeit*) all the palaver that goes with it (*coll.*)

**drum-** (*ugs.*) ⇨ **darum-**

**Drum·herum** *das;* **~s** everything that goes/went with it

**Drummer** /ˈdramɐ/ *der;* **~s, ~, Drummerin** *die;* **~, ~nen** (*Musik*) drummer

**Drums** /drams/ *Pl.* (*Musik*) drums; **an den ~:** on [the] drums

**drunten** /ˈdrʊntn̩/ *Adv.* (*südd., österr.*) down there

**drunter** /ˈdrʊntɐ/ *Adv.* (*ugs.*) underneath; **es** *od.* **alles geht ~ und drüber** everything is topsy-turvy; things are completely chaotic; **das Drunter und Drüber** the confusion

**drunter-** (*ugs.*) ⇨ **darunter-**

**Drusch** /drʊʃ/ *der;* **~[e]s, ~e** **A** threshing; **B** (*Ertrag*) threshed corn; grain

**Druse**[1] /ˈdruːzə/ *der;* **~n, ~n** Druze

**Druse**[2] *die;* **~, ~n** **A** (*Geol.*) geode; druse; **B** (*Pferdekrankheit*) strangles *sing.*

**Drüse** /ˈdryːzə/ *die;* **~, ~n** gland

**Drüsen-:** **~funktion** *die* glandular function; **~schwellung** *die* glandular swelling

**Drusin** *die;* **~, ~nen** ⇨ **Druse**[1]

**drusisch** *Adj.* Druze

**DSB** *Abk.* **Deutscher Sportbund**

**Dschingis Khan** /ˈdʒɪŋɡɪsˈkaːn/ (*der*) Genghis Khan

**Dschungel** /ˈdʒʊŋl̩/ *der;* **~s, ~** (*auch fig.*) jungle; (*von Konflikten, Leidenschaften*) tangle

**Dschungel-:** **~fieber** *das* jungle yellow fever; **~krieg** *der* jungle war; (*Kriegsführung*) jungle warfare

**Dschunke** /ˈdʒʊŋkə/ *die;* **~, ~n** junk

**DSF** *Abk.* (*DDR*) **Gesellschaft für Deutsch-Sowjetische Freundschaft**

**DSG** *Abk.* **Deutsche Schlafwagen- und Speisewagen-Gesellschaft**

**dt.** *Abk.* **deutsch** G.

**Dtzd.** *Abk.* **Dutzend** doz.

**du** /duː/ *Personalpron.*; *2. Pers. Sg. Nom.* you; thou (*arch.*); **Du zueinander sagen** use the familiar form in addressing one another; say 'du' to each other; **[mit jmdm.] per Du sein** be on familiar terms *or* use the familiar form of address [with sb.]; **mit jmdm. auf Du und Du stehen** be on familiar terms with sb.; **~ Glücklicher/Idiot!** you lucky thing/you idiot!; **unser Vater, der ~ bist im Himmel** (*bibl.*) our Father which art in heaven; **~, ich kann nicht länger warten** [listen,] I can't wait any longer; **du bist es** it's 'you; **mach du das doch** 'you do it; ⇨ *auch* (*Gen.*) **deiner**, (*Dat.*) **dir**, (*Akk.*) **dich**

**Du** *das;* **~[s], ~[s]** 'du' *no art.*; the familiar form 'du'; **jmdm. das ~ anbieten** suggest to sb. that he/she use [the familiar form] 'du' *or* the familiar form of address

**dual** /duˈaːl/ *Adj.* dual

**Dual** *der;* **~s, ~e, Dualis** /duˈaːlɪs/ *der;* **~, Duale** (*Sprachw.*) dual

**Dualismus** *der;* **~** (*Philos., geh.*) dualism

**dualistisch** *Adj.* (*Philos., geh.*) dualistic

**Dualität** /dualiˈtɛːt/ *die;* **~:** duality

**Dual·system** *das* (*Math.*) binary system

**Dübel** /ˈdyːbl̩/ *der;* **~s, ~:** plug; (*Holz~*) dowel

**dübeln** *tr. V.* **etw. ~:** fix sth. using a plug/plugs

**dubios** /duˈbi̯oːs/, **dubiös** /duˈbi̯øːs/ *Adj.* (*geh.*) dubious; **ich finde es ~, dass ...:** I find it suspicious that ...

**Dublee** /duˈbleː/ *das;* **~s, ~s** rolled gold [plate]

**Dublette** /duˈblɛtə/ *die;* **~, ~n** **A** duplicate; **B** (*bei Edelsteinen*) doublet; **C** (*Boxen*) one-two

**dublieren** /duˈbliːrən/ *tr. V.* **A** plate with gold; **B** (*Spinnerei*) double; ply; **C** (*Kunstwiss.*) reline

**ducken** /ˈdʊkn̩/ **1** *refl. V.* duck; (*fig. abwertend*) humble oneself (**vor** + *Dat.* before); (*vor Angst*) cower; **sich vor jmds. Fäusten ~:** duck to avoid sb.'s fists. **2** *tr. V.* **A** duck ‹head [and shoulders]›; **B** (*abwertend*) (*einschüchtern*) intimidate; (*demütigen*) humiliate. **3** *itr. V.* humble oneself (**vor** + *Dat.* before)

**Duckmäuser** /ˈdʊkmɔyzɐ/ *der;* **~s, ~, Duckmäuserin** *die;* **~, ~nen** (*abwertend*) moral coward

**duckmäuserisch** (*abwertend*) **1** *Adj.* ‹behaviour etc.› showing moral cowardice. **2** *adv.* ‹behave› in a way that shows moral cowardice

**Duckmäusertum** *das;* **~s** (*abwertend*) moral cowardice

**Dudelei** *die;* **~, ~en** (*ugs. abwertend*) (*auf einem Blasinstrument*) tootling; (*aus dem Radio, Fernsehen usw.*) drone; droning

**Dudel·kasten** *der* (*salopp abwertend*) (*Radio*) radio; (*Plattenspieler*) record player

**dudeln** /ˈduːdl̩n/ **1** *tr. V.* (*auf Blasinstrument*) tootle; (*singen*) sing tunelessly. **2** *itr. V.* ‹radio, television, etc.› drone on; ‹barrel organ› grind away

**Dudel·sack** *der* bagpipes *pl.*

**Dudelsack·pfeifer** *der;* **~s, ~, Dudelsack·pfeiferin** *die;* **~, ~nen** piper; bagpipe player

**Duell** /duˈɛl/ *das;* **~s, ~e** **A** duel; **jmdn. zum ~ [heraus]fordern** challenge sb. to a duel; **ein ~ auf Pistolen** a duel with pistols; **B** (*Sport*) contest (*Gen.* between); **C** (*Wortgefecht*) duel of words

**Duellant** /dueˈlant/ *der;* **~en, ~en** duellist

**duellieren** *refl. V.* fight a duel (**um** over)

**Duett** /duˈɛt/ *das;* **~[e]s, ~e** **A** (*Musik*) duet; **im ~ singen** sing a duet; **etw. im ~ singen** sing sth. as a duet; **im ~ schreien/heulen** (*fig. ugs.*) scream/weep in unison; **B** (*Duo, Paar*) duo; pair

**Dufflecoat** /ˈdʌfəlkoʊt/ *der;* **~s, ~s** duffle coat

**Duft** /dʊft/ *der;* **~[e]s, Düfte** /ˈdʏftə/ **A** pleasant smell; scent; (*Zool.*) scent; (*von Parfüm, Blumen*) scent; fragrance; (*von Kaffee, frischem Brot, Tabak*) aroma; (*iron.*) beautiful smell (*iron.*); **den ~ der großen, weiten Welt schnuppern** (*fig.*) get a taste of the big, wide world; **B** (*schweiz.: Raureif*) hoar frost

**-duft** *der:* **Flieder~/Veilchen~/Jasmin~** *usw.* scent of lilac/violets/jasmine *etc.*

**Düftchen** /ˈdʏftçən/ *das;* **~s, ~:** pleasant aroma *or* smell; (*iron.*) beautiful whiff *or* smell

**Duft·drüse** *die* (*Zool.*) scent gland

**dufte** /ˈdʊftə/ (*ugs.*) **1** *Adj.* great (*coll.*). **2** *adv.* ‹dressed, behave› smashingly (*coll.*); ‹taste› great (*coll.*)

d

**duften** /ˈdʊftn̩/ *itr. V.* smell (**nach** of); **nicht ~:** not smell; have no smell; **die Rosen ~ gut** the roses smell lovely *or* have a lovely scent; **es duftet nach Kaffee** it smells of coffee; there's a smell of coffee

**duftend** *Adj.* sweet-smelling; fragrant; **angenehm/stark ~:** pleasant-/strong-smelling

**duftig** *Adj.* Ⓐ gossamer-fine ‹dress, material›; soft and fine ‹hair›; Ⓑ (*dichter.*) hazy

**Duft-:** **~marke** *die* (*Zool.*) scent mark; **~note** *die* fragrance; **~stoff** *der* Ⓐ (*Biol.*) scent; Ⓑ (*bei Kosmetika*) aromatic substance *or* essence; **~wasser** *das; Pl.* **~wässer** Ⓐ (*scherzh.: Parfüm*) perfume; scent; Ⓑ (*Eau de Toilette*) toilet water; **~wolke** *die* cloud of perfume

**duhn** /duːn/ ⇒ **dun**

**Dukaten** /duˈkaːtn̩/ *der;* **~s, ~** (*hist.*) ducat

**Dukaten-:** **~esel** *der* (*ugs. scherzh.*) **ein ~esel sein** be made of money; **~gold** *das* fine gold; **~scheißer** *der* (*salopp*) ⇒ **~esel**

**Duktus** /ˈdʊktʊs/ *der;* **~** (*geh.*) characteristic style; (*eines Gemäldes*) characteristic lines *pl.* *or* style; (*einer Handschrift*) characteristic shape *or* appearance

**dulden** /ˈdʊldn̩/ ❶ *tr. V.* Ⓐ tolerate; put up with; **keinen Widerspruch ~:** tolerate *or* (*literary*) brook no contradiction; **die Arbeit duldet keinen Aufschub** the work will admit no delay; Ⓑ (*Aufenthalt gestatten*) **jmdn. ~:** tolerate *or* put up with sb.'s presence; **er war nur geduldet** his presence was only tolerated; he was here/there only on sufferance; Ⓒ (*geh.: er~*) endure. ❷ *itr. V.* (*geh.*) suffer

**Dulder** *der;* **~s, ~, Dulderin** *die;* **~, ~nen** patient sufferer

**Dulder·miene** *die* (*iron.*) martyred expression; **mit ~:** with a martyred expression

**duldsam** /ˈdʊltzaːm/ ❶ *Adj.* tolerant (**gegen** towards); (*geduldig*) patient. ❷ *adv.* tolerantly; (*geduldig*) patiently

**Duldsamkeit** *die;* **~:** tolerance; (*Geduld*) patience

**Duldung** *die;* **~:** toleration; **stillschweigende ~:** tacit permission; connivance

**Dumdum** /dʊmˈdʊm/ *das;* **~s, ~s, Dumdum·geschoss**, ***Dumdum·geschoß** *das* dumdum [bullet]

**dumm** /dʊm/, **dümmer** /ˈdʏmɐ/, **dümmst...** /ˈdʏmst.../ ❶ *Adj.* Ⓐ (*nicht intelligent*) stupid; stupid, thick, dense ‹person›; **jmdn. wie einen ~en Jungen behandeln** treat sb. like a stupid child; **[nicht] so ~ sein, wie man aussieht** [not] be as stupid as one looks; **sich ~ stellen** act stupid; **~ geboren, nichts dazugelernt** (*salopp*) stupid idiot! (*coll.*); **sich nicht für ~ verkaufen lassen** (*ugs.*) not be taken in; **du willst mich wohl für ~ verkaufen!** you're trying to have me on (*Brit. coll.*) *or* (*Amer. coll.*) put me on; **sich ~ und dämlich** *od.* **dusselig reden/verdienen/essen** (*ugs.*) talk till one is blue in the face/earn a fortune/eat oneself silly; Ⓑ (*unvernünftig*) foolish; stupid; daft; **so etwas Dummes!** how stupid!; Ⓒ (*ugs.: töricht, albern*) idiotic; silly; stupid; **eine ~e Gans** a silly goose; **das ist mir [einfach] zu ~** (*ugs.*) I've had enough of it; Ⓓ (*ugs.: unangenehm*) nasty ‹feeling, suspicion›; annoying ‹habit›; awful (*coll.*) ‹experience, business, coincidence›; **so etwas Dummes!** how annoying!; **mir ist etwas Dummes passiert** something awful happened to me (*coll.*); Ⓔ (*ugs.: benommen*) **mir ist ganz ~ im Kopf** my head is swimming.
❷ *adv.* Ⓐ (*ugs.: töricht*) foolishly; stupidly; **frag nicht so ~:** don't ask such silly *or* stupid questions; Ⓑ (*ugs.: unangenehm*) ‹end› badly *or* unpleasantly; **jmdm. ~ kommen** be cheeky *or* insolent to sb.

**Dummchen** /ˈdʊmçən/ *das;* **~s, ~** ⇒ **Dummerchen**

**dumm·dreist** ❶ *Adj.* brashly impertinent. ❷ *adv.* in a brashly impertinent manner

**Dumme** *der/die; adj. Dekl.* fool; **einen ~n finden, der etw. macht** find somebody stupid enough to do sth.; **die ~n werden nicht alle** there's one born every minute; **der ~ sein** (*ugs.*) be the loser

**Dumme·jungen·streich** *der* (*ugs.*) silly prank

**Dummen·fang** *der* (*abwertend*) duping of unsuspecting people; **auf ~ gehen/aus sein** go looking/be out looking for unsuspecting people to dupe

**Dummerchen** /ˈdʊmɐçən/ *das;* **~s, ~** (*fam.*) nitwit (*coll.*); ninny; silly little boy/girl

**dummer·weise** *Adv.* Ⓐ (*leider*) unfortunately; (*ärgerlicherweise*) annoyingly; irritatingly; Ⓑ (*törichterweise*) foolishly; like a fool; stupidly

**Dummheit** *die;* **~, ~en** Ⓐ stupidity; **wenn ~ weh täte, müsste er den ganzen Tag schreien** (*salopp*) he's as thick as two short planks (*Brit. coll.*) *or* (*Amer.*) as dumb as an ox; Ⓑ (*unkluge Handlung*) stupid *or* foolish thing; **es war eine große ~, deine Warnung nicht ernst zu nehmen** it was extremely stupid not to heed your warning; **[mach] keine ~en!** don't do anything stupid *or* foolish; **lauter** *od.* **nur ~en im Kopf haben** have a head full of silly ideas

**Dumm·kopf** *der* (*ugs.*) nitwit (*coll.*); [silly] fool *or* idiot; blockhead

**dümmlich** /ˈdʏmlɪç/ ❶ *Adj.* simple-minded. ❷ *adv.* ‹grin, smile› [rather] foolishly *or* stupidly

**Dümmling** /ˈdʏmlɪŋ/ *der;* **~s, ~e** (*ugs.*) dimwit (*coll.*)

**Dumms·dorf** (*das*) (*scherzh.*) **ich bin doch nicht aus ~!** I wasn't born yesterday!; **du bist wohl aus ~!** you must be stupid!

**dümpeln** /ˈdʏmpl̩n/ *itr. V.* (*Seemannsspr.*) roll [gently]

**dumpf** /dʊmpf/ ❶ *Adj.* Ⓐ dull ‹thud, rumble of thunder›; muffled ‹sound, thump›; Ⓑ (*muffig*) musty; Ⓒ (*stumpfsinnig*) dull; dull and expressionless ‹look›; numb ‹indifference›; stifling ‹small-town atmosphere›; Ⓓ (*undeutlich*) dull ‹pain, anger›; dim ‹memory, recollection›; vague, hazy ‹conception, idea›; Ⓔ (*veralt.: benommen*) dazed; stupefied ‹half-sleep›. ❷ *adv.* Ⓐ ‹echo› hollowly; **~ auf etw.** (*Akk.*) **aufschlagen** land with a dull thud on sth.; Ⓑ (*stumpfsinnig*) apathetically; numbly; **~ vor sich hin blicken** gaze dully *or* apathetically into space; Ⓒ (*undeutlich*) vaguely ‹remember›

**Dumpfheit** *die;* **~** Ⓐ (*Stumpfsinn*) torpor; apathy; Ⓑ (*Benommenheit*) numbness

**dumpfig** *Adj.* (*muffig*) musty; (*moderig*) fusty; mouldy; (*stickig*) stuffy ‹atmosphere›

**Dumping** /ˈdampɪŋ/ *das;* **~s** (*Wirtsch.*) dumping

**Dumping·preis** *der* dumping price

**dun** /duːn/ *Adj.* (*nordd. salopp*) plastered (*sl.*); well oiled (*coll.*)

**Düne** /ˈdyːnə/ *die;* **~, ~n** [sand] dune

**Dung** /dʊŋ/ *der;* **~[e]s** dung; manure

**Dünge·mittel** *das* fertilizer

**düngen** /ˈdʏŋən/ ❶ *tr. V.* fertilize ‹soil, lawn, etc.›; spread fertilizer on ‹field›; scatter fertilizer around ‹plants›. ❷ *itr. V.* ‹person› put on fertilizer; **gut ~** ‹substance› be a good fertilizer

**Dünger** *der;* **~s, ~:** fertilizer

**Dung·haufen** *der* dunghill; dung *or* manure heap

**Düngung** *die;* **~, ~en** Ⓐ use of fertilizers; **die ~ mit Chemikalien** the use of chemical fertilizers; Ⓑ (*Dünger*) fertilizer

**dunkel** /ˈdʊŋkl̩/ ❶ *Adj.* Ⓐ dark; **es wird ~:** it's getting dark; **es wird um 22 h ~:** it gets dark about 10 o'clock; **im Dunkeln** in the dark; **im Dunkeln bleiben** (*fig.*) ‹person› remain unidentified; ‹sb.'s identity etc.› remain a mystery; ‹future events› remain uncertain; **im Dunkeln tappen** (*fig.*) grope around *or* about in the dark; Ⓑ (*unerfreulich*) dark ‹chapter in one's life›; black ‹day›; darker ‹side of life›; Ⓒ (*fast schwarz*) dark; **dunkles Brot** brown bread; **dunkles Bier** dark beer (*darker than bitter*); **eine dunkle Brille** dark glasses *pl.*; Ⓓ (*tief*) deep ‹voice, note›; Ⓔ (*unbestimmt*) vague; dim, faint, vague ‹recollection›; dark ‹hint, foreboding, suspicion›; **in dunkler Vorzeit** in the dim and distant past; **jmdn. [über etw.** (*Akk.*)**] im Dunkeln lassen** (*fig.*) leave sb. in the dark [about sth.]; Ⓕ (*abwertend: zweifelhaft*) dubious; shady; **dunkle Geschäfte machen** be involved in shady transactions *or* deals.
❷ *adv.* Ⓐ (*tief*) ‹speak› in a deep voice; Ⓑ (*unbestimmt*) vaguely; ‹remember› vaguely, dimly

**Dunkel** *das;* **~s** Ⓐ (*geh.*) darkness; **im ~ der Nacht** (*geh.*) in the darkness of the night; Ⓑ (*Rätselhaftigkeit*) obscurity, mystery (**um** surrounding); **in ~ gehüllt sein** be shrouded in mystery

**Dünkel** /ˈdʏŋkl̩/ *der;* **~s** (*geh. abwertend*) (*Überheblichkeit*) arrogance; haughtiness; (*Einbildung*) conceit[edness]; **einen ungeheuren ~ haben** be immensely arrogant *or* conceited

**dunkel-:** **~äugig** *Adj.* dark-eyed; **~blau** *Adj.* dark blue; **~blond** *Adj.* light brown ‹hair›; ‹person› with light brown hair; **~blond sein** have light brown hair; **~braun** *Adj.* dark brown; **~grau** *Adj.* dark grey; **~grün** *Adj.* dark green; **~haarig** *Adj.* dark-haired

**dünkelhaft** ❶ *Adj.* (*überheblich*) arrogant; haughty; (*eingebildet*) conceited. ❷ *adv.* (*hochmütig*) arrogantly; haughtily; (*eingebildet*) conceitedly

**Dunkel·haft** *die* confinement in a darkened cell

**dunkel·häutig** *Adj.* dark-skinned

**Dunkelheit** *die;* **~** Ⓐ darkness; **bei ~:** during the hours of darkness; **bei Einbruch der ~:** at nightfall; ⇒ *auch* **Einbruch**; Ⓑ (*geh.: dunkle Tönung*) darkness

**Dunkel-:** **~kammer** *die* darkroom; **~mann** *der* (*abwertend*) Ⓐ shady character; Ⓑ (*veralt.: Obskurant*) obscurantist

**dunkeln** ❶ *itr. V.* Ⓐ (*unpers.*) **es dunkelt** (*geh.*) it is growing dark; Ⓑ *mit sein* grow *or* go darker; darken; Ⓒ (*dichter.*) ‹evening, night› fall. ❷ *tr. V.* make darker; darken

**dunkel-, Dunkel-:** **~rot** *Adj.* dark red; (*tiefrot*) deep red; **~werden** *das;* **~~s** nightfall; **vor dem ~werden** before nightfall; **~ziffer** *die* number of unrecorded cases

**dünken** /ˈdʏŋkn̩/ (*geh. veralt.*) ❶ *unr. tr. V.* **mich dünkt, er hat Recht** methinks he is right (*arch.*). ❷ *refl. V.* **er dünkt sich etwas Besseres/ein Held [zu sein]** he regards himself as superior/a hero; he thinks that he is superior/a hero

**Dünkirchen** /ˈdyːnkɪrçn̩/ (*das*); **~s** ▶700 Dunkirk

**dünn** /dʏn/ ❶ *Adj.* Ⓐ thin ‹slice, layer, etc.›; slim ‹book›; Ⓑ (*mager*) thin ‹person›; **sich ~ machen** (*scherzh.*) squash *or* (*Amer.*) scrunch up [a bit]; Ⓒ (*leicht*) thin, light ‹clothing, fabric›; fine ‹stocking›; (*fig.*) thin, rarefied ‹air›; fine ‹mist, rain›; Ⓓ (*spärlich*) thin ‹hair›; sparse ‹cover, vegetation›; Ⓔ (*wenig gehaltvoll*) thin ‹soup›; weak, watery ‹coffee, tea›; watery ‹beer›; Ⓕ (*~flüssig*) thin ‹paint, lubricating oil›; runny ‹batter›; Ⓖ (*schwach*) thin ‹voice›; weak, faint ‹smile›; faint ‹scent›.
❷ *adv.* Ⓐ **~ geschnittene Wurst/~ geschnittener Käse** thinly sliced sausage/cheese; **etw. ~ auftragen** apply sth. thinly; Ⓑ (*leicht*) lightly ‹dressed›; Ⓒ (*spärlich*) **~ besiedelt/bevölkert** thinly *or* sparsely populated *or* inhabited; **~ gesät** (*ugs.*) rare; ⇒ *auch* **säen**; Ⓓ (*schwach*) ‹smile› weakly, faintly

**dünn-, Dünn-:** ***~besiedelt** *usw.* ⇒ **dünn 2c**; **~bier** *das* (*veralt.*) small beer; **~brett·bohrer** *der*, **~brett·bohrerin** *die;* **~~, ~~nen** (*salopp abwertend*) **er ist ein ~brettbohrer** he likes to take the easy way out; **~darm** *der* ▶471 (*Anat.*) small intestine; **~druck** *der Pl.* **~~e** thin-paper *or* India paper edition; **~druck·aus·gabe** *die* thin-paper *or* India paper edition; **~druck·papier** *das* India paper

**Dünne**[1] *die;* **~** (*Technik*) thinness

**Dünne**[2] *der/die; adj. Dekl.* (*ugs.*) thin man/woman; **die ~n** thin people

**dünne|machen** ⇒ **dünnmachen**

**dunnemals** /ˈdʊnəmaːls/ ⇒ **anno**

**dünn-, Dünn-:** **~flüssig** *Adj.* thin; runny ‹batter etc.›; ***~gesät** ⇒ **dunn 2c**; **~häutig** *Adj.* (*auch fig.*) thin-skinned; **~|machen**

*old spelling (see note on page 1707)

*refl. V.* (*ugs.*) make oneself scarce (*coll.*); **~pfiff** *der* (*salopp*), **~schiss**, ***~schiß** *der* (*derb*) the runs *pl.* (*coll.*); the shits *pl.* (*coarse*); **~wandig** *Adj.* thin-walled

**Dunst** /dʊnst/ *der;* **~[e]s, Dünste** /ˈdʏnstə/ A haze; (*Nebel*) mist; B (*Geruch*) smell; (*Ausdünstung*) fumes *pl.;* (*stickige, dumpfe Luft*) fug (*coll.*); **jmdm. blauen ~ vormachen** (*ugs.*) pull the wool over sb.'s eyes; **keinen [blassen] ~ von etw. haben** (*ugs.*) have not the foggiest *or* faintest idea about sth.

**Dunst·abzugs·haube** *die* extractor hood

**dunsten** *itr. V.* (*geh.*) A smell, give off a smell (**nach** of); B (*dampfen*) steam

**dünsten** /ˈdʏnstn̩/ *tr. V.* steam ‹fish, vegetables›; braise ‹meat›; stew ‹fruit›

**Dunst·glocke** *die* pall of haze

**dunstig** *Adj.* A hazy; (*neblig*) misty; B (*verräuchert*) smoky; (*stickig*) stuffy

**Dunst·kreis** *der* (*fig.*) orbit

**Dunst·obst** (*österr.*), **Dunst·obst** *das* stewed fruit

**Dunst-:** **~schicht** *die* layer of haze; (*Nebelschicht*) layer of mist; **~schleier** *der* veil of haze; (*Nebelschleier*) veil of mist; **~wolke** *die* cloud of smog; (*stickige, dumpfe Luft*) fug (*coll.*)

**Dünung** *die;* **~, ~en** swell

**Duo** /ˈduːo/ *das;* **~s, ~s** (*Musik*) A (*Stück*) duet; B (*Ausführende*) ‹piano etc.› duet; (*fig. scherzh.*) duo; pair

**Duodez-** /duoˈdeːts/: **~band** *der* duodecimo *or* twelvemo edition; **~fürst** *der* (*abwertend*) princeling; petty *or* minor prince; **~fürstentum** *das* (*abwertend*) petty *or* minor princedom; **~staat** *der* (*abwertend*) minor state

**Duo·dezimal·system** *das* duodecimal system

**düpieren** /dyˈpiːrən/ *tr. V.* (*geh.*) dupe

**Duplikat** /dupliˈkaːt/ *das;* **~[e]s, ~e** duplicate

**Duplikation** /duplikaˈtsi̯oːn/ *die;* **~, ~en** (*geh., Genetik*) duplication

**Duplizität** /duplitsiˈtɛːt/ *die;* **~, ~en** (*geh.*) duplication

**Dur** /duːɐ̯/ *das;* **~** (*Musik*) major [key]; **in ~ enden** finish in a major key

**Dur·akkord** *der* (*Musik*) major chord

**durativ** /ˈduːratiːf/ *Adj.* (*Sprachw.*) durative

**durch** /dʊrç/ ❶ *Präp. mit Akk.* A (*räumlich*) through; **~ die Straßen/die Stadt bummeln** stroll through the streets/the town; **~ ganz Europa reisen** travel all over *or* throughout Europe; **~ einen Fluss waten** wade across a river; ⇒ *auch* **Kopf**; B (*modal*) by; **etw. ~ Boten/die Post schicken** send sth. by courier/post (*Brit.*) *or* mail; **etw. ~ Lautsprecher/das Fernsehen bekannt geben** announce sth. over the loudspeakers/on television; **sie ist ~ das Fernsehen bekannt geworden** she became famous through television; **etw. ~ jmdn. bekommen** get *or* obtain sth. through sb.; **zehn [geteilt] ~ zwei** ten divided by two; C (*österr.: zeitlich*) **~ Wochen/Jahre** for weeks/years; **~ sein ganzes Leben** throughout *or* all his life. ❷ *Adv.* A (*hin~*) **das ganze Jahr ~:** throughout the whole year; all year; **die ganze Zeit ~:** the whole time; all the time; B (*ugs.: vorbei*) **es war 3 Uhr ~:** it was past *or* gone 3 o'clock; C **~ und ~ nass/überzeugt** wet through [and through]/completely *or* totally convinced; **jmdm. ~ und ~ gehen** go right through sb.; **er ist ein Lügner ~ und ~:** he's an out and out liar; D **[durch etw.] ~ sein** be through *or* have got through [sth.]; **durch den Fluss ~ sein** be across *or* have got across the river; **ist die Post/der Briefträger schon ~?** has the mail arrived/has the postman (*Brit.*) *or* (*Amer.*) mailman been?; E **~ sein** (*vorbeigefahren sein*) ‹train, cyclist› have gone through; (*abgefahren sein*) ‹train, bus, etc.› have gone; (*fertig sein*) have finished; **durch etw. ~ sein** have got through sth.; **mit etw. ~ sein** have got through sth.; F **~ sein** (*durchgescheuert sein*) have worn through; G **~ sein** (*reif sein*) ‹cheese› be ripe; H **~ sein** (*durchgebraten sein*) ‹meat› be well done; I **~ sein** (*angenommen sein*) ‹law, regulation› have gone through; ‹35-hour week etc.› have been adopted; J **~ sein** (*gerettet sein*) ‹sick or injured person› be out of danger; K **~ sein, bei jmdm. unten ~ sein** be in sb.'s bad books; L **~ sein** (*bestanden haben*) have got through

**durch|ackern** (*ugs.*) ❶ *tr. V.* plough through. ❷ *refl. V.* **sich durch etw. ~:** plough [one's way] through sth.

**durch|arbeiten** ❶ *tr. V.* A **die Nacht/Pause** *usw.* **~:** work through the night/break *etc.;* B (*lesen und auswerten*) work *or* go through ‹book, article›; C (*ausarbeiten*) work out ‹speech, essay›; D (*durchkneten*) work *or* knead thoroughly ‹dough›; massage *or* knead thoroughly ‹muscles›. ❷ *itr. V.* work through. ❸ *refl. V.* (*auch fig.*) work one's way through

**durch|atmen** *itr. V.* take a deep breath/deep breaths; breathe deeply

**durch·aus** *Adv.* A **~ mitkommen wollen** [absolutely] insist on coming too; **das ist ~ nötig/zu empfehlen** it is absolutely necessary/definitely to be recommended; **Muss das sein? — Ja, ~:** Is that necessary? — Yes, absolutely; **wenn du ~ willst** if you really insist; B (*völlig*) perfectly, quite ‹correct, possible, understandable›; **das ist ~ richtig** that is entirely right; **ich bin ~ Ihrer Meinung** I am entirely of your opinion; **man kann ~ vermuten, dass ...** one can quite reasonably suppose *or* assume that ...; **ein ~ annehmbarer Vorschlag/gelungener Abend** an eminently acceptable suggestion/thoroughly successful evening; C (*verneint*) **das hat ~ nichts damit zu tun** that's got nothing at all *or* whatsoever to do with it; **~ nicht ins Wasser/darüber sprechen wollen** absolutely refuse to go into the water/talk about it; **es ist ~ nicht so einfach wie ...** it is by no means as easy as ...; **das ist ~ kein Scherz** it is certainly no joke; **für so etwas habe ich ~ kein Verständnis** I have absolutely no time for that sort of thing

**durch|backen** ❶ *itr. V.* bake through. ❷ *tr. V.* **etw. richtig ~:** bake sth. right the way through

**durch|beißen**[1] ❶ *unr. tr. V.* bite through. ❷ *unr. refl. V.* (*ugs.*) [manage to] struggle through

**durch·beißen**[2] *unr. tr. V.* bite through; **jmdm. die Kehle ~:** tear *or* rip sb.'s throat open

**durch|bekommen** *unr. tr. V.* **etw. ~:** get sth. through; (*zerlegen*) get *or* cut through sth.

**durch|betteln** *refl. V.* **sich überall ~:** beg one's way through life

**durch|biegen** ❶ *unr. tr. V.* **etw. ~:** bend sth. as far as possible; **seinen Rücken/sein Kreuz ~:** straighten one's back. ❷ *unr. refl. V.* sag

**durch|blasen** ❶ *unr. tr. V.* A (*durch Hindurchblasen reinigen*) **etw. ~:** clear sth. by blowing through it; B (*treiben*) **etw. durch etw. ~:** blow sth. through sth.; C (*durchdringen*) ‹wind› blow right through ‹person›. ❷ *unr. itr. V.* **~ durch** ‹wind› blow through ‹cracks, thin coat, etc.›

**durch|blättern**[1], **durch·blättern**[2] *tr. V.* leaf through ‹book, file, etc.›

**durch|bläuen**, ***durch|bleuen** *tr. V.* (*ugs.*) **jmdn. ~:** give sb. a good hiding (*coll.*) *or* thrashing

**Durch·blick** *der* A (*ugs.*) **den [absoluten] ~ haben** know [exactly] what's going on; **den ~ verlieren** no longer know what's going on; lose track of what's going on; B (*Ausblick*) view (**auf** + *Akk.* of)

**durch|blicken** *itr. V.* A look through; **durch etw. ~:** look through sth.; B (*ugs.*) **ich blicke da nicht durch** I can't make head or tail of it; **blickst du bei dieser Aufgabe durch?** can you make head or tail of this exercise?; C **~ lassen, dass .../wie ...** hint that .../at how ...; **etw. ~ lassen** hint at sth.

**durch|bluten**[1] *itr. V.* A **die Wunde blutete durch** blood from the wound soaked through [the bandage/dressing *etc.*]; B *mit sein* ‹bandage etc.› become soaked with blood

**durch·bluten**[2] *tr. V.* A supply ‹body, limb, etc.› with blood; **seine Beine sind schlecht durchblutet** the circulation in his legs is poor; B (*mit Blut tränken*) **etw. ~:** soak sth. with blood

**Durch·blutung** *die* flow *or* supply of blood (+ *Gen.* to); [blood] circulation

**durchblutungs·fördernd** *Adj.* ‹substance› which stimulates the [blood] circulation; **~ sein** stimulate the [blood] circulation

**Durchblutungs·störung** *die* disturbance of the blood supply

**durch|bohren**[1] ❶ *tr. V.* drill *or* bore through ‹wall, plank›; drill, bore ‹hole›. ❷ *itr. V.* **durch etw. ~:** drill *or* bore through sth. ❸ *refl. V.* **sich durch etw. ~** ‹woodworm etc.› bore its way through sth.; ‹spear, iron paling› go right through sth.

**durch·bohren**[2] *tr. V.* pierce; **jmdn. mit ~den Blicken ansehen** (*fig.*) look piercingly *or* penetratingly at sb.

**durch|boxen** (*ugs.*) ❶ *refl. V.* fight one's way through; (*fig.*) battle through. ❷ *tr. V.* force *or* push through ‹law, measure, bill, etc.›; **einen Kandidaten ~:** bring pressure to bear to get a candidate appointed

**durch|braten** *unr. tr. V.* **etw. ~:** cook *or* roast sth. till it is well done; **ich möchte mein Steak durchgebraten** I'd like my steak well done

**durch|brechen**[1] ❶ *unr. tr. V.* A (*zerbrechen*) **etw. ~:** break sth. in two; B (*eine Öffnung brechen*) **eine Tür/ein Fenster ~:** make a door/window. ❷ *unr. itr. V.;* *mit sein* A break in two; **der Blinddarm/das Magengeschwür ist durchgebrochen** (*Med.*) the appendix has burst/the gastric ulcer has perforated; B (*hervorkommen*) ‹sun› break through; ‹new tooth› come through; ‹bud› appear; (*fig.*) ‹rage, hatred› erupt; C (*einbrechen*) fall through ‹ice, floor, etc.›; **durch etw. ~:** fall through sth.; D (*Milit.: sich einen Weg bahnen*) break through

**durch·brechen**[2] *unr. tr. V.* break through ‹sound barrier›; break *or* burst through ‹crowd barrier›; ‹car› crash through ‹railings etc.›; (*fig.*) break ‹law, convention›

**durch|brennen** *unr. itr. V.; mit sein* A ‹heating coil, light bulb› burn out; ‹fuse› blow; **da ist ihm die Sicherung durchgebrannt** (*fig. salopp*) he blew a fuse (*sl.*) *or* his top (*coll.*); B (*ugs.: weglaufen*) (*von zu Hause*) run away; (*mit der Kasse*) run off; abscond; (*mit dem Geliebten/der Geliebten*) run off; C (*glühen*) ‹coals, logs› glow

**durch|bringen** *unr. tr. V.* A ⇒ **durchbekommen;** B (*durch eine Kontrolle, über eine Grenze*) **etw. ~:** get sth. through; C (*bei Wahlen*) **jmdn. ~:** get sb. elected; D (*durchsetzen*) get ‹bill› through; get ‹motion› passed; get ‹proposal› accepted; E (*versorgen*) **seine Familie/sich ~:** support one's family/oneself; F (*verschwenden*) get through

**durch·brochen** ❶ *2. Part. v.* **durchbrechen**[2]. ❷ *Adj.* openwork *attrib.* ‹stockings, shoes, etc.›

**Durch·bruch** *der* A (*Milit., Geol., fig.*) breakthrough; **einer Idee** (*Dat.*) **zum ~ verhelfen** get an idea generally accepted; B (*Öffnung*) opening; (*durch Gewalteinwirkung*) breach

**durch|buchstabieren** *tr. V.* spell out

**durch|bummeln**[1] *itr. V.* (*ugs.*) A **bis zum Morgen ~:** live it up till morning (*coll.*); B *mit sein* **~ durch** wander through ‹park, exhibition, etc.›

**durch·bummeln**[2] *tr. V.* **die Nacht ~:** be on the spree all night (*coll.*); **eine durchbummelte Nacht** a night on the spree (*coll.*)

**durch|bürsten** *tr. V.* brush ‹hair› thoroughly

**durch|checken** *tr. V.* check ‹list, documents› thoroughly; check ‹car› over thoroughly

**durch·dacht** ❶ *2. Part. v.* **durchdenken.** ❷ *Adj.* **ein wenig/gut ~er Plan** a badly/well thought-out plan; **nicht [genügend] ~ sein** not be sufficiently well thought-out

**durch·denken** *unr. tr. V.* think over *or* through

**durch|diskutieren** *tr. V.* discuss thoroughly

**durch|drängen** *refl. V.* **sich [durch etw.] ~:** push *or* force one's way through [sth.]

**durch|drehen** **1** *tr. V.* put ‹meat etc.› through the mincer *or* (*Amer.*) grinder; chop ‹nuts etc.› in the blender. **2** *itr. V.* **A** *auch mit sein* (*ugs.*) crack up (*coll.*); go to pieces; **B** ‹wheels› spin

**durch|dringen**[1] *unr. itr. V.; mit sein* **A** ‹rain, sun› come through; **durch etw. ~:** penetrate sth.; come through sth.; **bis zu jmdm. ~** (*fig.*) ‹rumour, story› get through to sb.; **B** (*sich durchsetzen*) **mit einem Vorschlag bei der Geschäftsleitung ~:** succeed in getting the management to accept one's suggestion; **der Redner drang mit seiner Stimme nicht durch** the speaker couldn't make himself heard

**durch·dringen**[2] *unr. tr. V.* **A** penetrate; **kaum zu ~ sein** be almost impenetrable; **B** (*erfüllen*) **jmdn. ~** ‹idea› take hold of sb. [completely]; **von der Wahrheit einer Behauptung durchdrungen sein** be totally convinced of the truth of a statement; **seine Schriften sind von diesen Ideen durchdrungen** his writings are imbued with these ideas

**durch·dringend** **1** *Adj.* **A** (*intensiv*) piercing, penetrating ‹voice, look, scream, sound›; **mit ~em Blick** with a piercing *or* penetrating look; **B** (*penetrant*) pungent, penetrating ‹smell›. **2** *adv.* **A** **jmdn. ~ ansehen** look at a person piercingly *or* penetratingly; give sb. a piercing *or* penetrating look; **B** (*penetrant*) **~ riechen/stinken** have a pungent *or* penetrating smell/stench

**Durchdringung** *die;* **~** **A** penetration; (*Verschmelzung*) fusion; **B** (*Erfassung*) comprehension

**durch|drücken** *tr. V.* **A** **Püree** *usw.* **[durch ein Sieb/Tuch] ~:** press *or* pass purée *etc.* through a sieve/cloth; **B** (*strecken*) straighten ‹limb, back›; **die Knie ~:** straighten one's legs; **C** (*ugs.: durchsetzen*) manage to get ‹extra holiday etc.›; **seinen Antrag ~:** manage to force one's application through; **ein Gesetz im Parlament ~:** force a bill through Parliament

**durch|dürfen** *unr. itr. V.* (*ugs.*) be allowed through; **darf ich mal [hier] durch?** can I get through here?

**durch·einander** *Adv.* **~ sein** ‹papers, desk, etc.› be in a mess *or* a muddle; (*verwirrt sein*) be confused *or* in a state of confusion; (*aufgeregt sein*) be flustered *or* (*coll.*) in a state; **~ bringen** (*in Unordnung bringen*) get ‹room, flat› into a mess; get ‹papers, file› into a muddle; muddle up ‹papers, file›; (*verwirren*) confuse; (*verwechseln*) confuse ‹names etc.›; get ‹names etc.› mixed up; get ‹names etc.› muddled; **im Hause geht alles ~:** the whole house is in a muddle; **mir geht alles ~** (*fig.*) I'm getting everything muddled up; **~ geraten** get in a muddle; **~ kommen** ‹pictures, papers, etc.› get into a muddle; ‹person› get into a muddle, get confused; **~ laufen** run [around] in all directions; **~ reden** all talk at once *or* at the same time; **etw. ~ werfen** (*durcheinander bringen*) muddle *or* jumble sth. up; (*verwechseln*) mix *or* muddle sth. up; get sth. mixed *or* muddled up; **alles ~ essen/trinken** eat/drink everything indiscriminately

**Durcheinander** *das;* **~s** **A** muddle; mess; **in wirrem ~** (*fig.*) in wild confusion; **B** (*Wirrwarr*) confusion

***durcheinander|bringen** *usw.* ⇒ **durcheinander**

**durch|essen** *unr. refl. V.* **A** **sich bei jmdm. ~:** live on sb.'s hospitality; **B** (*scherzh.*) **sich durch etw. ~:** eat one's way through sth.

**durch|exerzieren** *tr. V.* (*ugs.*) go through, practise ‹rules, multiplication tables›; rehearse ‹situation›

**durch|fahren**[1] *unr. itr. V.; mit sein* **A** **[durch etw.] ~:** drive through [sth.]; **B** (*nicht anhalten*) go straight through; (*mit dem Auto*) drive straight through; (*fahren, ohne umsteigen zu müssen*) travel direct; go straight through; **durch eine Stadt ~:** go/drive straight through a town; go/drive through a town without stopping; **der Zug fährt [in H.] durch** the train doesn't stop [at H.]; **der Zug fährt bis München durch** the train is non-stop to Munich; **die [ganze] Nacht ~:** travel/drive [right] through the night

**durch·fahren**[2] *unr. tr. V.* **A** travel through; ‹train› pass through; (*mit dem Auto*) drive through; **B** (*zurücklegen*) cover ‹distance›; complete ‹course, lap›; **C** (*durchzucken*) **plötzlich durchfuhr ihn ein Schreck** he was seized with sudden fright; **auf einmal durchfuhr mich [der Gedanke], dass ...** suddenly the thought *or* it flashed through my mind that ...

**Durch·fahrt** *die* **A** (*das Durchfahren*) **„~ verboten"** 'no entry except for access'; **die ~ durch den Kanal** the passage through the canal; **bei der ~ durch den Tunnel** when passing through the tunnel; **B** (*Durchreise*) **auf der ~ sein** be passing through; be on the way through; **C** (*Weiterfahrt*) **die ~ freigeben** allow vehicles through; **freie ~ haben** have right of way; **D** (*Weg*) thoroughfare; **„bitte [die] ~ freihalten"** 'please do not obstruct'

**Durchfahrts·straße** *die* main road through

**Durch·fall** *der* **A** ▸ **474** diarrhoea *no art.*; **B** (*ugs.: Versagen*) failure; **in der Prüfung einen ~ erleben** fail the exam (*coll.*)

**durch|fallen** *unr. itr. V.; mit sein* **A** fall through; **durch etw. ~:** fall through sth.; **B** (*ugs.: nicht bestehen*) fail; flunk (*Amer. coll.*); **bei etw./in etw.** (*Dat.*)**/durch etw.** (*Akk.*) **~:** fail *or* flunk sth.; **C** (*ugs.: erfolglos sein*) ‹play, performance› flop (*sl.*); be a flop (*sl.*) *or* failure; **bei der Kritik ~:** be a flop with (*sl.*) *or* fail to please the critics; **D** (*ugs.: verlieren*) lose; not get in; be defeated; **bei der Wahl ~:** lose the election; be defeated in the election

**durch|faulen** *itr. V.; mit sein* rot through

**durch|faxen** *tr. V.* fax through; **jmdm. etw. ~:** fax sth. through to sb.

**durch|fechten** **1** *unr. tr. V.* **seine Ansprüche/Forderungen ~:** fight successfully to establish one's claims/get one's demands accepted. **2** *refl. V.* **sich [im Leben] ~:** battle one's way through [life]

**durch|fegen** *tr. V.* sweep ‹room› [out] thoroughly

**durch|feiern**[1] *itr. V.* **[die ganze Nacht] ~:** celebrate all night

**durch·feiern**[2] *tr. V.* **die [ganze] Nacht ~:** spend all night celebrating; celebrate all night; **nach durchfeierter Nacht** after celebrating all night

**durch|feilen** *tr. V.* **A** file through; **B** (*bearbeiten*) polish ‹essay, speech, etc.›

**durch|finden** *unr. refl. V.* find one's way through; **sich durch etw. ~:** find one's way through sth.; **sich durch das U-Bahn-System/in der Stadt ~:** find one's way around the underground (*Brit.*) *or* (*Amer.*) subway system/the town; **ich finde mich in diesem Kuddelmuddel nicht mehr durch** I can't make head or tail of this muddle

**durch|fliegen**[1] *unr. itr. V.; mit sein* **A** **[durch etw.] ~:** fly through [sth.]; **unter der Brücke ~:** fly under the bridge; **B** (*nicht zwischenlanden*) fly non-stop; **C** (*ugs.: nicht bestehen*) **[in einem Examen/bei einer Prüfung] ~:** fail [an exam (*coll.*)]

**durch·fliegen**[2] *unr. tr. V.* **A** fly through; fly over ‹country›; fly along ‹air corridor›; **B** (*zurücklegen*) fly, cover ‹distance›; **C** (*lesen*) glance through ‹newspaper, post›; skim through ‹novel›

**durch|fließen**[1] *unr. itr. V.; mit sein* **[durch etw.] ~:** flow through [sth.]

**durch·fließen**[2] *unr. tr. V.* flow through

**Durch·flug** *der* flight through; **der ~ durch den Luftkorridor/das Gebiet** the flight along the air corridor/over the area; **Passagiere auf dem ~:** transit passengers; **auf dem ~ [nach Kanada] sein** be in transit [to Canada]

**Durch·fluss,** ***Durch·fluß** *der* **A** (*das Durchfließen*) flow; **B** (*Öffnung in einem Damm*) [discharge] opening; outlet; (*zwischen Becken*) connection channel

**durch·fluten** *tr. V.* (*geh.*) ‹river› flow through ‹country›; ‹warmth, pleasant feeling› flood through ‹person›; **Licht durchflutete den Raum** light flooded the room; the room was flooded with light

**durch|formen** *tr. V.* **etw. ~:** get sth. into its final shape; **etw. bis ins Einzelne ~:** work sth. out down to the last detail

**durch|formulieren** *tr. V.* finalize the [exact] wording of ‹essay, thesis›; **eine Rede ~:** prepare the wording of a speech in detail

**durch·forschen** *tr. V.* **A** search ‹pocket, room, area, etc.› thoroughly; **B** (*untersuchen*) make a thorough investigation *or* examination of ‹sources, literature on a subject›; carry out research into ‹subject›

**durch|forsten**[1], **durch·forsten**[2] *tr. V.* **A** (*Forstw.*) thin; **B** (*durchsehen*) sift through ‹archives, regulations, etc.›

**durch|fragen** *refl. V.* **sich [nach dem Bahnhof/zum Museum] ~:** find one's way [to the station/museum] by asking

**durch|fressen**[1] **1** *unr. tr. V.* **A** **ein Loch durch etw. ~:** eat a hole through *or* in sth.; **B** (*zerstören, zersetzen*) eat through; ‹moths› eat holes in ‹pullover etc.›. **2** *unr. refl. V.* **A** ‹maggot, woodworm› eat [its way] through; ‹rust› eat through; **B** (*ugs. abwertend*) **sich bei jmdm. ~:** live on sb.'s hospitality; **C** (*durcharbeiten*) plough through ‹book, statistics, etc.›

**durch·fressen**[2] *Adj.* **von Motten ~ sein** be moth-eaten *or* full of moth-holes; **ein von Säure ~er Kittel** a lab coat full of acid holes

**durch|frieren** *unr. itr. V.; mit sein* **A** get frozen stiff; get *or* become chilled to the marrow *or* bone; **durchgefroren sein** be frozen stiff *or* chilled to the bone; **B** (*gefrieren*) ‹water, lake› freeze solid

**durchfroren** *Adj.* frozen ‹face, hands›; **~ sein** ‹person› be frozen stiff

**durch|fühlen** *tr. V.* **etw. durch etw. ~:** feel sth. through sth.; **jmds. Bitterkeit ~** (*fig.*) sense sb.'s bitterness

**durchführbar** *Adj.* practicable; feasible; workable; **ein leicht/schwer ~er Plan** a plan that is easy/difficult to carry out

**Durchführbarkeit** *die;* **~:** practicability; feasibility; workability

**durch|führen** **1** *tr. V.* **A** (*verwirklichen*) carry out ‹intention›; put into effect, implement ‹decision, programme›; carry out, put into effect, implement ‹plan›; put into practice ‹idea›; **B** (*ausführen*) carry out ‹work, installation, investigation›; perform, carry out ‹operation›; take ‹measurement›; **C** (*veranstalten*) make ‹charity collection›; hold ‹meeting, election, examination›; carry out ‹census›; **D** (*zu Ende führen*) complete, finish ‹task›; carry through ‹method, system›; maintain, keep up ‹role›. **2** *itr. V.* **durch etw./unter etw.** (*Dat.*) **~** ‹track, road› go *or* run *or* pass through/under sth.

**Durchfuhr-: ~handel** *der* (*Wirtsch.*) transit trade; **~land** *das* (*Wirtsch.*) country of transit

**Durch·führung** *die* **A** (*Verwirklichung*) (*einer Absicht*) carrying out; (*eines Plans, Programms*) carrying out, implementation; **zur ~ kommen** *od.* **gelangen** (*Papierdt.*) ‹decision, regulation› be implemented; **zur ~ bringen** (*Papierdt.*) enforce ‹regulation, law›; **B** (*Ausführung*) (*einer Arbeit*) carrying out; (*einer Operation*) performing; (*einer Messung*) taking; **C** (*Einhaltung*) (*einer Idee*) carrying through; (*von Richtlinien*) putting into practice; **D** (*Veranstaltung*) (*eines Kongresses usw.*) holding; (*eines Wettbewerbs*) staging

**Durchführungs·verordnung** *die* implementing order

**durch|füttern** *tr. V.* (*ugs.*) feed; support; **sich von jmdm. ~ lassen** live off sb.

**Durch·gabe** *die* (*von Nachrichten, Meldungen*) announcement; (*von Gewinnzahlen*)

*old spelling (see note on page 1707)

reading; **bei der ~ des Telegramms** when telephoning the telegram through

**Durch·gang** *der* Ⓐ **„kein ~", „ ~ verboten"** 'no thoroughfare'; Ⓑ (*Weg*) passage [way]; Ⓒ (*Phase*) stage; (*einer Versuchsreihe*) run; (*Sport, bei Wahlen, Wettbewerb*) round; Ⓓ (*Astron.*) transit

**durch·gängig** ❶ *Adj.* general; (*universell*) universal; constant ‹feature›; general ‹principle›; continual, constant ‹use›. ❷ *adv.* generally, universally ‹accepted›; **~ mit Maschine geschrieben sein** be typed throughout

**Durchgangs-:** **~bahn·hof** *der* through station; **~lager** *das* transit camp; **~station** *die* (*fig.*) transitional stage; **~straße** *die* through road; thoroughfare; **~verkehr** *der* Ⓐ through traffic; Ⓑ (*Transitverkehr*) transit traffic

**durch|geben** *unr. tr. V.* announce ‹news›; give ‹results, weather report, winning numbers›; **eine Meldung im Radio/Fernsehen ~:** make an announcement on the radio/on television; **etw. in den Nachrichten ~:** announce sth. on the news; **telefonisch** *od.* **per Telefon ~:** telephone ‹telegram› through; give ‹traffic information› over the telephone; pass on ‹report, results› by telephone

**durch|gehen** ❶ *unr. itr. V.; mit sein* Ⓐ **[durch etw.] ~:** go *or* walk through [sth.]; **„bitte weiter ~!"** 'pass *or* move right down, please'; Ⓑ (*hindurchdringen*) **[durch etw.] ~** ‹rain, water› come through [sth.]; ‹wind› go through [sth.]; Ⓒ (*direkt zum Ziel führen*) ‹train, bus, flight› go [right] through (**bis** to); go direct; Ⓓ (*andauern*) ‹meeting, party, etc.› go on (**bis zu** until); Ⓔ (*verlaufen*) ‹path etc.› go *or* run through (**bis zu** to); ‹stripe› go *or* run right through; Ⓕ (*angenommen werden*) ‹application, claim› be accepted; ‹law› be passed; ‹motion› be carried; ‹bill› be passed, get through; Ⓖ (*hingenommen werden*) ‹discrepancy› be tolerated; ‹mistake, discourtesy› be allowed to *or* let pass, be overlooked; **[jmdm.] etw. ~ lassen** let sb. get away with sth.; Ⓗ (*davonstürmen*) ‹horse› bolt; Ⓘ (*ugs.: davonlaufen*) **mit etw./jmdm. ~:** run off with sth./sb.; **sie ist ihrem Mann durchgegangen** she ran off and left her husband; Ⓙ (*außer Kontrolle geraten*) **die Nerven gehen mit ihm durch** he loses his temper; **ihr Temperament/ihre Begeisterung geht mit ihr durch** her temperament/enthusiasm gets the better of her; Ⓚ (*ugs.: durchgebracht werden können*) **[durch etw.] ~:** go through [sth.]; **hinter etw.** (*Dat.*) **~:** go through behind sth.; Ⓛ (*ohne Unterbrechung zu Fuß gehen*) walk without a break; Ⓜ (*gehalten werden für*) **für neu/30 Jahre** *usw.* **~:** be taken to be *or* pass for new/thirty *etc.* ❷ *unr. tr. V.; mit sein* go through ‹newspaper, text›; **etw. Punkt für Punkt/Wort für Wort ~:** go through sth. point by point/word by word

**durch·gehend** ❶ *Adj.* Ⓐ continuous ‹line, pattern, etc.›; constantly recurring ‹motif›; Ⓑ (*direkt*) through *attrib.* ‹train, carriage›; direct ‹flight, connection›. ❷ *adv.* Ⓐ **~ geöffnet haben/bleiben** be/stay open all day; (*Tag und Nacht*) be/stay open 24 hours a day; Ⓑ (*in einer Linie*) **~ geknöpft werden/gefüttert sein** button all the way down/be lined throughout *or* fully lined

**durch·geistigt** *Adj.* spiritual ‹person, appearance›

**durchgeknallt** *Adj.* (*ugs.*) crazy

**durch·geschwitzt** ❶ *2. Part. v.* **durchschwitzen.** ❷ *Adj.* ‹person› soaked *or* bathed in sweat; ‹clothes› soaked with sweat; sweat-soaked *attrib.* ‹clothes›

**durch|gestalten** *tr. V.* work ‹theme, motif› out in detail; portray ‹experience› in detail

**durch|gießen** *unr. tr. V.;* **etw. [durch etw.] ~:** pour sth. through [sth.]; **etw. durch ein Tuch ~:** strain sth. through a cloth

**durch|gliedern** *tr. V.* structure

**durch|glühen¹** ❶ *itr. V.; mit sein* Ⓐ (*entzweigehen*) ‹heating coil, light bulb› burn out; ‹fuse› blow; Ⓑ (*vollständig glühen*) ‹coals, log› glow right through. ❷ *tr. V.* **etw. ~:** heat sth. until it glows right through

**durch·glühen²** *tr. V.* (*dichter.*) **von etw. durchglüht sein** be aglow with sth.

**durch|graben** ❶ *unr. tr. V.* **einen Tunnel/Gang** *usw.* **[durch etw.] ~:** dig a tunnel/passage through [sth.]. ❷ *unr. refl. V.* **sich [durch etw.] ~** ‹miner› dig his way through [sth.]; ‹mole› tunnel its way through [sth.]

**durch|greifen** *unr. itr. V.* Ⓐ **[hart] ~:** take drastic measures *or* steps; **rücksichtslos/strenger ~:** take ruthless/more drastic measures *or* steps; **gegen die Demonstranten hart ~:** take drastic action against the demonstrators; Ⓑ **~ durch** reach through

**durch|gucken** *itr. V.* (*ugs.*) **[durch etw.] ~:** peep *or* look through [sth.]; **durch jmds. Fernglas ~:** have a look through sb.'s binoculars

**durch|haben** *unr. tr. V.* (*ugs.*) Ⓐ have finished with ‹book, newspaper›; have got through ‹song, discussion point›; Ⓑ (*zerteilt haben*) have got through; Ⓒ (*hindurchbewegt haben*) **etw. [durch etw.] ~:** have got sth. through [sth.]

**durch|hacken** *tr. V.* hack *or* chop through; (*mit einem Schlag*) chop through

**Durchhalte·appell** *der* (*bei einem Kampf*) appeal to hold out; (*bei einer schwierigen Aufgabe*) appeal to see it through

**durch|halten** ❶ *unr. itr. V.* (*bei einem Kampf*) hold out; (*bei einer schwierigen Aufgabe*) see it through; (*beim Rennen*) stay the course. ❷ *unr. tr. V.* stand ‹strain, difficult working conditions›; stand, keep up ‹pace›; **eine Diät ~:** keep to a diet

**Durchhalte-:** **~parole** *die* (*abwertend*) exhortation to hold out; **~vermögen** *das* staying power; stamina; [power of] endurance

**durch|hängen** *unr. itr. V.* Ⓐ sag; Ⓑ (*ugs.*) be washed out *or* drained

**durch|hauen** ❶ *regelm.* (*auch unr.*) *tr. V.* Ⓐ **etw. ~:** chop *or* split sth. in half; Ⓑ (*bahnen*) **sich** (*Dat.*) **einen Weg durch etw. ~:** hack one's *or* a way through sth. ❷ *tr. V.* (*ugs.*) Ⓐ (*verprügeln*) **jmdn. ~:** give sb. a good hiding (*coll.*) *or* (*coll.*) walloping; Ⓑ (*zerstören*) blow ‹fuse›; wreck ‹power line›. ❸ *unr. refl. V.* **sich [durch etw.] ~:** hack one's way through [sth.]

**durch|hecheln** *tr. V.* (*ugs. abwertend*) gossip about ‹person, behaviour›

**durch|heizen** ❶ *tr. V.* Ⓐ heat ‹house, offices, etc.› through; Ⓑ (*ohne Pause heizen*) heat ‹house, offices, etc.› continuously *or* day and night. ❷ *itr. V.* have *or* keep the heating on

**durch|helfen** *unr. itr. V.* **jmdm. [durch etw.] ~:** help a person through [sth.]; **ich werde mir schon ~:** I'll manage *or* get by

**durch|hören** *tr. V.* Ⓐ **etw. [durch etw.] ~:** hear sth. [through sth.]; Ⓑ (*heraushören*) sense, detect ‹bitterness, envy, etc.›

**durch|hungern** *refl. V.* get by *or* struggle along on very little to eat

**durch·irren** *tr. V.* wander *or* roam [aimlessly] through

**durch|ixen** *tr. V.* (*ugs.*) x out ‹typing error›

**durch|kämmen¹** *tr. V.* Ⓐ comb ‹hair› through; Ⓑ (*durchsuchen*) comb ‹area etc.›

**durch·kämmen²** *tr. V.* comb ‹area etc.›

**durch|kämpfen** ❶ *tr. V.* Ⓐ fight ‹case› [right] to the end; fight one's way through ‹adversity›; Ⓑ (*durchsetzen*) force through. ❷ *refl. V.* Ⓐ **sich [durch etw.] ~:** fight *or* battle one's way through [sth.]; Ⓑ (*durchstehen*) battle *or* struggle through; Ⓒ (*sich überwinden*) **sich dazu ~, etw. zu tun** bring oneself to do sth.

**durch|kauen** *tr. V.* Ⓐ **etw. [gut] ~:** chew sth. thoroughly *or* well; Ⓑ (*ugs.: besprechen*) go over and over

**durch|klettern** *itr. V.; mit sein* **[durch etw.] ~:** climb *or* clamber through [sth.]

**durch|kneten** *tr. V.* Ⓐ knead ‹dough etc.› thoroughly; Ⓑ (*ugs.: massieren*) knead ‹muscles etc.› thoroughly; **jmdn. ~:** give sb. a good hard massage

**durch|knöpfen** *tr. V.* button ‹dress, coat› all the way down; **das Kleid wird hinten durchgeknöpft** the dress buttons all the way up the back; **ein durchgeknöpftes Kleid** a button-through dress

**durch|kochen** *tr. V.* boil ‹stock, jam› thoroughly

**durch|kommen** *unr. itr. V.; mit sein* Ⓐ come through; (*mit Mühe hindurchgelangen*) get through; **durch etw. ~:** come/get through sth.; **es gab kein Durchkommen** there was no way through; Ⓑ (*ugs.: beim Telefonieren*) get through; Ⓒ (*durchgehen, -fahren usw.*) **durch etw. ~:** come *or* pass through sth.; **um fünf Uhr kommt der Zug [hier] durch** the train comes through [here] at five o'clock; **wenn du hier durchkommst, ...** when you're passing through ...; Ⓓ (*sich zeigen*) ‹sun› come out; ‹character trait, upbringing› come through, become apparent; **manchmal kommt sein Dialekt durch** (*fig.*) sometimes his dialect becomes noticeable; **bei ihm kommt der Lehrer durch** (*fig.*) the teacher in him comes through; Ⓔ (*erfolgreich sein*) **mit dieser Einstellung wird er [im Leben] nicht ~:** he won't get anywhere *or* far [in life] with an attitude like that; **mit Freundlichkeit und Verbindlichkeit kann man überall besser ~:** you'll get a lot further by being friendly and obliging; **damit kommst du bei mir nicht durch** you won't get anywhere with me like that; **mit so einer Entschuldigung kommt man bei ihm nicht durch** you won't get away with an excuse like that with him; Ⓕ (*ugs.: überleben*) pull through; Ⓖ (*ugs.: durchdringen*) **[durch etw.] ~** ‹water, sand, etc.› come through [sth.]; Ⓗ (*durchgesagt werden*) be announced; **die Nachricht kam im Fernsehen/Radio durch** the news was announced on television/the radio; Ⓘ (*bestehen*) get through; pass; **in einer Prüfung ~:** get through *or* pass an examination; Ⓙ (*auskommen*) manage; get by; **mit seiner Rente ~:** get by *or* manage on one's pension

**durch|komponieren** *tr. V.* Ⓐ work ‹story, play› out in detail; Ⓑ (*Musik*) compose ‹song› with an individual setting for each verse; set ‹poem› to music with an individual setting for each stanza; **die Ballade ist durchkomponiert** the ballad is through-composed *or* durchkomponiert

**durch|können** *unr. itr. V.* (*ugs.*) Ⓐ (*durchgehen, -kommen dürfen*) **[durch etw.] ~:** be able to go/come through [sth.]; **Sie können hier nicht durch** you can't go/come through here; **kann ich mal durch, bitte?** can I get by, please?; excuse me, please; Ⓑ (*durchkommen*) **[durch etw.] ~:** be able to get through [sth.]

**durch|konstruieren** *tr. V.* **etw. ~:** design and construct sth. with great attention to detail

**durch|kreuzen¹** *tr. V.* cross through *or* out ‹mistake, irrelevant information›

**durch·kreuzen²** *tr. V.* Ⓐ (*vereiteln*) thwart, frustrate ‹plan, intention, ambition, policy›; Ⓑ (*geh.: durchfahren*) cross ‹continent, sea, etc.›

**durch|kriechen** *unr. itr. V.; mit sein* **[durch etw.] ~:** crawl through [sth.]; **unter etw.** (*Dat.*) **~:** crawl [through] under sth.

**durch|kriegen** *tr. V.* (*ugs.*) ⇒ **durchbekommen**

**durch|laden** ❶ *unr. tr. V.* cock ‹pistol etc.› and rotate the cylinder. ❷ *unr. itr. V.* cock the trigger and rotate the cylinder

**Durchlass, *Durchlaß** /ˈdʊrçlas/ *der;* **Durchlasses, Durchlässe** /ˈdʊrçlɛsə/ Ⓐ (*geh.*) permission to pass; (*Einlass*) admittance; **sich** (*Dat.*) **~ verschaffen** obtain permission to pass/gain admittance; Ⓑ (*Öffnung*) gap; opening; (*für Wasser*) duct; conduit

**durch|lassen** *unr. tr. V.* Ⓐ **jmdn. [durch etw.] ~:** let *or* allow sb. through [sth.]; **den Ball ~** (*Sport*) ‹goalkeeper› let a goal in; Ⓑ (*durchlässig sein*) let ‹light, water, etc.› through; (*eindringen lassen*) let ‹light, water, etc.› in; Ⓒ (*ugs.: dulden*) **jmdm. etw. ~:** let sb. get away with sth.

**durchlässig** /ˈdʊrçlɛsɪç/ *Adj.* Ⓐ permeable; (*porös*) porous; (*undicht*) leaky; ‹raincoat, shoe› that lets in water; **B** (*offen*) open ‹system, border›; **die Grenzen müssen ~er werden** the borders must be opened up further; **im Verteidigungsministerium gab es eine ~e Stelle** (*fig.*) there had been a leak/leaks at the defence ministry

**-durchlässig** *Adj.* **gas-/luft-/wasser~** *usw.* **sein** be permeable to gas/air/water *etc.*

**Durchlässigkeit** *die;* ~ **A** permeability; (*Porosität*) porosity; (*Undichte*) leakiness; **B** (*Offenheit*) free interchange (+ *Gen.*, **zwischen** between)

**Durchlaucht** /ˈdʊrçlauxt/ *die;* ~, **~en: Ihre/Seine ~:** Her/His [Serene] Highness; **[Euer] ~:** Your [Serene] Highness

**Durch·lauf** *der* **A** (*Sport, DV*) run; **B** (*von Wasser*) flow; **während des ~s des Wassers** while the water is flowing through; **C** (*Ferns.*) preview (*of programme to gain approval for broadcast*); (*Rundf.*) scrutiny

**durch|laufen**[1] **1** *unr. itr. V.; mit sein* **A** **[durch etw.] ~:** run through [sth.]; **B** (*durchrinnen*) **[durch etw.] ~:** trickle through [sth.]; **der Kaffee ist durchgelaufen** the coffee is filtered; **C** (*passieren*) ‹runners› run *or* pass through; **D** (*ohne Pause laufen*) run without stopping; **E** (*fortlaufen*) ‹balcony, frieze› run all the way along. **2** *unr. tr. V.* go through ‹socks, soles of shoes›

**durch·laufen**[2] *unr. tr. V.* **A** go *or* pass through ‹phase, stage›; **B** (*geh.: hindurchgehen durch*) ‹shudder, feeling, etc.› run through; **C** (*zurücklegen*) run, cover ‹distance›

**durchlaufend** **1** *Adj.* continuous. **2** *adv.* ‹numbered, marked› in sequence

**Durchlauf-: ~erhitzer** *der;* **~s, ~:** geyser; instantaneous water heater; **~zeit** *die* processing time; (*DV*) run duration

**durch|lavieren** *refl. V.* (*ugs. abwertend*) get along by dint of some smart manœuvring

**durch·leben** *tr. V.* live through; experience; experience ‹moments of bliss, terror, fright›; **etw. wieder ~:** relive sth.

**durch|legen** *tr. V.* (*ugs.*) **die Straße/Leitung wird hier durchgelegt** the road/pipe will be laid through here

**durch·leiden** *unr. tr. V.* (*geh.*) endure; suffer

**durch|leiten** *tr. V.* **den Verkehr durch die Stadt ~:** direct the traffic through the town; **den Strom [durch das Gebiet] ~:** run electricity cables through [the area]

**durch|lesen** *unr. tr. V.* **etw. [ganz] ~:** read sth. [all the way] through; **wenn du das Buch durchgelesen hast** when you've finished reading the book; **sich** (*Dat.*) **etw. ~:** read sth. through; **etw. auf Fehler hin ~:** read sth. for errors

**durch·leuchten** *tr. V.* **A** x-ray ‹patient, part of body›; **sich ~ lassen** have an x-ray; **jmdm. den Magen ~:** x-ray sb.'s stomach; **B** (*fig.: analysieren*) investigate ‹case, matter, problem, etc.› thoroughly *or* in depth; **jmds. Vergangenheit ~:** probe into *or* investigate sb.'s past; **jmdn. ~:** vet sb.

**Durchleuchtung** *die;* **~, ~en** **A** (*das Röntgen*) x-ray examination; **jmdn. zur ~ ins Krankenhaus schicken** send sb. to hospital for an x-ray; **B** (*fig.: Analyse*) [thorough] investigation; (*von Bewerbern usw.*) vetting

**durch|liegen** **1** *unr. tr. V.* wear out ‹mattress, bed› [so that it sags in the middle]; **eine durchgelegene Matratze** a worn-out mattress. **2** *refl. V.* ‹patient› develop *or* get bedsores

**durch·löchern** *tr. V.* **A** make holes in; wear holes in ‹socks, shoes›; ‹rust› eat holes in; **jmdn./etw. mit Schüssen ~:** riddle sb./sth. with bullets; **völlig durchlöchert sein** be full of holes; **B** (*fig.: schwächen*) undermine ‹system› completely; render ‹principle› meaningless

**durch|lotsen** *tr. V.* (*ugs.*) **ein Schiff [durch etw.] ~:** pilot a ship through [sth.]; **jmdn. [durch die Stadt] ~:** guide sb. through [the town]

**durch|lüften**[1] **1** *tr. V.* air ‹room, flat, etc.› thoroughly. **2** *itr. V.* air the place

**durch·lüften**[2] *tr. V.* (*fachspr.*) aerate ‹soil›; ventilate ‹grain, woodpile›

**durch|machen** (*ugs.*) **1** *tr. V.* **A** undergo ‹change›; complete ‹training course›; go through ‹stage, phase›; serve ‹apprenticeship›; **B** (*erleiden*) go through; **sie hat schlimme Zeiten/viel durchgemacht** she's been through some bad times/a lot; **eine schwere Krankheit ~:** suffer *or* have a serious illness; **C** (*durcharbeiten*) work through ‹lunch break, weekend, etc.›. **2** *itr. V.* (*durcharbeiten*) work [right] through; (*durchfeiern*) celebrate all night/day *etc.*; keep going all night/day *etc.*

**durch|manövrieren** *tr. V.* **etw. [durch etw.] ~:** manœuvre sth. through [sth.]; **jmdn. sicher durch alle Schwierigkeiten ~** (*fig.*) bring *or* lead sb. safely through all the difficulties

**Durch·marsch** *der* **A** **der ~ zur Grenze** the march through to the frontier; **auf dem ~ sein** be marching through; **B** (*salopp: Durchfall*) **~ haben/bekommen** have/get the runs (*coll.*); **C** (*Skat*) **einen ~ machen** *take all the tricks when ramsch is called*

**durch|marschieren** *itr. V.; mit sein* **[durch etw.] ~:** march through [sth.]

**durch|mengen** *tr. V.* **[gut] ~:** mix ‹ingredients etc.› thoroughly

**durch·messen** *unr. tr. V.* (*geh.*) cross ‹room›; traverse ‹time and space›; **das Zimmer mit großen Schritten ~:** stride across the room; cross the room with long strides

**Durchmesser** *der;* **~s, ~:** diameter; **das misst 3 m im ~:** it measures 3 m in diameter

**durch|mischen**[1] *tr. V.* **[gut/gründlich] ~:** mix ‹ingredients etc.› thoroughly

**durch·mischen**[2] *tr. V.* **etw. mit etw. ~:** mix sth. with sth.

**durch|mogeln** *refl. V.* (*ugs. abwertend*) cheat one's way through; (*sich hineinmogeln*) wangle one's way in (*sl.*); **sich bei einer Prüfung** *usw.* **~:** get through an examination *etc.* by cheating

**durch|müssen** *unr. itr. V.* (*ugs.*) **[durch etw.] ~:** have to go through [sth.]; **da werden wir ~** (*fig.*) we'll have to see it *or* the thing through

**durch·mustern** *tr. V.* (*geh.*) examine closely; scrutinize

**durch|nagen** *tr. V.* gnaw through

**Durchnahme** /ˈdʊrçnaːmə/ *die;* **~: bei ~ des Stoffes** while we/they *etc.* are/were going through the material

**durch·nässen** *tr. V.* soak; drench; **[völlig] durchnässt sein** be soaking wet *or* wet through; **mit durchnässten Kleidern** with soaking wet clothes

**durch|nehmen** *unr. tr. V.* deal with, do ‹subject, topic›; go through ‹material›

***durch|numerieren**, **durch|nummerieren** *tr. V.* number ‹pages, seats, etc.› consecutively from beginning to end

**durch|organisieren** *tr. V.* organize sth. well; **etw. perfekt ~:** organize sth. down to the last detail

**durch|pauken** *tr. V.* (*ugs.*) **A** force through ‹law, regulation, etc.›; **B** (*lernen*) swot up (*Brit.*); bone up on (*Amer.*)

**durch|pausen** *tr. V.* trace

**durch|peitschen** *tr. V.* **A** **jmdn. ~:** give sb. a flogging; flog sb.; **B** (*ugs. abwertend*) railroad ‹law, application, etc.› through

**durch|pennen** *itr. V.* (*salopp*) sleep through; **ich habe bis 11 Uhr durchgepennt** I kipped till 11 o'clock (*coll.*)

**durch·pflügen** *tr. V.* plough through

**durch|planen** *tr. V.* **etw. ~:** plan sth. well

**durch|plumpsen** *itr. V.; mit sein* (*ugs.*) **A** **[durch etw.] ~** ‹person› fall through [sth.]; ‹small object› drop *or* fall through [sth.]; **B** (*bei einer Prüfung*) fail; flunk (*Amer. coll.*); **bei/in etw.** (*Dat.*) **~:** fail *or* flunk sth.

**durch|pressen** *tr. V.* mash ‹potatoes›; purée ‹fruit› (*by pressing through a sieve*); crush ‹garlic› (*in a press*); **Kartoffeln/Obst durch ein Sieb ~:** press *or* pass potatoes/fruit through a sieve

**durch|proben** *tr. V.* **etw. ~:** run through *or* rehearse sth. from beginning to end

**durch|probieren** *tr. V.* taste *or* try ‹wines, cakes, etc.› one after another; try on ‹dresses, suits, etc.› one after another

**durch|prügeln** *tr. V.* (*ugs.*) give sb. a real beating *or* (*coll.*) walloping; give ‹naughty child› a good hiding *or* (*coll.*) walloping

**durch·pulsen** *tr. V.* (*geh.*) ‹blood› pulse through; **buntes Leben durchpulste die Straßen** (*fig.*) the streets pulsated with life

**durch|pusten** *tr. V.* (*ugs.*) **etw. ~:** clear sth. by blowing through it

**durch·queren** *tr. V.* cross; travel across ‹country›; ‹train› pass *or* go through ‹country›

**durch|quetschen** *refl. V.* (*ugs.*) **sich [durch etw.] ~:** squeeze one's way through [sth.]

**durch|rasen** *itr. V.; mit sein* **[durch etw.] ~:** tear through [sth.]

**durch|rasseln** *itr. V.; mit sein* (*salopp*), **durch|rauschen** *itr. V.; mit sein* (*ugs.*) ⇒ **durchfallen B**

**durch|rechnen** *tr. V.* calculate ‹costs etc.› [down to the last penny]; check ‹bill› thoroughly

**durch|regnen** *itr. V.* (*unpers.*) **in der Küche** *usw.* **regnet es durch** the rain is coming through in the kitchen *etc.*; **es regnet durchs Dach durch** the rain is coming [in] through the roof; **die ganze Nacht ~:** rain all [through the] night; ⇒ *auch* **durchgeregnet**

**Durchreiche** *die;* **~, ~n** [serving] hatch

**durch|reichen** *tr. V.* **etw. [durch etw.] ~:** pass *or* hand sth. through [sth.]

**Durch·reise** *die* journey through; **auf der ~ sein** be on the way through *or* passing through

**durch|reisen**[1] *itr. V.; mit sein* travel *or* pass through

**durch·reisen**[2] *tr. V.* travel through *or* across ‹area, continent›

**Durch·reisende** *der/die* person travelling through; **~ auf dem Weiterflug nach Rom** passengers travelling through *or* on to Rome

**Durchreise·visum** *das* transit visa

**durch|reißen** **1** *unr. tr. V.* **etw. ~:** tear sth. in two *or* in half. **2** *unr. itr. V.; mit sein* ‹fabric, garment› rip, tear; ‹thread, rope› snap *or* break [in two]

**durch|reiten** *unr. itr. V.; mit sein* **[durch etw.] ~:** ride through [sth.]; **die ganze Nacht ~:** ride all night without stopping

**durch|rennen** *unr. itr. V.; mit sein* **[durch etw.] ~:** run through [sth.]

**durch|rieseln**[1] *itr. V.; mit sein* **[durch etw.] ~:** trickle through [sth.]

**durch·rieseln**[2] *tr. V.* ‹feeling of horror or pleasure› run through; **es durchrieselte sie kalt/heiß** a cold shiver ran through her/she felt a hot flush come over her

**durch|ringen** *unr. refl. V.* **sie hat sich endlich [zu einem Entschluss] durchgerungen** finally she managed to come to a decision; **wann wirst du dich dazu ~, es zu tun?** when are you going to bring yourself to do it?

**durch|rinnen** *unr. itr. V.; mit sein* **[durch etw.] ~:** run through [sth.]; **das Geld rinnt ihm zwischen den Fingern durch** (*fig.*) money burns a hole in his pocket

**durch|rosten** *itr. V.; mit sein* rust through

**durch|rufen** *unr. itr. V.* (*ugs.*) **[bei jmdm.] ~:** ring [sb.] up (*Brit.*)

**durch|rühren** *tr. V.* **etw. [gut] ~:** stir sth. [well]

**durch|rutschen** *itr. V.; mit sein* **A** **[durch etw.] ~** ‹object› slip through [sth.]; ‹person› slide through [sth.]; **B** (*ugs.: durchkommen*) manage to get through without doing any work

**durch|rütteln** *tr. V.* **jmdn. ~:** shake sb. about badly

**durchs** /dʊrçs/ *Präp.* + *Art.* = **durch das**

**durch|sacken** *itr. V.; mit sein* ‹aeroplane› drop suddenly; (*bei zu geringer Geschwindigkeit*) stall

*old spelling (see note on page 1707)

**Dụrch·sage** *die* announcement; (*an eine bestimmte Person*) message; **eine ~ machen** make an announcement

**dụrch|sagen** *tr. V.* ⇒ **durchgeben**

**dụrch|sägen¹, durch·sägen²** *tr. V.* saw through

**dụrch|saufen** *unr. itr. V.* (*derb*) **die ganze Nacht ~:** booze all night (*sl.*)

**dụrch|sausen** *itr. V.*; *mit sein* (*ugs.*) Ⓐ **[durch etw.] ~:** shoot through [sth.]; Ⓑ (*ugs.: durchfallen*) **[durch eine Prüfung] ~:** fail *or* (*Amer. coll.*) flunk [an examination]

**dụrch|schalten** ❶ *tr. V.* (*Technik*) connect ‹telephone line› through; put ‹telephone call› through; switch ‹signal, current, etc.› through. ❷ *itr. V.* (*beim Autofahren*) ‹car driver› change up [quickly]

**durchschaubar** *Adj.* transparent; **leicht/schwer ~ sein** be easy/difficult to see through; (*verständlich*) be easy/difficult to understand; **leicht ~** ‹lie, plan, intention› that is easy to see through *or* is easily seen through; **ein leicht/schwer ~er Mensch** a person who is easy/difficult to see through; **etw. ~ machen** make sth. easy to understand

**dụrch|schauen¹** *itr. V.* ⇒ **durchsehen**

**durch·schauen²** *tr. V.* Ⓐ see through ‹lie, plan, intention, person, etc.›; see ‹situation› clearly; **du bist durchschaut** I've/we've seen through you; I/we know what you're up to; **~, worum es wirklich geht** see what it's really all about; Ⓑ (*verstehen*) understand

**dụrch|scheinen¹** *unr. itr. V.* **[durch etw.] ~** ‹sun, light› shine through [sth.]; ‹colour, pattern› show through [sth.]

**durch·scheinen²** *unr. tr. V.* (*geh.*) ‹sun› fill ‹room› with light; **von Sonnenlicht durchschienen** filled with sunlight

**dụrchscheinend** *Adj.* (*lichtdurchlässig*) translucent; (*durchsichtig*) transparent; diaphanous ‹fabric›; translucent ‹skin etc.›

**dụrch|scheuern** ❶ *tr. V.* wear through; **ein durchgescheuertes Kabel** a worn cable. ❷ *refl. V.* wear through

**dụrch|schieben** *unr. tr. V.* **etw. [durch etw.] ~:** push sth. through [sth.]; **einen Brief unter der Tür ~:** push a letter under the door

**dụrch|schießen¹** *unr. tr. V.* **durch etw. ~:** shoot through sth.; **den Ball zwischen den Bäumen ~:** shoot the ball [through] between the trees

**durch·schießen²** *unr. tr. V.* Ⓐ **etw. ~:** shoot sth. through; Ⓑ (*Buchbinderei*) interleave; Ⓒ (*Druckw.*) space out; Ⓓ (*Textilind.*) interweave (**mit** with)

**dụrch|schimmern** *itr. V.* Ⓐ **[durch etw.] ~** ‹light› shimmer through [sth.]; ‹colour› gleam through [sth.]; Ⓑ (*fig.*) ‹qualities, emotions› show through

**dụrch|schlafen** *unr. itr. V.* sleep [right] through; **die ganze Nacht ~:** sleep all night [without waking]

**Dụrch·schlag** *der* Ⓐ (*Kopie*) carbon [copy]; Ⓑ (*Küchengerät*) colander; strainer; Ⓒ (*Kfz-W.*) puncture; Ⓓ (*Werkzeug*) punch; Ⓔ (*Elektrot.*) disruptive discharge

**dụrch|schlagen¹** ❶ *unr. tr. V.* Ⓐ **etw. ~:** chop *or* split sth. in two; Ⓑ (*schlagen*) **ein Loch/einen Nagel [durch etw.] ~:** knock a hole through [sth.]/knock *or* drive a nail through [sth.].
❷ *unr. itr. V.* Ⓐ *mit sein* **[durch etw.] ~** ‹dampness, water› come through [sth.]; **das schlägt auf die Preise durch** (*fig.*) it has an effect on prices; **bei ihm schlägt die Mutter durch** (*fig.*) he takes after his mother; **der Aristokrat in ihm schlägt durch** the aristocrat in him comes out; Ⓑ *mit sein* ‹fuse› blow; Ⓒ (*abführen*) have a strong laxative effect; **bei jmdm. ~:** go straight through sb.
❸ *refl. V.* Ⓐ struggle along; Ⓑ (*ein Ziel erreichen*) (*mit Gewalt*) fight one's way through; (*mit List*) make one's way through

**durch·schlagen²** *unr. tr. V.* smash

**dụrchschlagend** *Adj.* resounding ‹success›; decisive ‹effect, measures›; conclusive ‹evidence›

**Dụrchschlag·papier** *das* copy paper

**Dụrchschlags·kraft** *die* Ⓐ (*Ballistik*) penetrating power; Ⓑ (*fig.: Wirkung*) power; force

**dụrch|schlängeln** *refl. V.* **sich [durch etw.] ~** (*auch fig.*) thread one's way through [sth.]

**dụrch|schleichen** *unr. refl. V.* **sich [durch etw.] ~:** slip *or* creep through [sth.]

**dụrch|schleppen** *tr. V.* (*ugs.*) carry ‹loss-making concern, non-productive worker›; keep ‹needy relation etc.›

**dụrch|schleusen** *tr. V.* Ⓐ (*ugs.*) **jmdn./etw. [durch etw.] ~:** guide sb./sth. through [sth.]; (*durchschmuggeln*) get sb./sth. through [sth.]; Ⓑ (*Schifffahrt*) **ein Schiff ~:** pass a ship through a lock

**Dụrchschlupf** /ˈdʊrçʃlʊpf/ *der;* **~[e]s, ~e** gap; (*Loch*) hole

**dụrch|schlüpfen** *itr. V.*; *mit sein* **[durch etw.] ~:** slip through [sth.]

**dụrch|schmecken** ❶ *tr. V.* be able to taste (**bei** in). ❷ *itr. V.* come through [too strongly]

**dụrch|schmoren** *itr. V.*; *mit sein* (*ugs.*) ‹cable› burn through; ‹element› burn out

**dụrch|schmuggeln** *tr. V.* **etw. [durch etw.] ~:** smuggle sth. through [sth.]

**dụrch|schneiden¹** *unr. tr. V.* cut through ‹thread, cable›; cut ‹ribbon, sheet of paper› in two; cut ‹throat, umbilical cord›; **etw. in der Mitte ~:** cut sth. in half

**durch·schneiden²** *unr. tr. V.* Ⓐ ⇒ **durchschneiden¹**; Ⓑ (*geh.*) ‹road, river, valley› cut through; ‹bow of boat› slice through ‹waves›; **das Land ist von Kanälen durchschnitten** the country is criss-crossed by canals

**Dụrch·schnitt** *der* Ⓐ average; **im ~:** on average; **im ~ 110 km/h fahren** average 110 k.p.h.; do 110 k.p.h. on average; Ⓑ (*Mittelmaß*) **über/unter dem ~ liegen, guter/unterer ~ sein** be above/below average; **vom ~ abweichen** deviate from the norm; Ⓒ (*ugs.: Mehrheit*) majority; **der ~ ist ...** the majority [of people] *or* people in general are ...; Ⓓ (*Math.*) mean; Ⓔ (*fachspr.*) [cross] section

**dụrchschnittlich** ❶ *Adj.* Ⓐ average ‹growth, performance, output›; Ⓑ (*ugs.: mehrheitlich*) ordinary ‹life, person, etc.›; Ⓒ (*mittelmäßig*) modest ‹intelligence, talent, performance, achievements›; ordinary ‹appearance›. ❷ *adv.* ‹produce, spend, earn, etc.› on [an] average; **~ groß sein** be of average height; **~ begabt sein** be moderately talented

**Dụrchschnitts-: ~alter** *das* average age; **~bürger** *der*, **~bürgerin** *die* average citizen; **~ehe** *die* ordinary marriage; (*Statistik*) average marriage; **~einkommen** *das* average income; **~geschwindigkeit** *die* average speed; **~gesicht** *das* ordinary face; **~leser** *der*, **~leserin** *die* average reader; **~lohn** *der* average wage; **~mensch** *der* average person; (*Alltagsmensch*) ordinary person; **für uns ~menschen** for ordinary people like ourselves; **~note** *die* (*Schulw.*) average grade; **~temperatur** *die* average temperature; **~wert** *der* average *or* mean value; **~zensur** *die* ⇒ **~note**

**dụrch|schnüffeln¹, durch·schnüffeln²** *tr. V.* (*abwertend*) poke *or* nose around in

**Dụrchschreibe·block** *der; Pl.* **~s** *od.* **Durchschreibeblöcke** duplicate pad

**dụrch|schreiben** *unr. tr. V.* make a carbon copy of

**durch·schreiten** *unr. tr. V.* (*geh.*) stride across ‹room›; stride through ‹door, hall›

**Dụrch·schrift** *die* carbon [copy]

**Dụrch·schuss, *Dụrch·schuß** *der* Ⓐ bullet *or* gunshot wound (*where the bullet has passed right through*); Ⓑ (*Schuss*): *shot in which the bullet passes through and emerges on the other side;* Ⓒ (*Druckw.*) (*Zwischenraum*) space; (*Blindmaterial*) lead; Ⓓ (*Textilw.*) weft; woof

**dụrch|schütteln** *tr. V.* **jmdn. ~:** give sb. a good shaking; **wir wurden im Bus tüchtig durchgeschüttelt** we were shaken about all over the place in the bus

**durch·schweifen** *tr. V.* (*dichter.*) roam *or* wander through; (*fig.*) ‹gaze› rove *or* wander

**dụrch|schwimmen¹** *unr. itr. V.*; *mit sein* **[durch etw.] ~:** swim through [sth.]; **unter etw.** (*Dat.*) **~:** swim through under sth.

**durch·schwimmen²** *unr. tr. V.* swim ‹the Channel, course, etc.›

**dụrch|schwindeln** *refl. V.* get along by cheating and lying

**dụrch|schwitzen, durch·schwitzen** *tr. V.* **ich habe mein Hemd** *usw.* **durchgeschwitzt** *od.* **durchschwitzt** my shirt *etc.* is soaked in sweat; ⇒ *auch* **durchgeschwitzt**

**dụrch|segeln** *itr. V.*; *mit sein* Ⓐ **[durch etw.] ~:** sail through [sth.]; **zwischen den Felsen ~:** sail [through] between the rocks; Ⓑ (*Schülerspr.: durchfallen*) **[durch etw.] ~:** fail *or* (*Amer. coll.*) flunk sth.; **bei/in etw.** (*Dat.*) **~:** fail *or* flunk sth.

**dụrch|sehen** ❶ *unr. itr. V.* Ⓐ **[durch etw.] ~:** look through [sth.]; **durch dieses Glas kann man nicht ~:** you can't see through this type of glass; Ⓑ ⇒ **durchblicken** B. ❷ *unr. tr. V.* Ⓐ look *or* check through *or* over ‹essay, homework, etc.›; **etw. auf Fehler ~:** look *or* check through sth. for mistakes; Ⓑ (*lesen*) look through ‹newspaper, magazine›

**dụrch|seihen** *tr. V.* (*Kochk.*) strain; pass ‹sauce, gravy› through a sieve

***dụrch|sein** ⇒ **durch** 2 D-L

**dụrchsetzbar** *Adj.* enforceable ‹demand, claim›; **diese Rentenerhöhung/Reform ist nicht ~:** it will be impossible to get this pension increase approved/to carry this reform through

**dụrch|setzen¹** ❶ *tr. V.* carry *or* put through ‹programme, reform›; carry through ‹intention, plan›; accomplish, achieve ‹objective›; enforce ‹demand, claim›; get ‹resolution› accepted; **~, dass etw. geschieht** succeed in getting sth. done; **seinen Willen ~:** have one's [own] way. ❷ *refl. V.* assert oneself; ‹idea› find *or* gain acceptance, become generally accepted *or* established; ‹fashion› catch on (*coll.*), find *or* gain acceptance; **sich gegen jmdn. ~:** assert oneself against sb.; **sich den Schülern gegenüber ~** ‹teacher› assert one's authority over the pupils

**durch·setzen²** *tr. V.* **eine Gruppe mit Spitzeln/ein Land mit Spionen ~:** infiltrate informers into a group/spies into a country; **mit Nadelbäumen durchsetzt sein** be interspersed with conifers

**Dụrchsetzung** *die;* **~** ⇒ **durchsetzen¹**: carrying through; putting through; accomplishment; achievement; enforcement; **zur ~ unserer Forderungen** to enforce our demands

**Dụrchsetzungs-: ~kraft** *die*, **~vermögen** *das* ability to assert oneself

**Dụrch·sicht** *die* look *or* check through; **nach [einer] ~ der Unterlagen** after looking *or* checking through the documents; **jmdm. etw. zur ~ geben** give sb. sth. to look *or* check through

**dụrchsichtig** *Adj.* Ⓐ transparent; see-through, transparent ‹nightdress, blouse›; clear ‹air, water›; Ⓑ (*durchschaubar*) transparent; **etw. ~ machen** make sth. comprehensible

**dụrch|sickern** *itr. V.*; *mit sein* Ⓐ seep through; Ⓑ (*bekannt werden*) ‹news› leak out; **es ist durchgesickert, dass ...** news has leaked out that ...

**dụrch|sieben¹** *tr. V.* sift, sieve ‹flour etc.›; strain ‹tea etc.›; (*fig.*) sift [through] ‹applicants etc.›

**durch·sieben²** *tr. V.* ‹bullets› riddle; **von Kugeln durchsiebt** riddled with bullets

**dụrch|sitzen** ❶ *unr. tr. V.* wear out ‹chair, seat›; **seine Hose ~:** wear through *or* out the seat of one's trousers. ❷ *unr. refl. V.* ‹chair, seat› wear out, become worn out

**durchsọffen** *Adj.* (*derb*) **eine ~e Nacht** a night on the booze (*sl.*)

**dụrch|sollen** *itr. V.* (*ugs.*) **[durch etw.] ~** ‹cupboard, cable› be supposed to go through [sth.]; **soll der Schrank hier durch?** is the cupboard to go through here?

**durchsonnt** /dʊrçˈzɔnt/ *Adj.* (*dichter.*) sundrenched; sunny; sunny, sun-filled ‹room, clearing›

d

**durch|spielen** *tr. V.* Ⓐ act ‹scene› through; play ‹piece of music› through; Ⓑ (*fig.: durchgehen*) go through ‹alternatives, options›; play ‹part, role› to the end; ‹footballer› play right through; **die ganze Nacht ~** ‹card players etc.› play all night [long]

**durch|sprechen** *unr. tr. V.* talk ‹matter etc.› over; discuss ‹matter etc.› thoroughly

**durch|springen** *unr. itr. V.; mit sein* **[durch etw.] ~:** jump *or* leap through [sth.]

**durch|spülen** *tr. V.* **etw. [gut/gründlich] ~:** rinse sth. thoroughly

**durch|starten** *itr. V.; mit sein* Ⓐ (*Flugw.*) begin climbing again (*instead of landing*); Ⓑ (*Kfz-W.*) accelerate away again

**durch|stechen**[1] *unr. itr. V.* **mit einer Nadel** *usw.* **[durch etw.] ~:** stick a needle *etc.* through [sth.]

**durch·stechen**[2] *unr. tr. V.* pierce; cut through ‹isthmus›; **sich** (*Dat.*) **die Ohrläppchen ~ lassen** have one's ears pierced

**durch|stecken** *tr. V.* **etw. [durch etw.] ~:** put *or* (*coll.*) stick sth. through [sth.]

**durch|stehen** *unr. tr. V.* Ⓐ stand ‹pace, boring job, living with sb.›; come through ‹adventure, difficult situation›; pass ‹test›; get over ‹illness›; Ⓑ (*Ski*) complete ‹jump, run› without falling

**Durchsteh·vermögen** *das* staying power; stamina; [power of] endurance

**durch|steigen** *unr. itr. V.; mit sein* Ⓐ **[durch etw.] ~:** climb through [sth.]; Ⓑ (*salopp: verstehen*) get it (*coll.*); **da steige ich nicht durch** I don't get it (*coll.*)

**durch|stellen** *tr. V.* put ‹call› through (**in** + *Akk.*, **auf** + *Akk.* to)

**durch|stemmen** *tr. V.* chisel through, chisel a hole in ‹wall›

**Durch·stich** *der* Ⓐ (*Vorgang*) cutting through; **der ~ der Landenge** *usw.* cutting through the isthmus *etc.*; Ⓑ (*Verbindung*) cut; cutting

**Durchstieg** /ˈdʊrçʃtiːk/ *der;* **~[e]s, ~e einen ~ in den Zaun schneiden** cut a hole in the fence [through which one can/could climb]

**durch|stöbern**[1] *tr. V.* (*ugs.*) search all through ‹house›; rummage through ‹cupboard, case, etc.›; scour ‹wood, area›

**durch·stöbern**[2] *tr. V.* (*ugs.*) Ⓐ ⇒ **durchstöbern**[1]; Ⓑ (*durchsuchen*) rummage around ‹shop› (**nach** in search of); rummage through ‹archives› (**nach** in search of)

**Durch·stoß** *der* (*Milit.*) breakthrough

**durch|stoßen**[1] *unr. itr. V.* Ⓐ **durch etw. ~:** knock a hole through sth.; break through sth.; Ⓑ *mit sein* (*Milit.*) break through (**bis zu** to)

**durch·stoßen**[2] *unr. tr. V.* break through; go through ‹cloud layer›; rupture ‹hymen›; smash ‹pane of glass›; **die feindlichen Linien ~** (*Milit.*) break through the enemy lines

**durch|streichen**[1] *unr. tr. V.* Ⓐ cross through *or* out; delete; (*in Formularen*) delete; Ⓑ (*passieren*) **Gemüse/die Sauce [durch ein Sieb] ~:** pass vegetables through a sieve/strain the sauce [through a sieve]

**durch·streichen**[2] *unr. tr. V.* (*geh.*) roam ‹area›; rove, roam ‹foreign parts›

**durch·streifen** *tr. V.* Ⓐ (*geh.*) roam, wander through ‹fields, countryside›; Ⓑ (*kontrollieren*) patrol

**durch|strömen**[1] *itr. V.; mit sein* **[durch etw.] ~:** flow through [sth.]; (*fig.*) ‹people, crowd› stream *or* pour through [sth.]

**durch·strömen**[2] *tr. V.* flow through

**durch|strukturieren** *tr. V.* **etw. ~:** structure sth. well; **ein gut durchstrukturierter Artikel** a well-structured article

**durch|stylen** *tr. V.* give a completely integrated design/style to ‹premises, rooms etc.›

**durch|suchen**[1] *tr. V.* search through

**durch·suchen**[2] *tr. V.* search ‹house, car› (**nach** for); frisk, search ‹person› (**nach** for); search, scour ‹area› (**nach** for)

**Durchsuchung** *die;* **~, ~en** search; **zur ~ einer Wohnung** in order to search a flat

*old spelling (see note on page 1707)

**Durchsuchungs·befehl** *der* search warrant

**durch|tanzen**[1] ❶ *itr. V.* **die ganze Nacht ~:** dance all night; dance the night away; **bis zum Morgen ~:** dance until morning. ❷ *tr. V.* wear out ‹shoes› [by] dancing

**durch·tanzen**[2] *tr. V.* **die Nacht ~:** spend the night dancing; dance all night; **nach einer durchtanzten Nacht** after a night of *or* spent dancing

**durch|testen** *tr. V.* Ⓐ **jedes einzelne Gerät ~:** test each device individually; Ⓑ (*gründlich testen*) **etw. ~:** test sth. thoroughly

**durch·toben** *tr. V.* (*geh.*) rage through

**durch|trainieren** *tr. V.* get ‹athlete, team, body› into condition; **ein gut durchtrainierter Körper** a body in peak condition

**durch·tränken** *tr. V.* (*geh.*) soak *or* saturate [completely]; soak, steep ‹fruit›

**durch|treiben** *unr. tr. V.* Ⓐ **Menschen/Tiere [durch etw.] ~:** drive people/animals through [sth.]; Ⓑ (*durchschlagen*) **einen Nagel** *usw.* **[durch etw.] ~:** drive a nail *etc.* through [sth.]

**durch|trennen**[1], **durch·trennen**[2] *tr. V.* cut [through] ‹wire, rope›; sever ‹nerve, umbilical cord›

**durch|treten** ❶ *unr. tr. V.* press ‹clutch pedal, brake pedal› right down; depress ‹clutch pedal, brake pedal› completely. ❷ *unr. itr. V.* Ⓐ *mit sein* **[durch etw.] ~** ‹liquid, gas› come through [sth.]; Ⓑ *mit sein* (*ugs.: weitergehen*) ‹passenger› move along down (*in bus, train*)

**durchtrieben** (*abwertend*) ❶ *Adj.* crafty; sly. ❷ *adv.* craftily; slyly

**Durchtriebenheit** *die;* **~:** craftiness; slyness

**durch|trinken** *unr. itr. V.* **die ganze Nacht ~:** drink all night; **bis zum Morgen ~:** drink right through till morning

**durch|tropfen** *itr. V.; mit sein* **[durch etw.] ~** ‹water› drip through [sth.]

**durch|wachen**[1] *itr. V.* stay awake; **die ganze Nacht ~:** stay awake all night

**durch·wachen**[2] *tr. V.* **die Nacht/mehrere Nächte ~:** stay awake all night/[for] several nights running; **die Nacht am Bett des Kranken ~:** keep watch through the night at the patient's bedside

**durch|wachsen**[1] *unr. itr. V.; mit sein* **[durch etw.] ~** ‹plant› grow through sth.

**durch·wachsen**[2] ❶ *Adj.* Ⓐ **mit Unkraut ~ sein** ‹lawn› have weeds growing in it; **~er Speck** streaky bacon; Ⓑ (*ugs. scherzh.*) so-so. ❷ *adv.* **ihr geht es ~:** she has her ups and downs

**durch|wagen** *refl. V.* (*ugs.*) **sich [durch etw.] ~:** dare to go through sth.; venture through sth.

**Durchwahl** *die* Ⓐ direct dialling; Ⓑ **mein Apparat ist mit/hat keine ~:** I have/don't have an outside line; Ⓒ ⇒ **Durchwahlnummer**

**durch|wählen** *itr. V.* Ⓐ dial direct; **direkt nach Nairobi ~:** dial Nairobi direct; **in ein Land ~:** dial a country direct; Ⓑ (*bei Nebenstellenanlagen*) dial straight through

**Durchwahl·nummer** *die* number of the/one's direct line

**durch|walken** *tr. V.* Ⓐ (*durchkneten*) **jmdn. ~** ‹masseur› give sb. a good, hard massage; **die Wäsche ~:** use a vigorous kneading action to get the washing clean; Ⓑ (*ugs.: verprügeln*) **jmdn. ~:** give sb. a good belting; (*als Strafe*) give sb. a good hiding

**durch|wandern**[1] *itr. V.; mit sein* walk *or* hike without a break; **den ganzen Tag ~:** walk *or* hike all day

**durch·wandern**[2] *tr. V.* walk *or* hike through

**durch|wärmen**[1], **durch·wärmen**[2] *tr. V.* **jmdn. ~:** warm sb. up

**durch|waschen** *unr. tr. V.* (*ugs.*) **etw. ~:** wash sth. through

**durch|waten**[1] *itr. V.; mit sein* **[durch etw.] ~:** wade through [sth.]

**durch·waten**[2] *tr. V.* wade across

**durch·weben** *regelm.* (*dichter. auch unr.*) *tr. V.* interweave (**mit** with)

**durchweg** /ˈdʊrçvɛk/, (*österr. ugs.*) **durchwegs** /ˈdʊrçvɛːks/ *Adv.* without exception; **er umgibt sich ~ mit Leuten, die ...** he surrounds himself exclusively with people who ...; **die Vegetation ist ~ öde** the vegetation is uniformly dreary

**durch|wehen**[1] *itr. V.* **durch etw. ~** ‹wind› blow through sth.

**durch·wehen**[2] *tr. V.* (*geh.*) ‹breeze› waft through; (*fig.*) pervade

**durch|weichen**[1] *itr. V.; mit sein* ‹cardboard, paper› become *or* go [soft and] soggy

**durch·weichen**[2] *tr. V.* make ‹earth, path, etc.› sodden; **völlig durchweicht sein** (*fig.*) be drenched; be sopping wet

**durch|werfen** *unr. tr. V.* **etw. [durch etw.] ~:** throw sth. through [sth.]

**durch|wetzen** wear out ‹clothes›; wear through ‹sleeves›; **eine durchgewetzte Hose** a worn-out pair of trousers

**durch|winden** *unr. refl. V.* **sich [durch etw.] ~** ‹river› wind its way through [sth.]; ‹person› thread one's way through [sth.]

**durch·wirken** *tr. V.* ⇒ **durchweben**

**durch|witschen** *itr. V.* (*ugs.*) **[durch etw.] ~:** slip through [sth.]; **jmdm. ~** ‹word› escape sb.

**durch|wollen** *unr. itr. V.* (*ugs.*) Ⓐ **[durch etw.] ~** (*durchgehen wollen*) want to go through [sth.]; (*durchkommen wollen*) want to come through [sth.]; **unter etw.** (*Dat.*) **~:** want to go through under sth.; Ⓑ (*ein Hindernis durchqueren*) **[durch etw.] ~:** want to get through [sth.]

**durch|wühlen**[1] ❶ *tr. V.* rummage through, ransack ‹drawers, cupboard, case› (**nach** in search of, looking for); turn ‹room, house› upside down (**nach** in search of, looking for). ❷ *refl. V.* (*ugs.*) **sich durch das Blumenbeet/die Erde ~** ‹mole› dig up the flower bed/burrow through the earth; **sich durch einen Aktenstoß ~** (*fig.*) plough through a pile of documents

**durch·wühlen**[2] *tr. V.* Ⓐ ⇒ **durchwühlen**[1] 1; Ⓑ (*aufwühlen*) churn up

**durch|wurschteln**, **durch|wursteln** *refl. V.* (*salopp*) muddle through

**durch|zählen** *tr. V.* count; count up ‹money, people›

**durch|zechen**[1] *itr. V.* **bis zum Morgen ~:** drink until morning

**durch·zechen**[2] *tr. V.* **die Nacht ~:** spend all night drinking; **eine durchzechte Nacht** a night of drinking

**durch|zeichnen** *tr. V.* ⇒ **durchpausen**

**durch|ziehen**[1] ❶ *unr. tr. V.* Ⓐ **jmdn./etw. [durch etw.] ~:** pull sb./sth. through [sth.]; **ein Gummiband [durch etw.] ~:** draw an elastic through [sth.]; Ⓑ (*ugs.: durchführen*) get through ‹syllabus, programme›; **wir müssen die Sache ~:** we must see the matter through; Ⓒ (*bis zum Anschlag ziehen*) pull ‹oar, saw blade› right through; Ⓓ (*salopp: rauchen*) smoke; **einen [Joint] ~:** smoke a joint (*sl.*); Ⓔ (*erstellen*) dig ‹ditch› through; **eine Mauer [durch den Saal] ~:** build a wall across [the room].
❷ *unr. itr. V.; mit sein* Ⓐ **[durch ein Gebiet** *usw.*] **~:** pass through [an area *etc.*]; ‹soldiers› march through [an area *etc.*]; Ⓑ (*Kochk.*) ‹fruit, meat, etc.› soak; **gut durchgezogen sein** be well soaked

**durch·ziehen**[2] *unr. tr. V.* Ⓐ pass through ‹land, area›; Ⓑ (*durchsetzen*) ‹river, road, ravine› run through, traverse ‹landscape›; **von blauen Adern durchzogener Marmor** marble veined with blue; Ⓒ (*enthalten sein in*) ‹theme, motif, etc.› run through ‹book etc.›; Ⓓ (*durchdringen*) ‹pain› shoot through ‹person›; ‹smell, scent› suddenly fill ‹room›; (*fig.*) ‹feeling, awareness› come over ‹person›

**durch·zucken** *tr. V.* ‹lightning, beam of light› flash across; **jmdn. ~** (*fig.*) ‹thought› flash through *or* cross sb.'s mind

**Durch·zug** *der* Ⓐ draught; **~ machen** create a draught; **auf ~ schalten** (*ugs.*), **die Ohren auf ~ stellen** (*ugs.*) let it go in one ear and out the other; Ⓑ (*das Durchziehen*) passage through; (*von Truppen*) march through; **nach dem ~ des Schlechtwettergebietes** (*Met.*) once the area of bad weather has moved through

# dürfen

## 1. Erlaubnis

***ich darf***
= I may *od.* can

***Wann darf ich nach Hause gehen?***
= When may *od.* can I go home?

***Er sagte mir, ich dürfte sofort nach Hause gehen***
= He told me I could go home right away

Bei der Übersetzung von *dürfte* in dieser Konstruktion (indirekter Rede) ist **could** vorzuziehen, da **might** sich etwas gespreizt anhört.

In der Vergangenheit und in Fällen, wo *dürfen* qualifiziert wird, arbeitet man am besten mit **be allowed to**:

***Sie durfte die Katze streicheln***
= She was allowed to stroke the cat

***Ich darf nur bis hierher kommen***
= I am only allowed to come this far

***Ich darf nie meine Meinung sagen***
= I'm never allowed to say what I think, I can never speak my mind

***Er darf nicht reiten, weil er es mit dem Rücken hat***
= He isn't allowed to *od.* he can't ride because he has back trouble

(Weiteres zum negativen Gebrauch finden Sie unter **2.**).

Wenn *dürfen* ohne zweites Verb allein steht, übersetzt man auch am besten mit **be allowed [to]**:

***Wir haben nicht gedurft***
= We weren't allowed to

***Darf man das?***
= Is that allowed?

Bei Höflichkeitsformeln mit *darf/dürfte ich* ... handelt es sich um höfliche Bitten um Erlaubnis, logischerweise ist die Übersetzung also **may/might I ...** :

***Darf/Dürfte ich Sie begleiten?***
= May/Might I accompany you?

Lediglich bei der Formel *darf ich Sie bitten* ... kommen andere Übersetzungen in Betracht:

***Darf ich Sie bitten, hereinzukommen?***
= Would you please come in?

Im erweiterten Sinne von "Grund haben zu" = **can**:

***Wir dürfen annehmen, dass ...***
= We can assume that ...

***Ich darf mich nicht beklagen***
= I can't *od.* mustn't complain

## 2. Verbot

*Das darf man/darfst du/dürfen Sie nicht tun*

Solche Beispiele lassen sich auf verschiedene Art übersetzen, je nachdem, welcher Aspekt betont wird. Will man betonen, dass die Handlung nicht erlaubt ist, sagt man "That's not allowed". Ist man entsetzt über einen Verstoß gegen die Sitten, sagt man "You can't do that!". Aber vor allem wenn man ein Verbot ausspricht oder jemandem von etwas abrät, heißt es "You mustn't do that":

***Das darfst du unter keinen Umständen erwähnen***
= You mustn't mention that under any circumstances

Das gilt aber nicht nur für die Anrede in der zweiten Person:

***Sie darf nicht alleine fahren***
= She mustn't go on her own

***Er darf es nicht wissen***
= He must not know about it

Auch bei Vorschriften oder dergleichen sagt man **must not**:

***Hier darf man nicht rauchen***
= You must not smoke here, There's no smoking here

***Dieser Stoff darf nicht nass werden***
= This material must not get wet

Ähnliche Beispiele in der Vergangenheit, die Missbilligung ausdrücken, werden mit **should not have** übersetzt:

***Das hätte sie nicht sagen dürfen***
= She shouldn't have said that

## 3. dürfte

Außer in Höflichkeitsformeln, wird dieser Konjunktiv 2 meist mit **should** oder **ought to** übersetzt:

***Jetzt dürften sie dort angekommen sein***
= They should be there by now

***Das dürfte schon möglich sein***
= That should *od.* ought to be possible

Bei einer Schätzung sagt man aber **must**:

***Sie dürfte in den Achtzigern sein***
= She must be in her eighties

Und bei einer Vorhersage kann man **will probably** sagen:

***Es dürfte ein Gewitter geben***
= There will probably be a storm

**Durchzügler** /-tsy:klɐ/ *der;* **~s, ~** (*Zool.*) bird of passage

**Durchzugs·recht** *das* (*Völkerr.*) right to march troops through

**durch|zwängen** ❶ *tr. V.* **etw. [durch etw.] ~:** force *or* squeeze [sth.] through [sth.]. ❷ *refl. V.* **sich [durch etw.] ~:** force *or* squeeze one's way through [sth.]

**Dur·drei·klang** *der* (*Musik*) major triad

**dürfen** /ˈdʏrfn̩/ ❶ *unr. Modalverb; 2. Part.* **dürfen:** Ⓐ (*Erlaubnis haben zu*) **etw. tun ~:** be allowed *or* permitted to do sth.; **darf ich [das tun]?** may I [do that]?; **das darf man nicht tun** that is not allowed; one mustn't do that; **nein, das darfst du nicht** no you may not; **hier darf man nicht rauchen** smoking is prohibited here; **ich darf morgen nicht verschlafen** I mustn't oversleep tomorrow; **du darfst nicht lügen/jetzt nicht aufgeben!** you mustn't tell lies/give up now!; **ihm darf nichts geschehen** nothing must happen to him; **das darf nicht wahr sein** (*ugs.*) that's incredible; **das hätte nicht kommen ~** (*ugs.*) he/you *etc.* shouldn't have said that; Ⓑ (*in Höflichkeitsformeln*) **darf ich rauchen?** may I smoke?; **darf ich Sie bitten, das zu tun?** could I ask you to do that?; **darf** *od.* **dürfte ich mal Ihre Papiere sehen?** may I see your papers?; **darf ich um diesen Tanz bitten?** may I have [the pleasure of] this dance?; **was darf es sein?** (*im Laden*) can I help you?; (*was möchten Sie zum Trinken haben?*) what can I get you to drink?; **darf ich bitten?** (*um einen Tanz*) may I have the pleasure?; (*einzutreten*) won't you come in?; **Ruhe, wenn ich bitten darf!** will you please be quiet!; Ⓒ (*Grund haben zu*) **ich darf Ihnen mitteilen, dass ...** I am able to inform you that ...; **darf ich annehmen, dass ...?** can I assume that ...?; **sie darf sich nicht beklagen** she can't complain; she has no reason to complain; **da darf sie sich nicht wundern** that shouldn't surprise her; **das darfst du mir glauben** you can take my word for it; Ⓓ *Konjunktiv II + Inf.* **das dürfte der Grund sein** that is probably the reason; (*ich nehme an, dass das der Grund ist*) that must be the reason; **es dürfte einfach sein, das zu tun** it should be *or* ought to be easy to do it; **das dürfte reichen** that should be enough.
❷ *unr. tr., itr. V.* **er hat nicht gedurft** he was not allowed *or* permitted to; **darf ich ins Theater?** may I go to the theatre?; **darfst du das?** are you allowed to?; **Darf ich? — Ja, Sie ~:** May I? — Yes, you may

**durfte** /ˈdʊrftə/, *1. u. 3. Pers. Sg. Prät. v.* **dürfen**

**dürfte** /ˈdʏrftə/ *1. u. 3. Pers. Sg. Konjunktiv II v.* **dürfen**

**dürftig** /ˈdʏrftɪç/ ❶ *Adj.* Ⓐ (*ärmlich*) poor; scanty, meagre ‹meal›; scanty, poor ‹clothing›; Ⓑ (*abwertend: unzulänglich*) poor ‹substitute, performance, light›; feeble, poor ‹explanation›; lame, feeble ‹excuse›; scanty ‹knowledge, evidence, results›; sparse ‹growth of hair›; paltry, meagre ‹income›; Ⓒ (*kümmerlich, unansehnlich*) puny ‹tree, person›. ❷ *adv.* Ⓐ ‹live› poorly; scantily ‹dressed›; Ⓑ (*abwertend: unzulänglich*) skimpily, scantily ‹furnished›; poorly ‹attended›; ‹report, formulate› sketchily; thinly ‹concealed›

**Dürftigkeit** *die;* **~** ⇒ **dürftig**: Ⓐ (*Ärmlichkeit*) poorness; scantiness; meagreness; Ⓑ (*abwertend: Unzulänglichkeit*) poorness; feebleness; lameness; scantiness; sparseness; paltriness; meagreness

**dürr** /dʏr/ *Adj.* Ⓐ withered ‹branch›; dry, dried up, withered ‹grass, leaves›; arid, barren ‹ground, earth›; Ⓑ (*mager*) skinny, scraggy, scrawny ‹legs, arms, body, person›; Ⓒ (*unergiebig*) lean ‹years›; bare ‹words, description›

**Dürre** *die;* **~, ~n** Ⓐ (*Trockenheit*) drought; Ⓑ (*Dürrheit*) aridity; barrenness; (*fig.: der Sprache*) dryness

**Dürre-:** **~jahr** *das* year of drought; **~katastrophe** *die* catastrophic drought; **~periode** *die* period of drought

**Durst** /dʊrst/ *der;* ~**[e]s** thirst; ~ **haben** be thirsty; ~ **bekommen** get *or* become thirsty; **seinen** ~ **löschen** *od.* **stillen** quench *or* slake one's thirst; **ich habe** ~ **auf ein Bier** *od.* **nach einem Bier** I could just drink a beer; ~ **nach Ruhm/Wissen** (*fig. geh.*) a thirst for fame/knowledge; **ein Glas** *od.* **einen/etliche über den** ~ **trinken** (*ugs. scherzh.*) have one/a few too many; **Fisch macht** ~: fish makes one thirsty

**dursten** *itr. V.* (*geh.*) **A** thirst; ~ **müssen** have to go thirsty; **B** ⇒ **dürsten**

d

**dürsten** /ˈdʏrstn̩/ (*dichter.*) **1** *tr. V.* (*unpers.*) **mich dürstet** *od.* **es dürstet mich** I am thirsty; **ihn dürstete nach Rache** (*fig.*) he thirsted *or* was thirsty for revenge. **2** *itr. V.* **nach Rache/Gerechtigkeit** *usw.* ~: thirst for revenge/justice *etc.*

**durstig** *Adj.* thirsty; **das macht** ~: it makes you thirsty; it gives you a thirst

**durst-, Durst-:** ~**löschend**, ~**stillend** *Adj.* thirst-quenching; ~**strecke** *die* lean period *or* time; ~**streik** *der* refusal of fluids (*as a means of protest*); **in einen** ~**streik treten** refuse fluids

**Dur-:** ~**ton·art** *die* (*Musik*) major key; ~**ton·leiter** *die* (*Musik*) major scale

**Dusch·bad** *das* shower [bath]

**Dusche** /ˈdʊʃə/ *die;* ~, ~**n** shower; **unter die** ~ **gehen** take *or* have a shower; **unter der** ~ **sein** be in the shower; **eine heiße/kalte** ~ **nehmen** take *or* have a hot/cold shower; **eine kalte** ~ **[für jmdn.] sein, wie eine kalte** ~ **[auf jmdn.] wirken** (*ugs.*) be like a cold douche *or* a douche of cold water [on sb.]

**duschen** **1** *itr., refl. V.* take *or* have a shower; **[sich] warm/kalt** ~: take *or* have a warm/cold shower. **2** *tr. V.* **jmdn.** ~: give sb. a shower

**Düse** /ˈdyːzə/ *die;* ~, ~**n** (*Technik*) nozzle; (*eines Vergasers*) jet

**Dusel** /ˈduːzl̩/ *der;* ~**s** **A** (*ugs.*) luck; ~ **haben** be jammy (*Brit. coll.*) *or* lucky; **sie hat [einen]** ~ **gehabt** her luck was in (*coll.*); she was jammy (*Brit. coll.*) *or* lucky; **so ein** ~: that was lucky; **B** (*nordd.: Schwindelgefühl*) daze; **einen** ~ **haben** feel dizzy; **C** (*nordd.: Rausch*) fuddle; **im** ~ **sein** be in a fuddle

**duselig** *Adj.* (*ugs.*) (*angetrunken*) fuddled; tipsy; muzzy; (*benommen*) muzzy; (*schlaftrunken*) drowsy

**duseln** *itr. V.* (*ugs.*) doze

**düsen** *itr. V.; mit sein* (*ugs.*) dash

**Düsen-:** ~**an·trieb** *der* jet propulsion; **mit** ~**antrieb** jet-propelled; ~**bomber** *der* jet bomber; ~**clipper** *der* jet airliner; ~**flug·zeug** *das* jet aeroplane *or* aircraft *or* plane; ~**jäger** *der* jet fighter; ~**maschine** *die* jet [aeroplane *or* aircraft *or* plane]; ~**motor** *der* jet engine; ~**trieb·werk** *das* jet power plant; jet engine

**Dussel** /ˈdʊsl̩/ *der;* ~**s**, ~ (*ugs.*) dope (*coll.*); idiot; clot (*Brit. coll.*)

**Dusselei** *die;* ~ (*ugs.*) stupidity

**dusselig, dusslig, *dußlig** (*ugs.*) **1** *Adj.* **A** gormless (*Brit. coll.*); stupid; idiotic; **B** (*nordd.: benommen*) dopey (*coll.*); muzzy. **2** *adv.* gormlessly (*Brit. coll.*); stupidly

**duster** /ˈduːstɐ/ *Adj.* (*nordd.*) dark

**düster** /ˈdyːstɐ/ **1** *Adj.* **A** dark; gloomy; dim ‹light›; dark ‹background›; **B** (*bedrückend*) gloomy, dismal ‹day, weather, surroundings›; sombre ‹colour, music›; gloomy, sombre ‹atmosphere, picture›; **C** (*unheilvoll*) gloomy ‹forecast, conception, etc.›; dark ‹foreboding›; **D** (*schwermütig*) gloomy ‹expression, look, person›; gloomy, depressing ‹atmosphere›; gloomy, dark ‹thoughts›; **E** (*obskur*) shady ‹business, affair›; **F** (*unklar*) hazy ‹idea›; dim, hazy ‹conception›. **2** *adv.* (*schwermütig*) gloomily

**Düsterheit, Düsterkeit** *die;* ~, **Düsternis** *die;* ~ (*geh.*) **A** ⇒ **düster** A: darkness; gloom; dimness; **B** ⇒ **düster** B: gloominess; dismalness; sombreness; **C** ⇒ **düster** D: gloominess; depressingness; darkness

**Dutt** /dʊt/ *der;* ~**[e]s**, ~**e** *od.* ~**s** bun

**Dutte** *die;* ~, ~**n** (*österr. ugs.*) teat

**Dutyfree·shop, Duty-free-Shop** /ˈdjuːtɪˈfriːʃɔp/ *der* duty-free shop

**Dutzend** /ˈdʊtsn̩t/ *das;* ~**s**, ~**e** **A** *Pl.* ~: dozen; **ein [ganzes]/halbes** ~: a dozen/half a dozen; **zwei** ~: two dozen; **ein** ~ **Eier** a dozen eggs; **das** ~ **Schnecken kostet** *od.* **kosten 16 Mark** snails cost 16 marks a dozen; **davon gehen 12 auf ein** ~ (*ugs.*) there is nothing special about it; **B** ~**e** (*eine Menge*) dozens; **sie kamen in** *od.* **zu** ~**en** they came in [their] dozens (*coll.*)

**dutzend-, Dutzend-:** ~**fach** **1** *Adj.* dozens of *attrib.*; **2** *adv.* a dozen times; dozens of times; ~**gesicht** *das* (*abwertend*) nondescript face; *****~**mal** ⇒ **Mal**[1]; ~**mensch** *der* (*abwertend*) nondescript *or* run-of-the-mill person; ~**typ** *der* (*abwertend*) nondescript *or* run-of-the-mill type; ~**ware** *die* (*abwertend*) cheap mass-produced item; ~**ware sein** be a cheap mass-produced item; ~**weise** *Adv.* ‹arrive, leave› in [their] dozens (*coll.*); **Artikel** ~**weise kaufen/verkaufen** buy/sell articles by the dozen

**Duz·bruder** *der* (*veralt.*) ⇒ **Duzfreund**

**duzen** /ˈduːtsn̩/ *tr. V.* call 'du' (*the familiar form of address*); **sich** ~: call each other 'du'; **sich mit jmdm.** ~: call sb. 'du'

**Duz-:** ~**freund** *der,* ~**freundin** *die* good friend (*whom one addresses with 'du'*); ~**fuß** *der: in* **mit jmdm. auf [dem]** ~**fuß stehen** (*ugs. veralt.*) use [the familiar form] 'du' *or* the familiar form of address with sb.

**DVP** *Abk.* (*DDR*) **Deutsche Volkspolizei**

**dwars** /dvars/ *Adv.* (*Seemannsspr.*) abeam

**Dynamik** /dyˈnaːmɪk/ *die;* ~ **A** (*Physik*) dynamics *sing., no art.*; **B** (*Triebkraft*) dynamism; **C** (*Musik*) dynamics; **D** (*Versicherungsw.*) **eine Lebensversicherung mit** ~: ≈ index-linked life insurance (*linked to changes in the national product*)

**dynamisch** /dyˈnaːmɪʃ/ **1** *Adj.* **A** (*auch fig.*) dynamic; ~**e Renten** ≈ index-linked pensions (*linked to changes in the national product*); **eine** ~**e Lebensversicherung** ≈ index-linked life insurance (*linked to changes in the national product*); **B** (*Physik*) dynamic; ~**e Gesetze** laws of dynamics; **C** (*Musik*) dynamic. **2** *adv.* dynamically

**dynamisieren** *tr. V.* **A** **etw.** ~: make sth. dynamic; give sth. dynamism; **B** (*anpassen*) adjust ‹pension›

**Dynamisierung** *die;* ~, ~**en** **A** **eine** ~ **der Agrarpolitik** making the agricultural policy more dynamic; **die** ~ **einer Bewegung auslösen** give a movement dynamism; **B** (*Anpassung*) adjustment (*of pension*)

**Dynamismus** *der;* ~: dynamism

**Dynamit** /dynaˈmiːt/ *das;* ~**s** dynamite; ~ **in den Fäusten/Beinen haben** (*fig.*) pack a powerful punch/have a powerful shot

**Dynamo** /dyˈnaːmo/ *der;* ~**s**, ~**s** dynamo

**Dynast** /dyˈnast/ *der;* ~**en**, ~**en** (*hist.*) dynast

**Dynastie** *die;* ~, ~**n** dynasty

**dynastisch** *Adj.* dynastic

**Dys·funktion** /dʏs-/ *die* ▶ **474** (*Med., Psych., Soziol.*) dysfunction

**Dystonie** /dʏstoˈniː/ *die;* ~, ~**n** ▶ **474** (*Med.*) dystonia; **vegetative** ~: neurodystonia

**D-Zug** /ˈdeː-/ *der* fast *or* express train; **ein alter Mann/eine alte Frau ist doch kein** ~**!** (*salopp*) I'm too old to hurry

**D-Zug-:** ~**-Tempo** *das* (*ugs.*) **im** ~**-Tempo** in double-quick time; ~**-Zuschlag** *der* fast train supplement

# E e



**e, E** /e:/ *das;* ~, ~ **A** (*Buchstabe*) e/E; **B** (*Musik*) [key of] E; ⇒ *auch* **a,** A

**E** *Abk.* **Europastraße**

**Eau de Cologne** /'o: də ko'lɔnjə/ *das od. die;* ~, **Eaux de Cologne** /'o:-/ eau de Cologne

**Ebbe** /'ɛbə/ *die;* ~, ~**n** **A** (*Bewegung*) ebb tide; **nach Eintritt der ~:** once the tide starts/had started to go out; **~ und Flut** ebb and flow; **B** (*Zustand*) low tide; **es ist ~:** the tide is out; **bei ~:** at low tide; when the tide is/was out; **es herrschte ~ in seinem Geldbeutel** *od.* **in seiner Kasse** (*fig. ugs.*) he was short of cash (*coll.*)

**Ebbe-und-Flut-Kraftwerk** *das* tidal power station

**ebd.** *Abk.* **ebenda, ebendort** ibid.

**eben** /'e:bn̩/ ❶ *Adj.* **A** (*flach*) flat; **B** (*glatt*) level ‹ground, path, stretch›; **C** (*veralt.: gleichmäßig*) even, smooth ‹gait›.
❷ *adv.* **A** (*gerade jetzt*) just; **hast du ~ etwas gesagt?** did you just say something?; **B** (*kurz*) [for] a moment; **kann ich Sie ~ sprechen?** can I speak to you [for] a moment *or* minute?; **C** (*gerade noch*) just [about]; **etw. ~ noch schaffen** only just manage sth.; **D** (*genau*) precisely; **aus ~ diesem Grunde** for this very reason; for precisely this reason; **aus ~ diesem Grunde brauchen wir das Geld** that is exactly *or* precisely why we need the money; **ja, ~:** yes, exactly *or* precisely; **ja, ~ das meine ich auch** yes, that's just *or* exactly what I think.
❸ *Partikel* **A** **nicht ~:** not exactly; **B** (*nun einmal*) simply; **das ist ~ so** that's just the way it is; **so gut ich ~ kann** as well as I can in the circumstances

**eben-, Eben-:** **~bild** *das* image; **ganz jmds. ~bild sein** be the spitting image of sb.; **~bürtig** /-bʏrtɪç/ *Adj.* equal; **jmdm. ein ~bürtiger Gegner sein** be sb.'s equal; be a match for sb.; **jmdm. ~bürtig sein** be equal to sb.; be sb.'s equal; **die beiden waren sich ~bürtig** they were [both] equal; **~da** *Adv.* ibid. *abbr.*; ibidem; **~der, ~die, ~das** *Demonstrativpron.* **~das meine ich** that's exactly what I mean; **~die, von der wir sprachen** the very one we were talking about; **~der war krank** he was the very one who was ill; **~derselbe, ~dieselbe, ~dasselbe** *Demonstrativpron.* the very same ‹person, thing›; **~dieselbe meine ich** she's just the one I mean; **~dasselbe wollte ich auch kaufen** I wanted to buy the very same thing; **~deshalb, ~deswegen** *Adv.* that is/was precisely [the reason] why; **~dieser, ~diese, ~dieses** *Demonstrativpron.* **~dieses Thema wurde behandelt** this very topic was discussed; **~diese Regeln gelten in allen Abteilungen** these same rules apply in all departments; **~dieser wurde genannt** he was the very one who was mentioned

**Ebene** *die;* ~, ~**n** **A** (*flaches Land*) plain; **in der ~:** on the plain; **B** (*Geom., Physik*) plane; **zwei sich schneidende ~n** two intersecting planes; **C** (*Stufe*) level; **auf einer rein wissenschaftlichen ~:** on a purely scientific plane *or* level; **auf höchster ~:** at the highest level; ⇒ *auch* **schief**

**eben-:** **~erdig** ❶ *Adj.* ground level; (*in Gebäuden*) ground-floor; one-storey ‹house›; **~erdig sein** be on ground level/on the ground floor *or* (*Amer.*) first floor; ❷ *adv.* at ground level; (*in Gebäuden*) on the ground floor *or* (*Amer.*) first floor; **~falls** *Adv.* likewise; as well; **der Botschafter war ~falls eingeladen** the ambassador was likewise invited; the ambassador was invited as well; **danke, ~falls** thank you, [and] [the] same to you

**Eben·holz** *das* ebony

**ebenholz·farben** *Adj.* ebony

**eben-, Eben-:** **~maß,** *das* (*der Gesichtszüge*) regularity; (*des Körperbaus*) symmetry; even proportions *pl.*; (*von Versen*) regularity; harmony; **~mäßig** ❶ *Adj.* regular ‹features›; well-proportioned ‹figure›; regular, harmonious ‹verse›; **von ~mäßigem Wuchs** of even proportions; ❷ *adv.* **~mäßig geformt** *od.* **gestaltet** regularly shaped; **~mäßigkeit** *die;* ~ ⇒ **Ebenmaß**

**eben·so** *Adv.* **A** *mit Adjektiven, Adverbien, Indefinitpronomina* just as; **~ groß/schön/gut wie ... sein** be just as big/beautiful/good as ...; **ein ~ frecher wie dummer Kerl** a fellow who is/was as impudent as he is/was stupid; **er ist/arbeitet ~ fleißig wie geschickt** he is as diligent as he is skilful/works as diligently as he does skilfully; **~ gern mag ich Erdbeeren [wie ...]** I like strawberries just as much [as ...]; **~ gern würde ich an den Strand gehen** I would just as soon go to the beach; **~ gut hätte er zu Hause bleiben können** he might just as well have stayed at home; **ich kann ~ gut ein Taxi nehmen** I can just as easily take a taxi; **~ lange** for the same length of time; **~ sehr/viel** just as much; **~ wenig** just as little; **man kann dieses ~ wenig wie jenes tun** one cannot do this, any more than that; **er aß kein Gemüse, ~ wenig mochte er Obst** he didn't eat vegetables and he didn't like fruit either; he didn't eat vegetables, nor did he like fruit; **B** *mit Verben* in exactly the same way; (*in demselben Maße*) just as much; **ich glaube, er wird es ~ machen wie wir** I think he'll do exactly the same as we [do]; **bei Tag ~ wie bei Nacht** in the daytime as well as by night; **er ist dagegen, und ich denke ~:** he's against it, and so am I; **mir geht es ~:** it's just the same for me

***ebenso·gern** *usw.* ⇒ **ebenso** A

**eben·solch...** *Demonstrativpron.* the same; **ich habe ebensolche Angst/Kopfschmerzen wie du** I am just as afraid as you are/I have a headache too

***ebenso·sehr** *usw.* ⇒ **ebenso** A

**Eber** /'e:bɐ/ *der;* ~**s**, ~**:** boar; **wie ein angestochener ~** (*salopp*) like a [raving] maniac

**Eber·esche** *die* rowan; mountain ash

**ebnen** *tr. V.* level ‹ground›; **jmdm. den Weg** *od.* **die Bahn ~** (*fig.*) smooth the way for sb.; **das Geld seines Vaters ebnete ihm alle Wege** (*fig.*) his father's money opened [up] all doors for him

**echauffieren** /eʃɔ'fi:rən/ *tr. V.* (*geh.*) **A** make hot; **sich ~:** get hot; **B** (*aufregen*) excite; **sich ~:** get excited

**echauffiert** *Adj.* (*geh.*) **A** hot; **B** (*aufgeregt*) excited

**Echo** /'ɛço/ *das;* ~**s**, ~**s** echo; **das ~ auf die Ankündigung/den Vorschlag** (*fig.*) the response to the announcement/the suggestion; **das ~ in der Presse** (*fig.*) the press reaction; the reaction in the press; **ein breites ~ finden** meet with a wide response

**Echo·effekt** *der* echo effect

**echoen** /'ɛçoən/ ❶ *itr. V.* (*unpers.*) **es echot** there is an echo. ❷ *tr. V.* (*gedankenlos wiederholen*) echo

**Echo-:** **~lot** *das* **A** (*Seew.*) echo sounder; sonic depth finder; **B** (*Flugw.*) sonic altimeter; **~lotung** *die* (*Seew.*) echo-sounding

**Echse** /'ɛksə/ *die;* ~, ~**n** (*Zool.*) **A** saurian; **B** (*Eidechse*) lizard

**echt** /ɛçt/ ❶ *Adj.* **A** (*nicht nachgemacht*) genuine ‹gold, fur, coin, Scotch whisky, Persian carpet›; authentic, genuine ‹signature, document›; **ist das ~?** is that real gold/fur *etc.?*; **ein ~er Picasso** a genuine Picasso; **B** (*wahr*) true, real ‹love, friendship›; real, genuine ‹concern, sorrow, emergency, need›; **sind seine Gefühle ~?** is he sincere?; **sie hat noch ~e Gefühle** her emotions are still natural ones; **C** (*typisch*) real, typical ‹Bavarian, American, etc.›; **D** (*Math.*) proper ‹fraction›; **E** (*Textilw., Chemie*) fast ‹dye›; **F** (*reinrassig*) thoroughbred ‹horse›; pedigree ‹dog, cattle›.
❷ *adv.* **A** (*ugs. verstärkend*) really; **ich habe mich ~ gefreut** I was really pleased; **das ist ~ wahr/blöd** that's absolutely true/stupid; **das war eine Frechheit, aber ~:** it was a piece of downright cheek; **B** (*typisch*) typically; **das ist ~ amerikanisch/Frau/Klaus** that's typically American/just like a woman/Klaus all over; **C** (*unverfälscht*) **das Armband ist ~ golden** the bracelet is real gold

**echt-, Echt-:** **~gold** *das* real *or* genuine gold; **~golden** *Adj.* real *or* genuine gold; **~haar·perücke** *die* [real] hair wig

**Echtheit** *die;* ~ **A** genuineness; (*einer Unterschrift, eines Dokuments*) authenticity; genuineness; **B** (*Textilw., Chemie*) fastness

**echt-, Echt-:** **~silber** *das* real silver; genuine silver; **~silbern** *Adj.* real silver; genuine silver; **~zeit** *die* (*DV*) real time

**Eck** /ɛk/ *das;* ~**s**, ~**e** **A** (*südd., österr.:* ~*e*) corner; **über(s) ~:** diagonally; **B** (*Sport: Torecke*) **das lange/kurze ~:** the far/near corner [of the goal]

**Eckart** /'ɛkart/ *der: in* **der getreue ~** (*fig.*) a faithful supporter

**Eck-:** **~ball** *der* (*Sport*) corner [kick/hit/throw]; **einen ~ball treten** take a corner; **einen ~ball verwandeln** score from a corner; **~bank** *die; Pl.* **~bänke** corner seat; **~daten** *Pl.* basic information *sing.*

**Ecke** /'ɛkə/ *die;* ~, ~**n** **A** corner; **am liebsten hätte ich mich in eine ~ verkrochen** I felt like creeping off into a corner; **an der ~:** on *or* at the corner; **Nietzschestr., ~ Goethestr.** on the corner of Nietzschestrasse and Goethestrasse; Nietzschestrasse at Goethestrasse (*Amer.*); **um die ~:** round the corner; **um die ~ biegen** turn the corner; go/come round the corner; **jmdn. in die ~ drängen** (*fig.*) get sb. in a corner (*fig.*); **es brennt an allen ~n [und Enden** *od.* **Kanten]** (*fig.*) there's a terrible commotion everywhere (*coll.*); **das Auto klapperte an allen ~n [und Enden** *od.* **Kanten]** every nut and bolt in the car rattled; **jmdn. um die ~ bringen** (*salopp*) bump sb. off (*coll.*); **mit jmdm. um** *od.* **über sieben ~n verwandt sein** (*ugs.*) be distantly related to sb.; ⇒ *auch* **fehlen** F; **B** (*Ballspiele*) corner; **eine ~ treten** take a corner; **den Ball zur ~ schlagen** put the ball over for a corner; **in die lange/kurze ~:** in[to] the far/near corner; **eine lange/kurze ~ treten** take a long/short corner; **C** (*Boxen*) corner; **D** (*ugs.: Gegend*) corner; **ihr wohnt in einer schönen ~:** you live in a lovely spot; **E** (*ugs., bes. nordd.: Strecke*) **ich komme noch eine ~ mit** I'll come a little way/a bit further with you; **bis dahin ist es noch eine ganze ~:** it's still quite some way there; **er ist eine ganze ~ besser als du** (*fig.*) he is a whole lot better than you are; **F** (*keilförmiges Stück*) wedge; **eine ~ Käse** a wedge of cheese

**Ecken·steher** *der (ugs.)* street loafer

**Ecker** /ˈɛkɐ/ *die;* ~, ~**n** [A] *(Buch~)* beech nut; [B] *(selten: Eichel)* acorn

**Eck-:** ~**fahne** *die (Sport)* corner flag; ~**fenster** *das* corner window; ~**grund·stück** *das* corner site; ~**haus** *das* corner house; house on the/a corner; *(einer Häuserreihe)* end house

**eckig** ❶ *Adj.* [A] square; angular ‹features›; [B] *(ruckartig)* jerky ‹movement, walk, gait›. ❷ *adv.* **sich ~ bewegen** move jerkily

**Eck-:** ~**kneipe** *die: small friendly pub on a street corner;* ~**laden** *der; Pl.* ~**läden** corner shop; ~**lohn** *der (Wirtsch.)* basic *or* minimum wage; ~**pfeiler** *der* corner pillar; *(fig.)* cornerstone; ~**platz** *der* end seat; ~**schrank** *der* corner cupboard; ~**sitz** *der* ⇨ ~**platz**; ~**sofa** *das* corner sofa; ~**stein** *der* [A] cornerstone; head stone; *(fig.)* cornerstone; [B] *(Kartenspiel)* ⇨ **Karo**; ~**stoß** *der (Fußball)* corner kick; ~**tisch** *der* corner table; ~**turm** *der* angle tower; ~**wert** *der (Wirtsch.)* standard [of value]; ~**zahn** *der* ▶**471** canine tooth; ~**zimmer** *das* corner room; ~**zins** *der; Pl.* ~~**en** *(Finanzw.) official minimum interest rate on savings*

**Eclair** /eˈklɛːɐ̯/ *das;* ~**s**, ~**s** éclair

**Economy·klasse** /ɪˈkɔnəmɪ-/ *die* economy class; tourist class; **in der ~ fliegen** fly economy [class]

**Ecstasy** /ˈɛkstəsi/ *das;* ~**s** Ecstasy

**Ecuador** /ekuaˈdoːɐ̯/ *(das);* ~**s** Ecuador

**Ecuadorianer** /ekuadoˈri̯aːnɐ/ *der;* ~**s**, ~, **Ecuadorianerin** *die;* ~, ~**nen** Ecuadorean

**Edamer Käse** /ˈeːdamɐ-/ *der* Edam cheese

**Edda** /ˈɛda/ *die;* ~**:** [Elder] Edda; **die jüngere ~:** the Younger Edda

**edel** /ˈeːdl̩/ ❶ *Adj.* [A] *(reinrassig)* thoroughbred ‹horse›; species ‹rose›; [B] *(großmütig)* noble[-minded], high-minded ‹person›; noble ‹thought, gesture, feelings, deed›; honourable ‹motive›; **seine edle Gesinnung** his nobility of mind *or* noble-mindedness; [C] *(geh.: wohlgeformt)* finely shaped; **von edlem Wuchs** of noble stature; [D] *(geh.: vortrefflich)* fine ‹wine›; high-grade ‹wood, timber›; **die edlen Teile** *(scherzh.)* the vital parts [of the body]; [E] *(veralt.: adlig)* noble; **aus edlem Geschlecht** of noble stock. ❷ *adv.* **~ handeln** act nobly; **~ geformt** finely fashioned

**Edel-:** ~**fäule** *die (Winzerspr.)* noble rot; ~**frau** *die (hist.)* noblewoman; ~**fräulein** *das (hist.)* [unmarried] noblewoman; ~**gas** *das (Chemie)* noble *or* inert *or* rare gas; ~**hirsch** *der* ⇨ **Rothirsch**; ~**holz** *das* high-grade wood; high-grade timber

**Edeling** /ˈeːdəlɪŋ/ *der;* ~**s**, ~**e** *(hist.)* ⇨ **Edelmann**

**edel-, Edel-:** ~**kastanie** *die* sweet chestnut; Spanish chestnut; ~**kitsch** *der* grandly pretentious kitsch; ~**mann** *der; Pl.* ~**leute** *od.* ~**männer** *(hist.)* nobleman; noble; ~**metall** *das* [A] precious metal; [B] *(Chem.)* noble metal; ~**mut** *der (geh.)* nobility of mind; noble-mindedness; magnanimity; ~**mütig** *Adj. (geh.)* noble-minded; magnanimous; ~**nutte** *die (salopp)* high-class tart *(sl.)*; ~**pilz·käse** *der* blue[-veined] cheese; ~**reis** *das* scion; ~**rost** *der* patina; ~**schnulze** *die (abwertend)* example of pretentious schmaltz; **der Film/Roman war eine ~schnulze** the film/novel was pretentious schmaltz; ~**stahl** *der (rostfreier Stahl)* stainless steel; *(Sonderstahl)* special steel

**Edel·stein** *der* precious stone; gem[stone]; **mit ~en besetzt** set with precious stones; **ein synthetischer ~:** a synthetic stone; an artificial stone

**Edelstein·schleifer** *der,* **Edelstein·schleiferin** *die* gem cutter

**Edel-:** ~**tanne** *die* silver fir; ~**weiß** *das;* ~~**[es]**, ~~**e** edelweiss; ~**wild** *das* ⇨ **Rotwild**; ~**zwicker** *der* Edelzwicker *(fine Alsatian wine)*

**Eden** /ˈeːdn̩/ [A] *in* **der Garten ~** *(bibl.)* the Garden of Eden; [B] *das;* ~**[s]** *(Paradies)* earthly paradise

*old spelling (see note on page 1707)

**edieren** /eˈdiːrən/ *tr. V.* edit

**Edikt** /eˈdɪkt/ *das;* ~**[e]s**, ~**e** *(hist.)* edict

**Edition** /ediˈtsi̯oːn/ *die;* ~, ~**en** *(das Herausgeben)* editing; *(Ausgabe)* edition

**E-Dur** *das (Musik)* E major; ⇨ *auch* **A-Dur**

**EDV** *Abk.* **elektronische Datenverarbeitung** EDP

**EEG** *Abk.* **Elektroenzephalogramm** EEG; **ein EEG machen lassen** have an EEG

**Efeu** /ˈeːfɔy̆/ *der;* ~**s** ivy

**efeu·bewachsen** *Adj.* ivy-covered; ivy-clad

**Efeu·ranke** *die* ivy twine; ivy bind

**Effeff** /ɛfˈ|ɛf/ *in* **etw. aus dem ~ beherrschen** *od.* **verstehen** know sth. inside out; **etw. aus dem ~ machen/können** do/be able to do sth. just like that *(coll.)*

**Effekt** /ɛˈfɛkt/ *der;* ~**[e]s**, ~**e** effect; **im ~:** in the end; **im ~ läuft beides auf das Gleiche hinaus** in effect the two *or* both come to the same thing

**Effekten** /ɛˈfɛktn̩/ *Pl. (Finanzw.)* securities

**Effekten-:** ~**bank** *die; Pl.* ~~**en** investment bank *(also acting as an issuing house)*; ~**börse** *die* stock exchange; ~**geschäft** *das* dealing in securities; ~**makler** *der,* ~**maklerin** *die* stockbroker

**Effekt·hascherei** /-haʃəˈrai̯/ *die;* ~, ~**en** *(abwertend)* straining for effect; showiness; **ohne jede ~:** without any showiness; **billige ~:** cheap straining for effect

**effektiv** /ɛfɛkˈtiːf/ ❶ *Adj.* [A] *(wirksam)* effective; **ein ~er Schutz** an effective form of protection; [B] *(tatsächlich)* effective ‹profit, price, benefit›. ❷ *adv.* [A] effectively; [B] *(ugs.: ganz bestimmt)* really; **ich weiß ~ nichts** I really haven't a clue *(coll.)*; **da ist ~ nichts zu machen** there's really nothing that can be done about it

**Effektivität** /ɛfɛktiviˈtɛːt/ *die;* ~**:** effectiveness

**Effektiv·lohn** *der* real wage[s]

**effekt·voll** ❶ *Adj.* effective ‹speech, poem, contrast, pattern›; dramatic ‹pause, gesture, entrance›. ❷ *adv.* effectively

**Effet** /ɛˈfeː/ *der;* ~**s**, ~**s** spin; *(Billard)* side; **den Ball mit ~ schlagen** put spin/side on the ball

**effizient** /ɛfiˈtsi̯ɛnt/ ❶ *Adj. (geh.)* efficient. ❷ *adv.* efficiently

**Effizienz** /ɛfiˈtsi̯ɛnts/ *die;* ~, ~**en** *(geh.)* efficiency; *(Wirksamkeit)* effectiveness

**EFTA** /ˈɛfta/ *die;* ~ *Abk.* **Europäische Freihandelsassoziation** EFTA; European Free Trade Association

**EG** *Abk.* [A] **Europäische Gemeinschaft[en]; die ~-Länder** the countries of the European Communities; [B] **Erdgeschoss**

**egal** /eˈgaːl/ ❶ *Adj.* [A] *(ugs.: einerlei)* **es ist jmdm. ~:** it makes no difference to sb.; it's all the same to sb.; *(es kümmert ihn nicht)* sb. couldn't care less; it's all the same to sb.; **das ist ~:** that doesn't make any difference; **das kann dir doch ~ sein** that's none of your business; that's no concern of yours; **[ganz] ~, wie/wer/warum/wo/ob ...** no matter how/who/why/where/whether ...; [B] *(ugs.: gleich[artig])* identical; **~ sein** be the same *or* identical; **sie hat nicht zwei ~e Stühle** *(ugs.)* she hasn't got two chairs the same. ❷ *adv.* [A] **Bretter ~ schneiden** cut planks to the same size; [B] *(bes. ostm.: fortwährend)* constantly

**egalisieren** *tr. V.* [A] *(Sport)* equal ‹record›; **den Vorsprung des Gegners ~:** wipe out the opponent's lead; **den Punktvorsprung ~:** level the scores; [B] *(Textilw.)* level ‹colour›; [C] *(Technik, Handw.)* smooth; dress ‹leather›

**egalitär** /egaliˈtɛːɐ̯/ ❶ *Adj.* egalitarian. ❷ *adv.* in an egalitarian way

**Egalität** *die;* ~**:** equality

**Egel** /ˈeːgl̩/ *der;* ~**s**, ~**:** leech

**Egge** /ˈɛgə/ *die;* ~, ~**n** *(Landw.)* harrow

**eggen** *tr. V. (Landw.)* harrow

**Ego** /ˈeːgo/ *das;* ~, ~**s** *(Psych.)* ego

**Egoismus** /egoˈɪsmʊs/ *der;* ~, **Egoismen** [A] *(Selbstsucht)* egoism; **gesunder ~:** healthy self-esteem; [B] *Pl. (egoistische Eigenschaften)* egoistic traits; **wo persönliche Egoismen aufeinander stoßen** where individual egos clash

**Egoist** /egoˈɪst/ *der;* ~**en**, ~**en**, **Egoistin** *die;* ~, ~**nen** egoist

**egoistisch** ❶ *Adj.* egoistic[al]. ❷ *adv.* egoistically

**Ego·trip** /ˈeːgo-/ *der (ugs.)* ego trip

**Egozentrik** /egoˈtsɛntrɪk/ *die;* ~**:** egocentric attitude

**Egozentriker** *der;* ~**s**, ~, **Egozentrikerin**, *die;* ~, ~**nen** egocentric

**egozentrisch** ❶ *Adj.* egocentric. ❷ *adv.* egocentrically; **~ denken** be egocentric in the way one thinks

**eh**[1] /eː/ *Interj. (ugs.)* [A] hey; [B] *(was?)* **das hast du nicht erwartet, ~?** you didn't expect that, did you [,eh]?

**eh**[2] *Adv.* [A] *(bes. südd., österr.: sowieso)* anyway; in any case; **es ist ~ alles zu spät** it's too late anyway *or* in any case; [B] **seit ~ und je** for as long as anyone can remember; for donkey's years *(coll.)*; **wie ~ und je** just as before; **es sieht aus wie ~ und je** it looks the same as ever *or* the same as it always 'has done

**ehe** /ˈeːə/ *Konj.* before; **~ ihr nicht still seid, kann ich euch das Märchen nicht vorlesen** I can't read you the fairy story until you're quiet; **~ ich das tue, gehe ich lieber ins Gefängnis** I would rather go to prison than do it

**Ehe** /ˈeːə/ *die;* ~, ~**n** marriage; **eine glückliche ~ führen** be happily married; lead a happy married life; **die ~ brechen** *(geh. veralt.)* commit adultery; **jmdm. die ~ versprechen** promise to marry sb.; **mit jmdm. eine ~ eingehen** marry sb.; **ihre ~ wurde vor dem Standesamt/in der Kirche geschlossen** they were married in a registry office/in church; **Geld/Kinder in die ~ mitbringen** bring money/children into the marriage; **in erster ~ war sie mit einem Arzt verheiratet** her first husband was a doctor; **aus erster ~:** from his/her first marriage; **in wilder ~ leben** *(veralt.)* live in sin *(dated)*; **eine ~ zur linken Hand** *(hist.)* a morganatic *or* left-handed marriage; ⇨ *auch* **Hafen**[1] F; **Stand**; **wild** 1 B

**ehe-, Ehe-:** ~**ähnlich** *Adj.* **ein ~ähnliches Verhältnis** a common law marriage; **in einem ~ähnlichen Verhältnis leben** live [together] as man and wife; cohabit; ~**anbahnung** *die* ⇨ ~**vermittlung**; ~**berater** *der,* ~**beraterin** *die* marriage guidance counsellor; ~**beratung** *die* [A] marriage guidance *(Brit.)*; marriage counselling; [B] ⇨ ~**beratungsstelle**; ~**beratungs·stelle** *die* marriage guidance centre *(Brit.)*; marriage counseling center *(Amer.)*; ~**bett** *das* marriage bed; *(Doppelbett)* double bed; ~**brechen** *unr. itr. V.; nur im Inf. u. 1. Part. gebr. (geh. veralt.)* commit adultery; **du sollst nicht ~brechen** *(bibl.)* thou shalt not commit adultery; ~**brecher** *der* adulterer; ~**brecherin** *die;* ~~, ~~**nen** adulteress; ~**brecherisch** *Adj.* adulterous; ~**bruch** *der* adultery

**ehe·dem** *Adv. (geh.)* formerly; in former times; **wie ~:** as in former times; **von ~:** of former times

**ehe-, Ehe-:** ~**feindlich** *Adj.* [A] *(der Ehe abgeneigt)* misogamic ‹attitude, tendencies›; [B] *(die Ehe erschwerend)* **ein ~feindlicher Beruf** an occupation which is difficult to combine with marriage; ~**frau** *die (im Verhältnis zum ~mann)* wife; *(im Verhältnis zu anderen)* married woman; ~**freuden** *Pl. (scherzh.)* joys of married life; ~**gatte** *der (geh.)* husband; spouse; **beide ~gatten** both husband and wife; ~**gattin** *die (geh.)* wife; spouse; ~**gelübde** *das (geh.)* marriage vows *pl.*; ~**gemeinschaft** *die* marriage partnership; ~**glück** *das* wedded *or* married bliss; ~**hälfte** *die (scherzh.)* better half *(joc.)*; ~**hindernis** *das (Rechtsw.)* impediment to marriage; ~**joch** *das (scherzh.)* yoke of marriage *or* matrimony; **sich ins ~joch begeben** get hitched *(coll.)*; ~**kandidat** *der,*

**~kandidatin** *die* (*scherzh.*) marriage candidate; **~krach** *der* (*ugs.*) row; quarrel; **er hat immer ~krach zu Hause** he is always having rows at home with his wife; **sie hatten ihren ersten ~krach** they had the first row of their married life; **~krise** *die* marital crisis; **~leben** *das* married life; **~leute** *Pl.* married couple *sing.*; **die beiden ~leute** the husband and wife

**ehelich** ❶ *Adj.* Ⓐ (*die Ehe betreffend*) marital; matrimonial; conjugal ‹rights, duties›; **~es Gemeinschaft** marriage partnership; **~es Zusammenleben** married life; Ⓑ (*aus einer Ehe stammend*) legitimate ‹child›; **ein Kind für ~ erklären** declare a child legitimate; legitimate a child. ❷ *adv.* **sich ~ verbinden** (*geh.*) enter into [holy] wedlock

**ehelichen** *tr. V.* (*veralt.*, *scherzh.*) wed

**ehe·los** *Adj.* celibate

**Ehelosigkeit** *die*; **~:** celibacy

**ehemalig** /ˈeːəmalɪç/ *Adj.* former; **ein ~er Offizier** a former *or* one-time officer; **meine ~e Wohnung** my old flat (*Brit.*) *or* (*Amer.*) apartment; **seine ~e Frau** his ex-wife; **seine Ehemalige/ihr Ehemaliger** (*ugs.*) his/her ex (*coll.*)

**ehemals** /ˈeːəmals/ *Adv.* (*geh.*, *veralt.*) formerly; in former times

**ehe-, Ehe-: ~mann** *der* husband; **als ~mann** as a married man; **~müde** *Adj.* tired of married life *postpos.*; **~mündig** *Adj.* (*Rechtsspr.*) of marriageable age *postpos.*; **~mündig sein** be of marriageable age *or* of an age to marry; **~mündigkeit** *die* (*Rechtsspr.*) being of marriageable age; **vor Eintritt der ~mündigkeit** before attaining marriageable age; **~paar** *das* married couple; **ein älteres ~paar** an elderly [married] couple; **~partner** *der*, **~partnerin** *die* marriage partner

**eher** /ˈeːɐ/ *Adv.* Ⓐ (*früher*) earlier; sooner; **ich war ~ da als er** I was there earlier *or* sooner than he was; **je ~, desto lieber** *od.* **besser** the sooner the better; Ⓑ (*lieber*) rather; sooner; **~ will ich sterben als mit ihr zusammenwohnen** I'd rather *or* sooner die than live with her; **alles ~ als das** anything but that; Ⓒ (*wahrscheinlicher*) more likely; (*leichter*) more easily; **das ist schon ~ möglich** that's more likely; **er ist schon ~ mein Typ** he's more my type; **umso ~, als ...** [all] the more so as *or* because ...; Ⓓ (*mehr*) **er ist ~ faul als dumm** he is lazy rather than stupid; he's more lazy than stupid (*coll.*); **~ wie ein Beamter als wie ein Künstler aussehen** look more like a civil servant than an artist; **seine Wohnung ist ~ klein** his flat (*Brit.*) *or* (*Amer.*) apartment is rather on the small side; **es geht ihm ~ besser** he's rather better; **alles ~ sein als ...** be anything but ...

**Ehe-: ~recht** *das* (*Rechtsw.*) marriage law; laws governing marriage; **~ring** *der* wedding ring

**ehern** /ˈeːɐn/ *Adj.* (*dichter.*) bronze; (*eisern*) iron; (*fig.*: *unbeugsam*) iron ‹will, law›; **mit ~er Stirn** brazenly

**Ehe-: ~sakrament** *das* (*kath. Rel.*) sacrament of marriage; **~scheidung** *die* divorce; **~schließung** *die* wedding *or* marriage ceremony; **standesamtliche ~schließung** registry office wedding

**ehest...** /ˈeːəst/ ❶ *Adj.* **zum ~en Termin** at the earliest possible date; **bei ~er Gelegenheit** at the earliest opportunity. ❷ *adv.* Ⓐ (*noch am liebsten*) best of all; **am ~en wäre er nach Peru gefahren** best of all he'd have liked to go to Peru; Ⓑ (*noch am wahrscheinlichsten*) most likely; **am ~en möglich sein** be most likely *or* the most likely possibility; **mit diesem Werkzeug wirst du es noch am ~en schaffen** you'll manage it easiest with this tool; **am ~en könnte man ihn/es mit ... vergleichen** he/it could be most nearly compared to ...

**Ehe·stand** *der* marriage *no art.*; matrimony *no art.*; **in den ~ treten** (*geh.*) enter into matrimony

**Ehestands·darlehen** *das*: *low-interest government-backed loan available to young married couples*

**ehestens** /ˈeːəstn̩s/ *Adv.* Ⓐ (*frühestens*) at the earliest; **~ [am] Dienstag** [on] Tuesday at the earliest; **~ in drei Wochen** in three weeks at the earliest; Ⓑ (*österr.*: *baldmöglichst*) as soon as possible

**ehe-, Ehe-: ~stifter** *der*, **~stifterin** *die* matchmaker; **~streit** *der* marital *or* matrimonial dispute; **~vermittlung** *die* Ⓐ arrangement of introductions between people wishing to marry; **~vermittlung durch Computer** matching prospective marriage partners by computer; Ⓑ (*Institut*) marriage bureau; **~vermittlungs·institut** *das* marriage bureau; **~versprechen** *das* promise of marriage; **~vertrag** *der* (*Rechtsw.*) marriage contract; **~weib** *das* (*veralt.*, *scherzh.*) spouse (*arch.*, *joc.*); **~widrig** (*Rechtsspr.*) ❶ *Adj.* extramarital ‹relations›; **~widriges Verhalten** behaviour constituting a matrimonial offence; ❷ *adv.* **sich ~widrig verhalten** commit a matrimonial offence; **~zwist** *der* ⇒ **~streit**

**Ehr-: ~ab·schneider** *der*, **~ab·schneiderin** *die* calumniator; vilifier; **~auf·fassung** *die* conception of honour

**ehrbar** ❶ *Adj.* (*geh.*) respectable, worthy ‹person, occupation›; honourable ‹intentions›; **~e Leute** respectable *or* worthy people. ❷ *adv.* respectably

**Ehrbarkeit** *die*; **~:** respectability; worthiness

**Ehr·begriff** *der* conception of honour

**Ehre** /ˈeːrə/ *die*; **~, ~n** Ⓐ (*Ansehen*) honour; **seine ~ verlieren/bewahren** lose/preserve one's self-respect; **jmdm./einer Sache [alle] ~ machen** do sb./sth. [great] credit; **in ~n alt werden** (*geh.*) grow old without dishonour; **jmds. Andenken** (*Akk.*) **in ~n halten** honour sb.'s memory; **etw. um der ~ willen tun** do sth. for the honour of it; **zu ihrer ~ sei gesagt, ...** in fairness to her *or* to do her justice it should be said ...; **[ich] hab** *od.* **habe die ~** (*österr.*, *südd.*) pleased to meet you; **auf ~ und Gewissen** in all truthfulness *or* honesty; **er fragte mich auf ~ und Gewissen, ob ich ...** he asked me whether in all truthfulness *or* honesty I ...; **auf ~!, bei meiner ~!** upon my [word of] honour!; **dein Eifer in [allen] ~n, aber ...** your enthusiasm is not in doubt *or* in question, but ...; **deine Meinung in [allen] ~n, aber ich halte das nicht für richtig** with [all] due respect to your opinion, I still think that it is wrong; **~ verloren, alles verloren** (*Spr.*) take away my good name and take away my life (*prov.*); Ⓑ (*Zeichen der Wertschätzung*) **jmdm./einer Sache ~ antun** pay tribute to sb./sth.; **jmdm./einer Sache zu viel ~ antun** overvalue sb./sth.; **die ~ haben, etw. zu tun** (*geh.*) have the honour of doing sth.; **wir geben uns die ~, die Vermählung unserer Tochter bekannt zu geben** (*geh.*) we have much pleasure in announcing *or* are very pleased to announce the marriage of our daughter; **wir geben uns die ~, Sie zu einem Gartenfest einzuladen** (*geh.*) we request the pleasure of your company at a garden party; we have the honour of inviting you to a garden party; **sich** (*Dat.*) **etw. zur ~ anrechnen** give oneself credit for sth.; regard sth. as being to one's credit; **jmdm. zur ~ gereichen** (*geh.*) bring honour to sb.; **etw. zur ~ Gottes tun** do sth. to the glory of God; **~, wem ~ gebührt** [give] credit where credit is due; **jmdm. die letzte ~ erweisen** pay one's last respects to sb.; **mit ihr kannst du ~/keine ~ einlegen** she's a/no credit to you; **damit kannst du [keine] ~ einlegen** that does you [no] credit; **mit diesen Manieren legst du keine ~ ein** you won't get very far with manners like that; **der Wahrheit** (*Dat.*) **die ~ geben** tell the truth; **um der Wahrheit die ~ zu geben** to tell the truth; to be [perfectly] honest; **mit ~n** with honour; **mit ~n überhäuft** loaded with honours; **er wurde in ~n entlassen** he went into an honourable retirement; **zu ~n des Staatsbesuchs/des Königs** in honour of the state visit/of the king; **wieder zu ~n kommen** come back into favour; Ⓒ (*Ehrgefühl*) sense of honour; (*Selbstachtung*) self-esteem; pride; **jmdm. gegen die ~ gehen** offend sb.'s sense of honour; **ein Mann von ~** (*geh.*) a man of honour; **er hat keine ~ im Leib[e]** he doesn't have an ounce of integrity in him; **jmdn. bei seiner ~ packen** *od.* **fassen** appeal to sb.'s sense of honour; Ⓓ (*veralt.*: *Jungfräulichkeit*) honour; Ⓔ (*Golf*) honour

**ehren** *tr. V.* Ⓐ (*Ehre erweisen*) honour; **ihre Einladung ehrt uns sehr** we are greatly honoured by her invitation; **für seine Verdienste wurde er mit einem Orden geehrt** he was awarded a medal in recognition of his services; **man ehrte den ausländischen Gast mit einem Empfang** a reception was held in honour of the foreign guest; **sehr geehrter Herr Müller!/sehr geehrte Frau Müller!** Dear Herr Müller/Dear Frau Müller; **hoch geehrt** highly honoured; Ⓑ (*Ehre machen*) **deine Hilfsbereitschaft ehrt dich** your willingness to help does you credit; **sein Vertrauen ehrt mich** I'm honoured by his confidence in me; Ⓒ (*veralt.*: *achten*) respect; **du sollst Vater und Mutter ~** (*bibl.*) honour thy father and thy mother

**ehren-, Ehren-: ~ab·zeichen** *das* medal; **~amt** *das* honorary position *or* post; **~amtlich** ❶ *Adj.* honorary ‹position, membership›; voluntary ‹help, worker›; ❷ *adv.* in an honorary capacity; (*freiwillig*) on a voluntary basis; **~bezeigung** *die* salute

**Ehren·bürger** *der*, **Ehren·bürgerin** *die* honorary citizen; **ein ~/eine ~in der Stadt** a freeman of the town/city; **jmdn. zum ~ der Stadt ernennen** give sb. the freedom of the town/city

**Ehren·bürger-: ~recht** *das*, **~würde** *die*: **jmdm. das ~recht** *od.* **die ~würde verleihen** admit sb. as a freeman

**Ehren-: ~dame** *die* lady-in-waiting; **~dienst** *der* (*geh.*) **seinen ~dienst leisten** have the privilege of serving; **~doktor** *der* Ⓐ honorary doctor; Ⓑ (*Titel*) honorary doctorate; **~doktor·würde** *die* honorary doctorate; **~erklärung** *die*: **eine ~erklärung [für jmdn.]** a statement that aspersions cast on sb. are without foundation; **~formation** *die* (*Milit.*) guard of honour; **~fried·hof** *der* war cemetery; **~garde** *die* guard of honour; **~gast** *der* guest of honour; **~geleit** *das* official escort; **~gericht** *das* disciplinary tribunal *or* court; (*Standesgericht*) professional tribunal

**ehrenhaft** ❶ *Adj.* honourable ‹intentions, person›; **ein ~er Mann** an honourable man; a man of honour. ❷ *adv.* ‹act› honourably

**Ehrenhaftigkeit** *die*; **~:** sense of honour; **die ~ seiner Absichten** the honourableness of his intentions

**ehren-, Ehren-: ~halber** *Adv.* **jmdm. den Doktortitel ~halber verleihen** confer an honorary doctorate on sb.; **Doktor ~halber** honorary doctor; **~handel** *der*; *Pl.* **~händel** (*veralt.*) affair of honour; **~karte** *die* complimentary ticket; **~kodex** *der* code of honour; **~kompanie** *die* guard of honour; **~kränkung** *die* (*Rechtsspr.*) affront; insult; **~legion** *die* Legion of Honour; **~loge** *die* VIP box; box reserved for VIPs; **~mal** *das*; *Pl.* **~~e** *od.* **~mäler** monument; **~mann** *der* man of honour; **~mit·glied** *das* honorary member; **~nadel** *die* badge of honour (*in the form of a lapel-pin*); **~name** *der*: **den ~namen ... erhalten/tragen** be honoured by being given/by bearing the name ...; **~pflicht** *die* bounden duty; **es ist meine ~pflicht, diese Aufgabe zu erfüllen** I'm honour bound to perform this task; **~platz** *der* place of honour; **die ~plätze** the seats of honour; **~präsident** *der*, **~präsidentin** *die* honorary president; **~preis** *der* special prize; special award; **~rechte** *Pl.* **die bürgerlichen ~rechte** civil rights *or* liberties; ⇒ *auch* **Aberkennung**; **~rettung** *die*: **zu jmds. ~rettung etw. sagen** say sth. to clear sb.'s name; **zu ihrer ~rettung muss ich sagen, dass ...** it must be said in her defence that ...; **~rührig** *Adj.* defamatory ‹allegations›; insulting ‹behaviour›; **etw. ist ~rührig** sth. is an insult to sb.'s honour; **~runde**

*die* lap of honour; **eine ~runde laufen/fahren** *usw.* do a lap of honour; **eine ~runde drehen** (*Schülerspr.*) repeat *or* (*Brit.*) stay down a year [at school]; **~sache** *die* **A** (*~pflicht*) **das ist ~sache** that is a point of honour; **Verschwiegenheit ist ~sache** I/we feel honour bound to stay silent; **~sache!** you can count on me!; **B** (*Angelegenheit der Ehre*) **es handelt sich um eine ~sache** my/our *etc.* reputation *or* good name is at stake; **~salut** *der* salute; **man begrüßte ihn mit einem ~salut** a salute was fired to welcome him; **~schuld** *die* debt of honour; **~senator** *der* honorary member of the/a university senate; **~spalier** *das* guard of honour; **~tag** *der* (*geh.*) special day; **~titel** *der* **A** (*für besondere Dienste*) [honorary] title; **B** (*~de Anrede, Bezeichnung*) title; **~tor** *das*, **~treffer** *der* (*Sport*) consolation goal; **~tribüne** *die* VIP stand; **~urkunde** *die* certificate; **~voll** **1** *Adj.* honourable ‹peace, death, compromise, occupation›; creditable, gallant ‹attempt, conduct›; **2** *adv.* ‹act› honourably; **~vorsitzende** *der/die* honorary chairman; **~wache** *die* **A** (*Wachtposten*) guard of honour; **B** (*Dienst*) **Soldaten zur ~wache abkommandieren** detail soldiers to form a guard of honour; **~wache halten** keep vigil; **~wert** *Adj.* (*geh.*) worthy, honourable ‹person, occupation›; **die ~werte Gesellschaft** the Mafia; **~wort** *das Pl.* **~~e:** **~wort[!/?]** word of honour[!/?]; **sein ~wort brechen** break one's word; **auf [mein] ~wort** [I] promise; **großes ~wort!** (*scherzh.*) scout's honour! (*joc.*); **Urlaub auf ~wort** (*Milit.*) parole; **~wörtlich** **1** *Adj.* solemn ‹agreement, promise›; ‹agreement, promise› on one's honour; **2** *adv.* **es war ~wörtlich ausgemacht, dass ...** he/they *etc.* had promised faithfully *or* made a solemn promise that ...; **~zeichen** *das* decoration

**ehrerbietig** /ˈeːɐ̯|ɛɐ̯biːtɪç/ **1** *Adj.* (*geh.*) respectful; **sein ~es Gehabe** his deferential manner. **2** *adv.* ‹greet› respectfully

**Ehrerbietung** *die;* ~ (*geh.*) respect

**Ehr·furcht** *die* reverence (**vor** + *Dat.* for); **[große] ~ vor jmdm./etw. haben** have [a great] respect for sb./sth.; **~ vor dem Leben** reverence for life; **jmdm. ~ einflößen** fill sb. with awe; **er hat vor nichts ~:** he has no respect for anything; nothing is sacred to him

**ehrfurchtgebietend** **1** *Adj.* awe-inspiring ‹personality, cathedral›; awesome ‹silence›; authoritative ‹voice›. **2** *adv.* **~ auftreten** have an imposing presence

**ehrfürchtig** **1** *Adj.* reverent. **2** *adv.* reverently

**ehrfurchts-: ~los** **1** *Adj.* irreverent; **2** *adv.* irreverently; **~voll** (*geh.*) **1** *Adj.* reverent; **mit ~voller Miene** with a reverential expression; **2** *adv.* reverently

**ehr-, Ehr-: ~gefühl** *das* sense of honour; (*Selbstachtung*) self-esteem; pride; **falsches ~gefühl** a misplaced sense of honour; **~geiz** *der* ambition; **sie hatte den ~geiz, Pilotin zu werden** her ambition was *or* it was her ambition to become a pilot; **seinen ~geiz dareinsetzen, etw. zu tun** make it one's ambition to do sth.; **~geizig** **1** *Adj.* ambitious; **wenig ~geizig sein** be lacking in ambition; **2** *adv.* ambitiously; **~geizling** /-gai̯tslɪŋ/ *der;* **~~s, ~~e** (*ugs. abwertend*) pushy individual (*coll.*); pusher

**ehrlich** **1** *Adj.* **A** honest ‹person, face, answer, deal›; genuine ‹concern, desire, admiration›; upright ‹character›; honourable ‹intentions›; (*wahrheitsgetreu*) truthful ‹answer, statement›; **wenn ich ~ bin** if you want my honest opinion; **der ~e Finder gab die Brieftasche beim Fundbüro ab** the person who found the wallet handed it in (*Brit.*) *or* (*Amer.*) turned it in at the lost-property office; **dem ~en Finder winkt eine Belohnung von 10% der Gesamtsumme** a reward of 10% is offered [for the return of the money]; **~ währt am längsten** (*Spr.*) honesty is the best policy (*prov.*); **B** (*veralt.: anständig*) **seinen Namen wieder ~ machen** restore one's good name; **ein ~es Handwerk** an honest trade. **2** *adv.* honestly; **etw. ~ teilen** share sth.; **~ spielen** play fairly; **es ~ mit jmdm. meinen** play straight with sb.; **~ gesagt** quite honestly; to be honest

**ehrlicherweise** *Adv.* **A** in all honesty; **etw. ~ zugeben** own up and admit sth.; **B** (*selten: ehrlich*) honestly

**Ehrlichkeit** *die;* ~ ⇒ **ehrlich** 1 A: honesty; genuineness; uprightness; honourableness; truthfulness

**ehr-, Ehr-: ~los** **1** *Adj.* dishonourable; **2** *adv.* dishonourably; **~los aus dem Leben scheiden** depart this life in dishonour; **~losigkeit** *die;* **~~:** dishonourableness; **~pusselig**, **~pusslig**, ***~pußlig** *Adj.* (*ugs.*) ‹person› who is pompously concerned about his/her reputation

**ehrsam** *Adj.* (*geh. veralt.*) respectable, worthy ‹people, occupation›

**Ehrsamkeit** *die;* **~:** respectability

**ehr-, Ehr-: ~sucht** *die* (*veralt.*) inordinate ambition; **~süchtig** *Adj.* (*veralt.*) inordinately ambitious; overambitious

**Ehrung** *die;* ~, **~en** **A** (*das Ehren*) **die ~ der Preisträger** the prize-giving (*Brit.*) *or* (*Amer.*) awards ceremony; **bei der ~ der Sieger** when the winners were awarded their medals/trophies; **für jmdn. die höchste ~ sein** be the supreme accolade for sb.; **B** (*Ehrenerweisung*) honour

**ehr-, Ehr-: ~verlust** *der* (*Rechtsw.*) loss of civil rights; (*hist.*) attainder; **~würden** (*der*); **~~s** (*kath. Kirche, veralt.*) **Euer ~würden** Reverend Father; **~würden Bruder Martin/Schwester Notburga** brother Martin/sister Notburga; **~würdig** *Adj.* **A** (*Ehrfurcht gebietend*) venerable ‹person›; **ein ~würdiges Alter haben** ‹person› have reached a grand old age; ‹building› be of great age; **B** (*kath. Kirche*) **~würdiger Vater/~würdige Mutter** Reverend Father/Mother

**ei** /ai̯/ *Interj.* **A** hey; (*abschätzig*) oho; ⇒ *auch* **Daus**; **B** (*Kinderspr.*) **ei [ei] machen** stroke sb. [affectionately]; **mach mal ei!** stroke me!

**Ei** /ai̯/ *das;* **~[e]s, ~er** **A** egg; (*Physiol., Zool.*) ovum; **aus dem ~ schlüpfen** hatch [out]; **verlorene** *od.* **pochierte ~er** poached eggs; **russische ~er** egg mayonnaise; Russian eggs; **sie geht wie auf [rohen] ~ern** (*fig.*) she is walking very carefully; **das ist ein [dickes] ~!** (*ugs.*) that's terrible; **ach, du dickes ~!** (*ugs.*) dash it! (*Brit. coll.*); darn it! (*Amer. coll.*); **das ~ des Kolumbus** (*fig.*) an inspired discovery; **wie aus dem ~ gepellt sein** (*fig.*) be dressed to the nines; **sich gleichen wie ein ~ dem anderen** be as like as two peas in a pod; **das ~ will klüger sein als die Henne** (*fig.*) stop trying to teach your grandmother to suck eggs; **ein ~ legen** lay an egg; (*ugs.: einen Plan ausbrüten*) hatch [out] a plan; (*derb: seine große Notdurft verrichten*) have (*Brit.*) *or* (*Amer.*) take a shit (*coarse*); ⇒ *auch* **Apfel**; **bewerfen**; **Pfanne**; **roh**; **ungelegt**; **B** **~er** (*derb: Hoden*) balls (*coarse*); nuts (*Amer. coarse*); **C** (*salopp*) **zwölf ~er** twelve marks; (*zwölf Pfund*) twelve quid (*coll.*); (*zwölf Dollar*) twelve bucks (*coll.*); **D** (*Sportjargon: Ball*) ball

**eia** /ˈai̯a/ ⇒ **ei** B

**eiapopeia** /ai̯apoˈpai̯a/ *Interj.* (*Kinderspr.*) hushaby[e]; **~ machen** lull the baby to sleep

**Eibe** /ˈai̯bə/ *die;* ~, **~n** yew [tree]

**Eibisch** /ˈai̯bɪʃ/ *der;* **~[e]s, ~e** (*Bot.*) marsh mallow

**Eich-: ~amt** *das* local weights and measures office (*Brit.*); local bureau of standards (*Amer.*); **~baum** *der* oak tree; **~behörde** *die* ≈ Weights and Measures Inspectorate (*Brit.*); ≈ National Bureau of Standards (*Amer.*)

**Eiche** /ˈai̯çə/ *die;* ~, **~n** oak [tree]; (*Holz*) oak [wood]

**Eichel** /ˈai̯çl̩/ *die;* ~, **~n** **A** (*Frucht*) acorn; **B** ▸ **471** (*Anat.*) glans; **C** *Pl.* (*Spielkartenfarbe*) acorns *pl.*; ⇒ *auch* **Pik**[2]

**Eichel·häher** *der* jay

**eichen**[1] *tr. V.* calibrate ‹measuring instrument, thermometer›; standardize ‹weights, measures, containers, products›; adjust ‹weighing scales›; **darauf bin ich geeicht** (*ugs.*) that's in my line (*coll.*)

**eichen**[2] *Adj.* oak[en] ‹furniture›

**Eichen-: ~baum** *der* oak tree; **~blatt** *das* oak leaf; **~holz** *das* oak [wood]; **ein Schreibtisch aus ~holz** an oak writing desk; **~laub** *das* **A** oak leaves *pl.*; **B** (*Auszeichnung*) garland of oak [leaves]; **~sarg** *der* oak[en] coffin *or* (*Amer.*) casket; **~wald** *der* oak wood; (*größer*) oak forest

**Eich·gewicht** *das* standard weight

**Eich·hörnchen** *das*, **Eich·kätzchen** *das* (*landsch.*), **Eich·katze** *die* (*landsch.*) squirrel

**Eich-: ~maß** *das* standard measure; **~stempel** *der* verification stamp; **~strich** *der* [engraved] line showing the correct measure; **ein Glas bis zum ~strich füllen** fill a glass up to the line

**Eid** /ai̯t/ *der;* **~[e]s, ~e** oath; **einen ~ leisten** *od.* **ablegen** swear *or* take an oath; **einen ~ auf die Bibel schwören** swear an oath on the [Holy] Bible; **einen ~ auf die Verfassung schwören** solemnly swear to preserve, protect, and defend the constitution; **unter ~ [stehen]** [be] under *or* on oath; **etw. auf seinen ~ nehmen** swear to sth.; **ich nehme es auf meinen ~, dass ...** I swear that ...; **der ~ des Hippokrates** the Hippocratic oath; **an ~es statt erklären, dass ...** (*Rechtsspr.*) attest in an statutory declaration that ...

**Eidam** /ˈai̯dam/ *der;* **~s, ~e** (*veralt.*) son-in-law

**Eid·bruch** *der* breach of one's oath; (*Rechtsw.*) perjury *no indef. art.;* **einen ~ begehen** break one's oath

**eid·brüchig** *Adj.* treacherous ‹allies›; **~ werden** break one's oath; (*Rechtsw.*) perjure oneself

**Eidechse** /ˈai̯dɛksə/ *die;* ~, **~n** lizard

**Eider-** /ˈai̯dɐ-/: **~daune** *die* eider down; **~ente** *die* eider [duck]

**eides-, Eides-: ~belehrung** *die* (*Rechtsw.*) *caution to those about to take the oath;* **~formel** *die* (*jur.*) wording of the oath; **die ~formel nachsprechen** repeat the [words of the] oath; **~stattlich** **1** *Adj.* (*Rechtsw.*) **eine ~stattliche Erklärung** a statutory declaration; **2** *adv.* **~stattlich erklären** *od.* **versichern, dass ...** attest in a statutory declaration that ...

**Eidetik** /ai̯ˈdeːtɪk/ *die;* ~ (*Psych.*) eidetic ability

**eidetisch** *Adj.* (*Psych.*) eidetic

**eid-, Eid-: ~genosse** *der* Swiss; (*Verbündeter*) confederate; **~genossenschaft** *die:* **die Schweizerische ~genossenschaft** the Swiss Confederation; **~genössisch** *Adj.* Swiss

**eidlich** **1** *Adj.* made under oath *postpos.* **2** *adv.* on oath

**Ei·dotter** *der od. das* egg yolk

**eier-, Eier-: ~becher** *der* eggcup; **~brikett** *das* ovoid; **~farbe** *die: paint for decorating eggs as Easter gifts;* **~frucht** *die* eggplant; aubergine; **~hand·granate** *die* Mills bomb *or* grenade; **~kohle** *die* eggcoal; **~kopf** *der* **A** (*salopp*) egg-shaped head; **B** (*ugs.: Intellektueller*) egghead (*coll.*); **~kuchen** *der* pancake; (*Omelett*) omelette; **~laufen** *das* egg-and-spoon race; **~legend** *Adj.* (*Biol.*) oviparous; egg-laying; **~likör** *der* egg flip; egg nog; **~löffel** *der* egg spoon

**eiern** *itr. V.* **A** (*ugs.: ungleichmäßig rotieren*) wobble; **B** *mit sein* (*salopp: sich wackelnd fortbewegen*) roll

**eier-, Eier-: ~nudel** *die* egg noodle; **~pfann·kuchen** *der* ⇒ **~kuchen**; **~pflaume** *die* egg-plum; **~punsch** *der* egg flip; egg nog; **~salat** *der* egg salad; **~schale** *die* eggshell; **er hat noch die ~schalen hinter den Ohren** (*fig.*) he's still wet behind the ears (*fig.*); **~schalen·farben** *Adj.* off-white; **~schwamm** *der*

*old spelling (see note on page 1707)

(*bes. österr.*) chanterelle; **~speise** *die* **A** egg dish; **B** (*österr.*) scrambled egg; **~stich** *der* (*Kochk.*) cooked-egg garnish; royale; **~stock** *der* ▶ 471 (*Physiol., Zool.*) ovary; **~stock·entzündung** *die* (*Med.*) ovaritis; **~tanz** *der* (*ugs.*) (*um eine heikle Angelegenheit*) intricate manœuvring *no indef. art.*; (*zwischen unangenehmen Alternativen*) treading carefully *no art.*; **einen [richtigen] ~tanz aufführen** *od.* **vollführen** engage in [really] intricate manœuvring/tread [very] carefully; **~uhr** *die* egg timer; **~wärmer** *der* egg cosy

**Eifer** /ˈai̯fɐ/ *der;* **~s** enthusiasm; (*Eifrigkeit*) eagerness; (*Emsigkeit*) zeal; **etw. voller ~ tun** do sth. with great enthusiasm; **in ~ geraten** become excited *or* heated; **etw. im ~ [des Gefechts] vergessen** forget sth. in the excitement; ⇒ *auch* **blind** 1 c

**Eiferer** *der;* **~s, ~, Eiferin** *die;* **~, ~nen** (*geh.*) zealot

**eifern** *itr. V.* **A** (*abwertend*) **für etw. ~:** agitate for sth.; **gegen etw. ~:** rail *or* agitate against sth.; **B** (*geh.: heftig streben*) strive; **nach Macht ~:** strive for power

**Eifer·sucht** *die* jealousy (**auf** + *Akk.* of); **etw. aus ~ tun** do sth. out of jealousy

**Eifersüchtelei** /-zʏçtəˈlai̯/ *die;* **~, ~en** petty jealousy

**eifer·süchtig** ❶ *Adj.* jealous (**auf** + *Akk.* of). ❷ *adv.* jealously

**Eifersuchts-: ~szene** *die* display of jealousy; **sie machte ihm eine ~szene** in a fit of jealousy she made a scene; **~tragödie** *die* tragedy due to jealousy; **es handelte sich um eine ~tragödie** the tragedy was the result of jealousy

**Eiffel·turm** /ˈai̯fl-/ *der* Eiffel Tower

**ei·förmig** *Adj.* egg-shaped

**eifrig** ❶ *Adj.* eager; constant ‹reader›; enthusiastic ‹supporter, collector›; (*fleißig*) assiduous; **die ganz Eifrigen** the really keen ones; **~ bei einer Sache sein** show keen interest in doing sth. ❷ *adv.* eagerly; **~ dabei sein, etw. zu tun** be busy doing sth.; **sich ~ um etw. bemühen** set about sth. eagerly; **sich ~ bemühen, etw. zu tun** set about doing sth. eagerly; **~ bemüht sein, etw. zu tun** be eager to do sth.

**Ei·gelb** *das;* **~[e]s, ~e** egg yolk; **drei ~:** the yolks of three eggs; three [egg] yolks

**eigen** /ˈai̯gn̩/ *Adj.* **A** (*jmdm. selbst gehörend*) own; (*selbstständig*) separate; **mein ~er Bruder** my own brother; **eine ~e Wohnung haben** have one's own flat (*Brit.*) *or* (*Amer.*) apartment; **ein Zimmer mit ~em Eingang** a room with a separate entrance; **etw. mit ~en Augen sehen** see sth. with one's [very] own eyes; **seine ~e Meinung** his own opinion; **auf ~en Füßen** *od.* **Beinen stehen** stand on one's own two feet; **sich** (*Dat.*) **etw. zu *~** *od.* **Eigen machen** adopt sth.; **etw. sein *~** *od.* **Eigen nennen** (*geh., iron.*) call sth. one's own; **meinem Lehrer zu *~** *od.* **Eigen** (*geh.*) [dedicated] to my teacher; **B** (*kennzeichnend*) characteristic; **mit einer ihr ~en Gebärde** with a gesture characteristic of her; with a characteristic gesture; **mit allem ihr ~en Charme** with all her characteristic charm; **C** (*landsch.: gewissenhaft*) particular; **mit etw. ~ sein** be particular about sth.; **D** (*veralt.: seltsam*) peculiar; strange; odd; **mir ist so ~ zumute** I feel so strange; I have the strangest feeling

**Eigen** ⇒ **eigen** A

**-eigen** *Adj.* **A** (*im Besitz von*) belonging to the ‹school, company, community›; **B** (*zugehörig*) intrinsic to the ‹body, language›; inherent in the ‹system, period›

**eigen-, Eigen-: ~art** *die* (*Wesensart*) particular nature; (*Zug*) peculiarity; **eine ~art dieser Stadt** one of the characteristic features of this city; **ihre merkwürdigen ~arten** her strange peculiarities; **~artig** *Adj.* peculiar; strange; odd; **~artigerweise** *Adv.* strangely [enough]; oddly [enough]; **~artigkeit** *die* **A** peculiarity; strangeness; oddness; **B** (*~artige Verhaltensweise*) peculiarity; eccentricity; oddity; **~bau** *der; Pl.* **~~ten** **A** (*das Selbstbauen*) **Möbel/ein Haus im ~bau herstellen** make one's own furniture/build one's own house; **eine Anleitung zum ~bau einer Solaranlage** instructions for building one's own solar array; **das Haus ist im ~bau entstanden** I built the house myself/he built the house himself *etc.*; **B** (*das Selbstanbauen*) **der ~bau ist ...:** growing your own is ...; **Gemüse/Tabak im ~bau produzieren** grow one's own vegetables/tobacco; **C** (*etw. Selbstgebautes*) **das Haus ist ein ~bau** *od.* **ist Marke ~bau** I built the house myself/he built the house himself *etc.*; **D** (*etw. Selbstangebautes*) **probier doch mal unseren ~bau** try one/some we grew ourselves; **Marke ~bau sein** be home-grown; **~bedarf** *der* own requirements *pl.*; (*eines Landes*) domestic requirements *pl.*; **~bericht** *der:* „**~bericht**" 'report from our own correspondent'; **nur die Lokalberichte sind ~berichte** only the local news reports are by staff reporters; **~besitz** *der* (*Rechtsspr.*) personal property; **~brötelei** /-brø:təˈlai̯/ *die;* **~~, ~~en** taking an [unduly] independent line; **~brötler** /-brø:tlɐ/ *der;* **~~s, ~~, ~brötlerin** *die;* **~~, ~~nen** loner; lone wolf; **~brötlerisch** ❶ *Adj.* solitary; ❷ *adv.* **sich ~brötlerisch verhalten** behave like a loner *or* a lone wolf; **~dynamik** *die* inherent dynamism; **eine ~dynamik entwickeln** develop a momentum of its own; **~finanzierung** *die* self-financing *no art.*; **etw. in ~finanzierung tun** finance sth. oneself; **~funktion** *die* (*Math., Phys.*) eigenfunction; **~gesetzlich** ❶ *Adj.* **die ~gesetzliche Entwicklung der Wirtschaft** the development of the economy according to its own laws; ❷ *adv.* according to its/their own laws; **~gesetzlichkeit** *die* inherent laws *pl.*; **~gewicht** *das* **A** own weight; **B** (*Wirtsch.: Nettogewicht*) net weight; **~goal** *das* (*österr.*) ⇒ **~tor**; **~händig** ❶ *Adj.* personal ‹signature›; personally inscribed ‹dedication›; holographic ‹will, document›; ❷ *adv.* **etw. ~händig unterschreiben/übergeben** sign/present sth. personally; „**~händig abzugeben**" 'to be delivered to the addressee in person'; **~heim** *das* house of one's own; **der Trend zum ~heim** the trend towards owning a house of one's own

**Eigenheit** *die;* **~, ~en** peculiarity

**eigen-, Eigen-: ~initiative** *die* initiative of one's own; **auf ~initiative** on one's own initiative; **~interesse** *das* personal interest; **~kapital** *das* (*Wirtsch.*) equity capital; **~leben** *das* life of one's own; **ein ~leben haben** *od.* **führen** live one's own life; **sein ~leben bewahren** continue to live a life of one's own; **~liebe** *die* amour propre; **~lob** *das* self-praise; **~lob stinkt!** (*ugs.*) self-praise is no recommendation; **~mächtig** ❶ *Adj.* unauthorized ‹decision›; (*selbstherrlich*) high-handed; ❷ *adv.* **~mächtig handeln** act on one's own authority; (*selbstherrlich*) act high-handedly; **er ist ~mächtig mit meinem Auto gefahren** he took my car without permission; **etw. ~mächtig tun** do sth. without asking; **~mächtiger·weise** *Adv.* ⇒ **~mächtig** 2; **~mächtigkeit** *die; Pl.* **~~en** **A** high-handedness; **B** (*~mächtige Handlung*) unauthorized action; **~mittel** *Pl.* own resources; **aus ~mitteln** out of *or* from one's own resources; **~name** *der* proper name; (*Ling.*) proper noun; **~nutz** *der;* **~~es** self-interest; **~nützig** /-nʏtsɪç/ ❶ *Adj.* self-interested, self-seeking ‹person›; selfish ‹motive›; ❷ *adv.* selfishly; **~produktion** *die:* **aus ~produktion** home-made; home-grown ‹fruit, vegetables, etc.›; **das ist eine ~produktion** I/they *etc.* made it myself/themselves *etc.*; **~regie** *die:* **etw. in ~regie tun** undertake sth. oneself

**eigens** *Adv.* specially; **~ für diesen Zweck** specifically for this purpose; **~ aus diesen Gründen** just *or* solely for these reasons

**Eigenschaft** *die;* **~, ~en** (*von Menschen, Tieren, Pflanzen*) quality; characteristic; (*von Sachen, Stoffen*) property; **in seiner ~ als Mann/Vorsitzender** as a man/in his capacity as chairman

**Eigenschafts·wort** *das; Pl.* **Eigenschaftswörter** adjective

**eigen-, Eigen-: ~sinn** *der* obstinacy; stubbornness; **~sinnig** ❶ *Adj.* obstinate; stubborn; ❷ *adv.* obstinately; stubbornly; **~sinnigkeit** *die;* **~~:** obstinacy; stubbornness; **~sinnigkeiten** obstinate *or* stubborn behaviour *sing.*; **~staatlich** *Adj.* **A** (*souverän*) sovereign; **B** (*den ~en Staat betreffend*) national; **~staatlichkeit** *die;* **~~:** sovereignty; (*von Bundesstaaten*) statehood; **~ständig** ❶ *Adj.* independent; ❷ *adv.* independently; **~ständigkeit** *die;* **~~:** independence; **~sucht** *die* selfishness; **~süchtig** ❶ *Adj.* selfish; ❷ *adv.* selfishly

**eigentlich** /ˈai̯gn̩tlɪç/ ❶ *Adj.* (*wirklich*) actual; real; (*wahr*) true; (*ursprünglich*) original; **die ~e Bedeutung eines Wortes** the original meaning of a word; **das Eigentliche** the essential thing. ❷ *Partikel* **A** (*tatsächlich, genau genommen*) actually; really; **~ nicht** not really; **B** (*Verstärkung*) **wann erscheint ~ der letzte Band?/warum kommst du ~ nicht mehr zu uns?** tell me, when will the last volume come out/why have you stopped coming to see us?; **~ müsste ich ja jetzt gehen, aber ...** really, I ought to go now, but ...; **es ist ~ schade, dass ...** actually, it's a pity that ...; **sind sie ~ verheiratet?** are they in fact married?; **wohnen Sie ~ in Köln oder in Bonn?** is it in Cologne or Bonn that you live?; **wussten Sie ~ schon, dass ...?** were you actually aware that ...?; **warst du ~ schon [ein]mal da?** have you in fact ever been there?; **ist daraus ~ was geworden?** (*ugs.*) did it ever come to anything?; **was soll das ~?** what's it all about?; **wer sind Sie ~?** who do you think you are?; **wissen Sie ~, wer ich bin?** do you know who 'I am?; **rauchen Sie ~ viel?** do you actually smoke a lot?; **was muss ~ noch alles passieren, bevor ...?** what else has got to happen before ...?; **was denkst du dir ~?** what do you think you're doing?; **was willst du ~?** what exactly do you want?

**Eigentlichkeit** *die;* **~** (*geh.*) authenticity

**Eigen·tor** *das* (*Ballspiele, fig.*) own goal; **ein ~ schießen** score an own goal; **zum ~ für jmdn. werden** (*fig.*) backfire on sb.

**Eigentum** *das;* **~s** **A** property; (*einschließlich Geld usw.*) assets *pl.*; **geistiges ~:** [one's own] intellectual creation; **sie haben sein geistiges ~ verwendet** they used his idea/ideas; **sich an fremdem ~ vergreifen** steal; **B** (*Recht des Eigentümers*) ownership (**an** + *Dat.* of); **C** (*veralt.: Grundbesitz*) property

**Eigentümer** /ˈai̯gn̩ty:mɐ/ *der;* **~s, ~:** owner; (*Hotel~, Geschäfts~*) proprietor; owner

**Eigentümerin** *die* owner; (*Hotel~, Geschäfts~*) proprietress; proprietor; owner

**eigentümlich** /ˈai̯gn̩ty:mlɪç/ ❶ *Adj.* **A** (*typisch*) peculiar; characteristic; **eine ihm ~e Geste** a gesture peculiar to him *or* characteristic of him; **B** (*eigenartig*) peculiar; strange; odd. ❷ *adv.* peculiarly; strangely; oddly

**eigentümlicherweise** *Adv.* strangely enough; oddly enough

**Eigentümlichkeit** *die;* **~, ~en** **A** (*Eigenartigkeit*) peculiarity; strangeness; **B** (*typischer Zug*) peculiarity

**Eigentums-: ~bildung** *die* the acquisition of assets; **~delikt** *das* offence against property; **~recht** *das* right of ownership; **~rechte geltend machen** claim one's proprietary rights; **~streuung** *die* distribution of assets; **~vorbehalt** *der* (*Rechtsw.*) reservation of proprietary rights; **~wohnung** *die* owner-occupied flat (*Brit.*); condominium *or* co-op apartment (*Amer.*); **eine ~wohnung kaufen** buy a flat (*Brit.*) *or* (*Amer.*) an apartment

**eigen-, Eigen-: ~verantwortlich** ❶ *Adj.* responsible; **eine ~verantwortliche Tätigkeit** a job with responsibility; a responsible job; ❷ *adv.* **~verantwortlich handeln** act on one's own authority; **etw. ~verantwortlich bestimmen/entscheiden** decide sth. on one's own responsibility; **~wärme** *die* (*Biol.*) body temperature;

e

**~wert** *der* intrinsic value; (*Math., Phys.*) eigenvalue; **~willig** *Adj.* [A] self-willed ‹person›; individual ‹style, idea›; [B] (*~sinnig*) obstinate; stubborn; **~willigkeit** *die; ~~, ~~en* [A] (*von Menschen*) individualism; independence of mind; (*einer Behauptung, eines Kunstwerks, eines Stils usw.*) originality; unconventionality; [B] (*Handlung*) display of self-will

**eigne, eigner** ⇒ eigen

**eignen** ❶ *refl. V.* be suitable; **sich als** *od.* **zum Lehrer ~:** be suitable as a teacher; **er würde sich gut als** *od.* **zum Handwerker ~:** he would make a good craftsman; **das Buch eignet sich gut als Geschenk** this book makes a good present; **für solche Arbeiten eignet er sich besonders** he is particularly well suited for that kind of work; ⇒ *auch* **geeignet**. ❷ *itr. V.* (*geh., veralt.: eigen sein*) **jmdm. eignet etw.** sb. possesses sth.

**Eigner** *der; ~s, ~,* **Eignerin** *die; ~, ~nen* owner

**Eignung** *die; ~:* suitability; aptitude; **seine ~ für diesen Beruf/als Lehrer** his suitability for this profession/as a teacher; **seine ~ zum Fliegen** his aptitude for flying

**Eignungs-: ~prüfung** *die,* **~test** *der* aptitude test

**Ei·klar,** *das; ~s, ~* (*österr.*) ⇒ **Eiweiß A**

**Eiland** /ˈailant/ *das; ~[e]s, ~e* (*veralt., dichter.*) isle (*poet.*)

**Eil-** /ail-/: **~bote** *der* special messenger; **etw. durch einen ~boten zustellen lassen** send sth. by special delivery *or* express; **„durch** *od.* **per ~boten“** (*veralt.*) ‘express’; **~brief** *der* express letter

**Eile** /ˈailə/ *die; ~:* hurry; **ich habe [große] ~:** I'm in a [great] hurry; **ich habe keine ~:** I'm not in a *or* any hurry; **die Sache hat ~:** it's urgent *or* a matter of urgency; **die Sache hat keine ~:** there's no hurry; it's not urgent; **[immer] in ~ sein** [always] be in a hurry; **in der ~:** in her/our *etc.* hurry; **in aller ~:** in great haste; **jmdn. zur ~ antreiben** hurry sb. up

**Ei·leiter** *der* ▶ 471 (*Anat.*) Fallopian tube

**Eileiter-: ~entzündung** *die* salpingitis; **~schwangerschaft** *die* tubal pregnancy

**eilen** ❶ *itr. V.* [A] *mit sein* hurry; hasten; (*besonders schnell*) rush; **nach Hause ~:** hurry/rush home; **jmdm. zu Hilfe ~:** rush to sb.'s aid; **eile mit Weile** (*Spr.*) more haste, less speed (*prov.*); [B] (*dringend sein*) ‹matter› be urgent; **„eilt!“** ‘urgent’; **„eilt sehr!“** ‘immediate’; **es eilt mir damit** it's urgent; I'm in a hurry; **es eilt ihm mit dem Umzug** he is in a hurry to move. ❷ *refl. V.* hurry; make haste

**eilends** *Adv.* (*unverzüglich*) immediately; without delay; (*geh.: geschwind*) hastily

**eil-, Eil-: ~fertig** (*geh.*) ❶ *Adj.* [A] (*vorschnell*) rash; [B] (*dienstbeflissen*) zealous; ❷ *adv.; s. Adj.* rashly; zealously; **~fertigkeit** *die* ⇒ **~fertig**: rashness; zeal; **~fracht** *die* express freight; express goods *pl.;* **etw. per** *od.* **als ~fracht senden** send sth. express freight; **~gut** *das* fast freight; express goods *pl.;* **etw. als ~gut schicken** send sth. by fast freight

**eilig** ❶ *Adj.* [A] (*schnell*) hurried; **mit ~en Schritten** hurriedly; **es ~ haben** be in a hurry; **es weniger ~ haben** be in less of a hurry; [B] (*dringend*) urgent ‹news›; **~ sein** be urgent; **es [sehr] ~ mit etw. haben** be in a [great] hurry about sth.; **etw. Eiliges** sth. urgent; an urgent matter; **nichts Eiligeres zu tun haben, als ...** (*iron*) have nothing better to do than...; **er hatte nichts Eiligeres zu tun, als allen davon zu erzählen** he couldn't wait to tell everybody about it. ❷ *adv.* hurriedly; **~ laufen** run hurriedly; hurry

**Eil-: ~marsch** *der* (*Milit.*) forced march; **~paket** *das* express parcel; **~schritt** *der:* **im ~schritt laufen** walk with short, quick steps; **~sendung** *die* express consignment; (*Brief*) express letter; (*Paket*) express parcel; **~tempo** *das* (*ugs.*) **im ~tempo** in a rush; **im ~tempo ging es zum Bahnhof** we/they *etc.* rushed to the station; **~verfahren** *das* (*jur.*) summary proceedings *pl.;* **etw. im ~verfahren erledigen** (*fig. ugs.*) do sth. in a rush; **~zug** *der* semi-fast train; stopping train (*Brit.*); **~zustellung** *die* (*Postw.*) express delivery

**Eimer** /ˈaimɐ/ *der; ~s, ~* [A] bucket; (*Milch~*) pail; (*Abfall~*) bin; **ein ~ [voll] Wasser** a bucket of water; **es gießt wie aus ~n** (*ugs.*) it's raining cats and dogs (*coll.*); it's coming down in buckets (*coll.*); **im ~ sein** (*salopp*) be up the spout (*coll.*); **mein Wagen ist im ~** (*salopp*) my car is a total wreck; **unsere Stimmung war im ~** (*salopp*) the atmosphere was totally ruined; **seine Gesundheit ist im ~** (*salopp*) he's a physical wreck; [B] (*ugs. abwertend: altes Schiff*) tub

**Eimer·bagger** *der* bucket dredger

**eimer·weise** *Adv.* by the bucketful; in bucketfuls

**ein**[1] /ain/ ▶ 841 ❶ *Kardinalz.* one; **~ Dollar/~e Mark/~ Jahr** one dollar/mark/year; **in ~em Tag** in one day; in a single day; **~ einziger Tag/Mensch** one single day/person; **ich will dir noch ~[e]s sagen** there's one more thing I'd like to tell you; **~[e]s gefällt mir daran/an ihr nicht** there's one thing I don't like about it/her; **das ~e Gute daran ist ...** the only good thing about it is ...; **das ~e, das ich brauche** the one thing I need; **~er von beiden** one of the two; one or the other; **~er für alle, alle für ~en** one for all and all for one; **~ für alle Mal, *~ für allemal** once and for all; **~ und derselbe** one and the same; **er war ihr Ein und Alles** he was everything to her; **das Buch bietet alles in ~em** the book has everything in one volume; **in ~em fort** (*geh.*) continuously; all the time.

❷ *unbest. Art.* a/an; **~ Kleid/Apfel/Mensch/Hotel** a dress/an apple/a human being/a[n] hotel; **~ Held/~ ehrlicher Mensch** a hero/an honest man/woman; **~ bisschen** *od.* **wenig** a little [bit]; **~ anderer** somebody else; **~ jeder** (*geh.*) each and every one; **~e Kälte ist das hier!** it's freezing here!; **~e Frechheit ist das!** what absolute cheek!; **was für ~ Wein!** what superb wine!; **was für ~e Unordnung!** what a mess!; **was für ~ Kleid hast du gekauft?** what sort of dress did you buy?; **das konnte nur ~ Beethoven schaffen** only a Beethoven could do that; **er besaß ~en Klee und ~en Picasso** he owned a Klee and a Picasso.

❸ *Indefinitpron.* [A] (*irgendeiner*) one; [B] (*man*) one; (*jemand*) someone; somebody; **wie soll das ~er wissen?** how is one supposed to know that?; **das mach mal ~em verständlich** try explaining that to anybody; **~e/~er/~[e]s der besten** one of the best [people/things]; **~s war offen und ~s zu** one was open and one shut; **kaum ~er** hardly anybody; **~er von uns/euch** one of us/you; **~er namens Mayer** (*meist abwertend*) a certain Mayer; **ist ~er bereit, mir zu helfen?** is anyone willing to help me?; **~er nach dem anderen** one after the other; one by one; **der ~e kommt, der andere geht** one comes, the other goes; **die ~en ..., die anderen ...** some ..., the others ...; **er trinkt ganz gerne ~en** (*ugs.*) he likes [to have] a drink; **sieh [mal] ~er an!** (*ugs.*) [now just] look at that!; **du bist [mir] ~e/~er!** (*iron.*) you are a [right] one (*coll.*); **das ist ~e/~er!** (*ugs.*) she's/he's quite a one (*coll.*); **er ist belesen wie selten ~er** he's uncommonly well read; [C] (*der-/die-/dasselbe*) **~er Meinung sein** be of the same opinion; **es kommt alles auf ~[e]s heraus** it all comes to the same thing [in the end]

**ein**[2] (*elliptisch*) **~ — aus** (*an Schaltern*) on — off; **~ und aus gehen** go in and out; **bei jmdm. ~ und aus gehen** be a regular visitor at sb.'s house; **ich wusste nicht ~ noch aus** I didn't know where to turn *or* what to do

**ein·achsig** *Adj.* single-axle

**ein·adrig** *Adj.* (*Elektrot.*) single-core

**Einakter** /ˈain|aktɐ/ *der; ~s, ~:* one-act play

**einander** /aiˈnandɐ/ *reziprokes Pron.* (*geh.*) each other; one another; **sie grüßten ~:** they greeted each other *or* one another; **liebet ~** (*bes. bibl.*) love one another; **~ widersprechende Behauptungen** mutually contradictory statements

**ein|arbeiten** *tr. V.* [A] (*ausbilden*) train ‹employee›; **er arbeitet sich gerade ein** he is training at present; **sich in etw.** (*Akk.*) **~:** become familiar *or* familiarize oneself with sth.; [B] (*einfügen*) incorporate ‹quotation etc.› (**in** + *Akk.* into); **sie arbeitete einige Verzierungen in die Decke ein** she worked some patterns into the cover

**Einarbeitung** *die; ~, ~en* training; **die ~ in das neue Sachgebiet fiel ihm schwer** he found it difficult to familiarize himself with the new subject

**Einarbeitungs·zeit** *die* training period

**ein·armig** ❶ *Adj.* one-armed; **ein Einarmiger** a one-armed man. ❷ *adv.* **~ Gewichte stemmen** lift weights with one hand

**ein|äschern** /ˈain|ɛʃɐn/ *tr. V.* [A] (*niederbrennen*) **ein Gebäude ~:** burn a building to the ground *or* down; reduce a building to ashes; **eine Stadt ~:** reduce a town to ashes; [B] cremate ‹corpse›; **ich werde mich ~ lassen** I am going to be cremated

**Einäscherung** *die; ~, ~en* [A] (*das Niederbrennen*) **die ~ des Gebäudes** the burning down of the building; **die ~ der Stadt** the destruction of the town by fire; [B] (*Leichenverbrennung*) cremation

**Einäscherungs·halle** *die* crematorium

**ein|atmen** *tr., itr. V.* breathe in

**einatomig** /ˈain|ato:mɪç/ *Adj.* (*Chemie, Physik*) monatomic

**ein·äugig** *Adj.* one-eyed; single-lens ‹camera›; **unter Blinden ist der Einäugige König** (*Spr.*) in the kingdom of the blind the one-eyed man is king (*prov.*)

**Ein·bahn·straße** *die* one-way street; **eine ~, aus der es kein Zurück mehr gab** (*fig.*) a path from which there could be no turning back (*fig.*); **das Verhältnis darf keine ~ sein** there must be give and take on both sides

**ein|balsamieren** *tr. V.* embalm ‹corpse›; **du kannst dich ~ lassen** (*fig. ugs.*) you might as well give up

**Ein·band** *der* binding; [book] cover

**Einband-: ~deckel** *der* (*Buchw.*) board; **~entwurf** *der* cover design

**ein·bändig** *Adj.* one-volume

**ein·basisch** *Adj.* (*Chemie*) monobasic

**Ein·bau** *der; Pl.* **~ten** [A] (*das Einbauen*) fitting; (*eines Motors*) installation; [B] (*Einfügung*) incorporation; insertion; [C] *Pl.* (*Eingebautes*) fitted shelves/cupboards

**ein|bauen** *tr. V.* [A] build in, fit ‹cupboard, kitchen›; [B] (*Technik*) install ‹engine, motor›; [C] (*einfügen*) insert, incorporate ‹chapter›

**Einbau·küche** *die* fitted kitchen

**Ein·baum** *der* dugout [canoe]

**Einbau-: ~möbel** *das* piece of built-in furniture; (*Schrank*) built-in cupboard; (*Regal*) fitted shelves *pl.;* **teure ~möbel** expensive built-in furniture *sing.;* (*Schränke*) expensive built-in cupboards; (*Regale*) expensive fitted shelves **~schrank** *der* built-in cupboard; (*für Kleidung*) built-in wardrobe

**ein|begreifen** *unr. tr. V.* (*geh.*) include; **MWSt einbegriffen** including VAT

**ein|behalten** *unr. tr. V.* [A] (*zurückbehalten*) withhold; [B] (*Amtsspr.: festsetzen*) detain

**ein·beinig** *Adj.* one-legged

**ein|bekennen** *unr. tr. V.* (*geh., bes. österr.*) ⇒ **eingestehen**

**Ein·bekenntnis** *das* (*geh., bes. österr.*) ⇒ **Eingeständnis**

**ein|berechnen** *tr. V.* ⇒ **einkalkulieren**

**ein|berufen** *unr. tr. V.* [A] summon; call; **eine Versammlung/Sitzung ~:** call *or* convene a meeting; **den Bundestag ~:** summon the

*old spelling (see note on page 1707)

Bundestag; **eine Versammlung nach Berlin/eine Sitzung für den 30. Mai ~:** call a meeting in Berlin/for 30 May; **B** (*zur Wehrpflicht*) call up; conscript; draft (*Amer.*); **~ werden** be called up *or* conscripted; be drafted (*Amer.*)

**Ein·berufene** *der/die; adj. Dekl.* conscript; draftee (*Amer.*)

**Ein·berufung** *die* **A** (*das Einberufen*) calling; **die ~ des Parlaments** the summoning of Parliament; **B** (*zur Wehrpflicht*) call-up; conscription; draft (*Amer.*)

**Einberufungs-: ~befehl** *der*, **~bescheid** *der* call-up papers *pl.*; draft card (*Amer.*)

**ein|beschreiben** *unr. tr. V.* (*Geom.*) inscribe ‹circle›; **einem Dreieck einen Kreis ~:** inscribe a circle in a triangle

**ein|bestellen** *tr. V.* (*Amtsspr.*) summon

**ein|betonieren** *tr. V.* concrete in; **etw. in etw.** (*Akk.*) **~:** concrete sth. into sth.

**ein|betten** *tr. V.* **A** embed (**in** + *Akk.* in); **das Haus liegt eingebettet in ein Tal** the house nestles in a valley; **B** (*Sprachw.*) **eingebettete Sätze** embedded sentences

**Einbett-: ~kabine** *die* single-berth cabin; **~zimmer** *das* single room

**ein|beulen** **1** *tr. V.* **etw. ~:** dent sth.; make a dent in sth.; **ein eingebeulter Kotflügel** a dented mudguard. **2** *refl. V.* become dented

**ein|beziehen** *unr. tr. V.* include; **etw. in etw.** (*Akk.*) **~:** include sth. in sth.; **jmdn. in eine Diskussion ~:** involve sb. *or* get sb. involved in a discussion

**Ein·beziehung** *die*, (*schweiz.*) **Ein·bezug** *der* inclusion; **unter ~ aller Faktoren** taking all factors into account

**ein|biegen** **1** *unr. itr. V.* ▶ 818 ; *mit sein* turn; **in eine Straße ~:** turn into a street; **[nach] links/rechts ~:** turn left/right. **2** *unr. tr. V.* bend. **3** *unr. refl. V.* bend inwards

**ein|bilden** *refl. V.* **A** **sich** (*Dat.*) **etw. ~:** imagine sth.; **sich** (*Dat.*) **~, dass ...** imagine that ...; **ich bilde mir ein, dass ich ihn in der Stadt gesehen habe** (*ugs.*) I think I saw him in town; **eine eingebildete Krankheit** an imaginary illness; **was bildest du dir eigentlich ein?** (*ugs.*) what do you think you are doing?; **B** (*ugs.: übermäßig stolz sein*) **er bildet sich** (*Dat.*) **ganz schön viel ein** he thinks no end of himself (*coll.*); he fancies himself no end (*coll.*); **sich** (*Dat.*) **ziemlich viel auf etw. ~:** be terribly conceited about sth. (*coll.*); **darauf brauchst du dir nichts einzubilden** there's no need to be stuck-up about it

**Ein·bildung** *die;* **~, ~en** **A** (*Fantasie*) imagination; **B** (*falsche Vorstellung*) fantasy; **das ist alles nur ~:** it's all in the mind; **C** (*Hochmut*) conceitedness; **~ ist auch eine Bildung** (*ugs.*) you're kidding yourself/he's kidding himself *etc.* (*coll.*)

**Einbildungs-: ~kraft** *die*, **~vermögen** *das* [powers *pl.* of] imagination; imaginative powers *pl.*

**ein|bimsen** *tr. V.* (*ugs.*) **jmdm. etw. ~:** drum sth. into sb.

**ein|binden** *unr. tr. V.* **A** bind ‹book›; **etw. neu ~:** rebind sth.; **B** (*einfügen*) **er war in bestimmte Konventionen/Wertvorstellungen eingebunden** (*fig.*) he was bound by certain conventions/subject to certain values; **in die Verantwortung eingebunden** constrained by responsibility; **C** (*integrieren*) **das Dorf muss in das Verkehrsnetz eingebunden werden** the village must be linked into the transport system; **den Einzelnen in ein Kollektiv ~:** make the individual part of a group; **in ein System eingebunden bleiben** remain part of a system; **D** (*einhüllen*) wrap; bandage ‹limb›

**Ein·bindung** *die* **A** (*Integration*) integration; **die ~ der Bundesrepublik in die EG** the fact that the Federal Republic forms part of the European Community; **B** (*Bindung, Festgelegtsein*) **gegen die zu starke ~ durch den Vertrag setzte er sich zur Wehr** he fought against being bound *or* tied too closely by the contract

**ein·blätt[e]rig** *Adj.* (*Bot.*) monophyllous

**ein|bläuen** *tr. V.* **jmdm. etw. ~:** drum *or* hammer sth. into sb.

**ein|blenden** (*Rundf., Ferns., Film*) **1** *tr. V.* insert; **eine Nachricht in eine Sendung ~:** interrupt a programme with a news flash; **Geräusche/Musik/Szenen nachträglich ~:** dub in sounds/music/scenes. **2** *refl. V.* **sich in ein Fußballspiel ~:** go over to a football match; **sich in eine Direktübertragung ~:** link up with a live transmission

**Ein·blendung** *die* (*Rundf., Ferns., Film*) insertion; (*Rückblende*) flashback (**in** + *Akk.* to)

***ein|bleuen** ⇒ **einbläuen**

**Ein·blick** *der* **A** (*Sicht*) **den ~ in den Garten verhindern** obstruct the view of the garden; **~ in etw.** (*Akk.*) **haben** be able to see into sth.; **B** (*Durchsicht*) **~ in etw. nehmen** take a look at *or* examine sth.; **jmdm. ~ in etw.** (*Akk.*) **gewähren** allow *or* permit sb. to look at *or* examine sth.; **keinen ~ in etw.** (*Akk.*) **haben** not be permitted to look at *or* examine sth.; **C** (*Kenntnis*) insight; **[einen] ~ in etw. haben/gewinnen** have/gain an insight into sth.

**ein|bohnern** *tr. V.* wax ‹floor, stairs›

**ein|bohren** **1** *tr. V.* drill; bore. **2** *refl. V.* **sich in etw.** (*Akk.*) **~:** bore into sth.

**ein|brechen** **1** *unr. itr. V.* **A** *mit haben od. sein* break in; **in eine Bank/ein Geschäft ~:** break into a bank/shop; **bei jmdm. ~:** burgle sb.; **bei uns wurde eingebrochen** we were burgled; we had a break-in; **B** *mit sein* (*einstürzen*) ‹roof, ceiling› fall in, cave in; **C** *mit sein* (*durchbrechen*) fall through; **beim Eislaufen ~:** fall *or* go through the ice while skating; **D** *mit sein* (*eindringen*) **in ein Land ~:** invade a country; **in die Verteidigungslinie ~:** break through the line of defences; **E** *mit sein* (*geh.: beginnen*) ‹night, darkness› fall; ‹winter› set in; **F** *mit sein* (*salopp: scheitern*) **[ganz schön] ~:** come [badly] unstuck (*coll.*); come a [fearful] cropper (*coll.*); **G** *mit sein* (*hineinstürzen*) burst in; **in etw.** (*Akk.*) **~:** burst into sth.
**2** *unr. tr. V.* break down ‹door, wall›; demolish ‹chimney›

**Einbrecher** *der;* **~s, ~:** burglar

**Einbrecher·bande** *die* gang of burglars

**Einbrecherin** *die;* **~, ~nen** burglar

**Einbrenne** /ˈainbrɛnə/ *die;* **~, ~n** (*Kochk.: bes. südd., österr.*) roux

**ein|brennen** **1** *unr. tr. V.* **ein Zeichen in Holz/auf eine Platte ~:** burn a design into wood/bake a design on to a plate; **einem Tier das Brandzeichen ~:** brand an animal. **2** *unr. refl. V.* (*geh.*) **das Erlebnis hatte sich tief in sein** *od.* **seinem Gedächtnis eingebrannt** the experience had engraved itself on his memory

**ein|bringen** **1** *unr. tr. V.* **A** (*hineinschaffen*) bring *or* gather in ‹harvest›; **ein Schiff in den Hafen ~:** bring a ship into port; **das Werkstück in die Maschine ~:** put the workpiece into the machine; **B** (*verschaffen*) **jmdm. viel Geld ~:** bring sb. [in] a lot of money; **Gewinn/Zinsen ~:** yield a profit/bring in interest; **jmdm. Ruhm/Ehre ~:** bring sb. fame/honour; **das hat nichts als Ärger eingebracht** that's caused nothing but trouble; **das bringt nichts ein** it isn't worth it; **C** (*Parl.: vorlegen*) introduce ‹bill›; **einen Antrag im Parlament ~:** introduce a bill into parliament; bring a bill before parliament; **D** (*in eine Gemeinschaft, Gesellschaft usw.*) invest ‹capital, money›; **etw. in eine Ehe ~:** bring sth. into a marriage; **etw. [in eine Situation] ~:** contribute sth. [to a situation]; **E** (*festsetzen*) catch, capture ‹escaped prisoners›; **F** (*Druckw.*) take in ‹lines›.
**2** *unr. refl. V.* **sich in eine Beziehung ~:** make one's own contribution to a relationship

**Einbringung** *die;* **~** **A** (*Festsetzung*) capture; **B** (*Parl.: von Gesetzen*) introduction

**ein|brocken** *tr. V.* (*ugs.*) **sich/jmdm. etw. [Schönes] ~, sich/jmdm. eine schöne Suppe ~:** land oneself/sb. in the soup *or* in it (*coll.*); **das hast du dir selbst eingebrockt** you've only yourself to thank for that (*coll.*)

**Ein·bruch** *der* **A** burglary; break-in; **ein ~ in eine Bank** a break-in at a bank; **einen ~ verüben** commit a burglary; **B** (*das Einstürzen*) collapse; **ein ~ der Börsenkurse** (*fig.*) a slump in stock market prices; **C** (*Vorstoß*) breakthrough; **der ~ des Feindes in ein Land** the enemy invasion of a country; **der ~ einer Kälte-/Hitzewelle** (*fig.*) the onset of a cold wave *or* spell/a heat wave; **D** (*Beginn*) **vor ~ der Dunkelheit** before it gets dark; **der ~ des Winters** the onset of winter; **bei ~ der Nacht** at nightfall; when night closes/closed in; **bei ~ des Winters** when winter sets/set in; **E** (*salopp: das Scheitern*) **einen ~ erleiden** take a drubbing *or* hiding (*coll.*); **F** (*Geol.*) area of subsidence

**einbruch[s]-, Einbruch[s]-: ~diebstahl** *der* burglary; breaking and entering; **~gefahr** *die:* **„~gefahr"** 'danger — thin ice'; **~sicher** *Adj.* burglar-proof

**ein|buchten** *tr. V.* (*salopp*) **jmdn. ~:** lock sb. up (*coll.*); put sb. away (*coll.*); ⇒ *auch* **eingebuchtet**

**Einbuchtung** *die;* **~, ~en** **A** **eine ~ der Straße** a bend in the road; **eine ~ der Küste** a bay; an inlet; **B** (*Delle*) dent; **die ~ der Autotür** the dent in the car door

**ein|buddeln** *tr. V.* (*ugs.*) bury; **sich ~:** dig oneself in

**einbürgern** ▶ 553 **1** *tr. V.* naturalize ‹person, plant, animal›; introduce ‹custom, practice›. **2** *refl. V.* ‹custom, practice› become established; ‹person, plant, animal› become naturalized; **sich in einer Sprache ~:** become established as part of a language; **das hat sich hier so eingebürgert** it has become the practice here

**Einbürgerung** *die;* **~, ~en** naturalization

**Ein·buße** *die* loss; **schwere ~n erleiden** suffer heavy losses; **eine ~ an etw.** (*Dat.*) a loss of sth.; **das bedeutet eine [finanzielle] ~ für mich** I shall be worse off financially

**ein|büßen** **1** *tr. V.* lose; (*durch eigene Schuld*) forfeit; **sein Geld/seine Freiheit/sein Leben ~:** lose/forfeit one's money/one's freedom/one's life. **2** *itr. V.* **sie büßte an Ansehen ein** her reputation suffered

**ein|checken** *tr., itr. V.* (*Flugw.*) check in

**ein|cremen** *tr. V.* put cream on ‹hands, back›; **sich ~:** put cream on; **jmdm./sich die Hände/den Rücken ~:** put cream on sb.'s/one's hands/back

**ein|dämmen** *tr. V.* **A** dam ‹river›; embank, dike ‹land›; **B** (*aufhalten*) check; stem

**ein|dämmern** *itr. V.; mit sein* doze off

**Eindämmung** *die;* **~, ~en** ⇒ **eindämmen**: damming; diking; checking, stemming; **eine ~ des Drogenhandels scheint unmöglich** it seems impossible to stem the flow of drugs

**ein|dampfen** *tr. V.* (*Chemie*) evaporate

**ein|decken** **1** *refl. V.* stock up; **sich [für den Winter] mit etw. ~:** stock up with sth. [for the winter]. **2** *tr. V.* (*ugs.: überhäufen*) **jmdn. mit Arbeit/Fragen ~:** swamp sb. with work/questions; **mit etw. eingedeckt sein** be swamped with sth.

**Eindecker** *der;* **~s, ~** (*Flugw.*) monoplane

**ein|deichen** *tr. V.* dike ‹land›; dike, embank ‹river›

**ein|dellen** *tr. V.* (*ugs.*) dent [in]

**eindeutig** /ˈaindɔytɪç/ **1** *Adj.* **A** (*klar*) clear; clear, definite ‹proof›; **B** (*nur eine Deutung zulassend*) unambiguous ‹concept›. **2** *adv. s. Adj.* clearly; unambiguously

**Eindeutigkeit** *die;* **~, ~en** **A** ⇒ **eindeutig**: clarity; unambiguity; **B** (*scherzh.: unanständiger Witz*) crudity

**ein|deutschen** *tr. V.* Germanize

**Eindeutschung** *die;* **~, ~en** **A** Germanization; **B** (*eingedeutschtes Wort*) Germanized word

**ein|dicken** *tr., itr. V.* thicken

**ein·dimensional** *Adj.* one-dimensional; unidimensional; (*fig.*) one-dimensional ‹personality›

e

**ein|docken** *tr. V.* (*Schiffbau*) dock

**ein|dosen** *tr. V.* can; tin (*Brit.*)

**ein|dösen** *itr. V.* (*ugs.*) *mit sein* doze off

**ein|drängen** ❶ *itr. V.*; *mit sein* **auf jmdn. ~:** crowd around sb.; **Eindrücke/Erinnerungen drängten auf ihn ein** (*fig.*) impressions/memories crowded in [up]on him. ❷ *refl. V.* push one's way in; force one's way in

**ein|drecken** /ˈaindrɛkn̩/ *tr. V.* (*ugs.*) **etw./sich ~:** get sth./oneself filthy; (*mit Schlamm usw.*) get sth./oneself covered in *or* with muck (*coll.*)

**ein|drehen** *tr. V.* Ⓐ (*hin~*) screw in ‹light bulb› (**in** + *Akk.* into); Ⓑ **sich** (*Dat.*) **die Haare ~:** put one's hair in curlers *or* rollers; **sich** (*Dat.*) **die Haare ~ lassen** have one's hair curled

**ein|dreschen** *unr. itr. V.* (*ugs.*) **auf jmdn. ~:** lay into sb. (*coll.*)

**ein|dringen** *unr. itr. V.*; *mit sein* Ⓐ **in etw.** (*Akk.*) **~:** penetrate into sth.; ‹vermin› get into sth.; ‹bullet› pierce sth.; (*allmählich*) ‹water, sand, etc.› seep into sth.; **er drang in sie ein** he penetrated her (*sexually*); **die ~de Kaltluft** the cold air that blows in; Ⓑ (*einbrechen*) **in ein Gebäude ~:** force an entry *or* one's way into a building; **Feinde sind in das Land eingedrungen** (*geh.*) enemies invaded the country; **in eine Gesellschaft ~** (*fig.*) be an uninvited guest; Ⓒ (*bedrängen*) set upon, attack ‹person›; **mit Fragen auf jmdn. ~:** besiege *or* ply sb. with questions; **auf jmdn. ~[, etw. zu tun]** (*fig.*) press *or* urge sb. [to do sth.]

**ein·dringlich** ❶ *Adj.* urgent ‹warning, entreaty›; impressive ‹voice›; forceful, powerful ‹speech, words›. ❷ *adv.* ‹urge› strongly; ‹talk› insistently; **jmdn. auf das Eindringlichste warnen** warn sb. most urgently

**Ein·dringlichkeit** *die*; ~ ⇒ **eindringlich**: urgency; impressiveness; forcefulness

**Eindringling** /ˈaindrɪŋlɪŋ/ *der*; **~s, ~e** intruder

**Ein·druck** *der*; **~[e]s, Eindrücke** Ⓐ (*Vorstellung, Wirkung*) impression; **einen ~ haben/gewinnen** have/get *or* gain an impression; **jmdn. nach dem ersten ~ beurteilen** judge sb. by first impressions; **einen guten ~ machen** make a good impression; **~ auf jmdn. machen** make an impression on sb.; **Eindrücke gewinnen** receive impressions; **er macht den ~ eines sehr gewissenhaften Menschen** he gives the impression of being a very conscientious person; **er konnte sich des ~s nicht erwehren, dass ...** (*geh.*) he had the strong impression that ...; he could not help thinking *or* feeling that ...; **sie stand noch unter dem ~ dieses schrecklichen Erlebnisses** she was still haunted by this terrible experience; **er stand noch ganz unter dem ~ seiner Indienreise** he was still under the spell of his journey to India; **er tat es nur, um [bei ihr] ~ zu schinden** (*ugs.*) he only did it to impress [her]; Ⓑ (*Spur*) impression

**ein|drücken** *tr. V.* Ⓐ (*verbiegen, zerbrechen*) smash in ‹mudguard, bumper›; stave in ‹side of ship›; smash ‹pier, column, support›; break ‹window›; crush ‹ribs›; flatten ‹nose›; **der Wind drückte alle Fenster ein** the wind blew all the windows in; Ⓑ (*hineindrücken*) **etw. [in etw.** (*Akk.*)**] ~:** press *or* push sth. in[to sth.]

**eindrucks-:** **~los** ❶ *Adj.* unimpressive; ❷ *adv.* unimpressively; **~voll** ❶ *Adj.* impressive; ❷ *adv.* impressively

**ein|dübeln** *tr. V.* **etw. in die Wand ~:** fix sth. into the wall with a plug/dowel

**eine** ⇒ **ein¹**

**ein|ebnen** *tr. V.* level; **der Unterschied ist eingeebnet worden** (*fig.*) the difference has been eliminated

**Einebnung** *die*; **~, ~en** levelling; (*fig.*) elimination; **bei der ~ des Grundstücks** during the levelling of the site

*old spelling (see note on page 1707)

**Ein·ehe** *die* monogamy *no art.*

**eineiig** /ˈain|aiɪç/ *Adj.* identical ‹twins›

**ein·eindeutig** *Adj.* one-to-one ‹correspondence, relationship›; **eine ~e Abbildung** a representation having a one-to-one correspondence with its original

**ein·ein·halb** *Bruchz.* ▸ **841** | one and a half; **~ Stunden/Jahre** an hour/a year and a half; one and a half hours/years

**ein·ein·halb·fach** *Vervielfältigungsz.* one and a half times; **die ~e Anzahl/Menge** one and a half times the number/amount

**einen** *tr. V.* (*geh.*) unite

**ein|engen** *tr. V.* Ⓐ **jmdn. ~:** restrict sb.'s movement[s]; **sich eingeengt fühlen** feel hemmed in *or* shut in; Ⓑ (*fig.: einschränken*) restrict; restrict, narrow down ‹concept›; **jmdn. in seiner Freiheit ~:** restrict *or* curb sb.'s freedom

**einer** ⇒ **ein¹**

**Einer** *der*; **~s, ~** Ⓐ (*Math.*) unit; Ⓑ (*Sport*) single sculler; **im ~:** in the single sculls

**einerlei** /ˈainɐlai/ ❶ *Adj.* (*unwichtig*) **~, ob/wo/wer** *usw.* no matter whether/where/who *etc.*; **es ist ~:** it makes no difference; **es ist ihm ~:** it is all the same *or* all one to him; (*es kümmert ihn nicht*) he does not care at all. ❷ *indekl. Gattungsz.* **von ~ Sorte** of one *or* of the same kind; **mit ~ Maß gemessen werden** be assessed according to one *or* the same standard

**Einerlei** *das*; **~s** monotony; **das tägliche ~:** the monotony of everyday life; the daily grind (*coll.*)

**einerseits** /ˈainɐˈzaits/ *Adv.* on the one hand; **~ ..., andererseits ...** on the one hand ..., on the other hand ...

**Einer·stelle** *die* (*Math.*) units place

**eines** ⇒ **ein¹**

**eines·teils** *Adv.* on the one hand; **~ ..., ander[e]nteils ...** on the one hand ..., on the other hand ...

**ein|exerzieren** *tr. V.* drill, train ‹soldier, pupil, etc.›; **jmdm. etw. ~:** drill *or* train sb. in sth.

**ein·fach** ❶ *Adj.* Ⓐ (*nicht mehrfach*) single ‹knot, ticket, journey›; **zweimal ~ [nach] Köln** two singles to Cologne; Ⓑ (*nicht schwierig*) simple, easy ‹task›; **das ist ~:** that is simple *or* easy; **sich** (*Dat.*) **etw. [zu] ~ machen** make sth. [too] easy for oneself; **warum ~, wenn es auch kompliziert geht!** (*scherzh.*) the other way would be too simple, I suppose!; Ⓒ (*einleuchtend*) simple ‹explanation, reason›; **aus dem ~en Grund, weil ...** for the simple reason that ...; Ⓓ (*bescheiden*) simple ‹person, manner, life, dress, etc.›; plain, simple ‹food›; **er war nur ein ~er Mann** he was just an ordinary man; ⇒ *auch* **Verhältnis**.
❷ *adv.* Ⓐ (*bescheiden, einleuchtend*) simply; **sich betont ~ kleiden** dress very simply; Ⓑ (*nicht mehrfach*) **etw. ~ falten** fold sth. once.
❸ *Partikel* (*verstärkend*) simply; just; **das ist ~ unmöglich** that is simply *or* just impossible; **ich begreife es ~ nicht** I simply *or* just cannot understand it; **es ist ~ nicht zu begreifen, dass ...** it's simply incomprehensible that ...

**Einfachheit** *die*; **~** Ⓐ (*einfache Gestaltung*) simplicity; **von verblüffender ~ sein** be of astonishing simplicity; **der ~ halber** for the sake of simplicity; for simplicity's sake; Ⓑ (*Bescheidenheit*) simplicity; (*der Nahrung*) plainness; simplicity

**ein|fädeln** ❶ *tr. V.* Ⓐ thread ‹needle, tape› (**in** + *Akk.* into); thread up ‹sewing machine›; **einen [neuen] Faden ~:** [re]thread the needle; Ⓑ (*ugs.: geschickt einleiten*) engineer ‹scheme, plot›; **das hat sie fein/schlau eingefädelt** she worked that nicely/craftily (*coll.*). ❷ *refl. V.* (*Verkehrsw.*) filter in; **sich in den fließenden Verkehr ~:** filter into the flow of traffic. ❸ *itr. V.* (*Skisport*) become entangled in the gate

**ein|fahren** ❶ *unr. itr. V.*; *mit sein* come in; ‹train› come *or* pull in; **in den Bahnhof ~:** come *or* pull into the station; **der Zug nach Hamburg ist soeben auf Gleis 5 eingefahren** the Hamburg train has just arrived at platform 5. ❷ *unr. tr. V.* Ⓐ bring in ‹harvest›; Ⓑ (*beschädigen*) knock down ‹wall›; smash in ‹mudguard›; Ⓒ (*Kfz-W.*) run in ‹car›; Ⓓ (*Technik*) retract ‹undercarriage, antenna›; Ⓔ (*Wirtsch.*) make ‹profit, loss›; set up ‹record›. ❸ *unr. refl. V.* Ⓐ **sich mit einem Fahrzeug ~:** get used to a vehicle; Ⓑ (*sich einspielen*) **der neue Produktionsprozess hat sich eingefahren** the new production process is now running smoothly; ⇒ *auch* **eingefahren**

**Einfahr·signal** *das* (*Eisenb.*) home signal

**Ein·fahrt** *die* Ⓐ (*das Hineinfahren*) entry; **Vorsicht bei der ~ des Zuges!** stand clear [of the edge of the platform], the train is approaching; Ⓑ (*Zufahrt*) entrance; (*Autobahn~*) slip road; **„keine ~"** 'no entry'; **der Zug hat noch keine ~/hat ~ auf Gleis 5** the train is not yet able to pull in/is now approaching platform 5

**Ein·fall** *der* Ⓐ (*Idee*) idea; **ein sonderbarer ~:** a strange notion *or* idea; **auf den ~ kommen, etw. zu tun** have *or* get the idea of doing sth.; **sie hat Einfälle wie ein altes Haus** (*scherzh.*) she gets some strange ideas; Ⓑ (*Licht~*) incidence (*Optics*); Ⓒ (*in ein Land usw.*) invasion (**in** + *Akk.* of); Ⓓ (*geh.: plötzliches Einsetzen*) (*des Winters*) onset; **bei ~ der Nacht** at nightfall

**ein|fallen** *unr. itr. V.*; *mit sein* Ⓐ **jmdm. fällt etw. ein** sb. thinks of sth.; sth. occurs to sb.; **fällt dir etwas ein, was wir tun könnten?** can you think of anything we can do?; **ihm fallen immer wieder neue Ausreden ein** he can always think of *or* (*coll.*) come up with new excuses; **was fällt dir denn ein!** what do you think you're doing?; how dare you?; **lass dir das ja nicht ~!** don't you dare!; **sich** (*Dat.*) **etw. ~ lassen [müssen]** [have to] think of sth.; **das fällt mir nicht im Schlaf** *od.* **im Traum[e] ein** I wouldn't dream of it *or* such a thing; Ⓑ (*in Erinnerung kommen*) **ihr Name fällt mir nicht ein** I cannot think of her name; **plötzlich fiel ihm seine Frau ein** suddenly he thought of his wife; **es wird dir schon [wieder] ~:** it will come [back] to you; **plötzlich fiel ihr ein, dass ...** (*merkte sie*) suddenly she realized that ...; (*erinnerte sie sich daran*) suddenly she remembered that ...; Ⓒ (*von Licht*) come in; Ⓓ (*gewaltsam eindringen*) **in ein Land ~:** invade a country; Ⓔ (*einstimmen, mitreden usw.*) join in; **in den Gesang ~:** join in the singing; **in ein Gespräch ~:** break into a conversation; **„Ja, natürlich", fiel er ein** 'Yes, of course,' he put in; Ⓕ (*geh.: plötzlich beginnen*) ‹winter› set in; ‹night› fall; ‹storm› break

**einfalls-, Einfalls-:** **~los** ❶ *Adj.* unimaginative; lacking in ideas; ❷ *adv.* unimaginatively; without imagination; **~losigkeit** *die*; **~~:** unimaginativeness; lack of ideas; **~reich** ❶ *Adj.* imaginative; full of ideas; ❷ *adv.* imaginatively; with imagination; **~reichtum** *der* imaginativeness; wealth of ideas; **~tor** *das* gateway

**Einfall·straße** *die* (*Verkehrsw.*) access road

**Einfall[s]·winkel** *der* (*Physik*) angle of incidence

**Einfalt** /ˈainfalt/ *die*; **~** Ⓐ (*Beschränktheit*) simpleness; simple-mindedness; Ⓑ (*geh.: Reinheit*) simplicity; innocence; **~ des Herzens** simplicity of heart

**einfältig** /ˈainfɛltɪç/ *Adj.* Ⓐ (*arglos*) simple; naïve; artless; naïve ‹remarks›; **sei nicht so ~!** don't be so naïve!; Ⓑ (*beschränkt*) simple; simple-minded

**Einfältigkeit** *die*; **~** Ⓐ (*Arglosigkeit*) simplicity; naïvety; artlessness; Ⓑ (*Beschränktheit*) simpleness; simple-mindedness

**Einfalts·pinsel** *der* (*ugs. abwertend*) nincompoop

**Ein·familien·haus** *das* house (*as opposed to block of flats etc.*)

**ein|fangen** ❶ *unr. tr. V.* Ⓐ catch, capture ‹fugitive, animal›; Ⓑ (*geh.: wiedergeben*) capture ‹atmosphere, aura, etc.›. ❷ *unr. refl. V.* (*ugs.: bekommen*) **sich** (*Dat.*) **eine Erkältung** *usw.* **~:** catch *or* get a cold *etc.*; **sich** (*Dat.*) **eine Tracht Prügel ~:** get a beating

**ein|färben** *tr. V.* Ⓐ dye ‹material, hair›; **eine kommunistisch eingefärbte Zeitung** (*fig.*) a newspaper with a communist slant; Ⓑ (*Druckw.*) ink

**ein·farbig**, (*österr.*) **ein·färbig** ❶ *Adj.* ‹material, dress› of one colour; plain ‹material, dress›. ❷ *adv.* **das Sofa ~ beziehen** cover the sofa in material of one colour; **die Wände ~ streichen** paint the walls all one colour

**ein|fassen** *tr. V.* border, hem, edge ‹material, dress, tablecloth›; frame ‹picture›; set ‹gem›; edge ‹lawn, flower bed, grave›; curb ‹source, spring›

**Ein·fassung** *die* ⇒ **einfassen**: border; hem; edging; frame; setting; (*von Brunnen, Quellen*) enclosure

**ein|fetten** *tr. V.* grease; dubbin ‹leather›; **sich** (*Dat.*) **die Haut/Hände ~:** rub cream into one's skin/hands

**ein|finden** *unr. refl. V.* (*eintreffen*) arrive; (*sich treffen*) meet; (*zusammenkommen*) gather; (*sich melden*) be present; (*fig.*) ‹opportunity etc.› occur; **sich bei jmdm. ~:** report to sb.

**ein|flechten** *unr. tr. V.* **sich** (*Dat.*) **Bänder ins Haar ~:** plait *or* braid ribbons into one's hair; **ein Muster in einen Korb ~:** weave a pattern into a basket; **in eine Rede ein paar Scherze ~:** work a couple of jokes into a speech; **Episoden in einen Roman ~:** weave episodes into a novel; **wenn ich das kurz ~ darf** if I could turn to this for a moment

**ein|flicken** *tr. V.* (*ugs.*) stitch on; (*fig.*) shove in (*coll.*)

**ein|fliegen** ❶ *unr. tr. V.* Ⓐ fly in ‹supplies, troops›; Ⓑ flight-test, test-fly ‹aircraft›; Ⓒ (*Wirtsch.*) make ‹profit, loss›. ❷ *unr. itr. V.*; *mit sein* Ⓐ fly in; **eingeflogen kommen** come over by air; **in ein Gebiet ~:** fly into *or* enter a territory; Ⓑ (*in einen geschlossenen Raum*) ‹bees, doves, etc.› fly in; **in etw.** (*Akk.*) **~:** fly into sth.

**ein|fließen** *unr. itr. V.*; *mit sein* flow in; **von Norden fließt Kaltluft nach Westeuropa ein** (*fig.*) a cold northerly airstream is moving into Western Europe; **etw. in ein Gespräch ~ lassen** (*fig.*) slip sth. into a conversation; **~de Kalt-/Warmluft** (*Met.*) an inflow of cold/warm air

**ein|flößen** *tr. V.* Ⓐ **jmdm. Tee/Medizin ~:** pour tea/medicine into sb.'s mouth; **jmdm. mit Gewalt Alkohol ~:** force alcohol *or* drink down sb.['s throat]; Ⓑ (*fig.*) **jmdm. Angst ~:** put fear into sb.; arouse fear in sb.; **jmdm. Vertrauen ~:** inspire sb. with confidence; **jmdm. Ehrfurcht/Mut ~:** fill sb. with awe/courage; inspire awe/courage in sb.

**Ein·flug** *der*: **~ einer feindlichen Maschine** an incursion by an enemy aircraft; **beim ~ in feindliches Hoheitsgebiet** while flying into enemy territory

**Einflug-: ~loch** *das* (*Zool.*) entrance [hole]; **~schneise** *die* (*Flugw.*) approach path

**Ein·fluss**, ***Ein·fluß** *der* Ⓐ influence; **~ auf jmdn./etw. haben/ausüben** have/exert an influence on sb./sth.; **das entzieht sich meinem ~:** I have no influence over that; that is beyond my control; **unter jmds. ~** (*Dat.*) **stehen** be under sb.'s influence; **unter dem ~ von Alkohol** under the influence of alcohol; **~ auf etw.** (*Akk.*) **nehmen** influence sth.; **[einen] großen ~ besitzen** have a great deal of influence or sway; Ⓑ (*Met.*) inflow; Ⓒ (*fig.: von Kapital usw.*) influx

**einfluss-**, ***einfluß-**, **Einfluss-**, ***Einfluß-**: **~bereich** *der*, **~gebiet** *das* sphere of influence; **~los** *Adj.* uninfluential; lacking in influence *postpos.*; **~nahme** *die*; **~~:** exertion of influence (**auf** + *Akk.* on); (*Versuch*) **~nahme auf jmdn.** attempt to influence sb.; **~reich** *Adj.* influential; **~sphäre** *die* sphere of influence

**ein|flüstern** ❶ *tr. V.* (*oft abwertend*) **wer hat dir denn diesen Unsinn eingeflüstert?** who has put this nonsense into your head?; **lass dir nicht solche albernen Gerüchte ~:** don't be taken in by such silly gossip. ❷ *itr. V.* (*flüsternd sprechen*) whisper

**Einflüsterung** *die*; **~**, **~en** (*geh. abwertend*) blandishment

**ein|fordern** *tr. V.* demand ‹payment›; demand payment of ‹money, outstanding debts›; **ein Gutachten ~:** ask for a report

**ein·förmig** ❶ *Adj.* monotonous. ❷ *adv.* monotonously

**Ein·förmigkeit** *die*; **~**, **~en** monotony

**ein|fressen** *unr. refl. V.* **sich in etw.** (*Akk.*) **~:** eat into sth.

**ein|frieden**, **ein|friedigen** *tr. V.* (*geh.*) enclose ‹plot of land›

**Einfriedung**, **Einfriedigung** *die*; **~**, **~en** means of enclosure; (*Zaun*) fence; (*Hecke*) hedge; (*Mauer*) wall

**ein|frieren** ❶ *unr. itr. V.*; *mit sein* Ⓐ ‹water› freeze, turn to ice; ‹pond› freeze over; ‹pipes› freeze up; ‹ship› be frozen in; **ihr Lächeln war eingefroren** (*fig.*) her smile had frozen (*fig.*); Ⓑ (*fig.*) ‹wages, credit› be frozen; ‹negotiations› break down. ❷ *unr. tr. V.* Ⓐ deep-freeze ‹food›; Ⓑ (*beenden*) freeze ‹credit, project, plan›; break off, suspend ‹negotiations›; suspend ‹inquiry›

**ein|frosten** *tr. V.* ⇒ **einfrieren** 2 A

**ein|fuchsen** *tr. V.* (*ugs.*) **jmdn. auf etw.** (*Akk.*) **~:** drill sb. in sth.; **ein eingefuchster Spezialist/Trainer** an experienced specialist/trainer; **auf etw.** (*Akk.*) **eingefuchst sein** be well practised in sth.

**ein|fügen** ❶ *tr. V.* fit in; **etw. in etw.** (*Akk.*) **~:** fit sth. into sth.; **etw. in einen Text ~:** insert sth. into a text; **ich möchte noch ~, dass ...** (*fig.*) I would like to add that .... ❷ *refl. V.* adapt; **sich in etw.** (*Akk.*) **~:** adapt oneself to sth.; **sich überall gut ~:** fit in well anywhere

**Ein·fügung** *die* insertion

**ein|fühlen** *refl. V.* **sich in jmdn. ~:** empathize with sb.; **ich kann mich gut in deine Lage ~:** I know exactly how you feel; I can well understand how you feel; **er kann sich gut in eine Rolle/in einen anderen ~:** he is good at getting into a part/putting himself in another person's place; **sich in die Atmosphäre des alten Moskau ~:** get the feel of the atmosphere in old Moscow

**einfühlsam** *Adj.* understanding; sensitive ‹interpretation, performance›

**Einfühlsamkeit** *die*; **~:** sensitivity

**Ein·fühlung** *die*; **~:** empathy (**in** + *Akk.* with)

**Einfühlungs·vermögen** *das* ability to empathize; **mit ausgesprochenem ~ spielen/übersetzen** play/translate with great sensitivity for the work

**Ein·fuhr** *die*; **~**, **~en** Ⓐ (*das Einführen*) import; importing; Ⓑ (*das Eingeführte*) import

**ein|führen** ❶ *tr. V.* Ⓐ (*importieren*) import ‹goods, technology›; Ⓑ (*als Neuerung*) introduce ‹fashion, method, technology›; Ⓒ (*ein-, unterweisen*) introduce; initiate; **jmdn. in etw.** (*Akk.*) **~:** introduce sb. to sth.; initiate sb. into sth.; **jmdn. in sein Amt ~:** install sb. in office; **der neue Kollege wurde eingeführt** our *etc.* new colleague was introduced to *or* initiated into his new job; Ⓓ (*hineinschieben*) introduce, insert ‹catheter etc.› (**in** + *Akk.* into); Ⓔ (*vorstellen*) introduce; **jmdn. bei seinen Eltern ~:** introduce sb. to one's parents; **eine junge Dame in die Gesellschaft ~:** bring a young lady out; **jmdn. bei Hofe ~:** present sb. at court. ❷ *refl. V.* Ⓐ (*sich vorstellen*) introduce oneself; **du hast dich nicht sehr gut eingeführt** you didn't make a very good first impression; Ⓑ (*Kaufmannsspr.*) ‹shop, company› become established

**Einfuhr-: ~erlaubnis**, **~genehmigung** *die* import licence; **~hafen** *der* port of entry; **~kontingent** *das* import quota; **~land** *das* importing country; importer; **~lizenz** *die* import licence; **~sperre** *die*, **~stopp** *der* embargo *or* ban on imports

**Ein·führung** *die* Ⓐ introduction; **eine ~ in die Naturwissenschaften** an introduction to the natural sciences; **ihre ~ in die Gesellschaft/bei Hof** her introduction to society/her presentation at court; **die ~ in sein Amt** his installation in office; Ⓑ (*Einarbeitung*) introduction; initiation; induction; Ⓒ (*das Hineinschieben*) introduction; insertion

**Einführungs-: ~kurs[us]** *der* (*Schulw.*) introductory course; **~preis** *der* (*Kaufmannsspr.*) introductory price

**Einfuhr-: ~verbot** *das* ⇒ **~sperre**; **~zoll** *der* import duty

**ein|füllen** *tr. V.* **etw. in etw.** (*Akk.*) **~:** pour *or* put sth. into sth.; **Wasser in eine Flasche ~:** fill a bottle with water

**Einfüll·stutzen** *der* (*an Tanks*) filler pipe; (*an Haushaltsgeräten*) filling spout

**ein|füttern** *tr. V.* (*DV*) feed in; **einem Computer Daten ~:** feed data into a computer

**Ein·gabe** *die* Ⓐ (*Gesuch*) petition; (*Beschwerde*) complaint; Ⓑ (*das Verabreichen*) administration; **die ~ der Tabletten sollte alle zwei Stunden erfolgen** the tablets are to be taken every two hours; Ⓒ (*DV*) input

**Eingabe·gerät** *das* (*DV*) input device

**Ein·gang** *der* Ⓐ (*Tür, Pforte, Portal usw.*) entrance; **der ~ eines Hauses/eines Parks** the entrance of *or* to a house/a park; **„kein ~"** 'no entry'; **in etw.** (*Akk.*) **~ finden** (*fig.*) become established in sth.; Ⓑ (*von Post, Geld*) receipt; Ⓒ (*eingetroffene Post*) incoming mail Ⓓ (*Elektrot.*) input

**ein·gängig** ❶ *Adj.* catchy ‹song, melody›; **ihr war das [nicht] ~** (*geh.*) it was [in]comprehensible to her. ❷ *adv.* **etw. ~ erklären** explain sth. simply and clearly

**eingangs** ❶ *Adv.* at the beginning; at the start. ❷ *Präp.* + *Gen.* **~ der Kurve/Fußgängerzone** where the bend/pedestrian precinct begins *or* starts; **~ des Jahres** at the beginning *or* start of the year

**Eingangs-: ~buch** *das* (*Buchf.*) 'goods inward' book; **~datum** *das* (*Bürow.*) date of receipt; **~formel** *die* preamble; **~halle** *die* entrance hall; (*eines Hotels, Theaters*) foyer; **~pforte** *die* gateway; **~stempel** *der* (*Bürow.*) date stamp; **~tür** *die* (*von Kaufhaus, Hotel usw.*) [entrance] door; (*von Wohnung, Haus usw.*) front door

**ein|geben** *unr. tr. V.* Ⓐ (*verabreichen*) give; **jmdm. Medizin ~:** give *or* administer medicine to sb.; Ⓑ (*DV*) feed in; **etw. in den Computer ~:** feed sth. into the computer; Ⓒ (*geh.: zu denken veranlassen*) **jmdm. eine Idee ~:** inspire sb. with an idea; **jmdm. den Wunsch ~, etw. zu tun** prompt sb. to do sth.

**ein·gebildet** ❶ *2. Part. v.* **einbilden**. ❷ *Adj.* Ⓐ (*imaginär*) imaginary ‹illness›; **ein ~er Kranker** a malade imaginaire; **~e Schwangerschaft** false pregnancy; Ⓑ (*arrogant*) conceited; **auf etw.** (*Akk.*) **~ sein** be conceited about sth.; ⇒ *auch* **Affe**

**ein·geboren** *Adj.* Ⓐ native ‹population etc.›; Ⓑ (*geh.: angeboren*) inborn; innate; Ⓒ (*Rel.*) **Gottes ~er Sohn** the only begotten Son of God

**Eingeborene** *der/die*; *adj. Dekl.* (*veralt.*) native

**eingebuchtet** ❶ *2. Part. v.* **einbuchten**. ❷ *Adj.* indented ‹coastline›

**Eingebung** *die*; **~**, **~en** inspiration; **es muss eine glückliche ~ gewesen sein** the idea was an inspiration; **einer ~ folgend** acting on a sudden impulse

**eingedenk** /'aingədɛŋk/ *Adj.* **einer Sache** (*Gen.*) **~ sein/bleiben** (*geh.*) be mindful of sth.; **~ dieser Sache ...** bearing this in mind ...; **~ der Tatsache, dass ...** bearing in mind that ...

**ein·gefahren** ❶ *2. Part. v.* **einfahren**. ❷ *Adj.* long-established; deep-rooted ‹prejudice›; **sich auf** *od.* **in ~en Bahnen** *od.* **Gleisen bewegen** go on in the same old way

**ein·gefallen** ❶ *2. Part. v.* **einfallen**. ❷ *Adj.* gaunt ‹face›; sunken, hollow ‹cheeks›

**eingefleischt** /'aingəflaiʃt/ *Adj.* confirmed ‹bachelor›; inveterate ‹smoker›; deep-rooted, ingrained ‹habit, prejudice›

**ein|gehen** ❶ *unr. itr. V.*; *mit sein* Ⓐ (*eintreffen*) arrive; be received; **der Brief ist nicht bei uns eingegangen** we have not received the letter; Ⓑ (*aufgenommen werden*) **in die**

e

Geschichte ~: go down in history; **in die Weltliteratur ~:** find one's/its place in world literature; **in die ewige Ruhe ~** (*dichter.*) pass away; **in das Reich Gottes ~:** enter the kingdom of Heaven; Ⓒ (*schrumpfen*) shrink; Ⓓ (*Bezug nehmen*) **auf eine Frage/ein Problem ~/nicht ~:** go into *or* deal with/ignore a question/problem; Ⓔ (*entgegenkommen, sich widmen*) **auf jmdn. ~:** be responsive to sb.; **auf jmdn. nicht ~:** ignore sb.'s wishes; Ⓕ **auf ein Angebot ~/nicht ~:** accept/reject an offer; Ⓖ (*sterben*) ‹animal, plant› die; **ihm war die Kuh eingegangen** the cow had died on him (*coll.*); **die Blumen gehen eine nach der anderen ein** the flowers are dying off; Ⓗ (*Bankrott gehen*) ‹shop› close down; ‹newspaper, business› close down, fold [up]; Ⓘ (*einleuchten*) **ihm geht alles leicht ein** he's quick on the uptake (*coll.*); he cottons on to things quickly (*coll.*); **es will ihr nicht ~, dass ...** she can't grasp the fact that ... ❷ *unr. tr. V.* enter into ‹contract, matrimony›; take ‹risk›; accept ‹obligation›; **darauf gehe ich jede Wette ein** (*ugs.*) I'll bet you anything on that (*coll.*)

**eingehend** ❶ *Adj.* detailed ‹discussion, explanation, report›; **~e Verhandlungen** negotiations on every detail. ❷ *adv.* in detail; **~er** in more detail

**ein·gekeilt** ❶ *2. Part. v.* **einkeilen.** ❷ *Adj.* (*von beiden Seiten*) wedged in (**in, zwischen** + *Dat.* between); (*von allen Seiten*) hemmed in (**in** among); **mein Auto war ~:** my car was boxed in

**Ein·gekochte** *das;* **~n** ⇒ **Eingemachte** A

**Ein·gemachte** *das;* **~n** Ⓐ preserved fruit/vegetables; Ⓑ (*fig.: Substanz*) **ans ~ gehen** (*ugs.*) draw on one's reserves; **jetzt gehts ans ~** (*ugs.*) now comes the crunch

**ein|gemeinden** *tr. V.* incorporate ‹village› (**in** + *Akk.*, **nach** into)

**Eingemeindung** *die;* **~, ~en** incorporation

**ein·genommen** ❶ *2. Part. v.* **einnehmen.** ❷ *Adj.* Ⓐ (*eingebildet*) **von sich ~ sein** be conceited; **von etw. ~ sein** be conceited about sth.; Ⓑ (*begeistert*) **von jmdn./etw. ~ sein** be taken with sb./sth.; (*dauerhaft*) like sb. very much/be very fond of sth.

**ein·geschlechtig** *Adj.* (*Bot.*) unisexual

**ein·geschnappt** ❶ *2. Part. v.* **einschnappen.** ❷ *Adj.* (*ugs.: beleidigt*) huffy

**ein·geschossig** *Adj.* single-storey; one-storey; ⇒ *auch* **achtstöckig; einstöckig**

**ein·geschränkt** ❶ *2. Part. v.* **einschränken.** ❷ *Adj.* **~es Haltverbot** prohibition of stopping except for certain purposes; **in ~en Verhältnissen leben** live in reduced circumstances. ❸ *adv.* **~ leben** live in reduced circumstances

**ein·geschrieben** ❶ *2. Part. v.* **einschreiben.** ❷ *Adj.* registered ‹letter, member›; enrolled ‹student›

**ein·geschworen** ❶ *2. Part. v.* **einschwören.** ❷ *Adj.* dedicated (**auf** + *Akk.* to); **ein ~er Freund/Gegner** a sworn friend/enemy; **die beiden waren darauf ~:** the two had agreed on it

**ein·gesessen** ❶ *2. Part. v.* **einsitzen.** ❷ *Adj.* established

**Ein·gesessene** *der/die; adj. Dekl.* established resident

**ein·gespannt** ❶ *2. Part. v.* **einspannen.** ❷ *Adj.* **stark ~:** very busy

**ein·gespielt** ❶ *2. Part. v.* **einspielen.** ❷ *Adj.* in practice; **aufeinander ~:** playing well together

**ein·gesprengt** ❶ *2. Part. v.* **einsprengen.** ❷ *Adj.* **mit ~en Kiefern/Heideflächen/Fremdwörtern** with a sprinkling of conifers/a few areas of heathland/occasional foreign words

**eingestandenermaßen** *Adv.* admittedly

**Ein·geständnis** *das* confession; admission

**ein|gestehen** *unr. tr. V.* admit, confess ‹guilt›; admit, confess to ‹mistake, theft›; **[sich] ~, dass ...** admit [to oneself] that ...

**ein·gestellt** ❶ *2. Part. v.* **einstellen.** ❷ *Adj.* **fortschrittlich/modern ~:** progressively minded/not at all old-fashioned in one's views; **ich weiß nicht, wie er [politisch] ~ ist** I don't know what his [political] views are

**ein·gestrichen**[1] *2. Part. v.* **einstreichen**

**ein·gestrichen**[2] *Adj.* (*Musik*) **das ~e A** the A above middle C; **das ~e C** middle C

**Eingeweide** /ˈaingəvaidə/ *das;* **~s, ~:** entrails *pl.;* innards *pl.;* **der Hunger wühlte in seinen ~n** (*geh.*) raging hunger gnawed his insides

**Eingeweide·bruch** *der* (*Med.*) hernia

**Ein·geweihte** *der/die; adj. Dekl.* initiate

**ein|gewöhnen** ❶ *refl. V.* get used *or* accustomed to one's new surroundings; accustom oneself to one's new surroundings; **er hat sich hier gut eingewöhnt** he's settled down here very well; **sich an seinem neuen Arbeitsplatz/in eine neue Tätigkeit ~:** settle in at one's new place of work/get used to a new job. ❷ *tr. V.* **jmdn. in etw.** (*Akk.*) **~:** get sb. used *or* accustomed to sth.

**Ein·gewöhnung** *die* (*am Arbeitsplatz usw.*) settling in *no art.;* **die ~ in seiner neuen Umgebung/an seinem neuen Arbeitsplatz fiel ihm schwer** he found it difficult to get used to his new surroundings/place of work

**ein·gewurzelt** ❶ *2. Part. v.* **einwurzeln.** ❷ *Adj.* ingrained; **ein tief ~es Misstrauen** a deeply rooted *or* deep-seated mistrust

**ein|gießen** *unr. tr.* (*auch itr.*) *V.* pour in; **etw. in etw.** (*Akk.*) **~:** pour sth. into sth.; **den Kaffee/die Limonade ~:** pour [out] the coffee/lemonade

**ein|gipsen** *tr. V.* Ⓐ (*Handw.*) **einen Nagel/Haken ~:** fix a nail/hook in with plaster; Ⓑ (*Med.*) **ein Bein/einen Arm ~:** put *or* set a leg/arm in plaster

**Ein·glas** *das* (*veralt.*) monocle

**eingleisig** /ˈainglaizɪç/ ❶ *Adj.* single-track ‹railway line›. ❷ *adv.* **eine ~ befahrene Strecke** a single-track line; **~ denken/ausgerichtet sein** (*fig.*) be narrow in one's outlook; be narrow-minded

**Eingleisigkeit** *die* **~** (*fig.*) narrowness

**ein|gliedern** ❶ *tr. V.* integrate (**in** + *Akk.* into); incorporate ‹village, company› (**in** + *Akk.* into); (*einordnen*) include (**in** + *Akk.* in). ❷ *refl. V.* **sich in etw.** (*Akk.*) **~:** fit into sth.

**Ein·gliederung** *die* ⇒ **eingliedern**: integration; incorporation; inclusion

**ein|graben** *unr. tr. V.* Ⓐ bury ‹box, treasure› (**in** + *Akk.* in); sink ‹pile, pipe› (**in** + *Akk.* into); **sich in etw.** (*Akk.*) **~** ‹claws› dig into sth.; **der Krebs grub sich in den Sand ein** the crab buried itself in the sand; Ⓑ (*einpflanzen*) plant ‹tree, bush› (**in** + *Akk.* in); Ⓒ (*eindrücken*) make, leave ‹imprint, hole› (**in** + *Akk.* in); Ⓓ (*geh.: einmeißeln*) engrave ‹inscription, epitaph, etc.› (**in** + *Akk.* on); **der Fluss hatte sich tief ins Tal eingegraben** (*fig.*) the river had carved a deep channel in the valley

**ein|gravieren** *tr. V.* engrave (**in** + *Akk.* on)

**ein|greifen** *unr. itr. V.* Ⓐ (*Einfluss nehmen*) intervene (**in** + *Akk.* in); **entschieden ~:** take decisive action; **das Eingreifen** intervention; Ⓑ (*Technik*) **in etw.** (*Akk.*) **~:** mesh with sth.

**eingreifend** *Adj.* drastic, radical ‹change›; far-reaching ‹consequences›

**Eingreif·truppe** *die* (*Milit.*) strike force

**ein|grenzen** *tr. V.* Ⓐ enclose; **von** *od.* **mit etw. eingegrenzt werden** be enclosed by sth.; Ⓑ (*fig.: beschränken*) limit, restrict ‹topic, discussion, etc.› (**auf** + *Akk.* to); restrict, circumscribe ‹freedom, rights, etc.›

**Ein·griff** *der* Ⓐ intervention (**in** + *Akk.* in); **ein staatlicher ~ in die Wirtschaft** state intervention in the economy; **ein ~ in jmds. Intimsphäre** (*Akk.*) an intrusion upon sb.'s privacy; **ein ~ in jmds. Rechte** an infringement of sb.'s rights; Ⓑ (*Med.*) operation; Ⓒ (*Schlitz*) fly

**ein|gruppieren** *tr. V.* **jmdn. in eine Gehaltsstufe ~:** place sb. on a step on the salary scale

**Ein·gruppierung** *die* grading

**ein|hacken** *itr. V.* **auf jmdn./aufeinander/etw. ~:** peck at sb./each other/sth.; **auf jmdn. ~** (*fig. ugs.*) pick on sb.

**ein|haken** ❶ *tr. V.* Ⓐ (*mit Haken befestigen*) fasten; Ⓑ **jmdn. ~:** take sb.'s arm; link arms with sb.; **die Demonstranten hakten sich ein** the demonstrators linked arms; **sie gingen eingehakt** they walked arm in arm. ❷ *refl. V.* **sich bei jmdm. ~:** link arms with sb.; take sb.'s arm. ❸ *itr. V.* (*ugs.*) butt in; **bei einem Punkt ~:** [butt in and] take up a point

**ein·halb·mal** *Wiederholungsz., Adv.* half; **~ so viel/groß/teuer** half as much/big/expensive

**Ein·halt** *der:* *in* **jmdm./einer Sache ~ gebieten** *od.* **tun** (*geh.*) stop *or* halt sb./sth.

**ein|halten** ❶ *unr. tr. V.* keep ‹appointment›; meet ‹deadline, commitments›; keep to ‹diet, speed limit, agreement›; observe ‹regulation›; **die Gesetze ~:** obey the laws; **den Kurs ~:** stay on course. ❷ *unr. itr. V.* (*geh.*) stop; (*vorübergehend*) pause; stop; **mit/in etw.** (*Dat.*) **~:** stop doing sth.

**Ein·haltung** *die* (*einer Verabredung*) keeping; (*einer Vorschrift*) observance; **die ~ der Diät/Geschwindigkeitsbegrenzung/Vereinbarung** keeping to the diet/speed limit/agreement; **die ~ eines Termins** meeting a deadline; **die ~ des Kurses** staying on course

**ein|hämmern** ❶ *itr. V.* **auf etw.** (*Akk.*) **~:** hammer on sth.; **auf jmdn. ~** (*fig.*) pummel *or* pound sb. ❷ *tr. V.* **jmdm. etw. ~:** hammer *or* drum sth. into sb. *or* sb.'s head

**ein|handeln** ❶ *tr. V.* **etw. für/gegen etw. ~:** barter sth. for sth. ❷ *refl. V.* Ⓐ (*ugs.: hinnehmen müssen*) **sich** (*Dat.*) **etw. ~:** let oneself in for sth. (*coll.*); Ⓑ (*ugs.: sich zuziehen*) catch, get ‹disease›

**einhändig** /ˈainhɛndɪç/ ❶ *Adj.* one-handed. ❷ *adv.* with [only] one hand

**ein|händigen** *tr. V.* **jmdm. etw. ~:** hand sth. over to sb.

**Einhand·segler** *der* single-handed yachtsman; (*Boot*) single-hander; single-handed dinghy/yacht

**Einhand·seglerin** *die* single-handed yachtswoman

**ein|hängen** ❶ *tr. V.* hang ‹door›; fit ‹window›; put down ‹receiver›. ❷ *itr. V.* (*Fernspr.: auflegen*) hang up. ❸ *refl. V.* **sich bei jmdm. ~:** take sb.'s arm; link arms with sb.; **sie gingen eingehängt** they walked arm in arm

**ein|hauchen** *tr. V.* (*dichter.*) **jmdm./einer Sache etw. ~:** breathe sth. into sb./sth.

**ein|hauen** ❶ *unr. tr. V.* Ⓐ (*zertrümmern*) smash [in] ‹window›; break down ‹door›; **jmdm. den Schädel ~** (*ugs.*) bash sb.'s head in (*coll.*); Ⓑ (*hineinschlagen*) drive in, knock in ‹nail›; Ⓒ (*einmeißeln*) carve. ❷ *unr. itr. V.* Ⓐ (*einschlagen*) **auf jmdn. ~:** lay into sb.; Ⓑ (*ugs.: essen*) stuff oneself (*coll.*)

**ein|heben** *unr. tr. V.* Ⓐ hang, fit ‹door›; fit ‹window›; put *or* lift ‹wagon, train› back on the rails; Ⓑ (*südd., österr.*) levy ‹tax, fine›; charge ‹sum, fee›

**Einhebung** *die;* **~, ~en** (*südd., österr.*) ⇒ **einheben** B: levying; charging

**ein|heften** *tr. V.* file

**ein|heilen** *itr. V.* (*Med.*) ‹graft› take

**ein·heimisch** *Adj.* native, indigenous ‹population, plant›; native ‹culture, traditions›; home *attrib.* ‹team›

**Einheimische** *der/die; adj. Dekl.* local

**ein|heimsen** /ˈainhaimzn̩/ *tr. V.* (*ugs.*) collect ‹medals, good marks›; rake in (*coll.*) ‹money, profits›

**Ein·heirat** *die* marriage (**in** + *Akk.* into); **durch ~ in die Familie** by marrying into the family

**ein|heiraten** *itr. V.* **in eine Familie ~:** marry into a family

**Einheit** *die;* **~, ~en** Ⓐ unity; Ⓑ (*Maß~, Milit.*) unit

*old spelling (see note on page 1707)

**einheitlich** ❶ *Adj.* Ⓐ (*in sich geschlossen*) unified; integrated; **der Film hatte keine ~e Handlung** there was no unity of action in the film; Ⓑ (*unterschiedslos*) uniform ‹dress›; standardized ‹education›; standard ‹procedure, practice›. ❷ *adv.* **~ gekleidet sein** be dressed the same; **die Prüfungsbestimmungen ~ regeln** standardize the examination regulations; **~ gestaltet sein** be designed along the same lines; **alle waren ~ ausgebildet** they had all had the same training

**Einheitlichkeit** *die;* ~ (*der Kleidung*) uniformity; (*der Ausbildung, des Verfahrens*) standard nature

**Einheits-:** **~essen** *das* institutional food; **~format** *das* standard size; **~front** *die* united front; **~gewerkschaft** *die* general trade union; **~kleidung** *die* uniform; **~kurz·schrift** *die* unified shorthand [system]; **~liste** *die* (*Politik*) unified list [of candidates]; single list [of candidates]; **~partei** *die* united party; **Sozialistische ~partei Deutschlands** (*DDR*) Socialist Unity Party of Germany; **~preis** *der* standard *or* fixed price; **~staat** *der* centralized state; **~tarif** *der* standard tariff; **~wert** *der* (*Steuerw.*) rateable value

**ein|heizen** ❶ *tr. V.* put on ‹stove, boiler›; heat ‹room›. ❷ *itr. V.* Ⓐ (*ugs.: zur Eile antreiben*) **jmdm. ~:** chivvy sb. along (*coll.*); Ⓑ (*ugs.: bedrängen*) **jmdm. ~:** go on at sb. (*coll.*)

**einhellig** /ˈainhɛlɪç/ ❶ *Adj.* unanimous. ❷ *adv.* unanimously

**Einhelligkeit** *die;* **~:** unanimity

**ein·her|gehen** *unr. itr. V.; mit sein* Ⓐ (*geh.: gemächlich gehen*) walk about *or* around; Ⓑ (*fig.: begleitet sein*) **mit etw. ~:** be accompanied by sth.

**einhöck[e]rig** *Adj.* one-humped

**ein|holen** ❶ *tr. V.* Ⓐ (*erreichen*) **jmdn./ein Fahrzeug ~:** catch up with sb./a vehicle; Ⓑ make up ‹arrears, time›; pull back ‹lead›; Ⓒ (*einziehen*) haul in, pull in ‹nets›; lower ‹flag›; Ⓓ (*ugs.: einkaufen*) buy, get ‹groceries›; Ⓔ (*erbitten*) ask for, seek ‹reference, advice›; make ‹enquiries›. ❷ *itr. V.* (*ugs.*) **~ gehen** go shopping

**Einhol-:** **~netz** *das* (*ugs.*) string bag; **~tasche** *die* (*ugs.*) shopping bag

**Ein·horn** *das* unicorn

**Einhufer** /ˈainhu:fɐ/ *der;* **~s, ~** (*Zool.*) soliped; solidungulate

**ein|hüllen** *tr. V.* **sich/jmdn. in etw.** (*Akk.*) **~:** wrap oneself/sb. up in sth.; **der Schnee/Nebel hatte die Gipfel eingehüllt** snow blanketed the peaks/the peaks were shrouded in mist

**ein·hundert** *Kardinalz.* ▶ 841 | a *or* one hundred; ⇒ *auch* **hundert**; **Hundert**

**einig** /ˈainɪç/ *Adj.* Ⓐ (*einmütig*) **sich** (*Dat.*) **~ sein** be agreed *or* in agreement; **sich** (*Dat.*) **~ werden** reach agreement; **mit jmdm. über etw.** (*Akk.*) **~ sein** be in agreement *or* agree with sb. about *or* on sth.; **mit jmdm. über etw.** (*Akk.*) **~ werden** reach agreement *or* agree with sb. about *or* on sth.; **in seiner Sache ~ gehen** agree *or* be agreed about *or* on a matter; Ⓑ (*geeint*) united ‹nation›

**einig...** /ˈainɪg.../ *Indefinitpron. u. unbest. Zahlwort* Ⓐ *Sg.* (*etwas*) some ‹effort, hope, courage›; **bei ~em guten Willen** with a measure of good will; **in ~er Entfernung** some distance away; Ⓑ *Pl.* (*mehrere*) some; **~e wenige** a few; **~e Hundert** several hundred; **~e Dreißig** thirty or so; Ⓒ *Sg. u. Pl.* (*beträchtlich*) **~er Ärger** quite a bit *or* quite a lot of trouble; **ich könnte dir über ihn ~es erzählen** I could tell you a thing *or* two about him; **dazu gehört schon ~es** it takes something to do that

**ein|igeln** /ˈain|i:gl̩n/ *refl. V.* Ⓐ (*sich einrollen*) curl up into a ball; Ⓑ (*sich zurückziehen*) hide oneself away; Ⓒ (*Milit.*) take up a position of all-round defence

***einige·mal** ⇒ **Mal**[1]

**einigen** ❶ *tr. V.* unite. ❷ *refl. V.* come to an agreement; reach an agreement; **sich auf jmdn./etw. ~:** agree on sb./sth.; **sich mit jmdm. [über etw.]** (*Akk.*) **~:** come to *or* reach an agreement with sb. [about sth.]

**einigermaßen** *Adv.* rather; somewhat; **~ zufrieden** fairly *or* reasonably satisfied; **Wie gehts dir? — ~:** How are you? — Not too bad; **das Essen war ~** (*ugs.*) the meal was OK (*coll.*) *or* all right

***einig|gehen** ⇒ **einig** A

**Einigkeit** *die;* ~ Ⓐ (*Einheit, Eintracht*) unity; Ⓑ (*Übereinstimmung*) agreement

**Einigung** *die;* **~, ~en** Ⓐ (*Übereinkunft*) agreement; **[über etw.** (*Akk.*)**] eine ~ erzielen** come to *or* reach [an] agreement [on sth.]; Ⓑ (*Vereinigung*) unification

**Einigungs-:** **~vertrag** *der* (*Politik*) unification treaty; **~versuch** *der* attempt to reach [an] agreement

**ein|impfen** *tr. V.* Ⓐ (*ugs.*) **jmdm. etw. [immer wieder] ~:** drum sth. into sb. [over and over again]; Ⓑ (*Med.: einspritzen*) **jmdm./einem Tier etw. ~:** inject sb./an animal with sth.

**ein|jagen** *tr. V.* **jmdm. Angst/einen Schrecken ~:** give sb. a fright

**ein·jährig** *Adj.* Ⓐ (*ein Jahr alt*) one-year-old *attrib.;* one year old *pred.;* (*ein Jahr dauernd*) **eine ~e Strafe** a one-year sentence; **eine ~e Abwesenheit** an absence of a *or* one year; a year's absence; **eine ~e Frist** a period of a *or* one year; Ⓑ (*Bot.*) annual

**Einjährige**[1] *das; adj. Dekl.* (*Schulw. veralt.*) *school-leaving examination taken after six years at secondary school*

**Einjährige**[2] *der/die; adj. Dekl.* one-year-old

**ein|kalkulieren** *tr. V.* Ⓐ (*einplanen*) take into account; Ⓑ (*mitberechnen*) take into account; include

**Ein·kammer·system** *das* (*Politik*) unicameral system

**ein|kapseln** ❶ *tr. V.* encapsulate. ❷ *refl. V.* encapsulate oneself; (*fig.*) withdraw into one's shell

**Einkaräter** /ˈainkarɛ:tɐ/ *der;* **~s, ~:** one-carat gem

**einkarätig** /ˈainkarɛ:tɪç/ *Adj.* one-carat

**ein|kassieren** *tr. V.* Ⓐ (*einnehmen*) collect; Ⓑ (*ugs.: entwenden*) pinch (*coll.*); nick (*Brit. coll.*); Ⓒ (*salopp: festnehmen*) pinch (*coll.*); nab (*coll.*)

**Ein·kauf** *der* Ⓐ (*Besorgung*) buying; **[einige] Einkäufe machen** *od.* **erledigen** do some shopping; Ⓑ (*eingekaufte Ware*) purchase; **ein guter/schlechter ~:** a good/bad buy; Ⓒ (*für ein Unternehmen*) buying; purchasing; **einen ~ tätigen** make a purchase; Ⓓ (*Kaufmannsspr.*) buying *or* purchasing department; **die Abteilung ~:** the buying *or* purchasing department; Ⓔ (*Sport*) (*von Spielern*) purchase; (*eingekaufter Spieler*) new signing; **der Verein tätigte einige Einkäufe** the club bought some players; Ⓕ (*einer Teilhaberschaft*) **der ~ in eine Firma** buying oneself into a firm

**ein|kaufen** ❶ *itr. V.* Ⓐ (*Einkäufe machen*) shop; **~ gehen** go shopping; do the *or* some shopping; **beim Bäcker/im Supermarkt ~:** shop at the baker's/the supermarket; **da hast du aber teuer eingekauft** you paid high prices there; Ⓑ (*Kaufmannsspr.*) do the buying *or* purchasing. ❷ *tr. V.* Ⓐ buy; purchase; buy in ‹stores, provisions›; **etw. billig/günstig ~:** buy sth. cheaply/at a favourable price; Ⓑ (*Sport*) buy ‹player›. ❸ *refl. V.* **sich in ein Seniorenheim ~:** buy a place in an old people's home; **sich in eine Firma ~:** buy oneself into a firm

**Ein·käufer** *der*, **Ein·käuferin** *die* ▶ 159 | (*Berufsbez.*) buyer; purchaser

**Einkaufs-:** **~abteilung** *die* ⇒ **Einkauf** D; **~bummel** *der* [leisurely] shopping expedition; **einen ~bummel machen** go on a shopping expedition; **~genossenschaft** *die* purchasing cooperative; **~korb** *der* shopping basket; (*im Geschäft*) [wire] basket; **~netz** *das* string bag; **~passage** *die* shopping arcade *or* (*Amer.*) mall; **~preis** *der* (*Kaufmannsspr.*) wholesale price; **~quelle** *die:* **eine gute ~quelle für etw. sein** a good place to buy sth.; **~tasche** *die* shopping bag; **~wagen** *der* [shopping] trolley (*Brit.*) *or* (*Amer.*) cart; **~zentrum** *das* shopping centre; (*Großmarkt*) hypermarket; **~zettel** *der* shopping list

**Einkehr** /ˈainke:ɐ̯/ *die;* ~ Ⓐ (*geh. veralt.*) stop; **~ halten** stop; make a stop; Ⓑ (*geh.: Sammlung*) **~ halten** take stock of oneself and one's attitudes; **eine Stunde der ~:** time for reflection and taking stock

**ein|kehren** *itr. V.; mit sein* Ⓐ stop; **in einem Wirtshaus ~:** stop at an inn; Ⓑ (*geh.: sich einstellen*) come

**ein|keilen** *tr. V.* **mein Auto ist eingekeilt** my car is boxed in; **die Fans keilten die Spieler ein** the fans mobbed the players; ⇒ *auch* **eingekeilt**

**ein·keim·blättrig** *Adj.* (*Bot.*) monocotyledonous

**ein|kellern** *tr. V.* store in the/a cellar

**ein|kerben** *tr. V.* cut *or* carve a notch/notches in; notch; **Zeichen in etw.** (*Akk.*) **~:** carve signs on sth.

**Einkerbung** *die;* **~, ~en** (*Kerbe*) notch

**ein|kerkern** *tr. V.* (*geh.*) incarcerate

**Einkerkerung** *die;* **~, ~en** incarceration

**ein|kesseln** *tr. V.* (*bes. Milit.*) surround; encircle

**Einkesselung** *die;* **~, ~en** (*bes. Milit.*) encirclement

**ein|kitten** *tr. V.* fix in with putty

**einklagbar** *Adj.* legally recoverable ‹debts›; **nicht alle Rechte sind ~:** not all rights can be obtained through legal action

**ein|klagen** *tr. V.* sue for ‹damages, compensation, etc.›; **etw. ~:** take legal action in order to gain *or* obtain sth.; **Schulden ~:** sue for the recovery of debts

**ein|klammern** *tr. V.* **etw. ~:** put sth. in brackets; bracket sth.

**Ein·klang** *der* Ⓐ (*Übereinstimmung*) harmony; **im ~ mit jmdm. sein** be in accord *or* agreement with sb.; **im** *od.* **in ~ mit etw. stehen** accord with sth.; **zwei Dinge in ~ [miteinander] bringen** harmonize two things; **die Hausarbeit mit einem Beruf in ~ bringen** combine housework and a career; Ⓑ (*Musik*) unison

**ein|klappen** *tr. V.* fold up; shut, close ‹knife›

**ein|klarieren** *tr. V.* (*Zollw., Seew.*) clear

**Ein·klassen·schule** *die* one-room school

**ein·klassig** *Adj.* (*Schulw.*) one-room ‹school›; **der ~e Unterricht** the teaching of children of different age groups in one class

**ein|kleben** *tr. V.* stick in; **Fotos ins Album ~:** stick photos into the album

**ein|kleiden** *tr. V.* Ⓐ **sich/jmdn. ~:** clothe oneself/sb.; **sich/jmdn. neu ~:** fit oneself/sb. out with a new set of clothes; **sich/jmdn. völlig neu ~:** buy oneself/sb. a complete new wardrobe; Ⓑ (*mit einer Uniform versehen*) kit out ‹soldier›; clothe ‹priest, nun›; Ⓒ (*fig.: umschreiben*) couch; **Ermahnungen in Fabeln ~:** couch warnings in the form of fables

**ein|klemmen** *tr. V.* Ⓐ (*quetschen*) catch; **jmdm./sich die Hand [in etw.** (*Dat.*)**] ~:** catch *or* trap sb.'s/one's hand [in sth.]; ⇒ *auch* **Schwanz** A; Ⓑ (*fest einfügen*) clamp

**ein|klicken** *refl. V.* (*DV*) **sich in eine Homepage/eine Webseite ~:** visit *or* access a home page/a Web site; **sich in das Netz ~:** go online

**ein|klinken** ❶ *tr. V.* latch ‹door›; engage ‹latch›. ❷ *itr. V.; mit sein* ‹door› click to *or* shut

**ein|klopfen** *tr. V.* knock in ‹nail›; pat in ‹cream›

**ein|kneifen** *unr. tr. V.* ⇒ **Schwanz** A

**ein|knicken** ❶ *tr. V.* bend; crease over ‹paper›; (*brechen*) snap; **mit eingeknickten Knien** with knees bent. ❷ *itr. V.; mit sein* bend; (*brechen*) snap; **sie knickte beim Gehen ein** she went over on her ankle while walking along

**ein|knöpfen** *tr. V.* **etw. in etw.** (*Akk.*) **~:** button sth. into sth.

**ein|kochen** ❶ *tr. V.* preserve ‹fruit, vegetables›. ❷ *itr. V.* thicken; **eine eingekochte Soße** a thickened sauce

**ein|kommen** *unr. itr. V.; mit sein* Ⓐ (*geh.: nachsuchen*) **[bei jmdm.] um etw. ~** (*geh.*)

apply [to sb.] for sth.; Ⓑ (*veralt.: eingehen*) ‹money› come in; Ⓒ (*Sport, Seemannsspr.*) come in; **als Ersterl/Letzter ~:** come in first/last

**Einkommen** *das;* **~s, ~:** income; **~ aus Grundbesitz/unselbstständiger Arbeit** income from property/from employment

**einkommens-, Einkommens-: ~grenze** *die* income limit; **~los** *Adj.* without an income *postpos.;* **~los sein** have no income; be without an income; **~schwach** *Adj.* low-income *attrib.;* **~stark** *Adj.* high-income *attrib.*

**Einkommen·steuer** *die* income tax

**Einkommensteuer·erklärung** *die* income tax return

**einkommensteuerpflichtig** /-pflıçtıç/ *Adj.* liable for income tax *postpos.*

**ein|köpfen** *tr., itr. V.* (*Fußball*) head in; **er köpfte zum 1:0 ein** he headed in to make it *or* the score 1-0

**ein|kreisen** *tr. V.* Ⓐ (*durch einen Kreis markieren*) **etw. ~:** put a circle round sth.; Ⓑ (*umzingeln*) surround ‹person›; surround, encircle ‹house, town, troops›; Ⓒ (*fig.: eingrenzen*) circumscribe ‹problem›

**Einkreisung** *die;* **~, ~en** encirclement

**ein|kriegen** (*ugs.*) ❶ *tr. V.* ⇒ **einholen** 1 A. ❷ *refl. V.* control oneself; **sie konnte sich vor Lachen nicht ~:** she couldn't stop laughing

**Einkünfte** /'ainkynftə/ *Pl.* income *sing.* (**aus** from); **feste ~:** a regular income

**ein|kuppeln** *itr. V.* (*Kfz-W.*) engage the clutch

**ein|laden[1]** *unr. tr. V.* load (**in** + *Akk.* into) ‹goods›

**ein|laden[2]** *unr. tr. V.* invite; **jmdn. zum Essen ~:** invite sb. for a meal; (*im Restaurant*) invite sb. out for a meal; **jmdn. in sein Landhaus/auf sein Boot ~:** invite sb. to one's country house/on to one's boat; **ich lade euch alle ein** this is on me; **sich ~** (*scherzh.*) invite oneself; **jmdn. auf ein Bier/einen Kaffee ~:** invite sb. for a beer/a coffee; **jmdn. zu sich nach Hause ~:** invite sb. over

**einladend** ❶ *Adj.* inviting ‹impression, atmosphere›; tempting, appetizing ‹meal›; **~e Worte** words of invitation. ❷ *adv.* invitingly

**Ein·ladung** *die* invitation; **einer ~** (*Dat.*) **folgen** accept an invitation

**Einladungs-: ~karte** *die* invitation [card]; **~schreiben** *das* [written] invitation

**Ein·lage** *die* Ⓐ (*in einem Brief*) enclosure; Ⓑ (*Kochk.*) *vegetables, meat balls, dumplings, etc. added to a clear soup;* **eine Brühe mit ~:** a clear soup with meat balls/dumpling *etc.;* Ⓒ (*Schuh~*) arch support; Ⓓ (*Einschiebsel*) **eine witzige ~:** a witty *or* humorous aside; **eine musikalische ~:** a musical interlude; Ⓔ (*eingelegte Verzierung*) inlay; Ⓕ (*Zahnmed.*) temporary filling; Ⓖ (*Finanzw.*) (*Guthaben*) deposit; (*Beteiligung*) investment; **die ~n bei den Banken** bank deposits; Ⓗ (*Schneiderei*) padding; (*Versteifung*) interfacing

**ein|lagern** ❶ *tr. V.* store; lay in ‹stores›. ❷ *refl. V.* **sich [in etw.** (*Akk.*)**] ~:** be deposited [in sth.]

**Ein·lagerung** *die* Ⓐ (*Aufbewahren*) storage; Ⓑ (*das Abgelagerte*) deposit

**ein|langen** *itr. V.; mit sein* (*österr.*) arrive

**Einlass, *Einlaß** /'ainlas/ *der;* **Einlasses, Einlässe** /'ainlɛsə/ Ⓐ admission, admittance (**in** + *Akk.* to); **sich** (*Dat.*) **~ verschaffen** gain admission *or* admittance; **~ fordern** demand entry *or* admission; **jmdm. ~ gewähren** grant sb. admission *or* admittance; Ⓑ (*veralt.: Eingang*) entrance

**ein|lassen** ❶ *unr. tr. V.* Ⓐ (*hereinlassen*) admit; let in; Ⓑ (*einfüllen*) run ‹water›; Ⓒ (*einpassen*) **etw. in etw.** (*Akk.*) **~:** set sth. into sth.
❷ *unr. refl. V.* Ⓐ (*meist abwertend*) **sich mit jmdm. ~:** get mixed up *or* involved with sb.; **sie lässt sich mit vielen Männern ein** she goes with lots of different men (*coll.*); Ⓑ **sich auf etw.** (*Akk.*) **~:** get involved in sth.; **sich auf einen Streit ~:** be drawn into *or* get involved in an argument; **auf dein Vorhaben lasse ich mich nicht ein** I don't want anything to do with your plan; Ⓒ (*Rechtsw.*) testify; **sich dahin gehend ~, dass ...** testify that ...; make a statement to the effect that ...

**Einlass·karte, *Einlaß·karte** *die* admission ticket

**Einlassung** *die;* **~, ~en** (*Rechtsw.*) testimony; statement; **nach eigenen ~en** according to his/her *etc.* own testimony

**Ein·lauf** *der* Ⓐ (*Med.*) enema; **jmdm. einen ~ machen** give sb. an enema; Ⓑ (*Sport: Passieren der Ziellinie*) finish; **beim ~:** at the finish; Ⓒ (*Sport: Beginn einer Rennphase*) **beim ~ in die Gerade/das Stadion** entering the straight/the stadium; Ⓓ (*Sport: Reihenfolge*) placings *pl.;* **es gab folgenden ~:** the placings were as follows

**ein|laufen** ❶ *unr. itr. V.; mit sein* Ⓐ (*Sport*) **ins Stadion ~:** run into *or* enter the stadium; **in die letzte Runde ~:** start the last lap; Ⓑ (*ankommen*) **der Zug/das Schiff läuft ein** the train/ship is coming in; **das Schiff läuft in den Hafen ein** the ship is coming into *or* entering port; Ⓒ (*kleiner werden*) ‹clothes› shrink; Ⓓ (*hineinfließen*) run in; Ⓔ (*eingehen*) ‹news, information› come in. ❷ *unr. tr. V.* Ⓐ wear in ‹shoes›; Ⓑ **jmdm. das Haus** *od.* **die Tür** *od.* **die Bude ~** (*ugs.*) pester sb. all the time. ❸ *unr. refl. V.* (*Sport*) warm up

**Einlauf·wette** *die* (*Pferdesport*) place bet

**ein|läuten** *tr. V.* ring in ‹Sunday, New Year›; **die letzte Runde ~** (*Sport*) ring the bell to signal *or* for the start of the last lap; (*Boxen*) ring the bell for the [start of the] last round

**ein|leben** *refl. V.* settle down; **sich an einem Ort ~:** settle down in a place; **sich in einem Haus ~:** settle in in a house; **sich gut ~:** settle down well

**Einlege·arbeit** *die* (*Kunsthandwerk*) inlaid work; (*Gegenstand*) piece of inlaid work

**ein|legen** *tr. V.* Ⓐ **etw. in etw.** (*Akk.*) **~:** put sth. in sth.; **einen Film in eine Kamera ~:** put *or* load a film into a camera; **den ersten Gang ~:** engage first gear; **einen schnelleren Gang** *od.* **ein schnelleres Tempo ~** (*fig.*) get a move on (*coll.*); Ⓑ (*Kochk.*) pickle; **eingelegte Zwiebeln/Heringe** pickled onions/herrings; Ⓒ (*Kunsthandwerk*) **in die Truhe waren Blumenmuster eingelegt** the chest had been inlaid with flower patterns; Ⓓ (*Friseurhandwerk*) set ‹hair›; **sich/jmdm. die Haare ~:** set one's/sb.'s hair; Ⓔ (*einschieben*) put in, insert ‹film extracts etc.›; put on ‹trains, buses›; **eine Pause ~:** take a break; Ⓕ (*geltend machen*) lodge ‹protest›; **sein Veto gegen etw. ~:** use one's veto against sth.; veto sth.; **ein gutes Wort für jmdn. ~:** put in a good word for sb.; ⇒ *auch* **Ehre** B

**Einleger** *der;* **~s, ~, Einlegerin** *die;* **~, ~nen** (*Bankw.*) depositor

**Einlege·sohle** *die* insole

**ein|leiten** *tr. V.* Ⓐ (*beginnen*) institute, start ‹search›; introduce, take ‹measures, steps›; open ‹negotiations, investigation, inquest›; induce ‹birth›; launch, open ‹campaign›; Ⓑ (*eröffnen*) introduce ‹chapter›; **der Roman leitete eine neue Epoche ein** the novel ushered in a new epoch; **einige ~de Worte sprechen** say a few words of introduction; make a few introductory remarks; Ⓒ (*hineinleiten*) lead ‹water› (**in** + *Akk.* into); discharge ‹effluent›

**Ein·leitung** *die* Ⓐ (*einleitender Teil*) introduction; **die ~ eines Aufsatzes/Buches** the introduction to an essay/book; Ⓑ (*einer Suche*) institution; (*von Maßnahmen*) introduction; (*einer Untersuchung, von Verhandlungen*) opening; (*einer Geburt*) induction; (*einer Kampagne*) launching; opening; Ⓒ (*Eröffnung*) **als** *od.* **zur ~ des Empfanges** to open *or* start the reception; **ein Feuerwerk bildete die ~:** the opening event was a firework display; Ⓓ **die ~ giftiger Abwässer in etw.** (*Akk.*) the discharge of poisonous effluents into sth.

**ein|lenken** ❶ *itr. V.* Ⓐ (*nachgeben*) give way; make concessions; **sein Einlenken führte zu einem Kompromiss** by giving way *or* making concessions he enabled a compromise to be reached; Ⓑ *mit sein* (*einbiegen*) **in eine Straße ~:** turn into a street. ❷ *tr. V.* steer ‹boat, rocket, etc.›

**ein|lesen** ❶ *unr. refl. V.* **sich in ein Buch ~:** get into a book. ❷ *unr. tr. V.* (*DV*) feed in; input; **etw. in den Speicher ~:** read sth. into the memory

**ein|leuchten** *tr. V.* **jmdm. ~:** be clear to sb.; **es leuchtet ihr nicht ein, dass sie es allein machen soll** she doesn't see why she should do it by herself; **das will mir nicht ~:** I don't see that

**ein·leuchtend** ❶ *Adj.* plausible. ❷ *adv.* plausibly

**ein|liefern** *tr. V.* **einen Brief bei der Post ~:** take a letter to the post office; **jmdn. ins Krankenhaus/Gefängnis ~:** take sb. to hospital/jail; **wir mussten unsere Großmutter ins Krankenhaus ~ [lassen]** we had to have our grandmother admitted to hospital

**Ein·lieferung** *die* admission (**in** + *Akk.* to); **die ~ eines Verurteilten [ins Gefängnis]** taking a convicted prisoner to jail; **er wehrte sich gegen seine ~ ins Krankenhaus** he fought against being admitted to hospital

**Einlieferungs·schein** *der* Ⓐ receipt; Ⓑ (*Postw.*) certificate of posting

**ein·liegend** *Adj.* (*Papierdt.*) enclosed; **~ übersenden wir Ihnen ...** please find enclosed ...

**Einlieger·wohnung** *die* ≈ granny flat

**ein|lochen** ❶ *tr. V.* (*salopp*) **jmdn. ~:** put sb. away (*coll.*); put sb. behind bars (*coll.*). ❷ *tr., itr. V.* (*Golf*) hole; (*Billard*) pot ‹ball›

**ein|loggen** *refl. V.* (*DV*) log in *or* on

**einlösbar** *Adj.* redeemable; **das Versprechen ist nicht ~:** the promise can't be kept

**ein|lösen** *tr. V.* Ⓐ cash ‹cheque›; cash [in] ‹token, voucher, bill of exchange›; redeem ‹pledge, pawned article›; **man wollte [mir] den Scheck nicht ~:** they wouldn't cash the cheque [for me]; Ⓑ (*geh.: erfüllen*) redeem ‹pledge›; **sein Wort ~:** keep one's word

**Ein·lösung** *die* (*von Schecks*) cashing; (*von Pfändern, Versprechen*) redemption

**ein|lullen** *tr. V.* (*ugs.*) **jmdn. ~:** lull sb. to sleep; (*fig.*) lull sb.'s suspicions

**ein|machen** *tr. V.* preserve ‹fruit, vegetables›; (*in Gläser*) bottle

**Einmach·glas** *das* preserving jar

**einmal** ❶ *Adv.* Ⓐ (*ein Mal*) once; **noch ~ so groß [wie]** twice as big [as]; **etw. noch ~ tun** do sth. again; **~ mehr** once more *or* again; **~ sagt er dies, ein andermal das** first he says one thing, then another; **~ ist keinmal** (*Spr.*) just once won't matter; it won't matter just this once; **auf ~:** all at once; suddenly; (*zugleich*) at once; Ⓑ /'-'-/ (*später*) some day; one day; (*früher*) once; **es war ~ ein König, der ...** once upon a time there was a king who ...
❷ *Partikel* Ⓐ **daran ist nun ~ nichts mehr zu ändern** there's nothing more that can be done about it; **nicht ~:** not even; **wieder ~:** yet again; **wir wollen die Sache erst ~ in Ruhe besprechen** let's discuss the matter quietly first; Ⓑ **alle ~ zuhören!** listen everybody!; **hör ~ auf zu reden!** stop talking, will you!

**Einmal·eins** *das;* **~:** [multiplication] tables *pl.;* **das kleine/große ~:** tables from 1 to 10/11 to 20; **das ~ der Kochkunst/Politik** (*fig.*) the fundamentals *pl.* of cookery/politics

**Einmal·handtuch** *das* disposable towel

**einmalig** ❶ *Adj.* Ⓐ unique ‹opportunity, chance›; one-off, single ‹payment, purchase›; Ⓑ (*hervorragend*) superb ‹film, book, play, etc.›; (*ugs.*) fantastic (*coll.*) ‹girl, woman›. ❷ *adv.* (*ugs.*) really fantastic *or* superb (*coll.*); **das Fest war ~ schön** the party was really superb *or* really fantastic (*coll.*)

**Einmaligkeit** *die;* **~:** uniqueness

**Ein·mann-: ~betrieb** *der* Ⓐ (*Firma*) one-man business; Ⓑ (*Arbeitsweise*) one-man

*old spelling (see note on page 1707)

operation; **~bus** *der* one-man bus; **~wagen** *der* one-man bus/tram (*Brit.*) *or* (*Amer.*) trolley

**Ein·mark·stück** *das* ▸337 one-mark piece

**Ein·marsch** *der* Ⓐ entry; **der ~ ins Stadion** the march into the stadium; Ⓑ (*Besetzung*) invasion (**in** + *Akk.* of)

**ein|marschieren** *itr. V.; mit sein* Ⓐ march in; **ins Stadion ~:** march into the stadium; Ⓑ (*gewaltsam besetzen*) **in ein Land ~:** march into *or* invade a country

**ein|massieren** *tr. V.* massage *or* rub in

**Einmaster** /ˈainmastɐ/ *der;* **~s, ~** (*Seemannsspr.*) single-master

**ein|mauern** *tr. V.* Ⓐ immure ‹prisoner, traitor›; wall in ‹relic, treasure›; Ⓑ (*ins Mauerwerk einfügen*) **etw. in die Wand** *usw.* **~:** set sth. into the wall *etc.*

**ein|meißeln** *tr. V.* **etw. in etw.** (*Akk.*) **~:** carve sth. into *or* on sth. [with a chisel]

**Ein·meter·brett** *das* one-metre board

**ein|mieten** *refl. V.* **sich in einer Villa ~:** rent a villa; **sich in einer Pension ~:** rent a room in a boarding house

**ein|mischen** ❶ *refl. V.* interfere (**in** + *Akk.* in); **wenn ich mich kurz ~ darf** if I may butt in for a moment. ❷ *tr. V.* mix in

**Ein·mischung** *die* interference (**in** + *Akk.* in); **verzeihen Sie meine ~:** excuse my butting in

**einmonatig** *Adj.* Ⓐ (*einen Monat alt*) one-month-old *attrib.;* Ⓑ (*einen Monat dauernd*) one-month *attrib.;* ⇒ *auch* **achtmonatig**

**ein·monatlich** ❶ *Adj.* monthly; ⇒ *auch* **achtmonatlich** 1. ❷ *adv.* monthly; once a month

**ein·motorig** *Adj.* single-engined

**ein|motten** *tr. V.* **etw. ~:** put sth. into mothballs; (*fig.*) mothball sth.

**ein|mumme[l]n** *tr. V.* (*ugs.*) wrap up; **sich [warm] ~:** wrap up *or* wrap oneself up [warmly]

**ein|münden** *itr. V.; auch mit sein* Ⓐ flow in; enter; **in einen Fluss ~:** flow into *or* enter a river; Ⓑ (*enden*) **in etw.** (*Akk.*) **~:** lead into sth.

**Ein·mündung** *die* Ⓐ **die ~ der Mosel in den Rhein** the confluence of the Rhine and the Moselle; **die ~ des Kanals in den Fluss** the point where the canal flows into the river; Ⓑ (*von Straßen*) **die ~ der Straße in die Hauptstraße/den Platz** the junction of the street and the main road/the point where the road comes out into the square

**einmütig** /ˈainmy:tɪç/ ❶ *Adj.* unanimous. ❷ *adv.* unanimously

**Einmütigkeit** *die;* **~:** unanimity (**über** + *Akk.* on)

**ein|nachten** *itr. V.* (*unpers.*) (*schweiz.*) get dark

**ein|nähen** *tr. V.* Ⓐ (*festnähen*) sew in; **etw. in etw.** (*Akk.*) **~:** sew sth. into sth.; Ⓑ (*enger nähen*) take in

**Einnahme** *die;* **~, ~en** Ⓐ income; (*Staats~*) (*Kassen~*) takings *pl.;* Ⓑ (*von Arzneimitteln*) taking; **wir empfehlen die ~ einer leichten Mahlzeit** it is advisable to take a light meal; **die ~ der Tabletten muss regelmäßig erfolgen** the tablets must be taken regularly; Ⓒ (*einer Stadt, Burg*) capture; taking; **die ~ Berlins** the capture *or* taking of Berlin

**Einnahme·quelle** *die* source of income; (*des Staates*) source of revenue

**ein|nässen** *tr., itr. V.* wet ‹bed›; **er nässt noch ein** he's still wetting the bed

**ein|nebeln** ❶ *tr. V.* shroud; blanket. ❷ *refl. V.* Ⓐ (*Milit.*) put up a smokescreen; Ⓑ (*unpers.*) **es hat sich eingenebelt** a mist has come down

**ein|nehmen** *unr. tr. V.* Ⓐ (*kassieren*) take; (*verdienen*) earn; **er hat nicht viel an Trinkgeld eingenommen** he didn't make much by way of tips; Ⓑ (*zu sich nehmen*) take ‹medicine, tablets›; **eine Mahlzeit ~** (*geh.*) take a meal; partake of a meal (*literary*); Ⓒ (*besetzen*) capture, take ‹town, fortress›; Ⓓ **seinen Platz ~:** take one's place; (*sich setzen*) take one's seat *or* place; **eine Haltung/einen Standpunkt ~** (*fig.*) take up *or* adopt an attitude/a position; **eine wichtige Stellung in der Kunst/Literatur ~** (*fig.*) occupy an important place in the artistic/literary world; Ⓔ (*ausfüllen*) take up ‹amount of room›; Ⓕ (*beeinflussen*) **jmdn. für sich ~:** win sb. over; **jmdn. gegen sich ~:** turn sb. against one; **gegen jmdn. eingenommen sein** be prejudiced against sb.; **von sich eingenommen sein** think a lot of oneself (*coll.*); be very taken with oneself

**einnehmend** *Adj.* winning ‹manner›; **ein ~es Wesen haben** (*scherzh.*) take everything one can get

**ein|nicken** *itr. V.; mit sein* (*ugs.*) nod off (*coll.*)

**ein|nisten** *refl. V.* Ⓐ (*meist abwertend: sich niederlassen*) **sich bei jmdm. ~:** park oneself on sb. (*coll.*); Ⓑ (*ein Nest bauen*) build a nest/their nests; nest; Ⓒ (*Med.*) **das befruchtete Ei nistet sich im Uterus ein** the fertilized ovum is implanted in the uterus

**Ein·öde** *die* barren *or* featureless waste; (*Einsamkeit*) isolation; **die weißen ~n Alaskas** the white wastes of Alaska

**Einöd·hof** *der* (*südd., österr.*) isolated farm

**ein|ölen** *tr. V.* Ⓐ (*mit Öl einreiben*) **sich/jmdn. ~:** put *or* rub oil on oneself/sb.; Ⓑ (*ölen*) oil

**ein|ordnen** ❶ *tr. V.* Ⓐ (*einfügen*) arrange; put in order; **etw. in Aktenordner ~:** sort sth. into files; file sth.; **Briefe in Fächer ~:** sort letters and place them in their correct pigeon-holes; Ⓑ (*klassifizieren*) classify; categorize, classify ‹writer, thinker, artist›. ❷ *refl. V.* Ⓐ (*Verkehrsw.*) get into the correct lane; **sich nach rechts/links ~:** get into the right-hand/left-hand lane; „~" 'get in lane'; Ⓑ (*sich einfügen*) **sich [in die Gemeinschaft] ~:** fit in[to the community]

**Ein·ordnung** *die* (*in Karteien usw.*) arranging; (*Klassifizierung*) classification

**ein|packen** ❶ *tr. V.* Ⓐ pack (**in** + *Akk.* in); (*einwickeln*) wrap [up]; Ⓑ (*ugs.: warm anziehen*) wrap up; **jmdn./sich warm/gut ~:** wrap sb./oneself up warmly. ❷ *itr. V.* (*ugs.*) **er kann ~:** he's had it (*coll.*); **pack ein!** (*hör auf!*) pack it in! (*coll.*); give it a rest! (*coll.*); (*verschwinde!*) get lost! (*coll.*)

**ein|parken** *tr., itr. V.* park

**Ein·parteien-:** one-party

**ein|passen** ❶ *tr. V.* fit; install; **etw. in etw.** (*Akk.*) **~:** fit sth. into sth. ❷ *refl. V.* fit in

**ein|pauken** *tr. V.* **etw. ~:** mug up (*Brit.*) *or* (*Amer.*) bone up on sth. (*coll.*); **jmdm. etw. ~:** drum *or* hammer sth. into sb.

**Einpeitscher** /ˈainpaitʃɐ/ *der;* **~s, ~, Einpeitscherin** *die;* **~, ~nen** Ⓐ (*Agitator*) rabble-rouser; Ⓑ (*Parl.*) whip

**ein|pendeln** ❶ *refl. V.* settle down; cease to fluctuate ❷ *itr. V.; mit sein* commute; **die aus dem Umland ~den Beschäftigten** the workers commuting in from the surrounding area

**Ein·pendler** *der* commuter; ⇒ *auch* **Auspendler**

**ein|pennen** *itr. V.; mit sein* (*salopp*) drop *or* doze off

**Ein·personen-: ~haushalt** *der* single-person household; **~stück** *das* (*Theater*) monodrama

**Ein·pfennig·stück** *das* ▸337 one-pfennig piece

**ein|pferchen** *tr. V.* Ⓐ (*zusammendrängen*) **eingepfercht stehen/sein** stand/be crammed *or* crushed together; Ⓑ pen in ‹animals›

**ein|pflanzen** *tr. V.* Ⓐ plant ‹flowers, shrubs, etc.›; **jmdm. einen Sinn für Gerechtigkeit ~** (*fig.*) implant in sb. a sense of justice; Ⓑ (*Med.*) implant; **jmdm. ein Organ ~:** implant an organ in[to] sb.

**ein|pfropfen** *tr. V.* graft (**in** + *Akk.* on)

**Ein·phasen-Wechselstrom** *der* (*Physik, Elektrot.*) single-phase current

**einphasig** *Adj.* (*Physik, Elektrot.*) single-phase

**ein|pinseln** *tr. V.* brush; paint ‹wound›

**ein|planen** *tr. V.* **etw. ~:** include sth. in one's plans; **diese Verzögerung war nicht eingeplant** we/they *etc.* didn't plan on this delay

**ein|pökeln** *tr. V.* (*Kochk.*) salt

**ein·polig** *Adj.* (*Physik, Elektrot.*) single-pole

**ein|prägen** ❶ *tr. V.* Ⓐ stamp (**in** + *Akk.* into, on); Ⓑ (*fig.*) **sich** (*Dat.*) **etw. ~:** memorize sth.; commit sth. to memory; **jmdm. ~, pünktlich zu sein** impress on sb. the importance of being punctual. ❷ *refl. V.* **das prägte sich ihm [für immer] ein** it made an [indelible] impression on him; **Werbetexte prägen sich einem leicht ein** advertising slogans are catchy

**einprägsam** ❶ *Adj.* easily remembered; catchy, easily remembered ‹tune, melody, slogan›. ❷ *adv.* **er hat das sehr ~ dargelegt** he expounded it in a way that made it easy to remember

**ein|prasseln** *itr. V.; mit sein* **auf jmdn./etw. ~:** rain down on sb./sth.; **die Fragen der Zuhörer prasselten auf ihn ein** the audience showered him with questions

**ein|pressen** *tr. V.* press in; **etw. in etw.** (*Akk.*) **~:** press sth. into sth.

**ein|programmieren** *tr. V.* (*DV*) input ‹data, figures, etc.›; programme in ‹function, property›

**ein·prozentig** *Adj.* one per cent *attrib.;* of one per cent *postpos.*

**ein|prügeln** ❶ *itr. V.* **auf jmdn./ein Tier ~:** beat sb./an animal. ❷ *tr. V.* **jmdm. etw. ~** (*fig.*) drub *or* beat sth. into sb.

**ein|pudern** *tr. V.* powder; **sich** (*Dat.*) **das Gesicht ~:** powder one's face

**ein|quartieren** ❶ *tr. V.* quarter, billet ‹troops›; **die Opfer wurden vorläufig in Hotels einquartiert** the victims were given temporary accommodation in hotels; **sie quartierten ihre Freunde bei ihren Eltern ein** they put their friends up with their parents. ❷ *refl. V.* **sich bei jmdm. ~** (*Milit.*) be quartered with *or* billeted on sb.; **sich auf einem Bauernhof/bei seinen Eltern ~:** stay on a farm/with one's parents

**Einquartierung** *die;* **~, ~en** Ⓐ (*Milit.*) quartering; billeting; Ⓑ **[sechs Mann] ~ haben** have [six] soldiers billeted on one

**ein|quetschen** *tr. V.* ⇒ **einklemmen**

**Ein·rad** *das* unicycle

**einräd[e]rig** *Adj.* one-wheeled

**ein|rahmen** *tr. V.* frame; **sich** (*Dat.*) **etw. ~ lassen** have sth. framed; **er saß da, von zwei Damen eingerahmt** (*fig.*) he sat flanked by two ladies; **den Brief solltest du dir ~ lassen** (*iron.*) you ought to *or* should get that letter framed

**ein|rammen** *tr. V.* Ⓐ ram in; **etw. in den Boden ~:** ram sth. into the ground; Ⓑ (*zertrümmern*) smash up ‹car›; break *or* batter down ‹door›

**ein|rasten** *itr. V.; mit sein* (*Technik*) engage

**ein|räuchern** *tr. V.* envelope in smoke; **ein Zimmer ~:** fill a room with smoke; **die Gardinen ~:** get *or* make the curtains smoky; **jmdn. mit Tränengas ~:** use tear gas against sb.

**ein|räumen** *tr. V.* Ⓐ (*einordnen*) put away; **etw. in etw.** (*Akk.*) **~:** put sth. away in sth.; **Bücher wieder [ins Regal] ~:** put books back [on the shelf]; Ⓑ (*füllen*) **er musste seinen Schrank ~:** he had to put his things away in his cupboard; **das Zimmer wieder ~:** put everything *or* all the furniture back into the room; Ⓒ (*zugestehen*) admit; concede; **jmdm. etw. ~:** admit sth. to sb.; **jmdm. einen Platz ~:** reserve sb. a seat; **jmdm. ein Recht/einen Kredit ~:** give *or* grant sb. a right/loan; **jmdm. das Recht ~, etw. zu tun** give *or* grant sb. the right to do sth.; Ⓓ (*Sprachw.*) **~de Konjunktion** concessive conjunction

**ein|rechnen** *tr. V.* include, take account of ‹costs etc.›; **nicht eingerechnet die Trinkgelder** not including the tips

**ein|reden** ❶ *tr. V.* **jmdm. etw. ~:** talk sb. into believing sth.; **er redete ihr ein, es zu kaufen** he persuaded her to buy it; he talked her into buying it; **sich** (*Dat.*) **~, dass ...**

e

persuade oneself that...; **das redest du dir bloß ein** you're just imagining it. ❷ *itr. V.* **auf jmdn. ~:** talk insistently to sb.; **laut/beruhigend auf jmdn. ~:** keep talking to sb. loudly/soothingly

**ein|regnen** ❶ *refl. V.* (*unpers.*) **es hat sich eingeregnet** it's begun to rain steadily. ❷ *itr. V.; mit sein* get soaked [to the skin]

**ein|regulieren** *tr. V.* (*Technik*) set ‹temperature› (**auf** + *Akk.* at); **ein falsch einreguliertes Hörgerät** a wrongly adjusted hearing aid

**ein|reiben** *unr. tr. V.* **Salbe [in die Haut] ~:** rub ointment in[to one's skin]; **jmdm. den Rücken ~:** rub lotion/ointment *etc.* into sb.'s back; **sich** (*Dat.*) **den Nacken/das Gesicht mit etw. ~:** rub sth. into one's neck/face

**ein|reichen** *tr. V.* [A] submit ‹application›; hand in, submit ‹piece of work, dissertation, thesis›; lodge, make ‹complaint›; tender ‹resignation›; [B] (*jur.*) file ‹suit, petition for divorce›

**ein|reihen** ❶ *refl. V.* **sich in etw.** (*Akk.*) **~:** join sth. ❷ *tr. V.* **jmdn. in eine Kategorie/Gruppe ~:** place sb. in a category/group; **sich in eine Gruppe** *usw.* **~:** become part of a group *etc.*

**Einreiher** *der;* **~s, ~:** single-breasted suit/jacket

**einreihig** /ˈainraiıç/ ❶ *Adj.* single-breasted ‹suit›. ❷ *adv.* in a single row *or* line; **ein ~ geknöpfter Mantel** a single-breasted overcoat

**Ein·reise** *die* entry; **bei der ~ nach Frankreich/in die ČSSR** on entry into France/Czechoslovakia; **jmdm. die ~ verweigern** refuse sb. entry

**Einreise·erlaubnis** *die* entry permit

**ein|reisen** *itr. V.; mit sein* enter; **nach Schweden ~:** enter Sweden

**Einreise-: ~verbot** *das:* **jmdm. ~verbot erteilen** refuse sb. entry; **~visum** *das* entry visa

**ein|reißen** ❶ *unr. tr. V.* [A] (*abreißen*) pull *or* tear down ‹building›; [B] (*einen Riss machen in*) tear; rip; [C] **sich** (*Dat.*) **einen Dorn ~:** prick oneself on a thorn; **sich** (*Dat.*) **einen Splitter ~:** get a splinter in one's hand/foot *etc.* ❷ *unr. itr. V.; mit sein* [A] (*einen Riss bekommen*) tear; rip; [B] (*ugs.: sich verbreiten*) become a habit; **etw. ~ lassen** allow sth. to *or* let sth. become a habit; **eine Gewohnheit ~ lassen** allow a habit to catch on (*coll.*) *or* spread

**Einreiß·haken** *der* ceiling hook

**ein|reiten** ❶ *unr. itr. V.; mit sein* ride in; **in etw.** (*Akk.*) **~:** ride into sth.. ❷ *unr. refl. V.* warm up; **sich mit einem Pferd ~:** get used to riding a horse

**ein|renken** *tr. V.* [A] (*Med.*) set; reduce (*Med.*); **jmdm. den Fuß/Arm [wieder] ~:** [re]set sb.'s foot/arm; [B] (*ugs.: bereinigen*) **etw. ~:** sort *or* straighten sth. out; **das renkt sich ein** that will sort *or* straighten itself out

**ein|rennen** ❶ *unr. tr. V.* (*aufbrechen*) break down ‹door›; **jmdm. [wegen etw.] das Haus** *od.* **die Bude ~** (*ugs.*) pester sb. all the time [for sth.]; ⇨ *auch* **offen**. ❷ *unr. refl. V.* (*ugs.: sich verletzen*) **sich** (*Dat.*) **den Kopf an etw.** (*Dat.*) **~:** bash *or* bang one's head on *or* against sth.

**ein|richten** ❶ *refl. V.* [A] **sich gemütlich/schön ~:** furnish one's home comfortably/beautifully; **sich an einem Ort häuslich ~:** make oneself at home in a place; [B] (*auskommen*) **sich [mit seinem Gehalt] ~:** get by *or* make ends meet [on one's salary]; [C] (*sich vorbereiten*) **sich auf jmdn./etw. ~:** prepare for sb./sth.; **darauf war sie nicht eingerichtet** she was not prepared for that. ❷ *tr. V.* [A] furnish ‹flat, house›; fit out ‹shop, restaurant, hobby room›; equip ‹laboratory›; [B] (*ermöglichen*) arrange; **das lässt sich ~:** that can be arranged; **es so ~, dass ...** arrange things so that ...; [C] (*eröffnen*) open ‹branch, shop›; set up ‹advisory centre›; start, set up ‹business›; **sich** (*Dat.*) **ein Geschäft/eine Modeboutique ~:** start a business/open a fashion boutique; [D] (*Med.*) set; reduce (*Med.*); [E] (*umformen*) arrange ‹piece of music›; adapt ‹play, novel, etc.›; [F] (*Math.*) **eine gemischte Zahl ~:** reduce a mixed number

**Ein·richter** *der,* **Ein·richterin** *die* fitter

**Ein·richtung** *die* [A] (*das Einrichten*) (*einer Wohnung*) furnishing; (*eines Musikstücks*) arrangement; (*eines Theaterstücks*) adaptation; (*Med.*) setting; reducing (*Med.*); [B] (*Mobiliar*) furnishings *pl.;* [C] (*Geräte*) **~en** (*Geschäfts~*) fittings; (*Labor~*) equipment *sing.;* **sanitäre ~en** sanitary facilities; sanitation *sing.;* [D] (*Institution, Gewohnheit*) institution; **öffentliche/staatliche ~en** public/state institutions

**Einrichtungs-: ~gegen·stand** *der* piece of furniture; **~haus** *das* [large] furniture store

**ein|ritzen** *tr. V.* carve; **seinen Namen in einen Stamm ~:** carve one's name on a tree trunk

**ein|rollen** ❶ *tr. V.* roll up ‹carpet etc.›; **sich/jmdm. die Haare ~:** put one's/sb.'s hair in curlers *or* rollers; **sich ~** ‹hedgehog, cat› curl up. ❷ *itr. V.; mit sein* [A] roll in; **der Zug rollt ein** the train is coming in

**ein|rosten** *itr. V.; mit sein* go rusty; rust up; **er ist/seine Knochen sind eingerostet** (*fig.*) his joints have stiffened up

**ein|rücken** ❶ *itr. V.; mit sein* [A] (*Milit.: einmarschieren*) move in; **in ein Land ~:** march into a country; **wieder in die Kaserne ~:** return to barracks; [B] (*Milit. veralt.: eingezogen werden*) report for duty. ❷ *tr. V.* [A] (*Schriftw.*) indent ‹line, heading, etc.›; [B] (*Zeitungsw.*) insert ‹advertisement, article›

**ein|rühren** *tr. V.* stir in; **etw. in etw.** (*Akk.*) **~:** stir sth. into sth.

**ein|rüsten** *tr. V.* (*Bauw.*) put up *or* erect scaffolding around ‹building›

**eins** /ains/ ❶ *Kardinalz.* ▶76|, ▶752|, ▶841| one; **es ist ~:** it is one o'clock; **Punkt ~:** on the stroke of one; at one o'clock precisely; **halb ~:** half past twelve; **Viertel nach/vor ~:** [a] quarter past/to one; **gegen/vor ~:** around/before one; **~ zu null** one-nil; **~ zu ~:** one all; **~ zu null für dich!** (*ugs.*) that's one up to you!; **die Nummer ~ sein** (*fig.*) be number one; „**~, zwei, drei!**" 'ready, steady, go'; **... und ~, zwei, drei, weg war er** and in a jiffy (*coll.*) *or* in no time he was gone; **~ a,** (*Kaufmannsspr. meist*) **1 a** top-quality; **seine Arbeit ~ a erledigen** (*ugs.*) do a first-class job; ⇨ *auch* **acht**[1]. ❷ *Adj.* **mir ist alles ~:** it's all the same *or* all one to me; **den Schrei hören und zu Hilfe eilen war für sie ~:** the moment she heard the cry, she was hurrying to help; **mit jmdm. über etw.** (*Akk.*) **~ sein/werden** be in/reach agreement with sb. about *or* on sth.; **sich mit jmdm. ~ wissen/fühlen** be/feel at one with sb. ❸ *Indefinitpron.* ⇨ **ein**[1] 3 B, C

**Eins** *die;* **~, ~en** [A] one; **wie eine ~ stehen** (*ugs.*) stand as straight as a ramrod; **sie kocht/spielt Klavier wie eine ~** (*ugs.*) she's a fantastic cook/piano player (*coll.*); ⇨ *auch* **Acht**[1] A, E, G; [B] (*Schulnote*) one; A; ⇨ *auch* **Zwei** B

**Ein·saat** *die* sowing

**ein|sacken**[1] *tr. V.* [A] (*in Säcke füllen*) **etw. ~:** put sth. into sacks; [B] (*ugs.: einstecken*) grab; pocket ‹money›

**ein|sacken**[2] *itr. V.; mit sein* sink in; ‹building, pavement› subside

**ein|sagen** *itr. V.* (*südd., österr.*) **er sagte ihr ein** he whispered the answer to her

**ein|sägen** *tr. V.* **etw. ~:** saw into sth.

**ein|salben** *tr. V.* **den Arm ~:** rub ointment on *or* into one's arm; **sich/jmdn. ~:** rub ointment on [oneself]/rub ointment on sb.

**ein|salzen** *tr. V.* salt ‹fish, meat›

**einsam** *Adj.* [A] (*verlassen*) lonely ‹person, decision›; **~ leben** live a lonely *or* solitary life; **sich ~ fühlen** feel lonely; [B] (*einzeln*) solitary ‹rock, tree, wanderer›; **~e Spitzenklasse sein** (*ugs.*) be in a class of its/his/her own; [C] (*abgelegen*) isolated; **~ liegen** be situated miles from anywhere; [D] (*menschenleer*) empty; deserted; **~ und verlassen [da]liegen** lie [there] lonely and deserted

**Einsamkeit** *die;* **~, ~en** [A] (*Verlassenheit*) loneliness; [B] (*Alleinsein*) solitude; [C] (*Abgeschiedenheit*) isolation

**ein|sammeln** *tr. V.* [A] (*auflesen*) pick up; gather up; **die Kinder/Betrunkene ~** (*ugs.*) pick up *or* collect the children/pick up drunks; [B] (*sich aushändigen lassen*) collect in; collect ‹tickets›

**ein|sargen** *tr. V.* **einen Toten ~:** put the body of a dead person into a coffin; **lass dich doch ~!** (*salopp*) [go and] get stuffed! (*Brit. sl.*); go to hell! (*sl.*)

**Ein·satz** *der* [A] (*eingesetztes Teil*) (*in Tischdecke, Kopfkissen usw.*) inset; (*in Kochtopf, Nähkasten usw.*) compartment; [B] (*eingesetzter Betrag*) stake; **den ~ erhöhen** raise the stakes *pl.;* [C] (*das Einsetzen*) (*von Maschinen, Gewehren, Wasserwerfern, Schlagstöcken*) use; (*von Truppen*) deployment; **unter ~ seines Lebens** at the risk of his life; **zum ~ kommen** *od.* **gelangen** (*Papierdt.*) ‹machine› come into operation; ‹police, troops› be brought into action, be used; ‹reserve player› be brought on *or* used; **jmdn./etw. zum ~ bringen** use sb./sth.; [D] (*Engagement*) commitment; dedication; **~ zeigen** show commitment *or* dedication; **der ~ hat sich gelohnt** the effort was worthwhile; [E] (*Milit.*) **im ~ sein/fallen** be in action *or* on active service/die in action; **einen ~ fliegen** (*Luftwaffe*) fly a mission; [F] (*Musik*) **der ~ der Instrumente** the entry of the instruments; **der ~ der Violinen kam zu spät** the violins came in too late

**einsatz-, Einsatz-: ~befehl** *der* [A] (*Befehl zum ~*) order to go into action; [B] (*Verantwortung*) **den ~befehl haben** have operational command; **~bereit** *Adj.* [A] (*bereit, sich einzusetzen*) ‹worker› ready to work; ‹athlete› fit to compete; [B] (*bereit, eingesetzt zu werden*) ready for use; [C] (*Milit.*) combat-ready *attrib.;* ready for action *postpos.;* **~bereitschaft** *die* ⇨ **~bereit**: readiness to work; fitness to compete; readiness for use; combat-readiness; readiness for action; **~fähig** *Adj.* [A] (*fähig, sich einzusetzen*) ‹athlete› fit to compete; [B] (*verfügbar*) fit ‹player›; ‹washing machine etc.› in working order; **~freudig** *Adj.* enthusiastic; **~gruppe** *die,* **~kommando** *das* task force; **~leiter** *der,* **~leiterin** *die* [A] (*des ~kommandos*) head of operations; [B] (*des ~es*) leader of the task force; **~plan** *der* plan of action; **~wagen** *der* (*der Polizei*) police car; (*der Feuerwehr*) fire engine; (*Notarztwagen*) ambulance; (*der Straßenbahn*) relief; **~zentrale** *die* operations centre

**ein|sauen** *tr. V.* (*derb*) **sich/etw. ~:** get oneself/sth. covered in muck (*coll.*)

**ein|saugen** *unr.* (*auch regelm.*) *tr. V.* suck in ‹air, liquid›; breathe [in] ‹fresh air›; **die Bienen saugen den Nektar ein** the bees suck the nectar

**ein|säumen** *tr. V.* [A] (*Schneiderei*) hem; [B] (*einfassen*) edge ‹flower bed, vegetable-patch›; surround ‹property›

**ein|schalten** ❶ *tr. V.* [A] switch *or* turn on ‹radio, TV, electricity, etc.›; **einen anderen Sender ~:** switch *or* tune to another station; [B] (*fig.: beteiligen*) call in ‹press, police, expert, etc.›; **jmdn. in die Verhandlungen ~:** bring sb. into the negotiations; [C] (*einfügen*) take ‹break›. ❷ *refl. V.* [A] switch [itself] on; come on; [B] (*eingreifen*) intervene (**in** + *Akk.* in)

**Einschalt·quote** *die* (*Rundf.*) listening figures *pl.;* (*Ferns.*) viewing figures *pl.*

**Ein·schaltung** *die* [A] (*Einschalten*) switching *or* turning on; [B] (*Beteiligung*) calling in; [C] (*Sprachw.*) parenthesis

**ein|schärfen** *tr. V.* **jmdm. etw. ~:** impress sth. [up]on sb.; **jmdm. ~, etw. zu tun** impress upon sb. that he/she must do sth.

**ein|scharren** *tr. V.* (*vergraben*) bury; (*lieblos begraben*) **jmdn. ~:** bury sb. hurriedly

**ein|schätzen** *tr. V.* [A] judge ‹person›; assess ‹situation, income, damages›; (*schätzen*) estimate; **jmdn./eine Situation falsch ~:** misjudge sb./a situation; **jmdn./eine Leistung hoch/niedrig ~:** think highly/not think highly of sb./an achievement; **wie ich die**

*old spelling (see note on page 1707)

**Lage einschätze** as I see the situation; Ⓑ (*Steuerw.*) assess

**Ein·schätzung** *die* Ⓐ ⇒ **einschätzen**: judging; assessment; estimation; **nach seiner/meiner ~:** in my estimation *or* judgement; Ⓑ (*Steuerw.*) assessment

**ein|schäumen** *tr. V.* Ⓐ (*mit Schaum bedecken*) lather; **sich/jmdm. die Haare ~:** lather one's/sb.'s hair; Ⓑ (*mit Schaumstoff umhüllen*) **etw. ~:** wrap sth. in foam [material]

**ein|schenken** *tr., itr. V.* Ⓐ (*eingießen*) pour [out]; **jmdm. etw. ~:** pour out sth. for sb.; Ⓑ (*füllen*) fill [up] ‹glass, cup›; **er schenkte immer wieder ein** he kept on filling up my glass/cup/our/their *etc.* glasses/cups

**ein|scheren** *itr. V.; mit sein* (*Verkehrsw.*) **in** *od.* **auf eine Fahrspur ~:** get *or* move into a lane; **nach links/rechts ~:** get *or* move into the left-hand/right-hand lane; **in eine Lücke ~:** move into a space; **er scherte vor mir ein** he cut in in front of me

**ein|schicken** *tr. V.* send in; **etw. zur Reparatur ~:** send sth. [in] to be repaired

**ein|schieben** *unr. tr. V.* Ⓐ (*hineinschieben*) push in; **den Ball zum 1:0 ~** (*Fußballjargon*) put the ball away to make it *or* the score 1-0; Ⓑ (*einfügen*) put in; insert; put on ‹trains, buses›; fit in ‹client, patient›; **etw. in etw.** (*Akk.*) **~:** put *or* insert sth. into sth.

**Ein·schienen·bahn** *die* monorail

**ein|schießen** ❶ *unr. tr. V.* Ⓐ (*zerstören*) demolish ‹wall, building› by gunfire; **das Fenster [mit einem Ball] ~** (*fig.*) smash the window [with a ball]; Ⓑ (*treffsicher machen*) try out, test ‹gun etc.›; Ⓒ (*hineinschießen*) insert ‹dowel, plug›; Ⓓ (*Sport*) kick in ‹ball›; **den Ball zum 1 : 1 ~:** shoot a goal to make it *or* the score 1-1; Ⓔ (*einzahlen*) inject ‹capital, cash, etc.› (**in** + *Akk.* into); Ⓕ (*Druckw.*) interleave; insert; Ⓖ (*Weberei*) **den Faden ~:** shoot the weft; pick. ❷ *unr. refl. V.* Ⓐ (*treffsicher werden*) **sich [auf etw.** (*Akk.*)**] ~:** find *or* get the range [of sth.]; Ⓑ (*Sport*) find *or* get the range; Ⓒ (*angreifen*) **sich [immer mehr] auf jmdn./etw. ~:** make sb./sth. the target of [increasingly frequent] attacks

**ein|schiffen** ❶ *tr. V.* embark ‹passengers›; load ‹cargo›. ❷ *refl. V.* embark (**nach** for)

**Einschiffung** *die;* ~, **~en** ⇒ **einschiffen**: embarkation; loading

**Einschiffungs·hafen** *der* port of embarkation

**ein|schlafen** *unr. itr. V.; mit sein* Ⓐ fall asleep; go to sleep; **über der Zeitung ~:** fall asleep over the paper; **beim Fernsehen ~:** fall asleep while watching television *or* in front of the television; **ich kann nicht ~:** I can't get to sleep; Ⓑ (*verhüll.: sterben*) pass away (*euphem.*); Ⓒ (*gefühllos werden*) go to sleep; **mein Bein ist eingeschlafen, mir ist das Bein eingeschlafen** my leg has gone to sleep; Ⓓ (*aufhören*) peter out

**ein|schläfern** *tr. V.* Ⓐ (*in Schlaf versetzen*) **jmdn. ~:** send sb. to sleep; Ⓑ (*betäuben*) **jmdn. ~:** put sb. to sleep; Ⓒ (*schmerzlos töten*) **ein Tier ~:** put an animal to sleep; Ⓓ (*beruhigen*) soothe, salve ‹conscience›; dull ‹critical faculties›

**einschläfernd** ❶ *Adj.* soporific. ❷ *adv.* **~ wirken** have a soporific effect

**Einschläferung** *die;* ~, **~en** Ⓐ (*Betäubung*) anaesthesia *no art.;* Ⓑ (*Tötung*) **der Tierarzt empfahl die ~:** the vet recommended putting the animal to sleep; Ⓒ (*Beruhigung*) ⇒ **einschläfern** D: soothing; salving; dulling

**Ein·schlag** *der* Ⓐ (*Einschlagen*) **wir sahen den ~ des Blitzes/der Bomben** we saw the lightning strike/the bombs land; Ⓑ (*Stelle*) **wir sahen die Einschläge der Kugeln/der Bomben** we saw the bullet holes/where the bombs had fallen *or* landed; Ⓒ (*Anteil*) element; **eine Familie mit südländischem ~:** a family with southern blood in it; **mit nihilistischem ~:** with an element of nihilism; Ⓓ (*Kfz-W.*) (*des Lenkrads*) turning; (*der Räder*) lock; Ⓔ (*Forstw.*) felling

**ein|schlagen** ❶ *unr. tr. V.* Ⓐ (*hin~*) knock in; hammer in; **etw. in etw.** (*Akk.*) **~:** knock *or* hammer sth. into sth.; Ⓑ (*zertrümmern*) smash [in]; Ⓒ (*einwickeln*) wrap up ‹present›; cover ‹book›; **ein Kind in eine warme Decke ~:** wrap a child up in a warm blanket; Ⓓ (*wählen*) take ‹route, direction›; take up ‹career›; adopt ‹policy›; **einen Kurs ~:** follow a course; (*fig.*) follow *or* pursue a course; **einen anderen Kurs ~** (*auch fig.*) change *or* alter course; Ⓔ (*Kfz-W.*) turn ‹[steering] wheel›; Ⓕ (*Schneiderei: umlegen*) take in; take up ‹trousers›; Ⓖ (*Forstw.*) fell ‹trees›. ❷ *unr. itr. V.* Ⓐ (*auftreffen*) ‹bomb› land; ‹lightning› strike; **bei uns hat es eingeschlagen** our house was struck by lightning; Ⓑ (*einprügeln*) **auf jmdn./etw. ~:** rain blows on *or* beat sb./sth.; Ⓒ (*durch Händedruck*) shake [hands] on it; (*fig.*) accept; **schlag ein!** shake on it!; Ⓓ (*Kfz-W.*) **nach links/rechts ~:** steer to the left/right; Ⓔ (*sich erfolgreich entwickeln*) come along *or* on well; Ⓕ (*Erfolg haben*) be a success

**einschlägig** /ˈainʃlɛːgɪç/ ❶ *Adj.* specialist ‹journal, shop›; relevant ‹literature, passage›. ❷ *adv.* **er ist ~ vorbestraft** he has previous convictions for a similar offence/similar offences; **der ~ vorbestrafte Angeklagte** the accused, who has/had previous convictions for a similar offence/similar offences

**ein|schleichen** *unr. refl. V.* steal *or* sneak *or* creep in; (*fig.*) creep in; **sich in etw.** (*Akk.*) **~:** steal *or* sneak *or* creep into sth.; **der Verdacht schleicht sich ein, dass ...** one has a sneaking suspicion that ...

**ein|schleifen** ❶ *unr. tr. V.* Ⓐ (*eingraben*) cut in; **etw. in etw.** (*Akk.*) **~:** cut sth. into sth.; Ⓑ (*Technik: einpassen*) grind in. ❷ *unr. refl. V.* (*bes. Psych.*) become established

**ein|schleppen** *tr. V.* tow in ‹ship, yacht, etc.›; bring in, introduce ‹disease, pest›; **Typhus in ein Land ~:** bring *or* introduce typhus into a country

**ein|schleusen** *tr. V.* smuggle in; **Agenten in ein Land/eine Terroristengruppe ~:** infiltrate agents into a country/a terrorist group

**ein|schließen** *unr. tr. V.* Ⓐ **etw. in etw.** (*Dat.*) **~:** lock sth. up [in sth.]; **jmdn./sich ~:** lock sb./oneself in; **jmdn. in ein[em] Zimmer ~:** lock sb. [up] in a room; **sich in ein[em] Zimmer ~:** lock oneself in a room; Ⓑ (*umgeben*) ‹wall› surround, enclose; ‹people› surround, encircle; Ⓒ (*einbegreifen*) **etw. in etw.** (*Akk.*) **~:** include sth. in sth.

**einschließlich** ❶ *Präp. mit Gen.* (*stark dekl. Substantiv im Sg. ohne Artikel od. Attribut bleibt ungebeugt*) including; inclusive of; **~ der Unkosten** including expenses; **die Kosten ~ Porto** costs including *or* inclusive of postage; **sie verlor ihre Handtasche ~ aller Papiere** she lost her handbag and all the papers which were in it. ❷ *adv.* **bis ~ 30. Juni** up to and including 30 June; **bis Montag ~:** up to and including Monday

**ein|schlummern** *itr. V.; mit sein* Ⓐ (*geh.: einschlafen*) fall asleep; Ⓑ (*verhüll.: sterben*) pass away (*euphem.*)

**Ein·schluss**, ***Ein·schluß** *der* Ⓐ (*Einbeziehung*) inclusion; **alle Staaten unter** *od.* **mit ~ dieses Landes** all states, including this country; Ⓑ (*Geol.*) inclusion

**ein|schmeicheln** *refl. V.* **sich bei jmdm. ~:** ingratiate oneself with sb.

**einschmeichelnd** *Adj.* beguiling ‹music, voice›; ingratiating ‹manner›

**ein·schmeißen** *unr. tr. V.* (*salopp*) smash [in] ‹window›

**ein|schmelzen** *unr. tr. V.* melt down

**ein|schmieren** *tr. V.* (*ugs.*) Ⓐ (*einfetten*) (*mit Creme*) cream ‹face, hands, etc.›; (*mit Fett*) grease; (*mit Öl*) oil; **die Kinder schmierten meine Schuhe mit Zahncreme ein** the children smeared toothpaste on my shoes *or* smeared my shoes with toothpaste; Ⓑ (*schmutzig machen*) **sich/etw. ~:** make *or* get oneself/sth. mucky (*coll.*) *or* dirty; **sich mit Eis ~:** get oneself covered in ice cream

**ein|schmuggeln** *tr. V.* Ⓐ (*unerlaubt einführen*) smuggle in; **etw. in ein Land** (*Akk.*) **~:** smuggle sth. into a country; Ⓑ (*ugs.: unerlaubt Zutritt verschaffen*) **sich in etw.** (*Akk.*) **~:** sneak into sth.; **jmdn. in etw.** (*Akk.*) **~:** smuggle *or* sneak sb. into sth.

**ein|schnappen** *itr. V.; mit sein* Ⓐ ‹door, lock› click to; Ⓑ (*ugs.: schmollen*) go into a huff; ⇒ *auch* **eingeschnappt** 2

**ein|schneiden** ❶ *unr. tr. V.* Ⓐ (*hin~*) make a cut in; cut; ‹rope› cut into ‹wrists›; **das Papier an den Ecken ~:** make a cut at each of the corners of the paper; Ⓑ (*einritzen*) carve; **ein tief eingeschnittenes Tal** a deeply carved valley. ❷ *unr. itr. V.* **das Kleid schneidet an den Schultern ein** the dress cuts into my shoulders

**einschneidend** *Adj.* drastic, radical ‹measure, change›; drastic, far-reaching ‹effect›

**ein|schneien** *itr. V.; mit sein* ‹person, car› get snowed in; become snowbound; ‹village, farm› get snowed in, be cut off by snow; ‹mountain pass› be closed by snow; **eingeschneit sein** be snowed in

**Ein·schnitt** *der* Ⓐ (*Schnitt*) cut; incision (*Med.*); **einen ~ machen** make a cut *or* (*Med.*) incision; Ⓑ (*eingeschnittene Stelle*) cut; (*Med.*) incision; (*im Gebirge*) cleft; Ⓒ (*Zäsur*) break; Ⓓ (*einschneidendes Ereignis*) [decisive] turning point; decisive event

**ein|schnüren** *tr. V.* Ⓐ **sich/jmdm. die Taille ~:** lace one's/sb.'s waist; **sich ~:** lace oneself up [in one's corset]; Ⓑ (*einengen*) cut in; **es schnürt mich ein** it cuts into me

**ein|schränken** ❶ *tr. V.* Ⓐ (*verringern*) reduce, curb ‹expenditure, consumption, power›; **das Trinken/Rauchen/Essen ~:** cut down on the amount one drinks/smokes/eats; Ⓑ (*einengen*) limit; restrict; **jmdn. in seinen Rechten/seiner Bewegungsfreiheit ~:** limit *or* restrict sb.'s rights/freedom of movement; Ⓒ (*relativieren*) qualify, modify ‹remark›. ❷ *refl. V.* economize; cut back on spending; **sich finanziell ~ müssen** have to cut back on one's spending; **sich im Rauchen/Trinken sehr ~:** cut down drastically on the amount one smokes/drinks; ⇒ *auch* **eingeschränkt**

**Einschränkung** *die;* ~, **~en** Ⓐ restriction; limitation; **jmdm. ~en auferlegen** impose restrictions on sb.; **sich** (*Dat.*) **erhebliche finanzielle ~en auferlegen müssen** have to make considerable economies; Ⓑ (*Vorbehalt*) reservation; **nur mit ~[en]** only with reservations *pl.;* **ohne ~[en]** without reservation; **mit der ~, dass ...** with the [one] reservation that ...

**ein|schrauben** *tr. V.* screw in

**Einschreibe-: ~brief** *der* registered letter; **~gebühr** *die* Ⓐ (*Postw., Hochschulw.*) registration fee; Ⓑ (*in Vereinen usw.*) membership fee

**ein|schreiben** *unr. tr. V.* Ⓐ (*hineinschreiben*) write up; Ⓑ (*Postw.*) register ‹letter›; **einen Brief ~ lassen** register a letter; send a letter by registered mail; ⇒ *auch* **eingeschrieben** 2; Ⓒ (*eintragen*) **sich/jmdn. [in eine Liste] ~:** write sb.'s/one's name down [on a list]; enter sb.'s/one's name [on a list]; **sich an einer Universität ~:** register at a university; **sich für einen Abendkurs ~:** enrol for an evening class; ⇒ *auch* **eingeschrieben**; Ⓓ (*DV*) input

**Ein·schreiben** *das* (*Postw.*) registered letter; **per ~:** by registered mail

**Ein·schreibung** *die* (*Hochschulw.*) registration; (*für einen Abendkurs*) enrolment

**ein|schreien** *unr. itr. V.* **auf jmdn. ~:** shout at sb.

**ein|schreiten** *unr. itr. V.* intervene; **gegen jmdn./etw. ~:** take action against sb./sth.; **das Einschreiten der Polizei** intervention by the police

**ein|schrumpfen** *itr. V.; mit sein* shrivel up; (*fig.*) dwindle

**Ein·schub** *der* (*Schrift- u. Druckw.*) insertion

**ein|schüchtern** *tr. V.* intimidate; **sich ~ lassen** let oneself be intimidated; **wir lassen uns nicht ~:** we won't be intimidated

e

**Einschüchterungs·versuch** *der* attempt at intimidation

**ein|schulen** *tr. V.* **eingeschult werden** start school; **Sie müssen Ihr Kind mit 6 Jahren ~ lassen** you must ensure that your child starts school when he or she reaches the age of 6

**Ein·schulung** *die:* **die Anforderungen für die ~ erfüllen** meet the requirements for starting school; **wir müssen die ~ verlegen** we must postpone the date on which he/she starts school

**Einschulungs·alter** *das* age at which children start school

**Ein·schuss, *Ein·schuß** *der* **A** bullet wound; wound at point of entry; **B** (*Raumf.*) **nach dem ~ in die Mondumlaufbahn** after the rocket has/had been put into orbit around the moon *or* into moon orbit; **C** (*Weberei*) weft; woof; **D** (*Sport*) **zum ~ kommen** shoot a goal

**Einschuss-, *Einschuß-: ~loch** *das* bullet hole; **~stelle** *die* wound at point of entry; bullet wound

**ein|schütten** *tr. V.* pour in; **etw. in etw.** (*Akk.*) **~:** pour sth. into sth.; **den Schweinen das Futter ~:** pour the pigs their feed

**ein|schweben** *itr. V.; mit sein* glide in

**ein|schweißen** *tr. V.* **A** weld in; **etw. in etw.** (*Akk.*) **~:** weld sth. into sth.; **B** (*in Klarsichtfolien*) **etw. ~:** seal sth. in transparent film

**ein|schwenken** *itr. V.; mit sein* **A** turn in; **in die Toreinfahrt ~:** turn into the gateway; **nach links ~:** wheel left; **B** (*fig.*) fall into line; **er schwenkte auf einen neuen politischen Kurs ein** he changed course politically

**ein|schwören** *unr. tr. V.* **A** (*durch Treueschwur binden*) **jmdn. ~:** swear sb. in; **B** (*verpflichten*) **jmdn. auf etw.** (*Akk.*) **~:** swear sb. to sth.; ⇒ **eingeschworen**

**ein|segnen** *tr. V.* **A** (*ev. Religion landsch.: konfirmieren*) confirm; **B** (*kath. Religion: weihen*) consecrate

**Ein·segnung** *die* ⇒ **einsegnen**: confirmation; consecration

**ein|sehen** *unr. tr. V.* **A** (*überblicken*) see into ‹building, garden, etc.›; **B** (*prüfend lesen*) look at, see ‹files›; **C** (*erkennen*) see; realize; **D** (*begreifen*) understand, see

**Einsehen** *das;* **~s: ein ~ haben** have *or* show [some] understanding; **kein ~ haben** have *or* show no understanding

**ein|seifen** *tr. V.* **A** **jmdn./sich/etw. ~:** lather sb./oneself/sth.; **jmdn. mit Schnee ~** (*ugs.*) rub snow in sb's face; **B** (*ugs.: betrügen*) **jmdn. ~:** con sb. (*coll.*); put one over on sb. (*coll.*)

**ein·seitig** ❶ *Adj.* **A** on one side *postpos.;* unrequited ‹love›; one-sided ‹friendship›; **er hat eine ~e Lähmung** he's paralysed down one side; **B** (*tendenziös*) one-sided, biased ‹view, statement, etc.›; one-sided ‹person›; **C** (*nicht abwechslungsreich*) unbalanced ‹diet›; one-sided ‹education›; **ein sehr ~er Mensch** a person with narrow interests. ❷ *adv.* **A** **etw. ~ bedrucken** print sth. on one side; **B** (*tendenziös*) one-sidedly; **C** (*nicht abwechslungsreich*) **sich ~ ernähren** have an unbalanced diet; **sehr ~ ausgebildet sein** have had a very one-sided education

**Einseitigkeit** *die;* **~, ~en** (*Voreingenommenheit*) one-sidedness; bias

**ein|senden** *unr.* (*auch regelm.*) *tr. V.* send [in]; **etw. einem Verlag** *od.* **an einen Verlag ~:** send sth. to a publisher

**Ein·sender** *der,* **Ein·senderin** *die;* **~, ~nen** sender; (*bei einem Preisausschreiben*) entrant; **die Einsender von Fotos werden gebeten ...** we [would] ask all those who send in photographs ...

**Einsende·schluss, *Einsende·schluß** *der* closing date

**Ein·sendung** *die* letter/card/contribution/article *etc.;* (*bei einem Preisausschreiben*) entry

*old spelling (see note on page 1707)

**ein|senken** *tr. V.* sink ‹pile etc.›; **etw. in etw.** (*Akk.*) **~:** sink sth. into sth.

**Einser** *der;* **~s, ~** (*ugs.*) **A** (*Schulnote*) one; A; ⇒ *auch* **Zweier A**; **B** (*Buslinie*) number one [bus]

**ein|setzen** ❶ *tr. V.* **A** (*hineinsetzen*) put in; put in, fit ‹window›; insert, put in ‹tooth, piece of fabric, value, word›; **etw. in etw.** (*Akk.*) **~:** put/fit/insert sth. into sth.; **Karpfen in einen Teich ~:** stock a pond with carp; **B** (*Verkehrsw.*) put on ‹special train etc.›; **C** (*ernennen, in eine Position setzen*) appoint; **jmdn. zum** *od.* **als Erben ~:** appoint *or* name sb. one's heir; **jmdn. in ein Amt ~:** appoint sb. to an office; **der Monarch glaubte sich von Gott eingesetzt** the monarch believed he held his office by divine right; **D** (*in Aktion treten lassen*) use ‹weapon, machine›; bring into action, use ‹troops, police›; bring on, use ‹reserve player›; **seine ganze Kraft ~:** use all one's strength; **E** (*aufs Spiel setzen*) stake ‹money›; **F** (*riskieren*) risk; put at risk; **sein Leben/seinen Ruf ~:** risk one's life/reputation; put one's life/reputation at risk.
❷ *itr. V.* start; begin; ‹storm› break; **mit etw. ~:** start *or* begin sth.; **dann setzte Regen ein** then it started *or* began to rain; **wenn [die] Ebbe/Flut einsetzt** when the tide begins to ebb/flow.
❸ *refl. V.* **A** (*sich engagieren*) **ich werde mich dafür ~, dass Sie mehr Geld bekommen** I shall do what I can to see that you get more money; **sich für die Annahme des Gesetzes/die Rettung der Flüchtlinge ~:** do what one can to see that the law is passed/the refugees are saved; **sich selbstlos für die Armen ~:** lend aid unselfishly to the poor; **der Schüler/Minister setzt sich nicht genug ein** the pupil is lacking application/the minister is lacking in commitment; **B** (*Fürsprache einlegen*) **sich für jmdn. ~:** support sb.'s cause

**Einsetzung** *die;* **~, ~en** appointment (**in +** *Akk.* to)

**Ein·sicht** *die* **A** (*das Einsehen*) view (**in +** *Akk.* into); **B** (*Einblick*) **~ in die Akten nehmen** take *or* have a look at the files; **jmdm. ~ in etw.** (*Akk.*) **gewähren** allow sb. to look at *or* see sth.; **C** (*Erkenntnis*) insight; **zu der ~ kommen, dass ...** come to realize that ...; come to the realization that ...; **D** (*Vernunft*) sense; reason; (*Verständnis*) understanding; **~ mit jmdm. haben** show [some] understanding for sb.; **zur ~ kommen** come to one's senses

**einsichtig** ❶ *Adj.* **A** (*verständnisvoll*) understanding; **jeder Einsichtige muss zugeben, dass ...** anyone with any understanding of the situation must concede that ...; **B** (*verständlich*) comprehensible, understandable, clear; **ihm war nicht ~, warum ...** it was not clear to him why ...; he was not clear why ... ❷ *adv.* **sehr ~ vorgehen** show a great deal of understanding

**Einsichtnahme** *die;* **~, ~n** (*Papierdt.*) **nach ~ in die Akten** after studying the files; **die Baupläne liegen zur ~ aus** the building plans are available for inspection

**einsichts-: ~los** *Adj.* **A** (*verständnislos*) lacking in understanding *postpos.;* **B** (*reuelos*) without remorse *postpos.;* **~voll** *Adj.* understanding

**ein|sickern** *itr. V.; mit sein* seep in; (*fig.*) trickle in

**Einsiedelei** /ainzi:də'lai/ *die;* **~, ~en** hermitage; (*fig.*) [country] retreat

**Ein·siedler** *der,* **Ein·siedlerin** *die* hermit; (*fig.*) recluse

**einsiedlerisch** *Adj.* hermit-like; solitary

**Einsiedler-: ~klause** *die* hermitage; **~krebs** *der* hermit crab

**ein·silbig** ❶ *Adj.* **A** monosyllabic ‹word›; **B** (*fig.*) taciturn ‹person›; monosyllabic ‹answer›. ❷ *adv.* (*fig.*) ‹answer› in monosyllables

**Einsilbigkeit** *die;* **~** (*fig.*) taciturnity

**ein|singen** *unr. refl. V.* get oneself into voice; ‹choir› get itself into voice

**ein|sinken** *unr. itr. V.* **A** sink in; **in etw.** (*Dat.*) **~:** sink into sth.; **B** (*zusammenfallen*) ‹roof› sag; **eingesunkene Wangen** sunken cheeks

**ein|sitzen** *unr. itr. V.* (*Rechtsw.*) serve a prison sentence; **er sitzt für drei Jahre ein** he is serving three years *or* a three-year sentence

**Einsitzer** *der;* **~s, ~:** single-seater

**einsitzig** *Adj.* single-seater *attrib.*

**ein|sortieren** *tr. V.* sort ‹books, papers, etc.› and put them away; **Briefmarken/Fotos in ein Album ~:** put stamps/photos into an album; **Karteikarten ~:** file cards; **Briefe in Fächer ~:** sort letters into pigeon-holes

**ein·spaltig** (*Druckw.*) ❶ *Adj.* single-column *attrib.* ❷ *adv.* ‹print, set› in one column

**ein|spannen** *tr. V.* **A** harness ‹horse›; **B** (*in etw. spannen*) **den Bogen [in die Schreibmaschine] ~:** put the sheet of paper in[to the typewriter]; **Stoff in einen Stickrahmen ~:** fix cloth into an embroidery frame; **das Werkstück [in den Schraubstock] ~:** clamp the work [in the vice]; **C** (*ugs.: heranziehen*) rope in (*coll.*); **er wollte uns für seine Zwecke ~:** he wanted to use us for his own ends; ⇒ *auch* **eingespannt 2**

**Einspänner** /'ainʃpɛnɐ/ *der;* **~s, ~** **A** one-horse carriage; **B** (*österr. Gastr.*) black coffee with whipped cream (*served in a glass*)

**einspännig** ❶ *Adj.* one-horse *attrib.* ‹carriage›. ❷ *adv.* **~ fahren** drive a one-horse carriage

**ein|sparen** *tr. V.* save, cut down on ‹costs, expenditure›; save ‹time›; save, economize on ‹energy, electricity, gas, materials›; **Stellen/Arbeitsplätze ~:** cut down on the number of posts/cut down on staff

**Einsparung** *die;* **~, ~en** saving (**an +** *Dat.* in); **~en an Kosten/Energie/Material** savings *or* economies in costs/energy/materials; **durch ~ an** *od.* **von Material** by economizing on *or* saving materials

**Einsparungs·maßnahme** *die* economy measure

**ein|speicheln** *tr. V.* insalivate

**ein|speichern** *tr. V.* (*DV*) feed in; input; **einem Computer etw. ~:** feed sth. into a computer

**ein|speisen** *tr. V.* (*Technik, DV*) feed in; **etw. in etw.** (*Akk.*) **~:** feed sth. into sth.

**ein|sperren** *tr. V.* **jmdn. ~:** lock sb. up

**ein|spielen** ❶ *refl. V.* **A** ‹musician, athlete, team, etc.› warm up; (*zum Saisonbeginn*) ‹athlete, team› get into practice; **sich aufeinander ~** (*fig.*) get used to each other's ways *or* one another; ⇒ *auch* **eingespielt 1**; **B** (*funktionieren*) get going [properly]. ❷ *tr. V.* **A** (*einbringen*) make; bring in; **der Film hat seine Unkosten eingespielt** the film has covered its costs; **B** play *or* break in ‹musical instrument›; **C** (*aufnehmen*) record

**Einspiel·ergebnis** *das* (*Film, Theater*) box office takings *pl.*

**ein|spinnen** *unr. refl. V.* (*Zool.*) ‹insect› spin a cocoon around itself

**einsprachig** /'ainʃpra:xɪç/ ❶ *Adj.* monolingual. ❷ *adv.* **~ aufwachsen** grow up speaking only one language; ⇒ *auch* **zweisprachig**

**ein|sprechen** *unr. itr. V.* ⇒ **einreden 2**

**ein|sprengen** *tr. V.* **etw. ~:** sprinkle sth. with water; damp sth.; ⇒ *auch* **eingesprengt**

**Einsprengsel** /'ainʃprɛŋsl/ *das;* **~s, ~:** embedded particles *pl.;* **mit einigen philosophischen** *usw.* **~n** (*fig.*) with a sprinkling of philosophy *etc.*

**ein|springen** ❶ *unr. itr. V.; mit sein* **A** (*als Stellvertreter*) stand in; (*fig.: aushelfen*) step in and help out; **für jmdn. ~:** stand in for sb./step in and help sb. out; **B** (*Turnen*) **in den Handstand ~:** perform a dive to handstand. ❷ *unr. refl. V.* (*Ski*) do practice jumps

**Einspritz|düse** *die* injection nozzle

**ein|spritzen** *tr. V.* (*auch Kfz-W.*) inject; **jmdm. etw. ~:** inject sb. with sth.

**Einspritz-: ~motor** *der* fuel-injection engine; **~pumpe** *die* injection pump

**Ein·spruch** *der* **A** (*Einwand*) objection (**gegen** to); **~ gegen etw. erheben** raise an objection to sth.; B (*Rechtsw.*) objection; (*gegen Urteil, Entscheidung*) appeal; **[gegen etw.] ∼ einlegen** raise an objection [to sth.]; (*gegen Urteil, Entscheidung*) lodge an appeal [against sth.]

**ein|sprühen** *tr. V.* **die Windschutzscheibe mit einem Entfroster ∼:** spray de-icer on [to] the windscreen (*Brit.*) *or* (*Amer.*) windshield; **sich** (*Dat.*) **das Haar ∼:** put hairspray on one's hair

**einspurig** /ˈainʃpu:rɪç/ ❶ *Adj.* single-track ‹road›. ❷ *adv.* **die Autobahn ist nur ∼ befahrbar** only one lane of the motorway is open

**Eins·sein** *das* (*geh.*) oneness

**einst** /ainst/ *Adv.* (*geh.*) A (*früher*) once; B (*der∼*) some *or* one day; **∼ wird kommen der Tag, da ...** (*dichter., veralt.*) the day will come when ...

**ein|stampfen** *tr. V.* pulp ‹books›

**Ein·stand** *der* A (*zum Dienstantritt*) **seinen ∼ geben** celebrate starting a new job; B (*Sport: erstes Spiel*) début; **seinen ∼ geben** make one's début; play one's first match; C (*Tennis*) deuce

**ein|stanzen** *tr. V.* (*Technik*) stamp in; **etw. auf etw.** (*Akk.*)**/in etw.** (*Akk.*) **∼:** stamp sth. into *or* on sth.

**ein|stauben** *itr. V.; mit sein* get dusty; get covered in dust; **eingestaubt sein** be dusty; be covered in dust

**ein|stäuben** *tr. V.* (*mit Mehl*) dust

**ein|stechen** ❶ *unr. itr. V.* A (*mit einer Stichwaffe*) **auf jmdn. ∼:** stab sb.; B (*Kartenspiel*) trump; play a trump. ❷ *unr. tr. V.* pierce, make ‹hole›; **eine Nadel in etw.** (*Akk.*) **∼:** stick *or* push a needle into sth.; **den Teig mit einer Gabel ∼:** prick the dough with a fork

**ein|stecken** *tr. V.* A (*in etw. stecken*) put in; **etw. in etw.** (*Akk.*) **∼:** put sth. into sth.; **das Bügeleisen ∼:** plug in the iron; **er steckte die Pistole/das Messer wieder ein** he put the pistol back in the holster/the knife back in the sheath; B (*mitnehmen*) **[sich** (*Dat.*)**] etw. ∼:** take sth. with one; put sth. in one's pocket/case *etc.*; C mail ‹letter›; D (*abwertend: für sich behalten*) pocket ‹money, profits›; E (*hinnehmen*) take ‹criticism, defeat, etc.›; take, swallow ‹insult›; F (*ugs.: übertreffen*) outclass ‹competitors, opponents›

**Einsteck-: ∼kamm** *der* comb; **∼tuch** *das; Pl.* **∼tücher** dress handkerchief

**ein|stehen** *unr. itr. V.* A (*garantieren*) **für jmdn. ∼:** vouch for sb.; **dafür ∼, dass ...** vouch [for the fact] that ...; B (*verantwortlich gemacht werden*) **für etw. ∼:** take responsibility for *or* assume liability for sth.; **für jmdn. ∼:** take responsibility for *or* assume liability for sb.'s debts/misdeeds *etc.*; (*jmdm. treu bleiben*) stand by sb.

**Einsteige·diebstahl** *der* (*Rechtsw.*) *burglary involving entering, but not breaking into, a property*

**ein|steigen** *unr. itr. V.; mit sein* A (*in ein Fahrzeug*) get in; **in ein Auto ∼:** get into a car; **in den Bus ∼:** get on the bus; **vorn/hinten ∼** (*ins Auto*) get into the front/back; (*in den Bus*) get on at the front/back; B (*eindringen*) **durch ein Fenster/über den Balkon ∼:** climb in *or* get in through a window/over the balcony; C (*ugs.: sich engagieren*) **in ein Geschäft/die Politik ∼:** go into a business/into politics; **in die Frauenbewegung ∼:** get involved in the women's movement; **[mit zwei Millionen] in ein Unternehmen ∼:** take a [two million pound *etc.*] stake in a company; D (*Bergsteigen*) **in eine Felswand ∼:** tackle a rock face; E (*Sport*) tackle; **hart ∼:** go in hard

**einstellbar** *Adj.* adjustable; **das ist genau ∼:** it can be adjusted *or* set exactly

**ein|stellen** ❶ *tr. V.* A (*einordnen*) put away ‹books etc.›; B (*unterstellen*) put in ‹car, bicycle›; **das Auto [in die Garage] ∼:** put the car in [the garage]; C (*auch itr.*) (*beschäftigen*) take on, employ ‹workers›; **„VW stellt wieder ein"** 'VW is taking on new workers again'; **„wir stellen ein: Schweißer"** 'we have vacancies for welders'; D (*regulieren*) adjust; set; focus ‹camera, telescope, binoculars›; adjust ‹headlights›; **die Kamera auf die richtige Entfernung ∼:** set the camera to the correct distance; **das Radio laut/leiser ∼:** put the radio on loud/turn the radio down; **ein Radio auf einen Sender ∼:** tune a radio to a station; tune in to a station; **ein Programm [an der Waschmaschine] ∼:** select a programme [on the washing machine]; E (*beenden*) stop; call off ‹search, strike›; **das Feuer ∼:** cease fire; **die Zeitung hat ihr Erscheinen eingestellt** the newspaper has ceased publication; **ein Gerichtsverfahren ∼:** abandon court proceedings; **die Arbeit ∼** ‹factory› close; ‹workers› stop work; F (*Sport*) equal ‹record›; G (*Sport: vorbereiten*) **eine Mannschaft defensiv/offensiv ∼:** train a team to play defensive/attacking football.
❷ *refl. V.* A (*ankommen, auch fig.*) arrive; B (*eintreten*) ‹pain, worry› begin; ‹success› come; ‹symptoms, consequences› appear; **starkes Erbrechen stellte sich ein** he/she began to vomit violently; C (*einrichten*) **sich auf etw.** (*Akk.*) **∼:** prepare oneself *or* get ready for sth.; **sich schnell auf neue Situationen ∼:** adjust quickly to new situations; **sie war nicht auf Gäste eingestellt** she was not prepared for guests; **sich auf jmdn. ∼:** adapt to sb.

**Einstell·hebel** *der* adjusting lever

**ein·stellig** *Adj.* single-figure *attrib.* ‹number›

**Einstell·platz** *der* parking space; (*auf eigenem Grundstück*) carport

**Ein·stellung** *die* A (*von Arbeitskräften*) employment; taking on; B (*Regulierung*) adjustment; setting; (*eines Fernglases, einer Kamera*) focusing; (*von Scheinwerfern*) adjustment; C (*Beendigung*) stopping; (*einer Suchaktion, eines Streiks*) calling off; **die ∼ der Produktion veranlassen** order that production be stopped; **er drohte mit der ∼ der Zahlungen** he threatened to stop the payments; D (*Sport*) **die ∼ eines Rekordes** the equalling of a record; E (*Ansicht*) attitude; **ihre politische/religiöse ∼:** her political/religious views *pl.*; F (*Film*) take

**Einstellungs-: ∼bedingung** *die* requirement [for appointment]; **∼gespräch** *das* interview; **∼sperre** *die*, **∼stopp** *der* freeze on recruitment; **∼termin** *der* starting date

**einstens** /ˈainstn̩s/ (*geh., veralt.*) ⇒ **einst**

**Ein·stich** *der* A insertion; B (*∼stelle*) puncture; prick

**ein|sticken** *tr. V.* embroider (**in** + *Akk.* on)

**Ein·stieg** *der;* **∼[e]s, ∼e** A (*Eingang*) entrance; (*Tür*) door/doors; B (*das Einsteigen*) entry; **„kein ∼"** 'exit only'; C (*Bergsteigen*) **der ∼ in die Nordwand** the start of the assault on the north face; **beim ∼ in den Kamin** at the start of the climb up the chimney; **ein guter ∼:** a good point to start the climb; D (*fig.*) **der ∼ in diese Problematik ist schwierig** these are difficult problems to approach

**Einstieg·luke** *die* hatch

**Einstiegs·droge** *die* come-on drug

**einstig** *Adj.* former

**ein|stimmen** ❶ *itr. V.* join in; (*veralt.: zustimmen*) agree; **in den Gesang ∼:** join in the singing; **in das [allgemeine] Lachen ∼** (*fig.*) join in the [general] laughter. ❷ *tr. V.* **jmdn. auf etw.** (*Akk.*) **∼:** get sb. in the [right] mood for sth.

**einstimmig** ❶ *Adj.* A (*Musik*) **ein ∼es Lied** a song for one voice; B (*einmütig*) unanimous ‹decision, vote›. ❷ *adv.* A (*Musik*) **∼ singen** sing in unison; B (*einmütig*) unanimously

**Einstimmigkeit** *die;* **∼:** unanimity; **∼ erzielen** achieve unanimity; reach unanimous agreement

**Ein·stimmung** *die:* **zur** *od.* **als ∼ auf etw.** to get in the [right] mood for sth.

**ein|stippen** *tr. V.* (*bes. nordd.*) dip; dunk

**einst·mals** *Adv.* (*geh., veralt.*) formerly; in former times

**ein·stöckig** ❶ *Adj.* single-storey *attrib.;* one-storey *attrib.;* **hier sind die meisten Häuser ∼:** most of the houses here have one storey. ❷ *adv.* **hier darf nur ∼ gebaut werden** single-storey *or* one-storey buildings only may be built here

**ein|stöpseln** *tr. V.* A plug in ‹telephone, electrical device›; B put in, push in ‹cork etc.›

**ein|stoßen** *unr. tr. V.* A (*gewaltsam öffnen*) break down ‹door, wall›; smash [in] ‹window›; smash ‹mirror›; B (*durch Anstoßen verletzen*) break ‹nose, ribs›; **sich** (*Dat.*) **den Kopf ∼:** bang one's head

**ein|strahlen** ❶ *itr. V.* A (*hineinscheinen*) shine in; **das ∼de Licht** the light shining in; B **auf etw.** (*Akk.*) **∼** ‹sun› irradiate sth. ❷ *tr. V.* (*Physik, Technik*) direct ‹beam etc.›

**Ein·strahlung** *die* irradiation; (*Sonnen∼*) insolation

**ein|streichen** *unr. tr. V.* A **Brot mit Butter** *usw.* **∼:** spread butter *etc.* on bread; B (*ugs.: für sich behalten*) pocket ‹money, winnings, etc.›; (*ugs. abwertend*) rake in (*coll.*) ‹money, profits, etc.›; C (*Theater*) cut ‹script, play›

**ein·streifig** (*Verkehrsw.*) ❶ *Adj.* single-lane. ❷ *adv.* in a single lane

**ein|streuen** *tr. V.* A **etw. mit Sand ∼:** strew *or* scatter sand on sth.; B (*einfügen*) **er streute witzige Bemerkungen in seinen Vortrag ein** he sprinkled his lecture with witty remarks

**ein|strömen** *itr. V.* ‹water› pour *or* flood *or* stream in; ‹air, light› stream in; (*fig.*) ‹crowd, supporters› stream *or* pour in

**ein·strophig** *Adj.* one-verse *attrib.* ‹poem, song›; ‹poem, song› consisting of one verse; **das Gedicht ist ∼:** the poem consists of *or* has one verse *or* stanza

**ein|studieren** *tr. V.* rehearse

**ein·studiert** *Adj.* (*abwertend*) studied

**Einstudierung** *die;* **∼, ∼en** A rehearsal; B (*Inszenierung*) production

**ein|stufen** *tr. V.* classify; categorize; **jmdn. in eine Kategorie/eine höhere Steuerklasse ∼:** put sb. in a category/a higher income-tax bracket

**ein·stufig** *Adj.* single-stage ‹rocket›

**Einstufung** /ˈainʃtu:fʊŋ/ *die;* **∼, ∼en** classification; categorization

**ein|stülpen** *tr. V.* push in

**ein·stündig** *Adj.* one-hour *attrib.* ‹wait, delay›; **nach ∼em Warten** after a wait of one hour; after an hour's wait; ⇒ *auch* **achtstündig**

**ein|stürmen** *itr. V.* **mit Fragen/Bitten auf jmdn. ∼:** besiege sb. with questions/requests

**Ein·sturz** *der* collapse

**ein|stürzen** *itr. V.; mit sein* A collapse; **eine Welt stürzte für sie ein** (*fig.*) her whole world collapsed *or* fell apart; B (*fig.*) **auf jmdn. ∼** ‹worries, problems› crowd in [up]on sb.

**Einsturz·gefahr** *die* danger of collapse; **„Achtung, ∼!"** 'danger — building unsafe'

**einst·weilen** *Adv.* A (*vorläufig*) for the time being; temporarily; B (*inzwischen*) in the mean time; meanwhile

**einstweilig** *Adj.* (*Amtsspr.*) temporary; **eine ∼e Verfügung/Anordnung** (*Rechtsw.*) a temporary injunction/order; **in den ∼en Ruhestand versetzt werden** be suspended from duty

**ein|suggerieren** *itr. V.* **jmdm. etw. ∼:** instil sth. into sb. by suggestion

**Eins·werden** *das* (*geh.*) becoming one *no art.*; **das ∼ der Liebenden** the union of the lovers

**ein·tägig** *Adj.* one-day *attrib.*; **ein ∼er Ausflug** a day tour; ⇒ *auch* **achttägig**

**Eintags·fliege** *die* (*Zool.*) mayfly; (*fig. ugs.*) seven-day wonder; (*kein Dauerzustand*) passing phase

**ein|tanzen** *refl. V.* warm up

**Ein·tänzer** *der* (*veralt.*) gigolo

**ein|tasten** *tr. V.* (*Technik*) key in

**ein|tauchen** ❶ *tr. V.* immerse; **den Pinsel in die Farbe ∼:** dip the brush in the paint; **den Zwieback in den Tee ∼:** dunk *or* dip the rusk in the tea. ❷ *itr. V.; mit sein* dive in; ‹submarine› dive

**Ein·tausch** *der* exchange; **im ∼ gegen etw.** in exchange for sth.

**ein|tauschen** *tr. V.* exchange (**gegen** for)
**ein·tausend** *Kardinalz.* ▶ 841 a *or* one thousand; ⇒ *auch* **acht**[1]
**ein|teilen** *tr. V.* **A** divide up; classify ‹plants, species›; **den Kuchen in zwölf Stücke ~:** divide *or* cut the cake [up] into twelve pieces; **B** (*disponieren, verplanen*) organize; plan [out]; **sein Geld [besser] ~:** plan *or* organize one's finances [better]; **sich** (*Dat.*) **seine Arbeit ~:** organize *or* plan [out] one's work; **sich seine Vorräte ~:** plan out how to make one's provisions last; **C** (*delegieren, abkommandieren*) **jmdn. für etw.** *od.* **zu etw. ~:** assign sb. to sth.
**Einteiler** *der;* **~s, ~** (*Mode*) one-piece bathing suit
**einteilig** /'ai̯ntai̯lɪç/ *Adj.* one-piece ‹dress, bathing suit›
**Ein·teilung** *die* **A** (*Gliederung*) division; dividing up; (*Biol.*) classification; **B** (*planvolles Disponieren*) organization; planning; **bei besserer ~ seines Gehalts würde er …** if he planned out better how to spend his salary, he would…; **C** (*Delegierung, Abkommandierung*) assignment
**Eintel** /'ai̯ntl̩/ *das* (*schweiz. meist der*); **~s, ~:** whole
**ein|tippen** *tr. V.* (*in die Kasse*) register; (*in einen Rechner*) key in
**eintönig** /'ai̯ntøːnɪç/ **1** *Adj.* monotonous ‹landscape, work, life›. **2** *adv.* monotonously; ‹read› in a monotone
**Eintönigkeit** *die;* **~:** monotony
**Ein·topf** *der,* **Eintopf·gericht** *das* (*Kochk.*) stew
**Ein·tracht** *die* harmony; concord; **in ~ leben** live in harmony
**ein·trächtig** **1** *Adj.* harmonious. **2** *adv.* harmoniously; **~ zusammenleben** live together in harmony
**Eintrag** /'ai̯ntraːk/ *der;* **~[e]s, Einträge** /'ai̯ntrɛːgə/ **A** (*das ~en*) entering; **B** (*Aktennotiz*) entry; **ein ~ ins Register** an entry in the register
**ein|tragen** *unr. tr. V.* **A** (*einschreiben*) enter; copy out ‹essay›; **einen Aufsatz in sein Heft ~:** copy an essay into one's exercise book; (*einzeichnen*) mark in; enter; **seinen Namen** *od.* **sich [in eine Liste] ~:** enter one's name [on a list]; **B** (*Amtsspr.*) register; **sich ~ lassen** register; **etw. auf seinen Namen ~ lassen** have sth. registered in one's name; **ein eingetragenes Warenzeichen** a registered trade mark; ⇒ *auch* **Verein**; **C** (*einbringen*) bring in ‹money›; bring ‹criticism›; win ‹goodwill›; **das Geschäft trägt [einen] Gewinn ein** the business makes a profit; **das hat ihm nur Undank eingetragen** that only brought him ingratitude
**einträglich** /'ai̯ntrɛːklɪç/ *Adj.* profitable, lucrative ‹business, sideline›; lucrative ‹work, job›
**Eintragung** *die;* **~, ~en** **A** (*das Eintragen*) entering; **die ~ der Zinsen vornehmen lassen** have the interest entered [in one's account book]; **eine ~ ins Grundbuch bezahlen** pay to have a property *etc.* entered in the land register; **B** (*Eingetragenes*) entry
**ein|träufeln** *tr. V.* **sich/jmdm. Augentropfen ~:** put drops in one's/sb.'s eyes; **jmdm. ein Medikament ~:** administer *or* give a medicine to sb. in drops
**ein|treffen** *unr. itr. V.; mit sein* **A** (*ankommen*) arrive; **B** (*verwirklicht werden*) ‹prophecy› come true
**Ein·treffen** *das* arrival; **ich glaube nicht an das ~ dieser Prophezeiung** I don't believe that this prophecy will come true
**ein|treiben** *unr. tr. V.* **A** (*kassieren*) collect ‹taxes, debts›; (*durch Gerichtsverfahren*) recover ‹debts, money›; **das Geld ~ lassen** take action to obtain the money; **B** (*hineintreiben*) drive in ‹nail, stake›
**Eintreibung** *die;* **~, ~en** (*von Steuern, Schulden*) collection; (*durch Gerichtsverfahren*) recovery
**ein|treten** **1** *unr. itr. V.* **A** *mit sein* (*einen Raum betreten*) enter; **in ein Zimmer ~:** enter a room; **bitte, treten Sie ein!** please come in; **die Eintretenden** those entering; **B** *mit sein* (*Mitglied werden*) **in einen Verein/einen Orden ~:** join a club/enter a religious order; **C** *mit sein* (*Raumfahrt*) **in die Erdumlaufbahn/Erdatmosphäre ~:** enter Earth orbit/the Earth's atmosphere; **D** *mit sein* **in eine neue/schwierige Phase ~:** be entering a new/difficult phase; **in Verhandlungen ~:** enter into negotiations; **in die Beweisaufnahme ~** (*Rechtsw.*) proceed to hearing the evidence; **E** *mit sein* (*sich ereignen*) occur; ‹silence› descend; ‹thaw› set in; ‹darkness, night› set in, fall; **bald trat eine Besserung ein** there was soon an improvement; **bei Eintreten der Dunkelheit** at nightfall; when darkness sets/set in; **das Unerwartete war eingetreten** the unexpected had occurred *or* happened; **F** *mit sein* (*sich einsetzen*) **für jmdn./etw. ~:** stand up for sb./sth.; (*vor Gericht*) speak in sb.'s defence; **G** **auf jmdn./etw. ~:** kick sb./sth.
**2** *unr. tr. V.* kick in ‹door, window, etc.›.
**3** *unr. refl. V.* **sich** (*Dat.*) **etw. ~:** get sth. in one's foot
**ein|trichtern** *tr. V.* (*salopp*) **jmdm. etw. ~:** drum sth. into sb.; **jmdm. ~, dass …** drum into sb. that …
**Ein·tritt** *der* **A** entry; entrance; **sich** (*Dat.*) **[in etw. (*Akk.*)] ~ verschaffen** gain entry [to sth.]; **beim ~ in die Adoleszenz** (*fig.*) when entering adolescence; **vor dem ~ in die Verhandlungen** (*fig.*) before entering into negotiations; **B** (*Beitritt*) **der ~ in einen Verein/einen Orden** joining a club/entering a religious order; **C** (*von Raketen*) entry; **beim ~ [in die Erdatmosphäre]** on entry [into the Earth's atmosphere]; **D** (*Zugang, ~sgeld*) admission; **[der] ~ [ist] frei** admission [is] free; **jmdm. den ~ [in etw. (*Akk.*)] verwehren** refuse sb. admission [to sth.]; **E** (*Beginn*) (*des Winters*) onset; **vor/nach ~ der Dunkelheit** before/after nightfall *or* dusk; **F** (*eines Ereignisses*) occurrence; (*der Menstruation, Wehen*) onset; **bei ~ des Todes** when death occurs
**Eintritts-:** **~geld** *das* admission charge *or* fee; entrance charge *or* fee; **~karte** *die* admission *or* entrance ticket; **~preis** *der* admission *or* entrance charge
**ein|trocknen** *itr. V.; mit sein* **A** ‹paint, blood› dry; ‹water, toothpaste› dry up; **B** (*verdorren*) ‹leather› dry out; ‹berry, fruit› shrivel
**ein|trüben** *refl. V.* (*Met.*) cloud over; become overcast; **es trübt sich ein** it's clouding over
**Ein·trübung** *die* cloudy spell
**ein|trudeln** *itr. V.; mit sein* (*ugs.*) drift in (*coll.*)
**ein|tunken** *tr. V.* (*landsch.*) **etw. in etw.** (*Akk.*) **~:** dip *or* dunk sth. in sth.
**ein|tüten** *tr. V.* bag
**ein|üben** *tr. V.* **A** (*sich aneignen*) practise; **jede einzelne seiner Gesten wirkt sorgfältig eingeübt** all of his gestures seem carefully rehearsed; **B** (*proben, trainieren*) **mit jmdm. etw. ~:** practise sth. with sb.
**Ein·übung** *die* **A** (*Aneignung*) acquisition; **B** (*Proben, Trainieren*) practising
**Ein·uhr-:** one o'clock ‹news, train›
**ein·und·ein·halb** ▶ 841 ⇒ **anderthalb**
**ein·und·zwanzig** *Kardinalz.* twenty-one
**Einung** *die;* **~, ~en** (*dichter.*) ⇒ **Einigung** B
**ein|verleiben** /-fɛɐ̯lai̯bn̩/ **1** *tr. V.* annex ‹land, country›. **2** *refl. V.* (*sich zu Eigen machen*) assimilate, absorb ‹knowledge, experience›; (*scherzh.: zu sich nehmen*) put away (*coll.*)
**Einvernahme** *die;* **~, ~n** (*Rechtsw., bes. österr. u. schweiz.*) examination
**ein|vernehmen** *unr. tr. V.* (*Rechtsw., bes. österr. u. schweiz.*) examine
**Ein·vernehmen** *das;* **~s** harmony; (*Übereinstimmung*) agreement; **in freundschaftlichem/gutem ~ [mit jmdm.]** on friendly/good terms [with sb.]; ⇒ *auch* **setzen** 1 C
**ein·vernehmlich** (*Amtsspr.*) **1** *Adv.* conjointly. **2** *adj.* conjoint
**einverstanden** *Adj.* **mit jmdm. ~ sein** (*einer Meinung*) be in agreement with sb.; agree with sb.; **mit jmdm./etw. ~ sein** (*zufrieden*) approve of sb./sth.; **sich [mit etw.] ~ erklären** agree [to sth.]; express one's agreement [to sth.]; **~!** (*ugs.*) okay! (*coll.*); agreed!
**ein·verständlich** (*geh.*) **1** *Adj.* mutually agreed; ‹divorce› by mutual consent. **2** *adv.* by mutual consent
**Ein·verständnis** *das* **A** (*Billigung*) consent (**zu** to), approval (**zu** of); **im ~ mit jmdm. handeln** act with sb.'s consent; **Ihr ~ vorausgesetzt** with your approval; if you are agreed; **B** (*Übereinstimmung*) agreement; **zwischen ihnen herrscht ~:** there is agreement between them
**Ein·waage** *die* (*Kaufmannsspr.*) contents *pl.*
**ein|wachsen**[1] *unr. itr. V.; mit sein* grow into the flesh; **eingewachsen** ingrown ‹toenail›
**ein|wachsen**[2] *tr. V.* wax
**Einwand** *der;* **~[e]s, Einwände** /'ai̯nvɛndə/ objection (**gegen** to)
**Ein·wanderer** *der,* **Ein·wanderin** *die* immigrant
**ein|wandern** *itr. V.; mit sein* immigrate (**in** + *Akk.* into)
**Ein·wanderung** *die* immigration; **eine Zunahme der ~en** an increase in the number of immigrants
**Einwanderungs-:** **~behörde** *die* immigration authorities *pl.*; **~land** *das* country of immigration; **~quote** *die* immigration quota; **~welle** *die* wave of immigrants
**einwand·frei** **1** *Adj.* **A** (*ohne Fehler*) flawless; perfect; impeccable ‹behaviour›; **das Fleisch ist noch ~:** the meat is still perfectly fresh; **B** (*eindeutig*) indisputable, definite ‹proof›; watertight ‹alibi›. **2** *adv.* **A** perfectly; flawlessly; ‹behave› impeccably; **B** beyond question *or* doubt; **es ist ~ erwiesen, dass …** it has been proved beyond question *or* doubt that …
**einwärts** /'ai̯nvɛrts/ *Adv.* inwards; **~ gebogen** concave
***einwärts·gebogen** ⇒ **einwärts**
**ein|weben** *tr. V.* weave *or* work in; **etw. in etw.** (*Akk.*) **~:** weave *or* work sth. into sth.
**ein|wechseln** *tr. V.* **A** (*wechseln, umtauschen*) change ‹money›; **B** (*Sport*) substitute ‹player›
**ein|wecken** *tr. V.* preserve; preserve, bottle ‹fruit, vegetables›
**Einweck-:** **~glas** *das* preserving jar; **~gummi** *der,* **~ring** *der* rubber seal (*for preserving jar*); **~topf** *der* preserving pan
**Ein·weg-:** **~flasche** *die* non-returnable bottle; **~packung** *die* disposable pack; **~spiegel** *der* one-way mirror; **~spritze** *die* disposable [hypodermic] syringe
**ein|weichen** *tr. V.* soak
**ein|weihen** *tr. V.* **A** open [officially] ‹bridge, road›; dedicate ‹monument›; consecrate ‹church›; **B** (*ugs. scherzh.: zum ersten Mal benutzen*) christen (*coll.*); **C** (*vertraut machen*) **jmdn. in etw.** (*Akk.*) **~:** let sb. in on sth.; **jmdn. in die Kunst des Strickens/in das Schachspiel ~:** initiate sb. into the art of knitting/the mysteries of chess
**Einweihung** *die;* **~, ~en** [official] opening
**ein|weisen** *unr. tr. V.* **A** **jmdn. in ein Krankenhaus ~:** have sb. admitted to hospital; **die Flüchtlinge wurden in eine Wohnung/ein Lager eingewiesen** the refugees were assigned a flat (*Brit.*) *or* (*Amer.*) apartment/sent to a camp; **B** (*in eine Tätigkeit*) **jmdn. [in eine/die Arbeit] ~:** introduce sb. to a/the job; show sb. what a/the job involves; **C** (*in ein Amt*) install; **jmdn. in sein Amt ~:** install sb.; **D** (*Verkehrsw.*) direct
**Ein·weisung** *die* **A** (*Unterbringung*) **~ in ein Krankenhaus** admission to a hospital; **sich gegen die ~ in ein Lager wehren** fight against being sent to a camp; **B** introduction; **er wurde mit der ~ der neuen Mitarbeiter betraut** he was given the task of introducing the new members of staff to their jobs; **C** (*Amtseinführung*) installation
**ein|wenden** *unr.* (*auch regelm.*) *tr. V.* **dagegen lässt sich manches/vieles ~:** there

*old spelling (see note on page 1707)

are a number of things/is a lot to be said against that; **dagegen ist nichts einzuwenden** there can be no objection to that; **„...", wandte er ein** '...,' he objected; **gegen etw. nichts einzuwenden haben** have no objection to sth.; have nothing against sth.

**Ein·wendung** *die* objection [**gegen** to]

**ein|werfen** ❶ *unr. tr. V.* A mail ‹letter, mail›; put in, insert ‹coin›; B (*zertrümmern*) smash, break ‹window›; C (*Ballspiele*) throw in ‹ball›; D (*bemerken, sagen*) throw in ‹remark›; **„...", warf sie ein** '...,' she interjected. ❷ *unr. itr. V.* (*Ballspiele*) (*vom Rand*) take the throw-in; (*ins Tor*) score

**ein·wertig** *Adj.* A (*Chemie*) monovalent ‹atom›; B (*Sprachw.*) one-place ‹verb›

**ein|wickeln** *tr. V.* A wrap [up] ‹article, present›; **jmdn./sich in etw.** (*Akk.*) **~:** wrap sb./oneself [up] in sth.; B (*ugs.*) **jmdn. ~** (*überreden*) get round sb.; (*überlisten*) take sb. in

**Einwickel·papier** *das* wrapping paper

**ein|wiegen**[1] *tr. V.* **jmdn. ~:** lull sb. to sleep; (*in der Wiege*) **ein Kind ~:** rock a child to sleep

**ein|wiegen**[2] *unr. tr. V.* (*Kaufmannsspr.*) weigh out

**ein|willigen** *itr. V.* agree, consent (**in** + *Akk.* to); **in ein Angebot ~:** accept an offer

**Einwilligung** *die;* **~, ~en** agreement; consent; **seine ~ zu etw. geben** give one's consent to sth.; **ihre ~ in das Angebot** her acceptance of the offer

**ein|winken** *tr. V.* (*Verkehrsw.*) guide in ‹aircraft›; guide *or* direct in ‹car›; **ein Auto in eine Parklücke ~:** guide *or* direct a car into a parking space

**ein|wirken** ❶ *itr. V.* A (*beeinflussen*) **auf jmdn. ~:** influence sb.; exert *or* have an influence on sb.; **beruhigend auf jmdn. ~:** exert a soothing *or* calming influence on sb.; B (*eine Wirkung ausüben*) have an effect (**auf** + *Akk.* on); **man lasse die Creme ~:** let the cream work in. ❷ *tr. V.* (*Handarb., Textilw.*) work in; **etw. in etw.** (*Akk.*) **~:** work sth. into sth.

**Ein·wirkung** *die* (*Einfluss*) influence; (*Wirkung*) effect; **unter ~ von Drogen stehen** be under the influence of drugs

**ein·wöchig** *Adj.* one-week *attrib.;* week-old ‹baby›; week-long ‹conference›

**Einwohner** *der;* **~s, ~, Einwohnerin** *die;* **~, ~nen** inhabitant; **die Stadt hat 3 Millionen ~:** the town has 3 million inhabitants *or* a population of 3 million

**Einwohner·meldeamt** *das: local government office for registration of residents*

**Einwohnerschaft** *die;* **~:** population; inhabitants *pl.*

**Einwohner·zahl** *die* population

**Ein·wurf** *der* A (*Einwerfen*) insertion; (*von Briefen*) mailing; B (*Ballspiele*) throw-in; **ein falscher ~:** a foul throw; C (*Öffnung*) (*eines Briefkastens*) slit; (*einer Tür*) letter box; D (*Zwischenbemerkung*) interjection; (*kritisch*) objection; **einen kritischen ~ machen** raise an objection

**ein|wurzeln** *itr.* (*auch refl.*) *V.* root; (*fig.*) take root

**Ein·zahl** *die* (*Sprachw.*) singular

**ein|zahlen** *tr. V.* pay in; deposit; **Geld auf sein Konto ~:** pay *or* deposit money into one's account; **die Miete ~:** pay in the rent

**Ein·zahlung** *die* payment; deposit; (*Überweisung*) payment

**Einzahlungs-:** **~beleg** *der* counterfoil; **~schalter** *der* paying-in counter (*Brit.*); deposit counter (*Amer.*); **~schein** *der* pay[ing]-in slip (*Brit.*); deposit slip

**ein|zäunen** *tr. V.* fence in; enclose; **ein Grundstück [mit etw.] ~:** fence a property in [with sth.]

**Einzäunung** *die;* **~, ~en** A (*das Einzäunen*) fencing-in; enclosure; B (*Zaun*) fence; enclosure

**ein|zeichnen** *tr. V.* draw *or* mark in; **etw. in eine Karte ~:** draw *or* mark sth. in on a map

**ein·zeilig** *Adj.* A one-line *attrib.;* ⇒ *auch* achtzeilig; B **eine ~e Küche** a fitted kitchen arranged along one wall

**Einzel** /'aintsl/ *das;* **~s, ~** (*Sport*) singles *pl.;* **der Sieger im ~:** the winner in the singles; **~ spielen** to play a singles match

**Einzel-:** **~aktion** *die* independent action; **~an·fertigung** *die* custom-made article; (*Fahrzeug*) custom-built model; **~ausgabe** *die* separate edition; **~band** *der* individual *or* single volume; **~bett** *das* single bed; **~buchstabe** *der* (*Druckw.*) single [piece of] type; single sort; **~darstellung** *die* (*eines Themas*) individual treatment; (*Abhandlung*) monograph; **~disziplin** *die* (*bes. Leichtathletik*) single event; **~erscheinung** *die* isolated occurrence; **~fahrer** *der,* **~fahrerin** *die* (*Motorsport*) solo rider; **~fahr·schein** *der* single; **~fall** *der* A particular case; **im ~fall** in particular cases; B (*Ausnahme*) isolated case; exception; **~feuer** *das* (*Milit.*) independent fire; **~frage** *die* individual question

**Einzelgänger** /-gɛŋɐ/ *der;* **~s, ~** A solitary person; loner; B (*Tier*) lone animal

**Einzelgängerin** *die;* **~, ~nen** solitary person; loner

**Einzelgängertum** *das;* **~s** solitariness

**Einzel-:** **~gehöft** *das* solitary farm; **~gewerkschaft** *die* member union; **~grab** *das* separate *or* individual grave; **~haft** *die* solitary confinement

**Einzel·handel** *der* retail trade; **das kostet im ~ 200 DM** it retails at 200 marks; **etw. im ~ kaufen** buy sth. retail

**Einzelhandels-:** **~geschäft** *das* retail shop; retail store (*Amer.*); **~kauffrau** *die* retail saleswoman; **~kaufmann** *der* retail salesman; **~preis** *der* retail price

**Einzel-:** **~händler** *der,* **~händlerin** *die* retailer; retail trader; **~haus** *das* detached house

**Einzelheit** *die;* **~, ~en** A detail; B (*einzelner Umstand*) particular; **bis in alle ~en** down to the last detail; **in ~en gehen** go into detail

**Einzel-:** **~interesse** *das* individual interest; **~kind** *das* only child

**Einzeller** /'aintsɛlɐ/ *der;* **~s, ~** (*Biol.*) unicellular organism

**einzellig** /'aintsɛlɪç/ *Adj.* (*Biol.*) unicellular; single-cell *attrib.*

**einzeln** *Adj.* A (*für sich allein*) individual; **die ~en Bände eines Werkes** the individual *or* separate volumes of a work; **jede ~e Insel** each individual island; **ein ~er Schuh/Handschuh** an odd shoe/glove; **jede ~e ist ein Kunstwerk** each individual one is a work of art; **schon ein ~es von diesen Gläsern** just one of these glasses on its own; **„bitte ~ eintreten"** 'please enter one [person] at a time'; **alle Teile ~ verpacken** pack each piece individually; **~ reisen** travel alone *or* on one's own; **wir sind alle ~ gekommen** we all came separately; **sich um jeden ~en Gast kümmern** look after each guest individually; **~ stehend** solitary; B (*allein stehend*) solitary ‹building, tree›; **eine ~e Dame/ein ~er Herr** a single lady/gentleman; C *Pl.* (*wenige*) a few; (*einige*) some; **~e Regenschauer** scattered *or* isolated showers; D *substantivisch* (*~er Mensch*) **der/jeder Einzelne** the/each individual; **als Einzelner** as an individual; **jeder Einzelne der Betroffenen wurde angehört** every [single] one of those concerned was given a hearing; **ein Einzelner** one individual; **für einen Einzelnen geeignet** suitable for one person; E *substantivisch* **Einzelnes** (*manches*) some things *pl.;* **das Einzelne** the particular; **vom Einzelnen zum Allgemeinen** from the particular to the general; **etw. im Einzelnen besprechen** discuss sth. in detail; **ins Einzelne gehen** go into detail[s *pl.*]; **bis ins Einzelne** right down to the last detail

***einzeln·stehend** ⇒ **einzeln** A

**Einzel-:** **~person** *die* one person; individual; **als ~person** as an individual; **~preis** *der* individual price; **~rad·aufhängung** *die* (*Kfz-W.*) independent suspension; **~richter** *der,* **~richterin** *die* judge sitting singly; **~schicksal** *das* individual fate *or* destiny; **~staat** *der* individual state; **~stück** *das* individual piece *or* item; **~stunde** *die* private lesson; **~teil** *das* individual *or* separate part; **etw. in [seine] ~teile zerlegen** take sth. to pieces; **~therapie** *die* (*Med.*) individual therapy; **~unterricht** *der* individual tuition; **~wertung** *die* (*Sport*) individual placings *pl.;* **~wesen** *das* individual [being]; **der Mensch als ~wesen** man as an individual; **~wettbewerb** *der* (*Sport*) individual event; **~zelle** *die* A (*für ~haft*) single cell; B (*Biol.*) single cell; **~zimmer** *das* single room

**ein|zementieren** *tr. V.* cement in

**einziehbar** *Adj.* A (*Technik*) retractable; B (*Finanzw.*) recoverable

**Einzieh·decke** *die* duvet (*Brit.*); continental quilt (*Brit.*); stuffed quilt (*Amer.*)

**ein|ziehen** ❶ *unr. tr. V.* A put in ‹duvet›; thread in ‹tape, elastic›; B (*einbauen*) put in ‹wall, ceiling›; C (*einholen*) haul in, pull in ‹net›; retract, draw in ‹feelers, claws›; **den Kopf ~:** duck; **der Hund zog den Schwanz ein** the dog put its tail between its legs; ⇒ *auch* **Schwanz** A; D (*einatmen*) breathe in ‹scent, fresh air›; inhale ‹smoke›; E (*einberufen*) call up, conscript ‹recruits›; F (*beitreiben*) collect; **er lässt die Miete vom Konto ~:** he pays his rent by direct debit; G (*beschlagnahmen*) confiscate; seize; H (*aus dem Verkehr ziehen*) withdraw, call in ‹coins, banknotes›; I (*Amtsspr.: einholen*) **Informationen/Erkundigungen ~:** gather information/make enquiries; J (*Druckw.*) indent ‹paragraph›. ❷ *unr. itr. V.; mit sein* A (*eindringen*) ‹liquid› soak in; B (*einkehren*) enter; **der Frühling zieht ein** (*geh.*) spring comes *or* arrives; **dann zog bei uns wieder Ruhe ein** then we had peace and quiet again; **ins Parlament ~:** enter parliament; C (*in eine Wohnung*) move in

**Ein·ziehung** *die* A (*Einberufung*) call-up; conscription; drafting (*Amer.*); B (*Beitreibung*) collection; C (*von Eigentum*) confiscation, seizure; (*von Münzen, Banknoten usw.*) withdrawal

**einzig** /'aintsɪç/ ❶ *Adj.* A (*alleinig*) only; single; (*intensivierend nach „ein" od. „kein"*) single; **der ~e Sohn** the only son; **unser Einziger/unsere Einzige** our only son/daughter; **nur ein Einziger** only one; **nicht ein ~es Stück** not one single piece; **es blieb nur ein ~er Ausweg** there was only one way out; **ihre ~e Freude war ihre Tochter** her daughter was her one and only joy; **das Einzige, was er sah, war ...** the only thing he saw was ...; B (*völlig*) complete; absolute; one long ‹torment›; C (*geh.: unvergleichlich*) unique; unparalleled; **~ in ihrer/seiner Art** unique in her/his/its [own] way.
❷ *adv.* A (*ganz besonders*) singularly; extraordinarily; **ein ~ schöner Tag** an extraordinarily beautiful day; B (*ausschließlich*) only; **das ~ Wahre** the only thing; **das ~ Vernünftige/Richtige** the only sensible/right thing [to do]; **~ und allein** nobody/nothing but; solely; **~ ihm wollte sie sich anvertrauen** he was the only one she would confide in

**einzig·artig** ❶ *Adj.* unique. ❷ *adv.* uniquely; **~ schön** extraordinarily beautiful

**Einzigartigkeit** *die,* **Einzigkeit** *die* uniqueness

**einzigst...** *Adj.* (*ugs.*) ⇒ **einzig** 1

**Ein·zimmer-:** **~apartment** *das,* **~appartement** *das,* **~wohnung** *die* one-room flat *or* (*Amer.*) apartment

**ein|zuckern** *tr. V.* sprinkle with sugar

**Ein·zug** *der* A entry (**in** + *Akk.* into); **der ~ des Winters** (*geh.*) the advent of winter; **[seinen] ~ halten** make one's entrance; **mit strahlendem Sonnenschein hielt der Frühling [seinen] ~:** glorious sunshine marked the beginning of spring; **der ~ ins Parlament** entry into parliament; B (*in eine Wohnung*) move; C (*Druckw.*) indentation

e

**Einzugs-: ~bereich** *der,* **~gebiet** *das* catchment area

**ein|zwängen** *tr. V.* squeeze *or* hem in; ‹corset› constrict

**Ein·zylinder·motor** *der* single-cylinder engine

**Eis** /ais/ *das;* **~es** Ⓐ ice; **eine Flasche auf ~ legen** put a bottle on ice; **ein Whisky mit ~:** a whisky with ice *or* on the rocks; **etw. auf ~ legen** (*fig. ugs.*) put sth. on ice; shelve sth.; **jmdn. auf ~ legen** (*fig. salopp*) put sb. out of harm's way; **~ laufen** ice-skate; Ⓑ (*Speise~*) ice cream; **ein ~ am Stiel** an ice lolly (*Brit.*) *or* (*Amer.*) ice pop

**Eis-: ~bahn** *die* ice rink; **~bär** *der* polar bear; **~behälter** *der* ice bucket; **~becher** *der* Ⓐ (*~portion*) ice cream sundae; Ⓑ (*Gefäß*) [ice cream] sundae dish; **~bein** *das* Ⓐ (*Kochk.*) knuckle of pork; Ⓑ **ich habe ~beine** (*ugs. scherzh.*) my feet are like ice; **~berg** *der* iceberg; **die Spitze eines ~bergs** the tip of an iceberg; **~beutel** *der* ice bag; ice pack; **~blume** *die* frost flower; **~bombe** *die* (*Gastr.*) bombe glacée; **~brecher** *der* ice-breaker; **~café** *das* ice cream parlour

**Ei·schnee** *der* stiffly beaten egg white

**Eis-: ~creme** *die* ice cream; **~diele** *die* ice cream parlour

**Eisen** /'aizn̩/ *das;* **~s, ~** Ⓐ iron; **aus ~ sein** be made of iron; **die ~ verarbeitende Industrie** the iron-processing industry; **die ~ schaffende Industrie** the iron-and-steel-producing industry; Ⓑ (*Werkzeug, Werkstück usw., Golf~*) iron; (*Jägerspr.*) trap; **jmdn. in ~ legen** (*veralt.*) put sb. in irons; (*fig.*) **ein heißes ~ anfassen** *od.* **anpacken** grasp the nettle; **das ist ein heißes ~:** that is a hot potato; **noch ein/mehrere ~ im Feuer haben** have another iron/several irons in the fire; **man muss das ~ schmieden, solange es heiß ist** (*Spr.*) strike while the iron is hot (*prov.*); Ⓒ **jmdn./etw. zum alten ~ werfen** (*ugs.*) throw sb./sth. on [to] the scrap heap; **zum alten ~ gehören** belong on the scrap heap; **jmdn. zum alten ~ zählen** write sb. off [as too old]

**Eisen·bahn** *die* Ⓐ railway; railroad (*Amer.*); **mit der ~ fahren** go *or* travel by train *or* rail; **es ist [die] [aller]höchste ~** (*ugs.*) it's high time; it's getting late; Ⓑ (*Bahnstrecke*) railway line; railroad track (*Amer.*); Ⓒ (*Verwaltung*) railway[s]; railroad (*Amer.*); Ⓓ (*Spielbahn*) train *or* railway set

**Eisenbahn-: ~abteil** *das* railway *or* (*Amer.*) railroad compartment; **~bau** *der* railway *or* (*Amer.*) railroad construction

**Eisenbahner** *der;* **~s, ~** ▶159 railwayman; railway worker; railroader (*Amer.*)

**Eisenbahner·gewerkschaft** *die* railwaymen's union;

**Eisenbahnerin** *die;* **~, ~nen** ▶159 railway worker; railroader (*Amer.*)

**Eisenbahner·streik** *der* railway *or* (*Amer.*) railroad strike

**Eisenbahn-: ~fähre** *die* train ferry; **~gesellschaft** *die* railway *or* (*Amer.*) railroad company; **~knotenpunkt** *der* railway *or* (*Amer.*) railroad junction; **~netz** *das* railway *or* (*Amer.*) railroad network; **~schaffner** *der,* **~schaffnerin** *die* railway guard; railroad conductor (*Amer.*); **~tunnel** *der* railway *or* (*Amer.*) railroad tunnel; **~unglück** *das* train crash; **~wagen** *der* railway carriage; railroad car (*Amer.*); (*Güterwagen*) railway wagon; railroad car (*Amer.*); **~waggon** *der* (*veralt.*) ⇨ **~wagen**

**eisen-, Eisen-: ~berg·werk** *das* iron mine; **~beschlag** *der* piece of ironwork; **~beschläge** ironwork *sing.;* **~erz** *das* iron ore; **~farbe** *die* ferric oxide paint; **~feil·späne** *Pl.* iron filings; **~fresser** *der* (*ugs. abwertend*) big mouth (*coll.*); **~gerüst** *das* iron scaffolding *no indef. art.;* **~gießerei** *die* (*Verfahren*) iron smelting; (*Betrieb*) iron foundry; **~guss,** ***~guß** *der* (*das Gießen*) iron casting; (*Guss~guss*) cast iron; **~haltig** *Adj.* iron-bearing ‹stone›; ‹food› containing iron; **~hammer** *der* Ⓐ steam hammer; Ⓑ (*bild. Kunst*) trimming hammer; **~hart** *Adj.* as hard as iron *or* as a rock; (*fig.*) ‹person› as hard as nails; iron ‹will›; **~hut** *der* Ⓐ (*Bot.*) monkshood; wolfsbane; Ⓑ (*Hist.*) iron hat

**Eisen·hütte** *die* ironworks *sing. or pl.;* iron foundry

**Eisenhütten-: ~industrie** *die* iron industry; **~werk** *das* ⇨ Eisenhütte

**eisen-, Eisen-: ~industrie** *die* iron industry; **~kern** *der* (*Elektrot.*) ferrite core; **~kette** *die* iron chain; **~kitt** *der* iron cement; **~kraut** *das* (*Bot.*) vervain; **~kur** *die* course of iron treatment; **~legierung** *die* iron alloy; **~mangel** *der* (*Med.*) iron deficiency; **~nagel** *der* iron nail; **~oxid, ~oxyd** *das* (*Chemie*) iron oxide; **~präparat** *das* iron preparation; **~ring** *der* iron ring; **~säge** *die* hacksaw; ***~schaffend** ⇨ Eisen A; **~schwamm** *der* (*Metall.*) sponge iron; **~span** *der* iron filing; **~spat** *der* (*Mineral.*) siderite; **~stange** *die* iron bar; **~staub** *der* iron filings *pl.;* **~sulfat** *das* (*Chemie*) ferrous sulphate; **~teil** *das* iron part; **~träger** *der* iron girder; ***~verarbeitend** ⇨ Eisen A; **~verhüttung** *die* iron smelting; **~vitriol** *das* (*Chemie*) green vitriol; copperas; ferrous sulphate; **~waren** *Pl.* ironmongery *sing.;* **~waren·händler** *der,* **~waren·händlerin** *die* ▶159 ironmonger; **~zeit** *die* Iron Age

**eisern** /'aizɐn/ ❶ *Adj.* Ⓐ (*aus Eisen*) iron; **~e Lunge** (*Med.*) iron lung; **der ~e Vorhang** (*Theater*) the safety curtain; **der Eiserne Vorhang** (*Pol.*) the Iron Curtain; **das Eiserne Kreuz** the Iron Cross; **die Eiserne Jungfrau** the Iron Maiden; Ⓑ (*unerschütterlich*) iron ‹discipline›; unflagging ‹energy›; **mit ~em Willen** with a will of iron; **Eiserne Hochzeit** 65th wedding anniversary; Ⓒ (*unerbittlich*) iron; unyielding; iron ‹discipline›; **mit ~em Besen [aus]kehren** *od.* **[aus]fegen** make a ruthlessly clean sweep; **der Eiserne Kanzler** the Iron Chancellor; Ⓓ (*bleibend*) **~er Bestand** emergency stock; **eine ~e Reserve** emergency reserves *pl.;* **die ~e Ration** the iron rations *pl.;* (*fig.*) one's last reserves *pl. or* standby. ❷ *adv.* Ⓐ (*unerschütterlich*) resolutely; **~ bei etw. bleiben** stick tenaciously to sth.; **~ schweigen** remain resolutely silent; **sich ~ an etw.** (*Akk.*) **halten** keep resolutely to sth.; **~ sparen/trainieren** save/train with iron determination; Ⓑ (*unerbittlich*) **~ Widerstand leisten** put up steadfast resistance; **~ durchgreifen** take drastic measures *or* action; **~ auf Disziplin bedacht sein** insist on iron discipline

**Eises·kälte** *die* icy cold

**eis-, Eis-: ~fach** *das* freezing compartment; **~fischerei** *die* ice fishing; **~fläche** *die* sheet *or* surface of ice; **~frau** *die* (*ugs.*) ice cream woman; **~frei** *Adj.* ice-free; free of ice *postpos.;* **~gang** *der* drift ice; **~gekühlt** *Adj.* iced ‹drink›; **~glatt** *Adj.* Ⓐ icy ‹road›; Ⓑ /'-'-/ (*ugs.*) ‹floor, steps› as slippery as ice; **~glätte** *die* black ice; **~grau** *Adj.* steely grey; **eine ~graue Alte** a hoary old woman; **~heilige** *in* **die ~heiligen** [*feast days of*] *Three Saints* (*12, 13, 14 May*); **~hockey** *das* ice hockey

**eisig** ❶ *Adj.* Ⓐ (*kalt wie Eis*) icy ‹wind, cold›; icy [cold] ‹water›; **es ist ~:** it's icy cold; it's freezing; Ⓑ (*kalt ablehnend*) frosty, icy ‹atmosphere›; frosty ‹smile›. ❷ *adv.* Ⓐ **~ kalt** ice-cold ‹drink›; freezing cold ‹weather›; Ⓑ (*ablehnend*) ‹smile› frostily; **~ schweigen** maintain an icy silence; **jmdn. ~ empfangen** give sb. a frosty *or* icy reception

***eisig·kalt** ⇨ **eisig** 2 A

**eis-, Eis-: ~kaffee** *der* iced coffee; **~kalt** ❶ *Adj.* Ⓐ ice-cold ‹drink›; freezing cold ‹weather›; **sich ~kalt anfühlen** feel freezing cold; Ⓑ (*völlig gefühllos*) icy; ice-cold ‹technocrat, businessman›; **ein ~kalter Blick** a cold look. ❷ *adv.* Ⓐ **es lief mir ~kalt über den Rücken** a cold shiver went down my spine; Ⓑ **etw. ~kalt tun** (*kaltblütig*) do sth. in cold blood; (*lässig*) do sth. without turning a hair; **jmdn. ~kalt ansehen/abweisen** give sb. an icy *or* frosty look/coldly reject sb.'s request; **er ging ~kalt hin und sagte ...** he went over there, cool as you like, and said ...; **~kanal** *der* (*Sportjargon*) toboggan run; **~karte** *die* (*Gastron.*) ice cream menu; **~kraut** *das* (*Bot.*) ice plant; **~kristall** *der* ice crystal; **~kübel** *der* ice bucket

**Eis·kunst-: ~lauf** *der* figure skating; **~laufen** *das* figure skating; **~läufer** *der,* **~läuferin** *die* figure skater

**eis-, Eis-: ~lauf** *der* ice skating; ***~|laufen** ⇨ Eis A; **~laufen** *das;* **~~s** ice skating; **~läufer** *der,* **~läuferin** *die* ice skater; **~mann** *der* (*ugs.*) ice cream man; **~maschine** *die* ice cream maker; freezer (*Amer.*); **~meer** *das:* **das Nördliche/Südliche ~meer** the Arctic/Antarctic Ocean; **~pickel** *der* (*Bergsteigen*) ice pick

**Ei·sprung** *der* (*Physiol.*) ovulation

**eis-, Eis-: ~regen** *der* sleet; **~revue** *die* ice show; **~schicht** *die* layer of ice; **~schießen** *das* (*Sport*) ⇨ **~stockschießen**; ***~schnellauf** *usw.* ⇨ **~schnelllauf** *usw.*; **~schnell·lauf** *der,* **~schnell·laufen** *das;* **~~s** speed skating; **~schnell·läufer** *der,* **~schnell·läuferin** *die* speed skater; **~scholle** *die* ice floe; **~schrank** *der* refrigerator; **~spalte** *die* crevasse; **~sport** *der* ice sports *pl.;* **~stadion** *das* ice rink; **~stock** *der* (*Sport*) ice stick; **~stock·schießen** *das;* **~~s** (*Sport*) ice stick shooting; Bavarian curling; **~tanz** *der* (*Sport*) ice dancing; **~vogel** *der* Ⓐ kingfisher; Ⓑ (*Falter*) white admiral; **~waffel** *die* [ice cream] wafer; **~wasser** *das* Ⓐ (*~kaltes Wasser*) ice-cold water; Ⓑ (*Wasser mit ~stücken*) iced water; Ⓒ (*Schmelzwasser*) meltwater; **~wein** *der: wine made from grapes frozen on the vine;* **~würfel** *der* ice cube; **~zapfen** *der* icicle; **~zeit** *die* ice age; **~zeitlich** *Adj.* ice-age *attrib.*, of the ice age *postpos.*

**eitel** /'aitl̩/ *Adj.* Ⓐ (*abwertend*) vain; **~ wie ein Pfau [sein]** [be] as proud as a peacock; Ⓑ (*veralt.: nichtig*) vain ‹hope›; futile, vain ‹endeavour›; empty, idle ‹talk›; Ⓒ *indekl.* (*veralt.: rein*) pure; **~ Freude** pure joy

**Eitelkeit** *die;* **~, ~en** vanity

**Eiter** /'aitɐ/ *der;* **~s** pus

**Eiter-: ~beule** *die* boil; abscess; **~herd** *der* pus focus; suppurative focus; **~pickel** *der* spot; pimple

**eitern** *itr. V.* suppurate

**eitrig** *Adj.* suppurating; festering

**Ei·weiß** *das* Ⓐ (*des Hühnereis*) egg white; albumen; **~ und Dotter trennen** separate the egg white and the yolk; **drei ~:** the whites of three eggs; Ⓑ (*Chemie, Biol.*) protein

**eiweiß-, Eiweiß-: ~arm** *Adj.* low-protein *attrib.;* low in protein *postpos.;* **~bedarf** *der* protein requirement; **~haltig** *Adj.* ‹food› containing protein; **~mangel** *der* protein deficiency; **~reich** *Adj.* high-protein *attrib.;* rich in protein *postpos.*

**Ejakulation** /ejakula'tsi̯o:n/ *die;* **~, ~en** (*Physiol.*) ejaculation

**EK** *Abk.* **Eisernes Kreuz** Iron Cross

**EKD** *Abk.* **Evangelische Kirche in Deutschland**

**ekel** /'e:kl̩/ *Adj.* (*veralt.*) Ⓐ nauseating; disgusting; vile; Ⓑ (*verwerflich*) nasty; odious

**Ekel**[1] *der;* **~s** Ⓐ (*Abscheu*) disgust; loathing; revulsion; **[einen] ~ vor etw.** (*Dat.*) **haben** have a loathing *or* revulsion for sth.; **[ein] ~ packte/erfüllte ihn** he was seized by/filled with disgust *etc.;* **ein ~ stieg in ihr hoch** she was overcome by a feeling of disgust *etc.;* **~ erregend** disgusting; nauseating; revolting; **~ erregende Krankheiten** diseases which could cause offence; Ⓑ (*Überdruss*) loathing; **einen ~ vor etw.** (*Dat.*) **entwickeln** come to loathe sth.

**Ekel**[2] *das;* **~s, ~** (*ugs. abwertend*) horror; **er ist ein [altes] ~:** he is a perfect horror *or* quite obnoxious

***ekel·erregend** *Adj.* ⇨ **Ekel**[1] A

**ekelhaft** ❶ *Adj.* disgusting, revolting, nauseating ‹sight›; nasty (*coll.*), horrible ‹weather, person›; **~ riechen/schmecken** smell/taste disgusting *or* revolting. ❷ *adv.* Ⓐ in a

*old spelling (see note on page 1707)

disgusting *or* revolting *or* nauseating way; Ⓑ (*ugs.: sehr*) terribly (*coll.*), dreadfully (*coll.*) ‹cold, hot›

**ekeln** /ˈe:kl̩n/ ❶ *refl. V.* be *or* feel disgusted *or* sickened; **sie ekelt sich vor Schlangen/Spinnen** *usw.* she finds snakes/spiders *etc.* repulsive; **sich vor jmdm./etw. ~:** find sb./sth. disgusting *or* revolting. ❷ *tr., itr. V.* (*unpers.*) **es ekelt mich** *od.* **mir ekelt davor** I find it disgusting *or* revolting. ❸ *tr. V.* Ⓐ **Hunde ~ ihn** he finds dogs repulsive; Ⓑ (*vertreiben*) **jmdn. aus dem Haus ~:** hound sb. out of the house

**EKG** *Abk.* **Elektrokardiogramm** ECG; **ein ~ machen lassen** have an ECG

**Eklat** /eˈkla(:)/ *der;* **~s, ~s** (*geh.*) (*Aufsehen, Skandal*) sensation; stir; (*Konfrontation*) row; altercation; **es kam zum ~:** it came to a row *or* [major] confrontation

**eklatant** /eklaˈtant/ (*geh.*) ❶ *Adj.* Ⓐ (*offensichtlich*) striking ‹difference›; flagrant, scandalous ‹offence›; Ⓑ (*sensationell*) sensational; spectacular. ❷ *adv.* flagrantly; **~ gegen etw. verstoßen** be in flagrant breach of sth.

**Eklektiker** /eˈklɛktikɐ/ *der;* **~s, ~, Eklektikerin** *die;* **~, ~nen** eclectic

**eklektisch** ❶ *Adj.* eclectic. ❷ *adv.* eclectically

**Eklektizismus** /eklɛktiˈtsɪsmʊs/ *der;* **~:** eclecticism

**eklig** /ˈe:klɪç/ ❶ *Adj.* Ⓐ disgusting, revolting, nauseating ‹sight›; nasty (*coll.*), horrible ‹weather, person›; **~ riechen/schmecken** smell/taste disgusting *or* revolting; Ⓑ (*ugs.: gemein*) mean; nasty; **sich ~ benehmen** be mean *or* nasty. ❷ *adv.* Ⓐ in a disgusting *or* revolting *or* nauseating way; Ⓑ (*ugs.: sehr*) terribly (*coll.*), dreadfully (*coll.*) ‹hot, cold›

**Eklipse** /eˈklɪpsə/ *die;* **~, ~n** (*Astron.*) eclipse

**Ekliptik** /eˈklɪptɪk/ *die;* **~, ~en** (*Astron.*) ecliptic

**Ekstase** /ɛkˈsta:zə/ *die;* **~, ~n** ecstasy; **in ~ geraten** go into ecstasies; become ecstatic; **jmdn. in ~ versetzen** send sb. into ecstasies; make sb. ecstatic

**ekstatisch** /ɛkˈsta:tɪʃ/ ❶ *Adj.* ecstatic. ❷ *adv.* ecstatically

**Ektoderm** /ˈɛktodɛrm/ *das;* **~s, ~e** (*Zool.*) ectoderm

**Ekto·plasma** /ɛkto-/ *das* (*Biol.; Parapsychologie*) ectoplasm

**Ekzem** *das;* **~s, ~e** (*Med.*) eczema

**ekzematös** /ɛktsemaˈtø:s/ *Adj.* (*Med.*) eczematous

**Elaborat** /elaboˈra:t/ *das;* **~[e]s, ~e** (*geh. abwertend*) pathetic concoction

**elaboriert** *Adj.* (*geh.*) elaborate ‹style›; elaborated; **ein ~er Code** (*Sprachw.*) an elaborated code

**Elan** /eˈla:n/ *der;* **~s** zest; vigour

**elan·voll** ❶ *Adj.* zestful; vigorous. ❷ *adv.* zestfully; vigorously

**Elaste** /eˈlastə/ *Pl.* (*Chemie*) elastomers

**Elastik** /eˈlastɪk/ *das;* **~s, ~s** *od. die;* **~, ~en** elasticated material; stretch fabric

**elastisch** ❶ *Adj.* Ⓐ (*dehnbar*) elasticated ‹material›; springy, resilient ‹surface›; Ⓑ (*geschmeidig*) supple, lithe ‹person, body›; Ⓒ (*flexibel*) flexible ‹tactics, rules›. ❷ *adv.* Ⓐ (*geschmeidig*) supply; lithely; **sein ~ federnder Gang** his supple *or* lithe walk; Ⓑ (*flexibel*) flexibly

**Elastizität** /elastitsiˈtɛ:t/ *die;* **~** Ⓐ (*Dehnbarkeit*) elasticity; (*Federkraft*) springiness; Ⓑ (*Geschmeidigkeit*) suppleness; Ⓒ (*Flexibilität*) flexibility

**Elativ** /ˈe:lati:f/ *der;* **~s, ~e** (*Sprachw.*) absolute superlative; elative

**Elb-Florenz** /ˈɛlp-/ *das* Dresden

**Elb·kähne** *Pl.* (*nordd. scherzh.*) clodhoppers (*coll.*)

**Elch** /ɛlç/ *der;* **~[e]s, ~e** elk; (*in Nordamerika*) moose

**Elch-:** **~bulle** *der* bull elk; **~kuh** *die* cow elk; **~test** *der* elk test

**Eldorado** /ɛldoˈra:do/ *das;* **~s, ~s** eldorado; **ein ~ der** *od.* **für Taucher** (*fig.*) a divers' paradise

**Elefant** /eleˈfant/ *der;* **~en, ~en** elephant; **wie ein ~ im Porzellanladen** (*ugs.*) like a bull in a china shop; ⇒ *auch* **Mücke**

**Elefanten-:** **~baby** *das* baby elephant; ⇒ *auch* **~küken**; **~bulle** *der* bull elephant; **~haut** *die* elephant skin; **eine ~haut haben** (*fig. ugs.*) be thick-skinned; **~herde** *die* elephant herd; **~hochzeit** *die* (*Wirtsch. scherzh.*) giant merger; **~kuh** *die* cow elephant; **~küken** *das:* **er ist ein richtiges ~küken** (*ugs. scherzh.*) he looks just like a baby elephant

**Elefantiasis** /elefanˈti:azɪs/ *die;* **~** (*Med.*) elephantiasis

**elegant** /eleˈgant/ ❶ *Adj.* Ⓐ (*geschmackvoll*) elegant, stylish ‹dress, appearance›; elegant ‹society›; **die ~e Welt** elegant society; Ⓑ (*harmonisch*) elegant, graceful ‹movement›; neat ‹solution›; Ⓒ (*kultiviert*) elegant, civilized ‹taste›; elegant ‹style›; civilized ‹manner›. ❷ *adv.* elegantly, stylishly ‹dressed›; **sich ~ aus der Affäre ziehen** get oneself gracefully out of it

**Eleganz** /eleˈgants/ *die;* **~:** elegance; stylishness; **zeitlose/sportliche/lässige ~:** timeless/sporty/casual elegance

**Elegie** /eleˈgi:/ *die;* **~, ~n** elegy

**elegisch** /eˈle:gɪʃ/ ❶ *Adj.* Ⓐ (*Dichtk.*) elegiac; Ⓑ (*fig.: wehmütig*) elegiac; mournful; plaintive. ❷ *adv.* **~ gestimmt sein** feel in a mournful mood

**elektrifizieren** /elɛktrifiˈtsi:rən/ *tr. V.* electrify

**Elektrifizierung** *die;* **~, ~en** electrification

**Elektrik** /eˈlɛktrɪk/ *die;* **~, ~en** electrics *pl.*

**Elektriker** *der;* **~s, ~, Elektrikerin** *die;* **~, ~nen** electrician

**elektrisch** ❶ *Adj.* electric ‹current, light, heating, shock›; electrical ‹resistance, wiring, system›; **der ~e Stuhl** the electric chair. ❷ *adv.* **~ kochen** cook with electricity; **~ geladen sein** be electrically charged; be charged with electricity; **sich ~ rasieren** use an electric shaver

**Elektrische** *die;* **~n, ~n** (*veralt.*) tram (*Brit.*); streetcar (*Amer.*)

**elektrisieren** ❶ *tr. V.* Ⓐ (*Med.*) treat using electricity; Ⓑ (*fig.: entflammen*) electrify. ❷ *refl. V.* give oneself *or* get an electric shock

**Elektrizität** /elɛktritsiˈtɛ:t/ *die;* **~** (*Physik*) electricity; (*elektrische Energie*) electricity; [electric] power

**Elektrizitäts-:** **~erzeugung** *die* generation of electricity; **~gesellschaft** *die* electricity company; **~versorgung** *die* [electric] power supply; **~werk** *das* power station; **~zähler** *der* electricity meter

**elektro-, Elektro-:** **~antrieb** *der* electric drive; **~artikel** *der* electrical appliance; **~auto** *das* electric car; **~chemie** *die* electrochemistry *no art.*; **~chemisch** ❶ *Adj.* electrochemical; ❷ *adv.* electrochemically; **~chirurgie** *die* electrosurgery *no art.*

**Elektrode** /elɛkˈtro:də/ *die;* **~, ~n** electrode

**elektro-, Elektro-:** **~dynamik** *die* (*Physik*) electrodynamics *sing., no art.*; **~dynamisch** (*Physik*) ❶ *Adj.* electrodynamic; ❷ *adv.* electrodynamically; **~enzephalogramm** *das* (*Med.*) electroencephalogram; **~fahrzeug** *das* electric vehicle; **~gerät** *das* electrical appliance; **~geschäft** *das* electrical shop *or* (*Amer.*) store; **~handwerk** *das* electrical trade; **~herd** *der* electric cooker; **~industrie** *die* electrical goods industry; **~ingenieur** *der,* **~ingenieurin** *die* ▶ 159 electrical engineer; **~installateur** *der,* **~installateurin** *die* ▶ 159 electrical fitter; electrician; **~kardiogramm** *das* (*Med.*) electrocardiogram; **~karren** *der* electric trolley; **~konzern** *der* electrical company

**Elektrolyse** /elɛktroˈly:zə/ *die;* **~, ~n** (*Chemie, Physik*) electrolysis

**elektrolysieren** *tr. V.* (*Chemie*) electrolyse

**Elektrolyt** /elɛktroˈly:t/ *der;* **~en** *od.* **~s, ~en** *od.* **~e** electrolyte

**elektrolytisch** *Adj.* electrolytic

**elektro-, Elektro-:** **~magnet** *der* electromagnet; **~magnetisch** ❶ *Adj.* electromagnetic; ❷ *adv.* electromagnetically; **~magnetismus** *der* electromagnetism *no art.*; **~mechanik** *die* electrical engineering *no art.*; **~mechanisch** ❶ *Adj.* electromechanical; ❷ *adv.* electromechanically; **~meter** *der* electrometer; **~mobil** *das;* **~~s, ~~e** electric car; **~monteur** *der,* **~monteurin** *die* ⇒ **~installateur**; **~motor** *der* electric motor

**Elektron** /eˈlɛktrɔn/ *das;* **~s, ~en** /-ˈtro:nən/ (*Kernphysik*) electron

**Elektronen-:** **~blitz** *der* electronic flash; **~blitz·gerät** *das* (*Fot.*) electronic flash; **~[ge]hirn** *das* (*ugs.*) electronic brain (*coll.*); **~hülle** *die* electron shell; **~mikroskop** *das* electron microscope; **~optik** *die* electron optics *sing., no art.*; **~rechner** *der* electronic computer; **~röhre** *die* electron tube *or* valve; **~strahl** *der* (*Physik*) electron beam; **~theorie** *die* electron theory; **~volt** *das* electron volt

**Elektronik** /elɛkˈtro:nɪk/ *die;* **~** Ⓐ electronics *sing., no art.*; Ⓑ (*Bestandteile*) electronic parts *pl.*; electronics *pl.*

**Elektroniker** *der;* **~s, ~, Elektronikerin** *die;* **~, ~nen** ▶ 159 electronics engineer

**Elektronik·schrott** *der* scrapped electrical appliances *pl.*

**elektronisch** ❶ *Adj.* electronic. ❷ *adv.* electronically

**Elektro-:** **~ofen** *der* (*Technik*) electric furnace; **~rasierer** *der* electric shaver *or* razor; **~rasur** *die* shaving *no art.* with an electric shaver *or* razor; **~schock** *der* (*Med.*) electric shock; **~schweißer** *der,* **~schweißerin** *die* arc welder

**Elektroskop** /elɛktroˈsko:p/ *das;* **~s, ~e** electroscope

**elektro-, Elektro-:** **~smog** *der* (*Jargon*) electronic smog; **~statisch** ❶ *Adj.* electrostatic; ❷ *adv.* electrostatically; **~technik** *die* electrical engineering *no art.*; **~techniker** *der,* **~technikerin** *die* Ⓐ electronics engineer; Ⓑ (*Elektriker[in]*) electrician; **~technisch** ❶ *Adj.* electrotechnical; **~technische Industrie** electrical *or* electrotechnical industry; ❷ *adv.* electrotechnically; **~therapie** *die* (*Med.*) electrotherapy; **~wagen** *der* electric vehicle

**Element** /eleˈmɛnt/ *das;* **~[e]s, ~e** Ⓐ element; **die vier ~e** the four elements; **die entfesselten ~e** (*geh.*) the raging elements; **er war/fühlte sich in seinem ~:** he was/felt in his element; **zwielichtige/kriminelle ~e** shady/criminal elements; **die ~e der Mathematik/Grammatik** *usw.* the elements *or* rudiments of mathematics/grammar *etc.*; Ⓑ (*Bauteil*) element; (*einer Schrankwand*) unit; Ⓒ (*Elektrot.*) cell; battery

**elementar** /elemɛnˈta:ɐ̯/ ❶ *Adj.* Ⓐ (*grundlegend*) fundamental ‹requirement, right, condition, insight, significance›; Ⓑ (*einfach*) elementary, rudimentary ‹knowledge›; **ihm fehlen die ~sten Kenntnisse** he lacks the most elementary *or* rudimentary knowledge; Ⓒ (*naturhaft*) elemental ‹force, forces›. ❷ *adv.* with elemental force

**Elementar-:** **~begriff** *der* elementary *or* basic concept; **~gewalt** *die* elemental force; **~kenntnisse** *Pl.* elementary *or* rudimentary knowledge *sing.*; **~mathematik** *die* elementary mathematics *sing., no art.*; **~stufe** *die* (*Schulw.*) preschool level; **~teilchen** *das* (*Physik*) elementary particle; **~unterricht** Ⓐ (*Einführungsunterricht*) elementary instruction; Ⓑ (*Unterricht in der ~stufe*) preschool teaching

**Elen** /ˈe:lɛn/ *das od. der;* **~s, ~** ⇒ **Elch**

**elend** /ˈe:lɛnt/ ❶ *Adj.* Ⓐ wretched, miserable ‹existence, life, conditions, environment›; **eines ~en Todes sterben** die a miserable death; Ⓑ (*krank*) **sich ~ fühlen** feel wretched *or* (*coll.*) awful; **mir ist/wird ~:** I feel/I am beginning to feel awful *or* terrible (*coll.*); Ⓒ

(*gemein*) despicable ‹person, coward, allegation›; Ⓓ (*ugs.: besonders groß*) dreadful (*coll.*) ‹hunger, pain›. ❷ *adv.* Ⓐ (*jämmerlich*) wretchedly; miserably; **~ zugrunde gehen** come to a miserable *or* wretched end; Ⓑ (*ugs.: intensivierend*) dreadfully (*coll.*)

**Elend** *das;* **~s** Ⓐ (*Leid*) misery; wretchedness; **das ganze Leben ist ein ~:** life is just a complete misery; **es ist ein ~ mit ihm** (*ugs.*) he's enough to drive you to despair; **das heulende ~ kriegen** (*ugs.*) start blubbering hysterically; **..., da kann man das heulende ~ kriegen** it's enough to make you weep; **wie das leibhaftige ~ aussehen** (*ugs.*) look like death warmed up (*coll.*); **ein langes ~** (*ugs. scherzh.*) a beanpole; ⇒ *auch* **Häufchen**; Ⓑ (*Armut*) misery; destitution; **jmdn. ins ~ stürzen** plunge sb. into misery

**elendig, elendiglich** *Adv.* (*geh.*) miserably; wretchedly; **~ zugrunde gehen** perish miserably; come to a wretched *or* miserable end

**Elends-: ~gestalt** *die* [poor] wretch; wretched figure; **~quartier** *das* slum [dwelling]; **~viertel** *das* slum area

**Eleve** /e'le:və/ *der;* **~n, ~n, Elevin** *die;* **~, ~nen** Ⓐ (*Theater, Ballett*) student; Ⓑ (*Land- und Forstwirtsch.*) trainee; Ⓒ (*veralt. geh.: Schüler, Jünger*) acolyte; disciple

**elf** /ɛlf/ *Kardinalz.* ▶ 76, ▶ 752, ▶ 841 eleven; ⇒ *auch* **acht**[1]

**Elf**[1] *die;* **~, ~en** Ⓐ eleven; ⇒ *auch* **Acht**[1] A, E, G; Ⓑ (*Sport*) team; side

**Elf**[2] *der;* **~en, ~en** elf

**Elfe** /'ɛlfə/ *die;* **~, ~n** fairy

**Elfen·bein** *das* ivory; **schwarzes ~** (*fig.*) black ivory

**Elfenbein·arbeit** *die* ivory piece

**elfen·beinern** *Adj.* ivory

**elfenbein-, Elfenbein-: ~farben** *Adj.* ivory-coloured; **~küste** *die* Ivory Coast; **~schnitzerei** *die* Ⓐ ivory carving; Ⓑ (*Gegenstand*) ivory carving; **~turm** *der* (*fig.*) ivory tower

**elfenhaft** *Adj.* elfish; elfin

**Elfen-: ~königin** *die* elfin queen; fairy queen; **~reigen** *der* fairy dance

**Elfer** *der;* **~s, ~** Ⓐ (*Fußballjargon*) penalty; Ⓑ (*landsch.: Zahl Elf*) eleven; Ⓒ (*Buslinie*) number eleven

**elferlei** *indekl. Gattungsz.* Ⓐ *attr.* eleven kinds *or* sorts of; eleven different ‹sorts, kinds, sizes, possibilities›; Ⓑ *subst.* eleven [different] things

**Elfer-: ~rat** *der: carnival committee consisting of eleven members;* **~wette** *die* (*Sport*) *football pools [entry] requiring eleven selections;* **er hat sieben Richtige in der ~wette** he's got seven out of eleven on the pools

**elf-: ~fach** *Vervielfältigungsz.* elevenfold; **die ~fache Menge** eleven times the amount; ⇒ *auch* **achtfach**; **~mal** *Wiederholungsz.* eleven times; ⇒ *auch* **achtmal**

**Elf·meter** *der* (*Fußball*) penalty; **einen ~ schießen** take a penalty

**Elfmeter-: ~punkt** *der* (*Fußball*) penalty spot; **~schießen** *das;* **~~s** (*Fußball*) **durch ~schießen** by *or* on penalties; **es gab ein ~schießen** it was decided on penalties; **~schütze** *der,* **~schützin** *die* (*Fußball*) penalty taker; **~tor** *das* (*Fußball*) penalty

**elft** *in* **wir waren zu ~:** there were eleven of us; ⇒ *auch* **acht**[2]

**elft...** *Ordinalz.* ▶ 207, ▶ 841 eleventh; ⇒ *auch* **acht...**

**elf·tausend** *Kardinalz.* eleven thousand

**Elftel** /'ɛlftl̩/ *das;* **~s, ~:** eleventh

***elfte·mal, *elftenmal** ⇒ **Mal**[1]

**elftens** *Adv.* eleventh

**elidieren** /eli'di:rən/ *tr. V.* Ⓐ (*geh.: streichen*) delete; Ⓑ (*Sprachw.*) elide

**Elimination** /elimina'tsi̯o:n/ *die;* **~, ~en** elimination

**eliminieren** /elimi'ni:rən/ *tr. V.* eliminate

**Eliminierung** *die;* **~, ~en** elimination

**Elisabeth** /e'li:zabɛt/ (*die*) Elizabeth

**elisabethanisch** *Adj.* Elizabethan

**Elision** /eli'zi̯o:n/ *die;* **~, ~en** elision

**elitär** /eli'tɛ:ɐ̯/ ❶ *Adj.* Ⓐ élitist; **ein ~es Bewusstsein** an élite-awareness; Ⓑ (*zu einer Elite gehörend*) élite *attrib.* ❷ *adv.* **er denkt/verhält sich ~:** he thinks/behaves in an élitist fashion

**Elite** /e'li:tə/ *die;* **~, ~n** élite; **die ~ der Sportler** the sporting élite

**Elite-: ~denken** *das* élitist thinking; élitism; **~truppe** *die* (*Milit.*) élite *or* crack force

**Elixier** /elɪ'ksi:ɐ̯/ *das;* **~s, ~e** elixir

**Ell·bogen** *der;* **~s, ~** ▶ 471 elbow; **er/sie hat keine ~** (*fig. ugs.*) he/she isn't pushy enough (*coll.*)

**Ellbogen-: ~freiheit** *die* elbow room; **~gesellschaft** *die* (*abwertend*) society where the weakest go to the wall; **~mensch** *der* (*abwertend*) pushy individual (*ugs.*)

**Elle** /'ɛlə/ *die;* **~, ~n** Ⓐ ▶ 471 (*Anat.*) ulna; Ⓑ (*frühere Längeneinheit*) cubit; Ⓒ (*veralt.: Maßstock*) ≈ yardstick; **alles mit einer ~ messen** (*fig.*) measure everything by the same yardstick

**Ellen·bogen** ⇒ **Ellbogen**

**ellen·lang** *Adj.* (*ugs.*) ‹list› as long as your arm; interminable ‹lecture, sermon›; terribly long (*coll.*) ‹letter›

**Ellipse** /ɛ'lɪpsə/ *die;* **~, ~n** ellipse; (*Sprachw., Rhet.*) ellipsis

**Ellipsen·bahn** *die* elliptical orbit

**ellipsen·förmig** ❶ *Adj.* elliptical. ❷ *adv.* elliptically

**elliptisch** /ɛ'lɪptɪʃ/ ❶ *Adj.* elliptical. ❷ *adv.* elliptically

**Elms·feuer** /'ɛlms-/ *das* (*Met.*) St. Elmo's fire

**Eloge** /e'lo:ʒə/ *die;* **~, ~n** (*geh.*) eulogy

**E-Lok** *die* (*veralt.*) electric locomotive *or* engine

**eloquent** /elo'kvɛnt/ (*geh.*) ❶ *Adj.* eloquent. ❷ *adv.* eloquently

**Eloquenz** *die;* **~** (*geh.*) eloquence

**Elritze** /'ɛlrɪtsə/ *die;* **~, ~n** (*Zool.*) minnow

**Elsass, *Elsaß** /'ɛlzas/ *das;* **~** *od.* **Elsasses** Alsace; **im/aus dem ~:** in/from Alsace

**Elsässer** /'ɛlzɛsɐ/ ❶ *indekl. Adj.* Alsatian. ❷ *der;* **~s, ~:** Alsatian

**Elsässerin** *die;* **~, ~nen** Alsatian; ⇒ *auch* **-in**

**elsässisch** *Adj.* Alsatian

**Elsass-Lothringen, *Elsaß-Lothringen** (*das*) (*hist.*) Alsace-Lorraine

**Elster** /'ɛlstɐ/ *die;* **~, ~n** (*Zool.*) magpie; **wie eine ~ stehlen** be light-fingered; **eine diebische ~** (*fig.*) a pilferer

**Elter** /'ɛltɐ/ *das od. der;* **~s, ~n** (*Biol.*) parent

**elterlich** *Adj.* parental

**Eltern** *Pl.* parents; **nicht von schlechten ~ sein** (*fig. ugs.*) be quite something

**eltern-, Eltern-: ~abend** *der* (*Schulw.*) parents' evening; **~aktiv** *das* (*DDR: Schulw.*) parents' committee; **~bei·rat** *der* (*Schulw.*) parents' association; **~haus** *das* parental home; **aus einem armen/katholischen ~haus kommen** come from a poor/Catholic home; **~liebe** *die* parental love; **~los** ❶ *Adj.* parentless; orphaned; **ein ~loses Kind** a child without parents; an orphan; ❷ *adv.* **~los aufwachsen** grow up an orphan *or* without parents

**Elternschaft** *die;* **~** Ⓐ (*Schulw.*) parents' association; Ⓑ (*Elternsein*) parenthood; **geplante ~:** planned parenthood

**Eltern-: ~sprech·tag** *der* parents' day; **~teil** *der* parent; **~versammlung** *die* parents' meeting

**elysäisch** /ely'zɛ:ɪʃ/, **elysisch** /e'ly:zɪʃ/ *Adj.* (*dichter.*) Elysian

**Elysium** /e'ly:zi̯ʊm/ *das;* **~s, Elysien** /e'ly:zi̯ən/ (*dichter.*) Elysium

**EM** *Abk.* **Europameisterschaft[en]**

**Email** /e'mai̯/ *das;* **~s, ~s, Emaille** /e'malјə/ *die;* **~, ~n** enamel

**Email[le]-: ~arbeit** *die* (*Kunst*) Ⓐ enamel; Ⓑ (*~malerei*) enamel painting; **~geschirr** *das* enamelware; **~waren** *Pl.* enamelware *sing.*

**emaillieren** *tr. V.* enamel

**Emanation** /emana'tsi̯o:n/ *die;* **~, ~en** (*Philos.*) emanation

**Emanze** /e'mantsə/ *die;* **~, ~n** (*ugs., auch abwertend*) women's libber (*coll.*)

**Emanzipation** /emantsipa'tsi̯o:n/ *die;* **~, ~en** emancipation; **die ~ der Frau** the emancipation *or* liberation of women

**Emanzipations·bewegung** *die* liberation movement

**emanzipatorisch** /emantsipa'to:rɪʃ/ *Adj.* (*geh.*) emancipatory ‹education›

**emanzipieren** /emantsi'pi:rən/ ❶ *refl. V.* **sich [von jmdm./etw.] ~:** emancipate oneself [from sb./sth.]. ❷ *tr. V.* emancipate

**emanzipiert** *Adj.* emancipated; emancipated, liberated ‹woman›

**Embargo** /ɛm'bargo/ *das;* **~s, ~s** embargo

**Emblem** /ɛm'ble:m/ *das;* **~s, ~e** emblem

**Embolie** /ɛmbo'li:/ *die;* **~, ~n** (*Med.*) embolism

**Embonpoint** /ãbõ'po̯ɛ̃:/ *der od. das;* **~s** (*geh. scherzh.*) embonpoint

**Embryo** /'ɛmbryo/ *der;* **~s, ~nen** /-y'o:nən/ *od.* **~s** embryo

**Embryoblast** *der;* **~en, ~en** (*Biol.*) cyst

**embryonal** *Adj.* (*Med., Biol., fig.*) embryonic

**Emendation** /emɛnda'tsi̯o:n/ *die;* **~** (*Literaturw.*) emendation

**emeritieren** /emeri'ti:rən/ *tr. V.* confer emeritus status on; **ein emeritierter Professor** an emeritus professor; a professor emeritus

**Emeritierung** *die;* **~, ~en seit seiner ~:** since he has been an emeritus professor

**Emeritus** /e'me:ritʊs/ *der;* **~, Emeriti** (*geh.*) emeritus professor

**Emigrant** /emi'grant/ *der;* **~en, ~en** emigrant; (*Flüchtling*) emigré

**Emigranten·presse** *die* emigré press

**Emigrantin** *die;* **~, ~nen** ⇒ **Emigrant**

**Emigration** /emigra'tsi̯o:n/ *die;* **~, ~en** Ⓐ (*das Emigrieren*) emigration; **die innere ~:** inner emigration (*particularly during the Nazi period in Germany*); Ⓑ (*die Fremde*) exile; **in der ~ leben** live in exile; Ⓒ (*die Emigranten*) emigrés *pl.*

**emigrieren** /emi'gri:rən/ *itr. V.; mit sein* emigrate

**eminent** /emi'nɛnt/ ❶ *Adj.* (*geh.*) eminent; **von ~er Bedeutung sein** be of the utmost significance. ❷ *adv.* eminently; **das ist ~ wichtig** that is of the utmost importance

**Eminenz** /emi'nɛnts/ *die;* **~, ~en** ▶ 91 (*kath. Kirche*) eminence; **Eure/Seine ~:** Your/His Eminence; **eine graue ~:** an éminence grise; a grey eminence

**Emir** /'e:mɪr/ *der;* **~s, ~e** emir

**Emirat** *das;* **~[e]s, ~e** emirate

**Emissär** /emɪ'sɛ:ɐ̯/ *der;* **~s, ~e** emissary

**Emission** /emɪ'si̯o:n/ Ⓐ (*Physik, Ökologie*) emission; Ⓑ (*Ausgabe [von Briefmarken, Wertpapieren]*) issue

**Emissions·schutz·gesetz** *das* anti-pollution law

**Emitter** /e'mɪtɐ/ *der;* **~s, ~** (*Technik*) emitter

**emittieren** *tr. V.* Ⓐ (*Finanzw.*) issue; Ⓑ (*in die Luft abblasen*) emit

**Emmchen** /'ɛmçən/ *Pl.* (*ugs. veralt.*) marks

**Emmentaler** /'ɛmənta:lɐ/ *der;* **~s, ~:** Emmenthal [cheese]

**e-Moll** *das* E minor; ⇒ *auch* **a-Moll**

**Emotion** /emo'tsi̯o:n/ *die;* **~, ~en** emotion

**emotional** ❶ *Adj.* emotional ‹person, reaction, etc.›; emotive ‹topic, question›. ❷ *adv.* emotionally

**emotionalisieren** *tr. V.* (*geh.*) arouse emotions in, emotionalize ‹person›; emotionalize ‹issue›

**Emotionalität** *die;* **~:** emotionalism; emotionality

---

*old spelling (see note on page 1707)

**emotionell** *Adj.* ⇒ **emotional**
**emotions·geladen** *Adj.* emotionally charged
**E-Motor** *der* electric motor
**Empathie** /ɛmpa'ti:/ *die;* ~ (*Psych.*) empathy
**empfahl** /ɛm'pfa:l/ *1. u. 3. Pers. Sg. Prät. v.* **empfehlen**
**empfand** /ɛm'pfant/ *1. u. 3. Pers. Sg. Prät. v.* **empfinden**
**Empfang** /ɛm'pfaŋ/ *der;* ~**[e]s, Empfänge** Ⓐ (*Entgegennahme*) receipt; **bei ~:** on receipt; **etw. in ~ nehmen** accept sth.; **mit einer Strafpredigt in ~ genommen werden** (*iron.*) be welcomed *or* greeted with a dressing-down; **zahlbar bei ~:** payable on receipt; Ⓑ (*Funkw., Rundf., Ferns.*) reception; **auf ~ gehen/bleiben** (*Funkw.*) switch over to 'receive'/stay on 'receive'; Ⓒ (*geh.: Begrüßung*) reception; Ⓓ (*festliche Veranstaltung*) reception; Ⓔ (*Rezeption*) reception [desk]
**empfangen** ❶ *unr. tr. V.* Ⓐ (*geh.*) receive; **einen Gast bei sich ~:** receive a guest at home; **die Sakramente ~** (*Rel.*) receive the sacraments; Ⓑ (*Funkw., Rundf., Ferns.*) receive; Ⓒ (*begrüßen*) receive, greet ‹person›; **jmdn. mit Blumen ~:** greet sb. with flowers; Ⓓ (*geh.: angeregt werden zu*) conceive ‹idea›; **eine Anregung [von jmdm.] ~:** receive a stimulus from sb.; Ⓔ (*geh.*) **ein Kind ~:** conceive a child. ❷ *unr. itr. V.* (*geh.: schwanger werden*) conceive
**Empfänger** /ɛm'pfɛŋɐ/ *der;* ~**s,** ~ Ⓐ recipient; (*eines Briefs*) addressee; **~ unbekannt/verzogen/unbekannt verzogen** not known at this address/gone away/gone away, address unknown; Ⓑ (*Empfangsgerät*) receiver
**-empfänger** *der* (*Renten~ usw.*) recipient of ...
**Empfängerin** *die;* ~, ~**nen** ⇒ **Empfänger** A
**empfänglich** *Adj.* Ⓐ (*leicht zugänglich*) receptive (**für** to); Ⓑ (*beeinflussbar*) susceptible; **für jmds. Charme/Schönheit ~ sein** be susceptible to sb.'s charm/beauty
**Empfänglichkeit** *die;* ~ Ⓐ (*Zugänglichkeit*) receptivity, receptiveness (**für** to); Ⓑ (*Beeinflussbarkeit*) susceptibility (**für** to)
**Empfängnis** *die;* ~**:** conception
**empfängnis·verhütend** *Adj.* **ein ~es Mittel** a contraceptive; **~ wirken** act as a contraceptive
**Empfängnis·verhütung** *die* contraception
**Empfängnisverhütungs·mittel** *das* contraceptive
**Empfängnis·zeit** (*Rechtsw.*) time of conception
**empfangs-, Empfangs-: ~antenne** *die* (*Rundf., Ferns.*) [receiving] aerial (*Brit.*) *or* (*Amer.*) antenna; **~berechtigt** *Adj.* authorized to receive payment/goods *postpos.;* **eine ~berechtigte Person** an authorized recipient; **~bereich** *der* (*Rundf., Ferns.*) reception area; **~bestätigung** *die* receipt; **~chef** *der* head receptionist; **~dame** *die* receptionist; **~gerät** *das* (*Funkw., Rundf., Ferns.*) receiver; **~halle** *die* reception lobby; **~saal** *der* reception hall; **~station** *die* (*Funkw., Rundf., Ferns.*) receiving station; (*Raumfahrt*) tracking station; **~zimmer** *das* reception room
**empfehlen** /ɛm'pfe:lən/ ❶ *unr. tr. V.* Ⓐ **jmdm. etw./jmdn. ~:** recommend sth./sb. to sb.; **der empfohlene Richtpreis** (*Wirtsch.*) the recommended price; **~ Sie mich Ihrer Gattin** (*geh.*) convey my respects to your wife; **dieser Arzt/dies ist sehr zu ~:** this doctor/this is to be highly recommended; Ⓑ (*veralt.: anvertrauen*) commend (*Dat.* to).
❷ *unr. refl. V.* Ⓐ (*geh.: sich verabschieden und gehen*) take one's leave; **darf ich mich ~?** may I take my leave?; Ⓑ (*unpers.*) **es empfiehlt sich, ... zu ...** it's advisable to ...; Ⓒ (*geh.: sich als geeignet erweisen*) **sich [durch/wegen etw.] ~:** commend oneself/itself [because of sth.]
**empfehlens·wert** *Adj.* Ⓐ to be recommended *postpos.;* recommendable; Ⓑ (*ratsam*) advisable
**Empfehlung** *die;* ~, ~**en** Ⓐ recommendation; **sie kam auf ~:** she came on somebody's recommendation; Ⓑ (*~sschreiben*) letter of recommendation; testimonial; Ⓒ (*höflicher Gruß*) **„eine ~ an Ihre Frau Mutter"** '[kind] regards to your mother'; **„mit freundlicher ~"** 'with kindest regards'
**Empfehlungs·schreiben** *das* letter of recommendation; testimonial
**empfiehl** /ɛm'pfi:l/ *Imperativ Sg. v.* **empfehlen**
**empfiehlst** *2. Pers. Sg. Präsens v.* **empfehlen**
**empfiehlt** *3. Pers. Sg. Präsens v.* **empfehlen**
**empfinden** /ɛm'pfɪndn̩/ *unr. tr. V.* Ⓐ (*wahrnehmen*) feel ‹pain, pleasure, bitterness, etc.›; **etwas/nichts für jmdn. ~:** feel something/nothing for sb.; Ⓑ (*auffassen*) **etw. als Beleidigung ~:** feel sth. to be an insult; **jmdn. als Eindringling ~:** feel sb. to be an impostor; **das empfinde ich nicht so** I feel differently about it
**Empfinden** *das;* ~**s** feeling; **für mein** *od.* **nach meinem ~:** to my mind
**empfindlich** ❶ *Adj.* Ⓐ (*sensibel, feinfühlig, auch fig.*) sensitive; **hoch ~:** highly sensitive; fast ‹film›; **eine ~e Stelle** a tender spot; Ⓑ (*leicht beleidigt*) sensitive, touchy ‹person›; Ⓒ (*anfällig*) **zart und ~:** delicate; **~ gegen Viruserkrankungen** prone to virus infections; Ⓓ (*spürbar*) severe ‹punishment, shortage›; harsh ‹punishment, measure›; sharp ‹increase›.
❷ *adv.* Ⓐ **~ auf etw.** (*Akk.*) **reagieren** (*sensibel*) be susceptible to sth.; (*beleidigt*) react oversensitively to sth.; Ⓑ (*spürbar*) ‹punish› severely, harshly; ‹increase› sharply; Ⓒ (*intensivierend*) ‹hurt› badly; bitterly ‹cold›; **der Streik machte sich für die Verbraucher sofort ~ bemerkbar** the strike had an immediate effect on the consumers
**Empfindlichkeit** *die;* ~, ~**en** ⇒ **empfindlich**: sensitivity; touchiness; severity; harshness; (*eines Films*) speed; **ihre ~ gegen Infektionen** her proneness *or* susceptibility to infections
**empfindsam** ❶ *Adj.* sensitive ‹nature›; (*gefühlvoll*) sentimental. ❷ *adv.* sensitively; (*gefühlvoll*) sentimentally
**Empfindsamkeit** *die;* ~**:** sensitivity; (*Literaturw.*) sentimentality
**Empfindung** *die;* ~, ~**en** Ⓐ (*sinnliche Wahrnehmung*) sensation; sensory perception; Ⓑ (*Gefühl*) feeling; emotion
**empfindungs-, Empfindungs-: ~los** *Adj.* Ⓐ (*körperlich*) numb; without sensation *pred.;* Ⓑ (*seelisch*) insensitive; unfeeling; **~losigkeit** *die;* ~~ Ⓐ (*körperlich*) numbness; lack of sensation; Ⓑ (*Gefühlskälte*) insensitivity; lack of feeling; **~nerv** *der* sensory nerve; **~vermögen** *das* Ⓐ (*physisch*) sensory perception; Ⓑ (*seelisch*) sensitivity
**empfing** /ɛm'pfɪŋ/ *1. u. 3. Pers. Sg. Prät. v.* **empfangen**
**empfohlen** /ɛm'pfo:lən/ ❶ *2. Part. v.* **empfehlen.** ❷ *Adj.* recommended
**empfunden** /ɛm'pfʊndn̩/ *2. Part. v.* **empfinden**
**Emphase** /ɛm'fa:zə/ *die;* ~, ~**n** (*geh.*) emphasis
**emphatisch** /ɛm'fa:tɪʃ/ ❶ *Adj.* (*geh.*) emphatic. ❷ *adv.* emphatically
**Empire[1]** /ã'pi:ɐ̯/ *das;* ~**[s]** Empire
**Empire[2]** /'ɛmpaɪə/ *das;* ~**[s]** (*Hist.*) Empire
**Empire·stil** /ã'pi:ɐ̯-/ *der* Empire style
**Empirie** /ɛmpi'ri:/ *die;* ~ Ⓐ (*Methode*) empirical method; Ⓑ (*Erfahrungswissen*) empirical knowledge
**Empiriker** *der;* ~**s,** ~, **Empirikerin** *die;* ~, ~**nen** empiricist
**empirisch** ❶ *Adj.* empirical. ❷ *adv.* empirically
**Empirismus** *der;* ~**:** empiricism
**empor** /ɛm'po:ɐ̯/ *Adv.* (*geh.*) upwards; up
**empor-: ~|arbeiten** *refl. V.* (*geh.*) work one's way up; **~|blicken** *itr. V.* (*geh.*) look upwards *or* (*literary*) heavenwards; **zum Himmel ~blicken** raise one's eyes heavenwards (*literary*)
**Empore** *die;* ~, ~**n** gallery
**empören** /ɛm'pø:rən/ ❶ *tr. V.* fill with indignation; incense; outrage. ❷ *refl. V.* Ⓐ (*zornig werden*) **sich über jmdn./etw. ~:** become indignant *or* incensed *or* outraged about sb./sth.; Ⓑ (*geh.: sich auflehnen*) **sich gegen jmdn./etw. ~:** rebel *or* rise against sb./sth.
**empörend** ❶ *Adj.* outrageous. ❷ *adv.* outrageously
**Empörer** *der;* ~**s,** ~, **Empörerin** *die;* ~, ~**nen** (*geh.*) rebel
**empörerisch** *Adj.* (*geh.*) rebellious
**empor-: ~|heben** *unr. tr. V.* (*geh.*) raise; **~|kommen** *unr. itr. V.; mit sein* (*geh.*) Ⓐ (*nach oben kommen*) come up; Ⓑ (*fig.: aufsteigen*) rise
**Emporkömmling** /-kœmlɪŋ/ *der;* ~**s,** ~**e** (*abwertend*) upstart; parvenu
**empor-: ~|ragen** *itr. V.* (*geh.*) rise [up]; **über etw.** (*Akk.*) **~ragen** tower above sth.; **~|recken** ❶ *tr. V.* (*geh.*) raise; ❷ *refl. V.* rise; **~|schauen** *itr. V.* (*geh.*) raise one's eyes; **~|schwingen** *unr. refl. V.* (*geh.*) **sich ~schwingen** swing oneself aloft; **sich zu großen Taten ~schwingen** (*fig.*) rise to great deeds; **~|steigen** *unr. itr. V.; mit sein* (*geh.*) Ⓐ climb up; **an etw.** (*Dat.*) **~steigen** climb [up] sth.; **einen Berg/die Treppe ~steigen** climb a mountain/the stairs; Ⓑ ‹balloon, kite› rise aloft; **~|streben** *itr. V.; mit sein* (*geh.*) soar upwards; **ein ~strebender Künstler** an aspiring artist
**empört** ❶ *Adj.* outraged ‹letter, look›; **über jmdn./etw. ~ sein** be outraged about sb./at *or* about sth. ❷ *adv.* **jmdn./etw. ~ zurückweisen** reject sb./sth. indignantly *or* angrily
**Empörung** *die;* ~, ~**en** Ⓐ outrage; Ⓑ (*geh.: Aufstand*) rebellion; uprising
**empor|züngeln** *itr. V.; mit sein* (*geh.*) ‹flames› leap up
**emsig** /'ɛmzɪç/ ❶ *Adj.* (*fleißig*) industrious, busy ‹person›; (*geschäftig*) bustling ‹activity›; (*übereifrig*) sedulous; **ein ~es Treiben** bustling activity; a hustle and bustle; **~ wie die Ameisen** *od.* **Bienen sein** be busy as bees. ❷ *adv.* (*fleißig*) industriously; busily; (*übereifrig*) sedulously
**Emsigkeit** *die;* ~ (*Fleiß*) industriousness; business; (*Übereifer*) sedulousness
**Emu** /'e:mu/ *der;* ~**s,** ~**s** (*Zool.*) emu
**Emulgator** /emʊl'ga:tɔr/ *der;* ~**s,** ~**en** /-ga'to:rən/ (*Chemie*) emulsifying agent; emulsifier
**Emulsion** /emʊl'zi̯o:n/ *die;* ~, ~**en** (*Chemie, Fot., Kosmetik*) emulsion
**E-Musik** *die;* ~**:** serious music
**en bloc** /ã'blɔk/ *Adv.* en bloc
**end-, End-: ~abnehmer** *der,* **~abnehmerin** *die* (*Wirtsch.*) ultimate buyer; **~ab·rechnung** *die* final account; **~achtziger** *der* man in his late eighties; **~achtzigerin** *die* woman in her late eighties; **~bahn·hof** *der* terminus; **~betont** *Adj.* (*Sprachw.*) ‹word› with final stress; **das Wort „Berlin" ist ~betont** the word 'Berlin' is stressed on the final syllable; **~betonung** *die* (*Sprachw.*) final stress; **~betrag** *der* final amount
**Endchen** *das;* ~**s,** ~**:** little bit; small piece
**End·darm** *der* ▶ 471 (*Anat.*) (*Dickdarm*) large intestine; colon; (*Afterdarm*) rectum
**Ende** /'ɛndə/ *das;* ~**s,** ~**n** ▶ 76, ▶ 207 Ⓐ end; **am ~ der Straße/Stadt** at the end of the road/town; **am ~ der Welt** (*scherzh.*) at the back of beyond; **etw. am richtigen/falschen ~ anfassen** (*fig.*) go about sth. the right/wrong way; **am/bis/gegen ~ des Monats/der Woche/des Jahres/des Jahrhunderts** at/by/towards the end of the month/week/year/century; **~ April** at the end of April; **bis ~ der Woche** by the end of the week; **am ~ des Buchs/Films** at the

end of the book/film; **das ~ des Films hat mir nicht gefallen** I didn't like the ending of the film; **~ zwanzig** *od.* **der Zwanziger/fünfzig** *od.* **der Fünfziger sein** be in one's late twenties/fifties; **wenn die beiden sich zanken, finden sie kein ~:** once those two start quarrelling they never stop; **zu ~ sein** ‹patience, hostility, war› be at an end; **die Schule/das Kino/das Spiel ist zu ~:** school is over/the film/game has finished; **zu ~ gehen** ‹period of time› come to an end; ‹supplies, savings› run out; ‹contract› expire; **etw. zu ~ führen** *od.* **bringen** finish sth.; **ein Buch zu ~ lesen** read a book to the end; **alles hat ein ~** *od.* **muss ein ~ haben** everything has to [come to an] end sometime; **~ gut, alles gut** all's well that ends well (*prov.*); **ein/kein ~ nehmen** come to an end/never come to an end; **einer Sache/seinem Leben ein ~ machen** *od.* **setzen** (*geh.*) put an end to sth./take one's life; **am ~ sein** (*ugs.*) be at the end of one's tether; **ich bin mit meiner Geduld am ~:** my patience is at an end; **mit etw. am ~ sein** be at *or* have reached the end of sth.; **mit ihm geht es zu ~** (*verhüll.*) he is nearing his end; **das ~ vom Lied** (*ugs.*) the end of the story; **am ~** (*schließlich*) when all is said and done; **am ~ wird er der Täter sein** (*nordd.*) he's probably the culprit; **das ~ der Wurst** the end [piece] of the sausage; [B] (*ugs.: kleines Stück*) bit; piece; **ein ~ Schnur** a bit *or* piece of string; [C] (*ugs.: Strecke*) **ein ganzes ~:** a pretty long way; [D] (*Jägerspr.*) point; [E] (*Seemannsspr.*) rope

**End·effekt** *der:* **im ~:** in the end; in the final analysis

**endeln** /'ɛndl̩n/ *tr. V.* (*bayr., österr.*) turn in [and oversew] ‹hem, seam›

**endemisch** /ɛn'de:mɪʃ/ ❶ *Adj.* (*Biol., Med.*) endemic. ❷ *adv.* endemically

**enden** *itr. V.* [A] end; ‹programme› end, finish; **der Zug endet in Berlin/hier** this train terminates in Berlin/here; **gut ~:** end well; **das wird nicht gut ~:** it's bound to end in disaster; **nicht ~ wollender Beifall** unending applause; [B] (*sterben*) *mit sein* **in der Gosse/im Gefängnis ~:** end up in the gutter/in prison; (*dort sterben*) die in the gutter/end one's days in prison

**End·ergebnis** *das* final result

**en détail** /ãde'taj/ *Adv.* [A] (*im Einzelnen*) in detail; [B] (*Kaufmannsspr. veralt.*) retail

**end-, End-: ~geschwindigkeit** *die* ⇒ **Höchstgeschwindigkeit**; **~gültig** ❶ *Adj.* final ‹consent, answer, decision›; conclusive ‹evidence›; **etwas/nichts ~gültiges sagen/hören** say/hear something/nothing definite; ❷ *adv.* **das ist ~gültig vorbei** that's all over and done with; **sich ~gültig trennen** separate for good; **das ist jetzt ~gültig entschieden** it's been decided once and for all; **~gültigkeit** *die* finality; (*von Beweisen*) conclusiveness; **~halte·stelle** *die* terminus

**endigen** /'ɛndɪɡn̩/ *itr. V.* (*veralt.*) ⇒ **enden**

**Endivie** /ɛn'di:vi̯ə/ *die;* **~, ~n** endive

**End-: ~kampf** *der* (*Sport*) final; (*Milit.*) final battle; **~lager** *das* [permanent] disposal site; [permanent] depository; **~|lagern** *tr. V.* dispose of [permanently]; **~lagerung** *die* permanent disposal (*of nuclear waste*); **~lauf** *der* (*Sport*) final; **~lauf·teilnehmer** *der*, **~lauf·teilnehmerin** *die* finalist

**endlich** ❶ *Adv.* [A] (*nach langer Zeit*) at last; **na ~ [kommst du]!** [so you've arrived] at [long] last; **bist du ~ so weit?** are you ready at last?; **siehst du ~ ein, dass du unrecht hattest?** do you see now that you were wrong?; **halt ~ den Mund!** why don't you shut up?; **lass mich ~ in Ruhe mit deinem Geschwätz!** stop your babbling and leave me in peace; [B] (*schließlich*) in the end; eventually; **wir kamen ~ doch zu einer Einigung** we did reach an agreement in the end *or* eventually. ❷ *Adj.* finite ‹size, number›

**Endlichkeit** *die;* **~:** finiteness

**end·los** ❶ *Adj.* [A] (*ohne Ende*) infinite; (*ringförmig*) endless, continuous ‹belt, chain›; [B] (*nicht enden wollend*) endless ‹road, desert, expanse, etc.›; endless, infinite ‹patience›; interminable ‹speech›. ❷ *adv.* **~ lange dauern** be interminably long; go on and on; **~ lange reden** talk interminably; **~ warten** wait for ages

**Endlos·formular** *das:* **ein ~:** continuous stationery; form paper (*Amer.*)

**Endlosigkeit** *die;* **~:** infinity; endlessness

**End-: ~lösung** *die* [A] (*selten: endgültige Lösung*) final solution; [B] (*ns. verhüll.*) Final Solution (*to the Jewish question*); **~moräne** *die* terminal moraine

**Endogamie** /ɛndoga'mi:/ *die;* **~** (*Völkerk.*) endogamy *no art.*

**endogen** /ɛndo'ge:n/ *Adj.* (*Med., Psych., Bot.*) endogenous

**Endoskop** /ɛndo'sko:p/ *das;* **~s, ~e** (*Med.*) endoscope

**endotherm** /ɛndo'tɛrm/ *Adj.* (*Physik, Chemie*) endothermic

**End-: ~phase** *die* final stages *pl.*; **~produkt** *das* final *or* end product; **~punkt** *der* end; (*einer Reise*) last stop; **~reim** *der* end rhyme; **~resultat** *das* final result; **~runde** *die* (*Sport*) final; **~runden·teilnehmer** *der*, **~runden·teilnehmerin** *die* (*Sport*) finalist; **~sieg** *der* (*bes. ns.*) final *or* ultimate victory; **~silbe** *die* [word-]final syllable; **~spiel** *das* [A] (*Sport*) final; [B] (*Schach*) endgame; **~spurt** *der* (*bes. Leichtathletik*) final spurt; **einen guten ~spurt haben** have a good finish; be good in the final spurt; **~stadium** *das* final stage; (*Med.*) terminal stage; **Krebs im ~stadium** terminal cancer; **~stand** *der* (*Sport*) final result; **~station** *die* terminus; **~station Krankenhaus** (*fig.*) finishing up in hospital; **~stück** *das* end; (*eines Brotes*) crust; **~summe** *die* [sum] total

**Endung** *die;* **~, ~en** (*Sprachw.*) ending

**endungs·los** *Adj.* (*Sprachw.*) without an ending *postpos., not pred.*; uninflected

**end-, End-: ~verbraucher** *der*, **~verbraucherin** *die* (*Wirtsch.*) consumer; **~verbraucher·preis** *der* retail price; **~zeit** *die* (*Rel.*) last days [of the world]; **~zeitlich** *Adj.* (*Rel.*) apocalyptic; **~ziel** *das* (*einer Reise*) final destination; (*Zweck*) ultimate aim *or* goal; **~ziffer** *die* final number; **das Los mit der ~ziffer 4** the coupon with a number ending in 4; **~zustand** *der* final state; **~zweck** *der* ultimate purpose *or* object

**Energie** /enɛr'gi:/ *die;* **~, ~n** [A] (*Physik*) energy; [B] (*Tatkraft*) energy; vigour

**energie-, Energie-: ~arm** *Adj.* ‹country› lacking in energy resources; **~bedarf** *der* energy requirement; **~bewusst**, ***~bewußt** *Adj.* energy-conscious; **~bündel** *das* (*ugs.*) bundle of energy; **~form** *die* form of energy; **~geladen** *Adj.* energetic, dynamic ‹person›; **~gewinnung** *die* energy production; **~haushalt** *der* (*Physiol.*) energy balance; (*Wirtsch.*) control of the use of energy; **~intensiv** *Adj.* energy-intensive; **~krise** *die* energy crisis; **~los** *Adj.* lacking [in] energy *postpos.*; sluggish; **~politik** *die* energy policy; **~politisch** ❶ *Adj.* **~politische Maßnahmen/Programme** energy measures/programmes; ❷ *adv.* in terms of energy policy; **~quelle** *die* energy source; source of energy; **neuzeitliche ~quellen** modern sources of energy; **~reich** *Adj.* energy-rich; **~reichtum** *der* energy wealth; **~satz** *der* (*Physik*) principle of the conservation of energy; **~sparer** *der*, **~sparerin** *die* energy-saver; **~spar·lampe** *die* energy-saving lamp; **~spender** *der* energy-giving substance; **~träger** *der* energy source; **~verbrauch** *der* energy consumption; **~verschwendung** *die* [A] wasting of energy; [B] (*Verschwendung von Tatkraft*) waste of energy; **~versorgung** *die* energy supply; **der ~versorgung** (*Dat.*) **dienen** serve to supply energy; **~wirtschaft** *die* energy sector; **~zufuhr** *die* supply of energy

**energisch** /e'nɛrgɪʃ/ ❶ *Adj.* [A] (*tatkräftig*) energetic, vigorous ‹person›; firm ‹action›; **~ werden** put one's foot down; [B] (*von starkem Willen zeugend*) determined; forceful; **ein ~es Kinn** a strong chin; [C] (*entschlossen*) forceful, firm ‹voice, words›. ❷ *adv.* [A] (*tatkräftig*) **~ durchgreifen** take drastic action; **etw. ~ verteidigen** defend sth. vigorously; [B] (*entschlossen*) ‹reject, say› forcefully, firmly; ‹stress› emphatically; ‹deny› strenuously

**enervieren** /enɛr'vi:rən/ *tr. V.* (*geh.*) enervate

**Enfant terrible** /ãfãtɛ'ribl/ *das;* **~ ~, ~s ~s** (*geh.*) enfant terrible

**eng** /ɛŋ/ ❶ *Adj.* [A] (*schmal*) narrow ‹valley, road, bed›; **einen ~en Horizont** *od.* **Gesichtskreis haben** (*fig.*) have a narrow *or* limited outlook; [B] (*dicht*) close ‹writing›; [C] (*fest anliegend*) close-fitting, tight; **ein ~es Kleid** a close-fitting dress; **der Anzug/Rock ist zu ~:** the suit/skirt is too tight; [D] (*beschränkt*) narrow, restricted ‹interpretation, concept›; cramped, constricted ‹room, space›; [E] *im Komp. u. Sup.* (*begrenzt*) **in die ~ere Wahl kommen** be short-listed (*Brit.*); **in der ~eren Wahl sein** be on the shortlist (*Brit.*); **im ~eren Sinne** in the stricter sense; [F] (*nahe*) close ‹friend›; **im ~sten Freundeskreis** among close friends; **die Hochzeit fand im ~sten Kreis der Familie statt** the wedding was attended by close relatives [only]; **die ~ere Verwandtschaft/Heimat** one's immediate relatives/home [area]. ❷ *adv.* [A] (*dicht*) **~ schreiben** write closely together; **~ [zusammen]sitzen/-stehen** sit/stand close together; **~ bedruckt/beschrieben** closely-printed/closely-written ‹page›; [B] (*fest anliegend*) **~ anliegen/sitzen** fit closely; **~ anliegend** tight-fitting, close-fitting ‹dress etc.›; [C] (*beschränkt*) **etw. zu ~ auslegen** interpret sth. too narrowly; **das siehst du zu ~** (*ugs.*) there's more to it than that; **~ begrenzt** limited; restricted; [D] (*nahe*) closely ‹related›; **mit jmdm. ~ befreundet sein** be a close friend of sb.; **die beiden ~ befreundeten Herren/Ehepaare** the two gentlemen/[married] couples, who are/were close friends

**Engadin** /'ɛŋgadi:n/ *das;* **~s** Engadine

**Engagement** /ãgaʒə'mã:/ *das;* **~s, ~s** [A] (*Einsatz*) involvement; **sein ~ für etw.** his commitment to sth.; **sein ~ gegen etw.** his committed stand against sth.; [B] (*eines Künstlers*) engagement

**engagieren** /ãga'ʒi:rən/ ❶ *refl. V.* commit oneself, become committed (**für** to); **sich politisch ~:** become politically involved; **sich in einer Organisation ~:** be active in an organization; **sich in einem Land/Geschäft ~** (*verhüllend*) become involved in a country/business. ❷ *tr. V.* (*unter Vertrag nehmen*) engage ‹artist, actor, etc.›

**engagiert** *Adj.* [A] (*entschieden für etw. eintretend*) committed ‹literature, film, director›; **politisch/sozial ~ sein** be politically/socially committed *or* involved; [B] (*angestellt*) engaged ‹artist, actor, etc.›

**Engagiertheit** *die;* **~:** commitment; involvement

***eng·anliegend** *usw.* ⇒ **eng** 2

**Enge** /'ɛŋə/ *die;* **~, ~n** [A] confinement; restriction; [B] (*veralt.: Engpass*) (*Meeres~*) strait; (*Kanal~*) narrows *pl.*; **jmdn. in die ~ treiben** (*fig.*) drive sb. into a corner

**Engel** /'ɛŋl̩/ *der;* **~s, ~:** angel; **ich habe die ~ [im Himmel] singen** *od.* **pfeifen hören** (*ugs.*) it hurt like hell; **sie ist mein guter/ein rettender/ein wahrer ~:** she is my good/a guardian/a real angel; **er ist [auch] nicht gerade ein ~:** he's not exactly an angel

**Engelchen** *das;* **~s, ~, Engelein** *das;* **Engeleins, Engelein** little angel

**engel-, Engel-: ~haft** *Adj.* angelic; **~macher** *der*, **~macherin** *die* backstreet abortionist; **~schar** *die* heavenly host; host of angels

**Engels-: ~geduld** *die* patience of a saint; **~gesicht** *das* angelic face

**engel[s]·gleich** *Adj.* angelic

**Engels·haar** *das* angel's hair

**Engel[s]·kopf** *der* cherub

**Engels-: ~miene** *die* innocent look; **~musik** *die* heavenly music; **~zungen** *Pl.* **in mit**

*old spelling (see note on page 1707)

**~zungen auf jmdn. einreden** use all one's powers of persuasion on sb.

**Engerling** /'ɛŋɐlɪŋ/ *der;* **~s, ~e** grub

**eng·herzig** ❶ *Adj.* petty. ❷ *adv.* in a petty way

**Eng·herzigkeit** *die;* **~:** pettiness

**England** *(das);* **~s** Ⓐ England; Ⓑ *(ugs.: Großbritannien)* Britain

**Engländer** /'ɛŋlɛndɐ/ *der;* **~s, ~** ▶553 Ⓐ Englishman/English boy; **er ist ~:** he is English *or* an Englishman; **die ~:** the English; Ⓑ *(ugs.: Brite)* British person/man; Britisher *(Amer.)*; **die ~:** the British; Ⓒ *(Schraubenschlüssel)* monkey wrench

**Engländerin** *die;* **~, ~nen** ▶553 Ⓐ Englishwoman/English girl; **sie ist ~:** she is English *or* an Englishwoman; Ⓑ *(ugs.: Britin)* British person/woman; **die ~nen sind ...** British women are ...

**england·freundlich** *Adj.* anglophile

**englisch[1]** ▶553, ▶696 ❶ *Adj.* English; **~-deutsch** Anglo-German; English-German ‹dictionary›; ‹book› in English and German; **die ~e Sprache/Literatur** the English language/English literature; **die ~e Krankheit** *(veralt.)* rickets; **Englisch Horn** *(fachspr.)* ⇒ **Englischhorn**; **~e Bulldogge** bulldog. ❷ *adv.* **~ sprechen** speak English; **~ [gebraten]** rare; underdone; **ein ~ abgefasster Artikel** an article in English; ⇒ *auch* **deutsch, Deutsche[2]**

**englisch[2]** *Adj.* **der Englische Gruß** the Angelic Salutation; the Ave Maria; the Hail Mary; **die Englischen Fräulein** *Institute of the Blessed Virgin Mary;* the 'English Ladies'; the 'English Virgins'

**Englisch** *das;* **~[s]** ▶696 English; **ein gutes/fehlerfreies ~ sprechen** speak good/perfect English; **das moderne ~/~ Chaucers** present day/Chaucerian English; ⇒ *auch* **Deutsch**

**englisch-, Englisch-: ~horn** *das (Musik)* cor anglais; **~lehrer** *der,* **~lehrerin** *die* 'English teacher; **~sprachig** *Adj.* Ⓐ *(in ~er Sprache)* English-language ‹book, magazine›; **die ~sprachige Literatur** English literature; Ⓑ *(~sprachig sprechend)* English-speaking ‹population, country›; **~unterricht** *der* English teaching; *(Unterrichtsstunde)* English lesson; **er gibt ~unterricht** he teaches English; **sie arbeitet im ~unterricht gut mit** she always pays attention in English lessons; **das habe ich im ~unterricht gelernt** I learnt that in English

**Englishwaltz** /'ɪŋglɪʃ 'wɔ(:)l(t)s/ *der;* **~, ~:** slow waltz

**eng·maschig** ❶ *Adj.* Ⓐ close-meshed ‹fabric›; Ⓑ *(Sport)* tight. ❷ *adv.* Ⓐ **~ stricken/gestrickt sein** knit/be knitted tightly; Ⓑ *(Sport)* **~ spielen** play tightly

**Eng·pass, *Eng·paß** *der* Ⓐ [narrow] pass; defile; Ⓑ *(fig.: in der Versorgung usw.)* bottleneck

**en gros** /ã'gro/ *(Kaufmannsspr.)* wholesale

**eng-, Eng-: ~stirnig** ❶ *Adj. (abwertend)* narrow-minded ‹person›; ❷ *adv.* **~stirnig denken/handeln** be narrow-minded in the way one thinks/acts; **~stirnigkeit** *die;* **~~:** narrow-mindedness; ***~verwandt** ⇒ **eng** 2D; **~zeilig** *Adv.* with the lines closely spaced

**Enjambement** /ãʒãbə'mã:/ *das;* **~s, ~s** *(Verslehre)* enjambment

**Enkel[1]** /'ɛŋkl̩/ *der;* **~s, ~** *(nordd.)* ankle

**Enkel[2]** *der;* **~s, ~** Ⓐ grandson; Ⓑ *(Nachfahr)* grandchild; **selbst unsere ~ werden sich daran erinnern** even our grandchildren and great-grandchildren will remember it

**Enkelin** *die;* **~, ~nen** granddaughter

**Enkel-: ~kind** *das* grandchild; **~sohn** *der* grandson; **~tochter** *die* granddaughter

**Enklave** /ɛn'kla:və/ *die;* **~, ~en** enclave

**enkodieren** /ɛnko'di:rən/ *tr. V.* encode

**en masse** /ã'mas/ *(ugs.)* en masse

**en miniature** /ãminja'ty:r/ in miniature; **der Eiffelturm ~:** the Eiffel Tower in miniature; a miniature Eiffel Tower

**enorm** /e'nɔrm/ ❶ *Adj.* enormous ‹sum, costs›; tremendous *(coll.)* ‹effort›; immense ‹strain›; vast ‹knowledge, sum›. ❷ *adv.* tremendously *(coll.)* ‹expensive, practical›; **~ verdienen** earn an enormous amount *or* vast sums [of money]; **~ viel/viele** a tremendous *(coll.) or* an enormous amount/a tremendous *(coll.) or* an enormous number; **sich ~ freuen** *(ugs.)* be tremendously *(coll.)* pleased

**en passant** /ãpa'sã/ Ⓐ *(beiläufig)* en passant; in passing; Ⓑ *(Schach)* en passant

**Enquete** /ã'kɛ:t(ə)/ *die;* **~, ~n** Ⓐ survey; Ⓑ *(österr.: Arbeitstagung)* meeting for discussion

**Ensemble** /ã'sã:bl̩/ *das* Ⓐ *(Gruppe)* ensemble; **das ~ eines Theaters** the company of a theatre; Ⓑ *(Auftritt)* ensemble; Ⓒ *(Kleidungsstück)* outfit; ensemble; Ⓓ *(geh.: Gesamtheit)* ensemble

**Ensemble-: ~mitglied** *das* member of the ensemble/company; **~musik** *die* light music

**entarten** *itr. V.; mit sein* degenerate; **entartet** degenerate; **zu** *od.* **in** *(Akk.)* **etw. ~:** degenerate into sth.

**Entartung** *die;* **~, ~en** degeneration

**Entartungs·erscheinung** *die* sign of degeneration; **das führte zu ~en** this led to degeneracy

**entasten, entästen** *tr. V. (Forstw.)* disbranch

**entäußern** *refl. V. (geh.)* Ⓐ **sich einer Sache** *(Gen.)* **~** *(entsagen)* renounce sth.; *(weggeben)* relinquish *or* give up sth.; Ⓑ *(Philos.)* be realized

**Entäußerung** *die* Ⓐ *(geh.: Verzicht)* renunciation; Ⓑ *(Weggabe)* giving up; Ⓒ *(Philos.)* realization

**entbehren** /ɛnt'be:rən/ ❶ *tr. V.* Ⓐ *(geh.: vermissen)* miss ‹person›; Ⓑ *(verzichten)* do without; spare; **etw./jmdn. nicht ~ können** not be able to spare sth./sb.; not be able to do without sth./sb.; **viel[es] ~ müssen** have to go without [a lot of things]. ❷ *itr. V. (geh.: ermangeln)* **einer Sache** *(Gen.)* **~:** lack *or* be without sth.

**entbehrlich** *Adj.* dispensable; unnecessary ‹action›

**Entbehrlichkeit** *die;* **~:** superfluousness; dispensability

**Entbehrung** *die;* **~, ~en** privation; **große ~en auf sich** *(Akk.)* **nehmen** make great sacrifices

**entbehrungs-: ~reich, ~voll** *Adj.* ‹life, years› of privation

**entbeinen** *tr. V.* bone

**entbieten** *unr. tr. V. (geh.)* Ⓐ offer ‹best wishes, greetings›; **jmdm. seine Grüße ~:** present one's compliments to sb.; Ⓑ *(veralt.: kommen lassen)* summon

**entbinden** ❶ *unr. tr. V.* Ⓐ *(befreien)* **jmdn. von einem Versprechen ~:** release sb. from a promise; **seines Amtes** *od.* **von seinem Amt entbunden werden** be relieved of [one's] office; Ⓑ *(Geburtshilfe leisten)* **jmdn. ~:** deliver sb.; deliver sb.'s baby; **von einem Jungen/Mädchen entbunden werden** give birth to a boy/girl. ❷ *unr. itr. V. (gebären)* give birth; **zu Hause ~:** have one's baby at home

**Entbindung** *die* Ⓐ *(das Gebären)* **eine schwere/schmerzfreie ~:** a difficult/painless delivery *or* birth; **zur ~ in die Klinik müssen** have to go to hospital for the delivery *or* to have the baby; **bei der ~ anwesend sein** be present at the birth; Ⓑ *(Befreiung)* release; **um die ~ von seinem Amt bitten** ask to be relieved of one's duties

**Entbindungs-: ~saal** *der* delivery room; **~station** *die* maternity ward

**entblättern** ❶ *refl. V.* Ⓐ ‹trees, shrubs› shed its/their leaves; Ⓑ *(scherzh.: sich ausziehen)* strip; take one's clothes off. ❷ *tr. V.* strip ‹trees› [of leaves]

**entblöden** *refl. V.* **sich nicht ~, etw. zu tun** *(geh. abwertend)* have the effrontery to do sth.

**entblößen** ❶ *refl. V.* take one's clothes off; ‹exhibitionist› expose oneself; *(sein wahres Gesicht zeigen)* show oneself as one really is/was. ❷ *tr. V.* Ⓐ **den Arm ~:** uncover one's arm; **entblößt** bare; **mit entblößtem Kopf** without a hat; **sein Schwert ~** *(dichter.)* unsheathe one's sword; Ⓑ *(fig.)* reveal ‹feelings, thoughts›

**entbrennen** *unr. itr. V.; mit sein (geh.)* Ⓐ *(beginnen)* ‹battle› break out; ‹quarrel› flare up; Ⓑ *(ergriffen werden)* **in Liebe entbrannt sein** be passionately in love; **in Zorn entbrannt sein** be inflamed with anger

**Entchen** /'ɛntçən/ *das;* **~s, ~:** duckling

**entdecken** ❶ *tr. V.* Ⓐ *(finden)* discover; **eine Insel/ein chemisches Element ~:** discover an island/a chemical element; Ⓑ *(ausfindig machen)* **jmdn. ~:** find *or* spot sb.; **wir konnten ihn in dem Gewühl nicht ~:** we couldn't find him in the crowd; **etw. ~:** find *or* discover sth.; Ⓒ *(überraschend bemerken)* discover ‹theft›; come across ‹acquaintance›; Ⓓ *(veralt.: offenbaren)* **jmdn. etw. ~:** reveal *or (arch.)* discover sth. to sb. ❷ *refl. V. (veralt.: anvertrauen)* **sich jmdm. ~:** confide in sb.

**Entdecker** *der;* **~s, ~:** discoverer; *(Forschungsreisender)* explorer

**Entdecker·freude** *die* joy of discovery

**Entdeckerin** *die;* **~, ~nen** ⇒ **Entdecker**

**Entdeckung** *die;* **~, ~en** discovery

**Entdeckungs·reise** *die* voyage of discovery; *(zu Lande)* expedition; **auf ~/~n gehen** *(fig. scherzh.)* go exploring

**Ente** /'ɛntə/ *die;* **~, ~n** Ⓐ *(Vogel, Fleisch)* duck; **eine lahme ~** *(ugs.)* a slowcoach *(coll.)*; **sein Wagen ist eine richtige lahme ~** *(ugs.)* his car totally lacks oomph *(coll.) or* has no pick-up *(Amer. sl.)*; Ⓑ *(ugs.: Falschmeldung)* canard; spoof *(coll.)*; Ⓒ **kalte ~:** [cold] punch; Ⓓ *(ugs.: Auto)* Citroën 2 CV car; Ⓔ *(ugs.: Uringefäß)* [bed] bottle

**entehren** *tr. V.* dishonour; **~d** degrading

**Entehrung** *die* dishonouring

**enteignen** *tr. V.* expropriate

**Enteignung** *die* expropriation

**enteilen** *itr. V.; mit sein (geh.)* hasten away; *(fig.)* ‹hours, years, etc.› fly by

**enteisen** *tr. V.* de-ice

**enteisenen** *tr. V.* remove the iron from; **stark/schwach enteisent** with a very low/slightly reduced iron content

**Entelechie** /ɛntelɛ'çi:/ *die;* **~, ~n** *(Philos.)* entelechy

**Enten-: ~braten** *der* roast duck; **~ei** *das* duck's egg; **~feder** *die* duck's feather; **~flott** *das;* **~~s** *(nordd.)* ⇒ **~grütze**; **~gericht** *das* duck dish; **~grütze** *die* duckweed; **~jagd** *die* duck shooting; **eine ~jagd** a duck shoot; **~junge** *das* duckling; **~klein** *das;* **~s** *(Kochk.)* duck's giblets *pl;* **~küken** *das* duckling; **~schnabel** *der* Ⓐ duck's bill; Ⓑ *(Schuh)* duckbill

**Entente** /ã'tã:t(ə)/ *die;* **~, ~n** *(Politik)* entente

**Enten-: ~teich** *der* duck pond; **~wal** *der* bottle-nosed whale

**Enter·beil** *das* boarding pike

**enterben** *tr. V.* disinherit

**Enter·brücke** *die* boarding bridge

**Enterbung** *die;* **~, ~en** disinheritance

**Enter·haken** *der* grapnel; grappling iron

**Enterich** /'ɛntərɪç/ *der;* **~s, ~e** drake

**entern** /'ɛntɐn/ ❶ *tr., itr. V.* board ‹ship›. ❷ *itr. V.; mit sein* **in die Masten ~** *(Seemannsspr.)* climb the rigging. ❸ *tr. V. (ugs.: erklettern)* climb ‹fence, wall, etc.›; climb on to ‹lorry, etc.›

**Enter·säbel** *der (hist.)* cutlass

**Entertainer** /'ɛntɐteɪnɐ/ *der;* **~s, ~, Entertainerin** *die;* **~, ~nen** ▶159 entertainer

**entfachen** *tr. V. (geh.)* Ⓐ kindle, light ‹fire›; **einen Brand ~:** start a fire; Ⓑ *(fig.: hervorrufen)* provoke, start ‹quarrel, argument›; arouse ‹passion, enthusiasm›

**entfahren** *unr. itr. V.; mit sein* **ihm entfuhr ein Fluch/ein Seufzer** he swore inadvertently/he let out a sigh

**entfallen** *unr. itr. V.; mit sein* Ⓐ *(aus dem Gedächtnis)* **der Name/das Wort ist mir ~:** the name/word escapes me *or* has slipped my mind; **das ist mir ~:** I have forgotten; Ⓑ

(*zugeteilt werden*) **auf jmdn./etw. ~:** be allotted to sb./sth.; **auf jeden Erben entfielen 10 000 Mark** each heir received 10,000 marks; **auf jeden Miteigentümer ~ 50 000 Mark** (*müssen bezahlt werden*) each of the joint owners has to pay 50,000 marks; C (*wegfallen*) lapse; **für Kinder ~ diese Gebühren** these charges do not apply *or* are not applicable to children; **aus Zeitmangel ~:** be omitted for lack of time; D (*geh.*) **jmds. Händen ~:** slip *or* fall from sb.'s hands

**entfalten** ❶ *tr. V.* A (*auseinander falten*) open [up]; unfold, spread out ‹map etc.›; ‹plant› open ‹leaves›; B (*zeigen*) show, display ‹ability, talent›; C (*darlegen*) expound ‹ideas, thoughts›; present ‹plan›; D (*entwickeln*) begin to show *or* display ‹interest, enthusiasm, etc.›. ❷ *refl. V.* A (*sich entwickeln*) ‹personality, talent› develop; **sich frei ~:** develop one's own personality to the full; B (*sich öffnen*) ‹flower, parachute› open [up]

**Entfaltung** *die; ~, ~en* A (*Entwicklung*) development; **die ~ der Persönlichkeit** the development of one's personality; **zur ~ kommen** *od.* **gelangen** develop; B (*Darstellung*) display; (*eines Plans*) exposition; presentation

**entfärben** ❶ *tr. V.* take the colour out of ‹material, clothing›. ❷ *refl. V.* ‹material, clothing, etc.› fade

**Entfärber** *der* colour *or* dye remover

**entfernen** ❶ *tr. V.* A remove ‹stain, wart, etc.›; take out ‹tonsils etc.›; **jmdn. von** *od.* **aus der Schule ~:** expel sb. [from school]; **jmdn. aus seinem Amt ~:** dismiss sb. from his office; B (*geh.: fortbringen*) remove. ❷ *refl. V.* go away; **sich vom Weg ~:** go off *or* leave the path; **sich unerlaubt von der Truppe ~:** go absent without leave; **sich aus der Stadt/dem Büro ~:** leave [the] town/the office; **langsam entfernten sich die Schritte** the footsteps slowly receded

**entfernt** ❶ *Adj.* A ▶265 (*fern*) remote; **das ist** *od.* **liegt weit ~ von der Stadt** it is a long way from the town *or* out of town; **er ist weit davon ~, das zu tun** (*fig.*) he does not have the slightest intention of doing that; **10 km/zwei Stunden [von einem Punkt] ~:** 10 km/two hours away [from a place]; B (*weitläufig*) slight ‹acquaintance›; distant ‹relation›; C (*schwach*) slight, vague ‹resemblance›.
❷ *adv.* A (*fern*) remotely; **das stört mich nicht im Entferntesten** that does not bother me in the slightest *or* in the least; **er dachte nicht ~** *od.* **im Entferntesten daran, das zu tun** he did not have the slightest intention of doing that; B (*weitläufig*) slightly ‹acquainted›; distantly ‹related›; **mit jmdm. ~ verwandt sein** be distantly related to sb.; C (*schwach*) slightly, vaguely; **sich ~ an etw.** (*Akk.*) **erinnern** remember sth. vaguely; have a vague recollection of sth.

**Entfernung** *die; ~, ~en* A ▶265 (*Abstand*) distance; (*beim Schießen*) range; **in einer ~ von 100 m** at a distance/range of 100 m.; 100 m. away; **auf eine ~ von 100 m** from a distance of 100 m.; **aus der ~:** from a distance; B (*das Beseitigen*) removal; C (*das Weggehen*) **unerlaubte ~ von der Truppe** absence without leave

**Entfernungs·messer** *der; ~s, ~* (*Gerät*) rangefinder

**entfesseln** *tr. V.* unleash ‹war, riot, etc.›; raise ‹laughter etc.›; **die entfesselten Elemente** *od.* **Naturgewalten** the raging elements; **entfesselte Leidenschaften** (*geh.*) unbridled passions

**Entfesselungs·künstler** *der*, **Entfesselungs·künstlerin** *die* escapologist

**entfetten** *tr. V.* skim ‹milk›; scour ‹wool›; dry ‹skin›

**Entfettungs·kur** *die* diet to remove one's excess fat

**entflammbar** *Adj.* A inflammable; B (*begeisterungsfähig*) easily roused

*old spelling (see note on page 1707)

**entflammen** ❶ *tr. V.* arouse ‹enthusiasm etc›; **jmdn. für etw. ~:** arouse sb.'s enthusiasm for sth. ❷ *itr. V.*; *mit sein* A ‹hatred etc.› flare up; ‹battle, strike› break out; **er ist [in Liebe] für sie entflammt** he became enraptured with her; (*Zustand*) he is passionately in love with her

**entflechten** *unr.* (*auch regelm.*) *tr. V.* A (*entwirren*) disentangle; B (*Wirtsch.*) break up ‹cartel etc.›

**Entflechtung** *die; ~, ~en* (*Wirtsch.*) breaking-up; break-up

**entfleuchen** *itr. V.*; *mit sein* (*altertümelnd scherzh.*) get *or* run away

**entfliegen** *unr. itr. V.*; *mit sein* fly away; **gestern ist uns** (*Dat.*) **unser Kanarienvogel entflogen** yesterday our canary got away; **„Wellensittich entflogen"** 'budgerigar lost'

**entfliehen** *unr. itr. V.*; *mit sein* A escape; **jmdm. ~:** escape from sb.; **dem Alltag ~** (*geh.*) escape from the daily routine; B (*geh.: entschwinden*) ‹time› fly by

**entfremden** ❶ *tr. V.* A (*fremd machen*) **jmdn. einer Sache** (*Dat.*) **~:** alienate *or* estrange sb. from sth.; **etw. seinem Zweck ~:** use sth. for a different purpose; B (*Philos., Soziol.*) **entfremdet** alienated ‹person, work, etc.›. ❷ *refl. V.* **sich jmdm./einer Sache ~:** become estranged from sb./unfamiliar with sth.

**Entfremdung** *die; ~, ~en* A alienation; estrangement; **die ~ von jmdm./etw.** alienation *or* estrangement from sb./sth.; **die ~ zwischen Regierung und Volk** the government's alienation from the people; B (*Philos., Soziol.*) alienation

**entfrosten** *tr. V.* defrost ‹refrigerator etc.›; defrost, de-ice ‹windscreen etc.›

**Entfroster** *der; ~s, ~:* defroster; de-icer

**entführen** *tr. V.* A kidnap, abduct ‹child etc.›; hijack ‹plane, lorry, etc.›; B (*scherzh.: mitnehmen*) steal; make off with

**Entführer** *der*, **Entführerin** *die* ⇒ **entführen** A: kidnapper; abductor; hijacker

**Entführung** *die* ⇒ **entführen** A: kidnap; kidnapping; abduction; hijack; hijacking; **„Die ~ aus dem Serail"** 'Il Seraglio'

**entgegen** ❶ *Adv.* A (*auf … zu*) towards; **der Sonne ~!** on towards the sun!; B (*zuwider*) **alles, was ihnen ~ war** everything they did not like. ❷ *Präp. mit Dat.* **~ meinem Wunsch** against my wishes; **~ dem Befehl** contrary to orders

**entgegen-, Entgegen-: ~|arbeiten** *itr. V.* **jmdm./einer Sache** (*Dat.*) **~arbeiten** work against sb./sth.; **~|blicken** *itr. V.* (*geh.*) A **jmdm. freudig/böse ~blicken** happily/angrily watch sb. coming; B (*fig.: ~sehen*) **der Zukunft froh/mit Bangen ~blicken** look towards the future with joy/fear; **~|branden** *itr. V.*; *mit sein* (*geh.*) **dem Künstler brandete Beifall ~:** the artist received *or* was greeted with a great wave of applause; **~|bringen** *unr. tr. V.* (*fig.*) **jmdm. Liebe/Verständnis ~bringen** show sb. love/understanding; **~|eilen** *itr. V.*; *mit sein* A **jmdm. ~eilen** hurry to meet sb.; B (*fig.: ~gehen*) **einer Sache** (*Dat.*) **~eilen** rush towards sth.; **~|fahren** *unr. itr. V.*; *mit sein* **jmdm. ~fahren** come/go to meet sb.; **~|fiebern** *itr. V.* **einem Ereignis ~fiebern** look forward to an event with nervous anticipation; **~|gehen** *unr. itr. V.*; *mit sein* A **jmdm. [ein Stück] ~gehen** go [a little way] to meet sb.; B (*fig.*) **einer Katastrophe/schweren Zeiten ~gehen** be heading for *or* towards a catastrophe/hard times; **der Vollendung/dem Ende ~gehen** be approaching completion/its end; **~gesetzt** ❶ *Adj.* A (*umgekehrt*) opposite ‹end, direction›; **sie gingen in ~gesetzter Richtung davon** they went off in opposite directions; B (*gegensätzlich*) opposing; **~gesetzter Meinung sein** hold opposing views; **das ~gesetzte tun** do the opposite; ❷ *adv.* **genau ~gesetzt handeln/denken** do/think exactly the opposite; **~|halten** *unr. tr. V.* A **jmdm. etw. ~halten** offer sth. to sb.; B (*fig.: einwenden*) **einem Argument ein anderes ~halten** counter an argument with another; **~halten, dass …** counter that …; **~|kommen** *unr. itr. V.*; *mit sein* A (*zukommen auf*) **jmdm. ~kommen** come to meet sb.; **der ~kommende Verkehr** oncoming traffic; B (*Zugeständnisse machen*) **jmdm. ~kommen** be accommodating towards sb.; **dem Verhandlungspartner ~kommen** make concessions to one's opposite number in the negotiations; **sie/das kam unseren Wünschen ~:** she complied with our wishes/it was what we wanted; C (*entsprechen*) **einer Sache** (*Dat.*) **~kommen** comply with *or* fit in with sth.; **~kommen** *das; ~~s, ~~* A (*Konzilianz*) cooperation; **wenn er etwas mehr ~kommen gezeigt hätte** if he had shown a little more willingness to cooperate; B (*Zugeständnis*) concession; **zu keinem ~kommen bereit sein** be unwilling to make any concessions; **~kommend** *Adj.* obliging; **~kommenderweise** *Adv.* obligingly; **~|laufen** *unr. itr. V.*; *mit sein* A **jmdm. ~laufen** run to meet sb.; B (*sich widersprechen*) **einander ~laufen** conflict with each other; **~nahme** *die; ~~* (*Amtsdt.*) receipt; **bei ~nahme** on receipt; **~|nehmen** *unr. itr. V.* receive; **ein Paket ~nehmen** accept a parcel; **~|schlagen** *unr. itr. V.* A *mit sein* **eine Rauchwolke/ein übler Geruch schlug mir ~:** I encountered a cloud of smoke/a foul smell; **ihm schlug eine Welle der Entrüstung ~:** he was met by a wave of indignation; B (*geh.*) **die Herzen schlugen ihm ~:** their/our *etc.* hearts went out to him; **~|sehen** *unr. itr. V.* A **einer Sache** (*Dat.*) **~sehen** look forward to sth.; **einem Ereignis freudig ~sehen** look forward eagerly to an event; B (*~blicken*) **den eintreffenden Gästen ~sehen** watch the guests arriving; **~|setzen** *tr. V.* A **einer Sache** (*Dat.*) **etw. ~setzen** oppose sth. with sth.; **einer Sache** (*Dat.*) **Widerstand ~setzen** resist sth.; B (*gegenüberstellen*) **einer Behauptung/einem Argument etw. ~setzen** counter a claim/an argument with sth.; **~|stehen** *unr. itr. V.* A (*hinderlich sein*) **einer Sache** (*Dat.*) **~stehen** stand in the way of sth.; **dem steht nichts ~:** there's no reason why not; B (*im Gegensatz stehen zu*) **einer Sache** (*Dat.*) **~stehen** conflict with sth.; **~|stellen** *tr. V.*: ⇒ **~setzen** B; **~|strecken** *tr. V.* **jmdm. etw. ~strecken** hold sth. out towards sb.; **~|treten** *unr. itr. V.*; *mit sein* A (*in den Weg treten*) go/come up to; **einem Angreifer ~treten** go into action against an attacker; **Schwierigkeiten** (*Dat.*) **~treten** stand up to difficulties; **einem Angriff ~treten** answer an attack; B (*sich wehren gegen*) **Vorwürfen/Anschuldigungen ~treten** answer reproaches/accusations; **~|wirken** *itr. V.* **einer Sache** (*Dat.*) **~wirken** [actively] oppose sth.; **die Regierung sollte diesem Missbrauch ~wirken** the Government should do something to halt this abuse

**entgegnen** /ɛnt'ge:gnən/ *tr. V.* retort; reply; **einer Sache** (*Dat.*) **etw. ~:** say sth. in reply to sth.; **jmdm. ~, dass …** reply that …

**Entgegnung** *die; ~, ~en* retort; reply; **als ~ darauf** in reply

**entgehen** *unr. itr. V.*; *mit sein* A (*entkommen*) escape; **einer Gefahr/Strafe** (*Dat.*) **~:** escape *or* avoid danger/punishment; B (*versäumt, ausgelassen werden*) miss; **das darf man sich** (*Dat.*) **nicht ~ lassen** that is not to be missed; C (*nicht bemerkt werden*) **jmdm. entgeht etw.** sb. misses sth.; sb. fails to see sth.; **ihm ist nicht entgangen, dass …** it has not escaped his notice that …

**entgeistert** /ɛnt'gaistɐt/ *Adj.* dumbfounded; **jmdn. ~ anstarren** stare at sb. in amazement *or* astonishment

**Entgelt** /ɛnt'gɛlt/ *das; ~[e]s, ~e* payment; fee; **gegen** *od.* **für ein geringes ~:** for a small fee; **ohne ~:** free of charge

**entgelten** *unr. tr. V.* (*geh.*) pay for (*also fig.*); **jmdm. eine Arbeit ~:** pay sb. for a job; **jmdn. etw. ~ lassen** make sb. pay for sth.

## Entfernung

***1 Meter*** = one metre = 3 feet 3.4 inches *od.* 1.094 yards
***1 Kilometer*** = one kilometre = 1094 yards *od.* 0.6214 mile

***Wie weit ist es von A nach B?***
= How far is it *od.* What's the distance from A to B?
***Es sind/Die Entfernung beträgt beinahe 600 Kilometer***
= It's/The distance is nearly 600 kilometres
≈ It's/The distance is nearly 370 miles
***Es ist ziemlich weit [entfernt]***
= It's quite a long way [away]
***Hannover liegt weiter vom Meer entfernt als Bremen***
= Hanover is further from the sea than Bremen
***Magdeburg liegt näher an Berlin als Braunschweig***
= Magdeburg is closer to Berlin than Brunswick
***A und B sind gleich weit entfernt***
= A and B are the same distance away
***Er traf das Ziel aus einer Entfernung von 50 Metern***
= He hit the target from a distance of 50 metres
***eine Autofahrt von achtzig Kilometern/zwanzig Minuten***
= an eighty-kilometre *od.* ≈ a fifty-mile/twenty-minute drive
***eine Stunde/zwei Stunden Fahrt [mit dem Auto]***
= an hour's/two hours' drive, a one-hour/two-hour drive
***Es sind nur zehn Minuten zu Fuß***
= It's only a ten-minute walk *od.* ten minutes on foot

**entgeltlich** (*Papierdt.*) ❶ *Adj.* payable. ❷ *adv.* on payment of a fee

**entgiften** *tr. V.* decontaminate ‹substance etc.›; detoxicate ‹body etc.›

**Entgiftung** *die;* ~, ~**en** decontamination; detoxication

**entgleisen** *itr. V.; mit sein* **A** be derailed; **der Zug ist entgleist** the train was derailed; **das Entgleisen** the derailment; **B** (*in Gesellschaft*) make *or* commit a/some faux pas

**Entgleisung** *die;* ~, ~**en** ⇒ **entgleisen**: **A** derailment; **B** faux pas

**entgleiten** *unr. itr. V.; mit sein* (*geh.*) **A** slip; **jmds. Händen** ~: slip from sb.'s hands; **B** (*fig.*) **jmdm. entgleitet etw.** sb. loses his/her grip on sth.

**entgräten** *tr. V.* fillet; bone; **entgräteter Fisch** filleted fish

**enthaaren** *tr. V.* remove hair from; depilate (*formal*)

**Enthaarungs·mittel** *das* hair remover; depilatory

**enthalten**[1] ❶ *unr. tr. V.* contain. ❷ *unr. refl. V.* **sich einer Sache** (*Gen.*) ~: abstain from sth.; **sich der Stimme** ~: abstain; **sich jeder Meinung/Äußerung** ~: refrain from giving any opinion/making any comment

**enthalten**[2] *Adj.* **in etw.** (*Dat.*) ~ **sein** be contained in sth.; **die im Wasser** ~**en Stoffe** the substances contained in water; **wie oft ist 4 in 12** ~? how many times does 4 go into 12?; **das ist im Preis** ~: that is included in the price

**enthaltsam** ❶ *Adj.* abstemious; (*sexuell*) abstinent. ❷ *adv.* **in Bezug auf etw.** (*Akk.*) ~ **sein** be moderate regarding sth.; ~ **leben** live in abstinence

**Enthaltsamkeit** *die;* ~: abstinence

**Enthaltung** *die* abstention; **mit 20 Stimmen bei 3** ~**en gewählt werden** be elected by 20 votes with 3 abstentions

**enthärten** *tr. V.* soften ‹water›

**Enthärtungs·mittel** *das* [water] softener

**enthaupten** *tr. V.* (*geh.*) behead

**Enthauptung** *die;* ~, ~**en** (*geh.*) beheading

**enthäuten** *tr. V.* skin

**entheben** *unr. tr. V.* (*geh.*) relieve; **jmdn. seines Amtes** ~: relieve sb. of his/her office; **aller Sorgen enthoben sein** be relieved of all one's cares; **einer Verpflichtung enthoben werden** be released from an obligation

**entheiligen** *tr. V.* desecrate, profane ‹sabbath›

**enthemmen** *tr., itr. V.* **jmdn.** ~: make sb. lose his/her inhibitions; free sb. from his/her inhibitions; **Alkohol enthemmt** alcohol takes away one's inhibitions

**enthemmend** ❶ *Adj.* disinhibitory ‹effect, etc.›. ❷ *adv.* ~ **wirken** take away sb.'s inhibitions

**enthemmt** ❶ ⇒ **enthemmen**. ❷ *Adj.* uninhibited

**Enthemmtheit** *die;* ~, **Enthemmung** *die* loss of inhibition[s]; disinhibition (*Psych.*)

**enthüllen** ❶ *tr. V.* **A** unveil ‹monument etc.›; reveal ‹face, etc.›; **B** (*offenbaren*) reveal ‹truth, secret›; disclose ‹secret›; (*Zeitungsw.*) expose ‹scandal›. ❷ *refl. V.* (*sich offenbaren*) **sich [jmdm.]** ~: be revealed [to sb.]; **sich als etw.** ~: be revealed as *or* turn out to be sth.

**Enthüllung** *die;* ~, ~**en** ⇒ **enthüllen**: **A** (*das Enthüllen*) unveiling; revelation; disclosure; exposé; **B** (*das Enthüllte*) revelation; disclosure

**enthülsen** *tr. V.* shell; pod

**Enthusiasmus** /ɛntu'zi̯asmʊs/ *der;* ~: enthusiasm

**Enthusiast** *der;* ~**en**, ~**en**, **Enthusiastin** *die;* ~, ~**nen** enthusiast

**enthusiastisch** ❶ *Adj.* enthusiastic. ❷ *adv.* enthusiastically

**Entität** /ɛnti'tɛ:t/ *die;* ~, ~**en** (*Philos.*) entity

**entjungfern** *tr. V.* deflower

**Entjungferung** *die;* ~, ~**en** defloration

**entkalken** *tr. V.* decalcify

**entkeimen** *tr. V.* **A** (*keimfrei machen*) sterilize ‹water etc.›; **B** (*Triebe entfernen von*) remove the shoots from ‹potatoes etc.›

**entkernen** *tr. V.* **A** core ‹apple etc.›; stone, remove stone from ‹plum etc.›; remove pips from ‹grape etc.›; **B** (*Städtebau*) reduce the density of ‹town›

**entkleiden** *tr. V.* (*geh.*) **A** **jmdn./sich** ~: undress sb./undress; **die entkleidete Leiche einer Unbekannten** the unclothed body of an unknown woman; **B** (*berauben*) strip; **jmdn. einer Sache** (*Gen.*) ~: strip sb. of sth.

**Entkleidung** *die* undressing

**entknoten** ❶ *tr. V.* untie, undo ‹string etc.›; unravel ‹wool etc.›. ❷ *refl. V.* (*fig.*) ‹plot etc.› unravel itself

**entkoffeiniert** /ɛntkɔfei'ni:ɐ̯t/ *Adj.* decaffeinated

**Entkolon[ial]isierung** *die* decolonization

**entkommen** *unr. itr. V.; mit sein* escape; **jmdm./einer Sache** ~: escape *or* get away from sb./sth.; **es gibt kein Entkommen:** there is no escape

**entkorken** *tr. V.* uncork ‹bottle›

**entkräften** /ɛnt'krɛftn̩/ *tr. V.* **A** weaken; **völlig** ~: exhaust; **von etw. [völlig] entkräftet sein** be [utterly] exhausted by sth.; **B** (*widerlegen*) refute, invalidate ‹argument etc.›; remove ‹suspicion etc.›

**Entkräftung** *die;* ~, ~**en** **A** debility; **völlige** ~: exhaustion; **an** *od.* **vor** ~ (*Dat.*) **sterben** die of exhaustion; **B** (*Widerlegung*) refutation; invalidation

**entkrampfen** ❶ *tr. V.* **A** relax ‹body etc.›; loosen, relax ‹muscles etc.›; **B** (*fig.*) ease ‹situation, tension›; ❷ *refl. V.* **A** relax; **B** (*fig.*) ‹atmosphere etc.› become relaxed

**Entkrampfung** *die;* ~, ~**en** ⇒ **entkrampfen**: relaxation; loosening; easing

**entkriminalisieren** *tr. V.* decriminalize

**entladen** ❶ *unr. tr. V.* unload ‹vehicle, ship, luggage, gun›; discharge ‹battery›; ⇒ *auch* **beladen**[1] A. ❷ *unr. refl. V.* **A** ‹storm› break; **B** (*fig.: hervorbrechen*) ‹anger etc.› erupt; ‹aggression etc.› be released; **sich in etw.** (*Dat.*) ~: release itself in sth.; **C** (*Elektrot.*) ‹battery› run down; **D** ‹gun› go off

**Entladung** *die* ⇒ **entladen** 1, 2 B: unloading; discharge; eruption; release; **etw. zur** ~ **bringen** (*fig.*) cause sth. to erupt

**entlang** ❶ *Präp. mit Akk. u. Dat.* along; **den Weg** ~, ~ **dem Weg** along the path. ❷ *Adv.* along; **hier/dort** ~, **bitte!** this/that way please!

**entlang-:** ~**|fahren** *unr. itr. V.; mit sein* **A** drive along; **die Straße/den** *od.* **am Fluss** ~**fahren** drive *or* go down the street/along the river; **B** (*streichen*) go along; **er fuhr mit dem Finger die** *od.* **an der Tischkante** ~: he ran his finger along the edge of the table; ~**|führen** ❶ *tr. V.* lead along; **jmdn. die Straße** ~**führen** lead sb. along *or* down the street; ❷ *itr. V.* (*verlaufen*) run *or* go along; **die Straße führt am** *od.* **den Fluss** ~: the road runs *or* goes along the river; ~**|gehen** *unr. itr. V.; mit sein* ‹person› go *or* walk along; **bitte gehen Sie hier** ~: [go] this way please; ~**|kommen** *unr. itr. V.; mit sein* come along; ~**|laufen** *unr. itr. V.; mit sein* **A** go *or* walk/run along; **B** (*verlaufen*) go *or* run along

**entlarven** *tr. V.* expose; **jmdn. als Schwindler** ~: expose sb. as *or* show sb. to be a swindler

**Entlarvung** *die;* ~, ~**en** exposure

**Entlass-**, ***Entlaß-** (*südd.*) ⇒ **Entlassungs-**

**entlassen** *unr. tr. V.* **A** (*aus dem Gefängnis*) release; (*aus dem Krankenhaus, der Armee*) discharge; **jmd. wird aus der Schule** ~: sb. leaves school; **jmdn. aus der** *od.* **seiner Staatsbürgerschaft** ~: release sb. from citizenship; **B** (*aus einem Arbeitsverhältnis*) dismiss; (*wegen Arbeitsmangels*) make redundant (*Brit.*); lay off; **bei einer Firma** ~ **werden** be dismissed from/be made redundant (*Brit.*) *or* laid off by a company; **C** (*geh.: gehen lassen*) release

**Entlassung** *die;* ~, ~**en** **A** (*aus dem Gefängnis*) release; (*aus dem Krankenhaus, der Armee*) discharge; (*aus der Schule*) leaving; ~ **aus der Staatsbürgerschaft** release from citizenship; **B** (*aus einem Arbeitsverhältnis*) dismissal; (*wegen Arbeitsmangels*) redundancy (*Brit.*); laying off; **C** (~*schreiben*) notice of dismissal; (*wegen Arbeitsmangels*) redundancy notice (*Brit.*); pink slip (*Amer.*)

**Entlassungs-:** ~**feier** *die* (*Schulw.*) school-leaving *or* (*Amer.*) graduation ceremony; ~**gesuch** *das* resignation; ~**papiere** *Pl.* (*eines Soldaten*) discharge papers; (*eines Häftlings*) release papers; ~**schreiben** *das*

(*Arbeitsw.*) notice of dismissal; (*wegen Arbeitsmangels*) redundancy notice (*Brit.*); pink slip (*Amer.*)

**entlasten** *tr. V.* **A** (*Rechtsspr.*) exonerate ‹defendant›; **B** (*Beanspruchung mindern*) **jmdn. ~:** relieve *or* take the load off sb.; **den Verkehr ~:** ease the traffic; **den Kreislauf ~:** relieve the strain on the circulation; **C** (*erleichtern*) **sein Gewissen ~:** ease *or* relieve one's conscience; **D** (*Finanzw.*) **sein Konto ~:** pay off the amount owed on one's account; **E** (*Kaufmannsspr.*) approve the actions of ‹chairman, board, etc.›

**Entlastung** *die; ~, ~en* **A** (*Rechtsw.*) exoneration; defence; **zu jmds. ~:** in sb.'s defence; **B** (*Minderung der Belastung*) relief; **die ~ eines Menschen/des Körpers/der Straßen** relief of the burden on a person/the body/the roads; **C** (*Person od. Sache*) **eine große ~ für seinen Vater** a great help to his father; **eine ungeheure ~ für den Ortsverkehr** an enormous relief for local traffic; **D** (*Erleichterung*) easing; relief; **wir senden Ihnen Ihre Unterlagen zu unserer ~ zurück** we are returning your documents for safe keeping; **E** (*Finanzw.*) **die ~ eines Kontos** paying off the amount owed on an account; **F** (*Kaufmannsspr.*) approval of the actions of ‹chairman, board, etc.›

**Entlastungs-: ~material** *das* (*Rechtsw.*) evidence for the defence; **~zeuge** *der* (*Rechtsw.*) witness for the defence; defence witness; **~zug** *der* (*Eisenb.*) relief train

**entlauben 1** *tr. V.* strip ‹branch›; defoliate ‹forest, area›. **2** *refl. V.* ‹tree› shed its leaves; **entlaubte Äste** bare branches

**Entlaubung** *die; ~, ~en* defoliation

**Entlaubungs·mittel** *das* defoliant

**entlaufen** *unr. itr. V.; mit sein* run away; **jmdm. ~:** run away from sb.; **ein ~er Sträfling/Sklave** an escaped convict/a runaway slave; **„Hund ~"** 'dog missing *or* lost'

**entlausen** *tr. V.* delouse

**Entlausung** *die; ~, ~en* delousing

**entledigen** *refl. V.* (*geh.*) **A sich jmds./einer Sache** (*Gen.*) **~:** dispose of *or* rid oneself of sb./sth.; **B sich eines Kleidungsstücks ~:** remove an item of clothing; **C** (*erledigen*) **sich einer Aufgabe/einer Schuld/seiner Pflichten ~:** carry out a task/discharge a debt/one's duty

**entleeren 1** *tr. V.* **A** empty ‹ashtray etc.›; **B** evacuate ‹bowels, bladder›. **2** *refl. V.* **A** (*leer werden*) empty; become empty; **B** (*fig.: seinen Sinn verlieren*) ‹concept, tradition› lose its meaning

**Entleerung** *die* **A** (*das Leermachen*) emptying; **B** (*fig.: von Werten, Begriffen*) erosion; **C** (*Med.*) evacuation

**entlegen** *Adj.* **A** (*entfernt*) out-of-the-way ‹place›; **B** (*abwegig*) remote, little-known ‹word, expression›; out-of-the-way, odd ‹theory etc.›

**entlehnen** *tr. V.* borrow (*Dat.*, **aus** from)

**Entlehnung** *die; ~, ~en* borrowing; **das Wort ist eine ~ aus dem Lateinischen** the word is borrowed *or* a borrowing from the Latin

**entleiben** *refl. V.* (*geh. veralt.*) take one's own life

**entleihen** *unr. tr. V.* borrow; **entliehene Bücher** borrowed books

**Entleiher** *der; ~s, ~,* **Entleiherin** *die; ~, ~nen* borrower

**Entlein** /ˈɛntlain/ *das; ~s, ~:* duckling; **ein hässliches ~** (*ugs. scherzh.*) an ugly duckling

**entloben** *refl. V.* break off one's *or* the engagement

**Entlobung** *die; ~, ~en* breaking off [of] one's *or* the engagement

**entlocken** *tr. V.* (*geh.*) **jmdm. etw. ~:** elicit sth. from sb.; **jmdm. Begeisterung ~:** arouse enthusiasm in sb.; **jmdm. ein Geheimnis ~:** worm a secret out of sb.; **jmdm. ein Lächeln ~:** draw a smile from sb.

*old spelling (see note on page 1707)

**entlohnen,** (*bes. schweiz.*) **entlöhnen** *tr. V.* pay; **jmdn. [für etw.] ~:** pay sb. [for sth.]

**Entlohnung** *die; ~, ~en* payment; (*Lohn*) pay

**entlüften** *tr. V.* **A** ventilate; **B** (*Technik*) bleed ‹brakes, radiator, etc.›

**Entlüfter** *der; ~s, ~* **A** ventilator; **B** (*Technik*) bleeder

**Entlüftung** *die* ventilation; (*Anlage*) ventilation [system]

**Entlüftungs-: ~an·lage** *die* ventilation system; **~ventil** *das* air-release valve

**entmachten** *tr. V.* deprive of power

**Entmachtung** *die; ~, ~en* deprivation of power

**entmannen** *tr. V.* castrate; (*fig.*) emasculate

**Entmannung** *die; ~, ~en* castration; (*fig.*) emasculation

**entmaterialisieren** *tr. V.* (*bes. Philos.*) dematerialize

**entmenschen, entmenschlichen** *tr. V.* **A** dehumanize; **B** (*verrohen*) brutalize

**entmenscht** *Adj.* brutalized

**entmieten** *tr. V.* (*Amtsspr.*) drive out the tenants of

**entmilitarisieren** *tr. V.* demilitarize; **eine entmilitarisierte Zone** a demilitarized zone

**Entmilitarisierung** *die* demilitarization

**entminen** *tr. V.* clear of mines

**entmisten** *tr. V.* muck out

**entmotten** *tr. V.* (*Technik*) de-mothball

**entmündigen** *tr. V.* (*Rechtsw.*) incapacitate; (*fig.*) deprive of the right of decision

**Entmündigung** *die; ~, ~en* (*jur.*) incapacitation; (*fig.*) deprivation of the right of decision

**entmutigen** *tr. V.* discourage; dishearten; **lass dich nicht ~:** don't be discouraged

**Entmutigung** *die; ~, ~en* discouragement

**Entmythologisierung** *die* demythologization

**Entnahme** *die; ~, ~n* (*von Wasser*) drawing; (*von Geld, Blutprobe*) taking; (*von Blut*) extraction; (*von Organen*) removal

**entnazifizieren** /ɛntnatsifiˈtsiːrən/ *tr. V.* denazify

**Entnazifizierung** *die; ~, ~en* denazification

**entnehmen** *unr. tr. V.* **A** (*herausnehmen aus*) **etw. [einer Sache** (*Dat.*)**] ~:** take sth. [from sth.]; **der Kasse Geld ~:** take money out of the till; **jmdm. Blut/eine Blutprobe ~:** take a blood sample from sb.; **Organe ~:** remove organs; **B** (*ersehen aus*) gather; **einer Sache** (*Dat.*) **etw. ~ können** be able to gather sth. from sth.; **wie wir Ihrem Schreiben ~, ...** we gather from your letter that ...

**entnerven** *tr. V.* **jmdn. ~:** wear sb. down

**entnervend** *Adj.* wearing; **eine ~e Warterei** a nerve-racking wait; **der Lärm ist ~:** the noise is wearing on the nerves

**entnervt** *Adj.* **~ sein** be worn down; have reached *or* be at the end of one's tether; **von etw. ~ sein** have been worn down by sth.; **der ~e Beamte/Lehrer sagte ...:** the official/teacher, who had reached the end of his tether, said ...; **er gab ~ auf** he had reached the end of his tether and gave up

**entölen** *tr. V.* remove fat from ‹cocoa›; **stark/schwach entölt** with very low/slightly reduced fat content *postpos., not pred.*

**Entomologe** *der; ~, ~n* ▶ 159 entomologist

**Entomologie** /ɛntomoloˈgiː/ *die; ~:* entomology *no art.*

**Entomologin** *die; ~, ~nen* ▶ 159 entomologist

**entpflichten** *tr. V.* release

**entprivatisieren** *tr. V.* nationalize; take out of the private sector

**entpuppen** *refl. V.* **sich als etw./jmd. ~:** turn out to be sth./sb.

**entquellen** *unr. itr. V.; mit sein* (*geh.*) **einer Sache** (*Dat.*) **~:** pour from sth.; **Tränen entquollen ihren Augen** tears streamed from her eyes

**entrahmen** *tr. V.* skim ‹milk›

**entraten** *unr. itr. V.* (*geh.*) **jmds./einer Sache ~:** dispense with sb./sth.; **einer Sache** (*Gen.*) **~ müssen** have to do without sth.

**enträtseln 1** *tr. V.* decipher ‹code etc.›; understand, fathom ‹behaviour etc.›. **2** *refl. V.* ‹mystery, secret, etc.› be solved

**entrechten** *tr. V.* **jmdn. ~:** deprive sb. of his/her rights

**Entrechtete** *der/die; adj. Dekl.* person deprived of his/her rights

**Entrecote** /ãtrəˈkoːt/ *das; ~s, ~s* (*Kochk.*) entrecôte

**Entree** /ãˈtreː/ *das; ~s, ~s* **A** (*Kochk.*) entrée; **B** (*Eingang*) [entrance] hall; **C** (*Erscheinen*) entrance; **D** (*bes. österr.: Eintrittsgeld*) entrance *or* admission fee

**entreißen** *unr. tr. V.* **A** (*wegnehmen*) **jmdm. etw. ~:** snatch sth. from sb.; **B** (*retten vor*) **jmdn. dem Tod ~:** save sb. from imminent death; **C** (*geh.: befreien von*) **jmdn./etw. dem Vergessen ~:** rescue sb./sth. from oblivion

**entrichten** *tr. V.* (*Amtsspr.*) pay ‹fee›; **jede Familie musste dem Krieg ihren Tribut ~** (*fig.*) the war took its toll of every family

**entriegeln** *tr. V.* unbolt

**entrinden** *tr. V.* strip the bark off; decorticate

**entringen** (*geh.*) **1** *unr. tr. V.* (*wegnehmen*) **jmdm. etw. ~:** wrest sth. from sb. **2** *unr. refl. V.* **sich [einer Sache** (*Dat.*)**] ~:** escape [from sth.]; **ein Seufzer entrang sich ihrer Brust** she heaved a sigh

**entrinnen** *unr. itr. V.; mit sein* (*geh.*) **A** (*entgehen*) **einer Sache** (*Dat.*) **~:** escape sth.; **B** (*dichter.*) ‹time› fly by

**entrollen 1** *tr. V.* (*geh.*) unroll. **2** *refl. V.* (*fig.*) unfold

**Entropie** /ɛntroˈpiː/ *die; ~, ~n* (*fachspr.*) entropy

**entrosten** *tr. V.* derust

**entrücken** *tr. V.* (*geh.*) **jmdn. ~:** carry sb. [far] away (*fig.*) (*Dat.* from); **entrückt** carried away; transported; (*gedankenverloren*) lost in reverie; **jmdm./einer Sache entrückt sein** be far away from sb./sth.; **in eine bessere Welt entrückt** transported to a better world

**Entrücktheit** *die; ~, ~en* (*geh.*) reverie; **in völliger ~:** completely lost in reverie

**entrümpeln** /ɛntˈrʏmpl̩n/ *tr. V.* clear out

**Entrümpelung** *die; ~, ~en* clear-out; clearing out

**entrußen** *tr. V.* clear of soot

**entrüsten 1** *refl. V.* **sich [über etw.** (*Akk.*)**] ~:** be indignant [at *or* about sth.]. **2** *tr. V.* (*empören*) **jmdn. ~:** make sb. indignant; **über etw.** (*Akk.*) **entrüstet/aufs Höchste entrüstet sein** be indignant/outraged at sth.; **etw. entrüstet tun** do sth. indignantly

**Entrüstung** *die* indignation (**über** + *Akk.* at, about)

**entsaften** *tr. V.* extract the juice from

**Entsafter** *der; ~s, ~:* juice extractor

**entsagen** *itr. V.* (*geh.*) **einem Genuss ~:** renounce *or* forgo a pleasure; **der Welt ~:** renounce the world; **sie musste lernen zu ~:** she had to learn self-denial

**Entsagung** *die; ~, ~en* (*geh.*) renunciation; **viele ~en auf sich** (*Akk.*) **nehmen** renounce many things

**entsagungs·voll** *Adj.* **A** full of self-denial *postpos.*; **B** (*Entsagungen verlangend*) full of privation *postpos.*

**entsalzen** *tr. V.* desalinate

**Entsalzung** *die; ~, ~en* desalination

**Entsalzungs·anlage** *die* desalination plant; (*bei Erdölgewinnung*) brine separator

**Entsatz** *der* (*Milit.*) **A** relief; **B** (*~truppe*) relief troops *pl.*

**entsäuern** *tr. V.* deacidify; disacidify

**entschädigen** *tr. V.* compensate (**für** for); **jmdn. für etw. ~** (*fig.*) make up for sth.

**Entschädigung** *die* compensation *no indef. art.*

**entschädigungs-, Entschädigungs-: ~los** *Adj., adv.* without compensation; **~summe** *die* compensation *no indef. art.*

**entschärfen** *tr. V.* [A] defuse, deactivate ‹bomb etc.›; control ‹avalanche›; blunt ‹edge etc.›; make ‹hill, slope› less steep; alleviate ‹disaster, crisis›; [B] (*fig.*) defuse ‹situation›; tone down ‹discussion, criticism›

**Entschärfung** *die; ~, ~en* [A] (*von Bomben usw.*) defusing; deactivation; [B] (*fig.*) defusing; toning down

**Entscheid** /ɛnt'ʃait/ *der; ~[e]s, ~e* decision

**entscheiden** ❶ *unr. refl. V.* [A] decide; **sich für/gegen jmdn./etw. ~:** decide on *or* in favour of/against sb./sth.; **sich nicht ~ können** be unable to make up one's mind; [B] (*unpers.*) **morgen entscheidet es sich, ob ...** I/we/you will know tomorrow whether ... ❷ *unr. itr. V.* **über etw.** (*Akk.*) **~:** decide on *or* settle sth. ❸ *unr. tr. V.* [A] (*bestimmen*) decide on ‹dispute›; **der Richter entschied, dass ...** the judge decided *or* ruled that ...; [B] (*den Ausschlag geben für*) decide ‹outcome, result›

**entscheidend** ❶ *Adj.* crucial ‹problem, question, significance›; decisive ‹action›; **die ~e Stimme** the deciding vote; **etwas/nichts Entscheidendes** something/nothing crucial *or* decisive. ❷ *adv.* **jmdn./etw. ~ beeinflussen** have a crucial *or* decisive influence on sb./sth.; **sich/etw. ~ verändern** change/change sth. decisively

**Entscheidung** *die* decision; (*Gerichts~*) ruling; (*Schwurgerichts~*) verdict; **etw. steht vor der ~:** sth. is just about to be decided; **einer ~** (*Dat.*) **ausweichen** avoid making a decision; **jmdn. vor die ~ stellen, etw. zu tun** leave the decision to sb. to do sth.

**entscheidungs-, Entscheidungs-: ~befugnis** *die* decision-making powers *pl.*; **~frage** *die* (*Sprachw.*) yes-no *or* polar question; **~gewalt** *die* power of decision; **~hilfe** *die* help *or* assistance in reaching a decision; **~kampf** *der* decisive struggle; (*Milit.*) decisive battle; **~schlacht** *die* decisive battle; **~spiel** *das* (*Sport*) deciding match; (*bei gleichem Rang*) play-off; **~träger** *der*, **~trägerin** *die* decision-maker

**entschieden** ❶ *2. Part. v.* **entscheiden.** ❷ *Adj.* [A] (*entschlossen*) determined; resolute; [B] (*eindeutig*) definite. ❸ *adv.* resolutely; **etw. ~** *od.* **auf das Entschiedenste ablehnen** reject sth. emphatically *or* categorically; **jmdm. sehr ~ antworten** give sb. a very definite answer; **das geht ~ zu weit** that is going much too far

**Entschiedenheit** *die; ~:* decisiveness; **etw. mit ~ behaupten/verneinen** state/deny sth. categorically; **etw. mit ~ fordern** demand sth. emphatically

**entschlacken** *tr. V.* cleanse

**Entschlackung** *die; ~, ~en* cleansing

**entschlafen** *unr. itr. V.; mit sein* [A] (*verhüll.: sterben*) pass away; fall asleep (*euphem.*); **sanft ~:** pass away peacefully; [B] (*geh.: einschlafen*) fall asleep

**entschleiern** *tr. V.* (*geh.*) [A] (*fig.*) reveal; uncover; **ein Geheimnis ~:** reveal a secret; [B] unveil ‹face›

**entschließen** *unr. refl. V.* decide; make up one's mind; **sich ~, etw. zu tun** decide *or* resolve to do sth.; **sich dazu ~:** decide to do it; **sich zu einer Reise/zur Heirat ~:** decide to make a journey/to marry; **ich kann mich zu nichts ~:** I can't make up my mind; **sich anders ~:** change one's mind

**Entschließung** *die* resolution

**entschlossen** ❶ *2. Part. v.* **entschließen.** ❷ *Adj.* determined, resolute ‹person›; determined ‹look etc.›; **fest ~ [sein], etw. zu tun** [be] absolutely determined to do sth. ❸ *adv.* **~ handeln/durchgreifen** act resolutely *or* with determination/take determined action; **kurz ~:** on the spur of the moment; (*als Reaktion*) immediately

**Entschlossenheit** *die; ~:* determination; resolution; **in wilder ~:** fiercely determined; with fierce determination

**entschlummern** *itr. V.; mit sein* [A] (*dichter.: einschlafen*) fall asleep; [B] ⇒ **entschlafen** A

**entschlüpfen** *itr. V.; mit sein* [A] escape; slip away; [B] ‹remarks, words› slip out

**Entschluss, *Entschluß** *der* decision; **seinen ~ ändern** change one's mind; **aus eigenem ~:** on one's own initiative; of one's own volition

**entschlüsseln** *tr. V.* decipher; decode

**Entschlüsselung** *die; ~, ~en* deciphering; decoding

**entschluss-, *entschluß-, Entschluss-, *Entschluß-: ~freudig** *Adj.* decisive; **~kraft** *die* decisiveness; **~los** ❶ *Adj.* indecisive; ❷ *adv.* indecisively

**entschuldbar** *Adj.* excusable; pardonable

**entschulden** *tr. V.* free of debts; **einen Betrieb ~:** write off a business's debts

**entschuldigen** ▶ 268 ❶ *refl. V.* apologize; **sich bei jmdm. wegen** *od.* **für etw. ~:** apologize to sb. for sth.; **sich in aller Form ~:** apologize formally; make a formal apology. ❷ *tr.* (*auch itr.*) *V.* excuse ‹person›; **die Mutter entschuldigte ihren Sohn in der Schule** the mother had her son excused from school; **sich ~ lassen** ask to be excused; **sein Verhalten ist durch nichts zu ~:** his behaviour is inexcusable; **~ Sie [bitte]!** (*bei Fragen, Bitten*) excuse me; (*bedauernd*) excuse me; I'm sorry; **Sie müssen ~, dass ...** I'm sorry, but ...

**entschuldigend** ❶ *Adj.* apologetic; **~e Worte** words of apology. ❷ *adv.* apologetically

**Entschuldigung** *die; ~, ~en* [A] (*Rechtfertigung*) excuse; **etw. zu seiner ~ sagen/anführen** say sth. in one's defence; [B] (*schriftliche Mitteilung*) [excuse] note; letter of excuse; [C] ▶ 268 (*Höflichkeitsformel*) **~!** (*bei Fragen, Bitten*) excuse me; (*bedauernd*) excuse me; [I'm] sorry; **jmdn. für** *od.* **wegen etw. um ~ bitten** apologize to sb. for sth.; [D] (*entschuldigende Äußerung*) apology

**Entschuldigungs-: ~grund** *der* excuse; **~schreiben** *das* letter of apology

**entschweben** *itr. V.; mit sein* (*geh., häufig iron.*) waft away

**entschwefeln** *tr. V.* (*Chemie*) desulphurize

**entschwinden** *unr. itr. V.; mit sein* (*geh.*) [A] disappear; vanish; **jmds. Blicken ~:** disappear *or* vanish from sb.'s view *or* sight; [B] (*vergehen*) ‹time› fly by

**entseelt** /ɛnt'ze:lt/ *Adj.* (*geh.*) lifeless, dead (*also fig.*)

**entsenden** *unr.* (*auch regelm.*) *tr. V.* dispatch

**Entsendung** *die* (*geh.*) dispatch

**entsetzen** ❶ *refl. V.* be horrified; **sich vor** *od.* **bei dem Anblick von etw. ~:** be horrified at the sight of sth. ❷ *tr. V.* [A] (*erschrecken*) horrify; **über etw.** (*Akk.*) **entsetzt sein** be horrified by sth.; **entsetzt starren** stare in horror; [B] (*Milit.*) relieve

**Entsetzen** *das; ~s* horror; **vor ~ stumm** speechless with horror; **mit ~ bemerken** notice to one's horror; **ihn befiel lähmendes ~:** he was paralysed with horror

**Entsetzens·schrei** *der* cry of horror

**entsetzlich** ❶ *Adj.* [A] horrible, dreadful ‹accident, crime, etc.›; [B] (*ugs.: stark*) terrible ‹thirst, hunger›; **einen ~en Durst haben** have a terrible thirst; be terribly thirsty. ❷ *adv.* terribly (*coll.*); awfully; **es ist ~ kalt/warm/dunkel** it is terribly (*coll.*) *or* awfully cold/warm/dark

**Entsetzlichkeit** *die; ~, ~en* horribleness; dreadfulness

**entseuchen** *tr. V.* decontaminate

**entsichern** *tr. V.* **eine Pistole ~:** release the safety catch of a pistol; **das Gewehr war entsichert/nicht entsichert** the rifle had the safety catch off/on

**entsinnen** *unr. refl. V.* **sich jmds./einer Sache ~:** remember sb./sth.; **sich an jmdn./etw. ~:** remember sb./sth.

**entsorgen** *tr. V.* (*Amtsspr., Wirtsch.*) dispose of ‹waste etc.›; **eine Stadt/ein Kernkraftwerk ~:** dispose of a town's/a nuclear power station's waste

**Entsorgung** *die; ~, ~en* (*Amtsspr., Wirtsch.*) waste disposal

**entspannen** ❶ *tr. V.* [A] (*lockern*) relax ‹body etc.›; relax, loosen ‹muscles›; [B] (*von Spannung befreien*) relax the tension of ‹spring›; reduce the surface tension of ‹water›. ❷ *refl. V.* [A] ‹person› relax; [B] (*fig.*) ‹situation, tension› ease

**Entspannung** *die* [A] relaxation; [B] (*politisch*) easing of tension; détente

**Entspannungs-: ~politik** *die* policy of détente; **~übung** *die* relaxation exercise

**entspiegeln** *tr. V.* bloom; **entspiegeltes Glas** coated glass

**entspinnen** *unr. refl. V.* develop; arise

**entsprechen** *unr. itr. V.* [A] (*übereinstimmen mit*) **einer Sache** (*Dat.*) **~:** correspond to sth.; **der Wahrheit/den Tatsachen ~:** be in accordance with the truth/the facts; **den Erwartungen ~:** live up to one's expectations; **sich** (*Dat.*) *od.* (*geh.*) **einander ~:** correspond; [B] (*nachkommen*) **einem Wunsch/einer Bitte ~:** comply with a wish/request; **den Anforderungen ~:** meet the requirements; **dem Anlass ~:** be appropriate for the occasion; **dem Zweck ~:** suit the purpose

**entsprechend** ❶ *Adj.* [A] corresponding; (*angemessen*) appropriate ‹payment, reply, etc.›; [B] (*dem~*) in accordance *postpos.*; **das Wetter war schlecht und die Stimmung ~:** the weather was bad and the mood was the same; [C] (*zuständig*) relevant ‹department etc.›; ‹person› concerned. ❷ *adv.* [A] (*angemessen*) appropriately; [B] (*dem~*) accordingly. ❸ *Präp. mit Dativ:* **~ einer Sache** in accordance with sth.; **der Anweisung ~ handeln** act in accordance with *or* according to instructions; **es geht ihm den Umständen ~:** he is as well as can be expected [in the circumstances]

**Entsprechung** *die; ~, ~en* [A] (*Übereinstimmung*) correspondence; [B] (*Analogie*) parallel; **in einer Sache seine ~ haben** *od.* **finden** have its counterpart in sth.; **für dieses Wort gibt es keine deutsche ~:** there is no German equivalent for this word

**entsprießen** *unr. itr. V.; mit sein* (*geh.*) **einer Sache** (*Dat.*) **~:** spring from sth.; (*fig.: hervorgehen aus*) come from sth.

**entspringen** *unr. itr. V.; mit sein* [A] ▶ 306 ‹river› rise, have its source; [B] (*entstehen aus*) **einer Sache** (*Dat.*) **~:** spring from sth.; [C] (*entweichen aus*) escape; **ein entsprungener Häftling** an escaped prisoner; **dem Irrenhaus entsprungen sein** (*scherzh.*) be crazy

**entstaatlichen** *tr. V.* denationalize

**Entstalinisierung** /ɛntʃtalini'zi:rʊŋ/ *die; ~:* destalinization

**entstammen** *itr. V.; mit sein* come from; (*herrühren von*) derive from; **einer Sache** (*Dat.*) **~:** come/derive from sth.

**entstauben** *tr. V.* dust; remove the dust from; (*fig.*) bring up to date

**entstehen** *unr. itr. V.; mit sein* [A] originate; ‹quarrel, friendship, etc.› arise; ‹work of art› be created; ‹building, town, etc.› be built; ‹industry› emerge; ‹novel etc.› be written; **im Entstehen [begriffen] sein** be being created/built/written/be emerging; [B] (*gebildet werden*) be formed (**aus** from, **durch** by); [C] (*sich ergeben*) occur; (*als Folge*) result; **jmdm. ~ Kosten** sb. incurs costs; **hoffentlich ist nicht der Eindruck entstanden, dass ...** I/we hope I/we have not given the impression that ...

**Entstehung** *die; ~:* origin; **die ~ des Lebens/der Arten** the origin of life/species; **die ~ dieser Stadt/Industrie** the building of this town/the emergence of this industry

**Entstehungs-: ~geschichte** *die* history of the origin[s]; **~ort** *der* place of origin; **~ursache** *die* [original] cause; **~zeit** *die* time of origin; (*Datum*) date of origin

**entsteigen** *unr. V.; mit sein* (*geh.*) **einer Kutsche** (*Dat.*) *usw.* **~:** alight from a coach *etc.*

**entsteinen** *tr. V.* stone

**entstellen** *tr. V.* [A] disfigure ‹person›; distort ‹face›; [B] (*verfälschen*) distort ‹text, facts›

# Entschuldigungen

## Ziemlich formell

***Wir bedauern, Ihnen mitteilen zu müssen, dass ...***
= We regret to have to inform you that ...
***Ich muss Ihnen leider mitteilen, dass ...***
= I am sorry to have to inform you that ...
***Ich bedaure sehr, dass ich Sie enttäuschen musste***
= I greatly *od.* very much regret that I have had to disappoint you
***Es tut mir aufrichtig Leid, dass ich Sie im Stich gelassen habe***
= I am really sorry to have let you down *od.* that I have let you down
***Ich muss mich bei Ihnen [in aller Form] entschuldigen, dass ich Sie fälschlich beschuldigt habe***
= I owe you an [unreserved] apology *od.* I must apologize [unreservedly] for accusing you wrongly
***Ich muss Sie für meinen Fehler um Entschuldigung/ Verzeihung bitten***
= I must ask you to excuse/forgive my mistake
***Wir bitten Sie für unser Versehen um Entschuldigung***
= We apologize for our oversight
***Sie müssen entschuldigen, dass ich erst heute schreibe***
= You must forgive me *od.* Please forgive me for not writing earlier
***Bitte entschuldigen Sie unser Versehen***
= Please excuse our oversight
***Entschuldigen Sie bitte, können Sie mir sagen, wie spät es ist?***
= Excuse me, can you tell me the time?
***Entschuldigen Sie die Störung, aber haben Sie meine Uhr gesehen?***
= I'm sorry to bother you, but have you seen my watch?

## Weniger formell

***Tut mir Leid, da kann ich nicht helfen***
= Sorry, I can't help you there
***Tut mir Leid, dass ich dir so viel Mühe mache***
= [I'm] sorry to be such a nuisance
***Verzeihung!*** od.***Tut mir Leid! Es war alles nur ein dummes Missverständnis!***
= Sorry! It was all a stupid misunderstanding
***Leider muss ich jetzt gehen***
= I'm afraid I'll have to go now
***Sei mir nicht böse! Ich konnte nichts dafür***
= Don't be cross [with me]! I couldn't help it

**Entstellung** *die* Ⓐ(*Entstelltsein*) disfigurement; Ⓑ(*Verfälschung*) distortion
**entstielen** *tr. V.* remove the stalks from
**entstören** *tr. V.* (*Elektrot.*) suppress ‹engine, distributor, electrical appliance›
**Entstörungs·stelle** *die* fault repair service
**entströmen** *tr. V.*; *mit sein* (*geh.*) pour out; ‹gas› escape; (*fig.*) ‹crowd› pour *or* stream out
**enttabuisieren** *tr. V.* (*geh.*) free from taboos
**enttarnen** *tr. V.* uncover; (*fig.*) discover; **etw. als etw. ~:** reveal sth. as sth.
**Enttarnung** *die* uncovering
**enttäuschen** ❶ *tr. V.* disappoint; **unsere Hoffnungen wurden enttäuscht** our hopes were dashed; **jmdn. angenehm ~:** come as a pleasant surprise to sb. ❷ *itr. V.* **etw./jmd. enttäuscht** sth./sb. is disappointing *or* a disappointment
**enttäuscht** *Adj.* disappointed; dashed ‹hopes›; **von jmdm. ~ sein** be disappointed in sb.; **von** *od.* **über etw. ~ sein** be disappointed by *or* at sth.
**Enttäuschung** *die* disappointment (**für** to); **jmdm. eine ~ bereiten** be a disappointment to sb.
**entthronen** *tr. V.* Ⓐ(*geh.*) dethrone ‹monarch›; Ⓑ(*fig.: verdrängen*) take the title away from ‹champion etc.›; remove ‹magnate› from power
**Entthronung** *die; ~, ~en* (*auch fig.*) dethronement
**entvölkern** /ɛnt'fœlkɐn/ ❶ *tr. V.* depopulate. ❷ *refl. V.* become depopulated *or* deserted
**Entvölkerung** *die; ~, ~en* depopulation
**ent·wachsen** *unr. itr. V.*; *mit sein* **einer Sache** (*Dat.*) **~:** grow out of *or* outgrow sth.; ⇒ *auch* **Kinderschuh**
**entwaffnen** *tr. V.* (*auch fig.*) disarm
**entwaffnend** ❶ *Adj.* disarming. ❷ *adv.* disarmingly
**Entwaffnung** *die; ~:* disarming; (*der Bevölkerung, eines Landes*) disarmament
**entwalden** *tr. V.* deforest
**entwarnen** *itr. V.* sound *or* give the all-clear
**Entwarnung** *die* [sounding of the] all-clear
**entwässern** ❶ *tr. V.* Ⓐdrain ‹meadow, area›; Ⓑ(*Med.*) dehydrate. ❷ *itr. V.* (*abfließen*) flow

*old spelling (see note on page 1707)

**Entwässerung** *die; ~, ~en* Ⓐdrainage; Ⓑ(*Kanalisation*) drainage [system]
**Entwässerungs-: ~an·lage** *die* drainage system; **~graben** *der* drainage ditch; **~netz** *das* drainage network
**entweder** *Konj.* **~ ... oder** either ... or
**Entweder-oder**, ***Entweder-Oder** *das; ~, ~:* **es gibt kein ~:** there is no alternative *or* are no alternatives; **es gibt nur ein ~:** a choice has to be made
**entweichen** *unr. itr. V.*; *mit sein* Ⓐ(*ausströmen*) escape; **ihrem Gesicht entwich alles Blut** (*geh.*) the blood drained from her face; Ⓑ(*geh.: entfliehen*) escape
**entweihen** *tr. V.* desecrate; profane
**Entweihung** *die; ~:* desecration; profanation
**entwenden** *tr. V.* (*geh.*) purloin (*Dat.* **from**)
**entwerfen** *unr. tr. V.* Ⓐdesign ‹furniture, dress›; (*fig.*) draw ‹picture›; Ⓑ(*ausarbeiten*) draft ‹novel etc.›; draw up ‹plans etc.›
**entwerten** *tr. V.* Ⓐcancel ‹ticket, postage stamp›; Ⓑ(*Finanzw.*) devalue ‹currency›
**Entwerter** *der; ~s, ~:* ticket-cancelling machine
**Entwertung** *die* ⇒ **entwerten**: cancellation; cancelling; devaluation
**entwesen** *tr. V.* (*Amtsspr.*) disinfest
**Entwesung** *die; ~, ~en* (*Amtsspr.*) disinfestation
**entwickeln** ❶ *refl. V.* develop (**aus** from, **zu** into); **sie ist körperlich voll entwickelt** she is [physically] fully developed. ❷ *tr. V.* give off, produce ‹vapour, smell›; show, display ‹ability, characteristic›; develop ‹weapons, equipment, process, photograph, film›; elaborate ‹theory, ideas›; **hoch entwickelt** highly developed
**Entwickler** *der; ~s, ~* (*Fot.*) developer
**Entwickler·bad** *das* (*Fot.*) developing bath
**Entwicklung** *die; ~, ~en* Ⓐdevelopment; (*von Dämpfen usw.*) production; **in der ~ sein** ‹young person› be adolescent *or* in one's adolescence; **in seiner [körperlichen] ~ zurückbleiben** be physically underdeveloped; **eine bestimmte ~ nehmen** show certain developments; **eine positive ~ zeichnet sich ab** positive developments *pl.* can be seen; **die ~ geht dahin, dass ...** the trend is that ...; **etw. befindet sich in der ~:** sth. is [still] in the development stage; Ⓑ(*Darlegung*) elaboration; Ⓒ(*Fot.*) developing
**entwicklungs-, Entwicklungs-: ~ab·schnitt** *der* stage of development; **~alter** *das* adolescence; **~dienst** *der* development aid service; **~fähig** *Adj.* capable of development; **~geschichte** *die* history of the development; **die ~geschichte der Menschheit/der Meerestiere** the evolution of man/of marine animals; **~ge·schichtlich** ❶ *Adj.* historical; (*stammesgeschichtlich*) evolutionary. ❷ *adv.* **~geschichtlich bedeutsam** important historically/as regards evolution; **sich ~geschichtlich verändert haben** have evolved; **~helfer** *der*, **~helferin** *die* development aid worker; **~hilfe** *die* [development] aid; **~jahre** *Pl.* adolescence *sing.*; **in die ~jahre kommen** reach adolescence; **~kosten** *Pl.* development costs; **~land** *das* developing country; **~ministerium** *das* ministry of development aid; **~phase** *die* stage of development; **~politik** *die* development aid policy; **~roman** *der* (*Literaturw.*) novel showing the development of an individual's character; **~stand** *der* level of development; **~störung** *die* developmental disturbance; **~stufe** *die* stage of development; **~zeit** *die* Ⓐ ⇒ **~alter**; Ⓑ(*~zeitraum*) period of development
**entwinden** (*geh.*) ❶ *unr. tr. V.* **jmdm. etw. ~:** wrest sth. from sb.. ❷ *unr. refl. V.* **sich jmdm./einer Sache ~:** wrest *or* free oneself from sb./sth.
**entwirrbar** *Adj.* **das Garnknäuel war kaum ~:** the ball of thread could scarcely be unravelled; **die vielen Handlungsstränge waren kaum ~:** the strands of the plot could scarcely be untangled
**entwirren** ❶ *tr. V.* Ⓐunravel, disentangle ‹wool etc.›; Ⓑ(*fig.*) unravel, sort out ‹situation etc.›. ❷ *refl. V.* sort itself out
**entwischen** *itr. V.*; *mit sein* (*ugs.*) get away; **aus dem Gefängnis ~:** get out of jail; **jmdm. ~:** give sb. the slip (*coll.*)
**entwöhnen** /ɛnt'vø:nən/ *tr. V.* Ⓐwean ‹baby›; Ⓑ(*geh.*) **jmdn. einer Sache** (*Dat.*) **~:** break sb. of the habit of [doing] sth.; **jmdn. [von einer Sucht] ~:** cure sb. [of an addiction]

**entwürdigen** *tr. V.* degrade

**entwürdigend** ❶ *Adj.* degrading. ❷ *adv.* ‹treat sb.› in a degrading manner; degradingly ‹low›

**Entwürdigung** *die* degradation

**Entwurf** *der* A design; B (*Konzept*) draft; **der ~ zu einem Roman** the outline *or* draft of a novel

**entwurmen** *tr. V.* worm

**entwurzeln** *tr. V.* uproot ‹tree etc., person›; **ein entwurzelter Mensch** a rootless person

**Entwurzelung** *die; ~, ~en* uprooting

**entzaubern** *tr. V.* (*geh.*) A free ‹person› from the spell; break the spell on ‹person›; B **entzaubert werden** (*die Poesie, den Zauber verlieren*) lose its magic

**entzerren** *tr. V.* A (*Technik*) correct; rectify; B (*Fot.*) rectify

**Entzerrer** *der; ~s, ~* A (*Technik*) equalizer; B (*Fot.*) rectifier;

**entziehen** ❶ *unr. tr. V.* A take away; **etw. jmdm./einer Sache ~:** take sth. away from sb./sth.; **jmdm. den Führerschein ~:** take sb.'s driving licence away; **jmdm. das Wort ~:** ask sb. to stop [speaking]; B (*nicht zugestehen*) withdraw; **jmdm. das Vertrauen ~:** withdraw one's confidence in sb.; C (*entfernen von, aus*) **etw. einer Sache** (*Dat.*) **~:** remove sth. from sth.; D (*herausziehen aus*) **etw. einer Sache** (*Dat.*) **~:** extract sth. from sth.; E (*ugs.: entwöhnen*) get ‹addict› off drugs; dry ‹alcoholic› out (*coll.*).
❷ *unr. refl. V.* **sich jmds. Armen/Umklammerung ~:** free oneself from sb.'s arms/embrace; **ihrem Reiz konnte ich mich nicht ~:** I could not resist her/their charms; **sich der Gesellschaft** (*Dat.*) **~** (*geh.*) withdraw from society; **sich seinen Pflichten** (*Dat.*) **~:** shirk *or* evade one's duty; **sich einer Untersuchung** (*Dat.*) **~** (*geh.*) elude an investigation; **das entzieht sich meiner Kontrolle/Kenntnis** that is beyond my control/knowledge

**Entziehung** *die* A withdrawal; loss; B (*~skur*) withdrawal treatment *no indef. art.*; **eine ~ machen** take withdrawal treatment

**Entziehungs-: ~anstalt** *die* treatment centre; clinic; **~kur** *die* course of withdrawal treatment; withdrawal programme

**entzifferbar** *Adj.* decipherable

**entziffern** *tr. V.* A decipher ‹writing›; B (*entschlüsseln*) decipher, decode ‹message›

**Entzifferung** *die; ~, ~en* ⇒ **entziffern**: deciphering; decoding

**entzücken** ❶ *tr. V.* delight; **etw. entzückt jmdn.** sth. delights sb. *or* fills sb. with delight. ❷ *refl. V.* (*geh.*) **sich an etw.** (*Dat.*) **~:** be enraptured by sth.

**Entzücken** *das; ~s* (*geh.*) delight, joy (**an** + *Dat.* in)

**entzückend** ❶ *Adj.* delightful; **das ist ja ~!** (*iron.*) [that's] charming! ❷ *adv.* delightfully

**entzückt** *Adj.* delighted; **von/über etw.** (*Akk.*) **~ sein** be delighted by/at sth.

**Entzückung** *die; ~, ~en* (*geh.*) joy; rapture

**Entzug** *der; ~[e]s* A withdrawal; (*das Herausziehen*) extraction; B ⇒ **Entziehung B**

**Entzugs·erscheinung** *die* withdrawal symptom

**entzündbar** *Adj.* A (*brennbar*) [in]flammable; B (*fig.: erregbar*) easily roused

**entzünden** ❶ *tr. V.* A (*geh.: anzünden*) light ‹fire›; strike, light ‹match›; B (*geh.: erregen*) kindle, arouse ‹passion›; arouse ‹hatred›. ❷ *refl. V.* A catch fire; ignite; B (*anschwellen*) become inflamed; **entzündete Augen haben** have inflamed eyes; C (*geh.: entstehen*) **sich an etw.** (*Dat.*) **~** ‹quarrel› be sparked off by sth.; ‹temper› flare at sth.

**entzündlich** *Adj.* A [in]flammable ‹substance›; B (*Med.*) inflammatory

**Entzündlichkeit** *die; ~:* [in]flammability

**Entzündung** *die; ~, ~en* inflammation

**entzündungs·hemmend** *Adj.* anti-inflammatory; antiphlogistic (*Med.*)

**Entzündungs·herd** *der* focus of inflammation

**entzwei** *Adj.* (*geh.*) in pieces

**entzwei|brechen** (*geh.*) ❶ *unr. tr. V.* break into pieces. ❷ *unr. itr. V.; mit sein* break into pieces

**entzweien** ❶ *refl. V.* **sich [mit jmdm.] ~:** fall out [with sb.]. ❷ *tr. V.* cause ‹persons› to fall out

**entzwei-** (*geh.*): **~|gehen** *unr. itr. V.; mit sein* (*zerbrechen*) break; (*nicht mehr funktionieren*) cease to function; **~|machen** *tr. V.* break; **~|schlagen** *unr. tr. V.* smash to pieces

**Entzweiung** *die; ~, ~en:* **eine ~ herbeiführen** cause the two friends/countries *etc.* to fall out

**en vogue** /ã'vo:k/ (*geh.*) **~ sein** be fashionable *or* in vogue

**Enzephalogramm** /ɛntsefalo'gram/ *das; ~s, ~e* (*Med.*) encephalogram

**Enzian** /'ɛntsi̯a:n/ *der; ~s, ~e* A (*Bot.*) gentian; B (*Schnaps*) enzian liqueur

**enzian·blau** *Adj.* gentian-blue

**Enzyklika** /ɛn'tsy:klika/ *die; ~, Enzykliken* encyclical

**Enzyklopädie** /ɛntsyklopɛ'di:/ *die; ~, ~n* encyclopaedia

**enzyklopädisch** ❶ *Adj.* encyclopaedic. ❷ *adv.* encyclopaedically

**Enzyklopädist** *der; ~en, ~en* encyclopaedist

**Enzym** /ɛn'tsy:m/ *das; ~s, ~e* (*Chemie*) enzyme

**eo ipso** /'e:o 'ɪpso/ (*geh.*) ipso facto

**Eolithikum** /eo'li:tikʊm/ *das; ~s* eolithic period

**Epaulett** /epo'lɛt/ *das; ~s, ~s*, **Epaulette** *die; ~, ~n* epaulette

**Epen** ⇒ **Epos**

**ephemer** /efe'me:ɐ̯/ *Adj.* (*geh.*) ephemeral

**Epidemie** /epide'mi:/ *die; ~, ~n* (*auch fig.*) epidemic

**epidemisch** ❶ *Adj.* epidemic. ❷ *adv.* as/like an epidemic

**Epidermis** /epi'dɛrmɪs/ *die; ~, Epidermen* (*Biol.*) epidermis

**Epidiaskop** /epidia'sko:p/ *das; ~s, ~e* epidiascope

**epigonal** /epigo'na:l/ *Adj.* (*geh.*) ⇒ **epigonenhaft**

**Epigone** /epi'go:nə/ *der; ~n, ~n* (*geh.*) imitator

**epigonenhaft** *Adj.* (*geh.*) imitative; unoriginal

**Epigonentum** *das; ~s* (*geh.*) imitativeness; unoriginality

**Epigonin** *die; ~, ~nen* ⇒ **Epigone**

**Epigramm** /epi'gram/ *das; ~s, ~e* (*Literaturw.*) epigram

**Epigrammatik** *die; ~* (*Literaturw.*) epigrammatism

**epigrammatisch** *Adj.* epigrammatic

**Epik** /'e:pɪk/ *die; ~* (*Literaturw.*) epic poetry

**Epiker** *der; ~s, ~*, **Epikerin** *die; ~, ~nen* epic poet

**Epikureer** /epiku're:ɐ/ *der; ~s, ~*, **Epikureerin** *die; ~, ~nen* A (*Philos.*) Epicurean; B (*geh.*) epicurean

**epikureisch** *Adj.* A (*Philos.*) Epicurean; B (*geh.*) epicurean

**Epilepsie** /epilɛ'psi:/ *die; ~, ~n* (*Med.*) epilepsy *no art.*

**Epileptiker** /epi'lɛptikɐ/ *der; ~s, ~*, **Epileptikerin** *die; ~, ~nen* epileptic

**epileptisch** *Adj.* epileptic

**Epilog** /epi'lo:k/ *der; ~s, ~e* epilogue

**Epiphanias** /epi'fa:ni̯as/ *das; ~:* Epiphany *no art.*

**Epiphanie** /epifa'ni:/ *die; ~* (*Rel.*) epiphany

**episch** /'e:pɪʃ/ ❶ *Adj.* epic. ❷ *adv.* in epic terms

**Episkop** /epi'sko:p/ *das; ~s, ~e* episcope

**Episkopal·kirche** *die* A Episcopal church; B (*ev. Kirche*) Protestant church

**Episkopat** /epɪsko'pa:t/ *das od. der; ~[e]s, ~e* (*Theol.*) A (*Amt*) episcopate; B (*Gesamtheit der Bischöfe*) episcopate; episcopacy

**Episode** /epi'zo:də/ *die; ~, ~n* episode

**episodenhaft, episodisch** ❶ *Adj.* episodic. ❷ *adv.* episodically

**Epistel** /e'pɪstl̩/ *die; ~, ~n* A (*bibl.*) epistle; B (*kath. Kirche*) epistle; lesson; **jmdm. die ~ lesen** (*fig. veralt.*) read sb. a lesson

**Epitaph** /epi'ta:f/ *das; ~s, ~e* (*geh.*) A epitaph; B (*Gedenktafel*) memorial plaque

**Epithel** /epi'te:l/ *das; ~s, ~e* (*Biol.*) epithelium

**Epitheton** /e'pi:tetɔn/ *das; ~s, Epitheta* (*Sprachw.*) epithet

**Epizentrum** *das* (*Geol.*) epicentre

**epochal** /epɔ'xa:l/ *Adj.* epochal; epoch-making; epoch-making ‹invention›; (*fig. iron.*) world-shattering; monumental

**Epoche** /e'pɔxə/ *die; ~, ~n* epoch; **~ machen** be epoch-making

**epoche·machend** *Adj.* epoch-making

**Epos** /'e:pɔs/ *das; ~, Epen* epic [poem]; epos

**Eprouvette** /epru'vɛt/ *die; ~, ~n* (*österr.*) test tube

**Equipage** /ekvi'pa:ʒə/ *die; ~, ~n* (*veralt.*) equipage

**Equipe** /e'kɪp/ *die; ~, ~n* team

**er** /e:ɐ̯/ *Personalpron. 3. Pers. Sg. Nom. Mask.* he; (*betont*) him; (*bei Dingen/Tieren*) it; (*bei männlichen Tieren*) he/him; it; **„Er"** (*auf Handtüchern, an Türen*) 'His'; **~ war es, nicht sie** it was him, not her; **ich weiß mehr als ~:** I know more than he does; I know more than him (*coll.*); **„Er, 42, Witwer ..."** 'widower, 42 ...'; **bring Er den Wein!** (*veralt.*) fetch the wine!; ⇒ *auch* **ihm**; **ihn**; **seiner**

**Er** *der; ~, ~s* (*ugs.*) he; **ist es ein ~ oder eine Sie?** is it a he or a she?

**erachten** *tr. V.* (*geh.*) consider; **etw. als** *od.* **für seine Pflicht ~:** consider sth. [to be] one's duty; **etw. als** *od.* **für notwendig ~:** consider *or* think sth. necessary

**Erachten** *das: in* **meinem ~ nach, meines ~s** in my opinion

**erahnen** *tr. V.* imagine; guess

**erarbeiten** *tr. V.* A (*erwerben*) work for; **[sich** (*Dat.*)**] ein Vermögen ~:** make [oneself] a fortune; B (*zu Eigen machen*) work on; study; **[sich** (*Dat.*)**] einen Text ~:** understand a text by working on it; C (*erstellen*) work out ‹plan, programme, etc.›

**Erb-** /'ɛrp-/: **~adel** *der* hereditary nobility; (*Titel*) hereditary title; **~an·lage** *die* (*Biol.*) hereditary disposition; **~an·spruch** *der* claim to an/the inheritance; **~an·teil** *der* share of an/the inheritance

**erbarmen** /ɛɐ̯'barmən/ ❶ *refl. V.* (*geh.*) **sich jmds./einer Sache ~:** take pity on sb./sth.; **Herr, erbarme dich unser!** Lord, have mercy upon us. ❷ *tr. V.* **jmdn. ~:** arouse sb.'s pity; move sb. to pity

**Erbarmen** *das; ~s* pity; **mit jmdm. ~ haben** take pity on *or* feel pity for sb.; **er kennt kein ~:** he knows no pity or mercy; **zum ~:** pitifully; pathetically; **zum ~ sein** be pitiful *or* pathetic

**erbarmens·wert** *Adj.* pitiful

**erbärmlich** /ɛɐ̯'bɛrmlɪç/ ❶ *Adj.* A (*elend*) wretched; B (*unzulänglich*) pathetic; C (*abwertend: gemein*) mean; wretched; D (*sehr groß*) terrible ‹hunger, thirst, fear, etc.›. ❷ *adv.* (*intensivierend*) terribly ‹cold, hot, thirsty, hungry, etc.›

**Erbärmlichkeit** *die; ~* A (*Elend*) wretchedness; B (*abwertend: Gemeinheit*) meanness; wretchedness

**erbarmungs-, Erbarmungs-: ~los** ❶ *Adj.* merciless; ❷ *adv.* mercilessly; **~losigkeit** *die; ~~:* mercilessness; **~würdig** *Adj.* pitiful

**erbauen** ❶ *tr. V.* A build; B (*geh.: erheben*) uplift; edify; **wir waren von seinen Plänen wenig erbaut** we were not exactly delighted about his plans. ❷ *refl. V.* (*geh.: sich erfreuen*) **sich an etw.** (*Dat.*) **~:** be uplifted *or* edified by sth.

**Erbauer** *der; ~s, ~*, **Erbauerin** *die; ~, ~nen* architect

e

**erbaulich** *Adj.* edifying
**Erbauung** *die;* ~ (*Freude*) edification
**Erbauungs·literatur** *die* devotional literature
**erb-, Erb-:** **~bauer** *der;* ~~**n**, ~~**n** Ⓐ *farmer owning property by hereditary right;* Ⓑ (*in ~pacht*) *farmer with hereditary right of tenure;* **~begräbnis** *das* Ⓐ *right to be buried in the family grave;* Ⓑ ⇒ **Familiengrab**; **~berechtigt** *Adj.* entitled to inherit; entitled to an/the inheritance; **die ~berechtigten** the heirs; **~biologisch** *Adj.* genetic; **ein ~biologisches Gutachten** the opinion of an expert in genetics
**Erbe**[1] /'ɛrbə/ *das;* **~s** Ⓐ (*Vermögen*) inheritance; **das väterliche/mütterliche ~:** patrimony/maternal inheritance; **sein ~ antreten** come into one's inheritance; Ⓑ (*Vermächtnis*) heritage; legacy
**Erbe**[2] *der;* **~n**, **~n** heir; **der rechtmäßige/mutmaßliche ~:** the rightful heir/heir presumptive; **jmdn. zum** *od.* **als ~n einsetzen** appoint sb. as one's heir; **am Ende war alles nur für die lachenden ~n** (*ugs.*) in the end it was all just for others to inherit; **die ~n** (*fig.*) future generations
**Erbe·aneignung, Erbe·rezeption** *die* (*DDR*) acquainting oneself with the nation's cultural heritage
**erbeben** *itr. V.; mit sein* (*geh.*) Ⓐ shake; tremble; Ⓑ (*fig.: erregt werden*) shake; quiver
**erb-, Erb-:** **~eigen** *Adj.* inherited; **~eigenschaft** *die* (*Biol.*) hereditary characteristic; **~einsetzung** *die* (*Rechtsw.*) appointment of an/one's heir
**erben** *tr.* (*auch itr.*) *V.* inherit; **bei mir ist nichts zu ~** (*ugs.*) you won't get anything out of me
**Erben·gemeinschaft** *die* [community of] joint heirs
**erbetteln** *tr. V.* get by begging; **um eine Mahlzeit zu ~:** to beg for a meal
**erbeuten** /ɛɐ̯'bɔytn̩/ *tr. V.* carry off, get away with ‹valuables, prey, etc.›; capture ‹enemy plane, tank, etc.›
**erb-, Erb-:** **~fähig** *Adj.* (*Rechtsspr.*) heritable; **~faktor** *der* hereditary factor; **~fall** *der* (*Rechtsw.*) inheritance; **~fehler** *der* hereditary defect; **~feind** *der*, **~feindin** *die* Ⓐ traditional enemy; Ⓑ (*verhüll.: Teufel*) arch fiend
**Erb·folge** *die* Ⓐ succession; **die gesetzliche ~:** intestate succession; Ⓑ (*Thronfolge*) succession
**Erbfolge-:** **~krieg** *der* war of succession; **~recht** *das* law of succession
**Erb-:** **~forschung** *die* genetics *sing., no art.;* **~gut** *das* (*Biol.*) genotype; genetic make-up; **~hof** *der* ancestral estate; (*fig. Pol.*) perquisite
**erbieten** *unr. refl. V.* (*geh.*) **sich ~, etw. zu tun** offer to do sth.
**Erbin** *die;* **~, ~nen** heiress
**erbitten** ❶ *unr. tr. V.* (*geh.*) request; **„baldige Antwort erbeten"** 'early reply appreciated'. ❷ *unr. refl. V.* (*veralt.*) **sich ~ lassen, etw. zu tun** be prevailed upon to do sth.
**erbittern** *tr. V.* enrage; incense
**erbittert** ❶ *Adj.* bitter ‹resistance, struggle›. ❷ *adv.* **~ kämpfen** wage a bitter struggle
**Erbitterung** *die;* **~:** bitterness
**Erb·krankheit** *die* hereditary disease
**erblassen** /ɛɐ̯'blasn̩/ *itr. V.; mit sein* (*geh.*) go *or* turn pale; blanch (*literary*); ⇒ *auch* **Neid**
**Erblasser** /'ɛrplasɐ/ *der;* **~s, ~** (*Rechtsw.*) testator
**Erblasserin** *die;* **~, ~nen** (*Rechtsw.*) testatrix
**Erb-:** **~lehen** *das* (*hist.*) hereditary fief; **~lehre** *die* (*Biol.*) genetics *sing.*
**erbleichen** *itr. V.; mit sein* (*geh.*) go *or* turn pale; blanch (*literary*)
**erblich** ❶ *Adj.* hereditary ‹title, disease›. ❷ *adv.* **er ist ~ belastet** he suffers from a hereditary condition; (*scherzh.*) it runs in his family

*old spelling (see note on page 1707)

**Erblichkeit** *die;* **~** (*auch Biol.*) heritability
**erblicken** *tr. V.* (*geh.*) Ⓐ catch sight of; see; Ⓑ (*fig.*) see; **sie erblickte in mir eine Konkurrentin** she saw me as a rival; she saw a rival in me
**erblinden** *itr. V.; mit sein* Ⓐ go blind; lose one's sight; Ⓑ (*matt werden*) go *or* become dull
**Erblindung** *die;* **~:** loss of sight
**erblonden** *itr. V.; mit sein* (*scherzh.*) go blonde
**erblühen** *itr. V.; mit sein* (*geh.*) Ⓐ bloom; blossom; Ⓑ (*sich entfalten*) blossom
**Erb-:** **~masse** *die* Ⓐ (*Biol.*) genotype; genetic make-up; Ⓑ (*Rechtsspr.*) estate; **~monarchie** *die* hereditary monarchy; **~onkel** *der* (*ugs. scherzh.*) rich uncle
**erbosen** /ɛɐ̯'bo:zn̩/ (*geh.*) ❶ *tr. V.* infuriate. ❷ *refl. V.* **sich über etw.** (*Akk.*) **~:** become furious about sth.
**erbost** *Adj.* angry, furious (**über** + *Akk.* at)
**erbötig** /ɛɐ̯'bø:tɪç/ *Adj.* (*veralt.*) **sich ~ machen, etw. zu tun** offer to do sth.
**Erb-:** **~pacht** *die* Ⓐ (*Rechtsw.*) hereditary lease; Ⓑ (*hist.*) fee simple; **~prinz** *der*, **~prinzessin** *die* heir to the throne
**erbrechen** ❶ *unr. tr. V.* Ⓐ bring up ‹food›; Ⓑ (*geh.: aufbrechen*) break open ‹safe etc.›; Ⓒ (*veralt.: öffnen*) open ‹letter, seal›. ❷ *unr. itr., refl. V.* (*geh.: sich übergeben*) [**sich**] **~:** vomit; be sick
**Erbrechen** *das;* **~s** vomiting; **bis zum ~** (*ugs.*) ad nauseam
**Erb·recht** *das* (*Rechtsw.*) Ⓐ law of inheritance; Ⓑ (*Anspruch*) right of inheritance
**erbringen** *unr. tr. V.* Ⓐ produce ‹proof, evidence›; Ⓑ (*liefern*) produce ‹result etc.›; yield ‹amount›; result in ‹savings etc.›; **die vorgesehene Leistung ~:** do the required work; Ⓒ (*aufbringen*) raise ‹funds etc.›; put up ‹money etc.›
**Erbrochene** /ɛɐ̯'brɔxənə/ *das; adj. Dekl.* vomit
**Erb·schaden** *der* (*Genetik*) hereditary defect
**Erbschaft** *die;* **~, ~en** inheritance; **eine ~ machen** come into an inheritance; **die ~ des Kolonialismus** (*fig.*) the legacy of colonialism
**Erbschafts·anspruch** *der* claim to an/the inheritance
**Erbschaft[s]·steuer** *die* estate *or* death duties *pl.*
**Erb-:** **~schein** *der* certificate of inheritance; **~schleicher** *der* (*abwertend*) legacy hunter; **~schleicherei** *die;* **~~, ~~en** (*abwertend*) legacy hunting; **~schleicherin** *die* ⇒ **~schleicher**; **~schuld** *die* (*Rechtsw.*) inherited debt
**Erbse** /'ɛrpsə/ *die;* **~, ~n** pea; **grüne/getrocknete** *od.* **gelbe ~n** green/dried peas
**erbsen·groß** *Adj.* pea-size; the size of a pea *postpos.*
**Erbs[en]·püree** *das* pease pudding
**Erbsen·suppe** *die* Ⓐ pea soup; Ⓑ (*ugs.: Nebel*) pea souper
**Erb-:** **~stück** *das* heirloom; **~sünde** *die* original sin; **~tante** *die* (*ugs. scherzh.*) rich aunt; **~teil** *das* Ⓐ share of an/the inheritance; Ⓑ (*fig.: Anlage*) inherited trait; **~träger** *der* (*Biol.*) gene; **~vertrag** *der* testamentary contract; **~verzicht** *der* renunciation of the/an inheritance
**Erd-:** **~achse** *die* earth's axis; **~altertum** *das* (*Geol.*) Palaeozoic [era]; **~anziehung** *die* earth's gravitational pull; **~apfel** *der* (*bes. österr.*) ⇒ **Kartoffel**; **~arbeiten** *Pl.* (*Bauw.*) earth-moving *sing.;* **~atmosphäre** *die* earth's atmosphere; **~bahn** *die* earth's orbit; **~ball** *der* (*geh.*) globe; earth; **~beben** *das* earthquake
**erdbeben-, Erdbeben-:** **~gebiet** *das* earthquake area; **~herd** *der* seismic focus; hypocentre; **~messer** *der;* **~~s, ~~:** seismograph; **~sicher** *Adj.* earthquake-proof ‹building, construction›; ‹region etc.› free from earthquakes; **~warte** *die* seismological station; **~welle** *die* seismic wave

**Erdbeer·bowle** *die* strawberry punch
**Erd·beere** *die* strawberry
**erdbeer·farben** *Adj.* strawberry-coloured
**Erd-:** **~beschleunigung** *die* acceleration of gravity; **~bestattung** *die* burial; interment; **~bevölkerung** *die* earth's population; **~bewegung** *die* Ⓐ (*in der ~kruste*) tremor; Ⓑ (*Bauw.*) excavation; earthwork; **~bewohner** *der*, **~bewohnerin** *die* inhabitant of the earth; (*Science-Fiction*) earthling; **~boden** *der* ground; earth; **etw. dem ~boden gleichmachen** raze sth. to the ground; **sie ist wie vom ~boden verschluckt** it's as if the earth *or* ground had swallowed her up; **er wäre am liebsten in den ~boden versunken** he wished the earth *or* ground could have swallowed him up; **vom ~boden verschwinden** disappear from *or* off the face of the earth; **~bohrer** *der* (*Technik*) drill
**Erde** /'e:ɐ̯də/ *die;* **~, ~n** Ⓐ (*Erdreich*) soil; earth; **ein Klumpen ~:** a lump of earth; **etw. in die ~ rammen** ram sth. into the ground; **zu ~ werden** (*geh. verhüll.*) turn to dust; Ⓑ (*fester Boden*) ground; **etw. auf die ~ legen/stellen** put sth. down [on the ground]; **zu ebener ~:** on the ground floor *or* (*Amer.*) the first floor; **auf der ~ bleiben** (*fig.*) keep one's feet on the ground (*fig.*); **mit beiden Beinen** *od.* **Füßen fest auf der ~ stehen** (*fig.*) have one's feet firmly on the ground (*fig.*); **unter der ~ liegen** (*geh. verhüll.*) be in one's grave; **jmdn. unter die ~ bringen** (*ugs.*) bury sb.; (*fig.: töten*) be the death of sb. (*coll.*); Ⓒ (*Gebiet*) **ein ruhiges/idyllisches Fleckchen ~:** a peaceful/idyllic spot; **in heimatlicher/fremder ~ begraben werden** be buried in one's native soil/in foreign soil; ⇒ *auch* **Taktik**; Ⓓ (*Welt*) earth; world; **auf ~n** (*bibl.*), **auf der ~:** on earth; **die fernsten Winkel der ~:** the farthest corners of the globe; **auf der ganzen ~:** throughout the world; Ⓔ (*Planet*) Earth; **der Mars, der Jupiter und die ~:** Mars, Jupiter, and [the] Earth; Ⓕ (*Elektrot.*) earth
**erden** *tr. V.* (*Elektrot.*) earth
**Erden-:** **~bürger** *der*, **~bürgerin** *die* earth-dweller; **ein neuer/kleiner ~bürger** (*scherzh.*) a new arrival; **~da·sein** *das* (*geh.*) earthly existence; **~jammer** *der* (*dichter.*) earthly misery; misery of the world
**erdenkbar** *Adj.* ⇒ **erdenklich**
**erdenken** *unr. tr. V.* think *or* make up; **eine erdachte Geschichte** a made-up story
**Erden·kind** *das* (*geh.*) child of the earth (*literary*); mortal
**erdenklich** *Adj.* conceivable; imaginable; **alle** *od.* **jede ~e Mühe** every conceivable *or* the greatest possible trouble
**Erden-:** **~kloß** *der* (*veralt.: Mensch*) lump of clay; **~leben** *das* (*geh.*) earthly existence; **~wurm** *der* (*dichter. veralt.*) earthly being; mortal
**erd-, Erd-:** **~fern** *Adj.* Ⓐ (*Astron.*) remote, distant ‹planet›; distant ‹orbit›; Ⓑ (*dichter.*) spiritual ‹world etc.›; **~ferne** *die* Ⓐ (*Astron.*) apogee; Ⓑ (*dichter.*) remoteness [from the world]; **~gas** *das* natural gas; **~gebunden** *Adj.* (*geh.*) close to nature *postpos.;* **~geist** *der* earth spirit; **~geruch** *der* earthy smell; **~geschichte** *die* history of the earth; **~geschichtlich** ❶ *Adj.* relating to the earth's history *postpos., not pred.;* ❷ *adv.* in relation to the earth's history; **~geschoss**, ***~geschoß** *das* ground floor; first floor (*Amer.*); **im ~geschoss** on the ground floor; **~gravitation** *die* [earth's] gravitation; **~haufen** *der* mound of earth; **~hörnchen** *das;* **~s, ~** (*Zool.*) chipmunk; ground squirrel
**erdichten** *tr. V.* manufacture; **das ist alles erdichtet** it's all a pure fabrication
**erdig** *Adj.* Ⓐ earthy ‹mass, smell, taste›; Ⓑ (*geh.: mit Erde beschmutzt*) muddy
**erd-, Erd-:** **~innere** *das* interior of the earth; **~kabel** *das* underground cable; **~karte** *die* map of the earth; **~kern** *der* earth's core; **~klumpen** *der* lump of earth; clod [of earth]; **~kreis** *der* (*dichter.*) world; **~kröte** *die* toad; **~kruste** *die* earth's crust; **~kugel** *die* Ⓐ (*Planet*) terrestrial globe; earth; Ⓑ

(*Globus*) globe; **~kunde** *die* geography; **~kundlich** ❶ *Adj.* geographical; ❷ *adv.* geographically; **~leitung** *die* (*Elektrot.*) earth [connection]

**Erdling** /ˈeːɐ̯tlɪŋ/ *der;* **~s, ~e** (*Science-Fiction*) earthling

**erd-, Erd-: ~loch** *das* hole in the ground; (*Milit.*) foxhole; **~magnetismus** *der* terrestrial magnetism; **~massen** *Pl.* masses of earth; **~metall** *das* (*Chemie*) group III metal; **~mittel·alter** *das* (*Geol.*) Mesozoic [era]; **~mittel·punkt** *der* centre of the earth; **~nah** *Adj.* Ⓐ (*Astron.*) close to the earth *postpos.;* Ⓑ (*geh.*) down to earth; **~nuss, *~nuß** *die* peanut; groundnut; **~nuss·butter, *~nuß·butter** *die* peanut butter; **~nuss·öl, *~nuß·öl** *das* groundnut oil; **~ober·fläche** *die* earth's surface; **~öl** *das* oil; petroleum (*as tech. term*); **~öl exportierende/produzierende Länder** oil-exporting/oil-producing countries

**erdolchen** *tr. V.* (*geh.*) stab to death

**erdöl-, Erdöl-: *~exportierend** ⇨ **Erdöl**; **~feld** *das* oilfield; **~förder·land** *das* oil-producing country; **~gewinnung** *die* oil production; **~leitung** *die* oil pipeline; **~produkt** *das* oil product; **~produzent** *der* oil-producing country; ***~produzierend** ⇨ **Erdöl**; **~raffinerie** *die* oil refinery

**Erd-: ~pol** *der* terrestrial pole; **~reich** *das* soil

**erdreisten** *refl. V.* **sich ~, etw. zu tun** have the audacity to do sth.

**erdröhnen** *itr. V.; mit sein* Ⓐ (*ertönen*) roar; Ⓑ (*beben*) shake

**erdrosseln** *tr. V.* strangle

**Erdrosselung** *die;* **~, ~en** strangling

**Erd·rotation** *die* rotation of the earth

**erdrücken** *tr. V.* Ⓐ crush; Ⓑ (*fig.: belasten*) overwhelm; **die ständigen Geldsorgen erdrückten ihn** he was oppressed by the continual worries about money; Ⓒ (*fig.: nicht gelten lassen*) overshadow; **die Schrankwand erdrückt den kleinen Raum** these wall units are too overpowering in the small room

**erdrückend** ❶ *Adj.* overwhelming ‹evidence, superiority›; oppressive ‹heat, silence›. ❷ *adv.* overwhelmingly

**Erd-: ~rutsch** *der* landslide; landslip; **ein politischer ~rutsch** a political landslide; **~rutsch·sieg** *der* (*Politik*) landslide victory; **~satellit** *der* earth satellite; **~schatten** *der* shadow of the earth; **~schicht** *die* Ⓐ layer of earth; Ⓑ (*Geol.*) stratum; **~schluss, *~schluß** *der* (*Elektrot.*) accidental earth contact; **~scholle** *die* lump of earth; clod [of earth]; **~spalte** *die* fissure [in the ground]; **~stoß** *der* earth tremor; **~teil** *der* continent; **~trabant** *der* (*geh.*) earth satellite

**erdulden** *tr. V.* endure ‹sorrow, misfortune›; tolerate ‹insults›; (*über sich ergehen lassen*) undergo

**Erd-: ~um·drehung** *die* rotation of the earth; **eine ~umdrehung** one revolution of the earth; **~um·fang** *der* circumference of the earth; **~umkreisung** *die* orbit of the earth; **~um·lauf·bahn** *die* orbit [of the earth]; **in die ~umlaufbahn eintreten** enter into orbit; **~um·rundung** *die* (*eines Schiffs*) circumnavigation of the earth; (*eines Raumschiffs*) orbit of the earth; **~umseg[e]lung** *die* circumnavigation of the earth

**Erdung** *die;* **~, ~en** (*Elektrot.*) Ⓐ (*das Erden*) earthing; Ⓑ (*Leitung*) earth [connection]

**erd-, Erd-: ~verbunden, ~verhaftet, ~verwachsen** *Adj.* (*geh.*) close to nature *postpos.;* **~wall** *der* wall of earth; (*Milit., Straßenbau*) earthwork; **~wärts** *Adv.* (*geh.*) earthward[s]; **~zeit·alter** *das* geological era

**ereifern** *refl. V.* **sich über etw.** (*Akk.*) **~:** get excited about sth.; **sich schnell/unnötig ~:** quickly get worked up/get worked up about nothing

**Ereiferung** *die;* **~:** excitement

**ereignen** *refl. V.* happen; ‹accident, mishap› occur

**Ereignis** /ɛɐ̯ˈ|aiɡnɪs/ *das;* **~ses, ~se** event; occurrence; **ein aufregendes/historisches ~:** an exciting/historical event; **das fröhliche ~ eurer Hochzeit** the happy occasion of your marriage; **die ~se überstürzten sich** everything seemed to happen at once; **ein freudiges ~:** a happy event; **große ~se werfen ihren Schatten voraus** coming events cast their shadows before

**ereignis-: ~los** ❶ *Adj.* uneventful; ❷ *adv.* uneventfully; **~reich** ❶ *Adj.* eventful; ❷ *adv.* eventfully

**ereilen** *tr. V.* (*geh.*) **der Tod ereilte ihn** he died suddenly; **das gleiche Schicksal ereilte ihn** he met the same fate

**Erektion** /erɛkˈtsi̯oːn/ *die;* **~, ~en** erection

**Eremit** /ereˈmiːt/ *der;* **~en, ~en** hermit

**Eremitage** /eremiˈtaːʒə/ *die;* **~, ~n** hermitage

**Eremiten·leben** *das* hermit's life

**ererben** *tr. V.* (*veralt.*) inherit ‹money, characteristics›

**ererbt** *Adj.* inherited ‹fortune, ability›; inherited, hereditary ‹characteristic etc.›

**erfahrbar** *Adj.* **~ sein** be able to be experienced; **einem Kind etw. ~ machen** bring sth. within a child's experience

**erfahren**[1] *unr. tr. V.* Ⓐ find out; learn; (*hören*) hear; **etw. Wichtiges/Neues/Einzelheiten ~:** find out something important/new/some details; **etw. von jmdm. ~:** find sth. out from sb.; **etw. über jmdn./etw. ~:** find out *or* hear sth. about sb./sth.; **etw. von etw. ~:** find out *or* learn/hear sth. about sth.; **etw. durch jmdn./etw. ~:** learn of sth. from sb./sth.; Ⓑ (*geh.: erleben*) experience; **viel Leid/Kummer ~:** suffer much sorrow/anxiety; ⇨ *auch* **Leib** A; Ⓒ (*mitmachen*) undergo ‹change, experience, development, etc.›; suffer ‹setback›

**erfahren**[2] *Adj.* experienced

**Erfahrung** *die;* **~, ~en** experience; **über reiche/langjährige ~en verfügen** have extensive/years of experience; **eine Frau mit ~:** a woman of experience; **~en sammeln** gain experience *sing.;* **~en austauschen** share one's experiences; **bittere ~en sammeln müssen** have bitter experiences; **die ~ machen, dass ...** learn by experience that ...; **durch ~ lernen** learn through experience; **aus ~ sprechen** speak from experience; **wir haben schlechte ~en mit ihm/damit gemacht** our experience of him/it has not been very good; **etw. in ~ bringen** discover sth.

**erfahrungs-, Erfahrungs-: ~austausch** *der* exchange of experiences; **~bericht** *der* report; **~gemäß** *Adv.* in our/my experience; **~gemäß ist es so, dass ...** experience shows that ...; **~mäßig** ❶ *Adj.* empirical; ❷ *adv.* empirically; **~tat·sache** *die* empirical fact; **~wert** *der* figure drawn from past experience; **~wissenschaft** *die* empirical science

**erfassbar, *erfaßbar** *Adj.* ascertainable

**erfassen** *tr. V.* Ⓐ (*mitreißen*) catch; Ⓑ (*begreifen*) grasp ‹situation, implications, etc.›; **etw. intuitiv ~:** have an intuitive grasp of sth.; **du hast es erfasst!** (*meist iron.*) you've got it!; Ⓒ (*registrieren*) register; record; **einen repräsentativen Bevölkerungsdurchschnitt ~:** record information on *or* from a representative cross section of the population; Ⓓ (*einbeziehen*) cover; Ⓔ (*packen*) seize; **Angst/Freude erfasste ihn** he was seized by fear/overcome with joy

**Erfassung** *die* registration; **eine ~ der gesamten Bevölkerung/des Wohnraums** a survey of the whole population/of living space

**erfinden** *unr. tr. V.* Ⓐ invent; Ⓑ (*ausdenken*) make up ‹story, words›; make up, invent ‹excuse›; **sie hat die Arbeit [auch] nicht erfunden** (*iron.*) she is a lazy so-and-so (*coll.*); **das ist alles erfunden** it is pure fabrication; ⇨ *auch* **Pulver** B

**Erfinder** *der;* **~s, ~, Erfinderin** *die;* **~, ~nen** Ⓐ inventor; Ⓑ (*Urheber*) creator; **das ist nicht im Sinne des ~s** (*ugs.*) that's not what it was meant for

**Erfinder·geist** *der* inventive genius

**erfinderisch** *Adj.* inventive; (*schlau*) resourceful

**Erfinder·schutz** *der: protection of inventors;* ≈ patent law

**erfindlich** *Adj.* **nicht ~ sein** be unclear; **mir ist nicht ~, warum ...** I do not see why ...

**Erfindung** *die;* **~, ~en** Ⓐ invention; **die ~en der Raumfahrttechnik** inventions in the field of space technology; **eine ~ machen** invent something; **er hat viele ~en gemacht** he has many inventions to his credit; Ⓑ (*Ausgedachtes*) invention; fabrication

**erfindungs-, Erfindungs-: ~gabe** *die* inventiveness; **~reich** ❶ *Adj.* imaginative; ❷ *adv.* imaginatively; **~reichtum** *der* capacity for invention

**erflehen** *tr. V.* (*geh.*) beg; **jmds. Hilfe/Hilfe von jmdm. ~:** beg sb.'s help/beg help from sb.; **Vergebung ~:** beg for forgiveness

**Erfolg** /ɛɐ̯ˈfɔlk/ *der;* **~[e]s, ~e** ▶ 369 success; **viel/keinen ~ haben** be very successful/be unsuccessful; **etw. mit/ohne ~ tun** do something successfully/without success; **ohne ~ bleiben** remain unsuccessful; **der ~ blieb aus** success was not forthcoming; **einen ~ erzielen** *od.* **erringen** achieve success; **von ~ begleitet/gekrönt sein** be accompanied by/crowned with success; **der ~ war, dass ...** (*ugs.*) the upshot was that ...

**erfolgen** *itr. V.; mit sein* take place; occur; **nach erfolgtem Umbau** when reconstruction has/had been completed; **auf seine Beschwerden erfolgte keine Reaktion** there was no reaction to his complaints; **es erfolgte keine weitere Stellungnahme** no further statement was forthcoming

**erfolg-, Erfolg-: ~gekrönt** *Adj.* (*geh.*) crowned with success; **~los** ❶ *Adj.* unsuccessful; ❷ *adv.* unsuccessfully; **~losigkeit** *die;* **~~:** lack of success; **~reich** ❶ *Adj.* successful; ❷ *adv.* successfully

**Erfolgs-: ~aus·sicht** *die* prospect of success; **~autor** *der,* **~autorin** *die* successful author; **~beteiligung** *die* profit sharing; **~chance** *die* chance of success; **~denken** *das:* **das rücksichtslose ~denken** the thoughtless worship of success; **~erlebnis** *das* feeling of achievement; **dieses ~erlebnis tat ihm gut** this experience of success did him good; **~film** *der* successful film; **~honorar** *das* contingent fee; **~kurve** *die* path of success; (*eines Produkts*) sales graph; **~meldung** *die* report of success; **~mensch** *der* successful individual; **~prämie** *die* (*eines Vertreters*) commission; (*eines Arbeiters*) bonus; **~quote** *die* success rate; (*bei Prüfungen*) pass rate; **~rezept** *das* recipe for success; **~roman** *der* successful novel; **~stück** *das* (*Theater*) successful play; **~zahl** *die,* **~ziffer** *die* high success figure; (*Wirtsch.*) profit figure; **~zwang** *der* pressure to succeed

**erfolg·versprechend** *Adj.* promising

**erforderlich** *Adj.* required; necessary

**erforderlichenfalls** *Adv.* (*Amtsspr.*) should it be necessary

**erfordern** *tr. V.* require; demand; **wenn es die Umstände ~:** if circumstances require

**Erfordernis** *das;* **~ses, ~se** requirement

**erforschen** *tr. V.* discover ‹facts, causes, etc.›; explore ‹country›; find out ‹truth›; **sein Gewissen ~:** search one's conscience

**Erforscher** *der,* **Erforscherin** *die* researcher; (*Forschungsreisender*) explorer

**Erforschung** *die* research (+ *Gen.* into); (*der Erde, des Weltalls usw.*) exploration

**erfragen** *tr. V.* ascertain; **Einzelheiten zu ~ bei ...** further details can be obtained from ...

**erfrechen** *refl. V.* (*veralt., scherzh.*) **sich ~, etw. zu tun** have the audacity to do sth.

**erfreuen** ❶ *tr. V.* please; **wir möchten Sie mit einem kleinen Geschenk ~:** we should like to give you a small present; **diese gute Nachricht hat uns sehr erfreut** we

e

were very pleased to hear the good news; **sehr erfreut!** pleased to meet you. ❷ *refl. V.* [A] **sich an etw.** (*Dat.*) **~:** take pleasure in sth.; [B] (*geh.: genießen*) **sich einer Sache** (*Gen.*) **~:** enjoy sth.; **sich bester Gesundheit ~:** enjoy the best of health

**erfreulich** *Adj.* pleasant; **eine ~e Mitteilung** a piece of good news; **es ist sehr ~ zu hören, dass es Ihnen besser geht** it's very good to hear that you're better; **etwas/wenig/nichts Erfreuliches** something/hardly anything/nothing pleasant

**erfreulicherweise** *Adv.* happily

**erfrieren** ❶ *unr. itr. V.; mit sein* [A] ‹person, animal› freeze to death; ‹plant, harvest, etc.› be damaged by frost; suffer frost damage; **er ist ganz erfroren** (*ugs.*) he's absolutely frozen; [B] (*fig.: erstarren*) freeze; ‹feelings› cool. ❷ *unr. refl. V.* **sich** (*Dat.*) **die Finger/Ohren ~:** get frostbite in one's fingers/ears

**Erfrierung** *die;* **~, ~en** ▶ 474 frostbite *no pl.;* **~en an den Händen/Füßen** frostbitten hands/feet

**Erfrierungs·tod** *der* death from exposure

**erfrischen** ❶ *tr.* (*auch itr.*) *V.* [A] (*beleben*) refresh; **ein Abendspaziergang erfrischt sehr** an evening walk is very refreshing; [B] (*anregen*) stimulate. ❷ *refl. V.* freshen oneself up

**erfrischend** (*auch fig.*) ❶ *Adj.* refreshing. ❷ *adv.* refreshingly

**Erfrischung** *die;* **~, ~en** (*auch fig.*) refreshment

**Erfrischungs-: ~getränk** *das* soft drink; **eisgekühlter Tee ist ein herrliches ~getränk** iced tea is a wonderfully refreshing drink; **~raum** *der* refreshment room; **~stand** *der* refreshment stand; **~trunk** *der* (*geh.*) refreshing drink; **~tuch** *das; Pl.* **~tücher** tissue wipe; towelette

**erfühlen** *tr. V.* (*geh.*) sense

**erfüllbar** *Adj.* **~e Wünsche/Bedingungen** wishes which can be granted/conditions which can be met; **Ihre Wünsche/Bedingungen sind nicht ~:** your wishes cannot be granted/your conditions cannot be met

**erfüllen** ❶ *tr. V.* [A] grant ‹wish, request›; fulfil ‹contract›; carry out ‹duty›; meet ‹condition›; **seinen Zweck ~:** serve its purpose; **der Tatbestand des Totschlags ist erfüllt** this constitutes a case of manslaughter; [B] (*füllen*) fill; **die Luft war von süßem Duft erfüllt** a sweet perfume filled the air; **ein erfülltes Leben** (*geh.*) a full life; [C] (*stark beschäftigen*) overcome; **eine Sehnsucht erfüllte sein Herz** a longing came over him; **jmdn. mit etw. ~** (*geh.*) fill sb. with sth.; [D] (*Math.*) satisfy.
❷ *refl. V.* ‹wish› come true

**Erfüllung** *die:* **die ~ von Pflichten** the performance of duties; **sie glaubte nicht mehr an die ~ ihrer Wünsche** she no longer believed that her wishes would be granted; **in ~ gehen** come true; **in etw.** (*Dat.*) **~ finden** find fulfilment in sth.

**Erfüllungs-: ~gehilfe** *der* (*Rechtsw.*) agent of vicarious liability; **~ort** *der* (*Rechtsw.*) place of performance; **~politik** *die* (*bes. ns.*) *policy of unconditional fulfilment of the reparations and disarmament clauses of the Treaty of Versailles;* **~tag** *der* (*Rechtsw.*) day for settlement (*of debts*)

**erfunden** ❶ *2. Part. v.* **erfinden.** ❷ *Adj.* **eine ~e Geschichte** a fictional story; **das Abenteuer ist doch nur ~:** the adventure is just made up; **frei ~:** completely fictitious

**Erg** /ɛrk/ *das;* **~s, ~** (*Physik*) erg

**ergänzen** /ɛɐ̯ˈgɛntsn̩/ ❶ *tr. V.* [A] (*vervollständigen*) complete; (*erweitern*) add to; replenish ‹supply›; amplify ‹remark, statement, etc.›; amend ‹statute›; **etw. wieder ~:** make sth. up; **er ergänzte seine Sammlung durch** *od.* **um einige wertvolle Stücke** he added some valuable pieces to his collection; [B] (*hinzufügen*) **~[d hinzufügen]** add ‹remark›; [C] (*hinzukommen zu*) **eine Jacke ergänzte das Sommerkleid** a jacket complemented the summer dress; **der neue Mitarbeiter ergänzt das Team hervorragend** the new employee makes up the team admirably; [D] **sie ~ einander** *od.* **sich** they complement each other.
❷ *refl. V.* **sich durch etw. ~:** be augmented by sth.

**Ergänzung** *die;* **~, ~en** [A] (*Vervollständigung*) completion; (*Erweiterung*) enlargement; **die ~ der Arbeitsgruppen** making up the working groups; **zur ~ des Gesagten/einer Sammlung** to amplify what has been said/in order to enlarge a collection; **die ~ eines Gesetzes** the amendment of a statute; **die ~ der Vorräte** the replenishment of supplies; [B] (*Zusatz*) addition; (*zu einem Gesetz*) amendment; [C] (*zusätzliche Bemerkung*) further remark; [D] (*Sprachw.: Objekt*) object

**Ergänzungs-: ~ab·gabe** *die* (*Steuerw.*) surtax; **~band** *der* supplementary volume; **~bindestrich** *der* (*Sprachw.*) hyphen; **~frage** *die* [A] (*Sprachw.*) wh-question; [B] (*Zusatzfrage*) supplementary question

**ergattern** *tr. V.* (*ugs.*) manage to grab

**ergaunern** *tr. V.* get by underhand means; **wo hast du [dir] das Fahrrad ergaunert?** (*ugs.*) where did you pinch *or* swipe that bike? (*coll.*)

**ergeben**[1] ❶ *unr. refl. V.* [A] (*sich fügen*) **sich in etw.** (*Akk.*) **~:** submit to sth.; **sich in sein Schicksal ~:** resign oneself *or* become resigned to one's fate; [B] (*kapitulieren*) surrender (**jmdm.** to sb.); **sich [der Polizei** (*Dat.*)**] ~:** give oneself up [to the police]; [C] (*folgen, entstehen*) ‹opportunity, difficulty, problem› arise (**aus** from); **bald ergab sich ein angeregtes Gespräch** soon a lively discussion was taking place; **es ergab sich so** it just turned out that way; [D] (*sich hingeben*) **sich jmdm. ~:** give oneself to someone; **sich einer Sache** (*Dat.*) **~:** abandon oneself to sth.; **sich dem Alkohol/**(*ugs.*) **Suff ~:** take to alcohol/drink *or* the bottle.
❷ *unr. tr. V.* result in; **die Ernte ergab rund 400 Zentner Kartoffeln** the harvest produced about 400 hundredweight of potatoes; **eins und eins ergibt zwei** one and one makes two

**ergeben**[2] ❶ *Adj.* [A] (*zugeneigt*) devoted; [B] (*resignierend*) **mit ~er Miene** with an expression of resignation; [C] (*geh.: devot*) obsequious; **~sten Dank** (*veralt.*) humblest thanks; **Ihr sehr ~er ...** (*geh.*) yours most obediently, ...; **Ihr ~ster** *od.* **sehr ~er Diener** (*veralt.*) your most obedient servant (*arch.*). ❷ *adv.* [A] devotedly; [B] with resignation; [C] (*geh.*) obsequiously; **jmdm. ~st danken** (*veralt.*) thank sb. most humbly

**Ergebenheit** *die;* **~** [A] (*Treue*) devotion; [B] (*Sichfügen*) resignation

**Ergebenheits·adresse** *die* declaration of loyalty; (*an Monarchen*) loyal address

**Ergebnis** *das;* **~ses, ~se** result; **zu einem ~ kommen** reach a conclusion; **zu einem ~ führen** produce a result; **ohne ~ bleiben** lead to nothing

**ergebnis·los** ❶ *Adj.* fruitless ‹discussion›; **die Verhandlungen blieben/verliefen ~/wurden ~ abgebrochen** negotiations remained inconclusive/proceeded unprofitably/were broken off without a conclusion having been reached. ❷ *adv.* fruitlessly

**ergebnis·reich** *Adj.* fruitful

**Ergebung** *die;* **~:** resignation

**ergebungs·voll** ❶ *Adj.* humble. ❷ *adv.* humbly

**ergehen** ❶ *unr. refl. V.* [A] (*äußern*) **sich in etw.** (*Dat.*) **~:** indulge in sth.; **sich in endlosen Reden ~:** get carried away in endless speeches; [B] (*geh.: lustwandeln*) take a turn.
❷ *unr. itr. V.; mit sein* [A] (*geh.: erlassen werden*) ‹law› be enacted; **an ihn erging der Ruf einer bekannten Universität** he was offered a chair at a well-known university; **die Einladungen ergingen an alle Mitglieder** the invitations went to all members; [B] *unpers.* (*widerfahren*) **jmdm. ergeht es gut/schlecht** things go well/badly for sb. [C] **etw. über sich** (*Akk.*) **~ lassen** let sth. wash over one

**ergiebig** /ɛɐ̯ˈgiːbɪç/ *Adj.* rich ‹deposits, resources›; productive ‹mine›; fertile ‹fisheries, topic›; **der neue Kaffee ist nicht so ~/ist ~er** the new coffee does not go as far/goes further

**Ergiebigkeit** *die;* **~** ⇒ **ergiebig:** richness; productivity; fertility; **wegen der ~ des Kaffees/Tees** because the coffee/tea goes a long way

**ergießen** *unr. refl. V.* pour; **die Abwässer ~ sich in den Fluss** the effluent pours out into the river; **eine Menschenmasse ergoss sich in das Stadion** a mass of people poured into the stadium

**erglänzen** *itr. V.; mit sein* (*geh.*) ‹sun, light› appear; ‹sea, diamonds› begin to sparkle

**erglühen** *itr. V.; mit sein* (*geh.*) [A] glow; **in Liebe [zu jmdm.] erglüht sein** be passionately in love [with sb.]; [B] (*rot werden*) redden

**ergo** /ˈɛrgo/ *Adv.* ergo

**Ergo·meter** *das;* **~s, ~** (*Med.*) ergometer

**Ergonomie** /ɛrgonoˈmiː/ *die;* **~, Ergonomik** /ɛrgoˈnoːmɪk/ *die;* **~:** ergonomics *sing., no art.*

**ergonomisch** ❶ *Adj.* ergonomic. ❷ *adv.* ergonomically

**ergötzen** (*geh.*) ❶ *tr. V.* enthrall; captivate. ❷ *refl. V.* **sich an etw.** (*Dat.*) **~:** be delighted by sth.

**Ergötzen** *das;* **~s** (*geh.*) delight

**ergötzlich** (*geh.*) ❶ *Adj.* delightful. ❷ *adv.* delightfully

**ergrauen** *itr. V.; mit sein* go *or* turn grey; **in Ehren ergraut sein** (*fig.*) have grown old with honour; **ein im Dienst ergrauter Beamter** (*fig.*) an official of long standing

**ergreifen** *unr. tr. V.* [A] (*greifen*) grab; **jmds. Hand ~:** grasp sb.'s hand; [B] (*festnehmen*) catch ‹thief etc.›; [C] (*fig.: erfassen*) seize; **von blindem Zorn ergriffen** (*geh.*) in the grip of blind anger; [D] (*fig.: aufnehmen*) **einen Beruf ~:** take up a career; **die Initiative/eine Gelegenheit ~:** take the initiative/an opportunity; [E] (*fig.: bewegen*) move

**ergreifend** ❶ *Adj.* moving; **das ist ja ~** (*iron.*) how moving. ❷ *adv.* movingly

**Ergreifung** *die;* **~** [A] (*des Schuldigen*) capture; [B] (*der Macht*) seizure

**ergriffen** *Adj.* moved

**Ergriffenheit** *die;* **~: vor ~ schweigen** be too moved to speak; **vor ~ weinen** be moved to tears; **voller ~:** deeply moved

**ergrimmen** (*geh.*) ❶ *itr. V.; mit sein* be angry; **über etw.** (*Akk.*) **ergrimmt sein** be angry about something. ❷ *tr. V.* infuriate

**ergründbar** *Adj.* ⇒ **ergründen:** ascertainable; discoverable; graspable; fathomable

**ergründen** *tr. V.* ascertain; discover ‹cause›; grasp ‹concept›; fathom ‹mystery›

**Ergründung** *die* ⇒ **ergründen:** ascertainment; discovery; grasping; fathoming

**Erguss, *Erguß** *der* [A] (*Med.*) (*Blut~*) bruise; contusion; (*Samen~*) ejaculation; [B] (*geh. abwertend*) outburst; **ein poetischer ~:** a poetic outpouring; [C] (*Geol.*) eruption

**erhaben** *Adj.* [A] (*weihevoll*) solemn ‹moment›; awe-inspiring ‹sight›; sublime ‹beauty›; [B] (*überlegen*) **über etw.** (*Akk.*) **~ sein** be above sth.; **über jeden Zweifel ~:** beyond all criticism; [C] (*hervortretend*) uneven ‹surface›; embossed ‹pattern›

**Erhabenheit** *die;* **~:** grandeur; **eine Landschaft von solcher ~:** a landscape of such awe-inspiring grandeur; **die ~ des Augenblicks** the solemn grandeur of the moment

**Erhalt** *der;* **~[e]s** (*Amtsdt.*) [A] receipt; **den ~ eines Briefes bestätigen** acknowledge receipt of a letter; **bei ~ zahlen** pay on receipt; [B] ⇒ **Erhaltung**

**erhalten** ❶ *unr. tr. V.* [A] (*empfangen, bekommen*) receive ‹letter, news, gift›; be given ‹order›; get ‹good mark, impression›; **eine hohe Geldstrafe ~:** be fined heavily; **er erhielt 3 Jahre Gefängnis** he was sentenced to 3 years in prison; [B] (*bewahren*) preserve ‹town, building›; conserve ‹energy›; **diese Kleider sind noch gut ~:** these clothes are still

*old spelling (see note on page 1707)

in good condition; **jmdn. am Leben ~:** keep sb. alive; **er ist noch gut ~** (*scherzh.*) he is well preserved; **C** (*unterhalten*) support; **D** (*als Endprodukt gewinnen*) obtain ‹sugar, oil, etc.›. **2** *unr. refl. V.* (*überdauern*) survive

**Erhalter** *der*, **Erhalterin** *die* (*Bewahrer[in]*) preserver; (*der Familie*) breadwinner

**erhältlich** /ɛɐ̯'hɛltlɪç/ *Adj.* obtainable

**Erhaltung** *die;* ~ (*des Friedens*) maintenance; (*der Arten, von Kunstschätzen*) preservation; (*der Energie*) conservation

**Erhaltungs·satz** *der* (*Physik*) principle of conservation

**erhängen** *tr. V.* **jmdn./sich ~:** hang sb./oneself; **Tod durch Erhängen** death by hanging

**erhärten** *tr. V.* **A** strengthen ‹suspicion, assumption›; substantiate ‹claim›; **B** ⇒ **härten** 1

**Erhärtung** *die;* ~, **~en** **A** (*Bekräftigung*) substantiation; **B** ⇒ **Härtung**

**erhaschen** *tr. V.* (*geh., auch fig.*) catch

**erheben** **1** *unr. tr. V.* **A** (*emporheben*) raise ‹one's arm/hand›; **das Glas ~:** raise one's glass; **[hoch] erhobenen Hauptes** with head held high; **mit hoch erhobenen Armen** with arms raised *or* held high; **die Stimme ~:** raise one's voice; **B** (*verlangen*) levy ‹tax›; charge ‹fee›; **C** (*befördern*) **jmdn. in den Adelsstand ~:** elevate sb. to the nobility; **D** (*sammeln*) gather, collect ‹data, material›; **E** (*vorbringen*) **Anklage ~:** bring *or* prefer charges; **Protest ~:** make a protest; ⇒ *auch* **Einspruch** A; **F** *auch itr.* (*geh.: erbauen*) ‹art› edify; ‹music› uplift; **G** (*bes. südd., österr.: feststellen*) ascertain ‹cause etc.›. **2** *unr. refl. V.* **A** (*aufstehen*) rise; **sich von seinem Platz ~:** rise from one's seat; **B** (*rebellieren*) rise up (**gegen** against); **C** (*aufsteigen*) ‹bird, balloon› rise; **D** (*hinauswachsen*) **sich über etw.** (*Akk.*) **~:** rise above sth.; **E** (*emporragen*) ‹tower, mountain› rise; **F** (*geh.: sich besser dünken*) **sich über jmdn. ~:** feel superior to sb.; **G** (*geh.: beginnen*) ‹cry› ring out; ‹storm› rise

**erhebend** *Adj.* uplifting

**erheblich** /ɛɐ̯'he:plɪç/ **1** *Adj.* considerable. **2** *adv.* considerably

**Erhebung** *die;* ~, **~en** **A** (*Anhöhe*) elevation; **B** (*Aufstand*) uprising; **C** (*Umfrage*) survey; **D** (*Einziehen*) (*von Steuern*) levying; (*von Gebühren*) charging; **E** (*Beförderung*) elevation; **seine ~ in den Adelsstand** his elevation to the nobility; **F** (*seelische Erbauung*) uplift

**Erhebungs·zeitraum** *der* (*Statistik*) period during which information is/was collected

**erheischen** *tr. V.* (*geh.*) demand; command ‹admiration›

**erheitern** **1** *tr. V.* **jmdn. ~:** cheer sb. up. **2** *refl. V.* (*geh.*) be amused; **seine Züge erheiterten sich** his face brightened up

**Erheiterung** *die;* ~, **~en** amusement

**erhellen** **1** *tr. V.* **A** (*beleuchten*) light up, illuminate ‹room, sky›; **B** (*erklären*) shed light on, illuminate ‹reason, relationship›. **2** *refl. V.* (*geh.: sich aufheitern*) ‹eyes, face› brighten. **3** *itr. V.* (*veralt.: hervorgehen*) **daraus erhellt, dass ...** it follows *or* is evident from this that ...

**Erhellung** *die;* ~ (*Erklärung*) illumination

**erhitzen** **1** *tr. V.* **A** (*heiß machen*) heat ‹liquid›; **jmdn. ~:** make sb. hot; **B** (*fig.: erregen*) **die Gemüter ~:** make feelings run high. **2** *refl. V.* **A** heat up; ‹person› become hot; **B** (*fig.: sich erregen*) ‹feelings› become heated

**erhitzt** *Adj.* heated

**Erhitzung** *die;* ~, **~en** heating; (*Hitze*) heat

**erhoffen** *tr. V.* **sich** (*Dat.*) **viel/wenig von etw. ~:** expect a lot/little from sth.; **die erhoffte Änderung/Lohnerhöhung** the change/pay rise we/they etc. had expected

**erhöhen** **1** *tr. V.* **A eine Mauer [um einen Meter] ~:** make a wall [one metre] higher; **B** (*steigern*) increase, raise ‹prices, productivity, etc.›; **erhöhte/leicht erhöhte Temperatur haben** have a [high]/slight temperature; **erhöhter Blutdruck** somewhat high blood pressure; **erhöhte Gefahr** increased danger; **erhöhte Vorsicht** extra care; **C** (*Musik*) raise ‹note›. **2** *refl. V.* ‹rent, prices› rise

**Erhöhung** *die;* ~, **~en** **A** (*Höhermachen*) raising; **die ~ der Schornsteine/Deiche** increasing the height of the chimneys/dikes; **B eine ~ der Preise/Steuern** an increase in prices/taxes; **eine ~ des Blutdrucks** a rise in blood pressure; **die ~ einer Dosis** the increasing of a dose; **C** (*Musik*) raising [of a note]; **D** (*Anhöhe*) hill

**Erhöhungs-: ~winkel** *der* (*Waffent.*) angle of elevation; **~zeichen** *das* (*Musik*) sharp [sign]

**erholen** *refl. V.* ▶ **474** **A** (*sich ausruhen*) **sich [gut] ~:** have a [good] rest; (*entspannen*) relax [thoroughly]; **die Kurse haben/die Wirtschaft hat sich erholt** (*fig.*) the rates of exchange have/the economy has recovered; **B** (*genesen*) **sich von etw. ~:** recover from something

**erholsam** *Adj.* restful ‹weekend, holiday›; **wandern ist sehr ~:** walking is very refreshing

**Erholung** *die;* ~ ▶ **474** **A ~ brauchen** *od.* **nötig haben** need a rest; **nach der langen Krankheit hat er ~ nötig** he needs to recuperate after his long illness; **zur ~ fahren** go on holiday to rest/relax; (*nach einer Krankheit*) go on holiday to convalesce; **eine ~ sein** be relaxing; **~ suchende Menschen** people seeking relaxation; **B** (*fig.*) refreshing change

**erholungs-, Erholungs-: ~aufenthalt** *der* holiday; **~bedürftig** *Adj.* in need of a rest *postpos.*; **~bedürftig sein** need a rest; **~gebiet** *das* holiday area; **~heim** *das* holiday home; **~ort** *der* resort; **~pause** *die* break; **~reif** *Adj.* (*ugs.*) ⇒ **~bedürftig**; **~reise** *die* holiday trip; **~suchend** *Adj.* seeking relaxation *postpos.*; **~suchende** *der/die; adj. Dekl.* holidaymaker; **~urlaub** *der* holiday for convalescence; **~wert** *der* recreational value; **~zentrum** *das* leisure centre

**erhören** *tr. V.* (*geh.*) hear ‹plea, prayer›; **einen Liebhaber ~** (*veralt.*) yield to a lover

**erigieren** /eri'gi:rən/ *itr. V.*; *mit sein* become erect; **erigiert** erect

**Erika** /'e:rika/ *die;* ~, **~s** *od.* **Eriken** /-kən/ (*Bot.*) erica

**erinnerlich** *Adj.* **wie ~:** as will be recalled; **soviel mir ~ ist** as I recall; **das ist mir nicht mehr ~:** I cannot remember that any more

**erinnern** /ɛɐ̯'|ɪnɐn/ **1** *refl. V.* **sich an jmdn./etw. [gut/genau] ~:** remember sb./sth. [well/clearly]; **sich [daran] ~, dass ...** remember *or* recall that ...; **wenn ich mich recht erinnere** if I remember rightly; **sich jmds./einer Sache ~** (*geh.*) remember *or* recall sb./sth.

**2** *tr. V.* **A** (*ins Bewusstsein rufen*) **jmdn. an etw./jmdn. ~:** remind sb. of sth./sb.; **jmdn. daran ~, etw. zu tun** remind sb. to do sth.; **B** (*ugs., bes. nordd.*) **jmdn./etw. ~:** remember sb./sth.

**3** *itr. V.* **A jmd./etw. erinnert an jmdn./etw.** sb./sth. reminds one of sb./sth.; **B** (*zu bedenken geben*) **an etw.** (*Akk.*) **~:** remind sb. of sth.; **ich möchte daran ~, dass ...** let us not forget *or* overlook that ...

**Erinnerung** *die;* ~, **~en** **A** memory (**an** + *Akk.* of); **etw. [noch gut] in ~ haben** [still] remember sth. [well]; **etw. aus der ~ aufschreiben/sagen** write/say sth. from memory; **wenn mich die ~ nicht täuscht** if my memory does not deceive me; **sich** (*Dat.*) **etw. in die ~ zurückrufen** call something to mind again; **nach meiner ~, meiner ~ nach** as far as I remember; **seinen ~en nachhängen** lose oneself in one's memories; **jmdn./etw. in guter ~ behalten** have pleasant memories of sb./sth.; **zur ~ an jmdn./etw.** in memory of sb./sth.; **zur ~ an die Gefallenen wurde ein Denkmal errichtet** a monument was erected to the memory of those who had fallen; **B** (*~sstück*) remembrance; souvenir; **C** *Pl.* (*Autobiographie*) memoirs; **D** (*Zahlungsaufforderung*) reminder

**Erinnerungs-: ~bild** *das* memory; **~foto** *das* souvenir snapshot; **~lücke** *die* gap in one's memory; **da habe ich eine ~lücke** my mind is a blank about that; **~medaille** *die* commemorative coin; **~schreiben** *das* reminder; **~stück** *das* keepsake; (*von einer Reise*) souvenir; **~vermögen** *das* memory; **~wert** *der* sentimental value

**Erinnye** /e'rɪnỹə/ *die;* ~, **~n** (*Myth.*) Fury; Erinys

**erjagen** *tr. V.* **A** (*erbeuten*) catch; **B** (*gewinnen*) win ‹fame›; make ‹money, fortune›

**erkalten** *tr. V.*; *mit sein* cool; ‹limbs› grow cold; (*fig.*) ‹passion, feeling› cool

**erkälten** *refl. V.* ▶ **474** catch cold; **sich** (*Dat.*) **den Magen ~:** get a chill on one's stomach; ⇒ *auch* **Blase** C

**Erkältung** *die;* ~, **~en** ▶ **474** cold; **sich** (*Dat.*) **eine ~ zuziehen** *od.* (*ugs.*) **holen** catch a cold

**Erkältungs·krankheit** *die* cold

**erkämpfen** *tr. V.* win; **den Sieg ~:** gain a victory; **sich** (*Dat.*) **etw. ~ müssen** have to fight for sth.

**erkaufen** *tr. V.* **A** (*durch Opfer*) win; **etw. teuer ~:** win sth. at great cost; **B** (*durch Geld*) buy; **sich** (*Dat.*) **etw. ~:** buy oneself sth.

**erkennbar** **1** *Adj.* recognizable; (*sichtbar*) visible; (*schwach sichtbar*) discernible. **2** *adv.* recognizably; (*sichtbar*) visibly

**erkennen** **1** *unr. tr. V.* **A** (*deutlich sehen*) make out; **die Fingerabdrücke waren deutlich zu ~:** the fingerprints were clearly visible; **B** (*identifizieren*) recognize (**an** + *Dat.* by); **der Täter wurde nicht erkannt** the culprit was not identified; **sich zu ~ geben** reveal one's identity; **sich als etw. zu ~ geben** reveal oneself to be sth.; **C** (*einschätzen*) recognize; perceive; acknowledge ‹error, mistake›; **„erkenne dich selbst!“** 'know thyself!'; **D** (*geh. veralt: begatten*) know (*arch.*).

**2** *unr. itr. V.* **A** (*Rechtsspr.*) **auf Freispruch ~:** grant an acquittal; **das Gericht erkannte auf 6 Jahre Gefängnis** the court passed a sentence of six years' imprisonment; **B** (*Sport*) **auf Elfmeter/Freistoß ~:** award a penalty/free kick

**erkenntlich** *Adj.* **A sich [für etw.] ~ zeigen** show one's appreciation for sth.; **B** ⇒ **erkennbar**

**Erkenntlichkeit** *die;* ~, **~en** **A** (*Dankbarkeit*) gratitude; **B** (*Geschenk*) token of gratitude

**Erkenntnis** *die;* ~, **~se** **A** (*Einsicht*) discovery; **wissenschaftliche/wichtige/gesicherte ~se** scientific findings/important discoveries/firm insights; **zu der ~ kommen, dass ...** come to the realization that ...; **B** (*das Erkennen*) cognition; **der Baum der ~** (*bibl.*) the tree of knowledge

**erkenntnis-, Erkenntnis-: ~drang** *der* thirst for knowledge; **~kritik** *die* (*Philos.*) critique of knowledge; **~prozess**, ***~prozeß** *der* cognitive process; **~theoretisch** (*Philos.*) **1** *Adj.* epistemological; **2** *adv.* epistemologically; **~theorie** *die* (*Philos.*) theory of knowledge; epistemology *no art.*; **~vermögen** *das* powers *pl.* of cognition

**erkennungs-, Erkennungs-: ~dienst** *der* police records department; **~dienstlich** **1** *Adj.* **~dienstliche Behandlung** fingerprinting and photographing; **2** *adv.* **Personen ~dienstlich erfassen** investigate persons through the police records department; **jmdn. ~dienstlich behandeln** take sb.'s fingerprints and photograph; **~marke** *die* identification disc; **~melodie** *die* (*einer Sendung*) theme music; (*eines Senders*) signature tune; **~zeichen** *das* sign [to recognize sb. by]

**Erker** /'ɛrkɐ/ *der;* **~s, ~:** bay window

**Erker-: ~fenster** *das* bay window; **~zimmer** *das* room with a bay window

**erkiesen** *unr. tr. V.* (*veralt. geh.*) choose

**erklärbar** *Adj.* explicable; **etw. ist ~:** sth. can be explained; **aus ~en Gründen** for reasons which can easily be explained

**erklären** ❶ *tr. V.* [A] explain; **jmdm. etw. ~:** explain sth. to sb.; **etw. an einem Beispiel ~:** explain sth. with an example; [B] (*begründen*) explain (**durch** by); [C] (*mitteilen*) state; declare; announce ‹one's resignation›; **jmdm. den Krieg ~:** declare war on sb.; [D] (*bezeichnen*) **jmdn. für tot ~:** pronounce sb. dead; **etw. für ungültig/verbindlich ~:** declare sth. to be invalid/binding; **die Ehe wurde für ungültig erklärt** the marriage was declared void; **jmdn. zu etw. ~:** name sb. as sth.
❷ *refl. V.* [A] **sich einverstanden/bereit ~:** declare oneself [to be] in agreement/willing; **sich zu einer Sache ~:** make a statement on sth.; **sich für jmdn./etw. ~** (*geh.*) declare one's support for sb./sth.; **sich gegen jmdn./etw. ~:** declare one's opposition to sb./sth.; **sich jmdm. ~** (*geh. veralt.*) declare one's love to sb.; [B] (*seine Begründung finden*) be explained; **das erklärt sich einfach/von selbst** that is easily explained/self-evident

**erklärend** ❶ *Adj.* explanatory; **mit einigen ~en Worten** with a few words of explanation. ❷ *adv.* by way of explanation

**erklärlich** *Adj.* understandable; **es ist mir einfach nicht ~, wie ...** I just can't understand how ...

**erklärlicherweise** *Adv.* understandably

**erklärt** *Adj.* declared ‹opponent, intention›; **er war der ~e Mittelpunkt** he was regarded by all as the centre of attraction

**erklärtermaßen** *Adv.* on one's own admission

**Erklärung** *die;* **~, ~en** [A] (*Darlegung*) explanation; [B] (*Mitteilung*) statement; **eine ~ abgeben** make a statement

**Erklärungs·versuch** *der* attempt at an explanation

**erklecklich** /ɛɐ̯'klɛklɪç/ *Adj.* considerable ‹sum, profit›

**erklettern** *tr. V.* climb to the top of ‹rock, wall, mountain›; climb to ‹summit›

**erklimmen** *unr. tr. V.* (*geh.*) climb ‹wall, tree›; **die oberste Stufe der Erfolgsleiter ~** (*fig.*) reach the top of the ladder to success

**erklingen** *unr. itr. V.;* *mit sein* ring out; **Musik ~ hören** hear the sound of music; **es erklang die Nationalhymne** the national anthem was played

**erkoren** /ɛɐ̯'ko:rən/ *2. Part. v.* **erkiesen**

**erkranken** *itr. V.* ▶ **474** ; *mit sein* become ill (**an** + *Dat.* with); **er ist an einer Lungenentzündung erkrankt** he's got an inflammation of the lungs; **schwer erkrankt sein** be seriously ill; **ein erkrankter Kollege** a sick colleague

**Erkrankung** *die;* **~, ~en** ▶ **474** (*eines Menschen, Tieres*) illness; (*eines Körperteils*) disease

**Erkrankungs·fall** *der:* **im ~:** in event of illness; **die Versicherung schließt Erkrankungsfälle nicht ein** the insurance does not cover illness

**erkühnen** *refl. V.* (*geh.*) **sich ~, etw. zu tun** dare to do sth.

**erkunden** *tr. V.* reconnoitre ‹terrain›; **die Situation ~:** find out what the situation is

**erkundigen** *refl. V.* **sich nach jmdm./etw. ~:** ask after sb./enquire about sth.; **sich ~, ob/wann ...** enquire whether/when ...; ⇨ *auch* **Befinden**

**Erkundigung** *die;* **~, ~en** enquiry; **~en einholen** *od.* **einziehen** make enquiries

**Erkundung** *die;* **~, ~en** (*meist Milit.*) reconnaissance; **auf ~ gehen** go out on reconnaissance

**Erkundungs-: ~fahrt** *die* exploratory trip; **eine ~fahrt machen** go exploring; **eine ~fahrt durch die Umgebung machen** explore the area; **~flug** *der* reconnaissance flight; **~trupp** *der* reconnaissance party

**erkünstelt** /ɛɐ̯'kʏnstl̩t/ *Adj.* (*abwertend*) ⇨ **gekünstelt 1**

**Erlag·schein** /ɛɐ̯'la:k-/ *der* (*österr.*) ⇨ **Zahlkarte**

*old spelling (see note on page 1707)

**erlahmen** *itr. V.;* *mit sein* [A] tire; become tired; ‹strength› flag; [B] (*nachlassen*) ‹enthusiasm etc.› wane

**erlangen** *tr. V.* gain; obtain ‹credit, visa›; reach ‹age›

**Erlangung** *die;* **~:** attainment; (*eines Kredits, Visums*) obtaining; (*von Stimmen*) gaining; **zur ~ der Doktorwürde** for the degree of doctor

**Erlass, *Erlaß** /ɛɐ̯'las/ *der;* **Erlasses, Erlasse** [A] (*Anordnung*) decree; **der ~ eines Ministers** a decree by a minister; a ministerial decree; [B] (*Straf~, Schulden~ usw.*) remission; [C] (*Verfügung*) (*eines Gesetzes, einer Bestimmung*) enactment; (*eines Dekrets*) issue; (*eines Verbots*) imposition

**erlassen** *unr. tr. V.* [A] (*verkünden*) enact ‹law›; declare ‹amnesty›; issue ‹warrant›; [B] (*verzichten auf*) remit ‹sentence›; **~ Sie es mir, das zu schildern** (*geh.*) excuse me from having to describe it

**erlauben** ❶ *tr. V.* [A] allow; **jmdm. ~, etw. zu tun** allow sb. to do sth.; **~ Sie mir, das Fenster zu öffnen?** (*geh.*) would you mind if I opened the window?; **es ist nicht erlaubt, den Rasen zu betreten** it is forbidden to walk on the grass; **[na], ~ Sie mal!** (*ugs.*) do you mind! (*coll.*); **was ~ Sie sich!** how dare you!; **erlaubt ist, was gefällt** do what you feel like doing; **was nicht verboten ist, das ist erlaubt** if something's not forbidden then it's allowed; [B] (*ermöglichen*) permit; **meine Gesundheit erlaubt es mir nicht** my health does not permit me to do it; **meine Zeit erlaubt es mir nicht** time does not allow.
❷ *refl. V.* [A] (*sich die Freiheit nehmen*) **sich** (*Dat.*) **etw. ~:** permit oneself sth.; **du hast dir in letzter Zeit ziemlich viele Freiheiten erlaubt** you have been taking a lot of liberties recently; **sie erlaubt sich** (*Dat.*) **in letzter Zeit grobe Nachlässigkeiten** she's allowed herself to become extremely negligent recently; **über seine berufliche Leistung kann ich mir kein Urteil ~:** I do not feel free to comment on his professional competence; **sich** (*Dat.*) **alles ~:** do just as one pleases; **sich** (*Dat.*) **einen Scherz [mit jmdm.] ~:** play a trick [on sb.]; [B] (*sich leisten*) **sich** (*Dat.*) **etw. ~:** treat oneself to sth.; **das/solche teuren Geschenke kannst du dir nicht ~:** you cannot afford it/such expensive presents

**Erlaubnis** *die;* **~, ~se** permission; (*Schriftstück*) permit; **jmdn. um ~ bitten, etw. zu tun** ask sb.'s permission *or* sb. for permission to do sth.; **jmdm. die ~ erteilen/verweigern, etw. zu tun** give/refuse sb. permission to do sth.

**Erlaubnis·schein** *der* permit

**erlaucht** /ɛɐ̯'lauxt/ *Adj.* (*geh.*) illustrious

**Erlaucht** *die;* **~, ~en** (*veralt.*) **Ihre/Seine ~:** Her Ladyship/His Lordship; **Euer ~:** Your Ladyship/Lordship

**erläutern** *tr. V.* explain; comment on ‹picture etc.›; annotate ‹text›; **näher ~:** clarify; **~de Anmerkungen** explanatory notes

**Erläuterung** *die* explanation; (*zu einem Bild usw.*) commentary; (*zu einem Text*) [explanatory] note

**Erle** /'ɛrlə/ *die;* **~, ~n** alder

**erleben** *tr. V.* experience; **etwas Schönes/Schreckliches ~:** have a pleasant/terrible experience; **das habe ich noch nie erlebt!** I've never heard of such a thing!; **er hat viel erlebt** he has seen a lot of life; **große Abenteuer ~:** have great adventures; **er wollte erst etwas ~:** he wanted to live it up a bit first; **so ängstlich hatte er sie noch nie erlebt** he had never seen her so afraid before; **etw. bewusst/intensiv ~:** be fully aware of sth./experience sth. to the full; **sie wünschte sich nur, die Hochzeit ihrer Tochter noch zu ~:** her only remaining wish was to be at her daughter's wedding; **er wird das nächste Jahr nicht mehr ~:** he won't see next year; **dieser Film erlebte einen völligen Reinfall** this film was a complete flop (*coll.*); **du kannst was ~!** (*ugs.*) you won't know what's hit you!; **sich als etw. ~:** feel oneself to be sth.; ⇨ *auch* **erlebt**

**Erleben** *das* experience; **etw. aus eigenem ~ kennen** know sth. from one's own experience

**Erlebens·fall** *der* (*Versicherungsw.*) **im ~:** in the event of survival; **eine Versicherung auf den ~:** endowment assurance

**Erlebnis** *das;* **~ses, ~se** experience; **das war ein ~:** what an experience!

**Erlebnis-: ~auf·satz** *der* (*Schulw.*) essay based on personal experience; **~fähigkeit** *die* (*Psych.*) capacity for experience; **~hunger** *der* thirst for experience

**erlebt** *Adj.* **~e Rede** inner monologue; **~e Geschichte** a first-hand account

**erledigen** ❶ *tr. V.* [A] (*ausführen*) **einen Auftrag ~:** deal with a task; **ich muss noch einige Dinge ~:** I must see to a few things; **so, damit wäre die Angelegenheit endlich erledigt** so now the matter is finally settled; **sie hat alles pünktlich erledigt** she got everything done on time; **schon erledigt!** that's already done; [B] (*erschöpfen*) finish (*coll.*) ‹person›; **der Umzug hat ihn völlig erledigt** the move finished him off completely (*coll.*); [C] (*ugs.: töten*) knock off (*coll.*); (*fig.: zerstören*) destroy.
❷ *refl. V.* ‹matter, problem› resolve itself; **damit hat sich die Sache erledigt** that's that; **vieles erledigt sich von selbst** a lot of things sort them'selves out

**erledigt** *Adj.* closed ‹case›; (*ugs.*) worn out ‹person›

**Erledigung** *die;* **~, ~en** [A] (*Durchführung*) carrying out; (*Beendigung*) completion; (*einer Angelegenheit*) settling; **um baldige ~ wird gebeten** please give this matter your prompt attention; [B] (*Besorgung*) **er hat noch einige ~en zu machen** he's got one or two more things to see to

**erlegen** *tr. V.* [A] shoot ‹animal›; [B] (*österr.: entrichten*) pay ‹fee, charge›

**erleichtern** ❶ *tr. V.* [A] (*einfacher machen*) make easier; **jmdm./sich die Arbeit ~:** make sb.'s/one's work easier; [B] (*befreien*) relieve; **das hat ihn [sehr] erleichtert** that came as a [great] relief to him; **erleichtert aufatmen** breathe a sigh of relief; [C] (*Gewicht verringern, fig.*) lighten; **sein Herz/sein Gewissen ~:** open one's heart/unburden one's conscience; **jmdn. um etw. ~** (*ugs. scherzh.*) relieve sb. of sth. ❷ *refl. V.* (*verhüll.: seine Notdurft verrichten*) relieve oneself

**Erleichterung** *die;* **~, ~en** [A] (*Vereinfachung*) **zur ~ der Arbeit** to make the work easier; [B] (*Befreiung*) relief; **mit ~:** with relief; **voller ~:** with great relief; **~ empfinden** feel relieved; [C] (*Verbesserung, Milderung*) alleviation; **es gab weitere ~en im Reiseverkehr** there was a further easing of travel restrictions

**erleiden** *unr. tr. V.* suffer

**erlernbar** *Adj.* learnable; **es ist leicht ~:** it can be easily learnt *or* is easy to learn; **eine ~e Fähigkeit** a faculty which can be acquired

**erlernen** *tr. V.* learn

**erlesen**[1] *unr. tr. V.* (*geh. veralt.*) choose

**erlesen**[2] *Adj.* superior ‹wine›; choice ‹dish›; **ein ~er Geschmack** a discriminating taste

**Erlesenheit** *die;* **~:** exquisiteness

**erleuchten** *tr. V.* [A] light; **Blitze erleuchteten den Himmel** the sky was lit up by flashes of lightning; **hell erleuchtete Fenster** brightly lit windows; [B] (*geh.: mit Klarheit erfüllen*) inspire

**Erleuchtung** *die;* **~, ~en** inspiration; **ihm kam eine ~:** he had a flash of inspiration

**erliegen** *unr. itr. V.;* *mit sein* [A] succumb (*Dat.* to); **einem Irrtum ~:** be misled; **im Kampf ~** (*veralt.*) be vanquished in battle; **zum Erliegen kommen** come to a standstill; **etw. zum Erliegen bringen** bring sth. to a standstill; [B] (*zum Opfer fallen*) **einer Krankheit** (*Dat.*) **~:** die from an illness

**Erl·könig** /'ɛrl-/ *der* [A] **„Der ~"** 'The erl-king'; [B] (*Kfz-Jargon*) test model

**erlogen** *Adj.* made up; untruthful ‹story›

**Erlös** /ɛɐ̯ˈløːs/ *der;* **~es, ~e** proceeds *pl.;* **vom ~ seiner Bilder leben** live on the income from the sale of one's paintings

**erlöschen** *unr. itr. V.; mit sein* **A** ‹fire› go out; **ein erloschener Vulkan** an extinct volcano; **die Lichter waren schon erloschen** the lights were already out; **B** (*nachlassen*) ‹hope, feelings› wane; **C** (*aussterben*) ‹family, clan› die out; **D** (*zu bestehen aufhören*) ‹claim, obligation› cease; ‹firm, membership› cease to exist

**erlösen** *tr. V.* save, rescue (**von** from); **jmdn. von seinen Schmerzen ~:** release sb. from pain; **von einer Sorge erlöst sein** be relieved of a worry; **von einer Krankheit erlöst werden** (*verhüll.*) be released from an illness; **jmdn. ~** (*ugs. scherzh.*) take over from sb.; **und erlöse uns von dem Übel** *od.* **Bösen** (*bibl.*) and deliver us from evil

**erlösend** *Adj.* **das ~e Wort sprechen** say the magic word; **~ wirken** come as a relief

**Erlöser** *der;* **~s, ~** **A** saviour; **B** (*christl. Rel.*) redeemer

**Erlöserin** *die;* **~, ~nen** ⇒ **Erlöser A**

**Erlösung** *die* release (**von** from); (*christl. Rel.*) redemption; **es war eine ~ zu wissen, dass ...** it was a relief to know that ...

**ermächtigen** *tr. V.* authorize; **[dazu] ermächtigt sein, etw. zu tun** be authorized to do sth.

**Ermächtigung** *die;* **~, ~en** authorization

**Ermächtigungs·gesetz** *das* (*Politik, bes. ns.*) Enabling Act

**ermahnen** *tr. V.* admonish; tell (*coll.*); (*warnen*) warn

**Ermahnung** *die* admonition; (*Warnung*) warning

**ermangeln** *itr. V.* (*geh.*) **einer Sache** (*Gen.*) **~:** lack sth.

**Ermang[e]lung** *die;* **~:** *in* **in ~** (+ *Gen.*) (*geh.*) in the absence of; **in ~ eines Besseren** for lack of anything better

**ermannen** *refl. V.* (*geh.*) **sich ~, etw. zu tun** pluck up courage to do sth.

**ermäßigen** ❶ *tr. V.* reduce. ❷ *refl. V.* be reduced

**Ermäßigung** *die* reduction

**ermatten** (*geh.*) ❶ *itr. V.; mit sein* ‹person› become exhausted; (*fig.*) ‹enthusiasm› wane. ❷ *tr. V.* (*matt machen*) exhaust, tire ‹person›

**ermattet** *Adj.* exhausted

**Ermattung** *die;* **~:** weariness; fatigue

**ermessen** *unr. tr. V.* estimate, gauge ‹consequences, implications›; **daran können Sie ~, wie/ob ...** that will give you some idea of how/whether ...; **die Bedeutung von etw. ~:** appreciate the significance of sth.

**Ermessen** *das;* **~s** estimation; **nach eigenem ~:** in one's own estimation; **in jmds. ~** (*Dat.*) **liegen** be at sb.'s discretion; **nach menschlichem ~:** as far as anyone can judge; **etw. in jmds.** (*Akk.*) **~ stellen** leave sth. to sb.'s discretion

**Ermessens-: ~entscheidung** *die* discretionary decision; **~frage** *die* matter of discretion; **~missbrauch, *~mißbrauch** *der* abuse of one's powers of discretion; **~spiel·raum** *der* powers *pl.* of discretion; discretionary powers *pl.*

**ermitteln** ❶ *tr. V.* **A** (*herausfinden*) ascertain, determine ‹facts›; discover ‹culprit, hideout, address›; establish, determine ‹identity, origin›; decide ‹winner›; **B** (*errechnen*) calculate ‹quota, rates, data›. ❷ *itr. V.* (*Rechtsw.*) investigate; **gegen jmdn. ~:** investigate sb.; **in einer Sache ~:** investigate sth.

**Ermittlung** *die;* **~, ~en** **A** (*das Ermitteln*) ⇒ **ermitteln A**: ascertainment; determination; discovery; establishment; **die ~ eines Gewinners** deciding a winner; **B** (*Untersuchung*) investigation

**Ermittlungs-: ~arbeit** *die* investigatory work; **~aus·schuss, *~aus·schuß** *der* committee of inquiry; **~beamte** *der,* **~beamtin** *die* investigating officer; **~richter** *der,* **~richterin** *die* examining magistrate; **~verfahren** *das* (*Rechtsw.*) preliminary inquiry

**ermöglichen** *tr. V.* enable; **jmdm. etw. ~:** make sth. possible for sb.; **um einen besseren Gedankenaustausch zu ~:** to facilitate a better exchange of ideas

**ermorden** *tr. V.* murder; (*aus politischen Gründen*) assassinate

**Ermordung** *die;* **~, ~en** murder; (*aus politischen Gründen*) assassination

**ermüden** ❶ *itr. V.; mit sein* **A** (*müde werden*) tire; become tired; **B** (*Technik*) ‹metal› fatigue. ❷ *tr. V.* (*müde machen*) tire; make tired

**ermüdend** *Adj.* tiring

**Ermüdung** *die;* **~, ~en** **A** tiredness; **vor ~:** from tiredness; **B** (*Technik*) metal fatigue

**Ermüdungs-: ~erscheinung** *die* sign of fatigue; **~zustand** *der* state of fatigue

**ermuntern** *tr. V.* **A** **jmdn. [dazu] ~, etw. zu tun** encourage sb. to do sth.; **jmdn. zum Reden/zu einem Verbrechen ~:** encourage sb. to talk/to commit a crime; **B** (*veralt.: wach machen*) liven up ‹person›

**ermunternd** ❶ *Adj.* encouraging. ❷ *adv.* encouragingly

**Ermunterung** *die;* **~, ~en** **A** (*Aufheiterung*) enlivenment; **zur ~ der Anwesenden** to the amusement of those present; **B** (*Ermutigung*) encouragement; **C** (*ermunternde Worte*) words *pl.* of encouragement

**ermutigen** *tr. V.* **A** encourage; **B** ⇒ **ermuntern A**

**ermutigend** ❶ *Adj.* encouraging. ❷ *adv.* encouragingly

**Ermutigung** *die;* **~, ~en** **A** encouragement; **zur ~:** to encourage; **B** (*ermutigende Worte*) words *pl.* of encouragement

**ernähren** ❶ *tr. V.* **A** feed ‹young, child›; **mit der Flasche ernährt werden** be bottle-fed; **B** (*unterhalten*) keep ‹family, wife›; **das ernährt seinen Mann** it provides a good living. ❷ *refl. V.* feed oneself; **sich von etw. ~:** live on sth.; ‹animal› feed on sth.; **sich vegetarisch ~:** live on a vegetarian diet

**Ernährer** *der;* **~s, ~, Ernährerin** *die;* **~, ~nen** breadwinner; provider

**Ernährung** *die;* **~** **A** (*das Ernähren*) feeding; **B** (*Nahrung*) diet; **gesunde/ungesunde ~:** a healthy/an unhealthy diet; **C** (*Versorgung*) feeding; **zur ~ der Familie beitragen** contribute to feeding the family

**Ernährungs-: ~lage** *die* state of nutrition; **~lehre** *die* (*Med.*) dietetics *sing., no art.;* **~ministerium** *das* Ministry of Food; **~störung** *die* ▸ 474 (*Med.*) nutritional disorder; **~weise** *die* diet; **~wissenschaft** *die* dietetics *sing., no art.*

**ernennen** *unr. tr. V.* **A** **jmdn. zu etw. ~:** make sb. sth.; **B** (*bestimmen*) appoint ‹deputy, ambassador›

**Ernennung** *die* appointment (**zu** as)

**Ernennungs·urkunde** *die* certificate of appointment

**Erneu[e]rer** *der;* **~s, ~, Erneuerin** *die;* **~, ~nen** reviver

**erneuern** ❶ *tr. V.* **A** (*auswechseln*) replace; **B** (*wiederherstellen*) renovate ‹roof, building›; (*fig.*) thoroughly reform ‹system›; **C** (*beleben*) resume ‹relations›; **D** (*verlängern lassen*) extend, renew ‹permit, licence, contract›. ❷ *refl. V.* ‹nature, growth› renew itself

**Erneuerung** *die* **A** (*Auswechslung*) replacement; **B** (*Wiederherstellung*) renovation; (*fig.*) thorough reform; **demokratische/religiöse ~:** democratic/religious revival; **C** (*von Beziehungen*) resumption; **D** (*Verlängerung eines Vertrages usw.*) renewal; extension

**erneuerungs·bedürftig** *Adj.* in need of replacement *postpos.*

**Erneuerungs·schein** *der* (*Börsenw.*) talon

**erneut** ❶ *Adj.* renewed. ❷ *adv.* once again

**erniedrigen** *tr. V.* **A** (*demütigen*) humiliate; **sich [selbst] ~:** lower oneself; **wer sich selbst erniedrigt, wird erhöht werden** (*bibl.*) he that shall humble himself shall be exalted; **B** (*heruntersetzen*) lower, reduce ‹price, pressure›; **C** (*Musik*) lower ‹note›

**erniedrigend** *Adj.* humiliating

**Erniedrigung** *die;* **~, ~en** **A** (*Demütigung*) humiliation; **B** (*Senkung*) lowering; reduction (+ *Gen.* in); **C** (*Musik*) lowering

**Erniedrigungs·zeichen** *das* (*Musik*) flat sign

**ernst** /ɛrnst/ ❶ *Adj.* **A** serious ‹face, expression, music, doubts›; **~ bleiben** remain serious; keep a straight face (*coll.*); **B** (*aufrichtig*) genuine ‹intention, offer›; **C** (*gefahrvoll*) serious ‹injury›; grave ‹situation›; **etwas Ernstes** something serious. ❷ *adv.* seriously; **jmdn./etw. ~ nehmen** take sb./sth. seriously; **es ~ mit etw. meinen** be serious about sth.; **~ gemeint** serious ‹offer, reply›; sincere ‹wish›

**Ernst**[1] *der;* **~[e]s** **A** (*ernster Wille*) seriousness; **das ist mein [voller] ~:** I mean that [quite] seriously; **es ist mir [bitterer] ~ damit** I'm [deadly] serious about it; **etw. im ~ sagen** say sth. in all seriousness; **etw. im ~ meinen** mean sth. seriously; **allen ~es** in all seriousness; **etw. mit ~ betreiben** apply oneself seriously to sth.; **[mit etw.] ~ machen** be serious [about sth.]; **er will jetzt ~ machen und morgen nach Peru fliegen** now he wants to turn words into action and fly to Peru tomorrow; **B** (*Wirklichkeit*) **daraus wurde [blutiger/bitterer] ~:** it became [deadly] serious; **der ~ des Lebens** the serious side of life; **dann beginnt der ~ des Lebens** then life begins in earnest; **C** (*Gefährlichkeit*) **der ~ der Lage** the seriousness of the situation; **D** (*gemessene Haltung*) gravity

**Ernst**[2] (*der*); **~s** Ernest

**Ernst·fall** *der:* **eine Übung für den ~:** a practice for the real thing; **im ~:** when the real thing happens

***ernst·gemeint** ⇒ **ernst 2**

**ernsthaft** ❶ *Adj.* serious; **etwas/nichts Ernsthaftes** something/nothing serious. ❷ *adv.* seriously; **jmdn. ~ an etw.** (*Akk.*) **erinnern** give sb. a stern reminder about sth.

**Ernsthaftigkeit** *die;* **~:** seriousness

**ernstlich** ❶ *Adj.* **A** (*nachdrücklich*) serious ‹doubt, attempt, intention›; **B** (*aufrichtig*) genuine ‹wish›; **C** (*gefährlich*) serious ‹threat, danger, risk›. ❷ *adv.* **A** (*nachdrücklich*) seriously; **er hat ~ gefordert, dass ...** he has demanded in all seriousness that ...; **B** (*aufrichtig*) genuinely ‹sorry, repentant›; **jmdm. ~ böse sein** be seriously annoyed with sb.; **C** (*gefährlich*) seriously ‹ill, threatened›; **~ gefährdet sein** be in serious danger

**Ernte** /ˈɛrntə/ *die;* **~, ~n** **A** (*das ~n*) harvest; **bei der ~ sein** be bringing in the harvest; **während der ~:** at harvest time; **reiche/furchtbare ~ halten** (*fig. geh.*) take a heavy/terrible toll; **B** (*Ertrag*) crop; **die ~ einbringen** bring in the harvest; **die ~ an Getreide/Kartoffeln/Tabak** the grain/potato/tobacco crop; **ihm ist die ganze ~ verhagelt** (*fig.*) he's had a bad blow

**-ernte** *die;* **-~, -~n** ... harvest; (*Ertrag*) ... crop

**Ernte-: ~arbeit** *die* harvest work; **~arbeiter** *der,* **~arbeiterin** *die* harvester; **~aus·fall** *der* crop failure; **~dank·fest** *das* harvest festival; **~ein·satz** *der* assistance with the harvest; **jmdn. zum ~einsatz aufrufen** call upon sb. to help with the harvest; **~ertrag** *der* yield; **~maschine** *die* harvester; **~monat** *der* month of the harvest

**ernten** *tr. V.* harvest ‹cereal, fruit›; (*fig.*) get ‹mockery, ingratitude›; win ‹fame, praise›

**Ernte-: ~wagen** *der* harvest wagon; **~wetter** *das:* **gutes/schlechtes ~wetter haben** have good/bad weather for the harvest; **~zeit** *die* harvest time; **in der ~zeit** at harvest time

**ernüchtern** *tr. V.* **A** (*nüchtern machen*) sober up; **B** (*fig.*) **jmdn. [völlig] ~:** bring sb. down to earth [with a bang]; **~d** sobering

**Ernüchterung** *die;* **~, ~en** (*fig.*) disillusionment

**Eroberer** /ɛɐ̯ˈ|oːbərɐ/ *der;* **~s, ~, Eroberin** *die;* **~,~nen** conqueror

**erobern** *tr. V.* **A** conquer ‹country›; take ‹town, fortress›; **B** (*fig.*) conquer ‹woman, market›; seize ‹power›; **[sich** (*Dat.*)**] die Herzen ~:** win hearts; **eine Stadt/ein Land ~** (*scherzh.*) take a town/country by storm; ⇒ *auch* **Sturm B**

**Eroberung** *die;* ~, **~en** (*auch fig. scherzh.*) conquest; (*einer Stadt, Festung*) taking; **die ~ der Macht** the seizing of power; **~en machen** make conquests; ⇒ *auch* **ausgehen H**

**Eroberungs-: ~drang** *der* thirst for conquest; **~feld·zug** *der* campaign of conquest; **~krieg** *der* war of conquest

**eröffnen** ❶ *tr. V.* **A** open ‹shop, gallery, account›; start ‹business, practice›; **B** (*beginnen*) open ‹meeting, conference›; **das Feuer ~:** open fire; **eine Veranstaltung mit Musik ~:** begin an event with music; **C** (*mitteilen*) **jmdm. etw. ~:** reveal sth. to sb.; **D ein Testament ~:** read a will; **E** (*Rechtsw., Wirtsch.*) **den Konkurs ~:** institute bankruptcy proceedings; **das Verfahren ~:** begin proceedings; **F jmdm. neue Möglichkeiten ~:** open up new possibilities to sb. ❷ *itr. V.* (*Börsenw.*) ‹stock exchange› open. ❸ *refl. V.* (*sich bieten*) **sich jmdm. ~** ‹opportunity, possibility› present itself

**Eröffnung** *die* **A** opening; (*einer Sitzung*) start; (*einer Schachpartie*) opening [move]; **B** (*Mitteilung*) revelation; **ich muss dir eine ~ machen** I have something to tell you; **C** (*Testaments~*) reading; **D** (*Wirtsch.*) **die ~ des Konkurses** the institution of bankruptcy proceedings

**Eröffnungs-: ~an·sprache** *die* opening speech; **~beschluss, *~beschluß** *der* (*Rechtsw.*) decision to begin court proceedings; **~bilanz** *die* (*Wirtsch.*) opening balance; **~feier** *die* opening ceremony; **~kurs** *der* (*Börsenw.*) opening price; **~spiel** *das* (*Sport*) opening game; **~tag** *der* (*einer Ausstellung, eines Kongresses usw.*) first day; (*eines Geschäftes usw.*) first day of opening; **~variante** *die* (*Schach*) opening variation; **~wehen** *Pl.* (*Med.*) dilation pains

**erogen** /ero'ge:n/ *Adj.* erogenous ‹zone›

**erörtern** /ɛɐ̯'|œrtɐn/ *tr. V.* discuss

**Erörterung** *die;* ~, **~en** discussion

**Eros** /'e:rɔs/ *der;* ~ **A** (*Gott*) Eros; **B** (*sinnliche Liebe*) erotic love

**Eros·center, Eros-Center** *das* [licensed] brothel; eros centre

**Erosion** /ero'zi̯o:n/ *die;* ~, **~en** erosion

**Erosions·schutz** *der* protection against erosion

**Erotik** /e'ro:tɪk/ *die;* **~:** eroticism

**Erotika** /e'ro:tika/ ⇒ **Erotikon**

**Erotiker** *der;* **~s,** ~, **Erotikerin** *die;* ~, **~nen** **A** eroticist; **B** (*Autor[in]*) erotic writer

**Erotikon** /e'ro:tikɔn/ *das;* **~s, Erotika** **A** erotic work; **Erotika** erotica; **B** *Pl.* (*Mittel*) aphrodisiacs

**erotisch** ❶ *Adj.* erotic. ❷ *adv.* erotically

**erotisieren** *tr. V.* arouse sexual desire in; **~d wirken** have an erotic effect

**Erotomane** /eroto'ma:nə/ *der;* **~n, ~n** erotomaniac

**Erotomanie** *die;* **~:** erotomania

**Erotomanin** *die;* ~, **~nen** erotomaniac

**Erpel** /'ɛrpl̩/ *der;* **~s, ~:** drake

**erpicht** /ɛɐ̯'pɪçt/ *Adj.: in* **auf etw.** (*Akk.*) **~ sein** be keen on sth.

**erpressbar, *erpreßbar** *Adj.* blackmailable; susceptible to blackmail *postpos.*

**Erpressbarkeit, *Erpreßbarkeit** *die;* **~:** susceptibility to blackmail; **dem Verdacht der ~ begegnen** counter the suspicion of being susceptible to blackmail

**erpressen** *tr. V.* **A** (*nötigen*) blackmail; **jmdn. mit etw. ~:** blackmail sb. with sth.; **B** (*erlangen*) extort ‹money, confession› (**von** from)

**Erpresser** *der;* **~s, ~:** blackmailer

**Erpresser·brief** *der* blackmail letter

**Erpresserin** *die;* ~, **~nen** blackmailer

**erpresserisch** ❶ *Adj.* blackmailing *attrib.*; **diese Maßnahme ist ~:** this action amounts to blackmail; **in ~er Absicht** for the purpose of blackmail. ❷ *adv.* **~ vorgehen** use blackmail

**Erpresser·methoden** *Pl.* blackmail *sing.*

**Erpressung** *die* blackmail *no indef. art.*; (*von Geld, Geständnis*) extortion; ⇒ *auch* **räuberisch 1 A**

**Erpressungs·versuch** *der* blackmail attempt

**erproben** *tr. V.* test ‹medicine› (**an** + *Akk.* on); **jmds. Zuverlässigkeit ~:** put sb.'s reliability to the test; **ein erprobter Soldat** an experienced soldier; **das ist seit langem erprobt** it is tried and tested

**Erprobung** *die;* ~, **~en** testing

**Erprobungs·flug** *der* test *or* proving flight

**erquicken** /ɛɐ̯'kvɪkn̩/ *tr. V.* (*geh.*) refresh; **das Herz ~:** gladden one's heart; **ich will euch ~** (*bibl.*) and I will give you rest

**erquickend** *Adj.* (*geh.*) refreshing

**erquicklich** (*geh.*) ❶ *Adj.* pleasant. ❷ *adv.* pleasantly

**Erquickung** *die;* ~, **~en** (*geh.*) refreshment; **der Schlaf brachte ihm keine ~:** the sleep did not refresh him

**Errata** ⇒ **Erratum**

**erraten** *unr. tr. V.* guess; **du hast es ~!** (*iron.*) you've guessed it!

**erratisch** /ɛ'ra:tɪʃ/ *Adj.* (*Geol.*) erratic

**Erratum** /ɛ'ra:tʊm/ *das;* **~s, Errata** (*Druckw. u. Schriftw.*) erratum

**errechenbar** *Adj.* calculable; **leicht/genau ~ sein** be easily/accurately calculated

**errechnen** ❶ *tr.* (*auch itr.*) *V.* **A** (*ausrechnen*) calculate ‹sum›; **wie er errechnete** according to his calculations; **B** (*erwarten*) count on ‹chance, advantage›. ❷ *refl. V.* (*Papierdt.*) **sich aus etw. ~:** be calculated from sth.

**erregbar** *Adj.* excitable

**Erregbarkeit** *die;* **~:** excitability

**erregen** ❶ *tr. V.* **A** annoy; **B** (*sexuell*) arouse; **C** (*verursachen*) arouse; **Aufsehen/Ärgernis ~:** cause a stir/annoyance; ⇒ *auch* **öffentlich.** ❷ *refl. V.* **sich über etw.** (*Akk.*) **~:** get excited about sth.

**erregend** *Adj.* exciting; (*sexuell*) arousing

**Erreger** *der;* **~s,** ~ ▶ 474 (*Med.*) pathogen

**erregt** ❶ *Adj.* excited; (*sexuell*) aroused; **die ~en Gemüter** the hot tempers. ❷ *adv.* excitedly

**Erregung** *die* **A** excitement; (*sexuell*) arousal; **in starke ~ geraten** become extremely excited; **vor ~:** with excitement; **B** (*Verursachung*) **~ öffentlichen Ärgernisses** (*Rechtsspr.*) causing a public nuisance; **~ von Missfallen** incurring displeasure

**Erregungs·zustand** *der* state of excitement; (*sexuell*) [state of] arousal

**erreichbar** *Adj.* **A** within reach *postpos.*; **in ~er Höhe** at a reachable height; **B der Ort ist mit dem Auto/Zug ~:** the place can be reached by car/train; **leicht ~ sein** be easy to reach; be easily reachable; **C er ist [telefonisch] ~:** he can be contacted [by telephone]

**erreichen** *tr. V.* **A** reach; **den Zug ~:** catch the train; **etw. ist zu Fuß/mit dem Bus/schnell zu ~:** sth. can be reached on foot/by bus/quickly; **B** (*in Verbindung treten mit, ansprechen*) reach ‹viewers›; **er ist telefonisch/um 10 Uhr/zu Hause zu ~:** he can be contacted by telephone/at 10 o'clock/at home; **C** (*durchsetzen*) achieve ‹goal, aim›; **bei jmdm. etwas/nichts ~:** get somewhere/not get anywhere with sb.

**Erreichung** *die;* **~:** reaching *no art.*; **bei** *od.* **mit ~ der Altersgrenze/Volljährigkeit** on reaching the age limit/one's majority

**erretten** *tr. V.* (*geh.*) save

**Erretter** *der,* **Erretterin** *die* (*geh.*) saviour

**errichten** *tr. V.* **A** build ‹house, bridge, etc.›; **B** (*aufstellen*) erect, put up ‹rostrum, barrier, etc.›; **C** (*einrichten*) found ‹company›; set up ‹fund›

**erringen** *unr. tr. V.* gain ‹victory›; reach ‹first etc. place›; win ‹majority›; gain, win ‹sb.'s trust›

**erröten** *itr. V.; mit sein* blush (**vor** with); **jmdn. zum Erröten bringen** make sb. blush

**Errungenschaft** /ɛɐ̯'rʊŋənʃaft/ *die;* ~, **~en** achievement; **meine neueste ~** (*ugs. scherzh.*) my latest acquisition

**Ersatz** *der;* **~es** **A** replacement; **als ~ für jmdn.** in place of sb.; **B** (*Entschädigung*) compensation; **C** (*Milit.*) reserve

**ersatz-, Ersatz-: ~an·spruch** *der* claim for damages; **~ansprüche stellen** claim damages; **~ball** *der* (*Sport*) new ball; **~bank** *die; Pl.* **~bänke** (*Sport*) substitutes' bench; **~befriedigung** *die* (*Psych.*) vicarious satisfaction; **~dienst** *der: community service as an alternative to military service;* **~dienst·leistende** *der; adj. Dekl.: person carrying out alternative service;* **~frau** *die* replacement; (*Sport*) substitute; **~heer** *das* reserve army; **~kasse** *die* private health insurance company; **~los** ❶ *Adj.* without replacement *postpos.;* ❷ *adv.* **etw. ~los streichen** cancel sth.; **ein Gesetz ~los streichen** strike a law from the statute books; **~mann** *der; Pl.* **~männer** *od.* **~leute** replacement; (*Sport*) substitute; **~mine** *die* refill; **~mittel** *das* substitute; **~pflichtig** *Adj.* liable to pay compensation *postpos.;* **~rad** *das* spare wheel; **~reifen** *der* spare tyre; **~religion** *die* substitute religion; **~spieler** *der,* **~spielerin** *die* (*Sport*) substitute [player]

**Ersatz·teil** *das* (*bes. Technik*) spare part; spare (*Brit.*)

**Ersatzteil-: ~lager** *das* [spares] store; **~medizin** *die* spare-part surgery

**Ersatz-: ~truppe** *die* (*Milit.*) reserve troops *pl.;* **~weise** *Adv.* as an alternative

**ersaufen** *unr. itr. V.; mit sein* **A** (*salopp*) drown; **B** (*überflutet werden*) flood

**ersäufen** /ɛɐ̯'zɔy̆fn̩/ *tr. V.* drown; **seinen Kummer im Alkohol ~** (*fig.*) drown one's sorrows [in drink]

**erschaffen** *unr. tr. V.* create; **wie Gott ihn ~ hat** (*scherzh. verhüll.*) in his birthday suit

**Erschaffer** *der;* **~s,** ~, **Erschafferin** *die;* ~, **~nen** creator; (*Gott*) Creator

**Erschaffung** *die* creation

**erschallen** *unr. od. regelm. itr. V.; mit sein* ‹song, call› ring out; ‹music› sound

**erschaudern** *itr. V.; mit sein* (*geh.*) shudder (**bei** at)

**erschauern** *itr. V.; mit sein* (*geh.*) tremble (**vor** + *Dat.* with)

**erscheinen** *unr. itr. V.; mit sein* **A** (*sichtbar werden, sich zeigen, auftreten*) appear; **jmdm. ~:** appear to sb.; **in der Schule/am Arbeitsplatz ~:** put in an appearance at school/at work; **vor Gericht ~:** appear in court; **um frühzeitiges/rechtzeitiges/zahlreiches Erscheinen wird gebeten** an early/a punctual arrival/a full turnout is requested; **B** (*herausgegeben werden*) ‹newspaper, periodical› appear; ‹book› be published; **C** (*sich darstellen*) **jmdm. ratsam/unverständlich ~:** seem advisable/incomprehensible to sb.; ⇒ *auch* **Licht A**

**Erscheinung** *die;* ~, **~en** **A** (*Vorgang*) phenomenon; (*Alters~, Krankheits~ usw.*) symptom; **in ~ treten** become evident; **das Fest der ~ des Herrn** (*christl. Rel.*) [the Feast of the] Epiphany; **B** (*äußere Gestalt*) appearance; **eine stattliche/elegante ~ sein** be an imposing/elegant figure; **C** (*Vision*) apparition; **eine ~/~en haben** see a vision/visions

**Erscheinungs-: ~bild** *das* appearance; **vom ~bild her** judging by appearance; **~fest** *das* Epiphany *no art.;* **~form** *die* manifestation; **~jahr** *das* year of publication; **~ort** *der* place of publication; **~tag** *der* day of publication; publication day; **~weise** *die* **A** ⇒ **~form; B die ~weise einer Zeitung** the frequency of publication of a newspaper; **wöchentliche/monatliche ~weise** weekly/monthly publication; **„~weise: vierteljährlich"** 'published quarterly'; **~welt** *die* world perceived through the senses

*old spelling (see note on page 1707)

**erschießen** *unr. tr. V.* shoot dead; **Tod durch Erschießen** death by firing squad; **erschossen sein** (*fig. ugs.*) be completely whacked (*Brit. coll.*); **dann kann ich mich ~** (*ugs.*) I might as well end it all (*coll.*); ⇒ *auch* **Flucht** A, **standrechtlich** 2

**Erschießung** *die; ~, ~en* shooting; **eine sofortige/standrechtliche ~:** a summary execution [by firing squad]; **zur ~ abgeführt werden** be led away to be shot

**Erschießungs·kommando** *das* firing squad

**erschlaffen** *itr. V.; mit sein* **A** (*kraftlos werden*) ‹muscle, limb› become limp; (*fig.*) ‹resistance, will› weaken; **seine Spannkraft war erschlafft** he had lost his vigour; **B** (*welk werden*) ‹skin› grow slack

**Erschlaffung** *die; ~* **A** (*das Müdewerden*) weakening; **B** (*das Welkwerden*) **bei ~ der Haut** when the skin grows slack

**erschlagen**[1] *unr. tr. V.* strike dead; kill; (*ugs.: erschöpfen*) wear out; **vom Blitz ~ werden** be struck dead by lightning; **jmdn. mit Argumenten ~** (*fig.*) defeat sb. with arguments

**erschlagen**[2] *Adj.* (*ugs.*) **A** (*erschöpft*) worn out; **B** (*verblüfft*) **wie ~ sein** be flabbergasted (*coll.*) *or* thunderstruck

**erschleichen** *unr. refl. V.* (*abwertend*) **sich** (*Dat.*) **etw. ~:** get sth. by devious means; **sich** (*Dat.*) **jmds. Gunst/Vertrauen ~:** worm oneself into sb.'s favour/confidence

**erschließbar** *Adj.* ascertainable ‹facts›; **~e Rohstoffquellen** sources of raw materials which can be tapped; **~e Absatzmärkte** markets which can be opened up

**erschließen** ❶ *unr. tr. V.* **A** (*zugänglich machen*) develop ‹area, building land›; open up ‹market›; **jmdm. etw. ~** (*fig.*) make sth. accessible to sb.; **er hat mir ganz neue Welten erschlossen** he opened up a whole new world to me; **B** (*nutzbar machen*) tap ‹resources, energy sources›; **C** (*ermitteln*) deduce ‹meaning, wording›. ❷ *unr. refl. V.* **A** (*verständlich werden*) **sich jmdm. ~:** become accessible to sb.; **B** (*geh.: sich offenbaren*) **sich jmdm. ~:** confide in sb.

**Erschließung** *die* **A** (*von Bauland*) development; (*von Märkten*) opening up; **B** (*von Rohstoffen*) tapping; **C** **zur ~ des Textes** in order to grasp the meaning of the text

**Erschließungs·kosten** *Pl.* (*Bauw.*) development costs *pl.*

**erschöpfen** ❶ *tr. V.* (*auch fig.*) exhaust; **seine Kräfte ~:** drain one's strength. ❷ *refl. V.* **A** (*sich beschränken*) **darin ~ sich ihre Kenntnisse** her knowledge does not go beyond that; **B** (*zu Ende gehen*) ‹supplies, stores› run out; **seine Ideen haben sich erschöpft** he has run out of ideas

**erschöpfend** ❶ *Adj.* exhaustive. ❷ *adv.* exhaustively

**erschöpft** *Adj.* exhausted

**Erschöpfung** *die* exhaustion; **bis zur ~:** to the point of exhaustion; **vor ~ einschlafen/umfallen** fall asleep from exhaustion/drop with exhaustion

**Erschöpfungs-: ~tod** *der* death from exhaustion; **den ~tod sterben** die from exhaustion; **~zu·stand** *der* state of exhaustion; **Müdigkeit und ~zustände** tiredness and exhaustion

**erschrecken**[1] *unr. itr. V.; mit sein* be startled; **vor etw.** (*Dat.*) *od.* **über etw.** (*Akk.*) **~:** be startled by sth.; **erschrick nicht!** don't be startled; **er war zutiefst/zu Tode erschrocken** he was frightened out of his wits/frightened to death

**erschrecken**[2] *tr. V.* frighten; scare; **du hast mich aber erschreckt!** you really gave me a scare

**erschrecken**[3] *unr. od. regelm. refl. V.* get a fright; **erschrick dich nicht!** don't be frightened

**erschreckend** *Adj.* ❶ alarming. ❷ *adv.* alarmingly

**erschrocken** ❶ *2. Part. v.* **erschrecken**[1]. ❷ *Adj.* frightened; **sie wandte sich ~ ab** she turned away in fright

**erschüttern** *tr. V.* (*auch fig.*) shake; **die Nachricht hat uns erschüttert** we were shaken by the news; **über etw.** (*Akk.*) **erschüttert sein** be shaken by sth.; **das kann mich nicht ~** (*ugs.*) that doesn't worry me

**erschütternd** *Adj.* deeply distressing ‹account, picture, news›; deeply shocking ‹conditions›

**Erschütterung** *die; ~, ~en* **A** (*Bewegung*) (*durch LKWs usw.*) vibration; (*der Erde*) tremor; **wirtschaftliche ~en** (*fig.*) economic upheavals; **B** (*Ergriffenheit*) shock; (*Trauer*) distress; **C** **das trug zur ~ meines Glaubens/Vertrauens bei** that helped to shake my faith/confidence

**erschütterungs-: ~fest** *Adj.* shockproof; **~frei** ❶ *Adj.* vibrationless; free from *or* without vibration *postpos.*; **ein ~freier Transport von etw.** transporting sth. without jolting; ❷ *adv.* without vibration

**erschweren** ❶ *tr. V.* **etw. ~:** make sth. more difficult; **etw. durch etw. ~:** impede *or* hinder sth. by sth. ❷ *refl. V.* **sich [durch etw.] ~:** be hindered [by sth.]

**erschwerend** ❶ *Adj.* complicating ‹factor›; **~e Umstände** (*Rechtsw.*) aggravating circumstances. ❷ *adv.* **es kommt ~ hinzu, dass er ...** to make matters worse he ...; **das kommt ~ hinzu** that is an added problem

**Erschwernis** *die; ~, ~se* difficulty

**Erschwernis·zulage** *die: bonus for particularly hard work or shift work*

**Erschwerung** *die; ~, ~en:* **eine ~ für etw.** an impediment to sth.; **das ist eine ~ seiner Tätigkeit** that makes his job more difficult

**erschwindeln** *refl. V.* get by swindling; **sich** (*Dat.*) **etw. von jmdm. ~:** swindle sb. out of sth.

**erschwinglich** *Adj.* reasonable ‹price›; **für jmdn. nicht ~ sein** not be within sb.'s reach; **dort sind die Mieten noch ~:** the rents there are still affordable

**ersehen** *unr. tr. V.* see; **aus etw. zu ~ sein** be evident from sth.

**ersehnen** *tr. V.* (*geh.*) long for

**ersetzbar** *Adj.* replaceable

**ersetzen** *tr. V.* **A** replace; **etw./jmdn. durch etw./jmdn. ~:** replace sth./sb. by sth./sb.; **Talent durch Fleiß ~:** substitute hard work for talent; **ihn wird niemand ~ können** nobody will be able to take his place; **B** (*erstatten*) **jmdm. einen Schaden ~:** compensate sb. for damages; **die Fahrtkosten ~:** reimburse travel expenses

**Ersetzung** *die; ~, ~en* (*von Kosten usw.*) reimbursement; **die ~ von Schäden** compensation for damage

**ersichtlich** *Adj.* apparent; **ohne ~en Grund** for no apparent reason; **etw. ist klar/nicht ~:** sth. is quite obvious/not clear; **hieraus ist ~, dass ...** it is apparent from this that ...; **die Lieferbedingungen sind aus dem Kaufvertrag ~:** the conditions of delivery are contained in the contract of sale

**ersinnen** *unr. tr. V.* (*geh.*) devise

**ersitzen** ❶ *unr. refl. V.* (*abwertend*) **als Beamter ersitzt man sich eine ansehnliche Pension** as a civil servant you get a considerable pension just by staying in your job long enough. ❷ *unr. tr. V.* (*Rechtsspr.*) obtain by prescription

**erspähen** *tr. V.* (*geh.*) espy (*literary*); catch sight of; **einen Vorteil ~** (*fig.*) see an advantage

**ersparen** *tr. V.* **A** (*erwerben*) save ‹money›; **sein/ihr erspartes Geld** *od.* **Erspartes** his/her savings; **B** (*fern halten von*) save, spare ‹trouble, bother›; save ‹work›; **er konnte ihr diese peinlichen Fragen nicht ~:** he could not spare her these awkward questions; **es bleibt einem nichts erspart** (*ugs.*) at least I/you *etc.* could have been spared that

**Ersparnis** *die; ~, ~se* **A** (*österr. auch das; ~ses, ~se*) (*ersparte Summe*) savings *pl.*; **B** (*Einsparung*) saving

**Ersparnis·kasse** *die* (*schweiz.*) savings bank

**ersprießlich** *Adj.* (*geh.*) profitable, fruitful ‹contacts, collaboration›; **das ist nicht sehr ~:** that is not very pleasant

**erst** /eːɐ̯st/ ❶ *Adv.* **A** (*zu~*) first; **~ einmal** first [of all]; **wenn er ~ einmal in Wut gerät** once he becomes angry; **~ noch** first; **eine solche Frau muss ~ noch geboren werden** such a woman has not yet been born; **B** (*nicht eher als*) **eben ~:** only just; **er will ~ in vierzehn Tagen/einer Stunde zurückkommen** he won't be back for a fortnight (*Brit.*) *or* for two weeks/for an hour; **~ nächste Woche/um 12 Uhr** not until next week/12 o'clock; **er war ~ zufrieden, als ...** he was not satisfied until ...; **~ im 19. Jh. ...** it was not until the nineteenth century that ...; **C** (*nicht mehr als*) only; **~ eine Stunde/halb so viel** only an hour/half as much; **sie ist mit ihrer Arbeit ~ am Anfang** she is only just beginning her work. ❷ *Partikel* **so was lese ich gar nicht ~:** I don't even start reading that sort of stuff; **jetzt tue ich es ~ recht!** that makes me even more determined to do it; **er ist schon ziemlich arrogant, aber ~ seine Frau** he is quite arrogant but his wife is even worse

**erst...** *Ordinalz.* **A** ▶ 207, ▶ 841 first; **der ~e Stock** the first *or* (*Amer.*) second floor; **etw. das ~e Mal tun** do sth. for the first time; **am Ersten [des Monats]** on the first [of the month]; **am nächsten Ersten** on the first [day] of next month; **als Erstes** first of all; **der/die Erste** the first person; **als Erster/Erste etw. tun** be the first to do sth.; **Karl der Erste** Charles the First; **fürs Erste** for the moment; **der/die/das ~e beste ...** the first suitable ...; **sie kaufte das ~e beste Kleid, das sie sah** she bought the first dress she saw; ⇒ *auch* **zum** H; **B** (*best...*) **das ~e Hotel** the best hotel; **der/die Erste [der Klasse]** the top boy/girl [of the class]; **sie kam als Erste ins Ziel** she was the first to reach the finish; **die Erste** (*Sportjargon: erste Mannschaft*) the first team

**erstarken** *itr. V.; mit sein* (*geh.*) regain one's strength; (*fig.*) grow stronger

**Erstarkung** *die; ~* (*geh.*) strengthening

**erstarren** *itr. V.; mit sein* **A** (*starr werden*) ‹jelly, plaster› set; **ihm erstarrte das Blut in den Adern** (*fig.*) the blood ran cold in his veins; **B** (*steif werden*) ‹limbs, fingers› grow stiff; **C** **vor Schreck/Entsetzen ~:** be paralysed by fear/with horror; **D** (*geh.: leblos werden*) ossify

**Erstarrung** *die; ~* **A** (*Starrheit*) numbness; **B** (*von Lava*) solidification; (*von Eisen*) hardening; **C** (*von Gliedern*) stiffening; **D** (*fig.: Absterben*) ossification

**erstatten** *tr. V.* **A** reimburse ‹expenses›; **B** **Anzeige gegen jmdn. ~:** report sb. [to the police]; **jmdm. Bericht über etw.** (*Akk.*) **~:** report on sth. to sb.; **[über etw.** (*Akk.*)**] Meldung ~:** report [sth.]

**Erstattung** *die; ~, ~en* **A** (*von Kosten*) reimbursement; **B** **die ~ einer Anzeige** the reporting of something [to the police]; **er sah von der ~ einer Anzeige ab** he refrained from reporting it/us *etc.* to the police; **die ~ einer Meldung** the making of a report

**Erst-: ~auf·führung** *die* première; **~auflage** *die* first impression

**erstaunen** *tr. V.* astonish; amaze; **es erstaunte ihn nicht sonderlich** he wasn't particularly surprised

**Erstaunen** *das; ~s* astonishment; amazement; **jmdn. in ~ versetzen** astonish *or* amaze sb.

**erstaunlich** ❶ *Adj.* astonishing, amazing ‹achievement, number, amount›; **das Erstaunliche ist, dass ...** the astonishing *or* amazing thing is that ...; **das Erstaunliche an diesem Vorfall** the astonishing *or* amazing thing about this incident. ❷ *adv.* astonishingly; amazingly

**erstaunlicher·weise** *Adv.* astonishingly *or* amazingly [enough]

**erstaunt** *Adj.* astonished; amazed

**erst-, Erst-: ~aus·gabe** *die* first edition; **~aus·rüstung** *die* (*Kfz-W.*) original fittings *pl.*; **~ausstattung** *die* original furnishings *pl.*; **~best...** *Adj.* **der ~beste Wagen, der ihr angeboten wurde** the first car she was offered; **die ~beste Frau, die ihm über**

e

den Weg lief the first woman he met; bei ~bester Gelegenheit at the first opportunity; **~beste** *der/die/das; adj. Dekl.* ⇨ **Nächstbeste**; **~besteigung** *die* first ascent; **Hillary gelang die ~besteigung des Mount Everest** Hillary made the first successful ascent of Mount Everest; **~druck** *der; Pl.* **~~e** ⇨ **~ausgabe**

**erstechen** *unr. tr. V.* stab [to death]

**erstehen** ❶ *unr. tr. V. (geh.: kaufen)* purchase. ❷ *unr. itr. V.; mit sein (geh.)* Ⓐ *(entstehen)* ‹difficulties, problems› arise; Ⓑ *(auf~)* rise; **„Christ ist erstanden"** 'Christ is risen'

**Erste-Hilfe-Ausrüstung** *die* first-aid kit

**Erste-Hilfe-Leistung** *die* administering of first aid; **zur ~ verpflichtet sein** be obliged to give first aid

**ersteigen** *unr. tr. V.* climb

**ersteigern** *tr. V.* buy [at an auction]

**Ersteigung** *die* ascent

**erstellen** *tr. V. (Papierdt.)* Ⓐ *(bauen)* build; Ⓑ *(anfertigen)* make ‹assessment›; draw up ‹plan, report, list›

**Erstellung** *die* Ⓐ *(Bau)* construction; building; Ⓑ *(Anfertigung)* ⇨ **erstellen** B: making; drawing up

***erste mal**, ***ersten mal** ⇨ **Mal**[1]

**erstens** /'e:ɐ̯stn̩s/ *Adv.* firstly; in the first place

**erster...** /'e:ɐ̯stɐ.../ *Adj.* former; **Ersteres** *od.* **das Erstere trifft hier zu** the former is the case here

**ersterben** *unr. itr. V.; mit sein (geh.)* ‹flame› die down; ‹singing, murmuring› die away; ‹smile› fade

**Erste[r]-Klasse-Abteil** *das* first-class compartment

**erst-, Erst-: ~geboren** *Adj.* first-born; **der/die ~geborene** the first-born child; **~gebot** *das* first *or* opening bid; **~geburt** *die* Ⓐ first-born child; Ⓑ **[das Recht der] ~geburt** *(Rechtsw.)* [right of] primogeniture; **~geburts·recht** *das* right of primogeniture; **~genannt** *Adj.* mentioned first *postpos.*; **der ~genannte** the one mentioned first

**ersticken** ❶ *itr. V.; mit sein* suffocate; *(sich verschlucken)* choke; **an einem Knochen ~:** choke on a bone; **vor Lachen ~** *(ugs.)* choke with laughter; **zum Ersticken sein** ‹heat› be stifling; **in Arbeit ~** *(ugs.)* be swamped with work; **in Geld ~** *(ugs.)* be rolling in money. ❷ *tr. V.* Ⓐ *(töten)* suffocate; **die Tränen erstickten ihre Stimme** *(fig.)* she was choked by tears; **der Widerstand wurde erstickt** *(fig.)* resistance was suppressed; **etw. sofort** *od.* **im Keim ~** *(fig.)* nip sth. in the bud; Ⓑ *(löschen)* smother ‹flames›

**Erstickung** *die;* ~ Ⓐ *(Sterben)* suffocation; asphyxiation; Ⓑ *(Löschen)* smothering; **zur ~ der Flammen** to smother the flames

**Erstickungs-: ~gefahr** *die* danger of suffocation; **~tod** *der* death from suffocation; **den ~tod sterben** die from suffocation

**erst-, Erst-: ~instanz** *die (Rechtsw.)* court of first instance; **~klassig** ❶ *Adj.* first-class; **~klassige Bedingungen** excellent conditions; ❷ *adv.* superbly; **da kann man ~klassig essen** you can get a first-class meal there; **da wird man ~klassig bedient** the service there is first-class; **~klässler**, ***~kläßler** *der;* **~~s, ~~**, **~klässlerin**, ***~kläßlerin** *die;* **~~**, **~~nen** *(südd., schweiz.) pupil in first class of primary school;* first-year pupil; **~kommunion** *die (kath. Rel.)* first communion

**Erstling** *der;* **~s, ~e** first work

**Erstlings-: ~ausstattung** *die* first layette; **~film** *der* first film; **~roman** *der* first novel; **~werk** *das* first work

**erstmalig** ❶ *Adj.* first. ❷ *adv.* for the first time

**erstmals** *Adv.* for the first time

**Erst·platzierte**, ***Erst·plazierte** *der/die; adj. Dekl. (Sport) person gaining one of the first [three] places*

**erstrahlen** *itr. V.; mit sein* shine; **der ganze Park erstrahlte im Lichterglanz** the whole park was aglow with light

**erstrangig** *Adj.* Ⓐ *(vordringlich)* of top priority *postpos.*; **von ~er Bedeutung** of the utmost importance; Ⓑ ⇨ **erstklassig** 1

**erstreben** *tr. V.* strive for

**erstrebens·wert** *Adj.* ‹ideals etc.› worth striving for; desirable ‹situation›

**erstrecken** *refl. V.* Ⓐ *(sich ausdehnen)* stretch; **sich bis an etw.** *(Akk.)* **~:** extend as far as sth.; **sich über ein Gebiet ~:** extend over *or* cover an area; Ⓑ *(dauern)* **sich über 10 Jahre ~:** carry on for 10 years; Ⓒ *(betreffen)* **sich auf jmdn./etw. ~:** affect sb./sth.; ‹laws, regulations› apply to sb./sth.

**erstreiten** *unr. tr. V. (geh.)* gain; **sich** *(Dat.)* **etw. ~ müssen** have to fight to get sth.; **sich ein Recht ~ müssen** have to fight for a right

**Erst-: ~schlag** *der* first strike; **~schlag·waffe** *die* first-strike weapon; **~sendung** *die* first broadcast; **~stimme** *die* first vote

**Ersttags-: ~brief** *der (Philat.)* first-day cover; **~stempel** *der (Philat.)* first-day stamp

**Erst·täter** *der*, **Erst·täterin** *die (Rechtsw.)* first offender

**erstunken** /ɛɐ̯'ʃtʊŋkn̩/ *in* **~ und erlogen sein** *(salopp)* be a pack of lies

**erstürmen** *tr. V.* take ‹fortress, town› by storm; **den Gipfel ~** *(geh.)* conquer the summit

**Erstürmung** *die;* **~, ~en** storming

**Erst-: ~wagen** *der* main car; **~wähler** *der*, **~wählerin** *die* first-time voter

**ersuchen** *tr. V. (geh.)* ask; **jmdn. um etw. ~:** request sth. of sb.; **jmdn. ~, etw. zu tun** request sb. to do sth.

**Ersuchen** *das;* **~s, ~:** request **(an + Akk.** to); **auf ~ von .../des ...** at the request of ...

**ertappen** *tr. V.* catch ‹thief, burglar›; **jmdn. dabei ~, wie er etw. tut** catch sb. in the act of doing sth.; **jmdn. beim Mogeln ~:** catch sb. cheating; **sich bei etw. ~:** catch oneself doing sth.; ⇨ *auch* **frisch** 1 A

**ertasten** *tr. V.* **etw. ~:** make out sth. by touch; **sich** *(Dat.)* **seinen Weg ~:** feel one's way

**erteilen** *tr. V.* give ‹advice, information›; give, grant ‹permission›; **Unterricht ~:** teach; **Klavier-/Deutschunterricht ~:** give piano/German lessons; ⇨ *auch* **Auftrag** A; **Lektion**; **Wort** B

**Erteilung** *die* giving; **die ~ der Arbeitsgenehmigung** granting of a work permit

**ertönen** *itr. V.; mit sein* Ⓐ *(laut werden)* sound; **er ließ seine tiefe Stimme ~:** his deep voice rang out; Ⓑ *(geh.)* **von etw. ~:** resound with sth.

**Ertrag** /ɛɐ̯'tra:k/ *der;* **~[e]s, Erträge** /ɛɐ̯'trɛ:gə/ Ⓐ *(landwirtschaftliche Produkte)* yield; Ⓑ *(Gewinn)* return

**ertragen** *unr. tr. V.* bear ‹pain, shame, uncertainty›; **etw. mit Geduld/Fassung ~:** bear sth. patiently/take sth. calmly; **es ist nicht mehr zu ~:** I can't stand it any longer; **Frauen können mehr Schmerz ~ als Männer** women can stand *or* tolerate more pain than men; **er musste große Schmerzen ~:** he had to endure great pain

**ertrag·fähig** *Adj.* Ⓐ *(Gewinn bringend)* profitable ‹investment etc.›; Ⓑ *(fruchtbar)* fertile ‹soil›

**Ertrag·fähigkeit** *die* ⇨ **ertragfähig**: profitability; fertility

**erträglich** /ɛɐ̯'trɛ:klɪç/ ❶ *Adj.* Ⓐ bearable ‹pain›; tolerable ‹conditions, climate›; **die Grenze des Erträglichen erreichen** be as much as one can endure; Ⓑ *(ugs.: annehmbar)* tolerable. ❷ *adv. (ugs.: annehmbar)* tolerably

**ertrag-: ~los** *Adj.* unprofitable ‹business›; unproductive ‹land, soil›; **~reich** *Adj.* lucrative ‹business›; productive ‹land, soil›

**ertrags-, Ertrags-: ~arm** *Adj.* unprofitable ‹year›; poor ‹soil›; **~ein·buße** *die* decrease in profits; **~lage** *die* profit situation; profits; **~minderung** *die* decrease in profits

**Ertrag[s]-: ~steigerung** *die* increase in profits; **~steuer** *die (Wirtsch.)* tax on profits

**ertränken** *tr. V.* drown; **seinen Kummer/seine Sorgen im Alkohol ~** *(fig.)* drown one's sorrows [in drink]

**erträumen** *refl. V.* dream of; **sie ist die Frau, die er sich** *(Dat.)* **erträumt hat** she's the woman of his dreams; **erträumte Welten** imaginary worlds

**ertrinken** *unr. itr. V.; mit sein* be drowned; drown; *(fig.)* be inundated; **in einer Flut von Anfragen ~** *(fig.)* be inundated with inquiries

**Ertrinkende** *der/die; adj. Dekl.* drowning person

**ertrotzen** *tr. V.* **sich** *(Dat.)* **etw. ~:** obtain sth. by sheer defiance

**Ertrunkene** *der/die; adj. Dekl.* drowned person

**ertüchtigen** ❶ *tr. V.* toughen up ‹body›. ❷ *refl. V.* **sich körperlich ~:** get/keep oneself fit

**Ertüchtigung** *die;* **~, ~en** fitness; **jmdn. zur körperlichen ~ anhalten** encourage sb. to keep [himself/herself] physically fit

**erübrigen** ❶ *tr. V.* spare ‹money, time›; **etw. Geld/Zeit ~ können** have some money/time to spare. ❷ *refl. V.* be unnecessary; **es erübrigt sich, noch länger darüber zu sprechen** there's no point in talking about it any longer

**eruieren** /eru'i:rən/ *tr. V.* find out; **jmdn. ~** *(österr.)* trace sb.

**Eruierung** *die;* **~, ~en** investigation; **die ~ des Täters** *(österr.)* the tracing of the culprit

**Eruption** /erʊp'tsi̯o:n/ *die;* **~, ~en** *(Geol., Med.)* eruption

**Eruptiv·gestein** /erʊp'ti:f-/ *das (Geol.)* eruptive rock

**erwachen** *itr. V.; mit sein (geh.)* awake; wake up; *(fig.)* awake; **aus tiefem Schlaf ~:** awake from a deep sleep; **aus der Narkose ~:** come round; **aus seinen Tagträumen ~:** snap out of one's daydreams; **ein neuer Tag erwacht** *(geh.)* a new day dawns

**Erwachen** *das;* **~s** *(auch fig.)* awakening; **es wird ein böses ~ [für ihn] geben** *(fig.)* it'll be a rude awakening [for him]

**erwachsen**[1] *unr. itr. V.; mit sein* Ⓐ grow **(aus** out of); ‹rumour› spread; Ⓑ *(sich ergeben)* ‹difficulties, tasks› arise

**erwachsen**[2] ❶ *Adj.* grown-up *attrib.*; **~ sein** be grown up; **~ werden** reach adulthood. ❷ *adv.* ‹behave› in an adult way

**Erwachsene** *der/die; adj. Dekl.* adult; grown-up

**Erwachsenen-: ~alter** *das* adulthood; **~bildung** *die* adult education *no art.*

**Erwachsen·sein** *das* being an adult/adults *no art.*

**erwägen** *unr. tr. V.* consider

**erwägens·wert** *Adj.* worth considering *postpos.*; worthy of consideration *postpos.*

**Erwägung** *die;* **~, ~en** consideration; **etw. in ~ ziehen** consider sth.; take sth. into consideration

**erwählen** *tr. V. (geh.)* choose

**Erwählte** *der/die; adj. Dekl. (Freund[in])* sweetheart; *(Bevorrechtigte)* **er gehört zu den wenigen ~n** he belongs to the select few

**erwähnen** *tr. V.* mention; **etw. mit keinem Wort ~:** make no mention of sth.; **jmdn. lobend ~:** speak in praise of sb.; **es muss lobend erwähnt werden, dass ...** it must be said in his/her *etc.* praise that ...; **bereits erwähnt** aforementioned *attrib.*; **oben erwähnt** above mentioned *attrib.*

**erwähnens·wert** *Adj.* worth mentioning *postpos.*

**Erwähnung** *die;* **~, ~en** mention; **das verdient [keine] ~:** that is [not] worth mentioning

**erwandern** *tr., refl. V.* **er hat [sich** *(Dat.)***] ganz Frankreich erwandert** he's walked all round France

**erwärmen** ❶ *tr. V.* Ⓐ *(warm machen)* heat; **das erwärmte uns** *(Dat.)* **das Herz** *(fig.)*

*old spelling (see note on page 1707)

that warmed our hearts; **B** (*fig.: gewinnen*) **jmdn. für etw. ~:** win sb. over to sth. ❷ *refl. V.* (*warm werden*) ‹air, water› warm up; **sich für jmdn./etw. ~** (*fig.*) warm to sb./sth.; **für diese Idee kann ich mich nicht ~:** I cannot work up any enthusiasm for this idea

**Erwärmung** *die; ~:* **eine ~ der Luft/des Wassers** an increase in air/water temperature; **bei ~ der Flüssigkeit** when the liquid is heated

**erwarten** *tr. V.* **A** expect ‹guests, phone call, post›; **etw. ungeduldig/sehnlich ~:** wait impatiently/eagerly for sth; **jmdn. am Bahnhof ~:** wait for sb. at the station; **wir ~ ihn um 7 Uhr** we are expecting him at 7 o'clock; **ein Kind ~:** be expecting a baby; be expecting (*coll.*); **ich kann meinen Urlaub kaum ~:** I can hardly wait for my holiday; **B** (*rechnen mit*) **etw. von jmdm. ~:** expect sth. of sb.; **von jmdm. ~, dass er etw. tut** expect sb. to do sth.; **es ist** *od.* (*geh.*) **steht zu ~, dass ...** it is to be expected that ...; **wider Erwarten** contrary to expectation; **[sich (*Dat.*)] von etw. viel/wenig/nichts ~:** expect a lot/little/nothing from sth.

**Erwartung** *die; ~, ~en* expectation; **~en in etw.** (*Akk.*) **setzen** have expectations of sth.; **die in ihn gesetzten ~en erfüllten sich nicht** the hopes placed in him were not fulfilled; **in freudiger ~:** in joyful anticipation; **die ~en [nicht] erfüllen** [not] come up to one's expectations

**erwartungs-, Erwartungs-: ~gemäß** *Adv.* as expected; **~horizont** *der* level of expectations; **~voll** ❶ *Adj.* expectant; ❷ *adv.* expectantly

**erwecken** *tr. V.* **A** (*auf~*) wake; **jmdn. vom Tode ~:** bring sb. back to life; **B** (*erregen*) arouse ‹longing, mistrust, pity›; **den Eindruck ~, als ...** give the impression that ...

**Erweckung** *die; ~, ~en* **A** (*Auf~*) resurrection; **B** (*Erregung*) arousal; **C** (*Mystik*) religious awakening; **D** (*ev. Theol.*) religious revival

**Erweckungs·bewegung** *die* revivalist movement

**erwehren** *refl. V.* (*geh.*) **sich jmds./einer Sache ~:** fend *or* ward sb./sth. off; **sie konnte sich des Gefühls/des Eindrucks nicht ~, dass ...** she could not help feeling/thinking that ...

**erweichen** ❶ *tr. V.* soften; **jmdn./jmds. Herz ~** (*fig.*) soften sb.'s heart; **sich ~ lassen** (*fig.*) yield. ❷ *itr. V.; mit sein* (*aufweichen*) become soft

**Erweichung** *die; ~, ~en* softening

**erweisen** ❶ *unr. tr. V.* **A** prove; **es ist erwiesen, dass ...** it has been proved that ...; **B** (*bezeigen*) **jmdm. Achtung ~:** show respect to sb.; **jmdm. einen Gefallen ~:** do sb. a favour; **~ Sie mir die Ehre** (*geh.*) do me the honour. ❷ *unr. refl. V.* **sich als etw. ~:** prove to be sth.; **seine Behauptungen haben sich als falsch erwiesen** his assertions have proved false

**erweislich** *Adv.* (*geh.*) demonstrably

**erweitern** ❶ *tr. V.* widen ‹river, road›; expand ‹library, business›; enlarge ‹collection›; dilate ‹pupil, blood vessel›; extend ‹power›; **seinen Horizont/seine Kenntnisse ~:** broaden one's horizons/knowledge; **einen Bruch ~** (*Math.*) reduce a fraction to higher terms; **eine erweiterte Neuauflage** a new, expanded edition; **erweiterte Oberschule** (*DDR*) (*Stufe*) ≈ sixth form; (*Schule*) ≈ sixth-form college. ❷ *refl. V.* ‹road, river› widen; ‹pupil, blood vessel› dilate; **sich zu etw. ~:** widen into sth.

**Erweiterung** *die; ~, ~en* ⇒ **erweitern**: widening; expansion; enlargement; dilation; extension; **die ~ eines Bruchs** the reduction of a fraction; **zur ~ seiner Fremdsprachkenntnisse ...** to increase his knowledge of foreign languages ...

**Erweiterungs·bau** *der; Pl.* **Erweiterungs·bauten** extension

**Erwerb** /ɛɐ̯ˈvɛrp/ *der; ~[e]s* **A der ~ des Lebensunterhaltes** earning a living; **B** (*Arbeit*) occupation; **ohne ~ sein** be unemployed; **C** (*Aneignung*) acquisition; **D** (*Kauf*) purchase; **E** (*das Erworbene*) earnings *pl.*

**erwerben** *unr. tr. V.* **A** (*verdienen*) earn; (*fig.*) win ‹fame›; **sich** (*Dat.*) **großen Ruhm ~:** win great fame; **jmds. Vertrauen ~:** win *or* earn sb.'s trust; **B** (*sich aneignen*) gain ‹experience, influence›; acquire, gain ‹knowledge›; **C** acquire ‹property, works of art, etc.›; **etw. käuflich ~** (*Papierdt.*) purchase sth.; **D** (*Biol., Psych.*) acquire

**erwerbs-, Erwerbs-: ~fähig** *Adj.* capable of gainful employment *postpos.;* able to work *postpos.;* **~fähigkeit** *die* ability to work; **~leben** *das* working life; **im ~leben stehen** be working; **~los** *Adj.:* ⇒ **arbeitslos; ~lose** *der/die; adj. Dekl.:* ⇒ **Arbeitslose; ~minderung** *die:* **eine ~minderung** a reduction in one's/sb.'s capacity for work; **~mittel** *das* means of livelihood; **~quelle** *die* source of income; **~sinn** *der* business sense; **~tätig** *Adj.* gainfully employed; **~tätige** *der/die; adj. Dekl.* person in work; **die ~tätigen** those in work; **~unfähig** *Adj.* incapable of gainful employment *postpos.;* unable to work *postpos.;* **~unfähigkeit** *die* inability to work; **~zweig** *der* source of employment

**Erwerbung** *die* **A** (*Aneignung*) acquisition; **B** (*Erworbenes*) acquisition; (*Gekauftes*) purchase

**erwidern** /ɛɐ̯ˈviːdɐn/ *tr. V.* **A** reply; **etw. auf etw.** (*Akk.*) **~:** say sth. in reply to sth.; **auf diese Beleidigung wusste sie nichts zu ~:** she could not think of a reply to this insult; **B** (*reagieren auf*) return ‹greeting, visit›; reciprocate ‹sb.'s feelings›

**Erwiderung** *die; ~, ~en* **A** (*Antwort*) reply (**auf** + *Akk.* to); **B** ⇒ **erwidern B**: return; reciprocation

**erwiesen** ❶ *2. Part. v.* **erweisen.** ❷ *Adj.* proved; **eine ~e Tatsache** a proven fact; **das ist doch längst ~:** that has long since been proved

**erwiesener·maßen** *Adv.* as has been proved; **er hat ~ die Unwahrheit gesagt** it has been proved that he didn't tell the truth

**erwirken** *tr. V.* obtain ‹permit, release›

**erwirtschaften** *tr. V.* **etw. ~:** obtain sth. by careful management

**erwischen** *tr. V.* (*ugs.*) **A** (*fassen, ertappen, erreichen*) catch ‹culprit, train, bus›; **jmdn. beim Abschreiben ~:** catch sb. copying; **B** (*greifen*) grab; **jmdn. am Ärmel ~:** grab sb. by the sleeve; **C** (*bekommen*) manage to catch *or* get; **D** (*unpers.*) **es hat ihn erwischt** (*ugs.*) (*er ist tot*) he has bought it (*sl.*); (*er ist krank*) he has got it; (*er ist verletzt*) he's been hurt; (*scherzh.: er ist verliebt*) he's got it bad (*coll.*)

**erwünscht** /ɛɐ̯ˈvʏnʃt/ *Adj.* wanted; **das ~e Resultat** the desired result; **deine Anwesenheit ist dringend ~:** your presence is urgently required

**erwürgen** *tr. V.* strangle

**Erz** /ɛrts *od.* eːɐ̯ts/ *das; ~es, ~e* ore

**Erz-: ~abbau** *der* mining of ore; **~ader** *die* vein of ore

**erzählen** *tr.* (*auch itr.*) *V.* tell ‹joke, story›; **jmdm. etw. ~:** tell sb. sth.; **erzähl keine Märchen!** (*ugs.*) don't tell stories!; **dem werde ich was ~!** (*ugs.*) (*zurechtweisend*) I'll have something to say to him!; (*ablehnend*) I'll tell him where to get off! (*coll.*); **einen Traum/ein Erlebnis ~:** recount a dream/an experience; **jmdm. von etw. ~:** tell sb. about sth.; **von etw. ~:** talk about sth.; **etw. von jmdm.** *od.* **über jmdn. ~:** tell sth. about sb.; **das kannst du einem anderen** *od.* (*ugs.*) **deiner Großmutter ~!** tell that to the [horse] marines (*Brit. coll.*); pull the other leg *or* one (*coll.*); **du kannst mir viel ~** (*ugs.*) you can say what you like

**erzählens·wert** *Adj.* ‹things, stories› worth telling

**Erzähler** *der,* **Erzählerin** *die; ~, ~nen* **A** storyteller; **der Erzähler eines Romans** the narrator of a novel; **B** (*Autor*) writer [of stories]; narrative writer; **„Deutsche Erzähler"** 'Stories by German Authors'; 'German Narrative Writers'

**erzählerisch** *Adj.* narrative *attrib.*

**Erzähl-: ~gut** *das* narrative [writing]; **~kunst** *die* narrative art; **~technik** *die* narrative technique

**Erzählung** *die; ~, ~en* **A** account; **ich kenne sie nur aus ~en** I only know her from what other people have said about her; **B** (*literarischer Text*) story; (*märchenhafte, fantastische Geschichte*) tale; **die in die ~ eingebetteten Dialoge** the dialogue embedded in the narrative

**Erzähl-: ~weise** *die* **A** narrative style; **B** (*Literaturw.*) narrative form; **~zeit** *die* (*Literaturw.*) narrative time

**erz-, Erz-: ~bergbau** *der* ore mining *no art.;* **~bergwerk** *das* ore mine; **~bischof** *der* archbishop; **~bischöflich** *Adj.* archiepiscopal; **~bistum** *das,* **~diözese** *die* archbishopric; archdiocese

**erzen** *Adj.* (*geh.*) bronze

**Erz·engel** *der* archangel

**erzeugen** *tr. V.* **A** produce; generate ‹electricity›; **B** (*österr.: anfertigen*) manufacture; produce

**Erzeuger** *der; ~s, ~* **A** (*Vater*) father; **er ist zwar mein ~, aber ich betrachte ihn nicht als Vater** I may be his child, but I do not regard him as a father; **B** (*Produzent*) producer; **vom ~ zum Verbraucher** from producer to consumer; **C** (*österr.: Hersteller*) manufacturer

**Erzeugerin** *die; ~, ~nen* ⇒ **Erzeuger B, C**

**Erzeuger-: ~land** *das* country of origin; **~preis** *der* manufacturer's price

**Erzeugnis** *das* (*auch fig.*) product; **landwirtschaftliche ~se** agricultural products *or* produce

**Erzeugung** *die* **A** (*das Bewirken*) creation; **B** (*das Produzieren*) (*von Lebensmitteln usw.*) production; (*von Industriewaren*) manufacture; (*Strom~*) generation; **C** (*österr.: Herstellung*) manufacture

**erz-, Erz-: ~feind** *der,* **~feindin** *die* arch enemy; **~gang** *der* lode of ore; **~gauner** *der,* **~gaunerin** *die* (*ugs.*) arch villain; **~gehalt** *der* ore content; **~grube** *die* ore mine; **~haltig** *Adj.* ore-bearing; **~herzog** *der* archduke; **~herzogin** *die* archduchess; **~hütte** *die* ore-smelting works *sing.*

**erziehbar** *Adj.* educable; **der Junge ist sehr schwer ~:** the boy is a very difficult child

**erziehen** *unr. tr. V.* **A** (*bilden u. fördern*) bring up; (*in der Schule*) educate; **ein Kind streng/sehr frei ~:** give a child a strict/very liberal upbringing/education; **B** (*anleiten*) **jmdn. zum Verbrecher ~:** bring sb. up to criminal ways; **ein Kind zu Sauberkeit und Ordnung ~:** bring a child up to be clean and tidy; **jmdn./sich dazu ~, etw. zu tun** train sb./oneself to do sth.; ⇒ *auch* **erzogen 2**

**Erzieher** *der; ~s, ~,* **Erzieherin** *die; ~, ~nen* ▸ **159** educator; (*Pädagoge*) educationalist; (*Lehrer*) teacher

**erzieherisch** ⇒ **pädagogisch 1 A, 2 A**

**erziehlich** *Adj.* (*bes. österr.*) educational

**Erziehung** *die* **A** (*das Erziehen*) upbringing; (*Schul~*) education; **eine gute ~ genießen** enjoy a good education; **B** (*Manieren*) upbringing; breeding; **seine gute ~ vergessen** forget oneself

**erziehungs-, Erziehungs-: ~anstalt** *die* (*veralt.*) approved school; Borstal (*Brit.*); **~berater** *der,* **~beraterin** *die* (*Berufsbez.*) child guidance counsellor; **~beratung** *die* **A** (*Beraten*) child guidance; **B** (*Beratungsstelle*) child guidance clinic; **~berechtigt** *Adj.* having parental authority *postpos., not pred.;* **sein Großvater wurde ~berechtigt** his grandfather became his [legal] guardian; **~berechtigte** *der/die; adj. Dekl.* parent or [legal] guardian; **~frage** *die* question of upbringing; **~heim** *das* community home; **~maßnahme** *die* measure used in bringing up a child; **~methode** *die* educational method; teaching method; **~roman** *der* (*Literaturw.*) novel describing the development of an individual's character; **~wesen** *das* educational system; education;

**~wissenschaft** *die* education; **~wissenschaften studieren** study education *sing.*; **~wissenschaftler** *der*, **~wissenschaftlerin** *die* educationalist

**erzielen** *tr. V.* reach ‹agreement, compromise, speed›; achieve ‹result, effect›; make ‹profit›; obtain ‹price›; score ‹goal›

**erzittern** *itr. V.; mit sein* [A] [begin to] shake *or* tremble; **etw. ~ lassen** shake sth.; [B] (*geh.*) quiver; tremble

**erz-, Erz-: ~konservativ** *Adj.* ultra-conservative; **~lager·stätte** *die* ore deposit; **~lügner** *der*, **~lügnerin** *die* inveterate liar; **~lump** *der* (*abwertend*) [low-down] scoundrel

**erzogen** **1** *2. Part. v.* **erziehen**. **2** *Adj.* **gut/schlecht ~ sein** have been brought up/not have been brought up properly

**erz-, Erz-: ~reaktionär** *Adj.* ultra-reactionary; **~reaktionär** *der*, **~reaktionärin** *die* ultra-reactionary; **~schurke** *der*, **~schurkin** *die* (*abwertend*) ⇒ **Erzlump**

**erzürnen** (*geh.*) **1** *tr. V.* anger; (*stärker*) incense; **erzürne ihn nicht** don't make him angry. **2** *refl. V.* **sich über jmdn./etw. ~:** become *or* grow angry with sb./about sth.

**Erz-: ~vater** *der* (*Rel.*) patriarch; **~verhüttung** *die* ore smelting; **~vorkommen** *das* ore deposit

**erzwingen** *unr. tr. V.* force; **sich** (*Dat.*) **den Zutritt ~:** force an entry; **etw. von jmdm. ~:** force sth. out of sb.

**erzwungenermaßen** *Adv.* under duress

**es**[1] /ɛs/ *Personalpron.; 3. Pers. Sg. Nom. u. Akk. Neutr.* [A] (*s. auch Gen.* **seiner;** *Dat.* **ihm**) (*bei Dingen*) it; (*bei weiblichen Personen*) she/her; (*bei männlichen Personen*) he/him; [B] *bezieht sich auf ein Nomen mit beliebigem Genus* **Wer ist der Mann? — Es muss der Bruder des Gastgebers sein** Who is that man? — He/It must be the host's brother; **es waren Studenten** they were students; **keiner will es gewesen sein** no one will admit to it; **ich bin es** it's me; it is I (*formal*); **er/sie ist es** it's him/her; it is he/she (*formal*); **wir sind es** it's us; it is we (*formal*); **ich bin/wir sind es, der/die ...** I am the one/we are the ones who ...; (*förmlicher*) it is I/it is we who ...; [C] *bezieht sich auf ein Adj.* **wir sind traurig, ihr seid es auch** we are sad, and you are too *or* so are you; [D] *bezieht sich auf ein Prädikat* it; **er hat gelogen, will es aber nicht zugeben** he lied, but won't admit it; **er hatte es nicht anders erwartet** he hadn't expected anything else; **Wird man ihn dafür bestrafen? — Ich befürchte es** Will he be punished for it? — I fear so; [E] *kündigt Subjekt od. Subjekt- und Objektsatz an* **es war einmal ein König** once upon a time there was a king; there was once a king; **es gibt keinen anderen Weg** there is no other way; **es war Karl, der ...** it was Karl who ...; **es ist schön, dass ...** it is nice that ...; **es wundert mich, dass ...** I'm surprised that ...; **es sei denn, [dass] ...** unless ...; [F] *bezieht sich auf einen Sachverhalt* **es ist genug!** that's enough; **wir schaffen es** we'll manage it; [G] *bei unpersönlicher Witterungsangabe* **es regnet/schneit/donnert** it rains/snows/thunders; (*jetzt*) it is raining/snowing/thundering; **es blitzt** there is lightning; **es stürmt** it is blowing a gale; [H] *bei unpersönlicher Darstellung* **es hat geklopft** there was a knock; **es klingelte** there was a ring; **es klingelt** someone is ringing; **es knistert** there is something rustling; **in diesem Haus spukt es** this house is haunted; **es friert mich** I am cold; [I] *bei Zustands- u. Artsätzen* **es ist 9 Uhr/spät/Nacht** it is 9 o'clock/late/nighttime; **es wird schöner** the weather is improving; **es wird kälter** it's getting colder; **es wird Frühling** spring is on the way; **es geht ihm gut/schlecht** he is well/unwell; [J] *bei passivischer Konstruktion* **es wird gelacht** there is laughter; **es wird um 6 Uhr angefangen** we/they *etc.* start at 6 o'clock; **es wurde uns befohlen, das Gebäude zu verlassen** we were ordered to leave the building; [K] *bei reflexiver Konstruktion* **es lässt sich aushalten** it is bearable; **es lebt sich gut hier** it's a good life here; [L] *als formales Objekt* **er hat es gut** he has it good; it's all right for him; **er meinte es gut** he meant well; **sie hat es mit dem Herzen** (*ugs.*) she has got heart trouble *or* something wrong with her heart; **er hat es mit seiner Sekretärin** (*salopp*) he's making it with his secretary (*sl.*); ⇒ *auch* **haben** 1 N

**es**[2], **Es**[1] *das;* ~, ~ (*Musik*) E flat

**Es**[2] *das;* ~, ~ (*Psych.*) id

**Es**[3] *der;* ~, ~ (*österr., ugs.*) schilling

**E-Saite** *die* E-string

**Eschatologie** /ɛsçatolo'gi:/ *die;* ~, ~**n** /-ən/ (*Theol.*) eschatology *no art.*

**eschatologisch** *Adj.* eschatological

**Esche** /'ɛʃə/ *die;* ~, ~**n** (*Bot.*) ash

**Es-Dur** *das* E flat major; ⇒ *auch* **A-Dur**

**Esel** /'e:zl/ *der;* ~**s**, ~ [A] donkey; ass; **bepackt** *od.* **beladen wie ein ~ sein** be loaded down like a packhorse; **den hat der ~ im Galopp verloren** (*salopp*) he just appeared from nowhere (*coll.*); **wenn es dem ~ zu wohl wird, geht er aufs Eis** (*Spr.*) you'll/he'll *etc.* come unstuck one of these days; [B] (*ugs.: Dummkopf*) ass (*coll.*); idiot (*coll.*); **so ein alter ~:** what a stupid ass *or* idiot (*coll.*); **du ~:** you ass!; ⇒ *auch* **ich**

**Eselei** *die;* ~, ~**en** (*ugs.*) stupidity; **das war aber eine ~!** (*Handlung*) that was a stupid *or* silly thing to do; (*Bemerkung*) that was a stupid *or* silly thing to say

**Eselein** *das;* ~**s**, ~**:** little donkey

**Esel-: ~füllen** *das* ass-foal; **~hengst** *der* he-donkey; jackass

**Eselin** *die;* ~, ~**nen** she-donkey; jenny[-ass]

**Esels-: ~brücke** *die* (*ugs.*) mnemonic; **~milch** *die* ass's milk; **~ohr** *das* (*ugs.*) [A] **~ohren haben** (*fig.*) have donkey's ears; [B] (*umgeknickte Stelle*) dog-ear; **ein Buch voller ~ohren** a dog-eared book; **~stute** *die* she-donkey; jenny[-ass]

**Esel·treiber** *der*, **Esel·treiberin** *die* donkey driver

**Eskalation** /ɛskala'tsio:n/ *die;* ~, ~**en** escalation

**eskalieren** *tr., itr. V.* escalate

**eskamotieren** /ɛskamo'ti:rən/ *tr. V.* conjure away; **Fakten ~:** explain facts away by sleight of hand

**Eskapade** /ɛska'pa:də/ *die;* ~, ~**n** escapade; (*Seitensprung*) amorous adventure

**Eskapismus** /ɛska'pɪsmʊs/ *der;* ~ (*Psych.*) escapism *no art.*

**eskapistisch** *Adj.* escapist

**Eskimo** /'ɛskimo/ *der;* ~**[s]**, ~**[s]** ▶ 553 Eskimo

**Eskimo·frau** *die* Eskimo woman

**eskimoisch** *Adj.* ▶ 696 Eskimo

**Eskorte** /ɛs'kɔrtə/ *die;* ~, ~**n** escort; (*fig.*) entourage; **eine ~ der Polizei** a police escort

**eskortieren** *tr. V.* escort

**es-Moll** *das* E flat minor; ⇒ *auch* **a-Moll**

**esoterisch** /ezo'te:rɪʃ/ **1** *Adj.* esoteric. **2** *adv.* esoterically

**Espe** /'ɛspə/ *die;* ~, ~**n** aspen

**Espen·laub** *das: in* **wie ~ zittern** shake like a leaf

**Esperanto** /ɛspe'ranto/ *das;* ~**[s]** ▶ 696 Esperanto

**Esplanade** /ɛspla'na:də/ *die;* ~, ~**n** esplanade

**Espresso**[1] /ɛs'prɛso/ *der;* ~**s**, ~**s** [A] *dark blend of roasted coffee;* [B] (*Getränk*) espresso [coffee]

**Espresso**[2] *das;* ~**[s]**, ~**[s]** (*Lokal*) espresso [bar]

**Espresso·maschine** *die* espresso [machine]

**Esprit** /ɛs'pri:/ *der;* ~**s** esprit

**Essai** /'ɛse, ɛ'se:/ ⇒ **Essay**

**Ess·apfel**, ***Eß·apfel** *der* eating apple; eater (*Brit.*)

**Essay** /'ɛse/ *der od. das;* ~**s**, ~**s** essay

**Essayist** *der;* ~**en**, ~**en**, **Essayistin** *die;* ~, ~**nen** ▶ 159 essayist

**essayistisch** *Adj.* essayistic; **seine ~e Begabung** his talent as an essayist

**essbar**, ***eßbar** *Adj.* edible; **ist etwas Essbares im Haus?** (*ugs.*) is there anything to eat in the house?; **nicht ~ sein** be inedible

**Ess·besteck**, ***Eß·besteck** *das* knife, fork, and spoon; **unser ~:** our cutlery; **zwei ~e** two sets of knife, fork, and spoon

**Esse** /'ɛsə/ *die;* ~, ~**n** [A] (*bes. ostmd.*) chimney; [B] (*Herd*) hearth; forge

**Ess·ecke**, ***Eß·ecke** *die* dining area

**essen** /'ɛsn̩/ *unr. tr., itr. V.* eat; eat, drink ‹soup›; **mittags isst er meist im Restaurant** he usually lunches *or* has lunch at a restaurant; **etw. gern ~:** like sth.; **möchten Sie ein Stück Kuchen ~?** would you like a piece of cake?; **was gibt es zu ~?** what's for lunch/dinner/supper?; **von etw. ~:** eat some of sth.; **jmdm. etwas zu ~ machen** get sb. something to eat; **sich satt ~:** eat one's fill; **den Teller leer ~:** clear one's plate; **er isst mich noch arm!** he'll eat me out of house and home!; **gut ~:** have a good meal; (*immer*) eat well; **warm/kalt ~:** have a hot/cold meal; **das Kind isst schlecht** the child doesn't eat very much *or* has a poor appetite; **Kranke müssen gut ~:** you must eat properly when you're ill; **~ gehen** got out for a meal; **er isst bei seiner Tante** he has his meals with his aunt; **es wird nichts so heiß geg~, wie es gekocht wird** (*Spr.*) nothing is ever as bad as it seems; **selber ~ macht fett** (*ugs.*) I'm all right, Jack (*coll.*); ⇒ *auch* **Abend** A; **Mittag**[1] A; **Mittag**[2]

**Essen** *das;* ~**s**, ~ [A] **beim ~ sein** be having lunch/dinner/supper; **lasst euch nicht beim ~ stören** don't let me/us disturb your meal; **zum ~ gehen** go to lunch; **jmdn. zum ~ einladen** invite sb. for a meal; [B] (*Mahlzeit*) meal; (*Fest~*) banquet; **zehn ~:** ten meals; **ein ~ [für jmdn.] geben** give a banquet [in sb.'s honour]; [C] (*Speise*) food; **[das] ~ machen/kochen** get/cook the meal; **das ~ warm stellen** keep the lunch/dinner/supper hot; **das ~ wird kalt** lunch/dinner/supper is getting cold; the food is getting cold; **~ fassen!** (*Soldatenspr.*) come and get it!; **~ auf Rädern** meals on wheels; [D] (*Verpflegung*) food; **~ und Trinken** food and drink

**Essen·fassen** *das* (*Soldatenspr.*) **zum ~!** come and get it!; **beim ~:** at mess time

**Essen[s]-: ~ausgabe** *die* [A] (*das Ausgeben*) serving of meals; **die ~ausgabe ist zwischen 12 und 14 Uhr** meals are *or* lunch is served between 12 [o'clock] and 2 o'clock; [B] (*Stelle*) serving hatch; **~marke** *die* meal ticket; **~zeit** *die* mealtime; **während der ~zeit** during *or* at mealtimes

**essentiell** ⇒ **essenziell**

**Essenz** /ɛ'sɛnts/ *die;* ~, ~**en** essence

**essenziell** /ɛsɛn'tsiɛl/ **1** *Adj.* (*geh., auch Chemie, Biol.*) essential. **2** *adv.* (*geh.*) essentially

**Esser** *der;* ~**s**, ~, **Esserin** *die;* ~, ~**nen: sie ist eine gute/schlechte Esserin** she has a healthy/poor appetite; **ein zusätzlicher Esser, den es zu ernähren gilt** an extra mouth to feed

**Ess-**, ***Eß-: ~geschirr** *das* [A] pots and pans; [B] (*Milit.*) mess kit; **~gewohnheiten** *Pl.* eating habits

**Essig** /'ɛsɪç/ *der;* ~**s**, ~**e** vinegar; **~ und Öl** oil and vinegar; **es ist mit etw. ~** (*ugs.*) sth. has fallen through completely (*coll.*)

**essig-, Essig-: ~baum** *der* staghorn sumac; **~essenz** *die* vinegar essence; **~flasche** *die* vinegar bottle; **~gurke** *die* pickled gherkin; **~sauce** *die* vinaigrette; French dressing; **~sauer** *Adj.* acetic; **~saure Tonerde** basic aluminium acetate; **~säure** *die* (*Chemie*) acetic acid; **~soße** *die:* ⇒ **~sauce**; **~-und-Öl-Ständer** *der* cruet stand; **~wasser** *das* water with a little vinegar added

**ess-**, ***eß-**, **Ess-**, ***Eß-: ~kastanie** *die* sweet chestnut; **~kohle** *die* dry steam coal;

*old spelling (see note on page 1707)

**~kultur** *die* gastronomy; **~löffel** *der (Suppenlöffel)* soup spoon; *(für Nach-, Vorspeise)* dessert spoon; **~löffel·weise** *Adv. (abmessend)* in dessert-spoonfuls; *(steigernd)* by the spoonful; **~lokal** *das* restaurant; **~lust** *die* desire for something to eat; **~napf** *der* bowl; **~paket** *das* food parcel; **~platz** *der* dining area; **~stäbchen** *das* chopstick; **~teller** *der* dinner plate; **~tisch** *der* dining table; **~waren** *Pl.* food *sing.*; **~zimmer** *das* dining room; *(Möbel)* dining room suite

**Establishment** /ɪs'tɛblɪʃmənt/ *das;* **~s, ~s** Establishment

**Este** /'e:stə/ *der;* **~n, ~n** Estonian

**Ester** /'ɛstɐ/ *der;* **~s, ~** *(Chemie)* ester

**Estin** *die;* **~, ~nen** Estonian

**Estland** *(das);* **~s** Estonia

**Estländer** *der;* **~s, ~, Estländerin** *die;* **~, ~nen** ⇒ **Este, Estin**

**estländisch, estnisch** *Adj.* ▶696 Estonian; ⇒ *auch* **deutsch; Deutsch**

**Estrade** /ɛs'tra:də/ *die;* **~, ~n** Ⓐ *(veralt.)* estrade; dais; platform; Ⓑ *(DDR)* open-air show

**Estragon** /'ɛstragɔn/ *der;* **~s** tarragon

**Estrich** /'ɛstrɪç/ *der;* **~s, ~e** Ⓐ composition *or* jointless floor; Ⓑ *(schweiz.)* attic; loft

**Eszett** /ɛs'tsɛt/ *das;* **~, ~:** [the letter] ß

**Eta** /'e:ta/ *das;* **~[s], ~s** eta

**etablieren** /eta'bli:rən/ ❶ *tr. V. (gründen)* establish; set up. ❷ *refl. V.* Ⓐ *(sich niederlassen)* ‹shop› open up; ‹chain store› open up *or* set up branches; **sich als Juwelier ~:** set up as a jeweller; open up a jeweller's shop; Ⓑ *(sich einrichten)* settle in; Ⓒ *(gesellschaftlich)* become established

**etabliert** *Adj.* established; **er ist jetzt so entsetzlich ~** *(abwertend)* he is now so terribly conservative; **die Etablierten** the Establishment

**Etablissement** /etablɪs(ə)'mã:/ *das;* **~s, ~s** establishment

**Etage** /e'ta:ʒə/ *die;* **~, ~n** floor; storey; **in** *od.* **auf der dritten ~ wohnen** live on the third *or (Amer.)* fourth floor

**Etagen-: ~bett** *das* bunk bed; **~haus** *das* block of flats *(Brit.) or (Amer.)* apartments; **~heizung** *die: central heating serving one floor of a building;* **~wohnung** *die: flat (Brit.) or (Amer.) apartment occupying an entire floor*

**Etagere** /eta'ʒe:rə/ *die;* **~, ~n** *(veralt.)* étagère; whatnot

**Etappe** /e'tapə/ *die;* **~, ~n** Ⓐ *(Teilstrecke)* stage; leg; *(Rennsport)* stage; Ⓑ *(Stadium)* stage; Ⓒ *(Milit.)* back area; base; **jmdn. in die ~ versetzen** move sb. back behind the lines

**etappen-, Etappen-: ~hase** *der,* **~hengst** *der (Soldatenspr. salopp)* base wallah *(Mil. coll.)*; **~sieg** *der (Rennsport)* stage win; **der heutige ~sieg ging an ...** the winner of today's stage was ...; **~weise** *Adv.* by *or* in stages; **~wertung** *die (Rennsport)* daily points classification; **~ziel** *das (Sport)* finish of the stage

**Etat** /e'ta:/ *der;* **~s, ~s** budget

**etat-, Etat-: ~ausgleich** *der* balancing of the budget; **~defizit** *das* budgetary deficit; **~kürzung** *die* cut in the budget; **die ~kürzungen im Bildungswesen** the cuts in the education budget; the education cuts; **~mäßig** ❶ *Adj.* Ⓐ *(im ~)* budgetary ‹expenditure›; Ⓑ *(eingeplant)* budgeted ‹post, position›; **der ~mäßige Mittelstürmer** *(Fußballjargon)* the regular centre forward; ❷ *adv.* in the budget; **~stärke** *die (Milit.)* planned strength

**etc.** *Abk.* **et cetera** etc.

**et cetera** /ɛt'tse:tera/ et cetera; **~ pp.** /-'--pe'pe:/ *(ugs. scherzh.)* and so on and so forth *(coll.)*

**etepetete** /e:tape'te:tə/ *Adj. (ugs.)* fussy; finicky; pernickety *(coll.)*

**Eternit** Ⓦⓩ /etɛr'ni:t/ *das od. der;* **~s** asbestos cement

**ETH** *Abk.* **Eidgenössische Technische Hochschule** Swiss Federal Institute of Technology

**Ethik** /'e:tɪk/ *die;* **~, ~en** Ⓐ *(Sittenlehre)* ethics *sing.;* Ⓑ *(sittliche Normen)* ethics *pl.;* Ⓒ *(Werk über ~)* ethical work

**Ethiker** *der;* **~s, ~, Ethikerin** *die;* **~, ~nen** Ⓐ *(Philos.)* moral philosopher; Ⓑ *(Moralist)* moralist

**ethisch** ❶ *Adj.* ethical. ❷ *adv.* ethically

**Ethnie** /ɛt'ni:/ *die;* **~, ~n** *(Völkerk.)* ethnos

**ethnisch** /'ɛtnɪʃ/ ❶ *Adj.* ethnic; **~e Säuberung** ethnic cleansing. ❷ *adv.* ethnically

**Ethno** *der;* **~s** ethnic music

**Ethnograph** /ɛtno'gra:f/ *der;* **~en, ~en** ethnographer

**Ethnographie** *die;* **~, ~n** ethnography *no art.*

**Ethnographin** *die;* **~, ~nen** ethnographer

**Ethnologe** /ɛtno'lo:gə/ *der;* **~n, ~n** ethnologist

**Ethnologie** *die;* **~, ~n** ethnology *no art.*

**Ethnologin** *die;* **~, ~nen** ethnologist

**ethnologisch** ❶ *Adj.* ethnological. ❷ *adv.* ethnologically

**Ethno·pop** *der* ethnic pop [music]

**Ethologie** /etolo'gi:/ *die;* **~, ~n** ethology *no art.*

**Ethos** /'e:tɔs/ *das;* **~:** ethos; **das berufliche ~ der Ärzteschaft** doctors' professional ethics *pl.*

**Etikett** /eti'kɛt/ *das;* **~[e]s, ~en** *od.* **~e** *od.* **~s** label; **jmdn./etw. mit einem ~ versehen** *(fig.)* pin a label on sb./sth.

**Etikette**[1] *die;* **~, ~n** *(schweiz., österr.)* ⇒ **Etikett**

**Etikette**[2] *die;* **~, ~n** etiquette; **die ~ wahren** observe the proprieties; **gegen die ~ verstoßen** commit a breach of etiquette

**Etiketten·schwindel** *der (abwertend)* playing with names

**etikettieren** /etikɛ'ti:rən/ *tr. V.* label

**etlich...** /'ɛtlɪç.../ *Indefinitpron. u. unbest. Zahlwort* Ⓐ *(ugs. verstärkend) Sg.* quite a lot of; *Pl.* quite a few; a number of; **vor ~en Wochen** several *or* some weeks ago; Ⓑ *Sg. (veralt.: wenig)* a little; **Etliches bemerken** make a few remarks *or* comments; **Etliches sagen** say a few things; Ⓒ *Pl. (veralt.: einige)* a few; some; **~e der Gefangenen** a few *or* some of the prisoners

***etliche·mal** ⇒ **Mal**[1]

**Etrusker** /e'trʊskɐ/ *der;* **~s, ~, Etruskerin** *die;* **~, ~nen** Etruscan

**etruskisch** *Adj.* ▶696 Etruscan; ⇒ *auch* **deutsch**

**Etsch** *die;* **~:** Adige

**Etüde** /e'ty:də/ *die;* **~, ~n** *(Musik)* étude

**Etui** /ɛt'vi:/ *das;* **~s, ~s** case

**etwa** /'ɛtva/ ❶ *Adv.* Ⓐ *(ungefähr)* about; approximately; **~ 50 m/2 Wochen** about 50 m/2 weeks; **~ so groß wie ...** about as large as ...; **wie lange wird die Fahrt ~ dauern?** roughly how long will the journey take?; **~ so** roughly like this; **das lässt sich ~ so erklären** you could perhaps explain it like this; **in ~:** to some *or* a certain extent *or* degree; **können Sie mir in ~ sagen, wann ...?** can you give me any idea when ...?; Ⓑ *(beispielsweise)* for example; for instance; **vergleicht man ~ ...** for example, if one compares ...; **wie ~ ...** as, for example ...; Ⓒ *(schweiz.: bisweilen)* from time to time; now and then.
❷ *Part. (womöglich)* **hast du das ~ vergessen?** you haven't forgotten that, have you?; **störe ich ~?** am I disturbing you at all?; **falls sie ~ doch mitgeht, ...** if she does happen to go ...; **du glaubst doch nicht ~, dass ...?** surely you don't think that ...?; **sie darf nicht ~ glauben, dass ...** she mustn't think that ...

**etwaig...** /'ɛtva(:)ɪg.../ *Adj. (Papierdt.)* possible ‹delays›; **~e Mängel/Beschwerden** any faults/complaints [which might arise]; **bei ~en Beschwerden** in the event of any complaints

**etwas** /'ɛtvas/ *Indefinitpron.* Ⓐ something; *(fragend, verneinend)* anything; **~ sagen/hören/sehen** say/hear/see something; **hast du ~ gesagt?** did you say something?; **irgend~:** something; **erzähl ihm einfach irgend~:** just tell him anything!; **es muss ~ geschehen** something has to *or* must be done; **wenn sie es wagt, dir ~ zu tun** if she dares to do anything to you; **~ gegen jmdn. haben** have something against sb.; **sie haben ~ miteinander** *(ugs.)* there is something going on between them; **~ für sich haben** *(ugs.)* have something in it; **dein Argument hat ~ für sich** *(ugs.)* there's something in your argument; **so ~:** a thing like that; **[so] ~ wie ...** something like ...; **so ~ habe ich noch nie gesehen** I've never seen anything like it; **nein, so ~:** would you believe it!; Ⓑ *attr.* something; *(fragend, verneinend)* anything; **~ Schönes/Neues/Unangenehmes** something beautiful/new/unpleasant; **so ~ Schönes habe ich noch nie gesehen** I've never seen anything so beautiful before; **~ anderes** something else; *(fragend, verneinend)* anything else; **das ist ~ anderes** *(ugs.)* that's different; Ⓒ *(Bedeutsames)* **aus ihm wird ~:** he'll make something of himself *or* his life; **es zu ~ bringen** get somewhere; **~ gelten** count for something; **das will ~ heißen** that really is something; Ⓓ *(ein Teil)* some; *(fragend, verneinend)* any; **~ von dem Geld** some of the money; **kann ich auch ~ davon haben?** can I have some of it too?; **er weiß ~ von dieser Sache** he knows something about this matter; **sie hat ~ von einer Künstlerin an sich** *(Dat.)* she has *or* there is something of the artist about her; Ⓔ *(ein wenig)* a little; **noch ~ Milch** a little more *or* some more milk; **kannst du mir ~ Geld leihen?** can you lend me some money?; **~ lauter/besser** a little louder/better; **[noch] ~ spielen/lesen** play/read for a little while [longer]; **~ Englisch** a little *or* some English

**Etwas** *das;* **~, ~:** something; **ein hilfloses ~:** a helpless little thing; **das gewisse ~:** that certain something

**etwelch...** /'ɛtvɛlç.../ *Indefinitpron. (schweiz., österr.)* some

**Etymologe** /etymo'lo:gə/ *der;* **~n, ~n** etymologist

**Etymologie** *die;* **~, ~n** etymology

**Etymologin** *die;* **~, ~nen** etymologist

**etymologisch** *(Sprachw.)* ❶ *Adj.* etymological. ❷ *adv.* etymologically

**etymologisieren** *tr. V. (Sprachw.)* etymologize

**Et-Zeichen** /'ɛt-/ *das* ampersand

**Etzel** /'ɛts̩l/ *(der)* Attila the Hun

**EU** *Abk.* **Europäische Union** EU

**euch** /ɔyç/ ❶ *Dat. u. Akk. Pl. des Personalpron.* **ihr** you; ye *(Bibl./arch.)*; **ich gebe ~ das** I'll give you it; I'll give it to you. ❷ *Dat. u. Akk. Pl. des Reflexivpron. der 2. Pers. Pl.* yourselves

**Eucharistie** /ɔyçarɪs'ti:/ *die;* **~, ~n** *(kath. Rel.)* Eucharist

**eucharistisch** *Adj. (kath. Rel.)* Eucharistic

**euer**[1] /'ɔyɐ/ *Possessivpron.* your; **Grüße von eu[e]rer Helga/eu[e]rem Hans** Best wishes, Yours, Helga/Hans; **Eu[e]re** *od.* **Euer Exzellenz** Your Excellency; **ist das/sind das eure?** is that/are they yours?; **es ist der Eu[e]re** *(geh.)* it is yours; **die Eu[e]ren** *od.* **Euern** *(geh.)* your family; **nehmt euch das Eu[e]re** *(geh.)* take what is yours; **ihr müsst das Eu[e]re dazu tun** you must do your share; **ich verbleibe auf immer die Eu[e]re ...** *(veralt.)* I remain, yours for ever, ...; ⇒ *auch* **dein**[1]

**euer**[2] *Gen. des Personalpron.* **ihr** *(geh.)* **wir werden ~ gedenken** we will remember you

**euerseits** ⇒ **eurerseits**

**euersgleichen** ⇒ **euresgleichen**

**euert-: ~halben** ⇒ **eurethalben; ~wegen** ⇒ **euretwegen; ~willen** ⇒ **euretwillen**

**Eugenik** /ɔy'ge:nɪk/ *die;* **~** *(Med.)* eugenics *sing.*

**eugenisch** *Adj. (Med.)* eugenic

**Eukalyptus** /ɔyka'lʏptʊs/ *der;* **~, Eukalypten** *od.* **~:** eucalyptus

e

e

**Eukalyptus·bonbon** *das* eucalyptus cough sweet (*Brit.*); cough drop

**Euklid** /ɔy'kli:t/ (*der*) Euclid

**euklidisch** *Adj.* (*Math.*) Euclidean

**Eule** /'ɔylə/ *die;* ~, ~n **A** owl; **~n nach Athen tragen** carry coals to Newcastle; send owls to Athens; **B** (*salopp abwertend: Frau*) old boot (*sl.*)

**eulen-, Eulen-:** **~haft** *Adj.* owlish; owl-like; **~spiegel** *der* joker; ⇒ *auch* **Till**; **~spiegelei** *die;* ~~, ~~en caper; **~vogel** *der* (*Zool.*) owl

**Eumel** /'ɔyml/ *der;* ~s, ~ (*Jugendspr.*) twerp (*coll. derog.*)

**Eunuch** /ɔy'nu:x/ *der;* ~en, ~en, **Eunuche** *der;* ~en, ~en eunuch

**Eunuchen·stimme** *die* (*ugs.*) squeaky, high-pitched voice

**Euphemismus** /ɔyfe'mɪsmʊs/ *der;* ~, **Euphemismen** (*geh.*, *Sprachw.*) euphemism

**euphemistisch** (*geh.*, *Sprachw.*) **1** *Adj.* euphemistic. **2** *adv.* euphemistically

**euphonisch** /ɔy'fo:nɪʃ/ *Adj.* (*Sprachw.*, *Musik*) euphonic

**Euphorie** /ɔyfo'ri:/ *die;* ~, ~n (*bes. Med.*, *Psych.*) euphoria; **in [eine] ~ verfallen** go into a state of euphoria

**euphorisch** (*bes. Med.*, *Psych.*) **1** *Adj.* euphoric. **2** *adv.* euphorically

**Euphrat** /'ɔyfrat/ *der;* ~[s] ▶ 306 Euphrates

**Eurasien** /ɔy'ra:zi̯ən/ (*das*); ~s Eurasia

**Eurasier** *der;* ~s, ~, **Eurasierin** *die;* ~, ~nen Eurasian

**eurasisch** *Adj.* Eurasian

**Euratom** /ɔyra'to:m/ *die;* ~: Euratom

**eure** /'ɔyrə/ ⇒ **euer[1]**

**eurer·seits** *Adv.* (*von eurer Seite*) on your part; (*auf eurer Seite*) for your part

**eures·gleichen** *indekl. Pron.* people *pl.* like you; (*abwertend*) the likes *pl.* of you; your sort *or* kind; ⇒ *auch* **deinesgleichen**

**euret-:** **~halben** /-halbn̩/ (*veralt.*), **~wegen** *Adv.* (*wegen euch*) because of you; on your account; (*für euch*) on your behalf; (*euch zuliebe*) for your sake; **ich mache mir ~wegen keine Sorgen** I don't worry about you; **~willen** *Adv.* **um ~willen** for your sake

**Eurhythmie** /ɔyrʏt'mi:/ *die;* ~ **A** (*bes. Tanz*, *Gymnastik*) eurhythmics *sing.*, *no art.*; **B** (*Med.*) eurhythmia

**eurige** /'ɔyrɪgə/ *Possessivpron.* (*geh.*, *veralt.*) **der/die/das ~:** yours; **das ~** *od.* **Eurige** (*Angelegenheit*) your affairs; (*Besitz*) what is yours

**Euro** *der;* ~[s], ~[s] ▶ 337 Euro

**Eurocheque** /'ɔyroʃɛk/ *der;* ~s, ~s Eurocheque

**Eurocheque·karte** *die* Eurocheque card

**Euro-:** **~dollar** *der* (*Wirtsch.*) Eurodollar; **~kommunismus** *der* Eurocommunism; **~krat** /-'kra:t/ *der;* ~~en, ~~en, **~kratin** *die;* ~~, ~~nen Eurocrat; **~land** (*das*); ~s Euroland

**Europa** /ɔy'ro:pa/ (*das*); ~s Europe

**Europa·cup** *der* (*Sport*) European cup

**Europäer** /ɔyro'pɛ:ɐ/ *der;* ~s, ~, **Europäerin** *die;* ~, ~nen European

**Europa·flagge** *die* flag of the Council of Europe

**europäisch** /ɔyro'pɛ:ɪʃ/ *Adj.* European; **die Europäische Gemeinschaft/Europäischen Gemeinschaften** the European Community/European Communities; **Europäische Wirtschaftsgemeinschaft** European Economic Community

**europäisieren** *tr. V.* Europeanize

**Europäisierung** *die;* ~, ~en Europeanization

**europa-, Europa-:** **~meister** *der*, **~meisterin** *die* (*Sport*) European champion; **~meisterschaft** *die* (*Sport*) **A** (*Wettbewerb*) European Championship; **B** (*Sieg*) championship of Europe, European title; **~minister** *der*, **~ministerin** *die* minister for Europe; **~müde** *Adj.* disillusioned with the Common Market *postpos.*; **~parlament** *das* European Parliament *or* Assembly; **~pokal** *der* (*Sport*) ⇒ **Europacup**; **~politik** *die* policy towards the EEC; **~rat** *der* Council of Europe; **~rekord** *der* (*Sport*) European record; **~straße** *die* European long-distance road; **~wahlen** *Pl.* European elections

**Euro·scheck** *der* ⇒ **Eurocheque**

**Euro·vision** *die* Eurovision

**Eurythmie** ⇒ **Eurhythmie A**

**eustachische Röhre** /ɔys'taxɪʃə/ *die;* ~n ~, ~n ~n ▶ 471 (*Med.*, *Zool.*) Eustachian tube

**Euter** /'ɔytɐ/ *das od. der;* ~s, ~: udder

**Euthanasie** /ɔytana'zi:/ *die;* ~: euthanasia *no art.*

**ev.** *Abk.* **evangelisch** ev.

**e. V., E. V.** *Abk.* **eingetragener Verein**

**Eva[1]** /'e:fa *od.* 'e:va/ (*die*) Eve; ⇒ *auch* **Adam[1]**

**Eva[2]** *die;* ~, ~s (*ugs. scherzh.: Frau*) **sie ist eine richtige ~:** she's a real little Eve

**evakuieren** /evaku'i:rən/ *tr. V.* evacuate

**Evakuierte** *der/die; adj. Dekl.* evacuee

**Evakuierung** *die;* ~, ~en evacuation

**Evaluation** /evalu̯a'tsi̯o:n/ *die;* ~, ~en **A** (*geh.*) valuation; **B** (*Päd.*) evaluation

**Evangelien·buch** *das* Gospel

**evangelikal** /evaŋgeli'ka:l/ *Adj.* (*christl. Kirche*) evangelical

**evangelisch** /evaŋ'ge:lɪʃ/ *Adj.* **A** Protestant; **die ~e Kirche** the Protestant Church; **B** (*des Evangeliums*) evangelical

**evangelisch-lutherisch** *Adj.* Lutheran

**evangelisch-reformiert** *Adj.* Reformed

**evangelisieren** *tr. V.* evangelize

**Evangelist** *der;* ~en, ~en evangelist

**Evangelium** /evaŋ'ge:li̯ʊm/ *das;* ~s, **Evangelien** **A** (*auch fig.*) gospel; **alles, was ihr Mann sagte, war [ein] ~ für sie** she took everything her husband said as gospel; **B** (*christl. Rel.*) Gospel; **das ~ des Johannes** St. John's Gospel

**Evas-** /'e:fas- *od.* 'e:vas-/: **~kostüm** *das:* **in im ~kostüm** (*ugs. scherzh.*) in her birthday suit/their birthday suits (*coll. joc.*); in the altogether (*coll. joc.*); **~tochter** *die* (*scherzh.*) **eine echte ~tochter** a real little Eve

**Eventual-** /evɛn'tu̯a:l-/: **~fall** *der* eventuality; contingency; **für den ~fall** should the eventuality arise; **~haushalt** *der* (*Politik*) contingency reserve

**Eventualität** /evɛntu̯ali'tɛ:t/ *die;* ~, ~n eventuality; contingency

**eventuell** /evɛn'tu̯ɛl/ **1** *Adj.* possible ‹objections, difficulties, applicants›; ‹objections, difficulties› which might occur; **bei ~en Schäden** in the event *or* case of damage. **2** *adv.* possibly; perhaps; **wir werden ~ morgen kommen** we may [possibly] come tomorrow; **können wir ~ bei euch übernachten?** can we stay the night at your house, if necessary?

**Evergreen** /'ɛvəgri:n/ *der;* ~s, ~s old favourite

**evident** /evi'dɛnt/ *Adj.* (*geh.*) **A** (*einleuchtend*) convincing ‹argument, proof›; evident, self-evident ‹truth›; **B** (*offenkundig*) evident, obvious ‹disadvantage›

**Evidenz** /evi'dɛnts/ *die;* ~, ~en (*geh.*) (*einer Behauptung, eines Beweises*) convincingness; (*eines Satzes, einer Wahrheit*) self-evidence

**Evolution** /evolu'tsi̯o:n/ *die;* ~, ~en evolution

**evolutionär** /evolutsi̯o'nɛ:ɐ/ **1** *Adj.* evolutionary. **2** *adv.* by evolution

**Evolutions·theorie** *die* theory of evolution

**evozieren** /evo'tsi:rən/ *tr. V.* (*geh.*) evoke

**evtl.** *Abk.* **eventuell**

**EW** *Abk.* **Elektrizitätswerk**

**Ewer** /'e:vɐ/ *der;* ~s, ~ (*nordd.*) ketch-rigged sailing barge

**E-Werk** *das* ⇒ **Elektrizitätswerk**

**EWG** *Abk.* **Europäische Wirtschaftsgemeinschaft** EEC

**ewig** /'e:vɪç/ **1** *Adj.* eternal, everlasting ‹life, peace›; eternal, undying ‹love›; (*abwertend*) never-ending; **die Ewige Stadt** the Eternal City; **der Ewige Jude** the Wandering Jew; **ein ~er Student** (*scherzh.*) an eternal student; **das ~e Einerlei** the unending *or* never-ending monotony; **seit ~en Zeiten** for ages (*coll.*); for donkey's years (*coll.*); **das ~e Licht** (*kath. Rel.*) the Sanctuary Lamp. **2** *adv.* eternally; for ever; **~ warten** wait for ever; **~ dauern** take ages; **~ halten** last for ever *or* indefinitely; **auf ~:** for ever; **sein Name wird ~ leben** his name will live for ever; **~ und drei Tage** (*ugs.*) for ever and a day; **~ kommt er mit denselben Problemen an** (*ugs.*) he is for ever coming along with the same problems; ⇒ *auch* **immer A**

**Ewig·gestrige** *der/die; adj. Dekl.* (*abwertend*) **ein ~r sein** be an old reactionary

**Ewigkeit** *die;* ~, ~en **A** eternity; **in ~:** for ever and ever; **in die ~ eingehen** (*geh. verhüll.*) find eternal rest; **B** (*ugs.*) **es dauert eine [ganze] ~:** it takes [absolutely] ages (*coll.*); **es ist eine [kleine] ~ her** it was ages ago (*coll.*); **es muss ~en her sein, dass ...** it must be ages since ... (*coll.*); **seit ~en** for ages (*coll.*); **in alle ~:** for ever

**Ewigkeits-:** **~sonntag**, *der* ⇒ **Totensonntag**; **~wert** *der* (*geh.*) **es besitzt ~wert** it will last for ever

**ewiglich** *Adv.* (*dichter. veralt.*) for ever; till the end of time

**Ewig·weibliche** *das; adj. Dekl.* (*geh.*) **das ~:** the essential Feminine

**EWS** *Abk.* **Europäisches Währungssystem** EMS

**ex** /ɛks/ *Adv.* (*ugs.*) **A** **etw. ex trinken** drink sth. down in one (*coll.*); knock sth. back in one (*sl.*); **ex!** down in one! (*sl.*); **B** (*salopp: tot*) **der ist ex** he's snuffed it (*sl.*)

**Ex-** (*vor Personenbez.: vormalig*) ex-

**exakt** /ɛ'ksakt/ **1** *Adj.* exact; precise; **eine ~e Beschreibung** a precise description. **2** *adv.* ‹work etc.› accurately; **~ [um] 12 Uhr** at 12 o'clock precisely; **~!** exactly!; precisely!

**Exaktheit** *die;* ~: precision; exactness

**exaltieren** /ɛksal'ti:rən/ *refl. V.* get overexcited *or* worked up

**exaltiert** **1** *Adj.* (*hysterisch*) overexcited; (*überspannt*) exaggerated ‹behaviour, gestures›; (*überschwänglich*) effusive. **2** *adv.* (*hysterisch*) overexcitedly; (*überschwänglich*) effusively

**Exaltiertheit** *die;* ~, ~en ⇒ **exaltiert**: overexcitedness; exaggeratedness; effusiveness

**Examen** /ɛ'ksa:mən/ *das;* ~s, ~ *od.* **Examina** /ɛ'ksa:mina/ examination; exam (*coll.*); **ein ~ machen** *od.* **ablegen** sit *or* take an examination; **~ haben** (*ugs.*) have examinations; **im ~ sein** *od.* **stehen** be in the middle of one's examinations; **im ~ durchfallen** fail the examination

**Examens-:** **~angst** *die* examination nerves *pl.*; **~arbeit** *die: written work presented for an examination;* **~kandidat** *der*, **~kandidatin** *die* examination candidate

**examinieren** *tr. V.* **A** examine; **eine examinierte Krankenschwester** a qualified nurse; **B** (*ausfragen*) question; **C** (*veralt. geh.: prüfend untersuchen*) scrutinize ‹appearance›; investigate ‹affair, matter›

**ex cathedra** /ɛks'ka(:)tedra/ (*kath. Rel.*) ex cathedra

**Exegese** /ɛkse'ge:zə/ *die;* ~, ~n (*Theol.*) exegesis

**Exeget** /ɛkse'ge:t/ *der;* ~en, ~en (*Theol.*) exegete

**exekutieren** /ɛkseku'ti:rən/ *tr. V.* **A** execute; **B** (*österr.*) ⇒ **pfänden**

**Exekution** /ɛkseku'tsi̯o:n/ *die;* ~, ~en **A** execution; **B** (*österr.*) ⇒ **Pfändung**

**Exekutions·kommando** *das* firing squad

**exekutiv** /ɛkseku'ti:f/ *Adj.* (*bes. Politik*, *Rechtsw.*) executive

**Exekutiv·ausschuss**, ***Exekutiv·ausschuß** *der* executive committee

**Exekutive** /ɛkseku'ti:və/ *die;* ~, ~n (*Rechtsw.*, *Politik*) executive

**Exekutiv-:** **~gewalt** *die* (*Politik*) executive power; **~organ** *das* (*Politik*) executive body

**Exekutor** /ɛkse'ku:tɔr/ *der;* ~s, ~en, **Exekutorin** *die;* ~, ~nen (*österr.*) bailiff

*old spelling (see note on page 1707)

**Exempel** /ɛ'ksɛmpl̩/ *das;* **~s, ~:** example; **ein ~ [an jmdm.] statuieren** make an example [of sb.]; **zum ~** (*veralt.*) for example; ⇒ *auch* Probe A

**Exemplar** /ɛksɛm'pla:ɐ̯/ *das;* **~s, ~e** specimen; (*Buch, Zeitung, Zeitschrift*) copy

**exemplarisch** /ɛksɛm'pla:rɪʃ/ ❶ *Adj.* exemplary; **eine ~e Strafe** an exemplary punishment; a deterrent sentence; **~ für etw. sein** be typical of sth. ❷ *adv.* by means of an example/examples; **jmdn. ~ bestrafen** punish sb. as an example to others

**exemplifizieren** /ɛksɛmplifi'tsi:rən/ *tr. V.* (*geh.*) exemplify; **etw. an einem Beispiel ~:** illustrate sth. by an example

**Exequien** /ɛ'kse:kvi̯ən/ *Pl.* (*kath. Kirche*) exequies

**exerzieren** /ɛksɛr'tsi:rən/ ❶ *itr. V.* (*Milit.: Übungen machen*) drill. ❷ *tr. V.* Ⓐ (*Milit.: ausbilden*) drill ‹soldiers›; Ⓑ (*ugs.: üben*) practise; Ⓒ (*ausführen*) employ ‹technique, method›; follow ‹procedure›

**Exerzier-:** **~munition** *die* (*Milit.*) dummy ammunition; **~platz** *der* (*Milit.*) parade ground; **~reglement** *das* (*Milit.*) drill regulations *pl.*

**Exerzitien** /ɛksɛr'tsi:tsi̯ən/ *Pl.* (*kath. Rel.*) religious *or* spiritual exercises

**Exhaustor** /ɛks'haustɔr/ *der;* **~s, ~en** (*Technik*) extractor fan

**exhibitionieren** /ɛkshibitsi̯o'ni:rən/ *itr., refl. V.* (*Psych.*) expose oneself

**Exhibitionismus** *der;* **~** (*Psych., fig.*) exhibitionism

**Exhibitionist** *der;* **~en, ~en, Exhibitionistin** *die;* **~, ~nen** (*Psych., fig.*) exhibitionist

**exhibitionistisch** (*Psych.*) ❶ *Adj.* exhibitionist. ❷ *adv.* **er ist ~ veranlagt** he has exhibitionist tendencies

**exhumieren** /ɛkshu'mi:rən/ *tr. V.* exhume

**Exhumierung** *die;* **~, ~en** exhumation

**Exil** /ɛ'ksi:l/ *das;* **~s, ~e** exile; **ins ~ gehen** go into exile

**Exilant** /ɛksi'lant/ *der;* **~en, ~en, Exilantin** *die;* **~, ~nen** exile

**Exil·heimat** *die* home in exile

**exiliert** /ɛksi'li:ɐ̯t/ *Adj.* exiled

**Exilierte** *der/die; adj. Dekl.* exile

**Exil-:** **~literatur** *die* literature written in exile; **~regierung** *die* government in exile

**existent** /ɛksɪs'tɛnt/ *Adj.* existing; existent; **jmdn./etw. als nicht ~ betrachten** treat sb./sth. as if he/she/it did not exist

**Existentialismus** *usw.* ⇒ **Existenzialismus** *usw.*

**Existenz** /ɛksɪs'tɛnts/ *die;* **~, ~en** Ⓐ (*Dasein*) existence; **die nackte ~ retten** to escape with one's life; Ⓑ (*Lebensgrundlage*) livelihood; **sich** (*Dat.*) **eine ~ aufbauen** build a life for oneself; **jmdm. eine gesicherte ~ bieten** offer sb. a secure livelihood *or* living; Ⓒ (*Mensch*) **zweifelhafte ~en** dubious characters; **eine verkrachte ~** (*ugs.*) a deadbeat

**existenz-, Existenz-:** **~angst** *die* angst; existential fear; **~bedingungen** *Pl.* living conditions; conditions of life; **~berechtigung** *die* right to exist; **diese Institution hat keine ~berechtigung mehr** there is no longer any justification for the existence of this institution; **~fähig** *Adj.* able to exist *or* to survive *postpos.*; **~frage** *die* matter of life and death; **~grundlage** *die* basis of one's livelihood; **~gründung** *die* [business] start-up

**Existenzialismus** /ɛksɪstɛntsi̯a'lɪsmʊs/ *der;* **~** (*Philos.*) existentialism *no art.*

**Existenzialist** *der;* **~en, ~en, Existenzialistin** *die;* **~, ~nen** existentialist

**existenzialistisch** ❶ *Adj.* existentialist. ❷ *adv.* **~ beeinflusst** influenced by existentialism

**existenziell** /ɛksɪstɛn'tsi̯ɛl/ *Adj.* (*Philos.*) existential; **in etw.** (*Dat.*) **eine ~e Bedrohung sehen** see in sth. a threat to one's existence

**Existenz-:** **~kampf** *der* struggle for existence; **~minimum** *das* subsistence level; **am Rande des ~minimums leben** live at subsistence level; **die Löhne der Teepflücker liegen unter dem ~minimum** the tea pickers earn less than a living wage; **~philosophie** *die* existential philosophy *no art.*

**existieren** /ɛksɪs'ti:rən/ *itr. V.* exist

**Exitus** /'ɛksitʊs/ *der;* **~** (*Med.*) death; „**~**“, **konstatierte der Arzt** 'she's/he's dead,' confirmed the doctor

**exkl.** *Abk.* **exklusiv[e]** excl.

**Exklave** /ɛks'kla:və/ *die;* **~, ~n** exclave

**exklusiv** /ɛksklu'zi:f/ ❶ *Adj.* exclusive. ❷ *adv.* exclusively; **[über etw.** (*Akk.*)**] ~ berichten** run an exclusive report [on sth.]

**Exklusiv·bericht** *der* exclusive [report]

**exklusive** /ɛksklu'zi:və/ *Präp. + Gen.* (*Kaufmannsspr.*) exclusive of; excluding

**Exklusiv·interview** *das* exclusive interview

**Exklusivität** /ɛkskluzivi'tɛ:t/ *die;* **~:** exclusiveness; exclusivity

**Exklusiv·vertrag** *der* exclusive contract

**Ex·kommunikation** *die* (*kath. Kirche*) excommunication

**ex·kommunizieren** *tr. V.* (*kath. Kirche*) excommunicate

**Ex·könig** *der* ex-king

**Ex·königin** *die* ex-queen

**Exkrement** /ɛkskre'mɛnt/ *das;* **~[e]s, ~e** (*bes. Med., Zool.*) excrement; **menschliche ~e** human excrement *sing.*

**Exkret** /ɛks'kre:t/ *das;* **~[e]s, ~e** (*Med., Zool.*) excretion; **~e** excreta; excretions

**Exkulpation** /ɛkskʊlpa'tsi̯o:n/ *die;* **~, ~en** (*Rechtsw.*) exculpation

**exkulpieren** /ɛkskʊl'pi:rən/ *tr. V.* (*Rechtsw.*) exculpate

**Exkurs** /ɛks'kʊrs/ *der;* **~es, ~e** digression; (*in einem Buch*) excursus

**Exkursion** /ɛkskʊr'zi̯o:n/ *die;* **~, ~en** study trip *or* tour

**Exlibris** /ɛks'li:bri:s/ *das;* **~, ~** (*Buchw., Grafik*) ex libris; bookplate

**Exmatrikulation** /ɛksmatrikula'tsi̯o:n/ *die;* **~, ~en** (*Hochschulw.*) *removal of a student's name from the register on leaving a university*

**exmatrikulieren** /ɛksmatriku'li:rən/ *tr. V.* (*Hochschulw.*) **jmdn./sich ~:** remove sb.'s name/have one's name removed from the university register

**Ex·meister** *der,* **Ex·meisterin** *die* (*Sport*) ex-champion

**exmittieren** /ɛksmɪ'ti:rən/ *tr. V.* (*Rechtsw.*) evict

**Exmittierung** *die;* **~, ~en** (*Rechtsw.*) eviction

**Exodus** /'ɛksodʊs/ *der;* **~, ~se** (*geh.*) exodus

**exogen** /ɛkso'ge:n/ *Adj.* (*Med., Psych., Bot.*) exogenous

**exorbitant** /ɛksɔrbi'tant/ ❶ *Adj.* (*geh.*) exorbitant ‹price›. ❷ *adv.* exorbitantly

**Exorzismus** /ɛksɔr'tsɪsmʊs/ *der;* **~, Exorzismen** (*Rel.*) exorcism

**Exorzist** *der* (*Rel.*) exorcist

**Exot** /ɛ'kso:t/ *der;* **~en, ~en** Ⓐ (*Mensch*) strange foreigner; Ⓑ (*Tier, Pflanze*) exotic

**Exotin** *die;* **~, ~nen** ⇒ **Exot** A

**exotisch** ❶ *Adj.* exotic. ❷ *adv.* exotically

**Expander** /ɛks'pandɐ/ *der;* **~s, ~** (*Sport*) chest expander

**expandieren** /ɛkspan'di:rən/ *tr., itr. V.* expand

**Expansion** /ɛkspan'zi̯o:n/ *die;* **~, ~en** expansion

**expansionistisch** *Adj.* (*Politik*) expansionist

**expansions-, Expansions-:** **~freudig** *Adj.* Ⓐ (*Politik*) expansionist; Ⓑ (*Wirtsch.*) **~freudige Unternehmen** businesses which are eager to expand; **~kraft** *die* (*Physik, Technik*) expansive force; **~krieg** *der* expansionist war; **~politik** *die* Ⓐ expansionism; expansionist policy; Ⓑ (*Wirtsch.*) policy of expansion

**expansiv** /ɛkspan'zi:f/ ❶ *Adj.* Ⓐ (*Politik*) expansionist; Ⓑ (*Wirtsch.*) expansionary. ❷ *adv.* in an expansionary manner

**expatriieren** /ɛkspatri'i:rən/ *tr. V.* (*Politik, Rechtsw.*) expatriate

**Expedient** /ɛkspe'di̯ɛnt/ *der;* **~en, ~en, Expedientin** *die;* **~, ~nen** Ⓐ dispatch clerk; Ⓑ (*im Reisebüro*) travel agency clerk

**expedieren** /ɛkspe'di:rən/ *tr. V.* dispatch; send; **jmdn. an einen anderen Ort ~** (*ugs.*) pack sb. off somewhere else (*coll.*)

**Expedition** /ɛkspedi'tsi̯o:n/ *die;* **~, ~en** Ⓐ expedition; Ⓑ (*Versandabteilung*) dispatch department

**Expeditions-:** **~korps** *das* (*Milit.*) expeditionary force; **~leiter** *der,* **~leiterin** *die* leader of the/an expedition

**Experiment** /ɛksperi'mɛnt/ *das;* **~[e]s, ~e** experiment; **mach keine ~e!** (*ugs.*) (*sei vorsichtig*) don't take any unnecessary risks!; (*bleib bei dem, was du kennst*) why experiment unnecessarily?; **ein filmisches ~:** an experimental film

**Experimental-** /ɛksperimɛn'ta:l-/: **~film** *der* experimental film; **der ~film** experimental cinema; **~physik** *die* experimental physics

**experimentell** /ɛksperimɛn'tɛl/ ❶ *Adj.* experimental. ❷ *adv.* experimentally; **etw. ~ beweisen/bestätigen** prove/confirm sth. experimentally *or* by experiment

**experimentieren** *itr. V.* experiment; **mit etw. ~:** experiment on *or* with sth.

**experimentier-, Experimentier-:** **~freudig** *Adj.* keen to experiment; **~stadium** *das* experimental stage; **~theater** *das* experimental theatre

**Experte** /ɛks'pɛrtə/ *der;* **~n, ~n** expert (**für** in)

**Experten·system** *das* (*DV*) expert system

**Expertin** *die;* **~, ~nen** expert (**für** in)

**Expertise** /ɛkspɛr'ti:zə/ *die;* **~, ~n** expert's report; **eine ~ [über etw.] einholen** obtain an expert opinion [on sth.]

**explizieren** /ɛkspli'tsi:rən/ *tr. V.* (*geh.*) explicate

**explizit** /ɛkspli'tsi:t/ ❶ *Adj.* explicit. ❷ *adv.* ‹describe, define› explicitly

**explizite** /ɛks'pli:tsɪte/ *Adv.* (*geh.*) explicitly

**explodieren** /ɛksplo'di:rən/ *itr. V.; mit sein* (*auch fig.*) explode; ‹costs› rocket

**Explosion** /ɛksplo'zi̯o:n/ *die;* **~, ~en** explosion; **etw. zur ~ bringen** detonate sth.; **eine ~ der Rohstoffpreise** (*fig.*) an explosion in the price of raw materials

**explosions-, Explosions-:** **~artig** ❶ *Adj.* explosive, astronomical ‹growth, increase›; ❷ *adv.* ‹rise› astronomically; **~gefahr** *die* danger of explosion; „**~gefahr!**“ '[Danger,] Explosives!'; **~herd** *der* Ⓐ centre of the explosion; Ⓑ (*Unruheherd*) trouble spot; **~krater** *der* crater; (*Bombenkrater*) bomb crater; **~motor** *der* internal combustion engine; **~welle** *die* shock wave

**explosiv** /ɛksplo'zi:f/ ❶ *Adj.* Ⓐ (*auch fig.*) explosive; Ⓑ (*Sprachw.*) explosive; plosive; **~e Laute** plosives. ❷ *adv.* explosively; **~ reagieren** (*fig.*) react violently

**Explosiv-:** **~geschoss**, ***~geschoß** *das* explosive device; **~laut** *der* (*Sprachw.*) explosive; plosive; **~stoff** *der* ⇒ **Sprengstoff**

**Explosivität** /ɛksplozivi'tɛ:t/ *die* explosiveness

**Exponat** /ɛkspo'na:t/ *das;* **~[e]s, ~e** exhibit

**Exponent** /ɛkspo'nɛnt/ *der;* **~en, ~en** (*Math.*) exponent; (*fig.*) leading exponent

**Exponential-** /ɛksponɛn'tsi̯a:l-/ (*Math.*) exponential ‹function, equation, curve›

**Exponentin** *die;* **~, ~nen** leading exponent

**exponieren** /ɛkspo'ni:rən/ *tr. V.* (*geh.*) (*der Aufmerksamkeit aussetzen*) **jmdn./sich ~:** draw attention to sb./oneself; (*der Gefahr aussetzen*) lay sb./oneself open to attack

**exponiert** *Adj.* exposed

**Export**[1] /ɛks'pɔrt/ *der;* **~[e]s, ~e** Ⓐ (*das ~ieren*) export; exporting; **der ~ nach Afrika** exports to Africa Ⓑ (*das ~ierte*) export;

**Export**[2] *das;* **~s, ~s** export; **zwei ~:** two export

**Export-:** **~ab·teilung** *die* export department; **~artikel** *der* export; **~bier** *das* export beer

**Exporteur** /ɛkspɔr'tøːɐ̯/ *der;* **~s, ~e** (*Wirtsch.*) exporter

**Export-: ~firma** *die* exporter; **~geschäft** *das* (A) export business; (B) (*geschäftlicher Abschluss*) export deal; **~handel** *der* export trade; **~händler** *der,* **~händlerin** *die* exporter

**exportieren** *tr., itr. V.* export

**Export-: ~kauffrau** *die* export saleswoman; **~kaufmann** *der* export salesman; **~quote** *die: ratio of the value of exports to that of the national product*

**Exposé** /ɛkspo'zeː/ *das;* **~s, ~s** (A) exposé; report; (B) (*eines Drehbuchs, Romans usw.*) outline

**Exposition** /ɛkspozi'tsi̯oːn/ *die;* **~, ~en** exposition

**express, *expreß** /ɛks'prɛs/ *Adv.* (A) (*schnell*) express; (B) (*veralt.: absichtlich*) on purpose; deliberately

**Express, *Expreß** *der;* **~es, ~e** (*bes. österr.*) express [train]

**Express-, *Expreß-: ~brief** *der* (*veralt.*) express letter; **~gut** *das* express freight; express goods *pl.*; **etw. als ~gut schicken** send sth. by express goods

**Expressionismus** /ɛksprɛsi̯o'nɪsmʊs/ *der* expressionism *no art.*

**Expressionist** *der;* **~en, ~en, Expressionistin** *die;* **~, ~nen** expressionist

**expressionistisch** ❶ *Adj.* expressionist. ❷ *adv.* expressionistically; ‹influenced› by expressionism

**expressis verbis** /ɛks'prɛsiːs-/ (*geh.*) explicitly

**expressiv** /ɛksprɛ'siːf/ *Adj.* expressive; creative ‹dance›

**Express-, *Expreß-: ~reinigung** *die* express [dry-]cleaning service; **~zug** *der* (*bes. schweiz.*) express [train]

**Expropriation** /ɛksproprіa'tsi̯oːn/ *die;* **~, ~en** (*geh., Soziol.*) expropriation

**exquisit** /ɛkskvi'ziːt/ ❶ *Adj.* exquisite. ❷ *adv.* exquisitely

**Exquisit·geschäft** *das* (*DDR*) shop selling foreign and luxury goods (*for GDR currency*)

**ex tempore** /ɛks'tɛmpore/ *Adv.* (*Theater*) extempore

**Extempore** *das;* **~s, ~s** (*Theater*) improvisation; extemporization

**extemporieren** *itr. V.* (*Theater*) improvise; extemporize

**extensiv** /ɛkstɛn'ziːf/ ❶ *Adj.* (*auch Landw.*) extensive. ❷ *adv.* (A) (*auch Landw.*) extensively; (B) (*Rechtsw.*) **ein Gesetz ~ auslegen** give an extensive interpretation to a law

**Exterieur** /ɛkste'ri̯øːɐ̯/ *das;* **~s, ~s** *u.* **~e** (*geh.*) (*von Menschen*) appearance; (*von Gebäuden*) exterior

**extern** /ɛks'tɛrn/ (*Schulw.*) ❶ *Adj.* external; **ein ~er Schüler** a day boy/girl. ❷ *adv.* **eine Prüfung ~ ablegen** take an examination as an external candidate

**Externe** *der/die; adj. Dekl.* (*Schulw.*) day boy/girl; (*Prüfling*) external candidate

**exterritorial** /ɛkstɛrito'ri̯aːl/ *Adj.* (*Völkerr.*) extraterritorial

**Exterritorialität** /ɛkstɛritori̯ali'tɛːt/ *die* (*Völkerr.*) extraterritoriality

**extra** /'ɛkstra/ ❶ *Adv.* (A) (*gesondert*) ‹pay› separately; **Getränke werden ~ berechnet** drinks are extra; (*ugs. auch attr.*) **ein ~ Bett** a spare bed; (B) (*zusätzlich, besonders*) extra; **~ fein gemahlener Kaffee** extra-fine ground coffee; **dafür brauche ich aber noch 10 DM ~:** but I need another 10 marks for that; **etwas ~ Schönes** something particularly nice; (C) (*eigens*) especially; **etw. ~ für jmdn. tun** do sth. especially *or* just for sb.; **~ deinetwegen** just because of you; (D) (*ugs.: absichtlich*) **etw. ~ tun** do sth. on purpose.
❷ *Adj.* (*bayr., österr.*) **~ sein** be fussy *or* hard to please

**Extra** *das;* **~s, ~s** extra

**extra-, Extra-: ~aus·gabe** *die* (A) (*Zeitung*) special edition; extra; (B) (*Geldausgabe*) extra *or* additional expense; **~blatt** *das* special edition; extra; **~fahrt** *die* (*bes. schweiz.*) special excursion; **~fein** *Adj.* (*ugs.*) really good; superb; **~galaktisch** *Adj.* (*Astron.*) extragalactic

**extrahieren** /ɛkstra'hiːrən/ *tr. V.* (*Med., Chem.*) extract

**Extrakt** /ɛks'trakt/ *der;* **~[e]s, ~e** (A) *fachspr. auch das* extract; (B) (*Zusammenfassung*) summary; synopsis

**Extraktion** /ɛkstrak'tsi̯oːn/ *die;* **~, ~en** (*Med., Chem.*) extraction

**extra-, Extra-: ~ordinarius** *der* (*Hochschulw.*) extraordinary professor; **~polation** /-polatsi̯oːn/ *die;* **~~, ~~en** (*Math.*) extrapolation; **~polieren** *tr., itr. V.* (*Math.*) extrapolate; **~post** *die* (*hist.*) post-chaise; **mit ~post** (*veralt.*) by express post; **~ration** *die* extra ration; **~terrestrisch** /-tɛrɛstrɪʃ/ *Adj.* (*Astron.*) extraterrestrial; **~tour** *die* (*ugs. abwertend*) **sich** (*Dat.*) **ständig irgendwelche ~touren leisten** keep doing things off one's own bat (*Brit.*) *or* on one's own initiative

**extravagant** /-va'gant/ ❶ *Adj.* flamboyant; flamboyantly furnished ‹flat›. ❷ *adv.* flamboyantly

**Extravaganz** /-va'gants/ *die;* **~, ~en** (A) flamboyance; (B) *Pl.* **seine ~en** his flamboyance *sing.*

**extravertiert** /-vɛr'tiːɐ̯t/ *Adj.* (*Psych.*) extrovert[ed]

**Extravertiertheit** *die;* **~** (*Psych.*) extroversion

**Extra·wurst** *die* (A) (*fig. ugs.*) **eine ~ bekommen** get special treatment *or* special favours; **sie will immer eine ~ [gebraten] haben** she always expects to get special treatment; (B) (*österr.*) ⇒ **Lyoner**

**extrem** /ɛks'treːm/ ❶ *Adj.* extreme. ❷ *adv.* extremely; **das Unternehmen hat sich ~ vergrößert** the business has expanded enormously; **~ reagieren** react in an extreme manner

**Extrem** *das;* **~s, ~e** extreme; **von einem ~ ins andere fallen** go from one extreme to another

**Extrem·fall** *der* extreme case

**Extremismus** *der;* **~, Extremismen** extremism; **alle Extremismen** all forms of extremism

**Extremist** *der;* **~en, ~en, Extremistin** *die;* **~, ~nen** extremist

**extremistisch** *Adj.* extremist

**Extremität** /ɛkstremi'tɛːt/ *die;* **~, ~en** (A) extremity; (B) (*das Extremsein*) extremeness

**Extrem-: ~punkt** *der* (*Math.*) extremum; **~situation** *die* extreme situation; extremity; **~wert** *der* (*Math.*) extremum

**extrovertiert** /ɛkstrovɛr'tiːɐ̯t/ ⇒ **extravertiert**

**exzellent** /ɛkstsɛ'lɛnt/ (*geh.*) ❶ *Adj.* excellent. ❷ *adv.* excellently

**Exzellenz** /ɛkstsɛ'lɛnts/ *die;* **~, ~en** ▶ **91** Excellency; **Eure/Seine ~:** Your/His Excellency

**Exzenter** /ɛks'tsɛntɐ/ *der;* **~s, ~** (*Technik*) tappet

**Exzenter·welle** *die* (*Technik*) camshaft; tappet shaft

**Exzentriker** /ɛks'tsɛntrikɐ/ *der;* **~s, ~, Exzentrikerin** *die;* **~, ~nen** eccentric

**exzentrisch** ❶ *Adj.* eccentric. ❷ *adv.* eccentrically

**Exzentrizität** /ɛkstsɛntritsi'tɛːt/ *die;* **~, ~en** eccentricity

**exzeptionell** /ɛkstsɛptsi̯o'nɛl/ *Adj.* (*geh.*) unusual; exceptional ‹case, circumstances›; (*hervorragend*) exceptional

**exzerpieren** /ɛkstsɛr'piːrən/ *tr. V.* (*geh.*) extract ‹reference›; excerpt ‹book›

**Exzerpt** /ɛks'tsɛrpt/ *das;* **~[e]s, ~e** excerpt

**Exzess, *Exzeß** /ɛks'tsɛs/ *der;* **~es, ~e** excess; **etw. bis zum ~ treiben** carry sth. to excess

**exzessiv** /ɛkstsɛ'siːf/ ❶ *Adj.* excessive. ❷ *adv.* excessively

**Eyeliner** /'ailainɐ/ *der;* **~s, ~:** eyeliner

**E-Zug** *der* semi-fast train; stopping train (*Brit.*)

# Ff

f

**f, F** /ɛf/ *das;* ~, ~ Ⓐ (*Buchstabe*) f/F; **nach Schema F** according to a set pattern *or* routine; Ⓑ (*Musik*) [key of] F; ⇒ *auch* **a, A**

**f.** *Abk.* **folgend** f.

**F** *Abk.* **Fahrenheit** F

**Fa.** *Abk.* **Firma**

**Fabel** /ˈfa:bl̩/ *die;* ~, ~**n** Ⓐ (*Literaturw.*) (*Gattung*) fable; (*Kern einer Handlung*) plot; Ⓑ (*Erfundenes*) story; tale; fable; **[jmdm.] eine ~ auftischen** spin [sb.] a yarn; **ins Reich der ~ gehören** belong in the realm of fantasy

**Fabel-:** ~**buch** *das* book of fables; ~**dichter** *der,* ~**dichterin** *die* writer of fables

**fabelhaft** ❶ *Adj.* Ⓐ (*ugs.: großartig*) fantastic (*coll.*); **das ist ja ~:** that's [just] fantastic; Ⓑ (*unglaublich*) fabulous ‹riches›. ❷ *adv.* (*ugs.*) fantastically (*coll.*); fabulously (*coll.*)

**Fabel-:** ~**tier** *das* mythological *or* fabulous creature; ~**welt** *die* fairy tale world; fabulous world

**Fabrik** /faˈbri:k/ *die;* ~, ~**en** factory; (*Papier~, Baumwollspinnerei*) mill; **eine chemische ~:** a chemical works; **in die ~ gehen** (*ugs.*) work in a factory

**Fabrik·anlage** *die* factory; (*Maschinen*) factory plant

**Fabrikant** /fabriˈkant/ *der;* ~**en,** ~**en, Fabrikantin** *die;* ~, ~**nen** manufacturer

**Fabrik·arbeiter** *der,* **Fabrik·arbeiterin** *die* ▶ 159 factory worker

**Fabrikat** /fabriˈka:t/ *das;* ~**[e]s,** ~**e** product; (*Marke*) make

**Fabrikation** /fabrikaˈtsi̯o:n/ *die;* ~**:** production; **die ~ einstellen** stop production

**Fabrikations-:** ~**fehler** *der* manufacturing fault; factory fault; ~**prozess,** *~**prozeß** *der,* ~**verfahren** *das* manufacturing process

**fabrik-, Fabrik-:** ~**besitzer** *der,* ~**besitzerin** *die* factory owner; ~**direktor** *der,* ~**direktorin** *die* works *or* production manager; ~**gebäude** *das* factory building; ~**gelände** *das* factory site; ~**neu** *Adj.* brand-new

**fabriks-, Fabriks-** (*bes. österr.*) ⇒ **fabrik-, Fabrik-**

**Fabrik-:** ~**schiff** *das* factory ship; ~**schorn·stein** *der* factory chimney; ~**tor** *das* factory gate

**fabrizieren** /fabriˈtsi:rən/ *tr. V.* Ⓐ (*ugs. abwertend*) knock together (*coll.*); **Unsinn ~:** make a mess of things; Ⓑ (*veralt.: herstellen*) manufacture; produce

**fabulieren** /fabuˈli:rən/ *itr. V.* invent stories; spin yarns

**Fabulier·lust** *die* delight in making up stories

**Facette** /faˈsɛtə/ *die;* ~, ~**n** facet

**Facetten-:** ~**auge** *das* compound eye; ~**schliff** *der* faceting; **ein Schmuckstein mit ~schliff** a faceted gem

**Fach** /fax/ *das;* ~**[e]s, Fächer** /ˈfɛçɐ/ Ⓐ compartment; (*für Post*) pigeon-hole; **ein ~ für Wäsche** a shelf for linen; ⇒ *auch* **Dach** A; Ⓑ (*Studienrichtung, Unterrichtsfach*) subject; (*Wissensgebiet*) field; (*Berufszweig*) trade; **ein Meister seines ~es** a master of his trade; **das schlägt [nicht] in mein ~:** that is [not] my province; **vom ~ sein** be an expert; **ein Mann vom ~:** an expert

**fach-, Fach-:** ~**arbeiter** *der,* ~**arbeiterin** *die* skilled worker; craftsman; ~**arzt** *der,* ~**ärztin** *die* ▶ 159 specialist (**für** in); ~**ausdruck** *der,* ~**begriff,** *der* technical *or* specialist term; ~**bereich** *der* (*Hochschulw.*) faculty; school; (*in der Schule*) department; ~**bezogen** *Adj.* specialized ‹training›; ~**blatt** *das* specialist journal; ~**buch** *das* (*Abhandlung*) specialist book; (*Nachschlagewerk*) reference book; (*Lehrbuch*) textbook

**fächeln** /ˈfɛçl̩n/ ❶ *tr. V.* fan. ❷ *itr. V.* ‹breeze› blow gently

**Fächer** /ˈfɛçɐ/ *der;* ~**s,** ~**:** fan; (*fig.*) range

**fächer-, Fächer-:** ~**artig** ❶ *Adj.* fan-like; ❷ *adv.* like a fan; ~**besen** *der* (*Gartenbau*) wire-tooth rake; ~**gewölbe** *das* fan vault

**fächern** ❶ *refl. V.* fan out. ❷ *tr. V.* (*fig.*) diversify; **das Angebot ist breit gefächert** there is a wide range to choose from

**Fächer·palme** *die* fan palm

**Fächerung** *die;* ~, ~**en** (*fig.*) diversity

**fach-, Fach-:** ~**frau** *die* expert; ~**fremd** *Adj.* ~**fremde Methoden** methods alien to the subject; ~**fremde Ausdrücke/Vorstellungen** layman's terms/ideas; ~**gebiet** *das* field; ~**gelehrte** *der/die* specialist (**für** in); ~**gerecht** ❶ *Adj.* correct; ❷ *adv.* correctly; ~**geschäft** *das* specialist shop; **ein ~geschäft für Sportartikel/Eisenwaren** *usw.* a specialist sports shop/ironmonger's; ~**gespräch** *das* technical discussion; ~**gruppe** *die* section; ~**handel** *der* specialist shops *pl.;* ~**hoch·schule** *die* college (*offering courses in a special subject*); ~**hochschule für Musik** academy of music; ~**idiot** *der* (*abwertend*) *person who has no interests outside his/her subject;* ~**jargon** *der* (*abwertend*) technical jargon; ~**kenntnis** *die* specialized *or* specialist knowledge; ~**kraft** *die* skilled worker; ~**kreise** *Pl.* **in ~n** in specialist circles; ~**kundig** ❶ *Adj.* knowledgeable; ❷ *adv.* **jmdn. ~kundig beraten** give sb. informed *or* expert advice; ~**lehrer** *der,* ~**lehrerin** *die* subject teacher

**fachlich** ❶ *Adj.* specialist ‹knowledge, work›; technical ‹problem, explanation, experience›; ~**e Ausbildung/Qualifikation** training/qualification in the subject. ❷ *adv.* **etw. ~ beurteilen** give a professional opinion on sth.; ~ **qualifiziert** qualified in the subject

**fach-, Fach-:** ~**literatur** *die* specialist literature; (*bes. naturwissenschaftlich auch*) technical literature; **in der medizinischen ~literatur** in the specialist medical literature; ~**mann** *der; Pl.* ~**männer** *od.* ~**leute** expert; ~**männisch** ❶ *Adj.* expert; ❷ *adv.* **jmdn. ~männisch beraten** give sb. expert advice; ~**ober·schule** *die: college specializing in particular subjects;* ~**presse** *die* specialist/technical publications *pl.;* ⇒ *auch* ~**literatur;** ~**richtung** *die* ⇒ **Fach** B

**Fachschaft** *die;* ~, ~**en** Ⓐ (*einer Berufsgruppe*) professional association; Ⓑ (*von Studenten*) student body of the/a faculty

**fach-, Fach-:** ~**schule** *die* technical college; ~**simpelei** /-zɪmpəˈlai̯/ *die;* ~~, ~~**en** (*ugs. abwertend*) shop talk; ~**simpeleien** shop talk *sing.;* ~**simpeln** /-zɪmpl̩n/ *itr. V.* (*ugs. abwertend*) talk shop; ~**sprache** *die* technical terminology *or* language; ~**sprachlich** *Adj.* technical; ~**tagung** *die* [specialist] conference; ~**terminus** *der* specialist/technical term; ⇒ *auch* ~**literatur;** ~**text** *der* specialist text; ~**übergreifend** ❶ *Adj.* inter-disciplinary ‹teaching›; ❷ *adv.* ‹think, argue› along interdisciplinary lines; ‹teach› using interdisciplinary methods; ~**verband** *der* trade association; ~**welt** *die* experts *pl.;* **in der ~welt** among experts

**Fach·werk** *das* Ⓐ (*Bauweise*) half-timbered construction; Ⓑ (*Balkengerippe*) half-timbering

**Fachwerk·haus** *das* half-timbered house

**Fach-:** ~**wissenschaftler** *der,* ~**wissenschaftlerin** *die* specialist; ~**wort** *das; Pl.* ~**wörter** technical *or* specialist term; ~**wörter·buch** *das* specialist/technical dictionary; ⇒ *auch* ~**literatur;** ~**zeit·schrift** *die* specialist/technical journal; ⇒ *auch* ~**literatur**

**Fackel** /ˈfakl̩/ *die;* ~, ~**n** torch; **die ~ des Krieges** (*fig.*) the flames of war; **die ~ der Revolution/der Hoffnung** (*fig.*) the flame of revolution/hope; **von ~n erleuchtet sein** be torchlit *or* lit by torches; **wie lebende ~n** like human torches

**fackeln** *itr. V.* (*ugs.*) shilly-shally (*coll.*); dither; **nicht lange gefackelt!** no shilly-shallying! (*coll.*); don't dither about!

**Fackel-:** ~**schein** *der* torchlight; **im ~schein** by torchlight; ~**träger** *der,* ~**trägerin** *die* torch-bearer; ~**zug** *der* torchlight procession

**fad** /fa:t/ (*bes. südd., österr.*) ⇒ **fade**

**Fädchen** /ˈfɛ:tçən/ *das;* ~**s,** ~**:** short, thin thread

**fade** /ˈfa:də/ *Adj.* Ⓐ (*schal*) insipid; **ein ~r Beigeschmack** (*fig.*) a flat aftertaste; Ⓑ (*bes. südd., österr.: langweilig*) dull; Ⓒ (*südd., österr.: zimperlich*) **sei nicht ~!** don't be such a sissy!

**fädeln** /ˈfɛ:dl̩n/ *tr. V.* thread; **etw. auf eine Schnur ~:** thread sth. on to a string

**Faden**[1] /ˈfa:dn̩/ *der;* ~**s, Fäden** /ˈfɛ:dn̩/ Ⓐ (*Garn*) thread; **ein ~:** a piece of thread; **sich wie ein roter ~ durch etw. ziehen** run like a thread through sth.; **der rote ~** (*fig.*) the central theme; **den ~ verlieren** (*fig.*) lose the thread; **er hat** *od.* **hält alle Fäden in der Hand** (*fig.*) he holds the reins; **er hält alle Fäden fest in der Hand** (*fig.*) he keeps a tight rein on everything; **an einem dünnen** *od.* **seidenen ~ hängen** (*fig.*) hang by a single thread; **seine Fäden spinnen** (*fig.*) spin a web of intrigue; **keinen trockenen ~ mehr am Leibe haben** (*ugs.*) be wet through *or* soaked to the skin; ⇒ *auch* **Strich** H; Ⓑ (*fig.*) **ein schmaler ~ Blut** a thin trickle of blood; **graue Fäden im Haar haben** have a grey hair here and there; **Fäden ziehen** ‹cheese etc.› be soft and stringy; Ⓒ (*Med.*) suture; **die Fäden ziehen** remove the stitches

**Faden**[2] *der;* ~**s,** ~ (*Seemannsspr.*) fathom

**faden-, Faden-:** ~**kreuz** *das* cross hairs *pl.;* ~**lauf** *der* grain [of the cloth]; ~**molekül** *das* linear molecule; ~**nudeln** *Pl.* (*Kochk.*) vermicelli *sing.;* ~**scheinig** /-ʃainɪç/ *Adj.* Ⓐ (*fig. abwertend: nicht glaubhaft*) threadbare ‹morality›; flimsy ‹argument, reason, excuse›; Ⓑ (*abgewetzt*) threadbare ‹clothes›; ~**spiel** *das* cat's cradle; ~**stärke** *die* thickness (*of wool*); ~**wurm** *der* (*Zool.*) threadworm

**Fadheit** *die;* ~, ~**en** ⇒ **fade** A, B: insipidness; dullness

**Fagott** /faˈgɔt/ *das;* ~**[e]s,** ~**e** bassoon

**Fagottist** *der;* ~**en,** ~**en, Fagottistin** *die;* ~, ~**nen** bassoonist

**Fähe** /ˈfɛ:ə/ *die;* ~, ~**n** (*Jägerspr.*) (*Fuchsfähe*) vixen; bitch; (*Dachsfähe*) sow; bitch

**fähig** /ˈfɛ:ɪç/ *Adj.* Ⓐ (*begabt*) able; capable; **ich halte ihn für einen ~en Kopf** I think he has an able mind; Ⓑ (*bereit, in der Lage*) **zu etw. ~ sein** be capable of sth.; **er ist zu allem ~:** he is capable of anything; **~ sein, etw. zu tun** be capable of doing sth.

**Fähigkeit** *die;* ~, ~**en** Ⓐ ability; capability; **menschliche ~en** human faculties; **geistige ~en** intellectual faculties *or* abilities;

**praktische ~en** practical skills; **jmds. ~en wecken** awaken sb.'s talents; **seine ~en für etw. einsetzen** use one's abilities for sth.; **B** (*Imstandesein*) ability (**zu** to)

**Fähigkeits·nachweis** *der* certificate of proficiency

**fahl** /faːl/ *Adj.* pale; pallid; wan ‹light, smile›; **~ schien der Mond ins Zimmer** the moon shone wanly into the room

**fahl-: ~blau** *Adj.* pale blue; **~blond** *Adj.* ash-blond; **~gelb** pale yellow

**Fahlheit** *die;* **~:** paleness; pallor

**Fähnchen** /ˈfɛːnçən/ *das;* **~s, ~ A** little flag; **~ schwenken** wave flags; **B** (*ugs. abwertend: Kleid*) **ein billiges ~:** a cheap frock (*Brit.*) *or* dress

**fahnden** /ˈfaːndn̩/ *itr. V.* search (**nach** for)

**Fahndung** *die;* **~, ~en** search

**Fahndungs-: ~aktion** *die* search operation; **~apparat** *der:* **der gesamte ~apparat der Polizei ist eingesetzt worden** the police have committed all their available resources to the search; **~blatt** *das,* **~liste** *die* wanted list

**Fahne** /ˈfaːnə/ *die;* **~, ~n A** flag; **B** (*fig.*) **etw. auf seine ~n schreiben** espouse the cause of sth.; **seine ~ nach dem Wind[e] hängen** trim one's sails to the wind; **mit fliegenden ~n zu jmdm./etw. übergehen** *od.* (*abwertend*) **überlaufen** openly and suddenly turn one's coat; **zu den ~n eilen** (*veralt.*) join the colours; **jmdn. zu den ~n rufen** (*veralt.*) call sb. to the colours; **C** (*ugs.: Alkoholgeruch*) smell of alcohol on sb.'s breath; **eine ~ haben** reek of alcohol; **D** (*Druckw.*) galley

**fahnen-, Fahnen-: ~eid** *der* oath of allegiance; **~flucht** *die* desertion; **~flucht begehen** desert; **~flüchtig** *Adj.* **~flüchtig werden/sein** desert/be a deserter; **~geschmückt** *Adj.* decorated with flags *postpos.;* **~korrektur** (*Druckw.*) (*Fahne*) galley proof; (*Korrekturlesen*) **die ~korrektur muss bald erfolgen** the galley proofs will have to be read soon; **~mast** *der,* **~stange** *die* flagpole; **das Ende der ~stange ist erreicht** (*fig.*) that's as far as we/they *etc.* can go; **~träger** *der,* **~trägerin** *die* standard-bearer; **~weihe** *die* consecration of the flag

**Fähnlein** /ˈfɛːnlai̯n/ *das;* **~s, ~** (*hist.*) small troop

**Fähnrich** /ˈfɛːnrɪç/ *der;* **~s, ~e** (*Milit.*) **~,** (*Marine*) **~ zur See** ensign

**Fahr·ausweis** *der* **A** (*Amtsspr.: Fahrschein*) ticket; **B** (*schweiz.: Führerschein*) driving licence

**Fahr·bahn** *die* carriageway; **die linke/rechte ~:** the left-hand/right-hand side of the road; **beim Überqueren der ~:** when crossing the road *or* (*formeller*) carriageway

**Fahrbahn-: ~belag** *der* road surface; **~breite** *die* road width; **~markierung** *die* road marking

**fahrbar** *Adj.* ‹table, bed› on castors; mobile ‹crane, kitchen, etc.›; **ein ~er Untersatz** (*ugs.*) wheels *pl.* (*joc.*)

**fahr·bereit** *Adj.* ‹car etc.› in running order; **wir sind ~:** we're ready to go

**Fahr·bereitschaft** *die* motor pool

**Fähr·betrieb** *der* ferry service; (*von mehreren Fähren*) ferry services *pl.*

**Fahr-: ~bücherei** *die* mobile library; **~damm** *der* (*bes. berlin.*) ⇨ **~bahn**; **~dienst·leiter** *der,* **~dienst·leiterin** *die* (*Eisenb.*) train controller; **~draht** *der* overhead contact wire

**Fähre** /ˈfɛːrə/ *die;* **~, ~n** ferry

**Fahr·eigenschaft** *die* (*Kfz-W.*) handling characteristic; **~en** handling

**fahren** /ˈfaːrən/ **1** *unr. itr. V.; mit sein* **A** ▶ **348** (*als Fahrzeuglenker*) drive; (*mit dem Fahrrad, Motorrad usw.*) ride; (*mit dem Kinderroller*) scooter; (*auf Skiern*) ski; (*mit Rollschuhen*) [roller-]skate; (*mit Schlittschuhen*) [ice-]skate; (*mit dem Rodelschlitten*) toboggan; **mit dem Auto ~:** drive; (*her~ auch*) come by car; (*hin~ auch*) go by car; **mit dem Fahrrad/Motorrad ~:** cycle/motorcycle; come/go by bicycle/motorcycle; **mit 80 km/h ~:** drive/ride at 80 k.p.h.; **links/rechts ~:** drive on the left/right; (*abbiegen*) bear *or* turn left/right; **langsam ~:** drive/ride slowly; **langsamer ~:** slow down; **gegen etw. ~:** go into sth.; **wie fährt man am schnellsten zum Bahnhof?** what is the quickest route to the station [by car/motorcycle *etc.*]?; **B** (*mit dem Auto usw. als Mitfahrer; mit dem Bus, der Straßenbahn, U-Bahn, dem Taxi, Zug, Schiff, Luftschiff, Schlitten usw., ugs. mit dem Flugzeug*) go; (*mit dem Aufzug/der Rolltreppe/der Seilbahn/dem Skilift*) take the lift (*Brit.*) *or* (*Amer.*) elevator/escalator/cable car/ski lift; (*mit der Achterbahn, dem Karussell usw.*) ride (**auf** + *Dat.* on); (*per Anhalter*) hitch-hike; **mit dem Auto/Bus/Zug** *usw.* **~:** go by car/bus/train *etc.;* **erster/zweiter Klasse/zum halben Preis ~:** travel *or* go first/second class/at half-price; **ich fahre nicht gern [im] Auto/Bus** I don't like travelling in cars/buses; **fährst du mit mir?** are you coming with me?; **sollen wir ~ oder zu Fuß gehen?** shall we go by car/bus *etc.* or walk?; **mit Chauffeur ~:** be driven round by a chauffeur; **ich will noch mal ~!** (*auf der Achterbahn usw.*) I want to have another ride!; **C** (*reisen*) go; **in Urlaub ~:** go on holiday; **ins Wochenende gefahren sein** (*vom Arbeitsplatz aus gesehen*) have left for the weekend; (*von zu Hause*) have gone away for the weekend; ⇨ *auch* **Himmel** B; **Hölle** A; **D** (*los~*) go; leave; **E** ‹motor vehicle, train, lift, cable car› go; ‹ship› sail; **mein Auto fährt nicht** my car won't go; **der Wagen fährt sehr ruhig** the car is very quiet *or* runs very quietly; **der Aufzug fährt heute nicht** the lift (*Brit.*) *or* (*Amer.*) elevator is out of service today; **F** (*verkehren*) run; **der Bus fährt alle fünf Minuten/bis Goetheplatz** the bus runs *or* goes every five minutes/goes to Goetheplatz; **hier fährt dreimal täglich eine Fähre** there are three ferries a day from here; **von München nach Passau fährt ein D-Zug** there's a fast train from Munich to Passau; **G** (*mit bestimmtem Treibstoff*) **mit Diesel/Benzin ~:** run on diesel/petrol (*Brit.*) *or* (*Amer.*) gasoline; **mit Dampf/Atomkraft ~:** be steam-powered/atomic-powered; **H** (*schnelle Bewegungen ausführen*) **in die Kleider ~:** leap into one's clothes; **in die Höhe ~:** jump up [with a start]; **der Blitz ist in einen Baum gefahren** the lightning struck a tree; **jmdm. an die Kehle ~:** leap at sb.'s throat; **sich** (*Dat.*) **mit der Hand durch das Haar ~:** run one's fingers through one's hair; **was ist denn in dich gefahren?** (*fig.*) what's got into you?; **der Schreck fuhr ihm in die Glieder** (*fig.*) the shock went right through him; **ein Gedanke fuhr ihm durch den Kopf** (*fig.*) an idea flashed through his mind; **jmdm. über den Mund ~** (*fig.*) shut sb. up; **aus der Haut ~** (*ugs.*) blow one's top (*coll.*); **etw. ~ lassen** (*loslassen*) let sth. go; (*fig.: aufgeben*) abandon sth.; **I** (*Erfahrungen machen*) **gut/schlecht mit jmdm./einer Sache ~:** get on well/badly with sb./sth.; **er ist schlecht damit gefahren, den Arbeitsplatz zu wechseln** his change of job turned out badly for him.

**2** *unr. tr. V.* **A** (*fortbewegen*) drive ‹car, lorry, train, etc.›; ride ‹bicycle, motorcycle›; **ein Boot ~:** sail a boat; **Auto/Motorrad/Roller ~:** drive [a car]/ride a motorcycle/scooter; **Kahn** *od.* **Boot/Kanu ~:** go boating/canoeing; **Ski ~:** ski; **Schlitten ~:** toboggan; **Rollschuh ~:** [roller-]skate; **Schlittschuh ~:** [ice-]skate; **Aufzug/Rolltreppe ~:** ride up and down in the lift (*Brit.*) *or* (*Amer.*) elevator/on the escalator; **Sessellift ~:** ride in a/the chairlift; **U-Bahn ~:** ride on the underground (*Brit.*) *or* (*Amer.*) subway; **B** *mit sein* ([*als Strecke*] *zurücklegen*) drive; (*mit dem Motorrad, Fahrrad*) ride; take ‹curve›; **einen Umweg/eine Umleitung ~:** make a detour/follow a diversion; **der Zug fährt jetzt eine andere Strecke** the train takes a different route now; **er fährt seine 26. Runde** he is on his twenty-sixth lap; **C** (*befördern*) drive, take ‹person›; take ‹thing›; ‹vehicle› take; ‹ship, lorry, etc.› carry ‹goods›; (*zum Sprecher*) drive, bring ‹person›; bring ‹thing›; ‹vehicle› bring; **jmdn. über den Fluss ~:** ferry sb. across the river; **D** *mit sein* (*mit einer bestimmten Geschwindigkeit*) **50/80 km/h ~:** do 50/80 k.p.h.; **hier muss man 50 km/h ~:** you've got to keep to 50 k.p.h. here; **E** *meist mit sein* (*als Teilnehmer mit~ bei*) **ein Rennen ~:** take part in a race; **F** *meist mit sein* (*erzielen*) **einen Rekord ~:** set a record; **1:23:45/eine gute Zeit ~:** do *or* clock 1.23.45/a good time; **G** *mit sein* (*leisten*) **der Wagen fährt 210 km/h** the car will do 210 k.p.h.; **H** (*in einen schlechten Zustand bringen*) **ein Auto schrottreif** *od.* **zu Schrott ~:** write off a car; (*durch lange Beanspruchung*) run *or* drive a car into the ground; **eine Beule in den Kotflügel ~:** dent the wing; **jmdm. eine Schramme in den Kotflügel ~:** scratch sb.'s wing; **I** (*als Treibstoff benutzen*) use ‹diesel, regular, etc.›; **J** (*auf Roll-, Schlittschuhen ausführen*) skate; **K** (*Technik: bedienen*) operate; **einen Hochofen ~:** control a blast furnace; **L** (*Rundf.: senden*) broadcast ‹programme›; **M** (*arbeiten*) **eine Sonderschicht ~:** do *or* work an extra shift.

**3** *unr. refl. V.* **A** **sich gut ~** ‹car› handle well, be easy to drive; **wie fährt sich so ein Rennboot?** how does a power boat like that handle?; **B** *mit sein* (*unpers.*) **in dem Wagen fährt es sich bequem** the car gives a comfortable ride; **auf dieser Straße/mit dem Zug fährt es sich angenehm** this road is pleasant to drive on/it's pleasant travelling by train

**fahrend** *Adj.* itinerant; **~er Sänger** wandering minstrel; **~es Volk** travelling people *pl.*

**Fahrenheit** ⇨ **Grad** C

***fahren|lassen** ⇨ **fahren** 1H

**Fahrens·mann** *der; Pl.* **Fahrensmänner** *od.* **Fahrensleute** (*Seemannsspr.*) sailor

**Fahrer** *der;* **~s, ~** ▶ **159** driver; **„Nicht mit dem ~ sprechen!"** 'Passengers must not talk to the driver'

**Fahrerei** *die;* **~, ~en** (*Fahrweise*) driving; (*dauerndes Fahren*) driving/riding around

**Fahrer-: ~flucht** *die:* **wegen ~flucht** for failing to stop after [being involved in] an accident; **~flucht begehen** fail to stop after [being involved in] an accident; **~haus** *das* [driver's] cab

**Fahrerin** *die;* **~, ~nen** ▶ **159** driver; ⇨ *auch* **-in**

**fahrerisch 1** *Adj.* **~es Können** driving skill; skill as a driver. **2** *adv.* **jmdm. ~ überlegen sein** be a better driver than sb.

**Fahrer·kabine** *die* [driver's] cab

**Fahr-: ~erlaubnis** *die* (*Amtsspr.*) driving licence; **jmdm. die ~erlaubnis entziehen** disqualify sb. from driving; **~gast** *der* passenger; **~geld** *das* fare; **~geld·erstattung** *die* reimbursement of travelling expenses; **~gelegenheit** *die* means of transport; **~gemeinschaft** *die* car pool; **~geschwindigkeit** *die* speed; **~gestell** *das* **A** (*Kfz-W.*) chassis; **B** (*bei Kränen, Eisenbahnwagen, Maschinen*) bogie (*Brit.*); (*Lafette*) gun carriage; (*beim Flugzeug*) undercarriage; **C** (*scherzh.: Beine*) legs *pl.*

**Fähr·hafen** *der* ferry terminal

**fahrig** /ˈfaːrɪç/ *Adj.* nervous, agitated ‹movements›; nervous and fidgety ‹student, pupil›

**Fahrigkeit** *die;* **~:** nervousness and fidgetiness

**Fahr·karte** *die* ticket; **eine ~ schießen** (*ugs.*) miss completely

**Fahrkarten-: ~ausgabe** *die* ticket office; **~automat** *der* ticket machine; **~kontrolleur** *der,* **~kontrolleurin** *die* (*im Bus*) inspector; (*im Zug*) ticket inspector; **~schalter** *der* ticket window; **~verkäufer** *der,* **~verkäuferin** *die* ticket office clerk

**fahr-, Fahr-: ~kilometer** *der* (*im Bus*) kilometre [travelled]; (*eines Autos*) kilometre [covered]; **~komfort** *der* [passenger] comfort; **~kunst** *die* driving skills *pl.;* **~lässig**

*old spelling (see note on page 1707)

❶ *Adj.* negligent ‹behaviour›; **~lässige Tötung/Körperverletzung** (*Rechtsw.*) causing death/injury through *or* by [culpable] negligence; ❷ *adv.* negligently; **er hat den Tod des Fußgängers ~lässig verschuldet** he was responsible for *or* guilty of causing the death of the pedestrian through *or* by culpable negligence; **~lässigkeit** *die* negligence; **~lehrer** *der*, **~lehrerin** *die* ▶ 159 driving instructor; **~leistung** *die* performance

**Fähr·mann** *der; Pl.* **Fähr·männer** *od.* **Fähr·leute** ▶ 159 ferryman

**Fahrnis** *die;* ~, **~se** (*Rechtsw.*) chattels *pl.;* movables *pl.*

**Fährnis** *die;* ~, **~se** (*veralt.*) peril

**Fahr·personal** *das* crew

**Fahr·plan** *der* Ⓐ timetable; schedule (*Amer.*); **den ~ einhalten** run to schedule *or* on time; Ⓑ (*ugs.: Vorhaben*) plans *pl.;* **den ~ durcheinander bringen** upset the entire schedule *or* all the arrangements

**fahrplan·mäßig** ❶ *Adj.* scheduled ‹departure, arrival›; **der verspätete Schnellzug nach Köln, ~e Abfahrt 16.30 ...** the delayed fast train to Cologne, due to depart at 16.30, ... ❷ *adv.* ‹depart, arrive› according to schedule, on time

**Fahr·praxis** *die* driving experience

**Fahr·preis** *der* fare

**Fahrpreis-: ~anzeiger** *der* taximeter; **~erhöhung** *die* fare increase; increase in fares; **~ermäßigung** *die* reduction in fares; **eine ~ermäßigung erhalten** be given concessionary fares

**Fahr·prüfung** *die* driving test

**Fahr·rad** *das* bicycle; cycle; **mit dem ~ fahren** cycle; ride a bicycle

**Fahrrad-: ~computer** *der* cycle computer; **~fahrer** *der*, **~fahrerin** *die* cyclist; **~händler** *der*, **~händlerin** *die* bicycle dealer; **etw. beim ~händler kaufen** buy sth. from a/the bicycle shop; **~handlung** *die* bicycle shop; **~kette** *die* bicycle chain; **~kurier** *der* bicycle *or* bike messenger; bicycle *or* bike courier; **~lampe** *die* bicycle lamp; **~pumpe** *die* bicycle pump; **~schlüssel** *der* Ⓐ (*für das Schloss*) bicycle-lock key; Ⓑ (*Schraubenschlüssel*) bicycle spanner; **~ständer** *der* bicycle rack *or* stand; **~weg** *der* cycle path

**Fahr·rinne** *die* shipping channel; fairway

**Fahr·schein** *der* ticket

**Fahrschein-: ~automat** *der* ticket machine; **~entwerter** *der* ticket cancelling machine; **~heft** *das* book of tickets

**Fähr·schiff** *das* ferry

**Fahr-: ~schule** *die* Ⓐ (*Unternehmen*) driving school; Ⓑ (*ugs.: Unterricht*) driving lessons *pl;* **~schüler** *der*, **~schülerin** *die* Ⓐ learner driver; Ⓑ *pupil who must use transport to get to school;* **~sicherheit** *die* safe driving *no art.;* **die ~sicherheit erhöhen** make driving safer; **~spur** *die* traffic lane; **die ~spur wechseln/beibehalten** change lanes/stay in one's lane

**fährst** /fɛ:ɐst/ *2. Pers. Sg. Präsens v.* **fahren**

**Fahr-: ~stil** *der* style of driving; (*mit dem Rad*) style of riding; (*auf Skiern*) style of skiing; **~streifen** *der* ⇒ **~spur**

**Fahr·stuhl** *der* lift (*Brit.*); elevator (*Amer.*); (*für Lasten*) hoist; **mit dem ~ fahren** take the lift/elevator

**Fahrstuhl-: ~führer** *der*, **~führerin** *die* lift attendant (*Brit.*); elevator operator (*Amer.*); **~schacht** *der* lift shaft (*Brit.*); elevator shaft (*Amer.*)

**Fahr·stunde** *die* driving lesson

**Fahrt** /fa:ɐ̯t/ *die;* ~, **~en** Ⓐ ▶ 265 (*das Fahren*) journey; **„während der ~ nicht hinauslehnen!"** 'do not lean out of the window while the train is in motion'; **freie ~ haben** have a clear run; (*fig.*) have been given the green light; Ⓑ (*Reise*) journey; (*Schiffsreise*) voyage; **auf der ~:** on the journey; Ⓒ (*kurze Reise, Ausflug*) trip; (*Wanderung*) hike; **eine ~ [nach/zu X] machen** go on *or* take a trip [to X]; **eine ~ ins Blaue machen** (*mit dem Auto*) go for a drive; (*Veranstaltung*) go on a mystery tour; **auf ~ gehen** (*veralt.*) go hiking; Ⓓ (*Geschwindigkeit*) **in voller ~:** at full speed; **die ~ verlangsamen** slow down; decelerate; **die ~ beschleunigen** speed up; accelerate; **die ~ aufnehmen** gather speed; pick up speed; **kleine ~ machen** (*Seemannsspr.*) sail slowly; **in ~ kommen** *od.* **geraten** (*ugs.*) get going; (*böse werden*) get worked up; **jmdn. in ~ bringen** (*ugs.*) get sb. going; (*böse machen*) get sb. worked up; Ⓔ (*Seemannsspr.*) **Kapitän auf großer ~:** foreign trade master; **das Patent für kleine ~:** master's certificate for coastal trade *or* home trade

**-fahrt** *die;* ~, **~en: Frankreich~/Ostasien~:** trip to France/East Asia

**fährt** /fɛ:ɐt/ *3. Pers. Sg. Präsens v.* **fahren**

**fahr·tauglich** *Adj.* fit to drive *postpos.*

**Fahr·tauglichkeit** *die* fitness to drive

**fahrt-, Fahrt-: ~ausweis** *der* ⇒ **Fahrausweis**; **~bereit** ⇒ **fahrbereit**; **~dauer** *die* travelling time

**Fährte** /'fɛ:ɐ̯tə/ *die* tracks *pl.;* trail; **die ~ aufnehmen** pick up the trail *or* scent; **Hunde auf die ~ setzen** put hounds on the track; **jmds. ~ verfolgen** track sb.; **die richtige ~ finden** (*fig.*) get on the right track; **die falsche ~ verfolgen** (*fig.*) be on the wrong track; **jmdn. auf eine falsche ~ locken** (*fig.*) put sb. on the wrong track

**Fahrten-: ~buch** *das* Ⓐ (*Kontrollbuch*) logbook; Ⓑ (*Tagebuch*) [rambler's] diary; **~messer** *das* sheath knife; **~schreiber** *der* tachograph; **~schwimmer** *der*, **~schwimmerin** *die* advanced swimmer; **den ~schwimmer machen** (*ugs.*) take the advanced swimmer's test

**Fahrt·kosten** *Pl.* (*für öffentliche Verkehrsmittel*) fare/fares; (*für Autoreisen*) travel costs; **die ~ erstatten** pay travelling expenses

**Fahr·treppe** *die* escalator

**Fahrt·richtung** *die* direction; **in ~ Innenstadt** in the direction of the town centre; **die Autobahn ist in ~ Norden gesperrt** the northbound carriageway of the motorway is closed; **in ~ parken** park in the direction of the traffic; **die ~ ändern** change direction; **gegen die ~ sitzen** (*im Zug*) sit with one's back to the engine; (*im Bus*) facing backwards; **in ~ sitzen** (*im Zug*) sit facing the engine; (*im Bus*) facing forwards

**Fahrtrichtungs·anzeiger** *der* (*Kfz-W.*) Ⓐ (*Blinklicht*) [direction] indicator; Ⓑ (*Hinweistafel*) destination board

**Fahrt·schreiber** *der* ⇒ **Fahrtenschreiber**

**fahr·tüchtig** *Adj.* ‹driver› fit to drive; ‹vehicle› roadworthy

**Fahr·tüchtigkeit** *die* (*des Fahrers*) fitness to drive; (*des Fahrzeugs*) roadworthiness

**Fahrt-: ~unterbrechung** *die* break [in the journey]; stop; **eine ~unterbrechung ist [nicht] möglich** passengers may [not] break their journey; **~wind** *der* airflow; **~ziel** *das* destination

**fahr·untüchtig** *Adj.* ‹driver› unfit to drive; ‹vehicle› unroadworthy

**Fähr·verbindung** *die* ferry link

**Fahr-: ~verbot** *das* disqualification from driving; driving ban; **jmdm. [ein] ~verbot erteilen** ban *or* disqualify sb. from driving; **~verhalten** *das* Ⓐ (*des ~ers*) behaviour as a driver; Ⓑ (*des ~zeuges*) performance

**Fähr·verkehr** *der* ferry traffic

**Fahr-: ~wasser** *das* shipping channel; fairway; **in ein gefährliches ~wasser geraten** (*fig.*) get on to dangerous ground; **in ein politisches ~wasser geraten** (*fig.*) stumble into a political minefield; **in jmds. ~wasser schwimmen** *od.* **segeln** (*fig.*) follow [along] in sb.'s wake; **~weise** *die* way of driving; **seine ~weise** the way he drives; **~werk** *das* Ⓐ (*Flugw.*) undercarriage; Ⓑ (*Kfz-W.*) ⇒ **~gestell**; **~wind** *der* Ⓐ (*Segelfliegen*) wind; Ⓑ ⇒ **Fahrtwind**; **~zeit** *die* travelling time; **eine ~zeit von wenigen Minuten/Stunden** a few minutes'/hours' travelling time; **nach einer ~zeit von zwei Stunden** after travelling for two hours

**Fahr·zeug** *das* vehicle; (*Luft~*) aircraft; (*Wasser~*) vessel

**Fahrzeug-: ~bau** *der* motor manufacturing industry; **~brief** *der* ⇒ **Kraftfahrzeugbrief**; **~führer** *der*, **~führerin** *die* driver of a/the motor vehicle; **~halter** *der*, **~halterin** *die* registered keeper [of a/the vehicle]; **~kolonne** *die* convoy of vehicles; **~papiere** *Pl.* vehicle documents *pl.;* **~verkehr** *der* traffic

**Faible** /'fɛ:bl̩/ *das;* **~s**, **~s** liking; (*Schwäche*) weakness; **ein ~ für etw. haben** have a weakness for sth.

**fair** /fɛ:ɐ̯/ ❶ *Adj.* fair (**gegen** to). ❷ *adv.* fairly; **~ spielen** play fairly *or* (*coll.*) fair

**Fairness**, ***Fairneß** /'fɛ:ɐ̯nɛs/ *die;* **~:** fairness

**Fairness·pokal**, ***Fairneß·pokal** *der* (*Sport*) *cup for the most sporting competitor*

**Fairplay** /'fɛə'pleɪ/ *das;* **~:** fair play

**Fait accompli** /fɛtakõ'pli/ *das;* ~, **Faits accomplis** (*geh.*) fait accompli

**Fäkalien** /fɛ'ka:li̯ən/ *Pl.* faeces *pl.*

**Fakir** /'fa:ki:ɐ̯, *österr.:* fa'ki:ɐ̯/ *der;* **~s**, **~e** fakir

**Faksimile** /fak'zi:mile/ *das;* **~s**, **~s** facsimile

**Faksimile-: ~aus·gabe** *die* facsimile edition; **~druck** *der; Pl.* **~~e** printed facsimile

**Fakt** /fakt/ *das od. der;* **~[e]s**, **~en** *od.* **~s** fact

**Fakten** ⇒ **Faktum**

**Fakten-: ~material** *das* facts *pl.;* **~wissen** *das* factual knowledge

**Faktion** /fak'tsi̯o:n/ *die;* ~, **~en** (*veralt.*, *schweiz.*) faction

**faktisch** ❶ *Adj.* real; actual; **der ~e Nachteil/Nutzen** the practical disadvantage/usefulness. ❷ *adv.* Ⓐ **das bedeutet ~ ...** it means in effect ...; **es ist ~ möglich/unmöglich** it is in actual fact possible/impossible; Ⓑ (*bes. österr. ugs.: praktisch, eigentlich*) more or less; virtually

**Faktor** /'faktɔr/ *der;* **~s**, **~en** /-'to:rən/ Ⓐ (*auch Math.*) factor; **der auslösende ~:** the immediate cause; **ein konstanter ~** (*Math.*) a constant; Ⓑ (*Berufsbez.*) (*in einer Setzerei*) composing-room foreman *or* supervisor; (*in einer Druckerei*) [printing-room] foreman *or* supervisor

**Faktorei** *die;* ~, **~en** (*hist.*) foreign trading post; factory (*Hist.*)

**Faktotum** /fak'to:tʊm/ *das;* **~s**, **~s** *od.* **Faktoten** (*scherzh.*) factotum

**Faktum** /'faktʊm/ *das;* **~s**, **Fakten** fact

**Faktur** /fak'tu:ɐ̯/ *die;* ~, **~en** (*Kaufmannsspr. veralt.*) invoice

**fakturieren** *itr. V.* do invoicing

**Fakturier·maschine** *die* invoicing machine

**Fakturist** *der;* **~en**, **~en**, **Fakturistin** *die;* ~, **~nen** invoice clerk

**Fakultas** /fa'kʊltas/ *die;* ~, **Fakultäten** /fakʊl'tɛ:tn̩/ (*Schulw.*) qualification to teach; **die ~ für etw. haben** be qualified to teach sth.

**Fakultät** /fakʊl'tɛ:t/ *die;* ~, **~en** (*Hochschulw.*) Ⓐ (*Abteilung*) faculty; **die philosophische/medizinische/juristische ~:** the faculty of arts/medicine/law; **die ~ wechseln** change faculty; Ⓑ (*Lehrer und Studenten*) staff and students (*of a faculty*); Ⓒ (*Räumlichkeiten*) faculty building; Ⓓ (*Math.*) factorial; **5 ~:** factorial 5

**fakultativ** /fakʊlta'ti:f/ ❶ *Adj.* optional ‹subject, participation›. ❷ *adv.* optionally

**Falange** /fa'laŋge/ *die;* **~:** Falange

**Falangist** *der;* **~en**, **~en**, **Falangistin** *die;* ~, **~nen** Falangist

**falb** /falp/ *Adj.* (*geh.*) dun-coloured

**Falbe** /'falbə/ *der;* **~n**, **~n** dun [horse]

**Falbel** /'falbl̩/ *die;* ~, **~n** (*Textilw.*) furbelow; flounce

**Falke** /'falkə/ *der;* **~n**, **~n** (*auch Politik fig.*) hawk

**Falken·beize** *die* falconry

**Falkenier** /falkə'ni:ɐ̯/ *der;* **~s**, **~e** ⇒ **Falkner**

**Falkländer** /'falklɛndɐ/ *der;* **~s**, ~, **Falkländerin** *die;* ~, **~nen** Falklander

**Falkland·inseln** *Pl.* Falkland Islands; Falklands

f

**Falkner** *der;* **~s**, **~**, **Falknerin** *die;* **~**, **~nen** falconer

**Falknerei** *die;* **~**, **~en** **A** *(Falkenbeize)* falconry; **B** *(Anlage)* hawk house

**Fall**[1] /fal/ *der;* **~[e]s**, **Fälle** /'fɛlə/ **A** *(Sturz)* fall; **zu ~ kommen** have a fall; **durch** *od.* **über etw.** *(Akk.)* **zu ~ kommen** *(fig.)* come to grief because of sth.; **jmdn. zu ~ bringen** *(fig.)* bring about sb.'s downfall; **der ~ einer Stadt** *(fig.)* the fall of a town; ⇒ *auch* **Hochmut**; **B** *(das ~en)* descent; **der freie ~:** free fall; **C** *(Ereignis, Vorkommnis)* case; *(zu erwartender Umstand)* eventuality; **für den äußersten** *od.* **schlimmsten ~, im schlimmsten ~:** if the worst comes to the worst; **im besten ~:** at best; **es ist [nicht] der ~:** it is [not] the case; **gesetzt den ~:** assuming; supposing; **für den ~, dass es morgen schön ist** in case it's fine tomorrow; **im ~e einer Veränderung** in the event of a change; **auf jeden ~:** in any case; **auf alle Fälle** in any case; **auf keinen ~:** on no account; **das ist doch ein ganz klarer ~:** it's perfectly clear; **jmds. ~ sein** *(fig. ugs.)* be sb.'s cup of tea; **klarer ~** *(ugs.)* it goes without saying; **in jedem ~:** in any case; **der ~ ist [für mich] erledigt** [as far as I'm concerned] that's the end of it; **D** *(Rechtsw., Med., Grammatik)* case; **der 1./2./3./4. ~** *(Grammatik)* the nominative/genitive/dative/accusative case

**Fall**[2] *das;* **~[e]s**, **~en** *(Seemannsspr.)* halyard

**Fall-: ~beil** *das* guillotine; **~beschleunigung** *die (Physik)* gravitational acceleration

**Falle** /'falə/ *die;* **~**, **~n** **A** *(auch fig.)* trap; **in die ~ gehen** walk into the trap; **jmdm. eine ~ stellen** *(fig.)* set a trap for sb.; **jmdn. in eine ~ locken** *(fig.)* lure sb. into a trap; **jmdm. in die ~ gehen** *(fig.)* fall into sb.'s trap; **in der ~ sitzen** *(fig.)* be in a spot; **B** *(salopp: Bett)* **in die ~ gehen** turn in *(coll.)*; **sich in die ~ hauen** hit the sack *or* hay *(coll.)*; **C** *(Riegel am Türschloss)* catch; latch

**fallen** *unr. itr. V.; mit sein* **A** fall; **etw. ~ lassen** drop sth.; **immer [wieder] auf die Füße ~** *(fig. ugs.)* always land on one's feet; **sich ins Gras/Bett/Heu ~ lassen** fall on to the grass/into bed/into the hay; *(fig.)* **jmdn. ~ lassen** drop sb.; **einen Plan ~ lassen** abandon a plan; **eine Bemerkung ~ lassen** let fall a remark; **einen Hinweis ~ lassen** drop a hint; ⇒ *auch* **Decke** C; **Gewicht**; **Groschen** B; **Rahmen** B; **Schoß** A; **Schuppe** A; **stehen**; **Stein** B; **Stuhl** A; **Tür**; **Wasser** A; **Wolke**; **Würfel** B; **B** *(hin~, stürzen)* fall [over]; **auf die Knie/in den Schmutz ~:** fall to one's knees/in the dirt; **über einen Stein ~:** trip over a stone; **im Fallen hat er den Schirmständer umgerissen** he pulled the umbrella stand over as he fell; ⇒ *auch* **gefallen** 2; **Kopf** A; **Mund**; **Nase** A; **C** *(sinken)* ‹prices› fall; ‹temperature, water level› fall, drop; ‹fever› subside; **im Preis ~:** go down *or* fall in price; ⇒ *auch* **Arm** A; **Hals** A; **Knie** A; **Rücken** A; **Schloss** A; **Zügel** A; **D** *(an einen bestimmten Ort gelangen, dringen)* ‹light, shadow, glance, choice, suspicion› fall; **die Wahl fiel auf ihn** the choice fell on him; **E** *(abgegeben, erzielt werden)* ‹shot› be fired; *(Sport)* ‹goal› be scored; **F** *(nach unten hängen)* ‹hair› fall; **die Haare ~ ihr ins Gesicht/auf die Schulter** her hair falls over her face/to her shoulders; **G** *(im Kampf sterben)* die; fall *(literary)*; **im Krieg ~:** die in the war; **er ist bei Verdun gefallen** he died *or* fell at Verdun; **H** *(aufgehoben, beseitigt werden)* ‹ban› be lifted; ‹tax› be abolished; ‹obstacle› be removed; ‹limitation› be overcome; ⇒ *auch* **Opfer** B; **Tisch**; **I** *(zu einer bestimmten Zeit stattfinden)* **in eine Zeit ~:** occur at a time; **mein Geburtstag fällt auf einen Samstag** my birthday falls on a Saturday; **in diese Zeit fällt der Höhepunkt der romantischen Dichtung** that time saw the heyday of Romantic poetry; **J** *(zu einem Bereich gehören)* **in/unter eine Kategorie ~:** fall into *or* within a category; **unter ein Gesetz/eine Bestimmung ~:** come under a law/a regulation; **K** *(zu~, zuteil werden)* **eine Erbschaft/ein Gebiet fällt an jmdn.** an inheritance/a piece of territory falls to sb.; **er ist seinen Feinden in die Hände gefallen** he has fallen into the hands of his enemies; **L** *(geäußert werden)* ‹decision› be taken *or* made; **scharfe Worte/Bemerkungen fielen** harsh words were spoken/harsh remarks were made; **M** *(verfallen)* **in Trümmer ~:** collapse in ruins; **in Schwermut ~:** be overcome by melancholy; **in einen Dialekt ~:** lapse into a dialect; **in Trab ~:** break into a trot; ⇒ *auch* **Last** C; **Rolle** F; **Ungnade**; **N** *(erobert werden)* ‹town, stronghold› fall; **O** *(geh.: ab~)* slope; fall

**fällen** /'fɛlən/ *tr. V.* **A** fell ‹tree, timber›; **B** *(verkünden)* **ein Urteil ~** ‹judge› pass sentence; ‹jury› return a verdict; **einen Schiedsspruch ~:** make a ruling; **C** *(Milit.: zum Angriff senken)* lower ‹bayonet›; **D** *(Chemie)* precipitate

***fallen|lassen** ⇒ **fallen** A

**Fallen·steller** *der;* **~s**, **~**, **Fallen·stellerin** *die;* **~**, **~nen** trapper

**Fall-: ~geschwindigkeit** *die (Physik)* velocity of fall; **~gesetz** *das (Physik)* law of gravity; **~gitter** *das* portcullis; **~grube** *die* pitfall; **~höhe** *die* **A** *(Physik)* height of fall; **B** *(Literaturw.)* extent of a/the dramatic hero's fall

**fallieren** *itr. V. (Finanzw.)* go bankrupt

**fällig** /'fɛlɪç/ *Adj.* **A** due; **eine ~e Reform** an overdue reform; **der Kerl ist ~** *(ugs.)* he's in for it *(sl.)*; **B** *(zu bezahlen)* ‹sum of money› payable, due; **ein ~er Wechsel/~e Zinsen** a bill to mature/interest payable

**Fälligkeit** *die;* **~**, **~en** *(Wirtsch.)*, **Fälligkeits·termin** *der* settlement date; date of payment

**Fall·obst** *das* windfalls *pl.*

**Fall-out** /fɔːl'|aʊt/ *der;* **~s**, **~s** *(Kernphysik)* fallout

**Fall-: ~reep** *das (Seemannsspr.)* jack ladder; **~rückzieher** *der (Fußball)* bicycle kick

**falls** /fals/ *(Konj.)* **A** *(wenn)* if; **~ es regnet/schneit** if it rains/snows; **B** *(für den Fall, dass)* in case; **~ es regnen sollte** in case it should rain

**Fall·schirm** *der* parachute; **mit dem ~ abspringen** *(im Notfall)* parachute out; *(als Sport)* make a [parachute] jump; **mit dem ~ über Belgien abspringen** parachute out over Belgium; *(als Soldat, Spion)* parachute into Belgium

**Fallschirm-: ~jäger** *der (Luftwaffe)* paratrooper; **~springen** *das;* **~~s** parachuting *no art.*; **~springer** *der*, **~springerin** *die* parachutist

**Fall-: ~strick** *der* trap; snare; **jmdm. ~stricke legen** *(fig.)* set traps for sb.; **~studie** *die* case study; **~sucht** *die (veralt.)* falling sickness *(arch.)*; **~tür** *die* trapdoor

**Fällungs·mittel** *das (Chemie)* precipitant

**fall-, Fall-: ~weise** *Adv. (österr.)* ⇒ **gelegentlich** 2 A; **~wind** *der* katabatic wind; **~wurf** *der (Handball)* falling throw

**falsch** /falʃ/ **1** *Adj.* **A** *(unecht, imitiert)* false ‹teeth, plait›; imitation ‹jewellery›; **Falsche Akazie** *(Bot.)* false acacia; **~er Hase** *(Kochk.)* meat loaf; **B** *(gefälscht)* counterfeit, forged ‹banknote›; false, forged ‹passport›; assumed ‹name›; **C** *(irrig, fehlerhaft)* wrong ‹impression, track, pronunciation›; wrong, incorrect ‹answer›; **auf der ~en Fährte sein** be on the wrong track; **logisch ~ sein** be logically false; **an den Falschen geraten** come to the wrong man; **alle Aufgaben ~ [gelöst] haben** have got all one's exercises wrong; **etw. in die ~e Kehle** *od.* **den ~en Hals bekommen** *(fig. ugs.)* take sth. the wrong way; ⇒ *auch* **Licht** A, **Pferd** A; **D** *(unangebracht)* false ‹shame, modesty›; **E** *(irreführend)* false ‹statement, promise›; **unter Vorspiegelung ~er Tatsachen** under false pretences; **F** *(abwertend: hinterhältig)* false ‹friend›; **ein ~er Hund** *(salopp)* a two-faced so-and-so *(sl.)*; **eine ~e Schlange** *(fig.)* a snake in the grass; **ein ~es Spiel [mit jmdm.] treiben** play false with sb.; ⇒ *auch* **Fuffziger**; **G** *(bes. nordd.: erzürnt)* angry. **2** *adv.* **A** *(fehlerhaft)* wrongly; incorrectly; **~ singen** sing wrongly; **~ gehen/fahren** go the wrong way; **etw. ~ verstehen** misunderstand sth.; **die Uhr geht ~:** the clock is wrong; **~ informiert** *od.* **unterrichtet sein** be misinformed; **~ liegen** *(ugs.)* be mistaken; **~ herum** *(verkehrt)* back to front; the wrong way round; *(auf dem Kopf)* upside down; *(links)* inside out; ⇒ *auch* **herum** A, **verbinden** 1 H; **B** *(irreführend)* **~ schwören** lie on oath; **~ spielen** cheat

**Falsch** *der;* **~s** *(geh., veralt.)* **in an jmdm. ist kein ~:** sb. is guileless; **ohne ~ sein** be completely guileless

**Falsch-: ~aus·sage** *die (Rechtsspr.)* **[eidliche] ~aussage** false testimony *or* evidence; **uneidliche ~aussage** false statement [not on oath]; **~eid** *der (Rechtsspr.)* unintentional false statement under oath

**fälschen** /'fɛlʃn̩/ *tr. V.* forge, fake ‹signature, document, passport›; forge ‹painting›; forge, counterfeit ‹coin, banknote›; falsify ‹history›

**Fälscher** *der;* **~s**, **~**, **Fälscherin** *die;* **~**, **~nen** forger; counterfeiter

**Falsch-: ~fahrer** *der*, **~fahrerin** *die* ⇒ **Geisterfahrer**; **~geld** *das* counterfeit money

**Falschheit** *die;* **~** **A** *(Hinterhältigkeit)* duplicity; deceitfulness; **B** *(Unechtheit)* falseness; *(Fehlerhaftigkeit)* wrongness

**fälschlich** **1** *Adj.* false ‹claim, accusation›; *(irrtümlich)* mistaken, false ‹assumption, suspicion›. **2** *adv.* falsely, wrongly ‹claim, accuse›; mistakenly, falsely ‹assume, suspect›

**fälschlicher·weise** *Adv.* by mistake; mistakenly

**falsch-, Falsch-: *~|liegen** ⇒ **falsch** 2A; **~meldung** *die* false report; **~münzer** /'-mʏntsɐ/ *der;* **~s**, **~~:** forger; counterfeiter; **~münzerei** /-mʏntsə'rai/ *die;* **~~**, **~~en** forgery; counterfeiting; **~münzerin** *die;* **~~**, **~~nen** ⇒ **~münzer**; ***~|spielen** ⇒ **falsch** 2B; **~spieler** *der*, **~spielerin** *die* cheat; *(erwerbsmäßig)* card sharp[er]

**Fälschung** *die;* **~**, **~en** **A** fake; counterfeit; **B** *(das Fälschen)* forging; counterfeiting

**fälschungs·sicher** *Adj.* secure against forgery

**Falsett** /fal'zɛt/ *das;* **~[e]s**, **~e** *(Musik)* falsetto [voice]

**Falsifikat** /falzifi'kaːt/ *das;* **~[e]s**, **~e** forgery; fake

**Falsifikation** /falzifika'tsjoːn/ *die;* **~**, **~en** falsification

**falsifizieren** /falzifi'tsiːrən/ *tr. V.* falsify

**faltbar** *Adj.* collapsible ‹box, boat›

**Falt-: ~blatt** *das* leaflet; *(in Zeitungen, Zeitschriften, Büchern)* insert; **~boot** *das* collapsible boat

**Fältchen** /'fɛltçən/ *das;* **~s**, **~:** wrinkle

**Falte** /'faltə/ *die;* **~**, **~n** **A** crease; **~n schlagen** crease; **B** *(im Stoff)* fold; *(mit scharfer Kante)* pleat; **C** *(Hautfalte)* wrinkle; line; **die Stirn in ~n legen** *od.* **ziehen** *(nachdenklich)* knit one's brow; *(verärgert)* frown; **D** *(Geol.)* fold

**fälteln** /'fɛltl̩n/ *tr. V.* pleat

**falten** **1** *tr. V.* fold; **die Hände ~:** fold one's hands. **2** *refl. V. (auch Geol.)* fold; ‹skin› wrinkle, become wrinkled

**falten-, Falten-: ~bildung** *die (auch Geol.)* folding; *(der Haut)* wrinkling; **~frei** *Adj.* creaseless ‹fit›; **~gebirge** *das* [range of] fold mountains; **~los** *Adj.* uncreased ‹garment›; unwrinkled ‹skin›; **~reich** *Adj.* heavily pleated ‹robe›; heavily lined ‹face›; **~rock** *der* pleated skirt; **~wurf** *der* arrangement of the folds

**Falter** *der;* **~s**, **~** *(Nacht~)* moth; *(Tag~)* butterfly

**faltig** **A** *Adj.* ‹clothes› gathered [in folds]; wrinkled ‹skin, hands›; **B** *(zerknittert)* creased

**-fältig** /-fɛltɪç/ *Adj., adv.* -fold; **hundert~/tausend~:** hundredfold/thousandfold

*old spelling (see note on page 1707)

**Falt-: ~karte** *die* folding map; **~karton** *der* collapsible cardboard box; **~tür** *die* folding door

**Faltung** *die;* ~, **~en** (*Geol.*) fold

**Falz** /falts/ *der;* **~es, ~e** **A** (*Buchbinderei*) (*scharfe Faltlinie*) fold; (*Übergang zwischen Buchdeckel und -rücken*) groove; (*angehefteter Leinenstreifen*) guard; stub; **B** (*bei Briefmarken*) hinge; **C** (*Bauw., Holzverarb.*) rebate; rabbet; **D** (*Technik*) lock seam; double seam

**falzen** *tr. V.* (*Buchbinderei*) fold; (*Technik*) seam

**Falz·maschine** *die* **A** (*Buchbinderei*) folding machine; **B** (*Technik*) seaming machine

**Fama** /ˈfa:ma/ *die;* ~ (*geh.*) rumour; **es geht die ~, dass ...** there is a rumour that ...

**familial** /familiˈa:l/ *Adj.* (*Soziol.*) familial

**familiär** /famiˈliɛ:ɐ̯/ ❶ *Adj.* **A** family ‹problems, worries›; **aus ~en Gründen** for family reasons; **B** (*zwanglos*) familiar; informal; informal ‹tone, relationship›. ❷ *adv.* (*zwanglos*) **sich ~ ausdrücken** to talk in a familiar way

**Familiarität** /familiariˈtɛ:t/ *die;* ~, **~en** familiarity

**Familie** /faˈmi:li̯ə/ *die;* ~, **~n** **A** family; **~ Meyer** the Meyer family; **~ haben** have a family; **eine ~ gründen** (*heiraten*) marry; (*Kinder bekommen*) start a family; **das bleibt in der ~:** it will stay in the family; it will go no further; **das kommt in den besten ~n vor** it happens in the best families; **das liegt in der ~:** it runs in the family; **B** (*Biol.*) family

**familien-, Familien-: ~album** *das* family album; **~angehörige** *der/die* member of the family; **~angelegenheit** *die* family affair *or* matter; **in dringenden ~angelegenheiten** on urgent family business; **~anschluss, *~anschluß** *der* personal contact [with a/the family]; **~anzeigen** *Pl.* births, deaths, and marriages; **~besitz** *der* family property; **im ~besitz** in the family's possession; **dieses Stück ist aus altem ~besitz** this piece is a family heirloom; **~betrieb** *der* family business *or* firm; **~bibel** *die* family bible; **~bild** *das* (*Foto*) family photograph; (*Gemälde*) family picture; **~chronik** *die* family history; **~ehre** *die* family honour; **~feier** *die* family party; **~feindlich** *Adj.* ‹policy etc.› hostile to the family; **~flasche** *die* family-sized bottle; **~forschung** *die* genealogy; **~für·sorge** *die* family welfare service; **~gerecht** *Adj.* ‹accommodation etc.› suiting the needs of families; **~grab** *das* family grave; **~gruft** *die* family vault; **~krach** *der* (*ugs.*) family row; **bei uns gibt es oft ~krach** we often have family rows; **~kreis** *der* family circle; **im engsten ~kreis** in the immediate family; **~leben** *das* family life; **~minister** *der*, **~ministerin** *die: minister responsible for family matters;* **~mit·glied** *das* member of the family; **~name** *der* surname; family name; **~ober·haupt** *das* head of the family; **~pass, *~paß** *der* family passport; **~planung** *die* family planning *no art.;* **~politik** *die* policy/policies relating to the family; **~recht** *das* family law; **~roman** *der* family saga; **~schmuck** *der* family jewels *pl.;* family jewellery; **~sinn** *der* sense of commitment to the family; **~stand** *der* marital status; **~stück** *das* family heirloom; **~treffen** *das* family meeting; **~vater** *der:* **~vater sein** be the father of a family; **ein guter ~vater** a good husband and father; **~verhältnisse** *Pl.* family circumstances; family background; **aus geordneten ~verhältnissen kommen** have a stable family background; **~vorstand** *der* (*Amtsspr.*) head of the family; **~wappen** *das* family coat of arms; **~zusammen·führung** *die* re-uniting of families; **~zuwachs** *der* addition[s] to the family; **~zuwachs bekommen/erwarten** have/expect an addition to the family

**famos** /faˈmo:s/ (*veralt.*) ❶ *Adj.* splendid. ❷ *adv.* splendidly

**famulieren** /famuˈli:rən/ *itr. V.* (*Med.*) do one's clinical training

**Famulus** /ˈfa:mulʊs/ *der;* ~, **~se** *od.* **Famuli** /ˈfa:muli/ **A** (*Med.*) *medical student doing his/her clinical training;* intern (*Amer.*); **B** (*veralt., scherzh.: Assistent*) famulus

**Fan** /fɛn/ *der;* **~s, ~s** fan

**Fanal** /faˈna:l/ *das;* **~s, ~e** (*geh.*) torch; **ein ~ für etw. setzen** light a torch for sth.

**Fanatiker** /faˈna:tikɐ/ *der;* **~s,** ~, **Fanatikerin** *die;* ~, **~nen** fanatic; (*religiös*) fanatic; zealot

**-fanatiker** *der*, **-fanatikerin** *die:* **Frischluft~/Fußball~:** fresh air/football fanatic

**fanatisch** ❶ *Adj.* fanatical. ❷ *adv.* fanatically

**fanatisieren** *tr. V.* rouse to fanaticism; **der fanatisierte Mob** the fanatically excited mob

**Fanatismus** *der;* **~:** fanaticism

**fand** /fant/ *1. u. 3. Pers. Sg. Prät. v.* **finden**

**Fandango** /fanˈdaŋgo/ *der;* **~s, ~s** fandango

**Fanfare** /fanˈfa:rə/ *die;* ~, **~n** **A** herald's trumpet; **die ~ blasen** play the ceremonial trumpet; **B** (*Signal*) fanfare; flourish; **~n erklingen** fanfares are sounded; **C** (*Musikstück*) fanfare; **D** (*am Auto*) musical [air] horn

**Fanfaren-: ~klang** *der* sound of the fanfare; **~zug** *der* parade of trumpeters

**Fang** /faŋ/ *der;* **~[e]s, Fänge** /ˈfɛŋə/ **A** (*Tierfang*) trapping; (*von Fischen*) catching; **zum ~ auslaufen** put to sea [to fish]; **B** (*Beute*) bag; (*von Fischen*) catch; haul; **einen guten ~ machen** *od.* **tun** (*fig.*) make a good catch; **C** *Pl.* (*Jägerspr.: Fuß eines Raubvogels*) talons *pl.;* claws *pl.;* **was er einmal in den Fängen hat, rückt er nicht wieder heraus** (*fig. ugs.*) once something gets into his clutches, he doesn't let go; **D** *Pl.* (*Jägerspr.: ~zähne*) fangs *pl.*

**Fang-: ~arm** *der* (*Zool.*) tentacle; **~ball** *der* catch; **~eisen** *das* (*Jagdw.*) trap

**fangen** ❶ *unr. tr. V.* **A** (*ergreifen, fassen*) catch, trap ‹bird, animal›; catch ‹fish›; **die Katze fängt eine Maus** the cat catches a mouse; **eine ~** (*südd., österr. ugs.*) get a clip round the ear (*coll.*); **B** (*gefangen nehmen*) catch, capture ‹fugitive etc.›; **gefangene Soldaten** captured soldiers; **in Frankreich/Russland gefangen sein** be a prisoner of war in France/Russia; **von etw. [ganz] gefangen sein** (*fig.*) be [quite] enthralled by sth.; **sich gefangen geben** give oneself up; surrender; **jmdn./ein Tier gefangen halten** hold sb. prisoner *or* captive/keep an animal in captivity; **jmdn. gefangen nehmen** capture sb.; take sb. prisoner; (*fig.: begeistern*) captivate *or* enthral sb.; **jmds. Aufmerksamkeit gefangen halten** rivet sb.'s attention; **jmdn. gefangen halten** (*fig.: faszinieren*) hold sb. enthralled; **jmdn. gefangen setzen** (*geh.*) imprison sb.; **C** *auch itr.* (*auf~*) catch ‹ball›; **er kann gut/nicht ~:** he's good/not good at catching.
❷ *unr. refl. V.* **A** (*in eine Falle geraten, nicht mehr frei kommen*) get *or* be caught; **der Wind fängt sich in etw.** sth. catches the wind; ⇒ *auch* **Schlinge B**; **B** (*wieder in die normale Lage kommen*) **sich [gerade] noch ~:** [just] manage to steady oneself; **sich wieder ~** (*fig.*) recover

**Fangen** *das;* **~s: ~ spielen** play tag *or* catch

**Fänger** /ˈfɛŋɐ/ *der;* **~s,** ~, **Fängerin** *die;* ~, **~nen** catcher; (*von Großwild*) hunter

**fang-, Fang-: ~flotte** *die* fishing fleet; **~frage** *die* catch question; trick question; **~frisch** *Adj.* fresh; freshly caught ‹fish›; **~gebiet** *das* fishing ground; **~leine** *die* **A** (*Seemannsspr.*) (*eines Schiffs*) hawser; (*eines Bootes*) mooring rope; **B** (*Fallschirmspringen*) shroud line; **~netz** *das* **A** (*Fischereiw.*) [fishing] net; **B** (*Flugw.*) arrester gear; **C** (*Artistik*) safety net

**Fango·packung** /ˈfaŋgo-/ *die* (*Med.*) fango pack

**Fang-: ~prämie** *die* bounty; **~riemen** *der* [binding] strap; **~schaltung** *die* (*Fernspr.*) tracing device; interception circuit; **~schuss, *~schuß** *der* (*Jagdw.*) coup de grâce; **~zeit** *die* season

**Fan-** /fɛn-/: **~klub** *der* fan club; **~post** *die* fan mail

**Fantasie** /fantaˈzi:/ *die;* ~, **~n** **A** imagination; **mit [viel]/ohne [jede] ~:** [very] imaginatively *or* with [a lot of] imagination/[very] unimaginatively *or* without [any] imagination; **eine schmutzige ~ haben** have a dirty mind; **B** (*Produkt der ~;*) fantasy; **C** (*Musik*) fantasia

**fantasie·los** ❶ *Adj.* unimaginative. ❷ *adv.* unimaginatively

**Fantasielosigkeit** *die;* **~:** lack of imagination; (*Eintönigkeit*) dullness

**fantasieren** ❶ *itr. V.* **A** indulge in fantasies, fantasize (**von** about); **fantasierst du, oder sagst du die Wahrheit?** are you making it up or telling the truth?; **B** (*Med.: irrereden*) talk deliriously. ❷ *tr. V.* **was fantasierst du da?** what's all that nonsense?

**fantasie·voll** ❶ *Adj.* imaginative. ❷ *adv.* imaginatively

**Fantasie·vor·stellung** *die* figment of the imagination

**Fantast** /fanˈtast/ *der;* **~en, ~en** dreamer; starry-eyed idealist

**Fantasterei** *die;* ~, **~en** fantasy; (*Wunschtraum*) pipe dream

**Fantastin** *die;* ~, **~nen** ⇒ **Fantast**

**fantastisch** ❶ *Adj.* **A** fantastic; ‹idea› divorced from reality; **eine ~e Erzählung** a tale of fantasy; **B** (*ugs.: großartig*) fantastic (*coll.*); terrific (*coll.*). ❷ *adv.* (*ugs.*) fantastically (*coll.*); **~ tanzen/kochen** (*ugs.*) dance/cook fantastically (*coll.*) *or* incredibly well

**Faraday·käfig** /ˈfærədɪ-/ *der* (*Physik*) Faraday cage

**Farb-: ~ab·stimmung** *die* colour balance; colour harmony; **~band** *das; Pl.* **~bänder** [typewriter] ribbon; **~beutel** *der* paint bomb; **~bild** *das* **A** (*Aufnahme*) colour photo; **B** (*Illustration*) colour picture; **~dia** *das* colour slide; colour transparency; **~druck** *der; Pl.* **~~e** colour print *or* reproduction

**Farbe** /ˈfarbə/ *die;* ~, **~n** **A** colour; **~ bekommen/verlieren** get some colour/lose one's colour; **an ~ gewinnen/verlieren** (*fig.*) become more/less colourful; **die ~ wechseln** ‹person› blanch; **B** (*Farbstoff*) (*für Textilien*) dye; (*für Holz, Metall, Stein usw.*) paint; **~n mischen/auftragen** mix/apply paint; **die ~n laufen ineinander/verblassen** the colours are running together/are fading; **etw. in den schwärzesten/glühendsten ~n malen** *od.* **schildern** (*fig.*) paint the gloomiest possible picture/a rosy picture of sth.; **C** (*Buntheit*) colour; **der Film ist in ~:** the film is in colour; **D** (*Symbol eines Landes, einer Vereinigung*) **~n** colours; **die ~n seines Landes vertreten** represent one's country; **die ~ wechseln** (*fig.*) change sides; **E** (*Spielkarten*) suit; **eine ~ bedienen** follow suit; **~ bekennen** (*fig. ugs.*) come clean (*coll.*)

**farb-, Farb-: ~echt** *Adj.* colour-fast; **~effekt** *der* colour effect; **~empfindlich** *Adj.* **A** colour-sensitive ‹film›; **B** (*nicht ~echt*) non-colour-fast

**Färbe·mittel** *das* dye

**färben** /ˈfɛrbn̩/ ❶ *tr. V.* **A** dye ‹wool, material, hair›; **etw. grün/schwarz/beige ~:** dye sth. green/black/beige; **sich** (*Dat.*) **das Haar blond ~ lassen** have one's hair dyed blond; **B** *meist im 2. Part.* (*verändert darstellen*) **eine politisch gefärbte Rede** a speech with a political slant; **ein gefärbter Bericht** a biased report. ❷ *refl. V.* change colour; **sich schwarz/rot** *usw.* **~:** turn black/red *etc.* ❸ *itr. V.* (*ugs.: ab~*) **der Stoff/die Bluse färbt** the material/the blouse runs

**-farben** *Adj., adv.* **erd~/erdbeer~/creme~/haut~:** earth-/strawberry-/cream-/skin-coloured; **creme~ angestrichen** painted cream

**farben-, Farben-: ~blind** *Adj.* colour-blind; **~freudig** *Adj.,* **~froh** *Adj.* colourful; **~industrie** *die* paint industry; **~lehre** *die* theory of colour; **~pracht** *die* colourful splendour; **~prächtig** *Adj.* vibrant with colour *postpos.;* **~sinn** *der* colour sense; sense of colour; **~spiel** *das* play of colours; **~test**

f

der (*Psych.*) colour test; **~tragend** *Adj.* ‹student fraternity› using traditional colours

**Färber** *der;* ~s, ~ ▶ 159 dyer

**Färberei** *die;* ~, ~en **A** (*Betrieb*) dyeworks *sing.;* **B** (*Verfahren*) dyeing

**Färberin** *die;* ~, ~nen ▶ 159 dyer

**Farb-: ~fernsehen** *das* colour television; **~fernseher** *der* (*ugs.*) colour telly (*coll.*) *or* television; **~fernseh·gerät** *das* colour television [set]; **~film** *der* colour film; **~filter,** *der, fachspr. meist: das* colour filter; **~fleck** *der* paint spot; **~foto** *das* colour photo; **~fotografie** *die* **A** (*Verfahren*) colour photography; **B** (*Foto*) colour photograph; **~gebung** *die;* ~~, ~~en, **~gestaltung** *die* colouring; choice of colours

**farbig** ❶ *Adj.* **A** coloured; **B** (*bunt, fig.: anschaulich, lebhaft*) colourful ‹dress, picture, description, tale›; **~e [Kirchen]fenster** stained-glass [church] windows. ❷ *adv.* colourfully

**-farbig** *Adj., adv.* ⇒ **-farben**

**Farbige** *der/die; adj. Dekl.* coloured man/woman; coloured; **die ~n in Amerika/Südafrika** the coloured people in America/the Coloureds in South Africa

**Farbigkeit** *die;* ~ (*auch fig.*) colourfulness

**Farb-: ~karte** *die* colour chart *or* guide; **~klecks** *der* paint spot *or* splash; (*nicht aufgesogen*) blob of paint; paint spot; **~kombination** *die* colour combination; **~komposition** *die* colour composition

**farblich** ❶ *Adj.* in colour *postpos.;* as regards colour *postpos.* ❷ *adv.* **etw. ~ aufeinander abstimmen** match sth. in colour

**farb-, Farb-: ~los** *Adj.* (*auch fig.*) colourless; clear ‹varnish›; neutral ‹shoe polish›; **~losigkeit** *die;* ~~ (*auch fig.*) colourlessness; **~negativ** *das* (*Fot.*) colour negative; **~schicht** *die* layer of paint; (*beim Auftragen*) coat of paint; **~skala** *die* colour range; **~stift** *der* **A** (*Buntstift*) coloured pencil; **B** (*Filzstift*) coloured felt-tip *or* pen; **~stoff** *der* **A** (*Med., Biol.*) pigment; **B** (*für Textilien*) dye; **C** (*für Lebensmittel*) colouring; **~ton** *der; Pl.* **~töne** shade; **~tupfen, ~tupfer** *der* spot of colour

**Färbung** *die;* ~, ~en **A** (*Farbgebung*) colouring; colour; **B** (*das Färben*) dyeing; **C** (*fig.: Tendenz*) slant

**Farb-: ~walze** *die* (*Druckw.*) ink[ing] roller; **~wechsel** *der* **A** (*wechselndes Auftreten von ~en*) variation in colour; **B** (*Zool.*) ability to change skin colour

**Farce** /ˈfarsə/ *die;* ~, ~n **A** (*auch fig.*) farce; **B** (*Kochk.*) stuffing; (*mit Fleisch*) forcemeat

**farcieren** *tr. V.* (*Kochk.*) fill; stuff

**Farm** /farm/ *die;* ~, ~en farm

**Farmer** *der;* ~s, ~, **Farmerin** *die;* ~, ~nen farmer

**Farn** /farn/ *der;* ~[e]s, ~e fern

**Farn-: ~kraut** *das* fern; **~wedel** *der* fern frond

**Färse** /ˈfɛrzə/ *die;* ~, ~n heifer

**Fasan** /faˈza:n/ *der;* ~[e]s, ~e[n] pheasant

**Fasanerie** /fazanəˈri:/ *die;* ~, ~n pheasantry

**faschieren** *tr. V.* (*österr.*) mince

**Faschierte** *das; adj. Dekl.* (*österr.*) minced meat; mince

**Faschine** /faˈʃi:nə/ *die;* ~, ~n (*Straßenbau*) fascine; faggot

**Fasching** /ˈfaʃɪŋ/ *der;* ~s, ~e *od.* ~s [pre-Lent] carnival; **im ~:** at carnival time

**Faschings-: ~ball** *der* carnival ball; **~kostüm** *das* fancy-dress costume [for carnival]; **~zug** *der* carnival procession

**Faschismus** /faˈʃɪsmʊs/ *der;* ~: fascism *no art.;* **Opfer des ~:** victim of fascism

**Faschist** *der;* ~en, ~en, **Faschistin** *die;* ~, ~nen fascist

**faschistisch** *Adj.* fascist

**faschistoid** /faʃɪstoˈi:d/ *Adj.* fascistic

**Fase** /ˈfa:zə/ *die;* ~, ~n (*Technik*) bevel [edge]; chamfer [edge]

**Faselei** *die;* ~, ~en (*ugs. abwertend*) drivel; twaddle

**faseln** /ˈfa:zl̩n/ *itr. V.* (*ugs. abwertend*) drivel; blather

**fasen** /ˈfa:zn̩/ *tr. V.* (*Technik*) bevel; chamfer

**Faser** /ˈfa:zɐ/ *die;* ~, ~n fibre; **mit jeder ~ seines Herzens an etw.** (*Dat.*) **hängen** (*fig. geh.*) love sth. with every fibre of one's being

**Faser·glas** *das* (*Technik*) fibreglass

**faserig** *Adj.* fibrous ‹paper›; stringy ‹meat›

**fasern** *itr. V.* fray

**faser-, Faser-: ~pflanze** *die* fibre plant; **~schonend** *Adj.* gentle [to fabrics]; **~stoff** *der* fibrous material

**Fas·nacht** /ˈfas-/ *die* (*bes. südd.*) ⇒ **Fastnacht**

**Fass, *Faß** /fas/ *das;* **Fasses, Fässer** /ˈfɛsɐ/ barrel; (*Öl~, Benzin~ usw.*) drum; (*kleines Bier~*) keg; (*kleines Sherry~, Portwein~ usw.*) cask; (*Butter~*) churn; **Bier vom ~:** draught beer; **Wein vom ~:** wine from the wood; **er ist [so] dick wie ein ~** (*ugs.*) he's as fat as a barrel; **er säuft wie ein ~** (*ugs.*) he drinks like a fish; **das schlägt dem ~ den Boden aus** (*ugs.*) that takes the biscuit (*Brit. coll.*) *or* (*coll.*) cake; **das bringt das ~ zum Überlaufen** that's the last straw; **ein ~ ohne Boden sein** be an endless drain on sb.'s resources; **ein ~ aufmachen** (*ugs.*) paint the town red

**Fassade** /faˈsa:də/ *die;* ~, ~n **A** façade; frontage; **B** (*abwertend: äußere Erscheinung*) façade; front; **das ist nur [noch] ~:** it is just a façade *or* front; **sie hat eine hübsche ~:** she is pretty on the outside

**Fassaden-: ~kletterer** *der;* ~s, ~, **~kletterin** *die* cat burglar; **~lift** *der* [workmen's/window cleaners'] cradle

**fassbar, *faßbar** *Adj.* **A** (*greifbar, konkret*) tangible, concrete ‹results›; **B** (*verständlich*) comprehensible

**Fass-, *Faß-: ~bier** *das* draught beer; beer on draught; **~binder** *der,* **~binderin** *die;* ~~, ~~nen (*bes. südd., österr.*) cooper

**Fässchen, *Fäßchen** /ˈfɛsçən/ *das;* ~s, ~: small barrel; [small] cask

**fassen** /ˈfasn̩/ ❶ *tr. V.* **A** (*greifen*) grasp; take hold of; **jmdn. am Arm ~:** take hold of sb.'s arm; **jmdn. bei der Hand ~:** take hold of sb.'s hand; take sb. by the hand; **etw. zu ~ bekommen** get a hold on sth.; **fass!** get *or* grab it/him!; ⇒ *auch* **Ehre C; Fuß B; Kopf A; Nase A; Schopf A; Stier A; Wurzel A; B** (*festnehmen*) catch ‹thief, culprit›; **C** ▶ 611 (*aufnehmen können*) ‹hall, tank› hold; **D** (*begreifen*) **ich kann es nicht ~:** I cannot take it in; **das ist [doch] nicht zu ~!** it's incredible; **E** (*in verblasster Bedeutung*) make, take ‹decision›; **Vertrauen** *od.* **Zutrauen zu jmdm. ~:** begin to feel confidence in *or* to trust sb.; **Mut ~:** take courage; **er konnte keinen klaren Gedanken ~:** he could not think clearly; ⇒ *auch* **Auge A; Herz B; F** (*in eine Fassung bringen*) set, mount ‹jewel›; curb ‹spring, well›; **G** (*formulieren, gestalten*) **etw. in Worte/Verse ~:** put sth. into words/verse; **einen Begriff eng/weit ~:** define a concept narrowly/widely; **H** (*geistig erfassen*) grasp; **I** (*als Ladung aufnehmen*) take on ‹load, goods›; **J** (*Soldatenspr.*) draw ‹rations, supplies, ammunition›. ❷ *itr. V.* **A** (*greifen*) **nach etw. ~:** reach for sth.; **in etw.** (*Akk.*) **~:** put one's hand in sth.; **an etw.** (*Akk.*) **~:** touch sth.; **ins Leere ~:** grasp thin air; **B** (*einrasten*) ‹screw› bite; ‹cog› mesh. ❸ *refl. V.* **A** pull oneself together; recover [oneself]; **sich [schnell/allmählich] wieder ~:** recover [quickly/gradually]; **B sich kurz ~:** be brief; ⇒ *auch* **Geduld**

**fässer·weise** *Adv.* by the barrel

**fasslich, *faßlich** *Adj.* comprehensible; intelligible; **etw. in [leicht] ~er Form schreiben** write sth. in an easily comprehensible way

**Fasson** /faˈsõ:/ *die;* ~, ~s style; shape; **keine ~ mehr haben** have become shapeless; **jeder muss nach seiner [eigenen]** *od.* **auf seine [eigene] ~ selig werden** everyone has to work out his own salvation

**Fasson·schnitt** *der* short back and sides

**Fassung** *die;* ~, ~en **A** (*sprachliche, künstlerische Form*) version; **B** (*Selbstbeherrschung, Haltung*) composure; self-control; **die ~ bewahren** keep one's composure; **die ~ verlieren** lose one's self-control; **jmdn. aus der ~ bringen** upset *or* ruffle sb.; **etw. mit ~ tragen** bear sth. calmly; **nach ~ ringen** struggle to retain one's composure; **C** (*für Glühlampen*) holder; **D** (*von Juwelen*) setting; (*Bilder~, Brillen~*) frame

**fassungs-, Fassungs-: ~kraft** *die* ⇒ **Auffassungsgabe; ~los** *Adj.* stunned; **ich war einfach ~los** (*ugs.*) I was completely bewildered; **~los vor Schmerz sein** be beside oneself with grief; **jmdn. ~los anstarren** gaze at sb. in bewilderment; **~losigkeit** *die;* ~~: state of bewilderment; **~vermögen** *das* ▶ 611 capacity

**fast** /fast/ *Adv.* almost; nearly; **~ nie** almost never; hardly ever; **~ nirgends** hardly anywhere; **~ nichts** almost nothing; hardly anything

**fasten** *itr. V.* fast; **das lange/kurze Fasten** the long/short fast

**Fasten** *Pl.* **A** (*~zeit vor Ostern*) Lent *sing.;* **B** (*Bußübungen*) Lenten works of penance

**Fasten-: ~kur** *die* drastic reducing diet; **eine ~kur machen** be/go on a drastic reducing diet; **~predigt** *die* (*kath. Rel.*) Lent[en] sermon; **~zeit** *die* **A** (*Rel.*) time of fasting; **B** (*kath. Rel.*) Lent

**Fast·nacht** *die* **A** (*Faschingsdienstag*) Shrove Tuesday; **B** (*Karneval*) carnival; Shrovetide; **während der ~:** at Shrovetide; at carnival time; **~ feiern** celebrate Shrovetide *or* the carnival

**fast·nächtlich** *Adj.* Shrovetide; carnival

**Fastnachts-: ~brauch** *der* Shrovetide custom; **~dienstag** *der* Shrove Tuesday; **~kostüm** *das* [carnival] fancy dress; **~spiel** *das* (*Literaturw.*) Shrovetide play; **~treiben** *das* [carnival] hustle and bustle; **~zeit** *die* Shrovetide; **~zug** *der* carnival procession

**Faszikel** /fasˈtsi:kl̩/ *der;* ~s, ~: fascicle

**Faszination** /fastsinaˈtsi̯o:n/ *die;* ~: fascination; **eine ~ auf jmdn. ausüben** fascinate sb.

**faszinieren** /fastsiˈni:rən/ *tr. V.* fascinate

**faszinierend** ❶ *Adj.* fascinating; ❷ *adv.* fascinatingly

**fatal** /faˈta:l/ *Adj.* **A** (*peinlich, misslich*) awkward; embarrassing; **~e Folgen haben** have unfortunate consequences; **sich als ~ erweisen** prove [to be] rather unfortunate; **B** (*verhängnisvoll*) fatal

**fataler·weise** *Adv.* unfortunately

**Fatalismus** *der;* ~: fatalism

**Fatalist** *der;* ~en, ~en, **Fatalistin** *die;* ~, ~nen fatalist

**fatalistisch** ❶ *Adj.* fatalistic. ❷ *adv.* fatalistically

**Fata Morgana** /ˈfa:ta mɔrˈga:na/ *die;* ~, **Fata Morganen** *od.* ~s fata morgana; mirage; (*fig.*) illusion

**Fatum** /ˈfa:tʊm/ *das;* ~s, **Fata** (*geh.*) fate; destiny

**Fatzke** /ˈfatskə/ *der;* ~n *od.* ~s, ~n *od.* ~s (*ugs. abwertend*) twit (*Brit. coll.*); jerk (*coll.*)

**fauchen** /ˈfau̯xn̩/ *itr. V.* **A** ‹cat› hiss; ‹tiger› snarl; (*fig.*) ‹engine› hiss; **B** (*sich gereizt äußern*) snarl

**faul** /fau̯l/ ❶ *Adj.* **A** (*verdorben*) rotten, bad ‹food›; bad ‹tooth›; rotten ‹wood›; foul, stale ‹air›; foul ‹water›; **B** (*träge*) lazy; idle; **zu ~ zu etw. sein/zu ~ sein, etw. zu tun** be too lazy *or* idle for sth./to do sth.; **er hat heute seinen ~en Tag** (*ugs.*) he's having a lazy day today; **er, nicht ~, übernahm die Leitung** he was not slow in taking over; **auf der ~en Haut liegen/sich auf die ~e Haut legen** take it easy; **C** (*ugs.: nicht einwandfrei*) bad ‹joke›; dud ‹cheque›; false ‹peace›; lame ‹excuse›; shabby ‹compromise›; shady ‹business, customer›; **das ist doch [alles] ~er Zauber** it's [all] quite bogus; **etwas ist ~ im Staate Dänemark** something is

*old spelling (see note on page 1707)

rotten in the state of Denmark; D (*säumig*) bad ‹debtor›. ❷ *adv.* (*träge*) lazily; idly

**Faul·baum** *der* alder buckthorn; alder dogwood

**Fäule** /ˈfɔ̯ylə/ *die;* ~: foulness

**faulen** *itr. V.; meist mit sein* ‹vegetables, fruit, straw, leaves, wood› rot; ‹water› go foul, stagnate; ‹meat› go off, putrefy; ‹fish› go off, go bad

**faulenzen** /ˈfau̯lɛntsn̩/ *itr. V.* laze about; loaf about (*derog.*)

**Faulenzer** *der;* ~s, ~: idler; lazybones *sing.* (*coll.*)

**Faulenzerei** *die;* ~, ~en (*abwertend*) idleness; laziness

**Faulenzerin** *die;* ~, ~nen ⇒ **Faulenzer**

**Faulenzer·leben** *das* life of idleness

**Faul·gas** *das* sludge *or* sewage gas

**Faulheit** *die;* ~: laziness; idleness; **vor ~ stinken** (*ugs.*) be bone idle

**faulig** *Adj.* stagnating ‹water›; putrefying ‹meat›; ‹meat› which is going bad; rotting ‹vegetables, fruit›; foul, putrid ‹smell›; **~ schmecken/riechen** taste/smell bad *or* off

**Fäulnis** /ˈfɔ̯ylnɪs/ *die;* ~: rottenness; (*fig.*) decadence; degeneracy; **in ~ übergehen** begin to rot

**Fäulnis-:** **~bakterie** *die* putrefactive bacterium; **~erreger** *der* putrefactive agent; organism causing putrefaction

**Faul-:** **~pelz** *der* (*fam.*) lazybones *sing.* (*coll.*); **~schlamm** *der* sludge; **~tier** *das* A (*Zool.*) sloth; B (*ugs.: ~enzer*) ⇒ **Faulpelz**

**Faun** /faun/ *der;* ~[e]s, ~e faun

**Fauna** /ˈfauna/ *die;* ~, **Faunen** (*Zool.*) fauna

**faunisch** ❶ *Adj.* (*geh.*) A (*naturhaft*) faunlike; B (*sinnesfroh*) lascivious. ❷ *adv.* lasciviously

**Faust** /faust/ *die;* ~, **Fäuste** /ˈfɔ̯ystə/ fist; **eine ~ machen, die Hand zur ~ ballen** clench one's fist; **die ~ ballen/öffnen** clench/unclench one's fist; **mit den Fäusten auf jmdn. losgehen** fly at sb. with one's fists; **jmdm. mit der ~ ins Gesicht schlagen** punch sb. in the face; **das passt wie die ~ aufs Auge** (*ugs.*) (*passt nicht*) that clashes horribly; (*passt*) that matches perfectly; **er passt zu ihr wie die ~ aufs Auge** (*ugs.*) they are like chalk and cheese *or* like night and day; **die ~ im Nacken spüren** (*fig.*) begin to feel the pressure; **die ~/Fäuste in der Tasche ballen** (*fig.*) be seething inwardly; **auf eigene ~**: on one's own initiative; off one's own bat (*coll.*); **mit der ~ auf den Tisch schlagen** *od.* **hauen** (*fig.*) put one's foot down

**Faust-:** **~abwehr** *die* (*Ballspiele*) save with the fists; **~ball** *der* faustball

**Fäustchen** /ˈfɔ̯ystçən/ *das;* ~s, ~: fist; **sich** (*Dat.*) **ins ~ lachen** laugh up one's sleeve; (*aus finanziellen Gründen*) laugh all the way to the bank

**faust·dick** ❶ *Adj.* as thick as a man's fist *postpos.*; **eine ~e Lüge** (*fig.*) a barefaced lie. ❷ *adv.* **er hat es ~ hinter den Ohren** (*ugs.*) he's a crafty *or* sly one

**Fäustel** /ˈfɔ̯ystl̩/ *der;* ~s, ~: club hammer; stonemason's hammer

**fausten** *tr. V.* fist, punch ‹ball›

**faust-, Faust-:** **~groß** *Adj.* as big as a fist *postpos.*; **~hand·schuh** *der* mitten; **~hieb** *der* punch

**faustisch** *Adj.* (*geh.*) Faustian

**Faust-:** **~kampf** *der* (*geh.*) pugilism; boxing; (*Wettkampf*) boxing contest; **~kämpfer** *der* (*geh.*) pugilist; boxer; **~keil** *der* (*Archäol.*) hand-axe

**Fäustling** /ˈfɔ̯ystlɪŋ/ *der;* ~s, ~e mitten

**Faust-:** **~pfand** *das* security; (*fig.*) bargaining-counter; **ein ~pfand verlangen** demand security; **~recht** *das* rule of force; **~regel** *die* rule of thumb; **~schlag** *der* punch; **jmdm. einen ~schlag versetzen** punch sb.

**Fauteuil** /foˈtø:j/ *der;* ~s, ~s (*bes. österr., sonst veralt.*) armchair

**Fauvismus** /foˈvɪsmʊs/ *der;* ~ (*bild. Kunst*) fauvism *no art.*

**Fauxpas** /foˈpa/ *der;* ~, ~: faux pas

**favorisieren** /favoriˈzi:rən/ *tr. V.* A (*geh.: bevorzugen*) favour; B (*Sport*) **er ist klar favorisiert** he is the clear favourite

**Favorit** /favoˈri:t/ *der;* ~en, ~en favourite

**Favoriten·rolle** *die* position as favourite

**Favoritin** *die;* ~, ~nen favourite

**Fax** /faks/ *das;* ~, ~[e] fax

**Fax·anschluss**, ***Fax·anschluß** *der* fax line

**faxen** *tr. V.* fax

**Faxen** *Pl.* (*ugs.*) A (*dumme Späße*) fooling around; **nur ~ im Sinn** *od.* **Kopf haben** do nothing but fool around *or* play the fool; **lass die ~!** stop fooling around *or* playing the fool!; B (*Grimassen*) **~ machen** *od.* **schneiden** make *or* pull faces

**Fax·gerät** *das* fax machine

**Fax·nummer** *die* fax number

**Fazialis** /faˈtsi̯a:lɪs/ *der;* ~ ▶ **471** (*Anat.*) facial nerve

**Fazit** /ˈfa:tsɪt/ *das;* ~s, ~s *od.* ~e result; **das ~ [aus etw.] ziehen** sum [sth.] up

**FCKW** *Abk.* **Fluorchlorkohlenwasserstoff** CFC

**FCKW-frei** *Adj.* CFC-free

**FDGB** *Abk.* (*DDR*) **Freier Deutscher Gewerkschaftsbund**

**FDJ** *Abk.* (*DDR*) **Freie Deutsche Jugend** Free German Youth

**FDJler** /ɛfdeːˈjɔtlɐ/ *der;* ~s, ~, **FDJlerin** *die;* ~, ~nen (*DDR*) Free German Youth member

**FDP, F.D.P.** *Abk.* **Freie Demokratische Partei**

**F-Dur** /ˈɛf-/ *das* (*Musik*) [key of] F major; ⇒ *auch* **A-Dur**

**Feature** /ˈfi:tʃɐ/ *das;* ~s, ~s *od. die;* ~, ~s (*Rundf., Ferns., Zeitungsw.*) feature

**Feber** /ˈfe:bɐ/ *der;* ~[s], ~ (*österr.*) February

**Febr.** *Abk.* **Februar** Feb.

**Februar** /ˈfe:brua:ɐ̯/ *der;* ~[s], ~e ▶ **207** February; ⇒ *auch* **April**

**Fecht-:** **~bahn** *die* [fencing] piste; **~boden** *der* (*Studentenspr.*) fencing room

**fechten** /ˈfɛçtn̩/ *unr. itr., tr. V.* A fence; **für etw. ~** (*fig. geh.*) fight for sth.; B (*geh.: im Krieg kämpfen*) fight

**Fechten** *das;* ~s fencing *no art.*

**Fechter** *der;* ~s, ~: fencer

**Fechter·flanke** *die* (*Turnen*) flank vault

**Fechterin** *die;* ~, ~nen fencer; ⇒ *auch* **-in**

**Fecht-:** **~hand·schuh** *der* fencing glove; **~hieb** *der* cut; **~kampf** *der* rapier fight; (*Sport*) fencing bout; **~maske** *die* fencing mask; **~meister** *der*, **~meisterin** *die* fencing master; **~sport** *der* fencing; **~stellung** *die* fencing stance; **~waffe** *die* fencing weapon

**Fedajin** /fedaˈji:n/ *der;* ~[s], ~: fedayin

**Feder** /ˈfe:dɐ/ *die;* ~, ~n A (*Vogel~*) feather; (*Gänse~*) quill; (*lange Hut~*) plume; **leicht wie eine ~ sein** be as light as a feather; **in die ~n kriechen** (*ugs.*) turn in (*coll.*); **[noch] in den ~n liegen** (*ugs.*) [still] be in one's bed; **er ließ ~n** *od.* **musste ~n lassen** (*ugs.*) he did not come out [of it] unscathed; **sich mit fremden ~n schmücken** strut in borrowed plumes; B (*zum Schreiben*) nib; (*mit Halter*) pen; (*Gänse~*) quill [pen]; **ein Mann der ~** (*geh.*) a man of letters; **eine spitze ~ führen** (*geh.*) wield a sharp pen; **aus berufener ~ stammen** (*geh.*) come from an authoritative source; **jmdm. etw. in die ~ diktieren** dictate sth. to sb.; **zur ~ greifen** (*geh.*) take up one's pen; C (*Technik*) spring; D (*Tischlerei*) tongue

**Feder·antrieb** *der* (*Technik*) clockwork

**Feder·ball** *der* A (*Spiel*) badminton; B (*Ball*) shuttlecock

**Federball-:** **~schläger** *der* badminton racket; **~spiel** *das* A badminton; B (*Zubehör*) badminton rackets and shuttlecock

**feder-, Feder-:** **~bein** *das* (*Technik*) (*am Auto*) suspension strut; (*am Motorrad*) telescopic arm; **~bett** *das* duvet (*Brit.*); continental quilt (*Brit.*); stuffed quilt (*Amer.*); **~blume** *die* artificial flower [made of feathers]; **~boa** *die* feather boa; **~busch** *der* A (*Hutzierde*) plume; B (*eines Vogels*) crest; **~fuchser** /-fʊksɐ/ *der;* ~~s, ~~, **~fuchserin** *die;* ~~, ~~nen (*abwertend*) pen-pusher; **~führend** *Adj.* in charge *postpos.*; **der ~führende Redakteur** the chief editor; **~führung** *die:* **unter der ~führung des Ministers** under the overall control of the minister; **die ~führung haben** have overall control; be in overall charge; **~gewicht** (*Schwerathletik*) A (*Gewichtsklasse*) featherweight; ⇒ *auch* **Fliegengewicht** A; B (*Sportler*) featherweight; **~gewichtler** *der;* ~~s, ~~: featherweight; **~halter** *der* fountain pen; **~kiel** *der* quill; **~kissen** *das* feather cushion; (*im Bett*) feather pillow; **~kleid** *das* (*geh.*) plumage; **~kraft** *die* A tension [of a/the spring]; B (*Elastizität*) springiness; **~leicht** ❶ *Adj.* ‹person› as light as a feather; featherweight ‹object›; ❷ *adv.* as lightly as a feather; **~lesen** *das:* **nicht viel ~lesen[s] mit jmdm./etw. machen** give sb./sth. short shrift; make short work of sb./sth.; **ohne viel ~lesen[s], ohne langes ~lesen** without much ado; **viel zu viel ~lesen[s] machen** make far too much fuss; **~mappe** *die* pen and pencil case; **~messer** *das* penknife

**federn** ❶ *itr. V.* ‹springboard, floor, etc.› be springy; **in den Knien ~**: bend at the knees; **ein ~der Gang** a springy *or* bouncy walk; **mit ~den Schritten** with a spring in one's step. ❷ *tr. V.* A (*mit einer Federung versehen*) spring; **das Auto ist gut/schlecht gefedert** the car has good/poor suspension; **das Bett ist gut gefedert** the bed is well-sprung; B ⇒ *auch* **teeren**

**Feder-:** **~ohr** *das* ear tuft; plumicorn; **~schaft** *der* shaft of a/the feather; **~schmuck** *der* A (*Kopfschmuck*) feather headdress; B (*geh.: Gefieder*) plumage; **~spiel** *das* (*Jägerspr.*) lure; **~skizze** *die* pen-and-ink sketch; **~strich** *der* stroke of the pen; **du hast noch keinen ~strich getan** (*fig. ugs.*) you have not yet put pen to paper

**Federung** *die;* ~, ~en (*in Möbeln*) springs *pl.*; (*Kfz-W.*) suspension

**Feder-:** **~vieh** *das* (*ugs.*) poultry; **~waage** *die* spring balance; **~weiße** *der; adj. Dekl.* new wine; **~werk** *das* spring mechanism; **~wild** *das* game birds *pl.*; **~wisch** *der* feather duster; **~wolke** *die* wispy *or* fleecy cloud; **~zeichnung** *die* pen-and-ink drawing

**Fee** /fe:/ *die;* ~, ~n fairy

**Feed-back** /ˈfi:dbæk/ *das;* ~s, ~s feedback

**Feeling** /ˈfi:lɪŋ/ *das;* ~s, ~s feeling; (*Geschicklichkeit*) feel

**feenhaft** *Adj.* fairy-like

**Feen-:** **~königin** *die* fairy queen; queen of the fairies; **~reich** *das* Fairyland; **ins ~reich** to Fairyland

**Fege·feuer** *das* purgatory

**fegen** /ˈfe:gn̩/ ❶ *tr. V.* A (*bes. nordd.: säubern*) sweep; B (*schnell entfernen*) brush; **etwas vom Tisch ~**: brush sth. off the table; (*fig.*) brush sth. aside; **den Gegner vom Platz ~** (*Sportjargon*) wipe the floor with one's opponent/opponents; C (*schnell treiben*) sweep; drive; D (*bes. südd.: blank reiben*) scour ‹pots, pans›; E *auch itr.* (*Jägerspr.*) fray; **die Hirsche ~ [ihr Geweih]** the stags fray [their heads]. ❷ *itr. V.* A sweep up; B *mit sein* (*rasen, stürmen*) sweep; tear (*coll.*)

**Feger** *der;* ~s, ~ (*ugs.*) live wire

**Fehde** /ˈfe:də/ *die;* ~, ~n feud; **mit jmdm. in ~ liegen** be at feud with sb.; **literarische/politische ~n [mit jmdm.] austragen/ausfechten** (*fig. geh.*) carry on/fight out literary/political controversies [with sb.]

**Fehde·hand·schuh** *der* (*geh.*) **jmdm. den ~ hinwerfen** *od.* **vor die Füße werfen**

f

throw down the gauntlet to sb.; **den ~ aufnehmen** *od.* **aufheben** take up the gauntlet

**fehl** /fe:l/ *Adv.* **~ am Platz[e] sein** be out of place

**Fehl** *in* **ohne ~ [und Tadel] sein** (*geh.*) be faultless *or* beyond reproach

**Fehl·anzeige** *die* Ⓐ (*ugs.: Ausdruck der Verneinung*) no chance (*coll.*); Ⓑ (*Milit.*) nil return

**fehlbar** *Adj.* fallible

**Fehlbarkeit** *die;* **~:** fallibility

**Fehl-: ~bedienung** *die* incorrect operation; **~besetzung** *die:* **so viele ~besetzungen** so many examples of miscasting; **[als Ophelia] eine ~besetzung sein** be miscast [in the role of Ophelia]; **~bestand** *der* shortage; deficiency; **~betrag** *der* (*bes. Kaufmannsspr.*) deficit; **~bildung** *die* ▶474 (*Med.*) deformity; malformation; **~diagnose** *die* incorrect diagnosis; **~druck** *der; Pl.* **~~e** (*Philat.*) misprint; **~ein·schätzung** *die* false assessment; (*einer Entwicklung*) misjudgement

**fehlen** *itr. V.* Ⓐ (*nicht vorhanden sein*) **ihm fehlt der Vater/das Geld** he has no father/no money; **ihr fehlt der Sinn dafür** she lacks a *or* has no feeling for it; Ⓑ (*ausbleiben*) be missing; be absent; **[un]entschuldigt ~:** be absent with[out] permission; **du darfst bei dieser Party nicht ~:** you mustn't miss this party; **diese Zutat darf bei dieser Soße nicht ~:** this ingredient is a must in this sauce; Ⓒ (*verschwunden sein*) be missing; be gone; **in der Kasse fehlt Geld** money is missing *or* has gone from the till; Ⓓ (*vermisst werden*) **er/das wird mir ~:** I shall miss him/that; Ⓔ (*erforderlich sein*) be needed; **zwei Punkte ~ nur noch** only two points are still needed; **ihm ~ noch zwei Punkte zum Sieg** he needs only two points to win; **es fehlte nicht viel, und ich wäre eingeschlafen** I all but fell asleep; **das fehlte mir gerade noch [zu meinem Glück], das hat mir gerade noch gefehlt** (*ugs.*) that's all I needed; Ⓕ *unpers.* (*mangeln*) **es fehlt an Lehrern** there is a lack of teachers; **es fehlt am Nötigsten** what is most needed is lacking; **bei ihnen fehlt es am Nötigsten** they lack what is most needed; **es an nichts ~ lassen** provide everything that is needed; **an mir soll es nicht ~:** I shall do my part; **es fehlt an allen Ecken und Enden** *od.* **Kanten [bei jmdm.]** sb. is short of everything; Ⓖ (*krank sein*) **was fehlt Ihnen?** what seems to be the matter?; **fehlt dir etwas?** is there something wrong?; are you all right?; **mir fehlt nichts** I'm all right; there is nothing wrong with me; Ⓗ **weit gefehlt!** (*geh.*) far from it!; Ⓘ (*geh.: sündigen*) do wrong; sin

**Fehl-: ~entscheidung** *die* wrong decision; **~entwicklung** *die* abortive development

**Fehler** *der;* **~s, ~** Ⓐ (*Unrichtigkeit, Irrtum*) mistake; error; (*Sport*) fault; **der Schiedsrichter entschied** *od.* **erkannte auf ~:** the referee called a fault; Ⓑ (*schlechte Eigenschaft*) fault; shortcoming; (*Gebrechen*) [physical] defect; **sein ~ ist, dass er ...** it is a fault of his that ...; Ⓒ (*schadhafte Stelle*) flaw; blemish; **Textilien/Porzellan mit kleinen ~n** textiles/porcelain with small flaws *or* imperfections

**fehler·frei** ❶ *Adj.* faultless, perfect ‹piece of work, dictation, etc.›; correct ‹measurement›; **ein ~es Deutsch sprechen/schreiben** speak/write faultless *or* perfect German; (*Reiten*) **ein ~er Durchgang** a clear round. ❷ *adv.* without any mistakes; (*Reiten*) without any faults; **ich spreche französisch, aber nicht ~:** I can speak French, but not perfectly

**Fehler·grenze** *die* margin of error; tolerance; **die ~ liegt bei 30%** there's a 30% margin of error

**fehlerhaft** *Adj.* faulty; defective; imperfect ‹pronunciation›; incorrect ‹measurement›; **eine ~e Stelle im Material** a defect in the material

**fehler-, Fehler-: ~los** ❶ *Adj.* flawless; ❷ *adv.* flawlessly; without a mistake; **etw. ~los schreiben/aufsagen** write/recite sth. without a mistake; **~quelle** *die* source of error; **~quote** *die* (*Statistik, Schulw.*) error rate; **~rechnung** *die* calculus of accidental error; **~suche** *die* Ⓐ (*bei der Reparatur*) **ein Gerät zur ~suche** a device for detecting faults; Ⓑ (*zur Kontrolle*) **bei der ~suche** when checking for faults; (*DV: im Programm*) when checking for errors; **~zahl** *die* number of mistakes *or* errors

**fehl-, Fehl-: ~farbe** *die* (*Kartenspiel*) (*Farbe, die einem Spieler fehlt*) void suit; (*Farbe, die nicht Trumpf ist*) plain suit; **mit einer ~farbe bedienen** follow with a non-trump card; **~geburt** *die* miscarriage; **~|gehen** *unr. itr. V.; mit sein* (*geh.*) Ⓐ (*sich irren*) go *or* be wrong; **in einer Annahme ~gehen** be wrong in an assumption; Ⓑ (*sich verlaufen*) lose one's way; **Sie können nicht ~gehen** you cannot go [far] wrong; Ⓒ (*nicht treffen*) ‹shot› miss [the mark]; **~griff** *der* mistake; wrong choice; **einen ~griff tun** make a mistake *or* the wrong choice; **~information** *die* piece of wrong information; **einer ~information aufsitzen** (*ugs.*) have been given wrong information; **auf einer ~information beruhen** be based on [a piece of] incorrect information; **~interpretation** *die* misinterpretation; **~investition** *die* (*bes. Wirtsch.*) Ⓐ bad investment; Ⓑ (*ugs.: Gegenstand*) **eine [glatte] ~investition sein** be a [total] waste of money; **~kalkulation** *die* miscalculation; **~kauf** *der* (*ugs.*) bad buy; **~konstruktion** *die:* **eine ~konstruktion sein** be badly designed; **~leistung** *die* (*Psych.*) slip; mistake; **eine freudsche ~leistung** a Freudian slip; **~|leiten** *tr. V.* (*geh.*) misdirect; misdirect, misroute ‹transport, convoy›; **~pass**, ***~paß** *der* (*Ballspiele*) bad pass; **~planung** *die* [piece of] bad planning *no art.;* **~schlag** *der* failure; **~|schlagen** *unr. itr. V.; mit sein* fail; ‹hopes› come to nothing; **~schluss**, ***~schluß** *der* wrong conclusion; **~sichtig** /-zɪçtɪç/ *Adj.* ‹person› with defective vision; **~sichtigkeit** *die;* **~~:** defective vision; **~start** *der* Ⓐ (*Leichtathletik*) false start; Ⓑ (*Flugw.*) faulty start; Ⓒ (*Raumf.*) abortive launch; **~tritt** *der* Ⓐ (*falscher Tritt*) false step; Ⓑ (*geh.: Verfehlung*) slip; indiscretion; (*veralt.: gesellschaftlich verpönte Liebesbeziehung*) indiscretion; **einen ~tritt begehen, sich eines ~tritts schuldig machen** commit an indiscretion; **~urteil** *das* Ⓐ (*Rechtsw.*) **ein ~urteil fällen** ‹jury› return a wrong verdict; ‹judge› pass a wrong judgement; Ⓑ (*falsche Beurteilung*) error of judgement; **ein ~urteil über etw.** (*Akk.*) **abgeben** make an incorrect assessment of sth.; **~verhalten** *das* Ⓐ (*fehlerhaftes Verhalten*) incorrect conduct; **~verhalten beim Überholen** incorrect action when overtaking; Ⓑ (*anormales Verhalten*) aberrant behaviour; **~versuch** *der* (*Gewichtheben, Hochsprung*) unsuccessful attempt; failure; (*Weitsprung*) foul jump; **~zündung** *die* (*Technik*) misfire

**Fehn** /fe:n/ *das;* **~[e]s, ~e** fen; marsh

**Fehn·kultur** *die* (*Landw.*) *method of cultivation which puts marshland to agricultural use*

**feien** /ˈfaiən/ *tr. V.; meist im 2. Part.* (*geh.*) protect (**gegen** against); **gegen Tropenkrankheiten gefeit sein** be immune to tropical diseases

**Feier** /ˈfaiɐ/ *die;* **~, ~n** Ⓐ (*Veranstaltung*) party; (*aus festlichem Anlass*) celebration; **zu** *od.* **anlässlich einer Begebenheit eine ~ veranstalten** celebrate an occasion with a party; **eine ~ in kleinem Rahmen/im Familienkreis** a small/family celebration/party; **keine ~ ohne Meier** (*scherzh.*) he/she *etc.* never misses a party; Ⓑ (*Zeremonie*) ceremony; **die ~ des heiligen Abendmahls** the celebration of Holy Communion; **zur ~ des Tages** (*oft scherzh.*) to mark the day; in honour of the occasion

**Feier·abend** *der* Ⓐ (*Zeit nach der Arbeit*) evening; **den ~ genießen** enjoy one's evening; **schönen ~!** have a nice evening; Ⓑ (*Arbeitsschluss*) finishing time; **nach ~:** after work; **~ machen** finish work; knock off; **für mich ist ~, dann ist** *od.* **mache ich ~** (*fig. ugs.*) I'm finished; I've had enough (*coll.*)

**Feierabend-: ~beschäftigung** *die* leisure pursuit; spare-time interest; **~heim** *das* (*DDR*) old people's home; **~lektüre** *die* leisure-time reading

**Feierei** *die;* **~, ~en** (*ugs. abwertend*) **diese ständige ~:** these endless parties

**feierlich** ❶ *Adj.* Ⓐ ceremonial; solemn; **eine ~e Handlung** a ceremonial act; **eine ~e Stille** a solemn silence; **das ist ja [schon] nicht mehr ~** (*ugs.*) it's got beyond a joke; Ⓑ (*emphatisch*) solemn ‹declaration›. ❷ *adv.* Ⓐ solemnly; ceremoniously; **jmdm. ist ~ zumute** sb. is in a solemn mood *or* frame of mind; **~ verabschiedet werden** be given a ceremonious farewell; Ⓑ (*emphatisch*) solemnly ‹declare, swear, etc.›

**Feierlichkeit** *die;* **~, ~en** Ⓐ (*Würde, Ernst*) solemnity; Ⓑ (*feierliche Veranstaltung*) celebration; festivity

**feiern** ❶ *tr. V.* Ⓐ (*festlich begehen*) celebrate ‹birthday, wedding, etc.›; **man muss die Feste ~, wie sie fallen** you have to enjoy yourself while you can; Ⓑ (*ehren, umjubeln*) acclaim ‹artist, sportsman, etc.›; **ein gefeierter Sportler/Dichter** a celebrated sportsman/poet; **Triumphe ~:** win the highest acclaim. ❷ *itr. V.* (*lustig beisammen sein*) celebrate; have a party

**feier-, Feier-: ~schicht** *die* (*Arbeitswelt*) cancelled shift; **eine ~schicht einlegen müssen** have one's shift cancelled; **~stunde** *die* ceremony; **jmdn. in/mit einer ~stunde ehren** hold a ceremony in sb.'s honour; **~tag** *der* holiday; **ein gesetzlicher/kirchlicher ~tag** a public holiday/religious festival; **an Sonn- und ~tagen** on Sundays and public holidays; **jmdm. schöne ~tage wünschen** wish sb. a good holiday; **für mich ist heute ein ~tag** (*fig.*) today is a very special *or* a red letter day for me; **~täglich** *Adj.* solemn ‹silence, mood›; **~tags** *Adv.* **sonn- und ~tags** on Sundays and public holidays; **~tags·stimmung** *die* Sunday mood

**feig, feige** /faik, ˈfaigə/ ❶ *Adj.* cowardly. ❷ *adv.* like a coward/like cowards; in a cowardly way

**Feige** *die;* **~, ~n** fig

**Feigen-: ~baum** *der* fig tree; **~blatt** *das* Ⓐ (*Blatt*) fig leaf; Ⓑ (*fig.: Verhüllung*) front; cover; **~kaktus** *der* Indian fig; prickly pear

**Feigheit** *die;* **~:** cowardice; cowardliness; **~ vor dem Feind** (*Milit.*) cowardice in the face of the enemy

**Feigling** *der;* **~s, ~e** coward

**feil** /fail/ *Adj.* (*veralt.*) for sale *postpos.;* (*fig.*) venal; **eine ~e Dirne** (*veralt.*) a harlot; **für Geld ist nicht alles ~:** money can't buy everything

**feil|bieten** *unr. tr. V.* (*geh.*) offer ‹goods› for sale

**Feile** *die;* **~, ~n** file; **etw. mit einer ~ bearbeiten** file sth.

**feilen** *tr., itr. V.* file; **etw. passend/rund ~:** file sth. to fit/into a round shape; **sich** (*Dat.*) **die Fingernägel ~:** file one's [finger]nails

**feil|halten** *unr. tr. V.* (*veralt.*) offer ‹goods› for sale

**feilschen** /ˈfailʃn̩/ *itr. V.* haggle (**um** over); **nach langem/hartem Feilschen** after a long/hard bout of haggling

**Feil-: ~span** *der* filing; **~staub** *der* filings *pl.*

**fein** /fain/ ❶ *Adj.* Ⓐ (*zart*) fine ‹material, line, mesh, etc.›; Ⓑ (*aus kleinsten Teilchen bestehend*) fine ‹sand, powder›; finely ground ‹flour›; finely granulated ‹sugar›; **etw. ~ mahlen** grind sth. fine; **etw. ~ schleifen** fine-grind sth.; **~ gemahlen** finely ground; **~ geschnitten** finely chopped; (*fig.: schön geformt*) delicate, finely shaped ‹face, hands, etc.›; Ⓒ (*hochwertig*) high-quality ‹fruit, soap, etc.›; fine ‹silver, gold, etc.›; fancy ‹cakes, pastries, etc.›; **nur das Feinste vom Feinen kaufen**

*old spelling (see note on page 1707)

buy only the best; **vom Feinsten** of the finest *or* highest quality; **D** (*ugs.: erfreulich*) great (*coll.*); marvellous; **E** (*~ geschnitten*) finely shaped, delicate ‹hands, features, etc.›; **F** (*scharf, exakt*) keen, sensitive ‹hearing›; keen ‹sense of smell›; **eine ~e Nase für etw. haben** (*fig.*) have a good nose for sth.; **G** (*listig, gerissen*) cunning ‹move, scheme›; **H** (*ugs.: anständig, nett*) great (*coll.*), splendid ‹person›; **eine ~e Verwandtschaft/Gesellschaft** (*iron.*) a fine *or* nice family/crowd; **I** (*einfühlsam*) delicate ‹sense of humour›; keen ‹sense, understanding›; **ein ~es Gespür für etw. haben** have a good feeling for sth.; **J** (*gediegen, vornehm*) refined ‹gentleman, lady›; **du bist dir wohl zu ~ dafür!** (*ugs.*) I suppose you think it's beneath you; **sich ~ machen** (*ugs.*) dress up; ⇒ *auch* **Herr** A.

❷ *adv.* **A** (*gut, günstig*) **~ [he]raus sein** (*ugs.*) be sitting pretty (*coll.*); **Unterschiede ~ herausarbeiten** bring out subtle differences; **B** (*listig, gerissen*) **~ ausgeklügelt** cleverly thought out; **C** (*ugs.: bekräftigend*) **etw. ~ säuberlich aufschreiben** write sth. down nice and neatly; **~ brav sein** be a good boy/girl

**Fein-: ~ab·stimmung** *die* (*Technik*) fine tuning; **~arbeit** *die* detailed work; (*Technik*) precision work; **~bäckerei** *die* patisserie; **~bearbeitung** *die* (*Technik*) finishing; **~blech** *das* thin sheet metal

***feind, Feind** /faint/ (*geh.*) *in* **jmdm./einer Sache ~ sein** be hostile towards sb./sth.

**-feind** *der* ...hater; **ein Hunde~/Fernseh~ sein** be anti dogs/television

**Feind** *der;* **~[e]s, ~e** **A** enemy; **er ist ein ~ des Alkohols** he is opposed to alcohol; **sich** (*Dat.*) **~e machen** make enemies; **sich** (*Dat.*) **jmdn. zum ~ machen** make an enemy of sb.; **liebet eure ~e** (*bibl.*) love thine enemy; **„~ hört mit"** 'careless talk costs lives'; **B** (*feindliche Truppen*) enemy *constr. as pl.;* **[nichts wie] ran an den ~** (*fig. ugs.*) get/let's get going *or* (*coll.*) stuck in

**Feind-: ~berührung** *die* (*Milit.*) contact with the enemy; **~bild** *das* concept of the enemy

**Feindes-: ~hand** *die* (*veralt.*) **in ~hand geraten** *od.* **fallen** fall into the hands of the enemy; **von ~hand fallen** fall at the hands of the enemy; **~land** *das* (*veralt.*) enemy territory

**Feind·flug** *der* (*Luftwaffe*) operational flight [over enemy territory]

**Feindin** *die;* **~, ~nen** ⇒ **Feind** A

**feindlich** ❶ *Adj.* **A** hostile; **B** (*Milit.*) enemy ‹attack, broadcast, activity›. ❷ *adv.* in a hostile manner; with hostility

**-feindlich** *adj.* anti-‹Soviet, American, EU, government, etc.›; **familienfeindliche/kinderfeindliche Gesetze** laws which are hostile towards families/children

**Feindlichkeit** *die;* **~, ~en** hostility (**gegenüber** towards); **~en** hostilities

**Feind·mächte** *Pl.* enemy powers *pl.*

**Feindschaft** *die;* **~, ~en** enmity; **zwischen ihnen herrscht bittere ~:** they are bitter enemies; **sich** (*Dat.*) **jmds. ~ zuziehen** make an enemy of sb.

**feind·selig** ❶ *Adj.* hostile; **sich ~ gegen jmdn. zeigen** show hostility towards sb. ❷ *adv.* **sich ~ ansehen** look at each other in a hostile manner *or* with hostility

**Feind·seligkeit** *die;* **~, ~en** hostility; **~en** (*Milit.*) hostilities

**fein-, Fein-: ~einstellung** *die* fine adjustment; **~frost** *der* (*DDR*) deep-frozen foods *pl.;* **~fühlig** ❶ *Adj.* sensitive; ❷ *adv.* sensitively; **~fühligkeit** *die;* **~~:** sensitivity; **~gebäck** *das* [fancy] cakes and pastries *pl.;* **~gefühl** *das* sensitivity; **~gehalt** *der* fineness; ***~gemahlen** ⇒ **fein** 1B; ***~geschnitten** ⇒ **fein** 1B; **~gewicht** *das* fineness; **~glied[e]rig** *Adj.* delicate; slender; **~gold** *das* fine gold; **~guss, *~guß** *der* (*Metall*) precision casting

**Feinheit** *die;* **~, ~en** **A** (*zarte Beschaffenheit*) fineness; delicacy; **B** (*Nuance, Andeutung*) subtlety; **die stilistischen ~en** the stylistic subtleties *or* nuances; **C** (*Vornehmheit*) refinement

**fein-, Fein-: ~körnig** *Adj.* **A** fine-grained, fine ‹sand, gravel, etc.›; finely granulated ‹sugar›; **B** (*Fot.*) fine-grain ‹film›; **~kost** *die* delicatessen *pl.;* **~kost·geschäft** *das* delicatessen; ***~|machen** ⇒ **fein** 1 J; **~maschig** *Adj.* finely meshed, fine-mesh *attrib.* ‹net etc.›; **~mechanik** *die* precision engineering *no art.;* **~mechaniker** *der,* **~mechanikerin** *die* ▶159| precision engineer; **~mechanisch** *Adj.* precision ‹instrument›; **~mess·gerät, *~meß·gerät** *das* precision measuring instrument; **~nervig** *Adj.* sensitive; **~säuberlich** *Adj.* (*österr.*) ⇒ **säuberlich;** ***~|schleifen** ⇒ **fein** 1 B; **~schmecker** *der;* **~~s, ~~,** **~schmeckerin** *die;* **~~, ~~nen** gourmet; **~schmecker·lokal** *das* gourmet restaurant; **~schnitt** *der* **A** (*Tabak*) fine cut; **B** (*Film*) final editing; **~silber** *das* fine silver; **~sinnig** ❶ *Adj.* sensitive and subtle; ❷ *adv.* in a sensitive and subtle manner; **~sinnigkeit** *die;* **~~:** sensitivity and subtlety

**Feins·liebchen** *das* (*dichter. veralt.*) sweetheart

**Fein-: ~struktur** *die* (*Physik, Med.*) fine structure; **~strumpf·hose** *die* sheer tights *pl. or* pantihose; **~unze** *die:* **eine ~unze Gold/Silber** an ounce of fine gold/silver; **~wäsche** *die* delicates *pl.;* **~wasch·mittel** *das* mild detergent

**feist** *Adj.* (*meist abwertend*) fat ‹face, fingers, etc.›; **mit einem ~en Grinsen** (*fig.*) with a leer

**feixen** /ˈfaiksn̩/ *itr. V.* (*ugs.*) smirk

**Felchen** /ˈfɛlçn̩/ *der;* **~s, ~:** whitefish

**Feld** /fɛlt/ *das;* **~[e]s, ~er** **A** (*geh.: unbebaute Bodenfläche*) country[side]; **freies ~:** open country[side]; **B** (*bebaute Bodenfläche*) field; **auf dem ~ arbeiten** work in the field; **das ~ bestellen** till the field; **C** (*Sport: Spiel~*) pitch; field [of play]; **D** (*auf Formularen*) box; space; (*auf Brettspielen*) space; (*auf dem Schachbrett*) square; (*in Kassettendecken*) panel; **E** (*Tätigkeitsbereich*) field; sphere; **das ~ der Wissenschaften** the field of science; **ein weites ~ [sein]** (*fig.*) [be] a wide sphere; **F** (*veralt.: Schlacht~*) field [of battle]; **ins ~ rücken** *od.* **ziehen** (*veralt.*) go into battle; **gegen/für jmdn./etw. ins ~ ziehen** (*fig.*) crusade against/for sb./sth.; **das ~ behaupten** stand one's ground; **in der Politik behaupten nach wie vor Männer das ~:** politics is still dominated by men; **das ~ räumen** leave; get out; **jmdm. das ~ überlassen** hand over to sb.; leave sb. a clear field; **jmdn. aus dem ~[e] schlagen** eliminate sb.; get rid of sb.; **jmdm. das ~ streitig machen** compete with sb.; **etw. gegen jmdn./etw. ins ~ führen** bring up sth. against sb./sth.; **G** (*Sport: geschlossene Gruppe*) field; **H** (*Physik, Sprachw.*) field

**feld-, Feld-: ~ahorn** *der* field maple; **~arbeit** *die* **A** work in the field; **B** (*Wissensch.*) fieldwork; **~bahn** *die* narrow-gauge railway; light railway; **~bau** *der* agriculture; **~bett** *das* camp bed; **~blume** *die* field flower; wild flower; **~ein[wärts]** /-ˈ-(-)/ *Adv.* across the field/fields; **~flasche** *die* (*Milit.*) canteen; water bottle; **~forschung** *die* (*Wissensch.*) fieldwork; **~frucht** *die* arable crop; **~geistliche** *der* (*Milit. veralt.*) army chaplain; **~gottesdienst** *der* field service; **~grau** *Adj.* field-grey; **~hand·ball** *der* field handball; fieldball; **~hase** *der* common hare; European hare

**Feld·herr** *der* (*veralt.*) commander

**Feldherrn-: ~kunst** *die* (*veralt.*) strategy; **~stab** *der* (*veralt.*) field marshal's baton

**feld-, Feld-: ~hockey** *das* (*Sport*) [field] hockey; **~huhn** *das* partridge; **~hüter** *der,* **~hüterin** *die: guard protecting crops from birds, thieves, etc.;* **~jäger** *der* (*Polizist*) military policeman; **die ~jäger** the military police; **~küche** *die* (*bes. Milit.*) field kitchen; **~lager** *das* (*veralt.*) encampment; **~lazarett** *das* field hospital; **~linien** *Pl.* (*Physik*) field lines; **~marschall** *der* ▶91| Field Marshal; **~marsch·mäßig** ❶ *Adj.* in full marching order *postpos.;* ❷ *adv.* **~marschmäßig angetreten/ausgerüstet sein** be lined up/be in full marching order; **~maus** *die* [European] common vole

**Feld·post** *die* forces' (*Brit.*) *or* (*Amer.*) military postal service

**Feldpost-: ~brief** *der* forces' (*Brit.*) *or* (*Amer.*) military letter; **~nummer** *die* forces' (*Brit.*) *or* (*Amer.*) military postal code

**Feld-: ~prediger** *der* (*veralt.*) army chaplain; **~rain** *der* balk; baulk; **~salat** *der* corn salad; lamb's lettuce

**Feldscher** /ˈfɛltʃeːɐ̯/ *der;* **~s, ~e** (*Milit.*) **A** (*hist.: Wundarzt*) [unqualified] army doctor; **B** (*DDR*) medical orderly

**Feld-: ~schlacht** *die* (*veralt.*) battle [in the field]; **~schütz** *der;* **~~en, ~~en** field guard; **~spat** /-ʃpaːt/ *der* feldspar; **~spieler** *der,* **~spielerin** *die* player (*excluding goalkeeper*); **~stärke** *die* (*Physik*) field strength; **~stecher** *der;* **~~s, ~~:** binoculars *pl.;* field glasses *pl.;* **~stein** *der* stone; boulder; **~studie** *die* (*Wissensch.*) field study; **~theorie** *die* (*Sprachw.*) field theory; **~überlegenheit** *die* (*Sport*) superiority; **~versuch** *der* (*Wissensch.*) field experiment; **~verweis** *der* (*Sport*) sending-off; **einen ~verweis gegen jmdn. aussprechen** send sb. off [the field]

**Feld-Wald-und-Wiesen-** (*ugs.*) run-of-the-mill; common-or-garden

**Feld·webel** /-veːbl̩/ *der;* **~s, ~** ▶91| (*Milit.*) sergeant

**Feld·weg** *der* path; track

**Feld·weibel** /-vaibl̩/ *der;* **~s, ~** (*schweiz. Milit.*) sergeant

**Feld-: ~zeichen** *das* (*hist.*) standard; flag; **~zug** *der* (*Milit., fig.*) campaign

**Felg·auf·schwung** *der* (*Turnen*) upward circle forwards

**Felge** /ˈfɛlɡə/ *die;* **~, ~n** **A** (*Radkranz*) [wheel] rim; **die Reifen auf die ~n montieren** put the tyres on the wheels; **B** (*Turnen*) circle

**Felgen·bremse** *die* (*Technik*) rim brake

**Felg·um·schwung** *der* (*Turnen*) circle

**Fell** /fɛl/ *das;* **~[e]s, ~e** **A** (*Haarkleid*) fur; (*Pferde~, Hunde~, Katzen~*) coat; (*Schaf~*) fleece; skin; **ein weiches/glänzendes ~:** a soft/shiny coat; **einem Tier das ~ abziehen** skin an animal; **jmdm. das ~ über die Ohren ziehen** (*fig. salopp*) take sb. for a ride (*coll.*); **B** (*Material*) fur; furskin; **ein Mantel aus [braunem] ~:** a [brown] fur coat; **C** (*abgezogene behaarte Haut*) skin; hide; **ihm sind die** *od.* **alle ~e weg-** *od.* **davongeschwommen** (*fig.*) he has had all his hopes dashed; **D** (*salopp: Haut des Menschen*) skin; (*fig.*) **ihm** *od.* **ihn juckt das ~** (*ugs.*) he is asking for a good hiding (*coll.*); **sich** (*Dat.*) **ein dickes ~ anschaffen** (*ugs.*) become thick-skinned; **ein dickes ~ haben** (*ugs.*) be thick-skinned *or* have a thick skin; **jmdm. das ~ versohlen** (*ugs.*) tan sb.'s hide; give sb. a good hiding (*coll.*); **das ~ versaufen** (*ugs.*) have a good drink to sb.'s memory

**Fellache** /fɛˈlaxə/ *der;* **~n, ~n, Fellachin** *die;* **~, ~nen** fellah

**Fellatio** /fɛˈlaːtsio/ *die;* **~:** fellatio *no art.*

**Fell·eisen** *das* (*veralt.*) knapsack

**Fell-: ~handel** *der* skin trade; **~jacke** *die* fur jacket; **~mütze** *die* fur cap

**Fels** /fɛls/ *der;* **~en, ~en** **A** (*Gestein*) rock; **B** (*geh.: ~en*) rock; **wie ein ~ in der Brandung stehen** stand as firm as a rock; ⇒ *auch* **wachsen**[1] A

**Fels-: ~bild** *das* rock painting; **~block** *der; Pl.* **~blöcke** rock; boulder

**Felsen** /ˈfɛlzn̩/ *der;* **~s, ~:** rock; (*an der Steilküste*) cliff

**felsen-, Felsen-: ~bucht** *die* bay lined by cliffs; cliff-lined bay; **~fest** ❶ *Adj.* firm; unshakeable ‹opinion, belief›; ❷ *adv.* ‹believe, be convinced› firmly; **~grab** *das* rock tomb; **~grotte** *die* grotto; cave; **~höhle** *die* rock cave; **~klippe** *die* rocky cliff; **an einer ~klippe zerschellen** be dashed to pieces on a rock; ~**küste** *die* rocky coast *or* coastline; ~**riff** *das* rocky reef; ~**tor** *das* (*Geogr.*) rock arch

**Fels-:** ~**geröll** *das* rocks *pl.*; boulders *pl.*; ~**haken** *der* (*Bergsteigen*) piton

**felsig** *Adj.* rocky

**Fels-:** ~**massiv** *das* [rock] massif; ~**nase** *die* ledge; ~**schlucht** *die* gorge; ravine; ~**spalte** *die* crevice [in the rock]; ~**vorsprung** *der* ledge; ~**wand** *die* rock face; **in der ~wand** on the rock face

**fem.** *Abk.* **feminin** fem.

**Feme** /ˈfeːmə/ *die;* ~, ~**n** Ⓐ (*hist.*) vehmgericht; Ⓑ (*Geheimgericht*) kangaroo court

**Feme-:** ~**gericht** *das* ⇒ **Feme**; ~**mord** *der* lynching

**feminin** /femiˈniːn/ *Adj.* Ⓐ (*geh.: weiblich*) feminine ‹characteristic, behaviour›; Ⓑ (*abwertend: unmännlich*) effeminate ‹man, type›; Ⓒ (*Sprachw.*) feminine

**Femininum** /ˈfeːmininʊm/ *das;* ~**s**, **Feminina** feminine noun

**Feminismus** *der;* ~, **Feminismen** Ⓐ (*Frauenbewegung*) feminism *no art.*; Ⓑ ▶ **474** (*Med., Zool.*) feminism *no art.*

**Feminist** *der;* ~**en**, ~**en**, **Feministin** *die;* ~, ~**nen** feminist

**feministisch** *Adj.* feminist

**Femme fatale** /famfaˈtal/ *die;* ~, **Femmes fatales** (*geh.*) femme fatale

**Fenchel** /ˈfɛnçl̩/ *der;* ~**s** fennel

**Fenchel-:** ~**knolle** *die* fennel; ~**öl** *das* fennel oil; ~**tee** *der* fennel tea

**Fender** /ˈfɛndɐ/ *der;* ~**s**, ~ (*Seew.*) fender

**Fenn** /fɛn/ *das;* ~**[e]s**, ~**e** (*bes. nordd.*) fen

**Fennek** /ˈfɛnɛk/ *der;* ~**s**, ~**s** *od.* ~**e** fennec

**Fenster** /ˈfɛnstɐ/ *das;* ~**s**, ~ (*auch DV*) window; **im ~ liegen** be leaning out of the window; **[sein] Geld zum ~ hinauswerfen** (*fig.*) throw [one's] money down the drain; **weg vom ~ sein** (*ugs.*) be right out of it

**Fenster-:** ~**bank** *die; Pl.* ~**bänke** window sill; window ledge; ~**bogen** *der* (*Archit.*) window arch; ~**brett** *das* ⇒ ~**bank**; ~**brief[umschlag]** *der* window envelope; ~**brüstung** *die* window breast; ~**flügel** *der* [side of a/the] window; ~**front** *die* window frontage; ~**gips** *der* (*Med.*) fenestrated plaster; ~**gitter** *das* window grille *or* grating; ~**glas** *das; Pl.* ~**gläser** Ⓐ window glass; Ⓑ (*ungeschliffenes Glas*) plain glass; **eine Brille aus ~glas** glasses with plain glass lenses; ~**griff** *der* window catch; ~**heber** *der* (*Kfz.-W.*) window regulator; (*elektrisch*) window [regulator] mechanism; **das Auto hat elektrische ~heber** this car has electric windows; ~**kitt** *der* window putty; ~**klappe** *die* shutter opening; ~**kreuz** *das* mullion and transom; ~**kurbel** *die* window handle; ~**laden** *der; Pl.* ~**läden**, *auch* ~~**:** [window] shutter; ~**leder** *das* wash leather

**fensterln** /ˈfɛnstɐln/ *itr. V.* (*bes. südd., österr.*) climb through one's sweetheart's window

**fenster-, Fenster-:** ~**los** *Adj.* windowless; ~**nische** *die* window recess; ~**öffnung** *die* window opening; ~**platz** *der* window seat; seat by the window; ~**putzer** *der;* ~~**s**, ~~, ~**putzerin** *die;* ~~, ~~**nen** ▶ **159** window cleaner; ~**rahmen** *der* window frame; ~**ritze** *die* gap between window pane and frame; ~**rose** *die* (*Archit.*) rose window; ~**scheibe** *die* window pane; ~**sims** *der od. das* ⇒ ~**bank**; ~**sturz** *der* Ⓐ **der Prager ~sturz** (*Hist.*) the Defenestration of Prague; Ⓑ (~*abschluss*) [window] lintel; ~**verband** *der* (*Med.*) fenestrated dressing

**Ferial·tag** /feˈri̯aːl-/ *der* (*österr.*) ⇒ **Ferientag**

**Ferien** /ˈfeːri̯ən/ *Pl.* Ⓐ (*Arbeitspause*) holiday (*Brit.*); vacation (*Amer.*); (*Werks*~) shutdown; holiday (*Brit.*); (*Parlaments*~) recess; (*Hochschul*~) vacation; **in den großen/während der großen ~:** in/during the summer holidays/vacation; **~ haben** have a *or* be on holiday/vacation; **das Parlament geht in die ~:** parliament goes into recess; Ⓑ (*Urlaub*) holiday[s *pl.*] (*Brit.*); vacation (*Amer.*); **in die ~ fahren** go on holiday/vacation

**Ferien-** holiday... (*Brit.*); vacation... (*Amer.*); ⇒ *auch* **Urlaubs-**

**Ferien-:** ~**arbeit** *die* vacation work; **eine ~arbeit** a vacation job; ~**aufenthalt** *der* holiday (*Brit.*); vacation (*Amer.*); ~**beginn** *der* start of the school holidays/vacation; ~**dorf** *das* holiday/vacation village; ~**erlebnis** *das* holiday/vacation experience; ~**gast** *der* holiday/vacation guest; ~**haus** *das* holiday/vacation house; ~**heim** *das* holiday/vacation home; ~**kind** *das: child on a state-subsidized holiday/vacation in the country or at the seaside;* ~**kolonie** *die* [children's] holiday/vacation camp; ~**kurs** *der* vacation course; ~**lager** *das* holiday/vacation camp; ~**ordnung** *die* holiday/vacation dates *pl.*; ~**ort** *der* holiday/vacation resort; **ein idyllischer ~ort** an idyllic holiday/vacation spot *or* spot for a holiday/vacation; ~**paradies** *das* holiday[-maker's]/vacation[er's] paradise; ~**reise** *die* holiday/vacation trip; ~**sonder·zug** *der* special holiday/vacation train; holiday/vacation special; ~**tag** *der* day [of one's holiday (*Brit.*) *or* (*Amer.*) vacation]; ~**zeit** *die* holiday (*Brit.*); vacation (*Amer.*); **zu Beginn der ~zeit** at the beginning of the holidays/vacation; ~**zentrum** *das* holiday/vacation centre *or* resort

**Ferkel** /ˈfɛrkl̩/ *das;* ~**s**, ~ Ⓐ (*junges Schwein*) piglet; Ⓑ (*ugs. abwertend*) pig; **du [altes] ~!** you [dirty] pig!

**Ferkelei** *die;* ~, ~**en** (*ugs. abwertend*) (*Benehmen*) filthy behaviour; (*Bemerkung*) dirty remark; **seine ~en** his filth *sing. or* smut *sing.*

**ferkeln** *itr. V.* Ⓐ (*Ferkel werfen*) farrow; Ⓑ (*ugs. abwertend*) be filthy

**Fermate** /fɛrˈmaːtə/ *die;* ~, ~**n** (*Musik*) pause

**Ferment** /fɛrˈmɛnt/ *das;* ~**[e]s**, ~**e** (*veralt.*) ferment (*arch.*); enzyme

**Fermentation** /fɛrmɛntaˈtsi̯oːn/ *die;* ~, ~**en** fermentation

**fermentieren** *tr. V.* ferment

**fern** /fɛrn/ ❶ *Adj.* Ⓐ (*räumlich*) distant, far-off, faraway ‹country, region, etc.›; **jmdn./etw. von jmdm./etw. ~ halten** keep sb./sth. away from sb./sth.; **sich von jmdm./etw. ~ halten** keep away from sb./sth.; Ⓑ (*zeitlich*) distant ‹past, future›; **eine Geschichte aus ~en Tagen** a story from far-off days; **in [nicht allzu] ~er Zukunft** in the [not too] distant future; **der Tag ist nicht mehr ~:** the day is not far off; **der Frieden ist ~er denn je** peace is farther away than ever.

❷ *adv.* **~ von der Heimat [sein/leben]** [be/live] far from home; **etw. von ~ betrachten** look at sth. from a distance; **von ~ betrachtet** (*fig.*) looked at from a distance; **so von ~ betrachtet würde ich ...** looking at it from a distance, I should ...; **das liegt mir ~:** that is the last thing I want to do; **es liegt mir ~, das zu tun** I shouldn't dream of doing that; **das sei ~ von mir, dass ich dich jemals verraten werde** (*geh.*) heaven forbid that I should ever betray you; **jmdm. ~ stehen** (*geh.*) not be on close terms with sb.; ⇒ *auch* **Osten** C; **nahe** 2 A.

❸ *Präp. mit Dat.* (*geh.*) far [away] from; a long way from; **~ der Heimat [leben]** [live] far from home *or* a long way from home

**fern-, Fern-:** ~**ab** /-ˈ-/ (*geh.*) ❶ *Adv.* far away; **~ab von aller Zivilisation** far [away] from all civilization; ❷ *Präp. mit Dat.* **~ab aller Zivilisation** far [away] from all civilization; ~**amt** *das* (*veralt.*) telephone exchange; ~**auslöser** *der* (*Fot.*) remote shutter release; ~**bahn** *die* main-line railway; ~**bahn·hof** *der* main-line station; ~**beben** *das* (*Geol.*) distant earthquake; ~**bedienung** *die* remote control; ~**bereich** *der* (*bes. Fot.*) distance; ~**|bleiben** *unr. itr. V.; mit sein* (*geh.*) stay away; **dem Unterricht ~bleiben** stay away from lessons; ~**blick** *der* view

**ferne** *in* **von ~** (*geh.*) from far off *or* away

**Ferne** *die;* ~, ~**n** Ⓐ (*räumlich*) distance; **etw. in weiter ~ erblicken** see sth. in the far distance; **ein Gruß aus der ~:** greetings from afar *or* far away; **in die ~ ziehen** (*geh.*) travel to far-off parts [of the world]; Ⓑ (*Zukunft*) future; (*Vergangenheit*) past; **das liegt noch/schon in weiter ~:** that is still far off *or* a long time away/that was a long time ago

**ferner** *Adv.* Ⓐ in addition; furthermore; **er rangiert unter „~ liefen"** (*fig.*) he is an also-ran; Ⓑ (*geh.: künftig*) in [the] future; **auch ~ etw. tun** continue to do sth.

**ferner...** *Adj.* (*Papierdt.*) further

**ferner·hin** *Adv.* Ⓐ in [the] future; **wir werden ihn auch ~ unterstützen** we shall continue to support him. Ⓑ ⇒ **ferner** A

**fern-, Fern-:** ~**fahrer** *der*, ~**fahrerin** *die* ▶ **159** long-distance lorry driver (*Brit.*) *or* (*Amer.*) trucker; ~**fahrer·lokal** *das* transport café; ~**fahrt** *die* long run *or* trip; ~**flug** *der* long-distance *or* long-haul flight; ~**gelenkt** *Adj.* remote-controlled; (*fig.: durch Geheimdienste usw.*) controlled; **eine ~gelenkte Rakete** a guided missile; ~**geschoss**, *~**geschoß** *das* (*Milit.*) long-range missile; ~**gespräch** *das* long-distance call; trunk call; **ein ~gespräch mit jmdm./London führen** speak to *or* with sb./London long-distance; ~**gesteuert** *Adj.* ⇒ ~**gelenkt**; ~**glas** *das; Pl.* ~**gläser** binoculars *pl.*; **etw. mit dem ~glas erkennen** make sth. out with binoculars; ~**|gucken** *itr. V.* (*ugs.*) watch telly (*coll.*) *or* the box (*coll.*); *~**|halten** ⇒ **fern** 1A; ~**heizung** *die* district heating system; ~**her** *Adv.* (*geh.*) **[von] ~her** from afar; ~**hin** *Adv.* (*geh.*) far off; ~**kopierer** *der* fax machine; ~**kurs[us]** *der* correspondence course; ~**laster** *der* (*ugs.*) long-distance lorry (*Brit.*) *or* (*Amer.*) truck; ~**last·fahrer** *der*, ~**last·fahrerin** *die* long-distance lorry driver (*Brit.*) *or* (*Amer.*) trucker; ~**last·zug** *der* [long-distance] articulated lorry; ~**lehr·gang** *der* correspondence course; ~**leihe** *die* Ⓐ (*Dienststelle*) inter-library loans department; Ⓑ (*Leihverkehr*) inter-library loan system; **ein Buch über [die] ~leihe bestellen** order a book through inter-library loans; ~**leitung** *die* Ⓐ (*Postw.*) long-distance line; Ⓑ (*Energiewirtsch.*) long-distance cable; ~**|lenken** *tr. V.* operate by remote control; ~**lenkung** *die* remote control; ~**lenk·waffen** *Pl.* guided missiles; ~**licht** *das* (*Kfz-W.*) full beam; **das ~licht anhaben** drive on full beam; *~**|liegen** ⇒ **fern** 2

**Fern·melde-:** ~**amt** *das* telephone exchange; ~**gebühren** *Pl.* telephone charges; ~**netz** *das* telecommunications network; ~**satellit** *der* communications satellite; ~**technik** *die* telecommunications *sing., no art.*; ~**truppe** *die* (*Milit.*) signal corps; ~**turm** *der* telecommunications tower; ~**verkehr** *der* telecommunication; ~**wesen** *das* telecommunications *pl.*

**fern-, Fern-:** ~**mündlich** ❶ *Adj.* telephone ‹communication›; ❷ *adv.* by telephone; ~**ost** *in* **in/aus** *usw.* ~**ost** in/from etc. the Far East; **in/nach ~ost** in/to the Far East; ~**östlich** *Adj.* Far Eastern; **eine ~östliche Schönheit** an oriental beauty; ~**rohr** *das* telescope; ~**ruf** *der* telephone number; **~ruf: 45678** telephone *or* tel.: 45678; ~**schach** *das* correspondence chess; ~**schaltung** *die* remote control system; **durch ~schaltung** by remote control; ~**schreiben** *das* telex [message]; ~**schreiber** *der* telex [machine]; teleprinter; ~**schriftlich** ❶ *Adj.* telex ‹message›; ❷ *adv.* by telex; ~**schuss**, *~**schuß** *der* (*Ballspiele*) long-range shot

**Fernseh-:** ~**ansager** *der*, ~**ansagerin** *die* television announcer; ~**anstalt** *die* television organization; ~**antenne** *die* television aerial (*Brit.*) *or* (*Amer.*) antenna; ~**apparat** *der* television [set]; ~**aufzeichnung** *die* telerecording; ~**diskussion** *die* [television] discussion programme; ~**empfang** *der* television reception

**fern|sehen** *unr. itr. V.* watch television

**Fern·sehen** *das;* ~**s** television; **im ~:** on television; **vom** *od.* **im ~ übertragen werden** be televised; be shown on television; **das ~ brachte eine Sendung über ...** (*Akk.*)

*old spelling (see note on page 1707)

they showed a programme about ... on television

**Fern·seher** *der;* ∼**s**, ∼ (*ugs.*) **A** (*Gerät*) telly (*Brit. coll.*); TV; television; **B** (*Zuschauer*) [television] viewer

**Fernseh-:** ∼**fassung** *die* television version; ∼**film** *der* television film; ∼**gebühren** *Pl.* television licence fee; ∼**gerät** *das* television [set]; ∼**journalist** *der*, ∼**journalistin** *die* television reporter; ∼**kamera** *die* television camera; ∼**kanal** *der* television channel; ∼**lotterie** *die* television lottery; ∼**programm** *das* **A** (*Sendungen*) television programmes *pl.;* **B** (*Kanal*) television channel; **C** (*Blatt, Programmheft*) television [programme] guide; ∼**publikum** *das* viewing public; ∼**reporter** *der*, ∼**reporterin** *die* television reporter; ∼**satellit** *der* television satellite; ∼**schirm** *der* television screen; ∼**sender** *der* television transmitter; ∼**sendung** *die* television programme; ∼**serie** *die* television series; ∼**sessel** *der* television chair; ∼**spiel** *das* television play; ∼**spot** *der* television commercial; ∼**sprecher** *der*, ∼**sprecherin** *die* ⇒ ∼**ansager**; ∼**studio** *das* television studio; ∼**team** *das* television crew; ∼**techniker** *der*, ∼**technikerin** *die* television engineer; ∼**truhe** *die* cabinet television; ∼**turm** *der* television tower; ∼**übertragung** *die* television broadcast; ∼**werbung** *die* television advertising; ∼**zuschauer** *der*, ∼**zuschauerin** *die* television viewer

**Fern·sicht** *die* (*Aussicht*) view; (*gute Sicht*) visibility

**fern·sichtig** *Adj.* ⇒ **weitsichtig**

**Fern·sprech-** (*bes. Amtsspr.*) ⇒ **Telefon-**

**Fernsprech-:** ∼**amt** *das* telephone [area] office; ∼**ansage·dienst** *der* telephone information service; ∼**an·schluss**, *∼**an·schluß** *der* telephone line; **noch keinen ∼anschluss haben** not yet be connected to the telephone network; ∼**apparat** *der* telephone; ∼**auftrags·dienst** *der* telephone services *pl.;* **ich möchte mich vom ∼auftragsdienst wecken lassen** I'd like to book an alarm call; ∼**auskunft** *die* directory enquiries *sing., no art.;* **eine Telefonnummer über die** *od.* **von der ∼auskunft bekommen** get a [telephone] number from *or* through directory enquiries; ∼**automat** *der* coinbox telephone; pay phone; ∼**buch** *das* telephone book *or* directory

**Fern·sprecher** *der* telephone

**Fernsprech-:** ∼**gebühren** *Pl.* telephone charges; ∼**nummer** *die* telephone number; ∼**säule** *die* roadside telephone; ∼**teilnehmer** *der*, ∼**teilnehmerin** *die* telephone subscriber; telephone customer (*Amer.*); ∼**verbindung** *die* telephone connection *or* link; ∼**verkehr** *der* telephone communication; ∼**zelle** *die* telephone booth *or* (*Brit.*) box; call box (*Brit.*)

**fern-, Fern-:** *∼|**stehen** ⇒ **fern** 2; ∼|**steuern** *tr. V.* ⇒ ∼**lenken**; ∼**steuerung** *die* (*Technik*) remote control; (*fig.: durch Geheimdienste usw.*) control; ∼**straße** *die* [principal] trunk road; major road; ∼**studium** *das* **A** (*Studium ohne personale Medien*) correspondence course; ≈ Open University course (*Brit.*); **B** (*DDR*) extramural studies *pl.;* ∼**trauung** *die* marriage by proxy; ∼**universität** *die* ≈ Open University (*Brit.*); ∼**unterricht** *der* correspondence courses *pl.;* ∼**verkehr** *der* long-distance traffic; ∼**verkehrs·mittel** *das* form of long-distance transport; ∼**verkehrs·straße** *die* ⇒ ∼**straße**; ∼**wahl** *die* (*Postw.*) [automatic] trunk dialling; long-distance dialling; ∼**wärme** *die* district heating; ∼**weh** *das* (*geh.*) wanderlust; ∼**ziel** *das* **A** (*zeitlich*) long-term aim; **etw. als ∼ziel anstreben** aim for sth. in the long term; **B** (*räumlich*) distant destination; ∼**zug** *der* long-distance train

**Ferrit** /fɛ'ri:t/ *der;* ∼**s**, ∼**e** ferrite

**Ferrit·antenne** *die* ferrite-rod aerial *or* (*Amer.*) antenna

**Ferro-** /fɛro-/ ferro-

**Ferro·magnetismus** *der* ferromagnetism

**Ferse** /'fɛrzə/ *die;* ∼, ∼**n** ▶471 heel; **jmdm. in die ∼n treten** kick sb. in the heel; (*fig.*) **sich an jmds. ∼n** (*Akk.*)**/sich jmdm. an die ∼n heften** stick [hard] on sb.'s heels; **jmdm. [dicht] auf den ∼n sitzen** *od.* **sein** (*ugs.*) be [hard *or* close] on sb.'s heels; **jmdm. auf den ∼n bleiben** stick on sb.'s heels; stay on sb.'s tail; **ich habe die Polizei auf den ∼n** (*ugs.*) the police are on my tail; **er hatte Löcher in den ∼n** he had holes in the heels of his socks

**Fersen-:** ∼**bein** *das* ▶471 (*Anat.*) heel bone; calcaneum; ∼**geld** *in* ∼**geld geben** (*ugs. scherzh.*) take to one's heels

**fertig** /'fɛrtɪç/ *Adj.* **A** (*völlig hergestellt*) finished ‹manuscript, picture, etc.›; **etw. ∼ machen** finish sth.; **etw. ∼ stellen** complete *or* finish sth.; **das Essen ist ∼:** lunch/dinner *etc.* is ready; **und ∼ ist der Lack** *od.* **die Laube** (*ugs.*) and there you are; and bob's your uncle (*Brit. coll.*); **B** (*zu Ende*) finished; **[mit etw.] ∼ sein/werden** have finished/finish [sth.]; **bist du ∼?** have you finished?; **mit jmdm. ∼ sein** (*ugs.*) be finished *or* through with sb.; **mit etw. ∼ werden** (*fig.*) cope with sth.; **sie wird mit dem Jungen einfach nicht mehr ∼** (*ugs.*) she cannot cope with the boy any more; **C** (*bereit, verfügbar*) ready (**zu, für** for); **zum Abmarsch/Start ∼ sein** be ready to march/ready for take-off; **etw. ∼ machen** get sth. ready; **sich für etw. ∼ machen** get ready for sth.; **auf die Plätze — ∼ — los!** on your marks, get set, go! (*Sport*); (*bei Kindern auch:*) ready, steady, go!; **D** (*ugs.: erschöpft*) shattered (*coll.*); **mit den Nerven ∼ sein** be at the end of one's tether; **jmdn. ∼ machen** (*erschöpfen*) wear sb. out; (*schikanieren*) wear sb. down; (*deprimieren*) get sb. down; (*salopp: zusammenschlagen, töten*) do sb. in (*sl.*); (*ugs.: zurechtweisen*) tear sb. off a strip (*coll.*); **der Lärm macht mich [ganz] ∼:** that noise is getting me down; **E** (*reif*) mature ‹person, artist, etc.›; **F etw. ∼ bekommen** *od.* **bringen** *od.* (*ugs.*) **kriegen** manage sth; **so etwas bringst** *od.* **bekommst** *od.* (*ugs.*) **kriegst auch nur du ∼!** (*iron.*) only you could manage to do a thing like that!; **ich brächte** *od.* **bekäme** *od.* (*ugs.*) **kriegte es nicht ∼, jmdn. zu erschießen** I couldn't bring myself to shoot anybody; **der bringt** *od.* **bekommt** *od.* (*ugs.*) **kriegt das ∼!** (*iron.*) I wouldn't put it past him; **sie bringt** *od.* **bekommt** *od.* (*ugs.*) **kriegt es ∼ und sagt ihr das** she is capable of saying that to her

**fertig-, Fertig-:** ∼**bau** *der; Pl.* ∼∼**ten** **A** (*Gebäude*) prefabricated building; **B** (*Herstellung*) prefabricated building; prefabrication; ∼**bau·weise** *die* prefabricated construction; prefabrication; **etw. in ∼bauweise errichten** build sth. by the prefabricated method; *∼|**bekommen**, *∼|**bringen** ⇒ **fertig** F

**fertigen** *tr. V.* make; **von Hand/maschinell gefertigte Waren** hand-made/machine-produced goods

**Fertig-:** ∼**erzeugnis** *das*, ∼**fabrikat** *das* finished product; ∼**gericht** *das* ready-to-serve meal; **ein ∼gericht aus der Dose** a meal out of *or* from a tin (*Brit.*) *or* (*Amer.*) can; ∼**haus** *das* prefabricated house; prefab

**Fertigkeit** *die;* ∼, ∼**en** skill; **eine ∼ in etw.** (*Dat.*) **haben** be skilled in *or* at sth.; **∼ im Zeichnen** skill in *or* at drawing

**fertig-, Fertig-:** *∼|**kriegen** ⇒ **fertig** F; *∼|**machen** ⇒ **fertig** A, D; ∼**produkt** *das* finished product; *∼|**stellen** ⇒ **fertig** A; ∼**stellung** *die* completion; ∼**teil** *das* prefabricated part

**Fertigung** *die;* ∼**:** production; manufacture

**Fertigungs-** production

**Fertigungs-:** ∼**kosten** *Pl.* production *or* manufacturing costs; ∼**verfahren** *das* production *or* manufacturing process

**Fertig·ware** *die* finished product

**Fertilität** /fɛrtili'tɛ:t/ *die;* ∼ (*Biol., Med.*) fertility

**fes, Fes**[1] /fɛs/ *das;* ∼, ∼ (*Musik*) F flat

**Fes**[2] /fe:s/ *der;* ∼**[es]**, ∼**[e]** fez

**fesch** /fɛʃ/ *Adj.* **A** (*bes. österr.: hübsch*) smart ‹woman, suit, etc.›; **B** (*österr.: nett*) good; **sei ∼ und komm mit!** be a sport and come too!

**Fessel**[1] /'fɛsl̩/ *die;* ∼, ∼**n** (*auch fig.*) fetter; shackle; (*Kette*) chain; **jmdm. ∼n anlegen,** (*geh.*) **jmdn. in ∼n legen** fetter sb./put sb. in chains

**Fessel**[2] *die;* ∼, ∼**n** ▶471 (*Anat.*) **A** (*bei Huftieren*) pastern; **B** (*bei Menschen*) ankle

**Fessel-:** ∼**ballon** *der* captive balloon; ∼**gelenk** *das* (*Zool.*) pastern joint

**fesseln** *tr. V.* **A** tie up; (*mit Ketten*) chain up; **jmdn. an etw.** (*Akk.*) **∼:** tie/chain sb. to sth.; **jmdn. an Händen und Füßen ∼:** tie sb. hand and foot; **jmdm. die Hände auf den Rücken ∼:** tie sb.'s hands behind his/her back; **ans Bett/Haus/an den Rollstuhl gefesselt sein** (*fig.*) be confined to [one's] bed/tied to the house/confined to a wheelchair; **jmdn. an sich** (*Akk.*) **∼** (*fig.*) bind sb. to oneself; **B** (*faszinieren*) ‹book› grip; ‹work, person› fascinate; ‹personality› captivate; ‹idea› possess; **das Buch hat mich so gefesselt** I was so gripped by the book; **jmdn. durch etw. ∼:** captivate sb. with sth.

**fesselnd** ❶ *Adj.* compelling; ❷ *adv.* compellingly

**Fesselung, Fesslung,** ***Feßlung** *die;* ∼, ∼**en** (*Schach*) block

**fest** /fɛst/ ❶ *Adj.* **A** (*nicht flüssig od. gasförmig*) solid; **∼e Nahrung** solid food; **∼e Gestalt** *od.* **Form[en] annehmen** take on a definite shape; **B** (*straff*) firm, tight ‹bandage›; **C** (*kräftig*) firm ‹handshake›; (*tief*) sound ‹sleep›; **D** (*haltbar, solide*) sturdy ‹shoes›; tough, strong ‹fabric›; solid ‹house, shell›; **E** (*energisch*) firm ‹tread›; steady ‹voice›; **eine ∼e Hand brauchen** (*fig.*) need a firm hand; **F** (*unbeirrbar*) **der ∼en Überzeugung** *od.* **Meinung sein, dass ...** be firmly convinced *or* of the firm opinion that ...; **G** (*endgültig*) firm ‹appointment, date›; **eine ∼e Zusage machen** make a firm *or* definite commitment; ⇒ *auch* **Fuß** B; **H** (*konstant*) fixed, permanent ‹address›; fixed ‹income›; **einen ∼en Freund/eine ∼e Freundin haben** have a steady boyfriend/girlfriend; **in ∼en Händen sein** (*fig.*) be spoken for; **einen ∼en Platz in etw.** (*Dat.*) **haben** (*fig.*) be firmly established in sth.; **I** (*Milit. veralt.*) fortified ‹position›.
❷ *adv.* **A** (*straff*) ‹tie, grip› tight[ly]; **B** (*ugs. auch* **feste**) (*tüchtig*) ‹work› with a will; ‹eat› heartily; ‹sleep› soundly; **∼ zuschlagen** plant a solid punch; **er schläft [gerade] ∼:** he is fast asleep; **∼ zulangen** tuck in; **∼ feiern** have a real celebration; **immer ∼[e] drauf** *od.* **druff!** (*salopp*) get stuck in! (*coll.*); let him/them have it!; **C** (*unbeirrbar*) ‹believe, be convinced› firmly; **sich auf jmdn./etw. ∼ verlassen** rely one hundred per cent on sb./sth.; **D** (*endgültig*) firmly; definitely; **etw. ∼ vereinbaren** come to a firm *or* definite arrangement about sth.; **E** (*auf Dauer*) permanently; **∼ angestellt** permanent ‹employee›; **∼ angestellt sein** be permanently employed *or* a permanent member of staff; **∼ befreundet sein** be close friends; (*als Paar*) be going steady; **jmdn. ∼ einstellen** give sb. a permanent job; employ sb. as a permanent member of staff; **∼ besoldet** full-time [and] salaried

**Fest** *das;* ∼**[e]s**, ∼**e** **A** (*Veranstaltung*) celebration; (*Party*) party; **man muss die ∼e feiern, wie sie fallen** you don't get a chance for a celebration every day of the week; **es ist mir ein ∼** (*scherzh.*) [it's] my pleasure; **B** (*Feiertag*) festival; (*Kirchenfest*) feast; festival; **bewegliches/unbewegliches ∼:** movable/immovable feast; **frohes ∼!** happy Christmas/Easter!

**fest-, Fest-:** ∼**akt** *der* ceremony; *∼**angestellt** ⇒ **fest** 2E; ∼**angestellte** *der/die* permanent employee; ∼**ansprache** *die* address; ∼|**backen** *itr. V.* (*landsch.*) stick; ∼|**beißen** *unr. refl. V.* **sich in etw.** (*Dat.*) **∼beißen** ‹dog etc.› sink its teeth firmly into sth.; **sich an einem Problem ∼beißen** (*fig.*) get bogged down in a problem; ∼**beleuchtung** *die* festive lighting; **in ∼beleuchtung erstrahlen** be ablaze with

f

festive illuminations; ***~besoldet** ⇒ **fest** 2E; **~besoldete** *der/die; adj. Dekl.* full-time member of staff; **~|binden** *unr. tr. V.* tie [up]; **etw. an einem Baum/Pfosten ~binden** tie sth. to a tree/post; **~|bleiben** *unr. itr. V.; mit sein* stand firm; **~|drehen** *tr. V.* screw [up] tight

**feste** *Adv. (ugs.)* ⇒ **fest** 2 B

**Feste** *die; ~, ~n (veralt.)* fortress; castle

**fest-, Fest-: ~essen** *das* banquet; **~|fahren** *unr. itr., refl. V. (itr. V. mit sein)* get stuck; *(fig.)* get bogged down; **der Wagen hat sich** *od.* **ist ~gefahren** the car got stuck; **~|fressen** *unr. refl. V.* Ⓐ *(sich verklemmen)* ‹engine› seize up; ‹saw› get stuck; Ⓑ *(fig.: sich einprägen)* **sich in jmdm. ~fressen** become fixed in sb.'s mind; **~|frieren** *unr. itr. V.; mit sein* freeze up; freeze solid; **~gabe** *die (geh.)* gift; ***~gefügt** ⇒ **fügen** 1B; **~gelage** *das* ⇒ **Gelage**; **~geld** *das (Bankw.)* time deposit; **~gottes·dienst** *der* festival service; **~|haken** ❶ *tr. V. (befestigen)* hook up; **etw. an etw. (*Dat.*) ~haken** hook sth. to sth.; ❷ *refl. V.* get caught (**an** + *Dat.* on); **~halle** *die* festival hall; **~|halten** ❶ *unr. tr. V.* Ⓐ *(halten, packen)* hold on to; **jmdn. am Arm ~halten** hold on to sb.'s arm; **etw. mit den Händen ~halten** hold sth. in one's hands; Ⓑ *(nicht weiterleiten)* withhold ‹letter, parcel, etc.›; Ⓒ *(verhaftet haben)* hold, detain ‹suspect›; Ⓓ *(aufzeichnen, fixieren)* record; capture; **etw. in Bild und Ton ~halten** record *or* capture sth. in sound and vision; **etw. mit der Kamera ~halten** capture sth. with the camera; Ⓔ *(konstatieren)* record; **~halten, dass ...** record the fact that ...; ❷ *unr. refl. V. (sich anklammern)* **sich an jmdm./etw. ~halten** hold on to sb./sth.; **halt dich ~!** hold tight!; *(fig. ugs.)* brace yourself!; ❸ *unr. itr. V.* **an jmdm./etw. ~halten** stand by sb./sth.; **~|hängen** *unr. itr. V.* get caught; **[mit etw.] an/in etw. (*Dat.*) ~hängen** get [sth.] caught on/in sth.

**festigen** /ˈfɛstɪɡn̩/ ❶ *tr. V.* strengthen ‹friendship, alliance, marriage, etc.›; consolidate ‹position›; **in sich (*Dat.*) gefestigt sein** be strong. ❷ *refl. V.* ‹friendship, ties› become stronger

**Festigkeit** *die; ~* Ⓐ *(Entschlossenheit)* firmness; Ⓑ *(Standhaftigkeit)* steadfastness; resolution; **sein Ziel mit ~ verfolgen** pursue one's aim with [great] resolution; Ⓒ *(von Stoffen)* strength

**Festigkeits·lehre** *die* [theory of] strength of materials

**Festigung** *die; ~:* strengthening; *(einer Stellung)* consolidation

**Festival** /ˈfɛstivəl/ *das; ~s, ~s* festival

**Festival·besucher** *der,* **Festival·besucherin** *die* visitor to a/the festival

**Festivität** /fɛstiviˈtɛ:t/ *die; ~, ~en (veralt., scherzh.)* festivity; celebration

**fest-, Fest-: ~|klammern** ❶ *tr. V.* **etw. [an etw. (*Dat.*)] ~klammern** clip sth. on [to sth.]; **Wäsche an der Leine ~klammern** peg washing [up] on the line; ❷ *refl. V.* **sich an jmdm./etw. ~klammern** cling [on] to sb./sth.; **~|kleben** ❶ *itr. V.; mit sein* stick (**an** + *Dat.* to); ❷ *tr. V.* stick; **etw. an etw. (*Dat.*) ~kleben** stick sth. to sth.; **~kleid** *das* evening dress; **die Stadt legte ihr ~kleid an** *(fig. geh.)* the town took on a festive look; **~kleidung** *die* formal dress; **~|klemmen** ❶ *itr. V.; mit sein* **~geklemmt sein** be stuck *or* jammed; ❷ *tr. V.* wedge; jam; **~|klopfen** *tr. V.* bang ‹nail› in *or* home; bang ‹floorboard› down; *(fig.)* finalize ‹agreement›; **~|knoten** *tr. V.* **etw. an etw. (*Dat.*) ~knoten** tie sth. to sth.; **~komitee** *das* festival committee; **~komma** *das (DV)* fixed point; **~körper** *der (Physik)* solid; **~körper·physik** *die* solid-state physics *sing., no art.;* **~|krallen** *refl. V.* **sich in etw. (*Dat.*) ~krallen** dig its claws into sth.; **sich an jmdm. ~krallen** cling to sb. with its claws; ‹person› cling [on] to sb.; **~land** *das* Ⓐ *(Kontinent)* continent; *(im Gegensatz zu den Inseln)* mainland; **das europäische ~land** the continent of Europe/the European mainland; Ⓑ *(fester Boden)* land; **auf dem ~land** on dry land; **~ländisch** *Adj.* Ⓐ *(kontinental)* continental ‹climate, shelf, etc.›; Ⓑ *(im Gegensatz zu den Inseln)* mainland *attrib.;* **~land[s]·sockel** *der (Geogr.)* continental shelf; **~|laufen** ❶ *unr. itr., refl. V. (itr. V. mit sein)* ‹ship› run aground, get stuck; ‹wheels› jam, get jammed; *(fig.)* ‹negotiations› reach a deadlock; ‹policy› get bogged down; **das Schiff hat sich** *od.* **ist im Packeis ~gelaufen** the ship has got stuck in the pack ice; ❷ *refl. V. (Sport)* **die Stürmer liefen sich immer wieder ~:** the forwards could not find a way through [the defence]; **~legbar** *Adj.* **das ist [nicht] eindeutig ~legbar** it can[not] definitely be established; **~|legen** *tr. V.* Ⓐ *(verbindlich regeln)* fix ‹time, deadline, price›; arrange ‹programme›; **etw. gesetzlich ~legen** prescribe sth. by law; Ⓑ *(verpflichten)* **sich [auf etw. (*Akk.*)] ~legen [lassen]** commit oneself [to sth.]; **jmdn. [auf etw. (*Akk.*)] ~legen** tie sb. down [to sth.]; Ⓒ *(Bankw.)* tie up ‹money›; **~legung** *die; ~~, ~~en* ⇒ **Festlegen**: Ⓐ fixing; arrangement; Ⓑ commitment

**festlich** ❶ *Adj.* Ⓐ festive ‹atmosphere›; Ⓑ *(einem Fest gemäß)* formal ‹dress›. ❷ *adv.* Ⓐ festively; Ⓑ *(einem Fest gemäß)* formally; **etw. ~ begehen** celebrate sth.

**Festlichkeit** *die; ~, ~en* Ⓐ *(Feier)* celebration; Ⓑ *(der Stimmung, Atmosphäre)* festiveness; *(Feierlichkeit, Würde)* solemnity

**fest-, Fest-: ~|liegen** *unr. itr. V.* Ⓐ *(nicht weiterkommen)* be stuck; Ⓑ *(~stehen)* have been fixed; ‹programme› have been arranged; Ⓒ *(Bankw.)* ‹money› be tied up; **~|machen** ❶ *tr. V.* Ⓐ *(befestigen)* fix; *(fig.)* demonstrate ‹characteristic, fault›; Ⓑ *(~ vereinbaren)* arrange ‹meeting etc.›; Ⓒ *(Seemannsspr.)* moor ‹boat›; ❷ *itr. V. (Seemannsspr.)* ⇒ **anlegen** 2 A; **~mahl** *das (geh.)* banquet; **~meter** *der od. das* cubic metre *(of solid timber)*; **~|nageln** *tr. V.* Ⓐ *(befestigen)* nail (**an** + *Dat.* to); **wie ~genagelt dastehen** *(ugs.)* stand there as though rooted to the spot; Ⓑ *(ugs.: ~legen)* **jmdn. [auf etw. (*Akk.*)] ~nageln** tie sb. down [to sth.]; **sich auf etw. (*Akk.*) ~nageln lassen** let oneself be tied [down] to sth.; **~nahme** *die; ~~, ~~n* arrest; **bei seiner ~nahme** when he was/is arrested; **~|nehmen** *unr. tr. V.* arrest; **jmdn. vorläufig ~nehmen** take sb. into custody

**Feston** /fɛsˈtõ:/ *das; ~s, ~s* festoon

**fest-, Fest-: ~platte** *die (DV)* fixed disk; **~platz** *der* fairground; **~preis** *der (Wirtsch.)* fixed price; **~programm** *das* festival programme; **~rede** *die* speech; **~redner** *der,* **~rednerin** *die* speaker; **~|rennen** *unr. refl. V.* Ⓐ *(ugs.)* get tangled up; Ⓑ *(Sport)* ⇒ **~laufen** 2; **~saal** *der* banqueting hall; *(Ballsaal)* ballroom; **~|saugen** *regelm. (auch unr.) refl. V.* attach itself (**an** + *Dat.* to); **~schmaus** *der (veralt.)* banquet; feast; **~schmuck** *der* festive decorations *pl.;* **im ~schmuck erstrahlen** be festively decorated; **~|schnallen** *tr. V.* tie (**an** + *Dat.* to); **der Pilot schnallte sich am Sitz ~:** the pilot strapped *or* fastened himself in; **~|schrauben** *tr. V.* screw [up] tight; **~|schreiben** *unr. tr. V.* establish; **~|schrift** *die* commemorative volume; *(für Gelehrten)* Festschrift; **~|setzen** ❶ *tr. V.* Ⓐ *(~legen)* fix ‹time, deadline, price›; lay down ‹duties›; Ⓑ *(in Haft nehmen)* detain; ❷ *refl. V.* Ⓐ ‹dust› collect, settle; ‹idea› take root; **diese Idee hat sich bei ihm ~gesetzt** this idea has become fixed in his mind; Ⓑ *(ugs.: sich niederlassen)* establish oneself; **~setzung** *die; ~~, ~~en* ⇒ **~setzen** 1: Ⓐ fixing; laying down; Ⓑ *(selten)* detention; **~|sitzen** *unr. itr. V.* Ⓐ *(haften)* be stuck; Ⓑ *(nicht mehr weiterkommen)* be stuck; **~spiel** *das* Ⓐ *Pl.* festival; **die Bayreuther/Edinburger ~spiele** the Bayreuth/Edinburgh Festival *sing.;* Ⓑ *(Bühnenstück)* festival production; **~spiel·haus** *das* festival theatre; **~|stecken** ❶ *tr. V. (befestigen)* pin up; ❷ *regelm. (auch unr.) itr. V. (nicht weiterkommen)* be stuck; **~|stehen** *unr. itr. V.* Ⓐ *(~gelegt sein)* ‹order, appointment, etc.› have been fixed; Ⓑ *(unumstößlich sein)* ‹decision› be definite; ‹fact› be certain; **~ steht** *od.* **es steht ~, dass ...** it is certain *or* definite that ...; **es steht ~, dass sie keine Chance haben** they certainly have no chance; **~stellbar** *Adj.* Ⓐ *(zu ermitteln)* ascertainable; **die Ursache ist nicht mehr ~stellbar** the cause can no longer be ascertained *or* established; Ⓑ *(wahrnehmbar)* detectable; diagnosable ‹illness›; Ⓒ *(arretierbar)* lockable; securable ‹lock›; **~|stellen** *tr. V.* Ⓐ *(ermitteln)* establish ‹identity, age, facts›; **das lässt sich [nicht] mit Sicherheit ~stellen** it can[not] be established with certainty *or* for certain; Ⓑ *(wahrnehmen)* detect; diagnose ‹illness›; **er stellte ~, dass er sich geirrt hatte** he realized that he was wrong; **sie musste ~stellen, dass ...** she realized that ...; **die Ärzte konnten nur noch den Tod ~stellen** all the doctors could do was [to] confirm that the patient/victim *etc.* was dead; Ⓒ *(aussprechen)* state ‹fact›; **ich muss ~stellen, dass ...** I must *or* am bound to say that ...; Ⓓ *(arretieren)* secure, lock ‹moving part›; secure ‹lock›

**Feststell-: ~hebel** *der* locking lever; **~taste** *die* shift lock

**Fest·stellung** *die* Ⓐ *(Ermittlung)* establishment; Ⓑ *(Wahrnehmung)* realization; **die ~ machen, dass ...** realize that ...; Ⓒ *(Erklärung)* statement; **die ~ treffen, dass ...** observe that ...

**Fest-: ~stimmung** *die* festive atmosphere *or* mood; **~stoff·rakete** *die* solid-fuel rocket; **~tafel** *die (geh.)* banquet table

**Fest·tag** *der* Ⓐ holiday; *(Kirchenfest)* [religious] feast day; *(Ehrentag)* special day; Ⓑ *(Festspieltag)* [day of a/the] festival; **die Berliner ~e** the Berlin Festival *sing.*

**Festtags·stimmung** *die* festive atmosphere *or* mood

**fest-: ~|treten** *unr. tr. V.* tread down; **das tritt sich ~:** don't worry, it's good for the carpet *(iron.)*; ***~umrissen** ⇒ **umreißen²**

**Festung** *die; ~, ~en* Ⓐ *(Verteidigungsanlage)* fortress; Ⓑ *(hist.: Haft)* imprisonment [in a fortress]

**Festungs-: ~anlage** *die* fortification; **~graben** *der* moat; **~haft** *die (hist.)* imprisonment [in a fortress]; **~mauer** *die* wall of a/the fortress

**fest-, Fest-: ~veranstaltung** *die* official function; ***~verwurzelt** ⇒ **verwurzelt**; **~verzinslich** *Adj. (Bankw.)* fixed-interest *attrib.;* fixed-income *attrib.;* **~vortrag** *der* lecture; **~|wachsen** *unr. itr. V.; mit sein* **an** *od.* **auf etw. (*Dat.*) ~wachsen** grow on [to] sth.; **~wiese** *die* festival site; **~zeit** *die* holiday *(Brit.) or (Amer.)* vacation [period]; **~zelt** *das* marquee; **~|ziehen** *unr. tr. V.* pull tight; **~zug** *der* procession

**fetal** /feˈta:l/ *Adj. (Med.)* foetal

**Fete** /ˈfe:tə/ *die; ~, ~n (ugs.)* party; **eine ~ geben** *od.* **feiern** have *or* throw a party

**Fetisch** /ˈfe:tɪʃ/ *der; ~s, ~e (Völkerk., fig.)* fetish

**Fetischismus** *der; ~:* fetishism *no art.*

**Fetischist** *der; ~en, ~en,* **Fetischistin** *die; ~, ~nen* fetishist

**fett** /fɛt/ ❶ *Adj.* Ⓐ *(~reich)* fatty ‹food›; **~er Speck** fat bacon; **das Fleisch war zu ~:** there was too much fat on the meat; Ⓑ *(sehr dick)* fat; Ⓒ *(ugs.: üppig, reich)* fat ‹inheritance, wallet›; **~e Jahre/Zeiten** rich years/good times; **~e Beute machen** make a rich haul; Ⓓ *(ertragreich)* rich ‹soil›; luxuriant ‹vegetation›; Ⓔ *(Druckw.)* bold; *(breiter, größer)* extra bold; **etw. ~ drucken** print sth. in bold/extra bold [type]; **~ gedruckt** bold. ❷ *adv.* **~ essen** eat fatty foods; **~ kochen** use a lot of fat [in cooking]; **~ lachen** guffaw

**Fett** *das; ~[e]s, ~e* Ⓐ fat; **pflanzliche/tierische ~e** vegetable/animal fats; *(fig.)* **das ~ abschöpfen** *(ugs.)* cream off the best; **sein ~ [ab]bekommen** *od.* **[ab]kriegen** *(ugs.)* get one's comeuppance *(Amer.)*; **sein ~ [weg]haben** *(ugs.)* have been put in one's place *or* taught a lesson; **im ~ schwimmen** *(ugs.)* be rolling in it *(coll.)*; Ⓑ *(~gewebe)* fat; **~ ansetzen** ‹animal› fatten up; ‹person› put on weight; **die Gans hat viel ~:** the goose has a lot of fat on it; **~ schwimmt oben**

*old spelling (see note on page 1707)

(*Spr.*) fat people never drown!; (*fig.*) the rich never suffer

**fett-, Fett-: ~ansatz** *der* fat; **er neigt zu ~ansatz** he tends to get fat *or* to put on weight easily; **~arm** ❶ *Adj.* low-fat ‹food›; low in fat *pred.*; ❷ *adv.* **~arm essen** eat low-fat foods; **~auge** *das* speck of fat; **~bauch** *der* (*ugs.*) paunch; fat stomach; **~bedarf** *der* fat requirement; **~creme** *die* enriched [skim] cream; **~depot** *das* (*Physiol.*) fat depot; **~druck** *der* bold type; **in ~druck** in bold [type]

**fetten** ❶ *tr. V.* (*mit Fett einreiben*) grease. ❷ *itr. V.* (*Fett absondern*) be greasy

**fett-, Fett-: ~film** *der* greasy film; **~fleck[en]** *der* grease mark *or* spot; **~frei** *Adj.* non-fat; **~gebäck** *das*, **~gebackene** *das; adj. Dekl.* cakes *pl.* fried in fat; ***~gedruckt** ⇒ **fett** 1E; **~gehalt** *der* fat content; **~geschwulst** *die* fatty tumour; **~gewebe** *das* ▶ 471 fatty tissue; **~haltig** *Adj.* fatty; **[sehr] ~haltig sein** contain [a lot of] fat; **~henne** *die* (*Bot.*) stonecrop; **Große ~henne** orpine; **~herz** *das* fatty heart; fat heart

**fettig** *Adj.* greasy; oily; greasy ‹skin, saucepan, etc.›

**fett-, Fett-: ~kloß** *der* (*ugs. abwertend*) fatty; fatso (*sl.*); **~leber** *die* ▶ 474 (*Med.*) fatty liver; **~leibig** *Adj.* obese; **~leibigkeit** *die;* **~~:** obesity; **~löslich** *Adj.* fat-soluble; **~näpfchen** *das:* **in [bei jmdm.] ins ~näpfchen treten** (*scherzh.*) put one's foot in it [with sb.]; **~polster** *das* subcutaneous fat *no indef. art.;* fat pad; **~reich** ❶ *Adj.* high-fat ‹food›; ❷ *adv.* **~reich essen** eat high-fat foods; **~sack** *der* (*salopp abwertend*) fatso (*sl.*); **~säure** *die* (*Chemie*) fatty acid; **~schicht** *die* layer of fat; **~stift** *der* A (*Schreibgerät*) grease pencil; lithographic pencil; B (*Lippenstift*) lip salve; **~stoffwechsel** *der* fat metabolism; **~sucht** *die* ▶ 474 (*Med.*) obesity; **~triefend** *Adj.* dripping with fat *postpos.;* **~wanst** *der* (*salopp abwertend*) fatso (*sl.*); **~wulst** *der od. die* roll of fat

**Fetus** /ˈfe:tʊs/ *der;* ~ *od.* **~ses, ~se** *od.* **Feten** (*Med.*) foetus

**fetzen** /ˈfɛtsn̩/ *tr. V.* (*ugs.*) tear; **die Musik/Platte fetzt unheimlich** (*Jugendspr.*) the music/record is really mind-blowing (*coll.*)

**Fetzen** *der;* **~s, ~** A scrap; **die Tapete hängt in ~ von der Wand** the wallpaper is hanging [off the wall] in shreds; **das Kleid ist in ~:** the dress is in tatters; **etw. in ~ [zer]reißen** tear sth. to pieces *or* shreds; **in ~ gehen** (*ugs.*) fall apart *or* to pieces; **dass die ~ fliegen** (*ugs.*) like mad (*coll.*); B (*abwertend: billiges Kleid*) **ein billiger ~:** cheap rags *pl.*

**feucht** /fɔy̆çt/ *Adj.* damp ‹cloth, wall, hair›; tacky ‹paint›; humid ‹climate›; sweaty, clammy ‹hands›; moist ‹lips›; lubricated ‹condom›; **die ~e Schnauze des Hundes** the dog's wet nose; **Oberhemden müssen ~ gebügelt werden** shirts must be ironed damp; **Gardinen ~ aufhängen** hang curtains while [they are] still damp; **etw. ~ abwischen** wipe sth. with a damp cloth; **eine ~e Aussprache haben** (*scherzh.*) spit when one speaks; **ein ~er Abend** (*fig. ugs.*) a boozy evening (*coll.*); **~e Augen bekommen** be close to tears; **das geht dich einen ~en Schmutz** *od.* **Kehricht an** (*ugs.*) that's none of your business

**Feucht·biotop** *das* (*Ökol.*) wetland

**Feuchte** *die;* **~:** humidity

**feucht-, Feucht-: ~fröhlich** *Adj.* (*ugs. scherzh.*) merry ‹company›; boozy (*coll.*) ‹evening›; **~gebiet** *das* wet area; **~heiß** *Adj.* hot and humid

**Feuchtigkeit** *die* A (*leichte Nässe*) moisture; B (*das Feuchtsein*) dampness; **die ~ des Bodens/der Luft** the wetness of the soil/humidity of the air

**Feuchtigkeits-: ~creme** *die* (*Kosmetik*) moisturizing cream; moisturizer; **~gehalt** *der* moisture content; (*der Luft*) humidity; **~grad** *der* moisture level; (*der Luft*) humidity; **~messer** *der;* **~~s, ~~:** hygrometer; **~schutz** *der* (*Bauw.*) damp protection; protection against damp

**feucht-: ~kalt** *Adj.* cold and damp; **~warm** *Adj.* muggy; humid

**feudal** /fɔy̆ˈda:l/ ❶ *Adj.* A feudal ‹system›; B (*aristokratisch*) aristocratic ‹regiment etc.›; C (*ugs.: vornehm*) plush ‹hotel etc.›. ❷ *adv.* (*ugs.: vornehm*) **~ essen** have a slap-up meal (*coll.*); **~ Urlaub machen** have a plush holiday

**Feudal-: ~gesellschaft** *die* feudal society; **~herr** *der* feudal lord; **~herrschaft** *die* feudalism

**Feudalismus** *der;* **~:** feudalism *no art.*

**feudalistisch** *Adj.* feudalistic

**Feudal·staat** *der* feudal state

**Feuer** /ˈfɔy̆ɐ/ *das;* **~s, ~** A fire; **[ein Gegensatz] wie ~ und Wasser sein** be as different as chalk and cheese; **das Essen aufs ~ stellen/vom ~ nehmen** put the food on to cook/take the food off the heat; **jmdn. um ~ bitten** ask sb. for a light; **jmdm. ~ geben** give sb. a light; **das olympische ~:** the Olympic flame *or* torch; **mit dem ~ spielen** play with fire; **er ist ganz ehrlich, für ihn** *od.* **dafür lege ich die Hand ins ~:** he is totally honest, I'd swear to it; **~ speiend** fire-breathing ‹dragon›; ‹volcano› spewing fire; ⇒ *auch* **brennen** 2 A; B (*Brand*) fire; blaze; **~!** fire!; **[für etw.] ~ und Flamme sein** be full of enthusiasm [for sth.]; **~ fangen** catch fire; (*fig.: sich verlieben*) be smitten; (*fig.: sich schnell begeistern*) be fired with enthusiasm; **für jmdn. durchs ~ gehen** go through hell and high water for sb.; **zwischen zwei ~ geraten** be caught between the devil and the deep blue sea; **jmdm. ~ unter dem Hintern machen** (*salopp*) put a squib under sb.; C (*Milit.*) fire; **unter feindliches ~ geraten** come under enemy fire; **das ~ einstellen** cease fire; **jmdn./etw. unter ~ nehmen** fire on sb./sth.; **[gebt] ~!** fire!; **~ frei!** open fire!; D (*Leuchten, Funkeln*) sparkle; blaze; **ihre Augen sprühten ~:** her eyes blazed [with fire]; E (*innerer Schwung*) fire; passion; **das ~ der Jugend** the fire *or* passion of youth; **das Pferd/der Wein hat [viel] ~:** the horse has [a lot of] spirit/the wine is strong and full-bodied

**feuer-, Feuer-: ~alarm** *der* fire alarm; **~alarm geben** raise the [fire] alarm; **~anzünder** *der;* **~~s, ~~:** firelighter; **~befehl** *der* (*Milit.*) order to fire; **~bekämpfung** *die* firefighting; **~bereit** *Adj.* (*Milit.*) ready to fire *postpos.;* **~beständig** *Adj.* fire-resistant; **~bestattung** *die* cremation; **~bock** *der* firedog; andiron; **~bohne** *die* (*Bot.*) scarlet runner [bean]; **~büchse** *die* A (*Technik*) firebox; B (*veralt.: Gewehr*) musket; **~eifer** *der* enthusiasm; zest; **~einstellung** *die* cessation of fire; (*Waffenstillstand*) ceasefire; **~fest** *Adj.* heat-resistant ‹dish, plate›; fireproof ‹material›; **~flüssig** *Adj.* molten ‹rock, lava›; **~gefahr** *die* fire hazard *or* risk; **bei ~gefahr** when there is a risk of fire; **~gefährlich** *Adj.* [in]flammable; **~gefecht** *das* gun battle; **~haken** *der* poker; **~holz** *das* firewood; **~kult** *der* fire cult

**Feuerland** (*das*); **~s** Tierra del Fuego

**Feuerländer** *der;* **~s, ~,** **Feuerländerin** *die;* **~, ~nen** Fuegian

**Feuer-: ~leiter** *die* (*bei Häusern*) fire escape; (*beim ~wehrauto*) [fireman's] ladder; (*fahrbar*) turntable ladder; **~lösch·boot** *das* fireboat; **~löscher** *der* fire extinguisher; **~melder** *der* fire alarm

**feuern** ❶ *tr. V.* A (*ugs.: entlassen*) fire (*coll.*); sack (*coll.*); B (*ugs.: schleudern, werfen*) fling; **jmdm. eine ~** (*salopp*) belt sb. one; C (*heizen*) fire ‹stove›; **mit Holz ~:** have wood fires. ❷ *itr. V.* (*Milit.*) fire (**auf** + *Akk.* at)

**feuer-, Feuer-: ~patsche** *die* fire beater; **~pause** *die* (*Milit.*) lull in the fighting; **~polizei** *die: authorities responsible for fire precautions and firefighting;* **~probe** *die* A (*Prüfung*) test; **die ~probe bestehen** pass the [acid] test; B (*Gottesurteil*) ordeal by fire; **~qualle** *die* stinging jellyfish; **~rad** *das* A (**~***werkskörper*) Catherine wheel; B (*Wagenrad*) fire wheel; **~rot** *Adj.* fiery red; flaming red; **~rot werden** (*fig.*) turn crimson *or* scarlet; **~salamander** *der* fire salamander; **~säule** *die* column of fire

**Feuers·brunst** *die* (*geh.*) great fire; conflagration

**feuer-, Feuer-: ~schein** *der* fiery glow; glow of the/a fire; **~schiff** *das* lightship; **~schlucker** *der,* **~schluckerin** *die* fire-eater; **~schutz** *der* A (*Brandschutz*) fire prevention *or* protection; B (*Milit.*) covering fire; **jmdm. ~schutz geben** cover sb.; **~sicher** ❶ *Adj.* fireproof; ❷ *adv.* **etw. ~sicher in einem Safe deponieren** deposit sth. in a fireproof safe; **~sirene** *die* fire siren; ***~speiend** ⇒ **Feuer** A; **~spritze** *die* fire hose; **~stätte** *die* hearth; **~stein** *der* flint; **~stelle** *die* [camp]fire; **~stellung** *die* (*Milit.*) firing position; **~stuhl** *der* (*ugs. scherzh.*) [motor]bike (*coll.*); machine; **~taufe** *die* baptism of fire; **~teufel** *der* (*Pressejargon*) arsonist; **~tod** *der* (*geh.*) [death at] the stake; **den ~tod erleiden** be burnt at the stake; **~treppe** *die* fire escape; **~über·fall** *der* armed attack

**Feuerung** *die;* **~, ~en** A (*Verbrennungsvorrichtung*) firing [system]; B (*das Heizen*) heating; C (*Brennstoff*) fuel

**Feuer-: ~versicherung** *die* fire insurance; **~wache** *die* fire station; **~waffe** *die* firearm; **~wasser** *das* (*ugs.*) firewater (*coll.*)

**Feuer·wehr** *die;* **~, ~en** fire service; **das ging ja wie die ~** (*ugs.*) that was quick; **der fährt ja wie die ~** (*ugs.*) he drives like a maniac

**Feuerwehr-: ~auto** *das* fire engine; **~beil** *das* fireman's axe; **~mann** *der; Pl.* **~männer** *od.* **~leute** ▶ 159 fireman; **~übung** *die* fire service drill; firefighting exercise

**Feuer-: ~werk** *das* firework display; (**~***werkskörper*) fireworks *pl.;* (*fig.*) barrage; **~werks·körper** *der* firework; **~zangen·bowle** *die: burnt rum and red wine punch;* **~zeug** *das* lighter; **~zone** *die* (*Milit.*) firing zone

**Feuilleton** /fœjəˈtõ:/ *das;* **~s, ~s** A (*Teil einer Zeitung*) arts section; B (*literarischer Beitrag*) [literary] article

**Feuilletonismus** *der;* **~** (*oft abwertend*) literary journalese

**Feuilletonist** *der;* **~en, ~en, Feuilletonistin** *die;* **~, ~nen** arts writer *or* correspondent

**feuilletonistisch** ❶ *Adj.* (*unterhaltend*) literary journalistic ‹style›; (*abwertend*) glib, facile ‹essay etc.›. ❷ *adv.* in a literary journalistic style; (*abwertend*) glibly

**Feuilleton·teil** *der* arts section

**feurig** *Adj.* A fiery ‹horse, spice, wine›; passionate ‹speech›; B (*geh.: feuerrot*) flaming ‹sky, red, etc.›; C (*geh.: funkelnd*) blazing ‹precious stone›

**Fez** /fe:ts/ *der;* **~es** (*ugs.*) lark (*coll.*); **~ machen** lark about (*coll.*); **hört mit dem ~ auf!** stop larking about (*coll.*)

**ff** /ɛfˈɛf/ *Abk.* **sehr fein** superior-quality ‹sweets, cakes and pastries, etc.›

**ff.** *Abk.* **folgende [Seiten]** ff.

**Ffm.** *Abk.* **Frankfurt am Main**

**Fiaker** /ˈfi̯akɐ/ *der;* **~s, ~** (*österr.*) hackney carriage; cab

**Fiale** /ˈfi̯a:lə/ *die;* **~, ~n** (*Archit.*) pinnacle

**Fiasko** /ˈfi̯asko/ *das;* **~s, ~s** fiasco; **unser Urlaub war ein einziges ~:** our holiday was a total disaster (*coll.*)

**Fibel** /ˈfi:bl̩/ *die;* **~, ~n** A (*Lesebuch*) reader; primer; B (*Lehrbuch*) handbook; guide

**Fiber** /ˈfi:bɐ/ *die;* **~, ~n** fibre

**Fibrille** /fiˈbrɪlə/ *die;* **~, ~n** (*Med.*) fibril

**Fibrin** /fiˈbri:n/ *das;* **~s** (*Med.*) fibrin

**Fibrom** /fiˈbro:m/ *das;* **~s, ~e** ▶ 474 (*Med.*) fibroma

**Fiche** /fi:ʃ/ *der od. das;* **~s, ~s** (*Informationst.*) [micro]fiche

**ficht** /fɪçt/ *Imperativ Sg. u. 3. Pers. Sg. Präsens v.* **fechten**

**Fichte** *die;* ~, ~**n** (A) spruce; (B) (*Rottanne*) Norway spruce

**Fichten-:** ~**brett** *das* spruce board; ~**holz** *das* spruce [wood]; ~**nadel** *die* spruce needle; ~**nadel·öl** *das* spruce oil; pine needle oil; ~**wald** *der* spruce forest

**Fick** /fɪk/ *der;* ~**s,** ~**s** (*vulg.*) fuck (*coarse*)

**ficken** *tr., itr. V.* (*vulg.*) fuck (*coarse*); **mit jmdm. ~:** fuck sb. (*coarse*); **sie ließ sich von ihm ~:** she let him fuck her (*coarse*)

**Fickerei** *die;* ~, ~**en** (*vulg.*) (A) (*das Ficken*) fucking (*coarse*); (B) (*sexuelles Abenteuer*) fuck (*coarse*)

**fick[e]rig** /ˈfɪk(ə)rɪç/ *Adj.* (*landsch.: nervös*) nervous

**Fideikommiss,** ***Fideikommiß** /fidei kɔˈmɪs/ *das;* **Fideikommisses, Fideikommisse** (*Rechtsspr.*) entail; entailed estate

**fidel** /fiˈdeːl/ *Adj.* (*ugs.*) jolly, merry ‹company, person›; **ein ~es Haus sein** be a *or* the cheerful type

**Fidibus** /ˈfiːdibʊs/ *der;* ~ *od.* ~**ses,** ~ *od.* ~**se** (*scherzh.*) spill

**Fidschianer** /fiˈdʒi̯aːnɐ/ *der;* ~**s,** ~, **Fidschianerin** *die;* ~, ~**nen** Fijian

**Fidschi·inseln** /ˈfɪdʒi-/ *Pl.* **die ~:** Fiji; the Fiji Islands

**Fieber** /ˈfiːbɐ/ *das;* ~**s** (A) ▶ 474, ▶ 728 [high] temperature; (*über 38 °C*) fever; **~ haben** have a [high] temperature/a fever; **hohes/ansteigendes ~ haben** have a high/rising temperature; **~ messen/bei jmdm. ~ messen** take one's/sb.'s temperature; **im ~:** in one's fever; (B) (*geh.: Besessenheit*) fever; **vom ~ des Ehrgeizes gepackt sein** be consumed with ambition; **das ~ der Ungeduld hatte ihn ergriffen** he was in a fever of impatience; **im ~ der Erwartung** in a fever of anticipation; **im ~ des Wahlkampfs** in the heat of the election campaign

**fieber-, Fieber-:** ~**anfall** *der* attack *or* bout of fever; ~**fantasie** *die* [feverish] delirium; ~**flecke[n]** *Pl.* fever spots; fever rash *sing.;* ~**frei** *Adj.* ‹person› free from fever; **er ist wieder ~frei** his temperature is back to normal; ~**glänzend** *Adj.* (*geh.*) feverish ‹eyes›

**fieber·haft** ❶ *Adj.* (A) feverish, febrile ‹infection, state, condition›; (B) (*angestrengt, hektisch*) feverish ‹activity›; **eine ~e Tätigkeit entfalten** become feverishly active. ❷ *adv.* feverishly; **~ überlegen** think desperately hard

**fieberig** *Adj.* ⇒ **fiebrig**

**Fieber-:** ~**kurve** *die* temperature chart; ~**messer** *der;* ~~**s,** ~~ ⇒ ~**thermometer**; ~**mücke** *die* (*Zool.*) malaria mosquito

**fiebern** *itr. V.* (A) (*Fieber haben*) have *or* run a temperature; (B) (*sehr aufgeregt sein*) **vor Aufregung/Erwartung** (*Dat.*) **~:** be in a fever of excitement/anticipation; (C) (*heftig verlangen*) **nach etw. ~:** long desperately for sth.

**fieber-, Fieber-:** ~**phantasie** ⇒ ~**fantasie**; ~**senkend** *Adj.* antipyretic; ~**senkende Mittel** antipyretics; ~**thermometer** *das* [clinical] thermometer; ~**wahn** *der* (*geh.*) [feverish] delirium; **im ~wahn** in his/her delirium

**fiebrig** *Adj.* (*auch fig.*) feverish

**Fiedel** /ˈfiːdl̩/ *die;* ~, ~**n** (*veralt., scherzh.*) fiddle

**fiedeln** *tr., itr. V.* (*scherzh., abwertend*) fiddle; **eine Melodie ~:** play a tune on the fiddle

**Fiedler** /ˈfiːdlɐ/ *der;* ~**s,** ~, **Fiedlerin** *die;* ~, ~**nen** (*scherzh., abwertend*) fiddler

**fiel** /fiːl/ *1. u. 3. Pers. Sg. Prät. v.* **fallen**

**fiepen** /ˈfiːpn̩/ *itr. V.* (A) ‹dog› whimper; ‹bird› cheep; (B) (*Jägerspr.*) ‹deer› call

**fies** /fiːs/ ❶ *Adj.* (*ugs.*) (A) (*charakterlich*) nasty ‹person, character›; **das finde ich ~:** I think that's mean; (B) (*geschmacklich*) horrid (*coll.*); awful (*coll.*). ❷ *adv.* in a nasty way

**Fiesling** /ˈfiːslɪŋ/ *der;* ~**s,** ~**e** (*salopp abwertend*) creep (*coll.*)

**Fifa, FIFA** /ˈfiːfa/ *die;* ~: FIFA; International Football Federation

**fifty-fifty** /ˈfɪftɪˈfɪftɪ/ *Adv.* (*ugs.*) *in* **~ machen** go fifty-fifty; **die Sache wird am Ende wohl ~ ausgehen** things will no doubt work out even in the end

**Figaro** /ˈfiːgaro/ *der;* ~**s,** ~**s** (*scherzh.*) hairdresser

**Fight** /fai̯t/ *der;* ~**s,** ~**s** (*Sport*) fight

**fighten** /ˈfai̯tn̩/ *itr. V.* (*Sport*) fight

**Fighter** /ˈfai̯tɐ/ *der;* ~**s,** ~, **Fighterin** *die;* ~, ~**nen** fighter

**Figur** /fiˈguːɐ̯/ *die;* ~, ~**en** (A) (*Wuchs, Gestalt*) (*einer Frau*) figure; (*eines Mannes*) physique; **eine gute/schlechte ~ machen** cut a good/poor *or* sorry figure; (B) (*Bildwerk*) figure; (C) (*geometrisches Gebilde*) shape; (D) (*Spielstein*) piece; (E) (*Persönlichkeit*) figure; (F) (*literarische Gestalt*) character; **die komische ~** (*Theater*) the comic character *or* figure; **eine komische ~:** a figure of fun; (G) (*Tanzen, Eissport usw.*) figure; **~en laufen** skate figures; (H) (*salopp: Mensch*) character (*coll.*); (I) (*Musik, Sprachw.*) figure

**figural** /figuˈraːl/ *Adj.* figured

**Figural·musik** *die* figurate *or* florid music

**Figuration** /figuraˈtsi̯oːn/ *die;* ~, ~**en** (*Musik, Kunstwiss.*) figuration

**figurativ** /figuraˈtiːf/ (*Sprachw., Kunstw.*) ❶ *Adj.* figurative. ❷ *adv.* figuratively

**figurieren** *itr. V.* (*geh.*) figure

**Figurine** /figuˈriːnə/ *die;* ~, ~**n** (A) (*Kunstwiss.*) figurine; (B) (*bes. Theater*) costume design

**figürlich** /fiˈgyːɐ̯lɪç/ ❶ *Adj.* (*Kunstwiss.*) figured. ❷ *adv.* (*in Bezug auf die Figur*) as far as her figure/his physique is concerned

**Figur·problem** *das* (*ugs.*) weight problem

**Fiktion** /fɪkˈtsi̯oːn/ *die;* ~, ~**en** fiction

**fiktional** /fɪktsi̯oˈnaːl/ *Adj.* (*geh.*) fictional ‹significance›; ‹work› of fiction

**fiktiv** /fɪkˈtiːf/ *Adj.* (*geh.*) fictitious

**Filament** /filaˈmɛnt/ *das;* ~**s,** ~**e** (*Bot., Astron.*) filament

**Filet**[1] /fiˈleː/ *das;* ~**s,** ~**s** (*Textilw.*) filet; netting

**Filet**[2] *das;* ~**s,** ~**s** fillet; (*Rinder~, Schweine~*) fillet; filet

**Filet·arbeit** *die* (*Handarb.*) filet; netting

**filetieren** /fileˈtiːrən/ *tr. V.* (*Kochk.*) fillet

**Filet-:** ~**nadel** *die* netting needle; ~**steak** *das* fillet steak

**Filial·betrieb** *der* branch

**Filiale** /fiˈli̯aːlə/ *die;* ~, ~**n** branch

**Filial·generation** *die* (*Genetik*) filial generation

**Filialist** *der;* ~**en,** ~**en, Filialistin** *die;* ~, ~**nen** (*Wirtsch.*) chain-store owner

**Filial-:** ~**kirche** *die* daughter church; subsidiary church; ~**leiter** *der,* ~**leiterin** *die* branch manager

**Filibuster** /filiˈbastɐ/ *das;* ~**[s],** ~ (*Parl.*) filibuster

**filigran** /filiˈgraːn/ *Adj.* filigreed

**Filigran** *das;* ~**s,** ~**e** filigree

**Filigran-:** ~**arbeit** *die* [piece of] filigree work; ~**schmuck** *der* filigree [jewellery]

**Filipina** /filiˈpiːna/ *die;* ~, ~**s** Filipina

**Filipino** *der;* ~**s,** ~**s** Filipino

**Filius** /ˈfiːli̯ʊs/ *der;* ~, ~**se** (*scherzh.*) son

**Film** /fɪlm/ *der;* ~**[e]s,** ~**e** (A) (*Fot.*) film; (B) (*Kinofilm*) film; movie (*Amer. coll.*); **da ist bei ihm der ~ gerissen** (*fig. ugs.*) he's had a mental blackout; **der deutsche/brasilianische ~:** the German/Brazilian cinema; (C) (~*branche*) films *pl.;* **beim ~ sein** be in films; (D) (*dünne Schicht*) film

**Film-:** ~**amateur** *der,* ~**amateurin** *die* amateur film-maker; ~**archiv** *das* film library *or* archive; ~**atelier** *das* film studio; ~**aufnahme** *die* shot; **mit den ~aufnahmen beginnen** start filming *or* shooting; ~**aus·rüstung** *die* filming equipment; ~**bar** *die* [porno] film club; ~**bericht** *der* film report; ~**branche** *die* films *pl., no art.;* ~**bühne** *die* (A) (*Bildbühne*) film window; (B) ⇒ **Filmtheater**; ~**cutter** *der,* ~**cutterin** *die* film editor; ~**diva** *die* (*veralt.*) screen goddess

**Filme·macher** *der,* **Filme·macherin** *die* film-maker

**filmen** ❶ *tr. V.* (A) film; (B) (*ugs.: hereinlegen*) **jmdn. ~:** take sb. for a ride (*coll.*). ❷ *itr. V.* film; make a film/films

**Film-:** ~**festival** *das* film festival; ~**festspiele** *Pl.* film festival *sing.;* ~**fritze** *der* (*salopp*) film guy (*coll.*); ~**geschäft** *das* film business *or* industry; ~**groteske** *die* film grotesquerie; ~**held** *der* screen hero; ~**heldin** *die* screen heroine; ~**industrie** *die* film industry

**filmisch** ❶ *Adj.* cinematic ‹art etc.›. ❷ *adv.* cinematically

**Film-:** ~**kamera** *die* film camera; (*Schmalfilmkamera*) cine camera; ~**kassette** *die* (*Fot.*) film cassette *or* cartridge; ~**klub** *der* film club *or* society; ~**komödie** *die* film comedy; comedy film; ~**kopie** *die* [film] print; copy of a/the film; ~**kritik** *die* (A) (*Besprechung*) film review; (B) (~*kritiker*) film critics *pl.;* ~**kritiker** *der,* ~**kritikerin** *die* film critic; ~**kulisse** *die* film set; **das wäre eine ideale ~kulisse** that would be an ideal setting for a film; ~**kunst** *die* cinematic art; ~**kunst·theater** *das* film theatre; ~**lein·wand** *die* cinema screen; ~**material** *das* (A) (*Fot., Film: Aufnahmematerial*) film; (B) (~*é zu einem Thema*) film material; ~**musik** *die* film music; (*eines einzelnen ~s*) theme music

**Filmographie** /filmograˈfiː/ *die;* ~, ~**n** filmography *no art.*

**Film-:** ~**palast** *der* picture palace (*dated*); cinema; ~**preis** *der* film award; ~**produzent** *der,* ~**produzentin** *die* film producer; ~**projektor** *der* film projector; ~**regisseur** *der,* ~**regisseurin** *die* ▶ 159 film director; ~**riss,** ***~riß** *der: in* **einen ~riss haben** (*ugs.*) have a mental blackout; ~**rolle** *die* (A) (*schauspielerische Rolle*) film part *or* role; **jmdm. eine ~rolle anbieten** offer sb. a part in a film; (B) (*Spule*) reel of film; ~**schaffende** *der/die; adj. Dekl.* film-maker; ~**schau·spieler** *der* ▶ 159 film actor; ~**schauspielerin** *die* ▶ 159 film actress; ~**spule** *die* film reel; ~**stadt** *die* (A) (*Studiokomplex*) film studios *pl.;* (B) (*Zentrum*) centre of the film industry; ~**star** *der* ▶ 159 film star; ~**studio** *das* film studio; ~**technik** *die* film technology *no art.;* ~**theater** *das* cinema; ~**titel** *der* film title; ~**verleih** *der* film distributor[s]; ~**vorführer** *der;* ~~**s,** ~~, ~**vorführerin** *die;* ~~, ~~**nen** ▶ 159 film projectionist; ~**vorstellung** *die* film show; ~**wirtschaft** *die* film business *or* industry; ~**zensur** *die* film censorship; (*Gremium*) film censors *pl.;* censor (*coll.*)

**Filou** /fiˈluː/ *der* (*abwertend*) (A) (*Spitzbube*) dog (*derog.*); rogue; (B) (*Verführer*) devil (*derog.*)

**Filter** /ˈfɪltɐ/ *der,* (*fachspr. meist*) *das;* ~**s,** ~: filter; **Zigaretten ohne/mit ~:** plain/[filter-] tipped cigarettes

**filter-, Filter-:** ~**fein** *Adj.* finely ground *attrib.,* filter-fine *attrib.* ‹coffee›; **Kaffee ~fein mahlen** grind coffee fine[ly]; ~**kaffee** *der* filter coffee; ~**mund·stück** *das* filter tip

**filtern** *tr. V.* filter

**Filter-:** ~**papier** *das* filter paper; ~**presse** *die* (*Technik*) filter press; ~**tüte** *die* filter; ~**zigarette** *die* [filter-]tipped cigarette

**Filtrat** /fɪlˈtraːt/ *das;* ~**[e]s,** ~**e** (*Technik*) filtrate

**Filtration** /fɪltraˈtsi̯oːn/ *die;* ~, ~**en** (*Technik*) filtration

**filtrieren** *tr. V.* filter

**Filz** /fɪlts/ *der;* ~**es,** ~**e** (A) (*Material*) felt; (B) (*filzartig Verschlungenes*) mass; mat; (C) (*ugs. abwertend: geiziger Mensch*) miser; skinflint; (D) (*Bierdeckel*) beer mat; (E) (~*hut*) felt hat; (F) (*ugs. abwertend: Korruption*) corruption; graft (*coll.*)

**filzen** ❶ *itr. V.* felt. ❷ *tr. V.* (A) (*ugs.: durchsuchen*) search ‹room, car, etc.›; frisk ‹person›; (B) (*salopp: berauben*) do over (*sl.*); (C) (*salopp: schlafen*) kip (*Brit. coll.*)

*old spelling (see note on page 1707)

**Filz·hut** *der* felt hat

**filzig** *Adj.* **A** (*verfilzt*) felted ‹wool›; matted ‹hair›; **B** (*ugs.: geizig*) mean; tight-fisted

**Filz-:** **~latschen** *der* (*ugs.*) slipper; **~laus** *die* (*Zool.*) crab louse

**Filzokratie** /fɪltsokra'ti:/ *die;* **~**, **~n** (*abwertend*) corruption; graft (*coll.*)

**Filz-:** **~pantoffel** *der* slipper; **~schreiber** *der* felt-tip pen; **~stiefel** *der* felt boot; **~stift** *der* felt-tip pen

**Fimmel** /'fɪml/ *der;* **~s**, **~** (*ugs. abwertend*) **einen ~ für etw. haben** have a thing about sth. (*coll.*); **du hast wohl einen ~!** there must be something the matter with you; you must be dotty (*Brit.*); **das ist ein ~ von ihm** it's a strange habit of his; (*Idee*) it's a funny idea he has (*coll.*)

**final** /fi'na:l/ *Adj.* (*Philos.*, *Sprachw.*) final

**Finale** /fi'na:lə/ *das;* **~s**, **~[s]** **A** (*Sport: Endkampf*) final; **im ~ stehen** be in the final; **B** (*spektakulärer Abschluss; Musik: Schlusssatz, -szene*) finale

**Final·gegner** *der*, **Final·gegnerin** *die* (*Sport*) opponent in the final

**Finalist** *der;* **~en**, **~en**, **Finalistin** *die;* **~**, **~nen** (*Sport*) finalist

**Finalität** /finali'tɛ:t/ *die;* **~**, **~en** (*bes. Philos.*) finality

**Final·satz** *der* (*Sprachw.*) final clause

**Finanz** /fi'nants/ *die;* **~** **A** (*Geldwesen*) finance *no art.*; **B** (**~leute**) financial world

**Finanz-:** **~amt** *das* **A** (*Behörde*) ≈ Inland Revenue; **Ärger mit dem ~amt** trouble with the taxman; **B** (*Gebäude*) tax office; **~aristokratie** *die* financial aristocracy; **~ausgleich** *der: equalization of revenue and costs between government and local authorities;* **~beamte** *der*, **~beamtin** *die* tax officer; **~buch·halter** *der*, **~buch·halterin** *die* financial accountant; **~buch·haltung** *die* financial accountancy; **~dinge** *Pl.* financial matters

**Finanzen** *Pl.* **A** (*ugs.: finanzielle Verhältnisse*) finances; **B** (*Finanz- und Geldwesen*) finance *sing.*; **die Abteilung ~:** the finance department; **C** (*Einkünfte des Staates*) [government] finances

**Finanz-:** **~genie** *das* financial wizard; **~gericht** *das: court dealing with tax disputes;* **~gruppe** *die* [financial] syndicate; **~hilfe** *die* financial aid; **~hoheit** *die* fiscal prerogative

**finanziell** /finan'tsiɛl/ **1** *Adj.* financial. **2** *adv.* financially; **jmdn. ~ unterstützen** give sb. financial support; **~ gesichert sein** be financially secure

**Finanzier** /finan'tsie:/ *der;* **~s**, **~s** financier

**finanzieren** *tr. V.* **A** finance; (*fig.: bezahlen*) pay for; **frei/staatlich finanziert sein** be privately financed/financed by the state; **B** (*Kaufmannsspr.: auf Kredit kaufen*) buy on credit; **etw. langfristig ~:** obtain long-term credit for sth.

**Finanzierung** *die;* **~**, **~en** **A** financing; **B** (*Gewährung eines Kredits*) credit *no indef. art.*; **eine langfristige ~:** long-term credit

**Finanzierungs·plan** *der* financial plan

**finanz-, Finanz-:** **~kapital** *das* financial capital; **~kontrolle** *die* (*Wirtsch.*) financial control; **~kraft** *die* financial strength; **~kräftig** *Adj.* financially powerful; **~lage** *die* financial situation; **~minister** *der*, **~ministerin** *die* minister of finance; ≈ Chancellor of the Exchequer (*Brit.*); ≈ Secretary of the Treasury (*Amer.*); **~ministerium** *das* Ministry of Finance; (*in GB u. USA*) ≈ Treasury; **~not** *die* financial difficulties *pl.*; **~planung** *die* financial planning; **~politik** *die* (*des Staates, eines Unternehmens*) financial policy; (*allgemeine*) politics of finance; **~politisch** **1** *Adj.* ‹questions etc.› relating to financial policy; **2** *adv.* from the point of view of financial policy; **~reform** *die* financial reform; **~schwach** *Adj.* financially weak; **~spritze** *die* (*ugs.*) cash injection; **~stark** *Adj.* financially strong; **~verwaltung** *die: regional department with responsibility for settling fiscal matters;* ≈ Board of Inland Revenue (*Brit.*); ≈ Internal Revenue Service (*Amer.*); **~wesen** *das* **A** system of public finances; **ein Ausdruck aus dem ~wesen** a financial expression; **B** ⇒ **~verwaltung**; **~wirtschaft** *die* public finances *pl.*; **~wissenschaft** *die* public finance

**finassieren** /fina'si:rən/ *itr. V.* (*abwertend*) use trickery

**Findel·kind** /'fɪndl-/ *das* foundling

**finden** /'fɪndn/ **1** *unr. tr. V.* **A** (*entdecken*) find; **eine Spur von jmdm. ~:** get a lead on sb.; **keine Spur von jmdm. ~:** find no trace of sb.; **er/das ist nicht zu ~:** he/it is not to be found; **ich weiß nicht, was er an ihr findet** I don't know what he sees in her; **B** (*erlangen, erwerben*) find ‹work, flat, wife, etc.›; **Freunde ~:** make friends; **die Kraft/den Mut dazu ~, etw. zu tun** find the strength/the courage to do sth.; **C** (*heraus~*) find ‹solution, mistake, pretext, excuse, answer›; **einen Ausweg ~:** see a way out; **D** (*einschätzen, beurteilen*) **etw. gut/richtig ~:** think sth. is good/right; **wie ~ Sie dieses Bild?** what do you think of this painting?; **nichts bei etw. ~:** not mind sth.; **ich finde nichts dabei** I don't mind; **wie finde ich denn das?** (*ugs.*) well, really!; **E** (*erhalten*) **Hilfe [bei jmdm.] ~:** get help [from sb.]; ⇒ *auch* **Anklang** A; **Beifall** B; **Gefallen**[2]; **Gehör**; **Verwendung** A; **F** (*vor~*) find; **er fand das Haus verlassen** he found the house deserted.
**2** *unr. refl. V.* **sich ~:** turn up; **es fand sich niemand/jemand, der das tun wollte** nobody wanted to do that/there was somebody who wanted to do that; **das/es wird sich alles ~** (*das wird sich aufklären*) it will all work out all right; **sich in sein Schicksal/seine Lage/seine neue Rolle ~** (*geh.*) come to terms with one's fate/situation/new role.
**3** *unr. itr. V.* **zu jmdm. ~:** find sb.; **nach einem Ort ~:** find the way to a place; **nach Hause ~:** find the way home; **zu sich selbst ~** (*fig.*) come to terms with oneself; **er gehört zu diesen Nachtmenschen, die nicht ins Bett ~ können** he is one of these night owls who just will not go to bed; **das Kind findet schon allein zur Schule** the child knows the way to school by himself/herself

**Finder** *der;* **~s**, **~**, **Finderin** *die;* **~**, **~nen** finder; ⇒ *auch* **ehrlich** 1 A

**Finder·lohn** *der* reward [for finding sth.]

**Fin de Siècle** /fɛ̃d'sjɛkl/ *das;* **~:** fin de siècle; **die Kunst/Literatur des ~:** fin de siècle art/literature

**findig** *Adj.* resourceful; **ein ~er Kopf** a resourceful person; **er ist ~ im Aufspüren von Antiquitäten** he ist good at finding antiques

**Findling** /'fɪntlɪŋ/ *der;* **~s**, **~e** **A** (*Findelkind*) foundling; **B** (*Geol.*) erratic block

**Findlings·block** *der; Pl.* **Findlingsblöcke** (*Geol.*) erratic block

**Finesse** /fi'nɛsə/ *die;* **~**, **~n** **A** (*Kunstgriff*) trick; **alle ~n von etw. beherrschen** know all the tricks of sth.; **B** *meist Pl.* (*in der Ausstattung*) refinement; **mit allen ~n ausgestattet** equipped with every refinement; **C** (*Schlauheit*) flair

**fing** /fɪŋ/ *1. u. 3. Pers. Sg. Prät. v.* **fangen**

**Finger** /'fɪŋɐ/ *der;* **~s**, **~** **A** ▶ **471** finger; **mit dem ~ auf jmdn./etw. zeigen** (*auch fig.*) point one's finger at sb./sth.; **den ~ an die Lippen legen** put one's finger to one's lips; **einen Ring am ~ tragen** have a ring on one's finger; **den ~ am Abzug haben** have one's finger on the trigger; **mit den ~n schnippen** snap one's fingers; **sich** (*Dat.*) **die ~ wund schreiben** write one's fingers to the bone; **B** (*fig.*) **das Geld zerrinnt ihm unter** *od.* **zwischen den ~n** money just runs through his fingers; **wenn man ihm den kleinen ~ reicht, nimmt er gleich die ganze Hand** if you give him an inch he takes a mile; **die ~ davon lassen/von etw. lassen** (*ugs.*) steer clear of it/of sth.; **sie macht keinen ~ krumm** (*ugs.*) she never lifts a finger; **lange ~ machen** (*ugs.*) get itchy fingers; **er rührte keinen ~:** he wouldn't lift a finger; **ich würde mir alle [zehn] ~ danach lecken** (*ugs.*) I'd give my eye teeth for it; **die ~ in etw.** (*Dat.*)**/im Spiel haben** (*ugs.*) have a hand in sth./have one's finger in the pie; **sich** (*Dat.*) **die ~ schmutzig machen** get one's hands dirty; **sich** (*Dat.*) **die ~ verbrennen** (*ugs.*) burn one's fingers (*fig.*); **etw. an den ~n abzählen können** be able to count sth. on the fingers of one hand; **sich** (*Dat.*) **etw. an den [fünf** *od.* **zehn] ~n abzählen können** be able to see sth. straight away; **eine[n] an jedem ~ haben** (*ugs. scherz.*) have one for every day of the week; **jmdm. auf die ~ sehen** *od.* **gucken** (*ugs.*) keep a sharp eye on sb.; **jmdm. auf die ~ klopfen** (*ugs.*) rap sb. across the knuckles; **sich** (*Dat.*) **etw. aus den ~n saugen** (*ugs.*) make sth. up; **ihm** *od.* **ihn juckt es in den ~n [, etw. zu tun]** (*ugs.*) he is itching [to do sth.]; **dann juckts mir in den ~n** (*ugs.*) then I get restless; **jmdm. in die ~ fallen** *od.* **geraten** (*ugs.*) fall into sb.'s hands; **etw. in die ~ bekommen** *od.* **kriegen** (*ugs.*) get hold of sth.; **wenn ich den in die ~ kriege!** (*ugs.*) wait till I get my hands on him! (*coll.*); **sich** (*Dat.*) **in den ~ geschnitten haben** (*ugs.*) have another think coming (*coll.*); **etw. mit spitzen ~n anfassen** hold sth. at arm's length; **etw. mit dem kleinen ~ machen** (*ugs.*) do sth. with one's eyes shut; **jmdn. um den [kleinen] ~ wickeln** (*ugs.*) wrap sb. round one's little finger; **jmdm. unter die ~ kommen** *od.* **geraten** (*ugs.*) fall into sb.'s hands; **der elfte ~** (*salopp scherzh.*) one's third leg (*coll. joc.*); **C** (*Teil des Handschuhs*) finger

**finger-, Finger-:** **~abdruck** *der; Pl.* **~abdrücke** fingerprint; **jmdm. ~abdrücke abnehmen** take sb.'s fingerprints; **~beere** *die* ▶ **471** (*Anat.*) finger pad; **~breit** *Adj.* as wide as a finger *postpos.;* half an inch wide *postpos.;* **~breit** *der;* **~~**, **~~** (*Maßeinheit*) finger's width; (*fig.*) inch; **sie war nicht bereit, einen ~breit abzuweichen** (*fig.*) she was not prepared to budge an inch; **~dick** *Adj.* as thick as a finger *postpos.;* **Brot ~dick mit etw. bestreichen** spread bread thickly with sth.; **~druck** *der* touch of a finger; **~fertig** *Adj.* nimble-fingered; **~fertigkeit** *die* dexterity; **~gelenk** *das* ▶ **471** finger joint; **~glied** *das* ▶ **471** phalanx; **~hakeln** /-ha:kln/ *das;* **~~s** finger-wrestling; **~hand·schuh** *der* glove [with fingers]; **~hut** *der* **A** thimble; **ein ~hut [voll]** (*fig.*) a thimbleful; **B** (*Bot.*) foxglove; **~knochen** *der*, **~knöchel** *der* ▶ **471** knuckle; **~kuppe** *die* ▶ **471** fingertip

**fingern** **1** *itr. V.* fiddle; **an etw.** (*Dat.*) **~:** fiddle with sth.; **nach etw. ~:** fumble [around] for sth. **2** *tr. V.* **etw. aus der Tasche ~:** fish sth. out of one's pocket

**Finger-:** **~nagel** *der* ▶ **471** fingernail; **an den ~nägeln kauen** bite one's nails; **er gönnt ihr nicht das Schwarze unterm ~nagel** (*fig.*) he grudges her everything; **~rechnen** *das* counting on one's fingers *no art.;* **er beherrscht schon das ~rechnen** he can already count on his fingers; **~ring** *der* ring; **~satz** *der* (*Musik*) fingering; **~schale** *die* finger bowl; **~schnippen** *das;* **~~s** snapping one's fingers; **sich mit ~schnippen melden** attract attention by snapping one's fingers

**Finger·spitze** *die* ▶ **471** fingertip; **Künstler/musikalisch bis in die ~n sein** (*fig.*) be an artist/be musical to the tips of one's fingers; **das muss man in den ~n haben** (*fig.*) you have to have a feel for it

**Fingerspitzen·gefühl** *das* feeling; **ein [besonderes] ~ für etw. haben** have a [special] feeling for sth.

**Finger-:** **~sprache** *die* deaf-and-dumb language; (*alphabetische Zeichen*) deaf-and-dumb alphabet; **~übung** *die* (*Musik*) finger exercise; **~zeig** /-tsaik/ *der;* **~~s**, **~~e** tip-off; **einen ~zeig erhalten** be given a hint; ‹police› be tipped off, get a tip-off; **für sie war es ein ~zeig des Schicksals** she took it as a sign

**fingieren** /fɪn'gi:rən/ *tr. V.* fake ‹accident, break-in›; **ein fingierter Name** a false name; **ein**

**fingierter Briefwechsel** (*in der Literatur*) an imaginary correspondence

**Finish** /ˈfɪnɪʃ/ *das;* **~s, ~s** finish

**finit** /fiˈniːt/ *Adj.* (*Sprachw.*) finite

**Fink** /fɪŋk/ *der;* **~en, ~en** finch

**Finken-: ~schlag** *der* finch's song; **~vogel** *der* finch

**Finn-Ding[h]i** /ˈfɪndɪŋgi/ *das;* **~s, ~s** Finn dinghy

**Finne**[1] /ˈfɪnə/ *der;* **~n, ~n** ▶ 553 Finn

**Finne**[2] *die;* **~, ~n** Ⓐ (*Zool.*) fin; Ⓑ (*am Hammer*) peen

**Finnen·dolch** *der* [short, wide-bladed] dagger

**Finnin** *die;* **~, ~nen** Finn

**finnisch** *Adj.* ▶ 553, ▶ 696 Finnish; **der Finnische Meerbusen** the Gulf of Finland; ⇒ *auch* **deutsch, Deutsch, Deutsche**[2]

**Finnland** /ˈfɪnlant/ (*das*); **~s** Finland

**Finnlandisierung** /fɪnlandiˈziːrʊŋ/ *die;* **~** (*Pol.*) Finlandization

**Finn·wal** *der* (*Zool.*) fin whale; common rorqual

**finster** /ˈfɪnstɐ/ ❶ *Adj.* Ⓐ dark; **im Finstern** in the dark; Ⓑ (*düster*) dark ‹house, forest, alleyway›; dimly-lit ‹pub, district›; Ⓒ (*dubios*) shady ‹plan, affair›; **eine ~e Gestalt** a sinister figure; Ⓓ (*verdüstert, feindselig*) **eine ~e Miene [aufsetzen]** [assume] a black expression; **~e Gedanken gegen jmdn. hegen** have evil intentions against sb.; Ⓔ (*fig.*) **in diesen ~en Zeiten** in these dark times; **aus dem ~en Mittelalter** from the Dark Ages; **im Finstern tappen** be groping in the dark. ❷ *adv.* **jmdn. ~ ansehen** give sb. a black look; **~ entschlossen sein, etw. zu tun** be grimly determined to do sth.

**Finsternis** *die;* **~, ~se** Ⓐ darkness; (*auch bibl., fig.*) dark; **rabenschwarze ~:** pitch darkness; **in tiefer ~ liegen** be shrouded in darkness; **die Mächte/das Reich der ~:** the powers of darkness/the Kingdom of Darkness; **eine ägyptische ~:** stygian gloom; Ⓑ (*Astron.*) eclipse

**Finte** /ˈfɪntə/ *die;* **~, ~n** Ⓐ trick; **jmdn. durch eine ~ täuschen** deceive sb. by trickery; **alle ~n nützen Ihnen nichts** no trickery will help you; Ⓑ (*Fechten*) feint

**finten·reich** *Adj.* (*geh.*) skilful, tricky ‹opponent›

**finzelig, finzlig** /ˈfɪnts(ə)lɪç/ *Adj.* (*ugs.*) **~e Arbeit** fiddly work; **~e Schrift** tiny writing

**fipsig** /ˈfɪpsɪç/ *Adj.* (*ugs.*) undersized

**Firlefanz** /ˈfɪrləfants/ *der;* **~es** (*ugs. abwertend*) Ⓐ (*Tand, Flitter*) frippery; trumpery; Ⓑ (*Unsinn*) nonsense; **~ machen** fool around

**firm** /fɪrm/ *Adj.* **in etw.** (*Dat.*) **~ sein** be well up in sth.; know sth. thoroughly

**Firma** /ˈfɪrma/ *die;* **~, Firmen** Ⓐ firm; company; **in einer ~ arbeiten** work for a firm *or* company; **die ~ ist erloschen** the company has been struck from the register; **„Fa. W. Bert & Söhne“** 'W. Bert & Sons'; Ⓑ (*ugs. abwertend: Sippschaft*) bunch (*sl.*)

**Firmament** /fɪrmaˈmɛnt/ *das;* **~[e]s** (*dichter.*) firmament

**firmen** *tr. V.* (*kath. Rel.*) confirm

**firmen-, Firmen-: ~aufdruck** *der* company letter heading; **~chef** *der,* **~chefin** *die* ⇒ **~inhaber**; **~eigen** *Adj.* company *attrib.*; belonging to the company *postpos.*; **~eigen sein** belong to the company; **ein ~eigener LKW/eine ~eigene Kantine** a company lorry (*Brit.*) *or* truck/canteen; **~inhaber** *der,* **~inhaberin** *die* owner of the/a company; **~intern** ❶ *Adj.* internal; internal company *attrib.*; ❷ *adv.* internally; within the company; **~name** *der* name of a/the company *or* firm; **~schild** *das* company's name plate; **~stempel** *der* company stamp; firm's stamp; **~wagen** *der* company car; **~zeichen** *das* trademark

**firmieren** *itr. V.* trade

**Firmling** /ˈfɪrmlɪŋ/ *der;* **~s, ~e** (*kath. Rel.*) confirmation candidate

*old spelling (see note on page 1707)

**Firm·pate** *der,* **Firm·patin** *die* sponsor

**Firmung** *die;* **~, ~en** confirmation; **jmdm. die ~ erteilen** confirm sb.

**firn** /fɪrn/ *Adj.* mature ‹wine›

**Firn** *der;* **~[e]s** firn

**Firn·feld** *das* firn field

**Firnis** /ˈfɪrnɪs/ *der;* **~ses, ~se** varnish

**Firn·schnee** *der* firn snow

**First** /fɪrst/ *der;* **~[e]s, ~e** ridge

**First-: ~höhe** *die* height [to the ridge of the roof]; **eine ~höhe von 8,50 m aufweisen** be 8.50 m high; **~ziegel** *der* ridge tile

**Fis** /fɪs/ *das;* **~, ~** (*Musik*) [key of] F sharp

**Fisch** /fɪʃ/ *der;* **~[e]s, ~e** Ⓐ fish; **[fünf] ~e fangen** catch [five] fish; **sie hatten viele ~e im Netz** they had a good catch; **Fliegende ~e** flying fish; **gesund und munter wie ein ~ im Wasser** as fit as a fiddle; **stumm wie ein ~ sein** keep a stony silence; (*fig.*) **kleine ~e** (*ugs.*) small fry; **faule ~e** (*ugs.*) lame excuses; **die ~e füttern** (*ugs. scherzh.*) be seasick; Ⓑ (*Nahrungsmittel*) fish; **das ist weder ~ noch Fleisch** (*fig.*) that's neither fish nor fowl; Ⓒ (*Astrol.*) **die ~e** Pisces; the Fishes; **er ist [ein] ~:** he is a Piscean; **im Zeichen der ~e geboren sein** be born under [the sign of] Pisces; Ⓓ (*Druckerspr.*) *letter from the wrong fount*

**fisch-, Fisch-: ~abfälle** *Pl.* fish scraps; **~adler** *der* (*Zool.*) osprey; **~arm** *Adj.* poor as regards fish; **~auge** *das* Ⓐ fish eye; **er hat große, hervorquellende ~augen** (*fig.*) he's got big, protruding fish-like eyes; Ⓑ (*Fot.*) fisheye lens; **~becken** *das* fish pond; **~bein** *das* whalebone; **~bestand** *der* fish population; **~besteck** *das* fish knife and fork; **~blase** *die* Ⓐ (*Schwimmblase*) fish sound; Ⓑ (*Archit.*) vesica piscis; **~blut** *das* fish blood; **~blut in den Adern haben** (*fig.*) be a cold fish; **~brötchen** *das* fish roll; **~bude** *die: stall selling pickled and smoked fish;* **~bulette** *die* fishcake; **~dampfer** *der* steam trawler; **~ei** *das* fish egg

**fischen** ❶ *tr. V.* Ⓐ fish for; **Forellen/Aale ~:** fish for trout/eels; Ⓑ (*ugs.*) **etw. aus etw. ~:** fish sth. out of sth. ❷ *itr. V.* fish; **~ gehen** go fishing; **nach etw. ~:** fish for sth.; **nach Komplimenten ~** (*fig.*) fish for compliments; ⇒ *auch* **trüb** 1 A

**Fischer** *der;* **~s, ~** ▶ 159 Ⓐ fisherman; Ⓑ (*ugs.: Angler*) angler

**Fischer-: ~boot** *das* fishing boat; **~dorf** *das* fishing village

**Fischerei** *die;* **~:** fishing; **von der ~ leben** make a/one's living from fishing

**Fischerei-: ~fahrzeug** *das* fishing vessel; **~flotte** *die* fishing fleet; **~grenze** *die* fishing limit; **~hafen** *der* fish dock; (*Hafenort*) fishing port; **~recht** *das* Ⓐ fishing rights *pl.*; right of fishery (*Law*); Ⓑ (*Rechtsvorschriften*) fishing laws *pl.*; **~schiff** *das* fishing vessel; **~schutz·boot** *das* fishery protection vessel; **~wesen** *das* fisheries *pl.*

**Fischer·hütte** *die* fisherman's hut

**Fischerin** *die;* **~, ~nen** ▶ 159 Ⓐ fisherwoman; Ⓑ (*ugs.: Angler*) angler

**Fischer-: ~kate** *die* ⇒ **~hütte**; **~netz** *das* fishing net; **~ring** *der* (*kath. Rel.*) Fisherman's Ring

**Fisch-: ~fabrik** *die* fish cannery; **~fabrik·schiff** *das* factory ship

**Fisch·fang** *der* fishing; **vom ~ leben** make a/one's living by fishing; **auf ~ gehen** go fishing

**Fischfang-: ~flotte** *die* fishing fleet; **~gebiet** *das* fishing grounds *pl.*; fishery

**fisch-, Fisch-: ~filet** *das* fish fillet; **~frau** *die* fishwife; **~frikadelle** *die* fishcake; **~futter** *das* fish food; **~gabel** *die* fish fork; **~gang** *der* (*Gastr.*) fish course; **~gericht** *das* fish dish; **~geruch** *der* smell of fish; **~geschäft** *das* fishmonger's [shop] (*Brit.*); fish store (*Amer.*); **~gräte** *die* fish bone; **~grät[en]·muster** *das* (*Textilw.*) herringbone pattern; **ein Mantel/ein Anzug mit ~grätenmuster** a herringbone coat/suit; **~gräten·stich** *der* herringbone stitch; **~gründe** *Pl.* fishing grounds; **~guano** *der* fish guano; **~handel** *der* fish trade; **~händler** *der,* **~händlerin** *die* ▶ 159 fishmonger (*Brit.*); fish dealer (*Amer.*); (*Großhändler*) fish wholesaler; **~konserve** *die* canned fish; **~kutter** *der* fishing trawler; **~laden** *der; Pl.* **~läden** ⇒ **~geschäft**; **~laich** *der* (*Zool.*) fish spawn; **~lokal** *das* ⇒ **~restaurant**; **~markt** *der* fish market; **~mehl** *das* fishmeal; **~messer** *das* fish knife; **~milch** *die* (*Zool.*) milt; **~otter** *der* otter; **~pass,** ***~paß** *der* fish ladder; **~reich** *Adj.* rich in fish *postpos.*; **~reiher** *der* (*Zool.*) common heron; **~restaurant** *das* fish restaurant; seafood restaurant; **~reuse** *die* fish trap; **~schuppe** *die* fish scale; **~schwanz** *der* fish's tail; **~schwarm** *der* shoal of fish; **~stäbchen** *das* (*Kochk.*) fish finger; **~sterben** *das* death of the fish; **~suppe** *die* fish soup; **~teich** *der* fish pond; **~vergiftung** *die* fish poisoning; **~wanderung** *die* (*Zool.*) fish migration; **~weib** *das* (*meist abwertend*) fishwife; **~wilderei** *die* illicit fishing; **~wirt** *der,* **~wirtin** *die* fish farmer; **~wirtschaft** *die* fishing industry; **~zaun** *der* fish weir; fishgarth; **~zucht** *die* fish farming; **~zug** *der* Ⓐ (*ugs.: Gewinn bringendes Unternehmen*) killing; Ⓑ (*Fischereiw.*) draught

**Fis-Dur** *das* (*Musik*) F sharp major; ⇒ *auch* **A-Dur**

**Fisimatenten** /fizimaˈtɛntn̩/ *Pl.* (*ugs.*) messing about *sing.*; **mach keine ~!** stop messing about; **es ist besser, Sie machen keine ~:** it will be better if you don't try anything silly

**fiskalisch** /fɪsˈkaːlɪʃ/ *Adj.* fiscal

**Fiskus** /ˈfɪskʊs/ *der;* **~, Fisken** *od.* **~se** Government (*as managing the State finances*); **das Erbe fällt dem ~ zu** the estate falls to the Crown (*Brit.*)/the Government (*Amer.*)

**fis-Moll** *das* (*Musik*) F sharp minor; ⇒ *auch* **a-Moll**

**fisselig** /ˈfɪsəlɪç/ *Adj.* (*bes. nordd.*) Ⓐ (*dünn, fein*) fine ‹wool, material›; Ⓑ (*umständlich*) fiddly ‹work›

**fisseln** /ˈfɪsl̩n/ *itr. V.* (*unpers.*) (*bes. nordd.*) drizzle; **es fisselt** it is drizzling

**Fissur** /fɪˈsuːɐ̯/ *die;* **~, ~en** ▶ 474 (*Med.*) fissure

**Fistel** /ˈfɪstl̩/ *die;* **~, ~n** (*Med.*) fistula

**fisteln** /ˈfɪstl̩n/ *itr. V.* speak in a thin high-pitched voice

**Fistel·stimme** *die* Ⓐ (*hohe Stimme bei Männern*) thin high-pitched voice; Ⓑ (*Musik*) falsetto [voice]

**fit** /fɪt/ *Adj.* fit; **jmdn. ~ machen** get sb. fit; **sich ~ halten** keep fit; **das hält ~:** it keeps you fit

**Fitness, *Fitneß** /ˈfɪtnɛs/ *die;* **~:** fitness

**Fitness-, *Fitneß-: ~raum** *der* fitness room; **~training** *das* fitness training; **~zentrum** *das* fitness centre

**Fittich** /ˈfɪtɪç/ *der;* **~[e]s, ~e** (*dichter.*) wing; pinion; **jmdn. unter seine ~e nehmen** (*ugs. scherzh.*) take sb. under one's wing

**Fitting** /ˈfɪtɪŋ/ *das;* **~s, ~s** (*Technik*) fitting

**Fitzel** /ˈfɪtsl̩/ *der od. das;* **~s, ~** (*bes. nordd.*) morsel

**Fitzelchen** *das;* **~s, ~** (*ugs.*) scrap; **nicht ein ~ war von seinem Reichtum übrig geblieben** he did not have a penny of his fortune left

**fix** /fɪks/ ❶ *Adj.* Ⓐ (*ugs.: flink, wendig*) quick; **ein ~er Bursche** a bright lad; Ⓑ (*ugs.*) **~ und fertig** (*fertig vorbereitet*) quite finished; (*völlig erschöpft*) completely shattered (*coll.*); Ⓒ (*festgelegt*) fixed ‹cost, salary›; **eine ~e Idee** an idée fixe. ❷ *adv.* (*ugs.*) quickly; **das geht ganz ~:** it won't take a jiffy (*coll.*); **mach ~!** hurry up!

**Fixativ** /fɪksaˈtiːf/ *das;* **~s, ~e** fixative

**Fixe** /ˈfɪksə/ *die;* **~, ~n** (*Drogenjargon*) needle

**fixen** /ˈfɪksn̩/ *itr. V.* Ⓐ (*Drogenjargon: spritzen*) fix (*sl.*); Ⓑ (*Börsenw.*) bear

**Fixer** *der;* **~s, ~, Fixerin** *die;* **~, ~nen** Ⓐ (*Drogenjargon*) fixer; Ⓑ (*Börsenw.*) bear

# Fläche

***1 Quadratzentimeter*** = one square centimetre (sq. cm) = 0.155 square inch (sq. in.)
***1 Quadratmeter*** = one square metre (sq. m) = 10.764 square feet (sq. ft) *od.* 1.196 square yards (sq. yds)
***1 Hektar*** = one hectare (ha) = 2.471 acres
***1 Quadratkilometer*** = one square kilometre (sq. km) = 0.386 square mile

***Wie viel Wohnfläche hat die Wohnung?***
= What is the floor area of the flat *od.* (*amerik.*) apartment?

***Das Zimmer hat 16 m² [Fläche]***
= The room has an area of 16 sq. m, ≈ the room has an area of 170 sq. ft.

***ein Gebäude mit 8 000 m² Bürofläche***
= a building with 8,000 sq. m, ≈ a building with 86,000 sq. ft of office space

***Er bewirtschaftet 400 Hektar [Land]***
= He farms 400 hectares [of land], ≈ he farms 1,000 acres [of land]

***ein Gut von 400 ha***
= an estate of 400 ha, ≈ an estate of 1,000 acres

***eine Fläche von etwa 100 km²***
= an area of about 100 sq. km, ≈ an area of about 40 square miles

f

**Fix·geschäft** *das* (*Wirtsch.*) purchase for delivery at a fixed time

**Fixier·bad** *das* (*Fot.*) fixer

**fixierbar** *Adj.* definable

**fixieren** /fɪ'ksi:rən/ *tr. V.* Ⓐ (*scharf ansehen*) fix one's gaze on; **jmdn./etw. scharf/kühl ~:** gaze sharply/coldly at sb./sth.; Ⓑ (*geh.: schriftlich niederlegen*) take down ‹interview, report, statement›; Ⓒ (*geh.: verbindlich bestimmen*) fix ‹date›; **der Zeitpunkt ist auf den 12. Mai fixiert worden** the date has been fixed as the twelfth of May; Ⓓ (*Fot.*) fix; Ⓔ (*Med.: festmachen*) set; Ⓕ (*Psych.*) **er ist stark auf seine Mutter fixiert** he has a strong mother fixation; **sich auf** (*Akk.*)**/an** (*Dat.*) **etw. ~:** devote oneself *or* give oneself up entirely to sth.

**Fixier·salz** *das* (*Fot.*) hypo

**Fixierung** *die; ~, ~en* Ⓐ (*starres Festlegen, -halten*) **die ~ auf eine Frage** concentration on a question; **die ~ auf seine Mutter** his mother fixation; Ⓑ (*Festlegung*) determination

**Fixigkeit** *die; ~* (*ugs.*) speed

**Fix-: ~punkt** *der* fixed point; **~stern** *der* (*Astron.*) fixed star

**Fixum** /'fɪksʊm/ *das; ~s,* **Fixa** basic salary

**Fix·zeit** *die* core time

**Fjord** /fjɔrt/ *der; ~[e]s, ~e* fiord

**FKK** *Abk.* **Freikörperkultur** nudism *no art.*; naturism *no art.*

**FKK-: ~-Anhänger** *der,* **~-Anhängerin** *die* nudist; naturist; **~-Strand** *der* nudist beach

**Fla** /fla:/ *die; ~:* anti-aircraft defense; AA defence

**flach** /flax/ *Adj.* Ⓐ (*eben*) flat ‹countryside, region, roof›; **das ~e Land** the flat country; **sich ~ hinlegen** lay oneself [down] flat; **mit der ~en Hand** with the flat of one's hand; Ⓑ ▶ 411 (*niedrig*) low ‹heels, building›; flat ‹shoe›; Ⓒ ▶ 306, ▶ 411 (*nicht tief*) shallow ‹water, river, etc., dish›; Ⓓ (*abwertend: nichtssagend, unwesentlich*) shallow

**flach-, Flach-: ~bau** *der; Pl.* **~~ten** low building; **~bogen** *der* (*Archit.*) segmental arch; **~brüstig** *Adj.* flat-chested; **~dach** *das* flat roof; **~druck·verfahren** *das* planographic printing method

**Fläche** /'flɛçə/ *die; ~, ~n* Ⓐ (*ebenes Gebiet*) area; **auf einer ~ von x m²** over an area of x square metres; Ⓑ (*Ober~, Außenseite*) surface; Ⓒ ▶ 301 (*Math.*) area; (*einer dreidimensionalen Figur*) side; face; Ⓓ (*weite Land~, Wasser~*) expanse; Ⓔ (*von Kristallen*) facet

**Flach·eisen** *das* Ⓐ (*gewalztes Eisen*) flat bar; Ⓑ (*Werkzeug*) scorper

**flächen-, Flächen-: ~ausdehnung** *die* area; **~blitz** *der* sheet lightning; **~brand** *der* extensive blaze; **sich zu einem ~brand ausweiten** (*fig.*) spread like wildfire; **~gleich** *Adj.* of equal area *postpos.*; equal in area *postpos.*; **~haft** ❶ *Adj.* extensive; ❷ *adv.* extensively; **~inhalt** *der* (*Math.*) area; **~maß** *das* (*Math.*) unit of square measure; **~nutzungs·plan** *der* land development plan; **~staat** *der* territorial state; **~wirkung** *die* surface effect

**flach-, Flach-: ~|fallen** *itr. V.; mit sein* (*ugs.*) ‹trip› fall through; ‹event› be cancelled; **das Kino fällt für dich heute ~:** you won't be going to the cinema today; **diese Subventionen sollen ~fallen** these subsidies will not be continued; **~feile** *die* flat file; **~glas** *das* sheet glass; **~hang** *der* slip-off slope

**Flachheit** *die; ~, ~en* Ⓐ (*abwertend*) shallowness; Ⓑ (*Bemerkung*) platitude

**flächig** ❶ *Adj.* Ⓐ (*abgeflacht*) flat ‹features, shape›; Ⓑ (*ausgedehnt*) extensive ‹area›; Ⓒ (*Kunstw.*) two-dimensional ‹style, representation›. ❷ *adv.* extensively

**flach-, Flach-: ~kopf** *der* (*abwertend*) numskull; **~küste** *die* (*Geogr.*) beach; **~land** *das* lowland; **~länder** *der; ~~s, ~~,* **~länderin** *die; ~~, ~~nen* lowlander; **~|legen** ❶ *refl. V.* (*ugs.*) lie down; ❷ *tr. V.* (*zu Boden strecken*) floor ‹opponent›; **~|liegen** *unr. itr. V.* (*ugs.*) be flat on one's back; **~mann** *der* (*ugs. scherzh.*) hip flask; **~meißel** *der* flat chisel; **~moor** *das* (*Geog.*) lowmoor bog; **~pass, *~paß** *der* (*Fußball*) low pass; **einen ~pass [auf jmdn.] spielen** make a low pass [to sb.]; **~relief** *das* low relief; **~rennen** *das* (*Sport*) flat race

**Flachs** /flaks/ *der; ~es* Ⓐ flax; Ⓑ (*ugs.: Ulk*) **das war doch nur ~:** I/he *etc.* was just having you on (*Brit. coll.*) *or* (*Amer. coll.*) putting you on; **ganz ohne ~:** no kidding (*coll.*)

**flachs·blond** *Adj.* flaxen ‹hair›

**Flach·schuss, *Flach·schuß** *der* (*Fußball*) low shot

**flachsen** /'flaksn̩/ *itr. V.* **mit jmdm. ~** (*ugs.*) joke with sb.; **gerne ~:** like a joke

**Flachserei** *die; ~, ~en* (*ugs.*) joking; **das war doch nur ~:** it was just a joke

**Flachs·kopf** *der* flaxen-haired person; **beide Kinder waren ~köpfe** both of the children were flaxen-haired

**Flach-: ~strecke** *die* (*Leichtathletik*) flat race; **~zange** *die* flat tongs *pl.*; **~ziegel** *der* flat tile

**flackern** /'flakɐn/ *itr. V.* flicker; **~des Kaminfeuer/Licht/~de Augen** flickering fire/light/eyes; **Erregung flackerte in seinem Blick** his eyes glinted with excitement

**Flacker·schein** *der* flickering light

**Fladen** /'fla:dn̩/ *der; ~s, ~* Ⓐ *flat, round unleavened cake made with oat or barley flour;* ≈ [large] oatcake (*Scot.*); Ⓑ (*Kuh~*) cowpat

**Fladen·brot** *das* unleavened bread

**Flagellant** /flagɛ'lant/ *der; ~en, ~en,* **Flagellantin** *die; ~, ~nen* flagellant

**Flagellantismus** *der; ~* (*Med., Psych.*) flagellantism *no art.*

**Flagellation** /flagɛla'tsio:n/ *die; ~* (*Med., Psych.*) flagellation

**Flagellum** /fla'gɛlʊm/ *das; ~s,* **Flagellen** (*Biol.*) flagellum; (*Peitsche*) scourge

**Flagge** /'flagə/ *die; ~, ~n* flag; **unter neutraler ~ fahren** sail under a neutral flag; **die ~ streichen** (*fig.*) strike the flag (*fig.*); **~ zeigen** (*fig.*) show one's colours; **unter falscher ~ segeln** (*fig.*) sail under false colours

**flaggen** ❶ *itr. V.* put out the flags; **überall war geflaggt** the flags were flying everywhere. ❷ *tr. V.* **die Straßen sind geflaggt** the flags have been put out in the streets

**Flaggen-: ~alphabet** *das* international code of signals; **~ehrung** *die* ⇒ **~parade**; **~gala** *die* flag dressing; **~gruß** *der* flag salute; **~leine** *die* halyard; **~mast** *der* flagstaff; **~parade** *die* flag-raising/flag-lowering ceremony; **~signal** *das* code flag signal; **~tuch** *das; Pl.* **~~e** bunting

**Flagg-: ~leine** *die* halyard; **~offizier** *der* flag officer; **~schiff** *das* flagship

**flagrant** /fla'grant/ *Adj.* flagrant

**Flair** /flɛ:ɐ̯/ *das od. der; ~s* Ⓐ (*Fluidum, Aura*) air; **ein ~ von etw. haben** have an air of sth.; Ⓑ (*Talent*) flair; **ein ~ für etw. haben** have a flair for sth.

**Flak** /flak/ *die; ~, ~* (*Milit.*) anti-aircraft gun; AA gun

**Flak-: ~feuer** *das* anti-aircraft fire; flak; **wir wurden unter ~feuer genommen** we came under anti-aircraft fire *or* flak; **~geschütz** *das* anti-aircraft gun; AA gun; **~helfer** *der* anti-aircraft auxiliary; **~soldat** *der* anti-aircraft soldier; **~stellung** *die* anti-aircraft position; AA position

**Flakon** /fla'kõ:/ *das od. der; ~s, ~s* bottle

**flambieren** /flam'bi:rən/ *tr. V.* flambé; **flambiert** flambé; flambéed

**Flamboyant** /flɑ̃bo̯a'jɑ̃:/ *der; ~s, ~s* (*Bot.*) flamboyant tree; royal poinciana tree

**Flamboyant·stil** *der* (*Archit.*) Flamboyant style

**Flame** /'fla:mə/ *der; ~n, ~n* ▶ 553 Fleming

**Flamenco** /fla'mɛŋko/ *der; ~[s], ~s* flamenco

**Flamin, Flämin** /'flɛ:mɪn/ *die; ~, ~nen* ▶ 553 Fleming; ⇒ *auch* **-in**

**Flamingo** /fla'mɪŋgo/ *der; ~s, ~s* flamingo

**flämisch** /'flɛ:mɪʃ/ *Adj.* ▶ 553, ▶ 696 Flemish

**Flämmchen** /'flɛmçən/ *das; ~s, ~:* [small] flame

**Flamme** /'flamə/ *die; ~, ~n* Ⓐ flame; **etw. auf kleiner/großer ~ kochen** cook sth. on a low/high flame *or* gas; **in [hellen] ~n stehen** be in flames; **in ~n aufgehen** go up in flames; Ⓑ (*Brennstelle*) burner; **ein Gasherd mit drei ~n** a gas stove with three burners; Ⓒ (*ugs. veralt.: Freundin*) flame

**flammen** /'flamən/ *itr. V.* (*geh.*) blaze

**Flammen·blume** *die* (*Bot.*) phlox

**flammend** *Adj.* Ⓐ flaming; **~es Haar** flaming red hair; Ⓑ (*fig.*) fiery ‹speech›; **~e Anklagen und Protestaktionen** fervent accusations and protests

**Flammen-: ~meer** *das* (*geh.*) sea of flame[s]; **~tod** *der* (*geh.*) death by burning; **er konnte sie vor dem ~tod retten** he was able to save them from burning to death; **sie erlitt den ~tod** she was burnt to death; **~werfer** *der* (*Milit.*) flame-thrower

**Flammeri** /ˈflaməri/ *der;* **~[s]**, **~s** (*Kochk.*) flummery

**Flandern** /ˈflandɐn/ (*das*)*;* **~s** Flanders

**Flanell** /flaˈnɛl/ *der;* **~s**, **~e** flannel; **ein Anzug aus ~:** a flannel suit

**Flanell-:** **~anzug** *der* flannel suit; **~hose** *die* flannel trousers *pl.*

**Flaneur** /flaˈnøːɐ̯/ *der;* **~s**, **~e** (*geh.*) flâneur

**flanieren** /flaˈniːrən/ *itr. V.; mit Richtungsangabe mit sein* stroll

**Flanke** /ˈflaŋkə/ *die;* **~**, **~n** Ⓐ (*Weiche*) flank; Ⓑ (*Ballspiele*) centre; **eine ~ geben** *od.* **schlagen** centre the ball; **eine ~ direkt aufnehmen** pick up a centre; Ⓒ (*Teil des Spielfeldes*) wing; **über die [rechte/linke] ~ spielen** play on the [right/left] wing; Ⓓ (*Turnen*) flank vault; Ⓔ (*Milit.*) flank; Ⓕ (*Fechten*) lower outside target

**flanken** *itr. V.* Ⓐ (*Ballspiele*) **[in die Mitte] ~:** centre the ball; Ⓑ (*Turnen*) flank vault; **über etw.** (*Akk.*) **~:** flank vault over sth.

**Flanken-:** **~ball** *der* (*Ballspiele*) centre; **~deckung** *die* (*Milit.*) flank defence; **~schutz** *der* (*Milit.*) flank protection

**flankieren** *tr. V.* flank; **von jmdm./etw. flankiert werden** be flanked by sb./sth.; **~de Maßnahmen** (*fig.*) additional measures

**Flansch** /flanʃ/ *der;* **~[e]s**, **~e** (*Technik*) flange

**Flappe** /ˈflapə/ *die;* **~**, **~n** (*bes. nordd.; ugs.*) **eine ~ ziehen** sulk; **halt die ~!** shut up! (*coll.*)

**Flaps** /flaps/ *der;* **~es**, **~e** (*ugs.*) lout

**flapsig** /ˈflapsɪç/ (*ugs.*) ❶ *Adj.* rude. ❷ *adv.* rudely

**Flasche** /ˈflaʃə/ *die;* **~**, **~n** Ⓐ bottle; **eine ~ Wein/Bier/Milch** a bottle of wine/beer/milk; **etw. auf ~n abfüllen** *od.* **ziehen** bottle sth.; **gibst du deinem Kind immer noch die ~?** are you still bottle-feeding your child?; **ich muss dem Kind noch die ~ geben** I must just feed the baby; **ein Tier mit der ~ großziehen** rear an animal by bottle; **zur ~ greifen** (*fig.*) take to the bottle; Ⓑ (*ugs. abwertend*) (*Feigling*) wet (*coll.*); (*unfähiger Mensch*) **eine [richtige] ~ sein** be [completely] useless; **du ~!** you useless item! (*coll.*)

**flaschen-, Flaschen-:** **~batterie** *die* (*ugs.*) hoard of bottles; **~baum** *der* (*Bot.*) custard apple tree; sweetsop tree; **~bier** *das* bottled beer; **~bofist**, **~bovist** *der* (*Bot.*) devil's tobacco pouch; **~bürste** *die* bottle brush; **~etikett** *das* label [on a/the bottle]; **~gärung** *die* fermentation in the bottle; **~gas** *das* bottled gas; **~gestell** *das* bottle rack; **~grün** *Adj.* bottle-green; **~hals** *der* (*auch fig.*) bottleneck; **~halter** *der* bottle cage; **~kind** *das* bottle-fed baby; **waren Sie ein Brustkind oder ein ~kind?** were you breastfed or bottle-fed?; **~korken** *der* cork; **~kürbis** *der* (*Bot.*) bottle-gourd; **~milch** *die* Ⓐ (*abgefüllte Milch*) bottled milk; Ⓑ (*Nahrung*) [liquid] baby food; baby milk; **~öffner** *der* bottle opener; **~pfand** *das* deposit [on a/the bottle]; **~post** *die* message in a/the bottle; **~regal** *das* bottle rack; **~wein** *der* wine by the bottle; **offene und ~weine** wine by the bottle or by the glass; **~weise** *Adv.* by the bottleful; **~zug** *der* block and tackle

**Flaschner** /ˈflaʃnɐ/ *der;* **~s**, **~**, **Flaschnerin** *die* (*südd., schweiz.*) plumber

**Flatschen** /ˈfla(ː)tʃn̩/ *der;* **~s**, **~** (*ugs.*) (*Lehm~*) lump; (*Tapeten~*) strip

**Flatter** /ˈflatɐ/ *in* **die ~ machen** (*salopp*) beat it (*coll.*)

**Flatter-:** **~geist** *der* fickle person; **~gras** *das* millet grass

**flatterhaft** *Adj.* fickle

**Flatterhaftigkeit** *die;* **~:** fickleness

**Flatter·mann** *der* (*salopp*) Ⓐ (*nervöse Unruhe*) jitters *pl.* (*coll.*); **einen ~ haben** have the jitters; (*zitternde Hände*) be shaking all the time; Ⓑ (*scherzh.: Brathuhn*) roast chicken

**flattern** *itr. V.* Ⓐ *mit Richtungsangabe mit sein* flutter; **der Vogel flatterte in seinem Käfig** the bird fluttered its wings in its cage; Ⓑ (*zittern*) ‹hands› shake; ‹eyelids› flutter; **seine Nerven flatterten** (*fig.*) he got in a flap (*coll.*); Ⓒ *mit sein* (*vom Wind weitergetragen werden*) flutter; **zu Boden** *od.* **auf den Boden ~:** flutter to the ground; **plötzlich flattert mir eine Postkarte auf den Tisch** (*fig.*) suddenly a postcard appears on the table; Ⓓ (*die Haftung verlieren*) ‹ski, wheel› lose its grip

**Flatter-:** **~satz** *der* (*Druckw.*) unjustified setting; **~tier** *das* (*Zool.*) flying mammal; **~zunge** *die* (*Musik*) tonguing

**flau** /flau̯/ ❶ *Adj.* Ⓐ (*schwach, matt*) slack ‹breeze›; flat ‹atmosphere›; Ⓑ (*leicht übel*) queasy ‹feeling›; **mir ist ~ [vor Hunger]** I feel queasy [with hunger]. ❷ *adv.* (*Kaufmannsspr.*) **das Geschäft geht ~:** business is slack; **die Börse eröffnete ~:** the market got off to a slow start

**Flaum** /flau̯m/ *der;* **~[e]s** Ⓐ fuzz; Ⓑ (*~feder*) down

**Flaum·bart** *der* downy beard

**Flaumer** *der;* **~s**, **~** (*schweiz.*) mop

**Flaum-:** **~feder** *die* down feather; **~haar** *das* down

**flaumig** *Adj.* Ⓐ downy; Ⓑ (*österr.: schaumig, porös*) fluffy

**Flausch** /flau̯ʃ/ *der;* **~[e]s**, **~e** brushed wool

**flauschig** *Adj.* fluffy

**Flausch·jacke** *die* brushed-wool jacket

**Flause** /ˈflau̯zə/ *die;* **~**, **~n** (*ugs.*) Ⓐ (*Unsinn*) **er hat nur ~n im Kopf** he can never think of anything sensible; **jmdm. die ~n austreiben** knock some sense into sb.; **lass doch die albernen ~n** stop messing about (*coll.*); Ⓑ (*Ausflucht*) excuse; **~n machen** make excuses

**Flaute** /ˈflau̯tə/ *die;* **~**, **~n** Ⓐ (*Seemannsspr.*) calm; Ⓑ (*Kaufmannsspr.*) fall[-off] in trade; **in der ~:** in the doldrums; **es herrscht eine [allgemeine] ~:** trade is [generally] slack; Ⓒ (*Sport: Tiefpunkt*) **sie überwanden die ~:** they got over the bad patch [in the game]

**Fläz** /flɛːts/ *der;* **~es**, **~e** (*ugs. abwertend*) lout

**fläzen** *refl. V.* (*ugs. abwertend*) **sich in den/im Sessel ~:** flop into/lounge in the armchair

**Flebbe** /ˈflɛbə/ *die;* **~**, **~n** (*salopp*) identity card

**Flechse** /ˈflɛksə/ *die;* **~**, **~n** sinew

**Flecht·arbeit** *die* piece of wickerwork; **~en** wickerwork *sing.*

**Flechte** /ˈflɛçtə/ *die;* **~**, **~n** Ⓐ (*Bot.*) lichen; Ⓑ **▶ 474** (*Med.*) eczema; Ⓒ (*geh.: Zopf*) plait

**flechten** *unr. tr. V.* plait ‹hair›; weave ‹basket, mat›; **etw. zu einem Korb ~:** weave sth. into a basket; weave a basket out of sth.; **jmdn. aufs Rad ~** (*hist.*) break sb. on the wheel

**Flechter** *der;* **~s**, **~**, **Flechterin** *die;* **~**, **~nen** basket weaver

**Flecht-:** **~werk** *das* Ⓐ (*Geflecht*) wickerwork; Ⓑ (*Archit.*) wattle and daub; **~zaun** *der* wicker fence

**Fleck** /flɛk/ *der;* **~[e]s**, **~e** Ⓐ (*verschmutzte Stelle*) stain; **voller ~e sein** be covered in stains; **~e machen** leave stains; **das macht keine ~e** that does not leave stains *or* does not stain; **einen ~ auf der [weißen] Weste haben** (*fig. ugs.*) have blotted one's copybook; Ⓑ (*andersfarbige Stelle*) patch; **ein weißer ~ auf der Landkarte** a piece of uncharted territory; an uncharted region; ⇒ *auch* **blau**; Ⓒ (*Stelle, Punkt*) spot; **er rührte sich nicht vom ~:** he didn't move an inch; **auf demselben ~ stehen** stand in the same place; **wir brachten den Stein nicht vom ~:** we couldn't budge the stone; **ich bin nicht vom ~ gekommen** (*fig.*) I didn't get anywhere; **am falschen ~ sparen** (*fig.*) save on the wrong things; **vom ~ weg** (*fig.*) on the spot; ⇒ *auch* **Herz** A

**Fleckchen** *das;* **~s**, **~:** spot; **ein schönes ~ Erde** a lovely little spot

**flecken** *itr. V.* stain

**Flecken** *der;* **~s**, **~** Ⓐ ⇒ **Fleck** A, B; Ⓑ (*Ortschaft*) little place

**flecken-, Flecken-:** **~entfernungsmittel** *das* stain *or* spot remover; **~los** ❶ *Adj.* Ⓐ spotless; Ⓑ (*einwandfrei, tadellos*) without blemish *postpos.;* ❷ *adv.* spotlessly

**Fleck·entferner** *der;* **~s**, **~**, **Fleck·entfernungs·mittel** *das*, **Flecken·wasser** *das* stain *or* spot remover

**Fleckerl·teppich** *der* (*bayr., österr.*) patchwork rug

**Fleck·fieber** *das* **▶ 474** (*Med.*) typhus

**fleckig** /ˈflɛkɪç/ *Adj.* Ⓐ (*verschmutzt*) stained; **ganz ~:** full of stains; Ⓑ (*gepunktet*) speckled ‹apple›; blotchy ‹face, skin›

**fleddern** /ˈflɛdɐn/ *tr. V.* plunder, rob ‹person›; (*salopp*) ransack ‹desk etc.›

**Fleder·maus** /ˈfleːdɐ-/ *die* bat

**Fledermaus·ärmel** *der* (*Textilw.*) batwing sleeve

**Fleder·wisch** *der* feather duster

**Fleet** /fleːt/ *das;* **~s**, **~e** (*nordd.*) canal

**Flegel** /ˈfleːgl/ *der;* **~s**, **~** (*abwertend*) lout

**Flegel·alter** *das* ⇒ **Flegeljahre**

**Flegelei** *die;* **~**, **~en** (*abwertend*) loutish behaviour; **eine solche ~/solche ~en** such loutish behaviour

**flegelhaft** ❶ *Adj.* (*abwertend*) loutish; boorish ‹tone of voice›. ❷ *adv.* loutishly

**Flegel·jahre** *Pl.* uncouth adolescence *sing.;* **in die ~ kommen/aus den ~n heraus sein** reach/be past the awkward age *sing.*

**flegeln** *refl. V.* (*abwertend*) **sich auf ein Sofa/in einen Sessel ~:** flop on to a sofa/into an armchair

**flehen** /ˈfleːən/ *itr. V.* plead; **[bei jmdm.] um etw. ~:** plead [with sb.] for sth.; **mit ~der Stimme** with a pleading voice; **zu Gott/zum Himmel [um etw.] ~:** beg God/Heaven [for sth.]

**flehentlich** *Adv.* (*geh.*) pleadingly

**Fleisch** /flai̯ʃ/ *das;* **~[e]s** Ⓐ (*Muskelgewebe*) flesh; **das nackte ~:** one's bare flesh; **das rohe ~:** one's raw flesh; **viel ~ zeigen** (*ugs.*) show a lot of flesh; (*fig.*) **sein eigen[es] ~ und Blut** (*geh.*) his own flesh and blood; **jmdm. in ~ und Blut übergehen** become second nature to sb.; **sich** (*Dat.*) **ins eigene ~ schneiden** cut off one's nose to spite one's face; **vom ~ fallen** (*ugs.*) waste away; **~ fressend** (*Biol.*) carnivorous; Ⓑ (*Nahrungsmittel*) meat; Ⓒ (*Frucht~*) flesh; Ⓓ **den Weg allen ~es gehen** (*geh.*) go the way of all flesh; **~ geworden** (*dichter.*) incarnate (*Theol.*); ‹innocence, virtue, etc.› personified

**fleisch-, Fleisch-:** **~abfälle** *Pl.* meat scraps; **~arm** ❶ *Adj.* ‹diet› low in meat; ❷ *adv.* **ich esse sehr ~arm** I eat very little meat; **~beschau** *die* meat inspection; (*ugs. scherzh.*) cattle market; **~beschauer** *der*, **~beschauerin** *die* meat inspector; **~brocken** *der* chunk of meat; **~brühe** *die* (*mit Einlage*) meat soup; (*klar*) bouillon; consommé; **~einlage** *die* added meat; **mit ~einlage** with meat added; **~einwaage** *die* meat content

**Fleischer** /ˈflai̯ʃɐ/ *der;* **~s**, **~**, **Fleischerin** *die;* **~**, **~nen** **▶ 159** butcher; ⇒ *auch* **Bäcker**

**Fleischerei** *die;* **~**, **~en** butcher's shop; **in der ~:** at the butcher's; ⇒ *auch* **Bäckerei**

**Fleischer-:** **~geselle** *der*, **~gesellin** *die* butcher; **~haken** *der* meat hook; **~handwerk** *das* butchery trade; **~hund** *der* large fierce dog; **ein Gemüt wie ein ~hund haben** (*ugs.*) be a cold-blooded sort (*coll.*); **~laden** *der; Pl.* **~läden** ⇒ **Fleischerei**; **~meister** *der*, **~meisterin** *die* master butcher; **~messer** *das* butcher's knife

**Fleisches·lust** *die* (*geh.*) carnal lust

**fleisch-, Fleisch-:** **~esser** *der*, **~esserin** *die* meat eater; **~extrakt** *der* meat extract;

*old spelling (see note on page 1707)

~**farben**, ~**farbig** *Adj.* flesh-coloured; ~**fliege** *die* meat fly; ~**fondue** *das* (*Kochk.*) meat fondue; *~**fressend** ⇒ **Fleisch** A; ~**fresser** *der* (*Biol.*) carnivore; ~**füllung** *die* (*Kochk.*) meat stuffing; (*in Pasteten*) meat filling; ~**gang** *der* (*Gastr.*) meat course; ~**gericht** *das* meat dish; *~**geworden** ⇒ **Fleisch** D; ~**haken** *der* meat hook; ~**hauer** *der*, ~**hauerin** *die*; ~~, ~~**nen** (*österr.*) butcher

**fleischig** *Adj.* plump ‹hands, face›; fleshy ‹leaf, fruit›

**Fleisch-:** ~**käse** *der* meat loaf; ~**kloß** *der* Ⓐ (*Kochk.*) meat ball; Ⓑ ⇒ ~**klumpen**; ~**klößchen** *das* small meat ball; ~**klumpen** *der* (*ugs.*) Ⓐ (*großes Stück* ~*klumpen*) chunk of meat; Ⓑ (*abwertend: Mensch*) mound of flesh; ~**konserve** *die* tin of meat (*Brit.*); can of meat (*Amer.*); ~**konserven** tinned meat (*Brit.*); canned meat (*Amer.*)

**fleischlich** *Adj.* Ⓐ (*veralt.*) ~**e Kost** *od.* **Nahrung** meat; Ⓑ (*geh. veralt.*) carnal; **allem Fleischlichen entsagen** renounce the flesh

**fleisch-, Fleisch-:** ~**los** ❶ *Adj.* Ⓐ ‹meal› without meat; Ⓑ (*hager, mager*) bony ‹hands, face›; ❷ *adv.* ‹cook› without meat; ~**maschine** *die* (*südd., österr.*) ⇒ ~**wolf**; ~**messer** *das* carving knife; ~**pastete** *die* (*Kochk.*) pâté; ~**preis** *der* price of meat; **die** ~**preise** the meat prices; ~**ration** *die* meat ration; ~**salat** *der* (*Kochk.*) meat salad; ~**seite** *die* (*Gerberei*) flesh side; ~**stück** *das* piece of meat; ~**topf** *der* meat pot; **sich nach den** ~**töpfen Ägyptens sehnen/zurücksehnen** long for/long to return to the good life; ~**vergiftung** *die* food poisoning [from meat]; ~**waren** *Pl.* meat products; ~**- und Wurstwaren** meat and sausages; ~**werdung** *die*; ~~ (*dicht.*) incarnation; ~**wolf** *der* mincer; **etw. durch den** ~**wolf drehen** put sth. through the mincer; mince sth.; ~**wunde** *die* flesh wound; ~**wurst** *die* pork sausage

**Fleiß** /flais/ *der*; ~**es** Ⓐ (*eifriges Streben*) hard work; (*Eigenschaft*) diligence; **mit großem** ~: diligently; **mit ihrem beharrlichen** ~: with her unceasing application; **viel** ~ **auf etw.** (*Akk.*) **verwenden** put a lot of effort into sth.; **durch** ~ **etw. erreichen** achieve sth. by hard work; **im** ~ **nachlassen** become slack; **ohne** ~ **kein Preis** (*Spr.*) success never comes easily; Ⓑ (*veralt., südd.: Absicht*) **mit** ~: on purpose

**Fleiß·arbeit** *die* task requiring great diligence; **eine reine** ~ (*abwertend*) a [diligent but] routine piece of work

**fleißig** /ˈflaisɪç/ ❶ *Adj.* Ⓐ (*arbeitsam*) hard-working; ~**e Hände** willing hands; **sie sind** ~ **wie die Bienen** *od.* **Ameisen** they work like beavers; Ⓑ (*von Fleiß zeugend*) **eine** ~**e Arbeit** a diligent piece of work; Ⓒ (*regelmäßig, häufig*) **ein** ~**er Besucher** a frequent visitor (*Gen.* to); Ⓓ (*unermüdlich*) indefatigable ‹collector›; great ‹walker›. ❷ *adv.* Ⓐ ‹work, study› hard; ~ **lernen** learn as much as one can; Ⓑ (*unermüdlich*) ‹drink, spend› steadily; ‹collect› regularly; **immer** ~ **hauen** keep on hitting; Ⓒ (*regelmäßig*) frequently; **geh nur** ~ **spazieren** do as much walking as you can

**Fleiß·prüfung** *die: examination to assess application*

**flektierbar** *Adj.* (*Sprachw.*) inflectional

**flektieren** /flɛkˈtiːrən/ (*Sprachw.*) ❶ *tr. V.* inflect. ❷ *itr. V.* be inflected

**flennen** /ˈflɛnən/ *itr. V.* (*ugs. abwertend*) blubber

**fletschen** /ˈflɛtʃn̩/ *tr., itr. V.* **die Zähne** *od.* **mit den Zähnen** ~: bare one's teeth; **mit gefletschten Zähnen** with bared teeth

**fleucht** /flɔyçt/ ⇒ **kreucht**

**Fleurop** Ⓦⓩ /ˈflɔyrɔp/ *die* Interflora ®

**Flex** *die*; ~, ~**e** (*ugs.*) angle grinder [with cutting disc]

**flexibel** /flɛˈksiːbl̩/ ❶ *Adj.* flexible. ❷ *adv.* flexibly

**Flexibilität** /flɛksibiliˈtɛːt/ *die*; ~: flexibility

**Flexion** /flɛˈksi̯oːn/ *die*; ~, ~**en** Ⓐ (*Sprachw.*) inflexion; (*von Adjektiven, Substantiven*) declension; (*von Verben*) conjugation; Ⓑ ▶ 474 (*Med.*) flexion

**flexions-, Flexions-:** ~**endung** *die* (*Sprachw.*) inflectional suffix *or* ending; ~**los** *Adj.* (*Sprachw.*) uninflected

**Flexo·druck** /ˈflɛkso-/ *der* (*Druckw.*) flexographic printing

**flicht** *Imperativ Sg. u. 3. Pers. Sg. Präsens v.* **flechten**

**Flick·arbeit** *die* repair; **mit einer** ~ **beschäftigt sein** be repairing *or* mending something

**flicken** /ˈflɪkn̩/ *tr. V.* mend ‹trousers, dress›; repair ‹engine, cable›; mend, repair ‹wall, roof›; **etw. notdürftig** ~: patch sth. up

**Flicken** *der*; ~**s**, ~: patch

**Flicken-:** ~**decke** *die* patchwork quilt; ~**teppich** *der* patchwork rug

**Flickflack** /ˈflɪkflak/ *der*; ~**s**, ~**s** (*Turnen*) flik-flak

**Flick-:** ~**korb** *der* sewing basket; ~**schneider** *der*, ~**schneiderin** *die* (*veralt.*) mending tailor; ~**schuster** *der* Ⓐ (*veralt. abwertend*) mending shoemaker; cobbler; Ⓑ (*fig.: Nichtskönner*) bungler; ~**schusterei** *die* (*fig. abwertend*) bungling; ~**schusterin** *die* ⇒ ~**schuster**; ~**werk** *das* (*abwertend*) botched-up job; ~**wort** *das*; *Pl.* ~**wörter** filler; ~**zeug** *das* repair kit

**Flieder** /ˈfliːdɐ/ *der*; ~**s**, ~: lilac

**flieder-, Flieder-:** ~**duft** *der* scent of lilac; ~**farben**, ~**farbig** *Adj.* lilac; ~**strauch** *der* lilac bush; ~**tee** *der* elderberry tea

**Fliege** /ˈfliːɡə/ *die*; ~, ~**n** Ⓐ fly; **die Menschen starben wie die** ~**n** people were dying like flies; **er tut keiner** ~ **etwas zuleide/könnte keiner** ~ **etwas zuleide tun** he wouldn't/couldn't hurt a fly; (*fig.*) **ihn stört die** ~ **an der Wand** the least little thing annoys him; **zwei** ~**n mit einer Klappe schlagen** kill two birds with one stone; **die** *od.* **'ne** ~ **machen** (*salopp*) beat it (*coll.*); Ⓑ (*Schleife*) bow tie; Ⓒ (*Bärtchen*) shadow

**fliegen** ❶ *unr. itr. V.* Ⓐ *mit sein* fly; **das** ~**de Personal** the air crew; **im Wind** ~: be flying in the wind; **mit** ~**den Rockschößen** with flapping coat-tails; **die Funken flogen** sparks flew about; **in die Luft** ~: blow up; ⇒ *auch* **Fahne** B; Ⓑ *mit sein* (*ugs.: geworfen werden*) **aus der Kurve** ~: skid off a/the bend; **vom Pferd/Fahrrad** ~: fall off a/the horse/bicycle; Ⓒ *mit sein* (*ugs.: entlassen werden*) be sacked (*coll.*); get the sack (*coll.*); **auf die Straße/aus einer Stellung** ~: get the sack (*coll.*); be thrown out; **von der Schule** ~: be chucked out [of the school] (*coll.*); Ⓓ *mit sein* (*ugs.: hinfallen, stürzen*) fall; **in einen Graben** ~: fall into a ditch; **über etw.** (*Akk.*) ~: trip over sth.; **durch das Examen/eine Prüfung** ~ (*fig.*) fail the exam/a test; Ⓔ *mit sein* **auf jmdn./etw.** ~ (*ugs.*) go for sb./sth.; **er fliegt auf Blondinen** he makes a beeline for blondes; Ⓕ *meist mit sein* (*flattern, zittern*) ‹pulse› race; **sein Atem fliegt** he is gasping for breath; **er flog am ganzen Körper** he was trembling all over; Ⓖ *mit sein* (*eilen, rasen*) fly; race; **das Pferd flog wie ein Pfeil über die Bahn** the horse raced *or* flew over the track like a shot from a gun; **ihre Hand flog über das Papier** her hand flew over the paper; **in** ~**der Eile** *od.* **Hast** in a mad rush.

❷ *unr. tr. V.* Ⓐ (*steuern,* ~*d befördern*) fly ‹aircraft, passengers, goods›; Ⓑ *auch mit sein* (~*d ausführen*) **einen Einsatz** ~: fly a mission; **einen Umweg** ~: make a detour; **eine Kurve** ~: describe a curve; **einen Looping** ~: loop the loop; **einen Angriff** ~ (*Milit.*) make an attack.

❸ *refl. V.* **die Maschine fliegt sich gut/schlecht** the plane flies well/badly; **es fliegt sich gut/schlecht hier/heute** the flying is good/bad here/today

**fliegend** *Adj.* flying; **ein** ~**er Händler** a pedlar; ~**e Bauten** mobile buildings; **der Fliegende Holländer** the Flying Dutchman

**Fliegen-:** ~**draht** *der* fly screen; ~**dreck** *der* fly droppings *pl.*; ~**fänger** *der* flypaper; ~**fenster** *das* wire-mesh window; ~**gewicht** *das* (*Schwerathletik*) Ⓐ flyweight; **die Meisterschaften im** ~**gewicht** the flyweight championships; **im** ~**gewicht starten** compete at flyweight; Ⓑ ⇒ ~**gewichtler**; ~**gewichtler** /-ɡəvɪçtlɐ/ *der*; ~~**s**, ~~: flyweight; ~**klatsche** *die* fly swat; ~**kopf** *der* (*Druckw.*) *piece of type turned over to print as black oblong*; ~**pilz** *der* fly agaric; ~**schnäpper** *der*; ~~**s**, ~~ (*Zool.*) flycatcher; ~**schrank** *der* meat safe

**Flieger** *der*; ~**s**, ~ Ⓐ pilot; **er ist bei den** ~**n** (*Milit.*) he's in the air force; Ⓑ (*Radsport*) sprinter; Ⓒ (*Artistik*) trapeze artist; Ⓓ (*Zool.*) flyer

**Flieger-:** ~**abwehr** *die* ⇒ **Flugabwehr**; ~**abzeichen** *das* (*Milit.*) flying badge; ~**alarm** *der* air-raid warning; ~**angriff** *der* air raid

**Fliegerei** *die*; ~: flying *no art.*

**Flieger·horst** *der* (*Milit.*) military airfield

**Fliegerin** *die*; ~, ~**nen** [woman] pilot

**fliegerisch** *Adj.* aeronautical; ~**e Eigenschaften** handling characteristics; handling *sing.*

**Flieger-:** ~**jacke** *die* flying jacket; ~**krankheit** *die* altitude sickness; ~**rennen** *das* (*Radsport*) sprint; ~**schule** *die* flying school; ~**sprache** *die* airmen's jargon; ~**staffel** *die* (*Milit.*) [flying] squadron

**Flieh·burg** *die* refuge

**fliehen** /ˈfliːən/ ❶ *unr. itr. V.*; *mit sein* (*flüchten*) flee (**vor** + *Dat.* from); (*aus dem Gefängnis usw.*) escape (**aus** from); **ins Ausland/über die Grenze** ~: flee the country/escape over the border. ❷ *unr. tr. V.* (*geh.: meiden*) shun

**fliehend** *Adj.* sloping ‹forehead›; receding ‹chin›

**Flieh·kraft** *die* (*Physik*) centrifugal force

**Fliese** /ˈfliːzə/ *die*; ~, ~**n** tile; **etw. mit** ~**n auslegen** tile sth.

**fliesen** *tr. V.* tile

**Fliesenleger** /-leːɡɐ/ *der*; ~**s**, ~, **Fliesenlegerin** *die*; ~, ~**nen** ▶ 159 tiler

**Fließ-:** ~**arbeit** *die* assembly line production; ~**band** *das*; *Pl.* ~**bänder** conveyor belt; **am** ~**band arbeiten** *od.* (*ugs.*) **stehen** work on the assembly line; **am** ~**band gefertigt werden** be produced on the assembly line; ~**band·arbeit** *die* assembly-line work; ~**band·arbeiter** *der*, ~**band·arbeiterin** *die* assembly-line worker; ~**band·fertigung** *die* assembly-line production

**fließen** /ˈfliːsn̩/ *unr. itr. V.*; *mit sein* Ⓐ ▶ 306 flow; **ein Bach ist ein** ~**des Gewässer** a stream is a body of running water; **ein Zimmer mit** ~**dem [warmem und kaltem] Wasser** a room with [hot and cold] running water; **„Alles fließt", sagte Heraklit** 'All is flux', said Heraclitus; (*unpers.*) **es floss Blut** blood was shed; Ⓑ ▶ 696 (*fig.*) **viele Devisen flossen ins Land** a great deal of foreign currency flowed into the country; **die Gaben flossen reichlich** donations were pouring in; **die Nachrichten aus diesem Gebiet flossen nur spärlich** news from this area came in very infrequently; **der Verkehr war** ~**d** the traffic kept moving; **die Grenzen [zwischen zwei Gebieten] sind** ~**d** the dividing line [between two areas] is blurred; ~**de Übergänge** fluid transitions; **die Verse flossen ihm aus der Feder** the verses flowed from his pen; **eine Sprache** ~**d sprechen** speak a language fluently

**Fließ-:** ~**grenze** *die* (*Technik*) yield point; ~**heck** *das* (*Kfz-W.*) fastback; ~**komma** *das* (*DV*) floating point; ~**satz** *der* (*Druckw.*) undisplay

**Flimmer-:** ~**epithel** *das* (*Biol.*) ciliated epithelium; ~**kasten** *der*, ~**kiste** *die* (*ugs.*) telly (*coll.*); box (*coll.*)

**flimmern** /ˈflɪmɐn/ *itr. V.*; *mit Richtungsangabe mit sein* ‹water, air, surface› shimmer; ‹film› flicker; **ihm flimmerte es vor den Augen** everything was swimming in front of his eyes; **über den Bildschirm** ~ (*ugs.*) be served up on the box (*coll.*)

**flink** /flɪŋk/ ❶ *Adj.* nimble ‹fingers›; sharp ‹eyes›; quick ‹hands›; ~ **wie ein Wiesel** as quick as a flash; **er hat noch** ~**e Beine** *od.* **ist noch** ~ **auf den Beinen** (*ugs.*) he's still nippy on his pins (*coll.*). ❷ *adv.* quickly; **mit etw. ~ bei der Hand sein** be very ready to do sth.; **aber ein bisschen ~!** (*ugs.*) and be quick about it!

**Flinkheit** *die;* ~ ⇒ **flink** 1: nimbleness; sharpness; quickness

**flink·züngig** /-tsʏŋɪç/ ❶ *Adj.* eloquent. ❷ *adv.* eloquently

**Flinte** /ˈflɪntə/ *die;* ~, ~**n** shotgun; **alles, was ihm vor die ~ kommt** everything he gets in his sights; **der soll mir nur vor die ~ kommen!** (*fig. salopp*) if I can just get my hands on him; **die ~ ins Korn werfen** (*fig.*) throw in the towel

**Flinten-:** ~**knall** *der* gunfire; **ein ~knall** a gunshot; ~**kugel** *die* shotgun pellet; ~**lauf** *der* shotgun barrel; ~**weib** *das* (*abwertend*) soldier in skirts

**Flip** /flɪp/ *der;* ~**s**, ~**s** flip

**Flipchart** *das;* ~**s**, ~**s** flip chart

**Flipflop·schaltung** /ˈflɪpflɔp-/ *die* (*Elektrot.*) flip-flop circuit

**Flipper** /ˈflɪpɐ/ *der;* ~**s**, ~, **Flipper·automat** *der* pinball machine; ~ **spielen** play pinball

**flippern** /ˈflɪpɐn/ *itr. V.* (*ugs.*) play pinball

**flirren** /ˈflɪrən/ *itr. V.* (*geh.*) ‹heat, light, dust, etc.› shimmer

**Flirt** /flɪrt/ *der;* ~**s**, ~**s** flirtation; **einen ~ mit jmdm. anfangen/haben** start flirting with sb./flirt with sb.

**flirten** *itr. V.* flirt

**Flittchen** /ˈflɪtçən/ *das;* ~**s**, ~ (*ugs. abwertend*) floozie

**Flitter** /ˈflɪtɐ/ *der;* ~**s**, ~ Ⓐ (*täuschender Glanz*) frippery; trumpery; Ⓑ (*Metallplättchen*) sequin

**Flitter-:** ~**gold** *das* Dutch metal; ~**kram** *der* (*ugs. abwertend*) frippery; trumpery

**flittern** *itr. V.* (*ugs. scherzh.*) honeymoon

**Flitter-:** ~**wochen** *Pl.* honeymoon *sing.*; **in die ~wochen fahren** go on one's honeymoon; ~**wöchner** *der;* ~~**s**, ~~, ~**wöchnerin** *die* (*ugs. scherzh.*) honeymooner

**Flitz[e]·bogen** /ˈflɪts(ə)-/ *der* bow; (*fig.*) **gespannt sein wie ein ~:** be on tenterhooks; **ich bin gespannt wie ein ~, ob er kommen wird** I'm dying to see if he will come; **auf etw.** (*Akk.*) **gespannt sein wie ein ~:** be on tenterhooks waiting for sth.

**flitzen** /ˈflɪtsn̩/ *itr. V.; mit sein* (*ugs.*) shoot; dart; **ich flitze mal gerade zum Fleischer** I'll just dash to the butcher's; **nach rechts und links ~:** dart to either side

**Flitzer** *der;* ~**s**, ~ (*ugs.*) sporty job (*coll.*)

**floaten** /ˈfloʊtn̩/ *tr., itr. V.* (*Wirtsch.*) float

**Floating** /ˈfloʊtɪŋ/ *das;* ~**s**, ~**s** (*Wirtsch.*) floating

**F-Loch** /ˈɛf-/ *das* (*Musik*) F-hole

**flocht** /flɔxt/ *1. u. 3. Pers. Sg. Prät. v.* **flechten**

**Flöckchen** /ˈflœkçən/ *das;* ~**s**, ~ (*Schnee*~) flake; (*Staub*~) bit of fluff

**Flocke** /ˈflɔkə/ *die;* ~, ~**n** Ⓐ **eine ~ Watte/Wolle** a bit of cotton wool/tuft of wool; Ⓑ (*Schnee*~) flake; **es schneit in dicken ~n** it's snowing large flakes; Ⓒ (*Schaum*~) blob; (*Staub*~) piece of fluff

**Flocken-:** ~**blume** *die* (*Bot.*) centaury; ~**wirbel** *der* (*geh.*) whirl of snowflakes

**flockig** *Adj.* fluffy; ~**er Schaum** blobs *pl.* of foam; **Butter ~ rühren** cream butter

**flog** /flo:k/ *1. u. 3. Pers. Sg. Prät. v.* **fliegen**

**floh** /flo:/ *1. u. 3. Pers. Sg. Prät. v.* **fliehen**

**Floh** /flo:/ *der;* ~**[e]s**, **Flöhe** /ˈflø:ə/ Ⓐ flea; (*fig.*) **lieber einen Sack [voll] Flöhe hüten, als ...** even if you paid me a million pounds I wouldn't ...; **jmdm. einen ~ ins Ohr setzen** (*ugs.*) put an idea into sb.'s head; **die Flöhe husten** *od.* **niesen hören** (*ugs.*) know it all before it happens; Ⓑ *Pl.* (*salopp: Geld*) dough *sing.* (*coll.*); bread *sing.* (*coll.*)

*old spelling (see note on page 1707)

**Floh·biss**, ***Floh·biß** *der* flea bite

**flöhen** /ˈflø:ən/ *tr. V.* flea

**Floh-:** ~**hüpfen** *das;* ~~**s** (*Kinderspiel*) tiddlywinks; ~**kino** *das* (*ugs.*) fleapit (*coll.*); ~**kraut** *das* (*Bot.*) fleabane; ~**markt** *der* flea market; ~**zirkus** *der* flea circus

**Flom[en]** /ˈflo:m(ən)/ *der;* ~**s** (*nordd.*) leaf fat

**Flop** /flɔp/ *der;* ~**s**, ~**s** (*ugs.*) flop (*coll.*)

**Floppydisk** *die;* ~, ~**s** floppy disk; floppy

**Flor**[1] /flo:ɐ̯/ *der;* ~**s**, ~**e** (*geh.*) Ⓐ (*Blütenpracht*) **im ~ stehen** be in full bloom; **einen zweiten ~ entfalten** have a second flush; Ⓑ (*Blumenfülle*) display

**Flor**[2] *der;* ~**s**, ~**e**, *selten:* **Flöre** /ˈflø:rə/ Ⓐ (*zartes Gewebe*) gauze; Ⓑ (*Faserenden*) pile; Ⓒ ⇒ **Trauerflor**

**Flora** /ˈflo:ra/ *die;* ~, **Floren** flora

**Flor·band** *das; Pl.* **Florbänder** black band; mourning band

**Florentiner**[1] /florɛnˈti:nɐ/ *der;* ~**s**, ~ ▶ **700** Florentine

**Florentiner**[2] *der;* ~**s**, ~ Ⓐ (*Hut*) picture hat; Ⓑ (*Gebäck*) florentine

**Florentinerin** *die;* ~, ~**nen** Florentine

**florentinisch** *Adj.* Florentine

**Florenz** /floˈrɛnts/ (*das*); **Florenz'** ▶ **700** Florence

**Florett** /floˈrɛt/ *das;* ~**[e]s**, ~**e** Ⓐ (*Stoßwaffe*) foil; **mit dem ~ fechten** fence with a foil; Ⓑ (~*fechten*) foils *sing.*; foil fencing *no art.*

**Florett-:** ~**fechten** *das* foil fencing *no art.*; ~**fechter** *der*, ~**fechterin** *die* foil fencer

**Flor·fliege** *die* (*Zool.*) green lacewing

**florieren** /floˈri:rən/ *itr. V.* ‹business› flourish; **ein [gut] ~der Laden** a flourishing shop

**Florist** /floˈrɪst/ *der;* ~**en**, ~**en**, **Floristin** *die;* ~, ~**nen** ▶ **159** Ⓐ (*Blumenbinder*) [qualified] flower arranger; Ⓑ (*Kenner einer Flora*) botanist; Ⓒ (*Blumenhändler*) florist

**Flor·teppich** *der* pile carpet

**Floskel** /ˈflɔskl̩/ *die;* ~, ~**n** cliché; **der Brief enthält nichts außer abgedroschenen ~n** the letter is full of clichés *or* hackneyed phrases

**floskelhaft** ❶ *Adj.* cliché-ridden; clichéd. ❷ *adv.* **sich ~ ausdrücken** talk in clichés

**floss**, ***floß** /flɔs/ *1. u. 3. Pers. Sg. Prät. v.* **fließen**

**Floß** /flo:s/ *das;* ~**es**, **Flöße** /ˈflø:sə/ Ⓐ raft ; Ⓑ (*an der Angel*) float

**flöß·bar** *Adj.* navigable by raft *postpos.*

**Flosse** /ˈflɔsə/ *die;* ~, ~**n** Ⓐ (*Zool., Flugw.*) fin; Ⓑ (*zum Tauchen*) flipper; Ⓒ (*ugs. scherzh. od. abwertend: Hand*) paw

**flößen** /ˈflø:sn̩/ *tr., itr. V.* float; **Baumstämme [auf dem Fluss] ~:** raft tree trunks [on the river]

**Flossen·füß[l]er** *der* (*Zool.*) pinniped

**Flößer** /ˈflø:sɐ/ *der;* ~**s**, ~ ▶ **159** raftsman

**Flößerei** /flø:səˈrai/ *die;* ~**:** rafting

**Flößerin** *die;* ~, ~**nen** ▶ **159** raftswoman

**Floß-:** ~**fahrt** *die* voyage by raft; ~**gasse** *die* channel for rafts; ~**holz** *das* rafted wood

**Flotation** /flotaˈtsi̯o:n/ *die;* ~, ~**en** (*bes. Hüttenw.*) flotation

**Flöte** /ˈflø:tə/ *die;* ~, ~**n** Ⓐ (*Musik*) flute; (*Block*~) recorder; ~ **spielen** play the flute/recorder; **die ~ des Pan** the pipes of Pan; Ⓑ (*Skat*) **die [ganze] ~ herunterspielen** play a [straight] flush; Ⓒ (*hohes Glas*) flute

***flöten** /ˈflø:tn̩/ ❶ *itr. V.* Ⓐ ‹bird› flute; Ⓑ (*Flöte spielen*) play the flute/recorder; Ⓒ (*ugs.: affektiert sprechen*) pipe; **in den sanftesten Tönen ~:** speak in wheedling tones; Ⓓ ~ **gehen** (*ugs.*) go for a burton (*Brit. coll.*); ‹money› go down the drain; ‹time› be wasted. ❷ *tr. V.* whistle ‹song, tune›

**flöten-, Flöten-:** *~**|gehen** ⇒ **flöten** 1D; ~**kessel** *der* whistling kettle; ~**konzert** *das* Ⓐ (*Musikstück*) flute concerto; Ⓑ (*Veranstaltung*) flute concert; ~**musik** *die* flute music; ~**register** *das* (*Musik*) flute stop; ~**spiel** *das* flute-playing; ~**spieler** *der*, ~**spielerin** *die* flute player; ~**ton** *der; Pl.* ~**töne** sound of a flute; **jmdm. die ~töne beibringen** (*fig. ugs.*) teach sb. a thing or two (*coll.*)

**Flötist** /fløˈtɪst/ *der;* ~**en**, ~**en**, **Flötistin** *die;* ~, ~**nen** ▶ **159** flautist

**flott** /flɔt/ ❶ *Adj.* Ⓐ (*ugs.: schwungvoll*) lively ‹music, dance, pace, style›; snappy ‹dialogue›; **den ~en Otto haben** (*salopp*) have the runs (*coll.*); Ⓑ (*ugs.: schick, modisch*) smart ‹hat, suit, car›; Ⓒ (*munter, hübsch*) stylish; smart; ~ **aussehen** look attractive; Ⓓ (*leichtlebig*) **ein ~es Leben führen** be fast-living; Ⓔ (*fahrbereit, wiederhergestellt*) seaworthy ‹vessel›; (*ugs.*) roadworthy ‹vehicle›; airworthy ‹aircraft›; **mein Auto ist wieder ~:** my car ist back on the road again. ❷ *adv.* ‹work› quickly; ‹dance, write› in a lively manner; ‹be dressed› smartly

**flott|bekommen** *unr. tr. V.:* ⇒ **flottkriegen**

**Flotte** /ˈflɔtə/ *die;* ~, ~**n** fleet

**Flotten-:** ~**abkommen** *das* naval treaty; ~**chef** *der* commander-in-chief of the/a fleet; ~**kommando** *das* fleet command; ~**parade** *die* naval parade; ~**stützpunkt** *der* naval base; ~**verband** *der* naval unit

**Flottille** /flɔˈtɪl(j)ə/ *die;* ~, ~**n** flotilla

**Flottillen·admiral** *der* rear admiral

**flott-:** ~**|kommen** *unr. itr. V.* get afloat; ~**|kriegen** *tr. V.* get ‹boat› afloat; get ‹car› going; ~**|machen** *tr. V.* refloat ‹ship›; get ‹car› back on the road; ~**weg** *Adv.* (*ugs.*) ~**weg arbeiten** keep at it

**Flöz** /flø:ts/ *das;* ~**es**, ~**e** (*Bergbau*) seam

**Fluch** /flu:x/ *der;* ~**[e]s**, **Flüche** /ˈfly:çə/ Ⓐ (*Kraftwort*) curse; oath; **ein derber/lästerlicher ~:** a vulgar/blasphemous oath; **einen ~ ausstoßen/unterdrücken** utter/suppress an oath; Ⓑ (*Verwünschung*) curse; **einen ~ gegen jmdn. ausstoßen** utter a curse against sb.; Ⓒ (*Unheil, Verderben*) curse; **ein ~ liegt über/lastet auf jmdm.** there's a curse on sb.; **das ist der ~ der bösen Tat** that's the wages of sin

**fluch·beladen** *Adj.* (*geh.*) accursed

**fluchen** *itr. V.* Ⓐ (*Flüche ausstoßen*) curse; swear; **auf/über jmdn./etw. ~:** swear at *or* curse sb./sth.; Ⓑ (*verwünschen*) (*geh.*) curse; **jmdm./einer Sache ~:** curse sb./sth.

**Flucht**[1] /flʊxt/ *die;* ~ Ⓐ (*Fliehen, Flüchten*) flight; **auf/während der ~:** while fleeing; (*von Gefangenen*) on the run; **jmdn. auf der ~ erschießen** shoot sb. while he/she is trying to escape; **auf** *od.* **während der ~ erschossen werden** be shot while trying to escape; **in wilder ~ davonjagen** run away in mad panic; **die ~ aus dem Gefängnis/aus einem Land** the escape from prison/from a country; **den Bankräubern/Gefangenen gelang die ~:** the bank robbers/prisoners succeeded in escaping; **die ~ ergreifen** ‹prisoner› make a dash for freedom; (*fig.*) make a dash for it; **jmdn. in die ~ schlagen** put sb. to flight; ⇒ *auch* **Ägypten**; Ⓑ (*Ausweichen*) refuge; **ihr blieb nur noch die ~ in den Alkohol/das Rauschgift** the only thing left to her was to take refuge in alcohol/drugs; **die ~ in die Krankheit/Anonymität** taking refuge in illness/anonymity; **die ~ in die Krankheit antreten** take refuge in illness; **die ~ aus der Wirklichkeit/Verantwortung** escape from reality/responsibility; **die ~ nach vorn antreten** take the bull by the horns; **die ~ in die Öffentlichkeit antreten** make a public statement

**Flucht**[2] *die;* ~, ~**en** Ⓐ (*Bauw.: Häuser*~, *Arkaden*~) row; **die ~ der Fenster** the line of the windows; Ⓑ (*Zimmer*~) suite

**flucht-, Flucht-:** ~**artig** ❶ *Adj.* hurried; hasty; ❷ *adv.* hurriedly; hastily; ~**auto** *das* getaway car; ~**burg** *die* refuge

**flüchten** /ˈflʏçtn̩/ ❶ *itr. V.; mit sein* **vor jmdm./etw. ~:** flee from sb./sth.; **vor der Polizei ~:** run away from the police; (*mit Erfolg*) escape from the police; **zu jmdm. ~:** take refuge with sb.; **ins Ausland ~:** escape abroad; **unter ein schützendes Dach ~:** take shelter under a protective roof. ❷ *refl. V.* **sich in ein Bauernhaus ~:** take refuge in a farmhouse; **sich aufs Dach ~:** escape on to the roof

**Flucht-:** ~**fahrzeug** *das* getaway vehicle; ~**gefahr** *die* risk of an escape attempt; **es besteht** ~**gefahr/keine** ~**gefahr** there's a/no risk of an escape attempt; ~**helfer** *der*, ~**helferin** *die* person who aids/aided an/the escape; ~**hilfe** *die* aiding an escape

**flüchtig** /'flʏçtɪç/ **1** *Adj.* **A** *(flüchtend)* fugitive; **er ist noch** ~**:** he ist still at large; **ein** ~**er Dieb/Verbrecher** a wanted thief/criminal; **B** *(oberflächlich)* cursory; superficial ‹insight›; **eine** ~**e Arbeit** a hurried piece of work; **C** *(eilig, schnell)* quick; short ‹visit, greeting›; fleeting ‹glance›; **D** *(vergänglich)* fleeting ‹moment›; quickly changing ‹moods›; sudden ‹temper, whim›; **E** *(Chemie)* volatile. **2** *adv.* **A** *(oberflächlich)* cursorily; **B** *(eilig)* hurriedly

**Flüchtigkeit** *die;* ~, ~**en** **A** *(Oberflächlichkeit)* cursoriness; **B** ⇨ **Flüchtigkeitsfehler**; **C** *(Vergänglichkeit)* fleetingness; **D** *(Chemie)* volatility

**Flüchtigkeits·fehler** *der* slip; *(tadelnswert)* careless mistake

**Flucht·kapital** *das (Wirtsch.): capital which has been sent out of the country to evade tax*

**Flüchtling** /'flʏçtlɪŋ/ *der;* ~**s**, ~**e** refugee

**Flüchtlings-:** ~**ausweis** *der* refugee's identity card; ~**elend** *das* hardship among refugees; ~**lager** *das* refugee camp; ~**treck** *der* long stream of refugees

**Flucht-:** ~**linie** *die* vanishing line; ~**plan** *der* escape plan; ~**punkt** *der (Kunstwiss.)* vanishing point; ~**reaktion** *die (Verhaltensf.)* escape reaction; ~**verdacht** *der:* **es besteht [kein]** ~**verdacht** he/she is [not] likely to try to escape; ~**versuch** *der* escape attempt; **einen** ~**versuch unternehmen** *od.* **machen** attempt to escape; ~**weg** *der* escape route; **sich** *(Dat.)* **den** ~**weg offenhalten** keep a way out open; **sich** *(Dat.)* **den** ~**weg freischießen** shoot one's way out

**fluch·würdig** *Adj. (geh.)* monstrous

**Flug** /flu:k/ *der;* ~**[e]s**, **Flüge** /'fly:gə/ **A** flight; **im** ~**:** in flight; **die Urlaubstage/Stunden vergingen [wie] im** ~**e** the holiday/hours flew by; **B** *(*~*reise)* flight; **C** *(Skispringen)* jump; **einen** ~ **[sicher] stehen** land safely; **D** *(Jägerspr.)* flock

**flug-, Flug-:** ~**abwehr** *die (Milit.)* anti-aircraft defence; ~**abwehr·rakete** *die (Milit.)* anti-aircraft missile; ~**angst** *die* fear of flying; ~**asche** *die* fly ash; ~**bahn** *die* trajectory; ~**ball** *der (Tennis)* volley; ~**begleiter** *der* ▶ 159 steward; ~**begleiterin** *die* ▶ 159 stewardess; ~**benzin** *das* aviation fuel; ~**bereit** *Adj.* ready for take-off *postpos.;* ~**betrieb** *der* air traffic; ~**bild** *das (Zool.)* flight silhouette; ~**blatt** *das* pamphlet; leaflet; ~**boot** *das* flying boat; ~**daten·schreiber** *der* flight recorder; ~**dauer** *die* flight time; ~**dienst** *der* **A** *(*~*verkehr)* air service; **B** *(Überwachungsdienst)* air traffic control; ~**dienst·leiter** *der*, ~**dienst·leiterin** *die* air traffic controller; ~**drache** *der (Zool.)* flying dragon; ~**drachen** *der* hang-glider; ~**echse** *die (Zool.)* pterosaurian; ~**eigenschaft** *die* flying characteristic

**Flügel** /'fly:gl̩/ *der;* ~**s**, ~ **A** wing; **mit den** ~**n schlagen** flap its/their wings; **die** ~ **hängen lassen** *(fig. ugs.)* become disheartened; **jmdm. die** ~ **stutzen** *od.* **beschneiden** *(fig.)* clip sb.'s wings; **das verlieh ihm** ~ *(fig. geh.)* that gave *or* lent him wings *(literary)*; **B** *(Altar*~*)* wing; *(Fensterflügel)* casement; *(Nasen*~*)* nostril; **der linke/rechte** ~ **der Lunge** the left/right lung; **C** *(Klavier)* grand piano; **jmdn. auf dem** ~ **begleiten** accompany sb. on the piano; **D** *(Milit., Ballspiele)* wing; **über die** ~ **spielen/angreifen** play/attack on the wings; **E** *(Tragfläche, Partei*~*, Gebäude*~*)* wing; **F** *(Schrauben*~*)* vane; *(Windmühlen*~*)* sail

**flügel-, Flügel-:** ~**altar** *der* winged altar; ~**decke** *die (Zool.)* elytron; wing case; ~**fenster** *das* casement window; ~**horn** *das (Musik)* flugelhorn; ~**lahm** *Adj.* **A** ‹bird› with an injured wing; **einen Vogel** ~**lahm schießen** wing a bird; **B** *(fig.: mutlos, kraftlos)* lacking energy *postpos.;* limping ‹organization›; ~**mutter** *die; Pl.* ~~**n** wing nut; ~**pumpe** *die* rotary pump; ~**rad** *das* **A** impeller wheel; **B** *(als Symbol)* winged wheel; ~**ross**, *~**roß** *das (Myth.)* winged horse; ~**schlag** *der* beat of [its/their] wings; ~**schlagend** *Adj.* beating its/their wings; ~**spann·weite** *die (Flugw., Zool.)* wing span; ~**stürmer** *der*, ~**stürmerin** *die (Ballspiele)* wing forward; winger; ~**tür** *die* double door

**flug-, Flug-:** ~**entfernung** *die* distance by air; ~**erfahrung** *die* flying experience; ~**fähig** *Adj.* airworthy; ~**feld** *das* airfield; ~**gast** *der* [air] passenger

**flügge** /'flʏgə/ *Adj.* fully-fledged; *(fig.: selbstständig)* independent

**Flug-:** ~**geschwindigkeit** *die (eines Flugzeugs)* flying speed; *(eines Vogels)* speed of flight; ~**gesellschaft** *die* airline; ~**hafen** *der* airport; ~**hafen Frankfurt** Frankfurt airport; ~**hafen·restaurant** *das* airport restaurant; ~**hafer** *der (Bot.)* wild oat; ~**höhe** *die* altitude; **in einer** ~**höhe von ...** at an altitude of ...; ~**hund** *der (Zool.)* flying fox; ~**ingenieur** *der*, ~**ingenieurin** *die* flight engineer; ~**kapitän** *der*, ~**kapitänin** *die* ▶ 159 captain; ~**kilometer** *der* [air] kilometre; ~**körper** *der* space vehicle; ~**lärm** *der* aircraft noise; ~**lehrer** *der*, ~**lehrerin** *die* ▶ 159 flying instructor; ~**leiter** *der*, ~**leiterin** *die* flight controller; ~**linie** *die* **A** *(Strecke)* air route; **B** *(Gesellschaft)* airline; ~**loch** ⇨ **Einflugloch**; ~**lotse** *der*, ~**lotsin** *die* ▶ 159 air traffic controller; ~**motor** *der* aircraft engine; ~**objekt** *das* flying object; **ein unbekanntes** ~**objekt** an unidentified flying object; ~**personal** *das* flight personnel; ~**plan** *der* flight schedule; ~**platz** *der* airfield; aerodrome; ~**preis** *der* air fare; ~**reise** *die* air journey; ~**route** *die* air route

**flugs** /flʊks/ *Adv. (veralt.)* swiftly

**flug-, Flug-:** ~**sand** *der* wind-borne sand; ~**saurier** *der (Zool.)* pterosaurian; ~**schanze** *die (Skifliegen)* ski jump *(used for ski-flying)*; ~**schein** **A** pilot's licence; **B** *(*~*ticket)* air ticket; ~**schneise** *die* air corridor; ~**schreiber** *der* flight recorder; ~**schrift** *die* pamphlet; ~**schüler** *der*, ~**schülerin** *die* trainee pilot; ~**sicherung** *die* air traffic control; ~**simulator** *der* flight simulator; ~**sport** *der* aerial sports; ~**steig** *der* pier; *(Ausgang)* ~**steig 5** gate 5; ~**stunde** *die* hour's flying time; **zwei** ~**stunden entfernt** two hours away by air; ~**tauglich** *Adj.* ‹pilot› fit to fly; ~**technik** *die* **A** *(Technologie)* aeronautical engineering; **B** *(fliegerisches Können)* flying technique; ~**technisch** **1** *Adj.* aeronautical; **2** *adv.* aeronautically; ~**ticket** *das* air ticket; ~**touristik** *die* tourism by air; ~**tüchtig** *Adj.* ⇨ ~**fähig**; ~**unfähig** *Adj.* flightless ‹bird›; *(vorübergehend)* ‹bird› unable to fly; ‹aircraft› not airworthy; ~**verbindung** *die* air connection; ~**verkehr** *der* air traffic; **der** ~**verkehr nimmt ständig zu** the volume of air traffic is continually increasing; ~**wetter** *das* flying weather; ~**wetter·dienst** *der* meteorological service [for aviation]; ~**zeit** *die* flight time

**Flug·zeug** *das;* ~**[e]s**, ~**e** aeroplane *(Brit.)*; airplane *(Amer.)*; aircraft; **mit dem** ~ **reisen** travel by plane *or* air

**Flugzeug-:** ~**absturz** *der* plane crash; ~**bau** *der* aircraft construction; ~**besatzung** *die* crew; ~**entführer** *der*, ~**entführerin** *die* [aircraft] hijacker; ~**entführung** *die* [aircraft] hijack[ing]; ~**halle** *die* hangar; ~**industrie** *die* aircraft industry; ~**katastrophe** *die* air disaster; ~**konstrukteur** *der*, ~**konstrukteurin** *die* aircraft designer; ~**modell** *das* model aeroplane; ~**mutterschiff** *das* seaplane carrier; ~**träger** *der* aircraft carrier; ~**typ** *der* model of aircraft; ~**unglück** *das* plane crash; ~**wrack** *das* wreckage of the/a plane crash; **zwei** ~**wracks** the wreckage of two planes

**Fluidum** /'flu:idʊm/ *das;* ~**s**, **Fluida** aura; atmosphere; **von ihr/davon geht ein gewisses** ~ **aus** she/it exudes a certain aura; **das** ~ **des Künstlers** the aura *or* atmosphere surrounding the artist

**Fluktuation** /flʊktu̯a'ts̮i̯o:n/ *die;* ~, ~**en** *(bes. Wirtsch., Soziol.)* fluctuation *(Gen.* in)

**fluktuieren** /flʊktu'i:rən/ *itr. V. (bes. Wirtsch., Soziol.)* fluctuate

**Flunder** /'flʊndɐ/ *die;* ~, ~**n** flounder

**Flunkerei** /flʊŋkə'rai̯/ *die;* ~, ~**en** *(ugs.)* **A** *(Flunkern)* storytelling; **B** *(Lügengeschichte)* tall story

**flunkern** /'flʊŋkɐn/ *itr. V.* tell stories

**Flunsch** /flʊnʃ/ *der;* ~**[e]s**, ~**e** *od. die;* ~, ~**en** *(ugs.)* pout; **eine[n]** ~ **ziehen** *od.* **machen** pout

**Fluor**[1] /'flu:ɔr/ *das;* ~**s** *(Chemie)* fluorine

**Fluor**[2] *der;* ~**s** *(Med.)* vaginal discharge

**Fluor·chlor·kohlen·wasserstoff** *der (Chemie)* chlorofluorocarbon

**Fluoreszenz** /fluorɛs'ts̮ɛnts̮/ *die;* ~**:** fluorescence

**fluoreszieren** *itr. V.* fluoresce; be fluorescent; **das Wasser fluoresziert** the water is fluorescent; **eine** ~**de Flüssigkeit** a fluorescent liquid

**Fluor·gehalt** *der (Chemie)* fluorine content

**Fluorid** /fluo'ri:t/ *das;* ~**[e]s**, ~**e** *(Chemie)* fluoride

**Fluor·test** *der (Paläont.)* fluorine test

**Flur**[1] /flu:ɐ̯/ *der;* ~**[e]s**, ~**e** *(Korridor)* corridor; *(Diele)* [entrance] hall; **im/auf dem** ~**:** in the corridor/hall

**Flur**[2] *die;* ~, ~**en** **A** *(landwirtschaftliche Nutzfläche)* farmland *no indef. art.;* **die** ~ **bereinigen** reallocate land; **die** ~**en** the fields; **B** *(geh.: offenes Kulturland)* fields *pl.;* **allein auf weiter** ~ **sein** *od.* **stehen** *(fig.)* be all alone in the world; **er stand mit seiner Ansicht allein auf weiter** ~**:** he was a lone voice in the wilderness

**Flur-:** ~**begehung** *die* inspection of fields; ~**bereinigung** *die* reallocation of land; ~**fenster** *das* hall window/window in a/the corridor; ~**form** *die* layout of fields; ~**garderobe** *die* hall stand; ~**hüter** *der*, ~**hüterin** *die* field guard; ~**name** *der: name of a feature of the local landscape;* ~**schaden** *der* damage *no pl., no indef. art.* to farmland; ~**tür** *die* front door

**Fluse** /'flu:zə/ *die;* ~, ~**n** *(bes. nordd.)* bit of fluff

**flusen** *itr. V.* shed fluff

**Fluss**, ***Fluß** /flʊs/ *der;* **Flusses**, **Flüsse** /'flʏsə/ **A** ▶ 306 river; **die Stadt liegt am** ~**:** the town stands on the river; **am** ~ **sitzen** sit by the river; **B** *(fließende Bewegung)* flow; **der** ~ **des Verkehrs** the flow of traffic; **die Dinge sind noch im** ~**:** things are in a state of flux; **in** ~ **kommen** *od.* **geraten** get going; get under way; **etw. in** ~ **bringen** get sth. going

**fluss-**, ***fluß-**, **Fluss-**, ***Fluß-:** ~**aal** *der (Zool.)* freshwater eel; ~**ab[wärts]** *Adv.* ▶ 306 downstream; ~**arm** *der* river branch; river arm; ~**auf[wärts]** *Adv.* ▶ 306 upstream; ~**barsch** *der (Zool.)* perch; ~**bett** *das* river bed

**Flüsschen**, ***Flüßchen** /'flʏsçən/ *das;* ~**s**, ~**:** small river

**Fluss-**, ***Fluß-:** ~**dampfer** *der* river steamer; ~**diagramm** *das (DV, Arbeitswiss.)* flow chart; ~**ebene** *die* flood plain; ~**fisch** *der* freshwater fish; ~**gott** *der (Myth.)* river god; ~**göttin** *die* river goddess; ~**hafen** *der* river port

**flüssig** /'flʏsɪç/ **1** *Adj.* **A** liquid ‹nourishment, fuel›; molten ‹ore, glass›; melted ‹butter›; runny ‹honey›; **sie konnte nur** ~**e Nahrung zu sich nehmen** she could only take liquids; **etw.** ~ **machen** melt sth.; ~**es Brot** *(scherzh.)* beer; **B** *(fließend, geläufig)* fluent; ~**er Verkehr** free-flowing traffic; **C** *(verfügbar, solvent)* ~**es Kapital/Geld** ready capital/money; ~**es Vermögen** liquid assets; **einen Betrag** ~ **machen** make a sum of money available; **wieder** ~ **sein** *(ugs.)* have got some cash to play with again *(coll.)*; **nicht** ~ **sein** *(ugs.)* be skint *(Brit. coll.)* or *(coll.)* [flat] broke. **2** *adv.* ‹write, speak› fluently; **der Verkehr**

# Flüsse

Im Englischen gibt es nur das eine Wort **river**, das (oft großgeschrieben) vor dem Flussnamen eingesetzt werden kann:

***die Seine***
= the [river *od.* River] Seine

Eine Ausnahme im Englischen wie im Deutschen:

***der Sankt-Lorenz-Strom***
= the St Lawrence River

Bei Ortsnamen steht einfach **on** ohne Artikel:

Walton-on-Thames Stockton-on-Tees Ross-on-Wye

Heute fehlt oft der Bindestrich.

## Flusssprache

***flussaufwärts/flussabwärts fahren***
= to go upstream/downstream *od.* up/down [the] river

***rheinaufwärts/rheinabwärts fahren***
= to go up/down the Rhine

***die linksrheinischen Landesteile***
= the parts of the country on the left bank of the Rhine

***am rechten Weserufer***
= on the right bank of the Weser

***ein Haus am Fluss***
= a house by *od.* on the river

***Der Fluss führt Hochwasser***
= The river is in flood *od.* in full spate

***Der Fluss führt sehr wenig Wasser***
= The river is very low

***Die Drau, ein rechter Nebenfluss der Donau, ist in ihrem Unterlauf schiffbar***
= The Drava, a tributary of the Danube on its right bank, is navigable in its lower reaches

***Der Rhein entspringt in der Schweiz und mündet in die Nordsee***
= The Rhine rises in Switzerland and flows into the North Sea

***Das Schiff ist in der Elbmündung gesunken***
= The ship sank in the mouth of the Elbe *od.* the Elbe estuary

***An der Mündung der Mosel in den Rhein befindet sich das Deutsche Eck***
= At the point where the Moselle flows into the Rhine is the Deutsche Eck

***Münden liegt am Zusammenfluss von Werra und Fulda [zur Weser]***
= Münden lies at the confluence of the Werra and Fulda [which then become the Weser]

**lief ~:** the traffic was flowing freely; **~ ernährt werden müssen** be only able to take liquids

**Flüssig·gas** *das* liquid gas

**Flüssigkeit** *die;* **~, ~en** **A** liquid; (*auch Gas*) fluid; **B** (*Geläufigkeit*) fluency

**Flüssigkeits-: ~aufnahme** *die* intake of fluids; **~maß** *das* liquid measure

**Flüssig·kristall·anzeige** *die* (*Technik*) liquid crystal display

***flüssig|machen** ⇒ **flüssig** 1 C

**Flüssigseife** *die* liquid soap

**Fluss-, *Fluß-: ~krebs,** *der* (*Zool.*) crayfish; **~landschaft** *die* **A** (*Geogr.*) fluvial topography; **B** (*Gemälde*) river landscape; **~lauf** *der* course of a/the river; **~mittel** *das* (*Technik*) flux; **~mündung** *die* river mouth; (*mit Gezeiten*) estuary; **~name** *der* river name; **~niederung** *die* flood plain; **~pferd** *das* hippopotamus; **~regulierung** *die* river control; **~schifffahrt, *~schiffahrt** *die* river traffic; (*Navigation*) river navigation; **~spat** *der* fluorite; fluorspar; **~tal** *das* river valley; **~ufer** *das* river bank; **das diesseitige/jenseitige ~ufer** the near/opposite bank [of the river]; **~wasser** *das* river water

**Flüster-: ~gewölbe** *das* whispering gallery; **~laut** *der* whisper; **~laute von sich geben** whisper

**flüstern** /ˈflʏstɐn/ **1** *itr. V.* whisper; **sich ~d unterhalten/verständigen** speak/communicate in whispers; **leises, beschwörendes Flüstern** quiet, pleading whispers. **2** *tr. V.* whisper; **jmdm. etw. ins Ohr ~:** whisper sth. in sb.'s ear; **jmdm. [et]was ~** (*ugs.*) give sb. something to think about; **das kann ich dir ~** (*ugs.*) I can promise you that

**Flüster-: ~parole** *die* rumour; **~propaganda** *die* underground propaganda; **~ton** *der; Pl.* **~töne** whisper; **im ~ton sprechen** speak in whispers; **~tüte** *die* (*ugs.*) megaphone; **~witz** *der* underground joke

**Flut** /flu:t/ *die;* **~, ~en** **A** tide; **die ~ steigt/ebbt ab** the tide is coming in/going out; **die steigende ~:** the incoming *or* rising tide; **mit der ~ aus-/einlaufen** sail with the tide/come in on the tide; **B** (*geh.: Wassermasse*) flood; **aufgewühlte/schmutzige ~en** turbulent/dirty waters; **in den ~en umkommen** die in the floods; **eine ~ von Protesten** (*fig.*) a flood of protests

**fluten** **1** *itr. V.; mit sein* (*geh.*) flood; **in etw.** (*Akk.*) **~:** flood sth.; **Sonnenlicht flutete in den Raum** sunlight streamed into the room. **2** *tr. V.* (*Seemannsspr.: unter Wasser setzen*) flood

**Flut-: ~höhe** *die* height of the tide; **~katastrophe** *die* flood disaster; **~licht** *das* floodlight; **~licht·anlage** *die* floodlight installation; floodlights *pl.*

**flutschen** /ˈflʊtʃn̩/ *itr. V.* (*ugs., bes. nordd.*) **A** *mit sein* (*gleiten*) slip; **jmdm. aus den Fingern/Händen ~:** slip out of sb.'s fingers/hands; **B** (*glatt vonstatten gehen*) go smoothly; **es flutscht nur so** it's going extremely well

**Flut-: ~warnung** *die* flood warning; **~welle** *die* tidal wave

**fluvial** /fluˈvi̯a:l/ *Adj.* (*Geol.*) fluvial

**Flyer** /ˈflai̯ɐ/ *der;* **~s, ~:** flyer

**fm** *Abk.* **Festmeter** solid $m^3$

**f-Moll** /ˈɛf-/ F minor; ⇒ *auch* **a-Moll**

**focht** /fɔxt/ *1. u. 3. Pers. Sg. Prät. v.* **fechten**

**Fock** /fɔk/ *die;* **~, ~en** (*Seew.*) foresail; (*auf einer Jacht*) jib

**Fock·mast** *der* foremast

**föderal** /fødeˈra:l/ *Adj.* ⇒ **föderativ**

**Föderalismus** *der;* **~:** federalism *no art.*

**föderalistisch** *Adj.* federalist

**Föderation** /føderaˈtsi̯o:n/ *die;* **~, ~en** federation

**föderativ** /føderaˈti:f/ **1** *Adj.* federal. **2** *adv.* federally

**fohlen** /ˈfo:lən/ *itr. V.* foal

**Fohlen** *das;* **~s, ~:** foal

**Föhn** /fø:n/ *der;* **~[e]s, ~e** **A** (*Wind*) föhn; **es war ~:** the föhn was blowing; **bei ~:** when the föhn is/was blowing; **B** (*Haartrockner*) hairdryer; **sich** (*Dat.*) **die Haare mit dem ~ trocknen** blow-dry one's hair

**föhnen** /ˈfœ:nən/ *tr. V.* blow-dry

**Föhn·krankheit** *die* illness caused by föhn conditions

**Föhre** /ˈfø:rə/ *die;* **~, ~n** (*landsch.*) ⇒ **Kiefer**[2]

**Fokus** /ˈfo:kʊs/ *der;* **~, ~se** (*Optik, Med.*) focus

**fokussieren** *tr., itr. V.* (*Optik*) focus

**Folge** /ˈfɔlgə/ *die;* **~, ~n** **A** (*Auswirkung*) consequence; (*Ergebnis*) consequence; result; **das kann böse ~n nach sich ziehen** that could have dire consequences; **die ~n tragen müssen** have to take the consequences; **an den ~n eines Unfalls/eines Herzleidens sterben** die as a result of an accident/a heart condition; **etw. zur ~ haben** result in sth.; lead to sth.; **B** (*Aufeinander~*) succession; (*zusammengehörend*) sequence; (*einer Sendung*) episode; (*eines Romans*) instalment; (*einer Zeitschrift*) issue; **in rascher ~:** in quick succession; **in ~:** in a row; in succession; **das dritte Mal in ~:** the third time in a row *or* running; **eine ~ von Bildern/Tönen** a sequence of pictures/notes; **eine Fortsetzung in 10 ~n** a serialization in ten episodes; **C einem Aufruf/einem Befehl/einer Einladung ~ leisten** (*Amtsspr.*) respond to an appeal/obey *or* follow an order/accept an invitation

**Folge-: ~erscheinung** *die* consequence; **~kosten** *Pl.* resulting costs; **~kriminalität** *die: crime arising from the need to acquire drugs etc.;* **~lasten** ⇒ **~kosten**

**folgen** /ˈfɔlgn̩/ *itr. V.* **A** *mit sein* follow; **jmdm./einer Sache ~:** follow sb./sth.; **jmdm. im Amt/in der Regierung ~:** succeed sb. in office/in government; **auf etw.** (*Akk.*) **~:** follow sth.; come after sth.; **einer Rede/einem Vortrag ~ [können]** [be able to] follow a speech/a lecture; **kannst du mir ~?** (*oft scherzh.*) do you follow me?; **jmds. Beispiel** (*Dat.*) **~:** follow sb.'s example; **aus etw. ~:** follow from sth.; **daraus folgt, dass ...** it follows from this that ...; **B** (*gehorchen*) *auch mit sein* **jmds. Anordnungen/Befehlen ~:** follow *or* obey sb.'s orders; **seiner inneren Stimme/seinem Gefühl ~:** listen to one's inner voice/be ruled by one's feelings

**folgend...** *Adj.* following; **der/die/das Folgende** the next in order; **er sagte das Folgende ...** he said this ...; **Folgendes** *od.* **das Folgende** the following [words *pl.*/passage *etc.*]; **aus Folgendem** *od.* **dem Folgenden geht hervor, dass ...** it will be seen from what follows that ...; **alle Folgenden** all those who come/came after; **im Folgenden** *od.* **in Folgendem** in [the course of] the following discussion/passage *etc.*; **der/die Folgende** the one who follows/followed; **die Folgenden** those following

**folgendermaßen** *Adv.* as follows; (*so*) in the following way

*old spelling (see note on page 1707)

**folgen-:** **~los** *Adj.* without consequences *postpos.*; **das ist nicht ~los geblieben** that hasn't been without its consequences; **~reich** *Adj.* ‹decision, event› fraught with consequences; (*bedeutsam*) momentous; **~schwer** *Adj.* fateful ‹error, omission›; ‹error, omission, accident› with serious consequences

**folge·richtig** ❶ *Adj.* logical ‹decision, conclusion›; consistent ‹behaviour, action›. ❷ *adv.* ‹think, develop, conclude› logically; ‹act, behave› consistently

**Folge·richtigkeit** *die* (*einer Entscheidung, Schlussfolgerung*) logicality; (*eines Verhaltens, einer Handlung*) consistency

**folgern** /ˈfɔlgɐn/ ❶ *tr. V.* **~, dass ...** conclude that ...; **etw. aus etw. ~:** deduce *or* infer sth. from sth. ❷ *itr. V.* **richtig ~:** draw a/the correct conclusion; **voreilig ~:** jump to conclusions

**Folgerung** *die;* **~, ~en** conclusion

**Folge-:** **~satz** *der* (*Sprachw.*) consecutive clause; **~schaden** *der* Ⓐ damaging aftereffects; Ⓑ (*Versicherungsw.*) consequential damage

**folge·widrig** ❶ *Adj.* illogical ‹conclusion›; inconsistent ‹behaviour›. ❷ *adv.* ‹conclude› illogically; ‹behave› inconsistently

**Folge·zeit** *die* ensuing *or* following weeks/months/years *pl.*

**folglich** /ˈfɔlklɪç/ *Adv.* consequently; as a result; (*ugs.: deshalb*) consequently; therefore

**folgsam** ❶ *Adj.* obedient. ❷ *adv.* obediently

**Folgsamkeit** *die;* **~:** obedience

**Foliant** /foˈli̯ant/ *der;* **~en, ~en** folio

**Folie** /ˈfoːli̯ə/ *die;* **~, ~n** Ⓐ (*Metall~*) foil; (*Plastik~*) film; Ⓑ (*Druckw.: Farbschicht*) [blocking] foil

**Folio** /ˈfoːli̯o/ *das;* **~s, Folien** *od.* **~s** folio

**Folio·band** *der; Pl.* **~bände** folio volume

**Folklore** /fɔlkˈloːrə/ *die;* **~** Ⓐ (*Überlieferung*) folklore; Ⓑ (*Musik*) folk music

**Folklore·bluse** *die* peasant blouse

**Folkloristik** *die;* **~:** [study of] folklore

**folkloristisch** ❶ *Adj.* folkloric. ❷ *adv.* in a folkloric way

**Folk·song** /ˈfoʊk-/ *der* folk song

**Follikel** /fɔˈliːkl̩/ *der;* **~s, ~** ▶ 471 (*Med., Bot.*) follicle

**Follikel·sprung** *der* (*Med.*) ovulation

**Folter** /ˈfɔltɐ/ *die;* **~, ~n** Ⓐ torture; **bei jmdm. die ~ anwenden** use torture on sb.; **die ~ abschaffen** abolish the use of torture; Ⓑ (*~bank*) rack; **jmdn. auf die ~ legen** put sb. on the rack; **jmdn. auf die ~ spannen** (*fig.*) keep sb. in an agony of suspense; Ⓒ (*geh.: peinigende Qual*) torment

**Folter·bank** *die; Pl.* **Folterbänke** rack

**Folterer** *der;* **~s, ~, Folterin** *die;* **~, ~nen** torturer

**Folter-:** **~kammer** *die,* **~keller** *der* torture chamber; **~knecht** *der* torturer

**foltern** ❶ *tr. V.* Ⓐ torture; Ⓑ (*fig. geh.*) torment. ❷ *itr. V.* use torture

**Folter·qual** *die* Ⓐ agony of torture; Ⓑ (*fig. geh.*) torment; **~en erdulden** suffer torment; **jmdm. wahre ~en bereiten** be sheer torment to sb.

**Folterung** *die;* **~, ~en** torture; **nach tagelangen ~en** after days of torture

**Folter·werkzeug** *das* instrument of torture

**Fön** (Wz) /føːn/ *der;* **~[e]s, ~e** hairdrier; **sich** (*Dat.*) **die Haare mit dem ~ trocknen** blow-dry one's hair

**Fond**[1] /fõː/ *der;* **~s, ~s** (*geh.*) rear compartment; back; **im ~ sitzen** sit in the back [seat]

**Fond**[2] *der;* **~s, ~s** (*Kochk.*) juices *pl.*

**Fondant** /fõˈdãː/ *der od. das;* **~s, ~s** fondant

**Fonds** /fõː/ *der;* Fonds /fõː(s)/, **~** /fõːs/ Ⓐ (*Vermögensreserve*) fund; **einen ~ bilden** set up a fund; Ⓑ *Pl.* (*Finanzw.*) government stocks; government bonds

**Fondue** /fõˈdyː/ *die;* **~, ~s** *od.* **das; ~s, ~s** (*Kochk.*) fondue

**Fondue-:** **~gabel** *die* fondue fork; **~gerät** *das* fondue set

***fönen** ⇒ **föhnen**

**Fono-** ⇒ **Phono-**

**Fontäne** /fɔnˈtɛːnə/ *die;* **~, ~n** jet; (*Springbrunnen*) fountain

**Fontanelle** /fɔntaˈnɛlə/ *die;* **~, ~n** ▶ 471 (*Anat.*) fontanelle

**foppen** /ˈfɔpn̩/ *tr. V.* (*ugs.*) **jmdn. ~:** pull sb.'s leg (*coll.*); put sb. on (*Amer. coll.*); **jmdn. mit etw. ~:** make fun of sb. with sth.; **jmdn. mit einem Spitznamen ~:** make fun of sb. by calling him/her by his/her nickname

**forcieren** /fɔrˈsiːrən/ *tr. V.* Ⓐ step up ‹production›; redouble, intensify ‹efforts›; speed up, push forward ‹developments›; **das Tempo/Rennen ~** (*Sport*) force the pace; **er drängte auf eine forcierte Durchführung des Planes** he pressed for the plan to be forced through; Ⓑ (*Milit.*) force ‹pass, stronghold, etc.›

**Forcierung** *die;* **~, ~en** ⇒ **forcieren**: stepping up; redoubling; intensification; speeding up; pushing forward; forcing

**Förde** /ˈføːɐ̯də/ *die;* **~, ~n** long narrow inlet

**Förder-:** **~anlage** *die* (*Technik*) conveyor; **~band** *das; Pl.* **~bänder** (*Technik*) conveyor belt

**Förderer** /ˈfœrdərɐ/ *der;* **~s, ~** Ⓐ (*Gönner*) patron; Ⓑ ⇒ **Förderanlage**

**Förderin** *die;* **~, ~nen** ⇒ **Förderer** A

**Förder-:** **~korb** *der* (*Bergbau*) cage; **~leistung** *die* (*Bergbau, Technik*) output; production

**förderlich** *Adj.* beneficial; **für jmdn./etw. ~ sein** be beneficial *or* of benefit to sb./sth.; **guten Beziehungen ~ sein** be conducive to *or* promote good relations

**Förder·maschine** *die* (*Bergbau*) winding engine

**fordern** /ˈfɔrdɐn/ *tr. V.* Ⓐ (*verlangen*) demand; **sein Recht ~:** demand one's rights; **Rechenschaft von jmdm. ~:** call sb. to account; **das Unglück hat 200 Menschenleben gefordert** the disaster claimed 200 lives; Ⓑ (*in Anspruch nehmen*) make demands on; **gefordert werden** have demands made on one; **von etw. gefordert werden** be stretched by sth.; **jmdn. zu stark ~:** make excessive *or* too many demands on sb.; **von einem Gegner gefordert werden** be stretched by an opponent; Ⓒ (*zum Zweikampf*) **jmdn. [zum Duell] ~:** challenge sb. [to a duel]; **jmdn. auf Pistolen/Säbel ~** (*veralt.*) challenge sb. to a duel with pistols/sabres

**fördern** /ˈfœrdɐn/ *tr. V.* Ⓐ promote ‹trade, plan, project, good relations›; patronize, support ‹artist, art›; further ‹investigation›; foster ‹talent, tendency, new generation›; improve ‹appetite›; aid ‹digestion, sleep›; **~d auf etw.** (*Akk.*) **wirken** have a beneficial effect on sth.; Ⓑ (*Bergbau, Technik*) mine ‹coal, ore›; extract ‹oil›

**Förder-:** **~schacht** *der* (*Bergbau*) winding shaft; **~stufe** *die* (*Schulw.*): *phase of mixed-ability teaching intended to reveal the aptitudes and abilities of individual pupils;* **~turm** *der* (*Bergbau*) headframe; headgear

**Forderung** *die;* **~, ~en** Ⓐ (*Anspruch*) demand; (*in bestimmter Höhe*) claim; **eine ~ erfüllen** meet a demand/a claim; Ⓑ (*Kaufmannsspr.*) claim (**an** + *Akk.* against); **eine ~ einklagen** sue for payment of a debt; Ⓒ (*zum Duell*) challenge; **eine ~ auf Pistolen/Säbel** (*veralt.*) a challenge to a duel with pistols/sabres

**Förderung** *die;* **~, ~en** Ⓐ ⇒ **fördern** A: promotion; patronage; support; furthering; fostering; improvement; aiding; Ⓑ (*Bergbau, Technik*) output; (*das Fördern*) mining; (*von Erdöl*) extraction; **die ~ steigt** output is increasing

**-förderung** *die:* **Erdöl~/Erdgas~:** extraction of petroleum/natural gas; **Silber~/Kali~:** mining of silver/potash

**Förderungs·maßnahme** *die* supportive measure

**förderungs·würdig** *Adj.* worthy *or* deserving of support *postpos.*

**Förder·wagen** *der* (*Bergbau*) mine car

**Forelle** /foˈrɛlə/ *die;* **~, ~n** trout

**Forellen-:** **~teich** *der* trout pond; **~zucht** *die* trout farming

**forensisch** /foˈrɛnzɪʃ/ *Adj.* Ⓐ forensic; Ⓑ (*veralt.: rhetorisch*) oratorical

**Forke** /ˈfɔrkə/ *die;* **~, ~n** (*bes. nordd.*) fork

**Form** /fɔrm/ *die;* **~, ~en** Ⓐ (*Gestalt*) shape; **es hat die ~ einer Kugel/eines Rechtecks** it has the form of a sphere/rectangle; **[feste] ~[en] annehmen** take definite shape; **die Demonstration nahm hässliche ~en an** the demonstration began to look ugly; **in ~ von Tabletten/Briefmarken/Lebensmitteln/Subventionen** in the form of tablets/stamps/food/subsidies; **aus der ~ gehen** (*ugs. scherzh.*) lose one's figure; Ⓑ (*bes. Sport: Verfassung*) form; **in ~ sein** be on form; **in guter ~ sein** be in good form; **in schlechter ~ sein** be off form; **sich in ~ bringen** get on form; **zu großer ~ auflaufen** (*Jargon*) hit peak form; Ⓒ (*vorgeformtes Modell*) mould; (*Back~*) baking tin; Ⓓ (*Gestaltungsweise, Erscheinungs~, Darstellungs~*) form; **musikalische/künstlerische ~:** musical/artistic form; **~ und Inhalt** form and content; **etw. in angemessene ~ kleiden** present sth. in an appropriate form; Ⓔ (*Umgangs~*) form; **ein Mensch ohne ~en** an ill-mannered person; **die ~[en] wahren** observe the proprieties; **etw. der ~ halber tun** do sth. for the sake of form *or* as a matter of form; **in aller ~:** formally

**formal** /fɔrˈmaːl/ ❶ *Adj.* formal; **ein ~er Fehler** a technical error; (*Rechtsw.*) procedural error. ❷ *adv.* formally; **eine ~ gute Lösung** a good solution from the point of view of form; **~ im Recht sein** be technically in the right

**Formaldehyd** /ˈfɔrm|aldehyːt/ *der;* **~s** (*Biol., Med.*) formaldehyde

**Formalie** /fɔrˈmaːli̯ə/ *die;* **~, ~n** formality

**Formalin** (Wz) /fɔrmaˈliːn/ *das;* **~s** formalin

**formalisieren** *tr. V.* formalize

**Formalisierung** *die;* **~, ~en** formalization

**Formalismus** *der;* **~, Formalismen** formalism

**Formalist** *der;* **~en, ~en, Formalistin** *die;* **~, ~nen** formalist

**formalistisch** ❶ *Adj.* formalistic. ❷ *adv.* formalistically

**Formalität** /fɔrmaliˈtɛːt/ *die;* **~, ~en** formality

**formaliter** /fɔrˈmaːlitɐ/ *Adv.* (*geh.*) formally

**formal·juristisch, formal·rechtlich** ❶ *Adj.* technical; **ein rein ~er Standpunkt** a narrowly legalistic view. ❷ *adv.* technically

**Form·anstieg** *der* (*Sport*) improvement in form

**Format** /fɔrˈmaːt/ *das;* **~[e]s, ~e** Ⓐ size; (*Buch~, Papier~, Bild~*) format; Ⓑ (*Persönlichkeit*) stature; **ihm fehlt das menschliche ~:** he lacks real personal stature; **eine Frau von ~:** a woman of stature; Ⓒ (*besonderes Niveau*) quality; **etw. hat/ist ohne ~:** sth. has/lacks class

**formatieren** *tr. V.* (*DV*) format

**Formation** /fɔrmaˈtsi̯oːn/ *die;* **~, ~en** Ⓐ (*Herausbildung, Anordnung*) formation; (*einer Generation, Gesellschaft*) development; Ⓑ (*Gruppe*) group; **eine Hamburger ~** (*Tanzsport*) a team from Hamburg; Ⓒ (*Milit.*) (*von Flugzeugen*) formation; (*von Soldaten*) unit; Ⓓ (*Geol., Bot.*) formation

**Formations-:** **~flug** *der* Ⓐ (*Flug in Formation*) formation flying; Ⓑ (*Raumflug*) alignment of orbits; **~tanz** *der* (*Tanzsport*) formation dancing

**formbar** *Adj.* malleable; soft ‹bone›; (*fig.*) malleable, pliable ‹character, person›

**Formbarkeit** *die;* **~:** malleability; (*fig.*) malleability; pliability

**form-, Form-:** **~beständig** *Adj.* **~beständig sein** keep its/their shape; **~blatt** *das* form; **~brief** *der* form letter

**Formel** /ˈfɔrml̩/ *die;* **~, ~n** formula; **die ~ des Eides** the wording of the oath; **~ 1/2**

(*Motorsport*) Formula One/Two; **~-1-Fahrer/-Wagen** Formula One driver/car

**formelhaft** ❶ *Adj.* stereotyped ‹style, mode of expression›; **eine ~e Wendung** a stereotyped phrase. ❷ *adv.* **sich ~ ausdrücken** talk in stereotyped phrases

**Formelhaftigkeit** *die;* **~:** stereotyped character

**Formel·kram** *der* (*ugs.*) **die Chemie mit ihrem ~:** chemistry and its awful formulae *pl.*

**formell** /fɔr'mɛl/ ❶ *Adj.* formal. ❷ *adv.* formally; **die Einladung wurde rein ~ ausgesprochen** the invitation was made only as a matter of form; **er ist nur ~ im Recht** he's only technically in the right

**Formel-: ~sammlung** *die* formulary; **~sprache** *die:* **die ~sprache der Physik** the language of formulae as used in physics; **die mathematische ~sprache** the language of mathematical formulae; **~zeichen** *das* symbol

f

**formen** ❶ *tr. V.* Ⓐ (*gestalten*) form; shape; **etw. in Ton/Gips ~:** shape *or* form sth. in clay/plaster; **schön geformte Möbel/Hände** finely shaped furniture/hands; **Laute/Silben ~:** form sounds/syllables; Ⓑ (*bilden, prägen*) mould, form ‹character, personality›; mould ‹person›; **jmdn. zu etw. ~:** mould sb. into sth. ❷ *refl. V.* take on a shape; (*fig.*) form; take shape

**formen-, Formen-: ~lehre** *die* Ⓐ (*Sprachw., Biol.*) morphology; Ⓑ (*Musik*) theory of [musical] form; **~reich** *Adj.* with its/their great variety of forms; **~reich sein** display a great variety of forms; **~reichtum** *der* great variety of forms; wealth of forms

**Former** *der;* **~s, ~, Formerin** *die;* **~, ~nen** moulder

**Formerei** *die;* **~, ~en** moulding department

**form-, Form-: ~fehler** *der* Ⓐ (*in einem Verfahren, Dokument*) irregularity; Ⓑ (*Taktlosigkeit*) faux pas; breach of etiquette; **~frage** *die* formality; **~gebung** *die;* **~~, ~~en** design; **~gerecht** ❶ *Adj.* correct; proper; ❷ *adv.* correctly; properly; **~gestalter** *der,* **~gestalterin** *die* ⇒ **Designer**; **~gestaltung** *die* ⇒ **Design**

**formidabel** /fɔrmi'da:bl/ *Adj.* Ⓐ (*geh.: außergewöhnlich*) superb; Ⓑ (*veralt.: besorgniserregend*) formidable

**formieren** ❶ *tr. V.* form ‹team, party, organization›; **der Feldherr formierte seine Truppen auf dem Hügel** the commander drew up his troops on the hill. ❷ *refl. V.* Ⓐ (*sich aufstellen*) form; **wir formierten uns zu einer Gruppe** we formed ourselves into a group; **sich neben der Tribüne ~:** assemble beside the rostrum; Ⓑ (*sich zusammenschließen*) be formed; **die formierte Gesellschaft** (*hist.*) the aligned society

**Formierung** *die;* **~, ~en** formation; (*von Truppen*) drawing up

**-förmig** /-fœrmɪç/ -shaped; ⇒ *auch* **ei-, gabel-, kugelförmig** *usw.*

**Form·krise** *die* (*Sport*) bad patch; **in einer ~ sein** *od.* **stecken** be off form

**förmlich** /'fœrmlɪç/ ❶ *Adj.* Ⓐ formal; **warum denn so ~?** why [be] so formal?; Ⓑ (*regelrecht*) positive; **ein ~er Schreck durchfuhr ihn** he got a real fright; **einen ~en Abscheu verspüren** feel positive revulsion. ❷ *adv.* Ⓐ (*steif, unpersönlich, offiziell*) formally; Ⓑ (*geradezu*) **sich ~ fürchten** be really afraid; **~ außer sich sein** be quite beside oneself; **jmdn. ~ zwingen, etw. zu tun** positively force sb. to do sth.

**Förmlichkeit** *die;* **~, ~en** formality; **in aller ~ um etw. bitten** (*veraltend*) formally request sth.; **die juristischen ~en** the legal formalities; **bitte keine ~en!** please don't stand on ceremony!

**form-, Form-: ~los** ❶ *Adj.* Ⓐ informal; **einen ~losen Antrag stellen** make an application without the official form[s]; apply informally; Ⓑ (*gestaltlos*) shapeless; ❷ *adv.* informally; **~losigkeit** *die;* **~~** Ⓐ informality; Ⓑ (*Gestaltlosigkeit*) shapelessness; **~sache** *die* formality; **das ist [eine] reine ~sache** that is purely a formality; **~schön** *Adj.* elegant; **~tief** *das* (*Sport*) bad patch; **er steckt** *od.* **befindet sich in einem ~tief** he's badly off form

**Formular** /fɔrmu'la:ɐ̯/ *das;* **~s, ~e** form

**formulieren** /fɔrmu'li:rən/ *tr. V.* formulate; **eine Frage noch einmal ~:** reformulate *or* rephrase a question

**Formulierung** *die;* **~, ~en** Ⓐ (*das Formulieren*) formulation; (*eines Entwurfes, Gesetzes*) drafting; Ⓑ (*formulierter Text*) formulation; **politische/wissenschaftliche ~en** political/scientific phraseology *sing.*

**Formung** *die;* **~, ~en** Ⓐ (*Gestaltung*) design; **die strenge ~ des Sonetts** strict sonnet form; Ⓑ (*Bildung, Erziehung*) moulding; (*des Charakters*) moulding; forming

**form-, Form-: ~veränderung** *die* change in shape; **~verstoß** *der* ⇒ **~widrigkeit**; **~vollendet** ❶ *Adj.* perfectly executed ‹pirouette, bow, etc.›; ‹poem› perfect in form; ❷ *adv.* **etw. ~vollendet tun** do sth. faultlessly; **~vorschrift** *die* statutory form; **~widrig** ❶ *Adj.* improper ‹behaviour, expression›; ❷ *adv.* improperly; **~widrigkeit** *die* impropriety

**forsch** /fɔrʃ/ ❶ *Adj.* self-assertive; forceful; **einen ~en Eindruck machen** seem self-assertive *or* forceful; **mit ~en Schritten** with a brisk step; briskly. ❷ *adv.* self-assertively; forcefully

**forschen** *itr. V.* Ⓐ (*suchen*) **nach jmdm./etw. ~:** search *or* look for sb./sth.; **jmdn. ~d** *od.* **mit ~dem Blick betrachten** look at sb. searchingly; give sb. a searching look; Ⓑ (*als Wissenschaftler*) research; do research; **auf einem Gebiet ~:** research *or* do research in a field; **in [alten] Quellen ~:** research into [ancient] sources

**Forscher** *der;* **~s, ~** ▶ **159** Ⓐ (*Wissenschaftler*) researcher; research scientist; Ⓑ (*Forschungsreisender*) explorer

**Forscher-: ~drang** *der* Ⓐ (*Wissensdurst*) thirst for new knowledge; Ⓑ (*Entdeckerfreude*) urge to explore; **~geist** *der* inquiring mind

**Forscherin** *die;* **~, ~nen** ▶ **159** ⇒ **Forscher**

**forscherisch** ❶ *Adj.* research *attrib.*; **~e Arbeit** research work. ❷ *adv.* **~ arbeiten** do research [work]

**Forscher·team** *das* research team

**Forschheit** *die;* **~:** self-assertiveness; forcefulness

**Forschung** *die;* **~, ~en** research; **~en [auf einem Gebiet] betreiben** do research [in a field]; **~ und Lehre** teaching and research

**Forschungs-: ~anstalt** *die* research establishment; **~arbeit** *die* Ⓐ piece of research; Ⓑ ⇒ **Forschung**; **~auftrag** *der* research assignment; **~bericht** *der* research report; **~ergebnis** *das* result of the research; **~gebiet** *das* field of research; **~gegen·stand** *der* research topic; **~institut** *das* research institute; **~labor[atorium]** *das* research laboratory; **~methode** *die* research method; **~programm** *das* research programme; **~rakete** *die* research rocket; **~reaktor** *der* research reactor; **~reise** *die* expedition; **~reisende** *der/die* explorer; **~satellit** *der* research satellite; **~schiff** *das* research vessel; **~stipendium** *das* research grant; **~tätigkeit** *die* research work; **~vorhaben** *das* research project; **~zentrum** *das* research centre; **~zweck** *der* purpose of the research; **für ~zwecke** for research purposes

**Forst** /fɔrst/ *der;* **~[e]s, ~e[n]** forest

**Forst-: ~amt** *das* forestry office; **~beamte** *der,* **~beamtin** *die* forestry official

**Förster** /'fœrstɐ/ *der;* **~s, ~** ▶ **159** forest warden; forester; ranger (*Amer.*)

**Försterei** *die;* **~, ~en** ⇒ **Forsthaus**

**Försterin** *die;* **~, ~nen** ▶ **159** ⇒ **Förster**

**forst-, Forst-: ~frevel** *der* offence against the forest law; **~frevel begehen** break the forest law; **~haus** *das* forester's house; **~ingenieur** *der,* **~ingenieurin** *die* senior forestry official (*with academic qualifications*); **~nutzung** *die* [commercial] exploitation of forests; **~recht** *das* forest law; **~revier** *das* forest district; **~schaden** *der* damage *no pl.*, *no indef. art.* to the forest; **~schädling** *der* forest pest; **~verwaltung** *die* forestry commission; **~wesen** *das* forestry; **~wirtschaft** *die* forestry; **~wirtschaftlich** ❶ *Adj.* commercial; ❷ *adv.* commercially

**Forsythie** /fɔr'zy:tsi̯ə/ *die;* **~, ~n** Ⓐ forsythia; Ⓑ *Pl.* (*Zweige*) sprigs of forsythia

**fort** /fɔrt/ *Adv.* Ⓐ (*weg*) **sie ist schon ~:** she has already gone *or* left; **ihre Brille war ~:** her glasses had gone *or* had vanished; **~ mit dir!** be off with you!; away with you!; **~ mit ihr/damit!** take her/it away!; away with her/it!; **[schnell] ~!** run for it!; Ⓑ (*weiter*) **nur immer so ~:** just carry on as you are *or* like that; **und so ~:** and so on; and so forth; **in einem ~:** continuously

**Fort** /fo:ɐ̯/ *das;* **~s, ~s** fort

**fort-, Fort-: ~an** /-'-/ *Adv.* from now/then on; **~bestand** *der* continuation; (*eines Staates*) continued existence; **~|bestehen** *unr. itr. V.* remain; continue; ‹nation› remain in existence; (*beim Alten bleiben*) remain the same; remain as before; **~|bewegen** ❶ *tr. V.* move; shift; ❷ *refl. V.* move [along]; **~bewegung** *die* locomotion; **~bewegungs·mittel** *das* means of transport; **~|bilden** *tr. V.* **sich/jmdn. ~bilden** continue one's/sb.'s education; **die Lehrlinge wurden ~gebildet** the apprentices were given further training; **~bildung** *die* further education; (*beruflich*) further training; **~bildungs·kurs** *der* further education course; (*beruflich*) training course; **~|bleiben** *unr. itr. V.*; *mit sein* fail to come; **du bist so lange ~geblieben!** you've been away so long!; **sein Fortbleiben beunruhigte mich** I was worried when he didn't turn up; **~|bringen** *unr. tr. V.:* ⇒ **wegbringen**; **~dauer** *die* continuation; **~|dauern** *itr. V.* continue; **fortdauernder Widerstand** continuing/(*in der Vergangenheit*) continued resistance; **unter fortdauernden Beschuss geraten** come under continuous bombardment; **~|denken** *unr. itr. V.:* ⇒ **wegdenken**

**forte** /'fɔrtə/ *Adv.* (*Musik, Pharm.*) forte

**Forte** *das;* **~s, ~s** *od.* **Forti** (*Mus.*) forte

**fort-, Fort-: ~|eilen** *itr. V.*; *mit sein* (*geh.*) hurry off *or* away; hasten away; **~|entwickeln** ❶ *tr. V.* **etw. ~entwickeln** develop sth. further; ❷ *refl. V.* develop; **~|erben** *refl. V.* be passed on; be handed down; **sich auf jmdn. ~erben** pass to sb.; be handed down to sb.; **~|fahren** ❶ *unr. itr. V.* Ⓐ *mit sein* (*abreisen*) leave; (*einen Ausflug machen*) go out; Ⓑ *auch mit sein* (*weitermachen*) **~fahren [,etw. zu tun]** continue *or* go on [doing sth.]; **in seiner Rede ~fahren** continue *or* go on with one's speech; **bitte, fahren Sie ~:** please continue; please go on; ❷ *unr. tr. V.* drive away; **jmdn. [mit dem Auto] ~fahren** drive *or* take sb. away [in a car]; **etw. [mit einem Auto] ~fahren** take sth. away [in a car]; **~fall** *der* ending; discontinuation; **~|fallen** *unr. itr. V.*; *mit sein* ‹obstacle, misgiving› be removed; ‹words› be omitted; ‹conditions› no longer apply; ‹subsidy› be discontinued; ‹advantage› be lost; **ein Kapitel ~fallen lassen** delete a chapter; **~|fliegen** *unr. itr. V.*; *mit sein:* ⇒ **wegfliegen**; **~|führen** ❶ *tr. V.* Ⓐ lead away; Ⓑ (*~setzen*) continue, keep up ‹tradition, business›; continue, carry on ‹another's work›; ❷ *itr. V.* **von etw. ~führen** lead away from sth.; **~führung** *die* ⇒ **~führen** 1 B; continuation; keeping up; carrying on; **sich zur ~führung von jmds. Geschäften bereit erklären** declare one's readiness to carry on sb.'s business; **~gang** *der* Ⓐ departure (**aus** from); Ⓑ (*Weiterentwicklung*) progress; **seinen ~gang nehmen** progress; **~|geben** *unr. tr. V.* ⇒ **weggeben**; **~|gehen** *unr. itr. V.*; *mit sein* Ⓐ (*weggehen*) leave; **geh ~!** go away!; **geh nicht ~!** don't go away!; don't leave!; Ⓑ (*andauern, verlaufen*) continue; go

*old spelling (see note on page 1707)

on; **~geschritten** *Adj.* advanced; **in ~geschrittenem Alter** at an advanced age; **zu ~geschrittener Tageszeit** at a late hour; **die Krankheit befindet sich in einem ~geschrittenen Stadium** the disease has reached an advanced stage; **~geschrittene** *der/die; adj. Dekl.* advanced student/player; **ein Kurs[us] für ~geschrittene** a course for advanced students; an advanced course; **~geschrittenen·kurs[us]** *der* advanced course; **~gesetzt** ❶ *Adj.* continual; constant; **~gesetzter Betrug/~gesetzte Untreue** repeated fraud/embezzlement; ❷ *adv.* continually; constantly; **~|haben** *unr. tr. V.:* ⇒ **weghaben** A; **~hin** *Adv.* (*veralt.*) henceforth; henceforward

**fortissimo** /fɔr'tɪsimo/ *Adv.* (*Musik*) fortissimo

**Fortissimo** *das;* **~s, ~s** *od.* **Fortissimi** (*Musik*) fortissimo

**fort-, Fort-:** **~|jagen** *tr. V.:* ⇒ **wegjagen**; **~|kommen** *unr. itr. V.; mit sein* Ⓐ ⇒ **wegkommen** A, B, D, F; Ⓑ (*Erfolg haben*) get on; do well; **in der Schule/im Beruf ~kommen** get on at school/in one's job; **~kommen** *das;* **~~s** Ⓐ (*das Vorwärtskommen, auch beruflich*) progress; **das wird für mein ~kommen nützlich sein** that will help me get ahead *or* get on; Ⓑ (*Lebensunterhalt*) living; **sein ~kommen finden** make a living; **das Gehalt reichte gerade für sein ~kommen** the money was just enough for him to get by on; **~|können** *unr. itr. V.:* ⇒ **wegkönnen**; **~|lassen** *unr. tr. V.:* ⇒ **weglassen**; **~|laufen** *unr. itr. V.; mit sein* Ⓐ ⇒ **weglaufen**; Ⓑ (*sich ~setzen*) continue; **~laufend** ❶ *Adj.* continuous; **die ~laufende Handlung der Fernsehserie** the ongoing plot of the television series; **~laufende Hefte** consecutive issues; ❷ *adv.* continuously; **~laufend nummeriert** numbered consecutively; **~|leben** *itr. V.:* ⇒ **weiterleben**; **~|legen** *tr. V.* put down *or* aside; **~|loben** *tr. V.:* ⇒ **wegloben**; **~|machen** (*ugs.*) ❶ *refl. V.* get away; ❷ *itr. V.:* ⇒ **weitermachen** 1; **~|müssen** *unr. itr. V.:* ⇒ **wegmüssen**; **~|nehmen** *unr. tr. V.* take away; **~|pflanzen** *refl. V.* Ⓐ (*sich vermehren*) reproduce [oneself/itself]; Ⓑ (*sich verbreiten*) ‹idea, mood› spread; ‹sound, light› travel, propagate; **~pflanzung** *die* Ⓐ (*Vermehrung*) reproduction; Ⓑ (*Verbreitung*) transmission; (*von Schall, Licht*) propagation; (*von Ideen*) spread; **~pflanzungs·fähig** *Adj.* capable of reproduction *postpos.*; **~pflanzungs·trieb** *der* reproductive instinct; **~|räumen** *tr. V.:* ⇒ **wegräumen**; **~|reisen** *itr. V.; mit sein:* ⇒ **abreisen**; **~|reißen** *unr. tr. V.* Ⓐ (*wegreißen*) tear away; **die Fluten rissen alles mit sich ~:** the floods swept everything away; Ⓑ (*begeistern*) **jmdn. ~reißen** carry *or* sweep sb. along; **jmdn. zu Beifallsstürmen ~reißen** rouse sb. to tumultuous applause; **~|rennen** *unr. itr. V.; mit sein* (*ugs.*) run off *or* away; **~satz** *der* (*Biol.*) process; **~|schaffen** *tr. V.* take *or* carry away; **~|scheren** *refl. V.* (*ugs.*) **scher dich ~!** clear off! (*coll.*); **~|scheuchen** *tr. V.* shoo *or* chase away; **~|schicken** *tr. V.:* ⇒ **wegschicken**; **~|schieben** *unr. tr. V.:* ⇒ **wegschieben**; **~|schleichen** *unr. itr., refl. V.:* ⇒ **wegschleichen**; **~|schleppen** *refl., tr. V.:* ⇒ **wegschleppen**; **~|schleudern** *tr. V.* fling away; **~|schreiben** *unr. tr. V.* update; (*in die Zukunft*) project forward; **~schreibung** *die* updating; (*in die Zukunft*) forward projection; **~|schreiten** *unr. itr. V.; mit sein* ‹process› progress, continue; ‹time› move on; **die Zeit ist [weit] ~geschritten** it is getting on *or* late; **der Sommer ist [weit] ~geschritten** we are well into summer; **das ~schreiten** progress; **~schreitend** *Adj.* progressive; **mit ~schreitender Jahreszeit** as the year goes/went on; **mit ~schreitendem Alter** with advancing age; with the passing of the years; **~schritt** *der* progress; **~schritte** progress *sing.*; **ein ~schritt** a step forward; **das ist schon ein ~schritt** that is some progress at least; **große ~schritte machen** make great progress; **~schrittlich** ❶ *Adj.* progressive; ❷ *adv.* progressively; **~schrittlichkeit** *die;* **~~:** progressiveness; **~schritts·feindlich** *Adj.* anti-progressive; **~schritts·gläubig** *Adj.* **~schrittsgläubig/zu ~schrittsgläubig sein** put one's/too much faith in progress; **das ~schrittsgläubige 19. Jahrhundert** the nineteenth century with its implicit faith in progress; **~schritts·gläubigkeit** *die* belief *or* faith in progress; **~|schwemmen** *tr. V.* sweep away; **~|sehnen** *refl. V.* long to go; **~|setzen** ❶ *tr. V.* continue; carry on; **den Weg zu Fuß/mit dem Auto ~setzen** continue by foot/car; ❷ *refl. V.* continue; **~setzung** *die;* **~setzung, ~setzungen** Ⓐ (*das ~setzen*) continuation; **[s]eine ~setzung finden** resume; Ⓑ (*anschließender Teil*) instalment; **in ~setzungen erscheinen** be published in instalments; **~setzung von S. 7** continued from p. 7; **~setzung folgt** to be continued; **~setzungs·roman** *der* serial; serialized novel; **~|spülen** *tr. V.:* ⇒ **wegspülen**; **~|stehlen** *unr. refl. V.* steal *or* sneak away; **~|stoßen** *unr. tr. V.:* ⇒ **wegstoßen**; **~|stürzen** *itr. V.; mit sein* rush off *or* away; **~|tragen** *unr. tr. V.:* ⇒ **wegtragen**; **~|treiben** ❶ *unr. tr. V.* Ⓐ (*ver-, wegtreiben*) drive off *or* away; **er hat seinen Sohn ~getrieben** he made it impossible for his son to stay; **es trieb mich bald ~:** I soon felt I had to leave; Ⓑ (*vorwärts treiben*) sweep away; ❷ *itr. V.; mit sein* float away

**Fortuna** /fɔr'tu:na/ (*die*) Fortune; **~ lachte** *od.* **lächelte ihm** (*geh.*) Fortune smiled upon him

**Fortune** /fɔr'ty:n/ *die;* **~**, *eingedeutscht:* **Fortüne** /fɔr'ty:nə/ *die;* **~:** luck; **keine/wenig ~ haben** have no/not much luck

**fort-:** **~|währen** *itr. V.* (*geh.*) ⇒ **~dauern**; **~|während** ❶ *Adj.* continual; incessant; ❷ *adv.* continually; incessantly; **~|werfen** *unr. tr. V.:* ⇒ **wegwerfen**; **~|wirken** *itr. V.* continue to have an effect; **das wirkt in uns ~:** the effect of it persists in us; **sein Vorbild wirkt in ihnen ~:** his example continues to exert an influence on them; **das Fortwirken antiker Motive** the continuing influence of ancient motifs; **~|wollen** *unr. itr. V.* Ⓐ ⇒ **wegwollen**; Ⓑ (*vorwärts wollen*) want to move; **seine Füße wollten nicht recht ~:** his feet did not seem to be able to carry him; **~|zaubern** *tr. V.* **etw. ~zaubern** make sth. disappear; **~|zerren** *tr. V.:* ⇒ **wegzerren**; **~|ziehen** *unr. tr., itr. V.:* ⇒ **wegziehen**

**Forum** /'fo:rum/ *das;* **~s, Foren** *od.* **Fora** Ⓐ (*Personenkreis, Plattform, röm. Marktplatz*) forum; Ⓑ *Pl. nur* **Foren** (*Aussprache*) (*über Literatur*) symposium; (*über Politik*) forum discussion

**fossil** /fɔ'si:l/ *Adj.* fossilized; fossil *attrib.*

**Fossil** *das;* **~s, ~ien** fossil

**Foto**[1] /'fo:to/ *das;* **~s, ~s,** (*schweiz.:*) *die;* **~, ~s** photo; **~s machen** *od.* (*ugs.:*) **schießen** take photos; **auf einem ~:** in a photo

**Foto**[2] *der;* **~s, ~s** (*bes. südd. ugs.*) camera

**Foto-:** **~album** *das* photo album; **~apparat** *der* camera; **~atelier** *das* photographic studio; **~ecke** *die* [mounting] corner

**fotogen** /foto'ge:n/ *Adj.* photogenic

**Foto·geschäft** *das* photographic shop

**Foto·graf** *der;* **~en, ~en** ▶ 159 photographer

**Fotografie** *die;* **~, ~n** Ⓐ photography *no art.*; Ⓑ (*Lichtbild*) photograph

**fotografieren** ❶ *tr. V.* photograph; take a photograph/photographs of; **sie lässt sich gern/ungern ~:** she likes/does not like being photographed *or* having her photograph taken; **Katzen lassen sich gut ~:** cats photograph well. ❷ *itr. V.* take photographs; **er fotografiert gut** *od.* **kann gut ~:** he is a good photographer; **[das] Fotografieren [ist] verboten!** photography prohibited

**Fotografin** *die;* **~, ~nen** ▶ 159 photographer

**fotografisch** ❶ *Adj.* photographic. ❷ *adv.* photographically

**foto-, Foto-:** **~kopie** *die* photocopy; **~kopieren** *tr., itr. V.* photocopy; **~kopierer** *der,* **~kopier·gerät** *das* photocopier; photocopying machine

**Foto-:** **~labor** *das* photographic laboratory; **~modell** *das* ▶ 159 Ⓐ photographic model; Ⓑ (*verhüll.: Prostituierte*) model; **~montage** *die* photomontage; **~papier** *das* photographic paper; **~realismus** *der* (*bild. Kunst*) photorealism *no art.*; **~reporter** *der,* **~reporterin** *die* ▶ 159 press photographer; newspaper photographer; **~safari** *die* photographic safari; **~satz** *der* (*Druckw.*) ⇒ **Lichtsatz**; **~tasche** *die* camera bag; **~wettbewerb** *der* photographic competition; **~zeitschrift** *die* photographic magazine

**Fötus** ⇒ **Fetus**

**Fotze** /'fɔtsə/ *die;* **~, ~n** Ⓐ (*vulg.: Vulva*) cunt (*coarse*); Ⓑ (*vulg.: Frau*) cunt (*coarse*); Ⓒ (*bayr. u. österr. ugs.: Mund*) gob (*sl.*)

**foul** /faul/ *Adv.* (*Sport*) **~ spielen** play dirty; be a dirty player; **er hat gerade ~ gespielt** he has just committed a foul

**Foul** *das;* **~s, ~s** (*Sport*) foul (**an** + *Dat.* on)

**Foul·elf·meter** *der* (*Fußball*) penalty [for a foul]; **einen ~ verhängen** *od.* **geben** award *or* give a penalty

**foulen** /'faulən/ (*Sport*) ❶ *tr. V.* foul. ❷ *itr. V.* commit a foul

**Fox** /fɔks/ *der;* **~[es], ~e** Ⓐ ⇒ **Foxterrier**; Ⓑ ⇒ **Foxtrott**

**Fox·terrier** *der* fox terrier

**Fox·trott** /-trɔt/ *der;* **~s, ~e** *od.* **~s** foxtrot; **~ tanzen** foxtrot

**Foyer** /foa'je:/ *das;* **~s, ~s** foyer

**FPÖ** *Abk.* **Freiheitliche Partei Österreichs**

**Fr.**[1] *Abk.* **Franken** SFr.

**Fr.**[2] *Abk.* **Frau**

**Fr.**[3] *Abk.* **Freitag** Fri.

**Fracht** /fraxt/ *die;* **~, ~en** Ⓐ (*Schiffs~, Luft~*) cargo; freight; (*Bahn~, LKW-~*) goods *pl.*; freight; **volle/halbe ~ führen** carry full/half freight; Ⓑ (*~kosten*) (*Schiffs~, Luft~*) freight; freightage; (*Bahn~, LKW-~*) carriage

**Fracht-:** **~brief** *der* consignment note; waybill; **~dampfer** *der* (*veralt.*) steam freighter

**Frachten·bahnhof** *der,* **Frachtenstation** *die* (*österr.*) ⇒ **Güterbahnhof**

**Frachter** *der;* **~s, ~:** freighter

**fracht-, Fracht-:** **~flugzeug** *das* cargo *or* freight plane; **~frei** ❶ *Adj.* carriage-free ‹delivery›; ❷ *adv.* ‹deliver› carriage free; **~führer** *der,* **~führerin** *die* carrier; **~geld** *das* ⇒ **Fracht** B; **~gut** *das* slow freight; slow goods *pl.*; **etw. als ~gut schicken** send sth. by slow goods; **~kosten** *Pl.:* ⇒ **Fracht** B; **~raum** *der* [cargo] hold; (*Platz*) [cargo] space; **~schiff** *das* cargo ship

**Frack** /frak/ *der;* **~[e]s, Fräcke** /'frɛkə/ tails *pl.*; evening dress; **einen ~ tragen** wear tails *or* evening dress; **im ~ erscheinen** turn up in tails *or* evening dress; **jmdm. saust der ~** (*fig. ugs. scherzh.*) sb. gets the wind up (*coll.*)

**Frack-:** **~hemd** *das* dress shirt; **~sausen** *das: in* **~sausen haben** (*ugs.*) get the wind up (*coll.*); **~schoß** *der* coat-tail; **~weste** *die* waistcoat (*worn with evening dress*)

**Frage** /'fra:gə/ *die;* **~, ~n** Ⓐ question; **jmdm.** *od.* **an jmdn. eine ~ stellen** put a question to sb.; **jmdm. eine ~ beantworten/auf jmds. ~** (*Akk.*) **antworten** reply to *or* answer sb.'s question; **eine ~ [zu etw.] haben** have a question [on sth.]; **sind noch ~n?** are there any questions?; **an jmdn. eine ~ richten** direct a question to sb.; **darf ich Ihnen eine ~ stellen?** may I put a question?; **eine ~ verneinen/bejahen** give a negative/positive answer to a question; **auf eine dumme ~ bekommt man eine dumme Antwort** ask a silly question [and you get a silly answer]; Ⓑ (*Problem*) question; (*Angelegenheit*) issue; **es erhebt sich/bleibt die ~, ob ...** the question arises/remains whether ...; **eine soziale/politische ~:** a social/political issue; **die deutsche ~:** the German problem; **das ist [nur] eine ~ der Zeit** that is [only] a question *or* matter of time; [C] *in* **das ist noch sehr die ~:** that is still very much the question; **das ist die große ~:** that is the big question; **das ist gar keine ~:** there's no doubt *or* question about it; **es ist** *od.* **steht außer ~, dass ...** there is no doubt that ...; there is no question but that ...; **in ~:** ⇒ **infrage; ohne ~:** without question

**Frage-: ~bogen** *der* questionnaire; (*Formular*) form; **~bogen·aktion** *die* poll; **~fürwort** *das* ⇒ **Interrogativpronomen**

**fragen** ❶ *tr., itr. V.* [A] ask; **er fragt immer so klug** he always asks *or* puts such astute questions; **neugierig/erstaunt ~:** ask inquisitively/in amazement; **gezielt ~:** ask *or* put well-aimed questions; **frag nicht so dumm!** (*ugs.*) don't ask such silly questions; **das fragst du noch?** (*ugs.*) need you ask?; **~ Sie lieber nicht** (*ugs.*) don't ask!; **da fragst du mich zu viel** that I don't know; I really can't say; **jmdn. ~d ansehen** look at sb. inquiringly; give sb. a questioning look; **~ kostet nichts** there is no harm in asking; [B] (*sich erkundigen*) **nach etw. ~:** ask *or* inquire about sth.; **jmdn. nach/wegen etw. ~:** ask sb. about sth.; **nach dem Weg ~:** ask the way; **nach Einzelheiten ~:** ask for details; **nach jmds. Meinung ~:** ask [for] sb.'s opinion; **nach jmdm. ~** (*jmdn. suchen*) ask for sb.; (*über jmdn. Fragen stellen*) ask about sb.; (*nach jmds. Befinden ~*) ask after *or* about sb.; **wenn ich ~ darf** if you don't mind my asking; (*ungeduldig*) may I ask?; [C] (*nach~*) ask for; **jmdn. um Rat/Erlaubnis ~:** ask sb. for advice/permission; [D] (*verneint: sich nicht kümmern*) **nach jmdm./etw. nicht ~:** not care about sb./sth.; **ich frage den Teufel** *od.* **einen Dreck danach** (*salopp*) I couldn't care less [about it] (*coll.*); I don't give a damn about it (*sl.*).

❷ *refl. V.* **sich ~, ob ...** wonder whether ...; **das frage ich mich auch** I was wondering that, too; (*unpers.*) **es fragt sich [nur], ob/wann ...** the [only] question is whether/when ...

**Fragen·komplex** *der* set of problems

**Fragerei** *die;* ~, **~en** (*abwertend*) questions *pl.*

**Frage-: ~satz** *der* interrogative sentence/clause; **ein direkter/indirekter ~satz** a direct/an indirect question; **~stellung** *die* [A] (*Formulierung*) formulation of a/the question; **durch eine geschickte ~stellung** by skilled questioning; [B] (*Problem*) problem; **~stunde** *die* (*Parl.*) question time; **~-und-Antwort-Spiel** *das* question-and-answer game; **~zeichen** *das* question mark; **ein ~zeichen setzen** put a question mark; **etw. mit einem [dicken/großen] ~zeichen versehen** (*fig.*) put a [big] question mark over sth. (*fig.*); **dastehen/dasitzen wie ein ~zeichen** (*ugs.*) stand/sit like a hunchback

**fragil** /fra'gi:l/ *Adj.* (*geh.*) fragile

**fraglich** /'fra:klɪç/ *Adj.* [A] (*unsicher*) doubtful; [B] (*betreffend*) in question *postpos.;* relevant; **zur ~en Zeit** at the time in question; at the relevant time

**fraglos** *Adv.* without question; unquestionably

**Fragment** /fra'gmɛnt/ *das;* **~[e]s, ~e** fragment

**fragmentarisch** /fragmɛn'ta:rɪʃ/ ❶ *Adj.* fragmentary. ❷ *adv.* **ein ~ überlieferter Text** a text preserved only as fragments/a fragment; **es ist nur ~ erhalten** it is preserved only in fragmentary form

**frag·würdig** *Adj.* [A] questionable; [B] (*zwielichtig*) dubious

**Fragwürdigkeit** *die;* ~, **~en** [A] questionableness; [B] (*Zwielichtigkeit*) dubiousness

**fraktal** *Adj.* (*Math.*) fractal

**Fraktion** /frak'tsi̯o:n/ *die;* ~, **~en** [A] (*Parl.*) parliamentary party; (*mit zwei Parteien*) parliamentary coalition; [B] (*Sondergruppe*) faction; [C] (*Chemie*) fraction

**fraktionell** /fraktsi̯o'nɛl/ *Adj.* within a/the party/group *postpos.;* internal ‹conflict, agreement›

**fraktions-, Fraktions-: ~beschluss, *~beschluß** *der* party/coalition decision; **~führer** *der,* **~führerin** *die* leader of the parliamentary party/coalition; **~kollege** *der,* **~kollegin** *die* fellow parliamentary party/coalition member; **~los** *Adj.* independent; **~mit·glied** *das* member of a/the parliamentary party/coalition; **~sitzung** *die* meeting of the parliamentary party/coalition; **~stärke** *die* [A] *minimum number of elected members necessary for a party to be allowed to form a parliamentary group;* [B] (*Größe der Fraktion*) size of the parliamentary party; **~vorsitzende** *der/die* ⇒ **~führer**; **~zwang** *der* obligation to vote in accordance with party policy; **den ~zwang aufheben** allow a free vote

**Fraktur** /frak'tu:ɐ̯/ *die;* ~, **~en** [A] ▶ 474 (*Med.*) fracture; [B] (*Schriftart*) Fraktur; **mit jmdm. ~ reden** (*ugs.*) talk straight with sb.

**Franc** /frã:/ *der;* ~, **~s** ▶ 337 franc

**Franchise** /'fræntʃaɪz/ *das;* ~ (*Wirtsch.*) franchise

**frank** /fraŋk/ *Adv.* **~ und frei** frankly and openly; openly and honestly

**Franke** *der;* **~n, ~n** [A] Franconian; [B] (*hist.*) Frank

**Franken**[1] (*das*)*;* **~s** Franconia

**Franken**[2] *der;* **~s,** ~ ▶ 337 [Swiss] franc

**Frankfurter**[1] /'fraŋkfʊrtɐ/ *die;* ~, ~ (*Wurst*) frankfurter

**Frankfurter**[2] ▶ 700 ❶ *indekl. Adj.* Frankfurt. ❷ *der;* **~s, ~:** Frankfurter; ⇒ *auch* **Kölner**

**Frankfurterin** *die;* ~, **~nen** ⇒ **Frankfurter**[2] 2

**frankieren** /fraŋ'ki:rən/ *tr. V.* frank

**Frankier·maschine** *die* franking machine

**Fränkin** *die;* ~, **~nen** ⇒ **Franke**

**fränkisch** /'frɛŋkɪʃ/ *Adj.* [A] Franconian; [B] (*hist.*) Frankish; ⇒ *auch* **deutsch, Deutsch, badisch**

**franko** /'fraŋko/ *Adv.* (*Kaufmannsspr. veralt.*) carriage paid; (*mit der Post*) post-free

**Franko·kanadier** *der,* **Franko·kanadierin** *die* French Canadian

**frankophil** /-'fi:l/ *Adj.* Francophile

**frankophon** /-'fo:n/ *Adj.* Francophone

**Frank·reich** (*das*)*;* **~s** France

**Franktireur** /frãti'rø:ɐ̯/ *der;* **~s, ~e** *od.* **~s** (*hist.*) franc tireur

**Franse** /'franzə/ *die;* ~, **~n** strand [of a/the fringe]; **die ~n der Decke/des Teppichs** the fringe of the rug/the carpet

**fransen** *itr. V.:* ⇒ **ausfransen** 1

**fransig** ❶ *Adj.* frayed ‹shirt, trousers›; straggly ‹hair›. ❷ *adv.* **das Haar hing ihr ~ ins Gesicht** her hair hung down over her face in untidy strands

**Franz**[1] /frants/ (*der*) Francis

**Franz**[2] *das;* ~ (*Schülerspr.*) French

**Franz·branntwein** *der* (*veralt.*) alcoholic liniment

**Franziskaner** /frantsɪs'ka:nɐ/ *der;* **~s,** ~, **Franziskanerin** *die;* ~, **~nen** Franciscan

**Franziskaner-: ~kloster** *das* Franciscan monastery; **~orden** *der* (*kath.*) Franciscan Order

**Franzose** /fran'tso:zə/ *der;* **~n, ~n** [A] ▶ 553 Frenchman; **er ist ~:** he is French *or* a Frenchman; **die ~n** the French; [B] (*ugs.: Schraubenschlüssel*) screw wrench

**Franzosen·krankheit** *die* (*veralt.*) French disease (*dated*); syphilis

**Französin** /fran'tsø:zɪn/ *die;* ~, **~nen** ▶ 553 Frenchwoman

**französisch** ▶ 553, ▶ 696 ❶ *Adj.* French; **ein ~es Bett** a double bed; **die Französische Schweiz** French-speaking Switzerland; **die Französische Revolution** the French Revolution; **die ~e Krankheit** (*veralt.*) ⇒ **Franzosenkrankheit**. ❷ *adv.* **es ~ machen** (*salopp*) have oral sex; **sich [auf] ~ empfehlen** *od.* **verabschieden** (*ugs.*) take French leave; ⇒ *auch* **deutsch, Deutsche**[2]

**Französisch** *das;* **~[s]** ▶ 696 French; ⇒ *auch* **Deutsch**

**frappant** /fra'pant/ *Adj.* striking ‹similarity›; remarkable ‹success, discovery›

**frappieren** /fra'pi:rən/ *tr. V.* (*geh.*) astonish; astound

**frappierend** *Adj.* astonishing; remarkable

**Fräse** /'frɛ:zə/ *die;* ~, **~n** [A] (*für Holz*) moulding machine; (*für Metall*) milling machine; [B] ⇒ **Fräser** A; [C] (*Boden~*) rotary cultivator

**fräsen** *tr. V.* [A] shape ‹wood›; mill ‹metal›; form ‹groove, thread›; [B] (*Landw.*) hoe [with a rotary cultivator]

**Fräser** *der;* **~s,** ~ [A] (*Werkzeug*) cutter; [B] ▶ 159 (*Metallbearb.*) milling-machine operator; (*Holzverarb.*) moulding-machine operator

**Fräserin** *die;* ~, **~nen** ⇒ **Fräser** B

**Fräs·maschine** *die* ⇒ **Fräse** A

**fraß** /fra:s/ *1. u. 3. Pers. Sg. Prät. v.* **fressen**

**Fraß** *der;* **~es** [A] (*Tiernahrung*) food; **einem Tier etw. als** *od.* **zum ~ vorwerfen** feed an animal with sth.; **jmdm. etw. zum ~ hin-** *od.* **vorwerfen** (*fig. abwertend*) let sb. have sth.; [B] (*derb: schlechtes Essen*) muck; swill; **ein abscheulicher/widerlicher ~:** disgusting/repulsive muck; [C] **vom ~ befallen sein** have been eaten away

**Frater** /'fra:tɐ/ *der;* **~s, Fratres** /'fra:tre:s/ (*kath. Kirche*) lay brother

**fraternisieren** /fratɛrni'zi:rən/ *itr. V.* (*geh.*) fraternize

**Fraternisierung** *die;* **~:** fraternization

**Fratz** /frats/ *der;* **~es, ~e,** (*österr.:*) **~en, ~en** [A] (*ugs.: niedliches Kind*) [little] rascal; **ein süßer ~:** a sweet little rascal; [B] (*bes. südd., österr.: ungezogenes Kind*) brat

**Fratze** /'fratsə/ *die;* ~, **~n** [A] (*hässliches Gesicht*) hideous face; hideous features *pl.;* **sein Gesicht war zu einer ~ deformiert** his face was hideously deformed; [B] (*ugs.: Grimasse*) grimace; **jmdm. ~n schneiden** pull faces at sb.; [C] (*abwertend: Gesicht*) mug (*coll.*)

**fratzenhaft** *Adj.* grotesque; hideous

**Frau** *die;* ~, **~en** ▶ 91 [A] woman; **zur ~ werden** (*verhüll.*) lose one's virginity; **typisch** *od.* **echt ~** (*ugs.*) typical of a woman; **die Gleichberechtigung der ~:** equal rights for women; **von ~ zu ~:** woman to woman; [B] (*Ehefrau*) wife; **wie Mann und ~ zusammenleben** live together as man *or* husband and wife; **jmdn. zur ~ nehmen** (*veralt.*) take sb. to wife (*arch.*); **er hat eine Französin zur ~:** his wife is French; **willst du meine ~ werden?** will you be my wife?; [C] ▶ 187 (*Titel, Anrede*) **~ Schulze** Mrs Schulze; **~ Professor/Dr. Schulze** Professor/Dr. Schulze; **~ Ministerin/Direktorin/Studienrätin Schulze** Mrs/Miss/Ms Schulze; **~ Ministerin/Professor/Doktor** Minister/Professor/doctor; **~ Vorsitzende/Präsidentin** Madam Chairman/President; (*in Briefen*) **Sehr geehrte ~ Schulze** Dear Madam; (*bei persönlicher Bekanntschaft*) Dear Mrs/Miss/Ms Schulze; **[Sehr verehrte] gnädige ~:** [Dear] Madam; **gute ~** (*veralt.*) good lady; **Ihre ~ Gemahlin/Mutter** (*geh.*) your lady wife/lady mother (*dated*); your wife/mother; [D] (*Herrin*) lady; mistress; **die ~ des Hauses** the lady of the house; **Unsere Liebe ~** (*kath. Rel.*) Our Lady

**Frauchen** /'frau̯çən/ *das;* **~s,** ~ [A] (*ugs.: Ehefrau*) wifie; [B] (*Herrin eines Hundes*) mistress

**frauen-, Frauen-: ~arbeit** *die* [A] (*Erwerbstätigkeit*) women's employment; [B] (*für Frauen geeignete Arbeit*) women's work; [C] (*gesellschaftspolitisch*) work for the women's movement; **in der ~arbeit tätig sein** work in the women's movement; **~arzt** *der,* **~ärztin** *die* gynaecologist; **~beruf** *der* women's occupation; **~bewegung** *die* women's movement; **~emanzipation** *die* female emancipation; women's emancipation; **~fachschule** *die* women's technical college; **~farn** *der* (*Bot.*) lady fern; **~feind** *der*

*old spelling (see note on page 1707)

misogynist; **~feindlich** *Adj.* anti-women; **~frage** *die* issue of women's rights; **~funk** *der* women's [radio] programmes *pl.*; **~fuß·ball** *der* women's football; **~gefängnis** *das* women's prison; **~geschichten** *Pl.* (*ugs.*) affairs with women; **~gestalt** *die* female character; **~haar** *das* **A** woman's hair; **B** (*Bot.*) haircap moss; **~haar·farn** *der* (*Bot.*) maidenhair fern; **~hand** *die: in* **von zarter ~hand** from the fair hand of a lady; **von zarter ~hand gepflegt** nursed by a woman's tender care; **~haus** *das* **A** battered wives' refuge; **B** (*veralt.*) brothel; **C** (*Völkerk.*) unmarried girls' dormitory; **~heil·kunde** *die* gynaecology; **~held** *der* ladykiller; **~herz** *das* female heart; **sich auf ~herzen verstehen** know the way to a woman's heart; **~kleider** *Pl.* women's clothes; **~klinik** *die* gynaecological hospital *or* clinic; **~kloster** *das* convent; nunnery; **~krankheit** *die*, **~leiden** *das* gynaecological disorder; **Facharzt für ~krankheiten** gynaecologist; **~liebling** *der* favourite with the ladies; **~lohn** *der* women's pay *no indef. art.*; **~los** *Adj.* all-male; **~mörder** *der* killer of women; **~orden** *der* (*kath. Rel.*) women's order; **~recht** *das* women's right; **~rechtlerin** /-rɛçtlərɪn/ *die;* **~~**, **~~nen** feminist; Women's Libber (*coll.*); **~sache** *die:* **das ist ~sache** that's a woman's job; **~schänder** *der;* **~~s**, **~~:** rapist; **~schuh** *der* (*Bot.*) lady's slipper; **~seite** *die* women's page

**Frauens·person** *die* (*veralt.*) female

**Frauen-: ~sport** *der* women's sport; **~station** *die* women's ward; **~stimme** *die* **A** woman's voice; **B** (*Parl.*) **die ~stimmen** the women's vote *sing.*; **~stimmrecht** *das* ⇒ **~wahlrecht**; **~tausch** *der* (*Völkerk.*) exchange of wives

**Frauentum** *das;* **~s** (*geh.*) womanhood

**Frauen-: ~turnen** *das* ladies' *or* women's gymnastics *sing.*; **~über·schuss**, ***~über·schuß** *der* surplus of women; **~verband** *der* women's association; **~wahl·recht** *das* women's franchise; women's right to vote; **~zeitschrift** *die* women's magazine; **~zimmer** *das* **A** (*abwertend*) female; **B** (*veralt.*, *landsch.*) woman

**Fräulein** /ˈfrɔylain/ *das;* **~s**, **~** (*ugs.* **~s**) ▶ 91 **A** (*junges* **~**) young lady; (*ältliches* **~**) spinster; **B** ▶ 187 (*Titel, Anrede*) **~ Mayer/Schulte** Miss Mayer/Schulte; **[sehr verehrtes] gnädiges ~ [X]** Dear Miss X; **C** (*veralt.: Angestellte*) **~**, **wollen Sie ...** Miss, would you ...; **das ~ hat uns schlecht bedient** the girl gave us bad service; **D** (*Kellnerin*) **~**, **wir möchten zahlen** [Miss,] could we have the bill (*Brit.*) *or* (*Amer.*) check, please?; **das ~ kommt gleich** the waitress is just coming; **E das ~ vom Amt** (*veralt.*) the operator

**fraulich** ❶ *Adj.* feminine; (*reif*) womanly. ❷ *adv.* in a feminine/womanly way; **sich ~ kleiden** dress femininely/in a womanly way

**Fraulichkeit** *die;* **~:** femininity; (*reifes Wesen*) womanliness

**frech** /frɛç/ ❶ *Adj.* **A** (*respektlos, unverschämt*) impertinent; impudent; cheeky; barefaced ‹lie›; **ein ~er Kerl** an impertinent chap; **~ werden/sein** become/be impertinent; **etw. mit ~er Stirn behaupten** (*fig.*) have the barefaced cheek to say sth.; **~ wie Dreck** *od.* **Oskar sein** (*bes. berlin.*) be a cheeky devil (*coll.*); **B** (*keck, kess*) saucy. ❷ *adv.* (*respektlos, unverschämt*) impertinently; impudently; cheekily; **jmdn. ~ anlügen** tell sb. barefaced lies; **jmdm. etw. ~ ins Gesicht sagen** say sth. quite unashamedly to sb.'s face; **jmdm. ~ ins Gesicht lachen** laugh in sb.'s face

**Frech·dachs** *der* (*ugs.*, *meist scherzh.*) cheeky little thing

**Frechheit** *die;* **~**, **~en** **A** impertinence; impudence; cheek; **die ~ haben, etw. zu tun** have the impertinence *etc.* to do sth.; **das ist der Gipfel der ~!** that is the height of impertinence!; **B** (*Äußerung*) impertinent *or* impudent *or* cheeky remark; **sich** (*Dat.*) **~en erlauben** be impertinent; **was erlauben Sie sich für ~en?** how dare you be so impertinent?

**Frechling** *der;* **~s**, **~e** (*geh.*) impudent rascal

**Freesie** /ˈfreːzi̯ə/ *die;* **~**, **~n** freesia

**Fregatte** /freˈgatə/ *die;* **~**, **~n** **A** (*Marine*) frigate; **B** (*abwertend: Frau*) **eine alte/aufgetakelte ~:** an old bag/overdressed old bag

**Fregatten·kapitän** *der* commander

**frei** /frai/ ❶ *Adj.* **A** (*unabhängig*) free ‹man, will, life, people, decision, etc.›; **eine ~e Reichsstadt/Hansestadt** (*hist.*) a free imperial/Hanseatic city; **B** (*nicht angestellt*) freelance ‹writer, worker, etc.›; **die ~en Berufe** the independent professions; **C** (*ungezwungen*) free and easy; lax (*derog.*); **ein ~es Benehmen haben** behave in a free and easy/lax way; **es herrschte ein ~er Ton** there was an informal atmosphere; **~e Liebe** free love; **D** (*in Freiheit*) free; at liberty *pred.*; **~ lebende Tiere** animals living in the wild; **~ herumlaufen** ‹person› run around scot-free; **E** (*offen*) open; **ein ~es Gelände/~er Platz** open ground/an open square; **unter ~em Himmel** in the open [air]; outdoors; **auf ~er Strecke** (*Straße*) on the open road; (*Eisenbahn*) between stations; **ins Freie gehen** walk out into the open; **im Freien sitzen/übernachten** sit out of doors/spend the night in the open; **ständig im Freien übernachten** sleep rough; **F** (*unbesetzt*) vacant; unoccupied; free; **ein ~er Stuhl/Platz** a vacant *or* free chair/seat; **Entschuldigung, ist hier noch ~?** excuse me, is this anyone's seat *etc.?*; **eine ~e Stelle** a vacancy; **ein Bett ist [noch] ~:** one bed is [still] free *or* not taken; **ist der Tisch ~?** is this table free?; **sind Sie ~?** are you free?; **den Weg/die Kreuzung ~ machen** clear the path/junction; **[jmdm.] Platz ~ lassen** leave [sb.] some space; **einige Seiten ~ lassen** leave some pages blank; **Ring ~!** (*Boxen*) seconds out!; **G** (*kostenlos*) free ‹food, admission›; **~e Verpflegung** free board; **der Eintritt ist ~:** admission is free [of charge]; **20 kg Gepäck ~ haben** have *or* be allowed a 20 kilogram baggage allowance; **Lieferung ~ Haus** carriage free; **~e Kost und Logis** (*veralt.*) free board and lodging; **H** (*ungenau*) **eine ~e Übersetzung** a free *or* loose translation; **~ nach einer Vorlage** based [loosely] on a source; **I** (*ohne Vorlage*) improvised; **in ~er Improvisation** in spontaneous improvisation; **J** (*uneingeschränkt*) free; **~e Meinungsäußerung/Religionsausübung** free expression of opinion/practice of religion; **die ~e Arzt-/Berufswahl** the free choice of doctor/profession; **der Zug hat ~e Fahrt** the train can proceed; **der ~e Fall** (*Physik*) free fall; **K von etw. ~/~ von etw. sein** be free of sth.; **~ von Schuld/Schmerzen sein** be free of guilt/pain; **~ von Fehlern** without faults; **nicht ~ von Überheblichkeit** not without arrogance; **L** (*verfügbar*) spare; free; **jede ~e Minute/Stunde** every spare *or* free minute/hour; **ich habe heute ~:** I've got today off; **er hat seinen ~en Sonnabend/Abend** this is his Saturday/evening off; **sich** (*Dat.*) **~ nehmen** (*ugs.*) take some time off; **er ist noch/nicht mehr ~:** he is still/no longer unattached; **M** (*ohne Hilfsmittel*) **eine ~e Rede** an extempore speech; **aus ~er Hand zeichnen** draw freehand; **N** (*unbekleidet*) bare; **das Kleid lässt die Schultern ~:** the dress leaves the shoulders bare; ⇒ *auch* **freimachen** 2A; **O** (*bes. Fußball*) unmarked; **der ~e Mann** the sweeper; **~ stehen** be [standing] unmarked; **P** (*Chemie, Physik*) free; **~ werden** (*bei einer Reaktion*) be given off; **Elektronen werden ~:** electrons are released; **Q** (*in festen Wendungen*) **~e Hand haben** have a free hand; **jmdm. ~e Hand lassen** give sb. a free hand; **aus ~en Stücken** (*ugs.*) of one's own accord; voluntarily; **jmdn. auf ~en Fuß setzen** set sb. free; **auf ~em Fuß** (*von Verbrechern etc.*) at large; **~ ausgehen** get away scot-free; get away with it; **ich bin so ~!** if I may ...
❷ *adv.* ‹act, speak, choose› freely; ‹translate› freely, loosely; **etw. ~ heraus sagen** say sth. freely; **eine Rede ~ halten** make a speech without notes; **ein ~ praktizierender Arzt** a doctor in private practice; **die Personen sind/die Geschichte ist ~ erfunden** the characters are/the story is entirely fictional; **~ in der Luft schweben** hang in mid-air

**frei-, Frei-: ~aktie** *die* (*Börsenw.*) bonus share; **~bad** *das* open-air *or* outdoor swimming pool; **~ballon** *der* free balloon; **~bank** *die; Pl.* **~bänke** *place in slaughterhouse where lower-grade meat is sold;* **~|bekommen** ❶ *unr. itr. V.* (*ugs.*) get time off; **ich habe nachmittags ~bekommen** I've got the afternoon off; ❷ *unr. tr. V.* **jmdn./etw. ~bekommen** get sb./sth. released; **~beruflich** ▶ 159 ❶ *Adj.* self-employed; freelance ‹journalist, editor, architect, etc.›; ‹doctor, lawyer› in private practice; ❷ *adv.* **~beruflich tätig sein/arbeiten** work freelance/practise privately; **~betrag** *der* (*Steuerw.*) [tax] allowance; **~beuter** /-bɔytɐ/ *der;* **~~s**, **~~** **A** (*hist.: Pirat*) freebooter; **B** (*abwertend*) exploiter; **~beuterei** *die;* **~~** **A** (*hist.: Piraterie*) freebootery; **B** (*abwertend*) exploitation; **~beuterin** *die;* **~~**, **~~nen** ⇒ **~beuter**; **~bier** *das* free beer; **~bleibend** (*Kaufmannsspr.*) ❶ *Adj.* **~bleibendes Angebot** provisional offer; ❷ *adv.* **die Preise verstehen sich ~bleibend** prices are subject to alteration; **~bord** *der* (*Schifffahrt*) freeboard; **~brief** *der* **A** *in* **kein ~brief für etw. sein** be no excuse for sth.; **jmdm. einen ~brief für etw. geben** *od.* **ausstellen** give sb. a licence for sth.; **einen ~brief haben, etw. zu tun** have authority for sth./to do sth.; (*fig.*) have a licence for sth./to do sth.; **etw. als ~brief für etw. ansehen/betrachten** regard sth. as a charter for sth.; **B** (*hist.: Urkunde*) charter; **~demokrat** *der*, **~demokratin** *die* Free Democrat; **~denker** *der*, **~denkerin** *die* free thinker; **~denkertum** *das;* **~~s** free thought; freethinking

**Freie** *der/die; adj. Dekl.* (*hist.*) freeman/freewoman

**freien** ❶ *tr. V.* (*veralt.*) marry; wed; **jung gefreit hat nie gereut** (*Spr.*) marry young and you won't regret it. ❷ *itr. V.* **um ein Mädchen ~:** court *or* woo a girl

**Freier** *der;* **~s**, **~** **A** (*veralt.*) suitor; **B** (*salopp: Kunde einer Dirne*) punter (*coll.*)

**Freiers·füße** *Pl. in* **auf ~n gehen** (*scherzh.*) be courting

**frei-, Frei-: ~exemplar** *das* (*Buch*) free copy; (*Zeitung*) free issue; **~fahr·schein** *der* free ticket; **~fahrt** *die* free trip; (*auf Karussell*) free turn *or* ride; **~fläche** *die* open space; **~flug** *der* free flight; **~frau** *die*, **~fräulein** *das* baroness; **~gabe** *die* **A** release; **die ~gabe der Wechselkurse** the lifting of controls on exchange rates; **B** (*Übergabe*) opening [to the public]; **~|geben** ❶ *unr. tr. V.* **A** release ‹prisoner, footballer›; decontrol ‹exchange rates›; **jmdm. den Weg ~geben** let sb. through; **B** open ‹motorway›; pass ‹film›; **etw. für den Verkehr/die Öffentlichkeit ~geben** open sth. to traffic/to the public; **der Film ist ab 18 ~gegeben** the film has been passed 18; ❷ *unr. tr., itr. V.* **jmdm. ~geben** give sb. time off; **sich** (*Dat.*) **zwei Tage ~geben lassen** take two days off; **~gebig** /-geːbɪç/ *Adj.* generous; open-handed; **~gebig gegen jmdn. sein** (*veralt.*) be generous to sb.; **[nicht] sehr ~gebig mit etw. sein** be [not] very generous *or* open-handed with sth.; **~gebigkeit** *die;* **~~:** generosity; open-handedness; **~gehege** *das* outdoor *or* open-air enclosure; **~geist** *der* free thinker; **~geistig** *Adj.* freethinking; **~gelände** *das* piece of open ground; (*Film*) studio lot; **~gelassene** *der/die; adj. Dekl.* (*hist.*) freedman/freedwoman; **~gepäck** *das* baggage allowance; **~grenze** *die* (*Steuerw.*) tax exemption limit; **~gut** *das* (*Zollw.*) duty-free goods *pl.*; **~|haben** *unr. tr., itr. V.* (*ugs.*) **ich habe [am** *od.* **den] Montag ~:** I've got Monday off; **~hafen** *der* free port; ~|halten *unr. tr. V.* [A] treat; **er hielt das ganze Lokal ~:** he stood drinks for everyone in the pub (*Brit.*) *or* (*Amer.*) bar; [B] (*offenhalten*) keep ‹entrance, roadway› clear; **Einfahrt ~halten!** no parking in front of entrance; keep clear; [C] (*reservieren*) **jmdm.** *od.* **für jmdn. einen Platz ~halten** keep a place for sb.; **sich ~halten** keep oneself free of engagements; **~hand·bücherei** *die* open-access library; **~handel** *der* free trade; **~handels·zone** *die* free-trade zone; **~händig** /-hɛndɪç/ ❶ *Adj.* [A] freehand ‹drawing›; offhand ‹shooting›; [B] (*Amtsspr.*) private ‹sale›; ❷ *adv.* [A] ‹cycle› without holding on; ‹draw› freehand; ‹shoot› offhand; [B] (*Amtsspr.*) ‹sell› privately; **~hand·zeichnen** *das* freehand drawing

**Freiheit** *die;* ~, ~en [A] freedom; **~, Gleichheit, Brüderlichkeit** Liberty, Equality, Fraternity; **die persönliche ~:** personal freedom *or* liberty; **die ~ der Presse** Press freedom; the freedom of the Press; **die akademische ~:** academic freedom; **jmdm. völlige ~ lassen** give sb. a completely free hand; **die ~ der Meere** (*Rechtsw.*) the freedom of the seas; **einem Gefangenen/Tier die ~ schenken** give a prisoner his/an animal its freedom; **jmdn. in ~ setzen** set sb. free; [B] (*Vorrecht*) freedom; privilege; **[besondere] ~en genießen** enjoy [special] privileges; **sich** (*Dat.*) **gegen jmdn. ~en herausnehmen** take liberties with sb.; **die dichterische ~:** poetic licence; **sich** (*Dat.*) **die ~ nehmen, etw. zu tun** take the liberty of doing sth.

**-freiheit** *die;* **-~: Gebühren~/Porto~:** freedom from dues/postal charges; **Bewegungs~:** freedom of movement; **Entscheidungs~:** freedom of decision *or* choice

**freiheitlich** ❶ *Adj.* liberal ‹philosophy, conscience›; **~ und demokratisch** free and democratic. ❷ *adv.* liberally; **~ gesinnt sein** have liberal ideas

**Freiheitliche** *der/die; adj. Dekl.* (*Politik*) member of the Freedom Party; **die ~n** the Freedom Party

**freiheits-, Freiheits-: ~beraubung** *die* (*jur.*) wrongful detention; **~bewegung** *die* liberation movement; **~drang** *der* desire for freedom; **~entzug** *der* imprisonment; **jmdn. zu zwei Jahren ~entzug verurteilen** sentence sb. to two years' imprisonment; **~kampf** *der* struggle for freedom; **~kämpfer** *der,* **~kämpferin** *die* freedom fighter; **~krieg** *der* war of liberation; **die ~kriege** (*hist.*) the War of Liberation; **~liebe** *die* love of freedom *or* liberty; **~liebend** *Adj.* freedom-loving; **~rechte** *Pl.* civil rights; **~statue** *die* Statue of Liberty; **~strafe** *die* (*Rechtsw.*) term of imprisonment; prison sentence; **er wurde zu einer ~strafe von fünf Jahren/zu einer lebenslänglichen ~strafe verurteilt** he was sentenced to five years' imprisonment/given a life sentence

**frei-, Frei-: ~heraus** *Adv.* frankly; openly; **~heraus gesagt ...** to put it frankly ...; **~herr** *der* ▶91 baron; **~herrlich** *Adj.* baronial

**Freiin** /ˈfraiɪn/ *die;* ~, ~nen baroness

**frei-, Frei-: ~|kämpfen** *tr. V.* liberate; **sich ~kämpfen** fight one's way out; **~karte** *die* complimentary *or* free ticket; **~|kaufen** *tr. V.* ransom ‹hostage›; buy the freedom of ‹slave›; **sich von der Verantwortung/Schuld ~kaufen** (*fig.*) buy off one's responsibility/guilt; **~kirche** *die* Free Church; **~|kommen** *unr. itr. V.; mit sein* **aus dem Gefängnis ~kommen** be released from prison; leave prison; **aus jmds. Fängen ~kommen** escape from sb.'s clutches; **~körper·kultur** *die* nudism *no art.;* naturism *no art.;* **~korps** *das* (*hist.*) volunteer corps

**Freiland** *das* open ground; **etw. im ~ anbauen** grow sth. outdoors *or* in the open

**Freiland-: ~anbau** *der* (*Landw.*) **der ~anbau von Gemüse** growing vegetables outdoors *or* in the open; **Gemüse aus ~anbau** crops grown outdoors *or* in the open; **~ei** *das* free-range egg; **~gemüse** *das* outdoor vegetables *pl.;* **~hähnchen** *das* free-range chicken; **~haltung** *die* (*Landw.*) keeping of animals on free range; **Fleisch aus ~haltung** free-range meat; **~henne** *die* free-range hen; **~huhn** *das* free-range chicken; **~tomate** *der* outdoor tomato; **~versuch** *der* (*Landw., Biol.*) outdoor trial

**frei-, Frei-: ~|lassen** *unr. tr. V.* set free; release; **~lassung** *die;* ~~, ~~en release; **~lauf** *der* (*Technik*) neutral gear; (*beim Fahrrad*) free wheel; **im ~lauf fahren** ‹driver› coast in neutral; ‹cyclist› freewheel; **~|laufen** *unr. refl. V.* (*bes. Fuß- und Handball*) run into *or* find space; ***~lebend** ⇒ **frei** 1D; **~|legen** *tr. V.* uncover; **~leitung** *die* (*Technik*) overhead cable

**freilich** *Adv.* [A] (*einschränkend*) **er arbeitet schnell, ~ nicht sehr gründlich** he works quickly, though admittedly he's not very thorough; **deine Theorie klingt zwar überzeugend, ~ ist eine wichtige Einschränkung zu machen** your theory sounds convincing, it's true, but there is one important reservation to be made; **ich werde morgen einmal bei dir vorbeischauen, lange bleiben kann ich ~ nicht** I'll call in on you tomorrow, though I shan't be able to stay long; **sie hat sehr viel Talent, ~ fehlt es ihr an Ausdauer** she has a great deal of talent, but she does lack staying power; [B] (*einräumend*) **man muss ~ bedenken, dass ...** one must of course bear in mind that ...; **~ scheinen die Tatsachen gegen meine Überlegungen zu sprechen ...** admittedly the facts seem to contradict my ideas, but ...; **sie war sehr wütend auf ihren Mann, wozu sie ~ auch allen Grund hatte** she was furious with her husband, and of course she had every reason to be; [C] (*bes. südd.: selbstverständlich*) of course; **ja ~:** [why] yes; of course

**Frei·licht-: ~bühne** *die* ⇒ **~theater**; **~museum** *das* open-air *or* outdoor museum; **~theater** *das* open-air *or* outdoor theatre

**frei-, Frei-: ~los** *das* [A] free [lottery] ticket; [B] (*Sport*) bye; **durch ~los die nächste Runde erreichen** get a bye into the next round; **~|machen** ❶ *refl. V.* (*ugs.: ~nehmen*) **sich [für etw.] ~machen** take time off [for sth.]; ❷ *tr. V.* [A] (*entkleiden*) **den Oberkörper ~machen** strip to the waist; **sich ~machen** strip; [B] (*Postw.*) put a stamp on; (*freistempeln*) frank; **etw. mit 0,50 DM ~machen** put a 50-pfennig stamp on sth.; **~machung** *die;* ~~ (*Postw.*) franking; **~marke** *die* postage stamp; **~maurer** *der* Freemason; **~maurerei** *die;* **~~:** Freemasonry; **~maurer·loge** *die* Freemasons' lodge; **~mut** *der* candidness; frankness; **mit ~mut sprechen** speak candidly *or* frankly; **~mütig** ❶ *Adj.* candid; frank; ❷ *adv.* candidly; frankly; **~mütigkeit** *die;* **~~:** candidness; frankness; **~platz** *der* [A] ([*Hoch*]*schulw.*) scholarship; [B] (*Sitzplatz*) free seat; **~|pressen** *tr. V.* **jmdn. ~pressen** obtain sb.'s release by threats; **~raum** *der* (*Psych., Soziol.*) space *no indef. art.* to be oneself; **unpolitische ~räume** areas where politics is not involved; **~religiös** *Adj.* non-denominational; **~sass, *~saß, ~sasse** *der;* **~sassen, ~sassen** (*hist.*) yeoman; tenant farmer; **~schaffend** *Adj.* freelance; **Steuervergünstigungen für Freischaffende** tax concessions to self-employed persons; **~schar** *die* (*hist.*) corps of irregulars; **~schärler** /-ʃɛːɐ̯lɐ/ *der;* ~~s, ~~, **~schärlerin** *die;* ~~, ~~nen irregular [soldier]; **~|schaufeln** *tr. V.* clear ‹road› by shovelling; dig ‹person› free; **~|schießen** *unr. tr., refl. V.* **sich** (*Dat.*) **den Weg ~schießen** shoot one's way out; **jmdn. ~schießen** free sb. [in a gun battle]; **~|schwimmen** *unr. refl. V.* **sich ~schwimmen** pass the 15-minute swimming test; **inzwischen hat er sich ~geschwommen** (*fig.*) he has now got over his initial difficulties; **~|setzen** *tr. V.* [A] (*Physik, Chemie, Med.*) release ‹energy›; emit ‹rays, electrons, neutrons›; release, give off ‹gas›; [B] (*Arbeitsw.*) release ‹staff›; (*verhüll.*) make ‹staff› redundant; **~setzung** *die;* ~~, ~~en [A] (*Physik, Chemie, Med.*) (*von Energie, Gas*) release; (*von Strahlung usw.*) emission; [B] (*Arbeitsw.*) release (*of staff*); (*verhüll.*) redundancy; **~sinn** *der* (*veralt.*) liberalism; **~sinnig** *Adj.* (*veralt.*) liberal; broad-minded; **~spiel** *das* free turn; **~|spielen** ❶ *tr. V.* (*Ballspiele*) **jmdn./sich ~spielen** create space for sb./oneself; ❷ *refl. V.* (*auf der Bühne*) settle into the performance; **~sprech·anlage** *die* hands-free kit; **~|sprechen** *unr. tr. V.* [A] (*Rechtsw.*) acquit; **jmdn. von einer Anklage ~sprechen** acquit sb. of a charge; [B] (*für unschuldig erklären*) exonerate (**von** from); [C] (*Handw.*) release ‹apprentice›; **~sprechung** *die;* ~~, ~~en [A] (*Rechtsw.*) acquitting; [B] (*Handw.*) release; **~spruch** *der* (*Rechtsw.*) acquittal; **~staat** *der* (*veralt.*) free state; **der ~staat Bayern** the Free State of Bavaria; **~statt, ~stätte** *die* (*geh.*) sanctuary; **~|stehen** *unr. itr. V.* [A] **es steht jmdm. ~, etw. zu tun** sb. is free to do sth.; [B] ‹flat, house› be empty *or* vacant; ‹storeroom etc.› be empty; **~stelle** *die* ⇒ **~platz** A; **~|stellen** *tr. V.* [A] **jmdm. etw. ~stellen** leave sth. up to sb.; let sb. decide sth.; [B] (*befreien*) release ‹person›; **jmdn. vom Wehrdienst ~stellen** exempt sb. from military service; **~stellung** *die* release; (*befristet*) leave; **~stempel** *der* (*Postw.*) postmark

**Frei·stil** *der* (*Sport*) [A] ⇒ **~ringen**; [B] ⇒ **~schwimmen**

**Freistil-: ~ringen** *das* freestyle wrestling; **~schwimmen** *das* freestyle swimming

**Frei-: ~stoß** *der* (*Fußball*) free kick; **einen ~stoß schießen** take a free kick; **~stunde** *die* free hour; (*Schulstunde*) free period

**Frei·tag** *der* ▶207, ▶833 Friday; **ein schwarzer ~:** a black day; ⇒ *auch* **Dienstag, Dienstag-**

**freitags** *Adv.* ▶833 on Friday[s]; ⇒ *auch* **dienstags**

**frei-, Frei-: ~tod** *der* (*verhüll.*) suicide *no art.;* **den ~tod wählen** choose to take one's own life; **~tragend** *Adj.* (*Bauw.*) suspended ‹floor›; cantilever ‹bridge›; **~treppe** *die* [flight of] steps; **~übung** *die* (*Sport*) keep-fit exercise; **~übungen machen** do keep-fit exercises; **~umschlag** *der* stamped addressed envelope; s.a.e.; **~verkehr** *der* (*Bankw.*) unofficial market; kerb dealings *pl.;* **~wache** *die* (*Seemannsspr.*) watch below; **~weg** *Adv.* (*ugs.*) **wir können ~weg reden** we can talk freely *or* openly; **sag es ~weg** say it straight out; **~wild** *das* fair game; **zum ~wild werden** become fair game; **~willig** ❶ *Adj.* voluntary ‹decision›; optional ‹subject›; **~willige Feuerwehr** volunteer fire brigade; ❷ *adv.* voluntarily; of one's own accord; **sich ~willig melden** volunteer; **~willig aus dem Leben scheiden** choose to end one's life; **~willige** *der/die; adj. Dekl.* volunteer; **~willige vor!** volunteers take one step forward!; **sich als ~williger zu etw. melden** volunteer for sth.; **~wurf** *der* free throw; **~zeichen** *das* [A] (*volkst.*) dialling tone; [B] (*Nachrichtenw.*) ringing tone; **~zeichnungs·klausel** *die* (*Rechtsw.*) exemption clause

**Frei·zeit** *die* [A] spare time; leisure time; (*Arbeitsw.*) time off in lieu; **in** *od.* **während der ~:** in/during one's spare time; [B] (*Zusammenkunft*) [holiday/weekend] course; (*der Kirche*) retreat

**Freizeit-: ~anzug** *der* leisure suit; **~beschäftigung** *die* hobby; leisure pursuit; **~gesellschaft** *die* (*Soziol.*) leisure society; **~gestaltung** *die* (*Soziol., Päd.*) leisure activity; **~hemd** *das* sports shirt; **~industrie** *die* leisure industry; **~kleidung** *die* casual clothes *pl.;* leisure wear (*Commerc.*); **~park** *der* amusement park; **~wert** *der:* **eine Stadt mit hohem ~wert** a town with many leisure amenities

**frei-, Frei-: ~zügig** ❶ *Adj.* [A] (*großzügig*) generous, liberal ‹dosage, spending›; liberal, flexible ‹interpretation of rule etc.›; **~zügig im Geldausgeben** generous with one's money; [B] (*gewagt, unmoralisch*) risqué, daring ‹remark, film, dress›; permissive ‹attitude›; [C] (~ *in*

*old spelling (see note on page 1707)

*der Wahl des Wohnsitzes*) **~zügig sein** enjoy freedom of domicile; **ein ~zügiges Leben führen** live a nomadic life; be always on the move; ❷ *adv.* **Geld ~zügig ausgeben** be generous with one's money; **ein Gesetz ~zügig auslegen** interpret a law flexibly; **~zügigkeit** *die;* **~~** (A) (*Großzügigkeit*) liberalness; (*in Geldsachen*) generosity; (*von Interpretation*) flexibility; (B) permissiveness; (C) (*~e Wahl des Wohnsitzes*) freedom of domicile

**frẹmd** /frɛmt/ *Adj.* (A) foreign ‹country, government, customs, language›; (B) (*nicht eigen*) other people's; of others *postpos.;* **~es Eigentum** other people's property; the property of others; **sich in ~e Angelegenheiten mischen** interfere in other people's business; **etw. ohne ~e Hilfe schaffen** do sth. without anyone else's help; **unter ~em Namen** under an assumed name; **unter ~em Namen schreiben** write under a nom de plume *or* pseudonym; **~e Welten** other worlds; ⇒ *auch* **Feder** A; (C) (*unbekannt*) strange; **eine ~e Umgebung** strange *or* unknown surroundings *pl.;* **Rockmusik war ihr ~:** she knew nothing about rock music; **Hinterhältigkeit ist ihm ~:** underhandedness is foreign to his nature; **er fühlte sich sehr ~:** he felt very much a stranger; **sich** (*Dat.*) *od.* **einander ~ werden** become estranged; grow apart; **die Anziehungskraft des Fremden** the attraction of the unfamiliar; (D) (*anders geartet*) strange

**frẹmd-, Frẹmd-: ~arbeiter** *der,* **~arbeiterin** *die* (*veralt., schweiz.*) foreign worker; **~artig** *Adj.* strange; (*exotisch*) exotic; **~artigkeit** *die* strangeness; (*Exotik*) exoticness; **~bestimmt** *Adj.* (*Politik, Wirtsch., Soziol.*) heteronomous; **~bestimmung** *die* (*Politik, Wirtsch., Soziol.*) heteronomy

**Frẹmde**[1] /ˈfrɛmdə/ *der/die; adj. Dekl.* (A) (*Unbekannte[r]*) stranger; (B) (*Ausländer*) foreigner; alien (*Admin. lang.*); (C) (*Besucher, Tourist*) visitor

**Frẹmde**[2] *die;* ~ (*geh.*) foreign parts *pl.;* abroad; **in die ~ ziehen** go off to foreign parts; go abroad

**Frẹmd·einwirkung** *die* (*Rechtsspr.*) **ohne ~:** without any other person *or* vehicle being involved; **der Unfall passierte ohne ~:** no other vehicle was involved in the accident; **liegt ~ vor?** was any other person involved?

**frẹmdeln,** (*schweiz.*) **frẹmden** *itr. V.* be afraid of strangers

**frẹmden-, Frẹmden-: ~bett** *das* hotel bed; **~buch** *das* hotel register; **~feindlich** *Adj.* hostile to strangers/foreigners *postpos.;* **~feindlichkeit** *die* xenophobia; **~führer** *der,* **~führerin** *die* tourist guide; **~heim** *das* guest house; boarding house; **~industrie** *die* tourist industry; tourist trade; **~legion** *die* foreign legion; **~legionär** *der* legionnaire; **~pass,** ***~paß** *der* alien's passport; **~polizei** *die: police department dealing with aliens;* **~verkehr** *der* tourism *no art.;* **~zimmer** *das* (A) (*Hotelzimmer*) room; **~zimmer frei!** vacancies (*Brit.*); vacancy (*Amer.*); (B) (*Gastzimmer*) guest room

**frẹmd-, Frẹmd-: ~erregung** *die* (*Technik*) separate excitation; **~finanzierung** *die* (*Finanzw.*) financing from outside sources; **~|gehen** *unr. itr. V.; mit sein* (*ugs.*) be unfaithful

**Frẹmdheit** *die;* **~:** strangeness; (*Zurückhaltung*) reserve

**frẹmd-, Frẹmd-: ~herrschaft** *die* foreign domination *no art. or* rule *no art.;* **~kapital** *das* (*Wirtsch.*) outside capital; **~körper** *der* (A) (*Med., Biol.*) foreign body; (B) (*fig.*) **ein ~körper sein/ sich** (*Dat.*) **wie ein ~körper vorkommen** be/feel out of place; **~ländisch** /-lɛndɪʃ/ *Adj.* foreign; (*exotisch*) exotic

**Frẹmdling** *der;* **~s, ~e** (*veralt.*) stranger

**Frẹmd·sprache** *die* foreign language

**Frẹmdsprachen-: ~korrespondentin** *die* ▶ 159 | bilingual/multilingual secretary; **~unterricht** *der* teaching of foreign languages

**frẹmd-, Frẹmd-: ~sprachig** *Adj.* bilingual/ multilingual ‹staff, secretary›; foreign ‹literature›; foreign-language ‹edition, teaching›; **~sprachlich** *Adj.* foreign-language ‹teaching›; foreign ‹word›; **~stoff** *der* (*Med.*) foreign substance; **~verschulden** *das* involvement of another person; **ein ~verschulden an diesem Unfall ist unwahrscheinlich** it is unlikely that anyone else was involved in the accident; **~wort** *das; Pl.* **~wörter** foreign word; **Liebe ist für ihn ein ~wort** (*fig.*) he doesn't know the meaning of the word love; **~wörter·buch** *das* dictionary of foreign words

**frenetisch** /freˈneːtɪʃ/ ❶ *Adj.* frenetic ‹applause›. ❷ *adv.* ‹applaud› frenetically

**frequentieren** *tr. V.* frequent ‹pub, café›; use ‹library›; **eine stark frequentierte Straße** a heavily used road

**Frequenz** /freˈkvɛnts/ *die;* **~, ~en** (A) (*Physik*) frequency; (*Med.: Puls~*) rate; (B) (*Besucherzahl*) **die Schule hat eine geringe ~:** the school has low numbers; **die ~ der Touristen** (*bes. österr., schweiz.*) the number of tourists; **die ~ des Elternabends war gut** attendance at the parents' evening was good; (C) (*Verkehrsdichte*) traffic density

**Frequẹnz-: ~bereich** *der* frequency range; **~modulation** *die* frequency modulation

**Fresko** /ˈfrɛsko/ *das;* **~s, Frẹsken** (*Kunstwiss.*) fresco

**Frẹsko·malerei** *die* (*Kunstwiss.*) fresco; fresco painting

**Fressalien** /frɛˈsaːli̯ən/ *Pl.* (*ugs. scherzh.*) grub (*coll.*)

**Frẹss·beutel,** ***Freß·beutel** *der* (A) (*ugs.: Brotbeutel*) lunch bag; (B) (*für Pferde*) nosebag

**Frẹsse** /ˈfrɛsə/ *die;* **~, ~n** (*derb*) (A) (*Mund*) gob (*sl.*); trap (*sl.*); **eine große ~ haben** (*fig.*) have a big mouth (*coll.*); **die ~ weit aufreißen** (*fig.*) shoot one's mouth off (*sl.*); **[ach] du meine ~!** bloody hell! (*sl.*); **die ~ halten** keep one's trap *or* gob shut (*sl.*); (B) (*Gesicht*) mug (*coll.*); **jmdm. die ~ polieren** smash sb.'s face in (*sl.*); **jmdm. eins vor** *od.* **auf die ~ geben** smash sb. in the face (*sl.*)

**frẹssen** ❶ *unr. tr. V.* (A) ‹animal› eat; (*sich ernähren von*) feed on; **einem Tier zu ~ geben** feed an animal; **sich satt ~:** eat its/ her/his fill; **sich dick [und rund] ~:** get fat by overeating; (B) (*ugs.: verschlingen*) swallow up ‹money, time, distance›; drink ‹petrol›; (C) (*zerstören*) eat away; (D) (*derb: von Menschen*) guzzle; (*fig.*) **er wird dich schon nicht ~** (*salopp*) he won't eat you (*coll.*); **etw. ge~ haben** (*ugs.*) have understood sth.; **jmdn. ge~ haben** (*ugs.*) hate sb.'s guts (*coll.*); **jmdn. zum Fressen gern haben** like sb. so much one could eat him/her. ❷ *unr. itr. V.* (A) (*von Tieren*) feed; **friss, Vogel, oder stirb!** (*fig.*) you've got no option; (B) (*zerstören*) **an etw.** (*Dat.*) **~** ‹rust› eat away at sth.; ‹fire› begin to consume sth.; **Ärger und Sorgen fraßen an ihm** irritation and worry gnawed at him; (C) (*derb: von Menschen*) stuff oneself *or* one's face (*sl.*); **er frisst für drei** he eats enough for three. ❸ *unr. refl. V.* **sich durch/in etw.** (*Akk.*) **~:** eat one's way through/into sth.

**Frẹssen** *das;* **~s** (A) (*Futter*) (*für Hunde, Katzen usw.*) food; (*für Vieh*) feed; (B) (*derb, oft abwertend: Essen*) grub (*coll.*); **das ist ein gefundenes ~ für sie** (*fig.*) that's just what she needed; that's a real gift for her; **erst kommt das ~, dann kommt die Moral** you can't moralize on an empty stomach

**Frẹsser** *der;* **~s, ~** (A) (*Tier*) **ein guter/ langsamer ~:** a good/slow eater; (B) (*derb: Mensch*) hungry mouth to feed

**-fresser** *der;* **~s, ~** (*ugs. abwertend*) **Kommunisten~:** Communist-hater

**Fresserei** *die;* **~, ~en** (*derb abwertend*) guzzling; stuffing; **eine große ~:** a big blowout (*sl.*)

**Frẹsserin** *die;* **~, ~nen** ⇒ **Fresser** B

**frẹss-, *freß-, Frẹss-, *Freß-: ~gier** *die* (*abwertend*) (*bei Tieren*) voracity; (*bei Menschen*) greed; gluttony; **~gierig** *Adj.* voracious ‹animal›; greedy, gluttonous ‹person›; **~korb** *der* (*ugs.*) (A) (*Verpflegungskorb*) picnic basket; (B) (*Geschenkkorb*) hamper; **~lust** *die* (*ugs.*) desire for food; **~napf** *der* feeding bowl; **~paket** *das* (*ugs.*) food parcel; **~sack** *der* (*derb*) greedy pig (*sl.*); **~sucht** *die* [morbid] craving for food; **~trog** *der* [feeding] trough; **~welle** *die* (*scherzh.*) wave of gluttony *or* overeating; **~werk·zeuge** *Pl.* (*Zool.*) trophi

**Frettchen** /ˈfrɛtçən/ *das;* **~s, ~** (*Zool.*) ferret

**Freude** /ˈfrɔydə/ *die;* **~, ~n** (A) joy; (*Vergnügen*) pleasure; (*Wonne*) delight; **~ an etw.** (*Dat.*) **haben** take pleasure in sth.; **~ am Leben haben** enjoy life; **die ~ an der Natur** enjoyment of nature; **das war eine große ~ für uns** that was a great pleasure for us; **eine wahre/reine ~:** a real pleasure *or* joy; **das war nicht gerade eine reine ~ für mich** it was not exactly fun for me; **jmdm. eine ~ machen** *od.* **bereiten** make sb. happy; **etw. aus lauter** *od.* **reiner ~ tun** do sth. out of sheer joy; (*aus Spaß*) do sth. just for the pleasure oft it; **vor ~ hüpfen/in die Hände klatschen** jump for joy/ clap one's hands with joy; **zu unserer ~:** to our delight; **zu meiner ~ kann ich Ihnen mitteilen, dass …** I am pleased to be able to inform you that …; **jmdm. die ~ verderben** spoil sb.'s enjoyment; **seine helle ~ an etw.** (*Dat.*) **haben** be delighted about sth.; **herrlich und in ~n leben** live happily; **geteilte ~ ist doppelte ~** (*Spr.*) a pleasure shared is a pleasure doubled; **Freud und Leid** (*geh.*) joy and sorrow; **mit ~n** with pleasure; (B) *Pl.* (*Annehmlichkeit*) **die ~n des Alltags/der Liebe** the pleasures of everyday life/the joys of love

**Freuden-: ~botschaft** *die* glad news; **~fest** *das* celebration; **ein ~fest feiern** hold a celebration; **~feuer** *das* bonfire; **~gebrüll** *das,* **~geheul** *das,* **~geschrei** *das* cries *or* shouts of joy *pl.;* **~haus** *das* house of pleasure; **~mädchen** *das* (*verhüll.*) woman of easy virtue; **~rausch** *der* transport of joy; **~schrei** *der* cry *or* shout of joy; **einen ~schrei ausstoßen** shout for joy; **~spender** *der* (*geh.*) source of pleasure; **~sprung** *der* joyful leap; **einen ~sprung machen** jump for joy; **~tag** *der* joyous *or* happy day; **~tanz** *der: in* **einen [wilden** *od.* **wahren] ~tanz aufführen** *od.* **vollführen** dance for joy; **~taumel** *der* transport of delight *or* joy; **~träne** *die:* **~tränen weinen** *od.* **vergießen** cry *or* weep tears of happiness *or* joy

**freude-: ~strahlend** *Adj.* beaming with joy; radiant with joy; **mit ~strahlendem Gesicht** beaming with delight *or* joy; **~trunken** *Adj.* (*dichter.*) delirious with joy

**Freudianer** /frɔyˈdi̯aːnɐ/ *der;* **~s, ~, Freudianerin** *die;* **~, ~nen** Freudian

**freudianisch** *Adj.* Freudian

**freudig** ❶ *Adj.* (A) joyful, happy ‹face, feeling, greeting›; joyous ‹heart›; **in ~er Erwartung** in joyful anticipation; (B) (*erfreulich*) delightful ‹surprise›; **ein ~es Ereignis** (*verhüll.*) a happy event; **eine ~e Nachricht** good news; glad tidings (*literary*). ❷ *adv.* **~ erregt** happy and excited; **von etw. ~ überrascht sein** be surprised and delighted about sth.; **etw. ~ tun** do sth. gladly *or* with pleasure; **etw. ~ erwarten** look forward to sth. with pleasure; **jmd./etw. ~ begrüßen** give sb./sth. a warm welcome; **~ arbeiten/seine Pflicht tun** work cheerfully/do one's duty willingly

**-freudig** *Adj.* (A) (*Freude an etw. zeigend*) **lese~:** fond of reading; (B) (*schnell bereit, etw. zu tun*) **experimentier~/kauf~:** keen *or* eager to experiment/buy; **beifalls~/entscheidungs~:** very ready to applaud/take decisions

**Freudigkeit** *die;* **~:** joyfulness; (*Begeisterung*) enthusiasm

**freud·los** ❶ *Adj.* joyless ‹days, existence›; cheerless ‹surroundings›. ❷ *adv.* joylessly; **~ arbeiten** work unenthusiastically

**freudsch, *Freudsch** /frɔytʃ/ *Adj.* Freudian

**freud·voll** ❶ *Adj.* joyful; joyous; happy. ❷ *adv.* joyfully; joyously; happily

**freuen** /ˈfrɔyən/ ❶ *refl. V.* be pleased *or* glad (**über** + *Akk.* about); (*froh sein*) be happy; **ich freue mich über das Geschenk** I am pleased with the present; **sich zu früh ~:** get carried away *or* rejoice too soon; **sich an jmdm./etw. ~** (*geh.*) take pleasure in sb./sth.; **sich auf etw.** (*Akk.*) **~:** look forward to sth.; **sich auf jmdn. ~:** look forward to seeing sb.; **sich mit jmdm. ~:** rejoice with sb.; **sich für jmdn. ~:** be pleased *or* glad for sb.; **ich freue mich, Ihnen mitteilen zu können, dass ...** I am pleased to be able to inform you that ...
❷ *tr. V.* please; **es freut mich, dass ...** I am pleased *or* glad that ...; **freut mich!** pleased to meet you; **es hat mich aufrichtig gefreut, Ihre Bekanntschaft zu machen** I'm delighted *or* very pleased to have met you; **das hat ihn sehr gefreut** he was very pleased about it

f

***freund, Freund** /frɔynt/ (*geh. veralt.*) *in* **jmdm. ~ sein/bleiben** be/remain friends with sb.; **jedem Menschen ~ sein** be a friend to all men

**Freund** *der;* **~es, ~e** Ⓐ friend; **unter ~en sein** be among friends; **jmdn. zu seinen ~en rechnen** regard *or* count sb. as a friend; **~e in der Not gehen hundert** *od.* **tausend auf ein Lot** (*Spr.*) friends are hard to find when you really need them; **~ und Feind** friend and foe; **dicke ~e sein** (*ugs.*) be bosom pals *or* buddies (*coll.*); **du bist mir ja ein feiner ~!** (*iron.*) you're a fine friend!; Ⓑ (*Verehrer, Geliebter*) boyfriend; (*älter*) gentleman friend; Ⓒ (*Anhänger, Liebhaber*) lover; **ein ~ der Musik/Kunst/des Weines** a lover of music/art/wine; **ich bin kein ~ von großen Worten** (*fig.*) I am not one for fine words; Ⓓ (*Anrede*) **~[e]!** my friend[s]!; **hallo, alter ~!** hello, old friend!

**Freundchen** *das;* **~s, ~** (*Anrede;* [*scherzh.*] *drohend*) my friend

**Freundes-: ~hand** *die* (*geh.*) hand of friendship; **~kreis** *der* circle of friends; **im engen ~kreis** among close friends; **~treue** *die* (*geh.*) loyalty as a friend

**Freund-Feind-Denken** *das* us-and-them attitude

**Freundin** *die;* **~, ~nen** Ⓐ friend; Ⓑ (*Geliebte*) girlfriend; (*älter*) lady friend

**freundlich** ❶ *Adj.* Ⓐ (*liebenswürdig*) kind ‹face›; kind, friendly ‹reception›; friendly ‹smile›; fond ‹farewell›; **zu jmdm. ~ sein** be kind to sb.; **er war so ~, mir zu helfen** he was kind *or* good enough to help me; **würden Sie so ~ sein, mir den Weg zum Bahnhof zu zeigen?** would you be so kind *or* good as to show me the way to the station?; **bitte recht ~!** smile, please!; Ⓑ (*angenehm*) pleasant ‹weather, surroundings›; pleasant, congenial ‹atmosphere›; pleasant, mild ‹climate›; **eine ~e Stimmung/Tendenz an der Börse** (*Kaufmannsspr.*) a favourable mood/trend on the Stock Exchange; Ⓒ (*freundschaftlich*) friendly, amiable ‹person, manner›; friendly ‹disposition, attitude, warning›.
❷ *adv.* Ⓐ (*freundschaftlich*) **jmdn. ~ anhören/begrüßen** listen to/greet sb. amiably; **jmdm. ~ danken** thank sb. kindly; **jmdm. ~ gesinnt sein** be well-disposed towards sb.; Ⓑ (*angenehm*) **die Morgensonne schien ~ in das Zimmer** the morning sun cast its friendly light into the room

**-freundlich** *adj.* Ⓐ (*wohlgesinnt*) pro-; **regierungs~:** pro-government; **presse~:** friendly to the press *postpos.;* Ⓑ (*-gerecht*) **familien~/fußgänger~:** catering for the interests of families/pedestrians *postpos., not pred.;* **haut~:** kind to the skin *postpos.;* **benutzer~:** user-friendly

**freundlicher·weise** *Adv.* kindly; **sie hat mich ~ mit dem Auto mitgenommen** she was kind enough to take me in the car

**Freundlichkeit** *die;* **~, ~en** Ⓐ (*Liebenswürdigkeit, Gefälligkeit*) kindness; **würden Sie die ~ haben, mit uns mitzukommen?** would you be so kind as to come with us?; **jmdm. ein paar ~en sagen** to make a few kind remarks to sb.; **jmdm. ~en erweisen** show kindness to sb.; be kind to sb.; Ⓑ (*angenehme Art*) pleasantness; friendliness; (*eines Zimmers, Hauses*) cheerfulness

**freund·nachbarlich** *Adj.* good-neighbourly

**Freundschaft** *die;* **~, ~en** Ⓐ friendship; **die ~ zwischen uns/ihnen** the friendship between us/them; **mit jmdm. ~ schließen** make *or* become friends with sb.; **jmdm. etw. in aller ~ sagen** tell sb. sth. as a friend; Ⓑ (*DDR: Gruß der FDJ*) **~!** *greeting of the Free German Youth organization;* Ⓒ (*DDR: Pioniergruppe*) *school branch of the Pioneer organization*

**freundschaftlich** ❶ *Adj.* friendly; amicable; **ein ~er Hinweis** a friendly piece of advice; **mit jmdm. auf ~em Fuße stehen** be on friendly *or* amicable terms with sb. ❷ *adv.* in a friendly way; amicably; **jmdm. ~ auf die Schulter klopfen** give sb. a friendly pat on the shoulder

**Freundschafts-: ~bande** *Pl.* (*geh.*) bonds of friendship; **~besuch** *der* (*bes. Politik*) goodwill visit; **~bezeigung** *die;* **~~, ~~en** (*geh.*) gesture of friendship; **~dienst** *der* service rendered out of friendship; **jmdm. einen ~dienst erweisen** render sb. a service out of friendship; **~pakt** *der* (*Politik*) pact of friendship; **~preis** *der:* **etw. zu einem ~preis verkaufen** sell sth. at a specially reduced price; **~ring** *der* ring given as a token of friendship; **jmdm. einen ~ring schenken** give sb. a ring as a token of friendship; **~spiel** *das* (*Sport*) friendly match *or* game; friendly (*coll.*); **~treffen** *das* (*bes. DDR*) friendly meeting; **~vertrag** *der* (*Politik*) treaty of friendship

**Frevel** /ˈfreːfl̩/ *der;* **~s, ~** (*geh., veralt.*) crime; outrage; **einen ~ an jmdm./etw. begehen** commit a crime against sb./sth.; **~ gegen Gott** sacrilege

**frevelhaft** (*geh.*) ❶ *Adj.* wicked ‹deed, rebellion, person›; criminal ‹stupidity›. ❷ *adv.* wickedly

**freveln** *itr. V.* (*geh.*) **an jmdm./gegen etw. ~:** commit a crime against sb./sth.; **gegen das Gesetz ~:** violate the law

**Frevel·tat** *die* (*geh.*) wicked deed; heinous crime

**freventlich** /ˈfreːfn̩tlɪç/ *Adj.* (*veralt.*) ⇒ **frevelhaft**

**Frevler** *der;* **~s, ~, Frevlerin** *die;* **~in, ~innen** evildoer; wicked person; (*gegen Gott*) sacrilegious person; (*Lästerer*) blasphemer

**frevlerisch** *Adj.* ⇒ **frevelhaft**

**friderizianisch** /frideriˈtsi̯aːnɪʃ/ of Frederick the Great *postpos., not pred.*

**Friede** /ˈfriːdə/ *der;* **~ns, ~n** Ⓐ (*älter, geh.*) ⇒ **Frieden;** Ⓑ (*geh.*) **~ sei mit euch** peace be with you; **~ seiner Asche** (*Dat.*) God rest his soul; **~ auf Erden** peace on earth; **ruhe in ~n** Rest in Peace

**Frieden** *der;* **~s, ~** Ⓐ peace; **[mit dem Feind] ~ schließen** make peace [with the enemy]; **mit jmdm. ~ schließen** make one's peace with sb.; **mitten im ~:** in the middle of peacetime; **der eheliche/häusliche ~:** marital/domestic peace; **zwischen Gegnern ~ stiften** make peace between opponents; **um des lieben ~s willen** for the sake of peace and quiet; **er kann keinen ~ finden** he can find no peace; **der ~ der Natur** the peace *or* tranquillity of nature; **lass mich in ~!** (*ugs.*) leave me in peace!; leave me alone!; **seinen ~ mit jmdm. machen** make one's peace with sb.; **ich traue dem ~ nicht** (*ugs.*) it's too good to be true; Ⓑ (*~sschluss*) peace settlement; **den ~ diktieren** dictate the terms for peace *or* the terms of the peace settlement

**friedens-, Friedens-: ~angebot** *das* peace offer; **~apostel** *der* (*spött.*) peacemaker; **~appell** *der,* **~auf·ruf** *der* appeal for peace; **einen ~appell** *od.* **~aufruf an die Völker richten** call upon the nations to make peace; **~bedingungen** *Pl.* peace terms; terms for peace; **~bemühungen** *Pl.* efforts to bring about peace; **~bewegung** *die* peace movement; **~bruch** *der* violation of the peace; **~demonstration** *die* peace demonstration; **~diktat** *das* dictated peace terms *pl.;* **das ~diktat der Siegermächte** the peace terms dictated by the victorious nations; **~engel** *der* angel of peace (*poet.*); messenger of peace; **~fahrt** *die* (*DDR*) Peace Race; **~forschung** *die* peace studies *pl., no art.;* **~freund** *der,* **~freundin** *die* lover of peace; **~fürst** *der* (*bibl.*) Prince of Peace; **~garantie** *die* guarantee of peace; **~gefährdend** *Adj.* representing a threat to peace *postpos., not pred.;* **~gespräche** *Pl.* peace talks; **~glocken** *Pl.* **die ~glocken läuten** the bells are ringing to proclaim the peace; **~göttin** *die* goddess of peace; **~grenze** *die* (*DDR*) *frontier serving as guarantee of peace, esp. Oder-Neisse-Line;* **~kämpfer** *der,* **~kämpferin** *die* pacifist; **~konferenz** *die* peace conference; **~kundgebung** *die* peace rally; **~kuss, *~kuß** *der* (*kath. Rel.*) kiss of peace; pax; **~lager** *das* (*DDR*) *bloc of peace-loving nations;* **~liebe** *die* love of peace; **~nobel·preis** *der* Nobel Peace Prize; **~pfeife** *die* pipe of peace; **mit jmdm. die ~pfeife rauchen** (*fig.*) make one's peace with sb.; **lasst uns die ~pfeife rauchen!** (*fig.*) let us make peace; **~pflicht** *die* (*Arbeitswelt*) *obligation on employers and unions to avoid conflicts resulting in industrial action while a/the wages agreement is in force;* **~politik** *die* policy of peace; **~richter** *der,* **~richterin** *die: lay magistrate dealing with minor offences;* ≈ Justice of the Peace; **~schluss, *~schluß** *der* peace settlement; **nach dem ~schluss** after the peace settlement had been reached; **~sehnsucht** *die* longing for peace; **~sicherung** *die* peacekeeping; **~stärke** *die* (*Milit.*) peacetime strength; **~stifter** *der,* **~stifterin** *die* peacemaker; **~symbol** *das* symbol of peace; **~taube** *die* dove of peace; **~truppe** *die* peacekeeping force; **~verhandlungen** *Pl.* peace negotiations; peace talks; **~vertrag** *der* peace treaty; **~wille** *der* desire for peace; **~wirtschaft** *die* peacetime economy; **~zeiten** *Pl.* peacetime *sing.*

**fried·fertig** *Adj.* peaceable ‹person, character›; peaceful ‹intentions›; **selig sind die Friedfertigen** (*bibl.*) blessed are the peacemakers

**Fried·fertigkeit** *die;* **~:** peaceableness

**Fried·hof** *der* cemetery; (*Kirchhof*) graveyard; churchyard

**Friedhofs-: ~gärtner** *der,* **~gärtnerin** *die* cemetery gardener; **~kapelle** *die* cemetery chapel; **~ruhe** *die,* **~stille** *die* stillness *or* quiet of the graveyard; (*fig.*) deathly stillness; deathly quiet; **~wärter** *der,* **~wärterin** *die* cemetery attendant

**friedlich** /ˈfriːtlɪç/ ❶ *Adj.* Ⓐ (*nicht kriegerisch*) peaceful; **auf ~em Wege** by peaceful means; Ⓑ (*ruhig, verträglich*) peaceable, peaceful ‹character, person›; peaceful, tranquil ‹life, atmosphere, valley›; **sei ~!** (*ugs.*) be quiet! ❷ *adv.* ‹live, sleep› peacefully; **einen Streit ~ schlichten/beilegen** settle an argument peaceably *or* peacefully

**Friedlichkeit** *die;* **~:** peaceableness; peacefulness; (*der Atmosphäre, eines Tals*) peacefulness; tranquillity

**fried·liebend** *Adj.* peace-loving

**fried·los** ❶ *Adj.* Ⓐ (*geh.: ruhelos*) **er entsagte der ~en Welt** he renounced the unquiet world; Ⓑ (*hist.: geächtet*) outlawed ‹person›. ❷ *adv.* Ⓐ (*geh.: ruhelos*) **~ durchwanderte er die Welt** he wandered through the world, never finding peace; Ⓑ (*hist.: geächtet*) ‹live› as an outlaw

**Friedrich** /ˈfriːdrɪç/ (*der*) Frederick; **~ der Große** Frederick the Great

**Friedrich Wilhelm** *der;* **~~s, ~~s** (*ugs. scherzh.: Unterschrift*) monicker (*coll. joc.*)

**fried·voll** *Adj.* (*geh.*) peaceful; tranquil

**frieren** /ˈfriːrən/ *unr. itr. V.* Ⓐ (*Kälte empfinden*) be *or* feel cold; **erbärmlich/sehr ~:** be freezing/terribly cold; **er fror an den Händen/Beinen** he had [freezing] cold hands/legs; Ⓑ *mit sein* (*gefrieren*) freeze; **das Wasser/der Boden ist gefroren** the water/the ground is *or* has frozen; **steif gefroren sein**

*old spelling (see note on page 1707)

be frozen stiff; **blau gefroren sein** be blue with cold; **C** (*unpers.: Kälte empfinden*) **mich/ihn/sie friert [es]** I am/he/she is cold; **D** (*unpers.: ge~*) **es friert/hat gefroren** it is/was freezing; ⇒ *auch* **Stein**

**Fries** /fri:s/ *der;* **~es, ~e** (*Archit., Textilw.*) frieze

**Friese** /'fri:zə/ *der;* **~n, ~n, Friesin** *die;* **~, ~nen** Frisian

**friesisch** *Adj.* ▶ **696** [East] Frisian

**frigid[e]** /fri'gi:d(ə)/ *Adj.* frigid

**Frigidität** /frigidi'tɛ:t/ *die;* **~:** frigidity

**Frikadelle** /frika'dɛlə/ *die;* **~, ~n** rissole

**Frikandeau** /frikan'do:/ *das;* **~s, ~s** (*Kochk.*) fricandeau

**Frikassee** /frika'se:/ *das;* **~s, ~s** (*Kochk.*) fricassee; **aus jmdm. ~ machen** (*salopp, scherzh.*) make mincemeat of sb. (*coll.*)

**frikassieren** *tr. V.* fricassee

**Frikativ** /frika'ti:f/ *der;* **~s, ~e** (*Sprachw.*) fricative

**Friktion** /frɪk'tsi̯o:n/ *die;* **~, ~en** friction

**frisch** /frɪʃ/ **1** *Adj.* **A** fresh; new-laid ‹egg›; fresh, clean ‹linen›; clean ‹underwear›; wet ‹paint›; **~e Luft schöpfen** *od.* (*ugs.*) **schnappen** get some fresh air; **mit ~en Kräften** with renewed strength; **~en Mut fassen** take heart again; **sich ~ machen** freshen oneself up; **jmdn. auf ~er Tat ertappen** catch sb. red-handed; **die Erinnerung daran ist noch ganz ~:** the memory of it is still quite fresh [in sb.'s mind]; **B** (*munter*) fresh; **~ und munter sein** (*ugs.*) be bright and cheerful; **~, fromm, fröhlich, frei** fresh, pious, cheerful, free (*motto of 19th century physical education enthusiasts*); **C** (*kühl*) fresh ‹wind, breeze›; chilly ‹night, air›; **D** (*leuchtend*) lively ‹colours›.
**2** *adv.* freshly; **~ gelegte Eier** new-laid eggs; **~ gebackenes Brot/gefallener Schnee** freshly baked bread/fallen snow; **Bier, ~ vom Fass** beer straight from the barrel; **~ gewaschen sein** ‹person› have just had a wash; ‹garment› have just been washed; **~ rasiert sein** have just had a shave; **er kommt ~ von der Universität** he has come straight from the university; **er kommt ~ vom Friseur** he has just been to the hairdresser's; **~ geputzte Schuhe/ausgehobene Gräber/gestrichene Bänke** newly cleaned shoes/dug graves/painted seats; **„Vorsicht, ~ gestrichen!"** 'wet paint'; **etw. ~ verputzen lassen** have sth. replastered; **die Betten ~ beziehen** put fresh *or* clean sheets on the beds; **ein ~ gebackenes Ehepaar** (*ugs.*) a newly-wed couple; newly-weds *pl.*; **ein ~ gebackener Doktor** (*ugs.*) a newly qualified doctor; **~ gewagt ist halb gewonnen** (*Spr.*) nothing ventured, nothing gained (*prov.*)

**frisch·auf** *Adv.* (*veralt.*) let us be off

**Frische** *die;* **~ A** freshness; **B** (*Lebhaftigkeit, frisches Aussehen*) **jugendliche ~:** youthful freshness; **geistige ~:** mental alertness; **körperliche ~:** physical fitness; vigour; **in voller körperlicher und geistiger ~:** hale and hearty in mind and body; **in erstaunlicher ~:** with amazing sprightliness; **in rosiger ~:** with a rosy freshness; **bis morgen in alter ~!** (*ugs.*) see you tomorrow!; **C** (*Kühle, Reinheit*) freshness; **~ für den ganzen Tag** all-day freshness; **D** (*von Farben*) liveliness

**Frisch·ei** *das* new-laid egg

**frischen** *tr. V.* (*Hüttenw.*) refine

**frisch-, Frisch-: ~fisch** *der* fresh fish; **~fleisch** *das* fresh meat; ***~gebacken** ⇒ **frisch** 2; **~gemüse** *das* fresh vegetables *pl.*; **~gewaschen** *Adj.* (*präd. getrennt geschrieben*) ⇒ **frisch** 2; **~gewicht** *das* weight when packed; **~halte·beutel** *der* airtight bag; **~halte·packung** *die* airtight pack; **~käse** *der* curd cheese

**Frischling** *der;* **~s, ~e A** (*Jägerspr.*) young boar; **B** (*scherzh.*) new boy *or* girl

**frisch-, Frisch-: ~luft** *die* fresh air; **~luft·zufuhr** *die* fresh air supply; **~milch** *die* fresh milk; **~obst** *das* fresh fruit; **~wasser** *das* fresh water; **~weg** *Adv.* uninhibitedly; **~weg antworten** answer right away; **~zelle** *die* (*Med.*) living cell; **~zellen·therapie** *die* (*Med.*) Niehans's therapy

**Friseur** /fri'zø:ɐ̯/ *der;* **~s, ~e** ▶ **159** **A** hairdresser; (*Herren~*) hairdresser; barber; **B** (*~salon*) (*für Frauen*) hairdresser's (*Brit.*); beauty salon (*Amer.*); (*für Herren*) hairdresser's; barber's; ⇒ *auch* **Bäcker**

**Friseurin** *die;* **~, ~nen** ▶ **159** ⇒ **Friseur** A

**Friseur·salon** *der* hairdressing *or* hairdresser's salon (*Brit.*); (*für Frauen*) beauty salon (*Amer.*); (*für Herren*) barber shop (*Amer.*)

**Friseuse** /fri'zø:zə/ *die;* **~, ~n** ▶ **159** hairdresser

**Frisier·creme** *die* hair cream

**frisieren** /fri'zi:rən/ *tr. V.* **A** **jmdn./sich ~:** do sb.'s/one's hair; **sich ~ lassen** have one's hair done; **[sich** (*Dat.*)**] die Haare ~:** do one's hair; **eine elegant frisierte Dame** an elegantly coiffured lady; **er war immer sorgfältig frisiert** he was always well-groomed; **B** (*ugs.: verfälschen*) doctor ‹reports, statistics›; fiddle (*coll.*) ‹accounts›; **C** (*Kfz-W.*) soup up (*coll.*) ‹engine, vehicle›

**Frisier-: ~haube** *die* (*hood-type*) hairdrier; **~kommode** *die* dressing table; **~salon** *der* ⇒ **Friseursalon**; **~spiegel** *der* dressing table mirror; **~stab** *der* curling tongs *pl.*; **~um·hang** *der* cape

**Frisör** ⇒ **Friseur**

**Frisöse** ⇒ **Friseuse**

**friss, *friß** /frɪs/ *Imperativ Sg. v.* **fressen**

**frisst, *frißt** *2. u. 3. Pers. Sg. Präsens v.* **fressen**

**Frist** /frɪst/ *die;* **~, ~en A** (*Zeitspanne*) time; period; **die ~ für die Anmeldung läuft ab** the time allowed for registration is running out; **[sich** (*Dat.*)**] eine ~ von 3 Wochen setzen** set [oneself] a time limit of 3 weeks; **die ~ verlängern** extend the deadline; **in kürzester ~:** within a very short time; **B** (*begrenzter Aufschub*) extension; **jmdm. drei Tage [als] ~ geben** give sb. three days' time; **eine letzte ~ von einem Monat** a final extension of one month; **C** (*Zeitpunkt*) date; deadline; **[bis] zu dieser ~:** by that date

**fristen** *tr. V.* **ein kümmerliches Dasein** *od.* **Leben ~:** eke out a wretched existence; barely manage to survive

**Fristen-: ~lösung** *die,* **~regelung** *die* abortion limit

**frist-, Frist-: ~gemäß, ~gerecht** *Adj., adv.* within the specified time *postpos.*; (*bei Anmeldung usw.*) before the closing date *postpos.*; **wir bitten Sie um eine ~gerechte Wahrnehmung der Liefertermine** it is requested that delivery dates should be met; **~los 1** *Adj.* instant ‹dismissal›; **2** *adv.* without notice; **jmdn.** *od.* **jmdm. ~los kündigen, jmdn. ~los entlassen** dismiss sb. without notice; **jmdm. ~los die Wohnung kündigen** ask sb. to quit without notice; **~verlängerung** *die* extension [of the/a time limit]

**Frisur** /fri'zu:ɐ̯/ *die;* **~, ~en** hairstyle; hairdo (*coll.*)

***Friteuse** ⇒ **Fritteuse**

***fritieren** ⇒ **frittieren**

**Frittate** /frɪ'ta:tə/ *die;* **~, ~n** (*bes. österr.*) pancake

**Fritte** /'frɪtə/ *die;* **~, ~n** (*ugs.*) chip

**Fritteuse** /fri'tø:zə/ *die;* **~, ~n** deep fryer

**frittieren** /fri'ti:rən/ *tr. V.* deep-fry

**-fritze** /'frɪtsə/ *der;* **~n, ~n** (*ugs., abwertend*) man

**frivol** /fri'vo:l/ *Adj.* **A** (*schamlos*) suggestive ‹remark, picture, etc.›; risqué ‹joke›; earthy ‹man›; flighty ‹woman›; **B** (*leichtfertig*) frivolous; irresponsible

**Frivolität** /frivoli'tɛ:t/ *die;* **~, ~en A** ⇒ **frivol** A: suggestiveness; risqué nature; earthiness; flightiness; **B** (*frivole Bemerkung*) risqué remark

**Frivolitäten·arbeit** *die* (*Handarb.*) tatting

**Frl.** *Abk.* **Fräulein**

**froh** /fro:/ **1** *Adj.* **A** ▶ **369** (*glücklich*) happy; cheerful ‹person, mood›; **jmdn. ~ machen** make sb. happy; cheer sb. up; **~e Ostern** happy Easter; **~e Weihnachten** happy *or* merry Christmas; **~es Fest** happy Christmas/Easter *etc.*; **~en Herzens** with a glad heart; **B** (*ugs.: erleichtert*) pleased, glad (**über** + *Akk.* about); **du kannst ~ sein, dass ...** you can be thankful *or* glad that ...; **da bin ich aber ~ [, dass ...]** I am glad [that ...]; **seines Lebens nicht mehr ~ werden** not enjoy life any more; **der soll seines Lebens nicht mehr ~ werden** we'll make his life a misery; **C** (*erfreulich*) good ‹news›; happy ‹event›.
**2** *adv.* **~ gelaunt** cheerful

**froh-, Froh-: ~botschaft** *die* (*geh.*) glad tidings *pl.*; ***~gelaunt** ⇒ **froh** 2; **~gemut 1** *Adj.* happy; **2** *adv.* happily; in good spirits

**fröhlich** /'frø:lɪç/ **1** *Adj.* ▶ **369** cheerful; happy; **~e Ostern** happy Easter; **~e Weihnachten** happy *or* merry Christmas; **eine ~e Gesellschaft** a happy crowd of people; **~es Treiben** merrymaking; **~e Spiele** fun and games; **~e Tänze** dancing and merrymaking. **2** *adv.* (*unbekümmert*) blithely; cheerfully

**Fröhlichkeit** *die;* **~:** cheerfulness; (*eines Festes, einer Feier*) gaiety

**froh·locken** *itr. V.* (*geh.*) **A** (*Schadenfreude empfinden*) rejoice; gloat; **heimlich ~:** secretly rejoice; **B** (*jubeln*) rejoice; exult; **frohlocket dem Herrn** sing joyfully unto the Lord

**Froh-: ~natur** *die* **A** happy *or* cheerful nature; **B** (*Mensch*) cheerful person; **~sinn** *der* cheerfulness; gaiety

**fromm** /frɔm/, **frommer** *od.* **frömmer** /'frœmɐ/, **frommst...** *od.* **frömmst... 1** *Adj.* **A** pious, devout ‹person›; devout ‹Christian›; **ein ~es Leben führen** lead a devout life; **~e Reden führen** talk piously; **B** (*scheinheilig*) **ein ~er Augenaufschlag** a look of wide-eyed innocence; **~es Getue** pious affectation; **C** (*wohl gemeint*) **eine ~e Lüge** a white lie; **einer ~en Täuschung unterliegen** deceive oneself; **ein ~er Wunsch** a pious hope; **D** (*brav*) docile; **~ wie ein Lamm** meek as a lamb; **E** (*veralt.: rechtschaffen*) worthy ‹person›.
**2** *adv.* (*gläubig*) piously; (*brav*) docilely; **~ und rechtschaffen leben** (*veralt.*) live a worthy life

**Frömmelei** *die;* **~, ~en** (*abwertend*) **A** affected piety; **B** (*Handlung*) sanctimonious act; **~en** sanctimonious behaviour *sing.*

**frömmeln** /'frœml̩n/ *itr. V.* (*abwertend*) affect piety; **eine ~de Betschwester** an over-pious woman; **~des Geschwätz** sermonizing

**frommen** *itr. V.* (*unpers.*) (*veralt.*) **das frommt uns [nicht]** it will avail us [nothing]; ⇒ *auch* **Nutz**

**frömmer** ⇒ **fromm**

**Frömmigkeit** /'frœmɪçkai̯t/ *die;* **~:** piety; devoutness

**Frömmler** /'frœmlɐ/ *der;* **~s, ~, Frömmlerin** *die;* **~, ~nen** (*abwertend*) [pious] hypocrite

**frömmst ...** ⇒ **fromm**

**Fron** /fro:n/ *die;* **~, ~en A** (*hist.*) corvée; **schwere ~ leisten** do hard forced labour; **B** (*geh.: aufgezwungene Mühsal*) drudgery

**Fron·arbeit** *die* ⇒ **Fron** A

**Fronde** /'frõ:də/ *die;* **~, ~n** (*geh.*) [political] faction

**Fron·dienst** *der* **A** ⇒ **Fron** A; **B** (*schweiz.*) voluntary work

**fronen** *itr. V.* **A** (*hist.*) do forced labour; **B** (*geh.: unter Zwang arbeiten*) slave; toil

**frönen** /'frø:nən/ *itr. V.* (*geh.*) **einer Neigung/einem Laster ~:** indulge an inclination/in a vice; **dem Alkohol ~:** indulge one's craving for alcohol; **einem Hobby ~:** devote oneself to a hobby

**Fron·leichnam** (*das*); **~s** [the feast of] Corpus Christi

**Fronleichnams·prozession** *die* Corpus Christi procession

f

**Front** /frɔnt/ *die;* ~, **~en** Ⓐ (*Gebäude~*) front; façade; Ⓑ (*Kampfgebiet*) front [line]; **an die ~ gehen** go to the front; **er war an der ~:** he fought at the front; Ⓒ (*Milit.: vorderste Linie*) front line; **auf breiter ~:** on a broad front; **in vorderster ~ kämpfen** fight at the very front; **die ~en haben sich verhärtet** (*fig.*) attitudes have hardened; **zwischen die ~en geraten** (*fig.*) be caught in the crossfire; **an zwei ~en kämpfen** (*fig.*) fight on two fronts; **klare ~en schaffen** clarify one's position; Ⓓ (*Milit.: einer Truppe*) **die ~ abnehmen/abschreiten** inspect the troops/guard of honour *etc.*; **gegen jmdn./etw. ~ machen** (*fig.*) make a stand against sb./sth.; Ⓔ (*Sport*) **in ~ [liegen]** [be] in front *or* in the lead; **in ~ gehen** go in front; **die Mannschaft lag mit 5:0 in ~:** the team was leading 5-0; Ⓕ (*Gruppe*) front; **die Nationale ~** (*DDR*) the National Front; Ⓖ (*Met.*) front

**Front·abschnitt** *der* (*Milit.*) sector of the front

**frontal** /frɔnˈtaːl/ ❶ *Adj.* Ⓐ (*von vorn*) head-on ‹collision›; Ⓑ (*nach vorn*) frontal ‹attack›. ❷ *adv.* ‹collide› head-on; ‹attack› from the front

**Frontal-:** **~an·griff** *der* frontal attack; **zum ~angriff übergehen** go over into a frontal attack; **~unterricht** *der* (*Päd.*) teacher-centred teaching; **~zusammenstoß** *der* head-on collision

**Front-:** **~an·trieb** *der* (*Kfz-W.*) front-wheel drive; **~begradigung** *die* (*Milit.*) straightening of the front; **~bericht** *der* (*Milit.*) report *or* dispatch from the front; **~dienst** *der* (*Milit.*) front-line service; service at the front; **~ein·satz** *der* (*Milit.*) front-line action; **~erfahrung** *die* (*Milit.*) experience of the front; **~frau** *die* frontwoman

**Frontispiz** /frɔntiˈspiːts/ *das;* **~es, ~e** Ⓐ (*Archit.*) pediment; frontispiece; Ⓑ (*Buchw.*) frontispiece

**Front-:** **~kämpfer** *der* (*Milit.*) front-line soldier; **~linie** *die* (*Milit.*) front line; **~mann** *der* frontman; **~scheibe** *die* windscreen (*Brit.*); windshield (*Amer.*); **~seite** *die* front page; **~soldat** *der* (*Milit.*) front-line soldier; **~stellung** *die* Ⓐ (*entschiedene Gegnerschaft*) hostile stance; Ⓑ (*Fechten*) guard position; **~urlaub** *der* (*Milit.*) leave from the front; **~wechsel** *der* (*fig.*) U-turn; volte-face

**fror** /froːɐ̯/ *1. u. 3. Pers. Sg. Prät. v.* **frieren**

**Frosch** /frɔʃ/ *der;* **~[e]s, Frösche** /ˈfrœʃə/ Ⓐ frog; **einen ~ in der Kehle** *od.* **im Hals haben** have a frog in one's throat; **sei kein ~** (*ugs.*) don't be a spoilsport; Ⓑ (*Musik*) nut; Ⓒ ⇒ **Knallfrosch**

**Frosch-:** **~auge** *das* [frog's] eye; **[richtige] ~augen haben** (*fig.*) have [real] goggle-eyes; **~hüpfen** *das;* **~~s** leapfrog; **~klemme** *die* (*Technik*) stone tongs; nippers *pl.;* **~könig** *der* Frog Prince; **~laich** *der* frogspawn; **~löffel** *der* (*Bot.*) water plantain; **~lurch** *der* (*Zool.*) anuran; salientian; **~mann** *der* frogman; **~perspektive** *die* worm's-eye view; **etw. aus der ~perspektive fotografieren** make a low-angle shot of sth.; **etw. aus der ~perspektive betrachten** (*fig.*) take a very narrow view of sth.; **~schenkel** *der* frog's leg; **~teich** *der* frog pond; **~test** *der* (*Med.*) male frog test

**Frost** /frɔst/ *der;* **~[e]s, Fröste** /ˈfrœstə/ Ⓐ frost; **es herrscht** *od.* **ist [strenger] ~:** there is a [severe] frost; it is [very] frosty; Ⓑ (*Kälteempfindung*) fit of shivering

**frost-, Frost-:** **~anfällig** *Adj.* sensitive *or* susceptible to frost *postpos.;* **~auf·bruch** *der* frost damage *no indef. art.;* **wegen der ~aufbrüche** because of the frost damage; **~beständig** *Adj.* frost-resistant; **~beule** *die* chilblain; **~boden** *der* frozen soil; (*ständig*) permafrost; **~ein·bruch** *der* sudden frost

**frösteln** /ˈfrœstl̩n/ *itr. V.* Ⓐ feel chilly; **vor Kälte/Müdigkeit ~:** shiver with cold/tiredness; **mich überkommt** *od.* **durchläuft ein Frösteln:** I feel a sudden chill; Ⓑ (*unpers.*) **es fröstelt ihn, ihn fröstelt** he feels chilly

**frosten** *tr. V.* (*fachspr.*) deep-freeze

**Froster** *der;* **~s, ~:** freezing compartment

**frost-, Frost-:** **~frei** *Adj.* **ein ~freier Winter** a winter without frost; **die Nacht war ~frei** there was no frost during the night; **~gefahr** *die* danger of frost; **~grenze** *die* (*Met.*) 0 °C isotherm; (*Geol.*) frost line

**frostig** /ˈfrɔstɪç/ ❶ *Adj.* (*auch fig.*) frosty. ❷ *adv.* frostily; **sie lächelte ~:** she smiled frostily *or* icily; **jmdn. ~ empfangen** give sb. a frosty reception

**Frostigkeit** *die;* **~:** frostiness

**frost-, Frost-:** **~klirrend** *Adj.* crisp and frosty; **~salbe** *die* chilblain ointment; **~schaden** *der* frost damage; **durch die vielen ~schäden** due to extensive frost damage; **~schutz** *der* frost protection; protection from frost; **~schutz·mittel** *das* Ⓐ frost protection agent; Ⓑ (*Kfz-W.*) antifreeze; **~sicher** *Adj.* frostproof; **~warnung** *die* (*Met.*) frost warning; **~wetter** *das* freezing weather; frost

**Frottee** /frɔˈteː/ *das u. der;* **~s, ~s** terry towelling

**Frottee-:** **~handtuch** *das* terry towel; **~kleid** *das* towelling dress

**Frottier-** /frɔˈtiːɐ̯-/ ⇒ **Frottee-**

**frottieren** /frɔˈtiːrən/ *tr. V.* rub; towel; **sich ~:** rub oneself down

**Frotzelei** *die;* **~, ~en** (*ugs.*) Ⓐ teasing; Ⓑ (*Bemerkung*) teasing remark

**frotzeln** /ˈfrɔtsl̩n/ ❶ *tr. V.* tease; **jmdn. wegen einer Sache ~:** tease sb. about sth. ❷ *itr. V.* **über jmdn./etw. ~:** make fun of sb./sth.

**Frucht** /frʊxt/ *die;* **~, Früchte** /ˈfrʏçtə/ Ⓐ fruit; **Früchte tragen** (*auch fig.*) bear fruit; **Früchte ansetzen** start to fruit; **jmdm. wie eine reife ~ in den Schoß fallen** drop into sb.'s lap; **verbotene Früchte** (*fig.*) forbidden fruits; **die ~ ihres Leibes** (*fig. geh.*) the fruit of her womb; Ⓑ (*geh.: Ertrag*) fruit; **reiche Früchte tragen** bear rich fruit; Ⓒ (*landsch.: Getreide*) corn; crops *pl.;* **die ~ steht gut/schlecht [auf dem Halm]** the corn is coming on well/looks bad

**frucht·bar** *Adj.* fertile ‹soil, field, man, woman›; prolific ‹breed›; fruitful ‹work, idea›; fruitful, rewarding ‹conversation›; **eine Idee** *usw.* **für etw. ~ machen** allow sth. to benefit from an idea *etc.*

**Fruchtbarkeit** *die;* **~** ⇒ **fruchtbar**: fertility; prolificness; fruitfulness

**Fruchtbarkeits·kult** *der* fertility cult

**frucht-, Frucht-:** **~becher** *der* Ⓐ (*Eisbecher*) fruit sundae; Ⓑ (*Bot.*) cupule; **~blase** *die* ▶ 471 (*Anat.*) amniotic sac; **~bonbon** *das od. der* fruit drop; **~bringend** *Adj.* fruitful; rewarding

**Früchtchen** /ˈfrʏçtçən/ *das;* **~s, ~** (*ugs. abwertend: Tunichtgut*) good-for-nothing; **ein nettes/sauberes ~:** a right good-for-nothing

**Frucht-:** **~ein·waage** *die* net weight [of fruit]; **~eis** *das* fruit ice cream

**fruchten** *tr. V.* **nichts ~:** be no use; be of no avail; **[bei jmdm.] nicht[s] ~:** have no effect [on sb.]

**Frucht-:** **~fleisch** *das* flesh; pulp; **~fliege** *die* fruit fly; **~folge** *die* (*Landw.*) rotation of crops

**fruchtig** *Adj.* fruity

**frucht-, Frucht-:** **~joghurt** *der od. das* fruit yoghurt; **~kapsel** *die* (*Biol.*) capsule; **~knoten** *der* (*Bot.*) ovary; **~los** *Adj.* fruitless, vain ‹efforts›; **alle Anstrengungen blieben ~los** all efforts proved in vain; **~losigkeit** *die;* **~~:** fruitlessness; **~presse** *die* fruit squeezer; **~saft** *der* fruit juice; **~salat** *der* fruit salad; **~säure** *die* fruit acid; **~stand** *der* (*Bot.*) multiple fruit; **~wasser** *das; Pl.* **~wässer** ▶ 471 (*Anat.*) amniotic fluid; waters *pl.* (*coll.*); **~zucker** *der* fruit sugar; fructose

**Fructose** /frʊkˈtoːzə/ *die;* **~** (*Chemie*) fructose

**frugal** /fruˈgaːl/ ❶ *Adj.* frugal. ❷ *adv.* frugally

**früh** /fryː/ ❶ *Adj.* Ⓐ early; **am ~en Morgen/Abend** early in the morning/evening; **von ~er Kindheit an** from early childhood; Ⓑ (*vorzeitig*) premature; **ein ~es Ende finden** come to an untimely end; **einen ~en Tod sterben** die an untimely *or* premature death.
❷ *adv.* Ⓐ early; **~ am Tage/morgens** early in the day/morning; **~ genug kommen** arrive in [good] time; **~er oder später** sooner or later; **seine ~ verstorbene Mutter** his mother, who died young; **der ~ vollendete Dichter Keats** the poet Keats, whose life ended so soon; **ein ~ Vollendeter** one whose genius was cut off by his untimely death; Ⓑ (*morgens*) **heute/morgen/gestern ~:** this/tomorrow/yesterday morning; **um fünf Uhr ~:** at five o'clock in the morning; **von ~ bis spät** from morning till night; from dawn to dusk; ⇒ *auch* **aufstehen**; **früher**

**früh-, Früh-:** **~auf** *in* **von ~auf** from early childhood on[wards]; **~aufsteher** *der;* **~~s, ~~, ~aufsteherin** *die;* **~~, ~~nen** early riser; early bird (*coll.*); **~beet** *das* cold frame; (*geheizt*) [heated] frame; **~christlich** *Adj.* early Christian; **~diagnose** *die* (*Med.*) early diagnosis; **~dienst** *der* early duty; (*im Betrieb*) early shift; **~dienst haben** be on early duty/shift

**Frühe** *die;* **~: in der ~** (*geh.*) in the early morning; **in aller ~:** at the crack of dawn

**Früh·ehe** *die* early marriage

**früher** /ˈfryːɐ/ ❶ *Adj.* Ⓐ (*vergangen*) earlier; former; **in ~en Zeiten** in the past; in former times; **aus ~en Zeiten/Jahrhunderten** from the past/from past centuries; **eine ~e Auflage** an earlier edition; Ⓑ (*ehemalig*) former ‹owner, occupant, friend›. ❷ *adv.* formerly; **~ war er ganz anders** he used to be quite different at one time; **meine Bekannten von ~:** my former acquaintances; **ich kenne ihn [noch] von ~ [her]** I know him from some time ago; **diese Dinge waren ihm von ~ [her] vertraut** he had already been familiar with such things; **an ~ denken** think back

**Früh·erkennung** *die* (*Med.*) early recognition *or* diagnosis

**frühestens** /ˈfryːəstn̩s/ *Adv.* at the earliest; **~ in einer Woche/morgen** in a week/tomorrow at the earliest

**frühest·möglich** /ˈfryːəstˈmøːklɪç/ *Adj.* earliest possible

**früh-, Früh-:** **~geburt** *die* Ⓐ premature birth; Ⓑ (*Kind*) premature baby; **~gemüse** *das* early vegetables *pl.;* **~geschichte** *die* ancient history; **die ~geschichte Europas** the early history of Europe; early European history; **~geschichtlich** *Adj.* **~geschichtliche Funde** finds dating back to early history; **aus ~geschichtlicher Zeit** dating back to early history; **~gottes·dienst** *der* early service; **~herbst** *der* early autumn; **~invalide** *der/die* premature invalid

**Früh·jahr** *das* ▶ 431 spring; **im ~:** in spring

**Frühjahrs-:** **~kollektion** *die* spring collection; **~messe** *die* (*Wirtsch.*) spring trade fair; **~müdigkeit** *die* springtime tiredness; **~putz** *der* spring-cleaning

**früh-, Früh-:** **~kapitalismus** *der* early capitalism *no art.;* **~kapitalistisch** *Adj.* early capitalist; **~kartoffel** *die* early potato; **~kindlich** *Adj.* (*Psych.*) in early childhood *postpos.;* **~konzert** *das* [early] morning concert; **~kultur** *die* Ⓐ (*Geschichte*) early culture; Ⓑ (*Gartenbau*) forcing; **bei der ~kultur wachsen die Pflanzen schneller** when forced, plants grow more quickly

**Frühling** /ˈfryːlɪŋ/ *der;* **~s, ~e** ▶ 431 spring; **im ~:** in [the] spring; **[im] ~ vergangenen/nächsten Jahres** last/next spring; in spring last/next year; **der ~ kommt** spring is coming; **vor dem nächsten ~:** before next spring; **im ~ 1979** in the spring of 1979; **im ~ des Lebens** (*geh.*) in the springtime of one's life; **seinen zweiten ~ erleben** (*fig. iron.*) relive one's youth

*old spelling (see note on page 1707)

**frühlings-, Frühlings-: ~anfang** *der* first day of spring; **~gefühl** *das:* **~gefühle haben/bekommen** (*ugs. scherzh.*) feel/get frisky (*coll.*); **~haft** *Adj.* ▶431 springlike; **~lied** *das* song about spring; **~punkt** *der* (*Astron.*) vernal equinox; **~rolle** *die* (*Kochk.*) spring roll; **~tag** *der* spring day; **~wetter** *das* spring weather; **~zeit** *die* (*geh.*) spring [time]; springtide (*literary*)

**früh-, Früh-: ~messe, ~mette** *die* (*kath. Kirche*) early [morning] mass; **~morgens** /-ˈ--/ *Adv.* early in the morning; **~nebel** *der* early morning fog/mist; **~neu·hoch·deutsch** *das* Early New High German; **~reif** *Adj.* precocious ‹child›; early ‹fruit, vegetables›; **~rente** *die* early retirement pension; **~rentner** *der*, **~rentnerin** *die: person who has retired early;* **~rentner werden/sein** retire/have retired early; **~schicht** *die* early shift; **~schicht haben** be on the early shift; **~schoppen** *der* morning drink; (*um Mittag*) lunchtime drink; **~sommer** *der* early summer; **~sport** *der* early-morning exercise; **~stadium** *das* early stage; **im ~stadium** at an early stage; **~start** *der* (*Sport*) false start

**Früh·stück** *das;* **~s, ~e** Ⓐ breakfast; **das erste ~:** breakfast; **das zweite ~:** mid-morning snack; Ⓑ (*ugs.: Pause*) morning break; coffee break

**frühstücken** ❶ *itr. V.* breakfast; have breakfast; **gut/ausgiebig ~:** have a good/hearty breakfast. ❷ *tr. V.* **Brot/Eier ~:** breakfast on bread/eggs; have bread/eggs for breakfast

**Frühstücks-: ~brot** *das* sandwiches *pl.* [for morning snack]; **~fernsehen** *das* breakfast television; **~fleisch** *das* luncheon meat; **~kartell** *das* (*Wirtsch. Jargon*) informal, illegal cartel; **~pause** *die* morning break; coffee break; **~speck** *der* bacon; bacon rashers *pl.;* **~teller** *der* tea plate

**früh-, Früh-:** ***~verstorben** ⇒ **früh** 2A; ***~vollendet** ⇒ **früh** 2A; **~warn·system** *das* early warning system; **~werk** *das* early work; (*gesamtes*) early works *pl.;* **~zeit** *die* (*einer Kulturstufe*) early period; (*eines Künstlers*) early life; **~zeitig** ❶ *Adj.* Ⓐ (*früh*) early; Ⓑ (*vorzeitig*) premature; untimely ‹death›; **der ~zeitige Winter** the early onset of winter; ❷ *adv.* Ⓐ (*früh*) early; (*im Leben, in der Entwicklung*) at an early stage; **das Verbrechen wurde ~zeitig aufgedeckt** the crime was uncovered at an early stage; **jmdn. ~zeitig benachrichtigen** let someone know in good time; Ⓑ (*vorzeitig*) prematurely; **~zug** *der* early [morning] train; **~zündung** *die* (*Technik*) pre-ignition

**Fruktose** ⇒ **Fructose**

**Frust** /frʊst/ *der;* **~[e]s** (*ugs.*) frustration; **ihre Arbeit war der absolute ~:** her work was a real drag (*coll.*); **der große ~ überkam ihn** he began to feel really browned off (*coll.*)

**Frustration** /frʊstraˈtsi̯oːn/ *die;* **~, ~en** (*Psych.*) frustration

**frustrieren** /frʊsˈtriːrən/ *tr. V.* frustrate

**frustrierend** *Adj.* frustrating

**FS** *Abk.* **Fernschreiben**

**F-Schlüssel** *der* (*Musik*) bass clef; F-clef

**FU[B]** *Abk.* **Freie Universität [Berlin]**

**Fuchs** /fʊks/ *der;* **~es, Füchse** /ˈfʏksə/ Ⓐ fox; **dort sagen sich ~ und Hase** *od.* **die Füchse gute Nacht** (*scherzh.*) it's in the middle of nowhere *or* at the back of beyond; Ⓑ (*ugs.: schlauer Mensch*) **ein schlauer ~:** a sly *or* cunning devil; Ⓒ (*Fell, Pelz*) fox [fur]; Ⓓ (*Pferd*) chestnut; (*heller*) sorrel; Ⓔ (*ugs.: rothaariger Mensch*) carrot-top; Ⓕ (*Tagfalter*) tortoiseshell; Ⓖ (*Studentenspr.*) *first-year member of a student fraternity*

**Fuchs·bau** *der; Pl.* **~e** fox den

**Füchschen** /ˈfʏksçən/ *das;* **~s, ~:** little fox

**fuchsen** ❶ *tr. V.* annoy; vex. ❷ *refl. V.* **sich [über etw.** (*Akk.*)**] ~:** be annoyed [about sth.]

**Fuchs-: ~falle** *die* fox trap; **~fell** *das* fox fur

**Fuchsie** /ˈfʊksi̯ə/ *die;* **~, ~n** (*Bot.*) fuchsia

**fuchsig** *Adj.* Ⓐ (*ugs.: wütend*) mad (*coll.*); furious; Ⓑ ginger ‹hair›

**Füchsin** /ˈfʏksɪn/ *die;* **~, ~nen** vixen

**fuchs-, Fuchs-: ~jagd** *die* fox hunt; (*Schleppjagd*) drag-hunt; **~loch** *das* ⇒ **Fuchsbau**; **~pelz** *der* fox fur; **~rot** *Adj.* ginger; **~schwanz** *der* Ⓐ [fox's] brush; [fox] tail; Ⓑ (*Bot.*) amaranth; love-lies-bleeding; Ⓒ (*Werkzeug*) hand saw; **~teufels·wild** *Adj.* (*ugs.*) livid (*coll.*); hopping mad (*coll.*)

**Fuchtel** /ˈfʊxtl̩/ *die;* **~, ~n** Ⓐ (*ugs.: strenge Zucht*) **jmdn. unter der/seiner ~ haben/halten** have/keep sb. under one's thumb; Ⓑ (*österr.: zänkische Frau*) shrew

**fuchteln** *itr. V.* (*ugs.*) **mit etw. ~:** wave sth. about; **mit etw. vor jmds. Gesicht/Nase ~:** wave sth. in sb.'s face

**fuchtig** /ˈfʊxtɪç/ *Adj.* (*ugs.*) mad (*coll.*); furious

**Fuder** /ˈfuːdɐ/ *das;* **~s, ~** Ⓐ (*Wagenladung*) cartload; Ⓑ (*ugs.: große Menge*) load (*coll.*); Ⓒ (*fachspr.: Weinfass*) tun

**fuder·weise** *Adv.* (*ugs.*) by the ton; **er isst das ~:** he eats tons of it

**fuffzehn** /ˈfʊf-/ (*ugs.*) ⇒ **fünfzehn**

**fuffzig** /ˈfʊftsɪç/ (*ugs.*) ⇒ **fünfzig**

**Fuffziger** *der;* **~s, ~** (*ugs.*) fifty-pfennig piece; **ein falscher ~** (*salopp*) a real crook

**Fug** /fuːk/ *der: in* **mit ~ [und Recht]** rightly; justifiably

**Fuge**[1] /ˈfuːɡə/ *die;* **~, ~n** Ⓐ joint; (*Zwischenraum*) gap; **der Stuhl/Tisch kracht in allen ~n** (*ugs.*) every joint in the chair/table creaks; **aus den ~n gehen** *od.* **geraten/sein** (*fig.*) be turned completely upside down (*fig.*); Ⓑ (*Sprachw.*) juncture

**Fuge**[2] *die;* **~, ~n** (*Musik*) fugue

**fugen** /ˈfuːɡn̩/ *tr. V.* Ⓐ (*verbinden*) join, joint ‹timber›; Ⓑ (*ausfüllen*) point ‹brickwork›; grout ‹tiles›

**fügen** /ˈfyːɡn̩/ ❶ *tr. V.* Ⓐ (*hinzu~*) place; set; **etw. zu etw. ~** (*fig.*) add sth. to sth.; **Wort an Wort ~:** string words together; **sie fügte Masche an Masche** she joined up the stitches one by one; Ⓑ (*geh.: zusammen~*) put together; **aus roten Ziegeln gefügt** built with red bricks; **lose gefügte Bretter** loosely jointed boards; **Bestandteile zu einem Ganzen ~** (*fig.*) join parts together to form a whole; **fest gefügt** (*fig.*) firmly established; Ⓒ (*geh.: bewirken*) ‹fate› ordain, decree; ‹person› arrange; **der Zufall hat es gefügt, dass …** fate decreed that …

❷ *refl. V.* Ⓐ (*sich ein~*) **sich in etw.** (*Akk.*) **~:** fit into sth.; **im Garten fügte sich ein Beet an das andere** in the garden one flower bed followed the next; Ⓑ (*gehorchen*) **sich ~:** fall into line; **sich jmdm./einer Sache** (*Dat.*) **~:** fall into line with sb./sth.; **er muss lernen, sich zu ~:** he must learn to toe the line; **sich in sein Schicksal ~:** submit to *or* accept one's fate; Ⓒ (*geh.: geschehen*) **es fügt sich gut, dass …** it is fortunate that …; **die Umstände scheinen sich günstig zu ~:** circumstances seem to be favourable

**fugenlos** ❶ *Adj.* smooth ‹concrete wall›; **eine ~e Trockenmauer** a dry stone wall with no gaps. ❷ *adv.* **die Tür schließt ~:** the door fits exactly

**Fugen·zeichen** *das* (*Sprachw.*) juncture marker

**füglich** *Adv.* (*veralt.*) with reason; justifiably

**fügsam** ❶ *Adj.* obedient. ❷ *adv.* obediently

**Fügsamkeit** *die;* **~:** obedience

**Fügung** *die;* **~, ~en** Ⓐ **eine ~ Gottes** divine providence; **eine ~ des Schicksals** a stroke of fate; **in etw.** (*Dat.*) **eine glückliche ~ sehen** see providence at work in sth.; Ⓑ (*Sprachw.*) construction

**fühlbar** ❶ *Adj.* Ⓐ noticeable ‹lack, improvement, change, difference›; Ⓑ (*wahrnehmbar*) perceptible ‹touch, sound›. ❷ *adv.* Ⓐ noticeably; Ⓑ (*wahrnehmbar*) perceptibly

**fühlen** /ˈfyːlən/ ❶ *tr., itr. V.* feel ‹pain, warmth, etc.›; **jmdm. den Puls ~:** feel sb.'s pulse; **einen Drang/eine Kraft in sich** (*Dat.*) **~:** feel in oneself an urge/a strength; **jmdn. seine Verachtung ~ lassen** show sb. one's contempt; **[Mitleid] mit jmdm. ~:** feel [sympathy] for sb.

❷ *refl. V.* **sich krank/matt ~:** feel sick/weary; **sich bedroht/verfolgt ~:** feel threatened/persecuted; **sich zu jmdm. hingezogen/von jmdm. abgestoßen ~:** feel drawn to/repelled by sb.; **sich schuldig/betrogen ~:** feel guilty/betrayed; **sich zu etw. berufen ~:** feel called to be sth.; **sich zu etw. verpflichtet ~:** feel obliged *or* an obligation to do sth.; **sich als Künstler ~:** feel oneself to be an artist; feel one is an artist; **der fühlt sich aber** (*ugs.*) he's really pleased with himself.

❸ *itr. V.* (*tastend prüfen*) **nach etw. ~:** feel for sth.

**Fühler** *der;* **~s, ~** Ⓐ (*Tentakel*) feeler; antenna; **seine/die ~ ausstrecken** put out feelers; Ⓑ ⇒ **Mess~**

**Fühl[er]·lehre** *die* feeler gauge

**fühl·los** *Adj.* (*geh. veralt.*) unfeeling

**Fühlung** *die;* **~:** contact; **mit jmdm. ~ bekommen/[auf]nehmen** get into contact with sb.; **mit einer Organisation/Regierung ~ haben** be in contact with an organization/a government

**Fühlungnahme** *die;* **~:** initial contact; **die diplomatische ~ ist erfolgt** diplomatic contact has been established

**fuhr** /fuːɐ̯/ *1. u. 3. Pers. Sg. Prät. v.* **fahren**

**Fuhrbetrieb** *der* ⇒ **Fuhrunternehmen**

**Fuhre** /ˈfuːrə/ *die;* **~, ~n** Ⓐ (*Wagenladung*) load; **eine ~ Sand/Kies** a load of sand/gravel; Ⓑ (*Transport*) (*Taxi*) fare; (*Laster*) trip; journey

**führen** /ˈfyːrən/ ❶ *tr. V.* Ⓐ (*geleiten, bringen*) lead; **jmdn. an der Hand ~/zum Tisch ~:** lead sb. by the hand/to the table; **ein Tier an der Leine ~:** walk an animal on a lead; **jmdn. durch ein Haus/eine Stadt ~:** show sb. around a house/town; **jmdn. ins Theater/zu einem Ball ~:** take sb. to the theatre/to a ball; **durch das Programm führt [Sie] Klaus Frank** Klaus Frank will present the programme; **jmdn. auf die richtige Spur ~:** put sb. on the right track; **eine Klasse zum Abitur ~:** take a class through to Abitur level; **ein Land ins Chaos ~:** plunge a country into chaos; Ⓑ (*verkaufen*) stock, sell ‹goods›; Ⓒ (*durch~*) **Gespräche/Verhandlungen ~:** hold conversations/negotiations; **ein Orts-/Ferngespräch ~:** make a local/long-distance call; **ein unruhiges Leben ~:** lead a turbulent life; **eine glückliche Ehe ~:** be happily married; **einen Prozess [gegen jmdn.] ~:** take legal action [against sb.]; Ⓓ (*verantwortlich leiten*) manage, run ‹company, business, pub, etc.›; lead ‹party, country›; command ‹regiment›; chair ‹committee›; **eine Reisegruppe ~:** be courier to a group of tourists; Ⓔ (*gelangen lassen*) take; **die Straße/Reise führte uns durch einen Wald** the road/journey took us through a forest; **was führt Sie zu mir?** what brings you to me?; Ⓕ (*Amtsspr.*) drive ‹train, motor, vehicle›; navigate ‹ship›; fly ‹aircraft›; Ⓖ (*bewegen*) **die Hand an die Mütze/Stirn ~:** raise one's hand to one's cap/forehead; Ⓗ (*verlaufen lassen*) take; **die neue Autobahn um die Stadt ~:** take the new motorway round the city; Ⓘ (*als Kennzeichnung, Bezeichnung haben*) bear; **etw. in seinem Wappen ~:** have *or* bear sth. on one's coat of arms; **das Auto führt das Kennzeichen …** the car bears the registration number …; **das Schiff führt die schwedische Flagge** the ship is flying the Swedish flag; **einen Titel/Künstlernamen ~:** have a title/use a stage name; **den Titel „Professor" ~:** use the title of professor; Ⓙ (*angelegt haben*) keep ‹diary, list, file›; Ⓚ (*befördern*) carry; **die Leitung führt Gas** the pipe carries gas; **der Lkw führt Kohle** the truck *or* (*Brit.*) lorry is carrying coal; **der Zug führt einen Speisewagen** the train has a dining car; **der Fluss führt Hochwasser** the river is in flood; Ⓛ (*registrieren*) **jmdn. in einer Liste/Kartei ~:** have sb. on a list/on file; **in einer Liste geführt werden** appear on a list; **wir ~ hier keinen Müller** there is no Müller here; Ⓜ (*tragen*) **etw. bei** *od.* **mit sich ~:**

have sth. on one; **eine Waffe/einen Ausweis bei sich ~:** carry a weapon/a pass; Ⓝ (*handhaben*) wield ‹weapon›.
❷ *itr. V.* Ⓐ lead; **die Straße führt nach .../durch ...** the road leads *or* goes to .../goes through ...; **die Brücke führt über den Bach** the bridge goes over the stream; **das Rennen führt über zehn Runden** the race is over ten laps; **das führt zu weit** (*fig.*) that would be taking things too far; Ⓑ (*an der Spitze liegen*) lead; be ahead; **nach Punkten ~:** be ahead on points; **in der Tabelle ~:** be the league leaders; be at the top of the league; **mit 3:1 ~:** be leading 3-1; Ⓒ (*ein Ergebnis haben*) **zu etw. ~:** lead to sth.; **zum Ziel ~:** bring the desired result; **das führt zu nichts** (*ugs.*) that won't get you/us *etc.* anywhere (*coll.*).
❸ *refl. V.* **sich gut/schlecht ~:** conduct oneself *or* behave well/badly; **er wurde frühzeitig aus dem Gefängnis entlassen, weil er sich gut geführt hatte** he got remission for good behaviour

**führend** *Adj.* leading ‹politician, figure, role›; high-ranking ‹official›; prominent ‹position›; **auf einem Gebiet/in einer Sache ~ sein** be a leader in a field/in sth.

**Führer** *der;* **~s, ~** Ⓐ (*Leiter*) leader; **der ~** (*ns.*) the Führer; Ⓑ (*Fremden~*) guide; Ⓒ (*Handbuch*) guide[book] (**durch** to); Ⓓ (*Amtsspr., schweiz.: Fahrer*) driver

**Führer-: ~befehl** *der* (*ns.*) Führer's order; **~eigenschaft** *die* quality of leadership; **~hauptquartier** *das* (*ns.*) Führer's headquarters *pl.;* Hitler's headquarters *pl.;* **~haus** *das* driver's cab

**Führerin** *die;* **~, ~nen** ⇒ **Führer** A, B, D

**führer-, Führer-: ~kult** *der* leader cult; **~los** ❶ *Adj.* Ⓐ (*ohne An~*) leaderless; Ⓑ (*ohne Lenker*) driverless ‹car›; pilotless ‹aircraft›; unmanned ‹boat›; ❷ *adv.* Ⓐ (*ohne An~*) without a leader; Ⓑ (*ohne Lenker*) ⇒ 1 B: without a driver; without a pilot; unmanned; **~natur** *die* Ⓐ leader figure; Ⓑ (*Wesensart*) **er hat eine starke ~natur** he is clearly a born leader; **~persönlichkeit** *die* ⇒ **~natur** A; **~prinzip** *das* (*bes. ns.*) leadership principle

**Führerschaft** *die;* **~:** leadership

**Führer-: ~schein** *der* driving licence (*Brit.*); driver's license (*Amer.*); **den ~schein machen** (*ugs.*) learn to drive; **jmdm. den ~schein entziehen** take away sb.'s licence; ban *or* disqualify sb. from driving; **~schein·entzug** *der* disqualification from driving; driving ban; **~sitz** *der* driving seat; driver's seat; **~stand** *der* driver's cab

**Führ·hand** *die* (*Boxen*) leading hand

**Fuhr-: ~lohn** *der* (*an die Spedition*) carriage charge; (*an den Fahrer*) carriage money; **~mann** *der; Pl.* **~leute** Ⓐ carter; (*einer Kutsche*) driver; Ⓑ (*Astron.*) **der ~mann** the Charioteer; **~park** *der* transport fleet

**Führ·ring** *der* (*Pferdesport*) paddock

**Führung** *die;* **~, ~en** Ⓐ ⇒ **führen** 1 D: management; running; leadership; command; chairmanship; **die politische ~ übernehmen** take over political control *or* the political leadership; Ⓑ (*Fremden~*) guided tour; **an einer ~ teilnehmen** go on a guided tour; Ⓒ (*führende Position*) lead; **auf einem Gebiet/in etw.** (*Dat.*) **die ~ haben** be leading *or* the leader/leaders in a field/in sth.; **in ~ liegen/gehen** (*Sport*) be in/go into the lead; Ⓓ (*Erziehung*) guidance; **eine feste ~:** a firm hand; firm guidance; Ⓔ (*leitende Gruppe*) leaders *pl.;* (*einer Partei*) leadership; (*einer Firma*) directors *pl.;* (*eines Regiments*) commanders *pl.;* Ⓕ (*Betragen*) conduct; **wegen guter ~ vorzeitig entlassen werden** get remission for good behaviour; Ⓖ (*eines Registers, Protokolls usw.*) keeping; Ⓗ (*das Handhaben von Waffen*) wielding; Ⓘ (*Amtsspr.*) (*eines Kfz*) driving; (*eines Flugzeugs*) flying; Ⓙ (*eines Titels usw.*) use; Ⓚ (*Technik*) guide

**Führungs-: ~an·spruch** *der* claim to leadership; **einen ~anspruch erheben** lay claim to the leadership; **~auf·gabe** *die* (*im Betrieb*) management function; (*Politik*) leadership function; **~gremium** *das* executive committee; **~kraft** *die* manager; **~krise** *die* (*Politik*) leadership crisis; (*Wirtsch.*) boardroom crisis; **~rolle** *die* role as leader; **~schiene** *die* (*Technik*) guide rail; **~spitze** *die* (*Politik*) top leadership; (*im Betrieb*) top management; **~stab** *der* (*Milit.*) high command; (*im Betrieb*) top management; **~tor** *das,* **~treffer** *der* (*Sport*) *goal which puts the/a team in the lead;* **das ~tor erzielen** score the goal which puts one's team in the lead; **~wechsel** *der* (*Politik*) change of leadership; (*Wirtsch.*) change of director/directors; **~zeugnis** *das document issued by police certifying that holder has no criminal record*

**fuhr-, Fuhr-: ~unternehmen** *das* haulage business; **~unternehmer** *der,* **~unternehmerin** *die* haulage contractor; **~werk** *das* cart (*drawn by horse[s], ox[en], etc.*); (*veralt.: Wagen*) (*horse-drawn*) carriage; **~werken** *itr. V.* (*ugs.*) **mit etw. ~werken** wave sth. about; **sie ~werkte nervös mit ihrer Handtasche** she fumbled nervously with her handbag

**Fülle** /ˈfʏlə/ *die;* **~** Ⓐ (*große Menge*) wealth; abundance; **eine ~ von Arbeit** an enormous amount of work; **in ~:** in plenty; in abundance; Ⓑ (*Intensität*) **die ganze ~ des Lebens** the fullness *or* richness of life; **die ~ seines Glücks** the extent of his happiness; Ⓒ (*Körper~*) corpulence; (*von Wein*) full-bodiedness; (*von Haar*) fullness; **zur ~ neigen** tend to corpulence; **sie ließ sich mit ihrer ganzen ~ auf das Sofa fallen** she let her whole weight drop on to the sofa

**füllen** ❶ *tr. V.* Ⓐ (*voll machen, an~*) fill; **eine Flasche/ein Glas [mit etw.] ~:** fill a bottle/a glass with sth.; **bis zum Rand gefüllt sein** be full to the brim; **der Saal ist bis auf den letzten Platz/halb gefüllt** the hall is completely/half full; ⇒ *auch* **gefüllt** 2; Ⓑ (*fig.*) fill in ‹gap, time›; Ⓒ (*mit einer Füllung versehen*) stuff ‹fowl, tomato, apple, mattress, toy›; fill ‹tooth›; ⇒ *auch* **gefüllt** 2; Ⓓ (*schütten*) pour; **etw. in Flaschen ~:** bottle sth.; **etw. in Säcke ~:** put sth. into sacks; Ⓔ (*einnehmen*) fill ‹space etc.›. ❷ *refl. V.* (*voll werden*) fill [up]; **sich mit etw. ~:** fill up with sth.

**Füllen** *das;* **~s, ~** (*geh.*) foal

**Füller** *der;* **~s, ~** Ⓐ (*ugs.*) [fountain] pen; Ⓑ (*Zeitungsw.*) filler

**Füll-: ~feder·halter** *der* fountain pen; **~gewicht** *das* net weight; **~horn** *das* horn of plenty; (*fig.*) cornucopia

**füllig** *Adj.* corpulent, portly ‹person›; ample, portly ‹figure›; full ‹face›; ample ‹bosom›

**Füll-: ~masse** *die* filler; **~material** *das* (*Druckw.*) furniture; spacing material

**Füllsel** /ˈfʏlzl̩/ *das;* **~s, ~** Ⓐ (*Lückenfüller*) padding; Ⓑ (*in Lebensmitteln*) filling; (*in Geflügel*) stuffing

**Füllung** *die;* **~, ~en** Ⓐ (*in Geflügel, Paprika*) stuffing; (*in Pasteten, Kuchen*) filling; (*in Schokolade, Pralinen*) centre; (*in Kissen, Matratzen*) stuffing; Ⓑ (*Zahnmed.*) filling; Ⓒ (*Teil der Tür*) panel; Ⓓ (*das Vollmachen*) filling

**Füll·wort** *das; Pl.* **Füllwörter** filler; (*Sprachw., Literaturw.*) expletive

**fulminant** /fʊlmiˈnant/ *Adj.* brilliant

**Fummel** /ˈfʊml̩/ *der;* **~s, ~** (*salopp*) Ⓐ rags *pl.;* Ⓑ (*von Transvestiten*) drag [outfit]; **im ~:** in drag

**Fummelei** *die;* **~, ~en** (*ugs.*) Ⓐ twiddling; **das ist eine furchtbare ~:** it's terribly fiddly; Ⓑ (*Petting*) petting; groping (*coll.*); Ⓒ (*Fußballjargon*) dribbling

**fummeln** ❶ *itr. V.* Ⓐ (*ugs.: fingern*) fiddle; **an etw.** (*Dat.*) **~:** fiddle [around] with sth.; **nach etw. ~:** grope for *or* feel for sth.; Ⓑ (*ugs.: erotisch*) pet; Ⓒ (*Fußballjargon*) dribble. ❷ *tr. V.* **etw. in etw.** (*Akk.*)**/aus etw. ~** (*ugs.*) get sth. in sth./out of sth.

**Fund** /fʊnt/ *der;* **~[e]s, ~e** (*auch Archäol.*) find; (*wissenschaftliche Entdeckung*) discovery

**Fundament** /fʊndaˈmɛnt/ *das;* **~[e]s, ~e** Ⓐ (*Bauw.*) foundations *pl.;* **das ~ legen** *od.* **mauern** lay the foundations; **etw. bis auf die ~e abreißen** raze sth. to the ground; **etw. in seinen ~en erschüttern** (*fig.*) strike at the very foundations of sth.; **das ~ zu etw. legen** (*fig.*) lay the foundations for sth.; **an den ~en rütteln** (*fig.*) rock the very foundations; Ⓑ (*Basis*) base; basis; **ein solides ~ haben** have a solid base

**fundamental** /fʊndamɛnˈtaːl/ *Adj.* fundamental

**Fundamentalismus** *der;* **~:** fundamentalism

**Fundamentalist** *der;* **~en, ~en, Fundamentalistin** *die;* **~, ~nen** fundamentalist; ⇒ *auch* **-in**

**Fundamental·satz** *der* fundamental theorem

**fundamentieren** *tr. V.* (*Bauw.*) **ein Gebäude ~:** lay the foundations of a building; **schlecht fundamentiert sein** (*auch fig.*) have weak foundations

**Fund-: ~amt** *das* (*bes. österr.*), **~büro** *das* lost property office (*Brit.*); lost and found office (*Amer.*); **~gegenstand** *der* Ⓐ ⇒ **~sache**; Ⓑ (*Archäol.*) find; **~grube** *die* treasure house

**Fundi** /ˈfʊndi/ *der;* **~s, ~s,** *die;* **~, ~s** (*ugs.*) fundamentalist

**fundieren** /fʊnˈdiːrən/ *tr. V.* Ⓐ (*geistig begründen, untermauern*) underpin; **ein wissenschaftlich fundierter Vortrag** a scientifically sound lecture; Ⓑ (*geh.: festigen*) sustain; Ⓒ (*finanziell sichern*) strengthen [financially]; **ein gut fundiertes Unternehmen** a [financially] sound business

**fündig** /ˈfʏndɪç/ *Adj.* **~ sein** yield something; **~ werden** make a find; (*bei Bohrungen*) make a strike

**Fund-: ~ort** *der* place *or* site where sth. is/was found; **~sache** *die* article found; **~sachen** lost property *sing.;* **~stätte** *die,* **~stelle** *die* ⇒ **Fundort**; **~unterschlagung** *die* (*Rechtsw.*) larceny by finding

**Fundus** /ˈfʊndʊs/ *der;* **~, ~** Ⓐ (*Requisition*) equipment store; Ⓑ (*Grundstock, -lage*) **einen [reichen] ~ von/an etw.** (*Dat.*) **haben** have a [rich] fund of sth.; **kein eigentlicher geistiger ~:** no real intellectual resources *pl.*

**fünf** /fʏnf/ *Kardinalz.* ▸ **76**, ▸ **752**, ▸ **841** five; **~[e] gerade sein lassen** (*fig. ugs.*) let sth. pass; **man muss manchmal ~[e] gerade sein lassen** (*ugs.*) one has to turn a blind eye sometimes; **es ist ~ Minuten vor zwölf** it is five minutes to twelve; **~ Minuten vor zwölf** (*fig.*) at the eleventh hour; at the last minute; ⇒ *auch* **acht**[1]; **Finger** B; **Sinn** A

**Fünf** *die;* **~, ~en** five; **eine ~ schreiben/bekommen** (*Schulw.*) get an E; ⇒ *auch* **Acht**[1] A, D, E, G; **Zwei** B

**fünf-, Fünf-: ~akter** /-aktɐ/ *der;* **~~s, ~~:** five-act play; **~eck** *das* pentagon; **~eckig** *Adj.* pentagonal; five-cornered

**Fünfer** *der;* **~s, ~** (*ugs.*) Ⓐ (*Geldschein, Münze*) five; Ⓑ (*ugs.: Ziffer*) five; Ⓒ (*Lottogewinn*) five out of six; Ⓓ (*ugs.: Sprungturm*) five-metre board; ⇒ *auch* **Achter** C, D

**fünferlei** *indekl. Gattungsz.* Ⓐ *attr.* five kinds *or* sorts of; five different *attrib.* ‹sorts, kinds, sizes, possibilities›; Ⓑ *subst.* five [different] things

**fünf-, Fünf-: ~fach** *Vervielfältigungsz.* fivefold; quintuple; ⇒ *auch* **achtfach**; **~fache** *das; adj. Dekl.* five times as much; quintuple; ⇒ *auch* **Achtfache**; **~fältig** *Adj.* (*veralt.*) ⇒ **~fach**; **~flach** *das;* **~~s, ~~e, ~flächner** *der;* **~~s, ~~:** pentahedron; **~franken·stück** *das* five-franc piece; **~füßig** *Adj.* (*Verslehre*) five-foot; **~füßiger Jambus/Trochäus** iambic/trochaic pentameter; **~gang·getriebe** *das* five-speed gearbox; **~hebig** *Adj.* (*Verslehre*) ⇒ **~füßig**; **~hundert** *Kardinalz.* ▸ **841** five hundred; ⇒ *auch* **hundert**; **~hundert·jahr·feier** *die* quincentenary; **~jahr[es]·plan** *der* five-year plan; **~jährig** *Adj.* (*5 Jahre alt*)

*old spelling (see note on page 1707)

five-year-old; (*5 Jahre dauernd*) five-year; ⇒ *auch* **achtjährig**; **~jährlich** ❶ *Adj.* five-yearly; quinquennial; ❷ *adv.* every five years; ⇒ *auch* **achtjährlich**; **~kampf** *der* (*Sport*) pentathlon; **der moderne ~kampf** the Modern Pentathlon; **~kämpfer** *der*, **~kämpferin** *die* (*Sport*) pentathlete; **~köpfig** *Adj.* ‹family, crew› of five; five-headed ‹monster›

**Fünfling** /ˈfʏnflɪŋ/ *der;* **~s, ~e** quintuplet; quin (*coll.*)

**fünf-, Fünf-: ~mal** *Adv.* five times; ⇒ *auch* **achtmal**; **~malig** *Adj.* **eine ~malige Wiederholung** five repeats; ⇒ *auch* **achtmalig**; **~mark·schein** *der* ▶ 337 five-mark note; **~mark·stück** *das* ▶ 337 five-mark piece; **~meter·plattform** *die* (*Wasserspringen*) five-metre platform; **~meter·raum** *der* (*Fußball*) goal area; **~pfennig·stück** *das* ▶ 337 five-pfennig piece; **~prozentig** *Adj.* five per cent; **~prozent·klausel** *die: constitutional clause laying down that only parties with more than five per cent of the vote may be represented in parliament;* five per cent clause; **~seitig** *Adj.* five-page ‹letter, leaflet›; ⇒ *auch* **achtseitig**; **~silber** *der;* **~~s, ~~** ⇒ **Fünfsilbler**; **~silbig** *Adj.* five-syllable; pentasyllabic; **~silbler** *der;* **~~s, ~~** (*Verslehre*) five-syllable line; **~stellig** *Adj.* five-figure ‹number, sum›; ⇒ *auch* **achtstellig**; **~stöckig** *Adj.* five-storey *attrib.;* ⇒ *auch* **achtstöckig**; **~strophig** /-ʃtroːfɪç/ *Adj.* of five stanzas *or* verses *postpos., not pred.*

**fünft** /fʏnft/ *in* **wir/sie waren zu ~:** there were five of us/them; ⇒ *auch* **acht**[2]

**fünft...** *Ordinalz.* ▶ 207, ▶ 841 fifth; ⇒ *auch* **acht...**

**fünf-, Fünf-: ~tage·woche** *die* five-day [working] week; **~tägig** *Adj.* five-day; ⇒ *auch* **achttägig**; **~tausend** *Kardinalz.* ▶ 841 five thousand; ⇒ *auch* **tausend**

**Fünfte** *der/die; adj. Dekl.* fifth; **Kaiser Karl V.** *od.* **der ~:** the Emperor Charles V; ⇒ *auch* **Achte**

**fünfteilig** *Adj.* five-part; ⇒ *auch* **achtteilig**

**fünftel** /ˈfʏnftl̩/ *Bruchz.* ▶ 841 fifth; ⇒ *auch* **achtel**

**Fünftel** *das* (*schweiz. meist der*); **~s, ~:** ▶ 841 fifth

***fünfte·mal**, ***fünften·mal** ⇒ **Mal**[1]

**fünftens** /ˈfʏnftn̩s/ *Adv.* fifthly; in the fifth place

**fünf-, Fünf-: ~tonner** *der;* **~~s, ~~:** five-tonner; **~uhr·tee** *der* [afternoon] tea; **~viertel·takt** /-ˈ--/ *der* five-four time; **~zehn** *Kardinalz.* ▶ 76, ▶ 752, ▶ 841 fifteen; ⇒ *auch* **achtzehn**; **~zehn·jährig** *Adj.* (*15 Jahre alt*) fifteen-year-old *attrib.;* (*15 Jahre dauernd*) fifteen-year *attrib.;* ⇒ *auch* **achtjährig**; **~zehnt...** *Ordinalz.* ▶ 207 fifteenth; ⇒ *auch* **acht...**

**fünfzig** /ˈfʏnftsɪç/ *Kardinalz.* ▶ 76, ▶ 841 fifty; ⇒ *auch* **achtzig**

**Fünfzig** *die;* **~:** fifty

**fünfziger** *indekl. Adj.* **die ~ Jahre** the fifties; ⇒ *auch* **achtziger**

**Fünfziger**[1] *der;* **~s, ~** Ⓐ (*ugs.*) fifty-pfennig piece; Ⓑ (*50-jähriger*) fifty-year-old; ⇒ *auch* **Achtziger**[1] B, C

**Fünfziger**[2] *die;* **~, ~** (*ugs.*) Ⓐ (*Briefmarke*) fifty-pfennig/shilling *etc.* stamp; Ⓑ (*Zigarre*) fifty-pfennig cigar

**Fünfziger**[3] *Pl.* fifties; ⇒ *auch* **Achtziger**[3]

**Fünfzigerin** *die;* **~, ~nen** ⇒ **Fünfziger**[1] B

**Fünfziger·jahre** *Pl.* ▶ 76, ▶ 207 fifties *pl.*

**fünfzig-, Fünfzig-: ~jährig** *Adj.* (*50 Jahre alt*) fifty-year-old *attrib.;* (*50 Jahre dauernd*) fifty-year *attrib.;* ⇒ *auch* **achtjährig**; **~pfennig·stück** *das* fifty-pfennig piece

**fünfzigst...** /ˈfʏnftsɪçst.../ *Ordinalz.* ▶ 841 fiftieth; ⇒ *auch* **acht...**; **achtzigst...**

**fungieren** /fʊŋˈgiːrən/ *itr. V.* **als etw. ~** ‹person› act as sth.; ‹word etc.› function as sth.

**Funk** /fʊŋk/ *der;* **~s** Ⓐ (*drahtlose Übermittlung*) radio; **jmdn./etw. über ~** (*Akk.*) **anfordern** ask for sb./sth. by radio; Ⓑ (*Rund~*) radio; **beim ~ sein** (*ugs.*) *od.* **arbeiten** be (*coll.*) *or* work in radio

**Funk-: ~amateur** *der*, **~amateurin** *die* ▶ 159 radio ham; **~anlage** *die* radio set; **~ausstellung** *die* radio and television exhibition; **~bake** *die* radio beacon; **~bearbeitung** *die* radio adaptation; adaptation for radio; **~bericht** *der* radio report; **~bild** *das* radio photograph

**Fünkchen** /ˈfʏŋkçən/ *das;* **~s, ~** ⇒ **Funke** B

**Funk·dienst** *der* radio communication service

**Funke** /ˈfʊŋkə/ *der;* **~ns, ~n** Ⓐ (*glühendes Teilchen*) spark; **~n sprühen** send out a shower of sparks; (*fig.*) ‹eyes› flash; **ein ~n sprühendes Feuer** a fire sending out showers of sparks; **~n sprühend raste die Lok vorbei** the engine thundered past, giving off showers of sparks; Ⓑ (*fig.*) **der ~ der Begeisterung/Revolution** the spark of enthusiasm/revolution; **der auslösende ~ für meinen Entschluss war ...** what finally triggered my decision was ...; **ein/kein ~ *od.* Fünkchen [von] Verstand/Ehrgefühl/Mitleid** a/not a glimmer of understanding/shred of honour/scrap of sympathy; **arbeiten, dass die ~n stieben *od.* fliegen** (*fig.*) work like mad (*coll.*)

**funkeln** /ˈfʊŋkl̩n/ *itr. V.* ‹light, star› twinkle, sparkle; ‹gold, diamonds› glitter, sparkle; ‹eyes› blaze

**funkel·nagel·neu** *Adj.* (*ugs.*) brand new; spanking new (*coll.*)

**funken** /ˈfʊŋkn̩/ ❶ *tr. V.* radio; ‹transmitter› broadcast; **SOS ~:** send out an SOS. ❷ *itr. V.; unpers.* (*fig. ugs.*) **es hat gefunkt** (*es hat Streit gegeben*) the sparks flew; (*die Sache geht in Ordnung*) it's worked out OK (*coll.*); (*man hat sich verliebt*) something clicked between them/us (*coll.*); **es hat bei ihm gefunkt** the penny's dropped [with him] (*coll.*)

**funken-, Funken-: ~bildung** *die* sparking *no art.;* **~entladung** *die* spark discharge; **~fänger** *der* (*Eisenb.*) spark arrester; **~flug** *der* flying sparks *pl.;* **~mariechen** *das;* **~~s, ~~:** red-coat girl (*in Rhenish carnival*); **~regen** *der* shower of sparks; ***~sprühend** ⇒ **Funke** A

**funk·entstören** *tr. V.* fit with a suppressor/suppressors; suppress

**Funk·entstörung** *die* suppression of interference

**Funker** *der;* **~s, ~, Funkerin** *die;* **~, ~nen** ▶ 159 radio operator

**Funk-: ~fern·steuerung** *die* radio control; **~feuer** *das* ⇒ **~bake**; **~gerät** *das* radio set; (*tragbar*) walkie-talkie; **~haus** *das* broadcasting centre; **~kolleg** *das* radio-based [adult education] course; **~meldung** *die* radio message *or* report; **~mess·technik**, ***~meß·technik** *die* radar; **~navigation** *die* radio navigation; **~ortung** *die* radio position-finding; **~peiler** *der;* **~~s, ~~, ~peilerin** *die;* **~~, ~~nen** [radio] direction-finder; **~peilung** *die* [radio] direction-finding; **~sprech·gerät** *das* radiophone; (*tragbar*) walkie-talkie; **~sprech·verkehr** *der* radio telephony; **~spruch** *der* radio signal; (*Nachricht*) radio message; **~station** *die*, **~stelle** *die* radio station; **~stille** *die* radio silence; **bei ihm herrscht ~stille** (*fig.*) he's keeping quiet; **~störung** *die* [radio] interference; (*mit Absicht*) jamming; **~streife** *die* [police] radio patrol; **~streifen·wagen** *der* radio patrol car; **~taxi** *das* radio taxi; **~technik** *die* radio technology; **~telegramm** *das* radio telegram

**Funktion** /fʊnkˈtsi̯oːn/ *die;* **~, ~en** Ⓐ function; Ⓑ (*Tätigkeit, Arbeiten*) functioning; working; **außer/in ~ sein** be out of/in operation; **in ~** (*Akk.*) **treten** come into operation; **jmdn./etw. außer ~ setzen** put sb./sth. out of operation; Ⓒ (*Amt, Stellung*) function; **in seiner ~ als ...** in his function as ...; Ⓓ (*Math., Sprachw.*) function

**funktional** /fʊŋktsi̯oˈnaːl/ ❶ *Adj.* functional. ❷ *adv.* functionally

**Funktionalismus** *der;* **~:** functionalism

**Funktionär** /fʊŋktsi̯oˈnɛːɐ̯/ *der;* **~s, ~e, Funktionärin** *die;* **~, ~nen** official; functionary

**funktionell** /fʊŋktsi̯oˈnɛl/ ❶ *Adj.* functional. ❷ *adv.* functionally

**Funktionen·theorie** *die* (*Math.*) theory of functions

**funktionieren** *itr. V.* work; function; **die gut ~de Organisation** the smooth organization

**funktions-, Funktions-: ~fähig** *Adj.* able to function *or* work *pred.;* **~gerecht** ❶ *Adj.* functional; ❷ *adv.* functionally; **~los** *Adj.* ‹person› without a job to do; functionless ‹equipment, object›; **~los werden** become unnecessary; **~sicher** ❶ *Adj.* operatively sound; ❷ *adv.* properly; **~störung** *die* ▶ 474 (*Med.*) functional disorder; dysfunction; **~tüchtig** *Adj.* working ‹equipment, part›; sound ‹organ›; **~verb** *das* (*Sprachw.*) empty verb; **~wechsel** *der* change in function

**Funk-: ~turm** *der* radio tower; **~verbindung** *die* radio contact; **~verkehr** *der* radio communication; **~wagen** *der* radio patrol car; **~weg** *der:* **auf dem ~weg** by radio

**Funzel** /ˈfʊntsl̩/ *die;* **~, ~n** (*ugs. abwertend*) useless lamp *or* light; **bei dieser ~:** in this gloomy light

**für** /fyːɐ̯/ ❶ *Präp. mit Akk.* Ⓐ for; **~ etw. trainieren/kämpfen** train/fight for sth.; **~ jmdn. bestimmt sein** be meant for sb.; **das ist nichts ~ mich** that's not for me; **Lehrer/Professor/Minister ~ etw. sein** be a teacher/professor/minister of sth.; **zu jung/alt ~ etw. sein** be too young/old for sth.; **~ sich** by oneself; on one's own; **er ist am liebsten ganz ~ sich** he most prefers to be quite alone; **jetzt habe ich eine Küche ganz ~ mich** now I've a kitchen all to myself; **das ist gut ~ Husten** that's good for coughs; **sich ~ jmdn. freuen/schämen** be pleased/ashamed for sb.; **~ etw. verurteilt werden** be condemned for sth.; **etw. ~ 50 DM kaufen** buy sth. for 50 marks; **~ diese Jahreszeit ist es viel zu kalt** it's much too cold for this time of year; **~ 20 Minuten/drei Tage** for 20 minutes/three days; **~ morgen** for tomorrow; **~ immer** for ever; for good; **~ gewöhnlich** usually; **~ nichts und wieder nichts** for absolutely nothing; Ⓑ (*zugunsten*) for; **~ jmdn./etw. stimmen/sein** vote/be for *or* in favour of sb./sth.; **das hat etwas ~ sich** it has something to be said for it; **das Für und Wider** the pros and cons *pl.;* Ⓒ (*als*) **etw. ~ ungültig/zulässig erklären** declare sth. invalid/admissible; **jmdn. ~ tot erklären** declare sb. dead; Ⓓ (*anstelle*) for; **~ jmdn. einspringen** take sb.'s place; **~ zwei arbeiten** do the work of two people; Ⓔ (*als Stellvertreter*) for; on behalf of; **~ jmdn. eine Erklärung abgeben** make an announcement on sb.'s behalf; Ⓕ (*um*) **Jahr ~ Jahr/Tag ~ Tag** year after year/day after day; **Punkt ~ Punkt/Schritt ~ Schritt** point by point/step by step; **Wort ~ Wort** word for word; ⇒ *auch* **was** 1.
❷ *adv.* (*veralt.*) **~ und ~:** for ever [and ever]; unto all generations (*bibl.*)

**Furage** /fuˈraːʒə/ *die;* **~** (*Milit. veralt.*) Ⓐ (*Verpflegung*) rations *pl.;* Ⓑ (*Futter*) forage

**furagieren** *itr. V.* (*Milit. veralt.*) forage

**für·bass**, ***für·baß** *Adv.* (*veralt., noch scherzh.*) onwards; **~ gehen/schreiten** proceed on one's way

**Für·bitte** *die* intercession; **[bei jmdm.] für jmdn. ~ einlegen** intercede [with sb.] for sb.

**Furche** /ˈfʊrçə/ *die;* **~, ~n** Ⓐ furrow; **[mit dem Pflug] ~n ziehen** plough furrows; **~n im Gesicht/auf der Stirn haben** have a furrowed face/brow; Ⓑ (*Wagenspur*) rut; Ⓒ (*Rille*) groove

**furchen** *tr. V.* (*geh.*) Ⓐ (*Linien bilden*) furrow; **die Stirn/die Brauen ~:** furrow one's brow; Ⓑ (*Rillen ziehen*) make ‹ruts›; make ruts in ‹ground, track›

**Furcht** /fʊrçt/ *die;* **~:** fear; **~ vor jmdm./etw. haben** fear sb./sth.; **~ vor Gespenstern haben** be afraid of ghosts; **von ~ erfasst sein** (*geh.*) be seized by fear *or* dread; **jmdm. ~ einflößen** frighten sb.; **aus ~ vor jmdm./etw.** for fear of sb./sth.; **jmdn.**

f

in ~ und Schrecken versetzen fill sb. with terror; terrify sb.

**furchtbar** ❶ *Adj.* Ⓐ awful; frightful; dreadful; ~ aussehen look awful *or* frightful; es war mir ~, das tun zu müssen it was awful [for me] to have to do it; Ⓑ (*ugs.*: *unangenehm*) awful (*coll.*); terrible (*coll.*); ein ~er Angeber/Pedant an awful *or* frightful show-off/pedant (*coll.*). ❷ *adv.* (*ugs.*) awfully (*coll.*); terribly (*coll.*); ~ lachen [müssen] laugh oneself silly (*coll.*); das ist ~ einfach/teuer it's awfully simple/expensive; es dauerte ~ lange it took an awfully long time; jmdn. ~ beschimpfen/verprügeln give sb. an awful talking-to/beating

**furcht·einflößend** *Adj.* frightening; fearsome; es wirkte ~ auf uns it frightened us

**fürchten** ❶ *refl. V.* sich [vor jmdm./etw.] ~: be afraid *or* frightened [of sb./sth.]; es ist/war zum Fürchten: it is/was quite frightening; du siehst in diesem Anzug ja zum Fürchten aus (*scherzh.*) you look quite frightful in that suit.
❷ *tr. V.* fear; be afraid of; jmdn./etw. ~: fear *or* be afraid of sb./sth.; jmdn./etw. fcwegen etw. ~: fear sb./sth. because of sth.; er war als strenger Prüfer gefürchtet he was feared as a strict examiner; ein gefürchteter Kritiker a feared critic; der gefürchtete Augenblick the moment they/we *etc.* had been fearing; Gott ~: fear God; ich fürchte, [dass] ... I'm afraid [that] ...
❸ *itr. V.* für *od.* um jmdn./etw. ~: fear for sb./sth.

**fürchterlich** *Adj.* ⇒ furchtbar

**furcht·erregend** *Adj.* frightening

**furcht·los** ❶ *Adj.* fearless. ❷ *adv.* fearlessly

**Furcht·losigkeit** *die;* ~: fearlessness

**furchtsam** /ˈfʊrçtza:m/ ❶ *Adj.* timid; fearful. ❷ *adv.* timidly; fearfully

**Furchtsamkeit** *die;* ~, ~en timidity; fearfulness

**Furchung** *die;* ~, ~en (*Biol.*) cleavage; segmentation

**fürder[hin]** /ˈfʏrdɐ(hɪn)/ *Adv.* (*veralt.*) in future

**für·einander** *Adv.* for one another; for each other

**Furie** /ˈfu:ri̯ə/ *die;* ~, ~n Fury; er rannte wie von ~n gehetzt davon he ran off as if the devil were on his tail; sie wurde zur ~ (*fig.*) she started acting like a woman possessed; wie ~n gingen sie aufeinander los they went for each other like wildcats

**furios** /fuˈri̯o:s/ *Adj.* (*geh. veralt.*) rousing; stirring

***für·lieb|nehmen** *unr. itr. V.* (*veralt.*) ⇒ *vorliebnehmen

**fürnehm** /ˈfy:ɐ̯ne:m/ *Adj.* (*veralt., scherzh.*) ⇒ vornehm

**Furnier** /fʊrˈni:ɐ̯/ *das;* ~s, ~e veneer

**furnieren** *tr. V.* veneer; [mit] Eiche furniert sein have an oak veneer

**Furore** /fuˈro:rə/ in ~ machen cause a sensation *or* stir

**fürs** /fy:ɐ̯s/ *Präp.* + *Art.* Ⓐ = für das; Ⓑ ~ Erste for the time being

**Für·sorge** *die;* ~ Ⓐ (*umsorgende Hilfe*) care; Ⓑ (*veralt.*: *Sozialhilfe*) welfare; Ⓒ (*veralt.*: *Sozialamt*) social services *pl.*; Ⓓ (*ugs.*: *Unterstützungsgeld*) social security (*Brit.*); welfare (*Amer.*)

**Fürsorge-:** ~amt *das* (*veralt.*) welfare office; ~empfänger *der,* ~empfängerin *die* (*ugs.*) recipient of social security; ~empfänger sein receive social security; ~erziehung *die* upbringing in [local authority] care

**für·sorgend** ❶ *Adj.* caring; thoughtful. ❷ *adv.* caringly; thoughtfully

**Fürsorge·pflicht** *die* (*jur.*) *employer's obligation to ensure the welfare of his/her employees*

**Fürsorger** *der;* ~s, ~, **Fürsorgerin** *die;* ~, ~nen (*veralt.*) welfare worker

**Fürsorge·unterstützung** *die* (*veralt.*) social security (*Brit.*); welfare (*Amer.*)

**für·sorglich** ❶ *Adj.* considerate; thoughtful. ❷ *adv.* considerately; thoughtfully

*old spelling (see note on page 1707)

**Fürsorglichkeit** *die;* ~: considerateness; thoughtfulness

**Für·sprache** *die* support; bei jmdm. für jmdn. ~ einlegen put in a good word for sb. with sb.

**Fürsprech** /ˈfy:ɐ̯ʃprɛç/ *der;* ~s, ~e (*veralt., geh.*) ⇒ Fürsprecher

**Für·sprecher** *der,* **Für·sprecherin** *die* Ⓐ advocate; in jmdm. einen ~ haben have an advocate in sb.; Ⓑ (*schweiz.*) ⇒ Rechtsanwalt

**Fürst** /fʏrst/ *der;* ~en, ~en prince; der ~ der Hölle/Finsternis (*fig.*) the Prince of Hell/Darkness; gehe nie zu deinem ~, wenn du nicht gerufen wirst (*scherzh.*) do not meet trouble half way

**Fürst-:** ~abt *der* (*hist.*) prince-abbot; ~bischof *der* (*hist.*) prince-bishop

**Fürsten-:** ~geschlecht *das,* ~haus *das* royal house; ~hof *der* prince's palace; ~krone *die* prince's coronet; ~spiegel *der: novel giving guidance for the conduct of princes;* ~stand *der* rank of prince

**Fürstentum** *das;* ~s, **Fürstentümer** /-ty:mɐ/ principality; das ~ Liechtenstein/Monaco the Principality of Liechtenstein/Monaco

**Fürstin** *die;* ~, ~nen princess

**fürstlich** ❶ *Adj.* Ⓐ royal; Ⓑ (*fig.*: *üppig*) handsome; lavish. ❷ *adv.* handsomely; lavishly; ~ speisen enjoy a sumptuous meal

**Fürstlichkeit** *die;* ~, ~en royal personage

**Furt** /fʊrt/ *die;* ~, ~en ford

**Furunkel** /fuˈrʊŋkl̩/ *der od. das;* ~s, ~ ▶ 474 boil; furuncle

**Furunkulose** /furʊŋkuˈlo:zə/ *die;* ~, ~n ▶ 474 (*Med.*) furunculosis

**für·wahr** *Adv.* (*geh. veralt.*) of a truth (*arch.*); in truth (*literary*)

**Für·witz** *der;* ~es (*veralt.*) ⇒ Vorwitz

**Für·wort** *das; Pl.* **Fürwörter** pronoun

**Furz** /fʊrts/ *der;* ~es, **Fürze** /ˈfʏrtsə/ (*derb*) fart (*coarse*); einen ~ lassen let off a fart; jeder ~ (*fig.*) the slightest thing

**furzen** *itr. V.* (*derb*) fart (*coarse*)

**Fusel** /ˈfu:zl̩/ *der;* ~s, ~ (*ugs. abwertend*) rotgut (*coll. derog.*)

**Fusel-:** ~geruch *der* (*ugs. abwertend*) smell of cheap alcohol; ~öl *das* fusel oil

**Füsilier** /fyziˈli:ɐ̯/ *der;* ~s, ~e (*schweiz., sonst veralt.*) fusilier

**füsilieren** *tr. V.* (*veralt.*) execute by firing squad

**Fusion** /fuˈzi̯o:n/ *die;* ~, ~en Ⓐ amalgamation; (*von Konzernen*) merger; Ⓑ (*Naturw.*) fusion

**fusionieren** *itr. V.* merge

**Fusionmusic** /ˈfju:ʒənmju:zɪk/ *die;* ~: fusion

**Fusions·reaktor** *der* (*Physik*) fusion reactor

**Fuß** /fu:s/ *der;* ~es, **Füße** /ˈfy:sə/ Ⓐ ▶ 471 foot; (*südd., österr., schweiz.*) leg; sich (*Dat.*) den ~ verstauchen/brechen sprain one's ankle/break a bone in one's foot; mit bloßen Füßen barefoot; with bare feet; jmdm. auf den ~ treten tread on sb.'s foot; zu ~ gehen go on foot; walk; über seine eigenen Füße stolpern trip over one's own feet; gut/schlecht zu ~ sein be a good/bad walker; ich habe keinen ~ vor die Tür gesetzt I did not set foot outside the door; sich (*Dat.*) gegenseitig auf die Füße treten tread on each other's toes; jmdm. auf dem ~e folgen follow at sb.'s heels; bei ~! heel!; nimm die Füße weg! (*ugs.*) move your feet!; Gewehr bei ~ stehen stand with ordered arms; Ⓑ (*fig.*) stehenden ~es (*veralt., geh.*) without delay; instanter (*arch.*); [festen] ~ fassen find one's feet; kalte Füße kriegen (*ugs.*) get cold feet (*coll.*); sich (*Dat.*) die Füße nach etw. ablaufen *od.* wund laufen chase round everywhere for sth.; sich auf eigene Füße stellen stand on one's own feet; auf freiem ~ sein be at large; jmdn. auf freien ~ setzen set sb. free; auf großem ~ leben live in great style; mit jmdm. auf freundschaftlichem/gespanntem ~ stehen *od.* leben be on friendly/less than friendly terms with sb.; jmdm. auf die Füße treten (*ugs.*) give sb. a good talking-to; auf dem ~e folgen follow swiftly; jmdn. auf dem falschen ~ erwischen (*Sportjargon*) wrong-foot sb.; jmdn./etw. mit Füßen treten trample on sb./sth.; jmdm. etw. vor die Füße werfen throw sth. in sb.'s face; jmdm. zu Füßen liegen (*geh.*) (*bewundern*) adore *or* worship sb.; (*anflehen*) go on one's bended knee to sb.; jmdm. etw. zu Füßen legen (*geh.*) lay sth. at sb.'s feet; ⇒ *auch* eigen A; Erde B; fallen A; Gefängnis A; Grab *usw.*; Ⓒ (*tragender Teil*) (*einer Lampe*) base; (*eines Weinglases*) foot; (*eines Schranks, Sessels, Klaviers*) leg; auf tönernen *od.* schwachen *od.* schwankenden Füßen stehen (*fig.*) be unsoundly based; Ⓓ (*eines Berges*) foot; (*einer Säule*) base; Ⓔ *Pl.*: ~ ▶ 265, ▶ 411, ▶ 489 (*Längenmaß*) foot; zwei/drei ~: two/three feet *or* foot; Ⓕ (*Teil des Strumpfes*) foot

**fuß-, Fuß-:** ~abdruck *der; Pl.* ~abdrücke footprint; ~abstreifer, ~abtreter *der;* ~~s, ~~: shoe scraper; ~abwehr *die* (*Ballspiele*) kick save; ~angel *die* mantrap; (*fig.*) trap; er hat sich in den ~angeln dieser Paragraphen verstrickt he has got entangled in these legal clauses; ~bad *das* Ⓐ footbath; Ⓑ (*ugs. scherzh.*) pool in the saucer

**Fuß·ball** *der* Ⓐ (*Ballspiel*) football; soccer; Ⓑ (*Ball*) football; soccer ball

**Fuß·ballen** *der* ▶ 471 the ball of the/one's foot

**Fußballer** *der;* ~s, ~, **Fußballerin** *die;* ~, ~nen footballer; soccer player

**fußballerisch** *Adj.* footballing

**Fußball-:** ~klub *der* ⇒ ~verein; ~mannschaft *die* football team; ~meisterschaft *die* football championship; ~platz *der* football ground; (*Spielfeld*) football pitch; ~schuh *der* football boot; ~spiel *das* Ⓐ football match; Ⓑ (*Sportart*) football *no art.*; ~spieler *der,* ~spielerin *die* football player; ~tor *das* [football] goal; ~toto *das od. der* football pools *pl.*; ~verband *der* football association; ~verein *der* football club

**Fuß-:** ~bank *die; Pl.* ~bänke footstool; ~bekleidung *die* footwear; ~bett *das* footbed; ~boden *der* floor

**Fußboden-:** ~belag *der* floor covering; ~heizung *die* underfloor heating

**fuß-, Fuß-:** ~breit *Adj.* foot-wide; ~breit sein be a foot wide; ~breit *der;* ~~, ~~: foot; er wollte keinen ~breit nachgeben (*fig.*) he would not budge an inch; ~bremse *die* foot brake; ~brett *das* foot rest

**Füßchen** /ˈfy:sçən/ *das;* ~s, ~: [little] foot

**Fussel** /ˈfʊsl̩/ *die;* ~, ~n *od. der;* ~s, ~[n] fluff; ein[e] ~: a piece of fluff; some fluff

**fusselig** *Adj.* covered in fluff *postpos.*; (*ausgefranst*) frayed; sich (*Dat.*) den Mund ~ reden (*salopp*) talk till one is blue in the face (*coll.*)

**fusseln** *itr. V.* make fluff

**fußen** *itr. V.* auf etw. (*Dat.*) ~: be based on sth.

**Fuß·ende** *das* foot

**fuß-, Fuß-:** ~fall *der* kowtow; einen ~fall vor jmdm. machen (*fig.*) kowtow to sb.; ~fällig ❶ *Adj.* humble; ❷ *adv.* Ⓐ sie flehte den Fürsten ~fällig um Gnade an she fell on her knees before the prince, begging him for mercy; Ⓑ (*fig.*) humbly; ~fehler *der* Ⓐ (*bes. Hockey*) kick; Ⓑ (*Tennis*) foot fault; ~fesseln *Pl.* shackles (*on the feet*); ~frei *Adj.* ankle-length ‹dress, skirt, etc.›

**Fußgänger** /-gɛŋɐ/ *der;* ~s, ~: pedestrian

**Fußgänger·brücke** *die* footbridge;

**Fußgängerin** *die;* ~, ~nen ⇒ Fußgänger

**Fußgänger-:** ~tunnel *der* pedestrian subway; ~übergang *der,* ~über·weg *der* pedestrian crossing; ~unter·führung *die* pedestrian subway; ~verkehr *der* pedestrian traffic; ~zone *die* pedestrian precinct

**fuß-, Fuß-:** ~geher *der,* ~geherin *die* (*österr.*) pedestrian; ~gelenk *das* ▶ 471 ankle; ~gymnastik *die* foot exercises *pl.*; ~hebel *der* foot pedal; ~hoch ❶ *Adj.* ankle-high ‹grass etc.›; ankle-deep ‹water etc.›; ❷ *adv.* ‹rise, lie› ankle-deep

**-füßig** /-fyːsɪç/ *adj.* ▶471 -footed ‹animal›; -legged ‹chair, stool, insect›; -foot ‹line›

**fuß-, Fuß-: ~kalt** *Adj.* **das Zimmer ist ~kalt** the room has a cold floor; **~kettchen** *das* anklet; **~knöchel** *der* ▶471 ankle bone; **~krank** *Adj.* **~krank sein/werden** have/get bad feet; **~lage** *die* (*Med.*) footling presentation; **~lappen** *der* foot cloth; **~leiden** *das* foot complaint; **~leiste** *die* skirtingboard (*Brit.*); baseboard (*Amer.*)

**fusslig, *fußlig** ⇨ fusselig

**Füßling** /ˈfyːslɪŋ/ *der;* **~s, ~e** foot (*of sock, stocking*)

**Fuß-: ~marsch** *der* march; **ein ~marsch von zwei Stunden** (*fig.*) two hours' steady walk; **~matte** *die* doormat; **~nagel** *der* ▶471 toenail; **~note** *die* footnote; **~pfad** *der* footpath; **~pflege** *die* foot treatment; (*beruflich*) chiropody; **zur ~pflege gehen** go to the chiropodist's; **~pfleger** *der*, **~pflegerin** *die* ▶159 chiropodist; **~pilz** *der*, **~pilz·erkrankung** *die* ▶474 athlete's foot; **~puder** *der* foot powder; **~punkt** *der* Ⓐ (*Math.*) foot [of the perpendicular]; Ⓑ (*Astron.*) nadir; **~raste** *die* foot rest; **~ring** *der* leg ring; **~rücken** *der* instep; **~sack** *der* footmuff; **~schalter** *der* foot switch; **~schaltung** *die* foot gear change control; **~schemel** *der* footstool; **~schweiß** *der* foot perspiration; **~sohle** *die* ▶471 sole [of the/one's foot]; **meine ~sohlen** the soles of my feet; **~soldat** *der* (*veralt.*) foot soldier; **~spitze** *die:* ▶471 **auf den ~spitzen gehen/stehen** walk/stand on tiptoe; **~sprung** *der* (*ins Wasser*) feet-first jump; **einen ~sprung machen** jump feet first; **~spur** *die* footprint; (*Fährte*) line of footprints; tracks *pl.;* **~stapfen** *der* footprint; **in jmds. ~stapfen** (*Akk.*) **treten** (*fig.*) follow in sb.'s footsteps; **~steig** *der* Ⓐ (*veralt.*) footpath; Ⓑ (*Gehsteig*) pavement (*Brit.*); sidewalk (*Amer.*); **~stütze** *die* foot rest; **~tritt** *der* Ⓐ kick; **jmdm./einer Sache einen ~tritt geben** *od.* **versetzen** (*fig.*) give sb./sth. a kick; **einen ~tritt bekommen** (*fig.*) get a kick in the teeth (*coll.*); Ⓑ (*Auftreten*) **jmdn. an seinem ~tritt erkennen** recognize sb. by his/her step; **~truppe** *die* (*Milit.*) infantry; **~volk** *das* Ⓐ (*hist.*) footmen *pl.;* Ⓑ (*abwertend: Untergeordnete*) lower ranks *pl.;* dogsbodies *pl.* (*coll.*); **~wanderung** *die* ramble; **~waschung** *die* (*kath. Rel.*) pedilavium; foot washing; **~weg** *der* Ⓐ (*Gehweg, Bürgersteig*) footpath; Ⓑ (*Gehen zu ~weg*) walk; **eine Stunde/zwei Stunden ~weg** one hour's/two hours' walk; **~zehe** *die* (*ugs.*) toe

**Fut** /fʊt/ *die;* **~, ~en** (*vulg.*) ⇨ **Fotze** A

**Futon** /ˈfuːtɔn/ *der;* **~s, ~s** futon

**futsch** /fʊtʃ/ *Adj.* (*salopp*) **~ sein** have gone for a burton (*Brit. coll.*)

**Futter**[1] /ˈfʊtɐ/ *das;* **~s** (*Tiernahrung*) feed; (*für Pferde, Kühe*) fodder; **dem Vieh ~ geben** feed the cattle; **gut im ~ sein** *od.* **stehen** (*ugs.*) be well-fed

**Futter**[2] *das;* **~s** Ⓐ (*von Kleidungsstücken*) lining; Ⓑ (*Bauw.*) casing; Ⓒ (*Tech.*) chuck

**Futterage** /fʊtəˈraːʒə/ *die;* **~** (*ugs.*) grub (*coll.*)

**Futteral** /fʊtəˈraːl/ *das;* **~s, ~e** case

**Futter-: ~beutel** *der* nosebag; **~getreide** *das* fodder cereal; forage cereal; **~klee** *der* red clover; **~krippe** *die* manger; (*fig.*) **an der ~krippe sitzen** (*ugs.*) be in clover; **an die ~krippe kommen** (*ugs.*) get on the gravy train (*coll.*); **~mittel** *das* animal food

**futtern** (*ugs.*) ❶ *tr. V.* eat. ❷ *itr. V.* feed; **futtert nur ordentlich!** tuck in; have a good feed

**füttern**[1] /ˈfʏtɐn/ *tr. V.* feed; **Vieh mit etw. ~:** feed cattle on sth.; **„bitte nicht ~!"** 'please do not feed the animals'; **etw. ~:** use sth. for feed; (*für Haustiere*) use sth. for food; **einen Computer mit etw. ~** (*fig.*) feed a computer with sth.; **jmdn. mit Bonbons/Schokolade ~:** stuff sb. with sweets/chocolate

**füttern**[2] *tr. V.* Ⓐ (*mit Futter*[2] *ausstatten*) line; **mit Taft/Seide gefüttert** lined with taffeta/silk; Ⓑ (*ausmauern, auskleiden*) case

**Futter-: ~napf** *der* bowl; **~neid** *der* Ⓐ (*Verhaltensf.*) jealousy [as regards food]; Ⓑ (*fig. ugs.: Neid*) jealousy; envy; **~pflanze** *die* fodder plant; forage plant; **~rübe** *die* mangold; mangel-wurzel; **~silo** *der od. das* fodder silo; **~suche** *die* search for food; **auf ~suche/bei der ~suche** searching for food; **~trog** *der* feeding trough

**Fütterung**[1] *die;* **~, ~en** feeding

**Fütterung**[2] *die;* **~, ~en** (*von Kleidungsstücken*) lining

**Futter·verwerter** *der:* **ein guter/schlechter ~ sein** fatten up well/badly; (*fig. salopp*) ‹person› get fat easily/never get fat

**Futter·verwerterin** *die:* **eine gute/schlechte ~ sein** (*fig. salopp*) ‹person› get fat easily/never get fat

**Futur** /fuˈtuːɐ̯/ *das;* **~s, ~e** (*Sprachw.*) future [tense]; **das erste/zweite ~:** future/future perfect [tense]

**Futurismus** *der;* **~:** Futurism *no art.*

**futuristisch** Ⓐ Futurist; Ⓑ (*die Futurologie betreffend*) futuristic

**Futurologe** /futuroˈloːgə/ *der;* **~n, ~n**, **Futurologin** *die;* **~, ~nen** futurologist

**Futurologie** *die;* **~:** futurology

**Futurum** /fuˈtuːrʊm/ *das;* **~s, Futura** (*veralt.*) ⇨ **Futur**

**F-Zug** /ˈɛf-/ *der* [long-distance] express train

f

# Gg

**g, G** /ge:/ *das;* ~, ~ Ⓐ (*Buchstabe*) g/G; Ⓑ (*Musik*) [key of] G; ⇒ *auch* **a, A**

**g** *Abk.* Ⓐ **Gramm** g; Ⓑ **Groschen**

**gab** /ga:p/ *1. u. 3. Pers. Sg. Prät. v.* **geben**

**Gabardine** /'gabardi:n/ *der;* ~**s** *od. die;* ~**:** gabardine

**gäbe** /'gɛ:bə/ *1. u. 3. Pers. Sg. Konjunktiv II v.* **geben;** ⇒ *auch* **gang**

**Gabe** /'ga:bə/ *die;* ~, ~**n** Ⓐ (*geh.: Geschenk*) gift; present; **eine ~ Gottes** a gift of God; Ⓑ (*Almosen, Spende*) alms *pl.;* (*an eine Sammlung*) donation; **eine milde/fromme ~:** alms *pl.;* **um eine ~ bitten** beg for alms; Ⓒ (*geh.: Begabung, Talent*) gift; **die ~ haben, etw. zu tun** have the gift *or* (*iron.*) knack of doing sth.; Ⓓ (*Med.: Verabreichung*) administration; Ⓔ (*Med.: Dosis*) dose

**Gabel** /'ga:bl̩/ *die;* ~, ~**n** Ⓐ (*Essgerät*) fork; Ⓑ (*Heu~, Mist~*) pitchfork; Ⓒ (*Telefon~*) rest; cradle; Ⓓ (*Fahrrad~*) fork; Ⓔ (*Ast~*) fork; Ⓕ (*Jägerspr.*) fork; Ⓖ (*Deichsel*) shafts *pl.*

**gabel-, Gabel-:** ~**bissen** *der* Ⓐ piece of pickled herring; Ⓑ ⇒ **Appetithappen;** ~**bock** *der* (*Zool.*) pronghorn [antelope]; ~**deichsel** *die* shafts *pl.;* ~**förmig** ❶ *Adj.* forked; ❷ *adv.* **sich ~förmig teilen** fork; ~**frühstück** *das* cold buffet; fork lunch

**gabeln** ❶ *refl. V.* fork; (*fig.: sich teilen*) divide; **ein gegabelter Ast/Stock** a forked branch/stick. ❷ *tr. V.* fork ‹hay, straw›

**Gabel-:** ~**schlüssel** *der* flat spanner; ~**stapler** *der* forklift truck

**Gabelung** *die;* ~, ~**en** fork

**Gabel-:** ~**weihe** *die* (*Zool.*) red kite; ~**zinke** *die* prong

**Gaben·tisch** *der* gift table (*at Christmas and on birthdays*); **ein reich gedeckter ~:** a table overflowing with gifts

**Gabun** /ga'bu:n/ *das;* ~**s,** (*österr.*) **Gabon** /ga'bo:n/ (*das*); ~**s** Gabon

**gack, gack** /'gak 'gak/ *Interj.* cluck, cluck

**gackern** /'gakɐn/ *itr. V.* Ⓐ cluck; Ⓑ (*ugs.: kichern, lachen*) cackle

**Gaffel** /'gafl̩/ *die;* ~, ~**n** (*Seemannsspr.*) gaff

**Gaffel-:** ~**schoner** *der* (*Seemannsspr.*) fore-and-aft schooner; ~**segel** *das* (*Seemannsspr.*) gaff sail

**gaffen** /'gafn̩/ *itr. V.* (*abwertend*) gape; gawp (*coll.*)

**Gaffer** *der;* ~**s,** ~, **Gafferin** *die;* ~, ~**nen** gaper; starer

**Gag** /gɛk/ *der;* ~**s,** ~**s** Ⓐ (*Theater, Film*) gag; Ⓑ (*Besonderheit*) gimmick

**Gagat** /ga'ga:t/ *der;* ~**[e]s,** ~**e** jet

**Gage** /'ga:ʒə/ *die;* ~, ~**n** salary; (*für einzelnen Auftritt*) fee

**gähnen** /'gɛ:nən/ *itr. V.* Ⓐ yawn; **im Saal herrschte ~de Leere** the hall was totally empty; Ⓑ (*geh.: sich auftun*) ‹chasm, abyss› yawn; ‹hole› gape; **ein ~der Abgrund** a yawning abyss

**Gala** /'ga:la, *auch* 'gala/ *die;* ~ Ⓐ (*Festkleidung*) formal dress; gala dress; **sich in ~ werfen** (*ugs. scherzh.*) put on one's best bib and tucker (*coll.*); Ⓑ (~*vorstellung*) gala

**Gala-:** ~**abend** *der* ⇒ ~**vorstellung;** ~**diner** *das* formal dinner; banquet; ~**empfang** *der* gala reception; formal reception

**galaktisch** /ga'laktɪʃ/ *Adj.* galactic; ~**er Nebel** [galactic] nebula

**Galaktose** /galak'to:zə/ *die;* ~, ~**n** (*Biol.*) galactose

*old spelling (see note on page 1707)

**Galan** /ga'la:n/ *der;* ~**s,** ~**e** (*ugs. abwertend*) lover boy (*coll. derog.*)

**galant** /ga'lant/ ❶ *Adj.* Ⓐ (*veralt.*) gallant; Ⓑ (*amourös*) amorous ‹adventure›; ~**e Dichtung** galant poetry (*of the late 17th century*). ❷ *adv.* gallantly

**Galanterie** /galantə'ri:/ *die;* ~, ~**n** (*veralt.*) gallantry

**Galanterie·waren** *Pl.* (*veralt.*) fashion accessories *pl.*

**Gala-:** ~**uniform** *die* full-dress uniform; ~**vorstellung** *die* gala performance

**Galaxie** /gala'ksi:/ *die;* ~, ~**n** (*Astron.*) galaxy

**Galaxis** /ga'laksɪs/ *die;* ~ (*Astron.*) Galaxy

**Gäle** /'gɛ:lə/ *der;* ~**n,** ~**n** Gael

**Galeere** /ga'le:rə/ *die;* ~, ~**n** galley

**Galeeren-:** ~**sklave** *der* galley slave; ~**sträfling** *der* galley slave

**Galeone** /gale'o:nə/ *die;* ~, ~**n** (*hist.*) galleon

**Galerie** /galə'ri:/ *die;* ~, ~**n** Ⓐ gallery; Ⓑ (*scherzh.: beträchtliche Anzahl*) **eine [ganze] ~ von etw.** a [whole] array of sth.; Ⓒ (*bes. österr., schweiz.: Tunnel*) tunnel; Ⓓ (*Teppich*) runner

**Galerist** /galə'rɪst/ *der;* ~**en,** ~**en, Galeristin** *die;* ~, ~**nen** gallery owner

**Galgen** /'galgn̩/ *der* Ⓐ gallows *sing.;* gibbet; **jmdn. zum [Tode am] ~ verurteilen** condemn sb. to [death on] the gallows; **jmdn. an den ~ bringen** (*ugs.*) bring sb. to the gallows; **am ~ enden** end up on the gallows; Ⓑ (*Mikrofon~*) boom

**Galgen-:** ~**frist** *die* reprieve; ~**humor** *der* gallows humour; ~**strick** *der,* ~**vogel** *der* (*ugs. abwertend*) rogue

**Galicien** /ga'li:tsi̯ən/ (*das*); ~**s** Galicia (*in Spain*)

**Galiläa** /gali'lɛ:a/ (*das*); ~**s** Galilee

**Galiläer** /gali'lɛ:ɐ/ (*der*); ~**s,** ~, **Galiläerin** *die;* ~, ~**nen** Galilean

**Galilei** /gali'le:i/ (*der*) Galileo

**Gälin** *die;* ~, ~**nen** ⇒ **Gäle**

**Galions·figur** /ga'li̯o:ns-/ *die* figurehead

**gälisch** /'gɛ:lɪʃ/ *Adj.* ▶ **696** Gaelic

**Galizien** /ga'li:tsi̯ən/ (*das*); ~**s** Galicia (*in E. Europe*)

**Gall·apfel** *der* oak apple; gall

**Galle**[1] /'galə/ *die;* ~, ~**n** Ⓐ ▶ **471** (~*blase*) gall [bladder]; Ⓑ (*Sekret*) (*bei Tieren*) gall; (*bei Menschen*) bile; **bitter wie ~:** extremely bitter; **mir lief die ~ über** *od.* **kam die ~ hoch** (*fig.*) my blood boiled; **seine ~ verspritzen** (*fig.*) give bitter vent to one's feelings

**Galle**[2] *die;* ~, ~**n** (*Bot.*) gall

**galle·bitter** *Adj.* extremely bitter

**Gallen-:** ~**blase** *die* ▶ **471** gall bladder; ~**gang** *der* bile duct; ~**kolik** *die* ▶ **474** biliary colic; ~**leiden** *das* ▶ **474** gall-bladder complaint; ~**stein** *der* ▶ **474** gallstone; ~**wege** *Pl.* biliary tract *sing.;* bile ducts

**Gallert** /'galɐt/ *das;* ~**[e]s** jelly

**gallert·artig** *Adj.* jelly-like

**Gallerte** /ga'lɛrtə/ *die;* ~, ~**n** ⇒ **Gallert**

**Gallien** /'gali̯ən/ (*das*); ~**s** Gaul

**Gallier** /'gali̯ɐ/ *der;* ~**s,** ~, **Gallierin** *die;* ~, ~**nen** Gaul

**gallig** *Adj.* Ⓐ (*bitter*) **einen ~en Geschmack haben, ~ schmecken** taste of bile; Ⓑ (*verbittert*) caustic ‹remark, humour, person›

**Gallions·figur** *die* ⇒ **Galionsfigur**

**gallisch** *Adj.* Gallic

**Gallium** /'gali̯ʊm/ *das;* ~**s** (*Chemie*) gallium

**Gallizismus** /gali'tsɪsmʊs/ *der;* ~, **Gallizismen** Gallicism

**Gallone** /ga'lo:nə/ *die;* ~, ~**n** gallon

**Gall·wespe** *die* (*Zool.*) gall wasp

**Galopp** /ga'lɔp/ *der;* ~**s,** ~**s** *od.* ~**e** Ⓐ (*Gangart*) gallop; **im ~:** at a gallop; **in ~ fallen** break into a gallop; **in vollem** *od.* **gestrecktem ~:** at full gallop; **etw. im ~ machen** (*fig. ugs.*) race through sth.; Ⓑ (*Tanz*) galop

**Galopp·bahn** *die* (*Pferdesport*) racetrack; racecourse

**Galopper** *der;* ~**s,** ~ (*Pferd*) racehorse; (*Reiter*) jockey

**Galopperin** *die;* ~, ~**nen** jockey

**galoppieren** *itr. V.; meist mit sein* gallop; **die ~de Schwindsucht/Inflation** galloping consumption/inflation

**Galopp-:** ~**rennbahn** *die* ⇒ **Galoppbahn;** ~**rennen** *das* (*Pferdesport*) race

**Galosche** /ga'lɔʃə/ *die;* ~, ~**n** galosh

**galt** /galt/ *1. u. 3. Pers. Sg. Prät. v.* **gelten**

**galvanisch** /gal'va:nɪʃ/ *Adj.* galvanic

**Galvaniseur** /galvani'zø:ɐ̯/ *der;* ~**s,** ~**e, Galvaniseurin** *die;* ~, ~**nen** electroplater

**galvanisieren** *tr. V.* electroplate

**Galvano** /gal'va:no/ *das;* ~**s,** ~**s** (*graf. Technik*) electro[type]

**Galvano-:** ~**meter** *das* (*Technik*) galvanometer; ~**plastik** *die* Ⓐ electroforming; Ⓑ (*Druckw.*) electrotyping; ~**skop** *das;* ~~**s,** ~~**e** (*Technik*) galvanoscope

**Gamasche** /ga'maʃə/ *die;* ~, ~**n** gaiter; (*bis zum Knöchel reichend*) spat

**Gamaschen·hose** *die* [pair of] leggings *pl.*

**Gambe** /'gambə/ *die;* ~, ~**n** (*Musik*) viola da gamba

**Gambia** /'gambi̯a/ (*das*); ~**s** the Gambia

**Gambit** /gam'bɪt/ *das;* ~**s,** ~**s** (*Schach*) gambit

**Gamelan** /'ga:məlan/ *das;* ~**s,** ~**s, Gamelang** /'ga:məlaŋ/ *das;* ~**gs,** ~**gs** (*Musik*) gamelan

**Gamet** /ga'me:t/ *der;* ~**en,** ~**en** (*Biol.*) gamete

**Gamma** /'gama/ *das;* ~**[s],** ~**s** gamma

**Gamma-:** ~**funktion** *die* (*Math.*) gamma function; ~**strahlen** *Pl.* (*Physik, Med.*) gamma rays

**Gammel** /'gaml̩/ *der;* ~**s** (*ugs.*) junk (*coll.*)

**Gammelei** *die;* ~ (*ugs.*) drifting around; bumming around (*Amer. coll.*)

**gammelig** /'gam(ə)lɪç/ *Adj.* (*ugs.*) Ⓐ (*ungenießbar*) bad; rotten; **der Fisch/das Fleisch/der Käse ist ~:** the fish/meat/cheese has gone off; Ⓑ (*unordentlich*) scruffy; **~ aussehen/herumlaufen** look scruffy/go round looking scruffy

**Gammel-Look** *der* scruffy *or* untidy look; **sie erschien im ~:** she appeared dressed as a dropout (*coll.*)

**gammeln** /'gamln̩/ *itr. V.* Ⓐ (*ugs.*) (*verderben*) go bad; go off; Ⓑ (*nichts tun*) loaf around; bum around (*Amer. coll.*)

**Gammler** /'gamlɐ/ *der;* ~**s,** ~, **Gammlerin** *die;* ~, ~**nen** (*ugs.*) dropout (*coll.*)

**gammlig** ⇒ **gammelig**

**Gams** /gams/ *die;* ~, ~**en** (*Jägerspr., südd.*) ⇒ **Gämse**

**Gams·bart, Gäms·bart** /'gɛms-/ *der: tuft of chamois hair used as a hat decoration*

**Gams·bock** *der* chamois buck

**Gämse** /ˈgɛmzə/ *die:* ~, **~n** chamois

**gang** /gaŋ/ *in* ~ **und gäbe sein** be quite usual; be the usual *or* accepted thing

**Gang**[1] /gaŋ/ *der;* **~[e]s, Gänge** /ˈgɛŋə/ **A** (*Gehweise*) walk; gait; **jmdn. am ~ erkennen** recognise sb. by the way he/she walks; **gemessenen ~es einherschreiten** (*geh.*) walk with a measured step; **B** (*zu einem Ort*) **einen ~ in die Stadt machen** go to town; **sein erster ~ führte ihn in die Kneipe** the first place he went to was the pub; **jmdn. auf seinem letzten ~ begleiten** (*fig. geh.*) accompany sb. to his/her last *or* final resting place; **einen schweren ~ tun** *od.* **gehen [müssen]** (*fig.*) [have to] do a difficult thing; **C** (*Besorgung*) **ich habe noch einige Gänge zu machen** I still have some errands to do; **jmdm. einen ~ abnehmen** do an errand for sb.; **D** (*Bewegung*) running; **die Maschine hatte einen ruhigen ~:** the machine ran quietly; **etw. in ~ bringen** *od.* **setzen** get sth. going; **etw. in ~ halten** keep sth. going; **in ~ sein** be going; **die Maschine ist in ~:** the machine is running; **in ~ kommen** get going; get off the ground; **E** (*Verlauf*) course; **der ~ der Ereignisse/Verhandlungen** the course of events/negotiations; **seinen [gewohnten] ~ gehen** go on as usual; **im ~[e] sein** be in progress; **gegen ihn ist etwas im ~[e]** (*ugs.*) moves are being made against him; **F** (*Technik*) gear; **den ersten ~ einlegen** engage first gear; **in den ersten ~ [zurück]schalten** change [down] into first gear; **einen ~ zulegen** (*fig. ugs.*) get a move on (*coll.*); **einen ~ zurückschalten** (*fig. ugs.*) take things a bit easier; **G** (*Flur*) (*in Zügen, Gebäuden usw.*) corridor; (*Verbindungs~*) passage[way]; (*im Theater, Kino, Flugzeug*) aisle; **auf dem ~:** in the corridor/hall[-way]; **H** (*unterirdisch*) tunnel; passage[way]; (*im Bergwerk*) gallery; (*eines Tierbaus*) tunnel; (*von Insekten*) gallery; tunnel; **I** (*Kochk.*) course; **J** (*Fechten*) bout; **einen ~ ausfechten** *od.* **austragen** fight a bout; **K** (*Geol.*) vein; seam; **L** (*Technik*) ⇒ **Gewinde~**

**Gang**[2] /gɛŋ/ *die;* ~, **~s** (*Bande*) gang

**Gang·art** *die* walk; way of walking; gait; (*eines Pferdes*) gait; **eine schnellere ~ anschlagen** step up the pace; (*Pferdesport*) increase to a faster pace *or* gait; **eine langsamere ~ einlegen** (*fig.*) take things more easily

**gangbar** *Adj.* passable; **nicht ~:** impassable; **jmdm. einen ~en Weg zeigen** (*fig.*) show sb. a feasible *or* practicable way

**Gängel·band** /ˈgɛŋəl-/ *das: in* **jmdn. am ~ führen** keep sb. in leading reins; **am ~ gehen** be in leading reins

**Gängelei** *die;* ~, **~en** (*ugs.*) spoon-feeding; **sie war seine ~ leid** she was tired of being treated like a child by him

**gängeln** /ˈgɛŋl̩n/ *tr. V.* (*ugs.*) **jmdn. ~:** boss sb. around; tell sb. what to do

**gang·genau** *Adj.* accurate

**Gang·genauigkeit** *die* accuracy

**gängig** /ˈgɛŋɪç/ *Adj.* **A** (*üblich*) common; (*aktuell*) current; **B** (*leicht verkäuflich*) popular; in demand *postpos.*; **C** (*im Umlauf*) current; **D** (*beweglich*) **[wieder] ~ machen** get ‹mechanism› working [again]; loosen [again] ‹lock, screw, etc.›

**Ganglien·zelle** /ˈgaŋ(g)liən-/ *die* (*Med.*) ganglion cell

**Ganglion** /ˈgaŋ(g)liɔn/ *das;* **~s, Ganglien** /ˈgaŋ(g)liən/ (*Med.*) ganglion

**Gangrän** /gaŋˈgrɛːn/ *die;* ~, **~en** *od. das;* **~s, ~e** ▶ 474 (*Med.*) gangrene

**Gang·schaltung** *die* (*Technik*) gear system; (*Art*) gear change; **hat dein Auto Automatik oder ~?** has your car got an automatic or manual gearbox?; **ein Fahrrad mit ~:** a bicycle with gears

**Gangster** /ˈgɛŋstɐ/ *der;* **~s,** ~ (*abwertend*) gangster

**Gangster-:** **~bande** *die* gang [of criminals]; **~boss,** ***~boß** *der* (*ugs.*) gang boss; **~braut** *die* gangster's moll (*coll.*); **~methoden** *Pl.* (*abwertend*) gangster tactics; **~stück** *das* piece of villainy

**Gangstertum** *das;* **~s** gangsterism

**Gangway** /ˈgæŋweɪ/ *die;* ~, **~s** gangway

**Ganove** /gaˈnoːvə/ *der;* **~n, ~n** (*ugs. abwertend*) crook (*coll.*)

**Gans** /gans/ *die;* ~, **Gänse** /ˈgɛnzə/ **A** goose; **B** (*Braten*) [roast] goose; **C** (*abwertend: weibliche Person*) **eine [dumme/alberne/blöde] ~:** a silly goose

**Gänschen** /ˈgɛnsçən/ *das;* **~s,** ~ **A** (*junge Gans*) gosling; **B** (*kleine Gans, naives Mädchen*) little goose

**Gänse-:** **~blümchen** *das* daisy; **~braten** *der* roast goose; **~brust** *die* (*Kochk.*) breast of goose; **~ei** *das* goose egg; **~feder** *die* goose feather; goose quill; **~fett** *das* goose fat; **~füßchen** *das* (*ugs.*) ⇒ **Anführungszeichen**; **~geier** *der* griffon vulture; **~haut** *die* (*fig.*) gooseflesh; goose pimples *pl.*; **eine ~haut bekommen** *od.* **kriegen** get gooseflesh *or* goose pimples; **ihm läuft eine ~haut über den Rücken** a cold shiver runs down his spine; **~junge** *das* gosling; **~kiel** *der* goose quill; **~klein** *das;* **~s** (*Kochk.*) braised trimmings of goose; gänseklein; **~leber** *die* goose liver; **~leber·pastete** *die* pâté de foie gras; **~marsch** *in* **im ~marsch** in single *or* Indian file

**Ganser** /ˈganzɐ/ *der;* **~s,** ~ (*südd., österr.*), **Gänserich** /ˈgɛnzərɪç/ *der;* **~s, ~e** gander

**Gänse-:** **~schmalz** *das* goose dripping; **~wein** *der* (*ugs. scherzh.*) water; Adam's ale *or* wine (*coll. joc.*)

**Ganter** /ˈgantɐ/ *der;* **~s,** ~ (*nordd.*) ⇒ **Gänserich**

**ganz** /gants/ ▶ 841 **1** *Adj.* **A** (*gesamt*) whole; entire; **den ~en Tag/das ~e Jahr** all day/year; **die ~e Welt/Stadt** the whole world/town; **~ Europa/Afrika** the whole of Europe/Africa; **wir fuhren durch ~ Frankreich** we travelled all over France; **diese Arbeit fordert den ~en Mann** this work requires all one's efforts; **~e Arbeit leisten** do a complete *or* proper job; **die ~e Geschichte** *od.* **Sache** (*ugs.*) the whole story *or* business; **B** (*ugs.: alle*) **die ~en Kinder/Leute/Gläser** *usw.* all the children/people/glasses *etc.*; **die ~e Stadt/Straße** everybody in the town/street; **C** (*vollständig*) whole; **~e Zahlen** whole numbers; **eine ~e Note** (*Musik*) a semibreve (*Brit.*); a whole note (*Amer.*); **im Ganzen sechs Tage/drei Jahre** six days/three years in all *or* altogether; **im Ganzen ist seine Leistung gut** on the whole *or* all in all his performance is good; **der ~e Shakespeare** (*ugs.*) the whole of Shakespeare (*coll.*); **D** (*ugs.: ziemlich [viel]*) **eine ~e Menge/ein ~er Haufen** quite a lot/quite a pile; **~e Nächte/Tage** whole nights/days; **E** (*ugs.: unversehrt*) intact; **etw. wieder ~ machen** mend sth.; **F** (*ugs.: nur*) all of; **~e 14 Jahre alt/10 Mark** all of fourteen [years old]/ten marks; **mit ~en drei Mann kann ich die Arbeit unmöglich schaffen** with only three men I can't possibly get the work done; **G** (*richtig*) **ein ~er Mann** a real man; ⇒ *auch* **groß** 1 K; **Herz** B.
**2** *adv.* **A** (*vollkommen*) quite; **etw. ~ Blödes sagen** say sth. really stupid; **das ist mir ~ egal** it's all the same to me; I don't care; **etw. ~ vergessen** completely *or* quite forget sth.; **du bist ja ~ nass!** you're all wet!; **etwas ~ anderes** something quite different; **etw. ~ allein tun** *od.* **machen** do sth. entirely on one's own; **nicht ~:** not quite; **~ deiner Meinung!** I quite agree [with you]; **~ besonders** especially; **er hat sich ~ besonders viel Mühe gegeben** he took particular trouble; **~ wie Sie wollen** just as you like; **sie ist ~ die Mutter/der Vater** she's the image of *or* just like her mother/father; **sie ist ~ Dame** she ist quite the lady; **~ und gar** totally; utterly; **es ist ~ und gar nicht wahr** it is utterly *or* totally untrue; **etw. ~ oder gar nicht machen** do sth. properly or not at all; **ein Buch ~ lesen** read a book from cover to cover *or* all the way through; **B** (*sehr, ziemlich*) quite; **es ist mir ~ recht** it's quite all right with me; **~ gut/nett** quite good/nice; ⇒ *auch* **Ohr**

**Ganze** *das; adj. Dekl.* **A** (*Einheit*) whole; **das ~ im Auge behalten** keep looking at the whole; **etw. als ~s betrachten** see sth. as a whole; **B** (*alles*) **das ~:** the whole thing; **das ~ gefällt mir gar nicht** I don't like anything about it; **aufs ~ gehen** (*ugs.*) go the whole hog (*coll.*); **es geht ums ~:** everything's at stake

**Gänze** /ˈgɛntsə/ *in* **in seiner/ihrer ~** (*geh.*) in its/their entirety; **zur ~** (*bes. österr.*) entirely; completely

**Ganzheit** *die;* ~, **~en** entirety; (*Einheit*) unity; **etw. in seiner ~ erfassen** grasp sth. in its entirety

**ganzheitlich** *Adj.* (*Päd.*) integrated

**Ganzheits-:** **~medizin** *die* holistic medicine; **~methode** *die* (*Päd.*) 'look and say' method; **~psychologie** *die* 'Ganzheit' psychology; holism; **~unterricht** *der* (*Päd.*) integrated teaching

**ganz·jährig** **1** *Adj.* **die ~e Trockenperiode** the dry period lasting all year. **2** *adv.* **~ geöffnet** open throughout the year *or* all the year round

**Ganz·leder** *das* (*Buchw.*) **in ~ [gebunden]** bound in [full] leather

**Ganzleder·band** *der* (*Buchw.*) [full-]leather-bound volume

**ganz·leinen** *Adj.* **A** (*Textilw.*) pure linen; **B** (*Buchw.*) **ein ~er Einband** a cloth binding

**Ganzleinen·band** *der* (*Buchw.*) cloth-bound book

**gänzlich** /ˈgɛntslɪç/ **1** *Adv.* completely; entirely; **~ unangebracht** quite inappropriate *or* out of place. **2** *Adj.* complete; total

**Ganz·massage** *die* whole-body massage

**ganz-, Ganz-:** **~sache** *die* (*Postw., Philat.*) entire; **~seitig** **1** *Adj.* whole-page; **2** *adv.* **~seitig inserieren** (*einmal*) take a whole-page advertisement; (*auf Dauer*) use whole-page advertising; **~tägig** **1** *Adj.* all-day; **eine ~tägige Arbeit** a full-time job; **2** *adv.* all day

**ganz·tags** *Adv.* **~ arbeiten** work full-time

**Ganztags-:** **~beschäftigung** *die* full-time job; **~schule** *die* all-day school; (*System*) all-day schooling *no art.*

**Ganz·wort·methode** *die* (*Päd.*) 'look and say' method

**gar**[1] /gaːɐ̯/ *Adj.* **A** cooked; done *pred.*; **etw. ist ~ [gekocht]/erst halb ~:** sth. is cooked *or* done/only half-cooked *or* half-done; **etw. ~ kochen** cook sth. [until it is done]; **B** (*Landw.*) ready for cultivation *postpos.*; **der Kompost ist ~:** the compost is ready for use

**gar**[2] *Partikel* **A** (*überhaupt*) **~ nicht [wahr]** not [true] at all; **sie konnte ~ nicht anders handeln** there was nothing else at all that she could do; **~ nicht so übel** not bad at all; **das habe ich ~ nicht gewusst** I had no idea that that was so; **~ nichts** nothing at all *or* whatsoever; **ich habe ~ keinen Hunger** I'm not at all *or* not in the least hungry; **~ niemand** *od.* **keiner** nobody at all *or* whatsoever; **~ keines** not a single one; **~ kein Geld** no money at all; **B** (*südd., österr., schweiz.: verstärkend*) **~ zu** only too; **es waren ~ zu viele Leute da** there were just too many people there; **er wäre ~ zu gern gekommen** he would so much have liked to come; **~ so** so very; **sei doch nicht ~ so stur!** don't be so [damned] stubborn; **C** (*geh.: so~*) even; **die Zeitungen setzten sich ~ für den Attentäter ein** the papers even came out in support of the assassin; **ich glaube ~, sie weint** I do believe she's crying; **D** (*geh. veralt.: erst*) **er ist unangenehm genug, und ~ sein Bruder!** he's unpleasant enough, and as for his brother!; **E** (*veralt.: sehr*) very; **du bist ~ früh gekommen** you have indeed come early; **~ mancher** many a one *or* person; ⇒ *auch* **ganz** 2 A

**Garage** /gaˈraːʒə/ *die;* ~, **~n** garage

**Garagen-:** **~einfahrt** *die* garage entrance; **~wagen** *der* garaged car

**garagieren** *tr. V.* (*österr.*, *schweiz.*) park

**Garant** /ga'rant/ *der;* **~en, ~en** guarantor

**Garantie** /garan'ti:/ *die;* **~, ~n** (A) (*Gewähr*) guarantee; **eine ~ für etw.** a guarantee of sth.; **für etw. keine ~ übernehmen** not guarantee sth.; **wir haben unter ~ nicht genug Geld** (*ugs.*) we're dead certain not to have enough money (*coll.*); (B) (*Kaufmannsspr.*) guarantee; warranty; **die ~ auf** *od.* **für das Auto ist abgelaufen** the guarantee on the car has run out; **eine ~ auf etw.** (*Akk.*) **geben** guarantee sth.; **für** *od.* **auf etw.** (*Akk.*) **ein Jahr ~ erhalten** get a one year guarantee on sth.; (C) (*Sicherheit*) guarantee; surety

**Garantie-:** **~anspruch** *der* right to claim under [the] guarantee; **~frist** *die* guarantee period; **~lohn** *der* guaranteed minimum wage

**garantieren** ❶ *tr. V.* guarantee; **jmdm. etw. ~:** guarantee sb. sth. ❷ *itr. V.* **für etw. ~:** guarantee sth.; **ich kann für den Hund nicht ~:** I can't say for sure what the dog will do

**garantiert** *Adv.* (*ugs.*) **wir kommen ~ zu spät** we're dead certain to arrive late (*coll.*)

**Garantie·schein** *der* guarantee [certificate]

**Garantin** *die;* **~, ~nen** ⇒ **Garant**

**Garaus** /'ga:ɐ̯|aus/ *in* **jmdm. den ~ machen** do sb. in (*coll.*); **dem Ungeziefer/Unkraut den ~ machen** get rid of the vermin/weeds; **einem Gerücht den ~ machen** scotch a rumour

**Garbe**[1] /'garbə/ *die;* **~, ~n** (A) (*Getreide~*) sheaf; (B) (*Geschoss~*) burst of fire; **eine ~ abfeuern** fire a burst

**Garbe**[2] *die;* **~, ~n** ⇒ **Schafgarbe**

**Gär·bottich** *der* fermenter

**Garçonnière** *die;* **~, ~n** (*österr.*) bedsitter

**Garde** /'gardə/ *die;* **~, ~n** (A) (*Leib~*) guard; (B) (*Gruppe*) team; **von der alten ~ sein** (*ugs.*) be one of the old guard; (C) (*Milit.: Elitetruppe*) the Guards *pl.;* **bei der ~:** in the Guards

**Garde·maß** *das* (A) (*hist.*) *minimum height for belonging to the Prussian Guards;* (B) (*scherzh.*) **~ haben** be as tall as a tree; **mit deinem ~ solltest du Basketballspieler werden** with your height you ought to be a basketball player

**Gardenie** /gar'de:ni̯ə/ *die;* **~, ~n** (*Bot.*) gardenia

**Garde·regiment** *das* Guards regiment

**Garderobe** /gardə'ro:bə/ *die;* **~, ~n** (A) (*Oberbekleidung*) wardrobe; clothes *pl.;* **für diesen Anlass fehlt ihm die passende ~:** he hasn't got suitable clothes for this occasion; **für ~ wird nicht gehaftet!** clothes are left at the owner's risk; (B) (*Flur~*) coat rack; **etw. an die ~ hängen** hang sth. up on the coat rack; (C) (*Raum*) clothes cupboard *or* (*Amer.*) closet; (D) (*im Theater o. Ä.*) cloakroom; checkroom (*Amer.*); **etw. an der ~ abgeben** hand sth. in at the cloakroom; (E) (*Ankleideraum*) dressing room

**Garderoben-:** **~frau** *die* ▶ 159 cloakroom *or* (*Amer.*) checkroom attendant; **~marke** *die* cloakroom *or* (*Amer.*) checkroom ticket; **~spiegel** *der* hall mirror; **~ständer** *der* coat stand

**Garderobier** /gardəro'bi̯e:/ *der;* **~s, ~s** ▶ 159 dresser

**Garderobiere** /gardəro'bi̯e:rə/ *die;* **~, ~n** ▶ 159 (A) dresser; (B) (*veralt.*) ⇒ **Garderobenfrau**

**Gardine** /gar'di:nə/ *die;* **~, ~n** (A) net curtain; (B) (*landsch.*, *veralt.*) curtain; ⇒ *auch* **schwedisch**

**Gardinen-:** **~leiste** *die* curtain rail; **~predigt** *die* (*ugs.*) telling-off (*coll.*); (*einer Ehefrau zu ihrem Mann*) curtain lecture; **jmdm. eine ~predigt halten** give sb. a [good] telling-off (*coll.*)/a curtain lecture; **~ring** *der* curtain ring; **~röllchen** *das* curtain runner; **~stange** *die* curtain rail; **~stoff** *der* curtain material

*old spelling (see note on page 1707)

**Gardist** *der;* **~en, ~en** guardsman

**garen** /'ga:rən/ *tr.*, *itr. V.* cook; **Fleisch/Gemüse ~ [lassen]** cook meat/vegetables

**gären** /'gɛ:rən/ ❶ *regelm.* (*auch unr.*) *itr. V.* ferment; (*fig.*) seethe; **es gärt in ihm/der Masse** he/the crowd is seething [with anger]/afire [with hatred/passion]. ❷ *regelm.* (*auch unr.*) *tr. V.* ferment ‹beer, tobacco›

**Gär·futter** *das* (*Landw.*) silage *no pl.*

**gar-, Gar-:** ***~gekocht** ⇒ **gar**[1] A; **~küche** *die* snackbar

**Gär·mittel** *das* ferment; fermenting agent

**Garn** /garn/ *das;* **~[e]s, ~e** (A) (*Faden*) thread; (*zum Weben*, *Stricken*) yarn; (*Näh~*) cotton; (B) (*Seew.*) yarn; (C) (*Seemannsspr.: Geschichte*) *in* **[s]ein ~ spinnen** spin a yarn; (D) (*Jagdw.*, *Fischereiw.: Netz*) net; **jmdm. ins ~ gehen** (*fig.*) fall *or* walk into sb.'s trap

**Garnele** /gar'ne:lə/ *die;* **~, ~n** shrimp

**Gar·nichts** *der od. das;* **~, ~e** (*abwertend*) [absolute] nonentity

**garnieren** /gar'ni:rən/ *tr. V.* (A) (*schmücken*) decorate (*mit* with); (B) (*Gastr.*) garnish

**Garnierung** *die;* **~, ~en** (A) garnish; (B) (*Vorgang*) garnishing

**Garnison** /garni'zo:n/ *die;* **~, ~en** garrison

**Garnison·stadt** *die* garrison town

**Garnitur** /garni'tu:ɐ̯/ *die;* **~, ~en** (A) (*zusammengehörige Stücke*) set; (*Wäsche*) set of [matching] underwear; (*Schreibtisch~*) desk set; (*Möbel*) suite; **eine zwei-/dreiteilige ~:** a two-piece/three-piece suite; (B) (*ugs.*) **die erste/zweite ~:** the first/second-rate people *pl.;* **zur ersten/zweiten ~ gehören, erste/zweite ~ sein** be first-/second-rate; (C) (*Gastr.*) garnishing; garniture

**Garn-:** **~knäuel** *das od. der* ball of thread; (*zum Weben*) ball of yarn; **~rolle** *die* reel; bobbin; (*von Nähgarn*) cotton reel; **~spule** *die* spool

**Gär·prozess**, ***Gär·prozeß** *der* ⇒ **Gärungsprozess**

**Garrotte** /ga'rɔtə/ *die;* **~, ~n** garrotte

**garstig** /'garstɪç/ *Adj.* (A) (*boshaft*) nasty (**zu** to); bad ‹behaviour›; nasty, naughty, (*coll.*) horrid ‹child›; (B) (*abscheulich*) horrible; nasty

**Garstigkeit** *die;* **~, ~en** (A) nastiness; (*eines Kindes*) naughtiness, (*coll.*) horridness; (B) (*Handlung*) piece of nastiness; **~en** nastiness *sing.;* horridness *sing.* (*coll.*); (C) (*Äußerung*) nasty *or* (*coll.*) horrid remark

**Gärtchen** /'gɛrtçən/ *das;* **~s, ~:** little garden

**Garten** /'gartn̩/ *der;* **~s, Gärten** /'gɛrtn̩/ garden; **ein [kleines] Stück ~:** a [small] bit of garden; **der ~ Eden** the Garden of Eden; **quer durch den ~** (*ugs.: verschiedene Sorten Gemüse*) all sorts of different vegetables; (*oft spöttisch: in bunter Vielfalt*) all sorts; a real mixture; ⇒ *auch* **botanisch**; **zoologisch**

**Garten-:** **~anlage** *die* garden; (*öffentlich*) park; gardens *pl.;* **~arbeit** *die* gardening; **~architekt** *der*, **~architektin** *die* landscape gardener; **~bank** *die; Pl.* **~bänke** garden seat

**Garten·bau** *der* horticulture

**Gartenbau-:** **~betrieb** *der* market garden; **~ingenieur** *der*, **~ingenieurin** *die* horticulturist

**Garten-:** **~blume** *die* garden flower; **~erde** *die* garden mould; **~fest** *das* garden party; **~freund** *der*, **~freundin** *die* amateur gardener; **~gerät** *das* garden tool; **~gestaltung** *die* landscaping; **~haus** *das* (A) (*Haus im Garten*) summerhouse; garden house; (B) (*Hinterhaus*) *dwelling situated at or forming the rear of a house and having its own garden;* **wir wohnen in der Goethestr. 10, im ~haus** we live at 10, Goethestrasse, at the back; **~hecke** *die* garden hedge; **~land** *das* gardening land; **~laube** *die* summerhouse; garden house; **~lokal** *das* beer garden; (*Restaurant*) open-air café; **~mauer** *die* garden wall; **~möbel** *das* piece of garden furniture; **~möbel** expensive garden furniture *sing.;* **~party** *die* ⇒ **~fest**; **~schau** *die* horticultural show; **~schirm** *der* sunshade; **~schlauch** *der* garden hose; **~stadt** *die* garden city; **~stuhl** *der* garden chair; **~wirtschaft** *die* ⇒ **~lokal**; **~zaun** *der* garden fence; **~zwerg** *der* (A) garden gnome; (B) (*salopp abwertend*) little runt

**Gärtner** /'gɛrtnɐ/ *der;* **~s, ~** ▶ 159 gardener

**Gärtnerei** *die;* **~, ~en** (A) nursery; (B) (*Gartenarbeit*) gardening

**Gärtnerin** *die;* **~, ~nen** ▶ 159 gardener

**Gärtnerin·art** *die: in* **Schweinefleisch** *usw.* **nach ~** (*Gastr.*) pork *etc.* jardinière

**gärtnerisch** ❶ *Adj.* **der ~e Pflanzenbau** the growing of garden plants; **~er Betrieb** nursery. ❷ *adv.* **sich gern ~ betätigen** enjoy gardening

**Gärung** *die;* **~, ~en** (A) fermentation; **etw. zur ~ ansetzen** start sth. fermenting; (B) (*Erregung*) ferment; **in ~ sein** be in [a state of] ferment

**Gärungs-:** **~mittel** *das* ⇒ **Gärmittel**; **~prozess**, ***~prozeß** *der* fermentation process

**Gar·zeit** *die* (*Kochk.*) cooking time

**Gas** /ga:s/ *das;* **~es, ~e** (A) gas; **jmdn. mit ~ vergiften** gas sb.; **mit ~ heizen** have gas heating; **mit ~ kochen** cook with gas; use gas for cooking; **jmdm. das ~ abdrehen** (*fig. salopp*) force sb. out of business; **etw. aufs ~ stellen** put sth. on the cooker *or* the gas; (B) (*Treibstoff*) petrol (*Brit.*); gasoline (*Amer.*); gas (*Amer. coll.*); **ohne ~ den Berg hinunterfahren** drive down the mountain without using any petrol *etc.;* **~ wegnehmen** decelerate; take one's foot off the accelerator; **~ geben** accelerate; put one's foot down (*coll.*); (*ugs. fig.: schneller gehen*) step on it (*coll.*); (C) (*ugs.: ~pedal*) accelerator; gas pedal (*Amer.*); **aufs ~ treten** put one's foot down (*coll.*); **vom ~ gehen** take one's foot off the accelerator

**gas-, Gas-:** **~anschluss**, ***~anschluß** *der* gas connection; (*~hahn*) gas tap; **~anstalt** *die* ⇒ **~werk**; **~anzünder** *der* gas lighter; **~austausch** *der* (*Biol.*, *Med.*) gaseous exchange; **~automat** *der* coin-in-the-slot gas meter; **~bade·ofen** *der* gas water heater; **~behälter** *der* gasholder; gasometer; **~beheizt** *Adj.* gas-heated; **ein ~beheizter Backofen** a gas oven; **~beleuchtung** *die* gas lighting; **~beton** *der* (*Bauw.*) cellular *or* aerated concrete; **~bombe** *die* gas bomb; **~brand** *der* (*Med.*) gas gangrene; **~brenner** *der* gas burner; **~dicht** *Adj.* gas-tight; **~druck** *der; Pl.* **~drücke** gas pressure; **~entladung** *die* (*Physik*) gas discharge; **~entwicklung** *die* formation of gas; **~explosion** *die* gas explosion; **~fabrik** *die* gasworks *sing.;* **~feuerung** *die* gas firing; **~feuerzeug** *das* gas lighter; **~flamme** *die* gas flame; **~flasche** *die* gas cylinder; (*für einen Herd*, *Ofen*) gas bottle; gas container; **~förmig** *Adj.* gaseous; **~fuß** *der* (*ugs.*) **einen nervösen ~fuß haben** rev up impatiently at the lights (*coll.*); **~gemisch** *das* mixture of gases; **~gerät** *das* gas appliance; **~geruch** *der* smell of gas; **~hahn** *der; Pl.* **~hähne**, (*fachspr.*) **~~en** gas tap; **den ~hahn aufdrehen** (*ugs. verhüll.*) end it all (*coll. euphem.*); **jmdm. den ~hahn abdrehen** (*salopp*) force sb. out of business; **~hebel** *der* accelerator pedal; gas pedal (*Amer.*); **~heizung** *die* gas heating; **~herd** *der* gas cooker; **~hülle** *die* atmosphere; **~kammer** *die* gas chamber; **~kessel** *der* gasholder; gasometer; **~kocher** *der* camping stove; **~koks** *der* gas coke; **~krieg** *der* gas war; (*Kriegführung*) gas warfare; **~lampe**, **~laterne** *die* gas lamp; **~leitung** *die* gas pipe; (*Hauptrohr*) gas main; **~-Luft-Gemisch** *das* (*Kfz-W.*) fuel-and-air mixture; **~mann** *der* (*ugs.*) gas man; **~maske** *die* gas mask; **~ofen** *der* gas heater

**Gasolin** /gazo'li:n/ *das;* **~s** gasoline

**Gasometer** /gazo'me:tɐ/ *der* (*veralt.*) gasometer; gasholder

**Gas-:** **~pedal** *das* accelerator [pedal]; gas pedal (*Amer.*); **~pistole** *die* pistol that fires gas cartridges; **~rechnung** *die* gas bill; **~rohr** *das* gas pipe; (*Hauptrohr*) gas main; **~schlauch** *der* gas hose

**Gasse** /'gasə/ *die;* **~, ~n** (A) lane; narrow street; (*österr.*) street; **auf der ~:** in the lane *or* narrow street; **die Salzburger Altstadt**

**ist von kleinen, engen ~n durchzogen** the old part of Salzburg is a maze of little, narrow streets and alleyways *or* passages; **[für jmdn.] eine ~ bilden** (*fig.*) make way *or* clear a path [for sb.]; **wir machten eine ~ für das Brautpaar** (*fig.*) we lined up to make a passage for the bride and groom; **jmdm./sich eine ~ durch die Menge bahnen** (*fig.*) clear a path for sb./force one's way through the crowd; **B** (*Fußball*) opening; **eine ~ öffnen** make an opening; **C** (*Rugby*) line-out; **D** (*Kegeln*) **in die rechte/linke ~ zielen/werfen** *aim/throw at the right-hand/left-hand gap between the lines of skittles*

**gassen-, Gassen-: ~hauer** *der* (*ugs.*) popular song; **~junge** *der* (*abwertend*) street urchin; **~seitig** *Adj.* (*österr.*) ‹room etc.› facing the street; **~seitig sein** face the street; **~wohnung** *die* (*österr.*) flat facing the street; **~wort** *das; Pl.* **~wörter** coarse word; **er benutzt die ordinärsten ~wörter** he uses the most vulgar gutter language

**Gassi** /'gasi/ *in* **~ gehen** (*ugs.*) go walkies (*Brit. coll.*)

**Gast**[1] /gast/ *der;* **~[e]s, Gäste** /'gɛstə/ **A** (*auch zahlender ~*) guest; **ungebetene Gäste** (*auch fig.*) uninvited guests; (*bei einer Party usw. auch*) gatecrashers; **das Glück war ein seltener ~ bei ihr** (*fig.*) she hadn't known much happiness; **bei jmdm. zu ~ sein** be sb.'s guest/guests; **jmdn. zu ~ haben** have sb. as one's guest/guests; **jmdn. zu ~ laden** *od.* **bitten** (*geh.*) request the pleasure of sb.'s company; **B** (*Besucher eines Lokals*) patron; **C** (*Besucher*) visitor; **ein ~ in einem Land** a visitor to a country; **als ~ im Studio war X** the studio guest was X; **D** (*Künstler[in]*) guest star

**Gast**[2] *der;* **~[e]s, ~en** *od.* **Gäste** (*Seemannsspr.*) man; (*Boots~*) crewman; (*Signal~*) signalman

**Gas·tanker** *der* gas tanker

**Gast-: ~arbeiter** *der,* **~arbeiterin** *die* immigrant *or* foreign *or* guest worker; **~bett** *das* (*im Hotel*) bed; (*im Haus*) spare bed; **~dozent** *der,* **~dozentin** *die* (*Hochschulw.*) visiting lecturer

**Gäste-: ~buch** *das* guest book; **~handtuch** *das* guest towel; **~haus** *das* guest house; **~zimmer** *das* (*privat*) guest room; spare room; (*im Hotel*) room

**gast-, Gast-: ~frei** *Adj.* hospitable; **~freiheit** *die* hospitality; **~freund** *der* (*veralt.*) **A** (*~geber*) host; **B** (*Besucher*) guest; **~freundin** *die* (*veralt.*) **A** (*~geberin*) hostess; **B** (*Besucher*) guest; **~freundlich** *Adj.* hospitable; **~freundschaft** *die* hospitality; **~gebend** *Adj.* host ‹city, nation, etc.›; **die ~gebende Mannschaft** the home team *or* side; **~geber** *der* **A** host; **B** (*Sport*) **der/die ~geber** the home team *or* side; **~geberin** *die* hostess; **~geschenk** *das* gift [for one's host/hostess]; **~haus** *das,* **~hof** *der* inn; **~hörer** *der,* **~hörerin** *die: student who with permission attends lectures and seminars at a university without working for a degree;* auditor (*Amer.*)

**gastieren** *itr. V.* appear as a guest; give a guest performance; **das Orchester gastiert in N.** the orchestra is giving a guest performance in N; **der ~de Tenor** the guest tenor

**Gast-: ~konzert** *das* guest concert; **~land** *das* host country

**gastlich** ❶ *Adj.* hospitable; **~e Aufnahme finden** have a hospitable reception; be received hospitably. ❷ *adv.* hospitably

**Gastlichkeit** *die;* **~:** hospitality

**Gast-: ~mahl** *das* (*geh.*) banquet; **Platons „~mahl"** Plato's 'Symposium'; **~mannschaft** *die* (*Sport*) visiting team

**Gas·tod** *der* death by gassing; **den ~ erleiden** be gassed

**Gast-: ~professor** *der,* **~professorin** *die* visiting professor; **~recht** *das* right to hospitality; **jmdm. ~recht gewähren/das ~recht verweigern** grant/refuse sb. hospitality; **~recht genießen** enjoy the privileges of a guest; **das ~recht missbrauchen** abuse one's position as a guest; **~redner** *der,* **~rednerin** *die* guest speaker

**Gastritis** /gas'tri:tɪs/ *die;* **~, Gastritiden** ▶ 474 (*Med.*) gastritis

**Gast·rolle** *die* guest role *or* part; **in einer ~ auftreten** make a guest appearance; appear as a guest

**gastro-, Gastro-** /gastro:-/**: ~nom** /-'no:m/ *der;* **~~en, ~~en** restaurateur; **~nomie** /-no'mi:/ *die;* **~~ A** (*Gaststättengewerbe*) restaurant trade; (*Versorgung, Service*) catering *no art.;* **B** (*Kochk.*) gastronomy; **~nomin** *die;* **~~, ~~nen** restaurateur; **~nomisch** /-'no:mɪʃ/ *Adj.* gastronomic; **~skopie** /-sko'pi:/ *die;* **~~** (*Med.*) gastroscopy

**Gast·spiel** *das* guest performance; **ein [kurzes] ~ geben** (*fig. scherzh.*) stay for a short time

**Gastspiel·reise** *die* tour; **eine ~ durch Japan** a tour of Japan; **auf ~:** on tour

**Gast·stätte** *die* public house (*Brit.*); (*Speiselokal*) restaurant

**Gaststätten·gewerbe** *das* pub/restaurant trade

**Gast·stube** *die* bar; (*in einem Speiselokal*) restaurant

**Gas·turbine** *die* gas turbine

**Gast-: ~vorlesung** *die* guest lecture; **~vorstellung** *die* guest performance; **~wirt** *der* ▶ 159 publican; landlord; (*eines Restaurants*) [restaurant] proprietor *or* owner; (*Pächter*) restaurant manager; **~wirtin** *die* ▶ 159 ⇒ **~wirt:** publican; landlady; [restaurant] proprietress *or* owner; restaurant manageress; **~wirtschaft** *die* ⇒ **~stätte**; **~zimmer** *das* ⇒ **Gästezimmer**

**Gas-: ~uhr** *die* gas meter; **~verbrauch** *der* gas consumption; **~verflüssigung** *die* (*Technik, Physik*) liquefaction of gases; **~vergiftung** *die* gas-poisoning *no indef. art.;* **~versorgung** *die* gas supply; **~wasch·flasche** *die* (*Technik*) gas washer; (*Chemie*) gas-washing bottle; **~werk** *das* gasworks *sing.;* **~wolke** *die* cloud of gas; **~zähler** *der* gas meter

**Gatt** /gat/ *das;* **~[e]s, ~en** *od.* **~s** (*Seemannsspr.*) eyelet hole

**GATT** /gat/ *das;* **~:** GATT

**Gatte** /'gatə/ *der;* **~n, ~n A** (*geh.: Ehemann*) husband; **B** *Pl.* (*veralt.: Eheleute*) couple; husband and wife

**Gatten-: ~liebe** *die* (*geh.*) conjugal love; love of one's husband/wife; **~mord** *der* (*Rechtsw., sonst geh.*) murder of one's husband/wife

**Gatter** /'gatɐ/ *das;* **~s, ~ A** (*Zaun*) fence; (*Lattenzaun*) fence; paling; **B** (*Tor*) gate; **C** (*Jägerspr.: Gehege*) [game] preserve; **D** (*Pferdesport*) rails *pl.;* **E** (*Textilw.*) creel; **F** (*Elektronik*) gate

**Gatter-: ~säge** *die* (*Technik*) gang saw; **~tor** *das* gate

**Gattin** /'gatɪn/ *die;* **~, ~nen** (*geh.*) wife; **die besten Grüße an Ihre ~:** my regards to your lady wife

**Gattung** /'gatʊŋ/ *die;* **~, ~en A** kind; sort; (*Kunst~*) genre; form; **Menschen/Dinge verschiedener ~:** all sorts of people/things of different kinds *or* sorts; **B** (*Biol.*) genus; **C** (*Milit.*) service

**Gattungs-: ~begriff** *der* generic concept; **~name** *der* generic name; **~zahlwort** *das* (*Sprachw.*) *numeral showing how many different kinds ('achterlei' etc.);* variative numeral

**Gau** /gau/ *der;* **~[e]s, ~e A** *tribal district in Germanic times;* **B** (*ns.: Organisationseinheit*) *administrative district during the Nazi period;* **C** (*Gebiet*) region

**Gäu** /gɔy/ *das;* **~[e]s, ~e** (*österr., schweiz.*) ⇒ **Gau A**

**GAU** *der;* **~s, ~s: größter anzunehmender Unfall** MCA; maximum credible accident

**Gaube** /'gaubə/ *die;* **~, ~n** dormer [window]

**Gauchheil** /'gauxhail/ *der;* **~[e]s, ~e** (*Bot.*) anagallis; pimpernel

**Gaucho** /'gautʃo/ *der;* **~[s], ~s** gaucho

**Gaudi** /'gaudi/ *das;* **~s** (*bayr., österr.: die;* **~**) (*ugs.*) bit of fun; **eine große ~ haben** have a lot of *or* great fun; **eine ~ sein** be a lot of *or* great fun

**Gaudium** /'gaudiʊm/ *das;* **~s** amusement; entertainment; **zum allgemeinen ~:** to everyone's amusement; to the amusement of everyone *or* all

**Gaukel·bild** *das* (*veralt.*) phantasm; **ein ~ deiner Fantasie** a figment of your imagination

**Gaukelei** *die;* **~, ~en** (*geh.*) **A** (*Vorspiegelung*) trickery *no indef. art., no pl.;* **~en** trickery *sing.; tricks;* **B** (*Possenspiel*) trick

**gaukeln** /'gaukl̩n/ *itr. V.; mit sein* (*dichter.*) ‹glow-worm› flicker; ‹butterfly› flutter; **der ~de Flug der Fledermäuse** the dancing flight of the bats

**Gaukel·spiel** *das* (*geh.*) deception

**Gaukler** *der;* **~s, ~ A** (*veralt.: Taschenspieler*) itinerant entertainer; **B** (*geh.: Betrüger*) charlatan; mountebank; trickster; **C** (*Zool.*) bateleur [eagle]

**Gauklerin** *die;* **~, ~nen** ⇒ **Gaukler A, B**

**Gaul** /gaul/ *der;* **~[e]s, Gäule** /'gɔylə/ **A** (*abwertend*) nag (*derog.*); hack (*derog.*); **B** (*veralt.*) horse; **einem geschenkten ~ schaut man nicht ins Maul** (*Spr.*) never look a gift-horse in the mouth

**Gau·leiter** *der* (*ns.*) gauleiter

**Gaullismus** /go'lɪsmʊs/ *der;* **~:** Gaullism

**Gaumen** /'gaumən/ *der;* **~s, ~ A** ▶ 471 palate; roof of the mouth; **der weiche/harte ~:** the soft/hard palate; **B** (*geh.: Geschmacksorgan*) palate; **das ist etw. für einen verwöhnten ~:** this is sth. for the real gourmet

**Gaumen-: ~freude** *die* (*geh.*), **~kitzel** *der* (*geh.*) delicacy; **~laut** *der* guttural; **~mandel** *die* ▶ 471 (*Anat.*) [palatine] tonsil; **~platte** *die* upper [dental] plate; **~segel** *das* ▶ 471 (*Anat.*) soft palate; velum (*Anat.*); **~spalte** *die* ▶ 474 (*Med.*) cleft palate; **~zäpfchen** *das* uvula

**Gauner** /'gaunɐ/ *der;* **~s, ~ A** (*abwertend*) crook (*coll.*); rogue; **ein ausgemachter/kleiner ~:** an out-and-out crook (*coll.*) *or* rogue/a small-time crook (*coll.*); **B** (*ugs.: schlauer Mensch*) cunning devil (*coll.*); sly customer (*coll.*)

**Gauner·bande** *die* gang *or* band of crooks (*coll.*)

**Gaunerei** *die;* **~, ~en** swindle; (*das Gaunern*) swindling

**Gaunerin** *die;* **~, ~nen** ⇒ **Gauner**

**Gauner·komödie** *die* comedy thriller

**gaunern** ❶ *itr. V.* swindle; cheat. ❷ *refl. V.* **sich durchs Leben ~:** cheat one's way through life

**Gauner-: ~sprache** *die* thieves' cant *or* Latin; **~streich** *der,* **~stück** *das* swindle; piece of roguery

**gautschen** /'gautʃn̩/ *tr. V.* **A** (*Papierherstellung*) couch; **B** (*Druckw.*) **jmdn. ~:** give sb. a ducking (*initiation ceremony for those finishing an apprenticeship in the printing trade*)

**Gautscher** *der;* **~s, ~, Gautscherin** *die;* **~, ~nen** (*Papierherstellung*) coucher

**Gaza·streifen** /'ga:za-/ *der* Gaza Strip

**Gaze** /'ga:zə/ *die;* **~, ~n** gauze; (*Draht~*) gauze; [wire] mesh

**Gaze-: ~bausch** *der* gauze swab; **~binde** *die* gauze bandage

**Gazelle** /ga'tsɛlə/ *die;* **~, ~n** gazelle

**Gaze·schleier** *der* gauze veil

**Gazette** /ga'tsɛtə/ *die;* **~, ~n** newspaper; rag (*coll. derog.*)

**Gaze·tupfer** *der* ⇒ **Gazebausch**

**G-Dur** /'ge:-/ *das* (*Musik*) G major; ⇒ *auch* **A-Dur**

**geachtet** ❶ *2. Part. v.* **achten.** ❷ *Adj.* respected; **hoch ~:** highly respected *or* regarded; **~ und respektiert** esteemed and respected; **bei jmdm. ~ sein** be respected *or* held in esteem by sb.

g

**Geächtete** *der/die; adj. Dekl.* outlaw
**Geächze** *das;* **~s** groaning; groans *pl.*
**Geäder** /gə'|ɛ:dɐ/ *das;* **~s** venation; veins *pl.; (beim Menschen)* veins *pl.*
**geädert, geädert** *Adj.* veined
**Geäfter** /gə'|ɛftɐ/ *das;* **~s, ~** *(Jägerspr.)* dewclaws *pl.*
**Gealbere** *das;* **~s** *(ugs. abwertend)* messing about *or* around *(coll.)*
**geartet** *Adj.* **es ist [ganz] anders ~, als ich mir vorgestellt hatte** it is [quite] different [in kind] from what I'd imagined; **wie [auch] immer die Situation ~ ist** whatever the situation may be; **kein wie auch immer ~er Reiz** no stimulus of any kind; **dieses besonders ~e Material** this special material; **sie ist so ~, dass ...** her nature is such that ...; **gutmütig ~:** good-natured; **sie ist ganz anders ~:** she is quite different; she has quite a different nature
**Geäst** /gə'|ɛst/ *das;* **~[e]s** branches *pl.;* boughs *pl.*
**geb.** *Abk.* Ⓐ **geboren;** Ⓑ **geborene**
**Gebäck** /gə'bɛk/ *das;* **~[e]s, ~e** cakes and pastries *pl.; (Kekse)* biscuits *pl.; (Törtchen)* tarts *pl.*
**gebacken** *2. Part. v.* **backen**
**Gebäck-: ~schale** *die* cake dish; **~zange** *die* cake tongs *pl.*
**Gebälk** /gə'bɛlk/ *das;* **~[e]s, ~e** Ⓐ *(Balkenwerk)* beams *pl.; (Dach~)* rafters *pl.;* **es knistert** *od.* **kracht im ~** *(fig.)* there are signs that things are beginning to fall apart *(fig.);* Ⓑ *(antike Archit.)* entablature
**Geballere** *das;* **~s** *(ugs. abwertend)* banging
**geballt** /gə'balt/ ❶ *2. Part. v.* **ballen.** ❷ *Adj.* concentrated; **mit ~er Kraft einen neuen Angriff starten** concentrate one's forces in a new attack; **eine ~e Ladung** *(Milit.)* a concentrated charge; **jmdm. eine ~e Ladung Sand ins Gesicht werfen** *(fig. ugs.)* chuck a load of sand in sb.'s face *(coll.)*
**gebar** *1. u. 3. Pers. Sg. Prät. v.* **gebären**
**Gebärde** /gə'bɛ:ɐ̯də/ *die;* **~, ~n** gesture; **mit vielen ~n** with much gesticulation
**gebärden** *refl. V.* **sich seltsam/wie ein Rasender/wie toll ~:** behave *or* act oddly/like a madman/as if one were mad
**Gebärden-: ~spiel** *das* gestures *pl.;* gesticulation[s *pl.*]; **~sprache** *die (Zeichensprache)* sign language; *(Taubstummensprache)* deaf-and-dumb language
**gebären** /gə'bɛ:rən/ *unr. tr. V.* bear; give birth to; **jmdm. ein Kind ~** *(geh.)* bear sb. a child; **wo bist du geboren?** where were you born?; **einen Gedanken/eine Idee ~** *(fig.)* generate a thought/give birth to an idea; ⇒ *auch* **geboren**
**Gebaren** *das;* **~s** *(oft abwertend)* conduct; behaviour
**gebär·freudig** *Adj.* prolific
**Gebär·mutter** *die; Pl.* **Gebärmütter** ▶ **471** womb
**Gebärmutter·krebs** *der* ▶ **474** *(Med.)* cancer of the womb
**gebauchpinselt** /gə'bauxpɪnzl̩t/ *in* **sich ~ fühlen** *(ugs. scherzh.)* feel flattered
**Gebäude** /gə'bɔydə/ *das;* **~s, ~** Ⓐ *(Bauwerk)* building; Ⓑ *(Gefüge)* structure; **kunstvolles ~:** edifice; **das ~ einer Theorie/Wissenschaft** the structure of a theory/of a science; **ein ~ von Lügen** a tissue of lies
**Gebäude-: ~komplex** *der* complex of buildings; **~teil** *der* part of the building
**gebaut** ❶ *2. Part. v.* **bauen.** ❷ *Adj.* **gut ~ sein** have a good figure; **gut ~e Mannequins** models with good figures; **so wie du ~ bist ...** *(ugs.)* with a figure like yours ...; *(fig.)* you being what you are ... *(coll.)*
**gebe·freudig** *Adj.* generous; open-handed
**Gebein** *das;* **~[e]s, ~e** Ⓐ *Pl. (geh.: Skelett)* bones *pl.; (sterbliche Reste)* [mortal] remains; Ⓑ **ihr fuhr der Schreck durchs ~** *(veralt.)* her whole body shook with fear
**Gebell** *das;* **~[e]s** barking; *(der Jagdhunde)* baying; *(fig.: von Geschützen)* booming

*old spelling (see note on page 1707)

**geben** /'ge:bn̩/ ❶ *unr. tr. V.* Ⓐ give; *(reichen)* give; hand; pass; **jmdm. zu essen/trinken ~:** give sb. sth. to eat/drink; **jmdm. [zur Begrüßung] die Hand ~:** shake sb.'s hand [in greeting]; **~ Sie mir bitte Herrn N.** please put me through to Mr N.; **ich gäbe viel darum, wenn ich das machen könnte** I'd give a lot to be able to do that; **jmdm. etw. in die Hand ~:** give sb. sth.; **etw. [nicht] aus der Hand ~:** [not] let go of sth.; **ich gebe Ihnen die Vase für 130 Mark** I'll let you have the vase for 130 marks; **~ Sie mir bitte eine Schachtel Zigaretten/ein Bier** I'll have a packet of cigarettes/a beer, please; **können Sie mir zwei Plätze ~?** can you give me *or* let me have two seats?; **jmdm. seine ganze Liebe ~** *(fig.)* give sb. all one's love; **Geben ist seliger denn Nehmen** *(Spr.)* it is more blessed to give than to receive *(prov.);* Ⓑ *(über~)* **jmdn. zu jmdm. in die Lehre ~:** apprentice sb. to sb.; **etw. in Druck** *(Akk.)* *od.* **zum Druck ~:** send sth. to press *or* to be printed; **jmdm. etw. als** *od.* **zum Pfand ~:** give sb. sth. as [a] security; **etw. [bei jmdm.] in Verwahrung ~:** hand sth. in [to sb.] for safe keeping; **etw. zur Reparatur ~:** take sth. [in] to be repaired; **etw. zur Post ~:** post sth.; ⇒ *auch* **Pflege;** Ⓒ *(gewähren)* give; **jmdm. eine Genehmigung/ein Interview ~:** give sb. permission/an interview; **einen Elfmeter/eine Ecke ~** *(Sport)* award a penalty/corner; Ⓓ *(bieten)* give; **es hat mir nichts ge~:** I didn't gain anything from *or* get anything out of it; **jmdm. ein gutes/schlechtes Beispiel ~:** set sb. a good/bad example; Ⓔ *(versetzen)* give; **jmdm. einen Klaps/Tritt ~:** give sb. a slap/kick; **es jmdm. ~** *(ugs.: jmdm. die Meinung sagen)* give sb. what for *(coll.); (jmdn. verprügeln)* let sb. have it; **gib [es] ihm!** *(ugs.)* let him have it!; Ⓕ *(erteilen)* give; **Unterricht ~:** teach; **eine Lektion ~:** give a lesson; **Französisch ~:** teach French; **jmdm. Antwort ~:** give sb. an answer; **jmdm. Auskunft/Aufschluss ~:** give sb. information; Ⓖ *(hervorbringen)* give ‹milk, shade, light›; **etw. gibt Flecken** *(ugs.)* sth. stains; Ⓗ *(veranstalten)* give, throw ‹party›; give, lay on ‹banquet›; give ‹dinner party, ball›; **ein Fest ~:** give *or* hold a party *or* celebration; Ⓘ *(aufführen)* give ‹concert, performance›; **das Theater gibt nächste Woche den „Faust"** the theatre is putting on 'Faust' next week; **was wird heute ge~?** what's on today?; **die Schauspielerin gibt ihr Debüt** the actress is making her debut; Ⓙ *(er~)* **drei mal drei gibt neun** three threes are nine; three times three is *or* makes nine; **eins plus eins gibt zwei** one and one is *or* makes two; **das gibt [k]einen Sinn** that makes [no] sense; **ein Wort gab das andere** one word led to another; Ⓚ *(vermitteln)* give; **jmdm./einer Sache neue Impulse/Anregungen ~:** give sb./sth. a fresh impulse/stimulus; **etw. ist jmdm. nicht ge~:** sb. just hasn't got sth.; **es ist ihm nicht ge~, eine gute Rede zu halten** he just hasn't got what it takes to be a good speaker; Ⓛ *(äußern)* **etw. von sich ~:** utter sth.; **Unsinn/dummes Zeug von sich ~** *(abwertend)* talk nonsense/rubbish; **keinen Laut/Ton von sich ~:** not make a sound; Ⓜ **viel/wenig auf etw.** *(Akk.)* **~:** set great/little store by sth.; Ⓝ *(hinzu~)* add; put in; **etw. an das Essen ~:** add sth. to *or* put sth. into the food; Ⓞ *(ugs.: erbrechen)* **alles wieder von sich ~:** bring *or* *(coll.)* sick everything up again; Ⓟ *(Ballspiele: ab~)* pass; **den Ball nach links ~:** pass the ball [to the] left; Ⓠ *(darstellen)* play ‹role›.
❷ *unr. tr. V. (unpers.)* Ⓐ *(vorhanden sein)* **es gibt** there is/are; **es gibt einen/keinen Gott** God exists/does not exist; **das gibt es wohl häufiger** it happens all the time; **dass es so etwas heutzutage überhaupt noch gibt!** I'm surprised that such things still go on nowadays; **zu meiner Zeit gab es das nicht** it wasn't like that in my day; **gibt es noch etwas?** *(ugs.)* is there anything else?; **das gibt es ja gar nicht** I don't believe it; you're joking *(coll.);* **Ein Hund mit fünf Beinen? Das gibt es ja gar nicht** A dog with five legs? There's no such thing!; **was gibt es Neues?** what's new? *(coll.);* **bei mir gibts nichts Neues** I haven't got any news; **Kommen Sie herein. Was gibt es?** Come in. What's the matter *or* *(coll.)* what's up?; **was gibts denn da?** what's going on over there?; **was es nicht alles gibt!** *(ugs.)* what will they think of next?; **gibt es dich auch noch?** *(ugs.)* are you still around? *(coll.);* **da gibts nichts** *(ugs.)* there's no denying it *or* no doubt about it; **da gibts nichts, da würde ich sofort protestieren** there's nothing else for it, I'd protest immediately in that case; Ⓑ *(angeboten werden)* **was gibt es zu essen/trinken?** what is there to eat/drink?; **was gibt es denn zum Mittagessen?** what's for lunch?; **heute gibts Schweinefleisch** we're having pork today; **im Theater/Fernsehen gibt es heute Abend ...** ... is on at the theatre/on television this evening; Ⓒ *(einsetzen)* **morgen gibt es Schnee/Sturm** it'll snow tomorrow/there'll be a storm tomorrow; **es gibt Scherereien/Streit** there'll be trouble/a row; **gleich/sonst gibts was** *(ugs.)* there'll be trouble in a minute/otherwise.
❸ *unr. itr. V.* Ⓐ *(Karten austeilen)* deal; **wer gibt?** whose deal is it?; Ⓑ *(Sport: aufschlagen)* serve.
❹ *unr. refl. V.* Ⓐ **sich [natürlich/steif] ~:** act *or* behave [naturally/stiffly]; **er gab sich nach außen hin gelassen** he gave the appearance of being relaxed; **deine Art, dich zu ~:** the way you behave; Ⓑ *(nachlassen)* **das Fieber wird sich ~:** his/her *etc.* temperature will drop; **sein Eifer wird sich bald ~:** his enthusiasm will soon wear off *or* cool; **das gibt sich/wird sich noch ~:** it will get better
**gebenedeit** /gəbene'dait/ *Adj. (christl. Rel.)* blessed; **die ~e Jungfrau** the Blessed Virgin Mary
**Geber** *der;* **~s, ~** Ⓐ *(veralt.: Gebender)* giver; donor; Ⓑ *(Technik)* transducer
**Geberin** *die;* **~, ~nen** ⇒ **Geber** A
**Geber·laune** *die* generous mood; **in ~:** in a generous mood
**Gebet** /gə'be:t/ *das;* **~[e]s, ~e** prayer; **ein ~ sprechen** say a prayer; **sein ~ verrichten** say one's prayers *pl.;* **das ~ des Herrn** *(geh.)* the Lord's Prayer; **jmdn. ins ~ nehmen** *(ugs.)* give sb. a dressing down; take sb. to task
**Gebet·buch** *das* prayer book
**gebeten** *2. Part. v.* **bitten**
**Gebets-: ~mühle** *die* prayer wheel; **~teppich** *der (islam. Rel.)* prayer mat
**gebeut** /gə'bɔyt/ *(veralt.) 3. Pers. Sg. Präsens v.* **gebieten**
**gebiert** /gə'bi:ɐ̯t/ *3. Pers. Sg. Präsens v.* **gebären**
**Gebiet** /gə'bi:t/ *das;* **~[e]s, ~e** Ⓐ *(Landstrich)* region; area; Ⓑ *(Staats~)* territory; Ⓒ *(Bereich)* field; sphere; **auf dem ~ der Wirtschaft/Politik** in the field *or* sphere of economics/politics; Ⓓ *(Fach)* field; **auf einem ~ führend sein** be the leader in a field
**gebieten** *(geh.)* ❶ *unr. tr. V.* Ⓐ *(befehlen, fordern)* command; order; **jmdm. ~, etw. zu tun** command *or* order sb. to do sth.; **eine Respekt ~de Persönlichkeit** a figure who commands/commanded respect; Ⓑ *(erfordern)* demand; bid; ⇒ *auch* **Einhalt.** ❷ *unr. itr. V.* Ⓐ **über etw.** *(Akk.)* **~:** command sth.; have command over sth.; **über ein Land/Volk ~:** hold sway over a country/people; Ⓑ *(verfügen)* **über Geld ~:** have money at one's disposal; **er gebietet über beträchtliche Körperkräfte** he is a man of considerable strength
**Gebieter** *der;* **~s, ~** *(veralt.)* master; **~ über 400 Sklaven** master of 400 slaves
**Gebieterin** *die;* **~, ~nen** *(veralt.)* mistress
**gebieterisch** *(geh.)* ❶ *Adj.* imperious; *(herrisch)* domineering; overbearing; peremptory ‹tone›. ❷ *adv.* imperiously; **die Lage erfordert ~, dass ...** the situation makes it [absolutely] imperative that ...

**gebiets-, Gebiets-: ~abtretung** *die* cession *or* ceding of territory; **~anspruch** *der* territorial claim; **~körperschaft** *die* (*Rechtsw.*) regional authority; **~reform** *die* local government reorganization; **~weise** *Adv.* locally; in some areas

**Gebilde** /gəˈbɪldə/ *das;* **~s, ~** (*Gegenstand*) object; (*Bauwerk*) construction; structure; (*Form*) shape; **ein kompliziertes geistiges ~** (*fig.*) a complicated intellectual construct; **diese Dinge sind ~ seiner Fantasie** (*fig.*) these things are products of his imagination

**gebildet** ❶ *2. Part. v.* **bilden.** ❷ *Adj.* educated; (*kultiviert*) cultured; **er ist sehr ~:** he is very well educated; **vielseitig ~:** broadly educated; **er ist vielseitig ~:** he has a broad education; **akademisch ~ sein** have had an academic training. ❸ *adv.* **sich ~ unterhalten** have a cultured conversation

**Gebimmel** *das;* **~s** (*ugs.*) ringing; (*von kleinen Glocken*) tinkling

**Gebinde** *das;* **~s, ~** (*Blumenarrangement*) arrangement; (*Bund, Strauß*) bunch; (*von kleinen Blumen*) posy

**Gebirge** /gəˈbɪrgə/ *das;* **~s, ~** [A] mountain range; range of mountains; **ein ~ von Schutt** (*fig.*) a mountain of rubble (*fig.*); [B] (*Gebirgsgegend*) mountains *pl.;* [C] (*Bergbau*) rock

**gebirgig** *Adj.* mountainous

**Gebirgs-: ~ausläufer** *der* foothill; **~bach** *der* mountain stream; **~bahn** *die* mountain railway; **~bewohner** *der*, **~bewohnerin** *die* mountain dweller; **~jäger** *der* (*Milit.*) [A] (*Soldat*) mountain soldier; [B] *Pl.* (*Waffengattung*) mountain troops *pl.;* **~kamm** *der* mountain ridge *or* crest; **~kette** *die* mountain chain *or* range; **~klima** *das* mountain climate; **~landschaft** *die* mountainous region; (*Ausblick*) mountain scenery; (*Gemälde*) mountain landscape; **~massiv** *das* massif; **~pass, *~paß** *der* mountain pass; **~stock** *der* massif; **~truppe** *die* (*Milit.*) ⇒ **~jäger** B; **~volk** *das* mountain people; (*Stamm*) mountain tribe; **~zug** *der* mountain range

**Gebiss, *Gebiß** *das;* **Gebisses, Gebisse** [A] ▶ 471 (*Zähne*) set of teeth; teeth *pl.;* **sein ~ zeigen/entblößen** bare one's teeth; [B] (*Zahnersatz*) denture; plate (*coll.*); (*für die Zähne beider Kiefer*) dentures *pl.;* set of false teeth; false teeth *pl.;* **ein [künstliches] ~ anpassen** fit a denture/dentures *or* [a set of] false teeth; [C] (*am Pferdezaum*) bit

**gebissen** /gəˈbɪsn̩/ *2. Part. v.* **beißen**

**Gebläse** /gəˈblɛːzə/ *das;* **~s, ~** (*Technik*) fan; (*Kfz-W.: am Vergaser*) supercharger

**Gebläse·motor** *der* (*Kfz-W.*) supercharged engine

**geblasen** *2. Part. v.* **blasen**

**geblichen** /gəˈblɪçn̩/ *2. Part. v.* **bleichen**

**Geblödel** *das;* **~s** (*ugs.*) silly chatter; twaddle (*coll.*)

**geblümt** /gəˈblyːmt/ *Adj.* [A] flowered; [B] (*geziert*) flowery ‹style etc.›

**Geblüt** /gəˈblyːt/ *das;* **~[e]s** (*geh.*) blood; **von königlichem ~ sein** be of royal blood; **eine Prinzessin von ~:** a princess of the blood

**gebogen** ❶ *2. Part. v.* **biegen.** ❷ *Adj.* bent; **eine aufwärts ~e Nase** an upturned nose

**geboren** /gəˈboːrən/ ❶ *2. Part. v.* **gebären.** ❷ *Adj.* **blind/taub ~ sein** be born blind/deaf; **Frau Anna Schmitz ~e Meyer** Mrs Anna Schmitz née Meyer; **sie ist eine ~e von Schiller** she is a von Schiller by birth; **der ~e Schauspieler** *usw.* **sein** be a born actor *etc.*; **zum Musiker** *usw.* **~ sein** be born to be a musician *etc.*; be a born musician *etc.*

**geborgen** ❶ *2. Part. v.* **bergen.** ❷ *Adj.* safe; secure; **sich bei jmdm. ~ fühlen** feel safe and secure with sb.; **sicher und ~ sein** be safe and secure

**Geborgenheit** *die;* **~:** security

**geborsten** /gəˈbɔrstn̩/ *2. Part. v.* **bersten**

**gebot** *1. u. 3. Pers. Sg. Prät. v.* **gebieten**

**Gebot** *das;* **~[e]s, ~e** [A] (*Grundsatz*) precept; **das ~ der Fairness/Höflichkeit verlangt es, dass ...** fairness/politeness demands that ...; **das oberste/erste ~:** the highest precept; **die Zehn ~e** (*Rel.*) the Ten Commandments; [B] (*Vorschrift*) regulation; [C] (*geh.: Befehl*) command; (*Verordnung*) decree; **auf jmds. ~** (*Akk.*) **[hin]** at sb.'s command; [D] *in* **jmdm. zu ~[e] stehen** (*geh.*) be at sb.'s command/disposal; [E] (*Erfordernis*) **ein ~ der Vernunft/Klugheit** a dictate of reason/good sense; **es ist ein ~ der Vernunft/Klugheit, etw. zu tun** reason/good sense dictates that one does sth.; **es ist das ~ der Stunde, nicht länger zu zögern** (*geh.*) our present predicament demands that we hesitate no longer; **etw. ist das ~ der Stunde** (*geh.*) sth. is the order of the day; [F] (*Kaufmannsspr.*) bid; **verkaufe X gegen ~:** offers [are] invited for X

**geboten** ❶ *2. Part. v.* **bieten, gebieten.** ❷ *Adj.* (*ratsam*) advisable; (*notwendig*) necessary; (*unbedingt ~*) imperative; **mit der ~en Sorgfalt** with [all] due care; **mit dem ~en Respekt** with all due respect

**Gebots·schild** *das* (*Verkehrsw.*) regulatory sign

**Gebr.** *Abk.* **Gebrüder** Bros.

**gebracht** /gəˈbraxt/ *2. Part. v.* **bringen**

**gebrandmarkt** *2. Part. v.* **brandmarken**

**gebrannt** /gəˈbrant/ *2. Part. v.* **brennen**

**gebraten** *2. Part. v.* **braten**

**Gebräu** /gəˈbrɔy/ *das;* **~[e]s, ~e** (*meist abwertend*) brew; concoction (*derog.*)

**Gebrauch** *der* [A] (*Benutzung*) use; **für den persönlichen/täglichen ~:** for personal/daily use; **vor ~ gut schütteln!** shake well before use; **von etw. ~ machen** make use of sth.; **von seinem Recht ~ machen** avail oneself of *or* exercise one's rights *pl.;* **außer ~ kommen** fall into disuse; **etw. in ~ nehmen** start using sth.; **etw. in** *od.* **im ~ haben** be using sth.; **in** *od.* **im ~ sein** be in use; [B] (*Brauch*) custom

**gebrauchen** *tr. V.* use; **das kann ich gut ~:** I can make good use of that; I can just do with that (*coll.*); **er ist zu nichts zu ~** (*ugs.*) he is useless; **sie ist zu allem zu ~:** she is always a useful person to have around; **den Verstand/eine List ~:** use one's common sense/a subterfuge; **er könnte einen neuen Mantel ~** (*ugs.*) he could do with *or* (*coll.*) use a new coat; **ich kann jetzt keine Störung ~** (*ugs.*) I don't want to be disturbed just now

**gebräuchlich** /gəˈbrɔyçlɪç/ *Adj.* [A] (*üblich*) normal; usual; customary; [B] (*häufig*) common

**gebrauchs-, Gebrauchs-: ~anleitung** *die*, **~anweisung** *die* instructions *pl. or* directions *pl.* [for use]; **~artikel** *der* basic consumer item; **~artikel** *Pl.* basic consumer goods; **~fähig** *Adj.* usable; in working order *pred.;* **etw. ~fähig machen** make sth. usable; put sth. in working order; **~fertig** *Adj.* ready for use *pred.;* **~gegen·stand** *der* item of practical use; **~grafik, ~graphik** *die* commercial art; **~grafiker, ~graphiker** *der*, **~grafikerin, ~graphikerin** *die* commercial artist; **~gut** *das* consumer item; **~güter** consumer goods; **langlebige ~güter** consumer durables; **~muster** *das* (*Rechtsw.*) registered design; **~muster·schutz** *der* (*Rechtsw.*) protection of designs; **~wert** *der* utility value

**gebraucht** ❶ *2. Part. v.* **brauchen, gebrauchen.** ❷ *Adj.* second-hand ‹bicycle, clothes, etc.›; used, second-hand ‹car›; used ‹handkerchief›; **etw. ~ kaufen** buy sth. second-hand

**Gebraucht-: ~wagen** *der* used *or* second-hand car; **~wagen·händler** *der*, **~wagen·händlerin** *die* used-car dealer; second-hand car dealer; **~ware** *die* second-hand item; **~waren** second-hand goods

**Gebrause** *das;* **~s** (*des Meeres, der Wellen*) thundering; roar[ing]; booming; (*des Sturms, Windes*) roar[ing]; (*des Verkehrs*) roar

**gebrechen** *unr. itr. V.* (*unpers.*) (*geh.*) **jmdm. gebricht etw., jmdm. gebricht es an etw.** (*Dat.*) sb. is lacking in *or* lacks sth.

**Gebrechen** *das;* **~s, ~** (*geh.*) affliction

**gebrechlich** *Adj.* infirm; frail; **die Alten und Gebrechlichen** the aged and infirm

**Gebrechlichkeit** *die;* **~:** infirmity; frailty

**gebrochen** /gəˈbrɔxn̩/ ❶ *2. Part. v.* **brechen.** ❷ *Adj.* [A] (*fehlerhaft*) **~es Englisch/Deutsch** broken English/German; [B] (*niedergedrückt*) broken; **er ist ein ~er Mensch** he is a broken man; [C] (*gestört*) **ein ~es Verhältnis zu jmdm./etw. haben** have a disturbed relationship to sb./sth. ❸ *adv.* **~ Deutsch sprechen** speak broken German

**Gebrodel** *das;* **~s** boiling; bubbling; (*fig.*) turmoil

**Gebrüder** *Pl.* [A] (*Kaufmannsspr.*) **die ~ Meyer** Meyer Brothers; [B] (*veralt.*) **die ~ Schulze** the brothers Schulze

**Gebrüll** *das;* **~[e]s** [A] roaring; (*von Rindern*) bellowing; [B] (*ugs.*) (*lautes Schreien*) bellowing; yelling; (*einer Menschenmenge*) roaring; **auf sie mit ~!** (*scherzh.*) go for *or* get them!; [C] (*ugs.: lautes Weinen*) bawling

**Gebrumm** *das;* **~[e]s** (*von Bären*) growling; (*von Flugzeugen, Bienen*) droning; (*von Insekten*) buzz[ing]; **ein zustimmendes ~** (*fig.*) a growl of assent

**Gebrumme** *das;* **~s** (*ugs. abwertend*) (*von Flugzeugen, Motorrädern, Bienen*) droning; (*von Insekten*) buzz[ing]

**gebückt** ❶ *2. Part. v.* **bücken.** ❷ *Adj.* **in ~er Haltung** bending forward; **~ gehen** walk with a stoop

**gebügelt** *2. Part. v.* **bügeln;** ⇒ *auch* **geschniegelt**

**Gebühr** /gəˈbyːɐ̯/ *die;* **~, ~en** [A] charge; (*Maut*) toll; (*Anwalts~*) fee; (*Fernseh~*) licence fee; (*Vermittlungs~*) commission *no pl.;* fee; (*Post~*) postage *no pl.;* **~ bezahlt Empfänger** postage will be paid by addressee; [B] **jmds. Leistungen nach ~ anerkennen** give due recognition to sb.'s achievements; **ich werde dich nach ~ belohnen** I shall reward you appropriately; **über ~** (*Akk.*) unduly; excessively

**gebühren** (*geh.*) ❶ *itr. V.* **jmdm. gebührt Achtung** *usw.* **[für etw.]** sb. deserves respect *etc.* [for sth.]; respect *etc.* is due to sb. [for sth.]. ❷ *refl. V.* **wie es sich gebührt** as is fitting *or* proper; **er bewahrte die Haltung, wie es sich für einen König gebührt** he kept his composure, as befitted a king

**Gebühren·anzeiger** *der* (*Fernspr.*) telephone meter

**gebührend** ❶ *Adj.* fitting; proper; (*angemessen*) fitting; suitable; **in ~em Abstand** at a proper distance; **mit ~er Sorgfalt** with due care; **jmdm. die ~e Achtung erweisen** show sb. due *or* proper respect; show sb. the respect due to him/her. ❷ *adv.* fittingly; in a fitting manner

**gebührender·maßen, gebührender·weise** *Adv.* fittingly; in a fitting manner

**gebühren-, Gebühren-: ~einheit** *die* (*Fernspr.*) [tariff] unit; **~erhöhung** *die* ⇒ **Gebühr** A: increase in charges/fees; (*Erhöhung der Fernsehgebühren*) licence fee increase; **~erlass, *~erlaß** *der* ⇒ **Gebühr** A: remission of charges/fees; (*der Fernsehgebührenerlass*) remission of the licence fee; **~ermäßigung** *die* ⇒ **Gebühr** A: reduction of charges/fees; **~frei** ❶ *Adj.* free of charge *pred.;* post-free ‹letter, packet, etc.›; ❷ *adv.* free of charge; **einen Brief ~frei schicken** send a letter post-free; **~marke** *die* revenue stamp; fiscal stamp; **~ordnung** *die* ⇒ **Gebühr** A: scale of charges/fees; **~pflichtig** ❶ *Adj.* **eine ~pflichtige Verwarnung** a fine and a caution; ❷ *adv.* **jmdn. ~pflichtig verwarnen** fine and caution sb.; **~vignette** *die* [Swiss] motorway fee sticker

**gebührlich** *Adj.* (*veralt.*) ⇒ **gebührend**

**gebunden** ❶ *2. Part. v.* **binden.** ❷ *Adj.* [A] (*verpflichtet*) bound; **an ein Versprechen/das Haus ~ sein** be bound by a promise/tied to one's home; **sich [an etw.** (*Akk.*)**] ~ fühlen** feel bound by sth.; [B] (*verlobt*) engaged; (*verheiratet*) married; [C] (*festgesetzt*) fixed ‹book prices›

**Gebundenheit** *die;* **~: ein Gefühl der ~:** a feeling of being tied [down]

**Geburt** /gə'bu:ɐ̯t/ *die;* **~, ~en** ▶ 553 birth; **von ~ an** from birth; **vor/nach Christi ~:** before/after the birth of Christ; **von hoher ~ sein** (*geh.*) be of noble birth; **ein Deutscher/Engländer von ~:** a German/Englishman by birth; **das war eine schwere ~** (*fig. ugs.*) it wasn't easy; it took some doing (*coll.*)

**geburten-, Geburten-: ~beschränkung** *die* population control; **~kontrolle** *die,* **~regelung** *die* birth control; **~rückgang** *der* decrease in the birth rate; **~schwach** *Adj.* **ein ~schwacher Jahrgang** a year with a low birth rate; **~stark** *Adj.* **ein ~starker Jahrgang** a year with a high birth rate; **~überschuss,** ***~überschuß** *der* excess of births over deaths; **~ziffer** *die* birth rate

**gebürtig** /gə'bʏrtɪç/ *Adj.* **ein ~er Schwabe** a Swabian by birth; **aus Ungarn/Paris ~ sein** be Hungarian/Parisian by birth

**Geburts-: ~anzeige** *die* birth announcement; **~datum** *das* date of birth; **~fehler** *der* congenital defect; **~haus** *das:* **das ~haus Beethovens** the house where Beethoven was born; Beethoven's birthplace; **~helfer** *der* ▶ 159 (*Arzt*) obstetrician; (*Laie*) assistant [at a/the birth]; **~helferin** *die* ▶ 159 obstetrician; (*Hebamme*) midwife; **~hilfe** *die* (*Med.*) obstetrics *sing.;* (*von einer Hebamme*) midwifery; **~jahr** *das* year of birth; **1848 ist das ~jahr der Demokratie in Deutschland** (*fig.*) the year 1848 marks the birth of democracy in Germany; **~ort** *der* place of birth; birthplace; **~schein** *der* ⇒ **~urkunde**; **~stadt** *die* native town/city; **~stunde** *die* hour of birth; **die ~stunde des Reiches schlug, als er den Thron bestieg** (*fig.*) with his accession to the throne the empire was born

**Geburts·tag** *der* Ⓐ ▶ 369 birthday; **jmdm. zum ~ gratulieren** wish sb. [a] happy birthday *or* many happy returns of the day; **sich** (*Dat.*) **etw. zum ~ wünschen** want sth. for one's birthday; **er hat morgen ~:** it's his birthday tomorrow; Ⓑ (*Geburtsdatum*) date of birth

**Geburtstags-: ~feier** *die* birthday party; **~geschenk** *das* birthday present; **~kind** *das* (*scherzh.*) birthday boy/girl; **~torte** *die* birthday cake; **~überraschung** *die* birthday surprise

**Geburts-: ~trauma** *das* (*Med., Psych.*) birth trauma; **~ur·kunde** *die* birth certificate; **~wehen** *Pl.* labour pains; (*fig.*) birth pangs; **~zange** *die* obstetric forceps *pl.*

**Gebüsch** /gə'bʏʃ/ *das;* **~[e]s, ~e** bushes *pl.;* clump of bushes; **ein niedriges ~:** a clump of low bushes; some low bushes *pl.;* **sich im ~ verstecken** hide in the bushes

**Geck** /gɛk/ *der;* **~en, ~en** (*abwertend*) dandy; fop

**geckenhaft** ❶ *Adj.* dandyish; foppish. ❷ *adv.* **er kleidet sich ~:** he dresses like a dandy

**Gecko** /'gɛko/ *der;* **~s, ~s** *od.* **~nen** /-'--/ (*Zool.*) gecko

**gedacht** /gə'daxt/ ❶ *2. Part. v.* **denken, gedenken.** ❷ *Adj.* **für jmdn./etw. ~ sein** be meant *or* intended for sb./sth.; **so war das nicht ~:** that wasn't what I intended

**Gedächtnis** /gə'dɛçtnɪs/ *das;* **~ses, ~se** Ⓐ memory; **den Alten lässt sein ~ im Stich** the old man's memory fails him; **sich** (*Dat.*) **etw. ins ~ [zurück]rufen** recall sth.; **etw. aus dem ~ aufsagen** recite sth. from memory; **jmdm. etw. aus dem ~ sagen** tell sb. sth. from memory; **das ist meinem ~ entfallen** it has slipped my mind; **das ist mir noch frisch im ~:** it is still fresh in my memory; **du hast ein kurzes ~** (*ugs.*) you have a short memory; **jmds. ~** (*Dat.*) **nachhelfen** jog sb.'s memory; **ein ~ wie ein Sieb haben** (*ugs.*) have a memory like a sieve (*coll.*); Ⓑ (*Andenken*) memory; remembrance; **zum ~ an jmdn.** in memory *or* remembrance of sb.

**Gedächtnis-: ~feier** *die* ⇒ **Gedenkfeier**; **~gottes·dienst** *der* service of remembrance; memorial service; **~hilfe** *die* ⇒ **~stütze**; **~lücke** *die* gap in one's memory; **~rede** *die* ⇒ **Gedenkrede**; **~schwäche** *die* weak *or* poor memory; (*Med., Psych.*) defective *or* weakened memory; **~schwund** *der* loss of memory; amnesia; **~störung** *die* (*bes. Med., Psych.*) defect of memory; memory defect; **~stütze** *die* memory aid; mnemonic

**gedämpft** ❶ *2. Part. v.* **dämpfen.** ❷ *Adj.* subdued ‹mood›; subdued, soft ‹light›; subdued, muted ‹colour›; muffled ‹sound›; **mit ~er Stimme** in a low *or* hushed voice; **~e Schwingungen** (*Physik*) damped vibrations

**Gedanke** *der;* **~ns, ~n** Ⓐ thought; **ein guter/vernünftiger ~:** a good/sensible idea; **einen ~n aufgreifen** take up an idea; **einen ~n zu Ende denken** follow a thought through; **seinen ~n nachhängen** abandon oneself to one's thoughts; **jmdn. auf andere ~n bringen** take sb.'s mind off things; **in ~n verloren** *od.* **versunken [sein]** [be] lost *or* deep in thought; **er war ganz in ~n** he was lost in thought; **in ~n ganz woanders sein** have one's mind on something completely different; be miles away (*coll.*); **mit seinen ~n nicht bei der Sache sein** have one's mind on something else; **ich bin in ~n immer bei dir** I'm always with you in my thoughts; **sich mit einem ~n vertraut machen** get used to an idea; **~n sind frei** thoughts are free; **jmds. ~n lesen** read sb.'s thoughts *or* mind; **~n lesen können** be able to read people's thoughts *or* to mind-read; **sich** (*Dat.*) **[um jmdn./etw.** *od.* **wegen jmds./etw.] ~n machen** be worried [about sb./sth.]; **mach dir keine ~n** (*ugs.*) don't worry; **sich über etw.** (*Akk.*) **~n machen** (*länger nachdenken*) think about *or* ponder sth.; Ⓑ **der ~ an etw.** (*Akk.*) the thought of sth.; **bei dem ~n, hingehen zu müssen** at the thought of having to go; **kein ~ [daran]!** (*ugs.*) out of the question!; no way! (*coll.*); **kein ~ daran, dass ich rechtzeitig fertig werde** (*ugs.*) there's no chance that I'll be finished on time; Ⓒ *Pl.* (*Meinung*) ideas; **seine eigenen ~n über etw. haben** have one's own ideas about sth.; **seine ~n [über etw.** (*Akk.*)**] austauschen** exchange views [about sth.]; Ⓓ (*Einfall*) idea; **das bringt mich auf einen ~n** that gives me an idea; **mir kommt ein ~:** I've had an idea; **mir kam der ~, wir könnten ...** it occurred to me that we could ...; **auf dumme ~n kommen** (*ugs.*) get silly ideas (*coll.*); **sich mit dem ~n tragen, etw. zu tun** entertain the idea of *or* consider doing sth.; **mit dem ~n spielen[, etw. zu tun]** be toying with the idea [of doing sth.]; Ⓔ (*Idee*) idea; **der ~ des Friedens** the idea of peace

**gedanken-, Gedanken-: ~armut** *die* paucity of ideas; unoriginality; **~austausch** *der* exchange of ideas; **~blitz** *der* (*ugs. scherzh.*) brainwave (*coll.*); **~flug** *der* flight of intellect; **~freiheit** *die* freedom of thought; **~gang** *der* train of thought; **~gebäude** *das* edifice of ideas; **~gut** *das* thought; **christliches ~gut** Christian thought; **staatszersetzendes ~gut** subversive ideas *pl.;* **~lesen** *das* mind-reading; **~los** ❶ *Adj.* (*unüberlegt*) unconsidered; thoughtless; (*oberflächlich*) thoughtless; (*zerstreut*) absent-minded; ❷ *adv.* (*zerstreut*) absent-mindedly; (*unüberlegt*) without thinking; thoughtlessly; **~losigkeit** *die;* **~~:** (*Zerstreutheit*) absent-mindedness; (*Unüberlegtheit*) lack of thought; thoughtlessness; **~lyrik** *die* (*Literaturw.*) philosophical poetry; **~reichtum** *der* (*eines Menschen*) fertility of ideas; (*eines Werkes*) wealth of ideas; **~schritt** *der* logical step; **~spiel** *das* intellectual pastime *or* game; **~splitter** *der* ⇒ **Aphorismus**; **~sprung** *der* mental leap; jump from one idea to another; **~strich** *der* dash; **~übertragung** *die* telepathy *no indef. art.;* thought transference *no indef. art.;* **~verloren** *Adv.* lost in thought; **~voll** ❶ *Adj.* pensive; thoughtful; ❷ *adv.* pensively; thoughtfully; **~vorbehalt** *der* (*Rechtsw.*) mental reservation; **~welt** *die* intellectual world

**gedanklich** /gə'daŋklɪç/ ❶ *Adj.* intellectual; **ein ~er Fehler** an error in reasoning; **die ~e Klarheit in diesem Werk** the clarity of thought in this work. ❷ *adv.* intellectually

**Gedärm** /gə'dɛrm/ *das;* **~[e]s, ~e** ▶ 471 intestines *pl.;* bowels *pl.,* (*eines Tieres*) entrails *pl.*

**Gedeck** *das;* **~[e]s, ~e** Ⓐ place setting; cover; **ein ~ auflegen** lay *or* set a place; Ⓑ (*Menü*) set meal; Ⓒ (*Getränk*) drink [with a cover charge]

**gedeckt** ❶ *2. Part. v.* **decken.** ❷ *Adj.* subdued; muted; ⇒ *auch* **Apfelkuchen**

**Gedeih** *in* **auf ~ und Verderb** for good or ill; for better or [for] worse; **jmdm. auf ~ und Verderb ausgeliefert sein** be entirely at sb.'s mercy

**gedeihen** /gə'daiən/ *unr. itr. V.; mit sein* Ⓐ thrive; (*wirtschaftlich*) flourish; prosper; **gut/schlecht gediehen sein** have/not have thrived; Ⓑ (*fortschreiten*) progress; **noch nicht sehr weit gediehen sein** have not yet progressed very far

**gedeihlich** ❶ *Adj.* (*geh.*) thriving, flourishing, successful ‹business›; successful ‹development, cooperation›; beneficial ‹effect etc.›. ❷ *adv.* successfully

**ge·denken** *unr. itr. V.* Ⓐ (*geh.: zurückdenken, sich erinnern*) **jmds./einer Sache** *od.* (*schweiz.*) **jmdm./einer Sache** (*Dat.*) **~:** remember sb./sth.; (*erwähnen*) recall sb./sth.; (*in einer Feier*) commemorate sb./sth.; Ⓑ (*beabsichtigen*) intend

**Gedenken** *das;* **~s** (*geh.*) remembrance; memory; **Worte des ~s** words of remembrance; **zum ~ an jmdn./etw.** in memory *or* remembrance of sb./sth.

**Gedenk-: ~feier** *die* commemoration; commemorative ceremony; **~gottesdienst** *der* ⇒ **Gedächtnisgottesdienst**; **~marke** *die* (*Philat.*) commemorative stamp; **~minute** *die* minute's silence; **eine ~minute einlegen** observe a minute's silence; **~münze** *die* commemorative coin; **~rede** *die* commemorative speech; **~stätte** *die* memorial; **~stein** *der* memorial *or* commemorative stone; **~stunde** *die* hour of commemoration; **~tafel** *die* commemorative plaque; **~tag** *der* day of remembrance; commemoration day

**Gedicht** *das;* **~[e]s, ~e** poem; **Goethes ~e** Goethe's poetry *sing. or* poems; **das Steak/Kleid ist ein ~** (*fig. ugs.*) the steak is just superb/the dress is just heavenly

**Gedicht-: ~interpretation** *die* interpretation of a poem; **~sammlung** *die* collection of poems; (*von mehreren Dichtern*) anthology of poetry *or* verse; poetry anthology

**gediegen** /gə'di:gn̩/ ❶ *Adj.* Ⓐ (*solide*) solid, solidly made ‹furniture›; sound, solid ‹piece of work›; well-made ‹clothing›; **~e Kenntnisse/ein ~es Wissen** sound knowledge; **ein ~er Charakter** a sterling character; Ⓑ (*rein*) pure ‹gold, silver, etc.›; (*in der Natur rein vorkommend*) native ‹metal›; Ⓒ (*ugs.: komisch*) hilarious; **eine ~e Marke/Type sein** be good fun (*coll.*); Ⓓ (*wunderlich*) odd; peculiar. ❷ *adv.* **~ gebaut/verarbeitet** solidly built/made

**Gediegenheit** *die;* **~:** solidity; (*von Kleidung*) sound manufacture; (*von Metall*) purity

**gedieh** /gə'di:/ *1. u. 3. Pers. Sg. Prät. v.* **gedeihen**

**gediehen** *2. Part. v.* **gedeihen**

**gedient** /gə'di:nt/ ❶ *2. Part. v.* **dienen.** ❷ *Adj.* **ein ~er Soldat** a former soldier

**Gedinge** *das;* **~s, ~** (*Bergmannsspr.: Akkordlohn*) piece rate pay; (*Vereinbarung*) piecework agreement; **im ~ arbeiten** work on a piecework basis

**Gedöns** /gə'dø:ns/ *das;* **~es** (*landsch.*) fuss; **ein ~ machen** make a fuss

**Gedränge** *das;* **~s** Ⓐ (*das Drängeln*) pushing and shoving; (*Menschenmenge*) crush; crowd; **vor der Theaterkasse herrschte ein großes ~:** there was a big crush in front

*old spelling (see note on page 1707)

of the box office; **B** *in* **ins ~ kommen** *od.* **geraten** get into difficulties; **C** **mit dem Termin/der Zeit ins ~ kommen** *od.* **geraten** have problems meeting the deadline/get into difficulties through lack of time; **D** (*Rugby*) scrum; scrummage

**gedrängt** **1** *2. Part. v.* **drängen**. **2** *Adj.* compressed, condensed ‹account›; terse, succinct ‹style, description›; crowded ‹timetable, agenda›. **3** *adv.* **~ schreiben** write succinctly *or* tersely; **etw. ~ behandeln** treat sth. in a condensed form

**gedroschen** /gəˈdrɔʃn̩/ *2. Part. v.* **dreschen**

**gedrückt** **1** *2. Part. v.* **drücken**. **2** *Adj.* dejected, depressed ‹mood›

**gedrungen** /gəˈdrʊŋən/ **1** *2. Part. v.* **dringen**. **2** *Adj.* stocky; thickset

**Gedrungenheit** *die;* **~:** stockiness

**Gedudel** *das;* **~s** (*ugs. abwertend*) tootling; (*im Radio*) noise

**Geduld** /gəˈdʊlt/ *die;* **~:** patience; **meine ~ ist erschöpft/am Ende** my patience is exhausted/at an end; **die ~ verlieren** lose one's patience; **keine ~ [zu etw.] haben** have no patience [with sth.]; **mit jmdm. ~ haben** be patient with sb.; **haben Sie bitte noch ein wenig ~:** please bear with me/us *etc.* a little while longer; **ihm riss die ~:** his patience snapped *or* gave way; **mir reißt die ~:** my patience is wearing thin; I'm losing all patience; **sich in ~ fassen** exercise *or* have patience; **mit ~ und Spucke** (*fig. salopp*) with a little patience [and ingenuity]

**gedulden** *refl. V.* be patient; **~ Sie sich bitte ein paar Minuten** please be so good as to wait a few minutes

**geduldig** **1** *Adj.* patient; **ein ~er Patient** a good patient; **~ wie ein Lamm** meek as a lamb. **2** *adv.* patiently

**Gedulds-:** **~faden** *der:* **in mir/ihm** *etc.* **reißt der ~faden** (*ugs.*) my/his *etc.* patience is wearing thin; **~probe** *die* trial of one's patience; **das ist eine harte ~probe für mich** that sorely tries my patience; **auf eine harte ~probe gestellt werden** have one's patience sorely tried; **~spiel** *das* puzzle; (*fig.*) Chinese puzzle

**gedungen** /gəˈdʊŋən/ *2. Part. v.* **dingen**

**gedunsen** /gəˈdʊnzn̩/ *Adj.* ⇒ **aufgedunsen**

**gedurft** /gəˈdʊrft/ *2. Part. v.* **dürfen**

**geeignet** **1** *2. Part. v.* **eignen**. **2** *Adj.* suitable; (*richtig*) right; **er ist der ~e Mann für diese Aufgabe** he's the right man for this job; **im ~en Augenblick** at the right moment; **ich war für diese Arbeit nicht ~:** I wasn't suited to the work

**Geest** /geːst/ *die;* **~:** *sandy heathland on N. German coast*

**Gefahr** *die;* **~, ~en** **A** (*gefährliche Lage*) danger; (*Bedrohung*) danger; threat; **die ~en meines Berufs** the hazards of my job; **die ~en des Dschungels** the perils of the jungle; **eine ~ für jmdn./etw.** a danger to sb./sth.; **in ~ kommen/geraten** get into danger; **jmdn./etw. in ~ bringen** put sb./sth. in danger; **sich in ~ begeben** put oneself in danger; expose oneself to danger; **in ~ sein** be in danger; ‹rights, plans› be in jeopardy *or* peril; **außer ~ sein** be out of danger; **bei ~:** in case of emergency; **sie liebt die ~:** she likes living dangerously; **B** (*Risiko*) risk; **jmdn./sich einer ~ aussetzen** run *or* take a risk; **es besteht die ~, dass …** there is a danger *or* risk that …; **auf die ~ hin, dass das passiert** at the risk of that happening; **~ laufen, etw. zu tun** risk *or* run the risk of doing sth.; **auf eigene ~:** at one's own risk; **wer sich in ~ begibt, kommt darin um** if you keep on taking risks, you'll come to grief eventually

**gefahr·bringend** *Adj.* dangerous

**gefährden** /gəˈfɛːɐ̯dn̩/ *tr. V.* endanger; jeopardize ‹enterprise, success, position, etc.›; (*aufs Spiel setzen*) put at risk; **sich ~:** put oneself in danger

**gefährdet** *Adj.* ‹people, adolescents, etc.› at risk *postpos.*

**Gefährdung** *die;* **~, ~en** **A** endangering; (*eines Unternehmens, einer Position usw.*) jeopardizing; **B** (*Gefahr*) threat (+ *Gen.* to)

**gefahren** *2. Part. v.* **fahren**

**Gefahren-:** **~bereich** *der* danger area *or* zone; **~herd** *der* source of danger; **~quelle** *die* source of danger; **~zone** *die* danger zone *or* area; **~zulage** *die* danger money *no indef. art.*

**gefährlich** /gəˈfɛːɐ̯lɪç/ **1** *Adj.* dangerous; (*gewagt*) risky; **ein Mann im ~en Alter** (*fig.*) a man at a dangerous age; **[für jmdn./etw.] ~ sein** be dangerous [for sb./sth.]; **er könnte mir ~ werden** he could be a threat *or* a danger to me; (*fig.*) I could fall for him [in a big way]; **das ist [alles] nicht so ~:** it's not disastrous; **ein ~er Plan/~es Unternehmen** a risky plan/enterprise; **ein ~es Spiel treiben** play a dangerous game. **2** *adv.* dangerously

**Gefährlichkeit** *die;* **~:** dangerousness; (*Gewagtheit*) riskiness

**gefahr·los** **1** *Adj.* safe. **2** *adv.* safely

**Gefahr·losigkeit** *die;* **~:** safety; safeness

**Gefährt** *das;* **~[e]s, ~e** (*geh.*) vehicle

**Gefährte** *der;* **~n, ~n, Gefährtin** *die;* **~, ~nen** (*geh.*) companion; (*Ehemann/Ehefrau*) partner in life

**gefahr·voll** *Adj.* dangerous; perilous

**Gefälle** /gəˈfɛlə/ *das;* **~s, ~** **A** (*Neigungsgrad*) slope; incline; (*eines Flusses*) drop; (*einer Straße*) gradient; **ein ~ von fünf Prozent** a gradient of one in twenty *or* of five per cent; **das Gelände hat ein leichtes ~:** the land slopes gently; **B** (*Unterschied*) difference; **das geistige/soziale ~:** the difference in intellect/social class

**gefallen**[1] *unr. itr. V.* **A** **das gefällt mir** I like it; **das gefällt ihm gut/gar nicht** he likes it very much *or* (*coll.*) a lot/doesn't like it at all; **es gefiel ihr, wie er sich bewegte** she liked the way he moved; **zu ~ wissen** know how to make oneself liked [by everyone]; **weißt du, was mir an dir/dem Bild so gut gefällt?** do you know what I like so much about you/the picture?; **mir gefällt es hier** I like it here; **er gefällt mir [ganz und gar] nicht** (*ugs.: sieht krank aus*) he looks in a bad way to me (*coll.*); **die Sache gefällt mir nicht** (*ugs.*) I don't like [the look of] it (*coll.*); **wenn es dem Herrn gefällt** (*geh.*) if it please God; if it is God's will; **B** (*ugs.*) *in* **sich (*Dat.*) etw. ~ lassen** put up with sth.; **das lasse ich mir nicht länger ~:** I won't put up with it *or* stand for it any longer; **das lasse ich mir ~!** there's nothing I like better; that's just the job (*coll.*); **C** (*abwertend*) **sich (*Dat.*) in einer Rolle ~:** enjoy *or* like playing a role; fancy oneself in a role (*coll.*); **er gefällt sich in der Rolle des Intellektuellen** he likes playing the intellectual; **er gefällt sich in Übertreibungen** he likes to exaggerate

**gefallen**[2] **1** *2. Part. v.* **fallen, ~**. **2** *Adj.* fallen ‹angel etc.›; **ein ~es Mädchen** (*veralt.*) a fallen woman

**Gefallen**[1] *der;* **~s, ~:** favour; **jmdm. einen ~ tun** *od.* **erweisen** do sb. a favour; **tu mir den** *od.* **einen ~, und …!** (*ugs.*) do me a favour and …; **jmdn. um einen ~ bitten** ask a favour of sb.

**Gefallen**[2] *das;* **~s** pleasure; **etw. mit ~ betrachten** get pleasure from *or* enjoy looking at sth.; **~ an jmdm./aneinander finden** like sb./each other; **an etw. (*Dat.*) ~ finden** get *or* derive pleasure from sth.; enjoy sth.; **jmdm. etw. zu ~ tun** do sth. to please sb.

**Gefallene** *der; adj. Dekl.* soldier killed in action; **die ~n** the fallen; those killed *or* those who fell in action

**Gefallenen·denkmal** *das* war memorial

**Gefälle·strecke** *die* incline

**ge·fällig** **1** *Adj.* **A** (*hilfsbereit*) obliging; helpful; **jmdm. ~ sein** oblige *or* help sb.; **sich ~ zeigen/[als] ~ erweisen** show oneself willing to oblige *or* help; **B** (*anziehend*) pleasing; agreeable; pleasant, agreeable ‹programme, behaviour›; **C** (*gewünscht*) **folgen Sie mir, wenns ~ ist!** follow me, if you please; **noch ein Kaffee ~?** would you like *or* care for another coffee?. **2** *adv.* pleasingly; agreeably

**Gefälligkeit** *die;* **~, ~en** **A** (*Hilfeleistung*) favour; **jmdm. eine [kleine] ~ erweisen** do sb. a [small] favour; **B** (*Hilfsbereitschaft*) obligingness; helpfulness; **etw. aus reiner ~ tun** do sth. just to be obliging; **C** (*ansprechende Art*) agreeableness; pleasantness

**Gefälligkeits·akzept** *das*, **Gefälligkeits·wechsel** *der* (*Bankw.*) accommodation bill

**gefälligst** /gəˈfɛlɪçst/ *Adv.* (*ugs.*) kindly; **lass das ~!** kindly stop that

**Gefäll·strecke** *die* ⇒ **Gefällestrecke**

**Gefall·sucht** *die* (*veralt.*) vanity

**gefall·süchtig** *Adj.* (*veralt.*) vain

**gefangen** *2. Part. v.* **fangen**

**Gefangene** *der/die; adj. Dekl.* **A** prisoner; captive; **~ machen** take prisoners; **B** (*Häftling, Kriegs~*) prisoner

**Gefangenen-:** **~austausch** *der* exchange of prisoners; **~befreiung** *die* (*Rechtsw.*) aiding and abetting the escape of a prisoner; **~haus** *das* (*österr.*) ⇒ **Gefängnis**; **~lager** *das* prisoner of war camp; prison camp

**gefangen-, Gefangen-:** ***~|halten** ⇒ **fangen** 1B; **~nahme** *die;* **~, ~~nen** capture; **bei seiner ~nahme** when he was captured; ***~|nehmen** ⇒ **fangen** 1B

**Gefangenschaft** *die;* **~, ~en** captivity; **in ~ sein/geraten** be a prisoner/be taken prisoner; **in russischer ~ sein** be a prisoner of the Russians

***gefangen|setzen** ⇒ **fangen** 1B

**Gefängnis** /gəˈfɛŋnɪs/ *das;* **~ses, ~se** **A** (*Strafanstalt*) prison; gaol; **jmdn. ins ~ bringen/werfen** put/throw sb. in[to] prison; **im ~ sein** *od.* **sitzen** be in prison; **ins ~ kommen** be sent to prison; **mit einem Bein** *od.* **Fuß im ~ stehen** be only just on the right side of the law; **B** (*Strafe*) imprisonment; **darauf steht ~:** that is punishable by imprisonment *or* a prison sentence; **ein Vergehen mit ~ bestrafen** punish an offence with imprisonment; **jmdn. zu zwei Jahren ~ verurteilen** sentence sb. to two years' imprisonment *or* two years in prison

**Gefängnis-:** **~arzt** *der*, **~ärztin** *die* prison doctor; **~direktor** *der*, **~direktorin** *die* prison governor; **~geistliche** *der/die* prison chaplain; **~haft** *die* imprisonment; **~hof** *der* prison yard; **~kleidung** *die* prison uniform; **~mauer** *die* prison wall; **~strafe** *die* prison sentence; **eine ~strafe verbüßen** *od.* (*ugs.*) **absitzen** serve a prison sentence; **eine ~strafe von sechs Monaten** six months' imprisonment; six months in prison; **jmdn. zu einer ~strafe [von acht Monaten] verurteilen** send sb. to prison [for eight months]; **~wärter** *der*, **~wärterin** *die* ▶ **159** prison officer; [prison] warder; **~zelle** *die* prison cell

**Gefasel** *das;* **~s** (*ugs. abwertend*) twaddle (*coll.*); drivel (*derog.*)

**Gefäß** /gəˈfɛːs/ *das;* **~es, ~e** **A** (*Behälter*) vessel; container; **B** ▶ **471** (*Med.*) vessel; **C** (*Fechten*) coquille

**gefäß-, Gefäß-:** **~erweiternd** (*Med.*) **1** *Adj.* vaso-dilating; **2** *adv.* **~erweiternd wirken** have a vaso-dilating effect; **~erweiterung** *die* ▶ **474** (*Med.*) vascular dilation; **~leiden** *das* ▶ **474** (*Med.*) vascular complaint

**gefasst**, ***gefaßt** /gəˈfast/ **1** *2. Part. v.* **fassen**. **2** *Adj.* **A** (*beherrscht*) calm; composed; **mit ~er Haltung** with composure; **mit ~er Stimme** in a calm voice; **B** *in* **auf etw. (*Akk.*) [nicht] ~ sein** [not] be prepared for sth.; **sich auf etw. (*Akk.*) ~ machen** prepare oneself for sth.; **der kann sich auf was ~ machen** (*ugs.*) he'll catch it *or* be for it (*coll.*). **3** *adv.* calmly; with composure

**Gefasstheit**, ***Gefaßtheit** *die* calmness; composure

**gefäß-, Gefäß-:** **~verengend** (*Med.*) **1** *Adj.* vaso-constrictive; **2** *adv.* **~verengend wirken** have a vaso-constrictive effect; **~verengung** *die* ▶ **474** (*Med.*) vaso-constriction; vascular constriction; **~wand** *die* ▶ **471** (*Med.*) vascular wall

**Gefecht** *das;* **~[e]s, ~e** **A** battle; engagement (*Milit.*); **ein schweres/kurzes ~:**

fierce fighting/a skirmish; **sich** (*Dat.*)**/dem Feind ein ~ liefern** engage each other/the enemy in battle; **die Truppen ins ~ führen** lead the troops into battle; **ein hitziges ~** (*fig.*) a heated exchange; **jmdn./etw. außer ~ setzen** put sb./sth. out of action; **klar zum ~!** (*Marine*) clear for action!; [B] (*Fechten*) bout; ⇒ *auch* **Eifer**

**gefechts-, Gefechts-: ~ausbildung** *die* (*Milit.*) combat training; battle training; **~bereich** *der* (*Milit.*) battle zone; battle area; combat zone (*Amer.*); **~bereit** *Adj.* (*Milit.*) ready for action *or* battle *postpos.*; combat-ready; **~bereitschaft** *die* (*Milit.*) readiness for action; readiness for battle; **sich in ~bereitschaft befinden** be ready for action *or* battle; **~einheit** *die* (*Milit.*) fighting unit; **~klar** *Adj.* ⇒ **~bereit**; **~kopf** *der* (*Milit.*) warhead; **~mäßig** (*Milit.*) ❶ *Adj.* ‹equipment› for active service; combat ‹firing practice, formation, etc.›; ❷ *adv.* **~mäßig ausgerüstet** equipped for active service *or* for battle; **~pause** *die* lull in the fighting; **~stand** *der* (*Milit.*) battle headquarters *pl.*; command post; (*Luftw.*) operations room; **~stärke** *die* (*Milit.*) fighting strength; **~turm** *der* (*Milit.*) turret; **~übung** *die* (*Milit.*) combat exercise; field exercise

**gefedert** *2. Part. v.* **federn**

**gefehlt** ❶ *2. Part. v.* **fehlen**. ❷ *Adj.* **weit ~!** wide of the mark!

**Gefeilsche** *das;* **~s** haggling

**gefeit** *2. Part. v.* **feien**

**gefestigt** ❶ *2. Part. v.* **festigen**. ❷ *Adj.* assured ‹beliefs›; secure ‹person›; established ‹tradition›

**Gefiedel** *das;* **~s** (*abwertend*) fiddling

**Gefieder** /gəˈfi:dɐ/ *das;* **~s, ~:** plumage; feathers *pl.*

**gefiedert** *Adj.* [A] (*mit Federn*) feathered; **unsere ~en Freunde** our feathered friends; [B] (*Bot.*) pinnate; **paarig/unpaarig ~:** abruptly pinnate/odd-pinnate

**Gefilde** /gəˈfɪldə/ *das;* **~s, ~** (*geh.*) **anmutige/sonnige ~:** pleasant/sunny climes (*literary*); **die ~ der Seligen** (*griech. Myth.*) the Elysian Fields; **wieder in heimatlichen ~n sein** (*scherzh.*) be back under one's native skies

**gefingert** ❶ *2. Part. v.* **fingern**. ❷ *Adj.* (*Bot.*) digitate[d]; palmate

**gefinkelt** /gəˈfɪŋkl̩t/ *Adj.* (*österr.*) cunning; crafty; shrewd

**geflammt** ❶ *2. Part. v.* **flammen**. ❷ *Adj.* mottled, wavy-grained ‹wood›; mottled ‹tile›; watered, moiré ‹silk, fabric›

**Geflatter** *das;* **~s** fluttering

**Geflecht** *das;* **~[e]s, ~e** [A] (*Flechtwerk*) wickerwork *no art.*; **ein ~ aus Binsen** interlaced rushes *pl.*; [B] (*fig.: dichtes Netz*) tangle; **ein wirres/dichtes ~ von Zweigen und Wurzeln** a tangled/dense network of twigs and roots

**gefleckt** ❶ *2. Part. v.* **flecken**. ❷ *Adj.* spotty, blotchy ‹skin, face›; spotted ‹leopard skin›

**Geflenne** *das;* **~s** (*ugs. abwertend*) bawling; blubbering

**Geflimmer** *das;* **~s** (*auf dem Bildschirm, auf der Filmleinwand*) flickering; (*von Sternen*) twinkling

**geflissentlich** /gəˈflɪsn̩tlɪç/ ❶ *Adj.* [A] (*absichtlich*) deliberate; [B] (*Amtsspr. veralt.: freundlich*) **zu Ihrer ~en Kenntnisnahme/Beachtung** for your information/for your esteemed consideration. ❷ *adv.* deliberately; **jmdm. ~ aus dem Wege gehen** studiously avoid sb.

**geflochten** /gəˈflɔxtn̩/ *2. Part. v.* **flechten**

**geflogen** /gəˈflo:gn̩/ *2. Part. v.* **fliegen**

**geflohen** /gəˈflo:ən/ *2. Part. v.* **fliehen**

**geflossen** /gəˈflɔsn̩/ *2. Part. v.* **fließen**

**Gefluche** *das;* **~s** (*ugs. abwertend*) swearing; cursing

**Geflügel** *das;* **~s** (*Federvieh, Fleisch*) poultry

**Geflügel-: ~farm** *die* poultry farm; **~haltung** *die* poultry farming; **~händler** *der*, **~händlerin** *die* poulterer; **~handlung** *die* poulterer's [shop]; **~salat** *der* chicken salad/turkey salad *etc.*; **~schere** *die* poultry shears *pl.*

**geflügelt** *Adj.* winged ‹insect, seed›; **ein ~es Wort** (*fig.*) a standard *or* familiar quotation

**Geflügel-: ~zucht** *die* poultry breeding; **~züchter** *der*, **~züchterin** *die* poultry breeder

**Geflunker** *das;* **~s** (*ugs.*) fibbing (*coll.*)

**Geflüster** *das;* **~s** whispering

**gefochten** /gəˈfɔxtn̩/ *2. Part. v.* **fechten**

**Gefolge** *das;* **~s, ~** [A] (*Begleitung*) entourage; retinue; **etw. im ~ haben** lead to sth.; bring sth. in its wake; [B] (*Trauergeleit*) cortège

**Gefolgschaft** *die;* **~, ~en** [A] (*Gehorsam*) **jmdm. ~ leisten** obey *or* follow sb.; give one's allegiance to sb.; **jmdm. die ~ aufsagen** *od.* **kündigen** refuse to obey sb. any longer; renounce one's allegiance to sb.; **jmdm. die ~ verweigern** refuse to obey *or* follow sb.; refuse to give sb. one's allegiance; [B] (*hist.*) *band of young nobles bound to a peer leader by an oath of fealty;* ≈ followers *pl.*

**Gefolgs·mann** *der; Pl.* **Gefolgsmänner** *od.* **Gefolgsleute** *member of a Gefolgschaft;* ≈ follower; (*fig.*) follower

**Gefrage** *das;* **~s** (*abwertend*) questions *pl.*

**gefragt** ❶ *2. Part. v.* **fragen**. ❷ *Adj.* ‹artist, craftsman, product› in great demand; sought-after ‹artist, craftsman, product›; **~ sein** *od.* **werden** be in great demand

**gefräßig** /gəˈfrɛ:sɪç/ *Adj.* (*abwertend*) greedy; gluttonous; voracious ‹animal, insect›

**Gefräßigkeit** *die;* **~** (*abwertend*) greediness; gluttony; (*von Tieren*) voracity

**Gefreite** /gəˈfraitə/ *der; adj. Dekl.* ▶ **91** (*Milit.*) lance corporal (*Brit.*); private first class (*Amer.*); (*Marine*) able seaman; (*Luftw.*) aircraftman first class (*Brit.*); airman third class (*Amer.*)

**gefressen** *2. Part. v.* **fressen**

**Gefrier-: ~anlage** *die* freezing plant; **~apparat** *der* freezing unit; freezer

**gefrieren** ❶ *unr. itr. V.; mit sein* (*auch fig.*) freeze; ⇒ *auch* **Blut**. ❷ *unr. tr. V.* (*einfrieren*) freeze

**gefrier-, Gefrier-: ~fach** *das* freezing compartment; **~fleisch** *das* frozen meat; **~gemüse** *das* frozen vegetables *pl.*; **~getrocknet** *2. Part. v.* **~trocknen**; **~gut** *das* frozen food; **~punkt** *der* ▶ **728** freezing point; **Temperaturen über/unter dem ~punkt** temperatures above/below freezing; **~raum** *der* freezer; deep-freeze room; **~schrank** *der* [upright] freezer; **~schutz·mittel** *das* ⇒ **Frostschutzmittel**; **~|trocknen** *tr. V.; meist im Inf. u. 2. Part.* freeze-dry; **~truhe** *die* [chest] freezer

**gefroren** /gəˈfro:rən/ *2. Part. v.* **frieren, gefrieren**

**Gefror[e]ne** *das; adj. Dekl.* (*südd., österr.*) ice cream

**Gefrotzel** *das;* **~s** (*ugs.*) ribbing (*coll.*)

**gefrustet** *Adj.* (*ugs.*) frustrated

**Gefuchtel** *das;* **~s** gesticulating

**Gefüge** *das;* **~s, ~** [A] (*Zusammengefügtes*) structure; construction; **ein ~ aus Balken/Steinen** a construction of beams/stones; [B] (*Struktur*) structure; **das syntaktische ~:** the syntactical structure; **das wirtschaftliche/soziale ~:** the economic/social fabric

**gefügig** *Adj.* submissive; compliant; docile ‹animal›; **ein ~es Werkzeug** (*fig.*) a willing tool; **sich** (*Dat.*) **jmdn. ~ machen/jmdn. seinen Wünschen ~ machen** make sb. submit to one's will/one's wishes

**Gefügigkeit** *die;* **~:** submissiveness; compliance; (*von Tieren*) docility

**Gefühl** *das;* **~s, ~e** [A] (*Wahrnehmung*) sensation; feeling; **ein ~ für Wärme und Kälte haben** be able to feel *or* tell the difference between hot and cold; **kein ~ im Arm haben** have no feeling in one's arm; **ein ~ des Schmerzes/der Kälte** a sensation of pain/cold; [B] (*Gemütsverfassung*) feeling; **ein ~ der Einsamkeit/der Scham** a sense *or* feeling of loneliness/shame; **ein beglückendes/beängstigendes ~ überkam/ergriff sie** she was filled with a feeling of happiness/gripped by a feeling of anxiety; **kein ~ haben** have no feelings; **mit gemischten ~en** with mixed feelings; **drei Mark sind das höchste der ~e** (*ugs.*) three marks is the most I'm prepared to pay; (*was man dafür verlangen kann*) it won't fetch more than three marks; [C] (*Ahnung*) feeling; **ein/das ~ haben, als ob ...** have a/the feeling that ...; **etw. im ~ haben** have a feeling *or* a premonition of sth.; [D] (*Verständnis, Gespür*) sense; instinct; **ein ~ für Rhythmus/Gut und Böse** a sense of rhythm/right and wrong; **sich auf sein ~ verlassen** trust one's feelings *or* instinct; **etw. nach ~ tun** do sth. by instinct

**gefühlig** *Adj.* (*abwertend*) mushy, mawkish ‹play, film, etc.›; mawkish ‹person›

**gefühl·los** *Adj.* [A] (*ohne Wahrnehmung*) numb; **~ gegen Schmerzen** insensitive to pain; [B] (*herzlos, kalt*) unfeeling; callous

**Gefühllosigkeit** *die;* **~** [A] numbness; lack of sensation; [B] (*Mangel an Mitleid*) unfeelingness; callousness

**gefühls-, Gefühls-: ~aktiv** *Adj.* supersensitive, extra sensitive ‹condom›; **~arm** *Adj.* lacking in feeling; **~armut** *die* lack of feeling; **~ausbruch** *der* outburst [of emotion]; **~betont** ❶ *Adj.* emotional ‹speech, argument›; ❷ *adv.* **~betont handeln** be guided by one's emotions; **~dinge** *Pl.* emotional matters *pl.*; **~duselei** /-du:zəˈlai/ *die;* **~~** (*ugs. abwertend*) mawkishness; mawkish sentimentality; **~kalt** *Adj.* [A] cold; unfeeling; [B] (*frigide*) frigid; **~kälte** *die* [A] coldness; unfeelingness; [B] (*Frigidität*) frigidity; **~leben** *das* emotional life; **~mäßig** ❶ *Adj.* emotional ‹reaction›; ‹action› based on emotion; ❷ *adv.* **es hat sich ~mäßig auf ihn stark ausgewirkt** it has affected him deeply; **rein ~mäßig würde ich sagen, dass ...** my own, purely instinctive, feeling would be to say that ...; **~mensch** *der* emotionalist; person guided by his/her emotions; **~nerv** *der* sensory nerve; **~regung** *die* emotion; ***~roheit**, **~rohheit** *die* callousness; **~sache** *die* matter of feel *or* instinct; **~tiefe** *die* (*geh.*) depth of feeling; **~überschwang** *der* flood of emotion; **in seinem ~überschwang** carried away by emotion; **~welt** *die* emotions *pl.*

**gefühl·voll** ❶ *Adj.* [A] (*empfindsam*) sensitive; [B] (*ausdrucksvoll*) expressive. ❷ *adv.* sensitively; expressively; with feeling

**gefüllt** ❶ *2. Part. v.* **füllen**. ❷ *Adj.* **~e Bonbons** sweets (*Brit.*) *or* (*Amer.*) candies with centres; **~e Tomaten/Paprikaschoten** stuffed tomatoes/peppers; **~er Flieder/~e Geranien** double lilac/geraniums; **eine [gut] ~e Brieftasche** a well-stuffed *or* bulging wallet

**Gefummel** *das;* **~s** (*ugs. abwertend*) [A] fiddling (*coll.*); **lass doch das ~ an der Tischdecke!** stop fiddling with the tablecloth!; [B] (*erotisch*) pawing (*coll.*)

**gefunden** /gəˈfʊndn̩/ *2. Part. v.* **finden;** ⇒ *auch* **Fressen** B

**gefurcht** ❶ *2. Part. v.* **furchen**. ❷ *Adj.* lined; wrinkled

**gefürchtet** ❶ *2. Part. v.* **fürchten**. ❷ *Adj.* dreaded; feared ‹despot, opponent›

**gefüttert** *2. Part. v.* **füttern**

**gegabelt** ❶ *2. Part. v.* **gabeln**. ❷ *Adj.* forked ‹branch, stick, tail›

**Gegacker** *das;* **~s** [A] (*dauerndes Gackern*) cackling; [B] (*ugs.: Kichern*) giggling

**gegangen** *2. Part. v.* **gehen**

**gegeben** ❶ *2. Part. v.* **geben**. ❷ *Adj.* [A] (*vorhanden*) given; **etw. als ~ voraussetzen/hinnehmen** take sth. for granted; **aus ~em Anlass** for certain reasons (*specified or not*); **aus ~em Anlass kann ich nicht umhin, auch einige Worte der Kritik zu äußern** [there are reasons why] I cannot refrain from offering some criticisms; **unter den ~en Umständen** in these circumstances; **eine ~e Größe/Zahl** (*Math.*) a given magnitude/number; [B] (*passend*)

*old spelling (see note on page 1707)

right; proper; das ist das Gegebene that's the best thing; zu ~er Zeit in due course; at the appropriate time

**gegebenen·falls** *Adv.* should the occasion arise; (*wenn nötig*) if necessary; (*auf einem Formular*) if applicable

**Gegebenheit** *die;* ~, ~en condition; (*Tatsache*) fact; die wirtschaftlichen und sozialen ~en the economic and social conditions

**gegen** /ˈgeːgn̩/ ❶ *Präp. mit Akk.* (A) towards; (*an*) against; das Dia ~ das Licht halten hold the slide up to *or* against the light; ~ die Tür schlagen bang on the door; ~ etw. stoßen knock into *or* against sth.; das ist [nicht] ~ Sie gerichtet that is [not] aimed against you; ein Mittel ~ Husten/Krebs a cough medicine/a cure for cancer; ~ jmdn. spielen/gewinnen play [against] sb./win against sb.; etwas/nichts ~ jmdn. haben have something/nothing against sb.; ~ die Abmachung contrary to *or* against the agreement; ~ alle Vernunft/bessere Einsicht against all reason/one's better judgement; ~ jmds. Willen/Befehl against *or* contrary to sb.'s wishes/orders; (B) ▶ 752 (*ungefähr um*) ~ Abend/Morgen towards evening/dawn; ~ 4[00] nachts around 4 a. m. *or* 4 o'clock in the morning; (C) (*im Vergleich zu*) compared with; in comparison with; ~ gestern compared with yesterday; ich wette hundert ~ eins, dass er ... I'll bet you a hundred to one he ...; (D) (*im Ausgleich für*) for; etw. ~ bar verkaufen/tauschen sell/exchange sth. for cash; etw. ~ Quittung erhalten receive sth. against a receipt; (E) (*veralt.: gegenüber*) ~ jmdn. freundlich/höflich sein be pleasant/polite to *or* towards sb.; ~ jmdn./sich streng sein be strict with sb./oneself.
❷ *Adv.* ▶ 752 (*ungefähr*) about; around

**Gegen-:** ~angebot *das* counter-offer; ~angriff *der* counter-attack; zum ~angriff ansetzen mount *or* launch a counter-attack; ~antrag *der* (*im Parlament*) countermotion; ~anzeige *die* (*Med.*) contraindication; ~argument *das* counter-argument; ~beispiel *das* example to the contrary; counter-example; ~beschuldigung *die* counter-charge; counter accusation; ~besuch *der* return visit; ~bewegung *die* (A) countermovement; (B) (*Musik*) (*bei der Melodie*) inversion; (*bei Tonleitern usw.*) contrary motion; ~beweis *der* evidence to the contrary, counter-evidence *no indef. art., no pl.;* den ~beweis antreten *od.* führen produce evidence to the contrary *or* counter-evidence; ~buchung *die* (*Buchf.*) cross-entry

**Gegend** /ˈgeːgn̩t/ *die;* ~, ~en (A) (*Landschaft*) landscape; (*geographisches Gebiet*) region; die ~ ist flach/gebirgig the region is flat/mountainous; durch die ~ latschen/kurven (*salopp*) traipse around (*coll.*)/drive around; in der ~ herumbrüllen (*salopp*) bawl one's head off (*coll.*); (B) (*Umgebung*) area; neighbourhood; (*Stadtviertel*) district; neighbourhood; (*Einwohnerschaft*) neighbourhood; in der ~ von/um Hamburg in the Hamburg area; in der ~ des Parks in the neighbourhood of the park; ein Einbrecher/eine Jugendbande macht die ~ unsicher (*ugs.*) there is a burglar about in the neighbourhood/a gang of youths are making a nuisance of themselves in this area; (C) in der ~ des Magens/der Leber in the region of the stomach/the liver; (D) (*Richtung*) direction

**Gegen-:** ~darstellung *die:* eine ~darstellung [der Sache] an account [of the matter] from an opposing point of view; ~demonstration *die* counterdemonstration; ~dienst *der* service in return; (*Gefälligkeit*) favour in return; ~druck *der; Pl.* ~drücke counter-pressure; (*fig.*) resistance

**gegen·einander** *Adv.* (A) against each other *or* one another; (*im Austausch*) man tauschte die Geiseln ~ aus the hostages were exchanged; es ist schwierig, diese beiden Begriffe/Epochen ~ abzugrenzen it is difficult to distinguish these two concepts/to divide these two periods from each other; die beiden haben etwas ~: those two have got something against each other; zwei Dinge ~ halten hold two things up together *or* side by side; (*vergleichen*) compare two things; put two things side by side; ~ prallen collide; Bretter/Fahrräder ~ stellen stand planks/bicycles [up] against one another; (B) (*zueinander*) to[wards] each other *or* one another

**Gegen·einander** *das;* ~s conflict

***gegeneinander|halten** *usw.:* ⇒ gegeneinander

**gegen-, Gegen-:** ~entwurf *der* alternative draft; ~erklärung *die* counter-statement; rebuttal; ~fahrbahn *die* opposite carriageway; ~forderung *die* (A) countercondition; (B) (*Forderung eines Schuldners*) counterclaim; ~frage *die* question in return; counterquestion; auf eine Frage mit einer ~frage antworten answer a question with another question; ~gabe *die* (*geh.*) present *or* gift in return; ~gerade *die* (*Leichtathletik*) back straight; ~gewalt *die* counter-violence; ~gewicht *das* counterweight; ein ~gewicht zu *od.* ~ etw. bilden (*fig.*) counterbalance sth.; ~gift *das* antidote; ~grund *der* ⇒ Grund C; ~|halten *unr. tr., itr. V.* (*nordd. ugs.*) [die Hand/den Finger] ~halten hold one's hand/finger against it; ~kandidat *der,* ~kandidatin *die* opposing candidate; rival candidate; ~klage *die* (*Rechtsw.*) counterclaim; countercharge; ~klage [gegen jmdn.] erheben bring a counterclaim *or* countercharge/countercharges *pl.* [against sb.]; ~kläger *der,* ~klägerin *die* (*Rechtsw.*) counterclaimant; ~könig *der,* ~königin *die* (*hist.*) rival claimant to the throne; ~kraft *die* opposing force; counterforce; ~kultur *die* counterculture; alternative culture; ~kurs *der* (*Flugw.*) reciprocal course; auf ~kurs gehen set a reciprocal course; (*fig.*) steer an opposite course; ~läufig ❶ *Adj.* opposed ‹pistons›; contra-rotating ‹propellers›; eine ~läufige Entwicklung/Tendenz (*fig.*) a reverse development/trend; ❷ *adv.* sich ~läufig bewegen ‹pistons› be opposed; ‹propellers› contra-rotate; ~leistung *die* service in return; consideration; als ~leistung für etw. in return for sth.; zu einer ~leistung bereit sein be prepared to do sth. in return; ~|lenken *itr. V.* turn the wheel to correct the line; ~|lesen *unr. tr. V.* read as a check

**Gegen·licht** *das* (*bes. Fot.*) back-lighting

**Gegenlicht·aufnahme** *die* (*Fot.*) photograph taken/taking a picture against the light; contre-jour photograph

**gegen-, Gegen-:** ~liebe *die:* in [bei jmdm.] ~liebe finden *od.* auf ~liebe stoßen find favour [with sb.]; ~maßnahme *die* countermeasure; ~meinung *die* opposing *or* dissenting view; ~mittel *das* (*gegen Gift*) antidote; (*gegen Krankheit*) remedy; ein ~mittel für ein Gift/~ eine Krankheit an antidote for *or* to a poison/a remedy for a disease; ~mutter *die; Pl.* ~~n (*Technik*) locking nut; locknut; ~offensive *die* (*Milit.*) counteroffensive; ~papst *der* (*hist.*) antipope; ~part *der* (*geh.*) counterpart; (*Gegner*) opponent; ~partei *die* opposing side; other side; (*Sport*) opposing side *or* team; ~plan *der* (*DDR Wirtsch.*) counterplan (*to supplement the national economic plan*); ~pol *der* (*auch fig.*) opposite pole; (*Math.*) antipole; ~probe *die* (A) (*einer Behauptung, These*) cross-check; durch die ~probe by cross-checking; die ~probe machen carry out a cross-check; (*bei einer Rechnung*) work the sum the other way round; (B) (*bei Abstimmungen durch Handzeichen od. Aufstehen*) recount in which the opposite motion is put; ~propaganda *die* counter-propaganda; ~rechnung *die* contra account; check account; [jmdm.] die ~rechnung aufmachen make out a contra account for sb.; (*fig.*) reply with one's own set of figures; ~rede *die* (A) (*geh.: Erwiderung*) reply; rejoinder; Rede und ~rede dialogue; ein amüsantes Spiel von Rede und ~rede an amusing series of exchanges; (B) (*Widerrede*) contradiction; (*Einspruch*) objection; ~reformation *die* (*hist.*) Counter-Reformation; ~revolution *die* counter-revolution; ~richtung *die* opposite direction; ~ruder *das* (*Flugw.*) (A) (*zur Erleichterung des Steuerns*) servo tab; (B) (*zur Einhaltung der Fluglage*) trim tab; ~satz *der* (A) (~*teil*) opposite; einen schroffen/diametralen ~satz zu etw./jmdm. bilden contrast sharply with/be diametrically opposed to sth./sb.; im ~satz zu in contrast to *or* with; unlike; ~sätze ziehen sich an opposites attract; (B) (*Widerspruch*) conflict; im krassen/scharfen ~satz zu etw. stehen be in stark/sharp conflict with sth.; (C) *Pl.* (*Meinungsverschiedenheiten*) ~sätze abbauen/überbrücken reduce/reconcile differences; ~sätzlich ❶ *Adj.* conflicting ‹views, opinions, etc.›; ~sätzliche Fronten opposing alignments; ❷ *adv.* etw. ~sätzlich beurteilen judge sth. completely differently; ~schlag *der* counterstroke; zum ~schlag ausholen prepare to counter-attack *or* strike back; ~seite *die* (A) (*einer Straße, eines Flusses usw.*) other side; far side; (B) ⇒ ~partei; ~seitig ❶ *Adj.* (A) (*wechselseitig*) mutual ‹aid, consideration, love, consent, services›; reciprocal ‹aid, obligation, services›; in ~seitiger Abhängigkeit stehen be mutually dependent; be dependent on each other *or* one another; (B) (*beide Seiten betreffend*) eine ~seitige Abmachung a bilateral arrangement; in ~seitigem Einvernehmen by mutual agreement; ❷ *adv.* sich ~seitig helfen/überbieten help/outdo each other *or* one another; ~seitigkeit *die;* ~~: reciprocity; auf ~seitigkeit (*Dat.*) beruhen be mutual; ~sinn *der:* in im ~sinn in the opposite direction; ~spieler *der,* ~spielerin *die* (A) (*Widersacher*) opponent; (B) (*Sport*) opposite number; (C) (*Theater*) antagonist; ~spionage *die* counter-espionage; ~sprechanlage *die* intercom [system]; (*Fernspr.*) duplex system; ~sprech·verkehr *der* two-way communication

**Gegen·stand** *der* (A) (*Ding, Körper*) object; Gegenstände des täglichen Gebrauchs/Bedarfs objects *or* articles of everyday use; (B) (*Thema*) subject; topic; etw. zum ~ haben deal with sth.; be concerned with sth.; (C) (*Objekt, Ziel*) der ~ seiner Zuneigung/seines Hasses the object of his affections/of his hatred; zum ~ der Kritik werden become the target *or* butt of criticism; (D) (*österr.: Schulfach*) subject

**gegenständlich** /ˈgeːgn̩ʃtɛntlɪç/ *Adj.* (*Kunst*) representational; (*Philos.*) objective

**gegenstands·los** *Adj.* (A) (*hinfällig*) invalid; das hat unsere Pläne ~ gemacht that's made nonsense of our plans; (B) (*grundlos, unbegründet*) unsubstantiated, unfounded ‹accusation, complaint›; baseless ‹fear›; unfounded ‹jealousy›; (C) (*abstrakt*) non-representational; abstract

**Gegenstands·wort** *das; Pl.* **Gegenstands·wörter** (*Sprachw.*) concrete noun

**gegen-, Gegen-:** ~|steuern *itr. V.* (A) ⇒ ~lenken; (B) (*fig.*) take countermeasures; ~stimme *die* (A) vote against; ohne ~stimme unanimously; das Gesetz passierte mit 380 Jastimmen und 80 ~stimmen das Parlament the law was passed by Parliament by 380 votes to 80; (B) (~*teilige Meinung*) dissenting voice; (C) (*Musik*) counterpart; ~stoß *der* (A) ⇒ ~schlag; (B) ⇒ ~angriff; ~strömung *die* countercurrent; ~stück *das* (A) (*Pendant*) companion piece; (*fig.*) counterpart; (B) ⇒ ~teil; ~teil *das* opposite; im ~teil on the contrary; ganz im ~teil far from it; quite the reverse; die Stimmung schlug ins ~teil um the mood changed completely; ~teilig *Adj.* opposite; contrary; ~teiliger Meinung/Ansicht sein hold the opposite opinion *or* view; be of the opposite opinion; ~teilige Aussagen contradictory statements; ~tor *das,* ~treffer *der* (*Sport*) goal for the other side; ein ~tor *od.* einen ~treffer hinnehmen müssen concede a goal

**gegen·über** ❶ *Präp. mit Dat.* (A) ▶ 818 (*auf der entgegengesetzten Seite*) opposite; ~ dem Bahnhof/Rathaus, dem Bahnhof/Rathaus ~: opposite the station/town hall; (B)

(*in Bezug auf*) ~ **jmdm.** *od.* **jmdm.** ~ **freundlich/streng sein** be kind to/strict with sb.; ~ **einer Sache** *od.* **einer Sache** ~ **skeptisch sein** be sceptical about sth.; ~ **uns** *od.* **uns** ~ **brauchst du wirklich keine Hemmungen zu haben** you really needn't have any inhibitions with us; **C** (*im Vergleich zu*) compared with; in comparison with; ~ **jmdm. im Vorteil sein** have an advantage over sb.
**2** *Adv.* ▶ 818 opposite; **er wohnt schräg** ~: he lives diagonally opposite

**Gegen·über** *das;* ~**s,** ~ **A** (*gegenübersitzende/-stehende Person*) person [sitting/standing] opposite; (*Gesprächspartner*) person one is talking to; **B** (*Bewohner eines gegenüberliegenden Gebäudes*) person living opposite; **kein** ~ **haben** have no one living opposite

**gegenüber-, Gegenüber-:** ~|**liegen** *unr. itr. V.* **sich** (*Dat.*) *od.* **einander** ~**liegen** face each other *or* one another; **auf der** ~**liegenden Seite/am** ~**liegenden Ufer** on the opposite side/bank; ~|**sehen** *unr. refl. V.* **sich jmdm./etw.** ~**sehen** find oneself facing sb./sth.; **sich einer Sache** (*Dat.*) ~**sehen** (*fig.*) be faced with sth.; ~|**sitzen** *unr. itr. V.* **jmdm./sich** ~**sitzen** sit opposite *or* facing sb./each other; ~|**stehen** *unr. itr. V.* **A** (*zugewandt stehen*) **jmdm./einer Sache** ~**stehen** stand facing sb./sth.; **jmdm. Auge in Auge** ~**stehen** confront sb. face to face; **Schwierigkeiten/Problemen** ~**stehen** (*fig.*) be faced *or* confronted with difficulties/problems; **B** (*eingestellt sein*) **jmdm./einer Sache feindlich/wohlwollend** ~**stehen** be ill/well disposed towards sb./sth.; **jmdm./einer Sache misstrauisch** ~**stehen** be mistrustful of sb./sth.; ⇒ *auch* **ablehnend**; **C** (*Sport*) **sich** ~**stehen** face each other *or* one another; meet; **D** (*im Widerstreit stehen*) **sich** ~**stehen** stand directly opposed to each other *or* one another; ~|**stellen** *tr. V.* **A** (*konfrontieren*) confront; **jmdn. einem Zeugen** ~**stellen** to confront sb. with a witness; **B** (*in Beziehung bringen*) compare; ~**stellung** *die* **A** (*Konfrontation*) confrontation; **B** (*Vergleich*) comparison; ~|**treten** *unr. itr. V.; mit sein* face; **Schwierigkeiten** (*Dat.*) ~**treten** face [up to] difficulties

**Gegen-:** ~**verkehr** *der* oncoming traffic; ~**vorschlag** *der* counter-proposal

**Gegenwart** /-vart/ *die;* ~ **A** present; (*heutige Zeit*) present [time *or* day]; **bis in die** ~ **fortwirken** continue [down] to the present day; **die Literatur/Musik der** ~: contemporary literature/music; **B** (*Anwesenheit*) presence; **in** ~ **von anderen** in the presence of others; **C** (*Grammatik*) present [tense]

**gegenwärtig** /-vɛrtɪç/ **1** *Adj.* **A** present; (*heutig*) present[-day]; current; **B** (*geh.: erinnerlich*) **ich habe die Begebenheit nicht** ~: I cannot recall the event; **sich** (*Dat.*) **etw.** ~ **halten** keep sth. in mind; **C** (*veralt.: anwesend, zugegen*) present; **bei etw.** ~ **sein** be present at sth.; **in dieser mittelalterlichen Stadt ist die Geschichte überall** ~ (*fig.*) history is all around one in this medieval town. **2** *adv.* at present; at the moment; (*heute*) at present; currently

**gegenwarts-, Gegenwarts-:** ~**bezogen** *Adj.* relevant to the present day *or* to today *postpos.;* ~**fern** *Adj.* remote from the present *postpos.;* ~**fremd** *Adj.* out of touch with the present *or* with today; ~**kunde** *die* (*Schulw.*) political and social studies *sing., no art.;* ~**kunst** *die* contemporary art *no art.;* ~**literatur** *die* contemporary literature *no art.;* ~**nah[e]** **1** *Adj.* relevant to the present day *or* to today *postpos.;* (*aktuell*) topical; **2** *adv.* ~**nah denken** be up to date in one's thinking; ~**nah unterrichten** teach in accordance with contemporary ideas; ~**sprache** *die* present-day language; **die deutsche** ~**sprache** modern German; ~**stück** *das* contemporary play

**gegen-, Gegen-:** ~**wehr** *die* resistance; **[keine]** ~**wehr leisten** put up [no] resistance; ~**wert** *der* equivalent; **der volle** ~**wert für das gestohlene Auto** the full replacement value of the stolen car; ~**wind** *der* head wind; ~**winkel** *der* (*Math.*) opposite angle; ~**wirkung** *die* reaction; ~|**zeichnen** *tr. V.* countersign; ~**zug** *der* **A** (*Brettspiele, fig.*) countermove; (*Polit.*) reciprocal gesture; **im** ~**zug** (*fig.*) in return for; **B** (*entgegenkommender Zug*) train in the opposite direction; **C** ⇒ ~**angriff**

**gegessen** /gəˈgɛsn̩/ *2. Part. v.* **essen**

**geglichen** /gəˈglɪçn̩/ *2. Part. v.* **gleichen**

**geglitten** /gəˈglɪtn̩/ *2. Part. v.* **gleiten**

**Geglitzer** *das;* ~**s** (*von Edelsteinen*) glitter; sparkle; (*von Sternen*) twinkling

**geglommen** /gəˈglɔmən/ *2. Part. v.* **glimmen**

**Geglucks[e]** *das;* ~**[e]s** chuckling; (*lauter*) chortling; **lass doch mal dein** ~: stop [that] chuckling/chortling

**Gegner** /ˈgeːgnɐ/ *der;* ~**s,** ~ **A** adversary; opponent; (*Rivale*) rival; **ein** ~ **der Todesstrafe sein** oppose *or* be an opponent of; **B** (*Sport*) opponent; (*Mannschaft*) opposing team; **der** ~ **war für uns viel zu stark** the opposition was far too strong for us; **C** (*feindliches Heer*) enemy

**Gegnerin** *die;* ~, ~**nen A** ⇒ **Gegner A**; **B** (*Sport*) opponent

**gegnerisch** *Adj.* **A** opposing; **B** (*Sport*) opposing ‹team, player, etc.›; opponents' ‹goal›; **C** (*Milit.*) enemy

**Gegnerschaft** *die;* ~ **A** (*Einstellung*) hostility; antagonism; **B** (*Gesamtheit der Gegner*) opposition

**gegolten** /gəˈgɔltn̩/ *2. Part. v.* **gelten**

**gegoren** /gəˈgoːrən/ *2. Part. v.* **gären**

**gegossen** /gəˈgɔsn̩/ *2. Part. v.* **gießen**

**gegriffen** /gəˈgrɪfn̩/ *2. Part. v.* **greifen**

**Gegrinse** *das;* ~**s** (*abwertend*) grinning

**Gegröle** *das;* ~**s** (*ugs. abwertend*) [raucous] bawling and shouting; (*Gesang*) raucous singing

**Gegrunze** *das;* ~**s** (*abwertend*) grunting

**Gehabe** *das;* ~**s** (*abwertend*) affected behaviour; **ihr wichtigtuerisches** ~: her pompous behaviour

**gehaben** *refl. V.* (*veralt., noch scherzh.*) *in* **gehab dich wohl!/gehabt euch wohl!/** ~ **Sie sich wohl!** farewell!

**Gehaben** *das;* ~**s** (*geh. veralt.*) behaviour; demeanour

**gehabt** **1** *2. Part. v.* **haben. 2** *Adj.* (*ugs.: schon da gewesen*) same old (*coll.*); usual; **wie** ~: as before; **[es ist] alles wie** ~: everything's just the same *or* just as before

**Gehackte** /gəˈhaktə/ *das; adj. Dekl.* mince[-meat]; ~**s vom Rind/Schwein** minced beef/pork

**Gehalt**[1] *der;* ~**[e]s,** ~**e A** (*gedanklicher Inhalt*) meaning; **intellektueller/religiöser** ~: intellectual/religious content; **B** (*Anteil*) content; **ein hoher** ~ **an Gold/Blei** a high gold/lead content

**Gehalt**[2] *das, österr. auch: der;* ~**[e]s, Gehälter** /gəˈhɛltɐ/ salary; **ein hohes/niedriges** ~ **beziehen** draw a large/small salary; **1 000 DM** ~, **ein** ~ **von 1 000 DM** a salary of 1,000 marks

**gehalten** **1** *2. Part. v.* **halten. 2** *Adj.* **A** (*geh.*) ~ **sein, etw. zu tun** be obliged *or* required to do sth.; **B** (*Mus.*) held; tenuto

**gehalt·los** *Adj.* unnutritious ‹food›; ‹wine› lacking in body; (*fig.*) vacuous; empty; lacking in substance *postpos., not pred.*

**Gehaltlosigkeit** *die;* ~ (*von Nahrungsmitteln*) lack of nutritional value; (*fig.*) vacuousness; emptiness; lack of substance

**Gehalts-:** ~**abrechnung** *die* salary statement; payslip; ~**abzug** *der* deduction from salary; ~**anspruch** *der* salary claim; pay claim; ~**aufbesserung** *die* increase in salary; **zur** ~**aufbesserung** in order to increase one's salary; ~**auszahlung** *die* payment of salary/salaries; ~**empfänger** *der,* ~**empfängerin** *die* salary earner; ~**erhöhung** *die* salary increase; rise [in salary]; (*regelmäßig*) increment; ~**forderung** *die* salary claim; pay claim; ~**gruppe** *die* salary group *or* bracket; (*innerhalb einer Firma*) grade; ~**konto** *das: account into which the/one's salary is paid;* ~**kürzung** *die* salary cut; cut in salary; ~**liste** *die* payroll; **auf jmds.** ~**liste** (*Dat.*) **stehen** (*fig.*) be on sb.'s payroll; be in sb.'s pocket; ~**pfändung** *die* attachment of earnings; ~**streifen** *der* payslip; ~**stufe** *die* salary bracket; ~**vorrückung** *die;* ~~, ~~**en** (*österr.*) increment; ~**vorschuss**, *~**vorschuß** *der* advance [on one's salary]; ~**zahlung** *die* payment of salary/salaries; ~**zulage** *die* salary increase; (*regelmäßig*) increment; (*zusätzlich*) bonus

**gehalt·voll** *Adj.* nutritious, nourishing ‹food›; full-bodied ‹wine›; ‹novel, speech› rich in substance *postpos.*

**Gehänge** *das;* ~**s,** ~ **A** (*Girlande*) festoon; (*Kranz*) garland; (*Ohrring*) ear pendant; **B** (*österr.: Bergabhang*) slope; **C** (*Jagdw., sonst veralt.*) belt (*with scabbard for hunting knife, sword, etc.*); **D** (*vulg.: Hoden*) balls (*coarse*)

**gehangen** *2. Part. v.* **hängen**[1]

**Gehängte** /gəˈhɛŋtə/ *der/die; adj. Dekl.* hanged man/woman; **die** ~**n** the hanged

**geharnischt** /gəˈharnɪʃt/ **1** *Adj.* **A** (*scharf, energisch*) sharp, sharply-worded, strongly-worded ‹letter, protest, reply›; strongly-worded ‹speech, article›; **B** (*hist.: gepanzert*) **ein** ~**er Ritter** a knight in armour. **2** *adv.* sharply

**gehässig** /gəˈhɛsɪç/ *Adj.* (*abwertend*) spiteful; ~ **von jmdm. reden/sprechen** be spiteful about sb.

**Gehässigkeit** *die;* ~, ~**en A** (*Wesen*) spitefulness; **B** (*Äußerung*) spiteful remark

**gehauen** *2. Part. v.* **hauen**

**gehäuft** **1** *2. Part. v.* **häufen. 2** *Adj.* **ein** ~**er Teelöffel/Esslöffel** a heaped teaspoon/tablespoon. **3** *adv.* in large numbers

**Gehäuse** /gəˈhɔyzə/ *das;* ~**s,** ~ **A** (*einer Maschine, Welle*) casing; housing; (*einer Kamera, Uhr*) case; casing; (*einer Lampe*) housing; (*Pistolen*~, *Gewehr*~) casing; **B** (*Schnecken*~ *usw.*) shell; **C** (*Kern*~) core; **D** (*Sportjargon: Tor*) goal

**geh·behindert** *Adj.* able to walk only with difficulty *postpos.*; disabled; **sie ist stark** ~: she can walk only with great difficulty

**Geh·behinderung** *die* disability [which makes walking difficult]

**Gehege** *das;* ~**s,** ~ **A** (*Jägerspr.: Revier*) preserve; **jmdm. ins** ~ **kommen** (*fig.*) poach on sb.'s preserve; **sich** (*Dat.*) **[gegenseitig] ins** ~ **kommen** (*fig.*) encroach on each other's territory; **B** (*im Zoo*) enclosure

**geheim** **1** *Adj.* **A** secret; **streng** ~: top *or* highly secret; **etw.** ~ **halten** keep sth. secret; ~ **tun** (*ugs. abwertend*) be secretive (**mit** about); **im Geheimen** in secret; secretly; **Geheimer Rat** (*hist.*) (*Gremium*) Privy Council; (*Mitglied*) privy councillor; **B** (*mysteriös*) mysterious. **2** *adv.* ~ **abstimmen** vote by secret ballot

**geheim-, Geheim-:** ~**abkommen** *das* secret agreement; ~**agent** *der,* ~**agentin** *die* secret agent; ~**befehl** *der* secret order; ~**bund** *der* secret society; ~**bündelei** *die;* ~~ (*veralt.*) membership of an illegal secret society; ~**code** *der* ⇒ ~**kode**; ~**dienst** *der* secret service; ~**diplomatie** *die* secret diplomacy; (*neben der offiziellen Diplomatie*) behind-the-scenes diplomacy; ~**fach** *das* secret compartment; (*Schublade*) secret drawer; ~**gang** *der* secret passage; *~|**halten** ⇒ **geheim 1 A**

**Geheim·haltung** *die* the observance of secrecy; **zur** ~ **verpflichtet sein** be pledged to secrecy

**Geheimhaltungs·pflicht** *die* obligation to maintain secrecy

**Geheim-:** ~**kode** *der* secret code; ~**lehre** *die* esoteric doctrine; ~**material** *das* secret papers *pl. or* documents *pl.*; **militärisches** ~**material** secret military papers *or* documents

**Geheimnis** *das;* ~**ses,** ~**se A** secret; **ein** ~ **lüften/enträtseln** unravel a secret; **vor jmdm. [keine]** ~**se haben** have [no] secrets from sb.; **jmdn. in die** ~**se einer Sache einweihen** initiate *or* let sb. into the

*old spelling (see note on page 1707)

secrets of sth.; **ein/kein ~ aus etw. machen** make a big/no secret of sth.; **das ist das ganze ~:** that's all there is to it; **ein offenes** *od.* **öffentliches ~:** an open secret; **B** (*Unerforschtes*) mystery; secret; **die ~se der Natur/des Lebens** the mysteries *or* secrets of nature/life

**geheimnis-, Geheimnis-: ~krämer** *der* (*ugs.*) mystery-monger; **~krämerei** *die;* **~~** ⇒ **~tuerei**; **~krämerin** *die* ⇒ **~krämer**; **~träger** *der*, **~trägerin** *die* person cleared for access to secret information; **~tuerei** *die;* **~~** (*ugs. abwertend*) secretiveness; mystery-mongering; **~tuerisch** (*ugs. abwertend*) **1** *Adj.* secretive; **2** *adv.* secretively; **~umwittert**, **~umwoben** *Adj.* (*geh.*) shrouded in mystery *postpos.;* mysterious; **~verrat** *der* (*Rechtsspr.*) betrayal of secrets; **~voll** **1** *Adj.* mysterious; **auf ~volle Weise** in a mysterious way; mysteriously; **2** *adv.* mysteriously; **~voll tun** be mysterious; act mysteriously

**Geheim·nummer** *die* **A** (*Bankw.*) personal identification number; PIN; **B** (*Telefonnummer*) ex-directory number; unlisted number (*Amer.*)

**Geheim-: ~polizei** *die* secret police; **~polizist** *der*, **~polizistin** *die* member of the secret police

**Geheim·rat** *der* Privy Councillor (*purely honorary title*)

**Geheimrats·ecken** *Pl.* (*ugs. scherzh.*) receding hairline *sing.;* **er hat schon ~:** he's receding *or* going bald [at the temples] already

**geheim-, Geheim-: ~rezept** *das* secret recipe; **~sache** *die* classified information *no indef. art., no pl.;* **~schrift** *die* secret writing *no indef. art., no pl.;* cipher; **~sender** *der* secret transmitter; **~sitzung** *die* secret session; closed meeting; **~sprache** *die* secret language; **~tinte** *die* invisible ink; ***~tip**, **~tipp** *der* inside tip; ***~|tun** ⇒ **geheim** 1A; **~tür** *die* secret door; **~vertrag** *der* secret treaty *or* agreement; **~waffe** *die* (*Milit.*) secret weapon; **~wissenschaft** *die* occult science; **~zeichen** *das* secret sign

**Geheiß** *das;* **~es** (*geh.*) behest (*literary*); command; **auf jmds. ~:** at sb.'s behest *or* command

**gehemmt** **1** *2. Part. v.* **hemmen**. **2** *Adj.* inhibited

**gehen** /ˈgeːən/ **1** *unr. itr. V.; mit sein* **A** (*sich zu Fuß fortbewegen*) walk; go; **auf und ab ~:** walk up and down; **über die Straße ~:** cross the street; **wo er geht und steht** wherever he goes *or* is; no matter where he goes *or* is; **etw. geht durch die Presse** (*fig.*) sth. is in the papers; **B** (*sich irgendwohin begeben*) go; **schwimmen/tanzen ~:** go swimming/dancing; **schlafen ~:** go to bed; **zu jmdm. ~:** go to see sb.; go and see sb. (*coll.*); **zum Arzt ~:** go to the doctor; **nach London/Mannheim ~:** move to London/Mannheim; **aufs Amt/auf den Markt ~:** go to the office/the market; **an die Arbeit ~** (*fig.*) get down to work; **er geht auf die 60** (*fig.*) he is approaching *or* (*coll.*) pushing 60; **in sich** (*Akk.*) **~:** take stock of oneself; **C** (*regelmäßig besuchen*) attend; **in die** *od.* **zur Schule ~:** be at *or* attend school; **wieviel Jahre musst du noch in die Schule ~?** how many more years have you got at school?; **D** (*weg~*) go; leave; **ich muss jetzt/bald ~:** I must leave now/soon; **Sie können ~:** you may go; **gegangen werden** (*ugs. scherzh.*) be sacked (*coll.*); **der Minister/Offizier musste ~:** the Minister/officer had to resign; **er ist von uns gegangen** (*verhüll.*) he has passed away *or* passed over (*euphem.*); **jmdn. lieber ~ als kommen sehen** be always glad to see the back of sb.; **geh mir mit deinen politischen Schlagworten** spare me the political slogans; **jmdn. gehen lassen** (*ugs.: in Ruhe lassen*) leave sb. alone; **E** (*ugs.: [ab]fahren*) leave; **der Zug geht um zehn Uhr** the train leaves at ten o'clock; **F** (*in Funktion sein*) work; **etw. geht wieder/nicht mehr** sth. is working again/has stopped working; **meine Uhr geht falsch/richtig** my watch is wrong/right; **das Telefon/die Klingel geht ununterbrochen** the telephone/the bell never stops ringing; **G** (*möglich sein*) **ja, das geht** yes, I/we can manage that; **das geht nicht** that can't be done; that's impossible; (*ist nicht zulässig*) that's not on (*Brit. coll.*); no way (*coll.*); **Donnerstag geht auch** Thursday's a possibility *or* all right too; **es geht einfach nicht, dass du so spät nach Hause kommst** it simply won't do for you to come home so late; **es geht leider nicht anders** unfortunately there's nothing else for it; **das wird schwer/schlecht ~:** that will be difficult; **auf diese Weise geht es nicht/sicher** it won't/is bound to work this way; **H** (*ugs.: gerade noch an~*) **es geht so** it could be worse; **das Essen ging ja noch, aber der Wein war ungenießbar** the food was passable, but the wine was undrinkable; **Wie war die Feier? — Es ging so** How was the party? — [It was] all right *or* [It] could have been worse; **Hast du gut geschlafen? — Es geht** Did you sleep well? — Not too bad *or* So-so; **der Anfang ging, aber der Schluss des Films war idiotisch** the film began fairly well, but the end was absolutely stupid; **I** (*sich entwickeln*) **der Laden/das Geschäft geht gut/gar nicht** the shop/business is doing well/not doing well at all; **schief ~** (*ugs.: schlecht ausgehen*) go wrong; **es wird schon schief ~** (*iron.*) it'll all turn out OK (*coll.*); **gut ~** (*gut ausgehen*) turn out well; **es ist noch einmal gut gegangen** it worked out all right again this time; **es geht alles nach Wunsch/Plan** everything is going according to plan; **alles geht drunter und drüber** (*ugs.*) everything's at sixes and sevens; **die Anfangszeile geht …** (*fig.*) the first line goes *or* runs …; **wie geht die Melodie?** (*fig.*) how does the tune go?; what's the tune?; **vor sich ~:** go on; happen; **J** (*sich ausdehnen bis*) **das Wasser geht mir bis an die Knie** the water comes up to *or* reaches my knees; **ich gehe ihm bis zu den Schultern** I come up to his shoulders; **in die Hunderte/Tausende ~:** run into [the] hundreds/thousands; **das geht über mein Vermögen/meinen Horizont** (*fig.*) that is beyond me; **diese Nachricht würde über ihre Kräfte ~** (*fig.*) this news would be too much for her; **es geht [doch] nichts über …** (+ *Akk.*) (*fig.*) there is nothing like *or* nothing to beat …; nothing beats …; **das geht zu weit** (*fig.*) that's going too far; **K** (*unpers.*) **jmdm. geht es gut/schlecht** (*gesundheitlich*) sb. is well *or* (*coll.*) fine/not well; (*geschäftlich*) sb. is doing well/badly; **wie geht es dir/Ihnen?** how are you?; **mir geht es ähnlich** it's the same with me; same here (*coll.*); **wie gehts, wie stehts?** (*ugs.*) how are things?; **wenn sie das rausfindet, gehts dir schlecht!** (*ugs.*) if she finds out, you'll be [in] for it; **L** (*unpers.*) (*sich um etw. handeln*) **es geht um mehr als …** there is more at stake than …; **jmdm. geht es um etw.** sth. matters to sb.; **ihr geht es nur um Geld** she only thinks about money; **worum geht es hier?** what is this all about?; **bei dieser Sache geht es um viel Geld** this involves a great deal of money; **wenn es ums Geld geht, versteht er keinen Spaß** he takes money matters very seriously; **Ich hätte eine Frage. — Worum geht es denn?** I have a question. — What [is it] about?; ⇒ *auch* **darum** B; **M** (*tätig werden*) **in den Staatsdienst/in die Industrie/die Politik ~:** join the Civil Service/go into industry/politics; **zum Film/Theater ~:** go into films/on the stage; **ins Kloster ~:** enter a monastery/convent; **als Kellner/Prostituierte ~:** work as *or* be a waiter/prostitute; **N** (*ugs.: sich kleiden*) **gut/schlecht gekleidet ~:** be well/badly dressed; **in Kurz/Lang ~:** wear a short/long dress/skirt; **als Zigeuner/Matrose ~:** go as a gypsy/a sailor; **O** (*ugs.: sich zu schaffen machen an*) **du sollst nicht an meine Sachen ~:** you must not mess around with my things; (*benutzen*) you must not take my things; **die Kinder sind an den Kuchen/das Geld gegangen** the children have been at the cake/money (*coll.*); **P** (*ein Liebespaar sein*) **mit jmdm. ~:** go out with sb.; **Q** (*absetzbar sein*) **[gut/schlecht] ~:** sell [well/slowly]; **R** (*passen*) go; **in den Kofferraum geht nur ein Koffer** only one case will go into the boot; **S** (*aufgeteilt werden*) **etw. geht in zwei/drei Teile** sth. is shared out *or* divided two/three ways; **T** (*verlaufen*) go; **die Straße geht geradeaus/nach links** the road goes *or* runs straight ahead/turns to the left; **wohin geht diese Straße?** where does this road go *or* lead to?; **U** (*gerichtet sein auf*) **nach der Hauptstraße ~:** face the main road; **die Fenster ~ alle nach Süden** all the windows face south; **gegen jmdn./etw. ~** (*fig.*) be aimed *or* directed at sb./sth.; **das geht gegen meine Überzeugung** that goes against my convictions; **V** (*als Maßstab nehmen*) **nach jmdm./etw. ~:** go by sb./sth.; **wenn es nach mir geht, fangen wir jetzt an** I'd be quite happy if we began now; **W** ⇒ **aufgehen** D; **X** **sich ~ lassen** lose control of oneself; (*sich vernachlässigen*) let oneself go.
**2** *unr. tr. V.* (*zurücklegen*) **eine Strecke ~:** cover *or* do a distance; **er ist eine Strecke mit uns gegangen** he walked with us for some of the way; **einen Umweg ~:** make a detour; **10 km ~:** walk 10 km.; **einen Weg in 30 Minuten ~:** do a walk in 30 minutes; **seine eigenen Wege ~** (*fig.*) go one's own way; **lerne doch, deine eigenen Wege zu ~** (*fig.*) learn to stand on your own two feet.
**3** *unr. refl. V.* (*unpers.*) **in diesen Schuhen geht es sich sehr bequem** these shoes are very comfortable [to walk in]; **auf dem Weg ging es sich schlecht** the going on the track was difficult

**Gehen** *das;* **~s** **A** walking; **er hat Schmerzen beim ~:** it hurts him to walk; **B** (*Leichtathletik*) walking; **der Sieger im 50-km-~:** the winner of the 50 km walk

**Gehenkte** /gəˈhɛŋktə/ *der/die; adj. Dekl.* hanged man/woman; **die ~n** the hanged

***gehen|lassen** ⇒ **gehen** 1 D, X

**Geher** /ˈgeːɐ/ *der;* **~s**, **~**, **Geherin** *die;* **~**, **~nen** **A** (*Leichtathletik*) walker; **B** (*Bergsteigen*) hill/mountain walker

**geheuer** /gəˈhɔyɐ/ *Adj.* **A** **in diesem Gebäude ist es nicht ~:** this building is eerie; this building feels as if it's haunted (*coll.*); **in der Ruine soll es nicht ganz ~ sein** there is said to be something eerie about the ruins; **B** **ihr war doch nicht [ganz] ~:** she felt [a little] uneasy; **C** **diese Angelegenheit ist nicht ganz ~:** there's something odd *or* suspicious about this business

**Geheul** *das;* **~[e]s** **A** (*auch fig.*) howling; **B** (*ugs. abwertend: Weinen*) bawling; wailing

**Geheule** *das;* **~s** ⇒ **Geheul** B

**geh·fähig** *Adj.* ⟨patient⟩ who is able to walk *postpos., not pred.;* walking ⟨wounded⟩; **~ sein** be able to walk

**Geh·gips** *der: plaster which allows the patient to walk*

**Gehilfe** /gəˈhɪlfə/ *der;* **~n**, **~n**, **Gehilfin** *die;* **~**, **~nen** **A** qualified assistant; **B** (*veralt.: Helfer/Helferin*) helper; assistant

**Gehirn** *das;* **~[e]s**, **~e** **A** ▶ 471 brain; **B** (*ugs.: Verstand*) mind; **sein ~ anstrengen** *od.* **sich** (*Dat.*) **das ~ zermartern** rack one's brain[s]

**Gehirn-: ~blutung** *die* ▶ 474 (*Med.*) cerebral haemorrhage; encephalorrhagia (*Med.*); **~chirurgie** *die* brain surgery; **~erschütterung** *die* ▶ 474 (*Med.*) concussion; **~erweichung** *die* ▶ 474 (*Med.*) softening of the brain; encephalomalacia (*Med.*); **~haut** *die* ⇒ **Hirnhaut**; **~haut·entzündung** *die* ⇒ **Hirnhautentzündung**; **~kasten** *der* (*salopp scherzh.*) [thick] skull; **~schlag** *der* ▶ 474 (*Med.*) stroke; [cerebral] apoplexy *no art.* (*Med.*); **~substanz** *die* brain matter; **graue/weiße ~substanz** grey/white matter; **~tätigkeit** *die* brain activity; **~tumor** *der* ⇒ **Hirntumor**; **~wäsche** *die* brainwashing *no indef. art.;* **jmdn. einer ~wäsche unterziehen** brainwash sb.; **~zelle** *die* brain cell

g

**gehoben** /gəˈhoːbn̩/ ❶ *2. Part. v.* **heben.** ❷ *Adj.* Ⓐ higher ‹income›; senior ‹position›; **der ~e Dienst** the higher [levels of the] Civil Service; **die ~e Beamtenlaufbahn einschlagen** ≈ enter the Civil Service as an Administrative Trainee (*Brit.*); **der ~e Mittelstand** the upper middle class; Ⓑ (*anspruchsvoll*) **Kleidung für den ~en Geschmack** clothes for those with discerning taste; **Artikel für den ~en Bedarf** luxury goods; **die ~e Unterhaltungsliteratur** upmarket popular literature; Ⓒ (*gewählt*) elevated, refined ‹language, expression›; Ⓓ (*feierlich*) festive ‹mood›; **in ~er Stimmung sein** be in high spirits. ❸ *adv.* **sich ~ ausdrücken** use elevated *or* refined language

**Gehöft** /gəˈhœft, -ˈhøːft/ *das;* **~[e]s, ~e** farm[stead]

**geholfen** /gəˈhɔlfn̩/ *2. Part. v.* **helfen**

**Gehölz** /gəˈhœlts/ *das;* **~es, ~e** Ⓐ (*Wäldchen*) copse; spinney (*Brit.*); Ⓑ *Pl.* (*Holzgewächse*) woody plants

**Gehör** /gəˈhøːɐ̯/ *das;* **~[e]s** [sense of] hearing; **ein scharfes/gutes ~ haben** have acute/good hearing; **[etw.] nach dem ~ singen/spielen** sing/play [sth.] by ear; **das absolute ~ [haben]** (*Musik*) [have] absolute pitch; **~/kein ~ finden** meet with *or* get a/no response; **jmdm./einer Sache [kein] ~ schenken** [not] listen to sb./sth.; **sich** (*Dat.*) **~ verschaffen** make oneself heard; **um ~ bitten** ask for a hearing; **ein Lied/Gedicht/Musikstück zu ~ bringen** (*geh.*) sing a song/recite a poem/perform a piece of music

**gehorchen** /gəˈhɔrçn̩/ *itr. V.* Ⓐ (*Gehorsam leisten*) **jmdm. ~:** obey sb.; Ⓑ (*sich leiten, lenken lassen*) **einer Sache** (*Dat.*) **~:** respond to sth.; **das Auto gehorchte dem Fahrer nicht mehr** the car wouldn't respond when the driver turned the wheel; **einer Laune/Stimmung** (*Dat.*) **~:** yield to a caprice/mood

**gehören** ❶ *itr. V.* Ⓐ (*Eigentum sein*) **jmdm. ~:** belong to sb.; **das Haus gehört uns nicht** the house doesn't belong to us; we don't own the house; **der Jugend gehört die Zukunft** the future belongs to the young; **dir will ich ~** (*dichter.*) I want to be yours; **ihr Herz gehört einem anderen** (*geh.*) her heart belongs to another; Ⓑ (*Teil eines Ganzen sein*) **zu jmds. Freunden ~:** be one of sb.'s friends; **zu jmds. Aufgaben ~:** be part of sb.'s duties; Ⓒ (*passend sein*) **dein Roller gehört doch nicht in die Küche!** your scooter does not belong in the kitchen!; **das gehört nicht/durchaus hierher** that is not to the point/is very much to the point; **dieses Problem/Thema gehört nicht/durchaus hierher** this problem/topic is not relevant/certainly relevant here; **du gehörst ins Bett** you should be in bed; Ⓓ (*nötig sein*) **es hat viel Fleiß dazu gehört, dieses Projekt durchzuführen** it took *or* called for a lot of hard work to carry through this project; **dazu gehört sehr viel/einiges** that takes a lot/something; **dazu gehört nicht viel** that doesn't take much; **auf diese Weise sein Geld zu verdienen, dazu gehört nicht viel** earning one's living like this is nothing to be proud of; Ⓔ (*bes. südd.*) **er gehört geohrfeigt** he deserves *or* (*coll.*) needs a box round the ears; **du gehörst eingesperrt** (*ugs.*) you ought to be locked up. ❷ *refl. V.* (*sich schicken*) be fitting; **es gehört sich [nicht], ... zu ...** it is [not] good manners to ...; **wie es sich gehört** comme il faut; **benimm dich, wie es sich gehört** behave properly

**Gehör·gang** *der* ▶ 471 (*Anat.*) auditory canal

**gehörig** ❶ *Adj.* Ⓐ (*gebührend*) proper; **jmdm. den ~en Respekt/die ~e Achtung erweisen** show sb. proper *or* due respect; Ⓑ (*ugs.: beträchtlich*) **ein ~er Schrecken/eine ~e Portion Mut/Ausdauer** a good fright/a good deal of courage/perseverance; Ⓒ (*zu~*) **zu etw. ~ sein** be part of sth.; belong to sth.; **jmdm. ~ sein** (*geh.*) belong to sb.; be owned by sb.; **[nicht] zur momentanen Fragestellung ~:** [not] relevant to the question [under discussion]. ❷ *adv.* Ⓐ (*gebührend*) properly; Ⓑ (*ugs.: beträchtlich*) **~ essen/trinken** eat/drink properly *or* heartily; **er hat ~ geschimpft** he didn't half grumble (*coll.*); ⇒ *auch* **Marsch¹** B; **Meinung**

**Gehör·knöchelchen** *Pl.* ▶ 471 (*Anat.*) auditory ossicles

**gehör·los** *Adj.* deaf

**Gehörn** /gəˈhœrn/ *das;* **~[e]s, ~e** Ⓐ horns *pl.;* Ⓑ (*Jägerspr.*) antlers *pl.*

**Gehör·nerv** *der* ▶ 471 auditory nerve

**gehörnt** *Adj.* Ⓐ (*mit einem Gehörn*) horned; (*mit einem Geweih*) antlered; Ⓑ (*scherzh. verhüll.: betrogen*) cuckolded; **ein ~er Ehemann** a cuckold

**Gehör·organ** *das* organ of hearing

**gehorsam** /gəˈhoːɐ̯zaːm/ ❶ *Adj.* Ⓐ (*artig, brav*) obedient; **jmdm. ~ sein** (*geh.*) be obedient to sb.; Ⓑ (*veralt. als Höflichkeitsformel*) humble; (*als Briefschluss*) **Ihr ~ster Diener** your most obedient servant. ❷ *adv.* (*veralt. als Höflichkeitsformel*) humbly

**Gehorsam** *der;* **~s** obedience; **~ gegenüber jmdm.** obedience to sb.; **jmdm. ~ leisten/den ~ verweigern** obey/refuse to obey sb.

**Gehorsamkeit** *die* obedience

**Gehorsams-: ~pflicht** *die* (*Milit.*) duty to obey orders; **~verweigerung** *die* (*Milit.*) insubordination; refusal to obey orders

**Gehör·sinn** *der* [sense of] hearing

**Geh·rock** *der* frock coat

**Gehrung** /ˈgeːrʊŋ/ *die;* **~, ~en** (*Handw., Technik*) mitre [joint]

**Geh·steig** *der* pavement (*Brit.*); sidewalk (*Amer.*)

**Geht·nicht·mehr** *das: in* **bis zum ~** (*salopp*) ad nauseam; **das habe ich bis zum ~ erklärt/gehört** I've explained it ad nauseam *or* till I'm blue in the face (*coll.*)/I've heard it so often I'm sick of it (*coll.*)

**Gehupe** *das;* **~s** honking; hooting

**Geh-: ~versuch** *der* (*eines Kindes*) attempt at walking; (*nach einem Unfall*) attempt at walking again; **~weg** *der* ⇒ **~steig; ~werkzeuge** *Pl.* (*ugs. scherzh.*) legs

**Geier** /ˈgaiɐ/ *der;* **~s, ~:** vulture; **hol dich/hols der ~** (*ugs.*) to hell with you/it (*coll.*); **weiß der ~** (*salopp*) God only knows (*coll.*); Christ knows (*sl.*)

**Geifer** /ˈgaifɐ/ *der;* **~s** Ⓐ (*Speichel*) slaver; spittle; slobber; (*von Tieren*) slaver; slobber; (*schäumend*) foam; froth; Ⓑ (*geh. abwertend: Gehässigkeit*) venom; vituperation

**Geiferer** *der;* **~s, ~, Geiferin** *die;* **~, ~nen** (*geh. abwertend*) vituperator; venomous speaker/writer *etc.*

**geifern** *itr. V.* Ⓐ slaver; slobber; Ⓑ (*abwertend: gehässig reden*) **gegen jmdn./über etw.** (*Akk.*) **~:** discharge one's venom at sb./sth.

**Geige** /ˈgaigə/ *die;* **~, ~n** violin; fiddle (*coll./derog.*); **~ spielen** play the violin; **die erste ~ spielen** (*ugs.*) play first fiddle; call the tune; **die zweite ~ spielen** (*ugs.*) play second fiddle

**geigen** ❶ *itr. V.* Ⓐ (*ugs.: Geige spielen*) play the fiddle (*coll.*) *or* the violin; Ⓑ (*ugs.: von Insekten*) chirp; chirr. ❷ *tr. V.* Ⓐ (*ugs.: auf der Geige spielen*) **einen Walzer/ein Solo ~:** play a waltz/a solo on the fiddle (*coll.*) *or* violin; **jmdm. die Meinung ~:** give sb. a piece of one's mind; Ⓑ (*salopp: koitieren mit*) lay (*sl.*); shag (*sl.*); have it off with (*sl.*)

**Geigen-: ~bau** *der* violin making; **~bauer** *der;* **~~s, ~~, ~bauerin** *die;* **~~, ~~nen** ▶ 159 violin-maker; **~bogen** *der* violin bow; **~hals** *der* neck of the/a violin; **~kasten** *der* violin case; **~musik** *die* violin music; **~saite** *die* violin string; **~spiel** *das* violin-playing; **~spieler** *der,* **~spielerin** *die* violin player

**Geiger** *der;* **~s, ~, Geigerin** *die;* **~, ~nen** ▶ 159 violin player; violinist

**Geiger·zähler** *der* (*Physik*) Geiger counter

**geil** /gail/ ❶ *Adj.* Ⓐ (*oft abwertend: sexuell erregt*) randy; horny (*sl.*); (*lüstern*) lecherous; **auf jmdn. ~ sein** lust for *or* after sb.; **~e alte Männer** old lechers; dirty old men; Ⓑ (*Landw.*) rank ‹vegetation, growth, plant›; over-rich, over-manured ‹soil›; Ⓒ (*Jugendspr.*) great (*coll.*); fabulous (*coll.*). ❷ *adv.* Ⓐ (*oft abwertend*) lecherously; Ⓑ (*Landw.*) **~ wuchern/emporschießen** grow rank; Ⓒ (*Jugendspr.*) fabulously (*coll.*)

**Geilheit** *die;* **~** ⇒ **geil** 1: Ⓐ randiness; horniness (*sl.*); lecherousness; Ⓑ (*Landw.*) rankness; overrichness

**Geisel** /ˈgaizl̩/ *die;* **~, ~n** hostage; **jmdn. als ~ behalten** *od.* **festhalten** hold sb. hostage; **jmdn. als** *od.* **zur ~ nehmen** take sb. hostage

**Geisel-: ~drama** *das* (*Pressejargon*) hostage drama; **~gangster** *der* (*Pressejargon*) ⇒ **~nehmer; ~nahme** *die;* **~~, ~~n** taking of hostages; **„Bankraub mit ~nahme zweier Kunden"** 'Bank raid. Two customers taken hostage'; **~nehmer** *der;* **~~s, ~~, ~nehmerin** *die;* **~~, ~~nen** terrorist/guerrilla *etc.* holding the hostages

**Geisha** /ˈgeːʃa/ *die;* **~, ~s** geisha

**Geiß** /gais/ *die;* **~, ~en** Ⓐ (*südd., österr., schweiz.: Ziege*) [nanny] goat; Ⓑ (*Jägerspr.*) doe

**Geiß-: ~bart** *der* Ⓐ (*Bot.*) goat's beard; Ⓑ (*österr.: Spitzbart*) goatee; **~blatt** *das* (*Bot.*) honeysuckle; woodbine

**Geißel** /ˈgaisl̩/ *die;* **~, ~n** Ⓐ (*hist., auch fig.*) scourge; Ⓑ (*Biol.*) flagellum; Ⓒ (*bes. südd.: Peitsche*) whip

**geißeln** *tr. V.* Ⓐ (*anprangern, tadeln*) castigate; Ⓑ (*plagen*) plague; Ⓒ (*hist.: züchtigen*) scourge

**Geißel·tierchen** *das* (*Biol.*) flagellate

**Geißelung** *die;* **~, ~en** Ⓐ (*Anprangern*) castigation; Ⓑ (*hist.: Züchtigung*) scourging

**Geiß·fuß** *der* Ⓐ (*Bot.*) Aegopodium; **gewöhnlicher ~:** ground elder; goutweed; Ⓑ (*Handw., Technik*) V-shaped gouge

**Geißlein** *das;* **~s, ~:** little goat

**Geißler** /ˈgaislɐ/ *der;* **~s, ~, Geißlerin** *die;* **~, ~nen** ⇒ **Flagellant**

**Geist** /gaist/ *der;* **~[e]s, ~er** Ⓐ (*Verstand*) mind; **jmds. ~ ist verwirrt/gestört** sb. is mentally deranged/disturbed; **jmdm. mit etw. auf den ~ gehen** (*salopp*) get on sb.'s nerves with sth.; **den** *od.* **seinen ~ aufgeben** (*geh./ugs. scherzh., auch fig.*) give up the ghost; **im ~[e]** in my/his *etc.* mind's eye; **im ~ werde ich dabei sein** I shall be there in spirit; **den** *od.* **seinen ~ aushauchen** (*geh. verhüll.*) breathe one's last; pass away; **der ~ ist willig, aber das Fleisch ist schwach** (*bibl.*) the spirit is willing, but the flesh is weak; Ⓑ (*Scharfsinn*) wit; **einen sprühenden ~ haben** have a sparkling wit; **Mangel an ~:** lack of intellect *or* intelligence; Ⓒ (*innere Einstellung*) spirit; **im ~ der Zeit** in the spirit of the age; **ein schlechter ~ in der Mannschaft** poor morale in the team; **wes ~es Kind er/sie** *usw.* **ist** the kind of person he/she *etc.* is; Ⓓ (*denkender Mensch*) mind; intellect; **ein großer/kleiner ~:** a great mind/a person of limited intellect; **hier** *od.* **da scheiden sich die ~er** this is where opinions differ; **große ~er stört das nicht** (*ugs. scherzh.*) it doesn't worry me/her *etc.*; not to worry (*coll.*); Ⓔ (*Mensch mit bestimmten Eigenschaften*) spirit; **ein dienstbarer ~** (*ugs. scherzh.*) a servant; Ⓕ (*überirdisches Wesen*) spirit; **der Heilige ~** (*christl. Rel.*) the Holy Ghost *or* Spirit; **der böse ~:** the evil spirit; Ⓖ (*Gespenst*) ghost; **~er gehen im Schloss um/spuken im Schloss** the castle is haunted; **von allen guten ~ern verlassen sein** have taken leave of one's senses; be out of one's mind

**Geister-: ~bahn** *die* ghost train; **~beschwörer** *der;* **~~s, ~~, ~beschwörerin** *die;* **~~, ~~nen** exorcist; (*der die ~ heraufbeschwört*) necromancer; **~beschwörung** *die* exorcism; (*das Heraufbeschwören*) necromancy; **~erscheinung** *die* apparition; phantom; **~fahrer** *der,*

*old spelling (see note on page 1707)

**~fahrerin** *die: person driving on the wrong side of the road or the wrong carriageway;* **~geschichte** *die* ghost story

**geisterhaft** ❶ *Adj.* ghostly; spectral; eerie ‹atmosphere›. ❷ *adv.* eerily

**Geister·hand** *die: in* **wie von** *od.* **durch ~:** as if by an invisible hand

**geistern** /ˈgaistɐn/ *itr. V.; mit sein* ‹ghost› wander; (*fig.*) wander like a ghost; **Irrlichter geisterten über das Moor** will o' the wisps drifted eerily across the moor; **diese Idee geisterte immer noch durch seinen Kopf** he still had this idea in his head

**Geister-: ~seher** *der,* **~seherin** *die* ghost-seer; (*Hellseher*) visionary; **~stadt** *die* ghost town; **~stunde** *die* witching hour

**geistes-, Geistes-: ~abwesend** ❶ *Adj.* absent-minded; ❷ *adv.* absent-mindedly; **~abwesenheit** *die* absent-mindedness; **~anlage** *die* intellectual ability *or* gift; **~arbeiter** *der,* **~arbeiterin** *die* brainworker; **~armut** *die* poverty of mind; **~art** *die* cast of mind; **~blitz** *der* (*ugs.*) brainwave; flash of inspiration; **~gaben** *Pl.* intellectual gifts; **~gegenwart** *die* presence of mind; **~gegenwärtig** ❶ *Adj.* quick-witted; ❷ *adv.* with great presence of mind; **~geschichte** *die* history of ideas; intellectual history; **~geschichtlich** ❶ *Adj.* ‹work, method, etc.› relating to the history of ideas, relating to intellectual history; **eine ~geschichtliche Tradition** an intellectual tradition; a tradition of ideas; ❷ *adv.* **etw. ~geschichtlich einordnen** place sth. in the history of ideas; **~gestört** *Adj.* mentally disturbed; **~größe** *die* Ⓐ (*Kraft des ~*) greatness of mind; Ⓑ (*Mensch*) genius; intellectual giant; **~haltung** *die* attitude [of mind]; **~kraft** *die* mental ability; **~kräfte** *Pl.* mental powers; **~krank** *Adj.* mentally ill; [mentally] deranged; **~kranke** *der/die* mentally ill person; (*im Krankenhaus*) mental patient; **~krankheit** *die* mental illness; **~leben** *das* intellectual life; **~richtung** *die* school of thought; **~riese** *der,* **~riesin** *die* (*ugs.*) great genius; **~schaffende** *der/die; adj. Dekl.* (*bes. DDR*) intellectual; **~schärfe** *die* keenness of intellect; **~schwäche** *die* feeble-mindedness; mental deficiency; **~störung** *die* mental disturbance *or* disorder; **~strömung** *die* current of thought; **~tätigkeit** *die* mental activity; **~verfassung** *die* state of mind; mental state; **~verwandt** *Adj.* spiritually akin; **wir sind ~verwandt** we are kindred spirits; **~verwirrung** *die* mental confusion; (*~gestörtheit*) [mental] derangement; **~welt** *die* (*geh.*) Ⓐ (*Welt des ~es*) world of the mind; Ⓑ (*Gesamtheit der geistig Interessierten*) intelligentsia; **~wissenschaften** *Pl.* arts; humanities; **~wissenschaftler** *der,* **~wissenschaftlerin** *die* arts scholar; scholar in the humanities; **~wissenschaftlich** ❶ *Adj.* **~wissenschaftliche Fächer** arts subjects; ❷ *adv.* ‹interested, be distinguished› in arts subjects; **~zustand** *der* mental condition; mental state; **jmdn. auf seinen ~zustand untersuchen lassen** have sb.'s mental condition examined; **du solltest dich mal auf deinen ~zustand untersuchen lassen** (*ugs.*) you need your head examined (*coll.*)

**geistig** ❶ *Adj.* Ⓐ intellectual; (*Psych.*) mental; **~e und körperliche Arbeit** physical work and brainwork; **er verlebte seine Rentnerjahre in ~er Frische** he remained mentally alert throughout the years of his retirement; **der ~e Vater/Urheber** the spiritual father/author; **in ~er Umnachtung** (*geh.*) in a state of mental derangement; **das ~e Erbe** the spiritual legacy; **~es Eigentum** intellectual property; **~er Diebstahl** plagiarism; **ein ~es Band** (*fig. geh.*) a spiritual bond; **~-kulturell** intellectual and cultural; **das ~-kulturelle Leben** (*bes. DDR*) the intellectual and cultural scene; **ein ~-kulturelles Zentrum** (*bes. DDR*) a centre of learning and the arts; **~-schöpferische Arbeit** (*bes. DDR*) intellectual and creative work; Ⓑ (*alkoholisch*) **~e Getränke** alcoholic drinks *or* beverages. ❷ *adv.* **~ träge/rege sein** be mentally lazy/active; **~ überlegen** intellectually superior; **~ zurückgeblieben** mentally retarded; **~ weggetreten sein** (*ugs.*) be miles away (*coll.*)

**Geistigkeit** *die; ~:* intellectuality

**geistlich** *Adj.* sacred ‹song, music›; religious ‹order›; religious, devotional ‹book, writings›; spiritual ‹matter, support›; spiritual, religious ‹leader›; ecclesiastical ‹office, dignitary›; **der ~e Stand** the clergy; **in den ~en Stand eintreten** take holy orders

**Geistliche[1]** *der; adj. Dekl.* ▶ 159 clergyman; priest; (*einer Freikirche*) minister; (*Militär~, Gefängnis~*) chaplain

**Geistliche[2]** *die* ▶ 159 [woman] priest

**Geistlichkeit** *die; ~:* clergy

**geist-, Geist-: ~los** *Adj.* (*dumm*) dim-witted; witless; (*ohne ernsten Gehalt*) trivial; shallow ‹conversation›; **~losigkeit** *die; ~~* (*Dummheit*) dim-wittedness; witlessness; (*Trivialität*) triviality; **~reich** ❶ *Adj.* (*amüsant*) witty; (*elegant*) elegant; (*klug*) clever; (*unterhaltsam*) entertaining; **nicht gerade ~reich aussehen** (*ugs.*) look pretty stupid (*coll.*); ❷ *adv.; s. Adj.:* wittily; elegantly; cleverly; entertainingly; **~sprühend** *Adj.* brilliantly witty; **~tötend** *Adj.* soul-destroying ‹work, job›; stupefyingly boring ‹chatter, drivel›; **~voll** *Adj.* brilliantly witty ‹joke, satire›; brilliant ‹idea›; intellectually stimulating ‹conversation, book›

**Geiz** /gaits/ *der; ~es* (*abwertend*) meanness; (*Knauserigkeit*) miserliness

**geizen** *itr. V.* Ⓐ (*übertrieben sparsam sein*) be mean; **mit etw. ~:** be mean *or* stingy with sth.; **mit Lob ~** (*fig.*) be sparing with one's praise; **sie geizt nicht mit ihren Reizen** (*fig. iron.*) she doesn't mind displaying her charms; Ⓑ (*veralt.: heftig verlangen*) **nach etw. ~:** crave [for] sth.; (*gierig*) be greedy for sth.

**Geiz·hals** *der* (*abwertend*) skinflint

**geizig** *Adj.* mean; (*knauserig*) miserly

**Geiz·kragen** *der* (*ugs. abwertend*) skinflint

**Gejammer[e]** *das; ~s* (*abwertend*) yammering (*coll.*); bellyaching (*sl.*)

**Gejauchze** *das; ~s* rejoicing; jubilation; **ihr ~ hallte durch das ganze Haus** their joyful cheers echoed through the house

**Gejaul[e]** *das; ~s* (*abwertend*) howling

**Gejohl[e]** /gəˈjo:l(ə)/ *das; ~s* (*abwertend*) howling; **mit lautstarkem ~:** with loud howls *pl.*

**gekannt** /gəˈkant/ *2. Part. v.* **kennen**

**Gekeif[e]** /gəˈkaif(ə)/ *das; ~s* scolding; nagging

**Gekicher** *das; ~s* giggling

**Gekläff[e]** *das; ~[e]s* (*abwertend; auch fig.*) yapping

**Geklapper** *das; ~s* clatter[ing]

**Geklatsch[e]** *das; ~s* (*abwertend*) Ⓐ (*Beifallklatschen*) clapping; Ⓑ (*Tratsch*) gossiping

**gekleidet** ❶ *2. Part. v.* **kleiden.** ❷ *Adj.* dressed; **gut/schlecht ~ sein** be well/badly dressed

**Geklimper** *das; ~s* (*abwertend*) plunking

**Geklingel** *das; ~s* (*abwertend*) ringing

**geklungen** /gəˈklʊŋən/ *2. Part. v.* **klingen**

**Geknall[e]** *das; ~s* (*ugs. abwertend*) banging; (*von Schüssen, einer Peitsche*) cracking; (*von Korken*) popping

**Geknatter** *das; ~s* (*eines Autos, Motors, Motorrades*) clattering; (*eines Maschinengewehrs*) rattling; (*eines Segels*) flapping; (*eines Radios*) crackle

**geknickt** ❶ *2. Part. v.* **knicken.** ❷ *Adj.* (*ugs.*) dejected; downcast

**gekniffen** *2. Part. v.* **kneifen**

**Geknister** *das; ~s* rustling; rustle; (*von Holz, Feuer*) crackling; crackle

**gekommen** *2. Part. v.* **kommen**

**gekonnt** /gəˈkɔnt/ ❶ *2. Part. v.* **können.** ❷ *Adj.* accomplished; (*hervorragend ausgeführt*) masterly. ❸ *adv.* in an accomplished manner; (*hervorragend*) in masterly fashion

**gekoren** /gəˈko:rən/ *2. Part. v.* **küren, kiesen**

**Gekrächz[e]** *das; ~s* cawing; (*einer heiseren Stimme*) croaking; (*von Papageien*) squawking

**Gekrakel** *das; ~s* (*ugs. abwertend*) scrawl; scribble

**Gekreisch[e]** *das; ~s* (*von Vögeln*) screeching; (*von Menschen*) shrieking; squealing; (*von Rädern, Bremsen*) squealing

**gekrischen** /gəˈkrɪʃn̩/ *2. Part. v.* **kreischen**

**Gekritzel[e]** *das; ~s* (*abwertend*) scribble; scrawl

**gekrochen** *2. Part. v.* **kriechen**

**Gekröse** /gəˈkrø:zə/ *das; ~s, ~* Ⓐ (*Kochk.*) (*vom Kalb*) tripe; (*vom Schwein*) chitterlings *pl.*; (*von Geflügel*) giblets *pl.*; Ⓑ ▶ 471 (*Anat.*) mesentery

**gekünstelt** /gəˈkʏnstl̩t/ ❶ *Adj.* artificial; **ein ~es Lächeln** a forced smile; **ein ~es Benehmen** affected behaviour. ❷ *adv.* **er lächelte ~:** he gave a forced smile; **sie spricht immer so ~:** she always talks so affectedly

**Gel** /ge:l/ *das; ~s, ~e* (*Chemie*) gel

**Gelaber[e]** *das; ~s* (*ugs. abwertend*) rabbiting (*coll.*) *or* babbling on

**Gelächter** /gəˈlɛçtɐ/ *das; ~s, ~:* laughter; **ein lautes/schallendes ~:** loud/ringing laughter; **in ~ ausbrechen** burst out laughing; ⇒ *auch* **homerisch**

**gelackmeiert** /gəˈlakmaiɐt/ *Adj.* (*salopp scherzh.*) had (*sl.*); conned (*coll.*); **ich bin/du bist** *usw.* **der/die Gelackmeierte** I'm/you're *etc.* the one who's been had (*sl.*)

**geladen** ❶ *2. Part. v.* **laden.** ❷ *in* **~ sein** be furious *or* (*coll.*) livid; **[auf jmdn./etw.] ~ sein** be furious *or* (*Brit. coll.*) livid [with sb./about sth.]

**Gelage** *das; ~s, ~:* feast; banquet; (*abwertend*) orgy of eating and drinking

**Gelähmte** *der/die; adj. Dekl.* paralytic

**Gelände** /gəˈlɛndə/ *das; ~s, ~* Ⓐ (*Landschaft*) ground; terrain; **das ~ steigt an/fällt ab** the ground rises/falls; **das ~ durchkämmen/erkunden** comb/reconnoitre the ground; Ⓑ (*Grundstück*) site; (*von Schule, Krankenhaus usw.*) grounds *pl.*; **das ~ absperren** cordon off the area; Ⓒ (*Milit.*) **~ gewinnen/verlieren** gain/lose ground

**gelände-, Gelände-: ~darstellung** *die* (*Geogr.*) relief mapping; **~fahrt** *die* cross-country drive; (*das Fahren*) cross-country driving; **~fahrzeug** *das* cross-country vehicle; **~gängig** *Adj.* cross-country *attrib.* ‹vehicle›; ‹vehicle› suitable for cross-country driving; **~lauf** *der* (*Leichtathletik*) cross-country run; (*Wettbewerb*) cross-country race; (*das Laufen*) cross-country running

**Geländer** /gəˈlɛndɐ/ *das; ~s, ~:* banisters *pl.*; handrail; (*am Balkon, an einer Brücke*) railing[s *pl.*]; (*aus Stein*) balustrades; parapet

**Gelände-: ~reifen** *der* cross-country tyre; **~ritt** *der* Ⓐ cross-country ride; Ⓑ (*Reitsport*) endurance competition; **~spiel** *das* scouting game; **~sport** *der* scrambling; **~übung** *die* (*Milit.*) field exercise; **~wagen** *der* ⇒ **~fahrzeug**

**gelang** *3. Pers. Sg. Prät. v.* **gelingen**

**gelänge** *3. Pers. Sg. Konjunktiv II v.* **gelingen**

**gelangen** *itr. V.; mit sein* Ⓐ **an etw.** (*Akk.*)/**zu etw. ~:** arrive at *or* reach sth.; **ans Ziel ~:** arrive at *or* reach one's destination; **an die Öffentlichkeit ~:** reach the public; leak out; **in jmds. Besitz ~:** come into sb.'s possession; **in den Besitz von etw. ~:** gain possession of sth.; Ⓑ (*fig.*) **zu Geld ~** (*durch Arbeit*) make money; (*durch Erbe*) come into money; **zu Ansehen ~:** gain esteem *or* standing; **zu Ehre ~:** attain honour; **zu Ruhm ~:** achieve fame; **an die Macht ~:** come to power; **zu der Erkenntnis ~, dass ...** come to the realization that ...; realize that ...; Ⓒ *als Funktionsverb* **zur Aufführung ~:** be presented *or* performed; **zur Auszahlung/Verteilung ~:** be paid [out]/distributed

g

**Gelass**, ***Gelaß** /gəˈlas/ *das;* **Gelasses, Gelasse** (*geh.*) [small, dark] room *or* chamber; (*Verlies*) dungeon

**gelassen** ❶ *2. Part. v.* **lassen**. ❷ *Adj.* calm; (*gefasst*) composed; **~ bleiben** keep calm *or* cool. ❸ *adv.* calmly

**Gelassenheit** *die;* **~:** calmness; (*Gefasstheit*) composure

**Geläster** *das;* **~s** (*abwertend*) making malicious remarks

**Gelatine** /ʒelaˈtiːnə/ *die;* **~:** gelatine

**Geläuf** *das;* **~[e]s, ~e** Ⓐ (*Jägerspr.*) tracks *pl.;* track; spoor; Ⓑ (*Sport*) track, course

**gelaufen** *2. Part. v.* **laufen**

**geläufig** ❶ *Adj.* Ⓐ (*vertraut*) familiar, common ‹expression, concept›; **etw. ist jmdm. ~:** sb. is familiar with sth.; Ⓑ (*fließend, perfekt*) fluent. ❷ *adv.* fluently; **~ Englisch sprechen** speak fluent English; speak English fluently; be fluent in English

**Geläufigkeit** *die;* **~** Ⓐ (*Bekanntheit*) familiarity; Ⓑ (*Perfektion*) fluency

**gelaunt** /gəˈlaunt/ **gut ~:** good-humoured; cheerful; **froh ~:** cheerful; **schlecht ~:** ill-tempered; bad-tempered; **übel ~:** ill-tempered; ill-humoured; **gut/schlecht ~ sein** be in a good/bad mood; **wie ist sie ~?** what sort of mood is she in?; **zu etw. ~ sein** (*veralt.*) be in the mood for sth.

**Geläut** *das;* **~[e]s, ~e** Ⓐ (*Glocken*) chime; Ⓑ ⇒ **Geläute**

**Geläute** *das;* **~s** ringing; (*harmonisch*) chiming

**gelb** /gɛlp/ *Adj.* yellow; **die ~e Gefahr** (*abwertend*) the yellow peril; **die ~e Karte** (*Fußball*) the yellow card; **vor Neid ~ werden** turn green with envy; **der Gelbe Fluss/das Gelbe Meer** the Yellow River/Sea; **das Gelbe vom Ei** the egg yolk; **das ist nicht das Gelbe vom Ei** (*fig. ugs.*) that's no great shakes (*sl.*)

**Gelb** *das;* **~s, ~** *od.* (*ugs.*) **~s** yellow; **bei ~ über die Ampel fahren** go through *or* crash the lights on amber; ⇒ *auch* **Blau**

**gelb·braun** *Adj.* yellowish-brown

**Gelbe** /ˈgɛlbə/ *der/die; adj. Dekl.* (*abwertend*) Oriental

**gelb-, Gelb-: ~fieber** *das* ▶ 474 (*Med.*) yellow fever; **~filter** *der od.* (*fachspr. meist*) *das* (*Fot.*) yellow filter; **~grün** *Adj.* yellowish-green; **~körper** *der* ▶ 471 (*Anat.*) corpus luteum; **~kreuz** *das* mustard gas

**gelblich** ❶ *Adj.* yellowish; yellowed ‹paper›; sallow ‹skin›. ❷ *adv.* **~ grün** yellowish-green

**gelb-, Gelb-: ~sucht** *die* ▶ 474 (*Med.*) jaundice; icterus (*Med.*); **~süchtig** *Adj.* jaundiced; **~wurz[el]** *die* (*Bot.*) turmeric

**Geld** /gɛlt/ *das;* **~es, ~er** ▶ 337 Ⓐ money; **großes ~:** large denominations *pl.;* **kleines/bares ~:** change/cash; **etw. bedeutet bares ~:** sth. is worth hard cash; **~ scheffeln** rake in the money; **etw. für teures ~ erwerben** pay a lot of money for sth.; **es ist für ~ nicht zu haben** money cannot buy it; **mit ~ nicht umgehen können** be hopeless about money; **das ist hinausgeworfenes ~:** that is a waste of money *or* (*coll.*) money down the drain; **ohne ~ dastehen** be left penniless; **ins ~ gehen** (*ugs.*) run away with the money (*coll.*); **~ stinkt nicht** (*Spr.*) money has no smell; **~ regiert die Welt** (*Spr.*) money makes the world go round; **~ allein macht nicht glücklich** [(*scherzh.*), **aber es hilft**] (*Spr.*) money isn't everything[, but it helps]; **~ und Gut** (*geh.*) all one's wealth and possessions; **hier liegt das ~ auf der Straße** (*fig.*) the streets here are paved with gold; **das große ~ machen** make a lot of money; **sein ~ unter die Leute bringen** spend one's money; **jmdm. das ~ aus der Tasche ziehen** get *or* wheedle money out of sb.; **~ wie Heu haben, im ~ schwimmen** be rolling in money *or* in it (*coll.*); **nicht für ~ und gute Worte** (*ugs.*) not for love or money; **zu ~ kommen** get hold of [some] money; **etw. zu ~ machen** turn sth. into money *or* cash; Ⓑ (*größere Summe*) money; **öffentliche/staatliche ~er** public/state money *sing. or* funds; Ⓒ (*Börsenw.*) ⇒ **Geldkurs**

**geld-, Geld-: ~adel** *der* financial aristocracy; **~angelegenheit** *die* money *or* financial matter; **seine ~angelegenheiten regeln** settle one's affairs; **~anlage** *die* investment; **~automat** *der* cash dispenser; **~betrag** *der* sum *or* amount [of money]; **~beutel** *der* (*bes. südd.*) purse; **auf dem** *od.* **seinem ~beutel sitzen** (*ugs. abwertend*) be tight-fisted; **~bombe** *die* night-safe box; **~börse** *die* purse; **~briefträger** *der,* **~briefträgerin** *die: postman/postwoman who delivers items containing money or on which money is payable;* **~buße** *die* fine; **~entwertung** *die* depreciation of the/a currency; **~erwerb** *der* Ⓐ **zum ~erwerb arbeiten** work [in order] to earn money; **seine Malerei dient nicht dem ~erwerb** he does not paint for the money; Ⓑ (*Tätigkeit*) **seinem ~erwerb nachgehen** earn one's living; **~forderung** *die* claim [for money]; **eine ~forderung an jmdn. haben** have a claim against sb.; **~frage** *die* question of money; **~geber** *der,* **~geberin** *die* financial backer; (*für Forschungen usw.*) sponsor; **~geschäft** *das* financial transaction; money transaction; **~geschenk** *das* gift of money; **~gier** *die* (*abwertend*) greed; avarice; **~gierig** *Adj.* (*abwertend*) greedy; avaricious; **~hahn** *der: in* **[jmdm.] den ~hahn ab-** *od.* **zudrehen** (*ugs.*) cut off sb.'s supply of money; **~heirat** *die:* **das ist eine reine ~heirat** he just married her for her money/she just married him for his money; **~herrschaft** *die* plutocracy

**geldig** *Adj.* (*österr.*) rich; wealthy

**Geld-: ~institut** *das* financial institution; **~katze** *die* (*hist.*) *large leather purse worn on or as a belt;* **~klemme** *die* (*ugs.*) financial straits *pl. or* difficulties *pl.;* **~knappheit** *die* shortage of money; **~kurs** *der* (*Börsenw.*) bid price; **~leute** ⇒ **~mann**

**geldlich** *Adj.* financial

**Geld-: ~mangel** *der* lack of money; **~mann** *der; Pl.* **~leute** financier; **~markt** *der* (*Wirtsch.*) money market; **~mittel** *Pl.* financial resources; funds; **~not** *die* financial straits *pl. or* difficulties *pl.;* **~politik** *die* monetary policy; **~prämie** *die* cash bonus; (**~preis**) cash prize; **~preis** *der* cash prize; (*bei einem Turnier*) prize money; **~quelle** *die* source of income; (*für den Staat*) source of revenue; **~sache** *die* ⇒ **~angelegenheit**; **~sack** *der* Ⓐ money bag; Ⓑ (*veralt.*) ⇒ **~beutel**; Ⓒ (*ugs. abwertend: geiziger Mensch*) money bags *sing.;* **~schein** *der* ▶ 337 banknote; bill (*Amer.*); **~schöpfung** *die* (*Finanzw.*) creation of money; **~schrank** *der* safe; **~schrank·knacker** *der,* **~schrank·knackerin** *die* (*ugs.*) safe-breaker; safe-cracker; **~schuld** *die* [money *or* financial] debt; **~schwemme** *die* (*ugs.*) glut of money; **~schwierigkeiten** *Pl.* financial difficulties *or* straits; **~sorgen** *Pl.* money troubles; financial worries; **~sorte** *die* (*Bankw.*) currency; **~spende** *die* donation; contribution; **~spritze** *die* ⇒ **Finanzspritze**; **~strafe** *die* fine; **jmdn. zu einer ~strafe verurteilen** fine sb.; **~stück** *das* ▶ 337 coin; **~summe** *die* sum [of money]; **~tasche** *die* purse; **~umlauf** *der* circulation of money; **~umtausch** *der* ⇒ **~wechsel**; **~verlegenheit** *die* (*verhüll.*) financial embarrassment; **in ~verlegenheit sein** be financially embarrassed; **~verleiher** *der,* **~verleiherin** *die* moneylender; **~verlust** *der* financial loss; **~verschwendung** *die* waste of money; **das wäre reinste ~verschwendung** that would be a sheer waste of money; **~wasch·anlage** *die* (*ugs.*) moneylaundering scheme; **~wechsel** *der* exchanging of money; **„~wechsel"** 'bureau de change'; 'change'; **~wert** *der* Ⓐ (*Wert eines Gegenstandes*) cash value; Ⓑ (*innerer ~wert*) value of money; (*äußerer ~wert*) value of the/a currency; **~wesen** *das* finance *no art.;* **~zuwendung** *die* allowance [of money]; (**~geschenk**) gift of money

**geleckt** ❶ *2. Part. v.* **lecken²**. ❷ *Adj. in* **wie ~ aussehen** (*ugs.*) look all spruced up

**Gelee** /ʒeˈleː/ *der od. das;* **~s, ~s** jelly; **Aale in ~:** jellied eels

**Gelege** *das;* **~s, ~** (*von Vögeln*) clutch of eggs; (*von Reptilien, Insekten*) batch of eggs

**gelegen** ❶ *2. Part. v.* **liegen**. ❷ *Adj.* Ⓐ (*passend*) convenient; **das kommt mir ~:** that comes just at the right time for me; Ⓑ (*liegend*) situated; **hoch ~:** high-lying

**Gelegenheit** *die;* **~, ~en** Ⓐ (*günstiger Augenblick*) opportunity; **jmdm. [die] ~ geben, etw. zu tun** give sb. the opportunity of doing *or* to do sth.; **die ~ nutzen** make the most of the opportunity; **bei nächster ~:** at the next opportunity; **bei ~:** some time; **~ macht Diebe** opportunity makes the thief (*prov.*); **die ~ beim Schopf[e] fassen** *od.* **ergreifen** grab *or* seize the opportunity with both hands; Ⓑ (*Anlass*) occasion; **ein Anzug für alle ~en** a suit that can be worn on any occasion

**Gelegenheits-: ~arbeit** *die* casual work; **~arbeiter** *der,* **~arbeiterin** *die* casual worker; **~dieb** *der,* **~diebin** *die* opportunist thief; **~dichtung** *die* occasional poetry; **~kauf** *der* bargain

**gelegentlich** ❶ *Adj.* occasional. ❷ *adv.* Ⓐ (*manchmal*) occasionally; Ⓑ (*bei Gelegenheit*) some time. ❸ *Präp. + Gen.* (*Amtsspr.*) on the occasion of

**gelehrig** /gəˈleːrɪç/ ❶ *Adj.* ‹child› who is quick to learn *or* quick at picking things up; ‹animal› that is quick to learn. ❷ *adv.* **sich ~ anstellen** be quick to learn

**Gelehrigkeit** *die;* **~:** quickness to learn

**gelehrsam** *Adj.* Ⓐ ⇒ **gelehrig**; Ⓑ (*veralt.: gelehrt*) learned; erudite

**Gelehrsamkeit** *die;* **~:** learning; erudition

**gelehrt** ❶ *2. Part. v.* **lehren**. ❷ *Adj.* Ⓐ (*kenntnisreich*) learned; erudite; Ⓑ (*auf gründlichen Kenntnissen beruhend*) scholarly; Ⓒ (*abwertend: schwer verständlich*) highbrow. ❸ *adv.* Ⓐ learnedly; eruditely; Ⓑ (*abwertend: schwer verständlich*) in a highbrow way

**Gelehrte** *der/die; adj. Dekl.* scholar; **darüber streiten sich die ~n** *od.* **sind sich die ~n noch nicht einig** the experts disagree on that; (*fig.*) that's a moot point

**Gelehrten-: ~dasein** *das* scholarly life *or* existence; **~streit** *der* dispute among scholars

**Geleise** *das;* **~s, ~** (*österr., sonst geh.*) ⇒ **Gleis**

**Geleit** *das;* **~[e]s, ~e** Ⓐ (*geh.: das Begleiten*) **sie bot uns ihr ~ an** she offered to accompany *or* escort us; **freies** *od.* **sicheres ~** (*Rechtsw.*) safe conduct; **jmdm. das ~ geben** (*geh.*) accompany *or* escort sb.; **jmdm. das letzte ~ geben** (*geh. verhüll.*) attend sb.'s funeral; **zum ~:** as a preface; **„zum ~"** 'preface'; Ⓑ (*Eskorte*) escort; (*Gefolge*) entourage; retinue

**geleiten** *tr. V.* (*geh.*) escort; (*begleiten*) accompany; escort; **jmdn. zur Tür ~:** see sb. to the door; show sb. out

**Geleit-: ~schiff** *das* (*Milit.*) escort vessel; **~schutz** *der* (*Milit.*) escort; **jmdm. ~schutz geben** provide an escort for sb.; **~wort** *das; Pl.* **~~e** (*geh.*) preface; **~zug** *der* (*Milit.*) convoy

**Gelenk** /gəˈlɛŋk/ *das;* **~[e]s, ~e** Ⓐ ▶ 471 joint; **es kracht** *od.* **knackt in den ~en** my/your *etc.* joints creak; Ⓑ (*Technik*) joint; (*Scharnier~*) hinge

**Gelenk-: ~entzündung** *die* ▶ 474 (*Med.*) arthritis; **~fahrzeug** *das* articulated vehicle

**gelenkig** ❶ *Adj.* agile ‹person›; (*geschmeidig*) supple ‹limb›. ❷ *adv.* Ⓐ agilely; Ⓑ (*Technik*) **~ gelagert** (*mittels Scharnier*) hinge-mounted; (*mittels Drehzapfen*) swivel-mounted

**Gelenkigkeit** *die;* **~:** agility; (*von Gliedmaßen*) suppleness

**Gelenk-: ~kapsel** *die* ▶ 471 (*Anat.*) joint capsule; articular capsule; **~kopf** *der* (*Anat.*) head of a/the bone; **~pfanne** *die* ▶ 471

*old spelling (see note on page 1707)

g

# Geld

## Britisches Geld

| GESCHRIEBEN | GESPROCHEN |
|---|---|
| 1p | one p |
| 2p | two p *od.* pence |
| 50p | fifty p *od.* pence |
| £1 | one pound, a pound |
| £1.03 | one pound three p *od.* three pence* |
| £1.20 | one pound twenty [p *od.* pence*] |
| £1.99 | one pound ninety-nine |
| £20 | twenty pounds |
| £100 | one hundred *od.* a hundred pounds |
| £1,000 | one thousand *od.* a thousand pounds |
| £1,000,000 | one million *od.* a million pounds |
| £5,000,000 | five million pounds |

***100 Pence sind ein Pfund***
= 100 pence make one pound, there are 100 pence in a pound

* Normalerweise sagt man immer 'p' bzw 'pence' nach einer Zahl zwischen 1 und 19, die auf eine Pfundzahl folgt; bei 20 Pence oder mehr wird das 'p' bzw 'pence' hier meist weggelassen.

## Amerikanisches Geld

| GESCHRIEBEN | GESPROCHEN |
|---|---|
| 1c | one cent, a cent |
| 10c | ten cents, a dime* |
| 25c | twenty-five cents, a quarter* |
| $1 | one dollar, a dollar |
| $1.50 | one dollar fifty [cents] |
| $5.99 | five dollars ninety-nine |
| $200 | two hundred dollars |
| $1,000 | one thousand *od.* a thousand dollars |
| $1,000,000 | one million *od.* a million dollars |
| $100,000,000 | one hundred *od.* a hundred million dollars |

***100 Cent sind ein Dollar***
= 100 cents make one dollar, there are 100 cents in a dollar

* Diese Bezeichnungen beziehen sich meist auf die Münzen mit diesen Werten.

## Deutsches Geld

| GESCHRIEBEN | GESPROCHEN |
|---|---|
| 1Pf | one pfennig, a pfennig |
| 25Pf | twenty-five pfennigs |
| DM1 | one [Deutsch]mark, a [Deutsch]mark* |
| DM1.50 | one mark fifty [pfennigs] |
| DM2 | two marks |
| DM2.75 | two marks seventy-five [pfennigs] |
| DM100 | one hundred *od.* a hundred marks |
| DM200 | two hundred marks |
| DM1,000 | one thousand *od.* a thousand marks |
| DM1,000,000 | one million *od.* a million marks |
| DM50,000,000 | fifty million marks |

***100 Pfennig sind eine Mark***
= 100 pfennigs make one mark, there are 100 pfennigs in a mark

* Die Bezeichnung 'Deutschmark' wird meist für die Währung verwendet, z.B.

***der Wert des Pfundes gegenüber der Deutschen Mark***
= the value of the pound against the Deutschmark

## Österreichisches Geld

| GESCHRIEBEN | GESPROCHEN |
|---|---|
| 90g | ninety groschen |
| 1S, 1 Sch. | one schilling, a schilling |
| 100S, 100 ATS | one hundred *od.* a hundred schillings |

## Schweizerisches Geld

| GESCHRIEBEN | GESPROCHEN |
|---|---|
| 90c | ninety centimes |
| 1 SF | one [Swiss] franc, a [Swiss] franc |
| 2,000 SF | two thousand [Swiss] francs |

*Allgemeine Bemerkungen*: 1. Im Englischen steht bei Zahlen über tausend ein Komma dort, wo im Deutschen ein Spatium steht. 2. Das Wort 'million' ist kein Substantiv (wie *Million* im Deutschen), sondern ein Adjektiv. Deshalb kein **s** bei mehreren Millionen (zwei Millionen Pfund = two million pounds).

····➤ Zahlen

## Münzen und Scheine

■ **GB:**

***ein Zwanzigpencestück***
= a 20p *od.* 20 pence piece

***ein Fünfzigpencestück***
= a 50p *od.* 50 pence piece

***ein Pfundstück***
= a pound coin

***ein Fünfpfundschein***
= a five-pound note

■ **USA:**

***ein Fünfcentstück***
= a nickel

***ein Zehncentstück***
= a dime

***ein Vierteldollarstück***
= a quarter

***ein Dollarstück***
= a dollar coin

***ein Dollarschein***
= a dollar bill

***ein Zehndollarschein***
= a ten-dollar bill

Man sieht, dass für die kleineren Werte (unter 1 Pfund bzw. 1 Dollar) *Stück* durch 'piece' übersetzt wird, sonst durch 'coin'. Auch dass die Währungseinheit (pound, dollar, mark usw.) vor 'piece', 'coin', 'note' oder 'bill' im Singular bleibt. Das gilt ebenfalls für deutsche Münzen:

***ein Fünfzigpfennigstück***
= a 50 pfennig piece

***ein Markstück***
= a one-mark coin

***ein Fünfmarkstück***
= a five-mark coin

***ein Zwanzigmarkschein***
= a twenty-mark note *od.* (*amerik.*) bill

## Sonstige Ausdrücke

***Was*** od. ***Wie viel kostet das?***
= What *od.* How much does it cost?

***Es kostet knapp 200 DM/etwas über 200 DM***
= It costs just under/just over 200 DM

***Die Kartoffeln kosten 30p das Pfund***
= The potatoes are 30p a pound

***100 Mark in bar***
= 100 marks in cash

***etwas bar/in Pfund bezahlen***
= to pay for something in cash/in pounds

***Kann ich mit Scheck/mit Kreditkarte zahlen?***
= Can I pay by cheque/by credit card?

***ein Scheck über 50 Pfund***
= a cheque for £50

***ein Reisescheck in Dollar/Pfund [Sterling]***
= a dollar/sterling traveller's cheque *od.* (*amerik.*) traveler's check

***Können Sie auf einen Zwanzigmarkschein herausgeben?***
= Can you change *od.* give me change for a twenty-mark note *od.* (*amerik.*) bill?

***Ich will Mark in Dollar wechseln***
= I want to change marks into dollars

***Es gehen ... Mark auf ein Pfund***
= There are ... marks to the pound

(*Anat.*) socket of a/the joint; **~rheumatismus** *der* ▶474 (*Med.*) articular rheumatism; **~schmiere** *die* (*Anat.*) synovial fluid; **~welle** *die* (*Kfz-W.*) cardan shaft

**gelernt** ❶ *2. Part. v.* **lernen**. ❷ *Adj.* qualified

**gelesen** *2. Part. v.* **lesen**

**Gelichter** *das;* **~s** (*veralt. abwertend*) rabble; riff-raff

**Geliebte** /gə'li:ptə/ *der/die; adj. Dekl.* Ⓐ lover/mistress; Ⓑ (*geh. veralt.*) beloved

**geliefert** ❶ *2. Part. v.* **liefern**. ❷ *Adj. in* **~ sein** (*salopp*) be sunk (*coll.*); have had it (*coll.*)

**geliehen** /gə'li:ən/ *2. Part. v.* **leihen**

**gelieren** /ʒe'li:rən/ *itr. V.* set

**Gelier·zucker** *der* preserving sugar

**gelind[e]** ❶ *Adj.* Ⓐ (*schonend*) mild; Ⓑ (*geh. veralt.: mild, sanft*) mild ‹climate›; light ‹punishment›; slight ‹pain›. ❷ *adv.* mildly; **~ gesagt** to put it mildly

**gelingen** /gə'lɪŋən/ *unr. itr. V.; mit sein* succeed; **es gelang ihr, es zu tun** she succeeded in doing it; **es gelang ihr nicht, es zu tun** she did not succeed in doing it; she failed to do it; **möge dir dein Vorhaben ~:** I hope you succeed with *or* accomplish your plan; **das wollte ihr nicht ~:** she couldn't seem to manage it; **eine gelungene Arbeit** a successful piece of work; ⇨ *auch* **gelungen 2**

**Gelingen** *das;* **~s** success; **auf ein gutes ~ hoffen** hope for success; **jmdm. gutes ~ wünschen** wish sb. every success; **gutes ~!** the best of luck!

**gelitten** /gə'lɪtn̩/ *2. Part. v.* **leiden**

**gell**[1] /gɛl/ ❶ *Adj.* (*geh.*) piercing; shrill. ❷ *adv.* **~ aufschreien** let out *or* give a piercing scream *or* shriek

**gell[e]**[2] /'gɛl(ə)/ *Interj.* (*südd.*) ⇨ **gelt**

**gellen** /'gɛlən/ *itr. V.* Ⓐ (*hell schallen*) ring out; **ein Schrei gellte durch die Nacht** a scream *or* shriek pierced the night; **jmdm. in den Ohren ~:** make sb.'s ears ring; **~des Gelächter** shrill peals of laughter; **~d aufschreien** let out *or* give a piercing scream *or* shriek; Ⓑ (*nachhallen*) ring; **uns gellten die Ohren** our ears rang; **von etw. ~:** ring with sth.

**geloben** *tr. V.* (*geh.*) vow; **Besserung/Armut ~:** promise solemnly to improve/take a vow of poverty; **jmdm. Treue ~:** vow to be faithful to sb.; **sich** (*Dat.*) **~, etw. zu tun** vow to oneself *or* make a solemn resolve to do sth.; **das Gelobte Land** the Promised Land

**Gelöbnis** /gə'lø:pnɪs/ *das;* **~ses, ~se** (*geh.*) vow; **ein ~ ablegen** *od.* **leisten** make *or* take a vow

**gelogen** *2. Part. v.* **lügen**

**gelöst** /gə'lø:st/ ❶ *2. Part. v.* **lösen**. ❷ *Adj.* relaxed

**Gelöstheit** *die;* **~:** relaxed mood

**Gelse** /'gɛlzə/ *die;* **~, ~n** (*österr.*) mosquito, gnat

**gelt** /gɛlt/ *Interj.* (*südd., österr. ugs.*) **~, du bist mir doch nicht böse?** you're not angry with me, are you?; **er kommt doch morgen zurück, ~?** he'll be coming back tomorrow, won't he *or* (*coll.*) right?

**gelten** /'gɛltn̩/ ❶ *unr. itr. V.* Ⓐ (*gültig sein*) be valid; ‹banknote, coin› be legal tender; ‹law, regulation, agreement› be in force; ‹price› be effective; **etw. gilt für jmdn.** sth. applies to sb.; **das gilt auch für dich/Sie!** (*ugs.*) that includes you!; that goes for you too!; **das gilt nicht!** that doesn't count!; **~de Preise** current prices; **nach ~dem Recht** in accordance with the law as it [now] stands; **die ~de Meinung** the generally accepted opinion; **etw. [nicht] ~ lassen** [not] accept sth.; Ⓑ (*angesehen werden*) **als etw. ~:** be regarded as sth.; be considered [to be] sth.; **er galt als klug/Favorit** he was regarded as clever/the favourite; he was considered [to be] clever/the favourite; Ⓒ (+ *Dat.*) (*bestimmt sein für*) be directed at; **die Bemerkung gilt dir** the remark is aimed at you; **der Beifall galt auch dem Regisseur** the applause was also for the director.
❷ *unr. tr. V.* Ⓐ (*wert sein*) **sein Wort gilt viel/wenig** his word carries a lot of/little weight; **was gilt die Wette?** what do you bet?; **etw. gilt jmdm. mehr als …** sth. is worth *or* means more to sb. than …; Ⓑ *unpers.* (*darauf ankommen, dass*) **es gilt, Zeit zu gewinnen/rasch zu handeln** it is essential to gain time/act swiftly; **es gilt einen Versuch** the only thing to do is to make an attempt; Ⓒ *unpers.* (*geh.: auf dem Spiel stehen*) **es gilt dein Leben** *od.* **deinen Kopf** your life is at stake

**geltend** *in* **etw. ~ machen** assert sth.; **einige Bedenken/einen Einwand ~ machen** express some doubts/raise an objection; **sich ~ machen** begin to show; begin to make itself/themselves felt; ⇨ *auch* **gelten 1 A**

**Geltendmachung** *die;* **~** (*Amtsspr.*) assertion

**Geltung** *die;* **~** Ⓐ (*Gültigkeit*) validity; **~ haben** ‹banknote, coin› be legal tender; ‹law, regulation, agreement› be in force; ‹price› be effective; **für jmdn. ~ haben** apply to sb.; Ⓑ (*Wirkung*) recognition; **jmdm./sich/einer Sache ~ verschaffen** gain *or* win recognition for sb./oneself/sth.; **an ~ verlieren** ‹value, principle, etc.› lose its importance, become less important; **etw. zur ~ bringen** show something to its best advantage; **zur ~ kommen** show to [its best] advantage

**Geltungs-: ~bedürfnis** *das* need for recognition; **~bereich** *der* scope; **unter den ~bereich eines Gesetzes fallen** come within the scope of a law; **~bereich dieser Verordnung ist Hessen** the area in which the regulation is in force is Hesse; **~dauer** *die* period of validity; **die ~dauer des Vertrags/Gesetzes** the period during which the agreement/law is in force; **~drang** *der* ⇨ **~sbedürfnis**; **~sucht** *die* [pathological] craving for recognition; **~trieb** *der* (**~bedürfnis**) need for recognition; (**~sucht**) craving for recognition

**Gelump[e]** /gə'lʊmp(ə)/ *das;* **~s** (*ugs. abwertend*) Ⓐ (*Plunder*) junk; rubbish; Ⓑ (*Gesindel*) riff-raff; rabble

**gelungen** /gə'lʊŋən/ ❶ *2. Part. v.* **gelingen**. ❷ *Adj.* Ⓐ (*ugs.: spaßig*) priceless; **das finde ich ~:** what a laugh!; Ⓑ (*ansprechend*) inspired

**Gelüst** *das;* **~[e]s, ~e, Gelüste** *das;* **~es, ~e** (*geh.*) longing; strong desire; (*zwingend, krankhaft*) craving; **ein ~ nach** *od.* **auf etw.** (*Akk.*) **haben** have a longing *or* a strong desire/a craving for sth.

**gelüsten** *tr. V.* (*unpers.*) **es gelüstet ihn nach …** he has a longing for …; (*zwingend, krankhaft*) he has a craving for …

**gemach** /gə'ma(:)x/ *Adv.* (*veralt.*) **[nur/immer] ~!** not so fast!; take it easy!

**Gemach** /gə'ma(:)x/ *das;* **~[e]s, Gemächer** /gə'mɛ(:)çɐ/ (*veralt. geh.*) apartment

**gemächlich** /gə'mɛ(:)çlɪç/ ❶ *Adj.* leisurely; **ein ~es Leben führen** take life easily. ❷ *adv.* in a leisurely manner; **~ wandern** stroll

**Gemächlichkeit** *die;* **~:** leisureliness; **etw. mit ~ machen** do sth. at a leisurely pace

**gemacht** ❶ *2. Part. v.* **machen**. ❷ *in* **ein ~er Mann sein** (*ugs.*) be a made man; **zu** *od.* **für etw. [nicht] ~ sein** (*ugs.*) [not] be made for sth.; **ich bin nicht dazu ~, einen solchen Posten auszufüllen** I'm not cut out for a job like this

**Gemächt** *das;* **~[e]s, Gemächte** *das;* **~es** (*scherzh., veralt.*) privy parts *pl.* (*arch.*)

**Gemahl** *der;* **~s, ~e** (*geh.*) consort; husband; **bitte grüßen Sie Ihren Herrn ~:** please give my regards to your husband

**Gemahlin** *die;* **~, ~nen** (*geh.*) consort; wife; **eine Empfehlung an die Frau ~:** my compliments to your wife

**gemahnen** *tr., itr. V.* (*geh.*) **jmdn. an etw.** (*Akk.*) **~:** remind sb. of sth.; **diese Gedenktafel soll an die Opfer beider Weltkriege ~:** this memorial plaque is to commemorate the dead of two World Wars

**Gemälde** /gə'mɛ:ldə/ *das;* **~s, ~:** painting

**Gemälde-: ~ausstellung** *die* exhibition of paintings; **~galerie** *die* picture gallery; **~sammlung** *die* collection of paintings

**gemäß** /gə'mɛ:s/ ❶ *Präp.* + *Dat.* in accordance with; **~ Paragraph 15/Artikel 12** under section 15/article 12. ❷ *Adj.* **jmdm./einer Sache ~ sein** be appropriate for sb./to sth.; **eine deinen Leistungen ~e Arbeit** a job suited to your abilities

**-gemäß** *Adj.* in accordance with ‹tradition etc.›; **berufs~:** in accordance with the standards of the profession; **art~:** appropriate [for the species *postpos.*]

**gemäßigt** ❶ *2. Part. v.* **mäßigen**. ❷ *Adj.* moderate; modest ‹lifestyle›; more restrained ‹version›; qualified ‹optimism›; temperate ‹climate›

**Gemäuer** /gə'mɔyɐ/ *das;* **~s, ~:** walls *pl.*; (*Ruine*) ruin

**Gemauschel** *das;* **~s** (*ugs. abwertend*) underhand dealing

**Gemecker[e]** *das;* **~s** Ⓐ (*von Schafen, Ziegen*) bleating; Ⓑ (*abwertend: Lachen*) cackling; Ⓒ (*ugs. abwertend: Nörgelei*) griping (*coll.*); grousing (*sl.*); moaning

**gemein** ❶ *Adj.* Ⓐ (*abstoßend*) coarse, vulgar ‹joke, expression›; nasty ‹person›; Ⓑ (*niederträchtig*) mean; base, dirty ‹lie›; mean, dirty ‹trick›; **du bist ~!/das ist ~ [von dir]!** you're mean *or* nasty!/that's mean *or* nasty [of you]!; Ⓒ (*ärgerlich*) infuriating; damned annoying (*coll.*); Ⓓ (*Bot., Zool., sonst veralt.: allgemein vorkommend*) common; **der ~e Mann** the ordinary man; the man in the street; **ein ~er Soldat** a common soldier; Ⓔ (*veralt.: all~*) general; **das ~e Wohl** the common good; **etw. mit jmdm./etw. ~ haben** have sth. in common with sb./sth.; **sich mit jmdm. ~ machen** associate with sb.; **das ist ihnen ~:** they have that in common; they share that.
❷ *adv.* Ⓐ (*niederträchtig*) **jmdn. ~ behandeln** treat sb. in a mean *or* nasty way; Ⓑ (*ugs.: sehr*) **sich ~ verletzen** injure oneself badly; **es hat ganz ~ weh getan** it hurt like hell (*coll.*); **~ kalt** terribly *or* hellish cold (*coll.*)

**Gemein·besitz** *der* common property

**Gemeinde** /gə'maində/ *die;* **~, ~n** Ⓐ (*staatliche Verwaltungseinheit*) municipality; (*ugs.: ~amt*) local authority; **die ~ X** the municipality of X; **einen Zug durch die ~ machen** (*fig. ugs.*) go an a pub crawl (*Brit. coll.*); go barhopping (*Amer. coll.*); Ⓑ (*Seelsorgebezirk*) (*christlich*) parish; (*nichtchristlich*) community; (*Mitglieder*) parish; parishioners *pl.*; Ⓒ (*Bewohner*) community; local population; Ⓓ (*Gottesdienstteilnehmer*) congregation; Ⓔ (*Anhängerschaft*) body of followers; **die ~ seiner Anhänger** his following

**gemeinde-, Gemeinde-: ~abgaben** *Pl.* rates [and local taxes] (*Brit.*); local taxes (*Amer.*); **~amt** *das* local authority; (*Gebäude*) municipal offices *pl.*; **~beamte** *der*, **~beamtin** *die* local government official; **~behörde** *die* local authority; **~bezirk** *der* Ⓐ municipality; district; Ⓑ (*österr.*) ward; **~eigen** *Adj.* municipal ‹swimming pool, sports centre, etc.›; **~eigen sein** be municipally owned; **~haus** *das* parish hall; **~mitglied** *das* parishioner; **~ordnung** *die* [state] law governing local authorities; **~pflege** *die* parish welfare work; **~rat** *der* Ⓐ (*Gremium*) local council; Ⓑ (*Mitglied*) local councillor; **~rätin** *die* ⇨ **~rat** B; **~schwester** *die* district nurse; **~steuer** *die* local tax

**gemein·deutsch** *Adj.* standard German

**Gemeinde-: ~verwaltung** *die* local administration; **~vor·stand** *der* local council; **~wahl** *die* ⇨ **Kommunalwahl**; **~zentrum** *das* community centre

**gemein-, Gemein-: ~eigentum** *das* (*Politik, Wirtsch.*) public property; **~gefährlich** *Adj.* dangerous to the public; **~gefährlich sein** be a danger to the public; **ein ~gefährlicher Verbrecher** a dangerous criminal; **~gültig** *Adj.* ⇨ **allgemein gültig**; **~gültigkeit** *die* ⇨ **Allgemeingültigkeit**; **~gut** *das* (*geh.*) common property

*old spelling (see note on page 1707)

**Gemein·heit** *die;* ~, ~**en** Ⓐ (*niederträchtige Gesinnung*) meanness; nastiness; **etw. aus ~ tun/sagen** do/say sth. out of meanness *or* nastiness; Ⓑ (*gemeine Handlung*) mean *or* nasty *or* dirty trick; **das war eine ~:** that was a mean *or* nasty thing to do/say; Ⓒ (*unerfreulicher Umstand*) **so eine ~!** (*ugs.*) what a damned nuisance!

**gemein-, Gemein-:** ~**hin** *Adv.* commonly; generally; **wie man ~hin vermutet/annimmt** as is commonly *or* generally supposed/assumed; ~**kosten** *Pl.* (*Wirtsch.*) overheads; overhead expenses; ~**nutz** *der;* ~~**es** public good; ~**nutz geht vor Eigennutz** the public interest comes first; ~**nützig** /-nʏtsɪç/ *Adj.* serving the public good *postpos., not pred.;* (*wohltätig*) charitable; **eine ~nützige Institution** a charitable *or* non-profit-making institution; ~**platz** *der* platitude; commonplace

**gemeinsam** ❶ *Adj.* Ⓐ common ‹interests, characteristics›; mutual ‹acquaintance, friend›; joint ‹property, account›; shared ‹experience›; **der Gemeinsame Markt** the Common Market; ~**e Interessen/Merkmale haben** have interests/characteristics in common; ~**e Kasse machen** pool funds *or* resources; **größter ~er Teiler** (*Math.*) highest common denominator; **kleinstes ~es Vielfaches** (*Math.*) lowest common multiple; Ⓑ (*miteinander unternommen*) joint ‹undertaking, consultations›; joint, concerted ‹efforts, action, measures›; **[mit jmdm.] ~e Sache machen** join forces *or* up [with sb.]; Ⓒ (*übereinstimmend*) **ihnen ist nur das ~:** that's the only thing they have in common; **das blonde Haar ist ihnen ~:** they both have blond hair; **viel Gemeinsames haben** have a lot in common.
❷ *adv.* together; **es gehört ihnen ~:** it is owned by them jointly

**Gemeinsamkeit** *die;* ~, ~**en** Ⓐ (*gemeinsames Merkmal*) common feature; point in common; **zwischen den beiden Parteien gab es keine ~en** there was no common ground between the two parties; Ⓑ (*Einheit*) community of interest; **ein Gefühl der ~:** a sense of community

**Gemeinschaft** *die;* ~, ~**en** Ⓐ community; **die ~ der Heiligen** (*Rel.*) the communion of saints; **die Europäische ~:** the European Community; Ⓑ (*Verbundenheit*) coexistence; **in unserer Klasse herrscht keine echte ~:** there is no real sense of community in our class; **in ~ mit jmdm.** together *or* jointly with sb.

**gemeinschaftlich** ❶ *Adj.* common ‹interests, characteristics›; joint ‹property, undertaking›; mutual ‹acquaintance, friend›; joint, concerted ‹efforts, action›. ❷ *adv.* together; **wir führen die Firma ~:** we run the firm jointly *or* together

**Gemeinschafts-:** ~**anschluss**, *~**anschluß** *der* (*Fernspr.*) party line; ~**antenne** *die* community aerial (*Brit.*) *or* (*Amer.*) antenna; ~**arbeit** *die* Ⓐ (*gemeinschaftliches Arbeiten*) joint work; **etw. in ~arbeit tun** do sth. jointly; **sozialistische ~arbeit** (*DDR*) collective socialist work *or* efforts *pl.;* Ⓑ (*Ergebnis der Zusammenarbeit*) joint product *or* effort; ~**aufgabe** *die* Ⓐ common *or* shared task; Ⓑ (*Bundesrepublik Deutschland*) *major project for which Land and Federation are jointly responsible;* ~**beichte** *die* (*christl. Rel.*) public confession; ~**gefühl** *das* community spirit; ~**küche** *die* (*in einem Wohnheim usw.*) shared kitchen; ~**kunde** *die* social studies *sing.;* ~**leben** *das* communal life; ~**produktion** *die* (*von einem Film, Buch usw.*) co-production; ~**raum** *der* common room (*Brit.*); ~**schule** *die* non-denominational school; ~**sendung** *die* (*Rundf., Ferns.*) joint transmission; ~**sinn** *der* community spirit; ~**werbung** *die* joint advertising; ~**werbung machen** run a joint advertisement; ~**wesen** *das* social being *or* animal; ~**zelle** *die* shared cell

**gemein-, Gemein-:** ~**schuldner** *der,* ~**schuldnerin** *die* (*Rechtsw.*) [declared] bankrupt; ~**sinn** *der* public spirit; ~**sprache** *die* (*Sprachw.*) standard language; ordinary language; ~**verständlich** ❶ *Adj.* generally comprehensible *or* intelligible; ❷ *adv.* **sich ~verständlich ausdrücken** make oneself generally comprehensible *or* intelligible; ~**wesen** *das* community; (*staatlich*) political unit; polity; ~**wohl** *das* public *or* common good; **etw./jmd. dient dem ~wohl** sth. is/sb. acts in the public interest

**Gemenge** *das;* ~**s**, ~ Ⓐ (*Gemisch*) mixture (**aus, von** of); Ⓑ (*Durcheinander*) jumble; (*von Menschen*) crowd; Ⓒ (*Landw.*) mixed crop

**Gemengsel** /gəˈmɛŋzl̩/ *das;* ~**s**, ~**:** mixture; (*von Gerüchen, Düften*) medley

**gemessen** ❶ *2. Part. v.* **messen.** ❷ *Adj.* Ⓐ (*würdevoll*) measured ‹steps, tones, language›; deliberate ‹words, manner of speaking›; ~**en Schrittes** with measured tread *or* steps *pl.;* Ⓑ (*an*~) **in ~em Abstand** *od.* ~**er Entfernung** at a respectful distance; **in ~er Bescheidenheit** with due modesty; Ⓒ (*veralt.: zurückhaltend*) reserved. ❸ *adv.* ~ **schreiten** walk with measured tread *or* steps *pl.;* ~ **sprechen** speak in measured tones

**Gemessenheit** *die;* ~ Ⓐ (*Würde*) ⇒ **gemessen** 2 A: measuredness; deliberateness; **in aller ~:** slowly and with all due solemnity; Ⓑ (*An*~) respectfulness; Ⓒ (*veralt.: Zurückhaltung*) reserve

**Gemetzel** *das;* ~**s**, ~ (*abwertend*) bloodbath; massacre

**gemieden** /gəˈmiːdn̩/ *2. Part. v.* **meiden**

**Gemisch** *das;* ~**[e]s**, ~**e** (*auch fig.*) mixture (**aus, von** of); mix (*coll.*); (*Kfz-W.*) mixture

**gemischt** ❶ *2. Part. v.* **mischen.** ❷ *Adj.* Ⓐ mixed; ~**e Kost** a varied diet; **eine ~e Klasse** a mixed *or* coeducational *or* (*coll.*) coed class; Ⓑ (*abwertend: anrüchig*) **eine ~e Gesellschaft** a disreputable crowd. ❸ *adv.* (*abwertend: anrüchig*) **es geht sehr ~ zu** there are all sorts of goings-on

**gemischt-, Gemischt-:** ~**rassig**, ~**rassisch** *Adj.* multiracial; ~**rassige Badestrände** desegregated bathing beaches; ~**waren·handlung** *die* (*veralt.*) general store

**Gemme** /ˈgɛmə/ *die;* ~, ~**n** Ⓐ (*Edelstein*) engraved gem; (*Intaglio*) intaglio; (*Kamee*) cameo; Ⓑ (*Biol.: Zelle*) gemma

**gemocht** /gəˈmɔxt/ *2. Part. v.* **mögen**

**gemolken** *2. Part. v.* **melken**

**gemoppelt** /gəˈmɔpl̩t/ ⇒ **doppelt** 2 A

**Gemotze** *das;* ~**s** (*salopp*) grumbling; fault-finding; crabbing (*coll.*)

***Gems·bart**, ***Gems·bock**, ***Gemse** ⇒ **Gäms·bart** *usw.*

**Gemunkel** *das;* ~**s** rumours *pl.;* whispers *pl.*

**Gemurmel** *das;* ~**s** murmuring

**Gemüse** /gəˈmyːzə/ *das;* ~**s**, ~**:** vegetables *pl.;* **ein ~:** a vegetable; **frisches/gekochtes ~:** fresh/cooked vegetables; **junges ~** (*fig. ugs.*) youngsters *pl.;* **dieses junge ~ kann man doch nicht ernst nehmen** (*fig. ugs.*) these young whippersnappers *pl.* can't be taken seriously

**Gemüse-:** ~**anbau** *der* growing of vegetables; (*Handelsgärtnerei*) market gardening; ~**beet** *das* vegetable patch *or* plot; ~**beilage** *die* vegetables *pl.;* ~**eintopf** *der* vegetable stew; ~**frau** *die* vegetable seller; ~**garten** *der* vegetable *or* kitchen garden; (*Teil eines Gartens*) vegetable patch *or* plot; ~**händler** *der,* ~**händlerin** *die* ▶ 159 greengrocer; ~**konserve** *die* canned *or* (*Brit.*) tinned vegetables *pl.;* (*in einem Glas*) preserved vegetables *pl.;* ~**laden** *der; Pl.* ~**läden** greengrocer's [shop]; ~**mann** *der* vegetable seller; ~**pflanze** *die* vegetable; ~**platte** *die* vegetable dish; (*als Beilage*) dish of assorted vegetables; ~**saft** *der* vegetable juice; ~**suppe** *die* vegetable soup

**gemusst**, ***gemußt** /gəˈmʊst/ *2. Part. v.* **müssen**

**Gemüt** /gəˈmyːt/ *das;* ~**[e]s**, ~**er** Ⓐ (*Gefühlsleben*) nature; disposition; **ein sonniges/kindliches ~ haben** (*iron.*) be [really] naive; Ⓑ (*Empfindungsvermögen*) heart; soul; **viel/wenig ~ haben** be soft-hearted/hard-hearted; **das rührt ans** *od.* **ist etw. fürs ~:** that touches the heart *or* tears at one's heartstrings; **jmdm. aufs ~ schlagen** *od.* **gehen** make sb. depressed; **sich** (*Dat.*) **etw. zu ~e führen** (*beherzigen*) take sth. to heart; (*essen od. trinken*) treat oneself to sth.; Ⓒ (*Mensch*) soul; **einfache/romantische ~er** simple/romantic souls; **etw. erhitzt/erregt die ~er** sth. makes feelings run high; **die ~er haben sich beruhigt** feelings have cooled down

**gemütlich** ❶ *Adj.* Ⓐ (*behaglich*) snug; cosy; gemütlich (*literary*); (*bequem*) comfortable; **mach es dir ~!** make yourself comfortable *or* at home!; Ⓑ (*ungezwungen*) informal; **ein ~es Beisammensein** an informal get-together; Ⓒ (*umgänglich*) sociable; friendly; (*gelassen*) easygoing; Ⓓ (*gemächlich*) leisurely; **ein ~es Tempo** a leisurely *or* comfortable pace. ❷ *adv.* Ⓐ (*behaglich*) cosily; (*bequem*) comfortably; Ⓑ (*ungezwungen*) ~ **beisammensitzen** sit pleasantly together; **sich ~ unterhalten** have a pleasant chat; Ⓒ (*gemächlich*) at a leisurely *or* comfortable pace; unhurriedly

**Gemütlichkeit** *die;* ~ Ⓐ (*Behaglichkeit*) snugness; Ⓑ (*Zwanglosigkeit*) informality; **die ~ stören** disturb the atmosphere *or* mood of informality; Ⓒ (*Gemächlichkeit*) **in aller ~:** quite unhurriedly; **da hört [sich] doch die ~ auf** (*fig. ugs.*) that's going too far

**gemüts-, Gemüts-:** ~**arm** *Adj.* insensitive; cold; ~**art** *die* nature; disposition; ~**bewegung** *die* emotion; ~**krank** *Adj.* (*Med., Psych.*) emotionally disturbed; ~**krankheit** *die* emotional disorder; ~**lage** *die* emotional state; ~**mensch** *der* (*ugs.*) (*gutmütiger Mensch*) good-natured *or* even-tempered person; (*etwas langsamer Mensch*) phlegmatic person; **du bist [vielleicht] ein ~mensch!** (*iron. abwertend*) you're the soul of tact, I must say!; (*du bist naiv*) you'll be lucky!; ~**regung** *die* emotion; ~**ruhe** *die* peace of mind; **in aller ~ruhe** (*ugs.*) (*ohne Sorge*) completely unconcerned; (*ohne Hast*) as if there were all the time in the world; ~**verfassung** *die,* ~**zustand** *der* emotional state

**gemüt·voll** *Adj.* warm-hearted; (*empfindsam*) sentimental

**gen** /gɛn/ *Präp. + Akk.* (*veralt., bibl., noch dichter.*) towards; toward; ~ **Süden/Osten** *usw.* southwards/eastwards, *etc.;* **einen Blick ~ Himmel werfen** throw a glance heavenwards

**Gen** /geːn/ *das;* ~**s**, ~**e** (*Biol.*) gene

**genagelt** /gəˈnaːgl̩t/ ❶ *2. Part. v.* **nageln.** ❷ *Adj.* ~**e Schuhe** hobnailed boots

**genannt** /gəˈnant/ *2. Part. v.* **nennen**

**genant** /ʒeˈnant/ *Adj.* Ⓐ (*veralt.: peinlich*) embarrassing; Ⓑ (*bes. südd.: schüchtern*) shy; bashful

**genas** /gəˈnaːs/ *1. u. 3. Pers. Sg. Prät. v.* **genesen**

**genäschig** /gəˈnɛʃɪç/ *Adj.* ⇒ **naschhaft**

**genau** /gəˈnau/ ❶ *Adj.* Ⓐ (*exakt*) exact; precise; **eine ~e Waage** accurate scales *pl.;* **die ~e Uhrzeit** the exact *or* right time; ~**e Untersuchungen** accurate *or* precise investigations; **Genaues/Genaueres wissen** know the/more exact *or* precise details; **ich weiß nichts Genaues/Genaueres** I don't know anything definite/more definite; Ⓑ (*sorgfältig, gründlich*) meticulous, painstaking ‹person›; careful ‹study›; precise ‹use of language›; detailed, thorough ‹knowledge›.
❷ *adv.* Ⓐ exactly; precisely; ~ **um 8⁰⁰** at 8 o'clock precisely; at exactly 8 o'clock; **die Uhr geht [auf die Minute] ~:** the watch/clock keeps perfect time; **die Schuhe passten ihm ~:** the shoes fitted him perfectly; Ⓑ (*gerade, eben*) just; ~ **reichen** be just enough; Ⓒ (*als Verstärkung*) just; exactly; precisely; ~ **das habe ich gesagt** that's just *or* exactly what I said; Ⓓ (*als Zustimmung*) exactly; precisely; quite [so]; Ⓔ (*sorgfältig*) ~ **arbeiten/etw. ~ durchdenken** work/think sth. out carefully *or* meticulously; **jmdn. ~ kennen** know exactly what sb. is like; **etw. ~ beachten** observe sth.

meticulously *or* painstakingly; **es mit etw. [nicht so] ~ nehmen** be [not too] particular about sth.; **~ genommen** strictly speaking

***genau·genommen** ⇒ **genau** 2 E

**Genauigkeit** *die;* ~ Ⓐ (*Exaktheit*) exactness; exactitude; precision; (*einer Waage*) accuracy; Ⓑ (*Sorgfalt*) meticulousness

**genau·so** ⇒ **ebenso**

**genaustens** *Adv.* **etw. ~ durchdenken/beachten** think sth. out/observe sth. most meticulously

**Gendarm** /ʒan'darm/ *der;* **~en, ~en** (*österr., sonst veralt.*) village *or* local policeman *or* constable

**Gendarmerie** /ʒandarmə'ri:/ *die;* **~, ~n** (*österr., sonst veralt.*) village *or* local constabulary

**Genealoge** /genea'lo:gə/ *der;* **~n, ~n** ▶ **159** genealogist

**Genealogie** /genealo'gi:/ *die;* **~, ~n** genealogy

**Genealogin** *die;* **~, ~nen** ▶ **159** ⇒ **Genealoge**

**genealogisch** *Adj.* genealogical

**genehm** /gə'ne:m/ *Adj.*: *in* **jmdm. ~ sein** (*geh.*) (*jmdm. passen*) be convenient to *or* suit sb.; (*jmdm. angenehm sein*) be acceptable to sb.

**genehmigen** *tr. V.* approve ‹plan, alterations›; grant, approve ‹application›; authorize ‹stay›; grant, agree to ‹request›; give permission for ‹demonstration›; **sich** (*Dat.*) **etw. ~** (*ugs.*) treat oneself to sth.; **sich** (*Dat.*) **einen ~** (*ugs.*) have a drink

**Genehmigung** *die;* **~, ~en** Ⓐ (*eines Plans, Antrags, einer Veränderung*) approval; (*eines Aufenthalts*) authorization; (*einer Bitte*) granting; (*einer Demonstration*) permission (*Gen.* for); **jmdm. die ~ zur Eröffnung einer Gaststätte verweigern** refuse [to grant] sb. a licence to open a restaurant/pub; Ⓑ (*Schriftstück*) permit; (*Lizenz*) licence

**genehmigungs-, Genehmigungs-: ~pflicht** *die* (*Rechtsspr.*) obligation to obtain official approval; **der ~pflicht unterliegen** require official approval; **~pflichtig** *Adj.* requiring official approval *postpos.*; **~pflichtig sein** require official approval; **Demonstrationen sind ~pflichtig** demonstrations require official permission

**geneigt** /gə'naikt/ ❶ *2. Part. v.* **neigen.** ❷ *Adj. in* **~ sein** *od.* **sich ~ zeigen, etw. zu tun** be inclined to do sth.; (*bereit sein*) be ready *or* willing to do sth.; **jmdm./einer Sache ~ sein** (*geh.*) be well-disposed towards sb./sth.; **~er Leser** (*veralt.*) gentle reader

**Geneigtheit** *die;* ~ Ⓐ inclination; disposition; (*Bereitschaft*) readiness; willingness; Ⓑ (*Wohlwollen*) goodwill (**gegenüber, für** towards)

**Genera** ⇒ **Genus**

**General** /genə'ra:l/ *der;* **~s, ~e** *od.* **Generäle** ▶ **91** /genə'rɛ:lə/ (*auch kath. Rel.*) general; **Herr ~:** General

**General-: ~amnestie** *die* general amnesty; **~angriff** *der* general offensive; **~bass,** ***~baß** *der* (*Musik*) [basso] continuo; thorough bass; **~beichte** *die* (*kath. Rel.*) general confession; **~bevollmächtigte** *der/die* (*Rechtsw.*) general agent; universal agent [with full powers of attorney]; (*Politik*) plenipotentiary; (*in einer Firma*) general manager; **~bundes·anwalt** *der,* **~bundes·anwältin** *die* Chief Federal Prosecutor; **~direktion** *die* top management; **~direktor** *der* chairman; president (*Amer.*); **~direktorin** *die* chairwoman; president (*Amer.*); **~feld·marschall** /---'--/ *der* (*Milit.*) ⇒ **Feldmarschall**; **~gouverneur** *der* Governor-General; **~inspekteur** *der* (*Milit.*) inspector general; **~intendant** *der,* **~intendantin** *die* artistic director

**generalisieren** *tr., itr. V.* generalize

**Generalisierung** *die;* **~, ~en** generalization

***old spelling (see note on page 1707)**

**Generalissimus** /genəra'lɪsimʊs/ *der;* **~, ~se** *od.* **Generalissimi** /-'lɪsimi/ (*Milit.*) generalissimo

**Generalist** *der;* **~en, ~en, Generalistin** *die;* **~, ~nen** generalist

**Generalität** /genərali'tɛ:t/ *die;* **~, ~en** (*Milit.*) **die ~:** the generals *pl.*

**general-, General-: ~klausel** *die* (*Rechtsw.*) blanket *or* general clause; **~konsul** *der,* **~konsulin** *die* consul general; **~konsulat** *das* consulate general; **~leutnant** *der* (*Milit.*) lieutenant general; (*Luftw.*) air marshal (*Brit.*); **~major** *der* (*Milit.*) major-general; (*Luftw.*) air vice-marshal (*Brit.*); **~musik·direktor** /----'---/ *der,* **~musik·direktorin** *die* musical director; **~nenner** *der* ⇒ **Hauptnenner**; **~präventiv** *Adj.* (*Rechtsspr.*) ‹judgement› acting as a general deterrent; **~probe** *die* Ⓐ (*auch fig.*) dress *or* final rehearsal; Ⓑ (*Sport: letztes Testspiel*) final trial; **~sekretär** *der,* **~sekretärin** *die* Secretary General; (*einer Partei*) general secretary; **~staatsanwalt** /---'--/ *der,* **~staatsanwaltin** *die* chief public prosecutor (*in a Higher Regional Court*)

**Generals·rang** *der* rank of general

**General·stab** *der* (*Milit.*) general staff

**Generalstabs-: ~chef** *der* chief of the general staff; **~karte** *die* (*hist.*) ordnance survey map (*scale 1 : 100,000*); **~offizier** *der* general staff officer

**general-, General-: ~streik** *der* general strike; **~überholen** *tr. V.; nur im Inf. und 2. Part. gebr.* (*bes. Technik*) **etw. ~überholen** give sth. a general overhaul; **etw. ~überholen lassen** have sth. generally overhauled; **~überholung** *die* general overhaul; **~versammlung** *die* general meeting; **die ~versammlung der Vereinten Nationen** the General Assembly of the United Nations; **~vertreter** *der,* **~vertreterin** *die* general representative; **~vertretung** *die* ⇒ **Alleinvertretung**; **~vollmacht** *die* (*Rechtsw.*) full *or* unlimited power of attorney

**Generation** /genəra'tsio:n/ *die;* **~, ~en** generation

**Generations-: ~konflikt** *der* generation gap; **~problem** *das* generation problem; **~unterschied** *der* generation gap; **~wechsel** *der* Ⓐ new generation; **ein ~wechsel ist notwendig** new blood is needed; Ⓑ (*Biol.*) alternation of generations

**generativ** /genəra'ti:f/ *Adj.* Ⓐ (*Biol.*) generative ‹cell, nucleus, etc.›; sexual ‹reproduction›; Ⓑ (*Sprachw.*) generative

**Generator** /genə'ra:tɔr/ *der;* **~s, ~en** /---'--/ Ⓐ generator; Ⓑ (*Gas~*) producer

**Generator·gas** *das* producer gas

**generell** /genə'rɛl/ ❶ *Adj.* general. ❷ *adv.* generally; **man kann ganz ~ sagen, dass ...** generally speaking *or* in general, it can be said that ...; **es sollte sonnabends ~ schulfrei sein** all schools should close on Saturdays

**generieren** *tr. V.* (*geh.; Sprachw.*) generate

**Generikum** /ge'ne:rikʊm/ *das;* **~s, Generika** generic product; (*Pharm.*) generic drug

**generisch** ❶ *Adj.* generic. ❷ *adv.* generically

**generös** /genə'rø:s/ (*geh.*) ❶ *Adj.* generous. ❷ *adv.* generously

**Generosität** /genərozi'tɛ:t/ *die;* ~ (*geh.*) generosity

**genervt** *Adj.* annoyed

**Genese** /ge'ne:zə/ *die;* **~, ~n** genesis

**genesen** /gə'ne:zn̩/ *unr. itr. V.; mit sein* Ⓐ (*geh.*) recover; recuperate; (*fig.*) recover; **von einer Krankheit ~:** recover from an illness; Ⓑ (*veralt. dichter.*) **eines Knaben ~:** be delivered of a son

**Genesende** *der/die; adj. Dekl.* convalescent

**Genesis** /'ge:nezɪs/ *die;* **~:** genesis; **die ~** (*bibl.*) [the Book of] Genesis

**Genesung** *die;* **~, ~en** (*geh.*) recovery

**Genesungs-: ~heim** *das* convalescent home; **~prozess,** ***~prozeß** *der* [process of] recovery; **~urlaub** *der* (*Milit.*) convalescent leave

**Genetik** /ge'ne:tɪk/ *die;* ~ (*Biol.*) genetics *sing., no art.*

**Genetiker** *der;* **~s, ~, Genetikerin** *die;* **~, ~nen** ▶ **159** geneticist

**genetisch** (*Biol.*) ❶ *Adj.* genetic. ❷ *adv.* genetically

**Genezareth** /ge'ne:tsarɛt/ (*das*)*;* **~s** Gennesaret; **der See ~:** the Sea of Galilee

**Genf** /gɛnf/ (*das*)*;* **~s** ▶ **700** Geneva

**Genfer** ▶ **700** ❶ *der;* **~s, ~:** Genevese. ❷ *Adj.* Genevese; **der ~ See** Lake Geneva; **die ~ Konvention** the Geneva Convention; ⇒ *auch* **Kölner**

**Genferin** *die;* **~, ~nen** ⇒ **Genfer** 1

**Genfer·see** *der;* **~s** (*schweiz.*) Lake Geneva

**Gen·forschung** *die* (*Biol.*) genetic research

**genial** /ge'nia:l/ ❶ *Adj.* brilliant ‹idea, invention, solution, etc.›; **ein ~er Mensch** a [man/woman of] genius; **ein ~er Künstler/Musiker** an inspired artist/musician; an artist/musician of genius. ❷ *adv.* brilliantly

**genialisch** ❶ *Adj.* Ⓐ brilliant; **ein ~er Musiker** a brilliant musician; a musical genius; Ⓑ (*exaltiert*) **ein ~er Hauch** a touch of the eccentric genius. ❷ *adv.* Ⓐ like a genius; Ⓑ (*exaltiert*) like an eccentric genius

**Genialität** /geniali'tɛ:t/ *die;* **~:** genius

**Genick** /gə'nɪk/ *das;* **~[e]s, ~e** ▶ **471** back *or* nape of the neck; **sich das ~ brechen** (*auch fig.*) break one's neck; **jmdn. beim ~ packen** grab sb. by the scruff of the neck; **ein Schlag ins ~:** a blow to the back of the neck; **jmdm./einer Sache das ~ brechen** (*ugs.*) ruin sb./sth.; **jmdm. im ~ sitzen** (*ugs.*) haunt sb.

**Genick-: ~schlag** *der* blow to the back of the neck; rabbit punch; **~schuss,** ***~schuß** *der* shot through the base of the skull; **~starre** *die* stiffness of the neck

**Genie**[1] /ʒe'ni:/ *das;* **~s, ~s** genius; **sie ist ein ~ im Kochen** she is a brilliant cook

**Genie**[2] /-/ *die;* **~, ~s** (*schweiz. Milit.*) ⇒ **Genietruppe**

**genieren** /ʒe'ni:rən/ ❶ *refl. V.* be *or* feel embarrassed (**wegen** about); **sich vor jmdm. ~:** be *or* feel embarrassed *or* shy in sb.'s presence; **greifen Sie zu, ~ Sie sich nicht!** help yourself — don't be shy! ❷ *tr. V.* (*veralt.*) disturb

**genierlich** *Adj.* (*ugs.*) Ⓐ (*peinlich*) embarrassing; Ⓑ (*schüchtern*) shy

**genießbar** *Adj.* (*essbar*) edible; (*trinkbar*) drinkable; **er ist heute nicht ~** (*fig. ugs.*) he is unbearable today

**genießen** /gə'ni:sn̩/ *unr. tr. V.* Ⓐ enjoy; **er hat eine gute Ausbildung genossen** he had [the benefit of] a good education; **er genießt Vertrauen in der Partei** he has the confidence of the Party; Ⓑ (*geh.: essen/trinken*) eat/drink; **das Fleisch ist nicht/nicht mehr zu ~:** the meat is inedible/no longer edible; **er ist heute nicht zu ~** (*fig. ugs.*) he is unbearable today

**Genießer** *der;* **~s, ~, Genießerin** *die;* **~, ~nen er ist ein richtiger Genießer** he is a regular 'bon viveur'; he really knows how to enjoy life [to the full]; **sie ist eine stille Genießerin** she enjoys life [to the full] in her own quiet way

**genießerisch** ❶ *Adj.* appreciative; sensuous ‹lips›. ❷ *adv.* appreciatively; ‹drink, eat› with relish

**Genie-: ~streich** *der* (*auch iron.*) stroke of genius; **~truppe** *die* (*schweiz. Milit.*) engineer corps; **~zeit** *die* (*Literaturw.*) Storm and Stress Period

**genital** /geni'ta:l/ *Adj.* genital

**Genital·apparat** *der* ⇒ **Geschlechtsapparat**

**Genitale** *das;* **~s, Genitalien** /geni'ta:liən/, **Genital·organ** *das* ▶ **471** genital organ; **die männlichen/weiblichen Genitalien** the male/female genitals *or* genital organs *or* genitalia

**Genitiv** /'ge:niti:f/ *der;* **~s, ~e** (*Sprachw.*) genitive [case]; (*Wort im ~*) genitive; **im/mit dem ~ stehen** be in/take the genitive [case]

**Genitiv-:** ~**attribut** *das* genitive attribute; ~**objekt** *das* genitive object

**Genius** /ˈgeːni̯ʊs/ *der;* ~, **Genien** /ˈgeːni̯ən/ Ⓐ (*Geist*) guardian spirit; genius; ~ **loci** /- ˈloːtsi/ (*geh.*) genius loci; Ⓑ (*geh.: Schöpferkraft*) [creative] genius; Ⓒ (*Mensch, Gottheit*) genius

**Gen-:** ~**manipulation** *die* genetic manipulation; ~**manipuliert** *Adj.* genetically engineered; genetically manipulated; ~**mutation** *die* gene mutation

**Genom** /geˈnoːm/ *das;* ~**s**, ~**e** (*Biol.*) genome

**genommen** /gəˈnɔmən/ *2. Part. v.* **nehmen**

**genoppt** /gəˈnɔpt/ ❶ *2. Part. v.* **noppen.** ❷ *Adj.* knop ‹yarn, wool›; pimpled ‹rubber›; ‹suit› made of knop yarn

**Genörgel** /gəˈnœrgl̩/ *das;* ~**s** (*abwertend*) grumbling; moaning; (*Krittelei*) carping

**genoss**, ***genoß** /gəˈnɔs/ *1. u. 3. Pers. Sg. Prät. v.* **genießen**

**Genosse** /gəˈnɔsə/ *der;* ~**n**, ~**n** Ⓐ ▶ 91 comrade; „~ **General/Professor**" *usw.* 'Comrade General/Professor' *etc;* **er ist kein ~ der Partei** he is not a party member; Ⓑ (*veralt.: Kamerad*) comrade; companion; **... und ~n** (*abwertend*) ... and his/her/their ilk; Ⓒ (*Wirtsch. veralt.*) member of a/the cooperative

**genossen** /gəˈnɔsn̩/ *2. Part. v.* **genießen**

**Genossenschaft** *die;* ~, ~**en** cooperative

**Genossenschaftler** *der;* ~**s**, ~, **Genossenschaftlerin** *die;* ~, ~**nen** member of a/the cooperative

**genossenschaftlich** ❶ *Adj.* cooperative; collective ‹ownership›; jointly owned ‹property›. ❷ *adv.* on a cooperative basis

**Genossenschafts-:** ~**bank** *die; Pl.* ~~**en** credit cooperative *or* union; ~**bauer** *der;* ~~**n**, ~~**n** (*bes. DDR*) member of a/the farming cooperative; ~**betrieb** *der* cooperative

**Genossin** *die;* ~, ~**nen** Ⓐ ⇨ **Genosse** A: comrade; Ⓑ (*veralt.: Kameradin*) companion

**Geno·typ** /geno-/, **Geno·typus** *der* (*Biol.*) genotype

**Genozid** /-ˈtsiːt/ *der od. das;* ~**[e]s**, ~**e** *od.* ~**ien** /-ˈtsiːdi̯ən/ genocide; **der** *od.* **das ~ der Nazis an den Juden** the genocide perpetrated by the Nazis against the Jews

**Genre** /ˈʒãːrə/ *das;* ~**s**, ~**s** genre

**Genre-:** ~**bild** *das* genre picture; genre painting; ~**malerei** *die* genre painting

**Gent**[1] /dʒɛnt/ *der;* ~**s**, ~**s** (*iron.*) dandy

**Gent**[2] /gɛnt/ (*das*); ~**s** ▶ 700 Ghent

**Gen-:** ~**technik** *die*, ~**technologie** *die* genetic engineering *no art.;* ~**technisch** ❶ *Adj.* genetic engineering ‹techniques, research etc.›; ‹research, developments etc.› in genetic engineering; ❷ *adv.* by genetic engineering; ~**technisch verändert** genetically modified

**Genua** /ˈgeːnu̯a/ (*das*); ~**s** ▶ 700 Genoa

**Genuese** /geˈnueːzə/ *der;* ~**n**, ~**n** Genoese

**Genueser** ▶ 700 ❶ *der;* ~**s**, ~: Genoese. ❷ *Adj.* Genoese; ⇨ *auch* **Kölner**

**Genueserin** *die;* ~, ~**nen**, **Genuesin** *die;* ~, ~**nen** Genoese

**genuesisch** *Adj.* Genoese

**genug** /gəˈnuːk/ *Adv.* enough; **er hat ~ Geld/Geld ~:** he has enough *or* sufficient money; **das ist ~:** that's enough *or* sufficient; **er hat ~ gearbeitet** he has done enough work; **ich habe jetzt ~ [davon]** now I've had enough [of it]; **~ davon!** enough of that!; **nicht ~ damit, dass er faul ist, er ist auch frech** not only is he lazy, he is cheeky as well; **~ der Worte** (*geh.*) I/we/you have talked long enough; **er ist Manns ~, um zu ...** he is man enough to ...; **das ist ihm nicht gut ~:** that is not good enough for him; **sich** (*Dat.*) **selbst ~ sein** be quite happy in one's own company; **er kann nicht ~ kriegen** (*ugs.*) he is very greedy; **davon kann er nicht ~ kriegen** (*ugs.*) he can't get enough of it (*fig. coll.*); **von Bach kann ich nicht ~ kriegen** (*ugs.*) I can always listen to Bach's music

**Genüge** /gəˈnyːgə/ (*geh.*) *in* **jmdm. ~ tun** *od.* **leisten** satisfy sb.; **einer Anordnung/einer Pflicht ~ tun** *od.* **leisten** comply with an order; fulfil a duty *or* an obligation; **der Gerechtigkeit wurde ~ getan** justice was done; **zur ~** (*ausreichend*) enough; sufficiently; (*im Übermaß*) quite enough; **etw. zur ~ kennen** know sth. only too well; be only too familiar with sth.

**genügen** *itr. V.* Ⓐ be enough *or* sufficient; **diese Wohnung genügt für uns** this flat is adequate for us; **das genügt mir** that is enough *or* sufficient [for me]; that will do [for me]; (*das befriedigt mich*) that satisfies me; Ⓑ (*erfüllen*) satisfy; **den Anforderungen ~:** satisfy *or* meet *or* fulfil the requirements; **den Bestimmungen ~:** comply with the regulations; **einer Pflicht ~:** fulfil a duty *or* an obligation

**genügend** ❶ *Adj.* Ⓐ enough; sufficient; Ⓑ (*befriedigend*) satisfactory. ❷ *adv.* enough; sufficiently; **~ lange** long enough; **~ Geld/Zeit haben** have enough *or* sufficient money/time

**genugsam** *Adv.* (*geh.*) sufficiently; **das Thema dürfte ~ diskutiert sein** the subject has probably been adequately discussed

**genügsam** /gəˈnyːkzaːm/ ❶ *Adj.* modest ‹life›; **ein ~er Mensch** a person who lives modestly; **Schafe sind sehr ~e Tiere** sheep can live *or* subsist on very little; **in Bezug auf Kleidung ist sie sehr ~:** she does not spend a great deal on clothes. ❷ *adv.* **~ leben** live modestly

**Genügsamkeit** *die;* ~: **sie weiß, was ~ heißt** she knows what it means to live modestly; **wegen ihrer ~ sind Schafe ...** as they can live *or* subsist on very little, sheep are ...

**genug|tun** *unr. itr. V.* (*veralt.*) *in* **er konnte sich** (*Dat.*) **nicht ~, sie/es zu loben** he couldn't praise her/it enough

**Genugtuung** /-tuːʊŋ/ *die;* ~, ~**en** satisfaction; **es ist mir eine ~, das zu hören** it gives me satisfaction to hear that; **~ über etw.** (*Akk.*) **empfinden** feel satisfied *or* a sense of satisfaction about sth.; **[für etw.] ~ verlangen** demand satisfaction [for sth.]

**genuin** /genuˈiːn/ *Adj.* (*geh.*) genuine

**Genus** /ˈgɛnʊs/ *das;* ~, **Genera** /ˈgɛnera/ (*Sprachw.*) gender

**Genuschel** /gəˈnʊʃl̩/ *das;* ~**s** (*meist abwertend*) mumbling

**Genuss**, ***Genuß** /gəˈnʊs/ *der;* **Genusses**, **Genüsse** /gəˈnʏsə/ Ⓐ consumption; **der ~ von schmerzstillenden Mitteln/Heroin** the use *or* taking of painkillers/heroin; Ⓑ (*Wohlbehagen*) **etw. mit/ohne ~ essen/trinken** eat/drink sth. with/without relish; **etw. mit ~ lesen** enjoy reading sth.; **das Konzert/der Kuchen ist ein ~:** the concert is thoroughly enjoyable/the cake is delicious; **die Genüsse des Lebens** the pleasures *or* good things of life; **in den ~ von etw. kommen** enjoy sth.; **in den ~ einer Rente kommen** receive a pension

**genuss·freudig**, ***genuß·freudig** *Adj.* pleasure-loving

**Genuss·gift**, ***Genuß·gift** *das* (*Amtsspr.*) *stimulant etc.* (*see* **Genussmittel**) *dangerous to health*

**genüsslich**, ***genüßlich** /gəˈnʏslɪç/ ❶ *Adj.* appreciative; comfortable ‹feeling›; (*schadenfroh*) gleeful. ❷ *adv.* appreciatively; ‹eat, drink› with relish; (*schadenfroh*) ‹smile› gleefully; **sich ~ im Sessel zurücklehnen** lie back luxuriously in the armchair

**genuss-**, ***genuß-**, **Genuss-** ***Genuß-:** ~**mensch** *der* hedonist; ~**mittel** *das: tea, coffee, alcoholic drinks, tobacco, etc.;* ~**reich** *Adj.* very *or* highly enjoyable; ~**sucht** *die* (*oft abwertend*) craving for pleasure; ~**süchtig** *Adj.* (*oft abwertend*) pleasure-seeking; ~**voll** ❶ *Adj.* (*erfreulich*) very *or* highly enjoyable; (*genüsslich*) appreciative; ❷ *adv.* appreciatively; ‹eat, drink› with relish

**Geodäsie** /-dɛˈziː/ *die;* ~: geodesy *no art.*

**Geodät** *der;* ~**en**, ~**en**, **Geodätin** *die;* ~, ~**nen** ▶ 159 geodesist

**geodätisch** *Adj.* geodetic

**Geo·dreieck** Ⓦⓩ *das* geometry set square

**Geograph** /-ˈgraːf/ *der;* ~**en**, ~**en** ▶ 159 geographer

**Geographie** *die;* ~: geography *no art.*

**Geographin** *die;* ~, ~**nen** ▶ 159 geographer

**geographisch** ❶ *Adj.* geographic[al]. ❷ *adv.* geographically

**Geologe** /-ˈloːgə/ *der;* ~**n**, ~**n** ▶ 159 geologist

**Geologen·hammer** *der* geologist's hammer

**Geologie** *die;* ~: geology *no art.*

**Geologin** *die;* ~, ~**nen** ▶ 159 geologist

**geologisch** ❶ *Adj.* geological; ❷ *adv.* geologically

**Geo·meter** *der;* ~**s**, ~ Ⓐ ⇨ **Geodät**; Ⓑ (*veralt.*) geometer; geometrician

**Geometrie** *die;* ~: geometry *no art.*

**geometrisch** ❶ *Adj.* geometric[al]. ❷ *adv.* geometrically

**Geo·morphologie** *die* geomorphology *no art.*

**Geo·physik** *die* geophysics *sing., no art.*

**Geo·politik** *die* geopolitics *sing., no art.*

**geo·politisch** *Adj.* geopolitical

**geordnet** ❶ *2. Part. v.* **ordnen.** ❷ *Adj.* **in ~en Verhältnissen leben** live a settled life; **~e Verhältnisse schaffen** put things on a proper footing; **ein ~er Rückzug** (*Milit.*) an orderly retreat

**Georg** /geˈɔrk, ˈgeːɔrk/ (*der*) George

**Georgien** /geˈɔrgi̯ən/ (*das*); ~**s** Georgia

**Georgier** /geˈɔrgi̯ɐ/ *der;* ~**s**, ~, **Georgierin** *die;* ~, ~**nen** Georgian

**Geo·wissenschaft** *die* geoscience *no art.*

**Geozentrik** /geoˈtsɛntrɪk/ *die;* ~ (*Astron.*) geocentric system

**geozentrisch** *Adj.* (*Astron.*) geocentric

**Gepäck** /gəˈpɛk/ *das;* ~**[e]s** Ⓐ luggage (*Brit.*); baggage (*Amer.*); (*am Flughafen*) baggage; **mit leichtem ~ reisen** travel light; **das ~ aufgeben/einchecken** hand in *or* check in the luggage; check the baggage (*Amer.*); Ⓑ (*Milit.*) kit

**Gepäck-:** ~**abfertigung** *die* Ⓐ ⇨ **Gepäck** A: checking in the luggage/baggage; Ⓑ (*Schalter*) (*am Bahnhof*) luggage office (*Brit.*); baggage office (*Amer.*); (*am Flughafen*) baggage check-in; ~**ablage** *die* luggage rack (*Brit.*); baggage rack (*Amer.*); ~**annahme** *die* Ⓐ ⇨ **Gepäck** A: checking in the luggage/baggage; **bei der ~annahme** when checking in the luggage/baggage; Ⓑ (*Schalter*) [in-counter of the] luggage office (*Brit.*) *or* baggage office (*Amer.*); (*zur Aufbewahrung*) [in-counter of the] left-luggage office (*Brit.*) *or* checkroom (*Amer.*); (*am Flughafen*) baggage check-in; ~**aufbewahrung** *die* Ⓐ **Schäden, die während der ~aufbewahrung entstanden sind** damage to items in left luggage (*Brit.*) *or* the checkroom (*Amer.*); Ⓑ (*Schalter*) left-luggage office (*Brit.*); checkroom (*Amer.*); (*Schließfächer*) luggage lockers (*Brit.*); baggage lockers (*Amer.*); ~**aufbewahrungs·schein** *der* left-luggage ticket (*Brit.*); baggage check (*Amer.*); ~**aufgabe** *die* ⇨ ~**abfertigung** A, B; ~**ausgabe** *die* Ⓐ (*am Bahnhof*) returning the luggage (*Brit.*) *or* (*Amer.*) baggage; (*am Flughafen*) reclaiming of baggage; Ⓑ (*Schalter*) [out-counter of the] luggage office (*Brit.*) *or* (*Amer.*) baggage office; (*zur Aufbewahrung*) [out-counter of the] left-luggage office (*Brit.*) *or* (*Amer.*) checkroom; (*am Flughafen*) baggage reclaim; ~**beförderung** *die* (*mit der Bahn*) conveyance of luggage (*Brit.*) *or* (*Amer.*) baggage; (*mit einem Flugzeug*) conveyance of baggage; ~**karren** *der* ⇨ ~ A: luggage/baggage trolley; ~**kontrolle** *die* baggage check; ~**marsch** *der* (*Milit.*) route march with full kit; ~**netz** *das* ⇨ ~**ablage**; ~**raum** *der* ⇨ **Gepäck** A: luggage/baggage compartment; ~**schalter** *der* ⇨ ~**annahme** B; ~**schein** *der* luggage ticket (*Brit.*); baggage check (*Amer.*); ~**schließfach** *das* luggage locker (*Brit.*); baggage locker (*Amer.*); ~**stück** *das* ⇨ ~ A: piece *or* item of luggage/baggage;

**~träger** *der* **A** porter; **B** *(am Fahrrad)* carrier; rack; **~versicherung** *die* ⇒ **Gepäck A**: luggage/baggage insurance; **~wagen** *der* luggage van *(Brit.)*; baggage car *(Amer.)*

**Gepard** /'ge:part/ *der;* **~s, ~e** cheetah; hunting leopard

**gepfeffert** ❶ *2. Part. v.* **pfeffern.** ❷ *Adj. (ugs.)* **A** *(unverschämt)* steep *(coll.)* ‹price, rent, etc.›; **B** *(hart)* tough ‹question, problem, speech›; tough, harsh ‹words, criticism›; **C** *(derb)* crude ‹joke, oath, language, talk›; spicy ‹story›

**Gepfeife** *das;* **~s** *(ugs. abwertend)* [continuous, tuneless] whistling

**gepfiffen** /gə'pfɪfn̩/ *2. Part. v.* **pfeifen**

**gepflegt** ❶ *2. Part. v.* **pflegen.** ❷ *Adj.* **A** well-groomed, spruce ‹appearance›; neat ‹clothing›; cultured ‹conversation›; cultured, sophisticated ‹atmosphere, environment›; stylish ‹living›; well-kept, well-tended ‹garden, park›; well-kept ‹street›; well cared-for ‹hands, house›; **B** *(hochwertig)* choice ‹food, drink›. ❸ *adv.* **~ essen** dine in style; **~ essen gehen** dine at a good restaurant; **sich ~ ausdrücken** express oneself in a cultured manner

**Gepflegtheit** *die;* **~ A die [äußere] ~:** a well-groomed appearance; smartness of appearance; **B** *(Kultiviertheit)* **die ~ seines Stils** his cultured style

**gepflogen** /gə'pflo:gn̩/ *2. Part. v.* **pflegen 4**

**Gepflogenheit** *die;* **~, ~en** *(geh.)* *(Sitte, Brauch)* custom; tradition; *(Gewohnheit)* habit; *(Verfahrensweise)* practice

**Geplänkel** /gə'plɛŋkl̩/ *das;* **~s, ~ A** *(Wort~)* banter *no indef. art.*; **B** *(Milit. veralt.)* skirmish

**Geplapper** *das;* **~s** *(ugs., oft abwertend)* prattling; **das ~ des Babys** the baby's babbling

**Geplärr[e]** *das;* **~s** *(ugs. abwertend)* bawling

**Geplätscher** *das;* **~s** splashing; **das seichte ~ der Unterhaltung** *(fig.)* the superficial *or* polite exchange of pleasantries

**geplättet** ❶ *2. Part. v.* **plätten.** ❷ *Adj. (salopp)* flabbergasted

**Geplauder** *das;* **~s** *(geh.)* chatting

**Gepolter** *das;* **~s A** clatter; **sie rannten mit ~ die Treppe hinunter** they clattered down the stairs; **B** *(Schimpfen)* grumbling; moaning

**Gepräge** *das;* **~s, ~ A** *(Münzk.)* strike; **B** *(geh.: Merkmal)* [special] character; *(Aura, Ambiente)* aura; **einer Sache** *(Dat.)* **ihr ~ geben** give sth. its character

**Geprahle** *das;* **~s** *(abwertend)* bragging; boasting

**Gepränge** /gə'prɛŋə/ *das;* **~s** *(geh.)* pomp; splendour; **mit festlichem/feierlichem ~:** with pomp and pageantry/in solemn splendour

**Geprassel** *das;* **~s** *(von Kies usw.)* rattle; *(von Feuer)* crackle; crackling

**gepriesen** *2. Part. v.* **preisen**

**gepunktet** ❶ *2. Part. v.* **punkten.** ❷ *Adj.* spotted ‹tie, blouse, etc.›; *(regelmäßig)* polka-dot; dotted ‹line›

**Gequake** *das;* **~s** *(ugs.)* croaking; *(von Enten)* quacking

**Gequäke** *das;* **~s** *(ugs.)* bawling

**gequält** ❶ *2. Part. v.* **quälen.** ❷ *Adj.* forced ‹smile, gaiety›; pained ‹expression›

**Gequassel, Gequatsche** *das;* **~s** *(ugs. abwertend)* jabbering

**Gequengel[e]** *das;* **~s** *(ugs. abwertend)* whimpering; *(Drängelei)* nagging; *(Nörgelei)* carping

**Gequieke** *das;* **~s** *(ugs.)* squealing

**Gequietsche** *das;* **~s** *(ugs.)* squeaking; *(von Bremsen, Reifen, Kränen)* squealing; screeching; *(von Menschen)* squealing, shrieking

**gequollen** *2. Part. v.* **quellen**

**Ger** /ge:ɐ̯/ *der;* **~[e]s, ~e** *(hist.)* spear, javelin *(of ancient Germanic peoples)*

**gerade** /gə'ra:də/, *(ugs.)* **grade** /'gra:də/ ❶ *Adj.* **A** straight; **~ geschnitten** cut straight; **in ~r Linie von jmdm. abstammen** *(fig.)* be descended in a direct line from sb.; **den ~n Weg verfolgen** *(fig.)* keep to the straight and narrow; **B** *(nicht schief)* upright; **~ gewachsen sein** ‹plant› have grown straight; ‹person› have grown up straight; **~ sitzen/stehen** sit up/stand up straight; **etw. ~ halten** hold sth. straight; **den Kopf ~ halten** hold one's head up; **sich bei Tisch ~ halten** sit up straight at the table; **etw. ~ legen** put *or* set sth. straight; **etw. ~ klopfen** hammer sth. straight; **etw. ~ machen** straighten sth. [out]; **etw. ~ richten** straighten sth. [out]; put *or* set sth. straight; **C** *(aufrichtig)* forthright; direct; **D** *(genau)* **das ~ Gegenteil** the direct *or* exact opposite; **E** *(Math.)* even ‹number›. ❷ *Adv.* **A** *(soeben, ugs.: für kurze Zeit)* just; **halt ~ [mal] fest!** just hold this [for a moment]; **haben Sie ~ Zeit?** do you have time just now?; **~ erst** only just; **wir wollten diese Sache ~ noch besprechen** we were just going to discuss the matter; **B** *(direkt)* right; **~ gegenüber/um die Ecke** right opposite/just round the corner; **jmdm. ~ in die Augen schauen** look sb. straight in the eyes; **C** *(knapp)* just; **~ noch** only just; **er hat das Examen ~ so bestanden** he just scraped through the examination; **~ so viel, dass ...** just enough to ...; **~ noch rechtzeitig** only just in time; **D** *(eben)* just; **~ diese Angelegenheit** precisely *or* just this matter; **E** *(ausgerechnet)* **~ du/dieser Idiot** you/this idiot, of all people; **warum ~ ich/heute?** why me of all people/today of all days?; **~ seine Toleranz wurde ihm als Schwäche angerechnet** it was precisely his tolerance which was regarded as a weakness.
❸ *Partikel* **A** *(besonders)* particularly; **nicht ~:** not exactly; **B** *(ugs.: erst recht)* **nun** *od.* **jetzt [tue ich es] ~:** [you] just watch me; [you] just try and stop me now; **nun** *od.* **jetzt [tue ich es] ~ nicht** now I certainly shan't [do it]

**Gerade** *die;* **~n, ~n A** *(Geom.)* straight line; **B** *(Leichtathletik)* straight; **C** *(Boxen)* straight-arm punch; **linke/rechte ~:** straight left/right

**gerade·aus** ▶ 818 ❶ *Adv.* straight ahead; ‹walk, drive› straight on, straight ahead; **immer ~ gehen/fahren** carry straight on. ❷ *adj.* **er ist sehr ~** *(fig.)* he is very straightforward *or* direct

**gerade-: ~|biegen** *unr. tr. V. (ugs.: bereinigen)* straighten out; put right; ***~|halten** ⇒ **gerade 1B**; **~heraus** /----'-/ *(ugs.)* ❶ *Adv.* **etw. ~heraus sagen** say sth. straight out; **jmdm. ~heraus sagen/jmdn. ~heraus fragen** tell/ask sb. straight; **~heraus gesagt** quite frankly; to be quite frank; ❷ *adj.* straightforward; direct; ***~|klopfen** *usw.* **gerade 1B**

**geraden·wegs** ⇒ **geradewegs**

***gerade|richten** ⇒ **gerade 1B**

**gerädert** ❶ *2. Part. v.* **rädern.** ❷ *Adj. (ugs.)* whacked *(coll.)*; tired out; **wie ~ sein/sich wie ~ fühlen** be/feel whacked *(coll.)* *or* tired out

**gerade-: *~|sitzen** ⇒ **gerade 1B**; **~so** ⇒ **ebenso**; **~|stehen** *unr. itr. V. (fig.: einstehen)* **für etw. ~stehen** accept responsibility for sth.; **für jmdn. ~stehen** answer for sb.; **~wegs** *Adv.* **A** straight; **B** *(ohne Umschweife)* straight away; directly; **er kam ~wegs zum Thema** he came straight to the point; **~zu** ❶ *Adv.* **A** really; perfectly; *(beinahe)* almost; **das ist ~zu lächerlich** that is downright ridiculous; **ein ~zu ideales Beispiel** an absolutely perfect example; **B** *(landsch.: unverblümt)* bluntly; directly; ❷ *adj. (landsch.: unverblümt)* blunt; direct

**Gerad·heit** *die;* **~:** straightforwardness

**gerad-, Gerad-: ~linig** /-li:nɪç/ ❶ *Adj.* **A** straight; direct, lineal ‹descent, descendant›; **B** *(aufrichtig)* straightforward; ❷ *adv.* **A ~linig verlaufen** run in a straight line; **B** *(aufrichtig)* **~linig handeln/denken** be straightforward; **~linigkeit** *die;* **~~ A** straightness; **B** *(Aufrichtigkeit)* straightforwardness; **~sinnig** *Adj.* straightforward; honest

**gerammelt** ❶ *2. Part. v.* **rammeln.** ❷ *Adv.: in* **~ voll** *(ugs.)* [jam-]packed *(coll.)*; packed out *(coll.)*

**gerändert** *Adj.* **rot ~e Augen** red-rimmed eyes; **schwarz ~es Papier** black-edged paper

**Gerangel** /gə'raŋl̩/ *das;* **~s** *(ugs.)* **A** scrapping *(coll.)*; **B** *(abwertend: Kampf)* free-for-all; scramble; **ein ~ um etw.** a scramble for sth.; a free-for-all for sth.

**Geranie** /ge'ra:ni̯ə/ *die;* **~, ~n** geranium

**gerann** /gə'ran/ *3. Pers. Sg. Prät. v.* **gerinnen**

**gerannt** /gə'rant/ *2. Part. v.* **rennen**

**Geraschel** *das;* **~s** *(ugs.)* rustling

**Gerassel** /gə'rasl̩/ *das;* **~s** rattling; rattle

**gerät** /gə'rɛ:t/ *3. Pers. Sg. Präsens v.* **geraten**

**Gerät** /gə'rɛ:t/ *das;* **~[e]s, ~e A** piece of equipment; *(Fernseher, Radio)* set; *(Garten~)* tool; *(Küchen~)* utensil; *(Mess~)* instrument; **landwirtschaftliche ~e** agricultural implements; **elektrische ~e** electrical appliances; **B** *(Turnen)* piece of apparatus; **an den ~en turnen** do gymnastics on the apparatus; **C** *(Ausrüstung)* equipment *no pl.*; *(des Anglers)* tackle; *(des Handwerkers)* tools *pl.*

**Geräte·haus** *das (Feuerwehr)* appliance room

**geraten**[1] *unr. itr. V.; mit sein* **A** get; **in ein Unwetter ~:** be caught in a storm; **unter ein Auto ~:** be run over by a car; **an jmdn. ~:** meet sb.; **an den Richtigen/Falschen ~:** come to the right/wrong person; **in Panik/Wut/Ekstase ~:** panic *or* get into a panic/fly into a rage/go into a state of ecstasy; ⇒ *auch* **Gesellschaft A**; **Verdacht**; **Verruf** *usw.*; **B** *(gelingen)* turn out well; **das Essen ist [ihr] gut ~:** the meal [she cooked] turned out well; **sie ist zu kurz/lang ~** *(scherzh.)* she has turned out on the short/tall side; **die Tapeten sind zu bunt ~:** the wallpaper turned out to be too colourful; **C** *(ähneln)* **nach jmdm. ~:** take after sb.; **D** *(werden)* **zu etw. ~:** turn into *or* become sth.

**geraten**[2] ❶ *2. Part. v.* **raten, geraten**[1]. ❷ *Adj.* advisable; **es scheint mir ~, ...** I think it advisable ...

**Geräte-: ~raum** *der* **A** [sports] equipment store; **B** *(für Gartengeräte usw.)* tool shed; **~schuppen** *der* tool shed; **~turnen** *das* apparatus gymnastics *sing.*

**Geratewohl** *in* **wir fuhren aufs ~ los** *(ugs.)* we went for a drive just to see where we ended up; **er hat sich aufs ~ einige Firmen ausgewählt** *(ugs.)* he selected a few firms at random; **sie ist aufs ~ in die Prüfung gegangen** *(ugs.)* she took the examination on the off chance [of passing]

**Gerätschaften** /gə'rɛ:tʃaftn̩/ *Pl. (Werkzeug)* tools; *(Küchengeräte)* utensils

**gerätst** *2. Pers. Sg. Präsens v.* **geraten**

**Geratter** *das;* **~s** *(ugs.)* clatter; *(von Schüssen)* rattle

**Geräucherte** /gə'rɔyçɐtə/ *das;* **~n;** *adj. Dekl.* smoked *or* cured meat *(usually ham or bacon)*

**geraum** *Adj. (geh.)* considerable; **nach ~er Zeit** after some [considerable] time

**geräumig** /gə'rɔymɪç/ *Adj.* spacious ‹room›; roomy ‹cupboard, compartment›

**Geräumigkeit** *die;* **~** *(eines Zimmers)* spaciousness; *(eines Schrankes, Kofferraums)* roominess

**Geraune** *das;* **~s** *(geh.)* whispering; *(Gemurmel)* murmuring

**Geraunze** *das;* **~s** *(österr., südd. abwertend)* grumbling; moaning; grousing *(coll.)*

**Geräusch** /gə'rɔyʃ/ *das;* **~[e]s, ~e** sound; *(unerwünscht)* noise

**geräusch-, Geräusch-: ~arm** ❶ *Adj.* quiet; ❷ *adv.* quietly; **~empfindlich** *Adj.* sensitive to noise *pred.*; **~empfindliche Menschen** people who are sensitive to noise; **~kulisse** *die* **A** background noise; **B** *(akustische Untermalung)* [background]

*old spelling (see note on page 1707)

sound effects; **~los** ❶ *Adj.* silent; noiseless; ❷ *adv.* Ⓐ silently; without a sound; noiselessly; Ⓑ (*fig. ugs.: ohne Aufsehen*) without [any] fuss; quietly; **~losigkeit** *die;* ~~: quietness; noiselessness; **~pegel** *der* noise level; **~voll** ❶ *Adj.* noisy; ❷ *adv.* noisily

**Geräusper** /gəˈrɔyspɐ/ *das;* **~s** noise of throat-clearing

**gerben** /ˈgɛrbn̩/ *tr. V.* tan ‹hides, skins›; **von Wind und Wetter gegerbte Haut** (*fig.*) skin tanned by wind and sun

**Gerber** *der;* **~s, ~:** tanner

**Gerbera** /ˈgɛrbəra/ *die;* **~, ~[s]** gerbera

**Gerberei** *die;* **~, ~en** Ⓐ tannery; Ⓑ (*das Gerben*) tanning

**Gerberin** *die;* **~, ~nen** ⇒ **Gerber**

**Gerber·lohe** *die* tanning bark

**Gerbung** *die;* **~, ~en** tanning

**gerecht** ❶ *Adj.* Ⓐ just ‹verdict, punishment›; (*unparteiisch*) just; fair; **ein ~er Richter/Lehrer** an impartial judge/a just teacher; **~ gegen jmdn. sein** be fair *or* just to sb.; **eine ~e Sache** a just cause; **~er Zorn** righteous anger; **jmdm./einer Sache ~ werden** do justice to sb./sth.; **einer Aufgabe/der Belastung ~ werden** cope with a task/the strain; Ⓑ (*bibl.*) **der ~e Gott** our righteous Lord; **die Gerechten** the righteous. ❷ *adv.* justly; ‹judge, treat› fairly

**-gerecht** *Adj.* Ⓐ (*passend*) **kind~/behinderten~:** suitable for children/the disabled *postpos.*; **umwelt~:** harmless to the environment *postpos.*; Ⓑ (*entsprechend*) **protokoll~:** in accordance with protocol *postpos.*; **leistungs~:** productivity- *or* output-related

**gerechterweise** *Adv.* in [all] fairness; to be fair

**gerechtfertigt** ❶ *2. Part. v.* **rechtfertigen.** ❷ *Adj.* justified

**Gerechtigkeit** *die;* **~** Ⓐ justice; **~ üben** (*geh.*) act justly; be just; **jmdm. ~ widerfahren lassen** (*geh.*) treat sb. justly; **um der ~ willen** in order that justice be done; Ⓑ (*Recht*) **die ~ nimmt ihren Lauf** the law takes its course; Ⓒ (*christl. Rel.*) **die ~ Gottes** the righteousness of God; Ⓓ (*geh.: Justiz*) **jmdn. den Händen der ~ übergeben** hand sb. over to be dealt with by the courts

**gerechtigkeits-, Gerechtigkeits-: ~fanatiker** *der,* **~fanatikerin** *die* stickler for the law; **~fimmel** *der* (*ugs. abwertend*) exaggerated concern for justice; **~gefühl** *das* sense of justice; **~liebend** *Adj.* **~liebend sein** have a love of justice; **ein ~liebender Mensch** a person with a love of justice; **~sinn** *der* sense of justice

**Gerede** *das;* **~s** (*abwertend*) Ⓐ (*ugs.*) talk; **das ewige ~ darüber ändert doch nichts** talking about it all the time won't change anything; Ⓑ (*Klatsch*) gossip; **jmdn. ins ~ bringen** bring sb. into disrepute; **ins ~ kommen** get into disrepute

**geregelt** ❶ *2. Part. v.* **regeln.** ❷ *Adj.* regular, steady ‹job›; orderly, well-ordered ‹life›; **~er Katalysator** computer-controlled catalytic converter

**gereichen** *itr. V.* (*geh.*) **jmdm. zur Ehre/zum Vorteil ~:** redound to sb.'s honour *or* credit/advantage

**gereift** ❶ *2. Part. v.* **reifen.** ❷ *Adj.* mature; **sie ist jetzt geistig ~:** she has now matured as a person

**gereizt** ❶ *2. Part. v.* **reizen.** ❷ *Adj.* irritable; touchy. ❸ *adv.* irritably; **~ reagieren** react angrily; **~ lächeln** smile wearily

**Gereiztheit** *die;* **~:** irritability; touchiness

**Gerenne** /gəˈrɛnə/ *das;* **~s** (*ugs.*) running *or* racing about

**gereuen** *tr. V.* (*geh. veralt.*) **sein Zornesausbruch gereute ihn** he regretted his angry outburst; (*unpers.*) **es gereute ihn, dass ...** he regretted that ...; **es gereute ihn** he was sorry

**Geriater** /geˈriaːtɐ/ *der;* **~s, ~, Geriaterin** *die;* **~, ~nen** ▶ 159 (*Med.*) geriatrician; geriatrist

**Geriatrie** *die;* **~:** geriatrics *sing., no art.*

**geriatrisch** *Adj.* geriatric

**Gericht**[1] /gəˈrɪçt/ *das;* **~[e]s, ~e** Ⓐ (*Institution*) court; **jmdn. dem ~** *od.* **den ~en übergeben** *od.* **ausliefern** hand sb. over to be dealt with by the courts; **jmdn. vor ~ laden** *od.* **zitieren** summon sb. to appear in court; **vor ~ erscheinen/aussagen** appear/testify in court; **vor ~ stehen** be on *or* stand trial; **mit einem Fall vor ~ gehen** take a case to court; Ⓑ (*Richter*) bench; **Hohes ~!** Your Honour!; **das ~ zieht sich zur Beratung zurück** the bench retires for discussion; Ⓒ (*Gebäude*) court [house]; Ⓓ *in* **das Jüngste** *od.* **Letzte ~** (*Rel.*) the Last Judgement; **mit jmdm. [hart** *od.* **scharf] ins ~ gehen** (*zurechtweisen*) take sb. [severely] to task; (*bestrafen*) punish sb. [severely]; **über jmdn. ~ halten** *od.* **zu ~ sitzen** sit in judgement on sb.

**Gericht**[2] *das;* **~[e]s, ~e** dish; **~e aus der Dose** canned *or* (*Brit.*) tinned food *sing.*

**gerichtlich** ❶ *Adj.* judicial; forensic ‹psychology, medicine›; legal ‹proceedings›; court ‹order›; **~e Zuständigkeit** [legal] jurisdiction; **eine ~e Vorladung** a summons from the court; **ein ~es Nachspiel haben** have legal consequences; **die Sache wird ein ~es Nachspiel haben** the matter will end up in court. ❷ *adv.* **jmdn. ~ verfolgen** prosecute sb.; take sb. to court; **gegen jmdn. ~ vorgehen** take legal action against sb.; take sb. to court; **etw. ~ bezeugen/beeiden** testify/swear to sth. in court; **jmdn. ~ für tot erklären** pronounce sb. legally dead

**gerichts-, Gerichts-: ~akte** *die* court record; **~arzt** *der,* **~ärztin** *die* specialist in forensic medicine; **~ärztlich** *Adj.* forensic [medical] ‹report, test, investigation›; **~assessor** *der,* **~assessorin** *die: law student appointed as judge or court official for trial period after his/her second state examination*

**Gerichtsbarkeit** *die;* **~, ~en** jurisdiction; **der staatlichen ~ nicht unterliegen** be immune from legal proceedings by the State

**gerichts-, Gerichts-: ~beschluss, *~beschluß** *der* decision of the/a court; the/a court's decision; **~bezirk** *der* jurisdictional district; **~diener** *der,* **~dienerin** *die* ▶ 159 [court] usher; **~dolmetscher** *der,* **~dolmetscherin** *die* court interpreter; **~entscheid** *der,* **~entscheidung** *die* decision of the/a court; the/a court's decision; **~ferien** *Pl.* recess *sing.;* vacation *sing.;* **~gebäude** *das* court house; **~herr** *der* (*hist.*) [highest] judicial authority; **der oberste ~herr** the supreme judicial authority; **~hof** *der* Ⓐ Court of Justice; **der Oberste/Internationale/Europäische ~hof** the Supreme/International/European Court of Justice; Ⓑ (*früher: Kollegialgericht*) tribunal, Court of Justice (*with more than one judge*); **Hoher ~hof!** if it please the court; **~hoheit** *die* supreme legal authority; **~kosten** *Pl.* legal costs; costs of the case; **~kundig** *Adj.* ⇒ **~notorisch; ~medizin** *die* forensic medicine *no art.;* **~mediziner** *der,* **~medizinerin** *die* specialist in forensic medicine; **~medizinisch** ❶ *Adj.* forensic [medical] ‹examination, report›; ❷ *adv.* **etw. ~medizinisch feststellen** establish sth. by forensic [medical] tests; **~notorisch** *Adj.* (*Rechtsspr.*) ‹person, event, fact› known to the court; **~präsident** *der* senior judge; **~referendar** *der,* **~referendarin** *die: law student who has passed his/her first state examination;* **~reporter** *der,* **~reporterin** *die* legal correspondent; **~saal** *der* courtroom; **Ruhe im ~saal!** silence in court!; **~schreiber** *der,* **~schreiberin** *die* clerk of the court; **~stand** *der* (*Rechtsspr.*) place of jurisdiction; **~tag** *der* court day; **Mittwoch ist ~tag** the court sits on Wednesdays; **~termin** *der* (*strafrechtlich*) date of the/a trial; (*zivil*) date of the/a hearing; **~urteil** *das* judgement [of the court]; **~verfahren** *das* legal proceedings *pl.;* **ein ~verfahren einleiten** institute legal *or* court proceedings; **ohne ~verfahren** without trial; **~verfassung** *die* constitution of the courts; **~verhandlung** *die* (*strafrechtlich*) trial; (*zivil*) hearing; **~verwaltung** *die* administration of the courts; **~vollzieher** *der;* **~~s, ~~, ~vollzieherin** *die;* **~~, ~~nen** bailiff; **~weg** *der:* **auf dem ~weg** through the courts; by taking legal proceedings; **~weibel** *der;* **~~s, ~~** (*schweiz.*) court usher; **~wesen** *das* judicial system

**gerieben** ❶ *2. Part. v.* **reiben.** ❷ *Adj.* (*ugs.*) artful

**Geriebenheit** *die;* **~** (*ugs.*) artfulness

**gerieren** /geˈriːrən/ *refl. V.* (*geh.*) **sich als etw. ~:** talk and act as if one were sth.

**Geriesel** *das;* **~s** trickling; trickle; (*von Schnee*) gentle fall

**geriffelt** ❶ *2. Part. v.* **riffeln.** ❷ *Adj.* corrugated ‹surface, sheet metal›; fluted ‹column›; ribbed ‹glass›

**gering** /gəˈrɪŋ/ ❶ *Adj.* Ⓐ (*nicht groß, niedrig*) low ‹temperature, pressure, price›; low, small ‹income, fee›; little ‹value›; small ‹quantity, amount›; short ‹distance, time›; **in ~er Entfernung** a short distance away; **von/in ~er Höhe** low/low down; **der Abstand wird ~er** the gap is closing *or* getting smaller; **um ein Geringes** (*veralt.*) a little [bit]; (*um wenig Geld*) for a trifle *or* a mere bagatelle; (*fast*) nearly; almost; Ⓑ (*unbedeutend*) slight; minor ‹role›; **meine ~ste Sorge** the least of my worries; **das Geringste** the least; **nicht das Geringste** nothing at all; **nicht im Geringsten** not in the slightest *or* least; Ⓒ (*veralt.: niedrig stehend*) humble ‹origin, person›; **kein Geringerer als ...** no less a person than ...; Ⓓ (*geh.: schlecht*) poor, low, inferior ‹quality, opinion›; poor ‹knowledge›. ❷ *adv.* **~ von jmdm. sprechen/denken** speak badly/have a low opinion of sb.; **~ achten** *od.* **schätzen** +*Akk.* (*verachten*) have a low opinion of, think very little of ‹person, achievement›; set little store by ‹success, riches›; (*missachten*) disregard ‹warning›; make light of ‹danger›; **sein eigenes Leben ~ achten** *od.* **schätzen** have scant regard for one's own life

***gering|achten** ⇒ **gering** 2

**Gering·achtung** *die* ⇒ **Geringschätzung**

**geringelt** ❶ *2. Part. v.* **ringeln.** ❷ *Adj.* curly; ‹hair› in ringlets; ‹pattern, socks, jumper› with horizontal stripes

**gering·fügig** /-fyːgɪç/ ❶ *Adj.* slight ‹difference, deviation, improvement›; slight, minor ‹alteration, injury›; small, trivial ‹amount›; minor, trivial ‹detail›. ❷ *adv.* slightly

**Geringfügigkeit** *die;* **~, ~en** Ⓐ triviality; insignificance; **eine Beschwerde wegen ~ ablehnen** dismiss a complaint because of its trivial nature; Ⓑ (*Kleinigkeit*) triviality; trifle; (*Angelegenheit auch*) trivial matter

***gering|schätzen** ⇒ **gering** 2

**gering·schätzig** /-ʃɛtsɪç/ ❶ *Adj.* disdainful; contemptuous; disparaging ‹remark›. ❷ *adv.* disdainfully; contemptuously; **von jmdm. ~ sprechen** speak disparagingly of sb.

**Geringschätzigkeit** *die;* **~:** disdain[fulness]; contempt[uousness]

**Gering·schätzung** *die* Ⓐ (*Verachtung*) disdain; contempt; Ⓑ (*Missachtung*) disregard; **die ~ des Lebens** a scant regard for life

**geringsten·falls** *Adv.* (*geh.*) at the very least

**gerinnen** *unr. itr. V.;* *mit sein* Ⓐ coagulate; ‹blood› coagulate, clot; ‹milk› curdle; ⇒ *auch* **Blut;** Ⓑ (*fig. geh.*) **zu etw. ~:** develop into *or* become sth.

**Gerinnsel** /gəˈrɪnzl̩/ *das;* **~s, ~** Ⓐ (*Blut*) clot; Ⓑ (*veralt.: Rinnsal*) streamlet; rivulet

**Gerinnung** *die;* **~, ~en** coagulating; (*von Blut auch*) clotting; (*von Milch*) curdling

**gerinnungs-: ~fähig** *Adj.* coagulable; **sein Blut ist nicht ~fähig** his blood does not clot properly; **~hemmend** *Adj.* anticoagulant

**Gerippe** *das;* **~s, ~** Ⓐ skeleton; **sie ist bis zum ~ abgemagert** (*fig.*) she has lost so much weight that she is only skin and bones; Ⓑ (*fig.*) framework; (*von Schiffen, Gebäuden*) skeleton; (*Grundriss, Entwurf*) outline

**gerippt** /gəˈrɪpt/ *Adj.* ribbed ‹fabric, garment›; fluted ‹glass, column›; laid ‹paper›

**gerissen** /gəˈrɪsn̩/ ❶ *2. Part. v.* **reißen.** ❷ *Adj. (ugs.)* crafty

**Gerissenheit** *die; ~:* craftiness

**geritten** *2. Part. v.* **reiten**

**geritzt** ❶ *2. Part. v.* **ritzen.** ❷ *Adj. (salopp) in* **etw. ist ~:** sth. is [all] settled; **ist ~!** will do! *(coll.)*

**Germ** /gɛrm/ *der; ~[e]s, österr. auch: die; ~ (südd., österr.)* yeast

**Germane** /gɛrˈmaːnə/ *der; ~n, ~n (hist.)* ancient German; Teuton; *(scherzh.)* Teutonic type; **die alten ~n** the ancient Germanic peoples *or* Teutons; **die Skandinavier sind ~n** the Scandinavians are of Germanic *or* Teutonic origin

**Germanentum** *das; ~s (Kultur)* Germanic *or* Teutonic culture; *(germanische Völker)* Germanic *or* Teutonic world

**Germania** /gɛrˈmaːni̯a/ *(die)* Germania

**Germanien** /gɛrˈmaːni̯ən/ *(das); ~s (hist.)* Germania

**Germanin** *die; ~, ~nen* ancient German; Teuton

**germanisch** *Adj. (auch fig.)* Germanic; Teutonic; **Germanisches Seminar** Institute of Germanic Studies

**germanisieren** *tr. V.* Germanize

**Germanisierung** *die; ~:* Germanization

**Germanismus** *der; ~, Germanismen (Sprachw.)* Germanism

**Germanist** *der; ~en, ~en* Germanist; German scholar

**Germanistik** *die; ~:* German studies *pl., no art.*

**Germanistin** *die; ~, ~nen* Germanist; German scholar

**germanistisch** *Adj.* **~e Studien** German studies; **eine ~e Zeitschrift** a periodical on *or* devoted to German studies; **Germanistisches Seminar** Institute of German Studies

**Germanium** /gɛrˈmaːni̯ʊm/ *das; ~s (Chemie)* germanium

**germanophil** /gɛrmanoˈfiːl/ *Adj.* Germanophile

**germanophob** /gɛrmanoˈfoːp/ *Adj.* Germanophobe

**gern[e]** /ˈgɛrn(ə)/; **lieber** /ˈliːbɐ/, **am liebsten** /-ˈliːpstn̩/ *Adv.* Ⓐ *(mit Vergnügen)* **etw. ~ tun** like *or* enjoy *or* be fond of doing sth.; **er spielt lieber Tennis als Golf** he prefers playing tennis to golf; **etw. ~ essen/trinken** like sth.; **am liebsten trinkt er Wein** he likes wine best; **ja, ~/aber ~:** yes, of course; certainly!; **Kommst du mit? — Ja, ~!** Are you coming too? — Yes I'd like to!; **[das ist] ~ geschehen** it is *or* was a pleasure; **jmdn. ~ haben** like *or* be fond of sb.; **er hat sie lieber als dich** he likes her more than he does you; **sie hat ihn am liebsten** she likes him best; **sie hat** *od.* **sieht es lieber/am liebsten, wenn ...** she likes it better/likes it best if ...; **~ gesehen sein/werden** be welcome; **der kann mich ~ haben!** *(ugs.)* he can go to hell! *(coll.)*; he can get stuffed! *(sl.)*; Ⓑ *(drückt Billigung aus: durchaus)* **das glaube ich ~:** I can quite *or* well believe that; **das kannst du ~ tun/haben** you are welcome to do/have that; Ⓒ *(drückt Wunsch aus)* **ich hätte ~ einen Apfel** I would like an apple; **er wäre ~ mitgekommen** he would have liked to come along; **ich wäre lieber [zu Fuß] gegangen** I would rather have walked; **das hättest du lieber nicht tun sollen** it would have been better if you had not done that; **lass das lieber** better not do that; **noch ein Stück Kuchen? — Lieber nicht** Another piece of cake? — I'd rather not; *(aus Vernunftsgründen)* I'd better not; **ich bleibe heute lieber im Bett** I'd better stay in bed today; Ⓓ *(gewöhnlich)* **etw. ~ tun** usually do sth.; Ⓔ *(ugs.: leicht, oft)* soon

**Gerne·groß** *der; ~, ~e (ugs. scherzh.)* **er ist ein [kleiner] ~:** he likes to act big *(coll.)*

**Geröchel** *das; ~s* rattle in the throat; *(eines Sterbenden)* [death] rattle

**gerochen** *2. Part. v.* **riechen**

**Geröll** /gəˈrœl/ *das; ~s, ~e* detritus; debris; *(größer)* boulders *pl.*; *(im Gebirge auch)* scree

**Geröll-: ~halde** *die* scree [slope]; **~schutt** *der* detritus; debris; **~wüste** *die* boulder-strewn wilderness; *(Geogr.)* rock desert

**geronnen** /gəˈrɔnən/ *2. Part. v.* **rinnen, gerinnen**

**Gerontokratie** /gerɔntokraˈtiː/ *die; ~, ~n (hist., Völkerk.)* gerontocracy

**Gerontologie** *die; ~ (Med.)* gerontology *no art.*

**Geröstete** /gəˈrøːstətə, gəˈrœstətə/ *Pl.; adj. Dekl. (südd., österr.)* sauté potatoes

**Gerste** /ˈgɛrstə/ *die; ~:* barley

**Gersten-: ~grütze** *die* Ⓐ barley groats; Ⓑ *(Brei)* porridge *or* gruel made from barley; **~kaffee** *der: coffee substitute produced from malted barley;* **~korn** *das* Ⓐ *(Frucht)* barleycorn; Ⓑ *(Augenentzündung)* sty; **~saft** *der (scherzh.)* beer; **~schrot** *der od. das* bruised *or* ground barley; **~zucker** *der* barley sugar

**Gerte** /ˈgɛrtə/ *die; ~, ~n* switch

**gerten·schlank** *Adj.* slim *or* slender and willowy

**Geruch** /gəˈrʊx/ *der; ~[e]s, Gerüche* /gəˈrʏçə/ Ⓐ smell; odour; *(von Blumen)* scent; fragrance; *(von Brot, Kuchen)* smell; aroma; **ein ~ nach/der ~ von frischem Brot** a/the smell of freshly-baked bread; **einen unangenehmen ~ verbreiten** give off an unpleasant smell *or* odour *or* a stench; Ⓑ *(Geruchssinn)* sense of smell; Ⓒ *(geh.: Ruf)* reputation; **im ~ stehen, etw. zu sein/getan zu haben** be reputed to be sth./to have done sth.

**geruch·los** *Adj.* odourless; *(ohne Duft)* unscented, scentless ⟨flower etc.⟩

**geruchs-, Geruchs-: ~belästigung** *die* nuisance caused by the smell *or* stench; **~bindend** *Adj.* deodorant; **~empfindlich** *Adj.* sensitive to smells *postpos.*; **~empfindung** *die* Ⓐ olfactory sensation; Ⓑ ⇒ **~sinn**; **~nerv** *der* ▶ 471 olfactory nerve; **~organ** *das* olfactory organ; **~sinn** *der* sense of smell; olfactory sense; **~stoff** *der* aromatic essence; *(von Tieren)* scent; **~verschluss, *~verschluß** *der* [anti-siphon] trap

**Gerücht** /gəˈrʏçt/ *das; ~[e]s, ~e* rumour; **ein ~ in die Welt** *od.* **in Umlauf setzen** start a rumour; **es geht das ~, dass ...** there's a rumour going round that ...; **das halte ich für ein ~!** *(ugs.)* I can't believe that!

**Gerüchte-: ~küche** *die (ugs. abwertend)* hotbed of rumours; **~macher** *der,* **~macherin** *die (abwertend)* rumour-monger

**geruch·tilgend** *Adj.* deodorant

**gerücht·weise** *Adv.* **ich habe ~ vernommen** *od.* **gehört, dass ...** I've heard a rumour that ...; I've heard it rumoured that ...; **~ verlautet, er sei ...** rumour has it *or* it is rumoured that he is ...

**gerufen** *2. Part. v.* **rufen**

**geruhen** *tr. V. (geh. veralt.; sonst iron.)* ~, **etw. zu tun** condescend *or* deign to do sth.

**gerührt** ❶ *2. Part. v.* **rühren.** ❷ *Adj.* touched *(also iron.)*; moved

**geruhsam** ❶ *Adj.* peaceful; quiet; leisurely ⟨stroll⟩; **jmdm. eine ~e Nacht wünschen** wish sb. a restful night. ❷ *adv.* leisurely; *(ungestört)* quietly

**Geruhsamkeit** *die; ~:* peacefulness; quietness; *(eines Spaziergangs)* leisureliness

**Gerumpel** *das; ~s* bumping and banging; *(von Lastwagen usw.)* rumbling

**Gerümpel** /gəˈrʏmpl̩/ *das; ~s (abwertend)* junk; [useless] rubbish

**Gerundium** /geˈrʊndi̯ʊm/ *das; ~s, Gerundien (Sprachw.)* gerund

**Gerundiv** /gerʊnˈdiːf/ *das; ~s, ~e* /-ˈdiːvə/ *(Sprachw.)* gerundive

**gerundivisch** *Adj. (Sprachw.)* gerundival

**gerungen** /gəˈrʊŋən/ *2. Part. v.* **ringen**

**Gerüst** /gəˈrʏst/ *das; ~[e]s, ~e* scaffolding *no pl., no indef. art.*; *(fig.: eines Romans usw.)* framework

**Gerüst-: ~bau** *der* erection of the scaffolding; **„~bau: H. Müller, Mannheim"** 'scaffolding by H. Müller, Mannheim'; **~bauer** *der; ~~s, ~~,* **~bauerin** *die; ~~, ~~nen* scaffolder

**gerüttelt** ❶ *2. Part. v.* **rütteln.** ❷ *Adj.: in* **~ voll** *(veralt.)* [jam-]packed; **ein ~ Maß** *(veralt.)* a good measure

**ges, Ges** /gɛs/ *das; ~, ~ (Musik)* [key of] G flat; ⇒ *auch* **a, A**

**Gesabber** /gəˈzabɐ/ *das; ~s* Ⓐ slavering; slobbering; *(eines Babys)* dribbling; Ⓑ *(salopp: Gerede)* rabbiting *(Brit. sl.)*; babbling

**Gesalbte** /gəˈzalptə/ *der/die; adj. Dekl. (Rel., hist.)* **er/sie kehrte als ~r/~ von Rom zurück** he/she returned anointed from Rome; **Christus, der ~:** Christ, the Lord's Anointed

**gesalzen** ❶ *2. Part. v.* **salzen.** ❷ *Adj. (salopp)* Ⓐ *(sehr hoch) steep (coll.)* ⟨price, bill⟩; Ⓑ *(derb ausgedrückt)* crude ⟨joke, language⟩; spicy ⟨story⟩

**Gesalzene** *das; adj. Dekl.* salt[ed] meat

**gesammelt** ❶ *2. Part. v.* **sammeln.** ❷ *Adj.* concentrated ⟨attention, energy⟩; intense ⟨fear⟩; **~e Werke** collected works

**gesamt** *Adj.* whole; entire; **das ~e Vermögen** the entire *or* total wealth; **die ~en Werke** the complete works

**Gesamt** *das; ~s* ⇒ **Gesamtheit**

**gesamt-, Gesamt-: ~ansicht** *die* general *or* overall view; **~auflage** *die (Druckw.)* total edition; *(einer Zeitung)* total circulation; **~ausgabe** *die (Druckw.)* complete edition; **~betrag** *der* total amount; **~bild** *das* general *or* overall view; *(fig.)* general *or* overall picture; **~darstellung** *die* general account *or* description; **~deutsch** *Adj.* all-German; **~deutschland** *(das)* all Germany; **~eindruck** *der* general *or* overall impression; **~einkommen** *das* total income; **~ergebnis** *das* overall result; **~erscheinung** *die* general appearance; **~fläche** *die* total area; **~gesellschaftlich** *Adj. (Soziol.)* of society *or* the community as a whole *postpos.*; **~gewicht** *das* total weight; **das zulässige ~gewicht** the permissible maximum weight

**gesamthaft** *(schweiz.)* ❶ *Adj.* ⇒ **gesamt.** ❷ *adv.* ⇒ **insgesamt**

**Gesamtheit** *die; ~* Ⓐ **die ~ der Beamten** all civil servants; **die ~ der Bevölkerung** the whole of the *or* the entire population; **die Verleger in ihrer ~:** publishers as a whole; Ⓑ ⇒ **Allgemeinheit**

**gesamt-, Gesamt-: ~hoch·schule** *die (Hochschulw.) institution with colleges teaching at various levels, so that students can more readily extend their courses;* **die integrierte ~hochschule** *centrally administrated, fully integrated ~hochschule;* **~kapital** *das* total capital; **~katalog** *der* complete catalogue; *(Katalog der Bestände mehrerer Bibliotheken)* union catalogue; **~lage** *die* general *or* overall situation; **~note** *die* overall mark; **~produktion** *die* total production *or* output; **~schaden** *der* total damage; **ein ~schaden von 1 000 DM** total damage amounting to 1,000 marks; **~schuldner** *Pl. (Rechtsw.)* joint debtors; **~schule** *die* comprehensive [school]; **eine integrierte ~schule** an all-ages comprehensive [school]; **eine kooperative ~schule** *a comprehensive [school] which retains ability bands corresponding to the traditional types of school: Hauptschule, Realschule, and Gymnasium;* **~sieg** *der (Sport)* overall victory; **~sieger** *der,* **~siegerin** *die (Sport)* overall winner; **~stärke** *die* total strength; **~strafe** *die (Rechtsw.)* concurrent sentence; **~summe** *die* ⇒ **~betrag**; **~umsatz** *der* total turnover; **~unterricht** *der (Schulw.)* interdisciplinary teaching *no art.*; **~verband** *der (Wirtsch.)* general *or* national association; **~volumen** *das (Wirtsch.)* total volume; **das ~volumen des Verteidigungsetats** the total size of the defence budget; **~werk** *das* œuvre; *(Bücher)* complete works *pl.*; **~wert** *der* total value; **~wirtschaft** *die* economy as a whole; national economy; **~wirtschaftlich** ❶ *Adj.*

*old spelling (see note on page 1707)

overall economic ‹development etc.›; ‹development etc.› of the economy as a whole; ❷ *adv.* **~wirtschaftlich vertretbar** justifiable from the point of view of the economy as a whole; **~zahl** *die* total number; **~zusammenhang** *der* general *or* overall context

**gesandt** /gəˈzant/ *2. Part. v.* **senden**

**Gesandte** *der/die; adj. Dekl.* envoy; **der päpstliche ~:** the papal legate *or* nuncio

**Gesandtin** *die;* **~, ~nen** envoy

**Gesandtschaft** *die;* **~, ~en** legation

**Gesandtschafts·rat** *der,* **Gesandtschafts·rätin** *die* counsellor at a/the legation

**Gesang** /gəˈzaŋ/ *der;* **~[e]s, Gesänge** /gəˈzɛŋə/ Ⓐ singing; Ⓑ *(Lied)* song; ⇒ *auch* **gregorianisch**; Ⓒ *(Literaturw.)* canto

**Gesang·buch** *das* hymn book; **das richtige/falsche ~buch haben** *(ugs. scherzh.)* belong to the right/wrong [religious] denomination; *(in der Politik)* belong to the right/wrong [political] party

**gesanglich** ❶ *Adj.* vocal; **großes ~es Talent haben** have great talent as a singer. ❷ *adv.* vocally

**Gesang[s]-: ~lehrer** *der,* **~lehrerin** *die* singing teacher; **~stunde** *die* singing lesson; **~unterricht** *der* singing instruction; **~unterricht nehmen/geben** take/give singing lessons *pl.*

**Gesang·verein** *der* choral society; **mein lieber Herr ~!** *(salopp)* my godfathers!; ye gods [and little fishes]!

**Gesäß** /gəˈzɛːs/ *das;* **~es, ~e** ▶ 471 | backside; buttocks *pl.*

**Gesäß-: ~falte** *die* ▶ 471 | *(Anat.)* gluteal fold; gluteal furrow; **~muskel** *der* ▶ 471 | *(Anat.)* gluteal muscle; **~tasche** *die* back pocket

**gesättigt** ❶ *2. Part. v.* **sättigen.** ❷ *Adj.* *(Chemie)* **~e Fettsäuren** saturated fatty acids

**Gesäusel** /gəˈzɔyzl̩/ *das;* **~s** *(von Wind)* whispering; murmuring; *(von Blättern)* rustling; whispering; *(ugs. abwertend: Schmeichelei)* flannel *(coll.)*

**gesch.** *Abk.* **geschieden**

**Geschädigte** /gəˈʃɛːdɪçtə/ *der/die; adj. Dekl.* injured party

**geschaffen** *2. Part. v.* **schaffen** 1

**geschafft** ❶ *2. Part. v.* **schaffen** 2, 3. ❷ *Adj.* *(ugs.)* all in *(coll.)*

**Geschäft** /gəˈʃɛft/ *das;* **~[e]s, ~e** Ⓐ business; *(Abmachung)* [business] deal *or* transaction; **die ~e gehen gut** business is good; **mit jmdm. ~e/ein ~ machen** do business with sb./strike a bargain *or* do a deal with sb.; **in ein ~ einsteigen** go into a business; **in ~en reisen/unterwegs sein** travel/be travelling on business; **mit jmdm. ins ~ kommen** go into business with sb.; **~ ist ~:** business is business; **das ~ mit der Angst** trading on people's fears; Ⓑ *(Absatz)* business *no art.*; **das ~ blüht** business *or* trade is booming; Ⓒ *(Profit)* profit; **mit etw. ein gutes/schlechtes ~ machen** make a good/poor profit on sth.; **diese Unternehmung war für uns [k]ein ~:** this venture was [not] a financial success for us; Ⓓ *(Firma)* business; **ein ~ führen** run *or* manage a business; **ins ~ gehen** *(südd.)* go to work; Ⓔ *(Laden)* shop; store *(Amer.)*; *(Kaufhaus)* store; Ⓕ *(Aufgabe)* task; duty; **seinen ~en nachgehen** go about one's business; Ⓖ **sein großes/kleines ~ erledigen** *od.* **machen** *(ugs. verhüll.)* do big jobs *or* number two/small jobs *or* number one *(child language)*

**-geschäft** *das* Ⓐ *(Laden)* **Schuh~/Lebensmittel~/Feinkost~:** shoe shop/food shop/delicatessen [shop]; shoe store/food store/delicatessen [store] *(Amer.)*; Ⓑ *(Transaktion)* **Bank~/Kompensations~:** bank/barter transaction; *(Absatz)* **Weihnachts~:** Christmas trade; Ⓒ *(Aufgabe)* **Amts~e/Staats~e** official/state duties

**geschäfte-, Geschäfte-: ~halber** *Adv.* *(in Geschäften)* on business; *(wegen Geschäften)* because of business; **~macher** *der* *(abwertend)* profit-seeker; **~macherei** *die;* **~~** *(abwertend)* profit-seeking *no pl.*; **~macherin** *die* ⇒ **~macher**

**geschäftig** ❶ *Adj.* bustling; **ein ~es Treiben** bustling activity; hustle and bustle. ❷ *adv.* **~ hin und her laufen** bustle about

**Geschäftigkeit** *die;* **~:** bustle

**Geschaftlhuber** /gəˈʃaftl̩huːbɐ/ *der;* **~s, ~** *(bes. südd., österr. abwertend)* officious meddler

**geschäftlich** ❶ *Adj.* Ⓐ business *attrib.* ‹conference, appointment›; **das Geschäftliche besprechen** discuss business [matters]; Ⓑ *(sachlich, kühl)* businesslike. ❷ *adv.* Ⓐ on business; **er hat dort ~ zu tun** he has [some] business to do there; **ich habe nächste Woche ~ in Hamburg zu tun** I have to be in Hamburg next week on business; **Wie geht es Ihnen? — Meinen Sie ~ oder privat?** How are you doing? — Do you mean how's business or how am I personally?; Ⓑ *(sachlich, kühl)* in a businesslike way *or* manner

**geschäfts-, Geschäfts-: ~ablauf** *der* business *no art.*; **~abschluss,** ***~abschluß** *der* conclusion of the/a business transaction *or* deal; **einen ~abschluss tätigen** conclude a business transaction *or* deal; **~anteil** *der* share in the/a business; **~aufgabe** *die* closure of the/a business; **zur ~aufgabe gezwungen werden** be forced to close down; **„Ausverkauf wegen ~aufgabe!"** 'closing-down sale'; 'going-out-of-business sale' *(Amer.)*; **~auto** *das* ⇒ **~wagen**; **~bedingungen** *Pl.* terms [and conditions] of trade; **~beginn** *der* opening time; **eine Schlange hatte sich vor ~beginn gebildet** a queue *(Brit.)* *or* *(Amer.)* line had formed before the shop opened; **~bereich** *der* portfolio; **Minister ohne ~bereich** Minister without portfolio; **~bericht** *der* company report; *(jährlich)* annual report; **~beziehungen** *Pl.* business dealings; **in ~beziehungen mit einer Firma stehen** have business dealings with a firm; **~beziehungen zu China** business contacts with China; **~brief** *der* business letter; **~bücher** *Pl.* books; accounts; **~eröffnung** *die* opening of a/the shop *or* *(Amer.)* store; **~fähig** *Adj.* *(Rechtsspr.)* legally competent; **~fähigkeit** *die* *(Rechtsspr.)* legal competence; **~frau** *die* ▶ 159 | businesswoman; **~freund** *der,* **~freundin** *die* business associate; **~führend** *Adj.* managing ‹director›; executive ‹chairman›; **die ~führende Regierung** the caretaker government; **~führer** *der* Ⓐ *(leitender Angestellter)* manager; Ⓑ *(Vereinswesen)* secretary; **~führerin** *die* Ⓐ *(leitende Angestellte)* manageress; manager; Ⓑ *(Vereinswesen)* secretary; **~führung** *die* management; **~gang** *der* Ⓐ business *no art.*; Ⓑ *(Dienstweg)* **den normalen ~gang gehen** go through the normal channels; Ⓒ *(Besorgung)* errand; **~gebaren** *das* business *no art.*; business practices *pl.*; **~geheimnis** *das* business secret; **~geist** *der* business acumen *or* sense; **~haus** *das* Ⓐ business [house]; firm; Ⓑ *(Gebäude)* office block *(with or without shops)*; **~inhaber** *der,* **~inhaberin** *die* owner *or* proprietor of the/a business; **~interesse** *das:* **das ~interesse/die ~interessen** the interests *pl.* of the business; **~jahr** *das* financial year; **~jubiläum** *das* anniversary of the firm; **die Firma feiert ihr fünfzigjähriges ~jubiläum** the firm is celebrating its fiftieth anniversary; **~kapital** *das* working capital; **~kosten** *Pl.*: *in* **auf ~kosten [gehen]** [be] on expenses; **~kundig** *Adj.* ‹person› with business experience; **~lage** *die* Ⓐ *(wirtschaftliche Lage)* **die ~lage der Firma** the [business] position of the firm; **die allgemeine ~lage** the general business situation; Ⓑ *(Ort)* **in guter ~lage** well situated [for business]; **~leben** *das* business [life]; **er steht seit vierzig Jahren im ~leben** he's been active in business [life] for forty years; **~leitung** *die* ⇒ **~führung**; **~leute** ⇒ **~mann**; **~mann** *der; Pl.* **~leute** ▶ 159 | businessman; **~mäßig** *Adj.* businesslike; **~methoden** *Pl.* business methods; **~ordnung** *die* standing orders *pl.*; *(im Parlament)* [rules *pl.* of] procedure; **Antrag zur ~ordnung** procedural motion; **Fragen zur ~ordnung** questions on points of order; **zur ~ordnung!** point of order!; **~papiere** *Pl.* business documents *or* papers; **~partner** *der,* **~partnerin** *die* business partner; **~politik** *die* business *or* trading policy; **~räume** *Pl.* business premises; *(Büroräume)* offices; **~reise** *die* business trip; **auf ~reise sein** be on a business trip; **~rück·gang** *der* decline *or* fall-off in business; **~schädigend** *Adj.* bad for business; ‹conduct› damaging to the interests of the company; **~schluss,** ***~schluß** *der* closing time; **nach ~schluss** after business hours; *(im Büro)* after office hours; **~sinn** *der* business sense *or* acumen; **~sitz** *der* place of business; **eingetragener ~sitz** registered office[s]; **~stelle** *die* Ⓐ *(einer Bank, Firma)* branch; *(einer Partei, eines Vereins)* office; Ⓑ *(Rechtsspr.)* court office; **~straße** *die* shopping street; **~stunden** *Pl.* business hours; *(im Büro)* office hours; **~tätigkeit** *die* business activity *no indef. art.*; **~träger** *der,* **~trägerin** *die* *(Dipl.)* chargé d'affaires; **~tüchtig** *Adj.* able, capable, efficient ‹businessman, landlord, etc.›; **eine ~tüchtige Frau** an able *or* capable businesswoman; **~tüchtigkeit** *die* business ability *or* efficiency; **~über·gabe** *die* transfer of the business; **~übernahme** *die* takeover of the business; **~unfähig** *Adj.* *(Rechtsspr.)* legally incompetent; **~unfähigkeit** *die* *(Rechtsspr.)* legal incompetence; **~verbindung** *die* business connection; **~verkehr** *der* business; business dealings *pl.*; **~viertel** *das* business quarter; *(Einkaufszentrum)* shopping district; **~wagen** *der* company car; **~welt** *die* Ⓐ business world *or* community; Ⓑ ⇒ **~leben**; **~zeit** *die* business hours *pl.*; *(im Büro)* office hours *pl.*; **~zentrum** *das* ⇒ **~viertel**; **~zimmer** *das* office; **~zweig** *der* branch of the/a business

**geschah** /gəˈʃaː/ *3. Pers. Sg. Prät. v.* **geschehen**

**Geschäker** /gəˈʃɛːkɐ/ *das;* **~s** flirting

**Gescharre** *das;* **~s** *(abwertend)* scraping; *(mit den Füßen)* scraping of feet; *(von Hühnern)* scratching

**Geschaukel** *das;* **~s** rocking; *(auf See)* rolling

**gescheckt** /gəˈʃɛkt/ *Adj.* spotted ‹cow, bull, rabbit, etc.›; skewbald ‹horse›; *(mit weißen Flecken auf schwarzem Fell)* piebald ‹horse›

**geschehen** /gəˈʃeːən/ *unr. itr. V.; mit sein* Ⓐ *(passieren)* happen; occur; **so tun, als wäre nichts ~:** act as if nothing had happened; **~ ist ~:** what's done is done; **so ~ ...** *(veralt.)* this came to pass ...; Ⓑ *(ausgeführt werden)* be done; **die Tat/der Mord geschah aus Eifersucht** the deed was done/the murder was committed out of jealousy; **es muss etwas ~:** something must be done; **was geschieht damit?** what's to be done with it?; **er ließ es ~:** he let it happen; Ⓒ *(widerfahren)* **jmdm. geschieht etw.** sth. happens to sb.; **es geschieht dir nichts** nothing will happen to you; **das geschieht ihm recht** it serves him right; Ⓓ **ihm ist ein Unrecht ~:** he's been wronged; Ⓔ **es ist um ihn ~:** it's all up with him; **es ist um seine Gesundheit/Stellung ~:** his health is ruined/he has lost his job; **als er sie sah, war es um ihn ~:** he was lost the moment he saw her

**Geschehen** *das;* **~s, ~** *(geh.)* Ⓐ *(Ablauf der Ereignisse)* events *pl.*; happenings *pl.*; **das politische ~:** political events *pl.*; Ⓑ *(Vorgang)* action

**Geschehnis** *das;* **~ses, ~se** *(geh.)* event

**gescheit** /gəˈʃait/ ❶ *Adj.* Ⓐ *(intelligent)* clever; **daraus werde ich nicht ~:** I can't make head or tail of it; Ⓑ *(ugs.: vernünftig)* sensible; **sei doch ~:** be sensible; **nichts/etwas Gescheites** nothing/something sensible; **gibt es etwas Gescheites zu essen?** is there anything decent to eat?; **du bist wohl nicht ganz** *od.* **nicht recht ~:** you can't be quite right in the head; you must be off your head *(coll.)*. ❷ *adv.* cleverly

g

**Gescheitheit** *die;* **~:** cleverness

**Geschenk** /gəˈʃɛŋk/ *das;* **~[e]s, ~e** present; gift; **jmdm. ein ~ machen** give sb. a present; **jmdm. etw. zum ~ machen** make sb. a present of sth.; give sth. to sb. as a present; **kleine ~e erhalten die Freundschaft** (*Spr.*) small gifts preserve friendships; **ein ~ des Himmels** a godsend

**Geschenk-: ~artikel** *der* gift; **~packung** *die* gift pack; **~papier** *das* gift wrapping paper; **~sendung** *die* (*Postw.*) parcel containing a gift/gifts; „**~sendung**" 'gift [only]'

**Gescherr** /gəˈʃɛr/ ⇒ **Herr** c

**geschert** /gəˈʃeːɐ̯t/ *Adj.* (*südd., österr. salopp*) stupid; idiotic

**Gescherte** *der; adj. Dekl.* (*südd., österr. salopp*) stupid git (*sl.*)

**Geschichte** /gəˈʃɪçtə/ *die;* **~, ~n** **A** (*auch Wissenschaft, Darstellung*) history; **die ~ Frankreichs** the history of France; **die englische ~:** English history; **Alte/Mittlere/Neue ~:** ancient/medieval/modern history; **~ machen** make history; **in die ~ eingehen** (*geh.*) go down in history; **etw. gehört der ~ (*Dat.*) an** sth. belongs to *or* is part of history; **B** (*Erzählung*) story; (*Fabel, Märchen*) story; tale; **C** (*ugs.: Sache*) **das sind alte ~n** that's old hat (*coll.*); **das ist [wieder] die alte ~:** it's the [same] old story [all over again]; **das sind ja schöne ~n!** (*iron.*) that's a fine thing *or* state of affairs! (*iron.*); **die ganze ~:** the whole business *or* thing; **mach keine ~n!** don't do anything silly; **Du wirst doch nicht krank werden. Mach keine ~n!** You won't fall ill. Don't be [so] silly!; **mach keine langen ~n** don't make a [great] fuss

**Geschichten-: ~buch** *das* story book; **~erzähler** *der*, **~erzählerin** *die* storyteller

**geschichtlich** **1** *Adj.* **A** historical; **B** (*bedeutungsvoll*) historic. **2** *adv.* historically; **etw. ~ betrachten** consider sth. from a historical point of view *or* perspective

**Geschichtlichkeit** *die;* **~** (*Philos.*) historicity

**geschichts-, Geschichts-: ~atlas** *der* historical atlas; **~auffassung** *die* conception *or* view of history; **~bewusstsein**, ***~bewußtsein** *das* awareness of history; historical awareness; **~bild** *das* ⇒ **~auffassung**; **~buch** *das* history book; **~drama** *das* (*Literaturw.*) historical drama; **~epoche** *die* historical epoch; **~fälschung** *die* falsification of history; **~forscher** *der*, **~forscherin** *die* historian; **~forschung** *die* historical research; **~klitterung** *die;* **~~, ~~en** deliberately biased account of history; **~lehrer** *der*, **~lehrerin** *die* history teacher; **~los** *Adj.* ‹country, society, people, etc.› without a history *or* past; (*ohne ~bewusstsein*) with no sense of its own history; **~philosophie** *die* philosophy of history; **~philosophisch** **1** *Adj.* ‹writings› on/‹studies› in/‹interpretation› according to/‹view of the world› based on the philosophy of history; **2** *adv.* **etw. ~philosophisch interpretieren** interpret sth. from the point of view of the philosophy of history; **~schreiber** *der*, **~schreiberin** *die* historian; (*Chronist*) chronicler; **~schreibung** *die* historiography; **~unterricht** *der* history teaching; (*Unterrichtsstunde*) history lesson; **im ~unterricht nehmen sie den Dreißigjährigen Krieg durch** in history they are doing the Thirty Years War; ⇒ *auch* **Englischunterricht**; **~werk** *das* historical work; **~wissenschaft** *die* [science of] history; **~wissenschaftler** *der*, **~wissenschaftlerin** *die* [academic] historian; **~zahl** *die* [historical] date

**Geschick**[1] /gəˈʃɪk/ *das;* **~[e]s, ~e** **A** (*geh.: Schicksal*) fate; **ihn ereilte sein ~:** he met his fate; **ein glückliches/gutes ~:** a kindly Providence; **B** *Pl.* (*Lebensumstände*) destiny *sing.*

**Geschick**[2] *das;* **~[e]s** skill; **ein ~ für etw. haben** be skilled at sth.

**Geschicklichkeit** *die;* **~:** skilfulness; skill; **es zu großer ~ in etw. (*Dat.*) bringen** become very skilful at sth.

**Geschicklichkeits-: ~fahren** *das;* **~~s** (*Motorsport*) manoeuvring tests *pl.;* **~spiel** *das* game of skill

**geschickt** **1** *2. Part. v.* **schicken.** **2** *Adj.* **A** (*gewandt*) skilful; (*fingerfertig*) skilful; dexterous; **~ im Klettern sein** be an agile climber; **B** (*klug*) clever; adroit; **C** (*südd.: geeignet*) suitable (**für** for). **3** *adv.* **A** (*gewandt*) skilfully; (*fingerfertig*) skilfully; dexterously; **B** (*klug*) cleverly; adroitly

**Geschicktheit** *die;* **~** ⇒ **Geschicklichkeit**

**Geschiebe** *das;* **~s, ~** **A** (*ugs.*) pushing and shoving; **B** (*Geol.*) debris

**geschieden** *2. Part. v.* **scheiden**

**Geschiedene** *der/die; adj. Dekl.* divorcee; **seine ~:** his ex-wife; **ihr ~r** her ex-husband

**geschienen** *2. Part. v.* **scheinen**

**Geschimpfe** *das;* **~s** (*ugs.*) cursing; (*das Tadeln*) scolding

**Geschirr** /gəˈʃɪr/ *das;* **~[e]s, ~e** **A** (*Riemenzeug*) harness; **dem Pferd das ~ anlegen** harness the horse; put the harness on the horse; **sich ins ~ legen** (*kräftig ziehen*) pull hard; (*angestrengt arbeiten*) work like a slave; **B** (*Teller, Tassen usw.*) crockery; (*benutzt*) dishes *pl.;* (*zusammenpassend*) [dinner/tea] service; (*Küchen~*) pots and pans *pl.;* kitchenware; **das gute/beste ~:** the good/best china; **feuerfestes ~:** ovenware set; **das ~ abwaschen** wash up *or* do the dishes; **C** (*veralt.: Gefäß*) pot

**Geschirr-: ~aufzug** *der* dumb waiter; **~reiniger** *der* dishwasher detergent; **~schrank** *der* china cupboard; **~spülen** *das;* **~~s** washing-up; **~spüler** *der;* **~~s, ~~** **A** washer-up; **B** ⇒ **~spülmaschine;** **~spülerin** *die;* **~~, ~~nen** ⇒ **~spüler** A; **~spül·maschine** *die* dishwashing machine; dishwasher; **~spülmittel** *das* washing-up liquid; **~tuch** *das; Pl.* **~tücher** tea towel; drying-up cloth (*Brit.*); dish towel (*Amer.*)

**Geschiss, *Geschiß** /gəˈʃɪs/ *das;* **Geschisses** (*derb*) fuss and bother (*coll.*)

**geschissen** /gəˈʃɪsn̩/ *2. Part. v.* **scheißen**

**Geschlabber** *das;* **~s** (*ugs.*) **A** (*das Schlabbern*) slurping; **B** (*bei Kleidern*) **das ~ ihres langen Rocks** the flapping of her long skirt; **C** (*Brei, Pudding usw.*) mush

**geschlafen** *2. Part. v.* **schlafen**

**geschlagen** *2. Part. v.* **schlagen**

**Geschlecht** *das;* **~[e]s, ~er** **A** sex; **männlichen/weiblichen ~s sein** be male/female; **Jugendliche beiderlei ~s** young people of both sexes; **das starke ~** (*ugs. scherzh.*) the stronger sex; **das schwache/schöne/zarte ~** (*ugs. scherzh.*) the weaker/fair/gentle sex; **B** (*Generation*) generation; **die nachfolgenden ~er** future generations; **C** (*Sippe*) family; **von altem ~:** of ancient lineage; **das ~ der Habsburger** the house of Habsburg; **ein edles ~:** a noble house; **D** (*Sprachw.*) gender; **E** (*Geschlechtsteil*) sex; **F** (*dichter.: Gattung*) **das menschliche ~** *od.* **das ~ der Menschen** the human race; **das ~ der Götter** the gods

**Geschlechter-: ~folge** *die* succession of generations; **die ~folgen** the generations; **~trennung** *die* segregation of the sexes

**geschlechtlich** **1** *Adj.* sexual. **2** *adv.* **mit jmdm. ~ verkehren** have sexual intercourse with sb.

**Geschlechtlichkeit** *die;* **~:** sexuality

**geschlechts-, Geschlechts-: ~akt** *der* sex[ual] act; **~apparat** *der* (*Fachspr.*) genital organs *pl.;* genitals *pl.;* **~bestimmung** *die* **A** (*Festlegung*) sex determination; **B** (*Feststellung*) determination of sex; (*von Tieren auch*) sexing; **eine ~bestimmung vornehmen** determine the sex of a baby/an animal; **~chromosom** *das* (*Biol.*) sex chromosome; **~drüse** *die* ▶ 471 (*Anat., Zool.*) gonad; **~erziehung** *die* sex education; **~gebunden** **1** *Adj.* sex-linked; **2** *adv.* **~gebunden weitervererbt werden** be passed on in a way which shows sex-linkage; **~hormon** *das* sex hormone; **~krank** *Adj.* ‹person› suffering from VD *or* a venereal disease; **~krank sein** have VD; be suffering from a venereal disease; **~krankheit** *die* ▶ 474 venereal disease; **~leben** *das* sex life; **~los** *Adj.* (*Biol.*) asexual; (*fig.*) sexless; **~lust** *die* sexual desire *or* lust; **~merkmal** *das* sex[ual] characteristic; **~organ** *das* ▶ 471 sex[ual] organ; genital organ; **~partner** *der*, **~partnerin** *die* sex partner; **~reif** *Adj.* sexually mature; **~reife** *die* sexual maturity; **~rolle** *die* (*Soziol.*) sex role; **~spezifisch** *Adj.* (*Soziol.*) sex-specific; **~teil** *das:* ▶ 471 **die ~teile/das ~teil** the genitals *pl.;* **~trieb** *der* sex[ual] drive *or* urge; **~umwandlung** *die* sex change; change of sex; **~unterschied** *der* difference between the sexes; **~verkehr** *der* sexual intercourse; **~wort** *das; Pl.* **~wörter** ⇒ **Artikel**; **~zelle** *die* gamete

**geschlichen** *2. Part. v.* **schleichen**

**geschliffen** **1** *2. Part. v.* **schleifen.** **2** *Adj.* polished, refined ‹style, manners, etc.›; polished ‹sentence›. **3** *adv.* in a polished manner

**Geschliffenheit** *die;* **~, ~en** refinement; (*des Stils*) polish

**geschlissen** /gəˈʃlɪsn̩/ *2. Part. v.* **schleißen**

**geschlossen** **1** *2. Part. v.* **schließen.** **2** *Adj.* **A** (*gemeinsam*) united ‹action, front›; unified ‹procedure›; ⇒ *auch* **Gesellschaft**; **B** (*zusammenhängend*) **eine ~e Ortschaft** a built-up area; **eine ~e Linie von Demonstranten** a solid line of demonstrators; **C** (*abgerundet*) **eine [in sich] ~e Persönlichkeit** a well-rounded personality; **ein ~es Bild/~er Eindruck** a full *or* complete picture/impression. **3** *adv.* **~ für etw. stimmen/sein** vote/be unanimously in favour of sth.; **wir verließen ~ unser Büro** we walked out in a body *or* en masse; **~ gegen etw. vorgehen** take concerted action against sth.; **~ hinter jmdm. stehen** be solidly behind sb.; **die ganze Gruppe stand ~ auf** the whole group rose with one accord

**Geschlossenheit** *die;* **~** **A** (*Gemeinschaft*) unity; **B** (*Einheitlichkeit*) unity; uniformity; **C** **die ~ der Handlung** the tight construction of the plot

**Geschluchze** *das;* **~s** (*ugs.*) sobbing; **hör mit dem ~ auf!** stop your blubbering *or* (*sl.*) blubbing

**geschlungen** /gəˈʃlʊŋən/ *2. Part. v.* **schlingen**

**Geschlürfe** *das;* **~s** (*ugs. abwertend*) slurping

**Geschmack** /gəˈʃmak/ *der;* **~[e]s, Geschmäcke** /gəˈʃmɛkə/ *od. ugs. scherzh.:* **Geschmäcker** /gəˈʃmɛkɐ/ **A** taste; **einen schlechten ~ im Munde haben** have a bad *or* nasty taste in one's mouth; **einen guten/schlechten ~ haben** have good/bad taste; **das ist [nicht] mein** *od.* **nach meinem ~:** that is [not] to my taste; **jmds. ~ (*Akk.*) treffen** guess sb.'s taste exactly; **das verstößt gegen den guten ~:** that offends against good taste; **im ~ jener Zeit eingerichtet** furnished in the style of that period; **von erlesenem ~:** exquisitely tasteful; showing exquisite taste; **die Geschmäcker sind verschieden** (*ugs. scherzh.*) tastes differ; **über ~ lässt sich nicht streiten** there's no accounting for taste[s]; **an etw. (*Akk.*) ~ finden** *od.* **gewinnen** acquire a taste for sth.; take a liking to sth.; **einer Sache (*Dat.*) ~ abgewinnen** come *or* grow to like sth.; **sie kann solchen Bildern keinen ~ abgewinnen** she cannot appreciate such pictures; **auf den ~ kommen** acquire the taste for it; get to like it; **B** (*Geschmackssinn*) sense of taste

**geschmacklich** **1** *Adj.* as regards taste *postpos.;* **zur ~en Verfeinerung** to improve the taste *or* flavour. **2** *adv.* as regards taste

**geschmacklos** **1** *Adj.* **A** (*ohne Geschmack*) tasteless; insipid; **B** (*unschön, taktlos*) tasteless; **~ sein** be in bad taste; ‹person› be lacking in taste. **2** *adv.* tastelessly

*old spelling (see note on page 1707)

**Geschmacklosigkeit** *die;* ~, ~**en** Ⓐ lack of [good] taste; bad taste; **diese Gebäude sind** ~**en** these buildings are examples of bad taste; Ⓑ (*Unverschämtheit*) tastelessness; bad taste; **das ist eine** ~ **ersten Ranges!** that is the height of bad taste!; Ⓒ (*Äußerung*) tasteless remark; (*Handlung*) tasteless behaviour *sing., no indef. art.*

**geschmacks-, Geschmacks-:** ~**empfindung** *die* sense of taste; ~**frage** *die* question *or* matter of taste; ~**knospe** *die* ▶ 471 (*Zool., Anat.*) taste bud; ~**neutral** *Adj.* tasteless; flavourless; ~**richtung** *die* Ⓐ flavour; Ⓑ (*Geschmack, Vorliebe*) taste

**Geschmack[s]·sache** *die: in* **das ist** ~**:** that is a question *or* matter of taste

**Geschmacks-:** ~**sinn** *der* sense of taste; ~**stoff** *der* flavouring; ~**verirrung** *die* (*abwertend*) lapse of taste; **an** *od.* **unter** ~**verirrung** (*Dat.*) **leiden** (*ugs.*) suffer from a lapse in taste; ~**verstärker** *der* flavour enhancer

**geschmack·voll** ❶ *Adj.* tasteful; **die Bemerkung war nicht sehr** ~**:** the remark was not in very good taste. ❷ *adv.* tastefully

**Geschmatze** *das;* ~**s** (*ugs. abwertend*) smacking one's lips *no art.;* (*beim Essen*) noisy eating *no art.;* **hör mit dem** ~ **auf!** stop making so much noise when you're eating!

**Geschmeide** /gəˈʃmaidə/ *das;* ~**s**, ~ (*geh.*) jewellery *no pl.;* (*einzelnes Schmuckstück*) piece of jewellery

**geschmeidig** ❶ *Adj.* Ⓐ (*schmiegsam*) sleek ‹hair, fur›; supple, soft ‹leather, boots, skin›; smooth ‹dough›; Ⓑ (*gelenkig*) supple ‹fingers›; supple, lithe ‹body, movement, person›; Ⓒ (*fig.: anpassungsfähig*) adaptable. ❷ *adv.* Ⓐ (*gelenkig*) agilely; Ⓑ (*fig.*) adaptably

**Geschmeidigkeit** *die;* ~ ⇒ **geschmeidig** 1: sleekness; suppleness; softness; smoothness; litheness; adaptability

**Geschmeiß** *das;* ~**es** Ⓐ (*veralt., auch fig.*) vermin; Ⓑ (*Jägerspr.*) droppings *pl.*

**Geschmiere** *das;* ~**s** (*ugs. abwertend*) Ⓐ [filthy] mess; Ⓑ (*Geschriebenes*) scribble; scrawl; Ⓒ (*Machwerk*) rubbish; bilge (*sl.*)

**geschmissen** /gəˈʃmɪsn̩/ *2. Part. v.* **schmeißen**

**geschmolzen** *2. Part. v.* **schmelzen**

**Geschmorte** /gəˈʃmoːɐ̯tə/ *das; adj. Dekl.* (*ugs.*) braised meat

**Geschmunzel** *das;* ~**s** (*ugs.*) smiling; **allgemeines** ~ **auslösen** make everyone smile

**Geschmuse** *das;* ~**s** (*ugs.*) cuddling; (*eines Pärchens*) kissing and cuddling

**Geschnäbel** *das;* ~**s** (*ugs.*) Ⓐ (*von Vögeln*) billing; Ⓑ (*ugs. scherzh.: Geküsse*) billing and cooing

**Geschnatter** *das;* ~**s** (*ugs.*) Ⓐ (*das Schnattern*) cackling; cackle; Ⓑ (*abwertend: das Sprechen*) chatter[ing]; nattering (*coll.*)

**Geschnetzelte** *das; adj. Dekl. small, thin slices of meat* [*cooked in sauce*]

**geschniegelt** ❶ *2. Part. v.* **schniegeln.** ❷ *Adj.* (*ugs. abwertend*) nattily dressed; ~ **und gebügelt** *od.* **gestriegelt** all spruced up

**geschnitten** /gəˈʃnɪtn̩/ *2. Part. v.* **schneiden**

**geschnoben** *2. Part. v.* **schnauben**

**geschoben** /gəˈʃoːbn̩/ *2. Part. v.* **schieben**

**geschollen** *2. Part. v.* **schallen**

**gescholten** /gəˈʃɔltn̩/ *2. Part. v.* **schelten**

**Geschöpf** /gəˈʃœpf/ *das;* ~**[e]s**, ~**e** Ⓐ creature; **ein** ~ **Gottes** one of God's creatures; Ⓑ (*erfundene Gestalt*) creation

**geschoren** *2. Part. v.* **scheren**

**Geschoss**[1], ***Geschoß** *das;* **Geschosses, Geschosse** projectile; (*Kugel*) bullet; (*Rakete*) rocket; missile; (*Granate*) shell; grenade

**Geschoss**[2], ***Geschoß** *das;* **Geschosses, Geschosse** (*Etage*) floor; (*Stockwerk*) storey; **im ersten** ~**:** on the first (*Brit.*) *or* (*Amer.*) second floor

**Geschoss·bahn, *Geschoß·bahn** *die* trajectory

**geschossen** /gəˈʃɔsn̩/ *2. Part. v.* **schießen**

**Geschoss·hagel, *Geschoß·hagel** *der* hail of bullets

**-geschossig** ❶ *Adj.* -storey; **ein**~/**zwei**~/**mehr**~**:** single-storey/two-storey/multi-storey; **unser Wohnhaus ist zwei**~**:** our house has two storeys. ❷ *adv.* **drei**~ **bauen** build three storeys high

**geschraubt** ❶ *2. Part. v.* **schrauben.** ❷ *Adj.* (*ugs. abwertend*) stilted ‹language, construction›; (*schwülstig*) affected, pretentious ‹way of speaking, style›. ❸ *adv.* **sich** ~ **ausdrücken** express oneself in an affected *or* a pretentious manner *or* way

**Geschraubtheit** *die;* ~**:** stiltedness; (*Schwulst*) affectedness; pretentiousness

**Geschrei** *das;* ~**s** Ⓐ shouting; shouts *pl.;* (*durchdringend*) yelling; yells *pl.;* (*schrill*) shrieking; shrieks *pl.;* (*von Verletzten, Tieren*) screaming; screams *pl.;* **hört mit dem** ~ **auf** stop that shouting *or* yelling; Ⓑ (*ugs.: das Lamentieren*) fuss; to-do; **ein großes** ~ **wegen etw. machen** make *or* kick up a great fuss about sth.; make a great to-do about sth.

**Geschreibsel** /gəˈʃraipsl̩/ *das;* ~**s** (*ugs. abwertend*) rubbish; bilge (*sl.*)

**geschrieben** *2. Part. v.* **schreiben**

***geschrieen, geschrien** /gəˈʃriː(ə)n/ *2. Part. v.* **schreien**

**geschritten** *2. Part. v.* **schreiten**

**geschunden** *2. Part. v.* **schinden**

**Geschütz** *das;* ~**es**, ~**e** [big] gun; piece of artillery; **die** ~**e** the artillery *sing.;* the [big] guns; **grobes** *od.* **schweres** ~ **auffahren** (*fig. ugs.*) bring up the big guns *or* heavy artillery (*fig.*)

**Geschütz-:** ~**bedienung** *die* (*Milit.*) gun crew; ~**donner** *der* roar *or* booming of the [big] guns *or* the artillery; ~**feuer** *das* artillery fire; shellfire; ~**stand** *der,* ~**stellung** *die* (*Milit.*) gun emplacement

**geschützt** ❶ *2. Part. v.* **schützen.** ❷ *Adj.* Ⓐ sheltered; Ⓑ (*unter Naturschutz*) protected

**Geschwader** /gəˈʃvaːdɐ/ *das;* ~**s**, ~ (*Marine*) squadron; (*Luftwaffe*) wing (*Brit.*); group (*Amer.*)

**Geschwafel** *das;* ~**s** (*ugs. abwertend*) waffle

**Geschwätz** *das;* ~**es** (*ugs. abwertend*) Ⓐ (*Gerede*) prattle; prattling; Ⓑ (*Klatsch*) gossip; tittle-tattle

**Geschwatze, Geschwätze** *das;* ~**s** (*ugs. abwertend*) chatter[ing]; nattering (*coll.*)

**geschwätzig** *Adj.* (*abwertend*) talkative

**Geschwätzigkeit** *die;* ~ (*abwertend*) talkativeness; **sie neigt ein bisschen zur** ~**:** she tends to be rather talkative

**geschweift** ❶ *2. Part. v.* **schweifen.** ❷ *Adj.* (*gebogen*) curved; ~**e Klammern** (*Druckw.*) braces

**geschweige** *Konj.* ~ **[denn]** let alone; never mind

**geschwiegen** *2. Part. v.* **schweigen**

**geschwind** /gəˈʃvɪnt/ (*bes. südd.*) ❶ *Adj.* swift; quick. ❷ *adv.* swiftly; quickly; ~**!** be quick!; **ich laufe** ~ **zum Kaufmann** I'm just dashing to the grocer's

**Geschwindigkeit** *die;* ~, ~**en** ▶ 348 speed; **mit großer/hoher** ~**:** at great/high speed; **mit einer** ~ **von 50 km/h** at a speed of 50 kmh; **überhöhte** ~**:** excessive speed; **die** ~ **erhöhen/drosseln** *od.* **verringern** increase/reduce speed; speed up/slow down

**Geschwindigkeits-:** ~**abfall** *der* loss of speed; drop in speed; ~**begrenzung** *die,* ~**beschränkung** *die* speed limit; **die** ~**beschränkung nicht beachten** exceed the speed limit; ~**kontrolle** *die* speed check; ~**messer** *der;* ~~**s**, ~~**:** speedometer; ~**überschreitung** *die* exceeding the speed limit *no art.;* speeding; ~**zunahme** *die* increase in speed; increase in velocity (*Phys.*)

**Geschwirr** *das;* ~**s** (*von Pfeilen*) whizzing; (*von Insekten*) buzzing

**Geschwister** /gəˈʃvɪstɐ/ *das;* ~**s**, ~ Ⓐ *Pl.* brothers and sisters; **Hans und Maria sind** ~**:** Hans and Maria are brother and sister; Ⓑ (*bes. Biol., Psych.*) sibling

**Geschwister·kind** *das* (*veralt.*) Ⓐ (*Neffe/Nichte*) nephew/niece; Ⓑ (*Cousin/Cousine*) cousin

**geschwisterlich** ❶ *Adj.* brotherly/sisterly ‹affection, love›. ❷ *adv.* **das Geld** ~ **teilen** divide the money fairly among everybody

**Geschwister-:** ~**liebe** *die* Ⓐ brotherly/sisterly love *or* affection; Ⓑ (*Inzest*) love affair between a brother and [a] sister; ~**paar** *das* brother and sister; **zwei** ~**paare** two sets of brother and sister

**geschwollen** ❶ *2. Part. v.* **schwellen.** ❷ *Adj.* Ⓐ swollen; Ⓑ (*fig. abwertend*) pompous; bombastic. ❸ *adv.* pompously; bombastically

**geschwommen** /gəˈʃvɔmən/ *2. Part. v.* **schwimmen**

**geschworen** ❶ *2. Part. v.* **schwören.** ❷ *Adj. in* **ein** ~**er Feind** *od.* **Gegner von etw. sein** be a sworn enemy of sth.

**Geschworene,** (*österr.:*) **Geschworne** *der/die; adj. Dekl.* juror; **die** ~**n** the jury

**Geschworenen-:** ~**bank** jury box; (*fig.*) jury; ~**gericht** *das* ⇒ **Schwurgericht**

**Geschwulst** /gəˈʃvʊlst/ *die;* ~, **Geschwülste** /gəˈʃvʏlstə/ tumour

**geschwunden** *2. Part. v.* **schwinden**

**geschwungen** ❶ *2. Part. v.* **schwingen.** ❷ *Adj.* curved

**Geschwür** /gəˈʃvyːɐ̯/ *das;* ~**s**, ~**e** ▶ 474 ulcer; (*Furunkel*) boil; (*fig.*) running sore

**Ges-Dur** *das* (*Musik*) G major; ⇒ *auch* **C-Dur**

**gesehen** /gəˈzeːən/ *2. Part. v.* **sehen**

**Geselchte** /gəˈzɛlçtə/ *das; adj. Dekl.* (*südd., österr.*) smoked meat

**Gesell** /gəˈzɛl/ *der;* ~**en**, ~**en** (*veralt.*), **Geselle** /gəˈzɛlə/ *der;* ~**n**, ~**n** Ⓐ journeyman; Ⓑ (*Kerl*) fellow

**-geselle** *der:* **Tischler**~/**Fleischer**~**:** journeyman-carpenter/-butcher

**gesellen** *refl. V.* **sich zu jmdm.** ~**:** join sb.; (*fig.: hinzukommen*) **dazu gesellten sich noch Krankheit und finanzielle Unsicherheit** together with this came illness and financial insecurity

**Gesellen-:** ~**brief** *der* journeyman's diploma *or* certificate; ~**prüfung** *die* examination to become a journeyman; apprentice's final examination; ~**stück** *das: piece of work produced by an apprentice in order to qualify as a journeyman*

**gesellig** ❶ *Adj.* Ⓐ sociable; gregarious; **ein** ~**er Abend**/~**es Beisammensein** a convivial *or* sociable evening/a friendly get-together; Ⓑ (*Biol.*) gregarious. ❷ *adv.* ~ **leben** live gregariously; be gregarious; ~ **zusammensitzen** sit [together] and chat [sociably]

**Geselligkeit** *die;* ~, ~**en** Ⓐ (*Umgang*) **die** ~ **lieben** enjoy [good] company; Ⓑ (*geselliger Abend*) social gathering

**Gesellin** *die;* ~, ~**nen** journeyman; journeywoman (*rare*)

**Gesellschaft** *die;* ~, ~**en** Ⓐ society; **eine geschlossene** ~**:** a closed community *or* society; **die** ~ **verändern** change society; ~ **bekommen** get company; **in schlechte** ~ **geraten** get into bad company; **jmdm.** ~ **leisten** keep sb. company; **die Damen der** ~**:** society ladies; **zur** ~ **gehören** belong to society; **jmdn. in die** ~ **einführen** introduce sb. into society; **die** ~ **Jesu** (*kath. Rel.*) the Society of Jesus; **zur** ~**:** to be sociable; **sich in guter** ~ **befinden** (*fig. scherzh.*) be in good company; Ⓑ (*Veranstaltung*) party; **eine** ~ **geben** give a party; **eine geschlossene** ~**:** a private function *or* party; Ⓒ (*Kreis von Menschen*) group of people; crowd; (*abwertend*) crew; lot (*coll.*); Ⓓ (*Wirtschaft*) company; ~ **mit beschränkter Haftung** limited liability company

**Gesellschafter** *der;* ~**s**, ~ Ⓐ (*Unterhalter*) **ein glänzender** ~**:** a brilliant conversationalist; **ein guter** ~ **sein** be good company; Ⓑ (*verhüll.: Callboy*) [male] escort (*euphem.*); Ⓒ (*Wirtsch.*) partner; (*Teilhaber*) shareholder; **stiller** ~**:** sleeping partner; silent partner (*Amer.*)

**Gesellschafterin** *die;* ~, ~**nen** Ⓐ [lady] companion; Ⓑ (*verhüll.: Callgirl*) escort (*euphem.*); Ⓒ (*Wirtsch.*) partner; (*Teilhaber*) shareholder

# Geschwindigkeiten

In Großbritannien und den USA werden Geschwindigkeiten im Straßenverkehr sowie im Schienenverkehr und im Luftverkehr noch meist in Meilen in der Stunde (**miles per hour** *oder* **miles an hour, mph**) gemessen.

***100 km/h***
= 62,14 Meilen in der Stunde

Aber immer öfter werden diese Geschwindigkeiten auch als Kilometer in der Stunde (**kilometres** *od.* (*amerik.*) **kilometers per hour, kph**) angegeben.

Das britische Tempolimit in geschlossenen Ortschaften liegt bei 30 Meilen in der Stunde (ungefähr 50 km/h). Andere Grenzen liegen bei 40 (≈ 65 km/h), 50 (= 80 km/h), 60 (≈ 100 km/h), und auf der Autobahn 70 Meilen in der Stunde (≈ 110 km/h).

***Wie schnell*** od. ***Mit welcher Geschwindigkeit fuhr der Wagen?***
= How fast was the car going?, What speed was the car doing?

***Der Wagen fuhr mit 120 Stundenkilometern***
≈ The car was going at *od.* doing 75 [miles an hour]

***Sie fuhr mit Vollgas/mit Höchstgeschwindigkeit***
= She was driving flat out/at full speed

***Das Auto fährt 200 Kilometer Spitze***
≈ The car will do 125 [miles an hour] flat out, The car's top speed is 125 [miles an hour]

***Du hast das Tempolimit überschritten***
= You were exceeding the speed limit

***Sie rasten dahin/fuhren in rasendem Tempo***
= They were tearing along/going at a crazy speed

***Wir mussten im Kriechtempo fahren***
= We had to go at a crawl *od.* were reduced to a crawl

## Lichtgeschwindigkeit, Schallgeschwindigkeit

***Die Schallgeschwindigkeit beträgt 330 Meter pro Sekunde***
= The speed of sound is 330 metres per second (m/s)

***die Schallmauer durchbrechen***
= to break the sound barrier

***Die Lichtgeschwindigkeit beträgt 300 000 Kilometer pro Sekunde***
= The speed of light is 186,300 miles per second

***mit Lichtgeschwindigkeit***
= at the speed of light

**gesellschaftlich** ❶ *Adj.* [A] social; **die ~en Verhältnisse** social conditions; [B] (*Soziol.*) society; **die ~e Produktion** production by society; **~es Eigentum an etw.** (*Dat.*) social ownership of sth.; [C] (*DDR*) ‹work etc.› in the service of the community. ❷ *adv.* [A] socially; **sich ~ unmöglich machen** put oneself beyond the pale of society; [B] (*DDR*) **~ nützliche Tätigkeit** socially useful activity; **~ aktiv sein** *od.* **sich ~ betätigen** be actively involved in service to the community

**gesellschafts-, Gesellschafts-: ~abend** *der* social evening; **~anzug** *der* dress suit; **~dame** *die* (*veralt.*) ⇒ **Gesellschafterin** A; **~fähig** *Adj.* (*auch fig.*) socially acceptable; **~feindlich** *Adj.* anti-social; **~form** *die* form of society; social system; **~formation** *die* (*Soziol.*) social system; **~kapital** *das* (*Wirtsch.*) capital of a/the company; **~klasse** *die* social class; **~kritik** *die* social criticism; **~kritiker** *der*, **~kritikerin** *die* critic of society; **~kritisch** ❶ *Adj.* critical of society *postpos.*; **die ~kritischen Elemente bei Fontane** the elements of social criticism in Fontane; ❷ *adv.* **etw. ~kritisch interpretieren** interpret sth. from the point of view of social criticism; **~lehre** *die* (*veralt.*) sociology; (*Schulfach*) social studies *pl.*, *no art.*; **~ordnung** *die* social order; **~politik** *die* social policy; **~politisch** ❶ *Adj.* socio-political; ❷ *adv.* socio-politically; **~raum** *der* function room; (*auf Schiffen*) saloon; **~reise** *die* group tour; **~roman** *der* social novel; **~schicht** *die* stratum of society; **~spiel** *das* parlour *or* party game; **~struktur** *die* structure of society; **die japanische ~struktur** the structure of Japanese society; **~stück** *das* [A] (*Theater*) comedy of manners; [B] (*Malerei*) genre painting; **~system** *das* social system; **~tanz** *der* ballroom dance; (*das Tanzen*) ballroom dancing; **~vertrag** *der* [A] (*Philos.*) social contract; [B] (*Rechtsw.*) memorandum *or* articles of association; **~wissenschaften** *Pl.* social sciences; **~wissenschaftlich** *Adj.* sociological ‹studies, analyses›; **~wissenschaftliche Fächer** social-science subjects

**gesessen** /gəˈzɛsn̩/ *2. Part. v.* **sitzen**

**Gesetz** /gəˈzɛts/ *das;* **~es, ~e** [A] law; (*geschrieben*) statute; **ein ~ verabschieden/einbringen** pass/introduce a bill; **[zum] ~ werden** become law; **vor dem ~:** in [the eyes of the] law; **das ~ der Serie** *the expectation that future events will continue the pattern of past ones;* **das ~ des Handelns** the need *or* necessity to act; **das ~ des Handelns an sich reißen** seize the initiative; **etw. hat seine eigenen ~e** (*fig.*) sth. is a law unto itself; [B] (*Regel*) rule; law; **jmdm. höchstes ~ sein** be sb.'s golden rule; ⇒ *auch* **aufheben** C; **einhalten** 1

**Gesetz-: ~blatt** *das* law gazette; **~buch** *das* statute book; **das Bürgerliche ~buch** the Civil Code; **~entwurf** *der* bill

**gesetzes-, Gesetzes-: ~brecher** *der*, **~brecherin** *die;* **~~, ~~nen** lawbreaker; **~hüter** *der*, **~hüterin** *die* (*iron.*) guardian of the law; **~kraft** *die* force of law; legal force; **~kraft haben** have the force of law *or* legal force; **~kraft erlangen** become law; be placed on the statute book; **~kundig** *Adj.* well versed in the law *postpos.*; **~lücke** *die* loophole in the law; **~novelle** *die* amendment; **~sammlung** *die* legal digest; **~tafel** *die* (*hist.*) tablet on which laws are written; **die ~tafeln** (*bibl.*) the Tables of the Law; the Two Tables; **~text** *der* wording of the/a law; **~treu** ❶ *Adj.* law-abiding; ❷ *adv.* in accordance with the law; **~treue** *die* law-abidingness; **~übertretung** *die* violation of the law; **~vorlage** *die* bill; **~werk** *das* corpus *or* body of laws

**gesetz-, Gesetz-: ~gebend** *Adj.* legislative; **die ~gebende Versammlung/Gewalt** the legislative assembly *or* the legislature/the legislative power; **~geber** *der* legislator; lawmaker; (*Organ*) legislature; **~gebung** *die;* **~:** legislation; law-making; **~gebungs·hoheit** *die* supreme authority to make *or* enact laws; supreme legislative power *or* authority; **~kundig** *Adj.:* ⇒ **gesetzeskundig**

**gesetzlich** ❶ *Adj.* legal ‹requirement, definition, representative, interest›; legal, statutory ‹obligation›; statutory ‹holiday›; lawful, legitimate ‹heir, claim›; **~es Zahlungsmittel** legal tender; **~e Kündigungsfrist** statutory period of notice. ❷ *adv.* legally; **~ verankert sein** be established in law; **~ geschützt** registered ‹patent, design›; ‹symbol› registered as a trade mark; **~ geschützt/verboten sein** be protected/forbidden by law

**Gesetzlichkeit** *die;* **~** [A] (*Gesetzmäßigkeit*) conformity to a [natural] law/[natural] laws; **einer ~ folgen** obey a law/laws; [B] (*geregelter Zustand*) **~ wieder herstellen** restore law and order; **außerhalb der ~ liegen** be illegal

**gesetz-, Gesetz-: ~los** *Adj.* lawless; **~losigkeit** *die;* **~~:** lawlessness; **~mäßig** ❶ *Adj.* [A] law-governed ‹development, process›; **~mäßig sein** be governed by *or* obey a [natural] law/ [natural] laws; [B] (**~lich**) legal; (*rechtmäßig*) lawful; legitimate; ❷ *adv.* in accordance with a [natural] law/[natural] laws; **~mäßigkeit** *die* [A] conformity to a [natural] law/[natural] laws; **~mäßigkeiten im Verhalten von Tieren entdecken** discover laws governing animal behaviour; [B] (**~lichkeit**) legality; (*Rechtmäßigkeit*) lawfulness; legitimacy

**gesetzt** ❶ *2. Part. v.* **setzen.** ❷ *Adj.* staid; **eine Dame ~en Alters** a woman of mature years

**Gesetztheit** *die;* **~:** staidness

**gesetz·widrig** ❶ *Adj.* illegal; unlawful. ❷ *adv.* illegally; unlawfully

**Gesetz·widrigkeit** *die* [A] illegality; unlawfulness; [B] *Pl.* (*Handlungen*) unlawful acts

**Geseufze** *das;* **~s** sighing

**Gesicht**[1] /gəˈzɪçt/ *das;* **~[e]s, ~er** [A] ▸ 471 face; **das ~ abwenden** turn one's face away; **ein fröhliches ~ machen** look pleasant *or* cheerful; **über das ganze ~ strahlen** (*ugs.*) beam all over one's face; **sich** (*Dat.*) **eine Zigarette ins ~ stecken** (*ugs.*) stick a cigarette in one's mouth (*coll.*); (*fig.*) **sein wahres ~ zeigen** show oneself in one's true colours; show one's true character; **jmdm. wie aus dem ~ geschnitten sein** be the [very *or* dead] spit [and image] of sb.; **ihm fiel das Essen aus dem ~** (*ugs. scherzh.*) he threw up (*coll.*); **das ist ein Schlag ins ~:** that is a slap in the face; **jmdm. ins ~ lachen** laugh in sb.'s face; **jmdm. ins ~ lügen** lie to sb.'s face; **jmdm. etw. ins ~ sagen** say sth. to sb.'s face; **jmdm. nicht ins ~ sehen können** be unable to look sb. in the face; **den Tatsachen ins ~ sehen** face the facts; **jmdm. [nicht] zu ~[e] stehen** [not] become sb.: **solche Unhöflichkeit steht dir nicht zu ~[e]** such impoliteness ill becomes you; **jmdm. ins ~ springen** (*ugs.*) go for sb.; **ein bekanntes/fremdes ~:** a familiar *or* well-known/unknown *or* strange face; **ein anderes ~ aufsetzen** *od.* **machen** put on a different expression; **das ~ wahren** *od.* **retten** save one's face; **das ~ verlieren** lose face; **ein ~ machen wie**

*old spelling (see note on page 1707)

**drei** *od.* **acht** *od.* **vierzehn Tage Regenwetter** look as miserable as sin; **ein langes ~/lange ~er machen** pull a long face; **ein schiefes ~ machen** make a wry face; **ein ~ ziehen** *od.* **machen** make *or* pull a face; **~er schneiden** pull *or* make faces; **das stand ihm im ~ geschrieben** it was written all over his face; **B** (*fig.: Aussehen*) **das ~ einer Stadt** the appearance of a town; **die vielen ~er Chinas** the many faces of China; **diese Pläne haben noch kein ~:** these plans still have no definite shape *or* form; **ein anderes ~ bekommen** take on a different complexion *or* character; **C** (*geh., veralt.: Sehvermögen*) sight; **das zweite ~ [haben]** [have] second sight; **jmdn./etw. aus dem ~ verlieren** lose sight of sb./sth.; **jmdn./etw. zu ~ bekommen** set eyes on *or* see sb./sth.; **jmdm. zu ~ kommen** (*Amtsspr.*) be seen by sb.

**Gesicht**[2] *das;* **~[e]s, ~e** (*geh.*) vision; **ein ~/~e haben** have a vision/visions

**gesichts-, Gesichts-: ~ausdruck** *der; Pl.* **~ausdrücke** expression; look; **~creme** *die* face cream; **~erker** *der* (*ugs. scherzh.*) conk (*coll.*); hooter (*Brit. coll.*); schnozzle (*Amer. sl.*); **~farbe** *die* complexion; **~feld** *das* field of vision *or* view; **~hälfte** *die* side of the face; **seine rechte ~hälfte** the right side of his face; **~haut** *die* ▶ 471 facial skin; **~kontrolle** *die* identity check (*before granting admittance to nightclub etc.*); **~kreis** *der* (*veralt.*) **A** field of view; field *or* range of vision; **jmdn. aus dem ~kreis verlieren** (*fig.*) lose touch with sb.; **B** (*Horizont*) horizon; outlook; **seinen ~kreis erweitern** broaden one's horizons *pl.;* **~lähmung** *die* facial paralysis; **~los** *Adj.* faceless; **~lotion** *die* face lotion; **~maske** *die* **A** (*Larve*) mask; **B** (*Med.*) face mask; **C** (*Kosmetik*) face mask; face pack; **D** (*Sport*) face guard; **~muskel** *der* ▶ 471 facial muscle; **~nerv** *der* ▶ 471 facial nerve; **~partie** *die* part of the face; **ihre untere ~partie** the lower part of her face; **~pflege** *die* care of one's face; **ihre tägliche ~pflege** her daily facial; **zur ~pflege benutzt sie nur Wasser und Seife** all she uses on her face is soap and water; **~plastik** *die* (*Med.*) plastic surgery *no art.* on the face; **~puder** *der* face powder; **~punkt** *der* point of view; **etw. unter einem anderen/neuen ~punkt betrachten** consider sth. from a different/new point of view; **~rose** *die* ▶ 474 (*Med.*) facial erysipelas; **~schnitt** *der* [cast *sing.* of] features *pl.;* **~sinn** *der* visual faculty; **~verlust** *der* loss of face; **~wasser** *das; Pl.* **~wässer** face lotion; **~winkel** *der* **A** angle of vision; visual angle; **B** ⇒ **~punkt**; **~züge** *Pl.* features

**Gesims** *das;* **~es, ~e** cornice

**Gesinde** /gəˈzɪndə/ *das;* **~s, ~** (*veralt.*) [domestic] servants *pl.;* (*auf einem Bauernhof*) [farm]hands *pl.*

**Gesindel** /gəˈzɪndl̩/ *das;* **~s** (*abwertend*) rabble; riff-raff *pl.;* **lichtscheues ~:** shady characters *pl.*

**Gesinde·stube** *die* (*veralt.*) servants' quarters *pl.;* (*auf einem Bauernhof*) quarters *pl.* for the farmhands

**Gesinge** *das;* **~s** (*ugs. abwertend*) singing

**gesinnt** /gəˈzɪnt/ *Adj.* **christlich/sozial ~ [sein]** [be] Christian-minded/public-spirited; **jmdm. freundlich/übel ~ sein** be well-disposed/ill-disposed towards sb.

**Gesinnung** *die;* **~, ~en** [basic] convictions *pl.;* [fundamental] beliefs *pl.;* **eine niedrige ~:** a low cast of mind

**gesinnungs-, Gesinnungs-: ~freund** *der,* **~freundin** *die,* **~genosse** *der,* **~genossin** *die* like-minded person; **seine ~freunde** *od.* **~genossen** people of the same mind as himself; **~los** (*abwertend*) **1** *Adj.* unprincipled; **2** *adv.* in an unprincipled manner; **~losigkeit** *die;* **~~:** lack of principle; **~lump** *der* (*ugs. abwertend*) time-server; **~schnüffelei** *die* (*abwertend*) snooping around to find out people's political convictions; political snooping; **~täter** *der,* **~täterin** *die* lawbreaker motivated by moral *or* political convictions; **~treu** *Adj.* loyal; **~treue** *die* loyalty; **~wandel** *der,* **~wechsel** *der* change *or* shift of attitude *or* views

**gesittet** /gəˈzɪtət/ **1** *Adj.* **A** well-behaved; well-mannered ‹behaviour›; **B** (*zivilisiert*) civilized. **2** *adv.* **A** **sich ~ benehmen** *od.* **aufführen** be well-behaved; **B** (*zivilisiert*) in a civilized manner

**Gesittung** *die;* **~** (*geh.*) cultured behaviour

**Gesocks** /gəˈzɔks/ *das;* **~** (*salopp abwertend*) riff-raff; rabble

**Gesöff** /gəˈzœf/ *das;* **~[e]s, ~e** (*salopp abwertend*) muck (*coll.*); awful stuff (*coll.*)

**gesogen** /gəˈzoːgn̩/ *2. Part. v.* **saugen**

**gesondert** /gəˈzɔndɐt/ **1** *Adj.* separate. **2** *adv.* separately

**gesonnen** /gəˈzɔnən/ **1** *2. Part. v.* **sinnen.** **2** *Adj.* **~ sein, etw. zu tun** feel disposed to do sth.

**gesotten** /gəˈzɔtn̩/ *2. Part. v.* **sieden**

**Gesottene** *das; adj. Dekl.* (*landsch.*) boiled meat

**Gespann** /gəˈʃpan/ *das;* **~[e]s, ~e** **A** (*Zugtiere*) team; **ein ~ Ochsen** a yoke *or* team of oxen; **B** (*Wagen*) horse and carriage; (*zur Güterbeförderung*) horse and cart; **C** (*Menschen*) couple; pair

**gespannt** **1** *2. Part. v.* **spannen.** **2** *Adj.* **A** (*erwartungsvoll*) eager; expectant; rapt ‹attention›; **ich bin ~, ob ...** I'm keen *or* eager to know/see whether ...; ⇒ *auch* **Flitz[e]bogen**; **B** (*konfliktbeladen*) tense ‹situation, atmosphere›; strained ‹relations, relationships›. **3** *adv.* eagerly; expectantly; **die Kinder hörten seinen Erzählungen ~ zu** the children listened with rapt attention to his stories

**Gespanntheit** *die* **A** eager expectancy; **voller ~ die Entwicklung verfolgen** follow the developments with tense interest; **B** (*Gereiztheit*) tenseness

**gespaßig** (*bayr., österr.*) ⇒ **spaßig**

**Gespenst** /gəˈʃpɛnst/ *das;* **~[e]s, ~er** **A** ghost; **~er sehen** (*fig.*) be imagining things; **B** (*geh.: Gefahr*) spectre

**Gespenster-: ~geschichte** *die* ghost story; **~glaube** *der* belief in ghosts

**gespensterhaft** *Adj.* ghostly

**gespenstern** *itr. V.* **in etw.** (*Dat.*) **~:** haunt sth.

**Gespenster·stunde** *die* witching hour

**gespenstig, gespenstisch** *Adj.* ghostly; ghostly, eerie ‹appearance›; eerie ‹building, atmosphere›

***gespieen, gespien** /gəˈʃpiː(ə)n/ *2. Part. v.* **speien**

**Gespiele** *der;* **~n, ~n, Gespielin** *die;* **~, ~nen** (*geh. veralt.*) **A** playmate; **B** (*abwertend: Geliebte[r]*) lover

**Gespinst** /gəˈʃpɪnst/ *das;* **~[e]s, ~e** gossamer-like material; **das ~ der Seidenraupe** the cocoon of the silkworm; **ein ~ von Lügen** (*fig.*) a tissue of lies

**gesplissen** /gəˈʃplɪsn̩/ *2. Part. v.* **spleißen**

**gesponnen** /gəˈʃpɔnən/ *2. Part. v.* **spinnen**

**Gespons**[1] /gəˈʃpɔns/ *der;* **~es, ~e** (*veralt., noch scherzh.*) spouse; (*Bräutigam*) bridegroom

**Gespons**[2] *das;* **~es, ~e** (*veralt., noch scherzh.*) spouse; (*Braut*) bride

**gespornt** **1** *2. Part. v.* **spornen.** **2** *Adj.* ⇒ **gestiefelt**

**Gespött** /gəˈʃpœt/ *das;* **~[e]s** mockery; ridicule; **jmdn./sich zum ~ machen** make sb./oneself a laughing stock

**Gespräch** /gəˈʃprɛːç/ *das;* **~[e]s, ~e** **A** conversation; (*Diskussion*) discussion; **das ~ auf etw.** (*Akk.*) **bringen** bring *or* steer the conversation round to sth.; **ein ~ über etw.** (*Akk.*) a conversation *or* talk about sth.; **~e** (*Politik*) talks; discussions; **der Gegenstand des ~[e]s** the subject *or* topic under discussion; **ein ~ mit jmdm. führen** have a conversation *or* talk with sb.; **jmdn. in ein ~ verwickeln** engage sb. in conversation; **mit jmdm. ins ~ kommen** (*sich unterhalten*) get into *or* engage in conversation with sb.; (*fig.: sich annähern*) enter into a dialogue with sb.; **im ~ sein** be under discussion; **als neuer Vorsitzender ist Herr X im ~:** Mr X's name is being discussed in connection with the chairmanship; **B** (*Telefongespräch*) call (**mit** to); **ein ~ anmelden** make *or* place a call; **ein ~ für Sie!** there's a call for you!; **C** (*ugs.:* **~sgegenstand**) **das ~ der Stadt/der Familie** the talk of the town/the whole family; **das ~ der letzten Wochen** the talking point for the last few weeks

**gesprächig** *Adj.* talkative; **der Alkohol machte ihn ~:** the alcohol loosened his tongue

**Gesprächigkeit** *die;* **~:** talkativeness

**gesprächs-, Gesprächs-: ~bereit** *Adj.* ready to talk *postpos.;* (*zu Verhandlungen bereit auch*) ready for discussions *postpos.;* (*Telefon*) **sind Sie jetzt ~bereit?** are you ready to speak now?; **~bereitschaft** *die* readiness for discussions; **~dauer** *die* (*Fernspr.*) call time; **~einheit** *die* ⇒ **Gebühreneinheit**; **~fetzen** *der* fragment *or* snatch of conversation; **~form** *die* **in ~form** in the form of a dialogue; in dialogue form; **~gegenstand** *der* topic of conversation; (*Diskussionsgegenstand*) subject of the discussion; **~gegenstand war ...** the subject *or* topic of conversation/the subject of the discussion was ...; **~kreis** *der* discussion group; **~leiter** *der,* **~leiterin** *die* discussion leader; chairman; **~partner** *der,* **~partnerin** *die:* **wer war ihr ~partner?** who was she talking to?; **meine heutige ~partnerin wird die Innenministerin sein** today I shall be talking to the Minister of the Interior; **der Kanzler und seine ~partner** the Chancellor and his partners in the talks; **~pause** *die* break in the discussions *or* talks; **~stoff** *der* subjects *pl. or* topics *pl.* of conversation; **ihr geht nie der ~stoff aus** she never runs out of things to talk about; **~teilnehmer** *der,* **~teilnehmerin** *die* participant in the discussion; **~thema** *das* topic of conversation; **~therapie** *die* (*Psych.*) therapy by means of conversation; **~weise** *Adv.* in [the course of] conversation; **~zeit** *die* (*Fernspr.*) call time; **Ihre ~zeit ist abgelaufen** the time allowed for your call has run out

**gespreizt** **1** *2. Part. v.* **spreizen.** **2** *Adj.* (*abwertend*) stilted; affected. **3** *adv.* (*abwertend*) in a stilted *or* an affected manner

**Gespreiztheit** *die;* **~** (*abwertend*) stiltedness; affectedness

**gesprenkelt** **1** *2. Part. v.* **sprenkeln.** **2** *Adj.* mottled; speckled ‹egg›

**Gespritzte** *der; adj. Dekl.* (*südd.*) wine with soda water

**gesprochen** /gəˈʃprɔxn̩/ *2. Part. v.* **sprechen**

**gesprossen** /gəˈʃprɔsn̩/ *2. Part. v.* **sprießen**

**Gesprudel** *das;* **~s** bubbling

**gesprungen** *2. Part. v.* **springen**

**Gespür** /gəˈʃpyːɐ̯/ *das;* **~s** feel; **sie hat ein feines ~ für Unaufrichtigkeiten** she quickly senses when somebody is being insincere

**gest.** *Abk.* **gestorben** d.

**Gestade** /gəˈʃtaːdə/ *das;* **~s, ~** (*dichter.*) shore(s)

**Gestagen** /gɛstaˈgeːn/ *das;* **~s, ~e** (*Med.*) gestagen

**Gestalt** /gəˈʃtalt/ *die;* **~, ~en** **A** build; **von kräftiger ~, kräftig von ~:** of powerful *or* strong build; **zierlich von ~:** petite; **klein von ~:** small in stature; of small build; **B** (*Mensch, Persönlichkeit*) figure; **eine zwielichtige ~:** a shady character; **C** (*in der Dichtung*) character; **D** (*Form*) form; **die ~ des neuen Hochhauses** the shape of the new tower block; **~ annehmen** *od.* **gewinnen** take shape; **einer Sache** (*Dat.*) **~ geben** *od.* **verleihen** give shape [and form] to sth.; (*etw. ausdrücken*) express sth.; **in ~ von einer Sache** *od.* **einer Sache** (*Gen.*) in the form of sth.; **sich in seiner wahren ~ zeigen** show one's true character; show [oneself in] one's true colours

**gestalten** **1** *tr. V.* fashion, shape, form ‹vase, figure, etc.›; design ‹furnishings, stage set, etc.›; lay out ‹public gardens›; dress ‹shop window›; mould,

g

shape ‹character, personality›; arrange ‹party, conference, etc.›; frame ‹sentence, reply, etc.›; **etw. moderner ~:** modernize sth.; **etw. künstlerisch/literarisch ~:** give artistic/literary form to sth. ❷ *refl. V.* turn out; **sich schwieriger ~ als erwartet** turn out *or* prove to be more difficult than had been expected; **er fragte sich, wie sich seine Zukunft ~ würde** he wondered what the future would hold for him

**Gestalter** *der;* **~s, ~, Gestalterin** *die;* **~, ~nen** creator

**gestalterisch** *Adj.* creative; artistic; **vom ~en Standpunkt** creatively; artistically

**gestalt·los** *Adj.* shapeless; formless; **eine ~e Masse** an amorphous mass

**Gestalt·psychologie** *die* Gestalt psychology

**Gestaltung** *die;* **~, ~en** Ⓐ ⇒ **gestalten**: fashioning; shaping; forming; designing; laying out; dressing; moulding; shaping; arranging; framing; **die literarische ~ dieses historischen Ereignisses** the literary representation of this historic event; **Hochschule für ~:** academy of art and design; **die künstlerische ~ des Films** the artistic direction of the film; Ⓑ (*Gestaltetes*) form

**Gestaltungs-: ~form** *die* form; **~kraft** *die* creative power; **~prinzip** *das* formal principle

**Gestammel** *das;* **~s** stammering; stuttering; **seine Antwort war nur ein ~:** he was only able to stammer *or* stutter out a reply

**Gestampfe** *das;* **~s** stamping; **das ~ der Baumaschinen** the pounding *or* thumping of the construction plant

**gestand** *1. u. 3. Pers. Sg. Prät. v.* **gestehen**

**gestanden** ❶ *2. Part. v.* **stehen, gestehen.** ❷ *Adj.* **ein ~er Mann** a grown man; **ein ~er Parlamentarier** an experienced *or* seasoned parliamentarian

**geständig** *Adj.* **~ sein** have confessed; **wenn Sie ~ wären** if you confessed; **der ~e Entführer** the self-confessed kidnapper

**Geständnis** /gəˈʃtɛntnɪs/ *das;* **~ses, ~se** confession; **ein ~ ablegen** make a confession; **ich muss dir ein ~ machen** I must make a confession to you

**Gestänge** /gəˈʃtɛŋə/ *das;* **~s, ~** Ⓐ (*Stangen*) struts *pl.;* Ⓑ (*Technik*) linkage; (*des Kolbens*) connecting rod

**Gestank** /gəˈʃtaŋk/ *der;* **~[e]s** (*abwertend*) stench; stink

**Gestänker** /gəˈʃtɛnkɐ/ *das;* **~s** (*ugs.*) trouble-making

**Gestapo** /geˈsta:po/ *die;* **~** (*ns.*) Gestapo

**Gestapo·methoden** *Pl.* (*abwertend*) Gestapo methods

**gestatten** /gəˈʃtatn̩/ ❶ *tr., itr. V.* permit; allow; **jmdm. ~, etw. zu tun** permit *or* allow sb. to do sth.; **„Rauchen nicht gestattet!"** 'no smoking'; **~ Sie eine Bemerkung** allow *or* permit me to make a remark; **~ Sie, dass ich ...** may I ...?; **wenn Sie ~:** if I may; **wenn es die Umstände ~:** if circumstances permit *or* allow; circumstances permitting.

❷ *refl. V.* (*geh.*) **sich** (*Dat.*) **etw. ~:** allow oneself sth.; **wenn ich mir eine Bemerkung ~ darf** if I may be so bold as to make a remark; **sich** (*Dat.*) **~, etw. zu tun** take the liberty of doing sth.; **ich gestatte mir, Sie zu diesem Fest einzuladen** I have pleasure in inviting you to this celebration

**Geste** /ˈgɛstə, ˈge:stə/ *die;* **~, ~n** (*auch fig.*) gesture

**Gesteck** /gəˈʃtɛk/ *das;* **~[e]s, ~e** flower arrangement

**gestehen** *tr., itr. V.* confess; **die Tat** *usw.* **~:** confess to the deed *etc.;* **jmdm. seine Gefühle ~:** confess one's feelings to sb.; **ich muss ~, dass ...** I must confess that ...; **offen gestanden ...** frankly *or* to be honest ...

**Gestehungs·kosten** *Pl.* (*Wirtsch.*) production costs

*old spelling (see note on page 1707)

**Gestein** *das;* **~[e]s, ~e** rock

**Gesteins-: ~ader** *die* rock seam; **~art** *die* type of rock; **~brocken** *der* rock; **~formation** *die* rock formation; **~kunde** *die* petrology; **~masse** *die* rock mass; mass of rock; **~probe** *die* rock sample; **~schicht** *die* stratum *or* layer of rock

**Gestell** /gəˈʃtɛl/ *das;* **~[e]s, ~e** Ⓐ (*für Weinflaschen*) rack; (*zum Wäschetrocknen*) horse; (*für Pflanzen*) planter; Ⓑ (*Unterbau*) frame; (*eines Wagens*) chassis; (*fig. salopp*) legs *pl.;* Ⓒ (*salopp: dünne Person*) scarecrow; **sie ist ein dünnes ~:** she's as skinny as a rake

**Gestellung** *die;* **~, ~en** Ⓐ (*Milit., hist.*) reporting *no art.* for military service; Ⓑ (*Amtsspr.*) provision; **er bat um die ~ weiterer LKWs** he requested that more trucks *or* (*Brit.*) lorries be made available

**Gestellungs·befehl** *der* (*Milit., hist.*) call-up papers *pl.*

**gestelzt** ❶ *2. Part. v.* **stelzen.** ❷ *Adj.* stilted; affected. ❸ *adv.* in a stilted *or* an affected manner

**gestern** /ˈgɛstɐn/ *Adv.* ▶833 Ⓐ yesterday; **~ Morgen/Abend/Mittag** yesterday morning/evening/[at] midday yesterday; **seit ~:** since yesterday; **~ vor einer Woche** a week ago yesterday; **die Zeitung von ~:** yesterday's [news]paper; **die Welt/die Mode von ~:** the world of yesterday *or* yesteryear/yesterday's fashions *pl.;* **das Gestern:** yesterday; the past; **im Gestern leben** live in the past; **von ~ sein** be outdated *or* outmoded; **sie ist nicht von ~** (*ugs.*) she wasn't born yesterday (*coll.*)

**Gestichel** /gəˈʃtɪçl̩/ *das;* **~s** (*ugs. abwertend*) snide remarks *pl. or* comments *pl.* (*coll.*)

**gestiefelt** *Adj.* booted; **der ~e Kater** Puss in Boots; **~ und gespornt** (*ugs. scherzh.*) ready and waiting

**gestiegen** *2. Part. v.* **steigen**

**gestielt** *Adj.* (*Bot.*) stemmed, petiolate ‹leaf›; stemmed, pedunculate ‹flower›; stalked ‹fruit›

**Gestik** /ˈgɛstɪk/ *die;* **~:** gestures *pl.*

**Gestikulation** /gɛstikulaˈtsi̯o:n/ *die;* **~, ~en** gesticulation

**gestikulieren** /gɛstikuˈli:rən/ *itr. V.* gesticulate

**gestimmt** ❶ *2. Part. v.* **stimmen.** ❷ *Adj.* **freudig/heiter ~:** in a joyful/cheerful mood *pred.*

**Gestimmtheit** *die;* **~, ~en** mood

**Gestirn** *das;* **~[e]s, ~e** heavenly body; (*Stern*) star

**gestirnt** *Adj.* (*geh.*) starry

**gestoben** /gəˈʃto:bn̩/ *2. Part. v.* **stieben**

**Gestöber** /gəˈʃtø:bɐ/ *das;* **~s, ~:** snowstorm

**gestochen** /gəˈʃtɔxn̩/ ❶ *2. Part. v.* **stechen.** ❷ *Adj.* **eine ~e Handschrift** extremely neat *or* careful handwriting. ❸ *adv.* **~ scharfe Bilder** crystal clear photographs

**gestohlen** /gəˈʃto:lən/ ❶ *2. Part. v.* **stehlen.** ❷ *Adj.* **der/das kann mir ~ bleiben** (*ugs.*) he can get lost (*coll.*)/you can keep it (*coll.*)

**Gestöhne** *das;* **~s** groaning

**gestorben** /gəˈʃtɔrbn̩/ *2. Part. v.* **sterben**

**gestört** /gəˈʃtø:ɐ̯t/ ❶ *2. Part. v.* **stören.** ❷ *Adj.* disturbed; **ein ~es Verhältnis zu jmdm./etw. haben** have a disturbed relationship with sb./sth.; **geistig ~ sein** be mentally disturbed *or* unbalanced

**gestoßen** *2. Part. v.* **stoßen**

**Gestotter** /gəˈʃtɔtɐ/ *das;* **~s** (*ugs., meist abwertend*) stuttering; stammering; **das ~ des Motors** (*fig.*) the spluttering of the engine

**Gestrampel** *das;* **~s** (*ugs.*) kicking about; (*beim Radfahren*) pedalling

**Gesträuch** /gəˈʃtrɔyç/ *das;* **~[e]s, ~e** shrubbery; bushes *pl.*

**gestreckt** ❶ *2. Part. v.* **strecken.** ❷ *Adj.* full ‹gallop›; 180° ‹angle›; flat ‹trajectory›

**gestreift** ❶ *2. Part. v.* **streifen.** ❷ *Adj.* striped; **längs ~:** with vertical stripes *postpos.*; vertically striped; ‹material› with lengthwise stripes; **quer ~:** diagonally striped; (*horizontal*) horizontally striped

**Gestreite** *das;* **~s** (*ugs.*) quarrelling; squabbling; bickering

**gestreng** *Adj.* (*veralt.*) strict; severe; stern

**gestrichen** ❶ *2. Part. v.* **streichen.** ❷ *Adj.* level ‹measure›; **ein ~er Teelöffel [Zucker** *usw.*] a level teaspoon[ful] [of sugar *etc.*]. ❸ *adv.* **~ voll** full to the brim; ⇒ *auch* **Hose** B; **Nase** B

**gestrig** /ˈgɛstrɪç/ *Adj.* yesterday's; **der ~e Abend** yesterday evening; (*spät*) last night; **der ~e Tag** yesterday; **unser ~es Gespräch** our conversation yesterday; **die ewig Gestrigen** (*fig.*) those who live in the past

**gestritten** /gəˈʃtrɪtn̩/ *2. Part. v.* **streiten**

**Gestrüpp** /gəˈʃtrʏp/ *das;* **~[e]s, ~e** undergrowth

**gestuft** ❶ *2. Part. v.* **stufen.** ❷ *Adj.* stepped ‹gable, façade›; terraced ‹landscape, slope›; graduated ‹colours, shades›; (*fig.: ab~*) staggered ‹working hours›

**Gestühl** /gəˈʃty:l/ *das;* **~[e]s, ~e** seats *pl.;* (*Kirchen~*) pews *pl.*

**Gestümper** /gəˈʃtʏmpɐ/ *das;* **~s** (*ugs. abwertend*) ham-fisted performance; **das ist kein literarisches Kunstwerk, das ist abgeschmacktes ~:** that's no work of literature, it's banal rubbish; **ihr ~ auf der Violine** her amateurish efforts *pl.* on the violin

**gestunken** /gəˈʃtʊŋkn̩/ *2. Part. v.* **stinken**

**Gestus** /ˈgɛstʊs/ *der;* **~** (*geh.*) Ⓐ (*Attitüde*) air; Ⓑ ⇒ **Gestik**

**Gestüt** /gəˈʃty:t/ *das;* **~[e]s, ~e** stud [farm]

**Gesuch** /gəˈzu:x/ *das;* **~[e]s, ~e** request (**um** for); (*Antrag*) application (**um** for); **ein ~ einreichen/zurückziehen** submit/withdraw a request/an application

**Gesuchsteller** /-ʃtɛlɐ/ *der;* **~s, ~, Gesuchstellerin** *die;* **~, ~nen** (*Amtsspr. veralt.*) petitioner

**gesucht** ❶ *2. Part. v.* **suchen.** ❷ *Adj.* Ⓐ (*begehrt*) [much] sought-after; **einer der ~esten Dirigenten** one of the most sought-after conductors; Ⓑ (*gekünstelt*) affected ‹style›; laboured ‹expression›; far-fetched ‹comparison›. ❸ *adv.* ‹express oneself› affectedly

**Gesudel** /gəˈzu:dl̩/ *das;* **~s** (*abwertend*) scrawl; (*fig.: schlechte Literatur*) rubbish

**Gesülze** /gəˈzʏltsə/ *das;* **~s** (*salopp*) drivel (**von** about ‹topic›, from ‹speaker›)

**Gesumm** /gəˈzʊm/ *das;* **~[e]s** buzzing; humming

**Gesums** /gəˈzʊms/ *das;* **~es** (*ugs.*) fuss (**um** about); **dein ~:** the fuss you make

**gesund** /gəˈzʊnt/; **gesünder** /gəˈzʏndɐ/, *seltener:* **gesunder, gesündest...** /gəˈzʏndəst.../, *seltener:* **gesundest...** *Adj.* Ⓐ ▶474 healthy; healthy, strong ‹constitution›; (*fig.*) viable, financially sound ‹company, business›; **wieder ~ werden** get better; recover; **~ sein** ‹person› be healthy; (*im Augenblick*) be in good health; **jmdn. ~ pflegen** nurse sb. back to health; **~ und munter** hale and hearty; **frisch und ~:** fit and well; **aber sonst bist du ~?** (*ugs. iron.*) [are] you sure you're feeling all right? (*coll.*); **bleib ~!** look after yourself!; **das ist ~ für ihn** (*fig.*) that will do him good; Ⓑ (*natürlich, normal*) healthy ‹mistrust, ambition, etc.›; sound ‹construction›; healthy, sound ‹attitude, approach›; **der ~e Menschenverstand** common sense

**gesund-, Gesund-: ~|beten** *tr. V.* **jmdn. ~beten** heal sb. *or* restore sb. to health by prayer; **~beten** *das;* **~~s** faith healing *no art.;* healing by prayer; **~beter** *der;* **~~s, ~~, ~beterin** *die;* **~~, ~~nen** faith healer; **~beterei** *die;* **~beterei** ⇒ **~beten**; **~brunnen** *der* (*geh.*) **die Beschäftigung mit der Jugend/dieser Urlaub ist für mich der reinste ~brunnen** working with young people keeps me young and healthy/this holiday is doing wonders to restore me to health

**Gesunde** /gəˈzʊndə/ *der/die; adj. Dekl.* healthy person

**gesunden** *itr. V.; mit sein* ‹person› recover, get well, regain one's health; ‹tissue› heal; (*fig.*) ‹economy etc.› recover

**Gesundheit** *die;* ~ ▶474 health; **von zarter ~ sein** have a delicate constitution; **bei bester ~ sein** be in the best of health; **auf jmds. ~** (*Akk.*) **trinken/anstoßen** drink sb.'s health; **~ und ein langes Leben!** your very good health!; (*als Geburtstagswunsch*) many happy returns!; **~!** (*ugs.: Zuruf beim Niesen*) bless you!

**gesundheitlich** ❶ *Adj.* **~e Betreuung** health care; **sein ~er Zustand** [the state of] his health; **aus ~en Gründen** for reasons of health. ❷ *adv.* **wie geht es Ihnen ~?** how are you?; **~ geht es ihm nicht sehr gut** he is not in very good health

**gesundheits-, Gesundheits-: ~amt** *das* [local] public health department; **~apostel** *der* (*spött.*) health fanatic; **~attest** *das* certificate of health; health certificate; **~behörde** *die* public health authority; **~fabrik** *die* (*abwertend*) *large, impersonal hospital dispensing assembly-line treatment;* **~fördernd** *Adj.* conducive to health *postpos.;* good for one's health *postpos.;* healthy ‹food, diet, climate, etc.›; **~fürsorge** *die* medical welfare services *pl.;* **~gefährdung** *die* risk to health; **~halber** *Adv.* for reasons of health; for health reasons; **~lehre** *die* ⇒ **Hygiene** c; **~lenker** *der* (*ugs. scherzh.*) 'sit up and beg' handlebars; **~pflege** *die* health care; **~schaden** *der* ▶474 damage *no pl., no indef. art.* to [one's] health; **das kann ~schäden bewirken** that can damage one's health; **einen bleibenden ~schaden davontragen** suffer permanent damage to one's health as a result; **trotz eines leichten ~schadens ...** despite a slight disability ...; **~schädlich** *Adj.* detrimental to [one's] health *postpos.;* unhealthy; **Rauchen ist ~schädlich** smoking can damage your health; **~schutz** *der* (*DDR*) [system of] preventive health care; **~wesen** *das* [public] health service; **~zeugnis** *das* certificate of health; health certificate; **~zustand** *der* state of health

**gesund-: ~|machen** *refl. V.* (*ugs.*) make a pile (*coll.*); **~|schreiben** *unr. tr. V.* pass ‹person› fit; **~|schrumpfen** *itr.* (*auch refl.*) *V.* (*ugs.*) ‹industry, firm› be slimmed down; **eine Firma ~schrumpfen lassen** slim a firm down; **~|stoßen** *unr. refl. V.* (*salopp*) grow fat (*coll.*)

**Gesundung** *die;* ~ (*geh., auch fig.*) recovery

**gesungen** /gəˈzʊŋən/ *2. Part. v.* **singen**

**gesunken** /gəˈzʊŋkn̩/ *2. Part. v.* **sinken**

**Gesurre** /gəˈzʊrə/ *das;* **~s** (*von Insekten*) buzzing; (*einer Filmkamera*) whirring

**Getäfel** /gəˈtɛːfl̩/ *das;* **~s** panelling

**getäfelt** *2. Part. v.* **täfeln**

**getan** /gəˈtaːn/ *2. Part. v.* **tun**

**Getändel** *das;* **~s** (*veralt.*) dalliance

**geteilt** ❶ *2. Part. v.* **teilen.** ❷ *Adj.* (*Bot.*) **~e Blätter** compound leaves

**Getier** *das;* **~[e]s** (*geh.*) Ⓐ (*Tiere*) animals *pl.;* wildlife; Ⓑ (*einzelnes Tier*) animal/insect

**getigert** /gəˈtiːgɐt/ *Adj.* Ⓐ (*mit ungleichen Flecken*) patterned like a tiger *postpos.;* Ⓑ (*mit Querstreifen*) striped

**Getobe** *das;* **~s** romping *or* charging about

**Getose** *das;* **~s** roar

**Getöse** *das;* **~s** [thunderous] roar; (*von vielen Menschen*) din; **mit ~:** with a roar

**getragen** ❶ *2. Part. v.* **tragen.** ❷ *Adj.* solemn ‹music, voice, etc.›. ❸ *adv.* solemnly

**Geträller** *das;* **~s** (*von Vögeln*) trilling; (*von Menschen*) warbling

**Getrampel** *das;* **~s** (*ugs.*) tramping; (*als Zeichen des Beifalls, der Ablehnung*) stamping

**Getränk** /gəˈtrɛŋk/ *das;* **~[e]s, ~e** drink; beverage (*formal*)

**Getränke-: ~automat** *der* drinks machine *or* dispenser; **~bude** *die* drinks stand *or* kiosk; **~karte** *die* list of beverages; (*in einem Restaurant*) wine list; **~stand** *der* drinks stand *or* kiosk; **~steuer** *die: tax on alcoholic drinks*

**Getrappel** *das;* **~s** (*von Hufen, Pferden*) clatter; (*von Füßen*) patter; **das ~ der Tänzer** the patter of the dancers' feet

**Getratsch[e]** *das;* **~s** (*ugs. abwertend*) gossip; gossiping

**getrauen** *refl. V.* dare; **sich [nicht]** *od.* (*seltener:*) **sich** (*Dat.*) **es [nicht] ~, etw. zu tun** [not] dare to do sth.; **ich getraue mich nicht über die Straße** I dare not cross the road; **ich getraue mir den doppelten Salto noch nicht** I dare not attempt the double somersault yet

**Getreide** /gəˈtraidə/ *das;* **~s** grain; corn; **~ anbauen** grow cereals *pl. or* grain

**Getreide-: ~anbau** *der* growing of cereals *or* grain; **~art** *die* kind of grain *or* cereal; **~börse** *die* corn exchange; **~ernte** *die* grain harvest; **~feld** *das* cornfield; **~halm** *der* corn stalk; **~handel** *der* corn trade; **~korn** *das* [cereal] grain; **~land** *das* Ⓐ corn-growing country; Ⓑ (*Ackerland*) corn land; **~produkt** *das* cereal *or* grain product; **~schädling** *der* grain pest; **~speicher** *der* grain silo

**getrennt** ❶ *2. Part. v.* **trennen.** ❷ *Adj.* separate; **~e Kasse führen** pay separately. ❸ *adv.* ‹pay› separately; ‹sleep› in separate rooms; **[von jmdm.] ~ leben** live apart [from sb.]

**Getrennt·schreibung** *die: writing a lexical item as two or more separate words;* **beachten Sie bitte die ~ von „so viel"** please remember that 'so viel' is written as two words

**getreten** *2. Part. v.* **treten**

**getreu** ❶ *Adj.* (*geh.*) Ⓐ (*genau entsprechend*) exact ‹wording›; true, faithful ‹image›; Ⓑ (*treu*) faithful, loyal ‹friend, servant›; **~ bis in den Tod** faithful unto death. ❷ *adv.* (*geh.*) Ⓐ (*genau entsprechend*) ‹report, describe› faithfully, accurately; Ⓑ (*treu*) faithfully, loyally. ❸ *präpositional* (*geh.*) **~ einem Versprechen/einer Abmachung handeln** act in accordance with a promise/an agreement

**Getreue** *der/die; adj. Dekl.* faithful *or* loyal follower

**getreulich** *Adv.* ⇒ **getreu** 2

**Getriebe** *das;* **~s, ~** Ⓐ gears *pl.;* (*in einer Maschine*) gear system; (**~kasten**) gearbox; Ⓑ (*Betriebsamkeit*) hustle and bustle

**Getriebe-: ~bremse** *die* transmission brake; **~gehäuse** *das* gearbox casing; **~kasten** *der* gearbox

**getrieben** *2. Part. v.* **treiben**

**Getriebe·schaden** *der* gearbox damage

**Getriller** /gəˈtrɪlɐ/ *das;* **~s** trilling

**getroffen** *2. Part. v.* **treffen, triefen**

**getrogen** /gəˈtroːgn̩/ *2. Part. v.* **trügen**

**Getrommel** *das;* **~s** (*ugs.*) drumming

**getrost** ❶ *Adj.* confident; **sei ~!** take heart! ❷ *adv.* Ⓐ (*zuversichtlich*) confidently; Ⓑ (*ruhig*) **du kannst das Kind ~ allein lassen** you need have no qualms about leaving the child on its own; **du kannst mir ~ glauben, dass ...** you can take my word for it that ...; **man kann ~ behaupten, dass ...** one can safely say that ...

**getrüffelt** *Adj.* ‹pheasant etc.› [served *or* garnished] with truffles

**getrunken** *2. Part. v.* **trinken**

**Getto** /ˈgɛto/ *das;* **~s, ~s** ghetto

**Getto·bildung** *die* creation of a ghetto/of ghettos

**Getue** /gəˈtuːə/ *das;* **~s** (*ugs. abwertend*) fuss (**um** about); **ein ~ machen** kick up *or* make a fuss; (*sich wichtig machen*) put on airs

**Getümmel** /gəˈtʏml̩/ *das;* **~s** tumult; **das fröhliche/dichte ~:** the merry/crowded bustle; **mitten im dichtesten** *od.* **dicksten ~:** in the thick of it

**getupft** ❶ *2. Part. v.* **tupfen.** ❷ *Adj.* speckled ‹garment, fabric, etc.›

**Getuschel** *das;* **~s** (*ugs.*) whispering

**geübt** /gəˈ|yːpt/ ❶ *2. Part. v.* **üben.** ❷ *Adj.* experienced, accomplished, proficient ‹horseman, speaker, etc.›; trained, practised ‹eye, ear›; **in etw.** (*Dat.*) **~ sein** be proficient at sth.

**Gevatter** /gəˈfatɐ/ *der;* **~s** *od.* (*älter:*) **~n, ~n** (*veralt.*) Ⓐ (*Pate*) godfather; **[bei jmdm.] zu ~ stehen** act as *or* be [sb.'s] godfather; **jmdn. zu ~ bitten** ask sb. to act as *or* be godfather; **~ Tod** (*dicht. veralt.*) (*im Märchen*) Godfather Death; (*fig.*) the Grim Reaper; **bei etw. ~ stehen** (*scherzh.*) be the inspiration behind sth.; Ⓑ (*veralt., noch scherzh.*) **Grüß Gott, ~!** greetings, friend!

**Gevatterin** *die;* **~, ~nen** Ⓐ (*Patin*) godmother; Ⓑ (*veralt., noch scherzh.*) ⇒ **Gevatter** B

**Geviert** *das;* **~[e]s, ~e** Ⓐ (*veralt.*) ⇒ **Quadrat**; Ⓑ (*Druckw.*) quadrat; quad

**GEW** *Abk.* **Gewerkschaft Erziehung und Wissenschaft** Educators' Union

**Gewächs** /gəˈvɛks/ *das;* **~es, ~e** Ⓐ (*Pflanze*) plant; Ⓑ (*Weinsorte*) wine; (*Weinjahrgang*) vintage; Ⓒ ▶474 (*Med.: Geschwulst*) growth

**gewachsen** ❶ *2. Part. v.* **wachsen.** ❷ *in* **jmdm./einer Sache ~ sein** be a match for sb./be equal to sth.

**Gewächs·haus** *das* greenhouse; glasshouse; (*Treibhaus*) hothouse

**gewagt** ❶ *2. Part. v.* **wagen.** ❷ *Adj.* Ⓐ (*kühn*) daring; (*gefährlich*) risky; Ⓑ (*fast anstößig*) risqué ‹joke, song, etc.›; daring ‹neckline etc.›

**gewählt** ❶ *2. Part. v.* **wählen.** ❷ *Adj.* refined, elegant ‹style, manner of expression, etc.›; refined ‹taste›. ❸ *adv.* in a refined manner; elegantly

**Gewähltheit** *die;* ~ (*des Ausdrucks*) refinement; (*der Kleidung*) elegance

**gewahr** /gəˈvaːɐ̯/ *in* **jmdn./etw.** *od.* (*geh.*) **jmds./einer Sache ~ werden** catch sight of sb./sth.; **etw.** (*Akk.*) *od.* (*geh.*) **einer Sache** (*Gen.*) **~ werden** (*etw. erkennen, feststellen*) become aware of sth.

**Gewähr** /gəˈvɛːɐ̯/ *die;* **~:** guarantee; **für etw. ~ leisten/die ~ geben** guarantee sth.; **die ~ für etw. übernehmen/bieten** guarantee sth.; **keine ~ übernehmen** be unable to guarantee sth.; **die Angaben erfolgen ohne ~:** no responsibility is accepted for the accuracy of this information; **ohne ~** (*auf Fahrplänen usw.*) subject to change

**gewahren** *tr. V.* (*geh.*) become aware of

**gewähren** ❶ *tr. V.* Ⓐ (*zugestehen*) give; grant, give ‹asylum, credit, loan›; **jmdm. einen Aufschub ~:** grant *or* allow sb. a period of grace; Ⓑ (*erfüllen*) grant; **jmdm. seinen Wunsch/seine Bitte** *usw.* **~:** grant sb.'s wish/request *etc.;* Ⓒ (*bieten*) offer ‹advantage›; give ‹pleasure, joy›. ❷ *itr. V.: in* **jmdn. ~ lassen** let sb. do as he/she likes; **lass ihn nur ~:** leave him alone

**gewähr·leisten** *tr. V.* guarantee; ensure ‹safety›

**Gewähr·leistung** *die* Ⓐ guarantee; (*von Sicherheit*) ensuring; Ⓑ ⇒ **Mängelhaftung**

**Gewahrsam** /gəˈvaːɐ̯zaːm/ *der;* **~s** Ⓐ (*Obhut*) safe keeping; **etw. in ~ nehmen/behalten** take sth. into safe keeping/keep sth. safe; **jmdm. etw. in ~ geben** give sth. to sb. for safe keeping; Ⓑ (*Haft*) custody; **jmdn. in ~ bringen** take sb. into custody; **jmdn. in polizeilichen ~ bringen** hand sb. over to the police; **sich in [polizeilichem] ~ befinden** be in [police] custody

**Gewährs-: ~mann** *der; Pl.* **~männer** *od.* **~leute, ~person** *die* informant; source

**Gewährung** *die;* ~ ⇒ **gewähren** 1: granting; giving; offering

**Gewalt** /gəˈvalt/ *die;* **~, ~en** Ⓐ (*Macht, Befugnis*) power; **die elterliche/richterliche ~:** parental/judicial power *or* authority; **jmdn. in seiner ~ haben** have sb. in one's power; **jmdn./ein Land in seine ~ bekommen/bringen** catch sb./bring a country under one's control; **in** *od.* **unter jmds. ~** (*Dat.*) **stehen** be in sb.'s power; **die ~ über sein Fahrzeug verlieren** (*fig.*) lose control of one's vehicle; **sich/seine Beine in der ~ haben** have oneself under control/have control over one's legs; Ⓑ (*Willkür*) force; **der ~ weichen** yield to force; **etw. mit ~ zu erreichen suchen** try to achieve sth. by force; **sich** (*Dat.*) **~ antun [müssen]** [have to] force oneself; **er versuchte mit aller ~, seinen Ehrgeiz zu befriedigen** he did everything he could to achieve his ambition; **etw. mit [aller] ~ wollen** want sth. desperately; Ⓒ (*körperliche Kraft*) force; violence;

~ **anwenden** use force *or* violence; **etw. mit ~ öffnen** force sth. open; **mit roher/brutaler ~:** with brute force; **einer Frau ~ antun** (*geh. verhüll.*) violate a woman; **D** (*geh.: elementare Kraft*) force; **die ~ der Leidenschaft/Rede** (*fig.*) the power of passion/oratory; **höhere ~ [sein]** [be] an act of God; **im Falle höherer ~:** in the case of an act of God/acts of God

**Gewalt-: ~akt** *der* act of violence; **~androhung** *die* threat of violence; **~anwendung** *die* use of force *or* violence; **~einwirkung** *die:* **keinerlei Spuren von ~einwirkung aufweisen** show no signs of violence; **durch ~einwirkung sterben** die as a result of violence

**Gewalten-: ~teilung** *die*, **~trennung** *die* separation of powers

**Gewalt-: ~herrschaft** *die* tyranny; despotism; **~herrscher** *der*, **~herrscherin** *die* tyrant; despot

**gewaltig** **1** *Adj.* **A** (*immens*) enormous, huge ‹sum, amount, difference, loss›; tremendous ‹progress›; **B** (*imponierend*) mighty, huge, massive ‹wall, pillar, building, rock›; monumental ‹literary work etc.›; mighty ‹spectacle of nature›; **C** (*mächtig; auch fig.*) powerful. **2** *adv.* (*ugs.: sehr, überaus*) **sich ~ irren/täuschen** be very much mistaken; **es wundert mich/imponiert mir ~:** I'm amazed/tremendously impressed; **etw. ist ~ gestiegen/gesunken** sth. has risen/dropped sharply

**-gewaltige** *der/die; adj. Dekl.* boss; **die Zeitungs~n** the press barons

**Gewaltigkeit** *die;* ~ (*von Mauern, Felsen, Gebäuden usw.*) mightiness; massiveness

**gewalt-, Gewalt-: ~kur** *die* (*ugs.*) drastic measures *pl. or* methods *pl.;* drastic treatment *no indef. art.;* **~los** **1** *Adj.* non-violent; **2** *adv.* without violence; **~losigkeit** *die;* **~~:** non-violence; **~marsch** *der* forced march; **~maßnahme** *die* violent measure; **er schreckte vor ~maßnahmen nicht zurück** he was not afraid to use force; **~mensch** *der* brutal person; brute

**gewaltsam** **1** *Adj.* forcible ‹expulsion›; enforced ‹separation›; violent ‹death›; **ein ~es Ende nehmen** meet a violent death. **2** *adv.* forcibly; **~ die Tür öffnen** open the door by force; **sich ~ zurückhalten/wach halten** exercise the utmost restraint/force oneself to keep awake; **~ ums Leben kommen** meet a violent death

**Gewaltsamkeit** *die;* **~:** violence

**gewalt-, Gewalt-: ~streich** *der* bold surprise action; **~tat** *die* ⇒ **~verbrechen**; **~tätig** *Adj.* violent; **~tätigkeit** *die* **A** (*gewalttätige Art*) violence; **B** ⇒ **~akt**; **~verbrechen** *das* crime of violence; **~verbrecher** *der*, **~verbrecherin** *die* violent criminal; **~verzicht** *der* renunciation of the use of force; **~verzichts·abkommen** *das* non-aggression treaty

**Gewand** *das;* **~[e]s, Gewänder** /gəˈvɛndɐ/ (*geh.*) robe; gown; (*Abendkleid*) gown; **geistliche Gewänder** vestments; **im neuen ~** (*fig.*) dressed up as new; **ab nächster Woche erscheint die Zeitung in einem neuen ~** (*fig.*) from next week the newspaper will have a new look

**gewandet** *Adj.* (*veralt./scherzh.*) clad; apparelled (*arch.*)

**Gewand-: ~haus** *das* (*hist.*) cloth hall; **~meister** *der* wardrobe master; **~meisterin** *die* wardrobe mistress

**gewandt** /gəˈvant/ **1** *2. Part. v.* **wenden.** **2** *Adj.* skilful; (*körperlich*) agile; expert ‹skier›; **ein ~es Auftreten/~e Umgangsformen** an easy, confident manner/easy social manners. **3** *adv.* skilfully; (*körperlich*) agilely

**Gewandtheit** *die;* ~ ⇒ **gewandt** 2: skill; skilfulness; agility; expertness; easiness

**gewann** /gəˈvan/ *1. u. 3. Pers. Sg. Prät. v.* **gewinnen**

**gewärtig** /gəˈvɛrtɪç/ *in* **einer Sache** (*Gen.*) **~ sein** (*geh.*) be prepared for sth.; **~ sein, dass ...** expect that ...

*old spelling (see note on page 1707)

**gewärtigen** *tr. V.* (*geh.*) (*erwarten*) expect; (*gefasst sein auf*) be prepared for

**Gewäsch** /gəˈvɛʃ/ *das;* **~[e]s** (*ugs. abwertend*) twaddle; garbage (*Amer. coll.*)

**gewaschen** *2. Part. v.* **waschen**

**Gewässer** /gəˈvɛsɐ/ *das;* **~s, ~** stretch of water; **ein fließendes/stehendes ~:** a stretch of running/standing water; **sich in arktische ~ wagen** venture into Arctic waters

**Gewässer-: ~kunde** *die* hydrography *no art.;* **~schutz** *der* prevention of water pollution

**Gewebe** *das;* **~s, ~** **A** (*Stoff*) fabric; **B** ▶ 471 (*Med., Biol.*) tissue

**Gewebs-: ~transplantation** *die*, **~verpflanzung** *die* (*Med.*) tissue graft

**Gewehr** /gəˈveːɐ̯/ *das;* **~[e]s, ~e** rifle; (*Schrot~*) shotgun; **mit dem ~ auf jmdn./etw. zielen** aim [one's rifle/shotgun] at sb./sth.; **~ ab!** (*Milit.*) order arms!; **das ~ über!** (*Milit.*) shoulder arms!; **präsentiert das ~!** (*Milit.*) present arms!; **~ bei Fuß stehen** be at the ready

**Gewehr-: ~feuer** *das* rifle fire; **~kolben** *der* rifle/shotgun butt; **~kugel** *die* rifle bullet; **~lauf** *der* rifle/shotgun barrel; **~riemen** *der* rifle/shotgun sling; **~schloss, *~schloß** *das* lock of a rifle/shotgun; **~schuss, *~schuß** *der* rifle shot

**Geweih** /gəˈvai/ *das;* **~[e]s, ~e** antlers *pl.;* **~e/ein ~:** sets of antlers/a set of antlers

**Geweih·stange** *die* (*Jägerspr.*) beam; main trunk

**Gewerbe** *das;* **~s, ~** **A** business; (*Handel, Handwerk*) trade; **ein dunkles/schmutziges ~:** a shady/dirty business; **in einem ~ tätig sein** be in a trade/business; **das horizontale ~** (*ugs. scherzh.*), **das älteste ~ der Welt** (*verhüll. scherzh.*) the oldest profession [in the world] (*joc.*); **B** (*kleine Betriebe*) [small and medium-sized] businesses and industries

**Gewerbe·aufsicht** *die: enforcement of laws governing health and safety and conditions of work*

**Gewerbe·aufsichts·amt** *das* ≈ factory inspectorate (*authority with responsibility for* **Gewerbeaufsicht**)

**Gewerbe-: ~betrieb** *der* (*des Handels*) commercial enterprise; business; (*der Industrie*) industrial enterprise; business; **~freiheit** *die* right to carry on a business *or* trade; **~gebiet** *das* trading estate; **~lehrer** *der*, **~lehrerin** *die* teacher in a trade school; **~ordnung** *die* laws *pl.* governing trade and industry; **~schein** *der* licence to carry on a business *or* trade; **~schule** *die* trade school; **~steuer** *die* trade tax; **~tätigkeit** *die* business activities *pl.;* **~treibende** *der/die; adj. Dekl.* tradesman/tradeswoman; **~zweig** *der* branch of trade

**gewerblich** **1** *Adj.* commercial; business *attrib.;* (*industriell*) industrial; trade *attrib.* ‹union, apprentice›; **~e Nutzung** use for commercial *or* business/industrial purposes. **2** *adv.* **~ tätig sein** work; **etw. ~ nutzen** use sth. for commercial *or* business/industrial purposes

**gewerbs·mäßig** **1** *Adj.* professional; **~e Unzucht** prostitution; **ein ~er Hehler** a receiver of stolen goods. **2** *adv.* **etw. ~ betreiben** do sth. professionally *or* for gain

**Gewerkschaft** /gəˈvɛrkʃaft/ *die;* **~, ~en** **A** trade union; **B** (*veralt.: Bergbauunternehmen*) *mining company whose capital is divided into shares of no par value*

**Gewerkschaft[l]er** *der;* **~s, ~, Gewerkschaft[l]erin** *die;* **~, ~nen** trade unionist

**gewerkschaftlich** **1** *Adj.* [trade] union *attrib.;* ‹rights, duties› as a [trade] union member; **~er Vertrauensmann/~e Vertrauensfrau** shop steward; **der ~e Kampf** the struggle of the trade union movement. **2** *adv.* **~ organisiert sein** belong to a [trade] union; **sich ~ engagieren** devote oneself to trade union work

**gewerkschafts-, Gewerkschafts-: ~arbeit** *die* work for *or* on behalf of the/a [trade] union; **~bewegung** *die* [trade] union movement; **~boss, *~boß** *der* (*ugs. abwertend*) [trade] union boss; **~bund** *der* federation of trade unions; ≈ Trades Union Congress (*Brit.*); ≈ AFL-CIO (*Amer.*); **~eigen** *Adj.* owned by a [trade] union *postpos.;* **~führer** *der*, **~führerin** *die* [trade] union leader; **~funktionär** *der*, **~funktionärin** *die* [trade] union official; **~kongress, *~kongreß** *der* ⇒ **~tag**; **~mitglied** *das* member of a [trade] union; **~tag** *der* [trade] union conference

**Gewese** *das;* **~s** (*ugs.*) fuss; **ein großes ~ um etw. machen** kick up *or* make a lot of fuss about sth.

**gewesen** **1** *2. Part. v.* **sein**[1]. **2** *Adj.* (*bes. österr.*) former

**gewichen** *2. Part. v.* **weichen**

**gewichst** /gəˈvɪkst/ **1** *2. Part. v.* **wichsen.** **2** *Adj.* (*ugs.*) smart

**Gewicht** /gəˈvɪçt/ *das;* **~[e]s, ~e** ▶ 353 (*auch Physik, auch fig.*) weight; **ein ~ von 75 kg/ein großes ~ haben** weigh 75 kg/be very heavy; **das zulässige ~:** the maximum permitted weight; the weight limit; **das spezifische ~** (*Physik*) the specific gravity; **sein ~ halten** stay the same weight; **etw. nach ~ verkaufen** sell sth. by weight; **seine Meinung/eine adlige Abstammung hat noch großes ~:** his opinion still carries a great deal of weight/it still counts for a great deal to be of noble descent; **einer Sache** (*Dat.*) **[kein] ~ beimessen** *od.* **beilegen** attach [no] importance to sth.; **sein ganzes ~ in die Waagschale werfen** throw one's whole weight behind it; **auf etw.** (*Akk.*) **~ legen** attach importance to sth.; **[nicht] ins ~ fallen** be of [no] consequence

**gewichten** *tr. V.* **A** (*Statistik*) weight; **B** (*Schwerpunkte festsetzen*) evaluate

**Gewicht-: ~heben** *das;* **~~s** weightlifting; **~heber** *der;* **~~s, ~~, ~heberin** *die;* **~~, ~~nen** weightlifter

**gewichtig** *Adj.* **A** (*veralt.: schwer*) heavy; weighty; **jmd. ist ~** (*scherzh.*) sb. is impressively large; **B** (*bedeutungsvoll*) weighty, important ‹reason, question, decision, etc.›; **eine ~e Persönlichkeit** an important person *or* figure; **~ tun** act pompously; **ein ~es Gesicht machen** (*iron.*) put on *or* assume an air of importance

**Gewichtigkeit** *die;* ~ ⇒ **gewichtig** B: importance; weightiness

**gewichts-, Gewichts-: ~abnahme** *die* decrease *or* reduction in weight; (*~verlust*) loss of weight; **~angabe** *die* indication of weight; **~klasse** *die* **A** (*Sport*) weight [division *or* class]; **B** (*Kaufmannsspr.*) weight class; **Eier nach ~klassen sortieren** grade eggs according to weight; **~los** *Adj.* **A** ⇒ **schwerelos** 1; **B** (*bedeutungslos*) lacking in substance *postpos.;* **~verlagerung** *die* shift *or* transfer of weight; (*fig.*) shift in *or* of emphasis; **~verlust** *der* loss of weight; **~zunahme** *die* increase in weight

**Gewichtung** *die;* **~, ~en** evaluation

**gewieft** /gəˈviːft/ *Adj.* (*ugs.*) cunning; wily

**gewiegt** **1** *2. Part. v.* **wiegen**[2]. **2** *Adj.* ⇒ **gewieft**

**Gewieher** /gəˈviːɐ/ *das;* **~s** **A** (*Wiehern*) neighing; **B** (*salopp: Gelächter*) guffawing; braying laughter

**gewiesen** *2. Part. v.* **weisen**

**gewillt** /gəˈvɪlt/ *Adj.: in* **~/nicht ~ sein, etw. zu tun** be willing/unwilling to do sth.

**Gewimmel** *das;* **~s** throng; milling crowd; (*von Insekten*) teeming mass

**Gewimmer** *das;* **~s** whimpering

**Gewinde** *das;* **~s, ~** **A** (*Technik*) thread; **B** (*veralt.: Girlande*) garland

**Gewinde-: ~bohrer** *der* [screw] tap; **~gang** *der* turn [of a thread]; **~schneiden** *das;* **~~s** thread-cutting; (*innen*) tapping; **~stift** *der* grub screw

**Gewinn** /gəˈvɪn/ *der;* **~[e]s, ~e** **A** (*Reinertrag*) profit; **aus etw. ~ schlagen** *od.* **ziehen** make a profit out of sth.; **mit ~ wirtschaften** operate at a profit *or* profitably; **etw. mit ~ verkaufen** sell sth. at a

g

# Gewichte

***1 Gramm*** = one gram = 0.035 ounce (oz)
***1 Kilogramm*** = one kilogram = 2.205 pounds (lb)
***1 Tonne*** = one tonne = 2, 205 lb *od.* 19.684 hundredweight (cwt)

Es ist zu beachten, dass das britische Pfund (**pound**) nur 454 Gramm hat. Dagegen ist die britische Tonne (**ton**) einige Kilogramm mehr als die metrische (1 016 kg).

## Personen

***Wie viel wiegen Sie?***
= How much do you weigh?, What's your weight?

***Ich wiege 76 Kilo***
≈ I weigh 12 stone (*brit.*) *od.* 168 pounds (*amerik.*)

***Er hat zugenommen***
= He has put on weight

***Sie hat stark abgenommen***
= She has lost a lot of weight

***Mit mehr als 114 Kilo hat er Übergewicht***
= At over 18 stone (*brit.*) *od.* 250 pounds (*amerik.*) he is overweight

## Dinge

***Wie viel wiegt das Paket?***
= How much does the parcel weigh?, What's the weight of the parcel?

***Es wiegt ungefähr zwei Kilo***
= It weighs about two kilograms, ≈ It weighs about four pounds

***Mein Gepäck hat fünf Kilo Übergewicht***
= My baggage is five kilograms over weight, ≈ My baggage is ten pounds over weight

***A hat das gleiche Gewicht wie B***
= A is the same weight as B

***A und B sind gleich schwer***
= A and B are the same weight

***125 Gramm Leberwurst***
= 125 grams of liver sausage, ≈ 4 oz of liver sausage

***6 Pfund Kartoffeln***
≈ 6 pounds of potatoes

***Sie werden kiloweise verkauft***
= They are sold by the kilo

***eine 500-Gramm-Schachtel Pralinen***
≈ a pound box of chocolates

profit; Ⓑ (*Preis einer Lotterie*) prize; (*beim Wetten, Kartenspiel usw.*) winnings *pl.*; **die ∼e auslosen** draw the winners *or* winning numbers; **jedes zweite Los ist ein ∼:** every other ticket is a winner; Ⓒ (*Nutzen*) gain; profit; **das war ein großer ∼ für uns** we gained a great deal *or* profited greatly from it; **der neue Spieler ist ein [großer] ∼ für unsere Mannschaft** the new player is a valuable addition to our team; Ⓓ (*Sieg*) win; **auf ∼ stehen** (*Schach*) be in a winning position

**gewinn-, Gewinn-: ∼anteil** *der* (*Wirtsch.*) share of the profits; **∼beteiligung** *die* (*Wirtsch.*) profit sharing; (*Betrag*) profit-sharing bonus; **gegen ∼beteiligung** in return for a share of the profits; **∼bringend** *Adj.* Ⓐ profitable; lucrative; Ⓑ (*nutzbringend*) profitable; valuable ‹knowledge, information›; **∼chance** *die* chance of winning

**gewinnen** /gəˈvɪnən/ ❶ *unr. tr. V.* Ⓐ (*siegen in*) win ‹contest, race, etc.›; **es [nicht] über sich ∼, etw. zu tun** (*geh. veralt.*) [not] bring oneself to do sth.; ⇒ *auch* **Spiel** B; Ⓑ (*erringen, erreichen, erhalten*) gain, win ‹respect, sympathy, etc.›; gain ‹time, lead, influence, validity, confidence›; win ‹prize›; **Klarheit über etw.** (*Akk.*) **∼:** become clear in one's mind about sth.; **wie gewonnen, so zerronnen** (*Spr.*) easy come, easy go; ⇒ *auch* **Abstand** C; **Oberhand**; Ⓒ (*Unterstützung erlangen*) **jmdn. für etw. ∼:** win sb. over [to sth.]; **jmdn. als Kunden/Freund ∼:** win sb. as a customer/friend; Ⓓ (*abbauen, fördern*) mine, extract ‹coal, ore, metal›; recover ‹oil›; Ⓔ (*erzeugen*) produce (**aus** from); (*durch Recycling*) reclaim; recover.
❷ *unr. itr. V.* Ⓐ win (**bei** at); **in der Lotterie ∼:** win [a prize] in the lottery; **jedes zweite Los gewinnt!** every other ticket [is] a winner!; Ⓑ (*sich vorteilhaft verändern*) improve; Ⓒ (*zunehmen*) **an Höhe/Fahrt ∼:** gain height/gain *or* pick up speed; **an Bedeutung ∼:** gain in importance

**gewinnend** ❶ *Adj.* winning, engaging, winsome ‹manner, smile, way›; charming ‹manners›. ❷ *adv.* ‹smile› winningly, engagingly, winsomely

**Gewinner** *der;* **∼s, ∼** , **Gewinnerin** *die;* **∼, ∼nen** winner

**Gewinner·straße** *die* (*Sport, Jargon*) **auf der ∼ sein** be set *or* heading for victory

**gewinn-, Gewinn-: ∼los** *das* winning ticket; **∼nummer** *die* winning number; **∼quote** *die* share of prize money; **∼satz** *der* (*Sport*) **über fünf ∼sätze spielen** (*Tennis*) play the best of five sets; (*Tischtennis*) play the best of five games; **der fünfte Satz war ihr ∼satz** (*Tennis*) she won in the fifth set; (*Tischtennis*) she won in the fifth game; **∼spanne** *die* profit margin; **∼streben** *das* pursuit of profit; **∼sucht** *die* greed for profit; **∼süchtig** *Adj.* greedy for profits *pred.*; **in ∼süchtiger Absicht** (*Rechtsspr.*) with the intention of making unreasonably high profits; **∼trächtig** *Adj.* profitable; lucrative

***Gewinnummer** *die* ⇒ **Gewinnnummer**

**Gewinn-und-Verlust-Rechnung** *die* (*Wirtsch.*) profit and loss account

**Gewinnung** *die;* **∼** Ⓐ (*von Kohle, Erz usw.*) mining; extraction; (*von Öl*) recovery; (*von Metall aus Erz*) extraction; Ⓑ (*Erzeugung*) production

**Gewinn·zahl** *die* winning number

**Gewinsel** *das;* **∼s** (*abwertend*) Ⓐ whimpering; whining; Ⓑ (*das Klagen, Bitten*) whining

**Gewirr** *das;* **∼[e]s** Ⓐ (*wirres Knäuel*) tangle; Ⓑ (*Durcheinander*) **ein ∼ von Ästen** a maze of branches; **ein ∼ von Paragraphen** a maze *or* jungle of regulations; **ein ∼ von Stimmen** a [confused] babble of voices

**Gewisper** *das;* **∼s** whispering

**gewiss, *gewiß** /gəˈvɪs/ ❶ *Adj.* Ⓐ (*nicht sehr viel/groß*) certain; **in gewisser Beziehung** in some respects; **eine gewisse Ähnlichkeit/Distanz** a certain resemblance/distance; ⇒ *auch* **Etwas**; **Maß**[1] D; Ⓑ (*sicher*) certain (+ *Gen.* of); **etw. ist jmdm. ∼:** sb. is certain *or* sure of sth.; **wir können seiner Hilfe ∼ sein** we can be certain *or* sure of his help; we can count on his help; **man weiß nichts Gewisses** nothing certain *or* definite is known. ❷ *adv.* certainly; **ja** *od.* **aber ∼ [doch]!** but of course!; **du hast ∼ nichts dagegen, wenn ...** I'm sure you won't mind if ...; **ich weiß es ganz ∼:** I'm sure *or* certain of it

**Gewissen** *das;* **∼s, ∼** conscience; **ein gutes/schlechtes ∼:** a clear/guilty *or* bad conscience; **ruhigen ∼s etw. tun** do sth. with a clear conscience; **mit gutem ∼:** with a clear conscience; **ein gutes ∼ ist ein sanftes Ruhekissen** (*Spr.*) one can sleep more easily with a clear conscience; **sich** (*Dat.*) **kein ∼ daraus machen, etw. zu tun** have no scruples *or* qualms about doing sth.; **etw./jmdn. auf dem ∼ haben** have sth./sb. on one's conscience; **jmdm. ins ∼ reden [, etw. zu tun]** have a serious talk with sb. [and persuade him/her to do sth.]; ⇒ *auch* **Wissen**

**gewissenhaft** ❶ *Adj.* conscientious. ❷ *adv.* conscientiously

**Gewissenhaftigkeit** *die;* **∼** conscientiousness

**gewissen·los** ❶ *Adj.* conscienceless; unscrupulous; **er ist vollkommen ∼:** he is completely without conscience. ❷ *adv.* **∼ handeln** act with a complete lack of conscience

**Gewissenlosigkeit** *die;* **∼** Ⓐ (*gewissenloses Wesen*) lack of conscience; Ⓑ (*gewissenloses Handeln*) unscrupulous act; **wie konntest du eine solche ∼ begehen?** how could you show such a lack of conscience?

**Gewissens-: ∼bisse** *Pl.* pangs of conscience; **sich** (*Dat.*) **∼bisse über etw.** (*Akk.*) **machen** have a guilty conscience about sth.; **∼entscheidung** *die* decision on a matter of conscience; **∼frage** *die* question *or* matter of conscience; matter for one's conscience; **∼freiheit** *die* freedom of conscience; **∼gründe** *Pl.* reasons of conscience; **aus ∼gründen** for reasons of conscience; **∼konflikt** *der* moral conflict; **∼not** *die* moral dilemma; **∼qual** *die:* **∼qual[en]** agonies *pl.* of conscience

**gewissermaßen** *Adv.* (*sozusagen*) as it were; (*in gewissem Sinne*) to a certain extent

**Gewissheit, *Gewißheit** *die;* **∼, ∼en** certainty; **wir haben noch keine ∼, ob ...** we still do not know for certain whether ...; **sich** (*Dat.*) **∼ verschaffen** find out for certain; **zur ∼ werden** turn into certainty

**gewisslich, *gewißlich** *Adv.* (*veralt.*) ⇒ **gewiss** 2

**Gewitter** /gəˈvɪtɐ/ *das;* **∼s, ∼** thunderstorm; (*fig.*) storm

**Gewitter·front** *die* storm front

**gewitterig** *Adj.* ⇒ **gewittrig**

**gewittern** *itr. V.* (*unpers.*) **es gewitterte/wird bald ∼:** there was/will soon be thunder and lightning

**Gewitter-: ∼neigung** *die* likelihood of thunderstorms; **∼regen** *der,* **∼schauer** *der*

g

thundery shower; **~sturm** *der* thunderstorm; **~wolke** *die* thundercloud

**gewittrig** /gə'vɪtrɪç/ *Adj.* thundery; **~e Schwüle** sultry heat

**gewitzigt** /gə'vɪtsɪçt/ *Adj.* [A] (*klüger geworden*) wiser; **durch Erfahrung/Schaden ~ sein** have learnt from experience/one's mistakes; [B] ⇒ **gewitzt**

**gewitzt** /gə'vɪts:t/ *Adj.* shrewd; **ein ~er Junge** a smart lad

**gewoben** /gə'vo:bn̩/ *2. Part. v.* **weben**

**Gewoge** *das;* **~s** (*von einem Kornfeld usw.*) waving; (*von Gedanken*) surge; **das ~ der Menschenmenge** the surging back and forth of the crowd

**gewogen** ❶ *2. Part. v.* **wiegen**. ❷ *Adj.* (*geh.*) well disposed, favourably inclined (+ *Dat.* towards)

**Gewogenheit** *die;* ~ (*geh.*) favourable attitude; **bei aller ~, die ich Ihnen entgegenbringe, kann ich nicht ...** although I'm favourably disposed towards you, I can't ...

**gewöhnen** /gə'vø:nən/ ❶ *tr. V.* **jmdn. an jmdn./etw. ~:** get sb. used *or* accustomed to sb./sth.; accustom sb. to sb./sth.; **Kinder an Sauberkeit ~:** get children used to being clean and tidy; **an jmdn./etw. gewöhnt sein** be used *or* accustomed to sb./sth.. ❷ *refl. V.* **sich an jmdn./etw. ~:** get used *or* get *or* become accustomed to sb./sth.; accustom oneself to sb./sth.; **sich daran ~ müssen, dass ...** have to get used to the fact that ...

**Gewohnheit** /gə'vo:nhai:t/ *die;* ~, **~en** habit; **die ~ haben, etw. zu tun** be in the habit of doing sth.; **das ist ihm zur ~ geworden** this has become a habit with him; **sich** (*Dat.*) **etw. zur ~ machen** make a habit of sth.; **nach alter ~:** from long-established habit; **etw. aus ~ tun** do sth. out of habit *or* from force of habit; **die Macht der ~:** the force of habit

**gewohnheits-, Gewohnheits-: ~gemäß** *Adv.* as is/was his/her *etc.* custom; **~mäßig** ❶ *Adj.* habitual ‹drinker etc.›; automatic ‹reaction etc.›; ❷ *adv.* [A] (*regelmäßig*) habitually; [B] (*einer Gewohnheit folgend*) as is/was my/his *etc.* habit; **~mensch** *der* creature of habit; **~recht** *das* (*Rechtsw.*) [A] (*System*) common law; [B] (*einzelnes Recht*) established right; **~sache** *die* matter *or* question of habit; **~tier** *das* (*scherzh.*) creature of habit; **der Mensch ist ein ~tier** man is a creature of habit; **~trinker** *der*, **~trinkerin** *die* habitual drinker; **~verbrecher** *der*, **~verbrecherin** *die* (*Rechtsw.*) habitual criminal

**gewöhnlich** /gə'vø:nlɪç/ ❶ *Adj.* [A] (*alltäglich*) normal; ordinary; **im ~en Leben** in ordinary *or* everyday life; **ein ~er Sterblicher** an ordinary mortal; [B] (*gewohnt, üblich*) usual; normal; customary; [C] (*abwertend: ordinär*) common. ❷ *adv.* [A] **[für] ~:** usually; normally; **wie ~:** as usual; [B] (*abwertend: ordinär*) in a common way

**Gewöhnlichkeit** *die;* ~ (*abwertend*) commonness

**gewohnt** ❶ *2. Part. v.* **wohnen**. ❷ *Adj.* [A] (*vertraut*) usual; **zur ~en Zeit/Stunde** at the usual *or* normal *or* customary time; **in ~er** *od.* **auf ~e Weise** in the/one's usual manner *or* way; [B] **etw.** (*Akk.*) **~ sein** be used *or* accustomed to sth.; **es ~ sein, etw. zu tun** be used *or* accustomed to doing sth.

**gewohntermaßen** *Adv.* as usual

**Gewöhnung** *die;* ~ [A] habituation (**an** + *Akk.* to); [B] (*Sucht*) habit; addiction

**Gewölbe** /gə'vœlbə/ *das;* **~s**, ~ vault; **das blaue ~ des Himmels** (*fig.*) the blue vault of the sky; **das ~ der Burg** the vaults *pl.* of the castle

**Gewölk** /gə'vœlk/ *das;* **~[e]s** clouds *pl.*

**gewonnen** /gə'vɔnən/ *2. Part. v.* **gewinnen**

**geworben** /gə'vɔrbn̩/ *2. Part. v.* **werben**

**geworfen** /gə'vɔrfn̩/ *2. Part. v.* **werfen**

**gewrungen** /gə'vrʊŋən/ *2. Part. v.* **wringen**

**Gewühl** *das;* **~[e]s** [A] milling crowd; **das ~ der Menschenmassen** the milling crowd [of people]; [B] (*das Wühlen*) rooting about

**gewunden** *2. Part. v.* **winden**

**gewunken** /gə'vʊŋkn̩/ *2. Part. v.* **winken**

**gewürfelt** ❶ *2. Part. v.* **würfeln**. ❷ *Adj.* (*kariert*) check; checked

**Gewürm** /gə'vʏrm/ *das;* **~[e]s**, **~e** (*oft abwertend*) worms *pl.*; (*fig. geh.*) swarm of diminutive creatures

**Gewürz** *das;* **~es**, **~e** spice; (*würzende Zutat*) seasoning; condiment; (*Kraut*) herb; **verschiedene ~e** various herbs *or* spices

**Gewürz-: ~essig** *der* ⇒ **Kräuteressig**; **~gurke** *die* pickled gherkin; **~mischung** *die* mixed spices *pl.*/herbs *pl.*; **~nelke** *die* clove; **~traminer** *der* Gewürztraminer

**Gewusel** /gə'vu:zl̩/ *das;* **~s** (*landsch.*) ⇒ **Gewimmel**

**gewusst**, ***gewußt** *2. Part. v.* **wissen**

**Geysir** /'gai:zɪr/ *der;* **~s**, **~e** geyser

**gez.** *Abk.* **gezeichnet** sgd.

**gezähnt** /gə'tsɛ:nt/ *Adj.* (*Bot.*) dentate

**Gezänk** /gə'tsɛŋk/ *das;* **~[e]s**, **Gezanke** /gə'tsaŋkə/ *das;* **Gezankes** (*abwertend*) quarrelling

**Gezappel** *das;* **~s** (*ugs., oft abwertend*) wriggling

**Gezeiten** *Pl.* tides

**Gezeiten-: ~kraft·werk** *das* tidal power station; **~strom** *der* tidal current; **~tafel** *die* tide table

**Gezerre** *das;* **~s** wrangling

**Gezeter** *das;* **~s** (*abwertend*) scolding; nagging

**Geziefer** /gə'ts:i:fɐ/ *das;* **~s** (*veralt.*) ⇒ **Ungeziefer**

**geziehen** /gə'ts:i:ən/ *2. Part. v.* **zeihen**

**gezielt** ❶ *2. Part. v.* **zielen**. ❷ *Adj.* specific ‹questions, measures, etc.›; deliberate ‹insult, indiscretion›; well-directed ‹advertising campaign›. ❸ *adv.* ‹proceed, act› purposefully, in a purposeful manner; **~ nach etw. forschen** search specifically for sth.

**geziemen** (*geh. veralt.*) ❶ *itr. V.* **jmdm. [nicht] ~:** [ill] befit sb. ❷ *refl. V.* be proper *or* right; **sich für jmdn. ~:** befit sb.; **es geziemt sich nicht, so mit deiner Mutter zu reden** it isn't proper *or* right for you to talk to your mother like that

**geziemend** (*geh.*) ❶ *Adj.* fitting; proper, due ‹respect›; **in ~er Weise** in a proper manner; **mit ~en Worten** with a few fitting remarks; **mit der ihr ~en Bescheidenheit** with fitting modesty. ❷ *adv.* in a fitting manner

**geziert** ❶ *2. Part. v.* **zieren**. ❷ *Adj.* (*abwertend*) affected. ❸ *adv.* (*abwertend*) affectedly

**Geziertheit** *die;* ~ (*abwertend*) affectedness

**Gezirp[e]** *das;* **~s** (*oft abwertend*) chirping; chirruping

**gezogen** /gə'ts:o:gn̩/ *2. Part. v.* **ziehen**

**Gezücht** *das;* **~[e]s**, **~e** (*geh. abwertend*) riff-raff *pl.*; rabble

**Gezüngel** /gə'tsʏŋl̩/ *das;* **~s das ~ der Schlange** the flicking *or* darting of the snake's tongue; **das ~ der Flammen** (*fig.*) the flickering of the flames

**Gezweig** *das;* **~[e]s** (*geh.*) branches *pl.*

**Gezwitscher** *das;* **~s** twittering; chirping; chirruping

**gezwungen** /gə'ts:vʊŋən/ ❶ *2. Part. v.* **zwingen**. ❷ *Adj.* forced ‹laugh, smile, etc.›; stiff ‹behaviour›. ❸ *adv.* ‹laugh› in a forced way *or* manner; ‹behave› stiffly

**gezwungenermaßen** *Adv.* of necessity; **etw. ~ machen** be forced to do sth.

**GG** *Abk.* **Grundgesetz**

**ggf.** *Abk.* **gegebenenfalls**

**Ghana** /'ga:na/ *(das);* **~s** Ghana

**Ghanaer** *der;* **~s**, ~, **Ghanaerin** *die;* ~, **~nen** Ghanaian

**Ghetto** ⇒ **Getto**

**Ghostwriter** /'gəʊstraɪtə/ *der;* **~s**, ~ ghost writer; **von ~n geschrieben werden** be ghosted

**gib** /gi:p/ *Imperativ Sg. Präsens v.* **geben**

**Gibbon** /'gɪbɔn/ *der;* **~s**, **~s** (*Zool.*) gibbon

**gibst** /gi:pst/ *2. Pers. Sg. Präsens v.* **geben**

**gibt** /gi:pt/ *3. Pers. Sg. Präsens v.* **geben**

**Gicht**[1] /gɪçt/ *die;* ~, **~en** (*Metall.*) [A] (*Öffnung*) throat [of the/a furnace]; [B] (*Oberteil des Hochofens*) top [of the/a furnace]; [C] (*Menge*) charge

**Gicht**[2] *die;* ~ ▸ **474** gout

**gicht·brüchig** *Adj.* (*veralt.*) gouty; **die Gichtbrüchigen** (*bibl.*) those that had the palsy

**gichtig**, **gichtisch** *Adj.* gouty

**Gicht·knoten** *der* gouty concretion

**gicht·krank** *Adj.* gouty

**gicksen** /'gɪksn̩/ (*bes. md.*) ❶ *itr. V.* (*einen Schrei ausstoßen*) squeak. ❷ *tr. V.* (*stechen, stoßen*) **jmdn. ~:** jab sb.; **jmdn.** *od.* **jmdm. in die Seite ~:** jab sb. in the side

**Giebel** /'gi:bl̩/ *der;* **~s**, ~ [A] gable; [B] (*von Portalen*) pediment

**Giebel-: ~dach** *das* gable roof; **~feld** *das* (*Archit.*) tympanum; **~fenster** *das* gable window; **~seite** *die* gable end; **~wand** *die* gable wall

**Gier** /gi:ɐ̯/ *die;* ~ [A] greed (**nach** for); **mit solcher ~:** so greedily; **~ nach Macht/Ruhm** lust *or* craving for power/craving for fame; **~ nach Zigaretten** greedy desire for cigarettes; **~ nach Leben** passionate desire for life; [B] (*Lüsternheit*) lust

**gieren**[1] *itr. V.* (*geh.*) **nach etw. ~:** crave for sth.; **nach Macht/Rache ~:** lust for power/revenge

**gieren**[2] *itr. V.* (*Seemannsspr.*) yaw

**gierig** ❶ *Adj.* greedy; avid ‹reader, desire›; **nach etw. ~ sein** be greedy for sth. ❷ *adv.* greedily

**Gieß·bach** *der* [mountain] torrent; (*nach starkem Regen*) swollen [mountain] stream

**gießen** /'gi:sn̩/ ❶ *unr. tr. V.* [A] (*rinnen lassen/schütten*) pour (**in** + *Akk.* into, **über** + *Akk.* over); [B] (*verschütten*) spill (**über** + *Akk.* over); [C] (*be~*) water ‹plants, flowers, garden›; [D] cast ‹machine part, statue, candles, etc.›; cast, found ‹metal›; found ‹glass›; **Blei zu Kugeln ~:** cast lead into bullets. ❷ *unr. itr. V.* [A] **ich muss im Garten noch ~:** I still have to water the garden; [B] *unpers.* (*ugs.*) pour [with rain]; **es gießt in Strömen** it is coming down in buckets; it's raining cats and dogs

**Gießer** *der;* **~s**, ~, **Gießerin** *die;* ~, **~nen** caster; founder

**Gießerei** *die;* ~, **~en** [A] (*Betrieb*) foundry; [B] (*Zweig der Metallindustrie*) casting; founding

**Gieß-: ~form** *die* (*Gießerei*) [casting] mould; **~grube** *die* (*Gießerei*) casting pit; **~harz** *das* (*Technik*) cast resin; **~kanne** *die* watering can

**Gießkannen·prinzip** *das* (*scherzh.*) principle of 'equal shares for all'

**Gieß-: ~kelle** *die* (*Gießerei*) casting ladle; **~pfanne** *die* (*Gießerei*) pouring *or* teeming ladle

**Gift** /gɪft/ *das;* **~[e]s**, **~e** [A] poison; (*Schlangen~*) venom; **jmdm. ~ [ein]geben** poison sb.; **~ [aus]legen** put poison down; [B] (*fig.*) **~ für jmdn./etw. sein** be extremely bad for sb./sth.; **sein ~ verspritzen** (*ugs.*) spit venom (*fig.*); **~ und Galle speien** *od.* **spucken** (*sehr wütend sein*) be in a terrible rage; (*gehässig reagieren*) give vent to one's spleen; **du kannst ~ darauf nehmen** (*ugs.*) you can bet your life on it; ⇒ *auch* **blond**

**Gift-: ~becher** *der* (*hist.*) cup of poison; **~drüse** *die* (*Zool.*) poison gland

**giften** (*ugs.*) ❶ *tr. V.* (*böse machen*) rile (*coll.*); infuriate. ❷ *refl. V.* (*sich ärgern*) be furious. ❸ *itr. V.* (*gehässig reden*) **gegen jmdn./etw. ~:** be nasty about sb./sth.

**gift-, Gift-: ~frei** *Adj.* non-toxic; non-poisonous; **~gas** *das* poison gas; **~grün** *Adj.* garish green

**giftig** ❶ *Adj.* [A] poisonous; venomous, poisonous ‹snake›; toxic, poisonous ‹substance, gas, chemical›; [B] (*ugs.: bösartig*) venomous,

*old spelling (see note on page 1707)

spiteful ‹remark, person, words, etc.›; venomous ‹look›; **~ werden** turn nasty; (C) (*grell, schreiend*) garish, loud ‹colour›. ❷ *adv.* venomously

**Gift-: ~küche** *die* (*scherzh.*) chemical laboratory (*with its unpleasant products*); **~mischer** *der*, **~mischerin** *die*; **~~, ~~nen** (A) (*ugs. abwertend*) maker of poisons; (B) (*ugs. scherzh.: Apotheker*) chemist; **~mord** *der* [murder by] poisoning; **~mörder** *der*, **~mörderin** *die* poisoner; **~müll** *der* toxic waste; **~müll·deponie** *die* toxic [waste] tip *or* dump; **~pfeil** *der* poisoned arrow; **~pflanze** *die* poisonous plant; **~pilz** *der* poisonous mushroom; [poisonous] toadstool; **~schlange** *die* poisonous *or* venomous snake; **~schrank** *der* poison cabinet *or* cupboard; **~spinne** *die* poisonous spider; **~stachel** *der* poisonous sting; **~stoff** *der* poisonous *or* toxic substance; **~trank** *der* (*geh.*) poisoned drink; **~zahn** *der* poison fang; **~zwerg** *der* (*ugs. abwertend*) [nasty] spiteful little man

**Giga-** /giga-/ giga‹hertz etc.›

**Gigant** /gi'gant/ *der;* **~en, ~en** (A) (*geh.: Riese*) giant; (B) (*sehr beeindruckende Sache, Person*) giant; titan; **~en der Landstraße/des Meeres** (*fig.*) juggernauts of the road/leviathans of the ocean

**gigantisch** *Adj.* gigantic; huge ‹success›

**Gigantomanie** /gigantoma'ni:/ *die;* **~** (*geh.*) craze for the huge and spectacular

**Gigerl** /'gi:gɐl/ *der od. das;* **~s, ~n** (*südd., österr. ugs.*) dandy; fop

**Gigolo** /'ʒi:golo/ *der;* **~s, ~s** gigolo

**Gilde** /'gɪldə/ *die;* **~, ~n** (A) (*hist.*) guild; (B) (*Interessengruppe*) fraternity

**gilt** /gɪlt/ *3. Pers. Sg. Präsens v.* **gelten**

**Gimpel** /'gɪmpl̩/ *der;* **~s, ~** (A) (*Vogel*) bullfinch; (B) (*ugs. abwertend: einfältiger Mensch*) ninny; simpleton

**Gin** /dʒɪn/ *der;* **~s,** (*Sorten:*) **~s** gin

**Ginfizz** /'dʒɪnfɪs/ *der;* **~, ~** gin fizz

**ging** /gɪŋ/ *1. u. 3. Pers. Sg. Prät. v.* **gehen**

**Ginseng** /'gɪnzɛŋ/ *der;* **~s, ~s** ginseng

**Ginster** /'gɪnstɐ/ *der;* **~s, ~** broom; (*Stechginster*) gorse; furze

**Gipfel** /'gɪpfl̩/ *der;* **~s, ~** (A) peak; (*höchster Punkt des Berges*) summit; **den ~ besteigen/bezwingen** climb the peak/conquer the peak *or* summit; (B) (*Höhepunkt*) height; (*von Begeisterung, Glück, Ruhm, Macht auch*) peak; **auf dem ~ der Macht/des Ruhmes** at the height of one's power/fame; **der ~ der Geschmacklosigkeit/Dummheit** (*ugs.*) the height of bad taste/stupidity; **das ist [doch] der ~!** (*ugs.*) that's the limit!; (C) (*veralt.: Wipfel*) top; (D) (**~***konferenz*) summit

**Gipfel-: ~gespräch** *das* summit talks *pl.;* **~konferenz** *die* summit conference; **~kreuz** *das* cross on the summit of a/the mountain

**gipfeln** *itr. V.* **in etw.** (*Dat.*) **~:** culminate in sth.

**Gipfel·punkt** *der* highest point; top; (*fig.*) high point; **der ~ seines künstlerischen Schaffens** the peak of his artistic powers

**Gips** /gɪps/ *der;* **~es,** (*Sorten:*) **~e** plaster; gypsum (*Chem.*); (*zum Modellieren*) plaster of Paris; **einen Arm in ~ legen** put an arm in plaster; **drei Monate im ~ liegen** be laid up in plaster for three months

**Gips-: ~abdruck** *der; Pl.* **~abdrücke, ~abguss,** ***~abguß** *der* plaster cast; **~bein** *das* (*ugs.*) **ich komme mit meinem ~bein nicht mit** I can't keep up, with this plaster on my leg; **durch ein ~bein behindert werden** be hindered by having one's leg in plaster

**gipsen** *tr. V.* (A) plaster ‹wall, ceiling›; put ‹leg, arm, etc.› in plaster; (B) (*ausbessern*) repair with plaster

**Gipser** *der;* **~s, ~, Gipserin** *die;* **~, ~nen** ▶ 159 plasterer

**Gips-: ~figur** *die* plaster [of Paris] figure; **~korsett** *das* (*Med.*) plaster jacket; **~modell** *das* plaster model; **~verband** *der* plaster cast

**Giraffe** /gi'rafə/ *die;* **~, ~n** giraffe

**Girant** /ʒi'rant/ *der;* **~en, ~en, Girantin** *die;* **~, ~nen** (*Finanzw.*) endorser

**girieren** /ʒi'ri:rən/ *tr. V.* (*Finanzw.*) endorse

**Girl** /gø:ɐ̯l/ *das;* **~s, ~s** (A) (*ugs., oft scherzh.: Mädchen*) girl; (B) (*Tänzerin*) chorus girl

**Girlande** /gɪr'landə/ *die;* **~, ~n** festoon

**Girlie** /'gœrli/ *das;* **~s, ~s** girlie

**Giro** /'ʒi:ro/ *das;* **~s, ~s,** *österr. auch* **Giri** (*Finanzw.*) (A) (*Überweisung*) giro; (B) (*Vermerk*) endorsement

**Giro-: ~bank** *die; Pl.* **~~en** (*Finanzw.*) clearing bank; **~konto** *das* (*Finanzw.*) current account

**girren** /'gɪrən/ *itr. V.* (*auch fig.*) coo

**Gis, gis** /gɪs/ *das;* **~, ~** (*Musik*) G sharp

**Gischt** /gɪʃt/ *der;* **~[e]s, ~e** *od. die;* **~, ~en** (A) (*Schaumkronen*) foam; surf; (B) (*Sprühwasser*) spray

**gischten** *itr. V.* (*geh.*) spray up

**Gis-Dur** *das* (*Musik*) G sharp major; ⇒ *auch* **A-Dur**

**gis-Moll** *das* (*Musik*) G sharp minor; ⇒ *auch* **a-Moll**

**Gitarre** /gi'tarə/ *die;* **~, ~n** guitar

**Gitarren·spieler** *der*, **Gitarren·spielerin** *die* guitar player; guitarist

**Gitarrist** *der;* **~en, ~en, Gitarristin** *die;* **~, ~nen** ▶ 159 guitarist

**Gitter** /'gɪtɐ/ *das;* **~s, ~** (A) (*parallele Stäbe*) bars *pl.;* (*Drahtgeflecht vor Fenster-, Türöffnungen*) grille; (*in der Straßendecke, im Fußboden*) grating; (*Geländer*) railing[s *pl.*]; (*Spalier*) trellis; (*feines Draht~*) mesh; (*Kamin~*) [fire]guard; **hinter ~n** (*ugs.*) behind bars; (B) (*Physik, Chemie*) lattice; (C) (*Math., Elektronik, auf Landkarten*) grid

**Gitter-: ~bett** *das* cot; **~fenster** *das* barred window; **~mast** *der* (*Technik*) pylon; lattice tower; **~netz** *das* (*Kartographie*) grid; **~rost** *der* grating; **~stab** *der* bar; **~struktur** *die* (*Physik*) lattice structure; **~tor** *das* iron-barred gate; **~werk** *das* ironwork; (*kunstvoller*) wrought-iron work; **~zaun** *der* railing[s *pl.*]; (*mit gekreuzten Stäben*) lattice[-work] fence

**Glace** /'glasə/ *die;* **~, ~n** (*schweiz.*) ice cream

**Glacé-**/gla'se:/**: ~hand·schuh** *der* kid glove; **jmdn./etw. mit ~handschuhen anfassen** (*ugs.*) handle sb./sth. with kid gloves; **~leder** *das* glacé leather

**glacieren** /gla'si:rən/ *tr. V.* (*Kochk.*) glaze

**Glacis** /gla'si:/ *das;* **~, ~** (*Milit.*) glacis

**Gladiator** /gla'di̯a:tɔr/ *der;* **~s, ~en** /-'to:rən/ gladiator

**Gladiole** /gla'di̯o:lə/ *die;* **~, ~n** gladiolus

**Glamour** /'glæmə/ *der od. das;* **~s** glamour

**Glamour·girl** *das* glamour girl

**Glanz** /glants:/ *der;* **~es** (A) (*von Licht, Sternen*) brightness; brilliance; (*von Haar, Metall, Perlen, Leder usw.*) shine; lustre; sheen; (*von Augen*) shine; brightness; lustre; **den ~ verlieren** ‹diamonds, eyes› lose their sparkle; ‹metal, leather› lose its shine; **etw. auf ~ polieren** polish sth. till it shines; **welch ~ in meiner Hütte!** (*scherzh. iron.*) to what do I owe the honour of this visit? (*iron.*); (B) (*der Jugend, Schönheit*) radiance; (*des Adels usw.*) splendour; **zu neuem ~ kommen** acquire new splendour; **mit ~** (*ugs.*) with flying colours; **mit ~ und Gloria** (*ugs. iron.*) in grand style

**Glanz·abzug** *der* (*Fot.*) glossy print

**glänzen** /'glɛnts:n̩/ *itr. V.* (A) (*Glanz ausstrahlen*) shine; ‹car, hair, metal, paintwork, etc.› gleam; ‹elbows, trousers, etc.› be shiny; **vor Sauberkeit ~:** be so clean [that] it shines; **sein Gesicht glänzte vor Freude** his face shone with joy *or* pleasure; (B) (*Bewunderung erregen*) shine (**bei** at); **durch Wissen/Können ~:** be outstanding for one's knowledge/ability; **in einer Rolle ~:** shine in a role; **durch Abwesenheit ~** (*iron.*) be conspicuous by one's absence

**glänzend** (*ugs.*) ❶ *Adj.* (A) shining; gleaming ‹car, hair, metal, paintwork, etc.›; shiny ‹elbows, trousers, etc.›; (B) (*bewundernswert*) brilliant ‹idea, career, victory, pupil, prospects, etc.›; splendid, excellent, outstanding ‹references, marks, results, etc.›; **in ~er Laune/Form sein** be in a splendid mood/in splendid form. ❷ *adv.* **~ mit jmdm. auskommen** get on very well with sb.; **es geht mir/uns ~:** I am/we are very well; (*finanziell*) I am/we are doing very well *or* very nicely; **eine Aufgabe ~ lösen** solve a problem brilliantly

**glanz-, Glanz-: ~kohle** *die* glance coal; **~leistung** *die* (*auch iron.*) brilliant performance; **~licht** *das; Pl.* **~~er** (*bild. Kunst*) highlight; **einer Sache** (*Dat.*) **[noch einige] ~lichter aufsetzen** give sth. [more] sparkle; **~los** *Adj.* dull; lacklustre; **~nummer** *die* star turn; **diese Rezitation ist seine ~nummer** this recitation is his pièce de résistance; **~papier** *das* glossy paper; **~parade** *die* (*Sport*) superb *or* outstanding save; **~politur** *die* high-gloss polish; **~punkt** *der* high spot; highlight; **~rolle** *die* star role; **~stück** *das* (A) (*Meisterwerk*) pièce de résistance; (B) (*der kostbarste Gegenstand*) showpiece; **~voll** ❶ *Adj.* (A) (*ausgezeichnet*) brilliant; sparkling ‹variety number›; (B) (*prachtvoll*) magnificent; ❷ *adv.* (A) (*ausgezeichnet*) brilliantly; **eine Prüfung ~voll bestehen** pass an examination with flying colours; do brilliantly in an examination; (B) (*prachtvoll*) **Louis XIV pflegte ~voll Hof zu halten** Louis XIV used to hold court in glittering style; **~zeit** *die* heyday; **ihre ~zeit ist vorüber** she's had her day

**Glas** /gla:s/ *das;* **~es, Gläser** /'glɛ:zɐ/ (A) glass; **unter ~:** behind glass; ‹plants› under glass; **„Vorsicht, ~!"** 'glass — handle with care'; **du bist nicht aus ~** (*ugs.*) you make a better door than you do window (*coll.*); (B) (*Trinkgefäß*) glass; **zwei ~** *od.* **Gläser Wein/Bier** two glasses of wine/beer; **ein ~ über den Durst trinken** (*ugs. scherzh.*), **zu tief ins ~ gucken** (*ugs. scherzh.*) have one too many *or* (*coll.*) one over the eight; (C) (*Behälter aus ~*) jar; **ein ~ Marmelade/Honig** a jar of jam/honey; (D) (*geh.: Brillen~*) lens; **Gläser** (*veralt.: Brille*) spectacles; glasses; (E) (*Fern~*) binoculars *pl.;* [field] glasses *pl.;* (*Opern~*) opera glasses *pl.*

**glas-, Glas-: ~artig** *Adj.* vitreous; glassy; **~auge** *das* glass eye; **~ballon** *der* carboy; **~baustein** *der* glass brick *or* block; **~bläser** *der* ▶ 159 glass-blower; **~bläserei** /-blɛ:zə'rai:/ *die;* **~~, ~~en** (A) glass-blowing; (B) (*Betrieb*) glass-blowing works *sing. or pl.;* **~bläserin** *die* ⇒ **~bläser**

**Gläschen** /'glɛ:sçən/ *das;* **~s, ~** (A) (*kleines Trinkglas*) [little] glass; (B) (*kleines Gefäß aus Glas*) [little] [glass] jar

**Glas·dach** *das* glass roof

**Glaser** *der;* **~s, ~** ▶ 159 glazier

**Glaserei** *die;* **~, ~en** (A) (*Betrieb*) glazing business; (*Werkstatt*) glazier's workshop; (B) glazier's trade

**Glaserin** *die;* **~, ~nen** ▶ 159 ⇒ **Glaser**

**gläsern** /'glɛ:zɐn/ *Adj.* (A) (*aus Glas*) glass; **ein ~er Abgeordneter** (*fig.*) a member of parliament who has no secrets; (B) (*dichter.: wie Glas*) glassy

**glas-, Glas-: ~fabrik** *die* glassworks *sing. or pl.;* **~faser** *die* glass fibre; **~fenster** *das* [glass] window; **bemalte ~fenster** stained-glass windows; **~fiber** *die* ⇒ **~faser**; **~fiber·stab** *der* (*Leichtathletik*) glass-fibre pole; **~flasche** *die* glass bottle; **~flügler** *der;* **~~s, ~~** (*Zool.*) clearwing; **~fluss,** ***~fluß** *der* paste; **~geschirr** *das* glassware; **~hart** ❶ *Adj.* (A) /'--/ (*hart*) solid ‹ice›; rigid ‹plastic›; (*spröde*) brittle; (B) /'-'-/ (*Sport*) cracking ‹shot›; solid ‹punch›; ❷ *adv.* (A) **~hart gefroren** frozen hard; (B) (*Sport*) **seine Rechte ~hart schlagen** have a solid right; **~haus** *das* greenhouse; glasshouse; **wer [selbst] im ~haus sitzt, soll nicht mit Steinen werfen** (*Spr.*) those who live in glass houses shouldn't throw stones (*prov.*); **~hütte** *die* glassworks *sing. or pl.*

**glasieren** *tr. V.* (A) (*glätten und haltbar machen*) glaze; (B) (*Kochk.*) ice ‹cake etc.›; glaze ‹meat›

**glasig** *Adj.* (A) (*starr*) glassy ‹stare, eyes, etc.›; (B) (*Kochk.: durchsichtig*) transparent

**glas-, Glas-: ~kasten** *der* [A] glass case; (*kleiner*) glass box; [B] (*ugs.: Raum*) glass box; **~keramik** *die* devitrified glass; **~kinn** *das* (*Sportjargon*) vulnerable chin; **~klar** *Adj.* (*auch fig.*) crystal clear; **~kolben** *der* glass flask; (*einer Glühbirne*) glass bulb; **~körper** *der* ▸ 471 (*Anat.*) vitreous body; **~kugel** *die* glass ball; (*einer Wahrsagerin*) crystal ball; (*Murmel*) marble; **~malerei** *die* stained glass; (*Verfahren*) glass staining; **~papier** *das* glass *or* sand paper; **~perle** *die* glass bead; **~platte** *die* glass plate; (*eines Tisches*) glass top; (*im Fenster*) pane of glass; **~röhrchen** *das* small glass tube; **~scheibe** *die* sheet of glass; (*im Fenster*) pane of glass; **~scherbe** *die* piece of broken glass; **~scherben** [pieces of] broken glass; **~schleifer** *der*, **~schleiferin** *die* [A] glass cutter; [B] (*Optik*) glass grinder; **~schneider** *der* glass-cutter; **~schrank** *der* glass-fronted cabinet; (*mit Wänden aus Glas*) glass cabinet; **~splitter** *der* splinter of glass; **~stein** *der* ⇒ **~baustein**; **~tür** *die* glass door

**Glasur** /gla'zu:ɐ̯/ *die*; ~, **~en** [A] (*Schmelz*) glaze; [B] (*Kochk.*) (*auf Kuchen*) icing; (*auf Fleisch*) glaze

**glas-, Glas-: ~veranda** *die* glassed-in veranda; **~vitrine** *die* glass showcase; **~waren** *Pl.* glassware *sing.*; **~watte** *die* ⇒ **~wolle**; **~weise** *Adv.* by the glass; **~wolle** *die* glass wool; **~ziegel** *der* glass tile

**glatt** /glat/ ❶ *Adj.* [A] smooth; straight ‹hair›; **etw. ~ bügeln/hobeln** iron/plane sth. smooth; **etw. ~ machen** smooth sth. out; **den Boden ~ machen** level the ground; **sich** (*Dat.*) **die Haare ~ kämmen** comb one's hair straight; **etw. ~ ziehen** pull sth. straight; **~ rasiert** clean shaven; **eine ~e Eins/Fünf** a clear A/E; [B] (*rutschig*) slippery; [C] (*komplikationslos*) smooth ‹landing, journey›; clean, straightforward ‹fracture›; [D] (*ugs.: offensichtlich*) downright, outright ‹lie›; outright ‹deception, fraud›; sheer, utter ‹nonsense, madness, etc.›; pure, sheer ‹invention›, flat ‹refusal›; complete ‹failure›; **~er Mord sein** be tantamount to murder; [E] (*allzu gewandt*) smooth. ❷ *adv.* [A] **die Rechnung geht ~ auf** the calculation works out exactly; **stricken Sie die ersten zehn Reihen ~ rechts** start with ten rows of plain knitting; [B] (*komplikationslos*) smoothly; **jmdn. ~ schlagen/besiegen** beat/defeat sb. decisively; **~ gehen** (*ugs.*) go smoothly; [C] (*ugs.: rückhaltlos*) **jmdm. etw. ~ ins Gesicht sagen** tell sb. sth. straight to his/her face; **etw. ~ ablehnen/leugnen** reject/deny sth. flatly; **etw. ~ vergessen** completely *or* clean forget sth.; [D] (*abwertend: allzu gewandt*) smoothly

***glatt|bügeln** ⇒ **glatt** 1A

**Glätte** /'glɛtə/ *die*; ~ [A] (*ebene Beschaffenheit*) smoothness; [B] (*Rutschigkeit*) slipperiness; [C] (*abwertend: allzu große Gewandtheit*) smoothness

**Glatt·eis** *das* glaze; ice; (*auf der Straße*) black ice; **jmdn. aufs ~ führen** (*fig.*) catch sb. out; **aufs ~ geraten** (*fig.*) get on to tricky ground

**Glatteis·bildung** *die* formation of black ice

**Glätt·eisen** *das* (*schweiz.*) ⇒ **Bügeleisen**

**Glatteis·gefahr** *die* danger of black ice

**glätten** ❶ *tr. V.* smooth out ‹piece of paper, banknote, etc.›; smooth [down] ‹feathers, fur, etc.›; plane ‹wood etc.›; **jmds. Zorn/aufgebrachte Stimmung ~** (*fig.*) calm sb.'s anger/smooth sb.'s ruffled feathers. ❷ *refl. V.* ‹waves› subside; ‹sea› become calm *or* smooth; (*fig.*) subside; die down; **ihre Stirn glättete sich** her frown vanished. ❸ *tr., itr. V.* (*schweiz.*) ⇒ **bügeln**

**Glätterin** *die*; ~, **~nen** (*schweiz.*) ⇒ **Büglerin**

**glatt-: *~|gehen** *usw.*: ⇒ **glatt** 2B, 1A; **~|machen** *tr. V.* (*ugs.: begleichen*) settle ‹account etc.›; ***~rasiert** ⇒ **glatt** 1A; **~weg** *Adv.* (*ugs.*) **etw. ~weg ablehnen/ignorieren** turn sth. down flat/just *or* simply ignore sth.; **das ist ~weg erlogen/erfunden** that's a downright lie/that's pure invention; ***~|ziehen** ⇒ **glatt** 1A; **~züngig** /-ts:ʏŋɪç/ *Adj.* (*geh. abwertend*) smooth-tongued; glib

**Glatze** /'glatsə/ *die*; ~, **~n** bald head; (*kahle Stelle*) bald patch; **eine ~ haben/bekommen** be/go bald; **sich eine ~ schneiden lassen** (*ugs.*) have one's hair cropped very short all over; **ein Mann mit ~:** a man with a bald head; a bald-headed man

**Glatz·kopf** *der* [A] (*Kopf*) bald head; [B] (*ugs.: Person*) baldhead

**glatz·köpfig** *Adj.* bald[-headed]

**Glaube** /'glaubə/ *der*; **~ns** [A] (*gefühlsmäßige Bindung*) faith (**an** + *Akk.* in); (*Überzeugung, Meinung*) belief (**an** + *Akk.* in); **den ~n an jmdn./etw. verlieren** lose faith in sb./sth.; **jmdm./jmds. Worten ~n schenken** believe sb./what sb. says; **[bei jmdm.] ~n finden** be believed [by sb.]; **guten ~ns sein, dass ...** be quite convinced that ...; **in dem ~n leben, dass ...** live in the belief that ...; **lass ihn in seinem ~n** don't disillusion him; **jmdn. bei** *od.* **in dem ~n lassen, dass ...** let sb. believe that ...; **[der] ~ versetzt Berge** *od.* **kann Berge versetzen** faith can move mountains; **sich in dem ~n wiegen, dass ...** labour under the illusion that ...; **in gutem** *od.* **im guten ~n** in good faith; [B] (*religiöse Überzeugung, Religion, Bekenntnis*) faith; **den ~n verlieren** lose one's [religious] faith; **den ~n an Gott verlieren** lose one's faith *or* belief in God

**glauben** ❶ *tr. V.* [A] (*annehmen, meinen*) think; believe; **ich glaube, ja** I think *or* believe so; **ich glaube, nein** *od.* **nicht** I don't think so; I think *or* believe not; **jmdn. etw. ~ machen wollen** try to make sb. believe sth.; [B] (*für wahr halten*) believe; **jmdm. [etw.] ~:** believe sb.; **ich glaube ihm seine Geschichte** I believe his story; **das glaubst du doch selbst nicht!** [surely] you can't be serious; **sie glaubt ihm jedes Wort** she believes every word he says; **ob du es glaubst oder nicht ...** believe it or not ...; **wer hätte das [je] geglaubt?** who would [ever] have thought it?; **wer hätte [je] geglaubt, dass ...** who would [ever] have believed *or* thought that ...; **du glaubst [gar] nicht, wie ...** you have no idea how ...; **wers glaubt, wird selig** (*ugs. scherzh.*) if you believe that, you'll believe anything; **das ist doch kaum zu ~** (*ugs.*) it's incredible; [C] (*fälschlich annehmen*) **wir glaubten ihn tot/in Sicherheit** we thought *or* believed him [to be] dead/safe; **sich allein/unbeobachtet ~:** think *or* believe oneself [to be] alone/unobserved. ❷ *itr. V.* [A] (*vertrauen*) **an jmdn./etw./sich [selbst] ~:** believe in *or* have faith in sb./sth./oneself; [B] (*gläubig sein*) hold religious beliefs; believe; **fest/unbeirrbar ~:** have a strong/unshakeable religious belief; [C] (*von der Existenz von etw. überzeugt sein*) believe (**an** + *Akk.* in); **an Gott ~:** believe in God; [D] **dran ~ müssen** (*salopp: getötet werden*) buy it (*coll.*); (*salopp: sterben*) peg out (*coll.*); kick the bucket (*sl.*); **heute muss sie dran ~ und Küchendienst machen** (*ugs.: ist an der Reihe*) today it is her turn to be lumbered with working in the kitchen (*coll.*)

**Glauben** *der*; **~s** ⇒ **Glaube**

**glaubens-, Glaubens-: ~artikel** *der* article of faith; **~bekenntnis** *das* [A] (*auch fig.: Überzeugung*) creed; ⇒ *auch* **apostolisch** A; [B] (*Konfessionsangehörigkeit*) religion; **~bruder** *der* co-religionist; fellow-believer; **~dinge** *Pl.* matters of faith; **~eifer** *der* religious zeal; **~frage** *die* question of faith *or* belief; **~freiheit** *die* religious freedom; freedom of worship; **~gemeinschaft** *die* religious sect; denomination; **~kampf** *der* religious war; war of religion; **~lehre** *die* doctrine; (*Dogma*) dogma; (*Dogmatik*) dogmatics *sing.*; **~sache** *die* (*ugs.*) matter of faith *or* belief; **~satz** *der* doctrine; dogma; **~schwester** *die* ⇒ **~bruder**; **~spaltung** *die* schism; **~stark** *Adj.* deeply religious; **~streit** *der* religious dispute; **~wahrheit** *die* religious truth; **~wechsel** *der* change of religion

**Glauber·salz** /'glaubɐ-/ *das* (*Chemie*) Glauber's salt

**glaubhaft** ❶ *Adj.* credible; believable. ❷ *adv.* convincingly

**Glaubhaftigkeit** *die*; ~ credibility

**Glaubhaft·machung** *die*; ~ (*Rechtsspr.*) substantiation

**gläubig** /'glɔyːbɪç/ ❶ *Adj.* [A] (*religiös*) devout; **sehr/zutiefst ~ sein** be very/deeply religious; [B] (*vertrauensvoll*) trusting; **~e Anhänger** faithful followers. ❷ *adv.* [A] (*religiös*) devoutly; [B] (*vertrauensvoll*) trustingly

**-gläubig** *Adj.* having a blind trust in ‹authority, drugs, Hitler, the Party, etc.›

**Gläubige** *der/die*; *adj. Dekl.* believer; **die ~n** the faithful

**Gläubiger** *der*; **~s**, ~, **Gläubigerin** *die*; ~, **~nen** creditor

**Gläubigkeit** *die*; ~ [A] (*religiöse Überzeugung*) religious faith; [B] (*Vertrauen*) trustfulness

**glaublich** *Adj.* **es ist kaum ~:** it is scarcely *or* hardly credible

**glaub·würdig** ❶ *Adj.* credible; believable; **von ~er Seite/aus ~er Quelle** from reliable quarters/a reliable source. ❷ *adv.* convincingly

**Glaubwürdigkeit** *die* credibility

**Glaukom** /glau'ko:m/ *das*; **~s**, **~e** ▸ 474 (*Med.*) glaucoma

**glazial** /gla'ts:ja:l/ *Adj.* (*Geol.*) glacial

**Glazial** *das*; **~s**, **~e** (*Geol.*) glacial epoch

**gleich** /glaiç/ ❶ *Adj.* [A] (*identisch, von derselben Art*) same; (*~berechtigt, ~wertig, Math.*) equal; **~ bleiben** remain *or* stay the same; ‹speed, temperature, etc.› remain *or* stay constant *or* steady; ‹prices› remain unchanged, stay the same; **sich** (*Dat.*) **~ bleiben** stay the same; **das bleibt sich [doch] ~** (*ugs.*) it makes no difference; **~ bleibend** constant, steady ‹temperature, speed, etc.›; **in ~ bleibendem Abstand** at a steady distance; **zur ~en Zeit/im ~en Augenblick** at the same time/at the same moment; **~er Lohn für ~e Arbeit** equal pay for equal work; **~es Recht für alle** equal rights for all; **dreimal zwei [ist] ~ sechs** three times two equals *or* is six; **das Gleiche wollen/beabsichtigen** have the same objective[s *pl.*]/intentions *pl.*; **das Gleiche gilt auch für dich** the same applies to *or* goes for you too; **das kommt auf das Gleiche** *od.* **aufs Gleiche heraus** it amounts *or* comes to the same thing; **der/die Gleiche bleiben** remain *or* stay the same; **Gleiches mit Gleichem vergelten** pay sb. back in his/her own coin *or* in kind; **Gleich und Gleich gesellt sich gern** (*Spr.*) birds of a feather flock together (*prov.*); [B] (*ugs.: ~gültig*) **es ist mir völlig** *od.* **ganz ~:** it's all the same to me; I couldn't care less (*coll.*); **ganz ~, wer anruft, ...** no matter who calls, ...
❷ *adv.* [A] (*übereinstimmend*) **~ groß/alt** *usw.* **sein** be the same height/age *etc.*; **~ gut/schlecht** *usw.* equally good/bad *etc.*; [B] (*in derselben Weise*) **~ aufgebaut/gekleidet** having the same structure/wearing identical clothes; **alle Menschen ~ behandeln** treat everyone alike; **~ denkend** *od.* **gesinnt** like-minded; **~ lautend** identical, identically worded ‹texts etc.›; homonymous ‹words› (*Ling.*); [C] (*sofort*) at once; right *or* straight away; (*bald*) in a moment *or* minute; **ich komme ~:** I'm just coming; **es muss nicht ~ sein** there's no immediate hurry; **ich bin ~ wieder da** I'll be back in a moment *or* minute; I'll be right back; **es ist ~ zehn Uhr** it is almost *or* nearly ten o'clock; **das habe ich [euch] ~ gesagt** I told you so; what did I tell you?; **warum nicht ~ so?** why didn't you do that/say so in the first place?; **bis ~!** see you later!; [D] (*räumlich*) right; immediately; just; **~ rechts/links** just *or* immediately on the right/left; **~ um die Ecke** just round the corner; [E] (*geh.: schon, auch*) **wenn er ~ reich war, ...** rich though he was, ...; **ob er ~ unschuldig war, ...** although he was innocent, ...
❸ *Präp.* + *Dat.* (*geh.*) like; **einem silbernen Band ~:** like a silver ribbon.
❹ *Partikel* [A] **nun wein nicht ~/sei**

*old spelling (see note on page 1707)

**nicht ~ böse** don't start crying/don't get cross; **da könnte man doch ~ in die Luft gehen/aus der Haut fahren** it's enough to drive you up the wall (*coll.*); Ⓑ (*in Fragesätzen*) **wie hieß er ~?** what was his name [again]?; **was wollte ich ~ sagen?** what was I going to say?

**gleich-, Gleich-: ~alt[e]rig** /-alt[ə]rɪç/ *Adj.* of the same age (**mit** as); **die beiden sind ~alt[e]rig** they are both the same age; **~alt[e]rige** *Pl.* people/children of the same age; **~artig** ❶ *Adj.* of the same kind *postpos.* (+ *Dat.* as); (*sehr ähnlich*) very similar (+ *Dat.* to); ❷ *adv.* in the same way; **~artigkeit** *die* great similarity; **~bedeutend** *Adj.* **~bedeutend mit** synonymous with; ‹action› tantamount to; **~berechtigt** *Adj.* having *or* enjoying *or* with equal rights *postpos.*; **~berechtigte Partner/Mitglieder** equal partners/members; **~berechtigt sein** have *or* enjoy equal rights; **~berechtigt mit jmdm. sein** have the same rights as sb.; **~berechtigte** *Pl.* people who have *or* enjoy equal rights; **~berechtigung** *die* equal rights *pl.*; equality; **für die ~berechtigung der Frauen kämpfen** fight for equal rights *or* equality for women; ***~|bleiben** ⇒ **gleich** 1 A; ***~bleibend** *Adj.* ***~bleibend sein** remain *or* stay the same; ‹temperature, speed, etc.› remain *or* stay constant *or* steady; ⇒ *auch* **gleich** 2 B; ***~denkend** ⇒ **gleich** 2 B

**gleichen** *unr. itr. V.* **jmdm./einer Sache ~:** be like *or* resemble sb./sth.; (*sehr ähnlich aussehen*) closely resemble sb./sth.; **sich** (*Dat.*) **~:** be alike; (*sehr ähnlich aussehen*) closely resemble each other; **nichts gleicht dem Zauber dieser Musik** nothing can equal *or* there is nothing to equal the enchanting quality of this music

**gleichen·orts** *Adv.* (*schweiz.*) in the same place

**gleichermaßen** *Adv.* equally

**gleich-, Gleich-: ~falls** *Adv.* (*auch*) also; (*ebenfalls*) likewise; **danke ~falls!** thank you, [and] the same to you; **~farbig** *Adj.* of the same colour *postpos.*; **~förmig** ❶ *Adj.* Ⓐ (*einheitlich*) uniform; uniform, even ‹light›; steady ‹development›; Ⓑ (*langweilig, monoton*) monotonous; ❷ *adv.* Ⓐ (*einheitlich*) uniformly; Ⓑ (*langweilig, monoton*) monotonously; **~förmig sprechen** speak in a monotone; **~förmigkeit** *die;* ~~ Ⓐ (*Einheitlichkeit*) uniformity; Ⓑ (*Monotonie*) monotony; **~geschlechtlich** *Adj.* homosexual; ***~gesinnt** ⇒ **gleich** 2B; **~gesinnte** *der/die; adj. Dekl.* like-minded person; **mit ~gesinnten** with like-minded people

**Gleich·gewicht** *das* Ⓐ balance; **das ~ halten/verlieren** keep/lose one's balance; **aus dem ~ kommen** lose one's balance; **im ~ sein** be in equilibrium; **ihr ~ ist leicht gestört** her sense of balance is slightly impaired; Ⓑ (*Ausgewogenheit*) balance; **das europäische ~:** the balance of power in Europe; **das ~ der Kräfte** the balance of power; Ⓒ (*innere Ausgeglichenheit*) equilibrium; **aus dem ~ geraten** lose one's equilibrium; **sein ~ bewahren/verlieren** keep *or* retain/lose one's equilibrium; **jmdn. aus dem ~ bringen** throw sb. off balance

**Gleichgewichts-: ~lage** *die* equilibrium; **~organ** *das* ▶471 (*Anat.*) organ of equilibrium; **~sinn** *der* sense of balance; **~störung** *die* disturbance of one's sense of balance; **~störungen** impaired balance *sing.*

**gleich·gültig** ❶ *Adj.* Ⓐ (*teilnahmslos*) indifferent (**gegenüber** towards); **sie war ihm [nicht] ~** (*verhüll.*) he was [by no means] indifferent to her; Ⓑ (*belanglos*) trivial, unimportant ‹matter, question, etc.›; trivial ‹conversation›; **es ist ~, ob ...** it does not matter whether ...; **das ist mir [vollkommen] ~:** it's a matter of [complete] indifference to me. ❷ *adv.* indifferently; ‹look on› with indifference

**Gleich·gültigkeit** *die* indifference (**gegenüber** towards)

**Gleichheit** *die;* ~, **~en** Ⓐ (*Identität*) identity; (*Ähnlichkeit*) similarity; **bei ~ der Punktzahl** if the teams/players *etc.* are level on points; Ⓑ (*gleiche Rechte*) equality

**Gleichheits-: ~[grund]satz** *der* principle of equality before the law; **~zeichen** *das* equals sign

**gleich-, Gleich-: ~klang** *der* harmony; **~|kommen** *unr. itr. V.; mit sein* Ⓐ (*entsprechen*) amount to; be tantamount to; Ⓑ (*die gleiche Leistung erreichen*) **jmdm./einer Sache [an etw.** (*Dat.*)**] ~kommen** equal sb./sth. [in sth.]; **jmdm. an Erfolg/Schnelligkeit ~kommen** equal *or* match sb.'s success/match sb. for speed; **~lauf** *der* (*Technik*) synchronism; **~laufend** *Adj.* parallel (**mit** with); ***~lautend** *Adj.* ⇒ **gleich** 2 B; **~|machen** *tr. V.* make equal; **der Tod macht alle Menschen ~:** Death is the great leveller; ⇒ *auch* **Erdboden**; **~macherei** *die;* ~~, ~~**en** (*abwertend*) levelling down (*derog.*); egalitarianism; **~macherisch** *Adj.* (*abwertend*) egalitarian; **~maß** *das* Ⓐ (*Ebenmaß*) (*von Bewegung, Strophen*) regularity; (*von Zügen, Proportionen*) symmetry; Ⓑ (*Ausgeglichenheit*) equilibrium; **~mäßig** ❶ *Adj.* regular ‹interval, rhythm›; uniform ‹acceleration, distribution›; even ‹heat›; **~mäßige Atemzüge** regular breathing *sing.*; ❷ *adv.* ‹breathe› regularly; **etw. ~mäßig verteilen/auftragen** distribute sth. equally/apply sth. evenly; **~mäßig hohe Temperaturen** constantly high temperatures; **~mäßigkeit** *die* ⇒ **~mäßig**: regularity; uniformity; evenness; **~mut** *der* (*veralt., landsch. auch: die;* **~mut**) equanimity; calmness; composure; **etw. mit ~mut hinnehmen/ertragen** accept/bear sth. with equanimity; **~mütig** ❶ *Adj.* calm; composed; unruffled ‹calm›; ❷ *adv.* with equanimity; calmly; **~mütigkeit** *die;* ~~ ⇒ **~mut**; **~namig** /-na:mɪç/ *Adj.* Ⓐ of the same name *postpos.*; Ⓑ (*Math.*) **~namige Brüche** fractions with a common denominator; **Brüche ~namig machen** reduce fractions to a common denominator; Ⓒ (*Physik*) like ‹charges, poles›

**Gleichnis** *das;* **~ses, ~se** (*Allegorie*) allegory; (*Parabel*) parable

**gleichnishaft** ❶ *Adj.* (*allegorisch*) allegorical; (*parabolisch*) parabolic. ❷ *adv.* allegorically/parabolically

**gleich-, Gleich-: ~rangig** /-raŋɪç/ ❶ *Adj.* ‹principle, problem, etc.› of equal importance *or* status; equally important ‹principle, problem, etc.›; ‹official, job› of equal rank; ❷ *adv.* **alle Punkte ~rangig behandeln** give all points equal treatment; **~|richten** *tr. V.* (*Elektrot.*) rectify; **~richter** *der* (*Elektrot.*) rectifier

**gleichsam** *Adv.* (*geh.*) as it were; so to speak; **~ als [ob] ...** just as if ...

**gleich-, Gleich-: ~|schalten** *tr. V.* (*abwertend*) force *or* bring into line; **~schaltung** *die* (*abwertend*) Gleichschaltung; **~schenk[e]lig** *Adj.* (*Math.*) isosceles; **~schritt** *der* marching in step; **im ~schritt** in step; **im ~schritt marsch!** forward march!; **~schritt halten** keep in step; **~|sehen** *unr. itr. V.* **jmdm./einer Sache ~sehen** look like sb./sth.; **~seitig** *Adj.* (*Math.*) equilateral; **~|setzen** *tr. V.* **zwei Dinge ~setzen** equate two things; **etw. einer Sache** (*Dat.*) *od.* **mit etw. ~setzen** equate sth. with sth.; **sich mit jmdm. ~setzen** put oneself on the same level as *or* on a level with sb.; **Ludwig XIV. setzte sich mit seinem Staat ~:** Ludwig XIV identified himself with his state; **~setzung** *die;* ~~, ~~**en: die ~setzung von sozialistischen und fortschrittlichen Ideen** equating socialist and progressive ideas; **die ~setzung der Arbeiter mit den Vertretern der Intelligenz** placing the workers on the same level as the members of the intelligentsia; **~silbig** *Adj.* having the same number of syllables *postpos., not pred.*; **~silbig sein** have the same number of syllables; **~sinnig** ❶ *Adj.* ‹fluctuations etc.› in the same direction; ❷ *adv.* in the same direction; **~stand** *der* Ⓐ (*Sport: gleicher Spielstand*) **den ~stand herstellen/erzielen** level the score; **beim ~stand von 1:1** with the scores level at 1 all; **das Spiel wurde beim ~stand von 1:1 beendet** the match ended in a 1 all draw; Ⓑ (*Politik*) balance of forces; **~|stehen** *unr. itr. V.* be equal (*Dat.* to, with); (*Sport*) be level; **~|stellen** *tr. V.* **zwei Dinge ~stellen** equate two things; **etw. einer Sache** (*Dat.*) *od.* **mit etw. ~stellen** equate sth. with sth.; **jmd. [mit] jmdm. ~stellen** put sb. on the same level as *or* on a level with sb.; (*gleiche Rechte zugestehen*) put sb. on an equal footing with sb.; **~stellung** *die:* **die rechtliche ~stellung unehelicher Kinder** giving equal rights to illegitimate children; **soziale ~stellung** social equality; **~strom** *der* (*Elektrot.*) direct current; **~|tun** *unr. tr. V.* **es jmdm. ~tun** match *or* equal sb.; (*nachahmen*) copy sb.; **es jmdm. an** *od.* **in etw.** (*Dat.*) **~tun** match *or* equal sb. in sth.; **es jmdm. an Schnelligkeit ~tun** match *or* equal sb. for speed

**Gleichung** *die;* ~, **~en** equation; **die ~ ging nicht auf** (*fig.*) things did not work out as planned

**gleich-, Gleich-: ~viel** /-'- *od.* '--/ *Adv.* no matter; **~viel wohin** no matter where; **~viel ob es leicht oder schwer geht/du darüber böse bist** regardless of whether it's easy or difficult/even if you are angry about it; **~wertig** *Adj.* Ⓐ (*Sport: gleich stark*) evenly matched ‹opponents, teams›; Ⓑ (*von gleichem Wert*) of equal *or* the same value *postpos.*; ‹performances› of the same standard; Ⓒ (*Chemie*) equivalent; **~wertigkeit** *die:* **wie ist ~wertigkeit der Arbeit zu definieren?** how can you define what constitutes equal work?; **die ~wertigkeit beider Inszenierungen steht außer Frage** that the two productions are of an equal standard is beyond question; **~wink[e]lig** *Adj.* (*Geom.*) equiangular; **~wohl** /-'- *od.* '--/ ❶ *Adv.* nevertheless; nonetheless; ❷ *Konj.* (*selten, noch landsch.*) although; **~zeitig** ❶ *Adj.* simultaneous; ❷ *adv.* Ⓐ (*zur gleichen Zeit*) simultaneously; at the same time; Ⓑ (*auch noch*) at the same time; **~zeitigkeit** *die;* ~~ simultaneity; simultaneousness; (*von historischen Ereignissen*) contemporaneity; contemporaneousness; **~|ziehen** *unr. itr. V.* catch up; draw level

**Gleis** /glai:s/ *das;* **~es, ~e** Ⓐ (*Fahrspur*) track; line; rails *pl.*; permanent way *as Brit. tech. term;* (*Bahnsteig*) platform; (*einzelne Schiene*) rail; **auf ~ 5 einlaufen** ‹train› arrive at platform 5; **„das Überschreiten der ~e ist verboten!"** 'passengers must not cross the line'; **aus dem ~ springen/kommen** jump/leave the rails; **ein totes ~:** an unused siding; Ⓑ (*fig.*) **auf** *od.* **in ein falsches ~ geraten** get on [to] the wrong track; **jmdn. aufs tote ~ schieben** put sb. out of harm's way (*fig.*); **etw. auf ein totes ~ schieben** shelve sth. indefinitely; **jmdn. aus dem ~ bringen** *od.* **werfen** put sb. off [his/her stroke]; (*von jmdm. psychisch nicht bewältigt werden*) upset *or* affect sb. deeply; **sie/alles wird wieder ins rechte ~ kommen** she'll be all right/everything will sort itself out; **alles wieder ins [rechte] ~ bringen** put things *or* matters right again; **aus dem ~ kommen** go off the rails (*fig.*); **er/alles ist wieder im ~:** he's/everything's all right again; **sich in ausgefahrenen ~en bewegen** be in a rut

**Gleis-: ~anlage** *die* [railway] lines *pl. or* tracks *pl.*; **~anschluss, *~anschluß** *der* siding; **~bau** *der* track laying; construction of permanent way (*Brit.*); **~bremse** *die* (*Eisenb.*) rail brake; **~kette** *die* (*Technik*) caterpillar track

**Gleisner** /'glai:snɐ/ *der;* **~s,** ~, **Gleisnerin** *die;* ~, **~nen** (*veralt.*) hypocrite

**gleisnerisch** *Adj.* (*veralt.*) hypocritical

**gleißen** /'glai:sn̩/ *itr. V.* (*dichter.*) blaze

**Gleis-: ~sperre** *die* (*Eisenb.*) scotch block; **~waage** *die* weighbridge

**Gleit-: ~bahn** *die* (*Flugw.*) glide path; **~boot** *das* hydroplane

**gleiten** /'glai:tn̩/ *unr. itr. V.; mit sein* Ⓐ glide; ‹hand› slide; **ein Lächeln glitt über ihr Gesicht** a smile passed over her face; **aus dem Sattel/ins Wasser ~:** slide out of the saddle/slide *or* slip into the water; **jmdm.**

**aus den Händen ~:** slip from sb.'s hands; **er ließ das Geld in seine Tasche ~:** he slipped the money into his pocket; Ⓑ (*ugs.: in Bezug auf Arbeitszeit*) work flexitime

**gleitend** *Adj.* **~e Arbeitszeit** flexitime; flexible working hours *pl.*; **~e Lohnskala** index-linked wage scale

**Gleiter** *der;* **~s, ~** glider

**gleit-, Gleit-: ~fläche** *die* slide; (*für Schiffe*) slipway; (*am Ski*) sole [of the ski]; **~flug** *der* glide; **im ~flug landen** glide-land; **zum ~flug ansetzen** go into a glide; **~flugzeug** *das* glider; **~klausel** *die* (*Rechtsw.*) escalator clause; **~kufe** *die* (*Fliegerspr.*) skid; **~laut** *der* (*Sprachw.*) glide; **~schiene** *die* guide *or* slide rail; **~schutz** *der* (*Kfz-W.*) anti-skid protection; (*Bauteil*) anti-skid device; **~sicher** *Adj.* non-slip ‹shoe, surface, etc.›; non-skid ‹tyre›; **~zeit** *die* Ⓐ (*Zeitspanne*) flexible working hours *pl. or* starting and finishing times *pl.*; Ⓑ **drei Stunden ~zeit** three hours flexitime; Ⓒ (*ugs.: gleitende Arbeitszeit*) flexitime; flexible working hours *pl.*

**Glencheck** /ˈglɛntʃɛk/ *der;* **~[s], ~s** Ⓐ (*Material*) glen-check cloth; Ⓑ (*Anzug*) glen-check suit

**Gletscher** /ˈglɛtʃɐ/ *der;* **~s, ~** glacier

**Gletscher-: ~bach** *der* glacial stream; **~brand** *der* glacier burn; **~eis** *das* glacial ice; **~mühle** *die* glacier mill; moulin; **~spalte** *die* crevasse; **~tisch** *der* (*Geol.*) glacier table; **~tor** *das* (*Geol.*) glacier snout

**glibberig** /ˈglɪbərɪç/ *Adj.* (*bes. nordd.*) slippery; (*schleimig*) slimy

**glich** /glɪç/ *1. u. 3. Pers. Sg. Prät. v.* **gleichen**

**Glied** /gliːt/ *das;* **~[e]s, ~er** Ⓐ ▸471 (*Körperteil*) limb; (*Finger~, Zehen~*) joint; phalanx (*Anat.*); **kein ~ rühren können** be unable to move a muscle; **der Schreck sitzt** *od.* **steckt ihm noch in den ~ern** he is [still] shaking with the shock; **der Schreck fuhr ihr in die** *od.* **durch alle ~er** the shock made her shake all over; Ⓑ (*Ketten~, auch fig.*) link; Ⓒ (*Teil eines Ganzen*) section; part; (*Mit~*) member; (*eines Satzes*) part; (*einer Gleichung*) term; **ein nützliches ~ der Gesellschaft** a useful member of society; Ⓓ ▸471 (*Penis*) penis; Ⓔ (*Mannschaftsreihe*) rank; Ⓕ (*geh. veralt.: Generation*) generation

**glieder-, Glieder-: ~bau** *der* limb structure; **~füßer** *der;* **~~s, ~~** (*Zool.*) arthropod; **~lahm** *Adj.* stiff-limbed

**gliedern** /ˈgliːdɐn/ ❶ *tr. V.* structure; organize ‹thoughts›; **nach Eigenschaften ~:** classify according to properties; **in Teile ~:** arrange in parts; **einen Aufsatz in drei Teile ~:** divide an essay into three sections; **hierarchisch gegliedert** hierarchically structured. ❷ *refl. V.* **sich in Gruppen/Abschnitte** *usw.* **~:** divide *or* be divided into groups/sections *etc.*

**Glieder-: ~puppe** *die* jointed doll; (*als Modell für Maler o. Ä.*) lay figure; **~reißen** *das;* **~~s** (*ugs.*), **~schmerz** *der* rheumatic pains *pl.*; **~tier** *das* (*Zool.*) member of the Articulata; **die ~tiere** the Articulata

**Gliederung** *die;* **~, ~en** Ⓐ (*Aufbau, Einteilung*) structure; **in militärischer ~:** in military formation; **die ~ eines Buches in Kapitel** the division of a book into chapters; Ⓑ (*das Gliedern*) structuring; (*von Gedanken*) organization; (*nach Eigenschaften*) classification; (*in Teile*) arrangement; Ⓒ (*ns.: Gruppe*) section

**Glieder·zucken** *das;* **~~s** twitching of the limbs

**glied-, Glied-: ~maße** /-maːsə/ *die;* **~, ~n** limb; **~satz** *der* (*Sprachw.*) subordinate clause; **~staat** *der* member *or* constituent state; **~weise** *Adv.* in ranks

**glimmen** /ˈglɪmən/ *unr. od. regelm. itr. V.* glow; **in seinen Augen glomm ein gefährlicher Funke** (*fig.*) there was a dangerous glint in his eyes

**Glimmer** *der;* **~s, ~** mica

**glimmern** *itr. V.* glimmer; ‹lake etc.› glisten

**Glimm-: ~lampe** *die* (*Elektrot.*) glow lamp; **~stängel**, ***~stengel** *der* (*ugs. scherzh.*) fag (*coll.*); ciggy (*coll.*)

**glimpflich** /ˈglɪmpflɪç/ ❶ *Adj.* Ⓐ **der Unfall nahm ein ~es Ende** the accident turned out not to be too serious; **sie war über den ~en Ausgang der Angelegenheit erfreut** she was glad to have got off so lightly; Ⓑ (*mild*) lenient ‹sentence, punishment›. ❷ *adv.* Ⓐ (*ohne Schaden*) **~ davonkommen** get off lightly; **es ist ~ abgegangen** it turned out not to be too bad; Ⓑ (*mild*) mildly; leniently

**glitschen** /ˈglɪtʃn̩/ *itr. V.; mit sein* (*ugs.*) slip; **jmdm. aus der Hand ~:** slip out of sb.'s hand

**glitschig** /ˈglɪtʃɪç/ *Adj.* (*ugs.*) slippery

**glitt** /glɪt/ *1. u. 3. Pers. Sg. Prät. v.* **gleiten**

**glitz[e]rig** /ˈglɪts(ə)rɪç/ *Adj.* (*ugs.*) glistening ‹snow›; sparkling, glittering ‹diamond, decorations›

**glitzern** /ˈglɪtsɐn/ *itr. V.* ‹star› twinkle; ‹diamond, decorations› sparkle, glitter; ‹snow, eyes, tears› glisten

**glitzrig** ⇒ **glitz[e]rig**

**global** /gloˈbaːl/ ❶ *Adj.* Ⓐ (*weltweit*) global; worldwide; Ⓑ (*umfassend*) general, allround ‹education›; overall ‹control, planning, etc.›; Ⓒ (*allgemein*) general. ❷ *adv.* Ⓐ (*weltweit*) worldwide; globally; Ⓑ (*umfassend*) in overall terms; **~ gesteuert werden** be subject to overall control; Ⓒ (*allgemein*) in general terms; **~ gerechnet** in round figures

**globalisieren** *tr. V.* globalize

**Globalisierung** *die;* **~, ~en** globalization

**Global-: ~steuerung** *die* (*Wirtsch.*) overall control; **~strategie** *die* global *or* worldwide strategy

**Globen** ⇒ **Globus**

**Globetrotter** /ˈgloːbətrɔtɐ/ *der;* **~s, ~, Globetrotterin** *die;* **~, ~nen** globetrotter

**Globus** /ˈgloːbʊs/ *der;* **~** *od.* **~ses, Globen** /ˈgloːbn̩/ Ⓐ globe; Ⓑ (*salopp: Kopf*) nut (*coll.*); bonce (*Brit. sl.*)

**Glöckchen** /ˈglœkçən/ *das;* **~s, ~** [little] bell

**Glocke** /ˈglɔkə/ *die;* **~, ~n** Ⓐ (*auch: Tür~, Taucher~, Blüte*) bell; **etw. an die große ~ hängen** (*ugs.*) tell the whole world about sth.; **wissen, was die ~ geschlagen hat** (*ugs.*) know what one is in for (*coll.*); Ⓑ (*Hut*) cloche; Ⓒ (*Käse~, Butter~, Kuchen~*) cover; bell; Ⓓ (*Fechten*) coquille

**glocken-, Glocken-: ~balken** *der* [bell] yoke; **~blume** *die* (*Bot.*) bell flower; campanula; **~förmig** ❶ *Adj.* bell-shaped; widely flared ‹skirt etc.›; ❷ *adv.* **~förmig geschnitten** widely flared; **~geläute** *das* pealing *or* ringing of bells; **~gießer** *der* bell-founder; **~gießerei** /----ˈ-/ *die* bell foundry; **~gießerin** *die* ⇒ **~gießer**; **~guss**, ***~guß** *der* bell-founding *no art.*; **~heide** *die* (*Bot.*) bell heather; **~hell** ❶ *Adj.* bell-like; **eine ~helle Stimme** a high, clear voice; ❷ *adv.* **~hell lachen** give a high, clear laugh; **~klang** *der* pealing *or* ringing of bells; **~klöppel** *der* [bell-]clapper; **~läuten** *das;* **~~s** pealing *or* ringing of bells; **~mantel** *der* (*Gussform*) cope; **~rein** ❶ *Adj.* as clear as a bell *postpos.*; ❷ *adv.* as clear as a bell; **~rock** *der* widely flared skirt; **~schlag** *der* stroke; **beim ~schlag um acht Uhr** on the stroke of eight o'clock; **mit dem** *od.* **auf den ~schlag** (*ugs.*) on the dot (*coll.*); **~seil** *das* bell rope; **~spiel** *das* Ⓐ carillon; (*mit einer Uhr gekoppelt auch*) chimes *pl.*; Ⓑ (*Instrument*) glockenspiel; **~strang** *der* ⇒ **~seil**; **~stube** *die* belfry; **~stuhl** *der* bell cage; **~ton** *der; Pl.* **~töne** stroke of a/the bell; **~töne** the sound of a/the bell/of bells; **~turm** *der* bell tower; belfry; **~weihe** *die* (*kath. Rel.*) baptism *or* blessing of a/the bell; **~zeichen** *das* ring of a/the bell; **auf das ~zeichen** when the bell rings/rang; **~zug** *der* (*Klingelschnur*) bell pull; (**~seil**) bell rope

**glockig** /ˈglɔkɪç/ ⇒ **glockenförmig**

**Glöckner** /ˈglœknɐ/ *der;* **~s, ~** (*veralt.*) bell-ringer; **der ~ von Notre Dame** the Hunchback of Notre Dame

**glomm** /glɔm/ *1. u. 3. Pers. Sg. Prät. v.* **glimmen**

**Gloria**[1] /ˈgloːri̯a/ *das;* **~s** *od. die;* **~** (*iron.*) glory

**Gloria**[2] *das;* **~s, ~s** (*Rel.*) gloria; **das große/kleine ~:** the greater/lesser doxology

**Glorie** /ˈgloːri̯ə/ *die;* **~, ~n** Ⓐ (*geh.: Ruhm*) glory; Ⓑ (*geh.: Lichtschein*) glory; (*um den Kopf, um einen Stern*) halo

**Glorien·schein** *der* glory; (*um den Kopf, fig.*) halo

**Glorifikation** /glorifikaˈtsi̯oːn/ *die;* **~, ~en** glorification

**glorifizieren** /glorifiˈtsiːrən/ *tr. V.* glorify

**Glorifizierung** *die;* **~, ~en** glorification

**Gloriole** /gloˈri̯oːlə/ *die;* **~, ~n** Ⓐ (*auch fig.*) glory; Ⓑ (*um den Kopf*) halo; aura

**glorios** /gloˈri̯oːs/ (*iron.*) ❶ *Adj.* brilliant. ❷ *adv.* brilliantly

**glor·reich** /ˈgloːɐ̯-/ ❶ *Adj.* glorious. ❷ *adv.* gloriously

**glosen** /ˈgloːzn̩/ *itr. V.* (*landsch./dichter.*) ⇒ **glimmen**

**Glossar** /glɔˈsaːɐ̯/ *das;* **~s, ~e** glossary

**Glosse** /ˈglɔsə/ *die;* **~, ~n** Ⓐ (*in den Medien*) commentary; Ⓑ (*spöttische Bemerkung*) sneering *or* (*coll.*) snide comment; Ⓒ (*Sprachw., Literaturw.*) gloss

**Glossen·schreiber** *der*, **Glossen·schreiberin** *die* commentator

**glossieren** *tr. V.* Ⓐ commentate on; Ⓑ (*bespötteln*) sneer at; Ⓒ (*Sprachw., Literaturw.*) gloss

**Glottal** /glɔˈtaːl/ *der;* **~s, ~e** (*Phon.*) glottal stop

**Glottis** /ˈglɔtɪs/ *die;* **~, Glottides** /ˈglɔtideːs/ (*Anat.*) glottis

**Glotz·auge** *das* Ⓐ *Pl.* (*salopp abwertend*) goggle eyes; **~n machen/bekommen** go goggle-eyed; goggle; Ⓑ ▸474 (*Med.*) exophthalmus

**glotz·äugig** *Adj.* goggle-eyed

**Glotze** /ˈglɔtsə/ *die;* **~, ~n** (*salopp*) box (*coll.*); goggle-box (*Brit. coll.*)

**glotzen** *itr. V.* (*abwertend*) goggle; gawk, gawp (*coll.*)

**Glotz·kiste** *die* (*salopp*) box (*coll.*); goggle-box (*Brit. coll.*)

**Glotzophon** /glɔtsoˈfoːn/ *das;* **~s, ~e** (*salopp scherzh.*) ⇒ **Glotze**

**Gloxinie** /glɔˈksiːni̯ə/ *die;* **~, ~n** (*Bot.*) gloxinia

**Glubsch·augen** /ˈglʊpʃ-/ *Pl.* (*nordd.*) ⇒ **Glupschaugen**

**gluck** /glʊk/ *Interj.* Ⓐ (*für das Glucken*) cluck; Ⓑ (*für das Gluckern*) glug; **~, ~, weg war er** (*scherzh.*) glug, glug, and he went under; **~, ~ machen** (*ugs. scherzh.*) have a few (*sl.*)

**Glück** /glʏk/ *das;* **~[e]s** Ⓐ luck; **ein großes/unverdientes ~:** a great/an undeserved stroke of luck; **[es ist/war] ein ~, dass ...** it's/it was lucky that ...; **er hat [kein] ~ gehabt** he was [un]lucky; **sie hatte das ~, zu ...** she was lucky enough to ...; **bei jmdm. ~ mit etw. haben** succeed in getting sb. to agree to sth.; **bei jmdm. kein ~ haben** get no joy out of sb.; **~ bei Frauen haben** be successful with women; **bei der Auslosung kein ~ haben** have no luck in the draw; **~ im Unglück haben** be quite lucky in the circumstances; **jmdm. ~ wünschen** wish sb. [good] luck; **jmdm. viel ~ zum Geburtstag wünschen** wish sb. a very happy birthday; **viel ~!** [the] best of luck!; good luck!; **~ bringen** bring [good] luck; **~ muss der Mensch haben** my/his *etc.* luck must have been in; **mehr ~ als Verstand haben** have more luck than judgement; **er weiß noch nichts von seinem ~** (*iron.*) he doesn't know what's in store for him yet; **sein ~ versuchen** *od.* **probieren** try one's luck; **sein ~ machen** make one's fortune; **auf gut ~:** trusting to luck; **er hatte sich auf gut ~ beworben** he had applied on the off chance; **sie wählte ein Buch auf gut ~:** she chose a book at random; **von ~ sagen** *od.* **reden**

*old spelling (see note on page 1707)

**können** consider *or* count oneself lucky; **zum ~** *od.* **zu meinem/seinem** *usw.* **~:** luckily *or* fortunately [for me/him *etc.*]; **~ auf!** (*Bergmannsgruß*) good luck!; **~ ab!** (*Fliegergruß*) happy landings!; good luck!; **B** (*Hochstimmung*) happiness; **das häusliche ~:** domestic bliss; **sie ist sein ganzes ~:** she means everything to him; **jmdn. zu seinem ~ zwingen** make sb. do what is good for him/her; **man kann niemanden zu seinem ~ zwingen** you can lead a horse to water but you can't make him drink; **du hast/das hat mir gerade noch zu meinem ~ gefehlt** (*iron.*) you're/that's all I needed; **jeder ist seines ~es Schmied** (*Spr.*) life is what you make it; **~ und Glas, wie leicht bricht das** (*Spr.*) happiness is such a fragile thing; **C** (*Fortuna*) fortune; luck; **das ~ ist launisch** fortunes change; **er ist ein Liebling des ~s** fortune has always smiled upon him; **das ~ war ihm hold** (*geh.*) fortune smiled [up]on him

**glück·bringend** *Adj.* lucky

**Glucke** /ˈglʊkə/ *die;* ~, **~n** brood-hen; mother hen

**glucken** *itr. V.* **A** (*brüten*) brood; **B** (*ugs.: herumsitzen*) sit around; **C** (*Laut hervorbringen*) cluck

**glücken** *tr. V.; mit sein* succeed; be successful; **etw. glückt jmdm.** sb. is successful with sth.; **ein geglückter Versuch** a successful attempt; **die Flucht ist nicht geglückt** the escape [attempt] failed; **es glückt jmdm., etw. zu tun** sb. manages to do sth.

**gluckern** /ˈglʊkɐn/ *itr. V.* gurgle; glug

**glück·haft** *Adj.* (*geh.*) happy

**Gluck·henne** *die* ⇒ **Glucke**

**glücklich** ❶ *Adj.* **A** ▶ 369 (*von Glück erfüllt*) happy (**über** + *Akk.* about); **wunschlos/unsagbar ~ sein** be perfectly happy; **Geld allein macht nicht ~:** money by itself won't bring happiness; **du Glücklicher!** you lucky thing!; lucky you!; **wer ist denn der/die Glückliche?** who is the lucky man/woman/girl *etc.?*; **B** (*erfolgreich*) lucky ‹winner›; successful ‹outcome›; safe ‹journey›; happy ‹ending›; **C** (*vorteilhaft*) fortunate; **ein ~er Zufall** a happy coincidence; a lucky chance; ⇒ *auch* **Hand F**.
❷ *adv.* **A** (*erfolgreich*) successfully; **B** (*vorteilhaft, zufrieden*) happily ‹chosen, married›; **C** (*endlich*) eventually; at last

**glücklicher·weise** *Adv.* fortunately; luckily

**glück·los** *Adj.* luckless ‹enterprise›; unhappy ‹existence etc.›

**Glück·sache** ⇒ **Glückssache**

**Glücks-:** **~bote** *der,* **~botin** *die* bearer of good news *or* glad tidings; **~botschaft** *die* good news *sing.;* glad tidings *pl.;* **~bringer** *der;* **~~s, ~~:** lucky *or* good-luck charm; [lucky] mascot; (*Person*) [lucky] mascot; **~bringerin** *die;* **~~, ~~nen** [lucky] mascot

**glück·selig** ❶ *Adj.* blissfully happy ‹person›; blissfully happy, blissful ‹time, experience, etc.›. ❷ *adv.* blissfully

**Glück·seligkeit** *die;* **~:** bliss; blissful happiness

**glucksen** /ˈglʊksn̩/ *itr. V.* **A** ⇒ **gluckern**; **B** (*lachen*) chuckle; ‹baby› gurgle

**Glücks-:** **~fall** *der* piece *or* stroke of luck; **~fee** *die:* **sie war seine ~fee** she [always] brought him good luck; **~gefühl** *das* feeling of happiness; **~göttin** *die* goddess of fortune; Fortune *no art.;* **~güter** *Pl.* (*geh.*) riches; **~käfer** *der* ⇒ **Marienkäfer**; **~kind** *das* lucky person; **er/sie ist ein ~kind** he/she was born lucky; **~klee** *der* four-leaf *or* four-leaved clover; **~linie** *die* line of fortune; **~pfennig** *der* lucky penny; **~pilz** *der* (*ugs.*) lucky devil (*coll.*) *or* beggar (*coll.*); **~rad** *das* wheel of fortune; **~ritter** *der* (*abwertend*) adventurer; fortune hunter; **~ritterin** *die;* **~~, ~~nen** (*abwertend*) adventuress; fortune hunter

**Glück[s]·sache** *die:* **das ist ~:** it's a matter of luck

**Glücks-:** **~schwein** *das: model of a pig as a symbol of good luck or as a good-luck charm;* **~spiel** *das* **A** game of chance; **dem ~spiel verfallen sein** be addicted to gambling; **B** (*fig.*) matter of luck; lottery; **~spieler** *der,* **~spielerin** *die* gambler; **~stern** *der* lucky star; **~strähne** *die* lucky streak; **eine ~strähne haben** have hit a lucky streak; have a run of good luck; **~tag** *der* lucky day

**glück·strahlend** ❶ *Adj.* radiant; radiantly happy. ❷ *adv.* **sie verkündete uns ~, dass sie heiraten werde** she was radiant with happiness *or* radiantly happy as she told us she was going to get married

**Glücks-:** **~treffer** *der* **A** (*Gewinn*) bit *or* piece of luck; **B** (*beim Schießen*) lucky hit; fluke; **~umstand** *der* fortunate circumstance; **~zahl** *die* lucky number

**glück·verheißend** *Adj.* (*geh.*) auspicious, propitious ‹sign, omen›; ‹smile› which holds/held out the promise of happiness

**Glück·wunsch** *der* ▶ 369 congratulations *pl.;* **herzlichen ~ zur Beförderung!** [many] congratulations on your promotion!; **herzlichen ~ zum Geburtstag!** happy birthday!; many happy returns of the day!; **jmdm. die herzlichsten Glückwünsche übermitteln/senden** convey/send one's congratulations to sb.

**Glückwunsch-:** **~adresse** *die* message of congratulation; congratulatory message; **~karte** *die* congratulations card; (*zum Geburtstag, zu Weihnachten usw.*) greetings card; **~schreiben** *das* letter of congratulation; congratulatory letter; **~telegramm** *das* telegram of congratulations; congratulatory telegram; (*zum Geburtstag, zu Weihnachten usw.*) greetings telegram

**Glucose** /gluˈkoːzə/ *die;* ~ (*Chemie*) glucose

**Glüh-:** **~birne** *die* light bulb; **~draht** *der* filament

**glühen** /ˈglyːən/ ❶ *itr. V.* **A** (*leuchten*) glow; (*fig.*) ‹eyes, cheeks, etc.› be aglow, glow; **heiß glühte die Sonne über der Wüste** (*fig.*) the sun was burning down on the desert; **ihr Körper glühte im Fieber** (*fig.*) her body was burning with fever; **B** (*geh.: erregt sein*) burn; **in Liebe/Leidenschaft ~:** burn with love/passion; **vor Begeisterung ~:** be fired with enthusiasm. ❷ *tr. V.* (*zum Leuchten bringen*) heat until red-hot

**glühend** ❶ *Adj.* **A** (*heiß*) red-hot ‹metal etc.›; (*fig.*) blazing ‹heat›; burning ‹hatred›; flushed, burning ‹cheeks›; **B** (*begeistert*) ardent ‹admirer etc.›; passionate ‹words, letter, etc.›. ❷ *adv.* **A** (*heiß*) **~ heiß** scorching *or* blazing hot; **~ rot** red-hot; **B** (*begeistert*) ‹love› passionately; ‹admire› ardently; **jmdn. ~ beneiden** be intensely envious of sb.

***glühend·heiß** *usw.* ⇒ **glühend 2A**

**Glüh-:** **~faden** *der* filament; **~kerze** *die* (*Kfz-W.*) glow plug; **~lampe** *die* light bulb; **~ofen** *der* (*Technik*) annealing furnace; **~strumpf** *der* gas mantle; **~wein** *der* mulled wine; glühwein; **~würmchen** *das* (*ugs.*) (*weiblich*) glow-worm; (*männlich*) firefly

**Glukose** ⇒ **Glucose**

**Glupsch·augen** /ˈglʊpʃ-/ *Pl.* (*nordd.*) goggle-eyes; **~ machen** *od.* **bekommen** go goggle-eyed; goggle

**Glut** /gluːt/ *die;* ~, **~en** **A** embers *pl.;* (*von einer Zigarette*) [burning] ash; (*fig.*) [blazing] heat; (*des Fiebers*) [burning] heat; **die ~ ihrer Wangen** the flush on her cheeks; **die ~ des Abendhimmels** the glow of the evening sky; **B** (*geh.: Leidenschaft*) passion; **die ~ seiner Leidenschaft** the ardour of his passion; **die ~ seines Hasses** the fire of his hatred

**Glutamat** /glutaˈmaːt/ *das;* **~[e]s, ~e** (*Chemie*) glutamate

**Glutamin** /glutaˈmiːn/ *das;* **~s, ~e** (*Chemie*) glutamine

**Glutamin·säure** *die* (*Chemie*) glutamic acid

**glut-, Glut-:** **~äugig** *Adj.* fiery-eyed; **~hauch** *der* (*dichter.*) scorching *or* sweltering heat; **~heiß** *Adj.* blazing *or* swelteringly hot; **~hitze** *die* blazing *or* sweltering heat; **~rot** *Adj.* fiery red; **~voll** ❶ *Adj.* passionate; ❷ *adv.* passionately

**Glycerin** (*fachspr.*) ⇒ **Glyzerin**

**Glykogen** /glykoˈgeːn/ *das;* **~s** (*Med., Biol.*) glycogen

**Glykol** /glyˈkoːl/ *das;* **~s, ~e** (*Chemie*) [ethylene] glycol

**Glyzerin** /glytsəˈriːn/ *das;* **~s** glycerine; glycerol (*Chem.*)

**Glyzerin·creme** *die* glycerine cream

**Glyzine, Glyzinie** /glyˈtsiːn(i̯)ə/ *die;* ~, **~n** wisteria

**GmbH** *Abk.* **Gesellschaft mit beschränkter Haftung** ≈ Plc, plc

**g-Moll** /ˈgeː-/ *das* (*Musik*) G minor; ⇒ *auch* **a-Moll**

**Gnade** /ˈgnaːdə/ *die;* ~, **~n** **A** (*Gewogenheit*) favour; **die ~ [des Königs] erlangen/verlieren** gain/lose [the king's] favour; **die ~ haben, etw. zu tun** (*iron.*) graciously consent to do sth. (*iron.*); **vor jmdm.** *od.* **vor jmds. Augen ~ finden** find favour with sb. *or* in sb.'s eyes; **jmdm. auf ~ und** *od.* **oder Ungnade ausgeliefert sein** be [completely] at sb.'s mercy; **etw. aus ~ [und Barmherzigkeit] tun** do sth. out of the kindness of one's heart; **in ~n wieder aufgenommen werden** be restored to favour; **bei jmdm. in [hohen] ~n stehen** (*geh.*) stand high in sb.'s favour; **von jmds. ~n** by the grace of sb.; **B** (*Rel.: Güte*) grace; **C** (*Milde*) mercy; **~ walten lassen** show mercy; be lenient; **~ vor** *od.* **für Recht ergehen lassen** temper justice with mercy; **D** (*veraltete Anrede*) **Euer** *od.* **Ihro** *od.* **Ihre ~n** Your Grace

**gnaden** *itr. V. in* **gnade mir/dir Gott!** God *or* Heaven help me/you!

**gnaden-, Gnaden-:** **~akt** *der* act of mercy; **~beweis** *der,* **~bezeigung** *die;* **~~, ~~en** token of [his/her *etc.*] favour; **~bild** *das* (*kath. Rel.*) *picture of Christ, the Virgin Mary, or a saint, possessing miraculous powers;* **~brot** *das:* **jmdm./einem Tier das ~brot geben** keep sb./an animal in his/her/its old age; **einem Pferd das ~brot geben** put a horse out to grass; **~erweis** *der;* **~~es, ~~e** (*Rechtsw.*) pardon; **~frist** *die* reprieve; **jmdm. eine ~frist von 4 Wochen gewähren** give sb. four weeks' grace; **ihm bleibt eine ~frist von einer Woche** he has a week left; **~gesuch** *das* plea for clemency; **~instanz** *die: person in whom or authority in which the right of pardon is vested;* **~los** (*auch fig.*) ❶ *Adj.* merciless; ❷ *adv.* mercilessly; **~losigkeit** *die;* **~~:** mercilessness; **~reich** *Adj.* (*geh.*) gracious; **~schuss, *~schuß** *der* coup de grâce (*by shooting*); **einem Pferd den ~schuss geben** put a horse out of its misery [by shooting it]; **~stoß** *der* coup de grâce (*with sword etc.*); **~tod** *der* euthanasia; mercy killing; **jmdm. den ~tod gewähren** allow sb. to die; **~voll** *Adj.* (*geh.*) gracious; **~weg** *der:* **auf dem ~weg** by a pardon; **ihm steht der ~weg offen** he can ask *or* has the right to ask for a pardon

**gnädig** /ˈgnɛːdɪç/ ❶ *Adj.* **A** (*oft iron.*) gracious; **er war so ~, mich nach Hause zu begleiten** (*iron.*) he condescended to take me home; (*Anrede*) **~es Fräulein/~e Frau** madam; **~er Herr** (*veralt.*) sir; **die ~e Frau/das ~e Fräulein/der ~e Herr** (*veralt.*) madam/the young lady/the master; **die Gnädige** (*spött.*) her ladyship; **B** (*glimpflich*) lenient, light ‹sentence etc.›; **C** (*Rel.*) gracious ‹God›; **Gott ist allen Sündern ~:** God is merciful to *or* has mercy on all sinners; **Gott sei uns ~:** [may] the good Lord preserve us.
❷ *adv.* **A** (*oft iron.*) graciously; **B** (*glimpflich*) **das ist ~ abgegangen** it turned out not to be too bad; **machen Sie es ~ mit mir** (*scherzh.*) have mercy on me (*joc.*)

**Gneis** /gnais/ *der;* **~es, ~e** (*Geol.*) gneiss

**Gnom** /gnoːm/ *der;* **~en, ~en** gnome; (*fig.: ugs.*) little twerp (*coll.*)

**gnomen·haft** *Adj.* gnome-like

**Gnosis** /ˈgnoːzɪs/ *die;* ~ (*Rel.*) gnosis

**Gnostiker** /ˈgnɔstikɐ/ *der;* **~s, ~, Gnostikerin** *die;* **~, ~nen** (*Rel.*) gnostic

g

**gnostisch** *Adj.* (*Rel.*) gnostic

**Gnostizismus** /gnɔsti'tsɪsmʊs/ *der;* ~ (*Rel.*) gnosticism *no art.*

**Gnu** /gnu:/ *das;* **~s, ~s** gnu

**Go** /go:/ *das;* **~:** go

**Goal** /go:l/ *das;* **~s, ~s** (*österr., schweiz. Sport*) goal

**Goal-: ~getter** /-gɛtɐ/ *der;* **~~s, ~~** (*Sport*) goal scorer; **~keeper** /-ki:pɐ/ *der;* **~~s, ~~** (*Sport, bes. österr. u. schweiz.*) goalkeeper

**Gobelin** /gobə'lɛ̃:/ *der;* **~s, ~s** Gobelin [tapestry]

**Gobelin·stickerei** *die* Gobelin embroidery

**Go-cart** ⇨ **Gokart**

**Gockel** /'gɔkl/ *der;* **~s,** ~ (*bes. südd., sonst ugs. scherzh.*) cock; **stolz wie ein ~:** [as] proud as a peacock; **ein verliebter alter ~** (*fig.*) an amorous old goat (*coll.*)

**Gockel·hahn** *der; Pl.* **Gockel·hähne** ⇨ **Gockel**

**Godemiché** /go:dmi'ʃe:/ *der;* **~, ~s** dildo

**Goetheana** /gøte'a:na/ *Pl.* works by and on Goethe

**goethesch, *Goethesch** /'gø:təʃ/, **goethisch, *Goethisch** /'gø:tɪʃ/ *Adj.* Goethean; **die ~en Gedichte** Goethe's poems; the poems of Goethe

**Go-go-Girl** /'go:gogø:ɐ̯l/ *das* go-go girl *or* dancer

**Goi** /'go:i/ *der;* **~[s], Gojim** /'go:jɪm/ goy

**Go-in** /go:'ɪn/ *das;* **~s, ~s: ein ~ veranstalten** disrupt the/a meeting

**Gokart** /'go:kart/ *der;* **~s, ~s** go-kart (*Brit.*); kart

**Golan·höhen** /go'la:n-/ *Pl.* Golan Heights

**gold** /gɔlt/ *Adj.: in* **uns geht's ja noch ~** (*ugs.*) we're still doing just marvellously

**Gold** *das;* **~[e]s** gold; **etw. ist aus ~:** sth. is [made of] gold; **ein Barren ~:** a gold bar *or* ingot; **das schwarze ~** (*fig.*) black gold (*fig.*); **das flüssige ~** (*fig.*) liquid gold (*fig.*); **es ist nicht alles ~, was glänzt** (*Spr.*) all that glitters *or* glistens is not gold (*prov.*); **treu wie ~ sein** be absolutely loyal *or* faithful; **etw. in ~ bezahlen** pay for sth. in gold; **~ in der Kehle haben** (*fig.*) have a golden voice; **jmd. ist nicht mit ~ zu bezahlen** sb. is worth his/her weight in gold (*fig.*); **etw. ist nicht mit ~ zu bezahlen** *od.* **aufzuwiegen** sth. is invaluable; **olympisches ~:** Olympic gold; **er hat bereits dreimal olympisches ~ geholt** he has already won three Olympic gold medals *or* golds

**gold-, Gold-: ~ader** *die* vein of gold; **~ammer** *die* yellowhammer; **~arbeit** *die* goldwork; (*Gegenstand*) piece of goldwork; **~auflage** *die* gold plating *no indef. art.;* **~barren** *der* gold bar *or* ingot; **~barsch** *der* ⇨ **Rotbarsch**; **~bestand** *der* gold reserves *pl.;* **~bestickt** *Adj.* embroidered with gold [thread] *postpos.;* **~betresst, *~betreßt** *Adj.* trimmed with gold braid *postpos.;* **~blech** *das* rolled gold; **~blond** *Adj.* golden ‹hair etc.›; **~borte** *die* gold braid; **~braun** *Adj.* golden brown; **~broiler** *der* (*DDR*) spit-roasted chicken; **~brokat** *der* gold brocade; **~deckung** *die* gold cover; **~doublé** *das* ⇨ **~dublee**; **~druck** *der* gold tooling; **~dublee** *das* rolled gold; **~echt** *Adj.* (*ugs.*) completely genuine ‹person›

**golden** ❶ *Adj.* [A] gold ‹bracelet, watch, etc.›; **das Goldene Kalb** (*bibl.*) the golden calf; **der Tanz ums Goldene Kalb** the worship of the golden calf *or* Mammon; **eine ~e Schallplatte** a gold disc; **die Goldene Bulle** (*hist.*) the Golden Bull; **das Goldene Vlies** (*Myth.*) the Golden Fleece; (*Orden*) the [order of the] Golden Fleece; **das Goldene Buch [der Stadt]** the [town's] visitors' book; **die Goldene Stadt** the Golden City (*Prague*); [B] (*dichter.: goldfarben*) golden; [C] (*herrlich*) golden ‹days, memories, etc.›; blissful ‹freedom etc.›; **der ~e Westen** the promised land in the West; **~e Worte/Lehren** words of wisdom/wise teachings; **einen ~en Humor haben** have a wonderful sense of humour; **ein ~es Herz haben** have a heart of gold; **die ~e Mitte** *od.* **den ~en Mittelweg finden/wählen** find/strike a happy medium; **das goldene Zeitalter** the Golden Age; **die ~en zwanziger [Jahre]** the roaring twenties; **der goldene Schnitt** (*Math.*) the golden section. ❷ *adv.* like gold

**gold-, Gold-: ~esel** *der* (*ugs.*) **ich bin auch kein ~esel** I'm not made of money (*coll.*); **~faden** *der* gold thread; **~farben, ~farbig** *Adj.* gold-coloured; golden; **~fasan** *der* golden pheasant; **~feder** *die* gold nib; **~fieber** *das* gold fever; **~folie** *die* gold foil; **~fuchs** *der* [A] (*Pferd*) golden chestnut [horse]; [B] (*veralt.: ~stück*) gold coin *or* piece; **~füllung** *die* gold filling; **~fund** *der* gold find *or* strike; **~gefasst, *~gefaßt** *Adj.* gold-rimmed ‹glasses›; ‹jewel› mounted in gold; **~gehalt** *der* gold content; **~gelb** *Adj.* golden yellow; **~gerändert** *Adj.* ‹plate etc.› edged with gold; gold-rimmed ‹glasses›; **~glänzend** *Adj.* shining gold; **~gräber** *der;* **~~s, ~~, ~gräberin** *die;* **~~, ~~nen** gold-digger; **~grube** *die* (*auch fig.*) gold mine; **~haltig** *Adj.* gold-bearing; auriferous; **~hamster** *der* golden hamster

**goldig** ❶ *Adj.* (*niedlich, landsch.: nett*) sweet. ❷ *adv.* sweetly

**Gold-: ~junge** *der* [A] (*Kosewort*) good [little] boy; [B] (*Sportjargon*) gold medallist; gold-medal winner; **~käfer** *der* [A] rose chafer; rose beetle; [B] (*ugs.: reiches Mädchen*) rich girl; **~kette** *die* gold chain; **~kind** *das* (*ugs. Kosew.*) little treasure (*coll.*); **mein ~kind** my precious (*coll.*); my pet; **~klumpen** *der* gold nugget; **~krone** *die* (*Zahnmed.*) gold crown; **~kurs** *der* (*Börsenw.*) price of gold; gold price; **~küste** *die;* **~~** (*Geogr.*) Gold Coast; **~lack** *der* [A] gold lacquer; [B] (*Bot.*) wallflower; **~lagerstätte** *die* gold deposit; **~legierung** *die* gold alloy; **~leiste** *die* gilt strip *or* fillet; **~macher** *der* alchemist; **~mädchen** *das* (*Sportjargon*) gold medallist; gold-medal winner

**Gold·medaille** *die* gold medal

**Goldmedaillen-: ~gewinner** *der,* **~gewinnerin** *die* gold medallist; gold-medal winner

**gold-, Gold-: ~mine** *die* gold mine; **~münze** *die* gold coin; **~papier** *das* gold[-coloured] paper; **~parität** *die* (*Wirtsch.*) gold parity; **~pool** *der* (*Wirtsch.*) gold pool; **~preis** *der* price of gold; gold price; **~probe** *die* gold assay; **~rahmen** *der* gold *or* gilt frame; **~rausch** *der* gold fever; **~regen** *der* [A] (*Bot.*) laburnum; golden rain; [B] (*Feuerwerk*) golden rain; [C] (*Reichtum*) riches *pl.*; wealth; **~reif** *der* (*geh.*) gold ring; (*Armband*) gold bracelet; **~reserve** *die* gold reserve; **~richtig** (*ugs.*) ❶ *Adj.* absolutely *or* dead right; **du bist ~richtig, so wie du bist** you're perfectly all right as you are; ❷ *adv.* absolutely right; **~schatz** *der* [A] (*Schatz*) gold treasure; (*verborgen auch*) hoard of gold; [B] (*Kosew.*) treasure

**Gold·schmied** *der* ▶ 159 goldsmith

**Goldschmiede-: ~arbeit** *die* piece of goldwork; **~handwerk** *das* goldsmith's craft; goldwork *no art.;* **~kunst** *die* goldsmith's art; goldwork *no art.*

**Gold-: ~schmiedin** *die* ▶ 159 ⇨ **Goldschmied**; **~schmuck** *der* gold jewelry *or* (*Brit.*) jewellery; **~schnitt** *der* gilt edging; **~schrift** *die* gold lettering; **~staub** *der* gold dust; **~stück** *das* (*hist.*) gold piece; **sie ist ein ~stück** (*fig.*) she is a [real] treasure; **~sucher** *der,* **~sucherin** *die* gold prospector; **~ton** *der; Pl.* **~töne** golden colour; **~topas** *der* yellow topaz; **~tresse** *die* gold braid; **~überzug** *der* layer of gold plate; **~uhr** *die* gold watch; **~vorkommen** *das* gold deposit; **~waage** *die* gold balance; **alles** *od.* **jedes Wort auf die ~waage legen** (*wörtlich nehmen*) take everything *or* every word [too] literally; (*vorsichtig äußern*) weigh one's words very carefully; **~währung** *die* (*Wirtsch.*) currency tied to the gold standard; **~waren** *Pl.* gold articles; **~wäscher** *der;* **~~s, ~~:** gold washer; **~wert** *der* [A] (*Wert des ~es*) value of gold; [B] (*Wert in ~*) value in gold; **~zahn** *der* (*ugs.*) gold tooth

**Golem** /'go:lɛm/ *der;* **~s** golem

**Golf**[1] /gɔlf/ *der;* **~[e]s, ~e** gulf; **der ~ von Neapel** the Bay of Naples

**Golf**[2] *das;* **~s** (*Sport*) golf

**Golf·ball** *der* golf ball

**Golfer** *der;* **~s, ~, Golferin** *die;* **~, ~nen** golfer

**Golf-: ~hose** *die* golf[ing] trousers *pl.;* **~mütze** *die* golf[ing] cap; **~platz** *der* golf-course; **~schläger** *der* golf club; **~schuh** *der* golf[ing] shoe; **~spieler** *der,* **~spielerin** *die* golfer; **~staat** *der* Gulf State; **~strom** *der* Gulf Stream; **~turnier** *das* golf tournament

**Golgatha** /'gɔlgata/ *das;* **~[s]** (*bibl.*) Golgotha; **für ihn war diese Niederlage/dieser Verlust ein ~** (*fig. geh.*) this defeat/loss caused him much pain and suffering

**Goliath** /'go:ljat/ *der;* **~s, ~s** Goliath

**Gomorrha** /go'mɔra/ ⇨ **Sodom**

**Gondel** /'gɔndl̩/ *die;* **~, ~n** gondola

**Gondel-: ~bahn** *die* [A] (*Seilbahn*) cable railway; [B] (*schweiz.*) ⇨ **Sessellift**; **~fahrt** *die* trip in a gondola; gondola trip

**gondeln** *itr. V.; mit sein* (*ugs.*) [A] (*mit einem Boot*) cruise; [B] (*reisen*) travel around; [C] (*herumfahren*) drive *or* cruise around; **durch die Stadt ~:** drive *or* cruise around town

**Gondoliere** /gɔndo'lje:rə/ *der;* **~s, Gondolieri** gondolier

**Gong** /gɔŋ/ *der;* **~s, ~s** gong

**gongen** *itr. V.* **es hat gegongt** the gong has sounded; **der Butler gongte zum Abendessen** the butler sounded the gong for dinner

**Gong·schlag** *der* stroke of the/a gong; **beim ~:** when the gong sounds/sounded

**gönnen** /'gœnən/ *tr. V.* [A] (*zugestehen*) **jmdm. etw. ~:** not begrudge sb. sth.; **ich gönne ihm diesen Erfolg von ganzem Herzen** I'm delighted *or* very pleased for him that he has had this success; **jmdm. den Misserfolg ~** (*iron.*) delight in sb.'s misfortune; [B] (*zukommen lassen*) **sich/jmdm. etw. ~:** give *or* allow oneself/sb. sth.; **sie gönnte sich** (*Dat.*) **einen großen Cognac** she treated herself to a large cognac; **sie gönnte ihm keinen Blick/kein Wort** she didn't spare him a single glance/she didn't say a single word to him

**Gönner** *der;* **~s, ~:** patron

**gönnerhaft** (*abwertend*) ❶ *Adj.* patronizing; **mit ~er Miene** with a patronizing expression [on his/her face]. ❷ *adv.* patronizingly; in a patronizing manner

**Gönnerin** *die;* **~, ~nen** patroness

**Gönner·miene** *die* (*abwertend*) patronizing expression; **mit ~:** with a patronizing expression [on his/her face]

**Gonokokkus** /gono'kɔkʊs/ *der;* **~, Gonokokken** (*Med.*) gonococcus

**Gonorrhö[e]** /gonɔ'rø:/ *die;* **~, Gonorrhöen** ▶ 474 /gonɔ'rø:ən/ (*Med.*) gonorrhoea

**Goodwill** /'gʊd'wɪl/ *der;* **~s** [A] (*Ansehen*) good name; [B] (*Wohlwollen*) goodwill

**Goodwill-: ~reise** *die* goodwill trip **(nach** to); **~tour** *die* goodwill tour **(durch** of)

**Göpel** /'gø:pl̩/ *der;* **~s, ~:** whim

**Gopher** /'goʊfɐ/ *der;* **~s, ~** (*DV*) gopher

**gor** /go:ɐ̯/ *3. Pers. Sg. Prät. v.* **gären**

**Gör** /gø:ɐ̯/ *das;* **~[e]s, ~en** (*nordd., oft abwertend*) ⇨ **Göre**

**gordisch** /'gɔrdɪʃ/ *Adj.* **der Gordische Knoten** the Gordian knot; **ein ~er Knoten** (*fig.*) a Gordian knot (*fig.*)

**Göre** /'gø:rə/ *die;* **~, ~n** (*nordd., oft abwertend*) [A] (*Kind*) child; kid (*coll.*); brat (*coll. derog.*); [B] (*freches Mädchen*) [cheeky *or* saucy] little madam (*coll.*)

**Gorilla** /go'rɪla/ *der;* **~s, ~s** [A] gorilla; [B] (*ugs.: Leibwächter*) heavy (*coll.*)

**Gosch[e]** /'gɔʃ(ə)/ *die;* **~, Goschen, Goschen** /'gɔʃn̩/ *die;* **~, ~** (*südd., österr. meist*

*old spelling (see note on page 1707)

*abwertend*) mouth; **eine große/freche Gosche** *od.* **Goschen haben** (*derb*) have a big mouth (*coll.*)/be a cheeky so-and-so (*coll.*); **die Gosche** *od.* **Goschen halten** (*derb*) shut one's gob *or* trap (*sl.*)

**Gospel** /ˈgɔspl̩/ *das od. der;* **~s, ~s, Gospelsong** *der;* **~s, ~s** gospel song

**goss, *goß** /gɔs/ *1. u. 3. Pers. Sg. Prät. v.* **gießen**

**Gosse** /ˈgɔsə/ *die;* **~, ~n** gutter; (*fig. abwertend*) **aus der ~ kommen** come from the gutter; **in der ~ enden** end up in the gutter; **jmdn.** *od.* **jmds. Namen durch die ~ ziehen** drag sb.'s name through the mud

**Gossen-: ~jargon** *der,* **~sprache** *die* (*abwertend*) gutter language; language of the gutter

**Gote[1]** /ˈgoːtə/ *der;* **~n, ~n** Goth

**Gote[2]** *der;* **~n, ~n** (*bes. südd.: Pate*) godfather

**Gote[3]** *die;* **~, ~n** (*bes. südd.: Patin*) godmother

**Gotha** /ˈgoːta/ *der;* **~:** *almanac containing information on the nobility of Europe*

**Gotik** /ˈgoːtɪk/ *die;* **~** (*Stil*) Gothic [style]; (*Epoche*) Gothic period

**Gotin** *die;* **~, ~nen** ⇒ **Gote[1]**

**gotisch** *Adj.* Gothic; **die ~e Schrift** Gothic [script]

**Gott** /gɔt/ *der;* **~es, Götter** /ˈgœtɐ/ **A** God; **~ Vater** God the Father; **hier ruht in ~ ...** here lies ...; **~ segne dich!** God bless you!; **~es Mühlen mahlen langsam** (*Spr.*) the mills of God grind slowly; **bei ~ ist kein Ding unmöglich** (*Spr.*) with God all things are possible; **grüß [dich] ~!** (*landsch.*) hello!; **behüt dich ~!** (*südd., österr.*) goodbye! God bless!; **vergelts ~!** (*landsch.*) thank you! God bless you!; **großer** *od.* **mein ~!** good God!; **o** *od.* **ach [du lieber] ~!** goodness me!; **weiß ~:** God *or* heaven knows; **~ behüte** God *or* Heaven forbid; **~ steh mir bei** God help me; **gebe ~, dass alles gut ausgeht** please God, may everything turn out all right; **wie ~ ihn/sie geschaffen hat** (*scherzh.*) in his/her birthday suit (*joc.*); in the altogether (*joc.*); **~ und die Welt** all the world and his wife; **über ~ und die Welt quatschen** (*ugs.*) talk about everything under the sun (*coll.*); **~ sei Dank!** (*ugs.*) thank God!; **~ seis geklagt!** alas; **um ~es Willen** (*bei Erschrecken*) for God's sake; (*bei einer Bitte*) for heaven's *or* goodness' sake; **tue es in ~es Namen** (*ugs.*) do it and have done with it; **da sei ~ vor!** God forbid!; **~ soll mich strafen, wenn ...** may God strike me down if ...; **so ~ will** (*ugs.*) God willing; **~ hab ihn selig** God rest his soul; **wie ~ in Frankreich leben** (*ugs.*) live in the lap of luxury; **den lieben ~ einen guten Mann sein lassen** (*ugs.*) take things as they come; **ein Wetter, dass [es] ~ erbarm** (*ugs.*) abominable weather; **er spielt/kocht, dass [es] ~ erbarm** his playing/cooking is abominable; **dem lieben ~ den Tag stehlen** laze the day away; **er/sie ist ganz und gar von ~ verlassen** (*ugs.*) he/she has quite taken leave of his/her senses; **B** (*übermenschliches Wesen*) god; **wie ein junger ~ spielen/tanzen** play/dance divinely; **das wissen die Götter** (*ugs.*) God *or* heaven only knows; **es war ein Bild für die Götter** (*ugs.*) it was priceless (*coll.*)

**gott·ähnlich** *Adj.* godlike

**Gottchen** *in* **[ach] ~!** oh dear!

**Gott·erbarmen** *das: in* **zum ~ sein** (*mitleiderregend*) be pitiful; (*schlecht*) be pathetic; **zum ~ schreien** cry out pitifully; **zum ~ spielen/singen** play/sing pathetically

**Götter-: ~bild** *das* idol; **~bote** *der* messenger of the gods; **~dämmerung** *die* (*nord. Myth.*) twilight of the gods; (*fig.*) end of civilization; götterdämmerung; **~gatte** *der* (*ugs. scherzh.*) lord and master (*coll. joc.*)

**gott·ergeben** **1** *Adj.* meek. **2** *adv.* meekly

**Gott·ergebenheit** *die* meekness

**götter-, Götter-: ~gestalt** *die* god; **~gleich** *Adj.* godlike; **~sage** *die* **A** (*Myth.*) mythology of the gods; **B** (*Sage von einem Gott*) myth about a god/the gods; **~speise** *die* **A** (*Myth.*) food of the gods; **B** (*Kochk.*) jelly; **~trank** *der* (*Myth.*) drink of the gods; **~vater** *der* (*Myth.*) father of the gods

**gottes-, Gottes-: ~acker** *der* (*geh.*) God's Acre *no art.* (*literary*); graveyard; **~begriff** *der* conception of God; **~beweis** *der* proof of the existence of God; **~dienst** *der* service; **den ~dienst besuchen** go to church; **~erkenntnis** *die* knowledge of God; **~friede** *der* (*hist.*) Truce of God; **~furcht** *die* fear of God; **~fürchtig** *Adj.* god-fearing; **~gabe** *die* gift from God; **~gelehrte** *der* (*veralt.*) theologian; **~gnadentum** *das;* **~~s** (*hist.*) divine right [of kings]; **~haus** *das* (*geh.*) house of God; **~lästerer** *der,* **~lästerin** *die* blasphemer; **~lästerlich** **1** *Adj.* blasphemous; **2** *adv.* blasphemously; **~lästerung** *die* blasphemy; **~lohn** *der* God's reward; **um ~lohn** for love; **~mann** *der* (*geh.*) man of God; **~sohn** *der* Son of God; **~staat** *der* theocracy; **~urteil** *das* (*hist.*) trial by ordeal

**gott-: ~gefällig** *Adj.* (*geh.*) pleasing to God *postpos.;* **~gegeben** *Adj.* God-given; **~gesandt** *Adj.* sent by God *postpos.;* **~geweiht** *Adj.* dedicated to God *postpos.;* **~gewollt** *Adj.* ordained by God *postpos.;* **~gläubig** *Adj.* **A** (*veralt.*) religious; **B** (*ns.*) **~gläubig sein** be a theist but of no particular denomination

**Gottheit** *die;* **~, ~en** **A** (*Gott, Göttin*) deity; **B** (*geh.: Gottsein*) divinity; **C** (*geh.: Gott*) **die ~:** the Godhead

**Göttin** /ˈgœtɪn/ *die;* **~, ~nen** goddess

**göttlich** /ˈgœtlɪç/ **1** *Adj.* **A** (*Gott eigen od. ähnlich; herrlich*) divine ‹grace, beauty, etc.›; **die ~e Gerechtigkeit** divine justice; **B** (*einem Gott zukommend*) god-like ‹status etc.›; **jmdm. ~e Verehrung entgegenbringen** worship sb. as if he/she were a God. **2** *adv.* (*herrlich*) divinely

**gott-, Gott-: ~lob** *adv.* thank goodness; **es hat ~lob nicht geschneit** it didn't snow, thank goodness; **~los** **1** *Adj.* **A** (*verwerflich*) ungodly, wicked ‹life etc.›; impious ‹words, speech, etc.›; (*pietätlos*) irreverent; **B** (*~ leugnend*) godless ‹theory etc.›; **2** *adv.* (*verwerflich*) irreverently; **~losigkeit** *die;* **~~** **A** (*Verwerflichkeit*) ungodliness; wickedness; (*von der Rede*) impiety; **B** (*Unglauben*) godlessness; **~mensch** *der* God-man; **~sei·bei·uns** *der;* **~~** (*verhüll.*) **der ~seibeiuns** the Evil One

**gotts·erbärmlich, gotts·jämmerlich** **1** *Adj.* (*salopp*) **A** (*erbärmlich*) dreadful (*coll.*); **B** (*stark*) dreadful (*coll.*); terrible (*coll.*); God-awful (*sl.*). **2** *adv.* terribly (*coll.*); dreadfully (*coll.*)

**gott-, Gott-: ~vater** *der* God the Father; **~verdammich** /-fɛɐ̯ˈdamɪç/ *Interj.* (*derb*) God damn it (*sl.*); God Almighty (*coll.*); **~verdammt** *Adj.* (*salopp*), **~verflucht** *Adj.* (*salopp*) goddamn[ed] (*sl.*); **~vergessen** *Adj.* **A** (*~los*) godless; **B** ⇒ **gottverlassen**; **~verlassen** *Adj.* **A** (*ugs.: abseits*) godforsaken; **B** (*von ~ verlassen*) forsaken by God *postpos.;* **sich ~verlassen fühlen** feel that God has forsaken one; **~vertrauen** *das* trust in God; **~voll** **1** *Adj.* **A** (*ugs.: komisch*) priceless (*coll.*); **B** (*herrlich*) divine; **2** *adv.* divinely

**Götze** /ˈgœtsə/ *der;* **~n, ~n** (*auch fig.*) idol

**Götzen-: ~anbeter** *der* ⇒ **~diener**; **~anbeterin** *die* ⇒ **~dienerin**; **~bild** *das* idol; graven image (*bibl.*); (*fig.*) idol; **~diener** *der* idolater; (*fig.*) worshipper; **~dienerin** *die* idolatress; (*fig.*) worshipper; **~dienst** *der* idolatry *no art.;* (*fig.*) worship; **~dienst leisten** practise idolatry; **~verehrung** *die* idolatry *no art.*

**Götz·zitat** /ˈgœts-/ *das: the insulting remark 'du kannst mich am Arsch lecken' or the like, frequently used in altercations; a verbal equivalent of the V-sign*

**Gouache** /gu̯a[ː]ʃ/ *die;* **~, ~n** gouache

**Gouda** /ˈgau̯da/ *der;* **~s, ~s, Gouda·käse** *der* Gouda [cheese]

**Goulasch** ⇒ **Gulasch**

**Gourmand** /gʊrˈmãː/ *der;* **~s, ~s** gourmand

**Gourmet** /gʊrˈmɛ/ *der;* **~s, ~s** gourmet

**goutieren** /guˈtiːrən/ *tr. V.* (*geh.*) appreciate

**Gouvernante** /guvɛrˈnantə/ *die;* **~, ~n** ▶ **159** governess

**gouvernanten·haft** **1** *Adj.* schoolmarmish (*coll.*). **2** *adv.* like a schoolmarm (*coll.*)

**Gouvernement** /guvɛrnəˈmãː/ *das;* **~s, ~s** **A** (*Regierung*) government; (*Verwaltung*) administration; **B** (*Verwaltungsbezirk*) province

**Gouverneur** /guvɛrˈnøːɐ̯/ *der;* **~s, ~e** governor

**Grab** /graːp/ *das;* **~[e]s, Gräber** /ˈgrɛːbɐ/ grave; **das ~ meiner Träume/Hoffnungen** (*fig.*) the end of my dreams/hopes; **er würde sich im ~[e] herumdrehen** (*fig. ugs.*) he would turn in his grave; **das Heilige ~:** the Holy Sepulchre; **das ~ des Unbekannten Soldaten** the tomb of the Unknown Soldier *or* Warrior; **verschwiegen wie ein** *od.* **das ~ sein** (*ugs.*) keep absolutely mum (*coll.*); **ein feuchtes** *od.* **nasses ~ finden,** (*geh.*) **sein ~ in den Wellen finden** go to a watery grave; meet a watery end; **sich** (*Dat.*) **selbst sein ~ schaufeln** (*fig.*) dig one's own grave (*fig.*); **mit einem Fuß** *od.* **Bein im ~[e] stehen** (*fig.*) have one foot in the grave (*fig.*); **jmdn. an den Rand des ~es bringen** (*fig. geh.*) drive sb. to distraction; **jmdn. ins ~ bringen** be the death of sb.; **jmdm. ins ~ folgen** (*geh.*) follow sb. to the grave; **etw. mit ins ~ nehmen** (*geh.*) take sth. with one to the grave; **bis ins** *od.* **ans ~** (*fig. geh.*) [right up] to the end; **jmdn. zu ~e tragen** (*geh.*) bury sb.; **seine Pläne/Hoffnungen zu ~e tragen** (*fig. geh.*) abandon one's plans/hopes

**Grab·beigabe** *die* burial object

**grabbeln** /ˈgrabl̩n/ *itr. V.* (*ugs., bes. nordd.*) grope [about]; rummage [about]

**Grab·denkmal** *das* ⇒ **Grabmal**

**graben** **1** *unr. tr. V.* **A** dig ‹hole, grave, etc.›; dig, carve ‹groove›; **Furchen/Falten in jmds. Gesicht ~** (*fig.*) carve *or* etch lines/wrinkles in sb.'s face; **B** (*gewinnen*) cut ‹turf›; mine ‹coal etc.›; **C** (*geh.: ein~*) carve; engrave. **2** *unr. itr. V.* dig (**nach** for); **seine Zähne/Hände in etw.** (*Akk.*) **~** (*geh.*) sink *or* bury one's teeth/hands in sth. **3** *unr. refl. V.* (*geh.*) **sich in etw. ~:** dig into sth.; **es grub sich ihm ins Gedächtnis** (*fig.*) it became imprinted *or* engraved in his memory

**Graben** *der;* **~s, Gräben** /ˈgrɛːbn̩/ **A** ditch; **B** (*Schützengraben*) trench; **im ~ liegen** lie in the trenches; **C** (*Festungsgraben*) moat; **D** (*Geol.*) rift valley; graben

**Graben-: ~bruch** *der* (*Geol.*) graben; **~kampf** *der,* **~krieg** *der* trench warfare *no pl., no indef. art.*

**Gräber-: ~feld** *das* [large] cemetery; **~fund** *der* grave find

**Grabes-: ~kälte** *die* (*geh.*) deathly cold; **~luft** *die* (*geh.*) grave-like *or* tomb-like air *no pl., no indef. art.;* **~ruhe** *die,* **~stille** *die* deathly silence *or* hush; **~stimme** *die* (*ugs.*) sepulchral voice

**Grab-: ~fund** *der* ⇒ **Gräberfund**; **~geläut[e]** *das* [death] knell; **~gesang** *der* dirge; funeral hymn; (*fig.*) death knell; **~gewölbe** *das* vault; (*in Kirche, Dom*) crypt; **~hügel** *der* grave mound; **~inschrift** *die* inscription [on a/the gravestone]; epitaph; **~kammer** *die* burial chamber; **~kreuz** *das* cross [on the/a grave]; **~legung** *die;* **~~, ~~en** **A** (*christl. Rel.*) entombment of Christ; **B** (*Kunst*) **die ~legung Christi** the Entombment of Christ; **~licht** *das; Pl.* **~er** grave light; **~mal** *das; Pl.* **~mäler,** *geh.* **~~e** monument; (*~stein*) gravestone; **das ~mal des Unbekannten Soldaten** the tomb of the Unknown Soldier *or* Warrior; **~platte** *die* memorial slab; (*aus Metall*) memorial plate; **~rede** *die* funeral oration *or* speech; **~schänder** *der;* **~~s, ~~, ~schänderin** *die;* **~~, ~~nen** desecrator of a/the grave/of [the] graves; **~schändung** *die* desecration of a/the grave/of [the] graves

**grabschen** /ˈgrapʃn̩/ ❶ *tr. V.* grab; snatch. ❷ *itr. V.* **nach etw. ∼:** grab at sth.

**Grab-:** **∼spruch** *der* epitaph; **∼stätte** *die* tomb; grave; **∼stein** *der* gravestone; tombstone; **∼stelle** *die* burial plot

**gräbst** /grɛːpst/ *2. Pers. Sg. Präsens v.* **graben**

**gräbt** *3. Pers. Sg. Präsens v.* **graben**

**Grabung** *die;* ∼, **∼en** (*bes. Archäol.*) excavation

**Grabungs·fund** *der* archaeological find

**Grab·urne** *die* funeral urn

**Gracht** /graxt/ *die;* ∼, **∼en** canal

**Grad** /graːt/ *der, als Maßeinheit: das;* **∼[e]s, ∼e** Ⓐ degree; **Verbrennungen ersten/zweiten ∼es** first-/second-degree burns; **ein Verwandter ersten/zweiten ∼es** an immediate relation/a relation once removed; **Vettern ersten ∼es** first cousins; **bis zu einem gewissen ∼[e]** to a [certain] degree; **in hohem ∼e** to a great *or* large extent; **er ist mir in höchstem ∼e unsympathisch** I dislike him intensely; **in geringem ∼e** to a slight extent; slightly; Ⓑ (*akademischer ∼*) degree; (*Milit.*) rank; Ⓒ ▶ 728 (*Maßeinheit, Math., Geogr.*) degree; **20 ∼ Celsius/Fahrenheit** *usw.* 20 degrees Centigrade *or* Celsius/Fahrenheit *etc.*; **10 ∼ Wärme/Kälte** 10 degrees above zero/below [zero]; **39 ∼ Fieber haben** have a temperature of 39 degrees; **minus 5 ∼/5 ∼ minus** minus 5 degrees; **null ∼:** zero; **etw. auf 90 ∼ erhitzen** heat sth. to [a temperature of] 90 degrees; **Gleichungen zweiten ∼es** equations of the second degree; quadratic equations; **sich um hundertachtzig ∼ drehen** (*fig.*) completely change [one's views]; **der 50. ∼ nördlicher Breite** [latitude] 50 degrees North; **die Insel liegt auf dem 42. ∼ östlicher Länge** the longitude of the island is 42 degrees East

**grad.** *Abk.* **graduiert**

**grad-, Grad-¹** ⇒ **gerad[e]-, Gerad[e]-**

**Grad-²:** **∼bogen** *der* graduated arc; **∼einteilung** *die* graduation

**Gradient** /graˈdi̯ɛnt/ *der;* **∼en, ∼en** (*bes. Math., Physik*) gradient

**gradieren** *tr. V.* graduate; calibrate

**Gradier·werk** *das* thorn-house; graduation-house

**grad-, Grad-:** **∼mäßig** ⇒ **graduell**; **∼messer** *der;* **∼s, ∼:** gauge, yardstick (**für** of); **∼netz** *das* network of parallels and meridians

**graduell** /graˈdu̯ɛl/ ❶ *Adj.* gradual ‹development etc.›; slight ‹difference etc.›. ❷ *adv.* gradually; by degrees; ‹different› in degree

**graduieren** ❶ *tr. V.* Ⓐ (*an Hochschulen*) award a degree to; graduate (*Amer.*); Ⓑ ‹in Grade einteilen› graduate; calibrate. ❷ *itr. V.* (*an Hochschulen*) graduate

**graduiert** *Adj.* graduate; **ein ∼er Ingenieur/eine ∼e Ingenieurin** an engineering graduate

**Graduierte** *der/die; adj. Dekl.* graduate

**Graduierung** *die;* ∼, **∼en** graduation

**Grad·unterschied** *der* difference of *or* in degree

**grad·weise** *Adv.* gradually; by degrees

**Graecum** /ˈgrɛːkʊm/ *das;* **∼s** (*Prüfung*) examination in Greek; (*Qualifikation*) qualification in Greek

**Graf** /graːf/ *der;* **∼en, ∼en** Ⓐ count; (*britischer ∼*) earl; Ⓑ (*Titel*) Count; (*britischer ∼*) Earl; **∼ Koks [von der Gasanstalt]** (*salopp scherzh.*), **∼ Rotz [von der Backe]** (*salopp abwertend*) Lord Muck (*Brit. joc.*)

**Grafen·stand** *der* Ⓐ (*Rang eines Grafen*) rank of count; (*in Großbritannien*) rank of earl; earldom; **jmdn. in den ∼ erheben** confer the rank of count/earl upon sb.; Ⓑ (*Gesamtheit der Grafen*) counts *pl.*; (*in Großbritannien*) earls *pl.*

**Graffito** /graˈfiːto/ *der od. das;* **∼[s], Graffiti** Ⓐ (*Kunst*) graffito; Ⓑ *Pl.* (*Kritzelei*) graffiti

**Grafik** /ˈgraːfɪk/ *die;* ∼, **∼en** Ⓐ (*Gestaltung, grafisches Schaffen*) graphic art[s *pl.*]; Ⓑ (*Kunstwerk*) graphic; (*Druck*) print; Ⓒ (*Illustration*) diagram

**Grafiker** ⇒ **Graphiker**

**Gräfin** /ˈgrɛːfɪn/ *die;* ∼, **∼nen** countess; (*Titel*) Countess

**grafisch** ⇒ **graphisch**

**Grafit** ⇒ **Graphit**

**gräflich** /ˈgrɛːflɪç/ *Adj.* count's *attrib.*; of the count *postpos.*, *not pred.*; (*in Großbritannien*) earl's; of the earl

**Grafschaft** *die;* ∼, **∼en** Ⓐ (*Amtsbezirk des Grafen*) count's land; (*in Großbritannien*) earldom; Ⓑ (*Verwaltungsbezirk*) county

**Graham·brot** /ˈgraːham-/ *das* wholemeal (*Brit.*) *or* (*Amer.*) wheatmeal bread

**gräko-** /ˈgrɛːko-/ Graeco-; **∼lateinisch** Graeco-Latin

**Gral** /graːl/ *der;* **∼[e]s: der [Heilige] ∼:** the [Holy] Grail

**Grals-:** **∼hüter** *der* keeper of the [Holy] Grail; (*fig.*) guardian; **∼hüterin** *die* (*fig.*) guardian; **∼ritter** *der* knight of the [Holy] Grail

**gram** /graːm/ *in* **jmdm. ∼ sein** be aggrieved at sb.

**Gram** *der;* **∼[e]s** (*geh.*) grief; sorrow; **aus ∼ um** *od.* **über etw.** (*Akk.*) out of grief *or* sorrow at sth.; **vom** *od.* **von ∼ gebeugt sein** be bowed down with grief *or* sorrow

**grämen** /ˈgrɛːmən/ ❶ *tr. V.* grieve. ❷ *refl. V.* grieve (**über** + *Akk.*, **um** over); **sich wegen etw. ∼:** worry about sth.

**gram·erfüllt** ❶ *Adj.* grief-stricken; sorrowful. ❷ *adv.* sorrowfully

**Gram·färbung** *die* (*Bakteriol.*) Gram's method

**gram·gebeugt** *Adj.* bowed down with grief *or* sorrow *postpos.*

**grämlich** /ˈgrɛːmlɪç/ ❶ *Adj.* morose; sullen; morose ‹thought›. ❷ *adv.* morosely; sullenly

**Gramm** /gram/ *das;* **∼s, ∼e** ▶ 353 gram; **250 ∼ Käse** 250 grams of cheese

**Grammatik** /graˈmatɪk/ *die;* ∼, **∼en** Ⓐ grammar; Ⓑ (*Lehrbuch*) grammar [book]

**grammatikalisch** /gramatiˈkaːlɪʃ/ *Adj.* ⇒ **grammatisch**

**Grammatik·regel** *die* grammatical rule; rule of grammar

**grammatisch** ❶ *Adj.* grammatical. ❷ *adv.* grammatically

**Gramm·atom** *das* (*Chemie, Physik*) gram-atom

**Grammel** /ˈgraml̩/ *die;* ∼, **∼n** (*bayr., österr.*) ⇒ **Griebe**

**Grammophon** Ⓦⓩ /gramoˈfoːn/ *das;* **∼s, ∼e** gramophone; phonograph (*Amer.*); **auf dem ∼ spielen** (*ugs.*) play records

**Grammophon·trichter** *der* gramophone *or* (*Amer.*) phonograph horn

**gram-:** **∼negativ** *Adj.* (*Bakteriol.*) Gram-negative; **∼positiv** *Adj.* (*Bakteriol.*) Gram-positive

**Granat** /graˈnaːt/ *der;* **∼[e]s, ∼e** Ⓐ (*Schmuckstein*) garnet; Ⓑ (*Garnele*) [common] shrimp

**Granat·apfel** *der* pomegranate

**Granat·[apfel]baum** *der* pomegranate [tree]

**Granate** /graˈnaːtə/ *die;* ∼, **∼n** shell; (*Hand∼*) grenade

**granaten·voll** *Adj.* (*ugs.*) absolutely plastered (*sl.*); totally canned (*Brit. sl.*)

**Granat-:** **∼feuer** *das* shellfire *no pl.*, *no indef. art.*; **∼splitter** *der* shell splinter; **∼trichter** *der* shell crater; **∼werfer** *der* (*Milit.*) mortar

**Grand** /grɑ̃ː *od.* graŋ/ *der;* **∼s, ∼s** (*Skat*) grand; **∼ Hand** grand solo; **∼ ouvert** open grand

**Grande** /ˈgrandə/ *der;* **∼n, ∼n** (*hist.*) grandee

**Grandeur** /grɑ̃ˈdøːɐ̯/ *die;* **∼:** grandeur

**Grandezza** /granˈdɛtsːa/ *die;* **∼:** grandeur; **mit ∼:** with a grand air

**Grand·hotel** /ˈgrɑ̃ː-/ *das* luxury *or* five-star hotel

**grandios** /granˈdi̯oːs/ ❶ *Adj.* magnificent. ❷ *adv.* magnificently

**Grand Prix** /grɑ̃ˈpriː/ *der;* ∼ /-priː(s)/, ∼ /-priːs/ Grand Prix

**Grandseigneur** /grɑ̃sɛnˈjøːɐ̯/ *der;* **∼s, ∼s** *od.* **∼e** (*geh.*) grand seigneur

**Granit** /graˈniːt/ *der;* **∼s, ∼e** granite; **auf ∼ beißen** (*fig.*) bang one's head against a brick wall (*fig.*); **bei jmdm. auf ∼ beißen** (*fig.*) get nowhere with sb. (*fig.*)

**Granit·block** *der; Pl.* **Granitblöcke** block of granite; granite block

**graniten** *Adj.* Ⓐ granite; granitic (*Geol.*); Ⓑ (*geh.: hart*) granitic; granite; (*fig.*) rigid; inflexible; granitic

**Granit·gestein** *das* granitic rock

**Granne** /ˈgranə/ *die;* ∼, **∼n** awn; beard

**Grant** /grant/ *der;* **∼s** (*südd., österr. ugs.*) **[wegen etw.] einen ∼ haben/bekommen** be in/get into a bad mood [because of sth.]

**grantig** /ˈgrantɪç/ (*südd., österr. ugs.*) ❶ *Adj.* bad-tempered; grumpy. ❷ *adv.* bad-temperedly; grumpily

**Granulat** /granuˈlaːt/ *das;* **∼[e]s, ∼e** (*bes. Chemie*) granules *pl.*

**granulieren** *itr., tr. V.* (*bes. Chemie*) granulate

**Grapefruit** /ˈgreːpfruːt/ *die;* ∼, **∼s** grapefruit

**Grapefruit·saft** *der* grapefruit juice

**Graph¹** /graːf/ *der;* **∼en, ∼en** (*Math., Naturw.*) graph

**Graph²** *das;* **∼s, ∼e** (*Sprachw.*) graph

**Graphem** /graˈfeːm/ *das;* **∼s, ∼e** (*Sprachw.*) grapheme

**Graphie** /graˈfiː/ *die;* ∼, **∼n** (*Sprachw.*) written form

**Graphik** /ˈgraːfɪk/ *die;* ∼, **∼en** Ⓐ (*Gestaltung, graphisches Schaffen*) graphic art[s *pl.*]; Ⓑ (*Kunstwerk*) graphic; (*Druck*) print; Ⓒ (*Illustration*) diagram

**Graphiker** *der;* **∼s,** ∼, **Graphikerin** *die;* ∼, **∼nen** [graphic] designer; (*Künstler[in]*) graphic artist

**graphisch** ❶ *Adj.* Ⓐ graphic; **das ∼e Gewerbe** (*veralt.*) the printing trade; Ⓑ (*schematisch*) graphic; diagrammatic; **eine ∼e Darstellung** a diagram; (*Math.: ein Graph*) a graph; Ⓒ (*Sprachw.*) graphic. ❷ *adv.* graphically

**Graphit** /graˈfiːt/ *der;* **∼s, ∼e** graphite

**graphit·grau** *Adj.* dark grey

**Graphit·stift** *der* lead pencil

**Graphologe** /grafoˈloːgə/ *der;* **∼n, ∼n** ▶ 159 graphologist

**Graphologie** *die;* **∼:** graphology *no art.*

**Graphologin** *die;* ∼, **∼nen** ▶ 159 graphologist

**graphologisch** ❶ *Adj.* graphological. ❷ *adv.* graphologically; ‹analysed, interpreted› by a graphologist

**grapschen** /ˈgrapʃn̩/ ⇒ **grabschen**

**Gras** /graːs/ *das;* **∼es, Gräser** /ˈgrɛːzɐ/ grass; **wo er hinhaut, da wächst kein ∼ mehr** (*fig. ugs.*) one blow from him and you'd be out cold (*coll.*); **das ∼ wachsen hören** (*ugs. spött.*) read too much into things; **über etw.** (*Akk.*) **∼ wachsen lassen** (*ugs.*) let the dust settle on sth.; **ins ∼ beißen [müssen]** (*salopp*) bite the dust (*coll.*)

**gras-, Gras-:** **∼bahn** *die* (*Sport*) grass track; **∼bedeckt, ∼bewachsen** *Adj.* grass-covered; grassy; **∼büschel** *das* tuft of grass; **∼decke** *die* covering of grass

**grasen** *itr. V.* Ⓐ graze; Ⓑ (*ugs.: suchen*) **nach etw. ∼:** search for sth.

**gras-, Gras-:** **∼fläche** *die* area of grass; (*Rasen*) lawn; **∼fleck** *der* Ⓐ patch of grass; Ⓑ (*auf der Kleidung*) grass stain; **∼fresser** *der* (*Zool.*) herbivore; **∼frosch** *der* grass frog; **∼grün** *Adj.* grass-green; **∼halm** *der* blade of grass; **∼hüpfer** *der* (*ugs.*) grasshopper; **∼land** *das* grassland; **∼mäher** *der*, **∼mäh·maschine** *die* grass mower; [grass-]mowing machine; **∼mücke** *die* warbler; **∼narbe** *die* turf; **∼nelke** *die* thrift; **∼pflanze** *die* gramineous plant (*Bot.*); grass

**Grass** /graːs/ *das;* ∼ (*Drogenjargon*) grass (*sl.*)

**grassieren** /graˈsiːrən/ *itr. V.* ‹disease etc.› rage, be rampant; ‹craze etc.› be [all] the rage; ‹rumour› be rife

*old spelling (see note on page 1707)

**Gras·ski** *der* grass ski

**grässlich, *gräßlich** /ˈɡrɛslɪç/ ❶ *Adj.* Ⓐ (*abscheulich*) horrible; terrible ‹accident›; Ⓑ (*ugs.: unangenehm*) dreadful (*coll.*); awful; Ⓒ (*ugs.: sehr stark*) terrible (*coll.*); awful. ❷ *adv.* Ⓐ (*abscheulich*) horribly; terribly; Ⓑ (*ugs.: unangenehm*) terribly (*coll.*); Ⓒ (*ugs.: sehr*) terribly (*coll.*); dreadfully (*coll.*); **~ frieren** be terribly *or* dreadfully cold (*coll.*)

**Grässlichkeit, *Gräßlichkeit** *die;* ~, **~en** Ⓐ (*Abscheulichkeit*) horribleness; (*eines Unfalls*) terribleness; Ⓑ (*unangenehme Art*) dreadfulness (*coll.*); awfulness; Ⓒ (*grässliche Handlung*) atrocity

**Gras-: ~steppe** *die* (*Geogr.*) [grassy] steppe; **~streifen** *der* strip of grass; (*längs einer Straße*) grass verge; **~teppich** *der* (*geh.*) sward (*literary*)

**Grat** /ɡraːt/ *der;* **~[e]s, ~e** Ⓐ (*Bergrücken*) ridge; Ⓑ (*Archit.*) hip; Ⓒ (*Technik*) burr

**Gräte** /ˈɡrɛːtə/ *die;* ~, **~n** Ⓐ [fish] bone; Ⓑ (*salopp: Knochen*) bone; **sich** (*Dat.*) **die ~n brechen** get badly smashed up (*sl.*); **jmdm. alle** *od.* **sämtliche ~n brechen** break every bone in sb.'s body (*coll.*)

**gräten-, Gräten-: ~los** *Adj.* boneless; **~muster** *das* herringbone [pattern]; **ein Jackett mit ~muster** a herringbone jacket; **~schritt** *der* (*Skifahren*) herringbone [step]

**Gratifikation** /ɡratifikaˈtsi̯oːn/ *die;* ~, **~en** bonus

**gratinieren** /ɡratiˈniːrən/ *tr. V.* (*Gastr.*) brown [the top of]; **gratinierter Blumenkohl** cauliflower au gratin

**gratis** /ˈɡraːtɪs/ *Adv.* free [of charge]; gratis; **~ und franko** (*ugs.*) for free (*coll.*)

**Gratis-: ~aktie** *die* (*Börsenw.*) bonus share; **~anzeiger** *der* (*schweiz.*) [free] advertisement paper; **~exemplar** *das* free copy; **~muster** *das,* **~probe** *die* free sample; **~vorstellung** *die* free performance

**Grätsche** /ˈɡrɛːtʃə/ *die;* ~, **~n** (*Turnen*) straddle; (*Sprung*) straddle vault; **in die ~ gehen** go into the straddle position

**grätschen** ❶ *tr. V.* **die Beine ~:** straddle one's legs. ❷ *itr. V.; mit sein* straddle; do *or* perform a straddle; **über ein Gerät ~:** do a straddle vault over a piece of apparatus

**Grätsch-: ~sitz** *der* (*Turnen*) straddle position; **~sprung** *der* (*Turnen*) astride jump; (*über ein Gerät*) straddle vault; **~stellung** *die* (*Turnen*) straddle position

**Gratulant** /ɡratuˈlant/ *der;* **~en, ~en, Gratulantin** *die;* ~, **~nen** well-wisher; **sie war die erste ~in** she was the first to offer her congratulations

**Gratulation** /ɡratulaˈtsi̯oːn/ *die;* ~, **~en** Ⓐ (*Glückwunsch*) congratulations *pl.;* **~en entgegennehmen** receive congratulations; **meine [herzliche] ~!** [many] congratulations!; Ⓑ (*das Gratulieren*) **sie kamen zur ~:** they came to congratulate him/her/them

**Gratulations-: ~besuch** *der* congratulatory visit; **~cour** *die;* **~~, ~~en** reception; **~schreiben** *das* letter of congratulation[s]; congratulatory letter

**gratulieren** *itr. V.* **jmdm. ~:** congratulate sb.; **jmdm. zum Geburtstag ~:** wish sb. many happy returns [of the day]; **jmdm. zum Examen ~:** congratulate sb. on passing his/her exam; **[ich] gratuliere!** congratulations!; **zu dieser Tochter kann ich Ihnen/er sich nur ~:** you are/he is lucky to have a daughter like her

**Grat·wanderung** *die* ridge walk; (*fig.*) balancing act

**grau** /ɡrau̯/ ❶ *Adj.* Ⓐ grey; **~ werden** go grey; **~ im Gesicht** grey- *or* ashen-faced; **eine ~e Stadt** (*fig.*) a grey *or* drab town; **deine ~en Zellen** (*ugs.*) your grey matter (*coll.*); **~ in ~:** grey and drab; Ⓑ (*trostlos*) dreary; drab; depressing; **der ~e Alltag** the dull routine *or* monotony of daily life; **alles ~ in ~ sehen** always see the gloomy side of things; **alles ~ in ~ malen** paint a gloomy *or* bleak picture of things; Ⓒ (*zwischen legal und illegal*) grey; **der ~e Markt** the grey market; Ⓓ (*unbestimmt*) vague; **in ~er Vorzeit/Ferne** in the dim and distant past/future. ❷ *adv.* **~ meliert** greying ‹hair›

**Grau** *das;* **~s, ~** Ⓐ grey; Ⓑ (*Trostlosigkeit*) dreariness; drabness

**grau-, Grau-: ~äugig** *Adj.* grey-eyed; **~bart** *der* (*ugs.*) greybeard; **~bärtig** *Adj.* grey-bearded; **~blau** *Adj.* grey-blue; **~brot** *das: bread made with rye- and wheat-flour*

**Grau·bünden** /-ˈbʏndn̩/ (*das*); **~s** the Grisons

**Gräuel** /ˈɡrɔy̯əl/ *der;* **~s, ~** (*geh.*) Ⓐ (*Abscheu*) horror; **~ vor etw.** (*Dat.*) **empfinden** have a horror of sth.; **er/sie/es ist mir ein ~:** I loathe *or* detest him/her/it; **es ist ihm ein ~, das zu tun** he loathes *or* detests doing it; Ⓑ (**~tat**) atrocity

**Gräuel-: ~geschichte** *die,* **~märchen** *das* horror story; **~meldung** *die* report of an/the atrocity/of atrocities; **~propaganda** *die* atrocity propaganda; stories *pl.* of atrocities; **~tat** *die* atrocity

**grauen**[1] *itr. V.* (*geh.*) **der Morgen/der Tag graut** morning is breaking; day is dawning *or* breaking

**grauen**[2] *itr. V.* (*unpers.*) **ihm graut [es] davor/vor ihr** he dreads [the thought of] it/he's terrified of her; **mir graut es, wenn ich nur daran denke** I dread the [mere] thought of it

**Grauen** *das;* **~s, ~** Ⓐ horror (**vor** + *Dat.* of); **ein Bild des ~s** a scene of horror; Ⓑ (*Schreckbild*) horror

**grauen·erregend** *Adj.* horrifying

**grauen·haft, grauen·voll** ❶ *Adj.* Ⓐ horrifying; Ⓑ (*ugs.: sehr unangenehm*) terrible (*coll.*); dreadful (*coll.*). ❷ *adv.* Ⓐ horrifyingly; Ⓑ (*ugs.: sehr unangenehm*) terribly (*coll.*); dreadfully (*coll.*)

**grau-, Grau-: ~gans** *die* grey goose; greylag [goose]; **~grün** *Adj.* grey-green; **~guss,** ***~guß** *der* (*Technik*) grey iron; **~haarig** *Adj.* grey-haired; **~kopf** *der* (*ugs.*) Ⓐ (**~es** *Haar*) grey hair; **einen ~kopf haben** have grey hair; Ⓑ (*Mensch*) grey-headed man/woman

**graulen** /ˈɡrau̯lən/ ❶ *tr. V.* drive out; **jmdn. aus dem Haus ~:** drive sb. out of the house. ❷ *refl. V.* **sich [vor jmdm./etw.] ~:** be scared *or* frightened [of sb./sth.]. ❸ *tr., itr. V.* (*unpers.*) **davor graulte [es] ihm/ihn** he dreaded it; **mir/mich grault bei dem Gedanken, dass ...** I shudder at the thought that ...

**graulich** *Adj.* scary

**gräulich**[1] /ˈɡrɔy̯lɪç/ *Adj.* greyish

**gräulich**[2] ❶ *Adj.* Ⓐ (*entsetzlich*) horrifying; Ⓑ (*unangenehm*) awful. ❷ *adv.* Ⓐ (*entsetzlich*) horrifyingly; Ⓑ (*unangenehm*) terribly

***grau·meliert** ⇒ **grau** 2

**Graupe** /ˈɡrau̯pə/ *die;* ~, **~n** Ⓐ (*Gerstenkorn*) grain of pearl barley; (*Weizenkorn*) grain of hulled wheat; **~n** pearl barley *sing.*/hulled wheat *sing.;* Ⓑ *Pl.* (*Gericht*) pearl barley *sing.*

**Graupel** /ˈɡrau̯pl̩/ *die;* ~, **~n** soft hail pellet; **~n** soft hail; graupel

**graupeln** *itr. V.* (*unpers.*) **es graupelt** there's soft hail falling

**Graupel-: ~regen** *der* shower of soft hail; **der ~regen behinderte den Verkehr** the soft hail impeded the flow of traffic; **~schauer** *der* shower of soft hail; **der Regen ging in ~schauer über** the rain turned to soft hail

**Graupen·suppe** *die* barley soup *or* broth

**Graus** /ɡrau̯s/ *der;* **~es** Ⓐ **es ist ein ~:** it's terrible; **es ist ein ~ mit dem Jungen** the boy's impossible (*coll.*); **o ~!** (*ugs. scherzh.*) oh horror! (*joc.*); Ⓑ (*veralt.:* **~en**) horror

**grausam** ❶ *Adj.* Ⓐ cruel; **~ gegen jmdn. sein** be cruel to sb.; Ⓑ (*furchtbar*) terrible; dreadful; Ⓒ (*ugs.: sehr schlimm*) terrible (*coll.*); dreadful (*coll.*). ❷ *adv.* Ⓐ cruelly; **sich ~ für etw. rächen** take cruel revenge for sth.; Ⓑ (*furchtbar*) terribly, dreadfully; **~ ums Leben kommen** die a horrible death; Ⓒ (*ugs.: sehr stark*) terribly (*coll.*); dreadfully (*coll.*)

**Grausamkeit** *die;* ~, **~en** Ⓐ cruelty; Ⓑ (*Handlung*) act of cruelty; (*Gräueltat*) atrocity

**grau-, Grau-: ~schimmel** *der* Ⓐ (*Pferd*) grey [horse]; Ⓑ (*Pilz*) grey mould; **~schwarz** *Adj.* grey-black

**grausen** ❶ *tr., itr. V.* (*unpers.*) **es grauste ihm** *od.* **ihn davor/vor ihr** he dreaded [the thought of] it/he was terrified of her; **es graust ihr** *od.* **sie, wenn sie nur an die Prüfung denkt** she dreads the [mere] thought of the exam; **uns grauste vor der langen Fahrt** we were dreading the long journey. ❷ *refl. V.* **sich vor etw./jmdm. ~:** be terrified by *or* dread sth./be terrified of sb.

**Grausen** *das;* **~s** horror; **das kalte ~ kriegen** (*ugs.*) be scared stiff *or* to death (*coll.*)

**grausig** ⇒ **grauenhaft**

**grauslich** (*bes. bayr., österr.*) ⇒ **grässlich**

**grau-, Grau-: ~specht** *der* grey-headed woodpecker; **~tier** *das* (*ugs. scherzh.*) (*Esel*) ass; donkey; (*Maultier*) mule; **~ton** *der; Pl.* **~töne** [shade of] grey; **~wal** *der* grey whale; **~weiß** *Adj.* greyish white; **~zone** *die* grey area (*fig.*)

**Graveur** /ɡraˈvøːɐ̯/ *der;* **~s, ~e, Graveurin** *die;* ~, **~nen** ▶ **159** engraver

**Gravier-: ~anstalt** *die* engraving establishment; engraver's; **~arbeit** *die* engraving

**gravieren** /ɡraˈviːrən/ *tr. V.* engrave; **etw. auf etw.** (*Akk.*) **~:** engrave sth. on sth.

**gravierend** *Adj.* serious, grave ‹matter, accusation, error, etc.›; important ‹difference, decision, etc.›; **~e Beweise** very strong evidence

**Gravier·nadel** *die* engraving needle

**Gravierung** *die;* ~, **~en** engraving

**Gravimetrie** /ɡravimeˈtriː/ *die;* ~ (*Chemie, Physik*) gravimetry *no art.*

**Gravis** /ˈɡraːvɪs/ *der;* ~, ~ (*Sprachw.*) grave [accent]

**Gravitation** /ɡravitaˈtsi̯oːn/ *die;* ~ (*Physik, Astron.*) gravitation

**Gravitations-: ~feld** *das* (*Physik, Astron.*) gravitational field; **~gesetz** *das* (*Physik, Astron.*) law of gravitation

**gravitätisch** ❶ *Adj.* grave; solemn. ❷ *adv.* gravely; solemnly

**gravitieren** /ɡraviˈtiːrən/ *itr. V.* (*Physik, Astron.*) gravitate

**Gravur** /ɡraˈvuːɐ̯/ *die;* ~, **~en, Gravüre** /ɡraˈvyːrə/ *die;* ~, **~n** engraving

**Grazie** /ˈɡraːtsi̯ə/ *die;* ~, **~n** Ⓐ (*Anmut*) grace; gracefulness; Ⓑ (*Myth.*) Grace; Ⓒ (*scherzh.: junges Mädchen*) beauty

**grazil** /ɡraˈtsiːl/ *Adj.* (*auch fig.*) delicate

**graziös** /ɡraˈtsi̯øːs/ ❶ *Adj.* graceful; (*anmutig*) charming. ❷ *adv.* gracefully; (*anmutig*) charmingly

**Gräzismus** /ɡrɛˈtsɪsmʊs/ *der;* ~, **Gräzismen** Graecism

**Gräzist** *der;* **~en, ~en, Gräzistin** *die;* ~, **~nen** expert on/student of ancient Greece

**Greenhorn** /ˈɡriːnhɔːn/ *das;* **~s, ~s** greenhorn

**Gregor** /ˈɡreːɡɔr/ (*der*) Gregory

**gregorianisch, *Gregorianisch** /ɡreɡoˈri̯aːnɪʃ/ *Adj.* Gregorian; **~er Gesang** Gregorian chant; **der ~e Kalender** the Gregorian calendar

**Greif** /ɡraiːf/ *der;* **~[e]s** *od.* **~en, ~en** Ⓐ (*Wappentier*) griffin; gryphon; Ⓑ ⇒ **~vogel**

**Greif-: ~arm** *der* (*Technik*) grasping arm; **~bagger** *der* grab-dredger

**greif·bar** ❶ *Adj.* Ⓐ **etw. ~ haben** have sth. to hand; **~ sein** be within reach; **in ~er Nähe** (*fig.*) within reach; **der Urlaub ist in ~e Nähe gerückt** (*fig.*) the holiday is just coming up [now]; Ⓑ (*deutlich*) tangible; concrete; Ⓒ (*ugs.: verfügbar*) available. ❷ *adv.* **~ nahe** (*fig.*) within reach

**Greif·bewegung** *die* grasping movement

**greifen** ❶ *unr. tr. V.* Ⓐ (**er~**) take hold of; grasp; (*rasch* ~) grab; seize; **sich** (*Dat.*) **etw. ~:** help oneself to sth.; **jmdn. an den Händen ~:** take sb. by the hand; **aus dem Leben gegriffen sein** be taken from real life; **von hier scheint der See zum Greifen nah[e]** from here the lake seems close

enough to reach out and touch; **zum Greifen nahe sein** ‹end, liberation› be imminent; ‹goal, success› be within sb.'s grasp; **B** (*fangen*) catch; **den werde ich mir mal ~** (*ugs.*) I'll sort (*Brit.*) *or* (*Amer.*) straighten him out (*coll.*); **Greifen spielen** play tag; **C einen Akkord ~** (*auf dem Klavier usw.*) play a chord; (*auf der Gitarre usw.*) finger a chord; **er kann noch keine Oktave ~:** he can't reach an octave yet; **D** (*schätzen*) **tausend ist zu hoch/niedrig gegriffen** one thousand is an overestimate/underestimate; **sein Ziel ist zu hoch gegriffen** (*fig.*) he has set his sights too high (*fig.*).
❷ *unr. itr. V.* **A in/unter/hinter etw./sich** (*Akk.*) **~:** reach into/under/behind sth./one; **nach etw. ~:** reach for sth.; (*hastig*) make a grab for sth.; **zu Drogen/zur Zigarette ~:** turn to drugs/reach for a cigarette; **zu strengen Maßnahmen ~** (*fig.*) resort to *or* use tough measures; **nach der Macht ~** (*fig.*) try to seize power; **[jmdm.] ans Herz ~** (*fig. geh.*) tug at sb.'s heartstrings; **seine Argumentation greift zu kurz** (*fig.*) his arguments do not go far enough; **etw. greift um sich** sth. is spreading; **B** (*Technik*) grip; **C** (*ugs.: spielen*) **in die Tasten/Saiten ~:** sweep one's hand over the keys/across the strings; **D** (*wirken*) take effect; **nicht mehr ~:** be no longer effective

**Greifer** *der;* **~s, ~ A** (*Technik*) grab[-bucket]; **B** (*salopp abwertend: Polizist*) cop (*coll.*)

**Greiferin** *die;* **~, ~nen** ⇒ **Greifer B**

**Greif-: ~fuß** *der* (*Zool.*) prehensile foot; **~vogel** *der* (*Zool.*) diurnal bird of prey; **~zange** *die* tongs *pl.*; **~zirkel** *der* [outside] callipers *pl.*

**greinen** /ˈgraiːnən/ *itr. V.* (*ugs. abwertend*) grizzle (*coll. derog.*); (*weinerlich klagen*) whine

**greis** /graiːs/ *Adj.* (*geh.*) aged; white ‹hair, head›; **~ werden** grow old

**Greis** *der;* **~es, ~e** old man

**Greisen·alter** *das* old age; **im [hohen] ~:** in old age

**greisen·haft** ❶ *Adj.* old man's/woman's *attrib.*; aged; (*von jüngerem Menschen*) ‹face etc.› like that of an old man/woman. ❷ *adv.* like an old man/woman

**Greisen·haupt** *das* (*geh.*) old head

**Greisin** *die;* **~, ~nen** old woman *or* lady

**grell** /grɛl/ ❶ *Adj.* **A** (*hell*) glaring, dazzling ‹light, sun, etc.›; **B** (*auffallend*) garish, gaudy ‹colour etc.›; flashy, loud ‹dress, pattern, etc.›; **C** (*schrill*) shrill, piercing ‹cry, voice, etc.›. ❷ *adv.* **A** (*hell*) with glaring *or* dazzling brightness; **~ beleuchtet** dazzlingly lit; **B** (*auffallend*) **gegen** *od.* **von etw. ~ abstechen** contrast sharply with sth.; **C** (*schrill*) shrilly; piercingly

**grell-: *~beleuchtet** ⇒ **grell 2 A**; **~bunt** *Adj.* gaudily coloured

**Grelle** /ˈgrɛlə/ *die;* **~, Grellheit** *die;* **~ A** (*Helligkeit*) dazzling brightness; **B** (*Auffälligkeit*) garishness; gaudiness; **C** (*Schrillheit*) shrillness; piercing quality

**grell·rot** *Adj.* garish *or* bright red

**Gremium** /ˈgreːmiʊm/ *das;* **~s, Gremien** committee

**Grenadier** /grenaˈdiːɐ̯/ *der;* **~s, ~e** (*Milit.*) **A** (*Infanterist*) infantryman; **er kam zu den ~en** he went into *or* joined the infantry; **B** (*hist.*) grenadier

**Grenz-: ~abfertigung** *die* (*Zollw.*) passport control and customs clearance [at the/a border]; **~baum** *der* ⇒ **Schlagbaum**; **~beamte** *der,* **~beamtin** *die* border official; **~befestigung** *die* (*Milit.*) border fortification; **~bereich** *der* **A** border *or* frontier zone *or* area; **B** (*äußerster Bereich*) limit[s *pl.*]; **~berichtigung** *die* adjustment to a/the border; **~bewohner** *der,* **~bewohnerin** *die* inhabitant of a/the border *or* frontier zone; **die ~bewohner** [the] people living near the border *or* frontier; **~bezirk** *der* border *or* frontier district

**Grenze** /ˈgrɛntsə/ *die;* **~, ~n A** (*zwischen Staaten*) border; frontier; **die ~ zu Italien** the border with Italy; **die ~ passieren/überschreiten** cross the border *or* frontier; **über die ~n hinaus** beyond the borders of this country; **an der ~ wohnen** live on the border *or* frontier; **über die grüne ~ gehen** (*ugs.*) cross the border *or* frontier illegally; **B** (*zwischen Gebieten*) boundary; **die ~ des Grundstücks** the boundary of the property; **C** (*gedachte Trennungslinie*) borderline; dividing line; **D** (*Schranke*) limit; **jmdm. [keine] ~n setzen** impose [no] limits on sb.; **einer Sache** (*Dat.*) **[keine] ~n setzen** set [no] limits to sth.; **alles hat seine ~n** there is a limit *or* are limits to everything; one must draw the line somewhere; **an seine ~n stoßen** reach its limit[s]; **an ~n stoßen** come up against limiting factors; **keine ~n kennen** know no bounds; **seine ~n kennen** know one's limitations; **jmdn. in seine ~n verweisen** put sb. in his/her place; **sich in ~n halten** (*begrenzt sein*) keep *or* stay within limits; **seine Leistungen hielten sich in ~n** his achievements were not [all that (*coll.*)] outstanding; **die ~n des Möglichen** the bounds of possibility

**grenzen** *itr. V.* **an etw.** (*Akk.*) **~:** border [on] sth.; (*fig.*) verge on sth.

**grenzen·los** ❶ *Adj.* boundless; endless; (*fig.*) boundless, unbounded ‹joy, wonder, jealousy, grief, etc.›; unlimited ‹wealth, power›; limitless ‹patience, ambition›; extreme ‹tiredness, anger, foolishness›. ❷ *adv.* endlessly; (*fig.*) beyond all measure

**Grenzen·losigkeit** *die;* **~:** boundlessness; immensity; **bis zur ~ steigern** (*fig.*) increase beyond all measure

**Grenzer** *der;* **~s, ~, Grenzerin** *die;* **~, ~nen** (*ugs.*) **A** ⇒ **Grenzbewohner**; **B** ⇒ **Grenzsoldat**

**grenz-, Grenz-: ~fall** *der* (*nicht eindeutiger Fall*) borderline case; (*Sonderfall*) limiting case; **~fluss, *~fluß** *der* river forming a/the border *or* frontier; **~formalitäten** *Pl.* passport and customs formalities [at the/a border]; **~gänger** *der;* **~~s, ~~, ~gängerin** *die;* **~~, ~~nen** [regular] commuter across the border *or* frontier; **~gebiet** *das* **A** border *or* frontier area *or* zone; **B** (*Sachgebiet zwischen Disziplinen*) adjacent field; **die Biochemie ist ein ~gebiet der Medizin** biochemistry is a field bordering on medicine; **im ~gebiet zwischen zwei Wissenschaften** in the area where two sciences meet; **~konflikt** *der* border *or* frontier conflict; **~kontrolle** *die* **A** border *or* frontier check; **B** (*Personen*) border officials *pl.*; **~land** *das* border *or* frontier area; **~linie** *die* **A** (*Grenze*) border; **B** (*Sport*) line (*marking edge of playing area*); **~mark** *die; Pl.* **~~en** (*hist.*) marches *pl.*; **~nah** *Adj.* close to the border *or* frontier *postpos.*; **~nutzen** *der* (*Wirtsch.*) marginal utility; **~polizei** *die* border *or* frontier police; **~posten** *der* border *or* frontier guard; **~schutz** *der* **A** border *or* frontier protection; **B** (*ugs.: Bundesgrenzschutz*) border *or* frontier police; **~situation** *die* borderline situation; **~soldat** *der,* **~soldatin** *die* border *or* frontier guard; **~stadt** *die* border *or* frontier town; **~stein** *der* boundary stone; **~streitigkeit** *die* boundary dispute; (*wegen einer Staatsgrenze*) border *or* frontier dispute; **~übergang** *der* **A** border crossing point; frontier crossing-point; [border] checkpoint; **B** (*das Passieren der ~e*) crossing of the border *or* frontier; **~überschreitend** *Adj.* across the/a border *or* frontier/across the borders *or* frontiers *postpos., not pred.*; **~verkehr** *der* [cross-]border traffic; frontier traffic; **der kleine ~verkehr** local [cross-]border *or* frontier traffic; **~verlauf** *der* frontier line; **~verletzung** *die* border *or* frontier violation; **~wacht** *die* (*schweiz.*) border *or* frontier guard[s *pl.*]; **~wall** *der* border *or* frontier rampart; **~wert** *der* (*Math.*) limit; **~zwischenfall** *der* border incident

**Gretchen-: ~frage** *die;* **~:** crucial question; sixty-four-thousand-dollar question (*coll.*); **~frisur** *die* chaplet hairstyle

***Greuel** *usw.* ⇒ **Gräuel** *usw.*

***greulich** ⇒ **gräulich²**

**Greyerzer** /ˈgraiːɐtsɐ/ *der;* **~s, ~** Gruyère

**Griebe** /ˈgriːbə/ *die;* **~, ~n** crackling *no indef. art.*; greaves *pl.*

**Grieben-: ~fett** *das* bacon dripping; **~schmalz** *das* dripping with crackling *or* greaves

**Grieche** /ˈgriːçə/ *der;* **~n, ~n** ▶ **553** Greek

**Griechenland** (*das*); **~s** Greece

**Griechentum** *das;* **~s** (*Zivilisation*) Hellenism *no art.*; Greek civilization; (*Kultur*) Greek culture

**Griechin** *die;* **~, ~nen** ▶ **553** Greek

**griechisch** ▶ **553**, ▶ **696** ❶ *Adj.* Greek ‹language, mythology, island, etc.›; Grecian, Greek ‹vase, style, etc.›; **die ~e Tragödie** Greek tragedy. ❷ *adv.* **~ sprechen/schreiben** speak/write in Greek; ⇒ *auch* **deutsch**

**Griechisch** *das;* **~[s]** ▶ **696** Greek *no art.*; ⇒ *auch* **Deutsch**

**Griechische** *das;* **~n A** (*Sprache*) Greek *no art.*; **B** (*Eigenart*) things Greek *pl.*; **alles ~:** all things *pl. or* everything Greek

**griechisch-: ~-orthodox** *Adj.* Greek Orthodox; **~-römisch** *Adj.* (*Ringen*) Graeco-Roman

**grienen** /ˈgriːnən/ *itr. V.* (*bes. nordd.*) grin

**Griesgram** /ˈgriːsgraːm/ *der;* **~[e]s, ~e** (*abwertend*) grouch (*coll.*)

**griesgrämig** /ˈgriːsgrɛːmɪç/ ❶ *Adj.* grouchy (*coll.*); grumpy. ❷ *adv.* in a grouchy (*coll.*) *or* grumpy manner

**Grieß** /griːs/ *der;* **~es, ~e** semolina

**Grieß-: ~brei** *der* semolina; **~kloß** *der,* **~klößchen** *das* semolina dumpling

**griff** /grɪf/ *1. u. 3. Pers. Sg. Prät. v.* **greifen**

**Griff** *der;* **~[e]s, ~e A** grip; grasp; **mit eisernem/festem ~:** with a grip of iron/a firm grip; **der ~ nach etw./in etw.** (*Akk.*)**/an etw.** (*Akk.*) reaching for sth./dipping into sth./taking hold of *or* grasping sth.; **der ~ zum Alkohol/zu Drogen** turning to alcohol/drugs; **[mit jmdm./etw.] einen guten/glücklichen ~ tun** make a good choice [with sb./sth.]; **einen ~ in die Ladenkasse tun** (*verhüll.*) put one's hand in the till; **der ~ nach der Macht** (*fig.*) the bid for *or* attempt to seize power; **B** (*beim Ringen, Bergsteigen*) hold; (*beim Turnen*) grip; (*bei der Arbeit*) **jeder ~ muss sitzen** every movement must be exactly right; **mit wenigen ~en** with very little effort; **~e kloppen** (*Soldatenspr.*) do rifle drill; **etw. im ~ haben** (*etw. routinemäßig beherrschen*) have the hang of sth. (*coll.*); (*etw. unter Kontrolle haben*) have sth. under control; **etw. in den ~ bekommen** *od.* (*ugs.*) **kriegen** get the hang *or* knack of sth. (*coll.*); acquire a grasp of *or* hold on sth.; **C** (*Knauf, Henkel*) handle; (*eines Gewehrs, einer Pistole*) butt; (*eines Schwerts*) hilt; **D** (*Musik*) finger placing; **schwierige ~e beherrschen** master difficult fingering; **E** (*Weberei*) hand; handle

**griff·bereit** *Adj.* ready to hand *postpos.*

**Griff·brett** *das* (*Musik*) fingerboard

**Griffel** /ˈgrɪfl/ *der;* **~s, ~ A** (*Schreibgerät*) slate pencil; **B** (*Bot.*) style; **C** (*salopp: Finger*) finger

**Griffel·kasten** *der* (*veralt.*) pencil box

**griffig** *Adj.* **A** (*handlich*) handy; ‹tool etc.› that is easy to handle; (*fig.*) handy, useful ‹word, expression, etc.›; **B** (*gut greifend*) that grips well *postpos., not pred.*; non-slip ‹surface, floor›; **ein ~er Reifen** a tyre with good roadholding characteristics; **C** (*fest gewebt*) ‹cloth› with a firm handle; **D** (*österr.: grobkörnig*) coarse ‹flour›

**Griffigkeit** *die;* **~ A** (*Handlichkeit*) handiness; **B** (*von Reifen, Straßen*) grip; **C** (*Festigkeit des Gewebes*) firm handle; **D** (*österr.: von Mehl*) coarseness

**Griff·loch** *das* (*Musik*) fingerhole

**Grill** /grɪl/ *der;* **~s, ~s A** (*Feuerstelle*) grill; (*Rost*) barbecue; **B** (*Kfz-W.*) radiator grille

**Grille** /ˈgrɪlə/ *die;* **~, ~n A** (*Insekt*) cricket; **B** (*sonderbarer Einfall*) whim; fancy; **er hat ~n im Kopf** (*hat seltsame*

*old spelling (see note on page 1707)

*Ideen*) his head is [stuffed] full of silly ideas; (*hat trübselige Gedanken*) he's in low spirits *or* (*coll.*) [down] in the dumps; (*fig.*) **~n fangen** (*veralt.*) be in low spirits *or* (*coll.*) down in the dumps; **jmdm. die ~n vertreiben** *od.* **austreiben** (*fig. veralt.*) knock some sense into sb.

**grillen** ❶ *tr. V.* grill. ❷ *itr. V.* **im Garten ~:** have a barbecue in the garden. ❸ *refl. V.* (*ugs.: bräunen*) **sich in der Sonne ~:** soak up the sun

**Grill-: ~platz** *der* barbecue area; **~spieß** *der* ≈ souvlaki

**Grimasse** /gri'masə/ *die;* ~, **~n** grimace; **eine ~ schneiden** *od.* **machen** grimace; pull a face

**Grimm** /grɪm/ *der;* **~[e]s** (*geh.*) fury

**Grimm·darm** *der* ▶ 471 (*Anat.*) colon

**grimmen** *tr., itr. V.* (*unpers.*) (*veralt.*) **es grimmt mir** *od.* **mich im Bauch/Magen** I have griping pains in my stomach

**Grimmen** *das;* **~s** colic; griping pains *pl.*

**grimmig** ❶ *Adj.* Ⓐ (*zornig*) furious ‹person›; grim ‹face, expression›; fierce, ferocious ‹enemy, lion, etc.›; Ⓑ (*heftig*) fierce, severe ‹cold, hunger, pain, etc.›. ❷ *adv.* Ⓐ (*wütend*) furiously; **~ lachen** laugh grimly; Ⓑ (*heftig*) fiercely; **~ kalt** bitterly *or* fiercely cold

**Grind** /grɪnt/ *der;* **~[e]s, ~e** Ⓐ (*Flechte*) impetigo; Ⓑ (*Wundschorf*) scab

**grindig** *Adj.* scabby

**grinsen** /'grɪnzn̩/ *itr. V.* grin; (*höhnisch*) smirk

**Grinsen** *das;* **~s ein fröhliches/unverschämtes ~:** a happy grin/an insolent smirk

**grippal** /grɪ'pa:l/ *Adj.* influenzal; grippal

**Grippe** /'grɪpə/ *die;* ~, **~n** Ⓐ ▶ 474 influenza; flu (*coll.*); Ⓑ (*volkst.: Erkältung*) cold

**Grippe-: ~epidemie** *die* influenza epidemic; **~impfung** *die* influenza *or* (*coll.*) flu immunization; **~welle** *die* wave of influenza *or* (*coll.*) flu

**Grips** /grɪps/ *der;* **~es** (*bes. nordd. u. md. ugs.*) brains *pl.;* nous (*coll.*); **streng deinen ~ an** use your brains *or* nous

**Grisli·bär, *Grisly·bär, Grizzly·bär** /'grɪsli-/ *der* grizzly bear

**grob** /gro:p/ ❶ *Adj.* Ⓐ coarse ‹sand, gravel, paper, sieve, etc.›; thick ‹wire›; rough, dirty ‹work›; **~e Gesichtszüge** coarse features; Ⓑ (*ungefähr*) rough; **in ~en Umrissen** in rough outline; Ⓒ (*schwerwiegend*) gross; flagrant ‹lie›; **ein ~er Fehler/Irrtum** a bad mistake *or* gross error; **~er Unfug** disorderly conduct; **das Gröbste** the worst; **aus dem Gröbsten heraus sein** (*ugs.*) be over the worst; Ⓓ (*barsch*) coarse; rude; **~ werden** become abusive *or* rude; Ⓔ (*nicht sanft*) rough; **~ [zu jmdm.] sein** be rough [with sb.]; Ⓕ (*heftig*) fierce ‹gust of wind›; **~e See** (*Seemannsspr.*) rough sea.
❷ *adv.* Ⓐ coarsely; **~ gemahlen** coarsely ground; coarse-ground; **~ gesponnen** coarsely spun; coarse-spun; **ein ~ geschnittenes Gesicht haben** have coarse features *pl.;* Ⓑ (*ungefähr*) roughly; **~ gerechnet** *od.* **geschätzt** at a rough estimate; **etw. ~ umreißen/darlegen** present a rough outline/exposition of sth.; Ⓒ (*schwerwiegend*) grossly; **~ fahrlässig handeln** (*Rechtsspr.*) be guilty of gross negligence; Ⓓ (*barsch*) coarsely; rudely; **jmdm. ~ kommen** (*ugs.*) get rude with sb.; Ⓔ (*nicht sanft*) roughly

**grob-, Grob-: ~blech** *das* thick *or* heavy [steel] plate; **~einstellung** *die* rough adjustment; **~faserig** *Adj.* coarse-fibred; ***~gemahlen** *usw.* ⇒ **grob** 2 A

**Grobheit** *die;* ~, **~en** Ⓐ (*Wesensart*) rudeness; coarseness; Ⓑ (*Äußerung*) rude remark; (*Handlung*) [piece of] rudeness; **jmdm. ~en sagen/**(*ugs.*) **an den Kopf werfen** be extremely rude to sb.; Ⓒ (*derbe Beschaffenheit*) coarseness

**Grobian** /'gro:bia:n/ *der;* **~[e]s, ~e** boor; lout

**grob-: ~knochig** *Adj.* big-boned; **~körnig** *Adj.* coarse ‹sand, flour, etc.›; (*Fot.*) coarse-grained ‹film›

**gröblich** /'grø:plɪç/ (*geh.*) ❶ *Adj.* gross. ❷ *adv.* grossly

**grob-, Grob-: ~maschig** *Adj.* wide-meshed ‹sieve, net, etc.›; loose-knit ‹pullover etc.›; **~schlächtig** /-ʃlɛçtɪç/ *Adj.* heavily built; **eine ~schlächtige Darstellung** (*fig.*) a simplistic account; **~schmied** *der* (*veralt.*) blacksmith

**Grog** /grɔk/ *der;* **~s, ~s** grog

**groggy** /'grɔgi/ *Adj.* Ⓐ (*Boxen*) groggy; Ⓑ (*ugs.: erschöpft*) whacked [out] (*coll.*); all in (*coll.*)

**grölen** /'grø:lən/ ❶ *tr. V.* (*ugs. abwertend*) bawl [out]; roar, howl ‹approval›. ❷ *itr. V.* bawl; **eine ~de Menge** a roaring crowd

**Groll** /grɔl/ *der;* **~[e]s** (*geh.*) rancour; resentment; **einen ~ auf jmdn./etw. haben** *od.* **gegen jmdn./etw. hegen** harbour resentment *or* a grudge against sb./sth.; **aus ~ über jmdn./etw.** from a grudge against sb./ out of resentment at sth.; **ohne ~:** without rancour; with no ill feelings

**grollen** *itr. V.* (*geh.*) Ⓐ (*verstimmt sein*) be sullen; **[mit] jmdm. ~:** bear a grudge against sb.; bear sb. a grudge; Ⓑ (*dröhnen*) rumble; ‹thunder› roll, rumble; **das Grollen des Donners** the roll *or* rumble of thunder

**Grönland** /'grø:n.../ (*das*); **~s** Greenland

**Grönländer** *der;* **~s,** ~, **Grönländerin** *die;* ~, **~nen** Greenlander

**Gros**[1] /gro:/ *das;* ~ /gro:(s)/, ~ /gro:s/ bulk; main body; **das ~ der Betriebe** the greater *or* major part of industry

**Gros**[2] /grɔs/ *das;* **~ses, ~se** gross; **zwei ~:** two gross

**Groschen** /'grɔʃn̩/ *der;* **~s,** ~ ▶ 337 Ⓐ (*österreichische Münze*) groschen; Ⓑ (*ugs.: Zehnpfennigstück*) ten-pfennig piece; (*fig.*) penny; cent (*Amer.*); **Bonbons für einen** *od.* **zu einem ~:** ten pfennigs' worth of sweets; **[sich (*Dat.*)] ein paar ~ verdienen** (*ugs.*) earn [oneself] a few pennies *or* pence; **die ~ zusammenhalten müssen** (*ugs.*) have to count every penny [one spends]; **der ~ ist [bei ihm] gefallen** (*fig.*) the penny has dropped; **bei ihr fällt der ~ pfennigweise** (*fig.*) she's a bit slow on the uptake

**Groschen-: ~blatt** *das* (*abwertend*) tabloid; cheap rag (*derog.*); **~roman** *der* (*abwertend*) cheap novel; dime novel (*Amer.*)

**groß** /gro:s/, **größer** /'grø:sɐ/, **größt...** /'grø:st.../ ❶ *Adj.* Ⓐ ▶ 411 big; big, large ‹house, window, area, room, etc.›; large ‹pack, size, can, etc.›; great ‹length, width, height›; tall ‹person›; **~e Eier/Kartoffeln** large eggs/potatoes; **der ~e Zeiger** the big *or* minute hand; **ein ~er Buchstabe** a big *or* capital letter; **eine ~e Terz/Sekunde** (*Musik*) a major third/second; **ein ~es Bier, bitte** a pint, please; **im Großen einkaufen** buy in bulk; **die Großen Seen/der Große Salzsee** the Great Lakes/Great Salt Lake; **ein/zwei Nummern zu ~:** one size/two sizes too big; Ⓑ ▶ 411 (*eine bestimmte Größe aufweisend*) **1 m$^2$/2 ha ~:** 1 m$^2$/2 ha in area; **sie ist 1,75 m ~:** she is 1.75 m tall; **doppelt/dreimal so ~ wie ...** twice/three times the size of ...; Ⓒ (*älter*) big ‹brother, sister›; **seine größere Schwester** his elder sister; **unsere Große/unser Großer** our eldest *or* oldest daughter/son; (*von zwei Kindern*) our elder *or* older daughter/son; Ⓓ (*erwachsen*) grown-up ‹children, son, daughter›; **[mit etw.] ~ werden** grow up [with sth.]; **die Großen** (*Erwachsene*) the grown-ups; (*ältere Kinder*) the older children; **Groß und Klein** old and young [alike]; Ⓔ (*lange dauernd*) long, lengthy ‹delay, talk, explanation, pause›; **ein ~er Zeitraum** a long period of time; **die ~en Ferien** (*Schulw.*) the summer holidays *or* (*Amer.*) long vacation *sing.;* **die ~e Pause** (*Schulw.*) [mid-morning] break; Ⓕ (*beträchtlich*) **eine ~e Zuhörerschaft/Kundschaft** a large audience/clientele; **~e Summen/Kosten** large sums/heavy costs; **eine ~e Familie** a big *or* large family; **eine ~e Auswahl** a wide selection *or* range; **~es Geld** notes *pl.;* **das ~e Geld machen** (*ugs.*) *od.* **verdienen** make big money; Ⓖ (*außerordentlich*) great ‹pleasure, pain, hunger, anxiety, hurry, progress, difficulty, mistake, importance›; intense ‹heat, cold›; high ‹speed›; **mit dem größten Vergnügen** with the greatest of pleasure; **eine ~e Freude empfinden** feel great pleasure; **ein ~er Lärm** a lot of noise; **~en Hunger haben** be very hungry; **ein ~er Esser/Bastler** a great *or* heavy eater/ great handyman; **ihre/seine ~e Liebe** her/ his great love; **~ im Geschäft sein** be in great demand; Ⓗ (*gewichtig*) great; major ‹producer, exporter›; great, major ‹event›; **ein ~er Augenblick/Tag** a great moment/day; **~e Worte/Gesten** grand *or* fine words/grand gestures; **[k]eine ~e Rolle spielen** [not] play a great *or* an important part; **sie hat Großes geleistet** she has achieved great things; **die Großen [der Welt]** the great figures [of our world]; Ⓘ (*glanzvoll*) grand ‹celebration, ball, etc.›; **in ~er Aufmachung/Garderobe** in all one's finery; **die ~e Dame/den ~en Herrn spielen** (*iron.*) play the fine lady/gentleman; Ⓙ (*bedeutend*) great, major ‹artist, painter, work›; **Otto der Große/Katharina die Große** Otto/Catherine the Great; ⇒ *auch* **Karl**; Ⓚ (*wesentlich*) **die ~e Linie/der ~e Zusammenhang** the basic line/the overall context; **in ~en Zügen** *od.* **Umrissen** in broad outline; **im Großen [und] Ganzen** by and large; on the whole; Ⓛ (*geh.: selbstlos*) noble ‹deed etc.›; **ein ~es Herz haben** be great-hearted; Ⓜ (*ugs.: ~artig*) great (*coll.*); **das finde ich** *od.* **das ist ganz ~** (*iron.*) that's just great (*coll. iron.*); **~ in etw.** (*Dat.*) **sein** be a great one for sth.; Ⓝ (*ugs.: ~spurig*) **~e Reden schwingen** *od.* (*salopp*) **Töne spucken** talk big (*coll.*).
❷ *adv.* Ⓐ **die Heizung** *usw.* **~/größer einstellen** turn the heating *etc.* up high/ higher; **~ geschrieben werden** (*fig.*) be stressed *or* emphasized; **bei ihm wird Geldverdienen ~ geschrieben** earning money comes high on his list of priorities; **jmdn. ~ ansehen** stare hard at sb.; **~ machen** (*Kinderspr.*) do number two (*child lang.*); **~ und breit** at great length; Ⓑ (*ugs.: aufwendig*) **~ ausgehen** go out for a big celebration; **etw. ~ feiern** celebrate sth. in a big way; **jmdn./etw. ~ herausbringen** publicize sb./sth. with a big splash; **ein ~ angelegtes Projekt** a large-scale project; **ein ~ angelegter Angriff** a full-scale attack; Ⓒ (*ugs.: besonders*) greatly; particularly; **es lohnt [sich] nicht ~, das zu tun** there is not much point in doing that; **sich nicht ~ um jmdn./etw. kümmern** not bother *or* concern oneself greatly about sb./sth.; **wir haben nicht ~ darauf geachtet** we didn't pay much attention to it; **was gibt es da noch ~ zu diskutieren?** why do we need all this long discussion?; **niemand freute sich ~:** nobody was very pleased *or* (*coll.*) exactly overjoyed; Ⓓ (*geh.: selbstlos*) **~ handeln** act nobly; **fähig sein, ~ zu fühlen** be capable of noble sentiments; Ⓔ (*ugs.: ~artig*) **sie steht ganz ~ da** she has made it big (*coll.*) *or* made the big time (*coll.*); Ⓕ (*ugs.: ~spurig*) **~ daherreden/auftreten** talk/act big (*coll.*)

**groß-, Groß-: ~abnehmer** *der,* **~abnehmerin** *die* bulk buyer *or* purchaser; **~admiral** *der* (*Milit. hist.*) Grand Admiral; **~aktion** *die* major campaign; big drive; **~aktionär** *der,* **~aktionärin** *die* (*Wirtsch.*) principal *or* major shareholder; **~alarm** *der* full-scale alarm; ***~angelegt** ⇒ **groß** 2B; **~angriff** *der* (*Milit.*) full-scale attack; **~artig** ❶ *Adj.* magnificent; splendid; wonderful ‹person›; ❷ *adv.* magnificently; splendidly; **wir haben uns ~artig amüsiert** we had a marvellous time; **~artigkeit** *die* magnificence; splendour; **~aufnahme** *die* Ⓐ (*Film*) close-up; **in ~aufnahme** in close-up; Ⓑ (*Fot.*) ⇒ **Nahaufnahme**; **~auftrag** *der* (*Wirtsch.*) large order; **~bank** *die; Pl.* **~~en** (*Finanzw.*) big bank; **die fünf ~banken** the Big Five; **~bauer** *der;* **~~n, ~~n** big farmer; **~betrieb** *der* large *or* big concern; large-scale enterprise; **~bourgeoisie** *die* (*marx.*) haute bourgeoisie; **~brand** *der* large fire *or* blaze

g

**Groß·britannien** *(das);* **~s** the United Kingdom; [Great] Britain

**groß-, Groß-:** **~buchstabe** *der* capital [letter]; upper-case letter *(Printing)*; **~bürgerlich** *Adj.* upper middle-class; **~bürgertum** *das* upper middle class; **~deutsch** *Adj.* *(bes. ns.)* Pan-German; **~deutschland** *(das)* *(bes. ns.)* *Germany after the anschluss of Austria*

**Größe** /ˈgrøːsə/ *die;* **~, ~n** Ⓐ size; *(Kleider~)* **in ~ 38** in size 38; **sie trägt ~ 44** she is *or* takes size 44; Ⓑ ▶411 *(Höhe, Körper~)* height; **der ~ nach** by height; Ⓒ *(Bedeutsamkeit, sittlicher Wert)* greatness; Ⓓ *(Ausmaß)* **die ~ der Katastrophe** the [full] scale *or* extent of the catastrophe; Ⓔ *(Genie)* outstanding *or* important figure; Ⓕ *(Math., Physik)* quantity; **eine gegebene/** *(auch fig.)* **unbekannte ~:** a given/an unknown quantity

**Groß-:** **~ein·kauf** *der* bulk purchase; **~einkauf machen** do all one's shopping at one time; **~ein·satz** *der* large-scale operation; **~eltern** *Pl.* grandparents; **~enkel** *der* great-grandchild; *(Junge)* great-grandson; **~enkelin** *die* great-granddaughter

**Größen-:** **~klasse** *die* Ⓐ size [group]; **Eier der ~klasse 2** class 2 eggs; Ⓑ *(Astron.)* magnitude; **~ordnung** *die* Ⓐ *(Dimension)* order [of magnitude]; **in einer ~ordnung von einer Milliarde Mark** in the order of a thousand million *or* a billion marks; Ⓑ *(Physik, Math.)* order of magnitude

**großen·teils** *Adv.* largely; for the most part

**größen-, Größen-:** **~verhältnis** *das* Ⓐ *(Maßstab)* scale; **im ~verhältnis 1:10** on a scale of 1:10; Ⓑ *(Proportion)* proportions *pl.;* **~wahn** *der* *(abwertend)* megalomania; delusions *pl.* of grandeur; **~wahnsinnig** *Adj.* megalomaniacal; **er ist ~wahnsinnig** he's a megalomaniac

**größer** ⇒ **groß**

**groß-, Groß-:** **~fahndung** *die* large-scale search *or* manhunt; **~familie** *die* *(Soziol.)* extended family; *(mehrere Kleinfamilien)* composite family; **~feuer** *das* large fire *or* blaze; **~flug·hafen** *der* large *or* major airport; **~folio** *das* *(Buchw.)* large folio; **~format** *das* large size; *(bei Büchern)* large format *or* size; **~fürst** *der* *(hist.)* Grand Duke; **~fürstin** *die* *(hist.)* Grand Duchess; **~grund·besitz** *der* ownership of large estates; **~grund·besitzer** *der,* **~grund·besitzerin** *die* big landowner; **~handel** *der* wholesale trade; **~händler** *der,* **~händlerin** *die* wholesaler; **~handlung** *die* wholesale business; **~herzig** *(geh.)* ❶ *Adj.* magnanimous; ❷ *adv.* magnanimously; **~herzigkeit** *die;* **~~** *(geh.)* magnanimity; **~herzog** *der* Grand Duke; **~herzogin** *die* Grand Duchess; **~herzoglich** *Adj.* grand-ducal; **~herzogtum** *das* grand duchy; **~herzogtum Luxemburg** Grand Duchy of Luxembourg; **~hirn** *das* ▶471 *(Anat.)* cerebrum; **~hirn·rinde** *die* ▶471 *(Anat.)* cerebral cortex; **~industrie** *die* big industry; **~industrielle** *der/die* big industrialist; **~inquisitor** *der* *(hist.)* Grand Inquisitor

**Grossist** *der;* **~en, ~en, Grossistin** *die;* **~, ~nen** *(Kaufmannsspr.)* wholesaler

**groß-, Groß-:** **~jährig** *Adj.* *(veralt.)* ‹person› who is of age; **~jährig werden/sein** come/be of age; **~jährigkeit** *die;* **~~** *(veralt.)* majority; **die ~jährigkeit erlangen** reach the age of majority; **~kampf·schiff** *das* *(Milit. veralt.)* capital ship; **~kapital** *das* *(Wirtsch.)* big business *or* capital; **~kapitalist** *der,* **~kapitalistin** *die* big capitalist; **~katze** *die* *(Zool.)* big cat; **~kauffrau** *die,* **~kaufmann** *der* merchant; **~kind** *das* *(schweiz.)* grandchild; **~klima** *das* *(Met.)* macroclimate; **~konzern** *der* big *or* large combine; **~kopfe[r]te** /-kɔpfɐtə/ *der; adj. Dekl.* *(ugs. abwertend)* high-up *(coll.)*; *(Intellektueller)* egghead *(coll.)*; **~kotzig** /-kɔtsɪç/ ❶ *Adj.* *(salopp abwertend)* pretentious ‹style›; swanky *(coll.)* ‹present etc.›; boastful ‹tone etc.›; ❷ *adv.* boastfully; **~kreuz** *das* Grand Cross; **~küche** *die* large kitchen *(of hotel, hospital, etc.)*; **~kundgebung** *die* mass rally *or* meeting; **~macht** *die* great power; **die ~macht USA** the USA, one of the great powers; **~macht·stellung** *die* great power status; **~mama** *die* *(ugs.)* grandma *(coll./child lang.)*; granny *(coll./child lang.)*; **~manns·sucht** *die* *(abwertend)* craving for status; **~markt** *der* central market; **~maschig** *Adj.* wide-meshed; **~mast** *der* *(Seemannsspr.)* mainmast; **~maul** *das* *(ugs. abwertend)* bigmouth *(coll.)*; braggart; **~mäulig** /-mɔyːlɪç/ *Adj.* *(ugs. abwertend)* big-mouthed *(coll.)*; **~meister** *der* Grand Master; *(Schach)* grand master; **~mut** *die;* **~~:** magnanimity; generosity; **~mütig** /-myːtɪç/ ❶ *Adj.* magnanimous; generous; ❷ *adv.* magnanimously; generously; **~mutter** *die; Pl.* **~mütter** Ⓐ grandmother; **~mutter werden** become a grandmother; **das kannst du deiner ~mutter erzählen** *(ugs.)* tell that to the marines; Ⓑ *(ugs.: alte Frau)* old lady; **~mütterlich** *Adj.* Ⓐ grandmother's; **das ~mütterliche Haus** one's grandmother's house; **jmds. ~mütterliches Erbe** sb.'s inheritance from his/her/their grandmother; Ⓑ *(wie eine ~mutter)* grandmotherly; **~neffe** *der* great-nephew; grandnephew; **~nichte** *die* great-niece; grandniece; **~offensive** *die* *(Milit.)* major *or* full-scale offensive; **~oktav** *das* *(Buchw.)* royal octavo; **~onkel** *der* great-uncle; granduncle; **~papa** *der* *(ugs.)* grandpa *(coll./child lang.)*; granddad *(coll./child lang.)*; **~rat** *der,* **~rätin** *die* *(schweiz.)* *member of a cantonal great council;* **~raum** *der* area; **im ~raum Hamburg** in the [Greater] Hamburg area; **~raum·abteil** *das* *(Eisenb.)* open carriage; **~raum·büro** *das* open-plan office; **~raum·flugzeug** *das* wide-bodied aircraft

**großräumig** /-rɔymɪç/ ❶ *Adj.* extensive; over a wide *or* large area *postpos., not pred.;* *(viel Platz bietend)* spacious, roomy ‹office, house, etc.›; wide-bodied ‹aircraft›. ❷ *adv.* over a wide *or* large area; **eine ~ gebaute Stadt** a town [built] with plenty of open space; **ein ~ konzipiertes Flugzeug** an aircraft designed for high-capacity air transport

**groß-, Groß-:** **~raum·wagen** *der* *(Verkehrsw.)* open car; **~rechner** *der* *(DV)* mainframe [computer]; **~reinemachen** *das* *(ugs.)* thorough cleaning; spring-clean; **ein ~reinemachen veranstalten** spring-clean the house; **~schanze** *die* *(Skisport)* ninety-metre hill; **~schnauze** *die* *(salopp)* bigmouth *(coll.)*; **~schnauzig** *Adj.* *(salopp)* big-mouthed *(coll.)*; **~|schreiben** *unr. tr. V.* write ‹word› with a capital [initial] letter; write ‹word› with a capital; ⇒ *auch* **groß** 2 A; **~schreibung** *die* capitalization; **~segel** *das* *(Seemannsspr.)* mainsail; **~sprecher** *der,* **~sprecherin** *die* *(abwertend)* braggart; boaster; **~sprecherisch** *Adj.* *(abwertend)* boastful ‹person›; bragging *attrib.,* boastful ‹words, manner, etc.›; **~spurig** *(abwertend)* ❶ *Adj.* boastful; *(hochtrabend)* pretentious ‹word, language›; grandiose ‹plan›; ❷ *adv.* boastfully; *(hochtrabend)* pretentiously; **~stadt** *die* city; large town; **~städter** *der,* **~städterin** *die* city-dweller; urbanite; **~städtisch** *Adj.* [big-]city *attrib.* ‹life›; **der ~städtische Autoverkehr** traffic in the [big] cities; **Genf ist in vielem ~städtischer als Bern** in many ways Geneva is more of a big city than Berne; **~stadt·luft** *die* city air; *(fig. ugs.: Atmosphäre)* atmosphere of the big city *(fig.)*; **~stadt·verkehr** *der* [big-]city traffic

**größt...** ⇒ **groß**

**Groß-:** **~tante** *die* great-aunt; grandaunt; **~tat** *die* *(geh.)* great feat; **~teil** *der* Ⓐ *(Hauptteil)* major part; **zum ~teil** mostly; for the most part; Ⓑ *(nicht unerheblicher Teil)* large part; **zu einem ~teil** largely

**größten·teils** *Adv.* for the most part

**Größt·maß** *das* Ⓐ *(zulässiges Maß)* maximum size *or* dimensions *pl.;* Ⓑ *(größtmöglicher Anteil)* maximum amount

**größt·möglich** *Adj.* greatest possible

**groß-, Groß-:** **~tuer** /-tuːɐ/ *der;* **~~s, ~~** *(abwertend)* braggart; boaster; **~tuerei** *die;* **~~** *(abwertend)* bragging; boasting; **~tuerin** *die;* **~~, ~~nen** ⇒ **~tuer**; **~tuerisch** *Adj.* *(abwertend)* boastful; bragging; **~|tun** ❶ *unr. itr. V.* boast; brag; **mit jmdm./etw. ~tun** boast *or* brag about sb./sth.; **mit seinen Kenntnissen ~tun** show off one's knowledge; ❷ *unr. refl. V.* **sich mit jmdm./etw. ~tun** boast *or* brag about sb./sth.; **~unternehmen** *das* *(Wirtsch.)* large-scale enterprise; big concern; **~unternehmer** *der* *(Wirtsch.)* big businessman; **~unternehmerin** *die* *(Wirtsch.)* big businesswoman; **~vater** *der* grandfather; **~väterlich** Ⓐ *Adj.* grandfather's; **das ~väterliche Haus** one's grandfather's house; **jmds. ~väterliches Erbe** sb.'s inheritance from his/her/their grandfather; Ⓑ *(wie ein ~vater)* grandfatherly; **~vater·stuhl** *der* *(ugs.)* easy chair; wing chair; **~veranstaltung** *die* mass rally *or* meeting; **~verbraucher** *der,* **~verbraucherin** *die* bulk *or* large consumer; **~verdiener** *der,* **~verdienerin** *die* big earner; **~versandhaus** *das* [large] mail order firm *or* house; **~vieh** *das* cattle and horses *pl.;* **~wesir** *der* *(hist.)* grand vizier; **~wetter·lage** *die* *(Met.)* macro weather situation; *(fig.)* general political situation; **~wild** *das* big game; **~wild·jagd** *die* big-game hunting *no art.;* **~wild·jäger** *der,* **~wild·jägerin** *die* big-game hunter; **~wörterbuch** *das* comprehensive dictionary; **~|ziehen** *unr. tr. V.* bring up; raise; rear ‹animal›; **~zügig** ❶ *Adj.* Ⓐ generous; generous, handsome ‹tip›; Ⓑ *(in ~em Stil)* grand and spacious ‹building, gardens, etc.›; generous, liberal ‹working conditions›; large-scale ‹measures›; ❷ *adv.* Ⓐ generously; **sich ~zügig über etw.** *(Akk.)* **hinwegsetzen** be broad-minded enough to disregard sth.; Ⓑ *(in ~em Stil)* **ein ~zügig eingerichtetes Büro** a handsomely equipped office; **die ~zügig angelegten Schlossgärten** the palace gardens, laid out on a grand scale; **~zügigkeit** *die* Ⓐ generosity; Ⓑ *(~es Ausmaß)* grand scale

**grotesk** /groˈtɛsk/ ❶ *Adj.* grotesque. ❷ *adv.* grotesquely

**Grotesk** *die;* **~** *(Druckw.)* Grotesque; sanserif

**Groteske** *die;* **~, ~n** Ⓐ *(Ornamentik)* grotesque; Ⓑ *(Literaturwiss.)* grotesque tale

**grotesker·weise** *Adv.* absurdly [enough]

**Grotte** /ˈgrɔtə/ *die;* **~, ~n** grotto

**grotten·doof** *Adj.* bloody stupid *(sl.)*

**Grotten·olm** *der* olm

**grub** /gruːp/ *1. u. 3. Pers. Sg. Prät. v.* **graben**

**Grubber** /ˈgrʊbɐ/ *der;* **~s, ~:** cultivator

**Grübchen** /ˈgryːpçən/ *das;* **~s, ~:** dimple

**Grube** *die;* **~, ~n** Ⓐ pit; hole; **wer andern eine ~ gräbt, fällt selbst hinein** *(Spr.)* take care that you are not hoist with your own petard; Ⓑ *(Bergbau)* mine; pit; **in der ~ arbeiten/in die ~ einfahren** work/go down the mine; Ⓒ *(veralt.: offenes Grab)* grave; **in die** *od.* **zur ~ fahren** *(veralt.)* yield up the ghost *(arch.)*

**Grübelei** *die;* **~, ~en** pondering; *(Melancholie)* brooding

**grübeln** /ˈgryːbl̩n/ *itr. V.* ponder **(über** + *Dat.* on, over); *(brüten)* brood **(über** + *Dat.* over, about)

**Gruben-:** **~arbeiter** *der,* **~arbeiterin** *die* miner; mineworker; **~bahn** *die* mine *or* pit tram *or* train; **~brand** *der* pit fire; **~gas** *das* firedamp; **~lampe** *die* miner's lamp; **~unglück** *das* pit *or* mine disaster; **~wasser** *das* pit *or* mine water

**Grübler** *der;* **~s, ~, Grüblerin** *die;* **~, ~nen** meditative person; *(Melancholiker)* brooder; brooding person

**grüblerisch** *Adj.* meditative; *(melancholisch)* brooding

**grüezi** /ˈgryːɛtsiː/ *Adv.* *(schweiz.)* hello

**Gruft** /grʊft/ *die;* **~, Grüfte** /ˈgrʏftə/ Ⓐ *(Gewölbe)* vault; *(in einer Kirche)* crypt; Ⓑ *(offenes Grab)* grave

**grummeln** /ˈgrʊml̩n/ *itr. V.* Ⓐ *(dröhnen)* rumble; **man hörte den Donner/die Geschütze ~:** one could hear the rumble of thunder/the guns; Ⓑ *(murmeln)* mumble

**Grummet** /ˈgrʊmət/ *das;* **~s, Grumt** /grʊmt/ *das;* **Grumt[e]s** aftermath

*old spelling (see note on page 1707)

**grün** /gry:n/ *Adj.* [A] green; **~er Salat** lettuce; **die Ampel ist ~** (*ugs.*) the lights are green; **wir haben ~e Weihnachten gehabt** we didn't have a white Christmas; **die Grüne Insel** the Emerald Isle; **~e Bohnen/Erbsen** French beans/green peas; **~es Holz** green timber; **~e Heringe** fresh herrings; **ein ~er Junge** (*abwertend*) a greenhorn; **~es Licht geben** give the go-ahead; **jmdn. ~ und blau** *od.* **gelb schlagen** (*ugs.*) beat sb. black and blue; **sich ~ und blau** *od.* **gelb ärgern** (*ugs.*) be livid (*coll.*) *or* furious; **du bist noch [zu] ~ hinter den Ohren** (*abwertend*) you're still [too] wet behind the ears (*coll.*); ⇒ *auch* **Welle** A; [B] (*ugs.: wohlgesinnt*) **ich bin ihr nicht ~:** she's not someone I care for; **die beiden sind sich** (*Dat.*) **nicht ~:** there's no love lost between them; [C] (*Politik*) ecological; **ein ~er Abgeordneter** a Member belonging to the Green party

**Grün** *das;* **~s, ~** *od.* (*ugs.*) **~s** [A] green; **die Ampel steht auf** *od.* **zeigt ~:** the lights *pl.* are at green; **das ist dasselbe in ~** (*ugs.*) it makes *or* there is no real difference; [B] (*Pflanzen*) greenery; [C] (*Golf*) green; [D] (*Spielkartenfarbe*) spades *pl.*; ⇒ *auch* **Pik**[2]

**Grün·anlage** *die* green space; (*Park*) park

**grün·blau** *Adj.* greenish blue

**Grund** /grʊnt/ *der;* **~[e]s, Gründe** /ˈgrʏndə/ [A] (*Erdoberfläche*) ground; **etw. bis auf den ~ abreißen** raze sth. to the ground; **etw. von ~ auf neu bauen** rebuild sth. from scratch; **den ~ zu etw. legen** (*fig.*) lay the foundations *pl.* of *or* for sth. (*fig.*); **sich in ~ und Boden schämen** be utterly ashamed; **etw. in ~ und Boden verdammen** condemn sth. outright; **jmdn. in ~ und Boden reden** shoot every one of sb.'s arguments to pieces; **etw. in ~ und Boden wirtschaften** bring *or* reduce sth. to rack and ruin; [B] (*eines Gewässers, geh.: eines Gefäßes*) bottom; **auf ~ laufen** run aground; **ein Glas bis auf den ~ leeren** (*geh.*) drain a glass [to the dregs]; **im ~e seines Herzens/seiner Seele** (*fig. geh.*) at heart *or* deep down/in his innermost soul; **der Sache** (*Dat.*) **auf den ~ gehen/kommen** get to the bottom *or* root of the matter; **im ~e [genommen]** basically; [C] (*Ursache, Veranlassung*) reason; (*Beweg~*) grounds *pl.*; reason; **es gibt keinen/nicht den geringsten ~ zu etw.** there is no/not the slightest reason for sth.; **allen ~ haben, etw. zu tun** have every *or* good reason to do *or* for doing sth.; **[k]einen ~ zum Feiern/Klagen haben** have [no] cause for [a] celebration/to complain *or* for complaint; **aus Gründen der Geheimhaltung/Sicherheit** for reasons of secrecy/security; **aus dem einfachen ~, weil ...** (*ugs.*) for the simple reason that ...; **ohne ersichtlichen ~:** for no obvious *or* apparent reason; **auf ~ ihrer Aussagen/dieser Lage** on the basis *or* strength of their statements/in view of this situation; **Gründe und Gegengründe** pros and cons; arguments for and against; [D] (*veralt., noch landsch.: Erdreich*) soil; ground; [E] (*bes. österr.: ~besitz*) land *no indef. art., no pl.*; (*Bau~*) plot [of land]; **~ und Boden** land; [F] (*veralt.: kleines Tal*) valley; [G] (*Unter~*) ground; [H] **zu ~e** ⇒ **zugrunde**

**grund-, Grund-: ~anschauung** *die* fundamental ideas *pl. or* attitudes *pl.*; **seine politische ~anschauung** his basic political outlook; **~anständig** *Adj.* thoroughly decent; **~anstrich** *der* priming coat; **~ausbildung** *die* (*Milit.*) basic training; **~ausstattung** *die* basic equipment; **~bedeutung** *die* [A] fundamental *or* basic *or* essential meaning; [B] (*Sprachw.*) original meaning; **~bedingung** *die* basic condition; **~begriff** *der* basic *or* fundamental concept; **die ~begriffe der lateinischen Sprache** the rudiments of Latin; **~besitz** *der* [A] (*Eigentum an Land*) ownership of land; [B] (*Land*) land; landed property; **~besitzer** *der,* **~besitzerin** *die* landowner; **~bestandteil** *der* [basic] element; **~buch** *das* land register; **~buch·amt** *das* land registry; **~ehrlich** *Adj.* thoroughly honest; **~eigentum** *das* ⇒ **~besitz** A; **~eigentümer** *der,* **~eigentümerin** *die* ⇒ **~besitzer**; **~einheit** *die* [A] (*Physik*) fundamental unit; [B] (*DDR: organisatorische Einheit*) local group; **~einstellung** *die* fundamental *or* basic attitude; **~eis** *das* anchor ice; ground ice; ⇒ *auch* **Arsch** A

**gründen** /ˈgrʏndn̩/ ❶ *tr. V.* [A] (*neu schaffen*) found, set up, establish ‹organization, party, etc.›; set up, establish ‹business›; start [up] ‹club›; **eine Familie/ein Heim ~:** start a family/set up home; [B] (*aufbauen*) base ‹plan, theory, etc.› (**auf** + *Akk.* on). ❷ *itr. V.* **auf** *od.* **in etw.** (*Dat.*) **~:** be based on sth. ❸ *refl. V.* **sich auf etw.** (*Akk.*) **~:** be based on sth.

**Gründer** *der;* **~s, ~, Gründerin** *die;* **~, ~nen** founder

**Gründer·jahre** *Pl.*: *period (1871-1873) when many industrial firms were founded in Germany*

**Grund-: ~erwerb** *der* (*Rechtsw.*) acquisition of land; (*Kauf*) purchase of land; **~erwerb[s]·steuer** *die* (*Steuerw.*) land transfer tax

**Gründer·zeit** *die* ⇒ **Gründerjahre**

**grund-, Grund-: ~falsch** *Adj.* utterly wrong; **~farbe** *die* [A] (*Malerei, Druckw.*) primary colour; [B] (*Untergrundfarbe*) ground colour; **~fehler** *der* basic *or* fundamental mistake *or* error; **~festen** *Pl.*: *in* **an den ~festen von etw. rütteln** shake the [very] foundations of sth.; **etw. in seinen** *od.* **bis in seine ~festen erschüttern** shake sth. to its [very] foundations; **~fläche** *die* [A] (*eines Zimmers*) [floor] area; [B] (*Math.*) base; **~form** *die* [A] (*Hauptform*) basic form; [B] (*Urform*) original form; [C] (*Sprachw.*) infinitive; (*Satzbauplan*) basic [grammatical] structure of a/the sentence; **~frage** *die* basic *or* fundamental issue *or* question; **die politischen ~fragen** the basic *or* fundamental political issues *or* questions; **~gebühr** *die* basic *or* standing charge; **~gedanke** *der* basic idea; **~gehalt**[1] *der* (*einer Theorie*) basic idea; (*eines Dramas*) basic theme; **~gehalt**[2] *das* basic salary; **~gescheit** *Adj.* extremely clever *or* bright; **~gesetz** *das* [A] (*Verfassung*) Basic Law; [B] (*wichtiges Gesetz*) fundamental *or* basic law; **~haltung** *die* [A] (*Sport: Körperhaltung*) basic position; [B] (*Einstellung*) basic *or* fundamental attitude; **~herr** *der* (*hist.*) lord of the manor

**Grundier·anstrich** *der* priming coat

**grundieren** /grʊnˈdi:rən/ *tr. V.* prime; (*Ölmalerei*) ground; apply the ground to

**Grundier·farbe** *die* primer

**Grundierung** *die;* **~, ~en** [A] (*das Grundieren*) priming; (*Ölmalerei*) grounding; applying the ground (*Gen.* to); [B] (*erster Anstrich*) priming coat; (*Ölmalerei*) ground coat

**Grund-: ~kapital** *das* (*Wirtsch.*) equity *or* share capital; **~kenntnis** *die* basic knowledge *no pl.* (**in** + *Dat.* of); **~konzeption** *die* basic *or* fundamental conception; **~kurs** *der* basic course

**Grund·lage** *die* basis; foundation; **auf der ~:** on the basis; **jeder ~ entbehren** be completely unfounded *or* without any foundation; **die geistigen/theoretischen ~n** the intellectual/theoretical foundations; **die ~n einer Wissenschaft** the basic principles of a science; **auf breiter ~ arbeiten** work *or* operate on a broad basis; **iss mal tüchtig, damit du eine gute ~ hast** (*ugs.*) get a good meal inside you to line your stomach with (*coll.*)

**Grundlagen·forschung** *die* basic research

**grund·legend** ❶ *Adj.* fundamental, basic (**für** to); seminal ‹idea, work›. ❷ *adv.* fundamentally; **sich ~ zu etw. äußern** make a statement of fundamental importance on sth.

**Grund·legung** *die;* **~** (*fig.*) laying of the foundations (*Gen.* for)

**gründlich** /ˈgrʏntlɪç/ ❶ *Adj.* thorough. ❷ *adv.* [A] (*gewissenhaft*) thoroughly; [B] (*ugs.: gehörig*) **sich ~ täuschen** be sadly *or* greatly mistaken; **sich ~ langweilen** be bored to tears (*coll.*); **~ mit etw. aufräumen** do away completely with sth.; **~ mit jmdm. abrechnen** really get even with sb.

**Gründlichkeit** *die;* **~:** thoroughness

**Gründling** /ˈgrʏntlɪŋ/ *der;* **~s, ~e** (*Zool.*) gudgeon

**grund-, Grund-: ~linie** *die* [A] (*Math.*) base; [B] (*Sport*) baseline; [C] (*Hauptzug*) main *or* principal feature *or* characteristic; **~linien·spiel** *das* (*Tennis*) baseline play; **~lohn** *der* basic salary; **~los** ❶ *Adj.* [A] (*unbegründet*) groundless; unfounded; [B] (*ohne festen Boden*) bottomless ‹sea, depths, etc.›; ❷ *adv.* **sich ~los aufregen/ängstigen** be needlessly agitated/alarmed; **~los lachen** laugh for no reason [at all]; **jmdn. ~los verdächtigen** be suspicious of sb. without reason; **~mauer** *die* foundation wall; **das Haus war bis auf die ~mauern abgebrannt** the house had burnt to the ground; **~nahrungs·mittel** *das* basic food[stuff]; **~norm** *die* basic standard

**Grün·donnerstag** *der* Maundy Thursday

**Grund-: ~ordnung** *die* basic fundamental [constitutional] order; **~pfeiler** *der* foundation *or* main pillar; (*einer Brücke*) main pier; (*fig.*) main pillar; **~prinzip** *das* fundamental *or* basic principle; **~rechen·art, ~rechnungs·art** *die* fundamental *or* basic arithmetical operation; **~recht** *das* basic *or* fundamental *or* constitutional right; **~regel** *die* fundamental *or* basic rule; **~rente** *die* [A] (*Wirtsch.: Bodenrente*) ground rent; [B] (*Sozialw.*) basic pension; **~riss,** ***~riß** *der* [A] (*Bauw.*) [ground] plan; [B] (*Leitfaden*) outline; **~satz** *der* principle; **aus ~satz** on principle; **sich** (*Dat.*) **etw. zum ~satz machen** make sth. a matter of principle; **ein Mann von ~sätzen** a man of principle; **~satz·entscheidung** *die* decision on fundamental principles; (*Rechtsw.*) ruling; **~satz·erklärung** *die* declaration of principle

**grund·sätzlich** ❶ *Adj.* [A] fundamental ‹difference, question, etc.›; [B] (*aus Prinzip*) ‹rejection, opponent, etc.› on principle; [C] (*allgemein*) ‹agreement, readiness, etc.› in principle. ❷ *adv.* [A] fundamentally; **zu etw. ~ Stellung nehmen** make a statement of principle on sth.; [B] (*aus Prinzip*) as a matter of principle; on principle; **es ist ~ verboten** it is absolutely forbidden; [C] (*allgemein*) in principle; **~ habe ich nichts dagegen einzuwenden, aber ...** basically *or* in principle I've nothing against it, but ...

**Grund-: ~satz·programm** *das* political programme; **~schnelligkeit** *die* (*Sport*) [A] maximum speed; [B] (*angeboren*) basic speed capability; **~schuld** *die* (*Rechtsw., Finanzw.*) land charge; encumbrance; **~schule** *die* primary school; **~schüler** *der* primary school pupil; **~schul·lehrer** *der,* **~schul·lehrerin** *die* ▶ 159 primary-school teacher; **~stein** *der* foundation stone; (*fig.*) foundation [stone]; **den ~stein zu etw. legen** lay the foundation stone of sth.; (*fig.*) lay the foundation[s *pl.*] for *or* of sth.; **~stein·legung** *die;* **~~, ~~en** laying of the foundation stone; **~stellung** *die* (*Sport*) basic position; **~steuer** *die* (*Steuerw.*) property tax [under German law]; **~stimmung** *die* prevailing mood; **eine pessimistische ~stimmung** a prevailing mood of pessimism; **~stock** *der* basis; foundation; (*einer Sammlung*) basis; nucleus; **~stoff** *der* [A] (*Chemie: Element*) element; [B] (*Rohstoff*) [basic] raw material; **~stoff·industrie** *die* basic industry

**Grund·stück** *das* plot [of land]; (*Baugrundstück*) plot of land; site; **ein bebautes ~:** a developed site *or* property; **~e kaufen/erben** buy/inherit property *sing.*

**Grundstücks-: ~makler** *der,* **~maklerin** *die* ▶ 159 estate agent; **~spekulant** *der,* **~spekulantin** *die* property speculator

**Grund-: ~studium** *das* basic course; **~tendenz** *die* basic trend; **~text** *der* original text; **~ton** *der; Pl.* **~töne** [A] (*Farbton*) basic colour; [B] (*~stimmung*) basic *or* prevailing tone *or* mood; **ein optimistischer ~ton** a basic *or* prevailing mood of optimism; [C] (*Musik*) fundamental [tone]; root; **~übel** *das* basic evil; **~umsatz** *der* (*Physiol.*) basal metabolic rate

**Gründung** *die;* ~, ~**en** (*Partei*~, *Vereins*~) foundation; establishment; setting up; (*Geschäfts*~) setting up; establishing; (*Klub*~) starting [up]; **die ~ einer Familie** starting a family

**Gründungs-:** ~**feier** *die* foundation ceremony; ~**jahr** *das* year of foundation *or* establishment; **das ~jahr unseres Vereins** the year of the foundation of our organization; ~**kapital** *das* (*Wirtsch.*) original *or* initial capital

**grund-, Grund-:** ~**verkehrt** *Adj.* completely *or* entirely wrong; ~**vermögen** *das* (*Finanzw.*) [landed] property; real estate; ~**verschieden** *Adj.* totally *or* completely different; ~**wahrheit** *die* fundamental *or* basic truth; ~**wasser** *das* (*Geol.*) groundwater; ~**wasser·spiegel** *der* water table; groundwater level; ~**wehr·dienst** *der* basic military service; national service; ~**wissen** *das* basic *or* elementary knowledge; ~**wissenschaft** *die* basic discipline; ~**wort** *das; Pl.* ~**wörter** (*Sprachw.*) basic component; ~**wort·schatz** *der* (*Sprachw.*) basic vocabulary; ~**zahl** *die* cardinal [number]; ~**zug** *der* essential feature; **etw. in seinen ~zügen darstellen** outline the essential features *or* essentials of sth.

**Grüne**[1] *das; adj. Dekl.* Ⓐ green; Ⓑ **im ~n/ins ~:** [out] in/into the country; Ⓒ (*ugs.: grüne Pflanzen*) greenery; (*Salat*) green salad; (*Gemüse*) greens *pl.*; green vegetables *pl.*

**Grüne**[2] *der/die; adj. Dekl.* (*Politik*) member of the Green Party; **die ~n** the Greens

**Grüne**[3] *der; adj. Dekl.* (*ugs.*) Ⓐ (*Polizist*) cop (*coll.*); Ⓑ (*20-Mark-Schein*) 20-mark note

**grünen** *itr. V.* (*geh.*) be green; (*grün werden*) turn green; (*fig. dichter.*) spring up anew

**grün-, Grün-:** ~**fink** *der* greenfinch; ~**fläche** *die* green space; (*im Park*) lawn; ~**futter** *das* (*Landw.*) green fodder; ~**gelb** *Adj.* greenish yellow; ~**gürtel** *der* green belt; ~**kern** *der: dried unripe spelt grains* (*used to thicken soup*); ~**kohl** *der* curly kale; ~**land** *das* (*Landw.*) (*Wiese*) meadow land; (*Weide*) pastureland; (*mit ~futter bebaut*) land used for growing green fodder

**grünlich** ❶ *Adj.* greenish. ❷ *adv.* ~ **gelb** greenish yellow

**grün-, Grün-:** ~**pflanze** *die* foliage plant; ~**schnabel** *der* (*abwertend*) [young] whippersnapper; (*Neuling*) greenhorn; ~**span** *der* verdigris; ~**specht** *der* green woodpecker; ~**stichig** *Adj.* (*Fot.*) with a green cast *postpos., not pred.*; ~**stichig sein** have a green cast; ~**streifen** *der* central reservation; centre strip (*grassed and often with trees and bushes*); (*am Straßenrand*) grass verge

**grunzen** /ˈgrʊntsn̩/ *tr., itr. V.* grunt

**Grün·zeug** *das* (*ugs.*) ⇒ **Grüne**[1] C

**Grunz·laut** *der* grunt

**Grüppchen** /ˈgrʏpçən/ *das;* ~**s**, ~: small group

**Gruppe** /ˈgrʊpə/ *die;* ~, ~**n** Ⓐ (*auch Sport, Math., Musik*) group; **eine ~ Jugendlicher/Erwachsener** *od.* **von Jugendlichen/Erwachsenen** a group of juveniles/adults; Ⓑ (*Klassifizierung*) class; category; **die ~ der starken/schwachen Verben** the class of strong/weak verbs; Ⓒ (*Milit.: kleine Einheit*) ≈ section; (*Luftwaffe*) ≈ squadron

**gruppen-, Gruppen-:** ~**arbeit** *die* group work; ~**aufnahme** *die* ⇒ ~**bild** A; ~**bild** *das* Ⓐ (*Fot.*) group photograph; Ⓑ (*Gemälde*) group portrait; ~**dynamik** *die* (*Sozialpsych.*) group dynamics *sing., no art.*; ~**führer** *der* Ⓐ (*Milit.*) ≈ section commander *or* leader; Ⓑ (*Wirtsch.*) team *or* group leader; Ⓒ (*ns.*) SS lieutenant general; ~**führerin** *die* ⇒ ~**führer** B; ~**mitglied** *das* member of the/a group; ~**reise** *die* (*Touristik*) group travel *no pl., no art.*; **eine ~reise nach London machen** travel to London with a group; ~**sex** *der* group sex; ~**sieg** *der* (*Sport*) top place in the group; **den ~sieg erreichen** win the group; ~**sieger** *der*, ~**siegerin** *die* (*Sport*) winner of the/a group; ~**therapie** *die* (*Psych.*) group therapy; ~**unterricht** *der* Ⓐ (*Päd.*) teaching of groups; **etw. im ~unterricht lernen** learn sth. as part of a group; Ⓑ (*erteilter Unterricht*) group instruction; ~**versicherung** *die* (*Versicherungsw.*) group insurance; ~**weise** *Adv.* in groups

**gruppieren** ❶ *tr. V.* arrange; **die Stühle um den Tisch ~:** arrange *or* set the chairs round the table; **Pflanzen nach verschiedenen Gesichtspunkten ~:** group plants according to different criteria. ❷ *refl. V.* form a group/groups; **sie gruppierten sich um den Tisch** they arranged themselves in a group around the table

**Gruppierung** *die;* ~, ~**en** Ⓐ (*Personengruppe*) grouping; group; (*Politik*) faction; Ⓑ (*Anordnung*) arrangement; grouping

**Grus** /gru:s/ *der;* ~**es**, ~**e** Ⓐ (*Kohlenstaub*) breeze; slack; Ⓑ (*Geol.*) detritus

**Grusel-:** ~**effekt** *der* horror effect; ~**film** *der* horror film; ~**geschichte** *die* horror story

**gruselig** /ˈgru:zəlɪç/, **gruslig** /ˈgru:slɪç/ *Adj.* eerie; creepy; blood-curdling ‹apparition, scream›; spine-chilling ‹story, film›

**gruseln** ❶ *tr., itr. V.* (*unpers.*) **es gruselt jmdn.** *od.* **jmdm.** sb.'s flesh creeps; **es hat mich** *od.* **mir vor diesem Anblick gegruselt** this sight made my flesh creep *or* (*coll.*) gave me the creeps. ❷ *refl. V.* be frightened; get the creeps (*coll.*); **mit leichtem Gruseln** with a small shiver of fear

**gruslig** ⇒ **gruselig**

**Gruß** /gru:s/ *der;* ~**es**, **Grüße** /ˈgry:sə/ ▶ 369 Ⓐ greeting; (*Milit.*) salute; **jmdm. die Hand zum ~ reichen** (*geh.*) shake hands with sb.; **jmdm. herzliche Grüße senden** send sb. one's best regards *or* wishes; **viele Grüße** best wishes (**an** + *Akk.* to); **bestell Barbara bitte viele Grüße von mir** please give Barbara my regards; please remember me to Barbara; **einen [schönen] ~ an jmdn./von jmdm.** [best] regards *pl.* to/from sb.; **der Deutsche ~** (*ns.*) the Nazi salute; Ⓑ (*im Brief*) **mit herzlichen Grüßen** [with] best wishes; **viele liebe Grüße euer Hans** love, Hans; **mit bestem ~/freundlichen Grüßen** Yours sincerely

**Gruß·adresse** *die* message of greetings

**grüßen** /ˈgry:sn̩/ ▶ 369 ❶ *tr. V.* Ⓐ greet; (*Milit.*) salute; **grüß [dich] Gott!** (*südd.*) hello; **er hat mich nie gegrüßt** he never said hello to me; **grüß dich!** (*ugs.*) hello *or* (*coll.*) hi [there]!; Ⓑ (*Grüße senden*) **grüße deine Eltern [ganz herzlich] von mir** please give your parents my [kindest] regards; **jmdn. ~ lassen** send one's regards to sb.; **grüß mir die Familie** remember me to your family. ❷ *itr. V.* say hello; (*Milit.*) salute; **Franz lässt ~:** Franz sends his regards

**gruß-, Gruß-:** ~**formel** *die* salutation; (*am Briefende*) [complimentary] close; ~**los** *Adv.* without a word of greeting/farewell; ~**wort** *das; Pl.* ~**worte** Ⓐ ⇒ ~**adresse**; Ⓑ (*Ansprache*) [short] welcoming speech *or* address; **einige ~worte** a few words of welcome

**Grütz·beutel** *der* sebaceous cyst

**Grütze** /ˈgrʏtsə/ *die;* ~, ~**n** Ⓐ groats *pl.*; **rote ~:** red fruit pudding (*made with fruit juice, fruit and cornflour, etc.*); Ⓑ (*ugs.: Verstand*) brains *pl.*; nous (*coll.*); **die hat [keine] ~ im Kopf** she's got [no] nous (*coll.*)

**G-Saite** /ˈge:-/ *die* (*Musik*) G-string

**Gschaftlhuber** ⇒ **Geschaftlhuber**

**gschert, Gscherte** ⇒ **geschert, Gescherte**

**G-Schlüssel** /ˈge:-/ *der* (*Musik*) ⇒ **Violinschlüssel**

**Gspusi** /ˈkʃpu:zi/ *das;* ~**s**, ~**s** (*südd., österr. ugs.*) Ⓐ (*Liebschaft*) [love] affair; Ⓑ (*Geliebte[r]*) sweetheart

**Guatemala** /gu̯ateˈma:la/ (*das*); ~**s** Guatemala

**Guatemalteke** /gu̯atemalˈte:kə/ *der;* ~**n**, ~**n**, **Guatemaltekin** *die;* ~, ~**nen** Guatemalan

**Guayana** /gu̯aˈja:na/ ⇒ **Guyana**

**gucken** /ˈgʊkn̩/ ❶ *itr. V.* (*ugs.*) Ⓐ look; (*heimlich*) peep; **jmdm. über die Schulter ~:** look *or* peer over sb.'s shoulder; **lass [mich] mal ~!** let's have a look! (*coll.*); ⇒ *auch* **Karte** G; Ⓑ (*hervorsehen*) stick out; Ⓒ (*dreinschauen*) look; **finster/freundlich ~:** look grim/affable. ❷ *tr. V.* (*ugs.*) **Fernsehen ~:** watch TV *or* (*coll.*) telly *or* (*coll.*) the box

**Guck·fenster** *das* judas [window]

**Gucki** /ˈgʊki/ *der;* ~**s**, ~**s** (*Fot.*) [slide] viewer

**Guck-:** ~**in·die·luft** ⇒ **Hans**; ~**kasten** *der* peep show; ~**loch** *das* spyhole; peephole

**Guerilla**[1] /geˈrɪlja/ *die;* ~, ~**s** Ⓐ (*Krieg*) guerrilla war; Ⓑ (*Einheit*) guerrilla unit

**Guerilla**[2] *der;* ~**s**, ~**s** (*Kämpfer*) guerrilla

**Guerilla-:** ~**kämpfer** *der*, ~**kämpferin** *die* guerrilla; ~**krieg** *der* guerrilla war; **eine Spezialausbildung für den ~krieg** special training in guerrilla warfare

**Guerillero** /-ˈje:ro/ *der;* ~**s**, ~**s** guerrilla

**Gugel·hupf** /-hʊpf:/ *der;* ~**[e]s**, ~**e** (*südd., österr.*) gugelhupf

**Güggeli** /ˈgʏgəli/ *das;* ~**s**, ~ (*schweiz.*) roast chicken

**Guillotine** /gijoˈti:nə/ *die;* ~, ~**n** guillotine

**guillotinieren** *tr. V.* guillotine

**Guinea** /giˈne:a/ (*das*); ~**s** Guinea

**Guineer** /giˈne:ɐ/ *der;* ~**s**, ~, **Guineerin** *die;* ~, ~**nen** Guinean

**Gulasch** /ˈgʊlaʃ, ˈgu:laʃ/ *das od. der;* ~**[e]s**, ~**e** *od.* ~**s** goulash

**Gulasch-:** ~**kanone** *die* (*Soldatenspr. scherzh.*) field kitchen; ~**suppe** *die* goulash soup

**gülden** /ˈgʏldn̩/ *Adj.* (*dichter.*) golden

**Gulden** /ˈgʊldn̩/ *der;* ~**s**, ~: guilder; florin

**Gülle** /ˈgʏlə/ *die;* ~ (*Landw.*) ⇒ **Jauche**

**Gulli, Gully** /ˈgʊli/ *der;* ~**s**, ~**s** drain

**gültig** /ˈgʏltɪç/ *Adj.* valid; current ‹note, coin›; **ein ~er Beweis** a valid proof; **das bisher ~e Gesetz** the law previously/hitherto in force; **diese Münze/dieser Geldschein ist nicht mehr ~:** this coin/note is no longer legal tender; **der Fahrplan ist ab 1. Oktober ~:** the timetable comes into operation on 1 October; **einen Vertrag als ~ anerkennen** recognize a contract as valid *or* legally binding; **eine Ehe für ~ erklären** declare a marriage [to be] legal *or* valid; **~ für zwanzig Fahrten sein** be valid *or* good for twenty journeys

**Gültigkeit** *die;* ~: validity; (*eines Gesetzes*) [legal] force; **~ haben/erlangen** be/become valid; ‹law› be in/come into force; **die ~ verlieren** become invalid; **wann verliert diese Münze ihre ~?** when does this coin cease to be legal tender?; **einem Dokument ~ verleihen** validate a document

**Gültigkeits-:** ~**dauer** *die* period of validity; ~**erklärung** *die* validation

**Gummi**[1] /ˈgʊmi/ *der od. das;* ~**s**, ~**[s]** Ⓐ [india] rubber; Ⓑ (~*ring*) rubber *or* elastic band

**Gummi**[2] *der;* ~**s**, ~**s** Ⓐ (*Radier*~) rubber; eraser; Ⓑ (*salopp: Präservativ*) rubber (*sl.*)

**Gummi**[3] *das;* ~**s**, ~**s** (~*band*) elastic *no indef. art.*

**gummi-, Gummi-:** ~**arabikum** /-aˈra:bikʊm/ *das;* ~~**s** gum arabic; ~**artig** *Adj.* rubbery; rubber-like ‹material›; ~**ball** *der* rubber ball; ~**band** *das; Pl.* ~**bänder** Ⓐ rubber *or* elastic band; Ⓑ (*in Kleidung*) elastic *no indef. art.*; **ein ~band einziehen** insert a piece of elastic; ~**bär** *der*, ~**bärchen** *das* jelly baby; ~**baum** *der* (*Zimmerpflanze*) rubber plant; ~**bereifung** *die* rubber tyres *pl.*; ~**bonbon** *das* gumdrop; ~**druck** *der* (*Druckw.*) flexography

**gummieren** *tr. V.* Ⓐ gum; Ⓑ (*Textilw.*) rubberize

**Gummierung** *die;* ~, ~**en** Ⓐ (*gummierte Fläche*) gummed surface; (*Textilw.*) rubberized surface; Ⓑ (*das Gummieren*) gumming; (*Textilw.*) rubberizing

**Gummi-:** ~**gutt** *das;* ~~**s** gamboge; ~**hand·schuh** *der* rubber glove; ~**harz** *das*

*old spelling (see note on page 1707)

## Grüße

**■ AUF EINER POSTKARTE**

***Schöne*** od. ***Herzliche Grüße aus Freiburg***
= Greetings *od.* Best wishes from Freiburg

***Es gefällt uns hier ausgezeichnet***
= We're having a wonderful time

***Bis bald***
= See you soon

***Es grüßen recht herzlich Stephan und Inge***
= All best wishes, Stephan and Inge

**■ ZUM GEBURTSTAG**

***Herzlichen Glückwunsch zum Geburtstag***
= Many happy returns [of the day], Happy birthday

***Alles Gute zum 60. Geburtstag***
= All best wishes on your 60th birthday

**■ ZU WEIHNACHTEN UND ZUM NEUEN JAHR**

***Frohe Weihnachten!***
= Happy Christmas!

***Ein gesegnetes Weihnachtsfest und viel Glück im neuen Jahr***
= Best wishes for a Happy *od.* Merry Christmas and a Prosperous New Year

***Glückliches neues Jahr!, Prost Neujahr!***
= Happy New Year!

**■ ZU OSTERN**

***Frohe Ostern!***
= [Best wishes for a] Happy Easter

**■ ZU EINER HOCHZEIT**

***Dem glücklichen Paar alles Gute am Hochzeitstag und viel Glück in der Zukunft***
= Every good wish to the happy couple *od.* to the bride and groom on their wedding day and in the years to come

**■ ZU EINER PRÜFUNG**

***Viel Erfolg bei der bevorstehenden Prüfung***
= Every success in your exams, The best of luck with your exams

***Alles Gute zum/Viel Glück beim Abitur***
≈ All good wishes/The best of luck with your A levels

**■ ZUM UMZUG**

***Viel Glück im neuen Heim***
= Every happiness in your new home

**■ BEI EINEM KRANKHEITSFALL**

***Gute Besserung!***
= Get well soon!

***Die besten Wünsche zur baldigen Genesung***
= Best wishes for a speedy recovery

### Gesprochene Grüße

Hier gibt es manchmal keine genauen bzw. gar keine richtigen Entsprechungen.

**■ BEI BEGEGNUNGEN**

***Guten Tag!***
= Good morning/afternoon/evening (*je nach Tageszeit*); Hello! (*wirkt ungezwungener*)

***Hallo!***
= Hello [there]!, Hi [there]!

***Guten Morgen!***
= Good morning!

***Guten Abend!***
= Good evening!

***Wie geht es Ihnen?/Wie gehts?***
= How are you?

***Freut mich!*** (bei Vorstellungen)
= How do you do?

**■ BEIM ABSCHIED**

***Auf Wiedersehen!***
= Goodbye!

***Tschüs!***
= 'Bye now!

***Bis bald!***
= See you soon!

***Machs gut!***
= Look after yourself!, Take care!

····➤ Briefeschreiben

gum resin; **~knüppel** *der* [rubber] truncheon; **~lack** *der* shellac; **~linse** *die* (*Fot.*) zoom lens; **~lösung** *die* rubber solution; **~mantel** *der* mackintosh (*Brit.*); raincoat; **~paragraph** *der* (*ugs.*) paragraph *or* section with an elastic interpretation; **~reifen** *der* rubber tyre; **~ring** *der* **A** rubber band; **B** (*Spielzeug*) rubber ring; quoit; **C** (*Weckglasring*) rubber seal; **~sauger** *der* rubber teat; **~schlauch** *der* rubber hose; **~schuh** *der* **A** rubber shoe; **B** ⇒ **~überschuh**; **~schutz** *der* (*veralt.*) sheath; condom; **~sohle** *die* rubber sole; **~stiefel** *der* rubber boot; (*für Regenwetter*) wellington [boot] (*Brit.*); (*bis zum Oberschenkel*) wader; **~strumpf** *der* elastic stocking; **~tier** *das* rubber animal; (*aufblasbar*) inflatable animal; **~über·schuh** *der* galosh; rubber overshoe; **~waren** *Pl.* rubber goods; **~zelle** *die* padded cell; **~zug** *der* ⇒ **~band** B

**Gunder·mann** /'gʊndɐ-/ *der;* **~[e]s** (*Bot.*) ground ivy

**Gunst** /gʊnst/ *die;* **~** **A** favour; goodwill; **jmds. ~ erlangen** win *or* gain sb.'s favour; **in jmds. ~** (*Dat.*) *od.* **bei jmdm. in ~** (*Dat.*) **stehen** (*geh.*) enjoy sb.'s favour; be in favour with sb.; **jmdm. seine ~ bezeugen** show one's favour to sb.; **die ~ der Stunde/Lage nutzen** (*fig.*) take advantage of the favourable *or* propitious moment/situation; **zu jmds. ~en** in sb.'s favour; **B** **zu ~en** ⇒ **zugunsten**

**Gunst·bezeigung** *die* mark of favour *or* goodwill

**günstig** /'gʏnstɪç/ **1** *Adj.* **A** (*vorteilhaft*) favourable; propitious ‹sign›; auspicious ‹moment›; beneficial ‹influence›; good, reasonable ‹price›; **bei ~em Wetter** if the weather is favourable; weather permitting; **der Zug um 10 Uhr ist ~er** the 10 o'clock train is better *or* more convenient; **B** (*wohlwollend*) well-disposed; favourably disposed; **das Glück war uns ~:** luck was on our side. **2** *adv.* **A** (*vorteilhaft*) favourably; **etw. ~ beeinflussen** have *or* exert a beneficial influence on sth.; **etw. ~ kaufen/verkaufen** buy/sell sth. at a good price; **das trifft sich ~:** that's a piece of luck; **B** (*wohlwollend*) **jmdn./etw. ~ aufnehmen** receive sb./sth. well *or* favourably; **jmdn. ~ stimmen** put sb. in a favourable mood; **jmdn. für etw. ~ stimmen** make sb. well-disposed towards sth.; **jmdm./einer Sache ~ gesinnt sein** be well *or* favourably disposed towards sb./sth.

**günstig[st]en·falls** *Adv.* at best

**Günstling** /'gʏnstlɪŋ/ *der;* **~s, ~e** favourite

**Günstlings·wirtschaft** *die* (*abwertend*) favouritism

**Guppy** /'gʊpi/ *der;* **~s, ~s** (*Zool.*) guppy

**Gurgel** /'gʊrgl̩/ *die;* **~, ~n** throat; **jmdm. die ~ zudrücken** strangle *or* throttle sb.; **jmdm. die ~ durchschneiden** cut sb.'s throat; **jmdm. an die ~ springen/fahren** jump *or* leap at/go for sb.'s throat; **jmdm. an die ~ wollen** fly at sb.; **jmdm. die ~ abdrehen** *od.* **zudrücken** (*fig. salopp*) force *or* send sb. to the wall; **sein ganzes Geld durch die ~ jagen** (*ugs.*) drink all one's money away (*coll.*); **sich** (*Dat.*) **die ~ ölen** *od.* **schmieren** (*ugs.*) wet one's whistle (*coll.*)

**gurgeln** *itr. V.* **A** (*spülen*) gargle; **B** (*blubbern*) gurgle

**Gürkchen** /'gʏrkçən/ *das;* **~s, ~** [cocktail] gherkin

**Gurke** /'gʊrkə/ *die;* **~, ~n** **A** cucumber; (*eingelegt*) gherkin; **saure ~n** pickled gherkins; **B** (*salopp scherzh.: Nase*) hooter (*coll.*); snout (*coll.*); **C** (*salopp abwertend: Auto*) [old] banger (*sl.*)

**Gurken-: ~hobel** *der* cucumber slicer; **~salat** *der* cucumber salad; **~truppe** *die* (*salopp*) useless *or* feeble bunch (*coll.*)

**gurren** /'gʊrən/ *itr. V.* (*auch fig.*) coo

**Gurt** /gʊrt/ *der;* **~[e]s, ~e** strap; (*Gürtel*) belt; (*im Auto, Flugzeug*) [seat] belt

**Gürtel** /'gʏrtl̩/ *der;* **~s, ~** belt; **den ~ enger schnallen** (*fig. ugs.*) tighten one's belt (*fig.*)

**Gürtel-: ~linie** *die* waist[line]; **ein Schlag unter die ~linie** (*Boxen*) a punch *or* blow below the belt; **das war ein Schlag unter die ~linie** (*fig. ugs.*) that was hitting below the belt (*fig. coll.*); **~reifen** *der* radial[-ply] tyre; **~rose** *die* ▶ 474 (*Med.*) shingles *sing. or pl.*; **~schnalle** *die* belt buckle; **~tier** *das* armadillo

**gürten** /'gʏrtn̩/ (*geh. veralt.*) **1** *tr. V.* gird (*arch./literary*); **jmdn. mit dem Schwert ~:** gird sb. with his sword. **2** *refl. V.* **sich [zum Kampf] ~:** gird oneself; **sich mit dem Schwert ~:** gird on one's sword

**Gurt·muffel** *der* (*ugs.*) person not wearing a safety belt

**Gurtstraffer** *der;* **~s, ~** (*Kfz.-W.*) [seat-]belt tensioner

**Guru** /'gʊru/ *der;* **~s, ~s** guru

**Guss**, ***Guß** /gʊs/ *der;* **Gusses, Güsse** /'gʏsə/ Ⓐ *(das Gießen)* casting; founding; **[wie] aus einem ~:** forming a unified *or* an integrated whole; fully coordinated ‹plan›; Ⓑ *(ugs.: Regenschauer)* downpour; **ein heftiger/wolkenbruchartiger ~:** a violent downpour/a cloudburst; Ⓒ *(gegossenes Erzeugnis)* casting; cast; Ⓓ *(das Begießen)* stream; *(Med.)* affusion; Ⓔ *(auf Backwaren)* icing; **eine Torte mit ~ überziehen** ice a gateau

**guss-**, ***guß-**, **Guss-**, ***Guß-:** **~beton** *der* cast concrete; **~eisen** *das* cast iron; **~eisern** *Adj.* cast-iron; **~form** *die* casting mould; **~naht** *die (Gießerei)* [casting] fin *or* flash; **~stahl** *der* cast steel

**Gusto** /'gʊsto/ *der;* **~s, ~s** Ⓐ *(Neigung)* taste; liking; **nach jmds. ~ sein** be to sb.'s taste *or* liking; Ⓑ *(Appetit)* **~ auf etw.** *(Akk.)* **haben** feel like *or* fancy sth.

**Gusto·stückerl** *das (österr.)* star turn

**gut** /gu:t/; **besser** /'bɛsɐ/, **best...** /'bɛst.../ ❶ *Adj.* Ⓐ good; fine ‹wine›; **in Französisch ~ sein** be good at French; **ist der Kuchen ~ geworden?** did the cake turn out all right?; **es wäre ~, wenn ...** it would be as well if ...; **also ~:** very well; all right; **schon ~:** [it's] all right *or (coll.)* OK; **nun ~:** very well *or* all right [then]; **wie ~, dass ...** it's good that ...; **jetzt ist es aber ~!** *(ugs.)* that's enough!; **das ist ja alles ~ und schön** that's all very well *or* all well and good; **es ~ sein lassen** *(ugs.)* leave it at that; **lass es ~ sein** *(ugs.)* let's say no more about it; **das·ist ~ gegen** *od.* **für Kopfschmerzen** it's good for headaches; **wer weiß, wozu das ~ ist** perhaps it's for the best; **das ist so ~ wie gewonnen** it's as good as won; **dieser Stürmer ist immer ~ für ein Tor** *(ugs.)* this forward is always likely to score goals; **~en Tag!** good morning/afternoon!; **~en Morgen!** good morning!; **~en Abend!** good evening!; **~e Nacht!** good night!; **etw. zu einem ~en Ende führen** bring sth. to a happy conclusion; **ein ~es neues Jahr** a happy new year; **Sie haben es noch nie so ~ gehabt** you've never had it so good; **er hat es doch ~ bei uns** he's well enough off with us; **ihr habt es ~:** it's all right for 'you; **mir ist nicht ~:** I'm not feeling well; I don't feel well; **alles Gute!** all the best!; **das bedeutet nichts Gutes** that's an ominous sign; **das ist zu viel des Guten** *(iron.)* that's overdoing it; **das Gute daran** the good thing about it; **~en Appetit!** enjoy your lunch/dinner *etc.!*; **ein ~ Teil von etw.** a good deal *or* part of sth.; **~e Frau/~er Mann** *(iron. Anrede)* dear lady/my good man; **sich** *(Dat.)* **zu ~ für etw. sein** consider sth. beneath one *or* beneath one's dignity; **du bist ~!** *(iron.)* you're joking!; you must be joking!; **im Guten wie im Bösen haben wir uns bemüht ...** we've done everything we can to try ...; **jmdm. ~ sein** *(ugs.)* feel a lot of affection for sb.; **wieder ~ [mit jmdm.] sein** be friends [with sb.] again; **sei [bitte] so ~ und reich mir das Buch** would you be good *or* kind enough to pass me the book?; **im Guten auseinander gehen** part amicably *or* on amicable terms; **[jmdm.] ~ tun** do [sb.] good; **ein Schnaps tut ~ bei der Kälte** schnapps is good for you when it's cold; Ⓑ *(besonderen Anlässen vorbehalten)* best; **sein ~er Anzug** his best suit; **die ~e Stube** the best room; **für ~** *(ugs.)* for best; for special occasions.

❷ *adv.* Ⓐ well; **~ reiten/schwimmen** be a good rider/swimmer; **etw. ~ können** be good at sth.; **seine Sache ~ machen** do well; **~ hören/sehen** [be able to] hear/see well *or* clearly; **[das hast du] ~ gemacht!** well done!; **du tätest ~ daran, darüber zu schweigen** you would do well *or* be wise to say nothing about it; **der Laden/das Geschäft geht ~:** the shop/business is doing well; **~ bezahlt** well-paid; **~ gehend** flourishing, thriving ‹business›; **~ gekleidet** well-dressed; **~ gemeint** well-meant; **~ unterrichtet** well-informed; **~ eine Stunde [von hier] entfernt** a good hour [from here]; **~ zwei Pfund wiegen** weigh a good two pounds; **~ und gern** *(ugs.)* easily; at least *(ugs.)*; **so ~ wie nichts** next to nothing; **so ~ ich kann** as best I can; **~ und richtig handeln** do the right thing; **jmdm. ~ zureden** coax sb. [gently]; **mit jmdm. ~ stehen** *od.* **auskommen** be on good *or* friendly terms with sb.; get on well with sb.; **es ~ meinen** mean well; **es ~ mit jmdm. meinen** have sb.'s interests at heart; ⇒ *auch* **anschreiben** 1 B; Ⓑ *(mühelos)* easily; **~ zu Fuß sein** *(ugs.)* be a strong walker; **hinterher hat** *od.* **kann man ~ reden** it's easy to be wise after the event; **du hast ~ lachen** it's all right for you to laugh; **es kann ~ sein, dass ...** it may well be that ...; **ich kann das nicht ~ tun** I can't very well do that; ⇒ *auch* **besser, best...**

**Gut** *das;* **~[e]s, Güter** /'gy:tɐ/ Ⓐ *(Eigentum)* property; *(Besitztum, auch fig.)* possession; **ererbtes/gestohlenes ~:** inherited/stolen property; **irdische Güter** earthly goods *or* possessions; **die geistigen Güter des Volkes** the intellectual wealth *sing.* of the people; **bewegliche/unbewegliche Güter** movables/immovables; **das höchste ~** *(fig.)* the greatest good; **unrecht ~ gedeihet nicht** *od.* **tut selten gut** *(Spr.)* ill-gotten goods *or* gains never *or* seldom prosper; Ⓑ *(landwirtschaftlicher Grundbesitz)* estate; Ⓒ *(Frachtgut, Ware)* item; **Güter** goods; *(Fracht~)* freight *sing.;* goods *(Brit.)*; Ⓓ *(das ~e)* **~ und Böse** good and evil; **jenseits von ~ und Böse sein** *(iron.)* be past it *(coll.)*; Ⓔ *(veralt.: Material)* material [to be processed]

**gut-**, **Gut-:** **~achten** *itr. V.* give an expert opinion; *(in einem Prozess)* act as an expert witness; **der ~de Arzt** the medical expert; **~achten** *das;* **~~s, ~~:** [expert's] report; **~achter** *der;* **~~s, ~~, ~achterin** *die;* **~~, ~~nen** expert; *(in einem Prozess)* expert witness; **~artig** *Adj.* Ⓐ good-natured; Ⓑ *(nicht gefährlich)* benign; **~artigkeit** *die* Ⓐ good nature; goodnaturedness; Ⓑ *(Ungefährlichkeit)* benignity; ***~aussehend** ⇒ **aussehen**; ***~bezahlt** ⇒ **gut** 2 A; **~bürgerlich** ❶ *Adj.* good middle class; **~bürgerliche Küche** good plain cooking; **~bürgerliches Zuhause** comfortable middle-class home; ❷ *adv.* in a good middle-class way; ‹grow up› in good middle-class circumstances; **~bürgerlich essen** eat good plain food; **~dünken** *das;* **~~s** discretion; judgement; **nach [eigenem] ~dünken** at one's own discretion; **nach [eigenem/seinem] ~dünken mit jmdm./etw. verfahren** use one's own discretion in dealing with sb./sth.

**Güte** /'gy:tə/ *die;* **~** Ⓐ goodness; kindness; *(~ Gottes)* loving kindness; goodness; **er ist die ~ selbst** he is goodness *or* kindness itself; **sich mit jmdm. in ~ einigen** come to an amicable agreement with sb.; **ein Vorschlag zur ~:** a suggestion for an amicable agreement; **hätten Sie die ~, mir zu helfen?** *(geh.)* would you be kind *or* good enough to help me?; **[ach] du meine** *od.* **liebe ~!** *(ugs.)* my goodness!; goodness me; Ⓑ *(Qualität)* quality

**Güte·klasse** *die* grade; class

**Gute·nacht·kuss**, ***Gute·nacht·kuß** *der* goodnight kiss

**Güter-:** **~abfertigung** *die* Ⓐ *(Abfertigung von Waren)* dispatch of freight *or (Brit.)* goods; Ⓑ *(Annahmestelle)* freight *or (Brit.)* goods office; **~austausch** *der* exchange of goods *or* commodities; **~bahnhof** *der* freight depot; goods station *(Brit.)*; **~fern·verkehr** /-'---/ *der* long-distance haulage *no art.;* **~gemeinschaft** *die (Rechtsw.)* community of property; **~nah·verkehr** /--'---/ *der* short-distance haulage *no art.;* **~recht** *das (Rechtsw.)* law of property; **~transport** *der* transport *or* carriage of goods *(Brit.) or* freight; **~trennung** *die (Rechtsw.)* separation of property; **~verkehr** *der* freight *or (Brit.)* goods traffic; **~wagen** *der* goods wagon *(Brit.)*; freight car *(Amer.)*; **~zug** *der* goods train *(Brit.)*; freight train *(Amer.)*

**Güte-:** **~siegel** *das* ⇒ **~zeichen**; **~verfahren** *das (Rechtsw.)* conciliation procedure; *(Verhandlung)* conciliation meeting; **~zeichen** *das* quality mark

**gut-**, **Gut-:** ***~|gehen** ⇒ **gehen** 1 I, 1 K; ***~gehend** ⇒ **gut** 2 A; ***~gekleidet** ⇒ **gut** 2 A; ***~gelaunt** ⇒ **gelaunt**; ***~gemeint** ⇒ **gut** 2 A; **~gläubig** *Adj.* innocently trusting; **~gläubigkeit** *die* innocent trust; **~|haben** *unr. tr. V.* **etw. bei jmdm. ~haben** be owed sth. by sb.; **~haben** *das* credit balance; **Sie haben ein ~haben von 450 DM auf Ihrem Konto** your account is 450 marks in credit; **~|heißen** *unr. tr. V.* approve of; **~herzig** *Adj.* kind-hearted; good-hearted; **~herzigkeit** *die;* **~~:** kind-heartedness; good-heartedness

**gütig** /'gy:tɪç/ ❶ *Adj.* kindly; kind ‹heart›; **mit Ihrer ~en Erlaubnis** *(geh./iron.)* with your kind permission. ❷ *adv.* **~ lächeln/nicken** give a kindly smile/nod

**gütlich** /'gy:tlɪç/ ❶ *Adj.* amicable. ❷ *adv.* amicably; **sich ~ an etw.** *(Dat.)* **tun** regale oneself with sth.

**gut-**, **Gut-:** **~|machen** *tr. V.* make good ‹damage›; put right, correct ‹omission, mistake, etc.›; **an jmdm. viel ~zumachen haben** have a lot to make up *or* make amends to sb. for; **wie soll/kann ich das ~machen?** how can I ever repay you?; **das ist nicht wieder gutzumachen** that cannot be put right; **ein nicht wieder gutzumachendes Unrecht** an irreparable injustice; **~mütig** ❶ *Adj.* good-natured; ❷ *adv.* good-naturedly; **~mütig veranlagt sein** be good-natured; **~mütigkeit** *die;* **~~:** good nature; goodnaturedness; **~nachbarlich** ❶ *Adj.* good-neighbourly ‹relations etc.›; ❷ *adv.* as good neighbours

**Guts·besitzer** *der*, **Guts·besitzerin** *die* owner of a/the estate; landowner

**gut-**, **Gut-:** **~schein** *der* voucher, coupon (**für**, **auf** + *Akk.* for); **~|schreiben** *unr. tr. V.* credit; **etw. jmdm./jmds. Konto ~schreiben** credit sb./sb.'s account with sth.; **~schrift** *die* Ⓐ *(Betrag)* credit; Ⓑ *(Bescheinigung)* credit slip *or* note; Ⓒ *(Vorgang)* crediting

**Guts-:** **~haus** *das* manor house; **~herr** *der* lord of the manor; **~herrin** *die* lady of the manor; **~hof** *der* estate; manor

**Guts·verwalter** *der*, **Guts·verwalterin** *die* steward; bailiff

***gut·tun** ⇒ **gut** 1 A

**Guttural[laut]** /gʊtu'ra:l(-)/ *der;* **~s, ~e** *(Sprachw. veralt.)* guttural

**gut-**, **Gut-:** ***~unterrichtet** ⇒ **gut** 2 A; **~willig** ❶ *Adj.* willing; *(entgegenkommend)* obliging; **sich ~willig zeigen** be obliging; show willing *(coll.)*; ❷ *adv.* **etw. ~willig herausgeben/versprechen** hand sth. over voluntarily/promise sth. willingly *or* freely; **~willigkeit** *die;* **~~:** willingness; *(Entgegenkommen)* obligingness

**Guyana** /gu'ja:na/ *(das);* **~s** Guyana

**gymnasial** /gymna'zi̯a:l/ *Adj.* ≈ grammar-school ‹education, syllabus›

**Gymnasial-** ≈ grammar-school ‹education, teacher›

**Gymnasiast** /gymna'zi̯ast/ *der;* **~en, ~en**, **Gymnasiastin** *die;* **~, ~nen** ≈ grammar-school pupil

**Gymnasium** /gym'na:zi̯ʊm/ *das;* **~s, Gymnasien** Ⓐ *(höhere Schule)* ≈ grammar school; **neusprachliches ~:** ≈ grammar school stressing modern languages; **aufs ~ gehen** ≈ be at *or* attend grammar school; Ⓑ *(in der Antike)* gymnasium

**Gymnastik** /gym'nastɪk/ *die;* **~:** physical exercises *pl.;* *(Turnen)* gymnastics *sing.*

**Gymnastiklehrer** *der*, **Gymnastiklehrerin** *die* teacher of physical exercises

**gymnastisch** *Adj.* gymnastic

**Gynäkologe** /gynɛko'lo:gə/ *der;* **~n, ~n** ▶ 159 gynaecologist

**Gynäkologie** *die;* **~:** gynaecology *no art.*

**Gynäkologin** *die;* **~, ~nen** ▶ 159 gynaecologist

**gynäkologisch** *Adj.* gynaecological

**Gyroskop** /gyro'sko:p/ *das;* **~s, ~e** gyroscope

# Hh

**h, H** /ha:/ *das;* ~, ~ Ⓐ (*Buchstabe*) h/H; Ⓑ (*Musik*) [key of] B; ⇨ *auch* **a, A**

**h** *Abk.* Ⓐ **Uhr** hrs; Ⓑ **Stunde** hr[s]

**H** *Abk.* Ⓐ **Herren;** Ⓑ **Haltestelle**

**H.** *Abk.* **Heft** No.

**ha¹** /ha(:)/ *Interj.* Ⓐ (*Überraschung*) ha!; oh!; ah!; Ⓑ (*Triumph*) aha!

**ha²** *Abk.* **Hektar** ha

**Haag** /ha:k/ *(das) od. der;* ~s ▶ 700 The Hague; ⇨ *auch* **Den Haag**

**Haar** /ha:ɐ̯/ *das;* ~[e]s, ~e Ⓐ ▶ 471 (*auch Zool., Bot.*) hair; **blonde ~e** *od.* **blondes ~ haben** have fair hair; **echtes ~:** real hair; **sein echtes ~:** his own hair; **[sich (*Dat.*)] das ~** *od.* **die ~e waschen** wash one's hair; **sich** (*Dat.*) **das ~** *od.* **die ~e schneiden lassen** have *or* get one's hair cut; **ihm geht das ~ aus** he's losing his hair; **sich** (*Dat.*) **die ~e [aus]raufen** (*ugs.*) tear one's hair [out]; Ⓑ (*fig.*) **ihr stehen die ~e zu Berge** *od.* **sträuben sich die ~e** (*ugs.*) her hair stands on end; **ein ~ in der Suppe finden** (*ugs.*) find something to quibble about *or* find fault with; **kein gutes ~ an jmdm./etw. lassen** (*ugs.*) pull sb./sth. to pieces (*fig. coll.*); **jmdm. die ~e vom Kopf fressen** (*ugs. scherzh.*) eat sb. out of house and home; **~e auf den Zähnen haben** (*ugs. scherzh.*) be a tough customer; **sich** (*Dat.*) **über** *od.* **wegen** *od.* **um etw. keine grauen ~e wachsen lassen** not lose any sleep over sth.; not worry one's head about sth.; **er wird dir kein ~ krümmen** (*ugs.*) he won't harm a hair of your head; **an einem ~ hängen** (*ugs.*) be touch-and-go; **das ist an den ~en herbeigezogen** (*ugs.*) that's far-fetched; **jmdm. aufs ~ gleichen** be the spitting image of sb.; **sie gleichen sich aufs ~:** they're as alike as two peas in a pod; **sich in die ~e geraten** *od.* **kriegen** (*ugs.*) quarrel, squabble (**wegen** over); **sich** (*Dat.*) **in den ~en liegen** (*ugs.*) be at loggerheads; **um ein ~** (*ugs.*) very nearly; **sie wäre um ein ~ abgestürzt** (*ugs.*) she came within an inch *or* an ace *or* a whisker of falling; **ich hätte sie um ein ~ verfehlt** (*ugs.*) I just missed her by a hair's breadth; **nicht [um] ein ~** *od.* **[um] kein ~ besser** (*ugs.*) not a whit *or* bit better

**Haar-:** **~ansatz** *der* Ⓐ hairline; Ⓑ (*unmittelbar an der Kopfhaut*) roots *pl.*; **~ausfall** *der* loss of hair; hair loss; **~balg** *der; Pl.* **~bälge** hair follicle; **~band** *das; Pl.* **~bänder** hairband; **~besen** *der* broom; **~breit** *das: in* **nicht [um] ein** *od.* **[um] kein ~breit** not an inch; **~bürste** *die* hairbrush; **~büschel** *das* tuft of hair

**haaren** *itr. V.* moult; lose *or* shed its hair

**Haar-:** **~entferner** *der;* **~~s, ~~:** hair remover; depilatory; **~ersatz** *der* hairpiece

**Haares·breite** *die: in* **um ~:** by a hair's breadth; **nicht um ~ von etw. abweichen** not budge an inch from sth.

**haar-, Haar-:** **~farbe** *die* hair colour; **mit seiner ~farbe nicht zufrieden sein** be unhappy with the colour of one's hair; **welche ~farbe hatte der Dieb?** what colour hair did the thief have?; **~färbe·mittel** *das* hair dye; **~fein** *Adj.* fine as a hair *postpos.*; **ein ~feiner Sprung** a hairline crack; **~festiger** *der;* **~~s, ~~:** setting lotion; **~garn** *das* (*Textilw.*) hair yarn; **~gefäß** *das* ▶ 471 (*Med.*) capillary [vessel]; **~genau** (*ugs.*) ❶ *Adj.* exact; ❷ *adv.* exactly; **die Beschreibung trifft ~genau auf sie zu** the description fits her to a T (*coll.*); **etw. ~genau erzählen** relate sth. in great detail; **das stimmt ~genau** that is absolutely right

**haarig** *Adj.* Ⓐ (*behaart*) hairy; Ⓑ (*ugs.: heikel*) tricky

**haar-, Haar-:** **~klammer** *die* hairgrip; **~kleid** *das* (*geh.*) coat; **~klein** ❶ *Adj.* minute; ❷ *adv.* in minute detail; **~klemme** *die* hairgrip; **~kranz** *der* Ⓐ fringe *or* circle of hair; Ⓑ (*Frisur*) chaplet [of plaited hair]; **~künstler** *der,* **~künstlerin** *die* (*oft scherzh.*) hair stylist; tonsorial artist (*joc.*); **~lack** *der* hair lacquer; **~los** *Adj.* hairless; (*glatzköpfig*) bald; **~mode** *die* hairstyle; **~nadel** *die* hairpin; **~nadel·kurve** *die* hairpin bend; **~netz** *das* hairnet; **~öl** *das* hair oil; **~pflege** *die* hair care; **~pflege·mittel** *das* hair-care product; **~pinsel** *der* fine animal-hair brush; **~pracht** *die* (*scherzh.*) magnificent head of hair; **~riss,** ***~riß** *der* hairline crack; **~röhrchen** *das* (*Physik*) capillary tube; **~scharf** ❶ *Adj.* (*sehr genau*) razor-sharp ‹remark›; very fine ‹distinction›; very good ‹memory›; ❷ *adv.* Ⓐ (*sehr nah*) **das Auto blieb ~scharf vor dem Kind stehen** the car stopped only a hair's breadth from the child; **die Kugel flog ~scharf an ihm vorbei** the bullet missed him by a hair's breadth; **~scharf an jmdm. vorbeizielen** aim to just miss sb.; Ⓑ (*sehr genau*) with great precision; **~schleife** *die* bow; hair ribbon; **~schmuck** *der* hair ornaments *pl.*; **~schneide·maschine** *die* electric clippers *pl.*; **~schnitt** *der* haircut; (*modisch*) hairstyle; **jmdm. einen ~schnitt machen** cut sb.'s hair; give sb. a haircut; **~schopf** *der* mop *or* shock of hair; **~schwund** *der* loss of hair; hair loss; **~seite** *die* Ⓐ (*Textilw.*) right side; front; Ⓑ (*Gerberei*) hair side; (*eines Pelzes*) fur side; **~sieb** *das* hair sieve; **~spalter** *der;* **~~s, ~~** (*abwertend*) hairsplitter; **~spalterei** *die;* **~~, ~~en** (*abwertend*) hair-splitting; **das ist doch ~spalterei** that's splitting hairs; **~spalterin** *die;* **~~, ~~nen** ⇨ **~spalter**; **~spalterisch** *Adj.* (*abwertend*) hair-splitting; **~spange** *die* hairslide; **~spitze** *die* end of a hair; **die ~spitzen** the ends of the hairs; **~spray** *der od. das* hair spray; **~sträubend** *Adj.* Ⓐ (*grauenhaft*) hair-raising; horrifying; Ⓑ (*empörend*) outrageous; shocking; **~teil** *das* hairpiece; **~tracht** *die* (*veralt.*) hairstyle; **~trockner** *der* hairdryer; **~wäsche** *die* shampoo; [hair] wash; **~wasch·mittel** *das* shampoo; **~wasser** *das; Pl.* **~wässer** hair lotion; **~wild** *das* (*Jägerspr.*) ground game; **~wuchs** *der* hair growth; growth of hair; **einen spärlichen/starken ~wuchs haben** have little/a lot of hair; **~wuchs·mittel** *das* hair restorer; **~wurzel** *die* root [of the/a hair]

**Hab** /ha:p/ *in* **~ und Gut** (*geh.*) possessions *pl.*; belongings *pl.*

**Habacht·stellung** *die* ⇨ **Habtachtstellung**

**Habe** /'ha:bə/ *die;* ~ (*geh.*) possessions *pl.*; belongings *pl.*; **bewegliche ~:** movables *pl.*

**Habeaskorpus·akte** /ha:beas'kɔrpʊs-/ *die* (*hist.*) Habeas Corpus Act

**haben** ❶ *unr. tr. V.* Ⓐ have; have got; **er hat nichts** (*ugs.*) he has nothing; **von ihm kannst du dir kein Geld borgen: er hat selber nichts** you can't borrow money from him: he hasn't got any himself; **wer hat, der hat** (*scherzh./iron.*) I/you *etc.* can afford it; **was man hat, das hat man** (*scherzh./iron.*) I'd rather have something than nothing; **da hast du das Geld** there's the money; **die ~s ja** (*ugs.*) they can afford it; **gute Kenntnisse ~:** be knowledgeable; **ich habe Zeit/keine Zeit** I have [got] [the] time/I have [got] no time *or* I haven't [got] any time; **die Sache hat Zeit** it's not urgent; it can wait (*coll.*); **wir ~ Mai/1998/den 15./Donnerstag/Sommer** it's May/1998/the 15th/Thursday/summer; **den Wievielten ~ wir heute?** what's the date today?; what's today's date?; **in Kalifornien ~ sie jetzt Nacht/fünf Uhr morgens** it's night-time/five o'clock in the morning now in California; **heute ~ wir schönes Wetter/30°** the weather is fine/it's 30° today; **wann hast du Urlaub?** when is your holiday?; ⇨ *auch* **Datum** A; **Schuld** B; Ⓑ (*empfinden*) **Hunger/Durst ~:** be hungry/thirsty; **Sehnsucht nach etw. ~:** long for sth.; **Heimweh/Furcht ~:** be homesick/afraid; **Husten/Fieber/Schmerzen ~:** have [got] a cough/a temperature/have pain; **es an der Leber/auf der Brust ~** (*ugs.*) have [got] liver trouble *or* something wrong with one's liver/have [got] a bad chest; **was hast du denn?** (*ugs.*) what's the matter?; what's wrong?; **hast du was?** (*ugs.*) is [there] something the matter?; is [there] something wrong?; **ich kann das nicht ~** (*ugs.*) I can't stand it; **dich hats wohl** (*ugs.*) you must be mad *or* crazy; Ⓒ *mit Adj. u. „es"* **es gut/schlecht/schwer/eilig ~:** have it good (*coll.*)/have a bad time [of it]/have a difficult *or* tough time/be in a hurry; **wir ~ es sehr gemütlich hier** we are very comfortable here; **möchten Sie es etwas wärmer ~?** are you warm enough?; Ⓓ *mit „zu" u. Inf.* **nichts zu essen/trinken ~:** have nothing to eat/drink; **habt ihr nichts zu trinken?** haven't you got anything to drink?; **er hat nichts mehr zu erwarten** he can expect nothing more; (*müssen*) **du hast zu gehorchen** you must obey; **etw. zu tun/erledigen ~:** have [got] sth. to do *or* that one must do; **er hat zu tun** he's busy; (*dürfen*) **er hat mir nichts zu befehlen** he has [got] no right to order me about; **du hast dich hier nicht einzumischen** you should mind your own business; Ⓔ (*sich zusammensetzen aus*) **das Jahr hat 12 Monate** there are 12 months in a year; **ein Kilometer hat 1 000 Meter** there are 1,000 metres in a kilometre; **diese Stadt hat 10 000 Einwohner** this town has 10,000 inhabitants; **die USA ~ 50 Bundesstaaten** the USA is made up of 50 states; Ⓕ (*bekommen*) have; **kann ich heute dein Auto ~?** can I have your car today?; **sind diese Puppen noch zu ~?** can you still get these dolls?; **zu ~ sein** (*ugs.*) be unattached; (*zum Beischlaf bereit sein*) be available; **dafür ist er immer zu ~:** he's always game for that; **er ist immer für ein gutes Essen zu ~:** he always likes *or* enjoys a good meal; **für so etw. bin ich nicht zu ~:** I'm not one for *or* keen on things like that; **da hast dus** (*ugs.*) there you are; Ⓖ (*ugs.: in der Schule*) **morgen ~ wir Geschichte** we've got history tomorrow; **wir ~ schon seit Monaten keine Chemie** we haven't done [any] chemistry for months; Ⓗ (*ugs.: gebrauchen*) **man hat das nicht mehr** it is no longer in use/in fashion; **hat man bei euch noch die alten Karbidlampen?** are you still using the old carbide lamps?; Ⓘ (*ugs.: gefasst* ~) have ‹thief etc.›; **jetzt hab' ich dich** now I've got you; Ⓙ (*bekommen* ~) **Nachricht von jmdm. ~:** have heard from sb.; **was** (*ugs.*)/**welche Note hast du diesmal in Physik?** what did you get in *or* for physics this time?; Ⓚ (*gefunden* ~) **~ Sie den Fehler?** have you found the mistake?; **ich habs!** (*ugs.*) I've got it!; **das werden wir gleich ~** (*ugs.*) we'll soon find out; Ⓛ (*ugs.: repariert,* *beendet* ~) **noch zwei Minuten, dann hab ichs** I'll be finished in a couple of minutes; **das werden wir gleich ~:** we'll soon fix that; **M** *mit Präp.* **sie hat einen guten Freund an ihm** he is a good friend to her; **er weiß ja gar nicht, was er an dir hat** he doesn't realize how lucky he is to have you; **wir ~ viele Bilder an der Wand [hängen]** we have quite a lot of pictures up; **er hat immer Blumen auf dem Tisch [stehen]** he has always [got] flowers on the table; **ich habe meinen Wagen auf dem Parkplatz [stehen]** I've got my car in the car park; **etwas/nichts gegen jmdn.** *od.* **etw. ~:** have something/nothing against sb. *or* sth.; **sie hat alle Kollegen gegen sich** all her colleagues are against her; **etwas mit jmdm. ~** (*ugs.*) have a thing *or* something going with sb. (*coll.*); **hast du es schon einmal mit einer Frau gehabt?** (*salopp*) have you ever had it off with a woman? (*sl.*); **viel/wenig von jmdm. ~:** see a lot/little of sb.; **er hat etwas von einem Tyrannen/Faulpelz** he is a bit of a tyrant/lazybones; **etw. von etw. ~:** get sth. out of sth.; **ihn würde ich gerne zum Freund ~:** I would like [to have] him as a friend; **er hat eine Adlige zur Frau** he has [got] an aristocratic wife; ⇒ *auch* **an, auf, bei** *usw.*; **N** *unpers.* (*bes. österr., südd.: vorhanden sein*) **es hat ...** there is/are ...

**2** *refl. V.* **A** (*ugs. abwertend: sich aufregen*) make a fuss; **hab dich nicht so!** don't make *or* stop making such a fuss!; **B** (*ugs.: sich erledigt* ~) **und damit hat es sich** *od.* **hat sich die Sache** then that's that; **hat sich was!** far from it!

**3** *Hilfsverb* have; **ich habe/hatte ihn eben gesehen** I have *or* I've/I had *or* I'd just seen him; **sie ~ gelacht** they laughed; **er hat das gewusst** he knew it; **wir suchten, bis wir ihn gefunden hatten** we kept looking until we [had] found him; **das hättest du früher machen können** you could have done that earlier

**Haben** *das;* **~s, ~** (*Kaufmannsspr.*) credit; (*~seite*) **etw. im ~ verbuchen** credit sth.; ⇒ *auch* **Soll** A

**Habe·nichts** *der;* **~, ~e** pauper

**Haben-: ~seite** *die* (*Kaufmannsspr.*) credit side; **~zinsen** *Pl.* interest *sing.* on deposits

**Haber** *der;* **~s** (*südd., österr., schweiz.*) ⇒ **Hafer**

**Hab·gier** *die* (*abwertend*) greed

**hab·gierig** **1** *Adj.* (*abwertend*) greedy. **2** *adv.* greedily

**habhaft** *in* **jmds./einer Sache ~ werden** catch *or* apprehend sb./get hold of sth.

**Habicht** /ˈhaːbɪçt/ *der;* **~s, ~e** **A** hawk; **B** (*Hühner~*) goshawk

**Habichts-: ~kraut** *das* (*Bot.*) hawkweed; **~nase** *die* hooked *or* aquiline nose

**Habilitand** /habiliˈtant/ *der;* **~en, ~en, Habilitandin** *die;* **~, ~nen** person working on his/her habilitation thesis

**Habilitation** /habilitaˈt͡si̯oːn/ *die;* **~, ~en** habilitation (*qualification as a university lecturer*)

**Habilitations·schrift** *die: postdoctoral thesis required in order to qualify as a university lecturer*

**habilitieren** /habiliˈtiːrən/ **1** *itr., refl. V.* habilitate (*qualify as a university lecturer*); **[sich] in Berlin/bei Prof. Schumacher ~:** habilitate at Berlin/under Professor Schumacher. **2** *tr. V.* **jmdn. ~:** habilitate sb.; confer on sb. his/her qualification as a university lecturer

**Habit**[1] /haˈbiːt/ *das od. der;* **~s, ~e** **A** (*abwertend, iron.*) outfit; **B** (*Amtskleidung*) habit

**Habit**[2] /ˈhæbɪt/ *das od. der;* **~s, ~s** (*Psych.: Gewohnheit*) habit

**Habitat** /habiˈtaːt/ *das;* **~s, ~e** (*Biol.*) habitat

**habituell** /habiˈtu̯ɛl/ *Adj.* habitual

**Habitus** /ˈha(ː)bitʊs/ *der;* **~** (*geh.*) **A** (*Gesamterscheinungsbild*) appearance and manner *or* bearing; **B** (*Haltung*) attitude; **C** (*Benehmen*) behaviour; **D** (*Med.*) habitus

**Habsburger** /ˈhaːpsbʊrgɐ/ *der;* **~s, ~, Habsburgerin** *die;* **~, ~nen** (*hist.*) Habsburg

**hab-, Hab-: ~seligkeiten** *Pl.* [meagre] possessions *or* belongings; **~sucht** *die* (*abwertend*) greed; avarice; **~süchtig** (*abwertend*) **1** *Adj.* greedy; avaricious; **2** *adv.* greedily; avariciously

**Habt·acht·stellung** *die* attention; **in ~ stehen** stand to attention

**hach** /hax/ *Interj.* oh!

**Haché** /[h]aˈʃeː/ ⇒ **Haschee**

**Hachse** /ˈhaksə/ *die;* **~, ~n** (*südd.*) **A** knuckle; **~ vom Kalb** knuckle of veal; **B** (*ugs. scherzh.*) leg

**Hack** /hak/ *das;* **~s** (*ugs., bes. nordd.*) mince; minced meat

**Hack-: ~beil** *das* chopper; cleaver; **~braten** *der* (*Kochk.*) meat loaf; **~brett** *das* (*Musik*) dulcimer

**Hacke**[1] *die;* **~, ~n** hoe; (*Pickel*) pick[axe]

**Hacke**[2] *die;* **~, ~n** ▶ 471 (*bes. nordd. u. md.*) heel; **sich** (*Dat.*) **die ~n nach etw. ablaufen** *od.* **abrennen** wear oneself out running around looking for sth.; ⇒ *auch* **Ferse**

**hacken** **1** *itr. V.* **A** (*mit der Hacke arbeiten*) hoe; **sich** (*Dat. od. Akk.*) **ins Bein ~:** cut one's leg [with a hoe/an axe *etc.*]; **B** (*picken*) peck; **nach jmdm./etw. ~:** peck at sb./sth.; **der Papagei hat mir in den Finger gehackt** the parrot pecked my finger. **2** *tr. V.* **A** (*mit der Hacke bearbeiten*) hoe ‹garden, flower bed, etc.›; **B** (*mit der Axt zerkleinern*) chop ‹wood etc.›; **etw. in Stücke ~:** chop sth. up; **C** (*ein Loch machen*) chop, hack ‹hole›; **D** (*zerkleinern*) chop [up] ‹meat, vegetables, etc.›

**Hacker** *der;* **~s, ~, Hackerin** *die;* **~, ~nen** (*DV-Jargon*) hacker

**Hack-: ~fleisch** *das* minced meat; mince; **aus jmdm. ~fleisch machen** (*fig. ugs.*) make mincemeat of sb.; **~frucht** *die* (*Landw.*) root crop; **~klotz** *der* chopping block; **~messer** *das* chopper; cleaver; **~ordnung** *die* (*Verhaltensf.*) pecking order

**Häcksel** /ˈhɛksl̩/ *der od. das;* **~s** (*Landw.*) chaff

**Häcks[e]ler** *der;* **~s, ~, Häcksel·maschine** *die* (*Landw.*) chaff-cutter

**häckseln** *tr. V.* chop [up] ‹straw, hay, etc.›

**Hader** /ˈhaːdɐ/ *der;* **~s** (*geh.*) discord

**hadern** *itr. V.* (*geh.*) **A** (*streiten*) quarrel; **B** (*unzufrieden sein*) **mit etw. ~:** be at odds with sth.; **er haderte mit seinem Schicksal** he railed against his fate

**Hadern·papier** *das* (*fachspr.*) rag paper

**Hades** /ˈhaːdɛs/ *der;* **~** (*griech. Myth.*) Hades *no art.*

**Hadschi** /ˈhaːd͡ʒi/ *der;* **~s, ~s** hadji

**Hafen**[1] /ˈhaːfn̩/ *der;* **~s, Häfen** harbour; port; (*~anlagen*) docks *pl.*; **der Hamburger ~:** the port of Hamburg; **ein Schiff läuft den ~ an/aus dem ~ aus/in den ~ ein** a ship is putting into/leaving/entering port *or* harbour; **in den ~ der Ehe einlaufen** (*fig. scherzh.*) taste the joys of married *or* wedded bliss

**Hafen**[2] *der;* **~s, ~** (*südd., schweiz., österr.*) pot; (*Schüssel*) bowl

**Hafen-: ~amt** *das* port *or* harbour authority; **~anlagen** *Pl.* docks; **~arbeiter** *der,* **~arbeiterin** *die* ▶ 159 dock worker; docker; **~aus·fahrt** *die* harbour mouth; **~bahn** *die* harbour railway; **~becken** *das* harbour basin; dock; **~behörde** *die* port *or* harbour authority; **~blockade** *die* blockade of a/the harbour *or* port; **~ein·fahrt** *die* harbour entrance *or* mouth; **~gebühren** *Pl.*, **~geld** *das* harbour charges *pl.*; port dues *pl.*; **~kneipe** *die* dockland pub (*Brit.*) *or* (*Amer.*) bar; **~meister** *der,* **~meisterin** *die* harbour master; **~polizei** *die* port *or* dock police; **~rund·fahrt** *die* trip round the harbour; **~stadt** *die* port; **~viertel** *das* dock area; dockland *no art.*

**Hafer** /ˈhaːfɐ/ *der;* **~s** oats *pl.*; **jmdn. sticht der ~** (*ugs.*) sb. is feeling his oats

**Hafer-: ~brei** *der* porridge; **~flocken** *Pl.* rolled oats; porridge oats; **~grütze** *die* **A** oat groats; **B** (*Brei*) porridge; **~mehl** *das* oatmeal; **~sack** *der* nosebag; **~schleim** *der* gruel

**Haff** /haf/ *das;* **~[e]s, ~s** *od.* **~e** lagoon

**Haflinger** /ˈhaːflɪŋɐ/ *der;* **~s, ~:** Haflinger [horse]

**Hafner** *der;* **~s, ~, Hafnerin** *die;* **~, ~nen** (*südd., österr., schweiz.*) **A** (*Töpfer*) potter; **B** (*Ofensetzer*) stove-fitter

**Haft** /haft/ *die;* **~** **A** (*Gewahrsam*) custody; (*aus politischen Gründen*) detention; **jmdn. aus der ~ entlassen** release sb. from custody/detention; **sich in ~ befinden** be [held] in custody/detention; **jmdn. in ~ nehmen** take sb. into custody; (*aus politischen Gründen*) detain sb.; **B** (*Freiheitsstrafe*) imprisonment; **jmdn. zu zwei Jahren ~ verurteilen** sentence sb. to two years in prison *or* two years' imprisonment

**-haft** *Adj., adv.* -like

**Haft-: ~anstalt** *die* prison; **~aussetzung** *die* (*Rechtsspr.*) **der Verteidiger beantragte ~aussetzung** the defence counsel requested that the defendant be released from custody

**haftbar** *Adj.* (*bes. Rechtsspr.*) *in* **für etw. ~ sein** be [legally] responsible *or* liable for sth.; **jmdn. für etw. ~ machen** make *or* hold sb. [legally] liable for sth.

**Haft-: ~befehl** *der* (*Rechtsw.*) warrant [of arrest]; **einen ~befehl gegen jmdn. ausstellen** issue a warrant for sb.'s arrest; **~beschwerde** *die* (*Rechtsw.*) appeal against a remand in custody; **~creme** *die* (*Pharm.*) fixative cream; **~dauer** *die* term of imprisonment

**haften**[1] *itr. V.* **A** (*festkleben*) stick (**an/auf** + *Dat.* to); **~ bleiben** stick (**an/auf** + *Dat.* to); **B** (*sich festsetzen*) ‹smell, dirt, etc.› cling (**an** + *Dat.* to); **~ bleiben** ‹mud, clay, dirt, etc.› stick, cling (**an/auf** + *Dat.* to); ‹smell, smoke› cling (**an/auf** + *Dat.* to); (*fig.: im Gedächtnis bleiben*) stick; **[einem] in der Erinnerung ~** (*fig.*) stick in one's memory *or* mind; **~de Eindrücke** lasting impressions; **an ihm haftet ein Makel** (*fig.*) he carries a stigma; **seine Augen hafteten/sein Blick haftete an ...** (*Dat.*) (*fig.*) his eyes were/gaze was fixed on ...; **C** ‹tyre› grip

**haften**[2] *itr. V.* **A** (*einstehen*) **für jmdn./etw. ~:** be responsible for sb./liable for sth.; (*verantwortlich sein*) **jmdm. für etw. ~:** be responsible *or* answerable to sb. for sth.; **für etw. nicht ~** ‹company› not accept liability for sth.; ⇒ *auch* **Garderobe** A; **B** (*Rechtsw., Wirtsch.*) be liable

***haften|bleiben** ⇒ **haften**[1] A, B

**haft-, Haft-: ~erleichterung** *die* special privilege; **~fähig**[1] *Adj.* (*Rechtsw.*) fit to be kept in prison *postpos.*; **~fähig**[2] *Adj.* (*klebend*) adhesive; **~fähigkeit**[1] *die* (*Rechtsw.*) fitness to be kept in prison; **~fähigkeit**[2] *die* (*von Materialien*) adhesion

**Häftling** /ˈhɛftlɪŋ/ *der;* **~s, ~e** prisoner

**Häftlings·kleidung** *die* prison clothing

**Haft·pflicht** *die* **A** liability (**für** for); **B** ⇒ **Haftpflichtversicherung**

**haftpflichtig** *Adj.* liable (**für** for)

**Haftpflicht·versicherung** *die* personal liability insurance; (*für Autofahrer*) third party insurance

**haft-, Haft-: ~prüfung** *die* (*Rechtsw.*) review of a/the remand in custody; **~psychose** *die* prison psychosis; **~reibung** *die* (*Physik*) static friction; **~richter** *der,* **~richterin** *die* (*Rechtsw.*) magistrate; **~schale** *die* contact lens; **~strafe** *die* (*Rechtsspr. veralt.*) prison sentence; **~unfähig** *Adj.* unfit to be kept in prison *postpos.*; **~unfähigkeit** *die* unfitness to be kept in prison

**Haftung**[1] *die;* **~:** adhesion; (*von Reifen*) grip

**Haftung**[2] *die;* **~, ~en** **A** (*Verantwortlichkeit*) liability; responsibility; ⇒ *auch* **Garderobe**; **B** (*Rechtsw., Wirtsch.*) liability; **Gesellschaft mit [un]beschränkter ~:** [un]limited [liability] company

*old spelling (see note on page 1707)

**Haft·verschonung** *die* (*Rechtsw.*) suspended sentence

**Hag** /ha:k/ *der;* **~[e]s, ~e** (*veralt., noch schweiz.*) Ⓐ (*Hecke*) hedge; Ⓑ (*Wald*) grove

**Hagebutte** /ˈha:gəbʊtə/ *die;* **~, ~n** Ⓐ (*Frucht*) rose hip; Ⓑ (*ugs.: Heckenrose*) dog rose

**Hagebutten·tee** *der* rose hip tea

**Hage·dorn** *der; Pl.* **~e** hawthorn

**Hagel** /ˈha:gl̩/ *der;* **~s, ~** (*auch fig.*) hail; **ein ~ von Drohungen** a stream of threats

**Hagel·korn** *das* hailstone

**hageln** ❶ *itr., tr. V.* (*unpers.*) hail; **es hagelt** it is hailing; **es hagelte Steine und leere Bierdosen** (*fig.*) there was a hail of stones and empty beer cans; **es hagelte Drohungen/Fragen** (*fig.*) there was a stream of threats/flood of questions. ❷ *itr. V.; mit sein* (*fig.*) **auf jmdn./etw. ~** ‹stones, bombs, etc.› rain down on sb./sth.

**Hagel-: ~schaden** *der* damage *no pl.* caused by hail; **~schauer** *der* [short] hailstorm; **~schlag** *der* hail; **~sturm** *der* hailstorm; **~zucker** *der* sugar crystals *pl.*

**hager** /ˈha:gɐ/ *Adj.* gaunt ‹person, figure, face›; thin ‹neck, arm, fingers›

**Hagerkeit** *die;* **~** ⇒ **hager**: gauntness; thinness

**Hage·stolz** *der;* **~es, ~e** (*veralt.*) confirmed bachelor

**haha** /haˈha(:)/ *Interj.* ha ha

**Häher** /ˈhɛ:ɐ/ *der;* **~s, ~:** jay

**Hahn¹** /ha:n/ *der;* **~[e]s, Hähne** /ˈhɛ:nə/ Ⓐ cock; (*junger* **~**) cockerel; **~ im Korb sein** (*ugs.*) be cock of the walk; **nach ihr/danach kräht kein ~** (*ugs.*) no one could care less about her/it; **jmdm. den roten ~ aufs Dach setzen** (*veralt.*) set sb.'s house on fire; Ⓑ (*Wetter***~**) weathercock

**Hahn²** *der;* **~[e]s, Hähne,** *fachspr.:* **~en** Ⓐ tap; faucet (*Amer.*); (*eines Fasses*) tap; spigot; ⇒ *auch* **abdrehen** 1 A; Ⓑ (*bei Waffen*) hammer; **den ~ spannen** cock a/the gun

**Hähnchen** /ˈhɛ:nçən/ *das;* **~s, ~:** chicken; (*junger Hahn*) cockerel

**Hahnen-: ~fuß** *der* buttercup; **~fuß·gewächs** *das* ranunculus; **~kamm** *der* cockscomb; **~kampf** *der* Ⓐ cockfighting; (*einzelner Wettkampf*) cockfight; Ⓑ (*Gymnastik*) *hopping-game in which players barge each other and attempt to push each other off balance;* **~schrei** *der* cockcrow; **beim ersten ~schrei** at cockcrow; **~tritt·muster** *das* dog-tooth *or* dog's tooth check

**Hahnrei** /ˈha:nrai/ *der;* **~s, ~e** (*geh., veralt.*) cuckold

**Hai** /hai/ *der;* **~s, ~e** (*auch fig.*) shark

**Hai·fisch** *der* shark

**Haifisch·flossen·suppe** *die* (*Kochk.*) shark-fin soup

**Hain** /hain/ *der;* **~[e]s, ~e** (*dichter. veralt.*) grove

**Hain·buche** *die* hornbeam

**Haiti** /haˈi:ti/ (*das*)*;* **~s** Haiti

**Haitianer** /haiˈti̯a:nɐ/ *der;* **~s, ~, Haitianerin** *die;* **~, ~nen** Haitian

**haitianisch** *Adj.* Haitian

**Häkchen** /ˈhɛ:kçən/ *das;* **~s, ~** Ⓐ [small] hook; **was ein ~ werden will, krümmt sich beizeiten** (*Spr.*) there's nothing like starting young; Ⓑ (*Zeichen*) mark; (*beim Abhaken*) tick

**Häkel-: ~arbeit** *die* crocheting; crochet work; (*etw. Gehäkeltes*) a piece of crochet work *or* crocheting; **~decke** *die* crocheted tablecloth; (*für ein Sofa, einen Stuhl usw.*) crocheted cover

**Häkelei** *die;* **~, ~en** ⇒ **Häkelarbeit**

**Häkel-: ~garn** *das* crochet thread *or* yarn; **~muster** *das* crochet pattern

**hakeln** /ˈha:kl̩n/ ❶ *itr. V.* Ⓐ (*landsch.*) finger-wrestle; Ⓑ (*Fußball*) trip the/an opposing player. ❷ *tr. V.* Ⓐ (*Fußball*) trip; Ⓑ (*Ringen*) **jmds. Bein/Fuß ~:** get sb. in a leg lock/foot lock

**häkeln** /ˈhɛ:kl̩n/ *tr., itr. V.* crochet

**Häkel·nadel** *die* crochet hook

**haken** /ˈha:kn̩/ ❶ *tr. V.* Ⓐ hook (**an** + *Akk.* on to); Ⓑ ([*Eis*]*hockey*) hook; Ⓒ (*Fußball*) ⇒ **hakeln** 2. ❷ *itr. V.* (*klemmen*) be stuck

**Haken** *der;* **~s, ~** Ⓐ hook; **~ und Öse** hook and eye; **einen ~ schlagen** dart sideways; **mit ~ und Ösen** (*fig. ugs.*) by fair means or foul; Ⓑ (*Zeichen*) tick; Ⓒ (*ugs.: Schwierigkeit*) catch; snag; **wo ist der ~?** where's the catch?; **der ~ an etw.** (*Dat.*) the catch in sth.; Ⓓ (*Boxen*) hook

**haken-, Haken-: ~förmig** ❶ *Adj.* hooked; hook-shaped; ❷ *adv.* **~förmig gebogen** hooked; hook-shaped; **~kreuz** *das* swastika; **~leiter** *die* hook ladder; **~nase** *die* hooked nose; hook nose

**Halali** /halaˈli:/ *das;* **~s, ~[s]** (*Jägerspr.*) Ⓐ (*Signal*) mort; Ⓑ (*Ende der Jagd*) mort; kill

**halb** /halp/ ❶ *Adj. u. Bruchz.* Ⓐ ▶ 752 |, ▶ 841 | (*die Hälfte von*) half; **eine ~e Stunde/ein ~er Meter/ein ~es Glas** half an hour/a metre/a glass; **zum ~en Preis** [at] half price; **~ Europa/die ~e Welt** half of Europe/half the world; **es ist ~ eins** it's half past twelve; **5 Minuten vor/nach ~:** 25 [minutes] past/to; ⇒ *auch* **Arm** C; **Höhe** B; **Note** A; **Weg** D; Ⓑ (*unvollständig, vermindert*) **die ~e Wahrheit** half [of] *or* part of the truth; **er macht keine ~en Sachen** he doesn't do things by halves; **er hat [nur] ~e Arbeit getan** he hasn't done the job properly; **nichts Halbes und nichts Ganzes [sein]** [be] neither one thing nor the other ; Ⓒ (*fast*) **[noch] ein ~es Kind sein** be hardly *or* scarcely more than a child; **eine ~e Ewigkeit warten** wait [for] ages; **die ~e Stadt** half the town.
❷ *adv.* Ⓐ (*zur Hälfte*) **~ voll/leer** half-full/-empty; **~ lachend, ~ weinend** half laughing, half crying; **~ link.../recht...** (*bes. Fußball*) inside left/right; **~ links/rechts** (*Fußball*) [at] inside left/right; **~ links/rechts abbiegen** fork left/right; Ⓑ (*unvollständig*) **~ gar/angezogen** *od.* **bekleidet/wach/fertig** half-done *or* -cooked/half dressed/half awake/half-finished; **~ offen** half-open ‹door etc.›; open ‹prison›; **~ verdaut** (*auch fig.*) half-digested; **~ reif** half-ripe; **die Pflaumen sind erst ~ reif** the plums aren't fully ripe; **er hat seine Arbeit ~ getan** he has done some of his work; **die Verletzung war nur ~ so schlimm, wie er erst dachte** the injury was not as serious as he at first thought; **etw. nur ~ verstehen** only half understand sth.; **nur ~ zuhören** be only half listening; **nur ~ bei der Sache sein** be only half with it (*coll.*); ⇒ *auch* **schlimm** 1 B; Ⓒ (*fast*) **~ blind/verhungert/tot/erfroren/nackt** half blind/starved/dead/frozen/naked; **~ roh** half-cooked; half-done; **~ verwest** partially decomposed; **~ wild** half-wild ‹animal, country›; half-savage ‹person›; **ich bin schon ~ fertig** I'm nearly *or* almost finished; **~ so klug** half as clever; **~ und ~** (*ugs.*) more or less; **Gefällt es dir? — Halb und ~** (*ugs.*) Do you like it? — Sort of (*coll.*)

**halb-, Halb-: ~affe** *der* (*Zool.*) half-ape; prosimian; **~amtlich** *Adj.* semi-official; **~automatisch** ❶ *Adj.* semi-automatic; ❷ *adv.* semi-automatically; ***~bekleidet** ⇒ **halb** 2 B; **~bildung** *die* (*abwertend*) superficial education; **~bitter** *Adj.* plain ‹chocolate›; ***~blind** ⇒ **halb** 2 C; **~blut** *das* Ⓐ (*bei Pferden*) cross-breed; Ⓑ (*Mischling*) half-caste; half-breed; **~bruder** *der* half-brother; **~dunkel** *Adj.* half-dark; **~dunkel** *das* semi-darkness

**Halbe¹** *der od. die od. das; adj. Dekl.* (*ugs.*) half litre (*of beer etc.*); **ein ~s** a half litre

**Halbe²** *die; adj. Dekl.* (*Musik*) minim (*Brit.*); half note (*Amer.*)

**Halb·edelstein** *der* (*veralt.*) semi-precious stone

**halbe-halbe** *in* **[mit jmdm.] ~ machen** (*ugs.*) go halves [with sb.]

**halber** /ˈhalbɐ/ *Präp. mit Gen.* (*wegen*) on account of; (*um ... willen*) for the sake of; **der Ordnung ~:** as a matter of form; **der Wahrheit ~:** to tell the truth

**halb-, Halb-: *~erfroren** ⇒ **halb** 2 C; **~fabrikat** *das* (*Wirtsch.*) semi-finished product; ***~fertig** ⇒ **halb** 2 B; **~fett** ❶ *Adj.* Ⓐ (*Druckw.*) bold ‹type›; (*schmaler, kleiner*) semibold; Ⓑ medium-fat ‹cheese›; ❷ *adv.* **etw. ~fett drucken** print sth. in bold/semibold [type]; **~finale** *das* (*Sport*) semi-final; ***~gar** ⇒ **halb** 2 B; **~gebildet** ❶ *Adj.* (*abwertend*) half-educated; ❷ *adv.* in a half-educated way; **~gebildete** *der/die; adj. Dekl.* (*abwertend*) half-educated person; **~gefror[e]ne** *das; adj. Dekl.* soft ice cream; ***~geschoß, ~geschoss** *das* (*Archit.*) mezzanine [floor]; **~geschwister** *Pl.* half-brothers/half-sisters/half-brother[s] and -sister[s]; **~gott** *der* (*Myth., fig. iron.*) demigod; **~götter in Weiß** (*ugs. iron.*) [hospital] doctors

**Halbheit** *die;* **~, ~en** (*abwertend*) half measure

**halb-, Halb-: ~herzig** ❶ *Adj.* half-hearted; ❷ *adv.* half-heartedly; **~herzigkeit** *die;* **~~:** half-heartedness; **~hoch** ❶ *Adj.* (*bes. Sport*) shoulder-high ‹shot, pass, etc.›; low ‹shelf etc.›; calf-length ‹boot›; ❷ *adv.* **der Ball kam ~hoch** the ball came at shoulder height

**halbieren** *tr. V.* cut/tear ‹object› in half; halve ‹amount, number›; (*Math.*) bisect

**halb-, Halb-: ~insel** *die* peninsula; **~jahr** *das* six months *pl.*; half year; **im ersten/zweiten ~jahr** in the first/last six months [of the year]; **~jahres·bilanz** *die* half-yearly figures *pl. or* results *pl.;* **~jahres·zeugnis** *das* half-yearly report; **~jährig** *Adj.* Ⓐ (*ein ~es Jahr alt*) six-month-old ‹baby, pony, etc.›; Ⓑ (*ein ~es Jahr dauernd*) six-month ‹contract, course, etc.›; **~jährlich** ❶ *Adj.* half-yearly; six-monthly; ❷ *adv.* every six months; twice a year; **~jude** *der,* **~jüdin** *die* (*bes. ns.*) half-Jew; **~jude sein** be half Jewish; **~kanton** *der* demicanton; **~kreis** *der* semicircle; **sich im ~kreis aufstellen** form a semicircle; **im ~kreis sitzen** sit in a semicircle; **~kreis·förmig** ❶ *Adj.* semicircular; ❷ *adv.* in a semicircle; **~kugel** *die* hemisphere; **~kugel·förmig** *Adj.* hemispherical; **~lang** *Adj.* mid-length ‹hair›; mid-calf length ‹coat, dress, etc.›; **[nun] mach [aber mal] ~lang!** (*ugs.*) hang on a minute! (*coll.*); **~laut** ❶ *Adj.* low; quiet; ❷ *adv.* in a low voice; in an undertone; **~leder** *das* (*Buchw.*) half-leather; ***~leer** ⇒ **halb** 2 A; **~leinen** *das* Ⓐ (*Gewebe*) fifty-per-cent linen material; Ⓑ (*Buchw.*) half-cloth; **~leiter** *der* (*Elektronik*) semiconductor; ***~link...** ⇒ **halb** 2 A; **~linke** /-ˈ--/ *der* (*bes. Fußball*) inside left; ***~links** ⇒ **halb** 2 A; **~mast** *Adv.* at half mast; **~mast flaggen** fly a flag/the flags at half mast; **~matt** *Adj.* (*Fot.*) semimatt; **~messer** *der;* **~~s, ~~** (*Math.*) radius; **~metall** *das* (*Chemie*) semi-metal; **~militärisch** *Adj.* paramilitary; **~monatlich** ❶ *Adj.* fortnightly; twice-monthly; ❷ *adv.* fortnightly; twice monthly; **~monats·schrift** *die* fortnightly periodical; **~mond** *der* Ⓐ (*Mond*) half-moon; **heute ist ~mond** there's a half-moon tonight; Ⓑ (*Figur*) crescent; Ⓒ (*an Fingernägeln*) half-moon; **~mond·förmig** *Adj.* crescent-shaped; ***~nackt** ⇒ **halb** 2 C; ***~offen** ⇒ **halb** 2 B; **~offiziell** *Adj.* semi-official; **~part** *Adv. in* **[mit jmdm.] ~part machen** (*ugs.*) go halves [with sb.]; **~pension** *die* half board; ***~recht...** ⇒ **halb** 2 A; **~rechte** /-ˈ--/ *der* (*bes. Fußball*) inside right; ***~rechts** ⇒ **halb** 2 A; ***~reif** ⇒ **halb** 2 B; **~rock** *der* waist petticoat; ***~roh** ⇒ **halb** 2 C; **~rund** *Adj.* semicircular; **~rund** *das* semicircle; **~schatten** *der* Ⓐ half shadow; Ⓑ (*Optik, Astron.*) penumbra; **~schlaf** *der* light sleep; **im ~schlaf liegen** be half asleep; doze; **~schuh** *der* shoe; **~schwer·gewicht** *das* (*Schwerathletik*) Ⓐ light-heavyweight; ⇒ *auch* **Fliegengewicht** A; Ⓑ ⇒ **~schwergewichtler**; **~schwergewichtler** *der* (*Schwerathletik*) light-heavyweight; **~schwester** *die* half-sister; **~seide** *die* fifty-per-cent silk [mixture]; **~seiden** *Adj.* Ⓐ fifty-per-cent silk; Ⓑ (*ugs. abwertend: unmännlich*) poofy (*coll.*); pansyish (*coll.*); Ⓒ (*ugs. abwertend: anrüchig*) dubious ‹business practice etc.›; fast ‹woman›; **~seitig**

h

❶ *Adv.* Ⓐ (*Med.*) **~seitig gelähmt sein** be hemiplegic; be paralysed down one side; Ⓑ **ein Blatt ~seitig beschreiben** write on the left-hand/right-hand side of a sheet only; ❷ *adj.* half-page ‹article etc.›; **~staatlich** *Adj.* (*DDR*) partially state-controlled *or* state-run; **~stark** *Adj.* (*ugs. abwertend*) rowdy; **~starke** *der; adj. Dekl.* (*ugs. abwertend*) young rowdy; [young] hooligan; **~stiefel** *der* half-boot; ankle boot; **~stündig** *Adj.* half-hour; lasting half an hour *postpos., not pred.*; **eine ~stündige Fahrt** a half-hour journey; half an hour's journey; **~stündlich** ❶ *Adj.* half-hourly; ❷ *adv.* half-hourly; every half an hour; **~stürmer** *der*, **~stürmerin** *die* (*bes. Fußball*) midfield player; **~tägig** ❶ *Adj.* half-day ‹excursion etc.›; part-time ‹work, worker, etc.›; (*morgens/nachmittags*) morning/afternoon ‹work etc.›; ❷ *adv.* ‹work› part-time; (*morgens/nachmittags*) ‹work› [in the] mornings/afternoons; **~täglich** ❶ *Adj.* twice daily; ❷ *adv.* twice a day; twice daily

**halb·tags** *Adv.* ▶ 159 ‹work› part-time; (*morgens/nachmittags*) ‹work› [in the] mornings/afternoons

**Halbtags-: ~arbeit** *die* **~beschäftigung** *die* part-time job; (*morgens/nachmittags*) morning/afternoon job; **~kraft** *die* part-time worker; part-timer; **~schule** *die* half-day school

**halb-, Halb-: ~ton** *der; Pl.* **~töne** Ⓐ (*Musik*) semitone; half step (*Amer.*); Ⓑ (*Malerei*) half-tone; ***~tot** ⇒ **halb** 2 C; **~totale** *die* (*Film*) medium shot; **~trauer** *die* half mourning; **~trauer tragen** be in half mourning; ***~verdaut** ⇒ **halb** 2 B; ***~verhungert** ⇒ **halb** 2 C; ***~verwest** ⇒ **halb** 2 C; **~vokal** *der* (*Phon.*) semivowel; ***~voll** ⇒ **halb** 2 A; ***~wach** ⇒ **halb** 2 B; **~wahrheit** *die* half-truth; **~waise** *die* fatherless/motherless child; **er/sie ist ~waise** he/she has lost one of his/her parents; **~wegs** /-'ve:ks/ *Adv.* Ⓐ to some extent; reasonably ‹good, clear, comprehensible, etc.›; **es geht mir ~wegs besser** I'm feeling a bit better; **kannst du dich nicht wenigstens ~wegs ordentlich benehmen?** can't you behave at all properly?; **ich kann ~wegs von meinem Einkommen leben** I can live fairly well on my income; Ⓑ (*veralt.: auf halbem Weg*) halfway; **~welt** *die* demi-monde; **~welt·dame** *die* demi-mondaine; **~weltergewicht** *das* Ⓐ (*Klasse*) light welterweight; Ⓑ (*Sportler*) light welterweight; **~werts·zeit** *die* (*Physik*) half-life; ***~wild** ⇒ **halb** 2 C; **~wilde** *der/die: in* **wie die ~wilden** (*ugs.*) like [a bunch of] savages; **~wissen** *das* (*abwertend*) superficial knowledge; smattering of knowledge; **sein medizinisches ~wissen** his smattering of medical knowledge; **~wüchsig** /-vy:ksɪç/ *Adj.* adolescent; teenage; **~wüchsige** *der/die; adj. Dekl.* adolescent; teenager; **~zeit** *die* (*bes. Fußball*) Ⓐ half; **die erste/zweite ~zeit** the first/second half; **während der ersten ~zeit seiner Amtsperiode** (*fig.*) during the first half of his period of office; Ⓑ (*Pause*) half-time; **zur ~zeit seiner Regierungszeit** (*fig.*) halfway through his period of office; **~zeit·pause** *die* (*Sport*) half-time; **~zeit·pfiff** *der* (*Sport*) half-time whistle; **~zeug** *das* (*Wirtsch.*) semi-finished product

**Halde** /'haldə/ *die;* ~, **~n** Ⓐ (*Bergbau*) slag heap; (*von Vorräten*) pile; (*fig.*) mountain; pile; **neue Wagen liegen massenhaft auf ~:** there are piles of unsold new cars; **Kartoffeln werden jetzt für die ~ produziert** the potatoes now being produced will simply go to swell existing stocks; Ⓑ (*geh.: Hang*) slope

**half** /half/ *1. u. 3. Pers. Sg. Prät. v.* **helfen**

**Hälfte** /'hɛlftə/ *die;* ~, **~n** Ⓐ half; **die ~ einer Sache** (*Gen.*) *od.* **von etw.** half [of] sth.; **Studenten bezahlen die ~ des Preises** students pay *or* (*coll.*) are half-price; **etw. in zwei gleiche ~n teilen** divide sth. in half *or* into two equal parts; **er füllte sein Glas nur bis zur ~:** he only half-filled his glass; **über die ~:** more than *or* over half; **um die ~ größer/kleiner** half as big/small again; **um die ~ zu viel/mehr** too much by half/half as much again; **etw. um die ~ steigern** increase sth. by half; **etw. zur ~ zahlen** pay half of sth.; **die gegnerische ~** (*Sport*) the opponents' half; **ich habe die ~ vergessen** I've forgotten half of it; **meine bessere ~** (*ugs. scherzh.*) my better half (*coll. joc.*); Ⓑ (*ugs.: Teil*) part; **die größere ~ ihres Gehalts/des Publikums** the greater part of her salary/the majority of the audience

**Halfter**[1] /'halftɐ/ *der od. das;* **~s**, ~, *veralt. auch die;* ~, **~n** halter

**Halfter**[2] *die;* ~, **~n**, *auch das;* **~s**, **~:** holster

**halftern** *tr. V.* halter

**Halfter·riemen** *der* halter strap

**Hall** /hal/ *der;* **~[e]s**, **~e** Ⓐ (*geh.*) reverberation; Ⓑ (*Echo*) echo

**Halle** /'halə/ *die;* ~, **~n** (*Saal, Gebäude*) hall; (*Fabrik~*) shed; (*Hotel~, Theater~*) lobby; foyer; (*Sport~*) [sports] hall; (*Schwimm~*) pool; **Tennis in der ~ spielen** play tennis indoors *or* on an indoor court; **in diesen heiligen ~n** (*iron.*) within these sacred halls (*iron.*)

**halleluja** /hale'lu:ja/ *Interj.* hallelujah!; (*scherzh.: hurra*) hurrah!

**Halleluja** *das;* **~s**, **~s** hallelujah; **das ~ aus Händels „Messias"** the Hallelujah Chorus from Handel's 'Messiah'

**hallen** *itr. V.* Ⓐ reverberate; ring; ‹shot, bell, cry› ring out; Ⓑ (*wider~*) echo; **von etw. ~:** reverberate *or* echo with sth.

**Hallen-** indoor ‹swimming pool, handball, football, hockey, tennis, championship, record, sport, etc.›

**Hallig** /'halɪç/ *die;* ~, **~en** small low island (*particularly one of those off Schleswig-Holstein*)

**Hallimasch** /'halimaʃ/ *der;* **~[e]s**, **~e** (*Bot.*) honey agaric; honey mushroom

**hallo** *Interj.* Ⓐ *meist* /'halo/ (*am Telefon*) hello; **~, warte doch mal auf mich!** hey! wait for me!; **~, gehört Ihnen diese Tasche?** excuse me! is this your bag?; Ⓑ *meist* /ha'lo:/ (*überrascht*) hello; Ⓒ (*ugs., bes. Jugendspr. als Gruß*) hi (*coll.*); hello

**Hallo** /ha'lo:/ *das;* **~s**, **~s** Ⓐ cheering; cheers *pl.*; **mit großem ~:** with loud cheering *or* cheers; Ⓑ (*Aufsehen*) hullabaloo

**Hallodri** /ha'lo:dri/ *der;* **~s**, **~[s]** (*bayr., österr. ugs. abwertend*) rogue

**Hallstatt·zeit** /'halʃtat-/ *die;* ~ (*Archäol.*) Hallstatt period

**Halluzination** /halutsina'tsio:n/ *die;* ~, **~en** hallucination; **du hast wohl ~en** you must be seeing things

**halluzinatorisch** /halutsina'to:rɪʃ/ *Adj.* (*Med., Psych.*) hallucinatory

**halluzinieren** *itr. V.* (*Med., Psych.*) hallucinate; have hallucinations

**halluzinogen** /halutsino'ge:n/ *Adj.* (*Med., Psych.*) hallucinogenic

**Halluzinogen** *das;* **~s**, **~e** (*Med., Psych.*) hallucinogen

**Halm** /halm/ *der;* **~[e]s**, **~e** stalk; stem; **das Getreide/die Ernte auf dem ~:** the standing corn

**Halma** /'halma/ *das;* **~s** halma

**Hälmchen** /'hɛlmçən/ *das;* **~s**, **~:** [small] stalk *or* stem

**Halm·frucht** *die* cereal

**Halo** /'ha:lo/ *der;* **~[s]**, **~s** *od.* **~nen** /-'--/ (*Physik*) halo

**Halogen** /halo'ge:n/ *das;* **~s**, **~e** (*Chemie*) halogen

**Halogen-** halogen ‹lamp, headlamp›

**Hals** /hals/ *der;* **~es**, **Hälse** /'hɛlzə/ Ⓐ ▶ 471 neck; **sich** (*Dat.*) **den ~ brechen** break one's neck; **jmdm. um den ~ fallen** throw *or* fling one's arms around sb.['s neck]; **~ über Kopf** (*ugs.*) in a rush *or* hurry: **sich ~ über Kopf verlieben** fall head over heels in love; **sich** (*Dat.*) **nach jmdm./etw. den ~ verrenken** crane one's neck to see sb./sth.; **einen langen ~/lange Hälse machen** (*ugs.*) crane one's neck/their necks; **jmdm. den ~ abschneiden** *od.* **umdrehen** *od.* **brechen** (*ugs.*) drive sb. to the wall; **das kostete ihn** *od.* **ihm den ~** (*ugs.*) that did for him (*coll.*); **jmdn./etw. auf dem** *od.* **am ~ haben** (*ugs.*) be saddled with sb./sth. (*coll.*); **zu viel am ~ haben** (*ugs.*) have too much on one's plate (*coll.*); **sich jmdm. an den ~ werfen** (*ugs.*) throw oneself at sb.; **jmdm. jmdn. auf den ~ schicken** *od.* **hetzen** (*ugs.*) get *or* put sb. on [to] sb.; **sich** (*Dat.*) **jmdn./etw. auf den ~ laden** (*ugs.*) lumber *or* saddle oneself with sb./sth. (*coll.*); **bis über den ~ in etw.** (*Dat.*) **stecken** (*ugs.*) be up to one's ears *or* eyes in sth.; **jmdm. steht** *od.* **geht das Wasser bis zum** *od.* **an den ~** (*ugs.: jmd. hat Schulden*) sb. is up to his/her eyes in debt; (*ugs.: jmd. hat Schwierigkeiten*) sb. is up to his/her neck in it; **jmdn. mit etw. vom ~[e] bleiben** (*ugs.*) not bother sb. with sth.; **sich** (*Dat.*) **jmdn. vom ~[e] halten** (*ugs.*) keep sb. away: **dem Chef alle Besucher vom ~e halten** (*ugs.*) keep all visitors away from the boss; Ⓑ ▶ 471 (*Kehle*) throat; **aus vollem ~[e]** at the top of one's voice; **er hat es in den falschen** *od.* **verkehrten ~ bekommen** (*ugs.: falsch verstanden*) he took it the wrong way; (*ugs.: sich verschluckt*) it went down [his throat] the wrong way; **er kann den ~ nicht voll [genug] kriegen** (*ugs.*) he can't get enough; he's insatiable; **das hängt/wächst mir zum ~[e] heraus** (*ugs.*) I'm sick and tired of it (*coll.*); Ⓒ (*einer Flasche*) neck; **einer Flasche** (*Dat.*) **den ~ brechen** (*ugs.*) crack [open] a bottle; Ⓓ (*Musik*) (*einer Note*) stem; (*eines Saiteninstruments*) neck; Ⓔ (*Anat.*) neck; collum (*Anat.*); (*Gebärmutter~*) neck; cervix (*Anat.*)

**hals-, Hals-: ~ab·schneider** *der*, **~ab·schneiderin** *die* (*ugs. abwertend*) shark; **~abschneiderisch** *Adj.* cutthroat ‹practice etc.›; extortionate ‹interest etc.›; **~aus·schnitt** *der* neckline; **~band** *das; Pl.* **~bänder** Ⓐ (*für Tiere*) collar; Ⓑ (*Samtband*) choker; neckband; Ⓒ (*veralt.: ~kette*) necklace; **~brecherisch** /-brɛçərɪʃ/ *Adj.* dangerous, risky ‹climb, action, etc.›; hazardous ‹road›; breakneck *attrib.* ‹speed›; **~bruch** *der* ⇒ **~- und Beinbruch**

**Hälschen** /'hɛlsçən/ *das;* **~s**, **~:** [little] neck

**halsen**[1] *tr. V.* (*veralt.*) embrace

**halsen**[2] *itr. V.* (*Seemannsspr.*) wear

**hals-, Hals-: ~entzündung** *die* ▶ 474 inflammation of the throat; **~kette** *die* necklace; (*für Hunde*) chain; **~kragen** *der* collar; **~krause** *die* ruff; **~länge** *die* (*Pferdesport*) neck; **um eine ~länge** by a neck; **~-Nasen-Ohren-Arzt** *der*, **~-Nasen-Ohren-Ärztin** *die* ear, nose, and throat specialist; **~-Nasen-Ohren-Krankheiten** *Pl.* (*Med.*) diseases of the ear, nose, and throat; **Facharzt für ~-Nasen-Ohren-Krankheiten** ear, nose, and throat specialist; **~schlagader** *die* ▶ 471 carotid [artery]; **~schmerzen** *Pl.* ▶ 474 sore throat *sing.*; **[starke] ~schmerzen haben** have a[n extremely] sore throat; **~starrig** /-ʃtarɪç/ ❶ *Adj.* (*abwertend*) stubborn; obstinate; ❷ *adv.* stubbornly; obstinately; **~starrigkeit** *die;* **~~:** (*abwertend*) stubbornness; obstinacy; **~stück** *das* (*Kochk.*) neck; **~tuch** *das* cravat; (*des Cowboys*) neckerchief; **~- und Beinbruch** *Interj.* (*scherzh.*) good luck!; best of luck!; **~weh** *das* (*ugs.*) ⇒ **~schmerzen**; **~wickel** *der* (*Med.*) compress (*applied to the throat*); **~wirbel** *der* ▶ 471 (*Anat.*) cervical vertebra

**halt**[1] /halt/ *Partikel* (*südd., österr., schweiz.*) ⇒ **eben** 3 B

**halt**[2] *Interj.* stop; (*Milit.*) halt; **~, ich habe etwas vergessen** wait a minute *or* (*coll.*) hold on, I've forgotten something

**Halt** *der;* **~[e]s**, **~e** Ⓐ (*Stütze*) hold; **seine Füße/Hände fanden keinen ~:** he couldn't find *or* get a foothold/handhold; **in diesen Schuhen haben meine Füße keinen ~:** these shoes don't give my feet any support; **den ~ verlieren** lose one's hold; **inneren ~ haben** be secure; **ohne jeden ~:** totally insecure; **er hat einen festen ~ an seinem Glauben** his faith gives him *or*

*old spelling (see note on page 1707)

provides him with a great sense of security; **B** (*Anhalten*) stop; **einen ~ machen** make a stop; **zum ~ kommen** come to a stop *or* halt; **ohne ~**: non-stop; without stopping; **~ machen** stop; **vor jmdm./etw. nicht ~ machen** (*fig.*) not spare sb./sth.; **vor nichts und niemandem ~ machen** stop at nothing

**haltbar** *Adj.* **A** (*nicht verderblich*) **~ sein** ‹food› keep [well]; **etw. ~ machen** preserve sth.; **~ bis 5. 3.** use by 5 March; **B** (*nicht verschleißend*) hard-wearing, durable ‹material, clothes›; **C** (*aufrechtzuerhalten*) tenable ‹hypothesis etc.›; **D** (*Ballspiele*) stoppable, savable ‹shot›; **der Ball war nicht ~**: the shot was unstoppable; **E** (*beizubehalten*) maintainable ‹position etc.›; **die Position war nicht ~**: the position could not be maintained

**Haltbarkeit** *die;* **~ A Lebensmittel von beschränkter ~**: perishable foods; **eine längere ~ haben** keep longer; **B** (*Strapazierfähigkeit*) durability; **ein Teppich von größter ~**: an extremely hard-wearing carpet; **C** (*Glaubhaftigkeit*) tenability

**Haltbarkeits·dauer** *die:* **Sahne, die eine ~ von 3 Monaten hat** cream which keeps for three months; **die ~ von verpackten Lebensmitteln muss auf der Packung angegeben werden** the date by which packed foodstuffs should be eaten must be shown on the pack

**Halte-: ~bogen** *der* (*Musik*) tie; **~bucht** *die* (*Verkehrsw.*) lay-by (*Brit.*); turnout (*Amer.*); **~griff** *der* **A** [grab] handle; (*Riemen*) [grab] strap; **B** (*Budo, Ringen*) pinning hold; **~gurt** *der* seat belt; **~linie** *die* (*Verkehrsw.*) stop line

**halten 1** *unr. tr. V.* **A** (*auch Milit.*) hold; **etw. an einem Ende/am Griff ~**: hold one end of sth./hold sth. by the handle; **jmdm. den Mantel ~**: hold sb.'s coat [for him/her]; **sich (*Dat.*) den Kopf/den Bauch ~**: hold one's head/stomach; **jmdn. an *od.* bei der Hand ~**: hold sb.'s hand; hold sb. by the hand; **jmdn./etw. im Arm ~**: hold sb./sth. in one's arms; **die Hand vor den Mund ~**: put one's hand in front of one's mouth; **etw. ins Licht/gegen das Licht ~**: hold sth. to/up to the light; **B** (*Ballspiele*) save ‹shot, penalty, etc.›; **C** (*bewahren*) keep; (*beibehalten, aufrechterhalten*) keep up ‹speed etc.›; maintain ‹temperature, equilibrium›; **einen Ton ~**: stay in tune; (*lange an~*) sustain a note; **den Takt ~**: keep time; **Diät ~**: keep to a diet; **den Kurs ~**: stay on course; **diese Forderungen lassen sich nicht ~ *od.* sind nicht zu ~**: these demands cannot be kept up *or* maintained; **diese Behauptung lässt sich nicht ~**: this statement does not hold up; **mit jmdm. Kontakt *od.* Verbindung ~**: keep in touch *or* contact with sb.; **Ordnung/Frieden ~**: keep order/the peace; **Ruhe in der Klasse ~** ‹teacher› keep the class quiet; ‹pupils› keep quiet in class; **D** (*erfüllen*) keep; **sein Wort/ein Versprechen ~**: keep one's word/a promise; **das Buch hielt nicht, was das Titelbild versprach** (*fig.*) the book didn't live up to the promise of the picture on its cover; **E** (*besitzen, beschäftigen, beziehen*) keep ‹chickens etc.›; take ‹newspaper, magazine, etc.›; **ein Auto ~**: run a car; **sich (*Dat.*) eine Putzfrau ~**: have a woman to come in and clean; **F** (*einschätzen*) **jmdn. für reich/ehrlich ~**: think sb. is *or* consider sb. to be rich/honest; **jmdn. für tot ~**: think sb. is dead; **ich halte es für das beste/möglich/meine Pflicht** I think it best/possible/my duty; **viel/nichts/wenig von jmdm./etw. ~**: think a lot/nothing/not think much of sb./sth.; **G** (*ab~, veranstalten*) give, make ‹speech›; give, hold ‹lecture›; **Unterricht ~**: give lessons; teach; **seinen Winterschlaf ~**: hibernate; **seinen Mittagsschlaf ~**: have one's *or* an afternoon nap; **eine Mahlzeit ~** (*veralt.*) have a meal; **H** (*Halt geben*) hold up, support ‹bridge etc.›; hold back ‹curtain, hair›; fasten ‹dress›; **I** (*zurück~*) keep; **ihn hält hier nichts** there's nothing to keep him here; **es hält dich niemand** nobody's stopping you; **J** (*bei sich be~*) **das Wasser ~**: hold one's water; **K** (*nicht aufgeben*) **ein Geschäft *usw.* ~**: keep a business *etc.* going; **L** (*behandeln*) treat; **jmdn. streng ~**: be strict with sb.; **M** (*vorziehen*) **es mit jmdm./etw. ~**: like sb./sth.; **es mehr *od.* lieber mit jmdm./etw. ~**: prefer sb./sth.; **N** (*verfahren*) **es mit einer Sache so/anders ~**: deal with *or* handle sth. like this/differently; **wie haltet ihr es in diesem Jahr mit eurem Urlaub?** what are you doing about holidays this year?; **O** (*lassen, be~*) keep; **für jmdn. das Essen warm ~**: keep sb.'s meal hot; **jmdn. jung/fit ~**: keep sb. young/fit; **jmdn. bei Laune/in Bewegung/in Atem ~**: keep sb. happy/on the go/in suspense; **P** (*gestalten*) **das Badezimmer ist in Grün ge~**: the bathroom is decorated in green; **sie wollten das Esszimmer ganz in Eiche ~**: they wanted all oak furniture in the dining room; **die Rede war sehr allgemein ge~**: the speech was very general.

**2** *unr. itr. V.* **A** (*stehen bleiben*) stop; **etw. zum Halten bringen** stop sth.; bring sth. to a stop; **halt [mal]** (*fig. ugs.*) hang *or* hold on [a minute] (*coll.*); **B** (*unverändert, an seinem Platz bleiben*) last; **der Nagel/das Seil hält nicht mehr länger** the nail/rope won't hold much longer; **die Tapete hält nicht** the wallpaper won't stay on; **diese Freundschaft hält nicht [lange]** (*fig.*) this friendship won't last [long]; **C** (*Sport*) save; **er hat gut ge~**: he made some good saves; **D** (*beistehen*) **zu jmdm. ~**: stand *or* stick by sb.; **E** (*zielen*) aim (**auf** + *Akk.* at); **F** (*Seemannsspr.*) head; **auf etw. (*Akk.*) ~**: head for *or* towards sth.; **G** (*sich beherrschen*) **an sich (*Akk.*) ~**: control oneself; **H** (*achten*) **auf Ordnung ~**: attach importance to tidiness; **auf sich (*Akk.*) ~**: take a pride in oneself.

**3** *unr. refl. V.* **A** (*sich durchsetzen, behaupten*) **wir werden uns/die Stadt wird sich nicht länger ~ können** we/the town won't be able to hold out much longer; **das Geschäft wird sich nicht ~ können** the shop won't keep going [for long]; **der neue Regisseur konnte sich nicht ~**: the new director didn't last; **B** (*sich bewähren*) **sich gut ~**: do well; make a good showing; **halte dich tapfer** be brave; **C** (*unverändert bleiben*) ‹weather, flowers, etc.› last; ‹milk, meat, etc.› keep; **D** (*Körperhaltung haben*) **sich schlecht/gerade/aufrecht ~**: hold *or* carry oneself badly/straight/erect; **E** (*bleiben*) **sich auf den Beinen/im Sattel ~**: stay on one's feet/in the saddle; **F** (*gehen, bleiben*) **sich links/rechts ~**: keep [to the] left/right; **sich südwärts/in Richtung Bahnhof ~**: keep going south/towards the station; **sich an jmds. Seite (*Dat.*)/hinter jmdm. ~**: stay *or* keep next to/behind sb.; **G** (*befolgen*) **sich an etw. (*Akk.*) ~**: keep to *or* follow sth.; **der Film hat sich nicht eng an den Roman ge~**: the film didn't keep *or* stick closely to the book; **H** (*sich wenden*) **sich an jmdn. ~**: ask sb.; **halte dich an Peter, der ist immer hilfsbereit** stay *or* stick with Peter — he's always helpful; **I** (*ugs.: jung, gesund bleiben*) **sie hat sich gut ge~**: she is well preserved for her age (*coll.*)

**Halte-: ~platz** *der* [taxi] rank (*Brit.*); [cab] stand (*Amer.*); **~punkt** *der* stop

**Halter** *der;* **~s, ~ A** (*Fahrzeug~*) keeper; **B** (*Tier~*) owner; **C** (*Vorrichtung*) holder; (*Handtuch~*) towel rail; **D** (*ugs.: Feder~*) pen; **E** (*österr.*) ⇒ **Viehhirt**

**Halterin** *die;* **~, ~nen** ⇒ **Halter** A, B

**Halterung** *die;* **~, ~en** support

**Halte-: ~seil** *das* supporting cable; (*eines Ballons*) mooring cable; **~signal** *das* stop signal; **~stelle** *die* stop; **~verbot** *das* **A „~verbot"** 'no stopping'; **auf dieser Straße besteht ~verbot** stopping is prohibited in this street; **„absolutes/eingeschränktes ~verbot"** 'no stopping/no waiting'; **B** (*Stelle*) no-stopping zone; **hier ist ~verbot** this is a no-stopping zone; **~verbots·schild** *das* no-stopping sign; **~vorrichtung** *die* ⇒ **Halterung**

**-haltig** /-haltɪç/, (*österr.*) **-hältig** /-hɛltɪç/ **vitamin~/silber~** *usw.* containing vitamins/silver *etc. postpos., not pred.*; **vitamin~ sein** contain vitamins

**halt-, Halt-: ~los** *Adj.* **A** (*labil*) **~los sein** be a weak character; **ein ~loser Mensch** a weak character; **B** (*unbegründet*) unfounded; **~losigkeit** *die;* **~~ A** (*Labilität*) weakness of character; **B** (*mangelnde Begründung*) unfoundedness; ***~|machen** ⇒ **Halt** B

**Haltung** *die;* **~, ~en A** (*Körper~*) posture; (*Sport*) stance; (*in der Bewegung*) style; **~ annehmen** (*Milit.*) stand to attention; **B** (*Pose*) manner; **C** (*Einstellung*) attitude; **D** (*Fassung*) composure; **~ zeigen/bewahren** keep one's composure; **E** (*Tier~*) keeping

**Haltungs-: ~fehler** *der* **A** (*Med.*) bad posture; **B** (*Sport*) style fault; **~schaden** *der* (*Med.*) bad posture; **~schäden** bad posture

**Halt·verbot** *das* ⇒ **Halteverbot**

**Halunke** /ha'lʊnkə/ *der;* **~n, ~n A** (*Schurke*) scoundrel; villain; **B** (*scherzh.: Lausbub*) rascal; scamp

**Hämatit** /hɛma'ti:t/ *der;* **~s, ~e** (*Geol.*) haematite

**Hämatologe** /hɛmato'lo:gə/ *der;* **~n, ~n** (*Med.*) haematologist

**Hämatologie** *die;* **~** (*Med.*) haematology *no art.*

**Hämatologin** *die;* **~, ~nen** ⇒ **Hämatologe**

**Hämatom** /hɛma'to:m/ *das;* **~s, ~e** (*Med.*) haematoma

**Hamburg** /'hambʊrk/ (*das*)*;* **~s ▶ 700** Hamburg

**Hamburger[1] ▶ 700 1** *der;* **~s, ~**: native of Hamburg; (*Einwohner*) inhabitant of Hamburg; **Schmidt ist ~**: Schmidt comes from Hamburg. **2** *indekl. Adj.* Hamburg; **der ~ Hafen** the harbour at Hamburg; Hamburg harbour; ⇒ *auch* **Kölner**

**Hamburger[2]** *der;* **~s, ~** *od.* **~s** (*Frikadelle*) hamburger

**hamburgern** *itr. V.* speak Hamburg dialect

**hamburgisch** *Adj.* Hamburg *attrib.*; of Hamburg *postpos.*

**Häme** /'hɛ:mə/ *die;* **~**: malice

**Hameln** /'ha:mln̩/ (*das*)*;* **~s** Hamelin; **der Rattenfänger von ~**: the Pied Piper of Hamelin

**hämisch** /'hɛ:mɪʃ/ **1** *Adj.* malicious. **2** *adv.* maliciously

**Hammel** /'haml̩/ *der;* **~s, ~ A** wether; **B** (*Fleisch*) mutton; **C** (*salopp abwertend*) oaf; dolt

**Hammel-: ~bein** *das:* **in jmdm. die ~beine lang ziehen** (*ugs.*) give sb. a good telling-off; **~fleisch** *das* mutton; **~herde** *die* (*salopp abwertend*) flock of sheep; **~keule** *die* leg of mutton; **~sprung** *der* (*Parl.*) division

**Hammer** /'hamɐ/ *der;* **~s, Hämmer** /'hɛmɐ/ **A** hammer; (*Holz~*) mallet; (*Eis~*) hammer axe; (*eines Auktionators*) hammer; gavel; **~ und Sichel** hammer and sickle; **~ und Zirkel** hammer and compasses (*on the GDR national flag*); **unter den ~ kommen** come under the hammer; **etw. unter den ~ bringen** auction sth.; **B** (*Technik*) tup; ram; **C** (*Musik*) hammer; **D** (*Leichtathletik*) hammer; **E** (*ugs.: Fehler*) bad mistake; (*in einer Aufgabe*) howler (*coll.*); **ein dicker ~**: an awful blunder; **er hat einen ~**: he must be round the bend (*coll.*) *or* (*sl.*) twist; **F** (*ugs.: Überraschung, Clou*) real surprise; **das ist ein ~!** (*großartig*) that's fantastic! (*coll.*); (*unerhört*) that's quite outrageous!; **G ▶ 471** (*Anat.*) hammer; malleus

**Hämmerchen** /'hɛmɐçən/ *das;* **~s, ~**: [small] hammer

**hammer-, Hammer-: ~förmig** *Adj.* hammer-shaped; **~hai** *der* hammerhead [shark]; **~klavier** *das* (*veralt.*) pianoforte; **~kopf** *der* (*auch Leichtathletik, Musik*) hammerhead

**hämmern** /'hɛmɐn/ **1** *itr. V.* **A** hammer; **es hämmert** sb. is hammering; **B** (*schlagen*) hammer; (*mit der Faust*) hammer; pound; **gegen die Wand/die Tür ~**: hammer/

pound on the wall/door; **C** (*klopfen*) pound; ‹pulse› race. **2** *tr. V.* **A** hammer; beat, hammer ‹tin, silver, etc.›; beat ‹jewellery›; **B** (*ugs.*) hammer *or* pound out ‹melody etc.›; **C** (*ugs.: einprägen*) **jmdm. etw. in den Schädel ~:** hammer *or* knock sth. into sb.'s head (*coll.*); **D** (*Fußballjargon*) hammer, slam ‹ball›

**Hammer-: ~schlag** *der* **A** hammer blow; blow from a/the hammer; **B** (*Boxen*) rabbit punch; **C** (*Faustball*) smash; **D** (*Technik*) hammer scale; **~stiel** *der* handle *or* shaft of a/the hammer; **~werfen** *das;* **~~s** (*Leichtathletik*) throwing the hammer; **er ist Weltmeister im ~werfen** he's world champion in the hammer; **~werfer** *der* (*Leichtathletik*) hammer-thrower; **~werk** *das* **A** (*veralt.*) hammer mill; **B** (*Musik*) striking mechanism; **~wurf** *der* (*Leichtathletik*) **A** ⇒ **~werfen**; **B** (*einzelner Wurf*) hammer throw; **~zehe** *die* hammer toe

**Hammond·orgel** /'hæmənd-/ *die* Hammond organ

**Hämoglobin** /hɛmoglo'bi:n/ *das;* **~s** (*Physiol.*) haemoglobin

**Hämorrhoiden** /hɛmɔro'i:dn̩/ *Pl.* (*Med.*) haemorrhoids; piles

**Hämozyt** /hɛmo'ts̮y:t/ *der;* **~en, ~en** (*Physiol.*) haemocyte

**Hampelei** *die;* **~** (*ugs. abwertend*) fidgeting

**Hampel·mann** /'hampl̩-/ *der* **A** jumping jack; **B** (*ugs. abwertend*) puppet; **jmdn. zu einem/seinem ~ machen** make sb. one's puppet; **C** (*Gymnastik*) side-straddle hop; jumping jack

**hampeln** *itr. V.* (*ugs.*) jump about

**Hamster** /'hamstɐ/ *der;* **~s, ~:** hamster

**Hamster·backen** *Pl.* chubby cheeks

**Hamsterer** *der;* **~s, ~** (*ugs.*) hoarder

**Hamster·fahrt** *die* foraging trip; **auf ~ gehen** go foraging

**Hamsterin** *die;* **~, ~nen** ⇒ **Hamsterer**

**Hamster·kauf** *der* panic-buying *no pl.;* **Hamsterkäufe machen** panic-buy

**hamstern** *tr., itr. V.* **A** (*horten*) hoard; (*Hamsterkäufe machen*) panic-buy; **B** (*Lebensmittel tauschen*) barter goods for food

**Hand** /hant/ *die;* **~, Hände** /'hɛndə/ **A** ▶ **471** hand; **mit der rechten/linken ~:** with one's right/left hand; **jmdm. die ~ geben** *od.* (*geh.*) **reichen** shake sb.'s hand; shake sb. by the hand; **jmdm. die ~ drücken/schütteln** press/shake sb.'s hand; **eine ~ frei haben** have a free hand; **ich habe keine ~ frei** my hands are full; **Hände hoch!** hands up!; **jmdm. die ~ küssen** kiss sb.'s hand; **jmdn. an die** *od.* (*geh.*) **bei der ~ nehmen** take sb. by the hand; **jmdm. etw. aus der ~ nehmen** take sth. out of sb.'s hand/hands; **etw. aus der ~ legen** put sth. down; **jmdm. aus der ~ lesen** read sb.'s hand *or* palm; **etw. in die/zur ~ nehmen** pick sth. up; **etw. in der ~/den Händen haben** *od.* (*geh.*) **halten** have got *or* hold sth. in one's hand/hands; **in die Hände klatschen** clap one's hands; **mit Händen und Füßen reden** use gestures to make oneself understood; **etw. mit der ~ schreiben/nähen** write/sew sth. by hand; **von ~:** by hand; **~ in ~ gehen** go *or* walk hand-in-hand; **eine Sonate für vier Hände** *od.* **zu vier Händen** a four-handed sonata; **jmdm. etw. in die ~ versprechen** promise sb. sth. faithfully; **eine ~/ein paar Hände voll Sand** a handful/a couple of handfuls of sand; **B** (*Fußball*) handball; **C** (*Boxen*) punch; **D** (*veralt., geh.: ~schrift*) hand; **E** (*österr. ugs.: Arm*) arm; **F** (*in Wendungen*) **was hältst du davon — ~ aufs Herz!** what do you think? — be honest; **~ aufs Herz, ich habe ihn nicht gesehen** I haven't seen him, word of honour *or* (*coll.*) cross my heart; **eine ~ wäscht die andere** you scratch my back and I'll scratch yours; **Zuschüsse von öffentlicher ~:** subsidies from government funds *or* from the government; **die öffentlichen Hände** the local/regional authorities; **jmds. rechte ~:** sb's right-hand man; **ihm rutschte die ~ aus** (*ugs.*) he couldn't stop himself [hitting her/him *etc.* ]; **jmdm. sind die Hände gebunden** sb.'s hands are tied; **~ und Fuß/weder ~ noch Fuß haben** (*ugs.*) make sense/no sense; **[bei etw. selbst mit] ~ anlegen** lend a hand [with sth.]; **die** *od.* **seine ~ aufhalten** *od.* **hinhalten** (*ugs.*) hold out one's hand; **jmds. ~ ausschlagen** (*veralt. geh.*) reject sb.; **keine ~ rühren** (*ugs.*) not lift a finger; **~ an sich legen** (*geh.*) take one's own life; **letzte ~ an etw.** (*Akk.*) **legen** put the finishing touches *pl.* to sth.; **jmdm. die ~ [zum Bund] fürs Leben reichen** (*geh.*) marry sb.; **sich** (*Dat.*) *od.* (*geh.*) **einander die ~ reichen können** be tarred with the same brush; **dann können wir uns die ~ reichen** snap!; shake!; **alle** *od.* **beide Hände damit voll haben, etw. zu tun** (*ugs.*) have one's hands full doing sth.; **er hat alle Hände voll zu tun** he's got his hands full; **sich** (*Dat.*) **die ~ für jmdn./etw. abhacken** *od.* **abschlagen lassen** (*ugs.*) do anything for sb./stake one's life on sth.; **jmdm. auf etw.** (*Akk.*) **die ~ geben** promise sb. sth.; **die Hände in den Schoß legen** sit back and do nothing; **bei etw. die** *od.* **seine Hände [mit] im Spiel haben** have a hand in sth.; **überall seine ~** *od.* **Hände im Spiel haben** have a finger in every pie; **die Hände über dem Kopf zusammenschlagen** (*ugs.*) throw up one's hands in horror; **die** *od.* **seine ~ über jmdn. halten** (*geh.*) protect sb.; **zwei linke Hände haben** (*ugs.*) have two left hands (*coll.*); **eine lockere** *od.* **lose ~ haben** (*ugs.*) hit out at the slightest provocation; **eine offene ~ haben** be open-handed; **eine glückliche ~ bei etw. haben** have a feel for the right choice in sth.; **dabei hat er eine glückliche ~ gehabt** he intuitively made the right choice; **eine glückliche ~ in etw.** (*Dat.*) **haben** have the right knack for sth.; **im Umgang mit Kindern hat er eine glückliche ~:** he's very good *or* has a way with children; **sie hat in solchen Dingen eine glückliche ~:** she has a [natural] flair for such things; **eine grüne ~ haben** (*ugs.*) have green fingers; **linker/rechter ~:** on *or* to the left/right; **an ~** (+ *Gen.*) with the help of; **an ~ dieses Berichts** from this report; **jmdm. etw. an die ~ geben** make sth. available to sb.; **jmdn. an der ~ haben** (*ugs.*) know [of] sb.; **[klar] auf der ~ liegen** (*ugs.*) be obvious; **jmdn. auf Händen tragen** lavish every kind of care and attention on sb.; **Möbel/ein Auto aus erster ~:** furniture/a car which has/had had one [previous] owner; **etw. aus erster ~ wissen** know sth. at first hand; have first-hand knowledge of sth.; **Kleidung aus zweiter ~:** second-hand clothes *pl.;* **das Auto ist aus zweiter ~:** the car has had two [previous] owners; **Leihgaben aus** *od.* **von privater ~:** loans from private collections; **jmdm. aus der ~ fressen** eat out of sb.'s hand (*fig.*); **etw. aus der ~ geben** (*weggeben*) let sth. out of one's hands; (*aufgeben*) give sth. up; **[aus der] ~ spielen** (*Skat*) play without using the widow *or* skat; **jmdm. etw. aus der ~ nehmen** relieve sb. of sth.; **etw. bei der ~ haben** (*greifbar haben*) have sth. handy; (*parat haben*) have sth. ready; **mit etw. schnell** *od.* **rasch bei der ~ sein** (*ugs.*) be ready with sth.; **[schon** *od.* **bereits] durch viele Hände gegangen sein** have been *or* have [been] passed through many hands; **die Vera ist schon durch viele Hände gegangen** (*ugs.*) she's been around a bit, has Vera (*coll.*); **~ in ~ arbeiten** work hand in hand; **Regierung und Rauschgifthändler arbeiteten ~ in ~:** the government and the drug dealers were working hand in glove; **mit etw. ~ in ~ gehen** go hand in hand with sth.; **hinter vorgehaltener ~:** off the record; **in die Hände spucken** spit on one's hands; (*fig. ugs.*) roll up one's sleeves (*fig.*); **jmdm./einer Sache in die Hände arbeiten** play into sb.'s hands/help bring sth. about; **jmdn./etw. in die ~** *od.* **Hände bekommen** *od.* **kriegen** lay *or* get one's hands on sb./get one's hands on sth.; **jmdm. in die Hände fallen** fall into sb.'s hands; **etw. in der ~ haben** have sth.; **jmdn. in der ~ haben** have *or* hold sb. in the palm of one's hand; **etw. in Händen halten** hold sth.; **etw. in jmds. ~** *od.* **Hände legen** (*geh.*) put sth. in sb.'s hands; **etw. in die ~ nehmen** take sth. in hand; **in jmds. ~** (*Dat.*) **sein** *od.* (*geh.*) **liegen** be in sb.'s hands; **in festen Händen sein** (*ugs.*) be spoken for *or* attached; **in sicheren** *od.* **guten Händen sein, sich in guten Händen befinden** be in safe *or* good hands; **jmdm. Informationen** *usw.* **in die ~** *od.* **Hände spielen** pass information *etc.* to sb.; **in jmds. ~** *od.* **Hände übergehen** pass into sb.'s hands; **mit Händen zu greifen sein** be as plain as a pikestaff; be perfectly obvious; **mit beiden Händen zugreifen** grab *or* seize the opportunity with both hands; **sich mit Händen und Füßen gegen etw. sträuben** *od.* **wehren** (*ugs.*) fight tooth and nail against sth.; **mit leeren Händen** empty-handed; **das mache ich mit der linken ~** (*ugs.*) I could do that with my eyes closed; **mit starker** *od.* **fester ~:** with a firm hand; **das Geld mit vollen Händen ausgeben** spend money like water; **um jmds. ~ anhalten** *od.* **bitten** (*geh. veralt.*) ask for sb.'s hand [in marriage]; **etw. unter den Händen haben** be working on sth.; **unter der ~:** on the quiet; **etw. unter der ~ erfahren** hear sth. through the grapevine; **jmdm. etw. unter der ~ mitteilen** tell sb. sth. secretly; **von jmds. ~ sterben** (*geh.*) die at sb.'s hand; **das geht ihm gut/leicht von der ~:** he finds that no trouble; **etw. von langer ~ vorbereiten** plan sth. well in advance; **die Nachteile/seine Argumente lassen sich nicht von der ~ weisen** *od.* **sind nicht von der ~ zu weisen** the disadvantages cannot be denied/his arguments cannot [simply] be dismissed; **von der ~ in den Mund leben** live from hand to mouth; **von ~ zu ~ gehen** be passed from hand to hand; **etw. zu treuen Händen nehmen** take sth. into one's care; **jmdm. etw. zu treuen Händen geben** give sth. to sb. for safe keeping; **zur linken/rechten ~:** on *or* to the left/right[-hand side]; **etw. zur ~ haben** have sth. handy; **ich habe kein Kleingeld zur ~:** I haven't got any change on me; **jmdm. zur ~ gehen** lend sb. a hand; **zu Händen [von] Herrn Müller** for the attention of Herr Müller; attention Herr Müller; ⇒ *auch* **öffentlich 1**

**hand-, Hand-: ~ab·zug** *der* **A** (*Druckw.*) proof pulled by hand; **B** (*Fot.*) print made by hand; **~akte** *die* file; **~apparat** *der* **A** (*Fernspr.*) handset; **B** (*Bücher*) set of reference books; reference collection; **~arbeit** *die* **A** handicraft; craft work; **etw. in ~arbeit herstellen** make sth. by hand; **B** (*Gegenstand*) handmade article; **das ist eine ~arbeit** that is handmade *or* made by hand; **C** (*Arbeit aus Stoff, Wolle usw.*) [piece of] needlework; (*gestrickt*) [piece of] knitting; (*gehäkelt*) [piece of] crocheting; **sie macht gerne ~arbeiten** she likes doing needlework/knitting/crocheting; **D** (*ugs.: ~arbeitsunterricht*) needlework; **~arbeiten** *itr. V.* do needlework; **ich kann nicht gut ~arbeiten** I am not very good at needlework; **~arbeiter** *der,* **~arbeiterin** *die* manual worker

**Handarbeits-: ~geschäft** *das* wool and needlework shop; **~korb** *der* workbasket; **~lehrerin** *die* needlework teacher

**Hand-: ~aufheben** *das* (*bei einer Wahl*) show of hands; **sich durch ~aufheben melden** put one's hand up to speak/answer; **~auflegen** *das;* **~~s** (*bes. Rel.*) laying on *or* imposition of hands

**Hand·ball** *der* **A** (*Spiel*) handball; **B** (*Ball*) handball

**Hand·ballen** *der* ▶ **471** ball of the thumb

**Hand·baller** *der;* **~s, ~, Hand·ballerin** *die;* **~, ~nen** (*ugs.*) handball player

**Handball-: ~mannschaft** *die* handball team; **~spiel** *das* **A** handball match; **B** (*Sportart*) **das ~spiel** the game of handball; **~spieler** *der,* **~spielerin** *die* handball player

*old spelling (see note on page 1707)

**hand-, Hand-: ~bedienung** *die* manual operation; **eine Maschine mit ~bedienung** a manually operated *or* hand-operated machine; **~besen** *der* brush; **~betrieb** *der* manual operation; **mit ~betrieb** manually operated; hand-operated; **~betrieben** *Adj.* manually operated; hand-operated; **~bewegung** *die* Ⓐ movement of the hand; Ⓑ (*Geste*) gesture; **~bibliothek** *die* Ⓐ reference library; Ⓑ (*~apparat*) set of reference books; reference collection; **~bohrer** *der* (*mit Kurbel*) hand-drill; (*zum Vorbohren*) gimlet; **~bohr·maschine** *die* hand-drill; (*elektrisch*) drill; **~brause** *die* shower handset; **~breit** ❶ *Adj.* ‹seam etc.› a few inches wide; **ein ~breiter Abstand** a gap of a few inches; ❷ *adv.* a few inches; **~breit** *die*; **~~, ~~: eine/zwei ~breit** a few/several inches; **keine ~breit** barely an inch; **~breite** *die*: **ein Abstand/Streifen von einer ~breite** a gap of a few inches/a strip a few inches wide; **~bremse** *die* handbrake; **~buch** *das* handbook; (*technisches ~buch*) manual

**Händchen** /ˈhɛntçən/ *das*; **~s, ~:** [little] hand; **~ halten** (*ugs. scherzh.*) hold hands; **ein ~ haltendes junges Paar** a young couple holding hands; **für etw. ein ~ haben** (*fig. ugs.*) have a knack for sth.; be good at sth.

**Händchen·halten** *das*; **~s** (*ugs. scherzh.*) holding hands *no art.*

***händchen·haltend** ⇨ **Händchen**

**Hand·creme** *die* hand cream

**Hände** ⇨ **Hand**

**Hände-: ~druck** *der*; *Pl.* **~drücke** handshake; **~klatschen** *das*; **~~s** clapping; applause

**Handel**[1] /ˈhandl̩/ *der*; **~s** Ⓐ (*Wirtschaft*) trade; commerce; **~ und Industrie/~ und Gewerbe** trade and industry; Ⓑ (*~n*) trade; **der ~ mit Waffen/Drogen** the traffic in arms/drugs; Ⓒ (*Geschäftsverkehr*) trade; **der internationale/überseeische ~:** international/overseas trade; **~ treiben** trade; **~ treibend** trading ‹nation›; ‹tribe› engaged primarily in trade; **ein Produkt aus dem ~ ziehen** take a product off the market; **in den ~ kommen** come on [to] the market; **das ist [nicht mehr] im ~:** it is [no longer] on the market; **~ und Wandel** (*veralt.*) commercial and social life; Ⓓ (*veralt.: Geschäft*) business; Ⓔ (*Vereinbarung*) deal

**Handel**[2] *der*; **~s, Händel** /ˈhɛndl̩/ (*geh.*) quarrel; **einen ~ [mit jmdm.] austragen** settle a quarrel [with sb.]; **Händel anfangen/suchen** start/ [try to] pick a quarrel

**Hand·elfmeter** *der* (*Fußball*) penalty for handball

**handeln** ❶ *itr. V.* Ⓐ trade; deal; **mit** *od.* **in Gemüse/Gebrauchtwagen ~:** deal in vegetables/second-hand cars; **mit Waffen/Drogen ~:** traffic in arms/drugs; **mit jmdm. ~:** trade *or* deal with sb.; **en gros/en detail ~:** be in the wholesale/retail trade; **wir ~ en gros mit Spielwaren** we are toy wholesalers; Ⓑ (*feilschen*) haggle; bargain; **um den Preis ~:** haggle over the price; **mit ihm lässt sich [nicht] ~:** he is [not] open to negotiation; **er lässt nicht mit sich ~:** it's impossible to bargain with him; Ⓒ (*eingreifen*) act; **auf Befehl/aus Überzeugung ~:** act on orders/out of conviction; **im Affekt/in Notwehr ~:** act in the heat of the moment/in self-defence; Ⓓ (*verfahren*) act; **eigenmächtig/richtig/fahrlässig ~:** act on one's own authority/correctly/carelessly; Ⓔ (*sich verhalten*) behave; **gut/schlecht an jmdm.** *od.* **gegen jmdn. ~:** behave well/badly towards sb.; Ⓕ **von etw.** *od.* **über etw.** (*Akk.*) **~** ‹book, film, etc.› be about *or* deal with sth. ❷ *refl. V.* (*unpers.*) **bei dem Besucher handelte es sich um einen entfernten Verwandten** the visitor was a distant relative; **es handelt sich um ...** it is a matter of ...; (*es dreht sich um*) it's about *or* it concerns ...; **es handelt sich darum, dass die Presse nichts davon erfährt** the important thing is that the press should not get wind of it. ❸ *tr. V.* sell (**für** at, for); **diese Papiere werden nicht an der Börse gehandelt** these securities are not traded on the stock exchange; **der US-Dollar wird jetzt zu 2 DM gehandelt** the US dollar is now valued at 2 marks

**Handeln** *das*; **~s** Ⓐ (*das Feilschen*) haggling; bargaining; Ⓑ (*das Eingreifen*) action; Ⓒ (*Verhalten*) action[s *pl.* ]

**handels-, Handels-: ~abkommen** *das* trade agreement; **~agent** *der*, **~agentin** *die* (*österr.*) ⇨ **~vertreter**; **~akademie** *die* (*österr.*) commercial college; **~artikel** *der* commodity; **~attaché** *der* commercial attaché; **~bank** *die*; *Pl.* **~~en** merchant bank; **~beschränkung** *die* trade restriction; **~beziehungen** *Pl.* trade relations; **~bilanz** *die* Ⓐ (*eines Betriebes*) balance sheet; Ⓑ (*eines Staates*) balance of trade; **eine aktive/passive ~bilanz** a balance of trade surplus/deficit; **~boykott** *der* trade boycott; **~delegation** *die* trade delegation; **~einig, ~eins** *in* **mit jmdm. ~einig** *od.* **~eins werden/sein** agree/have agreed terms *or* come/have come to an agreement with sb.; **~firma** *die* [business *or* commercial] firm; business concern; **~flagge** *die* merchant flag; **~flotte** *die* merchant fleet; **~geist** *der* business acumen *or* sense; **~gericht** *das* commercial court; **~gesellschaft** *die* company; **offene ~gesellschaft** general partnership; **~gesetz** *das* commercial law; **~gesetzbuch** *das* commercial code; **~größe** *die* (*Kaufmannsspr.*) commercial size; **~hafen** *der* commercial *or* trading port; **~haus** *das* (*veralt.*) business house; firm; **~kammer** *die* ⇨ **Industrie- und Handelskammer**; **~kette** *die* (*Kaufmannsspr.*) Ⓐ (*Weg der Ware*) channel of distribution; Ⓑ (*Zusammenschluss von Händlern*) voluntary chain; **~klasse** *die* grade; **~kontor** *das* (*hist.*) branch; **~korrespondenz** *die* business correspondence; **~lehrer** *der*, **~lehrerin** *die* teacher of commercial subjects; **~macht** *die* trading power; **~marine** *die* merchant navy; **~marke** *die* trade mark; **~messe** *die* trade fair; **~metropole** *die* commercial metropolis *or* centre; **~minister** *der*, **~ministerin** *die* minister of trade; (*in UK*) Secretary of State for Trade; Trade Secretary (*coll.*); **~ministerium** *das* ministry of trade; (*in UK*) Department of Trade; **~mission** *die* trade mission; **~monopol** *das* trading monopoly; **~name** *der* trade *or* business name; **~nation** *die* trading nation; **~niederlassung** *die* branch; **~organ** *das* (*DDR*) branch; **~organisation** *die* Ⓐ trading organization; Ⓑ (*DDR*) [*state-owned*] *commercial concern running shops, hotels, etc.*; **~partner** *der*, **~partnerin** *die* trading partner; **~politik** *die* trade *or* commercial policy; **~politisch** ❶ *Adj.* relating to trade *or* commercial policy *postpos.*; **vom ~politischen Standpunkt** from the point of view of trade *or* commercial policy; ❷ *adv.* as far as trade *or* commercial policy is concerned; **~recht** *das* commercial law; **~rechtlich** ❶ *Adj.* relating to commercial law *postpos.*; ‹offence› against commercial law; ❷ *adv.* from the point of view of commercial law; **es ist ~rechtlich nicht erlaubt** it is not allowed under commercial law; **~register** *das* register of companies; **~reisende** *der/die* ⇨ **~vertreter**; **~schiff** *das* merchant ship; trading vessel; ***~schiffahrt, ~schifffahrt** *die* merchant shipping; (*Schiffsverkehr*) movement of merchant shipping; **~schranke** *die* trade barrier; **~schule** *die* commercial college; **~schüler** *der*, **~schülerin** *die* student at a commercial college; **~schul·lehrer** *der*, **~schul·lehrerin** *die* teacher at a commercial college; **~spanne** *die* (*Kaufmannsspr.*) margin; **~sperre** *die* trade embargo; **~sprache** *die* trade language; language of commerce; **~stadt** *die* trading town; (*Großstadt*) trading city; **~straße** *die* (*hist.*) trade route; **~üblich** *Adj.* **~übliche Praktiken/Größen** normal *or* standard business practices/standard [commercial] sizes; **~üblich sein** be normal *or* standard business practice

**Händel·sucht** *die* (*geh. veralt.*) quarrelsomeness

**händel·süchtig** *Adj.* (*geh. veralt.*) quarrelsome

**Handels-: ~unternehmen** *das* trading concern; **~verbindung** *die* trade link; **~vertrag** *der* trade agreement; **~vertreter** *der*, **~vertreterin** *die* ▸ 159 [sales] representative; travelling salesmann/saleswoman; commercial traveller; **~vertretung** *die* ⇨ **~mission**; **~volumen** *das* (*Wirtsch.*) volume of trade; **~ware** *die* commodity; **„keine ~ware"** (*Postw.*) 'no commercial value'; **~weg** *der* Ⓐ commercial artery; Ⓑ (*Weg der Ware*) channel of distribution; **~wert** *der* (*Kaufmannsspr.*) commercial value; **~zentrum** *das* trading *or* commercial centre

***handel·treibend** ⇨ **Handel** C

**hände-, Hände-: ~ringend** *Adv.* Ⓐ wringing one's hands; Ⓑ (*ugs.: dringend*) **~ringend suchen** need urgently; **~ringend nach jmdm./etw. suchen** search desperately for sb./sth.; **~schütteln** *das*; **~~s** hand-shaking *no pl.*; **die ersten zehn Minuten vergingen mit ~schütteln** the first ten minutes were spent shaking hands; **~trockner** *der* hand-drier; **~waschen** *das*; **~~s** washing *no art.* one's hands; **sie ging zum ~waschen ins Bad** she went to the bathroom to wash her hands

**hand-, Hand-: ~feger** *der* brush; **herumlaufen wie ein wild gewordener ~feger** (*salopp*) (*zerzaust*) go round looking like a scarecrow; (*aufgeregt*) run around madly; **~fertigkeit** *die* [manual] dexterity; **~fest** ❶ *Adj.* Ⓐ (*kräftig*) robust; sturdy; Ⓑ (*deftig*) substantial ‹meal etc.›; **etwas ~festes** something substantial; Ⓒ (*gewichtig*) solid, tangible ‹proof›; concrete ‹suggestion›; full-blooded, violent ‹row›; complete ‹lie›; well-founded ‹argument›; real, thorough ‹beating›; ❷ *adv.* (*deutlich*) ‹criticize› severely; **er hat mich ~fest belogen/betrogen** he told me a complete lie/it was an out-and-out deception; **~feuerlöscher** *der* hand fire extinguisher; **~feuer·waffe** *die* handgun; **~feuerwaffen** small arms; **~fläche** *die* ▸ 471 palm [of one's/the hand]; flat of one's/the hand; **~galopp** *der* (*Reiten*) canter; hand gallop; **~gas** *das* (*Kfz-W.*) hand throttle; **mit ~gas fahren** drive using the hand throttle; **~gearbeitet** *Adj.* hand-made ‹furniture, jewellery, etc.›; **~gefertigt** *Adj.* hand-made; **~geknüpft** *Adj.* handwoven; **~geld** *das* lump sum [payment]; **~gelenk** *das* ▸ 471 wrist; **ein loses** *od.* **lockeres ~gelenk haben** (*ugs.*) lash out at the slightest provocation; **aus dem ~gelenk [heraus]** (*ugs.*) (*unvermittelt*) offhand; (*ohne Mühe*) effortlessly; as easily as anything (*coll.*); **etw. aus dem ~gelenk schütteln** (*ugs.*) do sth. just like that (*coll.*); **~gemacht** *Adj.* handmade; **~gemalt** *Adj.* hand-painted; **~gemenge** *das* Ⓐ fight; Ⓑ (*Milit.*) hand-to-hand fighting *no indef. art.*; **~gepäck** *das* hand baggage; **~geschliffen** *Adj.* hand-cut; **~geschmiedet** *Adj.* hand-wrought; **~geschöpft** *Adj.* handmade; **~geschrieben** *Adj.* handwritten; **~gesponnen** *Adj.* hand-spun; **~gesteuert** *Adj.* manually operated; manually controlled ‹vehicle›; **~gestrickt** *Adj.* hand-knitted; (*fig. abwertend*) half-baked ‹idea, theory, etc.›; **~gewebt** *Adj.* handwoven; **~granate** *die* hand grenade; **~greiflich** ❶ *Adj.* Ⓐ (*tätlich*) **eine ~greifliche Auseinandersetzung** a scuffle; **~greiflich werden** start using one's fists; Ⓑ tangible ‹success, advantage, proof, etc.›; palpable ‹contradiction, error›; obvious ‹fact›; ❷ *adv.* Ⓐ (*tätlich*) **sich ~greiflich auseinander setzen** come to blows; Ⓑ (*konkret fassbar*) clearly; **~greiflichkeit** *die*; **~~, ~~en** Ⓐ (*eines Beweises*) tangibility; (*eines Widerspruchs, Fehlers*) palpability; Ⓑ (*Tätlichkeit*) scuffle; fight; **es kam zu/nicht zu ~greiflichkeiten** a fight broke out/there was no violence; **~griff** *der* Ⓐ **ein falscher ~griff** a false move; **ein geschickter ~griff, und ...** one deft action and ...; **mit einem ~griff/wenigen ~griffen** in one movement/without much trouble; (*schnell*) in

h

no time at all/next to no time; **jeder ~griff muss sitzen** every movement must be exactly right; **keinen ~griff [für jmdn.] tun** (*fig.*) not do anything to help sb.; **B** (*am Koffer, an einem Werkzeug*) handle; **C** (*Haltegriff*) grab handle; **~groß** *Adj.* ‹hole, wound, etc.› the size of a hand; **~habbar** /-ha:pba:ɐ̯/ *Adj.* handy; **kaum ~habbar** very difficult *or* awkward to manage; very unwieldy; **~habe** *die;* **~~**, **~~n: eine [rechtliche] ~habe [gegen jmdn.]** a legal handle [against sb.]; **~haben** *tr. V.* **A** handle; operate ‹device, machine›; **B** (*praktizieren*) implement ‹law etc.›; **~habung** *die;* **~~**, **~~en A** handling; (*eines Gerätes, einer Maschine*) operation; **B** (*Durchführung*) implementation; **~harmonika** *die* accordion

**Handikap** /ˈhɛndikɛp/ *das;* **~s**, **~s** (*auch Sport*) handicap

**handikapen** /ˈhɛndikɛpn̩/ *tr. V.* handicap

**händisch** /ˈhɛndɪʃ/ (*österr. ugs.*) **1** *Adj.* manual. **2** *adv.* manually; by hand

**Hand-: ~kamera** *die* hand camera; **~kante** *die* edge of the/one's hand

**Handkanten·schlag** *der* chop

**hand-, Hand-: ~karre** *die*, **~karren** *der* handcart; **~käse** *der* (*landsch.*) *small, hand-formed curd cheese;* **~käse mit Musik** (*landsch.*) marinaded hand-formed curd cheese; **~koffer** *der* [small] suitcase; **~koloriert** *Adj.* hand-coloured; **~kurbel** *die* [hand-]crank; **~kuss**, ***~kuß** *der* kiss on sb.'s hand; **etw. mit ~kuss [an]nehmen/tun** accept/do sth. with [the greatest of] pleasure; **~lampe** *die* hand-lamp; inspection lamp

**Hand·langer** *der;* **~s**, **~**, **Hand·langerin** *die;* **~**, **~nen A** (*Hilfsarbeiter[in]*) labourer; **B** (*abwertend*) lackey; general dogsbody; **C** (*abwertend: Büttel*) henchman/henchwoman

**Handlanger·dienst** *der* (*abwertend*) **für jmdn. ~e leisten** do sb.'s dirty work for him/her

**Hand·lauf** *der* handrail

**Händler** /ˈhɛndlɐ/ *der;* **~s**, **~:** trader; tradesman/tradeswoman; **ein fliegender ~:** ▶ 159 a hawker *or* street trader

**-händler** *der* ‹cattle-, furniture-, scrap-, stamp-› dealer; ‹coal-, corn-, scrap-, timber, wine›merchant

**Händlerin** *die;* **~**, **~nen** tradeswoman; ⇒ *auch* **Händler**

**Hand-: ~lese·kunst** *die* palmistry *no art.;* **~lexikon** *das* concise encyclopaedia

**handlich** /ˈhantlɪç/ **1** *Adj.* handy; easily carried ‹parcel, suitcase›; easily portable ‹television, camera›; manœuvrable ‹car›. **2** *adv.* **~ verpackt** wrapped as a manageable parcel

**Handlichkeit** *die;* **~:** handiness; (*eines Buches*) handy size; (*eines Autos*) manœuvrability

**Hand-: ~linie** *die* line of the hand; **~linien·deutung** *die* palmistry

**Handlung** *die;* **~**, **~en A** (*Vorgehen*) action; (*Tat*) act; **eine symbolische/feierliche ~:** a symbolic/ceremonial act; **B** (*Fabel*) plot; **Einheit der ~:** unity of action; **C** (*veralt.: Geschäft*) business

**handlungs-, Handlungs-: ~ablauf** *der* action; **~arm** *Adj.* short on action *pred.;* **~bedarf** *der* need for action; **wir haben ~bedarf** we need action; **ein juristischer/politischer ~bedarf besteht** legal/political action is needed; **~bevollmächtigte** *der/die* authorized representative; **~fähig** *Adj.* **A** able to act *pred.;* working *attrib.* ‹majority›; **B** (*Rechtsw.*) able to act on one's own account *pred.;* **~fähigkeit** *die* **A** ability to act; **B** (*Rechtsw.*) ability to act on one's own account; **~freiheit** *die* freedom of action *or* to act; **~gehilfe** *der*, **~gehilfin** *die* (*Kaufmannsspr.*) employee (*on the business side of a firm*); **~reich** *Adj.* action-packed; **~reisende** *der/die* ⇒ **Handelsvertreter**; **~schema** *das* plot structure; **~spiel·raum** *der* scope for action; **~unfähig** *Adj.* **A** unable to act *pred.;* **B** (*Rechtsw.*) unable to act on one's own account *pred.;* **~unfähigkeit** *die* **A** inability to act; **B** (*Rechtsw.*) inability to act on one's own account; **~vollmacht** *die* authority to act; **~weise** *die* behaviour; conduct

**Hand-: ~mixer** *der* hand mixer; **~mühle** *die* hand mill

**Hand-out** /ˈhɛndaut/ *das;* **~s**, **~s** handout

**Hand-: ~presse** *die* hand press; **~pumpe** *die* hand pump; **~puppe** *die* glove *or* hand puppet; **~puppen·spiel** *das* glove puppet *or* hand puppet show; (*Technik*) glove *or* hand puppetry; **~rad** *das* handwheel; **~reichung** *die;* **~~**, **~~en: eine ~reichung/~reichungen machen** lend a hand; **sie konnte nur einige ~reichungen machen** she couldn't help very much; **~rücken** *der* ▶ 471 the back of the/one's hand; **auf beiden ~rücken tätowiert** with tattoos on the back of both hands; **~säge** *die* handsaw; **~satz** *der* (*Druckw.*) hand-setting; **etw. im ~satz herstellen** hand-set sth.; **~schelle** *die* handcuff; **jmdm. ~schellen anlegen** handcuff sb.; put handcuffs on sb.; **~schlag** *der* **A** handshake; **jmdn. mit ~schlag begrüßen** greet sb. by shaking hands; **etw. durch einen ~schlag besiegeln** shake hands on sth.; **B** *in* **er tat keinen ~schlag** (*ugs.*) he did not lift a finger

**Hand·schrift** *die* **A** handwriting; **eine deutliche/unleserliche ~:** clear/illegible handwriting; **B** (*Ausdrucksweise*) personal style; **C** (*Text*) manuscript

**Handschriften-: ~deutung** *die* graphology *no art.;* analysis of handwriting; **~kunde** *die* palaeography; **~probe** *die* sample of handwriting

**Handschrift·leser** *der* (*DV*) *optical character reader for reading handwritten block letters and numerals*

**hand·schriftlich 1** *Adj.* handwritten; **~e Quellen/Urkunden** manuscript sources/texts. **2** *adv.* by hand

**Hand·schuh** *der* glove

**Handschuh-: ~fach** *das* glove compartment *or* box; **~größe** *die* glove size; **welche ~größe haben Sie?** what size glove do you take?; **~macher** *der*, **~macherin** *die* glove maker

**hand-, Hand-: ~schutz** *der* hand guard; **~setzer** *der*, **~setzerin** *die* (*Druckw.*) hand compositor; **~signiert** *Adj.* signed; **~skizze** *die* freehand sketch; **~spiegel** *der* hand-mirror; **~spiel** *das* (*Fußball*) handball

**Hand·stand** *der* (*Turnen*) handstand; **einen ~ machen** do a handstand

**Handstand·überschlag** *der* (*Turnen*) handspring

**Hand-: ~steuerung** *die* **A** manual operation *or* control; **B** (*Apparatur*) manual control; **~streich** *der* (*bes. Milit.*) lightning *or* surprise attack; **in einem** *od.* **im ~streich** in a surprise *or* lightning attack; **~tasche** *die* handbag; **~teller** *der* ▶ 471 palm [of the/one's hand]; **~trommel** *die* hand drum

**Hand·tuch** *das; Pl.* **Handtücher** towel; (*Geschirrtuch*) tea towel; tea cloth; **dieser Raum ist nicht mehr als ein ~** (*ugs.*) this room is nowhere near wide enough; **das ~ werfen** *od.* (*ugs.*) **schmeißen** (*Boxen, fig.*) throw in the towel

**Handtuch·halter** *der* towel rail

**hand-, Hand-: ~umdrehen** *in* **im ~umdrehen** in no time at all; **~verlesen** *Adj.* hand-picked; **~vermittlung** *die* (*Fernspr.*) connection by the operator; **über ~vermittlung laufen** be connected by the operator; ***~voll** *die;* **~~** (*auch fig.*) handful; **ein paar ~voll** a couple of handfuls; **~waffe** *die* hand weapon; **~wagen** *der* handcart; **~warm 1** *Adj.* hand-hot; **2** *adv.* **etw. ~warm waschen** wash sth. in hand-hot water; **~wäsche** *die* washing by hand; **diese Pullover kommen in die ~wäsche** these pullovers will have to be washed by hand

**Handwerk** *das* **A** craft; (*als Beruf*) trade; **ein ~ ausüben/betreiben** carry on/ply a trade; **B** (*Beruf*) **sein ~ kennen** *od.* **verstehen/beherrschen** know one's job; ‹tradesman› know/be master of one's trade; **jmdm. das ~ legen** put a stop to sb.'s activities; **jmdm. ins ~ pfuschen** try to do sb.'s job for him/her; **C das ~:** the craft professions *pl.*

**-handwerk** *das:* **Töpfer~/Bäcker~/Schuhmacher~:** potter's / baker's / shoemaker's trade

**Handwerker** *der;* **~s**, **~:** tradesman; craftsman; **die ~ im Haus haben** have the workmen in; **er ist ein guter ~:** he's a good craftsman

**Handwerkerin** *die;* **~**, **~nen** tradeswoman; craftswoman

**Handwerkerschaft** *die;* **~:** skilled tradesmen *pl. or* craftsmen *pl.*

**Handwerker·stand** *der* artisan class

**handwerklich** *Adj.* **A** ‹training, skill, ability› as a craftsman; **ein ~er Beruf** a [skilled] trade; **B** (*fig.*) technical

**Handwerks-: ~beruf** *der* [skilled] trade; **~betrieb** *der* workshop; **~bursche** *der* (*veralt.*) travelling journeyman (*arch.*); **~kammer** *die* Chamber of Crafts; **~meister** *der* master craftsman; **~meisterin** *die* master craftswoman; **~rolle** *die* register of qualified craftsmen; **~zeug** *das* tools *pl.;* (*fig.*) tools *pl.* of the trade

**Hand·wörter·buch** *das* concise dictionary

**Hand·wurzel** *die* ▶ 471 wrist; carpus (*Anat.*)

**Handwurzel·knochen** *der* ▶ 471 (*Anat.*) wristbone; carpal bone (*Anat.*)

**Handy** /ˈhɛndi/ *das;* **~s**, **~s** mobile [phone]

**Hand-: ~zeichen** *das* **A** sign [with one's hand]; (*eines Autofahrers*) hand signal; **darf ich die Betroffenen um Ihr ~zeichen bitten?** will those concerned please raise their hands; **B** (*Abstimmung*) show of hands; **durch ~zeichen** by a show of hands; **~zeichnung** *die* drawing; (*Skizze*) sketch; **~zettel** *der* handbill; leaflet

**hanebüchen** /ˈha:nəby:çn̩/ **1** *Adj.* outrageous. **2** *adv.* outrageously; **~ lügen** tell the most outrageous lies

**Hanf** /hanf/ *der;* **~[e]s A** (*Pflanze, Faser*) hemp; **B** (*Samen*) hempseed

**Hanf·anbau** *der* growing *or* cultivation of hemp

**hanfen, hänfen** /ˈhɛnfn̩/ *Adj.* hempen; hemp

**Hänfling** /ˈhɛnflɪŋ/ *der;* **~s**, **~e A** (*Vogel*) linnet; **B** (*abwertend*) weakling

**Hanf-: ~seil** *das*, **~strick** *der* hempen *or* hemp rope

**Hang** /haŋ/ *der;* **~[e]s, Hänge** /ˈhɛŋə/ **A** (*Berg~*) slope; hillside/mountainside; (*Ski~*) slope; **das Haus am ~:** the house on the hillside; **das Haus ist an einen ~ gebaut** the house is built on a slope; **B** (*Neigung*) tendency; **einen ~ zum Träumen/Lügen** *usw.* **haben** have a tendency to dream/lie *etc.;* **einen ~ haben, etw. zu tun** tend to do sth.; **C** (*Turnen*) hang

**Hangar** /ˈhaŋga:ɐ̯/ *der;* **~s**, **~s** hangar

**Hänge-: ~arsch** *der* (*derb*) sagging backside (*coll.*); **~backe** *die* flabby cheek; **~bauch** *der* paunch; **~bauch·schwein** *das* pot-bellied pig; **~boden** *der* false *or* drop ceiling; **~brücke** *die* suspension bridge; **~brust** *die*, **~busen** *der* sagging breasts *pl.;* **~dach** *das* suspended roof; **~gleiter** *der* hang-glider; **~kleid** *das* tent dress; **~lampe** *die* pendant light; drop-light

**hangeln** /ˈhaŋl̩n/ **1** *itr. V.; meist mit sein* make one's way hand over hand; **an einem Seil über die Schlucht ~:** make one's way hand over hand along a rope over the ravine. **2** *refl. V.* **sich aufwärts/abwärts ~:** climb up/down hand over hand

**Hänge·matte** *die* hammock

**hangen** /ˈhaŋən/ (*schweiz., landsch.*) ⇒ **hängen**[1]

**hängen**[1] /ˈhɛŋən/ *unr. itr. V.; südd., österr., schweiz. mit sein* **A** hang; **die Bilder ~ [schon]** the pictures are [already] up; **der Schrank hängt voller Kleider** the wardrobe is full of clothes; **der Weihnachtsbaum hängt voller Süßigkeiten** the Christmas tree is laden with sweets; **sein Zimmer hängt voller Plakate** the walls of his room are covered with posters; **an einem**

*old spelling (see note on page 1707)

**Faden ~:** be hanging by a thread; **etw. ~ lassen** (*vergessen*) leave sth. behind; **die Nachbarn hingen aus den Fenstern** (*fig.*) the neighbours were hanging out of the windows; **B** (*sich festhalten*) hang, dangle (**an** + *Dat.* from); **jmdm. am Hals ~:** hang round sb.'s neck; **der Junge hing an ihrem Arm** the boy hung on to her arm; ⇒ *auch* **Rockzipfel**; **C** (*erhängt werden*) hang; be hanged; **D** (*an einem Fahrzeug*) be hitched *or* attached (**an** + *Dat.* to); **E** (*herab~*) hang down; **bis auf den Boden ~:** hang down to the ground; **die Pflanzen ließen ihre Blätter ~:** the leaves of the plants drooped; **die Beine ins Wasser ~ lassen** let one's legs dangle in the water; **der Anzug hängt ihm am Leib** the suit hangs loosely on him; **sich ~ lassen** (*fig.*) let oneself go; **lass dich nicht so ~!** (*fig.*) [you must] pull yourself together! **F** (*unordentlich sitzen*) **im Sessel ~** (*erschöpft, betrunken*) be *or* sit slumped in one's/the chair; (*flegelhaft*) lounge in one's/the chair; **G** (*geh.: schweben, auch fig.*) hang (**über** + *Dat.* over); **H** (*haften*) cling, stick (**an/auf** + *Dat.* to); **~ bleiben** stick (**an/auf** + *Dat.* to); **ihre Augen hingen an seinen Lippen** (*fig.*) her eyes were fixed on his lips; **das bleibt an mir ~** (*fig.*) I've been stuck *or* landed with it (*coll.*); **von dem Vortrag blieb [bei ihm] nicht viel ~** (*fig.*) not much of the lecture stuck (*coll.*); **ein Verdacht bleibt an ihr ~** (*fig.*) suspicion rests on her; **I** (*fest~*) **sie hing mit dem Rock am Zaun/in der Fahrradkette** her skirt was caught on the fence/in the bicycle chain; **mit dem Ärmel** *usw.* **an/in etw.** (*Dat.*) **~ bleiben** get one's sleeve *etc.* caught on/in sth.; **der Angriff blieb im Mittelfeld ~** (*fig.*) the attack broke down in mid-field; **sein Blick blieb an der Uhr ~** (*fig.*) his gaze rested on the clock; **ich bin bei Freunden ~ geblieben** (*fig. ugs.*) I got stuck talking to friends (*coll.*); **~ bleiben** (*ugs.: in der Schule nicht versetzt werden*) stay down; have to repeat a year; **J** (*ugs.: sich aufhalten, sein*) hang around (*coll.*); **[schon wieder] am Radio/Telefon/vorm Fernseher ~:** have got the radio on [again]/be on the telephone [again]/be in front of the television [again]; **K** (*sich nicht trennen wollen*) **an jmdm./etw. ~:** be very attached to sb./sth.; **am Geld/Leben ~:** love money/life; **L** (*sich neigen*) lean; ‹road› slope to one side; **M** (*ugs.: angeschlossen sein*) **an etw.** (*Dat.*) **~:** be on sth.; **N** (*ugs.: nicht weiterkommen*) be stuck; **die Verhandlungen ~:** the talks are deadlocked; **O** (*ugs.: zurück sein*) be behind; **P** (*verschuldet sein*) **bei ihr hänge ich mit 2 000 DM** I owe her 2,000 marks; **Q** (*entschieden werden*) **an/bei jmdm./etw. ~:** depend on sb./sth.; **R** (*Schach*) ‹man› be en prise; (*nicht beendet sein*) ‹game› be adjourned; **S** (*ugs.: verbunden sein*) **etw. hängt an etw.** (*Dat.*) sth. involves sth. **T** **jmdn. ~ lassen** (*ugs.: jmdm. nicht helfen*) let sb. down.

**hängen²** **1** *tr. V.* **A** **etw. in/über etw.** (*Akk.*) **~:** hang sth. in/over sth.; **etw. an/auf etw.** (*Akk.*) **~:** hang sth. on sth.; **den Hörer in die Gabel ~:** replace the receiver; **B** (*befestigen*) hitch up (**an** + *Akk.* to); couple on ‹railway carriage, trailer, etc.› (**an** + *Akk.* to); **C** (**~ lassen**) hang; **seinen Arm aus dem Fenster ~:** put one's arm out of the window; **die Beine ins Wasser ~:** let one's legs dangle in the water; **D** (*er~*) hang; **Tod durch Hängen:** death by hanging; **mit Hängen und Würgen** by the skin of one's teeth; **E** (*ugs.: aufwenden*) **an/in etw.** (*Akk.*) **~:** put ‹work, time, money› into sth.; spend ‹time, money› on sth.; **F** (*ugs.: anschließen*) **jmdn./etw. an etw.** (*Akk.*) **~:** put sb./sth. on sth.; ⇒ *auch* **Glocke** A; **Nagel** B.
**2** *refl. V.* **A** (*ergreifen*) **sich an etw.** (*Akk.*) **~:** hang on to sth.; **sich jmdm. an den Hals ~:** cling to sb.'s neck; **sich ans Telefon ~** (*fig. ugs.*) get on the telephone; **sich an den Wasserhahn ~** (*ugs. fig.*) turn the tap on and drink thirstily from it; **B** (*sich festsetzen*) ‹smell› cling (**an** + *Akk.* to); ‹burr, hairs, etc.› cling, stick (**an** + *Akk.* to); **C** (*anschließen*) **sich an jmdn. ~:** attach oneself to sb.; latch on to sb. (*coll.*); **sie hängt sich zu sehr an mich** she clings to me too much; **D** (*verfolgen*) **sich an jmdn./ein Auto ~:** follow *or* (*coll.*) tail sb./a car; **E** (*binden*) **sich an jmdn./etw. ~:** get *or* become attached to sb./sth.; **sie hängt sich zu sehr an materielle Werte** she's too attached to material values

**Hangen** *das;* **~s** *in* **mit ~ und Bangen** (*geh.*) in fear and trepidation

***hängen|bleiben** ⇒ **hängen¹** H, I

**hängend** *Adj.* hanging; **die Hängenden Gärten der Semiramis** the Hanging Gardens of Babylon; **mit ~em Kopf** with head hanging; **mit ~er Zunge** (*fig.*) gasping for breath

***hängen|lassen** ⇒ **hängen¹** A, E, T

**Hänge-:** **~ohr** *das* lop ear; **~partie** *die* (*Schach*) adjourned game; **~pflanze** *die* trailing plant

**Hänger** *der;* **~s, ~** **A** ⇒ **Anhänger** B; **B** ⇒ **Hängekleid**; **C** (*weiter Mantel*) loose[-fitting] coat; tent coat

**Hänge-:** **~schrank** *der* wall cupboard; **~schultern** *Pl.* round shoulders

**hängig** *Adj.* **A** (*schweiz. Rechtsspr.*) **~ sein** be in progress; continue; **ein ~er Prozess** a trial that is in progress; **B** (*fachspr.*) sloping; **in ~er Lage** on a slope *or* an incline

**Hang·lage** *die* hillside location; **in ~:** in a hillside location

**Hängolin** /hɛŋo'li:n/ *das;* **~s** (*salopp scherzh.*) *substance allegedly used in order to diminish sb.'s sex drive*

**Hang-:** **~täter** *der,* **~täterin** *die* (*Rechtsspr.*) compulsive criminal; **~wind** *der* slope wind

**Hannover** /ha'no:fɐ/ (*das*); **~s** ▶ 700 | Hanover

**Hannoveraner** ▶ 700 | **1** *der;* **~s, ~** (*Einwohner, Pferd*) Hanoverian. **2** *indekl. Adj.* Hanover; ⇒ *auch* **Kölner**

**Hannoveranerin** *die;* **~, ~nen** Hanoverian

**hannoversch** /ha'no:fɐʃ/ *Adj.* Hanoverian; **im Hannoverschen** in the Hanover area

**Hans** /hans/ *der;* **~, Hänse** /'hɛnzə/ **~ im Glück** lucky devil; (*Märchenfigur*) Hans in Luck; **~ Guckindieluft** dreamer; (*Märchenfigur*) Johnny-Head-in-[the-]Air; **jeder ~ findet seine Grete** every Jack shall have his Jill

**Hansaplast** Ⓦᴢ /hanza'plast/ *das;* **~[e]s** sticking plaster; Elastoplast ®

**Hänschen** /'hɛnsçən/ *das;* **~s, ~: was ~ nicht lernt, lernt Hans nimmermehr** what you don't learn as a child, you'll never learn as an adult

**Hans·dampf** *der;* **~[e]s, ~e: ~ [in allen Gassen]** Jack of all trades

**Hanse** /'hanzə/ *die;* **~** (*hist.*) Hanse; Hanseatic league

**Hanseat** /hanze'a:t/ *der;* **~en, ~en** **A** citizen of a Hanseatic city; **ein typischer ~** *someone with the dignified bearing regarded as typical of upper-class citizens of the Hanseatic cities;* **B** (*hist.*) member of the Hanseatic League

**Hanseatin** *die;* **~, ~nen** ⇒ **Hanseat** A

**hanseatisch** *Adj.* Hanseatic

**Hanse-:** **~bund** *der* ⇒ **Hanse**; **~kogge** *die* (*hist.*) Hansa cog

**Hänselei** *die;* **~, ~en** **A** teasing; **B** (*Bemerkung*) teasing remark

**hänseln** /'hɛnzl̩n/ *tr. V.* tease

**Hanse·stadt** *die* Hanseatic city

**Hans·wurst** *der;* **~[e]s, ~e** **A** (*dummer Mensch*) clown; **B** (*Theater*) fool; hanswurst

**Hans·wurstiade** /hansvʊrs'tia:də/ *die;* **~, ~n** **A** (*Scherz*) clowning; buffoonery; **B** (*Theater*) harlequinade

**Hantel** /'hantl̩/ *die;* **~, ~n** (*Sport*) (*kurz*) dumb-bell; (*lang*) barbell

**hanteln** *itr. V.* exercise with dumb-bells/barbells

**hantieren** /han'ti:rən/ *itr. V.* be busy; **sie hantierte mit einem Schraubenschlüssel an ihrem Auto** she was busy doing something to her car with a spanner

**hapern** /'ha:pɐn/ *itr. V.* (*unpers.*) **A** (*fehlen*) **es hapert an etw.** (*Dat.*) there's a shortage of sth.; **es hapert bei jmdm. an etw.** sb. is short of sth.; **ich wäre gerne mitgefahren, aber es hapert an der Zeit** I'd like to have gone, but I haven't got the time; **B** (*nicht klappen*) **es hapert mit etw.** there's a problem with sth.; **bei ihr hapert es in Latein** she's poor at *or* weak in Latin

**haploid** /haplo'i:t/ *Adj.* (*Biol.*) haploid

**Häppchen** /'hɛpçən/ *das;* **~s, ~** **A** [small] morsel; **B** (*Appetithappen*) canapé

**Happen** /'hapn̩/ *der;* **~s, ~:** morsel; **einen ~ essen** have a bite to eat; **ein fetter ~** (*fig.*) a real plum

**Happening** /'hɛpənɪŋ/ *das;* **~s, ~s** happening

**happig** /'hapɪç/ *Adj.* (*ugs.*) steep (*coll.*); **~e Preise** fancy prices (*coll.*); **das ist aber [ein bisschen] ~:** that's a bit much (*coll.*)

**happy** /'hɛpi/ (*ugs.*) **1** *Adj.* happy. **2** *adv.* happily

**Happyend** /'hɛpi'|ɛnt/ *das;* **~s, ~s** happy ending

**Harakiri** /hara'ki:ri/ *das;* **~[s], ~s** hara-kiri *no art.;* **politisches ~ begehen** (*fig.*) commit political suicide; **gesellschaftliches ~ begehen** (*fig.*) ruin one's reputation

**Härchen** /'hɛ:ɐ̯çən/ *das;* **~s, ~:** little *or* tiny hair; **die feinen ~ in ihrem Nacken** the fine down on her neck

**Hardcover** /'ha:d'kʌvə/ *das;* **~s, ~s** (*Buchw.*) hardback

**Hardtop** /'ha:dtɔp/ *das od. der;* **~s, ~s** hardtop

**Hardware** /'ha:dwɛə/ *die;* **~, ~s** (*DV*) hardware

**Harem** /'ha:rɛm/ *der;* **~s, ~s** (*auch ugs. scherzh.*) harem

**Harems-:** **~dame** *die* lady of the harem; **~wächter** *der* guardian of the harem

**hären** /'hɛ:rən/ *Adj.* (*geh.*) [made] of hair *postpos.;* hair

**Häresie** /hɛre'zi:/ *die;* **~, ~n** /-i:ən/ heresy

**Häretiker** /hɛ're:tikɐ/ *der;* **~s, ~, Häretikerin** *die;* **~, ~nen** heretic

**häretisch** *Adj.* heretical

**Harfe** /'harfə/ *die;* **~, ~n** harp

**harfen** **1** *itr. V.* play the harp; harp. **2** *tr. V.* **ein Lied** *usw.* **~:** play a song *etc.* on the harp

**Harfenist** *der;* **~en, ~en, Harfenistin** *die;* **~, ~nen** harpist; harp player

**Harfen·spiel** *das* harp playing; (*Musik*) harp music

**Harke** /'harkə/ *die;* **~, ~n** rake; **jmdm. zeigen, was eine ~ ist** (*fig. salopp*) give sb. what for (*coll.*)

**harken** *tr. V.* rake

**Harlekin** /'harleki:n/ *der;* **~s, ~e** harlequin

**Harlekinade** /harleki'na:də/ *die;* **~, ~n** ⇒ **Hanswurstiade**

**Harm** /harm/ *der;* **~[e]s** (*geh. veralt.*) distress; (*über Verlorenes*) grief

**härmen** /'hɛrmən/ *refl. V.* (*geh.*) grieve (**um** over)

**harm·los** **1** *Adj.* **A** (*ungefährlich*) harmless; slight ‹injury, cold, etc.›; mild ‹illness›; safe ‹medicine, bend, road, etc.›; **eine ~e Grippe** a mild bout of flu; **B** (*arglos*) innocent; harmless ‹fun, pastime, etc.›. **2** *adv.* **A** (*ungefährlich*) harmlessly; **B** (*arglos*) innocently; **ich bin ganz ~ hingegangen** I went there quite innocently; **er hatte nur ~ gefragt** he only asked an innocent *or* inoffensive question; **ganz ~ tun** act innocent

**Harmlosigkeit** *die;* **~** **A** (*Ungefährlichkeit*) harmlessness; (*einer Krankheit*) mildness; (*eines Medikamentes*) safety; **B** (*Arglosigkeit, harmloses Verhalten*) innocence; **in aller ~:** in all innocence

**Harmonie** /harmo'ni:/ *die;* **~, ~n** (*auch fig.*) harmony

**Harmonie-:** **~lehre** *die* theory of harmony; **~musik** *die* music for wind instruments

**harmonieren** *itr. V.* **A** (*zusammenpassen*) harmonize; go together; match; **mit etw. ~:** harmonize *or* go together with sth.; **B** (*miteinander auskommen*) get on well

**Harmonik** /har'mo:nɪk/ *die;* ~: harmony

**Harmonika** /har'mo:nika/ *die;* ~, ~s *od.* **Harmoniken** harmonica

**Harmonika-:** ~**spieler** *der,* ~**spielerin** *die* harmonica player; ~**tür** *die* folding door; accordion door

**harmonisch** ❶ *Adj.* Ⓐ (*Musik*) harmonic ‹tone, minor›; Ⓑ (*wohlklingend, zusammenpassend, übereinstimmend*) harmonious; Ⓒ (*Math.*) ~**e Teilung** harmonic division. ❷ *adv.* Ⓐ (*Musik*) harmonically; Ⓑ (*wohlklingend, zusammenpassend, übereinstimmend*) harmoniously; ~ **zusammenleben** live together in harmony

**harmonisieren** *tr. V.* Ⓐ (*Musik*) harmonize; Ⓑ (*in Einklang bringen*) coordinate; **etw. mit etw.** ~ (*Wirtsch.*) bring sth. into line with sth.

**Harmonisierung** *die;* ~, ~**en** (*Wirtsch.*) harmonization

**Harmonium** /har'mo:ni̯ʊm/ *das;* ~s, **Harmonien** harmonium

**Harn** /harn/ *der;* ~[e]s, ~e (*Med.*) urine; ~ **lassen** pass water; urinate

**Harn-:** ~**blase** *die* ▶ 471 bladder; ~**drang** *der* desire to urinate *or* to pass water

**Harnisch** /'harnɪʃ/ *der;* ~s, ~e Ⓐ armour; Ⓑ **in** ~ **sein** be in a furious temper; **jmdn. in** ~ **bringen** get sb.'s hackles up; make sb. see red; **in** ~ **geraten** get up in arms (**über** + *Akk.* over, about)

**harn-, Harn-:** ~**lassen** *das;* ~~s urination *no pl., no art.;* **Schmerzen beim** ~**lassen haben** find it painful to urinate *or* pass water; ~**leiter** *der* (*Med.*) ureter; ~**röhre** *die* ▶ 471 (*Anat.*) urethra; ~**säure** *die* (*Med., Chemie*) uric acid; ~**stein** *der* (*Med.*) urinary calculus; ~**stoff** *der* (*Med., Chemie*) urea; ~**treibend** ❶ *Adj.* diuretic; ❷ *adv.* ~**treibend wirken** have a diuretic effect; ~**vergiftung** *die* (*Med.*) uraemia; ~**wege** *Pl.* ▶ 471 (*Med.*) urinary tract *sing.*

**Harpune** /har'pu:nə/ *die;* ~, ~n harpoon

**Harpunier** /harpu'ni:ɐ̯/ *der;* ~s, ~e harpooner

**harpunieren** ❶ *tr. V.* harpoon. ❷ *itr. V.* throw/fire the harpoon

**Harpyie** /har'py:jə/ *die;* ~, ~n (*Myth.*) harpy

**harren** /'harən/ *itr. V.* (*geh.*) **jmds./einer Sache** *od.* **auf jmdn./etw.** ~: wait for *or* await sb./sth.; (*fig.*) await sb./sth.; **der Dinge** ~, **die da kommen sollen** wait and see what happens

**harsch** /harʃ/ ❶ *Adj.* Ⓐ (*vereist*) crusted ‹snow›; Ⓑ (*barsch*) harsh. ❷ *adv.* harshly

**Harsch** *der;* ~[e]s crusted *or* hard snow

**harschen** *itr. V.* ‹snow› freeze [over]

**harschig** *Adj.* ‹snow› frozen hard [on top]

**Harsch·schnee** *der* ⇒ **Harsch**

**hart** /hart/; **härter** /'hɛrtɐ/, **härtest...** /'hɛrtəst.../ ❶ *Adj.* Ⓐ hard ‹wood, bread, cheese, etc.›; ~**e** *od.* ~ **gekochte Eier** hard-boiled eggs; **Eier** ~ **kochen** hard-boil eggs; ~ **gefroren** frozen hard *or* solid; ~ **werden** go hard; harden; ‹cheese etc.› go hard; ⇒ *auch* **Brocken** B; **Nuss** A; **Schädel** A; Ⓑ (*abgehärtet*) tough; ~ **im Nehmen sein** (*Schläge ertragen können*) be able to take a punch; (*Enttäuschungen ertragen können*) be able to take the rough with the smooth; Ⓒ (*schwer erträglich*) hard ‹work, life, fate, lot, times›; tough ‹childhood, situation, job›; harsh ‹reality, truth›; bitter ‹disappointment›; heavy, severe ‹loss›; severe ‹hardship›; **jmds. Geduld** *usw.* **auf eine** ~**e Probe stellen** sorely try sb.'s patience *etc.;* **ein** ~**er Schlag für jmdn. sein** be a heavy *or* severe blow for sb.; **es war** ~ **für ihn, darauf zu verzichten** it was hard for him to go without; **es ist sehr** ~ **für ihn, dass er nicht mitkommen darf** it's very hard on him that he can't come too; Ⓓ (*streng*) severe, harsh ‹penalty, punishment, judgement›; tough ‹measure, law, course›; hard, harsh ‹words›; harsh ‹treatment›; severe, hard ‹features›; **durch eine** ~**e Schule gegangen sein** have been through a hard school; ~ **gegen jmdn. sein** be hard on sb.; Ⓔ (*heftig*) hard, violent ‹impact, jolt›; heavy ‹fall›; violent ‹argument›; Ⓕ (*rau*) rough ‹game, opponent›; Ⓖ (*stabil*) hard ‹currency›; Ⓗ (*kalkig*) hard ‹water›; Ⓘ hard, severe ‹winter, frost›; harsh ‹accent, light, colour, contrast›; hard ‹consonant, drink, drug, pornography›; Ⓙ (*Physik*) hard ‹rays etc.›. ❷ *adv.* Ⓐ ~ **schlafen/sitzen** sleep on a hard bed/sit on a hard chair; Ⓑ (*mühevoll*) ‹work› hard; **es kommt mich** ~ **an** it is hard for me; Ⓒ (*streng*) severely; harshly; ~ **durchgreifen** take tough measures; **jmdn.** ~ **anfassen** be tough with sb.; Ⓓ (*heftig*) ~ **aneinander geraten** have a violent argument; have a real set-to (*coll.*); **jmdm.** ~ **zusetzen, jmdn.** ~ **bedrängen** press sb. hard; ~ **bedrängt** hard-pressed; ~ **umkämpft** bitterly contested; **jmdn.** ~ **treffen** hit sb. hard; **es geht** ~ **auf** ~: the chips are down; Ⓔ (*nahe*) close (**an** + *Dat.* to); **die Kugel ging** ~ **an seinem Kopf vorbei** the bullet just missed his head; **das ist** ~ **an der Grenze der Legalität/des Machbaren** that is very close to being illegal/that's nearing the limits of what's possible; ~ **am Wind segeln** (*Seemannsspr.*) sail near *or* close to the wind; ~ **auf ein Ziel zuhalten** (*Seemannsspr.*) hold steady on course for sth.

***hart·bedrängt** ⇒ **hart** 2 D

**Hart·beton** *der* granolithic concrete

**Härte** /'hɛrtə/ *die;* ~, ~n Ⓐ (*auch Physik*) hardness; Ⓑ (*Widerstandsfähigkeit*) toughness; Ⓒ (*schwere Belastung*) hardship; **eine soziale** ~: a case of social hardship; Ⓓ (*Strenge*) severity; Ⓔ (*Heftigkeit*) (*eines Aufpralls usw.*) force; (*eines Streits*) violence; Ⓕ (*Rauheit*) roughness; Ⓖ (*Stabilität*) hardness; Ⓗ (*von Wasser*) hardness; Ⓘ (*von Licht, Farbe*) harshness; (*von Frost*) hardness

**Härte-:** ~**ausgleich** *der* (*Sozialw.*) hardship payment; ~**fall** *der* Ⓐ case of hardship; Ⓑ (*ugs.: Person*) hardship case; ~**fonds** *der* hardship fund; ~**grad** *der* degree of hardness; ~**mittel** *das* hardener

**härten** ❶ *tr. V.* harden; harden, temper ‹steel›; cure ‹plastic›. ❷ *itr. V.* harden

**härter** ⇒ **hart**

**Härter** *der;* ~s, ~ (*Chemie*) hardener

**Härte·skala** *die* (*Mineral.*) scale of hardness; hardness scale

**härtest...** ⇒ **hart**

**Härte·test** endurance test; (*fig.*) acid test

**Hart·faser·platte** *die* hardboard

**hart-, Hart-:** *~**gefroren**, *~**gekocht** ⇒ **hart** 1 A; ~**geld** *das* coins *pl.;* small change; ~**gesotten** *Adj.* Ⓐ (*gefühllos*) hard-bitten; hard-boiled; Ⓑ (*unbelehrbar*) hardened; ~**gummi** *das* hard rubber; ~**herzig** ❶ *Adj.* hard-hearted; ❷ *adv.* hard-heartedly; ~**herzigkeit** *die;* ~~: hard-heartedness; ~**holz** *das* hardwood; ~**käse** *der* hard cheese; ~**laub·gewächs** *das* (*Bot.*) sclerophyll [plant]; sclerophyllous plant; ~**löten** *tr., itr. V.* hard-solder; ~**metall** *das* hard metal; ~**näckig** /-nɛkɪç/ ❶ *Adj.* Ⓐ (*eigensinnig*) obstinate; stubborn; Ⓑ (*ausdauernd*) persistent; dogged; inveterate ‹liar›; stubborn, dogged ‹resistance›; persistent ‹questioning, questioner›; Ⓒ (*langwierig*) stubborn ‹illness, stain›; ❷ *adv.* Ⓐ (*eigensinnig*) obstinately; stubbornly; Ⓑ (*ausdauernd*) persistently; doggedly; ~**näckigkeit** *die;* ~~: Ⓐ (*Eigensinn*) obstinacy; stubbornness; Ⓑ (*Ausdauer*) persistence; doggedness; Ⓒ (*Langwierigkeit*) stubbornness; ~**packung** *die* cardboard packet; ~**papier** *das* (*Technik*) laminated paper; ~**pappe** *die* fibreboard; ~**platz** *der* (*Sport*) (*Tennis*) hard court; (*Fußball*) asphalt pitch; ~**schalig** /-ʃa:lɪç/ *Adj.* hardshell; hard-shelled; thick-skinned ‹apple, pear, etc.›; *~**umkämpft** ⇒ **hart** 2 D

**Härtung** *die;* ~, ~**en** hardening; (*von Stahl auch*) tempering; (*von Kunststoffen*) curing

**Hart-:** ~**weizen·grieß** *der* semolina; ~**wurst** *die* dry sausage

**Harz** /ha:ɐ̯ts/ *das;* ~es, ~e resin

**harzen** ❶ *itr. V.* exude resin. ❷ *tr. V.* resin; resinate ‹wine›

**Harzer** *der;* ~s, ~, **Harzer Käse** *der;* ~ **Käses,** ~ **Käse** Harz [Mountain] cheese

**Harzer Roller** *der;* ~ ~s, ~ ~ Ⓐ ⇒ **Harzer Käse;** Ⓑ (*Kanarienvogel*) Harz mountain roller

**Harz·geruch** *der* smell of resin

**harzig** *Adj.* Ⓐ resinous; Ⓑ (*schweiz.: zähflüssig*) slow-moving ‹traffic, queue›

**Harz·säure** *die* resin acid

**Hasard** /ha'zart/ *das;* ~s: ~ **spielen** (*auch fig.*) gamble

**Hasardeur** /hazar'dø:ɐ̯/ *der;* ~s, ~e (*abwertend*) gambler

**Hasard·spiel** *das* Ⓐ (*Glücksspiel*) game of chance; Ⓑ (*Wagnis*) gamble

**Hasch** /haʃ/ *das;* ~s (*ugs.*) hash (*coll.*)

**Haschee** /ha'ʃe:/ (*Kochk.*) *das;* ~s, ~s hash

**haschen**[1] (*veralt.*) ❶ *tr. V.* catch. ❷ *itr. V.* **nach etw.** ~: make a grab for sth.; **nach Komplimenten/Beifall** ~ (*fig.*) fish *or* angle for compliments/applause

**haschen**[2] *itr. V.* (*ugs.*) smoke [hash] (*coll.*)

**Haschen** *das;* ~s tag

**Häschen** /'hɛ:sçən/ *das;* ~s, ~: bunny

**Hascher** *der;* ~s, ~ (*ugs.*) hash smoker (*coll.*)

**Häscher** /'hɛʃɐ/ *der;* ~s, ~ (*geh. veralt.*) pursuer

**Hascherin** *die;* ~, ~**nen** ⇒ **Hascher**

**Hascherl** /'haʃɐl/ *das;* ~s, ~n (*südd., österr. ugs.*) **armes** ~! poor thing *or* soul!; (*Kind*) poor little thing *or* soul!

**Haschisch** /'haʃɪʃ/ *das od. der;* ~[s] hashish

**Haschmich** /'haʃmɪç/ *in* **einen** ~ **haben** (*salopp*) have a screw loose (*coll.*)

**Hase** /'ha:zə/ *der;* ~n, ~n Ⓐ hare; (*männlicher* ~) hare; buck; **ängstlich wie ein** ~: timid as a mouse; **ein alter** ~ **sein** (*ugs.*) be an old hand; **falscher** ~ (*Kochk.*) meat loaf; **da liegt der** ~ **im Pfeffer** (*ugs.*) that's the real trouble; **sehen/wissen wie der** ~ **läuft** (*ugs.*) see/know which way the wind blows; **mein Name ist** ~ (*ugs. scherzh.*) I'm not saying anything; Ⓑ (*landsch.*) ⇒ **Kaninchen**

**Hasel-:** ~**busch** *der* hazel [tree]; ~**huhn** *das* hazel grouse *or* hen; ~**kätzchen** *das* hazel catkin; ~**nuss**, *~**nuß** *die* Ⓐ hazelnut; Ⓑ hazel [tree]; ~[**nuss**]·**strauch**, *~[**nuß**]·**strauch** *der* hazel [tree]

**hasen-, Hasen-:** ~**braten** *der* roast hare; ~**fuß** *der* (*spöttisch abwertend*) coward; chicken (*sl.*); ~**füßig** *Adj.* (*spöttisch abwertend*) cowardly; ~**herz** *das* ⇒ ~**fuß**; ~**jagd** *die* hare shoot; **auf** ~**jagd gehen** go on a hare shoot; go hare shooting; ~**klein** *das;* ~~s trimmings *pl.* of hare; ~**panier** *in* **das** ~**panier ergreifen** take to one's heels; ~**pfeffer** *der* (*Kochk.*) marinaded and stewed trimmings *pl.* of hare; ~**rein** *Adj.* (*Jagdw.*) steady from hare; **er/das ist nicht ganz** ~**rein** (*fig.*) there's something fishy (*coll.*) about him/it; ~**scharte** *die* ▶ 474 (*Med.*) harelip

**Häsin** /'hɛ:zɪn/ *die;* ~, ~**nen** doe [hare]

**Haspel** /'haspl̩/ *die;* ~, ~n (*Technik*) Ⓐ (*für Garn*) reel; bobbin; (*für ein Seil, Kabel*) drum; Ⓑ (*Seilwinde*) windlass

**haspeln** ❶ *tr. V.* wind. ❷ *itr. V.* (*ugs.: hastig reden*) gabble

**Hass**, ***Haß** /has/ *der;* **Hasses** hate, hatred (**auf** + *Akk.*, **gegen** of, for); ~ **auf** *od.* **gegen jmdn. empfinden** feel hatred of *or* for sb.; **sich** (*Dat.*) **jmds.** ~ **zuziehen** incur sb.'s hatred

**hassen** *tr., itr. V.* hate; ⇒ *auch* **Pest**

**hassens·wert** *Adj.* hateful; odious

**hass·erfüllt**, ***haß·erfüllt** ❶ *Adj.* filled with hatred *or* hate *postpos.* ❷ *adv.* **jmdn.** ~ **ansehen** look at sb. with [one's] eyes full of hatred *or* hate

**Hass·gefühl**, ***Haß·gefühl** *das* feeling of hatred

**hässlich**, ***häßlich** /'hɛslɪç/ ❶ *Adj.* Ⓐ ugly; ~ **wie die Nacht** as ugly as sin (*coll.*); Ⓑ (*gemein*) nasty; hateful; ~ **zu jmdm. sein** be mean *or* hateful to sb.; **das war** ~ **von dir** that was mean *or* nasty of you; Ⓒ (*unangenehm*) terrible (*coll.*), awful ‹weather, cold,

*old spelling (see note on page 1707)

situation, etc.›. ❷ *adv.* Ⓐ ‹dress› unattractively; Ⓑ (*gemein*) nastily; hatefully; **~ von jmdm. sprechen** be mean *or* nasty about sb.; Ⓒ (*unangenehm*) terribly (*coll.*); awfully

**Hässlichkeit**, ***Häßlichkeit** *die;* ~, **~en** Ⓐ (*Aussehen*) ugliness; Ⓑ (*Gesinnung*) meanness; nastiness; hatefulness; Ⓒ (*Äußerung*) mean remark

**hass-**, ***haß-**, **Hass-**, ***Haß-**: **~liebe** *die* love-hate relationship; **~tirade** *die* (*abwertend*) tirade of hatred *or* hate; **~verzerrt** *Adj.* twisted with hatred *or* hate *postpos.*

**hast** /hast/ *2. Pers. Sg. Präsens v.* **haben**

**Hast** *die;* ~: haste; **etw. in** *od.* **mit größter ~ tun** do sth. in great haste; **ohne ~**: unhurriedly; without hurrying *or* haste

**haste** /ˈhastə/ (*ugs.*) = **hast du; [was] ~, was kannste** as fast as he/you/they *etc.* can/could; **~ was, biste was** money talks

**hasten** *itr. V.; mit sein* hurry; hasten

**hastig** ❶ *Adj.* hasty; hurried. ❷ *adv.* hastily; hurriedly; **sein Essen ~ herunterschlingen** gobble [down] one's food; **nur nicht so ~!** not so fast!

**hat** /hat/ *3. Pers. Sg. Präsens v.* **haben**

**Hätschelei** *die;* ~, **~en** (*abwertend*) Ⓐ **~[en]** fondling; caressing; Ⓑ (*das Verwöhnen*) pampering

**Hätschel·kind** *das* pampered child; (*fig.*) darling

**hätscheln** /ˈhɛtʃl̩n/ *tr. V.* Ⓐ (*liebkosen*) fondle; caress; Ⓑ (*verwöhnen*) pamper; (*fig.*) lionize; Ⓒ (*sich widmen*) cherish ‹idea, hope, etc.›; nurse ‹pain etc.›

**hatschen** /ˈhaːtʃn̩/ *itr. V.; mit sein* (*bayr., österr. ugs.*) Ⓐ (*schlendern*) stroll; saunter; Ⓑ (*hinken*) hobble; limp; Ⓒ (*mühselig gehen*) trudge

**hatschi** /haˈtʃiː/ *Interj.* atishoo; atchoo; **~ machen** (*Kinderspr.*) sneeze

**hatte** /ˈhatə/ *1. u. 3. Pers. Sg. Prät. v.* **haben**

**hätte** /ˈhɛtə/ *1. u. 3. Pers. Sg. Konjunktiv II v.* **haben**

***Hat-Trick**, **Hattrick** /ˈhættrɪk/ *der;* **~s, ~s** Ⓐ (*Fußball, Handball*) *three successive goals by the same player in the same half;* Ⓑ (*Sport*) hat trick

**Hatz** /hats/ *die;* ~, **~en** Ⓐ (*Hetzjagd, auch fig. ugs.*) hunt; Ⓑ (*ugs., bes. bayr.: Eile, Stress*) mad rush

**hatzi** /haˈtsiː/ ⇒ **hatschi**

**Hau** /hau/ *in* **einen ~ haben** (*salopp*) have a screw loose (*coll.*)

**Häubchen** /ˈhɔypçən/ *das;* **~s,** ~ ⇒ **Haube** A, E

**Haube** /ˈhaubə/ *die;* ~, **~n** Ⓐ bonnet; (*einer Krankenschwester*) cap; **unter die ~ kommen** (*ugs. scherzh.*) get hitched (*coll.*); **unter der ~ sein** (*ugs. scherzh.*) be married; **jmdn. unter die ~ bringen** (*ugs. scherzh.*) marry sb. off; Ⓑ (*Kfz-W.*) bonnet (*Brit.*); hood (*Amer.*); Ⓒ ⇒ **Trocken~**; Ⓓ (*südd., österr.: Mütze*) [woollen] cap; Ⓔ (*Zool.*) crest; Ⓕ (*Bedeckung*) cover; (*über Teekanne, Kaffeekanne, Ei*) cosy

**Hauben-**: **~lerche** *die* crested lark; **~taucher** *der* great crested grebe

**Haubitze** /hauˈbɪtsə/ *die;* ~, **~n** (*Milit.*) howitzer; **voll wie eine ~ sein** (*derb*) be as pissed as a newt (*sl.*)

**Hauch** /haux/ *der;* **~[e]s, ~e** (*geh.*) Ⓐ (*Atem, auch fig.*) breath; Ⓑ (*Luftzug*) breath of wind; breeze; Ⓒ (*leichter Duft*) delicate smell; waft; Ⓓ (*dünne Schicht*) [gossamer-]thin layer; **ein ~ von Reif** a [thin] film of hoar frost; Ⓔ (*Atmosphäre*) air; feeling; Ⓕ (*Anflug*) hint; trace; **der ~ eines Lächelns** a ghost *or* hint of a smile

**hauch·dünn** ❶ *Adj.* gossamer-thin ‹material, dress›; wafer-thin, paper-thin ‹layer, slice, majority›; **ein ~er Sieg** (*fig.*) the narrowest of victories. ❷ *adv.* **etw. ~ auftragen** apply sth. very sparingly; **etw. ~ schneiden** cut sth. wafer-thin *or* into wafer-thin slices

**hauchen** ❶ *itr. V.* breathe (**gegen, auf** + *Akk.* on). ❷ *tr. V.* (*auch fig.: flüstern*) breathe; **jmdm. etw. ins Ohr ~**: breathe sth. in sb.'s ear

**hauch-**, **Hauch-**: **~fein** *Adj.* extremely fine; **~laut** *der* (*Phon.*) aspirate; **~zart** *Adj.* extremely delicate; gossamer-thin

**Hau·degen** *der:* **[alter] ~**: old soldier *or* warhorse

**Haue** /ˈhauə/ *die;* ~, **~n** Ⓐ (*südd., österr.: Hacke*) hoe; Ⓑ (*ugs.: Prügel*) a hiding (*coll.*); **..., sonst gibts ~**: ... or you'll get a hiding

**hauen** ❶ *unr. tr. V.* Ⓐ (*ugs.: schlagen*) belt; clobber (*coll.*); beat; **jmdn. windelweich/grün und blau ~**: beat sb. black and blue; **jmdn. zu Brei ~** (*salopp*) beat sb.'s brains in (*sl.*); Ⓑ (*ugs.: auf einen Körperteil*) belt (*coll.*); hit; (*mit der Faust auch*) smash (*sl.*); punch; (*mit offener Hand auch*) slap; smack; **jmdn. ins Gesicht ~**: hit/belt/slap sb. in the face; **jmdm. das Heft um die Ohren ~**: clout (*coll.*) *or* hit sb. round the ears with the exercise book; Ⓒ (*ugs.: hineinschlagen*) knock; **einen Nagel in die Wand ~**: knock a nail into the wall; Ⓓ (*herstellen*) carve ‹figure, statue, etc.› (**in** + *Akk.* in); cut, chop ‹hole›; (*mit einem Hammer*) knock ‹hole›; **Stufen in den Fels ~**: cut steps in the rock; Ⓔ (*mit einer Waffe schlagen*) **jmdn. aus dem Sattel/vom Pferd ~**: knock sb. out of the saddle/off his/her horse; **das haut mich vom Stuhl** *od.* **aus dem Anzug** (*salopp*) I'm [absolutely] staggered (*coll.*); Ⓕ (*salopp: schleudern*) sling (*coll.*); fling; (*nachlässig schreiben*) stick (*coll.*), scrawl ‹comments, signature› (**in** + *Akk.* in, **unter** + *Akk.* underneath); **jmdm. eine 6 ins Zeugnis ~** (*fig.*) stick a 6 on sb.'s report (*coll.*); Ⓖ (*landsch.: fällen*) fell; cut down; Ⓗ (*Bergbau*) cut ‹coal, ore›.
❷ *unr. itr. V.* Ⓐ (*ugs.: prügeln*) **hau doch nicht schon wieder!** don't belt me again!; **er haut immer gleich** he's quick to hit out; Ⓑ *auch unr.* (*auf einen Körperteil*) belt; hit; (*mit der Faust auch*) punch; (*mit offener Hand auch*) slap; smack; **jmdm. auf die Schulter ~**: slap *or* clap sb. on the shoulder; **jmdm. ins Gesicht ~**: belt/slap sb. in the face; Ⓒ (*ugs.: auf/gegen etw. schlagen*) thump; **mit der Faust auf den Tisch ~**: thump the table [with one's fist]; **auf die Tasten ~**: thump on the keys; **auf den Putz** *od.* **Pudding ~** (*fig. salopp*) run riot; Ⓓ *mit sein* (*ugs.: stoßen*) bump; **mit dem Kopf/Bein gegen etw. ~**: bang *or* hit *or* bump one's head/leg against sth.; Ⓔ *mit sein* (*ugs.: auftreffen*) **auf etw.** (*Akk.*) **~**: hit sth.
❸ *unr. refl. V.* Ⓐ (*ugs.: sich prügeln*) have a punch-up (*coll.*) *or* a fight; fight; Ⓑ (*salopp: sich setzen, legen*) fling *or* throw oneself; **sich ins Bett ~**: hit the sack (*coll.*)

**Hauer** *der;* **~s,** ~ Ⓐ ▶ 159 (*Bergmannsspr.*) faceworker; Ⓑ (*Jägerspr.*) tusk; (*fig.*) fang; Ⓒ (*südd., österr.: Winzer*) winegrower

**Häufchen** /ˈhɔyfçən/ *das;* **~s, ~**: [small *or* little] pile *or* heap; **wie ein ~ Unglück** *od.* **Elend aussehen/dasitzen** (*ugs.*) look a/sit there looking a picture of misery; **nur noch ein ~ Unglück** *od.* **Elend sein** (*ugs.*) be nothing but a small bundle of misery

**Haufe** /ˈhaufə/ *der;* **~ns, ~n** (*veralt.*) ⇒ **Haufen**

**häufeln** /ˈhɔyfl̩n/ *tr. V.* Ⓐ (*Gartenbau*) earth *or* hill up; Ⓑ (*zu Häufchen schichten*) pile *or* heap up

**häufen** /ˈhɔyfn̩/ ❶ *tr. V.* heap, pile (**auf** + *Akk.* on to); (*aufheben*) hoard ‹money, supplies›. ❷ *refl. V.* (*sich mehren*) pile up; ⇒ *auch* **gehäuft**

**Haufen** /ˈhaufn̩/ *der;* **~s,** ~ Ⓐ heap; pile; **ein ~ Erde/trockenes Stroh** *od.* **trockenen Strohs** a heap *or* pile of earth/dry straw; **etw. zu ~ aufschichten** stack sth. up in piles; **alles auf einen ~ werfen** throw everything in a heap; **der Hund hat da einen ~ gemacht** (*ugs.*) the dog has done his business there (*coll.*); **etw. über den ~ werfen** (*ugs.*) (*aufgeben*) chuck sth. in (*coll.*); (*zunichte machen*) mess sth. up; **jmdn. über den ~ fahren/rennen** (*ugs.*) knock sb. down; run sb. over; **jmdn. über den ~ schießen** *od.* **knallen** (*ugs.*) gun *or* shoot sb. down (*coll.*); Ⓑ (*ugs.: große Menge*) heap (*coll.*); pile (*coll.*); load (*coll.*); **ein ~ Arbeit/Bücher** a load *or* heap *or* pile of work/books (*coll.*); loads *or* heaps *or* piles of work/books (*coll.*); **ein ~ Unsinn** a load of rubbish *or* nonsense (*coll.*); **ein ~ Geld** loads of money (*coll.*); **einen ~ Geld machen** make a packet (*coll.*); Ⓒ (*Ansammlung von Menschen*) crowd; **so viele Idioten auf einem ~** (*ugs.*) so many idiots in one place; Ⓓ (*Gruppe*) crowd (*coll.*); bunch (*coll.*); Ⓔ (*Soldatenspr.*) troop

**haufen-**, **Haufen-**: **~dorf** *das* Haufendorf (*irregular conglomerate village*); **~weise** *Adv.* (*ugs.*) **~weise Geld ausgeben/Eis essen** spend loads of money/eat heaps *or* loads of ice cream (*coll.*); **~wolke** *die* (*Met.*) cumulus [cloud]

**häufig** /ˈhɔyfɪç/ ❶ *Adj.* frequent. ❷ *adv.* frequently; often

**Häufigkeit** *die;* ~, **~en** frequency

**Häufigkeits·zahl** *die*, **Häufigkeits·ziffer** *die* frequency

**Häuflein** /ˈhɔyflain/ *das;* **~s,** ~ Ⓐ (*kleine Menge*) ⇒ **Häufchen**; Ⓑ (*kleine Gruppe*) handful

**Häufung** *die;* ~, **~en** increasing frequency; **in dieser ~**: in these large numbers; (*so oft*) with this high frequency

**Haupt** /haupt/ *das;* **~[e]s, Häupter** /ˈhɔyptɐ/ Ⓐ (*geh.: Kopf*) head; **bloßen** *od.* **entblößten ~es** with one's head bared; **erhobenen ~es** with one's head [held] high; **gesenkten ~es** with head bowed; **gekrönte Häupter** crowned heads; **an ~ und Gliedern** completely; **zu jmds. Häupten** (*in Kopfhöhe*) at head height; (*bei einem Liegenden*) at sb.'s head; **jmdn. aufs ~ schlagen** vanquish sb.; Ⓑ (*geh.: wichtigste Person*) head

**haupt-**, **Haupt-**: **~abnehmer** *der*, **~abnehmerin** *die* main *or* principal *or* chief customer; **der ~abnehmer eines Produktes** the main buyer of a product; **~achse** *die* Ⓐ (*beim Fahrzeug*) main axle; Ⓑ (*Geom.*) principal axis; **~aktion** *die* ⇒ **~- und Staatsaktion**; **~aktionär** *der* principal shareholder; **~akzent** *der* (*Phon.*) main *or* primary stress; (*fig.*) main emphasis; **~altar** *der* high altar; **~amtlich** ❶ *Adj.* full-time; ❷ *adv.* **~amtlich tätig sein** work full-time *or* on a full-time basis; **~angeklagte** *der/die* (*Rechtsw.*) main *or* principal defendant; **~anschluss**, ***~anschluß** *der* (*Fernspr.*) main exchange line; **~arbeit** *die* main part of the work; **~argument** *das* main *or* principal argument; **~augenmerk** *das* closest attention; **sein ~augenmerk galt ...** (+ *Dat.*) he paid closest attention to ...; **~bahnhof** *der* main station; **Amsterdam ~bahnhof** Amsterdam Central; **~belastungs·zeuge** *der* (*Rechtsw.*) principal *or* main *or* chief prosecution witness; **~beruf** *der* main occupation *or* job; **er ist im ~beruf Schreiner** his main occupation *or* job is that of carpenter; **~beruflich** ❶ *Adj.* **seine ~berufliche Tätigkeit** his main occupation; ❷ *adv.* **er ist ~beruflich als Elektriker tätig** his main occupation is that of electrician; **~beschäftigung** *die* main occupation; **~buch** *das* (*Kaufmannsspr.*) ledger; **~darsteller** *der* (*Theater, Film*) leading man; male lead; **~darstellerin** *die* (*Theater, Film*) leading lady; female lead; **~deck** *das* main deck; **~eingang** *der* main entrance; **~einnahme·quelle** *die* main *or* principal source of income; (*eines Staates*) main *or* principal source of revenue

**Häuptel** /ˈhɔyptl̩/ *das;* **~s, ~[n]** (*südd., österr.*) head (*of cabbage/lettuce*); **ein ~ Salat/Kohl** a [head of] lettuce/cabbage

**Haupt·erbe** *der* principal heir

**Hauptes·länge** *die: in* **jmdn. um ~ überragen** (*geh.*) be a head taller than sb.

**Haupt-**: **~fach** *das* Ⓐ (*Universität*) main subject; major; **etw. im ~fach studieren** study sth. as one's main subject; Ⓑ (*Schule*) main subject; **~farbe** *die* main *or* principal colour; **~fehler** *der* main *or* principal *or* chief error; (*im Charakter*) fault/(*in einer Theorie, einem Argument*) flaw; **~feind** *der*, **~feindin** *die* main *or* principal *or* chief enemy; **~feld** *das* (*Sport*) [main] bunch;

h

**~feldwebel** *der* ▶91 (*Milit.*) **A** ≈ staff sergeant (*Brit.*); ≈ sergeant first class (*Amer.*); **B** (*hist.*) company sergeant major; **~figur** *die* main *or* principal character; **~film** *der* main feature *or* film; **~forderung** *die* main *or* principal *or* chief demand; **~frage** *die* main question; (*Angelegenheit*) main question *or* issue; **~gang** *der* **A** main corridor; **B** ⇒ **~gericht**; **~gas·leitung** *die* gas main; **~gebäude** *das* main building; **~gegenstand** *der* main *or* principal *or* chief subject; **~gericht** *das* main course; **~geschäft** *das* **A** (*Laden*) main branch; **B** (*größter Umsatz*) peak sales *pl.*; (*wichtigster Geschäftszweig*) main line; **~geschäfts·stelle** *die* head office; **~geschäfts·straße** *die* main shopping street; **~geschäfts·zeit** *die* peak shopping hours *pl.*; **~gewicht** *das* main emphasis; **~gewinn** *der* first *or* top prize; **~grund** *der* main *or* principal *or* chief reason; **~hahn** *der; Pl.* **~hähne**, (*fachspr.*) **~~en** mains stopcock; **~interesse** *das* main interest; **~kampf·linie** *die* (*Milit.*) front [line]; **~kasse** *die* main cash desk; **~katalog** *der* main catalogue; **~last** *die* main burden; **~leitung** *die* (*Gas-, Wasserleitung*) main; (*Stromleitung*) main[s *pl.*]; **~leute** ⇒ **~mann**

**Häuptling** /ˈhɔyptlɪŋ/ *der;* **~s, ~e** chief[tain]; (*iron. abwertend*) bigwig (*coll.*)

**haupt-, Haupt-: ~macht** *die* (*veralt.*) main body [of the army]; **~mahlzeit** *die* main meal; **~mangel** *der* main *or* principal defect; **~mann** *der; Pl.* **~leute** **A** ▶91 (*Milit.*) captain; **B** (*hist.*) leader; **~masse** *die* bulk; **~merkmal** *das* main *or* principal *or* chief characteristic; **~mieter** *der*, **~mieterin** *die* [main] tenant; **~motiv** *das* **A** (*Gegenstand*) main *or* principal motif; **B** (*Beweggrund*) main *or* principal *or* chief motive; **~nahrung** *die* staple *or* main food; **~nenner** *der* (*Math.*) common denominator; **~person** *die* central figure; **sie will immer und überall die ~person sein** (*fig.*) she always wants to be the centre of everything *or* of attention; **~portal** *das* main portal; **~post** *die*, **~post·amt** *das* main post office; **~probe** *die* ⇒ **Generalprobe** A; **~problem** *das* main *or* chief problem; **~produkt** *das* main *or* chief product; **~punkt** *der* main point; **~quartier** *das* (*Milit., auch fig.*) headquarters *sing. or pl.*; **~quelle** *die* main *or* principal *or* primary source; **~redner** *der*, **~rednerin** *die* main *or* principal speaker; **~reise·zeit** *die* high season; peak [holiday] season; **~rolle** *die* leading *or* main role; lead; **die ~rolle spielen** play the leading role *or* the lead (**in** + *Dat.* in); **die ~rolle [in** *od.* **bei etw.] spielen** (*fig.*) play the leading role [in sth.]; **~runde** *die* (*Fußball*) main round; **~sache** *die* main *or* most important thing; **~sache, du bist gesund** (*ugs.*) the main thing is, you're in good health; **in der ~sache** mainly; in the main; **~sächlich** ❶ *Adv.* mainly; principally; chiefly; ❷ *adj.* main; principal; chief; **~saison** *die* high season; **~satz** *der* **A** (*Sprachw.*) main clause; (*allein stehend*) sentence; **B** (*Musik*) first subject; **C** (*grundlegender Satz*) first *or* basic principle; **~schalter** *der* **A** (*Elektrot.*) mains switch; **B** (*in der Bank, Post*) main counter; **~schiff** *das* (*Archit.*) nave; **~schlag·ader** *die* aorta; **~schlüssel** *der* master key; pass key; **~schul·abschluss**, ***~schul·abschluß** *der* ≈ secondary school leaving certificate; **~schuld** *die* main share of the blame; **die ~schuld an etw.** (*Dat.*) **haben** bear the main part of the blame for sth.; **~schuldige** *der/die* person mainly to blame; (*an einem Verbrechen*) main *or* chief offender; **~schule** *die* ≈ secondary modern school; **~schüler** *der*, **~schülerin** *die* ≈ secondary modern school pupil; **~schul·lehrer** *der*, **~schul·lehrerin** *die* ≈ secondary modern school teacher; **~schwierigkeit** *die* main *or* chief difficulty; **~segel** *das* (*Seemannsspr.*) mainsail; **~seminar** *das* (*Hochschulw.*) advanced seminar; **~sicherung** *die* (*Elektrot.*) mains fuse; **~sitz** *der* head office; headquarters *pl.*; **~sorge** *die* main worry; **~stadt** *die* capital [city]; **~städter** *der*, **~städterin** *die* citizen *or* inhabitant of the capital; **~städtisch** *Adj.* metropolitan; **~straße** *die* ▶818 **A** (*wichtigste Geschäftsstraße*) high *or* main street; **B** (*Durchgangsstraße*) main road; **~strecke** *die* (*Eisenb.*) main line; **~stütze** *die* main support; (*fig.*) mainstay; **~sünde** *die* (*kath. Rel.*) cardinal sin; **~tätigkeit** *die* main *or* principal activity; **~teil** *der* major part; **~thema** *das* main topic *or* theme; (*Musik*) main theme; **~ton** *der; Pl.* **~töne** **A** (*Musik*) principal note; **B** ⇒ **~akzent**; **~treffer** *der* ⇒ **~gewinn**; **~tribüne** *die* (*Sport*) main stand; **~übel** *das* main *or* chief evil; **~- und Staatsaktion** *die: in* **eine ~- und Staatsaktion aus etw. machen** make a big thing *or* a meal of sth. (*coll.*); **~unterschied** *der* main *or* principal *or* chief difference; **~ursache** *die* main *or* principal *or* chief cause; **~verantwortliche** *der/die* person mainly responsible; **~verdiener** *der*, **~verdienerin** *die* principal *or* main wage earner; breadwinner; **~verhandlung** *die* (*Rechtsw.*) main hearing

**Haupt·verkehr** *der* bulk of the traffic

**Hauptverkehrs-: ~straße** *die* main road; **~zeit** *die* rush hour

**Haupt-: ~versammlung** *die* (*Wirtsch.*) shareholders' meeting; **~verwaltung** *die* head office; **~wache** *die* main police station; **~wachtmeister** *der*, **~wachtmeisterin** *die* ⇒ **Polizeihauptwachtmeister**; **~werk** *das* **A** (*eines Künstlers*) major *or* most important work; **B** (*zentrales Werk mit mehreren Teilbetrieben*) main works *sing. or pl.*; **C** (*an der Orgel*) great organ; **~wohnsitz** *der* main place of residence; **~wort** *das; Pl.* **~wörter** (*Sprachw.*) noun; **~zeuge** *der*, **~zeugin** *die* principal *or* main *or* chief witness; **~zug** *der* **A** (*Eisenbahnw.*) scheduled train; **B** (*wichtigste Eigenschaft*) main *or* principal feature; **~zweck** *der* main *or* chief purpose *or* aim

**hau ruck** /ˈhauˈrʊk/ *Interj.* heave[-ho]

**Haus** /haus/ *das;* **~es, Häuser** /ˈhɔyzɐ/ **A** house; (*Firmengebäude*) building; **~ an ~ wohnen** be next-door neighbours; **~ an ~ mit jmdm. wohnen** live next door to sb.; **er ist gerade aus dem ~ gegangen** he has just gone out; **im ~ spielen** play indoors; **kommt ins ~, es regnet** come inside, it's raining; **Herrn X, im ~e** (*auf Briefen*) to Mr X (*living in the same block of flats, working in the same firm, etc.*); **das ~ Gottes** (*geh.*) the house of God; **das Weiße ~:** the White House; **~ und Hof** house and home; **jmdm. ins ~ stehen** (*ugs.*) be in store for sb.; ⇒ *auch* **öffentlich** 1; **B** (*Heim*) home; **jmdm. das ~ verbieten** not allow sb. in one's *or* the house; **etw. ins ~/frei ~ liefern** deliver sth. to sb.'s door/free of charge; **das ~ auf den Kopf stellen** (*ugs.*) turn the place upside down; **außer ~[e] sein/essen** be/eat out; **ist Ihre Frau im ~[e]?** is your wife at home?; **nach ~e** home; **zu ~e** at home; **ich bin für niemanden zu ~e** I'm not at home to anybody; **wie geht es zu ~e?** how are things at home?; **zu ~e anrufen** phone home; **fühlt euch wie zu ~e** make yourselves at home; **sich zu ~e fühlen** (*fig.*) feel at home; **schon dreißig, und er wohnt noch zu ~e** he's already thirty and he's still living with his parents; **bei ihnen zu ~e** in their house/flat; (*in ihrer Heimat*) where they come from; **dieser Brauch ist in Holstein zu ~e** this custom comes from Holstein; **zu ~e spielen** (*Sport*) play at home; **das ~ hüten** stay at home *or* indoors; **jmdm. das ~ einrennen** (*ugs.*) be constantly on sb.'s doorstep; **jmdm. ins ~ schneien** (*ugs.*) descend on sb.; **auf einem Gebiet/in etw.** (*Dat.*) **zu ~e sein** (*ugs.*) be at home in a field/in sth.; **C** (*Theater*) theatre; (*Publikum*) house; **das große/kleine ~:** the large/small theatre; **vor vollen/ausverkauften Häusern spielen** play to full *or* packed houses; **D** (*Gasthof, Geschäft*) **das erste ~ am Platze** the best shop of its kind/hotel in the town/village *etc.*; **eine Spezialität des ~es** a speciality of the house; **E** (*Firma*) firm; business house; **das ~ Meyer** the firm of Meyer; **F** (*geh.: Parlament*) **das Hohe ~:** the House; **beide Häuser [im Parlament]** both Houses [of Parliament]; **Hohes ~!** ≈ Mr Speaker, Sir; **G** (*geh.: Familie*) household; **der Herr/die Dame des ~es** the master/lady of the house; **aus gutem ~e kommen** come from a *or* be of good family; **der Herr im eigenen ~ sein** be master in one's own house; **Grüße von ~ zu ~:** regards from all of us to all of you; **von ~[e] aus** (*von der Familie her*) by birth; (*eigentlich*) really; actually; **H** (*~halt*) household; **jmdm. das ~ führen** keep house for sb.; **~ halten** (*veralt.*) keep house; **jmdn. ins ~ nehmen** take sb. in and look after him/her; **I** (*Dynastie*) house; **das ~ Tudor/[der] Hohenzollern** the House of Tudor/Hohenzollern; **J** (*ugs.: die ~bewohner*) occupants *pl.* [of the house]; **das ganze ~:** the whole house; **K** (*ugs. scherzh.: Mensch*) **ein gelehrtes/lustiges** *usw.* **~:** a scholarly/amusing *etc.* sort (*coll.*); **L** (*Schnecken~*) shell; **M** (*Astrol.*) house; **N ~ halten** (*sparsam sein*) be economical (**mit** with); **mit seinen Kräften ~ halten** conserve one's strength

**haus-, Haus-: ~altar** *der* domestic altar; **~angestellte** *der/die* domestic servant; **~antenne** *die* external aerial (*Brit.*) *or* (*Amer.*) antenna; **~anzug** *der* (*für Männer*) leisure suit; (*für Frauen*) pyjama suit; **~apotheke** *die* medicine cabinet; **~arbeit** *die* **A** housework; **B** (*Schulw.*) item of homework; **~arbeiten aufhaben** (*ugs.*) have homework *sing.*; **~arrest** *der* **A** house arrest; **B** (*in der Familie*) **er bestraft seinen Sohn mit ~arrest** he punishes his son by keeping him in; **mein Bruder hat ~arrest** my brother is being kept in; **~arzt** *der*, **~ärztin** *die* **A** family doctor; **B** (*eines Hotels, Heims*) resident doctor; **~aufgabe** *die* piece of homework; **~aufgaben aufhaben** (*ugs.*) have homework *sing.*; **~aufsatz** *der* homework essay; **~backen** ❶ *Adj.* plain; unadventurous, boring ‹clothes›; ❷ *adv.* ‹dress› unadventurously; **~ball** *der* [private] dance (*held at sb.'s house*); **~bar** *die* **A** (*Möbelstück*) cocktail cabinet; **B** (*kleine Bar*) [home] bar; **~bau** *der* housebuilding; **beim ~bau** when building a/one's house; **mit dem ~bau beginnen** start building a/one's house; **~besetzer** *der*, **~besetzerin** *die* squatter; **~besetzung** *die* (*Vorgang*) squatting; (*Ergebnis*) squat; **~besitzer** *der* houseowner; (*Vermieter*) landlord; **~besitzerin** *die* houseowner; (*Vermieterin*) landlady; **~besorger** *der;* **~~s, ~~, ~besorgerin** *die;* **~~, ~~nen** (*österr.*) ⇒ **Hausmeister[in]**; **~besuch** *der* house call; **~bewohner** *der*, **~bewohnerin** *die* occupant [of the house]; **~boot** *das* houseboat; **~brand** *der* **A** (*Material*) domestic fuel; **B** (*Prozess*) domestic heating; **~bursche** *der* pageboy

**Häuschen** /ˈhɔysçən/ *das;* **~s, ~** **A** little *or* small house; **B** **[ganz** *od.* **rein] aus dem ~ sein** (*ugs.*) be [completely] over the moon (*coll.*); **[ganz** *od.* **rein] aus dem ~ geraten** *od.* **fahren** (*ugs.*) go wild with excitement; **jmdn. aus dem ~ bringen** (*ugs.*) get sb. wildly excited; **C** (*ugs.: Toilette*) privy

**haus-, Haus-: ~dame** *die* housekeeper; **~detektiv** *der*, **~detektivin** *die* house detective; **~diener** *der*, **~dienerin** *die* domestic servant; **~drachen** *der* (*ugs. abwertend*) dragon (*coll.*); **~durchsuchung** *die* (*österr.*) ⇒ **~suchung**; **~ecke** *die* corner of the house; **~eigen** *Adj.* **der ~eigene Kindergarten** the company's/hotel's *etc.* own kindergarten; **das Hotel hat einen ~eigenen Swimmingpool/Strand** the hotel has its own swimming pool/[private] beach; **~eigentümer** *der*, **~eigentümerin** *die* ⇒ **~besitzer**; **~einfahrt** *die* **A** drive[way] [of the house]; **B** (*österr.*) ⇒ **~eingang**; **~eingang** *der* entrance [to the house]

**hausen** *itr. V.* **A** (*ugs. abwertend: wohnen*) live; **B** (*ugs. abwertend: Verwüstungen anrichten*) **[furchtbar] ~:** cause *or* wreak havoc; **wie die Wandalen ~:** behave like vandals; **C** (*schweiz.: sparen*) be economical

*old spelling (see note on page 1707)

**Häuser-: ~block** *der; Pl.* **~~s** *od.* **~blöcke** block [of houses]; **~makler** *der,* **~maklerin** *die* ▶ 159 estate agent; **~meer** *das* mass of houses; **~reihe** *die* row of houses; (*aneinander gebaut*) terrace [of houses]

**Haus-: ~fassade** *die* house front; **~flagge** *die* (*Seew.*) house flag; **~flur** *der* hall[way]; entrance hall; (*im Obergeschoss*) landing

**Haus·frau** *die* ▶ 159 A housewife; B (*südd., österr.*) ⇨ **~besitzerin**

**Hausfrauen-: ~art** *die: in* **nach** *od.* **auf ~art** home-made-style *attrib.*; **~pflicht** *die* housewifely duty

**hausfraulich** *Adj.* housewifely; **ihre ~en Fähigkeiten** her abilities as a housewife

**Haus·freund** *der* A friend of the family; family friend; B (*verhüll.: Liebhaber*) man friend (*euphem.*)

**Haus·freundin** *die* ⇨ **Hausfreund** A

**Haus·friede[n]** *der* (*in der Familie*) domestic peace; (*zwischen Hausbewohnern*) good relationships *pl.* between the tenants

**Hausfriedens·bruch** *der* (*Rechtsw.*) trespass

**haus-, Haus-: ~gans** *die* domestic goose; **~gast** *der* resident; guest; **~gebrauch** *der* domestic use; **das reicht für den ~gebrauch** (*ugs.*) it's good enough to get by (*coll.*); **Spielst du Klavier? — Ja, aber nur für den ~gebrauch** Do you play the piano? — Yes, but only well enough to get by (*coll.*); **~gehilfin** *die* [home] help; **~geist** *der* A (*Gespenst*) [resident] ghost; B (*scherzh.: ~angestellte*) **unser guter ~geist** our faithful housekeeper; **~gemacht** *Adj.* home-made; **~gemeinschaft** *die* A (*gemeinsamer Haushalt*) household; **in einer ~gemeinschaft mit jmdm. leben** live together with sb.; B (*Bewohner eines Hauses*) occupants *pl.* of the block; **~gerät** *das* A (*veralt.*) household articles *pl.*; B ⇨ **~haltsgerät**

**Haus·halt** *der* A household; **einen ~ gründen/auflösen** set up home/break up a household; B (*Arbeit im ~*) housekeeping; **jmdm. den ~ führen** keep house for sb.; **im ~ helfen** help with the housework; C (*Politik*) budget

**-haushalt** *der* (*bes. Biol., Med.*) balance

***haus|halten** ⇨ **Haus** H, N

**Haushälterin** *die;* **~, ~nen** housekeeper

**haushälterisch** ❶ *Adj.* economical. ❷ *adv.* **~ mit etw. umgehen** be economical with sth.; use sth. economically

**haushalts-, Haushalts-: ~artikel** *der* household article; **billige ~artikel** cheap household articles *or* goods; **~auflösung** *die* house clearance; **bei einer ~auflösung** when a house/flat is cleared; **~ausgleich** *der* (*Politik*) **den ~ausgleich garantieren** guarantee a balanced budget; **einen ~ausgleich herbeiführen** balance the budget; **~buch** *das* housekeeping book; **~debatte** *die* (*Politik*) budget debate; **~defizit** *das* budgetary deficit; **~frage** *die* budgetary question *or* issue; **~führung** *die* housekeeping; **~geld** *das* housekeeping money; **~gerät** *das* household appliance; **~gesetz** *das* (*Amtsspr.*) budget legislation; **~hilfe** *die* home help; **~jahr** *das* A (*Rechnungsjahr*) financial year; B (*Lehrzeit in einem Haushalt*) **sie machte ein ~jahr** she spent a year with a family, learning how to keep house; **~kasse** *die* housekeeping money; **die ~kasse war leer** there was no housekeeping money left; **diese alte Schachtel dient uns als ~kasse** we use this old box to keep the housekeeping money in; **~mittel** *Pl.* budgetary funds; **~packung** *die* family pack; **~plan** *der* budget; **~politik** *die* budgetary policy; **~politisch** ❶ *Adj.* related to budgetary policy *postpos.*; **~politische Erwägungen** considerations of budgetary policy; ❷ *adv.* **~politisch gesehen** from the point of view of the budget; **~volumen** *das* total budget; **~waage** *die* kitchen scales *pl.*; **~waren** *Pl.* household goods

**Haushaltung** *die* A ⇨ **Haushalt** A; B (*Haushaltsführung*) housekeeping

**Haushaltungs-: ~kosten** *Pl.* housekeeping costs; **~vorstand** *der* head of the household

**haus-, Haus-: ~herr** *der* A (*Familienoberhaupt*) head of the household; B (*als Gastgeber*) host; C (*Rechtsspr.*) (*Eigentümer*) owner; (*Mieter*) occupier; D (*südd., österr.*) ⇨ **~besitzer**; E (*Sportjargon*) **die ~herren** the hosts; the home team *sing.*; **~herrin** *die* A (*Familienoberhaupt*) lady of the house; B (*als Gastgeberin*) hostess; C (*südd., österr.*) ⇨ **~besitzerin**; **~hoch** ❶ *Adj.* ‹flames/waves etc.› as high as a house; (*fig.*) overwhelming ‹superiority etc.›; **die ~hohe Favoritin** the hot favourite; ❷ *adv.* **~hoch türmten sich die Wellen** the waves were mountainous; (*fig.*) **~hoch gewinnen/jmdn. ~hoch schlagen** win hands down/beat sb. hands down; **jmdm. ~hoch überlegen sein** be vastly superior to sb.; **~huhn** *das* domestic chicken; **~hund** *der* domestic dog

**hausieren** *itr. V.* **[mit etw.] ~:** hawk [sth.]; peddle [sth.]; **mit einer Idee ~ [gehen]** (*ugs. abwertend*) hawk an idea around; **„Hausieren verboten"** 'no hawkers'

**Hausierer** *der;* **~s, ~, Hausiererin** *die;* **~, ~nen** ▶ 159 pedlar; hawker

**haus-, Haus-: ~intern** ❶ *Adj.* internal ‹regulations, purposes, information›; ‹agreement, custom› within the company; ❷ *adv.* internally; within the company; **~jacke** *die* casual [wrapover] jacket (*worn at home*); **~jurist** *der,* **~juristin** *die* firm's lawyer; company lawyer; **~kapelle**[1] *die* private chapel; **~kapelle**[2] *die* resident band; **~katze** *die* domestic cat; **~kleid** *das* house dress; **~konzert** *das* concert given at home; **~lehrer** *der,* **~lehrerin** *die* private tutor

**häuslich** /ˈhɔyslɪç/ ❶ *Adj.* A domestic ‹bliss, peace, affairs, duties, etc.›; **am ~en Kaminfeuer** at one's own fireside; ⇨ *auch* **Herd** A; B (*das Zuhause liebend*) home-loving. ❷ *adv.* **sich [bei jmdm./irgendwo] ~ niederlassen** *od.* **einrichten** (*ugs.*) make oneself at home [in sb.'s house/somewhere]

**Häuslichkeit** *die;* **~:** domesticity

**Hausmacher-: ~art** *die: in* **nach ~art** home-made-style *attrib.*; **~wurst** *die* home-made sausage

**Haus-: ~macht** *die* (*hist.*) allodium; (*fig.*) power base; **~mädchen** *das* ▶ 159 [home] help

**Haus·mann** *der* ▶ 159 *man who stays at home and does the housework;* (*Ehemann*) househusband

**Hausmanns·kost** *die* plain cooking

**Haus-: ~mantel** *der* housecoat; **~märchen** *das* folk tale; **die ~märchen der Brüder Grimm** Grimms' Fairy Tales; **~marke** *die* A (*Wein, Sekt*) house wine; B (*ugs.: bevorzugtes Getränk*) usual *or* favourite tipple (*coll.*); C (*Markenfabrikat einer Firma*) own brand; **~maus** *die* house mouse; **~meier** *der* (*hist.*) mayor of the palace; **~meister** *der,* **~meisterin** *die* ▶ 159 A caretaker; B (*schweiz.*) ⇨ **Hausbesitzer[in]**; **~mitteilung** *die* A (*im Büro*) [internal] memo; B (*für Kunden*) company newsletter; **~mittel** *das* household remedy; **~musik** *die* music at home; **~musik machen** play music at home; **~mutter** *die; Pl.* **~mütter** housemother; **~mütterchen** *das* (*ugs. scherzh.*) little housewife; **~nummer** *die* ▶ 187 house number; **ihre ~nummer** the number of her house; **~ordnung** *die* house rules *pl.*; **~partei** *die* (*österr.*) tenant; **~postille** *die* (*hist.*): *collection of religious and devotional sayings and stories for the family;* (*fig. ugs.*) organ; **~putz** *der* spring-clean; (*regelmäßig*) clean-out; **beim ~putz helfen** help with the regular cleaning-out; **~putz halten** *od.* **machen** spring-clean the house

**Haus·rat** *der* household goods *pl.*

**Hausrat·versicherung** *die* [household *or* home] contents insurance

**Haus-: ~recht** *das* (*Rechtsw.*): *right of a householder or owner of a property to forbid sb. entrance or order sb. to leave;* **von seinem ~recht Gebrauch machen** forbid sb. entrance/order sb. to leave; **~rind** *das* domestic ox; **~sammlung** *die* house-to-house *or* door-to-door collection; **~schaf** *das* domestic sheep; **~schlachtung** *die* home slaughtering; **aus eigener ~schlachtung stammen** be home-slaughtered; **~schlüssel** *der* front-door key; house key; **~schneiderin** *die* visiting seamstress; **~schuh** *der* slipper; **~schwamm** *der* (*Pilz*) dry rot; **~schwein** *das* domestic pig

**Hausse** /ˈhoːs(ə)/ *die;* **~, ~n** (*Börsenw.*) rise [in prices]; (*fig.*) boom; **~ haben** rise [on the Stock Exchange]; **auf ~ spekulieren** bull; speculate for a rise

**Haus·segen** *der* house blessing (*devotional inscription placed in a house*); **bei ihnen hängt der ~ schief** (*ugs. scherzh.*) they've been having a row

**Haussier** /(h)oˈsi̯eː/ *der;* **~s, ~s** (*Börsenw.*) bull

**Haus·stand** *der* household; **einen [eigenen] ~stand gründen** set up home [on their own]; **sie führt einen eigenen ~stand** she lives independently

**Haussuchung** *die;* **~, ~en** house search

**Haussuchungs·befehl** *der* search warrant

**Haus-: ~telefon** *das* internal telephone; **~tier** *das* A pet; B (*Nutztier*) domestic animal; **~tochter** *die: young girl living with a family in order to learn how to keep house;* **~tor** *das* front entrance; **~tür** *die* front door; **etw. direkt vor der ~tür haben** (*ugs. fig.*) have sth. on one's doorstep; **~tyrann** *der,* **~tyrannin** *die* (*ugs.*) tyrant [in one's own home]; **~vater** *der* A (*in einem Heim*) housefather; (*in einer Jugendherberge*) warden; B (*veralt.: Familienvater*) paterfamilias; **~verbot** *das* ban on entering the house/pub/restaurant *etc.*; **~verbot haben/bekommen** be banned [from the house/pub/restaurant *etc.*]; **jmdm. ~verbot erteilen** ban sb. [from the house/pub/restaurant *etc.*]; **~versammlung** *die* (*DDR*) tenants' meeting; **~verwalter** *der,* **~verwalterin** *die* manager [of the block]; **~verwaltung** *die* management [of the block]; **~wand** *die* [house] wall; **~wart** *der;* **~~[e]s, ~~e, ~wartin** *die;* **~~, ~~nen** (*landsch.*) caretaker; **~wesen** *das* (*veralt.*) household; **~wirt** *der* landlord; **~wirtin** *die* landlady

**Haus·wirtschaft** *die* A domestic science and home economics; B (*DDR Landw.*) **individuelle** *od.* **persönliche ~:** *cooperative farmer's personal holding of land, buildings livestock, and equipment*

**hauswirtschaftlich** ❶ *Adj.* domestic; **~e Kenntnisse** knowledge of domestic matters. ❷ *adv.* **~ interessiert/begabt** interested/talented in domestic matters

**Hauswirtschafts-: ~lehrerin** *die* ▶ 159 domestic science and home economics teacher; **~leiterin** *die* housekeeper; **~schule** *die* college of domestic science and home economics

**Haus-: ~zelt** *das* ridge tent; **~zins** *der; Pl.* **~~e** (*südd., schweiz.*) ⇨ **Miete**[1] A

**Haut** /haut/ *die;* **~, Häute** /ˈhɔytə/ A ▶ 471 skin; **sich** (*Dat.*) **die ~ abschürfen** graze oneself; **viel ~ zeigen** (*ugs. scherzh.*) show a lot of bare flesh (*coll.*); **nass bis auf die ~:** soaked to the skin; wet through; **nur noch ~ und Knochen sein** (*ugs.*), **nur noch aus ~ und Knochen bestehen** (*ugs.*) be nothing but skin and bone; **seine eigene ~ retten** save one's own skin; **seine ~ zu Markte tragen** (*ugs.*) risk one's neck (*coll.*); **seine ~ so teuer wie möglich verkaufen** (*ugs.*) sell oneself as dearly as possible; **sich seiner ~** (*Gen.*) **wehren** (*ugs.*) stand up for oneself; **aus der ~ fahren** (*ugs.*) go up the wall (*coll.*); **es ist zum Aus-der-~-Fahren** it's enough to drive or send you up the wall (*coll.*); **er/sie kann nicht aus seiner/ihrer ~ heraus** (*ugs.*) a leopard cannot change its spots (*prov.*); **sich in seiner ~ nicht wohl fühlen** (*ugs.*) feel uneasy; (*unzufrieden sein*) feel discontented [with one's lot]; **sich in seiner ~ wohl fühlen** (*ugs.*) feel contented [with one's lot]; **ich möchte nicht in deiner ~ stecken** (*ugs.*) I shouldn't like to be in your shoes (*coll.*); **mit heiler ~ davonkommen** (*ugs.*) get away with it; **jmdm. mit ~ und Haar[en] verfallen sein** (*ugs.*) be head over heels in love with sb.; **sich einer Aufgabe** (*Dat.*) **mit ~ und Haar[en] verschreiben** (*ugs.*) devote oneself completely *or* wholeheartedly to a task; **jmdm. unter die ~ gehen** (*ugs.*) get under sb.'s skin (*coll.*); **B** (*Fell*) skin; (*von größerem Tier auch*) hide; **auf der faulen ~ liegen** (*ugs.*) sit around and do nothing; **sich auf die faule ~ legen** (*ugs.*) sit back and do nothing; **C** (*Schale*) skin; **D** (*dünne Schicht, Bespannung*) skin; **E** (*Mensch*) **eine gute/ehrliche ~:** a good/honest sort (*coll.*)

**Haut-: ~abschürfung** *die* graze; **~arzt** *der*, **~ärztin** *die* ▶ 159 skin specialist; dermatologist; **~atmung** *die* (*Med., Zool.*) cutaneous respiration; **~ausschlag** *der* [skin] rash

**Häutchen** /'hɔytçən/ *das;* **~s, ~** **A** ⇒ **Haut C**: piece of skin; **B** ⇒ **Haut D**: thin skin

**Haut·creme** *die* skin cream

**Haute Couture** /(h)o:tku'ty:ɐ̯/ *die;* **~:** haute couture

**häuten** /'hɔytn̩/ **1** *tr. V.* skin, flay ‹animal›; skin ‹tomato, almond, etc.›. **2** *refl. V.* shed its skin/their skins; ‹snake› shed *or* slough its skin

**haut·eng** *Adj.* skintight

**Hautevolee** /(h)o:tvo'le:/ *die;* **~** (*abwertend*) upper crust (*coll.*)

**haut-, Haut-: ~falte** *die* fold [of skin]; **~farbe** *die* [skin] colour; **wegen seiner ~farbe** because of the colour of his skin; **~farben** *Adj.* skin-coloured; flesh-coloured; **~freundlich** *Adj.* kind to the/one's skin *pred.*

**-häutig** /-'hɔytɪç/ *Adj.* -skinned

**haut-, Haut-: ~jucken** *das* itching *no indef. art.*; **~krankheit** *die* skin disease; **~krebs** *der* skin cancer; **~nah** **1** *Adj.* **A** (*unmittelbar*) immediate ‹contact›; eyeball-to-eyeball ‹confrontation›; **B** (*ugs.: packend, anschaulich*) realistic and gripping ‹description›; **C** (*Anat.*) close to *or* immediately below the skin *postpos.*; **2** *adv.* **A** (*unmittelbar*) **mit etw. ~nah in Berührung/Kontakt kommen** come into very close contact with sth.; **jmdn. ~nah decken** *od.* **bewachen** (*Sport Jargon*) mark sb. very tightly *or* closely; (*sehr eng*) **~nah tanzen** dance very close together; **B** (*ugs.: packend, anschaulich*) **etw. ~nah beschreiben** describe sth. in a realistic and gripping way; **~öl** *das* body oil; **~pflege** *die* skin care; **~pilz** *der* fungus parasitic on the skin; cutaneous fungus (*Med.*); **~reizung** *die* skin irritation; **~schere** *die* cuticle scissors *pl.*; **~schicht** *die* layer of skin; **~schonend** *Adj.* kind to the/one's skin *pred.*; **~transplantation** *die* (*Med.*) skin graft; **~typ** *der* skin type

**Häutung** *die;* **~, ~en** **A** ⇒ **häuten 1**: skinning; flaying; **B** (*das Sichhäuten*) **Schlangen machen viele ~en durch** snakes shed *or* slough their skin many times; **eine Eidechse bei der ~:** a lizard shedding its skin

**haut·verträglich** *Adj.* kind to the/one's skin *pred.*

**Havanna**[1] /ha'vana/ (*das*); **~s** ▶ 700 Havana

**Havanna**[2] *die;* **~, ~[s], Havanna·zigarre** *die* Havana [cigar]

**Havarie** /hava'ri:/ *die;* **~, ~n** (*Seew., Flugw., österr. auch:* **~** *eines Autos*) accident; (*Schaden*) damage *no indef. art.*; average (*Ins.*); (*fig.*) breakdown

**havarieren** *itr. V.* (*Seew., Flugw.*) ‹aircraft› crash; ‹ship› have an accident; **zwei Militärmaschinen/**(*österr.*) **Autos havarierten** two military planes/cars collided; **ein havariertes Schiff** a damaged ship

**Havarist** *der;* **~en, ~en** (*Seew.*) **A** (*Schiff*) damaged ship; **B** (*Eigentümer*) owner of a/the damaged ship

**Havaristin** *die;* **~, ~nen** ⇒ **Havarist B**

**Hawaii** /ha'vai/ (*das*); **~s** Hawaii

**Hawaii-: ~gitarre** *die* Hawaiian guitar; **~inseln, ~-Inseln** *Pl.* Hawaiian Islands

*old spelling (see note on page 1707)

**hawaiisch** *Adj.* Hawaiian

**Haxe** *die;* **~, ~n** ⇒ **Hachse**

**H-Bombe** /'ha:-/ *die* H-bomb

**H-Dur** /'ha:-/ *das* (*Musik*) B major; ⇒ *auch* **A-Dur**

**he** /he:/ *Interj.* (*ugs.*) **A** (*Zuruf, Ausruf*) hey; **~ [du], komm mal her!** hey [you], come here!; **B** (*zur Verstärkung einer Frage*) eh

**Hearing** /'hɪərɪŋ/ *das;* **~[s], ~s** (*bes. Politik*) hearing

**Heb·amme** *die* ▶ 159 midwife

**Hebe-: ~balken** *der,* **~baum** *der* lever; **~bühne** *die* hydraulic lift; **~figur** *die* (*Eis-, Rollkunstlauf*) lift

**Hebel** /'he:bl̩/ *der;* **~s, ~** (*auch Griff, Physik*) lever; **den ~ ansetzen** position the lever; **da müssen wir den ~ ansetzen** (*fig.*) that's where we've got to start (*coll.*); **alle ~ in Bewegung setzen** (*ugs.*) move heaven and earth; **am längeren ~ sitzen** (*ugs.*) have the whip hand

**Hebel-: ~arm** *der* (*Physik*) lever arm; **~gesetz** *das* (*Physik*) principle of the lever; **~griff** *der* (*Ringen*) lever [hold]; **~kraft** *die* leverage; **~wirkung** *die* leverage

**heben** /'he:bn̩/ **1** *unr. tr. V.* **A** (*nach oben bewegen*) lift; raise; raise ‹baton, camera, glass›; **eine Last ~:** lift a load; **die Hand/den Arm ~:** raise one's hand/arm; **schlurft nicht, hebt die Füße!** pick your feet up!; **100 kg/einen Rekord ~** (*Sport*) lift 100 kg./a record weight; **die Stimme ~** (*geh.*) raise one's voice; **einen ~** (*ugs.*) have a drink; **B** (*an eine andere Stelle bringen*) lift; **jmdn. auf die Schulter/von der Mauer ~:** lift sb. [up] on to one's shoulders/[down] from the wall; **C** (*heraufholen*) dig up ‹treasure etc.›; raise ‹wreck›; **D** (*verbessern*) raise, improve ‹standard, level›; increase ‹turnover, self-confidence›; improve ‹mood›; enhance ‹standing›; boost ‹morale›; **E** (*unpers.*) **es hebt jmdm. den Magen** sb.'s stomach heaves; **es hebt mich, wenn ich das sehe** it turns me over to see it (*coll.*).

**2** *unr. refl. V.* **A** (*geh.: sich recken, sich erheben*) rise; **sich auf die Zehenspitzen ~:** stand on tiptoe; **B** (*hochgehen, hochsteigen*) rise; ‹curtain› rise, go up; ‹mist, fog› lift; **sich ~ und senken** rise and fall; **C** ‹sea, chest› rise and fall, heave; **D** (*sich verbessern*) ‹mood› improve; ‹trade› pick up; ‹standard, level› rise, improve, go up; **E** (*geh.: emporragen*) rise [up]

**Heber** *der;* **~s, ~** **A** (*Technik*) jack; **B** (*Chemie*) pipette; **C** (*Sport: Gewicht~*) weightlifter

**-hebig** /-he:bɪç/ (*Verslehre*) **~:** -footed

**Hebräer** /he'brɛ:ɐ/ *der;* **~s, ~, Hebräerin** *die;* **~, ~nen** Hebrew

**Hebraicum** /he'bra:ikʊm/ *das;* **~s** qualifying examination in Hebrew (*taken by theology students*); **das ~ haben** have passed the Hebrew examination

**hebräisch** *Adj.* ▶ 696 Hebrew

**Hebung** *die;* **~, ~en** **A** (*Bergung*) **die ~ eines Schiffes** the raising of a ship; **bei der ~ des Schatzes ...** when the treasure is/was dug up ...; **B** (*Verbesserung*) raising; improvement; **zur ~ des Selbstvertrauens/der Moral** to improve sb.'s self-confidence/morale; **C** (*Geol.*) uplift; **D** (*Verslehre*) stressed syllable

**Hechel** /'hɛçl̩/ *die;* **~, ~n** (*Landw.*) card; hackle; heckle

**Hechelei** *die;* **~, ~en** (*ugs. abwertend*) backbiting *no pl.*; (*Klatsch*) gossip *no pl.*

**hecheln**[1] **1** *itr. V.* (*ugs. abwertend*) gossip. **2** *tr. V.* (*Landw.*) card; hackle; heckle

**hecheln**[2] *itr. V.* pant [for breath]

**Hecht** /hɛçt/ *der;* **~[e]s, ~e** **A** pike; **der ~ im Karpfenteich sein** (*ugs.*) be a new broom; be a live wire full of new ideas; (*die erste Rolle spielen*) be the kingpin; **B** (*ugs.: Bursche*) **ein toller ~:** an incredible fellow; **C** (*Tabaksqualm*) fug (*coll.*).

**hechten** *itr. V.; mit sein* dive headlong; make a headlong dive; (*schräg nach oben*) throw oneself sideways; (*Schwimmen*) perform *or* do a racing dive; (*vom Sprungturm*) perform *or* do a pike-dive; (*Turnen*) do a long fly

**Hecht-: ~rolle** *die* (*Turnen*) piked roll; **~sprung** *der* **A** (*Turnen*) Hecht vault; **B** (*Schwimmen*) racing dive; (*vom Sprungturm*) pike-dive; **~suppe** *die:* *in* **es zieht wie ~suppe** (*ugs.*) there's a terrible draught (*coll.*)

**Heck**[1] /hɛk/ *das;* **~[e]s, ~e** *od.* **~s** **A** (*Schiffs~*) stern; **B** (*Flugzeug~*) tail; **im ~ der Maschine** at the rear of the plane; **C** (*Auto~*) rear; back

**Heck**[2] *das;* **~[e]s, ~e** (*nordd.*) gate

**Heck·antrieb** *der* (*Kfz-W.*) rear-wheel drive

**Hecke** *die;* **~, ~n** **A** hedge; **B** (*wild wachsend*) thicket

**Hecken-: ~landschaft** *die* landscape of fields and hedgerows; **~rose** *die* dogrose; **~schere** *die* hedge shears *pl.*; (*elektrisch*) hedge trimmer; **~schütze** *der,* **~schützin** *die* sniper

**heck-, Heck-: ~fenster** *das* rear *or* back window; **~flosse** *die* tail fin; **~lastig** /-lastɪç/ **1** *Adj.* tail-heavy; **2** *adv.* **das Auto reagiert ~lastig** the car tends to be tail-heavy

**Heckmeck** /'hɛkmɛk/ *der;* **~s** (*ugs. abwertend*) **A** (*Getue*) fuss; **B** (*Unsinn*) rubbish

**Heck-: ~motor** *der* rear engine; **~scheibe** *die* rear *or* back window; **~tür** *die* back

**heda** /'he:da/ *Interj.* (*veralt.*) I say

**Hederich** /'he:dərɪç/ *der;* **~s, ~e** (*Bot.*) jointed charlock

**Hedonismus** /hedo'nɪsmʊs/ *der;* **~** (*Philos.*) hedonism *no art.*

**Hedonist** *der;* **~en, ~en, Hedonistin** *die;* **~, ~nen** (*Philos.*) hedonist

**hedonistisch** *Adj.* hedonistic

**Hedschra** /'hɛdʒra/ *die;* **~:** Hegira

**Heer** /he:ɐ̯/ *das;* **~[e]s, ~e** **A** (*Gesamtheit der Streitkräfte*) armed forces *pl.*; **das stehende ~:** the standing army; **in das ~ eintreten** join the services; **B** (*für den Landkrieg*) army; **C** (*fig.: große Anzahl*) army

**Heeres-: ~bericht** *der* (*Milit.*) military communiqué; **~bestände** *Pl.* army supplies *or* stores; **~dienst** *der* military service; **~leitung** *die* (*Milit.*) army command staff; **die oberste ~leitung** the high command; **~reform** *die* army reform

**Heer-: ~führer** *der* army commander; **~lager** *das* army camp; **~schar** *die* (*veralt., noch fig.*) host (*arch.*); ⇒ *auch* **himmlisch 1 A**; **~straße** *die* (*veralt.*) military road; **~wesen** *das* armed forces *pl.*

**Hefe** /'he:fə/ *die;* **~, ~n** **A** yeast; (*fig.*) driving force; **B** (*geh. abwertend: Abschaum*) scum

**Hefe-: ~gebäck** *das* pastry (*made with yeast dough*); **~kloß** *der* dumpling made with yeast dough; **aufgehen** *od.* **auseinander gehen wie ein ~kloß** (*ugs. scherzh.*) blow up like a balloon; **~kuchen** *der* yeast cake; **~pilz** *der* yeast fungus; **~teig** *der* yeast dough; **~zopf** *der* plaited bun

**Heft**[1] /hɛft/ *das;* **~[e]s, ~e** (*geh.*) (*am Dolch, Messer*) haft; handle; (*am Schwert*) hilt; **das ~ ergreifen** *od.* **in die Hand nehmen** (*geh.*) take control; **das ~ in der Hand haben/behalten** (*geh.*) be in/keep control; **jmdm. das ~ aus der Hand nehmen** (*geh.*) take control from sb.

**Heft**[2] *das;* **~[e]s, ~e** **A** (*bes. Schule*) exercise book; **B** (*Nummer einer Zeitschrift*) issue; **Jahrgang 10, ~ 12** Volume 10, No. 12; **C** (*kleines Buch*) (*small stapled*) book

**Heftchen** *das;* **~s, ~** **A** (*Comic*) comic; (*Groschenroman*) novelette; **B** (*Block*) book [of tickets/stamps *etc.*]

**heften** **1** *tr. V.* **A** (*mit einer Nadel*) pin; fix; (*mit einer Klammer*) clip; fix; (*mit Klebstoff*) stick; **etw. an/in etw.** (*Akk.*) **~:** pin/stick/clip sth. to/into sth.; **etw. in einen Ordner ~:** put *or* insert sth. in[to] a file; **B** (*richten*) **die Augen/den Blick auf jmdn./etw. ~:** fasten one's eyes/gaze on sb./sth.; **C** (*Schneiderei*) tack; baste; **D** (*Buchbinderei*) stitch; (*mit Klammern*) staple.

**2** *refl. V.* **A** (*verfolgen*) **sich an jmds. Fersen** (*Akk.*) **~:** stick hard on sb.'s heels; **sich**

an jmds. Spur (*Akk.*) ~: get on the track of sb.; **B** (*geh.: knüpfen*) **sich an etw.** (*Akk.*) ~: be linked with sth.; **C** (*richten*) ‹eyes, look› be fixed (**auf** + *Akk.* on)

**Hefter** *der;* ~**s**, ~: [loose-leaf] file

**Heft·garn** *das* tacking thread; basting thread

**heftig** **1** *Adj.* **A** violent ‹storm, explosion, struggle, collision, argument, movement, passion›; heavy ‹rain, shower, blow›; intense, burning ‹hatred, desire›; fierce ‹controversy, criticism, competition›; severe ‹pain, cold›; loud ‹bang›; rapid ‹breathing›; bitter ‹weeping›; **B** (*unbeherrscht*) violent ‹reaction, manner›; ‹person› with a violent temper; heated, vehement ‹tone, words›; ~ **werden/gleich** ~ **sein** fly into a temper/flare up. **2** *adv.* **A** ‹rain, snow, breathe› heavily; ‹hit› hard; ‹hurt› a great deal; ‹quarrel, shiver› violently; ~ **weinen** bawl; cry loudly; **sich** ~ **verlieben** fall passionately *or* (*coll.*) madly in love; **B** (*unbeherrscht*) ‹answer› angrily, heatedly; ‹react› angrily, violently

**Heftigkeit** *die;* ~ **A** ⇒ **heftig** A: violence; heaviness; intensity; fierceness; severity; loudness; rapidity; bitterness; **B** (*Unbeherrschtheit*) vehemence

**Heft-:** ~**klammer** **A** staple; **B** ⇒ **Büroklammer**; ~**maschine** *die* stapler; (*Buchbinderei*) stitcher; ~**pflaster** *das* sticking plaster; ~**zwecke** *die;* ~~, ~~**n** ⇒ **Reißzwecke**

**Hege** /ˈheːɡə/ *die;* ~ (*Forstw., Jagdw.*) care and protection; (*fig.*) care

**Hegelianer** /heːɡəˈli̯aːnɐ/ *der;* ~**s**, ~, **Hegelianerin** *die;* ~, ~**nen** Hegelian

**hegelianisch** *Adj.* Hegelian

**Hegelianismus** *der;* ~: Hegelianism *no art.*

**hegelsch**, ***Hegelsch** /ˈheːɡl̩ʃ/ *Adj.* Hegelian; **die** ~**e Staatsphilosophie** Hegel's political philosophy

**hegemonial** /hegemoˈni̯aːl/ *Adj.* hegemonic

**Hegemonie** /hegemoˈniː/ *die;* ~, ~**n** /-ən/ hegemony

**hegen** *tr. V.* **A** (*bes. Forstw., Jagdw.*) look after, tend ‹plants, animals›; **B** (*geh.: umsorgen*) look after; take care of; preserve ‹old customs›; **jmdn./etw.** ~ **und pflegen** lavish care and attention on sb./sth.; **C** (*in sich tragen*) feel ‹contempt, hatred, mistrust›; cherish ‹hope, wish, desire›; harbour, nurse ‹grudge, suspicion›; **eine Abneigung gegen/eine gewisse Achtung für jmdn.** ~: have a dislike/a certain respect for sb.; **ich hege den Verdacht, dass ...** I have a suspicion that ...; **große Zweifel [an etw.** (*Dat*)**]** ~: have *or* entertain grave doubts [about sth.]

**Hehl** /heːl/ *in* **kein[en]** ~ **aus etw. machen** make no secret of sth.; **er macht kein[en]** ~ **daraus, dass ...** he makes no secret of the fact that ...

**Hehler** *der;* ~**s**, ~: receiver [of stolen goods]; fence (*coll.*)

**Hehlerei** *die;* ~, ~**en** (*Rechtsw.*) receiving [stolen goods] *no art.*

**hehr** /heːɐ̯/ *Adj.* (*geh.*) majestic ‹sight›; glorious ‹moment›; noble ‹ideal›

**hei** /hai̯/ *Interj.* ~, **war das eine Fahrt!** wow, what a trip!; ~, **ist das ein Spaß!** oh *or* hey, what fun!

**heia** /ˈhai̯a/ (*Kinderspr.*) *in* ~ **machen** go bye-byes *or* beddy-byes (*child lang.*)

**Heia** *die;* ~, ~**[s]**, **Heia·bett** *das* (*Kinderspr.*) bye-byes, beddy-byes (*child lang.*); **ab in die** ~: off to bye-byes *or* beddy-byes

**heiapopeia** *Interj.* ⇒ **eiapopeia**

**Heide**[1] /ˈhai̯də/ *der;* ~**n**, ~**n** heathen; pagan; **das Kind ist ein kleiner** ~: the child is a little heathen

**Heide**[2] *die;* ~, ~**n** **A** moor; heath; (~*landschaft*) moorland; heathland; **die Lüneburger** ~: the Luneburg Heath; **B** ⇒ ~**kraut**

**Heide-:** ~**kraut** *das* heather; ling; ~**land** *das* moorland; heathland

**Heidel·beere** /ˈhai̯dl̩-/ *die* bilberry; blueberry; whortleberry; **in die** ~**n gehen** (*ugs.*) go picking bilberries *etc.*

**Heiden-:** ~**angst** *die* (*ugs.*) **eine** ~**angst vor etw.** (*Dat.*) **haben** be scared stiff of sth. (*coll.*); **er hatte eine** ~**angst vor der Fahrprüfung** he was in a blue funk about the driving test (*coll.*); ~**arbeit** *die* (*ugs.*) a heck of a lot of work (*coll.*); ~**geld** *das* (*ugs.*) a packet (*coll.*); a heck of a lot of money (*coll.*); ~**krach** *der* (*ugs.*) **A** ⇒ ~**lärm**; **B** (*Streit*) flaming row (*coll.*); ~**lärm** *der* (*ugs.*) unholy *or* dreadful din *or* row (*coll.*); dreadful racket (*coll.*); ~**mission** *die* missionary work; ~**respekt** *der* (*ugs.*) healthy respect (**vor** + *Dat.* for); ~**röschen** *das* ⇒ **Heideröschen** B; ~**schreck** *der* (*ugs.*) terrible fright (*coll.*); **ihr habt mir einen** ~**schreck eingejagt** you frightened the life out of me (*coll.*); ~**spaß** *der* (*ugs.*) terrific fun (*coll.*); **es macht einen** ~**spaß** it's terrific fun (*coll.*); ~**spektakel** *der* (*ugs.*) (*Lärm*) unholy *or* dreadful din *or* row (*coll.*); (*Aufregung*) great *or* (*coll.*) dreadful commotion; ~**tempel** *der* heathen *or* pagan temple

**Heidentum** *das;* ~**s** **A** (*Zustand*) heathenism; paganism; **B** (*die Heiden*) the heathen *pl. or* pagans *pl.*; **das westliche** ~: the infidels *pl.* in the West

**Heide·röschen** *das* **A** rock rose (*of genus Fumana*); **B** (*veralt.: Hundsrose*) dogrose

**heidi** /hai̯ˈdiː/ *Interj.* **[und]** ~ **begann die wilde Fahrt** away he/they *etc.* went; ~ **gings den Berg hinunter** away he/they *etc.* went down the hill

**Heidin** *die;* ~, ~**nen** heathen; pagan

**heidnisch** **1** *Adj.* heathen; pagan. **2** *adv.* ~ **leben** live a heathen *or* pagan life

**Heid·schnucke** *die;* ~, ~**n** German Heath [sheep]

**heikel** /ˈhai̯kl̩/ *Adj.* **A** (*schwierig*) delicate, ticklish ‹matter, subject›; ticklish, awkward, tricky ‹problem, question, situation›; **B** (*wählerisch, empfindlich*) finicky, fussy, fastidious (**in Bezug auf** + *Akk.* about); **in allen Dingen der Hygiene ist sie sehr** ~: she is very particular in all matters of hygiene

**heil** /hai̯l/ *Adj.* **A** (*unverletzt*) unhurt, unharmed ‹person›; **ein Wunder, dass seine Knochen** ~ **geblieben sind** it's a wonder he didn't break any bones; ~ **ankommen** arrive safely *or* safe and sound; **etw.** ~ **überstehen** survive sth. unscathed; **sollte ich diese Angelegenheit** ~ **überstehen** (*fig.*) if I come out of this affair without getting my fingers burned; **aus etw.** ~ **herauskommen** come through sth. safely *or* unscathed; (*fig.*) survive sth.; ⇒ *auch* **Haut** A; **B** (*wieder gesund*) ~ **werden/wieder** ~ **sein** ‹injured part› heal [up]/have healed [up]; **C** (*nicht entzwei*) intact; in one piece; **er hat nicht ein einziges** ~**es Hemd** he hasn't got a single shirt that doesn't need mending; **es gab nur noch wenige** ~**e Häuser** only a few houses were undamaged; **eine** ~**e Welt** (*fig.*) an ideal *or* a perfect world

**Heil** *das;* ~**s** **A** (*Wohlergehen*) benefit; **sein** ~ **in etw.** (*Dat.*) **suchen** seek one's salvation in sth.; **bei jmdm./irgendwo sein** ~ **versuchen** try one's luck with sb./somewhere; ~ **Hitler!** (*ns.*) heil Hitler!; **sein** ~ **in der Flucht suchen** seek refuge in flight; ⇒ *auch* **Berg** A; **Petri Heil**; **Ski**; **B** (*Rel.*) salvation

**Heiland** /ˈhai̯lant/ *der;* ~**[e]s**, ~**e** **A** (*Christus*) Saviour; Redeemer; **B** (*geh.: Retter*) saviour

**Heil-:** ~**anstalt** *die* **A** (*Anstalt für Kranke od. Süchtige*) sanatorium; **B** (*psychiatrische Klinik*) mental hospital *or* home; ~**bad** *das* **A** (*Kurort*) spa; watering place; **B** (*medizinisches Bad*) medicinal bath

**heilbar** *Adj.* curable

**Heilbarkeit** *die;* ~: curability

**heil·bringend** *Adj.* saving; redeeming; **die** ~**e Botschaft** the message of salvation *or* redemption

**Heil·butt** *der* halibut

**heilen** **1** *tr. V.* **A** ▶ 474 cure ‹disease›; heal ‹wound›; **jmdn.** ~: cure sb.; restore sb. to health; **B** (*befreien*) **jmdn. von etw.** ~: cure sb. of sth.; **davon/von ihm bin ich geheilt** (*ugs.*) I've been cured of it/my attachment to him. **2** ▶ 474 *itr. V.; mit sein* ‹wound› heal [up]; ‹infection› clear up; ‹fracture› mend

**heil-**, **Heil-:** ~**erde** *die: pulverized earth with therapeutic properties, used in treating skin diseases and intestinal complaints*; ~**erfolg** *der* success (*of cure etc.*); **zum** ~**erfolg führen** lead to a successful cure; ~**froh** *Adj.* very *or* (*Brit. coll.*) jolly glad; ~**gymnastik** *die* ⇒ **Krankengymnastik**

**heilig** *Adj.* **A** holy; **der Heilige Vater** the Holy Father; **der Heilige Stuhl** the Holy See; **die Heilige Jungfrau** the Blessed Virgin; **die** ~**e Barbara/der** ~**e Augustinus** Saint Barbara/Saint Augustine; **die Heilige Familie/Dreifaltigkeit** the Holy Family/Trinity; **der Heilige Geist** the Holy Spirit; **die Heiligen Drei Könige** the Three Kings *or* Wise Men; the Magi; **die** ~**e Taufe/Messe** Holy Baptism/Mass; **der** ~**e Sonntag** the Sabbath; **die Heilige Schrift** the Holy Scriptures *pl.*; **die Heilige Allianz** (*hist.*) the Holy Alliance; **das Heilige Römische Reich** (*hist.*) the Holy Roman Empire; **jmdn.** ~ **sprechen** canonize sb; **B** (*besonders geweiht*) holy; sacred; ~**e Stätten** holy *or* sacred places; **der Heilige Abend/die Heilige Nacht** Christmas Eve/Night; **das Heilige Land** the Holy Land; **C** (*geh.: unantastbar*) sacred ‹right, tradition, cause, etc.›; sacred, solemn ‹duty›; gospel ‹truth›; solemn ‹conviction, oath›; righteous ‹anger, zeal›; awed ‹silence›; **etw. ist jmdm.** ~: sth. is sacred to sb.; **bei allem, was mir** ~ **ist** by all that I hold sacred; **etw.** ~ **halten** keep *or* observe sth.; ⇒ *auch* **hoch** 2 D; **D** (*ugs.: groß*) incredible (*coll.*); healthy ‹respect›; **seine** ~**e Not mit jmdm. haben** have a lot of trouble *or* a hard time with sb.; **E** (*veralt.: fromm*) [extremely] devout *or* pious

**Heilig·abend** *der* Christmas Eve

**Heilige** *der/die; adj. Dekl.* saint; **ein sonderbarer** *od.* **komischer** ~**r** (*ugs. iron.*) a queer fish (*coll.*)

**heiligen** *tr. V.* **A** keep, observe ‹tradition, Sabbath, etc.›; **die geheiligten Räume** (*auch iron.*) the inner sanctum; the holy of holies; **der Zweck heiligt die Mittel** the end justifies the means; **B** (*geh.: weihen*) consecrate ‹church›; bless ‹house, field, etc.›

**Heiligen-:** ~**bild** *das* picture of a saint; ~**figur** *die* figure of a saint; ~**legende** *die* life of a saint; ~**schein** *der* gloriole; aureole; (*um den Kopf*) halo; **jmdn. mit einem** ~**schein umgeben** (*fig.*) be unable to see sb.'s faults; ~**verehrung** *die* veneration of the saints

***heilig|halten** ⇒ **heilig** C

**Heiligkeit** *die;* ~ **A** holiness; **Seine/Euere** ~ (*Anrede*) His/Your Holiness; **B** (*der Ehe, Taufe usw.*) sanctity; sacredness; (*geh.: des Zornes*) righteousness; **die** ~ **des Eigentums** (*geh.*) the sanctity *or* inviolability of property

**heilig-**, **Heilig-:** ~**mäßig** **1** *Adj.* saintly; **2** *adv.* ~**mäßig leben** lead a saintly life; *~**|sprechen** ⇒ **heilig** A; ~**sprechung** *die;* ~~, ~~**en** (*kath. Kirche*) canonization

**Heiligtum** *das;* ~**s**, **Heiligtümer** shrine; **ein** ~ **für jmdn. sein** (*fig.*) be a sacred object to sb.; **sein Arbeitszimmer ist sein** ~ (*fig.*) his study is his sanctuary *or* sanctum

**Heiligung** *die;* ~, ~**en** (*geh.*) **A** (*das Heilighalten*) observance; **B** (*Rechtfertigung*) justification

**heil-**, **Heil-:** ~**klima** *das* healthy climate; **ein gutes** ~**klima** a healthy climate; ~**kraft** *die* healing *or* curative power; ~**kräftig** *Adj.* medicinal ‹herb, plant, etc.›; curative ‹effect›; ~**kraut** *das* medicinal *or* officinal herb; ~**kunde** *die* medicine; ~**kundig** *Adj.* skilled in medicine *or* the art of healing *postpos.*; ~**los** **1** *Adj.* hopeless, awful ‹mess, muddle›; utter, (*coll.*) terrible ‹confusion›; **eine** ~**lose Angst haben** be terrified *or* (*coll.*) terribly frightened; **2** *adv.* hopelessly; ~**massage** *die* curative massage; ~**massagen** massage treatment *sing., no indef. art.*; ~**methode** *die* curative treatment; method of treatment; ~**mittel** *das* (*auch fig.*) remedy (**gegen** for); (*Medikament*) medicament; ~**pädagoge** *der*, ~**pädagogin** *die* teacher of children with special needs; ~**pädagogik** *die* special education *no art.*; ~**pflanze** *die* medicinal *or* officinal plant *or* herb; **~praktiker** *der*, **~praktikerin** *die* ▶159 non-medical practitioner; **~quelle** *die* mineral spring

**heilsam** *Adj.* salutary ‹lesson, effect, experience, etc.›

**Heils-: ~armee** *die* Salvation Army; **~botschaft** *die* message of salvation

**Heil-: ~schlaf** *der* (*Med.*) healing sleep; **~serum** *das* (*Med.*) [antitoxic] serum

**Heils-: ~geschichte** *die* (*Theol.*) Heilsgeschichte; salvation-history; **~lehre** *die* (*auch fig.*) doctrine of salvation

**Heil·stätte** *die* sanatorium; clinic

**Heilung** *die;* ~, ~en ▶474 (A) (*einer Wunde*) healing; (*von Krankheit, Kranken*) curing; **wenig Hoffnung auf ~ haben** have little hope of being cured; **~ suchen** seek a cure; (B) (*das Gesundwerden*) **die ~ dieser Fraktur dauert mehrere Wochen** this fracture will take several weeks to mend; **diese Salbe wird die ~ der Wunde beschleunigen** this ointment will help the wound to heal faster

**Heilungs-: ~prozess**, ***~prozeß** *der*, **~verlauf** *der* healing process; (*Rekonvaleszenz*) process of recovery

**Heil-: ~verfahren** *das* [course of] treatment; **~wirkung** *die* therapeutic *or* curative effect; **~zweck** *der: in* **zu ~zwecken** for therapeutic *or* medicinal purposes

**heim** /haim/ *Adv.* home

**Heim** *das;* ~[e]s, ~e (A) (*Zuhause*) home; **ein eigenes ~:** a home of his/their *etc.* own; (B) (*Anstalt, Alters~*) home; (*für Obdachlose*) hostel; (*für Studenten*) hall of residence; hostel; (C) ⇒ **Erholungsheim**

**Heim-: ~abend** *der* social evening; **~arbeit** *die* outwork; **eine ~arbeit suchen/bekommen** look for/get outwork; **etw. in ~arbeit herstellen lassen** have sth. produced by homeworkers; **~arbeiter** *der*, **~arbeiterin** *die* homeworker; outworker

**Heimat** /ˈhaimaːt/ *die;* ~, ~en (A) (*~ort*) home; home town/village; (*~land*) home; homeland; **ihr ist Frankreich zur zweiten ~ geworden** France has become her second home; (B) (*Ursprungsland*) natural habitat; **Frankreich ist die ~ des Champagners** France is the home of champagne

**Heimat-: ~an·schrift** *die* home address; **~dichter** *der*, **~dichterin** *die* regional writer; **~dichtung** *die* regional literature; **~erde** *die* native soil; **~film** *der* [sentimental] film in a[n idealized] regional setting; **~forschung** *die* research into local history; **~front** *die* (*bes. ns.*) home front; **~hafen** *der* home port; **~kunde** *die* local history, geography, and natural history; **~land** *das* homeland; native land; (*fig.*) home

**heimatlich** *Adj.* (A) (*zur Heimat gehörend*) native ‹dialect›; **die ~en Berge** the mountains of [one's] home; **die ~e Landschaft/die ~en Bräuche** the landscape/customs of one's native land/district; ⇒ *auch* **Gefilde**; (B) (*an die Heimat erinnernd*) nostalgic ‹emotions›; **~e Klänge** sounds which evoke memories of home

**heimat-, Heimat-: ~lied** *das* song of one's homeland; **~los** *Adj.* homeless; **durch den Krieg ~los werden** be displaced by the war; **~lose** *der/die; adj. Dekl.* homeless person; **die ~losen** the homeless; **~museum** *das* museum of local history; **~ort** *der* (A) home town/village; (B) ⇒ **~hafen**; **~recht** *das* right of domicile; **~sprache** *die* native language; (*Mundart*) native dialect; **~stadt** *die* home town; **~verein** *der* local history society; **~vertrieben** *Adj.* expelled from his/her homeland *postpos.*; **~vertriebene** *der/die* expellee [from his/her homeland]

**heim-: ~|begeben** *unr. refl. V.* (*geh.*) make one's way home; go home; **~|begleiten** *tr. V.* **jmdn. ~begleiten** take *or* see sb. home; **~|bringen** *unr. tr. V.* (A) ⇒ **~begleiten**; (B) bring home

*old spelling (see note on page 1707)

**Heimchen** *das;* ~s, ~ (A) (*ugs. abwertend: Frau*) **~ [am Herd]** little hausfrau *or* housewife; (B) (*Grille*) house cricket

**Heim·computer** *der* home computer

**heim|dürfen** *unr. itr. V.* be allowed [to go] home; **darf ich heim?** may I go home?

**heimelig** /ˈhaiməlɪç/ *Adj.* cosy

**heim-, Heim-: ~erzieher** *der*, **~erzieherin** *die* ▶159 *counsellor in a home for children or young people;* **~|fahren** ❶ *unr. itr. V.; mit sein* drive home; ❷ *unr. tr. V.* drive home; ⇒ *auch* **fahren** 1 A, 2 C; **~fahrt** *die* journey home; (*mit dem Auto*) drive home; **~|finden** *unr. itr. V.* find one's way home; **~|führen** *tr. V.* (A) (*geleiten*) take home; (B) (*geh. veralt.: heiraten*) **eine Frau ~führen** take a wife; **er führte sie ~:** he took her to wife (*arch.*); **er führte sie als seine Braut ~:** he took her for his bride; **~gang** *der* (*geh. verhüll.*) passing away; **nach dem ~gang ihres Mannes** after her husband passed away; **~gegangene** *der/die; adj. Dekl.* (*geh. verhüll.*) departed; **unser lieber ~gegangener** our dear departed friend/brother *etc.;* **~|gehen** *unr. itr. V.; mit sein* (A) go home; (B) (*geh. verhüll.: sterben*) pass away; (C) (*unpers.*) **es geht ~:** I/we *etc.* are going home; **~geschädigt** *Adj.* institutionalized; **~|holen** *tr. V.* (A) fetch home; (B) (*geh. verhüll.*) **Gott hat ihn [zu sich] ~geholt** he has been called to his Maker; **~industrie** *die* cottage industry

**heimisch** *Adj.* (A) (*ein~*) indigenous, native ‹plants, animals, etc.› (**in** + *Dat.* to); domestic, home ‹industry›; **die ~en Flüsse und Seen** the rivers and lakes of his/her *etc.* native land; **vor ~em Publikum** (*Sport*) in front of a home crowd; (B) (*zum Heim gehörend*) **an den ~en Herd zurückkehren** go back home; **vom ~en Herd flüchten** get away from the house; (C) **~ sein/sich ~ fühlen** be/feel at home; **~ werden** settle in; **~ werden in** (+ *Dat.*) settle into

**heim-, Heim-: ~kehr** *die;* ~~: return home; homecoming; **~|kehren** *itr. V.; mit sein* return home (**aus** from); **~kehrer** *der;* ~~s, ~~, **~kehrerin** *die;* ~~, ~~nen homecomer; **die ~kehrer aus dem Krieg/Urlaub** the soldiers returning from the war/the holidaymakers returning home; **~kind** *das* child brought up in a home; **ein ~kind adoptieren** adopt a child from a home; **~kino** *das* (A) home movies *pl.;* **eine Vorführung im ~kino** a home-movie show; (B) (*ugs. scherzh.: Fernsehen*) box (*coll.*); goggle-box (*Brit. coll.*); **~|kommen** *unr. itr. V.; mit sein* come *or* return home; **~|laufen** *unr. itr. V.; mit sein* run [back] home; **schnell ~laufen** dash home; **~leiter** *der* warden; (*eines Kinder-/Jugendheims*) superintendent; (*eines Pflegeheims*) director; **~leiterin** *die* warden; (*eines Kinder-/Jugendheims*) superintendent; (*eines Pflegeheims*) matron; **~leitung** *die* (A) warden's office; (*eines Kinder-/Jugendheims*) superintendent's office; (*eines Pflegeheims*) director's/matron's office; (B) (*Person*) ⇒ **~leiter**, **~leiterin**; **~|leuchten** *itr. V.* (*salopp*) **jmdm. ~leuchten** give sb. a piece of one's mind (*coll.*)

**heimlich** ❶ *Adj.* (A) secret; secret, clandestine ‹agreement, meeting›; (B) (*österr.*) ⇒ **heimelig.** ❷ *adv.* secretly; ‹meet› secretly, in secret; **sie schaute ~ auf die Uhr** she looked furtively at her watch; **er ist ~ weggelaufen** he slipped *or* stole away; **~, still und leise** (*ugs.*) on the quiet; quietly

**Heimlichkeit** *die;* ~, ~en secret; **in aller ~:** in secret; secretly

**Heimlichtuer** /-tuːɐ/ *der;* ~s, ~, **Heimlichtuerin** *die;* ~, ~nen (*abwertend*) secretive person

**heim-, Heim-: ~mannschaft** *die* (*Sport*) home team *or* side; **~|müssen** *unr. itr. V.* have to go home; **~niederlage** *die* (*Sport*) home defeat; **~ordnung** *die* rules of the/a home/hostel *etc.;* **~orgel** *die* home organ; **~platz** *der* place in a home/hostel *etc.;* **~recht** *das* (*Sport*) **~recht haben** be playing at home; **die Mannschaft mit ~recht** the home team *or* side; **~reise** *die* journey home; **~|schicken** *tr. V.* send home; **~schwach** *Adj.* (*Sport*) **~schwach sein** have a poor home record; **~sieg** *der* (*Sport*) home win; **~spiel** *das* (*Sport*) home match *or* game; **~stark** *Adj.* (*Sport*) **~stark sein** have a very good home record; **~statt** *die* (*geh.*) home; **~stätte** *die* (A) ⇒ **Heimstatt**; (B) (*Grundbesitz für Vertriebene*) homestead (*for refugees etc.*); **~|suchen** *tr. V.* (A) (*überfallen*) ‹storm, earthquake, epidemic› strike; ‹disease› afflict; ‹nightmares, doubts› plague; ‹catastrophe, fate› overtake; **von Streiks/Dürre ~gesucht** striketorn/drought-ridden; (B) (*aufsuchen*) ‹visitor, salesman, etc.› descend [up]on; **~suchung** *die;* ~~, ~~en affliction; visitation; **~|trauen** *refl. V.* dare to go home

**Heim·tücke** *die;* ~ (*Bösartigkeit*) [concealed] malice; (*Hinterlistigkeit, fig.: einer Krankheit*) insidiousness

**heim·tückisch** ❶ *Adj.* (*bösartig*) malicious; (*fig.*) insidious ‹disease›; (*hinterlistig*) insidious. ❷ *adv.* maliciously

**heim-, Heim-: ~vorteil** *der* (*Sport*) advantage of playing at home; home advantage; **~wärts** /-vɛrts/ (*nach Hause zu*) home; (*in Richtung Heimat*) homeward[s]; **~weg** *der* way home; **sich auf den ~weg machen** set off [for] home; **haben Sie einen weiten ~weg?** have you got a long way to go to get home?

**Heim·weh** *das* homesickness; **nach jmdm./einem Ort ~ haben** pine for sb./be homesick for a place; **~ bekommen** get homesick

**heimweh·krank** *Adj.* homesick

**heim-, Heim-: ~werker** *der;* ~~s, ~~: handyman; do-it-yourselfer; **~werkerin** *die;* ~~, ~~nen handywoman; do-it-yourselfer; **~|wollen** *unr. itr. V.* want to go home; **~|zahlen** *tr. V.* **jmdm. etw. ~zahlen** pay sb. back *or* get even with sb. for sth.; **jmdm. in gleicher Münze ~zahlen** pay sb. back in the same coin; **~|ziehen** ❶ *unr. itr. V.; mit sein* return home; ❷ *unr. tr. V.* (*unpers.*) **es zog ihn ~:** he wanted to go home; **~zögling** *der* ⇒ **~kind**

**Hein** /hain/ *in* **Freund ~** (*verhüll.*) [Angel of] Death

**Heini** /ˈhaini/ *der;* ~s, ~s (*ugs. Schimpfwort*) idiot; halfwit; clot (*Brit. coll.*)

**Heinzel·männchen** /ˈhaintsl̩-/ *das;* ~s, ~: brownie

**Heirat** /ˈhairaːt/ *die;* ~, ~en marriage

**heiraten** ❶ *itr. V.* marry; get married; **~ müssen** (*verhüll.*) have to get married; **das Heiraten:** marriage *no art.;* getting married *no art.;* **sie hat nach Amerika geheiratet** she got married and settled in America. ❷ *tr. V.* marry

**heirats-, Heirats-: ~absichten** *Pl.* marriage plans; **ernsthafte ~absichten haben** seriously intend to marry *or* get married; **~alter** *das* marrying age; **im ~alter sein** be of an age to marry; **~annonce** *die* advertisement for a marriage partner; **~antrag** *der* proposal *or* offer of marriage; **jmdm. einen ~antrag machen** propose to sb.; **~anzeige** *die* (A) (*Anzeige, dass jemand heiratet*) announcement of a/the forthcoming marriage; (B) ⇒ **~annonce**; **~fähig** *Adj.* ‹person› of marriageable age; **im ~fähigen Alter** of marriageable age; **~institut** *das* marriage bureau; **~kandidat** *der* (*scherzh.*) (A) (*jmd., der heiraten will*) husband-to-be; (B) (*unverheirateter Mann*) eligible bachelor; **~kandidatin** *die* (*scherzh.*) (A) bride-to-be; (B) (*unverheiratete Frau*) eligible single woman; **~lustig** *Adj.* (*scherzh.*) eager *or* keen to get married *postpos.;* **~markt** *der* (*scherzh.*) (A) (*Zeitungsrubrik*) matrimonial advertisements *pl.;* (B) (*Veranstaltung*) marriage market; **~schwindel** *der* fraud involving a spurious offer of marriage; **~schwindler** *der*, **~schwindlerin** *die: person who makes a spurious offer of marriage for purposes of fraud;* **~urkunde** *die* marriage certificate; **~vermittler** *der*, **~vermittlerin** *die* ▶159 marriage broker; **~versprechen** *das* promise of marriage; **Bruch eines**

**~versprechens** (*Rechtsw.*) breach of promise

**heisa** /ˈhaiza *od.* ˈhaisa/ *Interj.* (*veralt.*) hooray

**heischen** /ˈhaiʃn̩/ *tr. V.* (*geh.*) **A** (*fordern*) demand; **B** (*veralt.: bitten um*) ask for; (*inständig*) beg

**heiser** /ˈhaizɐ/ **1** *Adj.* hoarse; (*rauchig*) husky; **sich ~ schreien/reden** shout/talk oneself hoarse. **2** *adv.* hoarsely; in a hoarse voice

**Heiserkeit** *die;* ~ ⇒ **heiser**: hoarseness; huskiness

**heiß** /hais/ **1** *Adj.* **A** hot; hot, torrid ‹zone›; **brennend/glühend ~:** burning/scorching hot; **jmdm. ist ~:** sb. feels hot; **etw. ~ machen** heat sth. up; **ein Paar Heiße** (*ugs.*) a couple of hot sausages; **es überläuft mich ~ und kalt, es läuft mir ~ und kalt den Rücken hinunter** I feel hot and cold all over; **sie haben sich die Köpfe ~ geredet** the conversation/debate became heated; **dich haben sie wohl zu ~ gebadet?** (*salopp*) you must be off your rocker (*coll.*); **B** (*heftig*) heated ‹debate, argument›; impassioned ‹anger›; burning, fervent ‹desire›; fierce ‹fight, battle›; **C** (*innig*) ardent, passionate ‹wish, love›; **~e Tränen weinen** weep bitterly; cry one's heart out; **~en Dank** (*ugs.*) thanks a lot! (*coll.*); **D** (*aufreizend*) hot ‹rhythm etc.›; sexy ‹blouse, dress, etc.›; **eine ~e Nummer** (*ugs.*) a [red-]hot number (*coll.*); **was für'n ~er Typ!** (*salopp*) what a guy! (*coll.*); ⇒ *auch* **Sohle** A; **E** (*ugs.: gefährlich*) hot (*coll.*) ‹goods, money›; **das wird ein ~es Jahr** things are going to get pretty hot this year (*coll.*); **ein ~es Thema** a controversial subject; **ein ~es Geschäft** a risky business; **eine ~e Gegend** a rough district; ⇒ *auch* **Eisen** B; **F** (*ugs.: Aussichten habend*) hot ‹favourite, tip, contender, etc.›; **auf einer ~en Spur sein** be hot on the scent; **G** (*ugs.: schnell*) hot; ⇒ *auch* **Ofen** E; **H** (*ugs.: brünstig*) on heat; **I** (*salopp: aufgereizt*) **jmdn. ~ machen** turn sb. on (*coll.*); **J** (*Physik*) hot (*coll.*). **2** *adv.* **A** (*heftig*) ‹fight› fiercely; **die Stadt wurde ~ umkämpft** the town was the object of fierce fighting; **es ging ~ her** things got heated; sparks flew (*coll.*); (*auf einer Party usw.*) things got wild; **~ umkämpft** fiercely contested or disputed; **~ umstritten** hotly debated ‹matter, subject, etc.›; highly controversial ‹figure, director, etc.›; **B** (*innig*) **jmdn. ~ und innig lieben** love sb. dearly *or* with all one's heart; **etw. ~ ersehnen** long fervently for sth.; **~ geliebt** dearly beloved ‹husband, son, etc.›; beloved ‹doll, car, etc.›; **das ~ ersehnte Fahrrad** the bicycle he/she has longed for so fervently

**heißa** /ˈhaisa/ ⇒ **heisa**

**heiß·blütig** *Adj.* (*leidenschaftlich*) hot-blooded; ardent, passionate ‹lover›; (*leicht erregbar*) hot-tempered

**heißen**[1] **1** *unr. itr. V.* **A** (*den Namen tragen*) be called; **ich heiße Hans** I am called Hans; my name is Hans; **er heißt mit Nachnamen Müller** his surname is Müller; **früher hat sie anders ge~:** she used to have a different name; **nach jmdm. ~:** be named *or* called after sb.; **und wie sie alle ~:** and the rest [of them]; **wie kann man nur Traugott ~?** how can anyone have a name like Traugott?; **so wahr ich ... heiße** (*ugs.*) as sure as I'm standing here; **dann will ich Emil ~** (*ugs.*) then I'm a Dutchman (*coll.*); **B** (*bedeuten*) mean; **was heißt „danke" auf Französisch?** what's the French for 'thanks'?; **das will viel/nicht viel ~:** that means a lot/doesn't mean much; **was soll das denn ~?** what's that supposed to mean?; **was heißt hier: morgen?** what do you mean, tomorrow?; **das heißt** that is [to say]; **C** (*lauten*) ‹saying› go; **wie heißt das Buch?** what's [the title *or* name of] the book?; **der Titel/sein Motto heißt ...** the title/his motto is ...; **D** (*unpers.*) (*man sagt*) **es heißt, dass ...** they say *or* it is said that ...; **es heißt, dass sie unheilbar krank ist** she is said to be incurably ill; **wie es hieß, war sie unheilbar krank** they said *or* it was said [that] she was incurably ill; **es hieß allgemein, dass ...** everybody said that ...; **es soll nicht ~, dass ...** never let it be said that ...; **E** (*unpers.*) (*ist zu lesen*) **in dem Gedicht/Roman/Artikel heißt es ...** in the poem/novel/article it says that ...; **wie heißt es doch gleich bei Goethe?** what was it Goethe said?; **F** (*unpers.*) (*geh.: es gilt*) **jetzt heißt es aufgepasst!** you'd better watch out now!; **jetzt heißt es handeln!** now it's time to act *or* for action! **2** *unr. tr. V.* **A** (*geh.: auffordern*) tell; bid; **jmdn. etw. tun ~:** tell sb. to do sth.; bid sb. do sth.; **B** (*geh.: bezeichnen*) call; **jmdn. einen Lügner ~:** call sb. a liar; **jmdn. willkommen ~:** bid sb. welcome; **C** (*veralt.: einen Namen geben*) name; call

**heißen**[2] *tr. V.* ⇒ **hissen**

**heiß-, Heiß-: *~ersehnt, *~geliebt** ⇒ **heiß** 2B; **~getränk** *das* hot drink; **~getränke** (*auf Speisekarten*) hot beverages; **~hunger** *der:* **einen ~hunger auf etw.** (*Akk.*) *od.* **nach etw. [haben]** [have] a craving for sth.; **etw. mit [wahrem] ~hunger verschlingen** devour sth. ravenously; [absolutely (*coll.*)] wolf sth. down; **sich mit [wahrem] ~hunger auf etw.** (*Akk.*) **stürzen** (*fig.*) [absolutely (*coll.*)] devour sth.; **~hungrig 1** *Adj.* ravenous; **2** *adv.* ravenously; voraciously; **~|laufen 1** *unr. itr. V.; mit sein* run hot; ‹engine› run hot, overheat; **sie hat so viel telefoniert, dass die Drähte ~liefen** she made so many telephone calls that the wires were buzzing; **2** *unr. refl. V.* run hot; ‹engine› run hot, overheat

**Heiß·luft** *die* hot air

**Heißluft-: ~backofen** *der* fan oven; **~bad** *das* hot-air bath; **~ballon** *der* hot-air balloon; **~gerät** *das* (*Trockner*) hot-air dryer; (*Herd*) hot-air oven

**heiß-, Heiß-: ~mangel** *die* rotary ironer; **~sporn** *der* hothead; ***~umkämpft, *~umstritten** ⇒ **heiß** 2A

**Heiß·wasser-: ~bereiter** *der;* **~~s, ~~:** water heater; **~speicher** *der* hot-water tank with an immersion heater

**heiter** /ˈhaitɐ/ *Adj.* **A** (*fröhlich*) cheerful, happy ‹person, nature›; happy, merry ‹laughter›; **~ und zufrieden** happy and contented; **B** (*froh stimmend*) cheerful ‹music etc.›; cheerful, bright ‹colour, wallpaper, room, etc.›; (*amüsant*) funny, amusing ‹story etc.›; **einer Sache** (*Dat.*) **die ~e Seite abgewinnen** look on the bright side of sth.; **das ist ja ~!** (*ugs. iron.*) that's just great *or* wonderful (*iron.*); **das kann ja ~ werden!** (*ugs. iron.*) that'll be fun (*iron.*); **C** (*sonnig*) fine ‹weather›; bright, fine ‹day›; **~ bis wolkig** generally fine, though cloudy in places

**Heiterkeit** *die;* ~ **A** (*Frohsinn*) cheerfulness; **B** (*Belustigung*) merriment; **allgemeine ~ erregen** provoke *or* cause general merriment; **C** (*sonniges Wetter*) brightness

**Heiterkeits·ausbruch** *der* burst of merriment

**heizbar** *Adj.* heated ‹windscreen, room, etc.›; **das Zimmer ist nicht/schwer ~:** the room has no heating/is difficult to heat

**Heiz·decke** *die* electric blanket

**heizen** /ˈhaitsn̩/ **1** *itr. V.* have the heating on; **der Ofen heizt gut** the stove gives off *or* throws out a good heat; **mit Kohle** *usw.* **~:** use coal *etc.* for heating. **2** *tr. V.* **A** (*warm machen*) heat ‹room etc.›; **B** (*an~*) stoke ‹furnace, boiler, etc.›; **den Badeofen ~:** heat the bathwater; **sie ~ ihre Öfen mit Öl** their boilers are oil-fired; **C** (*als Brennstoff verwenden*) burn. **3** *refl. V.* **sich gut/schlecht ~:** be easy/difficult to heat

**Heizer** *der;* **~s, ~, Heizerin** *die;* **~, ~nen** ▶ 159 (*einer Lokomotive*) fireman; stoker; (*eines Schiffes*) stoker

**Heiz-: ~fläche** *die* heating surface; **~gerät** *das* heater; **~kessel** *der* boiler; **~kissen** *das* heating pad; **~körper** *der* radiator; **~kosten** *Pl.* heating costs; **~lüfter** *der* fan heater; **~material** *das* fuel [for heating]; **~ofen** *der* stove; heater; **ein elektrischer ~ofen** an electric heater; **~öl** *das* heating oil; fuel oil; **~periode** *die* heating period; **~platte** *die* hotplate; **~rohr** *das* heating pipe; **~sonne** *die* bowl fire; parabolic heater; **~strahler** *der* radiant heater

**Heizung** *die;* **~, ~en A** [central] heating *no pl., no indef. art.;* **B** (*ugs.: Heizkörper*) radiator

**Heizungs-: ~anlage** *die* heating system; **~keller** *der* boiler room (*in the basement*); **~monteur** *der,* **~monteurin** *die* ▶ 159 heating engineer; **~technik** *die* heating engineering

**Heiz·wert** *der* calorific value

**Hektar** /ˈhɛktaːɐ̯/ *das od. der;* **~s, ~e** ▶ 301 hectare

**Hektar·ertrag** *der* (*Landw.*) yield per hectare

**Hektik** /ˈhɛktɪk/ *die;* **~:** hectic rush; (*des Lebens*) hectic pace; **wozu die ~?** (*ugs.*) what's the rush?; **nur keine ~!** (*ugs.*) take it easy!

**hektisch 1** *Adj.* **A** (*fieberhaft*) hectic; **sie ist immer furchtbar ~:** she is always in a hectic rush; **nun mal nicht so ~!** take it easy!; **B** (*Med. veralt.*) hectic; **~e Flecken** (*fig.*) red blotches. **2** *adv.* ‹work, run to and fro› frantically; **~ zugehen** be hectic; **~ leben** lead a hectic life

**Hektographie** /hɛktograˈfiː/ *die;* **~, ~n A** (*veralt.: Verfahren*) hectography *no art.;* **B** (*Kopie*) hectographed *or* hectographic copy

**hektographieren** *tr. V.* **A** (*veralt.*) hectograph; **B** (*vervielfältigen*) duplicate; copy

**Hekto-: ~liter** *der od. das* hectolitre; **~pascal** *das* hectopascal; **~watt** *das* hundred watts

**Helanca** Ⓦⓩ /heˈlaŋka/ *das;* **~:** nylon stretch fabric

**helau** /heˈlau/ *Interj.*: *cheer or greeting used at Carnival time*

**Held** /hɛlt/ *der;* **~en, ~en** hero; **du bist mir ein schöner** *od.* **netter ~** (*scherzh.*) a fine one you are!; **den ~en spielen** (*abwertend*) play the hero; **kein ~ in etw.** (*Dat.*) **sein** (*ugs. scherzh. od. spött.*) be no great shakes at sth. (*coll.*); **du bist nicht gerade ein ~ in der Schule** (*ugs.*) you're not exactly doing brilliantly at school; **der ~ des Tages/des Abends** the hero of the hour; **~ der Arbeit** (*DDR*) Hero of Labour

**Helden-: ~brust** *die* (*scherzh./iron.*) manly chest; **~darsteller** *der* (*Theater*) actor of heroic roles; **~dichtung** *die* (*Literaturw.*) epic *or* heroic poetry; **~epos** *das* (*Literaturw.*) heroic epic; **~friedhof** *der* military *or* war cemetery; **~gedenktag** *der* (*veralt.*) ≈ Remembrance Day (*Brit.*); Memorial Day (*Amer.*); **~gestalt** *die* hero

**heldenhaft 1** *Adj.* heroic. **2** *adv.* heroically

**helden-, Helden-: ~lied** *das* (*Literaturw.*) heroic song *or* lay; **~mut** *der* heroism; **~mütig 1** *Adj.* heroic; **2** *adv.* heroically; **~pose** *die* (*abwertend*) heroic pose; **~rolle** *die* (*Theater*) part *or* role of the hero; **~sage** *die* (*Literaturw.*) heroic legend; (*aus Norwegen, Island*) heroic saga; **~stück** *das* (*iron.*) **das war kein ~stück** that was nothing to be proud of; **~tat** *die* heroic feat *or* deed; **das war keine ~tat** (*spött.*) that was nothing to be proud of; **~tenor** *der* **A** (*Sänger*) heroic *or* dramatic tenor; Heldentenor; **B** (*Stimmlage*) Heldentenor; **~tod** *der* (*geh. verhüll.*) death in action; **den ~tod sterben/finden** be killed in action

**Heldentum** *das;* **~s** heroism

**Heldin** *die;* **~, ~nen** heroine

**helfen** /ˈhɛlfn̩/ *unr. itr. V.* **A** (*behilflich sein*) **jmdm. ~ [etw. zu tun]** help *or* assist sb. [to do sth.]; lend *or* give sb. a hand [in doing sth.]; **jmdm. bei etw. ~:** help *or* assist sb. with sth.; **jmdm. in den/aus dem Mantel ~:** help sb. into *or* on with/out of *or* off with his/her coat; **jmdm. über die Straße/in den Bus ~:** help sb. across the road/on to the bus; **dem Kranken war nicht mehr zu ~:** the patient was beyond [all] help; **dir ist nicht zu ~** (*ugs.*) you're a hopeless case; **sich** (*Dat.*) **nicht mehr zu ~ wissen** be at one's wits' end; **sich immer zu ~ wissen** be able to take care of oneself; **dem werde ich ~, einfach die Schule zu schwänzen!** (*ugs.*) I'll teach him to play truant; **ich kann mir nicht ~, aber ...** I'm sorry, but [I have to say that] ...; **B** (*nützlich sein*) help;

h

**ein paar Tage Ruhe werden Ihnen sicher ~:** a couple of days' rest will certainly do you good; **das hilft gegen** *od.* **bei Kopfschmerzen** it is good for *or* helps to relieve headaches; **das hilft mir auch nichts** that's no help *or* good to me either; **hilf dir selbst, so hilft dir Gott** (*Spr.*) God helps those who help themselves; **da hilft alles nichts** there's nothing *or* no help for it; **da hilft kein Jammern und kein Klagen** it's no good *or* use moaning and groaning; **C** (*unpers.*) **es hilft nichts** it's no use *or* good; **was hilfts?** what's the use *or* good?; **damit ist uns nicht geholfen** that is no help to us; that doesn't help us; **es hilft dir wenig zu jammern** it's not much good *or* use moaning

**Helfer** *der;* **~s, ~:** helper; (*Mitarbeiter*) assistant; (*eines Verbrechens*) accomplice; **ein ~ in der Not** a friend in need

**Helferin** *die;* ~, **~nen** ⇒ **Helfer**

**Helfers·helfer** *der,* **Helfers·helferin** *die* (*abwertend*) accomplice

**Helikopter** /heli'kɔptɐ/ *der;* **~s, ~:** helicopter

**helio-, Helio-** /helio-/ helio-

**Heliograph** /-'gra:f/ *der;* **~en, ~en** (*Astron., Nachrichtenw.*) heliograph

**Heliographie** /-gra'fi:/ *die;* ~ (*Druckw., Nachrichtenw.*) heliography *no art.*

**Helioskop** /-'sko:p/ *das;* **~s, ~e** (*Astron.*) helioscope

**Heliostat** /-'sta:t/ *der;* **~[e]s** *od.* **~en, ~en** (*Astron.*) heliostat

**Heliotrop**[1] *das;* **~s, ~e** (*Pflanze, Farbe, Farbstoff*) heliotrope

**Heliotrop**[2] *der;* **~s, ~e** (*Schmuckstein*) bloodstone; heliotrope

**Helium** /'he:li̯ʊm/ *das;* **~s** helium

**Helix** /'he:lɪks/ *die;* ~, **Helices** /'he:lit̮se:s/ (*Chemie*) helix

**hell** /hɛl/ **1** *Adj.* **A** (*von Licht erfüllt*) light ‹room etc.›; well-lit ‹stairs›; **es wird ~:** it's getting light; **es war schon ~er Morgen/Tag** it was already broad daylight; **am ~en Tag** (*ugs.*) in broad daylight; **in ~en Flammen stehen** be in flames *or* ablaze; **B** (*klar*) bright ‹day, sky, etc.›; **eine ~ere Zukunft** (*fig. ugs.*) a brighter *or* more promising future; **C** (*viel Licht spendend*) bright ‹light, lamp, star, etc.›; **D** (*blass*) light ‹colour›; fair ‹skin, hair›; light-coloured ‹clothes›; **~es Bier** ≈ lager; **E** (*akustisch*) **ein ~er Ton/Klang** a high, clear sound; **eine ~e Stimme** a high, clear voice; **ein ~es Lachen** a ringing laugh; **F** (*klug*) bright; intelligent; **ein ~er Kopf sein** be bright; **dort fehlt ein ~er Kopf** what is needed there is somebody with brains; **G** (*voll bewusst*) lucid ‹moment, interval›; **H** (*ugs.: absolut*) sheer, utter ‹madness, foolishness, despair, nonsense›; unbounded, boundless ‹enthusiasm›; unrestrained ‹jubilation›; **in ~e Wut geraten** fly into a blind rage; **er hat seine ~e Freude an ihr/daran** she/it is his great joy; **daran wirst du deine ~e Freude haben** (*iron.*) you'll soon find out what you've let yourself in for; ⇒ *auch* **Schar**.
**2** *adv.* **A** brightly; **~ erleuchtet** brightly-lit; **~ leuchtend** bright; **~ lodernd** blazing; **~ lodernde Flammen** raging flames; **B** (*in hoher Tonlage*) **~ läuteten die Glocken** the bells rang out high and clear; **~ lachen** give a ringing laugh; **C** (*sehr*) highly ‹enthusiastic, delighted, indignant, etc.›; (*laut*) **über diesen Unsinn musste er ~ lachen** he had to laugh heartily at this nonsense

**hell-, Hell-: ~auf** *Adv.* highly ‹enthusiastic, indignant, etc.›; **~auf lachen** laugh out loud; **~äugig** *Adj.* ‹person› with light-coloured eyes; **~blau** *Adj.* light blue; **~blond** *Adj.* very fair; light blonde; **~braun** *Adj.* light brown; **~-Dunkel-Adap[ta]tion** *die* adaptation to light and dark; **~dunkel·malerei** *die* chiaroscuro

**helle** *Adj.* (*landsch.*) bright; intelligent; **sei ~!** use your head!

**Helle**[1] *die;* ~ (*geh.*) ⇒ **Helligkeit**

**Helle**[2] *das; adj. Dekl.* ≈ lager

**Hellebarde** /hɛlə'bardə/ *die;* **~, ~n** (*hist.*) halberd

**hellenisieren** /hɛleni'zi:rən/ *tr. V.* Hellenize *no art.*

**Hellenismus** *der;* **~:** Hellenism *no art.*

**Hellenist** *der;* **~en, ~en** Hellenist

**Hellenistik** *die;* **~:** classical Greek studies *pl., no art.*

**Hellenistin** *die;* ~, **~nen** ⇒ **Hellenist**

**hellenistisch** *Adj.* Hellenistic; **die ~en Staaten** the states of Ancient Greece

**Heller** *der;* **~s, ~:** heller; **bis auf den letzten ~/bis auf ~ und Pfennig** (*ugs.*) down to the last penny *or* (*Amer.*) cent; **das ist keinen [roten** *od.* **lumpigen] ~ wert** (*ugs.*) it's not worth a penny *or* (*Amer.*) one red cent; **sie hat keinen [roten** *od.* **lumpigen] ~** (*ugs.*) she doesn't have a penny to her name *or* (*Amer.*) have one [red] cent; **keinen [roten] ~ für jmdn./etw. geben** (*ugs.*) not care tuppence about sb./sth.

***hell·erleuchtet** ⇒ **hell** 2 A

***helleuchtend** ⇒ **hell** 2 A

**hell-: ~farben, ~farbig** *Adj.* light-coloured; **~gelb** *Adj.* light yellow; **~grau** *Adj.* light grey; **~grün** *Adj.* light green; **~haarig** *Adj.* fair[-haired]; **~häutig** *Adj.* fair[-skinned]; fair-skinned, pale-skinned ‹race›; **~hörig** *Adj.* **A** (*aufmerksam*) **~hörig werden** sit up and take notice (*coll.*); **jmdn. ~hörig machen** make sb. sit up and take notice (*coll.*); **B** (*schalldurchlässig*) badly *or* poorly soundproofed; **C** (*veralt.: gut hörend*) **~hörig sein** have keen hearing *or* sharp ears

***hellicht** ⇒ **helllicht**

**Helligkeit** *die;* ~, **~en** (*auch Physik*) brightness; **eine Lampe von größerer ~:** a brighter lamp

**Helligkeits·regler** *der* (*Elektrot.*) dimming control; dimmer; (*beim Fernsehgerät*) brightness control; **Lichtschalter mit ~:** dimmer switch

**hell·licht** /'hɛlɪçt/ *Adj.*: *in* **es ist ~er Tag** it's broad daylight; **am ~en Tag** in broad daylight

***hellodernd** /'hɛlo:dɛnt/ ⇒ **hell** 2 A

**hell-, Hell-: ~rot** *Adj.* light red; **~sehen** *unr. itr. V.; nur im Inf.* **~sehen können** have second sight; be clairvoyant; **~seher** *der,* **~seherin** *die* clairvoyant; **~seherisch** *Adj.* clairvoyant; **~seherische Begabung haben** have the gift of second sight; **~sichtig** *Adj.* **A** (*durchschauend*) perceptive; **B** (*weitblickend*) far-sighted; **~sichtigkeit** *die;* **~~:** perceptiveness; **~wach** *Adj.* **A** (*ganz wach*) wide awake; **B** (*ugs.: klug*) bright; **~werden** *das;* **~~s** daybreak *no art.*

**Helm**[1] /hɛlm/ *der;* **~[e]s, ~e** **A** (*Kopfschutz*) helmet; **~ ab zum Gebet!** (*Milit.*) helmets off for prayers!; **B** (*Archit.*) (*pyramidenförmig*) helm *or* pyramidal roof; (*kegelförmig*) conical roof

**Helm**[2] *der;* **~[e]s, ~e** (*einer Axt, eines Hammers usw.*) helve; (*eines Messers*) haft; handle

**Helm-: ~busch** *der* plume; crest; **~dach** *das* ⇒ **Helm**[1] B; **~zier** *die* crest

**Helot** /he'lo:t/ *der;* **~en, ~en** (*hist.*) Helot

**Helotentum** *das;* **~s** (*hist.*) helotism; helotry

**hem** /həm/ *Interj.* hem

**Hemd** /hɛmt/ *das;* **~[e]s, ~en** **A** (*Oberhemd*) shirt; **B** (*Unterhemd*) [under]vest; undershirt; **C** *in* **etw. wechseln wie das** *od.* **sein ~** (*ugs. abwertend*) change sth. as often as one changes one's clothes; **nass bis aufs ~ sein** be soaked to the skin; be wet through; **das ~ ist mir näher als der Rock** for me charity begins at home; **mach dir nicht ins ~** (*salopp*) don't get [all] uptight (*coll.*); **das zieht einem [ja] das ~ aus** (*ugs.*) that's terrible!; **für sie gibt er sein letztes** *od.* **das letzte ~ her** (*ugs.*) he'd sell the shirt off his back to help her; **jmdn. bis aufs ~ ausziehen** (*ugs.*) have the shirt off sb.'s back (*coll.*); **alles bis aufs ~ verlieren** (*ugs.*) lose almost everything

**Hemd-: ~ärmel** *der* (*österr.*) ⇒ **Hemdsärmel**; **~bluse** *die* shirt; **~blusen·kleid** *das* shirt-waist dress; **~brust** *die* shirt front; dicky (*coll.*)

**Hemden·matz** *der* (*ugs. scherzh.*) *small child wearing only a shirt or vest;* little bare-bum (*coll.*)

**Hemd-: ~knopf** *der* shirt button; **~kragen** *der* shirt collar

**Hemds·ärmel** *der* shirtsleeve; **in ~n** in [one's] shirtsleeves

**hemdsärmelig** /-ɛrməlɪç/ *Adj.* **A** (*im Hemd*) shirtsleeved *attrib.;* in [one's] shirtsleeves *postpos.;* **B** (*ugs.: leger*) casual ‹manner›; informal ‹style›; **sich ~ geben** behave in a casual manner; **er ist mir zu ~:** he's too pally for my liking (*coll.*)

**Hemd·zipfel** *der* shirt tail

**Hemisphäre** /hemi'sfɛ:rə/ *die;* **~, ~n** hemisphere

**hemmen** /'hɛmən/ *tr. V.* **A** (*verlangsamen*) slow [down]; retard; **seinen Schritt ~:** slow one's pace; slow down; **B** (*aufhalten*) check; stem ‹flow›; **C** (*beeinträchtigen*) hinder; hamper; **jmdn. in seiner Entwicklung ~:** inhibit sb.'s development; **D** (*behindern*) impede, hamper ‹person›; **die Verletzung hemmte sie beim Laufen** her injury made walking difficult

**Hemmnis** *das;* **~ses, ~se** obstacle, hindrance (**für** to)

**Hemm·schuh** *der* **A** (*Hemmnis*) obstacle, hindrance (**für** to); **B** (*Eisenb.*) slipper [brake]; **C** (*Bremsklotz*) chock; **D** (*Bremse*) skid; drag

**Hemmung** *die;* ~, **~en** **A** (*Gehemmtheit*) inhibition; **~en haben** have inhibitions; be inhibited; **ich hatte ~en, sie darum zu bitten** I felt awkward about asking her for it; **B** (*Bedenken*) scruple; **keine ~en haben, etw. zu tun** have no scruples about doing sth.; **C** (*Hemmen*) (*des Wachstums, einer Entwicklung*) inhibition

**hemmungs·los** **1** *Adj.* unrestrained; unrestrained, unbridled ‹passion›; (*skrupellos*) unscrupulous; **ein ~er Mensch** a person lacking in all restraint/an unscrupulous person. **2** *adv.* unrestrainedly; without restraint; ‹cry, laugh, scream› uncontrollably; (*skrupellos*) unscrupulously

**Hemmungslosigkeit** *die;* **~:** lack of restraint; (*Skrupellosigkeit*) unscrupulousness

**Hendl** /'hɛndl̩/ *das;* **~s, ~[n]** (*bayr., österr.*) chicken; (*Brathähnchen*) [roast] chicken

**Hengst** /hɛŋst/ *der;* **~[e]s, ~e** (*Pferd*) stallion; (*Kamel*) male; (*Esel*) male; jackass

**Hengst-: ~fohlen** *das,* **~füllen** *das* colt; [male] foal

**Henkel** /'hɛnkl̩/ *der;* **~s, ~:** handle; (*einer Kanne*) handle; ear

**Henkel-: ~kanne** *die* jug; (*größer*) pitcher; **~kreuz** *das* ansate cross; ankh; **~mann** *der* (*ugs.*): *portable set of stacked containers for taking a hot meal to one's work*

**henken** /'hɛŋkn̩/ *tr. V.* (*veralt.*) hang

**Henker** *der;* **~s, ~** **A** hangman; (*Scharfrichter, auch fig.*) executioner; **B** (*salopp*) **sich den ~ um etw. scheren** not give a damn about sth. (*coll.*); **scher dich** *od.* **geh zum ~!** go to blazes *or* to the devil! (*coll.*); **hols der ~!** damn [it]! (*coll.*); the devil take it! (*coll.*); **weiß der ~!** the devil only knows (*coll.*); **beim** *od.* **zum ~!** damn it! (*coll.*); hang it all! (*coll.*)

**Henker[s]-: ~beil** *das* executioner's axe; **~hand** *die:* **durch** *od.* **von ~hand** (*geh.*) at the hand of the executioner

**Henkers-: ~knecht** *der* hangman's assistant; (*eines Scharfrichters*) executioner's assistant; (*fig.*) henchman; **~mahlzeit** *die* last meal (*before execution*); (*scherzh.*) last slap-up meal (*before examination, operation, departure, etc.*)

**Henna** /'hɛna/ *die;* ~ *od. das;* **~[s]** henna

**Henne** /'hɛnə/ *die;* ~, **~n** hen

**Hepatitis** /hepa'ti:tɪs/ *die;* ~, **Hepatitiden** ▶ **474** (*Med.*) hepatitis

**her** /he:ɐ̯/ *Adv.* **A** **~ damit** give it to me; give it here (*coll.*); **~ mit dem Geld** hand over *or* give me the money; **Bier ~!** bring me/us some beer!; **vom Fenster ~:** from the

*old spelling (see note on page 1707)

window; **von weit ~:** from far away *or* a long way off; **sie ist von Köln ~:** she is or comes from Cologne; Ⓑ (*zeitlich*) **von ihrer Kindheit ~:** since childhood; **jmdn. von früher/von der Schulzeit ~ kennen** know sb. from earlier times/from one's schooldays; ⇒ *auch* **früher** 2; Ⓒ **von der Konzeption ~:** as far as the basic design is concerned; **das ist von der Sache ~ nicht vertretbar** it is unjustifiable in the nature of the matter; Ⓓ **eine Woche/einige Zeit/lange ~ sein** be a week/sometime/a long time ago; **es ist lange ~, dass ...** it is a long time since ...; **es ist schon einen Monat ~:** it was a month ago; Ⓔ **mit jmdm./etw. ist es nicht weit ~** (*ugs.*) sb./sth. isn't all that hot (*coll.*); Ⓕ **hinter jmdm./etw. ~ sein** (*ugs.*) be after sb./sth.

**herab** /hɛ'rap/ *Adv.* **vom Gipfel ~ bis ins Tal** from the summit down to the valley; **bis ~ auf etw.** (*Akk.*) down to sth.; **die Treppe/den Berg ~:** down the stairs/the mountain; **von oben ~** (*fig.*) condescendingly; **er ist immer so von oben ~:** he's always so superior

**herab-, Herab-** (⇒ *auch* **herunter-**): **~|blicken** *itr. V.* (*geh.*) ⇒ **~sehen**; **~|flehen** *tr. V.* (*geh.*) **Gottes Hilfe ~flehen** beseech God's help; **Gottes Segen auf jmdn. ~flehen** call down God's blessing on sb.; **~|fließen** *unr. itr. V.; mit sein* (*geh.*) flow down; **~|hängen** *unr. itr. V.* Ⓐ (*nach unten hängen*) hang [down] (**von** from); (*fig.*) ‹clouds› hang low [in the sky]; Ⓑ (*schlaff hängen*) ‹hair, arms, etc.› hang down; **~hängende Schultern** drooping shoulders; **~|klettern** *itr. V.; mit sein* (*geh.*) climb down; descend; **~|kommen** *unr. itr. V.; mit sein* (*geh.*) come down; descend; **~|lassen** ❶ *unr. tr. V.* let down; lower; ❷ *unr. refl. V.* Ⓐ (*iron.: bereit sein*) **sich ~lassen, etw. zu tun** condescend *or* deign to do sth.; Ⓑ (*iron. veralt.: leutselig sein*) **sich zu jmdm. ~lassen** come down to sb.'s level; **~lassend** ❶ *Adj.* condescending; patronizing (**zu** towards); ❷ *adv.* condescendingly; patronizingly; in a condescending *or* patronizing manner; **~lassung** *die;* **~~:** condescension; **~|mindern** *tr. V.* Ⓐ reduce; Ⓑ (*schlecht machen*) belittle, disparage ‹achievement, qualities, etc.›; **~minderung** *die* belittlement; disparagement; **~|regnen** *itr. V.; mit sein* ‹drops of rain› fall; (*fig.*) rain down; **~|rieseln** *itr. V.; mit sein* (*geh.*) trickle down; ‹snow› fall gently; ‹snowflakes› float down; **~|sehen** *unr. itr. V.* Ⓐ (*nach unten sehen*) look down (**auf** + *Akk.* on); Ⓑ (*geringschätzig betrachten*) **auf jmdn. ~sehen** look down on sb.; **~|senken** *refl. V.* (*geh.*) ‹night, evening› fall; ‹mist, fog› settle, descend (**auf** + *Akk.* on, over); **~|setzen** *tr. V.* Ⓐ (*reduzieren*) reduce, cut ‹cost, price, working hours, etc.›; reduce ‹speed›; **zu ~gesetzten Preisen** at reduced prices; **~gesetzte Waren** (*ugs.*) cut-price goods; Ⓑ (*abwerten*) belittle; disparage; **~setzung** *die;* **~~:** ⇒ **~setzen**: Ⓐ reduction, cut (*Gen.* in); Ⓑ belittling; disparagement; **~|sinken** *unr. itr. V.; mit sein* Ⓐ (*nach unten sinken*) sink [down]; (*fig.*) ‹night› fall; descend; ‹mist, fog› settle, descend (**auf** + *Akk.* on, over); Ⓑ (*moralisch absinken*) sink; **~|steigen** *unr. itr. V.; mit sein* (*geh.*) descend; climb down; (*vom Pferd*) dismount; **~|stoßen** (*geh.*) ❶ *unr. tr. V.* push down; **er hat ihn von der Klippe ~gestoßen** he pushed him off the cliff; ❷ *unr. itr. V.; mit sein* swoop down; **~|stürzen** ❶ *itr. V.; mit sein* plummet down; **er stürzte vom Gerüst ~:** he fell from *or* off the scaffolding; **~stürzende Felsbrocken** falling rocks; ❷ *refl. V.* throw oneself (**von** from *or* off); **~|würdigen** *tr. V.* belittle; disparage; **~würdigung** *die* belittling; disparagement; **~|ziehen** *unr. tr. V.* (*geh.*) Ⓐ pull down; Ⓑ (*moralisch*) **jmdn. zu sich/auf sein eigenes Niveau ~ziehen** drag sb. down to one's own level

**Heraklit** /hera'kli:t/ (*der*) Heraclitus

**Heraldik** /he'raldɪk/ *die;* **~:** heraldry *no art.*

**Heraldiker** *der;* **~s, ~, Heraldikerin** *die;* **~, ~nen** heraldist; expert in heraldry

**heraldisch** *Adj.* heraldic

**heran** /hɛ'ran/ *Adv.* **an etw.** (*Akk.*) **~:** close to *or* right up to sth.; **nur ~ zu mir!, immer ~!** come closer!

**heran-, Heran-: ~|arbeiten** *refl. V.* **sich an etw.** (*Akk.*) **~arbeiten** work one's way towards sth.; **~|bilden** ❶ *tr. V.* train [up]; (*auf der Schule, Universität*) educate; ❷ *refl. V.* (*sich entwickeln*) develop; **~|bringen** *unr. tr. V.* Ⓐ (*zu jmdm. bringen*) bring [up] (**an** + *Akk.*, **zu** to); Ⓑ (*vertraut machen*) **jmdn. an etw.** (*Akk.*) **~bringen** introduce sb. to sth.; **~|fahren** *unr. itr. V.; mit sein* drive up (**an** + *Akk.* to); **~|führen** ❶ *tr. V.* Ⓐ (*in die Nähe führen*) lead up; bring up ‹troops›; **aus dem Osten wird Kaltluft ~geführt** there is/will be a cold easterly airstream; Ⓑ (*nahe bringen*) bring up (**an** + *Akk.* to); Ⓒ (*vertraut machen*) **jmdn. an etw.** (*Akk.*) **~führen** introduce sb. to sth.; ❷ *itr. V.* **an etw.** (*Akk.*) **~führen** lead up to sth.; **~|gehen** *unr. itr. V.; mit sein* Ⓐ go up (**an** + *Akk.* to); **näher ~gehen** go [up] closer; Ⓑ (*anpacken*) **an ein Problem/eine Aufgabe/die Arbeit** *usw.* **~gehen** tackle a problem/a task/the work *etc.;* **an die Lösung eines Problems ~gehen** set about solving a problem; **~|holen** *tr. V.* fetch; **~|kommen** *unr. itr. V.; mit sein* Ⓐ **an etw.** (*Akk.*) **~kommen** come *or* draw near to sth.; approach sth.; **lass es erst an dich ~kommen** (*ugs.*) cross that bridge when you get to it; **wir waren fast an den Fluss ~gekommen** we had almost reached the river; **ganz nahe an etw.** (*Akk.*) **~kommen** come right up to sth.; Ⓑ (*zeitlich*) **der große Tag kam näher ~/war ~gekommen** the big day drew nearer/had arrived; Ⓒ **an etw.** (*Akk.*) **~kommen** (*erreichen*) reach sth.; (*erwerben*) obtain sth.; get hold of sth.; **an den Motor** *usw.* **~kommen** get at the engine *etc.;* **an jmdn. ~kommen** (*fig.*) get hold of sb.; **er ist so verschlossen, man kommt nur schwer an ihn ~:** he's so reserved, it's very hard to get to know him; **an diesen Wissenschaftler kommt keiner ~** (*fig.*) there is no one who can compare with this scientist; **an jmds. Erfolg/Rekord ~kommen** (*fig.*) equal sb.'s success/record; **~|machen** *refl. V.* (*ugs.*) Ⓐ (*beginnen*) **sich an etw.** (*Akk.*) **~machen** get down to *or* (*coll.*) get going on sth.; Ⓑ (*nähern*) **sich an jmdn. ~machen** chat sb. up (*coll.*); **~|nahen** *itr. V.; mit sein* (*geh.*) approach; draw near; **~|nehmen** *unr. tr. V.* **die Lehrlinge werden ganz schön ~genommen** the apprentices are really made to work [hard]; **der Lehrer nahm den Schüler tüchtig ~:** the teacher took the boy firmly in hand; **~|reichen** *itr. V.* Ⓐ (*erreichen*) reach; **an die oberen Schrankfächer ~reichen** reach [up to] the top shelves; Ⓑ (*von gleicher Qualität sein*) **an jmdn./etw. ~reichen** come *or* measure up to the standard of sb./sth.; **~|reifen** *itr. V.; mit sein* ‹fruit, crops› ripen; (*fig.*) ‹plan› mature; **zur Frau/zum Mann/zu einer großen Malerin ~reifen** mature into a woman/man/great painter; **in ihm reifte der Entschluss ~, ins Ausland zu gehen** (*fig.*) he became increasingly resolved to go abroad; **~|rücken** ❶ *tr. V.* pull up ‹table›; draw *or* pull *or* bring up ‹chair›; ❷ *itr. V.; mit sein* move *or* come closer *or* nearer; ‹troops› advance (**an** + *Akk.* towards); **dicht** *od.* **nah ~rücken** move up close (**an** + *Akk.* to); **mit seinem Stuhl ~rücken** draw *or* pull *or* bring one's chair up closer; **~|schaffen** *tr. V.* bring; (*liefern*) supply; **~|schleichen** *unr. itr. V. mit sein; refl. V.* **[sich an etw./jmdn.] ~schleichen** creep *or* sneak up [to sth./on sb.]; **~|tasten** *refl. V.* **sich [an etw.** *Akk.***] ~tasten** grope *or* feel one's way [over to sth.]; (*fig.*) feel one's way [towards sth.]; **~|tragen** *unr. tr. V.* Ⓐ bring [over]; Ⓑ (*vorbringen*) **eine Bitte/Beschwerde an jmdn. ~tragen** go/come to sb. with a request/complaint; **~|treten** *unr. itr. V.; mit sein* Ⓐ (*an eine Stelle treten*) come/go up (**an** + *Akk.* to); **treten Sie nur näher ~!** come along!; [just] step this way!; Ⓑ (*sich ergeben*) **Probleme/Fragen/Anfechtungen treten an jmdn. ~:** sb. is faced with problems/questions/accusations; **Zweifel treten an ihn ~:** he is assailed by doubts; Ⓒ (*sich wenden*) **an jmdn. ~treten** approach sb.; **~|wachsen** *unr. itr. V.; mit sein* grow up; (*fig.*) develop; **zum Mann/zur Frau ~wachsen** grow up into *or* to be a man/woman; **die ~wachsende Generation** the rising *or* up-and-coming generation; **~wachsende** *der/die; adj. Dekl.* Ⓐ young person; **viele ~wachsende** many young people; Ⓑ (*Rechtsw.*) adolescent; **~|wagen** *refl. V.* venture near; dare to go near; **sich an etw.** (*Akk.*) **~wagen** venture near sth.; dare to go near sth.; (*fig.*) venture *or* dare to tackle *or* attempt sth.; **er wagte sich nicht an das Mädchen ~:** he did not dare to approach the girl; **~|ziehen** ❶ *unr. tr. V.* Ⓐ (*an eine Stelle ziehen*) pull *or* draw over; pull *or* draw up ‹chair›; **etw. zu sich ~ziehen** pull *or* draw sth. towards one; **etw. näher ~ziehen** pull *or* draw sth. closer *or* near (**an** + *Akk.* to); Ⓑ (*beauftragen*) call *or* bring in; **weitere Arbeitskräfte ~ziehen** bring in more labour; Ⓒ (*in Betracht ziehen*) refer to; (*geltend machen*) invoke; quote; Ⓓ (*großziehen*) rear, raise ‹animal›; grow ‹plant›; (*ugs.*) rear, raise ‹child›; Ⓔ (*ausbilden*) **jmdn. zu etw. ~ziehen** make *or* turn sb. into sth.; ❷ *unr. itr. V.; mit sein* (*auch fig.*) approach; (*Milit.*) advance

**herauf** /hɛ'rauf/ *Adv.* up; **~ ist es beschwerlich** it's hard work coming up; **vom Tal ~:** up from the valley

**herauf-: ~|arbeiten** *refl. V.* Ⓐ work one's/its way up; Ⓑ (*hocharbeiten*) work one's way up; **~|bemühen** ❶ *tr. V.* **jmdn. ~bemühen** trouble sb. to come up; ❷ *refl. V.* take the trouble to come up; **würden Sie sich bitte ~bemühen?** (*geh.*) would you mind coming up?; **~|beschwören** *tr. V.* Ⓐ (*verursachen*) cause, bring about ‹disaster, war, crisis›; cause, provoke ‹dispute, argument›; give rise to ‹criticism›; Ⓑ (*erinnern*) evoke ‹memories etc.›; **~|bitten** *unr. tr. V.* **jmdn. ~bitten** ask sb. [to come] up; **~|bringen** *unr. tr. V.* bring up; **~|dämmern** *itr. V.; mit sein* ‹day, morning› dawn, break; (*fig.*) dawn; **~|dringen** *unr. itr. V.; mit sein* rise up [from below]; ‹smell› drift up [from below]; **von/aus etw. ~dringen** rise/drift up from sth.; **Lachen drang zu uns ~:** [the sound of] laughter reached our ears from below; **~|fahren** ❶ *unr. itr. V.; mit sein* drive up; (*mit einem Motorrad, Rad*) ride up; ❷ *unr. tr. V.* **jmdn. ~fahren** drive sb. up; **~|führen** ❶ *itr. V.* **es führen zwei Wege ~:** there are two paths up; ❷ *tr. V.* show ‹person› up; **~|kommen** *unr. itr. V.; mit sein* Ⓐ (*nach oben kommen*) come up; **auf den Baum/die Mauer ~kommen** climb *or* get up the tree/up on the wall; **in das obere Stockwerk ~kommen** come up to the top floor; Ⓑ (*aufsteigen*) rise; come up; Ⓒ (*bevorstehen*) ‹storm› be approaching *or* gathering *or* brewing; **~|lassen** *unr. tr. V.* (*ugs.*) **jmdn. ~lassen** allow sb. [to come] up; let sb. [come] up; **~|reichen** ❶ *tr. V.* hand *or* pass up; ❷ *itr. V.* (*ugs.: erreichen*) **bis zu etw. ~reichen** reach up to sth.; **~|sehen** *unr. itr. V.* look up; **~|setzen** *tr. V.* increase, raise, put up ‹prices, rents, interest rates, etc.›; **~|steigen** *unr. itr. V.; mit sein* Ⓐ (*nach [hier] oben kommen*) climb [up]; Ⓑ (*aufsteigen*) rise; come up; ‹mist, smoke› rise; Ⓒ (*geh.: beginnen*) ‹day, morning› dawn, break; ‹night› come on, fall; ‹dawn› break; ‹new age› dawn; **~|ziehen** ❶ *unr. tr. V.* pull up; ❷ *unr. itr. V.; mit sein* Ⓐ (*näher kommen*) ‹storm› be approaching *or* gathering *or* brewing; (*fig.*) ‹disaster› be approaching; Ⓑ ⇒ **~steigen** c

**heraus** /hɛ'raus/ *Adv.* out; **aus etw. ~ sein** be out of sth.; **aus der Schule ~ sein** have left school; **aus den Schulden/einem Dilemma** *usw.* **~ sein** have got *or* be out of debt/a dilemma *etc.*; **aus dem Gröbsten ~ sein** (*ugs.*) be over the worst; **fein ~ sein** (*ugs.*) be sitting pretty (*coll.*); **~ aus den Federn!/dem Bett!** rise and shine!/out of bed!; **~ mit dir!** get out of here!; **~ damit!** (*gib her!*) hand it over!; (*weg damit!*) get rid of it!; **~ mit der Sprache!** out with it!; **nach vorn ~ wohnen** live at the front; **aus**

**einem Gefühl der Einsamkeit ~:** out of a feeling of loneliness

**heraus-, Heraus-: ~|arbeiten** ❶ *tr. V.* [A] (*aus Stein, Holz*) fashion, carve (**aus** out of); [B] (*hervorheben*) bring out ‹difference, aspect, point of view, etc.›; develop ‹observation, remark›; ❷ *refl. V.* work one's way out (**aus** of); **~|bekommen** ❶ *unr. tr. V.* [A] (*entfernen*) get out (**aus** of); [B] (*ugs.: lösen*) work out ‹problem, answer, etc.›; solve ‹puzzle›; [C] (*ermitteln*) find out; **etw. aus jmdm. ~bekommen** get sth. out of sb.; [D] (*als Wechselgeld bekommen*) **5 DM ~bekommen** get back 5 marks change; **ich bekomme noch 5 DM ~:** I still have 5 marks [change] to come; [E] (*von sich geben*) ⇒ **~bringen** H; ❷ *unr. itr. V.* (*Wechselgeld bekommen*) **richtig/falsch ~bekommen** (*ugs.*) get the right/wrong change; **~|bilden** *refl. V.* develop; **~|bitten** *unr. tr. V.* **jmdn. ~bitten** ask sb. to come out[side]; **darf ich Sie einen Moment ~bitten?** would you mind coming outside for a moment?; **~|boxen** *tr. V.* [A] (*Fußball, Handball*) punch out; [B] (*befreien*) bail out; **~|brechen** ❶ *unr. tr. V.* knock out; (*mit brutaler Gewalt*) wrench out; pull up ‹paving stone›; **eine Tür/ein paar Fliesen aus der Wand ~brechen** knock out a hole [in the wall] for a doorway/knock a few tiles off the wall; ❷ *unr. itr. V.; mit sein* ‹anger, hatred› burst forth, erupt; **aus dem Glas ist ein großer Splitter ~gebrochen** there's a large chip out of the glass; **~|bringen** *unr. tr. V.* [A] (*nach außen bringen*) bring out (**aus** of); [B] (*nach draußen begleiten*) show out; [C] (*veröffentlichen*) bring out; publish; (*aufführen*) put on, stage ‹play›; screen ‹film›; [D] (*auf den Markt bringen*) bring out; launch; [E] (*populär machen*) make widely known; **jmdn./etw. ganz groß ~bringen** launch sb./sth. in a big way; [F] (*ugs.: ermitteln*) ⇒ **~bekommen** 1 C; [G] (*ugs.: lösen*) ⇒ **~bekommen** 1 B; [H] (*von sich geben*) utter; say; **~|drehen** *tr. V.* unscrew; **~|drücken** *tr. V.* [A] **etw. ~drücken** squeeze sth. out (**aus** of); squeeze *or* press ‹juice, oil› out (**aus** of); [B] (*vorwölben*) stick out ‹chest etc.›; **~|dürfen** *unr. itr. V.* be allowed [to come/go] out; **~|fahren** ❶ *unr. itr. V.; mit sein* [A] (*nach außen fahren*) **aus etw. ~fahren** drive out of sth.; (*mit dem Rad, Motorrad*) ride out of sth.; **der Zug fuhr aus dem Bahnhof ~:** the train pulled out of the station; [B] (*fahrend ~kommen*) come out; [C] (*ugs.: schnell ~kommen*) **aus dem Bett ~fahren** shoot *or* leap out of bed; **eilig fuhr sie aus dem Mantel ~:** she whipped off her coat; [D] (*ugs.: entschlüpfen*) ‹word, remark, etc.› slip out; ❷ *unr. tr. V.* [A] **den Wagen/das Fahrrad [aus dem Hof] ~fahren** drive the car/ride the bicycle out [of the yard]; **jmdn. ~fahren** drive sb. out (**zu** to); [B] (*Sport*) **eine gute Zeit/einen Sieg ~fahren** record a good *or* fast time/a victory; **den zweiten Platz ~fahren** take second place; **~|finden** ❶ *unr. tr. V.* [A] (*entdecken*) find out; trace ‹fault›; **man fand ~, dass ...** it was found *or* discovered that ...; [B] (*aus einer Menge*) pick out (**aus** from [among]); find (**aus** among); ❷ *unr. itr. V.* find one's way out (**aus** of); ❸ *unr. refl. V.* find one's way out (**aus** of); **~|fischen** *tr. V.* (*ugs.*) fish out (*coll.*) (**aus** of); **sie hat sich** (*Dat.*) **einige hübsche Sachen ~gefischt** she picked out some nice things [for herself]; **~|fliegen** ❶ *unr. itr. V.; mit sein* [A] fly out (**aus** of); [B] (*aus etw. fallen*) be thrown out (**aus** of); [C] (*ugs.: entlassen werden*) be fired *or* (*coll.*) sacked (**bei** from); ❷ *unr. tr. V.* fly out (**aus** of); **~forderer** *der;* **~~s, ~~, ~forderin** *die;* **~~, ~~nen** (*auch Sport*) challenger; **~|fordern** ❶ *tr. V.* [A] (*auch Sport*) challenge; [B] (*heraufbeschwören*) provoke ‹person, resistance, etc.›; invite ‹criticism›; court ‹danger›; **sein Schicksal ~fordern** tempt fate *or* providence; ❷ *itr. V.* (*provozieren*) **zu etw. ~fordern** provoke sth.; **~fordernd** ❶ *Adj.* provocative; (*verlockend*) provocative, inviting ‹glance, smile, etc.›; (*Streit suchend*) challenging, defiant ‹words, speech, look›; ❷ *adv.: s. Adj.:* provocatively; invitingly; challengingly; defiantly

**Heraus·forderung** *die* (*auch Sport*) challenge; (*Provokation*) provocation

**heraus-, Heraus-: ~|fühlen** *tr. V.* sense; feel; **~|führen** ❶ *tr. V.* [A] (*nach außen führen*) lead out; [B] (*nach draußen führen*) bring out; **was führt dich denn zu uns ~?** what brings you out to see us, then?; ❷ *itr. V.* lead out (**aus** of); **~gabe** *die* [A] (*von Eigentum, Personen, Geiseln usw.*) handing over; (*Rückgabe*) return; [B] (*das Veröffentlichen*) publication; (*Redaktion*) editing; **~|geben** ❶ *unr. tr. V.* [A] (*nach außen geben*) hand *or* pass out; [B] (*aushändigen*) hand over ‹property, person, hostage, etc.›; (*zurückgeben*) return; give back; [C] (*als Wechselgeld zurückgeben*) **5 DM/zu viel ~geben** give 5 marks/too much change; [D] (*veröffentlichen*) publish; (*für die Veröffentlichung bearbeiten*) edit [for publication]; [E] issue ‹stamp, coin, etc.›; [F] (*erlassen*) issue; ❷ *itr. V.* give change; **können Sie [auf 100 DM] ~geben?** do you have *or* can you give me change [for 100 marks]?; **jmdm. falsch/richtig ~geben** give sb. the wrong/right change; **~geber** *der,* **~geberin** *die;* publisher; (*Redakteur*) editor; **~|gehen** *unr. itr. V.; mit sein* [A] (*nach außen gehen*) go out; leave; **aus dem Saal ~gehen** go out of the hall; **aus sich ~gehen** come out of one's shell; [B] (*sich entfernen lassen*) ‹stain, cork, nail, etc.› come out; **~|greifen** *unr. tr. V.* pick out; select; **sich** (*Dat.*) **jmdn. ~greifen** pick *or* single sb. out (**aus** from); (*fig.*) take ‹example, aspect, etc.› (**aus** from); **~|haben** *unr. tr. V.* (*ugs.*) [A] (*entfernt haben*) have got ‹stain, nail, cork, etc.› out; **ich will ihn aus dem Verein ~haben** I want him out of the club; [B] (*verstanden haben*) have found out; **den Bogen** *od.* **Dreh ~haben[, wie man es macht]** have got the knack [of doing it]; [C] (*gelöst haben*) have worked out *or* solved ‹problem›; have solved ‹puzzle›; **er hat etwas anderes ~ als ich** we arrived at *or* got different answers; **ich habs ~!** I've done it!; [D] (*ermittelt haben*) know; have found out; **~|halten** ❶ *unr. tr. V.* [A] (*nach außen halten*) put *or* stick out (**aus** of); [B] (*ugs.: fernhalten, nicht verwickeln*) keep out (**aus** of); ❷ *unr. refl. V.* keep *or* stay out; **halte du dich da ~!** you keep *or* stay out of this *or* it!; **~|hängen¹** *unr. itr. V.* hang out (**aus** of); **~|hängen²** *tr. V.* hang out (**aus** of); **~|hauen** *unr. tr. V.* [A] chop *or* cut down and clear ‹tree›; [B] (*durch Hauen fertigen*) carve ‹figure, letters, relief, etc.› (**aus** from, out of); [C] (*ugs.: befreien*) get out; (*aus Schwierigkeiten*) bail out; **~|heben** ❶ *unr. tr. V.* [A] (*nach außen heben*) lift out (**aus** of); [B] (*hervorheben*) bring out; **es ist diese Eigenschaft, die ihn aus der Masse ~hebt** it is this quality that raises him above *or* sets him apart from the rest; **etw. durch Fettdruck aus dem übrigen Text ~heben** make sth. stand out from the rest of the text with bold type; ❷ *unr. refl. V.* stand out (**aus** from); **~|helfen** *unr. itr. V.* **jmdm. ~helfen** (*auch fig.*) help sb. out (**aus** of); **er half ihr aus dem Zug ~:** he helped her off the train; **~|holen** *tr. V.* [A] (*nach außen holen*) bring out; **etw. aus einem brennenden Haus ~holen** get sth. out of a burning house; [B] (*ugs.: abgewinnen*) get out; gain, win ‹victory, points›; gain, take ‹place›; **er holte das Letzte aus sich ~:** he made an all-out *or* supreme effort; [C] (*ugs.: erwirken*) gain, win ‹wage increase, advantage, etc.›; get, achieve ‹result›; [D] (*ugs.: durch Fragen*) get out; **etw. aus jmdm. ~holen** get sth. out of sb.; [E] (*ugs.: ~arbeiten*) bring out ‹difference, aspect, point of view›; [F] (*ausgleichen*) make up ‹time, points deficit, etc.›; [G] (*ugs.*) **Geld aus jmdm. ~holen** get money out of *or* extract money from sb.; **~|hören** *tr. V.* [A] hear; [B] (*erkennen*) detect, sense (**aus** in); **~|kehren** *tr. V.* parade; **den Vorgesetzten ~kehren** parade the fact that one is in charge; **die Dame der Gesellschaft ~kehren** act the society lady; **~kehren, dass ...** parade the fact that ...; **~|kommen** *unr. itr. V.; mit sein* [A] (*nach außen kommen*) come out (**aus** of); **nach/in zwei Jahren wieder ~kommen** (*ugs.*) be let out after/in two years; [B] (*ein Gebiet verlassen*) **er ist nie aus seiner Heimatstadt ~gekommen** he's never been out of *or* never left his home town; **du kommst viel zu wenig ~:** you don't get out nearly enough; **wir kamen aus dem Staunen/Lachen nicht ~** (*fig.*) we couldn't get over our surprise/stop laughing; [C] (*ugs.: einen Ausweg finden*) get out (**aus** of); **aus einer Situation/den Sorgen ~kommen** get out of a situation/get over one's worries; **aus den Schulden ~kommen** get out of debt; [D] (*ugs.: auf den Markt kommen*) come out; **mit einem Produkt ~kommen** bring out *or* launch a product; [E] (*erscheinen*) ‹book, timetable, etc.› come out, be published, appear; ‹coin, postage stamp› be issued; ‹play› be staged; [F] (*ugs.: bekannt werden*) come out; [G] (*ugs.: zur Sprache kommen*) **mit etw. ~kommen** come out with sth.; [H] (*ugs.: sich erfolgreich produzieren*) **ganz groß ~kommen** make a big splash; [I] (*deutlich werden*) come out; ‹colour› show up; [J] (*ugs.: ausgedrückt werden*) sound; [K] (*ugs.: sich als Resultat ergeben*) **bei etw. ~kommen** come out of *or* emerge from sth.; **auf dasselbe ~kommen** amount to the same thing; **was kommt bei der Aufgabe ~?** what is the answer to the question?; **dabei kommt nichts ~:** nothing will come of it; **was soll dabei ~kommen?** what's that supposed to achieve?; [L] (*ugs.: aus der Übung kommen*) get out of practice; [M] (*ugs.: ausspielen*) lead; **wer kommt ~?** whose lead is it?; **mit etw. ~kommen** lead sth.; [N] (*ugs.: gewinnen*) ‹number, person› come up; [O] (*schweiz.: ausgehen, enden*) turn out; **~|kriegen** *tr. V.* (*ugs.*) ⇒ **~bekommen**; **~|kristallisieren** ❶ *tr. V.* [A] (*Chemie*) crystallize [out]; [B] (*zusammenfassen*) extract; ❷ *refl. V.* [A] (*Chemie*) crystallize [out]; ‹crystal› form; [B] (*entwickeln*) crystallize (**aus** out of); **~|lassen** *unr. tr. V.* (*ugs.*) [A] (*nach außen kommen lassen*) let out (**aus** of); release (**aus** from); **abends lassen sie den Wachhund ~:** they let the guard dog loose in the evenings; [B] (*weglassen*) leave out (**aus** of); **~|laufen** ❶ *unr. itr. V.; mit sein* [A] run out (**aus** of); (*Fußball*) ‹goalkeeper› come out; [B] (*nach außen fließen*) run out (**aus** of); ❷ *unr. tr. V.* (*Sport*) win ‹victory›; build up ‹lead›; take ‹first place etc.›; **eine gute Zeit ~laufen** run *or* record a good time; **~|lesen** *unr. tr. V.* [A] (*entnehmen*) tell (**aus** from); [B] (*interpretieren*) **etw. aus etw. ~lesen** read sth. into sth.; [C] (*auswählen*) pick out (**aus** from); **~|locken** *tr. V.* [A] entice out (**aus** of); lure ‹enemy, victim, etc.› out (**aus** of); [B] (*durch List*) **Geld/ein Geheimnis aus jmdm. ~locken** wheedle money/worm a secret out of sb.; **jmdn. aus seiner Reserve ~locken** draw sb. out of his/her shell; **~|lügen** *unr. refl. V.* **sich aus etw. ~lügen** lie one's way out of sth.; **~|machen** (*ugs.*) ❶ *tr. V.* take out; get out ‹stain›; ❷ *refl. V.* come on well; (*nach einer Krankheit*) pick up; (*finanziell*) do well; **~|müssen** *unr. itr. V.* (*ugs.*) [A] **aus etw. ~müssen** have to leave sth.; **dieser Zahn muss ~:** this tooth has to come out; [B] (*aufstehen müssen*) have to get up; [C] (*gesagt werden müssen*) have to come out; **das musste einfach ~!** I simply had to get that off my chest (*coll.*); **~nehmbar** *Adj.* removable; detachable ‹lining›; **~|nehmen** *unr. tr. V.* [A] take out (**aus** of); [B] (*ugs.: entfernen*) take out, remove ‹appendix, tonsils, tooth, etc.›; **jmdm. den Blinddarm ~nehmen** take out *or* remove sb.'s appendix; **sich** (*Dat.*) **die Mandeln ~nehmen lassen** have one's tonsils out; **den Gang ~nehmen** (*fig.*) put the car into neutral; **ein Kind aus einer Schule ~nehmen** take a child away *or* remove a child from a school; [C] (*Ballspiele*) take off ‹player›; [D] (*ugs.: erlauben*) **sich** (*Dat.*) **Freiheiten ~nehmen** take liberties; **was nimmst du dir ~, mich so zu kritisieren!** how dare you criticize me like that!; **sich** (*Dat.*) **zu viel ~nehmen** go too far; **~|picken** *tr. V.* (*fig.*) pick out (**aus** of); **~|platzen** *itr. V.; mit sein* (*ugs.*) [A] (*~lachen*) burst out laughing; [B] (*spontan äußern*) **mit etw. ~platzen** blurt sth. out;

*old spelling (see note on page 1707)

~|**pressen** *tr. V.* Ⓐ (*aus etw. pressen*) ⇒ ~**drücken** A; Ⓑ (*erpressen*) squeeze out ‹money› (**aus** from); wring out ‹confession, concession› (**aus** from); ~|**putzen** *tr. V.* Ⓐ (*festlich kleiden*) dress up; **sich ~putzen** get dressed up; Ⓑ (*festlich schmücken*) deck out; **sich ~putzen** be decked out; ~|**ragen** *itr. V.* Ⓐ jut out, project (**aus** from); (*sich erheben über*) **aus etw. ~ragen** rise above sth.; Ⓑ (*hervortreten*) stand out (**aus** from); ~**ragend** *Adj.* outstanding; ~|**reden** *refl. V.* (*ugs.*) talk one's way out (**aus** of); ~|**reißen** *unr. tr. V.* Ⓐ tear *or* rip out (**aus** of); pull up *or* out ‹plant›; pull out ‹hair›; pull up ‹floor›; rip out ‹tiles›; Ⓑ (*aus der Umgebung, der Arbeit*) tear away (**aus** from); **die Krankheit hat ihn aus der Arbeit ~gerissen** the illness had interrupted his work; **jmdn. aus einem Gespräch/seiner Lethargie ~reißen** drag sb. away from a conversation/jolt *or* shake sb. out of his/her lethargy; **jmdn. aus seiner Traurigkeit ~reißen** take sb. out of himself/herself; Ⓒ (*ugs.: befreien*) save; ~|**rücken** ❶ *tr. V.* Ⓐ (*nach außen rücken*) move out (**aus** of); Ⓑ (*ugs.: hergeben*) hand over; cough up (*coll.*) ‹money›; ❷ *itr. V.*; *mit sein* **mit etw./der Sprache ~rücken** come out with sth./it; ~|**rufen** ❶ *unr. itr. V.* call *or* shout out (**aus** of); ❷ *unr. tr. V.* call out; **jmdn. aus einer Sitzung ~rufen** call sb. out of a meeting; **das Publikum rief den Sänger mehrmals ~:** the audience called the singer back several times; ~|**rutschen** *itr. V.*; *mit sein* Ⓐ slip out (**aus** of); **ihm rutscht immer das Hemd aus der Hose ~:** his shirt is always coming out of his trousers; Ⓑ (*ugs.: entschlüpfen*) ‹remark etc.› slip out; **die Bemerkung war ihr nur so ~gerutscht** the remark just slipped out somehow; ~|**saugen** *unr.* (*auch regelm.*) *tr. V.* suck out (**aus** of); ~|**schälen** *refl. V.* Ⓐ (*erkennbar werden*) emerge (**aus** from); Ⓑ (*sich erweisen*) **sich als etw. ~schälen** turn out *or* prove to be sth.; ~|**schauen** *itr. V.* (*landsch.*) Ⓐ look out (**aus/zu** of); Ⓑ (*hervorschauen*) ‹petticoat etc.› be showing; ‹shirt› be hanging out; Ⓒ (*ugs.: zu erwarten sein*) **dabei schaut etwas/nicht viel für ihn ~:** there's something/not much in it for him; **es schaut nichts dabei ~:** there's nothing to be gained by it; ~|**schießen** *unr. itr. V.* Ⓐ **aus einem Fenster/Auto ~schießen** shoot *or* fire from a window/car; Ⓑ *mit sein* (*sich schnell bewegen*) shoot out (**aus** of); **ein Blutstrahl schoss aus der Wunde ~:** blood spurted from the wound; **~geschossen kommen** (*ugs.*) shoot out (**aus** of); ~|**schlagen** ❶ *unr. tr. V.* Ⓐ knock out; Ⓑ (*ugs.: gewinnen*) get ‹discount, advantage, etc.›; make ‹money, profit›; ❷ *unr. itr. V.*; *mit sein* ‹flames› leap out (**aus** of); ~|**schleichen** ❶ *unr. itr. V.*; *mit sein* sneak *or* steal out (**aus** of); ❷ *unr. refl. V.* sneak *or* steal out (**aus** of); ~|**schleudern** *tr. V.* hurl *or* fling out (**aus** of); hurl ‹accusations etc.›; **die Straßenbahn wurde aus den Schienen ~geschleudert** the tram (*Brit.*) *or* (*Amer.*) streetcar was flung *or* thrown off the rails; ~|**schlüpfen** *itr. V.*; *mit sein* slip out (**aus** of); **eine Bemerkung schlüpfte ihm ~:** a remark slipped out; ~|**schmecken** ❶ *tr. V.* **etw. ~schmecken [können]** be able to taste sth.; ❷ *itr. V.* taste; ~|**schmeißen** ⇒ **rausschmeißen**; ~|**schmuggeln** *tr. V.* smuggle out (**aus** of); ~|**schneiden** *unr. tr. V.* cut out (**aus** of); ~|**schrauben** *tr. V.* unscrew ‹light bulb, screw›; unscrew, screw off ‹door handle, table leg, etc.›; ~|**schreiben** *unr. tr. V.* copy out (**aus** from); ~|**schreien** *unr. tr. V.* **seine Wut/seinen Zorn/seinen Hass ~schreien** vent *or* give vent to one's anger/rage/hatred in a loud outburst; *~|**sein** ⇒ **heraus**

**heraußen** /hɛˈrau̯sn̩/ *Adv.* (*südd.*, *österr.*) out here

**her<u>aus</u>-:** ~|**springen** *unr. itr. V.*; *mit sein* Ⓐ jump *or* leap out (**aus** of); Ⓑ (*sich lösen*) come out; Ⓒ ⇒ ~**schauen** C; ~|**sprudeln** ❶ *itr. V.*; *mit sein* bubble out (**aus** of); ❷ *tr. V.* **sie sprudelte die Worte ~:** the words tumbled from her lips; ~|**stehen** *unr. itr. V.* protrude; stick out; ~|**stellen** ❶ *tr. V.* Ⓐ put out[side]; **sie stellte das Geschirr zum Abendessen ~:** she got the china out ready for dinner; **einen Spieler ~stellen** (*Sport*) send a player off; Ⓑ (*hervorheben*) emphasize; bring out; present, set out ‹principles etc.›; **eine Nebenfigur ~stellen** give prominence to a minor character; ❷ *refl. V.* **es stellte sich ~, dass ...** it turned out *or* emerged that ...; **wie sich später ~stellte, hatte er ...** it turned out later that he had ...; **wer Recht hat, wird sich erst noch ~stellen müssen** it remains to be seen who is right; **es wird sich bald ~stellen, ob ...** we shall soon know *or* find out whether ...; **sich als falsch/wahr** *usw.* **~stellen** turn out *or* prove to be wrong/true *etc.*; ~|**strecken** *tr. V.* stick out (**aus** of); **jmdm. die Zunge ~strecken** stick *or* put one's tongue out at sb.; **seinen Arm/Kopf zum Fenster ~strecken** stick *or* put one's arm/head out of the window; ~|**streichen** *unr. tr. V.* Ⓐ (*ausstreichen*) cross out; delete (**aus** from); Ⓑ (*hervorheben*) point out; **er streicht gerne ~, dass ...** he likes everyone to know that ...; ~|**strömen** *itr. V.*; *mit sein* Ⓐ (*ausströmen*) ‹water etc.› pour out (**aus** of); ‹gas› escape (**aus** from); Ⓑ (~*kommen*) ‹Menschenmenge› pour out (**aus** of); ~|**stürzen** *itr. V.*; *mit sein* Ⓐ (~*fallen*) fall out (**aus** of); Ⓑ (*eilen*) rush *or* dash out (**aus** of); ~|**suchen** *tr. V.* pick out; look out ‹file›; ~|**tragen** *unr. tr. V.* carry outside; **die Kisten aus dem Haus ~tragen** carry the boxes out of the house; ~|**treten** *unr. itr. V.*; *mit sein* Ⓐ come out (**aus** of); **auf den Balkon ~treten** come *or* step out onto the balcony; Ⓑ (*sich abzeichnen*) ‹veins etc.› stand out; ~|**trommeln** *tr. V.* (*ugs.*) get out; ~|**wachsen** *unr. itr. V.*; *mit sein* grow out (**aus** of); ~|**werfen** *unr. tr. V.* Ⓐ throw out (**aus** of); Ⓑ ⇒ **hinauswerfen**; ~|**winden** *unr. refl. V.* wriggle out (**aus** of); ~|**wirtschaften** *tr. V.* make ‹profit etc.› (**aus** out of); ~|**wollen** *unr. itr. V.* want to come/go out (**aus** of); **er wollte nicht mit der Sprache ~:** he did not want to come out with it; ~|**ziehen** ❶ *unr. tr. V.* Ⓐ pull out (**aus** of); Ⓑ (*wegbringen*) pull out, withdraw ‹troops etc.›; Ⓒ (*exzerpieren, extrahieren*) extract (**aus** from); ❷ *unr. itr. V.*; *mit sein* move out (**aus** of)

**herb** /hɛrp/ ❶ *Adj.* Ⓐ [slightly] sharp *or* astringent ‹taste›; dry ‹wine›; [slightly] sharp *or* tangy ‹smell, perfume›; Ⓑ bitter ‹disappointment, loss›; severe ‹face, features›; austere ‹beauty›; Ⓒ (*unfreundlich*) harsh ‹words, criticism›; curt ‹greeting›. ❷ *adv.* bitterly ‹disappointed›

**Herbarium** /hɛrˈba:ri̯ʊm/ *das;* ~**s, Herbarien** /-ˈ-ri̯ən/ herbarium

**herbei** /hɛɐ̯ˈba̯i/ *Adv.* ~ **[zu mir]!** come [over] here!; **alle Mann** *od.* (*ugs.*) **alles ~!** come [over] here, everybody!

**herb<u>ei</u>-:** ~|**bringen** *unr. tr. V.* bring [over]; ~|**eilen** *itr. V.*; *mit sein* hurry over; come hurrying up; ~|**führen** *tr. V.* produce, bring about ‹decision›; bring about, cause ‹downfall›; cause ‹accident›; **wenn nicht bald eine Entscheidung ~geführt wird** if no decision is reached soon; **den Tod ~führen** cause death; ~|**holen** *tr. V.* fetch; **sich** (*Dat.*) **etw. ~holen lassen** have sth. brought to one; **einen Arzt ~holen/~holen lassen** fetch/send for a doctor; ~|**kommen** *unr. itr. V.*; *mit sein* come up *or* along; **die Menschen kamen aus allen Richtungen ~:** people came from all directions; ~|**lassen** *unr. refl. V.* (*iron.*) **sich ~lassen, etw. zu tun** condescend *or* deign to do sth.; ~|**laufen** *unr. itr. V.*; *mit sein* come running up; ~|**rufen** *unr. tr. V.* call over; **Hilfe/einen Arzt ~rufen** summon help/call a doctor; ~|**schaffen** *tr. V.* bring; (*besorgen*) get; ~|**sehnen** *tr. V.* long for; **sie hatte den Urlaub sehr ~gesehnt** she had been longing for the holidays to arrive; ~|**strömen** *itr. V.*; *mit sein* come in crowds; come flocking; ~|**winken** *tr. V.* **jmdn. ~winken** beckon sb. over; ~|**wünschen** *tr. V.* long for; **jmdn. ~wünschen** long for sb. to come; ~|**ziehen** *unr. tr. V.* **etw. ~ziehen** pull *or* draw sth. up; draw ‹crowd etc.›; **jmdn. ~ziehen** draw sb. to one; **sich** (*Dat.*) **etw. ~ziehen** pull *or* draw sth. to one; ⇒ *auch* **Haar** B; ~|**zitieren** *tr. V.* **jmdn. ~zitieren** send for *or* summon sb.

**h<u>e</u>r-:** ~|**bekommen** *unr. tr. V.* get; ~|**bemühen** (*geh.*) ❶ *tr. V.* **jmdn. ~bemühen** trouble sb. to come; ❷ *refl. V.* take the trouble to come; ~|**beordern** *tr. V.* summon; send for

**Herberge** /ˈhɛrbɛrgə/ *die;* ~, ~**n** Ⓐ (*veralt.: Gasthaus*) inn; Ⓑ (*Jugend~*) [youth] hostel; Ⓒ (*veralt.: Unterkunft*) accommodation *no indef. art.*

**H<u>e</u>rbergs-:** ~**mutter** *die; Pl.* ~**mütter**, ~**vater** *der* warden [of the/a youth hostel]

**h<u>e</u>r-:** ~|**bestellen** *tr. V.* **jmdn. ~bestellen** ask sb. to come; (~*beordern*) summon sb.; ~|**beten** ⇒ **herunterbeten**

**Herbheit** *die;* ~: ⇒ **herb** 1 A, B: [slight] sharpness *or* astringency; dryness; [slight] sharpness *or* tanginess; bitterness; severity; austerity

**h<u>e</u>r|bitten** *unr. tr. V.* **jmdn. ~:** ask sb. to come

**Herbizid** /hɛrbiˈt͜si:t/ *das;* ~**s,** ~**e** herbicide

**h<u>e</u>r|bringen** *unr. tr. V.* **etw. ~:** bring sth. [here]

**Herbst** /hɛrpst/ *der;* ~**[e]s,** ~**e** ▸ 431 | autumn; fall (*Amer.*); ⇒ *auch* **Frühling**

**H<u>e</u>rbst-:** ~**anfang** *der* beginning of autumn; ~**blume** *die* autumn flower

**h<u>e</u>rbsten** *itr. V.* (*unpers.*) (*geh.*) **es herbstet** autumn is coming *or* approaching

**H<u>e</u>rbst·ferien** *Pl.* autumn half-term holiday *sing.*

**h<u>e</u>rbstlich** ▸ 431 | ❶ *Adj.* autumn *attrib.*; autumnal; (*wie im Herbst*) autumnal; **es wird ~:** autumn is coming. ❷ *adv.* **sich ~ färben** take on the colours of autumn; **~ kühle Tage** cool autumn days; **es ist schon ~ kühl** there's already an autumn chill in the air

**H<u>e</u>rbst-:** ~**monat** *der* Ⓐ autumn month; Ⓑ (*veralt.*) **der ~monat** September; ~**tag** *der* autumn day; ~**wetter** *das* autumnal weather; ~**zeitlose** *die;* ~~, ~~**n** *od. adj. Dekl.* (*Bot.*) meadow saffron

**Herd** /he:ɐ̯t/ *der;* ~**[e]s,** ~**e** Ⓐ (*Kochstelle*) cooker; stove; **das Essen auf dem ~ haben** (*ugs.*) be cooking something; **den ganzen Tag am ~ stehen** (*ugs.*) slave over a hot stove all day; **am heimischen** *od.* **häuslichen ~:** by one's own fireside; **eigener ~ ist Goldes wert** there's no place like home (*prov.*); Ⓑ (*Ausgangspunkt*) centre (*of disturbance/rebellion*); (*Geol.*) focus; Ⓒ (*Med.*) focus; seat; Ⓓ (*Technik*) hearth

**H<u>e</u>rd·buch** *das* (*Landw.*) herd book

**Herde** /ˈhe:ɐ̯də/ *die;* ~, ~**n** Ⓐ (*von Tieren*) herd; **eine ~ Rinder** a herd of cattle; **eine ~ Schafe** a flock of sheep; Ⓑ (*abwertend: Menschenmenge*) crowd; **mit der ~ laufen, der ~ folgen** follow the herd *or* crowd; Ⓒ (*fig.: kirchliche Gemeinde*) flock

**H<u>e</u>rden-:** ~**mensch** *der* (*abwertend*) ⇒ ~**tier** B; ~**tier** *das* Ⓐ gregarious animal; Ⓑ (*abwertend: Mensch*) sheep; ~**trieb** *der* (*auch fig. abwertend*) herd instinct

**H<u>e</u>rd·platte** *die* (*eines Elektroherdes*) hotplate; (*eines Kohlenherds*) top

**herein** /hɛˈra̯in/ *Adv.* ~**!** come in!; **[immer] nur ~ mit dir!** come on in!

**her<u>ei</u>n-:** ~|**bekommen** *unr. tr. V.* (*ugs.*) get in ‹fresh stocks›; pick up ‹radio station›; recover ‹investment›; ~|**bemühen** (*geh.*) ❶ *tr. V.* **jmdn. ~bemühen** trouble sb. to come in; ❷ *refl. V.* take the trouble to come in; ~|**bitten** *unr. tr. V.* **jmdn. ~bitten** ask *or* invite sb. in; ~|**brechen** *unr. itr. V.*; *mit sein* Ⓐ (*geh.: hart treffen*) **über jmdn./etw. ~brechen** ‹fate, disaster, misfortune, etc.› befall *or* overtake sb./sth.; Ⓑ (*geh.: beginnen*) ‹night, evening, dusk› fall; ‹winter› set in; ‹storm› strike, break; Ⓒ (*überfluten*) **über etw.** (*Akk.*) **~brechen** break over sth.; **eine Flut von Beschimpfungen brach über ihn ~** (*fig.*) he was engulfed in a flood of abuse; ~|**bringen** *unr. tr. V.* Ⓐ bring in; **etw. in etw.** (*Akk.*) **~bringen** bring sth. into sth.; Ⓑ (*wettmachen*) make up ‹loss›; make up for ‹delay›; recoup ‹costs›; ~|**drängen** *itr. V.*; *mit sein* push one's way in; **in etw.** (*Akk.*) **~drängen** push one's way into sth.; ~|**dürfen** *unr. itr. V.* (*ugs.*) be allowed in; **in etw.** (*Akk.*) **~dürfen** be allowed into sth.; **darf er ~?** may *or* can he come in?; ~|**fallen** *unr. itr. V.*; *mit sein* **A** ‹light› shine in; **B** (*ugs.: betrogen werden*) be taken for a ride (*coll.*); be done (*coll.*); **bei/ mit etw. ~fallen** be taken for a ride with sth.; **auf jmdn./etw. ~fallen** be taken in by sb./sth.; ~|**führen** *tr. V.* **jmdn. ~führen** show sb. in; ~|**holen** *tr. V.* **A** bring in; **B** (*ugs.: verdienen*) make (*coll.*); ~|**kommen** *unr. itr. V.*; *mit sein* come in; **in das Haus/ zur Tür ~kommen** come into the house/in through the door; **wie sind sie ~gekommen?** how did they get in?; ~|**kriegen** *tr. V.* (*ugs.*) ⇒ **~bekommen**; ~|**lassen** *unr. tr. V.* let *or* allow in; **jmdn. ins Zimmer ~lassen** let *or* allow sb. into the room; ~|**legen** *tr. V.* (*ugs.*) **jmdn. ~legen** take sb. for a ride (*coll.*) (**mit, bei** with); ~|**nehmen** *unr. tr. V.* **A** bring in; **etw. ins Haus ~nehmen** bring sth. into the house; **B** (*in eine Liste*) include; **etw. in sein Sortiment ~nehmen** start selling sth. as well; ~|**platzen** *itr. V.*; *mit sein* (*ugs.*) burst in; come bursting in; **in den Saal ~platzen** burst *or* come bursting into the hall; ~|**rasseln** *itr. V.*; *mit sein* (*salopp*) **A** (*betrogen werden*) **mit/bei etw. ~rasseln** be taken for a ride with sth. (*coll.*); **B** (*in Schwierigkeiten geraten*) get into deep water (*coll.*); ~|**regnen** *itr. V.* (*unpers.*) **es regnet ~:** the rain's coming in; ~|**reichen** ❶ *tr. V.* hand *or* pass in; ❷ *itr. V.* **etw. reicht in das Zimmer ~:** sth. comes [right] in to the room; ~|**reißen** *unr. tr. V.* (*ugs.*) ⇒ **reinreißen**; ~|**reiten** ❶ *unr. itr. V.*; *mit sein* ride in; **in den Hof ~reiten** ride into the yard; ❷ ⇒ **reinreiten**; ~|**rufen** *unr. tr. V.* **jmdn. ~rufen** call sb. in; ~|**schauen** *itr. V.* (*landsch.*) ⇒ **~sehen**; ~|**schleichen** *unr. itr. V. mit sein; refl. V.* creep *or* steal in; **[sich] ins Haus ~schleichen** creep *or* steal into the house; ~|**schneien** *unr. itr. V.* **A** *mit sein* (*ugs.*) turn up out of the blue (*coll.*); **B** (*unpers.*) **es schneit ~:** the snow's coming in; ~|**sehen** *unr. itr. V.* **A** see in; (*~blicken*) look in; **in etw.** (*Akk.*) **~sehen** see/look into sth.; **B** (*kurz besuchen*) look *or* drop in (**bei** on); ~|**spazieren** *itr. V.*; *mit sein* (*ugs.*) walk in; stroll in; **er ist einfach in das Zimmer ~spaziert** he simply walked straight into the room; **nur ~spaziert!** come right in!; ~|**stecken** *tr. V.* **den Kopf zur Tür ~stecken** ⇒ **Tür**; ~|**strömen** *itr. V.*; *mit sein* ‹water etc.› pour in; ‹people› pour *or* stream in; **in etw.** (*Akk.*) **~strömen** pour *or* stream into sth.; ~|**stürmen** *itr. V.*; *mit sein* rush *or* dash in; come rushing *or* dashing in; (*wütend*) storm in; come storming in; **ins Zimmer ~stürmen** rush/storm into the room; ~|**stürzen** *itr. V.*; *mit sein* rush in; burst in; **ins Zimmer ~stürzen** rush *or* burst into the room; ~|**tragen** *unr. tr. V.* carry in; **etw. ins Haus ~tragen** carry sth. into the house; ~|**wagen** *refl. V.* venture to come in; ~|**wollen** *unr. itr. V.* (*ugs.*) want to come in; **ins Haus ~wollen** want to come into the house

**her-, Her-:** ~|**fahren** ❶ *unr. itr. V.*; *mit sein* come here; (*mit einem Auto*) drive *or* come here; (*mit einem [Motor]rad*) ride *or* come here; **hinter/vor jmdm./etw. ~fahren** drive/ride along behind/in front of sb./sth.; ❷ *unr. tr. V.* **jmdn. ~fahren** drive sb. here; **~fahrt** *die* journey here; ~|**fallen** *unr. itr. V.*; *mit sein* **A über jmdn. ~fallen** set upon *or* attack sb.; ‹animal› attack sb.; **mit Fragen/Vorwürfen über jmdn. ~fallen** (*fig.*) besiege sb. with questions/hurl reproaches at sb.; **B** (*gierig zu essen beginnen*) **über etw.** (*Akk.*) **~fallen** fall upon sth.; ~|**finden** *unr. itr. V.* find one's way here; ~|**führen** *tr. V.* **A** (*geleiten*) **jmdn. ~führen** bring sb. here; **ein Tier hinter/vor jmdm. ~führen** lead an animal along in front of/behind sb.; **B** (*an einen Ort gelangen lassen*) **was führt dich ~?** what brings you here?; **~gang** *der:* **der ~gang der Ereignisse** the sequence of events; **jmdn. über den ~gang befragen** question sb. about what happened; **schildern Sie den ~gang des Überfalls** describe what happened during the attack; ~|**geben** *unr. tr. V.* **A** hand over; (*weggeben*) give away; **sein Geld für etw. ~geben** put one's money into sth.; **seinen Namen für etw. ~geben** lend one's name to sth.; allow one's name to be associated with sth.; **er hat sein Letztes ~gegeben** he gave everything he had; **sich für etw. ~geben** get involved in sth.; **dazu gebe ich mich nicht ~:** I won't have anything to do with it; **B** (*reichen*) give; **gib es ~!** hand it over!; **C** (*erbringen*) **der Boden gibt wenig ~:** the soil is poor; **das Thema wird viel ~geben** there's a lot to this topic; **was seine Beine ~gaben** as fast as his legs could carry him; **~gebracht** ❶ *2. Part. v.* **~bringen**; ❷ *Adj.* time-honoured; ~|**gehen** *unr. itr. V.*; *mit sein* **A** (*begleiten*) **neben/ vor/hinter jmdm. ~gehen** walk along beside/in front of/behind sb.; **B** (*ugs.*) **~gehen und etw. tun** just [go and] do sth.; **C** (*südd., österr.: ~kommen*) come [here]; **D** *unpers.* (*ugs.*) **auf der Party ging es hoch/ lustig ~:** everyone had a whale of a time (*coll.*)/great fun at the party; **bei der Debatte ging es heiß ~:** the sparks really flew in the debate; ~|**gehören** ⇒ **hierher gehören**; **~gelaufen** ❶ *2. Part. v.* **~laufen**; ❷ *Adj.* **dieser ~gelaufene Strolch** this good-for-nothing rascal from Heaven knows where; ~|**haben** *unr. tr. V.* (*ugs.*) **wo hat er/ sie das ~?** where did he/she get that from?; ~|**halten** ❶ *unr. itr. V.* **~halten müssen [für jmdn./etw.]** be the one to suffer [for sb./sth.]; **als Beweis für die Theorie ~halten** serve as proof of the theory; **der Mantel wird diesen Winter noch einmal ~halten müssen** the coat will have to do for one more winter; ❷ *unr. tr. V.* hold out; ~|**holen** *tr. V.* fetch; **etw. von weit ~holen** get sth. from a long way away; **weit ~geholt** far-fetched; ~|**hören** *itr. V.* listen; **alle mal ~hören!** listen everybody

**Hering** /'he:rɪŋ/ *der;* **~s, ~e** **A** herring; **wie die ~e** (*fig.*) packed together like sardines; **B** (*Zeltpflock*) peg; **C** (*ugs.: sehr dünne Person*) **ein [richtiger] ~ sein** be as thin as a rake

**Herings-:** **~fänger** *der* (*Schiff*) herring boat; **~filet** *das* herring fillet; **~fischerei** *die* herring fishing; **~salat** *der* herring salad

**herinnen** /hɛ'rɪnən/ *Adv.* (*südd., österr.*) in here

**her-, Her-:** ~|**jagen** ❶ *tr. V.* **ein Tier ~jagen** drive *or* chase an animal here; **jmdn./ ein Tier vor sich** (*Dat.*) **~jagen** drive *or* chase sb./an animal along ahead of one; ❷ *itr. V.*; *mit sein* **hinter jmdm. ~jagen** chase *or* pursue sb.; **hinter etw. ~jagen** (*fig.*) pursue sth.; ~|**kommen** *unr. itr. V.*; *mit sein* **A** come here; **komm [mal] ~!** come here!; **sie wird mit Sicherheit ~kommen** she'll definitely come; **B** (*abstammen*) come; **wer weiß, wo das ~kommt** (*ugs.: warum das so ist*) who can tell the reason?; **C** (*~genommen werden*) **wo soll das Geld ~kommen?** where is the money coming from?; **~kommen** *das;* **~~s** **A** (*Brauch, Sitte*) tradition; **B** ⇒ **Herkunft A**; **~kömmlich** /-kœmlɪç/ *Adj.* conventional; traditional ‹custom›

**Herkules** /'hɛrkulɛs/ *der;* **~, ~se** Hercules

**Herkules·arbeit** *die* Herculean task

**herkulisch** /hɛr'ku:lɪʃ/ *Adj.* (*geh.*) Herculean

**Herkunft** /'he:ɐ̯kʊnft/ *die;* **~, Herkünfte** /'he:ɐ̯kʏnftə/ **A** (*soziale Abstammung*) origin[s *pl.*]; **einfacher** (*Gen.*) *od.* **von einfacher ~ sein** be of humble origin *or* stock; **sie ist ihrer ~ nach Amerikanerin** she is of American descent *or* extraction; **B** (*Ursprung*) origin

**Herkunfts-:** **~bezeichnung** *die* indication of country of origin; **~land** *das* country of origin

**her-:** ~|**laufen** *unr. itr. V.*; *mit sein* **A vor/ hinter/neben jmdm. ~laufen** run [along] in front of/behind/alongside sb.; **B** (*nachlaufen*) **hinter jmdm. ~laufen** run after sb.; (*fig.*) chase sb. up; **C** (*zum Sprechenden laufen*) come on foot; (*schneller*) come running up; **ich bin ~gelaufen** I walked here; (*schneller*) I ran here; ~|**leiten** ❶ *tr. V.* derive (**aus, von** from); **etw. von jmdm. ~leiten** derive sth. from sb.; ❷ *refl. V.* **sich von/aus etw. ~leiten** derive *or* be derived from sth.; ~|**locken** *tr. V.* **jmdn./ein Tier ~locken** lure *or* entice sb./an animal here; **ein Tier hinter sich** (*Dat.*) **~locken** entice an animal to follow one along; ~|**machen** (*ugs.*) ❶ *refl. V.* **A sich über etw.** (*Akk.*) **~machen** get stuck into sth. (*coll.*); **sich über das Essen/die Geschenke ~machen** fall upon the food/presents; **B** (*~fallen*) **sich über jmdn. ~machen** set on *or* attack sb.; ❷ *tr. V.* **wenig ~machen** not look much (*coll.*); **viel ~machen** look great (*coll.*); **nichts ~machen** not look much at all (*coll.*); **viel von jmdm./etw. ~machen** make a lot of fuss about sb./sth.; **wenig/ nichts von jmdm./etw. ~machen** not make a lot of/any fuss about sth.

**Hermaphrodit** /hɛrm|afro'di:t/ *der;* **~en, ~en** (*Biol., Med.*) hermaphrodite

**Hermelin**[1] /hɛrmə'li:n/ *das;* **~s, ~e** (*Tier*) ermine; (*im Sommerfell*) stoat

**Hermelin**[2] *der;* **~s, ~e** (*Pelz*) ermine

**Hermeneutik** /hɛrme'nɔy̆tɪk/ *die;* **~:** hermeneutics *sing., no art.*

**hermeneutisch** *Adj.* hermeneutic

**hermetisch** /hɛr'me:tɪʃ/ ❶ *Adj.* hermetic. ❷ *adv.* hermetically; **ein Dorf** *usw.* **~ abriegeln** seal a village *etc.* off completely

**her|müssen** *unr. itr. V.* (*ugs.*) **das muss her** I/we have to *or* must have it

**her·nach** *Adv.* (*veralt.*) after that

**her|nehmen** *unr. tr. V.* **A** (*beschaffen*) **wo soll ich das Geld ~?** where am I supposed to get the money from *or* find the money?; **B** (*bes. österr.: stark beanspruchen*) **die Arbeit/ Krankheit/der Schicksalsschlag hat sie hergenommen** the work/illness/blow of fate took it out of her; **C** (*ugs.: scharf tadeln*) **jmdn. ~:** give sb. a good talking-to

**her·nieder-** *in Zus.* (*geh.*) down

**heroben** /hɛ'ro:bn̩/ *Adv.* (*südd., österr.*) up here

**Heroe** /he'ro:ə/ *der;* **~n, ~n** (*geh.*) hero

**Heroen·kult** *der* (*geh.*) hero worship

**Heroin**[1] /hero'i:n/ *das;* **~s** heroin

**Heroin**[2] /he'ro:ɪn/ *die;* **~, ~nen** heroine

**Heroine** /hero'i:nə/ *die;* **~, ~n** (*Theater*) actress who plays heroine roles

**heroin·süchtig** *Adj.* addicted to heroin *postpos.*

**heroisch** *Adj.* heroic

**heroisieren** *tr. V.* make a hero of, heroize ‹person›; glorify ‹deed›

**Heroismus** *der;* **~:** heroism

**Herold** /'he:rolt/ *der;* **~[e]s, ~e** herald

**Herr** /hɛr/ *der;* **~n** (*selten:* **~en**), **~en** ▶91 **A** (*Mann*) gentleman; **ein feiner ~:** a refined gentleman; **ein feiner/sauberer ~** (*iron.*) a fine one; **das Kugelstoßen/Finale der ~en** (*Sport*) the men's shot-put/ final; **mein Alter ~** (*ugs. scherzh.: Vater*) my old man (*coll.*); **Alter ~** (*Studentenspr.*) former member; (*Sport*) veteran; **B** ▶187 (*Titel, Anrede*) **~ Schulze** Mr Schulze; **~ Professor/Dr. Schulze** Professor/Dr Schulze; **~ Minister/Direktor/Studienrat Schulze** Mr Schulze; **~ Minister/Professor/Doktor** Minister/Professor/doctor; **~ Vorsitzender/Präsident** Mr Chairman/ President; **Sehr geehrter ~ Schulze!** Dear Sir; (*bei persönlicher Bekanntschaft*) Dear Mr Schulze; **Sehr geehrte ~en!** Dear Sirs; **~ Ober!** waiter!; **mein ~:** sir; **meine ~en** gentlemen; **meine ~en!** (*salopp*) my God!; **bitte sehr, der ~!** there you are, sir; **womit kann ich dem ~n dienen?** (*veralt.*) can I help you, sir?; **Ihr ~ Vater/Sohn/ Gemahl** (*geh.*) your father/son/husband; **C** (*Gebieter*) master; **~! Gebt uns die Freiheit** Sire, give us our freedom; **er ist ~ über alle Menschen auf der Insel** he rules over the whole population of the island; **mein ~ und Gebieter** (*scherzh.*) my lord and master (*joc.*); **die ~en der Schöpfung** (*ugs. scherzh.*) their lordships (*coll.*

*old spelling (see note on page 1707)

*joc.*); **in diesem Land ist der König ~ über Leben und Tod** in this country the king has the power of life and death; **wie der ~, so's Gescherr** like master, like man; **sein eigener ~ sein** be one's own master; **~ der Lage sein/bleiben** be/remain master of the situation; **einer Sache** (*Gen.*) **~ werden** get sth. under control; **nicht mehr ~ seiner Sinne sein** be no longer in control of oneself; **aus aller ~en Länder[n]** (*geh.*) from the four corners of the earth; from all over the world; **D** (*Besitzer*) master (**über** + *Akk.* of); **E** (*christl. Rel.: Gott*) Lord; **Gott der ~:** Lord God; **Brüder und Schwestern im ~n** brothers and sisters in the Lord; **der ~ der Heerscharen** the Lord of Hosts; **er ist ein großer Jäger/Angler vor dem ~n** (*scherzh.*) he loves his hunting/angling

**Herrchen** *das;* **~s, ~:** master

**her|reichen** **1** *tr. V.* pass; hand. **2** *itr. V.* (*bes. südd.*) reach; be long enough

**Her·reise** *die* journey here

**herren-, Herren-: ~abend** *der* stag evening; **~artikel** *der* **A** *Pl.* (*Kleidung*) menswear *sing.;* **B** (*kleinere Bedarfsartikel*) accessories for men; **~ausstatter** *der;* **~~s, ~~:** [gentle]men's outfitter; **~begleitung** *die:* **in/ohne ~begleitung** in the company of a gentleman/unaccompanied; with/without a male companion; **~bekanntschaft** *die* gentleman acquaintance; **eine ~bekanntschaft machen** make the acquaintance of a gentleman; **~besuch** *der* gentleman visitor/visitors; **~besuch haben** have a gentleman visitor/gentlemen visitors; **~besuch ist ab $20^{00}$ untersagt** no male visitors after 8 p.m.; **~doppel** *das* (*Sport*) men's doubles *pl.;* **~einzel** *das* (*Sport*) men's singles *pl.;* **~fahrrad** *das* gent's *or* man's bicycle; **~friseur** *der* men's hairdresser; **~haus** *das* **A** (*großes Wohnhaus*) manor house; **B** (*hist.*) upper chamber; **~hemd** *das* ⇒ **Oberhemd**; **~konfektion** *die* menswear *no pl., no indef. art.;* **~leben** *das* life of luxury and ease; **~los** *Adj.* abandoned ‹car, luggage›; stray ‹dog, cat›; **~magazin** *das* men's magazine; magazine for men; **~mensch** *der* masterful person; (*ns.*) member of the master race; **~mode** *die* men's fashion; **~partie** *die* stag outing; **~rasse** *die* (*ns.*) master race; **~reiter** *der* (*Reiten*) amateur rider; **~salon** *der* men's hairdressing salon; **~sattel** *der* men's saddle; **~schnitt** *der* Eton crop; **~schuh** *der* man's shoe; **~schuhe** men's shoes; **~toilette** *die* [gentle]men's toilet; **~unterwäsche** *die* men's underwear; **~volk** *das* (*bes. ns.*) master race; **~zimmer** *das* smoking room

**Herr·gott** *der;* **~s** **A** (*ugs.: Gott*) **der [liebe]/unser ~:** the Lord [God]; God; **~ noch mal!** for Heaven's sake!; for God's sake!; **B** (*südd., österr.: Kruzifix*) crucifix

**Herrgotts-: ~frühe** *die: in* **in aller ~frühe** at the crack of dawn; **~schnitzer** *der,* **~schnitzerin** *die* (*südd., österr.*) carver of crucifixes (*and figures of Christ and saints*)

**her·richten** **1** *tr. V.* **A** (*bereitmachen*) get ‹room, refreshments, etc.› ready; dress ‹shop window›; arrange ‹table›; **B** (*in Ordnung bringen*) renovate; do up (*coll.*). **2** *refl. V.* get ready

**Herrin** *die;* **~, ~nen** mistress; (*als Anrede*) my lady

**herrisch** **1** *Adj.* overbearing; peremptory; imperious. **2** *adv.* peremptorily; imperiously; **~ auftreten** have a peremptory *or* imperious manner

**herr·je, herrjemine** /hɛr'je:mine/ *Interj.* (*ugs.*) goodness gracious [me]; heavens [above]

**herrlich** **1** *Adj.* marvellous; marvellous, glorious ‹weather›; magnificent, splendid ‹view›; magnificent, glorious ‹countryside›; magnificent, gorgeous ‹clothes›; marvellous, wonderful, splendid ‹meal›; ‹sth. tastes, looks, sounds› wonderful, marvellous. **2** *adv.* marvellously; **~ und in Freuden leben** live in clover

**Herrlichkeit** *die;* **~, ~en** **A** (*Schönheit*) magnificence; splendour; **die ~ Gottes** the glory of God; **ist das die ganze ~?** (*iron.*) is that all [there is]?; **B** (*herrliche Sache*) marvellous *or* wonderful thing; (*einer Sammlung*) treasure

**Herrschaft** *die;* **~, ~en** **A** rule; (*Macht*) power; **unter jmds. ~** (*Dat.*) **stehen** be under sb.'s rule; **die ~ an sich reißen/erringen** seize/gain power; **die ~ über jmdn./etw. ausüben/innehaben** rule over *or* hold sway over sb./sth.; **die ~ über sich/das Auto verlieren** (*fig.*) lose control of oneself/the car; **B** *Pl.* (*Damen u. Herren*) ladies and gentlemen; **die älteren/jüngeren ~en** the older/younger people; **meine ~en!** ladies and gentlemen!; **darf ich die ~en bitten, Platz zu nehmen** ladies and gentlemen/ladies/gentlemen, would you please take your seats; (*Mann und Frau*) would sir and madam care to take their seats, please; **Ruhe bitte, ~!** (*ugs.*) quiet please, all of you!; **meine Alten ~en** (*ugs. scherzh.*) my old man and old woman (*coll.*); **C** (*veralt.: Dienstherr[in]*) master/mistress; **D** **~ [noch mal]!** (*ugs.*) for Heaven's sake!

**herrschaftlich** *Adj.* **A** (*zu einer Herrschaft gehörend*) master's/mistress's ‹coach etc.›; **B** (*einer Herrschaft gemäß*) grand

**Herrschafts-: ~an·spruch** *der* claim to power; **~form** *die* system of government; **~system** *das* system of rule

**herrschen** /'hɛrʃn̩/ *itr. V.* **A** (*regieren*) rule; ‹monarch› reign, rule; **allein über jmdn./etw. ~:** have absolute power over sb./sth.; **B** (*vorhanden sein*) **draußen ~ 30° Kälte** it's 30° below outside; **überall herrschte große Freude/Trauer** there was great joy/sorrow everywhere; **in der Stadt herrschte reges Leben** the town was bustling with life; **jetzt herrscht hier wieder Ordnung** order has been restored here; **C** (*unpers.*) prevail; **es herrscht jetzt Einigkeit** there is now agreement; **es herrscht die Meinung, dass ...** the prevailing opinion is that ...

**herrschend** *Adj.* **A** ruling ‹power, party, etc.›; reigning ‹monarch›; **die Herrschenden** the rulers; those in power; **B** (*vorhanden*) prevailing ‹opinion, view, conditions, etc.›

**Herrscher** *der;* **~s, ~:** ruler; **~ über ein Volk sein** be [the] ruler of a people

**Herrscher-: ~geschlecht** *das* ruling dynasty; **~haus** *das* ruling house

**Herrscherin** *die;* **~, ~nen** ⇒ **Herrscher**

**Herrscher·paar** *das* ruler and his/her consort

**Herrsch·sucht** *die* thirst for power; (*herrisches Wesen*) domineering nature

**herrsch·süchtig** *Adj.* domineering

**her-: ~|rufen** *unr. tr. V.* call ‹dog›; **jmdn. ~rufen** call sb. [over]; **etw. hinter jmdm. ~rufen** call sth. after sb.; **~|rühren** *itr. V.* **von jmdm./etw. ~rühren** come from sb./stem from sth.; **~|sagen** *tr. V.* **etw. ~sagen** recite sth. mechanically; **~|schaffen** *tr. V.* **jmdn./etw. ~schaffen** bring sb./sth. here; **das Geld ~schaffen** get the money; **~|schenken** *tr. V.* (*landsch.*) give away; **~|schicken** *tr. V.* **jmdn./etw. ~schicken** send sb./sth. here; **jmdn./etw. hinter jmdm. ~schicken** send sb./sth. after sb.; **~|schieben** *unr. tr. V.* **etw. ~schieben** push sth. here; **etw. vor sich** (*Dat.*) **~schieben** push sth. along in front of one; (*fig.*) put sth. off; **~|schleichen** **1** *unr. itr. V.; mit sein* creep [over] here; **2** *unr. refl. V.* **sich hinter jmdm. ~schleichen** creep along behind sb.; **~|sehen** *unr. itr. V.* look [over] here *or* this way; **seht mal alle ~!** look here *or* this way, everyone!; **hinter jmdm. ~sehen** follow sb. with one's eyes; ***~|sein** ⇒ **her** A, D, E, F; **~|stellen** *tr. V.* **A** (*anfertigen*) produce; manufacture; make; **ein Auto von Hand ~stellen** build a car by hand; **in Deutschland ~gestellt** made in Germany; **etw. serienmäßig ~stellen** mass-produce sth.; **B** (*zustande bringen*) establish ‹contact, relationship, etc.›; bring about ‹peace, order, etc.›; **eine Verbindung zwischen der Insel und dem Festland ~stellen** connect the island to the mainland; **C** (*gesund machen*) **sie** *od.* **ihre Gesundheit ist [ganz] ~gestellt** she has [quite] recovered; **D** (*zum Sprechenden stellen*) **etw. ~stellen** put sth. [over] here; **stell dich ~ [zu mir]** [come and] stand over here [next to *or* by me]

**Her·steller** *der;* **~s, ~** ▶ **159** **A** (*Produzent*) producer; manufacturer; **B** (*Buchw.: Berufsbez.*) production department worker

**Hersteller·firma** *die* manufacturer

**Herstellerin** *die;* **~, ~nen** ▶ **159** ⇒ **Hersteller**

**Her·stellung** *die* **A** (*Anfertigung*) production; manufacture; **B** ⇒ **herstellen** B: establishment; bringing about

**Herstellungs-: ~kosten** *Pl.* production *or* manufacturing costs; **~land** *das* country of manufacture; **~verfahren** *das* production *or* manufacturing process

**her-: ~|stürzen** *itr. V.; mit sein* **A** (*nachlaufen*) **hinter jmdm. ~stürzen** rush after sb.; **B** (*zum Sprecher*) rush *or* come rushing here; **~|tragen** *unr. tr. V.* **A** (*zum Sprecher*) **etw. ~tragen** carry sth. here; **B** (*begleiten und tragen*) **etw. hinter/vor jmdm. ~tragen** carry sth. along behind/in front of sb.; **~|treiben** *unr. tr. V.* **A** (*zum Sprecher*) drive ‹animal› here; **jmdn. ~treiben** ‹yearning, hunger, worry, etc.› drive sb. here; **B** (*antreiben*) **etw. vor sich** (*Dat.*) **~treiben** drive sth. along in front of one; **der Spieler trieb den Ball vor sich** (*Dat.*) **~:** the player dribbled the ball; **der Wind trieb die Wolken vor sich** (*Dat.*) **~:** the wind drove *or* blew the clouds along

**Hertz** /hɛrts/ *das;* **~, ~** (*Physik*) hertz

**herüben** /hɛ'ry:bn̩/ *Adv.* (*südd., österr.*) over here

**herüber** /hɛ'ry:bɐ/ *Adv.* over; **die Fahrt von Amerika ~:** the journey over from America; **~ und hinüber** back and forth

**herüber-: ~|bitten** *unr. tr. V.* **jmdn. ~bitten** ask sb. [to come] over; **~|bringen** *unr. tr. V.* **jmdn./etw. ~bringen** bring sb./sth. over; **~|fahren** **1** *unr. itr. V.; mit sein* drive *or* come over; (*mit dem Motorrad, Rad*) come *or* ride over; **2** *unr. tr. V.* **jmdn./etw. ~fahren** drive sb./sth. over; **~|fliegen** **1** *unr. itr. V.; mit sein* fly over; **2** *unr. tr. V.* **jmdn./etw. ~fliegen** fly sb./sth. over; **~|geben** *unr. tr. V.* pass *or* hand over; **~|grüßen** *itr. V.* **[zu jmdm.] ~grüßen** call across to sb. in greeting; **~|holen** *tr. V.* **jmdn./etw. ~holen** bring sb./sth. over; **~|kommen** *unr. itr. V.; mit sein* come over; **über den Zaun/Fluss ~kommen** get over the fence/across the river; **kommt doch ~:** come over!; **~|lassen** *unr. tr. V.* **jmdn. ~lassen** let sb. come over; allow sb. to come over; **~|laufen** *unr. itr. V.; mit sein* run *or* come running over; **~|reichen** **1** *tr. V.* ⇒ **~geben**; **2** *itr. V.* **[über etw.** (*Akk.*)**] ~reichen** reach across [sth.]; **~|retten** **1** *tr. V.* retain; **etw. in die Gegenwart ~retten** preserve sth. [until the present day]; **2** *refl. V.* ‹customs, hopes, etc.› survive; **~|schicken** *tr. V.* **jmdn./etw. ~schicken** send sb./sth. over; **~|schwimmen** *unr. itr. V.; mit sein* swim over *or* across; ‹boat› float over *or* across; **~|sehen** *unr. itr. V.* **[zu jmdm.] ~sehen** look across [at sb.]; **~|wechseln** *itr. V.; mit sein od. haben* cross over; **er ist in unsere Partei ~gewechselt** he has swapped parties and joined ours; **~|wehen** **1** *itr. V.* **A** (*zum Sprecher*) **von Osten/Westen ~wehen** blow across from the East/West; **zu uns ~wehen** blow in our direction *or* towards us; **B** *mit sein* ‹scent› waft across; ‹sound› be blown across; **2** *tr. V.* **Blätter/den Duft ~wehen** blow leaves/waft the scent across here; **~|wollen** *unr. itr. V.* want to come over; **über den Zaun ~wollen** want to get over the fence; **~|ziehen** **1** *unr. tr. V.* **etw. ~ziehen** pull sth. over; **jmdn. ~ziehen** (*fig.*) win sb. over; **2** *unr. itr. V.; mit sein* ‹clouds, troops› move across; (*umziehen*) move here

**herum** /hɛ'rʊm/ *Adv.* **A** (*Richtung*) round; **im Kreis ~:** round in a circle; **verkehrt/richtig ~:** the wrong/right way round; (*mit Ober- und Unterseite*) upside down/the right way up; **etw. falsch** *od.* **verkehrt ~ anziehen** put sth. on back-to-front/(*Innenseite nach außen*) inside out; **B** (*Anordnung*) **um jmdn./etw. ~:** around sb./sth.; **um die Stadt ~ zog sich ein Grüngürtel** the

h

town was surrounded by a green belt; Ⓒ (*in enger Umgebung*) **um jmdn. ~ sein** be around sb.; **um München/Berlin ~:** around Munich/Berlin; Ⓓ (*ugs.: ungefähr*) **um Weihnachten/Ostern ~:** around Christmas/Easter; **um 100 DM/das Jahr 1050 ~:** around *or* about 100 marks/the year 1050; Ⓔ (*vorüber, vorbei*) over; **~ sein** be over; Ⓕ **~ sein** (*ugs.: überall bekannt geworden sein*) have got around

**herum-, Herum-:** ~|**albern** *itr. V.* (*ugs.*) fool around *or* about; ~|**ärgern** *refl. V.* (*ugs.*) **sich mit jmdm./etw. ~ärgern** keep getting annoyed with sb./sth.; **sich mit einem Problem ~ärgern müssen** be plagued by a problem; ~|**balgen** *refl. V.* **sich [mit jmdm.] ~balgen** keep scrapping (*coll.*) [with sb.]; ~|**basteln** *itr. V.* (*ugs.*) **an etw.** (*Dat.*) **~basteln** mess about with sth.; ~|**bekommen** *unr. tr. V.* (*ugs.*) Ⓐ (*überreden*) **jmdn. ~bekommen** talk sb. into it; **jmdn. ~bekommen, etw. zu tun** talk sb. into doing sth.; Ⓑ (*hinter sich bringen*) [manage to] pass *or* spend ‹time›; ~|**blättern** *itr. V.* **in etw.** (*Dat.*) **~blättern** keep leafing through sth.; ~|**bohren** *itr. V.* (*ugs.*) **[in etw.** (*Dat.*)**] ~bohren** keep poking [in sth.]; ~|**brüllen** *itr. V.* (*ugs.*) go on shouting one's head off (*coll.*); ~|**bummeln** *itr. V.* (*ugs.*) Ⓐ *mit sein* (*spazieren*) stroll *or* wander around; **in der Stadt ~bummeln** stroll *or* wander around the town; Ⓑ (*trödeln*) **[mit etw.] ~bummeln** dawdle [over sth.]; ~|**doktern** *itr. V.* (*ugs.*) **an jmdm./etw. ~doktern** have a go at treating sb./sth.; **an etw.** (*Dat.*) **~doktern** (*fig.*) fiddle *or* tinker around *or* about with sth.; ~|**drehen** ❶ *tr. V.* (*ugs.*) turn ‹key›; turn over ‹coin, mattress, hand, etc.›; **den Kopf ~drehen** turn one's head; ❷ *refl. V.* turn [a]round; **sich im Kreis ~drehen** turn right round; **sich [auf die andere Seite] ~drehen** turn over [on to one's other side]; ❸ *itr. V.* (*ugs.*) **an etw.** (*Dat.*) **~drehen** fiddle [around *or* about] with sth.; ~|**drücken** *refl. V.* Ⓐ (*ugs.: vermeiden*) **sich um etw. ~drücken** get out of *or* (*coll.*) dodge sth.; Ⓑ (*ugs.: sich aufhalten*) hang around; **wo hast du dich ~gedrückt?** where have you been?; ~|**drucksen** *itr. V.* (*ugs.*) hum and haw (*coll.*); ~|**erzählen** *tr. V.* (*ugs.*) **etw. ~erzählen** spread sth. around; **er erzählte überall ~, dass ...** he went around telling everyone that ...; ~|**experimentieren** *itr. V.* **[an jmdm./etw.] ~experimentieren** carry out experiments [on sb./sth.]; ~|**fahren** (*ugs.*) ❶ *unr. itr. V.*; *mit sein* Ⓐ **um etw. ~fahren** drive *or* go round sth.; (*mit einem Motorrad, Rad*) ride *or* go round sth.; (*mit einem Schiff*) sail round sth.; Ⓑ (*irgendwohin fahren*) drive/ride/sail around; Ⓒ (*sich plötzlich ~drehen*) spin round; Ⓓ (*hin und her bewegen*) **mit den Armen/dem Schirm** *usw.* **~fahren** wave one's arms/umbrella *etc.* about; ❷ *unr. tr. V.* **jmdn. [in der Stadt] ~fahren** drive sb. around the town; ~|**flattern** *itr. V.*; *mit sein* (*ugs.*) **[um jmdn./etw.] ~flattern** flutter around [sb./sth.]; ~|**fliegen** (*ugs.*) ❶ *unr. itr. V.*; *mit sein* Ⓐ **[um etw.] ~fliegen** fly around [sth.]; Ⓑ (*salopp: ~liegen*) ⇒ **rumfliegen** 1 B; ❷ *unr. tr. V.* **jmdn. ~fliegen** fly sb. around; ~|**fragen** *itr. V.* (*ugs.*) ask around (**bei** among); ~|**fuchteln** *itr. V.* (*ugs.*) **mit den Armen/einem Messer** *usw.* **~fuchteln** wave one's arms/a knife *etc.* around *or* about; ~|**führen** ❶ *tr. V.* Ⓐ **jmdn. [in der Stadt] ~führen** show sb. around the town; ⇒ *auch* **Nase**; Ⓑ (*rund um etw. führen*) **jmdn. um etw. ~führen** lead *or* take sb. round sth.; Ⓒ (*um etw. bauen*) **die Straße um die Stadt ~führen** take the road round the town; ❷ *itr. V.* **um etw. ~führen** ‹road etc.› go round sth.; ~|**fuhrwerken** *itr. V.* (*ugs.*) mess about; **mit einem Schraubenzieher an der Uhr ~fuhrwerken** fiddle around with the clock with the aid of a screwdriver; ~|**fummeln** *itr. V.* (*ugs.*) Ⓐ **an etw.** (*Dat.*) **~fummeln** fiddle about with sth.; Ⓑ (*sich handwerklich beschäftigen*) fiddle *or* mess around with sth.; Ⓒ (*betasten*) **an jmdm. ~fummeln** touch sb. up (*sl.*); ~|**geben** *unr. tr. V.*: ⇒ ~**reichen** 1; ~|**gehen** *unr. itr. V.*; *mit sein* Ⓐ **um etw. ~gehen** go *or* walk round sth.; Ⓑ (*ziellos gehen*) walk around; **im Garten ~gehen** walk around the garden; Ⓒ (*die Runde machen*) go around; (*~gereicht werden*) be passed *or* handed around; **etw. ~gehen lassen** circulate sth.; Ⓓ (*vergehen*) pass; go by; ~|**geistern** *itr. V.*; *mit sein* (*ugs.*) wander around *or* about; (*fig.*) ‹idea, rumour, etc.› go round; **im Haus ~geistern** wander around the house [like a ghost]; **jmdm. im Kopf ~geistern** go round in sb.'s mind; ~|**gondeln** *itr. V.*; *mit sein* (*salopp*) travel around; **in der Weltgeschichte ~gondeln** travel around all over the place; ~|**hacken** *itr. V.* (*ugs.*) Ⓐ (*kritisieren*) **auf jmdm. ~hacken** keep getting at sb. (*coll.*); Ⓑ (*mit einer Hacke bearbeiten*) **auf etw.** (*Dat.*) **~hacken** hack away at sth.; ~|**hängen** *unr. itr. V.* (*ugs.*) Ⓐ (*aufgehängt sein*) **überall ~hängen** be hung up all over the place; Ⓑ ⇒ **rumhängen** A; ~|**hantieren** *itr. V.* (*ugs.*) mess about; **an etw.** (*Dat.*) **~hantieren** mess about with sth.; ~|**hetzen** (*ugs.*) ❶ *tr. V.* **jmdn. ~hetzen** rush sb. off his/her feet; ❷ *itr. V.*; *mit sein* rush *or* chase around *or* about; ~|**horchen** *itr. V.* (*ugs.*) keep one's ears open; **horch mal ~, ob ...** keep your ears open and try and find out whether ...; ~|**irren** *itr. V.*; *mit sein* wander around *or* about; **im Wald ~irren** wander about the wood; ~|**kommandieren** (*ugs.*) ❶ *tr. V.* **jmdn. ~kommandieren** boss (*coll.*) *or* order sb. around *or* about; ❷ *itr. V.* boss (*coll.*) *or* order people around *or* about; ~|**kommen** *unr. itr. V.*; *mit sein* (*ugs.*) Ⓐ (*vorbeikommen können*) get round; **[mit etw.] um die Ecke** *usw.* **~kommen** get [sth.] round the corner *etc.*; Ⓑ (*sich ~bewegen*) come round; **um die Ecke ~kommen** come round the corner; Ⓒ (*vermeiden können*) **um etw. [nicht] ~kommen** [not] be able to get out of sth.; **um eine Operation/Entscheidung ~kommen** avoid having an operation/coming to a decision; **wir kommen nicht um die Tatsache ~, dass ...** we cannot get away *or* there is no getting away from the fact that ...; Ⓓ (*viel reisen*) get around *or* about; **in der Welt ~kommen** see a lot of the world; **viel ~kommen** get around *or* about a lot *or* a great deal; Ⓔ (*umschließen können*) **mit den Armen/der Hand/dem Seil um etw. ~kommen** get one's arms/hand/the rope [a]round sth.; ~|**kramen** *itr. V.* (*ugs.*) keep rummaging around *or* about; ~|**krebsen** *itr. V.* (*ugs.*) struggle; ~|**kriechen** *unr. itr. V.*; *mit sein* crawl around *or* about; **um etw. ~kriechen** crawl round sth.; ~|**kriegen** *tr. V.* Ⓐ (*salopp*) **jmdn. ~kriegen** talk sb. into it; (*verführen*) get sb. into bed (*coll.*); Ⓑ (*ugs.*) ⇒ ~**bekommen** B; ~|**kritisieren** *itr. V.* (*ugs.*) **an jmdm./etw. ~kritisieren** pick holes in sb./sth.; run sb./sth. down; ~|**kutschieren** (*ugs.*) ❶ *itr. V.*; *mit sein* drive around [aimlessly]; ❷ *tr. V.* drive ‹person› about [with no particular destination]; ~|**laborieren** *itr. V.* (*ugs.*) **an etw.** (*Dat.*) **~laborieren** try to get over sth.; ~|**laufen** *unr. itr. V.*; *mit sein* Ⓐ walk/(*schneller*) run around *or* about; **in der Stadt ~laufen** walk/(*schneller*) run around the town; Ⓑ (*umrunden*) **um etw. ~laufen** walk *or* go round sth.; Ⓒ (*gekleidet sein*) **wie ein Hippie ~laufen** go about looking *or* dressed like a hippie; **wie läufst du wieder ~!** what do you look like!; ~|**liegen** *unr. itr. V.* (*ugs.*) lie around *or* about; ~|**lümmeln** *refl. V.* (*ugs.*) lounge around; ~|**lungern** *itr. V.* (*salopp*) loaf around; ~|**machen** *itr. V.* (*ugs.*) be busy; (*abwertend*) mess about *or* around; **er fing an, an mir/meiner Bluse ~zumachen** he started trying to fondle me/undo my blouse; ~|**mäkeln** *itr. V.* (*ugs.*) **[an jmdm./etw.] ~mäkeln** pick holes [in sb./sth.]; **am Essen ~mäkeln** moan (*coll.*) *or* grumble about the food; ~|**nörgeln** *itr. V.* (*ugs. abwertend*) moan; grumble; **an jmdm./etw. ~nörgeln** moan *or* grumble about sb./sth.; ~|**pfuschen** *itr. V.* (*ugs. abwertend*) **[an jmdm./etw.] ~pfuschen** mess about [with sb./sth.]; ~|**posaunen** *tr. V.* (*ugs.*) broadcast; **sie posaunte im ganzen Dorf ~, dass ...** she broadcast to the whole village the fact that ...; ~|**quälen** *refl. V.* (*ugs.*) **sich [mit einem Problem] ~quälen** struggle [with a problem]; **sich mit Rheuma/finanziellen Sorgen ~quälen** be plagued by rheumatism/financial worries; ~|**rätseln** *itr. V.* (*ugs.*) **an etw.** (*Dat.*) **~rätseln** try to figure *or* puzzle sth. out; ~|**reden** *itr. V.* (*ugs.*) **um etw. ~reden** talk round sth.; **red nicht lange um die Sache ~!** don't beat about the bush!; ~|**reichen** (*ugs.*) ❶ *tr. V.* **etw. ~reichen** pass sth. round; **jmdn. [überall] ~reichen** (*fig.*) introduce sb. everywhere; ❷ *itr. V.* **[um etw.] ~reichen** reach round [sth.]; ~|**reisen** *itr. V.*; *mit sein* (*ugs.*) travel around *or* about; ~|**reißen** *unr. tr. V.* **den Wagen/das Pferd ~reißen** swing the car/horse round; ⇒ *auch* **Steuer**[1]; ~|**reiten** *unr. itr. V.*; *mit sein* Ⓐ (*ziellos reiten*) ride around *or* about; **in der Gegend ~reiten** ride around the area; Ⓑ (*salopp; auf dasselbe zurückkommen*) **auf etw.** (*Dat.*) **~reiten** go on about sth. (*coll.*); harp on sth.; Ⓒ (*salopp: kritisieren*) **auf jmdm. ~reiten** keep getting at sb. (*coll.*); ~|**rennen** *unr. itr. V.*; *mit sein* (*ugs.*) Ⓐ (*ziellos rennen*) run around *or* about; Ⓑ (*im Bogen rennen*) **um etw. ~rennen** run round sth.; **im Kreis ~rennen** run round in a circle; ~|**rutschen** *itr. V.*; *mit sein* (*ugs.*) slide around *or* about; ~|**scharwenzeln** *itr. V.*; *mit sein* (*ugs. abwertend*) **um jmdn. ~scharwenzeln** dance attendance on sb.; ~|**schlagen** ❶ *unr. tr. V.* **Papier/eine Decke** *usw.* **um etw. ~schlagen** wrap paper/a blanket *etc.* round sth.; ❷ *unr. refl. V.* (*ugs.*) Ⓐ (*sich schlagen*) **sich mit jmdm. ~schlagen** keep fighting *or* getting into fights with sb.; Ⓑ (*sich auseinander setzen*) **sich mit Problemen/Einwänden ~schlagen** grapple with problems/battle against objections; **sich mit jmdm. [wegen etw.] ~schlagen** conduct a running battle with sb. [about sth.]; ~|**schleichen** *unr. itr. V.*; *mit sein* (*ugs.*) creep around *or* about; **um etw. ~schleichen** creep round sth.; ~|**schlendern** *itr. V.*; *mit sein* (*ugs.*) stroll around *or* about; **in der Stadt ~schlendern** stroll around *or* about the town; ~|**schleppen** *tr. V.* (*ugs.*) **etw. um etw. ~schleppen** lug sth. round sth.; **eine Erkältung/ein Problem mit sich** (*Dat.*) **~schleppen** (*fig.*) go around with a cold/be worried by a problem; **die Probleme anderer mit sich** (*Dat.*) **~schleppen** (*fig.*) worry about other people's problems; ~|**schnüffeln** *itr. V.* (*ugs. abwertend*) nose *or* snoop around *or* about (*coll.*); **in jmds. Schreibtisch ~schnüffeln** poke around *or* about in sb.'s desk (*coll.*); **in anderer Leute Angelegenheiten ~schnüffeln** poke one's nose into other people's affairs; ~|**schubsen** *tr. V.* (*ugs.*) **jmdn. ~schubsen** push sb. around; *~|**sein** ⇒ **herum** C, E, F; ~|**sitzen** *unr. itr. V.* (*ugs.*) sit around *or* about; **um etw. ~sitzen** sit round sth.; **tatenlos ~sitzen** sit around *or* about doing nothing; ~|**spielen** *itr. V.* (*ugs.*) **an/mit etw. ~spielen** keep playing [around *or* about] with sth.; **an seinen Knöpfen ~spielen** fiddle with one's buttons; ~|**spionieren** *itr. V.* (*ugs.*) snoop *or* nose around *or* about (*coll.*); ~|**sprechen** *unr. refl. V.* get around *or* about; **schnell hatte sich ~gesprochen, dass ...** it had quickly got around that ...; ~|**spuken** *itr. V.* (*ugs.*) **in/auf etw.** (*Dat.*) **~spuken** haunt sth.; **ich möchte wissen, was in seinem Kopf ~spukt** (*fig.*) I'd like to know what's going on in his mind; ~|**stänkern** *itr. V.* (*ugs.*) keep complaining; ~|**stehen** *unr. itr. V.* (*ugs.*) stand around *or* about; **um etw. ~stehen** stand round sth.; ~|**stöbern** *itr. V.* (*ugs.*) (*in einem Schreibtisch usw.*) keep rummaging around *or* about (**in** + *Dat.* in); **die Jagdhunde stöberten im Dickicht ~:** the hounds were hunting around in the thicket; **ich habe in der ganzen Wohnung ~gestöbert** I've hunted all over the house; ~|**stochern** *itr. V.* poke around *or*

*old spelling (see note on page 1707)

about; **im Essen ~stochern** pick at one's food; **~|stoßen** *unr. tr. V. (ugs.)* **jmdn. ~stoßen** push sb. around; **~|streichen** *unr. itr. V.; mit sein (abwertend)* Ⓐ *(umherstreifen)* roam around *or* about; Ⓑ *(lauernd umkreisen)* **um jmdn./etw. ~streichen** prowl round sb./sth.; **~|streifen** *itr. V.; mit sein (ugs.)* roam around *or* about; **auf den Straßen ~streifen** roam the streets; **~|streiten** *unr. refl. V. (ugs.)* **sich [mit jmdm./etw.] ~streiten** keep quarrelling *or* wrangling [with sb.]; **~|streunen** *itr. V.; mit sein (abwertend)* roam around *or* about; **auf den Feldern ~streunen** roam the fields; **~|stromern** *itr. V.; mit sein (salopp abwertend)* roam around *or* about; **~|tanzen** *itr. V.; mit sein (ugs.)* Ⓐ dance around *or* about; **im Zimmer ~tanzen** dance around *or* about the room; Ⓑ *(im Bogen um etw. tanzen)* **um jmdn./etw. ~tanzen** dance round sb./sth.; **um jmdn. ~tanzen** *(fig.)* dance attendance on sb.; ⇒ *auch* **Kopf** A; **Nase** B; **~|tollen** *itr. V.; mit sein* romp around *or* about; **auf dem Hof ~tollen** romp around the yard; **~|tragen** *unr. tr. V. (ugs.)* Ⓐ *(überallhin tragen)* **jmdn./etw. ~tragen** carry sb./sth. around *or* about; **jmdn./etw. mit sich ~tragen** carry sb./sth. around with one; Ⓑ **eine Idee/einen Plan mit sich ~tragen** nurse an idea/a plan; Ⓒ *(abwertend: weitererzählen)* **etw. ~tragen** spread sth. around; **~|trampeln** *itr. V.; mit haben od. sein* **auf etw. (Dat.) ~trampeln** trample [around] on sth.; trample all over sth.; **auf jmdm. ~trampeln** *(fig.)* walk all over sb.; **auf jmds. Nerven/Gefühlen ~trampeln** *(fig.)* really get on sb.'s nerves/trample on sb.'s feelings; **~|treiben** *unr. refl. V. (ugs. abwertend)* Ⓐ *(kein geordnetes Leben führen)* **sich auf den Straßen/in Spelunken ~treiben** hang around the streets/*(coll.)* in dives; **sich mit Männern ~treiben** hang around with men; Ⓑ *(sich irgendwo aufhalten)* **sich in der Welt ~treiben** roam *or* move about the world; **wo hast du dich nur ~getrieben?** where have you been?; **ich möchte wissen, wo er sich ~treibt** I'd like to know where he's got to; **~treiber** *der,* **~treiberin** *die;* **~~, ~~nen** *(ugs.)* layabout; *(Streuner)* vagabond; **~|trödeln** *itr. V. (ugs.)* dawdle around *or* about (**mit** over); **~|wälzen** *(ugs.)* ❶ *tr. V.* **etw. ~wälzen** roll sth. over; ❷ *refl. V.* roll around *or* about; **sich im Bett ~wälzen** toss and turn in bed; **sich im Schlamm ~wälzen** wallow in the mud; **~|wandern** *itr. V.; mit sein* Ⓐ *(ugs.: umhergehen)* wander around *or* about; **im Garten ~wandern** wander around *or* about the garden; Ⓑ *(im Bogen um etw. wandern)* **um den Berg/See** *usw.* **~wandern** hike around the mountain/the lake *etc.;* **~|werfen** ❶ *unr. tr. V.* Ⓐ *(ugs.: umherwerfen)* **etw. ~werfen** chuck *(coll.) or* throw sth. around *or* about; **etw. im Zimmer ~werfen** chuck *(coll.) or* throw sth. around *or* about the room; Ⓑ *(in eine andere Richtung drehen)* throw ‹helm, steering wheel, etc.› [hard] over; **den Kopf ~werfen** turn one's head quickly; ❷ *unr. refl. V.* **sich im Bett ~werfen** toss and turn in bed; **~|wickeln** *tr. V.* **etw. um etw. ~wickeln** wrap sth. round sth.; **~|wirbeln** ❶ *tr. V.* **jmdn./etw. ~wirbeln** whirl *or* spin sb./sth. [a]round; **der Wind wirbelte die Blätter ~:** the wind whirled the leaves around *or* about; ❷ *itr. V.; mit sein* spin *or* whirl [a]round; **~|wühlen** *itr. V.* **in etw. (Dat.) ~wühlen** rummage *or* root around *or* about in sth.; **in jmds. Vergangenheit ~wühlen** *(fig.)* dig into sb.'s past; **~|wurschteln, ~|wursteln** *itr. V. (salopp)* **mit etw. ~wurschteln** *od.* **~wursteln** mess *or* fiddle around *or* about with sth.; **~|zanken** *refl. V. (ugs.)* ⇒ **~streiten**; **~|zeigen** *tr. V. (ugs.)* **etw. ~zeigen** show sth. round; **~|ziehen** ❶ *unr. itr. V.* move around *or* about; **im Land ~ziehen** move around *or* about the country; **um etw. ~ziehen** go round sth.; ❷ *unr. tr. V. (ugs.: mit sich ziehen)* **jmdn./etw. ~ziehen** drag sb./sth. round *(coll.)*; ❸ *unr. refl. V.* **sich um etw. ~ziehen** ‹fence, wall, river, etc.› go *or* run round sth.; ‹wood etc.› surround sth.

**herunten** /hɛˈrʊntn̩/ *Adv. (südd., österr.)* down here

**herunter** /hɛˈrʊntɐ/ *Adv.* Ⓐ *(nach unten)* down; **~ sein** *(unten sein)* be down; **von Kiel nach München ~** *(fig.)* from Kiel down to Munich; Ⓑ *(fort)* off; **~ vom Sofa!** [get] off the sofa!; **~ vom Baum/von der Mauer!** get *or* come down from that tree/wall!; Ⓒ **[körperlich] ~ sein** be in poor health; **er ist mit seiner Gesundheit/seinen Nerven ~:** he's in poor health/his nerves are in a bad state

**herunter-: ~|bekommen** *unr. tr. V. (ugs.)* Ⓐ *(essen können)* be able to eat; *(~schlucken)* swallow; Ⓑ *(entfernen können)* **etw. [von etw.] ~bekommen** be able to get sth. off [sth.]; **~|bemühen** ❶ *tr. V.* **jmdn. ~bemühen** trouble sb. to come down; ❷ *refl. V.* take the trouble to come down; **würden Sie sich bitte ~bemühen?** would you mind coming down?; **~|beten** *tr. V. (abwertend)* **etw. ~beten** recite sth. mechanically; **~|bitten** *unr. tr. V.* **jmdn. ~bitten** ask sb. [to come] down; **~|brennen** *unr. itr. V.* Ⓐ *mit sein (vollkommen abbrennen)* ‹house, fire, etc.› burn down; Ⓑ ‹sun› burn *or* beat down; **~|bringen** *unr. tr. V.* Ⓐ *(nach unten bringen)* bring down; Ⓑ *(zugrunde richten)* ruin; Ⓒ *(ugs.: ~schlucken)* ⇒ **~bekommen** A; **~|drücken** *tr. V.* Ⓐ *(nach unten drücken)* **etw. ~drücken** press sth. down; Ⓑ *(auf ein niedriges Niveau bringen, verringern)* force down ‹prices, wages, etc.›; bring down ‹temperature›; reduce ‹marks›; **~|fahren** ❶ *unr. itr. V.; mit sein* drive *or* come down; ‹skier› ski down; *(mit einem Motorrad, Rad)* ride down; ❷ *unr. tr. V.* Ⓐ **jmdn./etw. ~fahren** drive *or* bring sb. down/bring sth. down; Ⓑ *(DV)* shut down; **~|fallen** *unr. itr. V.; mit sein* fall down; **vom Tisch/Stuhl ~fallen** fall off the table/chair; **die Treppe ~fallen** fall down the stairs; **jmdm. fällt etw. ~:** sb. drops sth.; **~|fliegen** *unr. itr. V.; mit sein* Ⓐ *(nach unten fliegen)* fly down; Ⓑ *(ugs.)* ⇒ **~fallen**; **~|geben** *unr. tr. V. (ugs.)* pass *or* hand down; **~|gehen** *unr. itr. V.; mit sein* Ⓐ *(nach unten gehen)* come down; Ⓑ *(niedriger werden)* ‹temperature› go down, drop, fall; ‹prices› come down, fall; **im Preis ~gehen** come down in price; Ⓒ *(die Höhe senken)* **auf eine Flughöhe von 2 000 m ~gehen** descend to 6,000 ft.; **auf eine geringere Geschwindigkeit ~gehen** slow down; reduce speed; **mit den Preisen ~gehen** reduce one's/its prices; Ⓓ **von etw. ~gehen** *(ugs.: räumen)* get off sth.; Ⓔ *(ugs.: sich lösen)* come off; **~gekommen** ❶ *2. Part. v.* **~kommen**; ❷ *Adj.* poor ‹health›; dilapidated, run-down ‹building›; run-down ‹area›; down and out ‹person›; **ein [völlig] ~gekommenes Subjekt** a down-and-out; **~|handeln** *tr. V. (ugs.)* **einen Preis ~handeln** beat down a price; **100 DM vom Kaufpreis ~handeln** get 100 marks knocked off the price *(coll.)*; **~|hängen** *unr. itr. V.* hang down; **~|hauen** *unr. tr. V. (ugs.)* Ⓐ *(ohrfeigen)* **jmdm. eine ~hauen** give sb. a clout round the ear *(coll.)*; Ⓑ *(schlecht ausführen)* dash off; **~|heben** *unr. tr. V.* **etw. [von etw.] ~heben** lift sth. down [from sth.]; **~|helfen** *unr. itr. V. (ugs.)* **jmdm. ~helfen** help sb. down; **~|holen** *tr. V.* Ⓐ *(nach unten holen)* **jmdn./etw. ~holen** fetch sb./sth. down; Ⓑ *(ugs.: abschießen)* bring down; **~|klappen** *tr. V.* pull *or* put down ‹seat›; close ‹lid›; **seinen Kragen ~klappen** turn down one's collar; **~|klettern** *itr. V.; mit sein* climb down; **~|kommen** *unr. itr. V.; mit sein* Ⓐ *(kommen)* come down; *(nach unten kommen können)* manage to come down; Ⓑ *(ugs.: verfallen)* go to the dogs *(coll.)*; **er ist so weit ~gekommen, dass ...** he has sunk so low that ...; **er ist gesundheitlich ~gekommen** his health has deteriorated; Ⓒ *(ugs.: wegkommen)* **von Drogen/vom Alkohol ~kommen** come off drugs/alcohol; kick the habit *(coll.)*; **von einer [schlechten] Note ~kommen** improve on a [bad] mark; **~|können** *unr. itr. V. (ugs.)* be able to get down; **~|kriegen** *tr. V. (ugs.)* ⇒ **runterkriegen**; **~|laden** *unr. tr. V. (DV)* download; **~|lassen** *unr. tr. V. (schließen)* let down, lower ‹blind, shutter›; lower ‹barrier›; shut ‹window›; *(nach unten gleiten lassen)* wind down ‹car window›; **jmdn./etw. an etw. (Dat.) ~lassen** lower sb./sth. by sth.; **die Hose ~lassen** take one's trousers down; **~|leiern** *tr. V. (salopp)* Ⓐ *(abwertend)* drone out *(coll.)*; Ⓑ wind down ‹car window›; **~|machen** *tr. V. (salopp)* Ⓐ *(zurechtweisen)* **jmdn. ~machen** give sb. a rocket *(coll.)*; tear sb. off a strip *(coll.)*; Ⓑ *(herabsetzen)* slate *(coll.)*; run down *(coll.)*; **~|nehmen** *unr. tr. V.* take down; **die Arme ~nehmen** put one's arms down; **etw. von etw. ~nehmen** take sth. off sth.; **~|purzeln** *itr. V.; mit sein (ugs.)* **die Treppe ~purzeln** tumble down the stairs; **vom Stuhl ~purzeln** topple off the chair; **~|putzen** *tr. V. (salopp)* ⇒ **~machen** A; **~|rasseln** *(ugs.)* ❶ *tr. V.* rattle off; ❷ *itr. V.; mit sein* rattle down; come rattling down; **~|reißen** *unr. tr. V. (ugs.)* Ⓐ *(nach unten reißen)* pull down; Ⓑ *(abreißen)* pull off ‹plaster, wallpaper›; tear down ‹poster›; Ⓒ *(salopp: ableisten)* get through; **~|rutschen** *itr. V.; mit sein (ugs.)* slide down; ‹trousers, socks› slip down; **~|schalten** *itr. V. (Kfz-Jargon)* change down; **~|schießen** ❶ *unr. tr. V.* shoot down ‹bird, aircraft, etc.›; ❷ *unr. itr. V.* Ⓐ **von einem Fenster aus ~schießen** shoot *or* fire down from a window; Ⓑ *mit sein (~stürzen)* hurtle down; come hurtling down; **~|schlagen** *unr. tr. V.* Ⓐ knock off; **den Stuck von der Wand ~schlagen** knock the stucco off the wall; Ⓑ *(nach unten wenden)* turn ‹collar etc.› down; **~|schlucken** *tr. V.* swallow; **~|schrauben** *tr. V.* turn down ‹wick etc.›; **seine Ansprüche/Erwartungen ~schrauben** *(fig.)* reduce one's requirements/lower one's expectations; **~|sehen** *unr. itr. V.* Ⓐ *(nach unten sehen)* look down; Ⓑ *(geringschätzig betrachten)* **auf jmdn. ~sehen** look down [up]on sb.; ***~|sein** ⇒ **herunter** A, C; **~|setzen** *tr. V. (ugs.)* ⇒ **herabsetzen**; **~|spielen** *tr. V. (ugs.)* Ⓐ *(als unbedeutend darstellen)* play down *(coll.)*; Ⓑ *(ausdruckslos spielen)* **etw. ~spielen** play sth. through mechanically; **~|steigen** *unr. itr. V.; mit sein* climb down; **~|stürzen** ❶ *itr. V.; mit sein* fall down; *(steil herabfallen)* ‹aircraft, person, etc.› plunge down; *(~eilen)* rush down; **vom Dach ~stürzen** fall off the roof; ❷ *tr. V.* Ⓐ *(schnell trinken)* gulp down; Ⓑ **jmdn. ~stürzen** throw sb. down; **~|tragen** *unr. tr. V.* **etw. ~tragen** carry sth. down; **~|werfen** *unr. tr. V.* Ⓐ *(nach unten werfen)* **etw. ~werfen** throw sth. down; Ⓑ *(ugs.: ~fallen lassen)* drop; **~|wirtschaften** *tr. V. (ugs.)* **etw. ~wirtschaften** ruin sth./bring sth. to the brink *or* edge of ruin [by mismanagement]; **~|ziehen** ❶ *unr. tr. V.* pull down; **jmdn. [auf seine Ebene] ~ziehen** *(fig.)* drag sb. down [to one's own level]; ❷ *unr. itr. V.; mit sein* go *or* move down; *(umziehen)* move down

**her·vor** *Adv.* **aus etw. ~:** out of sth.; **aus der Ecke ~ kam ...** from out of the corner came ...

**hervor-, Hervor-: ~|brechen** *unr. itr. V.; mit sein (geh.)* Ⓐ *(zum Vorschein kommen)* ‹animal etc.› burst out; ‹sun› break through; ‹plant› come up *or* through; Ⓑ *(sich äußern)* ‹feelings› burst forth *or* out; **~|bringen** *unr. tr. V.* Ⓐ *(zum Vorschein bringen)* bring out (**aus** of); produce (**aus** from); Ⓑ *(wachsen, entstehen lassen; auch fig.)* produce; Ⓒ *(von sich geben)* say; produce ‹sound›; **er brachte kein Wort/keinen Ton ~:** he could not utter a word/sound; **~|dringen** *unr. itr. V.; mit sein (geh.)* ‹plant› come up *or* through; **~|gehen** *unr. itr. V.; mit sein (geh.)* Ⓐ *(seinen Ursprung haben)* **viele große Musiker gingen aus dieser Stadt ~:** this city produced many great musicians; **drei Kinder gingen aus der Ehe ~:** the marriage produced three children; there were three children from the marriage; **eines geht aus dem andern ~:** one thing evolves from another; Ⓑ *(herauskommen, sich ergeben)* emerge (**aus** from); **aus etw. siegreich/als Sieger ~gehen** emerge victorious from sth.; **aus seinem Brief geht klar ~, dass ...** it is clear from his letter that ...; Ⓒ *(zu folgern sein)*

h

follow; **daraus geht ~, dass ...** from this it follows that ...; **~|gucken** *itr. V.* (*ugs.*) look out; **unter etw.** (*Dat.*) **~gucken** peep out from under sth.; **~|heben** *unr. tr. V.* emphasize; stress; **etw. durch Kursivdruck ~heben** make sth. stand out by using italics; **~hebung** *die* emphasis; **der ~hebung dienen** be [used] for emphasis; **~|holen** *tr. V.* take out (**aus** of); **ich muss meine alten Schulbücher ~holen** I must get out my old school books; **~|kehren** *tr. V.* ⇒ **herauskehren**; **~|kommen** *unr. itr. V.*; *mit sein* come out (**aus** of, **unter** + *Dat.* from under); **~|locken** *tr. V.* lure *or* entice ‹person, animal› out (**aus** of); **~|quellen** *unr. itr. V.*; *mit sein* well up; ‹smoke› pour out; **aus etw. ~quellen** stream from sth.; **unter dem Hut quoll ihr Haar ~:** her hair spilled out from under her hat; **~quellende Augen** bulging eyes; **~|ragen** *itr. V.* **A** (*aus etw. ragen*) project; jut out; ‹cheekbones› stand out; **aus dem Häusermeer ragte der Kirchturm ~:** the church spire stood out above the sea of houses; **B** (*sich auszeichnen*) stand out; **~ragend** ❶ *Adj.* outstanding[ly good]; ❷ *adv.* **~ragend geschult** outstandingly well trained; **~ragend spielen/arbeiten** play/work outstandingly well *or* excellently; **~ruf** *der* curtain call; **~|rufen** *unr. tr. V.* **A** (*nach vorn rufen*) **jmdn. ~rufen** call for sb. to come out; (*Theater usw.*) call sb. back; **sie wurde sechsmal ~gerufen** she had to take six curtain calls; **B** (*verursachen*) elicit, provoke ‹response›; arouse ‹admiration›; cause ‹unease, disquiet, confusion, merriment, disease›; provoke ‹protest, displeasure›; **~|sehen** *unr. itr. V.* be visible; (*unerwünscht*) show; **~|springen** *unr. itr. V.*; *mit sein* **A** (*springend ~kommen*) leap *or* jump out (**hinter** + *Dat.* from behind); **B** (*vorspringen*) project; jut out; ‹nose› stick out; **~|stechen** *unr. itr. V.* **A** (*herausstehen*) stick out (**aus** of); **B** (*sich abheben*) stand out; **~stechend** *Adj.* outstanding; striking; **~|stehen** *unr. itr. V.* protrude; stick out; ‹cheekbones› stand out; **~|stürzen** *itr. V.*; *mit sein* rush *or* burst out (**hinter** + *Dat.* from behind); **~|suchen** *tr. V.* look out; **~|treten** *unr. itr. V.*; *mit sein* **A** emerge, step out (**hinter** + *Dat.* from behind); ‹veins, ribs, etc.› stand out; ‹similarity etc.› become apparent *or* evident; ‹eyes› bulge, protrude; **die Sonne trat aus den Wolken ~** (*fig. geh.*) the sun emerged *or* came out from behind the clouds; **B** (*bekannt werden*) make one's mark; make a name for oneself; **~|tun** *unr. refl. V.* **A** (*Besonderes leisten*) distinguish oneself; **sie hat sich nicht sonderlich ~getan** she did not exactly distinguish herself; **sich mit/als etw. ~tun** make one's mark with/as sth.; **B** (*wichtig tun*) show off; **~|wagen** *refl. V.* dare to come out (**aus** of); **du kannst dich wieder ~wagen** you can come out again; **~|zaubern** *tr. V.* conjure up; **er zauberte ein Päckchen Zigaretten ~:** as if by magic he produced a packet of cigarettes; **~|ziehen** *unr. tr. V.* pull out (**hinter** + *Dat.* from behind, **unter** + *Dat.* from under)

**her|wagen** *refl. V.* (*ugs.*) dare to come here

**Her·weg** *der:* **auf dem ~weg** on the way here

**Herz** /hɛrts/ *das;* **~ens, ~en** **A** ▶ 471 (*auch: herzförmiger Gegenstand, zentraler Teil*) heart; **sie hat es am ~en** (*ugs.*) she has a bad heart; (*fig.*) **komm an mein ~, Geliebter** come into my arms, my darling; **jmdm. das ~ zerreißen** break sb.'s heart; **dabei dreht sich mir das ~ im Leib[e] um** it makes my heart bleed; **mir blutet das ~** (*auch iron.*) my heart bleeds; **mir lacht das ~ im Leibe** my heart sings; **ihm rutschte** *od.* **fiel das ~ in die Hose[n]** (*ugs., oft scherzh.*) his heart sank into his boots; **jmds. ~ höher schlagen lassen** make sb.'s heart beat faster; **jmdm. das ~ brechen** (*geh.*) break sb.'s heart; **das ~ auf dem rechten Fleck haben** have one's heart in the right place; **das ~ in die Hand** *od.* **in beide Hände nehmen** take one's courage in both hands; **jmdn./etw. auf ~ und Nieren prüfen** (*ugs.*) grill sb./go over sth. with a fine toothcomb; **ein Kind unter dem ~en tragen** (*dichter.*) be with child; be great with child (*arch.*); ⇒ *auch* **drücken** A; **klopfen** 1 B; **B** (*meist geh.: Gemüt*) heart; **ein treues ~ haben** be true-hearted; **ein warmes/gutes ~ haben** have a warm/good *or* kind heart; **die ~en bewegen/rühren** touch people's hearts; **von ~en kommen** come from the heart; **im Grunde seines ~ens** in his heart of hearts; **man kann einem Menschen nicht ins ~ sehen** one cannot see *or* look into another man's heart; **wes das ~ voll ist, des geht der Mund über** (*prov.*) when you're excited about something, it's difficult to stop talking about it; **ein ~ und eine Seele sein** be bosom friends; **jmds. ~ hängt an etw.** (*Dat.*) (*jmd. möchte etw. sehr gerne behalten*) sb. is attached to sth.; (*jmd. möchte etw. sehr gerne haben*) sb.'s heart is set on sth.; **sein ~ gehört der Musik/Literatur** *usw.* (*geh.*) music/literature *etc.* is his first love; **ihm war/wurde das ~ schwer** his heart was/grew heavy; **alles, was das ~ begehrt** everything one's heart desires; **nicht das ~ haben, etw. zu tun** not have the heart to do sth.; **sich** (*Dat.*) **ein ~ fassen** pluck up one's courage; take one's courage in both hands; **sein ~ an jmdn./etw. hängen** (*geh.*) give one's heart to sb./devote oneself to sth.; **sein ~ für etw. entdecken** (*geh.*) discover a passion for sth.; **ein ~ für die Armen und Kranken haben** feel for the sick and the poor; **ein ~ für Kinder/die Kunst haben** have a love of children/art; **jmdm. sein ~ ausschütten** pour out one's heart to sb.; **jmdm. das ~ schwer machen** sadden sb.'s heart; **das ~ auf der Zunge haben** wear one's heart on one's sleeve; **die** *od.* **alle ~en im Sturm erobern** (*geh.*) capture everybody's heart; **seinem ~en einen Stoß geben** [suddenly] pluck up courage; **seinem ~en Luft machen** (*ugs.*) give vent to one's feelings; **leichten ~ens** easily; happily; **schweren ~ens** with a heavy heart; **jmd./etw. liegt jmdm. am ~en** sb. has the interests of sb./sth. at heart; **jmdm. etw. ans ~ legen** entrust sb. with sth.; **jmd./etw. ist jmdm. ans ~ gewachsen** sb. has grown very fond of sb./sth.; **etw. auf dem ~en haben** have sth. on one's mind; **aus seinem ~en keine Mördergrube machen** speak freely *or* frankly; **aus tiefstem ~en** (*geh.*) from the bottom of one's heart; **jmdn. ins** *od.* **in sein ~ schließen** take to sb.; **jmdn. ins ~ treffen** cut sb. to the quick; **mit halbem ~en** (*geh.*) half-heartedly; **es nicht übers ~ bringen, etw. zu tun** not have the heart to do sth.; **von ~en gern** [most] gladly; **von ganzem ~en** (*aufrichtig*) with all one's heart; (*aus voller Überzeugung*) wholeheartedly; **sich** (*Dat.*) **etw. zu ~en nehmen** take sth. to heart; **habt ein ~ [mit dem armen Kerl]!** have pity [on the poor fellow]!; **mit ganzem ~en** (*geh.*) wholeheartedly; **ein Mann** *usw.* **nach jmds. ~en** a man *etc.* after sb.'s own heart; **jmdm. aus dem ~en sprechen** express just what sb. is/was thinking; **jmdm. sein ~ schenken** (*geh.*) give sb. one's heart; **die Dame seines ~ens** (*geh., oft scherzh.*) the woman of his heart; **von ~en kommen** ‹present› be given with cordial feeling; ‹congratulations, thanks, etc.› come from the heart; **jmdm. zu ~en gehen** upset sb. deeply; ⇒ *auch* **golden** 1 C; **Luft** C; **Stein** B; **Stich** E; **Zentnerlast**; **C** (*Kartenspiel*) hearts *pl.*; ⇒ *auch* **Pik²**; **D** (*Speise*) heart; **ein Pfund ~ vom Schwein** a pound of pig's heart[s]; **E** (*Kosewort*) **mein ~:** my dear

**herz-, Herz-: ~allerliebste** *der/die; adj. Dekl.* (*veralt.*) beloved; **~allerliebster mein** my beloved; my darling; **~anfall** *der* heart attack; ***~as, ~ass** *das* ace of hearts; **~asthma** *das* ▶ 474 (*Med.*) cardiac asthma; cardiasthma; **~beklemmend** *Adj.* oppressive; **~beklemmung** *die* angina; **~beschwerden** *Pl.* heart trouble *sing.*; **~beutel** *der* ▶ 471 (*Anat.*) pericardium; **~binkerl** /-bɪŋkɐl/ *das;* **~~s, ~~** (*bayr., österr. ugs.*) pet (*coll.*); darling; **~blatt** *das* **A** (*Gartenbau*) new, inner leaf; **B** (*Kosewort*) darling; **~blut** *das:* **in sein ~blut für jmdn./etw. hingeben** (*geh. veralt.*) sacrifice everything for sb./sth.; **~bube** *der* jack of hearts

**Herzchen** *das;* **~s, ~** **A** (*abwertend: naive/unzuverlässige Person*) simpleton/unreliable person; **B** (*Kosewort*) darling; sweetheart; **C** (*kleines Herz*) little heart

**Herz-: ~chirurgie** *die* heart *or* cardiac surgery; **~dame** *die* queen of hearts

**Herzegowina** /hɛrtse'go:vina/ *die;* **~:** Herzegovina

**her|zeigen** *tr. V.* (*ugs.*) show; **zeig [es] mal her!** let me see [it]!

**Herze·leid** *das* (*veralt.*) heartbreak

**herzen** *tr. V.* (*veralt.*) hug

**herzens-, Herzens-: ~angelegenheit** *die* (*Liebesangelegenheit*) affair of the heart; (*Leidenschaft*) passion; **~angst** *die* (*geh.*) deep anxiety; (*bei unmittelbarer Bedrohung*) [mortal] fear; **~bedürfnis** *das:* **in jmdm. ein ~bedürfnis sein** (*geh.*) be very important to sb.; **~bildung** *die* (*geh.*) sensitivity; **~brecher** *der* ladykiller (*coll.*); heartbreaker; **~brecherin** *die;* **~~, ~~nen** heartbreaker; **~grund** *der:* **in aus ~grund** from the bottom of one's heart; **~gut** /'--'-/ *Adj.* kind-hearted; good-hearted; **~güte** *die* (*geh.*) kindness of heart; kind-heartedness; goodness of heart; **~lust** *die:* **in nach ~lust** to one's heart's content; **~wunsch** *der* dearest *or* fondest wish

**herz-, Herz-: ~entzündung** *die* ▶ 474 (*Med.*) ⇒ **Karditis**; **~erfreuend** *Adj.* heartwarming; **~erfrischend** ❶ *Adj.* refreshing; ❷ *adv.* refreshingly; **~ergreifend** ❶ *Adj.* heart-rending; ❷ *adv.* heart-rendingly; **~erquickend** *Adj.* ⇒ **~erfrischend**; **~fehler** *der* heart defect; **~flimmern** *das* ▶ 474 (*Med.*) (*Kammerflimmern*) ventricular fibrillation; (*Vorhofflimmern*) auricular fibrillation; **~förmig** *Adj.* heart-shaped; heart-shaped, cordate ‹leaf›; **~gegend** *die* area *or* region of the heart; **~geräusch** *das* ▶ 474 (*Med.*) heart murmur

**herzhaft** ❶ *Adj.* **A** (*kräftig*) hearty; **B** (*nahrhaft*) hearty, substantial ‹meal›; (*von kräftigem Geschmack*) tasty; **ein ~er Eintopf** a substantial/tasty stew; **C** (*veralt.: mutig*) bold. ❷ *adv.* **A** (*kräftig*) heartily; **~ gähnen** give a wide yawn; **B** (*nahrhaft*) **er isst gern ~:** he likes to have a hearty meal; **C** (*veralt.: mutig*) boldly

**her|ziehen** ❶ *unr. itr. V.* **A** *mit sein od. haben* (*ugs.: abfällig reden*) **über jmdn./etw. ~:** run sb./sth. down; pull sb./sth. to pieces; **B** *mit sein* (*mitgehen*) **vor/hinter/neben jmdm./etw. ~:** walk along in front of/behind/beside sb./sth.; (*marschieren*) march along in front of/behind/beside sb./sth.; **C** (*umziehen*) *mit sein* move here. ❷ *unr. tr. V.* **A** (*ugs.: zum Sprechenden bewegen*) **etw. ~:** pull sth. over [here]; **B** (*mit sich führen*) **jmdn./etw. hinter sich** (*Dat.*) **~:** pull sb./sth. along behind one

**herzig** ❶ *Adj.* sweet; dear; delightful. ❷ *adv.* sweetly; delightfully

**herz-, Herz-: ~infarkt** *der* ▶ 474 heart attack; cardiac infarction (*Med.*); **~innig** (*veralt.*), **~inniglich** (*veralt.*) ❶ *Adj.* heartfelt; ❷ *adv.* with heartfelt emotion; **jmdn. ~innig lieben** love sb. with all one's heart; **~insuffizienz** *die* ▶ 474 (*Med.*) cardiac insufficiency; **~kammer** *die* ▶ 471 (*Anat.*) ventricle; **~kirsche** *die* heart cherry; sweet cherry; **~klappe** *die* ▶ 471 (*Anat.*) heart valve; **~klappen·fehler** *der* ▶ 474 (*Med.*) valvular defect *or* insufficiency; **~klopfen** *das;* **~~s: jmd. hat ~klopfen** sb.'s heart is pounding; **jmd. bekommt ~klopfen** sb.'s heart starts to pound; **mit ~klopfen** with a pounding heart; **~kollaps** *der* ⇒ **~versagen**; **~könig** *der* king of hearts; **~krampf** *der* heart spasm; **~krank** *Adj.* ‹person› with *or* suffering from a heart condition; **[sehr] ~krank sein/werden** have/get a [serious] heart condition; **~kranke Patienten** cardiac patients; **~kranke** *der/die* person with *or* suffering from a heart condition; (*Patient*) cardiac patient; **~kranz·gefäß** *das* ▶ 471 coronary vessel; **~leiden** *das* heart condition

*old spelling (see note on page 1707)

**herzlich** ❶ *Adj.* Ⓐ (*warmherzig*) warm ‹smile, reception›; kind ‹words›; ~ **zu jmdm. sein** be cordial towards sb.; Ⓑ ▶ 369 (*ehrlich gemeint*) sincere; ~**e Grüße/~en Dank** kind regards/many thanks; **sein ~es Beileid zum Ausdruck bringen** express one's sincere condolences *pl.*; ~**[st] dein/euer Julius** (*als Briefschluss*) kind[est] regards, Julius; ⇒ *auch* **Glückwunsch**. ❷ *adv.* Ⓐ (*warmherzig*) warmly; **der Empfang fiel sehr ~ aus** the reception was very cordial; Ⓑ ▶ 369 (*ehrlich gemeint*) sincerely; ‹congratulate› heartily; **es grüßt euch ~ eure Viktoria** (*als Briefschluss*) kind regards, Victoria; Ⓒ (*sehr*) ~ **wenig** very *or* (*coll.*) precious little; ~ **schlecht** dreadful; ~ **gern!** gladly; **etw. ~ satt haben** be heartily sick of sth.

**Herzlichkeit** *die* Ⓐ ⇒ **herzlich** A: warmth; kindness; Ⓑ (*Aufrichtigkeit*) sincerity

**herz-, Herz-:** ~**liebste** *der/die* ⇒ ~**allerliebste**; ~**los** ❶ *Adj.* heartless; callous; ❷ *adv.* heartlessly; callously; ~**losigkeit** *die*; ~~, ~~**en** Ⓐ heartlessness; callousness; Ⓑ (~*lose Tat/Bemerkung*) heartless act/remark; ~**-Lungen-Maschine** *die* heart-lung machine; ~**massage** *die* cardiac massage; heart massage; ~**mittel** *das* (*ugs.*) heart pills *pl.*; ~**muskel** *der* ▶ 471 (*Anat.*) heart muscle; cardiac muscle

**Herzog** /ˈhɛrtso:k/ *der*; ~**s**, **Herzöge** /ˈhɛrtsø:gə/ duke; **[Herr] Friedrich ~ von Meiningen** Frederick, Duke of Meiningen

**Herzogin** *die*; ~, ~**nen** duchess

**herzoglich** *Adj.* ducal; of the duke *postpos.*, *not pred.*; **die ~e Familie** the family of the duke

**Herzogtum** *das*; ~**s**, **Herzogtümer** duchy

**Herz·rhythmus** *der* (*Med.*) heart rhythm; cardiac rhythm

**Herzrhythmus·störung** *die* ▶ 474 (*Med.*) disturbance of the heart *or* cardiac rhythm

**herz-, Herz-:** ~**schlag** *der* ▶ 474 Ⓐ heartbeat; **einen ~schlag lang** (*geh.*) for a *or* one fleeting moment; Ⓑ (*Abfolge der ~schläge*, *auch fig. geh.*) pulse; Ⓒ (~*versagen*) heart failure; **an einem ~schlag sterben** die of heart failure; ~**schmerz** *der* pain in the region of the heart; ~**schrittmacher** *der* (*Anat.*, *Med.*) [cardiac] pacemaker; ~**schwäche** *die* cardiac insufficiency; ~**spezialist** *der*, ~**spezialistin** *die* heart specialist; ~**stärkend** *Adj.* **ein ~stärkendes Mittel** a cardiac tonic; ~**stärkend sein/wirken** act as a cardiac tonic; ~**stillstand** *der* ▶ 474 (*Med.*) cardiac arrest; ~**stück** *das* (*geh.*) heart; ~**tätigkeit** *die* action of the heart; ~**ton** *der*; *Pl.* ~**töne** (*Med.*) heart sound; cardiac sound; ~**transplantation** *die* (*Med.*) heart transplantation

**herzu** /hɛɐ̯ˈtsu:/ *Adv.* (*geh.*) ⇒ **herbei**

**herz-, Herz-:** ~**verfettung** *die* fatty degeneration of the heart; ~**verpflanzung** *die* ⇒ ~**transplantation**; ~**versagen** *das*; ~~**s** ▶ 474 heart failure; ~**zerreißend** ❶ *Adj.* heart-rending; ❷ *adv.* heart-rendingly

**Hesse** /ˈhɛsə/ *der*; ~**n**, ~**n** Hessian

**Hessen** (*das*) Hesse

**Hessin** *die*; ~, ~**nen** ⇒ **Hesse**

**hessisch** *Adj.* Hessian

**Hetäre** /heˈtɛ:rə/ *die*; ~, ~**n** hetaera

**hetero-, Hetero-** /hetero-/ *in Zus.* hetero-

**Hetero** *der*; ~**s**, ~**s** (*ugs.*) hetero (*coll.*)

**heterodox** /-ˈdɔks/ *Adj.* (*Rel.*) heterodox

**Heterodoxie** /-dɔˈksi:/ *die*; ~, ~**n** (*Rel.*) heterodoxy

**heterogen** /-ˈge:n/ *Adj.* heterogeneous

**Heterogenität** /-geniˈtɛ:t/ *die*; ~: heterogeneity

**heteronom** /-ˈno:m/ *Adj.* (*geh.*; *Zool.*) heteronomous

**Hetero·sexualität** *die*; ~: heterosexuality *no art.*

**hetero·sexuell** *Adj.* heterosexual

**Hethiter** /heˈti:tɐ/ *der*; ~**s**, ~, **Hethiterin** *die*; ~, ~**nen** Hittite

**Hetz** /hɛts/ *die*; ~, ~**en** (*österr. ugs.*) **das war eine ~!** that was a [good] laugh; **seine ~ haben** have some fun; **aus ~**: for fun

**Hetz·blatt** *das* (*abwertend*) political smear-sheet

**Hetze** /ˈhɛtsə/ *die*; ~ Ⓐ (*große Hast*) [mad] rush; **in großer ~**: in a mad rush *or* hurry; **heute war eine fürchterliche ~**: today was one mad rush; Ⓑ (*abwertend: Aufhetzung*) smear campaign; (*gegen eine Minderheit*) hate campaign; **eine ~ betreiben** mount *or* run a smear/hate campaign; Ⓒ (*Jägerspr.*) ⇒ **Hetzjagd** A

**hetzen** ❶ *tr. V.* Ⓐ hunt; **ein Tier zu Tode ~**: hunt an animal to death; **die Hunde/die Polizei auf jmdn. ~**: set the dogs on [to] sb./get the police on to sb.; Ⓑ (*antreiben*) rush; hurry. ❷ *itr. V.* Ⓐ (*in großer Eile sein*) rush; **den ganzen Tag ~**: be in a rush all day long; Ⓑ *mit sein* (*hasten*) rush; hurry; (*rennen*) dash; race; Ⓒ (*abwertend: Hass entfachen*) stir up hatred; (*schmähen*) say malicious things; **gegen jmdn./etw. ~**: smear sb./agitate against sth.; **gegen eine Minderheit ~**: stir up hatred against a minority; **zum Krieg ~**: engage in warmongering; **bei jmdm. gegen jmdn. ~**: try to turn sb. against sb.

**Hetzer** *der*; ~**s**, ~: malicious agitator

**Hetzerei** *die*; ~, ~**en** Ⓐ (*Hast*) [mad] rush; Ⓑ (*ugs. abwertend: Aufwiegelei*) malicious agitation; Ⓒ (*ugs. abwertend: hetzerische Handlung/hetzerisches Wort*) inflammatory act/word

**Hetzerin** *die*; ~, ~**nen** ⇒ **Hetzer**

**hetzerisch** *Adj.* inflammatory

**Hetz-:** ~**hund** *der* hound; hunting dog; ~**jagd** *die* Ⓐ (*Jagdw.*) hunting (*with hounds*); (*einzelne Jagd*) hunt (*with hounds*); Ⓑ (*Hast*) [mad] rush; ~**kampagne** *die* (*abwertend*) smear campaign; (*gegen eine Minderheit*) hate campaign; ~**rede** *die* (*abwertend*) inflammatory speech

**Heu** /hɔy/ *das*; ~**[e]s** Ⓐ hay; ~ **machen** make hay; Ⓑ (*ugs.: Geld*) dough (*coll.*); **der hat vielleicht ~**: he's rolling in money *or* it (*coll.*); ⇒ *auch* **Geld** A

**Heu-:** ~**blumen** *Pl.*: *mixture of seeds, flowers, and grasses sieved from hay and used for medical purposes*; ~**boden** *der* hayloft

**Heuchelei** *die*; ~, ~**en** (*abwertend*) Ⓐ (*Verstellung*) hypocrisy; Ⓑ (*Äußerung*) piece of hypocrisy; hypocritical remark

**heucheln** /ˈhɔyçl̩n/ ❶ *itr. V.* be a hypocrite. ❷ *tr. V.* feign ‹joy, sympathy, etc.›

**Heuchler** *der*; ~**s**, ~, **Heuchlerin** *die*; ~, ~**nen** hypocrite

**heuchlerisch** ❶ *Adj.* Ⓐ (*unaufrichtig*) hypocritical; Ⓑ (*geheuchelt*) feigned ‹interest, sympathy, etc.›. ❷ *adv.* hypocritically

**heuen** *itr. V.* (*landsch.*) make hay

**heuer** /ˈhɔyɐ/ *Adv.* (*südd.*, *österr.*, *schweiz.*) this year

**Heuer** *die*; ~, ~**n** (*Seemannsspr.*) Ⓐ (*Lohn*) pay; wages *pl.*; Ⓑ (*Anstellung*) **auf einem Schiff [als Funker] ~ nehmen** join a ship [as wireless operator]; **auf einem Frachter ~ nehmen** ship on board a freighter; **eine ~ bekommen** get hired

**Heu·ernte** *die* Ⓐ hay harvest; haymaking; Ⓑ (*Ertrag*) hay crop

**Heuer·vertrag** *der* (*Seemannsspr.*) contract of employment

**Heu-:** ~**fieber** *das* ⇒ ~**schnupfen**; ~**forke** *die* (*nordd.*), ~**gabel** *die* hay fork; ~**haufen** *der* haystack; hayrick; ⇒ *auch* **Stecknadel**

**Heul·boje** *die* Ⓐ (*Seew.*) whistling buoy; Ⓑ (*ugs. abwertend: Sänger*) caterwauler

**heulen** /ˈhɔylən/ *itr. V.* Ⓐ ‹wolf, dog, jackal, etc.› howl; (*fig.*) ‹wind, gale› howl; ‹storm› roar; Ⓑ ‹siren, buoy, etc.› wail; Ⓒ (*ugs.: weinen*) howl; bawl; **vor Wut/Schmerz/Freude ~**: howl and weep with rage/pain/howl with delight; **das ist zum Heulen** (*ugs.*) it's enough to make you weep; **Heulen und Zähneklappern** *od.* **Zähneknirschen** wailing and gnashing of teeth

**Heuler** *der*; ~**s**, ~ Ⓐ (*ugs.: Heulton*) whine; Ⓑ (*Feuerwerkskörper*) wailing banshee; Ⓒ (*salopp: tolle Sache*) **das ist wirklich ein ~**: it's really great *or* fantastic (*coll.*); **das ist [ja] der letzte ~!** (*iron.*) it's bloody awful! (*Brit. sl.*); Ⓓ (*ugs.: Seehund*) seal

**Heulerei** *die*; ~, ~**en** (*abwertend*) Ⓐ (*einer Sirene, Boje*) wailing; Ⓑ (*ugs.: heftiges Weinen*) howling; bawling

**Heulsuse** /ˈhɔylzu:zə/ *die*; ~, ~**n** (*ugs. abwertend*) cry-baby

**Heu-:** ~**monat** *der*, ~**mond** *der* (*veralt.*) July; ~**pferd** *das* grasshopper; ~**reiter** *der* (*österr.*) ⇒ ~**reuter**

**heureka** /ˈhɔyreka/ *Interj.* (*geh.*) eureka

**Heu·reuter** *der*; ~**s**, ~ (*südd.*) drying rack for hay

**heurig** /ˈhɔyrɪç/ *Adj.* (*südd.*, *österr.*, *schweiz.*) this year's ‹harvest, crop, etc.›; new ‹potatoes, wine›; **der ~e Sommer** this summer

**Heurige** *der*; *adj. Dekl.* (*bes. österr.*) Ⓐ (*Wein*) new wine; **sie saßen beim ~n** they sat drinking the new wine; Ⓑ (*Weinlokal*) inn with new wine on tap

**Heuristik** /hɔyˈrɪstɪk/ *die*; ~: heuristics *sing.*

**heuristisch** *Adj.* heuristic

**Heu-:** ~**schnupfen** *der* ▶ 474 hay fever; ~**schober** *der* (*südd.*, *österr.*) haystack; hayrick; ~**schrecke** *die* grasshopper; (*in Afrika, Asien*) locust; grasshopper; ~**stadel** *der* (*südd.*, *österr.*, *schweiz.*) [hay] barn

**heut** /hɔyt/ (*ugs.*) ⇒ **heute**

**heute** /ˈhɔytə/ *Adv.* ▶ 833 today; ~ **früh** early this morning; ~ **Morgen/Abend** this morning/evening; ~ **Mittag** [at] midday today; ~ **Nacht** tonight; (*letzte Nacht*) last night; ~ **in einer Woche** a week [from] today; today week; ~ **vor einer Woche** a week ago today; **seit ~**: from today; **ab ~**, **von ~ an** from today [on]; **bis ~**: until today; **bis ~ nicht** (*erst ~*) not until today; (*überhaupt noch nicht*) not to this day; (*bis jetzt noch nicht*) not as yet; **für ~**: for today; **die Zeitung von ~**: today's paper; **das Brot ist von ~**: it is today's bread; **das kann sich ~ oder morgen schon ändern** (*ugs.*) that can change at any time; **lieber ~ als morgen** (*ugs.*) the sooner, the better; **von ~ auf morgen** from one day to the next; **von ~ auf morgen sterben** die suddenly; **das geht nicht von ~ auf morgen** it can't be done at such short notice; **das Heute** the present; today; **der Bauernhof/die Frau von ~**: the farm/woman of today

**heutig** *Adj.* Ⓐ (*von diesem Tag*) today's; **die ~e Post/Zeitung/Vorstellung** today's post/newspaper/performance; **der ~e Tag/am ~en Tage** today; **am ~en Abend** this evening; **bis zum ~en Tag** until the present day *or* today; Ⓑ (*gegenwärtig*) today's; of today *postpos.*; **die ~e Jugend/Generation** today's youth/generation; the youth/generation of today; **der ~e Stand der Forschung** the present state of research; **in der ~en Zeit** today; nowadays

**heut·zu·tage** *Adv.* nowadays

**Heu-:** ~**wagen** *der* hay cart; ~**wender** *der*; ~~**s**, ~~ (*Landw.*) tedder; tedding machine

**Hexagon** /hɛksaˈgo:n/ *das*; ~**s**, ~**e** (*Math.*) hexagon

**Hexa·gramm** /hɛksa-/ *das* hexagram

**Hexameter** /hɛˈksa:metɐ/ *der*; ~**s**, ~ (*Verslehre*) hexameter

**Hexe** /ˈhɛksə/ *die*; ~, ~**n** Ⓐ witch; Ⓑ (*abwertend*) **diese kleine ~**: this little minx

**hexen** ❶ *itr. V.* work magic; **ich kann doch nicht ~** (*ugs.*) I'm not a magician (*coll.*). ❷ *tr. V.* conjure up

**Hexen-:** ~**einmaleins** *das* magic formula; ~**haus** *das* witch's cottage; ~**jagd** *die* (*auch fig.*) witch-hunt; ~**kessel** *der*: **ein [wahrer] ~kessel sein** be [absolute] bedlam; **das Fußballstadion glich einem ~kessel** there was pandemonium *or* bedlam in the football ground; ~**meister** *der* sorcerer; ~**prozess**, *~**prozeß** *der* (*hist.*) witch trial; ~**ring** *der* Ⓐ (*von Pilzen*) fairy ring; Ⓑ (*Jägerspr.*) *circular run trodden by roedeer in the mating season*; ~**sabbat** *der* Ⓐ (*Zusammenkunft der ~*) witches' sabbath; Ⓑ (*wüstes Treiben*) orgy; ~**schuss**, *~**schuß** *der* lumbago *no indef. art.*; ~**verbrennung** *die* (*hist.*) burning of a witch/of

h

witches; **~verfolgung** *die* (*hist.*) witch-hunt
**Hexer** *der;* **~s, ~:** sorcerer
**Hexerei** *die;* **~, ~en** sorcery; witchcraft; (*von Kunststücken usw.*) magic; **das ist doch keine ~:** there's no magic about it
**Hexode** /hɛ'kso:də/ *die;* **~, ~n** (*Elektrot.*) hexode
**HGB** *Abk.* **Handelsgesetzbuch**
**hick** /hɪk/ *Interj.* (*ugs.*) hic
**Hickhack** /'hɪkhak/ *das od. der;* **~s, ~s** (*ugs.*) squabbling; bickering
**hie** /hi:/ *Adv.: in* **~ und da** (*stellenweise*) here and there; (*von Zeit zu Zeit*) now and then; from time to time; **~ ..., da ...** on the one hand ..., on the other [hand] ...
**hieb** /hi:p/ *1. u. 3. Pers. Sg. Prät. v.* **hauen**
**Hieb** *der;* **~[e]s, ~e** Ⓐ (*Schlag*) blow; (*mit der Peitsche*) lash; (*im Fechten*) cut; (*fig.*) dig (**gegen** at); **jmdm. einen ~ mit der Faust/einem Beil versetzen** punch sb./strike sb. with an axe; Ⓑ *Pl.* (*ugs.: Prügel*) hiding *sing.;* beating *sing.;* walloping *sing.* (*coll.*); **~e bekommen/kriegen** get a hiding *or* beating *or* (*coll.*) walloping; **es gibt/setzt ~e!** you'll get a hiding *or* beating *or* (*coll.*) walloping
**hieb·fest** *Adj.: in* **hieb- und stichfest** watertight; cast-iron
**Hieb·waffe** *die* cutting weapon
**hielt** /hi:lt/ *1. u. 3. Pers. Sg. Prät. v.* **halten**
**hienieden** /hi:'ni:dn̩/ *Adv.* (*bes. österr., sonst veralt.*) here below; here in this world [below]
**hier** /hi:ɐ̯/ *Adv.* Ⓐ (*an diesem Ort*) here; **~ sein/bleiben** be/stay here; **jmdn./etw. ~ behalten/lassen** keep/leave sb./sth. here; **[von] ~ oben/unten** [from] up/down here; **~ vorn** here in front; **~ draußen/drinnen** out/in here; **~ entlang** along here; **von ~ [aus]** from here; **wo ist ~ die nächste Tankstelle?** where is the nearest petrol station (*Brit.*) *or* (*Amer.*) gas station around here?; **er ist nicht von ~:** he's not from this area *or* around here; **das Buch ~:** this book [here]; **~ spricht Hans Schulze** this is Hans Schulze [speaking]; **~ und da** *od.* **dort** (*an manchen Stellen*) here and there; (*manchmal*) [every] now and then; **~ und jetzt** *od.* **heute** (*geh.*) here and now; **das Hier und Jetzt** *od.* **Heute** (*geh.*) the here and now; Ⓑ (*zu diesem Zeitpunkt*) now; **von ~ an** from now on; Ⓒ (*in diesem Zusammenhang, Punkt*) here; **was gibt es ~ zu lachen?** what's funny [about this]?
**hier-:** *Bei den aus* **hier** *und einer Präposition gebildeten Adverbien* (**hieran, hierauf, hierbei** *usw.*) *werden im Folgenden* this, these *oder* here *zur Übersetzung verwendet* (hold on to this; on here; among these; about this). *Dies ist im Allgemeinen die angemessene Form der Übersetzung. Wenn der Bestandteil* **hier-** *weniger stark betont ist, kann man* this *oder* here *durch* it *ersetzen* (hold on to it; on it; about it). *Beispiele:* **er suchte einen starken Ast und lehnte die Leiter hieran** he looked for a strong branch and leaned the ladder against it; **sie ging zum Schuppen, um ihr Fahrrad hierhinter zu stellen** she went to the shed to put her bicycle behind it. *Ähnlich:* **hierunter befanden sich auch einige Deutsche** there were some Germans among them.
**hieran** /'hi:'ran/ *Adv.* Ⓐ (*an dieser/diese Stelle*) here; **sich ~ festhalten** hold on to this; Ⓑ (*fig.*) **im Anschluss ~:** immediately after this; **~ wird deutlich, dass ...** this shows clearly that ...; ⇒ *auch* **hier-**
**Hierarchie** /hi̯erar'çi:/ *die;* **~, ~n** hierarchy
**hierarchisch** ❶ *Adj.* hierarchical. ❷ *adv.* hierarchically
**hierauf** /'hi:'rauf/ *Adv.* Ⓐ (*auf dieser/diese Stelle*) on here; Ⓑ (*darauf*) on this; **wir werden ~ zurückkommen** we'll come back to this; Ⓒ (*danach*) after that; then; Ⓓ (*infolgedessen*) whereupon; ⇒ *auch* **hier-**
**hierauf·hin** *Adv.* hereupon
**hieraus** /'hi:'raus/ *Adv.* Ⓐ (*aus dem eben Erwähnten*) out of *or* from here; Ⓑ (*aus dieser Tatsache, Quelle*) from this; Ⓒ (*aus diesem Material*) out of this; ⇒ *auch* **hier-**
***hier|behalten** ⇒ **hier** A
**hier·bei** *Adv.* Ⓐ (*bei dieser Gelegenheit*) **Diese Übung ist sehr schwierig. Man kann sich ~ leicht verletzen.** This exercise is very difficult. You can easily injure yourself doing it; **Ich habe ihn gestern getroffen. Hierbei habe ich gleich ...** I met him yesterday, and straightaway I ...; Ⓑ (*bei der erwähnten Sache*) here; ⇒ *auch* **hier-**
***hier|bleiben** ⇒ **hier** A
**hier·durch** *Adv.* Ⓐ (*hier hindurch*) through here; Ⓑ (*aufgrund dieser Sache*) because of this; as a result of this; Ⓒ ⇒ **hiermit**; ⇒ *auch* **hier-**
**hierein** /'hi:rain/ *Adv.* in here; ⇒ *auch* **hier-**
**hier·für** *Adv.* for this; **ich habe kein Interesse ~:** I have no interest in this; ⇒ *auch* **hier-**
**hier·gegen** *Adv.* Ⓐ (*gegen die erwähnte Sache*) against this; Ⓑ (*gegen diese Stelle*) against here; Ⓒ (*im Gegensatz hierzu*) in *or* by comparison with this; compared with this; ⇒ *auch* **hier-**
**hier·her** *Adv.* here; **jmdn. ~ bemühen** trouble sb. to come here; **sich ~ bemühen** take the trouble to come here; **darf ich Sie ~ bitten?** would you come here please?; **wie bist du ~ gekommen?** how did you get here?; **komm mal ~!** come here!; **ich gehe bis ~ und nicht weiter** I'm going this far and no further; **bis ~ und nicht weiter** (*als Warnung*) so far and no further; **das gehört nicht ~** (*fig.*) that is not relevant [here]
**hierher|bemühen** *usw.* ⇒ **hierher**
**hier·herum** *Adv.* Ⓐ (*an dieser Stelle herum*) round here; (*in diese Richtung*) round this way; Ⓑ (*ugs.: hier irgendwo*) around here
**hierher-:** **~|wagen** *refl. V.* dare to come here; **~|ziehen** ❶ *unr. tr. V.* **etw. ~ziehen** pull sth. here; ❷ *unr. itr. V.; mit sein* (*umziehen*) move here
**hier·hin** *Adv.* here; **sie blickte bald ~, bald dorthin** she looked this way and that; **bis ~:** up to here *or* this point
**hier·hinab** *Adv.* down here
**hier·hinauf** *Adv.* up here
**hier·hinaus** *Adv.* Ⓐ (*an dieser Stelle*) out here; Ⓑ (*aus diesem Raum*) out of here
**hier·hinein** *Adv.* in here
**hier·hinter** *Adv.* behind here; ⇒ *auch* **hier-**
**hier·hinunter** *Adv.* Ⓐ (*unter diesen Gegenstand*) under here; Ⓑ (*an dieser Stelle*) down here
**hierin** /'hi:'rɪn/ *Adv.* Ⓐ (*in diesem Gegenstand*) in here; Ⓑ (*in dieser Angelegenheit*) in this; ⇒ *auch* **hier-**
***hier|lassen** ⇒ **hier** A
**hier·mit** *Adv.* with this/these; **~ ist der Fall erledigt** that puts an end to the matter; **~ erkläre ich, dass ...** (*Amtsspr.*) I hereby declare that ...; **~ wird bestätigt/bescheinigt, dass ...** (*Amtsspr.*) this is to confirm/certify that ...; ⇒ *auch* **hier-**
**hier·nach** *Adv.* Ⓐ (*einer Sache entsprechend*) in accordance with this/these; Ⓑ (*demnach*) according to this/these; Ⓒ (*anschließend*) after that; ⇒ *auch* **hier-**
**hier·neben** *Adv.* beside this; next to this; ⇒ *auch* **hier-**
**Hieroglyphe** /hi̯ero'gly:fə/ *die;* **~, ~n** hieroglyph; **~n** hieroglyphics
**hier·orts** *Adv.* here
***hier|sein** ⇒ **hier** A
**hierüber** /'hi:'ry:bɐ/ *Adv.* Ⓐ (*über dem Erwähnten*) above here; Ⓑ (*über das Erwähnte*) over here; Ⓒ (*das Erwähnte betreffend*) about this/these; Ⓓ (*geh.: währenddessen*) **er war ~ eingeschlafen** he had fallen asleep while doing so; ⇒ *auch* **hier-**
**hierum** /'hi:'rʊm/ *Adv.* about this; (*um ... herum*) round here; **~ geht es gar nicht** that's not the point; it's not a question of that; ⇒ *auch* **hier-**
**hierunter** /'hi:'rʊntɐ/ *Adv.* Ⓐ (*unter diese[r] Stelle*) under here; Ⓑ (*unter der erwähnten Sache*) **~ leiden** suffer from this; **etw. ~ verstehen** *od.* **sich** (*Dat.*) **etw. ~ vorstellen** understand sth. by this; Ⓒ (*unter die genannte/der genannten Gruppe*) among these; ⇒ *auch* **hier-**
**hier·von** *Adv.* Ⓐ (*von dieser Stelle*) from here; Ⓑ (*von dieser Sache*) of this; **~ zeugen** bear witness to this; Ⓒ (*dadurch*) because of this; Ⓓ (*aus dieser Menge*) of this/these; Ⓔ (*aus diesem Material*) out of this; ⇒ *auch* **hier-**
**hier·vor** *Adv.* Ⓐ (*vor dieser/diese Stelle*) in front of this *or* here; Ⓑ (*vor der erwähnten Sache*) **Respekt ~ haben** have respect for this; **Angst ~ haben** be afraid of this; ⇒ *auch* **hier-**
**hier·zu** *Adv.* Ⓐ (*zu dieser Sache*) with this; **vgl. ~:** cf.; Ⓑ (*zu dieser Gruppe*) **~ gehört/gehören ...** this includes/these include; Ⓒ (*zu diesem Zweck*) **ich kann dir ~ nur raten** I can only recommend you to do this/buy this/go *etc.;* **ich wünsche dir ~ viel Erfolg** I wish you every success with this; **~ reicht mein Geld nicht** I haven't got enough money for that; Ⓓ (*hinsichtlich dieser Sache*) about this; ⇒ *auch* **hier-**
**hierzu·lande** *Adv.* (*in diesem Land*) [here] in this country; [here] in these parts; (*in dieser Gegend*) [here] in these parts
**hiesig** /'hi:zɪç/ *Adj.* local; **die ~e Gegend** this locality; **meine ~en Verwandten** my relatives here
**hieß** /hi:s/ *1. u. 3. Pers. Sg. Prät. v.* **heißen**
**hieven** /'hi:vn̩/ *tr. V.* heave
**Hi-Fi-Anlage** /'haifi-/ *die* (*Rundf.*) hi-fi system
**high** /haɪ/ *Adj.* (*ugs.*) high (*coll.*)
**Highlife** /'hailaif/ *das;* **~[s]** (*ugs.*) high life; **bei uns ist heute ~:** we're living it up today; **~ machen** live it up
**High Society** /hai sə'saɪətɪ/ *die;* **~ ~:** high society; **zur ~ ~ gehören** be a member of high society
**Hightech-, High-Tech-** /'hai'tɛk-/ *in Zus.* high-tech
**hihi** /hi'hi:/, **hihihi** /hihi'hi:/ *Interj.* hehe[-he]
**Hilfe** /'hɪlfə/ *die;* **~, ~n** Ⓐ help; (*für Notleidende*) aid; relief; **wirtschaftliche/finanzielle ~:** economic aid/financial assistance; **jmdm. ~ leisten** help sb.; **mit ~** (+ *Gen.*) with the help *or* aid of; **ohne fremde ~:** unaided; without help *or* assistance; **jmdn. um ~ bitten/**(*geh.*) **ersuchen** ask sb. for help *or* assistance/request sb.'s help *or* assistance; **sein ~ suchender Blick ging zum Fenster** he looked towards the window, seeking help; **sich ~ suchend umschauen** look round for help; **sich ~ suchend an jmdn. wenden** turn to sb. for help; **um ~ rufen** shout for help; **jmdn. zu ~ rufen** call on sb. for help; **jmdm. zu ~ kommen/eilen** come/hurry to sb.'s aid *or* assistance; **zu ~!** help!; **jmds. Gedächtnis zu ~ kommen** (*fig.*) refresh sb.'s memory [for him/her]; **etw. zu ~ nehmen** use sth.; make use of sth.; **jmdm. eine große ~ sein** be a great help to sb.; **jmdm. ~n geben** give sb. some help; **einem Pferd ~n geben** give a horse aids; **erste ~:** first aid; Ⓑ (*Hilfskraft*) help; (*im Geschäft*) assistant
**hilfe-, Hilfe-:** **~leistung** *die* help; assistance; **finanzielle ~leistung** financial aid *or* assistance; **unterlassene ~leistung** (*Rechtsspr.*) failure to render assistance in an emergency; **~ruf** *der* cry for help; (*Notsignal*) distress signal; **~stellung** *die* (*Turnen*) Ⓐ **jmdm. ~stellung geben** act as spotter for sb.; Ⓑ (*Person*) spotter; ***~suchend** ⇒ **Hilfe** A
**hilf-, Hilf-:** **~los** ❶ *Adj.* Ⓐ helpless; Ⓑ (*unbeholfen*) awkward; ❷ *adv.* Ⓐ helplessly; Ⓑ (*unbeholfen*) awkwardly; **~losigkeit** *die;* **~ ~** Ⓐ helplessness; Ⓑ (*Unbeholfenheit*) awkwardness; **~reich** (*geh.*) ❶ *Adj.* helpful; ❷ *adv.* **jmdm. ~reich zur Seite stehen** lend support to sb.; stand by sb.
**hilfs-, Hilfs-:** **~aktion** *die* relief programme; **~arbeiter** *der,* **~arbeiterin** *die* labourer; (*in einer Fabrik*) unskilled worker; **~bedürftig** *Adj.* Ⓐ (*schwach*) in need of help

*old spelling (see note on page 1707)

*postpos.;* Ⓑ *(Not leidend)* in need *postpos.;* needy; **~bedürftigkeit** *die* need; neediness; **~bereit** *Adj.* helpful; **~bereitschaft** *die* helpfulness; readiness *or* willingness to help; **~dienst** *der* Ⓐ *(Dienst zu Hilfszwecken)* community work; Ⓑ *(Organisation)* emergency service; *(bei Katastrophen)* [emergency] relief service; *(für Autofahrer)* [emergency] breakdown service; **~fonds** *der* aid *or* relief fund; **~geistliche** *der/die (ev. u. kath. Kirche)* curate; **~gelder** *Pl.* aid money *sing.;* **~konstruktion** *die (Geom.)* auxiliary construction; **~kraft** *die* assistant; **~lehrer** *der,* **~lehrerin** *die* assistant teacher; **~maßnahme** *die* aid *or* relief measure; **~mittel** *das* Ⓐ *(Mittel zur Erleichterung)* aid; Ⓑ *Pl. (finanzielle Mittel)* [financial] aid *sing.; (materielle Mittel)* aid *sing.;* supplies; **~motor** *der* auxiliary engine; **ein Fahrrad mit ~motor** a motor-assisted bicycle; **~organisation** *die* aid *or* relief organization; **~personal** *das* auxiliary staff; **~polizist** *der* reserve policeman; **~polizistin** *die* reserve policewoman; **~programm** *das* aid *or* relief programme; **~quelle** *die* Ⓐ *(Material)* source; Ⓑ *(finanziell)* source of [financial] aid; **~schule** *die (veralt., noch ugs.)* special school; **~schüler** *der (veralt., noch ugs.)* pupil at a special school; **~schul·lehrer** *der,* **~schul·lehrerin** *die (veralt., noch ugs.)* teacher at a special school; **~schwester** *die* nursing auxiliary; auxiliary nurse; **~sheriff** *der* deputy sheriff; **~truppe** *die (Milit.)* reserve unit; **~verb** *das (Sprachw.)* auxiliary [verb]; **~willig** *Adj.* helpful; willing to help *postpos.;* **~willige** *der/die; adj. Dekl.* Ⓐ person willing to help; **die ~willigen** the people willing to help; Ⓑ *(hist.) volunteer from German occupied territory serving in German army in Second World War;* **~wissenschaft** *die* ancillary science; **~zeitwort** *das* ⇒ **~verb**

**Himalaja** /hiˈma:laja/ *der;* **~[s] der/im ~:** the/in the Himalayas *pl.*

**Him·beere** /ˈhım-/ *die* raspberry

**Himbeer-: ~eis** *das* raspberry ice [cream]; **~marmelade** *die* raspberry jam; **~saft** *der* raspberry juice; **~strauch** *der* raspberry bush

**Himmel** /ˈhıml̩/ *der;* **~s, ~** Ⓐ sky; **hoch am ~ stehen** be high in the sky; **eher stürzt der ~ ein, als dass er dir Geld leiht** *(ugs.)* never in a million years will he lend you any money *(coll.)*; **unter freiem ~:** in the open [air]; outdoors; **~ und Erde** *(Kochk.) dish of puréed potato and apple with fried blood sausage and liver sausage;* **aus heiterem ~** *(ugs.)* out of the blue; **jmdn./etw. in den ~ heben** *(ugs.)* praise sb./sth. to the skies; **Fortschritte fallen nicht vom ~:** advances don't come overnight; Ⓑ *(Aufenthalt Gottes)* heaven; **in den ~ kommen** go to heaven; **im ~ sein** *(verhüll.)* be in heaven; **zum ~** *od.* **in den ~ auffahren,** *(geh.)* **gen ~ fahren** ascend into heaven; **Sohn des ~s** *(hist.: Titel des chinesischen Kaisers)* Son of Heaven; **~ und Hölle** *(Kinderspiel)* ≈ hopscotch; **jmdm. hängt der ~ voller Geigen** *(geh.)* sb. is walking on air; **~ und Hölle** *od.* **Erde in Bewegung setzen** move heaven and earth; **sie hat den ~ auf Erden** *(geh.)* life is heaven on earth for her; **jmdm. den ~ auf Erden versprechen** promise sb. the earth; **im sieb[en]ten ~ sein/sich [wie] im sieb[en]ten ~ fühlen** *(ugs.)* be in the seventh heaven; **etw. schreit zum ~:** sth. is scandalous *or* a scandal; **etw. stinkt zum ~** *(salopp)* sth. stinks to high heaven; Ⓒ *(verhüll.: Schicksal)* Heaven; **gerechter/gütiger/[ach] du lieber ~!** good Heavens!; Heavens above!; **dem ~ sei Dank** thank Heaven[s]; **das weiß der [liebe] ~** *od.* **das mag der liebe ~ wissen** Heaven [only] knows; **weiß der ~!** *(ugs.)* Heaven knows; **weiß der ~, wer .../wie .../wo .../wann ...** *(ugs.)* Heaven [only] knows who .../how .../where .../when ...; **um [des] ~s willen!** *(Ausruf des Schreckens)* good Heavens!; good God!; *(inständige Bitte)* for Heaven's sake; **~ noch [ein]mal!** for Heaven's *or* goodness' sake!; **~, Herrgott, Sakrament!** for Heaven's sake!; **~, Kreuz, Donnerwetter!** *(salopp)* damn and blast! *(sl.)*; **~, Arsch und Zwirn!** *(derb)* bloody hell! *(Brit. sl.)*; Ⓓ *(Baldachin)* canopy

**himmel-, Himmel-: ~an** *Adv. (dichter.)* heavenwards *(poet.)*; up towards the sky; **~angst** *Adj.: in* **mir ist/wird ~angst** I am scared to death; **~bett** *das* four-poster bed; **~blau** *Adj.* sky-blue; azure; clear blue ‹eyes›; **~donner·wetter** *Interj.: in* **~donnerwetter noch [ein]mal!** *(salopp)* hell's bells! *(coll.)*

**Himmel·fahrt** *die (Rel.)* Ⓐ *(Auffahrt in den Himmel)* ascent to heaven; **Christi/Mariä ~:** the Ascension of Christ/the Assumption of the Virgin Mary; Ⓑ *(Festtag)* **[Christi] ~:** Ascension Day *no art.*

**Himmelfahrts-: ~kommando** *das* Ⓐ *(Unternehmen)* suicide mission *or* operation; Ⓑ *(Personen)* suicide squad; **~nase** *die (ugs. scherzh.)* turned-up nose; **~tag** *der* Ascension Day *no art.*

**himmel-, Himmel-: ~herr·gott** *Interj.: in* **~herrgott noch [ein]mal!** *(salopp)* hell's bells! *(coll.)*; **~herr·gott·sakra** *Interj. (österr., südd. salopp)* bloody hell! *(Brit. sl.)*; **~hoch** ❶ *Adj.* soaring; towering; ❷ *adv.* ‹rise up etc.› high into the sky; **~hoch jauchzend, zu Tode betrübt** up one minute, down the next; on top of the world one minute, down in the dumps the next; **~hund** *der (derb)* unscrupulous bastard *(coll.)*; *(Draufgänger)* daredevil; **~reich** *das (christl. Rel.)* kingdom of heaven; **ein ~reich für ...** I'd give anything for ...; ⇒ *auch* **Mensch**[1] B

**Himmels-: ~achse** *die (Astron.)* celestial axis; **~äquator** *der (Astron.)* celestial equator; **~bahn** *die (dichter.)* path across the heavens

**himmel·schreiend** *Adj.* scandalous; outrageous; scandalous, appalling ‹conditions, disgrace›; arrant *attrib.* ‹nonsense›; **ihre Dummheit ist ~:** she is appallingly stupid; **eine ~e Ungerechtigkeit** an injustice that cries out to heaven

**Himmels-: ~erscheinung** *die* celestial phenomenon; **~fürst** *der (christl. Rel.)* King of heaven; **~gabe** *die (geh.)* gift from heaven; **~gegend** *die* ⇒ **~richtung**; **~gewölbe** *das* Ⓐ *(dichter.)* firmament; vault of heaven *or* the heavens; Ⓑ *(Astron.)* sky; **~globus** *der* celestial globe; **~karte** *die (Astron.)* star map; **~königin** *die (kath. Rel.)* Queen of heaven; **~körper** *der* celestial body; **~kugel** *die* celestial sphere; **~kunde** *die* astronomy; **~kuppel** *die* ⇒ **~gewölbe** A; **~labor** *das (Raumf., bes. DDR)* space lab[oratory]; **~macht** *die (geh.)* heavenly power; **~pforte** *die (dichter.)* gates *pl.* of heaven; Pearly Gates *(also joc.)*; **~pol** *der (Astron.)* celestial pole; **~richtung** *die* ▶ **400** point of the compass; cardinal point; **die vier ~richtungen** the four points of the compass; **aus allen ~richtungen** from all directions; **in alle ~richtungen verstreut sein** be scattered to all four corners of the earth; **von hier aus führen Wege in alle ~richtungen** from this point paths radiate in all directions; **~schlüssel** *der* cowslip; *(Waldschlüsselblume)* oxlip; **~sphäre** *die* celestial sphere; **~spion** *der (ugs.)* spy-in-the-sky satellite *(coll.)*; **~stürmer** *der,* **~stürmerin** *die (geh.)* unshakeable idealist; **~tor** *das,* **~tür** *die (dichter.)* gates *pl.* of heaven

**himmel·stürmend** *Adj. (geh.)* boundless ‹enthusiasm›; unbridled ‹feelings›; wildly ambitious ‹plan›

**Himmels·zelt** *das (dichter.)* firmament

**himmel-: ~wärts** *Adv. (geh.)* heavenwards; **~weit** ❶ *Adj.* enormous, vast ‹difference›; **zwischen uns besteht ein ~weiter Unterschied** there's a world of difference between us; ❷ *adv.* **~weit voneinander entfernt sein** be poles apart; **~weit von etw. entfernt sein** be nowhere near sth.

**himmlisch** ❶ *Adj.* Ⓐ *(den Himmel betreffend)* heavenly; **der ~e Vater** our Heavenly Father; **die ~en Heerscharen** the heavenly host[s]; Ⓑ *(göttlich)* divine; **eine ~e Fügung** divine providence; Ⓒ *(herrlich)* heavenly; divine; wonderful ‹weather, day, view›. ❷ *adv.* divinely; wonderfully, gloriously ‹comfortable, warm›

**hin** /hın/ *Adv.* Ⓐ *(räumlich)* **zur Straße ~ liegen** face the road; **nach rechts ~ verlaufen** ‹road› go off to the right; **nach Frankfurt ~:** in the direction of Frankfurt; **bis zu dieser Stelle ~:** [up] to this point; as far as here; **sich zu etw. ~ erstrecken** stretch as far as sth.; **zur Straße ~ sind es 500 m** *(landsch.)* it's 500 m to the road; **über die ganze Welt ~** *(veralt.)* all over the world; throughout the world; Ⓑ *(zeitlich)* **gegen Mittag ~:** towards midday; **zum Herbst ~:** towards the autumn; as autumn approaches/approached; **über einen Monat ~:** for a whole month; **durch viele Jahre ~:** for many years; Ⓒ *(in Verbindungen)* **nach außen ~:** outwardly; **auf meine Anweisung/meinen Rat ~:** on *or* in response to my instructions/advice; **auf seine Bitte/seinen Anruf/eine Annonce ~:** at his request/in response to his [telephone] call/an advertisement; **selbst/auch auf die Gefahr ~, einen Fehler zu begehen** even at the risk of making a mistake; **etw. auf eine spätere Erweiterung ~ planen** plan sth. with a view to future expansion; ⇒ *auch* **vor** 2; Ⓓ *(in Wortpaaren)* **~ und zurück** there and back; **einmal Köln ~ und zurück** a return [ticket] to Cologne; **Hin und zurück? — Nein, nur ~:** Return? — No, just a single; **~ und her** to and fro; back and forth; **~ und her beraten/reden** go backwards and forwards over the same old ground; **das Hin und Her** the toing and froing; **nach langem Hin und Her** after a great deal of argument; **das reicht/langt nicht ~ und nicht her** *(ugs.)* it's nowhere near enough; **Regen ~, Regen her** rain or no rain; **~ und wieder** [every] now and then; Ⓔ *(elliptisch)* **nichts wie ~!** what are we waiting for?; **~ zu ihm!** [hurry up,] to him!; **~ sein** *(ugs.: hingegangen, -gefahren sein)* have gone; Ⓕ **das ist noch lange ~:** that's not for a long time yet; **bis zu dem Termin ist es noch einige Zeit ~:** there's some time to go before the deadline; Ⓖ **von jmdm./etw. ganz ~ sein** *(ugs.: hingerissen sein)* be mad about sb./bowled over by sth.; Ⓗ **~ sein** *(ugs.: nicht mehr brauchbar sein)* have had it *(coll.)*; **das Auto ist ~** *(ugs.)* the car is a write-off; **er ist ~** *(salopp: tot)* he has snuffed it *or* has pegged out *(sl.)*; **wenn er richtig zuschlägt, bist du ~** *(salopp: tot)* if he really hits you you've had it *(coll.)*; Ⓘ **~ sein** *(ugs.: verloren sein)* be *or* have gone; **was ~ ist, ist ~:** what's done is done

**hinab** /hıˈnap/ *Adv.* down; **den Hang ~:** down the slope; **ins Tal ~:** down into the valley; **den Fluss ~:** downstream; down the river; **bis ~ zu** down to

**hinab-** (⇒ *auch* **hinunter-**)**: ~|blicken** *itr. V.* look down; **~|senken** ❶ *tr. V.* lower; sink ‹foundations›; ❷ *refl. V.* slope down; **~|steigen** *unr. itr. V.; mit sein* climb down; *(hinuntergehen)* go down; **~|ziehen** ❶ *unr. tr. V. (auch fig.)* **jmdn. ~ziehen** drag sb. down; ❷ *unr. itr. V.; mit sein (geh.)* move down

**hinan** /hıˈnan/ *Adv. (geh.)* ⇒ **hinauf**

**hin|arbeiten** *itr. V.* **auf etw.** *(Akk.)* **~:** work towards sth.; **auf eine Prüfung ~:** work for an examination; **auf einen Krieg ~:** work to bring about war

**hinauf** /hıˈnauf/ *Adv.* up; **den Hügel ~:** up the hill; **die Treppe ~:** up the stairs; upstairs; **bis ~ zu** up to

**hinauf-: ~|arbeiten** *refl. V.* ⇒ **hocharbeiten**; **~|begeben** *unr. refl. V. (geh.)* go up[stairs]; **~|begleiten** *tr. V.* **jmdn. ~begleiten** accompany sb. up[stairs]; **~|bemühen** ❶ *tr. V.* **jmdn. ~bemühen** trouble sb. to go up; ❷ *refl. V.* take the trouble to go up; **~|bitten** *unr. tr. V.* **jmdn. ~bitten** ask sb. to go up; **~|blicken** *itr. V.* look up; **~|bringen** *unr. tr. V.* **jmdn./etw. ~bringen** take sb./sth. up[stairs]; **~|fahren** ❶ *unr. itr. V.; mit sein* go up; *(im Auto)* drive up; *(mit einem Motorrad)* ride up; ❷ *unr. tr. V.* **jmdn. ~fahren** drive *or* take sb. up; **~|fallen** *unr. itr. V.;*

# Himmelsrichtungen

Die vier Himmelsrichtungen haben im Englischen nur die eine Form, die auch adjektivisch verwendet wird. (Es gibt andere Übersetzungen für die deutschen Adjektive *nördlich, südlich* usw.; s. unten):

| | |
|---|---|
| ***Nord, Norden, Nord-*** | north |
| ***Ost, Osten, Ost-*** | east |
| ***Süd, Süden, Süd-*** | south |
| ***West, Westen, West-*** | west |

Die weiteren, zusammengesetzten Bezeichnungen werden ähnlich wie im Deutschen gebildet:

| | |
|---|---|
| ***Nordost, Nordosten*** | north-east |
| ***Nordwest, Nordwesten*** | north-west |
| ***Südost, Südosten*** | south-east |
| ***Südwest, Südwesten*** | south-west |
| ***Nordnordost, Nordnordosten*** | north-north-east |
| ***Nordnordwest, Nordnordwesten*** | north-north-west |
| ***Südsüdost, Südsüdosten*** | south-south-east |
| ***Südsüdwest, Südsüdwesten*** | south-south-west |
| ***Ostnordost, Ostnordosten*** | east-north-east |
| ***Westnordwest, Westnordwesten*** | west-north-west |
| ***Ostsüdost, Ostsüdosten*** | east-south-east |
| ***Westsüdwest, Westsüdwesten*** | west-south-west |

## Richtung

***Der Wind kommt von Norden/Nordosten***
= The wind is from the north/north-east

***Wir fahren morgen nach Norden***
= We are going north tomorrow

***Die Nadel weist nach Norden***
= The needle points to the north

***der Zug nach Norden***
= the northbound train

***Das Schiff fährt nach Süden***
= The ship is southward bound

***Die Straße führt nach Südwesten***
= The road runs south-west/south-westwards

***Sie fuhren in Richtung Osten*** od. ***in östliche Richtung***
= They were travelling eastwards *od.* in an easterly direction

***Das Wohnzimmer geht nach Norden***
= The sitting room faces north

## Lage

***Sie wohnen im Südwesten***
= They live in the South-West

***im Süden Englands, in Südengland***
= in the South of England, in southern England

***Im Norden ballten sich Gewitterwolken zusammen***
= To the north storm clouds were gathering

***Sie stammt aus dem Nordosten***
= She comes from the North-East

***Es liegt ein paar Kilometer westlich***
= It's a few kilometres to the west

***Es liegt weiter östlich***
= It's further east

***30 Kilometer südlich von Passau***
= 30 kilometres [to the] south of Passau

***etwas westlich der Insel***
= a little to the west of the island

## Adjektive

*Nord-, Süd-, Ost-, West-* bei geographischen Namen werden durch **North, South, East, West** übersetzt, solange es sich um ein ziemlich genau umgrenztes Gebiet handelt, also:

***Nordamerika/Südamerika***
= North America/South America

***Westafrika/Ostafrika***
= West Africa/East Africa

***Nordkorea/Südkorea***
= North Korea/South Korea

***Westberlin/Ostberlin***
= West Berlin/East Berlin

Aber:

***Norditalien/Süditalien***
= Northern/Southern Italy,

da es sich hier nicht um ein genau umgrenztes Gebiet handelt. Man kann auch sagen 'the North/South of Italy'; vor allem *Südfrankreich* = the South of France. Allerdings:

***die Südstaaten***
= the southern States

***die Westmächte***
= the Western Powers

***Ostdeutschland/Westdeutschland***
= East *od.* Eastern Germany/West *od.* Western Germany

(*hierbei bezieht sich die jeweils erste Bezeichnung hauptsächlich auf die ehemalige DDR bzw. die alte BRD*)

Man beachte ferner:

***die Westküste***
= the West Coast

***die Südseite***
= the south side; (*eines Hauses*) the south front

***die Eigernordwand***
= the north face of the Eiger

Aber:

***die Westfront/Ostfront***
= the Western/Eastern Front

Da sie im Deutschen schon weniger spezifisch sind, liegt es nahe, die Adjektive *nördlich, südlich, westlich, östlich* mit **northern, southern, western, eastern** zu übersetzen, etwa in:

***das südliche Afrika***
= southern Africa (im Gegensatz zu *Südafrika* = South Africa)

Sofern die Adjektive eine politische Bedeutung haben, werden sie groß geschrieben:

***westliche Journalisten***
= Western journalists

***die westlichen Länder***
= the Western countries

Bei Winden (und Richtungen) hingegen verwendet man die Formen **northerly, southerly, westerly, easterly:**

***nördliche Winde***
= northerly winds, northerlies (im Gegensatz zu *der Nordwind* = the north wind)

***Winde aus östlicher Richtung***
= winds from an easterly direction, easterly winds

Für den Superlativ kann im Englischen auch eine mit den Adjektiven **northern, southern** usw. und dem Suffix **-most** gebildete Form stehen:

***der östlichste Punkt***
= the easternmost point, the most easterly point

*mit sein* ⇒ Treppe A; **~|führen** ❶ *itr. V.* lead up; ❷ *tr. V.* **jmdn. ~führen** show sb. up; **~|gehen** *unr. itr. V.; mit sein* Ⓐ (*nach oben gehen*) go up; **die Treppe ~gehen** go up the stairs *or* upstairs; **auf 1000 Meter ~gehen** ‹aircraft, pilot› climb to 1,000 metres; Ⓑ (*nach oben führen*) lead up; **es geht steil ~:** the road/path climbs steeply; Ⓒ (*ugs.: steigen*) ‹prices, taxes, etc.› go up; rise; Ⓓ **mit dem Preis/der Miete ~gehen** (*ugs.*) put the price/rent up; **~|gelangen** *itr. V.; mit sein* [manage to] get up; **auf etw.** (*Akk.*) **~gelangen** [manage to] get up sth.; **~|helfen** *unr. itr. V.* **jmdm. [die Treppe] ~helfen** help sb. up [the stairs]; **~|klettern** *itr. V.; mit sein* climb up; **[auf] den Baum ~klettern** climb up the tree; **~|kommen** *unr. itr. V.; mit sein* Ⓐ (*nach oben kommen*) come up; Ⓑ (*nach oben kommen können*) [manage

*old spelling (see note on page 1707)

to] get up; ~|**lassen** *unr. tr. V.* **jmdn. ~lassen** allow sb. to go up; let sb. go up; ~|**laufen** *unr. itr. V.; mit sein* run up; **die Treppe ~laufen** run up the stairs; ~|**reichen** ❶ *tr. V.* hand *or* pass up; **jmdm. etw. ~reichen** hand *or* pass sth. up to sb.; ❷ *itr. V.* **bis zu etw. ~reichen** reach up to sth.; ~|**schauen** *itr. V. (südd.)* look up; ~|**schicken** *tr. V.* send up; ~|**schnellen** *itr. V.; mit sein* shoot up; ~|**sehen** *unr. itr. V.* look up; ~|**setzen** *tr. V.* [A] *(erhöhen)* raise; increase; put up; **die Preise ~setzen** increase *or* raise prices; [B] *(nach oben setzen)* **etw. auf etw.** *(Dat.)* **~setzen** put sth. up on sth.; ~|**steigen** *unr. itr. V.; mit sein* climb up; (*~gehen*) go up; ~|**tragen** *unr. tr. V.* carry *or* take up; ~|**werfen** *unr. tr. V.* **etw. ~werfen** throw sth. up (**auf** + *Akk.* on to); ~|**winden** *unr. refl. V.* [A] **sich [an etw.** *(Dat.)***] ~winden** ‹plant› creep *or* climb up [sth.]; [B] *(nach oben verlaufen)* wind up; ~|**ziehen** ❶ *unr. tr. V.* pull up; ❷ *unr. itr. V.; mit sein* move up; ❸ *unr. refl. V. (sich erstrecken)* stretch up; ‹pain› spread up

**hinaus** /hɪˈnaus/ *Adv.* [A] *(räumlich)* out; ~ **[mit dir]!** out you go!; out with you!; **zum Fenster ~:** out of the window; **hier/dort ~:** this/that way out; **nach hinten/vorne ~ wohnen/liegen** live/be situated at the back/front; **durch die Tür ~:** out through the door; **über die Grenze ~:** beyond the frontier; [B] *(zeitlich)* **auf Jahre ~:** for years to come; **bis über die Achtzig ~:** well past *or* over eighty; well into one's eighties; [C] *(etw. überschreitend)* **über etw.** *(Akk.)* **~:** over and above *or* in addition to sth.; **über das Grab ~:** beyond the grave; [D] **über etw.** *(Akk.)* **~ sein** *(fig.)* be past *or* beyond sth.; ⇒ *auch* darüber

**hinaus-, Hinaus-:** ~|**befördern** *tr. V.* **jmdn. ~befördern** throw *or (coll.)* chuck sb. out; ~|**begeben** *unr. refl. V.* go out; ~|**begleiten** *tr. V.* **jmdn. ~begleiten** see sb. out; ~|**beugen** *refl. V.* lean out; **sich zum Fenster ~beugen** lean out of the window; ~|**bitten** *unr. tr. V.* **jmdn. ~bitten** ask sb. to go *or* step outside; ~|**blicken** *itr. V.* look out (**aus** of); ~|**bringen** *unr. tr. V.* [A] **jmdn./etw. ~bringen** take *or* see sb. out/take sth. out (**aus** of); [B] *(weiterbringen)* **es nie über den untersten Dienstgrad ~bringen** never make it *or* get beyond the lowest grade; ~|**bugsieren** *tr. V. (ugs.)* **jmdn. ~bugsieren** *(mit Geschick)* steer sb. out (**aus** of); (*~befördern*) hustle sb. out (**aus** of); ~|**drängen** ❶ *itr. V.; mit sein* push one's way out (**aus** of); ‹crowd› push its way out (**aus** of); ❷ *tr. V.* **jmdn. ~drängen** push sb. out (**aus** of); *(fig.)* push sb. out (**aus** of); oust sb. (**aus** from); ~|**dürfen** *unr. itr. V.* be allowed out (**aus** of); **darf ich bitte ~?** may I go out?; ~|**eilen** *itr. V.; mit sein* hurry out (**aus** of); ~|**ekeln** *tr. V. (ugs.)* **jmdn. ~ekeln** drive sb. out; ~|**fahren** ❶ *unr. itr. V.; mit sein* [A] **aus etw. ~fahren** *(mit dem Auto)* drive out of sth.; *(mit dem Zweirad)* ride out of sth.; ‹car, bus› go out of sth.; ‹train› pull out of sth.; **zum Flugplatz ~fahren** drive out to the airport; **aufs Meer ~fahren** head for the sea; [B] *(herauskommen)* shoot out (**aus** of); [C] *(weiterfahren)* **über etw.** *(Akk.)* **~fahren** go past sth.; ❷ *unr. tr. V.* **jmdn./etw. ~fahren** drive *or* take sb./take sth. out; ~|**fallen** *unr. itr. V.; mit sein* fall out (**aus** of); ‹light› come out (**aus** of); ~|**finden** *unr. itr. V.* find one's way out (**aus** of); **er wird alleine ~finden** he'll find his own way out; ~|**fliegen** ❶ *unr. itr. V.; mit sein* [A] fly out (**aus** of); [B] *(geworfen werden)* be thrown out (**aus** of); fly out; [C] *(ugs.: ~fallen)* fall out (**aus** of); [D] *(ugs.: ~geworfen werden)* be chucked out *(coll.)*; *(als Arbeitnehmer)* get the sack *(coll.)*; be fired *(coll.)*; *(als Mieter)* be thrown out *(coll.)*; ❷ *unr. tr. V.* fly out (**aus** of); ~|**führen** ❶ *tr. V.* [A] **jmdn. ~führen** show sb. out; [B] *(retten)* **die Partei aus der Krise ~führen** lead the party out of the crisis; **den Betrieb aus den roten Zahlen ~führen** get the business out of the red; [C] *(weiterführen)* **jmdn. über etw.** *(Akk.)* **~führen** take sb. beyond sth.; ❷ *itr. V.* [A] *(verlaufen)* lead out (**aus** of); [B] *(nach draußen gerichtet sein)* lead out; [C] *(weiter verlaufen, überschreiten)* **über etw.** *(Akk.)* **~führen** go beyond sth.; ~|**gehen** *unr. itr. V.; mit sein* [A] go out; **aus dem Zimmer ~gehen** go *or* walk out of *or* leave the room; [B] *(gerichtet sein)* **das Zimmer geht zum Garten/nach Westen ~:** the room looks out on to *or* faces the garden/faces west; **die Tür geht auf den Hof ~:** the door leads *or* opens into the yard; **die Schlafzimmer gehen nach hinten ~:** the bedrooms are at the back; [C] *(verlaufen)* lead; [D] *(überschreiten)* **über etw.** *(Akk.)* **~gehen** go beyond sth.; [E] *(gesendet werden)* go out; be sent out; [F] *(unpers.)* **wo geht es ~?** which is the way out?; **hier/da geht es ~:** this/that is the way out; ~|**gelangen** *itr. V.; mit sein* [A] *(nach draußen gelangen, auch fig.)* [manage to] get out (**aus** of); [B] *(weiter gelangen)* **über etw.** *(Akk.)* **~gelangen** progress *or* get beyond sth.; ~|**greifen** *unr. itr. V.* **über etw.** *(Akk.)* **~greifen** go beyond sth.; ~|**gucken** *itr. V. (ugs.)* ⇒ **~blicken**; ~|**halten** *unr. tr. V.* hold ‹lamp, flag, etc.› out; **den Kopf/die Hand [zum Fenster] ~halten** put *or* stick one's head/hand out [of the window]; ~|**hängen**[1] *unr. itr. V.* hang out (**aus** of); ~|**hängen**[2] *tr. V.* hang out (**aus** of); ~|**heben** *unr. tr. V.* [A] **jmdn./etw. ~heben** lift sb./sth. out (**aus** of); **etw. aus dem Bus ~heben** lift sth. down from the bus; [B] *(geh.: erheben)* **jmdn. über die anderen ~heben** raise sb. above the others; ~|**jagen** ❶ *tr. V.* drive *or* chase out; **jmdn. ~jagen** *(fig.: aus dem Haus)* drive *or* turn sb. out; ❷ *itr. V.; mit sein* rush *or* race out (**aus** of); ~|**katapultieren** *tr. V.* [A] *(mit dem Schleudersitz)* eject; [B] *(salopp: verdrängen)* **jmdn. ~katapultieren** push sb. out (**aus** of); ~|**kommen** *unr. itr. V.; mit sein* [A] come out (**aus** of); **ich bin schon seit zwei Tagen nicht mehr ~gekommen** I've not got *or* been out of the house for two days; [B] *(ein Gebiet verlassen)* **er ist nie aus dem Dorf/aus Europa ~gekommen** he has never been out of *or* outside his village/Europe; [C] *(ugs.: einen Ausweg finden)* get out (**aus** of); [D] **über etw.** *(Akk.)* **~kommen** *(auch fig.)* get beyond sth.; [E] ⇒ **~laufen** B; ~|**komplimentieren** *tr. V.* **jmdn. ~komplimentieren** show sb. the door; *(verabschieden)* usher sb. out [with a great show of courtesy]; ~|**lassen** *unr. tr. V.* **jmdn. ~lassen** let sb. out; ~|**laufen** *unr. itr. V.; mit sein* [A] run out (**aus** of); **zur Tür ~laufen** run out of the door; [B] *(als Ergebnis haben)* **auf etw.** *(Akk.)* **~laufen** lead to sth.; **das läuft auf dasselbe ~:** it comes to the same thing; ~|**lehnen** *refl. V.* lean out; **sich zum Fenster ~lehnen** lean out of the window; ~|**manövrieren** *tr. V.* **sich/jmdn./etw. aus etw. ~manövrieren** manoeuvre oneself/sb./sth. out of sth.; ~|**müssen** *unr. itr. V. (ugs.)* have to get out (**aus** of); ~|**nehmen** *unr. tr. V.* **jmdn./etw. ~nehmen** take sb./sth. out (**aus** of); **nimm den Mülleimer mit ~:** put *or* take the dustbin out when you go; ~|**posaunen** *tr. V. (ugs.)* broadcast; **~posaunen, dass ...** broadcast the fact that ...; ~|**ragen** *itr. V.* [A] *(vertikal)* rise up (**über** + *Akk.* above); *(horizontal)* jut out; project; [B] *(übertreffen)* **über seine Kollegen/die anderen Werke ~ragen** stand out from one's colleagues/the other works; ~|**reden** *refl. V. (südd., österr., schweiz.)* talk one's way out (**aus** of); ~|**reichen** ❶ *tr. V.* **etw. ~reichen** hand *or* pass sth. out (**aus** of); **etw. zum** *od.* **aus dem Fenster ~reichen** hand *or* pass sth. out through the window; ❷ *itr. V.* [A] *(bis nach draußen reichen)* reach *or* stretch (**bis zu** as far as); [B] *(weiter reichen)* **über etw.** *(Akk.)* **~reichen** go beyond sth.; ~|**rennen** *unr. itr. V.; mit sein* run out; **aus etw. ~rennen** run out of sth.; ~|**rücken** *tr. V.* [A] move out; [B] *(verschieben)* put off; postpone; ~|**schaffen** *tr. V.* **jmdn./etw. ~schaffen** get sb./sth. out (**aus** of); ~|**schauen** *itr. V. (südd.)* ⇒ **~blicken**; ~|**scheren** *refl. V.* **scher dich ~!** get out of here!; ~|**scheuchen** *tr. V.* chase out; ~|**schicken** *tr. V.* [A] **jmdn. ~schicken** send sb. out; [B] *(senden)* send out; ~|**schieben** ❶ *unr. tr. V.* [A] *(nach draußen schieben)* **jmdn./etw. ~schieben** push sb./sth. out (**aus** of); [B] *(aufschieben)* put off; postpone; **eine Entscheidung [um einen Tag] ~schieben** put off *or* postpone *or* defer a decision [by one day]; ❷ *unr. refl. V.* [A] *(sich nach draußen schieben)* push one's/its way out (**aus** of); [B] *(sich verschieben)* be put off *or* postponed; ~|**schießen** *unr. itr. V.* [A] **aus dem Auto/zum Fenster ~schießen** fire from the car/the window; [B] *mit sein (sich schnell ~bewegen)* shoot out (**aus** of); ‹water› rush out (**aus** of); [C] *(weiter bewegen)* **über etw.** *(Akk.)* **~schießen** shoot past sth.; **über das Ziel ~schießen** *(fig.)* go too far; ~|**schleichen** *unr. itr. V. mit sein; unr. refl. V.* creep *or* steal out (**aus** of); ~|**schmeißen** *unr. tr. V. (ugs.)* ⇒ **rausschmeißen**; ~|**schmuggeln** *tr. V.* smuggle out (**aus** of); ~|**schreien** ❶ *unr. itr. V.* shout out; ❷ *unr. tr. V. (geh.)* **seinen Hass/Zorn ~schreien** vent *or* give vent to one's hate/rage in a loud outburst; ~|**schwimmen** *unr. itr. V.; mit sein* ‹person› swim out; ‹object› float out; ~|**sehen** *unr. itr. V.* look out; **zum Fenster ~sehen** look out of the window; ***~|sein** ⇒ **hinaus**; ~|**setzen** ❶ *tr. V.* **etw. ~setzen** put sth. out[side]; ❷ *refl. V.* go and sit outside; ~|**stehlen** *unr. refl. V.* sneak *or* steal out (**aus** of); ~|**steigen** *unr itr. V.; mit sein* climb out (**aus** of); **zum Fenster ~steigen** climb out of the window; ~|**stellen** ❶ *tr. V.* [A] put out[side]; [B] *(Sport)* **einen Spieler ~stellen** send a player off; ❷ *refl. V.* go and stand outside; **~stellung** *die (Sport)* sending-off; ~|**strecken** *tr. V.* stick *or* put out (**aus** of); **den Arm/Kopf zum Fenster ~strecken** put *or* stick one's arm/head out of the window; ~|**strömen** *itr. V.; mit sein* pour out (**aus** of); ~|**stürzen** ❶ *itr. V.; mit sein* [A] *(~fallen)* fall (**aus** out of); **zum Fenster ~stürzen** fall out of the window; [B] *(~eilen)* rush *or* dash out (**aus** of); **zur Tür ~stürzen** rush *or* dash out of the door; ❷ *refl. V.* throw oneself out (**aus** of); ~|**tragen** *unr. tr. V.* [A] *(nach draußen tragen)* **jmdn./etw. ~tragen** carry sb./sth. out; [B] *(verbreiten)* **etw. in alle Welt ~tragen** spread sth. throughout the world; [C] *(weiter tragen)* **über etw.** *(Akk.)* **~getragen werden** be carried across sth.; **aufs Meer ~getragen werden** be carried out to sea; ~|**trauen** *refl. V.* venture out; dare to go out; ~|**treiben** ❶ *unr. tr. V.* drive out (**aus** of); **es treibt jmdn. in fremde Länder/die Welt ~:** sb. has an urge to travel to *or* see other countries/see the world; ❷ *unr. itr. V.; mit sein* drift out; ~|**treten** *unr. itr. V.; mit sein* step out (**aus** of); **ins Leben ~treten** go out into the world; ~|**trompeten** *tr. V.* ⇒ **~posaunen**; ~|**wachsen** *unr. itr. V.; mit sein* [A] *(größer werden)* **über etw.** *(Akk.)* **~wachsen** grow taller than *or* up above sth.; [B] *(~kommen)* **über etw.** *(Akk.)* **~wachsen** outgrow sth.; **über jmdn./sich ~wachsen** surpass sb./rise above oneself; ~|**wagen** *refl. V.* [A] venture out (**aus** of); **sich in die Dunkelheit ~wagen** dare [to] go out into the dark; [B] *(sich weiter wagen)* **sich über etw.** *(Akk.)* **~wagen** venture beyond *or* dare [to] go beyond sth.; ~|**weisen** ❶ *unr. tr. V.* **jmdn. ~weisen** order sb. out (**aus** of); ❷ *unr. itr. V.* **ein Symbol weist über sich ~** *(fig.)* a symbol implies something more than itself; ~|**werfen** *unr. tr. V.* [A] *(nach draußen werfen)* throw out (**aus** of); **etw. zur Tür ~werfen** throw sth. out of the door; [B] *(nach draußen richten)* **einen Blick ~werfen** take *or* have a look *or* glance outside; [C] *(ugs.: entfernen)* throw out; [D] *(ugs.: ausschließen, die Wohnung kündigen)* **jmdn. ~werfen** throw sb. out (**aus** of); *(ugs.: entlassen)* sack sb. *(coll.)*; ~|**wollen** *unr. itr. V. (ugs.)* want to get *or* go out (**aus** of); **[zu] hoch ~wollen** *(fig.)* aim [too] high; set one's sights [too] high; **worauf willst du ~?** *(fig.)* what are you getting *or* driving at?; **auf etwas Bestimmtes ~wollen** *(fig.)* have something particular in mind; **~wurf** *der (ugs.)* throwing out; *(eines Angestellten)* sacking *(coll.)*;

~|**ziehen** ❶ *unr. tr. V.* Ⓐ (*nach draußen ziehen*) **jmdn./etw. ~ziehen** pull *or* drag sb./sth. out (**aus** of); tow ‹ship› out; Ⓑ (*in die Ferne ziehen*) **das Fernweh zog ihn in die Welt ~:** his wanderlust drove him out into the world; Ⓒ (*hinziehen*) draw *or* drag out; prolong; protract; Ⓓ (*verzögern*) put off; delay; Ⓔ (*unpers.*) **es zog sie in die Natur ~:** she felt the urge to get out into the countryside; ❷ *unr. itr. V.; mit sein* Ⓐ (*umziehen*) move out; Ⓑ (*in die Ferne ziehen*) go out (**aus** of); ‹group, troops› move out (**aus** of); Ⓒ (*nach draußen dringen*) get out; ❸ *unr. refl. V.* Ⓐ (*sich erstrecken*) extend; Ⓑ (*sich hinziehen*) drag on; Ⓒ (*sich verzögern*) be delayed; ~|**zögern** ❶ *tr. V.* delay; put off; ❷ *refl. V.* be delayed; be put off

**hin-, Hin-:** ~|**bauen** *tr. V.* build; put up; ~|**begeben** *unr. refl. V.* **sich irgendwo ~begeben** go *or* proceed somewhere; **sich zu jmdm. ~begeben** go to see sb.; ~|**begleiten** *tr. V.* **jmdn. ~begleiten** accompany sb. [there]; ~|**bekommen** *unr. tr. V.* (*ugs.*) Ⓐ (*fertig bringen*) **das hast du gut ~bekommen** you made a good job of that; Ⓑ (*in Ordnung bringen*) **etw. ~bekommen** straighten sth. out; get sth. straightened out; put sth. right; ~|**bemühen** ❶ *tr. V.* **jmdn. ~bemühen** trouble sb. to go; ❷ *refl. V.* take the trouble to go; ~|**beordern** *tr. V.* **jmdn. ~beordern** order sb. [to go] there; ~|**bestellen** *tr. V.* **jmdn. ~bestellen** tell sb. to be there; ~|**biegen** *unr. tr. V.* (*ugs.*) **etw. ~biegen** sort sth. out; **wie hat er das bloß ~gebogen?** how did he manage *or* (*sl.*) wangle that?; **den werden wir schon ~biegen** we'll lick *or* knock him into shape (*coll.*); ~|**blättern** *tr. V.* (*ugs.*) fork *or* shell out (*coll.*), pay out ‹sum of money›; ~**blick** *der: in* **im** *od.* **in ~blick auf etw.** (*Akk.*) (*wegen*) in view of; (*~sichtlich*) with regard to; ~|**blicken** *itr. V.* look; **zu jmdm. ~blicken** look [across] at sb.; ~|**bringen** *unr. tr. V.* Ⓐ **jmdn./etw. ~bringen** take sb./sth. [there]; Ⓑ (*verbringen*) while away; (*müßig*) spend; Ⓒ (*ugs.: fertig bringen*) manage

**Hinde** /ˈhɪndə/ *die;* ~, ~**n** (*veralt.*) hind

**hin|denken** *unr. itr. V.* **wo denkst du hin?** (*ugs.*) whatever are you thinking of?; what an idea!

**hinderlich** *Adj.* **~ sein** get in the *or* sb.'s way; **ein ~er Verband/Mantel** a bandage/a coat that gets in the way *or* is restricting; **jmds. Karriere** (*Dat.*)/**für jmds. Karriere ~ sein** be an obstacle to sb.'s career; **jmdm.** *od.* **für jmdn. ~ sein** be a nuisance to sb.; **sich als ~ erweisen** prove to be a hindrance

**hindern** /ˈhɪndɐn/ *tr. V.* Ⓐ (*abhalten*) **jmdn. ~:** stop *or* prevent sb.; **jmdn. [daran] ~, etw. zu tun** prevent *or* stop sb. [from] doing sth.; **jmdn. am Sprechen ~:** prevent *or* stop sb. [from] speaking; **ich werde dich nicht ~** (*iron.*) I'm not stopping you; Ⓑ (*be~*) hinder, hamper ‹person›; impede, hamper, hinder ‹growth, progress, etc.›

**Hindernis** *das;* ~**ses,** ~**se** Ⓐ obstacle; **jmdm. ~se in den Weg legen** (*fig.*) put obstacles in sb.'s way; Ⓑ (*Leichtathletik, Geländeritt*) obstacle; (*Springreiten*) jump; obstacle; (*Pferderennen*) fence; Ⓒ (*Golf*) hazard

**Hindernis-:** ~**lauf** *der* (*Leichtathletik*) steeplechase; ~**rennen** *das* (*Pferdesport*) steeplechase

**Hinderung** *die;* ~, ~**en** hindrance

**Hinderungs·grund** *der:* **das ist kein ~ für mich** it does not prevent *or* stop me; **darin sehe ich keinen ~ für den Weiterbau** I do not see it as any reason why we should not continue with the construction

**hin|deuten** *itr. V.* Ⓐ **auf jmdn./etw.** *od.* **zu jmdm./etw. ~:** point to sb./sth.; Ⓑ (*aufmerksam machen*) **auf etw.** (*Akk.*) **~:** draw *or* call attention to sth.; point sth. out; **darauf ~, dass ...** draw *or* call attention to the fact that ...; point out that ...; Ⓒ (*anzeigen*) suggest; point to; **alles deutet darauf hin, dass ...** everything suggests that ...

*old spelling (see note on page 1707)

**Hindi** /ˈhɪndi/ *das;* ~ ▶ 696 Hindi

**Hindin** *die;* ~, ~**nen** (*veralt.*) hind

**hin|drängen** ❶ *tr. V.* **jmdn. zu etw. ~:** force sb. towards sth. ❷ *itr. V.; mit sein* **zu jmdm. ~:** push one's way towards sb. ❸ *refl. V.* **sich zu jmdm./etw. ~:** push [one's way] towards sb./sth.

**Hindu** /ˈhɪndu/ *der;* ~[**s**], ~[**s**] ▶ 553 Hindu

**Hinduismus** *der;* ~: Hinduism *no art.*

**hinduistisch** *Adj.* Hindu

**hin·durch** *Adv.* Ⓐ (*räumlich*) **durch den Wald ~:** through the wood; **mitten/quer durch etw. ~:** straight through sth.; Ⓑ (*zeitlich*) **das ganze Jahr ~:** throughout the year; **den ganzen Tag/die ganze Nacht ~:** all day/night [long]; throughout the day/night; all through the day/night; **die ganze Zeit ~:** all the time; **durch all die Schwierigkeiten ~** (*fig.*) through all the difficulties

**hindurch-:** ~|**finden** *unr. itr., refl. V.* [**sich**] **durch etw. ~finden** find one's way through sth.; ~|**gehen** *unr. itr. V.; mit sein* Ⓐ walk *or* go through; **durch etw. ~gehen** walk *or* go through sth.; (*fig.*) go through sth.; **unter der Brücke ~gehen** walk *or* go under the bridge; Ⓑ **durch etw. ~gehen** (*dringen*) go through sth.; (*verlaufen, auch fig.*) run through sth.; (*passen*) ‹person, vehicle› go *or* get through sth.; ‹object› go through sth.; ~|**müssen** *unr. itr. V.* **durch etw. ~müssen** have to go through sth.; ~|**sehen** *unr. itr. V.* Ⓐ [**durch etw.**] **~sehen** see through [sth.]; Ⓑ (*sichtbar sein*) peep through; ~|**ziehen** ❶ *unr. tr. V.* **etw. [durch etw.] ~ziehen** pull *or* draw sth. through [sth.]; ❷ *unr. itr. V.; mit sein* move through; ❸ *unr. refl. V.* **sich durch etw. ~ziehen** run through sth.

**hin-:** ~|**dürfen** *unr. itr. V.* (*ugs.*) be allowed to go (**zu** to); **dort dürft ihr nicht mehr ~:** you're not to go there any more; ~|**eilen** *itr. V.; mit sein* Ⓐ hurry (**zu** to); **alle eilten ~:** everyone hurried there; Ⓑ (*sich schnell bewegen*) ‹train etc.› speed (**über** + *Akk.* across); ‹person› rush (**über** + *Akk.* across)

**hinein** /hɪˈnain/ *Adv.* Ⓐ (*räumlich*) in; **~ mit euch!** in you go!; in with you!; **in etw.** (*Akk.*) **~:** into sth.; **nur ~!** go *or* walk right in!; Ⓑ (*zeitlich*) **bis in den Morgen/tief in die Nacht ~:** till morning/far into the night

**hinein-:** ~|**begeben** *unr. refl. V.* go in[side]; **sich in etw.** (*Akk.*) **~begeben** enter sth.; ~|**bekommen** *unr. tr. V.* (*ugs.*) **etw. [in etw.** (*Akk.*)**] ~bekommen** get sth. in[to sth.]; ~|**bemühen** ❶ *tr. V.* **jmdn. ~bemühen** trouble sb. to go in; ❷ *refl. V.* take the trouble to go in; ~|**bitten** *unr. tr. V.* **jmdn. ~bitten** ask *or* invite sb. in; ~|**blicken** *itr. V.* look in; **in etw.** (*Akk.*) **~blicken** look into sth.; ~|**bohren** ❶ *tr. V.* **Löcher in die Wand ~bohren** drill holes in the wall; **den Finger in den Kuchen ~bohren** stick *or* poke one's finger into the cake; ❷ *refl. V.* **sich in etw.** (*Akk.*) **~bohren** bore one's/its way into sth.; ~|**bringen** *unr. tr. V.* Ⓐ take in; **bringen Sie mir die Unterlagen ~:** bring me in the documents; **Ordnung in etw. ~bringen** (*fig.*) bring [some] order into sth.; **etw. in die Diskussion ~bringen** (*fig.*) introduce sth. into the discussion; **Schwung in etw.** (*Akk.*) **~bringen** put [some] life into sth.; liven sth. up; Ⓑ (*ugs.*) ⇒ **~bekommen;** ~|**denken** *unr. refl. V.* **sich in jmdn./in jmds. Lage ~denken** put oneself in sb.'s position; **sich in ein Problem ~denken** think one's way into a problem; ~|**drängen** ❶ *itr. V. mit sein; refl. V.* [**sich**] **in etw.** (*Akk.*) **~drängen** push one's way into sth.; [**sich**] **in den Bus ~drängen** push one's way on to the bus; ❷ *tr. V.* **jmdn. in etw.** (*Akk.*) **~drängen** push sb. into sth.; **jmdn. in eine Rolle ~drängen** (*fig.*) force sb. into a role; ~|**dürfen** *unr. itr. V.* be allowed in; **in etw.** (*Akk.*) **~dürfen** be allowed into sth.; ~|**fahren** ❶ *unr. itr. V.; mit sein* Ⓐ (*mit dem Auto*) drive in; (*mit dem Zweirad*) ride in; **in etw.** (*Akk.*) **~fahren** drive/ride into sth.; **der Zug fuhr [in den Bahnhof] ~:** the train pulled in[to the station]; Ⓑ (*ugs.*) **in ein anderes Auto ~fahren** run into another car; Ⓒ **in seine Kleider ~fahren** slip into one's clothes; ❷ *unr. tr. V.* Ⓐ **den Wagen in etw.** (*Akk.*) **~fahren** drive one's car into sth.; Ⓑ **jmdn. in die Stadt ~fahren** drive sb. into town; ~|**fallen** *unr. itr. V.; mit sein* fall in; **in etw.** (*Akk.*) **~fallen** fall into sth.; **sich in einen Sessel ~fallen lassen** drop into a chair; ~|**finden** *unr. refl. V.* **sich in etw.** (*Akk.*) **~finden** (*sich vertraut machen*) get used to sth.; (*sich abfinden*) come to terms with sth.; ~|**fliegen** ❶ *unr. itr. V.; mit sein* Ⓐ fly in; **in etw.** (*Akk.*) **~fliegen** fly into sth.; **zum Fenster ~fliegen** fly in through the window; Ⓑ (*geworfen werden*) **in etw.** (*Akk.*) **~fliegen** be thrown into sth.; ❷ *unr. tr. V.* fly in; **etw. in etw.** (*Akk.*) **~fliegen** fly sth. into sth.; ~|**fressen** ❶ *unr. tr. V.* **etw. in sich ~fressen** ‹animal, (*derb*) person› gobble sth. down *or* up, wolf sth. down; **seine Sorgen/seinen Ärger in sich ~fressen** (*fig.*) bottle up one's worries/anger; ❷ *unr. refl. V.* **sich in etw.** (*Akk.*) **~fressen** eat into sth.; ~**geboren** *Adj.* **in eine Zeit/Umwelt ~geboren** born into an age/environment; ~|**geheimnissen** *tr. V.* **etw. in etw.** (*Akk.*) **~geheimnissen** read sth. into sth.; ~|**gehen** *unr. itr. V.; mit sein* go in; **in etw.** (*Akk.*) **~gehen** go into sth.; **in den Eimer gehen 3 Liter ~:** the bucket holds three litres; ~|**geraten** *unr. itr. V.; mit sein* **in eine Schlägerei ~geraten** get into a fight; ~|**gießen** *unr. tr. V.* pour in; **etw. in etw.** (*Akk.*) **~gießen** pour sth. into sth.; ~|**grätschen** *itr. V.; mit sein* (*bes. Fußball*) [**in jmdn.**] **~grätschen** make a sliding tackle [on sb.]; ~|**gucken** *itr. V.* (*ugs.*) look in; **in etw.** (*Akk.*) **~gucken** look in[to] sth.; take a look in sth.; ~|**halten** ❶ *unr. tr. V.* **etw. in etw.** (*Akk.*) **~halten** put sth. into sth.; ❷ *unr. itr. V.* (*schießen*) **in die Menge ~halten** fire into the crowd; ~|**helfen** *unr. itr. V.* **jmdm. in den Mantel ~helfen** help sb. on with his/her coat; **jmdm. in den Bus ~helfen** help sb. on to the bus; ~|**interpretieren** *tr. V.* **etw. in etw.** (*Akk.*) **~interpretieren** read sth. into sth.; ~|**jagen** *tr. V.* drive *or* chase in; **jmdn./ein Tier in etw. ~jagen** drive *or* chase sb./an animal into sth.; ~|**knien** *refl. V.* (*ugs.*) **sich in etw.** (*Akk.*) **~knien** get one's teeth into sth.; ~|**kommen** *unr. itr. V.; mit sein* Ⓐ come in; **in etw.** (*Akk.*) **~kommen** come into sth.; Ⓑ (*gelangen, auch fig.*) get in; **in etw.** (*Akk.*) **~kommen** get into sth.; Ⓒ (*sich ~finden*) [**wieder**] **in eine Sprache/ein Fach ~kommen** get [back] into a language/subject; Ⓓ (*ugs.: hinzugefügt werden*) **in etw.** (*Akk.*) **~kommen** go into sth.; ~|**kriechen** *unr. itr. V.; mit sein* crawl in; **in etw.** (*Akk.*) **~kriechen** crawl into sth.; ⇒ *auch* **reinkriechen;** ~|**kriegen** *tr. V.* (*ugs.*) ⇒ **~bekommen;** ~|**lachen** *itr. V.* **in sich ~lachen** laugh to oneself; ~|**lassen** *unr. tr. V.* let *or* allow in; **jmdn. ins Zimmer ~lassen** let *or* allow sb. into the room; ~|**laufen** *unr. itr. V.; mit sein* Ⓐ run in; (*zu Fuß gehen*) walk in; **in etw.** (*Akk.*) **~laufen** run/walk into sth.; **in sein Verderben ~laufen** (*fig.*) be heading [straight] for disaster; **in ein Fahrzeug ~laufen** run under a vehicle; Ⓑ (*fließen*) **in etw.** (*Akk.*) **~laufen** run into sth.; ~|**legen** *tr. V.* Ⓐ **etw. [in etw.** (*Akk.*)**] ~legen** put sth. in[to sth.]; **seine ganze Liebe/sein ganzes Gefühl in etw.** (*Akk.*) **~legen** put all one's love/feeling into sth.; Ⓑ ⇒ **~interpretieren;** Ⓒ (*ugs.*) ⇒ **hereinlegen;** ~|**lesen** ❶ *unr. refl. V.* ⇒ **einlesen 1;** ❷ *unr. tr. V.* ⇒ **~interpretieren;** ~|**leuchten** *itr. V.* Ⓐ shine in; **in etw.** (*Akk.*) **~leuchten** shine into sth.; Ⓑ (*Licht ~werfen*) **mit einer Lampe in den Keller ~leuchten** shine a light into the cellar; Ⓒ (*fig.*) **in etw.** (*Akk.*) **~leuchten** throw light on sth.; ~|**manövrieren** *tr. V.* Ⓐ **etw. in etw.** (*Akk.*) **~manövrieren** manoeuvre sth. into sth.; Ⓑ (*in etw. bringen*) **jmdn./sich in eine verzwickte Lage ~manövrieren** get *or* put sb./oneself into a tricky situation; ~|**passen** *itr. V.* fit in; **in etw.** (*Akk.*) **~passen** fit into sth.; (*fig.*) fit in with sth.; ~|**pfuschen** *itr. V.* **jmdm. in seine Arbeit ~pfuschen** meddle *or* interfere in sb.'s work; ~|**platzen** *itr. V.; mit sein* (*ugs.*) burst in; **in etw.** (*Akk.*) **~platzen**

burst into sth.; **~|pressen** *tr. V.* Ⓐ (*durch Pressen erzeugen*) **etw. in etw.** (*Akk.*) **~pressen** stamp sth. into sth.; Ⓑ (*in etw. pressen*) **etw. in etw.** (*Akk.*) **~pressen** press sth. into sth.; **etw. in ein Schema ~pressen** (*fig.*) force sth. into a pattern; **~|projizieren** *tr. V.* **etw. in etw.** (*Akk.*) **~projizieren** project sth. into sth.; **~|pumpen** *tr. V.* Ⓐ pump in; **etw. in etw.** (*Akk.*) **~pumpen** pump sth. into sth.; Ⓑ (*fig. ugs.*) **Geld in etw./Drogen in jmdn. ~pumpen** pump money into sth./drugs into sb.; **~|ragen** *itr. V.* **in den Himmel ~ragen** rise up into the sky; **~|reden** *itr. V.* Ⓐ **ins Leere ~reden** talk to an empty hall/lecture theatre *etc.*; **in die Stille ~reden** break the silence with a remark/exclamation *etc.*; Ⓑ (*abwertend: sich einmischen*) **jmdm. in seine Angelegenheiten/Entscheidungen** *usw.* **~reden** meddle *or* interfere in sb.'s affairs/decisions *etc.*; **~|regnen** *itr. V.* (*unpers.*) **es regnet [ins Zimmer] ~:** the rain is coming in[to the room]; **es regnet bei uns ~:** the rain is coming in through our roof; **~|reichen** ❶ *tr. V.* **etw. [zum Fenster] ~reichen** hand *or* pass sth. in [through the window]; ❷ *itr. V.* Ⓐ (*lang genug sein*) **in etw.** (*Akk.*) **~reichen** reach into sth.; Ⓑ (*sich erstrecken*) **in etw.** (*Akk.*) **~reichen** extend into sth.; **~|reißen** *unr. tr. V.* **jmdn. in etw.** (*Akk.*) **~reißen** (*auch fig.*) drag sb. into sth.; **~|reiten** ❶ *unr. itr. V.*; *mit sein* ride in; **in etw.** (*Akk.*) **~reiten** ride into sth.; ❷ *unr. tr. V.* (*ugs.*) ⇒ **reinreiten**; **~|rennen** *unr. itr. V.*; *mit sein* (*ugs.*) run in; race in; **in etw.** (*Akk.*) **~rennen** run *or* race into sth.; **in sein Verderben ~rennen** (*fig.*) be heading [straight] for disaster; **~|riechen** *unr. itr. V.* (*ugs.*) **in eine Arbeit/eine Firma ~riechen** get a taste of a job/a firm; **~|rufen** ❶ *unr. tr. V.* **jmdn./etw. ~rufen** call sb./sth. in; ❷ *unr. itr. V.* **in etw.** (*Akk.*) **~rufen** call into sth.; **~|schaffen** *tr. V.* **jmdn./etw. [in etw.** (*Akk.*)**] ~schaffen** get sb./sth. in[to sth.]; **~|schauen** *itr. V.* Ⓐ (*bes. südd., österr.*) ⇒ **~sehen**; Ⓑ (*bes. südd., österr.: kurz besuchen*) **bei jmdm. ~schauen** look in on sb.; **~|schießen** *unr. itr. V.* Ⓐ **in etw.** (*Akk.*) **~schießen** fire into sth.; **in die Menge ~schießen** fire into the crowd; Ⓑ *mit sein* (*sich schnell ~bewegen*) ‹person, car› shoot in; ‹water› rush in; **in etw.** (*Akk.*) **~schießen** shoot/rush into sth.; **~|schlagen** *unr. tr. V.* **einen Nagel/Pfahl [in etw.** (*Akk.*)**] ~schlagen** knock *or* drive a nail/stake in[to sth.]; **ein Loch in etw.** (*Akk.*) **~schlagen** knock *or* cut a hole in sth.; **~|schleichen** ❶ *unr. itr. V.*; *mit sein* **[in etw.** (*Akk.*)**] ~schleichen** creep *or* steal in[to sth.]; ❷ *unr. refl. V.* **sich [in etw.** (*Akk.*)**] ~schleichen** creep *or* steal in[to sth.]; (*fig.*) ‹error› creep in[to sth.]; **~|schlingen** *unr. tr. V.* **etw. in sich ~schlingen** devour sth.; **~|schlittern** *itr. V.*; *mit sein* (*ugs.*) **in eine Situation** *usw.* **~schlittern** stumble into a situation *etc.*; **~|schlüpfen** *itr. V.*; *mit sein* slip in; **ins Zimmer/in seinen Mantel ~schlüpfen** slip into the room/one's coat; **~|schmuggeln** *tr. V.* smuggle in; **jmdn./etw. [in etw.** (*Akk.*)**] ~schmuggeln** smuggle sb./sth. in[to sth.]; **~|schneien** *itr. V.* Ⓐ (*unpers.*) **es schneit [in die Hütte] ~:** the snow is coming in[to the hut]; Ⓑ *mit sein* ⇒ **hereinschneien** A; **~|schreiben** *unr. tr. V.* write in; **etw. in etw.** (*Akk.*) **~schreiben** write sth. in sth.; **~|schütten** *tr. V.* pour in; **etw. in etw.** (*Akk.*) **~schütten** pour sth. into sth.; **etw. in sich ~schütten** (*fig.*) knock sth. back (*sl.*); pour sth. down one's throat; **~|sehen** *unr. itr. V.* look in; **in etw.** (*Akk.*) **~sehen** look into sth.; **in jmds. Zeitung ~sehen** have a look at sb.'s paper; **~|setzen** ❶ *tr. V.* (*auch ugs.: zuweisen*) **jmdn./etw. [in etw.** (*Akk.*)**] ~setzen** put sb./sth. in[to sth.]; ❷ *refl. V.* Ⓐ **sich in etw.** (*Akk.*) **~setzen** sit down in sth.; Ⓑ (*festsetzen*) **sich in die Ecken/die Teppiche ~setzen** ‹dust, dirt› get right into the corners/the carpet; **~|spazieren** *itr. V.*; *mit sein* walk *or* stroll in; **nur ~spaziert!** walk right [on] in!; **~|spielen** ❶ *itr. V.* **da spielen viele Dinge/Faktoren ~:** there are a lot of contributory factors; ❷ *tr. V.* (*Sport*) **den Ball [in den Strafraum** *usw.*] **~spielen** play the ball in[to the penalty area *etc.*]; **~|sprechen** *unr. itr. V.* **in etw.** (*Akk.*) **~sprechen** speak into sth.; **~|stecken** *tr. V.* Ⓐ **etw. [in etw.** (*Akk.*)**] ~stecken** put sth. in[to sth.]; Ⓑ (*ugs.: in etw. bringen*) **etw. [in etw.** (*Akk.*)**] ~stecken** stick (*coll.*) *or* put sth. in sth.; Ⓒ **viel Geld in etw.** (*Akk.*) **~stecken** (*ugs.*) put *or* sink a lot of money into sth.; **viel Arbeit in etw.** (*Akk.*) **~stecken** (*ugs.*) put a lot of work into sth.; **~|steigern** *refl. V.* **sich in große Erregung/seine Ängste/seine Wut ~steigern** work oneself up into a state of great excitement/anxiety/into a rage; **~|stoßen** ❶ *unr. tr. V.* Ⓐ thrust in; **etw. in etw.** (*Akk.*) **~stoßen** thrust sth. into sth.; Ⓑ (*~bringen*) **jmdn. in etw.** (*Akk.*) **~stoßen** push sb. into sth.; (*fig.*) plunge sb. into sth.; ❷ *unr. itr. V.*; *mit sein* **in etw.** (*Akk.*) **~stoßen** (*vordringen*) push *or* thrust into sth.; (*~steuern*) drive *or* turn into sth.; **~|stürzen** ❶ *itr. V.*; *mit sein* Ⓐ (*~fallen*) **in etw.** (*Akk.*) **~stürzen** fall *or* plunge into sth.; Ⓑ (*nach innen eilen*) rush *or* burst in; **ins Zimmer ~stürzen** rush *or* burst into the room; ❷ *tr. V.* **jmdn. in etw.** (*Akk.*) **~stürzen** hurl sb. into sth.; ❸ *refl. V.* **sich in etw.** (*Akk.*) **~stürzen** throw oneself *or* plunge into sth.; **sich in die Arbeit ~stürzen** (*fig.*) throw oneself into one's work; **~|tappen** *itr. V.*; *mit sein* (*ugs.*) **in etw.** (*Akk.*) **~tappen** grope one's way into sth.; (*~geraten*) walk [right] into sth.; **~|tragen** *unr. tr. V.* Ⓐ carry in; **etw. in etw.** (*Akk.*) **~tragen** carry sth. into sth.; **Schmutz ins Haus ~tragen** bring dirt into the house; Ⓑ (*verbreiten*) **etw. in etw.** (*Akk.*) **~tragen** bring sth. into sth.; **Unruhe in einen Betrieb ~tragen** spread unrest in a firm; **~|treiben** *unr. tr. V.* Ⓐ **jmdn./etw. in etw.** (*Akk.*) **~treiben** drive sb./sth. into sth.; ‹tide› carry sb./sth. into sth.; Ⓑ (*verwickeln*) **jmdn. in etw.** (*Akk.*) **~treiben** force sb. into sth.; Ⓒ (*in etw. schlagen*) **etw. [in etw.** (*Akk.*)**] ~treiben** drive sth. in[to sth.]; **~|tun** *unr. tr. V.* Ⓐ (*ugs.: in etw. tun*) **etw. [in etw.** (*Akk.*)**] ~tun** put sth. in[to sth.]; Ⓑ (*vollführen*) **einen Blick [in etw.** (*Akk.*)**] ~tun** take a look in[to sth.]; **~|versetzen** *refl. V.* **sich in jmdn.** *od.* **jmds. Lage ~versetzen** put oneself in sb.'s position; **~|wachsen** *unr. itr. V.*; *mit sein* Ⓐ **in das Haus/das Fleisch ~wachsen** grow into the house/the *or* one's flesh; Ⓑ (*ugs.: ~passen*) **in ein Kleid** *usw.* **~wachsen** grow into a dress *etc.*; **in die Uniform ~wachsen** (*fig.*) come to identify with the *or* one's uniform; Ⓒ (*vertraut werden*) **in eine Aufgabe/Rolle ~wachsen** get to know a job/get into *or* inside a part; **~|wagen** *refl. V.* venture in; dare to go in; **sich in etw.** (*Akk.*) **~wagen** venture into sth.; dare to go into sth.; **~|werfen** *unr. tr. V.* Ⓐ **etw. [in etw.** (*Akk.*)**] ~werfen** throw sth. in[to sth.]; Ⓑ (*fallen lassen*) **einen Blick [in etw.** (*Akk.*)**] ~werfen** glance [at sth.]; **~|wollen** *unr. itr. V.* (*ugs.: ~gelangen wollen*) want to get *or* go in; **in etw.** (*Akk.*) **~wollen** want to go/get into sth.; **das will mir nicht in den Kopf ~:** I just *or* simply can't understand it; **~|ziehen** ❶ *unr. tr. V.* Ⓐ (*nach drinnen ziehen*) pull *or* draw in; **etw./jmdn. in etw.** (*Akk.*) **~ziehen** pull *or* draw sth./sb. into sth.; Ⓑ (*verwickeln*) **jmdn. in eine Angelegenheit/einen Streit/Skandal ~ziehen** drag sb. into an affair/a dispute/scandal; ❷ *unr. itr. V.*; *mit sein* Ⓐ march in; **in etw.** (*Akk.*) **~ziehen** march into sth.; Ⓑ (*nach innen ziehen*) ‹smoke, fumes, etc.› drift in; **in etw.** (*Akk.*) **~ziehen** drift into sth.; **~|zwängen** ❶ *tr. V.* **etw. [in etw.** (*Akk.*)**] ~zwängen** squeeze *or* force sth. in[to sth.]; ❷ *refl. V.* squeeze in; **sich in die Hose ~zwängen** squeeze [oneself] into one's trousers; **~|zwingen** *unr. tr. V.* **jmdn. [in etw.** (*Akk.*)**] ~zwingen** force sb. to go in[to sth.]; **jmdn. in ein Schema/eine Rolle ~zwingen** force sb. into a rigid pattern/a role

**hin-, Hin-:** **~|fahren** ❶ *unr. itr. V.*; *mit sein* Ⓐ (*an einen Ort fahren*) go there; (*mit einem Auto*) drive *or* go there; (*mit einem Fahrrad, Motorrad*) ride *or* go there; **wo ist er ~gefahren?** where has he gone?; Ⓑ (*streichen*) **mit der Hand/den Fingern über etw.** (*Akk.*) **~fahren** run one's hand/fingers over sth.; ❷ *unr. tr. V.* **jmdn. ~fahren** drive *or* take sb. there; **jmdn. zum Bahnhof ~fahren** drive *or* take sb. to the station; **~fahrt** *die* journey there; (*Seereise*) voyage out; **auf der ~fahrt** on the way *or* journey there/the voyage out; **~|fallen** *unr. itr. V.*; *mit sein* Ⓐ (*stürzen*) fall down *or* over; **lang ~fallen** fall flat [on one's face/back]; Ⓑ (*herunterfallen*) **jmdm. fällt etw. ~:** sb. drops sth.; **etw. ~fallen lassen** drop sth.; **~fällig** *Adj.* Ⓐ (*schwächlich*) infirm; frail; Ⓑ (*ungültig*) invalid; **~fälligkeit** *die* Ⓐ (*Schwäche*) infirmity; frailty; Ⓑ (*Ungültigkeit*) invalidity; **~|finden** *unr. itr. V.* find one's way there; **zu jmdm./zu einem Ort ~finden** find one's way to sb./a place; **~|fläzen**, **~|flegeln** *refl. V.* (*ugs. abwertend*) loll around *or* about; **~|fliegen** ❶ *unr. itr. V.*; *mit sein* Ⓐ fly there; **er fliegt heute ~:** he's flying [out] there today; **wo fliegt sie ~?** where is she flying to?; Ⓑ (*ugs.: fallen*) come a cropper (*coll.*); fall over; **mit dem Fahrrad ~fliegen** come a cropper on one's bicycle (*coll.*); fall off one's bicycle; ❷ *unr. tr. V.* **jmdn./etw. ~fliegen** fly sb./sth. [out] there; **~flug** *der* outward flight

**hin·fort** *Adv.* (*geh.*) henceforth; henceforward

**hin|führen** ❶ *tr. V.* Ⓐ **jmdn. ~:** lead *or* take sb. there; Ⓑ (*zu etw. bringen*) **jmdn. zu etw. ~:** lead sb. to sth. ❷ *itr. V.* **zu etw. ~:** lead to sth.; **wo soll das ~?** what will it lead to?

**hing** /hɪŋ/ *1. u. 3. Pers. Sg. Prät. v.* **hängen**

**Hin·gabe** *die;* ~ Ⓐ devotion; (*Eifer*) dedication; **etw. mit ~ tun** do sth. with dedication; **mit ~ tanzen** put one's whole soul into one's dancing; Ⓑ (*geh.: das Opfern*) **unter ~ des Lebens** at the cost of one's life

**hin-, Hin-:** **~gang** *der* (*geh.*) decease; demise; **~|geben** ❶ *unr. tr. V.* (*geh.*) give; sacrifice; **sein Leben ~geben** lay down *or* sacrifice one's life; ❷ *unr. refl. V.* Ⓐ **sich einer Illusion/einem Genuss ~geben** entertain an illusion/abandon oneself to a pleasure; Ⓑ (*verhüll.*) **sich einem Mann ~geben** give oneself to a man; **~gebend** *Adj.* devoted

**Hingebung** *die;* **~:** devotion

**hingebungs·voll** ❶ *Adj.* devoted. ❷ *adv.* devotedly; with devotion; ‹listen› raptly, with rapt attention; ‹dance, play› with abandon

**hin·gegen** *Konj., Adv.* (*jedoch*) however; (*andererseits*) on the other hand

**hin-:** **~gegossen** *Adj.* (*ugs. scherzh.*) **wie ~gegossen auf der Couch liegen/sitzen** have draped oneself over the couch; **~|gehen** *unr. itr. V.*; *mit sein* Ⓐ go [there]; **zu jmdm./etw. ~gehen** go to sb./sth.; **wo gehst du ~?** where are you going?; Ⓑ (*verstreichen*) ‹years, time› pass, go by; **darüber gingen Jahre ~:** it took years; Ⓒ (*~gleiten*) **sein Blick ging über die Landschaft ~:** he *or* his eyes scanned the landscape; Ⓓ (*tragbar sein*) pass; **diesmal mag das noch ~gehen** I'll/we'll *etc.* let it pass this time; **~|gehören** *itr. V.* (*ugs.*) go; belong; ‹person› belong; **wo gehört das ~?** where does this go *or* belong *or* (*coll.*) live?; **~|gelangen** *itr. V.*; *mit sein* get there; **zu jmdm./etw. ~gelangen** get to sb./sth.; **~|geraten** *unr. itr. V.*; *mit sein* get there; **wie sind wir dort ~geraten?** how did we get there?; **wo ist er/der Brief ~geraten?** where has he/the letter got to?; **~gerissen** ❶ *2. Part. v.* **~reißen**; ❷ *Adj.* carried away; spellbound; **~gerissen der Musik lauschen** listen spellbound to the music; **~|gleiten** *unr. itr. V.*; *mit sein* Ⓐ glide along; **die Hand über etw.** (*Akk.*) **~gleiten lassen** run one's hand over sth.; **den Blick über etw. ~gleiten lassen** (*fig.*) let one's gaze sweep over sth.; Ⓑ (*geh.: vergehen*) slip away; **~|halten** *unr. tr. V.* Ⓐ hold out; **jmdm. etw. ~halten** hold sth. out to sb.; Ⓑ (*warten lassen*) **jmdn. ~halten** put sb. off; keep sb. waiting; Ⓒ (*Milit.: aufhalten*) hold off

**Hin·halte-: ~politik** *die* policy of procrastination; **~taktik** *die* delaying tactics *pl.*

**hin-: ~|hängen** *tr. V.* (*ugs.*) hang up; **~|hauen** ❶ *unr. tr. V.* (A) (*salopp: aufgeben*) chuck in (*sl.*); **den ganzen Kram ~hauen** chuck the whole thing in (*sl.*); (B) (*salopp abwertend: flüchtig anfertigen*) knock off (*coll.*); dash off; (C) (*unpers. salopp*) **es hat mich ~gehauen** I came a cropper (*coll.*); (D) (*salopp: ~werfen*) chuck down (*coll.*); ❷ *unr. itr. V.* (A) (*ugs.: schlagen*) **[mit etw.] ~hauen** take a swipe [with sth.] (*coll.*); (B) *mit sein* (*~fallen*) fall [down] heavily; (C) (*salopp: gut gehen*) ‹plan› work [all right]; **es wird schon ~hauen** it'll work out *or* be all right *or* (*coll.*) OK; (D) (*salopp: richtig sein*) ‹calculation› be right; **so haut das nicht ~:** it's wrong as it stands; ❸ *unr. refl. V.* (*salopp*) lie down and have a kip (*coll.*); **~|hören** *itr. V.* listen

**Hinke·bein** /ˈhɪŋkə-/ *das* (*ugs.*) (A) stiff *or* (*coll.*) gammy leg; (B) (*jmd., der hinkt*) person with a limp *or* (*coll.*) a gammy leg

**Hinkel·stein** *der* menhir; standing stone

**hinken** /ˈhɪŋkn̩/ *itr. V.* (A) limp; walk with a limp; **auf** *od.* **mit dem rechten Bein ~:** have a limp in one's right leg; (B) *mit sein* (*~d gehen*) limp; hobble; (C) (*fig.*) ‹line› be clumsy *or* halting; ‹rhyme› be clumsy; ‹comparison› be poor *or* feeble

**hin-, Hin-: ~|knallen** (*ugs.*) ❶ *tr. V.* slam down; ❷ *itr. V.; mit sein* fall [down] heavily; come a cropper (*coll.*); **~|knien** *refl. V.* kneel [down]; **~|kommen** *unr. itr. V.; mit sein* (A) get there; **nach Madrid ~kommen** get to Madrid; **wie kommt man zu ihm ~?** how do you get to his place?; (B) (*an einen Ort gehören*) go; belong; **wo kommen die Gläser ~?** where do the glasses go *or* belong?; **wo ist meine Uhr ~gekommen?** where has my watch got to *or* gone?; **wo kommen** *od.* **kämen wir ~, wenn ...** (*fig.*) where would we be if ...; (C) (*ugs.: auskommen*) **mit etw. ~kommen** manage with sth.; (D) (*ugs.: in Ordnung kommen*) work out *or* turn out all right *or* (*coll.*) OK; (E) (*ugs.: stimmen*) be right; **~|kriegen** *tr. V.* (*ugs.*) (A) (*fertig bringen*) **das hat sie toll ~gekriegt** she made a great job of that (*coll.*); **so genau wie auf der Vorlage kriege ich das nicht ~:** I won't be able to get it as accurate as it is on the pattern; **das wird er schon ~kriegen** he'll manage it all right *or* (*coll.*) OK; (B) (*in Ordnung bringen*) fix ‹radio etc.›; **jmdn. wieder ~kriegen** put sb. right; **~kunft** *die:* **in ~kunft** (*österr.*) in future; **~|langen** *itr. V.* (A) (*ugs.: fassen*) **er langte ~ und steckte einige Uhren in seine Tasche** he reached over and stuck some watches in his pocket (*coll.*); (B) (*salopp: zuschlagen*) **[kräftig] ~langen** take a [hefty] swipe (*coll.*); (C) (*salopp: sich bedienen*) help oneself; **schön/ordentlich ~langen** help oneself in a big way (*coll.*); (D) (*ugs.: ausreichen*) be enough; (E) (*ugs.: auskommen*) manage; **~länglich** ❶ *Adj.* sufficient; (*angemessen*) adequate; ❷ *adv.* sufficiently; (*angemessen*) adequately; **etw. ist ~länglich bekannt** sth. is sufficiently well known; **~|lassen** *unr. tr. V.* (*ugs.*) **jmdn. ~lassen** allow sb. to go there; let sb. go there; **jmdn. zu etw. ~lassen** allow sb. to go to sth.; let sb. go to sth.; **~|laufen** *unr. itr. V.; mit sein* (A) (*an einen Ort laufen*) run there; **zu jmdm./zu einer Stelle ~laufen** run to sb./a place; (B) (*zu Fuß gehen*) walk [there]; (C) (*zu jmdm./etw. gehen*) **zum Anwalt/Arzt/Chef ~laufen** run to *or* rush off to the lawyer/doctor/boss; **~|legen** ❶ *tr. V.* (A) (*an eine Stelle legen*) put; **sie legte den Kindern frische Wäsche ~:** she put out clean underwear for the children; (B) (*weglegen*) put down; (C) (*zu Bett bringen*) **jmdn. ~legen** lay sb. down; (D) (*ugs.: bezahlen*) pay *or* (*coll.*) shell out; (E) (*salopp: ausführen*) **eine hervorragende Rede ~legen** do a brilliant speech; **eine gekonnte Übung auf dem Trampolin ~legen** turn in a splendid performance on the trampoline; ❷ *refl. V.* (A) lie down; **da legst du dich [lang] ~** (*ugs.*) you won't believe your ears; (B) (*sich schlafen legen*) lie down; **sich zeitig ~legen** have an early night; **sich zum Sterben ~legen** (*geh.*) lie down to die; (C) (*ugs.: ~fallen*) come a cropper (*coll.*); fall [down *or* over]; **~|leiten** *tr. V.* lead there; **etw. zu etw. ~leiten** lead sth. to sth.; **~|lenken** *tr. V.* (A) **etw. [zu etw.] ~lenken** steer sth. [to sth.]; **seine Schritte zum Bahnhof ~lenken** direct one's steps towards the station; (B) (*fig.*) steer ‹conversation› (**auf** + *Akk.* round to); direct ‹attention› (**auf** + *Akk.* towards); turn ‹gaze› (**auf** + *Akk.* towards); **~|machen** (*salopp*) ❶ *tr. V.* (A) put up ‹curtain, picture, fence, etc.›; put on ‹paint, oil, cream›; put in ‹comma etc.›; put ‹cross, ring, etc.›; make ‹dirty mark etc.›; (B) (*töten*) do in (*sl.*); rub out (*sl.*); bump off (*coll.*); ❷ *itr. V.* (A) (*seine Notdurft verrichten*) do one's/its business (*coll.*); (B) (*landsch.: sich beeilen*) hurry up; get a move on (*coll.*); **~|marschieren** *itr. V.; mit sein* march there; **~|metzeln, ~|morden** *tr. V.* (*geh.*) massacre; slaughter; butcher; **~nahme** *die;* **~~:** acceptance; **~|nehmen** *unr. tr. V.* (A) (*annehmen*) accept; take; put up with, swallow; accept ‹insult›; **etw. als gegeben ~nehmen** take sth. for granted; accept sth. as a fact; (B) (*ugs.: mitnehmen*) **kannst du das Buch mit ~nehmen** can you take the book with you?; **~|neigen** ❶ *tr. V.* incline; **den Kopf zu jmdm. ~neigen** incline *or* bend one's head towards sb.; ❷ *refl. V.* lean [over]; ❸ *itr. V.* **zu einer Auffassung** *usw.* **~neigen** incline to a point of view *etc.*

**hinnen** /ˈhɪnən/ *in* **von ~** (*veralt. geh.*) [from] hence; **von ~ scheiden** (*verhüll.*) depart this life; pass away *or* on

**hin-, Hin-: ~|passen** *itr. V.* (*ugs.*) (A) (*an eine Stelle passen*) fit *or* go in; (B) (*in die Umgebung passen*) fit in; go; **~|pfeffern** *tr. V.* (*ugs.*) (A) (*~werfen*) fling *or* slam down; (B) (*äußern*) rap out; **~|pflanzen** ❶ *tr. V.* plant; ❷ *refl. V.* (*ugs.*) **sich vor jmdn. ~pflanzen** plant oneself in front of sb.; **~|reichen** ❶ *tr. V.* hand; pass; **jmdm. etw. ~reichen** hand *or* pass sth. to sb.; ❷ *itr. V.* (A) (*erstrecken*) reach; **bis zu etw. ~reichen** reach to *or* as far as sth.; (B) (*ausreichen*) be enough *or* sufficient; (C) (*ugs.: auskommen*) manage; **mit etw. ~reichen** manage on sth.; **~reichend** ❶ *Adj.* sufficient; (*angemessen*) adequate; ❷ *adv.* sufficiently; (*angemessen*) adequately; **~reise** *die* journey there; outward journey; (*mit dem Schiff*) voyage out; outward voyage; **die ~reise nach Rom** the journey to Rome; **[die] Hin- und Rückreise** the journey there and back; **~|reisen** *itr. V.; mit sein* travel there; **~|reißen** *unr. tr. V.* (A) **jmdn. zu sich ~reißen** pull sb. to one; (B) (*begeistern*) enrapture; **das Publikum zu Beifallsstürmen ~reißen** elicit thunderous *or* rapturous applause from the audience; (C) (*verleiten*) **jmdn. zu etw. ~reißen** drive sb. to sth.; **sich ~reißen lassen** let oneself get *or* be carried away; **~reißend** ❶ *Adj.* enchanting ‹person, picture, view›; captivating ‹speaker, play›; ❷ *adv.* enchantingly; **~|richten** *tr. V.* execute; **~richtung** *die* execution

**Hinrichtungs-: ~kommando** *das* firing squad; **~stätte** *die* place of execution

**hin-, Hin-: ~|rücken** ❶ *tr. V.* **etw. ~rücken** move *or* push sth. over; ❷ *itr. V.; mit sein* move over; **~|sagen** *tr. V.* say without thinking; (*nur beiläufig sagen*) say casually; **das hat er nur so ~gesagt** he just said it without thinking; **~|schaffen** *unr. tr. V.* **etw. ~schaffen** get sth. there; **etw. zum Bahnhof ~schaffen** get sth. to the station; **~|schauen** *itr. V.* (*bes. südd., österr.*) ⇒ **~sehen; ~|scheiden** *unr. itr. V.; mit sein* (*geh. verhüll.*) pass away *or* over; **der ~geschiedene** the deceased *or* departed; **~|scheiden** *das;* **~~s** (*geh. verhüll.*) decease; demise; **~|scheißen** *unr. itr. V.* (*derb*) crap (*coarse*); **~|schicken** *tr. V.* send; **~|schieben** *unr. tr. V.* **jmdm. etw. ~schieben** push sth. over to sb.; **~schied** *der;* **~~[e]s, ~~e** (*schweiz.*) ⇒ **~scheiden; ~|schielen** *itr. V.* steal a glance/glances (**zu** at); **~|schlachten** *tr. V.* (*geh.*) massacre; slaughter; butcher; **~|schlagen** *unr. itr. V.* (A) (*auf eine Stelle schlagen*) strike; hit; (B) *mit sein* (*ugs.: fallen*) **[der Länge nach** *od.* **lang] ~schlagen** fall flat on one's face/back; **da schlag einer lang ~!** (*ugs.*) well I never (*coll.*); would you believe it! (*coll.*); **~|schleichen** *unr. itr. V. mit sein; unr. refl. V.* creep *or* steal over; **~|schleppen** ❶ *refl. V.* (A) (*mühsam gehen*) drag oneself along; **sich zu etw. ~schleppen** drag oneself to sth.; (B) (*sich ~ziehen*) drag on; ❷ *tr. V.* (A) (*an einen Ort schleppen*) **etw. ~schleppen** drag sth. there; **etw. zu etw. ~schleppen** drag sth. to sth.; (B) (*verzögern*) drag out; **~|schmeißen** *unr. tr. V.* (*salopp*) (A) (*werfen*) chuck down (*coll.*); (B) (*aufgeben*) chuck in (*coll.*); **~|schmelzen** *unr. itr. V.; mit sein* (A) ⇒ **zerschmelzen;** (B) (*ugs. scherzh.: vergehen*) swoon; **vor Rührung ~schmelzen** be overcome with emotion; **~|schmieren** *tr. V.* (*ugs.*) (*~schreiben*) scrawl; scribble; (*~malen*) daub; **~|schreiben** ❶ *unr. tr. V.* write down; ❷ *unr. itr. V.* (*an eine Firma o. Ä. schreiben*) write; **~|schwinden** *unr. V.* ⇒ **dahinschwinden; ~|sehen** *unr. itr. V.* look; **ich kann nicht ~sehen** I can't [bear to] look; **bei genauerem ~sehen** on closer inspection; ***~|sein** ⇒ **hin; ~|setzen** ❶ *tr. V.* (A) (*an eine Stelle setzen*) put; seat, put ‹person›; **das Kind ~setzen** sit the child/baby down; (B) (*absetzen*) put *or* set down; ❷ *refl. V.* (A) sit down; **setzen Sie sich doch ~!** do sit down!; **wo soll ich mich ~setzen?** where should I sit?; **sich gerade ~setzen** sit up straight; **sich ~setzen und etw. tun** (*fig.*) sit down and do sth.; get down to doing sth.; (B) (*ugs.: fallen*) land on one's backside; (C) (*salopp: überrascht sein*) **er wird sich ~setzen** he won't believe his ears; **~sicht** *die:* **in gewisser ~sicht** in a way/in some respect *or* ways; **in mancher ~sicht** in some respects *or* ways; **in jeder ~sicht** in every respect; **in finanzieller ~sicht** financially; **in ~sicht auf** (+ *Akk.*) with regard to; **~sichtlich** *Präp. mit Gen.* (*Amtsspr.*) with regard to; (*in Anbetracht*) in view of; **~|sinken** *unr. itr. V.; mit sein* (*geh.*) sink down; sink to the ground; **~|sollen** *unr. itr. V.* (*ugs.*) **wo sollen die Sachen ~?** where do these things go?; where do you want these things [to go]?; **wo soll ich mit den Büchern ~?** where should I put the books?; what should I do with the books?; **sie weiß nicht, wo sie ~soll** she doesn't know where to go; **~spiel** *das* (*Sport*) first leg; **~|starren** *itr. V.* stare (**zu, nach** at); **~|stellen** ❶ *tr. V.* (A) (*an eine Stelle stellen*) put; put up ‹building›; put, park ‹car›; (B) (*absetzen*) put down; (C) (*bezeichnen*) **etw. als falsch ~stellen** make sth. out to be *or* represent sth. as false; **jmdn. als Lügner ~stellen** make sb. out to be *or* represent sb. as a liar; **jmdn. als Vorbild ~stellen** hold sb. up as an example; **er hat die Sache so ~gestellt, als seien wir die Schuldigen** he made it look as though it was our fault; ❷ *refl. V.* (A) (*sich an eine Stelle stellen*) stand; ‹driver› park; **sich gerade ~stellen** stand up straight; **sich vor jmdn. ~stellen** stand in front of sb.; (B) (*sich bezeichnen*) **sich als unschuldig ~stellen** make out that one is innocent; **~|steuern** ❶ *tr. V.* steer; **das Boot zum Ufer ~steuern** steer the boat towards the bank; ❷ *itr. V.; mit sein* (A) **zu etw. ~steuern** make *or* head for sth.; (B) (*eine Absicht verfolgen*) **auf etw.** (*Akk.*) **~steuern** aim at sth.; **~|strecken** ❶ *tr. V.* (A) stretch out; hold out; **jmdm. die Hand ~strecken** hold out one's hand to sb.; (B) (*geh. veralt.: töten*) fell; slay (*liter.*); ❷ *refl. V.* (A) (*sich ausgestreckt ~legen*) stretch [oneself] out; lie down full length; (B) (*sich erstrecken*) extend, stretch (**bis an** + *Akk.* as far as); **~|strömen** *itr. V.; mit sein* (A) ‹river› flow; (B) ‹people› flock there; **zu etw. ~strömen** flock to sth.; **~|stürzen** *itr. V.; mit sein* (A) (*~fallen*) fall down [heavily]; (B) (*~eilen*) rush *or* dash there; **zum Ausgang ~stürzen** rush *or* dash towards the exit

**hintan-, Hintan-** /hɪntˈ|an-/: **~|setzen** *tr. V.* **etw. ~setzen** put sth. last; **Differenzen**

*old spelling (see note on page 1707)

**~setzen** put *or* set aside differences; **~setzung** *die;* **~~: nur unter ~setzung persönlicher Interessen** only by putting personal interests last; **~|stellen** *tr. V.* ⇒ **~setzen**

**hinten** /'hɪntn̩/ *Adv.* **A** *(am rückwärtigen Ende)* at the back; in *or* at the rear; **~ im Bus sitzen** sit in the back of the bus; **~ in die Straßenbahn einsteigen** get on at the back of the tram (*Brit.*) *or* (*Amer.*) streetcar; **ganz ~ im Garten/in der Garage/im Schrank** right at the back of the garden/the garage/the cupboard; **sich ~ anstellen** join the back of the queue (*Brit.*) *or* (*Amer.*) line; **nach ~ abgehen** move [off] towards the back; exit upstage (*Theatre*); **~ im Buch** at the back *or* end of the book; **weiter ~:** further back; (*in einem Buch*) further on; **von ~ anfangen** start from the end; **von ~ nach vorne** backwards; (*in einem Buch*) from back to front; (*Bewegung*) towards the front; **nach ~ gehen** go *or* walk to the back/into the room behind; **B** *(an/auf/von der Rückseite)* **die Adresse steht ~ auf dem Brief** the address is on the back of the envelope; **~ auf der Münze** on the back *or* reverse of the coin; **~ am Haus** at the back *or* rear of the house; **nach ~ hinaus liegen/gehen** be at the back *or* rear; **von ~ kommen/jmdn. von ~ erstechen** come from behind/stab sb. from behind; **von ~ sah sie jünger aus** she looked younger from the back; **jmdn. von ~ erkennen** recognize sb. from the back; **jmdm. ~ drauffahren** (*ugs.*) run into the back of sb.; **~ und vorn[e] nichts haben** (*salopp*) be as flat as an ironing board (*coll.*); **C** *(entfernt)* **die anderen sind ganz weit ~:** the others are a long way back *or* behind; **~ in Sibirien** far away in Siberia; **~ im Wald** in the depths of the forest; deep in the forest; **ganz weit ~ konnte man die Bergspitzen erkennen** far away in the distance you could make out the mountain peaks; **D** *(in Wendungen)* **jetzt heißt es Herr Meier ~, Herr Meier vorn** now it's Herr Meier this, and Herr Meier that; **~ und vorn[e] bedient werden** be waited on hand and foot; **das kann ~ und vorn[e] nicht stimmen** that cannot possibly be true; there is no way that can be true; **~ und vorn[e] betrogen werden** be cheated right, left and centre; **nicht [mehr] wissen, wo ~ und vorn[e] ist** (*ugs.*) not know whether one is coming or going; **~ nicht mehr hochkönnen** (*ugs.*) be in desperate straits; **jmdn. am liebsten von ~ sehen** (*ugs.*) be glad to see the back of sb.; **von ~ durch die Brust ins Auge** (*salopp scherzh.*) in a roundabout fashion *or* way

**hinten-: ~dran** *Adv.* (*ugs.*) at the back; **~dran einen Anhänger hängen** hitch a trailer on behind; **~drauf** *Adv.* (*ugs.*) on the back; **jmdm. eins** *od.* **ein paar ~drauf geben** (*ugs.*) smack sb.'s bottom; **~drein** *Adv.* ⇒ **hinterher**; **~heraus** /'----/ *Adv.* **~heraus liegen/wohnen** be/live at the back; **~herum** /'----/ *Adv.* (*ugs.*) **A** *(um die hintere Seite herum)* round the back; **B** *(am Rücken)* **mir ist ~herum kalt** my back's cold; **C** (*ugs.: heimlich*) **etw. ~herum erfahren** hear sth. indirectly; **Waren ~herum besorgen** get goods under the counter; **~nach** *Adv.* (*südd., österr.*) ⇒ **hinterher**

**hinten·über** *Adv.* backwards

**hintenüber-: ~|fallen** *unr. itr. V.; mit sein* fall [over] backwards; **~|kippen** *itr. V.; mit sein* tip [over] backwards; **~|stürzen** *itr. V.; mit sein* ⇒ **~fallen**

**hinter** /'hɪntɐ/ ❶ *Präp. mit Dat.* **A** behind; **~ dem Haus sein** be behind *or* at the back of the house; **~ jmdm. zurückbleiben** lag behind sb.; **eine große Strecke ~ sich haben** have put a good distance behind one; **~ der Mauer hervortreten** step out from behind the wall; **~ jmdm. stehen** (*fig.*) be behind sb.; back *or* support sb.; **~ etw. (Dat.) stehen** (*fig.*) support sth.; **jmdn. ~ sich haben** (*fig.*) have sb.'s backing; **sich ~ etw. verbergen** (*fig.*) ‹person› hide behind sth.; ‹danger› lie concealed behind sth.; ‹purpose› lie behind sth.; **B** *(nach)* after; **3 km ~ der Grenze** 3 km beyond the frontier; **die nächste Station ~ Mannheim** the next stop after Mannheim; **C** *(in der Rangfolge)* **~ jmdm. zurückstehen** lag behind sb.; **~ der Entwicklung/der Zeit zurückbleiben** lag behind in development/be behind in times; **er ist ~ unseren Erwartungen zurückgeblieben** he has fallen short of our expectations; **D** *(bewältigt)* **eine Prüfung/Aufgabe ~ sich haben** (*fig.*) have got an examination/a job over [and done] with; **viele Enttäuschungen/eine Krankheit ~ sich haben** have experienced many disappointments/have got over an illness; **wenn er das Studium ~ sich hat** when he's finished his studies.
❷ *Präp. mit Akk.* **A** behind; **~ das Haus gehen** go behind the house; **sich ~ jmdn./etw. stellen** (*fig.*) stand *or* get behind sb./support sth.; **B ~ jmdn. zurückfallen** fall behind sb.; **C etw. ~ sich bringen** get sth. over [and done] with; **D** *(zeitlich)* **~ etw. gehen/reichen** go back to before sth.; **E** (*fig.*) **~ ein Geheimnis/die Wahrheit/seine Geschichte kommen** find out a secret/get to the truth/get to the bottom of his story

**hinter...** *Adj.* back; **das ~e Ende des Ganges/des Zimmers** the far end of the corridor/the far end *or* the back of the room; **das ~e Ende des Zuges** the back *or* rear [end] of the train; **die ~ste Reihe** the back row; **die Hinter[st]en** those [right] at the back

**Hinter-: ~achse** *die* rear *or* back axle; **~ansicht** *die* rear *or* back view; **~ausgang** *der* rear *or* back exit; **~backe** *die* ▶ **471** (*ugs.*) buttock; **auf seine ~backen fallen** fall over on one's backside; **~bänkler** /-bɛŋklɐ/ *der;* **~~s, ~~, ~bänklerin** *die;* **~~, ~~nen** (*ugs.*) inconspicuous back-bencher; **~bein** *das* hind leg; **sich auf die ~beine stellen** (*ugs.*) put up a fight; **sich auf die ~beine setzen** (*ugs.*) get *or* knuckle down and do some work

**Hinterbliebene** /-'bli:bənə/ *der/die; adj. Dekl.* **A** *(Familienangehörige)* **die ~n** the bereaved [family]; **B** (*jur.*) surviving dependant

**Hinterbliebenen·rente** *die* [surviving] dependant's pension

**hinter-, Hinter-: ~bringen**[1] /--'--/ *unr. tr. V.* **jmdm. etw. ~bringen** inform sb. [confidentially] of sth.; **~|bringen**[2] *unr. tr. V.* (*landsch.*) bring to the back; **~deck** *das* (*Seew.*) afterdeck

**hinter·einander** *Adv.* **A** *(räumlich)* one behind the other; **sie liefen dicht ~:** they were running close behind one another; **~ fahren** drive/ride one behind the other; **~ gehen** walk in a single file *or* one behind the other; **~ schalten** +*Akk.* (*Electrot.*) connect ‹lamps, etc.› in series; **B** *(zeitlich)* one after another *or* the other; **an drei Tagen ~:** for three days running *or* in succession

***hintereinander|fahren** *usw.* ⇒ **hintereinander**

**hintereinander·weg** *Adv.* (*ugs.*) one after the other

**hinter-, Hinter-: ~ein·gang** *der* rear *or* back entrance; **~fotzig** /-fɔtsɪç/ *Adj.* (*bayr.; sonst derb*) underhand[ed]; **~fragen** /--'--/ *tr. V.* examine; analyse; **~fuß** *der* hind foot; **~gebäude** *das* ⇒ **~haus**; **~gedanke** *der* ulterior motive; **einen ~gedanken bei etw. haben** have an ulterior motive for sth.; **~gehen**[1] /--'--/ *unr. tr. V.* deceive; **sie hat ihren Mann mit seinem besten Freund ~gangen** she deceived her husband by having an affair with his best friend; **~|gehen**[2] *unr. itr. V.; mit sein* (*landsch.*) go to the back; **ins Lager ~gehen** go to the back of the store room

**Hinterglas·malerei** *die* (*Kunst*) **A** *(Herstellung)* verre églomisé; **B** *(Bild)* verre églomisé picture

**Hinter·grund** *der* background; (*der Bühne*) back; (*Theater: Kulisse*) backcloth; backdrop; **der akustische/musikalische ~:** the background sounds/music; **im ~ der Bühne** at the back of the stage; **die Hintergründe dieser Verhaltensweise** (*fig.*) the background *sing.* to this behaviour; **jmdn./etw. in den ~ drängen** push sb./sth. into the background; **in den ~ treten/geraten** recede *or* fade into the background; **sich im ~ halten** keep in the background; **etw. im ~ haben** have sth. up one's sleeve

**hinter·gründig** ❶ *Adj.* enigmatic; cryptic. ❷ *adv.* enigmatically; cryptically

**Hintergründigkeit** *die;* **~, ~en A** *(Eigenschaft)* enigmaticness; crypticness; **B** *(Äußerung)* enigmatic *or* cryptic remark

**Hintergrund-: ~information** *die* item *or* piece of background information; **~informationen** [items *or* pieces of] background information *sing.;* **~musik** *die* background music

**hinter-, Hinter-: ~halt** *der* ambush; **in einen ~halt geraten** be ambushed; **jmdn. aus dem ~halt überfallen** ambush sb.; **im ~halt lauern** lie in ambush; **jmdn. aus dem ~halt angreifen** (*fig.*) attack sb. without warning; make a surprise attack on sb.; **etw. im ~halt haben** have sth. up one's sleeve *or* in reserve; **~hältig** ❶ *Adj.* underhand; ❷ *adv.* in an underhand fashion *or* manner; **~hältigkeit** *die;* **~~, ~~en A** *(Eigenschaft)* underhandedness; **B** *(Handlung)* underhand act; **~hand** *die* **A** *(bei Tieren)* hindquarters *pl.;* **B etw. in der ~hand haben** have sth. up one's sleeve *or* in reserve; **in der ~hand sein** *od.* **sitzen** (*Kartenspiel*) play last; **~haus** *das: dwelling situated at or forming the rear of a house* [*and accessible only from a courtyard*]

**hinter·her** *Adv.* **A** *(räumlich)* behind; **nichts wie ihm ~!** quick, after him!; **jmdm. ~ sein** (*ugs.*) be after sb.; ⇒ *auch* **nichts**; **B** *(nachher)* afterwards; **es ~ besser wissen** be wise after the event; **C ~ sein** (*fig. ugs.: zurückgeblieben sein*) be behind

**hinterher-: ~|blicken** *itr. V.* **jmdm. ~blicken** follow sb. with one's eyes; gaze after sb.; **~|fahren** *unr. itr. V.; mit sein* (*mit dem Auto/Fahrrad*) drive/ride [along] behind (**jmdm.** sb.); (*folgen*) follow (**jmdm.** sb.); **~|gehen** *unr. itr. V.; mit sein* walk [along] behind (**jmdm.** sb.); (*folgen*) follow (**jmdm.** sb.); **~|hinken** *itr. V.; mit sein* **A** limp *or* hobble [along] behind (**jmdm.** sb.); **B** (*fig.*) **einer Sache** (*Dat.*) **~hinken** lag behind sth.; **mit etw. ~hinken** be behind with sth.; **~|kommen** *unr. itr. V.; mit sein* **A** *(dahinter ankommen)* follow behind; **B** *(danach kommen)* follow; come after; **~|laufen** *unr. itr. V.; mit sein* **A** run [along] behind (**jmdm.** sb.); **B** ⇒ **~gehen**; **C** (*ugs.: für sich zu gewinnen suchen*) **jmdm./etw. ~laufen** run after sb./sth.; **~|schicken** *tr. V.* **jmdm. jmdn./etw. ~schicken** send sb. after sb./send sth. on to sb.; ***~sein** ⇒ **hinterher**; **~|spionieren** *itr. V.* **jmdm. ~spionieren** spy on sb.

**hinter-, Hinter-: ~hof** *der* courtyard; **~kopf** *der* ▶ **471** back of the/one's head; **etw. im ~kopf haben/behalten** (*ugs.*) have/keep sth. at the back of one's mind; **~lader** *der;* **~~s, ~~** (*Waffenkunde*) breech-loader; **~land** *das* hinterland; (*Milit.*) back area; **~lassen** /--'--/ *unr. tr. V.* **A** leave; (*testamentarisch*) leave; bequeath; **die ~lassenen Schriften** the posthumous works; **B** (*zurücklassen*) leave ‹message, telephone number, etc.›; **ein Zimmer in Unordnung ~lassen** leave a room in a muddle; **C** (*verursachen*) leave ‹fingerprints, impression, etc.›; **keine Spuren ~lassen** leave no trace[s] [behind]; **~lassene** /--'---/ *der/die; adj. Dekl.* (*schweiz.*) ⇒ **~bliebene**; **~lassenschaft** /--'---/ *die;* **~~, ~~en** estate; **jmds. ~lassenschaft antreten** inherit sb.'s estate; (*ugs. scherzh.*) take over from sb.; **jmds. literarische ~lassenschaft** the writings that sb. has left to posterity; **~lastig** *Adj.* tail-heavy ‹aircraft›; stern-heavy ‹ship›; **~lauf** *der* (*Jägerspr.*) hind leg; **~legen** /--'--/ *tr. V.* deposit (**bei** with); (*als Pfand*) deposit, leave (**bei** with)

**Hinterlegung** *die;* **~, ~en** ⇒ **hinterlegen**: depositing; leaving; **jmdn. gegen ~ einer Kaution freilassen** release sb. on bail

h

**Hinterlegungs·schein** *der* deposit receipt

**hinter-, Hinter-: ~list** *die* guile; deceit; (*Verrat*) treachery; **eine ~list** an underhand trick; a piece of deceit; **~listig** *Adj.* deceitful; (*verräterisch*) treacherous

**hinterm** /'hɪntɐm/ *Präp. + Art.* (*ugs.*) = **hinter dem**

**Hinter-: ~mann** *der* A person behind; **sein ~mann** the person behind [him]; B (*Gewährsmann*) [secret] informant; C (*jmd., der aus dem ~grund lenkt*) **der ~mann/die ~männer** the brains behind the operation; **~mannschaft** *die* (*Sport*) defence

**hintern** *Präp. + Art.* (*ugs.*) = **hinter den**

**Hintern** /'hɪntɐn/ *der;* **~s, ~** ▶ 471 (*ugs.*) behind; backside; bottom; **jmdm. den ~ verhauen** *od.* **versohlen** tan sb.'s hide; **jmdn.** *od.* **jmdm. in den ~ treten** kick sb. in the pants (*coll.*) *or* up the backside; (*fig.*) kick sb. in the teeth (*fig.*); **sich [vor Wut** *od.* **Ärger] in den ~ beißen** (*salopp*) kick oneself; **jmdm. in den ~ kriechen** (*derb*) lick sb.'s arse (*coarse*); suck up to sb. (*coll.*); **sich auf den ~ setzen** (*salopp*) (*sich anstrengen*) get *or* knuckle down to it; (*aufs Gesäß fallen*) fall on one's behind; (*überrascht sein*) be flabbergasted; **Hummeln** *od.* **Pfeffer im ~ haben** (*salopp*) have ants in one's pants (*coll.*); ⇒ *auch* **abwischen B**

**Hinter-: ~pfote** *die* hind paw; **~rad** *das* back *or* rear wheel; **~rad·antrieb** *der* rear-wheel drive; **~reifen** *der* back *or* rear tyre

**hinter·rücks** /'hɪntɐrʏks/ *Adv.* A (*von hinten*) from behind; B (*veralt.: hinter jmds. Rücken*) behind sb.'s back

**hinters** /'hɪntɐs/ *Präp. + Art.* (*ugs.*) = **hinter das**

**hinter-, Hinter-: ~schiff** *das* stern; **~seite** *die* ⇒ **Rückseite**; **~sinn** *der* deeper meaning; **~sinnig** *Adj.* ‹remark, story, etc.› with a deeper meaning; subtle ‹sense of humour›

**hinterst...** /'hɪntɐst.../ ⇒ **hinter...**

**hinter-, Hinter-: ~steven** *der* A (*Seemannsspr.*) sternpost; B (*ugs. scherzh.: Gesäß*) backside; behind; **~teil** *das* ▶ 471 (*ugs.: Gesäß*) backside; behind; (*eines Tieres*) rump; **~treffen** *das* (*ugs.*) *in* **ins ~treffen geraten** *od.* **kommen** fall behind; **jmdn./etw. ins ~treffen bringen** put sb./sth. behind; **~treiben** /--'--/ *unr. tr. V.* foil, thwart, frustrate ‹plan›; prevent ‹marriage, promotion›; block ‹law, investigation, reform›; **~treibung** *die;* **~~, ~~en** ⇒ **~treiben**: foiling; thwarting; frustration; prevention; blocking; **~treppe** *die* back stairs *pl.*; **~treppen·roman** *der* (*abwertend*) trashy novel; **~tupfingen** /-'tʊpfɪŋən/ (*das*); **~~s** (*ugs. spött.*) the back of beyond; **~tür** *die* back door; **durch die** *od.* **durch eine ~tür** (*auch fig.*) by the back door; **sich** (*Dat.*) **eine ~tür offen halten** (*fig.*) leave oneself a way out (*fig.*); **~wäldler** /-vɛltlɐ/ *der;* **~~s, ~~** (*spött.*) backwoodsman; **~wäldlerin** *die;* **~~, ~~nen** backwoods woman; **~wäldlerisch** *Adj.* (*spött.*) backwoods *attrib.* ‹views, attitudes, manners, etc.›; **~ziehen** /--'--/ *unr. tr. V.* misappropriate ‹materials, goods›; **Steuern ~ziehen** evade [payment of] tax; **~ziehung** *die* ⇒ **~ziehen**: misappropriation; evasion; **~zimmer** *das* back room

**hintnach** /hɪnt'na:x/ *Adv.* (*österr. ugs.*) ⇒ **hinterher**

**hin-: ~|tragen** *unr. tr. V.* **jmdn./etw. ~tragen** carry sb./take *or* carry sth. there; **etw. zu jmdm.** *od.* **jmdm. etw. ~tragen** take sth. to sb.; **~|treiben** ❶ *unr. tr. V.* A (*an eine Stelle treiben*) **die Schafe ~treiben/zur Weide ~treiben** drive the sheep there/to the pasture; **die Strömung/der Wind trieb das Boot zum Ufer ~:** the current carried/the wind blew the boat to the shore; B (*unpers.*) **es trieb ihn immer wieder zu ihr ~:** something always drove him back to her; ❷ *unr. itr. V.; mit sein* drift *or* float there; **~|treten** *unr. itr. V.* A *mit sein* **zu jmdm./etw. ~treten** step over to sb./sth.; **vor jmdn. ~treten** go up to sb.; B (*gegen jmdn./etw. treten*) kick him/her/it *etc.*

**hintüber** /hɪnt'|y:bɐ/ *Adv.* ⇒ **hintenüber**

**hin|tun** *unr. tr. V.* (*ugs.*) put; **wo soll ich ihn bloß ~?** (*fig.*) I can't place him

**hinüber** /hɪ'ny:bɐ/ *Adv.* A over; across; **bis zur anderen Seite ~:** over *or* across to the other side; **~ und herüber** back and forth; B (*ugs.*) **~ sein** (*tot/unbrauchbar sein*) have had it (*coll.*); (*verdorben sein*) be *or* have gone off; (*eingeschlafen sein*) have dropped off; (*bewusstlos sein*) be out for the count (*coll.*); (*betrunken sein*) be well away (*coll.*) *or* plastered (*sl.*)

**hinüber-** (*s. auch* **rüber-**)**: ~|blicken** *itr. V.* look across; **zu** *od.* **nach jmdm. ~blicken** look across at sb.; **~|bringen** *unr. tr. V.* **jmdn./etw. ~bringen** take sb./sth. across *or* over (**auf** + *Akk.*, **zu** to); **~|dämmern** *itr. V.; mit sein* A (*einschlafen*) drift off; B (*geh. verhüll.: sterben*) pass away in one's sleep; **~|fahren** ❶ *unr. itr. V.; mit sein* (*mit dem Auto/Fahrrad*) drive/ride *or* go over *or* across; **über den Fluss ~fahren** cross the river; ❷ *unr. tr. V.* **jmdn./ein Auto ~fahren** drive *or* take sb./drive a car over *or* across; **~|führen** ❶ *tr. V.* **jmdn. über die Straße/die Grenze/in den Saal ~führen** take sb. across the road/guide sb. over *or* across the frontier/take *or* show sb. across to the hall; ❷ *itr. V.* ‹street, path, etc.› lead *or* go over *or* across (**an** + *Akk.*, **nach** to); **über etw.** (*Akk.*) **~führen** lead *or* go over sth.; **~|gehen** *unr. itr. V.; mit sein* A walk *or* go over *or* across; **zu jmdm. ~gehen** go across *or* over to sb.; **ins Nebenzimmer ~gehen** go across into the next room; B (*geh. verhüll.: sterben*) pass away; **~|helfen** *unr. itr. V.* **jmdm. [über etw.** (*Akk.*)**] ~helfen** help sb. over *or* across [sth.]; **jmdm. auf die andere Seite ~helfen** help sb. over *or* across to the other side; **~|kommen** *unr. itr. V.; mit sein* A (*nach drüben kommen*) come over *or* across; (*~überkommen können*) get across; **über etw.** (*Akk.*) **~kommen** get across sth.; B (*ugs.: Besuch machen*) come over; pop over (*coll.*); **~|lassen** *unr. tr. V.* **jmdn. ~lassen** allow *or* let sb. over *or* across; **~|reichen** ❶ *tr. V.* **[jmdm.] etw. ~reichen** pass *or* hand sth. across [to sb.]; ❷ *itr. V.* A (*sich erstrecken*) extend [over *or* across]; B (*lang genug sein*) reach over *or* across; **über die Mauer ~reichen** reach over the wall; **~|retten** ❶ *tr. V.* A (*in Sicherheit bringen*) **sein Vermögen in die Schweiz ~retten** save one's fortune by getting it over *or* across the border into Switzerland; B (*bewahren*) keep alive, preserve ‹tradition etc.›; ❷ *refl. V.* A (*sich in Sicherheit bringen*) **sich ins Ausland ~retten** reach safety abroad; B (*sich erhalten*) ‹customs, hopes, etc.› survive; **~|rufen** ❶ *unr. tr. V.* **jmdn. ~rufen** call sb. over; ❷ *unr. itr. V.* call over; **~|schauen** *itr. V.* A (*landsch.*) ⇒ **~blicken**; B (*ugs.: besuchen*) **zu jmdm. ~schauen** look in on sb.; **~|schicken** *tr. V.* **jmdn./etw. ~schicken** send sb./sth. over; **~|schwimmen** *unr. itr. V.; mit sein* swim over *or* across; **~|sehen** *unr. itr. V.:* ⇒ **~blicken**; ***~|sein** ⇒ **hinüber**; **~|spielen** ❶ *tr. V.* (*Sport*) cross ‹ball›; ❷ *itr. V.* **das Weiß spielt ins Gelbliche ~:** the white is tinged with yellow *or* has a yellow tinge; **~|springen** *unr. itr. V.; mit sein* **über etw.** (*Akk.*)**/ein Hindernis ~springen** jump over sth./clear an obstacle; **~|steigen** *unr. itr. V.; mit sein* **[über etw.** (*Akk.*)**] ~steigen** climb over [sth.]; **~|wechseln** *itr. V.; mit haben od. sein* cross over; **zu einer anderen Partei ~wechseln** go over *or* switch to another party; **~|werfen** *unr. tr. V.* **etw. ~werfen** throw sth. over *or* across; **einen Blick ~werfen** (*fig.*) glance over *or* across; **~|ziehen** ❶ *unr. tr. V.* **jmdn./etw. ~ziehen** draw sb. over/pull *or* draw sth. over *or* across; ❷ *unr. itr. V.; mit sein* A (*wandern*) **über etw. ~ziehen** go over *or* across sth.; cross sth.; B (*umziehen*) move across

**hin- und her-: ~|bewegen** *tr. V.* **etw. ~bewegen** move sth. to and fro *or* back and forth; **~|fahren** ❶ *unr. itr. V.; mit sein* travel *or* go to and fro *or* back and forth; (*mit dem Auto*) drive to and fro *or* back and forth; (*mit dem Fahrrad*) ride to and fro *or* back and forth; ❷ *unr. tr. V.* **jmdn. ~fahren** drive sb. to and fro *or* back and forth; **~|gehen** *unr. itr. V.; mit sein* walk up and down *or* to and fro; (*aufgeregt*) pace up and down *or* to and fro; **im Zimmer ~gehen** walk/pace up and down the room

**Hinundher·gerede** *das:* **bei diesem ~ kommt doch nichts heraus** we're going backwards and forwards over the same old ground and getting nowhere

**hin- und her|pendeln** *itr. V.; mit sein* ‹person› commute; ‹bus› shuttle to and fro

**Hin- und Rück-: ~fahrt** *die* journey there and back; round trip (*Amer.*); **~flug** *der* outward and return flight; **~reise** *die*, **~weg** *der* journey there and back

**hinunter** /hɪ'nʊntɐ/ *Adv.* down; **den Berg ~:** down the mountain; **~ mit der Medizin!** (*ugs.*) get the medicine down!

**hinunter-: ~|begeben** *unr. refl. V.* **sich ~begeben** go down; **sich die Treppe ~begeben** go downstairs; **~|blicken** *itr. V.* look down; **auf jmdn. ~blicken** (*fig.*) look down on sb.; **~|bringen** *unr. tr. V.* **jmdn./etw. ~bringen** take sb./sth. down; **~|fahren** ❶ *unr. itr. V.; mit sein* go down; (*mit dem Auto*) drive down; (*mit dem Fahrrad*) ride down; ❷ *unr. tr. V.* **jmdn./ein Auto/eine Ladung ~fahren** drive *or* take sb. down/drive a car down/take a load down; **~|fallen** *unr. itr. V.; mit sein* fall down; **die Treppe ~fallen** fall down the stairs; **mir ist die Vase ~gefallen** I dropped the vase; **~|führen** ❶ *tr. V.* **jmdn. ~führen** lead *or* guide sb. down; ❷ *itr. V.* ‹path, road, etc.› lead *or* run down; **den Berg ~führen** lead *or* run down the mountain; **~|gehen** *unr. itr. V.; mit sein* A go down; (*zu Fuß*) go *or* walk down; ‹aircraft› descend; B ‹path, road, etc.› go *or* run down; **~|jagen** ❶ *tr. V.* **jmdn. ~jagen** chase sb. down; ❷ *itr. V.; mit sein* **die Treppe/Straße ~jagen** race down the stairs/street; **~|kippen** *tr. V.* A **etw. ~kippen** tip sth. down; B (*ugs.: trinken*) knock back (*sl.*); down; **~|klettern** *itr. V.; mit sein* climb down; **~|kommen** *unr. itr. V.; mit sein* come down; **die Treppe ~kommen** come downstairs; **~|lassen** *unr. tr. V.* A (*mit einem Seil usw.*) **jmdn./etw. ~lassen** lower sb./sth.; let sb./sth. down; B (*erlauben*) **jmdn. ~lassen** let sb. [go] down; **~|laufen** *unr. itr. V.; mit sein* A run down; (*zu Fuß ~gehen*) walk down; **die Treppe ~laufen** run/walk down the stairs *or* downstairs; B (*nach unten fließen*) run down; **an der Wand ~laufen** run down the wall; C (*fig.*) **ein Schauer lief ihm den Rücken ~:** a shiver ran down his spine; **~|reichen** ❶ *tr. V.* pass *or* hand down; ❷ *itr. V.* A (*sich bis ~ erstrecken*) reach down (**bis auf** + *Akk.* to); B (*bis zu einer Stufe reichen*) **bis zu jmdm. ~reichen** reach *or* extend down to sb.; **~|rutschen** *itr. V.; mit sein* slide down; **~|schauen** *itr. V.* (*landsch.*) ⇒ **~blicken**; **~|schlingen** *unr. tr. V.* gulp *or* gobble down; **~|schlucken** *tr. V.* A swallow; B (*hinnehmen*) swallow ‹insult etc.›; C (*unterdrücken*) bite back ‹remark, oath, etc.›; choke back ‹tears, anger›; **~|sehen** *unr. itr. V.* ⇒ **~blicken**; **~|springen** *unr. itr. V.; mit sein* A jump down; B (*ugs.: schnell ~laufen*) run down; **die Treppe ~springen** run down the stairs *or* downstairs; **~|spülen** *tr. V.* A **etw. [den Ausguss] ~spülen** swill sth. down [the sink]; **etw. [die Toilette] ~spülen** flush sth. down [the toilet]; B (*ugs.: ~schlucken*) wash down ‹tablets etc.›; **seinen Kummer [mit Alkohol] ~spülen** (*fig.*) drown one's sorrows [in drink]; **~|stürzen** ❶ *itr. V.; mit sein* A fall *or* plunge down; **die Treppe ~stürzen** fall down the stairs *or* downstairs; B (*ugs.: eilen*) rush *or* race down; ❷ *refl. V.* throw *or* fling oneself down; **sich von etw. ~stürzen** throw *or* fling oneself off sth.; ❸ *tr. V.* A **jmdn. ~stürzen** throw *or* hurl sb. down; **jmdn. von den Klippen/in den Abgrund ~stürzen** push sb. off the cliff/over the precipice; B (*ugs.: schnell trinken*) gulp down; knock back (*sl.*); **~|tragen** *unr. tr. V.* **etw. ~tragen** carry

*old spelling (see note on page 1707)

h

sth. down; ~|**werfen** *unr. tr. V.* throw down; **einen Blick ~werfen** (*fig.*) glance down; ~|**ziehen** ❶ *unr. itr. V.; mit sein* Ⓐ (*umziehen*) move down; Ⓑ (*sich nach unten bewegen*) move *or* go down; ❷ *unr. tr. V.* **jmdn./etw. ~ziehen** pull sb./sth. down; ❸ *unr. refl. V.* stretch *or* extend down

**hin-, Hin-:** ~|**wagen** *refl. V.* dare [to] go there; venture there; **~wärts** *Adv.* on the way there; **~weg** *der* way there; **auf dem ~weg** on the way there; **für den ~weg** for the journey there

**hin·weg** *Adv.* Ⓐ (*geh.*) **~ mit diesem Unrat!** away with this rubbish!; **~ mit dir!** away with you!; Ⓑ **über etw. ~:** over sth.; **über den Brillenrand ~:** over [the top of] his/her spectacles; **über alle Schwierigkeiten** *usw.* **~** (*fig.*) in spite of *or* despite all the difficulties *etc.*; **über jmdn. ~** (*fig.*) over sb.'s head; **über Jahre/lange Zeit ~:** for many years/a long time

**hinweg-:** ~|**brausen** *itr. V.; mit sein* **über etw.** (*Akk.*) **~brausen** roar over sth.; ~|**gehen** *unr. itr. V.; mit sein* (*nicht beachten*) **über etw.** (*Akk.*) **~gehen** pass over sth.; (*sich über etw. fortbewegen, auch fig.*) pass *or* sweep over sth.; ~|**helfen** *unr. itr. V.* **jmdm. über etw.** (*Akk.*) **~helfen** help sb. [to] get over sth.; ~|**kommen** *unr. itr. V.; mit sein* **über etw.** (*Akk.*) **~kommen** get over sth.; ~|**lesen** *unr. itr. V.* **über etw.** (*Akk.*) **~lesen** read past sth. without noticing it; ~|**raffen** *tr. V.* (*geh.*) carry off; ~|**sehen** *unr. itr. V.* Ⓐ **über jmdn./etw. ~sehen** see over sb. *or* sb.'s head/sth.; Ⓑ (*übersehen*) **über jmdn. ~sehen** look past sb.; Ⓒ (*unbeachtet lassen*) **über etw.** (*Akk.*) **~sehen** overlook sth.; ~|**setzen** ❶ *itr. V.; auch mit sein* **über etw.** (*Akk.*) **~setzen** leap *or* jump over sth.; ❷ *refl. V.* **sich über etw.** (*Akk.*) **~setzen** ignore *or* disregard sth.; ~|**täuschen** *tr. V.* **jmdn. über etw.** (*Akk.*) **~täuschen** blind sb. to sth.; deceive *or* mislead sb. about sth.; **darüber ~täuschen, dass ...** hide *or* obscure the fact that ...; ~|**trösten** *tr. V.* **jmdn. über etw.** (*Akk.*) **~trösten** console sb. for sth.

**Hinweis** /ˈhɪnvai̯s/ *der;* **~es, ~e** Ⓐ (*Wink*) hint; tip; **jmdm. einen ~ geben** give sb. a hint; **wenn ich mir den ~ erlauben darf** if I may [just] point something out *or* draw your attention to something; **~e für den Benutzer** notes for the user; **~e aus der Bevölkerung** leads provided by the public; Ⓑ **unter ~ auf** (+ *Akk.*) with reference to; Ⓒ (*Anzeichen*) hint; indication

**hin-:** ~|**weisen** ❶ *unr. itr. V.* Ⓐ (*zeigen*) **auf jmdn./etw. ~weisen** point to *or* indicate sb./sth.; Ⓑ **auf etw.** (*Akk.*) **~weisen** (*anzeigen*) point to *or* indicate sth.; (*verweisen*) point sth. out; refer to sth.; **darauf ~weisen, dass ...** point to the fact that *or* indicate that/point out that ...; ❷ *unr. tr. V.* **jmdn. auf etw.** (*Akk.*) **~weisen** point sth. out to sb.; draw sb.'s attention to sth.; **~weisend** *Adj.* (*Grammatik*) demonstrative ‹pronoun, adjective, etc.›

**Hinweis-:** **~schild** *das* sign; (*Straßenschild*) [road] sign; **~tafel** *die* information board

**hin-, Hin-:** ~|**wenden** ❶ *unr. tr. V.* turn **(zu** towards); ❷ *unr. refl. V.* turn **(zu** to, towards); **wo soll ich mich jetzt noch ~wenden?** (*ugs. fig.*) where shall I turn now?; **~wendung** *die* change of direction **(zu** towards); ~|**werfen** ❶ *unr. tr. V.* Ⓐ (*an eine Stelle werfen*) throw down; Ⓑ (*von sich werfen*) throw *or* fling down; Ⓒ (*ugs.: aufgeben*) chuck in (*coll.*); Ⓓ (*flüchtig schreiben*) jot down; (*flüchtig zeichnen*) dash off; Ⓔ (*beiläufig äußern*) drop [casually] ‹remark›; ask casually ‹question›; make casually ‹accusation›; say casually ‹words›; **eine [beiläufig] ~geworfene Bemerkung** a casual remark; Ⓕ (*ugs.: fallen lassen*) drop; ❷ *unr. refl. V.* **sich [vor jmdm.] ~werfen** throw oneself down [before sb.]

**hin·wieder, hin·wiederum** *Adv.* (*veralt.*) on the other hand

**hin|wirken** *itr. V.* **auf etw.** (*Akk.*) **~:** work towards sth.; **bei jmdm. darauf ~, dass er seine Meinung ändert** try to persuade sb. to change his opinion

**Hinz** /hɪnts/ *in* **~ und Kunz** (*ugs. abwertend*) every Tom, Dick and Harry

**hin-:** ~|**zählen** *tr. V.* count out; ~|**zaubern** *tr. V.* (*ugs.*) **etw. ~zaubern** produce sth. as if by magic; ~|**zeigen** *itr. V.* point **(zu** to, towards); ~|**ziehen** ❶ *unr. tr. V.* Ⓐ pull, draw **(zu** to, towards); Ⓑ (*zu etw., jmdm. treiben*) draw, attract **(zu** to); **sich zu jmdm./etw. ~gezogen fühlen** be *or* feel attracted to sb./sth.; Ⓒ (*in die Länge ziehen*) draw out; protract; Ⓓ (*verzögern*) delay; put off; ❷ *unr. itr. V.; mit sein* Ⓐ (*umziehen*) move there; **wo ist sie ~gezogen?** where did she move to?; Ⓑ (*an einen Ort ziehen*) move **(zu** towards); **am Himmel ~ziehen** (*dichter.*) sail across the sky; ❸ *unr. refl. V.* Ⓐ (*sich erstrecken*) drag on **(über** + *Akk.* for); Ⓑ (*sich verzögern*) be delayed; ~|**zielen** *itr. V.* **auf etw.** (*Akk.*) **~zielen** aim at sth.; ‹policies, efforts, etc.› be aimed at sth.

**hin·zu** *Adv.* in addition; besides; **dieses Gehalt und noch das Doppelte ~, dann wäre ich zufrieden** I'd be content with this salary and twice as much again *or* on top

**hinzu-, Hinzu-:** ~|**bekommen** *unr. tr. V.* get in addition; ~|**denken** *unr. refl. V.* **sich** (*Dat.*) **etw. ~denken** add sth. in one's imagination; ~|**dichten** *tr. V.* **etw. ~dichten** make sth. up and add it; add sth. out of one's head; ~|**fügen** *tr. V.* add; **~fügung** *die* addition; **unter ~fügung** (*Dat.*) **einer Sache** (*Gen.*) *od.* **von etw.** with the addition of sth.; ~|**geben** *unr. tr. V.* Ⓐ (*dazugeben*) **jmdm. etw. ~geben** give sth. to sb. in addition; Ⓑ (*hineingeben*) add; ~|**gesellen** *refl. V.* **sich [zu] jmdm./etw. ~gesellen** join sb./sth.; ~|**gewinnen** *unr. tr. V.* gain in addition; ~|**kommen** *unr. itr. V.; mit sein* Ⓐ (*zufällig kommen*) arrive *or* appear [on the scene]; come along; **er kam gerade** *od.* **genau in dem Moment ~, als ...** he arrived *or* happened to arrive at the very moment when *or* just as ...; Ⓑ (*hinkommen*) come along *or* up; Ⓒ (*sich anschließen*) join; **zu etw. ~kommen** join sth.; Ⓓ (*~gefügt werden*) **zu etw. ~kommen** be added to sth.; **zu der Grippe kam noch eine Lungenentzündung ~:** in addition to the flu he/she also contracted a lung infection; **es kommt noch ~, dass ...** there is also the fact that ...; ~|**nehmen** *unr. tr. V.* add; ~|**setzen** ❶ *refl. V.* **sich zu jmdm./einer Gruppe** *usw.* **~setzen** join sb./a group *etc.*; ❷ *tr. V.* add; ~|**treten** *unr. itr. V.; mit sein* Ⓐ come up; **zu jmdm./den anderen ~treten** come up to sb./join the others; Ⓑ ⇒ **~kommen** D; ~|**tun** *unr. tr. V.* (*ugs.*) add; ⇒ *auch* **dazutun**; ~|**verdienen** *tr. V.* **etwas ~verdienen** earn a bit extra; ~|**zählen** *tr. V.* add [on]; ~|**ziehen** *unr. tr. V.* consult; call in; **~ziehung** *die* consultation; **unter ~ziehung einschlägiger Literatur** by consulting the relevant literature

**Hiob** /ˈhiːɔp/ (*der*) Job

**Hiobs·botschaft** *die* bad news

**Hippe**[1] /ˈhɪpə/ *die;* **~, ~n** pruning knife; (*des Todes*) scythe

**Hippe**[2] *die;* **~, ~n** (*ugs. abwertend*) bitch (*derog.*)

**hipp, hipp, hurra** /ˈhɪpˈhɪphʊˈraː/ *Interj.* hip, hip, hooray *or* hurrah

**Hipphipphurra** /hɪphɪphʊˈraː/ *das;* **~s, ~s** cheer; **dem Sieger ein dreifaches ~:** three cheers for the winner

**Hippie** /ˈhɪpi/ *der;* **~s, ~s** hippie (*coll.*)

**Hippodrom** /hɪpoˈdroːm/ *der od. das;* **~s, ~e** hippodrome

**hippokratisch** /hɪpoˈkraːtɪʃ/ *Adj.* **der ~e Eid** the Hippocratic oath

**Hirn** /hɪrn/ *das;* **~[e]s, ~e** Ⓐ ▶471 brain; Ⓑ (*Speise; ugs.: Verstand*) brains *pl.*; **sein ~ anstrengen** exercise one's mental faculties; **sich** (*Dat.*) **das ~ zermartern** rack one's brains; **welchem ~ ist das entsprungen?** whose brainchild is that?

**hirn-, Hirn-:** **~anhangs·drüse** *die* ▶471 (*Anat.*) pituitary gland *or* body; **~gespinst** *das* (*abwertend*) fantasy; **~haut** ▶471 *die* (*Anat.*) meninges *Pl.*; **~haut·entzündung** *die* ▶474 (*Med.*) meningitis; **~kasten** *der* (*salopp scherzh.*) ⇒ **Gehirnkasten**; **~los** (*abwertend*) ❶ *Adj.* brainless; ❷ *adv.* brainlessly; **~rinde** *die* ▶471 (*Anat.*) cerebral cortex; **~rissig** *Adj.* (*abwertend*) crazy; crack-brained (*coll.*); **~stamm** *der* ▶471 (*Anat.*) brainstem; **~tod** *der* (*Med.*) brain death; **~tot** *Adj.* brain-dead; **~tumor** *der* ▶474 (*Med.*) brain tumour; **~verbrannt** *Adj.* (*abwertend*) crazy; crack-brained (*coll.*); **~windung** *die* ▶471 (*Med.*) convolution *or* (*Med.*) gyrus of the brain

**Hirsch** /hɪrʃ/ *der;* **~[e]s, ~e** Ⓐ deer; Ⓑ (*Rothirsch*) red deer; Ⓒ (*männlicher Rothirsch*) stag; hart; Ⓓ (*Speise*) venison; Ⓔ (*Schimpfwort*) bastard (*coll.*)

**Hirsch-:** **~brunft, ~brunst** *die* rut [of the stags]; **während der ~brunft** *od.* **~brunst** while the stags are in rut; **~fänger** *der* (*Jägerspr.*) [double-edged] hunting knife; **~geweih** *das* [stag's] antlers *pl.*; **ein ~geweih** a set of antlers; **~horn** *das* staghorn; **~horn·salz** *das* salt of hartshorn; ammonium carbonate; **~käfer** *der* stag beetle; **~kalb** *das* [male] deer calf; [male] fawn; **~kuh** *die* hind; **~leder** *das* buckskin; **~ragout** *das* (*Kochk.*) ragout of venison; **~steak** *das* (*Kochk.*) venison steak

**Hirse** /ˈhɪrzə/ *die;* **~, ~n** millet

**Hirse·brei** *der* millet gruel

**Hirt** /hɪrt/ *der;* **~en, ~en** herdsman; (*Schaf~*) shepherd

**Hirte** *der;* **~n, ~n** ▶159 (*geh.*) ⇒ **Hirt**; **der Gute ~:** the Good Shepherd

**Hirten-:** **~amt** *das* (*kath. Rel.*) pastorate; pastoral office; **~brief** *der* (*kath. Rel.*) pastoral letter; **~dichtung** *die* (*Literaturw.*) pastoral *or* bucolic poetry; **~hund** *der* sheepdog; **~junge** *der,* **~knabe** *der* (*dicht.*) shepherd boy; **~mädchen** *das* shepherd girl; **~spiel** *das* pastoral [play]; **~stab** *der* Ⓐ (*geh.*) shepherd's crook; Ⓑ (*kath. Rel.*) pastoral staff; crosier; **~täschel[-kraut]** *das;* **~~s** (*Bot.*) shepherd's purse; **~volk** *das* pastoral people

**Hirtin** *die;* **~, ~nen** ▶159 (*veralt. selten*) shepherdess

**his, His** /hɪs/ *das;* **~, ~** (*Musik*) B sharp; ⇒ *auch* **a**, A

**hispanisieren** /hɪspaniˈziːrən/ *tr. V.* Hispanicize

**Hispanist** *der;* **~en, ~en, Hispanistin** *die;* **~, ~nen** Hispanist; Hispanicist

**Hispanistik** *die;* **~:** study of Hispanic languages and literature; ≈ Hispanic studies

**hissen** /ˈhɪsn̩/ *tr. V.* hoist ‹sail›; hoist, run up ‹flag›

**Histamin** /hɪstaˈmiːn/ *das;* **~s** (*Chemie*) histamine

**Histologie** /hɪstoloˈgiː/ *die;* **~** (*Med.*) histology *no art.*

**histologisch** *Adj.* (*Med.*) histological

**Histörchen** /hɪsˈtøːɐ̯çən/ *das;* **~s, ~** (*scherzh.*) anecdote

**Historie** /hɪsˈtoːri̯ə/ *die;* **~, ~n** (*veralt.*) Ⓐ history; Ⓑ (*Erzählung*) story; tale

**Historien-:** **~maler** *der* painter of historical scenes; historical painter; **~malerei** *die* painting of historical scenes; historical painting; **~malerin** *die* ⇒ **~maler**

**Historiker** /hɪsˈtoːrikɐ/ *der;* **~s, ~, Historikerin** *die;* **~, ~nen** historian

**historisch** ❶ *Adj.* Ⓐ historical; Ⓑ (*geschichtlich bedeutungsvoll*) historic. ❷ *adv.* Ⓐ **das ist ~ belegt** this is historically attested; there is historical evidence for this; **etw. ~ erklären** explain sth. in historical terms; **~ erwiesen sein** be historically proven; **etw. ~ betrachten** see sth. in the light of history *or* in historical terms; Ⓑ **~ höchst bedeutsam** of historic importance

**historisieren** *itr. V.* (*geh.*) historicize

**Historismus** *der;* **~:** historicism

**Hit** /hɪt/ *der;* **~[s], ~s** (*ugs.*) hit

**Hitler-** /ˈhɪtlɐ-/: **~bärtchen** *das* (*ugs.*) Hitler moustache; **~faschismus** *der* Hitlerite fascism; **~gruß** *der* Nazi salute; **~jugend** *die*

Hitler Youth; ∼**junge** *der* member of the Hitler Youth; ∼**zeit** *die* Hitler era

**Hịt-:** ∼**liste** *die* top ten/twenty/thirty *etc.;* ∼**parade** *die* hit parade

**Hịtze** /ˈhɪtsə/ *die;* ∼, (*fachspr.:*) ∼**n** heat; **bei dieser** ∼: in this heat; **etw. bei mittlerer/mäßiger** ∼ **backen** bake sth. in a medium/moderate oven; **die fliegende** ∼ **haben** (*fig.*) have the [hot] flushes; **sich in** ∼ (*Akk.*) **reden** (*fig.*) get more and more excited as one talks; **in der** ∼ **des Gefechts** in the heat of the moment

**hịtze-, Hịtze-:** ∼**abweisend** *Adj.* heat-reflecting; ∼**beständig** *Adj.* heat-resistant, heat-resisting ‹metal etc.›; heatproof, heat-resistant ‹glass etc.›; ∼**bläschen** *das* heat spot; ∼**empfindlich** *Adj.* sensitive to heat *postpos.;* heat-sensitive ‹material›; ∼**frei** *Adj.* ∼**frei haben/bekommen** have/be given the rest of the day off [school/work] because of excessively hot weather; ∼**periode** *die* hot spell; spell *or* period of hot weather; (∼*welle*) heat wave; ∼**schild** *der* (*Raumf.*) heat shield; ∼**wallung** *die* hot flush; ∼**welle** *die* heat wave

**hịtzig** *Adj.* **A** (*heftig*) hot-tempered; quick-tempered; ∼ **werden** flare up; fly into a temper; **B** (*leidenschaftlich*) hot-blooded ‹person, race, etc.›; hot ‹blood›; passionate ‹supporter, advocate, etc.›; **C** (*erregt*) heated ‹discussion, argument, words, etc.›; **D** (*veralt.: fiebrig*) fevered ‹brow, cheeks, etc.›; feverish ‹red›; **E** (*läufig*) on *or* in heat *pred.*

**Hịtzigkeit** *die;* ∼ **A** (*Heftigkeit*) hot *or* quick temper; **B** (*Leidenschaftlichkeit*) hot-bloodedness

**hịtz-, Hịtz-:** ∼**kopf** *der* hothead; ∼**köpfig** *Adj.* hot-headed; ∼**pocke** *die* ⇒ **Hitzebläschen**; ∼**schlag** *der* heatstroke

**HIV** *Abk.* **humanes Immundefizienzvirus** HIV

**HIV-:** ∼**-infiziert** *Adj.* HIV-infected; ∼**-positiv** *Adj.* HIV-positive; ∼**-Test** *der* HIV test

**Hiwi** /ˈhiːvi/ *der;* ∼**s**, ∼**s** laboratory *or* (*coll.*) lab/departmental/library assistant

**HJ** *Abk.* (*ns.*) **Hitlerjugend**

**hl** *Abk.* **Hektoliter** hl

**hl.** *Abk.* **heilig** St.

**hm** /hm̩/ *Interj.* h'm; hem

**H-Milch** /ˈhaː-/ *die;* ∼: long-life *or* UHT milk

**h-Moll** /ˈhaː-/ *das* (*Musik*) B minor; ⇒ *auch* **a-Moll**

**HNO-Arzt** /haː|enˈ|oː-/ *der,* **HNO-Ärztin** *die* ENT specialist

**HO** /haː|ˈoː/ *die;* ∼ (*DDR*) **A** ⇒ **Handelsorganisation** B; **B** ⇒ ∼**-Geschäft**

**hob** /hoːp/ *1. u. 3. Pers. Sg. Prät. v.* **heben**

**Hobby** /ˈhɔbi/ *das;* ∼**s**, ∼**s** hobby

**Họbby-** amateur ‹gardener, archaeologist, astronomer, etc.›

**Họbby·raum** *der* hobby room

**Hobel** /ˈhoːbl̩/ *der;* ∼**s**, ∼ **A** plane; **B** (*Küchengerät*) [vegetable] slicer

**Ho̲bel-:** ∼**bank** *die; Pl.* ∼**bänke** carpenter's *or* woodworker's bench; ∼**eisen** *das,* ∼**messer** *das* plane iron

**ho̲beln** *tr., itr. V.* **A** plane; **an etw.** (*Dat.*) ∼: plane sth.; **B** (*schneiden*) slice

**Ho̲bel·span** *der* shaving

**hoch** /hoːx/, **höher**/ˈhøːɐ/, **höchst...** /ˈhøːçst.../ ❶ *Adj.* **A** ▶411 (*von beträchtlicher Höhe*) high; high, tall ‹building›; tall ‹tree, mast›; long ‹grass›; deep ‹snow, water›; long, tall ‹ladder›; high-ceilinged ‹room›; **10 m** ∼: 10 m high; **eine hohe Stirn** a high forehead; **er bekommt eine hohe Stirn** he's receding; **von hoher Gestalt** (*geh.*) tall in stature; of tall stature; **hohe Absätze** high heels; **hohe Schuhe** (*mit hohem Schaft*) high boots; (*mit hohen Absätzen*) high-heeled shoes; **B** (*mengenmäßig groß*) high ‹price, wage, rent, speed, pressure, temperature, sensitivity›; heavy ‹fine›; great ‹weight›; large ‹sum, amount›; high, large, big ‹profit›; severe, extensive ‹damage›; **einen hohen Blutdruck haben** have high blood pressure; **C** (*zeitlich fortgeschritten*) great ‹age›; **ein hohes Alter erreichen** live to *or* reach a ripe old age; **es ist höchste Zeit, dass ...** it is high time that ...; **D** (*oben in einer Rangordnung*) high ‹birth, office›; high-ranking ‹officer, civil servant›; senior ‹official, officer, post›; high-level ‹diplomacy, politics›; important ‹guest, festival›; **Verhandlungen auf höchster Ebene** top-level negotiations; **der hohe Adel** the higher ranks of the nobility; **eine hohe Ehre** a great honour; **mit höchster Diskretion/Eile** with the greatest discretion/urgency; **das Höchste Wesen** the Supreme Being; **sich zu Höherem berufen fühlen** feel called to higher things; **höchste Gefahr** extreme danger; **im höchsten Fall[e]** at the most; ⇒ *auch* **Blödsinn**; **Gefühl** B; **Gewalt** D; **Haus** F; **Jagd** A; **Tier**; **Tochter** A; **E** (*qualitativ* ∼ *stehend*) high ‹standard, opinion›; great ‹responsibility, concentration, talent, happiness, good, importance›; **die hohe Schule** (*Reiten*) haute école; **F** (*Musik*) high ‹voice, note›; **das hohe C** top C; **G** ▶841 (*Math.*) **vier** ∼ **zwei** four to the power [of] two; four squared; **H** (*in großer Höhe*) high ‹cloud, branch, etc.›; **der hohe Norden** (*fig.*) the far North; **I** (*auf dem Höhepunkt*) **das hohe Mittelalter** the High Middle Ages; **J** *in* **das ist mir zu** ∼ (*ugs.*) that's beyond me; that went over my head.

❷ *adv.* **A** (*in großer Höhe*) high; ∼ **oben am Himmel** high up in the sky; ∼ **über uns** high above us; **die Sonne steht** ∼: the sun is high in the sky; **wenn die Sonne am höchsten steht** when the sun is [at its] highest; ∼ **zu Ross** (*geh.*) on horseback; **er wohnt drei Treppen** ∼: he lives on the third (*Brit.*) *or* (*Amer.*) fourth floor; ∼ **auf etw.** (*Dat.*) **sitzen** sit high up on sth.; **B** (*nach oben*) up; **Kopf** ∼! chin up! **die Flammen loderten** ∼: the flames leapt up high; **zu** ∼ **zielen** aim too high; **ein** ∼ **aufgeschossener Junge** a very tall lad; **einen Ball** ∼ **in die Luft werfen** throw a ball high in the air; **die Nase** ∼ **tragen** walk around with one's nose in the air; **die Preise höher schrauben** (*fig.*) push up the prices; ∼ **gesteckt** (*fig.*) ambitious ‹goal, plan›; **C** (*zahlenmäßig viel*) highly ‹taxed, paid›; heavily ‹taxed›; ∼ **verschuldet/versichert** heavily in debt/insured for a large sum [of money]; ∼ **gewinnen/verlieren** (*Sport*) win/lose by a large margin; **wenn es** ∼ **kommt** at [the] most; **D** (*dem Rang nach oben*) **etw.** ∼ **und heilig versprechen** promise sth. faithfully; ∼ **hinauswollen** (*ugs.*) aim high; have great ambitions; **zu** ∼ **hinauswollen** (*ugs.*) aim too high; be too ambitious; ∼ **gestellt** ‹person› in a high position; important ‹person›; ∼ **stehend** ‹person› of high standing; **geistig** ∼ **stehend** intellectually distinguished; ‹person› of high intellect; **sittlich** ∼ **stehend** high-minded; **E** (*sehr*) highly ‹gifted, delighted, satisfied, respected, regarded›; most ‹welcome›; highly, greatly ‹esteemed›; **jmdm. etw.** ∼ **anrechnen** consider sth. [to be] greatly to sb.'s credit; **jmdn.** ∼ **verehren** esteem sb. highly *or* greatly; **F** (*zeitlich fortgeschritten*) ∼ **in den Siebzigern** well into his/her seventies; **G** (*Musik*) high; **H** (*in Wendungen*) **das Herz höher schlagen lassen** make sb.'s heart beat faster; **es ging** ∼ **her** things were pretty lively; **sie kamen drei Mann** ∼: three of them came; there were three of them; ⇒ *auch* **höchst**

**Ho̲ch** *das;* ∼**s**, ∼**s** **A** (∼*ruf*) **ein [dreifaches]** ∼ **auf jmdn. ausbringen** give three cheers for sb.; **ein** ∼ **dem Gastgeber!** three cheers for the host!; **B** (*Met.*) high

**ho̲ch-:** ∼**achtbar** *Adj.* highly respectable; *∼**|achten** ⇒ **achten** 1

**Ho̲ch·achtung** *die* great respect; high esteem; ∼ **vor jmdm. haben** have a great respect for sb.; hold sb. in high esteem; **meine** ∼! may I congratulate you; **mit vorzüglicher** ∼ (*veralt.: Briefschluss*) most respectfully yours (*dated*); yours faithfully

**ho̲chachtungs·voll** *Adv.* (*Briefschluss*) yours faithfully

**ho̲ch-, Ho̲ch-:** ∼**adel** *der* higher ranks *pl.* of the nobility; ∼**aktuell** *Adj.* highly topical; ∼**alpin** *Adj.* high alpine *attrib.* ‹landscape, flora, fauna, etc.›; ∼**altar** *der* high altar; ∼**amt** *das* (*kath. Rel.*) high mass; *∼**angesehen** *Adj.* ⇒ **hoch** 2E; ∼**anständig** ❶ *Adj.* very decent; ❷ *adv.* very *or* most decently; ∼**antenne** *die* roof aerial (*Brit.*) *or* (*Amer.*) antenna; ∼**|arbeiten** *refl. V.* work one's way up; ∼**bahn** *die* overhead railway; elevated railroad (*Amer.*); ∼**barren** *der* (*Sport*) parallel bars *pl.* (*set at international height of 180 cm.*); ∼**bau** *der* [building] construction *no art.;* ∼**- und Tiefbau** [building] construction and civil engineering *no art.;* ∼**befriedigt** *Adj.* highly satisfied; *∼**begabt** ⇒ **begabt**; ∼**beglückt** *Adj.* blissfully happy; ∼**beinig** *Adj.* long-legged ‹person, animal›; ‹table, sofa, etc.› with long legs; ∼**bejahrt** *Adj.* (*geh.*) ⇒ ∼**betagt**; ∼**|bekommen** *unr. tr. V.* [manage to] lift; [manage to] do up ‹zip›; *∼**beladen** ⇒ **beladen**[2]; ∼**berühmt** *Adj.* very famous; ∼**betagt** *Adj.* aged; ‹person› advanced in years *postpos.;* ∼**betrieb** *der* (*ugs.*) **es herrschte** ∼**betrieb im Geschäft** the shop was at its busiest; **heute herrschte** ∼**betrieb im Büro** the office was very busy today; *∼**bezahlt** ⇒ **bezahlen** 1; ∼**|biegen** ❶ *unr. tr. V.* **etw.** ∼**biegen** bend sth. up[wards]; ❷ *unr. refl. V.* bend up; ∼**|binden** *unr. tr. V.* tie up ‹plant›; put up ‹hair›; ∼**|blicken** *itr. V.* look up; ∼**blüte** *die* golden age; ∼**|bringen** *unr. tr. V.* **A** (*nach oben bringen*) bring up; **B** (*ugs.: in die Wohnung bringen*) bring in[to the flat (*Brit.*) *or* (*Amer.*) apartment]; **C** (*gesund machen*) **jmdn.** ∼**bringen** put sb. on his/her feet; **D** (*ugs.: ärgern*) **jmdn.** ∼**bringen** put sb.'s back up; ∼**burg** *die* stronghold; ∼**busig** *Adj.* high-bosomed; *∼**dekoriert** ⇒ **dekorieren** B; ∼**deutsch** *Adj.* standard *or* High German; **die** ∼**deutsche Lautverschiebung** the High German *or* second sound shift; **mit jmdm.** ∼**deutsch sprechen** *od.* **reden** (*ugs.*) give sb. a piece of one's mind; ∼**deutsch** *das,* ∼**deutsche** *das* standard *or* High German; ∼**|dienen** *refl. V.* work one's way up; *∼**dotiert** ⇒ **dotiert**; ∼**|drehen** *tr. V.* **A** (*in die Höhe drehen*) wind up ‹window, barrier, etc.›; **B** (*Technik*) rev [up] (*coll.*) ‹engine›

**Ho̲ch·druck**[1] *der; Pl.* **Ho̲ch·drücke** **A** (*Physik, Met.*) high pressure; **B** (*Geschäftigkeit*) **mit** *od.* **unter** ∼ **arbeiten** (*ugs.*) work flat out or at full stretch; **in allen Abteilungen herrschte** ∼: all departments were at full stretch; **C** ▶474 (*Med.*) high blood pressure; hypertension (*Med.*)

**Ho̲ch·druck**[2] *der; Pl.* ∼**e** (*Druckw.*) **A** (*Verfahren*) relief *or* letterpress printing; **etw. im** ∼ **herstellen/drucken** produce/print sth. by letterpress; **B** (*Erzeugnis*) piece of letterpress work; ∼**e** letterpress work

**Ho̲chdruck·gebiet** *das* high-pressure area

**ho̲ch-, Ho̲ch-:** ∼**ebene** *die* plateau; tableland; *∼**empfindlich** ⇒ **empfindlich** 1A; *∼**entwickelt** ⇒ **entwickeln** 2; *∼**erhoben** ⇒ **erheben** 1A; ∼**explosiv** *Adj.* (*auch fig.*) highly explosive; ∼**|fahren** ❶ *unr. itr. V.; mit sein* **A** (*ugs.: nach oben fahren*) go up; (*mit dem Auto*) drive up; (*mit dem Fahrrad, Motorrad*) ride up; **B** (*ugs.: nach Norden fahren*) drive up; **C** (*auffahren*) start up; **aus dem Sessel** ∼**fahren** start [up] from one's chair; **aus dem Schlaf** ∼**fahren** wake up with a start; **D** (*aufbrausen*) flare up; ❷ *unr. tr. V.* (*ugs.*) **jmdn./etw.** ∼**fahren** take sb./sth. up; **das Auto** ∼**fahren** drive the car up; ∼**fahrend** *Adj.* arrogant; supercilious; ∼**fein** *Adj.* of the finest quality *postpos.;* **aus** ∼**feiner Schokolade/**∼**feinem Batist** of the finest chocolate/batiste; ∼**finanz** *die* high finance; ∼**fläche** *die* plateau; tableland; ∼**|fliegen** *unr. itr. V.; mit sein* fly up [into the air]; ∼**fliegend** *Adj.* ambitious ‹plan, idea, etc.›; ∼**flut** *die* high water *or* tide; (*fig.*) flood; ∼**form** *die* peak *or* top form; ∼**format** *das* upright format; **ein Bild/Blatt in** ∼**format** a picture/sheet with an upright format; ∼**frequenz** *die* (*Physik*) high frequency; ∼**frequenz·technik** *die* radio-frequency engineering *no art.;* ∼**frisur** *die* upswept hairstyle; ∼**garage** *die* multi-storey car park; *∼**geachtet** ⇒ **geachtet** 2; ∼**gebildet** *Adj.* highly cultured; ∼**gebirge**

*old spelling (see note on page 1707)

*das* [high] mountains *pl.;* **∼gebirgs·land·schaft** *die* high-mountain region; **∼gebo·ren** *Adj.* (*veralt.*) high-born; ***∼geehrt** ⇨ **ehren** A; **∼gefühl** *das* [feeling of] elation; **im ∼gefühl des Erfolges/Sieges** in his/her *etc.* elation at success/victory; **∼|gehen** *unr. itr. V.; mit sein* Ⓐ (*steigen*) go up; rise; Ⓑ (*ugs.: hinaufgehen*) go up; **die Treppe ∼gehen** go up the stairs *or* upstairs; Ⓒ (*ugs.: zornig werden*) blow one's top (*coll.*); explode; Ⓓ (*ugs.: explodieren*) ‹bomb, mine› go off; ‹bridge, building, etc.› go up; **etw. ∼gehen lassen** (*salopp*) blow sth. up; Ⓔ (*ugs.: aufgedeckt werden*) get caught *or* (*coll.*) nabbed; **jmdn. ∼gehen lassen** ‹informer› grass *or* squeal on sb. (*sl.*); **die Polizei ließ den Rauschgiftring ∼gehen** the police smashed the drug ring; **∼geistig** *Adj.* highly intellectual; ***∼gelegen** ⇨ **gelegen** 2 B; **∼gelehrt** *Adj.* extremely *or* very learned *or* erudite; **∼gemut** /-gəmu:t/ (*geh.*) ❶ *Adj.* cheerful; ❷ *adv.* cheerfully; in good spirits; **∼genuss**, ***∼genuß** *der: in* **ein ∼genuss sein** be a real delight; ‹meal, concert, etc.› be a real treat; **ihm zuzuhören ist ein ∼genuss** he is a real delight to listen to; ***∼geschätzt** ⇨ **schätzen** 1B; **∼gescheit** *Adj.* ⇨ **∼intelligent**; **∼geschlossen** *Adj.* high-necked ‹dress›; **∼geschwindigkeits·zug** *der* high-speed train; **∼gesinnt** *Adj.* (*geh.*) high-minded; noble-minded; **∼gespannt** *Adj.* great, high ‹expectations›; ***∼gesteckt** ⇨ **hoch** 2 B; ***∼gestellt** ⇨ **hoch** 2 D; **∼gestimmt** *Adj.* (*geh.*) elated; **∼gestochen** (*ugs. abwertend*) ❶ *Adj.* Ⓐ (*anspruchsvoll*) highbrow; (*geschraubt*) stilted ‹style›; Ⓑ (*eingebildet*) conceited; stuck-up; ❷ *adv.* in a highbrow way (*coll.*); ***∼gewachsen** ⇨ **wachsen**[1] A; **∼gezüchtet** *Adj.* highly-bred ‹animal›; **ein ∼gezüchteter Motor** a very finely tuned engine

**Hoch·glanz** *der:* **ein Foto in ∼** (*Dat.*) a high-gloss print; **etw. auf ∼** (*Akk.*) **polieren** polish sth. until it shines *or* gleams; **etw. auf ∼** (*Akk.*) **bringen** give sth. a high polish; (*fig.*) make sth. spick and span

**Hochglanz·folie** *die* glazing sheet

**hoch-, Hoch-: ∼gradig** ❶ *Adj.* extreme; ❷ *adv.* extremely; **∼hackig** *Adj.* high-heeled ‹shoe›; **∼|halten** *unr. tr. V.* Ⓐ hold up ‹arms›; Ⓑ (*geh.: schützen*) uphold ‹truth, tradition, etc.›; **jmds. Andenken ∼halten** honour sb.'s memory; **∼haus** *das* high-rise building; **∼|heben** *unr. tr. V.* lift up; raise ‹arm, leg, etc.›; raise, hold up ‹hand›; **∼herrschaftlich** *Adj.* palatial ‹house, apartment›; **∼herzig** *Adj.* (*geh.*) magnanimous; generous; **∼herzigkeit** *die;* **∼∼:** magnanimity; generosity; **∼intelligent** *Adj.* highly intelligent; **∼interessant** *Adj.* extremely *or* most interesting; fascinating; **∼|jagen** *tr. V.* Ⓐ scare up ‹birds›; forcibly rouse ‹sleeper›; Ⓑ (*Jargon*) race, (*coll.*) rev up ‹engine›; Ⓒ (*ugs.: sprengen*) blow up; **∼|jubeln** *tr. V.* (*ugs.*) **jmdn./etw. ∼jubeln** build sb. up as a star/sth. up as a hit; **∼kant** *Adv.* Ⓐ on end; Ⓑ (*ugs.*) *in* **jmdn. ∼kant hinauswerfen** *od.* (*salopp*) **rausschmeißen** chuck sb. out (*sl.*); throw sb. out on his/her ear (*coll.*); **∼kant hinausfliegen** *od.* (*salopp*) **rausfliegen** be chucked out (*sl.*); be thrown out on one's ear (*coll.*); **∼kantig** *Adv.* ⇨ **∼kant**; **∼karätig** /-ka'rɛ:tɪç/ *Adj.* Ⓐ high-carat ‹gold, diamond›; Ⓑ (*fig.*) top-flight (*coll.*); **∼kirche** *die* High Church; **∼|klappen** ❶ *tr. V.* fold up ‹chair, table›; raise, lift up ‹lid, car bonnet›; turn up ‹collar›; ❷ *itr. V.; mit sein* fold up; **∼|klettern** *itr. V.; mit sein* (*ugs.*) climb up; **den Baum ∼klettern** climb [up] the tree; **∼|kommen** *unr. itr. V.; mit sein* (*ugs.*) Ⓐ come up; Ⓑ (*vorwärts kommen*) get on; Ⓒ (*aus dem Magen*) **ihr kam das Essen ∼:** she threw up (*coll.*) *or* brought up her meal; **es kommt einem ∼, wenn ...** (*fig.*) it makes you sick when ...; Ⓓ (*sich erheben*) get up; (*sich erheben können*) be able to get up; Ⓔ (*fig.*) **in jmdn. ∼kommen** rise up in sb.; **∼konjunktur** *die* (*Wirtsch.*) boom; **auf dem Automarkt herrscht ∼konjunktur** the car market is booming; there's a boom in car sales; **∼|können** *unr. V.* (*ugs.*) be able to get up; **∼konzentriert** *Adj.* highly concentrated; **∼|krempeln** *tr. V.* roll up ‹sleeve, trouser leg›; **∼|kriegen** *tr. V.* (*ugs.*) ⇨ **∼bekommen; einen ∼kriegen** (*salopp*) get it up (*sl.*); **∼kultur** *die* advanced civilization *or* culture; **∼|kurbeln** *tr. V.* wind up; **∼lage** *die* higher region; **∼land** *das* highlands *pl.;* **∼|leben** *itr. V.: in* **jmdn./etw. ∼leben lassen** cheer sb./sth.; **er/unser Verein lebe ∼!** three cheers for him/our club!; **der König lebe ∼!** long live the king!; **∼|legen** *tr. V.* **ein gebrochenes Bein ∼legen** support a broken leg in a raised position; **die Beine ∼legen** put one's feet up

**Hoch·leistung** *die* outstanding performance

**Hochleistungs·sport** *der* top-level sport

**höchlich[st]** /'hø:çlɪç(st)/ *Adv.* (*veralt.*) highly; greatly; most

**hoch-, Hoch-: ∼mittel·alter** *das* High Middle Ages; **∼modern** ❶ *Adj.* ultra-modern; ❷ *adv.* **∼modern gekleidet/eingerichtet sein** be extremely fashionably dressed *or* dressed in the very latest fashions/be furnished in the very latest style; **∼moor** *das* (*Geogr.*) high-moor bog; ***∼motiviert** ⇨ **motivieren** B; **∼mut** *der* arrogance; **∼mut kommt vor dem Fall** (*Spr.*) pride goes before a fall (*prov.*); **∼mütig** *Adj.* arrogant; **∼näsig** /-nɛ:zɪç/ *Adj.* (*abwertend*) stuck-up; conceited; **∼näsigkeit** *die;* **∼∼** (*abwertend*) conceitedness; **∼nebel** *der* low stratus [cloud]; **∼|nehmen** *unr. tr. V.* Ⓐ lift *or* pick up; Ⓑ (*ugs.: verspotten*) **jmdn. ∼nehmen** pull sb.'s leg; Ⓒ (*ugs.: nach oben nehmen*) **jmdn./etw. mit ∼nehmen** take sb./sth. up with one; Ⓓ (*salopp: verhaften*) run in; **∼not·peinlich** *Adj.* (*veralt.*) ‹interrogation› under torture; **ein ∼notpeinliches Verhör** (*fig.: scherzh.*) an inquisition; **∼ofen** *der* blast furnace; **∼offiziell** *Adj.* extremely formal; **∼|päppeln** *tr. V.* (*salopp*) feed up; **∼parterre** *das* upper ground floor; **∼plateau** *das* high plateau; **∼politisch** *Adj.* highly political; **∼prozentig** *Adj.* high-proof ‹spirits›; **∼punkt** *der* (*Math.*) maximum; ***∼qualifiziert** ⇨ **qualifiziert** 2 B; **∼rädrig** *Adj.* large-wheeled; **∼|ragen** *itr. V.* rise *or* tower up; **∼|rappeln** *refl. V.* ⇨ **aufrappeln**; **∼|rechnen** project; **∼rechnung** *die* (*Statistik*) projection; **∼reck** *das* (*Turnen*) high *or* horizontal bar; **∼|reißen** *unr. tr. V.* whip up; pull up ‹aircraft›; **die Arme ∼reißen** throw one's arms up; **∼relief** *das* high relief; **∼rot** *Adj.* bright red; **∼rot im Gesicht werden** (*aus Verlegenheit*) go as red as a beetroot; **∼ruf** *der* cheer; **∼|rutschen** *itr. V.; mit sein* (*ugs.*) ‹dress, shirt, etc.› ride up; **∼saison** *die* high season; **∼|schaukeln** *tr. V.* (*ugs.*) blow up ‹problem, incident, etc.›; **sich [gegenseitig] ∼schaukeln** goad each other; **∼|scheuchen** *tr. V.* ⇨ **aufscheuchen**; **∼|schieben** *unr. tr. V.* (*ugs.*) push up; **∼|schießen** ❶ *unr. tr. V.* send up, launch ‹rocket, space probe, etc.›; ❷ *unr. itr. V.; mit sein* (*auch fig.*) shoot up; **∼|schlagen** ❶ *unr. tr. V.* turn up ‹collar, brim›; ❷ *unr. itr. V.; mit sein* ‹water, waves› surge up; ‹flames› leap up; **Wellen der Begeisterung schlugen ∼** (*fig.*) there was a great surge of enthusiasm; **∼|schnellen** *itr. V.; mit sein* leap up; **∼schrank** *der* wardrobe; **∼|schrauben** ❶ *tr. V.* Ⓐ raise ‹seat› (*by screwing*); Ⓑ (*fig.*) force up ‹prices›; step up, increase ‹demands›; raise ‹expectations›; ❷ *refl. V.* circle up[wards]; **∼|schrecken** ⇨ **aufschrecken**

**Hochschul·bildung** *die* college/university education

**Hoch-: ∼schule** *die* college; (*Universität*) university; **∼schüler** *der,* **∼schülerin** *die* college/university student

**Hochschul-: ∼lehrer** *der,* **∼lehrerin** *die* ▶159 college/university lecturer *or* teacher; **∼studium** *das* college/university studies *pl., no art.;* **∼wesen** *das* university and college system; (*Bereich*) higher education

**hoch·schwanger** *Adj.* in an advanced stage of pregnancy *postpos.;* very pregnant (*coll.*)

**Hoch·see** *die* open sea

**hochsee-, Hochsee-: ∼fischerei** *die* deep-sea fishing *no art.;* **∼flotte** *die* deep sea fleet; **∼jacht** *die* ocean-going yacht; **∼tüchtig** *Adj.* seaworthy

**Hoch·seil** *das* high wire

**Hochseil-: ∼akrobat** *der,* **∼akrobatin** *die,* **∼artist** *der,* **∼artistin** *die* ▶159 performer on the high wire

**hoch-, Hoch-: ∼sicherheits·trakt** *der* high-security wing; **∼sitz** *der* (*Jagdw.*) raised hide; **∼sommer** *der* high summer; midsummer; **∼sommerlich** *Adj.* very summery ‹weather etc.›

**Hoch·spannung** *die* Ⓐ (*Elektrot.*) high voltage *or* tension; **Vorsicht, ∼spannung!** danger — high voltage; Ⓑ (*gespannte Stimmung*) high tension; **es herrscht ∼spannung** there's a great deal of tension

**Hochspannungs-: ∼leitung** *die* high voltage *or* high tension [transmission] line; power line; **∼mast** *der* electricity pylon

**hoch-, Hoch-: ∼|spielen** *tr. V.* blow up ‹incident, affair, etc.›; **∼sprache** *die* standard language; **∼sprachlich** ❶ *Adj.* standard; ❷ *adv.* **sich ∼sprachlich ausdrücken** speak the standard language; **∼|springen** *unr. itr. V.; mit sein* Ⓐ jump *or* leap up; **an jmdm. ∼springen** ‹dog etc.› jump up at sb.; Ⓑ *nur im Inf. u. Part. gebr.* (*Sport*) do the high jump; **∼springer** *der,* **∼springerin** *die* (*Sport*) high jumper; **∼sprung** *der* (*Sport*) high jump; (*einzelner Sprung*) jump; **∼sprung·anlage** *die* (*Sport*) high jump apparatus

**höchst** /hø:çst/ *Adv.* extremely; most

**höchst...** ⇨ **hoch**

**Höchstädt** /'hø:çʃtɛt/ (*das*); **∼s: die Schlacht bei ∼:** the Battle of Blenheim

**hoch-, Hoch-: ∼stämmig** *Adj.* standard ‹rose›; **∼stand** *der* (*Jagdw.*) raised stand; **∼stapelei** /-ʃta:pə'lai/ *die;* **∼∼, ∼∼en** Ⓐ fraud; **eine ∼stapelei** a confidence trick; Ⓑ (*Aufschneiderei*) empty boasting; **∼|stapeln** *itr. V.* Ⓐ perpetrate a fraud/frauds; Ⓑ (*aufschneiden*) make empty boasts; **∼stapler** *der* Ⓐ confidence trickster; conman (*coll.*); Ⓑ (*Aufschneider*) fraud; **∼staplerin** *die;* **∼∼, ∼∼nen** Ⓐ confidence trickster; Ⓑ (*Aufschneiderin*) fraud

**Höchst-: ∼belastung** *die* extreme strain *or* stress *no indef. art.;* (*Technik*) maximum [safe] load; **∼betrag** *der* maximum amount; **∼bietende** *der/die; adj. Dekl.* highest bidder

**hoch-: *∼stehend** ⇨ **hoch** 2 D; **∼|steigen** *unr. itr. V.; mit sein* Ⓐ climb; **die Treppe/Stufen ∼steigen** climb the stairs/steps; Ⓑ ‹bubbles, smoke, etc.› rise; ‹rocket› go up; Ⓒ (*langsam entstehen*) rise up; ‹tears› well up; **Freude/Wut stieg in ihr ∼:** joy rose in her heart/rage rose [up] inside her

**höchst·eigen** *Adj.* (*veralt.; noch scherzh.*) **in ∼er Person** in person

**hoch-: ∼|stellen** *tr. V.* Ⓐ put up; Ⓑ (*∼klappen*) turn up ‹collar›; Ⓒ (*Math.*) **eine ∼gestellte Zahl** a superior number; ⇨ *auch* **hochgestellt**; **∼|stemmen** *tr. V.* Ⓐ lift; Ⓑ (*aufrichten*) **sich/seinen Oberkörper ∼stemmen** raise oneself [up]

**höchsten·falls** /'hø:çstn̩-/ *Adv.* at [the] most *or* the outside; at the very most

**höchstens** *Adv.* Ⓐ (*nicht mehr als*) at most; (*bestenfalls*) at best; **in ∼** *od.* **∼ in drei Fällen** in three cases at most; Ⓑ (*außer*) **sie verreist nicht, ∼ dass sie einmal zu ihren Verwandten fährt** she never goes away anywhere, apart from *or* except for visiting her relations once in a while

**Höchst-: ∼fall** *der: in* **im ∼fall** at [the] most *or* the outside; at the very most; **∼form** *die* (*bes. Sport*) peak *or* top form; **∼gebot** *das* highest bid *or* offer; **etw. gegen ∼gebot verkaufen** sell sth. to the highest bidder; **„große Briefmarkensammlung gegen ∼gebot zu verkaufen"** 'offers invited for large stamp collection'; **∼geschwindig·keit** *die* ▶348 top *or* maximum speed; (*Geschwindigkeitsbegrenzung*) speed limit; **∼grenze** *die* maximum

**hoch|stilisieren** *tr. V.* (*abwertend*) build up (**zu** into)

**Hoch·stimmung** *die* festive mood; high spirits *pl.;* **in ∼ sein** be in a festive mood

h

**höchst-, Höchst-: ~leistung** *die* supreme performance; (*Ergebnis*) supreme achievement; (*Technik*) maximum performance; **~maß** *das:* **ein ~maß an etw.** (*Dat.*) a very high degree of sth.; **ein ~maß von etw.** (*Dat.*) a maximum [amount] of sth.; **~möglich** *Adj.* highest possible; **~persönlich** ❶ *Adj.* personal; ❷ *adv.* in person; **~preis** *der* (*~möglicher Preis*) highest price; (*~zulässiger Preis*) maximum price

**Hoch·straße** *die* overpass; flyover (*Brit.*)

**hoch|streifen** *tr. V.* pull up

**höchst-, Höchst-: ~richterlich** *Adj.* **eine ~richterliche Entscheidung** a ruling of the supreme court; **~satz** *der* maximum *or* top rate; **~stand** *der* highest level; **~strafe** *die* maximum penalty; **~wahrscheinlich** *Adv.* very probably; **~wert** *der* maximum value; **~zulässig** /*auch:* '-'--/ *Adj.* maximum [permissible] ‹weight, speed, etc.›

**hoch-, Hoch-: ~tal** *das* high[-lying] valley; **~tour** *die:* *in* **auf ~touren laufen** run at top *or* full speed; (*intensiv betrieben werden*) be in full swing; **einen Motor auf ~touren bringen** rev an engine up to full speed (*coll.*); **~tourig** /-tu:rɪç/ (*Technik*) ❶ *Adj.* fast-revving (*coll.*) ‹engine›; ❷ *adv.* **~tourig fahren** drive at high revs (*coll.*); **~trabend** (*abwertend*) ❶ *Adj.* pretentious; high-flown; ❷ *adv.* pretentiously; in a high-flown manner; **~|tragen** *unr. tr. V.* carry up; **~|treiben** *unr. tr. V.* Ⓐ (*ugs.: hinauftreiben*) drive up; **die Schafe den Berg ~treiben** drive the sheep up the mountain; Ⓑ (*fig.*) force *or* push up ‹prices etc.›; **~verdient** *Adj.* ‹scientist etc.› of outstanding merit; richly deserved ‹victory, success, etc.›; **~verehrt** *Adj.* highly respected *or* esteemed; (*als Anrede*) **meine ~verehrten Damen und Herren!** ladies and gentlemen!; **~verehrte Frau Schmidt** my dear Mrs Schmidt; **~verrat** *der* high treason; **~verräter** *der*, **~verräterin** *die* traitor; person guilty of high treason; **~verräterisch** *Adj.* traitorous; treasonable; ***~verschuldet** ⇒ **verschuldet**; **~verzinslich** *Adj.* (*Finanzw.*) ‹security etc.› yielding a high rate of interest; **~wald** *der* (*Forstw.*) high forest

**Hoch·wasser** *das* ▶ 306 | (*Flut*) high tide *or* water; (*Überschwemmung*) flood; **der Fluss hat** *od.* **führt ~:** the river is in flood; **er hat ~** (*ugs. scherzh.*) his trousers are at half mast (*coll.*)

**Hochwasser-: ~gefahr** *die* flood danger; danger of flooding; **~hose[n]** *die* (*scherzh.*) trousers *pl.* at half mast (*coll.*); **~schaden** *der* flood damage

**hoch-, Hoch-: ~|werfen** *unr. tr. V.* **etw. ~werfen** throw sth. up; **eine Münze ~werfen** toss a coin; **~wertig** *Adj.* high-quality ‹goods›; highly nutritious ‹food›; **~wild** *das* (*Jägerspr.*) *larger game animals, e.g. deer, boar, chamois;* **~willkommen** *Adj.* very *or* most welcome; **~|winden** ❶ *unr. tr. V.* wind up; weigh ‹anchor›; ❷ *unr. refl. V.* wind one's/its way up; **~wirksam** *Adj.* highly *or* extremely effective; **~wohlgeboren** *Adj.* ▶ 91 | (*veralt.*) high-born; **Euer Hochwohlgeboren** Your Honour; **~|wollen** *unr. itr. V.* (*ugs.*) want to get up; **~|wuchten** *tr. V.* (*ugs.*) heave up; **~würden** (*der*); **~~s** ▶ 91 | (*veralt.*) Reverend Father; **~zahl** *die* (*Math.*) exponent

**Hoch·zeit**[1] *die* (*geh.*) Golden Age

**Hochzeit**[2] /'hɔxtsait/ *die;* **~, ~en** ▶ 369 | wedding; **~ halten** *od.* **machen** (*veralt.*) get married; **grüne ~:** wedding day; **silberne/goldene ~:** silver/golden wedding [anniversary]; **man kann nicht auf zwei ~en tanzen** (*fig. ugs.*) you can't be in two places at once

**Hochzeiter** *der;* **~s, ~** (*landsch.*) [bride]groom; **die ~:** the bride and groom

**Hochzeiterin** *die;* **~, ~nen** (*landsch.*) bride

**Hochzeits-: ~anzeige** *die* wedding announcement; **~feier** *die* wedding; **~flug** *der* (*Zool.*) nuptial flight; **~geschenk** *das* wedding gift *or* present; **~kleid** *das* Ⓐ (*Brautkleid*) wedding dress; Ⓑ (*Zool.*) (*von Vögeln*) nuptial plumage; (*von Tieren*) nuptial coloration; **~kuchen** *der* wedding cake; **~nacht** *die* wedding night; **~reise** *die* honeymoon [trip]; **wir haben unsere ~reise nach Berlin gemacht** we went to Berlin for our honeymoon; **~tag** *der* ▶ 369 | Ⓐ wedding day; Ⓑ (*Jahrestag*) wedding anniversary; **~zug** *der* wedding procession

**hoch-, Hoch-: ~|ziehen** ❶ *unr. tr. V.* Ⓐ (*nach oben ziehen*) pull up; pull up, raise ‹shutters, blind›; hoist, raise, run up ‹flag›; hoist ‹sail›; **die Schultern/Brauen ~ziehen** hunch one's shoulders/raise one's eyebrows; **die Nase ~ziehen** sniff [loudly]; Ⓑ **ein Flugzeug ~ziehen** put an aircraft into a steep climb; Ⓒ (*mauern*) put up, build ‹wall, building›; ❷ *unr. refl. V.* **sich [an etw.** (*Dat.*)**] ~ziehen** pull oneself up [by hanging on to sth.]; **sich an etw.** (*Dat.*) **~ziehen** (*fig.*) latch on to sth.; **~zins·politik** *die* policy of keeping interest rates high

**Hocke** /'hɔkə/ *die;* **~, ~n** Ⓐ (*Körperhaltung*) squat; crouch; **in der ~ sitzen** squat; crouch; **in die ~ gehen** squat [down]; crouch down; Ⓑ (*Turnen*) squat vault

**hocken** ❶ *itr. V.* Ⓐ *mit haben od.* (*südd.*) *sein* squat; crouch; Ⓑ *mit haben od.* (*südd.*) *sein* (*ugs.: sich aufhalten*) sit around; **hinter einem Schreibtisch ~:** sit behind a desk; Ⓒ *mit sein* (*südd.: sitzen*) sit; Ⓓ *mit sein* (*Turnen*) perform *or* do a squat vault (**über** + *Akk.* over). ❷ *refl. V.* Ⓐ crouch down; squat [down]; Ⓑ (*südd.: sich setzen*) sit down

**Hocker** *der;* **~s, ~:** stool

**Höcker** /'hœkɐ/ *der;* **~s, ~** Ⓐ hump; (*auf der Nase*) bump; (*auf dem Schnabel*) knob; **er hat einen ~:** he's humpbacked; Ⓑ (*Hügel*) hillock; hump

**Hocker·grab** *das* (*Archäol.*) crouched burial

**höckerig** *Adj.* bumpy

**Höcker·schwan** *der* mute swan

**Hockey** /'hɔki/ *das;* **~s** hockey

**Hockey-: ~schläger** *der* hockey stick; **~spieler** *der*, **~spielerin** *die* hockey player

**Hock-: ~sitz** *der* (*Turnen*) squat; **~stand** *der* (*Turnen*) crouch

**Hoden** /'ho:dn̩/ *der;* **~s, ~** ▶ 471 | testicle

**Hoden-: ~bruch** *der* ▶ 474 | (*Med.*) scrotal hernia; **~sack** *der* ▶ 471 | scrotum

**Hoek van Holland** /'hʊk 'fan 'hɔlant/ (*das*); **Hoeks van Holland** Hook of Holland

**Hof** /ho:f/ *der;* **~[e]s, Höfe** /'hø:fə/ Ⓐ courtyard; (*Schul~*) playground; (*Gefängnis~*) [prison] yard; Ⓑ (*Bauern~*) farm; **in einen ~ einheiraten** marry into a farming family; Ⓒ (*Herrscher, ~staat*) court; **am ~ leben/verkehren** live at court/move in court circles; **die europäischen Höfe** the European royal courts; **jmdn. bei ~e einführen/vorstellen** present sb. at court; **~ halten** hold court; Ⓓ **jmdm. den ~ machen** (*veralt.*) pay court to sb.; Ⓔ (*Aureole*) corona; aureole; Ⓕ (*in Namen von Hotels, z. B. „Bayerischer ~"*) (*implying or suggesting a particular, e.g. Bavarian, style and a superior standard of accommodation*)

**hof-, Hof-: ~amt** *das* (*hist.*) [hereditary] office at court; **~ball** *der* court ball; **~dame** *die* lady of the court; (*Begleiterin der Königin*) lady-in-waiting; **~dichter** *der* (*hist.*) court poet; **~etikette** *die* court etiquette; **~fähig** *Adj.* presentable at court *pred.;* (*fig.*) [socially] acceptable

**Hoffart** /'hɔfart/ *die;* **~** (*veralt. abwertend*) overweening pride; haughtiness

**hoffärtig** /'hɔfɛrtɪç/ (*veralt. abwertend*) ❶ *Adj.* haughty. ❷ *adv.* haughtily

**hoffen** /'hɔfn̩/ ❶ *tr. V.* hope; **ich hoffe es/will es ~:** I hope so/can only hope so; **ich will es [doch wohl] ~:** I should hope so; **ich will nicht ~, dass sie das macht** I hope she doesn't do that; **ich will es nicht ~:** I hope not; **es bleibt zu ~, dass ...** let us hope that ...; **das wollen wir ~:** let's hope so; **~ wir das Beste** let's hope for the best. ❷ *itr. V.* Ⓐ (*vertrauen*) **auf etw.** (*Akk.*) **~:** hope for sth.; (*Vertrauen setzen auf*) **auf jmdn./etw. ~:** put one's trust *or* faith in sb./sth.; Ⓑ (*Hoffnung haben*) hope

**hoffentlich** /'hɔfn̩tlɪç/ *Adv.* hopefully; **~!** let's hope so; **~ ist ihr nichts passiert** I do hope nothing's happened to her; **es ist dir doch ~ recht** I hope it's all right with you

**-höffig** /-hœfɪç/ *adj.* promising to be rich in ‹oil, gas, uranium, etc.›

**Hoffnung** /'hɔfnʊŋ/ *die;* **~, ~en** hope; **seine ~ auf jmdn./etw. setzen** pin one's hopes *pl.* on sb./sth.; **keine ~ mehr haben, die ~ aufgegeben haben** have given up [all] hope; **sich** (*Dat.*) **[falsche] ~en machen** have [false] hopes; **jmdm. ~en machen** raise sb.'s hopes; **jmdm. auf etw.** (*Akk.*) **~en machen** lead sb. to expect sth.; **guter ~ sein** (*veralt.*) be expecting [a baby]; be with child (*dated*); **in der ~ auf etw.** (*Akk.*) in the hope of sth.

**hoffnungs-, Hoffnungs-: ~froh** (*geh.*) ❶ *Adj.* hopeful; ❷ *adv.* hopefully; ‹smile etc.› in happy anticipation; **~funke[n]** *der* (*geh.*) spark *or* glimmer of hope; **~lauf** *der* (*Sport*) repêchage; **~los** ❶ *Adj.* hopeless; despairing ‹person›; ❷ *adv.* hopelessly; **~losigkeit** *die;* **~~:** despair; (*der Lage*) hopelessness; **~schimmer** *der* (*geh.*) glimmer of hope; **~strahl** *der* (*geh.*) ray of hope; **~voll** ❶ *Adj.* Ⓐ hopeful; full of hope *pred.;* **jmdn. ~voll stimmen** give sb. cause to hope *or* make sb. hopeful; Ⓑ (*Erfolg versprechend*) promising; ❷ *adv.* Ⓐ full of hope; Ⓑ (*Erfolg versprechend*) promisingly

**Hof·gang** *der* exercise; **während des ~es** during the exercise period

**hof-, Hof-: ~gesellschaft** *die* court; ***~|halten** ⇒ **Hof** c; **~haltung** *die* running of the court; (*Haushalt*) court; **~hund** *der* watchdog

**hofieren** /ho'fi:rən/ *tr. V.* (*geh.*) pay court to

**höfisch** /'hø:fɪʃ/ *Adj.* courtly

**Hof-: ~knicks** *der* curtsy; **~kreise** *Pl.: in* **in/aus ~kreisen** in/from court circles; **~leben** *das* life at court; court life

**höflich** /'hø:flɪç/ ❶ *Adj.* polite; courteous; **etw. in ~em Ton fragen/sagen** ask/say sth. politely. ❷ *adv.* politely; courteously

**Höflichkeit** *die;* **~, ~en** Ⓐ politeness; courteousness; **etw. [nur] aus ~ tun/sagen** do/say sth. [only] to be polite *or* out of politeness; Ⓑ (*höfliche Redensart*) civility; courtesy

**höflichkeits-, Höflichkeits-: ~besuch** *der* courtesy visit; **~floskel, ~formel** *die* polite phrase; **~halber** *Adv.* to be polite; out of politeness

**Hof·lieferant** *der* (*veralt.*) supplier to the court; **königlicher ~:** supplier to the royal court; (*von Lebensmitteln*) purveyor to the royal court

**Höfling** /'hø:flɪŋ/ *der;* **~s, ~e** courtier

**Hof-: ~marschall** *der* ▶ 91 | major-domo; **~meister** *der* (*veralt.*) court tutor and master of ceremonies; **~narr** *der* (*hist.*) court jester; **~prediger** *der* court chaplain; **~rat** *der* ▶ 91 | (*veralt., noch österr.*) *honorary title conferred on senior civil servant;* **~sänger** *der* (*hist.*) court minstrel; **~schranze** *die od. der* (*veralt. abwertend*) fawning courtier; **~staat** *der* court; **~theater** *das* court theatre; **~tor** *das* courtyard gate; **~tür** *die* courtyard door

**HO-Geschäft** /ha:|'o:-/ *das* (*DDR*): *shop owned by the Handelsorganisation*

**hoh...** /'ho:ə.../ ⇒ **hoch**

**Höhe** /'hø:ə/ *die;* **~, ~n** Ⓐ ▶ 411 | (*Ausdehnung nach oben*) height; **das ist ja die ~!** (*ugs.*) that's the limit!; Ⓑ (*Entfernung nach oben*) height; altitude; **in einer ~ von 4 000 m fliegen/eine ~ von 4 000 m erreichen** fly at/reach a height *or* altitude of 4,000 m.; **an ~ gewinnen/verlieren** gain/lose height *or* altitude; **in großen ~n** at great heights *or* high altitudes; **auf halber ~:** at mid-altitude; Ⓒ (*Richtung*) **etw. in die ~ heben** lift sth. up; **in die ~ [auf]steigen** rise up[wards]; Ⓓ (*Gipfelpunkt*) height; **auf der ~ seines Ruhmes/Könnens/Erfolges sein** be at the height of one's fame/ability/success; **auf der ~ sein** (*fig.*

*old spelling (see note on page 1707)

# Höhe und Tiefe

## Höhe

***Wie hoch ist es?***
= How high *od.* What height is it?

***Es ist ungefähr neun Meter hoch***
= It's about nine metres *od.* ≈ thirty feet high *od.* in height

***A ist niedriger/höher als B***
= A is lower/higher than B

***A ist [genau]so hoch wie B***
= A is [just] the same height *od.* as high as B

***Die Türme sind gleich hoch***
= The towers are the same height

***Die Maschine flog in einer Höhe von 3 000 Metern***
≈ The aircraft was flying at a height *od.* an altitude of 10,000 feet

***Die Baumgrenze liegt bei etwa 2 000 Metern***
≈ The treeline is at [a height of] about 6,500 feet

***drei Meter hohe Wellen***
≈ waves ten feet high

***ein Berg von über 6 000 Metern*** od. ***von über 6 000 Meter Höhe***
≈ a mountain of over 20,000 feet *od.* over 20,000 feet in height

## Körpergröße

***Wie groß ist sie?***
= How tall *od.* What height is she?

***Sie ist ein*** od. ***einen Meter achtundsechzig groß***
≈ She's five foot six

***ein 1,80 Meter großer Athlet***
≈ an athlete six foot *od.* feet tall

***Er ist kleiner als sein Bruder***
= He's shorter *od.* smaller than his brother

***A ist [genau]so groß wie B***
= A is [just] the same height *od.* as tall as B

***Sie sind gleich groß***
= They are the same height

## Tiefe

***Wie tief ist*** od. ***Welche Tiefe hat der Fluss?***
= How deep *od.* What depth is the river?

***Er ist drei Meter tief*** od. ***hat eine Tiefe von drei Metern***
= It's three metres deep, ≈ It's ten feet deep

***Der Schatz liegt in einer Tiefe von fünfzehn Metern*** od. ***fünfzehn Meter tief***
= The treasure is at a depth of fifteen metres *od.* is fifteen metres down, ≈ The treasure is at a depth of fifty feet *od.* is fifty feet down

***A hat die gleiche Tiefe wie B***
= A is the same depth as *od.* as deep as B

***A und B sind gleich tief***
= A and B are the same depth

***A ist flacher*** od. ***seichter als B***
= A is shallower than B

***ein drei Meter tiefes Loch***
= a hole three metres deep, ≈ a hole ten feet deep

---

*ugs.*) (*gesund sein*) be fit; (*sich wohl fühlen*) feel fine; **nicht [ganz] auf der ~ sein** (*fig. ugs.*) be/feel a bit under the weather (*coll.*); not be/feel quite oneself; Ⓔ (*messbare Größe*) level; (*von Einkommen*) size; level; **die ~ der Geschwindigkeit/Temperatur** the speed/temperature level; **Unkosten/ein Stipendium in ~ von 5 000 DM** expenses/a grant of 5,000 DM; Ⓕ (*Linie*) **auf gleicher ~ sein/fahren** be in line abreast *or* be level/travel in line abreast; **die Pferde waren auf gleicher ~:** the horses were neck and neck; **auf ~ des Leuchtturms/von Hull sein** (*Seemannsspr.*) be level with *or* abreast of the lighthouse/be off Hull; Ⓖ (*hoher Grad*) high level; Ⓗ (*Anhöhe*) hill; **die ~n und Tiefen des Lebens** (*fig.*) the ups and downs of life; Ⓘ (*Math., Astron.*) altitude; Ⓙ *Pl.* (*Akustik*) treble *sing.*

**Hoheit** /'ho:hait/ *die;* ~, **~en** Ⓐ (*Souveränität*) sovereignty (**über** + *Akk.* over); **unter der ~ eines Staates stehen** be under the sovereignty of a state; Ⓑ ▶ 91 **Seine/Ihre ~:** His/Your Highness; Ⓒ (*geh.: Würde*) majestic dignity; majesty

**hoheitlich** *Adj.* Ⓐ sovereign; Ⓑ (*selten*) ⇒ **hoheitsvoll**

**hoheits-, Hoheits-: ~ab·zeichen** *das* national emblem; **~gebiet** *das* [sovereign] territory; **~gewässer** *Pl.* territorial waters; **~recht** *das* right of the state; **~voll** *Adj.* majestic; stately ‹gesture›; **~zeichen** *das* national emblem

**Hohe·lied** *das* Ⓐ (*bibl.*) Song of Songs; Ⓑ (*fig. geh.*) song of praise; **ein ~ der Liebe** a song in praise of love; ⇒ *auch* **Lied**

**höhen-, Höhen-: ~an·gabe** *die* altitude reading; (*auf Karten*) altitude marking; **~angst** *die* fear of heights; **~flug** *der* (*Flugw.*) high-altitude flight; (*fig.*) flight; **im ~flug** at high altitude; **~gleich** (*Verkehrsw.*) ❶ *Adj.* level ‹crossing›; ❷ *adv.* at the same level; **~klima** *das* mountain climate; **~krankheit** *die* altitude sickness; **~lage** *die* altitude; **in ~lage** at high altitude; **in ~lagen über 1 500 m** at altitudes over 1,500 m.; **~leitwerk** *das* (*Flugw.*) tailplane; **~linie** *die* (*Geogr.*) contour [line]; **~luft** *die* mountain air; air at high altitude; **~marke** *die* (*Vermessungsw.*) benchmark; **~messer** *der;* **~~s, ~~:** altimeter; **~messung** *die* measurement of height; **~rekord** *der* altitude record; **~ruder** *das* (*Flugw.*) elevator; **~sonne** *die* Ⓐ (*Med.: Quarzlampe*) ultraviolet lamp; sun lamp; Ⓑ (*Med.: Bestrahlung*) ultraviolet radiation treatment; sun lamp treatment; Ⓒ (*Met.*) high-altitude solar radiation; **~steuer** *das* (*Flugw.*) elevator control; **~strahlung** *die* (*Physik*) cosmic radiation; **~training** *das* (*Sport*) [high-]altitude training; **~unterschied** *der* altitude difference; difference in altitude; **~weg** *der* ridge path; **~winkel** *der* (*Geom.*) angle of elevation; **~zug** *der* (*Geogr.*) range of hills; (*Bergkette*) range of mountains; mountain range

**Hohe·priester** *der* (*bibl.*) high priest; ⇒ *auch* **Priester**

**Höhepunkt** *der* high point; (*einer Veranstaltung*) high spot; highlight; (*einer Laufbahn, des Ruhms*) peak; pinnacle; (*einer Krankheit*) crisis; critical point; (*einer Krise*) turning point; (*der Macht*) summit; pinnacle; (*des Glücks*) height; (*Orgasmus; eines Stückes*) climax; **auf dem ~ seiner Laufbahn stehen** be at the peak of one's career

**höher** /'hø:ɐ/ Ⓐ ⇒ **hoch**; Ⓑ **ein ~ gestellter Beamter** a senior official/civil servant; **die ~ gestellten Persönlichkeiten** the more prominent public figures

**höher-, Höher-:** ***~gestellt** ⇒ **höher** B; ***~|schrauben** ⇒ **hoch** 2 B; **~stufung** *die* upgrading

**hohl** /ho:l/ ❶ *Adj.* Ⓐ (*leer*) hollow; **sich innerlich ~ fühlen** (*fig.*) feel empty inside; Ⓑ (*nach innen gebogen*) cupped ‹hand›; sunken, hollow ‹cheeks, eyes›; concave ‹lens, mirror›; **ein ~es Kreuz** a hollow back; Ⓒ (*dumpf*) hollow ‹sound, voice, etc.›; Ⓓ (*abwertend: geistlos*) hollow, empty ‹phrases, slogans›; empty ‹talk, chatter›; shallow ‹person›. ❷ *adv.* Ⓐ (*dumpf*) hollowly; Ⓑ (*abwertend: geistlos*) inanely

**hohl·äugig** *Adj.* hollow-eyed; sunken-eyed

**Hohl·block·stein** *der* (*Bauw.*) hollow block

**Höhle** /'hø:lə/ *die;* ~, **~n** Ⓐ cave; (*größer*) cavern; Ⓑ (*Tierbau*) den; lair; (*von Höhlenbrütern*) nest; **sich in die ~ des Löwen begeben** (*scherzh.*) enter the lion's den; Ⓒ (*abwertend: Wohnung*) hole; Ⓓ (*Augenhöhle*) socket

**Hohl·eisen** *das* (*Handw.*) gouge; hollow chisel

**höhlen** /'hø:lən/ *tr. V.* hollow out; **steter Tropfen höhlt den Stein** (*Spr.*) these things take their toll eventually

**Höhlen-: ~bär** *der* cave bear; **~brüter** *der* (*Zool.*) bird that nests in holes; hole-nester; **~forscher** *der,* **~forscherin** *die* speleologist; (*Sportler[in]*) caver; **~forschung** *die* speleology; (*als Sport*) caving; **~malerei** *die* cave painting; **~mensch** *der* cave dweller; caveman; **~zeichnung** *die* cave painting

**Hohlheit** *die;* ~ Ⓐ hollowness; Ⓑ (*innere Leere, auch fig. abwertend*) emptiness

**hohl-, Hohl-: ~kopf** *der* (*abwertend*) idiot (*coll.*); dimwit; **~köpfig** *Adj.* (*abwertend*) idiotic (*coll.*); blockheaded; **~körper** *der* hollow body; **~kreuz** *das* ▶ 474 hollow back; lordosis (*Med.*); **~kugel** *die* hollow sphere; **~maß** *das* Ⓐ (*Maßeinheit*) measure of capacity; Ⓑ (*Gefäß*) dry/liquid measure; **~nadel** *die* (*Med.*) cannula; (*für Einspritzungen*) hypodermic needle; **~raum** *der* cavity; [hollow] space; **~raum·versiegelung** *die* (*Kfz-W.*) body-cavity sealing; **~saum** *der* (*Handarb.*) hem-stitch; **~schliff** *der* hollow grinding; **eine Klinge mit ~schliff** a hollow-ground blade; **~spiegel** *der* concave mirror; **~tier** *das* coelenterate

**Höhlung** *die;* ~, **~en** Ⓐ (*das Aushöhlen*) excavation; Ⓑ (*Vertiefung*) hollow

**hohl-, Hohl-: ~wangig** *Adj.* hollow-cheeked; sunken-cheeked; **~weg** *der* defile; (*Durchstich*) cutting; **~ziegel** *der* perforated tile; (*Dachziegel*) concave tile

**Hohn** /ho:n/ *der;* **~[e]s** scorn; derision; **jmdn. mit ~ und Spott überschütten** pour *or* heap scorn on sb.; **das ist der reine**

h

od. **der blanke ~** (*fig.*) it is just grotesque; **~ lächeln/lachen** smile/laugh scornfully *or* derisively; **einer Sache ~ sprechen** fly in the face of sth.

**höhnen** /'hø:nən/ *itr. V.* (*geh.*) jeer; sneer

**Hohn·gelächter** *das* derisive *or* scornful laughter

**höhnisch** /'hø:nɪʃ/ **1** *Adj.* scornful; derisive. **2** *adv.* scornfully; derisively

**hohn-: ~lächeln** *itr. V.* **er ~lächelte** he smiled scornfully *or* derisively; **ein Hohnlächeln** a scornful *or* derisive smile; ⇒ *auch* **Hohn**; **~lachen** *itr. V.* **A** laugh scornfully *or* derisively; **ein Hohnlachen** a scornful *or* derisive laugh; **B** (*geh.: zuwiderlaufen*) **einer Sache** (*Dat.*) **~lachen** fly in the face of sth.; ⇒ *auch* **Hohn**; ***~|sprechen** ⇒ **Hohn**

**Höker** /'hø:kɐ/ *der;* **~s, ~, Hökerin** *die;* **~, ~nen** (*veralt.*) (*auf dem Markt*) stallholder; (*auf der Straße*) street trader; street pedlar (*Amer.*)

**hökern** *itr. V.* (*auf dem Markt*) run a market stall; (*auf der Straße*) run a street stall

**Hokuspokus** /ho:kʊs'po:kʊs/ *der;* **~:** hocus-pocus; (*abwertend: Drum und Dran*) fuss

**hold** /hɔlt/ **1** *Adj.* **A** (*dichter. veralt.: anmutig*) fair; lovely; lovely ‹sight›; sweet, lovely ‹smile›; **die ~e Weiblichkeit** (*scherzh.*) the fair sex; **mein ~er Gatte/meine ~e Gattin** (*scherzh.*) my beloved spouse (*joc.*); **B** *in* **jmdm./einer Sache ~ sein** (*geh.*) be well-disposed towards sb./sth.; (*jmdn./etw. gern haben*) be fond of sb./sth.; **das Glück war uns** (*Dat.*) **~:** fortune smiled upon us. **2** *adv.* sweetly

**Holder** *der;* **~s, ~** (*bes. südd.*) ⇒ **Holunder**

**Holding·gesellschaft** /'ho:ldɪŋ-/ *die* (*Wirtsch.*) holding company

**Holdrio** /'hɔldrio/ *das;* **~s, ~s** halloo

**hold·selig** (*dichter. veralt.*) **1** *Adj.* sweet; lovely; lovely ‹sight, appearance›. **2** *adv.* sweetly

**holen** /'ho:lən/ **1** *tr. V.* **A** fetch; get; **jmdn. aus dem Bett ~:** get *or* (*coll.*) drag sb. out of bed; **da/bei ihr ist nichts/nichts mehr zu ~** (*fig.*) you won't get anything/any more there/out of her; **B** (*ab~*) fetch; pick up; collect; take away ‹suspect, prisoner, etc.›; **C** (*ugs.: erlangen*) get, win ‹prize›; get, carry off, win ‹medal, trophy, etc.›; get, score ‹points›; **den Sieg ~:** win; **D** (*landsch.: kaufen*) buy; get; **E** (*Seemannsspr.: herabziehen*) take in ‹sail›; haul ‹boat› alongside. **2** *refl. V.* **A** (*sich verschaffen*) get; **sich** (*Dat.*) **Hilfe/Rat** *usw.* **~:** get [some] help/advice *etc.*; **B** (*erlangen*) win, take ‹championship, prize, etc.›; **sich** (*Dat.*) **eine Niederlage ~:** be beaten; lose; **C** (*ugs.: sich zuziehen*) catch; **sich** (*Dat.*) **[beim Baden** *usw.*] **einen Schnupfen/die Grippe ~:** catch a cold/the flu [swimming *etc.*]; **sich** (*Dat.*) **den Tod ~** (*fig.*) catch one's death [of cold]

**holla** /'hɔla/ *Interj.* hallo; hello; hey

**Holland** /'hɔlant/ (*das*); **~s** Holland

**Holländer** /'hɔlɛndɐ/ ▶553 **1** *der;* **~s, ~** **A** Dutchman; **er ist ~:** he is Dutch *or* a Dutchman; **die ~:** the Dutch; **B** (*Käse*) Dutch cheese; **C** (*Papierherstellung*) Hollander. **2** *indekl. Adj.* **~ Käse** Dutch cheese

**Holländerin** *die;* **~, ~nen** ▶553 Dutchwoman/Dutch girl

**holländisch** *Adj.* ▶553 Dutch; ⇒ *auch* **deutsch**; **Deutsch**

**Holle** *in* **Frau ~ schüttelt die Betten [aus]** (*veralt.*) it is snowing; the old woman is plucking her geese (*dated*)

**Hölle** /'hœlə/ *die;* **~, ~n** **A** hell *no art.*; **in die ~ kommen** go to hell; **zur ~ fahren** (*geh.*) descend into hell; **jmdn. zur ~ wünschen** (*geh.*) wish sb. to hell; **zur ~ mit ihm/damit!** to hell with him/it (*coll.*); **B** (*fig.*) **die ~ ist los** (*ugs.*) all hell has broken loose (*coll.*); **es war die reinste ~:** it was pure hell (*coll.*); **die ~ auf Erden haben** suffer hell on earth; **jmdm. das Leben zur ~ machen** make sb.'s life hell (*coll.*); **jmdm. die ~ heiß machen** give sb. hell (*coll.*); **die grüne ~:** the jungle; ⇒ *auch* **Vorsatz**

**Höllen-: ~angst** *die* (*salopp*) terror; **eine ~angst vor etw.** (*Dat.*) **haben** be scared to death of sth. (*coll.*); be terrified of sth.; **~fahrt** *die* (*Myth., Rel.*) descent into hell; **~feuer** *das* hellfire; **das ~feuer** the fires *pl.* of hell; **~fürst** *der* Prince of Darkness; **~hund** *der* (*Myth.*) hellhound; hound of hell; **~lärm** *der* (*ugs.*) diabolical noise *or* row (*coll.*); **~maschine** *die* infernal machine (*arch.*); time bomb; **~pein, ~qual** *die* agony; **~qualen erleiden** suffer the torments of hell (*fig.*); suffer terrible agony *sing.*; **~spektakel** *das* (*ugs.*) ⇒ **~lärm**; **~stein** *der* lunar caustic; **~tempo** *das* (*ugs.*) breakneck speed; **in einem ~tempo** at breakneck speed

**Holler** /'hɔlɐ/ *der;* **~s, ~** (*bes. südd., österr.*) ⇒ **Holunder**

**höllisch** /'hœlɪʃ/ **1** *Adj.* **A** infernal; ‹spirits, torments› of hell; **B** (*schrecklich*) terrible ‹war, situation›; fiendish, diabolical ‹invention, laughter›; **~e Schmerzen** terrible agony *sing.*; **C** (*ugs.: sehr groß*) tremendous (*coll.*) ‹noise, shock, respect› (*coll.*); enormous (*coll.*) ‹pleasure›; **~e Angst vor etw.** (*Dat.*) **haben** be scared stiff of sth. (*coll.*). **2** *adv.* (*ugs.: sehr*) terribly, hellishly (*coll.*) ‹cold, difficult›; **sich ~ zusammennehmen** make a tremendous effort to control oneself (*coll.*); **~ [genau] aufpassen** be tremendously careful (*coll.*); **es tut ~ weh** it hurts like hell (*coll.*)

**Hollywood·schaukel** /'hɔlɪwʊd-/ *die* swinging garden hammock

**Holm** /hɔlm/ *der;* **~[e]s, ~e** **A** (*Turnen*) bar; **B** (*Leiter~*) upright; side piece; **C** (*Geländer~*) [banister] rail; **D** (*Flugw.*) spar

**Holocaust** /holo'kaust/ *der;* **~[s], ~s** Holocaust

**Hologramm** /holo'gram/ *das* (*Physik*) hologram

**Holographie** /hologra'fi:/ *die;* **~** (*Physik*) holography *no art.*

**Holozän** /holo'tsɛ:n/ *das;* **~s** (*Geol.*) Holocene

**holperig** ⇒ **holprig**

**holpern** /'hɔlpɐn/ *itr. V.* **A** *mit sein* (*fahren*) jolt; bump; **B** (*schütteln*) jolt; **C** (*stockend lesen*) stumble [over one's words]

**holprig** /'hɔlprɪç/ **1** *Adj.* **A** (*uneben*) bumpy; uneven; rough; **B** (*stockend*) stumbling, halting ‹speech›; clumsy ‹verses›; broken, halting ‹English etc.›. **2** *adv.* haltingly; **~ lesen** stumble over one's words when reading

**Hol·schuld** /'ho:l-/ *die* (*Rechtsw.*): *debt to be collected at the debtor's residence*

**Holster** /'hɔlstɐ/ *das;* **~s, ~:** holster

**holterdiepolter** /hɔltɐdi'pɔltɐ/ *Adv.* (*ugs.*) helter-skelter; **alles ging ~:** there was a mad rush

**holüber** /ho:l'|y:bɐ/ *Interj.* **[Fährmann] ~!** ferry[man]!

**Holunder** /ho'lʊndɐ/ *der;* **~s, ~** **A** (*Strauch*) elder; **B** (*Früchte*) elderberries *pl.*

**Holunder-: ~beere** *die* elderberry; **~strauch** *der* elder[berry] bush; **~tee** *der* elder tea

**Holz** /hɔlts/ *das;* **~es, Hölzer** /'hœltsɐ/ **A** wood; (*Bau~, Tischler~*) timber; wood; **bearbeitetes ~:** timber (*Brit.*); lumber (*Amer.*); **ein Stück/Festmeter ~:** a piece of wood *or* timber/cubic metre of timber; **viel ~** (*fig. ugs.*) a hell of a lot (*coll.*); **[viel] ~ vor der Hütte** *od.* **Tür haben** (*fig. ugs. scherzh.*) be well stacked (*coll.*) *or* well endowed; **ich bin nicht aus ~:** I've got feelings, you know; **die ~ verarbeitende Industrie** the timber processing industry; **B** (*~art*) wood; **aus dem ~ sein, aus dem man Minister/Helden macht** be cut out to be a minister/be of the stuff heroes are made of; **aus dem gleichen ~ [geschnitzt] sein** (*fig.*) be cast in the same mould; **aus anderem ~ [geschnitzt] sein** (*fig.*) be cast in a different mould; **C** (*Forstw.*) felled trunk; **D** (*Golf*) wood; **E** **den Ball mit dem ~ schlagen/treffen** (*Tennis, Badminton*) hit the ball with the wood; **F** *Pl.* **~** (*Kegeln*) skittle; ninepin; **gut ~!** have a good game! (*skittle-players' greeting*); **G** (*Musik*) woodwind; **H** (*Streich~*) match; **I** (*veralt., Jägerspr.: Wald*) wood

**holz-, Holz-: ~apfel** *der* **A** crab apple; **B** (*Baum*) crab apple tree; **~arbeiter** *der* ⇒ **~fäller**; **~arm** *Adj.* ‹country› with little timber of its own; **~arm sein** have little timber of its own; **~art** *die* kind of wood *or* timber; **~auge** *das: in* **~auge sei wachsam!** (*scherzh.*) better be careful; **~bearbeitung** *die* processing of timber; timber processing; (*in der Tischlerei*) woodworking; **~bein** *das* wooden leg; **~bläser** *der*, **~bläserin** *die* woodwind player; **~blas·instrument** *das* woodwind instrument; **~block** *der; Pl.* **~blöcke** block of wood; **~bock** *der* **A** (*Gestell*) wooden stand *or* trestle; **B** (*Zecke*) castor-bean tick; **C** (*Käfer*) poplar longhorn; **~bohrer** *der* **A** wood drill; **B** (*Schmetterling*) goat moth; carpenter moth; **~bündel** *das* bundle of wood

**Hölzchen** /'hœltsçən/ *das;* **~s, ~** **A** small piece of wood; (*Stöckchen*) stick; **B** (*Streichholz*) match

**Holz-: ~diele** *die* plank; (*für Fußböden*) [floor]board; **~dübel** *der* wooden dowel; (*in der Wand*) wooden plug

**holzen** *itr. V.* (*Fußballjargon*) play dirty (*coll.*)

**Holzerei** *die;* **~, ~en** **A** (*Fußballjargon*) dirty play; **eine ~:** a dirty game *or* match; **B** (*Prügelei*) brawl; free-for-all

**hölzern** /'hœltsɐn/ *Adj.* (*auch fig.*) wooden

**holz-, Holz-: ~essig** *der* wood vinegar; **~fäller** *der;* **~~s, ~~, ~fällerin** *die;* **~~, ~~nen** ▶159 woodcutter; lumberjack (*Amer.*); **~feuer** *das* wood fire; **~frei** *Adj.* wood-free ‹paper›; **~gas** *das* wood gas; **~geist** *der* wood spirit; **~geschnitzt** *Adj.* carved wooden *attrib.*; carved in wood *pred.*; **~hacker** *der*, **~hackerin** *die* **A** (*bes. österr.*) ⇒ **~fäller**; **B** (*Fußballjargon*) dirty player; **~haltig** *Adj.* woody ‹paper›; ‹paper› containing mechanical wood pulp

**Holz·hammer** *der* [wooden] mallet

**Holzhammer·methode** *die* (*ugs.*) sledgehammer method

**Holz-: ~handel** *der* timber trade; **~haus** *das* timber *or* wooden house

**holzig** *Adj.* woody

**holz-, Holz-: ~industrie** *die* timber industry; **~kitt** *der* plastic wood; **~klotz** *der* block of wood; (*als Spielzeug*) wooden block; **dasitzen wie ein ~klotz** (*fig.*) sit there like a stuffed dummy; **~kohle** *die* charcoal; **~kohlen·grill** *der* charcoal grill; **~kopf** *der* **A** wooden head; **B** (*salopp abwertend*) blockhead; numskull; **~kreuz** *das* wooden cross; **~lager** *das* timber yard; **~leim** *der* wood glue; **~leiste** *die* batten; **~malerei** *die* painting on wood; wood painting; **~nagel** *der* wooden nail; **~pantine** *die* (*landsch.*), **~pantoffel** *der* clog; **~pflock** *der* wooden stake; **~sandale** *die* wooden sandal; **~schädling** *der* wood pest; **~schale** *die* wooden bowl; **~scheit** *das* piece of wood; (*Brenn~*) piece of firewood; **~schläger** *der* (*Golf*) wood; **~schneider** *der*, **~schneiderin** *die* wood engraver; **~schnitt** *der* **A** woodcutting *no art.*; **B** (*Blatt*) woodcut; **~schnitt·artig** *Adj.* (*fig.*) simplistic; **~schnitzer** *der* wood carver; **~schnitzerei** *die* wood carving; **~schnitzerin** *die* ⇒ **~schnitzer**; **~schraube** *die* wood screw; **~schuh** *der* clog; **~schuh·tanz** *der* clog dance; **~schuppen** *der* **A** (*aus ~*) wooden shed; **B** (*für ~*) woodshed; **~span** *der* **A** (*zum Feueranzünden*) stick of firewood; (*zum Rühren usw.*) small stick [of wood]; **B** (*Hobelspan*) [wood] shaving; **~spielzeug** *das* wooden toy; **~spiritus** *der* wood alcohol; **~splitter** *der* splinter of wood; **~stab** *der* wooden rod; **~stich** *der* wood engraving; **~stift** *der* ⇒ **~nagel**; **~stock** *der* **A** [wooden] stick; **B** (*Grafik*) wood block; **~stoß** *der* pile of wood; **~täfelung** *die* wood[en] panelling; **~teer** *der* wood tar; **~treppe** *die* wooden steps *pl.*; ***~verarbeitend** ⇒ **Holz A**; **~verschlag** *der* **A** area divided off by a wooden partition; **B** (*Schuppen*) wooden shed; **~waren** *Pl.* wooden articles; **~weg** *der* (*fig.*): *in* **auf**

*old spelling (see note on page 1707)

dem ~weg sein *od.* **sich auf dem ~weg befinden** be on the wrong track (*fig.*); be barking up the wrong tree (*fig.*); **wenn du glaubst, du kannst das verhindern, so bist du auf dem ~weg** if you think you can prevent it, you're very much mistaken *or* (*coll.*) you've got another think coming; **~wirtschaft** *die* timber industry; **~wolle** *die* wood wool; **~wurm** *der* woodworm

**Homburg** /'hɔmbʊrk/ *der;* **~s, ~s** Homburg

**Homepage** /'hoʊmpeɪdʒ/ *die;* **~, ~s** (*DV*) home page

**homerisch** /ho'meːrɪʃ/ *Adj.* Homeric; **ein ~es Gelächter** Homeric laughter

**Home·trainer** /'hoʊm-/ *der* exerciser

**Hommage** /ɔ'maːʒ/ *die;* **~, ~n** (*geh.*) tribute (**für** to)

**homo** *Adj.* (*ugs.*) queer (*coll.*)

**Homo** /'hoːmo/ *der;* **~s, ~s** (*ugs.*) queer (*coll.*), homo (*coll.*)

**homo-, Homo-: ~erotisch** *Adj.* (*geh.*) homoerotic (*Psych.*); homosexual; **~gen** /-'geːn/ *Adj.* homogeneous; **~genisieren** *tr. V.* Ⓐ (*Chemie, Metallbearb.*) homogenize; Ⓑ (*geh.*) homogenize; integrate ‹groups›; **~genität** /-geni'tɛːt/ *die;* **~~** (*geh.*) homogeneity; **~log** /-'loːk/ *Adj.* (*Biol., Math., Chemie*) homologous; **~logieren** *tr. V.* (*Motorsport*) homologate; **~nym** /-'nyːm/ *Adj.* (*Sprachw.*) homonymous; **~nym** *das;* **~~s, ~~e** (*Sprachw.*) homonym; **~nymie** /homony'miː/ *die;* **~~** (*Sprachw.*) homonymy

**homöo-, Homöo-**/homøo-/ : **~path** /-'paːt/ *der;* **~~en, ~~en** homoeopath; **~pathie** *die;* **~~:** homoeopathy *no art.;* **~pathin** *die;* **~~, ~~nen** ⇒ **~path**; **~pathisch** *Adj.* homoeopathic

**homo-, Homo-: ~phil** /-'fiːl/ *Adj.* (*geh.*) homophile; **~phon** *das;* **~~s, ~~e** (*Sprachw.*) homophone; **~sexualität** *die;* **~~:** homosexuality; **~sexuell** ❶ *Adj.* homosexual; ❷ *adv.* **~sexuell veranlagt sein** have homosexual tendencies; **~sexuelle** *der/die; adj. Dekl.* homosexual

**Homunkulus** /ho'mʊŋkulʊs/ *der;* **~, ~se** *od.* **Homunkuli** homunculus

**Honduras** /hɔn'duːras/ *(das);* **~'** Honduras

**honen** /'hoːnən/ *tr. V.* (*Technik*) hone

**honett** /hɔ'nɛt/ *Adj.* (*geh.*) (*rechtschaffen*) honest; upright; (*anständig*) decent; (*ehrenhaft*) honourable

**Hongkong** /'hɔŋkɔŋ/ *(das);* **~s** ▶ **700** Hong Kong

**Honig** /'hoːnɪç/ *der;* **~s, ~e** honey; **jmdm. ~ um den Bart** (*ugs.*) *od.* (*salopp*) **ums Maul schmieren** (*fig.*) butter sb. up

**honig-, Honig-: ~biene** *die* honey bee; **~brot** *das* bread and honey; **ein ~brot** a slice of bread and honey; **~farben** *Adj.* honey-coloured; **~gelb** *Adj.* honey-yellow; **~kuchen** *der* honey cake; **~kuchen·pferd** *das:* **in lachen** *od.* **grinsen** *od.* **strahlen wie ein ~kuchenpferd** (*ugs. scherzh.*) grin like a Cheshire cat; **~lecken** *das:* **in das ist kein ~lecken** (*ugs.*) it is not a bed of roses; **~melone** *die* honeydew melon; **~schlecken** *das* ⇒ **~lecken**; **~süß** ❶ *Adj.* ‹grapes, taste, etc.› as sweet as honey; (*fig.*) honey-sweet ‹voice›; **ein ~süßes Lächeln** (*fig.*) the sweetest of smiles; **mit ~süßer Stimme** (*fig.*) in honeyed tones; ❷ *adv.* (*fig.*) **~süß lächeln/antworten** smile a honey-sweet smile/answer in honeyed tones; **~tau** *der* honeydew; **~wabe** *die* honeycomb; **~wein** *der* mead; **~zelle** *die* honey[comb] cell

**Honneur** /(h)ɔ'nøːɐ̯/ *in* **die ~s machen** (*veralt.*) do the honours

**Honorar** /hono'raːɐ̯/ *das;* **~s, ~e** fee; (*Autoren~*) royalty

**Honorar·professor** *der,* **Honorar·professorin** *die: professor who is not primarily an academic and has no voice in faculty matters*

**Honoratioren** /honora'tsi̯oːrən/ *Pl.* notabilities

**honorieren** *tr. V.* Ⓐ **jmdn. ~:** pay sb. [a/his/her fee]; **jmds. Leistung/Buch ~:** pay sb. [a/his/her fee] for his/her work/book; Ⓑ (*würdigen*) appreciate; (*belohnen*) reward; Ⓒ (*Finanzw.*) honour ‹cheque›

**Honorierung** *die;* **~, ~en** Ⓐ payment; Ⓑ (*Würdigung*) appreciation; (*Belohnung*) rewarding; Ⓒ (*Finanzw.*) honouring

**honorig** *Adj.* honourable; respectable

**honoris causa** /ho'noːrɪs 'kau̯za/ *Adv.* honoris causa; **Doktor ~:** honorary doctor

**hopfen** /'hɔpfn̩/ *tr. V.* hop ‹beer›

**Hopfen** *der;* **~s, ~:** hop; **bei ihm ist ~ und Malz verloren** (*ugs.*) he's a hopeless case

**Hopfen-: ~garten** *der* hop garden; **~stange** *die* hop pole

**hopp** /hɔp/ ❶ *Interj.* quick; look sharp. ❷ *Adv.* in double-quick time; **bei ihm muss alles ~ gehen** he likes everything done in double-quick time

**hoppe** /'hɔpə/ *Interj.: in* **~, ~, Reiter machen** (*Kinderspr.*) play gee-gees (*on sb.'s knee*)

**hoppeln** /'hɔpl̩n/ *itr. V.; mit sein* hop (**über** + *Akk.* across, over); (*fig.*) bump, jolt (**über** + *Akk.* across, over)

**Hoppelpoppel** /'hɔpl̩'pɔpl̩/ *das;* **~s, ~** Ⓐ (*bes. berlin.*) ⇒ **Bauernfrühstück**; Ⓑ (*Getränk*) ≈ egg flip

**hoppla** /'hɔpla/ *Interj.* oops; whoops

**hopp|nehmen** *unr. tr. V.* (*salopp*) nab (*coll.*); nick (*coll.*)

**hops** /hɔps/ ❶ *Interj.* up; jump. ❷ *Adj.* (*salopp*) **~ sein** be gone; ‹money› have gone down the drain (*coll.*); (*entzweigegangen sein*) be broken

**Hops** *der;* **~es, ~e** [little] jump

**hopsala** /'hɔpsala/, **hopsasa** /'hɔpsasa/ *Interj.* (*Kinderspr.*) oops-a-daisy (*coll.*); whoops-a-daisy (*coll.*)

**hopsen** *itr. V.; mit sein* (*ugs.*) (*springen*) jump; (*hüpfen*) ‹animal› hop; ‹child› skip; ‹ball› bounce

**Hopser** *der;* **~s, ~** (*ugs.*) Ⓐ (*kleiner Sprung*) [little] jump; Ⓑ (*Tanz*) écossaise

**Hopserei** *die;* **~, ~en** (*ugs. abwertend*) jumping about *or* around; (*Tanzen*) leaping about *or* around

**hops-: ~|gehen** *unr. itr. V.; mit sein* (*salopp*) Ⓐ (*umkommen*) buy it (*sl.*); Ⓑ (*entzweigehen*) get broken; (*abhanden kommen*) go missing; (*unbrauchbar werden*) ‹car, machine, etc.› pack up (*coll.*); **~|nehmen** *unr. tr. V.* ⇒ **hoppnehmen**

**Hör·apparat** *der* hearing aid

**hörbar** ❶ *Adj.* audible. ❷ *adv.* audibly; (*geräuschvoll*) noisily

**Hör-: ~bereich** *der* audible range; range of hearing; **~bild** *das* radio feature (*combining documentary and dramatic techniques*); **~brille** hearing aid spectacles *pl.*

**horchen** /'hɔrçn̩/ *itr. V.* listen (**auf** + *Akk.* to); (*heimlich zuhören*) eavesdrop; listen; **an der Tür/Wand ~:** listen at the door/through the wall

**Horcher** *der;* **~s, ~, Horcherin** *die;* **~, ~nen** ⇒ **Lauscher** A

**Horch-: ~gerät** *das* sound locator; (*Marine*) hydrophone; **~posten** *der* (*Milit., auch fig. scherzh.*) listening post

**Horde**[1] /'hɔrdə/ *die;* **~, ~n** (*auch Völkerk.*) horde; (*von Halbstarken*) mob; crowd; **eine ~ Kinder** *od.* **von Kindern** a horde of children

**Horde**[2] *die;* **~, ~n** (*Gestell*) rack

**hören** /'høːrən/ ❶ *tr. V.* Ⓐ hear; **jmdn. kommen/sprechen ~:** hear sb. coming/speaking; **ich habe sagen ~, dass ...** I have heard it said that ...; **ich höre nichts** I can't hear anything; ⇒ *auch* **Gras**; Ⓑ (*an~*) listen to, hear ‹programme, broadcast, performance, etc.›; hear ‹singer, musician›; **Rundfunk** *od.* **Radio ~:** listen to the radio; **den Angeklagten/Zeugen ~:** hear the accused/witness; **eine Vorlesung bei jmdm. ~:** go to *or* attend a lecture by sb.; **das lässt sich ~:** that's good news; Ⓒ (*erfahren*) hear; **etw. von jmdm. ~:** hear sth. from sb.; **er lässt nichts von sich ~:** I/we *etc.* haven't heard from him; **lass mal etwas von dir ~!** keep in touch; **etw. von jmdm. zu ~ bekommen** *od.* (*ugs.*) **kriegen** get a good talking-to from sb. (*coll.*); Ⓓ (*erkennen*) **an etw.** (*Dat.*) **~, dass ...** hear *or* tell by sth. that ... ❷ *itr. V.* Ⓐ hear; **gut ~:** have good hearing; **schlecht ~:** have bad hearing; be hard of hearing; **nur auf einem Ohr ~:** be deaf in one ear; **höre ich recht?** am I hearing things?; **ich geb' dir gleich eine, dass dir Hören und Sehen vergeht** (*ugs.*) I'll give you such a clout in a minute that you'll be seeing stars for a week (*coll.*); **er raste über die Autobahn, dass uns Hören und Sehen verging** (*ugs.*) he tore along the motorway so fast that we were scared out of our wits (*coll.*); Ⓑ (*aufmerksam verfolgen*) **auf etw.** (*Akk.*) **~:** listen to sth.; Ⓒ (*zu~*) listen; **ich höre** I'm listening; **hörst du!** listen [here]!; **hörst du?** are you listening?; **man höre und staune** would you believe it!; wonders will never cease (*iron.*); **hör mal!/~ Sie mal!** listen [here]!; **hört, hört!** aha, listen to this!; Ⓓ (*befolgen*) **auf jmdn./jmds. Rat ~:** listen to *or* heed sb./sb.'s advice; **alles hört auf mein Kommando!** (*Milit.*) I'm taking command; (*scherzh.*) everyone do as I say; **auf den Namen Monika ~:** answer to the name [of] Monika; Ⓔ (*Kenntnis erhalten*) **von jmdm./etw. ~:** hear of sb./sth.; **davon ~, dass ...** hear that ...; **von jmdm. ~** (*Nachricht bekommen*) hear from sb.; **Sie ~ noch von mir** you'll be hearing from me again; you haven't heard the last of this; **ich lasse wieder von mir ~:** I'll be in touch; Ⓕ (*ugs.: gehorchen*) do as one is told; **nicht ~ wollen** not do as one's told; **wer nicht ~ will, muss fühlen** (*Spr.*) if you don't do as you're told, you'll suffer for it

**Hören·sagen** *das;* **~s** hearsay; **vom ~:** by *or* from hearsay

**Hörer** *der;* **~s, ~** Ⓐ listener; Ⓑ (*Telefon~*) receiver

**Hörer·brief** *der* listener's letter; **~e** listeners' letters

**Hörerin** *die;* **~, ~nen** listener

**Hörer·kreis** *der* audience

**Hörerschaft** *die;* **~, ~en** audience

**Hör-: ~fehler** *der* Ⓐ **das war ein ~fehler** he/she *etc.* misheard; **~fehler ausschließen** exclude the possibility of mishearing [sth.]; Ⓑ (*Schwerhörigkeit*) hearing defect; **~folge** *die* radio series; (*in Fortsetzungen*) radio serial; **~funk** *der* radio; **im ~funk** on the radio; **~gerät** *das* hearing aid

**hörig** *Adj.* Ⓐ *in* **jmdm. ~ sein** be submissively dependent on sb.; (*sexuell*) be sexually dependent on *or* enslaved to sb.; be sb.'s sexual slave; Ⓑ (*hist.*) **die ~en Bauern** the serfs; **~ sein** be in bondage

**Hörige** *der/die; adj. Dekl.* (*hist.*) serf; bondsman/bondswoman

**Hörigkeit** *die;* **~** Ⓐ enslavement; (*sexuell*) sexual dependence; Ⓑ (*hist.*) bondage; serfdom

**Horizont** /hori'tsɔnt/ *der;* **~[e]s, ~e** (*auch Geol., fig.*) horizon; **am ~:** on the horizon; **einen engen** *od.* **kleinen ~ haben** (*fig.*) have narrow horizons *pl.*; **seinen ~ erweitern** (*fig.*) widen *or* expand one's horizons *pl.*; **hinter dem ~:** below the horizon; **über jmds. ~** (*Akk.*) **gehen** (*fig.*) be beyond sb.; go over sb.'s head

**horizontal** /horitsɔn'taːl/ ❶ *Adj.* horizontal; ⇒ *auch* **Gewerbe** A. ❷ *adv.* horizontally

**Horizontale** *die;* **~, ~n** Ⓐ (*Linie*) horizontal line; Ⓑ (*Lage*) **die ~:** the horizontal; **etw. in die ~ bringen** lay sth. flat; **sich in die ~ begeben** (*scherzh.*) lie down

**Hormon** /hɔr'moːn/ *das;* **~s, ~e** hormone

**hormonal** /hɔrmo'naːl/ ❶ *Adj.* hormonal. ❷ *adv.* hormonally

**Hormon·behandlung** *die* hormone treatment; **eine ~:** a course of hormone treatment

**hormonell** /hɔrmo'nɛl/ *Adj., adv.* ⇒ **hormonal**

**Hormon-: ~haushalt** *der* hormone balance; **~präparat** *das* hormone preparation; **~spiegel** *der* hormone level

**Hör·muschel** *die* earpiece

**Horn** /hɔrn/ *das;* **~[e]s, Hörner** /'hœrnɐ/ Ⓐ horn; **jmdm. Hörner aufsetzen**

h

(*fig. ugs.*) cuckold sb.; **sich** (*Dat.*) **die Hörner ablaufen** *od.* **abstoßen** (*fig.*) sow one's wild oats; **B** (*Blasinstrument*) horn; (*Milit.*) bugle; **ins gleiche ~ stoßen** (*fig.*) take the same line; **C** *Pl.* **~e** (*Substanz*) horn; **D** (*Signal~*) (*eines Autos usw.*) horn; hooter (*Brit.*); (*eines Zuges*) horn

**horn·artig** *Adj.* hornlike

**Hornberger** /ˈhɔrnbɛrgɐ/ *in* **wie das ~ Schießen ausgehen** all come to nothing

**Horn-: ~blende** *die* (*Mineral.*) hornblende; **~brille** *die* horn-rimmed spectacles *pl. or* glasses *pl.*

**Hörnchen** /ˈhœrnçən/ *das;* **~s, ~** **A** small *or* little horn; **B** (*Gebäck*) croissant; **C** (*Nagetier*) squirrel **D** ⇒ **Lenkerhörnchen**

**Hörner·klang** *der* sound of horns

**hörnern** *Adj.* horn ‹handle etc.›; ‹handle etc.› [made] of horn

**Horn·haut** *die* **A** callus; hard *or* callused skin *no indef. art.;* **B** ▶ 471 (*am Auge*) cornea

**Hornhaut-: ~entzündung** *die* ▶ 474 inflammation of the cornea; corneitis *no indef. art.* (*Med.*); keratitis *no indef. art.* (*Med.*); **~trübung** *die* corneal opacity; opacity of the cornea; **~übertragung** *die* corneal grafting

**hornig** *Adj.* horny

**Hornisse** /hɔrˈnɪsə/ *die;* **~, ~n** hornet

**Hornist** *der;* **~en, ~en, Hornistin** *die;* **~, ~nen** **A** horn player; **B** (*Milit.*) bugler

**Horn-: ~kamm** *der* horn comb; **~ochse** *der* (*ugs.*) stupid ass; **~signal** *das* blast on a/the horn; **~tier** *das* horned animal; **die ~tiere** the Bovidae

**Hornung** *der;* **~s, ~e** (*veralt.*) February

**Hör·organ** *das* ⇒ **Gehörorgan**

**Horoskop** /horoˈsko:p/ *das;* **~s, ~e** horoscope; **jmdm. das ~ stellen** cast sb.'s horoscope

**horrend** /hɔˈrɛnt/ *Adj.* shocking (*coll.*), horrendous (*coll.*) ‹price›; colossal (*coll.*) ‹sum, amount, rent›; shocking (*coll.*) ‹blunder, mistake, lack of discipline›

**horrido** /hɔriˈdo:/ *Interj.* (*Jägerspr.*) hurrah

**Hör·rohr** *das* **A** (*Stethoskop*) stethoscope; **B** (*Hörgerät*) ear trumpet

**Horror** /ˈhɔrɔr/ *der;* **~s** horror; **einen ~ vor jmdm./etw. haben** loathe and fear sb./have a horror of sth.

**Horror-: ~film** *der* horror film; **~trip** *der* (*ugs.*) bad trip; **der reinste ~trip sein** (*fig.*) be a nightmare

**Hör-: ~saal** *der* **A** lecture theatre *or* hall *or* room; **B** (*Zuhörerschaft*) audience; **~schwelle** *die* (*Akustik*) threshold of audibility *or* hearing

**Horsd'oeuvre** /ɔrˈdœ:vr/ *das;* **~s, ~s** (*Gastr.*) hors d'oeuvre

**Hör·spiel** *das* **A** radio play; **B** (*Gattung*) radio drama *no art.*

**Horst** /hɔrst/ *der;* **~[e]s, ~e** **A** (*Nest*) eyrie; **B** (*Forstw.*) (*Bäume*) group of trees; (*Gebüsch*) group of bushes; **C** (*Geol.*) horst; **D** ⇒ **Fliegerhorst**

**horsten** *itr. V.* nest

**Hör·sturz** *der* ▶ 474 (*Med.*) acute hearing loss

**Hort** /hɔrt/ *der;* **~[e]s, ~e** **A** (*dichter.: Goldschatz*) hoard [of gold]; **B** (*geh.: Schutz*) refuge; sanctuary; **ein ~ der Freiheit** a stronghold *or* bulwark of liberty; **C** (*geh.: Stätte*) **ein ~ des Lasters/des Geistes** a hotbed of vice/a centre of intellectual activity; **D** ⇒ **Kinderhort**

**horten** *tr. V.* hoard; stockpile ‹raw materials›

**Hortensie** /hɔrˈtɛnzi̯ə/ *die;* **~, ~n** hydrangea

**Hör·test** *der* hearing test

**Hortnerin** /ˈhɔrtnərɪn/ *die;* **~, ~nen** *supervisor in a day home for schoolchildren*

**Hortung** *die;* **~:** hoarding; (*von Rohstoffen*) stockpiling

**ho ruck** /ˈho:ˈrʊk/ ⇒ **hau ruck**

**Hör-: ~vermögen** *das* hearing; **~weite** *die* hearing range; **in/außer ~weite** in/out of hearing range *or* of earshot

*old spelling (see note on page 1707)

**hosanna** /hoˈzana/ ⇒ **hosianna**

**Höschen** /ˈhø:sçən/ *das;* **~s, ~** **A** trousers *pl.;* pair of trousers; (*kurzes ~*) short trousers *pl.;* shorts *pl.;* pair of shorts; **heiße ~** (*ugs. scherzh.*) hot pants; **B** (*Slip*) panties *pl.;* pair of panties

**Hose** /ˈho:zə/ *die;* **~, ~n** **A** trousers *pl.;* pants *pl.* (*Amer.*); (*Unter~*) pants *pl.;* (*Freizeit~*) slacks *pl.;* (*Bund~*) breeches *pl.;* (*Reit~*) jodhpurs *pl.;* riding breeches *pl.;* **eine ~:** a pair of trousers/pants/slacks *etc.;* **eine kurze/lange ~:** [a pair of] short trousers *or* shorts/long trousers; **ein/zwei Paar ~n** one/two pairs of trousers; **in die ~n schlüpfen/steigen** slip/get one's trousers on; slip/get into one's trousers; **das Kind hat in die ~[n] gemacht/die ~ vollgemacht** the child has made a mess in its pants; **B** (*fig.*) **[zu Hause** *od.* **daheim] die ~n anhaben** (*ugs.*) wear the trousers [at home]; **die ~n runterlassen** (*salopp*) come clean (*coll.*); **die ~[n] [gestrichen] voll haben** (*salopp*) be shitting oneself (*coarse*); be in a blue funk (*coll.*); **die ~n voll kriegen** (*ugs.*) get a good hiding (*coll.*); **jmdm. die ~n strammziehen** (*ugs.*) give sb. a good hiding (*coll.*); **in die ~[n] gehen** (*salopp*) be a [complete] flop (*coll.*); **sich [vor Angst] in die ~[n] machen** (*salopp*) shit oneself (*coarse*); get into a blue funk (*sl.*); **es ist tote ~** (*Jugendspr.*) there's nothing doing (*coll.*)

**Hosen-: ~an·zug** *der* trouser suit (*Brit.*); pant suit; **~aufschlag** *der* [trouser *or* (*Amer.*) pants] turn-up; **~band·orden** *der* Order of the Garter; **~bein** *das* trouser leg; pants leg (*Amer.*); **~boden** *der* seat of the/one's/sb.'s trousers *or* (*Amer.*) pants; **ein paar auf den ~boden bekommen** get a smacked bottom; **sich auf den ~boden setzen** (*fig.*) knuckle down to it; **jmdm. den ~boden stramm ziehen** (*fig. ugs.*) give sb. a good hiding (*coll.*); **~boje** *die* (*Seew.*) breeches buoy; **~bügel** *der* trouser hanger; **~bund** *der* waistband; **~klammer** *die* bicycle clip; **~knopf** *der* trouser button; pants button (*Amer.*); **~latz** *der* **A** (*an Leder~*) flap; (*an Trachten~, Matrosen~*) bib; **B** (*landsch.*) ⇒ **~schlitz**; **~matz** *der* (*ugs. scherzh.*) toddler; [tiny] tot; **~naht** *die* trouser seam; pants seam (*Amer.*); **Hände an die ~naht!** (*Milit.*) thumbs on your trouser seams!; **~rock** *der* culottes *pl.;* divided skirt; **~rolle** *die* (*Theater*) breeches part; **~scheißer** *der* **A** (*derb: Feigling*) chicken (*coll.*); **B** (*ugs. scherzh.*) ⇒ **~matz**; **~schlitz** *der* fly; flies *pl.;* **~spanner** *der* ⇒ **~bügel**; **~stall** *der* (*ugs. scherzh.*) ⇒ **~schlitz**; **~tasche** *die* trouser pocket; pants pocket (*Amer.*); **etw. wie seine ~tasche kennen** (*fig. ugs.*) know sth. like the back of one's hand; **~träger** *Pl.* braces; suspenders (*Amer.*); pair of braces/suspenders

**hosianna** /hoˈzi̯ana/ *Interj.* (*christl. Rel.*) hosanna

**Hospital** /hɔspiˈta:l/ *das;* **~s, ~e** *od.* **Hospitäler** /hɔspiˈtɛ:lɐ/ **A** hospital; **B** (*veralt.: Pflegeheim*) nursing home (*Brit.*)

**Hospitalismus** *der;* **~** (*Psych., Päd., Med.*) hospitalism *no art.*

**Hospitant** /hɔspiˈtant/ *der;* **~en, ~en, Hospitantin** *die;* **~, ~nen** **A** *person sitting in on a class/lecture;* **B** ⇒ **Gasthörer**

**hospitieren** *itr. V.* **bei jmdm. ~:** sit in on sb.'s lectures/seminars; **in einem Seminar/einer Vorlesung ~:** sit in on a seminar/lecture

**Hospiz** /hɔsˈpi:ts/ *das;* **~es, ~e** **A** hospice; **B** (*Hotel*) **[christliches] ~** *private hotel run in accordance with Protestant principles*

**Hostess, *Hosteß** /hɔsˈtɛs/ *die;* **~, ~en** ▶ 159 hostess

**Hostie** /ˈhɔsti̯ə/ *die;* **~, ~n** (*christl. Rel.*) host

**Hostien-** (*christl. Religion*)**: ~schrein** *der* tabernacle; **~teller** *der* paten

**Hotel** /hoˈtɛl/ *das;* **~s, ~s** hotel

**Hotel-: ~bar** *die* hotel bar; **~boy** *der* ▶ 159 page[boy]; bellboy (*Amer.*); **~direktor** *der* hotel manager; **~direktorin** *die* hotel manager[ess]; **~fach** *das* hotel trade; **~fachschule** *die* school of hotel management; **~führer** *der* hotel guide

**Hotel garni** /- garˈni:/ *das;* **~, Hotels garnis** bed-and-breakfast hotel

**Hotel-: ~gast** *der* hotel guest; **~halle** *die* hotel lobby

**Hotelier** /hotɛˈli̯e:/ *der;* **~s, ~s** ▶ 159 hotelier

**Hotel-: ~page** *der* ▶ 159 ⇒ **~boy**; **~portier** *der* ▶ 159 [hotel] commissionaire; **~zimmer** *das* hotel room

**Hotline** /ˈhɔtlaɪn/ *die;* **~, ~s** hotline

**hott** /hɔt/ *Interj.* gee[-up]; ⇒ *auch* **hü**

**HQ** *Abk.* **Hauptquartier** HQ.

**HR** *Abk.* **Hessischer Rundfunk** Hesse Radio

**hrsg.** *Abk.* **herausgegeben** ed.

**Hrsg.** *Abk.* **Herausgeber** ed.

**Hs.** *Abk.* **Handschrift** MS.

**hu** /hu:/ *Interj.* **A** ugh; **B** (*bei Kälte*) brrr; **C** (*zum Erschrecken*) boo

**hü** /hy:/ *Interj.* **A** (*vorwärts*) giddap; gee[-up]; **B** (*halt*) whoa; **einmal sagt sie ~ und einmal hott** (*fig. ugs.*) first she says one thing, then another

**Hub** /hu:p/ *der;* **~[e]s, Hübe** /ˈhy:bə/ (*Technik*) **A** (*das Heben*) lifting; **in einem ~:** in one lift; (*bei einem Bagger*) in one load; **B** (*Weg des Kolbens*) stroke

**Hubbel** /ˈhʊbl̩/ *der;* **~s, ~** (*bes. südd.*) bump

**hubbelig** *Adj.* (*bes. südd.*) bumpy

**Hub·brücke** *die* (*Technik*) lift bridge

**hüben** /ˈhy:bn̩/ *Adv.* on this side; over here; **~ und** *od.* **wie drüben** on both sides

**Hubertus·jagd** /huˈbɛrtʊs-/ *die;* **~, ~en** (*Jagdw.*) St. Hubert's Day hunt

**Hub-: ~höhe** *die* (*Technik*) (*eines Krans*) lifting height; (*einer Schleuse*) lift; (*eines Kolbens*) length of stroke; **~raum** *der* ▶ 611 (*Technik*) piston displacement; swept volume; (*Messgröße für die Leistungsfähigkeit eines Motors*) cubic capacity

**hübsch** /hʏpʃ/ ❶ *Adj.* **A** pretty; nice-looking ‹boy, person›; (*reizvoll*) nice, pleasant ‹area, flat, voice, tune, etc.›; nice ‹phrase, idea, present›; **ihr Hübschen** (*ugs.*) my pretty ones; **sich ~ machen** make oneself look nice; **B** (*ugs.: ziemlich groß*) **eine ~e Stange Geld kosten** cost a pretty penny; **ein ~es Sümmchen** a tidy sum (*coll.*); a nice little sum; **ein ~es Stück Arbeit** a fair amount *or* quite a lot of work; **C** (*ugs. iron.: unangenehm*) **das ist eine ~e Geschichte/hier herrschen ~e Zustände** this is a fine *or* pretty kettle of fish (*coll.*) *or* a fine state of affairs.
❷ *adv.* **A** prettily; **sich ~ anziehen** dress nicely; wear nice clothes; **~ eingerichtet/gekleidet** nicely *or* attractively furnished/dressed; **~ singen/spielen** sing/play nicely; **B** (*ugs.: sehr*) **~ kalt** perishing cold; **C** (*ugs.: ordentlich*) **immer ~ der Reihe nach** everybody must take his turn; **sei ~ brav** be a good boy/girl; **immer ~ langsam** take it nice and slowly

**Hub·schrauber** *der;* **~s, ~:** helicopter

**Hubschrauber·lande·platz** *der* heliport; (*kleiner*) helicopter pad; landing pad

**Hub-: ~stapler** *der* **A** stacker truck; **B** ⇒ **Gabelstapler**; **~volumen** *das* ⇒ **~raum**

**huch** /hʊx/ *Interj.* ugh; (*bei Kälte*) brrr

**Hucke** /ˈhʊkə/ *die;* **~, ~n** pannier; **jmdm. die ~ voll hauen** (*fig. ugs.*) give sb. a good hiding (*coll.*); (*bei einer Prügelei*) beat hell out of sb. (*coll.*); **jmdm. die ~ voll lügen** (*fig. ugs.*) tell sb. a pack of lies; **die ~ voll kriegen** (*fig. ugs.*) get a good hiding (*coll.*); (*bei einer Prügelei*) get a proper beating (*coll.*); ⇒ *auch* **saufen** 3

**huckepack** /ˈhʊkəpak/ *Adv.* (*ugs.*): *in* **jmdn. ~ tragen** carry sb. piggyback; give sb. a piggyback; **etw. ~ tragen** carry sth. piggyback; **jmdn./etw. ~ nehmen** take sb./sth. up on one's back

**Hudelei** *die;* **~, ~en** (*bes. südd., österr.*) **A** (*Arbeitsweise*) sloppiness; **B** (*Pfuscharbeit*) sloppy *or* slipshod *or* slapdash work *no indef. art.*

**hudelig** (*bes. südd., österr.*) ❶ *Adj.* sloppy; slapdash; slipshod ‹work›. ❷ *adv.* sloppily; in a sloppy *or* slipshod *or* slapdash manner

**hudeln** /ˈhuːdl̩n/ *itr. V.* (*bes. südd., österr.*) work sloppily; be sloppy *or* slapdash (**bei** in); **nur nicht ~!** don't be in such a hurry!; take it easy!

**hudlig** ⇒ **hudelig**

**Huf** /huːf/ *der;* **~[e]s, ~e** hoof; **einem Pferd die ~e beschlagen** shoe a horse

**huf-, Huf-: ~eisen** *das* horseshoe; **~eisen·form** *die:* **in ~eisenform** in [the shape of] a horseshoe; **~eisenförmig** ❶ *Adj.* horseshoe-shaped; ❷ *adv.* in [the shape of] a horseshoe

**Hufen·dorf** *das: linear village in which each house has its own fields behind it*

**Huf-: ~lattich** *der* coltsfoot; **~nagel** *der* horseshoe nail; **~schlag** *der* Ⓐ (*Klang*) hoofbeats *pl.;* Ⓑ (*Stoß*) kick [from a/the horse]; **~schmied** *der* farrier; blacksmith; **~schmiede** *die* farrier's *or* blacksmith's workshop

**Hüft·bein** *das* ▶471 (*Anat.*) hip bone; innominate bone (*Anat.*)

**Hüfte** /ˈhʏftə/ *die;* **~, ~n** ▶471 hip; **sie stand da, die Arme in die ~n gestemmt ...** she stood there, hands on hips *or* with arms akimbo; **sich in den ~n wiegen** swing one's hips; **aus der ~ schießen/feuern** shoot/fire from the hip

**hüft-, Hüft-: ~gelenk** *das* ▶471 (*Anat.*) hip joint; **~gelenk·entzündung** *die* coxitis; **~gürtel** *der,* **~halter** *der* girdle; **~hoch** ❶ *Adj.* **~hoch sein** ‹grass, wall› be almost waist-high; ‹water, snow, mud› be almost waist-deep; ❷ *adv.* **~hoch im Schlamm stehen** stand waist-deep in mud

**Huf·tier** *das* hoofed animal; ungulate (*Zool.*)

**Hüft-: ~knochen** *der* ⇒ **Hüftbein**; **~nerv** *der* ▶471 sciatic nerve; **~schwung** *der* (*Ringen*) cross-buttock; **~um·fang** *der,* **~weite** *die* (*Schneiderei*) hip size

**Hügel** /ˈhyːgl̩/ *der;* **~s, ~** Ⓐ hill; (*fig.*) heap; pile; Ⓑ (*dichter.*) grave mound

**hügel-, Hügel-: ~ab** *Adv.* (*geh.*) downhill; **~an, ~auf** *Adv.* (*geh.*) uphill; **~grab** *das* (*Archäol.*) barrow; tumulus

**hügelig** *Adj.* hilly

**Hügel-: ~kette** *die* chain *or* range of hills; **~land** *das* hill country

**Hugenotte** /hugəˈnɔtə/ *der;* **~n, ~n** Huguenot

**hüglig** ⇒ **hügelig**

**huh** ⇒ **hu**

**hüh** ⇒ **hü**

**Huhn** /huːn/ *das;* **~[e]s, Hühner** /ˈhyːnɐ/ Ⓐ chicken; [domestic] fowl; (*Henne*) chicken; hen; **gebratenes ~:** roast chicken; **herumlaufen wie ein aufgescheuchtes ~** (*ugs.*) run about in a great panic (*coll.*); **da lachen [ja] die Hühner** (*ugs.*) you/he/she *etc.* must be joking (*coll.*); **ein blindes ~ findet auch mal ein Korn** (*Spr.*) anyone can have a stroke of luck once in a while; **mit den Hühnern aufstehen/zu Bett gehen** (*scherzh.*) get up with the lark/go to bed early; Ⓑ (*ugs.: Mensch*) **ein verrücktes/dummes/fideles ~:** a nutcase (*coll.*) *or* idiot/stupid twit (*Brit. coll.*) *or* idiot/cheerful sort (*coll.*); Ⓒ (*Jägerspr.*) ⇒ **Rebhuhn**

**Hühnchen** /ˈhyːnçən/ *das;* **~s, ~:** little *or* small chicken; **mit jmdm. [noch] ein ~ zu rupfen haben** (*ugs.*) [still] have a bone to pick with sb.

**Hühner-: ~auge** *das* (*am Fuß*) corn; **jmdm. auf die ~augen treten** (*fig. ugs.*) tread on sb.'s corns *or* toes; **~augen·pflaster** *das* corn plaster; **~brühe** *die* chicken broth; **~brust** *die* ▶474 Ⓐ (*Med.*) chicken breast; pigeon breast; Ⓑ (*ugs.: flacher Brustkorb*) scrawny chest; **~dieb** *der* chicken thief; **~dreck** *der* (*ugs.*) chicken dirt; **~ei** *das* hen's egg; **~farm** *die* chicken farm; **~frikassee** *das* chicken fricassee; fricassee of chicken; **~futter** *das* chicken feed; **~habicht** *der* [northern] goshawk; **~hof** *der* chicken run; **~hund** *der* ⇒ **Vorstehhund**; **~klein** *das;* **~~s** trimmings *pl.* of chicken (*in stew etc.*); **~leiter** *die* chicken ladder; **~mist** *der* chicken droppings *pl.;* **~pest** *die* (*Tiermed.*) fowl pest; **~stall** *der* chicken coop; hen-coop; **~suppe** *die* chicken soup; **~vogel** *der* (*Zool.*) gallinaceous bird; **~zucht** *die* Ⓐ chicken rearing *no art.;* chicken farming *no art.;* Ⓑ (*Betrieb*) chicken farm

**hui** /hui:/ *Interj.* whoosh; **außen ~ und innen pfui** (*von Geräten usw.*) the outside's fine but inside it's a different story; (*von Personen*) he/she seems very nice on the surface, but underneath it's a different story

**Huld** /hʊlt/ *die;* **~** (*geh., veralt., noch iron.*) (*Gunst*) favour; (*Güte*) graciousness; **jmdm. seine ~ schenken** bestow one's favour on sb.

**huldigen** /ˈhʊldɪgn̩/ *itr. V.* Ⓐ **jmdm. ~:** pay tribute to *or* honour sb.; Ⓑ (*geh.: anhängen*) **einem Grundsatz/einer Ansicht/Mode ~:** hold [devotedly] to a principle/a point of view/follow a fashion; **dem Kartenspiel/Alkohol ~:** be addicted to cards/enjoy a few drinks; Ⓒ (*hist.: Treue geloben*) **jmdm. ~:** pay *or* render homage to sb.

**Huldigung** *die;* **~, ~en** Ⓐ (*Ehrung*) tribute; homage; **einer Dame seine ~ darbringen** pay one's addresses *pl.* to a lady; Ⓑ (*hist.: Treuegelöbnis*) homage

**Huldigungs·gedicht** *das* panegyric

**huld·reich, huld·voll** (*geh. veralt.*) ❶ *Adj.* gracious. ❷ *adv.* graciously

**Hülle** /ˈhʏlə/ *die;* **~, ~n** Ⓐ (*Umhüllung*) cover; (*für Ausweis, Zeitkarte*) cover; holder; (*für Füllhalter*) case; (*Schallplatten~*) cover; sleeve; (*fig.: eines Menschen*) **die leibliche ~** (*dicht.*) this mortal frame (*literary*); **die sterbliche ~** (*geh. verhüll.*) the mortal remains *pl.;* Ⓑ (*ugs. scherzh.: Kleidung*) **seine** *od.* **die ~ fallen lassen** strip off [one's clothes]; Ⓒ **in ~ und Fülle,** (*geh.*) **die ~ und Fülle** in abundance; in plenty; Ⓓ (*Bot.*) involucre

**hüllen** *tr. V.* (*geh.*) wrap; **jmdn./sich in etw.** (*Akk.*) **~:** wrap sb./oneself in sth.; **in Dunkel** (*Akk.*) **gehüllt** (*fig.*) shrouded *or* veiled in obscurity; **in Wolken** (*Akk.*) **gehüllt** (*fig.*) enveloped in clouds

**hüllenlos** *Adj.* Ⓐ (*unverhüllt*) plain; clear; Ⓑ (*scherzh.: nackt*) naked; in one's birthday suit *pred.* (*joc.*)

**Hülse** /ˈhʏlzə/ *die;* **~, ~n** Ⓐ (*Hülle*) (*für Füllhalter, Thermometer, Patrone*) case; (*für Film*) [cassette] container; (*für Impfstoff*) capsule; Ⓑ (*Bot.*) pod; hull

**Hülsen·frucht** *die* Ⓐ (*Frucht*) fruit of a leguminous plant; **Hülsenfrüchte** pulse *sing.;* Ⓑ (*Pflanze*) legume; leguminous plant

**human** /huˈmaːn/ ❶ *Adj.* Ⓐ (*menschenwürdig*) humane; **die modernen Großstädte müssen ~er werden** modern cities must provide a more humane environment for people to live in; Ⓑ (*nachsichtig*) considerate; Ⓒ (*Med.*) human. ❷ *adv.* Ⓐ (*menschenwürdig*) humanly; Ⓑ (*nachsichtig*) considerately

**Human-: ~biologie** *die* human biology *no art.;* **~genetik** *die* human genetics *sing., no art.*

**humanisieren** *tr. V.* humanize

**Humanisierung** *die;* **~:** humanization

**Humanismus** *der;* **~:** humanism; (*Epoche*) Humanism *no art.*

**Humanist** *der;* **~en, ~en, Humanistin** *die;* **~, ~nen** Ⓐ humanist; (*hist.*) Humanist; Ⓑ (*Altsprachler*) classical scholar; (*Student*) classics student

**humanistisch** *Adj.* Ⓐ humanist[ic]; (*hist.*) Humanist; Ⓑ (*altsprachlich*) classical; **ein ~es Gymnasium** *secondary school emphasizing classical languages*

**humanitär** /humaniˈtɛːɐ̯/ *Adj.* humanitarian

**Humanität** /humaniˈtɛːt/ *die;* **~:** respect for humanity

**Humanitäts·duselei** /-duːzəˈlai/ *die;* **~, ~en** (*abwertend*) **[eine] ~/~en** *Pl.* sentimental humanitarianism *sing.*

**Human-: ~medizin** *die* human medicine *no art.;* **~mediziner** *der,* **~medizinerin** *die* practitioner of human medicine; **~versuch** *der* (*Med.*) test on a human being/on human beings

**Humbug** /ˈhʊmbʊk/ *der;* **~s** (*ugs. abwertend*) humbug

**Hummel** /ˈhʊml̩/ *die;* **~, ~n** bumble-bee; humble-bee; **eine wilde ~** (*scherzh.*) a proper tomboy; ⇒ *auch* **Hintern**

**Hummer** /ˈhʊmɐ/ *der;* **~s, ~:** lobster

**Hummer-: ~cocktail** *der* (*Kochk.*) lobster cocktail; **~krabbe** *die* king prawn; **~majonäse, ~mayonnaise** *die* (*Kochk.*) lobster mayonnaise

**Humor** /huˈmoːɐ̯/ *der;* **~s, ~e** Ⓐ humour; (*Sinn für ~*) sense of humour; **etw. mit ~ tragen/nehmen** bear/take sth. with a sense of humour *or* cheerfully; **keinen [Sinn für] ~ haben** have no sense of humour; **er hat ~ — lässt mich mit der ganzen Arbeit allein hier sitzen** he's got a strange sense of humour, leaving me sitting here on my own with all the work; **~ ist, wenn man trotzdem lacht** it's not the end of the world; **der rheinische/englische ~:** Rhenish/English humour; the Rhinelander's/Englishman's sense of humour; **schwarzer ~:** black humour; Ⓑ (*gute Laune*) **den ~ nicht verlieren** remain good-humoured

**Humoreske** /humoˈrɛskə/ *die;* **~, ~n** Ⓐ (*Literaturwiss.*) humorous sketch; Ⓑ (*Musik*) humoresque

**humorig** *Adj.* humorous

**Humorist** *der;* **~en, ~en, Humoristin** *die;* **~, ~nen** Ⓐ (*Autor[in]*) humorist; Ⓑ (*Vortragskünstler[in]*) comedian

**humoristisch** ❶ *Adj.* humorous; **er ist ein großes ~es Talent** he has great talent to amuse. ❷ *adv.* with humour

**humor-, Humor-: ~los** ❶ *Adj.* humourless; ❷ *adv.* without humour; **~losigkeit** *die;* **~~:** humourlessness; lack of humour; **~voll** ❶ *Adj.* humorous; ❷ *adv.* humorously; in a humorous way

**Humpelei** *die;* **~** (*ugs.*) hobbling; **er übertreibt ein bisschen mit seiner ~:** he's overdoing the limp a bit

**humpeln** /ˈhʊmpl̩n/ *itr. V.* Ⓐ *auch mit sein* walk with *or* have a limp; Ⓑ *mit sein* (*sich ~d fortbewegen*) hobble; limp

**Humpen** /ˈhʊmpn̩/ *der;* **~s, ~:** tankard; [beer] mug; (*aus Ton auch*) stein

**Humus** /ˈhuːmʊs/ *der;* **~:** humus

**humus-, Humus-: ~boden** *der,* **~erde** *die* humus soil; **~reich** *Adj.* ‹soil› rich in humus; rich ‹soil›

**Hund** /hʊnt/ *der;* **~es, ~e** Ⓐ dog; (*Jagdhund*) hound; dog; **ein junger ~:** a puppy *or* pup; **bei diesem Wetter würde man keinen ~ vor die Tür schicken** I wouldn't turn a dog out in weather like this; **da liegt der ~ begraben** (*fig. ugs.*) (*Ursache*) that's what's causing it; (*Grund*) that's the real reason; **da wird der ~ in der Pfanne verrückt** (*salopp*) it's quite incredible; **das ist zum Junge-~e-Kriegen** (*ugs.*) it's enough to drive you to despair; it's enough to drive you spare (*Brit. coll.*); **viele ~e sind des Hasen Tod** (*Spr.*) it's one against many; **~e, die bellen, beißen nicht** (*Spr.*) barking dogs seldom bite; **den letzten beißen die ~e** (*fig.*) late-comers must expect to be unlucky; **ein dicker ~** (*ugs.: grober Fehler*) a real bloomer (*Brit. sl.*) *or* (*coll.*) goof; **das ist ein dicker ~** (*ugs.: Frechheit*) that's a bit thick (*coll.*); **kalter ~** (*ugs.*): *gateau consisting of layers of biscuit and chocolate-flavoured filling;* **der Große ~/der Kleine ~** (*Astron.*) the Great[er] Dog/the Little *or* Lesser Dog; **bekannt sein wie ein bunter** *od.* **scheckiger ~:** be a well-known figure; **wie ~ und Katze leben** (*ugs.*) lead a cat-and-dog life; **damit kannst du keinen ~ hinter dem Ofen hervorlocken** that won't tempt anybody; **auf den ~ kommen** (*ugs.*) go to the dogs (*coll.*); **mit allen ~en gehetzt sein** (*ugs.*) be up to (*coll.*) *or* know all the tricks; **vor die ~e gehen** (*ugs.*) go to the dogs (*coll.*); (*sterben*) die; kick the bucket (*coll.*); Ⓑ (*salopp: Mann*) bloke (*Brit. coll.*); (*abwertend*) bastard (*coll.*); **so ein blöder**

h

~! [what a] stupid bastard!; [C] (*Bergmannsspr.*) [mine] car; tub

**Hundchen, Hündchen** /ˈhʏntçən/ *das;* ~**s**, ~ (*kleiner Hund*) little dog; (*Koseform*) doggie (*coll.*); (*junger Hund*) puppy; pup

**hunde-, Hunde-:** ~**artige** *Pl.; adj. Dekl.* (*Zool.*) canines; **die ~artigen** the Canidae; ~**aus·stellung** *die* dog show; ~**blick** *der* (*fig. ugs.*) doglike look; (*ergeben*) look of doglike devotion; ~**blume** *die* dandelion; ~**deckchen** *das* [A] dog coat; [B] (*scherzh.: Gamasche*) gaiter; ~**dreck** *der* dog's mess *or* muck; ~**elend** *Adj.* [really] wretched *or* awful; ~**fänger** *der*, ~**fängerin** *die* dog catcher; ~**futter** *das* dog food; ~**gespann** *das* dog team; ~**halsband** *das* dog collar; ~**halter** *der*, ~**halterin** *die* (*Amtsspr.*) dog owner; ~**hütte** *die* (*auch fig. abwertend*) [dog] kennel; ~**kalt** *Adj.* (*ugs.*) freezing cold; ~**kälte** *die* (*ugs.*) freezing cold; ~**klo[sett]** *das* dogs' toilet *or* lavatory; ~**kot** *der* (*geh.*) dog dirt; ~**kuchen** *der* dog biscuit; ~**leben** *das* (*ugs.*) dog's life; ~**marke** *die* [A] dog licence disc; dog tag; [B] (*salopp scherzh.: Erkennungsmarke*) (*bei Soldaten*) identity disc; dog tag (*Amer. sl.*); (*bei der Polizei*) ⇒ **Kennmarke**; ~**müde** *Adj.* (*ugs.*) dog-tired; ~**narr** *der* fanatical dog lover; ~**rasse** *die* breed of dog; ~**rennen** *das* dog racing; greyhound racing; **ein Vermögen beim ~rennen verlieren** lose a fortune at the dog track *or* (*coll.*) on the dogs *pl.*

**hundert** /ˈhʊndɐt/ *Kardinalz.* [A] ▶ 76, ▶ 841 a *or* one hundred; **mehrere/einige ~** *od.* **Hundert Menschen** several/a few hundred people; **auf ~ kommen/sein** (*ugs.*) blow one's top (*coll.*)/be in a raging *or* (*coll.*) flaming temper; ⇒ *auch* **acht**; [B] (*ugs.: viele*) hundreds of; **~ Neuigkeiten** lots of news

**Hundert**[1] *das;* ~**s**, ~**e** *od.* (*nach unbest. Zahlwörtern*) ~ [A] hundred; **ein halbes ~:** fifty; **fünf vom ~:** five per cent; [B] *Pl.* (*große Anzahl*) **~e/hunderte von Menschen** hundreds of people; **von solchen Menschen gibt es unter ~en/hunderten nur einen** people like that are few and far between; **in die ~e/hunderte gehen** (*ugs.*) run into hundreds

**Hundert**[2] *die;* ~, ~**en** hundred

**hundert·ein[s]** *Kardinalz.* ▶ 76, ▶ 841 a *or* one hundred and one

**Hunderter** *der;* ~**s**, ~ [A] (*ugs.*) hundred-mark/-dollar *etc.* note; **das wird mich einige ~ kosten** that will cost me a few hundred [marks/dollars *etc.*]; [B] (*Math.*) hundred

**hunderterlei** *Gattungsz.; indekl.* (*ugs.*) [A] (*von verschiedener Art*) a hundred and one different ‹answers, kinds, etc.›; [B] (*viele*) a hundred and one; **ich muss noch ~ besorgen** I still have a hundred and one things to see to

**hundert·fach** *Vervielfältigungsz.* hundredfold; **die ~e Menge/der ~e Preis** a hundred times the amount/price; ⇒ *auch* **achtfach**

**Hundert·fünf·und·siebziger** *der;* ~**s**, ~ (*ugs. veralt.*) homo (*coll.*); queer (*sl.*)

**hundert·fünfzig·prozentig** *Adj.* (*ugs. iron.*) overzealous ‹official›; fanatical ‹nationalist, communist, etc.›

**Hundert·jahr·feier** *die* centenary; centennial; **die ~ unserer Organisation** the centenary *or* centennial of our organization

**hundert·jährig** *Adj.* [A] (*100 Jahre alt*) [one-]hundred-year-old; **ein ~er Greis** a centenarian; [B] (*100 Jahre dauernd*) **nach ~em Kampf** after a hundred years of war; **ihr/sein ~es Bestehen feiern** celebrate its centenary; **der Hundertjährige Krieg** (*hist.*) the Hundred Years' War; **der hundertjährige Kalender** the Century Almanac

**hundert·mal** *Adv.* a hundred times; **auch wenn du dich ~ beschwerst** (*ugs.*) however much *or* no matter how much you complain; ⇒ *auch* **achtmal**

**Hundert-:** ~**mark·schein** *der* ▶ 337 hundred-mark note; ~**meter·hürdenlauf** *der* (*Leichtathletik*) hundred-metres hurdles *sing.*; ~**meter·lauf** *der* (*Leichtathletik*) hundred metres *sing.*; **sie gehört zu den Weltbesten im ~meterlauf** she is among the world's best at a *or* the hundred metres

**hundert·prozentig** ❶ *Adj.* [A] [one-]hundred per cent *attrib.*; **~er Alkohol** pure alcohol; [B] (*ugs.: völlig*) a hundred per cent, complete, absolute ‹certainty, agreement, etc.›; [C] (*ugs.: ganz sicher*) completely *or* absolutely reliable; [D] (*ugs.: typisch*) **ein ~er Konservativer/eine ~e Amerikanerin** a conservative/an American through and through. ❷ *adv.* (*ugs.*) **ich bin nicht ~ sicher** I'm not a hundred per cent sure; **du kannst dich ~ auf ihn/darauf verlassen** you can rely on him/it absolutely *or* one hundred per cent; **~ Recht haben** be absolutely right; **etw. ~ wissen** know sth. for sure; **er wird das tun, ~:** he will do it, you can be a hundred per cent sure of that

**Hundertschaft** *die;* ~, ~**en** group of a hundred; **einige ~en der Polizei** several hundred police

**hundertst...** /ˈhʊndɐtst.../ *Ordinalz.* ▶ 841 hundredth; **zum ~en Mal fragen** (*ugs.*) ask for the hundredth time; **vom Hundertsten ins Tausendste kommen** get carried away so that one subject just leads another

**hundertstel** /ˈhʊndɐtstl/ *Bruchz.* ▶ 841 hundredth; ⇒ *auch* **achtel**

**Hundertstel** *das* (*schweiz. meist* **der**); ~**s**, ~: ▶ 841 hundredth

**Hundertstel·sekunde** *die* hundredth of a second

**hundert·tausend** *Kardinalz.* ▶ 841 a *or* one hundred thousand; **mehrere/viele ~** *od.* **Hunderttausend Menschen** several hundred thousand people/many hundreds of thousands of people

**hundert·und·ein[s]** *Kardinalz.* a *or* one hundred and one

**hundert·zehn** *Kardinalz.* ▶ 841 a *or* one hundred and ten

**Hundert·zehn·meter·hürden·lauf** *der* (*Leichtathletik*) 110 metres hurdles *sing.*

**Hunde-:** ~**salon** *der* poodle *or* dog parlour; ~**scheiße** *die* (*derb*) dog shit (*coarse*); ~**schlitten** *der* dog sledge; dog sled (*Amer.*); ~**schnauze** *die* dog's muzzle *or* snout; **kalt wie eine ~schnauze sein** (*fig. ugs.*) be as cold as ice (*fig.*); ~**sohn** *der* (*abwertend*) cur; ~**steuer** *die* dog licence fee; ~**streife** *die* dog patrol; ~**wetter** *das* (*ugs.*) filthy *or* (*coll.*) lousy weather; ~**zucht** *die* [A] dog breeding *no art.*; [B] (*Betrieb*) [breeding] kennels *pl.*; ~**zwinger** *der* dog run

**Hündin** /ˈhʏndɪn/ *die;* ~, ~**nen** bitch

**hündisch** /ˈhʏndɪʃ/ ❶ *Adj.* [A] (*würdelos*) doglike, servile ‹obedience›; doglike ‹devotion›; fawning, abject ‹submissiveness›; [B] (*gemein*) mean; nasty. ❷ *adv.* **jmdm. ~ ergeben sein** have a doglike devotion to sb.; **sich einer Sache** (*Dat.*) **~ unterwerfen** submit abjectly to sth.

**hunds-, Hunds-:** ~**erbärmlich** (*ugs.*) ❶ *Adj.* [A] [really] dreadful (*coll.*); [B] (*verabscheuenswürdig*) dirty *attrib.* ‹lie, coward›; **eine ~erbärmliche Gemeinheit** a dirty low-down thing to do/say; ❷ *adv.* [A] (*sehr*) terribly (*coll.*), dreadfully (*coll.*) ‹cold›; [B] (*sehr schlecht*) [really] abysmally (*coll.*) *or* dreadfully (*coll.*); ~**fott** /-fɔt/ *der;* ~~**[e]s**, ~~**e** *od.* ~**fötter** /fœtɐ/ (*derb abwertend*) low-down bastard (*coll.*); ~**föttisch** /-fœtɪʃ/ *Adj.* (*derb abwertend*) low-down *attrib.*; dirty *attrib.* ‹coward›; ~**gemein** (*ugs.*) ❶ *Adj.* [A] (*abwertend: überaus gemein*) really mean *or* shabby; dirty ‹liar›; **es war ~gemein, uns so hereinzulegen** it was a really mean *or* shabby trick to take us for a ride (*coll.*) like that; [B] (*sehr stark*) terrible (*coll.*), dreadful (*coll.*) ‹cold, weather, pain, etc.›; ❷ *adv.* [A] (*gemein*) ‹deceive, behave› really meanly *or* shabbily; [B] (*sehr stark*) **das tut ~gemein weh** it hurts like hell (*coll.*) *or* terribly (*coll.*); ~**gemeinheit** *die* (*abwertend*) really mean *or* shabby trick; ~**miserabel** (*salopp abwertend*) ❶ *Adj.* [really] lousy (*coll.*) *or* dreadful (*coll.*); ❷ *adv.* ‹behave› [really] appallingly (*coll.*) *or* dreadfully (*coll.*); ~**rose** *die* (*Bot.*) dog rose; wild briar; ~**stern** *der* (*Astron.*) dog star; ~**tage** *Pl.* dog days; ~**veilchen** *das* dog violet; ~**wut** *die* (*veralt.*) ⇒ **Tollwut**

**Hüne** /ˈhyːnə/ *der;* ~**n**, ~**n** giant

**Hünen·grab** *das* megalithic tomb; (*Hügelgrab*) barrow; tumulus

**hünenhaft** *Adj.* gigantic ‹build, stature›

**Hunger** /ˈhʊŋɐ/ *der;* ~**s** [A] **~ bekommen/haben** get/be hungry; **ich habe ~ wie ein Bär** *od.* **Wolf** I'm so hungry I could eat a horse; **sein ~ war groß** he was very hungry; **~ auf etw.** (*Akk.*) **haben** fancy sth.; feel like sth. (*coll.*); **~ leiden** go hungry; starve; **wissen, was ~ ist** know what it is to go hungry; **vor ~ sterben** die of starvation *or* hunger; starve to death; **seinen ~ stillen** satisfy one's hunger; **~ ist der beste Koch** (*Spr.*) hunger is the best sauce (*prov.*); **der ~ treibts rein** (*ugs. scherzh.*) if you're hungry enough, you'll eat anything; [B] (*Hungersnot*) famine; [C] (*geh.: Verlangen*) hunger; (*nach Ruhm, Macht*) craving; thirst; **~ nach Gerechtigkeit** powerful desire to see justice done

**Hunger-:** ~**blockade** *die* food blockade; ~**da·sein** *das* existence at starvation level *or* below subsistence level; ~**gefühl** *das* feeling of hunger; ~**jahr** *das* hungry year; ~**kur** *die* starvation diet; **eine ~kur machen** go on a starvation diet; ~**leider** *der;* ~~**s**, ~~, ~**leiderin** *die;* ~~, ~~**nen** (*ugs. abwertend*) starving pauper; ~**lohn** *der* (*abwertend*) starvation wage[s *pl.*]

**hungern** /ˈhʊŋɐn/ ❶ *itr. V.* [A] go hungry; starve; **~, um schlank zu werden** be on a starvation diet in order to get slim; **jmdn. ~ lassen** let sb. starve; (*als Strafe*) starve sb.; [B] (*verlangen*) **nach etw. ~:** hunger *or* be hungry for sth.; (*nach Macht, Ruhm*) crave sth.; thirst for sth. ❷ *refl. V.* **sich schlank ~:** go on a [slimming] diet; (*mit totalem Verzicht auf Nahrung*) slim by going on a starvation diet; **sich zu Tode ~:** starve oneself to death. ❸ *tr. V.* (*unpers.*) (*dichter.: verlangen*) **jmdn. hungert nach etw.** sb. craves [for] sth. *or* hungers for sth.

**Hunger-:** ~**ödem** *das* ▶ 474 (*Med.*) famine oedema; nutritional oedema; ~**ration** *die* (*ugs.*) starvation rations *pl.*

**hungers** *in* **~ sterben** die of starvation *or* hunger; starve to death

**Hungers·not** *die* famine

**Hunger-:** ~**streik** *der* hunger strike; **in den ~streik treten** go on hunger strike; ~**tod** *der* death from starvation; **den ~tod sterben** die of starvation; ~**tuch** *das: in* **am ~tuch nagen** (*ugs. scherzh.*) be on the breadline; ~**turm** *der* (*hist.*): *dungeon in which prisoners were starved to death*

**hungrig** *Adj.* [A] hungry; **das macht [einen] ~:** it makes you hungry *or* gives you an appetite; **~ nach etw. sein** fancy sth.; feel like sth. (*coll.*); [B] (*geh.: begierig*) hungry (**nach** for); **~ nach Anerkennung sein** crave recognition

**Hunne** /ˈhʊnə/ *der;* ~**n**, ~**n** (*hist.*) Hun

**Hupe** /ˈhuːpə/ *die;* ~, ~**n** horn; **auf die ~ drücken** sound the/one's horn

**hupen** *itr. V.* sound the *or* one's horn; **dreimal ~:** hoot three times; give three toots on the horn

**Huperei** *die;* ~: honking; hooting

**Hupf·dohle** *die* (*salopp*) chorus girl

**hupfen** /ˈhʊpfn̩/ *itr. V.; mit sein* (*südd., österr.*) hop; **das ist gehupft wie gesprungen** (*ugs.*) it doesn't make any difference; it doesn't matter either way

**hüpfen** /ˈhʏpfn̩/ *itr. V.; mit sein* hop; ‹ball› bounce; ‹lamb› gambol; **über die Straße ~:** skip across the road; **Hüpfen spielen** play [at] hopscotch; **mein Herz hüpfte vor Freude** my heart leapt for joy; **das ist gehüpft wie gesprungen** (*ugs.*) ⇒ **hupfen**

**Hupfer** *der;* ~**s**, ~ (*bes. südd., österr.*), **Hüpfer** *der;* ~**s**, ~ skip; (*auf einem Bein*) hop

**Hup-:** ~**konzert** *das* (*ugs. scherzh.*) chorus of hooting; ~**signal** *das* hoot; toot; ~**verbot** *das* ban on sounding one's horn

*old spelling (see note on page 1707)

**Hürde** /ˈhʏrdə/ *die;* ~, ~**n** Ⓐ (*Leichtathletik, Reitsport, fig.*) hurdle; **eine ~ nehmen/reißen** clear/knock over a hurdle; **eine ~ nehmen** (*fig.*) get over a hurdle

**Hürden-:** ~**lauf** *der* (*Leichtathletik*) hurdling; (*Wettbewerb*) hurdles *pl.*; hurdle race; ~**läufer** *der*, ~**läuferin** *die* (*Leichtathletik*) hurdler; ~**rennen** *das* (*Reitsport*) hurdle race; ~**rennen reiten** ride in a hurdle race

**Hure** /ˈhu:rə/ *die;* ~, ~**n** (*abwertend*) whore

**huren** *itr. V.* (*abwertend*) whore; fornicate; **mit jmdm. ~:** fornicate with sb.

**Huren-:** ~**bock** *der* (*abwertend*) whoremonger; fornicator; ~**kind** *das* (*Druckw.*) widow; ~**sohn** *der* (*abwertend*) bastard (*coll.*); son of a bitch (*derog.*)

**Hurerei** *die;* ~, ~**en** (*abwertend*) ~/~**en** *Pl.* whoring *sing.*; fornication *sing.*

**Huri** /ˈhu:ri/ *die;* ~, ~**s** (*islam. Rel.*) houri

**hurra** /hʊˈra:/ *Interj.* hurray; hurrah; ~/**Hurra schreien** cheer; ⇒ *auch* **hipp, hipp, hurra**

**Hurra** *das;* ~**s**, ~**s** cheer; **ein dreifaches ~:** three cheers *pl.*; **jmdn. mit ~ begrüßen** greet sb. with cheering *or* cheers *pl.*

**hurra-, Hurra-:** ~**gebrüll** *das*, ~**geschrei** *das* [loud] cheering *or* cheers *pl.*; ~**patriot** *der* (*ugs. abwertend*) flag-waving patriot; ~**patriotisch** *Adj.* (*ugs. abwertend*) flag-waving ‹speech etc.›; ~**patriotismus** *der* (*ugs. abwertend*) flag-waving patriotism; ~**ruf** *der* cheering; cheers *pl.*

**Hurrikan** /ˈhʌrɪkən/ *der;* ~**s**, ~**s** hurricane

**hurtig** /ˈhʊrtɪç/ ❶ *Adj.* rapid. ❷ *adv.* quickly; ‹work› fast, quickly

**Husar** /huˈza:ɐ̯/ *der;* ~**en**, ~**en** (*hist.*) hussar

**Husaren-:** ~**streich** *der*, ~**stück** *das* daring coup

**husch** /hʊʃ/ ❶ *Interj.* quick; quickly; ~, ~! away with you!; be off with you!; (*zu einem Tier*) shoo! ❷ *Adv.* **das geht nicht so ~, ~:** it can't be rushed; **bei ihr muss alles ~, ~ gehen** she wants everything done in a hurry

**Husch** *der;* ~[**e**]**s**, ~**e** *in* **in einem ~** (*ugs.*) in a flash; in no time at all

**Husche** /ˈhʊʃə/ *die;* ~, ~**n** (*ostmd.*) [sudden] shower

**huschen** *itr. V.; mit sein* (*lautlos u. leichtfüßig*) ‹person› slip, steal; (*lautlos u. schnell*) flit, dart; ‹mouse, lizard, etc.› dart; ‹smile› flit; ‹light› flash; ‹shadow› slide *or* glide quickly

**hussa** /ˈhʊsa/, **hussasa** /ˈhʊsasa/ *Interj.* (*bei der Jagd*) tally-ho; halloo; (*zum Pferd*) gee-up

**hüsteln** /ˈhy:stl̩n/ *itr. V.* cough slightly; give a slight cough; **verlegen/vornehm ~:** cough with embarrassment/politely

**husten** /ˈhu:stn̩/ ❶ *itr. V.* Ⓐ cough; **auf etw.** (*Akk.*) **~** (*salopp*) not give a damn for sth.; Ⓑ (*Husten haben*) have a cough; be coughing. ❷ *tr. V.* cough up ‹blood, phlegm›; **jmdm. etwas ~** (*salopp spött.*) tell sb. where he/she can get off (*coll.*)

**Husten** *der;* ~**s**, ~ ▶ 474 cough; **~ haben** have a cough

**Husten-:** ~**an·fall** *der* ▶ 474 coughing fit; fit of coughing; ~**bonbon** *das* cough sweet (*Brit.*); cough drop; ~**mittel** *das* cough medicine *or* mixture; ~**reiz** *der* tickling in the throat; **den ~reiz nicht unterdrücken können** be unable to suppress the urge *or* need to cough; ~**saft** *der* cough syrup; cough mixture; ~**tee** *der: herb tea which soothes coughs;* ~**tropfen** *Pl.* cough drops

**Hut**[1] /hu:t/ *der;* ~**es**, **Hüte** /ˈhy:tə/ Ⓐ hat; **den ~ abnehmen/aufsetzen** take off/put on one's hat; **vor jmdm. den ~ ziehen** (*abnehmen*) take off one's hat to sb.; (*zum Gruß*) raise one's hat to sb.; **in ~ und Mantel** wearing one's hat and coat; with one's hat and coat on; Ⓑ (*fig.*) **da geht einem/mir der ~ hoch** (*ugs.*) it makes you/me mad *or* wild (*coll.*); **~ ab!** (*ugs.*) hats off to him/her *etc.*; I take my hat off to him/her *etc.*; **ein alter ~ sein** (*ugs.*) be old hat; **seinen ~ nehmen [müssen]** (*ugs.*) [have to] pack one's bags and go; **vor jmdm./etw. den ~ ziehen** (*ugs.*) take off one's hat to sb./sth.; **das kann er sich** (*Dat.*) **an den ~ stecken** (*ugs. abwertend*) he can keep it (*coll.*) *or* (*sl.*) stick it; **mit etw. nichts am ~ haben** (*ugs.*) have nothing to do with sth.; **jmdm. eins auf den ~ geben** (*ugs.*) give sb. a dressing down *or* (*Brit. coll.*) rocket; **eins auf den ~ kriegen** (*ugs.*) get a dressing down *or* (*coll.*) rocket; **verschiedene Interessen/Personen unter einen ~ bringen** (*ugs.*) reconcile different interests/the interests of different people; Ⓒ (*Bot.*) cap

**Hut**[2] *die;* ~ (*geh.*) keeping; care; **bei jmdm. in guter ~ sein** be in good hands with sb.; **auf der ~ sein** be on one's guard

**Hut-:** ~**ab·lage** *die* hat rack; ~**band** *das; Pl.* ~**bänder** hatband; (*eines Damenhutes*) hat ribbon

**Hüte·junge** *der* shepherd boy

**hüten** /ˈhy:tn̩/ ❶ *tr. V.* look after; take care of; tend, keep watch over ‹sheep, cattle, etc.›; **etw. eifersüchtig ~:** guard sth. jealously; **ein Geheimnis ~** (*fig.*) keep *or* guard a secret; ⇒ *auch* **Bett** A. ❷ *refl. V.* (*vorsehen*) be on one's guard; **sich vor jmdm./etw. ~:** be on one's guard against sb./sth.; **sich ~, etw. zu tun** take [good] care not to do sth.; **ich werde mich ~!** (*ugs.*) no fear!; not likely! (*coll.*)

**Hüter** *der;* ~**s**, ~**:** guardian; custodian; **soll ich meines Bruders ~ sein?** (*bibl.*) am I my brother's keeper?; **ein ~ des Gesetzes** (*scherzh.*) a custodian of the law (*coll.*)

**Hüterin** *die;* ~, ~**nen** guardian; custodian

**Hut-:** ~**feder** *die* hat feather; (*größer*) plume; ~**geschäft** *das* hat shop; hatter's [shop]; (*für Damen*) hat shop; milliner's (shop); ~**größe** *die* hat size; size of hat; ~**krempe** *die* [hat] brim; ~**macher** *der* ▶ 159 hatter; hat maker; (*für Damen*) milliner; ~**macherin** *die;* ~, ~**nen** ▶ 159 ⇒ ~**macher**; ~**mode** *die* (*der Herren*) fashion in gents' *or* gentlemen's hats; (*der Damen*) fashion in ladies' hats; ~**nadel** *die* hatpin; ~**schachtel** *die* hat box

**Hutsche** /ˈhʊtʃə/ *die;* ~, ~**n** (*südd., österr. ugs.*) ⇒ **Schaukel**

**Hut·schnur** *die: in* **das geht mir über die ~** (*ugs.*) that's going too far

**Hutsch·pferd** *das* (*südd., österr.*) ⇒ **Schaukelpferd**

**Hütte** /ˈhʏtə/ *die;* ~, ~**n** Ⓐ hut; (*Holz~*) cabin; hut; (*ärmliches Haus*) shack; hut; Ⓑ (*Eisen~*) iron [and steel] works *sing. or pl.*; (*Glas~*) glassworks *sing. or pl.*; (*Blei~*) lead works *sing. or pl.*; Ⓒ (*Jagd~*) [hunting] lodge; Ⓓ (*Seemannsspr.*) poop

**Hütten-:** ~**abend** *der: evening social gathering or party in a mountain hut;* ~**arbeiter** *der*, ~**arbeiterin** *die* (*in der Eisenhütte*) worker in a/the iron/steel works; ironworker/steelworker; (*in der Glashütte*) glass worker; ~**industrie** *die* iron and steel industry; ~**käse** *der* cottage cheese; ~**kombinat** *das* (*DDR*) metallurgical combine; ~**schuh** *der* slipper sock; ~**werk** *das* ⇒ **Hütte** B; ~**wesen** *das* (*Technik*) metallurgical engineering *no art.*; (~*industrie*) iron and steel industry

**Hutzel** /ˈhʊtsl̩/ *die;* ~, ~**n** (*bes. südd.*) dried fruit; (*Birne*) dried pear

**Hutzel·brot** *das* (*bes. südd.*) fruit bread; **ein ~:** a fruit loaf

**hutzelig** *Adj.* (*ugs.*) wizened ‹person, face›; shrivelled, dried-up ‹fruit›

**Hutzel-:** ~**männchen** *das* brownie; ~**weib** *das* wizened old woman

**Hut·zucker** *der* loaf sugar (*in the shape of a cone*)

**Hyäne** /ˈhy̆ɛ:nə/ *die;* ~, ~**n** (*auch fig. ugs.*) hyena

**Hyazinthe** /hy̆aˈtsɪntə/ *die;* ~, ~**n** hyacinth

**hybrid** /hyˈbri:t/ *Adj.* (*bes. Biol.*) hybrid

**Hybride** *der;* ~**n**, ~**n** (*Biol.*) hybrid

**Hybrid-:** ~**rechner** *der* (*DV*) hybrid computer; ~**züchtung** *die* (*Biol.*) cross-breeding; crossing

**Hybris** /ˈhy:brɪs/ *die;* ~ (*geh.*) hubris

**Hydra** /ˈhy:dra/ *die;* ~, **Hydren** hydra

**Hydrant** /hyˈdrant/ *der;* ~**en**, ~**en** hydrant

**Hydrat** /hyˈdra:t/ *das;* ~[**e**]**s**, ~**e** (*Chemie*) hydrate

**Hydra[ta]tion** /hydra[ta]ˈtsi̯o:n/ *die;* ~ (*Chemie*) hydration

**Hydraulik** /hyˈdraulɪk/ *die;* ~ (*Technik*) Ⓐ (*Theorie*) hydraulics *sing., no art.*; Ⓑ (*Vorrichtungen*) hydraulics *pl.*; hydraulic system

**hydraulisch** (*Technik*) ❶ *Adj.* hydraulic. ❷ *adv.* hydraulically

**Hydrid** /hyˈdri:t/ *das;* ~[**e**]**s**, ~**e** (*Chemie*) hydride

**hydrieren** /hyˈdri:rən/ *tr. V.* (*Chemie*) hydrogenate

**Hydrierung** *die;* ~ (*Chemie*) hydrogenation

**hydro-, Hydro-** /hydro-/ : ~**biologie** *die* hydrobiology *no art.*; ~**dynamik** *die* (*Physik*) hydrodynamics *sing., no art.*; ~**dynamisch** *Adj.* (*Physik*) hydrodynamic; ~**kultur** *die* (*Gartenbau*) hydroponics *sing.*; ~**logie** *die;* ~~**:** hydrology; ~**logisch** ❶ *Adj.* hydrological; ❷ *adv.* hydrologically; ~**lyse** /-ˈly:zə/ *die;* ~~, ~~**n** (*Chemie*) hydrolysis; ~**meter** *das* current meter; (*Senkwaage*) hydrometer; ~**phil** /-ˈfi:l/ *Adj.* Ⓐ (*Biol.*) hydrophilous ‹plant, insect›; water-loving ‹animal›; Ⓑ (*Chemie*) hydrophilic; ~**phob** /-ˈfo:p/ *Adj.* Ⓐ (*Biol.*) ‹plant, animal› that avoids water; Ⓑ (*Chemie*) hydrophobic; ~**pneumatisch** *Adj.* (*Technik*) hydropneumatic; ~**technik** *die* hydraulic engineering *no art.*; ~**therapie** *die* (*Med.*) hydrotherapy

**Hydroxid, Hydroxyd** *das;* ~[**e**]**s**, ~**e** (*Chemie*) hydroxide

**Hygiene** /hyˈgi̯e:nə/ *die;* ~ Ⓐ (*Gesundheitspflege*) health care; Ⓑ (*Sauberkeit*) hygiene; Ⓒ (*Med.*) hygiene *no art.*; hygienics *sing., no art.*

**hygienisch** ❶ *Adj.* hygienic. ❷ *adv.* hygienically

**hygro-, Hygro-** /hygro-/: ~**meter** *das* (*Met.*) hygrometer; ~**skop** /-ˈsko:p/ *das;* ~~**s**, ~~**e** (*Met.*) hygroscope; ~**skopisch** *Adj.* (*Chemie*) hygroscopic

**Hymen** /ˈhy:mən/ *das od. der;* ~**s**, ~ ▶ 471 (*Anat.*) hymen

**Hymne** /ˈhʏmnə/ *die;* ~, ~**n** Ⓐ hymn; Ⓑ (*Nationalhymne*) national anthem

**hymnisch** *Adj.* hymnic; **ein ~er Gesang** a paean [of praise]

**Hymnus** /ˈhʏmnʊs/ *der;* ~, **Hymnen** (*geh.*) ⇒ **Hymne** A

**Hyperbel** /hyˈpɛrbl̩/ *die;* ~, ~**n** Ⓐ (*Geom.*) hyperbola; Ⓑ (*Rhet.*) hyperbole

**Hyperbel·funktion** *die* (*Math.*) hyperbolic function

**hyperbolisch** /hypɐˈbo:lɪʃ/ (*Math., Rhet.*) hyperbolic

**hyper-, Hyper-** /hypɐ-/ : ~**korrekt** (*ugs. abwertend, Sprachw.*) ❶ *Adj.* hypercorrect; ❷ *adv.* in a hypercorrect way; ~**kritisch** *Adj.* (*abwertend*) hypercritical; ~**link** *der* (*DV*) hyperlink; ~**modern** ❶ *Adj.* ultramodern; ultra-fashionable ‹clothes›; ❷ *adv.* ultra-modernly; ‹dress› ultra-fashionably; ~**sensibel** *Adj.* hypersensitive; ~**text** *der* (*DV*) hypertext ~**tonie** /-toˈni:/ *die;* ~~, ~~**n** ▶ 474 (*Med.*) Ⓐ hypertension; Ⓑ (*im Auge, Muskel*) hypertonia; ~**toniker** /-ˈto:nikɐ/ *der;* ~~**s**, ~~, ~**tonikerin** *die;* ~~, ~~**nen** (*Med.*) hypertensive; ~**troph** /-ˈtro:f/ *Adj.* (*Med.*) hypertrophic; ~**trophie** /-troˈfi:/ *die;* ~~ ▶ 474 (*Med.*) hypertrophy

**Hypnose** /hʏpˈno:zə/ *die;* ~, ~**n** hypnosis; **jmdn. in ~ versetzen** put sb. under hypnosis; **unter ~ stehen** be under hypnosis

**Hypno·therapie** *die* hypnotherapy

**Hypnotikum** /hʏpˈno:tikʊm/ *das;* ~**s**, **Hypnotika** (*Med.*) hypnotic; soporific

**hypnotisch** *Adj.* hypnotic; hypnotic, soporific ‹drug›

**Hypnotiseur** /hʏpnotiˈzø:ɐ̯/ *der;* ~**s**, ~**e**, **Hypnotiseurin** *die;* ~, ~**nen** hypnotist

**hypnotisieren** *tr. V.* hypnotize

**Hypnotismus** *der;* ~**:** hypnotism *no art.*

**Hypochonder** /hypoˈxɔndɐ/ *der;* ~**s**, ~, **Hypochonderin** *die;* ~, ~**nen** hypochondriac

**Hypochondrie** *die;* ~, ~n ▶474 (*Med.*) hypochondria *no art.*

**hypochondrisch** *Adj.* hypochondriac

**hypo-, Hypo-** /hypo-/: **~nym** /-'ny:m/ *das;* **~~s, ~~e** (*Sprachw.*) hyponym; **~physe** /-'fy:zə/ *die;* ~~, **~~n** ▶471 (*Anat.*) hypophysis; **~stase** /-'sta:zə/ *die;* ~~, **~~n** Ⓐ (*Philos.*) hypostasis; Ⓑ (*Sprachw.*) establishment as an independent word; **~taktisch** /-'taktɪʃ/ *Adj.* (*Sprachw.*) hypotactic; **~taxe** /-'taksə/ *die* (*Sprachw.*) hypotaxis; **~tenuse** /-te'nu:zə/ *die;* ~~, **~~n** (*Math.*) hypotenuse; **~thalamus** *der* ▶471 (*Anat.*) hypothalamus

**Hypothek** /-'te:k/ *die;* ~, **~en** Ⓐ (*Bankw.*) mortgage; **eine ~ aufnehmen** take out a mortgage; **etw. mit einer ~ belasten** encumber sth. with a mortgage; mortgage sth.; Ⓑ (*Bürde*) burden

**hypothekarisch** /-te'ka:rɪʃ/ ❶ *Adj.* **~e Sicherheiten bieten** offer a mortgage [on property] as security; **~e Belastungen** mortgage *sing.* ❷ *adv.* **etw. ~ belasten** mortgage sth.

**Hypotheken-: ~brief** *der* (*Bankw.*) mortgage deed; **~gläubiger** *der*, **~gläubigerin** *die* (*Bankw.*) mortgagee; **~pfand·brief** *der* (*Bankw.*) mortgage bond; **~schuldner** *der*, **~schuldnerin** *die* (*Bankw.*) mortgagor; **~zins** *der; Pl.* **~~en** mortgage interest

**hypo-, Hypo-: ~these** /-'te:zə/ *die* hypothesis; **das ist eine reine ~these** that's pure hypothesis; **~thetisch** ❶ *Adj.* hypothetical; ❷ *adv.* hypothetically; **~tonie** /-to'ni:/ *die;* ~~, **~~n** ▶474 (*Med.*) Ⓐ (*niedriger Blutdruck*) hypotension; Ⓑ (*im Auge, Muskel*) hypotonia; **~toniker** /-'to:nikɐ/ *der;* **~~s**, ~~, **~tonikerin** *die;* ~~, **~~nen** hypotensive; **~zykloide** *die* (*Math.*) hypocycloid

**Hysterie** /hyste'ri:/ *die;* ~, **~n** /-i:ən/ hysteria

**Hysteriker** /hys'te:rikɐ/ *der;* **~s**, ~, **Hysterikerin** *die;* ~, **~nen** hysterical person; hysteric

**hysterisch** ❶ *Adj.* hysterical; **einen ~en Anfall bekommen** have [a fit of] hysterics. ❷ *adv.* hysterically

**Hz** *Abk.* **Hertz** Hz

# I i

**i, I** /iː/ *das;* ~, ~: i/I; **das Tüpfelchen** *od.* **der Punkt auf dem** ~ (*fig.*) the final touch; ⇨ *auch* **a, A**

**i** *Interj.* ugh; **i bewahre, i wo** (*ugs*) [good] heavens, no!

**i. A.** *Abk.* **im Auftrag[e]** p.p.

**iah** /iˈaː/ *Interj.* hee-haw

**iahen** /iˈaːən/ *itr. V.* hee-haw; bray

**IAO** *Abk.* **Internationale Arbeitsorganisation** ILO

**ibd.** *Abk.* **ibidem** ibid.

**iberisch** /iˈbeːrɪʃ/ *Adj.* Iberian; **Iberische Halbinsel** Iberian Peninsula

**Ibero·amerika** /iˈbeːro-/ (*das*) Latin America

**IBFG** *Abk.* **Internationaler Bund Freier Gewerkschaften** ICFTU (*International Confederation of Free Trade Unions*)

**ibidem** /iˈbiːdɛm/ *Adv.* ibidem

**Ibis** /ˈiːbɪs/ *der;* ~**ses**, ~**se** (*Zool.*) ibis

**IC** *Abk.* **Intercity[zug]** IC

**ICE** *Abk.* **Intercityexpress[zug]** ICE

**ich** /ɪç/ *Personalpron.; 1. Pers. Sg. Nom.* I; **Wer ist da? — Ich bins!** Who's there? — It's me!; **Wer hat nun das gemacht? — Ich wars** Who did that? — I did *or* It was me; **Hat sie mich gerufen? — Nein,** ~**:** Was it she who called me? — No, I did; **und** ~ **Esel/Idiot habe es gemacht** and I, silly ass/idiot that I am, did it; and, like a fool, I did it; ~ **Idiot/Esel!** what an idiot I am!; I ˈam an idiot!; **immer** ~ (*ugs.*) [it's] always me; ~ **selbst** I myself; ~ **nicht** not me; **Menschen wie du und** ~**:** people like you and I *or* me; ⇨ *auch* (*Gen.*) **meiner,** (*Dat.*) **mir,** (*Akk.*) **mich**

**Ich** *das;* ~**[s]**, ~**[s]** Ⓐ self; **das eigene** ~**:** one's own self; Ⓑ (*Psych.*) ego

**ich-, Ich-:** ~**bewusstsein**, *~**bewußtsein** *das* self-awareness; ~**bezogen** ❶ *Adj.* egocentric; (*in der Kommunikation*) egotistic; ❷ *adv.* ~**bezogen denken** think in an egocentric way; ~**bezogenheit** *die;* ~~**:** egocentricity; (*in der Kommunikation*) egotism; ~**erzähler**, *~**Erzähler** *der*, ~**erzählerin**, *~**Erzählerin** *die* first-person narrator; ~**form**, *die* first person; ~**-laut**, *~**-Laut** *der* (*Sprachw.*) palatal fricative; ich-laut; ~**sucht** *die* (*geh.*) egoism; ~**süchtig** *Adj.* (*geh.*) egoistic[al]

**Ichthyo·saurier** /ɪçtÿo-/ *der* ichthyosaurus

**Icon** /ˈaikən/ *das;* ~**s**, ~**s** (*DV*) icon

**ideal** /ideˈaːl/ ❶ *Adj.* ideal. ❷ *adv.* ideally; **das Haus liegt** ~**:** the house is ideally situated

**Ideal** *das;* ~**s**, ~**e** ideal; **er ist das** ~ **eines Vorgesetzten** he is the ideal *or* perfect boss (*coll.*)

**Ideal-:** ~**besetzung** *die* Ⓐ (*Film, Theater*) ideal cast; Ⓑ (*Sport*) ideal line-up; ~**bild** *das* ideal; ~**fall** *der* ideal case; **im** ~**fall** in ideal circumstances *pl.;* ~**figur** *die* ideal figure; ~**gestalt** *die* ideal; ~**gewicht** *das* ideal weight

**idealisieren** *tr. V.* idealize; **ein** ~**des Bild von etw.** an idealized picture of sth.

**Idealisierung** *die;* ~, ~**en** idealization

**Idealismus** *der;* ~ (*auch Philos.*) idealism

**Idealist** *der;* ~**en**, ~**en**, **Idealistin** *die;* ~, ~**nen** (*auch Philos.*) idealist

**idealistisch** (*auch Philos.*) ❶ *Adj.* idealistic. ❷ *adv.* idealistically

**ideal-, Ideal-:** ~**konkurrenz** *die* (*Rechtsw.*) ⇨ **Tateinheit;** ~**linie** *die* (*Sport*) ideal line; ~**typisch** *Adj.* (*Soziol.*) ideal-typical; idealized; ~**typus** *der* (*Soziol.*) ideal type; ~**vorstellung** *die* ideal

**Idee** /iˈdeː/ *die;* ~, ~**n** Ⓐ idea; **du hast [vielleicht]** ~**n** (*iron.*) you do get some ideas, don't you!; **auf eine** ~ **kommen** hit [up]on an idea; **wie bist du nur auf die** ~ **gekommen?** whatever gave you ˈthat idea?; **jmdn. auf eine** ~ **bringen** give sb. an idea; **eine fixe** ~**:** an obsession; an idée fixe; **er ist von der fixen** ~ **besessen, Rennfahrer zu werden** he is obsessed with the idea of becoming a racing driver; Ⓑ (*ein bisschen*) **eine** ~**:** a shade *or* trifle; **eine** ~ **[Salz/Pfeffer]** a touch [of salt/pepper]

**ideell** /ideˈɛl/ ❶ *Adj.* non-material; (*geistig-seelisch*) spiritual. ❷ *adv.* **etw.** ~ **unterstützen** support sth. in non-material ways

**ideen-, Ideen-:** ~**arm** *Adj.* lacking in ideas *postpos.;* ~**armut** *die* lack of ideas; ~**austausch** *der* exchange of ideas; ~**drama** *das* (*Literaturw.*) drama of ideas; ~**gut** *das* ideas *pl.;* ~**los** *Adj.* devoid of *or* [completely] lacking in ideas *postpos.;* ~**losigkeit** *die;* ~~**:** [complete] lack of ideas; ~**reich** *Adj.* full of ideas *postpos.;* inventive; ~**reichtum** *der* inventiveness

**Iden** /ˈiːdn̩/ *Pl.* (*hist.*) **die** ~ **des März** the ides of March

**Identifikation** /idɛntifikaˈtsi̯oːn/ *die;* ~, ~**en** (*auch Psych.*) identification

**identifizierbar** *Adj.* identifiable; recognizable ‹handwriting›

**identifizieren** /idɛntifiˈtsiːrən/ ❶ *tr. V.* identify. ❷ *refl. V.* (*auch Psych.*) **sich mit jmdm./etw.** ~**:** identify with sb./sth.

**Identifizierung** *die;* ~, ~**en** (*auch Psych.*) identification

**identisch** /iˈdɛntɪʃ/ *Adj.* identical; **möglicherweise sind der Einbrecher und der entsprungene Häftling** ~**:** it's possible that the intruder and the escaped prisoner are one and the same person

**Identität** /idɛntiˈtɛːt/ *die;* ~**:** identity; **jmds.** ~ **feststellen** establish sb.'s identity; **die** ~ **dieser beiden Begriffe** the identity between these two concepts

**Identitäts-:** ~**krise** *die* identity crisis; ~**nachweis** *der* proof of identity; ~**verlust** *der* loss of identity

**Ideogramm** /ideoˈgram/ *das;* ~**s**, ~**e** ideogram

**Ideologe** /ideoˈloːgə/ *der;* ~**n**, ~**n** ideologue

**Ideologie** *die;* ~, ~**n** /-iːən/ ideology

**Ideologie-:** ~**begriff** *der* conception of ideology; ~**kritik** *die* (*Soziol.*) ideological criticism

**Ideologin** *die;* ~, ~**nen** ideologue

**ideologisch** ❶ *Adj.* ideological. ❷ *adv.* ideologically; **jmdn.** ~ **schulen** give sb. ideological instruction

**ideologisieren** *tr. V.* ideologize

**Ideologisierung** *die;* ~, ~**en** ideologization

**Idiom** /iˈdi̯oːm/ *das;* ~**s**, ~**e** (*Sprachw.*) idiom

**Idiomatik** /idi̯oˈmaːtɪk/ *die;* ~ (*Sprachw.*) idioms *pl.;* (*Gebiet der Lexikologie*) idiomology *no art.*

**idiomatisch** ❶ *Adj.* idiomatic. ❷ *adv.* idiomatically

**Idiosynkrasie** /idi̯ozʏnkraˈziː/ *die;* ~, ~**n** ▶ **474** Ⓐ (*Med.*) idiosyncrasy; Ⓑ (*Psych.*) pathological aversion

**Idiot** /iˈdi̯oːt/ *der;* ~**en**, ~**en** Ⓐ idiot; Ⓑ (*ugs. abwertend*) fool; (*stärker*) idiot (*coll.*)

**Idioten-:** ~**hang** *der*, ~**hügel** *der* (*ugs. scherzh.*) nursery slope

**idioten·sicher** *Adj.* (*ugs. scherzh.*) foolproof

**Idioten·test** *der* (*ugs.*) *range of medical and psychological tests designed to test suitability to hold a driving licence*

**Idiotie** /idi̯oˈtiː/ *die;* ~, ~**n** /-iːən/ Ⓐ idiocy; Ⓑ (*ugs. abwertend: Dummheit*) lunacy; madness; **seine** ~**n** his idiocies

**Idiotikon** /iˈdi̯oːtikɔn/ *das;* ~**s**, **Idiotiken** *od.* **Idiotika** dialect dictionary

**Idiotin** *die;* ~, ~**nen** Ⓐ idiot; Ⓑ (*ugs. abwertend*) fool; (*stärker*) idiot

**idiotisch** ❶ *Adj.* Ⓐ (*Psych.*) severely subnormal; idiotic (*as tech. term*); Ⓑ (*ugs. abwertend: unsinnig*) stupid; (*stärker*) idiotic. ❷ *adv.* Ⓐ (*schwachsinnig*) idiotically; Ⓑ (*ugs. abwertend: unsinnig*) stupidly; (*stärker*) idiotically

**Idiotismus** *der;* ~, **Idiotismen** Ⓐ (*Krankheit*) idiocy; Ⓑ (*Äußerung der Idiotie*) symptom of idiocy

**Idol** /iˈdoːl/ *das;* ~**s**, ~**e** (*auch bild. Kunst*) idol; **jmdn. als** ~ **vergöttern** idolize sb.

**Idolatrie** *die;* ~, ~**n** /-iːən/ (*geh.*) idolatry

**Idyll** /iˈdʏl/ *das;* ~**s**, ~**e** idyll; **ein** ~ **für Erholungssuchende** an idyllic place *or* spot for those seeking relaxation and recreation

**Idylle** *die;* ~, ~**n** (*auch Literaturw.*) idyll

**idyllisch** ❶ *Adj.* (*auch Literaturw.*) idyllic. ❷ *adv.* ~ **gelegen** in an idyllic spot

**i. e.** *Abk.* **id est** i.e.

**IG** *Abk.* **Industriegewerkschaft**

**Igel** /ˈiːgl̩/ *der;* ~**s**, ~**:** hedgehog

**Igel-:** ~**schnitt** *der* crew cut; ~**stellung** *die* (*Milit.*) hedgehog position

**igitt[igitt]** /iˈgɪt(iˈgɪt)/ *Interj.* ugh

**Iglu** /ˈiːglu/ *der od. das;* ~**s**, ~**s** igloo

**ignorant** /ɪgnoˈrant/ *Adj.* (*abwertend*) ignorant

**Ignorant** *der;* ~**en**, ~**en**, **Ignorantin** *die;* ~, ~**nen** (*abwertend*) ignoramus

**Ignoranz** /ɪgnoˈrants/ *die;* ~ (*abwertend*) ignorance

**ignorieren** *tr. V.* ignore

**ihm** /iːm/ *Dat. der Personalpron.* **er, es** Ⓐ (*nach Präpositionen*) (*bei Personen*) him; (*bei Dingen, Tieren*) it; (*bei männlichen Tieren*) him; it; Ⓑ **gib es** ~**:** give it to him; give him it; (*dem Tier*) give it to it/him; **ich sagte** ~, **dass ...** I told him that ...; I said to him that ...; ~ **geht es gut** he's well; ~ **war, als habe man** ~ **ins Gesicht geschlagen** he felt as if somebody had punched him in the face; **sie sah** ~ **ins Gesicht** she looked him in the face; **sie hat** ~ **etwas zu essen gekocht** she cooked him a meal; she cooked a meal for him; **sie kämmte** ~ **das Haar** she combed his hair [for him]; **ich bin zu** ~ **gegangen** I went to see him; **Freunde von** ~**:** friends of his

**ihn** /iːn/ *Akk. des Personalpron.* **er** (*bei Personen*) him; (*bei Dingen, Tieren*) it; (*bei männlichen Tieren*) him; it

**ihnen** /ˈiːnən/ *Dat. des Personalpron.* **sie,** *Pl.* Ⓐ (*nach Präpositionen*) them; Ⓑ **gib es** ~**:** give it to them; give them it; ~ **geht es gut** they're well; **Freunde von** ~**:** friends of theirs; ⇨ *auch* **ihm**

**Ihnen** *Dat. von* **Sie** (*Anrede*) Ⓐ (*nach Präpositionen*) you; Ⓑ **ich habe es** ~ **gegeben** I gave it to you; I gave you it; **geht es** ~ **gut?** are you well?; **Freunde von** ~**:** friends of yours; ⇨ *auch* **ihm**

**ihr**[1] /iːɐ̯/ *Dat. des Personalpron.* **sie,** *Sg.* (*nach Präpositionen*) (*bei Personen*) her; (*bei Dingen, Tieren*) it; (*bei weiblichen Tieren*) her; it; ⇨ *auch* **ihm**

i

**ihr**[2] *Personalpron.; 2. Pers. Pl. Nom.* (*Anrede an vertraute Personen*) you; **ihr Lieben** (*im Brief*) dear all; *s. auch* (*Gen.*) **euer**, (*Dat., Akk.*) **euch**

**ihr**[3] *Possessivpron.* Ⓐ (*einer Person*) her; **Ihre Majestät** Her Majesty; **das Buch dort, ist das ~[e]s?** that book there, is it hers?; is that book hers?; **das ist nicht mein Mann, sondern ~er** that is not my husband, but hers; **der/die/das ~e** hers; **die ~en** hers; **die ~en** *od.* **Ihren** her family; Ⓑ (*eines Tiers, einer Sache*) its; (*eines weiblichen Tiers*) her; its; **die Lok fährt glatt ~e 200 Sachen** (*ugs.*) the locomotive does a good 200 kilometres an hour; Ⓒ (*mehrerer Personen, Tiere, Sachen*) their; **das Haus am Ende der Straße ist ~es** the house at the end of the street is theirs; **der/die/das ~e** theirs; **die ~en** theirs; **die ~en** *od.* **Ihren** their family; **sie haben das ~e** *od.* **Ihre getan** they did their bit; **sie haben das ~e** *od.* **Ihre bekommen** they got their due *or* what was due to them

**Ihr** *Possessivpron.* (*Anrede*) your; **~ Hans Meier** (*Briefschluss*) yours, Hans Meier; **welcher Mantel ist ~er?** which coat is yours?; **der/die/das ~e** yours; **die ~en** yours; **Sie haben das ~e getan** you have done your bit; ⇒ *auch* **ihr**[3]

**ihrer** /ˈiːrɐ/ Ⓐ *Gen. des Personalpron.* **sie**, *Sg.* (*geh.*) **wir gedachten ~:** we remembered her; Ⓑ *Gen. des Personalpron.* **sie**, *Pl.* (*geh.*) **wir werden ~ gedenken** we will remember them; **es waren ~ zwölf** there were twelve of them

**Ihrer** *Gen. von* **Sie** (*Anrede*) (*geh.*) **wir werden ~ gedenken** we will remember you

**ihrerseits** /-zaịts/ *Adv.* Ⓐ *Sg.* (*von ihrer Seite*) on her part; (*auf ihrer Seite*) for her part; Ⓑ *Pl.* (*von ihrer Seite*) on their part; (*auf ihrer Seite*) for their part

**Ihrerseits** *Adv.* (*von Ihrer Seite*) on your part; (*auf Ihrer Seite*) for your part

**ihres·gleichen** *indekl. Pron.* Ⓐ *Sg.* people *pl.* like her; (*abwertend*) the likes of her; her sort *or* kind; **sie fühlt sich nur unter ~ wohl** she only feels at home among people like herself *or* her own kind; Ⓑ *Pl.* people like them; (*abwertend*) the likes of them; their sort *or* kind; **sie sollten unter ~ bleiben** they should stay among their own kind

**Ihresgleichen** *indekl. Pron.* people *pl.* like you; (*abwertend*) the likes of you; your sort *or* kind; **Sie sollten besser unter ~ bleiben** you should stay among your own kind

**ihret·halben** (*veralt.*), **ihret·wegen** *Adv.* Ⓐ *Sg.* (*wegen ihr*) because of her; on her account; (*für sie*) on her behalf; (*ihr zuliebe*) for her sake; **mach dir ~ keine Sorgen** don't worry about her; Ⓑ *Pl.* (*wegen ihnen*) because of them; on their account; (*für sie*) on their behalf; (*ihnen zuliebe*) for their sake[s]; (*um sie*) about them

**Ihrethalben** (*veralt.*), **Ihretwegen** *Adv.* (*wegen Ihnen*) because of you; on your account; (*für Sie*) on your behalf; (*Ihnen zuliebe*) for your sake; *Pl.* for your sake[s]; (*um Sie*) about you

**ihret·willen** *Adv.: in* **um ~** (*Sg.*) for her sake; (*Pl.*) for their sake[s]

**Ihret·willen** *Adv.: in* **um ~** (*Sg.*) for your sake; (*Pl.*) for your sake[s]

**ihrige** /ˈiːrɪɡə/ *Possessivpron.* (*geh. veralt.*) Ⓐ *Sg.* **der/die/das ~:** hers; Ⓑ *Pl.* **der/die/das ~:** theirs; ⇒ *auch* **deinige**

**Ihrige** *Possessivpron.* (*Anrede*) (*geh. veralt.*) **der/die/das ~:** yours

**Ihro** /ˈiːro/ *indekl. Pron.* (*veralt.*) your; **~ Gnaden** Your Grace

**Ikebana** /ikeˈbaːna/ *das;* **~[s]** ikebana

**Ikone** /iˈkoːnə/ *die;* **~, ~n** icon

**Ikonoklasmus** /ikonoˈklasmʊs/ *der;* **~, Ikonoklasmen** (*geh.*) iconoclasm

**Ikosaeder** /ikozaˈ|eːdɐ/ *das;* **~s, ~** (*Math.*) icosahedron

**Ilex** /ˈiːlɛks/ *die od. der;* **~, ~** (*Bot.*) holly

**Ilias** /ˈiːli̯as/ *die;* **~:** Iliad

**illegal** /ˈɪleɡaːl/ ❶ *Adj.* illegal. ❷ *adv.* illegally

**Illegalität** /ɪleɡaliˈtɛːt/ *die;* **~, ~en** illegality

**illegitim** /ˈɪleɡitiːm/ *Adj.* (*geh.*) illegitimate

**Illegitimität** *die;* **~** (*geh.*) illegitimacy

**illiquid** /ˈɪlikviːt/ *Adj.* (*Wirtsch.*) insolvent

**Illiquidität** *die;* **~** (*Wirtsch.*) insolvency

**illoyal** /ˈɪlo̯ajaːl/ *Adj.* (*geh.*) disloyal

**Illoyalität** *die;* **~** (*geh.*) disloyalty

**Illumination** /ɪluminaˈtsi̯oːn/ *die;* **~, ~en** Ⓐ (*Beleuchtung*) illumination; **die Stadt zeigte sich in festlicher ~:** the town was festively lit; Ⓑ (*von Handschriften*) illumination

**Illuminator** /ɪlumiˈnaːtɔr/ *der;* **~s, ~en** /-ˈtoːrən/, **Illuminatorin** *die;* **~, ~nen** illuminator

**illuminieren** *tr. V.* illuminate

**Illuminierung** *die;* **~, ~en** illumination

**Illusion** /ɪluˈzi̯oːn/ *die;* **~, ~en** illusion; **sich** (*Dat.*) **~en machen** delude oneself; **jmdm. die ~en rauben** rob sb. of his/her illusions; **gib dich doch nicht der ~ hin, du könntest damit irgendetwas erreichen** do not delude yourself that you could achieve anything by that

**illusionär** /ɪluzi̯oˈnɛːɐ̯/ *Adj.* (*geh.*) illusory ‹conception, expectation, thing›; fanciful ‹demand, procedure, attempt›

**Illusionist** *der;* **~en, ~en, Illusionistin** *die;* **~, ~nen** Ⓐ (*geh.*) dreamer; Ⓑ (*Zauberkünstler*) illusionist

**illusionistisch** *Adj.* (*Kunstw.*) illusionistic

**illusions·los** ❶ *Adj.* [sober and] realistic; **~ sein** have no illusions. ❷ *adv.* without any illusions

**illusorisch** /ɪluˈzoːrɪʃ/ *Adj.* Ⓐ (*trügerisch*) illusory; Ⓑ (*zwecklos*) pointless

**illuster** /ɪˈlʊstɐ/ *Adj.* (*geh.*) illustrious

**Illustration** /ɪlʊstraˈtsi̯oːn/ *die;* **~, ~en** illustration; **zur ~ von etw. [dienen]** (*fig.*) [serve] to illustrate sth.

**illustrativ** /ɪlʊstraˈtiːf/ ❶ *Adj.* (*auch fig.*) illustrative; **ein sehr ~er Vortrag** (*fig.*) a very illuminating lecture. ❷ *adv.* **etw. ~ schildern** describe sth. graphically

**Illustrator** /ɪlʊsˈtraːtɔr/ *der;* **~s, ~en** /-ˈtoːrən/, **Illustratorin** *die;* **~, ~nen** illustrator

**illustrieren** *tr. V.* (*auch fig.*) illustrate; **eine illustrierte Zeitschrift** a magazine; **jmdm. etw. ~:** illustrate sth. for sb.

**Illustrierte** *die; adj. Dekl.* magazine

**Illustrierung** *die;* **~, ~en** (*auch fig.*) illustration

**Iltis** /ˈɪltɪs/ *der;* **~ses, ~se** polecat; (*Pelz*) fitch

**im** /ɪm/ *Präp.* + *Art.* Ⓐ = **in dem;** Ⓑ (*räumlich*) in the; **er wohnt im vierten Stock** he lives on the fourth floor; **im Theater** at the theatre; **er tritt im Zirkus auf** he is appearing in *or* performing with the circus; **im Fernsehen** on television; **im Bett** in bed; **im Spessart/Schwarzwald** in the Spessart/the Black Forest; Ⓒ (*zeitlich*) **im Mai/Januar** in May/January; **im Jahre 1648** in [the year] 1648; **im letzten Jahr** last year; **im Alter von 50 Jahren** at the age of 50; Ⓓ (*Verlauf*) **etw. im Sitzen tun** do sth. [while] sitting down; **noch im Laufen** while still running; **im Gehen/Kommen sein** be going/coming

**i. m.** *Abk.* (*Med.*) **intramuskulär** IM

**Image** /ˈɪmɪtʃ/ *das;* **~[s], ~s** /ˈɪmɪtʃs/ image

**Image·pflege** *die* cultivation of one's image

**imaginär** /imaɡiˈnɛːɐ̯/ *Adj.* (*geh., Math.*) imaginary

**Imagination** /imaɡinaˈtsi̯oːn/ *die;* **~, ~en** (*geh.*) imagination

**imaginativ** /imaɡinaˈtiːf/ *Adj.* (*geh.*) imaginative

**Imagismus** /imaˈɡɪsmʊs/ *der;* **~** (*Literaturw.*) imagism *no art.*

**Imago** /iˈmaːɡo/ *die;* **~, Imagines** /-ɡineːs/ Ⓐ (*Psych., Biol.*) imago; Ⓑ (*Kunstwiss.*) *wax death mask of an ancestor*

**Imam** /iˈmaːm/ *der;* **~s, ~s** *od.* **~e** imam

**imbezil** /ɪmbeˈtsiːl/, **imbezill** /ɪmbeˈtsɪl/ *Adj.* (*Med.*) imbecile

**Imbiss, *Imbiß** /ˈɪmbɪs/ *der;* **Imbisses, Imbisse** Ⓐ (*kleine Mahlzeit*) snack; Ⓑ ⇒ **Imbisslokal**

**Imbiss-,* Imbiß-: ~bude** *die* (*ugs.*) ≈ hot-dog stall *or* stand; **~lokal** *das* café; **~stand** *der* ⇒ **~bude**; **~stube** *die* ⇒ **~lokal**

**-imitat** *das;* **-~s, -~e** imitation ‹leather, wood, etc.›

**Imitation** /imitaˈtsi̯oːn/ *die;* **~, ~en** imitation

**Imitator** /imiˈtaːtɔr/ *der;* **~s, ~en, Imitatorin** *die;* **~, ~nen** /-taˈtoːrən/ imitator; mimic; (*im Kabarett usw.*) impressionist

**imitieren** *tr. V.* imitate

**Imker** /ˈɪmkɐ/ *der;* **~s, ~** ▶ **159** bee-keeper; apiarist (*formal*)

**Imkerei** *die;* **~, ~en** Ⓐ (*Bienenzucht*) bee-keeping *no art.*; (*as tech. term*) apiculture *no art.*; Ⓑ (*Betrieb*) apiary

**Imkerin** *die;* **~, ~nen** ▶ **159** ⇒ **Imker**

**imkern** *itr. V.* keep bees

**immanent** /ɪmaˈnɛnt/ *Adj.* Ⓐ (*geh.*) inherent; **einer Sache** (*Dat.*) **~ sein** be inherent in sth.; Ⓑ (*Philos.*) immanent

**Immanenz** /ɪmaˈnɛnts/ *die;* **~** (*Philos.*) immanence

**immateriell** /ɪmateˈri̯ɛl/ *Adj.* (*geh.*) non-material

**Immatrikulation** /ɪmatrikulaˈtsi̯oːn/ *die;* **~, ~en** Ⓐ (*Hochschulw.*) registration; Ⓑ (*schweiz.: eines Fahrzeugs*) registration

**immatrikulieren** ❶ *tr. V.* Ⓐ (*Hochschulw.*) register; Ⓑ (*schweiz.*) register ‹vehicle›. ❷ *refl. V.* (*Hochschulw.*) register

**Imme** /ˈɪmə/ *die;* **~, ~n** (*dichter.*) bee

**immens** /ɪˈmɛns/ ❶ *Adj.* immense. ❷ *adv.* immensely; enormously ‹expensive›

**immer** /ˈɪmɐ/ *Adv.* Ⓐ always; **wie ~:** as always; as usual; **mach es wie ~!** do it the way you've/we've always done it; **~ dieser Nebel/dieser Streit** this fog never seems to lift/you're/they're *etc.* always arguing; **~ diese Kinder!** these wretched children!; **schon ~:** always; **~ und ewig** for ever; (*jedesmal*) always; **auf** *od.* **für ~ [und ewig]** for ever [and ever]; **sie haben sich für ~ getrennt** they've split up for good; **~ wieder** again and again; time and time again; **~ wieder von vorne anfangen** keep on starting from the beginning again; **~, wenn** every time that; whenever; **er ist ~ der Dumme** (*ugs.*) he's always the loser; **~ ich!** (*ugs.*) [it's] always me; Ⓑ **~** + *Komp.* (*nach u. nach*) **~ dunkler/häufiger** darker and darker/more and more often; **~ mehr** more and more; **~ mehr zunehmen** keep on increasing; Ⓒ (*ugs.: jeweils*) **es durften ~ zwei auf einmal eintreten** we/they were allowed in two at a time; **~ drei Stufen auf einmal** three steps at a time; Ⓓ (*auch*) **wo/wer/wann/wie [auch] ~:** wherever/whoever/whenever/however; Ⓔ (*verstärkend*) **~ noch, noch ~:** still; Ⓕ (*ugs.: bei Aufforderung*) **~ langsam!/mit der Ruhe!** take it easy!; **nur ~ zu!** keep it up!; **~ geradeaus!** keep [going] straight on; **~ der Nase nach!** keep following your nose!; **was treibst du denn ~?** what are you doing these days?; Ⓖ (*irgend*) **so schnell er ~ konnte** as fast as he possibly could

**immer-, Immer-: ~dar** /-ˈdaːɐ̯/ *Adv.* (*geh.*) forever; [for] evermore; **~fort** *Adv.* all the time; constantly; **~grün** *Adj.* evergreen; **~grün** *das* periwinkle; **~hin** *Adv.* Ⓐ (*wenigstens*) at any rate; anyhow; at least; **er hat es ~hin versucht** he tried, anyhow *or* at any rate; at least he tried; **er ist zwar nicht reich, aber ~hin!** he's not rich, it's true, but still; Ⓑ (*trotz allem*) nevertheless; all the same; Ⓒ (*schließlich*) after all

**Immersion** /ɪmɛrˈzi̯oːn/ *die;* **~, ~en** (*Physik, Astron.*) immersion

**immer-: *~während** ⇒ **währen**; **~zu** *Adv.* (*ugs.*) the whole time; all the time; constantly

**Immigrant** /ɪmiˈɡrant/ *der;* **~en, ~en, Immigrantin** *die;* **~, ~nen** immigrant

*old spelling (see note on page 1707)

**Immigration** /ɪmigra'tsi̯o:n/ *die;* ~, ~**en** immigration

**immigrieren** *itr. V.; mit sein* immigrate

**imminent** /ɪmi'nɛnt/ *Adj.* (*veralt.*) imminent

**Immission** /ɪmi'si̯o:n/ *die;* ~, ~**en** (*fachspr.*) *air pollution, noise, noxious substances, radiation, etc. constituting a private nuisance*

**Immissions·schutz** *der: protection against the effects of air pollution, noise, noxious substances, radiation, etc.*

**immobil** /'ɪmobi:l/ *Adj.* **A** (*geh.*) immobile; ~**es Vermögen** immovable property; real estate *or* property; **B** (*Milit.*) not on a war footing *postpos.*

**Immobilien** /ɪmo'bi:li̯ən/ *Pl.* [real] property *sing.*; real estate *sing.*; (*Rubrik in Zeitungen*) property *sing.*

**Immobilien-:** ~**handel** *der* dealing *no art.* in real estate *or* in property; ~**händler** *der*, ~**händlerin** *die* ▶ **159** estate agent

**immobilisieren** *tr. V.* (*Med.*) immobilize

**Immoralismus** /ɪmora'lɪsmʊs/ *der;* ~ (*geh.*) immoralism

**Immortelle** /ɪmɔr'tɛlə/ *die;* ~, ~**n** everlasting [flower]; immortelle

**immun** /ɪ'mu:n/ **A** (*Med., fig.*) immune (**gegen** to); **B** (*Rechtsspr.*) ~ **sein** have *or* enjoy immunity

**immunisieren** *tr. V.* immunize (**gegen** against)

**Immunisierung** *die;* ~, ~**en** immunization (**gegen** against)

**Immunität** /ɪmuni'tɛ:t/ *die;* ~, ~**en** **A** (*Med.*) immunity (**gegen** to); **B** (*Rechtsspr.*) immunity (**gegen** from)

**Immunologie** /ɪmunolo'gi:/ *die;* ~: immunology

**Immun-:** ~**schwäche** *die* (*Med.*) immunodeficiency; immune deficiency; **eine** ~**schwäche haben** be immunodeficient; ~**system** *das* (*Med.*) immune system

**Imp.** *Abk.* **A** **Imperfekt** imperf.; **B** **Imperativ** imper.

**Impedanz** /ɪmpe'dants/ *die;* ~, ~**en** (*Elektrot.*) impedance

**Imperativ** /'ɪmperati:f/ *der;* ~**s**, ~**e** **A** (*Sprachw.*) imperative; **B** (*Philos.*) [**kategorischer**] ~: [categorical] imperative

**imperativisch** (*Sprachw.*) **1** *Adj.* imperative. **2** *adv.* in the imperative

**Imperativ·satz** *der* imperative sentence

**Imperator** /ɪmpe'ra:tɔr/ *der;* ~**s**, ~**en** /-'to:rən/ (*hist.*) **A** (*römischer Oberfeldherr*) imperator; **B** (*Kaiser*) emperor; ~ **Rex** King Emperor

**Imperfekt** /'ɪmpɛrfɛkt/ *das;* ~**s**, ~**e**, **Imperfektum** /ɪmpɛr'fɛktʊm/ *das;* ~**s**, ~**Imperfekta** (*Sprachw.*) imperfect [tense]

**Imperialismus** /ɪmperi̯a'lɪsmus/ *der;* ~: imperialism *no art.*

**Imperialist** *der;* ~**en**, ~**en**, **Imperialistin** *die;* ~, ~**nen** imperialist

**imperialistisch** *Adj.* imperialistic

**Imperium** /ɪm'pe:ri̯ʊm/ *das;* ~**s**, **Imperien** (*hist., fig.*) empire

**impertinent** /ɪmpɛrti'nɛnt/ **1** *Adj.* impertinent; impudent. **2** *adv.* impertinently; impudently

**Impertinenz** /ɪmpɛrti'nɛnts/ *die;* ~, ~**en** impertinence; impudence; **diese** ~**en** this impertinence *or* impudence *sing.*

**Impetus** /'ɪmpetʊs/ *der;* ~ **A** (*Antrieb*) impetus; **B** (*Schwung*) verve; zest

**Impf-:** ~**aktion** *die* vaccination *or* inoculation programme; ~**arzt** *der*, ~**ärztin** *die* vaccinator; inoculator; ~**ausweis** *der* vaccination certificate

**impfen** /'ɪmpfn̩/ *tr. V.* ▶ **474** **A** vaccinate; inoculate; **sich** ~ **lassen** be vaccinated *or* inoculated; **B** (*Biol., Landw.*) inoculate

**Impfling** /'ɪmpflɪŋ/ *der;* ~**s**, ~**e** person who has been vaccinated; (*zu impfende Person*) person waiting to be vaccinated

**Impf-:** ~**pass**, *~**paß** *der* vaccination certificate; ~**pflicht** *die:* **die** ~**pflicht für die Pockenimpfung wurde aufgehoben** compulsory vaccination for smallpox was abolished; ~**pistole** *die* inoculation injector; ~**schaden** *der* vaccine damage *no pl., no indef. art.*; ~**schutz** *der* protection given by vaccination; ~**stoff** *der* vaccine

**Impfung** *die;* ~, ~**en** ▶ **474** vaccination; inoculation

**Impf-:** ~**zeugnis** *das* ⇒ ~**ausweis**; ~**zwang** *der* ⇒ ~**pflicht**

**Implantat** /ɪmplan'ta:t/ *das;* ~[**e**]**s**, ~**e** (*Med.*) implant

**Implantation** /ɪmplanta'tsi̯o:n/ *die;* ~, ~**en** (*Med.*) implantation

**implantieren** *tr. V.* (*Med.*) implant; **jmdm. etw.** ~: implant sth. in sb.

**implementieren** *tr. V.* (*DV*) implement

**Implikation** /ɪmplika'tsi̯o:n/ *die;* ~, ~**en** (*geh., Logik*) implication

**implizieren** /ɪmpli'tsi:rən/ *tr. V.* (*geh.*) imply

**implizit** /ɪmpli'tsi:t/ (*geh.*) **1** *Adj.* implicit. **2** *adv.* implicitly

**implizite** /ɪm'pli:tsite/ *Adv.* (*geh.*) implicitly

**implodieren** /ɪmplo'di:rən/ *itr. V.; mit sein* (*fachspr.*) implode

**Implosion** /ɪmplo'zi̯o:n/ *die;* ~, ~**en** (*fachspr.*) implosion

**Imponderabilien** /ɪmpɔndəra'bi:li̯ən/ *Pl.* (*geh.*) imponderables

**imponieren** /ɪmpo'ni:rən/ *itr. V.* impress; **jmdm. durch etw./mit etw.** ~: impress sb. by sth.; **am meisten imponiert uns an ihm seine Ruhe** what impresses us most about him is his calmness

**imponierend** **1** *Adj.* impressive. **2** *adv.* impressively

**Imponier·gehabe[n]** *das* (*Verhaltensf.*) display

**Import** /ɪm'pɔrt/ *der;* ~[**e**]**s**, ~**e** import; **den** ~ **erhöhen** increase imports; **eine Firma für** ~ **und Export** an import/export firm

**Importeur** /ɪmpɔr'tø:ɐ̯/ *der;* ~**s**, ~**e**, **Importeurin** *die;* ~, ~**nen** importer

**Import·geschäft** *das* **A** import business; **B** (*geschäftlicher Abschluss*) import deal

**importieren** *tr., itr. V.* import

**Import-:** ~**kauffrau** *die*, ~**kaufmann** *der* importer; ~**über·schuss**, *~**über·schuß** *der* import surplus

**imposant** /ɪmpo'zant/ **1** *Adj.* imposing; impressive ‹achievement›. **2** *adv.* imposingly

**impotent** /'ɪmpotɛnt/ *Adj.* impotent

**Impotenz** /'ɪmpotɛnts/ *die;* ~: impotence

**imprägnieren** /ɪmprɛ'gni:rən/ *tr. V.* **A** impregnate; (*wasserdicht machen*) waterproof; **B** (*fachspr.*) carbonate ‹wine›

**Imprägnierung** *die;* ~, ~**en** ⇒ **imprägnieren** A, B: impregnation; waterproofing; carbonation

**im·praktikabel** *Adj.* impracticable

**Impresario** /ɪmpre'za:ri̯o/ *der;* ~**s**, ~**s** *od.* **Impresari** (*veralt.*) impresario

**Impressen** ⇒ **Impressum**

**Impression** /ɪmprɛ'si̯o:n/ *die;* ~, ~**en** impression

**Impressionismus** *der;* ~: impressionism *no art.*

**Impressionist** *der;* ~**en**, ~**en**, **Impressionistin** *die;* ~**n**, ~**nen** impressionist

**impressionistisch** *Adj.* impressionistic

**Impressum** /ɪm'prɛsum/ *das;* ~**s**, **Impressen** imprint

**Imprimatur** /ɪmpri'ma:tʊr/ *das;* ~**s**, (*österr.:*) /---'-/ *die;* ~ **A** (*Buchw.*) **das** *od.* (*österr.*) **die** ~ [**für etw.**] **erteilen** pass sth. for press; **B** (*kath. Kirche*) imprimatur

**Improvisation** /ɪmproviza'tsi̯o:n/ *die;* ~, ~**en** improvisation

**Improvisations·talent** *das* gift *or* talent for improvisation

**improvisieren** *tr., itr. V.* improvise; **über ein Thema** ~ (*Musik*) improvise on a theme

**Impuls** /ɪm'pʊls/ *der;* ~**es**, ~**e** **A** (*Anstoß*) stimulus; **von etw. gehen wichtige** ~**e aus** sth. is an important stimulus *sing.*; **einer Sache** (*Dat.*) **neue** ~**e geben** give sth. fresh stimulus *sing. or* impetus *sing.*; **B** (*innere Regung*) impulse; **einem** ~ **folgen** act on [an] impulse; **etw. aus einem** ~ **heraus tun** do sth. on impulse; **C** (*Elektrot.*) pulse; **D** (*Physik*) impulse; (*Produkt aus Masse u. Geschwindigkeit*) momentum

**Impuls-:** ~**geber** *der*, ~**generator** *der* (*Elektrot.*) pulse generator

**impulsiv** /ɪmpʊl'zi:f/ **1** *Adj.* impulsive. **2** *adv.* impulsively

**Impulsivität** /ɪmpʊlzivi'tɛ:t/ *die;* ~: impulsiveness

**Impuls·satz** *der* (*Physik*) principle of the conservation of momentum

**imstande** /ɪm'ʃtandə/ *Adv.* ~ **sein, etw. zu tun** (*fähig sein*) be able to do sth.; be capable of doing sth.; (*die Möglichkeit haben*) be in a position to do sth.; **zu etw.** ~ **sein** be capable of sth.; **er ist** ~ **und schiebt mir die Schuld in die Schuhe** he's [quite] capable of putting the blame on to me

**in**[1] /ɪn/ **1** *Präp. mit Dat.* **A** (*auf die Frage: wo?*) in; **er hat in Tübingen studiert** he studied at Tübingen; **in Deutschland/der Schweiz** in Germany/Switzerland; **sind Sie schon mal in China gewesen?** have you ever been to China?; **in der Schule/Kirche** at school/church; **in der Schule/Kirche steht noch eine alte Orgel** there's still an old organ in the school/church; **in einer Partei** in a party; **B** (*auf die Frage: wann?*) in; **in zwei Tagen/einer Woche** in two days/a week; **in diesem Sommer** this summer; [**gerade**] **in dem Moment, als er kam** the [very] moment he came; **in diesem Jahr/Monat** this/that year/month; **C** (*auf die Frage: wie?*) in; **in Farbe/Schwarzweiß** in colour/black and white; **in Deutsch/Englisch** in German/English; **D** (*fig.*) **in Mathematik/Englisch** in mathematics/English; **sich in jmdm. täuschen** be wrong about sb.; **E** **er hat es in sich** (*ugs.*) he's got what it takes (*coll.*); **der Schnaps/diese Übersetzung hat es in sich** (*ugs.*) this schnapps packs a punch (*coll.*)/this translation is a tough one; **F** (*Kaufmannsspr.*) **in etw.** (*Dat.*) **handeln** deal in sth.; **er macht in Spirituosen** (*ugs.*) he deals in spirits **2** *Präp. mit Akk.* **A** (*auf die Frage: wohin?*) into; **in die Stadt/das Dorf** into town/the village; **in die Schweiz** to Switzerland; **in die Kirche/Schule gehen** go to church/school; **in eine Partei eintreten** join a party; **B** (*auf die Frage:* [*bis*] *wann?*) into; **bis in den Herbst** into the autumn; **C** (*fig.*) **in die Millionen gehen** run into millions; **sich in jmdn. verlieben** fall in love with sb.; **in etw. einwilligen** agree *or* consent to sth.; ⇒ *auch* **ins**

**in**[2] *Adj. in* ~ **sein** (*ugs.*) be in

**-in** *Bei der Übersetzung ins Englische wird das deutsche Suffix* **-in**, *mit dem feminine Substantive wie* **Lehrerin** *oder* **Kanadierin** *als Ableitungen von Maskulina gebildet werden, im Allgemeinen nicht übersetzt* (**Lehrerin** = teacher). *Soll jedoch betont werden, dass es sich um weibliche Personen im Gegensatz zu männlichen handelt, bieten sich folgende Übersetzungsmöglichkeiten an:* **Lehrerinnen gehen mit 60 in den Ruhestand** women teachers retire at sixty; **sie ist die bekannteste Kanadierin** she is the best-known Canadian woman; *gelegentlich sind Formulierungen wie* lady teachers *oder* Canadian lady *angebracht, wenn eine besonders höfliche Ausdrucksweise angestrebt wird. Sofern es sich um eine Nationalitätenbezeichnung handelt und die betreffende Person noch recht jung ist, findet man auch häufig die Form* Canadian girl. *In diesem Wörterbuch wurde aus Platzgründen auf die Darstellung solcher Möglichkeiten beim jeweiligen Einzelstichwort meist verzichtet*

**in·adäquat** **1** *Adj.* (*geh.*) inadequate. **2** *adv.* inadequately

**in·aktiv** **1** *Adj.* (*geh., auch Chemie, Med.*) inactive. **2** *adv.* **sich** ~ **verhalten** be inactive

**In·aktivität** *die;* ~ (*geh., auch Chemie, Med.*) inactivity

**in·akzeptabel** *Adj.* (*geh.*) unacceptable

**In·angriffnahme** /-na:mə/ *die;* ~, ~**n** (*Amtsspr.*) commencement; (*eines Problems*) tackling

**In·anspruchnahme** *die;* ~, ~n (A) (*Amtsspr.*) use; **bei häufiger ~ der Versicherung** if frequent [insurance] claims are made; **auf ~ seiner Rechte verzichten** waive one's rights; (B) (*starke Belastung*) demands *pl.*; **die große berufliche ~:** the heavy demands made on him/her by his/her job; (C) (*von Maschinen, Material*) use; (*von Einrichtungen*) utilization

**in·artikuliert** (*geh.*) ❶ *Adj.* inarticulate. ❷ *adv.* inarticulately

**In·augenscheinnahme** *die;* ~, ~n (*Amtsspr.*) inspection; **nach ~ mehrerer Wohnungen** after inspecting several flats

**Inaugural·dissertation** /ɪn|auguˈraːl-/ *die* (*doctoral*) thesis

**Inauguration** /ɪn|auguraˈtsi̯oːn/ *die;* ~, ~en (*geh.*) inauguration

**In·begriff** *der* quintessence; **der ~ des Gelehrten/Spießers** the epitome of the scholar/petit bourgeois; the quintessential scholar/petit bourgeois; **der ~ der Schönheit/des Schreckens** the quintessence of beauty/terror; **sie ist der ~ der Tugend/des Bösen** she is virtue personified *or* itself/the embodiment of evil

**inbegriffen** *Adj.* included

**In·besitznahme** *die;* ~, ~n (*Amtsspr.*) appropriation

**In·betriebnahme** *die;* ~, ~n, **In·betriebsetzung** /-zɛtsʊŋ/ *die;* ~, ~en (*Amtsspr.*) (A) (*von* [*öffentlichen*] *Einrichtungen*) opening; (B) (*von Maschinen*) bringing into service; **vor ~ der Maschine** before bringing the machine into service; (C) (*eines Kraftwerks*) commissioning

**In·brunst** *die;* ~ (*geh.*) fervour; (*der Liebe*) ardour; **mit ~:** with fervour; **jmdn. mit ~ lieben** love sb. ardently

**in·brünstig** (*geh.*) ❶ *Adj.* fervent; ardent ‹love›. ❷ *adv.* fervently; ‹love› ardently

**Inbus·schlüssel** (Wz) /ˈɪnbʊs-/ *der* (*Technik*) Allen key

**Indanthren** (Wz) /ɪndanˈtreːn/ *das;* ~s, ~e (*Textilind.*) indanthrene

**Indefinit·pronomen** /ɪndefiˈniːt-/ *das* (*Sprachw.*) indefinite pronoun

**in·deklinabel** *Adj.* (*Sprachw.*) indeclinable

**in·dem** *Konj.* (A) (*während*) while; (*gerade als*) as; (B) (*dadurch, dass*) **~ man etw. tut** by doing sth.; (C) (*bes. südd.*) **~ dass** because

**Indemnität** /ɪndɛmniˈtɛːt/ *die;* ~: ≈ parliamentary privilege

**Inder** /ˈɪndɐ/ *der;* ~s, ~, **Inderin** *die;* ~, ~nen ▶553 Indian

**in·des** (*selten*), **in·dessen** ❶ *Konj.* (*geh.*) (A) (*während*) while; (B) (*wohingegen*) whereas. ❷ *Adv.* (A) (*inzwischen*) meanwhile; in the meantime; (B) (*jedoch*) however

**Index** /ˈɪndɛks/ *der;* ~ *od.* ~es, ~e *od.* **Indizes** /ˈɪnditseːs/ (A) (*Register*) index; (B) (*kath. Kirche*) Index; (C) (*Math., Physik, Wirtsch.*) index

**Index·schaltung** *die* index gears *pl.*

**Index·zahl** *die* (*Wirtsch.*) index [number]

**in·dezent** *Adj.* (*geh.*) indelicate

**Indianer** /ɪnˈdi̯aːnɐ/ *der;* ~s, ~ ▶553 [American] Indian

**Indianer-:** **~geheul** *das* (*scherzh.*) **mit ~geheul** whooping and yelling like a Red Indian/[Red] Indians; **~häuptling** *der* Indian chief

**Indianerin** *die;* ~, ~nen ▶553 [American] Indian

**Indianer-:** **~krapfen** *der* (*österr.*) ⇒ **Mohrenkopf** A; **~reservat** *das* Indian reservation

**indianisch** *Adj.* ▶553 Indian

**Indien** /ˈɪndi̯ən/ (*das*); ~s India

**In·dienst·stellung** *die;* ~, ~en (*Amtsspr.*) commissioning

**in·different** ❶ *Adj.* (*geh., fachspr.*) indifferent. ❷ *adv.* (*geh.*) indifferently

**In·differenz** *die;* ~, ~en (*geh., auch Chemie, Med.*) indifference

*old spelling (see note on page 1707)

**Indignation** /ɪndɪgnaˈtsi̯oːn/ *die;* ~ (*geh.*) indignation

**indigniert** /ɪndɪˈgniːɐ̯t/ *Adj.* indignant

**Indigo** /ˈɪndigo/ *der od. das;* ~s, ~s indigo

**indigo·blau** *Adj.* indigo [blue]

**Indikation** /ɪndikaˈtsi̯oːn/ *die;* ~, ~en (A) (*Med.: Heilanzeige*) indication; (B) (*Rechtsw.*) **[medizinische/soziale/ethische] ~:** [medical/social/ethical] grounds *pl.* for abortion

**Indikativ** /ˈɪndikatiːf/ *der;* ~s, ~e /-iːvə/ (*Sprachw.*) indicative [mood]

**indikativisch** *Adj.* (*Sprachw.*) indicative

**Indikator** /ɪndiˈkaːtɔr/ *der;* ~s, ~en /-kaˈtoːrən/ (*auch Chemie, Technik*) indicator

**Indio** /ˈɪndi̯o/ *der;* ~s, ~s (*Central/South American*) Indian

**in·direkt** ❶ *Adj.* indirect; **~e Rede/eine ~e Frage** (*Sprachw.*) indirect *or* reported speech/an indirect question; **ein ~er Freistoß** (*Sport*) an indirect free kick. ❷ *adv.* indirectly; **einen Freistoß ~ ausführen** (*Sport*) take an indirect free kick

**indisch** /ˈɪndɪʃ/ ▶553 ❶ *Adj.* Indian. ❷ *adv.* **sie hat gestern ~ gekocht** she cooked an Indian meal yesterday

**in·diskret** *Adj.* indiscreet

**In·diskretion** *die;* ~, ~en indiscretion

**in·diskutabel** *Adj.* (*abwertend*) unworthy of discussion *pred.*

**in·disponiert** *Adj.* (*geh.*) indisposed

**In·disposition** *die* (*geh.*) indisposition

**individualisieren** *tr. V.* (*geh.*) individualize

**Individualismus** /ɪndividu̯aˈlɪsmʊs/ *der;* ~ (*Philos., geh.*) individualism

**Individualist** *der;* ~en, ~en, **Individualistin** *die;* ~, ~nen (*geh.*) individualist

**individualistisch** *Adj.* (*geh.*) individualistic

**Individualität** /ɪndividu̯aliˈtɛːt/ *die;* ~, ~en (*geh.*) (A) individuality; (B) (*Persönlichkeit*) personality

**Individual·verkehr** *der* private vehicle traffic; private vehicles *pl.*

**Individuation** /ɪndividu̯aˈtsi̯oːn/ *die;* ~, ~en (*Psych.*) individuation

**individuell** /ɪndiviˈdu̯ɛl/ ❶ *Adj.* (A) individual; (B) (*einem Einzelnen gehörend*) private ‹property, vehicle, etc.›. ❷ *adv.* individually; **etw. ~ gestalten** give sth. one's own personal touch; **das ist ~ verschieden** it varies from case to case

**Individuum** /ɪndiˈviːduʊm/ *das;* ~s, **Individuen** (*auch Chemie, Biol.*) individual; **ein fragwürdiges/verdächtiges ~** (*abwertend*) a dubious/suspicious individual *or* character

**Indiz** /ɪnˈdiːts/ *das;* ~es, ~ien (A) (*Rechtsw.*) piece of circumstantial evidence; **~ien** circumstantial evidence *sing.*; (B) (*Anzeichen*) sign (**für** of)

**Indizes** ⇒ **Index**

**Indizien·beweis** *der* (*Rechtsw.*) piece of circumstantial evidence; **~e** circumstantial evidence *sing.*

**indizieren** /ɪndiˈtsiːrən/ *tr. V.* (A) (*Med.*) indicate; (B) (*kath. Kirche*) **ein Buch ~:** place a book on the Index

**indo-, Indo-** /ɪndo-/: **~china** (*das*) Indo-China; **~europäer** *Pl.* ⇒ **~germanen**; **~europäisch** *Adj.* ⇒ **~germanisch**; **~germanen** *Pl.* Indo-Europeans; **~germanisch** *Adj.* ▶696 Indo-European; Indo-Germanic

**Indoktrination** /ɪndɔktrinaˈtsi̯oːn/ *die;* ~, ~en indoctrination

**indoktrinieren** *tr. V.* indoctrinate

**indolent** /ˈɪndolɛnt/ *Adj.* (*geh., Med.*) indolent

**Indonesien** /ɪndoˈneːzi̯ən/ (*das*); ~s Indonesia

**Indonesier** *der;* ~s, ~, **Indonesierin** *die;* ~, ~nen ▶553 Indonesian

**indonesisch** *Adj.* ▶553, ▶696 Indonesian

**Indossament** /ɪndɔsaˈmɛnt/ *das;* ~[e]s, ~e (*Finanzw.*) endorsement

**Indossant** /ɪndɔˈsant/ *der;* ~en, ~en, **Indossantin** *die;* ~, ~nen (*Finanzw.*) endorser

**Indossat** /ɪndɔˈsaːt/ *der;* ~en, ~en, **Indossatin** *die;* ~, ~nen (*Finanzw.*) endorsee

**indossieren** *tr. V.* (*Finanzw.*) endorse

**Induktanz** /ɪndʊkˈtants/ *die;* ~ (*Elektrot.*) inductance

**Induktion** /ɪndʊkˈtsi̯oːn/ *die;* ~, ~en (*Philos., Elektrot., Biol.*) induction

**Induktions-:** **~maschine** *die* (*Elektrot.*) induction machine; **~ofen** *der* (*Technik*) induction furnace; **~schleife** *die* (*Elektrot.*) induction control loop; **~spule** *die* (*Elektrot.*) induction coil; **~strom** *der* (*Elektrot.*) induced current

**induktiv** /ɪndʊkˈtiːf/ *Adj.* (*Philos., Elektrot.*) inductive

**Induktivität** /ɪndʊktiviˈtɛːt/ *die;* ~, ~en (*Elektrot.*) self-inductance; coefficient of self-induction

**industrialisieren** /ɪndʊstriali'ziːrən/ *tr. V.* industrialize

**Industrialisierung** *die;* ~: industrialization

**Industrie** /ɪndʊsˈtriː/ *die;* ~, ~n industry; **in die ~ gehen** (*ugs.*) go into industry; **in der ~ arbeiten** work in industry

**Industrie-:** **~aktie** *die* industrial share; **~anlage** *die* industrial plant; **~ansiedlung** *die* setting-up of industry; **~arbeiter** *der*, **~arbeiterin** *die* industrial worker; **~archäologie** *die* industrial archaeology *no art.*; **~ausstellung** *die* industrial exhibition; **~betrieb** *der* industrial company *or* firm; **~erzeugnis** *das* industrial product; **~gebiet** *das* industrial area; **~gesellschaft** *die* (*Soziol.*) industrial society; **~gewerkschaft** *die* industrial union; **~kapitän** *der* captain of industry; **~kauffrau** *die*, **~kaufmann** *der*: *person with three years' business training employed on the business side of an industrial company;* **~landschaft** *die* industrial landscape

**industriell** /ɪndʊstriˈɛl/ ❶ *Adj.* industrial; **die ~e Revolution** (*hist.*) the Industrial Revolution. ❷ *adv.* industrially; **~ überlegen/rückständig** industrially more/less advanced

**Industrielle** *der/die; adj. Dekl.* industrialist

**Industrie-:** **~magnat** *der* industrial magnate; **~müll** *der* industrial waste; **~produkt** *das* industrial product; **~spionage** *die* industrial espionage; **~staat** *der* industrial nation; **~stadt** *die* industrial town; (*größer*) industrial city

**Industrie- und Handels·kammer** *die* Chamber of Industry and Commerce

**Industrie-:** **~unternehmen** *das* industrial concern *or* company; **~zweig** *der* branch of industry

**induzieren** /ɪnduˈtsiːrən/ *tr. V.* (*Philos., Elektrot.*) induce

**in·effektiv** *Adj.* ineffective

**in·effizient** *Adj.* (*geh.*) inefficient

**In·effizienz** *die* (*geh.*) inefficiency

**in·einander** *Adv.* into each other; into one another; (*zusammen*) together; **die Farben fließen ~:** the colours run into each other *or* one another; **~ greifen** mesh or engage [with each other *or* one another]; mesh together; **sich ~ schieben** ‹vehicles› telescope; **~ verliebt sein** be in love with each other *or* one another; **~ verschlungene Ornamente** intertwined decorations; **ganz ~ aufgehen** be totally wrapped up in each other *or* one another; **~ übergehen** merge

***ineinander|fließen** *usw.*: ⇒ **ineinander**

**in·existent** *Adj.* (*geh.*) non-existent

**infam** /ɪnˈfaːm/ ❶ *Adj.* disgraceful; **~e Schmerzen** (*ugs.*) dreadful pain *sing.* (*coll.*). ❷ *adv.* disgracefully; **~ weh tun** (*ugs.*) hurt like mad *or* hell (*coll.*)

**Infamie** /ɪnfaˈmiː/ *die;* ~, ~n (A) disgracefulness; (B) (*Äußerung*) disgraceful remark; (*Handlung*) disgraceful action

**Infant** /ɪnˈfant/ *der;* ~en, ~en (*hist.*) infante; (*Thronfolger*) principe

**Infanterie** /ˈɪnfant(ə)riː/ *die;* ~, ~n (*Milit.*) infantry

**Infanterie-:** **~regiment** *das* (*Milit.*) infantry regiment; **~stellung** *die* (*Milit.*) infantry position

**Infanterist** *der;* **~en, ~en** (*Milit.*) infantryman

**infantil** /ɪnfan'ti:l/ (*Psych., Med., sonst abwertend*) ❶ *Adj.* infantile. ❷ *adv.* in an infantile way

**Infantilismus** *der;* **~, Infantilismen** (*Psych., Med.*) infantilism

**Infantilität** /ɪnfantili'tɛ:t/ *die;* **~** Ⓐ (*abwertend*) infantility; Ⓑ (*Psych., Med.*) infantilism

**Infantin** *die;* **~, ~nen** (*hist.*) infanta

**Infarkt** /ɪn'farkt/ *der;* **~[e]s, ~e** ▶474 (*Med.*) infarct; infarction

**infarktgefährdet** *Adj.* (*Med.*) ‹person› with a high risk of suffering a cardiac infarction

**Infekt** /ɪn'fɛkt/ *der;* **~[e]s, ~e** ▶474 (*Med.*) infection; **ein grippaler ~:** an influenzal infection

**Infektion** /ɪnfɛk'tsi̯o:n/ *die;* **~, ~en** ▶474 (*Med.*) Ⓐ (*Ansteckung*) infection; Ⓑ (*ugs.: Entzündung*) inflammation

**Infektions-:** **~gefahr** *die* (*Med.*) danger *or* risk of infection; **~herd** *der* (*Med.*) seat of the/an infection; **~krankheit** *die* ▶474 (*Med.*) infectious disease

**infektiös** /ɪnfɛk'tsi̯ø:s/ *Adj.* (*Med.*) infectious

**Inferiorität** /ɪnferi̯ori'tɛ:t/ *die;* **~** (*geh.*) inferiority

**Inferioritätskomplex** *der* (*Psych.*) ⇨ **Minderwertigkeitskomplex**

**infernalisch** /ɪnfɛr'na:lɪʃ/ (*geh.*) ❶ *Adj.* infernal; **~ schmecken** taste dreadful. ❷ *adv.* infernally; **~ stinken** stink dreadfully

**Inferno** /ɪn'fɛrno/ *das;* **~s** (*geh.*) inferno

**Infiltrat** /ɪnfɪl'tra:t/ *das;* **~[e]s, ~e** (*Med.*) infiltrate

**Infiltration** /ɪnfɪltra'tsi̯o:n/ *die;* **~, ~en** (*auch Med.*) infiltration

**infiltrieren** *tr. V.* (*auch Med.*) infiltrate; **jmdm. etw. ~** (*Med.*) infiltrate sth. into sb.

**infinit** *Adj.* (*Sprachw.*) infinite

**Infinitesimalrechnung** /ɪnfinitezi'ma:l-/ *die* (*Math.*) infinitesimal calculus

**Infinitiv** /'ɪnfiniti:f/ *der;* **~s, ~e** /-ti:və/ (*Sprachw.*) infinitive

**Infinitivsatz** *der* (*Sprachw.*) infinitive clause

**infizieren** /ɪnfi'tsi:rən/ ❶ *tr. V.* (*auch fig.*) infect. ❷ *refl. V.* become *or* get infected; **sich bei jmdm. ~:** be infected by sb.; catch an infection from sb.

**in flagranti** /ɪn fla'granti/ *Adv.* (*geh.*) in flagrante [delicto]

**Inflation** /ɪnfla'tsi̯o:n/ *die;* **~, ~en** (*Wirtsch.*) inflation; (*Zeit der* **~**) period of inflation; **eine schleichende ~:** creeping inflation

**inflationär** /ɪnflatsi̯o'nɛ:ɐ̯/, **inflationistisch** *Adj.* inflationary

**Inflations-:** **~ausgleich** *der* increase to allow for inflation; **~politik** *die* policy of inflation; **~rate** *die* rate of inflation

**inflexibel** *Adj.* Ⓐ (*auch fig.*) inflexible; Ⓑ (*Sprachw.*) uninflected

**Inflexibilität** *die;* **~** (*auch fig.*) inflexibility

**Influenz** /ɪnflu'ɛnts/ *die;* **~, ~en** (*Elektrot.*) [electrostatic] induction

**Influenza** /ɪnflu'ɛntsa/ *die;* **~** (*veralt.*) influenza

**Info** /'ɪnfo/ *das;* **~s, ~s** (*ugs.*) handout

**infolge** ❶ *Präp.* + *Gen.* as a result of; owing to. ❷ *Adv.* **~ von etw.** (*Dat.*) as a result of *or* owing to sth.

**infolgedessen** *Adv.* consequently; as a result of this

**Informant** /ɪnfɔr'mant/ *der;* **~en, ~en, Informantin** *die;* **~, ~nen** (*auch Sprachw.*) informant

**Informatik** /ɪnfɔr'ma:tɪk/ *die;* **~:** computer science *no art.*

**Informatiker** *der;* **~s, ~, Informatikerin** *die;* **~, ~nen** computer scientist

**Information** /ɪnfɔrma'tsi̯o:n/ *die;* **~, ~en** Ⓐ (*auch Kybernetik*) information *no pl., no indef. art.* (**über** + *Akk.* about, on); **eine ~:** [a piece of] information; **eine umfassende ~ der Öffentlichkeit zu diesen Vorfällen ist unbedingt notwendig** it is vital to inform the public fully about these incidents; **zu Ihrer ~:** for your information; **nach neuesten ~en** according to the latest information; **nähere ~en erhalten Sie ...** you can obtain more information ...; Ⓑ (*Büro*) information bureau; (*Stand*) information desk

**Informations-:** **~austausch** *der* exchange of information; **~büro** *das* information bureau *or* office; **~fluss, *~fluß** *der* flow of information; **~gespräch** *das* mutual briefing session; **~material** *das* informational literature; **~quelle** *die* source of information; **~stand** *der* Ⓐ information stand; Ⓑ (*Zustand*) **bei meinem jetzigen ~stand** with the information I have at present; **~theorie** *die* information theory *no art.*; **~vorsprung** *der* superior knowledge

**informativ** /ɪnfɔrma'ti:f/ ❶ *Adj.* informative. ❷ *adv.* informatively

**informatorisch** /ɪnfɔrma'to:rɪʃ/ *Adj.* informatory

**informell** *Adj.* informal

**informieren** ❶ *tr. V.* inform (**über** + *Akk.* about); **falsch/einseitig informiert sein** be misinformed/have biased information; **aus gut informierten Kreisen** from well-informed circles. ❷ *refl. V.* inform oneself, find out (**über** + *Akk.* about); **sich aus der Presse/in der Zeitung über etw.** (*Akk.*) **~:** inform oneself *or* find out about sth. from the press/the newspaper

**infrage** *in* **etw. ~ stellen** call sth. into question; question sth.; **jmdn. ~ stellen** cast doubt on sb.; **das stellt unsere Glaubwürdigkeit ~:** it casts doubt on our credibility; **~ kommen** be possible; **für ein Stipendium kommen nur gute Schüler ~:** only good pupils can be considered for a grant; **dieses Kleid kommt für mich nicht ~:** I couldn't possibly wear this dress; **die für die Tat ~ kommenden Personen** those suspected of the crime; **das kommt nicht ~** (*ugs.*) that is out of the question

**infrarot** /'ɪnfra-/ *Adj.* (*Physik*) infra-red

**Infrarot** *das;* **~s** (*Physik*) infra-red radiation; **im ~:** in the infra-red

**Infrarot-:** **~film** *der* infra-red film; **~strahler** *der* Ⓐ (*Heizgerät*) infra-red heater; Ⓑ (*Med.*) infra-red lamp

**Infra-:** **~schall** *der* (*Physik*) infrasound; **~struktur** *die* infrastructure

**Infusion** /ɪnfu'zi̯o:n/ *die;* **~, ~en** (*Med.*) infusion; (*durch den After*) enema

**Infusionstierchen** *das,* **Infusorium** /ɪnfu'zo:ri̯ʊm/ *das;* **~s, Infusorien** (*Biol.*) infusorium

**Ing.** *Abk.* **Ingenieur**

**Ingebrauchnahme** *die;* **~, ~n: vor ~ des Geräts** before operating the appliance

**Ingenieur** /ɪnʒe'ni̯ø:ɐ̯/ *der;* **~s, ~e** ▶159 [qualified] engineer

**Ingenieur-:** **~bau** *der; Pl.* **~~ten** civil engineering structure; **~büro** *das* firm of consulting engineers

**Ingenieurin** *die;* **~, ~nen** ▶159 [qualified] engineer

**Ingenieurschule** *die* college of engineering

**ingeniös** /ɪnge'ni̯ø:s/ (*geh.*) ❶ *Adj.* ingenious. ❷ *adv.* ingeniously

**Ingeniosität** /ɪngeni̯ozi'tɛ:t/ *die;* **~** (*geh.*) ingenuity

**Ingredienz** /ɪngre'di̯ɛnts/ *die;* **~, ~en** (*bes. Pharm., Kochk.*) ingredient

**Ingrimm** *der* (*geh.*) inward rage *or* wrath

**ingrimmig** (*geh.*) ❶ *Adj.* wrathful ‹look, expression›. ❷ *adv.* wrathfully

**Ingwer** /'ɪŋvɐ/ *der;* **~s, ~** Ⓐ ginger; Ⓑ (*Likör*) ginger liqueur

**Ingwerbier** *das* ginger beer

**Inhaber** /'ɪnha:bɐ/ *der;* **~s, ~** Ⓐ (*einer Aktie, einer Lizenz, eines Rekords, eines Patents, eines Passes*) holder; (*eines Schecks*) bearer; (*eines Amtes*) holder; incumbent; Ⓑ (*Besitzer*) owner; (*eines Hotels, Restaurants, Ladens*) owner; proprietor

**Inhaberin** *die;* **~, ~nen** Ⓐ ⇨ **Inhaber** A; Ⓑ ⇨ **Inhaber** B: owner; proprietress

**Inhaberpapier** *das* (*Wirtsch.*) bearer security

**inhaftieren** /ɪnhaf'ti:rən/ *tr. V.* take into custody; detain; **jmdn. zwei Tage lang ~:** keep sb. in custody *or* detain sb. for two days

**Inhaftierte** *der/die; adj. Dekl.* prisoner

**Inhaftierung** *die;* **~, ~en** detention

**Inhalation** /ɪnhala'tsi̯o:n/ *die;* **~, ~en** (*Med.*) inhalation

**inhalieren** ❶ *tr. V.* (*Med./ugs.*) inhale. ❷ *itr. V.* (*Med.*) use an inhalant

**Inhalt** *der;* **~[e]s, ~e** Ⓐ contents *pl.*; Ⓑ (*das Dargestellte/geistiger Gehalt*) content; **etw. zum ~ haben** deal with *or* concern sth.; **ein Buch politischen ~s** a political book; **der ~ eines Wortes** the meaning of a word; **wir erhielten eine Nachricht des ~s, dass ...** (*geh.*) we received a message to the effect that ...; Ⓒ (*bes. Math.*) (*Flächen~*) area; (*Raum~*) volume

**inhaltlich** ❶ *Adj.* **die ~e Struktur des Dramas** the plot structure of the drama; **an ~en Gesichtspunkten gemessen** from the point of view of content. ❷ *adv.* **~ ist der Aufsatz gut** the essay is good as regards content; **~ übereinstimmen** be the same in content

**inhalts-, Inhalts-:** **~angabe** *die* summary [of contents]; synopsis; (*eines Films, Dramas*) [plot] summary; synopsis; **~bezogen** *Adj.* (*Sprachw.*) **~bezogene Grammatik** content[-oriented] grammar; **~erklärung** *die* declaration of contents; **~leer, ~los** *Adj.* lacking in content *postpos.*; meaningless ‹word, phrase›; empty ‹life›; **~reich** *Adj.* full ‹life, discussion›; **~schwer** *Adj.* weighty; **~übersicht** *die* summary [of contents]; **~verzeichnis** *das* table of contents; (*auf einem Paket*) list of contents; (*als Überschrift*) [table of] contents; **~voll** *Adj.* ⇨ **~reich**

**inhärent** /ɪnhɛ'rɛnt/ *Adj.* (*geh., Philos.*) inherent (+ *Dat.* in)

**Inhärenz** /ɪnhɛ'rɛnts/ *die;* **~** (*Philos.*) inherence

**inhomogen** *Adj.* (*geh., fachspr.*) inhomogeneous

**Inhomogenität** *die;* **~** (*geh., fachspr.*) inhomogeneity

**inhuman** *Adj.* Ⓐ (*unmenschlich*) inhuman; Ⓑ (*rücksichtslos*) inhumane

**Inhumanität** *die;* **~:** inhumanity

**Initial** /ini'tsi̯a:l/ *das;* **~s, ~e** (*selten*), **Initiale** *die;* **~, ~n** initial [letter]

**Initial-:** **~zünder** *der* detonator; **~zündung** *die* detonation

**Initiation** /initsi̯a'tsi̯o:n/ *die;* **~, ~en** (*Soziol., Völkerk.*) initiation

**Initiationsritus** *der* (*Soziol., Völkerk.*) initiation rite

**initiativ** /initsi̯a'ti:f/ *Adj.* **~ werden** take the initiative

**Initiative** *die;* **~, ~n** Ⓐ (*erster Anstoß*) initiative; **die ~ ergreifen** take the initiative; **auf jmds. ~** (*Akk.*) **[hin]** on sb.'s initiative; Ⓑ (*Entschlusskraft*) initiative; **~ entwickeln/entfalten** develop initiative; **nur der ~** (*Dat.*) **der Opposition ist es zu verdanken, dass ...** it is only thanks to the Opposition that ...; Ⓒ ⇨ **Bürgerinitiative**; Ⓓ (*Parl.*) right to table *or* introduce a bill; (*das Einbringen*) tabling *or* introduction of a bill; Ⓔ (*schweiz.*) ⇨ **Volksbegehren**

**Initiator** /ini'tsi̯a:tɔr/ *der;* **~s, ~en, Initiatorin** *die;* **~, ~nen** initiator; (*einer Organisation*) founder

**initiieren** /initsi'i:rən/ *tr. V.* (*geh.*) initiate

**Injektion** /ɪnjɛk'tsi̯o:n/ *die;* **~, ~en** (*Med.*) injection

**Injektions-:** **~nadel** *die* hypodermic needle; **~spritze** *die* hypodermic syringe

**injizieren** /ɪnji'tsi:rən/ *tr. V.* (*Med.*) inject; **jmdm. etw. ~:** inject sb. with sth.

**Injurie** /ɪn'ju:ri̯ə/ *die;* **~, ~n** (*geh., Rechtsw.*) injury

**Inka** /'ɪŋka/ *der;* **~[s], ~[s]** Inca

**Inkarnation** /ɪnkarna'tsi̯o:n/ *die;* **~, ~en** incarnation

**Inkasso** /ɪn'kaso/ *das;* **~s, ~s** *od.* **Inkassi** (*Finanzw.*) collection

i

**In·kaufnahme** *die;* ~ (*Amtsspr.*) acceptance; **er konnte den Vertrag nur unter ~ von Verlusten abschließen** he could complete the contract only by accepting the losses involved

**inkl.** *Abk.* **inklusive** incl.

**inklusive** /ɪnklu'zi:və/ ❶ *Präp.* + *Gen.* (*bes. Kaufmannsspr.*) inclusive of; including; **der Preis versteht sich ~ der Verpackung** the price includes *or* is inclusive of packing; **wir bezahlten ~ Frühstück 40 DM** we paid 40 DM, breakfast included *or* including breakfast. ❷ *Adv.* inclusive

**inkognito** /ɪn'kɔgnito/ *Adv.* (*geh.*) incognito

**Inkognito** *das;* **~s, ~s** incognito

**in·kommensurabel** *Adj.* (*geh., Math.*) incommensurable

**in·kommodieren** /ɪnkɔmo'di:rən/ (*geh.*) ❶ *tr. V.* inconvenience; trouble; **jmdn. mit etw. ~:** trouble sb. with sth. ❷ *refl. V.* trouble oneself

**in·kompatibel** *Adj.* (*fachspr.*) incompatible

**In·kompatibilität** *die* (*fachspr.*) incompatibility

**in·kompetent** *Adj.* Ⓐ (*unfähig*) incompetent; Ⓑ (*bes. Rechtsspr.: nicht befugt*) not competent *postpos.;* incompetent

**In·kompetenz** *die* incompetence

**In·kongruenz** *die* (*Math.*) incongruence

**in·konsequent** ❶ *Adj.* inconsistent. ❷ *adv.* inconsistently

**In·konsequenz** *die* inconsistency

**in·konsistent** *Adj.* (*geh.*) inconsistent

**in·konstant** *Adj.* Ⓐ (*Physik*) inconstant; Ⓑ (*geh.*) inconsistent; [constantly] shifting ‹balance of power›

**in·konvertibel** *Adj.* (*Wirtsch.*) inconvertible ‹currency›

**in·korrekt** ❶ *Adj.* incorrect; incorrect, improper ‹dress, behaviour›. ❷ *adv.* incorrectly; **sich ~ kleiden/benehmen** dress/behave incorrectly *or* inproperly

**Inkorrektheit** *die;* **~, ~en** Ⓐ (*Fehlerhaftigkeit*) incorrectness; (*des Benehmens*) incorrectness; impropriety; Ⓑ (*Fehler*) mistake; (*inkorrektes Benehmen*) breach of propriety; impropriety

**In·kraftsetzung** /-zɛtsʊŋ/ *die;* **~, ~en** (*Amtsspr.*) **mit ~ dieses Gesetzes** when this law is/was brought *or* put into force

**In-Kraft-Treten, *Inkrafttreten** *das;* **~s: das ~ des Gesetzes erfolgt dann, wenn ...** the law comes into effect *or* force when ...

**In·kreis** *der* (*Geom.*) inscribed circle

**inkriminieren** /ɪnkrimi'ni:rən/ *tr. V.* (*bes. Rechtsspr.*) incriminate

**Inkubation** /ɪnkuba'tsi̯o:n/ *die;* **~, ~en** ▶ 474 (*Med., Biol.*) incubation

**Inkubations·zeit** *die;* **~, ~en** ▶ 474 (*Med.*) incubation period

**Inkubator** /ɪnku'ba:tɔr/ *der;* **~s, ~en** (*Med.*) incubator

**Inkubus** /'ɪnkubʊs/ *der;* **~, Inkuben** incubus

**in·kulant** *Adj.* (*Kaufmannsspr.*) unaccommodating; disobliging

**Inkulanz** /'ɪnkulants/ *die;* ~ (*Kaufmannsspr.*) disobligingness

**Inkunabel** /ɪnku'na:bl̩/ *die;* **~, ~n** (*Buchw., Literaturw.*) incunabulum

**In·land** *das* Ⓐ (*das eigene Land*) **im ~:** at home; **im ~ hergestellte Waren, Produktionen des ~es** home-produced goods; **für das ~ bestimmte Waren** goods for the home market; **wir werden unseren Urlaub diesmal im ~ verbringen** we're not going abroad for our holidays this year; **im In- und Ausland** at home and abroad; Ⓑ (*Binnenland*) interior; inland; **im/ins ~:** inland

**Inland·eis** *das;* **~es** inland ice

**Inländer** /'ɪnlɛndɐ/ *der;* **~s, ~, Inländerin** *die;* **~, ~nen** native citizen

**inländisch** *Adj.* domestic; internal, domestic ‹trade, traffic›; home, domestic ‹market›; home-produced, domestic ‹goods›

**Inlands-: ~ab·satz** *der* (*Wirtsch.*) domestic sales *pl.;* **~markt** *der* home *or* domestic market; **~porto** *das* inland postage; **~presse** *die* domestic press; **~verkehr** *der* internal *or* domestic traffic

**In·laut** *der;* **~[e]s, ~e** (*Sprachw.*) **im ~ stehen/vorkommen** occur in [word-]medial position *or* [word-]medially

**Inlett** /'ɪnlɛt/ *das;* **~[e]s, ~e** *od.* **~s** (*Stoff*) tick; ticking; (*Hülle*) tick

**in·liegend** *Adj.* (*Amtsspr., bes. österr.*) ⇒ **einliegend**

**Inliner** /'ɪnlaɪnɐ/ *der;* **~s, ~:** Rollerblade ®; in-liner

**Inlineskate** /'ɪnlaɪnske:t/ *der;* **~s, ~s** Rollerblade ®; in-line skate

**Inlineskater** /'ɪnlaɪnske:tɐ/ *der;* **~s, ~:** rollerblader; in-line skater

**in·mitten** ❶ *Präp.* + *Gen.* (*geh.*) in the midst of; surrounded by. ❷ *Adv.* **~ von** in the midst of; surrounded by

**inne** /'ɪnə/ *in* **einer Sache** (*Gen.*) **~ sein** (*geh.*) be [fully] aware of sth.

**inne-/'ɪnə-/: ~|haben** *unr. tr. V.* Ⓐ (*einnehmen*) hold, occupy ‹position›; hold ‹office›; **die Führung/Leitung ~haben** be in charge; **einen Lehrstuhl ~haben** hold a [professorial] chair; Ⓑ (*geh.: besitzen*) own; possess; **~|halten** *unr. itr. V.* pause; **in** *od.* **mit etw. ~halten** stop sth. for a moment; **er hielt in seiner Arbeit/im Laufen ~:** he stopped work/running for a moment; **er hielt mitten im Satz ~:** he stopped *or* paused in the middle of his sentence *or* in mid-sentence

**innen** /'ɪnən/ *Adv.* Ⓐ inside; (*auf/an der Innenseite*) on the inside; **etw. von ~ nach außen kehren** turn sth. inside out; **die Leitung verlief von ~ nach außen** the cable ran from the inside to the outside; **~ und außen** inside and out[side]; **nach ~ aufgehen** open inwards; **etw. von ~ besichtigen/ansehen** look round the/at the inside of sth.; **die Füße nach ~ setzen** turn one's feet in[wards]; **~ laufen** (*Sport*) run on the inside; **von ~ heraus** from within; Ⓑ (*österr.: drinnen*) inside; (*im Haus*) indoors

**innen-, Innen-: ~ansicht** *die* interior view; **~antenne** *die* indoor aerial; **~arbeiten** *Pl.* interior work *sing.;* **~architekt** *der,* **~architektin** *die* interior designer; **~aufnahme** *die* (*Fot.*) indoor photo[graph]; (*Film*) indoor *or* interior shot; **~ausstattung** *die:* **[eine] ~ausstattung** decoration and furnishings; (*eines Autos*) [an] interior trim; **~bahn** *die* (*Sport*) inside lane; **~beleuchtung** *die* Ⓐ (*eines Fahrzeugs*) interior light; (*beim Türöffnen aufleuchtend*) courtesy light; Ⓑ (*im Zug, Flugzeug*) interior lighting; **~dienst** *der:* **~dienst haben** be working in the office; ‹policeman› be on station duty; **im ~dienst tätig sein** work in the office; ‹policeman› do station duty; **~durchmesser** *der* internal diameter; **~einrichtung** *die* furnishings *pl.;* **~fläche** *die* inner surface; (*der Hand*) palm; **~geleitet** *Adj.* (*Soziol.*) self-directed; **~hof** *der* inner courtyard; (*eines Klosters, Colleges*) quadrangle; **~kurve** *die* inside bend; **die ~kurve nehmen** ‹driver› cut the corner; **~lager** *das* (*Jargon*) ⇒ **Tretlager**; **~leben** *das* Ⓐ [inner] thoughts and feelings *pl.;* Ⓑ (*oft scherzh.: Ausstattung*) inside; (*eines Hauses*) interior; (*eines Autos, Fernsehers usw.*) inner workings *pl.;* **~minister** *der,* **~ministerin** *die* ▶ 159 Minister of the Interior; ≈ Home Secretary (*Brit.*); ≈ Secretary of the Interior (*Amer.*); **~ministerium** *das* Ministry of the Interior; ≈ Home Office (*Brit.*); ≈ Department of the Interior (*Amer.*); **~pfosten** *der* (*Ballspiele*) inside of the post; **der rechte ~pfosten** the inside of the right-hand post; **~politik** *die* (*eines Staates*) home affairs *pl.;* (*einer Regierung*) domestic policy/policies *pl.;* **~politiker** *der,* **~politikerin** *die* politician concerned with home affairs; **~politisch** ⇒ **~politik:** ❶ *Adj.* **~politische Fragen** matters of domestic policy; **der ~politische Kurs der Regierung** the government's domestic policy; **eine ~politische Debatte** a debate on home affairs/domestic policy; ❷ *adv.* as regards home affairs/domestic policy; **~politisch betrachtet** from the point of view of home affairs/domestic policy; **~raum** *der* Ⓐ inner room; **die ~räume des Hauses** the interior of the house; Ⓑ (*Platz im Innern*) room inside; **ein Auto/Haus mit großem ~raum** a car/house with a spacious interior; **~rist** *der* (*bes. Fußball*) inside of the *or* one's foot; **~rolle** *die* hair curled under *no pl., no indef. art.;* **~seite** *die* inside; (*eines Stoffes*) wrong side; **~senator** *der,* **~senatorin** *die: minister for internal affairs* (*in Bremen, Hamburg, Berlin*); **~spiegel** *der* rear-view mirror; **~stadt** *die* town centre; downtown (*Amer.*); (*einer Großstadt*) city centre; **~stürmer** *der,* **~stürmerin** *die* (*Ballspiele*) inside forward; **~tasche** *die* inside pocket; **~temperatur** *die* inside temperature; **bei 22 °C ~temperatur** when the temperature inside is 22°C; when it's 22°C inside; **wir haben eine ~temperatur von 22 °C** the temperature inside is 22°C; **~wand** *die* interior wall; **~welt** *die* inner world; **sie hat sich ganz in ihre ~welt zurückgezogen** she withdrew completely into her own private world; **~winkel** *der* interior angle

**inner...** /'ɪnɐ.../ *Adj.* Ⓐ inner; inside ‹pocket, lane›; **die ~e Seite** the inside; Ⓑ (*Med.*) internal; **die ~en Organe** the internal organs; **eine ~e Blutung/~e Blutungen** *Pl.* internal bleeding; **die ~e Medizin** internal medicine; **die I~e** (*Med. Jargon*) the medical ward; Ⓒ (*im Innern gefühlt*) inner ‹calm, impatience, etc.›; Ⓓ (*einer Sache innewohnend*) internal ‹structure, stability, etc.›; Ⓔ (*inländisch*) internal

**inner-: ~betrieblich** ❶ *Adj.* internal ‹problem, question, regulation, agreement›; ❷ *adv.* internally; **~deutsch** *Adj.* Ⓐ (*Deutschland betreffend*) **~deutsche Angelegenheiten** the internal *or* domestic affairs of Germany; Germany's internal *or* domestic affairs; Ⓑ (*hist.: die beiden deutschen Staaten betreffend*) ‹trade, relations, border› between the two German states; **der Bundesminister für ~deutsche Beziehungen** the Federal Minister for Intra-German Relations

**Innere** /'ɪnərə/ *das; adj. Dekl.* Ⓐ inside; (*eines Gebäudes, Wagens, Schiffes*) interior; inside; (*eines Landes*) interior; **im ~n des Waldes** deep within the forest; **der Minister des Innern** the Minister of the Interior; ⇒ *auch* **Innenminister**; Ⓑ (*Empfindung*) inner being; **in seinem tiefsten ~n** in his heart of hearts; deep [down] inside; **wenn wir nur wüssten, was in ihrem ~n vorgeht** if only we knew what's going on inside her; Ⓒ (*Kern*) heart

**Innereien** /ɪnə'rai̯ən/ *Pl.* entrails; (*Kochk.*) offal *sing.*

**inner·halb** ❶ *Präp.* + *Gen.* Ⓐ (*im Innern*) within, inside; **~ der Familie/Partei** (*fig.*) within the family/party; Ⓑ (*binnen*) within; **~ einer Woche** within a week; **~ der Arbeitszeit** during *or* in working hours. ❷ *Adv.* Ⓐ (*im Innern*) **~ von** within; inside; Ⓑ (*im Verlauf*) **~ von zwei Jahren** within two years

**innerlich** ❶ *Adj.* Ⓐ (*geistig-seelisch*) inner; (*nicht nach außen gezeigt*) inward; Ⓑ (*geh.*) (*nach innen gewandt*) introvert[ed]; (*nicht oberflächlich*) inwardly directed; Ⓒ (*im Körper*) internal ‹use, effect›. ❷ *adv.* Ⓐ (*geistig-seelisch*) inwardly; **~ lachen** laugh inwardly *or* to oneself; Ⓑ (*im Körper*) **die Arznei muss ~ wirken/wird ~ angewendet** the medicine must work/is used internally

**Innerlichkeit** *die;* **~:** inwardness

**inner-: ~parteilich** *Adj.* **~parteiliche Auseinandersetzungen** internal [party] disputes; disputes within the party; **~parteiliche Diskussionen** discussions within the party; **~staatlich** *Adj.* internal; domestic; **~städtisch** *Adj.* urban

**innerst...** *Adj.* inmost; innermost; **ihre ~e Überzeugung** her deepest *or* most profound conviction

*old spelling (see note on page 1707)

**Innerste** *das; adj. Dekl.* innermost being; **in meinem ~n** in my heart of hearts; deep [down] inside

**innert** /ˈɪnɐt/ *Präp. + Gen. od. Dat. (schweiz., österr.)* within

**inne-:** ***~|sein** ⇒ inne; **~|werden** *unr. itr. V.; mit sein (Zusammenschreibung nur im Inf. u. Part.) (geh.)* **einer Sache** *(Gen.)* **~werden** become [fully] aware of sth.; **~|wohnen** *itr. V. (geh.)* **etw. wohnt jmdm./einer Sache ~:** sb./sth. possesses sth.

**innig** /ˈɪnɪç/ **1** *Adj.* **A** heartfelt, deep ‹affection, sympathy›; heartfelt, fervent ‹wish›; intimate ‹relation, relationship, friendship›; **mein ~ster Dank** my sincerest thanks; **unsere ~sten Wünsche begleiten euch** our warmest wishes go with you; **B** *(Chemie)* intimate. **2** *adv.* ‹hope› fervently; ‹love› deeply, with all one's heart; **~ verbunden sein** ‹friends, families› be very close

**Innigkeit** *die; ~:* depth; *(einer Beziehung, Freundschaft)* intimacy; **die ~ seiner Worte** the depth of feeling in his words

**inniglich** /ˈɪnɪklɪç/ *Adj., adv. (geh.)* ⇒ **innig**

**Innovation** /ɪnova'tsi̯o:n/ *die; ~, ~en (Soziol., Wirtsch.)* innovation

**Innung** /ˈɪnʊŋ/ *die; ~, ~en* [trade] guild; **die ganze ~ blamieren** *(ugs. scherzh.)* let the side down

**-innung** *die:* **Fleischer~/Bäcker~:** butchers'/bakers' guild

**in·offiziell** **1** *Adj.* unofficial. **2** *adv.* unofficially

**in·operabel** *Adj. (Med.)* inoperable

**in·opportun** *Adj. (geh.)* inopportune

**in petto** /ɪn ˈpɛto/ *in* **etw. ~ haben** *(ugs.)* have sth. up one's sleeve

**in puncto** /ɪn ˈpʊŋkto/ **~ Pünktlichkeit** *usw.* as regards punctuality *etc.;* where punctuality *etc.* is concerned

**Input** /ˈɪnpʊt/ *der od. das; ~s, ~s (fachspr.)* input

**Inquisition** /ɪnkvizi'tsi̯o:n/ *die; ~, ~en (hist.)* **A** Inquisition; **B** *(Untersuchung vor der ~)* inquisition

**Inquisitions·gericht** *das (hist.)* court of the Inquisition

**Inquisitor** /ɪnkvi'zi:tɔr/ *der; ~s, ~en* /-zi'to:rən/ *(hist.)* inquisitor

**ins** /ɪns/ *Präp. + Art.* **A** = **in das; B ~ Bett/Theater gehen** go to bed/the theatre; **er geriet ~ Stottern** he began to stutter; **etw. ~ Englische übersetzen** translate sth. into English

**Insasse** /ˈɪnzasə/ *der; ~n, ~n* **A** *(Fahrgast)* passenger; **die ~n eines Autos/Flugzeuges** the passengers in a car/an aircraft; **B** *(Bewohner)* inmate

**Insassen·versicherung** *die* passenger insurance

**Insassin** *die; ~, ~nen* ⇒ **Insasse**

**ins·besond[e]re** *Adv.* especially; particularly; in particular

**In·schrift** *die* inscription

**Insekt** /ɪn'zɛkt/ *das; ~s, ~en* insect; **~en fressend** *(Biol.)* insectivorous, insect-eating ‹animals›

**insekten-, Insekten-:** **~bekämpfung** *die* insect control; ***~fressend** ⇒ **Insekt**; **~fresser** *der* insectivore; insect eater; **~kunde** *die* entomology *no art.;* **~plage** *die* plague of insects; **~pulver** *das* insect powder; **~stich** *der (einer Wespe, Biene)* insect sting; *(einer Mücke)* insect bite; **~vertilgungs·mittel** *das* insecticide

**Insektizid** /ɪnzɛkti'tsi:t/ *das; ~s, ~e (fachspr.)* insecticide

**Insel** /ˈɪnzl̩/ *die; ~, ~n (auch fig.)* island; **die ~ Helgoland** the island of Heligoland; **die ~ Man** the Isle of Man

**Insel·bewohner** *der,* **Insel·bewohnerin** *die* islander

**Inselchen** *das; ~s, ~:* islet; little island

**Insel-:** **~gruppe** *die* group of islands; **~lage** *die* island position; position as an island; **~reich** *das* island kingdom; **~republik** *die* island republic; **~staat** *der* island state; **~volk** *das* island race *or* people; **~welt** *die* islands *pl.*

**Inserat** /ɪnze'ra:t/ *das; ~[e]s, ~e* advertisement *(in a newspaper)*; **sich auf ein ~ melden** reply to an advertisement; **ein ~ aufgeben** put in an advertisement; **am besten gibst du ein ~ auf** the best thing you can do is to put an advertisement in the paper

**Inseraten·teil** *der* advertisement section

**Inserent** /ɪnze'rɛnt/ *der; ~en, ~en,* **Inserentin** *die; ~, ~nen* advertiser

**inserieren** *itr., tr. V.* advertise; **[wegen etw.] in einer Zeitung ~:** advertise [sth.] in a newspaper

**ins·geheim** *Adv.* secretly

**ins·gemein** *Adv. (veralt.)* **die Naturwissenschaften ~ waren seine Leidenschaft** he had a passion for the natural sciences as a whole

**ins·gesamt** *Adv.* **A** in all; altogether; **es waren ~ 500** there were 500 in all *or* altogether; **B** *(alles in allem)* all in all; **~ gesehen** all in all

**Insider** /ˈɪnsaɪdə/ *der; ~s, ~:* insider; **~ der Rock-Szene** those in on the rock scene

**Insigne** /ɪn'zɪgnə/ *das; ~s,* **Insignien** insignia

**in·signifikant** *Adj. (geh.)* insignificant

**insistieren** /ɪnzɪs'ti:rən/ *itr. V. (geh.)* **auf etw.** *(Dat.)* **~:** insist on sth.

**inskribieren** /ɪnskri'bi:rən/ *(österr.)* **1** *itr. V.* register; **in Wien ~:** register at [the university of] Vienna. **2** *tr. V.* **Germanistik ~:** register to study German; **bei jmdm. Vorlesungen ~:** register to attend sb.'s lectures

**Inskription** /ɪnskrɪp'tsi̯o:n/ *(österr.) die; ~, ~en* registration

**insofern** **1** *Adv.* /ɪn'zo:fɛrn/ *(in dieser Hinsicht)* in this respect; to this extent; **~, als** in so far as; **die Vorstellung ist ~ irrig, als ...** this notion is wrong in so far as ... **2** *Konj.* /ɪnzo'fɛrn/ *(falls)* provided [that]; so *or* as long as

**in·solvent** *Adj.* insolvent

**In·solvenz** *die; ~, ~en (bes. Wirtsch.)* insolvency

***insonderheit** ⇒ **Sonderheit**

**insoweit** /ɪn'zo:vai̯t/ɪnzo'vai̯t/ *Adv./Konj.* ⇒ **insofern**

**in spe** /ɪn 'spe:/ future *attrib.;* **mein Schwiegersohn ~:** my future son-in-law

**Inspekteur** /ɪnspɛk'tø:ɐ̯/ *der; ~s, ~e (Milit.)* Chief of Staff

**Inspektion** /ɪnspɛk'tsi̯o:n/ *die; ~, ~en* **A** *(Kontrolle)* inspection; **B** *(Kfz-W.)* service; **das Auto zur ~ bringen** take the car in for a service; **C** *(Behörde)* inspectorate

**Inspektions·reise** *die* tour of inspection

**Inspektor** /ɪn'spɛktɔr/ *der; ~s, ~en* /-'to:rən/, **Inspektorin** *die; ~, ~nen* inspector; **das Gutachten des ~s Müller, ~ Müllers Gutachten** Inspector Müller's report; ⇒ *auch* **-in**

**Inspiration** /ɪnspira'tsi̯o:n/ *die; ~, ~en* inspiration

**inspirieren** *tr. V.* inspire; **das inspirierte ihn zu einem Roman** it inspired him to write a novel; **sich von jmdm./etw. ~ lassen** be inspired by sb./sth.

**Inspizient** /ɪnspi'tsi̯ɛnt/ *der; ~en, ~en,* **Inspizientin** *die; ~, ~nen (Theater)* stage manager; *(Ferns., Rundf.)* studio manager

**inspizieren** *tr. V.* inspect

**Inspizierung** *die; ~, ~en* inspection

**in·stabil** *Adj. (auch Physik, Technik)* unstable

**In·stabilität** *die; ~, ~en (auch Physik, Technik)* instability

**Installateur** /ɪnstala'tø:ɐ̯/ *der; ~s, ~e,* **Installateurin** *die; ~, ~nen* ▶ **159** **A** *(Klempner[in])* plumber; **B** *(Gas~)* [gas] fitter; **C** *(Heizungs~)* heating engineer; **D** *(Elektro~)* electrician

**Installation** /ɪnstala'tsi̯o:n/ *die; ~, ~en* **A** installation; **B** *(Anlage)* installation; *(Rohre)* plumbing *no pl.;* **C** *(schweiz., sonst veralt.: Amtseinführung)* installation

**installieren** **1** *tr. V.* **A** *(einbauen)* install; **B** *(geh.: in ein Amt einführen)* install; **C** *(einrichten)* set up. **2** *refl. V.* settle in

**in·stand** *Adv.* **etw. ist gut/schlecht ~:** sth. is in good/poor condition; **etw. ~ halten** keep sth. in good condition *or* repair *or (funktionsfähig)* in working order; **etw. ~ setzen/bringen** repair sth.; *(funktionsfähig machen)* get sth. into working order; **jmdn. ~ setzen, etw. zu tun** enable sb. to do sth.

**instand-, Instand-:** **~besetzen** *tr. V.* **ein Haus ~besetzen** occupy and renovate a house *(illegally, to prove that its demolition is not desirable)*; **~besetzung** *die: illegal occupation and renovation;* **~haltung** *die* maintenance; upkeep; **~haltungs·kosten** *Pl.* maintenance costs

**in·ständig** **1** *Adj.* urgent; insistent ‹invitation›. **2** *adv.* urgently; **~ um etw. bitten** beg for sth.; **jmdn. ~ bitten, etw. zu tun** beg *or* implore *or* beseech sb. to do sth.; **~ auf etw.** *(Akk.)* **hoffen** hope fervently for sth.

**Instandsetzung** *die; ~, ~en (Amtsspr.)* repair; *(Renovierung)* renovation; **eine ~ der Brücke hätte sich nicht gelohnt** it would not have been worth repairing the bridge

**Instanz** /ɪn'stants/ *die; ~, ~en* **A** authority; **durch alle ~en gehen** *od.* **alle ~en durchlaufen** go *or* pass through all the official channels; **in letzter ~ ist ... entscheidend** *(fig.)* in the final analysis, ... is decisive; **B** *(Rechtsw.)* **[die] erste/zweite/dritte ~:** the court of first instance *or* court of original jurisdiction/the appeal court/the court of final appeal; **durch alle ~en gehen** go through all the courts

**Instanzen·weg** *der* official channels *pl.; (Rechtsspr.)* stages *pl.* of appeal; **den ~ nehmen** go through the official channels/the various stages of appeal

**Instinkt** /ɪn'stɪŋkt/ *der; ~[e]s, ~e* instinct; **etw. aus ~ tun** do sth. instinctively; **den richtigen ~ für etw. haben** have a flair for sth.; **seinem ~ folgen** follow one's instincts *pl.*

**Instinkt·handlung** *die* instinctive action

**instinktiv** /ɪnstɪŋk'ti:f/ **1** *Adj.* instinctive. **2** *adv.* instinctively

**instinkt·los** **1** *Adj.* insensitive. **2** *adv.* insensitively; **politisch ~ handeln** act with political insensitivity

**Instinktlosigkeit** *die; ~, ~en* insensitivity; **eine ~ sein** be insensitive

**Institut** /ɪnsti'tu:t/ *das; ~[e]s, ~e* **A** institute; **das ~ für Kernphysik** the Institute of Nuclear Physics; **B** *(Rechtsspr.)* institution

**Institution** /ɪnstitu'tsi̯o:n/ *die; ~, ~en (auch fig.)* institution

**institutionalisieren** /ɪnstitutsi̯onali'zi:rən/ *tr. V. (geh.)* institutionalize

**institutionell** /ɪnstitutsi̯o'nɛl/ *Adj.* institutional

**Instituts-:** **~bibliothek** *die* institute library; **~leiter** *der,* **~leiterin** *die* director of the/an institute

**instruieren** /ɪnstru'i:rən/ *tr. V.* **A** *(in Kenntnis setzen)* inform; **jmdn. über etw.** *(Akk.)* **~:** inform sb. about sth.; **B** *(anleiten)* instruct; **jmdn. genau ~:** give sb. precise instructions

**Instrukteur** /ɪnstrʊk'tø:ɐ̯/ *der; ~s, ~e,* **Instrukteurin** *die; ~, ~nen* instructor

**Instruktion** /ɪnstrʊk'tsi̯o:n/ *die; ~, ~en* instruction

**instruktiv** /ɪnstrʊk'ti:f/ **1** *Adj.* instructive; informative. **2** *adv.* instructively; informatively

**Instrument** /ɪnstru'mɛnt/ *das; ~[e]s, ~e* instrument

**instrumental** /ɪnstrumɛn'ta:l/ *(Musik)* **1** *Adj.* instrumental. **2** *adv.* instrumentally; **~ musizieren** play instrumental music

**Instrumental·begleitung** *die* instrumental accompaniment

**Instrumentalismus** *der; ~ (Philos.)* instrumentalism

**Instrumental·musik** *die* instrumental music

i

**Instrumentarium** /ɪnstrumɛn'ta:ri̯ʊm/ *das;* **~s, Instrumentarien** Ⓐ (*Technik*) equipment; instruments *pl.;* Ⓑ (*Musik*) instruments *pl.;* **diese Oper verlangt ein großes ~:** this opera calls for a large number and range of instruments; Ⓒ (*geh.: Gesamtheit der Mittel*) apparatus

**instrumentell** /ɪnstrumɛn'tɛl/ ❶ *Adj.* (*mit Instrumenten*) using instruments *postpos.;* **~e Hilfsmittel/Ausrüstung** equipment; instruments *pl.* ❷ *adv.* **etw. ~ untersuchen** investigate sth. using instruments; **~ gut/schlecht ausgerüstet** well/poorly equipped

**Instrumenten-:** **~bau** *der* making of musical instruments; **~brett** *das* instrument panel; **~flug** *der* (*Flugw.*) flying on instruments; instrument-flying; **~kasten** *der* instrument housing; (*tragbar*) instrument case

**instrumentieren** ❶ *tr. V.* Ⓐ (*Musik: für das Orchester ausarbeiten*) instrument; (*für das Orchester umarbeiten*) orchestrate; Ⓑ (*Technik*) instrument; equip with instruments. ❷ *itr. V.* (*Med.*) **bei jmdm. ~:** assist sb. by handing him/her the instruments

**In·subordination** *die;* **~, ~en** (*geh.*) insubordination; **eine ~:** an act of insubordination

**Insuffizienz** /'ɪnzʊfitsi̯ɛnts/ *die;* **~, ~en** ▶ 474 (*Med.*) insufficiency

**Insulaner** /ɪnzu'la:nɐ/ *der;* **~s, ~, Insulanerin** *die;* **~, ~nen** (*veralt., noch scherzh.*) islander

**insular** /ɪnzu'la:ɐ̯/ *Adj.* insular

**Insulin** /ɪnzu'li:n/ *das;* **~s** insulin

**Insulin·schock** *der* ▶ 474 (*Med.*) insulin shock

**inszenatorisch** /ɪnstsena'to:rɪʃ/ *Adj.* directorial; **eine ~e Meisterleistung** a masterpiece of directing

**inszenieren** /ɪnstse'ni:rən/ *tr. V.* Ⓐ stage, put on ‹play, opera›; (*Regie führen bei*) direct; (*Ferns.*) direct; produce; Ⓑ (*oft abwertend*) (*einfädeln*) engineer; (*organisieren*) stage

**Inszenierung** *die;* **~, ~en** Ⓐ staging; (*Regie*) direction; Ⓑ (*Aufführung*) production; **Rigoletto in neuer ~:** a new production of 'Rigoletto'; Ⓒ (*oft abwertend*) (*das Einfädeln*) engineering; (*das Organisieren*) staging

**intakt** /ɪn'takt/ *Adj.* Ⓐ (*unbeschädigt*) intact; undamaged; unspoiled ‹region›; Ⓑ (*funktionsfähig*) in [proper] working order *postpos.;* healthy ‹economy›; **einen ~en Organismus haben** be physically healthy

**Intarsie** /ɪn'tarzi̯ə/ *die;* **~, ~n** intarsia

**integer** /ɪn'te:gɐ/ *Adj.* **eine integre Persönlichkeit** a person of integrity; **~ sein** be a person of integrity

**integral** /ɪnte'gra:l/ *Adj.* integral

**Integral** *das;* **~s, ~e** (*Math.*) integral; (*Zeichen*) integral sign

**Integral-:** **~helm** *der* integral helmet; **~rechnung** *die* Ⓐ integral calculus; Ⓑ (*einzelne Rechnung*) problem in integral calculus

**Integration** /ɪntegra'tsi̯o:n/ *die;* **~, ~en** (*auch Math.*) integration

**integrieren** *tr. V.* (*auch Math.*) integrate; ⇒ *auch* Gesamthochschule; Gesamtschule

**integrierend** *Adj.* integral ‹part, component, element›

**Integrierung** *die;* **~, ~en** (*auch Math.*) integration

**Integrität** /ɪntegri'tɛ:t/ *die;* **~:** integrity

**Intellekt** /ɪntɛ'lɛkt/ *der;* **~[e]s** intellect

**intellektuell** /ɪntɛlɛk'tu̯ɛl/ *Adj.* intellectual

**Intellektuelle** *der/die; adj. Dekl.* intellectual

**intelligent** /ɪntɛli'gɛnt/ ❶ *Adj.* intelligent. ❷ *adv.* intelligently

**Intelligenz** /ɪntɛli'gɛnts/ *die;* **~, ~en** Ⓐ intelligence; Ⓑ (*Gesamtheit der Intellektuellen*) intelligentsia; Ⓒ (*veralt.: intelligentes Wesen*) intelligence

**Intelligenz·bestie** *die* (*ugs.*) Ⓐ egghead (*coll.*); brain (*coll.*); Ⓑ (*abwertend*) clever-clever type

*old spelling (see note on page 1707)

**Intelligenzija** /ɪntɛli'gɛntsija/ *die;* **~:** intelligentsia

**Intelligenz·leistung** *die* instance of intelligent behaviour; **das war mal eine ~ von dir!** (*iron.*) that was bright of you, I must say

**Intelligenzler** *der;* **~s, ~, Intelligenzlerin** *die;* **~, ~nen** (*abwertend*) intellectual

**Intelligenz-:** **~quotient** *der* intelligence quotient; **~test** *der* intelligence test

**intelligibel** /ɪntɛli'gi:bl̩/ *Adj.* (*Philos.*) intelligible

**Intendant** /ɪntɛn'dant/ *der;* **~en, ~en, Intendantin** *die;* **~, ~nen** Ⓐ (*Theater*) manager and artistic director; (*Fernseh~, Rundfunk~*) director general

**Intendantur** /ɪntɛndan'tu:ɐ̯/ *die;* **~, ~en** ⇒ Intendanz A

**Intendanz** /ɪntɛn'dants/ *die;* **~, ~en** Ⓐ (*Amt*) management and artistic directorship; (*Ferns., Rundf.*) director-generalship; Ⓑ (*Büro*) office of the manager and artistic director; (*Ferns., Rundf.*) director-general's office

**intendieren** /ɪntɛn'di:rən/ *tr. V.* (*geh.*) intend

**Intensität** /ɪntɛnzi'tɛ:t/ *die;* **~** (*auch Physik*) intensity

**intensiv** /ɪntɛn'zi:f/ ❶ *Adj.* Ⓐ (*gründlich*) intensive ‹research, efforts, etc.›; Ⓑ (*kräftig*) intense; strong ‹smell, taste›; Ⓒ (*Landw.*) intensive ‹cultivation etc.›. ❷ *adv.* Ⓐ (*gründlich*) intensively; ‹think› hard; **sich ~ mit etw. beschäftigen** be deeply involved with sth.; Ⓑ (*kräftig*) intensely; ‹smell, taste› strongly; **~ leuchten** shine with intense brightness; Ⓒ (*Landw.*) ‹farm etc.› intensively

**-intensiv** -intensive; **geruchs~:** strong-smelling

**Intensiv-:** **~anbau** *der* (*Landw.*) intensive cultivation; **~haltung** *die* (*Landw.*) intensive rearing

**intensivieren** *tr. V.* intensify; increase ‹exports›; strengthen ‹connections›

**Intensivierung** *die;* **~, ~en** intensification; **bei einer ~ des Exports** by increasing exports *pl.*

**Intensiv-:** **~kurs** *der* intensive course; **~station** *die* intensive-care unit

**Intention** /ɪntɛn'tsi̯o:n/ *die;* **~, ~en** intention; **das liegt nicht in seinen ~en** that is not his intention

**intentional** /ɪntɛntsi̯o'na:l/ (*Philos.*) ❶ *Adj.* intentional. ❷ *adv.* intentionally

**Inter-**/ɪntɐ-/: **~aktion** *die* (*Psych., Soziol.*) interaction; **~aktiv** *Adj.* interactive; **~aktivität** *die;* **~~:** interactivity; **~brigaden** *Pl.* (*hist.*) International Brigades

**Inter·city** *der;* **~s, ~s** (*ugs.*) inter-city [train]

**Intercity-:** **~express, *~-Expreß** *der* inter-city express train; **~expresszug, *~-Expreßzug** *der* inter-city express train **~verkehr** *der* inter-city [railway] traffic; **~zug** *der* inter-city train

**inter-, Inter-:** **~dependent** *Adj.* (*geh.*) interdependent; **~dependenz** *die* (*geh.*) interdependence *no pl.;* **~disziplinär** ❶ *Adj.* interdisciplinary; ❷ *adv.* **~disziplinär forschen** do interdisciplinary research

**interessant** /ɪntərɛ'sant/ ❶ *Adj.* interesting; **sich ~ machen** attract attention to oneself; **das ist ja ~:** that's [very] interesting; **das Angebot ist für uns nicht ~:** the offer is of no interest to us *or* doesn't interest us. ❷ *adv.* **~ schreiben** write in an interesting way

**interessanterweise** *Adv.* interestingly enough

**Interesse** /ɪntə'rɛsə/ *das;* **~s, ~n** Ⓐ interest; **[großes] ~ an jmdm./etw. haben** be [very] interested in sb./sth.; **~ für jmdn./etw. haben/zeigen** have/show an interest in sb./sth.; Ⓑ (*Neigung*) interest; **gemeinsame ~n haben** have interests in common; **im eigenen ~ handeln** act in one's own interest; **jmds. ~n wahrnehmen** look after *or* represent sb.'s interests; **in jmds. ~** (*Dat.*) **liegen** be in sb.'s interest; **es liegt in unser aller ~:** it's in all our interests *pl.*

**interesse-, Interesse-:** **~halber** /-halbɐ/ *Adv.* out of interest; **~los** ❶ *Adj.* uninterested; ❷ *adv.* without interest; uninterestedly; **~losigkeit** *die;* **~~:** lack of interest

**Interessen-:** **~ausgleich** *der* reconciliation of [conflicting] interests; **~bereich** *der,* **~gebiet** *das* field of interest; **~gegensatz** *der* ⇒ **~konflikt**; **~gemeinschaft** *die* Ⓐ **sich in einer ~gemeinschaft zusammenfinden** join together with others to pursue common interests; Ⓑ (*Wirtsch.*) syndicate; **~gruppe** *die* interest group; **~kollision** *die* clash of interests; **~konflikt** *der* conflict of interests; **~lage** *die* interests *pl.;* **~sphäre** *die* sphere of influence

**Interessent** /ɪntərɛ'sɛnt/ *der;* **~en, ~en** Ⓐ interested person; **wenn es genug ~en gibt** if enough people are interested; **auf die Anzeige haben sich zahlreiche ~en gemeldet** the advertisement attracted a large response; **~en werden gebeten ...** those interested are asked ...; Ⓑ (*möglicher Käufer*) potential buyer

**Interessenten·kreis** *der* market

**Interessentin** *die;* **~, ~nen** ⇒ Interessent

**Interessen-:** **~verband** *der* [organized] interest group; **~vertretung** *die* Ⓐ representation; Ⓑ (*Vertreter von ~*) representative body

**interessieren** ❶ *refl. V.* **sich für jmdn./etw. ~:** be interested in sb./sth. ❷ *tr. V.* interest; **interessiert dich denn nicht, was passiert ist?** aren't you interested to know what happened?; **das interessiert mich nicht** I'm not interested [in it]; it doesn't interest me; **das hat dich zu ~:** you can't just ignore it; **das hat dich nicht zu ~:** it's none of your business; it's no concern of yours

**interessiert** *Adj.* interested; **an jmdm./etw. ~ sein** be interested in sb./sth.; **er ist daran ~, dass sie nichts davon erfahren** he doesn't want them to find out anything about it; **vielseitig ~ sein** have a wide range of interests; **~ zuhören** listen with interest

**Interessiertheit** *die;* **~:** **das Prinzip der materiellen ~** (*DDR*): *principle that the individual can directly improve his own standard of living by working harder and more efficiently to achieve the goals of socialism*

**inter-, Inter-:** **~ferenz** /-fe'rɛnts/ *die;* **~~, ~~en** (*Physik, Med., Sprachw.*) interference *no pl.;* **~feron** /-fe'ro:n/ *das;* **~~s, ~~e** (*Med.*) interferon; **~fraktionell** /-fraktsi̯o'nɛl/ ❶ *Adj.* inter-party *attrib.;* ❷ *adv.* **etw. ~fraktionell besprechen** discuss sth. on an inter-party basis; hold inter-party discussions about sth.; **~hotel** /'----/ *das* (*DDR*) Interhotel (*hotel intended mainly for visitors to the GDR*)

**Interieur** /ɛ̃te'ri̯ø:ɐ̯/ *das;* **~s, ~s** *od.* **~e** (*auch bild. Kunst*) interior

**Interim** /'ɪntərɪm/ *das;* **~s, ~s** (*geh.*) interim measure

**interimistisch** ❶ *Adj.* (*geh.*) interim *attrib.;* temporary; provisional. ❷ *adv.* on an interim basis

**Interims-:** **~lösung** *die* interim solution; **~regierung** *die* caretaker government; **~schein** *der* (*Wirtsch.*) scrip

**Interjektion** /ɪntɐjɛk'tsi̯o:n/ *die;* **~, ~en** (*Sprachw.*) interjection

**inter-, Inter-:** **~kantonal** ❶ *Adj.* inter-cantonal; ❷ *adv.* on an inter-cantonal basis; **~konfessionell** *Adj.* (*geh.*) interdenominational; interconfessional; **~kontinental** *Adj.* (*geh.*) intercontinental; **~kontinental·rakete** *die* (*Milit.*) intercontinental ballistic missile; **~linear** *Adj.* (*Literaturw.*) interlinear; **~linear·version** *die* interlinear version *or* translation; **~ludium** /-'lu:di̯ʊm/ *das;* **~~s, ~ludien** (*Musik*) interlude; **~mezzo** /-'mɛtso/ *das;* **~~s, ~~s** *od.* **~mezzi** (*Theat., Musik*) intermezzo; (*fig.*) interlude; intermezzo; **~ministeriell** ❶ *Adj.* inter-ministerial; ❷ *adv.* on an inter-ministerial basis; **~mittierend** /-mɪ'ti:rənt/ *Adj.* (*geh.*) intermittent; lightning ‹strike›

**intern** /ɪn'tɛrn/ ❶ *Adj.* Ⓐ internal; **diese Dinge müssen ~ bleiben** these matters must not become public knowledge; Ⓑ (*im Internat wohnend*) **ein ~er Schüler** a boarder. ❷ *adv.* internally; **wir haben das Jubiläum nur ~ gefeiert** we only celebrated the anniversary among ourselves

**-intern** ❶ *Adj.* **firmen~e/klub~e/abteilungs~e Dinge** internal [company/club/departmental] matters; **eine firmen~e/klub~e Regelung** an arrangement within the company/club. ❷ *adv.* **firmen~/klub~/abteilungs~:** within the company/club/department; internally

**Interna** ⇨ **Internum**

**internalisieren** /ɪntɐnali'zi:rən/ *tr. V.* (*Soziol., Psych.*) internalize

**Internalisierung** *die;* ~, ~**en** (*Soziol., Psych.*) internalization

**Internat** /ɪntə'na:t/ *das;* ~**[e]s**, ~**e** Ⓐ boarding school; Ⓑ (*einer Schule angeschlossenes Heim*) dormitory block

**inter-, Inter-:** ~**national** ❶ *Adj.* international; ❷ *adv.* internationally; ~**nationale** *die;* ~~, ~~**n** Ⓐ (*Internationale Arbeiterassoziation*) International; Internationale; Ⓑ (*Lied*) Internationale; ~**nationalisieren** *tr. V.* internationalize; ~**nationalismus** *der* Ⓐ (*Politik*) internationalism; **sozialistischer ~nationalismus** (*DDR*) socialist internationalism; Ⓑ (*Sprachw.*) internationalism; ~**nationalistisch** *Adj.* (*Politik*) internationalistic

**Internats-:** ~**schule** *die* boarding school; ~**schüler** *der*, ~**schülerin** *die* boarding school pupil; boarder

**Interne** *der/die; adj. Dekl.* boarder

**Internet** /'ɪntɐnɛt/ *das;* ~**s**, ~**s** Internet; **im ~:** on the Internet

**Internet·anschluss** *der*, ***Internet·anschluß** *der* Internet connection; connection to the Internet; **einen ~ haben** be connected to the Internet;

**internieren** *tr. V.* Ⓐ (*Milit.*) intern; Ⓑ (*Med.*) **jmdn. [in einem Krankenhaus] ~:** confine sb. to [a] hospital

**Internierte** *der/die; adj. Dekl.* Ⓐ (*Milit.*) internee; Ⓑ (*Med.*) patient confined to hospital

**Internierung** *die;* ~, ~**en** internment

**Internierungs·lager** *das* internment camp

**Internist** *der;* ~**en**, ~**en**, **Internistin** *die;* ~, ~**nen** (*Med.*) internist

**Internum** /ɪn'tɛrnʊm/ *das;* ~**s**, **Interna;** (*geh.*) internal matter

**inter-, Inter-:** ~**parlamentarisch** *Adj.* (*Politik*) inter-parliamentary; ~**planetar[isch]** *Adj.* (*Astron.*) interplanetary; ~**pol** /'---/ *die;* ~~: Interpol *no art.*; ~**polation** /-pola'tsi̯o:n/ *die;* ~~, ~~**en** (*Math., Sprachw.*) interpolation; ~**polieren** *itr.* (*auch tr.*) *V.* (*Math., Sprachw.*) interpolate

**Interpret** /ɪntɐ'prɛ:t/ *der;* ~**en**, ~**en** interpreter (*of music, text, events, etc.*)

**Interpretation** /ɪntɐpreta'tsi̯o:n/ *die;* ~, ~**en** interpretation (*of music, text, events, etc.*)

**interpretieren** *tr. V.* interpret ‹music, texts, events, etc.›; **etw. falsch ~:** misinterpret sth.; interpret sth. wrongly

**Interpretin** *die;* ~, ~**nen** ⇨ **Interpret**

**interpunktieren** *tr., itr. V.* (*Sprachw.*) punctuate

**Interpunktion** /ɪntɐpʊnk'tsi̯o:n/ *die;* ~ (*Sprachw.*) punctuation

**Interpunktions-:** ~**regel** *die* punctuation rule; ~**zeichen** *das* punctuation mark

**Interrail·karte** /'ɪntəreɪl-/ *die* (*Eisenbahnw.*) Interrail card

**Interregnum** /ɪntɐ'rɛgnʊm/ *das;* ~**s**, **Interregnen** *od.* **Interregna** (*Politik*) interregnum

**interrogativ** /ɪntɐroga'ti:f/ *Adj.* (*Sprachw.*) interrogative

**Interrogativ-:** ~**pronomen** *das* interrogative pronoun; ~**satz** *der* interrogative sentence

**Interruptus** /ɪntɐ'rʊptʊs/ *der;* ~ (*ugs.*) withdrawal

**Intershop** /'ɪntɐʃɔp/ *der;* ~**s**, ~**s** (*DDR*) Intershop (*shop where foreign goods and top-quality GDR goods were sold for freely convertible currency*)

**inter-:** ~**stellar** /-stɛ'la:ɐ̯/ *Adj.* (*Astron.*) interstellar; ~**subjektiv** *Adj.* (*Psych.*) intersubjective

**Intervall** /ɪntɐ'val/ *das;* ~**s**, ~**e** (*Musik, Math.*) interval

**Intervall·training** *das* (*Sport*) interval training

**intervenieren** /ɪntɐve'ni:rən/ *itr. V.* (*geh., Politik*) intervene; **bei jmdm. gegen etw. ~:** make representations to sb. about sth.; **für jmdn. ~:** intervene on sb.'s behalf

**Intervention** /ɪntɐvɛn'tsi̯o:n/ *die;* ~, ~**en** (*geh., Politik*) intervention; (*Protest*) representations *pl.*

**Interventions·krieg** *der* war of intervention

**Interview** /ɪntɐ'vju:/ *das;* ~**s**, ~**s** interview

**interviewen** /ɪntɐ'vju:ən/ *tr. V.* interview

**Interviewer** /ɪntɐ'vju:ɐ/ *der;* ~**s**, ~, **Interviewerin** *die;* ~, ~**nen** interviewer

**Intervision** *die;* ~: Intervision (*alliance of Eastern European television corporations for pooling of programmes*)

**Inter·zonen-:** ~**auto·bahn** *die* interzonal autobahn; ~**handel** *der* interzonal trade; ~**verkehr** *der* interzonal traffic; ~**zug** *der* interzonal train

**Inthronisation** /ɪntroniza'tsi̯o:n/ *die;* ~, ~**en** enthronement

**inthronisieren** *tr. V.* enthrone

**intim** /ɪn'ti:m/ ❶ *Adj.* Ⓐ intimate; **im ~en Kreis** among close friends; ~**e Beziehungen mit jmdm. haben** (*verhüll.*) have intimate relations with sb. (*euphem.*); **mit jmdm. ~ sein/werden** (*verhüll.*) be/become intimate with sb. (*euphem.*); ~**e Hygiene/Körperpflege** intimate personal hygiene; Ⓑ (*tiefinnerlich*) intimate; innermost. ❷ *adv.* ~ **befreundet sein** be intimate friends; **mit jmdm. ~ verkehren** (*verhüll.*) have intimate relations with sb. (*euphem.*)

**Intim-:** ~**bereich** *der* Ⓐ ⇨ ~**sphäre**; Ⓑ (*Genitalbereich*) genital area; ~**feind** *der*, ~**feindin** *die: person whom one knows well and dislikes intensely;* ~**hygiene** *die* intimate personal hygiene

**Intimität** /ɪntimi'tɛ:t/ *die;* ~, ~**en** intimacy; **es ist zu ~en gekommen** (*verhüll.*) intimacy took place (*euphem.*); ~**en austauschen** (*verhüll.*) be engaged in intimacy (*euphem.*)

**Intim-:** ~**kenner** *der*, ~**kennerin** *die:* **ein ~kenner von etw. sein** have an intimate knowledge of sth.; **von einem ~kenner der politischen Szene stammen** come from someone with an intimate knowledge of the political scene; ~**leben** *das* (*verhüll.*) intimate life; ~**pflege** *die* ⇨ ~**hygiene**; ~**sphäre** *die* private life; **jmds. ~sphäre verletzen** invade sb.'s privacy; **jmdn. wegen Verletzung seiner ~sphäre verklagen** sue sb. for invasion of privacy; ~**spray** *der od. das* intimate deodorant

**Intimus** /'ɪntimʊs/ *der;* ~, **Intimi** intimate friend; (*Vertrauter*) confidant

**Intim·verkehr** *der* (*verhüll.*) intimate relations *pl.* (*euphem.*)

**in·tolerant** ❶ *Adj.* intolerant (**gegenüber** of); **sich ~ zeigen** display *or* show intolerance. ❷ *adv.* intolerantly

**In·toleranz** *die;* ~, ~**en** intolerance (**gegenüber** of)

**Intonation** /ɪntona'tsi̯o:n/ *die;* ~, ~**en** (*Sprachw., Musik*) intonation

**intonieren** ❶ *tr. V.* Ⓐ (*Musik*) (*anstimmen*) **etw. ~:** sing/play the first few bars of sth.; start to sing/play sth.; (*Ton angeben*) play/sing; **bitte intoniere ein a** please give me/us an A; Ⓑ (*Musik: hervorbringen*) **die Melodie sauber/weich ~:** play/sing the melody with clean/soft intonation; Ⓒ (*Sprachw.*) **etw. richtig/falsch ~:** say sth. with the right/wrong intonation. ❷ *itr. V.* Ⓐ (*Musik*) **er hat sauber/weich intoniert** he played/sang with clean/soft intonation; Ⓑ (*Sprachw.*) **richtig/falsch ~:** use the right/wrong intonation

**Intoxikation** /ɪntɔksika'tsi̯o:n/ *die;* ~, ~**en** ▶ 474 (*Med.*) intoxication (*Med.*)

**intramuskulär** /ɪntramʊsku'lɛ:ɐ̯/ (*Med.*) ❶ *Adj.* intramuscular. ❷ *adv.* intramuscularly

**Intranet** *das* ~**s**, ~**s** (*DV*) Intranet

**intransitiv** ❶ *Adj.* (*Sprachw.*) intransitive. ❷ *adv.* intransitively

**Intrauterin·pessar** /ɪntra|ute'ri:n-/ *das* (*Med.*) intra-uterine device

**intravenös** /ɪntrave'nø:s/ (*Med.*) ❶ *Adj.* intravenous. ❷ *adv.* intravenously

**intrigant** /ɪntri'gant/ *Adj.* scheming

**Intrigant** *der;* ~**en**, ~**en**, **Intrigantin** *die;* ~, ~**nen** schemer; intriguer

**Intrige** /ɪn'tri:gə/ *die;* ~, ~**n** intrigue

**Intrigen-:** ~**spiel** *das* intrigue; ~**wirtschaft** *die* (*abwertend*) constant scheming and intriguing

**intrigieren** *itr. V.* intrigue; scheme; **gegen jmdn. ~:** intrigue *or* scheme against sb.; **er intrigierte beim Chef gegen sie** he attempted to turn the boss against her with hints and insinuations

**intro-, Intro-**/ɪntro-/**:** ~**duktion** /-dʊk'tsi̯o:n/ *die;* ~~, ~~**en** (*geh., Musik*) introduction; ~**spektion** /-spɛk'tsi̯o:n/ *die;* ~~ (*Psych.*) introspection; ~**vertiert** /-vɛr'ti:ɐ̯t/ *Adj.* (*Psych.*) introverted; **ein ~vertierter Mensch** an introvert; ~**vertiertheit** *die;* ~~ (*Psych.*) introversion

**Intuition** /ɪntui̯'tsi̯o:n/ *die;* ~, ~**en** intuition

**intuitiv** /ɪntui̯'ti:f/ ❶ *Adj.* intuitive. ❷ *adv.* intuitively

**intus** /'ɪntʊs/ *in* **etw. ~ haben** (*ugs.*) (*begriffen haben*) have got sth. into one's head; (*gegessen od. getrunken haben*) have put sth. away (*coll.*); **einen ~ haben** (*ugs.*) have had a few (*coll.*)

**invalid** /ɪnva'li:t/, **invalide** /ɪnva'li:də/ *Adj.* invalid *attrib.;* ~ **sein** be an invalid

**Invalide** *der;* ~**n**, ~**n** invalid

**Invaliden-:** ~**heim** *das* home for the disabled and infirm; ~**rente** *die* (*veralt./schweiz.*) invalidity *or* disability pension; ~**versicherung** *die* (*veralt., schweiz.*) invalidity *or* disability insurance

**Invalidin** *die;* ~, ~**nen** ⇨ **Invalide**

**Invalidität** /ɪnvalidi'tɛ:t/ *die;* ~: invalidity

**in·variabel** *Adj.* invariable

**Invasion** /ɪnva'zi̯o:n/ *die;* ~, ~**en** (*auch fig. scherzh.*) invasion

**Invasions·krieg** *der* war of invasion

**Invasor** /ɪn'va:zɔr/ *der;* ~**s**, ~**en**, **Invasorin** *die;* ~, ~**nen** invader

**Invektive** /ɪnvɛk'ti:və/ *die;* ~, ~**n** (*geh.*) invective

**Inventar** /ɪnvɛn'ta:ɐ̯/ *das;* ~**s**, ~**e** Ⓐ **[totes] ~** (*einer Firma*) fittings and equipment *pl.;* (*eines Hauses, Büros*) furnishings and fittings *pl.;* (*eines Hofes*) machinery and equipment; **lebendes ~:** livestock; **zum ~ gehören** (*fig.*) ‹person› be part of the scenery; Ⓑ (*Verzeichnis*) inventory

**inventarisieren** *tr. V.* inventory; draw up *or* make an inventory of

**Inventar·stück** *das* [inventoried] item

**Inventur** /ɪnvɛn'tu:ɐ̯/ *die;* ~, ~**en** stocktaking; ~ **machen** carry out a stocktaking; stocktake; (*fig.*) take stock

**Inventur·liste** *die* stock list; inventory list

**Inversion** /ɪnvɛr'zi̯o:n/ *die;* ~, ~**en** (*fachspr.*) inversion

**Invest-** /ɪn'vɛst-/ (*DDR*) ⇨ **Investitions-**

**investieren** *tr., itr. V.* (*auch fig.*) invest (**in** + *Akk.* in); **Gefühle in jmdn. ~** (*fig.*) become emotionally involved with sb.

**Investition** /ɪnvɛsti'tsi̯o:n/ *die;* ~, ~**en** investment; **die privaten ~en sind zurückgegangen** private investment has fallen

**Investitions-:** ~**güter** *Pl.* (*Wirtsch.*) capital goods; ~**güter·industrie** *die* capital-goods industry; ~**lenkung** *die* investment control; ~**tätigkeit** *die* investment activity

**Investitur** /ɪnvɛsti'tu:ɐ̯/ *die;* ~, ~**en** investiture

i

**Investiv·lohn** /ɪnvɛs'tiːf-/ *der (Wirtsch.) portion of worker's wages set aside for investment in the company's investment savings scheme*
**Investment** /ɪn'vɛstmɛnt/ *das;* **~s, ~s** *(Finanzw.)* ⇒ **Investition**
**Investment-: ~fonds** *der* investment fund; **~gesellschaft** *die* investment trust; **~papier** *das,* **~zertifikat** *das* investment fund certificate
**Investor** /ɪn'vɛstɔr/ *der;* **~s, ~en** /-'toːrən/ **Investorin** *die;* **~, ~nen** *(Wirtsch.)* investor
**involvieren** /ɪnvɔl'viːrən/ *tr. V. (geh.)* involve
**in·wendig** ❶ *Adj.* inside ‹pocket›; inner ‹part›; *(fig.)* inner, inward ‹happiness, strength›. ❷ *adv.* [on the] inside; *(fig.)* inwardly; deep down [inside]; **etw./jmdn. in- und auswendig kennen** *(ugs.)* know sb./sth. inside out
**in·wie·fern** *Adv. (in welcher Hinsicht)* in what way; *(bis zu welchem Grade)* to what extent; how far
**in·wie·weit** *Adv.* to what extent; how far
**In·zahlungnahme** *die;* **~, ~n** part exchange; trade in *(Amer.)*; **durch ~ Ihres Altgerätes ...** by taking your old appliance in part exchange ...; if you trade in your old appliance ...
**Inzest** /ɪn'tsɛst/ *der;* **~[e]s, ~e** incest
**Inzest·tabu** *das (Völkerk.)* incest taboo
**inzestuös** /ɪntsɛs'tu̯øːs/ *Adj.* incestuous
**In·zucht** *die;* **~:** inbreeding
**in·zwischen** *Adv.* Ⓐ *(seither)* in the meantime; since [then]; **es hatte sich ~ nichts geändert** nothing had changed in the meantime *or* since; Ⓑ *(bis zu einem Zeitpunkt) (in der Gegenwart)* by now; *(in der Vergangenheit)* by then; *(in der Zukunft)* by then; by that time; **er hat/hatte sich ~ daran gewöhnt** he has/had got used to it by now/then; **bestell ihm ~ einen schönen Gruß!** *(ugs.)* till then, give him my regards; Ⓒ *(währenddessen)* meanwhile; in the meantime
**IOK** *Abk.* **Internationales Olympisches Komitee** IOC
**Ion** /i̯oːn/ *das;* **~s, ~en** *(Physik, Chemie)* ion
**Ionen-: ~austauscher** *der;* **~~s, ~~** *(Physik, Chemie)* ion exchanger; **~beschleuniger** *der (Elektronik)* ion accelerator; **~bindung** *die (Physik, Chemie)* ionic bond; **~gitter** *das (Chemie)* ionic lattice; **~strahl** *der (Physik, Chemie)* ion beam
**Ionien** /i̯oːni̯ən/ *(das);* **~s** Ionia
**Ionisation** /ioniza'tsi̯oːn/ *die;* **~, ~en** *(Physik, Chemie)* ionization
**ionisch** *Adj.* Ⓐ Ionic ‹dialect, order, column›; **das Ionische Meer** the Ionian Sea; Ⓑ *(Musik)* Ionian ‹mode›
**ionisieren** *tr. V. (Physik, Chemie)* ionize
**Ionisierung** *die;* **~, ~en** ⇒ **Ionisation**
**Iono·sphäre** /i̯ono-/ *die* ionosphere
**Ionosphären-** ionospheric
**ionosphärisch** *Adj.* ionospheric
**i-Punkt, *I-Punkt** /'iː-/ *der* dot over *or* on the i; **ein i ohne ~:** a dotless i; **bis auf den ~** *(fig.)* down to the last detail
**IQ** *Abk.* **Intelligenzquotient** IQ
**i. R.** *Abk.* **im Ruhestand** retd.
**Irak** /i'raːk/ *(das);* **~s** *od. der;* **~[s]** Iraq; **in/nach/aus** *od.* **im/in den/aus dem ~:** in/to/from Iraq
**Iraker** *der;* **~s, ~, Irakerin** *die;* **~, ~nen** ▶553 Iraqi; ⇒ *auch* **-in**
**irakisch** *Adj.* 259, ▶696 Iraqi
**Iran** /i'raːn/ *(das);* **~s** *od. der;* **~[s]** Iran; ⇒ *auch* **Irak**
**Iraner** *der;* **~s, ~, Iranerin** *die;* **~, ~nen** ▶553 Iranian; ⇒ *auch* **-in**
**iranisch** *Adj.* ▶553, ▶696 Iranian; **I~/das I~e** Iranian; ⇒ *auch* **Deutsch**
**Iranistik** *die;* **~:** Iranian studies *pl., no art.*
**irden** /'ɪrdn̩/ *Adj.* earthen[ware] ‹bowl, pot, jug›; **~es Geschirr** earthenware
**Irden·ware** *die* earthenware
**irdisch** *Adj.* Ⓐ earthly ‹joys, paradise, love›; mortal, earthly ‹creature, being›; temporal ‹power, justice›; worldly ‹goods, pleasures, possessions›; **dieses ~e Jammertal** this vale of tears; **die Irdischen** *(dichter.)* the mortals; **den Weg alles Irdischen gehen** go the way of all flesh; ‹object› go the way of all things; **alles Irdische ist vergänglich** all earthly things must fade; Ⓑ *(zur Erde gehörig)* terrestrial; **das ~e Leben** life on earth
**Ire** /'iːrə/ *der;* **~n, ~n** ▶553 Irishman; **die ~n** the Irish; **er ist ~:** he is Irish *or* an Irishman
**irgend** /'ɪrgn̩t/ *Adv.* Ⓐ **~ so ein Politiker** *(ugs.)* some politician [or other]; **~ so etwas** something like that; something of the sort *or* kind; **führen Sie ~ so etwas?** do you stock anything like that?; Ⓑ *(~wie)* **wenn ~ möglich** if at all possible; **wenn ich Ihnen ~ helfen kann** if I can help you in any way; ⇒ *auch* **irgendetwas, irgendjemand**
**irgend-: ~ein** *Indefinitpron.* Ⓐ *(attr.)* some; *(fragend, verneinend)* any; **~ein Idiot** some idiot [or other]; **in ~einer Zeitung habe ich neulich gelesen, dass ...** I read in one of the papers recently that ...; **Welche Zeitung soll es sein? — Irgendeine** What newspaper do you want? — Just any; **~ein anderer Redakteur/~eine andere Zeitung/~ein anderes Buch** some other editor/newspaper/book; *(fragend, verneinend)* any other editor/newspaper/book; **~ein anderer/~eine andere** someone *or* somebody else; *(fragend, verneinend)* anyone *or* anybody else; **mehr als ~ein anderer** more than anyone *or* anybody else; Ⓑ *(subst.)* **~einer/~eine** someone; somebody; *(fragend, verneinend)* anyone; anybody; **~eines** *od. (ugs.)* **~eins** any one; **~einer muss es machen** someone *or* somebody [or other *(coll.)*] must do it; **nicht ~einer** not just anyone; **~einmal** *Adv.* sometime; [at] some time [or other *(coll.)*]; **hast du schon ~einmal solchen Unsinn gehört?** have you ever heard such nonsense before?; **~etwas** *Indefinitpron.* something; *(fragend, verneinend)* anything; **~jemand** *Indefinitpron.* someone; somebody; somebody or other *(coll.)*; *(fragend, verneinend)* anyone; anybody; **warum hast du nicht ~jemand[en] gefragt?** why didn't you ask someone *or* somebody?; **Haben Sie an jemand Bestimmtes gedacht? — Ach wo, ~jemand** Did you have anyone particular in mind? — Oh, anyone *or* anybody [will do]; **~wann** *Adv.* [at] some time [or other]; somewhen; *(zu jeder beliebigen Zeit)* [at] any time; **~wann einmal** [at] some time [or other]; **~was** *Indefinitpron. (ugs.)* something [or other]; *(fragend, verneinend)* anything; **[nimm] ~was** [take] anything [you like]; **ist ~was?** is [there] something wrong *or* the matter?; **~welch** *Indefinitpron.* some; *(fragend, verneinend)* any; **er raucht nicht ~welche Zigarren** he doesn't smoke just any *or (coll.)* any old cigars; **~wer** *Indefinitpron. (ugs.)* somebody or other *(coll.)*; someone; somebody; *(fragend, verneinend)* anyone; anybody; **~wie** *Adv.* Ⓐ somehow; somehow or other *(coll.)*; **ich glaube nicht, dass ihr das noch ~wie schaffen könnt** I don't think there's any way you could do it; **wer ~wie kann, sollte helfen** anyone who can help in any way should do so; **kann man das ~wie anders/besser machen?** is there some other/better way of doing this?; **er tut mir ~wie Leid, aber ...** I feel sorry for him in a way, but ...; **ihr Lächeln war ~wie kalt** her smile was somehow *or (coll.)* sort of cold; Ⓑ *(ugs.: als Füllwort)* **sie will ~wie auch kommen** I somehow think she wants to come too; **~wo** *Adv.* Ⓐ somewhere; some place [or other] *(coll.)*; *(fragend, verneinend)* anywhere; **ist hier ~wo ein Lokal?** is there a pub anywhere around here?; **~wo anders** somewhere/anywhere else; Ⓑ *(ugs.: ~wie)* **er tut mir ~wo Leid, aber ...** I feel sorry for him in a way, but ...; **~woher** *Adv.* from somewhere; from some place; from somewhere or other *(coll.)*; *(fragend, verneinend)* from anywhere; from any place; **Woher soll ich das nehmen? — [Von] ~woher** Where shall I get it from? — From anywhere *or* wherever you like; **~wohin** *Adv.* somewhere; somewhere or other *(coll.)*; *(fragend, verneinend)* anywhere; **wollen wir ~wohin gehen?** shall we go out somewhere?; **Wohin soll ich die Socken werfen? — Irgendwohin** Where should I throw these socks? — Anywhere [will do *or* you like]; **~wo·mit** *Adv.* with something; with something or other *(coll.)*; **~woran** *Adv.* **~woran erinnert mich dieses Gebäude** this building reminds me of something; **~woran werden wir es schon erkennen** we'll recognize it by something
**Iridium** /i'riːdi̯ʊm/ *das;* **~s** *(Chemie)* iridium
**Irin** *die;* **~, ~nen** ▶553 Irishwoman; **sie ist ~:** she is Irish *or* an Irishwoman
**Iris** /'iːrɪs/ *die;* **~, ~** ▶471 *(Bot., Anat.)* iris
**Iris·blende** *die (Fot.)* iris [diaphragm]
**irisch** *Adj.* ▶553, ▶696 Irish; **die Irische See** the Irish Sea; **Irisch-Republikanische Armee** Irish Republican Army; **~-römisches Bad** Turkish bath; ⇒ *auch* **Deutsch**
**Iris·diagnostik** *die (Med.)* iridodiagnosis
**irisieren** *itr. V.* iridesce; be iridescent; **~d** iridescent
**Irland** /'ɪrlant/ *(das);* **~s** Ireland; *(die Republik)* Ireland; Eire
**Ironie** /iro'niː/ *die;* **~, ~n** irony; **etw. mit ~ sagen** say sth. ironically; **das war ~:** that was meant ironically *or* meant to be ironic; **die ~ des Lebens hat es mit sich gebracht, dass ...** it was one of life's ironies that ...; **die ~ des Schicksals wollte es, dass ...** it was one of the ironies of fate *or* an irony of fate that ...
**ironisch** ❶ *Adj.* ironic; ironical; **das Ironische in der Literatur** irony *or* the ironic in literature; **sie zieht alles ins Ironische** she tends to be ironic about everything. ❷ *adv.* ironically
**ironischer·weise** *Adv.* ironically
**ironisieren** *tr. V.* ironize
**Ironisierung** *die;* **~, ~en** ironizing
**irr** /ɪr/ *Adj.* ⇒ **irre** 1
**irrational** /'ɪratsi̯onaːl/ ❶ *Adj.* irrational. ❷ *adv.* irrationally
**Irrationalismus** *der;* **~, Irrationalismen** irrationalism
**Irrationalität** *die;* **~:** irrationality
**irre** /'ɪrə/ ❶ *Adj.* Ⓐ *(geistesgestört)* mad, insane ‹person›; insane ‹laughter›; demented ‹grin, look›; insane, crazy ‹idea, thought, suggestion›; **davon kann man ja ~ werden** it's enough to drive you mad *or* crazy; **sich wie ~ gebärden** act *or* behave like a madman/madwoman; Ⓑ *(salopp: stark)* terrific *(coll.)*; terrible *(coll.)*; **eine ~ Arbeit** a hell of a job *(coll.)*; Ⓒ *(salopp: faszinierend)* amazing *(coll.)*; ⇒ *auch* **irrewerden**. ❷ *adv. (salopp)* terrifically *(coll.)*; terribly *(coll.)*; **sich ~ freuen** be thrilled to bits *(coll.)*
**Irre**[1] /'ɪrə/ *der/die; adj. Dekl.* madman/madwoman; lunatic; *(fig.)* fool; idiot; lunatic; **das sind alles ~:** they're all crazy *or* mad; **er fährt wie ein ~r** he drives like a maniac *or* lunatic; **er schreit/arbeitet wie ein ~r** he shouts/works like mad *(coll.)*
**Irre**[2] *die (geh.)* **in die ~ gehen** *(sich verirren)* go astray; *(fig.: sich irren)* make a mistake; **in die ~ führen** *(fig.)* be misleading; *(täuschen)* be deceptive; **jmdn. in die ~ führen** mislead sb.; *(täuschen)* deceive sb.
**irreal** /'ɪreaːl/ *Adj.* Ⓐ *(unwirklich)* unreal; Ⓑ *(unrealistisch)* unrealistic
**Irrealis** /'ɪreaːlɪs/ *der;* **~, Irreales** [-leːs] *(Sprachw.)* hypothetical subjunctive
**Irrealität** *die;* **~** Ⓐ unreality; Ⓑ *(Sprachw.)* **als Ausdruck der ~:** as an expression of the unreal *or* hypothetical
**irre-, Irre-: ~|führen** *tr. V.* mislead; *(täuschen)* deceive; **lassen Sie sich durch ... nicht ~führen** don't be misled *or* deceived by ...; **~führend** *Adj.* misleading; *(täuschend)* deceptive; **~führung** *die:* **das war eine bewusste ~führung** that was a deliberate attempt to mislead; **~führung der Öffentlichkeit** misleading the public; **~|gehen** *unr. V.; mit sein (geh.)* Ⓐ *(sich*

*old spelling (see note on page 1707)

*irren*) be mistaken; **B** (*sich verirren*) go astray

**irregulär** /ˈɪregulɛːɐ̯/ *Adj.* **A** (*regelwidrig, Milit.*) irregular; **B** (*abnorm*) abnormal

**irre|leiten** *tr. V.* (*geh.*) **A** (*verführen, täuschen*) lead astray; **irregeleitete Emotionen/Jugend** misguided emotions/youth; **B** (*falsch leiten*) **ein irregeleiteter Brief** a misdirected letter

**irrelevant** /ˈɪrelevant/ *Adj.* irrelevant (**für** to)

**Ir·relevanz** *die* irrelevance (**für** to)

**irreligiös** *Adj.* non-religious; unreligious ‹person, science, country›

**irre|machen** *tr. V.* **A** (*verwirren*) disconcert; put off; **lass dich durch ihn nicht ~:** don't be disconcerted *or* (*coll.*) put off by him; **B** (*zweifeln lassen*) **jmdn. in seinem Glauben ~:** shake sb.'s faith; **sie ließ sich in ihrer Hoffnung/ihrem Plan nicht ~:** she would not let anything confound her hopes/her plan

**irren** /ˈɪrən/ **1** *refl. V.* be mistaken; **man kann sich auch mal ~:** everybody makes *or* we all make mistakes [sometimes]; **Sie ~ sich, wenn ...** you are making a mistake if ...; **ich irre mich oft bei Namen** I often get names mixed up; **er hat sich in einigen Punkten geirrt** he got a few things wrong; **Sie haben sich in der Person/Hausnummer geirrt** you've got the wrong person/number; **sich um 1 DM ~:** be out by 1 DM; be 1 DM out; **ich habe mich in dir geirrt** I was wrong about you.
**2** *itr. V.* **A** (*sich ~*) **da ~ Sie** you are mistaken *or* wrong there; **die Zeitungsberichte ~ in diesem Punkt alle** the newspaper reports are all wrong on this point; **Irren ist menschlich** to err is human (*prov.*); **B** *mit sein* (*ziellos umherstreifen*) wander; **durch die Straßen/den Park ~:** wander the streets/about in the park

**irren-, Irren-: ~anstalt** *die* (*veralt. abwertend*) mental home; madhouse (*derog.*); **~arzt** *der*, **~ärztin** *die* (*veralt. abwertend*) mad-doctor (*arch.*); **~haus** *das* (*abwertend*) [lunatic] asylum; madhouse (*derog.*); **das war das reinste ~haus** (*ugs.*) it was bedlam *or* an absolute madhouse; **er ist reif fürs ~haus** (*ugs.*) he'll crack up soon (*coll.*); **~häusler** *der;* **~~s, ~~, ~häuslerin** *die;* **~~, ~~nen** (*veralt. abwertend*) lunatic (*derog.*); **~haus·reif** *Adj.* (*ugs.*) **sie ist bald ~hausreif** she'll crack up before long (*coll.*); **~witz** *der* (*ugs.*) loony joke (*coll.*); joke about lunatics

**irreparabel** /ɪrepaˈraːbl̩/ *Adj.* (*nicht reparabel*) irreparable; beyond repair *pred.;* (*nicht zu beheben, Med.*) irreparable ‹loss, damage›

**Irre·sein** *das* ⇒ **manisch-depressiv**

**irreversibel** *Adj.* (*fachspr.*) irreversible

**irre|werden** *unr. itr. V* (*geh.*) **an jmdm. ~:** lose faith in sb.; **an sich** (*Dat.*) **selbst ~:** doubt oneself; **am Glauben ~:** begin to have agonizing doubts about one's faith

**Irr-: ~fahrt** *die* wandering; **meine Reise wurde zu einer endlosen ~fahrt** my journey turned into an endless series of wanderings; **~flug** *der* aimless flight; **~garten** *der* maze; labyrinth; **~glaube[n]** *der* **A** misconception; **B** (*Rel.*) heresy; heterodoxy; **~gläubige** *der/die* heretic

**irrig** /ˈɪrɪç/ *Adj.* erroneous ‹impression, belief, assumption, etc.›; false ‹premise›

**Irrigation** /ɪrigaˈtsi̯oːn/ *die;* **~, ~en** irrigation; (*Med.: Spülung*) douche

**Irrigator** /ɪriˈgaːtɔr/ *der;* **~s, ~en** /-gaˈtoːren/ (*Med.*) irrigator

**irrigerweise** *Adv.* mistakenly; erroneously

**Irritation** /ɪritaˈtsi̯oːn/ *die;* **~, ~en** (*Med., geh.*) irritation

**irritieren** *tr., itr. V.* **A** (*verwirren*) bother; put off; **das irritiert** it's off-putting; **lass dich nicht dadurch ~:** don't be put off by it; **B** (*stören*) disturb; **C** (*befremden*) annoy; irritate

**irr-, Irr-: ~läufer** *der* (*Postw.*) misdirected letter/parcel; **~lehre** *die* (*Rel.*) heresy; heterodoxy; (*fig.*) false doctrine; **~licht** *das; Pl.* **~~er** will o' the wisp; jack o' lantern; **~lichter entstehen durch ...** will o' the wisp *or* jack o' lantern is caused by ...; **~sinn** *der* **A** (*Wahnsinn*) insanity; madness; **er war dem ~sinn nahe** he was on the brink of madness; **B** (*ugs. abwertend*) madness; lunacy; **so ein ~sinn!** what lunacy!; **~sinnig** **1** *Adj.* **A** (*geistig gestört*) insane; mad; (*absurd*) idiotic; **bist du ~sinnig?** are you mad?; **wie ~sinnig schreien/rasen** scream/rush like mad (*coll.*); **B** (*ugs.: extrem*) terrible (*coll.*), horrific (*coll.*) ‹pain, screams, prices, etc.›; terrific (*coll.*) ‹speed, heat, cold›; **2** *adv.* (*ugs.*) terribly (*coll.*); frightfully (*coll.*); **~sinnig schuften** slog away like mad *or* crazy (*coll.*); **~sinnige** *der/die; adj. Dekl.* madman/madwoman; lunatic; **sie schrie wie eine ~sinnige** she screamed like mad (*coll.*)

**Irrtum** *der;* **~s, Irrtümer** /ˈɪrtyːmɐ/ **A** (*falsche Vorstellung, Fehlhandlung*) fallacy; misconception; **im ~ sein** *od.* **sich im ~ befinden** be wrong *or* mistaken; **B** (*Fehler*) mistake; error; **~!** wrong!

**irrtümlich** /ˈɪrtyːmlɪç/ **1** *Adj.* incorrect; wrong. **2** *adv.* by mistake; **~ gemachte Angaben** inaccuracies; incorrect information *sing.*

**irrtümlicherweise** *Adv.* by mistake; **wie man oft ~ meint** as is often erroneously *or* mistakenly thought

**Irrung** *die;* **~, ~en** (*geh.*) **die ~en und Wirrungen seiner verfehlten Jugend** the vagaries of his misspent youth

**irr-, Irr-: ~weg** *der* error; **diese Methode hat sich als ~weg erwiesen** this method has proved to be wrong; **auf ~wege geraten** (*gedanklich*) go off on the wrong track; (*moralisch*) depart from the straight and narrow; **~|werden** *unr. itr. V.:* ⇒ **irrewerden**; **~wisch** *der* flibbertigibbet; **~witz** *der* (*geh.*) madness; lunacy; **~witzig** *Adj.* (*geh.*) mad

**Ischias** /ˈɪʃi̯as/ *der od. das od. Med. die;* **~** ▶ **474** sciatica

**Ischias·nerv** *der* ▶ **471** sciatic nerve

**Isegrim** /ˈiːzəgrɪm/ *der;* **~s, ~e** **A** (*Myth.*) **[Meister] ~:** Isegrim; Isgrin; **B** (*mürrischer Mann*) crusty old man

**Islam** /ɪsˈlaːm *od.* ˈɪslam/ *der;* **~[s]: der ~:** Islam; **die Welt des ~[s]** the Islamic world; the world of Islam

**islamisch** *Adj.* Islamic; Islamitic

**islamisieren** *tr. V.* Islamize

**Islamismus** *der;* **~:** Islamic fundamentalism; Islamism

**Islamist** *der;* **~en, ~en, Islamistin** *die;* **~, ~nen** Islamic fundamentalist; Islamist

**islamistisch** *Adj.* Islamic fundamentalist; Islamist

**Island** /ˈiːs-/ (*das*); **~s** Iceland

**Isländer** /ˈiːslɛndɐ/ *der;* **~s, ~, Isländerin** *die;* **~, ~nen** ▶ **553** Icelander

**isländisch** /ˈiːslɛndɪʃ/ *Adj.* ▶ **553**, ▶ **696** Icelandic; **I~/das I~e** Icelandic; ⇒ *auch* **Deutsch**

**Ismailit** /ɪsmaiˈliːt/ *der;* **~en, ~en** Ismaili

**Ismus** /ˈɪsmʊs/ *der;* **~, Ismen** (*abwertend*) ism

**iso-, Iso-,** (*vor Vokalen auch:*) **is-, Is-** [iz(o)-] iso-

**Iso·bar** *das;* **~s, ~e** (*Physik*) isobar

**Iso·bare** *die;* **~, ~n** (*Met.*) isobar

**Isogamie** /izogaˈmiː/ *die;* **~, ~n** /-iːən/ (*Biol.*) isogamy *no art.*

**Isolation** /izolaˈtsi̯oːn/ *die;* **~, ~en** ⇒ **Isolierung**

**Isolations-: ~folter** *die* torture by solitary confinement; **~haft** *die* solitary confinement

**Isolator** /izoˈlaːtɔr/ *der;* **~s, ~en** /-ˈtoːren/ insulator

**Isolier·band** *das; Pl.* **Isolierbänder** insulating tape

**Isolier·baracke** *die* isolation ward

**isolieren** *tr. V.* **A** isolate ‹prisoner, patient, bacterium, element›; **von der Umwelt isoliert** cut off from the outside world; **etw. isoliert betrachten** look at sth. out of context; **B** (*Technik*) insulate ‹wiring, wall, etc.›; lag ‹boilers, pipes, etc.›; (*gegen Schall*) soundproof; insulate ‹room, door, window, etc.›

**Isolierer** *der;* **~s, ~, Isoliererin** *die;* **~, ~nen** insulation engineer

**Isolier-: ~kanne** *die* Thermos jug ®; vacuum jug; **~schicht** *die* insulating layer; **~station** *die* (*Med.*) isolation ward

**Isolierung** *die;* **~, ~en** **A** (*Absonderung, auch fig.*) isolation; **in der ~:** in isolation; **in die ~ geraten** (*fig.*) become isolated *or* detached; **B** (*Technik*) (*das Isolieren*) insulation; insulating; (*von Kesseln, Röhren*) lagging; (*gegen Schall*) soundproofing; **C** (*Isoliermaterial*) insulation; (*für Kessel, Röhren*) lagging

**Isomer** /izoˈmeːɐ̯/ *das;* **~s, ~e, Isomere** *das; adj. Dekl.* (*Chemie*) isomer

**Isometrie** /izomeˈtriː/ *die;* **~** (*Biol., Geodäsie*) isometry

**isometrisch** **1** *Adj.* isometric. **2** *adv.* isometrically

**Isotherme** /izoˈtɛrmə/ *die;* **~, ~n** (*Met.*) isotherm

**Isotop** /izoˈtoːp/ *das;* **~s, ~e** isotope

**Isotopen·therapie** *die* (*Med.*) radiotherapy

**Israel** /ˈɪsraeːl/ (*das*); **~s** Israel; **das Volk ~** (*bibl.*) the Israelites; the people of Israel; **die Kinder ~[s]** (*bibl.*) the Children of Israel

**Israeli** *der;* **~[s], ~[s]/** *die;* **~, ~[s]** ▶ **553** Israeli

**israelisch** *Adj.* ▶ **553** Israeli

**Israelit** *der;* **~en, ~en, Israelitin** *die;* **~, ~nen** Israelite; ⇒ *auch* **-in**

**israelitisch** *Adj.* Israelite

**iss, *iß** /ɪs/ *Imperativ Sg. v.* **essen**

**isst, *ißt** /ɪst/ *2. u. 3. Pers. Sg. Präsens v.* **essen**

**ist** /ɪst/ *3. Pers. Sg. Präsens v.* **sein**

**Ist-: ~aufkommen, *~-Aufkommen** *das* (*Steuerw.*) actual *or* real yield; **~bestand, *~-Bestand** *der* (*Kaufmannsspr.*) actual stocks *pl.;* **~stärke, *~-Stärke** *die* (*Milit.*) actual strength

**Isthmus** /ˈɪstmʊs/ *der;* **~, Isthmen** isthmus

**Itaker** /ˈiːtakɐ/ *der;* **~s, ~, Itakerin** *die;* **~, ~nen** (*salopp abwertend*) Eyetie (*sl. derog.*); dago (*sl. derog.*)

**Italien** /iˈtaːli̯ən/ (*das*); **~s** Italy

**Italiener** /itaˈli̯eːnɐ/ *der;* **~s, ~, Italienerin** *die;* **~, ~nen** ▶ **553** Italian; ⇒ *auch* **-in**

**italienisch** *Adj.* Italian; **I~/das I~e** ▶ **553**, ▶ **696** Italian; ⇒ *auch* **Deutsch**

**Italo·western** /ˈiːtalo-/ *der* Italian-made Western; spaghetti western (*derog.*)

**iterativ** /iteraˈtiːf/ *Adj.* iterative

**i-Tüpfel[chen], *I-Tüpfel[chen]** *das;* **~s, ~,** (*österr.*) **i-Tüpferl, *I-Tüpferl** /ˈiːtypfɐl/ *das;* **~s, ~n** final *or* finishing touch; **bis aufs [letzte] ~:** down to the last detail

**i-Tüpfel-Reiter, *I-Tüpfel-Reiter** *der,* **i-Tüpfel-Reiterin, *I-Tüpfel-Reiterin** (*österr. ugs.*) nit-picker (*coll.*)

**i. v.** *Abk.* (*Med.*) **intravenös** IV

**i. V.** /iːˈfau̯/ *Abk.* **in Vertretung**

**Iwan** /ˈiːva(ː)n/ *der;* **~s, ~s** (*salopp abwertend*) Russki (*derog.*); Ivan (*derog.*); **der ~:** the Russkis *pl.;* Ivan

**i. w. S.** *Abk.* **im weiteren Sinne**

# J j

**j, J** /jɔt, *österr.:* je:/ *das;* ~, ~**:** j/J; ⇒ *auch* **a, A**

**ja** /ja:/ *Partikel* (A) (*zustimmend*) yes; **Wohnen Sie hier? — Ja** Do you live here? — Yes [, I do]; **Hast du ihm Bescheid gesagt? — Ja** Have you told him? — Yes [, I have]; **ja** *od.* **Ja zu etw. sagen** say yes to sth.; (B) (*bekräftigend*) yes; **ja natürlich** *od.* **sicher!** [yes,] of course; [yes,] certainly; **o ja!** oh, yes!; **aber ja doch!** yes, of course [I/you *etc.* can/do *etc.*]; (C) (*nachgestellt*) won't you/doesn't it *etc.*?; **du bleibst doch noch ein bisschen, ja?** but you'll stay on a bit, won't you *or* surely?; **das Kleid sieht doch gut aus, ja?** the dress looks nice, doesn't it?; (D) **ich komme ja schon** I'm [just] coming; **Sie wissen ja, dass ...** you know, of course, that ...; **du kennst ihn ja** you know what he's like; you know him; **es schneit ja!** it's [actually] snowing!; **da seid ihr ja!** there you are!; (E) (*einschränkend*) **er mag ja Recht haben** he may [well] be right; (F) (*unbedingt*) **lass ja die Finger davon!** [just you] leave it alone!; **sag das ja nicht weiter!** don't [you dare] pass it on, whatever you do!; **damit er ja alles mitbekommt** to make sure he knows all *or* everything that's going on; **damit wir ja nicht zu spät kommen** so that there's no risk of us being late; (G) (*sogar*) indeed; even; **ich schätze, ja bewundere ihn** I like him, indeed admire him *or* admire him even; (H) (*allerdings*) oh; **ja, das waren noch Zeiten!** [yes], those were the days!; (I) (*fragend*) (*am Telefon usw.*) **ja [bitte]?** yes?; **Sie kommen. — Ja?** They're coming. — Are they?; (*ungläubig*) **Der König ist tot. — Ja?** The King is dead. — [Is he] really?

**Ja** *das;* ~**[s]**, ~**[s]** yes; **mit ~ stimmen** vote yes

**Jacht** /jaxt/ *die;* ~, ~**en** yacht

**Jacht-:** ~**hafen** *der* yacht harbour; marina; ~**klub** *der* yacht club

**Jäckchen** /'jɛkçən/ *das;* ~**s**, ~**:** jacket; (*gestrickt*) cardigan

**Jacke** /'jakə/ *die;* ~, ~**n** jacket; (*gestrickt*) cardigan; **das ist ~ wie Hose** (*ugs.*) it makes no odds (*coll.*); ⇒ *auch* **saufen** 3

**Jacken-:** ~**kleid** *das* dress and jacket combination; ~**tasche** *die* jacket pocket

**Jacket·krone** /'dʒɛkɪt-/ *die* (*Zahnmed.*) jacket crown

**Jackett** /ʒa'kɛt/ *das;* ~**s**, ~**s** jacket

**Jade** /'ja:də/ *der;* ~**[s]** *od. die;* ~**:** jade

**jade·grün** *Adj.* jade-green

**Jagd** /ja:kt/ *die;* ~, ~**en** (A) (*Weidwerk*) **die ~:** shooting; hunting; (*Hetzjagd*) hunting; **die ~ auf Hasen** hare hunting; (*mit Hunden*) hare coursing; **die ~ auf Federwild** shooting game birds; **~ auf Fasanen/Wildschweine machen** shoot pheasant/hunt wild boar; **auf der ~ sein** be hunting/shooting; **auf die ~ gehen** go hunting/shooting; **die hohe/niedere ~** (*Jägerspr.*) hunting for Hochwild/Niederwild; (B) (*Veranstaltung*) shoot; (*Hetzjagd*) hunt; (C) (*Revier*) preserve; shoot; **eine ~ pachten** rent a hunting preserve *or* shoot; (D) (*Verfolgung*) hunt; (*Verfolgungsjagd*) chase; **auf jmdn./etw. ~ machen** hunt for sb./sth.; **die ~ nach Geld/Besitz** (*fig.*) the constant pursuit of money/possessions; (E) (~*gesellschaft*) shooting party; (*bei einer Hetzjagd*) hunt; field; **die Wilde ~:** the Wild Hunt

*old spelling (see note on page 1707)

**Jagd-:** ~**aufklärer** *der* (*Luftwaffe*) fighter-reconnaissance aircraft; ~**aufseher** *der*, ~**aufseherin** *die* game warden

**jagdbar** *Adj.* ~**e Tiere** animals that can be hunted/shot

**Jagd-:** ~**beute** *die* bag; kill; **eine reiche/magere ~beute** a good/poor bag; ~**bomber** *der* (*Luftwaffe*) fighter-bomber; ~**falke** *der* falcon; ~**fieber** *das* hunting fever; **vom ~fieber gepackt** in the fever of the hunt; ~**flieger** *der* (*Luftwaffe*) fighter pilot; ~**flugzeug** *das* (*Luftwaffe*) fighter aircraft; ~**frevel** *der* poaching; ~**gebiet** *das* hunting ground[s *pl.*]; ~**geschwader** *das* (*Luftwaffe*) fighter wing; ~**gesellschaft** *die* shooting party; hunting party; (*bei Hetzjagden*) hunting party; ~**gewehr** *das* sporting gun; ~**glück** *das:* **~glück/kein ~glück haben** be lucky/unlucky [in the hunt]; ~**grund** *der* hunting ground; **in die ewigen ~gründe eingehen** go to the happy hunting grounds; ~**haus** *das* hunting *or* shooting lodge; hunting *or* shooting box; ~**herr** *der*, ~**herrin** *die* owner of a/the preserve *or* shoot; ~**horn** *das* hunting horn; ~**hund** *der* gun dog; (*bei Hetzjagden*) hunting dog; hound; ~**hütte** *die* hunting *or* shooting box; ~**messer** *das* hunting knife; ~**pächter** *der*, ~**pächterin** *die* game-tenant; ~**panzer** *der* (*Milit.*) anti-tank vehicle; tank destroyer; ~**rennen** *das* (*Pferdesport*) steeplechase; ~**revier** *das* preserve; shoot; (*fig.*) hunting ground; ~**schein** *der* game licence; **er hat den** *od.* **einen ~schein** (*fig. ugs.*) he's certified — the courts can't do anything about him; ~**schloss**, *~**schloß** *das* hunting seat *or* lodge; ~**springen** *das;* ~~**s** (*Pferdesport*) showjumping; ~**staffel** *die* (*Luftwaffe*) fighter squadron; ~**stock** *der* shooting stick; ~**stück** *das* (*Malerei*) hunting piece; ~**stuhl** *der* ⇒ ~**stock**; ~**szene** *die* (*bild. Kunst*) hunting scene; ~**waffe** *die* hunting weapon; ~**wesen** *das* hunting; ~**wurst** *die* chasseur sausage; ~**zeit** *die* open *or* hunting *or* shooting season

**jagen** /'ja:gn̩/ ❶ *tr. V.* (A) (*verfolgen*) hunt ‹game, fugitive, criminal, etc.›; shoot ‹game, game birds›; (*hetzen*) chase, pursue ‹fugitive, criminal, etc.›; (*wegscheuchen*) chase; run after; **von Todesfurcht/Gewissensbissen gejagt** stricken by the fear of death/by pangs of conscience; **ein Gedanke jagte den anderen** thoughts raced through his/her *etc.* mind; (B) (*in eine bestimmte Richtung treiben*) drive ‹animals›; **den Ball ins Netz ~** (*Fußballjargon*) drive the ball into the net; (C) (*vertreiben*) **den Feind aus dem Land ~:** drive the enemy out of *or* from the country; **jmdn. aus dem Haus ~:** throw sb. out of the house; **jmdn. aus dem Bett ~:** turn sb. out of bed; **jmdn. in die Flucht ~:** put sb. to flight; **damit kannst du mich ~** (*ugs.*) I can't stand it/that/them; ⇒ *auch* **Gurgel**; (D) (*ugs.*) **sich/jmdm. eine Spritze in den Arm ~:** jab *or* stick a needle in one's/sb.'s arm; **sich/jmdm. eine Kugel durch den Kopf ~:** blow one's/sb.'s brains out.
❷ *itr. V.* (A) (*Jägerspr.*) **auf Rebhühner ~:** shoot partridge; **auf Hasen ~:** hunt *or* shoot hare; (B) (*die Jagd ausüben*) go shooting *or* hunting; (*auf Hetzjagd gehen*) go hunting; (C) **nach Geld/Glück ~:** chase after money/happiness; (D) *mit sein* (*eilen*) race; rush; **Wolken ~ am Himmel** (*fig.*) clouds race *or* scud across the sky; **mit ~dem Puls** (*fig.*) with his/her *etc.* pulse racing

**Jagen** *das;* ~**s**, ~ (*Forstw.*) compartment

**Jäger** /'jɛ:gɐ/ *der;* ~**s**, ~ (A) hunter; (*bei Hetzjagden*) huntsman; **~ und Sammler** (*Prähist.*) hunters and gatherers; (B) (*Milit.*) rifleman; jaeger; (C) (*Soldatenspr.: Jagdflugzeug*) fighter

**Jäger·art** *die* (*Kochk.*) **Schnitzel nach ~:** escalope chasseur

**Jägerei** *die;* ~ (A) (*das Jagen*) shooting; hunting; (*Hetzjagd*) hunting; (B) (*Jagdwesen*) hunting

**Jäger·hut** *der* huntsman's hat

**Jägerin** *die;* ~, ~**nen** huntress; huntswoman

**Jäger-:** ~**latein** *das* (*scherzh.*) [hunter's *or* huntsman's] tall story/stories; **das ist das reinste ~latein** that's all wild exaggeration; ~**rock** *der* hunting jacket; ~**schnitzel** *das* (*Kochk.*) escalope chasseur

**Jägers·mann** *der; Pl.* **Jägers·leute** (*ugs. veralt.*) ⇒ **Jäger** A

**Jäger·sprache** *die* hunting language

**Jag·hund** /'ja:k-/ *der* (*schweiz.*) ⇒ **Jagdhund**

**Jaguar** /'ja:gu̯a:ɐ̯/ *der;* ~**s**, ~**e** jaguar

**jäh** /jɛ:/ ❶ *Adj.* (*geh.*) (A) (*plötzlich, heftig*) sudden; sudden, abrupt ‹change, movement, stop›; sudden, sharp ‹pain›; **er fand einen ~en Tod** he met his death suddenly; **ein ~es Erwachen** a sudden awakening; (*fig.*) a rude awakening; (B) (*steil*) steep; precipitous ‹slope, ravine, ridge›. ❷ *adv.* (A) (*plötzlich*) **die Stimmung schlug ~ um** the mood changed suddenly *or* abruptly; (B) (*steil*) **dort ging es ~ in die Tiefe** the ground fell *or* dropped away steeply *or* abruptly at that point

**jählings** /'jɛ:lɪŋs/ *Adv.* (*geh.*) (A) (*plötzlich*) ‹change, end, stop› suddenly, abruptly; ‹die, understand, wake up› suddenly; (B) (*steil*) steeply; precipitously

**Jahr** /ja:ɐ̯/ *das;* ~**[e]s**, ~**e** (A) ▶ 207 (*12 Monate*) year; **ein halbes ~:** six months; **anderthalb ~e** eighteen months; a year and a half; **im ~[e] 1908** in [the year] 1908; **jedes ~:** every year; **jedes zweite ~:** [once] every two years; **alle halbe[n] ~ [mal]** (*ugs.*) [once] every six months; **alle ~e** every year; **1 000 Tonnen pro ~:** 1,000 tonnes per *or* a year; **100 000 DM pro ~:** DM 100,000 per annum; **lange ~e [hindurch]** for many years; **nach langen ~en** after many years; **vor langen ~en** many years ago; **~ für** *od.* **um ~:** year after year; **von ~ zu ~:** from one year to the next; from year to year; **ich war seit ~ und Tag nicht mehr dort** I haven't been there for many years; **zwischen den ~en** between Christmas and the New Year; **das Buch/der Sportler des ~es** the book/sportsman *or* sports personality of the year; **zu zehn ~en [Gefängnis] verurteilt werden** be sentenced to ten years [imprisonment]; **er ist Lehrling im zweiten ~:** he is an apprentice in his second year; **auf ~ und Tag** to the exact day; **nach ~ und Tag** after many years; **vor ~ und Tag** (*mit Präteritum*) many years ago; (*mit Plusquamperfekt*) many years before; (B) ▶ 76 (*Lebens~*) year; **er ist zwanzig ~e [alt]** he is twenty years old *or* of age; **Kinder bis zu zwölf ~en** children up to the age of twelve *or* up to twelve years of age; **Kinder über 14 ~e** children over the age of 14 *or* over 14 years of age; **Kinder ab zwei ~en** children of two years and over; **alle Männer zwischen 18 und 45 ~en** all men between the ages of 18 and 45; **mit 65 ~en** *od.* **im Alter von 65 ~en** at the age of 65; **seine ~e spüren** feel one's age; **das hat er schon in jungen ~en gelernt** he learned that at an early age *or* while he was still young; **für seine**

## Die Jahreszeiten

***der Frühling, das Frühjahr***
= spring

***der Herbst***
= autumn (*brit.*), fall (*amerik.*)

***der Sommer***
= summer

***der Winter***
= winter

Spricht man von einer Jahreszeit im Allgemeinen oder als Phänomen, verwendet man im Englischen oft keinen Artikel:

***Der Frühling ist früh eingetroffen***
= Spring came early

***Der Sommer ist meine Lieblingsjahreszeit***
= Summer *od.* The summer is my favourite time of year

***Im Winter bleibe ich die meiste Zeit zu Hause***
= In [the] winter I stay at home most of the time

***Sie blühen zu Anfang/zu Ende des Frühjahrs***
= They flower in [the] early/late spring

Eine Ausnahme bildet der amerikanische Ausdruck **fall**, der stets mit dem Artikel verwendet wird.

***Im Herbst verfärbt sich das Laub***
= The leaves change colour in [the] autumn *od.* (*amerik.*) in the fall

Spricht man aber von einem bestimmten Sommer usw., ist der Gebrauch ähnlich wie im Deutschen:

***Der Sommer war verregnet***
= The summer was wet

***nächsten/letzten Winter***
= next/last winter

***Er blieb den ganzen Sommer***
= He stayed all summer *od.* [for] the whole summer

***Sie kommen diesen Herbst***
= They are coming this autumn *od.* (*amerik.*) this fall

***Er macht jeden Winter Skiurlaub***
= He goes skiing every winter

***Die letzten beiden Sommer waren wir in Griechenland***
= The last two summers we were in Greece

### Adjektive

***frühlingshaft***
= springlike

***herbstlich***
= autumnal

***sommerlich***
= summery

***winterlich***
= wintry

In ganz wenigen Fällen lässt sich das Adjektiv durch ein attributives **summer, winter** usw. übersetzen. Bei Kleidung etwa unterscheidet man nicht zwischen *winterlich/sommerlich* und *Winter-/Sommer-*:

***Winterkleidung/winterliche Kleidung***
= winter clothing

***Sommerkleidung/sommerliche Kleidung***
= summer clothing

Allerdings:

***ein sommerliches Kleid***
= a summery dress

Beachten Sie auch:

***winterliche/sommerliche Temperaturen***
= winter/summer temperatures

**achtzig ~e ist er noch erstaunlich rüstig** he's amazingly sprightly for [a man of] eighty; **mit den ~en** as he/she *etc.* grows/grew older; **er ist um ~e gealtert** he's put on years; **in die ~e kommen** reach middle age

**jahr·aus** *Adv.* **~, jahrein** year in, year out

**Jahr·buch** *das* yearbook

**Jährchen** /ˈjɛːɐ̯çən/ *das;* **~s, ~** (*scherzh.*) year; **die paar ~, die ich noch zu leben habe!** the few short years I have left to live; **einige ~ auf dem Buckel haben** be knocking on a bit (*coll.*)

**jahr·ein** *Adv.;* ⇒ jahraus

**jahre·lang** ❶ *Adj.* [many] years of ‹practice, imprisonment, experience, etc.›; long-standing ‹feud, friendship›; **mit ~er Verspätung** years late. ❷ *adv.* for [many] years; **sie ist schon ~ tot** she has been dead for [many] years; **man sprach noch ~ darüber** people were talking about it for years afterwards

**jähren** /ˈjɛːrən/ *refl. V.* **heute jährt sich [zum fünften Male] sein Todestag** today is the [fifth] anniversary of his death; **heute jährt sich zum zehntenmal, dass ...** it is ten years ago today that ...; it is ten years since ...

**jahres-, Jahres-: ~abonnement** *das* annual *or* yearly subscription; **~abrechnung** *die* annual accounts *pl.;* (*Abrechnungsblatt*) annual [statement of] account; **~abschluss, *~abschluß** *der* Ⓐ (*Wirtsch., Kaufmannsspr.*) annual accounts *pl.;* Ⓑ ⇒ **~ende**; **~anfang** *der* beginning *or* start of the year; **~ausgleich** *der* (*Steuerw.*) end-of-year adjustment; **den ~ausgleich beantragen** send in one's tax return; **~ausklang** *der* close of the year; **Musik zum ~ausklang** music at the close of the year; **~ausstoß** *der* (*Wirtsch.*) annual production; **~beginn** *der* beginning *or* start of the new year; **den ~beginn feiern** celebrate New Year; **~beitrag** *der* annual *or* yearly subscription; **~bestleistung** *die* (*Sport*) best performance of the season; **~bestzeit** *die* (*Sport*) fastest *or* best time of the season; **~bezüge** *Pl.* annual income *sing.;* **~bilanz** *die* (*Wirtsch., Kaufmannsspr.*) annual balance [of accounts]; (*Dokument*) annual balance sheet; **~durchschnitt** *der* yearly *or* annual average; **~einkommen** *das* annual income; **~ende** *das* end of the year; **~etat** *der* annual budget; **~frist** *die:* **in** *od.* **innerhalb** *od.* **binnen ~frist** within [a period of] a *or* one year; **vor ~frist** in less than a year; within [a period of] a *or* one year; (*vor einem Jahr*) a year ago; **nach ~frist** after [a period of] a *or* one year; **~gehalt** *das* annual salary; **zwei ~gehälter** two years' salary; **~hälfte** *die* half of *or* six months of the year; **die erste/zweite ~hälfte** the first/second half *or* six months of the year; **~hauptversammlung** *die* (*Wirtsch.*) annual general meeting; **~kapazität** *die* (*Wirtsch.*) annual *or* yearly capacity; **~karte** *die* yearly season ticket; **~miete** *die* annual *or* yearly rent; **eine Kaution in Höhe einer ~miete** a deposit equivalent to a year's rent; **~mittel** *das* annual mean; **im ~mittel fallen 3,2 cm Niederschlag** the mean annual precipitation is 3.2 cm; **~plan** *der* [economic, financial] plan for the year; **~produktion** *die* annual *or* yearly production; **~ring** *der* (*Bot.*) annual ring; **~rückblick** *der* end-of-the-year review; **~schluss, *~schluß** *der* ⇒ **~ende**; **~schlussbilanz, *~schlußbilanz** *die* ⇒ **~abschluss** A; **~schrift** *die* annual; **~tag** *der* anniversary; **~tagung** *die* annual congress *or* conference *or* convention; **~temperatur** *die:* **die höchste/tiefste ~temperatur** the highest/lowest temperature of the year; **die mittlere ~temperatur** the mean temperature during the year; **eine mittlere ~temperatur von 9 °C** a mean annual temperature of 9°C; **~umsatz** *der* annual turnover; **~urlaub** *der* annual holiday *or* (*formal*) leave *or* (*Amer.*) vacation; **~versammlung** *die* annual [general] meeting; **~vertrag** *der* one-year contract; **~wechsel** *der* turn of the year; **zum ~wechsel die besten Wünsche** best wishes for the New Year; **~wende** *die* Ⓐ (*geh.*) ⇒ **~wechsel**; Ⓑ turn of the year; **um die ~wende 1976/1977** around the end of 1976; around the beginning of 1977; **~zahl** *die* date; **ohne Angabe der ~zahl** with no indication of the date *or* year; **~zeit** *die* season; **für die ~zeit ist es kalt** it's cold for the time of the year; **trotz der vorgerückten ~zeit** although it is/was late in the year; **~zeitlich** ❶ *Adj.* seasonal; ❷ *adv.* **~zeitlich schwanken** vary with the seasons *or* according to the time of year; **~zeitlich bedingt sein** be governed by seasonal factors

**Jahr·gang** *der* Ⓐ (*Altersklasse*) year; **der ~ 1900** those *pl.* born in 1900; **der ~ 1900 hat viele Gelehrte hervorgebracht** the year 1900 produced many scholars; **sie ist ~ 1943** she was born in 1943; **er ist mein ~:** he was born in the same year as I was; **welcher ~ sind Sie?** which year were you born in?; Ⓑ (*eines Weines*) vintage; **der 81er soll ein guter ~ werden** 81 should be a vintage year; **ein Edelzwicker ~ 1978** a 1978 Edelzwicker; Ⓒ (*einer Zeitschrift*) set [of issues] for a/the year; **die beiden letzten Jahrgänge** the sets of back numbers for the past two years; Ⓓ (*eines Autos usw.*) year; **ein Modell ~ 1950** a 1950 model

**Jahr·gänger** *der;* **~s, ~, Jahr·gängerin** *die;* **~, ~nen** (*südd., schweiz.*) **er ist mein Jahrgänger** he was born in the same year as I was

**Jahr·hundert** *das* ▶207 century; **das 18. ~:** the 18th century; **im 19. und 20. ~:** in the 19th and 20th centuries; **durch die ~e** over *or* through the centuries; **im ersten ~ vor/nach Christi Geburt** in the first century BC/AD; **die Literatur des 19. ~s** 19th-century literature; the literature of the 19th century

**jahrhunderte-: ~alt** *Adj.* centuries-old; **~lang** ❶ *Adj.* age-long. ❷ *adv.* for centuries; **das dauert noch ~lang** that will take centuries

**Jahrhundert-: ~hälfte** *die:* **die erste/zweite ~hälfte** the first/second half of the century; **~mitte** *die* middle of the century; **~sommer** *der* summer of the century; **~wein** *der* exceptional vintage wine; **~wende** *die* turn of the century; **aus der**

Zeit um die **~wende** from the turn of the century

**-jährig** /ˈjɛːrɪç/ [A] ▶ 76 (... *Jahre alt*) **ein elfjähriges/halbjähriges Kind** an eleven-year-old/a six-month-old child; **kaum acht~:** hardly eight years old; [B] (... *Jahre dauernd*) ... year's/years'; -year; **nach vierjähriger/halbjähriger Vorbereitung** after four years'/six months' preparation; **mit dreijähriger/halbjähriger Verspätung** three years/six months late

**jährlich** /ˈjɛːɐ̯lɪç/ ❶ *Adj.* annual; yearly. ❷ *adv.* annually; yearly; **einmal/zweimal ~:** once/twice a *or* per year; **ein Umsatz von 5 Millionen ~:** a turnover of five million per annum

**Jahr·markt** *der* fair; funfair; **ein ~ der Eitelkeit[en]** (*fig.*) a Vanity Fair

**Jahrmarkts·bude** *die* fairground booth

**Jahr·millionen** *Pl.* millions of years

**Jahr·schießet** *der;* **~s** (*schweiz.*) ⇒ **Schützenfest**

**Jahr·tausend** *das* thousand years; millennium; **vor ~en** thousands of years ago; **das dritte ~ nach Christi Geburt** the third millennium AD

**jahrtausende-:** **~alt** *Adj.* age-old; **ein ~altes Gebäude** a building dating back thousands of years; **~lang** ❶ *Adj.* age-long; ❷ *adv.* for thousands of years; **das dauert ~lang** that will take thousands of years

**Jahrtausend·wende** *die* turn of the millennium

**Jahr·zahl** *die* (*schweiz.*) ⇒ **Jahreszahl**

**Jahr·zehnt** *das* decade

**jahrzehnte·lang** ❶ *Adj.* **das macht die ~e Übung** that's the result of decades of practice; **mit ~er Verspätung** decades late; **nach ~er Abwesenheit** after being away for decades. ❷ *adv.* for decades

**Jahve**, (*ökum.:*) **Jahwe** /ˈjaːvə/ (*der*); **~s** Jehova; Yahweh

**Jäh·zorn** *der* violent anger; **er neigt zum ~:** he tends towards violent fits *or* outbursts of temper *or* anger; **in wildem ~ zuschlagen** lash out in blind anger *or* a blind rage

**jäh·zornig** ❶ *Adj.* violent-tempered; **ein ~er Charakter, ein ~es Temperament** a violent temper. ❷ *adv.* in blind anger; in a blind rage

**ja·ja** *Part.* (*ugs.*) [A] (*seufzend*) **~[, so ist das Leben]** oh well[, that's life]; [B] (*ungeduldig*) **~[, ich komme schon]!** OK, OK *or* all right, all right[, I'm coming]!

**Jak** /jak/ *der;* **~s, ~s** yak

**Jakob** /ˈjaːkɔp/ (*der*) James; (*in der Bibel*) Jacob; **ich weiß ja nicht, ob das der wahre ~ ist** I don't know if that is really quite the thing; **der billige ~:** the/a cheap jack

**Jakobi** /jaˈkoːbi/ (*das*); *indekl.* ⇒ **Jakobstag**

**Jakobiner** /jakoˈbiːnɐ/ *der;* **~s, ~** (*hist.*) Jacobin

**Jakobiner·mütze** *die* (*hist.*) cap of liberty; Phrygian cap

**Jakobinertum** *das;* **~s** Jacobinism *no art.*

**jakobinisch** *Adj.* Jacobin; Jacobinic

**Jakobit** /jakoˈbiːt/ *der;* **~en, ~en, Jakobitin** *die;* **~, ~nen** (*hist.*) Jacobite

**Jakobi·tag** *der* ⇒ **Jakobstag**

**Jakobs·leiter** *die* (*Seemannsspr., Bot.*) Jacob's ladder

**Jakobs·tag** *der* St. James's Day; Feast of St. James

**Jalousette** /ʒaluˈzɛtə/ *die;* **~, ~n, Jalousie** /ʒaluˈziː/ *die;* **~, ~n** venetian blind

**Jalta** /ˈjalta/ (*das*); **~s** Yalta

**Jamaika** /jaˈmaika/ (*das*); **~s** Jamaica

**Jamaikaner** *der;* **~s, ~, Jamaikanerin** *die;* **~, ~nen** Jamaican; ⇒ *auch* **-in**

**jamaikanisch** *Adj.* Jamaican

**Jamaika·rum** *der* Jamaica rum

**Jambe** /ˈjambə/ *die;* **~, ~n** ⇒ **Jambus**

**jambisch** *Adj.* (*Verslehre*) iambic

**Jamboree** /dʒæmbəˈriː/ *das;* **~[s], ~s** jamboree

*old spelling (see note on page 1707)

**Jambus** /ˈjambʊs/ *der;* **~, Jamben** (*Verslehre*) iambus; iamb; **ein Drama in Jamben** a drama in iambic verse *or* in iambics

**Jammer** /ˈjamɐ/ *der;* **~s** [A] (*Wehklagen*) [mournful] wailing; [B] (*Elend*) misery; **ein Bild des ~s** a picture of misery; **es ist ein ~, dass ...** (*ugs.*) it's a crying shame that ...

**Jammer-:** **~bild** *das* miserable sight; **~geschrei** *das* (*von Menschen*) wailing; moaning; (*von Vögeln*) squawking; squawks; **~gestalt** *die* [A] (*elender Mensch*) pitiful creature; [B] (*ugs. abwertend*) miserable wretch; **~lappen** *der* (*ugs. abwertend*) (*Feigling*) coward; (*Schwächling*) sniveller

**jämmerlich** /ˈjɛmɐlɪç/ ❶ *Adj.* [A] (*Jammer ausdrückend*) pathetic; pitiful; [B] (*beklagenswert*) miserable ‹existence, conditions, etc.›; wretched ‹appearance, existence, etc.›; [C] (*ärmlich*) pathetic; pitiful ‹conditions, clothing, housing›; paltry, meagre ‹quantity›; pitiful, sorry ‹state›; [D] (*abwertend: minderwertig*) contemptible ‹person›; pathetic, paltry ‹wages, sum›; pathetic, useless ‹piece of work etc.›; [E] (*sehr groß, stark*) awful; terrible (*coll.*). ❷ *adv.* [A] (*Jammer ausdrückend*) pathetically; pitifully; [B] (*beklagenswert*) miserably; hopelessly; pitifully; **~ versagen** fail miserably *or* hopelessly; [C] (*ärmlich*) pitifully; miserably; [D] (*abwertend: schlecht*) pathetically; hopelessly; [E] (*sehr, stark*) terribly (*coll.*); **~ frieren** be frozen stiff

**Jämmerlich·keit** *die;* **~** [A] (*Jammer*) mournfulness; [B] (*Elend*) wretchedness; [C] (*Ärmlichkeit*) pitifulness; wretchedness; [D] (*abwertend*) (*eines Menschen*) contemptibility; (*einer Arbeit usw.*) uselessness

**Jämmerling** /ˈjɛmɐlɪŋ/ *der;* **~s, ~e** (*ugs. abwertend*) (*Feigling*) chicken (*coll.*); (*Schwächling*) weakling

**jammern** ❶ *itr. V.* [A] wail; **ohne zu ~:** without so much as a groan; **Jammern und Klagen** groans and cries *pl.*; [B] (*sich beklagen*) moan; grumble; **über sein Schicksal ~:** bemoan one's fate; [C] (*verlangen*) cry [out]; **die Kinder jammerten nach einem Stück Brot** the children were crying out for *or* crying after a piece of bread. ❷ *tr. V.* (*geh.: Mitleid erregen*) grieve; distress; **er/sein Elend jammert mich** his distress grieves me; my heart goes out to him in his distress

**jammer-, Jammer-:** **~schade** *Adj.* (*ugs.*) **es ist ~schade, dass ...** it's a crying shame that ...; **es ist ~schade um ihn** it's a great pity about him; **~tal** *das* (*geh.*) vale of tears; **dieses irdische ~tal** this earthly vale of tears; **~voll** ❶ *Adj.* [A] (*Jammer ausdrückend*) pathetic; pitiful ‹cry etc.›; [B] (*beklagenswert*) miserable; ❷ *adv.* [A] (*Jammer ausdrückend*) pathetically; pitifully; [B] (*beklagenswert*) miserably; wretchedly

**Jan.** *Abk.* **Januar**

**Janker** /ˈjaŋkɐ/ *der;* **~s, ~** (*südd., österr.*) Alpine jacket

**Jänner** /ˈjɛnɐ/ *der;* **~s, ~** (*österr.*), **Januar** /ˈjanuaːɐ̯/ *der;* **~[s], ~e** ▶ 207 January; ⇒ *auch* **April**

**janus-, Janus-**/ˈjaːnʊs-/: **~gesicht** *das*, **~kopf** *der* Janus face; **~köpfig** *Adj.* Janus-faced

**Japan** /ˈjaːpan/ (*das*); **~s** Japan

**Japaner** *der;* **~s, ~, Japanerin** *die;* **~, ~nen** ▶ 553 Japanese; ⇒ *auch* **-in**

**japanisch** *Adj.* ▶ 553, ▶ 696 Japanese; **das Japanische Meer** the Sea of Japan; **Japanisch/das Japanische** Japanese; ⇒ *auch* **Deutsch**

**Japan·lack** *der* Chinese *or* Japanese lacquer

**Japan·papier** *das* rice paper

**Japs** /japs/ *der;* **~es, ~e** (*ugs. abwertend*) Jap (*derog.*)

**japsen** /ˈjapsn̩/ *itr. V.* (*ugs.*) pant; **ich kann kaum noch ~:** I'm gasping for breath

**Japser** *der;* **~s, ~** (*ugs.*) gasp of breath

**Jargon** /jarˈgõː/ *der;* **~s, ~s** [A] (*Gruppensprache*) jargon; **der ~ der Juristen/Mediziner** legal/medical jargon; **der ~ der Journalisten** journalese; **der Berliner ~:** Berlin slang; **im „Spiegel"-~:** in the jargon of the 'Spiegel'; [B] (*abwertend: ungepflegte Ausdrucksweise*) language; **er redet in einem ganz ordinären ~:** he uses very vulgar language

**Ja·sager** /-zaːgɐ/ *der;* **~s, ~, Ja·sagerin** *die;* **~, ~nen** (*abwertend*) yes-man

**Jasmin** /jasˈmiːn/ *der;* **~s, ~e** [A] (*Echter ~*) jasmine; [B] (*Falscher ~*) mock orange; syringa

**Jasmin·tee** *der* jasmine tea

**Jaspis** /ˈjaspɪs/ *der;* **~** *od.* **~ses, ~se** jasper

**Jass, *Jaß** /jas/ *der;* **Jasses** (*schweiz.*) jass

**jassen** *itr. V.* (*schweiz.*) play jass

**Ja·stimme** *die* yes-vote; **die ~n** the votes in favour; the ayes (*Brit. Parl.*)

**jäten** /ˈjɛːtn̩/ *tr., itr. V.* weed; **Unkraut ~:** weed; **Brennnesseln ~:** pull out *or* weed out stinging nettles

**Jauche** /ˈjauxə/ *die;* **~, ~n** [A] liquid manure; [B] (*ugs. abwertend*) muck

**Jauche·grube** *die* liquid-manure reservoir

**jauchen** *tr., itr. V.* (*Landw.*) manure

**jauchzen** /ˈjauxtsn̩/ *itr. V.* [A] (*laut jubeln*) cheer; **vor Freude ~:** shout for joy; **der Säugling jauchzte laut** the baby gurgled with pleasure; **das Publikum jauchzte** the audience was in raptures; [B] (*veralt.*) rejoice; **jauchzet dem Herrn** rejoice in the Lord

**Jauchzer** *der;* **~s, ~:** cry of delight

**jaulen** /ˈjaulən/ *itr. V.* ‹dog, cat, etc.› howl, yowl; ‹wind› howl; ‹engine› scream

**Jause** /ˈjauzə/ *die;* **~, ~n** (*österr.*) [A] snack; **eine ~ machen** have a snack; [B] (*Nachmittagskaffee*) [afternoon] tea

**Jausen·station** *die* (*österr.*) café

**jausnen** *itr. V.* (*österr.*) have a snack

**Java** /ˈjaːva/ (*das*); **~s** Java

**ja·wohl** *Part.* [A] certainly; **~, Herr Oberst!** yes, sir!; [B] (*verstärkend*) **Kant, ~ Kant** Kant, no less

**jawoll** /jaˈvɔl/ (*ugs.*) ⇒ **jawohl**

**Ja·wort** *das* consent; **jmdm. das ~ geben** consent to marry sb.; **sich** (*Dat.*) **das ~ geben** accept each other in marriage

**Jazz** /dʒæz *od.* dʒɛs *od.* jats/ *der;* **~:** jazz

**Jazz·band** *die* jazz band

**jazzen** /ˈdʒɛsn̩ *od.* ˈjatsn̩/ *itr. V.* play jazz

**Jazzer** /ˈdʒɛsɐ *od.* ˈjatsɐ/ *der;* **~s, ~, Jazzerin** *die;* **~, ~nen** jazz musician

**Jazz·fan** *der* jazz fan

**jazzig** /ˈjatsɪç/ *Adj.* (*ugs.*) jazzy

**Jazz-:** **~kapelle** *die* jazz band; **~keller** *der* jazz cellar; **~musik** *die* jazz music **~rock** *der* jazz-rock

**je**[1] /jeː/ ❶ *Adv.* [A] (*jemals*) ever; **mehr/besser denn je** more/better than ever; **seit** *od.* **von je** always; for as long as anyone can remember; ⇒ *auch* **eh**[2] B; [B] (*jeweils*) **je zehn Personen** ten people at a time; **die Gruppen bestehen aus je acht Mitgliedern** the groups consist of eight members each; **die Kinder stellen sich je zwei und zwei auf** the children arrange themselves in twos *or* in pairs; **die Schränke sind je zwei Meter breit** the wardrobes are each two metres wide; **sie kosten je 30 DM** they cost 30 DM each; **er gab den Mädchen je eine Birne** he gave each of the girls a pear; **in Schachteln mit** *od.* **zu je 10 Stück verpackt** packed in boxes of ten; [C] (*entsprechend*) **je nach Gewicht/Geschmack** according to weight/taste.
❷ *Präp. mit Akk.* per; for each; **je angebrochene Stunde** for each *or* per hour or part of an hour.
❸ *Konj.* [A] **je länger, je lieber** the longer the better; **je früher du kommst, desto** *od.* **um so mehr Zeit haben wir** the earlier you come, the more time we'll have; [B] **je nachdem** it all depends; **wir gehen hin, je nachdem [ob] wir Zeit haben oder nicht** we'll go, depending on whether we have the time or not; **Willst du mitgehen? — Je nachdem** (*ugs.*) Do you want to come too? — I'll see

**je**[2] ❶ *Interj.* **ach je, wie schade!** oh dear *or* dear me, what a shame!; ⇒ *auch* **oje**. ❷ *Adv.* (*veralt.*) **je nun** well now

**Jeans** /dʒi:nz/ *Pl. od. die;* ~, ~ **A** *(Hose)* jeans *pl.;* denims *pl.;* **B** *(Stoff)* denim; jean[s] material

**Jeans-:** **~hose** *die* [pair of] jeans; **~jacke** *die* denim jacket; **~stoff** *der* denim; jean[s] material

**jeck** /jɛk/ *Adj.* *(rhein., meist abwertend)* *(leicht verrückt)* stupid; daft; *(wahnsinnig)* crazy

**Jeck** *der;* **~en, ~en** *(rhein.)* **A** *(abwertend: Verrückter)* idiot; **B** *(Fastnachter)* carnival clown

**jede** ⇒ **jeder**

**jeden·falls** *Adv.* **A** *(gewiss)* certainly; definitely; **B** *(zumindest)* at any rate; **ich ~ habe keine Lust mehr** I at any rate *or* for one have had enough; **C** *(so viel steht fest)* in any case; at any rate; anyway; **das steht ~ fest** that much is certain, in any case *or* at any rate *or* anyway

**jeder** /ˈje:dɐ/,/ **jede, jedes** *Indefinitpron. u. unbest. Zahlwort* **1** *attr.* **A** ▶ **833** *(alle)* every; **jeder einzelne Schüler** every single pupil; **jeder zweite Bürger** one out of *or* in every two citizens; **der Zug fährt jeden Tag/viermal jeden Tag** the train runs every day/four times a day; **B** *(verstärkend)* **das kann Ihnen jedes Kind sagen** any child could tell you that; **ohne jeden Zweifel** without any doubt; **ohne jeden Grund** without any reason whatever; for no reason whatever; **C** *(alle einzeln)* each; **jeder Mitspieler bekommt sechs Karten** each player receives six cards; **D** *(jeglicher)* all; **jede Hilfe kam zu spät** all help came too late; **hier wurde jedes Maß überschritten** that went beyond all bounds; **Menschen jeden** *od.* **jedes Alters** people of all ages; **„nehme jede Arbeit an"** 'all offers of work accepted'.
**2** *allein stehend* **A** *(alle)* everyone; everybody; **jeder** *od.* *(geh.)* **ein jeder darf mitkommen** everyone *or* everybody can come; **hier kennt jeder jeden** everybody knows everybody else here; *(verstärkend)* **jeder, der Lust hat, ist willkommen** anyone who wants to come is welcome; **das kann ja jeder** anyone can do that; **B** *(alle einzeln)* **jedes der Kinder** every one *or* each of the children; **jeder für sich hat Recht** each of us/you/them *etc.* is right in his own way; **jeder von uns kann helfen** each *or* every one of us can help; **jedem nach seinem Verdienst** to each according to his merits

**jeder-:** **~art** *indekl. unbest. Gattungsz.; indekl.* any kind *or* sort *or* type of; **er ist bereit, ~art Arbeit anzunehmen** he is prepared to take any kind of work; **~lei** *indekl. unbest. Gattungsz.; (geh.)* all kinds *or* sorts of; **~mann** *Indefinitpron.* everyone; everybody; **hier kann ~mann mitmachen** everyone *or* everybody *or* anyone *or* anybody can come along and join in; **das ist ~manns Pflicht** that is everyone's *or* everybody's duty; **Schnecken sind nicht ~manns Sache/Geschmack** snails are not to everyone's *or* everybody's taste; **~zeit** *Adv.* [at] any time; **natürlich, ~zeit!** of course, any time!

**jedes** ⇒ **jeder**

***jedes·mal** ⇒ **Mal¹**

**je·doch** *Konj., Adv.* however; **es war ~ zu spät** it was too late, however; it was, however, too late

**jedweder** /ˈje:tˈve:dɐ/, **jedwede, jedwedes** *Indefinitpron. u. unbest. Zahlwort (nachdrücklich, veralt.)* **A** *attr.* every; **ohne jedwede Rücksicht** without any consideration whatsoever; **B** *allein stehend* everyone; everybody

**Jeep** Ⓦ /dʒi:p/ *der;* **~s, ~s** jeep ®

**jeglicher** /ˈje:klɪçɐ/, **jegliche, jegliches** *Indefinitpron. u. unbest. Zahlw.* ⇒ **jeder 1 C, 2 B**

**je·her** /od. ˈ-ˈ-/ *Adv.* **seit** *od.* **von ~:** always; since *or* from time immemorial; **es wurde seit** *od.* **von ~ so gehandhabt, dass ...** the procedure has always been that ...

**Jehova** /jeˈho:va/ ⇒ **Zeuge**

**jein** /jain/ *Adv.* *(scherzh.)* yes and no

**Je·länger·je·lieber** *das;* **~s, ~** *(Bot.)* honeysuckle; woodbine

**jemals** /ˈje:ma:ls/ *Adv.* ever

**jemand** /ˈje:mant/ *Indefinitpron.* someone; somebody; *(fragend, verneinend)* anyone; anybody; **ich kenne ~[en], der ...** I know someone *or* somebody who ...; **sich mit ~[em] treffen** to meet someone *or* somebody; **ist da ~?** is anybody there?; **ich glaube nicht, dass da ~ ist** I don't think there's anybody there; **~ anders/Fremdes** someone *or* somebody else/strange; **ein gewisser Jemand** *(scherzh.)* a certain somebody; **kaum ~:** hardly *or* scarcely anyone *or* anybody

**Jemen** /ˈje:mən/ *(das);* **~s** *od. der;* **~[s]** Yemen; ⇒ *auch* **Irak**

**Jemenit** /jeməˈni:t/ *der;* **~en, ~en, Jemenitin** *die;* **~, ~nen** Yemenite; Yemeni

**jemenitisch** *Adj.* Yemenite; Yemeni

**jemine** /ˈje:mine/ *Interj.* *(veralt.)* **ach ~!** oh dear; dear me!

**jener** /ˈje:nɐ/, **jene, jenes** *Demonstrativpron.* *(geh.)* **1** *attr.* that; *(im Pl.)* those; **in jenem Haus dort** in that house [over] there; **vergleichen Sie dieses mit jenem Bild** compare this picture and that one; **zu jenem Zeitpunkt** at that time; **in jenen Tagen** in those days. **2** *allein stehend* that one; *(im Pl.)* those; **jene, die ...** those who ...; **ein Roman Bölls, in dem jener schildert, wie ...** a novel by Böll in which he describes how ...

**jenseitig** /ˈje:n- *od.* ˈjɛn-/ *Adj.* **A** *(gegenüberliegend)* opposite; far, opposite ‹bank, shore›; **B** *(geh.)* **die ~e Welt** *od.* **das Jenseitige** the next world; the hereafter

**jenseits** /ˈje:n-/ **1** *Präp. mit Gen.* on the other side of; *(in größerer Entfernung)* beyond; **~ des Urals** beyond the Urals; **~ des Flusses** on the other *or* far *or* opposite side of the river; **sie ist schon ~ der Vierzig** she's already over *or* *(coll.)* the wrong side of forty. **2** *Adv.* beyond; on the other side; **~ vom Rhein** on the other side of *or* beyond the Rhine; **eine Welt ~ von Hass und Gewalt** a world free from hatred and violence; ⇒ *auch* **gut 4 B**

**Jenseits** *das;* **~:** hereafter; beyond; **ins ~ abgerufen** *od.* **abberufen werden** *(geh. verhüll.)* pass away; **jmdn. ins ~ befördern** *(salopp)* bump sb. off *(coll.)*

**Jeremia** /jereˈmi:a/ *(der);* **~s** Jeremiah

**Jeremiade** /jereˈmja:də/ *die;* **~** *(geh., veralt.)* jeremiad

**Jersey¹** /ˈdʒø:ɐ̯zi/ *der;* **~[s], ~s** *(Textilind.)* jersey

**Jersey²** *das;* **~s, ~s** *(Sport: Trikot)* jersey

**Jersey·kleid** *das* jersey dress

**jerum** /ˈje:rʊm/ *Interj.* ⇒ **ojerum**

**Jesaja** /jeˈza:ja/ *(der);* **~s** Isaiah

**Jessas [na]** /ˈjɛsas (na:)/ *Interj.* *(österr.)* my goodness

**Jesuit** /jeˈzu̯i:t/ *der;* **~en, ~en** *(Rel., auch abwertend)* Jesuit

**Jesuiten-:** **~general** *der* General of the Jesuits; **~orden** *der* order of Jesuits; Society of Jesus; **~schule** *die* Jesuit school

**Jesuitentum** *das;* **~s** Jesuitism

**Jesus** /ˈje:zʊs/ *(der);* **Jesu** /ˈje:zu/ Jesus; **~ Christus** Jesus Christ

**Jesus-:** **~kind** *das:* **das ~kind** the Infant Jesus; baby Jesus *(child lang.)*; **~knabe** *der* ⇒ **~kind**; **~latschen** *der* *(scherzh.)* Jesus sandal *(joc.)*

**Jesus[, Maria und Josef]** *Interj.* *(veralt.)* oh [my] Lord

**Jet** /dʒɛt/ *der;* **~[s], ~s** jet; **mit einem ~ fliegen/reisen** fly/travel by jet

**Jet·flug** *der* flight by jet

**Jeton** /ʒəˈtõ:/ *der;* **~s, ~s** **A** *(Spielmarke)* gaming chip *or* token; **B** *(für das Telefon usw.)* token

**Jetset, *Jet-set** /ˈdʒɛtsɛt/ *der;* **~s, ~s** jet set

**jetten** /ˈdʒɛtn̩/ *itr. V.; mit sein (ugs.)* jet

**jetzig** /ˈjɛtsɪç/ *Adj.* present; current; **in der ~en Zeit** at present; in present times

**jetzo** /ˈjɛtso/ *(veralt.)* ⇒ **jetzt**

**jetzt** /jɛtst/ *Adv.* **A** *(im Augenblick)* at the moment; just now; **bis ~:** up to now; **bis ~ noch nicht** not yet; not so far; **von ~ an** *od.* **ab** from now on[wards]; **~ noch** still; **was, ~ [so spät] noch?** what, now?; **das geht nicht von ~ auf nachher** *(ugs.)* it can't be done at a moment's notice; **~ oder nie!** it's now or never; **~ ist aber Schluss!** that's [quite] enough!; **B** *(nun, nunmehr)* now; **~ ist es aus mit uns** we've had it now; **sie ist gerade ~ weggegangen** she has just left; **~ endlich** [now,] at last; **~ erst [einmal]** just; **erst ~** *od.* **~ erst** only just; **schon ~:** already; **er ist ~ schon drei Wochen krank** he has been ill for three weeks now; **C** *(heutzutage)* now; these days; nowadays; **D** *(landsch.: wohl)* **von wem wird ~ der Brief sein?** now, who will that letter be from, I wonder?

**Jetzt** *das;* **~** *(geh.)* **das ~:** the present

**Jetzt·zeit** *die* present times *pl.;* **in der ~:** in present times; in our times

**je·weilen** *Adv.* *(schweiz.)* occasionally; once in a while

**jeweilig** /ˈje:vailɪç/ *Adj.* **A** *(in einem bestimmten Fall)* particular; **nach den ~en Umständen** according to the particular circumstances; **B** *(zu einer bestimmten Zeit)* current; of the time *postpos., not pred.;* **nach der ~en Mode** in the current fashion; in the fashion of the time; **C** *(zugehörig, zugewiesen)* respective

**jeweils** /ˈje:vails/ *Adv.* **A** *(jedesmal)* **~ am ersten/letzten Mittwoch des Monats** on the first/last Wednesday of each month; **B** *(zur jeweiligen Zeit)* currently; at the time; **die ~ amtierende Regierung** the government of the day

**Jg.** *Abk.* **Jahrgang**

**Jh.** *Abk.* **Jahrhundert** c.

**jiddeln** /ˈjɪdl̩n/ ⇒ **jüdeln**

**jiddisch** /ˈjɪdɪʃ/ *Adj.* ▶ **696** Yiddish; **Jiddisch/das Jiddische** Yiddish; ⇒ *auch* **Deutsch**

**Jitterbug** /ˈdʒɪtəbʌg/ *der;* **~:** jitterbug

**Jiu-Jitsu** /dʒi:uˈdʒɪtsu/ *das;* **~[s]** j[i]u-jitsu

**Jive** /dʒaɪv/ *der;* **~:** jive; **~ tanzen** jive

**Job¹** /jo:p/ ⇒ **Hiob**

**Job²** /dʒɔp/ *der;* **~s, ~s** ▶ **159** *(ugs.; auch DV)* job

**jobben** *itr. V.* *(ugs.)* do a job/jobs; **als Taxifahrer ~:** do [some] taxi-driving

**Jobber** *der;* **~s, ~, Jobberin** *die;* **~, ~nen** *(Börsenw.)* [stock] jobber; *(ugs. abwertend)* jobber *(derog.)*

**Joch** /jɔx/ *das;* **~[e]s, ~e** **A** *(bei Zugtieren)* yoke; **Ochsen/Kühe ins/unters ~ spannen** yoke oxen/cows; **das ~ der Tyrannei abschütteln** *(fig. geh.)* throw *or* cast off the yoke of tyranny; **B** *(Gespann, Feldmaß)* **zwei ~ Ochsen/Land** two yoke of oxen/land; **C** *(Geogr.)* col; saddle; **D** *(Archit.)* bay

**Joch·bein** *das* ▶ **471** *(Anat.)* zygomatic bone; malar bone

**Jockei, Jockey** /ˈdʒɔke *od.* ˈdʒɔki/ *der;* **~s, ~s** ▶ **159** jockey

**Jockey·mütze** *die* jockey cap

**Jod** /jo:t/ *das;* **~[e]s** iodine

**Jodel·lied** *das* yodelling song

**jodeln** /ˈjo:dl̩n/ *itr., tr. V.* yodel

**jod·haltig** *Adj.* iodiferous

**Jodler** *der;* **~s, ~** **A** *(Person)* yodeller; **B** *(kurzes Jodeln)* yodel; **C** ⇒ **Jodellied**

**Jodlerin** *die;* **~, ~nen** yodeller

**Jod-:** **~tinktur** *die* tincture of iodine; iodine tincture; **~zahl** *die* *(Chemie)* iodine number; iodine value

**Joga** /ˈjo:ga/ *der od. das;* **~[s]** yoga; **~ betreiben** *od.* *(ugs.)* **machen** practise *or* *(coll.)* do yoga

**Joga·übung** *die* yoga exercise

**joggen** /ˈdʒɔgn̩/ *itr. V.; mit Richtungsangabe mit sein* jog; **[zwei Kilometer] ~:** go jogging [for two km]

J

**Jogging** /ˈdʒɔgɪŋ/ *das;* ~s jogging *no art.*

**Joghurt** /ˈjo:gʊrt/ *der od. das;* ~[s], ~[s] yoghurt

**Joghurt·becher** *der* yoghurt pot (*Brit.*) *or* (*Amer.*) container

**Jogi** /ˈjo:gi/ *der;* ~s, ~s, **Jogin** /ˈjo:gɪn/ *der;* ~s, ~s yogi

**Johann** /ˈjo:han/ (*der*) John

**Johanna** /joˈhana/ (*die*): ~ von Orléans Joan of Arc

**Johannes** /joˈhanəs/ ❶ (*der*) John; ~ der Täufer John the Baptist. ❷ *der;* ~, ~se (*salopp*) ⇒ **Jonny**

**Johannes·evangelium** *das* St John's Gospel; Gospel according to St John

**Johanni** /joˈhani/ (*das*); *indekl.* ⇒ **Johannistag**

**Johannis·beere** *die* Ⓐ (*Frucht*) currant; rote/weiße/schwarze ~n redcurrants/white currants/blackcurrants; Ⓑ (*Strauch*) currant [bush]; rote/weiße/schwarze ~n redcurrant/white currant/blackcurrant bushes

**Johannisbeer-:** ~saft *der* currant juice; ~strauch *der* currant bush

**Johannis-:** ~brot *das* (*Bot.*) Saint-John's-bread; carob [bean]; ~brot·baum *der* (*Bot.*) Saint-John's-bread; carob [tree]; ~feuer *das* Saint John's fire; ~käfer *der* (*südd.*) ⇒ **Leuchtkäfer**; ~kraut *das* Saint John's wort; ~tag *der* Saint John's the Baptist's day; ~trieb *der* (*Bot.*) Ⓐ (*das Austreiben*) Lammas growth; Ⓑ (*Trieb*) Lammas shoot

**Johanniter** /jo:haˈni:tɐ/ *der;* ~s, ~: Knight of St. John of Jerusalem

**Johanniter·orden** *der* Order of [the Hospital of] St. John of Jerusalem

**johlen** /ˈjo:lən/ ❶ *itr. V.* yell; (*vor Wut*) howl. ❷ *tr. V.* die Menge johlte Beifall/Pfuirufe the crowd yelled *or* roared its approval/howled *or* roared its disapproval

**Joint** /dʒɔɪnt/ *der;* ~s, ~s (*ugs.*) joint (*sl.*); einen ~ kreisen lassen pass a joint round

**Jointventure, Joint Venture** /ˈdʒɔɪnt ˈventʃə/ *das;* ~s, ~s (*Wirtsch.*) joint venture

**Jo-Jo** /jo(:)ˈjo:/ *das;* ~s, ~s yo-yo

**Joker** /ˈjo:kɐ *od.* dʒo:kɐ/ *der;* ~s, ~ (*Kartensp.*) joker

**Jokus** /ˈjo:kʊs/ *der;* ~, ~se (*veralt.*) seinen ~ mit etw./jmdm. haben tease sth./sb.; make fun of sth./sb.

**Jolle** /ˈjɔlə/ *die;* ~, ~n Ⓐ (*Sportboot*) [sailing] yacht; Ⓑ (*mit Schwert*) keel-centreboard yawl; Ⓒ (*Beiboot*) yawl; jolly [boat]

**Jollen·kreuzer** *der* dinghy cruiser

**Jongleur** /ʒɔŋˈglø:ɐ/ *der;* ~s, ~e, **Jongleurin** *die;* ~, ~nen juggler

**jonglieren** *tr., itr. V.* juggle; Bälle *od.* mit Bällen ~: juggle with balls; mit Zahlen ~: juggle [about] with figures; ich werde das schon irgendwie ~ (*ugs.*) I'll wangle (*coll.*) *or* work it somehow

**Jonny** /ˈdʒɔni/ *der;* ~s, ~s (*salopp: Penis*) John Thomas (*sl.*)

**Joppe** /ˈjɔpə/ *die;* ~, ~n heavy jacket

**Jordan** /ˈjɔrdan/ *der;* ~[s] ▶306 Jordan; über den ~ gehen (*verhüll.*) go the way of all flesh

**Jordanien** /jɔrˈda:ni̯ən/ (*das*); ~s Jordan

**Jordanier** *der;* ~s, ~, **Jordanierin** *die;* ~, ~nen Jordanian; ⇒ *auch* -in

**jordanisch** *Adj.* Jordanian

**Josef, Joseph** /ˈjo:zɛf/ (*der*) Joseph

**Joseph[s]·ehe** *die* unconsumated marriage

**Jot** /jɔt/ *das;* ~, ~: j, J; ⇒ *auch* a, A

**Jota** /ˈjo:ta/ *das;* ~[s], ~s iota; kein/nicht ein/um kein ~ (*geh.*) not an iota; not one jot

**Joule** /dʒu:l *od.* dʒaul/ *das;* ~[s], ~ (*Physik*) joule

**Jour** /ʒu:ɐ/ *der;* ~s, ~s (*veralt.*) open house; ~ fixe at-home

**Journaille** /ʒʊrˈnaljə *od.* ʒʊrˈnail/ *die;* ~ (*veralt. abwertend*) Ⓐ (*verantwortungslose Presse*) yellow *or* gutter press; Ⓑ (*Sensationsjournalisten*) hacks *pl.* (*derog.*)

**Journal** /ʒʊrˈna:l/ *das;* ~s, ~e Ⓐ (*veralt.: Tageszeitung*) journal (*dated*); newspaper; Ⓑ (*geh.: Zeitschrift*) journal; periodical; ein ~ für Mode/Kunst a fashion/an art journal *or* periodical; Ⓒ (*veralt.: Tagebuch*) journal (*dated*); diary; Ⓓ (*Schiffstagebuch*) log[book]; Ⓔ (*Kaufmannsspr.*) daybook

**Journal·beamte** *der*, **Journal·beamtin** *die* (*österr.*) official *or* officer [on duty]

**Journalismus** *der;* ~: journalism *no art.*

**Journalist** *der;* ~en, ~en ▶159 journalist

**Journalisten·deutsch** *das* (*oft abwertend*) journalese

**Journalistik** *die;* ~: journalism *no art.*

**Journalistin** *die;* ~, ~nen ▶159 journalist

**journalistisch** ❶ *Adj.* journalistic; eine ~e Ausbildung a training in journalism. ❷ *adv.* journalistically; ~ tätig sein work as *or* be a journalist

**jovial** /joˈvi̯a:l/ *Adj.* jovial

**Jovialität** /jovi̯aliˈtɛ:t/ *die;* ~: joviality

**Joystick** /ˈdʒɔɪstɪk/ *der;* ~s, ~s (*DV*) joystick

**jr.** *Abk.* junior Jr.

**Jubel** /ˈju:bl̩/ *der;* ~s (*das Jauchzen*) rejoicing; jubilation; (*laut*) cheering; ein großer ~ brach aus a loud cheer went up; unter dem ~ der Zuschauer amid the cheering *or* cheers of the spectators; ~, Trubel, Heiterkeit an atmosphere of eat, drink, and be merry

**Jubel-:** ~feier *die* jubilee; anniversary; (*Feierlichkeiten*) jubilee *or* anniversary celebrations *pl.*; ~greis *der* (*scherzh.*) old swinger (*coll. joc.*); ~jahr *das* jubilee; alle ~jahre [einmal] once in a blue moon

**jubeln** ❶ *itr. V.* cheer; über etw. (*Akk.*) ~: rejoice over sth.; celebrate sth.; ~de Instrumente/Klänge (*dichter.*) joyful instruments/sounds. ❷ *tr. V.* Beifall ~: applaud; give applause; „Hurra!", jubelte er 'hurrah!' he cried delightedly

**Jubel-:** ~paar *das* couple celebrating their wedding anniversary; ~perser *der* (*ugs. abwertend*) person hired to cheer in the/a crowd; ~ruf *der* cheer; joyful shout; (*religiös*) exultation; shout of praise

**Jubilar** /jubiˈla:ɐ/ *der;* ~s, ~e man celebrating his anniversary/birthday

**Jubilarin** *die;* ~, ~nen woman celebrating her anniversary/birthday

**Jubiläum** /jubiˈlɛ:ʊm/ *das;* ~s, **Jubiläen** anniversary; (*eines Monarchen*) jubilee; fünfundzwanzigjähriges/fünfzigjähriges ~: twenty-fifth/fiftieth anniversary/jubilee; hundertjähriges ~: hundredth anniversary; centenary; 500jähriges/1 000jähriges ~: quincentenary/millenary; sein 25jähriges ~ bei der Firma begehen celebrate 25 years with the firm

**Jubiläums-:** ~ausgabe *die* jubilee edition; ~ausstellung *die* jubilee exhibition; ~heft *das* jubilee issue

**jubilieren** *itr. V.* (*geh. veralt.*) jubilate (*literary*); rejoice; die Lerche trällerte ~d the lark sang joyfully

**juchhe** /jʊxˈhe:/, **juchhei**/jʊxˈhai̯/, **juchheirassa[ssa]** /jʊxˈhai̯rasa(sa)/ (*veralt.*), **juchheißa** /jʊxˈhai̯sa/ *Interj.* (*veralt.*) hurrah

**Juchten** /ˈjʊxtn̩/ *der od. das;* ~s Ⓐ (*Leder*) Russia [leather]; Ⓑ (*Duftstoff*) Russian leather

**juchzen** /ˈjʊxtsn̩/ *itr. V.* (*ugs.*) shout with glee

**Juchzer** *der;* ~s, ~ (*ugs.*) shout of glee; einen ~ ausstoßen shout with glee

**jucken** /ˈjʊkn̩/ ❶ *tr., itr. V.* Ⓐ mir juckt die Haut I itch; es juckt mir *od.* mich auf dem Kopf my head itches; es juckt mich am ganzen Körper I itch all over; es juckt mich hier I've got an itch here; wens juckt, der kratze sich (*fig.*) anybody who does not like it should say something; Ⓑ (*Juckreiz verursachen*) irritate; die Wolle juckt ihn *od.* ihm auf der Haut the wool makes him itch; the wool irritates his skin; ein ~der Hautausschlag an itching rash; Ⓒ (*bes. nordd. salopp*) lass ~! get a move on! (*coll.*). ❷ *tr. V.* (*reizen, verlocken*) es juckt mich, das zu tun I am itching *or* dying to do it; ihn juckt das Geld he is tempted by the money; das juckt mich nicht (*ugs.*) I couldn't care less (*coll.*). ❸ *refl. V.* (*ugs.: sich kratzen*) scratch

**Jucken** *das;* ~s itching; ein ~ verspüren feel an itch

**Juck-:** ~pulver *das* itching powder; ~reiz *der* itch

**Judäa** /juˈdɛ:a/ (*das*); ~s Jud[a]ea

**Judaika** /juˈda:ika/ *Pl.* Judaica

**Judaist** *der;* ~en, ~en, **Judaistin** *die;* ~, ~nen specialist in Jewish studies; (*Student*) student of Jewish studies

**Judaistik** *die;* ~: Jewish studies *pl.*, *no art.*

**Judas** /ˈju:das/ ❶ (*der*); **Judas'** Judas; ~ Ischariot Judas Iscariot. ❷ *der;* ~, ~se (*fig.*) Judas

**Jude** /ˈju:də/ *der;* ~n, ~n Jew; er ist ~: he is a Jew; he is Jewish

**jüdeln** /ˈjy:dl̩n/ *itr. V.* speak half Yiddish

**Juden-:** ~frage *die* (*ns. verhüll.*) Jewish question; ~hass, *~haß *der* anti-Semitism; hatred of [the] Jews; ~hetze *die* Jew-baiting; ~pogrom *der od. das* pogrom against the Jews; ~stern *der* (*ns.*) Star of David

**Judentum** *das;* ~s Ⓐ (*Volk*) Jewry; Jews *pl.*; das gesamte ~: the whole of Jewry; Ⓑ (*Kultur u. Religion*) Judaism; Ⓒ (*jüdisches Wesen*) Jewishness

**Juden-:** ~verfolgung *die* persecution of [the] Jews; ~viertel *das* Jewish quarter; (*hist.*) Jewry

**Judikative** /judikaˈti:və/ *die;* ~, ~n (*Rechtsw., Politik*) judiciary

**Judikatur** /judikaˈtu:ɐ/ *die;* ~, ~en (*Rechtsw.*) judicature

**Jüdin** /ˈjy:dɪn/ *die;* ~, ~nen Jewess; sie ist ~: she is Jewish *or* a Jewess

**jüdisch** *Adj.* Jewish; ~ fühlen/denken feel/think like a Jew

**judizieren** /judiˈtsi:rən/ *itr. V.* (*Rechtsspr.*) administer justice

**Judo** /ˈju:do/ *das;* ~[s] judo *no art.*

**Judo·griff** *der* judo throw; (*Haltegriff*) judo hold

**Judoka** /juˈdo:ka/ *der;* ~[s], ~[s] judoka; judoist

**Jugend** /ˈju:gn̩t/ *die;* ~ Ⓐ youth; in ihrer ~: in her youth; when she was young; schon in früher ~: at an early age; seit früher ~, schon von ~ auf from an early age; from his/her *etc.* youth; Ⓑ (*Jugendliche*) young people; die ~ der Welt the youth *or* the young people of the world; die weibliche/männliche ~: girls *pl.*/boys *pl.*; er spielt in der ~ (*Sport*) he plays in the youth side *or* team; die reifere ~ (*scherzh.*) the over-forties *pl.*; Ⓒ (*Biol., Med.*) immature stage [of development]

**jugend-, Jugend-:** ~alkoholismus *der* alcoholism among young people; ~alter *das* adolescence; ~amt *das* youth office (*agency responsible for education and welfare of young people*); ~arbeit *die* Ⓐ (*Bildung und Erziehung*) youth work; Ⓑ (*Erwerbstätigkeit*) youth employment; employment of young people; ~arbeitslosigkeit *die* youth unemployment; ~arbeits·schutz *der* protection of young people at work; ~arrest *der* detention in a community home; zu vier Wochen ~arrest verurteilt werden be sentenced to four weeks in a community home; ~bewegt *Adj.* (*meist scherzh.*) boy-scoutish; ~bewegung *die* (*hist.*) [German] Youth Movement; ~bild *das:* ein ~bild seines Vaters/seiner Mutter a picture of his father/mother as a young man/woman; ~brigade *die* (*DDR*) youth brigade; ~buch *das* book for young people; ~erinnerung *die* memory of one's youth; (*Foto usw.*) memento of one's youth; ~film *der* film for young people; ~frei *Adj.* ‹film, book, etc.› suitable for persons under 18; nicht ~frei ‹film› 18 certificate *pred.*; (*scherzh.*) ‹joke, story, etc.› not for young ears *pred.*; ~freund *der*, ~freundin *die* Ⓐ friend of [the days of] one's youth; er ist ein ~freund von ihr he used to be a friend of hers when she was young; Ⓑ

*old spelling (see note on page 1707)

(*DDR*) FDJ member; **~frische** *die* youthfulness; **~funk** *der* programmes *pl.* for young people; **~gefährdend** *Adj.* liable to have an undesirable influence on the moral development of young people *postpos.;* **~gericht** *das* juvenile court; **~gruppe** *die* youth group; **~heim** *das* youth centre; **~herberge** *die* youth hostel; **~klub** *der* youth club; **~kriminalität** *die* juvenile delinquency

**jugendlich** /ˈjuːgn̩tlɪç/ ❶ *Adj.* [A] young ‹offender, customer, etc.›; **noch in ~em Alter sein** still be a youngster; still be young; [B] (*für Jugendliche charakteristisch*) youthful; **in ~er Begeisterung** fired by the spirit of youth *or* by youthful enthusiasm; [C] (*jung wirkend*) youthful ‹person, appearance›; **sie ist/wirkt noch sehr ~:** she still is/looks very young; [D] (*bes. Werbespr.*) young ‹fashions, dress, hairstyle, etc.›. ❷ *adv.* **sich ~ kleiden** dress young

**Jugendliche** /ˈjuːgn̩tlɪçə/ *der/die; adj. Dekl.* [A] young person; **die ~n** the young people; [B] (*Rechtsspr.*) juvenile; young person; **zwei ~:** two juveniles; two young persons; **ein 16jähriger ~r/eine 16jährige ~:** a 16-year-old youth/girl

**Jugendlichkeit** *die* youth; (*jugendliche Wirkung*) youthfulness

**Jugend-: ~liebe** *die* love *or* sweetheart of one's youth; **seine/ihre [alte] ~liebe** the love *or* sweetheart of his/her youth; **~mannschaft** *die* (*Sport*) youth team *or* side; **~meister** *der*, **~meisterin** *die* youth champion; (*Mannschaft*) youth champions; **~meisterschaft** *die* youth championship; **~objekt** *das* (*DDR*) youth project; **~pfleger** *der*, **~pflegerin** *die* youth worker; **~psychologie** *die* psychology of adolescence; adolescent psychology *no art.;* **~recht** *das* laws *pl.* relating to young persons; **~schutz** *der* protection of young people; **~schutz·gesetz** *das* laws *pl.* protecting young people; **~sprache** *die* young people's language *no art.;* **~stil** *der* art nouveau; (*in Deutschland*) Jugendstil; **Möbel im ~stil** art nouveau/Jugendstil furniture; **~straf·anstalt** *die* detention centre; **~strafe** *die* youth custody sentence; **sechs Monate ~strafe bekommen** get six months in a detention centre; **~sünde** *die*, **~torheit** *die* youthful folly; **~traum** *der* youthful dream; **es war sein ~traum gewesen, zu ...** when he was young, it had been his ambition to ...; **~verband** *der* youth organization; **~vorstellung** *die* performance for young people; **~weihe** *die* [A] (*DDR*) *ceremony in which fourteen-year-olds were given adult social status;* [B] *Freechurch ceremony for child of primary school leaving age, in place of confirmation;* **~werk** *das* early *or* youthful work; (*gesamtes*) early *or* youthful works *pl.;* juvenilia *pl.;* **~zeit** *die* youth; younger days *pl.;* **~zeitschrift** *die* magazine for young people; **~zentrum** *das* youth centre

**Jugo·slawe** /jugo-/ *der* ▶ 553 Yugoslav

**Jugo·slawien** (*das*); **~s** Yugoslavia

**Jugo·slawin** *die* ▶ 553 Yugoslav; ⇒ *auch* **-in**

**jugo·slawisch** *Adj.* ▶ 553 Yugoslav[ian]

**juhu** *Interj.* [A] /juˈhuː/ (*Ausruf des Jubels*) yippee; hooray; [B] /ˈjuˈhuː/ (*Zuruf*) yoo-hoo

**Juice** /dʒuːs/ *der od. das;* ~, **~s** /ˈdʒuːsɪs/ (*bes. österr., DDR: Fruchtsaft*) (*esp. citrus*) [fruit] juice; (*DDR: Gemüsesaft*) vegetable juice

**Julei** /juːˈlai/ *der;* **~[s]**, **~s** ⇒ **Juli**

**Jul·fest** /ˈjuːl-/ *das* Yuletide festival

**Juli** /ˈjuːli/ *der;* **~[s]**, **~s** ▶ 207 July; ⇒ *auch* **April**

**Jumbo·jet**, ***Jumbo-Jet** /ˈjʊmbo-/ *der* jumbo jet

**Jumelage** /ʒymˈlaːʒ/ *die;* ~, **~n zwischen Bonn und Oxford besteht eine ~:** Bonn and Oxford are twinned (*Brit.*) *or* (*Amer.*) are sister cities

**Jumper** /ˈdʒampɐ/ *der;* **~s**, **~:** jumper (*Brit.*); pullover

**jun.** *Abk.* **junior** Jr.

**jung** /jʊŋ/ *Adj.;* **jünger** /ˈjʏŋɐ/, **jüngst...** /ˈjʏŋst.../ [A] ▶ 76 young; **in ~en Jahren** at an early age; **er ist ~ gestorben** he died young; **in seinen ~en Jahren** in the days of his youth; **~ an Jahren sein** be young [in years]; **der jüngere Bruder** the younger brother; **die jüngste Tochter** the youngest daughter; **der ~e Meier** (*ugs.*) Meier junior; **Sport erhält ~:** sport keeps you young; [B] (*neu*) young ‹state, country, firm, foliage›; new ‹project, undertaking, sport, marriage, etc.›; **die Nacht ist noch ~:** the night is young; **der ~e Tag** (*geh.*) the new day; [C] (*letzt...*) recent; **in jüngster Zeit** recently; lately; **ein Ereignis der jüngeren/jüngsten Geschichte** an event in recent/very recent history; **die jüngsten Geschehnisse** the latest *or* [most] recent happenings; [D] (*ugs. scherzh.*) **er ist ganze 30 Jahre ~:** he's 30 years young; [E] **der Jüngste Tag** doomsday; ⇒ *auch* **Gericht**[1] D; **jünger**

**Jung-: ~akademiker** *der*, **~akademikerin** *die* newly-qualified [university] graduate; **~arbeiter** *der*, **~arbeiterin** *die* young worker; **~bauer** *der;* **~~n**, **~~n** young farmer; **~bäuerin** *die* young farmer's wife; **~brunnen** *der* Fountain of Youth; **das ist ein wahrer ~brunnen** (*fig.*) that's a real tonic; **~bürger** *der*, **~bürgerin** *die* (*bes. österr.*) first-time voter; new voter

**Jungchen** *das;* **~s**, ~ (*bes. ostd.*) little boy; little lad; **mein ~:** my boy *or* lad

**Jung·demokrat** *der*, **Jung·demokratin** *die* Young Democrat

**Junge**[1] /ˈjʊŋə/ *der;* **~n**, **~n** *od.* (*ugs.*) **Jung[en]s** [A] boy; (*Lauf~*, *Lehr~*) boy; lad; **Tag, alter ~!** (*ugs.*) hello, old pal! (*coll.*); **jmdn. wie einen dummen ~n behandeln** (*ugs.*) treat sb. like a child; **~, ~!** (*ugs.*) [boy,] oh boy!; ⇒ *auch* **schwer** 1 E; [B] (*ugs.: beim Kartenspiel*) jack; knave

**Junge**[2] *das; adj. Dekl.* **ein ~s** one of the young; **~ kriegen** give birth to young; **eine Löwin und ihr ~s** a lioness and her cub

**Jüngelchen** /ˈjʏŋl̩çən/ *das;* **~s**, ~ (*ugs. abwertend*) young puppy *or* cub

**jungen** *itr. V.* give birth; produce young; ‹cat› have kittens; ‹dog› have pups

**jungenhaft** ❶ *Adj.* boyish. ❷ *adv.* **seine Stimme klang ~ hell** his voice was high and clear like a boy's; **sie kleidet sich ~:** she dresses boyishly

**Jungen-: ~klasse** *die* boys' class; **wir waren eine reine ~klasse** our class was all boys; **~schule** *die* boy's school; school for boys; **~streich** *der* boyish prank

**jünger** /ˈjʏŋɐ/ *Adj.* youngish; **sie ist noch ~:** she is still quite young; ⇒ *auch* **jung**

**Jünger** *der;* **~s**, **~:** follower; disciple; (*der Kunst, Literatur*) devotee; **Jesus und seine ~:** Jesus and his disciples

**Jüngere** *der/die; adj. Dekl.* **die ~n unter Ihnen** the younger ones amongst you; **die ~n werden das nicht mehr wissen** younger people won't remember it; **Lucas Cranach der ~:** Lucas Cranach the younger

**Jüngerin** *die;* ~, **~nen** ⇒ **Jünger**

**Jungfer** /ˈjʊŋfɐ/ *die;* ~, **~n** [A] (*veralt.*) (*Fräulein*) young lady; (*als Anrede*) Mistress; [B] (*abwertend: ältere ledige Frau*) spinster; **eine alte ~:** an old maid

**Jungfern-: ~fahrt** *die* maiden voyage; **~flug** *der* maiden flight; **~häutchen** *das* hymen; **~kranz** *der* (*veralt.*) ⇒ **Brautkranz**; **~rede** *die* maiden speech; **~zeugung** *die* (*Biol.*) parthenogenesis

**Jung·frau** *die* [A] virgin; **sie ist noch ~:** she is still a virgin; **die Heilige ~:** the Holy Virgin; **die ~ Maria** the Virgin Mary; **die eiserne ~:** the iron maiden; **zu etw. kommen wie die ~ zum Kind[e]** get sth. by sheer chance or luck; **wir sind zu den Büchern gekommen wie die ~ zum Kind[e]** we have no idea how the books got here; [B] (*Astrol.*) Virgo; ⇒ *auch* **Fisch** C; [C] (*veralt.: junges Mädchen*) young maid *or* maiden (*arch.*)

**jung·fräulich** /-frɔylɪç/ *Adj.* (*geh.*, *auch fig.*) virgin; virginal ‹innocence, appearance›; **~ in die Ehe gehen** be a virgin bride; **ihr ~er Leib** (*dichter.*) her chaste body

**Jungfräulichkeit** *die* (*geh.*) virginity; (*fig.: von Wald, Erde usw.*) virgin state

**Jung·geselle** *der* bachelor; **~ bleiben** remain a bachelor

**Jung·gesellen-: ~bude** *die* (*ugs.*) bachelor pad (*coll.*); **~leben** *das* bachelor['s] life; **~wirtschaft** *die* (*ugs.*, *oft scherzh.*) **ich habe die ~wirtschaft satt** I've had enough of looking after myself; **~wohnung** *die* bachelor flat; **~zeit** *die* bachelor days *pl.;* bachelorhood

**Jung-: ~gesellin** *die* bachelor girl; **sie ist ~gesellin geblieben** she never married; **~lehrer** *der*, **~lehrerin** *die* probationary teacher (*teaching before second Staatsexamen*)

**Jüngling** /ˈjʏŋlɪŋ/ *der;* **~s**, **~e** (*geh./spött.*) youth; boy; **ein grüner** *od.* **unreifer ~** (*spött.*) a raw youth

**Jünglings-: ~alter** *das* (*geh.*) youth; **im zarten ~alter** as a tender youth; **~jahre** *Pl.* (*geh.*) years of one's youth; young years

**Jung-: ~mädel** *das* (*ns.*)**:** *girl member of the Hitler Youth, aged 10-14;* **~mann** *der* (*veralt.*) young man; **~sozialist** *der*, **~sozialistin** *die* Young Socialist

**jüngst** /jʏŋst/ *Adv.* (*geh.*) recently

**jüngst...** ⇒ **jung**

**Jüngste** *der/die; adj. Dekl.* youngest [one]; **die ~n** the youngest ones

**Jung-: ~steinzeit** *die* Neolithic period; New Stone Age; **~tier** *das* young animal; **~trieb** *der* new growth; **~verheiratete** *der/die; adj. Dekl.*, **~vermählte** *der/die; adj. Dekl.* (*geh.*) young married man/woman; **die ~verheirateten** the newly-weds; **~volk** *das* [A] (*veralt.*) young folk; [B] (*ns.*) *10-14-year-old members of the Hitler Youth;* **~wähler** *der*, **~wählerin** *die* first-time voter; new voter; **~wald** *der* (*Forstw.*) young forest/wood

**Juni** /ˈjuːni/ *der;* **~[s]**, **~s** ▶ 207 June; ⇒ *auch* **April**

**Juni·käfer** *der* summer chafer

**junior** /ˈjuːnjɔr/ *indekl. Adj.; nach Personennamen* junior

**Junior** *der;* **~s**, **~en** /-ˈnjoːrən/ [A] (*oft scherzh.*) junior (*joc.*); **mit seinem ~:** with junior; [B] (*Kaufmannsspr.*) junior partner; [C] (*Sport*) junior

**Junior·chef** *der*, **Junior·chefin** *die* owner's *or* (*coll.*) boss's son/daughter

**Junioren-: ~mannschaft** *die* youth team; **~meister** *der*, **~meisterin** *die* junior champion; (*Mannschaft*) junior champions; **~meisterschaft** *die* junior championship

**Juniorin** *die;* ~, **~nen** junior partner

**Junior·partner** *der*, **Junior·partnerin** *die* (*Kaufmannsspr.*) junior partner

**Junker** /ˈjʊŋkɐ/ *der;* **~s**, ~ [A] (*hist.*) junker; young nobleman; (*als Anrede*) young sir; [B] (*oft abwertend: Landadliger*) junker; squire

**Junkertum** *das;* **~s** (*hist.*) junkerdom; squirearchy

**Junkie** /dʒʌŋki/ *der;* **~s**, **~s** (*Drogenjargon*) junkie (*sl.*)

**Junktim** *das;* **~s**, **~s** package [deal]; **zwischen den beiden Abkommen besteht ein ~:** the two agreements form one package

**Juno** /juˈnoː/ *der;* **~[s]**, **~s** ⇒ **Juni**

**Junta** /ˈxʊnta/ *die;* ~, **Junten** junta

**Jupiter**[1] /ˈjuːpitɐ/ *der;* **~s** (*Astron.*), **[2]Jupiter** (*der*) (*Myth.*) Jupiter

**Jupon** /ʒyˈpõː/ *der;* **~[s]**, **~s** (*schweiz.*) petticoat; slip

**Jura**[1] /ˈjuːra/ *Pl.* law *sing.;* **~ studieren** read *or* study Law

**Jura**[2] *der;* **~s** (*Geol.*) Jurassic [period/system]

**juridisch** /juˈriːdɪʃ/ *Adj.* (*österr./veralt.*) ⇒ **juristisch**

**Jurisdiktion** /jurɪsdɪkˈtsi̯oːn/ *die;* ~, **~en** (*Rechtsw., kath. Kirche*) jurisdiction

**Jurisprudenz** /jurɪspruˈdɛnts/ *die;* ~ (*geh.*) jurisprudence *no art.*

**Jurist** *der;* **~en**, **~en** ▶ 159 lawyer; jurist

**Juristen·deutsch** *das* (*oft abwertend*) legal jargon

**Juristerei** *die;* ~ (*abwertend, oft scherzh.*) law *no art.*

**Juristin** *die;* ~, **~nen** ▶ 159 lawyer; jurist; ⇨ *auch* **-in**

**juristisch** ❶ *Adj.* legal ‹wrangle, term, training, career›; **eine ~e Staatsprüfung** a state law examination; **die Juristische Fakultät** the Law Faculty. ❷ *adv.* **~ denken** think in legal terms; **~ argumentieren** use legal arguments

**Juror** /'ju:rɔr/ *der;* **~s, ~en** /-'ro:rən/, **Jurorin** *die;* ~, **~nen** judge

**Jurte** /'jʊrtə/ *die;* ~, **~n** yurt

**Jury** /ʒy'ri:/ *die;* ~, **~s** Ⓐ (*Preisrichter*) panel [of judges]; jury; Ⓑ (*Sachverständige*) panel [of experts]

**Jus¹** /ju:s/ *das;* ~ (*österr., schweiz.*) ⇨ **Jura¹**

**Jus²** /ʒy:/ *die od. das od. der;* ~ Ⓐ (*Fleischsaft*) meat juices *pl.;* meat stock; Ⓑ (*schweiz.*) (*Fruchtsaft*) fruit juice; (*Gemüsesaft*) vegetable juice

**Juso** /'ju:zo/ *der;* **~s, ~s** Young Socialist

**just** /jʊst/ *Adv.* (*veralt., noch scherzh.*) just; **~ in diesem Augenblick** just at that moment; at that very moment; **~ an jenem Tag** on that very day

**justieren** *tr. V.* adjust

**Justierung** *die;* ~, **~en** adjustment

**Justitia** /jʊs'ti:tsi̯a/ *die;* ~**:** Justice *no art.;* (*Statue*) statue of Justice

**justitiabel** ⇨ **justiziabel**

**Justitiar** ⇨ **Justiziar**

**Justiz** /jʊs'ti:ts/ *die;* ~ Ⓐ justice; Ⓑ (*Behörden*) judiciary; **ein Vertreter der ~:** a representative of justice *or* of the law

**Justiz-: ~beamte** *der*, **~beamtin** *die* court official; **~behörde** *die* judicial authority

**justiziabel** /jʊsti'tsi̯a:bl̩/ *Adj.* (*geh.*) justiciable

**Justiziar** /jʊsti'tsi̯a:ɐ/ *der;* **~s, ~e, Justiziarin** *die;* ~, **~nen** company lawyer

**Justiz-: ~irrtum** *der* miscarriage of justice; **~minister** *der*, **~ministerin** *die* Minister of Justice; **~ministerium** *das* Ministry of Justice; **~mord** *der* judicial murder; **~vollzugsanstalt** *die* (*Amtsspr.*) penal institution (*formal*); prison; **~wachtmeister** *der*, **~wachtmeisterin** *die* court usher

**Jute** /'ju:tə/ *die;* ~**:** jute

**Jute·sack** *der* jute *or* gunny sack

**Jütland** /'jy:t-/ (*das*)*;* **~s** Jutland

**Juwel¹** /ju've:l/ *das od. der;* **~s, ~en** piece *or* item of jewellery; (*Edelstein*) jewel; gem; **Schmuck und ~en** jewellery

**Juwel²** *das;* **~s, ~e** (*Kostbarkeit*) gem; **ein ~ gotischer Baukunst** a gem *or* jewel of Gothic architecture

**Juwelen-: ~händler** *der*, **~händlerin** *die* dealer in precious stones; **~raub** *der* jewel robbery *or* theft

**Juwelier** /juvə'li:ɐ̯/ *der;* **~s, ~e, Juwelierin** *die;* ~, **~nen** ▶ 159 jeweller; ⇨ *auch* **Bäcker**

**Juwelier·geschäft** *das* jeweller's shop

**Jux** /jʊks/ *der;* **~es, ~e** (*ugs.*) joke; **aus ~:** as a joke; for fun; **sie machten sich** (*Dat.*) **einen ~ daraus, das zu tun** they did it as a joke *or* for a lark; **sich** (*Dat.*) **einen ~ mit jmdm. machen** play a [practical] joke on sb.; **aus [lauter] ~ und Tollerei** just for the fun *or* (*coll.*) hell of it

**Juxta·position** /'juksta-/ *die* (*Sprachw.*) juxtaposition

**jwd** /jɔtve:'de:/ *Adv.* (*ugs. scherzh.*) in *or* at the back of beyond; miles out

# Kk

**k, K** /ka:/ *das;* **~**, **~:** k/K; ⇒ *auch* **a**, **A**

**K** *Abk.* (*Physik*) **Kelvin** K

**Kabale** /ka'ba:lə/ *die;* **~**, **~n** (*veralt.*) cabal

**Kabarett** /kaba'rɛt/ *das;* **~s**, **~s** *od.* **~e** **A** satirical cabaret [show]; satirical revue; **ein politisches ~:** a satirical political revue; **B** (*Ensemble*) cabaret act; **C** (*Speiseplatte*) [revolvable] partitioned dish

**Kabarettist** *der;* **~en**, **~en**, **Kabarettistin** *die;* **~**, **~nen** revue performer

**kabarettistisch** *Adj.* [satirical] revue *attrib.*; **~e Szenen** scenes in the style of a [satirical] revue

**Kabäuschen** /ka'bɔysçən/ *das;* **~s**, **~** (*ugs.*) (*Zimmer*) cubbyhole; (*Häuschen*) little hut

**Kabbala** /'kabala/ *die;* **~:** cabbala

**Kabbalistik** *die;* **~:** cabbalism *no art.*

**Kabbelei** *die;* **~**, **~en** squabble

**kabbelig** *Adj.* (*Seemannsspr.*) choppy

**kabbeln** /'kabl̩n/ *refl. V.* (*ugs.*) squabble, bicker (**mit** with)

**Kabel** /'ka:bl̩/ *das;* **~s**, **~** **A** (*elektrische Leitung*) cable; (*für kleineres Gerät*) flex; **B** (*Stahltrosse*) cable; **C** (*veralt.: Telegramm*) cable

**Kabel-:** **~bericht** *der* (*veralt.*) cabled dispatch; **~fernsehen** *das* cable television

**Kabeljau** /'ka:bl̩jau/ *der;* **~s**, **~e** *od.* **~s** cod

**Kabel-:** **~länge** *die* (*Seew.*) cable['s length]; **~leger** *der;* **~~s**, **~~:** cable ship; **~mantel** *der* cable sheath

**kabeln** *tr., itr. V.* (*veralt.*) cable

**Kabel-:** **~rolle** *die* cable drum; **~schacht** *der* cable duct; (*in der Straße*) cable pit

**Kabine** /ka'bi:nə/ *die;* **~**, **~en** **A** (*auf Schiffen, in Flugzeugen*) cabin; **B** (*Umkleideraum, abgeteilter Raum*) cubicle; **in die ~n gehen** (*Fußball*) go back into the dressing rooms; **C** (*einer Seilbahn*) [cable] car

**Kabinen-:** **~bahn** *die* cableway; **~roller** *der* bubble car

**Kabinett** /kabi'nɛt/ *das;* **~s**, **~e** **A** (*Gesamtheit der Minister*) Cabinet; **B** (*veralt.: Arbeitszimmer*) cabinet (*arch.*); **C** (*österr.: kleines Zimmer*) small room with one window; boxroom (*Brit.*)

**Kabinetts-:** **~beschluss**, ***~beschluß** *der* Cabinet decision; **~bildung** *die* formation of a/the Cabinet; **~justiz** *die: interference by ruler or government in the process of law;* **~krise** *die* Cabinet crisis; **~liste** *die* list of Cabinet members; **~sitzung** *die* Cabinet meeting

**Kabinett-:** **~stück[chen]** *das* tour de force; **~wein** *der* Kabinett wine

**Kabis** /'ka:bɪs/ *der;* **~** (*südd., schweiz.*) cabbage

**Kabrio** /'ka:brio/ *das;* **~s**, **~s**, **Kabriolett** /kabrio'lɛt/ *das;* **~s**, **~s** **A** convertible; **B** (*veralt.: Kutsche*) cabriolet

**Kabuff** /ka'bʊf/ *das;* **~s**, **~s** (*ugs., oft abwertend*) [poky little] cubbyhole

**Kachel** /'kaxl̩/ *die;* **~**, **~n** [glazed] tile; **etw. mit ~n auslegen** tile sth.

**Kachel·bad** *das* tiled bathroom

**kacheln** *tr. V.* tile; **eine grün gekachelte Wand** a wall covered with green tiles

**Kachel·ofen** *der* tiled stove

**kack·braun** *Adj.* (*derb*) dirty brown; shit-coloured (*coarse*)

**Kacke** /'kakə/ *die;* **~** (*derb; auch fig.*) shit (*coarse*); crap (*coarse*); **so eine ~!** shit! (*coarse*); **dann/jetzt ist die ~ am Dampfen** then/now there'll be hell to pay (*coll.*)

**kacken** /'kakn̩/ *itr. V.* (*derb*) shit (*coarse*); crap (*coarse*)

**Kacker** *der;* **~s**, **~**, **Kackerin** *die;* **~**, **~nen** (*derb*) shit (*coarse*)

**Kadaver** /ka'da:vɐ/ *der;* **~s**, **~** (*auch fig., abwertend*) carcass

**Kadaver·gehorsam** *der* (*abwertend*) blind obedience

**Kadenz** /ka'dɛnts/ *die;* **~**, **~en** **A** (*Musik*) cadence; (*solistische Paraphrasierung*) cadenza; **B** (*Verslehre*) cadence

**Kader** /'ka:dɐ/ *der od.* (*schweiz.*) *das;* **~s**, **~** **A** cadre; **B** (*Sport*) squad

**kader-, Kader-:** **~abteilung** *die* (*DDR*) personnel department; **~akte** *die* (*DDR*) personal file; **~arbeit** *die* (*DDR*) cadre work; **~armee** *die* cadre army; **~leiter** *der*, **~leiterin** *die* (*DDR*) [chief] personnel officer; **~partei** *die* cadre party; **~politisch** *Adj.* (*DDR*) ‹matters, problems, measures, etc.› relating to the political development and function of the cadres; **~schmiede** *die* (*ugs.*) training ground for new cadres

**Kadett** /ka'dɛt/ *der;* **~en**, **~en** **A** (*hist., Milit.*) cadet; **B** (*ugs.: Bursche*) lad

**Kadetten·anstalt** *die* (*hist.*) cadet school

**Kadi** /'ka:di/ *der;* **~s**, **~s** **A** (*islam. Richter*) cadi; **B** (*ugs.: Gericht*) **jmdn. vor den ~ schleppen** haul sb. up before a judge *or* (*Brit. coll.*) the beak; **zum ~ laufen** go to court

**Kadmium** /'katmiʊm/ *das;* **~s** (*Chemie*) cadmium

**Käfer** /'kɛ:fɐ/ *der;* **~s**, **~** **A** (*Insekt; auch ugs.: VW*) beetle; **B** (*ugs.: junges Mädchen*) lass; girl; **ein flotter ~:** a nice bit of fluff (*coll.*)

**Kaff** /kaf/ *das;* **~s**, **~s** *od.* **Käffer** /'kɛfɐ/ (*ugs. abwertend*) dump (*coll.*); [dead-and-alive] hole (*coll.*)

**Kaffee** /'kafe *od.* (*österr.*) ka'fe:/ *der;* **~s**, **~s** **A** coffee; **~ kochen** make coffee; **~ mit Milch** white coffee (*Brit.*); coffee with milk/cream; **mir kam der ~ hoch** (*ugs.*) I felt like puking (*coarse*); **dir haben sie wohl was in den ~ getan?** (*ugs.*) have you gone soft in the head? (*coll.*); **das ist kalter ~** (*ugs.*) (*ist längst bekannt*) that's old hat (*coll.*); (*ist Unsinn*) that's a load of old rubbish (*coll.*); **B** (*Nachmittags~*) afternoon coffee; **~ trinken** have afternoon coffee; **jmdn. zum ~ einladen** invite sb. round for afternoon coffee

**kaffee-, Kaffee-:** **~automat** *der* coffee maker; **~bohne** *die* coffee bean; **~braun** *Adj.* coffee-coloured; **~durst** *der:* **~durst haben** feel like a [cup of] coffee; **~ersatz**, ***~-Ersatz** *der* coffee substitute; **~extrakt**, ***~-Extrakt** *der* coffee essence; **~fahrt** *die* **A** (*Fahrt*) trip [out] for afternoon coffee; **B** (*Werbefahrt*) *free trip for afternoon coffee during which goods are offered for sale to participants by sponsoring firm;* **~filter** *der* coffee filter; (*Filtertüte*) filter [paper]; **~geschirr** *das* coffee service *or* set (*including small plates*); **~haube** *die* ⇒ **~wärmer**

**Kaffee·haus** *das* (*bes. österr.*) coffee house

**Kaffee·haus-:** **~atmosphäre** *die* coffee house atmosphere; **~musik** *die* (*oft abwertend*) palm-court music

**Kaffee-:** **~kanne** *die* coffee pot; **~kirsche** *die* coffee cherry; **~klatsch** *der* (*ugs. scherzh.*) get-together and a chat over coffee; coffeeklatsch (*Amer.*); **heute ist bei ihr ~klatsch** she's having people round today for coffee and a chat; **~kränzchen** *das* (*veralt.*) **A** (*Zusammentreffen*) coffee afternoon; **B** (*Gruppe*) coffee circle; **~löffel** *der* coffee spoon; **~maschine** *die* coffee maker; **~mühle** *die* coffee grinder; **~pause** *die* coffee break; **~pflanze** *die* coffee plant; **~plantage** *die* coffee plantation; **~pulver** *das* coffee powder; **~rösterei** *die* coffee-roasting establishment; **~sahne** *die* coffee cream; **~satz** *der* coffee grounds *pl.*; **sich aus dem ~satz wahrsagen lassen** have one's fortune told from the coffee cup; **~schale** *die* (*österr.*) coffee cup; **~service** *das* coffee service *or* set; **~sieb** *das* coffee strainer; **~strauch** *der* coffee tree *or* plant; **~stube** *die* coffee shop; **~tante** *die* (*ugs. scherzh.*) coffee addict; **~tasse** *die* coffee cup; **~tisch** *der:* **sie saßen gerade am ~tisch** they were [sitting] having coffee and cakes; **den ~tisch decken** lay the table for coffee and cakes; **~trinker** *der*, **~trinkerin** *die* coffee drinker; **~wärmer** *der;* **~~s**, **~~:** coffee pot cosy *or* cover; **~wasser** *das* water for the coffee; **ich werde ~wasser/das ~wasser aufsetzen** I'll put on some water for coffee/the water for the coffee

**Kaffer** /'kafɐ/ *der;* **~s**, **~n** **A** Xhosa; **B** (*Schimpfwort*) blockhead; thickhead

**Kaffern·büffel** *der;* **~s**, **~:** African *or* Cape buffalo

**Käfig** /'kɛ:fɪç/ *der;* **~s**, **~e** cage; **in einem goldenen ~ sitzen** (*fig.*) be a bird in a gilded cage

**Käfig-:** **~haltung** *die* battery farming *no art.*; **~vogel** *der* cage bird

**kafkaesk** /kafka'ɛsk/ *Adj.* (*geh.*) Kafkaesque

**Kaftan** /'kaftan/ *der;* **~s**, **~e** caftan

**kahl** /ka:l/ *Adj.* **A** (*ohne Haare*) bald; (*ohne Federn*) bald; featherless; **~ werden** go bald; **jmdn. ~ scheren** shave sb.'s hair off; shave sb.'s head; **ein Schaf ~ scheren** shear a sheep completely bald; **sein ~ geschorener Kopf** his shaven head; **B** (*ohne Grün, schmucklos*) bare; **etw. ~ fressen** strip sth. bare; **eine Fläche ~ schlagen** clear-fell or clear-cut an area

**Kahl·fraß** *der* [complete] defoliation [by insects]

***kahl|fressen** ⇒ **kahl** B

**Kahlheit** *die;* **~** ⇒ **kahl** A, B: baldness; bareness

**kahl-, Kahl-:** **~hieb** *der* ⇒ **Kahlschlag** A; **~kopf** *der* **A** bald head; **B** (*ugs.: Person*) baldhead; **~köpfig** *Adj.* bald[-headed]; **~köpfig werden** go bald; **~köpfigkeit** *die;* **~~:** baldness; bald-headedness; ***~|scheren** ⇒ **kahl** A; **~schlag** *der* **A** clear-felling *no indef. art.*; clear-cutting *no indef. art.*; **B** (*Waldfläche*) clear-felled area; **C** (*fig.*) (*Beseitigung*) clearance; (*Kürzung*) massive cutbacks *pl.*; ***~|schlagen** ⇒ **kahl** B

**Kahm·haut** /'ka:m-/ *die* (*Biol.*) film of mould

**Kahn** /ka:n/ *der;* **~[e]s**, **Kähne** /'kɛ:nə/ **A** (*Ruder~*) rowing boat; (*Stech~*) punt; **~ fahren** go rowing/punting; **B** (*Lastschiff*) barge; **C** (*ugs., oft abwertend: Schiff*) tub; **D** *Pl.* (*ugs.: ausgetretene Schuhe*) old, worn-out shoes; **E** (*Soldatenspr.: Gefängnis*) glasshouse (*Mil. sl.*); **F** (*ugs. scherzh.: Bett*) bed; **in den ~ gehen** hit the hay (*coll.*)

**Kahn·fahrt** *die* trip in a rowing boat/punt

**Kai** /kai/ *der;* **~s**, **~s** quay

**Kai·anlage** *die* quays *pl.*

**Kaiman** /'kaiman/ *der;* **~s**, **~e** (*Zool.*) cayman

**Kai·mauer** *die* quay wall

**Kains·mal** /'kains-/ *das; Pl.* **~e**, **Kains·zeichen** *das* mark of Cain

k

**Kairo** /'kairo/ *(das);* **~s** ▶ 700 Cairo

**Kaiser** /'kaizɐ/ *der;* **~s, ~:** emperor; **sich um des ~s Bart streiten** engage in pointless argument; **dem ~ geben, was des ~s ist** render unto Caesar the things which are Caesar's; **er ist da/da hingegangen, wo auch der ~ zu Fuß hingeht** *(ugs. scherzh. verhüll.)* he's paying/he's gone to pay a call *(coll.)*

**Kaiser-: ~adler** *der* imperial eagle; **~haus** *das* imperial house *or* family

**Kaiserin** *die;* **~, ~nen** empress

**Kaiser: ~krone** *die* Ⓐ imperial crown; Ⓑ *(Zierpflanze)* crown imperial; **~krönung** *die* imperial coronation

**kaiserlich** ❶ *Adj.* imperial; **der ~e Hof** the imperial court. ❷ *adv.* **~ gesinnt sein** be loyal to the emperor; *(monarchistisch sein)* be monarchistic *or* imperialistic

**kaiserlich-königlich** *Adj.* imperial and royal; **die ~e Monarchie** the Austro-Hungarian monarchy

**Kaiser: ~pinguin** *der* emperor penguin; **~reich** *das* empire; **~schmarren** *der (österr., südd.): pancake pulled to pieces and sprinkled with powdered sugar and raisins;* **~schnitt** *der* Caesarean section

**Kaisertum** *das;* **~s** empire

**Kaiser·wetter** *das (scherzh.)* glorious, sunny weather *(for an event)*

**Kajak** /'ka:jak/ *der;* **~s, ~s** kayak

**Kajüt·boot** *das* cabin cruiser

**Kajüte** /ka'jy:tə/ *die;* **~, ~n** *(Seemannsspr.)* cabin

**Kakadu** /'kakadu/ *der;* **~s, ~s** cockatoo

**Kakao** /ka'kau/ *der;* **~s, ~s** cocoa; **jmdn./etw. durch den ~ ziehen** *(ugs.)* make fun of sb./sth.; take the mickey out of sb./sth. *(Brit. sl.)*

**Kakao-: ~baum** *der* cacao tree; **~bohne** *die* cocoa bean; **~pulver** *das* cocoa powder

**kakeln** /'ka:kl̩n/ *itr. V. (nordd.)* Ⓐ *(gackern)* cluck; Ⓑ *(schwatzen)* chat; natter *(sl.)*

**Kakerlak** /'ka:kɐlak/ *der;* **~s** *od.* **~en, ~en** cockroach; black beetle

**Kakophonie** /kakofo'ni:/ *die;* **~, ~n** cacophony

**Kaktee** /kak'te:ə/ *die;* **~, ~n, Kaktus** /'kaktʊs/ *der;* **~, Kakteen** cactus

**Kalamität** /kalami'tɛ:t/ *die;* **~, ~en** calamity; **sich in einer ~/in ~en befinden** be in [serious] difficulties *pl.*

**Kalander** /ka'landɐ/ *der;* **~s, ~** *(Technik)* calender

**Kalauer** /'ka:lauɐ/ *der;* **~s, ~:** laboured *or (coll.)* corny joke; *(Wortspiel)* atrocious *or (coll.)* corny pun

**kalauern** *itr. V.* tell laboured *or (coll.)* corny jokes; *(mit Wortspielen)* make atrocious *or (coll.)* corny puns

**Kalb** /kalp/ *das;* **~[e]s, Kälber** /'kɛlbɐ/ Ⓐ calf; *(Hirschkalb)* fawn; **glotzen** *od.* **Augen machen wie ein [ab]gestochenes ~** *(ugs.)* look pop-eyed; **das Goldene ~ anbeten/um das Goldene ~ tanzen** *(geh.)* worship the golden calf; Ⓑ *(ugs.: ~fleisch)* veal; Ⓒ *(dummer, alberner Mensch)* [silly] idiot

**Kälbchen** /'kɛlpçən/ *das;* **~s, ~:** little calf; *(Hirsch~)* little fawn

**kalben** *itr. V.* Ⓐ *(ein Kalb gebären)* calve; Ⓑ *(Geogr.)* ‹glacier, iceberg› calve

**Kalberei** *die;* **~, ~en** *(ugs.)* messing *or* fooling about *or* around *no pl.*

**kalbern** /'kalbɐn/ *itr. V. (ugs.)* mess *or* fool about *or* around

**Kalb-: ~fell** *das* ⇒ **Kalbsfell; ~fleisch** *das* veal; **~leder** *das* ⇒ **Kalbsleder**

**Kalbs-: ~braten** *der (Kochk.)* roast veal *no indef. art.; (Gericht)* roast of veal; **~brust** *die* breast of veal; **~fell** *das* calfskin; **~frikassee** *das (Kochk.)* fricassee of veal; **~hachse,** *(südd.:)* **~haxe** *die (Kochk.)* knuckle of veal; **~kotelett** *das* veal cutlet *(with bone)*; **~leder** *das* calfskin; calf leather; **~nieren·braten** *der (Kochk.)* loin of veal with kidneys; **~schnitzel** *das* veal cutlet

**Kaldaune** /kal'daunə/ *die;* **~, ~n** entrails *pl.*

**Kalebasse** /kale'basə/ *die;* **~, ~n** calabash

**Kaleidoskop** /kalaido'sko:p/ *das;* **~s, ~e** *(auch fig.)* kaleidoscope

**kalendarisch** /kalɛn'da:rɪʃ/ *Adj.* ‹age etc.› according to the calendar; **der ~e Beginn einer Jahreszeit** the beginning of a season according to the calendar

**Kalender** /ka'lɛndɐ/ *der;* **~s, ~** Ⓐ calendar; **sich** *(Dat.)* **etw./einen Tag im ~ [rot] anstreichen** *(oft iron.)* mark sth. in red on the calendar/mark a day as a red-letter day; **der julianische ~:** the Julian calendar; ⇒ *auch* **gregorianisch;** Ⓑ *(Taschen~)* diary

**Kalender-: ~blatt** *das* calendar sheet; **~geschichte** *die: edifying story or fable published on a calendar;* **~jahr** *das* calendar year; **~uhr** *die* calendar watch

**Kalesche** /ka'lɛʃə/ *die;* **~, ~n** *(hist.)* barouche

**Kalfaktor** /kal'faktɔr/ *der;* **~s, ~en** *(veralt., oft abwertend)* Ⓐ general factotum; general dogsbody *(coll. derog.)*; Ⓑ *(Strafgefangener)* trusty

**kalfatern** /kal'fa:tɐn/ *tr., itr. V. (Seemannsspr.)* caulk

**Kali** /'ka:li/ *das;* **~s, ~s** potash

**Kaliber** /ka'li:bɐ/ *das;* **~s, ~** Ⓐ *(Technik, Waffenkunde)* calibre; Ⓑ *(ugs., oft abwertend)* sort; kind; **älteren/jüngeren ~s sein** be older/younger

**Kali·dünger** *der* potash fertilizer

**Kalif** /ka'li:f/ *der;* **~en, ~en** *(hist.)* caliph

**Kalifat** /kali'fa:t/ *das;* **~[e]s, ~e** *(hist.)* caliphate

**Kalifornien** /kali'fɔrnjən/ *(das);* **~s** California

**kalifornisch** *Adj.* Californian

**Kaliko** /'kaliko/ *der;* **~s, ~s** calico

**Kali-: ~lauge** *die* caustic potash solution; **~salpeter** *der* saltpetre; potassium nitrate; **~salz** *das* potassium *or* potash salt

**Kalium** /'ka:liʊm/ *(Chemie) das;* **~s** potassium

**Kali·werk** *das* potash works *sing. or. pl.*

**Kalk** /kalk/ *der;* **~[e]s, ~e** Ⓐ *(Kalziumkarbonat)* calcium carbonate; Ⓑ *(Baustoff)* lime; quicklime; burnt lime; **die Wände mit ~ streichen** whitewash *or* limewash the walls; **bei ihm rieselt schon der ~** *(salopp)* he's going a bit senile; Ⓒ *(Knochensubstanz)* calcium

**Kalk-: ~ablagerung** *die* deposit of calcium carbonate; **~boden** *der* limy soil; lime soil; **~bruch** *der* ⇒ **~steinbruch**

**kalken** /'kalkn̩/ *tr. V.* Ⓐ *(tünchen)* whitewash; Ⓑ *(Kalk zuführen)* lime

**kalk-, Kalk-: ~erde** *die* Ⓐ *(gebrannter ~)* lime; quicklime; burnt lime; Ⓑ *(~haltige Erde)* lime *or* limy soil; **~grube** *die* lime pit; **~haltig** *Adj. (bes. Geol., Mineral.)* limy ‹soil›; calcareous ‹soil, rock› *(Geol., Min.)*; ‹water› containing calcium carbonate; **das Wasser ist sehr ~haltig** the water is high in calcium carbonate; **~mangel** *der* Ⓐ *(Mangel an Kalzium)* calcium deficiency; Ⓑ *(Mangel an ~)* deficiency of lime; **~milch** *die* limewash; **~sand·stein** *der* sand-lime brick; **~spat** *der* calcite; **~stein** *der* limestone; **~stein·bruch** *der* limestone quarry

**Kalkül**[1] /kal'ky:l/ *das od. der;* **~s, ~e** *(geh.)* calculation

**Kalkül**[2] *der;* **~s, ~e** *(Math.)* calculus

**Kalkulation** /kalkula'tsio:n/ *die;* **~, ~en** *(auch Wirtsch.)* calculation; **die ~ der Herstellungskosten eines Buches** the costing of a book; **in der ~ liegt ein Fehler** there's an error in the costings *pl.*; **nach meiner ~:** according to my calculations *pl.*

**Kalkulator** /kalku'la:tɔr/ *der;* **~s, ~en** /-la'to:rən/, **Kalkulatorin** *die;* **~, ~nen** cost accountant

**kalkulieren** ❶ *tr. V.* Ⓐ *(Kaufmannsspr.: veranschlagen)* calculate ‹cost, price›; cost ‹product, article›; **die Herstellungskosten eines Buches ~:** cost a book; Ⓑ *(abschätzen)* calculate; Ⓒ *(ugs.: annehmen)* reckon. ❷ *itr. V.* calculate; **falsch ~:** miscalculate

**Kalkutta** /kal'kʊta/ *(das);* **~s** ▶ 700 Calcutta

**kalk·weiß** *Adj.* Ⓐ *(weiß wie Kalk)* chalk-white; Ⓑ *(sehr bleich)* deathly pale; chalky white; **~ sein** be as white as a sheet

**Kalligraphie** /kaligra'fi:/ *die;* **~:** calligraphy *no art.*

**Kalme** /'kalmə/ *die;* **~, ~n** *(Met.)* calm

**Kalmen·gürtel** *der (Met.)* calm belt

**Kalorie** /kalo'ri:/ *die;* **~, ~n** calorie

**kalorien-, Kalorien-: ~arm** ❶ *Adj.* low-calorie *attrib.;* **~arm sein** be low in calories; ❷ *adv.* **~arm kochen/essen** cook low-calorie meals/eat low-calorie foods; **~bewusst, *~bewußt** ❶ *Adj.* calorie-conscious; ❷ *adv.* in a calorie-conscious way; **~bombe** *die (ugs.)* mountain of calories *(coll.)*; **~gehalt** *der* calorie content; **~reich** ❶ *Adj.* high-calorie *attrib.;* **~reich sein** be high in calories; ❷ *adv.* **~reich kochen/essen** cook high-calorie meals/eat high-calorie foods

**Kalori·meter** /kalori-/ *das;* **~s, ~** *(Physik)* calorimeter

**kalt** /kalt/; **kälter** /'kɛltɐ/, **kältest...** /'kɛltəst.../ ❶ *Adj.* cold; chilly, frosty ‹atmosphere, smile›; **ein ~es Buffet** a cold buffet; **mir ist/wird ~:** I am/am getting cold; **das Essen wird ~:** the food is getting cold; **im Kalten sitzen** sit in the cold; **~ und berechnend sein** be cold and calculating; **es packte uns das ~e Grausen/Entsetzen** our blood ran cold; **jmdm. die ~e Schulter zeigen** give sb. the cold shoulder; cold-shoulder sb.; **jmdn. ~ lassen** *(ugs.)* leave sb. unmoved; *(nicht interessieren)* leave sb. cold *(coll.)*; **~ bleiben** remain unmoved ❷ *adv.* Ⓐ **~ duschen** have *or* take a cold shower; **~ schlafen** sleep in a cold room; **Getränke/Sekt ~ stellen** cool drinks/chill champagne; **~ Zigarre/Pfeife rauchen** *(ugs.)* have an unlit cigar/pipe in one's mouth; **jmdn. ~ erwischen** *(bes. Sportjargon)* catch sb. on the hop; Ⓑ *(nüchtern)* coldly; Ⓒ *(abweisend, unfreundlich)* coldly; frostily; **jmdn. ~ anblicken** look at sb. coldly; **~ lächeln** smile coldly *or* frostily; **etw. ~ lächelnd tun** *(fig. ugs. abwertend)* take callous pleasure in doing sth.; Ⓓ **mich überlief** *od.* **durchrieselte es ~:** cold shivers ran down my spine

**kalt-, Kalt-: *~|bleiben** ⇒ **kalt** 1; **~blut** *das* heavy draught horse; **~blüter** /-bly:tɐ/ *der;* **~~s, ~~** *(Zool.)* cold-blooded animal; **~blütig** ❶ *Adj.* Ⓐ *(beherrscht)* cool-headed; Ⓑ *(abwertend: skrupellos)* cold-blooded; Ⓒ *(Zool.)* cold-blooded; ❷ *adv.* Ⓐ *(beherrscht)* coolly; calmly; **einer Gefahr ~blütig ins Auge sehen** face a danger coolly *or* calmly; Ⓑ *(abwertend: skrupellos)* cold-bloodedly; **~blütigkeit** *die;* **~~** ⇒ **~blütig** A, B: cool-headedness; cold-bloodedness

**Kälte** /'kɛltə/ *die;* **~** Ⓐ cold; **10 Grad ~:** 10 degrees of frost; 10 degrees below freezing; **vor ~ zittern** *od.* *(ugs.)* **bibbern** shiver with cold; **bei dieser ~:** in this cold; when it's as cold as this; Ⓑ *(Teilnahmslosigkeit, Unbehaglichkeit)* coldness

**kälte-, Kälte-: ~beständig** *Adj.* cold-resistant; **~beständig sein** be resistant to cold; **~ein·bruch** *der (Met.)* sudden onset of cold weather; **~empfindlich** *Adj.* sensitive to cold *pred.;* **~empfindliche Pflanzen** plants which are sensitive to cold; **~gefühl** *das* sensation *or* feeling of cold; chill; **~grad** *das (ugs.)* degree of frost; **~maschine** *die (Technik)* refrigerating machine; **~pol** *der* cold pole

**kälter** ⇒ **kalt**

**kältest...** ⇒ **kalt**

**Kälte-: ~sturz** *der (Met.)* sudden drop in temperature; **~technik** *die* refrigeration engineering *no art.;* **~tod** *der:* **den ~tod erleiden** freeze to death; die of cold; **~welle** *die* cold wave *or* spell

**kalt-, Kalt-: ~front** *die (Met.)* cold front; **~gepresst, *~gepreßt** *Adj.* cold-pressed;

*old spelling (see note on page 1707)

k

**~haus** *das (Gartenbau)* cold house; **~herzig** *Adj.* cold-hearted; ***~lächelnd** ⇒ **kalt** 2c; ***~|lassen** ⇒ **kalt** 1; **~leim** *der* [cold] woodworking adhesive; **~luft** *die (Met.)* cold air; **polare ~luft** cold polar air; **~|machen** *tr. V. (salopp)* **jmdn. ~machen** do sb. in *(sl.)*; **~mamsell** *die* ▶ 159 *girl/woman who prepares and serves cold dishes in a restaurant, hotel, etc.*; **~miete** *die* rent exclusive of heating; **~schale** *die: cold sweet soup made with fruit, beer, wine, or milk;* **~schnäuzig** /-ʃnɔytsɪç/ *(ugs.)* ❶ *Adj.* cold and insensitive; *(frech)* insolent; ❷ *adv.* coldly and insensitively; *(frech)* insolently; **~schnäuzigkeit** *die; ~~ (ugs.)* coldness and insensitivity; *(Frechheit)* insolence; **~start** *der (Kfz-W.)* cold start; **beim ~start** when starting from cold; **~|stellen** *tr. V. (ugs.)* **jmdn. ~stellen** put sb. out of the way *(coll. joc.)*; **den Mittelstürmer ~stellen** cut the centre forward out of the game

**Kalvarien·berg** /kal'va:ri̯ən-/ *der:* [Mount] Calvary

**Kalvinismus** /kalvi'nɪsmʊs/ *der; ~:* Calvinism *no art.*

**Kalvinist** *der; ~en, ~en,* **Kalvinistin** *die; ~, ~nen* Calvinist

**kalvinistisch** *Adj.* Calvinist

**Kalzium** /'kaltsi̯ʊm/ *das; ~s* calcium

**kam** /ka:m/ *1. u. 3. Pers. Prät. v.* **kommen**

**Kamarilla** /kama'rɪlja/ *die; ~,* **Kamarillen** *(geh.)* camarilla

**Kambodscha** /kam'bɔdʒa/ *(das); ~s* Cambodia

**Kambodschaner** /kambo'dʒa:nɐ/ *der; ~s, ~,* **Kambodschanerin** *die; ~, ~nen* Cambodian

**käme** /'kɛ:mə/ *1. u. 3. Pers. Konjunktiv II v.* **kommen**

**Kamel** /ka'me:l/ *das; ~s, ~e* A camel; **eher geht ein ~ durch ein Nadelöhr, als dass das geschieht** that will never happen in a million years; B *(salopp: dummer Mensch)* clot *(Brit. coll.)*; twit *(Brit. coll.)*; fathead

**Kamel-: ~haar** *das* camel['s] hair; **~haar·mantel** *der* camel['s]-hair coat

**Kamelie** /ka'me:li̯ə/ *die; ~, ~n* camellia

**Kamellen** /ka'mɛlən/ *Pl. (ugs.) in* **das sind alte** *od.* **olle ~:** that's old hat *(coll.)*; **es wurden nur alte** *od.* **olle ~ aufgewärmt** the same old stuff was dished up *(coll.)*

**Kamel·treiber** *der* A camel driver; B *(salopp abwertend)* smelly Arab *(sl. derog.)*

**Kamera** /'kamərа/ *die; ~, ~s* camera; **vor der ~ stehen** appear in front of the cameras *pl.*

**Kamera·assistent** *der,* **Kamera·assistentin** *die* camera assistant; assistant cameraman

**Kamerad** /kamə'ra:t/ *der; ~en, ~en (Lebens~, Gefährte)* companion; *(Freund)* friend; *(Mitschüler)* mate; friend; *(Soldat)* comrade; *(Sport)* teammate

**Kameraderie** /kamərаdə'ri:/ *die; ~ (meist abwertend)* loyalty to a/the clique; **falsch verstandene ~:** mistaken sense of comradeship and loyalty

**Kameradin** *die; ~, ~nen* ⇒ **Kamerad**

**Kameradschaft** *die; ~, ~en* A comradeship; **die ~ zwischen ihnen** the sense of comradeship between them; B *(Gruppe)* association

**kameradschaftlich** ❶ *Adj.* comradely. ❷ *adv.* in a comradely way

**Kameradschaftlichkeit** *die; ~:* comradeliness

**Kameradschafts-: ~abend** *der* social evening *(of youth group, ex-servicemen's association, etc.)*; **~ehe** *die: marriage based on feelings of companionship;* **~geist** *der* spirit of comradeship

**Kamera-: ~frau** *die* ▶ 159 camerawoman; **~führung** *die (Film)* camerawork *no indef. art.*; **~mann** *der Pl.* **~männer** *od.* **~leute** ▶ 159 cameraman; **~recorder, ~rekorder** *der* camcorder

**Kamerun** /'kaməru:n/ *(das); ~s* Cameroon; the Cameroons *pl.*

**Kameruner** *der; ~s, ~,* **Kamerunerin** *die; ~, ~nen* native of Cameroon *or* the Cameroons; Cameroonian

**Kamille** /ka'mɪlə/ *die; ~, ~n* camomile

**Kamillen·tee** *der* camomile tea

**Kamin** /ka'mi:n/ *der, schweiz.: das; ~s, ~e* A *(Feuerstelle)* fireplace; **sie saßen am ~:** they sat by the hearth *or* the fireside; B *(bes. südd.: Schornstein)* chimney; **er kann/muss das in den ~ schreiben** *(ugs.)* he can/will have to kiss goodbye to that *(coll.)*; C *(Bergsteigen: Felsspalt)* chimney

**Kamin-: ~feger** *der,* **~fegerin** *die; ~~, ~~nen* ▶ 159 *(bes. südd.)* ⇒ **Schornsteinfeger**; **~feuer** *das* [open] fire; **~kehrer** *der; ~~s, ~~,* **~kehrerin** *die; ~~, ~~nen* *(bes. südd.)* ⇒ **Schornsteinfeger**; **~sims** *der* mantelpiece; mantelshelf

**Kamm** /kam/ *der; ~[e]s,* **Kämme** /'kɛmə/ A comb; **alle/alles über einen ~ scheren** lump everyone/everything together; B *(bei Hühnern usw.)* comb; *(bei Reptilien, Amphibien)* crest; **ihm schwillt der ~** *(ugs.)* his hackles rise; *(er wird überheblich)* he gets cocky and big-headed *(coll.)*; C *(Gebirgs~)* ridge; crest; D *(Wellen~)* crest; E *(Rinder~)* neck; *(Schweine~)* spare rib; F *(beim Pferd)* crest

**kämmen** /'kɛmən/ *tr. V.* A comb; **jmdm./sich die Haare ~, jmdn./sich ~:** comb sb.'s/one's hair; **jmdm. einen Scheitel/Pony ~:** put a parting in sb.'s hair/comb sb.'s hair into a fringe; B *(Textilind.)* comb

**Kammer** /'kamɐ/ *die; ~, ~n* A storeroom; *(veralt.: Schlafraum)* chamber; B *(Biol., Med., Technik, Waffenkunde)* chamber; C *(Parl.)* chamber; House; **die erste/zweite ~:** the upper/lower chamber *or* House; D *(Rechtsw.)* court *(dealing with a particular branch of judicial business)*; E *(gewerbliche Vereinigung)* professional association; F *(Milit.)* stores *pl.*

**Kämmerchen** /'kɛmɐçən/ *das; ~s, ~:* small room; *(Abstellkammer)* [small] storeroom

**Kammer·chor** *der* chamber choir

**Kammer·diener** *der (veralt.)* valet

**Kämmerer** /'kɛmərɐ/ *der; ~s, ~ (veralt.)* [town/city] treasurer

**Kammer-: ~frau** *die (veralt.)* lady's maid; **die ~frau der Fürstin** the princess's maid; **~gericht** *das (hist.)* Supreme Court; **~herr** *der (hist.)* chamberlain

**Kämmerin** /'kɛmərɪn/ *die; ~, ~nen* ⇒ **Kämmerer**

**Kammer-: ~jäger** *der,* **~jägerin** *die* pest controller; **~konzert** *das* chamber concert

**Kämmerlein** /'kɛmɐlain/ *das; ~s, ~ (oft scherzh.) in* **ich muss mal im stillen ~ darüber nachdenken** I must [go away by myself and] think about that in peace and quiet; **das hat er sich im stillen ~ ausgedacht** he thought that up all by himself without anyone realizing

**Kammer-: ~musik** *die* chamber music; **~orchester** *das* chamber orchestra; **~sänger** *der,* **~sängerin** *die: title awarded to singer of outstanding merit;* **~spiel** *das* A *(kleines Theaterstück)* intimate chamber-drama; B *Pl. (kleines Theater)* studio theatre *sing.*; **~ton** *der; Pl.* **~töne** *(Musik)* standard pitch; **~zofe** *die (veralt.)* lady's maid

**Kamm-: ~garn** *das* worsted; **~griff** *der (Turnen)* undergrasp; **~muschel** *die* scallop

***Kammuschel** ⇒ **Kammmuschel**

**Kamm·wolle** *die (Textilw.)* worsted

**Kamp** /kamp/ *der; ~s,* **Kämpe** /'kɛmpə/ *(Forstw.)* [small] tree nursery

**Kampagne** /kam'panjə/ *die; ~, ~n* A *(größere Aktion)* campaign **(für** for, on behalf of; **gegen** against); B *(bestimmte Zeitspanne)* busy season; C *(Archäol.)* phase *(of an excavation)*

**Kampanile** /kampa'ni:lə/ *der; ~, ~:* campanile

**Kämpe** /'kɛmpə/ *der; ~n, ~n (veralt.)* [brave] warrior *or* fighter; **ein alter ~** *(scherzh.)* an old campaigner; a seasoned veteran

**Kampf** /kampf/ *der; ~[e]s,* **Kämpfe** A *(militärisch)* battle **(um** for); **nach wochenlangen erbitterten Kämpfen** after weeks of bitter fighting; **den ~ einstellen** stop fighting; **er ist im ~ gefallen** he fell *or* was killed in action *or* combat; B *(zwischen persönlichen Gegnern)* fight; *(fig.)* struggle; **ein ~ aller gegen alle** a free-for-all; **ein ~ Mann gegen Mann** a hand-to-hand fight; **ein ~ auf Leben und Tod** a fight to the death; **den ~ aufgeben** *od.* **verloren geben** give up the fight; **aus einem ~ als Sieger/Verlierer hervorgehen** emerge as victor *or* winner/loser from a fight; **sich dem ~ stellen** be prepared to fight; C *(Wett~)* contest; *(Boxen)* contest; fight; bout; **sich einen spannenden ~ liefern** produce an exciting contest; D *(Einsatz aller Mittel)* struggle, fight **(um, für** for; **gegen** against); **der ~ ums Dasein** the struggle for existence; **jmdm./einer Sache den ~ ansagen** declare war on sb./sth.; **~ dem Faschismus/Atomtod!** fight fascism/the nuclear menace!; E *(heftig ausgetragene Kontroverse)* battle; **der ~ zwischen den Geschlechtern** the battle of the sexes; **auf in den ~!** *(scherzh.)* into the fray!; F *(innerer Zwiespalt)* **ein ~ mit sich selbst** a struggle *or* battle with oneself

**kampf-, Kampf-: ~abschnitt** *der (Milit.)* combat *or* battle sector; **~abstimmung** *die (Politik)* crucial vote; **~ansage** *die* declaration of war; **~anzug** *der* combat uniform; **~bahn** *die (für Gladiatoren)* arena; *(für Stiere)* ring; *(veralt.: Sportstadion)* stadium; **~bereit** *Adj.* willing to fight *postpos.*; *(fertig)* ready to fight *postpos.*; ‹army› ready for battle; ‹troops› ready for battle *or* action; **~bereitschaft** *die* willingness to fight; *(eines Heeres)* readiness for battle; *(einer Truppe)* readiness for battle *or* action; **~boot** *das* fighting ship; warship; **~bündnis** *das* alliance; **~einheit** *die (Milit.)* combat unit

**kämpfen** /'kɛmpfn̩/ ❶ *itr. V.* A fight; **mit jmdm. ~:** fight [with] sb.; **gegen jmdn. ~:** fight [against] sb.; **um die Vorherrschaft/eine Stadt/Frau ~:** fight for supremacy/a town/over a woman; **um einen Titel ~:** compete for a title; **um seine Existenz ~:** fight *or* struggle for one's existence; **für jmdn./etw. ~:** fight for sb./sth.; **mit den Tränen ~** *(fig.)* fight back one's tears; **mit dem Schlaf ~** *(fig.)* struggle to keep awake; **mit dem Tod ~** *(fig.)* fight for one's life *or* to stay alive; **mit etw. zu ~ haben** *(fig.)* have to contend with sth.; **[lange] mit sich** *(Dat.)* **~:** have a [long] struggle with oneself; B *(Sport: sich messen)* ‹team› play; ‹wrestler, boxer› fight; **gegen jmdn. ~:** play/fight sb.

❷ *refl. V. (auch fig.)* fight one's way.

❸ *tr. V.* **einen Kampf ~** *(auch fig.)* fight a battle

**Kampfer** /'kampfɐ/ *der; ~s* camphor

**Kämpfer**[1] /'kɛmpfɐ/ *der; ~s, ~:* fighter

**Kämpfer**[2] *der; ~s, ~* A *(Archit.)* impost; B *(Bauw.)* transom

**Kämpferin** *die; ~, ~nen* fighter

**kämpferisch** ❶ *Adj.* A fighting ‹spirit, mood›; ‹person› full of fighting spirit; **eine ~e Natur sein** be full of fighting spirit; B *(Sport: mit großem Einsatz)* spirited. ❷ *adv.* A *(voller Kampfgeist)* in a fighting spirit; B *(Sport: mit großem Einsatz)* spiritedly

**Kämpfer·natur** *die* fighter

**kampf·erprobt** *Adj.* battle-tried; battle-tested ‹equipment›

**Kampfes·lust** *die* eagerness for the fray; **in wilder ~:** lusting for battle

**kampf-, Kampf-: ~fähig** *Adj.* ‹troops› fit for action *or* battle; ‹boxer etc.› fit to fight; **~fahrzeug** *das (Milit.)* combat vehicle; **~flieger** *der (Milit.)* bomber pilot; **~flugzeug** *das* bomber; **~gas** *das* war gas; **~gebiet** *das* battle area; combat zone; **~gefährte** *der,* **~gefährtin** *die (im militärischen ~)* comrade in arms; *(im politischen ~)* comrade in the struggle; **~geist** *der* fighting spirit; **~gemeinschaft** *die* action group; **~gericht** *das (Sport)* [panel of] judges *pl.*; **~geschehen** *das* fighting *no indef. art.*;

**~gruppe** *die* (*Milit.*) task force; **~hahn** *der; Pl.* **~hähne** A (*Hahn für Kämpfe*) fighting cock; B (*ugs.*) fighter; brawler; **~handlungen** *Pl.* fighting *sing.*; **die ~handlungen einstellen** cease hostilities *or* fighting; **~kraft** *die* fighting power *or* strength; (*einer Mannschaft*) strength; **~lied** *das* battle song; (*einer Bewegung*) battle anthem; **~los** ❶ *Adj.* peaceful; **an eine ~lose Übergabe der Stadt war nicht zu denken** to hand over the town without a fight was unthinkable; ❷ *adv.* without a fight; **~lustig** ❶ *Adj.* belligerent; ❷ *adv.* belligerently; **~maßnahme** *die* active measure; **~maßnahmen ergreifen** take action *sing.*; **~moral** *die* morale; **~panzer** *der* [battle] tank; **~platz** *der* battlefield; **~preis** *der* (*Wirtsch.*) cut price; **~richter** *der*, **~richterin** *die* (*Sport*) judge; **~schiff** *das* fighting ship; warship; **~schrift** *die* polemical document; **~spiel** *das* (*Sport*) contact sport; **~stark** *Adj.* powerful ‹army›; efficient ‹troops›; strong, powerful ‹team›; **~stärke** *die* (*eines Feindes, Heeres*) fighting strength *or* power; (*einer Mannschaft*) strength; **~stier** *der* fighting bull; **~stoff** *der* warfare agent; **~tag** *der* day of action; **~truppe** *die* (*Milit.*) fighting *or* combat unit; **~truppen** fighting *or* combat troops; **~unfähig** *Adj.* ‹troops› unfit for action *or* battle; ‹boxer etc.› unfit to fight; **jmdn./etw. ~unfähig machen** put sb./sth. out of action; **der Boxer schlug seinen Gegner ~unfähig** the boxer put his opponent out of the fight; **~verband** *der* (*Milit.*) combat unit; **~wagen** *der* chariot; **~ziel** *das* objective; **~zone** *die* (*Milit.*) battle zone; combat zone

**kampieren** /kam'pi:rən/ *itr. V.* camp; (*ugs.: wohnen*) camp down *or* out; **du kannst bei uns im Wohnzimmer ~:** you can bed down *or* (*Brit. sl.*) doss down in our living room

**Kamputschea** /kampʊ'tʃe:a/ (*das*); **~s** Kampuchea

**Kamuffel** /ka'mʊfl/ *das;* **~s,** ~ (*Schimpfwort*) [silly] fool

**Kanada** /'kanada/ (*das*); **~s** Canada

**Kanadier** /ka'na:di̯ɐ/ *der;* **~s,** ~ ▶553| A (*Einwohner Kanadas*) Canadian; B (*Boot*) Canadian canoe

**Kanadierin** *die;* ~, **~nen** ▶553| Canadian; ⇨ *auch* **-in**

**kanadisch** /ka'na:dɪʃ/ *Adj.* ▶553| Canadian

**Kanaille** /ka'naljə/ *die;* ~, **~n** (*abwertend*) A (*gemeiner Mensch*) scoundrel; villain; B (*Mob, Pöbel*) rabble; mob

**Kanake** /ka'na:kə/ *der;* **~n, ~n** A (*Polynesier*) kanaka; B (*derb abwertend: Südländer, Orientale*) dago (*sl. derog.*)

**Kanal** /ka'na:l/ *der;* **~s, Kanäle** /ka'nɛ:lə/ A (*künstlicher Wasserlauf*) canal; B (*Geogr.*) **der ~:** the [English] Channel; C (*für Abwässer*) sewer; D (*zur Entwässerung, Bewässerung*) channel; (*Graben*) ditch; E (*Rundf., Ferns., Weg der Information*) channel; F (*salopp*) **den ~ voll haben** (*betrunken sein*) be canned *or* plastered (*sl.*); (*überdrüssig sein*) have had a bellyful *or* as much as one can take

**Kanal-: ~arbeiter** *der*, **~arbeiterin** *die* A sewerage worker; B (*Politik Jargon*) back-room boy; **~bau** *der* canal/sewer building *or* construction; **~deckel** *der* manhole cover; **~gebühr** *die* canal toll; canal dues *pl.*; **~inseln** *Pl.* Channel Islands

**Kanalisation** /kanaliza'tsi̯o:n/ *die;* ~, **~en** A (*System der Abwasserkanäle*) sewerage system; sewers *pl.*; B (*Bau der Abwasserkanäle*) installation of a/the sewerage system; C (*Ausbau eines Flusses*) canalization

**Kanalisationssystem** *das* sewerage system; [system of] sewers *pl.*

**kanalisieren** *tr. V.* A (*mit Kanalisation versehen*) install a sewerage system in ‹area, village, etc.›; B (*lenken*) channel ‹energies, goods, etc.›; C (*schiffbar machen*) canalize

**Kanalisierung** *die;* ~, **~en** A installation of a/the sewerage system; **die ~ des Dorfes** the installation of a/the sewerage system in the village; B (*Lenkung*) channelling; C (*Schiffbarmachen*) canalization

**Kanal-: ~tunnel** *der* Channel Tunnel; **~zone** *die* Canal Zone

**Kanapee** /'kanape/ *das;* **~s, ~s** A (*veralt., noch scherzh.: Sofa*) sofa; settee; B (*belegtes Weißbrotschnittchen*) canapé

**Kanaren** /ka'na:rən/ *Pl.* Canaries

**Kanari** /ka'na:ri/ *der;* **~s,** ~ (*südd., österr. ugs.*), **Kanarienvogel** /ka'na:ri̯ən-/ *der* canary

**Kanarische Inseln** *Pl.* Canary Islands

**Kandare** /kan'da:rə/ *die;* ~, **~n** curb bit; **jmdn. an die ~ nehmen** (*fig.*) take sb. in hand; **jmdn. an der ~ haben** (*fig.*) keep sb. on a tight rein

**Kandelaber** /kande'la:bɐ/ *der;* **~s, ~:** candelabrum

**Kandidat** /kandi'da:t/ *der;* **~en, ~en** A candidate; **jmdn. als ~en aufstellen** nominate sb. *or* put sb. forward as a candidate; B (*beim Quiz usw.*) contestant; C (*an Hochschulen*) *person studying for the final examination for a doctorate;* **~ der Medizin/Philosophie** *usw.* 'Kandidat' in medicine/philosophy *etc.*

**Kandidatenliste** *die* list of candidates

**Kandidatin** *die;* ~, **~nen** ⇨ **Kandidat**; ⇨ *auch* **-in**

**Kandidatur** /kandida'tu:ɐ/ *die;* ~, **~en** candidature (**auf** + *Akk.* for)

**kandidieren** *itr. V.* stand [as a candidate] (**für** for)

**kandieren** /kan'di:rən/ *tr. V.* candy; **kandiert** crystallized ‹orange, petal›; glacé ‹cherry, pear›; candied ‹peel›

**Kandis** /'kandɪs/ *der;* ~, **Kandiszucker** *der* rock candy

**Kaneel** /ka'ne:l/ *der;* **~s, ~e** cinnamon

**Känguru, *Känguruh** /'kɛŋguru/ *das;* **~s, ~s** kangaroo

**Kanin** /ka'ni:n/ *das;* **~s, ~e** (*fachspr.*) rabbit [fur]

**Kaninchen** /ka'ni:nçən/ *das;* **~s, ~:** rabbit

**Kaninchen-: ~bau** *der; Pl.* **~e** rabbit burrow; rabbit hole; **~fell** *das* rabbit fur; **~fleisch** *das* rabbit [meat]; **~stall** *der* rabbit hutch

**Kanister** /ka'nɪstɐ/ *der;* **~s, ~:** can; [metal/plastic] container

**kann** /kan/ *1. u. 3. Pers. Sg. Präsens v.* **können**

**Kannbestimmung, *Kann-Bestimmung** *die* authorization

**Kännchen** /'kɛnçən/ *das;* **~s, ~:** [small] pot; (*für Milch*) [small] jug; **ein ~ Kaffee/Milch** a [small] pot of coffee/jug of milk

**Kanne** /'kanə/ *die;* ~, **~n** A (*Krug*) (*Tee~, Kaffee~*) pot; (*Milch~, Wein~, Wasser~*) jug; B (*Henkel~*) can; (*für Milch*) pail; (*beim Melken*) churn; (*für Essen*) container; (*Gieß~*) watering can; C (*Jazzjargon: Saxophon*) sax (*coll.*)

**Kannelierung** *die;* ~, **~en** (*Archit.*) fluting

**kannenweise** *Adv.* by the jugful

**Kannibale** /kani'ba:lə/ *der;* **~n, ~n, Kannibalin** *die;* ~, **~nen** cannibal

**kannibalisch** *Adj.* cannibalistic

**Kannibalismus** *der;* ~ (*auch Zool.*) cannibalism *no art.*

**kannst** /kanst/ *2. Pers. Sg. Präsens v.* **können**

**kannste** /'kanstə/ (*ugs.*) = **kannst du;** ⇨ *auch* **haste**

**kannte** /'kantə/ *1. u. 3. Pers. Sg. Prät. v.* **kennen**

**Kanon** /'ka:nɔn/ *der;* **~s, ~s** (*Musik, Lit., Theol., geh.*) canon

**Kanonade** /kano'na:də/ *die;* ~, **~n** (*Milit.*) cannonade; **eine ~ aufs Tor** (*fig.*) a barrage of shots [at goal]; **eine ~ von Flüchen** *usw.* (*fig. ugs.*) a barrage of curses *or* oaths *etc.*

**Kanone** /ka'no:nə/ *die;* ~, **~n** A (*Geschütz*) cannon; big gun; **mit ~n auf Spatzen** (*Akk.*) **schießen** (*fig.*) take a sledgehammer to crack a nut; **das ist unter aller ~** (*ugs.*) it's appallingly bad *or* indescribably dreadful (*coll.*); **unter aller ~ spielen** (*ugs.*) play appallingly badly (*coll.*); B (*ugs.: Könner*) ace; C (*salopp: Revolver*) shooting iron (*coll.*); rod (*Amer. sl.*)

**Kanonenboot** *das* gunboat

**Kanonenboot-: ~diplomatie** *die*, **~politik** *die* gunboat diplomacy

**Kanonen-: ~donner** *der* [rumble of] gunfire; **~futter** *das* (*ugs.*) cannon fodder; **~kugel** *die* cannon ball; **~ofen** *der* cylindrical [iron] stove; **~rohr** *das* gun barrel; **[ach du] heiliges ~rohr!** (*ugs.*) good grief!; **~schlag** *der* thunderflash; cannon cracker

**Kanonier** /kano'ni:ɐ/ *der;* **~s, ~e** (*Milit.*) gunner; artilleryman

**Kanoniker** /ka'no:nikɐ/ *der;* **~s,** ~, **Kanonikus** /ka'no:nikʊs/ *der;* ~, **Kanoniker** (*christl. Kirche*) canon

**kanonisch** ❶ *Adj.* A (*kath. Kirche*) canonical; **~es Recht** canon law; B (*mustergültig, klassisch*) canonical. ❷ *adv.* canonically

**kanonisieren** *tr. V.* canonize

**Kanossa** /ka'nɔsa/ *das;* **~s** (*geh.*) humiliation; **nach ~ gehen** eat humble pie; go to Canossa (*literary*)

**Kanossagang** *der* (*geh.*) humiliation; **einen ~ antreten/machen** eat humble pie; go to Canossa (*literary*)

**Kantate** /kan'ta:tə/ *die;* ~, **~n** (*Musik*) cantata

**Kante** /'kantə/ *die;* ~, **~n** A (*Schnittlinie zweier Flächen, Rand*) edge; (*bei Stoffen*) selvedge; **etw. auf die hohe ~ legen** (*ugs.*) put sth. away *or* by; **etw. auf der hohen ~ haben** (*ugs.*) have sth. put away *or* by; ⇨ *auch* **Ecke** A; B (*landsch.: Gegend*) part

**kanten** ❶ *tr. V.* A tilt; (*auf die Kante stellen*) stand on edge; **„Nicht ~!"** 'do not tilt!'; B (*Skisport*) edge ‹ski›. ❷ *itr. V.* (*Skisport*) edge

**Kanten** *der;* **~s,** ~ (*nordd.*) (*Anfangs- oder Endstück von Brot*) crust

**Kanter** *der;* **~s,** ~ (*Reiten*) canter

**Kantersieg** *der* (*Sport*) runaway *or* easy victory

**Kant-: ~haken** *der* A **jmdn. beim ~haken nehmen** *od.* **kriegen** (*salopp*) give sb. what for (*coll.*); **jetzt haben wir ihn beim ~haken** (*salopp*) now we've got him (*coll.*); B cant hook; **~holz** *das* squared timber; (*Stück*) piece of squared timber

**Kantianer** /kan'ti̯a:nɐ/ *der;* **~s,** ~, **Kantianerin** *die;* ~, **~nen** (*Philos.*) Kantian

**kantig** *Adj.* square-cut ‹timber, stone›; rough-edged ‹rock›; angular ‹face, figure, etc.›; sharp ‹nose›; square ‹chin›; jerky, awkward ‹movement›

**Kantine** /kan'ti:nə/ *die;* ~, **~n** canteen

**Kantinenessen** *das* canteen food *no indef. art.*

**kantisch** *Adj.* Kantian

**Kanton** /kan'to:n/ *der;* **~s, ~e** canton

**kantonal** /kanto'na:l/ ❶ *Adj.* cantonal. ❷ *adv.* on a cantonal basis

**Kantonist** /kanto'nɪst/ *der;* **~en, ~en** *in* **ein unsicherer ~ sein** (*ugs.*) be an unreliable type; be unreliable

**Kantons-: ~rat** *der* (*schweiz.*) cantonal great council; **~regierung** *die* (*schweiz.*) cantonal government

**Kantor** /'kantɔr/ *der;* **~s, ~en** /-'to:rən/ ▶159| choirmaster and organist

**Kantorei** *die;* ~, **~en** [church] choir

**Kantorin** *die;* ~, **~nen** choir mistress and organist

**Kantstein** *der* kerb

**Kanu** /'ka:nu/ *das;* **~s, ~s** canoe

**Kanufahrer** *der*, **Kanufahrerin** *die* canoeist

**Kanüle** /ka'ny:lə/ *die;* ~, **~n** (*Med.*) cannula; (*einer Injektionsspritze*) [hypodermic] needle

**Kanusport** *der* canoeing *no art.*

**Kanute** /ka'nu:tə/ *der;* **~n, ~n, Kanutin,** *die;* ~, **~nen** (*Sport*) canoeist

**Kanzel** /'kantsl̩/ *die;* ~, **~n** A pulpit; **auf der ~:** in the pulpit; **von der ~ herab** from the pulpit; B (*Flugw.*) cockpit; C (*Bergsteigen*) spur; D (*Jägerspr.*) raised hide; high seat

**Kanzel-: ~missbrauch, *~mißbrauch** *der* abuse *or* misuse of the pulpit [for political

*old spelling (see note on page 1707)

ends]; **~redner** *der*, **~rednerin** *die* preacher

**kanzerogen** /kantsero'ge:n/ *Adj.* (*Med.*) carcinogenic

**kanzerös** /kantse'rø:s/ *Adj.* (*Med.*) cancerous

**Kanzlei** /kants'lai/ *die*; ~, **~en** Ⓐ (*veralt.*: *Büro*) office; Ⓑ (*Anwalts~*) chambers *pl.* (*of barrister*); office (*of lawyer*); Ⓒ ⇒ **Staatskanzlei**

**Kanzlei-**: **~diener** *der*, **~dienerin** *die* (*veralt.*) messenger; **~kraft** *die* (*österr.*) ⇒ **Bürokraft**; **~sprache** *die* language of officialdom; officialese; **~stil** *der* (*abwertend*) officialese

**Kanzler** /'kantslɐ/ *der*; **~s**, ~ Ⓐ chancellor; Ⓑ (*an Hochschulen*) vice-chancellor; Ⓒ (*in diplomatischen Vertretungen*) chief secretary

**Kanzler·amt** *das* Ⓐ (*Kanzlerbüro*) chancellor's office; Ⓑ (*Amt des Kanzlers*) chancellorship; office of chancellor

**Kanzlerin** *die*; ~, **~nen** ⇒ **Kanzler**

**Kanzler·kandidat** *der*, **Kanzler·kandidatin** *die* candidate for the chancellorship

**Kanzlerschaft** *die*; ~, **~en** chancellorship

**Kaolin** /kao'li:n/ *das*, (*fachspr.*:) *der*; **~s**, **~e** kaolin

**Kap** /kap/ *das*; **~s**, **~s** cape; ~ **der Guten Hoffnung** Cape of Good Hope; ~ **Hoorn** Cape Horn

**Kapaun** /ka'paun/ *der*; **~s**, **~e** capon

**Kapazität** /kapatsi'tɛ:t/ *die*; ~, **~en** Ⓐ (*Wirtsch.*: *Leistung*) capacity; Ⓑ (*Wirtsch.*: *Gesamtheit der Einrichtungen*) capacity *no pl.*; Ⓒ (*Fassungsvermögen*) capacity; Ⓓ (*Experte*) expert; Ⓔ (*Physik*) capacitance

**Kapazitäts·auslastung** *die* (*Wirtsch.*) use *or* utilization of capacity

**Kapee** /ka'pe/ *in* **schwer von ~ sein** (*salopp*) be slow on the uptake

**Kapelle**[1] /ka'pɛlə/ *die*; ~, **~n** (*Archit.*) chapel

**Kapelle**[2] *die*; ~, **~n** (*Musik~*) band; [light] orchestra

**Kapell·meister** *der*, **Kapell·meisterin** *die* bandleader; bandmaster; (*im Orchester*) conductor; (*im Theater usw.*) musical director

**Kaper**[1] /'ka:pɐ/ *die*; ~, **~n** caper *usu. in pl.*

**Kaper**[2] *der*; **~s**, ~ (*hist.*: *Schiff, Freibeuter*) privateer

**Kaper·brief** *der* (*hist.*) letter[s *pl.*] of marque

**Kaperei** *die*; ~, **~en** (*hist.*) privateering *no art.*

**kapern** *tr. V.* Ⓐ (*hist.*) capture; seize; Ⓑ (*ugs.*) **jmdn. [für etw.] ~:** rope sb. in[to sth.]; **sich** (*Dat.*) **eine Frau/einen Mann ~:** hook [oneself] a wife/husband

**Kapern·soße** *die* caper sauce

**Kaper·schiff** *das* (*hist.*) privateer

**kapieren** /ka'pi:rən/ (*ugs.*) ❶ *tr. V.* (*ugs.*) get (*coll.*); understand; **kapier das endlich!** get that into your thick skull! (*coll.*). ❷ *itr. V.* **kapiert?** got it? (*coll.*); **sie hat schnell kapiert** she was quick to catch on (*coll.*)

**Kapillare** /kapɪ'la:rə/ *die*; ~, **~n** ▶ 471 (*Biol.*, *Med.*) capillary

**Kapillar·gefäß** *das* ▶ 471 (*Biol.*, *Med.*) capillary vessel

**kapital** /kapi'ta:l/ *Adj.* Ⓐ (*außergewöhnlich*) major ‹error, blunder, etc.›; **eine ~e Dummheit begehen** do something exceedingly foolish; Ⓑ (*Jägerspr.*: *sehr groß und stark*) large and powerful; royal ‹stag›; Ⓒ (*schwerwiegend*) serious, bad ‹accident etc.›

**Kapital** *das*; **~s**, **~e** *od.* **~ien** Ⓐ capital; Ⓑ (*fig.*) asset; **seine Hände sind sein einziges ~:** his capable hands are his only asset; **~ aus etw. schlagen** make capital out of sth.; capitalize on sth.; Ⓒ (*Kapitalisten*) capital

**Kapital-**: **~abwanderung** *die* (*Wirtsch.*) exodus of capital; **~anlage** *die* (*Wirtsch.*) capital investment; **~anteil** *der* (*Wirtsch.*) share; stake

**Kapitale** *die*; ~, **~n** (*geh.*) capital [city]

**Kapital-**: **~eigner** *der*, **~eignerin** *die* (*Wirtsch.*) share owner; **~ertrag** *der* (*Wirtsch.*) return on capital; **~ertrag[s]·steuer** *die* (*Steuerw.*) tax on capital income; **~flucht** *die* flight of capital; **~geber** *der*, **~geberin** *die* investor; **~gesellschaft** *die* joint-stock company

**kapitalisieren** *tr. V.* (*Wirtsch.*) capitalize

**Kapitalismus** *der*; **~:** capitalism *no art.*

**Kapitalist** *der*; **~en**, **~en**, **Kapitalistin** *die*; ~, **~nen** capitalist

**kapitalistisch** ❶ *Adj.* capitalistic. ❷ *adv.* capitalistically

**kapital-**, **Kapital-**: **~konto** *das* (*Wirtsch.*) capital account; **~kräftig** *Adj.* (*Wirtsch.*) financially strong; **~markt** *der* (*Wirtsch.*) capital market; **~verbrechen** *das* serious offence *or* crime; (*mit Todesstrafe bedroht*) capital offence *or* crime; **~verbrecher** *der*, **~verbrecherin** *die* serious/capital offender; **~verflechtung** *die* interlacing of capital interests

**Kapitän** /kapi'tɛ:n/ *der*; **~s**, **~e**, ▶ 91 **Kapitänin** *die*; ~, **~nen** Ⓐ (*Seew.*) captain; (*auf einem Handelsschiff*) master; captain; (*auf einem kleineren Schiff*) skipper; captain; **~ der Landstraße** (*ugs.*) knight of the road; [long-distance] truck driver *or* (*Brit.*) lorry driver; Ⓑ (*Flugw.*) captain; Ⓒ (*Sport*) captain; skipper

**Kapitän·leutnant** *der* (*Marine*) lieutenant commander

**Kapitäns·patent** *das* master's certificate

**Kapitel** /ka'pɪtl/ *das*; **~s**, ~ Ⓐ (*Abschnitt*, *auch fig.*) chapter; **das ist ein anderes ~** (*fig.*) that's another story; **ein dunkles ~ in jmds. Geschichte** (*fig.*) a black period in sb.'s history; **das ist ein ~ für sich** (*fig.*) that's an awkward subject; (*etwas Unklares*) that's a complicated subject; Ⓑ (*Geistliche einer Dom- oder Stiftskirche*) chapter

**Kapitell** /kapi'tɛl/ *das*; **~s**, **~e** capital

**Kapitulation** /kapitula'tsio:n/ *die*; ~, **~en** Ⓐ surrender; capitulation; **seine ~ erklären** admit defeat; Ⓑ (*fig.*: *das Aufgeben*) giving up; Ⓒ (*Vertrag*) surrender *or* capitulation document

**kapitulieren** *itr. V.* Ⓐ surrender; capitulate; **vor dem Feind ~:** surrender to the enemy; Ⓑ (*fig.*: *aufgeben*) give up; **vor etw.** (*Dat.*) **~:** give up in the face of sth.

**Kaplan** /ka'pla:n/ *der*; **~s**, **Kapläne** (*kath. Kirche*) Ⓐ (*Hilfsgeistlicher*) curate; Ⓑ (*Geistlicher mit besonderen Aufgaben*) chaplain

**Kapo** /'kapo/ *der*; **~s**, **~s** Ⓐ (*Soldatenspr.*) NCO; Ⓑ (*Lagerjargon*) prisoner acting as an overseer

**Kapok** /'kapɔk/ *der*; **~s** kapok

**Kapott·hut** /ka'pɔt-/ *der* capote; (*ugs. abwertend*: *old or old-fashioned*) hat

**Kappe** /'kapə/ *die*; ~, **~n** Ⓐ (*Kopfbedeckung*) cap; (*Flieger~*) helmet; **etw. auf seine [eigene] ~ nehmen** (*ugs.*) take the responsibility for sth.; Ⓑ (*Abdeckung*) cover; (*eines Rades*) hubcap; Ⓒ (*Verschluss*) cap; top; (*eines Füllers*) cap; Ⓓ (*am Schuh*) (*vorn*) [toe]cap; (*hinten*) counter

**kappen** *tr. V.* Ⓐ (*Seemannsspr.*) cut; Ⓑ (*beschneiden*) cut back ‹hedge etc.›; (*fig.*) cut; Ⓒ (*abschneiden*) cut off ‹branches, shoots, crown, etc.›; Ⓓ (*kastrieren*) caponize, castrate ‹cockerel›

**Kappen·abend** *der* (*landsch.*) carnival party (*at which funny hats are worn*)

**Kappes** /'kapəs/ *der*; ~ (*bes. westd.*) Ⓐ (*Weißkohl*) cabbage; Ⓑ (*ugs.*: *Unsinn*) rubbish; nonsense

**Käppi** /'kɛpi/ *das*; **~s**, **~s** overseas cap; garrison cap

**Kapp·naht** *die* (*Schneiderei*) flat-fell seam

**Kaprice** /ka'pri:sə/ *die*; ~, **~n** (*geh.*) caprice; whim

**Kapriole** /kapri'o:lə/ *die*; ~, **~n** Ⓐ (*Luftsprung*) caper; capriole; **~n schlagen** cut capers; Ⓑ (*Streich*) trick; Ⓒ (*Reiten*) capriole

**Kaprize** /ka'pri:tsə/ *die*; ~, **~n** (*österr.*) ⇒ **Kaprice**

**kaprizieren** *refl. V.* **sich darauf ~, etw. zu tun** be intent on doing sth.; **sich auf ein Land ~:** be utterly committed to a country

**kapriziös** /kapri'tsiø:s/ ❶ *Adj.* capricious. ❷ *adv.* capriciously

**Kapsel** /'kapsl/ *die*; ~, **~n** capsule

**Kapstadt** /'kap-ʃtat/ (*das*); **~s** Cape Town

**kaputt** /ka'pʊt/ *Adj.* Ⓐ (*entzwei*) broken ‹toy, cup, plate, arm, leg, etc.›; **die Maschine/das Auto ist ~:** the machine/car has broken down; (*ganz und gar*) the machine/car has had it (*coll.*); **irgendetwas ist am Auto ~:** there's something wrong with the car; **diese Jacke ist ~:** this jacket needs mending; (*ist zerrissen*) this jacket's torn; **die Birne ist ~:** the bulb has gone; (*ist zerbrochen*) the bulb is smashed; **das Telefon ist ~:** the phone is not working *or* is out of order; **der Fernseher ist ~:** the television has gone wrong; **sein Leben ist ~:** his life is in ruins; **eine ~e Ehe** (*ugs.*) a marriage that has broken up; **ein ~er Typ** (*fig. ugs.*) a down-and-out; **eine ~e Lunge/ein ~es Herz haben** (*ugs.*) have bad lungs/a bad heart; **die Ehe ist ~:** the marriage has failed *or* (*coll.*) is on the rocks; **was ist denn jetzt ~?** (*salopp*) what's wrong *or* the matter now?; **bei dir ist was ~** (*salopp*) there must be something wrong with you (*coll.*); Ⓑ (*ugs.*: *erschöpft*) shattered (*coll.*); whacked (*Brit. coll.*); pooped (*coll.*); Ⓒ (*salopp*: *krankhaft, abartig*) sick

**kaputt-**: **~|arbeiten** *refl. V.* (*ugs.*) work oneself into the ground (*coll.*); **~|fahren** *unr. tr. V.* (*ugs.*) run over ‹animal›; smash up ‹car etc.›; **~|gehen** *unr. itr. V.*; *mit sein* (*ugs.*) Ⓐ (*entzweigehen*) break; ‹machine› break down, (*coll.*) pack up; ‹clothes, shoes› fall to pieces; ‹lightbulb› go; (*zerbrechen*) be smashed; (*eingehen*) ‹plant› die; (*verderben*) ‹fish, fruit, etc.› go off; (*fig.*) ‹marriage› fail; ‹community, relationship, etc.› break up; Ⓑ (*zugrunde gehen*) ‹firm› go bust (*coll.*); ‹person› go to pieces; **er ist an Drogen ~gegangen** he was destroyed by drugs; **~|kriegen** *tr. V.* (*ugs.*) break; **wie hast du das ~gekriegt?** how did you [manage to] break it?; **~|lachen** *refl. V.* (*ugs.*) kill oneself [laughing] (*coll.*); **das ist ja zum Kaputtlachen!** that's a laugh!; **~|machen** (*ugs.*) ❶ *tr. V.* Ⓐ (*zerstören*) break ‹watch, spectacles, plate, etc.›; spoil ‹sth. made with effort›; ruin ‹clothes, furniture, etc.›; burst ‹balloon›; Ⓑ (*ruinieren*) drive ‹business, company› to the wall; destroy ‹political party›; finish ‹person› off; ❷ *refl. V.* wear oneself out; **~|schlagen** *unr. tr. V.* (*ugs.*) smash; **~|schmeißen** *unr. tr. V.* (*ugs.*) smash

**Kapuze** /ka'pu:tsə/ *die*; ~, **~n** hood; (*bei Mönchen*) cowl; hood

**Kapuzen·mantel** *der* coat with a hood

**Kapuziner** /kapu'tsi:nɐ/ *der*; **~s**, ~ Ⓐ (*Mönch*) Capuchin [friar]; Ⓑ (*österr.*: *Kaffee*) cappuccino

**Kapuziner·kresse** *die* nasturtium

**Kar** /ka:ɐ/ (*Geol.*) *das*; **~[e]s**, **~e** cirque; corrie; kar

**Karabiner** /kara'bi:nɐ/ *der*; **~s**, ~ Ⓐ (*Gewehr*) carbine; Ⓑ (*österr.*) ⇒ **Karabinerhaken**

**Karabiner·haken** *der* snap hook; spring hook; (*Bergsteigen*) karabiner

**Karacho** /ka'raxo/ *das*; **~s** *in* **mit ~** *od.* **in vollem ~** (*ugs.*) hell for leather (*coll.*)

**Karaffe** /ka'rafə/ *die*; ~, **~n** carafe; (*mit Glasstöpsel*) decanter

**Karakul·schaf** /kara'kʊl-/ *das* caracul [sheep]

**Karambolage** /karambo'la:ʒə/ *die*; ~, **~n** Ⓐ (*ugs.*) crash; collision; Ⓑ (*Billard*) cannon

**Karambole** /karam'bo:lə/ *die*; ~, **~n** (*Billard*) red [ball]

**karambolieren** *itr. V.* Ⓐ (*Billard*) cannon; Ⓑ *mit haben od. sein* (*zusammenstoßen*) crash; **mit etw. ~:** crash into sth.; collide with sth.

***Karamel** *usw.*: ⇒ **Karamell** *usw.*

**Karamell** /kara'mɛl/ *der* (*schweiz.*: *das*); **~s** caramel

k

**Karamell-: ~bonbon** *der od. das* caramel [toffee]; **~creme** *die* crème caramel
**Karamelle** /kara'mɛlə/ *die;* ~, **~n** caramel [toffee]
**Karaoke** *das;* **~[s]** karaoke
**Karat** /ka'ra:t/ *das;* **~[e]s, ~e** carat; **ein Diamant von 5 ~:** a 5-carat diamond; **reines Gold hat 24 ~:** pure gold is 24 carats
**Karate** /ka'ra:tə/ *das;* **~[s]** karate
**-karäter** /-karɛ:tɐ/ *die* **Zehn~/Fünf~:** ten-carat/five-carat diamond/stone
**Karate·schlag** *der* karate chop
**-karätig** /-karɛ:tɪç/ **zehn~/fünf~:** ten-carat/five-carat
**Karavelle** /kara'vɛlə/ *die;* ~, **~n** (*hist.*) caravel
**Karawane** /kara'va:nə/ *die;* ~, **~n** caravan; **~n von Autos** (*fig.*) long lines of cars
**Karawanen·straße** *die* caravan route
**Karawanserei** /karavanzə'rai/ *die;* ~, **~en** caravanserai
**Karbid** /kar'bi:t/ *das;* **~[e]s, ~e** (*Chem.*) carbide
**Karbid·lampe** *die* carbide lamp
**Karbol** /kar'bo:l/ *das;* **~s, Karbol·säure** *die* carbolic acid
**Karbol·seife** *die* carbolic soap
**Karbonat** /karbo'na:t/ *das;* **~[e]s, ~e** (*Chem.*) carbonate
**Karbunkel** /kar'bʊŋkl/ *der;* **~s,** ~ ▶ 474 (*Med.*) carbuncle
**Kardamom** /karda'mo:m/ *der od. das;* **~s, ~e[n]** cardamom
**Kardan-** /kar'da:n-/: **~antrieb** *der* (*Technik*) cardan drive; **~aufhängung** *die* (*Technik*) cardanic suspension; **~gelenk** *das* (*Technik*) cardan joint
**kardanisch** *Adj.*: *in* **~e Aufhängung** cardanic suspension
**Kardan-: ~tunnel** *der* (*Kfz-W.*) cardan tunnel; cardan-shaft housing; **~welle** *die* (*Technik*) cardan shaft
**Kardätsche** /kar'dɛ:tʃə/ *die;* ~, **~n** dandy brush; body brush
**kardinal** /kardi'na:l/ *Adj.* cardinal
**Kardinal** *der;* **~s, Kardinäle** /kardi'nɛ:lə/ **A** (*kath. Kirche*) cardinal; **B** (*Vogel*) cardinal [bird]
**Kardinal-: ~bischof** *der* cardinal bishop; **~fehler** *der* cardinal error
**Kardinals·kollegium** *das* college of cardinals; Sacred College
**Kardinal-: ~tugend** *die* cardinal virtue; **~zahl** *die* cardinal [number]
**Kardiogramm** /kardio'gram/ *das;* **~s, ~e** (*Med.*) **A** ⇨ **Elektrokardiogramm**; **B** (*Bild der Herzstoßkurven*) cardiogram
**Kardiologe** *der;* **~n, ~n** ▶ 159 cardiologist
**Kardiologie** *die;* ~ (*Med.*) cardiology *no art.*
**Kardiologin** *die;* ~, **~nen** ▶ 159 cardiologist
**Karditis** /kar'di:tɪs/ *die;* ~, **Karditiden** /kardi'ti:dn/ ▶ 474 (*Med.*) carditis
**Karenz** /ka'rɛnts/ *die;* ~, **~en, Karenz·zeit** *die* waiting period
**Karfiol** /kar'fio:l/ *der;* **~s** (*südd., österr.*) cauliflower
**Kar·freitag** /ka:ɐ-/ *der* Good Friday
**Karfunkel** /kar'fʊŋkl/ *der;* **~s,** ~ (*Edelstein; volkst.: Geschwür*) carbuncle
**karg** /kark/ **1** *Adj.* meagre ‹wages, pay, etc.›; frugal ‹meal etc.›; poor ‹light, accommodation›; scanty ‹supply›; meagre, scant ‹applause›; sketchy ‹report›; sparse ‹furnishings›; (*wenig fruchtbar*) barren, poor ‹soil›; barren ‹desert, land›; **~ mit Lob sein** be grudging *or* sparing in one's praise. **2** *adv.* **~ bemessen sein** ‹helping› be mingy (*Brit. coll.*); ‹supply› be scanty; **~ leben** live frugally; **~ möbliert** sparsely furnished; **~ ausgestattet** scantily equipped
**kargen** *itr. V.* **mit Geld ~:** be mean with one's money; **mit seinen Worten ~:** be a person of few words

*old spelling (see note on page 1707)

**Kargheit** *die;* ~ (*geh.*) ⇨ **karg 1**: meagreness; frugality; poorness; scantiness; sketchiness; sparseness; barrenness
**kärglich** /'kɛrklɪç/ **1** *Adj.* meagre, poor ‹wages, pension, etc.›; poor ‹light›; frugal ‹meal›; scanty ‹supply›; meagre ‹existence›; meagre, scant ‹applause›; sparse ‹furnishing›. **2** *adv.* sparsely ‹furnished›; poorly ‹lit, paid, rewarded›
**Kargo** /'kargo/ *der;* **~s, ~s** (*Seemannsspr.*) cargo
**Karibik** /ka'ri:bɪk/ *die;* **~:** Caribbean; **in die ~:** to the Caribbean
**karibisch** *Adj.* Caribbean; **die ~en Inseln** the Caribbean Islands
**kariert** /ka'ri:ɐt/ **1** *Adj.* check, checked ‹material, pattern›; check ‹jacket etc.›; squared ‹paper›. **2** *adv.* (*ugs.*) **~ reden** *od.* **quatschen** talk rubbish
**Karies** /'ka:riɛs/ *die;* ~ ▶ 474 (*Zahnmed.*) caries
**Karikatur** /karika'tu:ɐ/ *die;* ~, **~en** **A** cartoon; (*Porträt*) caricature; **B** (*abwertend: Zerrbild*) caricature
**Karikaturist** *der;* **~en, ~en, Karikaturistin** *die;* ~, **~nen** ▶ 159 cartoonist; (*Porträtist*) caricaturist
**karikaturistisch** **1** *Adj.* caricatural; **der Film gibt eine ~e Darstellung des Familienlebens** the film is a caricature of family life. **2** *adv.* **etw. ~ überzeichnen** caricature sth.
**karikieren** /kari'ki:rən/ *tr. V.* caricature
**kariös** /ka'riø:s/ *Adj.* (*Zahnmed.*) carious
**Karitas** /'ka:ritas/ *die;* ~ (*geh.*) charity
**karitativ** /karita'ti:f/ **1** *Adj.* charitable. **2** *adv.* **sich ~ betätigen** do work for charity
**Karkasse** /kar'kasə/ *die;* ~, **~n** (*Technik, Kochk.*) carcass
**Karl** /karl/ (*der*) Charles; **~ der Große** Charlemagne
**Karmeliter** /karme'li:tɐ/ *der;* **~s, ~:** Carmelite [friar]
**Karmelit[er]in** *die;* ~, **~nen** Carmelite [nun]
**Karmesin** /karme'zi:n/ *das;* **~s** ⇨ **Karmin**
**karmesin·rot** *Adj.* ⇨ **karminrot**
**Karmin** /kar'mi:n/ *das;* **~s** carmine
**karmin·rot** *Adj.* carmine
**Karneol** /karne'o:l/ *der;* **~s, ~e** cornelian
**Karneval** /'karnəval/ *der;* **~s, ~e** *od.* **~s** carnival; **im ~:** at carnival time; **~ feiern** join in the carnival festivities
**Karnevalist** *der;* **~en, ~en, Karnevalistin** *die;* ~, **~nen** carnival reveller; (*Vortragende[r] bei Karnevalssitzungen*) carnival performer
**karnevalistisch** **1** *Adj.* carnival *attrib.* ‹time, festivities, etc.›. **2** *adv.* **sich ~ verkleiden** dress up in a carnival costume/carnival costumes
**Karnevals-: ~kostüm** *das* carnival costume; **~sitzung** *die* carnival convention (*variety show organized by carnival society*); **~verein** *der* carnival society; **~zug** *der* carnival procession
**Karnickel** /kar'nɪkl/ *das;* **~s,** ~ **A** (*landsch.*) rabbit; **B** (*ugs.: Sündenbock*) **immer bin ich das ~!** I always get the blame!
**Karnickel-: ~bock** *der* (*bes. nordd.*) buck rabbit; **~stall** *der* (*bes. nordd.*) rabbit hutch
**karnivor** /karni'vo:ɐ/ *Adj.* (*Biol.*) carnivorous
**Kärnten** /'kɛrntn/ (*das*); **~s** Carinthia
**Kärnt[e]ner** *der;* **~s,** ~, **Kärntnerin** *die;* ~, **~nen** Carinthian
**Karo** /'ka:ro/ *das;* **~s, ~s** **A** (*Viereck*) square; (*auf der Spitze stehend*) diamond; **B** (~*muster*) check; **C** (*Kartenspiel: Farbe*) diamonds *pl.*; **D** (*Kartenspiel: Karte*) diamond; ⇨ *auch* **Pik²**
**Karo-: *~as, ~ass** *das* ace of diamonds; **~bube** *der* jack of diamonds; **~dame** *die* queen of diamonds; **~könig** *der* king of diamonds; **~muster** *das* check; check[ed] pattern
**Karolinger** /'ka:rolɪŋɐ/ *der;* **~s,** ~, **Karolingerin** *die;* ~, **~nen** (*hist.*) Carolingian

**Karosse** /ka'rɔsə/ *die;* ~, **~n** **A** (*Prunkwagen*) [state] coach; **B** (*scherzh. iron.: Auto*) limousine
**Karosserie** /karɔsə'ri:/ *die;* ~, **~n** bodywork; coachwork
**Karosserie·bauer** *der;* **~s, ~:** ▶ 159 coachbuilder
**Karotin** /karo'ti:n/ *das;* **~s** carotene
**Karotte** /ka'rɔtə/ *die;* ~, **~n** small carrot
**Karpaten** /kar'pa:tn/ *Pl.* Carpathians; Carpathian Mountains
**Karpfen** /'karpfn/ *der;* **~s, ~:** carp
**Karpfen·teich** *der* carp pond; ⇨ *auch* **Hecht A**
**Karre** /'karə/ *die;* ~, **~n** (*bes. nordd.*) **A** ⇨ **Karren**; **B** (*abwertend: Fahrzeug*) [old] heap (*coll.*)
**Karree** /ka're:/ *das;* **~s, ~s** **A** (*Viereck*) rectangle; (*Quadrat*) square; (*bes. Milit.: Formation*) square; **B** (*Häuserblock*) **ums ~ gehen/fahren** walk/drive round the block
**karren** **1** *tr. V.* **A** (*mit einer Karre*) cart; **etw./jmdn. nach Hause ~:** bring/take sth./sb. home in a cart; **B** (*salopp: mit einem Auto*) run (*coll.*). **2** *itr. V.*; *mit sein* (*ugs.*) drive [around]
**Karren** *der;* **~s,** ~ (*bes. südd., österr.*) cart; (*zweirädrig*) barrow; (*Schubkarren*) [wheel]barrow; (*für Gepäck*) trolley; **ein ~ voll Sand** a cartload/barrowload of sand; (*fig.*) **den ~ in den Dreck fahren** (*ugs.*) get things into a mess; mess things up; **den ~ [für jmdn.] aus dem Dreck ziehen** (*ugs.*) sort out the mess [for sb.]; **jmdm. an den ~ fahren** (*ugs.*) tell sb. where he gets off (*coll.*)
**Karrette** /ka'rɛtə/ *die;* ~, **~n** (*schweiz.*) **A** handcart; (*Schubkarren*) [wheel]barrow; **B** (*Einkaufswagen*) [shopping] trolley
**Karriere** /ka'rie:rə/ *die;* ~, **~n** **A** career; **~ machen** make a [successful] career for oneself; **B** (*Reiten*) [full *or* extended] gallop
**Karriere-: ~frau** *die* career woman/girl; **~knick** *der* career break; **~macher** *der*, **~macherin** *die* (*abwertend*) careerist
**Karrierist** *der;* **~en, ~en, Karrieristin** *die;* ~, **~nen** (*abwertend*) careerist
**karriolen** *itr. V.*; *mit sein* (*ugs.*) ride around
**Kärrner** /'kɛrnɐ/ *der;* **~s,** ~ (*veralt.*) labourer
**Kärrner·arbeit** *die* donkey work
**Kar·samstag** /ka:ɐ-/ *der* Easter Saturday; Holy Saturday
**Karst¹** /karst/ *der;* **~[e]s, ~e** (*landsch.*) [two-pronged] hoe
**Karst²** *der;* **~[e]s, ~e** (*Geol.*) karst
**karstig** *Adj.* karstic
**Karst·landschaft** *die* karst landscape
**Kartätsche** /kar'tɛ:tʃə/ *die;* ~, **~n** (*hist.*) case-shot
**Kartäuser** /kar'tɔyzɐ/ *der;* **~s,** ~ **A** (*Mönch*) Carthusian [monk]; **B** (*Likör*) chartreuse
**Kartäuserin** *die;* ~, **~nen** Carthusian [nun]
**Karte** /'kartə/ *die;* ~, **~n** **A** (*Kartei~, Loch~ usw.*) card; **die gelbe/rote ~** (*Fußball*) the yellow/red card; **die grüne ~** (*Verkehrsw.*) the green card; **B** (*Ansichts~, Post~, Glückwunsch~, Visiten~*) card; (*Einladungs~*) invitation [card]; **C** (*Speise~*) menu; (*Wein~*) wine list; **nach der ~ essen** eat à la carte; **D** (*Fahr~, Flug~, Eintritts~*) ticket; **E** (*Lebensmittel~*) ration card; **auf ~n** on coupons; **F** (*Land~*) map; (*See~*) chart; **~n lesen** map-read; **G** (*Spiel~*) card; **jmdm. die ~n legen** read sb.'s fortune from the cards; (*fig.*) **diese ~ sticht nicht [mehr]** that won't work [any more]; **die** *od.* **seine ~n aufdecken** *od.* **[offen] auf den Tisch legen** *od.* **offen legen** put one's cards on the table; **alles auf eine ~ setzen** stake everything on one chance; **auf die falsche ~ setzen** back the wrong horse; **jmdm. in die ~n sehen** *od.* (*ugs.*) **gucken** find out *or* see what sb. is up to; **sich** (*Dat.*) **nicht in die ~n sehen** *od.* (*ugs.*) **gucken lassen** play one's cards close to one's chest; not show one's hand; **mit offenen/verdeckten ~n spielen** put one's cards on the table/play

k

one's cards close to one's chest; (H) (*Anzahl von Spielkarten*) hand; **eine schlechte ~ [auf der Hand] haben** have a poor hand

**Kartei** /kar'tai/ *die;* ~, ~**en** card file *or* index

**Kartei-:** ~**karte** *die* file *or* index card; ~**kasten** *der* file-card *or* index-card box; ~**leiche** *die* (*scherzh.*) (A) dead card; (B) (*ugs.: passives Mitglied*) inactive member

**Kartell** /kar'tɛl/ *das;* ~**s**, ~**e** (*Wirtsch., Politik*) cartel

**Kartell-:** ~**amt** *das*, ~**behörde** *die: government body concerned with the control and supervision of cartels;* ≈ Monopolies and Mergers Commission (*Brit.*); ~**gesetz** *das*, ~**recht** *das* law relating to cartels; ≈ monopolies law (*Brit.*)

**Karten-:** ~**bestellung** *die* [ticket] reservation; booking; ~**brief** *der* letter-card; ~**gruß** *der* greeting *or* short message on a [post]card; **an jmdn. einen ~gruß verschicken** send sb. a card; ~**haus** *das* house of cards; ~**kunststück** *das* card trick; ~**legen** *das;* ~~**s** reading the cards *no art.;* cartomancy; ~**leger** *der;* ~~**s**, ~~, ~**legerin** *die;* ~~, ~~**nen** fortune teller (*who tells fortunes by reading the cards*); ~**lesen** *das;* ~~**s** map-reading; ~**spiel** *das* (A) (*Spiel mit* ~) card game; (B) (*Satz Spiel*~) pack *or* (*Amer.*) deck [of cards]; (C) (*das* ~*spielen*) card playing *no art.;* ~**spieler** *der*, ~**spielerin** *die* card player; ~**ständer** *der* map stand; ~**telefon** *das* cardphone; ~**tisch** *der* (A) (*bes. Milit.*) map table; (*Seew.*) chart table; (B) (*Spieltisch*) card table; ~**verkauf** *der* sale of tickets; ~**vorverkauf** *der* advance booking; **im ~vorverkauf sind die Karten billiger** the tickets are cheaper if you buy them in advance

**kartesianisch** /karte'zia:nɪʃ/, **kartesisch** /kar'te:zɪʃ/ *Adj.* Cartesian

**Karthager** /kar'ta:gɐ/ *der;* ~**s**, ~, **Karthagerin** *die;* ~, ~**nen** ▶ 553 Carthaginian

**Karthago** /kar'ta:go/ *(das);* ~**s** ▶ 700 Carthage

**Kartoffel** /kar'tɔfl̩/ *die;* ~, ~**n** (A) potato; **rin in die ~n, raus aus die ~n** (*salopp scherzh.*) it's 'do this' one minute and 'do that' the next; **jmdn. wie eine heiße ~ fallen lassen** (*ugs.*) drop sb. just like that (*coll.*); (B) (*ugs. scherzh.: Nase*) conk (*coll.*); hooter (*Brit. coll.*); (C) (*ugs. scherzh.: Loch im Strumpf*) large hole; potato (*coll.*)

**Kartoffel-:** ~**acker** *der* potato field; ~**brei** *der* mashed *or* creamed potatoes *pl.;* mash (*coll.*); ~**chips** *Pl.* [potato] crisps (*Brit.*) *or* (*Amer.*) chips; ~**ernte** *die* potato harvest; ~**ferien** *Pl.* (*ugs.*) autumn [school] holiday *sing.;* ~**feuer** *das* fire to dispose of potato leaves (*after the potato harvest*); ~**käfer** *der* Colorado beetle; potato beetle; ~**kloß** *der*, ~**knödel** *der* (*südd.*) potato dumpling; ~**mehl** *das* potato flour; ~**puffer** *der* potato pancake (*made from grated raw potatoes*); ~**püree** *das* ⇒ ~**brei**; ~**sack** *der* potato sack; ~**salat** *der* potato salad; ~**schale** *die* potato skin; (*abgeschält*) potato peel *or* peelings *pl.;* ~**suppe** *die* potato soup

**Kartograph** /karto'gra:f/ *der;* ~**en**, ~**en** ▶ 159 cartographer

**Kartographie** *die;* ~: cartography *no art.*

**kartographieren** *tr. V.* map

**Kartographin** *die;* ~, ~**nen** ▶ 159 cartographer

**kartographisch** *Adj.* cartographic

**Karton** /kar'tɔŋ/ *der;* ~**s**, ~**s** (A) (*Pappe*) card[board]; (B) (*Behälter*) cardboard box; (*kleiner und dünner*) carton; **zwei ~[s] Seife/Batterien** two boxes *or* packs of soap/batteries; (C) (*Kunstwiss.*) cartoon

**Kartonage** /karto'na:ʒə/ *die;* ~, ~**n** cardboard boxes [and cartons] *pl.;* cardboard packaging

**kartonieren** /karto'ni:rən/ *tr. V.* (*Buchw.*) bind in [paper] boards

**Kartothek** /karto'te:k/ *die;* ~, ~**en** ⇒ **Kartei**

**Kartusche** /kar'tʊʃə/ *die;* ~, ~**n** (A) (*Metallhülse*) cartridge; (B) (*Kunstwiss.*) cartouche

**Karussell** /karʊ'sɛl/ *das;* ~**s**, ~**s** *od.* ~**e** merry-go-round; carousel (*Amer.*); (*kleineres*) roundabout; ~ **fahren** have a ride on *or* go on the merry-go-round/roundabout; **mit jmdm. ~ fahren** (*fig. ugs.*) give sb. a good telling-off

**Kar·woche** /'ka:ɐ̯vɔxə/ *die* Holy Week; Passion Week

**Karyatide** /karya'ti:də/ *die;* ~, ~**n** (*bild. Kunst*) caryatid

**Karzer** /'kartsɐ/ *der;* ~**s**, ~ (*hist.*) (A) (*Arrestraum*) detention room (*in university, school*); (B) (*Strafe*) detention (*often lasting several days*)

**karzinogen** /kartsino'ge:n/ *Adj.* (*Med.*) carcinogenic

**Karzinologie** *die* (*Med.*) oncology *no art.*

**Karzinom** /kartsi'no:m/ *das;* ~**s**, ~**e** ▶ 474 (*Med.*) carcinoma

**Kasack** /'ka:zak/ *der;* ~**s**, ~**s** (*österr.: die;* ~, ~**s**) tunic

**Kaschemme** /ka'ʃɛmə/ *die;* ~, ~**n** (*abwertend*) [low] dive (*coll.*)

**kaschen** /'kaʃn̩/ *tr. V.* (*salopp*) (A) (*verhaften*) nab (*coll.*); nick (*coll.*); (B) (*sich aneignen*) pinch (*coll.*); nick (*Brit. coll.*)

**kaschieren** /ka'ʃi:rən/ *tr. V.* (A) (*verhüllen*) conceal; hide; disguise ‹fault›; (B) (*Buchw.*) laminate ‹jacket etc.›; line ‹cover etc.› [with paper]; (C) (*Textilw.*) bond [together]

**Kaschmir**[1] /'kaʃmi:ɐ̯/ *(das);* ~**s** Kashmir

**Kaschmir**[2] *der;* ~**s**, ~**e** (*Textilw.*) cashmere; **ein Pullover/Kleid aus ~:** a cashmere sweater/dress

**Käse** /'kɛ:zə/ *der;* ~**s**, ~ (A) cheese; (B) (*ugs. abwertend: Unsinn*) rubbish; nonsense; codswallop (*Brit. coll.*)

**Käse-:** ~**blatt** *das* (*salopp abwertend*) rag; ~**brot** *das* slice of bread and cheese; (*zugeklappt*) cheese sandwich; ~**fondue** *das* cheese fondue; ~**fuß** *der* (*salopp abwertend*) cheesy *or* smelly foot; ~**gebäck** *das* cheese savouries *pl.;* ~**glocke** *die* cheese dome

**Kasein** /kaze'i:n/ *das;* ~**s**, (*Chemie:*) **Casein** *das;* ~**s** casein

**Käse·kuchen** *der* cheesecake

**Kasematte** /kazə'matə/ *die;* ~, ~**n** (*Milit., Marine*) casemate

**Käse·platte** *die* (*Platte*) cheeseboard; (*Gericht*) [selection of] assorted cheeses *pl.*

**Käserei** /kɛ:zə'rai/ *die;* ~, ~**en** (A) (*Herstellung von Käse*) cheesemaking *no art.* (B) (*Betrieb*) cheese factory

**Kaserne** /ka'zɛrnə/ *die;* ~, ~**n** barracks *sing. or pl.*

**Kasernen-:** ~**hof** *der* barrack square; ~**sprache** *die* (*abwertend*) army lingo

**kasernieren** *tr. V.* quarter in barracks; (*fig.*) keep in isolation

**Kasernierung** *die;* ~, ~**en** quartering in barracks *no art.;* (*fig.*) keeping in isolation *no art.*

**käse-, Käse-:** ~**stange** *die* cheese straw; ~**torte** *die* cheesecake; ~**weiß** *Adj.* (*ugs.*) [as] white as a sheet; **sie war ~weiß im Gesicht** her face was as white as a sheet

**käsig** *Adj.* (A) (*ugs.: bleich*) pasty; pale; (*vor Schreck*) as white as a sheet; (B) (*wie Käse*) cheesy; cheeselike

**Kasino** /ka'zi:no/ *das;* ~**s**, ~**s** (A) (*Spiel*~) casino; (B) (*Offiziers*~) [officers'] mess; (C) (*Speiseraum*) canteen

**Kaskade** /kas'ka:də/ *die;* ~, ~**n** (A) (*Wasserfall, auch fig.*) cascade; **in ~n fallen** cascade [down]; **eine ~ von Verwünschungen/Flüchen** (*fig.*) a barrage of curses; (B) (*Sprung*) acrobatic leap (*in which the acrobat pretends to fall*); (C) (*Elektrot.*) cascade

**kasko·versichern** *tr. V.; nur im Inf. u. 2. Part. gebr.* (*mit Vollkasko*) insure comprehensively; (*mit Teilkasko*) insure against theft, fire, or act of God

**Kasko·versicherung** *die* (*Voll*~) comprehensive insurance; (*Teil*~) insurance against theft, fire, or act of God

**Kasper** /'kaspɐ/ *der;* ~**s**, ~ (A) ≈ Punch; (B) (*ugs.: alberner Mensch*) clown; fool

**Kasperl** /'kaspɐl/ *das;* ~**s**, ~**[n]** (*österr.*), **Kasperle** /'kaspɐlə/ *das od. der;* ~**s**, ~ ⇒ **Kasper**

**Kasperle-:** ~**puppe** *die* ≈ Punch and Judy puppet; ~**theater** *das* ≈ Punch and Judy show; (*Puppenbühne*) ≈ Punch and Judy theatre

**kaspern** *itr. V.* (*ugs.*) clown *or* fool around

**Kasper·theater** *das* ⇒ **Kasperletheater**

**Kaspische Meer** /'kaspɪʃə/ *das* Caspian Sea

**Kassa** /'kasa/ *die;* ~, **Kassen** (*österr.*) ⇒ **Kasse**

**Kassa-:** ~**geschäft** *das* (A) (*Börsenw.*) spot transaction; (B) (*Wirtsch.*) cash transaction; ~**kurs** *der* (*Börsenw.*) spot price; ~**markt** *der* (*Börsenw.*) spot market

**Kassandra·ruf** /ka'sandra-/ *der* (*geh.*) prophecy of doom

**Kassation** /kasa'tsio:n/ *die;* ~, ~**en** (A) (*von Urkunden*) annulment; (B) (*von Urteilen*) quashing; setting aside; (C) (*veralt.: unehrenhafte Entlassung*) cashiering

**Kassations·gericht** *das* (*schweiz. Rechtsw.*) court of appeal (*in a canton*)

**Kasse** /'kasə/ *die;* ~, ~**n** (A) (*Kassette*) cash box; (*Registrier*~) till; cash register; **in die ~ greifen** *od.* **einen Griff in die ~ tun** (*ugs.; auch fig.*) help oneself from the till; **er wurde beim Griff in die ~ ertappt** (*auch fig.*) he was caught with his fingers in the till; **die ~ klingelt** (*fig.*) the tills are ringing merrily; (B) (*Ort zum Bezahlen*) cash *or* pay desk; (*im Supermarkt*) checkout; (*in einer Bank*) counter; ~ **machen** (*Kaufmannsspr.*) cash up; **jmdn. zur ~ bitten** (*ugs.*) ask sb. to pay up; (C) (*Bargeld*) cash; **gemeinsame ~ führen** *od.* **machen** share expenses; **getrennte ~ haben** pay separately; **gut/knapp bei ~ sein** be well-off *or* flush/be short of cash *or* money; **bei ~ sein** be in the money; **etw. reißt ein Loch in die ~** (*ugs.*) sth. makes a hole in sb.'s pocket *or* a dent in sb.'s finances; **die ~ führen** be in charge of the money *or* finances *pl.;* (D) (*in Behörde, Unternehmen*) cashier's office; (E) (*Kassenraum*) cashier's office; (*in einer Bank*) counter hall; (F) (*Theater*~, *Kino*~, *Stadion*~) box office; (G) (*Spar*~) [savings] bank; (H) ⇒ **Krankenkasse**; (I) (*Kaufmannsspr.: Barzahlung*) [payment in] cash; **wir liefern nur gegen ~:** we deliver only if payment is made in cash

**Kasseler** /'kasəlɐ/ *das;* ~**s** smoked loin of pork; ⇒ *auch* **Rippenspeer**

**kassen-, Kassen-:** ~**arzt** *der*, ~**ärztin** *die: doctor who treats members of health insurance schemes;* ~**ärztlich** *Adj.* ~**ärztliche Behandlung** treatment under a health insurance scheme; ~**bericht** *der* (*Wirtsch.*) financial report *or* statement; ~**bestand** *der* cash [in hand]; ~**bon** *der* sales slip; receipt; ~**brille** *die* (*ugs.*) *glasses provided under a health insurance scheme;* ≈ National Health glasses *pl.* (*Brit.*); ~**buch** *das* cash book; ~**erfolg** *der* box office success; ~**führer** *der*, ~**führerin** *die* treasurer; ~**gestell** *das* (*ugs.*) *spectacle frame provided under a health insurance scheme;* ≈ National Health frame (*Brit.*); ~**magnet** *der* (*ugs.*) box office draw; ~**patient** *der*, ~**patientin** *die: patient who is a member of a health insurance scheme;* ~**raum** *der* counter hall; ~**schlager** *der* (*ugs.*) (A) (*Film, Theater*) box office hit; (B) (*von Waren*) top seller; ~**schrank** *der* safe; ~**stunden** *Pl.* hours of business, business hours (*of bank, cashier's office, etc.*); ~**sturz** *der* (*ugs.*) ~**sturz machen** check up on one's ready cash; ~**wart** *der;* ~~**s**, ~~**e**, ~**wartin** *die;* ~~, ~~**nen** ▶ 159 treasurer; ~**zettel** *der* (A) (*Quittung*) receipt; (B) (*Kassenbon*) sales slip

**Kasserolle** /kasə'rɔlə/ *die;* ~, ~**n** saucepan

**Kassette** /ka'sɛtə/ *die;* ~, ~**n** (A) (*für Geld u. Wertsachen*) box; case; (B) (*mit Büchern, Schallplatten*) boxed set; (C) (*Tonband*~) cassette; **etw. auf ~ aufnehmen** record *or* tape sth. on cassette; (D) (*Filmrolle*) cassette; (E) (*Behälter für Filmrollen*) can; (F) (*Archit.*) coffer; lacunar

**Kassetten-:** ~**deck** *das* cassette deck; ~**film** *der* film cassette; cassette of film; ~**recorder**, ~**rekorder** *der* cassette recorder *or* player

k

**Kassiber** /ka'si:bɐ/ *der;* **~s,** **~** (*Gaunerspr.*) [secret] message

**Kassier** /ka'si:ɐ̯/ *der;* **~s,** **~e** (*südd., österr., schweiz.*) ⇒ **Kassierer**

**kassieren**[1] ❶ *tr. V.* Ⓐ (*einziehen*) collect ‹rent etc.›; Ⓑ (*ugs.: einnehmen*) collect ‹money, fee, etc.›; (*fig.*) receive, get ‹recognition, praise, etc.›; **dafür hat er viel Geld kassiert** he got a lot of money for it *or* made a lot of money out of it; **bei der Transaktion hat er 100 000 DM kassiert** he made 100,000 marks on the deal; Ⓒ (*ugs.: hinnehmen müssen*) receive, get ‹penalty points, scorn, ingratitude, etc.›; Ⓓ (*ugs.: wegnehmen*) confiscate; take away ‹driving licence›; **er hat das Erbteil seiner Schwester kassiert** he appropriated his sister's share of the inheritance; Ⓔ (*ugs.: verhaften/gefangen nehmen*) pick up; nab (*coll.*); nick (*Brit. coll.*).
❷ *itr. V.* Ⓐ (*ab~*) **bei jmdm. ~:** give sb. his/her bill *or* (*Amer.*) check; (*ohne Rechnung*) settle up with sb.; **darf ich bei Ihnen ~?** would you like your bill?/can I settle up with you?; Ⓑ (*ugs.: Geld einnehmen*) collect the money; (*bezahlt werden*) make money; **[bei einem Geschäft] ganz schön ~:** make a packet *or* a bomb [on a deal] (*coll.*)

**kassieren**[2] *tr. V.* (*Rechtsw.*) quash ‹judgement etc.›

**Kassierer** *der;* **~s, ~, Kassiererin** *die;* **~, ~nen** ▶ 159 Ⓐ (*in Geschäften, Banken*) cashier; teller; Ⓑ (*bei einem Verein*) treasurer

**Kastagnette** /kastan'jɛtə/ *die;* **~, ~n** castanet

**Kastanie** /kas'ta:ni̯ə/ *die;* **~, ~n** chestnut; **[für jmdn.] die ~n aus dem Feuer holen** (*ugs.*) pull the chestnuts out of the fire [for sb.]

**kastanien-, Kastanien-: ~baum** *der* chestnut tree; **~braun** *Adj.* chestnut

**Kästchen** /'kɛstçən/ *das;* **~s, ~** Ⓐ small box; Ⓑ (*vorgedrucktes Quadrat*) square; (*auf Fragebögen*) box

**Kaste** /'kastə/ *die;* **~, ~n** caste

**kasteien** /kas'tai̯ən/ *refl. V.* Ⓐ (*als Bußübung*) chastise oneself; Ⓑ (*sich Entbehrungen auferlegen*) deny oneself

**Kasteiung** *die;* **~, ~en** Ⓐ (*als Bußübung*) self-chastisement; Ⓑ (*Auferlegung von Entbehrungen*) self-denial

**Kastell** /kas'tɛl/ *das;* **~s, ~e** Ⓐ (*hist.: röm. Lager*) fort; Ⓑ (*Burg*) castle

**Kastellan** /kastɛ'la:n/ *der;* **~s, ~e** (*hist.*) castellan

**Kasten** /'kastn̩/ *der;* **~s, Kästen** /'kɛstn̩/ Ⓐ box; Ⓑ (*für Flaschen*) crate; Ⓒ (*ugs.: Briefkasten*) postbox; letter box; Ⓓ (*ugs. abwertend: Gebäude*) barracks *sing. or pl.*; **das ist ja ein furchtbarer alter ~:** that's a terrible old barracks of a place; Ⓔ (*ugs. abwertend*) (*Flugzeug*) crate (*sl.*); (*Schiff*) tub; (*Auto*) heap (*coll.*); (*Fernseher, Radio*) box (*coll.*); Ⓕ (*ugs.: Kamera*) **ein Bild im ~ haben** have got a picture; **eine Szene im ~ haben** have a picture in the can; Ⓖ *in* **etw. auf dem ~ haben** (*ugs.*) have got it up top (*coll.*); have plenty of grey matter; Ⓗ (*Schaukasten*) showcase; display case; Ⓘ (*Soldatenspr.*) glasshouse (*Milit. sl.*); **vier Tage ~:** four days in the glasshouse *or* the cooler; Ⓙ (*Turnen*) box; Ⓚ (*Ballspiele Jargon*) goal; Ⓛ (*bes. nordd.: Schublade*) drawer; Ⓜ (*südd., österr., schweiz.: Schrank*) cupboard

**Kasten-: ~brot** *das* tin [loaf]; **~form** *die* [rectangular] tin; **~geist** *der* caste spirit; **~wagen** *der* cart; (*Lieferwagen*) van; **~wesen** *das* caste system

**Kastilien** /kas'ti:li̯ən/ (*das*)*;* **~s** Castile

**kastilisch** *Adj.* Castilian

**Kastrat** /kas'tra:t/ *der;* **~en, ~en** Ⓐ (*Eunuch*) eunuch; Ⓑ (*Musik hist.*) castrato

**Kastraten·stimme** *die* Ⓐ (*Musik*) castrato voice; Ⓑ (*abwertend*) falsetto voice

**Kastration** /kastra'tsi̯o:n/ *die;* **~, ~en** castration

**Kastrations-: ~angst** *die* (*Psych.*) castration anxiety; **~komplex** *der* (*Psych.*) castration complex

**kastrieren** *tr. V.* castrate; **eine Kastrierte** (*salopp scherzh.*) a filter cigarette

**Kasuistik** /ka'zu̯ɪstɪk/ *die;* **~** (*Philos., geh.*) casuistry

**kasuistisch** *Adj.* (*Philos., geh.*) casuistic

**Kasus** /'ka:zʊs/ *der;* **~, ~** /'ka:zu:s/ (*Sprachw.*) case

**Kasus-: ~bildung** *die* (*Sprachw.*) case formation; **~endung** *die* (*Sprachw.*) case ending

**Kat** /kat/ *der;* **~s, ~s** (*ugs.*) ⇒ **Katalysator** B

**Katafalk** /kata'falk/ *der;* **~s, ~e** catafalque

**Katakombe** /kata'kɔmbə/ *die;* **~, ~n** catacomb

**katalanisch** /kata'la:nɪʃ/ *Adj.* ▶ 696 Catalan

**Katalog** /kata'lo:k/ *der;* **~[e]s, ~e** (*auch fig.*) catalogue

**katalogisieren** *tr. V.* catalogue

**Katalonien** /kata'lo:ni̯ən/ (*das*)*;* **~s** Catalonia

**Katalysator** /kataly'za:tɔr/ *der;* **~s, ~en** /-za'to:rən/ Ⓐ (*Chemie, fig. geh.*) catalyst; Ⓑ (*Kfz-W.*) catalytic converter; ⇒ *auch* **geregelt** 2

**Katalyse** /kata'ly:zə/ *die;* **~, ~n** (*Chemie*) catalysis

**katalytisch** /kata'ly:tɪʃ/ *Adj.* (*Chemie*) catalytic

**Katamaran** /katama'ra:n/ *der od. das;* **~s, ~e** catamaran

**Katapult** /kata'pʊlt/ *das od. der;* **~[e]s, ~e** catapult

**katapultieren** *tr. V.* (*auch fig.*) catapult; eject ‹pilot›

**Katapult-: ~sitz** *der* ejector seat; **~start** *der* catapult launch

**Katarakt** /kata'rakt/ *der;* **~[e]s, ~e** (*Stromschnelle*) rapids *pl.*; (*Wasserfall*) cataract

**Katarrh** /ka'tar/ *der;* **~s, ~e** ▶ 474 (*Med.*) catarrh; **einen ~ haben** have catarrh

**Kataster** /ka'tastɐ/ *der od. das;* **~s, ~:** land register

**Kataster·amt** *das* land registry

**katastrophal** /katastro'fa:l/ ❶ *Adj.* disastrous; (*stärker*) catastrophic; (*entsetzlich*) appalling; atrocious. ❷ *adv.* disastrously; (*stärker*) catastrophically; **sich ~ auswirken** have a disastrous/catastrophic effect; **~ enden** end in disaster/catastrophe

**Katastrophe** /katas'tro:fə/ *die;* **~, ~n** Ⓐ (*Unglück*) disaster; (*stärker*) catastrophe; **jmd. ist eine ~** (*ugs.*) sb. is a disaster; Ⓑ (*Literaturw.*) catastrophe

**Katastrophen-: ~alarm** *der* emergency *or* disaster alert; **~dienst** *der* emergency services *pl.*; **~einsatz** *der:* **den ~einsatz üben** practise procedures in case of a disaster; **~fall** *der* disaster [situation]; **~gebiet** *das* disaster area; **~schutz** *der* Ⓐ (*Organisation*) emergency services *pl.*; Ⓑ (*Maßnahmen*) disaster procedures *pl.*; **dem ~schutz dienen** be useful in the event of a disaster

**Kate** /'ka:tə/ *die;* **~, ~n** (*bes. nordd.*) small cottage

**Katechese** /katɛ'çe:zə/ *die;* **~, ~n** (*christl. Kirche*) catechesis

**Katechet** /katɛ'çe:t/ *der;* **~en, ~en, Katechetin** *die;* **~, ~nen** (*christl. Kirche*) catechist

**Katechismus** /katɛ'çɪsmʊs/ *der;* **~, Katechismen** (*christl. Kirche*) catechism

**Katechist** *der;* **~en, ~en, Katechistin** *die;* **~, ~nen** catechist

**kategorial** /katego'ri̯a:l/ *Adj.* (*geh.*) categorial

**Kategorie** /katego'ri:/ *die;* **~, ~n** /-i:ən/ category; **diese ~ Mensch** that sort of person

**kategorisch** ❶ *Adj.* categorical; ⇒ *auch* **Imperativ** B. ❷ *adv.* categorically

**kategorisieren** *tr. V.* categorize

**Kater** /'ka:tɐ/ *der;* **~s, ~** Ⓐ tom cat; **wie ein verliebter ~:** like an amorous tom cat; ⇒ *auch* **gestiefelt**; Ⓑ (*ugs.: schlechte Verfassung*) hangover; **einen ~ haben** have a hangover; be hung-over

**Kater-: ~frühstück** *das: breakfast, usually of pickled herrings and gherkins, supposed to cure a hangover;* **~stimmung** *die* morning-after feeling; **er ist in der fürchterlichsten ~stimmung** he's got a terrible hangover

**Katharina** /kata'ri:na/ (*die*) Catherine; Katherine

**Katharsis** /'ka(:)tarzɪs/ *die;* **~** (*Literaturw.*) catharsis

**kathartisch** /ka'tartɪʃ/ (*geh.*) ❶ *Adj.* cathartic. ❷ *adv.* cathartically

**Katheder** /ka'te:dɐ/ *das od. der;* **~s, ~:** lectern; (*Pult des Lehrers*) teacher's desk

**Katheder·weisheit** *die* theoretical *or* academic knowledge *no pl., no indef. art.*

**Kathedrale** /kate'dra:lə/ *die;* **~, ~n** cathedral

**Kathete** /ka'te:tə/ *die;* **~, ~n** (*Math.*) leg (*of a right-angled triangle*)

**Katheter** /ka'te:tɐ/ *der;* **~s, ~** (*Med.*) catheter

**Kathode** /ka'to:də/ *die;* **~, ~n** (*Physik*) cathode

**Katholik** /kato'li:k/ *der;* **~en, ~en, Katholikin** *die;* **~, ~nen** [Roman] Catholic

**katholisch** *Adj.* [Roman] Catholic; **die Katholischen** (*ugs.*) the Catholics; ⇒ *auch* **taufen** A

**Katholizismus** /katoli'tsɪsmʊs/ *der;* **~:** [Roman] Catholicism *no art.*

**Katholizität** /katolitsi'tɛ:t/ *die;* **~:** Catholicism

**Katode** /ka'to:də/ *die;* **~, ~n** ⇒ **Kathode**

**Kattun** /ka'tu:n/ *der;* **~s, ~e** calico

**Kattun·kleid** *das* calico dress

**Katz** /kats/ *die:* in **~ und Maus [mit jmdm.] spielen** (*ugs.*) play cat and mouse [with sb.]; **für die ~ sein** (*salopp*) be a waste of time

**katzbalgen** *refl. V.* (*ugs.*) scrap; fight

**katzbuckeln** *itr. V.* (*abwertend*) bow and scrape; **vor jmdm. ~:** bow and scrape to sb.

**Kätzchen** /'kɛtsçən/ *das;* **~s, ~** Ⓐ (*kleine Katze*) little cat; (*liebkosend*) pussy; (*junge Katze*) kitten; Ⓑ (*Blüte der Birke, Erle u. a.*) catkin; Ⓒ (*ugs.: Mädchen*) kitten

**Kätzchen·zweig** *der* catkin twig

**Katze** /'katsə/ *die;* **~, ~n** Ⓐ cat; **die ~ lässt das Mausen nicht** (*Spr.*) a leopard cannot change its spots (*prov.*); **bei Nacht** *od.* **nachts sind alle ~n grau** it's impossible to see any details in the dark; **wenn die ~ aus dem Haus ist, tanzen die Mäuse [auf dem Tisch]** (*Spr.*) when the cat's away the mice will play (*prov.*); **da beißt sich die ~ in den Schwanz** (*fig.*) we've come round in a circle; **die ~ aus dem Sack lassen** (*ugs.*) let the cat out of the bag; **die ~ im Sack kaufen** (*ugs.*) buy a pig in a poke; **um etw. herumgehen wie die ~ um den heißen Brei** (*ugs.*) beat about the bush; ⇒ *auch* **Katz**; Ⓑ (*Jägerspr.*) female; Ⓒ (*temperamentvolle Frau*) cat

**Katzelmacher** *der;* **~s, ~** (*südd., österr.: salopp abwertend*) wop (*sl. derog.*)

**katzen-, Katzen-: ~auge** *das* Ⓐ (*ugs.: Rückstrahler*) reflector; Ⓑ (*Mineral.*) cat's-eye; **~buckel** *der* hunched back; **einen ~buckel machen** hunch one's back; **~fell** *das* cat's skin; **~freundlich** *Adj.* ingratiatingly friendly; **~haft** *Adj.* catlike; **~jammer** *der* Ⓐ (*Kater*) hangover; Ⓑ (*fig.*) mood of depression; **~klo** *das* (*ugs.*) cat's [litter] tray; **~kopf** *der* (*ugs.*) cobble[stone]; **~musik** *die* (*ugs. abwertend*) terrible row (*coll.*); cacophony; **~sprung** *der* ▶ 265 stone's throw; **bis zum Strand ist es nur ein ~sprung** the beach is only a stone's throw away; **~tisch** *der* (*ugs. scherzh.*) children's table; **~wäsche** *die* (*ugs.*) lick and a promise (*coll.*); catlick (*coll.*); **~wäsche machen** have a lick and a promise *or* a catlick; **~zunge** *die* langue de chat

**Kau·bewegung** *die* chewing movement

**Kauderwelsch** /'kaudɐvɛlʃ/ *das;* **~[s]** gibberish *no indef. art.*; double Dutch *no indef.*

*old spelling (see note on page 1707)

*art.;* **juristisches/medizinisches ~:** legal/medical jargon; **ein ~ aus Deutsch, Englisch und Französisch** an incomprehensible hotchpotch of German, English, and French

**kauderwelschen** *itr. V.* talk gibberish *or* double Dutch

**kauen** /'kauən/ ❶ *tr. V.* chew; masticate (*Med., formal*); **[die] Nägel ~:** bite *or* chew one's nails. ❷ *itr. V.* Ⓐ chew; **an etw.** (*Dat.*) **~:** chew [on] sth.; **an einem Problem ~** (*fig.*) wrestle *or* struggle with a problem; **an dieser Niederlage wird er noch einige Zeit zu ~ haben** (*fig.*) it will take him some time to get over this defeat; **mit vollen Backen ~** (*ugs.*) chew with one's mouth [stuffed] full; Ⓑ (*nagen, knabbern*) chew; bite; **an einem Bleistift/den Fingernägeln ~:** chew a pencil/bite *or* chew one's nails

**kauern** /'kauɐn/ ❶ *itr. V.* crouch [down]; (*ängstlich*) cower. ❷ *refl. V.* crouch [down]; (*ängstlich*) cower; **sich an jmdn. ~:** huddle up to sb.

**Kauf** /kauf/ *der;* **~[e]s, Käufe** /'kɔyfə/ Ⓐ (*das ~en*) buying; purchasing (*formal*); **den ~ vermitteln** arrange the purchase; **einen ~ abschließen/tätigen** complete/make a purchase; **jmdn. zum ~ ermuntern/veranlassen** encourage/induce sb. to buy; **jmdm. etw. zum ~ anbieten** offer sb. sth. for sale; **etw. in ~ nehmen** (*fig.*) accept sth.; **jmdn. in ~ nehmen** (*fig. ugs.*) put up with sb.; Ⓑ (*das käuflich Erworbene*) purchase

**Kauf-: ~auftrag** *der* order to buy *or* purchase; **~brief** *der* bill of sale; (*beim Hauskauf*) title deed

**kaufen** ❶ *tr. V.* Ⓐ (*erwerben*) buy; purchase; **etw. billig/zu teuer ~:** buy sth. cheaply/pay too much for sth.; **sich/jmdm. etw. ~:** buy sth. for oneself/sb.; buy oneself/sb. sth.; **etw. auf Raten** *od.* **Abzahlung ~:** buy sth. on hire purchase (*Brit.*) *or* (*Amer.*) the instalment plan; **etw. auf Stottern** *od.* **Pump ~** (*ugs.*) buy sth. on the never-never (*Brit. coll.*) *or* (*Amer. coll.*) on time; **etw. für viel** *od.* **teures Geld ~:** pay a lot of money for sth.; **das wird viel** *od.* **gern gekauft** it sells well; **dafür kann ich mir nichts ~** (*ugs.*) a [fat] lot of use that is to me (*coll.*); **sich** (*Dat.*) **jmdn. ~** (*ugs.*) give sb. what for (*coll.*); let sb. have *or* give sb. a piece of one's mind; Ⓑ (*ugs.: bestechen*) buy. ❷ *itr. V.* (*ein~*) shop; **in diesem Laden kaufe ich nicht mehr** I'm not getting anything in that shop again

**Käufer** /'kɔyfɐ/ *der;* **~s, ~, Käuferin** *die;* **~, ~nen** buyer; purchaser; (*Kunde/Kundin*) customer; ⇨ *auch* **-in**

**Käufer·schicht** *die* class of customer *or* consumer

**kauf-, Kauf-: ~fahrer** *der* (*veralt.*), **~fahrtei·schiff** /-fa:ɐ̯'tai-/ *das* (*veralt.*) merchantman; **~frau** *die* businesswoman; (*Händlerin*) trader; merchant; **~haus** *das* department store; **~haus·detektiv** *der*, **~haus·detektivin** *die* ▶159 store detective; **~kassette** *die* [commercially produced] video; **den Film/die Reihe gibt es auch als ~kassette** you can buy that film/series on video too; **~kraft** *die* (*Wirtsch.*) Ⓐ (*Wert des Geldes*) purchasing power; Ⓑ (*Zahlungsfähigkeit*) spending power; **~kräftig** *Adj.* **ein ~kräftiger Kunde/Interessent** a customer with money to spend/a wealthy potential buyer; **~kräftig sein** have money to spend; **~laden** *der; Pl.* **~läden** Ⓐ (*veralt.*) (*kleiner Laden*) [small] shop; (*Lebensmittelladen*) [small] grocer's shop; Ⓑ (*Kinderspielzeug*) toy shop

**käuflich** /'kɔyflɪç/ ❶ *Adj.* Ⓐ (*gegen Bezahlung erhältlich*) for sale *postpos.;* **~e Liebe** (*fig.*) prostitution; **ein ~es Mädchen** (*fig.*) a woman/girl of easy virtue; Ⓑ (*bestechlich*) venal; **~ sein** be easily bought. ❷ *adv.* **etw. ~ erwerben/erstehen** buy *or* purchase sth.; **~ zu erwerben sein** be for sale

**kauf-, Kauf-: ~lust** *die* inclination *or* desire to buy; **~lustig** *Adj.* eager to buy *pred.;* **die ~lustigen** the eager shoppers

**Kauf·mann** *der; Pl.* **Kaufleute** Ⓐ (*Geschäftsmann*) businessman; (*Händler*) trader; merchant; **gelernter ~:** *person who has completed a course of training in some branch of business;* Ⓑ (*Besitzer eines Kaufladens*) shopkeeper; (*Besitzer eines Lebensmittelladens*) grocer; **zum ~ gehen** go to the shop/grocer's

**kaufmännisch** ❶ *Adj.* commercial; business *attrib.;* commercial ‹bookkeeping›; **~er Angestellter** clerk; employee in business; **einen ~en Beruf ergreifen/erlernen** go into business/receive a business training; **~es Geschick/~e Erfahrung haben** possess business skill/experience. ❷ *adv.* **~ tätig sein** be in business; **~ denken** think along commercial lines

**Kaufmanns-: ~sprache** *die* business parlance; **~stand** *der* (*veralt.*) merchant class

**Kauf-: ~objekt** *das* article for sale; (*Haus usw.*) property for sale; **~preis** *der* purchase price; **~rausch** *der* frantic urge to spend; **~summe** *die* purchase price; **~vertrag** *der* contract of sale; (*beim Hauskauf*) title deed; **~zwang** *der* obligation to buy *or* purchase; **ohne ~zwang** without obligation [to buy *or* purchase]

**Kau·gummi** *der od. das;* **~s, ~s** chewing gum

**Kaukasien** /kau'ka:zi̯ən/ (*das*)**;** **~s** Caucasia

**Kaukasier** *der;* **~s, ~, Kaukasierin** *die;* **~, ~nen** Caucasian

**kaukasisch** *Adj.* Caucasian

**Kaukasus** /'kaukazʊs/ *der;* **~:** the Caucasus

**Kaulquappe** /'kaulkvapə/ *die;* **~, ~n** tadpole

**kaum** /kaum/ *Adv.* Ⓐ (*fast gar nicht*) hardly; scarcely; **~ jemand/etwas** hardly anybody *or* anyone/anything; **~ älter/größer/besser** hardly *or* scarcely any older/bigger/better; **wir haben ~ noch Zeit** we really haven't the time; **das war ~ noch zu erwarten** it was really too late to expect that; Ⓑ (*nur mit Mühe*) hardly; scarcely; barely; **ich kann es ~ glauben/erwarten** I can hardly believe it/wait; **ich konnte ~ rechtzeitig damit fertig werden** I could hardly *or* barely finish it in time; **diese Schrift ist ~ zu entziffern** this writing is barely decipherable; Ⓒ (*vermutlich nicht*) hardly; scarcely; **er wird [wohl] ~ zustimmen** he is hardly likely to agree; **ich glaube ~:** I hardly *or* scarcely think so; **es wird sich ~ lohnen** it is unlikely to be profitable; Ⓓ (*in dem Augenblick*) **~ hatte er Platz genommen, als ...** no sooner had he sat down than ...; Ⓔ (*nicht lange nachdem*) **~ dass er aus dem Gefängnis gekommen war ...** hardly *or* scarcely had he left prison when ...; **der Regen war, ~ dass er angefangen hatte, auch schon wieder vorüber** the rain had stopped almost as soon as it had started; Ⓕ (*geh.*) **~ dass ich mich an die Landschaft erinnere** I can hardly even remember the scenery

**Kau·muskel** *der* ▶471 (*Anat.*) masticatory muscle; **[äußerer] ~:** masseter

**kausal** /kau'za:l/ *Adj.* (*geh., Sprachw.*) causal

**Kausal·gesetz** *das* (*bes. Philos., Logik*) law of causality

**Kausalität** /kauzali'tɛ:t/ *die;* **~, ~en** causality

**Kausalitäts·gesetz** *das* ⇨ **Kausalgesetz**

**Kausal-: ~kette** *die* (*bes. Philos., Logik*) causal chain; **~satz** *der* (*Sprachw.*) causal clause; **~zusammenhang** *der* (*bes. Philos., Logik*) causal connection

**Kausativ** /'kauzati:f/ *das;* **~s, ~e** /-i:və/ (*Sprachw.*) causative verb

**Kau·tabak** *der* chewing tobacco

**Kautel** /kau'te:l/ *die;* **~, ~en** (*Rechtsw.*) proviso

**Kaution** /kau'tsi̯o:n/ *die;* **~, ~en** Ⓐ (*bei Freilassung eines Gefangenen*) bail; **eine ~ für jmdn. stellen** stand bail *or* surety for sb.; **gegen ~:** on bail; **jmdn. gegen ~ freibekommen** bail sb. out; Ⓑ (*beim Mieten einer Wohnung*) deposit

**Kautschuk** /'kautʃʊk/ *der;* **~s, ~e** [india] rubber

**Kautschuk-: ~milch** *die* rubber latex; **~paragraph** *der* (*ugs.*) ⇨ **Gummiparagraph**

**Kauz** /kauts/ *der;* **~es, Käuze** /'kɔytsə/ Ⓐ (*Wald~*) tawny owl; (*Stein~*) little owl; Ⓑ (*Sonderling*) odd *or* strange fellow; oddball (*coll.*); **ein komischer ~:** an odd *or* a queer bird (*coll.*)

**Käuzchen** /'kɔytsçən/ *das;* **~s, ~** ⇨ **Kauz** A

**kauzig** *Adj.* odd; queer; funny (*coll.*)

**Kavalier** /kava'li:ɐ̯/ *der;* **~s, ~e** Ⓐ (*höflicher Mann*) gentleman; **der ~ genießt und schweigt** a gentleman never talks about his amours; Ⓑ (*veralt., noch scherzh.: Freund*) beau (*dated*); young man; Ⓒ (*hist.: Edelmann*) cavalier; nobleman

**kavaliers-, Kavaliers-: ~delikt** *das* trifling offence; peccadillo; **~mäßig** ❶ *Adj.* gentlemanly; ❷ *adv.* like a gentleman; in a gentlemanly manner; **~start** *der* racing start

**Kavalkade** /kaval'ka:də/ *die;* **~, ~n** (*veralt.*) cavalcade

**Kavallerie** /kavalə'ri:/ *die;* **~, ~n** (*Milit. hist.*) cavalry

**Kavallerie·pferd** *das* cavalry horse

**Kavallerist** *der;* **~en, ~en** cavalryman; trooper

**Kavents·mann** /ka'vɛnts-/ *der* (*bes. nordd.*) (*übergroßes Exemplar*) monster

**Kaverne** /ka'vɛrnə/ *die;* **~, ~n** Ⓐ (*unterirdischer Hohlraum*) [artificial] cavern; Ⓑ (*Med.*) cavern

**Kaviar** /'ka:vi̯ar/ *der;* **~s, ~e** caviare

**Kaviar·brot** *das* French bread; **ein ~:** a French loaf

**kcal** *Abk.* **Kilo[gramm]kalorie** kcal

**KdF** *Abk.* (*ns.*) **Kraft durch Freude** Strength through Joy [movement]

**Kebse** /'ke:psə/ *die;* **~, ~n** (*hist.*), **Kebs·weib** *das* (*hist.*) concubine

**keck** /kɛk/ ❶ *Adj.* Ⓐ (*respektlos*) impertinent; cheeky; saucy (*Brit.*); Ⓑ (*veralt.: verwegen*) bold; Ⓒ (*flott*) jaunty, pert ‹hat etc.›. ❷ *adv.* Ⓐ (*respektlos*) impertinently; cheekily; saucily (*Brit.*); Ⓑ (*veralt.: verwegen*) boldly; Ⓒ (*flott*) jauntily

**Keckheit** *die;* **~, ~en** Ⓐ (*Respektlosigkeit*) impertinence; cheek; sauce (*Brit.*); Ⓑ (*veralt.: Kühnheit*) boldness

**Keeper** /'ki:pɐ/ *der;* **~s, ~, Keeperin** *die;* **~, ~nen** (*Fußball, bes. österr.*) [goal]keeper

**Kefir** /'ke:fɪr/ *der;* **~s** kefir

**Kegel** /'ke:gl̩/ *der;* **~s, ~** Ⓐ (*geometrischer Körper*) cone; Ⓑ (*Spielfigur*) skittle; (*beim Bowling*) pin; **~ schieben** play skittles *or* ninepins; Ⓒ (*Berg~*) peak; Ⓓ (*Licht~*) beam; Ⓔ (*Druckw.*) body size; point size

**kegel-, Kegel-: ~abend** *der* skittles night; **~bahn** *die* skittle alley; **~bruder** *der* skittle-club friend; **~förmig** *Adj.* conical; cone-shaped; **~klub** *der* skittle club; **~kugel** *die* [skittle] ball; **~mantel** *der* (*Geom.*) lateral surface of a/the cone

**kegeln** ❶ *itr. V.* Ⓐ (*eine Kegelpartie machen*) play skittles *or* ninepins; (*beim Bowling*) bowl; Ⓑ *mit sein* (*ugs.: hinfallen*) tumble. ❷ *tr. V.* Ⓐ (*durch Kegeln ausführen*) play; Ⓑ (*durch Kegeln erzielen*) bowl; score

**kegel-, Kegel-: ~rad** *das* (*Technik*) bevel wheel; ***~|schieben** ⇨ **Kegel** B; **~schieben** *das;* **~~s** skittles *sing.;* ninepins *sing.;* **~schnitt** *der* (*Geom.*) conic section; **~schwester** *die* ⇨ **~bruder**; **~sport** *der* skittles *sing.;* ninepins *sing.;* **~stumpf** *der* truncated cone; frustum of a cone

**Kegler** *der;* **~s, ~, Keglerin** *die;* **~, ~nen** skittle player; (*bei Bowling*) [tenpin] bowler

**Kehle** /'ke:lə/ *die;* **~, ~n** Ⓐ ▶471 throat; **jmdm. an die ~ springen/fahren** leap at sb.'s throat; **sich** (*Dat.*) **die ~ schmieren** *od.* **ölen** *od.* **anfeuchten** wet one's whistle (*coll.*); **sich** (*Dat.*) **die ~ aus dem Hals schreien** (*ugs.*) shout *or* yell one's head off; **aus voller ~:** at the top of one's voice; **sein ganzes Geld durch die ~ jagen** pour all one's money down one's throat; **etw. bleibt jmdm. in der ~ stecken** sth. sticks in sb.'s throat *or* gullet; **etw. in die falsche ~ bekommen** (*ugs.*) (*fig.: etw. missverstehen*) take sth. the wrong way; (*sich an etw. verschlucken*) have sth. go down the wrong way; ⇒ *auch* **Messer** A; Ⓑ(*Archit.*) hollow moulding; (*Dach~*) [roof] valley

**kehlig** ❶ *Adj.* guttural ‹language, speech, sound, etc.›; throaty, guttural ‹voice, laugh, etc.›. ❷ *adv.* throatily; gutturally; in a throaty *or* guttural voice

**Kehl·kopf** *der* ▶ 471 (*Anat.*) larynx

**Kehlkopf-:** **~entzündung** *die* laryngitis *no indef. art.*; **~krebs** *der* ▶ 474 (*Med.*) cancer of the larynx; **~mikrofon, ~mikrophon** *das* throat microphone; **~spiegel** *der* (*Med.*) laryngoscope

**Kehl·laut** *der* Ⓐ guttural sound; Ⓑ (*Sprachw.*) guttural

**Kehr-:** **~aus** *der;* **~~** Ⓐ(*letzter Tanz*) last dance; Ⓑ(*Schluss einer Veranstaltung*) **den ~aus machen** finish; call it a day (*coll.*); (*zumachen*) close; **~besen** *der* broom; (*Handfeger*) brush; **~blech** *das* (*bes. südd.*) small shovel (*used as dustpan*)

**Kehre** /ˈkeːrə/ *die;* **~, ~n** Ⓐ(*scharfe Kurve*) sharp bend *or* turn; (*Haarnadelkurve*) hairpin bend; Ⓑ(*geh.: Wende*) [abrupt] change of direction; Ⓒ(*Turnen*) back *or* rear vault

**kehren**[1] ❶ *tr. V.* turn; **die Innenseite von etw. nach außen ~:** turn sth. inside out; **jmdm. den Rücken ~:** turn one's back on sb.; **die Augen zum Himmel ~:** raise one's eyes to the sky *or* heavenwards; **etw./alles zum Besten ~:** make sure sth./everything turns out for the best.
❷ *refl. V.* turn; **sich gegen jmdn./etw. ~:** turn against sb./sth.; **etw./alles wird sich zum Besten ~:** sth./everything will turn out all right; **sich an etw.** (*Dat.*) **nicht ~:** pay no attention to *or* not care about sth.
❸ *itr. V.* Ⓐ(*selten: um~*) turn [round]; **Abteilung kehrt!** (*Milit.*) squad, about turn *or* (*Amer.*) face!; **rechtsum/linksum kehrt!** right/left turn *or* (*Amer.*) face!; Ⓑ *mit sein* (*geh.: zurück~/ein~*) return; **in sich** (*Akk.*) **gekehrt** lost in thought; in a brown study; **ein in sich** (*Akk.*) **gekehrter Mensch** an introverted person

**kehren**[2] ❶ *itr. V.* (*bes. südd.*) sweep; do the sweeping. ❷ *tr. V.* sweep; (*mit einem Handfeger*) brush; **den Staub von etw./auf etw.** (*Akk.*) **~:** sweep/brush the dust off sth./on to sth.

**Kehricht** /ˈkeːrɪçt/ *der od. das;* **~s** Ⓐ(*geh.: Schmutz, Unrat*) rubbish; **das geht dich einen feuchten ~ an!** (*salopp*) mind your own damned business!; Ⓑ(*schweiz.: Müll*) refuse; garbage (*Amer.*)

**Kehricht-:** **~eimer** *der* dustbin; garbage can (*Amer.*); **~haufen** *der* pile *or* heap of rubbish; **~schaufel** *die* ⇒ **Kehrschaufel**

**Kehr-:** **~maschine** *die* [mechanical] road sweeper; **~reim** *der* refrain; **~schaufel** *die* dustpan; **~seite** *die* Ⓐ(*Rückseite*) back; (*einer Münze, Medaille*) reverse; (*eines Stoffes*) back; wrong side; **die ~seite der Medaille** (*fig.*) the other side of the coin; Ⓑ (*scherzh.*) (*Gesäß*) backside; (*Rücken*) back; Ⓒ(*nachteiliger Aspekt*) drawback; disadvantage

**kehrt|machen** *itr. V.* (*ugs.*) (*sich umdrehen*) do an about-turn; (*umkehren*) turn [round and go] back; (*plötzlich*) turn in one's tracks; **auf dem Absatz ~:** turn on one's heel

**Kehrt·wendung** *die* (*bes. Milit. od. fig.*) about-turn; about-face (*Amer.*); **eine ~ machen** make *or* do an about-turn *or* (*Amer.*) about-face

**Kehr·wert** *der* (*Math.*) reciprocal

**keifen** /ˈkaifn̩/ *itr. V.* (*abwertend*) nag; scold; **das Keifen der Marktfrauen** the squabbling *or* bickering of the market women

**Keiferei** /kaifəˈrai/ *die;* **~, ~en** (*abwertend*) nagging; scolding

**Keil** /kail/ *der;* **~[e]s, ~e** Ⓐ(*zum Spalten*) wedge; **einen ~ in etw.** (*Akk.*) **treiben** drive a wedge into sth.; **einen ~ zwischen die beiden Freunde treiben** (*fig.*) drive a wedge between the two friends; Ⓑ(*zum Festklemmen*) chock; (*unter einer Tür*) wedge; Ⓒ (*bes. Milit.: keilförmige Formation*) wedge; Ⓓ(*Schneiderei*) [wedge-shaped] gusset

**Keil·absatz** *der* wedge [heel]

**Keile** /ˈkailə/ *die;* **~** (*nordd.*) walloping (*coll.*); thrashing; **~ bekommen** *od.* **kriegen** get a walloping (*coll.*) *or* thrashing

**keilen** ❶ *refl. V.* (*ugs.: sich prügeln*) fight; scrap; **sich um etw. ~:** fight over sth. ❷ *tr. V.* Ⓐ(*fachspr.: mit einem Keil spalten*) split with a wedge; Ⓑ(*fachspr.: als Keil hineinschlagen*) **etw. in etw.** (*Akk.*) **~:** drive sth. into sth.; Ⓒ(*ugs.: anwerben*) rope in (*coll.*); recruit. ❸ *itr. V.* (*ausschlagen*) kick

**Keiler** *der;* **~s, ~** (*Jägerspr.*) wild boar

**Keilerei** *die;* **~, ~en** (*ugs.*) punch-up (*coll.*); brawl; fight; **eine allgemeine ~:** a free-for-all

**keil-, Keil-:** **~förmig** wedge-shaped; cuneiform ‹lettering, script›; **~hose** *die* tapering trousers; (*Skihose*) tapering ski pants; **~kissen** *das* wedge-shaped bolster; **~riemen** *der* (*Technik*) V-belt; **~schrift** *die* cuneiform script

**Keim** /kaim/ *der;* **~[e]s, ~e** Ⓐ(*Bot.: erster Trieb*) shoot; Ⓑ(*Biol.: befruchtete Eizelle*) embryo; Ⓒ(*Ursprung, Ausgangspunkt*) seed[s *pl.*]; **etw. im ~ ersticken** nip sth. in the bud; **den ~ zu etw. legen** sow the seeds *pl.* of sth.; Ⓓ(*Biol., Med.: Krankheitserreger*) germ; Ⓔ(*Physik*) nucleus

**Keim-:** **~bahn** *die* (*Biol.*) germ line; **~bahn·therapie** *die* (*Med.*) germ-line therapy; **~blatt** *das* Ⓐ(*Bot.*) cotyledon; seed leaf; Ⓑ(*Biol., Med.*) germ layer; **~drüse** *die* ▶ 471 (*Zool., Med.*) gonad; **~drüsen·hormon** *das* sex hormone

**keimen** *itr. V.* Ⓐ(*zu sprießen beginnen*) germinate; sprout; Ⓑ(*innerlich entstehen*) ‹hope› stir; ‹thought, belief, decision› form; ‹love, yearning› awaken

**keim-, Keim-:** **~fähig** *Adj.* viable; capable of germinating *postpos.*; **~fähigkeit** *die* viability; ability to germinate; **~frei** *Adj.* germ-free; sterile; **etw. ~frei machen** sterilize sth.; **~freie Milch** sterilized milk; **~frei verpackt/gelagert** packed in sterile containers/stored in sterile conditions

**keimhaft** ❶ *Adj.* (*geh.*) incipient; (*noch nicht ausgeprägt*) embryonic. ❷ *adv.* **~ angelegt** embryonically present

**Keimling** /ˈkaimlɪŋ/ *der;* **~s, ~e** (*Bot.*) embryo

**keim-, Keim-:** **~scheibe** *die* (*Biol.*) blastodisc; germinal disc; **~tötend** *Adj.* germicidal; **~träger** *der*, **~trägerin** *die* (*Med.*) carrier

**Keimung** *die;* **~, ~en** germination

**Keim·zelle** *die* Ⓐ(*Ausgangspunkt*) nucleus; Ⓑ(*Bot.*) germ cell; Ⓒ ⇒ **Gamet**

**kein** /kain/ *Indefinitpron.* Ⓐ no; (*bei abstrakten Begriffen*) no; not any; **er hat ~ Wort gesagt** he didn't say a word; he said not a word; **er konnte ~e Arbeit finden** he could find no work; he could not find any work; **ich habe ~ Geld/~e Zeit** I have no money/time; I don't have any money/time; **hat er ~e Kinder?** has he no children?; **kennst du ~e Deutschen/~en Deutschen, der ...?** don't you know any Germans/a German who ...?; **~ Mensch/~ einziger** nobody *or* no one/not a single one; **in ~er Weise/unter ~en Umständen** in no way/in *or* under no circumstances; **das ist ~ dummer Vorschlag** that's not a bad suggestion; **er ist ~ Dichter** he is not a poet; (*er dichtet schlecht*) he is no poet; **zwischen den beiden Vorgängen besteht ~ großer Unterschied** there's no great difference between the two processes; **~ anderer als er kann es gewesen sein** it can't have been anybody else but him; Ⓑ(*ugs.: nicht ganz, nicht einmal*) less than; **es ist ~e drei Tage her, dass ich zuletzt dort war** it's not *or* it's less than three days since I was last there; **sie ist noch ~e zehn Jahre alt** she's not ten years old yet; **es dauert ~e fünf Minuten** it won't take five minutes; Ⓒ *allein stehend* (*niemand/nichts*) nobody; no one; **~er von uns** not one of us; none of us; **ich kenne ~en, der dir helfen kann** I don't know anyone who can help you; **~s von beiden** neither [of them]; **ich wollte ~es von beiden** I didn't want either of them; **mir kann ~er!** (*salopp*) I can look after myself!; **Kannst du mir Geld geben? — Ich habe selbst ~[e]s mehr** Can you give me some money? — No, I haven't any left either; Ⓓ *allein stehend* (*überhaupt nicht*) **Post kam ~e** there was no *or* wasn't any post *or* mail; **Lust habe ich ~e** I don't feel like it

**keinerlei** *indekl. unbest. Gattungsz.* no ... at all; no ... what[so]ever

**keiner·seits** *Adv.* (*selten*) **ihr Vorschlag fand ~ Zustimmung** her suggestion met with no support anywhere *or* from any side

**keines·falls** *Adv.* on no account; **die Aufgabe ist schwer, aber ~ unlösbar** the problem is difficult but by no means insoluble

**keines·wegs** *Adv.* by no means; not by any means; not at all; **sein Einfluss darf ~ unterschätzt werden** his influence must in no way be underestimated; **ich nehme euch eure Offenheit ~ übel** I'm not in any way *or* not in the least offended by your frankness

**kein·mal** *Adv.* not [even] once; ⇒ *auch* **einmal** A

**Keks** /keːks/ *der;* **~** *od.* **~es, ~** *od.* **~e** (*österr.:* **~, ~[e]**) biscuit (*Brit.*); cookie (*Amer.*); **~[e] essen/backen** eat/bake biscuits/cookies; **das/er geht mir auf den ~** (*salopp*) it/he gets up my nose (*coll.*)

**Kelch** /kɛlç/ *der;* **~[e]s, ~e** Ⓐ(*Trinkgefäß*) goblet; **den [bitteren] ~ bis auf den Grund** *od.* **bis zur Neige leeren [müssen]** (*geh.*) [have to] drain the [bitter] cup to the dregs; **der ~ ist an uns/ihm vorübergegangen** (*geh.*) we were/he was spared that ordeal; Ⓑ(*Rel.*) chalice; communion cup; Ⓒ(*Bot.*) calyx

**kelch-, Kelch-:** **~blatt** *das* (*Bot.*) sepal; **~förmig** *Adj.* goblet-shaped; **~glas** *das* goblet

**Kelim** /ˈkeːlɪm/ *der;* **~s, ~s** Kilim

**Kelle** /ˈkɛlə/ *die;* **~, ~n** Ⓐ(*Schöpflöffel*) ladle; Ⓑ(*Signalstab*) signalling disc; Ⓒ (*Maurer~*) trowel; Ⓓ(*ugs.*) (*Tischtennisschläger*) bat; (*Tennisschläger*) racket

**Keller** /ˈkɛlɐ/ *der;* **~s, ~** Ⓐ cellar; (*einer Burg usw.*) cellars *pl.*; (*~geschoss*) basement; **der Dollar/der Kurs des Dollars ist in den ~ gefallen** (*fig.*) the dollar has gone through the floor (*fig.*); **im ~ sein** (*Skatjargon*) have a minus score *or* minus points; Ⓑ (*~raum*) cellar; Ⓒ(*ugs.: Weinvorrat*) cellar; Ⓓ(*Luftschutz*) [air-raid] shelter; Ⓔ ⇒ **Kellerlokal**

**Keller·assel** *die* woodlouse

**Kellerei** *die;* **~, ~en** Ⓐ(*Betrieb*) winery; wine producer's; Ⓑ(*Kellerräume*) [wine] cellars *pl.*

**Keller-:** **~fenster** *das* cellar window; (*von ~geschoss*) basement window; **~geschoss**, ***~geschoß** *das* basement; **~gewölbe** *das* underground vault; **~kind** *das* (*ugs.*) slum child *or* (*sl.*) kid; **~lokal** *das* cellar bar/disco *etc.*; (*Restaurant*) cellar restaurant; **~meister** *der*, **~meisterin** *die* cellarmaster; maître de chai; **~treppe** *die* cellar stairs *pl.*; (*zum ~geschoss*) basement stairs *pl.*; **~wohnung** *die* basement flat (*Brit.*) *or* (*Amer.*) apartment

**Kellner** /ˈkɛlnɐ/ *der;* **~s, ~** ▶ 159 waiter

**Kellnerin** *die;* **~, ~nen** ▶ 159 waitress

**kellnern** *itr. V.* (*ugs.*) work as a waiter/waitress

**Kelte** /ˈkɛltə/ *der;* **~n, ~n** Celt

**Kelter** /ˈkɛltɐ/ *die;* **~, ~n** (*für Weintrauben*) winepress; (*für andere Obstarten*) fruit press

**Kelterei** *die;* **~, ~en** (*für Weintrauben*) grape crushing and pressing plant; (*für andere Obstarten*) fruit crushing and pressing plant

**keltern** *tr. V.* press ‹grapes etc.›

**Keltin** *die;* **~, ~nen** ⇒ **Kelte**

**keltisch** *Adj.* ▶ 696 Celtic

**Keltisch** *das;* **~[s]** ▶ 696 Celtic; ⇒ *auch* **Deutsch**

k

*old spelling (see note on page 1707)

**Kelvin** /ˈkɛlvɪn/ *das;* **~s,** **~** *(Phys.)* kelvin

**Kemenate** /kemeˈna:tə/ *die;* **~, ~n** [ladies'] heated apartments *pl.* *(in a medieval castle)*

**Kenia** /ˈke:ni̯a/ *(das);* **~s** Kenya

**Kenianer** /keˈni̯a:nɐ/ *der;* **~s, ~, Kenianerin** *die;* **~, ~nen** ▶553 Kenyan; ⇒ *auch* **-in**

**Kenn·daten** /ˈkɛn-/ *Pl.* *(fachspr.)* personal data *or* details

**kennen** /ˈkɛnən/ *unr. tr. V.* (A) know; **jmdn./etw. [näher] ~ lernen** get to know sb./sth. [better]; become [better] acquainted with sb./sth.; **jmdn. als etw. ~ lernen** come to know sb. as sth.; **jmdn. von einer bestimmten Seite ~ lernen** see a particular side of sb.; **du wirst mich noch ~ lernen!** you'll find out I don't stand for any nonsense; **das Leben ~:** know about life; know the ways of the world; **das ~ wir gar nicht anders** *(haben es nie anders gemacht)* we've always done it that way; *(haben es erfahren)* it's always been like that; **jmdn. als Schriftsteller/Feigling ~:** know sb. as a writer/know sb. to be a coward; **kennst du den?** *(diesen Mann)* do you know who he is?; *(bist du mit ihm bekannt)* are you acquainted with him?; *(diesen Witz)* have you heard this one?; **jmds. Bücher/Werk ~:** know *or* be acquainted with sb.'s books/work; **da kennst du mich aber schlecht** *(ugs.)* that just shows you don't know me very well; **das ~ wir [schon]** *(ugs. abwertend)* *(das ist nichts Neues)* we've heard all that before; *(diese Ausrede ~ wir)* we've heard that one before; **sich nicht mehr ~ [vor ...]** be beside oneself [with ...]; **einen guten Arzt/ein gutes Restaurant ~:** know [of] a good doctor/restaurant; **da kenne ich/da kennt er nichts** *(ugs.)* and to hell with everything else *(coll.)*; (B) *(bekannt sein mit)* know; be acquainted with; **jmdn. flüchtig/persönlich ~:** know sb. slightly/personally; **jmdn. ~ lernen** *(jmdm. erstmals begegnen)* meet sb.; **freut mich, Sie ~ zu lernen** pleased to meet you; pleased to make your acquaintance *(formal)*; **die beiden ~ sich nicht mehr** the two are no longer on speaking terms; **ich glaube, wir beide ~ uns noch nicht** I don't think we've been introduced; **er will mich nicht mehr ~:** he doesn't want to know me any more; (C) *(haben)* have; **keinen Winter/Sommer ~:** have no winter/summer; **er kennt keine Kopfschmerzen** he never gets a headache; **kein Mitleid ~:** know *or* have no pity; (D) *(wiedererkennen)* know; recognize; **na, kennst du mich noch?** well, do you remember me?; **jmdn. am Gang/an der Stimme ~:** know *or* recognize sb. by his/her walk/voice

***kennen|lernen** ⇒ **kennen** A, B

**Kenner** *der;* **~s, ~** (A) *(Fachmann)* expert, authority (+ *Gen.* on); (B) *(von Wein, Speisen)* connoisseur; **dieser Wein ist etwas für den ~:** this is a wine for the connoisseur

**Kennerblick** *der* expert eye; **mit ~:** with an expert eye; **er warf ~e auf die Ausstellungsstücke** he cast an expert eye over the exhibits

**Kennerin** *die;* **~, ~nen** ⇒ **Kenner**

**Kenner·miene** *die* air of an expert/connoisseur; **mit ~:** with the air of an expert/connoisseur

**Kennerschaft** *die;* **~:** connoisseurship; *(Sachkenntnis)* expertise

**Kenn-: ~karte** *die* identity card; **~marke** *die* [police] identification badge; ≈ [police] warrant card *or* *(Amer.)* ID card; **~melodie** *die* *(Rundf.)* signature tune; **~nummer** *die* reference number; code number

**kenntlich** /ˈkɛntlɪç/ *Adj.* **~ sein** be recognizable *or* distinguishable (**an** by); **etw./jmdn. ~ machen** mark sth./make sb. [easily] identifiable; **etw. als Gift ~ machen** mark *or* label sth. as a poison

**Kenntnis** /ˈkɛntnɪs/ *die;* **~, ~se** (A) *(das Kennen, Wissen)* knowledge; **von etw. ~ haben/erhalten** be informed on sth. *or* have knowledge of sth./learn *or* hear about sth.; **das entzieht sich meiner ~** *(geh.)* I have no knowledge of that; **von etw. ~ nehmen, etw. zur ~ nehmen** take note of sth.; **jmdn. von etw. in ~ setzen** inform *or* notify sb. of sth.; **jmdn. zur ~ nehmen** take notice of sb.; (B) *Pl.* *(Sach- und Erfahrungswissen)* knowledge *sing.*; **oberflächliche/gründliche ~se von etw. haben** have a superficial/thorough knowledge of sth.; **~se in Mathematik** *od.* **auf dem Gebiet der Mathematik** a knowledge of mathematics

**Kenntnisnahme** *die;* **~** *(Papierdt.)* **jmdm. etw. zur ~ vorlegen** submit sth. to sb. for his/her attention; **wir bitten um gefällige ~ der Akten** please give these documents your kind attention; **nach ~ der Akten** after giving the documents my/his *etc.* attention

**kenntnis·reich** *Adj.* well-informed; knowledgeable

***Kennummer** ⇒ **Kennnummer**

**kenn-, Kenn-: ~wort** *das; Pl.* **~wörter** (A) *(Erkennungszeichen)* code word; reference; (B) *(Parole)* password; code word; **~zahl** *die* (A) *(charakteristischer Zahlenwert)* index; (B) *(Fernspr.)* code; **~zeichen** *das* (A) *(Merkmal)* sign; mark; **ein ~zeichen für einen Witterungsumschlag** a sign of a change in the weather; **ein ~zeichen eines Genies** a [hall]mark of a genius; **besondere ~zeichen** distinguishing marks; (B) *(Erkennungszeichen)* badge; *(auf einem Behälter, einer Ware usw.)* label; **etw. als ~zeichen tragen** carry/wear sth. as a means of identification; *(einer Gruppe)* carry/wear sth. as an indication of membership; (C) *(am Fahrzeug)* registration number; **~zeichnen** *tr. V.* (A) *(mit einem ~zeichen versehen)* mark; label ‹container, goods, etc.›; mark, signpost ‹way›; tag ‹bird, animal›; **etw. als ... ~zeichnen** mark or identify sth. as ...; (B) *(charakterisieren)* characterize; **jmdn. als ... ~zeichnen** characterize sb. as ...; (C) *(in seiner Eigenart erkennen lassen)* typify; **jmdn. als ... ~zeichnen** mark sb. out as ...; **~zeichnend** *Adj.* typical, characteristic (**für** of); **~zeichnung** *die* (A) marking; *(von Behältern, Waren)* labelling; *(von Vögeln, Tieren)* tagging; (B) *(Charakterisierung)* characterization; (C) *(~zeichen)* label; **eine auffällige ~zeichnung von Fußgängerüberwegen** a conspicuous means of marking pedestrian crossings; (D) *(Logik)* definite description; **~ziffer** *die* (A) *(Ziffer zur Unterscheidung)* reference number; *(bei einem Zeitungsinserat)* box number; (B) *(Math.)* characteristic

**Kenotaph** /kenoˈta:f/ *das;* **~s, ~e** cenotaph

**Kentaur** /kɛnˈtau̯ɐ/ *der;* **~en, ~en** ⇒ **Zentaur**

**kentern** /ˈkɛntɐn/ *itr. V.* (A) *mit sein* ‹boat, ship, etc.› capsize; (B) *(Seemannsspr.)* ‹tide, wind› turn

**Keramik** /keˈra:mɪk/ *die;* **~, ~en** (A) *(gebrannter Ton)* ceramics *pl.*; pottery; (B) *(Keramikgegenstand)* ceramic; piece of pottery; (C) *(Material)* fired clay; (D) *(Technik)* ceramics *sing.*; pottery

**keramisch** *Adj.* ceramic

**Kerbe** /ˈkɛrbə/ *die;* **~, ~n** notch; **in dieselbe** *od.* **die gleiche ~ hauen** *od.* **schlagen** *(ugs.)* take the same line

**Kerbel** /ˈkɛrbl̩/ *der;* **~s** chervil

**kerben** *tr. V.* (A) *(mit Kerben versehen)* notch; cut a notch/notches in; (B) carve ‹pattern etc.›

**Kerb-: ~holz** *das: in* **etwas/einiges auf dem ~holz haben** *(ugs.)* have done a job/a job or two *(sl.)*; **~tier** *das* insect

**Kerker** /ˈkɛrkɐ/ *der;* **~s, ~** (A) *(hist.: Gefängnis)* dungeons *pl.*; *(einzelne Zelle)* dungeon; (B) *(österr., hist.: Freiheitsstrafe)* imprisonment

**Kerker-: ~haft** *die* *(hist.)* imprisonment; **~meister** *der* *(hist.)* jailer; **~strafe** *die* *(österr., hist.)* ⇒ **Gefängnisstrafe**

**Kerl** /kɛrl/ *der;* **~s, ~e** *(nordd., md. auch:* **Kerls)** (A) *(ugs.: männliche Person)* fellow *(coll.)*; chap *(coll.)*; bloke *(Brit. sl.)*; **ein ganzer** *od.* **richtiger ~:** a splendid fellow *(coll.)* *or* chap *(coll.)*; **ein gemeiner/frecher ~** *(abwertend)* a nasty so-and-so *(coll.)*/an impudent fellow *(coll.)*; (B) *(ugs.: sympathischer Mensch)* **er ist ein feiner ~:** he's a fine chap *(coll.)* *or* *(sl.)* a good bloke; **sie ist ein netter/feiner ~:** she's a nice/fine woman

**Kern** /kɛrn/ *der;* **~[e]s, ~e** (A) *(Fruchtsamen)* pip; *(von Steinobst)* stone; *(von Nüssen, Mandeln usw.)* kernel; **der ~ eines Problems/Vorschlags** *(fig.)* the crux *or* gist of a problem/gist of a suggestion; **er hat einen guten** *od.* **in ihm steckt ein guter ~** *(fig.)* he is good at heart; **das birgt einen wahren ~** *(fig.)* it contains a core of truth; **zum ~ einer Sache** *(Gen.)* **kommen** *(fig.)* get to the heart of a matter; (B) *(wichtigster Teil einer Gruppe)* core; nucleus; **der harte ~:** the hard core; (C) *(Physik: Atom~)* nucleus; (D) *(einer elektrischen Spule, eines Reaktors)* core; (E) *(Gießerei)* core; (F) *(Biol.: Zell~)* nucleus; *(Anat., Biol.: Nerven~)* centre; (G) *(Zentrum)* city/town centre; (H) *(Met.)* **mit seinem ~ über Schottland liegend** ‹depression etc.› centred over Scotland

**kern-, Kern-: ~beißer** *der* hawfinch; **~brenn·stoff** *der* nuclear fuel; **~chemie** *die* nuclear chemistry; **~energie** *die* nuclear energy *no art.*; **~explosion** *die* (A) *(von atomaren Sprengkörpern)* nuclear explosion; (B) *(Physik)* [complete] fragmentation of the nucleus; **~fach** *das* *(Schulw.)* core subject; **~fäule** *die* *(Forstw.)* heart rot; **~forschung** *die* nuclear research; **~frage** *die* central question; **~frucht** *die* *(Bot.)* pome; **~fusion** *die* *(Phys., Biol.)* nuclear fusion *no art.*; **~gedanke** *der* central idea; **~gehäuse** *das* core; **~gesund** *Adj.* fit as a fiddle *pred.*; sound as a bell *pred.*; **~haus** *das* ⇒ **~gehäuse**; **~holz** *das* *(Holzverarb.)* heartwood

**kernig** ❶ *Adj.* (A) *(urwüchsig, markig)* robust, earthy ‹language›; down-to-earth ‹remarks›; *(kraftvoll)* powerful, forceful ‹speech›; pithy ‹saying›; **ein ~er Mann/Typ** *(ugs.)* a robust and athletic man/type; (B) *(fest, haltbar)* robust, stout, sturdy ‹boots, shoes›; sound ‹wood›; robust ‹leather›; (C) *(gehaltvoll, kräftig)* full-bodied ‹wine›; (D) *(ugs.: vortrefflich)* great *(coll.)*; (E) *(voller Kerne)* full of pips *pred.* ❷ *adv.* (A) *(urwüchsig, markig)* robustly; *(kraftvoll)* forcefully; *(knapp)* pithily ‹expressed›; (B) *(ugs.: vortrefflich)* **wir haben ~ gezecht und geschwoft** we had a whale of a time drinking and dancing *(coll.)*

**Kern·kraft** *die* (A) *Pl.* *(Physik)* nuclear forces; (B) nuclear power *no art.*

**Kernkraft-: ~gegner** *der,* **~gegnerin** *die* opponent of nuclear power; **~werk** *das* nuclear power station *or* plant

**Kern·ladungszahl** *die* atomic number

**kern-, Kern-: ~los** *Adj.* seedless; **~obst** *das* pomaceous fruit; pomes *pl.*; **~pflichtfach** *das* *(Schulw.)* core-curriculum subject; **~physik** *die* nuclear physics *sing., no art.*; **~physiker** *der,* **~physikerin** *die* nuclear physicist; **~punkt** *der* central point; **~reaktion** *die* *(Physik)* nuclear reaction; **~reaktor** *der* nuclear reactor; **~satz** *der* (A) *(wesentlicher Satz)* key sentence *or* statement; (B) *(Sprachw.)* *basic structural form of the sentence, with the finite verb as the second idea;* kernel sentence; **~schatten** *der* *(Optik, Astron.)* umbra; total shadow; **~seife** *die* washing soap; hard soap; **~spaltung** *die* *(Physik)* nuclear fission *no art.*; **~spin·tomographie** /ˈkɛrnspɪn----/ *die* *(Med.)* [nuclear] magnetic resonance imaging; **~spruch** *der* wise saw *or* saying; **~stück** *das* centrepiece; *(einer Diskussion, eines Programms)* central *or* main item; *(eines Plans)* main point; **~technik** *die* nuclear engineering *no art.*; **~truppe** *die* crack unit; **~verschmelzung** *die* *(Physik, Biol.)* nuclear fusion *no art.*; **~waffe** *die* nuclear weapon; **~waffen·frei** *Adj.* nuclear-free; **~waffen·versuch** *der* nuclear [weapons] test; **~zeit** *die* core time

**Kerosin** /keroˈzi:n/ *das;* **~s** kerosene

**Kerze** /ˈkɛrt͡sə/ *die;* **~, ~n** (A) candle; **elektrische ~:** candle bulb; (B) *(Zünd~)* spark plug; sparking plug; (C) *(Turnen Jargon)* shoulder stand; (D) *(Physik veralt.)* candela

**kerzen-, Kerzen-: ~beleuchtung** *die* candlelight *no indef. art.*; **~docht** *der* [candle] wick; **~gerade,** *(ugs.)* **~grade**

k

❶ *Adj.* dead straight ‹tree, post, etc.›; very stiff ‹bow›; ❷ *adv.* bolt upright; ‹rise› straight upwards; **~halter** *der* candle holder; **~leuchter** *der* candlestick; (*für mehrere* ~) candelabrum; **~licht** *das* the light of a candle/of candles; **bei ~licht** by candlelight; **~schein** *der* candlelight *no pl.*; **~schlüssel** *der* (*Kfz-W.*) plug spanner; **~stummel** *der*, **~stumpf** *der* stump of a/the candle

**Kescher** /ˈkɛʃɐ/ *der;* **~s**, **~** (*für Fische*) hand net; fishing net; (*für Schmetterlinge*) butterfly net

**kess**, ***keß** /kɛs/ ❶ *Adj.* Ⓐ (*hübsch, flott*) pert; pert, jaunty ‹hat, dress, etc.›; ⇒ *auch* **Sohle** A; Ⓑ (*frech, vorlaut*) cheeky; Ⓒ (*salopp*) **kesser Vater** [bull]dyke (*sl.*); butch (*sl.*). ❷ *adv.* Ⓐ (*hübsch, flott*) jauntily; Ⓑ (*frech, vorlaut*) cheekily

**Kessel** /ˈkɛsl̩/ *der;* **~s**, **~** Ⓐ (*Tee~*) kettle; Ⓑ (*zum Kochen*) pot; (*für offenes Feuer*) cauldron; (*in einer Brauerei*) vat; (*Wasch~*) copper; wash boiler; Ⓒ (*Berg~*) basin-shaped valley; Ⓓ (*Milit.*) encircled area; (*kleiner*) pocket; Ⓔ (*Jägerspr.*) ring of hunters and beaters; Ⓕ (*Dampf~, Heiz~*) boiler; Ⓖ (*schweiz.: Eimer*) bucket

**Kessel-: ~fleisch** *das* ⇒ **Wellfleisch**; **~haus** *das* boilerhouse; **~jagd** *die* ⇒ **~treiben** A; **~pauke** *die* kettledrum; **~raum** *der* boiler room; **~schlacht** *die* battle of encirclement; **~schmied** *der*, **~schmiedin** *die* boilermaker; **~schmiede** *die* boiler shop; **~stein** *der* fur; scale; **~treiben** *das* Ⓐ (*Jägerspr.: Treibjagd*) battue (*using a circle of hunters and beaters*); Ⓑ (*Hetzkampagne*) witch-hunt; **~wagen** *der* (*Kfz-W.*) road tanker; tanker lorry (*Brit.*); tank truck (*Amer.*); (*Eisenbahn*) tank wagon; tank car

**Kessheit**, ***Keßheit** *die;* **~**, **~en** ⇒ **kess** 1: pertness; jauntiness; cheekiness

**Ketchup** ⇒ **Ketschup**

**Ketsch** /kɛtʃ/ *die;* **~**, **~en** (*Segeln*) ketch

**Ketschup** /ˈkɛtʃap/ *der od. das;* **~s**, **~s** ketchup

**Kettchen** /ˈkɛtçən/ *das;* **~s**, **~:** [neck] chain (*with cross etc. attached*); (*Fuß~*) anklet; (*Arm~*) bracelet

**Kette** /ˈkɛtə/ *die;* **~**, **~n** Ⓐ chain; (*von Kettenfahrzeugen*) track; **die ~ [an der Tür] vorlegen** put the chain across [the door]; **an der ~ liegen** ‹dog› be chained up; **jmdn. in ~n legen** put sb. in chains; **die ~n abwerfen/sprengen** *od.* **zerreißen** (*fig. geh.*) cast off *or* throw off/break one's chains *or* shackles; **jmdn. an die ~ legen** (*fig.*) keep sb. on a [tight *or* short] leash; Ⓑ (*Halsschmuck*) necklace; (*eines Bürgermeisters usw.*) chain; Ⓒ (*Reihe*) chain; (*von Autos*) line; **eine ~ bilden** form a chain; **eine ~ von Beweisen** a chain of evidence; **die ~ der Berge** the chain of mountains; **~ rauchen** (*ugs.*) chain-smoke; Ⓓ (*von Ereignissen*) string; series; Ⓔ (*Weberei*) warp

**Kettel·maschine** /ˈkɛtl̩-/ *die* (*Textilw.*) looper

**ketten** *tr. V.* Ⓐ (*mit einer Kette anbinden*) chain (**an** + *Akk.* to); Ⓑ (*unauflösbar binden*) bind; **jmdn. an sich** (*Akk.*) **~:** bind sb. to oneself; **sich an jmdn. ~:** tie oneself to sb.

**Ketten-: ~antrieb** *der* chain drive; chain transmission; **~armband** *das* (*für eine Armbanduhr*) [mesh-link/open-link] bracelet; (*Schmuck*) [chain] bracelet; **~blatt** *das* chain wheel; front sprocket; **~brücke** *die* chain bridge; **~fahrzeug** *das* ⇒ **Raupenfahrzeug**; **~glied** *das* [chain] link; **~hemd** *das* (*hist.*) coat of chain mail; **~hund** *der* Ⓐ watchdog *or* guard dog (*kept on a chain*); Ⓑ (*Milit. Jargon*) Military Policeman; **~laden** *der; Pl.* **~läden** chain store; **~panzer** *der* chain mail; chain armour; **~rad** *das* sprocket [wheel]; **~rauchen** *das;* **~~s** chain-smoking *no art.*; **~raucher** *der*, **~raucherin** *die* chain-smoker; **~reaktion** *die* chain reaction; **eine ~reaktion auslösen** trigger a chain reaction; **~ritzel** *das* [rear] sprocket; [rear] sprocket wheel; **~säge** *die* chain saw; **~schaltung** *die* derailleur gears *pl.*; **~schluss**, ***~schluß** *der* (*Logik*) chain syllogism; sorites; **~schutz** *der* chain guard; **~stich** *der* (*Handarb.*) chain stitch **~werfer** *der* ⇒ **Umwerfer**

**Ketzer** /ˈkɛtsɐ/ *der;* **~s**, **~** (*auch fig.*) heretic

**Ketzerei** *die;* **~**, **~en** (*auch fig.*) heresy

**Ketzer·gericht** *das* (*hist.*) Inquisition

**Ketzerin** *die;* **~**, **~nen** (*auch fig.*) heretic

**ketzerisch** (*auch fig.*) ❶ *Adj.* heretical. ❷ *adv.* heretically

**keuchen** /ˈkɔyçn̩/ *itr. V.* Ⓐ (*schwer atmen*) pant; gasp for breath; (*fig.*) ‹locomotive› chug; **mit ~dem Atem** gasping *or* panting for breath; Ⓑ *mit sein* (*sich ~d fortbewegen*) puff *or* pant one's way; come/go puffing *or* panting along

**Keuch·husten** *der* ▶ 474 whooping cough *no art.*

**Keule** /ˈkɔylə/ *die;* **~**, **~n** Ⓐ (*Schlagwaffe*) club; cudgel; **chemische ~:** Chemical Mace ®; Ⓑ (*Gymnastik*) [Indian] club; Ⓒ (*Kochk.*) leg; (*Reh~, Hasen~*) haunch; (*Gänse~, Hühner~*) drumstick; leg

**Keulen-: ~hieb** *der*, **~schlag** *der* blow with a club *or* cudgel; (*fig.*) terrible blow; **~schwingen** *das* (*Gymnastik*) club swinging; swinging [Indian] clubs

**keusch** /kɔyʃ/ ❶ *Adj.* Ⓐ (*sexuell enthaltsam*) chaste; pure; Ⓑ (*geh. veralt.*) (*sittsam*) modest; demure; (*sittlich und moralisch rein*) pure. ❷ *adv.* Ⓐ (*sexuell enthaltsam*) **~ leben** lead a chaste life; Ⓑ (*sittsam*) modestly; demurely; (*sittlich und moralisch rein*) in a pure manner

**Keuschheit** *die;* **~** Ⓐ (*sexuelle Enthaltsamkeit*) chastity; Ⓑ (*geh. veralt.*) (*Sittsamkeit*) modesty; (*sittliche und moralische Reinheit*) purity

**Keuschheits-: ~gelübde** *das* vow of chastity; **~gürtel** *der* chastity belt

**Kfz** *Abk.* **Kraftfahrzeug**

**kg** *Abk.* ▶ 353 **Kilogramm** kg

**KG** *Abk.* **Kommanditgesellschaft**

**K-Gruppe** /ˈka:-/ *die* (*Politik*) [*anti-Soviet*] *Communist organization*

**Khaki**[1] /ˈka:ki/ *der;* **~[s]** (*Stoff*) khaki

**Khaki**[2] *das;* **~[s]** (*Farbe*) khaki

**khaki·farben** *Adj.* khaki[-coloured]

**kHz** *Abk.* **Kilohertz** kHz

**Kibbuz** /kɪˈbu:ts/ *der;* **~**, **~im** /kɪbuˈtsi:m/ *od.* **~e** kibbutz

**Kibbuznik** /kɪˈbu:tsnɪk/ *der;* **~s**, **~s** kibbutznik

**Kicher·erbse** *die* chickpea

**kichern** /ˈkɪçɐn/ *itr. V.* giggle; **in sich hinein/vor sich hin ~:** giggle to oneself; **dass ich nicht kichere!** (*iron.*) don't make me laugh!

**Kick** /kɪk/ *der;* **~[s]**, **~s** (*Fußball, ugs.*) kick

**Kick·down, Kick-down** /kɪkˈdaun/ *das;* **~s**, **~s** (*Kfz-W.*) kick-down

**kicken** (*ugs.*) ❶ *itr. V.* play football. ❷ *tr. V.* kick

**Kicker** *der;* **~s**, **~**, **Kickerin** *die;* **~**, **~nen** (*ugs.*) footballer; [football] player

**Kick·starter** *der* (*Kfz-W.*) kick-starter; kick-start

**kidnappen** /ˈkɪtnɛpn̩/ *tr. V.* kidnap

**Kidnapper** /ˈkɪtnɛpɐ/ *der;* **~s**, **~**, **Kidnapperin** *die;* **~**, **~nen** kidnapper

**Kidnapping** /ˈkɪtnɛpɪŋ/ *das;* **~s**, **~s** kidnapping

**kiebig** /ˈki:bɪç/ *Adj.* (*bes. nordd.*) (*frech*) cheeky; impertinent; (*gereizt*) touchy

**Kiebitz** /ˈki:bɪts/ *der;* **~es**, **~e** Ⓐ (*Vogel*) lapwing; peewit; Ⓑ (*ugs.: Zuschauer beim Spiel*) kibitzer (*coll.*)

**kiebitzen** *itr. V.* (*ugs. scherzh.*) Ⓐ (*bei einem Spiel zuschauen*) kibitz (*coll.*); Ⓑ (*neugierig beobachten*) look on

**Kiefer**[1] /ˈki:fɐ/ *der;* **~s**, **~** ▶ 471 jaw; (*Kieferknochen*) jawbone

**Kiefer**[2] *die;* **~**, **~n** Ⓐ (*Baum*) pine [tree]; Ⓑ (*Holz*) pine [wood]

**Kiefer-: ~bruch** *der* ▶ 474 (*Med.*) fracture of the jaw; fractured jaw; **~chirurgie** *die* oral surgery *no art.*; **~höhle** *die* ▶ 471 (*Anat.*) maxillary sinus; **~höhlen·entzündung** *die* maxillary sinusitis *no art.*; **~klemme** *die* (*Med.*) lockjaw; trismus (*Med.*); **~knochen** *der* ▶ 471 jawbone

**Kiefern-: ~holz** *das* pine [wood]; **~nadel** *die* pine needle; **~wald** *der* pinewood; (*größer*) pine forest; **~zapfen** *der* pine cone

**Kiefer·orthopädie** *die* orthodontics *sing., no art.*

**kieken** /ˈki:kn̩/ *itr. V.* (*nordd.*) look

**Kieker** /ˈki:kɐ/ *der;* **~s**, **~** Ⓐ (*Seemannsspr.*) (*Fernglas*) binoculars *pl.*; (*Fernrohr*) telescope; Ⓑ *in* **jmdn. auf dem ~ haben** (*ugs.*) have it in for sb. (*coll.*); (*misstrauisch beobachten*) keep a careful eye *or* watch on sb.

**kieksen** /ˈki:ksn̩/ ⇒ **gicksen**

**Kiel**[1] /ki:l/ *der;* **~[e]s**, **~e** keel; **ein Schiff auf ~ legen** (*Schiffsbau*) lay down a ship; lay the keel of a ship

**Kiel**[2] *der;* **~[e]s**, **~e** Ⓐ (*Teil einer Vogelfeder*) quill; Ⓑ (*hist.: Schreibfeder*) quill [pen]

**kiel-, Kiel-: ~feder** *die* quill feather; **~holen** *tr. V.* (*Seemannsspr.*) Ⓐ (*auf die Seite legen*) careen ‹ship›; Ⓑ (*unter dem Schiff hindurchziehen*) keelhaul; **~oben** /-ˈ--/ *Adv.* bottom up; **~raum** *der* bilge; **~wasser** *das* wake; **in jmds. ~wasser segeln** *od.* **schwimmen** (*fig.*) follow in sb.'s wake

**Kieme** /ˈki:mə/ *die;* **~**, **~n** gill

**Kiemen-: ~atmer** /-|a:tmɐ/ *der;* **~~s**, **~~** (*Zool.*) gill-breathing animal; gill-breather; **~spalte** *die* (*Zool.*) gill slit

**Kien** /ki:n/ *der;* **~[e]s** resinous wood; (*Kiefernholz*) resinous pine wood

**Kien-: ~apfel** *der* ⇒ **Kiefernzapfen**; **~fackel** *die* pine [wood] torch; **~span** *der* pine wood chip; (*zum Anzünden*) pine wood spill

**Kiepe** /ˈki:pə/ *die;* **~**, **~n** (*nordd., md.*) dosser; pannier

**Kies** /ki:s/ *der;* **~es**, **~e** Ⓐ (*kleine, runde Steine*) gravel; (*auf dem Strand*) shingle; Ⓑ (*Mineral.*) pyrites *sing.*; Ⓒ (*salopp: Geld*) dough (*coll.*); bread (*coll.*)

**Kiesel** /ˈki:zl̩/ *der;* **~s**, **~:** pebble

**Kiesel-: ~erde** *die* siliceous earth; **~säure** *die* (*Chemie*) silicic acid; **~stein** *der* pebble

**kiesen** /ˈki:zn̩/ *unr., auch regelm. tr. V.* (*dichter. veralt.*) choose; select

**Kies·grube** *die* gravel pit

**Kies·weg** *der* gravel path

**Kiez** /ki:ts/ *der;* **~es**, **~e** Ⓐ (*nordostd., bes. berlin.*) (*Stadtteil*) neighbourhood; Ⓑ (*Jargon: Bordellgegend*) red-light district

**Kif** /kɪf/ *der;* **~[s]** (*ugs.*) pot (*sl.*); grass (*sl.*)

**kiffen** /ˈkɪfn̩/ *itr. V.* (*ugs.*) smoke pot (*sl.*) *or* grass (*sl.*)

**Kiffer** *der;* **~s**, **~**, **Kifferin** *die;* **~**, **~nen** (*ugs.*) pothead (*sl.*)

**kikeriki** /kikəriˈki:/ *Interj.* (*Kinderspr.*) cock-a-doodle-doo

**Kikeriki** *das;* **~s**, **~s** cock-a-doodle-doo

**Kilbi** /ˈkɪlbi/ *die;* **~**, **Kilbenen** /ˈkɪlbənən/ (*schweiz.*) ⇒ **Kirchweih**

**killekille** /ˈkɪləˈkɪlə/ *Interj.* (*Kinderspr.*) tickle-tickle; **bei jmdm. ~ machen** tickle sb.

**killen**[1] /ˈkɪlən/ *tr. V.* (*salopp*) do in (*sl.*); bump off (*coll.*)

**killen**[2] *itr. V.* (*Seemannsspr.*) ‹sail› shiver

**Killer** *der;* **~s**, **~**, **Killerin** *die;* **~**, **~nen** (*salopp*) killer; (*gegen Bezahlung*) hit man (*sl.*)

**Killer·satellit** *der* (*ugs.*) hunter-killer satellite

**Kilo** /ˈki:lo/ *das;* **~s**, **~[s]** ▶ 353 kilo

**Kilo-: ~gramm** *das* ▶ 353 kilogram; **~hertz** *das;* **~**, **~** (*Physik*) kilohertz; **~kalorie** *die* (*Physik veralt.*) kilocalorie

**Kilometer** *der;* **~s**, **~** ▶ 265, ▶ 348 kilometre; 75 **~ in der Stunde** 75 kilometres per hour

**kilometer-, Kilometer-: ~fresser** *der*, **~fresserin** *die* (*ugs. scherzh. od. abwertend*) **er ist ein ~fresser** he really burns up the miles (*coll.*); **~geld** *das* mileage allowance; **~lang** ❶ *Adj.* miles long *pred.*; **eine ~lange Autoschlange** a traffic jam stretching [back] for miles; ❷ *adv.* for miles [and

*old spelling (see note on page 1707)

k

miles]; **~pauschale** *die* (*Steuerw.*) mileage allowance (*to taxpayer driving to and from work*); **~stand** *der* mileage reading; **~stein** *der* milestone; **~weit** ❶ *Adj.* **in ~weiter Entfernung** miles away in the distance; **eine ~weite Aussicht** a view for miles; ❷ *adv.* for miles [and miles]

**Kilowatt·stunde** *die* (*Physik; bes. Elektrot.*) kilowatt-hour

**Kimbern** /ˈkɪmbɐn/ *Pl.* Cimbri

**Kimm** /kɪm/ *die;* ~ (*Seemannsspr.*) Ⓐ (*Horizontlinie*) apparent *or* visible horizon; Ⓑ (*von Schiffen*) bilge

**Kimme** /ˈkɪmə/ *die;* ~, **~n** Ⓐ (*Einschnitt im Visier*) sighting notch; Ⓑ (*salopp: Gesäßspalte*) cleft between the buttocks

**Kimmung** *die;* ~ (*Seemannsspr.*) mirage

**Kimono** /kiˈmoːno/ *der;* **~s**, **~s** kimono

**Kind** /kɪnt/ *das;* **~[e]s**, **~er** Ⓐ child; (*Klein~*) child; infant; (*Baby*) child; baby; **ein ~ erwarten/bekommen** *od.* (*ugs.*) **kriegen** be expecting/have a baby; **ich glaube, ihre Tochter kriegt ein ~:** I think her daughter's going to have a baby; **ein ~ zur Welt bringen** (*geh.*) give birth to a child; **ein ~/~er in die Welt setzen** bring a child/children into the world; **von einem ~ entbunden werden** be delivered of a child; **das ~ beim [rechten] Namen nennen** (*fig.*) call a spade a spade; **das ~ muss doch einen Namen haben** (*ugs.*) we need a good name for it; (*wir müssen einen Vorwand dafür finden*) we've got to dress it up somehow; **wir werden das ~ schon [richtig] schaukeln** (*ugs.*) we'll soon sort things out *or* have things sorted out; **unschuldig wie ein neugeborenes ~ sein** be as innocent as a newborn babe; **jmdm. ein ~ machen** *od.* **andrehen** (*ugs.*) put sb. in the family way (*coll.*) *or* in the club (*sl.*); **das ~ mit dem Bade ausschütten** (*fig.*) throw the baby out with the bathwater; **jmdn. wie ein [kleines] ~ behandeln** treat sb. like a [small] child; **das weiß/kann doch jedes ~:** any child *or* five-year old knows/can do that; **von ~ an** *od.* **auf** from childhood; **er ist ein großes ~:** he is a big baby; **sich wie ein ~ freuen** be [as] pleased as Punch; **über schöne Dinge kann er sich wie ein ~ freuen** he takes a childlike pleasure in beautiful things; **du bist als ~ [wohl] zu heiß gebadet worden** (*ugs.*) you [must] have a screw loose (*coll.*); **wie sag ichs meinem ~e?** I don't know the best way to put it; (*bei einer unangenehmen Nachricht*) how do I break the news?; **aus ~ern werden Leute** childhood passes [all too soon]; **dann kommt bei ihm das ~ im Manne durch** (*scherzh.*) then he shows that he is [still] a child at heart; **[seine/deine** *usw.*] **~er und ~eskinder** [his/your *etc.*] children and [his/your *etc.*] children's children; **bei jmdm. lieb ~ sein** (*ugs.*) be a favourite with sb.; **sich bei jmdm. lieb ~ machen** (*ugs.*) get on the right side of sb.; **einziges ~ sein** be an only child; **armer/reicher Leute ~ sein** be the child of poor/wealthy parents; come from a poor/wealthy family; **ein ~ seiner Zeit** (*fig.*) a child of one's times; **~er Gottes** (*fig.*) God's children; **ein ~ des Todes sein** (*fig. geh.*) be as good as dead; **ein [echtes] Wiener/Berliner ~:** a [true] Viennese/Berliner; **ein ~ der Liebe** (*geh. verhüll.*) a love child; **er ist/du bist** *usw.* **kein ~ von Traurigkeit** (*ugs.*) he knows/you know *etc.* how to enjoy himself/yourself *etc.*; **jmds. liebstes ~ sein** ‹person› be sb.'s pet; **das Auto/die Oberstufenreform ist sein liebstes ~:** the car is his first love/reform of the sixth form is his pet project; **jmdn. an ~es statt annehmen** (*veralt.*) adopt sb.; ⇒ *auch* **tot** A; Ⓑ (*ugs.: als Anrede*) **mein [liebes] ~:** my [dear] child; **~er, hört mal alle her!** listen to this, all of you (*coll.*); **[~er,] ~er!** my goodness!

**Kind·bett** *das* (*veralt.*) ⇒ **Wochenbett**

**Kindbett·fieber** *das* childbed *or* puerperal fever

**Kindchen** /ˈkɪntçən/ Ⓐ (*kleines Kind*) [small *or* little] child; Ⓑ (*Anrede*) dear child

**kinder-, Kinder-:** **~arbeit** *die* child labour; **~arm** *Adj.* with few children *postpos.*, *not pred.*; **~arzt** *der*, **~ärztin** *die* ▶ 159 paediatrician; **~auge** *das:* **mit sehnsüchtigen ~augen auf etw.** (*Akk.*) **blicken** look at sth. with the wistful eyes of a child; **~beihilfe** *die* (*österr.*) ⇒ **~geld**; **~bekleidung** *die* children's wear; **~besteck** *das* children's cutlery; **ein ~besteck** a set of children's cutlery; **~bett** *das* cot; (*für größeres Kind*) child's bed; **~bewahr·anstalt** *die* (*veralt.*) children's home; **~bild** *das* (*Foto*) photograph of a child; (*Malerei usw.*) portrait of a child; **~buch** *das* children's book; **~chor** *der* children's choir; **~dorf** *das* children's village; **~ehe** *die* child marriage

**Kinderei** *die;* ~, **~en** childishness *no indef. art.*, *no pl.*; **eine ~:** a childish prank; **~en** childishness *sing.*; childish behaviour *sing.*

**kinder-, Kinder-:** **~ermäßigung** *die* reduction for children; **~erziehung** *die* bringing up of children; **~fahrrad** *das* child's bicycle; **~feindlich** ❶ *Adj.* hostile to children *pred.*; anti-children *pred.*; (*für Kinder nicht förderlich*) ‹planning, policy› which does not cater for the needs of children; ❷ *adv.* **sich ~feindlich verhalten** act in a manner hostile to children; **~feindlichkeit** *die* hostility to children; (*von Planung, Politik*) failure to cater for children; **~fest** *das* children's party; children's fête; **~film** *der* children's film; **~fräulein** *das* ⇒ **Gouvernante**; **~freund** *der*, **~freundin** *die:* **ein [großer] ~freund/[große] ~freundin sein** be [very] fond of children; **~freundlich** ❶ *Adj.* fond of children *pred.*; ‹town, resort› which caters for children; ‹planning, policy› which caters for the needs of children; ❷ *adv.* **sich ~freundlich verhalten** act in a manner friendly to children; **~freundlich geplant werden** be planned with children in mind; **~freundlichkeit** *die* fondness for children; **~funk** *der* children's programme; (*Abteilung*) Children's Programmes *sing.*, *no art.*; **~garten** *der* kindergarten; nursery school; **~gärtnerin** *die* ▶ 159 kindergarten teacher; nursery-school teacher; **~geld** *das* child benefit; **~geschrei** *das* (*oft abwertend*) screaming *or* shouting of children; noise of children screaming *or* shouting; **~gesicht** *das* child's face; (*eines Erwachsenen*) childlike face; baby face; **~glaube** *der* childlike belief *or* faith; (*abwertend*) childish belief *or* faith; **~gottesdienst** *der* children's service; **~heilkunde** *die* paediatrics *sing.*, *no art.*; **~heim** *das* children's home; **~hort** *der* day home for schoolchildren; **~jahre** *Pl.* childhood years; **~karussell** *das* children's roundabout; **~kleidung** *die* children's clothes *pl.*; children's wear; **~krankheit** *die* Ⓐ (*Infektionskrankheit bei ~n*) children's disease *or* illness; **welche ~krankheiten hatten Sie?** what childhood diseases have you had?; Ⓑ *Pl.* (*Anfangsschwierigkeiten*) teething troubles; **~kreuzzug** *der* (*hist.*) Children's Crusade; **~kriegen** *das;* **~~s** (*ugs.*) having children; **~krippe** *die* crèche; day nursery; **~lähmung** *die* ▶ 474 poliomyelitis; infantile paralysis *no art.*; **~leicht** (*ugs.*) ❶ (*Adj.*) childishly simple *or* easy; dead easy; **das ist ~leicht** it's child's play *or* (*coll.*) kid's stuff; ❷ *adv.* **das kann ~leicht bedient werden** it's childishly simple to use; **~lieb** *Adj.* fond of children *pred.*; **~liebe** *die* love of children; **~lied** *das* nursery rhyme; **~los** *Adj.* childless; **~losigkeit** *die;* **~~:** childlessness; **~mädchen** *das* nursemaid; nanny; **~märchen** *das* [children's] fairy tale; **~mord** *der* child murder; **~mund** *der* child's mouth; **~mund tut Wahrheit kund** (*Prov.*) it takes a child to point out the truth; **~narr** *der:* **er ist ein ~narr** he adores children; **~närrin** *die:* **sie ist eine ~närrin** she adores children; **~pflegerin** *die* children's nurse; **~popo** *der* (*ugs.*) [baby's] bottom; **glatt wie ein ~popo** [as] smooth as a baby's bottom; **~porno** *der* (*ugs.*) child-porn *or* kiddy-porn film/video (*coll*); **~pornographie** *die* child pornography; **~psychologie** *die* child psychology *no art.*; **~puder** *der* baby powder; **~reich** *Adj.* with many children *postpos.*, *not pred.*; **eine ~reiche Familie** a large family; **~reichtum** *der* large number of children; **~reim** *der* nursery rhyme; **~schänder** *der;* **~~s**, **~~**, **~schänderin** *die;* **~~**, **~~nen** child abuser; **~schar** *die* crowd of children; **~schreck** *der* bogyman; **~schuh** *der* child's shoe; **ich bin/du bist den ~schuhen entwachsen** (*fig.*) I'm/you're not a child any more; **noch in den ~schuhen stecken** ‹process, technique, etc.› be still in its infancy; **~schutz** *der* child protection legislation; **~schwester** *die* children's nurse; **~segen** *der* (*oft scherzh.*) **eine Familie mit reichem ~segen** a family blessed with a large number of children; **~sitz** *der* child's seat; (*an einem Fahrrad*) child-carrier [seat]; (*im Auto*) child's safety seat; **~spiel** *das* children's game; **[für jmdn.] ein ~spiel sein** be child's play [to sb.]; **~spiel·platz** *der* [children's] playground; **~spiel·zeug** *das* [children's] toys *pl. or* playthings *pl.*; (*einzeln*) [child's] toy *or* plaything; **~sprache** *die* Ⓐ (*Sprache eines Kindes*) child language; children's language; Ⓑ (*kindliche Sprechweise Erwachsener*) nursery language; **~sterblichkeit** *die* child mortality; **~stimme** *die* child's voice; **~stube** *die:* **eine gute/schlechte ~stube gehabt** *od.* **genossen haben** have been well/badly brought up; **hast du gar keine ~stube?** didn't you ever learn any manners?; **~stuhl** *der* child's chair; (*Hochstuhl*) high chair; **~tages·heim** *das*, **~tages·stätte** *die* day nursery; **~teller** *der* Ⓐ child's plate; Ⓑ (*auf der Speisekarte*) children's menu; **~trommel** *die* toy drum; **~wagen** *der* pram (*Brit.*); baby carriage (*Amer.*); (*Sportwagen*) pushchair (*Brit.*); stroller (*Amer.*); **~wäsche** *die* [children's] underwear; (*für Neugeborene*) baby linen; **~zahl** *die* number of children per family; **~zeit** *die* childhood; **~zimmer** *das* Ⓐ children's room; (*für Kleinkinder*) nursery; Ⓑ (*Einrichtung*) furniture for the children's room/nursery; **~zuschlag** *der* child benefit

**Kindes-:** **~alter** *das* childhood; **im ~alter** at an early age; **~annahme** *die* ⇒ **Adoption**; **~aussetzung** *die* abandonment of [newborn] children; **~beine** *Pl.:* **in von ~beinen an** from *or* since childhood; from an early age; **~entführung** *die* kidnapping [of a child]; child abduction; **~kind** *das* (*veralt.*) grandchild; ⇒ *auch* **Kind** A; **~liebe** *die* (*geh.*) filial love *or* affection; **~misshandlung**, ***~mißhandlung** *die* (*Rechtsw.*) child abuse; **~mord** *der* child murder; (*Mord am eigenen Kind*) infanticide; **~mörderin** *die* infanticide; **~nöte** *Pl.* (*veralt.*) labour pains; **in ~nöten liegen** *od.* **sein** be in labour *sing.*; **~pflicht** *die* filial duty; **~raub** *der* ⇒ **~entführung**; **~tötung** *die* (*Rechtsw.*) infanticide

**Kind·frau** *die* Ⓐ (*frühreifes Mädchen*) precocious young lady; Ⓑ (*kindliche Frau*) childlike woman

**kind·gemäß** *Adj.* suitable for children *postpos.*

**kindhaft** *Adj.* childlike

**Kindheit** *die;* **~:** childhood; **seit frühester ~:** from earliest childhood; from infancy

**Kindheits·erinnerung** *die* childhood memory

**kindisch** ❶ *Adj.* childish, infantile ‹behaviour, enjoyment›; naïve ‹ideas›; **~ werden** become childish; **werd nicht ~!** do behave sensibly. ❷ *adv.* childishly; **sich ~ über etw.** (*Akk.*) **freuen** be absurdly pleased about sth.; **sich ~ an etw.** (*Dat.*) **freuen** take childish pleasure in sth.

**kindlich** ❶ *Adj.* childlike; **~er Gehorsam** filial obedience; **im ~en Alter** at an early age. ❷ *adv.* ‹behave› in a childlike way *or* manner; **sich ~ über etw.** (*Akk.*) **freuen** take a childlike pleasure in sth.

**Kindlichkeit** *die;* **~:** childlike quality

**Kinds·kopf** *der* overgrown child; **sei doch kein ~!** don't be so childish!; act your age!

k

**Kind·taufe** *die* christening
**Kinematographie** /kınematogra'fi:/ *die;* ~**:** cinematography *no art.*
**Kinetik** /ki'ne:tık/ *die;* ~ (A) (*Physik*) kinetics *sing., no art.;* (B) (*bild. Kunst*) kinetic art
**kinetisch** *Adj.* (*Physik, bild. Kunst*) kinetic
**King** /kıŋ/ *der;* **~s, ~s** (*ugs.*) boss (*coll.*); top dog (*coll.*)
**Kinkerlitzchen** /'kıŋkəlıtsçən/ *Pl.* (*ugs.*) trifles
**Kinn** /kın/ *das;* **~[e]s, ~e** ▶ 471 chin
**Kinn-: ~backe** *die,* **~backen** *der;* **~~s, ~~** (*südd.*) cheek; **~bart** *der* chin-beard; chin-tuft; **~haken** *der* hook to the chin; **~lade** *die* jaw; **~riemen** *der* chinstrap
**Kino** /'ki:no/ *das;* **~s, ~s** (A) (*Filmtheater*) cinema (*Brit.*); movie theatre *or* house (*Amer.*); **in die [deutschen] ~s kommen** go on general release [in Germany]; (B) (*Filmvorstellung*) film; movie (*Amer.*); **ins ~ gehen** go to the cinema (*Brit.*) *or* pictures (*Brit.*) *or* (*Amer.*) movies *pl.;* (C) (*Film als Medium*) cinema
**Kino-: ~besuch** *der* visit to the cinema (*Brit.*) *or* (*Amer.*) movies; **~besucher** *der,* **~besucherin** *die* cinema-goer (*Brit.*); movie-goer (*Amer.*); **~film** *der* cinema film (*Brit.*); movie film (*Amer.*); **~gänger** *der;* **~~s, ~~, ~gängerin** *die;* **~~, ~~nen** cinema-goer (*Brit.*); movie-goer (*Amer.*); **~karte** *die* cinema ticket (*Brit.*); movie ticket (*Amer.*); **~kasse** *die* cinema (*Brit.*) *or* (*Amer.*) movie box office; **~programm** *das* (A) (*Programm zu einem Film*) film programme; (B) (*Programmvorschau*) cinema guide; **~reklame** *die* (A) (*Reklame für einen Film*) publicity *no indef. art.* for the/a film; (B) (*Werbung vor einer Vorstellung*) cinema advertisements *pl.;* screen commercials *pl.;* **~vorstellung** *die* ⇒ **Filmvorstellung**
**Kintopp** /'ki:ntɔp/ *der od. das;* **~s, ~s** *od.* **Kintöppe** /'ki:ntœpə/ (*ugs.*) cinema
**Kiosk** /kiɔsk/ *der;* **~[e]s, ~e** kiosk
**Kipf** /kıpf/ *der;* **~[e]s, ~e** (*südd.*) long loaf
**Kipfel** /'kıpfl/ *das;* **~s, ~, Kipferl** /'kıpfel/ *das;* **Kipferls, Kipferln** (*bayr., österr.*) ⇒ **Hörnchen** B
**Kippe¹** /'kıpə/ *die;* **~, ~n** (*ugs.*) cigarette end; fag end (*coll.*); dog-end (*coll.*)
**Kippe²** *die;* **~, ~n** (A) (*Bergmannsspr.: Abraumhalde*) slag heap; (B) **in auf der ~ stehen** (*ugs.*) be balanced precariously; **etw. steht auf der ~** (*fig.*) (*etw. befindet sich in einer kritischen Lage*) it's touch and go with sth.; (*etw. ist noch nicht entschieden*) sth. hangs in the balance; (C) (*Turnen*) upstart; kip (*Amer.*); (D) (*Müll~*) tip; dump
**kippelig** /'kıpəlıç/ *Adj.* (*ugs.*) wobbly; rickety, wobbly ‹chair, table›
**kippeln** /'kıpln/ *itr. V.* (*ugs.*) (A) (*leicht wackeln*) wobble; ‹chair, table› wobble; be wobbly *or* rickety; (B) (*mit dem Stuhl wackeln*) **[mit seinem Stuhl] ~:** rock one's chair backwards and forwards
**kippen** ❶ *tr. V.* (A) (*schräg stellen, neigen*) tip [up]; tilt; (B) (*ausschütten*) tip [out]; (C) (*ugs.: trinken*) knock back (*sl.*); **einen ~:** have a quick one (*coll.*) *or* a drink; (D) (*ugs.: abbrechen*) give ‹project, series› the chop (*coll.*). ❷ *itr. V.; mit sein* tip over; ‹top-heavy object› topple over; ‹person› fall, topple; ‹boat› overturn; ‹car› roll over; **von etw. ~:** topple *or* fall off sth.
**Kipper** *der;* **~s, ~:** tipper lorry *or* truck; dump truck; (*Eisenb.*) tipper *or* tipping wagon; dump car (*Amer.*)
**Kipp-: ~fenster** *das* horizontally pivoted window; **~lore** *die* tipper *or* tipping wagon; **~schalter** *der* tumbler *or* toggle switch; **~wagen** *der* ⇒ **~lore**
**Kirche** /'kırçə/ *die;* **~, ~n** (A) (*Gebäude*) church; **die ~ im Dorf lassen** (*fig.*) keep a sense of proportion; **mit der ~ ums Dorf laufen** (*einen unnötigen Umweg machen*) go all round the houses; (*unnötig kompliziert vorgehen*) do things in a roundabout way; (B) (*Gottesdienst*) church *no art.;* **in der ~ sein** be at church; **in die ~ gehen** go to church; (C) (*Institution*) Church
**kirchen-, Kirchen-: ~älteste** *der* (*ev. Kirche*) [church] elder; **~amt** *das* (A) (*Stellung*) ecclesiastical office; (B) (*Verwaltungsstelle*) Church administrative offices *pl.;* **~austritt** *der* secession from the Church; **die Zahl der ~austritte** the number of people seceding from *or* leaving the Church; **~bank** *die; Pl.* **~bänke** [church] pew; **~bann** *der* (*kath. Kirche*) excommunication; **~besuch** *der* attendance at church; **~besucher** *der,* **~besucherin** *die* churchgoer; worshipper; **~blatt** *das* parish magazine; **~buch** *das* parish register; **~chor** *der* church choir; **~diebstahl** *der* theft from a/the church; **~diener** *der,* **~dienerin** *die* sexton; **~feindlich** *Adj.* hostile to the Church *postpos.;* **~fenster** *das* church window; **~fest** *das* religious festival; church festival; **~fürst** *der* (*geh.*) high ecclesiastical dignitary; high dignitary of the Church; (*kath. Kirche: Kardinal*) Prince of the Church; **~gebet** *das* (*veralt.*) collect; **~gemeinde** *die* parish; (*beim Gottesdienst*) congregation; **~geschichte** *die* ecclesiastical history *no art.;* Church history *no art.;* **~gestühl** *das* [church] pews *pl.;* **~glocke** *die* church bell; **~jahr** *das* ecclesiastical year; Church year; **~kampf** *der* struggle between the Church and the State (*e.g. in the period of Nazi rule*); **~leitung** *die* governing body of the Church; **~licht** *das; Pl.* **~~er** *in* **kein** *od.* **nicht gerade ein [großes] ~licht sein** (*ugs. scherzh.*) be not too *or* not all that bright; **~lied** *das* hymn; **~maus** *die: in* **arm sein wie eine ~maus** (*ugs. scherzh.*) be as poor as a church mouse; **~musik** *die* church music; sacred music; **~politik** *die* policy of the State towards the Church; **~portal** *das* portal *or* main door of the/a church; **~rat** *der* (*ev. Kirche*) (A) (*Verwaltungsorgan*) ecclesiastical council; (B) (*Mitglied*) member of the/an ecclesiastical council; **~rätin** *die* ⇒ **~rat** B; **~raub** *der* ⇒ **~diebstahl**; **~räuber** *der,* **~räuberin** *die* church-robber; **~recht** *das* ecclesiastical law; **~schändung** *die* sacrilege *no indef. art.;* profanation of a/the church; **~schiff** *das* (*Archit.*) nave; **~spaltung** *die* schism; **~staat** *der* (*hist.*) Papal States *pl.;* **~steuer** *die* church tax; **~tag** *der* Church congress; **~ton·art** *die* (*Musik*) ecclesiastical *or* church mode; **~tür** *die* church door; **~vater** *der* Father of the Church; **~vor·stand** *der* parochial church council
**Kirch-: ~gang** *der:* **der sonntägliche ~gang** going to church on Sunday; **~gänger** *der;* **~~s, ~~, ~gängerin** *die;* **~~, ~~nen** churchgoer; **~hof** *der* (*veralt.*) churchyard; graveyard
**kirchlich** ❶ *Adj.* (A) (*die Kirche betreffend*) ecclesiastical; Church *attrib.;* ecclesiastical ‹law, building›; religious, church ‹music, festival›; (B) (*den Riten der Kirche entsprechend*) church *attrib.* ‹wedding, funeral›. ❷ *adv.* **~ getraut/begraben werden** have a church wedding *or* be married in church/have a church funeral
**Kirch·spiel** *das* (*veralt.*) parish
**Kirch·turm** *der* (*mit Turmspitze*) [church] steeple; (*ohne Turmspitze*) church tower
**Kirchturm-: ~politik** *die* parish-pump politics *sing.;* **~spitze** *die* church spire; **~uhr** *die* church clock
**Kirch-: ~weih** *die;* **~~, ~~en** fair (*held on the anniversary of the consecration of a church*); **~weihe** *die* consecration of a/the church
**Kirmes** /'kırməs/ *die;* **~, ~sen** /'kırmɛsn/ (*bes. md., niederd.*) ⇒ **Kirchweih**
**kirre** /'kırə/ *Adj.* (*ugs.*) compliant; obedient; **jmdn. ~ machen/kriegen** bring sb. to heel
**Kirsch** /kırʃ/ *der;* **~[e]s, ~** ⇒ **Kirschwasser**
**Kirsch-: ~baum** *der* (A) cherry [tree]; (B) (*Holz*) cherry[wood]; **~blüte** *die* (A) (*Blüte des ~baums*) cherry blossom; (B) (*Zeit der ~blüte*) cherry blossom time
**Kirsche** /'kırʃə/ *die;* **~, ~n** (A) cherry; **mit ihm ist nicht gut ~n essen** (*ugs.*) it's best not to tangle with him; (B) ⇒ **Kirschbaum**
**kirsch-, Kirsch-: ~kern** *der* cherry stone; **~kuchen** *der* cake with cherry topping; **~likör** *der* cherry liqueur; (*Weinbrand*) cherry brandy; **~rot** *Adj.* cherry[-red]; **~saft** *der* cherry juice; **~stein** *der* ⇒ **~kern**; **~torte** *die* cherry gateau; (*mit Tortenboden*) cherry flan; **Schwarzwälder ~torte** Black Forest gateau; **~wasser** *das* kirsch
**Kissen** /'kısn/ *das;* **~s, ~:** cushion; (*Kopf~*) pillow
**Kissen-: ~bezug** *der* cushion cover; (*für Kopfkissen*) pillowcase; pillowslip; **~schlacht** *die* (*ugs.*) pillow fight
**Kiste** /'kıstə/ *die;* **~, ~n** (A) (*Behälter*) box; (*Truhe*) chest; (*Latten~*) crate; (*für Obst*) case; box; **eine ~ Wein/ Zigarren** a case of wine/box of cigars; **in die ~ gehen** (*fig. ugs.*) hit the hay (*coll.*); go to bed; (B) (*salopp*) (*Flugzeug, Auto*) bus (*coll.*); (*Boot*) tub; (C) (*ugs., bes. berlin.: Sache, Angelegenheit*) affair; business
**kisten·weise** *Adv.* **Wein/Obst ~ kaufen** buy wine by the case/fruit by the case *or* box; **Obst ~ wegwerfen** throw away fruit by the caseful *or* boxful
**Kita** *die;* **~, ~s** day nursery; crèche
**Kitsch** /kıtʃ/ *der;* **~[e]s** kitsch
**kitschig** *Adj.* kitschy
**Kitt** /kıt/ *der;* **~[e]s,** (*Arten:*) **~e** (*Fensterkitt*) putty; (*für Porzellan, Kacheln usw.*) cement; (*Füllmasse*) filler
**Kittchen** *das;* **~s, ~** (*ugs.*) clink (*sl.*); jug (*sl.*); jail; **im ~ sitzen** be inside (*coll.*); be in clink *or* jug (*sl.*)
**Kittel** /'kıtl/ *der;* **~s, ~** (A) overall; (*eines Arztes, Krankenpflegers, Laboranten*) white coat; (B) (*hemdartige Bluse*) smock; (C) (*südd.: Jackett*) jacket
**Kittel-: ~kleid** *das* [simple] button-through dress; **~schürze** *die* sleeveless overall
**kitten** *tr. V.* cement [together]; stick [together] with cement; (*fig.*) mend ‹breach›; patch up ‹broken marriage, friendship›
**Kitz** /kıts/ *das;* **~es, ~e** (*Reh~*) fawn; (*Ziegen~, Gämsen~*) kid
**Kitzel** /'kıtsl/ *der;* **~s, ~** (A) (*Juckreiz*) tickle; tickling feeling *or* sensation; (B) (*Reiz, Antrieb*) itch; urge; (*freudige Erregung*) thrill
**kitzelig** ⇒ **kitzlig**
**kitzeln** ❶ *tr. V.* (A) tickle; **es kitzelt mich in der Nase** my nose tickles; (B) (*einen Sinnenreiz hervorrufen*) tickle; **der Duft kitzelte sie in der Nase** the aroma tickled her nose; **jmds. Eitelkeit ~:** tickle sb.'s vanity; (C) (*reizen*) prompt; (*in freudige Erregung versetzen*) thrill; **es kitzelt jmdn., etw. zu tun** sb. is itching to do sth.; sb. feels an urge to do sth. ❷ *itr. V.* tickle; **auf der Haut ~:** tickle [the skin]
**Kitzler** *der;* **~s, ~** ▶ 471 (*Anat.*) clitoris
**kitzlig** *Adj.* (A) (*empfindlich gegen Kitzeln*) ticklish; (B) (*empfindlich reagierend*) touchy (**in** + *Dat.* about); (C) (*schwierig, heikel*) ticklish
**Kiwi** /'ki:vi/ *die;* **~, ~s** kiwi [fruit]
**KKW** *Abk.* **Kernkraftwerk**
**Kl.** *Abk.* **Klasse**
**Klabauter·mann** /kla'bautɐ-/ *der* (*nordd.*) *protective spirit of a/the ship*
**klack** /klak/ *Interj.* (A) click; (B) (*von Tropfen*) tap
**klacken** *itr. V.* (*ugs.*) click
**klackern** /'klakɐn/ *itr. V.* (*landsch.*) clatter
**Klacks** /klaks/ *der;* **~es, ~e** (*ugs.*) (~ *Schlagsahne, Kartoffelbrei*) dollop (*coll.*); (~ *Senf*) blob; dab; **etw. ist nur ein ~ [für jmdn.]** (*fig.*) sth. is no trouble at all [for sb.]
**Kladde** /'kladə/ *die;* **~, ~n** (A) (*Heft für erste Niederschrift*) rough book; **etw. in ~ schreiben** write sth. in rough; (B) (*dickes Schreibheft*) thick notebook
**kladderadatsch** /kladəra'da:tʃ/ *Interj.* crash bang wallop
**Kladderadatsch** *der;* **~[e]s, ~e** (*ugs.*) (A) (*Chaos, Durcheinander*) unholy mess (*coll.*); (B) (*Skandal*) scandal
**klaffen** /'klafn/ *itr. V.* ‹hole, wound› gape; ‹gap› yawn; **in der Mauer klaffte ein großes Loch** there was a gaping hole in the wall

*old spelling (see note on page 1707)

**kläffen** /ˈklɛfn̩/ *itr. V.* (*abwertend*) yap

**klaffend** *Adj.* gaping; yawning; gaping ‹hole, wound›; yawning ‹gap›

**Kläffer** *der;* ~**s,** ~ (*ugs. abwertend*) yapping dog; yapper

**Klafter** /ˈklaftɐ/ *der od. das;* ~**s,** ~ Ⓐ (*frühere Längeneinheit*) fathom; Ⓑ (*Raummaß für Holz*) cord

**klafter·tief** *Adj.* six feet deep; ‹water› a fathom deep; (*fig.*) very deep

**klagbar** *Adj.* (*Rechtsw.*) actionable ‹matter›; enforceable ‹claim›

**Klage** /ˈkla:gə/ *die;* ~, ~**n** Ⓐ (*Äußerung der Trauer*) lamentation; lament; (*Äußerung des Schmerzes*) complaint; **die ~n um jmdn./über den Verlust von etw.** the lamentations *pl.* for sb./over the loss of sth.; Ⓑ (*Beschwerde, Äußerung des Unmuts*) complaint; **~n werden laut** complaints are being voiced; **keinen Grund zur ~ geben/haben** give/have no grounds *pl. or* reason for complaint; **bei jmdm. über jmdn./etw. ~ führen** make a complaint to sb. *or* lodge a complaint with sb. about sb./sth.; Ⓒ (*Rechtsw.*) (*im Zivilrecht*) action; suit; (*im Strafrecht*) charge; **eine ~ auf etw.** (*Akk.*) an action for sth.; **eine ~ auf Scheidung** a petition for divorce; **[öffentliche] ~ gegen jmdn. einreichen/erheben** bring an action against sb.; institute [criminal] proceedings against sb.

**Klage-:** **~ab·weisung** *die* (*Rechtsw.*) dismissal of the action *or* suit; **~erhebung** *die* (*Rechtsw.*) institution of [legal] proceedings; bringing of an action *or* a suit; **~frau** *die* ⇒ **~weib**; **~laut** *der* plaintive cry; (*von Schmerzen verursacht*) cry of pain; (*stöhnend*) moan; **~lied** *das* lament; **ein ~lied [über jmdn./etw.] anstimmen/singen** start to moan/moan [about sb./sth.]; **~mauer** *die* Wailing Wall

**klagen** ❶ *itr. V.* Ⓐ (*geh.: jammern*) wail; (*stöhnend*) moan; ‹animal› cry plaintively; **der ~de Ruf des Käuzchens** the plaintive cry of the little owl; Ⓑ (*sich beschweren*) complain; **über etw.** (*Akk.*) **~:** complain about sth.; **über Rückenschmerzen/Kopfschmerzen ~:** complain of backache *sing.*/a headache; **[ich] kann nicht ~:** [I] can't complain; [I] mustn't grumble; Ⓒ (*geh.*) **um jmdn./jmds. Tod ~:** mourn sb./sb.'s death; **über den Verlust seines Vermögens ~:** lament *or* bewail the loss of one's fortune; Ⓓ (*bei Gericht*) sue; take legal action; **auf Schadenersatz ~:** sue for damages; bring an action for damages; **auf Scheidung ~:** petition for divorce; **gegen jmdn. ~:** sue sb.; take legal action against sb.
❷ *tr. V.* Ⓐ **jmdm. sein Leid/seine Not/sein Missgeschick ~:** pour out one's sorrows *pl.*/troubles *pl.*/tale of misfortune to sb.; **Gott seis geklagt** (*veralt.*) alas, alack (*arch.*); Ⓑ (*österr.: verklagen*) sue; take legal action against

**Klage·punkt** *der* (*Rechtsw.*) (*im Zivilrecht*) particular of the/a claim; (*im Strafrecht*) count of the/a charge

**Kläger** /ˈklɛ:gɐ/ *der;* ~**s,** ~, **Klägerin** *die;* ~, ~**nen** (*im Zivilrecht*) plaintiff; (*im Strafrecht*) prosecuting party; (*bei einer Scheidung*) petitioner; **wo kein ~ ist, ist auch kein Richter** (*Spr.*) if there's no law against it/if nobody complains, he/we *etc.* needn't worry

**Klage-:** **~ruf** *der* plaintive cry; (*von Schmerz verursacht*) cry of pain; (*stöhnend*) moan; **~schrift** *die* (*Rechtsw.*) (*im Zivilrecht*) statement of claim; (*im Strafrecht*) charge/list of charges; (*bei einer Scheidung*) petition; **~weg** *der* (*Rechtsw.*) **auf dem ~weg** *od.* **im ~weg** by [taking] legal action *or* proceedings; through the courts; **~weib** *das* [professional] mourner

**kläglich** /ˈklɛ:klɪç/ ❶ *Adj.* Ⓐ (*mitleiderregend*) pitiful ‹expression, voice, cry›; pitiful, wretched ‹condition, appearance›; **ein ~es Ende nehmen** come to a miserable end; Ⓑ (*minderwertig*) pathetic ‹achievement, result, etc.›; **ein ~er Rest** a few pathetic remains *pl.;* Ⓒ (*erbärmlich*) despicable, wretched ‹behaviour, role, compromise›; pathetic ‹result, defeat›.
❷ *adv.* Ⓐ ‹weep, sob› pitifully; Ⓑ (*erbärmlich*) ‹behave› wretchedly, despicably; ‹fail› miserably

**Kläglichkeit** *die;* ~ ⇒ **kläglich** 1 A-C: pitifulness; wretchedness; patheticness; despicableness

**klaglos** ❶ *Adj.* uncomplaining. ❷ *adv.* uncomplainingly; without complaint

**Klamauk** /klaˈmauk/ *der;* ~**s** (*ugs. abwertend*) fuss; to-do; (*Lärm, Krach*) row (*coll.*); racket; (*Reklamewirbel*) fuss; hullabaloo; (*im Theater*) slapstick

**klamm** /klam/ *Adj.* Ⓐ (*feucht*) cold and damp; Ⓑ (*steif*) numb; **~ vor Kälte** numb with cold; Ⓒ **~ sein** (*salopp*) be hard up

**Klamm** *die;* ~, ~**en** [deep and narrow] gorge; ravine

**Klammer** *die;* ~, ~**n** Ⓐ (*Wäsche~*) peg; Ⓑ (*Haar~*) [hair]grip; Ⓒ (*Zahn~*) brace; Ⓓ (*Wund~*) clip; Ⓔ (*Büro~*) paper clip; (*Heft~*) staple; Ⓕ (*Bau~*) cramp[-iron]; [timber-]dog; Ⓖ (*Schriftzeichen*) bracket; **runde ~n** round brackets; parentheses; **eckige/spitze ~n** square/angle *or* pointed brackets; **geschweifte ~n** braces; **~ auf/zu** open/close brackets; Ⓗ (*Text in Klammern*) bracketed material; material in [the] brackets; (*Math.*) bracket; bracketed expression; **die ~n auflösen** remove the brackets; Ⓘ (*Griff*) grip; Ⓙ (*fig.*) (*Verbindung*) bond; link; (*Fessel*) shackle; tie

**Klammer-:** **~affe** *der* (*Zool.*) spider monkey; **~ausdruck** *der; Pl.* **~ausdrücke** (*Math.*) bracket; bracketed expression; **~beutel** *der* peg bag; **dich haben sie wohl mit dem ~beutel gepudert!** (*berlin. salopp*) you must be off your rocker! (*coll.*)

**klammern** ❶ *refl. V.* **sich an jmdn./etw. ~** (*auch fig.*) cling to sb./sth.; **sich an Worte ~:** be pedantic about the words used. ❷ *tr. V.* Ⓐ **er klammerte seine Hände um das Geländer** he grasped the railing [with both hands]; Ⓑ (*zusammenhalten*) **eine Wunde ~:** close a wound with a clip/clips; Ⓒ (*befestigen*) (*mit einer Büroklammer*) clip; (*mit einer Heftmaschine*) staple; (*mit einer Wäscheklammer*) peg. ❸ *itr. V.* (*Boxen*) clinch

**klamm·heimlich** ❶ *Adj.* (*ugs.*) on the quiet *postpos.;* ‹meeting› held on the quiet. ❷ *adv.* on the quiet

**Klamotte** /klaˈmɔtə/ *die;* ~, ~**n** Ⓐ *Pl.* (*salopp: Kleidung*) clobber *sing.* (*coll.*); gear *sing.* (*coll.*); Ⓑ *Pl.* (*salopp: Kram*) junk *sing.;* stuff *sing.;* Ⓒ (*ugs. abwertend: Schwank*) rubbishy play/film *etc.*

**Klamotten·kiste** *die* (*ugs.*) *in* **etw. aus der ~ hervorholen** dig sth. up again; **ein Witz/eine Anekdote aus der ~:** an old chestnut

**Klampfe** /ˈklampfə/ *die;* ~, ~**n** Ⓐ (*volkst.: Gitarre*) guitar; Ⓑ (*österr.*) ⇒ **Klammer** F

**Klan** /kla:n/ *der;* ~**s,** ~**e** ⇒ **Clan**

**klang** /klaŋ/ *1. u. 3. Pers. Sg. Prät. v.* **klingen**

**Klang** *der;* ~**[e]s, Klänge** /ˈklɛŋə/ Ⓐ (*Ton*) sound; Ⓑ (*~farbe*) tone; **der Name dieser Familie/Firma hat einen guten/schlechten ~** (*fig.*) this family/firm has a good/bad name; **ihre Worte hatten einen bitteren ~** (*fig.*) there was a bitter note in *or* edge to her words; Ⓒ *Pl.* (*Melodie*) **das Orchester spielte alte, wohl bekannte Klänge** the orchestra played old familiar tunes; **nach den Klängen eines Walzers tanzen** dance to the strains of a waltz

**Klang-:** **~bild** *das* (*fachspr.*) sound; **~effekt** *der* sound effect; **~farbe** *die* tone colour *or* quality; (*einer Stimme*) tone; **~fülle** *die* (*eines Instruments*) richness *or* fullness of tone; (*eines Orchesters*) richness *or* fullness of sound; (*einer Stimme*) sonority

**klanglich** ❶ *Adj.* tonal ‹beauty, quality, etc.›; tonal, tone *attr.* ‹characteristics›. ❷ *adv.* tonally

**klanglos** ❶ *Adj.* toneless; **mit ~er Stimme** in a toneless voice; tonelessly. ❷ *adv.* tonelessly; ⇒ *auch* **sanglos**

**klang-, Klang-:** **~regler** *der* (*Technik*) ⇒ **Tonblende**; **~rein** ❶ *Adj.* **~rein sein** have a pure tone *or* sound; ❷ *adv.* **er spielte so ~rein, dass ...:** he played with such [a] purity of tone that ...; **~schön** *Adj.* **ein ~schönes Instrument** an instrument with a beautiful tone *or* sound; **~treu** *Adj.* faithful ‹reproduction›; high-fidelity ‹receiver, reception›; **~voll** *Adj.* Ⓐ sonorous ‹voice, language›; Ⓑ (*berühmt*) illustrious ‹name, title›

**klapp** /klap/ *Interj.* click

**Klapp-:** **~bett** *das* folding bed; **~brücke** *die* bascule bridge; **~deckel** *der* hinged lid

**Klappe** *die;* ~, ~**n** Ⓐ [hinged] lid; (*am Fenster*) [hinged] vent; (*am Briefkasten*) flap; (*am Tisch*) leaf; **~ zu, Affe tot** (*salopp*) there's an end to it; Ⓑ (*am LKW*) tailboard; tailgate; (*seitlich*) side gate; (*am Kombiwagen*) back; Ⓒ (*an Kleidertaschen*) flap; Ⓓ (*am Ofen*) [drop-]door; Ⓔ (*an Musikinstrumenten*) key; (*an einer Trompete*) valve; Ⓕ (*Herz~*) valve; Ⓖ (*Augen~*) [eye]patch; Ⓗ (*Achselstück*) shoulder strap; Ⓘ (*Filmjargon*) clapperboard; **das war die letzte ~:** that was the last take; Ⓙ (*salopp: Mund*) trap (*sl.*); **die** *od.* **seine ~ halten** shut one's trap (*sl.*); **eine große** *od.* **freche ~ haben** (*abwertend*) have a big mouth; Ⓚ (*ugs.: Bett*) **sich in die ~ hauen** hit the hay (*coll.*); get one's head down

**klappen** ❶ *tr. V.* **nach oben/unten ~:** turn up/down ‹collar, hat brim›; lift up/put down *or* lower ‹lid›; **nach vorne/hinten ~:** tilt forward/back ‹seat›. ❷ *itr. V.* Ⓐ ‹door, shutter› bang; **mit der Tür ~:** bang the door; Ⓑ (*stoßen*) bang; Ⓒ (*ugs.: gelingen*) work out all right; ‹rehearsal, performance, etc.› go [off] all right; **die Sache wird schon ~:** it *or* things will work out all right; **hat es mit den Karten geklappt?** did you get the tickets all right?

**Klappen-:** **~fehler** *der* ⇒ **Herzklappenfehler**; **~text** *der* (*Buchw.*) blurb

**Klapper** *die;* ~, ~**n** rattle

**klapper-, Klapper-:** **~dürr** (*ugs.*) all skin and bone *pred.;* **~gestell** *das* (*ugs.*) Ⓐ (*dünner Mensch*) bag of bones; Ⓑ (*scherzh.: Fahrzeug*) rattletrap; **~kasten** *der,* **~kiste** *die* (*ugs.*) rattletrap

**klappern** *itr. V.* Ⓐ rattle; ‹heels, knitting needles› click; **vor Kälte ~ ihr die Zähne** her teeth are chattering with cold; Ⓑ (*ein K~ erzeugen*) make a clatter; **vor Angst/Kälte klapperte er mit den Zähnen** his teeth were chattering with fear/cold; **auf der Schreibmaschine ~** (*ugs.*) clatter away on the typewriter; **mit den Augen ~** (*ugs.*) keep blinking; (*kokettieren*) flutter one's eyelashes; Ⓒ **mit sein** (*sich ~d fortbewegen*) ‹car› rattle along; ‹person› clatter along

**Klapper-:** **~schlange** *die* rattlesnake; **~storch** *der* (*Kinderspr.*) stork; **glaubst du noch an den ~storch?** do you still believe that babies are brought by the stork?

**Klapp-:** **~fahr·rad** *das* folding bicycle; **~fenster** *das* top-hung window; **~laden** *der; Pl.* **~läden,** *auch* **~~:** folding shutter; **~liege** *die* [folding] lounger *or* sunbed; **~messer** *das* clasp knife; **~rad** *das* folding bicycle

**klapprig** *Adj.* Ⓐ (*alt*) rickety; ramshackle; Ⓑ (*wenig stabil*) rickety; wobbly; Ⓒ (*ugs.: hinfällig*) decrepit; **er ist noch etwas ~:** he's still a bit shaky

**Klapp-:** **~sitz** *der* folding seat; tip-up seat; **~stuhl** *der* folding chair; **~stulle** *die* (*berlin.*) sandwich; **~tisch** *der* folding table; **~tür** *die* hinged door; **~verdeck** *das* collapsible *or* folding hood *or* top; **~zylinder** *der* opera hat; crush hat

**Klaps** /klaps/ *der;* ~**es,** ~**e** Ⓐ (*ugs.: leichter Schlag*) smack; slap; **jmdm. einen ~ geben** give sb. a slap *or* smack; Ⓑ (*salopp*) **einen ~ haben** have a screw loose (*coll.*); be a bit bonkers (*coll.*)

**Klaps·mühle** *die* (*salopp*) loony bin (*sl.*); nuthouse (*sl.*)

**klar** /kla:ɐ̯/ ❶ *Adj.* Ⓐ clear; **~e Brühe** clear soup; **mit ~en Augen** clear-eyed; **bei ~er Sicht** when it's clear; on a clear day; **einen ~en Moment haben** (*fig.*) have a lucid moment; **ein ~er Verstand** clear judgement *no art.;* **er ist nicht bei ~em Verstand** he's

k

not in his right mind; he's not in full possession of his faculties; **~ [im Kopf] sein** have a clear head; be able to think clearly *or* straight; **er ist nicht ganz ~ im Kopf** (*salopp*) he's not quite right in the head (*sl.*); **B** (*eindeutig*) clear ‹decision›; straight ‹question, answer›; **ein ~es Ziel vor Augen haben** have a clear aim *or* objective; **~e Verhältnisse schaffen** set things straight; **[ist] alles ~?** [is] everything clear?; **jetzt ist mir alles ~:** now I understand; **jmdm. wird etw. ~:** sth. becomes clear to sb.; **sich** (*Dat.*) **über etw.** (*Akk.*) **~ werden** realize *or* grasp sth.; **ich muss mir über meine Pläne für die Zukunft erst ~ werden** I must first get my plans for the future clear in my own mind; **na ~!** (*ugs.*), **aber ~!** (*ugs.*) of course!; **~, dass ...** naturally, ...; **Das werdet ihr nicht tun. Ist das ~?** You must not do that. Is that clear *or* Do I make myself clear?; **ist dir ~, dass ...?** are you aware that ...?; **das ist ~ wie Klärchen** *od.* **Kloßbrühe** *od.* **dicke Tinte** (*ugs.*) it's as plain as a pikestaff (*Brit.*) *or* as the nose on your face; **sich** (*Dat.*) **über etw.** (*Akk.*) **im Klaren sein** realize *or* be aware of sth.; **C** (*fertig*) ready; **~ zum Auslaufen** ready to sail.
**2** *adv.* clearly; **sie haben die gegnerische Mannschaft ~ besiegt** they won a clear[-cut] victory over the opposing team; **nicht ~ denken können** be unable to think clearly *or* straight; **~ auf der Hand liegen** (*ugs.*) be blindingly obvious; **etw. ~ und deutlich sagen** say sth. clearly and unambiguously; **ein ~ denkender Mann** a clear-thinking man; **~ sehen** (*fig.*) understand the matter

**Klar** *das;* **~s, ~** (*österr.*) ⇒ **Eiweiß A**

**Klär·anlage** *die* sewage treatment plant; (*einer Fabrik*) wastewater treatment plant

**klar-, Klar-: ~apfel** *der: type of early dessert apple;* ≈ White/Yellow Transparent; **~blick** *der* clear-sightedness; **~blickend** *Adj.* clear-sighted; ***~denkend** ⇒ **klar 2**

**Klare** *der;* **~n, ~n** schnapps

**klären** /ˈklɛːrən/ **1** *tr. V.* **A** (*auf~*) settle, resolve ‹question, issue, matter›; clarify ‹situation›; clear up ‹case, affair, misunderstanding›; **B** (*reinigen*) purify; treat ‹effluent, sewage›; clear ‹beer, wine›. **2** *refl. V.* **A** (*klar werden*) ‹situation› become clear; ‹question, issue, matter› be settled *or* resolved; **B** (*rein werden*) ‹liquid, sky› clear; ‹weather› clear [up]. **3** *itr. V.* (*Ballspiele*) clear [the ball]; **auf der Linie ~:** clear [the ball] off the line

**klar|gehen** *unr. itr. V.; mit sein* (*ugs.*) go OK (*coll.*); **geht das klar mit dem Antrag?** is the application going OK? (*coll.*); **es wird schon ~:** it'll be OK (*coll.*)

**Klarheit** *die;* **~, ~en A** clarity; **B** (*Eindeutigkeit*) clarity; (*von Ausführungen, Rede usw.*) clarity; lucidity; **C** (*Gewissheit*) **sich** (*Dat.*) **über etw.** (*Akk.*) **~ verschaffen** clarify sth.; **völlige ~ verlangen** demand full information *or* all the facts (**über** + *Akk.* about); **D** (*ugs. scherzh.*) **jetzt sind alle ~en beseitigt** now I'm/everyone's *etc.* totally confused

**klarieren** *tr. V.* (*Seemannsspr.*) **etw. ~:** clear sth. [through customs]

**Klarinette** /klariˈnɛtə/ *die;* **~, ~n** clarinet

**Klarinettist** *der;* **~en, ~en, Klarinettistin** *die;* **~, ~nen ▸ 159** clarinettist

**Klarisse** /klaˈrɪsə/ *die;* **~, ~n, Klarissin** *die;* **~, ~nen** nun of the order of St. Clare; **die Klariss[inn]en** the poor Clares

**klar-, Klar-: ~|kommen** *unr. itr. V.; mit sein* (*ugs.*) manage; cope; **mit jmdm. ~kommen** get on with sb.; **ich komme mit der neuen Waschmaschine/der Matheaufgabe nicht ~:** I can't get on with my new washing machine/sort out this maths exercise; **~lack** *der* clear varnish; **~|legen** *tr. V.* (*ugs.*) make clear; explain; **~|machen** *tr. V.* **A** (*ugs.: erklären*) make clear; **jmdm./sich etw. ~machen** make sth. clear to sb./realize sth.; **B** (*Seemannsspr.*) get ready; prepare

**Klär·schlamm** *der* (*Technik*) sludge

**Klar·schrift·leser** *der* (*DV*) optical character reader

***klar|sehen** ⇒ **klar 2**

**Klarsicht-: ~folie** *die* transparent film; **~packung** *die* transparent pack; **~umschlag** *der* transparent cover

**klar-, Klar-: ~|spülen** *itr. V.* rinse; **~spüler** *der,* **~spülmittel** *das* rinse aid; **~|stellen** *tr. V.* clear up; clarify; **ich möchte ~stellen, dass ...** I should like to make it clear that ...; **~stellung** *die* clarification; **~text** *der* (*auch DV*) clear *or* plain text; **im ~text** (*fig.*) in plain language; **[mit jmdm.] ~text reden** (*fig. ugs.*) talk turkey [to *or* with sb.] (*coll.*)

**Klärung** *die;* **~, ~en A** (*Beseitigung von Missverständnissen*) clarification; **B** (*Reinigung*) purification; (*von Abwässern*) treatment

***klar|werden** ⇒ **klar 1 B**

**Klär·werk** *das* sewage works *sing. or pl.*; (*einer Fabrik*) wastewater treatment works *sing. or pl.*

**klass, *klaß** /klas/ (*südd., österr.*) ⇒ **klasse**

**klasse** /ˈklasə/ (*ugs.*) **1** *indekl. Adj.* great (*coll.*); marvellous. **2** *adv.* marvellously

**Klasse** *die;* **~, ~n A** (*Schul~*) class; form (*esp. Brit.*); (*Raum*) classroom; (*Stufe*) year; grade (*Amer.*); **die vierte ~ besuchen** be in the fourth year *or* (*Amer.*) grade; **B** (*Bevölkerungsgruppe*) class; **die ~ der Werktätigen/der Besitzlosen** the working/propertyless class; **C** (*Sport*) league; (*Boxen*) division; class; **D** (*Fahrzeug~*) class; **PKWs der gehobenen ~:** upmarket cars; **ein Führerschein der ~ 1/2/3/4/5** ≈ a driving licence for a motorcycle/a heavy goods vehicle/a private car/a moped/a motor-assisted bicycle; **E** (*Boots~*) class; **F** (*Qualitätsstufe*) class; **ein Wagen/eine Fahrkarte erster ~:** a first-class carriage/ticket; **zweiter ~ liegen** occupy a second-class hospital bed; **er ist ein Künstler erster ~** (*ugs.*) he is a first-class *or* first-rate artist; **das ist [einsame** *od.* **ganz große] ~!** (*ugs.*) that's [just] great (*coll.*) *or* marvellous!; **der Verdienstorden erster ~:** the Order of Merit first-class; **G** (*Biol.*) class

**Klasse-: ~frau** *die* (*ugs.*) stunner (*coll.*); smasher (*coll.*); **~mann** *der* **A** (*ugs.*) marvellous man; fantastic guy (*coll.*); **B** (*Sportjargon*) top-class *or* first-rate player; **~mannschaft** *die* (*Sportjargon*) top-class *or* first-rate team

**Klassement** /klasəˈmãː/ *das;* **~s, ~s** (*Sport*) [list *sing.* of] rankings *pl.*

**klassen-, Klassen-: ~arbeit** *die* (*Schulw.*) [written] class test; **~aufsatz** *der* (*Schulw.*) essay written in class; class essay; **~ausflug** *der* (*Schulw.*) class outing; **~beste** *der/die; adj. Dekl.* top pupil in the class; **wer ist denn bei euch der oder die ~beste?** who is top of your class?; **~bewusstsein, *~bewußtsein** *das* (*Soziol.*) class consciousness; **~buch** *das* (*Schulw.*) *book recording details of pupils' attendance, behaviour, and of topics covered in each lesson* ≈ [class] register; **~durchschnitt** *der* (*Schulw.*) class average; **~erhalt** *der* (*Sport*) **um den ~erhalt kämpfen** struggle *or* battle to avoid relegation; **~fahrt** *die* (*Schulw.*) class outing; **~feind** *der* (*marx.*) class enemy; **~gegensatz** *der* class difference; **~geist** *der* (*Schulw.*) class spirit; **~gemeinschaft** *die* (*Schulw.*) (*~kollektiv*) class; (*~geist*) class spirit; **~gesellschaft** *die* (*Soziol.*) class society; **~hass, *~haß** *der* (*Sozialpsych.*) class hatred *no art.*; **~herrschaft** *die* (*Soziol.*) class rule *no art.*; **~justiz** *die* (*Soziol.*) legal system with a built-in class bias; **~kamerad** *der,* **~kameradin** *die* (*Schulw.*) class fellow; classmate; **~kampf** *der* (*marx.*) class struggle; **~kämpferisch** *Adj.* (*marx.*) **~kämpferische Parolen** slogans supporting the class struggle; **~keile** *die* (*Schülerspr.*) **~keile beziehen** *od.* **bekommen** be punched and pushed by the rest of the class; **~lehrer** *der,* **~lehrerin** *die,* **~leiter** *der,* **~leiterin** *die* (*Schulw.*) class *or* form teacher; form master/mistress; **~los** *Adj.* (*Soziol.*) classless; **~lotterie** *die: lottery in which draws are made on a number of different days and for which tickets can be bought for each individual draw;* **~raum** *der* ⇒ **~zimmer**; **~schranke** *die* (*Soziol.*) class barrier; **~sprecher** *der,* **~sprecherin** *die* (*Schulw.*) class spokesman; ≈ form leader *or* captain; **~stärke** *die* (*Schulw.*) size of the/a class/of classes; **~treffen** *das* (*Schulw.*) class reunion; **~unterschied** *der* **A** (*Soziol.*) class difference; **B** (*Sport*) difference in class; **~wahlrecht** *das* (*hist.*) class-based electoral system; class[-based] system of franchise; **~weise** *Adv.* (*Schulw.*) class by class; **~ziel** *das* (*Schulw.*) required standard (*for pupils in a particular class*); **das ~ziel erreichen** reach the required standard; (*fig.*) make the grade; come up to scratch; **~zimmer** *das* (*Schulw.*) classroom

**Klasse-: ~spieler** *der,* **~spielerin** *die* (*Sport Jargon*) [top-]class *or* first-rate player; **~weib** *das* (*ugs.*) stunner (*coll.*); smasher (*coll.*)

**Klassifikation** /klasifikaˈtsi̯oːn/ *die;* **~, ~en** classification

**klassifizieren** /klasifiˈtsiːrən/ *tr. V.* classify (**als** as)

**Klassifizierung** *die;* **~, ~en** classification

**-klassig** *Adj.* -class; **mehr~/zwei~:** with a number of/two classes

**Klassik** /ˈklasɪk/ *die;* **~ A** (*Antike*) classical antiquity *no art.*; **B** (*Zeit kultureller Höchstleistung*) classical period *or* age

**Klassiker** *der;* **~s, ~, Klassikerin** *die;* **~, ~nen A** (*der antiken Klassik*) classical writer; **B** (*einer Epoche*) classic; classical writer/composer *etc.*; **C** (*jmd., dessen Werk als mustergültig gilt*) classical exponent; classic

**klassisch** *Adj.* **A** classical; **B** (*vollendet, zeitlos; auch iron.*) classic; **C** (*herkömmlich*) classical; conventional ‹warfare›

**Klassizismus** /klasiˈtsɪsmʊs/ *der;* **~, Klassizismen A** (*Stilform*) classicism; **B** (*Stilmerkmal*) feature of the classical style

**klassizistisch** *Adj.* classical

**-klässler, *-kläßler** /-klɛslɐ/ *der;* **-~s, -~, -klässlerin, *-kläßlerin** *die;* **~, ~nen** -former; **Erst~/Zweit~:** first-former/second-former

**klatsch** *Interj.* smack; (*wenn etw. Weiches auf den Boden fällt*) splosh

**Klatsch** /klatʃ/ *der;* **~[e]s, ~e A** (*ugs. abwertend: Gerede*) gossip; tittle-tattle; **B** (*Geräusch*) smack; **es gab einen lauten ~, als er auf dem Wasser aufschlug** there was a loud splash *or* (*lauter und schärfer*) smack as he hit the water

**Klatsch·base** *die* (*ugs. abwertend*) gossip

**Klatsche** *die;* **~, ~n A** (*Fliegen~*) fly swatter; **B** (*Schülerspr.: Übersetzung*) crib; **C** (*abwertend*) ⇒ **Klatschbase**

**klatschen 1** *itr. V.* **A** *auch mit sein* ‹waves, wet sails› slap (**gegen** against); **der Regen klatscht gegen die Scheiben** the rain beats against the windows; **sie gab ihm eine Ohrfeige, dass es nur so klatschte** she gave him a resounding smack *or* slap round the face; **B** (*mit den Händen; applaudieren*) clap; **in die Hände ~:** clap one's hands; **lautes K~:** loud applause; **C** (*schlagen*) slap; **sich** (*Dat.*) **auf die Schenkel/gegen die Stirn ~:** slap one's thighs/clap one's hand to one's forehead; **D** (*ugs. abwertend: reden*) gossip (**über** + *Akk.* about).
**2** *tr. V.* **A** (*ugs.: werfen*) slap; chuck (*coll.*) ‹book etc.›; **B den Takt ~** ‹teacher› clap time; ‹audience› clap in time; **jmdm. Beifall ~:** clap *or* applaud sb.; **C** (*ugs.: schlagen*) **jmdm. eine ~:** slap sb. across the face; give sb. a slap across the face

**Klatscherei** *die;* **~, ~en** (*ugs. abwertend*) gossiping

**Klatsch·geschichte** *die* (*abwertend*) piece of gossip; **~n** gossip *sing.*

**klatschhaft** *Adj.* gossipy; fond of gossip *pred.*

**Klatschhaftigkeit** *die;* **~:** fondness for gossip

*old spelling (see note on page 1707)

**klatsch-, Klatsch-: ~kolumnist** *der,* **~kolumnistin** *die (abwertend)* gossip columnist; **~maul** *das (ugs. abwertend)* gossip; **~mohn** *der* corn poppy; field poppy; **~nass, *~naß** *Adj. (ugs.)* soaking *or* sopping wet ‹clothes›; dripping wet ‹hair›; **wir sind ~nass geworden** we got soaked [to the skin] *or* drenched; **~spalte** *die (ugs. abwertend)* gossip column; **~sucht** *die (abwertend)* passion for gossip *or* tittle-tattle; **~süchtig** *Adj.* extremely gossipy; **~süchtig sein** be a compulsive gossip/compulsive gossips; **~tante** *die (ugs. abwertend),* **~weib** *das (ugs. abwertend)* ⇒ **Klatschbase**

**klauben** /ˈklaubn̩/ *tr. V. (landsch.)* Ⓐ *(entfernen)* **die Flusen vom Teppich/die Rosinen aus dem Kuchen ~:** pick the fluff *sing.* off the carpet/the raisins out of the cake; Ⓑ *(auslesen)* pick over; Ⓒ *(bes. südd., österr. ugs.: sammeln)* pick ‹berries›; gather, collect ‹wood›; dig ‹potatoes›

**Klaue** /ˈklauə/ *die;* **~, ~n** Ⓐ claw; *(von Raubvögeln)* talon; *(fig. geh.)* **in den ~n eines Erpressers** in the clutches of a blackmailer; **jmdn. den ~n des Todes entreißen** snatch sb. from the jaws of death; Ⓑ *(Huf)* hoof; Ⓒ *(salopp: Hand)* mitt *(coll.)*; paw *(coll.)*; Ⓓ *(salopp abwertend: Handschrift)* handwriting; **seine ~ kann ich nicht entziffern** I can't decipher his scrawl

**klauen** *(ugs.)* ❶ *tr. V.* pinch *(coll.)*; nick *(Brit. coll.)*; *(fig.)* pinch *(coll.)*, nick *(Brit. coll.)*, crib ‹idea›; **jmdm. etw. ~:** pinch *or (Brit.)* nick/crib sth. from sb. ❷ *itr. V.* pinch *(coll.) or* nick *(Brit. coll.)* things

**Klauen·seuche** *die* ⇒ **Maul- und Klauenseuche**

**Klause** /ˈklauzə/ *die;* **~, ~n** Ⓐ *(Einsiedelei)* hermitage; Ⓑ *(Klosterzelle)* cell; *(fig.)* den; Ⓒ ⇒ **Klus**

**Klausel** /ˈklauzl̩/ *die;* **~, ~n** clause; *(Bedingung)* stipulation; condition; *(Vorbehalt)* proviso

**Klausner** /ˈklausnɐ/ *der;* **~s, ~:** hermit; recluse

**Klaustrophobie** /klaustrofoˈbiː/ *die;* **~, ~n** *(Psych.)* claustrophobia

**Klausur** /klauˈzuːɐ̯/ *die;* **~, ~en** Ⓐ *(Abgeschlossenheit)* **in ~ leben/tagen** live in seclusion/meet in private; Ⓑ *(~arbeit)* [examination] paper; *(Examen)* examination; **eine ~ schreiben** take a[n examination] paper/an examination; Ⓒ *(Klosterbereich)* enclosure

**Klausur-: ~arbeit** *die* [examination] paper; **~tagung** *die* private meeting

**Klaviatur** /klavjaˈtuːɐ̯/ *die;* **~, ~en** Ⓐ keyboard; Ⓑ *(Vielfalt)* [whole] gamut *or* range

**Klavichord** /klaviˈkɔrt/ *das;* **~[e]s, ~s** clavichord

**Klavier** /klaˈviːɐ̯/ *das;* **~s, ~e** piano

**Klavier-: ~auszug** *der* piano score; **~bauer** *der;* **~~s, ~~, ~bauerin** *die;* **~~, ~~nen** piano maker; **~bearbeitung** *die* piano arrangement; arrangement for the piano; **~begleitung** *die* piano accompaniment; **~hocker** *der* piano stool; **~konzert** *das* Ⓐ *(Musikstück)* piano concerto; Ⓑ *(Veranstaltung)* piano recital; **~lehrer** *der,* **~lehrerin** *die* piano teacher; **~schemel** *der* piano stool; **~schule** *die* piano tutor; **~sonate** *die* piano sonata; **~spiel** *das* piano playing; **~spieler** *der,* **~spielerin** *die* pianist; piano player; **~stimmer** *der;* **~~s, ~~, ~stimmerin** *die;* **~~, ~~nen** ▶ 159 piano tuner; **~stunde** *die* piano lesson; **~unterricht** *der* piano lessons *pl.*

**Klebe** /ˈkleːbə/ *die;* **~** *(ugs.)* glue

**Klebe-: ~band** *das; Pl.* **~bänder** adhesive *or* sticky tape; **~bindung** *die (Buchw.)* adhesive *or* perfect binding; **~folie** *die* adhesive film; *(für Regale)* self-adhesive plastic sheeting

**kleben** ❶ *itr. V.* Ⓐ stick **(an** + *Dat.* to); **~ bleiben** stick, remain stuck **(an** + *Dat.* to); **an allen Hauswänden klebten riesige Plakate** there were huge posters stuck on the walls of all the houses; **das Hemd klebte ihm am Körper** his shirt stuck *or* clung to his body; **an seinen Händen klebt Blut** *(fig.)* he has blood on his hands *(fig.)*; his hands are stained with blood *(fig.)*; **am Berghang ~** ‹hut etc.› cling to the mountainside; **jmdm. an der Stoßstange ~** *(fig. salopp)* ‹driver, vehicle› hang on sb.'s tail; **an jmdm. ~** *(salopp)* cling to sb.; Ⓑ *(ugs.: klebrig sein)* be sticky **(von, vor** + *Dat.* with); Ⓒ *(ugs.: an sich hängen haben)* **voller Fliegen/Kletten** *usw.* **~:** be covered in flies/burrs; Ⓓ *(ugs.: sich klammern)* **an seinem Stuhl/an der Theke ~:** stay put in one's chair *(coll.)*/prop the bar up *(coll.)*; **klebt nicht so an der Textvorlage** *(fig.)* don't stick so closely to the original text; Ⓔ *(verbunden sein)* **daran klebt ein Makel** there's a stigma attached to it; **diese Schande wird an ihr ~ bleiben** this disgrace will remain with her; Ⓕ *(ugs.: Sozialversicherungsbeiträge entrichten)* pay stamps; Ⓖ **~ bleiben** *(ugs.: in der Schule nicht versetzt werden)* stay down; have to repeat a year.
❷ *tr. V.* Ⓐ *(befestigen)* stick; *(mit Klebstoff)* stick; glue; *(mit Leim)* stick; paste; **jmdm. eine ~** *(salopp)* belt sb. one *(coll.)*; Ⓑ *(mit Klebstoff reparieren)* stick *or* glue ‹vase etc.› back together; Ⓒ *(zusammenfügen)* splice ‹tape, film›

***kleben|bleiben** ⇒ **kleben** 1A, E, G

**Klebe·pflaster** *das* adhesive plaster; sticking plaster

**Kleber** *der;* **~s, ~:** adhesive; glue

**Klebe-: ~streifen** *der* ⇒ **Klebstreifen**; **~verband** *der (Med.)* adhesive bandage

**Kleb-: ~fläche** *die* adhesive surface; sticky side; **~kraft** *die* adhesive strength; **~pflaster** *das* ⇒ **Klebepflaster**

**klebrig** *Adj.* Ⓐ *(klebend)* sticky; *(von Schweiß)* clammy ‹hands etc.›; Ⓑ *(abwertend: schmierig)* slimy

**Klebrigkeit** *die;* **~** ⇒ **klebrig**: stickiness; clamminess; sliminess

**Kleb-: ~stelle** *die* join; *(eines Films, Tonbandes)* splice; **~stoff** *der* adhesive; glue; **~streifen** *der* adhesive *or* sticky tape; *(zum Befeuchten auch)* gummed tape

**Kleckerei** *die;* **~, ~en** *(ugs.)* mess

**Klecker·kram** *der (ugs. abwertend)* peanuts *(coll.)*

**kleckern** /ˈklɛkɐn/ *(ugs.)* ❶ *itr. V.* Ⓐ *(Flecken machen)* make a mess; **oje, jetzt habe ich gekleckert** oh dear, now I've gone and spilled something *(coll.)*; Ⓑ *mit sein (heruntertropfen)* drip; spill; Ⓒ *(zögernd verlaufen)* ‹orders› come in dribs and drabs; Ⓓ *(ugs.: halbherzig handeln)* mess about with half measures; **nicht ~, sondern klotzen** stop messing about with half measures, and do the thing properly, whatever the cost. ❷ *tr. V.* spill; splash ‹paint›

**kleckerweise** *Adv. (ugs.)* in dribs and drabs; **der Umzug ging nur ~ vonstatten** the move went ahead in fits and starts

**Klecks** /klɛks/ *der;* **~es, ~e** Ⓐ stain; *(nicht aufgesogen)* blob; *(Tintenfleck)* [ink] blot; Ⓑ *(ugs.: kleine Menge)* spot; *(von Senf, Mayonnaise)* dab

**klecksen** ❶ *itr. V.* Ⓐ *(Klecks[e] machen)* make a stain/stains; *(mit Tinte)* make a blot/blots; ‹pen› blot; **er hat auf den Teppich gekleckst** he has made a stain/stains on the carpet; Ⓑ *(ugs. abwertend: schlecht malen)* daub. ❷ *tr. V. (ugs.)* daub ‹paint›; **Marmelade aufs Brot ~:** smear blobs of jam on the bread

**Kleckser** *der;* **~s, ~** *(ugs.)* Ⓐ *(abwertend)* *(Maler)* dauber; *(Schriftsteller)* scribbler; Ⓑ ⇒ **Klecks**

**Kleckserei** *die;* **~, ~en** *(ugs. abwertend)* Ⓐ *(dauerndes Klecksen)* making stains *no art.*; *(mit Tinte)* making blots *no art.*; Ⓑ *(Hingeschmiertes)* scribble; scrawl; *(schlecht gemaltes Bild)* daub; daubing

**Kledage** /kleˈdaːʒə/ *die;* **~, Kledasche** /kleˈdaːʃə/ *die;* **~** *(nordd., md. salopp)* clobber *(sl.) no indef. art.*

**Klee** /kleː/ *der;* **~s** clover; **jmdn./etw. über den grünen ~ loben** *(ugs.)* praise sb./sth. to the skies

**Klee·blatt** *das* Ⓐ *(Blatt des Klees)* cloverleaf; *(als Symbol Irlands)* shamrock; **ein vierblättriges ~:** a four-leaf *or* four-leaved clover; Ⓑ *(ugs.: drei Personen)* trio; threesome; Ⓒ *(Verkehrsw.: Straßenkreuz)* cloverleaf [intersection *or* junction]

**Kleiber** /ˈklaibɐ/ *der;* **~s, ~:** nuthatch

**Kleid** /klait/ *das;* **~es, ~er** Ⓐ dress; **ein zweiteiliges ~:** a two-piece [suit]; **die Natur trägt ein weißes ~** *(fig. geh.)* Nature is dressed *or* covered in a mantle of white *(literary)*; Ⓑ *Pl. (Kleidung)* clothes; **in den ~ern schlafen** sleep in one's clothes; **~er machen Leute** *(Spr.)* clothes make the man; the apparel oft proclaims the man *(literary)*; Ⓒ *(geh.)* *(Gefieder)* plumage; *(Fell)* coat; Ⓓ *(veralt. geh.: Uniform)* uniform; Ⓔ *(schweiz.: Anzug)* suit

**Kleidchen** *das;* **~s, ~** Ⓐ little dress; Ⓑ *(ugs.: leichtes Kleid)* plain little dress

**kleiden** ❶ *refl. V.* dress. ❷ *tr. V.* Ⓐ dress; **die Armen ~:** clothe the poor; Ⓑ suit; look well on; **die Farbe kleidet dich gut** the colour suits you *or* looks well on you; Ⓒ **etw. in Worte ~:** express sth. in words; put sth. into words; **etw. in schöne Worte ~:** clothe sth. in fine language

**Kleider-: ~ab·lage** *die* Ⓐ *(Ablage)* coat rack; Ⓑ *(Raum)* cloakroom; checkroom *(Amer.)*; **~bad** *das: dry-cleaning process in which the article is simply dipped in the cleaning fluid and not given any finishing treatment;* **~bügel** *der* clothes hanger; coat hanger; **~bürste** *die* clothes brush; **~größe** *die* size; **~haken** *der* coat hook; **~kammer** *die (bes. Milit.)* clothing store; **~kasten** *der (südd., österr., schweiz.)* ⇒ **~schrank**; **~macher** *der,* **~macherin** *die (österr./veralt.)* ⇒ **Schneider**; **~ordnung** *die (hist.)* laws *pl.* governing dress; **~puppe** *die* tailor's dummy; **~rock** *der* pinafore dress; **~sack** *der (bes. Milit.)* kitbag; **~schrank** *der* wardrobe; **er ist ein ~schrank** *(fig. ugs.)* he is a great hulk *or* a giant of a man; **~ständer** *der* coat stand; **~stange** *die* clothes rail; **~stoff** *der (Stoff für ein Kleid)* dress material; *(Stoff für Kleidungsstücke)* clothes material

**kleidsam** *Adj.* becoming

**Kleidung** *die;* **~:** clothes *pl.*; **leichte/warme ~:** light/warm clothes *pl. or* clothing

**Kleidungs·stück** *das* garment; article of clothing; **~e** clothes

**Kleie** /ˈklaiə/ *die;* **~:** bran

**klein** /klain/ ❶ *Adj.* Ⓐ ▶ 411 little; small; small ‹format, letter›; little ‹finger, toe›; **das Kleid ist mir zu ~:** the dress is too small for me; **ein ~es Bier** a small beer; ≈ a half[-pint]; **ein ~es Export** ≈ a half[-pint] of Export; **eine ~e Terz/Sekunde** *(Musik)* a minor third/second; **~e Schritte machen** take small *or* short steps; **sich ~ machen** make oneself small; **auf ~stem Raum** in the minimum of space; **sie ist ~ [von Gestalt/für ihr Alter]** she is small [in stature/for her age]; **er ist [einen Kopf] ~er als ich** he is [a head] shorter than me *or* shorter than I am [by a head]; **im Kleinen** in miniature; on a small scale; **Pippin der Kleine** *(hist.)* Pippin the Short; **~, aber oho** he/she may be small, but he/she certainly makes up for it; **~, aber fein** little, but very nice; **etw. ~ hacken** chop sth. up; **etw. ~ schneiden** cut sth. up small *or* in small pieces; **Zwiebeln ~ hacken/schneiden** chop up onions [small]; **etw. ~ machen** cut sth. up small; *(ugs.: aufbrauchen)* get through *or (sl.)* blow sth.; Ⓑ *(jung)* little; **sein ~er Bruder** his little brother; **als ich [noch] ~ war** when I was small *or* little; **unsere Kleine/unser Kleiner** our little girl/boy; **für die Kleinen** for the little ones; **von ~ auf** from an early age; Ⓒ *(von kurzer Dauer)* little, short ‹while›; short ‹walk, break, holiday›; short, brief ‹delay, introduction›; brief ‹moment›; Ⓓ *(von geringer Menge)* small ‹family, amount, audience, staff›; small, low ‹salary›; low ‹price›; **das Gas auf ~ stellen** turn the gas down [low]; **~es Geld**

k

**haben** have some [small] change; **haben Sie ~?** (*ugs.*) do you have the right money?; **~er habe ich es nicht** I don't have anything smaller; **einen Schein ~ machen** (*ugs.: wechseln*) change a note; **kann mir jemand ein 5-Mark-Stück ~ machen?** can anyone give me change for a five-mark piece?; **E** (*von geringem Ausmaß*) light ‹refreshment›; small ‹party, gift›; scant, little ‹attention›; slight ‹cold, indisposition›; slight, small ‹mistake, irregularity›; minor ‹event, error›; **die ~en Dinge des Alltags** the little everyday things; **einen ~en Schreck bekommen** get a bit of a shock; **das ~ere Übel** the lesser evil; the lesser of the two evils; **das ist meine ~ste Sorge** that's the least of my worries; **du ~er Schwindler!** you little twister!; **ein ~es Spielchen** a little game; **ein ~[es] bisschen** a little *or* tiny bit; **ein ~ wenig** a little bit; **ein ~ wenig Rücksichtnahme** a little bit of consideration; **im Kleinen wie im Großen** in little things as well as in big ones; **bis ins Kleinste** down to the smallest *or* tiniest detail; **F** (*unbedeutend*) lowly ‹employee, sales assistant›; minor ‹official›; **der ~e Mann** the ordinary citizen; the man in the street; **die ~en Leute** ordinary people; the man *sing.* in the street; **in ~en Verhältnissen leben** live in humble *or* modest circumstances; **~ anfangen** (*ugs.*) start off in a small way; **die Kleinen hängt man, die Großen lässt man laufen** it's always the small fry that get caught, while the big fish get away; **G ganz ~ [und hässlich] werden** become meek and subdued; **den mache ich so ~ mit Hut!** (*ugs.*) I'll bring him down a peg or two; **jetzt ist sie so ~:** she's come down a peg or two; **H ein ~er Geist** (*engstirnig*) a narrow-minded person; (*beschränkt*) a person of limited intellect.

**2** *adv.* **A die Heizung ~/~er einstellen** turn the heating down low/lower; **~ gedruckt** in small print (*postpos.*); **das klein Gedruckte** the small print; **~ gemustert** small-patterned; **~ kariert** with a small check or a small-checkered pattern (*postpos.*); **~ geblümt** with a small floral pattern (*postpos.*); **~ geschrieben werden** (*fig. ugs.*) count for [very] little (**bei** with); **~ machen** (*Kinderspr.*) do number one (*child lang.*); **B** (*engstirnig*) **~ von jmdm./etw. denken** think little *or* have a low opinion of sb./sth.; ⇒ *auch* **beigeben** 2

**Klein** *das;* **~s** (*Kochk.*) (*von Geflügel*) giblets *pl.;* (*von Hasen*) trimmings *pl.*

**klein-, Klein-: ~aktie** *die* (*Wirtsch.*) *minimum par-value (50-mark) share;* **~aktionär** *der,* **~aktionärin** *die* (*Wirtsch.*) small shareholder; **~anzeige** *die* (*Zeitungsw.*) small *or* classified advertisement *or* (*coll.*) ad; **~arbeit** *die* painstaking and detailed work; **~asien** (*das*) Asia Minor; **~bahn** *die* light [narrow-gauge] railway; **~bauer** *der;* **~~n, ~~n** small farmer; smallholder; **~|bekommen** *unr. tr. V.:* ⇒ **~kriegen**; **~betrieb** *der* **A** (*Industrie*) small business; **ein industrieller/handwerklicher ~betrieb** a small factory/small workshop; **B** (*Landw.*) small farm; smallholding; **~bild·kamera** *die* (*Fot.*) miniature camera; 35 mm camera; **~buchstabe** *der* small letter; lower-case letter (*Printing*); **~bürger** *der,* **~bürgerin** *die* lower middle-class person; (*abwertend: Spießbürger*) petit bourgeois; **die ~bürger** lower middle-class people; **~bürgerlich** **1** *Adj.* **A** (*das ~bürgertum betreffend*) lower middle class; **B** (*abwertend: spießbürgerlich*) petit bourgeois; **2** *adv.* (*abwertend: spießbürgerlich*) **~bürgerlich denken** have a petit bourgeois way of thinking; **~bürgerlichkeit** *die* (*abwertend*) petit bourgeois nature; **~bürgertum** *das* lower middle class; petite bourgeoisie; **~bus** *der* minibus; **~darsteller** *der,* **~darstellerin** *die* small-part *or* (*coll.*) bit-part actor/actress

**Kleine**[1] *der; adj. Dekl.* **A** (*kleiner Junge*) little boy; **B** (*ugs. Anrede*) little man; **na, ~r** (*Prostituierte zum Passanten*) hello, dearie

**Kleine**[2] *die; adj. Dekl.* **A** (*kleines Mädchen*) little girl; **B** (*ugs. Anrede*) love; (*abwertend*) little madam; **C** (*ugs.: Freundin*) girl[friend]

**Kleine**[3] *das; adj. Dekl.* **A** (*ugs. scherzh.*) little boy/girl (*joc.*); **das ~ der Familie** the baby of the family; **B** (*von Tieren*) baby; little one

**Kleine·leute·milieu** *das* world of simple, ordinary people

**Klein-: ~familie** *die* (*Soziol.*) nuclear family; **~format** *das* small size; (*bei Büchern*) small format *or* size

**Klein·garten** *der* ≈ allotment (*cultivated primarily as a garden*); **in ihrem ~:** on her allotment

**Kleingarten·anlage** *die* ≈ allotments *pl.*

**klein-, Klein-: ~gärtner** *der,* **~gärtnerin** *die* ≈ allotment holder; **~gebäck** *das* biscuits (*Brit.*) *or* (*Amer.*) cookies and small pastries; ***~geblümt** ⇒ **klein** 2 A; ***~gedruckt** ⇒ **klein** 2 A; **~gedruckte** *das; adj. Dekl.* small print; **~geist** *der* (*abwertend*) small-minded person; **~geistig** *Adj.* small-minded; petty-minded ‹official›; **~geld** *das* ▶ 337 [small] change; **würden Sie mir für 10 DM ~geld geben?** can you change a *or* give me change for a ten-mark note?; **über das nötige ~geld verfügen** (*iron.*) have the wherewithal (*coll.*); ***~gemustert** ⇒ **klein** 2 A; **~gläubig** *Adj.* (*unfähig zum festen Glauben*) of little faith *postpos.;* sceptical; (*ängstlich-zweifelnd*) faint-hearted; **o ihr Kleingläubigen!** (*bibl.*) o ye of little faith!; **die Kleingläubigen** the doubters/faint-hearts; **~gläubigkeit** *die* ⇒ **~gläubig**: lack of faith; scepticism; faint-heartedness; ***~|hacken** ⇒ **klein** 1 A

**Kleinheit** *die;* ~ **A** (*geringe Größe*) smallness; small size; **B** (*selten: Beschränktheit*) limitedness; restrictedness

**Klein-: ~hirn** *das* (*Anat.*) cerebellum; little brain; **~holz** *das* chopped wood; **~holz machen** chop wood; **~holz aus etw. machen, etw. zu ~holz machen** (*ugs.*) smash sth. to pieces; **~holz aus jmdm. machen, jmdn. zu ~holz machen** (*ugs.*) make mincemeat of sb.

**Kleinigkeit** *die;* **~, ~en** **A** (*kleine Sache*) small thing; (*Einzelheit*) [small] detail; minor point; **bis auf einige ~en habe ich alle Einkäufe gemacht** apart from a few small items *or* a few odds and ends I've done all the shopping; **ich habe noch eine ~ zu erledigen** I still have a small matter to attend to; **jmdm. eine ~ schenken** give sb. a small *or* little gift *or* present; **eine ~ essen** have a [small] bite to eat; **das kostet eine ~** (*ugs. iron.*) that costs a bob *or* two (*Brit. coll.*) *or* a tidy sum (*coll.*); **die ~ von 50 000 DM** (*ugs. iron.*) the small *or* little matter of 50,000 marks; **sich nicht mit ~en abgeben** not concern oneself with details *or* trifles; **B** (*leichte Aufgabe*) **eine ~ für jmdn. sein [, etw. zu tun]** be no trouble for sb. [to do sth.]; be a simple matter for sb. [to do sth.]; **es war eine ~ für sie, ihren Mann zu überreden** she had no trouble in persuading her husband; **es war keine ~ für ihn** it was no small matter for him; **das war eine ~:** it was nothing; **C** (*ugs.: ein Stückchen*) a little bit; (*noch kleiner*) a fraction; a shade

**Kleinigkeits·krämer** *der* (*abwertend*) pettifogger; pettifogging individual

**Kleinigkeits·krämerei** *die* (*abwertend*) pettifoggery; pettifogging

**Kleinigkeits·krämerin** *die* ⇒ **Kleinigkeitskrämer**

**klein-, Klein-: ~kaliber·gewehr** *das* small-bore rifle; **~kalibrig** *Adj.* small-bore *attrib.;* **~kariert** **1** *Adj.* (*ugs. abwertend: engstirnig*) narrow-minded; ⇒ *auch* **klein** 2 A; **2** *adv.* narrow-mindedly; in a narrow-minded way; **~kind** *das* small child; **~kleckersdorf** /-ˈklɛkɐs-/ (*das*) **~~s** (*ugs. spött.*) somewhere in the back of beyond (*coll.*); some tiny little place way out in the sticks (*coll.*); **~klima** *das* (*Met.*) microclimate; **~kram** *der* (*ugs.*) **A** (*~e Dinge*) odds and ends *pl.;* **B** (*unbedeutende Dinge*) trivial matters *pl.;* (*Einzelheiten*) trivial details; (*~ere Arbeiten*) trivial little jobs; **der tägliche ~kram** the trivial concerns *pl.* of everyday life; **~kredit** *der* (*Bankw.*) personal loan (*repayable within two years*); **~krieg** *der* **A** (*Guerillakrieg*) guerrilla warfare; **ein ~krieg** a guerrilla war; **B** (*ständiger Streit*) running battle; **~|kriegen** *tr. V.* (*ugs.*) **A** (*zerkleinern*) crush [to pieces]; get one's teeth through ‹tough meat›; **B** (*zerstören*) smash; break; **nicht ~zukriegen sein** be indestructible; **C** (*aufbrauchen*) get through, (*sl.*) blow ‹money›; get through, (*joc.*) demolish ‹sweets, cakes, etc.›; **D** (*entmutigen*) **jmdn. ~kriegen** get sb. down; (*durch Drohungen*) intimidate sb.; (*gefügig machen*) bring sb. into line; **sich nicht ~kriegen lassen** not allow oneself to be got down/intimidated

**Klein·kunst** *die* **A** cabaret; **B** (*Kunsthandwerk*) craftwork

**Kleinkunst·bühne** *die* cabaret ensemble

**klein·laut** **1** *Adj.* subdued; (*verlegen*) sheepish. **2** *adv.* in a subdued fashion; (*verlegen*) sheepishly

**kleinlich** (*abwertend*) **1** *Adj.* pernickety; (*ohne Großzügigkeit*) mean; (*engstirnig*) small-minded; petty; (*in Bezug auf Sauberkeit und Ordnung*) pernickety; fussy; petty ‹regulations›. **2** *adv.* meticulously; punctiliously; **~ denken** have a mean and petty cast of mind

**Kleinlichkeit** *die;* ~ (*abwertend*) ⇒ **kleinlich**: pernicketiness; meanness; small-mindedness; pettiness; fussiness

**klein-, Klein-: *~|machen** ⇒ **klein** 1 A; **~möbel** *das* smaller item of furniture; **teure ~möbel** expensive smaller furniture *sing.;* **~mut** *der* (*geh.*) faint-heartedness; timidity; **~mütig** *Adj.* (*geh.*) faint-hearted; timid

**Kleinod** /ˈklaino:t/ *das;* **~[e]s, ~e** *od.* **~ien** /-ˈno:djən/ (*geh.*) **A** (*Schmuckstück*) piece of jewellery; (*Edelstein*) jewel; **B** (*Kostbarkeit*) gem

**klein-, Klein-: ~rentner** *der,* **~rentnerin** *die* person living on a small pension; ***~|schneiden** ⇒ **klein** 1 A; **~|schreiben** *unr. tr. V* write ‹word etc.› with a small initial letter; ⇒ *auch* **klein** 2 A; **~schreibung** *die* use of small initial letters; **~sparer** *der,* **~sparerin** *die* (*Finanzw.*) small saver; **~staat** *der* small state; **~stadt** *die* small town; **~städter** *der,* **~städterin** *die* small-town dweller; **~städtisch** *Adj.* small-town *attrib.*

**Kleinst·betrag** *der* minimum *or* smallest sum *or* amount

**Kleinst·bild·kamera** *die* subminiature camera

**Kleinste** *der/die/das; adj. Dekl.* smallest *or* youngest boy/girl/child

**klein|stellen** *tr. V.* turn down [low]

**kleinst-, Kleinst-: ~kind** *das* very small child (*up to two years old*); **~lebewesen** *das* micro-organism; **~möglich** *Adj.* smallest possible

**Klein·tier** *das* pet; (*Nutztier*) small domestic animal

**Kleintier-: ~halter** *der,* **~halterin** *die* breeder of small animals; **~haltung** *die* breeding of small animals; **~zucht** *die* [professional] breeding of small animals; (*Betrieb*) establishment for breeding small animals

**Klein·verdiener** *der,* **Klein·verdienerin** *die* person on a low income

**Klein·vieh** *das* small farm *or* domestic animals *pl.;* small livestock; **~ macht auch Mist** (*ugs.*) many a mickle makes a muckle (*prov.*); every little helps

**Kleinvieh·zucht** *die* breeding of small farm *or* domestic animals

**Klein·wagen** *der* small car

**klein·wüchsig** /-vy:ksɪç/ *Adj.* ‹person› of small stature; small, short ‹person, race›; small ‹variety, species›

**Kleister** /ˈklaistɐ/ *der;* **~s, ~:** paste; (*ugs. abwertend: Brei*) goo (*coll.*)

**kleist[e]rig** *Adj.* (*ugs.*) gooey (*coll.*)

**kleistern** *tr. V.* (*ugs.*) **A** (*kleben*) paste, stick (**an** + *Akk.* on); **B** (*reparieren*) stick; **C**

*old spelling (see note on page 1707)

(*dick auftragen*) plaster (**auf** + *Akk.* on); **D** **jmdm. eine ~:** belt sb. one (*coll.*)

**Klementine** /klemɛn'ti:nə/ *die;* ~, ~**n** clementine

***Klemmappe** ⇒ **Klemmmappe**

**Klemme** /'klɛmə/ *die;* ~, ~**n** **A** (*Haar~*) [hair] clip; (*Papier~*) paper clip; (*Technik*) clip; (*Elektrot.*) terminal; (*Med.*) clip; **B** (*ugs.: schwierige Lage*) **in der ~ sein** *od.* **sitzen** be in a fix *or* jam (*coll.*); **jmdm. aus der ~ helfen** help sb. out of a fix *or* jam (*coll.*)

**klemmen** **1** *tr. V.* **A** (*befestigen*) tuck; stick (*coll.*); **etw. unter den Arm ~:** tuck *or* (*coll.*) stick sth. under one's arm; **B** (*quetschen*) **sich** (*Dat.*) **den Fuß/die Hand ~:** get one's foot/hand caught *or* trapped; catch *or* trap one's foot/hand; **C** (*salopp: stehlen*) swipe (*coll.*); pinch (*coll.*); nick (*Brit. coll.*). **2** *refl. V.* **sich hinter etw.** (*Akk.*) **~:** wedge oneself behind sth.; (*fig. ugs.: sich einsetzen*) put some hard work into sth.; **sich hinter jmdn. ~:** squeeze in behind sb.; (*fig. ugs.: antreiben*) get to work on sb. (*coll.*); **sich hinters Lenkrad ~** (*ugs.*) get behind the wheel. **3** *itr. V.* ‹door, drawer, etc.› stick

**Klemm·mappe** *die* spring *or* springback binder

**Klempner** /'klɛmpnɐ/ *der;* ~**s**, ~, **Klempnerin** *die;* ~, ~**nen** ▶ **159** tinsmith; (~ *und Installateur*) plumber

**Klepper** /'klɛpɐ/ *der;* ~**s**, ~ (*abwertend*) broken-down nag

**Kleptomane** /klɛpto'ma:nə/ *der;* ~**n**, ~**n** (*Psych.*) kleptomaniac; ~ **sein** be a kleptomaniac

**Kleptomanie** /klɛptoma'ni:/ *die;* ~ (*Psych.*) kleptomania *no art.*

**Kleptomanin** *die;* ~, ~**nen** kleptomaniac

**kleptomanisch** *Adj.* (*Psych.*) kleptomaniac

**klerikal** /kleri'ka:l/ *Adj.* (*auch abwertend*) clerical; church ‹property›

**Klerikale** *der/die; adj. Dekl.* (*auch abwertend*) cleric; **die ~n** the clergy *sing.*

**Klerikalismus** *der;* ~ (*oft abwertend*) clericalism

**Kleriker** /'kle:rikɐ/ *der;* ~**s**, ~**:** cleric

**Klerus** /'kle:rʊs/ *der;* ~**:** clergy

**Klette** /'klɛtə/ *die;* ~, ~**n** bur; (*Pflanze*) burdock; **sich wie eine ~ an jmdn. hängen** (*ugs.*) stick like a bur to sb.

**Kletter·affe** *der:* **ein ~ sein** be able to climb like a monkey

**Kletterei** *die;* ~, ~**en** (*ugs.*) **A** (*Herumklettern*) climbing [about]; **B** (*Bergsteigen*) climbing

**Kletterer** *der;* ~**s**, ~**:** climber

**Kletter·gerüst** *das* climbing frame

**Kletterin** *die;* ~, ~**nen** ⇒ **Kletterer**

**Klettermaxe** *der;* ~**n**, ~**n** (*ugs. scherzh.*) **A** (*Kind, das gerne klettert*) climbing-mad child; **B** (*Fassadenkletterer*) cat burglar

**klettern** /'klɛtɐn/ *itr. V.; mit sein* (*auch fig.*) climb; (*mit Mühe*) clamber; **auf einen Baum ~:** climb a tree; **aus dem Bett/Auto ~** (*ugs.*) climb out of bed/the car (*coll.*)

**Kletter-:** ~**partie** *die* **A** (*Bergsteigen*) climb; **B** (*ugs.: anstrengende Wanderung*) climbing expedition; ~**pflanze** *die* creeper; (*Bot.*) climbing plant; climber; ~**rose** *die* climbing *or* rambling rose; ~**seil** *das* climbing rope; ~**stange** *die* (*Turnen*) climbing pole; ~**tau** *das* ⇒ ~**seil**; ~**tour** *die* ⇒ ~**partie**; ~**wand** *die* (*Turnen*) climbing wall

**Klett·verschluss**, ***Klett·verschluß** *der* Velcro ® fastening

**Kletze** /'klɛtsə/ *die;* ~, ~**n** (*österr.*) dried pear

**klick** /klɪk/ *Interj.* click; ~ **machen** click; go click; **da machte es bei ihm ~** (*fig. ugs.*) and then the penny dropped (*coll.*)

**klicken** *itr. V.* **A** click; **es klickte** there was a click **B** (*DV*) click

**Klicker** *der;* ~**s**, ~ (*westmd.*) marble

**klickern** *itr. V.* (*westmd.*) play marbles

**Klient** /kli'ɛnt/ *der;* ~**en**, ~**en** client

**Klientel** /kliɛn'te:l/ *die;* ~, ~**en** clientele

**Klientin** *die;* ~, ~**nen** client

**klieren** /'kli:rən/ *tr., itr. V.* (*nordd.*) scrawl

**Kliff** /klɪf/ *das;* ~[**e**]**s**, ~**e** cliff

**Kliff·küste** *die* cliffed coast; cliffs *pl.*

**Klima** /'kli:ma/ *das;* ~**s**, ~**s** *od.* ~**te** /kli'ma:tə/ climate; **das politische/soziale ~** (*fig.*) the political/social climate; **im Büro herrscht ein angenehmes ~** (*fig.*) there's a pleasant atmosphere in the office

**Klima-:** ~**an·lage** *die* air conditioning *no indef. art.*; air-conditioning system; **mit ~anlage** air-conditione; ~**kammer** *die* (*Med., Biol.*) climatic chamber; ~**karte** *die* climatic map; ~**kunde** *die* climatology *no art.*; ~**technik** *die* air-conditioning engineering *no art.*

**Klimakterium** /klimak'te:ri̯ʊm/ *das;* ~**s** (*Med.*) menopause; change of life

**klimatisch** /kli'ma:tɪʃ/ **1** *Adj.* climatic. **2** *adv.* climatically

**klimatisieren** *tr. V.* air-condition

**Klimatologie** /klimatolo'gi:/ *die;* ~**:** climatology *no art.*

**Klima·wechsel** *der* change of climate

**Klimax** /'kli:maks/ *die;* ~**:** climax

**Klima·zone** *die* climatic zone

**Klimbim** /klɪm'bɪm/ *der;* ~**s** (*ugs.*) **A** (*Kram*) junk; odds and ends *pl.*; **B** (*Wirbel*) fuss; ~ **um etw. machen** make a fuss about sth.

**klimmen** /'klɪmən/ *unr. itr. V.; mit sein* (*geh.*) clamber; climb

**Klimm·zug** *der* (*Turnen*) pull-up; **geistige Klimmzüge machen** (*fig. ugs.*) do mental gymnastics

**Klimperei** *die;* ~, ~**en** (*ugs. abwertend*) [awful] plunking

**Klimper·kasten** *der* (*ugs. abwertend*) joanna (*sl.*); piano

**klimpern** /'klɪmpɐn/ **1** *itr. V.* jingle; tinkle; ‹coins, keys› jingle; **mit den Geldstücken/Schlüsseln ~:** jingle the coins/keys; **mit den Wimpern ~** (*scherzh.*) flutter one's eyelashes [seductively]; **auf dem Klavier/der Gitarre/dem Banjo ~** (*ugs.*) plunk away on the piano/guitar/banjo. **2** *tr. V.* (*ugs. abwertend*) plunk out ‹tune etc.›

**kling** /klɪŋ/ *Interj.* (*einer Glocke*) ding; (*von Gläsern*) chink; clink; ~ **machen** ding/chink *or* clink

**Klinge** *die;* ~, ~**n** **A** blade; **B** (*geh. veralt.: Waffe*) blade (*literary*); **mit jmdm. die ~n kreuzen** (*geh.*) cross swords with sb.; **eine [gute] ~ schlagen** (*geh.*) be a good swordsman; **eine scharfe ~ führen** (*fig. geh.*) be hard-hitting in debate; **jmdn. über die ~ springen lassen** (*fig.*) (*töten*) dispose of *or* kill sb.; (*ugs.: ruinieren*) ruin sb.; (*beruflich*) put paid to sb.'s career (*coll.*)

**Klingel** /'klɪŋl̩/ *die;* ~, ~**n** **A** bell; **B** (*kleine Glocke*) small bell

**Klingel-:** ~**beutel** *der* offertory bag; collection bag; ~**draht** *der* bell wire

**klinge[linge]ling** /klɪŋə(lɪŋə)'lɪŋ/ *Interj.* ting-a-ling

**Klingel·knopf** *der* bell button; bell push

**klingeln** *itr. V.* **A** ring; ‹alarm clock› go off; ring; **es klingelt** (*an der Tür*) somebody is ringing the doorbell; there is a ring at the door; (*Telefon*) the telephone is ringing; **es hat bei ihm/ihr** *usw.* **geklingelt** (*ugs.*) the penny's dropped (*coll.*); ⇒ *auch* **Kasse** A; **B** (*die Klingel betätigen*) ring [the bell]; **nach jmdm. ~:** ring for sb.; **der Radfahrer klingelte** the cyclist rang his/her bell; **es klingelte zur Pause** the bell went for the break; **jmdn. aus dem Schlaf ~:** ring [the bell] and wake sb. up; **C** (*Kfz-W.*) ‹engine› pink

**Klingel-:** ~**putzen** *das;* ~~**s** (*ugs.*) ringing doorbells [and running away]; ~**schnur** *die* bell pull; ~**zeichen** *das* ring; **das ist das ~zeichen für das Ende der Pause** that is the bell for the end of break/the interval (*Brit.*) *or* (*Amer.*) intermission; ~**zug** *der* bell pull

**klingen** *unr. itr. V.* **A** **die Glocken klangen** the bells were ringing; **aus dem Haus klangen fröhliche Stimmen** the sound of merry voices came from the house; **aus dem Wald klang der Ruf des Kuckucks** from the forest could be heard the call of the cuckoo; **die Gläser ~ lassen** clink glasses [in a toast]; **B** (*einen bestimmten Klang haben*) sound; **seine Worte klangen wie ein Vorwurf** his words sounded like a reproach; **es klang, als ob geschossen wurde** it sounded as if a shot had been fired

**klingend** **1** ⇒ **klingen**. **2** *Adj.* **ein ~er Reim** (*Verslehre*) a feminine rhyme; ~**e Münze** [hard] cash; **mit ~em Spiel** with the band playing

**klingling** /klɪŋ'lɪŋ/ *Interj.* ting-a-ling

**Klinik** /'kli:nɪk/ *die;* ~, ~**en** **A** hospital; (*spezialisiert*) clinic; **B** (*Med.: klinisches Studium*) clinical training

**Kliniker** *der;* ~**s**, ~ (*Med.*) **A** (*Arzt*) clinician; doctor teaching at a university hospital; **B** (*Student*) medical student doing his/her clinical training

**Klinikum** /'kli:nikʊm/ *das;* ~**s**, **Klinika** *od.* **Kliniken** **A** (*Med.: Ausbildung*) clinical training; **B** (*Zusammenschluss mehrerer Kliniken*) hospital complex (*usually teaching hospitals and clinics, with central administration*)

**klinisch** **1** *Adj.* (*Med.*) clinical; **sie ist jetzt im 5. ~en Semester** she is now in the fifth term of her clinical training. **2** *adv.* ~ **tot** clinically dead

**Klinke** /'klɪŋkə/ *die;* ~, ~**n** **A** (*an der Tür*) door handle; **sich** (*Dat.*) **die ~ in die Hand geben** (*ugs.*) come and go in a continuous stream; ~**n putzen** (*ugs. abwertend*) (*als Vertreter*) peddle one's goods from door to door; (*betteln*) go begging from door to door; **B** (*Technik*) catch; pawl

**Klinken·putzer** *der* (*ugs. abwertend*) (*Vertreter*) door-to-door salesman; (*Bettler*) beggar

**Klinker** *der;* ~**s**, ~**:** [Dutch] clinker

**Klinker-:** ~**bau** *der* building of clinker brick; ~**stein** *der* ⇒ **Klinker**

**klipp** /klɪp/ *Adv.* ~ **und klar** (*ugs.*) quite plainly *or* clearly

**Klippe** *die;* ~, ~**n** rock; **alle ~n umschiffen** (*fig.*) negotiate every obstacle [successfully]

**Klipper** *der;* ~**s**, ~ (*hist.*) clipper

**Klipp·fisch** *der: cod etc. split open, salted, and partly dried;* klipfish

**Klipp·schule** *die* (*nordd. abwertend*) second-rate school

**klirren** /'klɪrən/ *itr. V.* ‹glasses, ice cubes› clink; ‹weapons in fight› clash; ‹window pane› rattle; ‹chains, spurs› clank, rattle; ‹harness› jingle; **mit der Kette/den Sporen ~:** clank *or* rattle the chain/one's spurs; ~**der Frost** (*fig.*) sharp frost

**Klirr·faktor** *der* (*Elektrot.*) distortion factor

**Klischee** /kli'ʃe:/ *das;* ~**s**, ~**s** **A** cliché; **das ~ vom braven Hausmütterchen** the conventional picture *or* stereotype of the good little housewife; **B** (*Druckw.*) block; plate

**klischeehaft** **1** *Adj.* stereotyped, hackneyed ‹picture, description›; cliché-ridden ‹style›. **2** *adv.* in a stereotyped *or* hackneyed way *or* manner

**Klischee·vorstellung** *die* stereotyped idea

**klischieren** *tr. V.* (*Druckw.*) stereotype

**Klistier** /klis'ti:ɐ̯/ *das;* ~**s**, ~**e** (*Med.*) enema

**Klitoris** /'kli:tɔrɪs/ *die;* ~, ~ *od.* **Klitorides** /kli'to:ride:s/ ▶ **471** (*Anat.*) clitoris

**klitsch**, **klatsch** *Interj.* smack; ~, ~, **schlug der Regen gegen die Scheiben** pitter-patter went the rain on the window panes

**Klitsch** /klɪtʃ/ *der;* ~[**e**]**s**, ~**e** (*landsch.*) **A** (*Brei*) soggy mass; mush; **B** (*Schlag*) slap; smack

**Klitsche** *die;* ~, ~**n** (*ugs.*) **A** (*ärmlicher Bauernhof*) poor, run-down farm; **B** (*armseliges Dorf*) wretched little village *or* place; **C** (*kleiner Betrieb*) little shoestring outfit (*coll.*); **D** (*Schmierentheater*) third-rate little theatre

k

**klitsch·nass, *klitsch·naß** *Adj.* (*ugs.*) soaking *or* sopping wet; (*tropfnass*) dripping wet; **wir sind ~ geworden** we got soaked [to the skin] *or* drenched

**klitze·klein** /'klɪtsə-/ *Adj.* (*ugs.*) teeny [-weeny] (*coll.*)

**Klivie** /'kli:viə/ *die;* ~, **~n** (*Bot.*) clivia

**Klo** /klo:/ *das;* **~s, ~s** (*ugs.*) loo (*Brit. coll.*); john (*Amer. coll.*); **aufs ~ müssen** have to go to the loo; **etw. ins ~ schütten** tip sth. down the loo

**Kloake** /klo'a:kə/ *die;* ~, **~n** (*Senkgrube, auch fig.*) cesspit; (*Kanal*) sewer

**Kloben** /'klo:bn̩/ *der;* **~s**, ~ (*Holz~*) log

**klobig** *Adj.* **A** (*kantig*) heavy and clumsy [-looking] ‹shoes, furniture›; heavily-built, bulky ‹figure›; **B** (*plump*) clumsy; boorish; boorish ‹behaviour›

**Klo-:** **~bürste** *die* (*ugs.*) loo brush (*Brit. coll.*); toilet brush; **~frau** *die* (*ugs.*) loo attendant (*Brit. coll.*); bathroom attendant (*Amer.*)

**klomm** /klɔm/ *1. u. 3. Pers. Sg. Prät. v.* **klimmen**

**Klon** /klo:n/ *der;* **~s, ~e** (*Biol.*) clone

**klonen** *tr. V.* clone

**klönen** /'klø:nən/ *itr. V.* (*nordd.*) chat

**klonieren** *tr. V.:* ⇒ **klonen**

**Klo·papier** *das* (*ugs.*) loo paper (*Brit. coll.*); toilet paper

**klopfen** /'klɔpfn̩/ **1** *itr. V.* **A** (*schlagen*) knock; **an die Tür ~:** knock at the door; **es hat geklopft** there's somebody knocking at the door; **jmdm.** *od.* **jmdn. auf die Schulter ~:** slap sb. on the shoulder; **„bitte ~!"** 'please knock'; **„bitte zweimal ~!"** 'please give two knocks'; **B** (*pulsieren*) ‹heart› beat; ‹pulse› throb; **sein Herz schien ihm bis zum Hals zu ~:** his heart was in his mouth *or* was pounding wildly; **mit ~dem Herzen** with pounding *or* beating heart; **ein ~der Schmerz** a throbbing pain; **C** (*Kfz-W.*) ‹engine› knock.
**2** *tr. V.* beat ‹carpet›; **Beifall ~:** applaud by banging *or* rapping on the desk/table with one's fist; **den Takt [zur Musik] ~:** beat time [to the music]; **Fleisch ~:** beat *or* tenderize meat; **Steine ~:** break stones; (*pflastern*) lay cobbles; **Staub vom Mantel ~:** beat dust from one's coat; **die Asche aus der Pfeife ~:** knock *or* tap the ash out of one's pipe; **einen Nagel in die Wand ~:** knock *or* hammer a nail into the wall; **jmdn. aus dem Schlaf ~:** knock sb. up (*Brit.*); awaken sb. by knocking

**Klopfer** *der;* **~s**, ~ **A** (*Teppich~*) carpet beater; **B** (*Tür~*) [door] knocker; **C** (*Fleisch~*) meat mallet *or* tenderizer

**klopf-, Klopf-:** **~fest** *Adj.* antiknock ‹petrol, fuel›; **~festigkeit** *die* antiknock properties *pl.;* **~zeichen** *das* knock; (*leiser*) tap

**Kloppe** /'klɔpə/ *die;* ~ (*nordd., md.*) [good] hiding (*coll.*) *or* thrashing; **~ kriegen** get a [good] hiding (*coll.*) *or* thrashing

**Klöppel** /'klœpl̩/ *der;* **~s**, ~ **A** (*Glocken~*) clapper; **B** (*Musik*) beater; **C** (*Handarbeiten: Spule*) bobbin

**Klöppel·arbeit** *die* **A** bobbin-lace *or* pillow-lace making *no art.;* **B** (*Erzeugnis*) piece of pillow lace *or* bobbin lace

**klöppeln** *tr., itr. V.* [**etw.**] **~:** make *or* work [sth. in] pillow lace *or* bobbin lace

**Klöppel·spitze** *die* pillow lace; bobbin lace

**kloppen** (*nordd., md.*) **1** *tr. V.* hit. **2** *refl. V.* fight; scrap (*coll.*)

**Klopperei** *die;* ~, **~en** (*nordd., md.*) fight; scrap (*coll.*)

**Klöppler** *der;* **~s**, ~, **Klöpplerin** *die;* ~, **~nen** pillow-lace *or* bobbin-lace maker

**Klops** /klɔps/ *der;* **~es, ~e** (*nordostd.*) meat ball

**Klosett** /klo'zɛt/ *das;* **~s, ~s** *od.* **~e** lavatory; **etw. ins ~ schütten** tip sth. down the lavatory

**Klosett-:** **~becken** *das* lavatory pan; toilet bowl; **~brille** *die* (*ugs.*) loo seat (*Brit. coll.*); toilet seat; **~bürste** *die* lavatory brush; toilet brush; **~deckel** *der* toilet lid; **~frau** *die* lavatory attendant; **~papier** *das* toilet paper; lavatory paper; **~sitz** *der* toilet seat; lavatory seat

**Kloß** /klo:s/ *der;* **~es, Klöße** /'klø:sə/ dumpling; (*Fleisch~*) meat ball; **ihm sitzt ein ~ im Hals, er hat einen ~ im Hals** (*ugs.*) he has a lump in his throat

**Kloster** /'klo:stɐ/ *das;* **~s, Klöster** /'klø:stɐ/ (*Mönchs~*) monastery; (*Nonnen~*) convent; nunnery; **ins ~ gehen** enter a monastery/ convent

**Kloster-:** **~bruder** *der* lay brother; (*veralt.: Mönch*) monk; **~frau** *die* (*geh. veralt.*) nun; **~kirche** *die* monastery/convent church

**klösterlich** **1** *Adj.* **A** monastic; monastic/ convent ‹life›; **B** (*zum Kloster gehörend*) of the monastery/convent *postpos., not pred.;* monastery/convent *attrib.* **2** *adv.* **~ abgeschieden leben** live in monastic seclusion

**Kloster-:** **~regel** *die* rules *pl.* of the monastery/convent; **~schule** *die* monastery-school/convent-school; **~schüler** *der,* **~schülerin** *die* monastery-school/convent-school pupil

**Klotz** /klɔts/ *der;* **~es, Klötze** /'klœtsə/ **A** (*Stück Holz*) block [of wood]; (*Stück eines Baumstamms*) log; **schlafen wie ein ~** (*fig.*) sleep like a log; **ein ~ aus Beton [und Glas]** (*fig.*) a concrete [and glass] monstrosity; **jmdm. ein ~ am Bein sein** (*ugs.*) be a millstone round sb.'s neck; **mit ihm hast du dir einen ~ ans Bein gebunden** (*ugs.*) you have tied a millstone round your neck by getting involved with him; **auf einen groben ~ gehört ein grober Keil** (*Spr.*) rudeness can only be answered with rudeness; **B** (*salopp abwertend*) (*ungehobelter Mensch*) clod; oaf; (*roher Mensch*) lout

**Klötzchen** /'klœtsçən/ *das;* **~s, ~:** small block of wood

**klotzen** (*ugs.*) **1** *itr. V.* **A** (*großzügig vorgehen*) lash out in a big way (*coll.*); ⇒ *auch* **kleckern** 1 D; **B** (*hart arbeiten*) graft (*sl.*). **2** *tr. V.* stick up (*coll.*) ‹building, town›

**klotzig** *Adj.* **A** (*abwertend: unförmig*) large and ugly[-looking] ‹building›; large and clumsy[-looking] ‹furniture›; **B** (*ugs.: gewaltig*) massive great (*coll.*) ‹car, villa, etc.›

**Klub** /klʊp/ *der;* **~s, ~s** **A** (*Vereinigung*) club; **B** (*Gebäude*) club; **im ~:** at the club; **C** (*Clique*) crowd

**klub-, Klub-:** **~eigen** *Adj.* club's *attrib.;* the club's *pred.;* **~garnitur** *die* thickly upholstered three-piece suite; **~haus** *das* clubhouse; **~jacke** *die* blazer; **~mitglied** *das* club member; **~sessel** *der* club chair; **~zwang** *der* (*österr.*) ⇒ **Fraktionszwang**

**Kluft**[1] /klʊft/ *die;* ~, **~en** (*ugs.*) rig-out (*coll.*); gear (*coll.*); (*Uniform*) uniform; garb; **sich in seine beste ~ werfen** put on one's Sunday best *or* one's best things

**Kluft**[2] *die;* ~, **Klüfte** /'klʏftə/ **A** (*veralt.*) (*Spalte*) cleft; fissure; (*im Gletscher*) crevasse; (*Abgrund*) chasm; **B** (*Gegensatz*) gulf

**klug** /klu:k /;/ **klüger** /'kly:gɐ /,/ **klügst...** /'kly:kst.../ **1** *Adj.* **A** (*intelligent*) clever; intelligent; clever, bright ‹child, pupil›; intelligent ‹eyes›; **er ist ein ~er Kopf** he's clever *or* bright; he's got brains; **B** (*gelehrt, weise*) wise; **so ~ wie vorher** *od.* **zuvor sein** be none the wiser; **so ~ waren wir auch!** we know that as well as you do; **hinterher ist man immer klüger** it's easy to be wise after the event; **daraus werde ich nicht ~, daraus soll ein Mensch ~ werden** I can't make head or tail of it; **aus jmdm. nicht ~ werden** not know what to make of sb.; **C** (*vernünftig*) wise; wise, sound ‹advice›; wise, prudent ‹remark, course of action›; (*geschickt*) clever, shrewd ‹politician, negotiator, question›; shrewd, astute ‹businessman›; great ‹foresight›; **es wäre das Klügste, wenn wir ...** the wisest course *or* thing would be for us to ...; **der Klügere gibt nach** (*Spr.*) discretion is the better part of valour (*prov.*); **der ~e Mann baut vor** it pays to be prepared.
**2** *adv.* **A** (*intelligent*) cleverly; intelligently; **~ [daher]reden** talk as if one knows it all; **~ daherreden kann jeder!** anyone can talk!; **B** (*vernünftig*) wisely; (*geschickt*) cleverly; shrewdly

**Klügelei** *die;* ~, **~en** (*abwertend*) **~[en** *Pl.*] oversubtle reasoning *no pl.*

**klügeln** /kly:gl̩n/ *itr. V.* **an etw.** (*Dat.*) **~:** ponder [over] sth.

**klüger** ⇒ **klug**

**klugerweise** *Adv.* wisely

**Klugheit** *die;* ~, **~en** **A** ⇒ **klug** A, B, C: cleverness; intelligence; brightness; wisdom; soundness; prudence; shrewdness; astuteness; **B** (*iron.: weiser Spruch*) clever remark

**klüglich** *Adv.* (*geh.*) wisely

***klug|reden** ⇒ **klug** 2 A

**Klug·scheißer** *der,* **Klug·scheißerin** *die* (*salopp abwertend*) know-it-all (*coll.*); smart aleck (*coll.*)

**klügst...** ⇒ **klug**

**Klump** /klʊmp/ *der;* **~s** *in* **einen Wagen zu** *od.* **in ~ fahren** (*salopp*) smash up *or* write off a car; **jmdn. zu ~ schlagen** (*salopp*) beat the living daylights out of sb. (*coll.*)

**Klumpatsch** /'klʊmpatʃ/ *der;* **~[e]s** (*salopp abwertend*) junk

**klumpen** /'klʊmpn̩/ *itr. V.* go lumpy

**Klumpen** *der;* **~s**, ~ **A** lump; **ein ~ Erde** a lump *or* clod of earth; **ein ~ Gold** a gold nugget; **B** (*rhein.: Holzschuh*) clog

**Klump·fuß** *der* club foot

**klumpig** *Adj.* lumpy

**Klüngel** /'klʏŋl̩/ *der;* **~s**, ~ (*abwertend*) **A** (*Clique*) clique; **B** (*Cliquenwesen*) cliquism *no indef. art.*

**Klüngelei** *die;* ~, **~en** (*abwertend*) cliquism *no pl.;* (*Vetternwirtschaft*) nepotism *no pl.*

**klüngeln** *itr. V.* (*ugs.*) ⇒ **Klüngelei**: indulge in cliquism/nepotism

**Klunker** /'klʊŋkɐ/ *die;* ~, **~n** *od. der;* **~s**, ~ (*ugs.*) rock (*sl.*)

**Klus** /klu:s/ *die;* ~, **~en** (*schweiz.*) narrow gorge; cluse (*Geol.*)

**Klüse** /'kly:zə/ *die;* ~, **~n** ⇒ **Ankerklüse**

**Klüver** /'kly:vɐ/ *der;* **~s**, ~ (*Seemannsspr.*) jib

**Klüver·baum** *der* (*Seemannsspr.*) jib boom

**km** *Abk.* **Kilometer** km.

**knabbern** /'knabɐn/ **1** *tr. V.* nibble; **etw. zum K~:** sth. to nibble; **nichts mehr zu ~ haben** (*ugs. verhüll.*) be broke (*coll.*) *or* skint (*sl.*). **2** *itr. V.* **an etw.** (*Dat.*) **~:** nibble *or* gnaw [at] sth.; **an etw.** (*Dat.*) **[noch lange] zu ~ haben** (*ugs.*) (*sich anstrengen müssen*) have sth. to think about *or* chew on; (*leiden müssen*) take a long time to get over sth.; **an dieser Übersetzung hatten die Schüler ganz schön zu ~:** this translation really gave the pupils something to think about *or* chew on

**Knabe** /'kna:bə/ *der;* **~n, ~n** **A** (*geh. veralt./südd., österr., schweiz.*) boy; **B** (*ugs.: Bursche*) chap (*coll.*); **Na, alter ~! Wie gehts?** well, old boy *or* old chap, how are you? (*coll.*)

**Knaben-:** **~alter** *das* (*geh.*) boyhood; **~chor** *der* boys' choir

**knabenhaft** **1** *Adj.* boyish. **2** *adv.* boyishly

**Knaben-:** **~kraut** *das* orchis; wild orchid; **~liebe** *die* (*geh.*) pederasty; **~schule** *die* (*veralt.*) boys' school; **~stimme** *die* boy's voice; **~streich** *der* (*geh.*) boyish prank

**knack** /knak/ *Interj.* crack

**Knack** *der;* **~[e]s, ~e** crack

**Knäcke·brot** /'knɛkə-/ *das* crispbread; (*Scheibe*) slice of crispbread

**knacken** **1** *itr. V.* **A** (*krachen*) ‹bed, floor, etc.› creak; **es knackt im Telefon** the [telephone] line is crackling; **es knackte im Gebälk** the beams creaked; **mit den Fingern ~:** crack one's fingers; **B** *mit sein* (*ugs.: zerbrechen*) snap; ‹window› crack; **C** *in* **an etw.** (*Dat.*) **zu ~ haben** (*ugs.*) take a long time to get over sth. **2** *tr. V.* **A** (*zerbrechen*) crack ‹nut, shell›; **B** (*salopp: zerquetschen*) squash; **C** (*aufbrechen*) crack ‹safe› [open]; break into ‹car, bank, vending machine, etc.›; crack, break ‹code›

*old spelling (see note on page 1707)

k

**Knacker** *der;* **~s,** **~** Ⓐ **alter ~** (*salopp*) old fogey; Ⓑ (*ugs.: Geldschrankknacker*) safecracker; Ⓒ ⇒ **Knackwurst**

**knack·frisch** *Adj.* (*ugs.*) crispy fresh ‹rolls, crisps, etc.›; crisp fresh ‹fruit, vegetables›

**Knacki** /'knaki/ *der;* **~s,** **~s** (*salopp*) con (*coll.*); jailbird

**knackig** *Adj.* Ⓐ (*knusprig*) crisp; crisp, crunchy ‹apple›; Ⓑ (*ugs.: attraktiv*) luscious, delectable ‹girl›

**Knack·laut** *der* (*Phon.*) glottal stop

**knacks** *Interj.* crack

**Knacks** *der;* **~es,** **~e** (*ugs.*) Ⓐ (*Ton*) crack; Ⓑ (*Sprung*) crack; Ⓒ (*fig.: Defekt*) **einen ~ bekommen** ‹person› have *or* suffer a breakdown; ‹health› suffer; **die Ehe hatte einen ~:** the marriage was in difficulties

**Knack·wurst** *die:* [*smoked*] *sausage filled with minced meat and pieces of fat, the tight skin of which makes a cracking sound when bitten;* knackwurst

**Knall** /knal/ *der;* **~[e]s,** **~e** bang; (*fig.*) big row; **einen ~ haben** (*salopp*) be barmy (*sl.*) *or* off one's rocker (*coll.*); **auf ~ und Fall,** **~ auf Fall** (*ugs.*) without warning

**knall-, Knall-:** **~bonbon** *der od. das* cracker; **~bunt** *Adj.* gaudy; ‹car› painted in gaudy colours; **~effekt** *der* (*ugs.*) (*Überraschendes*) astonishing part; (*Sensation*) sensational part

**knallen** ❶ *itr. V.* Ⓐ (*einen Knall verursachen*) ‹shot› ring out; ‹firework› go bang; ‹cork› pop; ‹door› bang, slam; ‹whip, rifle› crack; **die Peitsche ~ lassen** crack the whip; **mit der Tür ~:** bang *or* slam the door; **an der Kreuzung hat es geknallt** (*ugs.*) there was a crash at the crossroads; **sei ruhig, oder es knallt!** (*fig. ugs.*) be quiet, or you'll get a good hiding; Ⓑ (*ugs.: schießen*) shoot, fire (**auf** + *Akk.* at); (*mehrere Male*) blaze *or* (*coll.*) bang away (**auf** + *Akk.* at); **Hände hoch, oder es knallt!** hands up, or I'll shoot!; Ⓒ (*Ballspiele ugs.*) **aufs Tor ~:** belt the ball/puck at the goal (*coll.*); Ⓓ *mit sein* (*ugs.: prallen*) **die Tür knallte ins Schloss** the door slammed *or* banged shut; **sie knallte mit dem Fahrrad gegen einen Laternenpfahl** she crashed into a lamp post on her bicycle; **mit dem Kopf gegen die Windschutzscheibe ~:** bang one's head against the windscreen; **der Ball knallte gegen die Latte** the ball slammed against the crossbar; Ⓔ (*ugs.: scheinen*) blaze *or* beat down.
❷ *tr. V.* Ⓐ (*ugs.*) (*hart aufsetzen*) slam *or* bang down; (*werfen*) sling (*coll.*); **den Hörer auf die Gabel ~:** slam *or* bang down the receiver; Ⓑ (*ugs.: schlagen*) **du kriegst gleich eine geknallt!** you're going to get a clout any minute (*coll.*); **jmdm. eine ~** (*salopp*) belt *or* clout sb. one (*coll.*); Ⓒ (*Ballspiele ugs.*) belt ‹ball›

**knall·eng** *Adj.* (*ugs.*) skintight

**Knaller** *der;* **~s,** **~:** banger

**Knall·erbse** *die* ≈ cap bomb

**Knallerei** *die;* **~,** **~en** (*ugs.*) (*von Korken*) popping; (*einer Peitsche*) cracking; (*von Gewehren*) banging, shooting; (*von Feuerwerk*) banging

**knall-, Knall-:** **~frosch** *der* jumping jack; **~gas** *das* (*Chemie*) oxy-hydrogen; **~gelb** *Adj.* (*ugs.*) bright *or* vivid yellow; **~hart** (*ugs.*) ❶ *Adj.* Ⓐ very tough ‹job, demands, action, measures, etc.›; ‹person› as hard as nails; hard [core] ‹pornography›; very sharp ‹criticism›; **ein ~harter Bursche** a thug; Ⓑ (*kraftvoll*) fierce ‹serve›; crashing ‹blow›; ❷ *adv.* Ⓐ (*rücksichtslos, brutal*) brutally; **gegen etw. ~hart vorgehen** take very tough action against sth.; **jmdm. etw. ~hart sagen** say sth. to sb. quite brutally; Ⓑ (*kraftvoll*) ‹serve, hit› really hard; **~heiß** *Adj.* (*ugs.*) boiling *or* baking hot (*coll.*)

**knallig** *Adj.* (*ugs.*) loud; gaudy

**knall-, Knall-:** **~kopf,** **~kopp** *der* (*salopp*) [stupid] berk (*Brit. coll.*) *or* (*Amer. coll.*) jerk; **~körper** *der* banger; (*bei Aufprall explodierend*) ≈ cap bomb; **~rot** *Adj.* bright *or* vivid red; **sie bekam einen ~roten Kopf** she *or* her face turned [bright] scarlet *or* as red as a beetroot; **~tüte** *die* (*ugs.*) nitwit (*coll.*); clot (*Brit. sl.*)

**knapp** /knap/ ❶ *Adj.* Ⓐ (*kaum ausreichend*) meagre, low ‹pension, wage, salary›; meagre ‹pocket money›; **Kaffee war ~:** coffee was scarce *or* in short supply; **das Geld wird ~:** money is getting tight; **die Vorräte wurden ~:** supplies ran short; **etw. ~ halten** keep sth. in short supply; **sie bekam nur ein sehr ~es Haushaltsgeld** she received very little housekeeping money; **~ mit etw. sein** be short of sth.; **..., und nicht zu ~!** ... and how!; Ⓑ (*gerade ausreichend*) narrow ‹victory, lead›; narrow, bare ‹majority›; close ‹result›; Ⓒ (*nicht ganz*) **vor einer ~en Stunde** almost *or* just under an hour ago; Ⓓ (*eng*) tight-fitting ‹garment›; (*zu eng*) tight ‹garment›; Ⓔ (*kurz*) terse ‹reply, greeting›; concise, succinct ‹description, account, report›; **mit ~en Worten** in a few brief words.
❷ *adv.* Ⓐ (*kaum ausreichend*) **~ bemessen sein** be meagre; **seine Zeit war ~ bemessen** his time was limited; **~ gerechnet** at the lowest estimate; **jmdn. ~ halten** (*ugs.*) keep sb. short (**mit** of); Ⓑ (*gerade ausreichend*) **~ gewinnen/verlieren** win/lose narrowly *or* by a narrow margin; **eine Prüfung ~ bestehen** just pass an examination; Ⓒ (*sehr nahe*) just; **~ über dem Knie enden** come to just above the knee; Ⓓ (*nicht ganz*) just under; not quite; **vor ~ einer Stunde** just under *or* not quite an hour ago; **er ist ~ fünfzig** he is not quite fifty *or* just this side of fifty; Ⓔ (*eng*) **~ sitzen** fit tightly; (*zu eng*) be a tight fit; **~ geschnitten/sitzend** tight-fitting; Ⓕ (*kurz*) ‹reply› tersely; ‹describe, summarize› concisely, succinctly

**Knappe** *der;* **~n,** **~n** Ⓐ (*Bergmann*) miner (*who has completed his apprenticeship*); Ⓑ (*hist.*) squire

***knapp|halten** ⇒ **knapp** 1 A, 2 A

**Knappheit** *die;* **~** Ⓐ (*Mangel*) shortage, scarcity (**an** + *Dat.* of); (*von Geld, Zeit*) shortage; Ⓑ (*Kürze*) (*einer Antwort, eines Grußes*) terseness; (*einer Beschreibung, eines Berichts*) conciseness, succinctness

**Knappschaft** *die;* **~,** **~en** (*Bergmannsspr.*) Ⓐ (*Gesamtheit der Knappen*) miners *pl.*; Ⓑ (*Organisation*) miners' guild

**knapsen** /'knapsn̩/ *itr. V.* (*ugs.*) skimp; scrimp

**Knarre** /'knarə/ *die;* **~,** **~n** Ⓐ (*Rassel*) rattle; Ⓑ (*salopp: Gewehr*) shooting iron (*coll.*)

**knarren** *itr. V.* creak; **mit ~der Stimme** in a rasping *or* grating voice

**Knast** /knast/ *der;* **~[e]s,** **Knäste** /'knɛstə/ *od.* **~e** (*ugs.*) Ⓐ (*Strafe*) bird (*sl.*); time; **man hat ihm zwei Jahre ~ gegeben** he got two years' bird (*sl.*); **~ schieben** (*salopp*) do bird (*sl.*) *or* time; Ⓑ (*Gefängnis*) clink (*sl.*); jug (*sl.*); prison; **im ~ sitzen** be in clink *or* jug (*sl.*)

**Knast·bruder** *der* (*ugs.*) Ⓐ jailbird; old lag (*sl.*); Ⓑ (*Mitgefangener*) fellow jailbird

**Knaster** *der;* **~s,** **~** Ⓐ (*veralt.: Tabak*) weed (*arch.*); Ⓑ (*ugs. abwertend: schlechter Tabak*) evil-smelling tobacco

**Knastologe** /knasto'lo:gə/ *der;* **~n,** **~n,** **Knastologin** *die;* **~,** **~nen** (*ugs. scherzh.*) jailbird; old lag (*sl.*)

**Knatsch** /kna:tʃ/ *der;* **~[e]s** (*ugs.: Ärger*) trouble; **die beiden haben schon wieder ~ miteinander** the two of them are already rowing again

**knatschig** *Adj.* (*ugs.*) grumpy; (*weinerlich*) fretful

**knattern** /'knatɐn/ *itr. V.* Ⓐ ‹machine gun› rattle, clatter; ‹sail› flap; ‹radio› crackle; ‹motor vehicle, engine› clatter; Ⓑ *mit sein* (*knatternd fahren*) clatter

**Knäuel** /'knɔy̆əl/ *der od. das;* **~s,** **~** Ⓐ ball; (*wirres ~*) tangle; **er knüllte den Brief zu einem ~ zusammen** he screwed the letter into a ball; Ⓑ (*fig.*) (*von Menschen*) knot; (*größer*) [milling] crowd; (*von Widersprüchen, Ereignissen*) tangle

**Knauf** /knau̯f/ *der;* **~[e]s,** **Knäufe** /'knɔy̆fə/ (*einer Tür, eines Gehstocks*) knob; (*eines Schwertes, Dolches*) pommel

**Knauser** *der;* **~s,** **~** (*ugs. abwertend*) Scrooge; skinflint; miser

**Knauserei** *die;* **~,** **~en** (*ugs. abwertend*) Ⓐ (*knauseriges Wirtschaften*) stinginess; penny-pinching; miserliness; Ⓑ (*Fall von ~*) piece of stinginess *or* miserliness

**knauserig** *Adj.* (*ugs. abwertend*) stingy; tight-fisted; close-fisted

**Knauserigkeit** *die;* **~,** **~en** ⇒ **Knauserei**

**knausern** /'knau̯zɐn/ *itr. V.* (*ugs. abwertend*) be stingy; skimp; scrimp; **mit etw. ~:** be stingy with sth.

**Knaus-Ogino-Methode** /'knaus|o'gi:no-/ *die* rhythm method (*with calendar-marking*)

**knautschen** /'knau̯tʃn̩/ (*ugs.*) ❶ *tr. V.* crumple; crumple, crease ‹dress›. ❷ *itr. V.* ‹dress, material› crease, get creased

**knautschig** *Adj.* (*ugs.*) crumpled ‹suit, dress, etc.›

**Knautsch-:** **~lack** *der,* **~lack·leder** *das,* **~leder** *das* patterned patent leather; (*Imitat*) imitation patterned patent leather; **~zone** *die* (*Kfz-W.*) crumple zone

**Knebel** /'kne:bl̩/ *der;* **~s,** **~** Ⓐ (*zum ~n*) gag; Ⓑ (*Griff*) toggle; (*am Schraubstock*) handle

**Knebel-:** **~bart** *der* Vandyke beard; (*Schnurrbart*) twisted moustache; **~knopf** *der* toggle

**knebeln** *tr. V.* gag; (*fig.*) gag, muzzle ‹the press, a people›

**Knecht** /knɛçt/ *der;* **~[e]s,** **~e** Ⓐ farm labourer; farmhand; (*fig.*) slave; vassal; Ⓑ **~ Ruprecht** *helper to St. Nicholas* [≈ *to Santa Claus*]

**knechten** *tr. V.* (*geh.*) (*versklaven*) reduce to servitude *or* slavery; enslave; (*unterdrücken*) oppress ‹people, nation›

**knechtisch** (*geh.*) ❶ *Adj.* servile, slavish ‹obedience, submissiveness›; servile, submissive ‹person, character›. ❷ *adv.* servilely; submissively

**Knechtschaft** *die;* **~,** **~en** (*geh.*) bondage; servitude; slavery

**Knechtung** *die;* **~,** **~en** (*geh.*) ⇒ **knechten:** enslavement; oppression

**kneifen** /'knai̯fn̩/ ❶ *unr. tr., itr. V.* pinch; **jmdm.** *od.* **jmdn. in den Arm ~:** pinch sb.'s arm. ❷ *unr. itr. V.* Ⓐ (*drücken*) ‹clothes› be too tight; Ⓑ (*ugs. abwertend: sich drücken*) chicken (*coll.*) *or* back out (**vor** + *Dat.* of); **vor einer Prüfung/Verantwortung ~:** funk an examination (*coll.*)/(*coll.*) duck [out of] a responsibility

**Kneifer** *der;* **~s,** **~:** pince-nez

**Kneif·zange** *die* pincers *pl.*; **eine ~:** a pair of pincers

**Kneip·abend** *der* [students'] drinking evening

**Kneipe** /'knai̯pə/ *die;* **~,** **~n** Ⓐ (*ugs.*) pub (*Brit.*); bar (*Amer.*); Ⓑ (*Studentenspr. veralt.*) [students'] drinking evening

**Kneipen·wirt** *der* (*salopp*) [pub] landlord (*Brit.*); barkeeper (*Amer.*)

**Kneipen·wirtin** *die* (*salopp*) [pub] landlady (*Brit.*); barkeeper (*Amer.*)

**Kneipier** /knai̯'pje:/ *der;* **~s,** **~s** (*salopp*) ⇒ **Kneipenwirt**

**kneippen** /'knai̯pn̩/ *itr. V.* (*ugs.*) take *or* undergo a Kneipp cure

**Kneipp·kur** *die* Kneipp cure

**knetbar** *Adj.* workable; kneadable ‹dough›

**Knete** *die;* **~** Ⓐ (*ugs.*) ⇒ **Knetmasse;** Ⓑ (*salopp: Geld*) dough (*coll.*)

**kneten** /'kne:tn̩/ *tr. V.* Ⓐ (*bearbeiten*) knead ‹dough, muscles›; work ‹clay›; Ⓑ (*formen*) model ‹figure›; **eine Figur aus Ton ~:** mould *or* fashion a figure in clay

**Knet-:** **~maschine** *die* kneading machine; **~masse** *die* plastic modelling material; Plasticine ®

k

**Knick** /knɪk/ *der;* **~[e]s, ~e/~s** A *Pl.* **~e** (*Biegung*) sharp bend; (*in einem Draht*) kink; **du hast wohl einen ~ in der Optik!** (*ugs. scherzh.*) are you blind?; B *Pl.* **~e** (*Falz*) crease; C *Pl.* **~s** (*nordd.: Hecke*) boundary hedge [with ditches and rampart]

**Knickebein** /ˈknɪkəbai̯n/ *der;* **~s** *egg liqueur used as a filling in sweets, Easter eggs, etc.*

**Knick·ei** *das* cracked egg

**knicken** ❶ *tr. V.* A (*brechen*) snap; B (*falten*) crease ‹page, paper, etc.›; **„Bitte nicht ~!"** (*auf einem Umschlag*) 'please do not bend'; (*auf einem Formular*) 'please do not fold'. ❷ *itr. V.; mit sein* snap

**Knicker** *der;* **~s, ~** A (*ugs. abwertend*) Scrooge; skinflint; miser; B (*niederd.: Murmel*) marble

**Knickerbocker** /-bɔkɐ/ *Pl.* knickerbockers; (*länger und breiter*) plus-fours

**knick[e]rig** *Adj.* (*ugs. abwertend*) stingy; tight-fisted

**Knick[e]rigkeit** *die;* **~** (*ugs. abwertend*) stinginess; tight-fistedness

**Knick·fuß** *der* club foot

**Knicks** /knɪks/ *der;* **~es, ~e** curtsy; **einen ~ machen** make *or* drop a curtsy (**vor** + *Dat.* to)

**knicksen** *itr. V.* curtsy (**vor** + *Dat.* to)

**Knie** /kniː/ *das;* **~s, ~** /ˈkniː(ə)/ A ▶ 471 knee; **jmdm. auf [den] ~n danken** go down on one's knees and thank sb.; **jmdn. auf ~n bitten** beg sb. on bended knees; **vor jmdm. auf die ~ fallen** go down on one's knees before sb.; **er hatte/bekam weiche ~** (*ugs.*) his knees trembled/started to tremble; **vor lauter Aufregung hatte ich ganz weiche ~:** I was weak at the knees with sheer excitement; **jmdn. auf** *od.* **in die ~ zwingen** (*geh.*) force sb. to his knees; **in die ~ gehen** (*umfallen*) sink to one's knees; (*eine* **~***beuge machen*) bend one's knees; (*sich unterordnen*) submit, bow (**vor** + *Dat.* to); **jmdn. übers ~ legen** (*ugs.*) put sb. across one's knee; **etw. übers ~ brechen** (*ugs.*) rush sth.; B (*an Hosen, Strümpfen*) knee; C (*Biegung*) sharp bend; (*eines Rohres*) elbow

**Knie·beuge** *die* ▶ 471 knee bend

**Knie·bund·hose** *die* knee breeches *pl.;* **eine ~:** a pair of knee breeches

**knie-, Knie-: ~fall** *der:* **einen ~fall tun** *od.* **machen** (*auch fig.*) go down on one's knees (**vor** + *Dat.* before); **~fällig** ❶ *Adj.* **sein ~fälliges Bitten** his pleading on bended knee; ❷ *adv.* on bended knees; on one's knees; **~frei** *Adj.* ‹skirt› worn above the knee; **wird die Mode wieder ~frei?** is the above-the-knee look coming back again?; **~gelenk** *das* ▶ 471 knee joint; **~hoch** *Adj.* knee-deep ‹water, snow›; knee-high ‹grass›; knee-length ‹boots›; **~hose** *die* knee breeches *pl.;* **~kehle** *die* ▶ 471 hollow of the knee; popliteal space (*Anat.*); **~lang** *Adj.* knee-length

**knien** /ˈkniː(ə)n/ ❶ *itr. V.* kneel; **diese Arbeit muss man ~d verrichten** this work has to be done on one's knees *or* kneeling. ❷ *refl. V.* kneel [down]; get down on one's knees; **sich in die Arbeit/die Akten ~** (*fig. ugs.*) get stuck into one's work/the files (*sl.*)

**Knies** /kniːs/ *der;* **~es** (*ugs.*) A (*Schmutzschicht*) layer of muck (*coll.*) *or* dirt; B (*Unstimmigkeit*) quarrel; **ständig ~ mit jmdm. haben** always be quarrelling with sb.

**knie-, Knie-: ~scheibe** *die* ▶ 471 kneecap; patella (*Anat.*); **~schützer** *der* (*Sport*) knee pad; **~strumpf** *der* knee-length sock; knee sock; **~tief** *Adj.* knee-deep

**Kniff** /knɪf/ *der;* **~[e]s, ~e** A (*das Kneifen*) pinch; B (*Falte*) crease; (*in Papier*) crease; fold; C (*Kunstgriff*) trick; dodge; **den ~ [bei etw.] heraushaben** have got the knack [of sth.]

**Kniffelei** *die;* **~, ~en** (*ugs.*) fiddly job

**kniff[e]lig** *Adj.* A (*schwierig*) fiddly; tricky ‹problem, crossword puzzle›; B (*heikel*) tricky

*old spelling (see note on page 1707)

**Knigge** /ˈknɪɡə/ *der;* **~[s], ~:** book on etiquette

**Knilch** /knɪlç/ *der;* **~s, ~e** (*salopp abwertend*) bastard (*coll.*)

**knipsen** /ˈknɪpsn̩/ ❶ *tr. V.* A (*entwerten*) clip; punch; B (*fotografieren*) snap; take a snap[shot] of; C (*wegschnellen*) flick. ❷ *itr. V.* A (*fotografieren*) take snapshots; B **mit den Fingern ~:** snap one's fingers

**Knipser** *der;* **~s, ~, Knips·schalter** *der* (*ugs.*) snap switch

**Knirps** /knɪrps/ *der;* **~es, ~e** A (Wz) *Taschenschirm*) telescopic umbrella; B (*ugs.: Junge*) nipper (*coll.*); C (*ugs. abwertend: kleiner Mann*) [little] squirt (*coll.*)

**knirschen** /ˈknɪrʃn̩/ *itr. V.* A crunch; B **mit den Zähnen ~:** grind one's teeth; (*fig.*) gnash one's teeth

**knistern** /ˈknɪstɐn/ *itr. V.* rustle; ‹wood, fire› crackle; **mit etw. ~:** rustle sth.; **eine ~de Atmosphäre** (*fig.*) a tense *or* charged atmosphere; ⇒ *auch* **Gebälk**

**Knittel·vers** /ˈknɪtl̩-/ *der* (*Metrik*) rhyming couplets of four-stress lines

**Knitter** /ˈknɪtɐ/ *der;* **~s, ~:** crease

**knitter·frei** *Adj.* non-crease; **[vollkommen] ~ sein** not crease [at all]

**knitt[e]rig** *Adj.* creased; crumpled; (*fig.*) wrinkled ‹face›

**knittern** *tr., itr. V.* crease; crumple

**Knobel·becher** *der* A (*Würfelbecher*) dice cup; B (*Soldatenspr.: Stiefel*) army boot

**knobeln** *itr. V.* A (*mit Würfeln*) play dice; (*mit Streichhölzern*) play spoof; (*mit Handzeichen*) play scissors, paper, stone; **um etw. ~:** play dice *etc.* to decide sth.; B (*ugs.: nachdenken*) puzzle (**an** + *Dat.* over)

**Knob·lauch** /ˈknoːp-/ *der* garlic

**Knoblauch-: ~butter** *die* (*Kochk.*) garlic butter; **~zehe** *die* clove of garlic; **~zwiebel** *die* garlic bulb

**Knöchel** /ˈknœçl̩/ *der;* **~s, ~** ▶ 471 A (*am Fuß*) ankle; **bis an/über die ~:** up to the *or* one's ankles/to above ankle level; **das Kleid reicht bis an die ~:** the dress reaches [down] to the ankles; B (*am Finger*) knuckle

**knöchel-, Knöchel-: ~bruch** *der* broken ankle; **~lang** *Adj.* ankle-length; **~tief** *Adj.* ankle-deep

**Knochen** /ˈknɔxn̩/ *der;* **~s, ~** A ▶ 471 bone; **Fleisch mit/ohne ~:** meat on/off the bone; **jmdm. alle ~ [einzeln] brechen** (*salopp*) break every [single] bone in sb.'s body; **die Wunde geht bis auf den ~:** the wound reaches to the bone; **mir tun sämtliche ~ weh** (*ugs.*) every bone in my body aches; **der Schreck fuhr ihm in die ~** (*ugs.*) he was shaken to the core; **eine Grippe in den ~ haben** (*ugs.*) feel the flu coming on (*coll.*); **keinen Mumm in den ~ haben** (*ugs.*) be a weed; **sich** (*Dat.*) **die ~ brechen** break something; **seine ~ für etw. hinhalten [müssen]** (*ugs.*) [have to] risk one's neck fighting for sth.; **die ~ zusammenreißen** (*Soldatenspr.*) stand up straight; **das geht auf die ~** (*salopp*) it's knackering (*Brit. sl.*); it burns you out (*Amer. coll.*); **sie hat mich bis auf die ~ blamiert** (*ugs.*) she made a complete *or* proper fool of me; B (*ugs. abwertend: Kerl*) so-and-so (*coll.*); C (*ugs.: Schraubenschlüssel*) double-ended ring spanner

**knochen-, Knochen-: ~arbeit** *die* (*ugs.*) back-breaking work; **~bau** *der* bone structure; **ein sehr kräftiger ~bau** a very powerful frame; **~bruch** *der* ▶ 474 fracture; **sich** (*Dat.*) **einen ~bruch zuziehen** sustain a fracture; **~erweichung** *die* ▶ 474 (*Med.*) softening of the bones; osteomalacia (*Med.*); **~gerüst** *das* A skeleton; B (*ugs. abwertend: magere Person*) bag of bones (*coll.*); **~hart** *Adj.* (*ugs.*) rock-hard; **der Kuchen ist ja ~hart** the cake is as hard as a rock; **~haut** *die* ▶ 471 (*Anat.*) periosteum; **~haut·entzündung** *die* ▶ 474 (*Med.*) periostitis; **~mann** *der* (*veralt.*) Death; **~mark** *das* ▶ 471 bone marrow; **~mehl** *das* bonemeal; **~mühle** *die* (*ugs.*) **diese Fabrik ist die reinste ~mühle** working in this factory is worse than the chain gang! (*joc.*); **~schinken** *der* ham on the bone; **~schwund** *der* ▶ 474 (*Med.*) bone atrophy; osteoporosis (*Med.*); **~trocken** *Adj.* (*ugs.*) bone dry; **~tuberkulose** *die* (*Med.*) tuberculosis of the bones

**knöchern** /ˈknœçɐn/ *Adj.* bony, (*formal*) osseous ‹material etc.›; bone *attrib.* ‹handle, tool, etc.›

**knochig** ❶ *Adj.* bony. ❷ *adv.* **sehr ~ gebaut sein** be very bony

**Knockdown** /nɔkˈdau̯n/ *der;* **~[s], ~** (*Boxen*) knock-down

***Knockout, Knock-out** /nɔk|ˈau̯t/ *der;* **~s, ~s** (*Boxen*) knockout

**Knödel** /ˈknøːdl̩/ *der;* **~s, ~** (*bes. südd., österr.*) dumpling

**Knöllchen** /ˈknœlçən/ *das;* **~s, ~** A ⇒ **Knolle**; **Knollen**; B (*ugs.: Strafzettel*) [parking] ticket

**Knolle** /ˈknɔlə/ *die;* **~, ~n** A (*einer Pflanze*) tuber; B (*ugs.: Auswuchs*) large round lump; (*Nase*) big fat conk (*coll.*) *or* (*Amer.*) schnozzle

**Knollen** *der;* **~s, ~** A (*Klumpen*) lump; clod; B (*ugs.: Strafzettel*) [parking] ticket

**Knollen-: ~begonie** *die* tuberous begonia; **~blätter·pilz** *der* amanita; **~nase** *die* large bulbous nose

**knollig** *Adj.* bulbous

**Knopf** /knɔpf/ *der;* **~[e]s, Knöpfe** /ˈknœpfə/ A (*an Kleidungsstücken, Geräten, Anlagen*) button; **[sich** (*Dat.*)**] etw. an den Knöpfen abzählen** (*ugs. scherzh.*) decide sth. by counting off one's buttons; B (*Knauf*) knob; (*eines Schwertes, Dolches*) pommel; C (*ugs. abwertend: kleiner Mann*) [little] squirt (*coll.*); D (*ugs.: Kind*) little thing (*coll.*); E (*südd., österr., schweiz.: Knoten*) knot; F (*südd., österr., schweiz.: Knospe*) bud

**Knopf-: ~auge** *das* [boot-]button eye; **~druck** *der; Pl.* **~drücke** touch of a/the button; **auf ~druck** at the touch of a/the button

**knöpfen** /ˈknœpfn̩/ *tr. V.* button [up]; **der Rock wird seitlich/vorn/hinten geknöpft** the skirt buttons up at the side/in front/at the back

**Knopf-: ~leiste** *die* button-facing; **ein Mantel mit verdeckter ~leiste** a coat with a fly front; **~loch** *das* buttonhole; **aus allen** *od.* **sämtlichen ~löchern platzen** (*ugs.*) be bursting at the seams; **aus allen** *od.* **sämtlichen ~löchern stinken** (*salopp*) stink *or* smell to high heaven (*coll.*); stink *or* smell something terrible (*sl.*)

**knorke** /ˈknɔrkə/ *Adj.* (*berlin. veralt.*) super (*coll.*); terrific (*coll.*)

**Knorpel** /ˈknɔrpl̩/ *der;* **~s, ~** A ▶ 471 (*Anat.*) cartilage; B (*im Steak o. Ä.*) gristle

**knorpelig, knorplig** *Adj.* A (*Anat.*) cartilaginous; B gristly ‹meat›

**Knorren** /ˈknɔrən/ *der;* **~s, ~** A (*Teil eines Astes*) gnarl; knot; B (*Baumstumpf*) [tree] stump; C (*im Holz*) knot

**knorrig** *Adj.* A (*krumm gewachsen*) gnarled ‹tree, branch›; B (*wenig umgänglich*) gruff

**Knospe** /ˈknɔspə/ *die;* **~, ~n** bud; **~n ansetzen** put forth buds; bud; **eine zarte ~** (*fig.*) a tender young bloom (*literary*)

**knospen** *itr. V.* bud; (*fig.*) burgeon

**Knötchen** /ˈknøːtçən/ *das;* **~s, ~** A (*scherzh.: Haartracht*) [little] bun *or* knot; B ▶ 474 (*Med.*) nodule; tubercle

**knoten** /ˈknoːtn̩/ *tr. V.* A (*zu einem Knoten schlingen*) knot; tie a knot in; **sich** (*Dat.*) **ein Tuch um den Hals ~:** tie a scarf round one's neck; B (*durch einen Knoten verknüpfen*) knot together; do *or* tie up ‹shoelace›

**Knoten** *der;* **~s, ~** A knot; **sich** (*Dat.*) **einen ~ ins Taschentuch machen** tie a knot in one's handkerchief; **der ~ der Handlung schürzt sich** (*fig.*) the plot thickens; ⇒ *auch* **gordisch**; B (*Haartracht*) bun; knot; C (*Maßeinheit*) knot; D (*Bot.*) node; E ▶ 474 (*Med.*) node (*Med.*); lump; (*Gicht*~) tophus (*Med.*); F (*Astron., Physik, Elektrot., Anat., Math., Sprachw.*) node; G ⇒ **~punkt** A

**Knoten-: ~punkt** *der* Ⓐ(*Verkehrsknotenpunkt*) junction; intersection; Ⓑ ⇒ **Knoten** F; **~stock** *der* knobby *or* knobbly *or* gnarled [walking] stick

**Knöterich** /ˈknøːtərɪç/ *der;* **~s, ~e** (*Gattung*) Polygonum; (*Vogel~*) knotgrass; (*Wiesen~*) bistort

**knotig** *Adj.* Ⓐ(*Knoten aufweisend*) knobby; knobbly; gnarled; knobbly ‹fabric›; Ⓑ(*knotenförmig*) nodular

**Know-how** /noʊˈhaʊ/ *das;* **~[s]** know-how

**Knubbel** /ˈknʊbl̩/ *der;* **~s, ~** (*bes. nordd.*) (*Verdickung*) small lump

**knubbelig** *Adj.* (*bes. nordd.*) podgy (*coll.*)

**knuddeln** /ˈknʊdl̩n/ *tr. V.* (*bes. nordd.*) hug and squeeze

**Knuff** /knʊf/ *der;* **~[e]s, Knüffe** /ˈknʏfə/ (*ugs.*) poke

**knuffen** /ˈknʊfn̩/ *tr. V.* poke; **jmdn. in den Arm/in die Rippen ~:** poke sb. in the arm/in the ribs

**knülle** /ˈknʏlə/ *Adj.* (*ugs.*) tight (*coll.*); pie-eyed (*coll.*)

**knüllen** ❶ *tr. V.* crumple [up] ‹paper›; crease, crumple ‹clothes, fabrics›. ❷ *itr. V.* crease; crumple

**Knüller** *der;* **~s, ~** (*ugs.*) sensation; (*Film, Buch usw.*) sensation; sensational success; (*Angebot, Verkaufsartikel*) sensational offer

**knüpfen** /ˈknʏpfn̩/ ❶ *tr. V.* Ⓐ tie (**an** + *Akk.* to); **Bande der Freundschaft ~** (*fig.*) establish ties *or* bonds of friendship; Ⓑ (*durch Knoten herstellen*) knot; make ‹net›; Ⓒ(*gedanklich verbinden*) **große Erwartungen/Hoffnungen an etw.** (*Akk.*) **~:** have great expectations/hopes of sth.; **Bedingungen an etw.** (*Akk.*) **~:** attach conditions to sth. ❷ *refl. V.* **sich an etw.** (*Akk.*) **~:** be connected with sth.; **an dieses Haus ~ sich nette Erinnerungen für mich** this house has pleasant memories for me

**Knüppel** /ˈknʏpl̩/ *der;* **~s, ~** Ⓐ cudgel; club; (*Polizei~*) truncheon; **da möchte man doch gleich mit dem ~ dreinschlagen** (*ugs.*) sb. ought to bang *or* knock their heads together; ⇒ *auch* **Bein**; Ⓑ ⇒ **Steuer~**; Ⓒ ⇒ **Schalt~**

**knüppel-, Knüppel-: ~damm** *der* log road; corduroy road; **~dick** *Adv.* (*ugs.*) **es kam ~dick** it was one disaster after the other; **~dick voll** full to bursting; **~hart** *Adj.:* ⇒ **knochenhart**

**knüppeln** ❶ *tr. V.* cudgel; club; beat with a cudgel *or* club/(*Polizeiknüppel*) truncheon. ❷ *itr. V.* Ⓐ use a/one's cudgel *or* club/truncheon; Ⓑ(*Sport Jargon*) play rough; Ⓒ(*unpers.*) (*ugs.*) **heute knüppelt es wieder** things are hectic again today

**Knüppel·schaltung** *die* (*Kfz-W.*) floor[-type] gear change

**knurren** /ˈknʊrən/ ❶ *itr. V.* Ⓐ ‹animal› growl; (*wütend*) snarl; **jmdm. knurrt der Magen** (*fig.*) sb.'s stomach is rumbling; **mit ~dem Magen** (*fig.*) with one's stomach rumbling; Ⓑ(*murren*) grumble (**über** + *Akk.* about); Ⓒ(*verärgert reden*) growl. ❷ *tr. V.* (*verärgert sagen*) growl

**Knurr·hahn** *der; Pl.* **Knurr·hähne** (*Zool.*) gurnard

**knurrig** ❶ *Adj.* grumpy. ❷ *adv.* grumpily

**Knusper·häuschen** *das* gingerbread house

**knusperig** ⇒ **knusprig**

**knuspern** /ˈknʊspɐn/ *tr., itr. V.* nibble; (*geräuschvoll*) crunch; **an etw.** (*Dat.*) **~:** nibble [at] sth.

**knusprig** ❶ *Adj.* Ⓐ crisp; crisp, crusty ‹roll›; crusty ‹bread›; **etw. ~ braten** roast/fry sth. crisp and brown; Ⓑ(*ugs.: frisch u. adrett*) delightfully fresh and attractive. ❷ *adv.* **~frisch** crunchy fresh ‹crisps, nuts›; crispy fresh ‹rolls›

**Knust** /knuːst/ *der;* **~[e]s, ~e** *od.* **Knüste** /ˈknyːstə/ (*bes. nordd.*) crust

**Knute** /ˈknuːtə/ *die;* **~, ~n** knout; **unter jmds. ~ [stehen]** (*fig.*) [be] under sb.'s heel

**knutschen** /ˈknuːtʃn̩/ (*ugs.*) ❶ *tr. V.* smooch with (*coll.*); neck with (*coll.*); (*sexuell berühren*) pet; **sich ~:** smooch (*coll.*) *or* neck (*coll.*)/pet. ❷ *itr. V.* smooch (*coll.*), neck (*coll.*) (**mit** with); (*sich sexuell berühren*) pet

**Knutscherei** *die;* **~, ~en** (*ugs.*) **~[en]** smooching (*coll.*); necking (*coll.*); (*sexuelle Berührung*) petting

**Knutsch·fleck** *der* (*ugs.*) love bite

**Knüttel** /ˈknʏtl̩/ *der;* **~s, ~** ⇒ **Knüppel**

**Knüttel·vers** *der* ⇒ **Knittelvers**

**k. o.** /kaːˈ|oː/ *Adj.* Ⓐ(*Boxen*) **jmdn. ~ schlagen** knock sb. out; **stehend ~ sein** be counted out on one's feet; **~ gehen** be knocked out; Ⓑ(*ugs.: übermüdet*) all in (*coll.*); whacked (*coll.*)

**K. o.** *der;* **~, ~** (*Boxen*) knockout; **[Sieger] durch ~:** [the winner] by a knockout

**koagulieren** /ko|aguˈliːrən/ (*Chemie*) ❶ *itr. V.; auch mit sein* coagulate. ❷ *tr. V.* coagulate

**Koala** /koˈaːla/ *der;* **~s, ~s** koala [bear]

**koalieren** /ko|aˈliːrən/ *itr. V.* (*Politik*) form a coalition (**mit** with)

**Koalition** /ko|aliˈtsi̯oːn/ *die;* **~, ~en** coalition; **die große/kleine ~:** the grand/little coalition

**Koalitions-: ~freiheit** *die* freedom of association (*of workers or employers*); **~partner** *der* coalition partner; **~recht** *das* right of freedom of association (*of workers or employers*); **~regierung** *die* coalition government

**Koaxial·kabel** /ko|aˈksi̯aːl-/ *das* (*Technik*) coaxial cable

**Kob** /kɔp/ *der;* **~s, ~s** (*ugs.*) ⇒ **Kontaktbereichsbeamte**

**Kobalt** /ˈkoːbalt/ *das;* **~s** (*Chemie*) cobalt

**kobalt·blau** *Adj.* cobalt blue

**Kobalt·bombe** *die* cobalt bomb

**Koben** /ˈkoːbn̩/ *der;* **~s, ~** (*Schweinestall*) pigsty; (*Verschlag*) pen

**Kober** /ˈkoːbɐ/ *der;* **~s, ~** (*ostmd.*) food basket

**Kobold** /ˈkoːbɔlt/ *der;* **~[e]s, ~e** goblin; kobold; (*fig.*) imp

**Kobolz** /koˈbɔlts/ *der: in* **~ schießen** *od.* **schlagen** (*bes. nordd.*) turn *or* do a somersault/somersaults

**Kobra** /ˈkoːbra/ *die;* **~, ~s** cobra

**Koch** /kɔx/ *der;* **~[e]s, Köche** ▶ **159** /ˈkœçə/ cook; (*Küchenchef*) chef; **viele Köche verderben den Brei** (*Spr.*) too many cooks spoil the broth (*prov.*)

**koch-, Koch-: ~an·leitung** *die* cooking instructions *pl.;* **~apfel** *der* cooking apple; **~buch** *das* cookery book; cookbook; **~echt** *Adj.* ‹fabric, garment› that is washable in boiling water; ‹colour, dye› that is fast in boiling water

**Köchel·verzeichnis** /ˈkœçl̩-/ *das* (*Musik*) Köchel Catalogue

**kochen** ❶ *tr. V.* Ⓐ boil; (*zubereiten*) cook ‹meal›; make ‹purée, jam›; **Suppe/Kaffee/Tee/Kakao ~:** make some soup/coffee/tea/cocoa; **sich** (*Dat.*) **Tee ~:** make some tea; **die Eier hart/weich ~:** hard-/soft-boil the eggs; **etw. weich/gar ~:** cook sth. until it is soft/[properly] done; **gar gekocht sein** be done; ⇒ *auch* **Flamme** A; Ⓑ(*waschen*) boil; Ⓒ(*verflüssigen*) heat ‹tar, glue, etc.› (*till it melts*). ❷ *itr. V.* Ⓐ(*Speisen zubereiten*) cook; (*das K~ übernehmen*) do the cooking; **gerne/gut ~:** like cooking/be a good cook; **fett/fettarm ~:** use a lot of fat/little fat in cooking; Ⓑ(*sieden*) ‹water, milk, etc.› boil; (*fig.*) ‹sea› boil, seethe; **das Wasser/die Milch kocht** the water/the milk is boiling; **~d heiß** boiling hot; piping hot ‹soup etc.›; **am Kochen sein** (*landsch.*) be on the boil; be boiling; **etw. zum Kochen bringen** bring sth. to the boil; Ⓒ(*in ~dem Wasser liegen*) be boiled; Ⓓ(*ugs.: wütend sein*) **vor Wut/innerlich ~:** be boiling *or* seething with rage/inwardly

***kochend·heiß** ⇒ **kochen** 2 B

**Kocher** *der;* **~s, ~** Ⓐ [small] stove; (*Kochplatte*) hotplate; Ⓑ(*Technik*) boiler

**Köcher** /ˈkœçɐ/ *der;* **~s, ~** Ⓐ(*für Pfeile*) quiver; Ⓑ(*für Fernglas o. Ä.*) case

**Kocherei** *die;* **~** (*ugs.*) cookery

**koch-, Koch-: ~fertig** *Adj.* ready-to-cook *attrib.;* ready to cook *pred.;* **~fest** *Adj.:* ⇒ **~echt**; **~fleisch** *das* stewing meat; **~gelegenheit** *die* cooking facilities *pl.;* **~geschirr** *das* (*Milit.*) mess tin; **~herd** *der* ⇒ **Herd** A

**Köchin** /ˈkœçɪn/ *die;* **~, ~nen** ▶ **159** cook

**Koch-: ~käse** *der* (*type of*) processed curd cheese; **~kunst** *die* Ⓐ culinary art; Ⓑ *Pl.* **~künste** (*ugs.: Fertigkeit im ~en*) culinary skill[s *pl.*]; **~kurs[us]** *der* cookery course; **~löffel** *der* wooden spoon; **den ~löffel schwingen** (*scherzh.*) do the cooking; **~nische** *die* kitchenette; **~platte** *die* Ⓐ hotplate; Ⓑ(*Kocher*) [small] stove; **~rezept** *das* recipe

**Koch·salz** *das* common salt; sodium chloride (*Chem.*)

**Kochsalz·lösung** *die* salt solution; sodium chloride solution (*Chem.*)

**Koch-: ~schinken** *der* boiled ham; **~topf** *der* [cooking] pot; **~wäsche** *die* washing that is to be boiled; **~zeit** *die* cooking time

**kodderig** /ˈkɔd(ə)rɪç/ *Adj.* (*nordd.*) Ⓐ *in* **jmdm. ist ~:** sb. feels sick; Ⓑ(*frech*) impertinent; impudent

**Kode** /koːt/ *der;* **~s, ~s** code

**Kodein** /kodeˈiːn/ *das;* **~s** (*Pharm.*) codeine

**Köder** /ˈkøːdɐ/ *der;* **~s, ~:** bait; (*fig.*) bait; lure; **einen/mehrere ~ auslegen** put out bait/a number of baits

**ködern** *tr. V.* lure; **jmdn. für eine Show ~** (*fig. ugs.*) entice sb. to appear on a show; **sich von jmdm./etw. nicht ~ lassen** (*fig. ugs.*) not be tempted by sb.'s offer/by sth.

**Kodex** /ˈkoːdɛks/ *der;* **~es** *od.* **~, ~e** *od.* **Kodizes** /ˈkoːditseːs/ Ⓐ(*Handschrift*) codex; Ⓑ(*hist.: Gesetzbuch*) code; codex; Ⓒ (*Verhaltensregel*) code

**kodieren** *tr. V.* code; encode

**kodifizieren** /kodifiˈtsiːrən/ *tr. V.* (*bes. Rechtsw.*) codify

**Kodizes** ⇒ **Kodex**

**Koedukation** /ko|edukaˈtsi̯oːn/ *die;* **~:** coeducation

**Koeffizient** /ko|ɛfiˈtsi̯ɛnt/ *der;* **~en, ~en** (*Math., Physik*) coefficient

**Koexistenz** *die;* **~:** coexistence

**Koffein** /kɔfeˈiːn/ *das;* **~s** caffeine

**koffein·frei** *Adj.* decaffeinated

**Koffer** /ˈkɔfɐ/ *der;* **~s, ~** Ⓐ [suit]case; (*Schrank~*) wardrobe trunk; **die ~ packen** pack one's bags [and leave]; **aus dem ~ leben** live out of a suitcase; Ⓑ(*Soldatenspr.*) heavy shell; Ⓒ(*Straßenbau*) roadbed

**Koffer·anhänger** *der* luggage tag *or* label

**Köfferchen** /ˈkœfɐçən/ *das;* **~s, ~:** small [suit]case

**Koffer-: ~gerät** *das* portable [radio/gramophone *etc.*]; **~kuli** *der* luggage trolley; **~radio** *das* portable radio; **~raum** *der* boot (*Brit.*); trunk (*Amer.*); **~schreibmaschine** *die* portable typewriter

**Kogel** /ˈkoːgl̩/ *der;* **~s, ~** (*südd., österr.*) rounded, wooded mountain top

**Kogge** /ˈkɔgə/ *die;* **~, ~n** cog

**Kognak** /ˈkɔnjak/ *der;* **~s, ~s** brandy; ⇒ *auch* **Cognac**

**Kognak-: ~bohne** *die: bean-shaped brandy-filled chocolate;* **~schwenker** *der* brandy glass

**kognitiv** /kɔgniˈtiːf/ *Adj.* (*bes. Psych., Päd.*) cognitive

**kohärent** /kohɛˈrɛnt/ *Adj.* (*Phys.*) coherent

**Kohäsion** /kohɛˈzi̯oːn/ *die;* **~** (*geh., Physik*) cohesion

**Kohl** /koːl/ *der;* **~[e]s** Ⓐ cabbage; **das macht den ~ [auch] nicht fett** (*ugs.*) that doesn't help a lot; Ⓑ(*ugs. abwertend: Unsinn*) rubbish; rot (*coll.*); **red/mach keinen ~!** don't talk rot! (*coll.*)/stop messing around (*coll.*)

**Kohl·dampf** *der* (*salopp*) **~ haben** be ravenously hungry; **~ schieben [müssen]** [have to] go hungry

**Kohle** /ˈkoːlə/ *die;* **~, ~n** Ⓐ(*Brennstoff*) coal; **glühende ~n** live coals; embers; **wir haben keine ~n mehr** we have run out of

k

coal; [wie] auf [glühenden] ~n sitzen (*gespannt warten*) be on tenterhooks; (*ungeduldig warten*) suffer agonies of impatience; **feurige ~n auf jmds. Haupt** (*Akk.*) **sammeln** (*geh.*) heap coals of fire upon sb.'s head; **B** *Pl.* (*salopp: Geld*) dough *sing.* (*coll.*); **Hauptsache, die ~n stimmen!** as long as the money's right; **C** (*Elektrot.*) ⇨ **Bürste** C; **D** (*Chemie*) ⇨ **Aktivkohle**; **E** ⇨ **Zeichenkohle**

**Kohle-: ~filter** *der*, (*fachspr. meist*) *das* charcoal filter; **~hydrat** ⇨ **Kohlenhydrat**; **~kraft·werk** *das* coal-fired power station

**kohlen**[1] *itr. V.* smoulder; ‹wick› smoke

**kohlen**[2] *itr. V.* (*fam.*) (*lügen*) tell fibs; (*übertreiben*) exaggerate; (*prahlen*) boast

**kohlen-, Kohlen-: ~bergbau** *der* coal mining *no art.*; **~bergwerk** *das* coal mine; colliery; **~bunker** *der* coal bunker; **~dioxid, ~dioxyd** /--'---/ *das* (*Chemie*) carbon dioxide; **~eimer** *der* coal scuttle; **~grube** *die* coal mine; [coal] pit; **~grus** *der* breeze; slack; **~halde** *die* coal heap; **~händler** *der*, **~händlerin** *die* ▶159 coal merchant; **~handlung** *die* coal merchant's; **~heizung** *die* coal-fired central heating *no indef. art.*; **~hydrat** *das* (*Chemie*) carbohydrate; **~kasten** *der* coal box; **~keller** *der* coal cellar; **~monoxid, ~monoxyd** /--'---/ *das* (*Chemie*) carbon monoxide; **~monoxid·vergiftung, ~monoxyd·vergiftung** /--'-----/ *die* carbon monoxide poisoning; **~ofen** *der* coal-burning stove; **~pott** *der* (*abwertend*) Ruhr [area]; **~sauer** *Adj.* (*Chemie*) carbonic; **~saures Natron/Kalzium** sodium/calcium carbonate; **~säure** *die* carbonic acid; **~säure·haltig** *Adj.* carbonated; **~schaufel** *die* coal shovel; **~staub** *der* coal dust; **~stoff** *der* carbon; **~wasserstoff** /--'--/ *der* (*Chemie*) hydrocarbon; **~zange** *die* coal tongs *pl.*

**Kohle-: ~ofen** ⇨ **Kohlenofen**; **~papier** *das* carbon paper

**Köhler** /'kø:lɐ/ *der*; **~s, ~:** charcoal burner

**Köhlerei** *die*; **~:** charcoal burning *no art.*

**Köhler·glaube** *der* (*geh. abwertend*) blind faith

**Kohle-: ~stift** *der* **A** (*Elektrot.*) carbon rod; **B** (*zum Zeichnen*) charcoal stick; **~tablette** *die* charcoal tablet; **~zeichnung** *die* charcoal drawing

**kohl-, Kohl-: ~kopf** *der* [head of] cabbage; **~meise** *die* great tit; **~räbchen** /-'--/ *das*; **~~s, ~~:** young kohlrabi; **~raben·schwarz** *Adj.* raven *attrib.*, raven-black, jet-black ‹hair›; jet-black ‹eyes›; ‹face, hands, etc.› as black as soot; **~rabi** /-'ra:bi/ *der*; **~~[s], ~~[s]** kohlrabi; **~roulade** *die* (*Kochk.*) stuffed cabbage; **~rübe** *die* swede; **~sprosse** *die* (*österr.*) [Brussels] sprout; **~weißling** *der*; **~~s, ~~e** cabbage white; cabbage butterfly

**Kohorte** /ko'hɔrtə/ *die*; **~, ~n** cohort

**Koinzidenz** /ko|ɪntsi'dɛnts/ *die*; **~** (*geh.*) coincidence

**koitieren** /koi'ti:rən/ *itr. V.* (*geh.*) engage in *or* have sexual intercourse

**Koitus** /'ko:itʊs/ *der*; **~, Koitus** (*geh.*) sexual intercourse; coitus (*formal*)

**Koje** /'ko:jə/ *die*; **~, ~n** **A** (*Seemannsspr.*) bunk; berth; **B** (*Ausstellungsstand*) stand; **C** (*ugs. scherzh.: Bett*) bed

**Kojote** /ko'jo:tə/ *der*; **~n, ~n** coyote

**Kokain** /koka'i:n/ *das*; **~s** cocaine

**kokain·süchtig** *Adj.* addicted to cocaine *postpos.*

**Kokarde** /ko'kardə/ *die*; **~, ~n** cockade

**Koka·strauch** /'ko:ka-/ *der* coca

**kokeln** /'ko:kl̩n/ *itr. V.* (*ugs.*) play with fire

**Kokerei** /ko:kə'rai/ *die*; **~, ~en** coking plant

**kokett** /ko'kɛt/ **1** *Adj.* coquettish. **2** *adv.* coquettishly

**Koketterie** /kokɛtə'ri:/ *die*; **~:** coquetry; coquettishness

**kokettieren** *itr. V.* **A** play the coquette; flirt; **B** (*kokett erwähnen*) **mit etw. ~:** make much play with sth.; **C** (*fig.*) **mit der Gefahr ~:** flirt with danger

**Kokke** /'kɔkə/ *die*; **~, ~n** (*Biol.*) coccus

**Kokolores** /koko'lo:rɛs/ *der*; **~** (*ugs.*) **A** (*Unsinn*) rubbish; nonsense; rot (*coll.*); **B** (*Getue*) fuss

**Kokon** /ko'kõ:/ *der*; **~s, ~s** cocoon

**Kokos-** /'ko:kɔs-/: **~fett** *das* coconut oil; **~faser** *die* coconut fibre; **~flocken** *Pl.* coconut ice *sing.*; (*als Füllung*) desiccated coconut *sing.*; **~läufer** *der* runner made of coconut matting; **~milch** *die* coconut milk; **~nuss**, ***~nuß** *die* coconut; **~palme** *die* coconut palm; coconut tree

**Kokotte** /ko'kɔtə/ *die*; **~, ~n** (*geh. veralt.*) cocotte (*arch.*)

**Koks**[1] /ko:ks/ *der*; **~es** **A** coke; **B** (*salopp scherzh.: Geld*) dough (*coll.*)

**Koks**[2] *der*; **~es** (*Drogenjargon: Kokain*) coke (*coll.*); snow (*sl.*)

**Koks**[3] *der*; **~es** (*salopp: Unsinn*) rubbish; nonsense; rot (*coll.*)

**koksen** *itr. V.* (*Jargon*) take coke (*sl.*)

**Kokser** *der*; **~s, ~, Kokserin** *die*; **~, ~nen** (*Drogenjargon*) [cocaine-]sniffer; snowbird (*Amer. sl.*)

**Koks-: ~heizung** *die* coke-fired heating; **~ofen** *der* **A** (*mit ~ geheizt*) coke-burning stove; **B** (*für die ~herstellung*) coke oven

**Kola** ⇨ **Kolon**

**Kola·baum** /'ko:la-/ *der* cola *or* kola [tree]

**Kolben** /'kɔlbn̩/ *der*; **~s, ~** **A** (*Technik*) piston; **B** (*Chemie: Glasgefäß*) flask; **C** (*Teil des Gewehrs*) butt; **D** (*Bot.*) spadix; (*Mais~*) cob; **E** (*salopp: dicke Nase*) hooter (*Brit. coll.*); conk (*coll.*); **F** (*der Glühlampe*) glass

**Kolben-: ~fresser** *der* (*ugs.*) piston seize-up; **einen ~fresser haben** have piston seizure *or* a seized[-up] piston; **~hub** *der* (*Technik*) piston stroke; **~ring** *der* (*Technik*) piston ring

**Kolchos·bauer** /'kɔlçɔs-/ *der*; **~n, ~n** kolkhoznik; worker on a Soviet collective farm

**Kolchose** /kɔl'ço:zə/ *die*; **~, ~n** kolkhoz; Soviet collective farm

**Kolibri** /'ko:libri/ *der*; **~s, ~s** hummingbird

**Kolik** /'ko:lɪk/ *die*; **~, ~en** colic

**Kolk·rabe** /'kɔlk-/ *der* (*Zool.*) raven

**kollabieren** /kɔla'bi:rən/ *itr. V.*; *mit sein* (*Med.*) collapse

**Kollaborateur** /kɔlabora'tø:ɐ̯/ *der*; **~s, ~e, Kollaborateurin** *die*; **~, ~nen** collaborator

**Kollaboration** /kɔlabora'tsi̯o:n/ *die*; **~:** collaboration

**kollaborieren** *itr. V.* collaborate (**mit** with)

**Kollagen** /kɔla'ge:n/ *das*; **~s, ~e** (*Med.*, *Biol.*) collagen

**Kollaps** /'kɔlaps/ *der*; **~es, ~e** ▶474 (*Med.*, *fig.*) collapse; **einen ~ erleiden** collapse

**kollationieren** /kɔlatsi̯o'ni:rən/ *tr. V.* **A** (*vergleichen*) collate, compare (**mit** with); (*Druckw.*) read (**mit** against); **B** (*bes. Buchbinderei*) collate

**Kolleg** /kɔ'le:k/ *das*; **~s, ~s** **A** (*Vorlesung*) lecture; (*Vorlesungsreihe*) course of lectures; **B** (*Institut*) *college offering full-time courses to prepare qualified adults for university entrance*; **C** (*kath. Kirche*) theological college

**Kollege** /kɔ'le:gə/ *der*; **~n, ~n** ▶91 **A** colleague; (*Arbeiter*) workmate; **die ~n vom Fach** professional colleagues; **~ kommt gleich!** (*im Restaurant*) somebody [else] will be with you in a moment; **Herr ~!** Mr. Smith/Jones *etc.!*; **Herr ~ [Müller** *usw.*] (*Abgeordneter*) ≈ the Honourable Gentleman; (*als Anrede*) **Herr ~ [Müller], Sie müssen ...** ≈ the Honourable Gentleman must ...; **B** (*Gewerkschaftsmitglied*) [union] member; **C** (*DDR: Werktätiger*) worker; **der ~ Werkleiter/Ober** the works manager/the waiter; **D** (*salopp: Freund*) mate (*coll.*)

**Kollegen-: ~kreis** *der*: **im ~kreis** among colleagues; **~rabatt** *der* trade discount (*in the publishing trade*)

**Kolleg-: ~geld** *das* (*Hochschulw.*) lecture fee; **~heft** *das* lecture notebook

**kollegial** /kɔle'gi̯a:l/ **1** *Adj.* helpful and considerate. **2** *adv.* ‹act etc.› like a good colleague/good colleagues

**Kollegialität** /kɔlegi̯ali'tɛ:t/ *die*; **~:** helpfulness and consideration

**Kollegin** *die*; **~, ~nen** ⇨ **Kollege** A, B, C; ⇨ *auch* **-in**

**Kollegium** /kɔ'le:gi̯ʊm/ *das*; **~s, Kollegien** **A** (*Gruppe*) group; (*unmittelbar zusammenarbeitend*) team; **B** (*Lehrkörper*) [teaching] staff; **C** (*Komitee*) committee

**Kolleg-: ~mappe** *die* document case; **~stufe** *die* (*Schulw.*) sixth-form college (*offering academic and vocational courses*)

**Kollekte** /kɔ'lɛktə/ *die*; **~, ~n** collection

**Kollektion** /kɔlɛk'tsi̯o:n/ *die*; **~, ~en** **A** (*Sortiment*) range; (*Mode*) collection; **B** (*Sammlung, Zusammenstellung*) collection

**kollektiv** /kɔlɛk'ti:f/ **1** *Adj.* collective; joint ‹collaboration›. **2** *adv.* collectively

**Kollektiv** *das*; **~s, ~e** *od.* **~s** **A** group; **als ~ auftreten** put up a united front; **B** (*Arbeitsgruppe*) collective; **C** (*Statistik*) population

**Kollektiv-: ~arbeit** *die* joint work; **~bewusstsein**, ***~bewußtsein** *das* collective consciousness; **~geist** *der* collective spirit; **~gesellschaft** *die* (*schweiz. Wirtsch.*) general partnership

**kollektivieren** *tr. V.* collectivize

**Kollektivismus** *der*; **~:** collectivism *no art.*

**kollektivistisch** *Adj.* collectivist

**Kollektiv-: ~schuld** *die* collective guilt; **~strafe** *die* collective punishment

**Kollektivum** /kɔlɛk'ti:vʊm/ *das*; **~s, Kollektiva** (*Sprachw.*) collective noun; collective

**Kollektiv·wirtschaft** *die* collective farm

**Kollektor** /kɔ'lɛktɔr/ *der*; **~s, ~en** /-'to:rən/ (*Elektrot., Physik*) collector

**Koller**[1] /'kɔlɐ/ *der*; **~s, ~** (*ugs.*) rage; **einen ~ haben/bekommen** be in/fly *or* get into a rage

**Koller**[2] *das*; **~s, ~** (*hist.*) cape collar

**kollern**[1] *itr. V.*; *mit sein* roll

**kollern**[2] *itr. V.* ‹turkey etc.› gobble; ‹stomach› rumble

**kollidieren** /kɔli'di:rən/ *itr. V.* **A** *mit sein* (*zusammenstoßen*) collide, be in collision (**mit** with); **B** (*im Widerspruch stehen*) clash, conflict (**mit** with); **miteinander ~** ‹meetings etc.› clash

**Kollier** /kɔ'li̯e:/ *das*; **~s, ~s** **A** (*Halskette*) necklace; **B** (*schmaler Pelz*) necklet

**Kollision** /kɔli'zi̯o:n/ *die*; **~, ~en** **A** (*Zusammenstoß*) collision; **B** (*Widerstreit*) conflict, clash (+ *Gen.* between); **mit etw. in ~ geraten** come into conflict with sth.

**Kollisions·kurs** *der* collision course; **gegen jmdn./etw. auf ~ gehen** (*fig.*) be heading for a confrontation with sb./sth.

**Kolloid** /kɔlo'i:t/ *das*; **~[e]s, ~e** (*Chemie*) colloid

**Kolloquium** /kɔ'lɔkvi̯ʊm/ *das*; **~s, Kolloquien** **A** (*Hochschulw.*) seminar; **B** (*Zusammenkunft*) colloquium; **C** (*österr.: Prüfung*) test

**Köln** /kœln/ (*das*); **~s** ▶700 Cologne

**Kölner** ▶700 **1** *indekl. Adj.* Cologne *attrib.*; (*in Köln*) in Cologne *postpos.*, *not pred.*; ‹suburb, archbishop, mayor, speciality› of Cologne; ‹car factory, river bank› at Cologne; **der ~ Dom/Karneval** Cologne Cathedral/the Cologne carnival; **meine ~ Freunde** (*in Köln*) my friends in Cologne; (*aus Köln*) my friends from Cologne; **seine ~ Heimat** his native Cologne; **meine ~ Zeit** my time in Cologne; **die ~ Innenstadt** Central Cologne; **alle ~ Bahnhöfe** every station in Cologne; **die 2 000 jährige ~ Geschichte** Cologne's 2000-year history. **2** *der*; **~s, ~:** inhabitant of Cologne; (*von Geburt*) native of Cologne; **er ist ~:** he is a native of Cologne; he comes from Cologne; **ein echter ~:** someone born and bred in Cologne; (*dem Naturell nach*) a true native of Cologne; **der ~** (*bestimmter Mann*) the man from Cologne; that chap from Cologne (*coll.*); (*das Kölner Auto usw.*) the car/bus *etc.* with

*old spelling (see note on page 1707)

k

the Cologne number plate; (*ugs.: die Kölner*) people *pl.* from Cologne; **wir ~:** we citizens of Cologne; **die ~:** the people of Cologne; (*die Kölner Mannschaft usw.*) Cologne *pl.*; (*die Kölner Fans usw.*) the Cologne supporters; (*die Kölner Firma usw.*) the Cologne works *sing. or pl.*/group *etc. sing.*; **die ~ haben einen Oberbürgermeister gewählt** Cologne has elected a mayor; ~ *Pl.* Cologne people; (*außerhalb Kölns*) people from Cologne; **das sind ~:** they are from Cologne; **er hatte als ~ eine tiefe Abneigung gegen Düsseldorf** coming from Cologne, he had a great dislike for Düsseldorf; **Sie als ~ mögen den Karneval nicht?** you come from Cologne, and you don't like the carnival?

**Kölnerin** *die;* ~, **~nen** ⇨ **Kölner** 2; ⇨ *auch* **-in**

**kölnisch** *Adj.* ▶ 700 Cologne *attrib.*; of Cologne *postpos.*, *not pred.*; **kölnisch Wasser** eau-de-Cologne

**Kolombine** /kolɔm'bi:nə/ *die;* ~, **~n** Columbine

**Kolon** /'ko:lɔn/ *das;* **~s**, **~s** *od.* **Kola** (*antike Metrik, Rhet. veralt.: Doppelpunkt*) colon

**Kolonel** /kolo'nɛl/ *die;* ~ (*Druckw.*) minion

**kolonial** /kolo'ni̯a:l/ *Adj.* colonial

**kolonialisieren** *tr. V.* colonialize

**Kolonialisierung** *die;* ~, **~en** colonialization

**Kolonialismus** *der;* **~:** colonialism *no art.*

**kolonialistisch** *Adj.* colonialist

**Kolonial-:** **~macht** *die* colonial power; **~politik** *die* colonial policy; **~stil** *der* colonial style; **~waren** *Pl.* (*veralt.*) groceries *pl.*; **~waren·händler** *der*, **~waren·händlerin** *die* (*veralt.*) grocer; **~zeit** *die* colonial era *or* period

**Kolonie** /kolo'ni:/ *die;* ~, **~n** Ⓐ (*auch Gruppe von Ausländern, Biol.*) colony; Ⓑ (*Siedlung*) colony; settlement

**Kolonisation** /koloniza'tsi̯o:n/ *die;* ~, **~en** colonization

**kolonisieren** *tr. V.* Ⓐ (*zur Kolonie machen*) colonize; Ⓑ (*besiedeln, erschließen*) settle and develop; (*urbar machen*) clear and cultivate ‹land›; reclaim ‹swampland›

**Kolonisierung** *die;* ~, **~en** colonization

**Kolonist** *der;* **~en**, **~en**, **Kolonistin** *die;* ~, **~nen** colonist; (*früher Siedler*) settler

**Kolonnade** /kolɔ'na:də/ *die;* ~, **~n** colonnade

**Kolonne** /ko'lɔnə/ *die;* ~, **~n** Ⓐ (*Truppe, Gruppe von Menschen, Zahlenreihe*) column; **die fünfte ~:** the fifth column; Ⓑ (*Fahrzeuge*) column; (*Schlange*) [long] line of traffic; (*Konvoi*) convoy; **~ fahren** drive in a [long] line of traffic; Ⓒ (*Arbeits~*) gang

**Kolonnen-:** **~fahren** *das;* **~~s** driving in a [long] line of traffic; **~springer** *der*, **~springerin** *die* (*ugs.*) *motorist who dodges in and out of a line of traffic in order to overtake*

**Kolophonium** /kolo'fo:ni̯ʊm/ *das;* **~s** colophony; rosin

**Koloratur** /kolora'tu:ɐ̯/ *die;* ~, **~en** (*Musik*) coloratura

**Koloratur·sängerin** *die* (*Musik*) coloratura

**kolorieren** /kolo'ri:rən/ *tr. V.* Ⓐ (*ausmalen*) colour; Ⓑ (*Musik*) decorate; embellish

**Kolorit** /kolo'ri:t/ *das;* **~[e]s**, **~e** *od.* **~s** Ⓐ (*Farbgebung*) colouring; Ⓑ (*Musik: Klangfarbe*) [tone] colour; Ⓒ (*Atmosphäre*) colour

**Koloss**, ***Koloß** /ko'lɔs/ *der;* **Kolosses**, **Kolosse** Ⓐ (*Standbild*) colossus; **der ~ von Rhodos** the Colossus of Rhodes; Ⓑ (*riesiges Gebilde, ugs. scherzh.: große Person*) colossus; giant

**kolossal** /kolɔ'sa:l/ ❶ *Adj.* Ⓐ (*riesenhaft*) colossal; gigantic; enormous; Ⓑ (*ugs.: sehr groß*) tremendous (*coll.*); incredible (*coll.*) ‹rubbish, nonsense›; **eine ~e Dummheit begehen** do something incredibly stupid; **~es Glück haben** be incredibly lucky (*coll.*). ❷ *adv.* (*ugs.*) tremendously (*coll.*); **~ viel Geld** a tremendous *or* vast amount of money (*coll.*)

**Kolossal-:** **~film** *der* [film] epic; **~gemälde** *das* huge painting; **~schinken** *der* (*salopp abwertend*) Ⓐ (*Film*) massive great epic (*coll.*); Ⓑ (*Gemälde*) whacking great painting (*coll.*)

**Kolportage** /kɔlpɔr'ta:ʒə/ *die;* ~, **~n** Ⓐ (*minderwertiger Bericht*) trashy writing; trash; Ⓑ (*Verbreitung von Gerüchten*) rumour-mongering

**Kolportage-:** **~literatur** *die* trashy literature; **~roman** *der* trashy novel

**Kolporteur** /kɔlpɔr'tø:ɐ̯/ *der;* **~s**, **~e**, **Kolporteurin** *die;* ~, **~nen** (*geh.*) rumour-monger

**kolportieren** *tr. V.* (*geh.*) spread, circulate ‹rumour, story›

**kölsch** /kœlʃ/ ⇨ **kölnisch**

**Kölsch** *das;* **~[s]** Ⓐ *strong very pale beer brewed in Cologne;* Ⓑ Cologne dialect; ⇨ *auch* **Deutsch** A

**Kolumbianer** /kolʊm'bi̯a:nɐ/ *der;* **~s**, ~, **Kolumbianerin** *die;* ~, **~nen** Colombian

**kolumbianisch** *Adj.* Colombian

**Kolumbien** /ko'lʊmbi̯ən/ (*das*)*;* **~s** Colombia

**Kolumbus** /ko'lʊmbʊs/ (*der*) Columbus; ⇨ *auch* **Ei** A

**Kolumne** /ko'lʊmnə/ *die;* ~, **~n** (*Druckw., Meinungsbeitrag*) column

**Kolumnen·titel** *der* (*Druckw.*) running title *or* head

**Kolumnist** *der;* **~en**, **~en**, **Kolumnistin** *die;* ~, **~nen** columnist

**Koma** /'ko:ma/ *das;* **~s**, **~s** *od.* **~ta** ▶ 474 (*Med.*) coma

**Kombattant** /kɔmba'tant/ *der;* **~en**, **~en** (*Völkerr.; geh. veralt.*) combatant

**Kombi** /'kɔmbi/ *der;* **~[s]**, **~s** ⇨ **Kombiwagen**

**Kombinat** /kɔmbi'na:t/ *das;* **~[e]s**, **~e** (*bes. DDR*) combine

**Kombination** /kɔmbina'tsi̯o:n/ *die;* ~, **~en** Ⓐ (*Verbindung*) combination; Ⓑ (*gedankliche Verknüpfung*) deduction; piece of reasoning; **unsere ~en** our reasoning *sing. or* deductions; Ⓒ (*Kleidungsstücke*) ensemble; suit; (*Herren~*) suit; (*Flieger~*) flying suit; Ⓓ (*Ballspiele*) combined move; Ⓔ (*Schach*) combination; Ⓕ (*Ski*) ⇨ **alpin**; **nordisch**

**Kombinations-:** **~gabe** *die* powers *pl.* of deduction *or* reasoning; **~schloss**, ***~schloß** *das* combination lock; **~sprung·lauf** *der* (*Ski*) jumping event (*of Nordic combination*)

**Kombinatorik** /kɔmbina'to:rɪk/ *die;* ~ (*Math.*) combinatorial analysis *no art.*

**kombinatorisch** *Adj.* deductive; **~e Fähigkeiten** powers of deduction *or* reasoning; deductive powers

**kombinieren** /kɔmbi'ni:rən/ ❶ *tr. V.* combine; **zwei Dinge zu etw. ~:** combine two things into sth.; **etw. mit etw. ~:** combine sth. with sth. ❷ *itr. V.* Ⓐ (*Zusammenhänge herstellen*) deduce; reason; **falsch/richtig ~:** come to the wrong/right conclusion; Ⓑ (*Ballspiele*) combine

**Kombi-:** **~wagen** *der* estate [car]; station wagon (*Amer.*); **~zange** *die* combination pliers *pl.*; **eine ~zange** a pair of combination pliers

**Kombüse** /kɔm'by:zə/ *die;* ~, **~n** (*Seemannsspr.*) galley

**Komet** /ko'me:t/ *der;* **~en**, **~en** comet

**kometen·haft** *Adj.* meteoric ‹rise, career›; extremely rapid ‹upturn, development›

**Komfort** /kɔm'fo:ɐ̯/ *der;* **~s** comfort; **mit allem ~** ‹flat, house› with all modern conveniences *pl.*; ‹car› with all the latest luxury features *pl.*

**komfortabel** /kɔmfɔr'ta:bl̩/ ❶ *Adj.* comfortable. ❷ *adv.* comfortably

**Komfort·wohnung** *die* [comfortable] flat (*Brit.*) *or* (*Amer.*) apartment with all modern conveniences

**Komik** /'ko:mɪk/ *die;* **~:** comic effect; (*komisches Element*) comic element *or* aspect; **die ~ der Situation** the funny side of the situation; **Sinn für ~ haben** have a sense of the comic; **etw. entbehrt nicht einer gewissen ~:** sth. is not without an element of comedy; **~ und Tragik** comedy and tragedy; the comic and the tragic

**Komiker** *der;* **~s**, ~, **Komikerin** *die;* ~, **~nen** ▶ 159 Ⓐ (*Vortragskünstler[in]*) comedian/comedienne; comic (*coll.*); Ⓑ (*Darsteller[in]*) comic actor/actress; Ⓒ (*salopp abwertend*) clown

**Kominform** /komɪn'fɔrm/ *das;* **~s** (*hist.*) Cominform

**Komintern** /komɪn'tɛrn/ *die;* ~ (*hist.*) Comintern

**komisch** /'ko:mɪʃ/ *Adj.* Ⓐ (*lustig*) comical; funny; **ich finde das gar nicht ~** (*ugs.*) I don't think that's at all funny; Ⓑ (*seltsam*) funny; strange; odd; **~, was?** (*ugs.*) [it's] funny *or* strange *or* odd, isn't it?; **~ [zu jmdm.] sein** act *or* behave strangely [towards sb.]; **~ [ist nur], dass ...** it's [just] funny *or* strange *or* odd that ...; **mir ist/wird so ~:** I'm feeling funny *or* peculiar; Ⓒ (*Theater*) comic ‹part›

**komischer·weise** *Adv.* (*ugs.*) strangely enough

**Komitee** /komi'te:/ *das;* **~s**, **~s** committee

**Komma** /'kɔma/ *das;* **~s**, **~s** *od.* **~ta** ▶ 841 Ⓐ (*Satzzeichen*) comma; Ⓑ (*Math.*) decimal point; **zwei ~ acht** two point eight; **zwei Stellen hinter dem ~:** two decimal places

**Komma·fehler** *der* mistake involving the use of the comma

**Kommandant** /kɔman'dant/ *der;* **~en**, **~en** (*einer Stadt, Festung*) commandant; (*eines Panzers, Raumschiffs*) commander; (*einer Militäreinheit*) commander; commanding officer; (*eines Flugzeugs, Schiffs*) captain

**Kommandantur** /kɔmandan'tu:ɐ̯/ *die;* ~, **~en** commandant's headquarters *sing. or pl.*

**Kommandeur** /kɔman'dø:ɐ̯/ *der;* **~s**, **~e** (*Milit.*) commander; commanding officer

**kommandieren** ❶ *tr. V.* Ⓐ (*befehligen*) command; be in command of; Ⓑ (*ab~*) **jmdn. an die Front ~:** order sb. to the front; Ⓒ order ‹retreat, advance›; Ⓓ (*ugs.: herum~*) **jmdn. ~:** order *or* (*sl.*) boss sb. about. ❷ *itr. V.* Ⓐ (*Milit.*) **Kommandierender General** Corps commander; Ⓑ (*ugs.*) order *or* (*sl.*) boss people about

**Kommandit·gesellschaft** /kɔman'di:t-/ *die* (*Wirtsch.*) limited partnership

**Kommanditist** *der;* **~en**, **~en**, **Kommanditistin** *die;* ~, **~nen** (*Wirtsch.*) limited partner

**Kommando** /kɔ'mando/ *das;* **~s**, **~s**, *österr. auch:* **Kommanden** Ⓐ (*Befehl*) command; **das ~ zum Schießen geben** give the command *or* order to shoot; **auf ~ gehorchen** obey [immediately] on command; **wie auf ~:** as if by command; ⇨ *auch* **hören** 2 D; Ⓑ (*Befehlsgewalt*) command; **das ~ haben** *od.* **führen/übernehmen** be in/assume *or* take command; Ⓒ (*Milit.*) (*Einheit*) detachment; (*Stoßtrupp*) commando; (*Dienststelle*) headquarters *sing. or pl.*

**Kommando-:** **~brücke** *die* bridge; **~sache** *die: in* **geheime ~sache** (*bes. Milit.*) military secret; **~stab** *der* (*Milit.*) headquarters *or* command staff; **~stand** *der* (*Milit.*) command post; **~stelle** *die* (*Milit.*) command post; **~stimme** *die* commanding [tone of] voice

**Kommata** ⇨ **Komma**

**kommen** /'kɔmən/ *unr. itr. V.; mit sein* Ⓐ come; (*eintreffen*) come; arrive; **der Kellner kommt sofort** the waiter will be with you directly; **zu spät ~:** be late; **zu Fuß/mit dem Auto ~:** come on foot/by car; **in einer halben Stunde/zwei Monaten ~:** come in half an hour/two months' time; **durch eine Gegend ~:** pass through a region; **von der Arbeit ~:** come [back] from work; **nach Hause ~:** come *or* get home; **ins Zimmer ~:** come into the room; **ich komme schon!** I'm coming!; **ich komme, Sie abzuholen** I've come to fetch you; **komm ich heut nicht, komm ich morgen** (*spött.*) you'll/he'll *etc.* get there eventually!; Ⓑ (*gelangen*)

k

get; **ans Ufer/Ziel ~:** reach the bank/finishing line; **komme ich hier zum Bahnhof?** can I get to the station this way?; **wie komme ich nach Paris?** how do I get to Paris?; **kaum noch aus dem Haus/ins Kino ~:** hardly ever get out of the house/to the cinema; **auf etw.** (*Akk.*) **zu sprechen ~** (*fig.*) turn to the discussion of sth.; **zum Schluss seiner Ausführungen ~** (*fig.*) come to the end of one's remarks; **C** + *Bewegungsverb im 2. Part.* **angelaufen/angebraust ~:** come running/roaring along; (*auf jmdn. zu*) come running/roaring up; **angekrochen ~** (*fig.*) come crawling up; **D** (*teilnehmen*) come; attend; **zu einer Tagung ~:** come to/attend a meeting; **E** (*besuchen*) come; **zu jmdm. ~:** come and see sb.; **er kommt zu uns zum Abendbrot** he's coming [to us] for supper; **F** (*gebracht werden*) come; **die Post/ein Paket ist ge~:** the post/a parcel has come; **ist keine Post für mich ge~?** is/was there no post for me?; **G ~ lassen** (*bestellen*) order ‹taxi›; **den Arzt/die Polizei ~ lassen** send for *or* call a doctor/the police; **Getränke** *usw.* **aufs Zimmer ~ lassen** have drinks *etc.* sent up to one's room; **H** (*aufgenommen werden*) **zur Schule/aufs Gymnasium ~:** go to *or* start school/grammar school; **ins Krankenhaus/Gefängnis ~:** go into hospital/to prison; **in die Lehre ~:** start an apprenticeship; **in den Himmel/in die Hölle ~** (*fig.*) go to heaven/hell; **I** (*auftauchen*) ‹seeds, plants› come up; ‹buds, flowers› come out; ‹peas, beans› form; ‹teeth› come through; **zur Welt ~:** be born; **ihr ist ein Gedanke/eine Idee ge~:** she had a thought/an idea; a thought/an idea came to her; **die Tränen ~ jmdm. in die Augen** tears come to sb.'s eyes; ⇒ *auch* **Herz** B; **J** (*seinen festen Platz haben*) go; belong; **in die Schublade/ins Regal ~:** go *or* belong in the drawer/on the shelf; **K** (*seinen Platz erhalten*) **in die Mannschaft ~:** get into the team; **auf den ersten Platz ~:** go into first place; **L** (*geraten*) get; **in Gefahr/Not/Verlegenheit ~:** get into danger/serious difficulties/get *or* become embarrassed; **unter ein Auto/zu Tode ~:** be knocked down by a car/be *or* get killed; **ins Schleudern ~:** go into a skid; ⇒ *auch* **Schwung; Stimmung; M** (*Gelegenheit haben*) **dazu ~, etw. zu tun** get round to doing sth.; **zum Einkaufen/Waschen ~:** get round to doing the shopping/washing; **kaum noch zum Schlafen ~:** hardly be able to find time to sleep; **N** (*nahen*) **ein Gewitter/die Flut kommt** a storm is approaching/the tide's coming in; **den Zeitpunkt für ge~ halten** think *or* consider the moment has come; **der Tag/die Nacht kommt** (*geh.*) day is breaking/night is falling; **dieses Unglück habe ich schon lange ~ sehen** I saw this disaster coming a long time ago; **im Kommen sein** ‹fashion etc.› be coming in; ‹person› be on the way up; **O** (*sich ereignen*) come about; happen; **was auch immer ~ mag** come what may; **das durfte [jetzt] nicht ~** (*ugs. spött.*) that's hardly the thing to say now; **es kam, wie es ~ musste** the inevitable happened; **es kam zum Streit/Kampf** there was a quarrel/fight; **es kam alles ganz anders** it all *or* everything turned out quite differently; **wies kommt, so kommts** *od.* **wies kommt, so wirds genommen** (*ugs.*) what will be will be; **so weit kommt es noch[, dass ich euern Dreck wieder wegräume]!** (*ugs. iron.*) that really is the limit[, expecting me to clear up your rubbish after you]!; **P** (*ugs.: erreicht werden*) **wann kommt der nächste Bahnhof?** when do we get to the next station? (*coll.*); **jetzt kommt gleich Mannheim** we'll be at Mannheim any moment; **da vorn kommt eine Tankstelle** there's a petrol station coming up (*coll.*); **Q zu Geld ~:** become wealthy; **zu Erfolg/Ruhm** *usw.* **~:** gain success/fame *etc.*; **nie zu etwas ~** (*ugs.*) never get anywhere; **wieder zu Kräften ~:** regain one's strength; **[wieder] zu sich ~:** regain consciousness; come round; **zu sich ~** (*sich fassen*) become one's normal self again; **R jmdm. auf die Spur/Schliche ~:** get on sb.'s trail/get wise to sb.'s tricks; **wie kommst du darauf?** what gives you that idea?; **hinter jmds. Geheimnis/Pläne ~:** find out sb.'s secret/plans; **S** (*an der Reihe sein; folgen*) **zuerst/zuletzt kam ...** first/last came ...; **als Erster/Letzter ~:** come first/last; **jetzt komme ich an die Reihe** it is my turn now; **wann ~ wir an die Reihe?** when do we get a turn?; **T** (*sich darstellen*) **gelegen/ungelegen ~** ‹offer, opportunity› come/not come at the right moment; ‹visit› be/not be convenient; **überraschend [für jmdn.] ~:** come as a surprise [to sb.]; **U** (*ugs.: sich verhalten*) **jmdm. frech/unverschämt/grob ~:** be cheeky/impertinent/rude to sb.; **so lasse ich mir nicht ~!** I don't stand for that sort of thing!; **so können Sie mir nicht ~!** don't take that line with me! (*coll.*); **V** (*ugs.: sich an jmdn. wenden*) **komm mir nicht mit ...!** don't give me ...; **da könnte ja jeder ~!** who do you think you are?/who does he think he is? *etc.*; **komm mir nicht damit, du hättest keine Zeit!** don't try and tell me you don't have the time!; **mit so etw. darfst du mir nicht ~:** don't try that sort of thing on with me (*coll.*); **W ich lasse auf ihn** *usw.* **nichts ~:** I won't hear anything said against him *etc.*; **X** + *Inf. mit* **zu** (*in eine Lage geraten*) **neben jmdn. zu sitzen ~:** get to sit next to sb.; **Y über jmdn. ~** (*erfassen*) ‹feeling› come over sb.; **Z** (*verlieren*) **um etw. ~:** lose sth.; **ums Leben ~:** lose one's life; **wir sind um unseren Theaterbesuch ge~:** we missed out on our visit to the theatre; **AA** (*entfallen*) **auf hundert Berufstätige ~ vier Arbeitslose** for every hundred people in employment, there are four people unemployed; **BB woher ~ diese Sachen?** where do these things come from?; **seine Eltern ~ aus Sachsen** his parents come *or* are from Saxony; **CC daher kommt es, dass ...** that's [the reason] why ...; **das kommt davon, dass ...** that's because ...; **vom vielen Rauchen/vom Vitaminmangel ~:** be due to smoking/vitamin deficiency; **wie kommt es, dass du/er** *usw.* **...** how is it that you/he *etc.* ...; how come that you/he *etc.* ... (*coll.*); **das kommt davon!** see what happens!; **das kommt davon, wenn du nicht aufpasst!** that's what happens when you don't pay attention; that's what comes of not paying attention; **DD** (*ugs.: kosten*) **auf 100 Mark ~:** cost 100 marks; **alles zusammen kam auf ...** altogether it came to ...; **wie teuer kommt der Stoff?** how much *or* dear is that material?; **etw. kommt [jmdn.] teuer** sth. comes expensive [for sb.]; **EE** (*ugs.: starten*) start; **FF** (*salopp: Orgasmus haben*) come (*sl.*); **es kommt jmdm.** sb. is coming (*sl.*); **GG** (*im Funkverkehr*) **[bitte] ~!** come in[, please]; **HH** (*ugs.: als Aufforderung, Ermahnung*) **komm/kommt/~ Sie** come on, now; **komm, komm** oh, come on; **II** (*Sportjargon: gelingen*) **[gut] ~/nicht ~** ‹serve, backhand, forehand, etc.› be going/not be going well; **JJ** *in festen Wendungen* ⇒ **Ausbruch** B; **Einsatz** C; **Entfaltung** A; **Fall**[1] A; **Gesicht**[1] C *usw.*

**kommend** *Adj.* **A** ▶ 207, ▶ 833 (*bevorstehend*) next; **das ~e Wochenende/am ~en Sonntag** next weekend/Sunday; **in der ~en Saison/Woche** next season/week; **~e Generationen** generations to come; future generations; **in den ~en Jahren** in years to come; **B** (*mit großer Zukunft*) **der ~e Mann/Meister** the coming man/future champion

**kommensurabel** /kɔmɛnzu'ra:bl̩/ *Adj.* (*Physik, Math.*) commensurable

**Komment** /kɔ'mã:/ *der;* **~s, ~s** (*Studentenspr.*) code of conduct (*in student fraternities*)

**Kommentar** /kɔmɛn'ta:ɐ̯/ *der;* **~s, ~e A** (*Erläuterung*) commentary; **B** (*Stellungnahme*) commentary; comment; **kein ~!** no comment!; **C** (*oft abwertend: Anmerkung*) comment; **~ überflüssig** no comment needed; **sich** (*Dat.*) **jedes ~s enthalten** refrain from commenting; **seinen ~ zu etw. geben** comment on sth.

**kommentarlos ❶** *Adj.* without comment *postpos.* **❷** *adv.* without comment

**Kommentator** /kɔmɛn'ta:tɔr/ *der;* **~s, ~en** /-ta'to:rən/, **Kommentatorin** *die;* **~, ~nen** commentator

**kommentieren** *tr. V.* **A** (*erläutern*) furnish with a commentary, annotate ‹text, work›; **eine kommentierte Ausgabe** an annotated edition; **B** (*Stellung nehmen zu; ugs.: Anmerkungen machen zu*) comment on

**Kommers** /kɔ'mɛrs/ *der;* **~es, ~e** (*Studentenspr.*) students' drinking evening (*to celebrate a particular occasion*)

**Kommers·buch** *das* book of students' drinking songs

**Kommerz** /kɔ'mɛrts/ *der;* **~es** (*abwertend*) business interests *pl.*

**kommerzialisieren** /kɔmɛrtsi̯ali'zi:rən/ *tr. V.* commercialize

**Kommerzial·rat** /kɔmɛr'tsi̯a:l-/ *der* (*österr.*) ⇒ **Kommerzienrat**

**kommerziell** /kɔmɛr'tsi̯ɛl/ **❶** *Adj.* commercial. **❷** *adv.* commercially

**Kommerzien·rat** /kɔ'mɛrtsi̯ən-/ *der* (*hist.*) *honorary title conferred on business magnates and financiers*

**Kommilitone** /kɔmili'to:nə/ *der;* **~n, ~n, Kommilitonin** *die;* **~, ~nen** [one's] fellow student; **der Kommilitone/die Kommilitonin Meyer** ≈ Mr/Ms Meyer

**Kommis** /kɔ'mi:/ *der;* **~** /kɔ'mi:(s)/, Kommis /kɔ'mi:s/ (*veralt.*) *employee on the business side of a commercial firm;* (*in einem Laden*) [shop] assistant

**Kommiss, *Kommiß** /kɔ'mɪs/ *der;* **Kommisses** (*Soldatenspr.*) army; **beim ~ sein** be in the army

**Kommissar** /kɔmɪ'sa:ɐ̯/ *der;* **~s, ~e A** (*Beamter der Polizei*) detective superintendent; **B** ▶ 91 (*staatlicher Beauftragter*) commissioner; **der Hohe ~:** the High Commissioner

**Kommissariat** /kɔmɪsa'ri̯a:t/ *das;* **~s, ~e A** (*Dienststelle*) (*der Polizei*) detective superintendent's office; (*allgemein*) commissioner's office; **B** (*Amt*) (*der Polizei*) rank of detective superintendent; (*allgemein*) commissionership; **C** (*österr.: Polizeistation*) police station

**Kommissarin** *die;* **~, ~nen** ▶ 91 **A** (*Beamte der Polizei*) detective superintendent; **B** (*staatliche Beauftragte*) commissioner; **die Hohe ~:** the High Commissioner

**kommissarisch ❶** *Adj.* acting. **❷** *adv.* in an acting capacity

**Kommiss·brot, *Kommiß·brot** *das* [coarse] wholemeal bread

**Kommission** /kɔmɪ'si̯o:n/ *die;* **~, ~en A** (*Gremium*) committee; (*Prüfungs~*) commission; **B** (*Kaufmannsspr. veralt.: Bestellung*) order; **C etw. in ~ nehmen/haben/geben** (*Wirtsch.*) take/have sth. on commission/give sth. to a dealer for sale on commission; **D** (*veralt.: Einkauf*) **~en machen** *od.* **tätigen** do some shopping

**Kommissionär** /kɔmɪsi̯o'nɛ:ɐ̯/ *der;* **~s, ~e, Kommissionärin** *die;* **~, ~nen A** (*Wirtsch.*) commission agent *or* merchant; **B** (*Buchhändler*) wholesale bookseller

**Kommissions-: ~buch·handel** *der* (*Wirtsch.*) wholesale book trade; **~geschäft** *das* (*Wirtsch.*) commission business

**Kommiss-, *Kommiß-: ~stiefel** *der* army boot; **~ton** *der* (*abwertend*) peremptory tone [of voice]

**kommod** /kɔ'mo:t/ *Adj.* (*bes. österr.*) ⇒ **bequem** 1 A, 2 A

**Kommode** /kɔ'mo:də/ *die;* **~, ~n** chest of drawers

**Kommodore** /kɔmo'do:rə/ *der;* **~s, ~n** *od.* **~s** (*Marine, Handelsmarine*) commodore; (*Luftwaffe*) wing commander

**kommunal** /kɔmu'na:l/ **❶** *Adj.* local; (*bei einer städtischen Gemeinde*) municipal; local.

*old spelling (see note on page 1707)

k

❷ *adv.* **etw. wird ~ verwaltet** sth. comes under local government

**Kommunal-: ~abgaben** *Pl.* rates [and local taxes]; **~anleihe** *die* municipal bond; **~politik** *die* local politics *sing.*; **~verwaltung** *die* local government; **~wahl** *die* local [government] elections *pl.*

**Kommunarde** /kɔmu'nardə/ *der;* **~n, ~n, Kommunardin** *die;* **~, ~nen** **A** (*hist.*) Communard; **B** (*einer Wohngemeinschaft*) member of a/the commune

**Kommune** /kɔ'mu:nə/ *die;* **~, ~n** **A** (*politische Gemeinde*) local authority area; (*städtische Gemeinde*) municipality; **B** **die Pariser ~** (*hist.*) the Paris Commune; **C** (*Wohngemeinschaft*) commune

**Kommunikant** /kɔmuni'kant/ *der;* **~en, ~en, Kommunikantin** *die;* **~, ~nen** **A** (*kath. Kirche*) communicant; **B** (*Sprachw., Soziol.*) participant in the communicative process

**Kommunikation** /'kɔmunika'tsio:n/ *die;* **~, ~en** (*Sprachw., Soziol.*) communication

**Kommunikations-: ~mittel** *das* communication medium; **~satellit** *der* communications satellite; **~schwierigkeit** *die* difficulty in communicating; **~wissenschaft** *die* communication science *no art.*; **~zentrum** *das* central meeting place (*for social and cultural activities*)

**kommunikativ** /kɔmunika'ti:f/ *Adj.* communicative

**Kommunikee** /kɔmuni'ke:/ ⇒ **Kommuniqué**

**Kommunion** /kɔmu'nio:n/ *die;* **~, ~en** (*kath. Kirche*) [Holy] Communion

**Kommunion-: ~bank** *die:* **auf der ~bank knien** ≈ kneel at the Communion rail; **~kleid** *das: dress worn to first Communion;* **~unterricht** *der: preparation for first Communion*

**Kommuniqué** /kɔmyni'ke:/ *das;* **~s, ~s** communiqué

**Kommunismus** *der;* **~:** communism; (*Bewegung*) Communism *no art.*

**Kommunist** *der;* **~en, ~en, Kommunistin** *die;* **~, ~nen** communist; (*Parteimitglied*) Communist

**kommunistisch** ❶ *Adj.* communist; (*die ~e Partei betreffend*) Communist; **das Kommunistische Manifest** the Communist Manifesto. ❷ *adv.* Communist-‹influenced, led, ruled, etc.›

**kommunizieren** /kɔmuni'tsi:rən/ *itr. V.* **A** (*geh.*) communicate; **~de Röhren** (*Physik*) communicating tubes; **B** (*kath. Kirche*) receive [Holy] Communion

**Kommutation** /kɔmuta'tsio:n/ *die;* **~, ~en** (*Math., Sprachw., Astron.*) commutation

**kommutativ** /kɔmuta'ti:f/ *Adj.* (*Math., Sprachw.*) commutative

**Komödiant** /komø'diant/ *der;* **~en, ~en** **A** (*veralt.: Schauspieler*) actor; player; **B** (*abwertend: Heuchler*) play-actor

**komödiantenhaft** *Adj.* theatrical

**Komödiantin** *die;* **~, ~nen** **A** (*veralt.: Schauspielerin*) actress; **B** (*abwertend: Heuchlerin*) play-actor

**komödiantisch** *Adj.* theatrical; acting ‹talent›

**Komödie** /ko'mø:diə/ *die;* **~, ~n** **A** comedy; (*fig.*) farce; **B** (*Theater*) comedy theatre; **C** (*Heuchelei*) play-acting; **~ spielen** put on an act

**Kompagnon** /kɔmpan'jõ:/ *der;* **~s, ~s** (*Wirtsch.*) partner; associate

**kompakt** /kɔm'pakt/ *Adj.* **A** (*massiv*) solid; **B** (*ugs.: gedrungen*) stocky

**Kompakt-: ~an·lage** *die* music centre; (*bei übereinander angeordneten Geräten*) compact stereo system; **~bau·weise** *die* compact design

**Kompanie** /kɔmpa'ni:/ *die;* **~, ~n** (*Milit., veralt.: Handelsgesellschaft*) company

**Kompanie·chef** *der,* **Kompanie·führer** *der* (*Milit.*) company commander

**Komparation** /kɔmpara'tsio:n/ *die;* **~, ~en** (*Sprachw.*) comparison

**Komparatistik** /kɔmpara'tɪstɪk/ *die;* **~:** comparative literature *no art.*

**Komparativ** /'kɔmparati:f/ *der;* **~s, ~e** (*Sprachw.*) comparative

**Komparse** /kɔm'parzə/ *der;* **~n, ~n** (*Theater*) supernumerary; super (*coll.*); (*Film*) extra

**Komparserie** /kɔmparzə'ri:/ *die;* **~, ~n** (*Theater*) supernumeraries *pl.*; supers *pl.* (*coll.*); (*Film*) extras *pl.*

**Komparsin** *die;* **~, ~nen** ⇒ **Komparse**

**Kompass, *Kompaß** /'kɔmpas/ *der;* **Kompasses, Kompasse** compass; **nach dem ~ marschieren** march by the compass

**Kompass-, *Kompaß-: ~häuschen** *das* (*Seew. hist.*) binnacle; **~nadel** *die* compass needle; **~rose** *die* compass card

**kompatibel** /kɔmpa'ti:bl/ *Adj.* (*Nachrichtenw., Sprachw.*) compatible

**Kompendium** /kɔm'pɛndiʊm/ *das;* **~s, Kompendien** (*geh.*) compendium

**Kompensation** /kɔmpɛnza'tsio:n/ *die;* **~, ~en** (*Wirtsch., Physik, geh.*) compensation

**kompensatorisch** *Adj.* (*Päd., Psych.*) compensatory

**kompensieren** *tr. V.* **A** (*ausgleichen*) **etw. mit etw.** *od.* **durch etw. ~:** compensate for *or* make up for sth. by sth.; **B** (*Wirtsch.: gegeneinander aufrechnen*) offset; **etw. durch etw. ~:** offset sth. against sth.

**kompetent** /kɔmpe'tɛnt/ *Adj.* **A** (*sachverständig*) competent; **ein ~er Sprecher** (*Sprachw.*) a person with native-speaker competence; **für diese Probleme/Fragen ist er nicht ~:** he's not competent to deal with these problems/answer these questions; **B** (*bes. Rechtsw.: zuständig*) competent, responsible ‹authority›; **das dafür ~e Gericht/der dafür ~e Kollege** the court which has jurisdiction in/the colleague who deals with these matters

**Kompetenz** /kɔmpe'tɛnts/ *die;* **~, ~en** **A** (*Sachverstand*) competence; **B** (*bes. Rechtsw.: Zuständigkeit*) authority; powers *pl.*; (*eines Gerichts*) jurisdiction; competence; **in jmds. ~** (*Dat.*) **liegen/in jmds. ~** (*Akk.*) **fallen** be/come within sb.'s authority *or* powers; **das liegt außerhalb meiner ~:** that doesn't lie within my authority *or* powers; **seine ~ überschreiten** exceed one's authority *or* powers; **die ~ haben/erhalten, etw. zu tun** have/receive the authority to do sth.; **C** (*Sprachw.*) competence

**Kompetenz-: ~bereich** *der* area of authority *or* responsibility/jurisdiction; **~konflikt** *der,* **~streitigkeit** *die* dispute over respective areas of authority *or* responsibility/jurisdiction

**Kompilation** /kɔmpila'tsio:n/ *die;* **~, ~en** (*geh., meist abwertend*) [mere] compilation

**kompilieren** *tr. V.* (*geh., meist abwertend*) [merely] compile

**Komplement** /kɔmple'mɛnt/ *das;* **~[e]s, ~e** (*Math.*) complement

**komplementär** /kɔmplemɛn'tɛ:ɐ̯/ ❶ *Adj.* complementary. ❷ *adv.* **sich ~ verhalten/~ zueinander stehen** complement one another; be complementary

**Komplementär** *der;* **~s, ~e, Komplementärin** *die;* **~, ~nen** (*Wirtsch.*) general partner

**Komplementär·farbe** *die* (*Optik*) complementary colour

**Komplement·winkel** *der* (*Math.*) complementary angle

**Komplet**[1] /kõ'ple:/ *das;* **~s, ~s** dress and matching jacket/coat

**Komplet**[2] /kɔm'ple:t/ *die;* **~, ~e** (*kath. Kirche*) compline

**komplett** /kɔm'plɛt/ ❶ *Adj.* **A** (*vollständig*) complete; **das kostet ~ 1 500 Mark** it costs 1,500 marks complete; **heute sind wir ~** (*ugs.*) today we are all here; **B** (*ugs.: ganz und gar*) complete; utter; **C** (*österr.: voll*) full ‹hotel, tram, etc.›. ❷ *adv.* **A** (*vollständig*) **~ möbliert/ausgerüstet** fully furnished/equipped; **B** (*ugs.: ganz und gar*) completely; totally

**komplettieren** *tr. V.* complete

**komplex** /kɔm'plɛks/ (*geh.*) ❶ *Adj.* **A** complex; **~e Zahl** (*Math.*) complex number; **B** (*allseitig*) full, complete ‹automation›; comprehensive ‹reconstruction, planning, provision›; ‹analysis, treatment› by several methods. ❷ *adv.* **etw. ~ vorbereiten** make comprehensive preparations for sth.

**Komplex** *der;* **~es, ~e** **A** (*Bereich*) complex; **Fragen im ~ lösen** solve questions as parts of an integrated whole; **B** (*Gebäudeblock*) complex; **in diesem ~ des Schlosses** in this complex of buildings in the castle; **C** (*Psych.*) complex

**Komplexität** /kɔmplɛksi'tɛ:t/ *die;* **~:** complexity

**Komplikation** /kɔmplika'tsio:n/ *die;* **~, ~en** (*auch Med.*) complication

**Kompliment** /kɔmpli'mɛnt/ *das;* **~[e]s, ~e** **A** compliment; **jmdm. ein ~ machen** pay sb. a compliment (**über** + *Akk.* on); **mein ~!** permit me to compliment you; my compliments!; **nicht gerade ein ~ für jmdn. sein** (*fig.*) not exactly do sb. credit; **B** (*veralt.: Gruß*) **meine ~e an die gnädige Frau** give my respects to your good wife

**komplimentieren** *tr. V.* (*geh.*) **jmdn. ins Haus/in den Sessel ~:** usher *or* show sb. into the house/help sb. into his/her seat with a great show of courtesy; **jmdn. aus dem Zimmer ~** (*verhüll.*) usher sb. out of the room

**Komplize** /kɔm'pli:tsə/ *der;* **~n, ~n** (*abwertend*) accomplice

**komplizieren** *tr. V.* complicate; **sich ~:** become more complicated

**kompliziert** ❶ *Adj.* complicated; complicated, intricate ‹device, piece of apparatus›; complicated, involved ‹problem, procedure›; **ein ~er Bruch** (*Med.*) a compound fracture. ❷ *adv.* **~ aufgebaut sein** have a complicated *or* complex structure; **sich ~ ausdrücken** express oneself in a complicated *or* an involved way *or* manner; ⇒ *auch* **einfach** 1 B

**Kompliziertheit** *die;* **~:** complexity; complicatedness

**Komplizin** *die;* **~, ~nen** ⇒ **Komplize**

**Komplott** /kɔm'plɔt/ *das;* **~[e]s, ~e** plot; conspiracy; **ein ~ zur Ermordung des Diktators** a plot *or* conspiracy to assassinate the dictator; **ein ~ schmieden** hatch a plot

**Komponente** /kɔmpo'nɛntə/ *die;* **~, ~n** **A** (*Bestandteil*) component; **B** (*Aspekt*) component; element

**komponieren** ❶ *tr. V.* (*auch geh.: gestalten*) compose. ❷ *itr. V.* compose

**Komponist** *der;* **~en, ~en, Komponistin** *die;* **~, ~nen** ▶ **159** composer

**Komposition** /kɔmpozi'tsio:n/ *die;* **~, ~en** (*Musik, geh.*) composition; **eine ~ kostbarer Essenzen** (*geh.*) a fusion *or* blend of expensive essential oils

**Kompositions·lehre** *die* (*Musik*) [theory of] composition

**kompositorisch** /kɔmpozi'to:rɪʃ/ *Adj.* compositional

**Kompositum** /kɔm'po:zitʊm/ *das;* **~s, Komposita** (*Sprachw.*) compound [word]

**Kompost** /kɔm'pɔst/ *der;* **~[e]s, ~e** compost

**Kompost-: ~erde** *die* [well-rotted] compost; **~haufen** *der* compost heap

**Kompott** /kɔm'pɔt/ *das;* **~[e]s, ~e** stewed fruit; compote; **Pflaumen~/Himbeer~:** stewed plums/raspberries *pl.*

**Kompott·schale** *die* fruit dish *or* bowl

**kompress, *kompreß** /kɔm'prɛs/ (*Druckw.*) ❶ *Adj.* solid. ❷ *adv.* ‹set› in solid type

**Kompresse** /kɔm'prɛsə/ *die;* **~, ~n** (*Med.*) **A** (*Umschlag*) [wet] compress; **B** (*Mull*) [gauze] pad

**Kompression** /kɔm'prɛ'sio:n/ *die;* **~, ~en** (*Physik, Technik, Med.*) compression

**Kompressions·verband** *der* (*Med.*) ⇒ **Druckverband**

**Kompressor** /kɔm'prɛsɔr/ *der;* **~s, ~en** /-'so:rən/ (*Technik*) compressor

**komprimieren** /kɔmpri'mi:rən/ *tr. V.* (*auch Physik, Technik*) compress; (*fig.*) condense ‹book, text›

k

**komprimiert** ❶ *Adj.* condensed ‹account etc.›. ❷ *adv.* **etw. ~ darstellen** present sth. in a condensed form

**Kompromiss**, ***Kompromiß** /kɔmpro'mɪs/ *der;* **Kompromisses, Kompromisse** compromise; **einen ~ schließen** make a compromise; compromise; **zu einem/keinem ~ bereit sein** be/not be ready to compromise; **ein fauler ~** (*ugs.*) a poor sort of compromise (*coll.*)

**kompromiss-**, ***kompromiß-**, **Kompromiss-**, ***Kompromiß-: ~bereit** *Adj.* ready *or* willing to compromise *pred.*; **~bereitschaft** *die* readiness *or* willingness to compromise; **~los** ❶ *Adj.* uncompromising; ❷ *adv.* uncompromisingly; **~lösung** *die* compromise solution; **~vorschlag** *der* compromise proposal *or* suggestion

**kompromittieren** /kɔmpromɪ'ti:rən/ *tr. V.* compromise; **sich ~:** compromise oneself

**Komsomolze** /kɔmzo'mɔltsə/ *der;* **~n, ~n, Komsomolzin,** *die;* **~, ~nen** Komsomol member

**Komtess**, ***Komteß**, **Komtesse** /kɔm'tɛs(ə)/ *die;* **~, Komtessen** (*veralt.*) count's [unmarried] daughter

**Komtur** /kɔm'tu:ɐ̯/ *der;* **~s, ~e** (*hist.*) commander (*of an honorary or a religious military order*)

**Kondensat** /kɔndɛn'za:t/ *das;* **~[e]s, ~e** (*Physik, Chemie*) condensate

**Kondensation** /kɔndɛnza'tsi̯o:n/ *die;* **~, ~en** (*Physik, Chemie*) condensation

**Kondensations·punkt** *der* (*Physik, Chemie*) condensation point

**Kondensator** /kɔndɛn'za:tɔr/ *der;* **~s, ~en** /-za'to:rən/ Ⓐ (*Elektrot.*) capacitor; condenser; Ⓑ (*Technik*) condenser

**kondensieren** *tr., itr. V.* (*itr. auch mit sein*) (*Physik, Chemie*) condense

**Kondens-: ~milch** *die* condensed milk; **~streifen** *der* condensation trail; vapour trail; **~wasser** *das* condensation

**Kondition** /kɔndi'tsi̯o:n/ *die;* **~, ~en** Ⓐ (*bes. Kaufmannsspr., Finanzw.*) condition; **die ~en** the terms *or* conditions; **zu günstigen ~en** on favourable terms; Ⓑ (*körperlich-seelische Verfassung, Leistungsfähigkeit*) condition; **eine gute/schlechte ~ haben** be/not be in good condition *or* shape; **keine ~ haben** be out of condition; (*fig.*) have no stamina

**konditional** /kɔnditsi̯o'na:l/ *Adj.* (*bes. Sprachw.*) conditional

**Konditional·satz** *der* (*Sprachw.*) conditional clause

**konditionieren** *tr. V.* (*Technik, Psych.*) condition

**Konditions-: ~mangel** *der*, **~schwäche** *die* lack of condition *or* fitness; **~training** *das* fitness training

**Konditor** /kɔn'di:tɔr/ *der;* **~s, ~en** /-di'to:rən/ ▶159 confectioner; pastry cook; **beim ~:** at the cake shop

**Konditorei** *die;* **~, ~en** Ⓐ cake shop; (*Lokal*) café; Ⓑ (*Herstellung*) confectionery

**Konditorin,** *die;* **~, ~nen** ▶159 ⇒ Konditor

**Konditor·waren** *Pl.* cakes and pastries

**Kondolenz-** /kɔndo'lɛnts-/: **~besuch** *der* visit of condolence; **~buch** *das* book of condolence

**kondolieren** /kɔndo'li:rən/ *itr. V.* offer one's condolences; **jmdm. [zu jmds. Tod] ~:** offer one's condolences to sb. *or* condole with sb. [on sb.'s death]

**Kondom** /kɔn'do:m/ *das od. der;* **~s, ~e** condom; [contraceptive] sheath

**Kondominium** /kɔndo'mi:ni̯ʊm/ *das;* **~s, Kondominien** (*Völkerr.*) condominium

**Kondor** /'kɔndɔr/ *der;* **~s, ~e** condor

**Kondukteur** /kɔndʊk'tø:ɐ̯/ *der;* **~s, ~e** ▶159 (*schweiz.*) (*in der Straßenbahn*) conductor; (*in der Eisenbahn*) ticket collector

**Kondukteurin** *die;* **~, ~nen** ▶159 (*schweiz.*) ⇒ **Kondukteur**: conductress/ticket collector

*old spelling (see note on page 1707)

**Konen** ⇒ Konus

**Konfekt** /kɔn'fɛkt/ *das;* **~[e]s** Ⓐ (*Süßigkeiten*) confectionery; sweets *pl.* (*Brit.*); candies *pl.* (*Amer.*); Ⓑ (*bes. südd., österr., schweiz.: Teegebäck*) [small] fancy biscuits *pl.* (*Brit.*) *or* (*Amer.*) cookies *pl.*

**Konfektion** /kɔnfɛk'tsi̯o:n/ *die;* **~, ~en** Ⓐ (*Anfertigung*) manufacture of ready-made *or* off-the-peg (*Brit.*) *or* (*Amer.*) off-the-rack clothes *or* garments; Ⓑ (*Kleidung*) ready-made *or* off-the-peg (*Brit.*) *or* (*Amer.*) off-the-rack clothes *pl. or* garments *pl.*; Ⓒ (*Industrie*) clothing industry

**Konfektionär** /kɔnfɛktsi̯o'nɛ:ɐ̯/ *der;* **~s, ~e** manufacturer of ready-made *or* off-the-peg (*Brit.*) *or* (*Amer.*) off-the-rack clothing; clothing manufacturer; (*Angestellter*) employee in a clothing factory

**Konfektions-: ~anzug** *der* ready-made *or* off-the-peg (*Brit.*) *or* (*Amer.*) off-the-rack suit; **~geschäft** *das* [ready-made *or* off-the-peg (*Brit.*) *or* (*Amer.*) off-the-rack] clothes shop; **~größe** *die* size; **~ware** *die* ready-made *or* off-the-peg (*Brit.*) *or* (*Amer.*) off-the-rack clothes *pl. or* garments *pl.*

**Konferenz** /kɔnfe'rɛnts/ *die;* **~, ~en** conference; (*Besprechung*) meeting

**Konferenz-: ~saal** *der* conference hall; **~schaltung** *die* (*Rundf., Ferns., Fernspr.*) conference circuit; **~teilnehmer** *der*, **~teilnehmerin** *die* conference participant; **~tisch** *der* conference table

**konferieren** /kɔnfe'ri:rən/ ❶ *itr. V.* Ⓐ (*beraten*) confer (**über** + *Akk.* on, about); Ⓑ (*ansagen*) act as compère. ❷ *tr. V.* (*ansagen*) compère

**Konfession** /kɔnfɛ'si̯o:n/ *die;* **~, ~en** Ⓐ denomination; religion; **die katholische ~:** the Catholic religion; **welche ~ haben Sie?** what denomination *or* religion are you?; Ⓑ (*geh.: Geständnis*) confession

**Konfessionalismus** /kɔnfɛsi̯ona'lɪsmʊs/ *der;* **~** (*geh.*) denominationalism *no art.*

**konfessionell** /kɔnfɛsi̯o'nɛl/ ❶ *Adj.* denominational. ❷ *adv.* as regards denomination; **~ [un]gebunden sein/sich ~ [un]gebunden fühlen** have/feel [no] denominational ties

**konfessions·los** *Adj.* not belonging to any denomination *or* religion *postpos., not pred.*

**Konfessions·schule** *die* denominational school

**Konfetti** /kɔn'fɛti/ *das;* **~[s]** confetti

**Konfident** /kɔnfi'dɛnt/ *der;* **~en, ~en, Konfidentin** *die;* **~, ~nen** (*österr.: Spitzel*) [police] informer

**Konfiguration** /kɔnfigura'tsi̯o:n/ *die;* **~, ~en** (*Physik, Chemie, Sprachw.*) configuration

**Konfirmand** /kɔnfɪr'mant/ *der;* **~en, ~en** (*ev. Rel.*) confirmand

**Konfirmanden·unterricht** *der* confirmation classes *pl.*

**Konfirmandin** *die;* **~, ~nen** ⇒ **Konfirmand**

**Konfirmation** /kɔnfɪrma'tsi̯o:n/ *die;* **~, ~en** (*ev. Rel.*) confirmation

**konfirmieren** *tr. V.* (*ev. Rel.*) confirm

**Konfiserie** /kɔnfizə'ri:/ *die;* **~, ~n** (*schweiz.*) ⇒ **Konditorei**

**Konfiskation** /kɔnfɪska'tsi̯o:n/ *die;* **~, ~en** (*Rechtsw.*) confiscation

**konfiszieren** /kɔnfɪs'tsi:rən/ *tr. V.* (*bes. Rechtsw.*) confiscate

**Konfitüre** /kɔnfi'ty:rə/ *die;* **~, ~n** jam (*made from whole fruit*)

**Konflikt** /kɔn'flɪkt/ *der;* **~[e]s, ~e** conflict; **ein offener/bewaffneter ~:** open/armed conflict; **mit etw. in ~ geraten** *od.* **kommen** come into conflict with sth.

**konflikt-, Konflikt-: ~fall** *der:* **im ~fall** in the event of conflict; **~forschung** *die* conflict studies *pl.*; **~los** *Adj.* conflict-free; **~situation** *die* conflict situation; **~stoff** *der* cause for conflict *or* dispute

**Konföderation** /kɔnfødera'tsi̯o:n/ *die;* **~, ~en** confederation; (*von kürzerer Dauer*) confederacy

**Konföderierte** *der/die; adj. Dekl.* confederate; **die ~n** (*hist.*) the Confederates

**konform** /kɔn'fɔrm/ *Adj.* concurring *attrib.* ‹views›; **mit jmdm./etw. ~ gehen** be in agreement with sb./sth.; **in etw.** (*Dat.*) **~ sein** agree *or* be in agreement on sth.

**Konformismus** *der;* **~:** conformism

**Konformist** *der;* **~en, ~en, Konformistin** *die;* **~, ~nen** (*auch Rel.*) conformist

**konformistisch** ❶ *Adj.* conformist. ❷ *adv.* in a conformist way

**Konformität** /kɔnfɔrmi'tɛ:t/ *die;* **~:** conformity

**Konfrater** /kɔn'fra:tɐ/ *der;* **~s, Konfratres** (*kath. Kirche*) fellow clergyman; brother-priest

**Konfrontation** /kɔnfrɔnta'tsi̯o:n/ *die;* **~, ~en** confrontation

**konfrontieren** *tr. V.* confront; **sich mit etw. konfrontiert sehen** be confronted with sth.

**konfus** /kɔn'fu:s/ ❶ *Adj.* confused; muddled; **jmdn. ~ machen** confuse *or* muddle sb. ❷ *adv.* in a confused *or* muddled fashion; confusedly

**Konfusion** /kɔnfu'zi̯o:n/ *die;* **~, ~en** confusion

**konfuzianisch** /kɔnfu'tsi̯a:nɪʃ/ *Adj.* Confucian

**Konfuzianismus** *der;* **~:** Confucianism *no art.*

**kongenial** /kɔnge'ni̯a:l/ *Adj.* (*geh.*) congenial, kindred ‹spirits›; ideally matched ‹translation›

**Kongenialität** /kɔngeni̯ali'tɛ:t/ *die;* **~** (*der Geister*) congeniality; (*einer Übersetzung*) well-matched quality

**Konglomerat** /kɔnglome'ra:t/ *das;* **~[e]s, ~e** Ⓐ conglomeration; Ⓑ (*Geol.*) conglomerate

**Kongo**[1] /'kɔŋgo/ *der;* **~[s]** ▶306 (*Fluss*) Congo

**Kongo**[2] /'kɔŋgo/ *(das);* **~s** *od. der;* **~[s]** (*Staat*) the Congo

**Kongolese** /kɔŋgo'le:zə/ *der;* **~n, ~n, Kongolesin** *die;* **~, ~nen** Congolese

**Kongregation** /kɔngrega'tsi̯o:n/ *die;* **~, ~en** (*kath. Kirche*) congregation

**Kongress**, ***Kongreß** /kɔn'grɛs/ *der;* **Kongresses, Kongresse** Ⓐ (*Tagung*) congress; conference; Ⓑ (*USA*) **der ~:** Congress

**Kongress-**, ***Kongreß-: ~halle** *die* conference hall; **~mit·glied** *das* (*USA*) Congressman/Congresswoman; **~teilnehmer** *der*, **~teilnehmerin** *die* congress *or* conference participant; **~zentrum** *das* conference centre

**kongruent** /kɔngru'ɛnt/ *Adj.* Ⓐ (*geh.*) identical; Ⓑ (*Math.*) congruent

**Kongruenz** /kɔngru'ɛnts/ *die;* **~, ~en** Ⓐ (*geh.*) identity; Ⓑ (*Math.*) congruence; Ⓒ (*Sprachw.*) agreement; concord

**kongruieren** *itr. V.* Ⓐ (*geh.*) coincide; Ⓑ (*Math.*) be congruent; Ⓒ (*Sprachw.*) agree

**K.-o.-Nieder·lage** *die* (*Boxen*) defeat by a knockout; **durch eine ~:** by a knockout

**Konifere** /koni'fe:rə/ *die;* **~, ~n** (*Bot.*) conifer

**König** /'kø:nɪç/ *der;* **~s, ~e** (*auch Schach, Kartenspiele, fig.*) king; **der ~ der Wüste/Lüfte** (*dicht.*)/**des Jazz** the king of beasts/birds/jazz; **der Kunde ist ~:** the customer is always right

**Königin** *die;* **~, ~nen** (*auch Bienen~*) queen; **die ~ des Festes/Balles** (*geh.*) the belle of the ball; **~ der Nacht** (*Bot.*) queen of the night

**Königin·mutter** *die; Pl.* **Königinmütter** queen mother

**königlich** ❶ *Adj.* Ⓐ royal; Ⓑ (*vornehm*) regal; Ⓒ (*reichlich*) princely ‹gift, salary, wage›; lavish ‹hospitality›; Ⓓ (*ugs.: außerordentlich*) tremendous (*coll.*) ‹fun›. ❷ *adv.* Ⓐ (*reichlich*) ‹entertain› lavishly; ‹pay› handsomely; **~ beschenkt werden** be showered with lavish presents; Ⓑ (*ugs.: außerordentlich*) ‹enjoy oneself› immensely (*coll.*); **sich über etw.** (*Akk.*) **~ freuen** be as pleased as Punch about sth.

**König·reich** *das* kingdom

**königs-, Königs-: ~blau** *Adj.* royal blue; **~haus** *das* royal house; **~hof** *der* royal court; king's court; **~kerze** *die* (*Bot.*) mullein; **~kind** *das* prince/princess; king's son/daughter; **~krone** *die* royal crown; **~macher** *der*, **~macherin** *die* (*ugs.*) kingmaker; **~paar** *das* royal couple; **~sohn** *der* prince; king's son; **~thron** *der* royal throne; **~tiger** *der* Bengal tiger; **~tochter** *die* princess; king's daughter; **~treu** *Adj.* loyal to the king *postpos.*; (*der Monarchie treu*) royalist; **~wasser** *das* (*Chemie, Technik*) aqua regia; **~weg** *der* (*geh.*) ideal way

**Königtum** *das;* **~s, Königtümer** Ⓐ (*Monarchie*) monarchy; Ⓑ (*veralt.: Reich*) kingdom

**konisch** /'ko:nɪʃ/ ❶ *Adj.* conical. ❷ *adv.* conically; **~ zugespitzt sein** taper to a point

**Konjektur** /kɔnjɛk'tu:ɐ̯/ *die;* **~, ~en** (*Literaturw.*) conjecture

**Konjugation** /kɔnjuga'tsi̯o:n/ *die;* **~, ~en** (*Sprachw.*) conjugation

**konjugieren** *tr. V.* (*Sprachw.*) conjugate

**Konjunktion** /kɔnjʊŋk'tsi̯o:n/ *die;* **~, ~en** (*Sprachw.*) conjunction

**Konjunktional·satz** *der* (*Sprachw.*) conjunctional clause

**Konjunktiv** /'kɔnjʊŋkti:f/ *der;* **~s, ~e** (*Sprachw.*) subjunctive; **~ I/II** present/imperfect subjunctive

**konjunktivisch** ❶ *Adj.* (*Sprachw.*) subjunctive. ❷ *adv.* in the subjunctive

**Konjunktur** /kɔnjʊŋk'tu:ɐ̯/ *die;* **~, ~en** (*Wirtsch.*) Ⓐ (*wirtschaftliche Lage*) [level of] economic activity; economy; (*Tendenz*) economic trend; **eine rückläufige/steigende ~:** declining/increasing economic activity; **die ~ beleben/bremsen** stimulate/slow down the economy; Ⓑ (*Hoch~*) boom; (*Aufschwung*) upturn [in the economy]; **~ haben** (*fig.*) be in great demand

**konjunktur-, Konjunktur-: ~abhängig** *Adj.* (*Wirtsch.*) dependent on economic trends *postpos.;* **~abschwächung** *die* (*Wirtsch.*) economic downturn; **~aufschwung** *der* (*Wirtsch.*) economic upturn; upturn in the economy; **~barometer** *das* (*Wirtsch.*) graph of leading economic indicators; (*fig.*) economic barometer; **~bedingt** *Adj.* (*Wirtsch.*) due to economic trends *postpos.;* cyclical; **~bericht** *der* (*Wirtsch.*) report on the economy

**konjunkturell** /kɔnjʊŋktu'rɛl/ ❶ *Adj.* economic; **die ~e Entwicklung** the development of the economy. ❷ *adv.* **~ bedingt** due to economic trends *postpos.*

**konjunktur-, Konjunktur-: ~entwicklung** *die* (*Wirtsch.*) economic trends *pl.;* **~flaute** *die* (*Wirtsch.*) [economic] recession; **~gerecht** *Adj.* (*Wirtsch.*) in keeping with the needs of the economy *postpos.;* **~politik** *die* (*Wirtsch.*) stabilization policy; measures *pl.* aimed at avoiding violent fluctuations in the economy; **~ritter** *der* (*Wirtsch. abwertend*) opportunist; **~rückgang** *der* (*Wirtsch.*) [economic] recession; decline in economic activity; **~schwankung** *die* (*Wirtsch.*) fluctuation in the level of economic activity; **~spritze** *die* (*Wirtsch. ugs.*) boost to the economy; **~zyklus** *der* (*Wirtsch.*) trade cycle

**konkav** /kɔn'ka:f/ (*Optik*) ❶ *Adj.* concave. ❷ *adv.* concavely

**Konkav·spiegel** *der* (*Optik*) concave mirror

**Konklave** /kɔn'kla:və/ *das;* **~s, ~n** (*kath. Kirche*) conclave

**Konklusion** /kɔnklu'zi̯o:n/ *die;* **~, ~en** (*bes. Philos.*) conclusion

**Konkordanz** /kɔnkɔr'dants/ *die;* **~, ~en** (*Wissensch.*) concordance

**Konkordat** /kɔnkɔr'da:t/ *das;* **~[e]s, ~e** concordat

**konkret** /kɔn'kre:t/ ❶ *Adj.* concrete; **~e Literatur/Musik** concrete poetry/music. ❷ *adv.* Ⓐ (*nicht abstrakt*) in concrete terms; **kannst du mal ~ sagen, was du damit meinst?** could you tell me exactly what you mean by that?; **kannst du dich etwas ~er ausdrücken?** could you be a bit more specific [about that]?; Ⓑ (*in der Praxis*) in practice

**konkretisieren** *tr. V.* **etw. ~:** put sth. in concrete terms

**Konkubinat** /kɔnkubi'na:t/ *das;* **~[e]s, ~e** (*Rechtsw.*) concubinage; **mit jmdm. im ~ leben** live in concubinage with sb.

**Konkubine** /kɔnku'bi:nə/ *die;* **~, ~n** Ⓐ (*hist.*) concubine; Ⓑ (*abwertend: Geliebte*) mistress

**Konkurrent** /kɔnkʊ'rɛnt/ *der;* **~en, ~en, Konkurrentin** *die;* **~, ~nen** rival; (*Sport, Wirtsch.*) competitor

**Konkurrenz** /kɔnkʊ'rɛnts/ *die;* **~, ~en** Ⓐ (*Rivalität*) rivalry *no indef. art.;* (*Sport, Wirtsch.*) competition *no indef. art.;* **jmdm. ~ machen** compete with sb.; **mit jmdm. in ~ treten/stehen** enter into/be in competition with sb.; Ⓑ (*Wettbewerb*) competition; **außer ~ starten/teilnehmen** take part as an unofficial competitor; Ⓒ (*die Konkurrenten*) competition

**konkurrenz-, Konkurrenz-: ~druck** *der* pressure of competition; **~fähig** *Adj.* competitive; **~kampf** *der* competition; (*zwischen zwei Menschen*) rivalry; **~los** *Adj.* ‹product, firm, etc.› that has no competition *or* competitors; (*unvergleichlich*) unrivalled; **~los sein** have no competition *or* competitors; **~unternehmen** *das* rival company *or* concern; **zwei ~unternehmen** two rival *or* competing companies *or* concerns

**konkurrieren** *itr. V.* compete; **mit jmdm./etw. [um etw.] ~:** compete with sb./sth. [for sth.]

**Konkurs** /kɔn'kʊrs/ *der;* **~es, ~e** Ⓐ (*Bankrott*) bankruptcy; **~ machen** *od.* **in ~ gehen** go bankrupt; **[den] ~ anmelden** file for bankruptcy; have oneself declared bankrupt; Ⓑ (*gerichtliches Verfahren*) bankruptcy proceedings *pl.*

**Konkurs-: ~masse** *die* (*Wirtsch.*) bankrupt's assets *pl.;* **~verfahren** *das* (*Wirtsch.*) bankruptcy proceedings *pl.;* **~verwalter** *der*, **~verwalterin** *die* (*Wirtsch.*) receiver

**können** /'kœnən/ ❶ *unr. Modalverb; 2. Part.* **~** ▶ 466 Ⓐ (*vermögen*) be able to; **er hat/hätte es machen ~:** he was able to *or* he could do it/he could have done it; **er kann es machen/nicht machen** he can do it *or* is able to do it/cannot *or* (*coll.*) can't do it *or* is unable to do it; **er kann gut reden/tanzen** he can talk/dance well; he is a good talker/dancer; **Auto fahren/Klavier spielen ~:** be able to drive [a car]/play the piano; **er kann Auto fahren** he can drive; **ich kann nicht schlafen** I cannot *or* (*coll.*) can't sleep; **er konnte das genau hören/sehen** he could hear/see everything; **er konnte nicht bleiben** he couldn't stay; **ich kann das nicht mehr hören/sehen** I can't stand *or* bear to hear it/can't stand *or* bear the sight of it any longer (*coll.*); **ich kann dir sagen!** (*ugs.*) I can tell you; **nirgends kann man besser jagen als in ...** nowhere is the hunting *or* shooting better than in ...;(*die Möglichkeit haben*) **kann das explodieren?** could it explode?; **er kann jeden Moment kommen** he may come at any moment; **wer kann es sein/gewesen sein?** who can it be/could it have been?; **man kann nie wissen** you never know; one never knows; **es kann sein, dass ...** it may be that ...; **das könnte [gut] sein** that could [well] be the case; **das kann nicht sein** that's not possible; **kann ich Ihnen helfen?** can I help you?; **~ Sie mir sagen, ...?** can you tell me ...?; **~ Sie nicht grüßen?** don't you know how to salute?; **kannst du nicht aufpassen?** can't you be more careful?; **kann sein** (*ugs.*) could be (*coll.*); **kann sein, kann nicht sein** (*ugs.*) might be, might not be (*coll.*); **Kommst du morgen? — Kann sein** Are you coming tomorrow? — Might do; Ⓑ (*Grund haben*) **du kannst ganz ruhig sein** you don't have to worry; **wir ~ uns/er kann sich freuen, dass ...** we can/he should be glad that ...; **er kann sie/es nicht leiden** he can't stand her/it; **er kann einem Leid tun** (*ugs.*) you have to feel sorry for him; **das kann man wohl sagen!** you could well say that; Ⓒ (*dürfen*) **kann ich gehen?** can I go?; **~ wir mitkommen?** can we come too?; **du kannst mich [mal]!** (*salopp verhüll.*) you can get stuffed (*sl.*); you know what you can do (*coll.*).
❷ *unr. tr. V.* Ⓐ (*beherrschen*) know ‹language›; be able to play, know how to play ‹game›; **sie kann das [gut]** she can do that [well]; **sie kann Mathe/kann keine Mathe** she can/can't do maths; **er kann etwas auf seinem Gebiet** he has quite a lot of know-how in his field; **hast du die Hausaufgabe gekonnt?** could you do the homework?; **ein Gedicht ~:** know a poem [by heart]; **er lief, was er konnte** he ran as fast as he could;**etwas/nichts für etwas ~:** be/not be responsible for sth.; **was kann ich dafür?** what am I supposed to do about it?
❸ *unr. itr. V.* Ⓐ (*fähig sein*) **er kann nicht anders** there's nothing else he can do; (*es ist seine Art*) he can't help it (*coll.*); **~ vor Lachen** (*ugs.*) I would if I could; Ⓑ (*Zeit haben*) **ich kann heute nicht** I can't today (*coll.*); Ⓒ (*ugs.: Kraft haben*) **kannst du noch?** can you go on?; **der Läufer konnte nicht mehr** the runner could not go on; Ⓓ (*ugs.: essen ~*) **für mich keinen Nachtisch, ich kann nicht mehr** no dessert for me, I couldn't manage any more; Ⓔ (*ugs.: umgehen ~*) **[gut] mit jmdm. ~:** get on *or* along [well] with sb.

**Können** *das;* **~s** ability; (*Kunstfertigkeit*) skill

**Könner** *der;* **~s, ~, Könnerin** *die;* **~, ~nen** expert

**Konnex** /kɔ'nɛks/ *der;* **~es, ~e** (*geh.*) Ⓐ (*Zusammenhang*) connection; link; Ⓑ (*Kontakt*) contact

**Konnossement** /kɔnɔsə'mɛnt/ *das;* **~[e]s, ~e** (*Seew.*) bill of lading

**Konnotation** /kɔnota'tsi̯o:n/ *die;* **~, ~en** (*Sprachw.*) connotation

**konnte** /'kɔntə/ *1. u. 3. Pers. Sg. Prät. v.* **können**

**könnte** /'kœntə/ *1. u. 3. Pers. Sg. Konjunktiv II v.* **können**

**Konrektor** /'kɔnrɛktɔr/ *der;* **~s, ~en** /-'to:rən/, **Konrektorin** *die;* **~, ~nen** (*Schulw.*) deputy head[master]

**Konsekration** /kɔnzekra'tsi̯o:n/ *die;* **~, ~en** (*kath. Kirche*) consecration

**konsekutiv** /kɔnzeku'ti:f/ *Adj.* (*auch Sprachw.*) consecutive; **~es Dolmetschen** consecutive interpreting

**Konsekutiv·satz** *der* (*Sprachw.*) consecutive clause

**Konsens** /kɔn'zɛns/ *der;* **~es, ~e** Ⓐ (*Übereinstimmung*) consensus; Ⓑ (*veralt.: Zustimmung*) consent

**konsequent** /kɔnze'kvɛnt/ ❶ *Adj.* Ⓐ (*folgerichtig*) logical; logically consistent, logical ‹thinking, argumentation›; Ⓑ (*unbeirrbar*) consistent; Ⓒ (*Sport*) close, tight ‹marking›. ❷ *adv.* Ⓐ (*folgerichtig*) logically; Ⓑ (*unbeirrbar*) consistently; **ein Ziel ~ verfolgen** resolutely and single-mindedly pursue a goal; **~ durchgreifen** take rigorous action; Ⓒ (*Sport*) ‹mark› closely, tightly

**konsequenter·maßen, konsequenter·weise** *Adv.* to be consistent

**Konsequenz** /kɔnze'kvɛnts/ *die;* **~, ~en** Ⓐ (*Folge*) consequence; **die ~en tragen** take the consequences; **[aus etw.] die ~en ziehen** draw the obvious conclusion [from sth.]; (*gezwungenermaßen*) accept the obvious consequences [of sth.]; Ⓑ (*Unbeirrbarkeit*) resolution; determination; **einer Sache** (*Dat.*) **mit ~ nachgehen** investigate sth. rigorously; Ⓒ (*Folgerichtigkeit*) logicality; (*eines Gedankenganges, einer Argumentation*) logical consistency; logicality

**konservativ** /kɔnzɛrva'ti:f/ ❶ *Adj.* (*auch Med.*) conservative; (*die ~e Partei betreffend*) Conservative. ❷ *adv.* (*althergebracht*) conservatively

**Konservative** *der/die; adj. Dekl.* conservative; **die ~n** (*Politik*) the Conservatives

**Konservativismus** *der;* **~:** conservativism

**Konservator** /kɔnzɛr'va:tɔr/ *der;* **~s, ~en** /-'to:rən/, **Konservatorin** *die;* **~, ~nen** curator; keeper

k

# können

Es kommen hauptsächlich zwei Übersetzungen in Betracht: **to be able to** (die einzige Möglichkeit im Infinitiv und im Futur und den anderen zusammengesetzten Zeiten) und **can/could**. Im Präsens ist **can** fast immer möglich und in vielen Fällen vorzuziehen. In der Vergangenheit dagegen ist **was able to** manchmal vorzuziehen, da **could** auch konditional sein kann (= *könnte*).

***Es ist wichtig, kochen zu können***
= It is important to be able to cook

***Wenn sie frei bekommt, wird sie hingehen können***
= If she gets time off she will be able to go there

***Er kann sie oft durch einen Freund bekommen***
= He can often get them *od.* is often able to get them through a friend

***Ich kann es nur mit einer Brille lesen***
= I can only read it with spectacles

***Er kann sie nicht leiden***
= He can't stand her

***Sie können** (= dürfen) **rauchen, wenn Sie wollen***
= You can smoke if you wish

***Ich konnte mit vier Jahren lesen***
= I could *od.* was able to read at the age of four

***Sie konnten nicht früher kommen***
= They couldn't *od.* were unable to come any earlier

In den beiden letzten Beispielen ist keine Verwechslung möglich.

***Er konnte sie durch einen Freund bekommen***
= He was able to get them through a friend

Aber:

***Er könnte sie durch einen Freund bekommen***
= He could get them through a friend

Im Perfekt, auch konditional:

***Glücklicherweise habe ich umbuchen können***
= Fortunately I was able/have been able to change the booking

***Sie hätten uns Bescheid sagen können***
= You could have let us know

Und schließlich im Plusquamperfekt:

***Sie hatte das Buch nicht finden können***
= She had been unable to find the book

## Bitten und Vorschläge

***Könntest du mir helfen?***
= Could you help me?

***Könnten Sie vielleicht Freitag kommen?***
= Perhaps you could come on Friday?

## Unpersönlicher Gebrauch: may, might

***Es kann sein, dass er es vergessen hat***
= It may be that he has forgotten it, He may have forgotten it

***Es könnte sein, dass wir es noch brauchen***
= We might still need it

***Es könnte ratsam sein, sie anzurufen***
= It might be advisable to telephone her

***Das kann nicht sein***
= That's not posssible, It can't be

k

**Konservatorium** /kɔnzɛrva'to:ri̯ʊm/ *das;* **~s, Konservatorien** conservatoire; conservatory (*Amer.*)

**Konserve** /kɔn'zɛrvə/ *die;* ~, **~n** Ⓐ (*Büchse*) can; tin (*Brit.*); **Musik aus der ~** (*fig. ugs.*) canned music (*coll.*); Ⓑ (*konservierte Lebensmittel*) preserved food; (*in Dosen*) canned *or* (*Brit.*) tinned food; **von ~n leben** eat out of cans *or* (*Brit.*) tins; live on canned *or* (*Brit.*) tinned food; Ⓒ (*Med.*: *Blut~*) stored blood

**Konserven-: ~büchse** *die*, **~dose** *die* can; tin (*Brit.*); **~fabrik** *die* canning factory; cannery; **~nahrung** *die* canned *or* (*Brit.*) tinned food

**konservierbar** *Adv.* preservable

**konservieren** *tr. V.* preserve; conserve, preserve ‹building, work of art›

**Konservierung** *die;* ~, **~en** preservation; (*von Gebäuden, Kunstwerken usw.*) conservation; preservation

**Konservierungs-: ~mittel** *das*, **~stoff** *der* preservative

**konsistent** /kɔnzɪs'tɛnt/ *Adj.* Ⓐ (*zähflüssig*) stiff; Ⓑ (*beständig*) stable; Ⓒ (*widerspruchsfrei*) consistent

**Konsistenz** /kɔnzɪs'tɛnts/ *die;* ~, **~en** Ⓐ (*Beschaffenheit*) consistency; Ⓑ (*Stabilität*) stability

**Konsistorium** /kɔnzɪs'to:ri̯ʊm/ (*kath. Kirche*) *das;* **~s, Konsistorien** consistory

**Konsole** /kɔn'zo:lə/ *die;* ~, **~n** Ⓐ (*Archit.*) console; Ⓑ (*Brett*) shelf; (*Tischchen*) console [table]

**konsolidieren** /kɔnzoli'di:rən/ ❶ *tr. V.* Ⓐ (*festigen*) consolidate; Ⓑ (*Wirtsch.*) (*in Anleihen umwandeln*) fund ‹debts›; (*vereinigen*) consolidate ‹debts›. ❷ *refl. V.* become consolidated

**Konsolidierung** *die;* ~, **~en** Ⓐ (*Festigung*) consolidation; Ⓑ (*Wirtsch.*) (*Umwandlung in Anleihen*) funding; (*Vereinigung*) consolidation

**Konsonant** /kɔnzo'nant/ *der;* **~en, ~en** consonant

**konsonantisch** (*Sprachw.*) ❶ *Adj.* consonantal. ❷ *adv.* ‹pronounce› as a consonant

**Konsorten** /kɔn'zɔrtn̩/ *Pl.* (*abwertend*) **Meier und ~:** Meier and his lot *or* crowd (*coll.*); Meier and Co. (*coll.*)

**Konsortium** /kɔn'zɔrtsi̯ʊm/ *das;* **~s, Konsortien** (*Wirtsch.*) consortium

**Konspekt** /kɔn'spɛkt/ *der;* **~[e]s, ~e** (*DDR*) synopsis; summary

**Konspiration** /kɔnspira'tsi̯o:n/ *die;* ~, **~en** conspiracy

**konspirativ** /kɔnspira'ti:f/ ❶ *Adj.* conspiratorial; **eine ~e Wohnung** a flat (*Brit.*) *or* (*Amer.*) an apartment used by persons engaged in subversive activities. ❷ *adv.* **sich ~ zusammenschließen** form a conspiracy

**konspirieren** *itr. V.* conspire, plot (**gegen** against)

**konstant** /kɔn'stant/ ❶ *Adj.* Ⓐ (*gleich bleibend, ständig*) constant; **eine ~e Größe** (*Math.*) a constant quantity; **eine ~e Leistung zeigen** maintain a consistent standard; Ⓑ (*beharrlich*) consistent; persistent. ❷ *adv.* Ⓐ (*gleich bleibend*) constantly; **wir hatten ~ schlechtes Wetter** we had consistently bad weather; Ⓑ (*beharrlich*) consistently; persistently

**Konstante** *die;* **~[n], ~n** (*Math., Physik*) constant; (*fig.*) constant factor (+ *Gen.* in)

**Konstantin** /'kɔnstanti:n/ (*der*) Constantine

**Konstantinopel** /kɔnstanti'no:pl̩/ (*das*); **~s** (*hist.*) Constantinople

**Konstanz** /kɔn'stants/ *die;* **~:** constancy

**konstatieren** /kɔnsta'ti:rən/ *tr. V.* Ⓐ (*feststellen*) establish ‹facts›; (*wahrnehmen*) detect ‹changes etc.›; Ⓑ (*erklären*) state

**Konstellation** /kɔnstɛla'tsi̯o:n/ *die;* ~, **~en** Ⓐ (*von Parteien usw.*) grouping; (*von Umständen*) combination; **die gesamte ~:** the whole situation; Ⓑ (*Astron., Astrol.*) constellation

**konsternieren** /kɔnstɛr'ni:rən/ *tr. V.* **jmdn. ~:** fill sb. with consternation

**konsterniert** ❶ ⇒ **konsternieren.** ❷ *Adj.* filled with consternation *pred.* ❸ *adv.* with consternation; **sie blickte ihn ~ an** she looked at him in consternation

**Konstituente** /kɔnsti'tu̯ɛntə/ *die;* ~, **~n** (*Sprachw.*) constituent

**konstituieren** /kɔnstitu'i:rən/ ❶ *tr. V.* (*gründen*) constitute; set up; (*für etw. konstitutiv sein*) constitute; **die ~de Versammlung** the constituent assembly. ❷ *refl. V.* be constituted

**Konstitution** /kɔnstitu'tsi̯o:n/ *die;* ~, **~en** (*auch Politik, Chemie*) constitution

**konstitutionell** /kɔnstitutsi̯o'nɛl/ (*Politik, Med.*) ❶ *Adj.* constitutional. ❷ *adv.* constitutionally

**konstitutiv** /kɔnstitu'ti:f/ *Adj.* (*geh.*) constitutive; **für etw. ~ sein** be a[n essential] constitutive element of sth.

**konstruieren** /kɔnstru'i:rən/ *tr. V.* Ⓐ (*entwerfen*) design; (*entwerfen und zusammenbauen*) design and construct; Ⓑ (*aufbauen, Geom.*) construct; Ⓒ (*Sprachw.*) construct; **dieses Verb wird mit dem Dativ konstruiert** this verb takes the dative *or* is construed with the dative; Ⓓ (*abwertend: künstlich aufbauen*) fabricate; **ein konstruierter Fall** a hypothetical *or* fictitious case; **die Handlung/seine Begründung wirkt sehr konstruiert** the plot seems/his reasons *pl.* seem very contrived

**Konstrukteur** /kɔnstrʊk'tø:ɐ̯/ *der;* **~s, ~e, Konstrukteurin** *die;* ~, **~nen** ▶ 159 designer; design engineer

**Konstruktion** /kɔnstrʊk'tsi̯o:n/ *die;* ~, **~en** Ⓐ (*Aufbau, Geom., Sprachw.*) construction; (*das Entwerfen*) designing; (*das Entwerfen und Zusammenbauen*) designing and construction; Ⓑ (*Entwurf*) design; (*Bau*) construction; structure

**Konstruktions-: ~büro** *das* drawing office; **~fehler** *der* design fault

**konstruktiv** /kɔnstrʊk'ti:f/ ❶ *Adj.* Ⓐ constructive; **ein ~es Misstrauensvotum**

*old spelling (see note on page 1707)

(*Parl.*) a constructive vote of no confidence; (B) (*Technik*) constructional. ❷ *adv.* (A) constructively; (B) (*Technik*) with regard to construction

**Konstruktivismus** *der;* ~ (*bild. Kunst*) constructivism *no art.*

**Konsul** /'kɔnzʊl/ *der;* **~s**, **~n** ▶91, ▶159 (*Dipl., hist.*) consul

**konsularisch** *Adj.* (*Dipl.*) consular

**Konsulat** /kɔnzu'la:t/ *das;* **~[e]s**, **~e** (*Dipl., hist.: Amt*) consulate

**Konsulin** *die;* **~**, **~nen** ⇒ **Konsul**

**Konsultation** /kɔnzʊlta'tsi̯o:n/ *die;* **~**, **~en** consultation; **sich zu ~en treffen** meet for consultations

**konsultieren** *tr. V.* (*auch fig.*) consult

**Konsum**[1] /kɔn'zu:m/ *der;* **~s** consumption (**an** + *Dat.* of); **der ~ von Alkohol steigt** alcohol consumption is on the increase

**Konsum**[2] /'kɔnzu:m/ *der;* **~s**, **~s** (A) (*Genossenschaft*) cooperative society; (B) (*Laden*) cooperative shop *or* store; co-op (*coll.*)

**-konsum** *der;* **-~s** ... consumption

**Konsum·artikel** *der* (*Wirtsch.*) consumer item *or* article; **~** *Pl.* consumer goods

**Konsumation** /kɔnzuma'tsi̯o:n/ *die;* **~**, **~en** (*österr., schweiz.*) consumption

**Konsument** /kɔnzu'mɛnt/ *der;* **~en**, **~en**, **Konsumentin** *die;* **~**, **~nen** consumer

**Konsum-:** **~genossenschaft** *die* (*Wirtsch.*) cooperative society; **~gesellschaft** *die* consumer society; **~gewohnheiten** *Pl.* (*Wirtsch.*) consumer habits

**Konsum·gut** *das* (*Wirtsch.*) ⇒ **Konsumartikel**

**Konsumgüter·industrie** *die* (*Wirtsch.*) consumer goods industry

**konsumieren** *tr. V.* consume; (*fig.*) devour ‹book›

**Konsum-:** **~terror** *der* (*abwertend*) pressure to buy (*generated in a consumer society*); **~verzicht** *der* reduction in consumption; **~zwang** *der* pressure to buy (*generated in a consumer society*)

**Kontakt** /kɔn'takt/ *der;* **~[e]s**, **~e** (A) (*auch fachspr.*) contact; **mit** *od.* **zu jmdm. ~ haben/halten** be/remain in contact *or* touch with sb.; **mit jmdm. [keinen] ~ bekommen** [not] get to know sb.; **[den] ~ mit jmdm./etw. finden/suchen** establish/try to establish contact with sb./sth.; **er findet keinen ~ zu seinen Zuhörern** he cannot establish a rapport with his audience; **in ~ mit jmdm. stehen** be in contact *or* touch with sb.; **den ~ zu jmdm. abbrechen/verlieren** break off contact/lose contact *or* touch with sb.; **mit jmdm. ~ aufnehmen** get into contact with sb.; contact sb.; (B) (*Elektrot.*) contact; **die Klingel hat/die Drähte haben keinen ~:** the bell is not connected up properly/the wires are not making contact

**kontakt-, Kontakt-:** **~abzug** *der* (*Fot.*) contact print; **~anzeige** *die* contact advertisement; **~arm** *Adj.* **~arm sein** not make friends easily; find it difficult to make friends; **~aufnahme** *die:* **unsere erste ~aufnahme mit dieser Firma** our first approach to this firm; **~bereichs·beamte** *der* community policeman

**kontakten** ❶ *tr. V.* contact. ❷ *itr. V.* make contacts

**kontakt-, Kontakt-:** **~fähig** *Adj.* **ein ~fähiger Mensch** a good mixer; **ein ~fähiger Mitarbeiter** a colleague who is able to communicate easily with people; **~feder** *die* (*Elektrot.*) contact spring; **~freudig** *Adj.* sociable; **~freudig sein** make friends easily; **~hof** *der:* [*inner*] *courtyard of an eros centre etc. where prostitutes wait for clients*

**kontaktieren** *tr. V.* contact

**kontakt-, Kontakt-:** **~linse** *die* contact lens; **~los** *Adj.* friendless; lonely; **~mangel** *der* lack of social contact; **~mann** *der; Pl.:* **~männer** *od.* **~leute** (*Agent*) contact; **~nahme** *die;* **~~**, **~~n** ⇒ **~aufnahme**; **~person** *die* (*Med.*) contact; **~pflege** *die:* **~pflege betreiben** be sociable; mix socially; **~schale** *die* ⇒ **~linse**; **~schwelle** *die* (*Verkehrsw.*) vehicle detector pad; **~schwierigkeiten** *Pl.* problems in mixing with others; **~sperre** *die* (*Rechtsw.*) ban on visits and letters; **~sperre über jmdn. verhängen** ban all sb.'s visits and letters; **~studium** *das* (*Hochschulw.*) *in-service study undertaken to keep up with the latest developments in one's field*

**Kontamination** /kɔntamina'tsi̯o:n/ *die;* **~**, **~en** (A) (*bes. Med., Biol., Milit.*) contamination; (B) (*Sprachw.*) contamination; blending; (*Wort*) blend

**kontaminieren** *tr. V.* (A) (*bes. Med., Biol., Milit.*) contaminate; (B) (*Sprachw.*) blend

**Kontemplation** /kɔntɛmpla'tsi̯o:n/ *die;* **~**, **~en** (*geh.*) contemplation

**kontemplativ** /kɔntɛmpla'ti:f/ (*geh.*) ❶ *Adj.* contemplative. ❷ *adv.* contemplatively

**Konten** ⇒ **Konto**

**Kontenance** ⇒ **Contenance**

**Konten·bewegung** *die* (*Bankw.*) change in the state of the/an account

**Konter** /'kɔntɐ/ *der;* **~s**, **~** (A) (*Boxen*) counter; (B) (*Ballspiele*) counter-attack

**Konter-:** **~admiral** *der* (*Marine*) rear admiral; **~bande** *die* (A) (*Völkerrecht*) contraband [of war]; (B) (*veralt.: Schmuggelware*) contraband

**Konterfei** /'kɔntɐfai̯/ *das;* **~s**, **~s** *od.* **~e** (*veralt., noch scherzh.*) likeness

**konterfeien** *tr. V.* (*veralt., noch scherzh.*) paint/draw a likeness of

**kontern** *tr., itr. V.* (*Boxen*) counter; (*Ballspiele*) counter-attack; (*fig.*) counter (**mit** with)

**konter-, Konter-:** **~revolution** *die* counter-revolution; **~revolutionär** *Adj.* counter-revolutionary; **~revolutionär** *der,* **~revolutionärin** *die* counter-revolutionary; **~schlag** *der* (*Boxen*) counter; (*Ballspiele, fig.*) counter-attack

**Kontext** /kɔn'tɛkst/ *der;* **~[e]s**, **~e** (*auch Sprachw.*) context

**Konti** ⇒ **Konto**

**Kontinent** /kɔnti'nɛnt/ *der;* **~[e]s**, **~e** continent

**kontinental** /kɔntinɛn'ta:l/ *Adj.* continental

**Kontinental-:** **~klima** *das* (*Geogr.*) continental climate; **~sockel** *der* (*Geogr.*) continental shelf; **~sperre** *die* (*hist.*) Continental System; **~verschiebung** *die* (*Geol.*) continental drift

**Kontingent** /kɔntɪŋ'gɛnt/ *das;* **~[e]s**, **~e** (A) (*Menge*) quota; (*fig.*) contingent; (B) (*Truppen~*) contingent

**kontingentieren** *tr. V.* (*bes. Wirtsch.*) limit by quotas; impose quotas on; (*rationieren*) ration

**Kontingentierung** *die;* **~**, **~en** (*bes. Wirtsch.*) imposition of quotas (*Gen.* on)

**kontinuierlich** /kɔntinu'i:ɐ̯lɪç/ ❶ *Adj.* steady; continuous; **eine ~e Außenpolitik** a consistent foreign policy. ❷ *adv.* steadily

**Kontinuität** /kɔntinui̯'tɛ:t/ *die;* **~:** continuity

**Kontinuum** /kɔn'ti:nuʊm/ *das;* **~s**, **Kontinua** *od.* **Kontinuen** continuum

**Konto** /'kɔnto/ *das;* **~s**, **Konten** *od.* **Konti** account; **ein laufendes ~:** a current account; **die nächste Runde geht auf mein ~** (*ugs.*) the next round is on me (*coll.*); **etw. geht auf jmds. ~** (*ugs.: jmd. ist schuld an etw.*) sb. is to blame *or* is responsible for sth.

**Konto-:** **~aus·zug** *der* (*Bankw.*) [bank] statement; statement of account; **~auszugsdrucker** *der* (*Bankw.*) statement machine *or* printer; **~buch** *das* (*Buchf.*) account book; **~führungsgebühr** *die* (*Bankw.*) bank charges *pl.;* **~inhaber** *der,* **~inhaberin** *die* (*Bankw.*) account holder; holder of an/the account; **~korrent** /-kɔ'rɛnt/ *das;* **~~s**, **~~e** (A) (*Wirtsch.*) open account; (B) (*Buchf.*) open accounting *no art.;* **~nummer** *die* account number

**Kontor** /kɔn'to:ɐ̯/ *das;* **~s**, **~e** (A) (*Niederlassung*) (*eines Handelsunternehmens*) branch; (*einer Reederei*) office; (B) (*DDR: Handelszentrale*) wholesale organization; (C) (*veralt.: Büro*) office; ⇒ *auch* **Schlag** A

**Kontorist** *der;* **~en**, **~en**, **Kontoristin** *die;* **~**, **~nen** [office] clerk; ⇒ *auch* **-in**

**Konto·stand** *der* (*Bankw.*) balance; state of an/one's account

**kontra** /'kɔntra/ ❶ *Präp. mit Akk.* (*Rechtsspr., auch fig.*) versus. ❷ *Adv.* against; **ich bin dazu ~ eingestellt** I am against it

**Kontra** *das;* **~s**, **~s** (*Kartenspiele*) double; **~ sagen** *od.* **geben** double; **jmdm. ~ geben** (*fig. ugs.*) flatly contradict sb.

**Kontra·bass**, ***Kontra·baß** *der* (*Musik*) double bass

**kontradiktorisch** /kɔntradɪk'to:rɪʃ/ ❶ *Adj.* contradictory. ❷ *adv.* in a contradictory way

**Kontra·fagott** *das* (*Musik*) double bassoon; contrabassoon

**Kontrahent** /kɔntra'hɛnt/ *der;* **~en**, **~en**, **Kontrahentin** *die;* **~**, **~nen** (A) (*Gegner[in]*) adversary; opponent; (B) (*Rechtsw., Kaufmannsspr.: Vertragspartner[in]*) contracting party

**kontrahieren** ❶ *itr., refl. V.* (*Biol., Med.*) contract. ❷ *tr. V.* (A) (*Biol., Med.*) contract; (B) (*Rechtsw., Kaufmannsspr.*) **Erdgaslieferungen ~:** contract to supply natural gas

**Kontrakt** /kɔn'trakt/ *der;* **~[e]s**, **~e** contract

**Kontraktion** /kɔntrak'tsi̯o:n/ *die;* **~**, **~en** (*Med., Sprachw.*) contraction

**kontraktlich** ❶ *Adj.* contractual. ❷ *adv.* contractually; by contract

**Kontra·punkt** *der* (*Musik, fig.*) counterpoint

**kontrapunktisch** (*Musik, fig.*) ❶ *Adj.* contrapuntal. ❷ *adv.* contrapuntally

**konträr** /kɔn'trɛ:ɐ̯/ ❶ contrary; opposite. ❷ *adv.* **zwei so ~ gesinnte Politiker** two politicians with such opposing views; **sich ~ entwickeln** develop in contrary *or* opposite ways

**Kontrast** /kɔn'trast/ *der;* **~[e]s**, **~e** (*auch Fot., Film, Fernsehen*) contrast; **etw. steht im/in ~ zu etw. anderem** sth. is in contrast with sth. else

**Kontrast-:** **~brei** *der* (*Med.*) opaque *or* test meal; **~farbe** *die* contrasting colour; **~filter** *der* (*Fot.*) contrast filter

**kontrastieren** *tr., itr. V.* contrast

**kontrastiv** /kɔntras'ti:f/ *Adj.* (*Sprachw.*) contrastive

**kontrast-, Kontrast-:** **~mittel** *das* (*Med.*) contrast medium; **~programm** *das* (*Rundf., Fernsehen*) alternative programme; **~reich** *Adj.* rich in *or* full of contrasts *pred.;* richly varied

**Kontrazeptivum** /kɔntratsɛp'ti:vʊm/ *das;* **~s**, **Kontrazeptiva** (*Med.*) contraceptive

**Kontribution** /kɔntribu'tsi̯o:n/ *die;* **~**, **~en** (*hist.*) contribution

**Kontroll·abschnitt** *der* stub

***Kontrollampe** ⇒ **Kontrolllampe**

**Kontroll-:** **~apparat** *der* supervisory apparatus; (*Polizei, Geheimdienst o. Ä.*) surveillance and control apparatus; **~beamte** *der,* **~beamtin** *die* inspector; (*an der Pass-/Zollkontrolle*) passport/customs officer; **~behörde** *die* monitoring authority

**Kontrolle** /kɔn'trɔlə/ *die;* **~**, **~n** (A) (*Überwachung*) surveillance; **unter ~ stehen** be under surveillance; **der ~ durch das Parlament unterliegen** be under the scrutiny of Parliament; **eine gegenseitige ~ ausüben** keep a check on each other; (B) (*Überprüfung*) check; (*bei Waren*) check; inspection; (*bei Lebensmitteln*) inspection; **~n durchführen** carry out checks/inspections; **jmdn./etw. einer ~ unterziehen** check sb./sth.; **Anwärter auf eine Stelle einer ~ unterziehen** screen candidates for a post; **in eine ~ kommen** be stopped at a police check; **zur ~:** as a check; (C) (*Herrschaft*) control; **die ~ über etw.** (*Akk.*) **verlieren** lose control of sth.; **die ~ über sich** (*Akk.*) **verlieren** lose control of oneself; **außer ~ geraten** get out of control; **etw. unter ~** (*Akk.*) **bringen/halten** get *or* bring/keep sth. under control; (D) (**~punkt**) checkpoint; (*an der Pass~/Zoll~*) passport control/customs

**Kontrolleur** /kɔntrɔ'lø:ɐ̯/ *der;* **~s**, **~e**, **Kontrolleurin** *die;* **~**, **~nen** inspector

**Kontroll-: ~funktion** *die* monitoring function; **~gang** *der* tour of inspection; (*eines Nachtwächters*) round; (*eines Polizisten*) patrol; **~gruppe** *die* (*Med., Psych., Soziol.*) control group

**kontrollierbar** *Adj.* ‹authority, body, decision, etc.› that is open to scrutiny; ‹statement, statistic, etc.› that is verifiable *or* checkable; demonstrable ‹progress›

**kontrollieren** ❶ *tr. V.* Ⓐ (*überwachen*) check; monitor; **die Regierung ~:** scrutinize the actions of the government; **die Lebensmittelproduktion wird streng kontrolliert** strict checks are kept *or* made on the production of food; Ⓑ (*überprüfen*) check; check, inspect ‹goods›; inspect ‹food›; **jmdn. auf etw.** (*Akk.*) **[hin] ~:** check sb. for sth.; **etw. auf etw.** (*Akk.*) **[hin] ~:** check/inspect sth. for sth.; Ⓒ (*beherrschen*) control. ❷ *itr. V.* carry out a check/checks

***Kontrolliste** ⇨ **Kontrollliste**

**Kontroll-: ~lampe** *die* pilot light; indicator light; (*Warnleuchte*) warning light; **~liste** *die* checklist; **~organ** *das* monitoring body; **~punkt** *der* checkpoint; (*bei einer Rallye*) control [point]; **~rat** *der* **Alliierter ~rat** Allied Control Commission; **~stempel** *der* (*auf Waren, Lebensmitteln*) inspection stamp; (*bei einer Rallye*) control stamp; **~turm** *der* control tower; **~uhr** *die* time clock; (*für Wächter*) telltale clock

**kontrovers** /kɔntro'vɛrs/ ❶ *Adj.* conflicting; (*strittig*) controversial. ❷ *adv.* **sich ~ zu etw. äußern** express conflicting opinions on sth.; **etw. ~ schildern** give conflicting accounts of sth.

**Kontroverse** *die;* **~, ~n** controversy (**um, über** + *Akk.* about)

**Kontur** /kɔn'tu:ɐ̯/ *die;* **~, ~en** contour; outline; **~ gewinnen/an ~ verlieren** (*fig.*) become clearer/fade

**Konturen·stift** *der* lip pencil

**konturieren** *tr. V.* (*auch fig.*) outline

**Konus** /'ko:nʊs/ *der;* **~, ~se** *od.* **Konen** (*Math., Technik*) cone

**Konvektor** /kɔn'vɛktɔr/ *der;* **~s, ~en** /-'to:rən/ convector [heater]

**konvenieren** /kɔnve'ni:rən/ *itr. V.* (*österr.*) **jmdm. ~:** be convenient for sb.; suit sb.

**Konvent** /kɔn'vɛnt/ *der;* **~es, ~e** Ⓐ (*kath. Kirche*) (*von Nonnen*) convent; (*von Mönchen*) monastery; Ⓑ (*Hochschulw.*) *qualified academic staff of a university*

**Konvention** /kɔnvɛn'tsi̯o:n/ *die;* **~, ~en** (*Verhaltensnorm, Völkerr.*) convention

**Konventional·strafe** *die* (*Rechtsw.*) liquidated damages *pl.*

**konventionell** ❶ *Adj.* Ⓐ (*herkömmlich*) conventional; **~e Waffen** (*Milit.*) conventional weapons; Ⓑ (*förmlich*) formal. ❷ *adv.* Ⓐ (*herkömmlich, Milit.*) conventionally; in a conventional way; Ⓑ (*förmlich*) formally; **hier geht es sehr ~ zu** things are very formal here

**konvergent** /kɔnvɛr'gɛnt/ (*geh., Math.*) ❶ *Adj.* convergent. ❷ *adv.* convergently

**Konvergenz** /kɔnvɛr'gɛnts/ *die;* **~, ~en** (*geh., Math.*) convergence

**Konvergenz·theorie** *die* (*Politik*) theory of convergence

**konvergieren** *tr. V.* (*geh., Math.*) converge

**Konversation** /kɔnvɛrza'tsi̯o:n/ *die;* **~, ~en** conversation; **~ in Französisch treiben** hold a conversation in French; **~ machen** make conversation

**Konversations·lexikon** *das* encyclopaedia

**Konversion** *die;* **~, ~en** (*Kirche, Sprachw., Psych., Kerntechnik, Börsenw.*) conversion

**Konverter** /kɔn'vɛrtɐ/ *der;* **~s, ~** Ⓐ (*Hüttenw., Rundfunk*) converter; Ⓑ (*Fot.*) converter [lens]

**konvertibel** /kɔnvɛr'ti:bl̩/, **konvertierbar** *Adj.* (*Wirtsch.*) convertible

**Konvertierbarkeit** *die;* **~** (*Wirtsch.*) convertibility

**konvertieren** ❶ *itr. V.; auch mit sein* (*Rel.*) be converted. ❷ *tr. V.* Ⓐ (*Wirtsch.*) convert; **sein Geld in Franken ~:** convert one's money into francs; Ⓑ (*DV*) convert

**Konvertit** /kɔnvɛr'ti:t/ *der;* **~en, ~en, Konvertitin** *die;* **~, ~nen** convert

**konvex** /kɔn'vɛks/ (*Optik*) ❶ *Adj.* convex. ❷ *adv.* convexly

**Konvex·spiegel** *der* (*Optik*) convex mirror

**Konvikt** /kɔn'vɪkt/ *das;* **~[e]s, ~e** Ⓐ (*Stift*) seminary; (*Wohnheim*) hall of residence (*for theology students*); Ⓑ (*österr.: kath. Internat*) [Roman Catholic] boarding school

**Konvoi** /kɔn'vɔy/ *der;* **~s, ~s** (*bes. Milit.*) convoy; **im ~ fahren** travel in convoy

**Konvolut** /kɔnvo'lu:t/ *das;* **~[e]s, ~e** bundle (*of letters, papers, etc.*)

**Konvulsion** /kɔnvʊl'zi̯o:n/ *die;* **~, ~en** (*Med.*) convulsion

**konvulsiv** /kɔnvʊl'zi:f/, **konvulsivisch** (*Med.*) ❶ *Adj.* convulsive. ❷ *adv.* convulsively

**konzedieren** /kɔntse'di:rən/ *tr. V.* (*geh.*) concede; **jmdm. etw. ~:** concede sb. sth.

**Konzentrat** /kɔntsɛn'tra:t/ *das;* **~[e]s, ~e** (*bes. Chemie*) concentrate; **ein ~ seiner früheren Werke** (*fig.*) a collection of his most important writings, chosen from his earlier works

**Konzentration** /kɔntsɛntra'tsi̯o:n/ *die;* **~, ~en** (*auch Chemie*) concentration

**Konzentrations-: ~fähigkeit** *die* ability to concentrate; powers *pl.* of concentration; **~lager** *das* (*bes. ns.*) concentration camp; **~mangel** *der* (*Med., Psych.*) lack of concentration; **~schwäche** *die* (*Med., Psych.*) poor powers *pl.* of concentration

**konzentrieren** ❶ *refl. V.* Ⓐ concentrate; **sich auf etw.** (*Akk.*) **~:** concentrate on sth.; Ⓑ (*richten*) be concentrated. ❷ *tr. V.* concentrate; **seine Gedanken auf etw.** (*Akk.*) **~:** concentrate one's thoughts on sth.

**konzentriert** ❶ ⇨ **konzentrieren**. ❷ *Adj.* (*auch Chemie*) concentrated. ❸ *adv.* with concentration; **sehr ~ arbeiten** work with great concentration

**konzentrisch** (*Math., fig.*) ❶ *Adj.* concentric. ❷ *adv.* concentrically

**Konzept** /kɔn'tsɛpt/ *das;* **~[e]s, ~e** Ⓐ (*Rohfassung*) [rough] draft; **es ist im ~ fertig** the [rough] draft is finished; **aus dem ~ kommen** *od.* **geraten** lose one's thread; **jmdn. aus dem ~ bringen** put sb. off his/her stroke; Ⓑ (*Programm*) programme; (*Plan*) plan; **jmdm. das ~ verderben** (*ugs.*) ruin sb.'s plans; **jmdm. nicht ins ~ passen** (*ugs.*) not suit sb.'s plans

**Konzeption** /kɔntsɛp'tsi̯o:n/ *die;* **~, ~en** Ⓐ central idea; (*Entwurf*) conception; Ⓑ (*Med.*) conception

**konzeptionslos** ❶ *Adj.* haphazard. ❷ *adv.* haphazardly; with no clear plan

**Konzeptionslosigkeit** *die;* **~:** haphazardness; lack of any clear plan

**Konzept·papier** *das* rough paper

**Konzern** /kɔn'tsɛrn/ *der;* **~[e]s, ~e** (*Wirtsch.*) group [of companies]

**-konzern** *der;* **-~[e]s, -~e** ... group

**Konzert** /kɔn'tsɛrt/ *das;* **~[e]s, ~e** Ⓐ (*Komposition*) concerto; Ⓑ (*Veranstaltung*) concert; **ins ~ gehen** go to a concert; Ⓒ (*geh.: Zusammenspiel*) concert

**Konzert-: ~abend** *der* concert evening; **~agentur** *die* concert artists' agency

**konzertant** /kɔntsɛr'tant/ *Adj.* (*Musik*) concert ‹performance etc.›; **~e Sinfonie** [sinfonia] concertante

**Konzert-: ~direktion** *die* concert promotion agency; **~flügel** *der* concert grand; **~führer** *der* concert guide

**konzertieren** *itr. V.* (*geh.*) give a concert

**konzertiert** ❶ ⇨ **konzertieren**. ❷ *Adj.* concerted; **die ~e Aktion** concerted action

**Konzertina** /kɔntsɛr'ti:na/ *die;* **~, ~s** concertina

**Konzert-: ~meister** *der,* **~meisterin** *die* ▶ 159 leader [of a/the orchestra]; concertmaster (*esp. Amer.*); **~pavillon** *der* bandstand; **~pianist** *der,* **~pianistin** *die* ▶ 159 concert pianist; **~reise** *die* concert tour; **~saal** *der* concert hall; **~sänger** *der,* **~sängerin** *die* concert singer

**Konzession** /kɔntsɛ'si̯o:n/ *die;* **~, ~en** Ⓐ (*Amtsspr.*) licence; Ⓑ (*Zugeständnis*) concession; **~en [an jmdn./etw.] machen** make concessions [to sb./sth.]

**Konzessionär** /kɔntsɛsi̯o'nɛ:ɐ̯/ *der;* **~s, ~e, Konzessionärin** *die;* **~, ~nen** (*Amtsspr.*) licensee

**konzessions·bereit** *Adj.* ready *or* willing *or* prepared to make concessions *pred.*

**konzessiv** /kɔntsɛ'si:f/ *Adj.* (*Sprachw.*) concessive

**Konzessiv·satz** *der* (*Sprachw.*) concessive clause

**Konzil** /kɔn'tsi:l/ *das;* **~s, ~e** *od.* **~ien** Ⓐ (*kath. Kirche*) council; Ⓑ (*Hochschulw.*) ≈ senate

**konziliant** /kɔntsi'li̯ant/ (*geh.*) ❶ *Adj.* accommodating; obliging. ❷ *adv.* accommodatingly; obligingly

**Konzilianz** /kɔntsi'li̯ants/ *die;* **~** (*geh.*) obligingness

**konzipieren** /kɔntsi'pi:rən/ ❶ *tr. V.* draft ‹speech, essay›; draw up, draft ‹plan, policy, etc.›; design ‹device, car, etc.›. ❷ *itr. V.* (*Med.*) conceive

**konzis** /kɔn'tsi:s/ ❶ *Adj.* concise. ❷ *adv.* concisely

**Koog** /ko:k/ *der;* **~[e]s, Köge** /'kø:gə/ (*niederd.*) polder

**Kooperation** *die;* **~, ~en** cooperation *no indef. art.*

**kooperations·bereit** *Adj.* ready *or* willing *or* prepared to cooperate *pred.*

**kooperativ** ❶ *Adj.* cooperative. ❷ *adv.* cooperatively

**Kooperativ** *das;* **~s, ~e, Kooperative** *die;* **~e, ~en** cooperative

**kooperieren** *tr. V.* cooperate

**Koordinate** *die;* **~, ~n** Ⓐ (*Geogr.*) coordinate; Ⓑ (*Math.*) coordinate

**Koordinaten-: ~achse** *die* (*Math.*) coordinate axis; **~kreuz** *das* (*Math.*) coordinate axes *pl.*; **~system** *das* (*Math.*) system of coordinates

**Koordination** *die;* **~, ~en** coordination

**Koordinations·störung** *die* (*Med.*) impaired coordination *no indef. art., no pl.*

**Koordinator** /ko|ɔrdi'na:tɔr/ *der;* **~s, ~en** /-'to:rən/, **Koordinatorin** *die;* **~, ~nen** coordinator

**koordinieren** *tr. V.* coordinate

**Koordinierung** *die;* **~, ~en** coordination

**Kopeke** /ko'pe:kə/ *die;* **~, ~n** copeck

**Kopenhagen** /ko:pn̩'ha:gn̩/ (*das*); **~s** ▶ 700 Copenhagen

**Köpenickiade** /kø:pənɪ'ki̯a:də/ *die;* **~, ~n** hoax (*involving impersonation of a uniformed official or military officer*)

**Köper** /'kø:pɐ/ *der;* **~s, ~:** twill

**kopernikanisch** /kopɛrni'ka:nɪʃ/ *Adj.* Copernican

**Kopernikus** /ko'pɛrnikʊs/ (*der*) Copernicus

**Kopf** /kɔpf/ *der;* **~[e]s, Köpfe** /'kœpfə/ Ⓐ ▶ 471 head; **jmdm. den ~ waschen** wash sb.'s hair; (*fig. ugs.: jmdn. zurechtweisen*) give sb. a good talking-to (*coll.*); give sb. what for (*coll.*); **[um] einen ganzen/halben ~ größer sein** be a good head/a few inches taller; **die Köpfe zusammenstecken** go into a huddle; **sie haben sich die Köpfe heiß geredet** the conversation/debate became heated; **~ an ~** (*dicht gedrängt*) shoulder to shoulder; (*im Wettlauf*) neck and neck; **~ weg!** (*ugs.*) mind your head!; **den ~ einziehen** duck; (*fig.: sich einschüchtern lassen*) be intimidated; **und wenn du dich auf den ~ stellst** you can talk until you're blue in the face; **~ ab!** off with his head!; **ich werde/er wird dir nicht gleich den ~ abreißen** (*ugs.*) I'm/he's not going to bite your head off; **auf dem ~ stehen** (*Kopfstand machen*) stand on one's head; (*ugs.: umgedreht sein*) be upside down; **~ stehen** (*Kopfstand machen*) stand on one's head; (*ugs.: überrascht sein*) be bowled over; (*fig.*) **auf seinen ~ ist eine Belohnung ausgesetzt** there is a price on

k

*old spelling (see note on page 1707)

his head; **jmdm. schwirrt/** (*ugs.*) **raucht der ~:** sb.'s head is spinning; **nicht wissen, wo einem der ~ steht** not know whether one is coming or going; **einen dicken** *od.* **schweren ~ haben** have a headache; (*vom Alkohol*) have a thick head (*coll.*) *or* a hangover; **jmdm.** *od.* **jmdn. den ~ kosten** cost sb. dearly; (*jmdn. das Leben kosten*) cost sb. his/her life; **~ hoch!** chin up!; **den ~ hängen lassen** become disheartened; **~ und Kragen riskieren** risk one's neck; **den ~ hinhalten [müssen]** (*ugs.*) [have to] face the music; [have to] take the blame *or* (*coll.*) rap; **sich** (*Dat.*) **[an etw.** (*Dat.*)**] den ~ einrennen** beat *or* run one's head against a brick wall [with sth.]; **den ~ aus der Schlinge ziehen** avoid any adverse consequences *or* (*sl.*) the rap; **den ~ in den Sand stecken** bury one's head in the sand; **den ~ hoch tragen** hold one's head high; **es gibt keinen Grund dafür, dass er den ~ so hoch trägt** (*überheblich ist*) there is no reason for him to act so superior; **jmdm. den ~ zurechtrücken** (*ugs.*) bring sb. to his/her senses; **sich [gegenseitig]** *od.* **einander die Köpfe einschlagen** be at each other's throats; **jmdn. [um] einen ~ kürzer** *od.* **kleiner machen** (*ugs.*) chop sb.'s head off; **sich** (*Dat.*) **an den ~ fassen** *od.* **greifen** (*ugs.*) throw up one's hands in despair; **jmdm. Beleidigungen an den ~ werfen** hurl insults at sb.; **sein Geld auf den ~ hauen** (*ugs.*) blow one's money (*coll.*); **etw. auf den ~ stellen** (*ugs.*) turn sth. upside down; **die Tatsachen/den Ablauf der Ereignisse auf den ~ stellen** get the facts/the order of events completely *or* entirely wrong; **jmdm. auf dem ~ herumtanzen** (*ugs.*) treat sb. just as one likes; do what one likes with sb.; **sich** (*Dat.*) **nicht auf den ~ spucken lassen** (*salopp*) not let people walk all over one (*coll.*); **jmdm. auf den ~ spucken können** (*salopp scherzh.*) be head and shoulders taller than sb.; **er ist nicht auf den ~ gefallen** (*ugs.*) there are no flies on him (*coll.*); **jmdm. etw. auf den ~ zusagen** say sth. to sb.'s face; **das hältst du im ~ nicht aus!** (*ugs.*) he/she/it really is the limit! (*coll.*); **jmdm. in den** *od.* **zu ~ steigen** go to sb.'s head; **mit dem ~ durch die Wand wollen** (*ugs.*) beat *or* run one's head against a brick wall; **etw. über jmds. ~ [hin]weg entscheiden** decide sth. over sb.'s head; **über die Köpfe der Zuhörer** *usw.* **hinwegreden** talk over the heads of the audience *etc.*; **jmdm. über den ~ wachsen** (*ugs.*) outgrow sb.; (*überfordern*) become too much for sb.; **bis über den ~ in etw. stecken** (*ugs.*) be up to one's ears in sth.; **es geht um ~ und Kragen** (*ugs.*) it's a matter of life and death; **sich um ~ und Kragen reden** (*ugs.*) risk one's neck with careless talk; (*sich belasten*) incriminate oneself as soon as one opens one's mouth; **von ~ bis Fuß** from head to toe *or* foot; **jmdn. vor den ~ stoßen** (*ugs.*) offend sb.; **wie vor den ~ geschlagen sein** (*ugs.*) be stunned; ⇒ *auch* **Hand** F; **B** (*Person*) person; **ein kluger/fähiger ~ sein** be a clever/able man/woman; **pro ~:** per head *or* person; **eine Familie mit acht Köpfen** a family of eight; **C** (*geistige Leitung*) **er ist der ~ der Firma** he's the brains of the firm; **die führenden Köpfe der Wirtschaft** the leading minds in the field of economics; **D** (*Wille*) **seinen ~ durchsetzen** make sb. do what one wants; **einen dicken ~ haben** have a mind of one's own; **muss es immer nach deinem ~ gehen?** why must 'you always decide?; **E** (*Verstand*) mind; head; **hast du noch im ~, wie ...?** can you still remember how ...?; **er hat die Zahlen im ~** (*ugs.*) he has the figures in his head; **er hat nur Autos im ~** (*ugs.*) all he ever thinks about is cars; **was wohl in ihrem ~ vorgeht?** what's going on in her mind?; **sie ist nicht ganz richtig im ~** (*ugs.*) she's not quite right in the head; **einen klaren/kühlen ~ bewahren** *od.* **behalten** keep a cool head; keep one's head; **ich habe den ~ voll mit anderen Dingen** I've got a lot of other things on my mind; **den ~ verlieren** lose one's head; **jmdm. den ~ verdrehen** (*ugs.*) steal sb.'s heart [away]; **sich** (*Dat.*) **den ~ zerbrechen** (*ugs.*) rack one's brains (**über** + *Akk.* over); (*sich Sorgen machen*) worry (**über** + *Akk.* about); **aus dem ~:** off the top of one's head; **das geht** *od.* **will ihm nicht aus dem ~:** he can't get it out of his mind; **sich** (*Dat.*) **etw. aus dem ~ schlagen** put sth. out of one's head; **sich** (*Dat.*) **etw. durch den ~ gehen lassen** think sth. over; **der Gedanke geht mir gerade durch den ~:** it just occurs to me; **jmdm. [plötzlich] durch den ~ schießen** [suddenly] occur to sb.; **jmdm. im ~ herumgehen** (*ugs.*) go round and round in sb.'s mind; **jmdm./sich etw. in den ~ setzen** put sth. into sb.'s head/get sth. into one's head; **etw. im ~ [aus]rechnen** work sth. out in one's head; **was man nicht im ~ hat, muss man in den Beinen haben** a short memory makes work for the legs; **jmdm. geht** *od.* **will etw. nicht in den ~ [hinein]** (*ugs.*) sb. can't get sth. into his/her head; **F** (*von Nadeln, Nägeln, Blumen*) head; (*von Pfeifen*) bowl; **G ein ~ Salat/Blumenkohl/Rotkohl** a lettuce/cauliflower/red cabbage; **H** (*oberer Teil*) (*eines Briefes, einer Tafel*) head; (*einer Zeitung*) heading; head; **I** (*auf Münzen*) **~ [oder Zahl?]** heads [or tails?]

**kopf-, Kopf-: ~-an-~-Rennen** *das* (*Sport*, *auch fig.*) neck-and-neck race (+ *Gen.* between); **~arbeit** *die* brainwork; intellectual work; **~arbeiter** *der*, **~arbeiterin** *die* brainworker; **~bahn·hof** *der* terminal station; **~ball** *der* (*Fußball*) header; **durch ~ball** with a header; **~ball·spiel** *das* (*Fußball*) heading; **~ball·stark** *Adj.* (*Fußball*) good at heading *pred.*; **der einzige ~ballstarke Spieler** the only good header of the ball; **~ball·tor** *das* (*Fußball*) headed goal; **ein ~balltor von Fischer** a goal headed by Fischer; **~bedeckung** *die* headgear; **ohne ~bedeckung** without anything on one's head; without a hat

**Köpfchen** /ˈkœpfçən/ *das;* **~s, ~ A** little head; **B** (*Findigkeit*) brains *pl.;* **~ muss man haben** you've got to have it up here (*coll.*); **~ haben** have brains *pl.;* **~, ~!** clever, eh? (*coll.*)

**köpfeln** /ˈkœpfl̩n/ (*südd., österr., schweiz.*) **1** *tr. V.:* ⇒ **köpfen** B. **2** *itr. V.* dive head first

**köpfen** /ˈkœpfn̩/ *tr. V.* **A** decapitate; (*hinrichten*) behead; (*fig.*) break *or* crack open ‹bottle›; slice the top off ‹egg›; **B** (*Fußball*) head; **das 2:0 ~:** head [in] the goal to make it 2-0

**Kopf-: ~ende** *das* head end; **~form** *die* head shape; shape of the head; **~freiheit** *die* headroom; **~füßer** *der;* **~~s, ~~** (*Zool.*) cephalopod; **~geld** *das* reward; bounty; **~grippe** *die* (*volkst.*) headachy cold; **~haar** *das* hair on the head; **~haltung** *die:* **die/eine ~haltung** the way one holds one's head; **~haut** *die* ▶ 471 [skin of the] scalp; **~höhe** *die:* **in ~höhe** at head height; **~hörer** *der* headphones *pl.*

**-köpfig** *Adj.* -headed; **drei~/fünf~:** three-headed/five-headed ‹monster›; **eine dreiköpfige/fünfköpfige Familie** a family of three/five

**kopf-, Kopf-: ~jäger** *der*, **~jägerin** *die* headhunter; **~kissen** *das* pillow; **~kissen·bezug** *der* pillow case; **~lage** *die* (*Med.*) cephalic *or* head presentation; **~länge** *die* head; **mit einer ~länge Vorsprung** by a head; **~lastig** *Adj.* down by the head *pred.;* nose-heavy ‹aircraft›; (*fig.*) top-heavy; **~laus** *die* head louse; **~los 1** *Adj.* **A** rash; (*in Panik*) panic-stricken; **seine ~lose Flucht** his headlong *or* panic-stricken flight; **B** (*ohne ~*) headless; **2** *adv.* rashly; **~los davonrennen/umherrennen** flee in panic/run round in a panic; **~losigkeit** *die;* **~~:** rashness; (*Panik*) panic; **~nicken** *das;* **~~s** nod [of the head]; **durch ~nicken** by nodding [one's head]; **~nuss**, ***~nuß** *die* (*ugs.*) rap on the head with one's *or* the knuckles; **~rechnen** *itr. V.; nur im Inf. gebr.* do mental arithmetic; **gut ~rechnen können** be good at mental arithmetic; **~rechnen** *das* mental arithmetic; **~salat** *der* cabbage *or* head lettuce; **~scheu** *Adj.* **in jmdn. ~scheu machen** (*ugs.*) unnerve sb.; **~scheu werden** lose one's nerve; **~schmerz** *der* ▶ 474 headache; **~schmerzen haben** have a headache *sing.;* **sich** (*Dat.*) **über etw.** (*Akk.*) *od.* **wegen etw. keine ~schmerzen machen** (*ugs.*) not worry about *or* concern oneself about sth.; **etw. bereitet** *od.* **macht jmdm. ~schmerzen** (*ugs.*) sth. weighs on sb.'s mind; **~schmuck** *der* headdress; **~schuppe** *die* flake of dandruff; **~schuppen** dandruff; **~schuss**, ***~schuß** *der* bullet wound in the head; **er wurde durch einen ~schuss getötet** he was killed by a bullet in the head; **~schütteln** *das;* **~~s** shake of the head; **ein allgemeines ~schütteln auslösen** cause everyone to shake their heads; **durch ~schütteln** by shaking one's head; **nicht ohne ~schütteln** not without some head-shaking; **~schüttelnd** *Adj.* **sich ~schüttelnd abwenden** turn away, shaking one's head; **~schutz** *der* (*Sport*) protective headgear; **~sprung** *der* header; **einen ~sprung machen** dive head first; **~stand** *der* headstand; ***~|stehen** ⇒ **Kopf** A; **~stein·pflaster** *das* cobblestones *pl.;* **~steuer** *die* (*hist.*) poll tax; **~stimme** *die* head voice; (*Falsett*) falsetto [voice]; **~stoß** *der* **A** (*Fußball*) header; **B** (*Boxen*) butt; **~stück** *das* (*Kochk.*) head end; **~stütze** *die* headrest; **~tuch** *das; Pl.* **~tücher** headscarf; **~über** /-ˈ--/ *Adv.* head first; (*fig.*) (*voller Tatendrang*) with a will; (*ohne Zögern*) headlong; **~verband** *der* head bandage; **~verletzung** *die* head injury; **~wäsche** *die* **A** hair wash; shampoo; **B** (*fig. ugs.*) dressing down; **~weh** *das* (*ugs.*) headache; **~weh haben** have a headache; **~weide** *die* pollarded willow; **~zerbrechen** *das;* **~~s: etw. bereitet** *od.* **macht jmdm. ~zerbrechen** sb. has to rack his/her brains about sth.; (*etw. macht jmdm. Sorgen*) sth. is a worry to sb.; **sich** (*Dat.*) **über etw.** (*Akk.*) **[kein] ~zerbrechen machen** [not] worry about sth.

**Kopie** /koˈpiː/ *die;* **~, ~n A** copy; (*Durchschrift*) carbon copy; (*Fotokopie*) photocopy; **B** (*Fot., Film*) print; **C** (*Nachbildung*) copy; **D** (*Abklatsch*) (*Werk*) pastiche; (*Person*) likeness

**Kopier·anstalt** *die* (*Fot.*) [photographic] processing laboratory

**kopieren** *tr. V.* **A** copy; (*foto~*) photocopy; **etw. mit Blaupapier ~:** take a carbon copy of sth.; **B** (*Fot., Film*) print; **C** (*nachbilden*) copy; (*imitieren*) imitate

**Kopierer** *der;* **~s, ~:** [photo]copier

**Kopier-: ~gerät** *das* photocopier; photocopying machine; **~papier** *das* **A** (*Fot.*) printing paper; **B** (*zum Fotokopieren*) photocopying paper; **~schutz** *der* (*DV*) copy protection; **~stift** *der* indelible pencil

**Kopilot** *der;* **~en, ~en, Kopilotin** *die;* **~, ~nen** (*Flugw.*) co-pilot; (*Motorsport*) co-driver

**Kopist** *der;* **~en, ~en, Kopistin** *die;* **~, ~nen A** (*Kunst*) copier; copyist; **B** (*Vervielfältiger[in]*) photocopying-machine operator; photocopier; (*Fot.*) [darkroom] printer

**Koppel**[1] /ˈkɔpl̩/ *das;* **~s, ~,** *österr.: die;* **~, ~n** (*Gürtel*) [leather] belt (*as part of a uniform*)

**Koppel**[2] *die;* **~, ~n A** (*Weide*) paddock; **auf** *od.* **in der ~:** in the paddock; **B** (*Hunde~*) pack; (*Pferde~*) string; **C** (*Musik*) coupler

**koppeln** *tr. V.* **A** (*aneinander binden*) string together ‹horses›; leash together ‹dogs›; couple ‹hounds›; **B** (*aneinander hängen*) dock ‹spacecraft›; couple [up] ‹railway carriage, trailers, etc.› (**an** + *Akk.* to); **C** (*verbinden*) link; couple ‹circuits, systems, etc.›; **etw. an etw.** (*Dat.*) **~:** link sth. to sth.; **mit etw. gekoppelt sein** be associated with sth.; **D** (*Sprachw.*) link

**Koppel-: ~rick** *das;* **~~s, ~~e A** (*Zaun*) paddock fence; **B** (*Hindernis*) post and rails; **~schloss**, ***~schloß** *das* belt buckle (*as part of a uniform*)

k

**Koppelung** ⇨ Kopplung
**Köpper** /ˈkœpɐ/ *der;* ~s, ~ (*ugs.*) header
**koppheister** /kɔpˈhaistɐ/ *Adv.* (*nordd.*) ⇨ kopfüber
**Kopplung** *die;* ~, ~en **A** (*Raumf.*) docking; (*von Eisenbahnwagen, Anhängern usw.*) coupling [up]; **B** (*Verbindung*) linking; (*von Schaltungen, Systemen*) coupling; **C** (*Sprachw.*) linking
**Kopplungs-:** **~geschäft** *das* (*Wirtsch.*) package deal; tie-in deal (*Amer.*); **~manöver** *das* (*Raumf.*) docking manoeuvre
**Kopra** /ˈkoːpra/ *die;* ~: copra
**Koproduktion** *die;* ~, ~en co-production; joint production
**Koproduzent** *der;* ~en, ~en, **Koproduzentin** *die;* ~, ~nen co-producer
**Kopte** /ˈkɔptə/ *der;* ~n, ~n Copt
**Koptin** *die;* ~, ~nen ⇨ Kopte
**koptisch** *Adj.* Coptic
**Kopula** /ˈkoːpula/ *die;* ~, ~s *od.* **Kopulae** /ˈkoːpulɛ/ (*Sprachw.*) copula
**Kopulation** /kopulaˈtsi̯oːn/ *die;* ~, ~en **A** (*Biol.*) copulation; **B** (*Gartenbau*) splice graft
**kopulativ** /kopulaˈtiːf/ *Adj.* (*Sprachw.*) copulative
**Kopulativum** /kopulaˈtiːvʊm/ *das;* ~s, **Kopulativa** (*Sprachw.*) copulative conjunction; copulative
**kopulieren** ❶ *itr. V.* copulate. ❷ *tr. V.* (*Gartenbau*) splice-graft
**kor** /koːɐ̯/ ⇨ küren; kiesen
**Koralle** /koˈralə/ *die;* ~, ~n coral
**korallen-, Korallen-:** **~bank** *die; Pl.* **~bänke** coral reef; **~bäumchen** *das* (*Bot.*) Jerusalem cherry; **~fischer** *der* coral fisherman; **~insel** *die* coral island; **~riff** *das* coral reef; **~rot** *Adj.* coral-red; **~schmuck** *der* coral jewellery
**Koran** /koˈraːn/ *der;* ~s, ~e Koran
**Korb** /kɔrp/ *der;* ~es, **Körbe** /ˈkœrbə/ **A** basket; (*für ein Baby*) wicker cradle; (*Last~ auf einem Tier*) pannier; (*Bienen~*) hive; (*Förder~*) cage; **ein ~ Kartoffeln** a basket[ful] of potatoes; **B** (*Gondel*) basket; **C** (*~ball*) net; (*Basketball*) basket; (*Treffer*) goal; **D** (*Flechtwerk*) wicker[work]; **E** (*Ablehnung*) **jmdm. einen ~ geben** turn sb. down; **einen ~ bekommen, sich** (*Dat.*) **einen ~ holen** be turned down
**Korb-:** **~ball** *der* netball; **~blütler** *der;* ~~s, ~~ (*Bot.*) composite flower; composite
**Körbchen** /ˈkœrpçən/ *das;* ~s, ~ **A** [little] basket; **husch, husch ins ~** (*fam.*) time for bye-bye[s] *or* beddy-byes (*child lang.*); **B** (*des Büstenhalters*) cup
**körbeweise** /ˈkœrbə-/ *Adv.* by the basketful
**Korb-:** **~flasche** *die* wicker bottle; **~geflecht** *das* wicker[work]; **~macher** *der,* **~macherin** *die* ▶ 159 basket-maker; **~möbel** *das* piece of wicker[work] furniture; **teure ~möbel** expensive wicker[work] furniture *sing.;* **~wagen** *der* wicker pram; **~waren** *Pl.* wickerwork *sing.;* basketry *sing.;* wickerwork articles; **~weide** *die* osier; basket willow; **~wurf** *der* (*Basketball*) throw *or* shot at goal *or* the basket
**Kord** /kɔrt/ *der;* ~[e]s **A** corduroy; cord; **B** ⇨ Kordsamt
**Kord·anzug** *der* corduroy suit
**Kordel** /ˈkɔrdl/ *die;* ~, ~n **A** cord; **B** (*landsch.: Bindfaden*) string
**Kord-:** **~hose** *die* corduroy *or* cord trousers *pl.;* **~jeans** *Pl.* corduroy *or* cord jeans
**Kordon** /kɔrˈdõ, *österr.:* -ˈdoːn/ *der;* ~s, ~s *od. österr.:* ~e **A** (*Absperrung*) cordon; **B** (*Ordensband*) cordon; ribbon
**Kord·samt** *der* cord velvet
**Korea** /koˈreːa/ (*das*); ~s Korea
**Korea·krieg** *der* Korean War
**Koreaner** /koreˈaːnɐ/ *der;* ~s, ~, **Koreanerin** *die;* ~, ~nen ▶ 553 Korean; ⇨ *auch* -in
**koreanisch** *Adj.* ▶ 553, ▶ 696 Korean; ⇨ *auch* **deutsch; Deutsch; Deutsche²**

*old spelling (see note on page 1707)

**Koreferat** ⇨ Korreferat
**kören** /ˈkøːrən/ *tr. V.* (*Landw.*) rank *or* classify ‹males› for breeding
**Korfu** /ˈkɔrfu/ (*das*); ~s Corfu
**Koriander** /koˈri̯andɐ/ *der;* ~s, ~: coriander
**Korinth** /koˈrɪnt/ (*das*); ~s ▶ 700 Corinth
**Korinthe** /koˈrɪntə/ *die;* ~, ~n currant
**Korinthen-:** **~brot** *das* currant bread; **~kacker** *der,* **~kackerin** *die* (*derb abwertend*) stupid rule-bound bastard (*sl.*); (*Pfennigfuchser[in]*) pettifogger (*coll.*)
**Korinther** *der;* ~s, ~, **Korintherin** *die;* ~, ~nen Corinthian
**korinthisch** *Adj.* (*Kunstwiss.*) Corinthian ‹column, order, etc.›
**Kork** /kɔrk/ *der;* ~s, ~e cork
**Kork·eiche** *die* cork oak
**Korken** *der;* ~s, ~: cork
**Korken·zieher** *der* corkscrew
**Korkenzieher·locke** *die* corkscrew *or* spiral curl
**korkig** *Adj.* corked, corky ‹wine›
**Kork·sohle** *die* cork sole
**Kormoran** /kɔrmoˈraːn/ *der;* ~s, ~e cormorant
**Korn¹** /kɔrn/ *das;* ~[e]s, **Körner** /ˈkœrnɐ/ **A** (*Frucht*) seed; grain; (*Getreide~*) grain [of corn]; (*Pfeffer~*) corn; **B** (*Getreide*) corn; grain; **das ~ steht gut** the grain harvest looks promising; **C** (*Salz~, Sand~*) grain; (*Hagel~*) stone; **D** *Pl.* **~e** (*an Handfeuerwaffen*) front sight; foresight; **etw. aufs ~ nehmen** take aim at *or* draw a bead on sth.; (*fig. ugs.*) attack sth.; **jmdn. aufs ~ nehmen** take aim at *or* draw a bead on sb.; (*fig. ugs.*) start to keep close tabs on sb. (*coll.*); **E** (*Fot.; von Papier, Stoff*) grain
**Korn²** *der;* ~[e]s, ~ (*ugs.*) corn schnapps; corn liquor (*Amer.*)
**korn-, Korn-:** **~ähre** *die* ear of corn; **~blume** *die* cornflower; **~blumen·blau** *Adj.* cornflower [blue]; (*fig. salopp*) paralytic (*coll.*); **~branntwein** *der* corn schnapps; corn liquor (*Amer.*)
**Körnchen** /ˈkœrnçən/ *das;* ~s, ~ (*Frucht*) tiny seed *or* grain; (*von Sand usw.*) [tiny] grain; granule; **an etw.** (*Dat.*) **ist ein ~ Wahrheit** (*fig.*) there's a grain of truth in sth.
**körnen** /ˈkœrnən/ *tr. V.* **A** (*zerkleinern, körnig machen*) granulate; **gekörnte Brühe** stock granules *pl.* (*for soup*); **B** (*Handw.: markieren*) punch
**Körner** ⇨ Korn
**Körner-:** **~fresser** *der* (*Ornith.*) seedeater; granivore; **~futter** *das* grain [feed]; (*für Vögel*) seed
**Kornett** /kɔrˈnɛt/ *das;* ~[e]s, ~e *od.* ~s (*Musik*) cornet
**Korn·feld** *das* cornfield
**körnig** /ˈkœrnɪç/ *Adj.* granular; (*Fot.*) grainy
**-körnig** *Adj.* -grained
**Korn-:** **~kammer** *die* granary; **~rade** *die;* ~~, ~~n corn cockle; corn campion; **~silo** *der od. das* grain silo
**Körnung** *die;* ~, ~en **A** (*Korngröße*) grain size; (*von Papier*) grain; **B** (*Jägerspr.*) ⇨ Körnerfutter
**Korona** /koˈroːna/ *die;* ~, **Koronen** **A** (*Astron.*) corona; **B** (*fig.*) crowd (*coll.*)
**Koronar·insuffizienz** /koroˈnaːɐ̯-/ *die* ▶ 474 (*Med.*) coronary insufficiency
**Körper** /ˈkœrpɐ/ *der;* ~s, ~ **A** body; **~ und Geist** body and mind; **am ganzen ~ frieren/zittern** be [freezing] cold/shake all over; **B** (*Rumpf*) trunk; body; **C** (*Gegenstand*) object; **D** (*Physik, Chemie*) body; **E** (*Geom.*) solid body; solid; **F** (*von Wein, Farbe*) body; **G** ⇨ Körperschaft
**körper-, Körper-:** **~bau** *der* physique; **~behaarung** *die* body hair *no indef. art.;* **~beherrschung** *die* body control; **~behindert** *Adj.* physically handicapped *or* disabled; **~behinderte** *der/die* physically handicapped *or* disabled person; **~behinderte** *Pl.* physically handicapped *or* disabled people; **die ~behinderten** (*als Kategorie*) the physically handicapped *or* disabled; **~behinderung** *die* physical handicap *or* disability; **~beschädigte** *der/die* (*Amtsspr.*) disabled person; **~betont** ❶ *Adj.* figure-hugging ‹clothes›; ‹clothes› that emphasize the figure; ❷ *adv.* **~betont geschnitten** cut to emphasize the figure; **~eigen** *Adj.* (*Biol.*) endogenous; **~erzieher** *der* (*bes. DDR*) physical education teacher; **~fremd** *Adj.* (*Biol.*) foreign; **~fülle** *die* corpulence; **~funktion** *die* bodily function; **~gerecht** *Adj.* shaped to fit the contours of the body *postpos.;* **~geruch** *der* body odour; BO (*coll.*); **~gewicht** *das* ▶ 353 body weight; **~größe** *die* ▶ 411 height; **~hälfte** *die* side of the body; **~haltung** *die* posture; **~hygiene** *die* ⇨ ~pflege; **~kontakt** *der* (*Psych.*) physical contact; **~kraft** *die* physical strength; **~kultur** *die* (*bes. DDR*) physical education *no art.;* **~länge** *die* (*bei Menschen*) height; (*bei Tieren*) length
**körperlich** ❶ *Adj.* physical; **~e Ertüchtigung** physical training; **~e Züchtigung** corporal punishment; **~e Liebe** carnal love. ❷ *adv.* physically; **~ [hart] arbeiten** do [hard] physical work
**körper-, Körper-:** **~los** *Adj.* incorporeal; **~maße** *Pl.* measurements; **~öffnung** *die* orifice of the body; **~pflege** *die* body care *no art.;* (*Reinigung*) personal hygiene; **~saft** *der* body fluid
**Körperschaft** *die;* ~, ~en **A** (*Rechtsw.*) corporation; corporate body; **~ des öffentlichen Rechts** public corporation; **B** (*Politik*) body
**Körperschaft[s]·steuer** *die* (*Steuerw.*) corporation tax
**Körper-:** **~schwäche** *die* physical weakness; **~sprache** *die* body language; **~spray** *der od. das* aerosol deodorant; deodorant spray; **~stärke** *die* physical strength; **~teil** *der* ▶ 471 part of the/one's body; **~temperatur** *die* body temperature; **~verletzung** *die* (*Rechtsw.*) bodily harm *no indef. art.;* **schwere/leichte ~verletzung** grievous/actual bodily harm; **~verletzung mit Todesfolge** *bodily harm resulting in death;* **~verletzung im Amt** bodily harm caused by a public servant when executing his/her duty; **~wärme** *die* body heat
**Korpora** ⇨ Korpus²
**Korporal** /kɔrpoˈraːl/ *der;* ~s, ~e *od.* **Korporäle** /kɔrpoˈrɛːlə/ (*Milit. veralt.*) corporal
**Korporation** /kɔrporaˈtsi̯oːn/ *die;* ~, ~en **A** (*veralt.: Körperschaft*) corporation; **B** (*Studentenverbindung*) student society
**korporiert** /kɔrpoˈriːɐ̯t/ *Adj.* ‹student› belonging to a student society
**Korporierte** *der; adj. Dekl.* member of a student society
**Korps** /koːɐ̯/ *das;* ~ /koːɐ̯(s)/, ~ /koːɐ̯s/ **A** (*Milit.*) corps; **B** (*Studentenverbindung*) student duelling society
**Korps-:** **~bruder** *der* (*Studentenspr.*) fellow member of a student duelling society; **~geist** *der* (*geh.*) esprit de corps; **~student** *der* student belonging to a duelling society
**korpulent** /kɔrpuˈlɛnt/ *Adj.* corpulent
**Korpulenz** /kɔrpuˈlɛnts/ *die;* ~: corpulence
**Korpus¹** /ˈkɔrpʊs/ *der;* ~, ~se **A** (*scherzh.*) body; **B** (*bild. Kunst*) figure of Christ (*on crucifix*); **C** (*fachspr.*) carcass
**Korpus²** *das;* ~, **Korpora** /ˈkɔrpora/ **A** (*Sprachw.*) corpus; **B** (*Musik*) body
**Korpus³** *die;* ~ (*Druckw.*) long primer
**Korpuskel** /kɔrˈpʊskl̩/ *das;* ~s, ~n *od. die;* ~, ~n (*Physik*) corpuscle; particle
**Korreferat** /kɔrefeˈraːt/ *das;* ~s, ~e *scholarly paper which supplements the main paper;* supplementary paper (*to a paper read at a seminar etc.*)
**Korreferent** /kɔrefeˈrɛnt/ *der;* ~en, ~en, **Korreferentin** *die;* ~, ~nen **A** (*Redner*) reader of a/the supplementary paper; **B** (*Prüfer*) second examiner
**korrekt** /kɔˈrɛkt/ ❶ *Adj.* correct; **es wäre ~ gewesen, …** the correct thing would have

## Körperteile

Im Englischen verwendet man ein Possessivum (**my, his, your** usw.) für Körperteile viel häufiger, auch zum Beispiel für die, die zum Subjekt des Satzes gehören:

***Er hob die Hand***
= He raised his hand

***Sie schloss die Augen***
= She closed her eyes

Ebenso in Fällen, wo man im Deutschen einen Dativ der Person (auch ein Reflexivum), gefolgt von einem Akkusativobjekt, verwendet:

***Sie schloss ihm die Augen***
= She closed his eyes

***Du hast ihm fast den Arm ausgerenkt***
= You nearly dislocated his arm

***Kannst du mir den Rücken eincremen?***
= Can you put some cream on my back [for me]?

***Ich habe mir das Bein gebrochen***
= I've broken my leg

***Er hat sich den Arm ausgerenkt***
= He dislocated his arm

***Sie hat sich den Kopf am Balken angestoßen***
= She hit her head on the beam

***Sie fuhr mir/sich mit der Hand über die Stirn***
= She passed her hand over my/her forehead

Verwendet man diese Konstruktion mit einem Substantiv statt dem Personalpronomen im Dativ, so entspricht dem Dativ im Englischen ein Genitiv:

***Sie massierte ihrem Sohn den Rücken***
= She massaged her son's back

Die deutsche unpersönliche Konstruktion hat keine direkte Entsprechung im Englischen. Auch hier verwendet man ein Possessivum:

***Mir dreht sich der Kopf***
= My head is spinning

***Es kribbelte mir in den Füßen***
= My feet were tingling

····➤ Krankheiten und Schmerzen

been to ...; **ein ~er Beamter** a very correct civil servant. **❷** *adv.* correctly

**korrekter·weise** *Adv.* to be [strictly] correct

**Korrektheit** *die;* **~:** correctness

**Korrektiv** /kɔrɛk'ti:f/ *das;* **~s, ~e** corrective (**gegen** to)

**Korrektor** /kɔ'rɛktɔr/ *der;* **~s, ~en** /-'to:rən/, **Korrektorin** *die;* **~, ~nen** ▶159 proof-reader

**Korrektur** /kɔrɛk'tu:ɐ̯/ *die;* **~, ~en** Ⓐ correction; (*von Ansichten usw.*) revision; Ⓑ (*Druckw.*) proof-reading; (*Verbesserung*) proof correction; **~ lesen** read/correct the proofs

**Korrektur-: ~ab·zug** *der,* **~fahne** *die* galley [proof]; **~zeichen** *das* proof-correction mark

**Korrelat** /kɔre'la:t/ *das;* **~[e]s, ~e** correlate

**Korrelation** /kɔrela'tsi̯o:n/ *die;* **~, ~en** (*auch Math.*) correlation

**korrelieren** *itr. V.* correlate (**mit** with, to)

**Korrepetitor** /kɔrepe'ti:tɔr/ *der;* **~s, ~en** /-ti'to:rən/, **Korrepetitorin** *die;* **~, ~nen** (*Musik*) répétiteur

**Korrespondent** /kɔrɛspɔn'dɛnt/ *der;* **~en, ~en**, **Korrespondentin** *die;* **~, ~nen** ▶159 Ⓐ (*Zeitungsw., veralt.: Briefpartner*) correspondent; Ⓑ (*Wirtsch.*) correspondence clerk

**Korrespondenz** /kɔrɛspɔn'dɛnts/ *die;* **~, ~en** Ⓐ correspondence; **die ~ erledigen** deal with the correspondence; **in ~ mit jmdm. stehen** correspond with sb.; Ⓑ (*Brief*) letter; **~en** correspondence *sing.*

**Korrespondenz-: ~büro** *das* press agency; **~karte** *die* (*österr., schweiz.*) *pre-stamped postcard*

**korrespondieren** *itr. V.* Ⓐ (*schreiben*) correspond (**mit** with); Ⓑ (*geh.: übereinstimmen*) **mit etw. ~:** correspond to *or* with sth.; ‹colour› match sth.

**Korridor** /'kɔrido:ɐ̯/ *der;* **~s, ~e** corridor; **der Polnische ~:** the Polish Corridor

**korrigierbar** *Adj.* correctable

**korrigieren** /kɔri'gi:rən/ *tr. V.* correct; revise ‹opinion, view›

**korrodieren** /kɔro'di:rən/ (*bes. Chemie, Geol.*) *tr., itr. V.* (*itr. mit sein*) corrode

**Korrosion** /kɔro'zi̯o:n/ *die;* **~, ~en** (*auch Geol., Med.*) corrosion

**korrosions-, Korrosions-: ~beständig** *Adj.,* **~fest** *Adj.* corrosion-resistant; **~schutz** *der* protection against corrosion

**korrosiv** /kɔro'zi:f/ *Adj.* Ⓐ corrosive; Ⓑ (*korrosionsbedingt*) ‹damage etc.› caused by corrosion

**korrumpieren** /kɔrʊm'pi:rən/ *tr. V.* corrupt

**Korrumpierung** *die;* **~, ~en** corruption

**korrupt** /kɔ'rʊpt/ *Adj.* corrupt

**Korruption** /kɔrʊp'tsi̯o:n/ *die;* **~, ~en** corruption

**Korsage** /kɔr'za:ʒə/ *die;* **~, ~n** strapless, tight-fitting corsage *or* bodice

**Korsar** /kɔr'za:ɐ̯/ *der;* **~en, ~en** Ⓐ (*hist.*) corsair; Ⓑ (*Segeln*) Korsar

**Korse** /'kɔrzə/ *der;* **~n, ~n** Corsican

**Korselett** /kɔrzə'lɛt/ *das;* **~s, ~s** *od.* **~e** corselette

**Korsett** /kɔr'zɛt/ *das;* **~s, ~s** *od.* **~e** corset; (*fig.*) straitjacket

**Korsett·stange** *die* corset bone

**Korsika** /'kɔrzika/ *(das);* **~s** Corsica

**Korsin** *die;* **~, ~nen** ⇒ **Korse**

**korsisch** *Adj.* ▶696 Corsican

**Korso** /'kɔrzo/ *der;* **~s, ~s** procession

**Kortison** /kɔrti'zo:n/ *das;* **~s** (*Med.*) cortisone

**Korund** /ko'rʊnt/ *der;* **~[e]s, ~e** corundum

**Körung** *die;* **~, ~en** (*Landw.*) ranking *or* classification for breeding

**Korvette** /kɔr'vɛtə/ *die;* **~, ~n** (*auch hist.*) corvette

**Korvetten·kapitän** *der* lieutenant commander

**Koryphäe** /kory'fɛ:ə/ *die;* **~, ~n** eminent authority; distinguished expert

**Kosak** /ko'zak/ *der;* **~en, ~en** (*hist.*) Cossack

**Kosaken·mütze** *die* Cossack hat

**Koschenille** /kɔʃə'nɪljə/ *die;* **~:** cochineal

**koscher** /'ko:ʃɐ/ *Adj.* Ⓐ kosher; Ⓑ (*ugs.: einwandfrei*) kosher (*coll.*)

**K.-o.-Schlag** *der* (*Boxen*) knockout punch

**Kose·form** *die* familiar form

**Kosekans** /'ko:zekans/ *der;* **~, ~** (*Math.*) cosecant

**kosen** /'ko:zn̩/ (*dichter. veralt.*) **❶** *tr. V.* caress. **❷** *itr. V.* **mit jmdm. ~:** caress sb.

**Kose·name** *der* pet name

**Kose·wort** *das; Pl.* **Kosewörter** term of endearment; **jmdm. Kosewörter ins Ohr flüstern** whisper endearments in sb.'s ear

**K.-o.-Sieg** *der* (*Boxen*) knockout victory; victory by a knockout

**Kosinus** /'ko:zinʊs/ *der;* **~, ~** *od.* **~se** (*Math.*) cosine

**Kosmetik** /kɔs'me:tɪk/ *die;* **~** Ⓐ beauty culture *no art.;* Ⓑ (*fig.*) cosmetic procedures *pl.*

**Kosmetika** ⇒ **Kosmetikum**

**Kosmetik·abteilung** *die* cosmetics department

**Kosmetiker** *der;* **~s, ~**, **Kosmetikerin** *die;* **~, ~nen** ▶159 Ⓐ cosmetician; beautician; Ⓑ (*Chemiker/Chemikerin*) cosmetics chemist

**Kosmetik-: ~salon** *der* beauty salon; **~tasche** *die* make-up bag; (*groß*) vanity case

**Kosmetikum** /kɔs'me:tikʊm/ *das;* **~s, Kosmetika** cosmetic

**kosmetisch** **❶** *Adj.* (*auch fig.*) cosmetic. **❷** *adv.* **jmdn. ~ beraten** give sb. advice on beauty care; **sich ~ behandeln lassen** have beauty treatment

**kosmisch** /'kɔsmɪʃ/ *Adj.* cosmic ‹ray, dust, etc.›; space ‹age, station, research, etc.›; meteoric ‹iron›

**Kosmodrom** /kɔsmo'dro:m/ *das;* **~s, ~e** cosmodrome

**Kosmologie** /kɔsmolo'gi:/ *die;* **~, ~n** cosmology

**Kosmonaut** /kɔsmo'naut/ *der;* **~en, ~en**, **Kosmonautin** *die;* **~, ~nen** ▶159 cosmonaut

**Kosmopolit** /kɔsmopo'li:t/ *der;* **~en, ~en**, **Kosmopolitin** *die;* **~, ~nen** (*geh.*) cosmopolitan

**kosmopolitisch** *Adj.* cosmopolitan

**Kosmos** /'kɔsmɔs/ *der;* **~** Ⓐ (*Weltall*) cosmos; Ⓑ (*geh.: Welt*) world

**Kosovo·albaner** /'kɔsovo.../ *der* Kosovo Albanian

**Kost** /kɔst/ *die;* **~** Ⓐ (*Nahrung*) food; **vegetarische ~:** vegetarian food; a vegetarian diet; **geistige ~** (*fig.*) intellectual nourishment; **leichte/schwere ~** (*fig.*) easy/heavy going; Ⓑ (*Verpflegung*) **~ und Logis** board and lodging

**kostbar** **❶** *Adj.* Ⓐ (*erlesen*) valuable; Ⓑ (*wichtig*) precious; **die Zeit ist ~:** time is precious. **❷** *adv.* expensively ‹dressed›; luxuriously ‹decorated›

**Kostbarkeit** *die;* **~, ~en** Ⓐ (*Sache*) treasure; precious object; Ⓑ (*Eigenschaft*) value

**kosten**[1] **❶** *tr. V.* Ⓐ (*probieren*) taste; try; sample; **jmdm. etw. zum K~ geben** give sb. sth. to taste *or* try *or* sample; Ⓑ (*geh.: empfinden*) taste; (*fig. iron.*) have a taste of. **❷** *itr. V.* (*probieren*) have a taste; **von etw. ~:** have a taste of *or* taste sth.

**kosten**[2] **❶** *tr. V.* Ⓐ ▶337 cost; **wie viel kostet .../was kostet ...?** how much/what does ... cost?; how much is ...?; **koste es** *od.* **es koste, was es wolle** whatever the cost; **sich** (*Akk. od. Dat.*) **eine Sache etw. ~ lassen** (*ugs.*) spend a fair bit of money on sth.; Ⓑ (*erfordern*) take; cost ‹lives›; **es kostet mich nur ein Wort** it would only take a word from me; **viel Arbeit ~:** take a

k

great deal of work; **C** (*Verlust nach sich ziehen*) **jmdn.** *od.* **jmdm. etw. ~:** cost sb. sth.; **jmdn. den Sieg ~:** cost sb. victory.
**2** *itr. V.* (*Geld ~*) **das kostet!** that will cost a bit!

**Kosten** *Pl.* cost *sing.*; costs; (*Auslagen*) expenses; (*Rechtsw.*) costs; **die ~ tragen, für die ~ aufkommen** bear the cost[s]; **keine ~ scheuen** spare no expense; **laufende ~:** running costs; **auf seine ~ kommen** cover one's costs; (*fig.*) get one's money's worth; **auf jmds. ~:** at sb.'s expense; **auf ~ von jmdm./etw.** at the expense of sb./sth.

**kosten-, Kosten-: ~aufwand** *der* expense; cost; **mit einem ~aufwand von ...** at a cost of ...; **~berechnung** *die* costing; **~beteiligung** *die* sharing of expenses; **~deckend** **1** *Adj.* that covers/cover [one's] costs *postpos., not pred.*; **2** *adv.* **~deckend kalkulieren** ensure that the estimates cover the true costs; **~druck** *der* (*Wirtsch.*) pressure of costs; **~ersparnis** *die* cost saving; **~erstattung** *die* reimbursement of costs; **~explosion** *die* cost explosion; **~frage** *die* question of cost; **~intensiv** *Adj.* (*Wirtsch.*) cost-intensive; **~los** **1** *Adj.* free; **2** *adv.* free of charge; **~pflichtig** (*Rechtsw.*) **1** *Adj.* **eine ~pflichtige Verwarnung** a fine and a caution; **2** *adv.* **eine Klage ~pflichtig abweisen** dismiss a case with costs; **ein Auto ~pflichtig abschleppen** tow a car away at the owner's expense; **~punkt** *der* (*ugs.*) **~punkt?** how much is it/are they?; **~punkt 25 DM** it costs/they cost 25 marks; **~rechnung** *die* (*Wirtsch.*) cost accounting; **~sparend** *Adj.* (*Wirtsch.*) cost-saving; **~stelle** *die* (*Wirtsch.*) cost centre; **~träger** *der* (*Wirtsch.*) cost unit; **~vor·an·schlag** *der* estimate

**Kost-: ~gänger** *der;* **~~s, ~~, ~gängerin** *die;* **~~, ~~nen** (*veralt.*) boarder; **~geld** *das* payment for [one's] board; **er gab seinen Eltern ~geld** he paid his parents for his board

**köstlich** /ˈkœstlɪç/ **1** *Adj.* **A** delicious; **B** (*unterhaltsam*) delightful; **der Witz war einfach zu ~:** the joke was simply priceless (*coll.*). **2** *adv.* **A** ‹taste› delicious; **B** **sich ~ amüsieren/unterhalten** enjoy oneself enormously (*coll.*)

**Köstlichkeit** *die;* **~, ~en** **A** (*Sache*) delicacy; **eine literarische ~:** a literary gem; **B** (*geh.: Eigenschaft*) deliciousness

**Kost·probe** *die;* **~, ~n** taste; (*fig.*) sample

**kost·spielig** /-ʃpiːlɪç/ **1** *Adj.* expensive; costly. **2** *adv.* expensively

**Kostüm** /kɔsˈtyːm/ *das;* **~s, ~e** **A** suit; **B** (*historisches ~, Theater~, Verkleidung*) costume

**Kostüm-: ~ball** *der* fancy-dress ball; **~bildner** *der;* **~~s, ~~, ~bildnerin** *die;* **~~, ~~nen** (*Theater, Film*) costume designer; **~film** *der* period picture *or* film

**kostümieren** *tr. V.* **A** (*verkleiden*) **jmdn./sich ~:** dress sb. up/dress [oneself] up; **wie hatte er sich kostümiert?** what was he dressed [up] as?; **alle erschienen kostümiert** they all came in fancy dress; **B** (*ugs. abwertend: unpassend anziehen*) **jmdn./sich ~:** get sb./oneself up

**Kostüm-: ~jacke** *die* jacket; **~probe** *die* (*Theater*) dress rehearsal; **~rock** *der* skirt; **~schneider** *der,* **~schneiderin** *die* ▶ 159 costumier; **~verleih** *der* [theatrical] costume agency

**Kost·verächter** *der:* **in kein ~ sein** (*scherzh.*) be fond of one's food; (*die Frauen lieben*) be one for the ladies

**K.-o.-System** *das* (*Sport*) knockout system

**Kot** /koːt/ *der;* **~[e]s, ~e** **A** (*Exkrement*) excrement; **B** (*veralt.: Schmutz*) mud; dirt

**Kotangens** /ˈkoːtaŋgɛns/ *der;* **~, ~** (*Math.*) cotangent

**Kotau** /koˈtau/ *der;* **~s, ~s** kowtow; **[vor jmdm.] einen** *od.* **seinen ~ machen** kowtow [to sb.]

---
*old spelling (see note on page 1707)

**Kotelett** /kɔtˈlɛt/ *das;* **~s, ~s** **A** chop; (*vom Nacken*) cutlet; **B** (*Teil des Tieres*) (*eines Schweins*) loin; (*eines Kalbs*) loin and rib

**Koteletten** *Pl.* side whiskers

**koten** /ˈkoːtn̩/ *itr. V.* (*Zool.*) defecate

**Köter** /ˈkøːtɐ/ *der;* **~s, ~** (*abwertend*) cur; tyke

**Kot·flügel** *der* (*Kfz-W.*) wing

**Kothurn** /koˈtʊrn/ *der;* **~s, ~e** cothurnus

**kotig** /ˈkoːtɪç/ *Adj.* **A** dirty ‹nappy, underpants›; **B** (*schmutzig*) muddy; filthy

**Kotz·brocken** *der* (*derb*) shit (*coarse*); turd (*coarse*)

**Kotze**[1] /ˈkɔtsə/ *die;* **~** (*derb*) vomit; puke (*coarse*)

**Kotze**[2] *die;* **~, ~n** (*südd., österr.*) **A** coarse woollen blanket; **B** (*Umhang*) cape

**kotzen** *itr. V.* (*derb*) puke (*coarse*); throw up (*coll.*); **das ist/ich finde ihn zum Kotzen:** it/he makes me sick; it/he makes me want to puke (*coarse*); **da kann man das [große] Kotzen kriegen** *od.* **bekommen** it makes you want to puke (*coarse*)

**kotz-: ~langweilig** *Adj.* (*derb abwertend*) bleeding boring (*coarse*); **~übel** *Adj.* (*derb*) **mir ist ~übel** I feel as if I'm going to throw up (*coll.*) *or* (*coarse*) puke

**KP** *Abk.* **Kommunistische Partei** CP

**Krabbe** /ˈkrabə/ *die;* **~, ~n** **A** (*Zool.*) crab; **B** (*ugs.: Garnele*) shrimp; (*größer*) prawn; **C** (*ugs. scherzh.: Kind*) [little] mite; (*älter*) kid (*coll.*); **D** (*bild. Kunst*) crochet

**Krabbel·alter** *das* (*ugs.*) crawling stage

**krabbeln** /ˈkrabl̩n/ **1** *itr. V.; mit sein* crawl. **2** *tr. V.* (*ugs.: kraulen*) tickle

**krach** *Interj.* crash; bang; (*wenn etw. zerbricht, einstürzt*) crash

**Krach** /krax/ *der;* **~[e]s, Kräche** /ˈkrɛçə/ **A** (*Lärm*) noise; row; **~ machen** make a noise *or* (*coll.*) a row; be noisy; **B** (*lautes Geräusch*) crash; bang; (*wenn etw. zerbricht, einstürzt*) crash; **mit** *od.* **unter lautem ~:** with a loud crash *or* bang/crash; **C** (*ugs.: Streit*) row; **mit jmdm. ~ anfangen/kriegen** start/have a row with sb. (*coll.*); **~ machen** *od.* **schlagen** (*ugs.*) kick up *or* make a fuss; **es gibt oft ~:** there are frequent rows; **D** (*ugs.: Börsen~*) crash

**krachen** **1** *itr. V.* **A** (*Krach auslösen*) ‹thunder› crash; ‹shot› ring out; ‹floorboard› creak; **in allen Fugen ~:** creak at the joints; **~de Kälte/~der Frost** (*fig.*) bitter cold/heavy frost; **B** *mit sein* (*ugs.: bersten*) ‹ice› crack; ‹bed› collapse; ‹trousers, dress, etc.› split; **C** *mit sein* (*ugs.: mit Krach auftreffen*) crash; **die Tür krachte ins Schloss** the door banged *or* slammed shut; **D** (*ugs.: Bankrott machen*) crash; **E** (*unpers.*) **an der Kreuzung kracht es dauernd** there are frequent crashes at that junction; **sonst kracht's!** (*fig. ugs.*) or there'll be trouble; (*es gibt Schläge*) or you'll get a beating; **etw. tun, dass es nur so kracht** (*ugs.*) do sth. with a vengeance.
**2** *refl. V.* (*ugs.*) row (*coll.*); have a row (*coll.*)

**Kracher** *der;* **~s, ~** (*ugs.: Knallkörper*) banger

**Kracherl** /ˈkraxɐl/ *das;* **~s, ~n** (*südd., österr.*) fizzy lemonade; pop (*coll.*)

**krach·ledern** *Adj.* rustic

**Krach·lederne** *die;* **~n, ~n** (*südd.*) Lederhosen *pl.*; leather shorts *pl.*

**Krach·macher** *der* (*ugs.*) (*Person*) noisy so-and-so (*coll.*); (*Gerät*) noise-maker

**Krach·macherin** *die* noisy so-and-so

**krächzen** /ˈkrɛçtsn̩/ *itr. V.* ‹raven, crow› caw; ‹parrot› squawk; ‹person› croak; (*fig.*) ‹loudspeaker etc.› crackle and splutter

**kracken** /ˈkrakn̩/ *tr. V.* (*Chemie*) crack

**Kräcker** /ˈkrɛkɐ/ *der;* **~s, ~** ⇒ **Cracker**

**Krad** /kraːt/ *das;* **~[e]s, Kräder** /ˈkrɛːdɐ/ (*bes. Milit.*) ⇒ **Kraftrad**

**Krad-: ~fahrer** *der* (*bes. Milit.*) motorcyclist; motorcycle rider; **~melder** *der* (*Milit.*) [motorcycle] despatch rider

**kraft** /kraft/ *Präp. + Gen.* (*Amtsspr.*) **~ [meines] Amtes** by virtue of my office; **~ Gesetzes** by law; **~ [des] Gesetzes hat der Richter ihn zum Tode verurteilt** as empowered by the law, the judge sentenced him to death

**Kraft** *die;* **~, Kräfte** /ˈkrɛftə/ **A** strength; **geistige/schöpferische Kräfte** mental/creative powers; **unter Aufbietung aller Kräfte** applying all one's energies; **jmds. Kräfte übersteigen** be too much for sb.; **wieder bei Kräften sein** have [got] one's strength back; **bei Kräften bleiben** keep one's strength up; **mit letzter ~:** with one's last ounce of strength; **mit frischer ~:** with renewed energy; **aus eigener ~:** by oneself *or* one's own efforts; **ich werde tun, was in meinen Kräften steht** I shall do everything [with]in my power; **mit vereinten Kräften sollte es gelingen** if we join forces *or* combine our efforts we should succeed; **nach [besten] Kräften** to the best of one's ability; **die militärische/wirtschaftliche ~ eines Landes** (*fig.*) the military/economic strength of a country; **B** (*Wirksamkeit*) power; **die treibende ~:** the driving force; **C** (*Arbeits~*) employee; (*in einer Fabrik*) employee; worker; **Kräfte** employees/workers; personnel *pl.*; (*Angestellte auch*) staff *pl.*; **D** *Pl.* (*Gruppe*) forces; **E** (*Physik*) force; **F** (*Seemannsspr.*) **mit voller/halber ~:** at full/half speed; **volle/halbe ~ voraus!** full/half speed ahead!; **G** *in* **außer ~ setzen** repeal ‹law›; countermand ‹order›; **außer ~ sein/treten** no longer be/cease to be in force; **in ~ treten/sein/bleiben** come into/be in/remain in force

**Kraft-: ~akt** *der* feat of strength; (*im Zirkus usw.*) strongman act; (*fig.*) show of strength; **~arm** *der* (*Physik*) [lever] arm to which force is applied; **~aufwand** *der* effort; **~ausdruck** *der; Pl.* **~ausdrücke** swear word; **~brühe** *die* strong meat broth; **~droschke** *die* (*veralt.*) hackney carriage; taxi

**Kräfte-: ~parallelogramm** *das* (*Physik*) parallelogram of forces; **~verhältnis** *das* (*bes. Politik*) balance of power; **~verschleiß** *der* loss of strength

**Kraft·fahrer** *der* ▶ 159 (*bes. Amtsspr.*) driver; motorist; (*Beruf*) driver

**Kraftfahrer·gruß** *der* ⇒ **Autofahrergruß**

**Kraft·fahrerin** *die* ▶ 159 ⇒ **Kraftfahrer**

**Kraft·fahrzeug** *das;* **~[e]s, ~e** (*bes. Amtsspr.*) motor vehicle

**Kraftfahrzeug-: ~bau** *der* automobile construction; **~brief** *der* vehicle registration document; logbook (*Brit.*); **~industrie** *die* motor industry; **~mechaniker** *der,* **~mechanikerin** *die* ▶ 159 motor mechanic; **~schein** *der* vehicle registration document (*containing detailed technical description of the vehicle and details of the owner*); **~steuer** *die* vehicle *or* road tax; **~zulassungs·stelle** *die* vehicle registration office

**Kraft-: ~feld** *das* (*Physik*) force field; **~futter** *das* concentrated feed

**kräftig** /ˈkrɛftɪç/ **1** *Adj.* **A** (*stark*) strong ‹person›; strong, powerful ‹arms, voice›; vigorous ‹plant, shoot›; **B** (*fest*) powerful, hefty, hard ‹blow, kick, etc.›; firm ‹handshake›; **C** (*ausgeprägt*) strong ‹breeze, high-pressure area›; deep ‹depression›; considerable ‹increase›; **einen ~en Schluck nehmen** take a deep drink *or* (*coll.*) good swig; **eine ~e Tracht [Prügel]** a good hiding (*coll.*); a sound beating; **D** (*intensiv*) strong, powerful ‹smell, taste, etc.›; bold ‹pattern›; strong ‹colour›; **E** (*~end*) nourishing ‹soup, bread, meal, etc.›; **etw. Kräftiges essen** eat a good nourishing meal; **F** (*grob*) strong ‹language›; coarse ‹expression, oath, etc.›.
**2** *adv.* **A** strongly, powerfully ‹built›; ‹hit, kick, press, push› hard; ‹sneeze› loudly; **~ entwickelt sein** strong, vigorous ‹plant›; sturdy ‹child›; **B** (*tüchtig*) ‹rain, snow› heavily; ‹eat› heartily; ‹sing› lustily; **etw. ~ schütteln** shake sth. vigorously; give sth. a good shake; **die Preise sind ~ gestiegen** prices have risen steeply; **der Flasche/dem Alkohol ~ zusprechen** hit the bottle in a big way (*coll.*); **C** (*mit Nachdruck*) **jmdm. ~ die** *od.* **seine Meinung sagen** give sb. a piece of one's mind

**kräftigen** *tr. V.* ‹holiday, air, etc.› invigorate; ‹food etc.› fortify; **sich ~:** build up one's strength; **~de Nahrung/Luft** nourishing food/bracing air

**Kräftigung** *die; ~, ~en* strengthening

**Kräftigungs·mittel** *das* tonic

**kraft-, Kraft-:** **~linien** *Pl.* (*Physik*) lines of force; **~los** *Adj.* weak; feeble; (*fig.*) weak ‹sun›; **~losigkeit** *die; ~~:* weakness; feebleness; **~maschine** *die* (*Technik*) engine; prime mover; **~meier** *der; ~~s, ~~* (*ugs. abwertend*) muscleman; **~meierei** *die; ~~* (*ugs. abwertend*) playing the muscleman; **~mensch** *der* strongman; muscleman; **~messer** *der; ~~s, ~~* **A** (*Physik*) dynamometer; **B** (*auf dem Jahrmarkt*) try-your-strength machine; **~paket** *das* (*Spieler*) powerhouse; (*Pferd*) powerful animal; (*Auto*) powerful machine; **ein ~paket von Spieler** a powerhouse of a player; **~post** *die* post-bus service; **~probe** *die* trial of strength; **~protz** *der* (*abwertend*) muscleman; **~rad** *das* (*Amtsspr.*) motorcycle; **~reserven** *Pl.* reserves of strength; **~sport** *der* ⇨ **Schwerathletik**; **~stoff** *der* (*Kfz-W.*) fuel; **~stoff·anzeiger** *der* (*Kfz-W.*) fuel gauge; **~stoff-Luft-Gemisch** *das* (*Kfz-W.*) air-fuel mixture; **~stoff·verbrauch** *der* fuel consumption; **~strotzend** *Adj.* vigorous; bursting with vigour *postpos.*; **~vergeudung** *die* waste of energy; **~verkehr** *der* (*Amtsspr.*) [motor] traffic; **~verschwendung** *die* ⇨ **~vergeudung**; **~voll** **1** *Adj.* powerful; **2** *adv.* powerfully; **~wagen** *der* motor vehicle; **~werk** *das* power station; **~wort** *das; Pl.* **~wörter** *od.* **~~e** ⇨ **~ausdruck**

**Kragen** /ˈkra:gn̩/ *der; ~s, ~, südd., österr. u. schweiz. auch:* **Krägen** /ˈkrɛ:gn̩/ **A** collar; **B** **ihm platzte der ~** (*salopp*) he blew his top (*coll.*); **jetzt platzt mir aber der ~!** (*salopp*) that's the last straw!; **es geht ihm an den ~** (*ugs.*) he's in for it now; **jmdn. am** *od.* **beim ~ packen** *od.* **nehmen** (*ugs.*) collar sb.; **jmdm. an den ~ wollen** (*ugs.*) get at *or* be after sb.; (*jmdn. verantwortlich machen*) try to hang something on sb. (*coll.*); ⇨ *auch* **Kopf** A; **C** (*Jägerspr.*) collar

**Kragen-:** **~bär** *der* [Himalayan] black bear; **~knopf** *der* collar stud (*Brit.*); (*oberster Knopf am Hemd*) top button; **~weite** *die* collar size; **[nicht] jmds. ~weite sein** (*salopp*) [not] be sb.'s cup of tea (*coll.*)

**Krag·stein** *der* (*Archit.*) bracket; (*Konsole*) console

**Krähe** /ˈkrɛ:ə/ *die; ~, ~n* crow; **eine ~ hackt der anderen kein Auge aus** (*Spr.*) dog does not eat dog (*prov.*)

**krähen** *itr. V.* (*auch fig.*) crow; ⇨ *auch* **Hahn**

**Krähen-:** **~füße** *Pl.* (*ugs.*) **A** (*Hautfalten*) crow's feet; **B** (*aus Eisen*) *devices with many sharp points scattered on the road to burst the tyres of a vehicle;* ≈ [tin] tacks; **~nest** *das* (*auch Seemannsspr.*) crow's nest

**Kräh·winkel** (*das*); **~s** (*spött.*) provincial backwater

**Krakau** /ˈkra:kau̯/ (*das*); **~s** **▶ 700** Cracow; Krakow

**Krakauer**[1] *der;* **~s, ~:** Cracovian

**Krakauer**[2] *die; ~, ~* (*Wurst*) *highly spiced, smoked beef and pork sausage*

**Krake** /ˈkra:kə/ *der; ~n, ~n* **A** (*Tintenfisch*) octopus; **B** (*Meeresungeheuer*) kraken

**Krakeel** /kraˈke:l/ *der;* **~s** (*ugs. abwertend*) row (*coll.*)

**krakeelen** **1** *itr. V.* (*ugs. abwertend*) kick up a row (*coll.*). **2** *tr. V.* scream

**Krakeeler** *der;* **~s, ~, Krakeelerin** *die; ~, ~nen* (*ugs. abwertend*) rowdy

**Krakel** /ˈkra:kl̩/ *der;* **~s, ~** (*ugs. abwertend*) scrawl; scribble

**krakelig** ⇨ **kraklig**

**krakeln** *tr., itr. V.* (*ugs. abwertend*) scrawl; scribble

**kraklig** *Adj.* (*ugs. abwertend*) scrawly

**Kral** /kra:l/ *der;* **~s, ~e** *od.* **~s** kraal

**Kralle** /ˈkralə/ *die; ~, ~n* claw; (*von Raubvögeln*) claw; talon; **die ~n des Todes** (*fig.*) the jaws of death; **jmdm. die ~n zeigen** (*ugs.*) show sb. one's claws; **etw. in die ~n bekommen** *od.* **kriegen** (*ugs.*) get sth. in one's clutches

**krallen** **1** *refl. V.* **sich an etw.** (*Akk.*) **~** ‹cat› dig its claws into sth.; ‹bird› dig its claws *or* talons into sth.; ‹person› clutch sth. [tightly]; **sich in/um etw.** (*Akk.*) **~:** dig into/clutch sth. **2** *tr. V.* **A** (*fest greifen*) **die Finger in/um etw.** (*Akk.*) **~:** dig one's fingers into sth./clutch sth. [tightly] with one's fingers; **B** (*krümmen*) **er krallte seine Finger/seine Hand** he bent his fingers into [the shape of] a claw; **C** (*salopp: stehlen*) pinch (*coll.*); nick (*Brit. coll.*); **D** (*salopp: ergreifen*) collar; (*verhaften*) nab (*coll.*)

**Kram** /kra:m/ *der;* **~[e]s** (*ugs.*) **A** stuff; (*Gerümpel*) junk; **den ganzen ~ hinschmeißen** (*fig. ugs.*) chuck the whole thing in (*coll.*); **B** (*Angelegenheit*) business; affair; **mach deinen ~ alleine!** do it yourself!; **jmdm. [genau] in den ~ passen** suit sb. [down to the ground (*coll.*)]

**kramen** **1** *itr. V.* **A** (*ugs.: herumwühlen*) **in etw.** (*Dat.*) **~:** rummage about in *or* rummage through sth.; **nach etw. ~:** rummage about looking for sth.; **B** (*schweiz.: einkaufen*) do some *or* a bit of shopping. **2** *tr. V.* (*ugs.*) **etw. aus etw. ~:** fish (*coll.*) *or* get sth. out of sth.

**Krämer** /ˈkrɛ:mɐ/ *der;* **~s, ~, Krämerin** *die; ~, ~nen* **A** (*veralt.: Lebensmittelhändler[in]*) grocer; **B** (*abwertend*) (*geiziger Mensch*) skinflint; stingy person; (*engstirniger Mensch*) petty-minded *or* small-minded person

**Krämer·seele** *die* (*abwertend*) **A** (*Geiz*) stingy nature; (*Engstirnigkeit*) petty-mindedness; small-mindedness; **B** (*geiziger Mensch*) skinflint; (*engstirniger Mensch*) petty-minded *or* small-minded person

**Kramladen** *der; Pl.* **Kramläden** (*ugs. abwertend*) junk shop

**Krampe** /ˈkrampə/ *die; ~, ~n* staple

**Krampen** *der;* **~s, ~** **A** ⇨ **Krampe**; **B** (*bayr., österr.: Spitzhacke*) pick[axe]

**Krampf** /krampf/ *der;* **~[e]s, Krämpfe** **▶ 474** /ˈkrɛmpfə/ **A** cramp; (*Zuckung*) spasm; (*bei Anfällen*) convulsion; **sich in Krämpfen winden** curl up in convulsions; **einen ~ bekommen** *od.* (*ugs.*) **kriegen** get cramp; **einen ~** *od.* **Krämpfe kriegen** (*fig. ugs.*) have a fit; **B** (*gequältes Tun*) painful strain; (*sinnloses Tun*) senseless waste of effort; **das ist doch alles ~:** it's all a senseless waste of effort

**Krampf·ader** *die* **▶ 474** varicose vein

**krampf·artig** **1** *Adj.* convulsive. **2** *adv.* convulsively

**krampfen** **1** *itr. V.* **A** be affected with cramp; (*bei Anfällen*) be convulsed; **sein Magen krampfte** he got stomach cramp; **B** (*schweiz.: sich anstrengen*) slave away. **2** *refl. V.* **A** be affected with cramp; (*bei Anfällen*) be convulsed; **B** (*umklammern*) **sich um/in etw.** (*Akk.*) **~:** clench sth./dig into sth. **3** *tr. V.* **A** (*schließen*) **die Fäuste/Finger um/in etw.** (*Akk.*) **~:** clench sth./dig one's hands/fingers into sth.; **B** (*ugs.: an sich bringen*) **sich** (*Dat.*) **etw. ~:** grab sth.

**krampfhaft** **1** *Adj.* **A** convulsive; **B** (*verbissen*) desperate; forced ‹cheerfulness›. **2** *adv.* **A** convulsively; **B** (*verbissen*) desperately

**krampf-, Krampf-:** **~husten** *der* **▶ 474** (*Med.*) whooping cough; **~lösend** *Adj.*, **~stillend** *Adj.* antispasmodic

**Kran** /kra:n/ *der;* **~[e]s, Kräne** /ˈkrɛ:nə/ **A** crane; **B** *Pl. auch* **~en** (*südwestd.: Wasserhahn*) tap; faucet (*Amer.*)

**Kran-:** **~brücke** *die* (*Technik*) gantry; **~führer** *der*, **~führerin** *die* **▶ 159** crane operator; (*~fahrer[in]*) crane driver

**Kranich** /ˈkra:nɪç/ *der;* **~s, ~e** crane

**krank** /kraŋk/, **kränker** /ˈkrɛŋkɐ/, **kränkst...** /ˈkrɛŋkst.../ *Adj.* **A** **▶ 474** ill *usu. pred.*; sick; bad ‹leg, tooth›; diseased ‹plant, organ›; (*fig.*) sick, ailing ‹economy, business›; **ein ~es Herz/eine ~e Leber haben** have a bad heart/a liver complaint; **[schwer] ~ werden** be taken *or* fall [seriously *or* very] ill; **er wurde immer kränker** he got steadily worse; **du siehst ~ aus** you don't look well; **sie liegt ~ zu/im Bett** she is ill in bed; **auf den Tod ~ sein** be critically *or* dangerously ill; **jmdn. ~ machen** make sb. ill; (*fig.*) get on sb.'s nerves; **vor Heimweh/Liebe ~ sein** be homesick/lovesick; ***sich ~ melden** let the office/boss *etc.* know that one is off sick; ***jmdn. ~ schreiben** give sb. a medical certificate; **B** (*Jägerspr.: angeschossen*) wounded

**Kranke** /ˈkraŋkə/ *der/die; adj. Dekl.* sick man/woman; (*Patient*) patient; **die ~n** the sick *pl.*; the patients

**kränkeln** /ˈkrɛŋkl̩n/ *itr. V.* be in poor health; not be well; (*fig.*) be in poor shape; **er kränkelt leicht** he is always ailing

**kranken** *itr. V.* (*leiden*) **an etw.** (*Dat.*) **~** ‹firm, project, etc.› suffer from sth.

**kränken** /ˈkrɛŋkn̩/ **1** *tr. V.* **jmdn. ~:** hurt *or* wound sb. *or* sb.'s feelings; **jmdn. in seiner Ehre/seinem Stolz/seiner Eitelkeit ~:** wound sb.'s honour/injure *or* wound sb.'s pride/vanity; **~d sein** be hurtful; **tief/schwer gekränkt sein** be deeply hurt. **2** *refl. V.* (*geh. veralt.*) **sich über jmdn./etw. ~:** be *or* feel hurt by sb./sth.

**kranken-, Kranken-:** **~anstalten** *Pl.* (*Amtsspr.*) hospital complex *sing.*; **~auto** *das* ⇨ **~wagen**; **~bericht** *der* case report; **~besuch** *der* visit to a sick person; **~blatt** *das* medical report [card]; **~fahrstuhl** *der* (*Amtsspr.*) wheelchair; **~geld** *das* sickness benefit; **~geschichte** *die* case history; **~gymnastik** *die* remedial *or* medical gymnastics *sing.*; physiotherapy; **~gymnastin** *die; ~~, ~~nen* **▶ 159** remedial gymnast; medical gymnast; physiotherapist; **~haus** *das* hospital; **jmdn. ins ~haus einliefern/aus dem ~haus entlassen** take sb. to hospital/discharge sb. from hospital; **im ~haus liegen** be in hospital; **ins ~haus [gehen] müssen** have to go [in]to hospital; **~haus·arzt** *der*, **~haus·ärztin** *die* hospital doctor; **~haus·aufenthalt** *der* stay in hospital; **~haus·reif** *Adj.* (*salopp*) **~hausreif aussehen** look like a hospital case; **jmdn. ~hausreif schlagen** make a real mess of sb. (*coll.*); **~kassa** *die* (*österr.*), **~kasse** *die* health insurance scheme; (*Körperschaft*) health insurance institution; (*privat*) health insurance company; **~kassen·beitrag** *der* health insurance contribution; **~lager** *das* (*geh.*) **A** (*Zeit des Krankseins*) illness; **B** (*~bett*) sickbed; **~pflege** *die* nursing; **in der ~pflege tätig sein** be a nurse; **~pfleger** *der* **▶ 159** male nurse; **~saal** *der* ward; **~salbung** *die* (*kath. Kirche*) extreme unction *no art.*; **~schein** *der* health insurance certificate; **~schwester** *die* **▶ 159** nurse; **~stand** *der* number of staff away sick; **im ~stand sein** (*österr.*) be away sick; **~stuhl** *der* ⇨ **~fahrstuhl**; **~transport** *der* transportation of sick/injured persons; **~versicherung** *die* **A** (*Versicherung*) health insurance; **B** (*Unternehmen*) health insurance company; **~versicherungs·pflichtig** *Adj.* ‹person› who is required to join a health insurance scheme; **~wagen** *der* ambulance; **~zimmer** *das* sickroom; (*im ~haus*) patients' room

**kränker** ⇨ **krank**

**krank|feiern** *itr. V.* (*ugs.*) skive off work (*coll.*) [pretending to be ill]; **ich glaube, ich feiere mal krank** I think I might just [have to] go sick (*joc.*)

**krankhaft** **1** *Adj.* **A** (*pathologisch*) pathological ‹change etc.›; morbid ‹growth, state, swelling, etc.›; **B** (*abnorm gesteigert*) pathological; pathological, morbid ‹fear, obsession›. **2** *adv.* **A** (*pathologisch*) pathologically; morbidly ‹swollen›; **B** (*abnorm gesteigert*) pathologically; pathologically, morbidly ‹obsessed, sensitive›

**Krankheit** *die; ~, ~en* **A** **▶ 474** illness; (*bestimmte Art, von Pflanzen, Organen*) disease; **von einer ~ befallen werden** contract *or* catch an illness/a disease; **an einer**

k

# Krankheiten und Schmerzen

## Verletzungen

***Wo haben Sie Schmerzen?, Wo tut es weh?***
= Where does it hurt?

***Mir tut der Arm weh***
= My arm is hurting

***Sie hat sich am Fuß wehgetan/verletzt***
= She has hurt her foot

***Ich habe mir den Fuß verstaucht/die Hand verbrannt***
= I have sprained my ankle/burnt my hand

***Er hat sich das Bein gebrochen***
= He has broken his leg

***ein Kieferbruch***
= a fracture of the jaw

***Sie hat einen Kieferbruch/Schädelbruch/Beckenbruch***
= She has a fractured jaw/skull/pelvis

Man sieht, dass das Possessivum im Englischen verwendet wird, wo im Deutschen der bestimmte Artikel mit dem Dativ der Person steht.

Siehe auch ····➤ **Körperteile**

## Schmerzen

***Ich habe Zahnschmerzen/Kopfschmerzen/Magenschmerzen*** od. (ugs.) ***Zahnweh/Kopfweh/Magenweh***
= I've got toothache/a headache/a stomach ache *od.* a pain in my stomach

***Sie hat Schmerzen im Rücken***
= (*allgemein*) She has back pain/(*dumpf*) backache; (*an verschiedenen Stellen*) She has pains in her back

***Sie hat Schmerzen***
= She is in pain

***ein stechender/bohrender Schmerz***
= a stab of pain/a gnawing pain

Ein starker Schmerz kann also nur **pain** sein, **ache** ist immer dumpf und anhaltend. Und *Schmerzen* sind auch meist **pain**; nur bei Schmerzen an verschiedenen Stellen sagt man **pains**.

## Das Kranksein

***Ich fühle mich krank/elend***
= I feel ill/wretched

***Mir ist schlecht/sauschlecht*** (ugs.)
= I don't feel well/I feel awful (*ugs.*)

***Ihnen war/wurde bei der Überfahrt übel***
= They felt/were sick on the crossing

***Sie ist schwer/unheilbar krank***
= She is seriously/terminally ill

***Er ist an Grippe erkrankt***
= He is ill with flu *od.* has [got] flu

***Sie hat sich erkältet/ist erkältet***
= She has caught a cold/has a cold

***Du holst dir eine Lungenentzündung***
= You'll catch pneumonia

***Sie leiden an Asthma/Bronchitis***
= They suffer from asthma/bronchitis

Mit Ausnahme von **cold** wird der unbestimmte Artikel bei Krankheiten nicht verwendet, auch dann nicht, wenn ein Adjektiv vor dem Substantiv steht:

***Ich habe eine schlimme Gelenkarthrose***
= I have bad arthritis

***Er bekommt immer eine leichte Bronchitis***
= He always gets slight bronchitis

Allerdings:

***eine schlimme Grippe***
= a nasty bout of flu

***ein schwerer Fall von Kehlkopfkrebs***
= a serious case of throat cancer

***eine hartnäckige Halsinfektion***
= a persistent throat infection

***ein Asthmaanfall***
= an attack of asthma

## Leiden und Leidende

***Er hat ein Herzleiden/ein Magenleiden/eine Hautkrankheit***
= He has a heart condition/a stomach complaint/a skin complaint

***Sie hat Rückenprobleme*** od. (ugs.) ***hats mit dem Rücken***
She suffers from back trouble

***Herzbeschwerden/Magenbeschwerden***
= heart/stomach trouble

In Zusammensetzungen wird *-kranke(r)* meist mit **sufferer** bzw. **patient** übersetzt:

***ein Aidskranker***
= an Aids sufferer

***ein Asthmakranker***
= an asthma sufferer

***Krebskranke***
= cancer patients

Aber:

***ein Epileptiker***
= an epileptic

***ein Diabetiker***
= a diabetic

## Behandlung

***Sie ist [bei einem Facharzt] in Behandlung***
= She is having *od.* receiving treatment [from a specialist]

***Er wird wegen Krebs/eines Magengeschwürs behandelt***
= He is being treated for cancer/a stomach ulcer

***Sie haben ihn auf ein Magengeschwür behandelt, aber es stellte sich heraus, dass er Krebs hatte***
= They treated him for a stomach ulcer, but it turned out he had cancer

***Ich bin wegen Gallensteinen operiert worden***
= I was operated on for gallstones

***Ich bin viermal operiert worden***
= I have had four operations

***mit Vollnarkose/Lokalanästhesie***
= under a general/local anaesthetic

***Die Krankenschwester gab mir eine Spritze***
= The nurse gave me an injection

***Sind Sie gegen Cholera geimpft [worden]?***
= Have you been vaccinated against cholera *od.* had a cholera vaccination?

## Heilmittel

***Haben Sie etwas gegen Verstopfung?***
= Have you got anything for constipation?

***Was kann ich gegen Heuschnupfen nehmen?***
What can I take for hay fever?

***Dreimal täglich einzunehmen***
= To be taken three times a day

***Es gibt kein Mittel gegen Aids***
= There is no cure for Aids

## Erholung

***Er ist auf dem Wege der Besserung***
= He is getting better *od.* is on the mend

***Es geht ihr*** od. ***Sie fühlt sich viel besser***
= She is [feeling] much better

***Ich habe mich vollständig erholt***
= I am fully recovered

~ **leiden/sterben** suffer from/die of an illness/a disease; **eine ~ heilen/einer ~ vorbeugen** cure/prevent an illness/a disease; **das ist doch kein Auto, das ist eine ~** (*fig. ugs. scherzh.*) that's just an apology for a car; **B** ▶ 474 (*Zeit des Krankseins*) illness; **nach langer/schwerer ~:** after a long/serious illness

**krankheits-, Krankheits-: ~bild** *das* clinical picture; **~erreger** *der* pathogen; disease-causing agent; **~fall** *der* case of illness; **im ~fall** in the event of illness; **~halber** *Adv.* due to illness; **~keim** *der* germ [causing the/a disease]

**krank|lachen** *refl. V.* (*ugs.*) laugh one's head off; laugh oneself silly

**kränklich** /ˈkrɛŋklɪç/ *Adj.* sickly; ailing

**krank-, Krank-: ~|machen** *itr. V.* (*ugs.*) ⇒ **~feiern**; ⇒ *auch* **krank** A; **~|melden** *refl. V.* let the office/boss *etc.* know that one is sick; **~meldung** *die* notification of absence through illness; **~|schreiben** *unr. tr. V.* give ‹person› a medical certificate

**kränkste** ⇒ **krank**

**Kränkung** *die*; ~, **~en eine ~:** an injury to one's/sb.'s feelings; **etw. als ~ empfinden** be hurt by sth.; take offence at sth.

**Kranz** /krants/ *der*; **~es, Kränze** /ˈkrɛntsə/ **A** wreath; garland; (*auf einem Grab, Sarg, an einem Denkmal*) wreath; **einen ~ niederlegen** lay a wreath; **B** (*Haar~*) chaplet (*of plaited hair*); **C** (*Kuchen*) ring cake; **D** (*geh.: Kreis*) circle; **ein ~ von Sagen** a cycle of legends

**Kränzchen** /ˈkrɛntsçən/ *das*; **~s, ~ A** (*zum Kaffeetrinken*) coffee circle; coffee klatch (*Amer.*); (*zum Handarbeiten*) sewing circle; **B** (*kleiner Kranz*) small wreath *or* garland

**Kranz-: ~gefäß** *das* ⇒ **Herzkranzgefäß**; **~geld** *das* (*Rechtsw.*) *damages for loss of virginity awarded against a woman's fiancé if he breaks off the engagement without good cause;* **~kuchen** *der* ⇒ **Kranz** C; **~niederlegung** *die* laying of a wreath; **~spende** *die* wreath; **„von ~spenden bitten wir abzusehen"** 'no flowers please'

**Krapfen** /ˈkrapfn̩/ *der*; **~s, ~ A** (*Berliner*) doughnut; **B** (*Kochkunst*) fritter

**krass, *kraß** /kras/ **1** *Adj.* **A** blatant ‹case›; gross, flagrant ‹injustice›; glaring, stark ‹contrast, contradiction›; sharp ‹difference›; gross ‹discrepancy, imbalance›; **B** rank, complete ‹outsider›; out-and-out ‹egoist›. **2** *adv.* **sich ~ ausdrücken** put sth. bluntly; **sich von etw. ~ unterscheiden** be in stark contrast to sth.

**Krassheit, *Kraßheit** *die*; ~, **~en** ⇒ **krass** A: blatancy; grossness, flagrancy; starkness; sharpness

**Krater** /ˈkraːtɐ/ *der*; **~s, ~:** crater

**Krater-: ~landschaft** *die* cratered landscape; **~see** *der* crater lake

**Kratz·bürste** *die* (*ugs. scherzh.*) stroppy (*Brit. coll.*) *or* prickly so-and-so

**kratzbürstig** *Adj.* (*ugs. scherzh.*) stroppy (*Brit. coll.*); prickly

**Kratze** *die*; ~, **~n** scraper

**Krätze** /ˈkrɛtsə/ *die*; ~ ▶ 474 scabies *sing.*

**kratzen** /ˈkratsn̩/ **1** *tr. V.* **A** scratch; **jmdm./sich den Arm blutig ~:** scratch sb.'s/one's arm and make it bleed; **B** (*scharren*) scratch; **seinen Namen in die Wand ~:** scratch one's name on the wall; **C** (*entfernen*) scrape; **etw. aus/von etw. ~:** scrape sth. out of/off sth.; **D** (*ugs.: stören*) bother; **jmdn. wenig ~:** not bother sb. all that much; **wen kratzt das schon?** who cares *or* who's bothered [about that]?.
**2** *itr. V.* **A** scratch; (*aus~*) scrape; **das Kratzen:** scratching; **an jmds. Ehre/Vormachtstellung** (*Dat.*) **~** (*fig.*) chip away at sb.'s honour/supremacy; **B** (*jucken*) itch; be scratchy *or* itchy; **C** (*brennen*) **im Hals ~** ‹wine› taste rough; ‹tobacco› be rough on the throat; ‹smoke› irritate the throat.
**3** *refl. V.* scratch [oneself]; **sich hinter dem Ohr/am Kopf ~:** scratch oneself behind the ear/scratch one's head

**Kratzer** *der*; **~s, ~ A** (*ugs.*) scratch; **B** (*Schaber*) scraper

**Krätzer** /ˈkrɛtsɐ/ *der*; **~s, ~** (*abwertend*) rough wine; plonk (*Brit. coll.*)

**kratz·fest** *Adj.* scratch-proof; non-scratch

**Kratz·fuß** *der* (*veralt.*) leg (*arch.*); **einen ~ machen** make a leg (*arch.*)

**kratzig** *Adj.* scratchy, itchy ‹material, pullover, etc.›; scratchy, rough ‹voice›

**krätzig** /ˈkrɛtsɪç/ *Adj.* scabious ‹skin›; mangy ‹dog›

**Krätz·milbe** *die* (*Zool.*) itch mite

**Kratz-: ~putz** *der* sgraffito; **~spur** *die* scratch [mark]; **~wunde** *die* scratch

**krauchen** /ˈkrauxn̩/ *itr. V.*; *mit sein* (*md.*) ⇒ **kriechen**

**krauen** /ˈkrauən/ *tr. V.* ⇒ **kraulen²**

**Kraul** /kraul/ *das*; **~s** (*Sport*) crawl

**kraulen¹ 1** *itr. V.* **A** do *or* swim the crawl; **B** *mit sein* **über den See/ans Ufer ~:** swim across the lake/to the bank using the crawl. **2** *tr. V.*; *auch mit sein* **eine Strecke ~:** cover a distance using the crawl

**kraulen²** *tr. V.* **jmdm. das Kinn ~:** tickle sb. under the chin; **jmdn. in den Haaren ~:** run one's fingers through sb.'s hair; **seinen Bart ~:** finger one's beard

**Kraul·schwimmen** *das* crawl; **beim ~:** when doing the crawl

**kraus** /kraus/ *Adj.* **A** frizzy ‹hair, beard›; creased ‹skirt etc.›; wavy ‹sea›; wrinkled ‹brow›; **die Stirn ~ ziehen** wrinkle one's brow; (*unmutig*) frown; **die Nase ~ ziehen** wrinkle one's nose; **B** (*abwertend: verworren*) muddled; confused

**Krause** *die*; ~, **~n A** (*Kragen*) ruff; (*am Ärmel*) ruffle; frill; **B** (*im Haar*) frizziness; **eine [starke] ~ haben/bekommen** ‹hair› be/go [very] frizzy; ‹person› be/go [very] frizzy-haired

**Kräusel-: ~band** *das*; *Pl.* **~bänder** Rufflette [tape] ®; **~krepp** *der* crêpe

**kräuseln** /ˈkrɔyzl̩n/ **1** *tr. V.* ruffle ‹water, surface›; gather ‹material etc.›; frizz ‹hair›; pucker [up] ‹lips›. **2** *refl. V.* ‹hair› go frizzy; ‹water› ripple; ‹smoke› curl up; ‹material› pucker up

**krausen 1** *tr. V.* gather ‹material etc.›; frizz ‹hair›; wrinkle [up] ‹forehead, nose›. **2** *itr. V.* ‹material, clothes› crease

**kraus·haarig** *Adj.* frizzy-haired ‹person›; curly-coated ‹dog etc.›

**Kraus·kopf** *der* frizzy hair; **einen ~ haben** have frizzy hair; be frizzy-haired; ⇒ *auch* **Wuschelkopf**

**Kraut** /kraut/ *das*; **~[e]s, Kräuter** /ˈkrɔytɐ/ **A** herb; **dagegen ist kein ~ gewachsen** (*ugs.*) there's nothing anyone can do about it; **B** (*Blätter*) foliage; stems and leaves *pl.*; (*von Kartoffeln, Bohnen usw.*) haulm; (*von Möhren, Rüben*) tops *pl.*; **ins ~ schießen** put on too much foliage; bolt; (*fig.*) run wild; **wie ~ und Rüben** (*ugs.*) all over the place; in a complete muddle; **C** (*bes. südd., österr.: Kohl*) cabbage; **D** (*ugs. abwertend: Tabak*) tobacco; **er raucht ein ganz elendes ~:** he is smoking some really foul stuff

**Kräutchen** /ˈkrɔytçən/ *das*; **~s, ~:** [small] herb; **ein ~ Rührmichnichtan sein** (*veralt.*) be oversensitive and easily upset

**Kräuter-: ~buch** *das* herbal; **~butter** *die* herb butter; **~essig** *der* herb vinegar; **~frau** *die* herbwoman; **~käse** *der* cheese flavoured with herbs; **~kissen** *das* herb pillow; **~likör** *der* herb liqueur; **~sammler** *der*, **~sammlerin** *die* herbalist; **~tee** *der* herb tea; **~weib** *das* (*veralt.*) ⇒ **~frau**

**krautig** *Adj.* herbaceous

**Kraut-: ~junker** *der* (*hist. abwertend*) large landowner; **~kopf** *der* ⇒ **Kohlkopf**

**Kräutlein** *das*; **~s, ~** ⇒ **Kräutchen**

**Kraut-: ~salat** *der* coleslaw; **~wickel** *der* (*südd., österr.*) ⇒ **Kohlroulade**

**Krawall** /kraˈval/ *der*; **~s, ~e A** (*Tumult*) riot; **B** (*ugs.: Lärm*) row (*coll.*); racket; **es gab ~:** there was a row (*coll.*) *or* racket; **~ machen** kick up *or* make a row (*coll.*) *or* racket; **~ schlagen** kick up *or* make a fuss

**Krawall·macher** *der*, **Krawall·macherin** *die* rowdy

**Krawatte** /kraˈvatə/ *die*; ~, **~n A** tie; **B** (*Catchen*) headlock; chancery

**Krawatten-: ~halter** *der* tie clip; **~knoten** *der* knot [of the/a/one's tie]; **~muffel** *der* (*ugs.*) stick-in-the-mud where ties are concerned; **~nadel** *die* tiepin; **~zwang** *der*: **hier herrscht [kein] ~zwang** you [do not] have to wear a tie here

**kraxeln** /ˈkraksl̩n/ *itr. V.*; *mit sein* (*bes. südd., österr. ugs.*) climb; (*mit Mühe*) clamber; **auf etw.** (*Akk.*) **~:** climb [up] sth.; (*mit Mühe*) clamber up sth.

**Kreation** /kreaˈtsi̯oːn/ *die*; ~, **~en** (*bes. Mode*) creation

**kreativ** /kreaˈtiːf/ **1** *Adj.* creative. **2** *adv.* **~ veranlagt sein** have a creative bent

**Kreativität** /kreativiˈtɛːt/ *die*; **~:** creativity

**Kreativ·urlaub** *der* [arts and crafts] activity holiday

**Kreatur** /kreaˈtuːɐ̯/ *die*; ~, **~en A** (*Geschöpf*) creature; **B** (*alle Lebewesen*) creation; **alle ~:** all creation; **Gott schuf alle ~:** God made all creatures *pl.*; **C** (*Mensch*) creature; wretch; **D** (*abwertend: willenloser Mensch*) minion; creature

**kreatürlich** /kreaˈtyːɐ̯lɪç/ *Adj.* (*geh.*) creaturely, natural ‹feeling, love, etc.›; animal *attrib.* ‹fear›

**Krebs** /kreːps/ *der*; **~es, ~e A** crustacean; (*Fluss~*) crayfish; (*Krabbe*) crab; **rot wie ein ~:** as red as a lobster; **einen ~ fangen** (*Rudererjargon*) catch a crab; **B** ▶ 474 (*Krankheit*) cancer; **C** (*Astrol.*) Cancer; the Crab; ⇒ *auch* **Fisch**

**krebs·artig 1** *Adj.* cancerous. **2** *adv.* cancerously; in the manner of a cancer

**krebsen** *itr. V.* **A** (*Flusskrebse fangen*) catch crayfish; (*Krabben fangen*) catch crabs; **B** (*ugs.: sich abmühen*) **mit etw. zu ~ haben** find sth. a real *or* uphill struggle

**krebs-, Krebs-: ~erregend, ~erzeugend** *Adj.* carcinogenic; cancer-producing *usu. attrib.*; **das Rauchen kann ~erregend** *od.* **~erzeugend sein** smoking can cause cancer; **~forschung** *die* cancer research; **~gang** *der* **A** (*rückläufige Entwicklung*) retrogression; **den ~gang gehen** ‹business› go downhill; **im ~gang gehen** go backwards; **B** (*Musik*) retrograde movement; retrogression; **~geschwulst** *die* cancerous growth *or* tumour; **~geschwür** *das* (*volkst.*) cancerous ulcer; (*fig. geh.*) cancer; **~krank** *Adj.* cancer *attrib.* ‹patient etc.›; **~krank sein** suffer from *or* have cancer; **~kranke** *der/die* person suffering from cancer; (*Patient*) cancer patient; **~leiden** *das* cancer *no def. art.*; **~rot** *Adj.* as red as a lobster *postpos.*; (*aus Verlegenheit*) as red as a beetroot *postpos.*; **~rot werden** *od.* **anlaufen** go *or* turn as red as a beetroot; **~suppe** *die* crab soup; (*aus Flusskrebsen*) crayfish soup; **~tier** *das* (*Zool.*) crustacean; **~vorsorge** *die* (*bes. Amtsspr.*) **[Maßnahmen zur] ~vorsorge** precautions *pl.* against cancer; **~zelle** *die* cancer cell

**Kredenz** /kreˈdɛnts/ *die*; ~, **~en** (*veralt.*) sideboard

**kredenzen** *tr. V.* (*geh.*) **[jmdm.] etw. ~:** serve [sb. with] sth.

**Kredit¹** /kreˈdiːt/ *der*; **~[e]s, ~e** ▶ 337 **A** (*Darlehen*) loan; credit; **jmdm. einen ~ gewähren** *od.* **einräumen** *od.* **geben** give *or* grant sb. a loan *or* a credit; **einen ~ kündigen** call in a loan; **B** (*Zahlungsaufschub*) credit; **er hat bei uns ~:** his credit is good with us; **jmdm. ~ geben** give *or* grant sb. credit; **auf ~:** on credit; **C** (*Kaufmannsspr.: Vertrauenswürdigkeit*) good reputation *or* name; **jmdm. großen politischen ~ verschaffen** give sb. considerable political standing

**Kredit²** /ˈkreːdɪt/ *das*; **~s, ~s** (*Finanzw.*) credit side

**kredit-, Kredit-: ~abteilung** *die* credit department; **~anstalt** *die* credit institution; **~aufnahme** *die*: **durch ~aufnahme** by means of a loan/loans; **~brief** *der* (*Finanzw.*) letter of credit; **~fähig** *Adj.* (*Finanzw.*) credit worthy; **~geber** *der*, **~geberin** *die* lender; **~geschäft** *das* credit transaction;

k

**~hai** *der* (*ugs. abwertend*) loan shark (*coll.*)

**kreditieren** *tr. V.* (*Kaufmannsspr.*) **jmdm. einen Betrag ~/jmdn. für einen Betrag ~:** advance sb. an amount *or* give sb. an amount on credit/credit sb. with an amount

**kredit-, Kredit-: ~institut** *das* credit institution; **~karte** *die* ▶337 credit card; **mit ~karte bezahlen** pay by credit card; **~kauf** *der* credit purchase; **~linie** *die* (*Finanzw.*) credit limit; **~nehmer** *der;* **~~s, ~~, ~nehmerin** *die;* **~~, ~~nen** borrower; **~schutz** *der* (*Finanzw.*) credit protection; **~würdig** *Adj.* (*Finanzw.*) credit worthy

**Kredo** /ˈkreːdo/ *das;* **~s, ~s** Ⓐ (*kath. Kirche*) creed; credo; Ⓑ (*fig. geh.*) credo

**kregel** /ˈkreːgl̩/ *Adj.* (*bes. nordd., md.*) lively

**Kreide** /ˈkraidə/ *die;* **~, ~n** Ⓐ (*Kalkstein*) chalk; Ⓑ (*zum Schreiben*) chalk; **mit ~ zeichnen/schreiben** draw/write in *or* with chalk; **ein Stück ~:** a piece of chalk; **bei jmdm. [tief] in der ~ stehen** *od.* **sitzen** *od.* **sein** be [deep] in debt to sb.; owe sb. [a lot of] money; Ⓒ (*Geol.*) Cretaceous [period]

**kreide-, Kreide-: ~bleich** *Adj.* as white as a sheet *postpos.;* **~felsen** *der* chalk cliff; **~haltig** *Adj.* chalky; cretaceous (*Geol.*); **~stift** *der* [piece of] chalk; (*bild. Kunst*) chalk; crayon; **~weiß** *Adj.:* ⇨ **~bleich**; **~zeichnung** *die* chalk drawing; **~zeit** *die* ⇨ **~ c**

**kreidig** *Adj.* Ⓐ (*voller Kreide*) chalky; Ⓑ (*kreidehaltig*) chalky; cretaceous (*Geol.*); Ⓒ (*geh.: bleich*) deathly pale ‹face›

**kreieren** /kreˈiːrən/ *tr. V.* (*auch Theater*) create

**Kreis** /krais/ *der;* **~es, ~e** Ⓐ circle; **einen ~ schlagen** *od.* **beschreiben** describe a circle; **jmds. ~e stören** (*geh.*) disturb sb.; Ⓑ (*Handball: Wurf~*) goal area; Ⓒ (*Ring*) circle; **einen ~ bilden** *od.* **schließen** form *or* make a circle; **in einem** *od.* **im ~ stehen/sitzen** stand/sit in a circle; **sich im ~ drehen** *od.* **bewegen** go *or* turn round in a circle; (*fig.*) go round in circles; **mir dreht sich alles im ~:** everything's going round and round; **der ~ hat sich geschlossen** the last piece has fallen into place; **~e ziehen** ‹court case› have [wide] repercussions; ‹movement› grow in size and influence; Ⓓ (*Gruppe*) circle; **der ~ meiner Freunde** my circle of friends; **im ~e der Freunde/Familie** among *or* with friends/within the family; **im kleinen** *od.* **engsten ~:** with a few close friends [and relatives]; **der ~ seiner Leser/Anhänger** his readers *pl.*/followers *pl.;* Ⓔ (*Teil der Gesellschaft*) circle; **in seinen ~en** in the circles in which he moves/moved; **in weiten** *od.* **breiten ~en der Bevölkerung** amongst wide sections of the population; **die besseren/besten ~e** the best circles; Ⓕ (*von Problemen, Lösungen usw.*) range; Ⓖ (*Verwaltungsbezirk*) district; (*Wahl~*) ward; **der ~ Heidelberg** the Heidelberg district *or* district of Heidelberg; Ⓗ (*Elektrot.*) circuit

**Kreis-: ~abschnitt** *der* (*Geom.*) segment [of a/the circle]; **~arzt** *der,* **~ärztin** *die* district medical officer; **~ausschnitt** *der* (*Geom.*) sector [of a/the circle]; **~bahn** *die* orbit; **~bewegung** *die* circular movement; **~bogen** *der* (*Geom.*) arc [of a/the circle]

**kreischen** /ˈkraiʃn̩/ *regelm.* (*veralt. auch unr.*) *itr. V.* ‹person› screech, shriek; ‹bird› screech; ‹brakes› squeal, screech; ‹door› creak; ‹saw› screech; **mit ~den Bremsen** with a squeal *or* screech of brakes

**Kreisel** /ˈkraizl̩/ *der;* **~s, ~** Ⓐ (*Technik*) gyroscope; Ⓑ (*Kinderspielzeug*) top; **den ~ schlagen** spin *or* whip the top; Ⓒ (*ugs.: Kreisverkehr*) roundabout

**Kreisel-: ~bewegung** *die* gyration; spinning movement; **~kompass, *~kompaß** *der* (*Schifffahrt*) gyrocompass

**kreiseln** *itr. V.* Ⓐ *auch mit sein* (*sich drehen*) spin [round]; gyrate; Ⓑ (*mit einem Kreisel spielen*) play with a top; spin a top

***old spelling (see note on page 1707)**

**Kreisel·pumpe** *die* (*Technik*) centrifugal pump

**kreisen** *itr. V.* Ⓐ *auch mit sein* ‹planet› revolve (**um** around); ‹satellite etc.› orbit; ‹aircraft, bird› circle; **der Satellit kreist um die Erde** the satellite orbits the Earth; **das Blut kreiste schneller in seinen Adern** (*fig.*) the blood coursed faster in his veins; **die Flasche [in der Runde] ~ lassen** (*fig.*) pass the bottle round; **seine Gedanken kreisten immer um dasselbe Thema** (*fig.*) his thoughts always revolved around the same subject; Ⓑ (*Sport*) **die Arme ~ lassen** swing one's arms round [in a circle]

**kreis-, Kreis-: ~fläche** *die* (*Geom.*) area of a/the circle; **~förmig** ❶ *Adj.* circular; ❷ *adv.* **ein ~förmig gebogenes Stück Draht** a piece of wire bent into a circle; **~frei** *Adj.* (*Amtsspr.*) **eine ~freie Stadt** a town that is administered as a district in its own right; **~klasse** *die* (*Sport*) district league; **~kolben·motor** *der* ⇨ **Wankelmotor**; **~lauf** *der* Ⓐ (*der Natur, der Wirtschaft, des Lebens usw.*) cycle; (*des Geldes; Technik*) circulation; Ⓑ (*Physiol.*) circulation; **~läufer** *der,* **~läuferin** *die* (*Hallenhandball*) ⇨ **~spieler**; **~lauf·kollaps** *der* ▶474 (*Med.*) circulatory collapse; **~lauf·mittel** *das* Ⓐ remedy to prevent faintness; Ⓑ (*Med.*) circulatory preparation; (*den ~lauf anregend*) circulatory stimulant; **~lauf·störung** *die* ▶474 Ⓐ *bes. im Pl.* faintness; Ⓑ (*Med.*) cardio-vascular disorder; circulatory disturbance; **~laufstörungen** *Pl.* circulatory trouble *sing.;* **~leitung** *die* (*DDR*) district committee; **~linie** *die* (*Geom.*) circumference [of a/the circle]; **~ring** *der* (*Geom.*) annulus; **~rund** ❶ *Adj.* [perfectly] circular *or* round; ❷ *adv.* ‹bent etc.› in[to] a [perfect] circle; **~säge** *die* Ⓐ (*Werkzeug*) circular saw; Ⓑ (*ugs. scherzh.: Strohhut*) boater

**kreißen** /ˈkraisn̩/ *itr. V.* (*veralt.*) be in labour

**Kreis·spieler** *der,* **Kreis·spielerin** *die* (*Hallenhandball*) pivot player

**Kreiß·saal** *der* (*Med.*) delivery room

**Kreis-: ~stadt** *die* the chief town of a/the district; **~tag** *der* district assembly; **~verkehr** *der* traffic on *or* going round a/the roundabout; (*Platz*) roundabout; **~verwaltung** *die* administration of a/the district; (*Behörde*) district authority; **~wehrersatz·amt** *das* district recruiting office; **~zahl** *die* (*Math.*) pi *no art.*

**Krem** /kreːm/ *die;* **~, ~s** ⇨ **Creme**

**Krematorium** /krema'toːri̯ʊm/ *das;* **~s, Krematorien** crematorium

**kremig** ⇨ **cremig**

**Kreml** /ˈkrɛml̩/ *der;* **~s** Kremlin

**Krempe** /ˈkrɛmpə/ *die;* **~, ~n** brim

**Krempel**[1] /ˈkrɛmpl̩/ *der;* **~s** (*ugs. abwertend*) stuff; (*Gerümpel*) junk; **den ganzen ~ hinwerfen** (*fig.*) chuck the whole thing in (*coll.*)

**Krempel**[2] *die;* **~, ~n** (*Textilind.*) carding machine

**krempeln**[1] *tr. V.* roll

**krempeln**[2] *tr. V.* (*Textilind.*) card

**Kremser** /ˈkrɛmzɐ/ *der;* **~s, ~** (*veralt.*) [covered] charabanc (*Brit. dated*)

**Kren** /kreːn/ *der;* **~[e]s** (*südd., bes. österr.*) ⇨ **Meerrettich**

**Kreole** /kreˈoːlə/ *der;* **~n, ~n, Kreolin** *die;* **~, ~nen** Creole

**kreolisch** *Adj.* ▶696 Creole

**krepieren** /kreˈpiːrən/ *itr. V.; mit sein* Ⓐ (*zerplatzen*) explode; go off; Ⓑ (*salopp: sterben*) ‹animal› die; ‹person› snuff it (*sl.*)

**Krepp** /krɛp/ *der;* **~s, ~s** *od.* **~e** crêpe

***Kreppapier** ⇨ **Krepppapier**

**Krepp-: ~papier** *das* crêpe paper; **~sohle** *die* crêpe sole

**Kresse** /ˈkrɛsə/ *die;* **~, ~n** (*Bot.*) cress

**Kreta** /ˈkreːta/ (*das*)**;** **~s** Crete

**Kreter** /ˈkreːtɐ/ *der;* **~s, ~, Kreterin** *die;* **~, ~nen** Cretan

**Krethi und Plethi** *Pl., auch Sg.* (*abwertend*) every Tom, Dick and Harry *sing.*

**Kretin** /kreˈtɛ̃ː/ *der;* **~s, ~s** Ⓐ (*Med.*) cretin; Ⓑ (*fig. abwertend*) imbecile

**Kretinismus** /kretiˈnɪsmʊs/ *der;* **~** (*Med.*) cretinism *no art.*

**kreucht** /krɔyçt/ *in* **alles, was da ~ und fleucht** all living creatures *or* things

**kreuz: ~ und quer durch die Stadt fahren** drive all over/round the town; **in die Kreuz und [in die] Quere fahren** drive all over the place

**Kreuz** /krɔyts/ *das;* **~es, ~e** Ⓐ cross; (*Symbol*) cross; crucifix; **etw. über ~ legen/falten** lay sth. down/fold sth. crosswise; **das ~ des Südens** (*Astron.*) the Southern Cross; **zu ~e kriechen** humble oneself; ⇨ *auch* **eisern** 1 A; **rot** 1; Ⓑ (*hist.*) cross; **jmdn. ans ~ schlagen** *od.* **nageln** nail sb. to the cross; Ⓒ (*~zeichen*) sign of the cross; **das/ein ~ schlagen** make the sign of the cross; (*sich bekreuzigen*) cross oneself; **drei ~e machen** (*ugs.*) heave a sigh of relief; Ⓓ (*Leid*) cross; **sein ~ auf sich nehmen/tragen** take up/bear one's cross; **es ist ein ~ mit jmdm./etw.** (*ugs.*) sb. is a real strain *or* is really trying/sth. is a real problem; Ⓔ (*Teil des Rückens*) small of the back; **ein steifes ~ haben** have a stiff back; **Schmerzen im ~:** pain in the small of the back; **ich habs im ~** (*ugs.*) I've got back trouble *or* a bad back; **jmdn. aufs ~ legen** (*salopp*) take sb. for a ride (*coll.*); **eine Frau aufs ~ legen** (*salopp: mit ihr schlafen*) lay a woman (*sl.*); **fast** *od.* **beinahe aufs ~ fallen** (*fig.*) almost fall through the floor; **jmdm. etw. aus dem ~ leiern** (*salopp*) talk sb. into handing sth. over; Ⓕ (*Kartenspiel*) (*Farbe*) clubs *pl.;* (*Karte*) club; ⇨ *auch* **Pik**[2]; Ⓖ (*Autobahn*) interchange; Ⓗ (*Musik*) sharp

**kreuz-, Kreuz-: ~abnahme** *die* (*bild. Kunst*) Descent *or* Deposition from the Cross; ***~as, ~ass** *das* ace of clubs; **~band** *das; Pl.* **~bänder** ▶471 (*Anat.*) cruciate ligament; **~bein** *das* ▶471 (*Anat.*) sacrum; **~blume** *die* Ⓐ (*Bot.*) milkwort; Ⓑ (*Archit.*) finial; **~blütler** *der;* **~~s, ~~** (*Bot.*) cruciferous plant; crucifer; **~brav** *Adj.* thoroughly good and honest ‹person›; very good *or* well-behaved ‹child›; **~bube** *der* jack of clubs; **~dame** *die* queen of clubs

**kreuzen** ❶ *tr. V.* (*auch Biol.*) cross; **die Arme/Beine [übereinander] ~:** cross *or* fold one's arms/cross one's legs; ⇨ *auch* **Klinge** B. ❷ *refl. V.* Ⓐ (*überschneiden*) cross; intersect; **ihre Wege ~ sich** (*fig.*) their paths cross; **ihre Blicke ~ sich** (*fig.*) their eyes meet; Ⓑ (*zuwiderlaufen*) clash (**mit** with). ❸ *itr. V.* Ⓐ *mit haben od. sein* (*hin und her fahren*) cruise; Ⓑ (*Seemannsspr.*) tack

**Kreuzer** *der;* **~s, ~** Ⓐ (*Milit.: Kriegsschiff*) cruiser; Ⓑ (*Segelsport*) cruising yacht; cruiser; Ⓒ (*hist.: Münze*) kreuzer

**Kreuzes·tod** *der* [death by] crucifixion; **den ~ sterben** die on the cross

**kreuz-, Kreuz-: ~fahrer** *der* (*hist.*) crusader; **~fahrt** *die* Ⓐ (*Seereise*) cruise; **eine ~fahrt machen** go on a cruise; Ⓑ (*hist.*) ⇨ **~zug**; **~feuer** *das* (*Milit., auch fig.*) crossfire; **etw. unter ~feuer nehmen** direct crossfire at sth.; **im ~feuer stehen** be under fire from all sides; **ins ~feuer geraten** come under fire from all sides; **~fidel** *Adj.* (*ugs.*) (*sehr gut gelaunt*) very cheerful; (*sehr lustig*) very jolly; **~förmig** ❶ *Adj.* cross-shaped; cruciform; ❷ *adv.* ‹built, arranged, etc.› in the shape of a cross; **~gang** *der* cloister; **~gelenk** *das* ⇨ **Kardangelenk**; **~gewölbe** *das* (*Archit.*) cross vault; **~griff** *der* (*Turnen*) cross grip; **~hacke** *die* pickaxe

**kreuzigen** /ˈkrɔytsɪgn̩/ *tr. V.* crucify; **der Gekreuzigte** Christ crucified

**Kreuzigung** *die;* **~, ~en** Ⓐ (*das Kreuzigen*) crucifixion; Ⓑ (*bild. Kunst*) Crucifixion

**kreuz-, Kreuz-: ~knoten** *der* (*Seemannsspr.*) reef knot; **~könig** *der* king of clubs; **~lahm** *Adj.* broken-backed ‹horse etc.›; **ich bin ganz ~lahm** (*ugs.*) my back is killing me (*coll.*); **~mast** *der* (*Seemannsspr.*) mizenmast; **~otter** *die* adder; [common] viper; **~reim** *der* (*Verslehre*) alternate rhyme; **~rippen·gewölbe** *das* (*Archit.*) ribbed vault; **~ritter** *der* (*hist.*) Ⓐ crusader; Ⓑ (*vom deutschen Ritterorden*) Teutonic Knight;

knight of the Teutonic Order; **~schlitz·schraube** *die* Phillips screw ®; **~schlitz·schrauben·dreher** *der* Phillips screwdriver ®; **~schlüssel** *der* four-way wheel brace; **~schmerzen** *Pl.* pain *sing.* in the small of the back; **~schnabel** *der* (*Zool.*) crossbill; **~spinne** *die* cross spider; garden spider; **~stich** *der* (*Handarb.*) cross stitch

**Kreuzung** *die;* ~, **~en** ▶ 818 **A** junction; crossroads *sing.*; **B** (*Biol.*) crossing; crossbreeding; (*Ergebnis*) cross; cross-breed; **eine ~ aus** *od.* **von ... und ...** a cross between ... and ...

**kreuz·unglücklich** *Adj.* (*ugs.*) terribly miserable (*coll.*)

**kreuzungs·frei** *Adj.* (*Verkehrsw.*) without [any] junctions *postpos.*

**Kreuzungs·punkt** *der* junction; (*von Autobahnen*) intersection

**kreuz-, Kreuz-: ~verband** *der* (*Bauw.*) English cross bond; **~verhör** *das* cross-examination; **jmdn. ins ~verhör nehmen** (*fig.*) cross-examine sb.; **~weg** *der* **A** (*Wegkreuzung*) crossroads *sing.*; **am ~weg stehen/an einen ~weg gekommen sein** (*geh.*) stand *or* be at/have reached a crossroads; **B** (*kath. Kirche: Darstellung, Gebete*) stations of the Cross, way of the Cross; **~weise** *Adv.* crosswise; crossways; **du kannst mich mal ~weise!** (*derb*) [you can] get stuffed! (*sl.*); **~wort·rätsel** *das* crossword [puzzle]; **~zeichen** *das* (*bes. kath. Kirche*) sign of the cross; **das ~zeichen machen** make the sign of the cross; (*sich bekreuzigen*) cross oneself; **~zug** *der* **A** (*hist.*) crusade; **B** (*Kampagne*) crusade

**Krevette** /kreˈvɛtə/ *die;* ~, **~n** palaemon prawn; leander

**kribbelig** *Adj.* (*ugs.*) **A** (*vor Ungeduld*) fidgety; (*nervös*) edgy; **B** (*kribbelnd*) **ein ~es Gefühl in der Hand** pins and needles in one's hand

**kribbeln** /ˈkrɪbl̩n/ *itr. V.* **A** (*jucken*) tickle; (*prickeln*) tingle; **es kribbelt mir** *od.* **mich in der Nase/in den Füßen/unter der Haut** I've got a tickle in my nose/my feet are tingling *or* I've got pins and needles in my feet/my skin is itching *or* prickling; **es kribbelt mir in den Fingern, es zu tun** (*fig.*) I'm just itching to do it; **B** (*wimmeln*) swarm [about]; **in dem Ameisenhaufen kribbelte und krabbelte es** the ants were swarming about in the anthill

**kribblig** ⇒ **kribbelig**

**Krickelkrakel** /ˈkrɪkl̩krakl̩/ *das;* **~s** (*ugs.*) scribble; scrawl

**Kricket** /ˈkrɪkət/ *das;* **~s** cricket

**Krida** /ˈkriːda/ *die;* ~ (*österr. Rechtsw.*) fraudulent bankruptcy; (*fahrlässig*) bankruptcy through negligence

**kriechen** /ˈkriːçn̩/ *unr. itr. V.* **A** *mit sein* ‹insect, baby› crawl; ‹plant› creep; ‹person, animal› creep, crawl; ‹car, train, etc.› crawl *or* creep [along]; **aus dem Ei/der Puppe ~:** hatch [out]/emerge from the chrysalis; **~de Pflanzen** creepers; **erschöpft ins Bett ~:** crawl exhausted into bed; **auf allen vieren/auf dem Bauch ~:** crawl on all fours/crawl [along] on one's stomach; **die Zeit/der Zeiger kriecht** (*fig.*) time creeps by/the hand creeps [around the dial]; ⇒ *auch* **Kreuz A**; **B** *mit sein* (*ugs.: sich fortbewegen*) walk; get about; **kaum noch ~ können** hardly be able to get about *or* walk; (*alt und gebrechlich sein*) be old and decrepit; **C** *auch mit sein* (*abwertend: sich unterwürfig verhalten*) crawl, grovel (**vor** + *Dat.* to)

**Kriecher** *der;* **~s**, ~, **Kriecherin** *die;* ~, **~nen** (*abwertend*) crawler; groveller

**kriecherisch** *Adj.* (*abwertend*) crawling; grovelling

**Kriech-: ~spur** *die* (*Verkehrsw.*) crawler lane; **~strom** *der* (*Elektrot.*) leakage current; **~tempo** *das* (*abwertend*) **im ~tempo** at a snail's pace; **~tier** *das* (*Zool.*) reptile

**Krieg** /kriːk/ *der;* **~[e]s, ~e** war; (*Kriegführung*) warfare; **[gegen jmdn.] ~ führen** wage war [on sb.]; **~ führend** warring; belligerent; **einem Land den ~ erklären** declare war on a country; **sich im ~ befinden** *od.* **im ~ stehen [mit ...]** be at war [with ...]; **in den ~ ziehen** go to war; **im ~ bleiben** *od.* **fallen** be killed in the war; **der kalte ~:** the cold war

**kriegen** *tr. V.* (*ugs.*) **A** (*bekommen*) get; **noch Geld von jmdm. ~:** be owed money by sb.; **Bescheid ~:** be told; **Schläge** *od.* **sie ~:** get a good hiding (*coll.*) *or* beating; **du kriegst gleich eine/ein paar!** I'll clout you in a moment!; **ein Jahr [Gefängnis] ~:** get a *or* one year [in prison]; **einen Schnupfen ~:** catch [a] cold; **Besuch ~:** have a visitor/visitors; **seinen Willen ~:** get one's own way; **ich kriege keine Verbindung** *od.* **keinen Anschluss** I can't get through; **am Ende des Films ~ sie sich** at the end of the film boy gets girl; **was ~ Sie?** what can I get you?; **ein Baby/Kind ~:** have a baby/child; **Junge ~:** have puppies/kittens *etc.*; **jmdn. dazu ~, etw. zu tun** get sb. to do sth.; **er ist nicht aus dem Haus** *od.* **vor die Tür zu ~:** nothing will get him out of the house *or* front door; **jmdn. satt/frei ~:** feed sb./get sb. free; **wir werden das** *od.* **es schon ~:** we'll soon sort it out; **zu viel ~** (*ugs.*) blow one's top (*coll.*); (*bei jmds. Worten*) see red; ⇒ *auch* **genug**; **Motte A**; **zu viel 1 A**; **B** (*befallen werden*) get; **die Wut/Angst/einen Schrecken ~:** get angry scared/have *or* get a shock; **Hunger/Durst ~:** get hungry/thirsty; **Heimweh/Fernweh ~:** get homesick/start suffering from wanderlust; **einen roten Kopf ~:** go red; blush; **Falten/eine Glatze ~:** get wrinkles/go bald; **C** (*erreichen*) catch ‹train, bus, etc.›; **D** (*fangen*) catch; **E** + *Inf. mit „zu"* (*die Möglichkeit haben*) **etw. zu essen ~:** get sth. to eat; **er kriegte den Ast zu fassen** he was able to *or* he managed to grab hold of the branch; **F** + *Inf. mit „zu"* (*ertragen müssen*) **etw. zu spüren/hören ~:** feel the force of sth./get a good talking-to; **es mit jmdm. zu tun ~:** have sb. to reckon with; **G** + *2. Part.* **etw. geschenkt ~:** get sth. as a present; **ein gutes Essen vorgesetzt ~:** get served with a good meal; **H** *in* **es nicht über sich ~, etw. zu tun** (*ugs.*) not be able to bring oneself to do sth.

**Krieger** *der;* **~s**, ~: warrior; (*nordamerikanischer Indianer*) brave; **die alten ~:** the veterans; **ein müder ~** (*fig.*) a tired old thing

**Krieger·denkmal** *das* (*veralt.*) war memorial

**Kriegerin** *die;* ~, **~nen** warrior

**kriegerisch** *Adj.* **A** (*kampflustig*) warlike; **B** (*militärisch*) military; **eine ~e Auseinandersetzung** an armed conflict

**Krieger·witwe** *die* war widow

***krieg·führend** ⇒ **Krieg**

**Krieg·führung** *die* warfare *no art.*; (*Leitung*) conduct of the war

**kriegs-, Kriegs-: ~anleihe** *die* war loan; **~aus·bruch** *der* outbreak of war; **bei/vor ~ausbruch** at/before the outbreak of war; **~bedingt** *Adj.* caused by the war *postpos.*; **~beginn** *der* beginning *or* start of the war; **~beil** *das* tomahawk; **das ~beil ausgraben/begraben** (*scherzh.*) start fighting/bury the hatchet; **~bemalung** *die* (*Völkerk.*) warpaint; **in voller ~bemalung** (*scherzh.*) in full warpaint; **~berichterstatter** *der*, **~berichterstatterin** *die* war correspondent; **~bericht·erstattung** *die* war reporting *no art.*; **~beschädigt** *Adj.* war-disabled; **~beschädigte** *der/die* war-disabled person; war invalid; **~beute** *die* spoils *pl.* of war; **~blinde** *der/die* person blinded in the war; **~dienst** *der* **A** (*im Krieg*) active service; **B** (*Wehrdienst*) military service; **den ~dienst verweigern** be a conscientious objector; **~dienst·verweigerer** *der* conscientious objector; **~dienst·verweigerung** *die* conscientious objection; **~einwirkung** *die:* **infolge von ~einwirkungen** as a result of the war; **~ende** *das* end of the war; **bei/vor ~ende** at/before the end of the war; **~entschädigung** *die* reparations *pl.*; **~entscheidend** *Adj.* decisive for the outcome of the war *postpos.*; **~erklärung** *die* declaration of war; **~erlebnis** *das* wartime experience; **~fall** *der:* **im ~fall[e]** in the event of war; **~film** *der* war film; **~flagge** *die* naval ensign; **~flotte** *die* navy; fleet; **~freiwillige** *der* [war] volunteer; **~führung** *die* ⇒ **Kriegführung**; **~fuß** *der:* in **mit jmdm. auf [dem] ~fuß stehen** *od.* **leben** (*scherzh.*) be at loggerheads with sb.; **mit etw. auf [dem] ~fuß stehen** (*scherzh.*) be totally lost when it comes to sth.; **~gebiet** *das* war zone; **~gefahr** *die* danger of war; **~gefangen** *Adj.* captured; **~gefangene** *der/die* prisoner of war; POW; **~gefangenschaft** *die* captivity; **in ~gefangenschaft sein/geraten** be a prisoner of war/be taken prisoner; **aus der ~gefangenschaft entlassen werden** be released from captivity; **~gegner** *der* **A** (*Gegner im Krieg*) enemy; **B** (*Gegner des Krieges*) opponent of the/a war; (*Pazifist*) opponent of war; **~gegnerin** *die* ⇒ **~gegner B**; **~gericht** *das* court martial; **jmdn. vor ein ~gericht stellen** court-martial sb.; **~geschrei** *das* war cries *pl.*; **~gewinnler** /-gəvɪnlɐ/ *der;* **~~s**, ~~, **~gewinnlerin** *die;* ~~, **~~nen** (*abwertend*) war profiteer; **~glück** *das* (*geh.*) fortune *or* luck in war; **~gott** *der* (*Myth.*) god of war; **~gräber·fürsorge** *die* **A** care of war graves; **B** (*Institution*) war graves commission; **~gräuel**, ***~greuel** *der* wartime atrocity; **~hafen** *der* naval port; **~handwerk** *das* (*geh. veralt.*) art of warfare; **~held** *der* (*geh.*) war hero; **~herr** *der* (*geh. veralt.*) commander; **oberster ~herr** supreme commander; commander-in-chief; **~hetze** *die* (*abwertend*) warmongering; **~hetze betreiben** stir up war; **~hinterbliebene** *der/die* war orphan/widow; **die ~hinterbliebenen** war widows and orphans; **~industrie** *die* armaments industry; **~invalide** *der* war-disabled person; war invalid; **~jahr** *das:* **im ersten/dritten ~jahr** in the first/third year of the war; **während der ~jahre/der letzten ~jahre** during the war years/the last years of the war; **~kamerad** *der* wartime comrade; **~knecht** *der* (*veralt.*) soldier; (*Söldner*) mercenary; **~kunst** *die* (*geh., veralt.*) art of war *or* warfare; **~list** *die* military stratagem; (*fig. scherzh.*) ruse; **~lüstern** *Adj.* bellicose; warlike; **~marine** *die* navy; **~maschine** *die* (*hist.*) engine [of war]; **~maschinerie** *die* (*abwertend*) machinery of war; **~minister** *der* (*hist.*) minister of *or* for war; **~ministerium** *das* (*hist.*) war ministry; (*in Großbritannien*) War Office (*Hist.*); **~müde** *Adj.* war-weary; **~opfer** *das* war victim; **~pfad** *der:* in **auf dem ~pfad** (*auch fig.*) on the warpath; **~propaganda** *die* wartime propaganda; **~rat** *der:* in **~rat [ab]halten** (*scherzh.*) have a powwow; **~recht** *das* **A** laws *pl.* of war; **B das ~recht verhängen** impose martial law; **~schaden** *der* (*bes. Amtsspr.*) war damage *no art.*; **~schäden** *Pl.* war damage *sing., no art.*; **~schauplatz** *der* theatre of war; **~schiff** *das* warship; **~schuld** *die* war guilt; **~schulden** *Pl.* war debts; **~spiel** *das* **A** (*Milit.*) war game; **B** (*Kinderspiel*) [game of] soldiers *sing.*; **~spiel·zeug** *das* war toys *pl.*; (*einzelnes*) war toy; **~stärke** *die* wartime strength; **~tanz** *der* (*Völkerk.*) war dance; **~tauglich** *Adj.* fit for active service *postpos.*; **~teilnehmer** *der* combatant; (*ehemaliger Soldat*) ex-serviceman; war veteran (*Amer.*); **~trauung** *die* war-marriage; **~treiber** *der*, **~treiberin** *die* (*abwertend*) warmonger; **~untauglich** *Adj.* unfit for active service *postpos.*; **~verbrechen** *das* (*Rechtsw.*) war crime; **~verbrecher** *der*, **~verbrecherin** *die* war criminal; **~verbrecher·prozess**, ***~verbrecher·prozeß** *der* war crimes trial; **~verbündet** *Adj.* co-belligerent; **~verbündete** *der* co-belligerent; **~verletzung** *die* war wound *or* injury; **~versehrt** *Adj.:* ⇒ **~beschädigt**; **~versehrte** *der/die* ⇒ **~beschädigte**; **~verwendungs·fähig** *Adj.* (*Amtsspr.*) fit for active service *postpos.*;

k

**~waise** *die* war orphan; **~wichtig** *Adj.* essential to the war effort *postpos.*; **~wirren** *Pl.* chaos *sing.* of war; **~wirtschaft** *die* war[time] economy; **~zeit** *die* wartime; **in ~zeiten** *Pl.* in wartime; **~ziel** *das* war aim; aim of a/the war; **~zustand** *der* state of war; **sich im ~zustand befinden** be at war

**Krill** /krɪl/ *der;* **~[e]s** krill

**Krim** /krɪm/ *die;* **~ die ~:** the Crimea

**Krimi** /'kri:mi/ *der;* **~[s], ~[s]** (*ugs.*) **A** (*Film, Stück*) crime thriller; whodunit (*coll.*); (*fig.: Fußballspiel, Quizsendung usw.*) thriller; cliffhanger; **B** (*Roman*) crime thriller; whodunit (*coll.*); (*mit Detektiv als Held*) detective story

**Kriminal·beamte** /krimi'na:l-/ *der,* **Kriminal·beamtin** *die* ▶ **159** [plain-clothes] detective

**Kriminale** *der; adj. Dekl.,* **Kriminaler** *der;* **~s, ~** (*ugs.*) detective

**Kriminal-: ~fall** *der* criminal case; crime; **~film** *der* crime film *or* thriller; **~gericht** *das* (*veralt.*) ⇒ **Strafgericht**; **~hörspiel** *das* radio crime thriller

**kriminalisieren** *tr. V.* **A** (*kriminell machen*) **jmdn. ~:** make sb. turn to crime; **B** (*als kriminell hinstellen*) **jmdn./etw. ~:** present sb. as a criminal/sth. as [being] criminal *or* a criminal act

**Kriminalist** *der;* **~en, ~en, Kriminalistin** *die* detective

**Kriminalistik** *die;* **~:** criminalistics *sing., no art.*

**kriminalistisch** ❶ *Adj.* ‹methods, practice› of criminalistics; ‹abilities› in the field of criminalistics. ❷ *adv.* ‹proceed etc.› using the methods of criminalistics

**Kriminalität** /kriminali'tɛ:t/ *die;* **~ A** crime *no art.*; **ein Absinken der ~:** a drop in the level of crime *or* in the crime rate; **B** (*Straffälligkeit*) criminality

**Kriminal-: ~kommissar** *der,* **~kommissarin** *die* ▶ **159** ≈ detective superintendent; **~komödie** *die* comedy thriller; **~polizei** *die* criminal investigation department; **~roman** *der* crime novel *or* thriller; (*mit Detektiv als Held*) detective novel

**kriminell** /krimi'nɛl/ ❶ *Adj.* (*auch ugs.: rücksichtslos*) criminal; **~ werden/sein** become a criminal *or* turn to crime/be a criminal. ❷ *adv.* **A ~ veranlagt sein** have criminal tendencies; **~ handeln** act illegally; break the law; **B** (*ugs.: rücksichtslos*) criminally; ‹drive› with criminal recklessness

**Kriminelle** *der/die; adj. Dekl.* criminal

**Kriminologe** *der;* **~n, ~n** ▶ **159** criminologist

**Kriminologie** /kriminolo'gi:/ *die* criminology *no art.*

**Kriminologin** *die;* **~, ~nen** ▶ **159** criminologist

**Krim·krieg** /'krɪm-/ *der;* **~[e]s** Crimean War

**Krimskrams** /'krɪmskrams/ *der;* **~[es]** (*ugs.*) stuff; **einigen ~ kaufen** buy a few bits and pieces

**Kringel** /'krɪŋl/ *der;* **~s, ~ A** (*Kreis*) [small] ring; (*Kritzelei*) round squiggle; **B** (*Gebäck*) [ring-shaped] biscuit; ring

**kringelig** *Adj.* crinkly ‹hair›; squiggly ‹shape, line, etc.›; **sich ~ lachen** (*ugs.*) laugh one's head off; kill oneself [laughing] (*coll.*)

**kringeln** ❶ *tr. V.* curl [up] ‹tail›; **jmds. Haar ~:** curl sb.'s hair; ‹wind, rain› make sb.'s hair go curly. ❷ *refl. V.* curl [up]; ‹hair› go curly; **sich [vor Lachen] ~** (*ugs.*) laugh one's head off; kill oneself [laughing] (*coll.*)

**Krinoline** /krino'li:nə/ *die;* **~, ~n** (*hist.*) crinoline

**Kripo** /'kri:po/ *die;* **~** (*ugs.*) **die ~:** ≈ the CID

**Krippe** /'krɪpə/ *die;* **~, ~n A** (*Futtertrog*) manger; crib; ⇒ *auch* **Futter~**; **B** (*Weihnachten*) model of a nativity scene; crib; **C** (*Kinder~*) crèche; day nursery

**Krippen·spiel** *das* nativity play

**Kris** /kri:s/ *der;* **~es, ~e** kris

**Krise** /'kri:zə/ *die;* **~, ~n** (*auch Med.*) crisis; **eine ~ durchmachen/überwinden** go through/overcome a crisis; **in eine ~ geraten** enter a state of crisis; **wenn sie das hört, kriegt sie die ~** (*ugs.*) she'll have a fit when she hears that (*coll.*)

**kriseln** /'kri:zl̩n/ *itr. V.* (*unpers.*) **es kriselt in ihrer Ehe/in der Partei** (*eine Krise droht*) their marriage is running into trouble/there is a crisis looming in the party; (*eine Krise ist vorhanden*) their marriage is in trouble/the party is in a state of crisis

**krisen-, Krisen-: ~anfällig** *Adj.* crisis-prone; **~fest** *Adj.* that is/are unaffected by crises *postpos., not pred.*; **~fest sein** be unaffected by crises; **~gebiet** *das* crisis area; **~herd** *der* trouble spot; **~management** *das* crisis management; **~stab** *der* crisis team

**Krisis** /'kri:zɪs/ *die;* **~, Krisen** (*veralt., Med.*) ⇒ **Krise**

**Kristall**[1] /krɪs'tal/ *der;* **~s, ~e** crystal

**Kristall**[2] *das;* **~s A** (*Material*) crystal *no indef. art.*; **Gläser aus ~:** crystal glasses; **B** (*Gegenstände*) crystal *no indef. art.*

**Kristall·bildung** *die* ⇒ **Kristallisation**

**kristallen** *Adj.* crystal

***Kristalleuchter** ⇒ **Kristallleuchter**

**Kristall-: ~gitter** *das* (*Chemie*) crystal lattice; **~glas** *das* **A** crystal glass; **B** (*Bleikristall*) crystal

**kristallin** /krɪsta'li:n/ *Adj.* (*bes. Mineral.*) crystalline

**Kristallisation** /krɪstaliza'tsi̯o:n/ *die;* **~, ~en** (*bes. Chemie*) crystallization

**kristallisieren** (*bes. Chemie*) ❶ *itr. V.* crystallize. ❷ *refl. V.* (*auch fig.*) crystallize

**kristall-, Kristall-: ~klar** *Adj.* (*auch fig.*) crystal clear; **~leuchter** *der,* **~lüster** *der* (*veralt.*) crystal chandelier; **~nacht** *die* (*ns.*) crystal night; kristallnacht; *National Socialist pogrom against Jews in November 1938;* **~schale** *die* crystal bowl

***Kristallüster** ⇒ **Kristalllüster**

**Kristall-: ~waren** *Pl.* crystal [glass] *sing.*; **~zucker** *der* (*bes. fachspr.*) refined sugar in crystals

**Kriterium** /kri'te:ri̯ʊm/ *das;* **~s, Kriterien A** criterion; **B** (*bes. Skisport*) race; **C** (*Radsport*) criterium

**Kritik** /kri'ti:k/ *die;* **~, ~en A** criticism *no indef. art.* (**an** + *Dat.* of); **an jmdm./etw. ~ üben** criticize sb./sth.; **auf ~ stoßen** meet with *or* come in for criticism; **unter aller** *od.* **jeder ~ sein** (*ugs.*) be absolutely hopeless; **B** (*Besprechung*) review; notice; **eine gute/schlechte ~** *od.* **gute/schlechte ~en bekommen** get good/bad reviews *or* notices; **C** (*die ~er*) critics *pl.*; reviewers *pl.*; **D** (*Philos., Analyse*) critique

**Kritikaster** /kriti'kastɐ/ *der;* **~s, ~, Kritikasterin** *die;* **~, ~nen** (*geh. abwertend*) criticaster; caviller

**Kritiker** /'kri:tikɐ/ *der;* **~s, ~, Kritikerin** *die;* **~, ~nen** ▶ **159** critic

**Kritik·fähigkeit** *die* critical faculties *pl.*

**kritik·los** ❶ *Adj.* uncritical; ❷ *adv.* uncritically; **etw. ~ hinnehmen** accept sth. without criticism

**kritisch** /'kri:tɪʃ/ ❶ *Adj.* **A** (*auch Kernphysik*) critical; **ein ~er Apparat** (*Wissensch.*) critical apparatus; **eine ~e Ausgabe** (*Wissensch.*) a critical edition; **B** (*entscheidend*) critical; **~er Punkt** (*Skisport*) critical point; **~e Temperatur** (*Physik, Chemie*) critical temperature. ❷ *adv.* critically; **sich mit etw. ~ auseinander setzen** make a critical study of sth.; **jmdm./etw. ~ gegenüber stehen** be critical of sb./sth.

**kritisieren** /kriti'zi:rən/ *tr. V.* criticize; review ‹book, play, etc.›; **immer etw. zu ~ haben** always find sth. to criticize

**Kritizismus** /kriti'tsɪsmʊs/ *der;* **~** (*Philos.*) critical philosophy

**Krittelei** *die;* **~, ~en** (*abwertend*) fault-finding; carping

**kritteln** /'krɪtl̩n/ *itr. V.* (*abwertend*) find fault (**an** + *Dat.*, **über** + *Akk.* with); carp (**an** + *Dat.*, **über** + *Akk.* at)

**Kritzelei** *die;* **~, ~en A** (*das Schreiben*) scribbling; (*das Zeichnen*) doodling; **B** (*Schrift*) scribble; (*Zeichnung*) doodle; (*an Wänden*) graffiti *sing. or pl.*

**kritzeln** /'krɪtsl̩n/ ❶ *itr. V.* (*schreiben*) scribble; (*zeichnen*) doodle. ❷ *tr. V.* scribble; **etw. auf/in etw.** (*Akk.*) **~:** scribble sth. on/in sth.

**Kroate** /kro'a:tə/ *der;* **~n, ~n** Croat; Croatian

**Kroatien** /kro'a:tsi̯ən/ (*das*) Croatia

**Kroatin** *die;* **~, ~nen** ⇒ **Kroate**; ⇒ *auch* **-in**

**kroatisch** *Adj.* ▶ **696** Croatian

**Kroatz·beere** /kro'ats-/ *die;* **~, ~n** (*ostmd.*) ⇒ **Brombeere**

**kroch** *1. u. 3. Pers. Sg. Prät. v.* **kriechen**

**Krocket** /'krɔkət/ *das;* **~s** croquet

**Krokant** /kro'kant/ *der;* **~s** praline

**Krokette** /kro'kɛtə/ *die;* **~, ~n** (*Kochk.*) croquette

**Kroki** /kro'ki:/ *das;* **~s, ~s** sketch map; (*künstlerische Skizze*) sketch

**Kroko** /'kro:ko/ *das;* **~[s]** crocodile [leather]

**Krokodil** /kroko'di:l/ *das;* **~s, ~e** crocodile

**Krokodil·leder** *das* crocodile skin *or* leather

**Krokodils·tränen** *Pl.* (*ugs.*) crocodile tears

**Kroko·tasche** *die* crocodile[-skin] [hand]bag

**Krokus** /'kro:kʊs/ *der;* **~, ~** *od.* **~se** crocus

**Krönchen** /'krø:nçən/ *das;* **~s, ~:** small crown; (*einer Welle*) small crest

**Krone** /'kro:nə/ *die;* **~, ~n A** crown; (*kleinere, eines Herzogs, eines Grafen*) coronet; **einer Sache** (*Dat.*)/**allem die ~ aufsetzen** cap sth./cap it all; **das setzt doch allem die ~ auf** that beats everything; **jmdm. in die ~ steigen** (*ugs.*) go to sb.'s head; **einen in der ~ haben** (*ugs.*) have had a drop too much (*coll.*); **die ~** (*fig.: Herrscherhaus*) the Crown; **dir wird keine Perle** *od.* **kein Stein aus der ~ fallen, wenn du uns mal hilfst** (*ugs.*) it won't hurt you to help us occasionally; **B** (*Spitze*) (*eines Baumes*) top; crown; (*einer Welle*) crest; **C** (*das Beste*) **die ~ der Schöpfung/meiner Sammlung** the pride of creation/my collection; **die ~ der Literatur** the highest form of literature; **D** (*Zahnmed.*) crown; **E** (*Jägerspr.*) (*beim Hirsch*) surroyals *pl.*; surroyal antlers *pl.*; (*beim Rehbock*) antlers *pl.*; **F** (*Rad an Uhren*) winder; [winding] crown; **G** (*Währungseinheit*) (*hist.*) crown; (*in Schweden, Island*) krona; (*in Dänemark, Norwegen*) krone; (*in der Tschechoslowakei*) koruna

**krönen** /'krø:nən/ *tr. V.* **A** crown; **jmdn. zum König/Kaiser ~:** crown sb. king/emperor; **gekrönte Häupter** crowned heads; **B** (*den Höhepunkt bilden*) crown; **von Erfolg gekrönt sein** *od.* **werden** be crowned with success; **der ~de Abschluss** the culmination; **C** (*oben abschließen*) crown

**Kronen-: ~korken** *der* crown cap *or* cork; **~mutter** *die; Pl.* **~~n** castle nut; castellated nut

**Kron-: ~erbe** *der,* **~erbin** *die* ⇒ **Thronfolger**; **~gut** *das* royal demesne; **~juwel** *das od. der* **A die ~juwelen** the crown jewels; **B** (*fig.*) gem; **~kolonie** *die* crown colony; **~land** *das* (*österr. hist.*) crownland; **~leuchter** *der* chandelier; **~prinz** *der* crown prince; **~prinzessin** *die* crown princess

**Krönung** *die;* **~, ~en A** coronation; **B** (*Höhepunkt*) culmination

**Kron·zeuge** *der,* **Kron·zeugin** *die* (*Rechtsw.*) person who turns Queen's/King's evidence; **als ~ auftreten** turn Queen's/King's evidence

**Kropf** /krɔpf/ *der;* **~[e]s, Kröpfe** /'krœpfə/ **A** ▶ **474** (*Med.*) goitre; **B** (*von Vögeln*) crop

**Kropf·taube** *die* pouter

**Kroppzeug** /'krɔp-/ *das;* **~s** (*ugs. abwertend*) **A** (*Gesindel*) rabble; riff-raff; **B** (*unnützes Zeug*) junk

**kross, *kroß** /krɔs/ *Adj.* (*nordd.*) ⇒ **knusprig**

*old spelling (see note on page 1707)

k

**Krösus** /'krø:zʊs/ *der;* ~ *od.* **~ses, ~se** (*oft scherzh.*) Croesus; **ich bin doch kein ~:** I'm not made of money

**Kröte** /'krø:tə/ *die;* ~, **~n** Ⓐ toad; Ⓑ *Pl.* (*salopp: Geld*) **ein paar/eine ganze Menge ~n verdienen** earn a few bob (*Brit. sl.*)/a fair old whack (*coll.*); **meine letzten paar ~n** my last few bob (*Brit. sl.*)/bucks (*Amer. sl.*); Ⓒ (*ugs. scherzh.: Kind*) **du kleine ~:** you little rascal; **eine süße kleine ~:** a sweet little thing; Ⓓ (*abwertend: Mensch*) creature

**Kröten·test** *der* (*Med.*) ⇒ **Froschtest**

**Krücke** /'krʏkə/ *die;* ~, **~n** Ⓐ (*Stock*) crutch; **an** *od.* **auf ~n** (*Dat.*) **gehen** walk on crutches; Ⓑ (*Griff*) crook; handle; Ⓒ (*ugs. abwertend*) (*Versager*) dead loss (*coll.*); wash-out (*coll.*); (*Gegenstand*) dead loss (*coll.*); **meine ~ von Auto** my old junk heap of a car (*coll.*)

**Krück·stock** *der* walking stick; ⇒ *auch* **Blinde**

**krude** /'kru:də/ ❶ *Adj.* rude. ❷ *adv.* rudely

**Krug** /kru:k/ *der;* **~[e]s, Krüge** /'kry:gə/ Ⓐ (*Gefäß für Flüssigkeiten*) jug; (*größer*) pitcher; (*Bier~*) mug; (*aus Ton*) mug; stein; (*Honig~*) jar; pot; **der ~ geht so lange zum Brunnen, bis er bricht** (*Spr.*) one day you'll come unstuck; you'll try it once too often; Ⓑ (*bes. nordd.: Wirtshaus*) inn

**Kruke** /'kru:kə/ *die;* ~, **~n** (*bes. nordd.*) Ⓐ (*Krug*) [earthenware] jug; (*zum Einlegen usw.*) [earthenware] jar; (*größer*) [earthenware] pitcher; Ⓑ (*kauziger Mensch*) **eine seltsame** *od.* **schrullige ~:** a queer fish

**Krüll·schnitt** /'krʏl-/ *der* shag

**Krümchen** /'kry:mçən/ *das;* **~s,** ~**:** [tiny] crumb; **ein ~ Erde** a grain of soil

**Krume** /'kru:mə/ *die;* ~, **~n** Ⓐ crumb; Ⓑ ⇒ **Ackerkrume**

**Krümel** /'kry:ml̩/ *der;* **~s,** ~ Ⓐ crumb; **ein ~ Zucker** a grain of sugar; Ⓑ (*scherzh.: kleines Kind*) little one

**krümelig** *Adj.* Ⓐ crumbly; Ⓑ (*voller Krümel*) covered in crumbs *postpos.*

**krümeln** *itr. V.* Ⓐ (*zerfallen*) crumble; be crumbly; Ⓑ (*Krümel machen*) make crumbs

**krumm** /krʊm/ ❶ *Adj.* Ⓐ bent ‹nail etc.›; crooked ‹stick, branch, etc.›; bandy ‹legs›; bent ‹back›; **eine ~e Nase** a crooked nose; (*Hakennase*) a hooked nose; **~ sein/werden** ‹person› stoop/develop a stoop; **etw. ~ biegen** bend sth.; **mach nicht so einen ~en Buckel** *od.* **Rücken** don't sit/stand with such a bent back; **~e Beine haben** have bandy legs; be bow-legged; **jmdn. ~ und lahm schlagen** beat sb. black and blue; ⇒ *auch* **krummlachen**; Ⓑ (*ugs.: unrechtmäßig*) crooked; **ein ~es Ding drehen** get up to sth. crooked; **auf die ~e Tour versuchen, etw. zu tun** try to do sth. by crooked means; Ⓒ **etw. ~ nehmen** (*ugs.*) take offence at sth.; take sth. the wrong way; **sich ~ legen** (*ugs.*) scrimp *or* pinch and scrape ❷ *adv.* crookedly; **~ gewachsen** crooked ‹tree etc.›; **~ dasitzen/gehen** slouch/walk with a stoop; **sitz nicht so ~ da!** sit up straight!; ⇒ *auch* **Finger B**

**krumm·beinig** *Adj.* bandy[-legged]; bow-legged

**Krumm·darm** *der* ▶ **471** (*Anat.*) ileum

**krümmen** /'krʏmən/ ❶ *tr. V.* bend; **in gekrümmter Haltung** stooping. ❷ *refl. V.* Ⓐ (*sich winden*) writhe; **sich vor Schmerzen/in Krämpfen ~:** double up with pain/cramp; **sich vor Lachen ~:** double up with laughter; **sich ~ wie ein Wurm** wriggle like a worm; **das Blech krümmte sich in der Hitze** the metal warped *or* buckled in the heat; Ⓑ (*krumm verlaufen*) ‹road, path, river› bend, curve; **eine gekrümmte Fläche** a curved surface

**krumm-, Krumm-:** **~horn** *das* (*Musik*) krummhorn; **~|lachen** *refl. V.* (*ugs.*) **sich über etw.** (*Akk.*) **~lachen** *od.* **~- und schieflachen** fall about laughing (*Brit.*) *or* laugh one's head off over sth.; ***~|legen** ⇒ **krumm 1C**; **~nasig** *Adj.* crooked-nosed; (*mit Hakennase*) hook-nosed; ***~|nehmen** ⇒ **krumm 1C**; **~säbel** *der* scimitar; **~stab** *der* ⇒ **Bischofsstab**

**Krümmung** *die;* ~, **~en** Ⓐ (*Biegung*) (*der Wirbelsäule*) curvature; (*der Nase usw.*) curve; (*eines Weges, Flusses usw.*) bend; turn; Ⓑ (*Geom.*) curvature

**krumpelig** /'krʊmpəlɪç/ *Adj.* (*westmd.*) creased

**krumpfen** /'krʊmpfn̩/ *tr. V.* (*Textilind.*) pre-shrink

**Kruppe** /'krʊpə/ *die;* ~, **~n** croup

**Krüppel** /'krʏpl̩/ *der;* **~s,** ~**:** cripple; **zum ~ werden** be crippled; **jmdn. zum ~ schlagen** beat sb. and leave him/her a cripple

**krüppelig** *Adj.* crippled ‹person›; stunted ‹tree, growth, etc.›

**Kruste** /'krʊstə/ *die;* ~, **~n** Ⓐ crust; (*vom Braten*) crisp; (*vom Schweinebraten*) crackling; Ⓑ (*Überzug*) coating; **mit ~:** with a coating; **eine ~ aus** *od.* **von Blut und Dreck/Blut** a crust of blood and dirt/a scab

**Krux** ⇒ **Crux**

**Kruzifix** /'kru:tsifɪks/ *das;* **~es, ~e** crucifix

**Krypta** /'krʏpta/ *die;* ~, **Krypten** (*Archit.*) crypt

**krypto-, Krypto-** /'krʏpto-/ crypto-

**Krypton** /'krʏptɔn/ *das;* **~s** (*Chemie*) krypton

**KSZE** *Abk.* **Konferenz für Sicherheit und Zusammenarbeit in Europa** CSCE

**Kuba** /'ku:ba/ (*das*); **~s** Cuba

**Kubaner** /ku'ba:nɐ/ *der;* **~s,** ~, **Kubanerin** *die;* ~, **~nen** ▶ **553** Cuban; ⇒ *auch* **-in**

**kubanisch** *Adj.* ▶ **553** Cuban

**Kübel** /'ky:bl̩/ *der;* **~s,** ~ Ⓐ pail; (*Wasser~, Abfall~*) pail; bucket; (*Pflanzen~*) tub; **Palmen in ~n** potted palms; **~ voll** *od.* **von Bosheit über jmdn. ausgießen** (*fig.*) pour torrents of abuse over sb.; **es gießt wie aus ~n** (*ugs.*) it's bucketing down; Ⓑ (*Toiletteneimer*) [latrine] bucket

**kübeln** *itr. V.* (*salopp: trinken*) booze (*coll.*)

**Kuben** ⇒ **Kubus**

**Kubik-** /ku'bi:k-/ ▶ **611** cubic ‹metre, foot, etc.›

**Kubik-:** **~wurzel** *die* (*Math.*) cube root; **~zahl** *die* (*Math.*) cube number

**kubisch** /'ku:bɪʃ/ *Adj.* Ⓐ (*würfelförmig*) cubical; cube-shaped; Ⓑ (*Math.*) cubic ‹equation etc.›

**Kubismus** *der;* ~ (*Kunstw.*) cubism *no art.*

**Kubist** *der;* **~en, ~en** (*Kunstw.*) cubist

**kubistisch** *Adj.* (*Kunstw.*) cubist

**Kubus** /'ku:bʊs/ *der;* ~, **Kuben** cube

**Küche** /'kʏçə/ *die;* ~, **~n** Ⓐ (*Raum*) kitchen; (*klein*) kitchenette; **was ~ und Keller zu bieten haben** the best food and drink in the house; Ⓑ (*Einrichtung*) kitchen furniture *no indef. art.*; **~n** kitchen furniture *sing.*; Ⓒ (*Kochk.*) cooking; cuisine; **die chinesische/französische** *usw.* **~:** Chinese/French *etc.* cooking; **kalte/warme ~:** cold/hot meals *pl. or* food; ⇒ *auch* **gutbürgerlich**

**Kuchen** /'ku:xn̩/ *der;* **~s,** ~**:** cake; (*Obst~*) flan; (*Torte*) gateau; cake

**Küchen-:** **~abfälle** *Pl.* kitchen scraps; **~bank** *die; Pl.* **~bänke** kitchen bench-seat; **~benutzung** *die:* **Zimmer mit ~benutzung** room and shared kitchen *or* use of kitchen

**Kuchen·blech** *das* baking sheet *or* -tray; (*mit höherem Rand*) baking tin

**Küchen-:** **~bulle** *der* (*Soldatenspr. salopp*) cookhouse wallah (*Mil. coll.*); **~chef** *der,* **~chefin** *die* ▶ **159** chef; **~dienst** *der* kitchen duty; **~dienst haben** be on kitchen duty; **~fee** *die* (*ugs. scherzh.*) cook

**Kuchen-:** **~form** *die* cake tin; **~gabel** *die* pastry fork

**Küchen-:** **~gerät** *das* kitchen utensil; (*als Kollektivum*) kitchen utensils *pl.*; **~geschirr** *das* kitchen crockery; **~handtuch** *das* kitchen towel; **~herd** *der* cooker; (*mit Holz- od. Kohlefeuer*) kitchen range; **~hilfe** *die* kitchen help; **~junge** *der* (*veralt.*) apprentice cook; **~latein** *das* (*iron.*) dog Latin; **~maschine** *die* food processor; **~meister** *der,* **~meisterin** *die* chef; ⇒ *auch* **Schmalhans**; **~messer** *das* kitchen knife; **~möbel** *das* piece of kitchen furniture; **teure ~möbel** expensive kitchen furniture *sing.*; **~personal** *das* kitchen staff; **~schabe** *die* cockroach; **~schrank** *der* kitchen cupboard; **~schürze** *die* kitchen apron

**Kuchen-:** **~teig** *der* cake mixture; **~teller** *der* Ⓐ (*mit ~*) plate of cakes; Ⓑ (*für ~*) cake plate

**Küchen-:** **~tisch** *der* kitchen table; **~uhr** *die* kitchen clock; **~waage** *die* kitchen scales *pl.*; **~zeile** *die: kitchen fittings along one wall of a room;* **~zettel** *der* menu

**Küchlein**[1] *das;* **~s,** ~ (*veralt.: Küken*) chick

**Küchlein**[2] *das;* **~s,** ~ (*kleiner Kuchen*) small cake

**kucken** /'kʊkn̩/ (*nordd.*) ⇒ **gucken**

**Kücken** /'kʏkn̩/ (*österr.*) ⇒ **Küken**

**kuckuck** /'kʊkʊk/ *Interj.* cuckoo; (*beim Versteckspiel mit Kindern*) yoo-hoo

**Kuckuck** *der;* **~s, ~e** Ⓐ cuckoo; **[das] weiß der ~** (*salopp*) heaven [only] knows; it's anybody's guess; **hol dich der ~!, der ~ soll dich holen!** (*salopp*) go to blazes! (*coll.*); **zum ~ [noch mal]!** (*salopp*) for crying out loud! (*coll.*); **wo, zum ~, hast du nur die Zeitung hingelegt?** (*salopp*) where the hell did you put the newspaper? (*coll.*); **das Geld ist zum ~** (*salopp*) the money's all gone; Ⓑ (*scherzh.: Siegel des Gerichtsvollziehers*) bailiff's seal (*placed on distrained goods*)

**Kuckucks-:** **~ei** *das* Ⓐ cuckoo's egg; Ⓑ (*ugs.: zweifelhafte Gabe*) **sich als ~ei erweisen** turn out to be more of a liability than an asset; **jmdm./sich ein ~ei ins Nest legen** do sb./oneself a dubious service; Ⓒ (*salopp: Kind eines anderen Vaters*) **ein ~ei** somebody else's *or* another man's child; **~uhr** *die* cuckoo clock

**Kuddelmuddel** /'kʊdl̩mʊdl̩/ *der od. das;* **~s** (*ugs.*) muddle; confusion

**Kufe**[1] /'ku:fə/ *die;* ~, **~n** Ⓐ (*von Schlitten, Schlittschuhen*) runner; Ⓑ (*von Flugzeugen, Hubschraubern*) skid

**Kufe**[2] (*landsch.*) *die;* ~, **~n** tub; (*zum Keltern, Brauen*) tun; vat

**Küfer** /'ky:fɐ/ *der;* **~s,** ~, **Küferin** *die;* ~, **~nen** Ⓐ (*südwestd., schweiz.*) cooper; Ⓑ (*Wein~*) cellarman

**Kugel** /'ku:gl̩/ *die;* ~, **~n** Ⓐ ball; (*Geom.*) sphere; (*Kegeln*) bowl; (*beim ~stoßen*) shot; (*eines ~lagers*) ball [bearing]; **die Erde ist eine ~:** the Earth is a sphere; **der Croupier ließ die ~ rollen** the croupier spun the wheel; **eine ruhige ~ schieben** (*ugs.*) take it *or* things easy; (*keine anstrengende Stellung haben*) have a cushy number (*coll.*); Ⓑ (*ugs.: Geschoss*) bullet; (*Kanonen~*) [cannon]ball; (*Luftgewehr~*) pellet; **sich** (*Dat.*) **eine ~ durch** *od.* **in den Kopf schießen** *od.* (*ugs.*) **jagen** blow one's brains out

**Kugel-:** **~abschnitt** *der* (*Geom.*) spherical segment [of one base]; **~ausschnitt** *der* (*Geom.*) spherical sector; **~blitz** *der* ball lightning

**Kügelchen** /'ky:gl̩çən/ *das;* **~s,** ~**:** small ball; (*aus Papier*) pellet

**kugel-, Kugel-:** **~fang** *der* butt; **ein Kind/eine Frau als ~fang benutzen** (*fig.*) use a child/woman as a shield; **~fest** *Adj.* bullet-proof; **~förmig** *Adj.* spherical; **~gelenk** *das* (*Anat., Technik*) ball-and-socket joint; **~hagel** *der* hail of bullets

**kugelig** *Adj.* spherical; ‹head› as round as a football; (*fig. scherzh.: dick*) rotund; plump; tubby; **sich ~ lachen** (*ugs.*) double *or* roll up [laughing *or* with laughter]; **ich hätte mich ~ lachen können** (*ugs.*) I could have died laughing

**Kugel-:** **~kopf** *der* golf ball; **~kopf·maschine** *die* golf-ball typewriter; **~lager** *das* (*Technik*) ball bearing

**kugeln** ❶ *tr. V.* roll. ❷ *refl. V.* roll [about]; **sich [vor Lachen] ~** (*ugs.*) double *or* roll up [laughing *or* with laughter]. ❸ *itr. V.*; *mit sein* roll

**kugel-, Kugel-:** **~oberfläche** *die* (*Geom.*) surface of a sphere; (*Flächeninhalt*) surface area of a sphere; **~regen** *der* ⇒ **~hagel**;

k

**~rund** /--'-/ *Adj.* [A] round as a ball *postpos.;* [B] *(scherzh.: dick)* rotund; plump; tubby; **~schreiber** *der* ballpoint [pen]; ball pen; Biro ®; **~schreiber·mine** *die* refill for a ballpoint [pen]; **~sicher** *Adj.* bulletproof; **~stoßen** *das;* **~~s** shot[-put]; *(Disziplin)* shot-putting *no art.;* putting the shot *no art.;* **~stoßer** *der;* **~~s,** **~~,** *(schweiz.)* **~stößer** /-ʃtøːsɐ/ *der;* **~~s,** **~~,** **~stoßerin** *die;* **~~,** **~~nen,** *(schweiz.)* **~stößerin** *die;* **~~,** **~~nen** shot-putter; **~wechsel** *der* exchange of shots

**Kuh** /kuː/ *die;* **~,** **Kühe** /'kyːə/ [A] cow; **heilige ~** *(ugs.)* sacred cow; **ich bin doch keine ~, die man melken kann** *(ugs.)* I am not made of money; ⇒ *auch* **dastehen** A; [B] *(Elefanten~, Giraffen~, Flusspferd~)* cow; *(Hirsch~)* hind; [C] *(salopp abwertend: Frau)* cow *(sl. derog.)*

**kuh-, Kuh-: ~augen** *Pl. (salopp)* cow-eyes; **~dorf** *das (salopp abwertend)* one-horse town *(coll.)*; **~fladen** *der* cowpat; **~fuß** *der (Technik)* crowbar; **~glocke** *die* cow bell; **~handel** *der (ugs. abwertend)* shady horse-trading *no indef. art.;* **ein ~handel** a bit of shady horse-trading; **~haut** *die* cowhide; **das geht auf keine ~haut** *(fig. salopp)* it's absolutely staggering *or* beyond belief; **~herde** *die* herd of cows; **~hirt** *der* cowherd

**kühl** /kyːl/ ❶ *Adj.* [A] cool; **mir ist/wird ~:** I feel/I'm getting chilly; **etw. ~ lagern** *od.* **aufbewahren** keep sth. in a cool place; [B] *(abweisend, nüchtern)* cool; **ein ~er Rechner** a cool, calculating person; **aus diesem ~en Grunde** *(scherzh.)* for this simple reason. ❷ *adv. (abweisend, nüchtern)* coolly

**Kühl-: ~aggregat** *das* refrigeration unit; **~an·lage** *die* refrigeration plant; cold-storage plant; **~box** *die* cool box

**Kuhle** /'kuːlə/ *die;* **~,** **~n** *(ugs.)* hollow

**Kühle** /'kyːlə/ *die;* **~** [A] *(Frische)* coolness; **die ~ des Morgens/Abends** the cool of the morning/evening; [B] *(Nüchternheit)* coolness

**kühlen** ❶ *tr. V.* cool; chill, cool ‹wine›; **seinen Zorn/seine Rache [an jmdm.] ~:** vent one's rage/revenge oneself [on sb.]. ❷ *itr. V.* ‹cold compress, ointment, breeze, etc.› have a cooling effect

**Kühler** *der;* **~s,** **~** [A] *(am Auto)* radiator; *(~haube)* bonnet *(Brit.)*; hood *(Amer.)*; **jmdn. auf den ~ nehmen** *(ugs.)* drive *or* run into *or* hit sb.; [B] *(Sekt~)* ice bucket; [C] *(Chem.)* condenser

**Kühler-: ~figur** *die* radiator mascot; **~haube** *die* bonnet *(Brit.)*; hood *(Amer.)*

**Kühl-: ~fach** *das* frozen food compartment; **~haus** *das* cold store; **~kette** *die (Wirtsch.)* cold chain; **~mittel** *das (Technik)* coolant; **~raum** *der* cold store; cold-storage room; **~rippe** *die* cooling fin *or* rib; **~schiff** *das* refrigerator ship; refrigerated ship; **~schlange** *die (Technik)* cooling coil; **~schrank** *der* refrigerator; fridge *(Brit. coll.)*; icebox *(Amer.)*; **~tasche** *die* cool bag; **~theke** *die* cold shelves *pl.;* **~truhe** *die* [chest] freezer; deep-freeze; *(im Lebensmittelgeschäft)* freezer [cabinet]; **~turm** *der (Technik)* cooling tower

**Kühlung** *die;* **~,** **~en** [A] cooling; **zur ~ der entzündeten Stellen** to cool the inflamed areas; **auch bei ~ sind die Waren nur begrenzt haltbar** even when refrigerated, the goods will keep only for a limited time; [B] *(Vorrichtung)* cooling system; *(für Lebensmittel)* refrigeration system; [C] *(Frische)* coolness; **sich** *(Dat.)* **~ verschaffen** cool down *or* off

**Kühl-: ~wagen** *der* [A] *(Eisenb.)* refrigerated *or* refrigerator car *or (Brit.)* wagon; [B] *(Lastwagen)* refrigerated *or* refrigerator truck *or (Brit.)* lorry; **~wasser** *das* cooling water

**Kuh-: ~milch** *die* cow's milk; **~mist** *der* cow dung

**kühn** /kyːn/ ❶ *Adj.* [A] *(mutig, eigenwillig)* bold; *(gewagt)* daring; brave, fearless ‹warrior›; **das übertraf meine ~sten Träume** that exceeded my wildest dreams; [B] *(dreist)* audacious; impudent. ❷ *adv.* [A] *(mutig, eigenwillig)* boldly; *(gewagt)* daringly; **eine ~ geschwungene Nase** an aquiline nose; [B] *(dreist)* audaciously; impudently

**Kühnheit** *die;* **~** [A] *(Mut, Eigenwilligkeit)* boldness; *(Gewagtheit)* daringness; [B] *(Dreistigkeit)* audacity; impudence

**kuh-, Kuh-: ~pocken** *Pl.* cowpox *sing., no art.;* **~schelle** *die (Bot.)* pasque flower; **~stall** *der* cowshed; **~warm** *Adj.* ‹milk› warm *or* fresh from the cow

**Kujon** /ku'joːn/ *der;* **~s,** **~e** *(veralt. abwertend)* scoundrel; rogue

**kujonieren** *tr. V. (veralt. abwertend)* bully; harass

**k. u. k.** /'kaː|ʊnt'kaː/ *Abk. (österr. hist.)* **kaiserlich und königlich** imperial and royal

**Küken** /'kyːkn̩/ *das;* **~s,** **~** [A] *(von Hühnern)* chick; [B] *(ugs.) (kleines Kind)* kiddie *(sl.)*; *(junges Mädchen)* young girl

**Ku-Klux-Klan** /kuklʊks'klaːn/ *der;* **~[s]** Ku-Klux-Klan

**kulant** /ku'lant/ ❶ *Adj.* obliging; accommodating; fair ‹terms›. ❷ *adv.* **sich ~ verhalten** be obliging *or* accommodating

**Kulanz** /ku'lants/ *die;* **~:** readiness *or* willingness to oblige; **aus ~:** out of good will; **eine Reparatur auf ~:** repair done free of charge out of good will

**Kuli** /'kuːli/ *der;* **~s,** **~s** [A] coolie; *(fig.)* slave; [B] *(ugs.: Kugelschreiber)* ballpoint; Biro ®

**kulinarisch** /kuli'naːrɪʃ/ *Adj.* culinary; **ein rein ~es Interesse an der Musik haben** *(fig.)* be interested in music purely as entertainment

**Kulisse** /ku'lɪsə/ *die;* **~,** **~n** piece of scenery; flat; wing; *(Hintergrund)* backdrop; **die ~n** the scenery *sing.;* **~n schieben** be a scene-shifter; **aus der ~ treten** step out from the wings *pl.;* **die ~ für etw. bilden** *(fig.)* form the backdrop to sth.; **hinter den ~n** *(fig.)* behind the scenes

**kulissenhaft** *Adj.* like a stage setting *pred.*

**Kulissen-: ~schieber** *der (ugs. scherzh.)* scene-shifter; **~wechsel** *der* scene change

**Kuller** *die;* **~,** **~n** *(ostmd.: Murmel)* marble

**Kuller·augen** *Pl. (ugs. scherzh.)* big, round eyes; **er machte ~:** his eyes nearly popped out of his head

**kullern** /'kʊlɐn/ *(ugs.)* ❶ *itr. V.* [A] *mit sein* roll; [B] **mit den Augen ~:** roll one's eyes. ❷ *tr. V.* roll

**Kuller·pfirsich** *der (ugs.)* peach served in a glass of champagne

**Kulmination** /kʊlmina'tsi̯oːn/ *die;* **~,** **~en** *(auch Astron.)* culmination

**Kulminations·punkt** *der* [A] culmination; culminating point; [B] *(Astron.)* point of culmination

**kulminieren** /kʊlmi'niːrən/ *itr. V. (auch Astron.)* culminate **(in** + *Dat.* in)

**Kult** /kʊlt/ *der;* **~[e]s,** **~e** [A] cult; **der ~ der Ahnen** ancestor worship; [B] *(fig.)* cult **(mit** of); **mit jmdm./etw. einen ~ treiben** make a cult [figure] out of sb./make a cult out of sth.

**-kult** *der:* **Motorrad~/Star~/Wagner~** *usw.* motorcycle/star/Wagner *etc.* cult

**Kult-: ~bild** *das* devotional image; **~figur** *die* cult figure; **~film** *der* cult film; **~handlung** *die* ritual; ritualistic act

**kultisch** ❶ *Adj.* cultic; ritual, cultic ‹object›. ❷ *adv.* ‹worship› cultically

**Kultivator** /kʊlti'vaːtɔr/ *der;* **~s,** **~en** /-va'toːrən/ *(Landw.)* cultivator

**kultivierbar** *Adj.* [A] cultivable; cultivatable; **leicht/schwer ~:** easy/hard to cultivate

**kultivieren** /kʊlti'viːrən/ *tr. V. (auch fig.)* cultivate

**kultiviert** ❶ ⇒ **kultivieren.** ❷ *Adj.* [A] *(gepflegt)* cultivated; cultured; [B] *(vornehm)* refined. ❸ *adv.* in a cultivated *or* cultured manner; *(vornehm)* in a refined manner; **with refinement; ~ essen** get a civilized meal

**Kultiviertheit** *die;* **~:** refinement

**Kultivierung** *die;* **~,** **~en** *(auch fig.)* cultivation; improvement

**Kult·stätte** *die* centre of cult worship

**Kultur** /kʊl'tuːɐ̯/ *die;* **~,** **~en** [A] *(geistiger und moralischer Überbau)* culture; [B] *(Zivilisation, Lebensform)* civilization; [C] *(Kultiviertheit, geistiges Niveau)* **ein Mensch von ~:** a cultured person; **sie hat [keine] ~:** she is [un]cultured; [D] *(kultivierte Lebensart, Verfeinerung)* refinement; **~ haben** be refined; [E] *(Landw., Gartenbau)* young crop; *(Forstw.)* young plantation; [F] *(Biol., Med.)* culture; [G] *(Landw., Gartenbau: Kultivierung)* cultivation

**Kultur-: ~abkommen** *das* cultural agreement; **~anthropologie** *die* cultural anthropology *no art.;* **~arbeit** *die* cultural activity *or* activities; **~attaché** *der* cultural attaché; **~aus·tausch** *der* cultural exchange; **~banause** *der (abwertend, oft scherzh.)* philistine; **~bei·lage** *die* arts supplement; **~betrieb** *der* culture industry; **~beutel** *der* sponge bag *(Brit.)*; toilet bag; **~boden** *der* [A] *(bearbeiteter Boden)* cultivated land; [B] *(Gebiet mit bedeutender ~boden)* **[ur]alter ~boden** the site of an ancient civilization; **~denkmal** *das* cultural monument

**kulturell** /kʊltu'rɛl/ ❶ *Adj.* cultural. ❷ *adv.* culturally; **die ehemals ~ führende Metropole** the metropolis, once cultural centre

**kultur-, Kultur-: ~epoche** *die* cultural epoch; **~erbe** *das* cultural heritage; **~feindlich** *Adj.* ‹atmosphere, policy, etc.› that is hostile to culture; **~feindlich sein** be hostile to culture; **~film** *der* documentary film; **~flüchter** *der;* **~~s,** **~~** *(Biol.)* plant/animal that does not survive in areas developed by man; **~föderalismus** *der: system of separate ministries for education and cultural affairs;* **~folger** *der;* **~~s,** **~~** *(Biol.)* plant/animal that survives in areas developed by man; **~geschichte** *die* [A] history of civilization; *(einer bestimmten ~)* cultural history; **die ~geschichte des Menschen** the history of human civilization; [B] *(Buch)* cultural history; **~geschichtlich** ❶ *Adj.* ‹importance› for *or* in the history of civilization/cultural history; ‹question, factor› connected with the history of civilization/cultural history; ‹essay, reflections› on the history of civilization/cultural history; *(die ~geschichte eines bestimmten Landes betreffend)* historico-cultural ‹law, phenomenon, standpoint, study, etc.›; ❷ *adv.* from the standpoint of the history of civilization/of cultural history; **~gut** *das* cultural possessions *pl.;* **~hauptstadt** *die* cultural capital; **~haus** *das* arts and leisure centre; **~historisch** *Adj., adv.:* ⇒ **~geschichtlich**; **~hoheit** *die* autonomy *or* independence in cultural and educational matters; **~industrie** *die (meist abwertend)* culture industry; **~kampf** *der (hist.)* kulturkampf *(struggle between the Prussian state and the Church 1872-87)*; **~kanal** *der* cultural channel; **~kreis** *der* [A] *(~raum)* cultural area; [B] *(Verein)* arts society; **~kritik** *die* critique of contemporary civilization *or* culture; **~kritiker** *der,* **~kritikerin** *die* critic of contemporary civilization *or* culture; **~landschaft** *die* [A] *(Agrargebiet)* cultivated area; area cultivated by man; *(Industrie-, Bergbaugebiet)* area developed by man; [B] *(kulturelles Leben)* cultural scene; **~leben** *das* cultural life; **~los** *Adj.* uncultured; lacking in culture *postpos.;* **~magazin** *das (Ferns.)* arts magazine; **~minister** *der,* **~ministerin** *die* minister for the arts; **~ministerium** *das* ministry for the arts; **~palast** *der (bes. DDR)* palace of culture; **~pessimismus** *der* cultural pessimism; **~pessimist** *der,* **~pessimistin** *die* cultural pessimist; **~pflanze** *die* cultivated plant; **~politik** *die* cultural and educational policy; **~politisch** ❶ *Adj.* ‹area, questions, aims, principles› of cultural and educational policy; ‹programme› of cultural and educational policies; ‹periodical› devoted to matters of cultural and educational policy; ❷ *adv.* in regard to cultural and educational policy;

*old spelling (see note on page 1707)

**~preis** *der* arts prize; **~psychologie** *die* psychology of culture; **~raum** *der* cultural area; **~revolution** *die* cultural revolution; **~schaffende** *der/die; adj. Dekl.* (*DDR*) creative artist; (*Intellektueller*) intellectual; **~schande** *die* (*abwertend*) disgrace in a civilized society; **~schock** *der* (*Soziol.*) culture shock; **~soziologie** *die* cultural sociology; **~sprache** *die* language of a civilized people; **in fast alle ~sprachen übersetzt** translated into nearly every civilized language; **~stätte** *die* (*geh.*) site of archaeological and cultural interest; **~steppe** *die* (*Geogr.*) cultivated steppe land; steppe [land] created by excessive cultivation of the soil; **~stufe** *die* level of civilization; **~szene** *die* (*ugs.*) cultural scene; **~träger** *der* vehicle of culture; **~volk** *das* civilized people *sing.*; **~voll** *Adj.* rich in culture *postpos.*; (*niveauvoll*) sophisticated; **~wissenschaften** *Pl.* ⇒ Geisteswissenschaften; **~zentrum** *das* **A** cultural centre; centre of cultural life; **B** (*Anlage*) arts centre

**Kultus** /'kʊltʊs/ *der;* ~ **A** (*geh.*) ⇒ Kult A; **B** (*Amtsspr.*) **Ministerium für Unterricht und ~** ⇒ Kultusministerium

**Kultus-: ~minister** *der*, **~ministerin** *die* minister for education and cultural affairs; **~ministerium** *das* ministry of education and cultural affairs; **~senator** *der*, **~senatorin** *die* minister for education and cultural affairs (*in Bremen, Hamburg, and West Berlin*)

**Kumarin** /kuma'ri:n/ *das;* **~s** coumarin

**Kumaron** /kuma'ro:n/ *das;* **~s** (*Chemie*) coumarone

**Kumme** /'kʊmə/ *die;* ~, **~n** (*nordd.*) bowl

**Kümmel** /'kʏml/ *der;* **~s**, ~ **A** (*Pflanze*) caraway; **B** (*Gewürz*) caraway [seed]; **C** (*Branntwein*) kümmel

**Kümmel-: ~brannt·wein** *der* caraway brandy; **~brötchen** *das* caraway[-seed] roll; **~käse** *der* caraway-seed[-flavoured] cheese; **~öl** *das* caraway oil; **~schnaps** *der* ⇒ **~branntwein**; **~türke** *der*, **~türkin** *die* **A** (*salopp abwertend: Türke/Türkin*) Turkish bastard (*derog.*); **B** **schuften wie ein ~türke/die ~türken** (*ugs.*) work like a slave/like slaves

**Kummer** /'kʊmɐ/ *der;* **~s** sorrow; grief; (*Ärger, Sorgen*) trouble; **~ um** *od.* **über jmdn.** grief for *or* over sb.; **hast du ~?** is there a problem?; **viel** *od.* **großen ~ haben** have a lot of trouble; **was hast du denn für ~?** what's bothering *or* troubling you?; **jmdm. ~ machen** give sb. trouble *or* bother; **ich bin ~ gewohnt** (*ugs.*) it happens all the time; I'm used to it

**Kummer·falte** *die* wrinkle [caused by worry]; **~n** lines of worry

**Kümmer·form** *die* (*Biol.*) degenerate form

**Kummer-: ~kasten** *der* (*scherzh.*) complaints box; **~kasten·tante** *die* (*scherzh.*) agony columnist *or* aunt (*coll.*)

**kümmerlich** **1** *Adj.* **A** (*schwächlich*) puny; stunted ‹vegetation, plants›; **B** (*ärmlich*) wretched; miserable; **C** (*abwertend: gering*) miserable; meagre, scanty ‹knowledge, leftovers›; very poor ‹effort›. **2** *adv.* **sich ~ ernähren** live on a poor *or* meagre diet; **sich ~ durchschlagen** eke out a bare/miserable existence

**Kümmerling** *der;* **~s**, **~e** stunted plant/animal

**kümmern** /'kʏmɐn/ **1** *refl. V.* **A** **sich um jmdn./etw. ~:** take care of *or* look after sb./sth.; **du solltest dich mal darum ~, dass ...** you should see to it that ...; **du kümmerst dich aber auch um gar nichts!** you don't bother to do anything!; **B** (*sich befassen mit*) **sich nicht um das Geschwätz** *usw.* **~:** not worry *or* mind about the gossip *etc.*; **sich nicht um Politik ~:** not care about *or* be interested in politics; **kümmere dich um deine eigenen Angelegenheiten** mind your own business.
**2** *tr. V.* concern; **was kümmert dich das?** what concern *or* business is it of yours?; what's it to you?; **Mach doch, was du willst! Was kümmerts mich?** Do what you like! What do I care?
**3** *itr. V.* (*ver~*) become stunted

**Kümmernis** *die;* ~, **~se** (*geh.*) trouble; worry

**Kummer·speck** *der* (*ugs.*) overweight caused by overeating as a result of emotional stress; **sie hat ~ angesetzt** all the worrying has made her eat too much, and she's [really] put on weight

**kummer·voll** **1** *Adj.* sorrowful; sad; sad ‹face›. **2** *adv.* sorrowfully; sadly

**Kummet** /'kʊmət/ *das, schweiz. auch der;* **~s**, **~e** [horse] collar

**Kümo** /'ky:mo/ *das;* **~s**, **~s** [motor-]coaster

**Kumpan** /kʊm'pa:n/ *der;* **~s**, **~e** (*ugs.*) **A** pal (*coll.*); mate; buddy (*coll.*); **B** (*abwertend: Mittäter*) accomplice

**Kumpanei** *die;* ~ (*ugs.*) chumminess (*coll.*)

**Kumpanin** *die;* ~, **~nen** ⇒ Kumpan

**Kumpel** /'kʊmpl̩/ *der;* **~s**, ~, *ugs. auch:* **~s** **A** (*Bergmannsspr.*) miner; collier; **B** (*salopp: Kamerad*) pal; mate; buddy (*coll.*)

**kumpelhaft** **1** *Adj.* matey; chummy (*coll.*). **2** *adv.* matily; chummily (*coll.*)

**Kumpen** /'kʊmpn̩/ *der;* **~s**, ~ (*nordd.*) bowl; basin

**Kumt** /kʊmt/ *das;* **~[e]s**, **~e** ⇒ Kummet

**Kumulation** /kumula'tsi̯o:n/ *die;* ~, **~en** cumulation; (*von Ämtern*) plurality

**kumulativ** /kumula'ti:f/ *Adj.* cumulative

**kumulieren** /kumu'li:rən/ *tr. V.* cumulate; **eine ~de Bibliographie** a cumulative bibliography

**Kumulierung** *die;* ~, **~en** cumulation

**Kumulus** /'ku:mulʊs/ *der;* ~, **Kumuli** (*Met.*) cumulus [cloud]

**Kumulus·wolke** *die* (*Met.*) cumulus cloud

**kund** /kʊnt/ *Adj. in* **jmdm. etw. ~ und zu wissen tun** (*veralt.*) make sth. known to sb.

**kündbar** *Adj.* terminable ‹contract›; redeemable ‹loan, mortgage›; **er hat eine nicht ~e Stellung** his employment cannot be terminated; **Beamte sind nicht ~:** established civil servants cannot be dismissed *or* given their notice

**Kündbarkeit** *die;* ~ (*von Verträgen*) terminability; (*von Anleihen, Hypotheken*) redeemability

**Kunde**[1] /'kʊndə/ *der;* **~n**, **~n** **A** customer; (*eines Architekten-, Anwaltbüros, einer Versicherung usw.*) client; **Dienst am ~n sein** be a service to the customer; ⇒ *auch* König; **B** (*ugs.: Kerl*) customer (*coll.*)

**Kunde**[2] *die;* ~ **A** (*geh.*) tidings *pl.* (*literary*); **jmdm. von etw. ~ geben** (*veralt.*) bring sb. tidings of sth.; **B** (*Lehre*) science

**Kunde**[3] *die;* ~ (*österr.*) ⇒ Kundschaft A

**-kunde** *die* science of ...; **Metall~/Vogel~:** metallurgy/ornithology

**künden** /'kʏndn̩/ **1** *tr. V.* (*geh.: ver~*) proclaim; **diese Zeichen ~ Unglück** these omens herald misfortune. **2** *itr. V.* (*geh.*) **von etw. ~:** bear witness to *or* tell of sth.

**Kunden-: ~beratung** *die* **A** customer advisory service; **~beratungen durchführen** advise customers; **B** (*Stelle*) customer advisory department; **~besuch** *der* call on a/the customer/client; **~dienst** *der* **A** service to customers; (*Wartung*) after-sales service; **B** (*Abteilung*) service department; **~fang** *der* (*abwertend*) touting for custom *or* customers; **auf ~fang gehen** go touting for custom *or* customers; **~kredit** *der* (*Wirtsch.*) credit terms *pl.*; **einen ~kredit in Anspruch nehmen** use the credit facilities which are available; **~kreis** *der* customers *pl.*; (*eines Architekten-, Anwaltbüros, einer Versicherung usw.*) clientele; **~stamm** *der* regular clientele *or* trade; **~werbung** *die* advertising aimed at attracting customers; **zu Zwecken der ~werbung** to attract custom *or* customers

**Künder** *der;* **~s**, ~, **Künderin** *die;* ~, **~nen** (*geh.*) herald

**Kund·gabe** *die* (*geh.*) announcement; (*von Gefühlen, Erfahrungen*) expression

**kund|geben** *unr. tr. V.* (*geh.*) declare; announce; express, make known ‹opinion, feelings›

**Kundgebung** *die;* ~, **~en** **A** rally; **B** (*geh.: Äußerung*) expression

**kundig** **1** *Adj.* (*kenntnisreich*) knowledgeable; well-informed; (*sachverständig*) expert; **mit ~er Hand** with an expert hand; **sich über etw.** (*Akk.*) **~ machen** (*Amtsspr.*) inform oneself about sth.; **einer Sache** (*Gen.*) **~/nicht ~ sein** (*geh.*) know about sth./have no knowledge of sth. **2** *adv.* expertly

**kündigen** /'kʏndɪgn̩/ **1** *tr. V.* call in, cancel ‹loan›; foreclose ‹mortgage›; cancel, discontinue ‹magazine subscription, membership›; terminate ‹contract, agreement›; denounce ‹treaty›; **seine Stellung ~:** give in *or* hand in one's notice (**bei** to); **jmdm. die Stellung** *od.* **jmds. Arbeitsverhältnis ~:** give sb. his/her notice; **ich bin gekündigt worden** (*ugs.*) I've been given my notice; **der Vermieter hat ihm die Wohnung gekündigt** the landlord gave him notice to quit the flat (*Brit.*) *or* (*Amer.*) apartment; **er hat seine Wohnung gekündigt** he's given notice that he's leaving his flat (*Brit.*) *or* (*Amer.*) apartment; **jmdm. die Freundschaft ~** (*fig.*) break off a friendship with sb.
**2** *unr. itr. V.* **A** (*ein Mietverhältnis beenden*) ‹tenant› give notice [that one is leaving]; **jmdm. ~** ‹landlord› give sb. notice to quit; **zum 1. Juli ~:** give notice for 1 July; **B** (*ein Arbeitsverhältnis beenden*) ‹employee› give in *or* hand in one's notice (**bei** to); **jmdm. ~** ‹employer› give sb. his/her notice

**Kündigung** *die;* ~, **~en** **A** (*eines Kredits*) calling-in; cancellation; (*einer Hypothek*) foreclosure; (*der Mitgliedschaft, eines Abonnements*) cancellation; discontinuation; (*eines Vertrags*) termination; **die Bank droht mit der ~ der Kredite** the bank is threatening to call in *or* cancel the loans; **B** (*eines Arbeitsverhältnisses*) **jmdm. die ~ aussprechen** give sb. his/her notice; dismiss sb.; **mit ~ drohen** ‹employee› threaten to give in *or* hand in one's notice *or* to quit; ‹employer› threaten dismissal; **ihm droht die ~:** he is threatened with dismissal; **eine fristlose ~:** dismissal without notice; **C** (*eines Mietverhältnisses*) **sie musste mit ~ rechnen** she had to reckon on being given notice to quit; **ich sah mich zur ~ gezwungen** I felt compelled to give notice; **D** ⇒ Kündigungsschreiben; **E** (*~sfrist*) [period *or* term of] notice; **bei jährlicher ~ betragen die Zinsen 9,5%** with one year's notice of withdrawal, interest is at 9.5%

**Kündigungs-: ~frist** *die* period of notice; **~grund** *der* (*Arbeitsrecht*) grounds *pl.* for dismissal; grounds *pl.* for giving sb. his/her notice; (*Mietrecht*) grounds *pl.* for giving sb. notice to quit; **~schreiben** *das* written notice; notice in writing; **~schutz** *der* protection against wrongful dismissal

**Kundin** *die;* ~, **~nen** customer/client; ⇒ *auch* Kunde[1] A

**kund|machen** *tr. V.* (*österr. Amtsspr.*) announce; make known; (*feierlich*) proclaim; promulgate ‹law›

**Kundschaft** *die;* ~, **~en** **A** ⇒ Kunde[1] A: customers *pl.*; clientele; **~!** service!; **ich habe gerade ~:** I've got a customer/customers at the moment; **B** (*veralt.: Erkundung*) **auf ~ ausgehen/jmdn. auf ~ ausschicken** go out on/send sb. out on reconnaissance *or* to reconnoitre; **C** (*veralt.: Nachricht*) news *sing.*; tidings *pl.* (*literary*)

**Kundschafter** *der;* **~s**, ~, **Kundschafterin** *die;* ~, **~nen** scout

**kund|tun** (*geh.*) **1** *unr. tr. V.* announce; make known. **2** *unr. refl. V.* be revealed; show itself

**kund|werden** *unr itr. V.; mit sein* (*veralt.*) become known; **ihm wurde der Verrat kund** he learned of the betrayal

**künftig** /'kʏnftɪç/ **1** *Adj.* future; **ihr ~er Mann** her future husband; her husband-to-be; **am 15. ~en Monats** (*geh.*) on the 15th of next month. **2** *adv.* in future

**künftig·hin** *Adv.* (*geh.*) henceforth; henceforward; in future

**Kungelei** *die;* ~, **~en** (*abwertend*) wheeling and dealing; **eine ~ um etw.** bargaining

k

over sth.; **große ~en** a great deal *sing.* of wheeling and dealing

**kungeln** /ˈkʊŋl̩n/ *itr. V.* **[mit jmdm.] um etw. ~:** bargain [with sb.] over sth.; **dort wird viel gekungelt** there is a lot of wheeling and dealing there

**Kunst** /kʊnst/ *die;* **~, Künste** /ˈkʏnstə/ Ⓐ art; **die schwarze ~** (*Magie*) the black art; (*Buchdruck*) [the art of] printing; **die schönen Künste** [the] fine arts; fine art *sing.*; **was macht die ~?** (*ugs.*) how are things?; how's tricks? (*sl.*); ⇒ *auch* **bilden** A; **darstellen** 1 A; **sieben²**; Ⓑ (*das Können*) skill; **die ärztliche ~:** medical skill; **die ~ des Reitens/der Selbstverteidigung** the art of riding/self-defence; **nach einer Vorlage zu stricken ist keine ~:** it's easy enough *or* it doesn't take anything to knit from a pattern; **~ kommt von können** (*meist iron.*) either you've got it or you haven't; **das ist keine/die ganze ~!** (*ugs.*) there's nothing 'to it/nothing more to it than that; **mit seiner ~ am Ende sein** be at a complete loss; ⇒ *auch* **brotlos**; **Regel** A

**Kunst-: ~akademie** *die* ⇒ **~hochschule**; **~ausstellung** *die* art exhibition; **~banause** *der* (*abwertend*) philistine; **~band** *der:* (*high-quality*) art book; **~besitz** *der* art collection; **~blatt** *das* art print; **~buch** *das* art book; **~darm** *der* artificial *or* synthetic sausage skin; **~denkmal** *das* artistic and cultural monument; **~denkmäler der Kelten/Griechen** *usw.* monuments of Celtic/Greek *etc.* art; **~diebstahl** *der* art theft; **~druck** *der; Pl.* **~~e** Ⓐ [fine] art print; Ⓑ (*Druckw.*) fine-art printing; **etw. im ~druck herstellen** produce sth. by fine-art printing methods; **~druck·papier** *das* art paper; **~dünger** *der* chemical *or* artificial fertilizer; **~eis·bahn** *die* artificial ice rink

**Künstelei** *die;* **~** (*abwertend*) affectation

**künsteln** ⇒ **gekünstelt**

**kunst-, Kunst-: ~erzieher** *der*, **~erzieherin** *die* ▶ 159 art teacher; **~erziehung** *die* art education; (*Schulfach*) art; **~fälschung** *die* art forgery; **~faser** *die* man-made *or* synthetic fibre; **~fehler** *der* professional error; (*fig. scherzh.: Versehen*) mistake; **ein ärztlicher ~fehler** a professional error on the part of a doctor; **~fertig** ❶ *Adj.* skilful; ❷ *adv.* skilfully; **~fertigkeit** *die* skill; skilfulness; **~flieger** *der*, **~fliegerin** *die* aerobatic pilot; stunt pilot (*coll.*); **~flug** *der* aerobatics *sing.*; stunt-flying (*coll.*); **ein ~flug** a piece of aerobatic flying *or* (*coll.*) stunt-flying; **~form** *die* art form; **~freund** *der*, **~freundin** *die* art lover; lover of the arts; **~führer** *der* guide to cultural and artistic monuments [of an/the area]; **~galerie** *die* art gallery; **~gegenstand** *der* work of art; **~genuss**, ***~genuß** *der* enjoyment of art; (*Ereignis*) artistic treat; **~gerecht** ❶ *Adj.* expert; skilful; ❷ *adv.* expertly; skilfully; **~geschichte** *die* Ⓐ art history; history of art; Ⓑ (*Buch*) art history book; book on the history of art; **~geschichtlich** ❶ *Adj.* art historical ‹studies, evidence, expertise, etc.›; ‹work› on art history *or* the history of art; ‹interest› in art history *or* the history of art; **~geschichtliches Museum** art-history museum; museum of art history; ❷ *adv.* **~geschichtlich interessiert/versiert** interested/well versed in art history *or* the history of art; **~geschichtlich bedeutsam** significant from an art-historical point of view; **~gewerbe** *das* arts and crafts *pl.*; **~gewerblich** ❶ *Adj.* craft *attrib.* ‹objects, skills, etc.›; **~gewerbliche Arbeiten** craftwork *sing.*; ❷ *adv.* **~gewerblich hergestellte Produkte** craft products; **~glied** *das* artificial limb; **~griff** *der* move; (*fig.*) trick; dodge; **~halle** *die* art gallery; **~handel** *der* [fine-]art trade; **~händler** *der*, **~händlerin** *die* [fine-]art dealer; **~handwerk** *das* craftwork; **Erzeugnisse des ~handwerks** craft products; craftwork *sing.*; **~harz** *das* (*Chemie*) synthetic resin; **~historiker** *der*, **~historikerin** *die* ▶ 159 art historian; **~historisch** ⇒ **~geschichtlich**; **~hochschule** *die* art college; college of art; **~honig** *der* artifical honey; honey substitute; **~kalender** *der* art calendar; **~kenner** *der*, **~kennerin** *die* art connoisseur *or* expert; **~kopf** *der* (*Tontechnik*) dummy head; **~kraftsport** *der* sports acrobatics *sing.*; **~kritik** *die* art criticism; (*die Kritiker*) art critics *pl.*; **~kritiker** *der*, **~kritikerin** *die* ▶ 159 art critic; **~lauf** *der* (*Sport*) figure skating; **~leder** *das* artificial *or* imitation leather

**Künstler** /ˈkʏnstlɐ/ *der;* **~s, ~, Künstlerin** *die;* **~, ~nen** ▶ 159 Ⓐ artist; (*Zirkus~, Varieté~*) artiste; **ein bildender ~:** a visual artist; Ⓑ (*Könner*) genius (**in** + *Dat.* at); **ein ~ in seinem Fach** a genius in one's field/at one's trade

**Künstler-: ~atelier** *das* studio; **~beruf** *der* artistic career; **~hand** *die: in* **von ~hand** by the artist's hand

**künstlerisch** ❶ *Adj.* artistic. ❷ *adv.* artistically; **etw. ~ darstellen** express sth. in artistic form; **ein ~ wertvoller Film** a film of great artistic worth

**Künstler-: ~kneipe** *die* pub (*Brit.*) *or* (*Amer.*) bar frequented by artists; **~kolonie** *die* artists' colony; colony of artists; **~mähne** *die* (*ugs. veralt. scherzh.*) mane of hair; **~name** *der* stage name; **~pech** *das* (*ugs. scherzh.*) hard luck

**Künstlertum** *das;* **~s** artistic genius

**künstlich** /ˈkʏnstlɪç/ ❶ *Adj.* Ⓐ artificial; artificial, glass ‹eye›; false ‹teeth, eyelashes, hair›; synthetic, man-made ‹fibre›; imitation, synthetic ‹diamond›; Ⓑ (*gezwungen*) forced ‹laugh, cheerfulness, etc.›; enforced ‹rest›. ❷ *adv.* Ⓐ artificially; **jmdn. ~ ernähren** feed sb. artificially; Ⓑ (*gezwungen*) **sich ~ aufregen** (*ugs.*) get worked up *or* excited about nothing

**Künstlichkeit** *die;* **~:** artificiality

**kunst-, Kunst-: ~licht** *das* artificial light; **bei ~licht** in artificial light; **~liebhaber** *der*, **~liebhaberin** *die* art lover; lover of the arts; **~lied** *das* art song; Kunstlied; **~los** ❶ *Adj.* plain; ❷ *adv.* plainly; **~maler** *der*, **~malerin** *die* ▶ 159 artist; painter; **~märchen** *das* (*Literaturw.*) literary fairy tale; **~pause** *die* pause for effect; (*iron.: Stockung*) awkward pause; **eine ~pause machen** pause for effect/pause awkwardly; **~post·karte** *die* art postcard; **~rasen** *der* artificial turf; **~reich** ⇒ **~voll**; **~reiter** *der*, **~reiterin** *die* circus rider; bareback rider; **~richtung** *die* trend in art; **neue ~richtungen** new directions in art; **~sammler** *der*, **~sammlerin** *die* art collector; **~sammlung** *die* art collection; **~schaffende** *der/die; adj. Dekl.* artist; **~schatz** *der* art treasure; **~schmied** *der*, **~schmiedin** *die* wrought-iron craftsman; **~schwimmen** *das* (*Sport*) synchronized swimming *no art.*; **~seide** *die* artificial silk; rayon; **~sinn** *der* artistic sense; feeling for art; **~sprache** *die* artificial language; **~springen** *das;* **~~s** (*Sport*) springboard diving; **~stein** *der* artificial stone

**Kunst·stoff** *der* synthetic material; plastic

***Kunststoffaser** ⇒ **Kunststofffaser**

**Kunststoff-: ~bahn** *die* (*Sport*) synthetic track; **~faser** *die* synthetic fibre; **~karosserie** *die* plastic body

**kunst-, Kunst-: ~stopfen** *tr. V.* (*nur im Inf. u. 2. Part. gebr.*) repair by invisible mending; invisibly mend; **~stück** *das* trick; **das ist kein ~stück** (*ugs.*) it's no great feat *or* achievement; **~stück!** (*ugs. iron.*) that's no great achievement; (*ist nicht verwunderlich*) it's hardly surprising; **~turnen** *das* gymnastics *sing.*; **~verstand** *der* artistic sense; feeling for art; **~voll** ❶ *Adj.* ornate *or* elaborate and artistic; (*kompliziert*) elaborate; ❷ *adv.* Ⓐ ornately *or* elaborately and artistically; Ⓑ (*geschickt*) skilfully; **~werk** *das* (*auch fig.*) work of art; **~wissenschaft** *die* aesthetics and art history; **~wort** *das; Pl.* **~wörter** (*Sprachw.*) made-up *or* invented word; **~szene** *die* art world

**kunter·bunt** /ˈkʊntɐ-/ ❶ *Adj.* Ⓐ (*vielfarbig*) multicoloured; Ⓑ (*abwechslungsreich*) varied; **wir laden Sie zu unserem ~en Abend mit ... ein** you are invited to our evening of varied entertainment with ...; Ⓒ (*ungeordnet*) jumbled ‹confusion, muddle, rows, etc.›. ❷ *adv.* Ⓐ ‹painted, printed› in many colours; Ⓑ (*abwechslungsreich*) **ein ~ gestalteter Abend** an evening of varied entertainment; **sein Leben verlief recht ~:** he had a very varied life; Ⓒ (*ungeordnet*) **~ durcheinander sein** be higgledy-piggledy *or* all jumbled up; **es ging ~ durcheinander** it was completely chaotic

**Kunterbunt** *das;* **~s** Ⓐ (*von Farben*) riotous profusion of colour; Ⓑ (*Gemisch*) potpourri; Ⓒ (*Durcheinander*) muddle

**Kunz** /kʊnts/ ⇒ **Hinz**

**Kupfer** /ˈkʊpfɐ/ *das;* **~s** Ⓐ copper; **etw. in ~** (*Akk.*) **stechen** engrave *or* etch sth. on copper; Ⓑ (*~geschirr*) copperware; (*~geld*) coppers *pl.*; Ⓒ ⇒ **Kupferstich** B

**kupfer-, Kupfer-: ~blech** *das* copper sheeting; **ein ~blech** a copper sheet; **~draht** *der* copper wire; **~druck** *der; Pl.* **~~e** Ⓐ copperplate printing *no art.*; **etw. in ~druck herstellen** produce sth. by copperplate printing; Ⓑ (*Abbildung*) copperplate [print]; **~erz** *das* copper ore; **~geld** *das* coppers *pl.*; **~haltig** *Adj.* containing copper *postpos.*, *not pred.*; cupriferous; **~kessel** *der* copper kettle; (*zum Bierbrauen*) copper vat; **~legierung** *die* copper alloy; **~münze** *die* copper coin; copper

**kupfern** *Adj.* (*geh.*) Ⓐ copper; **die ~e Hochzeit** the seventh wedding anniversary; Ⓑ (*wie Kupfer*) coppery

**kupfer-, Kupfer-: ~rot** *Adj.* copper-red; copper-coloured; **~schmied** *der*, **~schmiedin** *die* coppersmith; **~stecher** *der*, **~stecherin** *die;* **~~, ~~nen** copper[plate] engraver; **mein lieber Freund und ~stecher** (*ugs. scherzh.*) now then, my friend; **~stich** *der* Ⓐ copperplate engraving *no art.*; Ⓑ (*Blatt*) copperplate print *or* engraving; **~sulfat** *das* (*Chemie*) copper sulphate; **~vitriol** *das* (*Chemie*) blue vitriol

**kupieren** /kuˈpiːrən/ *tr. V.* Ⓐ crop, dock ‹tail›; crop ‹ears, hedge›; clip ‹wings›; prune ‹bush etc.›; Ⓑ (*Med.*) arrest; check

**Kupon** ⇒ **Coupon**

**Kuppe** /ˈkʊpə/ *die;* **~, ~n** Ⓐ [rounded] hilltop; Ⓑ (*Finger~*) tip; end

**Kuppel** /ˈkʊpl̩/ *die;* **~, ~n** dome; (*kleiner*) cupola; **die ~ der Bäume** the domed canopy of trees

**Kuppel-: ~bau** *der; Pl.* **~~ten** domed building; **~dach** *das* domed *or* dome-shaped roof

**Kuppelei** *die;* **~, ~en** Ⓐ (*veralt. abwertend*) matchmaking; Ⓑ (*Rechtsspr.*) procuring; procuration

**Kuppel·mutter** *die; Pl.* **Kuppel·mütter** (*abwertend*) procuress

**kuppeln** ❶ *itr. V.* Ⓐ (*bei einem Kfz*) operate the clutch; **hier muss man viel ~:** you have to use the clutch a great deal here; Ⓑ (*veralt.: Kuppelei betreiben*) matchmake; play the matchmaker. ❷ *tr. V.* Ⓐ (*koppeln*) couple (**an** + *Akk.*, **zu** [on] to); Ⓑ (*Technik*) couple; **gekuppelt** coupled ‹exposure meter, rangefinder›; **mit etw. gekuppelt sein** (*fig.*) be linked with sth.

**Kuppel·pelz** *der: in* **sich** (*Dat.*) **den ~ verdienen** (*abwertend*) arrange a/the match; play the matchmaker

**Kuppelung** ⇒ **Kupplung**

**Kuppler** *der;* **~s, ~** (*abwertend*) procurer

**Kupplerin** *die;* **~, ~nen** (*abwertend*) procuress

**Kupplung** *die;* **~, ~en** Ⓐ (*Kfz-W.*) clutch; Ⓑ (*Technik: Vorrichtung zum Verbinden*) coupling; Ⓒ (*das Verbinden*) coupling; (*fig.*) linking

**Kupplungs-: ~pedal** *das* (*Kfz-W.*) clutch pedal; **~scheibe** *die* (*Kfz-W.*) clutch plate; **~seil** *das* (*Kfz-W.*) clutch cable

**Kur** /kuːɐ̯/ *die;* **~, ~en** ▶ 474 [health] cure; (*ohne Aufenthalt im Badeort*) course of treatment; **eine ~ machen** take a cure/a course of treatment; **in ~ gehen** go to a health resort *or* spa [to take a cure]

*old spelling (see note on page 1707)

k

**Kür** /kyːɐ̯/ *die;* ~, ~**en** Ⓐ (*Eiskunstlauf*) free programme; (*Turnen*) optional exercises *pl.*; **eine ~ laufen/tanzen** skate/dance one's free programme; **eine ~ turnen** perform one's optional exercises; **die beste ~ laufen** skate the best free programme; Ⓑ (*veralt.: Wahl*) choosing

**Kurant** /kuˈrant/ *das;* ~**[e]s**, ~**e** (*veralt.*) *coin whose face value is equal to the value of its constituent metals*

**Kürass**, ***Küraß** /ˈkyːras/ *der;* **Kürasses, Kürasse** (*hist.*) cuirass

**Kürassier** /kyraˈsiːɐ̯/ *der;* ~**s**, ~**e** (*Milit. hist.*) cuirassier

**Kurat** /kuˈraːt/ *der;* ~**en**, ~**en** (*kath. Kirche*) curate

**Kuratel** /kuraˈteːl/ *die;* ~, ~**en** (*Rechtsspr. veralt.*) guardianship; **unter ~ stehen** be under the care of a guardian; **jmdn. unter ~ stellen** place sb. under the care of a guardian; (*jmdn. stärker kontrollieren*) place sb. under closer supervision

**Kurator** /kuˈraːtɔr/ *der;* ~**s**, ~**en**, /kuraˈtoːrən/ **Kuratorin** *die;* ~, ~**nen** Ⓐ (*einer Stiftung*) trustee; Ⓑ (*einer Universität*) *university officer dealing with financial and legal matters;* Ⓒ (*veralt.: Vormund*) guardian

**Kuratorium** /kuraˈtoːri̯ʊm/ *das;* ~**s**, **Kuratorien** board of trustees

**Kur-:** ~**aufenthalt** *der* stay at a health resort *or* spa; **ein ~aufenthalt am Meer** a stay at a seaside health resort; ~**bad** *das* health resort; spa

**Kurbel** /ˈkʊrbl̩/ *die;* ~, ~**n** (*bei Autos, Maschinen*) crank [handle]; (*an Fenstern, Spieldosen, Grammophonen*) winder; (*an einem Brunnen*) [winding] handle

**kurbeln** ❶ *tr. V.* Ⓐ **etw. nach oben/unten ~:** wind sth. up/down; **den Eimer aus dem Brunnen ~:** wind the bucket up out of the well; **sie kurbelte den Tisch so tief es ging** she wound the table down as far as it would go; Ⓑ (*ugs.: filmen*) film; shoot ‹film›. ❷ *itr. V.* turn *or* wind a/the handle; (*bei Autos*) turn a/the crank [handle]; crank; **er musste ziemlich ~, um aus der Parklücke herauszukommen** (*fig. ugs.*) he had to use a lot of lock (*Brit.*) to get out of the parking space

**Kurbel·welle** *die* (*Technik*) crankshaft

**Kürbis** /ˈkʏrbɪs/ *der;* ~**ses**, ~**se** Ⓐ pumpkin; Ⓑ (*salopp: Kopf*) nut (*coll.*); bonce (*Brit. coll.*)

**Kürbis-:** ~**flasche** *die* gourd; ~**kern** *der* pumpkin seed

**Kurde** /ˈkʊrdə/ *der;* ~**n**, ~**n**, **Kurdin** *die;* ~, ~**nen** Kurd

**kurdisch** *Adj.* ▶ 696 Kurdish; **das Kurdische** Kurdish; ⇒ *auch* **deutsch**; **Deutsch**

**Kurdistan** /ˈkʊrdɪstaːn/ *(das);* ~**s** Kurdistan

**kuren** *itr. V.* (*ugs.*) take a cure

**küren** *regelm.* (*veralt. auch unr.*) *tr. V.* choose (**zu** as)

**Kürettage** /kyrɛˈtaːʒə/ *die;* ~, ~**n** (*Med.*) curettage

**Kürette** /kyˈrɛtə/ *die;* ~, ~**n** (*Med.*) curette

**kur-**, **Kur-:** ~**fürst** *der* (*hist.*) Elector; ~**fürstentum** *das* (*hist.*) electorate; ~**fürstlich** *Adj.* (*hist.*) electoral; ~**gast** *der* visitor to a/the health resort *or* spa; (*Patient*) patient at a/the health resort *or* spa; ~**haus** *das* assembly rooms [at a health resort *or* spa]; ~**heim** *das* sanatorium

**Kurie** /ˈkuːri̯ə/ *die;* ~, ~**n** (*kath. Kirche*) Curia

**Kurien·kardinal** *der* (*kath. Kirche*) cardinal of the Roman Curia

**Kurier** /kuˈriːɐ̯/ *der;* ~**s**, ~**e** courier; messenger

**Kurier·dienst** *der* courier *or* messenger service; ~**e leisten** act as a courier/as couriers

**kurieren** *tr. V.* (*auch fig.*) cure (**von** of)

**Kurier·gepäck** *das* diplomatic bags *pl.*

**Kurierin** *die;* ~, ~**nen** ⇒ **Kurier**

**kurios** /kuˈri̯oːs/ ❶ *Adj.* curious; strange; odd. ❷ *adv.* curiously; strangely; oddly

**Kuriosa** ⇒ **Kuriosum**

**kurioser·weise** *Adv.* curiously *or* strangely *or* oddly enough

**Kuriosität** /kuri̯oziˈtɛːt/ *die;* ~, ~**en** Ⓐ strangeness; oddity; peculiarity; Ⓑ (*Gegenstand*) curiosity; curio; (*Ereignis*) curious occurrence

**Kuriositäten·kabinett** *das* gallery of curios

**Kuriosum** /kuˈri̯oːzʊm/ *das;* ~**s**, **Kuriosa** (*Gegenstand*) curiosity; curio; oddity; (*Situation*) curious *or* odd *or* strange situation

**Kur-:** ~**kapelle** *die* spa orchestra; ~**karte** *die* [visitor's] pass *or* season ticket (*allowing use of the facilities of a health resort*) *or* (*spa*); ~**klinik** *die* health clinic; ~**konzert** *das* concert [at a health resort *or* spa]; spa concert

**Kurkuma** /ˈkʊrkuma/ *das;* ~**[s]** turmeric

**Kurlaub** /ˈkuːɐ̯laup/ *der;* ~**[e]s**, ~**e** holiday [combined with cure] at a health resort *or* spa

**Kür·lauf** *der* (*Eiskunstlauf*) free programme; **er zeigte einen hervorragenden ~:** he gave an excellent display of free skating

**kur-**, **Kur-:** ~**mittel** *das* spa treatment; ~**mittel·haus** *das* spa house; ~**ort** *der* health resort; spa; ~**park** *der* gardens *pl.* [of a/the health resort *or* spa]; ~**pfalz** *die* (*hist.*) Electoral Palatinate; ~**pfälzisch** *Adj.* (*hist.*) of the Electoral Palatinate *postpos., not pred.*; ~**pfuscher** *der* (*ugs. abwertend*) quack; doctor; ~**pfuscherei** *die* (*ugs. abwertend*) quackery; ~**pfuscherin** *die* ⇒ ~**pfuscher**; ~**promenade** *die* [spa] promenade

**Kurrende** /kʊˈrɛndə/ *die;* ~, ~**n** (*ev. Kirche*) young people's choir

**Kurrent·schrift** /kʊˈrɛnt-/ *die* Ⓐ (*österr.*) Gothic handwriting *or* script; Ⓑ (*veralt.: Schreibschrift*) cursive writing *or* script; running hand

**Kurrikulum** ⇒ **Curriculum**

**Kurs** /kʊrs/ *der;* ~**es**, ~**e** Ⓐ (*Richtung*) course; **auf [nördlichen] ~ gehen** set [a northerly] course; **ein harter/weicher ~** (*fig.*) a hard/soft line; **den ~ ändern** (*auch fig.*) change *or* alter course; **seinen ~ beibehalten** (*auch fig.*) maintain course; **vom ~ abkommen** deviate from one's/its course; **den ~ halten** hold *or* maintain course; **~ auf Hamburg** (*Akk.*) **nehmen** set course for *or* head for Hamburg; **~ haben auf** (+ *Akk.*) be heading for; ⇒ *auch* **einschlagen** 1 D; Ⓑ (*von Wertpapieren*) price; (*von Devisen*) rate of exchange; exchange rate; **zum ~ von ...** at a rate of ...; **die ~e steigen/fallen** prices/rates are rising/falling; **der ~ des Dollars** the dollar rate; **hoch im ~ stehen** ‹securities› be high; (*fig.*) be very popular (**bei** with); **er steht hoch im ~ bei seinem Chef** his boss thinks very highly of him; **etw. außer ~ setzen** withdraw sth. from circulation; Ⓒ (*Lehrgang*) course; **ein ~ in Spanisch** (*Dat.*) a course in Spanish; a Spanish course; Ⓓ (*die Teilnehmer eines ~es*) class; Ⓔ (*Sport: Rennstrecke*) course

**Kurs-:** ~**änderung** *die* (*auch fig.*) change of course; ~**anstieg** *der* (*Börsenw.*) rise in prices/price; price rise; (*an Devisenbörsen*) rise in exchange rates/the exchange rate

**Kursant** /kʊrˈzant/ *der;* ~**en**, ~**en** ⇒ **Kursteilnehmer**

**Kurs-:** ~**bericht** *der* (*Börsenw.*) ⇒ ~**zettel**; ~**buch** *das* (*Eisenb.*) timetable

**Kur·schatten** *der* (*ugs. scherzh.*) lady friend/boyfriend at/from the spa

**Kürschner** /ˈkʏrʃnɐ/ *der;* ~**s**, ~ ▶ 159 furrier

**Kürschnerei** *die;* ~, ~**en** Ⓐ furriery; Ⓑ (*Werkstatt*) furrier's workroom

**Kürschnerin** *die;* ~, ~**nen** furrier

**Kurs-:** ~**einbuße** *die* (*Börsenw.*) fall in prices/price; price fall; (*bes. bei Devisen*) fall *or* decline in value; ~**gewinn** *der* (*Börsenw.*) Ⓐ market profit; (*bei Devisen*) profit on the foreign exchange market; Ⓑ (*Wertzuwachs*) market gain

**kursieren** *itr. V.; auch mit sein* circulate

**Kursist** *der;* ~**en**, ~**en**, **Kursistin** *die;* ~, ~**nen** ⇒ **Kursteilnehmer**

**kursiv** /kʊrˈziːf/ (*Druckw.*) ❶ *Adj.* italic. ❷ *adv.* **etw. ~ drucken** print sth. in italics; (*zur Hervorhebung*) italicize sth.

**Kursive** *die;* ~, ~**n**, **Kursiv·schrift** *die* (*Druckw.*) italics *pl.*; **in ~schrift** in italics

**Kurs-:** ~**korrektur** *die* (*auch fig.*) course correction; ~**leiter** *der* course leader

**kursorisch** /kʊrˈzoːrɪʃ/ ❶ *Adj.* cursory. ❷ *adv.* cursorily

**Kurs-:** ~**rück·gang** *der* (*Börsenw.*) fall in prices/price; price fall; (*bei Devisen*) fall in exchange rates/the exchange rate; ~**schwankung** *die* (*Börsenw.*) fluctuation in prices/price; (*bei Devisen*) fluctuation in exchange rates/the exchange rate; ~**system** *das* (*Schulw.*) course system; ~**teilnehmer** *der*, ~**teilnehmerin** *die* course participant

**Kursus** /ˈkʊrzʊs/ *der;* ~, **Kurse** ⇒ **Kurs** C, D

**Kurs-:** ~**verlust** *der* (*Börsenw.*) market loss; (*bei Devisen*) loss on the foreign exchange market; ~**wagen** *der* (*Eisenb.*) through carriage *or* coach; ~**wechsel** *der* (*auch fig.*) change of course; ~**wert** *der* (*Börsenw.*) market value *or* price; ~**zettel** *der* (*Börsenw.*) stock exchange list; list of [market] quotations; (*bei Devisen*) list of foreign exchange rates

**Kur·taxe** *die* visitors' tax (*at a health resort*)

**Kurtisane** /kʊrtiˈzaːnə/ *die;* ~, ~**n** (*hist.*) courtesan

**Kurve** /ˈkʊrvə/ *die;* ~, ~**n** Ⓐ (*einer Straße*) bend; curve; (*sehr scharf*) corner; **in dieser ~:** on this bend *or* curve; **die Straße macht eine [scharfe] ~:** the road bends *or* curves [sharply]; **die ~ kratzen** (*ugs.*) quickly make oneself scarce (*coll.*); **die ~ kriegen** (*ugs.*) manage to do it; (*etw. überwinden*) manage to do something decisive about it; ⇒ *auch* **schneiden**; Ⓑ (*Geom.*) curve; Ⓒ (*in der Statistik, Temperatur~ usw.*) graph; curve; Ⓓ (*Bogenlinie*) curve; **eine ~ fliegen** do a banking turn; Ⓔ *Pl.* (*ugs.: Körperformen*) curves

**kurven** *itr. V.; mit sein* Ⓐ ‹aircraft› circle; ‹tanks etc.› circle [round]; **um die Ecke ~:** turn the corner; Ⓑ (*ugs.: fahren*) drive around; (*mit dem Motorrad, Fahrrad*) ride around; **durch ganz Frankreich ~:** drive/ride all round France

**kurven-**, **Kurven-:** ~**diskussion** *die* (*Math.*) curve-tracing; ~**lineal** *das* French curve; ~**reich** *Adj.* Ⓐ winding; twisting; **„~reiche Strecke"** 'series of bends'; Ⓑ (*ugs. scherzh.*) curvaceous; ~**schreiber** *der* (*Technik*) graphic recording instrument; (*DV*) plotter; ~**verhalten** *das* (*Kfz-W.*) cornering characteristics *pl.*; ~**vorgabe** *die* (*Leichtathletik*) stagger

**Kur·verwaltung** *die* administrative office/offices of a/the health resort *or* spa

**kurvig** *Adj.* curved; winding, twisting ‹path, road, etc.›

**kurz** /kʊrts/; **kürzer** /ˈkʏrtsɐ/, **kürzest...** /ˈkʏrtsəst.../ ❶ *Adj.* Ⓐ (*räumlich*) short; ~**e Hosen** short trousers; shorts; **etw. kürzer machen** make sth. shorter; shorten sth.; **~ geschnitten** cropped short *postpos.*; **ein kürzerer Weg** a shorter *or* quicker way; **die Hundeleine ~ halten** keep the dog on a short lead; **etw./alles ~ und klein schlagen** *od.* **hauen** (*ugs.*) smash sth./everything to bits *or* pieces; **den Kürzeren ziehen** come off worst *or* second-best; get the worst of it; **nicht zu ~/zu ~ kommen** get one's/less than one's fair share; Ⓑ (*zeitlich*) short, brief ‹trip, journey, visit, reply›; short ‹life, break, time›; quick ‹look›; **nach einer ~en Weile** after a short *or* little while; **es ~ machen** make *or* keep it short; be brief; Ⓒ (*knapp*) short, brief ‹outline, note, report, summary, introduction›; **etw. in ~en Worten sagen** say sth. in a few brief words; **~ und bündig** *od.* **knapp** brief and succinct.
❷ *adv.* Ⓐ (*zeitlich*) briefly; for a short time *or* while; **~ gebratenes Fleisch** meat fried on high heat for a very short time; **die Freude währte nur ~** (*geh.*) his/her *etc.* joy was short-lived; **binnen ~em** shortly; soon; **er hatte binnen ~em das ganze Vermögen verjubelt** before long he had

k

frittered away the entire fortune; **über ~ oder lang** sooner or later; **vor ~em** a short time *or* while ago; recently; **sie lebt erst seit ~em in Bonn** she's only been living in Bonn [for] a short time *or* while; **B** (*knapp*) **~ gesagt** in a word; **~ angebunden sein** be curt *or* brusque (**mit** with); **sich ~ fassen** be brief; **~ gefasst** terse; succint; briefly worded; **~ und bündig** *od.* **knapp** briefly and succinctly; **~ und gut** in a word; **C** (*rasch*) **ich muss mal ~ weg** I must leave you for a few minutes; **er schaute ~ herein** he looked *or* dropped in for a short while; **kann ich Sie ~ sprechen?** can I speak to you *or* have a word with you for a moment?; **ich muss ~ etwas in der Stadt erledigen** I've just got something to do in town. I won't be long; **~ und schmerzlos** (*ugs.*) quickly and smoothly *or* without any hitches; ⇒ *auch* **entschlossen** 3; **D** (*in geringer Entfernung*) **~ vor/hinter der Kreuzung** just before/past the crossroads; **~ vor Bremen hatten wir eine Panne** just before we reached Bremen, we broke down; **E** (*mit geringem zeitlichem Abstand*) **~ vor/nach Pfingsten** just *or* shortly before/after Whitsun; **~ bevor .../nachdem ...** just *or* shortly before .../after ...; **F** **jmdn. ~ halten** (*jmdm. wenig Geld geben*) keep sb. short of money; (*jmdm. wenig erlauben*) keep sb. on a tight rein; **~ treten** (*sich schonen*) take things *or* it easy; (*sparsam sein*) retrench; cut back; **kürzer treten** (*sich mehr schonen*) take things *or* it easier; (*sparsam sein*) cut back; spend less; ⇒ *auch* **Atem**; **Kopf** A; **Prozess** C

**kurz-, Kurz-: ~arbeit** *die* short time; short-time working; **~|arbeiten** *itr. V.* work short time; **~arbeiter** *der*, **~arbeiterin** *die* short-time worker; worker on short time; **~ärm[e]lig** /-ɛrm(ə)lɪç/ *Adj.* short-sleeved; **~atmig** /-a:tmɪç/ **1** *Adj.* (*auch fig.*) short-winded; **~atmig sein** be short of breath; be short-winded; **2** *adv.* ‹speak› breathlessly; **~atmigkeit** *die;* **~~:** short-windedness; **~beinig** *Adj.* short-legged ‹breed, dog, etc.›; ‹person› with short legs; **~bericht** *der* brief *or* short report; **~biographie** *die* short *or* potted biography

**Kurze** *der; adj. Dekl.* (*ugs.*) **A** (*Kurzschluss*) short (*coll.*); **B** (*Schnaps*) schnapps

**Kürze** /ˈkʏrt͜sə/ *die;* **~, ~n** **A** shortness; **B** (*geringe Dauer*) shortness; short duration; brevity; **in ~:** shortly; soon; **C** (*Knappheit*) brevity; **in aller/gebotener ~:** very briefly/with due brevity; **in der ~ liegt die Würze** (*Spr.*) brevity is the soul of wit (*prov.*); **D** (*Verslehre*) short syllable; short

**Kürzel** /ˈkʏrt͜sl̩/ *das;* **~s, ~** **A** shorthand symbol; **B** (*Abkürzung*) abbreviation

**kürzen** *tr. V.* **A** shorten; shorten, take up ‹garment›; **ein Kleid um 5 cm ~:** shorten a dress by 5 cm; take a dress up 5 cm; **B** (*verringern*) shorten ‹speech›; shorten, abridge ‹article, book›; reduce, cut ‹pension, budget, etc.›; **jmdm. das Gehalt ~:** reduce *or* cut sb.'s salary; **eine gekürzte Fassung** a shortened *or* an abridged version; **C** (*Math.*) cancel

**kürzer** ⇒ **kurz**

**kurzer·hand** *Adv.* without more ado; **jmdn. ~ vor die Tür setzen** (*ugs.*) unceremoniously throw sb. out; **etw. ~ ablehnen** flatly reject sth.; reject sth. out of hand; **sich ~ entschließen, etw. zu tun** decide there and then to do sth.

***kürzer|treten** ⇒ **kurz** 2 F

**kürzest...** ⇒ **kurz**

**kurz-, Kurz-: ~fassung** *die* shortened *or* abridged version; **~film** *der* short; short film; **~form** *die* (*Sprachw.*) shortened *or* abbreviated form; **~fristig** **1** *Adj.* **A** (*plötzlich*) ‹refusal, resignation, etc.› at short notice; **B** (*für ~e Zeit*) short-term; **eine ~fristige Freiheitsstrafe** a short period of imprisonment; **C** (*rasch*) quick ‹solution›; **2** *adv.* **A** (*plötzlich*) at short notice; **sich ~fristig entschließen, etw. zu tun** make up one's mind within a short time to do sth.; **B** (*für ~e Zeit*) for a short time *or* period; (*auf ~e Sicht*) in the short term; **~fristig gesehen** looked at *or* viewed in the short term; **C** (*in ~er Zeit*) without delay; ***~gebraten** ⇒ **kurz** 2 A; ***~gefaßt** ⇒ **kurz** 2 B; **~geschichte** *die* (*Literaturw.*) short story; ***~geschnitten** ⇒ **kurz** 1 A; **~haar·frisur** *die* bob; bobbed hairstyle; **~haar·dackel** *der* short-haired dachshund; **~haarig** *Adj.* short-haired ‹dog, breed, etc.›; ‹person› with short hair; ***~|halten** ⇒ **kurz** 2 F; **~lebig** /-le:bɪç/ *Adj.* (*auch fig.*) short-lived; (*wenig haltbar*) non-durable ‹goods, materials›; with a short life *post-pos.*; **~lebigkeit** *die* short-livedness; (*von Gebrauchsgütern*) lack of durability; **~lehrgang** *der* short course

**kürzlich** *Adv.* recently; not long ago; **erst ~:** just *or* only recently; only a short time ago

**kurz-, Kurz-: ~meldung** *die* brief report; (*während einer anderen Sendung*) news flash; **~nachrichten** *Pl.* news *sing.* in brief; news summary *sing.*; **~parker** *der;* **~~s, ~~, ~parkerin** *die;* **~~, ~~nen** short-stay (*Brit.*) *or* short-term parker; **„nur für ~parker"** 'short-stay (*Brit.*) *or* short-term parking only'; **~referat** *das* short paper; **~|schließen** **1** *unr. tr. V.* short-circuit; **ein Auto ~schließen** short-circuit a car's ignition; **2** *unr. refl. V.* **sich mit jmdm./etw. ~schließen** contact sb./sth. directly; **~schluss**, ***~schluß** *der* **A** (*Elektrot.*) short-circuit; **B** (*fig. ugs.*) brainstorm; **C** (*falscher Schluss*) fallacy; **~schluss·handlung**, ***~schluß·handlung** *die* sudden irrational act; **~schrift** *die* shorthand; **~sichtig** (*auch fig.*) **1** *Adj.* short-sighted; **2** *adv.* short-sightedly; **~sichtigkeit** *die;* **~~** (*auch fig.*) short-sightedness; **~stielig** *Adj.* short-stemmed ‹glass, flower›; short-handled ‹axe, hammer, etc.›; **~strecke** *die* **A** short haul *or* distance; **auf ~strecken** over short distances; **B** (*Sport*) sprint distance; sprint; **auf [den] ~strecken** over sprint distances; in sprinting

**Kurzstrecken-: ~flug** *der* short-haul flight; **~lauf** *der* (*Sport*) short-distance race; sprint; (*Disziplin*) sprinting *no art.*; **~läufer** *der*, **~läuferin** *die* (*Sport*) sprinter; **~rakete** *die* short-range missile

**kurz-: *~|treten** ⇒ **kurz** 2F; **~um** /-ˈ-/ *Adv.* in short; in a word

**Kürzung** *die;* **~, ~en** **A** cut; reduction; **eine ~ des Gehaltes** a cut *or* reduction in salary; a salary cut; **B** (*Streichung*) cut; (*das Streichen*) abridgement

**kurz-, Kurz-: ~urlaub** *der* short holiday; (*Milit.*) short leave; **~wahl** *die* (*Fernspr.*) abbreviated dialling; **~waren** *Pl.* haberdashery *sing.* (*Brit.*); notions (*Amer.*); **~waren·abteilung** *die* haberdashery department (*Brit.*); notions department (*Amer.*); **~weg** /-ˈ-/ *Adv.* ⇒ **kurzerhand**; **~weil** *die;* **~~** (*veralt.*) amusement; **allerlei ~weil treiben** have fun; amuse oneself; **~weilig** *Adj.* entertaining; **~welle** *die* (*Physik, Rundf.*) short wave; **auf** *od.* **über ~welle** on short wave; **~wellen·empfänger** *der* (*Funkt., Rundf.*) short-wave receiver; **~wellen·sender** *der* (*Funkt., Rundf.*) short-wave transmitter; **~wort** *das; Pl.* **~wörter** (*Sprachw.*) abbreviation; **~zeit·gedächtnis** *das* (*Psych.*) short-term memory; **~zeitig** **1** *Adj.* brief; **2** *adv.* briefly; for a short time

**kusch** *Interj.* [lie] down; (*sei still*) quiet

**kuschelig** *Adj.* cosy

**kuscheln** /ˈkʊʃl̩n/ *refl. V.* **sich an jmdn. ~:** snuggle up *or* cuddle up to sb.; ‹cat etc.› snuggle up to sb.; **sich in etw.** (*Akk.*) **~:** snuggle up in sth.

**Kuschel·tier** *das* cuddly toy

**kuschel·weich** *Adj.* beautifully soft

**kuschen** /ˈkʊʃn̩/ *itr. V.* **A** knuckle under (**vor** + *Dat.* to); **B** ‹dog› lie down

**Kusine** /kuˈzi:nə/ *die;* **~, ~n** ⇒ **Cousine**

**Kuss**, ***Kuß** /kʊs/ *der;* **Kusses, Küsse** /ˈkʏsə/ kiss; **Gruß und ~ [dein ...]** love and kisses [from ...]

**Küsschen**, ***Küßchen** /ˈkʏsçən/ *das;* **~s, ~:** little kiss; **ein ~ in Ehren kann niemand verwehren** (*Spr.*) a friendly kiss can do no harm

**kuss·echt**, ***kuß·echt** *Adj.* kissproof

**küssen** /ˈkʏsn̩/ *tr., itr. V.* kiss; **jmdm. die Hand ~:** kiss sb.'s hand; **küss die Hand** (*südd., österr.*) (*beim Kommen*) how do you do?; good day; (*beim Gehen*) goodbye; **sich** *od.* (*geh.*) **einander ~:** kiss [each other]

**kuss·fest**, ***kuß·fest** *Adj.*: ⇒ **~echt**

**Kuss·hand**, ***Kuß·hand** *die:* **jmdm. eine ~ zuwerfen** blow sb. a kiss; **mit ~** (*ugs.*) gladly; with [the greatest] pleasure; **jmdn./etw. mit ~ nehmen** (*ugs.*) be only too glad *or* pleased to take sb./sth.

**Küste** /ˈkʏstə/ *die;* **~, ~n** coast

**Küsten-: ~bewohner** *der*, **~bewohnerin** *die* coastal inhabitant; **die deutschen ~bewohner** those living on the German coast; **~fischerei** *die* inshore fishing; **~gewässer** *das*, **~meer** *das* coastal waters *pl.*; ***~schiffahrt**, **~schifffahrt** *die* coastal shipping *no art.*; **~strich** *der* stretch of coast; coastal strip; **~wache** *die* coastguard [service]

**Küster** /ˈkʏstɐ/ *der;* **~s, ~**, **Küsterin** *die;* **~, ~nen** ▶ **159** sexton

**Kustos** /ˈkʊstɔs/ *der;* **~**, **Kustoden** ▶ **159** /kʊsˈto:dn̩/ curator

**Kutsch·bock** *der* coach box

**Kutsche** /ˈkʊt͜ʃə/ *die;* **~, ~n** **A** coach; carriage; **B** (*salopp: Auto*) jalopy (*coll.*)

**kutschen** ⇒ **kutschieren**

**Kutschen·schlag** *der* coach door; carriage door

**Kutscher** *der;* **~s, ~:** coachman; coach driver

**Kutscherin** *die;* **~, ~nen** coachwoman; coach driver

**kutschieren** **1** *itr. V.*; *mit sein* **A** drive, ride [in a coach *or* carriage]; **B** (*ugs.*) **durch die Gegend/durch Europa ~:** drive around/drive around Europe. **2** *tr. V.* **A** **jmdn. ~:** drive sb. [in a coach *or* carriage]; **B** (*ugs.*) **jmdn. nach Hause ~:** run sb. home; **C** (*ugs.: lenken*) drive ‹car, lorry›

**Kutsch·pferd** *das* coach horse; carriage horse

**Kutte** /ˈkʊtə/ *die;* **~, ~n** **A** [monk's/nun's] habit; **B** (*Jugendspr.*) (*Jacke*) jacket; (*Mantel*) coat

**Kutteln** /ˈkʊtl̩n/ *Pl.* (*südd., österr., schweiz.*) tripe *sing.*

**Kutter** /ˈkʊtɐ/ *der;* **~s, ~:** cutter

**Kuvert** /kuˈvɛ:ɐ̯/ *das;* **~s, ~s** **A** (*landsch., veralt.: Umschlag*) envelope; **B** (*geh.: Gedeck*) cover

**kuvertieren** /kuvɛrˈti:rən/ *tr. V.* **etw. ~:** put sth. into an envelope

**Kuvertüre** /kuvɛrˈty:rə/ *die;* **~, ~n** chocolate coating

**Kuwait** /kuˈvait/ (*das*)**; ~s** Kuwait

**Kuwaiter** *der;* **~s, ~, Kuwaiterin** *die;* **~, ~nen** Kuwaiti

**kuwaitisch** *Adj.* ▶ **553** Kuwaiti

**kV** *Abk.* (*Physik*) **Kilovolt** kV

**kW** *Abk.* (*Physik*) **Kilowatt** kW

**KW** *Abk.* **Kurzwelle** SW

**Kwass**, ***Kwaß** /kvas/ *der;* **~** *od.* **Kwasses** kvass

**kWh** *Abk.* (*Physik*) **Kilowattstunde** kWh

**Kybernetik** /kybɛrˈne:tɪk/ *die;* **~:** cybernetics *sing.*

**Kybernetiker** *der;* **~s, ~, Kybernetikerin** *die;* **~, ~nen** cybernetician; cyberneticist

**kybernetisch** *Adj.* cybernetic

**Kyrie** /ˈky:riə/ *das;* **~, ~s** kyrie; **~ eleison!** /eˈlaizɔn/ kyrie eleison

**kyrillisch** /kyˈrɪlɪʃ/ *Adj.* Cyrillic

**KZ** *Abk.* **Konzentrationslager**

**KZ-Häftling** *der*, **KZler** *der;* **~s, ~, KZlerin** *die;* **~, ~nen** concentration-camp prisoner

k

# L l

**l, L** /ɛl/ *das;* ~, ~: l/L; ⇒ *auch* **a, A**

**l** *Abk.* **Liter** l

**la** /la:/ la; **etw. auf la la singen** la-la sth.

**Lab** /la:p/ *das;* ~[e]s, ~e **A** (*Enzym*) rennin; **B** (*zur Käseherstellung*) rennet

**labberig** /ˈlabərɪç/ *Adj.* (*ugs. abwertend*) **A** (*fade*) wishy-washy; ~ **schmecken** taste of nothing; **B** (*weich*) floppy, limp ‹material›; floppy ‹trousers, dress, etc.›; slack ‹elastic›; **C** (*flau*) queasy

**labbern** /ˈlabɐn/ (*nordd. abwertend*) ❶ *tr. V.* slurp. ❷ *itr. V.* ‹sail› flap [about]

**labbrig** ⇒ **labberig**

**Labe** *die;* ~ (*dichter. veralt.*) refreshment *no indef. art.;* (~*trunk*) refreshing draught

**Label** /ˈle:bl̩/ *das;* ~s, ~s label

**laben** /ˈla:bn̩/ (*geh.*) ❶ *tr. V.* **jmdn.** ~: give sb. refreshment; **ein** ~**der Trunk** a refreshing drink; **das Auge** ~ (*fig.*) delight the eye. ❷ *refl. V.* refresh oneself (**an** + *Dat.*, **mit** with)

**labern** /ˈla:bɐn/ (*ugs. abwertend*) ❶ *tr. V.* talk; **was laberst du da?** what are you rabbiting (*Brit. coll.*) *or* babbling on about? ❷ *itr. V.* rabbit (*Brit. coll.*) *or* babble on

**labial** /laˈbi̯a:l/ (*Phon.*) ❶ *Adj.* labial. ❷ *adv.* labially

**Labial** *der;* ~s, ~e, **Labiallaut** *der* (*Sprachw.*) labial [sound]

**labil** /laˈbi:l/ *Adj.* **A** (*Med.*) delicate, frail ‹constitution, health›; poor ‹circulation›; **B** (*auch Psych.*) unstable ‹person, character, situation, equilibrium, etc.›

**Labilität** /labiliˈtɛ:t/ *die;* ~, ~en ⇒ **labil A, B**: delicateness; frailness; poorness; instability

**Labiodental** /labi̯o-/ *der* (*Sprachw.*) labiodental

**Lab-:** ~**kraut** *das* (*Bot.*) bedstraw; ~**magen** *der* (*Zool.*) abomasum; rennet stomach

**Labor** /laˈbo:ɐ̯/ *das;* ~s, ~s, *auch:* ~e laboratory

**Laborant** /laboˈrant/ *der;* ~en, ~en, **Laborantin** *die;* ~, ~nen ▶ **159** laboratory *or* (*coll.*) lab assistant *or* technician

**Laboratorium** /laboraˈto:ri̯ʊm/ *das;* ~s, **Laboratorien** laboratory

**laborieren** *itr. V.* (*ugs.*) **A** (*leiden*) suffer (**an** + *Dat.* from); **er laboriert schon seit Wochen an einer Grippe** he's been trying to shake off the flu for weeks (*coll.*); **B** (*sich abmühen*) **an etw.** (*Dat.*) ~: labour *or* toil away at sth.

**Labor-:** ~**platz** *der* place in a/the laboratory; ~**versuch** *der* laboratory experiment

**Labsal** /ˈlapza:l/ *das;* ~[e]s, ~e *od.* (*südd., österr.*) *die;* ~, ~e (*geh.*) refreshment; **ein** ~ **für jmdn. sein** refresh sb.

**Labskaus** /ˈlapskaus/ *das;* ~ (*Kochk.*) ≈ lobscouse; *stew made with beef, potatoes, onions, gherkins, and beetroot, eaten with a fried egg*

**Labung** *die;* ~, ~en (*geh.*) refreshment

**Labyrinth** /labyˈrɪnt/ *das;* ~[e]s, ~e **A** maze; labyrinth; **B** (*Anat.*) labyrinth

**labyrinthisch** ❶ *Adj.* labyrinthine. ❷ *adv.* ~ **verschlungene Wege** a maze of winding paths

**Lachanfall** *der* laughing fit; fit of laughing

**Lache¹** /ˈlaxə/ *die;* ~, ~n (*ugs.*) laugh

**Lache²** /ˈla(:)xə/ *die;* ~, ~n puddle; (*von Blut, Öl*) pool

**lächeln** /ˈlɛçl̩n/ *itr. V.* smile (**über** + *Akk.* at); **freundlich/verlegen** ~: give a friendly/an embarrassed smile

**Lächeln** *das;* ~s smile

**lachen** ❶ *itr. V.* **A** laugh; **da kann man** *od.* **ich doch nur** ~: that's a laugh; **jmdn. zum Lachen bringen** make sb. laugh; **die Clowns waren zum Lachen** the clowns were very amusing; **platzen/sterben vor Lachen** (*fig.*) split one's sides laughing/die laughing; **die Sonne** *od.* **der Himmel lacht** (*fig.*) the sun is shining brightly; **ihm lacht das Glück** (*dichter.*) Fortune smiled upon *or* favoured him; **wer zuletzt lacht, lacht am besten** (*Spr.*) he who laughs last, laughs longest; **zum Lachen sein** (*ugs. abwertend*) be laughable *or* ridiculous; **dass ich nicht lache!** (*ugs.*) don't make me laugh (*coll.*); **B** (*sich lustig machen*) laugh, make *or* poke fun (**über** + *Akk.* at); ⇒ *auch* **dritt...; Erbe²**.
❷ *tr. V.* **was gibt es denn zu** ~? what's so funny?; **es** *od.* **das wäre ja** *od.* **doch gelacht, wenn ...** (*ugs.*) it would be ridiculous if ...; **wenn dein Vater das erfährt, hast du nichts zu** ~: you won't think it funny if your father finds out about it; **da gibt es gar nichts zu** ~: it's no laughing matter; **nichts zu** ~ **haben** (*ugs.*) have a hard time of it (**bei** with); ⇒ *auch* **scheckig**

**Lachen** *das;* ~s laughter; **ein lautes** ~: a loud laugh; **sie konnte sich das** ~ **kaum verbeißen** she could hardly stop herself laughing; **ihm wird das** ~ **noch vergehen** he'll be laughing on the other side of his face

**Lacher** *der;* ~s, ~ **A** laugher; **die** ~: those who are/were laughing; **die** ~ **auf seiner Seite haben** score by making everybody laugh; **B** (*kurzes Lachen*) laugh

**Lacherfolg** *der:* **einen** ~ **haben, ein** ~ **sein** make everybody laugh; **einen großen** ~ **haben, ein großer** ~ **sein** bring the house down

**Lacherin** *die;* ~, ~nen ⇒ **Lacher A**

**lächerlich** /ˈlɛçɐlɪç/ (*abwertend*) ❶ *Adj.* **A** (*komisch*) ridiculous; **jmdn./sich [vor jmdm.]** ~ **machen** make a fool of sb./oneself *or* make sb./oneself look silly [in front of sb.]; **sich** (*Dat.*) ~ **vorkommen** feel ridiculous; **etw. ins Lächerliche ziehen** make a joke out of sth.; **B** (*töricht*) ridiculous; ludicrous ‹argument, statement›; **C** (*gering*) derisory, ridiculously *or* ludicrously small ‹sum, amount›; ridiculously low ‹price, payment›; **D** (*geringfügig*) ridiculously trivial *or* trifling; ~**e Kleinigkeiten** ridiculous trivialities. ❷ *adv.* ridiculously; ~ **wenig** ridiculously *or* ludicrously little

**lächerlicherweise** *Adv.* (*abwertend*) ridiculously enough

**Lächerlichkeit** *die;* ~, ~en (*abwertend*) **A** ridiculousness; (*von Argumenten, Behauptungen usw.*) ridiculousness; ludicrousness; **jmdn. der** ~ **preisgeben** make a laughing stock of sb.; make sb. look ridiculous; **B** ridiculous triviality

**Lach-:** ~**fältchen** *das* laughter line; ~**gas** *das* laughing gas

**lachhaft** (*abwertend*) ❶ *Adj.* ridiculous; laughable. ❷ *adv.* ridiculously

**Lach-:** ~**krampf** *der* paroxysm of laughter; violent fit of laughter; **einen** ~**krampf bekommen** go [off] into fits of laughter; **einen** ~**krampf haben** be in fits of laughter; be convulsed with laughter ~**möwe** *die* laughing gull; peewit gull; ~**nummer** *die* (*ugs.*) **eine** ~**nummer sein** be just a joke

**Lachs** *der;* ~es, ~e salmon

**Lachsalve** *die* roar *or* peal of laughter

**lachs-, Lachs-:** ~**ersatz** *der* rock salmon; ~**farben** *Adj.* salmon pink; salmon-coloured; ~**schinken** *der* lachsschinken (*rolled, smoked, and cured loin of pork*)

**Lack** /lak/ *der;* ~[e]s, ~e **A** varnish; (*für Metall,* ~*arbeiten*) lacquer; (*Auto*~) paint; (*transparent*) lacquer; (*Nagel*~) varnish; **der** ~ **ist ab** (*salopp: etw. hat seinen Reiz verloren*) the novelty has worn off; (*salopp: jmd. ist nicht mehr ganz jung*) he/she's no spring chicken any more; ⇒ *auch* **fertig**

**Lack-:** ~**affe** *der* (*ugs. abwertend*) dandy; ~**arbeit** *die* piece of lacquerwork

**Lackel** /ˈlakl̩/ *der;* ~s, ~ (*bes. südd., österr. abwertend*) oaf; **so ein** ~! stupid oaf!

**lacken** *tr. V.:* ⇒ **lackieren A**

**Lackfarbe** *die* lacquer paint; (*für Autos*) paint; (*Emaillelack*) enamel paint

**lackieren** *tr. V.* **A** varnish ‹wood›; varnish, paint ‹fingernails›; spray ‹car›; (*mit Emaillelack*) paint ‹metal›; **einen Wagen neu** ~: respray a car; **B** (*ugs.: täuschen*) **jmdn.** ~: take sb. for a ride (*coll.*); dupe sb.; **der Lackierte sein** have to carry the can (*Brit. coll.*)

**Lackierer** *der;* ~s, ~ (*Möbel*~) varnisher; (*Metall*~) painter; (*Auto*~) [paint] sprayer

**Lackiererei** *die;* ~, ~en varnisher's; (*für Autos*) paint shop

**Lackiererin** *die;* ~, ~nen ⇒ **Lackierer**

**Lackierung** *die;* ~, ~en **A** (*von Holz*) varnishing; (*von Autos*) [paint-]spraying; **B** (*Lackschicht*) (*auf Holz*) varnish; (*auf Metall, Autos*) paintwork; (*auf Lackarbeiten*) lacquer; **die zweite** ~: the second coat [of varnish/paint/lacquer]

**Lackleder** *das* patent leather

**lackmeiern** ⇒ **gelackmeiert**

**Lackmus** /ˈlakmʊs/ *das od. der;* ~ (*Chemie*) litmus

**Lackmuspapier** *das* (*Chemie*) litmus paper

**Lack-:** ~**reiniger** *der,* ~~s, ~~: original-colour restorer; ~**schaden** *der* damage to the paintwork; ~**schuh** *der* patent-leather shoe

**Lade** /ˈla:də/ *die;* ~, ~n (*landsch.*) **A** (*Schub*~) drawer; **B** (*veralt.: Truhe*) chest

**Lade-:** ~**baum** *der* derrick boom; cargo boom; ~**bühne** *die* ⇒ ~**rampe**; ~**fläche** *die* payload area; ~**gerät** *das* (*Elektrot.*) charger; ~**gewicht** *das* carrying capacity; maximum [permitted] load; ~**hemmung** *die* jam; stoppage; **[eine]** ~**hemmung haben** (*fig. scherzh.*) have a mental block; ~**klappe** *die* (*an einem LKW*) tailboard; tailgate; (*an einem Flugzeug*) taildoor; ~**kran** *der* loading crane; ~**luke** *die* cargo hatch; loading hatch; ~**mast** *der* derrick mast

**laden¹** ❶ *unr. tr. V.* **A** (*ver*~, *be*~) load; **B** (*aufnehmen*) **die Schiffe** ~ **Getreide** the ships are taking on *or* are being loaded with grain; **der LKW hat Sand ge**~: the truck is loaded up with sand; **der Tanker hat Flüssiggas ge**~: the tanker has a cargo of *or* is carrying liquid gas; **C** (*legen*) load; **sich** (*Dat.*) **einen Sack auf die Schultern** ~: load a sack on one's shoulders; **schwere Schuld auf sich** ~ (*fig.*) incur a heavy burden of guilt; **eine ziemliche Verantwortung auf sich** ~: shoulder quite a bit of responsibility; **D** (*Munition einlegen*) load ‹gun, pistol, etc.›; **E** (*Physik*) charge; **er ist ge**~ (*ugs.*) he's livid (*coll.*); he's hopping mad (*coll.*); **F** (*aus*~) unload (**aus** from).
❷ *unr. itr. V.* load [up]; **der LKW hat schwer ge**~: the truck is heavily loaded;

l

**schwer** *od.* **ganz schön ge~ haben** (*ugs. scherzh.*) be well tanked up (*sl.*); have had a skinful

**laden²** *unr. tr. V.* Ⓐ (*Rechtsspr.*) summon; Ⓑ (*geh.: ein~*) invite

**Laden** *der;* **~s, Läden** /ˈlɛ:dn̩/, **~** Ⓐ *Pl.* **Läden** shop; store (*Amer.*); Ⓑ *Pl.* **Läden** (*ugs.: Unternehmung*) **der ~ läuft** business is good; **wie ich den ~ kenne** (*fig.*) if I know how things go in this outfit (*coll.*); **den ~ dichtmachen** shut up shop; **den ~ schmeißen** manage *or* handle everything with no problem; **den ~ hinwerfen** *od.* **hinschmeißen** chuck the whole thing in (*coll.*); Ⓒ *Pl.* **Läden,** *auch* **~** (*Fenster~*) shutter

**Laden-: ~besitzer** *der,* **~besitzerin** *die* shopkeeper; storekeeper (*Amer.*); **~dieb** *der,* **~diebin** *die* shoplifter; **~diebstahl** *der* shoplifting; **[die] ~diebstähle** shoplifting offences; **~front** *die* shopfront; **~glocke** *die* shop bell; **~hüter** *der* (*abwertend*) (*sich schlecht verkaufend*) slow seller; slow-moving article/line; (*sich nicht verkaufend*) non-seller; article/line which isn't/wasn't selling; **~inhaber** *der,* **~inhaberin** *die* ⇒ **~besitzer; ~kasse** *die* till; **~preis** *der* shop price; **~schild** *das* shop sign

**Laden·schluss, *Laden·schluß** *der* shop *or* (*Amer.*) store closing time; **kurz vor/nach ~:** shortly before/after the shops *or* (*Amer.*) stores close/closed; **samstags ist um 14 Uhr ~:** the shops *or* (*Amer.*) stores close at two o'clock on Saturdays

**Ladenschluss-, *Ladenschluß-: ~gesetz** *das* law regulating shop *or* (*Amer.*) store closing times; **~zeit** *die* shop *or* (*Amer.*) store closing time

**Laden-: ~schwengel** *der* (*ugs. abwertend*) shop boy; **~straße** *die* shopping street; **~tisch** *der* [shop] counter; **unterm ~tisch** (*ugs.*) under the counter; **~tochter** *die* (*schweiz.*) salesgirl; shop *or* sales assistant

**Lade-: ~platz** *der* loading area; **~rampe** *die* loading ramp; **~raum** *der* Ⓐ (*beim Auto*) luggage space; Ⓑ (*beim Flugzeug, Schiff*) hold; Ⓒ (*bei LKWs*) payload space; **~stock** *der; Pl.* **~stöcke** (*hist.*) ramrod

**lädieren** /lɛˈdi:rən/ *tr. V.* damage; (*fig.*) damage, harm ‹reputation etc.›; undermine ‹confidence›; **lädiert aussehen** (*ugs. scherzh.*) look battered

**lädst** /lɛ:tst/ *2. Pers. Sg. Präsens v.* **laden**

**lädt** /lɛ:t/ *3. Pers. Sg. Präsens v.* **laden**

**Ladung** *die;* **~, ~en** Ⓐ (*Schiffs~, Flugzeug~*) cargo; (*LKW~*) load; **eine ~ Kohle** a cargo/load of coal; Ⓑ (*beim Sprengen, Schießen*) charge; **eine ~ Dynamit/Schrot** a charge of dynamite/shot; Ⓒ (*ugs.: Menge*) load (*coll.*); **eine ganze ~ Sand** a whole load of sand; Ⓓ (*Physik*) charge; Ⓔ (*Rechtsspr.: Vor~*) summons *sing.*

**Lady** /ˈleɪdɪ/ *die;* **~, ~s** Ⓐ (*Adlige*) Lady; Ⓑ (*Dame*) lady

**Lafette** /laˈfɛtə/ *die;* **~, ~n** gun carriage

**Laffe** /ˈlafə/ *der;* **~n, ~n** (*veralt. abwertend*) fop; dandy

**lag** /la:k/ *1. u. 3. Pers. Sg. Prät. v.* **liegen**

**Lage** /ˈla:gə/ *die;* **~, ~n** Ⓐ situation; location; **in ruhiger ~:** in a quiet location; **eine gute ~ haben** be peacefully/well situated; be in a good/peaceful location; **in höheren/tieferen ~n** (*Met.*) on high/low ground; Ⓑ (*Art des Liegens*) position; **jetzt habe ich eine bequeme ~:** now I'm lying comfortably; now I'm [lying] in a comfortable position; Ⓒ (*Situation*) situation; **jmdn./sich in eine dumme ~ bringen** get sb./get [oneself] into a stupid situation; **er war nicht in der ~, das zu tun** he was not in a position to do that; **versetzen Sie sich in meine ~:** put yourself in my position *or* place; **jmdn. in die ~ versetzen, etw. zu tun** put somebody in a position to do sth.; **nach ~ der Dinge** as matters stand/stood; **die ~ der Dinge erfordert es, dass ...** the situation requires that ...; **die ~ peilen** *od.* **spannen** (*ugs.*) see how the land lies; find out the lie of the land; ⇒ *auch* **Herr**; Ⓓ (*Schwimmen*) **die 400 m ~n** the 400 m. individual medley; **die 4 × 100 m ~n** the 4 × 100 m. medley relay; Ⓔ (*Schicht*) layer; Ⓕ (*Stimm~*) register; Ⓖ (*Musik: Stellung der Hand*) position; Ⓗ (*ugs.: Runde*) round; **eine ~ ausgeben** (*ugs.*) *od.* **schmeißen** (*salopp*) get *or* stand a round

**Lage-: ~bericht** *der* report; (*Milit.*) situation report; **~besprechung** *die* discussion of the situation; **eine ~besprechung abhalten** discuss the situation

**Lagen-: ~schwimmen** *das* (*Schwimmen*) individual medley; **~staffel** *die* (*Schwimmen*) Ⓐ (*Wettbewerb*) medley relay; Ⓑ (*Mannschaft*) medley relay team

**Lage·plan** *der* map of the area

**Lager** /ˈla:gɐ/ *das;* **~s, ~** Ⓐ camp; **ein ~ aufschlagen** set up *or* pitch camp; Ⓑ (*Gruppe, politischer Block*) camp; **ins andere ~ überwechseln** change camps *or* sides; join the other side; Ⓒ (*Raum*) storeroom; (*in Geschäften, Betrieben*) stockroom; **etw. auf** *od.* **am ~ haben** have sth. in stock; **am ~ sein** be in stock; **etw. auf ~ haben** (*fig. ugs.*) be ready with sth.; Ⓓ (*Warenbestand*) stock; **wir müssen das ~ auffüllen** we must replenish our stocks; Ⓔ (*geh.*) bed; **jmdn. aufs ~ werfen** force sb. to take to his/her bed; put sb. in bed; **an jmds. ~ treten** step up to sb.'s bedside; Ⓕ (*Geol.*) bed; Ⓖ (*Technik*) bearing

**lager-, Lager-: ~bestand** *der* (*Wirtsch.*) stock; **den ~bestand aufnehmen** do a stocktaking; **die ~bestände räumen** clear stocks; **~bier** *das* lager [beer]; **~fähig** *Adj.* suitable for storage *or* storing *postpos.;* **~feuer** *das* campfire; **~feuer·romantik** *die* romance of the great outdoors; **~gebühr** *die* (*Wirtsch.*) storage charge; **~halle** *die* warehouse; **~haltung** *die* Ⓐ storage; Ⓑ (*Wirtsch.*) holding stocks *no art.;* **~haus** *das* warehouse

**Lagerist** *der;* **~en, ~en** ▶ 159 storeman; storekeeper

**Lageristin** *die* ▶ 159 storekeeper

**Lager-: ~koller** *der:* **einen ~koller bekommen** *od.* **kriegen** be driven to a frenzy by life in the camp; **~leben** *das* camp life *no art.;* (*im Straflagerleben, KZ usw.*) life in the camp; **~leiter** *der,* **~leiterin** *die* (*im Jugend~, Ferien~*) camp leader; (*im Straf~, KZ usw.*) camp director

**lagern** ❶ *tr. V.* Ⓐ store; **etw. kühl/trocken ~:** keep *or* store sth. in a cool/dry place; Ⓑ (*hinlegen*) lay down; **jmdn. flach/bequem ~:** lay sb. flat/in a comfortable position; **die Beine hoch ~:** rest one's legs in a raised position; Ⓒ (*Technik*) support; mount ‹machine part, workpiece›; **drehbar gelagert sein** be mounted on a pivot.

❷ *itr. V.* Ⓐ camp; be encamped; **auf Luftmatratzen ~:** use air mattresses; Ⓑ (*liegen*) lie; ‹foodstuffs, medicines, etc.› be stored *or* kept; (*sich ab~*) have settled; (*fig.*) ‹mist, fog, stillness, heat, etc.› lie, hang; **ein guter Wein muss mehrere Jahre ~:** a good wine must be kept for several years; Ⓒ (*Geol.*) **hier ~ Eisenerze/Ölvorräte** there are deposits of iron ore/oil here; Ⓓ (*Technik*) be supported; ‹machine part, workpiece› be mounted; Ⓔ (*beschaffen sein, sich verhalten*) **ganz ähnlich/anders gelagert sein** be quite similar/different [in nature].

❸ *refl. V.* settle oneself/itself down; (*fig.*) ‹mist, fog› lie, hang

**Lager-: ~obst** *das* fruit for storing; **gutes ~obst sein** be good [fruit] for storing; [be fruit that] keep well; **~platz** *der* campsite; **~raum** Ⓐ storeroom; (*im Geschäft, Betrieb*) stockroom; Ⓑ (*Fläche*) storage space; (*in ~hallen*) warehouse space; **~schein** *der* (*Wirtsch.*) warehouse receipt; **~statt** *die* (*geh.*) bed; couch (*literary*); **~stätte** *die* Ⓐ (*Geol.*) deposit; Ⓑ ⇒ **~statt**

**Lagerung** *die;* **~, ~en** Ⓐ storage; **bei ~ im Tiefkühlfach** if *or* when stored in a deep-freeze; Ⓑ (*von Kranken*) **bei richtiger/falscher ~ des Verletzten** if the injured person is placed in the correct/wrong position

**Lager·verwalter** *der,* **Lager·verwalterin** *die* storekeeper; stores supervisor

**Lagune** /laˈgu:nə/ *die;* **~, ~n** lagoon

**Lagunen·stadt** *die:* **die ~ Venedig** Venice with its lagoons and islands

**lahm** /la:m/ ❶ *Adj.* Ⓐ (*gelähmt*) lame; crippled, useless ‹wing›; **ein ~es Bein haben** be lame in one leg; **auf dem linken Bein ~ sein** be lame in the *or* one's left leg; Ⓑ (*ugs.: unbeweglich*) stiff; **ihm wurde der Arm ~:** his arm became *or* got stiff; Ⓒ (*ugs. abwertend: unzureichend*) lame, feeble ‹excuse, explanation, etc.›; Ⓓ (*ugs. abwertend: matt*) dreary; dull; feeble ‹protest›; dull, dreary, lifeless ‹discussion›; **ein ~er Typ** a dull, lethargic [sort of] bloke (*Brit. coll.*) *or* (*coll.*) guy; Ⓔ **~ legen** + *Akk.* bring ‹traffic, production, industry› to a standstill; paralyse ‹industry› ⇒ *auch* **Ente** A.

❷ *adv.* Ⓐ (*kraftlos*) feebly; Ⓑ (*ugs. abwertend*) lethargically

**lahm-, Lahm-: ~arsch** *der* (*derb*) boring, lethargic old sod (*Brit. coarse*) *or* (*coll.*) bastard; **~arschig** (*derb*) ❶ *Adj.* bloody (*Brit. sl.*) *or* damned lethargic; ❷ *adv.* bloody (*Brit. sl.*) *or* damned lethargically; **~arschigkeit** *die;* **~~:** bloody (*Brit. sl.*) *or* damned lethargy

**Lahme** *der/die; adj. Dekl.* cripple

**lahmen** *itr. V.* be lame; **auf der rechten Hinterhand ~:** be lame in the right hind leg

**lähmen** /ˈlɛ:mən/ *tr. V.* Ⓐ paralyse; **an beiden Beinen gelähmt sein** be paralysed in both legs; **er ist durch einen Unfall gelähmt** he was paralysed in an accident; **einseitig gelähmt sein** be paralysed down one side of one's body; **vor Angst wie gelähmt sein** be paralysed with fear; Ⓑ (*fig.*) cripple, paralyse ‹economy, industry›; bring ‹traffic› to a standstill; deaden ‹enthusiasm›; numb ‹will›; **die Angst lähmte seine Schritte** (*geh.*) he was rooted to the spot with fear; **von ~der Müdigkeit/~dem Entsetzen befallen werden** be completely numbed with fatigue/paralysed with horror

***lahm|legen** ⇒ **lahm** 1 E

**Lahmlegung** *die;* **~: eine ~ des Verkehrs/der Wirtschaft zur Folge haben** bring traffic to a standstill/paralyse the economy

**Lähmung** *die;* **~, ~en** Ⓐ ▶ 474 paralysis; **eine halbseitige ~:** paralysis down one side of the body; Ⓑ (*fig.*) (*der Wirtschaft, Industrie*) paralysis; (*der Begeisterung*) deadening; (*des Willens*) numbing; **zu einer ~ des Verkehrs führen** bring traffic to a standstill

**Lähmungs·erscheinung** *die* symptom *or* sign of paralysis

**Lahn** /la:n/ *die;* **~, ~en** (*bayr., österr.*) ⇒ **Lawine**

**Laib** /laip/ *der;* **~[e]s, ~e** loaf; **ein [halber] ~ Brot** [half] a loaf of bread; **ein ~ Käse** a whole cheese

**Laibung** *die;* **~, ~en** (*Archit., Bauw.*) reveal; (*eines Bogens*) intrados; soffit

**Laich** /laiç/ *der;* **~[e]s, ~e** spawn

**laichen** *itr. V.* spawn

**Laich-: ~platz** *der* spawning ground; **~zeit** *die* spawning time

**Laie** /ˈlaiə/ *der;* **~n, ~n** Ⓐ (*Mann*) layman; (*Frau*) laywoman; **da staunt der ~ [und der Fachmann wundert sich]** it's incredible; Ⓑ (*Kirche*) (*Mann*) layman; (*Frau*) laywoman; **die ~n** the laity *pl.*

**Laien-: ~bruder** *der* (*kath. Kirche*) lay brother; **~bühne** *die* amateur theatre group

**laienhaft** ❶ *Adj.* amateurish; unprofessional; inexpert. ❷ *adv.* amateurishly; unprofessionally; inexpertly

**Laien-: ~investitur** *die* (*MA.*) lay investiture; **~prediger** *der,* **~predigerin** *die* (*Rel.*) lay preacher; **~richter** *der,* **~richterin** *die* lay judge; **~schauspieler** *der,* **~schauspielerin** *die* amateur actor; **~schwester** *die* (*kath. Kirche*) lay sister; **~spiel** *das* amateur performance; **~stand** *der* (*Rel.*) laity *pl.;* **~theater** *das* Ⓐ amateur theatre group; Ⓑ ⇒ **~spiel**

*old spelling (see note on page 1707)

l

**laisieren** /lai'zi:rən/ *tr. V.* (*kath. Kirche*) unfrock; defrock

**Laisierung** *die;* ~, ~**en** unfrocking; defrocking

**Laisser-faire** /lɛse'fɛ:r/ *das;* ~**:** laisser-faire *no art.*

**Laizismus** /lai'tsɪsmʊs/ *der;* ~ (*Politik, Geschichte*) laicism *no art.*

**Lakai** /la'kai/ *der;* ~**en**, ~**en** A lackey; liveried footman; B (*abwertend*) lackey

**lakaienhaft** (*abwertend*) ❶ *Adj.* servile. ❷ *adv.* servilely

**Lake** /'la:kə/ *die;* ~, ~**n** brine

**Laken** /'la:kn̩/ *das;* ~**s**, ~ (*bes. nordd.*) sheet

**lakonisch** /la'ko:nɪʃ/ ❶ *Adj.* laconic. ❷ *adv.* laconically

**Lakritz** /la'krɪts/ *der od. das;* ~**es**, ~**e**, **Lakritze** *die;* ~, ~**n** liquorice

**Laktation** /lakta'tsio:n/ *die;* ~, ~**en** (*Biol.*) lactation

**Laktose** /lak'to:zə/ *die;* ~ (*Biochemie*) lactose

**lala** /la'la/ *in* **so** ~ (*ugs.*) so-so; **es geht ihm so** ~**:** he's so-so *or* not too bad

**lallen** /'lalən/ *tr., itr. V.* ‹baby› babble; ‹drunk/drowsy person› mumble

**Lama**[1] /'la:ma/ *das;* ~**s**, ~**s** (*Zool.*) llama

**Lama**[2] *der;* ~**[s]**, ~**s** (*Rel.*) lama

**Lamaismus** *der;* ~**:** lamaism

**Lama·kloster** *das* lamasery

**Lamäng** /la'mɛŋ/ *die: in* **aus der** ~ (*ugs.*) just like that; off the top of one's head (*sl.*); (*ohne Besteck*) with one's fingers

**Lama·wolle** *die* llama [wool]

**Lambda·sonde** /'lambda-/ *die* (*Technik*) lambda probe

**Lambris** /lã'bri:/ *der;* ~, ~**:** wainscoting

**Lamé, Lamee** /la'me:/ *der;* ~**s**, ~**s** lamé

**Lamelle** /la'mɛlə/ *die;* ~, ~**n** A (*einer Jalousie*) slat; B (*eines Heizkörpers*) rib; C (*eines Pilzes*) lamella (*Bot.*); gill

**Lamellen·kupplung** *die* (*Technik*) multiplate clutch; multiple-disc clutch

**lamentieren** /lamɛn'ti:rən/ *itr. V.* (*ugs.*) moan, complain (**über** + *Akk.* about)

**Lamento** /la'mɛnto/ *das;* ~**s**, ~**s** (*ugs. abwertend*) loud regrets *pl.*; **ein [lautes** *od.* **großes]** ~ **[über etw.** (*Akk.*) *od.* **um etw.** *od.* **wegen etw.] anstimmen** kick up *or* make a [great] fuss [about sth.]

**Lametta** /la'mɛta/ *das;* ~**s** A lametta; B (*ugs. iron.: Orden*) gongs *pl.* (*coll.*)

**laminieren** /lami'ni:rən/ *tr. V.* A (*Buchw.*) laminate ‹material, book cover›; B (*Textilw.*) draw ‹fibres›

**Lamm** /lam/ *das;* ~**[e]s**, **Lämmer** /'lɛmɐ/ A lamb; **das** ~ **Gottes** the Lamb of God; B (~*fell*) lambskin

**Lamm·braten** *der* roast lamb *no indef. art.*; (*Gericht*) roast of lamb

**Lämmchen** /'lɛmçən/ *das;* ~**s**, ~**:** little lamb

**lammen** *itr. V.* lamb

**Lämmer-:** ~**geier** *der* bearded vulture; ~**wolke** *die* [light] fleecy cloud; cotton-wool cloud

**lamm-, Lamm-:** ~**fell** *das* lambskin; ~**fleisch** *das* lamb; ~**fromm** ❶ *Adj.* ‹horse› as gentle as a [little] lamb; ‹person› as meek as a [little] lamb; ❷ *adv.* ~**fromm antworten** answer like a lamb; ~**kotelett** *das* lamb chop

**Lämpchen** /'lɛmpçən/ *das;* ~**s**, ~**:** small *or* little light; **ein rotes** ~**:** a little red light

**Lampe** /'lampə/ *die;* ~, ~**n** A light; (*Tisch*~, *Öl*~, *Signal*~) lamp; (*Straßen*~) lamp; light; **[sich** (*Dat.*)**] einen auf die** ~ **gießen** (*fig. ugs.*) wet one's whistle (*coll.*); B (*bes. fachspr.: Glüh*~) bulb; ⇒ *auch* **Meister**

**Lampen-:** ~**fieber** *das* stage fright; ~**licht** *das* lamplight; **bei** ~**licht** by lamplight; by the light of a lamp/lamps; ~**schirm** *der* [lamp]shade

**Lampion** /lam'piɔŋ/ *der;* ~**s**, ~**s** Chinese lantern

**Lampion·blume** *die* Chinese-lantern plant; winter cherry

**lancieren** /lã'si:rən/ *tr. V.* A [deliberately] spread ‹report, rumour, etc.›; **eine Nachricht in die Presse** ~**:** get a report into the papers; B **jmdn. in eine Stellung** ~**:** get sb. into a position by pulling strings; C (*bes. Wirtsch., Werbung*) launch

**Land** /lant/ *das;* ~**es**, **Länder** /'lɛndɐ/ A (*Festland*) land *no indef. art.*; **an** ~**:** ashore; ~ **in Sicht!** (*Seemannsspr.*) land [ahead]!; „~ **unter!" melden** report that the land is flooded *or* under water; **auf dem** ~ **leben** live on [dry] land; **festes** ~ **unter den Füßen haben** be on dry land *or* terra firma; **[wieder]** ~ **sehen** (*fig.*) be able to see light at the end of the tunnel (*fig.*); **kein** ~ **mehr sehen** (*fig.*) be getting deeper and deeper into the mire (*fig.*); **[sich** (*Dat.*)**] eine Millionärin/antike Truhe/einen fetten Auftrag an** ~ **ziehen** (*ugs., oft scherzh.*) hook a millionairess/get one's hands on an antique chest/land a fat contract; B (*Ackerboden, Gelände*) land; **ein Stück/5 Hektar** ~**:** a plot *or* piece of land *or* ground/five hectares of land; **das** ~ **bebauen/bestellen** farm/till the land; C *Pl. auch* ~**e** (*Gegend*) country; land; **dies ist das** ~ **van Goghs** this is van Gogh country; **in deutschen** ~**en** (*veralt.*) in Germany; **durch die** ~**e ziehen** travel around *or* about; **Wochen/Jahre waren ins** ~ **gegangen** *od.* **gezogen** weeks/years had passed *or* gone by; D (*dörfliche Gegend*) country *no indef. art.*; **auf dem** ~ **wohnen** live in the country; **aufs** ~ **ziehen** move into the country; **über** ~ **fahren** (*veralt.*) travel from village to village; E (*Staat*) country; **andere Länder, andere Sitten** (*Spr.*) every nation has its own ways of behaving; ~ **und Leute kennen lernen** get to know the country and its people *or* inhabitants; **außer** ~**es gehen/sich außer** ~**es befinden** leave the country/be out of the country; **das** ~ **der unbegrenzten Möglichkeiten** the land of opportunity; **das** ~ **der aufgehenden Sonne** the land of the rising sun; **das** ~ **der tausend Seen** the land of a thousand lakes; **wieder im** ~**e sein** (*ugs.*) be back again; **das** ~ **meiner/seiner Väter** (*geh.*) the land of my/his fathers (*literary*); **hier/dort zu** ~**e** ⇒ **hierzulande/dortzulande**; **bei jmdm. zu** ~**e** where sb. comes from; in sb.'s country; F (*Bundesland*) Land; state; (*österr.*) province; **das** ~ **Bayern/Kärnten** the Land *or* state of Bavaria/the province of Carinthia

**-land** *das;* ~**es** (*geh.*) **[das] Bayern**~**:** Bavaria's fair land; **das große Sowjet**~**:** the mighty Soviet nation; **das schöne Schweizer**~**:** the lovely country of Switzerland

**land-, Land-:** ~**ab** /-'-/ ⇒ ~**auf**; ~**adel** *der* (*hist.*) landed aristocracy; ~**arbeit** *die* agricultural work; farm work; ~**arbeiter** *der*, ~**arbeiterin** *die* ▶ 159 agricultural worker; farm worker; ~**arzt** *der*, ~**ärztin** *die* country doctor

**Landauer** /'landauɐ/ *der;* ~**s**, ~ (*hist.*) landau

**land-, Land-:** ~**auf** /-'-/ *Adv. in* ~**auf**, ~**ab** (*geh.*) throughout the land; far and wide; ~**aus** /-'-/ *Adv. in* ~**aus**, ~**ein** throughout the [length and breadth of the] country; ~**bau** *der* ⇒ **Ackerbau**; ~**besitz** *der* ⇒ **Grundbesitz**; ~**bevölkerung** *die* rural population; ~**brot** *das* farm-baked bread; (*Laib*) *round loaf of farm-baked type;* ~**brücke** *die* (*Geogr.*) land bridge; ~**butter** *die* farm butter

**Lande-:** ~**an·flug** *der* (*Flugw.*) [landing] approach; ~**bahn** *die* (*Flugw.*) [landing] runway; ~**erlaubnis** *die* (*Flugw.*) permission to land *no art.*

**land-, Land-:** ~**ei** *das* farm egg; ~**ein** /-'-/ ⇒ ~**aus**; ~**einwärts** /-'--/ *Adv.* inland

**Lande·klappe** *die* (*Flugw.*) landing flap

**landen** ❶ *itr. V.*; *mit sein* A land; (*Schiff im Hafen*) arrive; **weich** ~**:** make a soft landing; **bei jmdm. nicht** ~ **[können]** (*fig. ugs.*) not get anywhere *or* very far with sb.; B (*ugs.: ankommen*) **zu Hause/in Paris** ~**:** get home/to Paris; C (*ugs.: gelangen*) land *or* end up; **im Krankenhaus/Zuchthaus/Papierkorb** ~**:** land up in hospital/end up in prison/the waste-paper basket. ❷ *tr. V.* A land ‹aircraft, troops, passengers, fish, etc.›; B (*ugs.: zustande bringen*) pull off ‹victory, coup›; have ‹smash hit›; C (*Boxen*) land ‹punch›

**länden** /'lɛndn̩/ *tr. V.* recover ‹corpse, wreck, etc.›

**Land·enge** *die* (*Geogr.*) isthmus

**Lande-:** ~**piste** *die* landing strip; ~**platz** *der* A (*Flugw.*) landing strip; airstrip; (*für Hubschrauber*) landing pad; (*nicht ausgebaut*) place to land; B ⇒ **Landungsplatz**

**Ländereien** /lɛndə'raiən/ *Pl.* estates

**Länder-:** ~**kammer** *die* second *or* upper chamber (*composed of representatives of the member states of a federation*); ~**kampf** *der* (*Sport*) international match; ~**kunde** *die* regional geography *no art.*; ~**spiel** *das* (*Sport*) international [match]

**landes-, Landes-:** ~**bank** *die; Pl.* ~**banken** regional bank; ~**behörde** *die* regional authority; ~**brauch** *der* custom of the country; national custom; ~**ebene** *die:* **auf [hessischer]** ~**ebene** at regional level [in Hessen]; at the level of the Land [of Hessen]; ~**farben** *Pl.* national colours; (*eines Bundeslandes*) colours of a Land/province; ~**fürst** *der* (*hist.*) ⇒ ~**herr**; ~**fürstin** *die* ⇒ ~**herrin**; ~**gericht** *das* (*österr.*) district court (*at a provincial capital*); ~**grenze** *die* national border *or* frontier; **die** ~**grenzen** the borders of the country; ~**haupt·frau** *die*, ~**hauptmann** *der; Pl.* ~**hauptleute** *od.* ~**hauptmänner** (*österr.*) prime minister of a province; ~**hauptstadt** *die* capital; ~**herr** *der* (*hist.*) sovereign prince; ~**herrin** *die* (*hist.*) sovereign princess; ~**innere** *das* interior [of the country]; ~**kind** *das* (*veralt., noch scherzh.*) citizen [of the country]; ~**kirche** *die* Land church; ~**kunde** *die* regional studies *pl., no art.; study of the geography, history, and civilization of a country/region;* ~**kundig** *Adj.* knowledgeable about country *postpos.*; ~**kundlich** *Adj.* ~**kundliche Forschungen** research into the geography, history, and civilization of a/the country/region; ~**liste** *die* (*Politik*) regional list; ~**mutter** *die*; *Pl.* ~**mütter** (*geh. veralt.*) sovereign lady; ~**recht** *das* (*Rechtsw.*) law of a/the Land/province; ~**regierung** *die* government of a/the Land/province; ~**rekord** *der* (*Sport*) national record; ~**sprache** *die* language of the country; **die drei belgischen** ~**sprachen** the three national languages of Belgium

**Lande·steg** *der* landing stage; jetty

**landes-, Landes-:** ~**tracht** *die* national costume *or* dress; ~**üblich** *Adj.* usual *or* customary in a/the country; **die** ~**übliche Kleidung** the costume of the country; ~**vater** *der* (*veralt.*) sovereign lord; ~**verrat** *der* (*Rechtsw.*) treason; ~**verteidigung** *die* national defence; ~**verweisung** *die* (*bes. österr.*) ⇒ **Ausweisung**; ~**währung** *die* currency of a/the country; ~**wappen** *das* national coat of arms

**land-, Land-:** ~**fahrer** *der*, ~**fahrerin** *die* vagrant; ~**fahrzeug** *das* land vehicle; ~**fein** *in* **sich** ~**fein machen** (*Seemannsspr.*) get spruced up *or* dressed up to go ashore; ~**flucht** *die* migration from the land *or* countryside [to the towns]; ~**frau** *die* countrywoman

**Land·friede[n]** *der* (*hist.*) general peace

**Landfriedens·bruch** *der* (*Rechtsw.*) breach of the peace

**land-, Land-:** ~**funk** *der* farming programme [on the radio]; (*Sendefolge*) farming programmes *pl.* [on the radio]; ~**gang** *der* (*Seemannsspr.*) shore leave; ~**gericht** *das* regional court; Land court; ~**gestützt** *Adj.* (*Milit.*) land-based; ~**gewinnung** *die* reclamation of land; ~**graf** *der* (*hist.*) landgrave; ~**gräfin** *die* (*hist.*) landgravine; ~**gut** *das* country estate; ~**haus** *das* country house; ~**jäger** *der* A (*veralt.: Polizist*) country policeman; B (*Wurst*) *small, highly seasoned, smoked, hard, flat sausage;* ~**karte** *die* map; ~**klima** *das* continental climate; ~**kreis** *der* district; ~**krieg** *der* land warfare; ~**läufig** *Adj.* widely held *or* accepted; (*nicht fachlich*) popular; **nach** ~**läufiger**

**Meinung/Auffassung** according to popular belief; **~leben** *das* country life

**Ländler** /ˈlɛntlɐ/ *der;* **~s, ~:** ländler

**Land·leute** *Pl.* Ⓐ (*veralt.*) country folk *or* people; Ⓑ ⇒ **Landmann**

**ländlich** /ˈlɛntlɪç/ *Adj.* rural; country *attrib.* ‹life›; **die ~e Ruhe** the quiet of the countryside

**ländlich-sittlich** *Adj.* (*scherzh.*) countrified; rustic; **hier herrschen noch ~e Zustände** people are still very countrified in their ways around here

**Land-: ~luft** *die* country air; **~macht** *die* land power; **~mann** *der; Pl.* **~leute** (*geh. veralt.*) husbandman (*arch.*); farmer; **~maschine** *die* agricultural machine; farm machine; **~maschinen** agricultural machinery; farm machinery; **~messer** *der;* **~~s, ~~, ~messerin** *die;* **~~, ~~nen** [land] surveyor; **~nahme** *die;* **~~:** occupation and settlement of land; **~partie** *die* (*veralt.*) outing into the country; **~pfarrer** *der,* **~pfarrerin** *die* country parson *or* priest; **~pfleger** *der* (*bibl.*) governor; **~plage** *die* plague [on the country]; (*fig.*) pest; nuisance; **dieses Jahr sind die Wespen eine wahre ~plage** there is an absolute plague of wasps all over the country this year; **~pomeranze** *die* (*ugs. abwertend*) country cousin (*derog.*); **~rat** *der* Ⓐ chief administrative officer of a/the district; Ⓑ (*schweiz.*) parliament of a/the canton; **~rätin** *die* ⇒ **~rat** A; **~ratte** *die* (*ugs., oft scherzh.*) landlubber; **~recht** *das* (*hist.*) common law; **~regen** *der* steady rain; **~rücken** *der* (*Geogr.*) ridge of land

**Landschaft** *die;* **~, ~en** Ⓐ landscape; (*ländliche Gegend*) countryside; **in die politische ~ passen** (*fig.*) fit in with the political mood; **in der ~ herumstehen** (*ugs.*) stand around; **die politische ~** (*fig.*) the political scene; Ⓑ (*Gemälde*) landscape; Ⓒ (*Gegend*) region

**-landschaft** *die* (*fig.*) scene; **in der Banken~:** on the banking scene

**landschaftlich** ❶ *Adj.* regional ‹accent, speech, expression, custom, usage, etc.›; **die ~en Gegebenheiten** the nature *sing.* of the landscape; the topography *sing.* ❷ *adv.* **~ herrlich gelegen sein** be in a glorious natural setting; **die Umgebung der Stadt ist ~ sehr schön** the town is in *or* has a beautiful natural setting; **eine ~ gefärbte Aussprache** an accent with a regional tinge; **~ verschieden sein** differ from one part of the country to another

**Landschafts-: ~bild** *das* Ⓐ (*Gemälde*) landscape [painting]; Ⓑ (*Aussehen*) landscape; **~gärtner** *der,* **~gärtnerin** *die* ▸159 landscape gardener; **~maler** *der* landscape painter; **~malerei** *die* landscape painting; **~malerin** *die* ⇒ **~maler**; **~pflege** *die* landscape conservation *no art.;* **~schutz·gebiet** *das* conservation area

**Land·schild·kröte** *die* land tortoise

**Landser** /ˈlantsɐ/ *der;* **~s, ~** (*veralt.*) [ordinary] soldier

**Land·sitz** *der* country seat

**Lands-: ~knecht** *der* (*hist.*) lansquenet; **~mann** *der; Pl.* **~leute** fellow countryman; compatriot; **~männin** *die;* **~~, ~~nen** fellow countrywoman; compatriot; **~mannschaft** *die* Ⓐ (*studentische Verbindung*) *association of students from the same country or region;* Ⓑ (*von Heimatvertriebenen*) *association of refugees and displaced Persons from a particular region*

**Land-: ~straße** *die* country road; (*im Gegensatz zur Autobahn*) ordinary road; **~streicher** *der* tramp; vagrant; **~streicherei** *die* vagrancy *no art.;* **~streicherin** *die* tramp; vagrant; **~streitkräfte** *Pl.* land forces; **~strich** *der* area; **ein bewaldeter ~strich** a wooded tract of land; a wooded area; **~sturm** *der* Ⓐ (*hist.*) landsturm; territorial reserve; Ⓑ (*schweiz.*) *territorial reserve consisting of men between the ages of 49 and 60;* **~tag** *der* Landtag; state parliament; (*österr.*) provincial parliament

*old spelling (see note on page 1707)

**Landung** *die;* **~, ~en** landing; **zur ~ ansetzen** begin one's/its landing approach; **den Piloten/das Flugzeug zur ~ zwingen** force the pilot/aircraft to land

**Landungs-: ~boot** *das* landing craft; **~brücke** *die* [floating] landing stage; **~platz** *der* landing place; **~steg** *der* landing stage

**land-, Land-: ~urlaub** *der* shore leave; **~vermesser** *der,* **~vermesserin** *die* ⇒ **~messer**; **~vermessung** *die* [land] surveying; **~vogt** *der* governor (*of an imperial province*); landvogt; **~wärts** *Adv.* landward; towards the land; **~weg** *der* Ⓐ (*über das Fest~*) overland route; **auf dem ~weg** overland; by the overland route; Ⓑ (*Feldweg*) track across the fields; **~wehr** *die* (*hist.: Reserveeinheit*) territorial reserve; **~wein** *der* ordinary local wine; vin du pays; **~wind** *der* land *or* offshore breeze; **~wirt** *der,* **~wirtin** *die* ▸159 farmer

**Land·wirtschaft** *die* Ⓐ agriculture *no art.;* farming *no art.;* Ⓑ (*Betrieb*) [small] farm

**land·wirtschaftlich** ❶ *Adj.* agricultural; agricultural, farm *attrib.* ‹machinery›. ❷ *adv.* **~ genutzt werden** be used for agricultural *or* farming purposes

**Landwirtschafts-: ~ministerium** *das* ministry of agriculture; **~schule** *die* agricultural college

**Land·zunge** *die* (*Geogr.*) tongue of land

**lang**[1] /laŋ/; **länger** /ˈlɛŋɐ/, **längst...** /ˈlɛŋst.../ ❶ *Adj.* Ⓐ ▸489 (*räumlich*) long; **eine Bluse mit ~en Ärmeln** a long-sleeved blouse; **etw. länger machen** make sth. longer; lengthen sth.; Ⓑ (*von bestimmter Länge*) **ein fünf Meter ~es Seil** a rope five metres long *or* in length; Ⓒ (*ugs.: groß*) tall; **komm mal her, Langer** come here, lofty (*coll.*); ⇒ *auch* **Latte** A; **Lulatsch**; Ⓓ (*ausführlich*) long; **des Langen und Breiten** (*geh.*) at great length; in great detail; Ⓔ (*zeitlich*) long; long, lengthy ‹speech, lecture, etc.›; prolonged ‹thought›; **seit ~er Zeit, seit ~em** for a long time; Ⓕ **ein vier Wochen ~es Seminar** a four-week seminar; **sein sechs Jahre ~es Studium** his six years of study. ❷ *adv.* Ⓐ (*zeitlich*) [for] a long time; **der ~ anhaltende Beifall** the lengthy *or* prolonged applause; **ein ~ gehegter Wunsch** a long-cherished wish; **~ ersehnt** long-awaited; longed-for; **etw. nicht länger ertragen können** be unable to bear *or* stand sth. any longer; **~ und breit** at great length; in great detail; Ⓑ (*von bestimmter Dauer*) **eine Sekunde/einen Augenblick/mehrere Stunden ~:** for a second/a moment/several hours; **den ganzen Winter ~:** all through the winter; **sein Leben ~:** all one's life; **ich werde das mein Leben ~ nicht vergessen** I won't forget it as long as I live Ⓒ **~ gestreckt** long; **~ gezogen** long drawn-out; ⇒ *auch* **länger** 2, 3

**lang**[2] (*bes. nordd.*) ❶ *Präp.:* ⇒ **entlang**. ❷ *Adv.* **[nicht] wissen, wo ~ es geht** (*fig.*) [not] know what it's all about; ⇒ *auch* **entlang**

**lang-, Lang-: ~ärm[e]lig** /-ɛrm(ə)lɪç/ *Adj.* long-sleeved; **~atmig** /-|a:tmɪç/ ❶ *Adj.* long-winded; ❷ *adv.* long-windedly; **etw. ~atmig erzählen** relate sth. at great length; **~atmigkeit** *die;* **~~:** long-windedness; **~beinig** *Adj.* long-legged

**lange; länger, am längsten** *Adv.* Ⓐ a long time; **er ist schon ~ fertig** he finished long ago; **~ schlafen/arbeiten** sleep/work late; **bist du schon ~ hier?** have you been here long?; **es ist schon ~/länger her, dass ...** it's a long time/some time since ...; **es ist noch gar nicht ~ her, dass ich ihn gesehen habe** it's not long since I saw him; I saw him not long ago; **[es dauert] nicht mehr ~, und es gibt Ärger** it won't be long before there's trouble; **da kannst du ~ warten** you can wait for ever; **sie wird es nicht mehr ~ machen** (*ugs.*) she won't last much longer; **was fragst du noch ~?** why do you keep asking questions?; ⇒ *auch* **länger** 3; Ⓑ (*bei weitem*) **das ist [noch] ~ nicht alles** that's not all by any means; that's not all, not by a long chalk *or* shot (*coll.*); **er spielt ~ nicht so gut Tennis wie du** he doesn't play tennis nearly *or* anything like as well as you; **er ist noch ~ nicht so weit** he's got a long time to go till then

**Länge** /ˈlɛŋə/ *die;* **~, ~n** Ⓐ ▸489 (*räumliche Ausdehnung*) length; **eine ~ von zwei Metern haben** be two metres in length; **auf einer ~ von zwei Kilometern** for two kilometres; **etw. der ~ nach falten** fold sth. lengthways; **der ~ nach hinschlagen** fall flat on one's face; measure one's length on the ground/floor; **sich der ~ nach hinwerfen** throw oneself flat on the ground/floor; Ⓑ (*hoher Wuchs*) tallness; **sich zu seiner ganzen ~ aufrichten** draw oneself up to one's full height; Ⓒ (*Ausführlichkeit*) length; Ⓓ (*Geogr.*) longitude; **die Insel liegt auf** *od.* **unter 15° östlicher ~:** the longitude of the island is 15° east; Ⓔ (*zeitliche Ausdehnung*) length; **ein Film von einer Stunde ~:** a film one hour in length; an hour-long film; **etw. in die ~ ziehen** drag sth. out; **sich in die ~ ziehen** drag on; go on and on; Ⓕ (*Sport*) length; **mit einer ~ [Vorsprung] siegen** win by a length; **um ~n gewinnen** (*ugs.*) win easily; Ⓖ *Pl.* (*in einem Film, Theaterstück usw.*) long drawn-out *or* tedious scene; (*in einem Buch*) long drawn-out *or* tedious passage; Ⓗ (*Verslehre*) long syllable; long

**länge·lang** *Adv.* at full length

**langen** (*ugs.*) ❶ *itr. V.* Ⓐ (*ausreichen*) be enough; **das Geld langt nicht** I/we *etc.* haven't got enough money; **das langt mir** that's enough for me; that'll do for me; **jetzt langts mir aber!** now I've had enough!; that's enough of that!; Ⓑ (*greifen*) reach (**in** + *Akk.* into; **auf** + *Akk.* on to; **nach** for); Ⓒ (*sich erstrecken*) **bis zu etw. ~:** reach sth.; Ⓓ (*erreichen*) reach; **bis zu etw. ~:** reach sth.. ❷ *tr. V.* **jmdm. etw. ~:** pass *or* hand sb. sth.; **jmdm. eine ~:** give sb. a clout [around the ear] (*coll.*)

**längen** *tr. V.* Ⓐ lengthen ‹garment›; Ⓑ (*strecken*) thin ‹soup, sauce›

**Längen-: ~grad** *der* (*Geogr.*) degree of longitude; **dieser Ort liegt auf dem 20. ~grad der östlichen Halbkugel** the longitude of this place is 20° east; **~kreis** *der* ⇒ **Meridian**; **~maß** *das* unit of length

**länger** /ˈlɛŋɐ/ ❶ ⇒ **lang**[1], **lange**. ❷ *Adj.* **eine ~e Abwesenheit/Behandlung** a fairly long *or* prolonged absence/period of treatment; **seit ~er Zeit** for quite some time; **es ist doch eine ~e Strecke** it's quite a long way; it's a longish way. ❸ *adv.* for some time; **es hat etwas ~ gedauert** it took/has taken some time

**länger·fristig** /-frɪstɪç/ ❶ *Adj.* fairly long-term. ❷ *adv.* on a fairly long-term basis

**Lange·weile** *die;* **~** *od.* **Langenweile** boredom; **~ haben** be bored; **aus ~** *od.* **Langerweile** out of boredom

**lang-, Lang-: ~fädig** /-fɛ:dɪç/ *Adj.* (*schweiz.*) long-winded; **~finger** *der* (*oft scherzh.*) (*Dieb*) thief; (*Taschendieb*) pickpocket; **~fristig** /-frɪstɪç/ ❶ *Adj.* long-term; long-dated ‹loan›; ❷ *adv.* on a long-term basis; **~fristig gesehen** in the long term; ***~gehegt** ⇒ **lang** 2 A; **~|gehen** *unr. itr. V.; mit sein* (*ugs.*) **an etw.** (*Dat.*) **~gehen** go along sth.; ⇒ *auch* **lang**[2]; ***~gestreckt** ⇒ **lang** 2 C; ***~gezogen** ⇒ **lang** 2 C; **~haardackel** *der* long-haired dachshund; **~haarig** *Adj.* long-haired; **~haus** *das* nave; (*mit Seitenschiffen*) nave and side aisles; **~holz** *das* (*Forstw.*) long timber; **~jährig** *Adj.* ‹customer, friend› of many years' standing; long-standing ‹friendship›; **~jährige Erfahrung** many years of experience; many years' experience; **eine ~jährige Strafe** a long sentence; **einer unserer ~jährigen Mitarbeiter** a colleague who has been with us for many years; **~lauf** *der* (*Skisport*) cross-country; **~läufer** *der,* **~läuferin** *die* cross-country skier

**Langlauf·ski** *der* cross-country ski

**lang-, Lang-: ~lebig** /-le:bɪç/ *Adj.* long-lived ‹animals, organisms›; durable ‹goods, materials›; **~lebige Gebrauchsgüter** consumer durables; **~lebigkeit** *die;* **~~** (*von Organismen*) longevity; long-livedness; (*von*

## Länge und Breite

***1 Millimeter*** = one millimetre* (1 mm) = 0.039 inch (in.)
***1 Zentimeter*** = one centimetre* (1 cm) = 0.394 inch (in.)
***1 Meter*** = one metre* (1 m) = 39.4 inches (ins), 3 feet (ft) 3.4 inches†
***1 Kilometer*** = one kilometre* (1 km) = 1094 yards (yds) *od.* 0.6214 mile

*Die amerikanische Schreibweise hat **-er** am Ende (**millimeter, centimeter, meter, kilometer**).

†Kann auch so geschrieben werden: 3' 3.4". Vergessen Sie nicht, dass bei Dezimalbrüchen ein Punkt gesetzt wird und kein Komma.

***Wie breit/lang ist es?***
= How wide/long is it?, What width/length is it?

***Das Zimmer ist vier mal fünf Meter [groß]***
= The room is four metres [wide] by five metres [long],
≈ The room is 12 feet [wide] by 15 feet [long]

***A hat die gleiche Länge/Breite wie B***
= A is the same length/width as B

***Sie haben die gleiche Länge*** od. ***sind gleich lang***
= They are the same length *od.* are equal in length

***Sie sind nicht gleich breit*** od. ***sind verschieden breit***
= They are not the same width *od.* are different widths

***eine 100 Meter lange Einfahrt***
= a drive 100 metres long *od.* in length

***ein fünf Zentimeter breites Brett***
= a plank five centimetres wide

***Der Stoff wird meterweise verkauft***
= The material is sold by the metre

***drei Meter Stoff zu 10 Mark das*** od. ***der Meter***
= three metres of material at 10 marks a *od.* the metre

***ein vier Meter langes Stück Seide***
= a four-metre length of silk

*Gebrauchsgütern*) durability; **~|legen** *refl. V. (ugs.)* [A] **sich eine Stunde/etwas ~legen** lie down *or* have a lie down for an hour/ a bit; [B] *(salopp: hinfallen)* fall flat [on one's face/back]

**länglich** /ˈlɛŋlɪç/ ❶ *Adj.* oblong; long narrow ‹opening›; long [narrow] ‹envelope›; long ‹box›; oval ‹roll›. ❷ *adv.* **~ rund** oval

***länglich·rund** ⇨ länglich 2

**lang-, Lang-: ~mähnig** /-mɛːnɪç/ *Adj.* long-maned ‹animal›; long-haired ‹person›; **~mut** *die;* **~~:** forbearance; **~mütig** /-myːtɪç/ *Adj.* forbearing; **~mütigkeit** *die;* **~~:** forbearance

**Langobarde** /laŋgoˈbardə/ *der;* **~n, ~n, Langobardin** *die;* **~, ~nen** Lombard

**langobardisch** *Adj.* Lombardic

**Lang-: ~ohr** *das (scherzh.)* [A] *(Hase)* hare; *(Kaninchen)* rabbit; bunny *(child lang.)*; [B] *(Esel)* donkey; **~pferd** *das (Turnen)* long horse

**längs** /lɛŋs/ ❶ *Präp. + Gen. od. (selten) Dat.* along; **~ des Flusses** *od.* **dem Fluss** along the river [bank]; **~ der Straße standen Apfelbäume** the road was lined with apple trees. ❷ *Adv.* [A] lengthways; **stellt das Sofa hier ~ an die Wand** put the sofa along here against the wall; [B] *(nordd.)* ⇨ **entlang**

**Längs·achse** *die* longitudinal axis

**langsam** ❶ *Adj.* [A] slow; low ‹speed›; [B] *(allmählich)* gradual. ❷ *adv.* [A] slowly; **geh [etwas] ~er!** go [a bit] more slowly; slow down [a bit]!; **~, aber sicher** *(ugs.)* slowly but surely; [B] *(allmählich)* gradually; **es wird ~ Zeit, dass du gehst** it's about time you left *or* went

**Langsamkeit** *die;* **~:** slowness

**Lang-: ~schäfter** /-ʃɛftɐ/ *der;* **~~s, ~~:** high boot; **~schläfer** *der*, **~schläferin** *die* late riser; **~seite** *die* long side

***längs·gestreift** ⇨ gestreift 2

**Langspiel·platte** *die* long-playing record; LP

**längs-, Längs-: ~richtung** *die* longitudinal direction; **in der ~richtung** lengthways; **~schnitt** *der* longitudinal section; **~seite** *die* long side; **~seits** *(Seemannsspr.)* ❶ *Präp. + Gen.* alongside; ❷ *Adv.* alongside; **~seits am Kai** alongside the quay

**längst** /lɛŋst/ *Adv.* [A] *(schon lange)* a long time ago; long since; **ich wusste das ~:** I've known that for a long time; I knew that long ago; **er ist ~ gestorben** he's been dead for a long time; he is long since dead; **seine ~ fälligen Schulden** his long overdue debts; [B] *(bei weitem)* **hier ist es ~ nicht so schön** it isn't nearly as nice here; **sie singt ~ nicht so gut wie du** she doesn't sing anything like as well as you; **ich bin ~ noch nicht fertig** I'm nowhere near finished

**längst...** ⇨ **lang¹**

**längstens** /ˈlɛŋstn̩s/ *Adv. (ugs.)* [A] *(höchstens)* at [the] most; **~ eine Woche** a week at the most; [B] *(spätestens)* at the latest

**lang·stielig** *Adj.* long-stemmed ‹glass, flower›; long-handled ‹axe, hammer, etc.›

**Lang·strecke** *die* [A] long haul *or* distance; **auf ~n** over long distances; [B] *(Sport)* long distance; **auf [den] ~n** over long distances; in long-distance running

**Langstrecken-: ~flug** *der* long-haul flight; **~lauf** *der (Sport)* long-distance race; *(Disziplin)* long-distance running *no art.*; **~läufer** *der*, **~läuferin** *die (Sport)* long-distance runner; **~rakete** *die* long-range missile

**Languste** /laŋˈgʊstə/ *die;* **~, ~n** spiny lobster; langouste

**lang-, Lang-: ~weile** *die:* ⇨ **Langeweile**; **~weilen** ❶ *tr. V.* bore; **er sah gelangweilt aus dem Fenster** he gazed out of the window, feeling bored. ❷ *refl. V.* be bored; **sich tödlich** *od.* **zu Tode ~weilen** be bored to death; **~weiler** *der*, **~weilerin** *die;* **~~, ~~nen** *(ugs. abwertend)* [A] bore; [B] *(schwerfälliger Mensch)* slowcoach; **~weilig** ❶ *Adj.* [A] boring; dull ‹place›; [B] *(ugs.: schleppend)* slow ‹person›; tedious ‹business›; **ein ~weiliger Kerl** a slowcoach; ❷ *adv.* boringly; **~weiligkeit** *die;* **~~** [A] boringness; [B] *(~samkeit)* slowness; **~welle** *die (Physik, Rundf.)* long wave; **auf** *od.* **über ~welle** on long wave; **~wierig** /-viːrɪç/ *Adj.* lengthy; prolonged ‹search›; protracted, lengthy, long ‹negotiations, treatment›; **~wierigkeit** *die;* **~~:** lengthiness; **~zeile** *die (Verslehre)* long line; **~zeit·gedächtnis** *das* long-term memory; **~zeit·programm** *das* long-term programme

**Lanolin** /lanoˈliːn/ *das;* **~s** lanolin

**Lanze** /ˈlantsə/ *die;* **~, ~n** lance; *(zum Werfen)* spear; **für jmdn. eine ~ brechen** *(fig.)* take up the cudgels on sb.'s behalf

**Lanzen-: ~spitze** *die* lance head; *(der Wurflanze)* spearhead; **~stoß** *der* lance thrust; *(mit der Wurflanze)* spear thrust

**Lanzette** /lanˈtsɛtə/ *die;* **~, ~n** *(Med.)* lancet

**Lanzett·fischchen** *das (Zool.)* lancelet

**Laos** /ˈlaːɔs/ *(das)* Laos

**Laote** /laˈoːtə/ *der;* **~n, ~n, Laotin** *die;* **~, ~nen** Laotian

**laotisch** *Adj.* Laotian

**lapidar** /lapiˈdaːɐ̯/ ❶ *Adj.* *(kurz, aber wirkungsvoll)* succinct; *(knapp)* terse; **in ~er Kürze** succinctly/tersely. ❷ *adv.* succinctly/ tersely

**Lapislazuli** /lapɪsˈlaːtsuli/ *der;* **~, ~:** lapis lazuli

**Lappalie** /laˈpaːli̯ə/ *die;* **~, ~n** trifle

**Lappe** /ˈlapə/ *der;* **~n, ~n** Lapp; Laplander

**läppen** /ˈlɛpn̩/ *tr. V. (Technik)* lap

**Lappen** *der;* **~s, ~** [A] cloth; *(Fetzen)* rag; *(Wasch~)* flannel; [B] *(salopp: Geldschein)* [large] note; **ein blauer ~:** a hundred-mark note; [C] *(Zool.)* flap of skin; *(eines Hahns)* wattle; [D] *in* **jmdm. durch die ~ gehen** *(ugs.)* slip through sb.'s fingers; [E] *(Anat.)* lobe

**läppern** /ˈlɛpɐn/ *tr. V. (ugs.) in* **es läppert jmdn. nach etw.** *(landsch.)* sb. has a sudden craving for sth.; **es läppert sich** it's mounting up

**lappig** *Adj. (ugs.)* limp; loosely sagging ‹skin›

**Lappin** *die;* **~, ~nen** ⇨ **Lappe**

**läppisch** /ˈlɛpɪʃ/ *Adj.* silly

**Lappland** *(das);* **~s** Lapland

**lappländisch** *Adj.* lapp

**Läpp·maschine** *die (Technik)* lapping machine

**Lapsus** /ˈlapsʊs/ *der;* **~, ~** *(geh.)* slip; *(gesellschaftlich)* faux pas; **mir ist ein ~ unterlaufen** I made a slip/committed a faux pas

**Laptop** /ˈlɛptɔp/ *der;* **~s, ~s** *(DV)* laptop

**Lärche** /ˈlɛrçə/ *die;* **~, ~n** larch

**Largo** /ˈlargo/ *das;* **~[s], ~s** *od.* **Larghi** /ˈlargi/ *(Musik)* largo

**larifari** /lariˈfaːri/ *(ugs.)* ❶ *Interj.* nonsense; rubbish; fiddlesticks. ❷ *Adj.* slipshod. ❸ *adv.* sloppily

**Larifari** *das;* **~s** *(ugs.)* nonsense; rubbish

**Lärm** /lɛrm/ *der;* **~[e]s** noise; *(Krach)* din; row *(coll.)*; *(fig.)* fuss; to-do; **um jmdn./etw. ~ machen** *(fig.)* make a fuss about sb./sth.; **„Viel ~ um Nichts"** 'Much Ado about Nothing'; **viel ~ um nichts machen** *(fig.)* make a big fuss *or* to-do about nothing; **~ schlagen** kick up *or* make a fuss

**lärm-, Lärm-: ~bekämpfung** *die* noise abatement; **~belästigung** *die* disturbance caused by noise; **~belastung** *die* noise pollution; **~empfindlich** *Adj.* sensitive to noise *postpos.*

**lärmen** *itr. V.* make a noise *or (coll.)* row; ‹radio› blare; **die ~de Menge** the noisy crowd; **~d vorbeigehen** go noisily past

**larmoyant** /larmoaˈjant/ *(geh.)* ❶ *Adj.* maudlin; tearfully sentimental. ❷ *adv.* in a maudlin way; in a tearful and sentimental manner

**Larmoyanz** /larmoaˈjants/ *die;* **~** *(geh.)* maudlin *or* tearful sentimentality

**Lärm-: ~pegel** *der* noise level; **~quelle** *die* source of noise; **~schutz** *der* [A] protection against noise; [B] *(Vorrichtung)* noise barrier; noise *or* sound insulation *no indef. art.*; **~schutz·wand** *die* sound-insulating wall

**Larve** /ˈlarfə/ *die;* ~, ~**n** Ⓐ grub; larva; Ⓑ (*veralt.: Maske*) mask; Ⓒ (*abwertend veralt.: Gesicht*) mask

**las** /la:s/ *1. u. 3. Pers. Sg. Prät. v.* **lesen**

**lasch** /laʃ/ ❶ *Adj.* limp ‹handshake›; feeble ‹action, measure›; listless ‹movement, gait›; lax ‹upbringing›. ❷ *adv. s. Adj.:* limply; feebly; listlessly; laxly; ~ **gewürzt sein** be insipid *or* tasteless

**Lasche** *die;* ~, ~**n** Ⓐ (*Gürtel*~) loop; (*eines Briefumschlags*) flap; (*Schuh*~) tongue; Ⓑ (*Technik*) (*von Eisenbahnschienen*) fish plate; (*Stoßplatte*) butt strap

**Laschheit** *die;* ~ ⇒ **lasch** 1: limpness; feebleness; listlessness; laxness

**Laser** /ˈleɪzə/ *der;* ~**s,** ~ (*Physik*) laser

**Laser-:** ~**drucker** *der* (*DV*) laser printer; ~**pointer** *der* (*DV*) laser pointer; ~**strahl** *der* (*Physik*) laser beam; ~**ziel·gerät** *das* laser sight

**lasieren** /laˈzi:rən/ *tr. V.* varnish

**lass,** ***laß** /las/ *Imperativ Sg. v.* **lassen**

**lassen** /ˈlasn̩/ ❶ *unr. tr. V.* Ⓐ *mit Inf. + Akk.* (*2. Part.* ~) (*veran*~) **etw. tun/machen/bauen/waschen** ~**:** have *or* get sth. done/made/built/washed; **von welcher Baufirma haben Sie Ihr Haus bauen** ~**?** which builder did you get to build your house?; **Essen kommen** ~**:** have some food sent in; **Wasser in die Wanne laufen** ~**:** run water into the bath; **das Licht über Nacht brennen** ~**:** keep the light on overnight; **sie ließ mir eine Nachricht zukommen** she sent me a message; **jmdn. warten/erschießen** ~**:** keep sb. waiting/have sb. shot; **jmdn. grüßen** ~**:** send one's regards to sb.; **jmdn. kommen/rufen** ~**:** send for sb.; **jmdm. etw. mitteilen/jmdn. etw. wissen** ~**:** let sb. know sth.; Ⓑ *mit Inf. + Akk.* (*2. Part.* ~) (*erlauben*) **jmdn. etw. tun** ~**:** let sb. do sth.; allow sb. to do sth.; **jmdn. ausreden** ~**:** let sb. finish speaking; allow sb. to finish speaking; **er lässt sich** (*Dat.*) **nichts sagen** you can't tell him anything; **ich lasse mich nicht beleidigen/einschüchtern** I won't be insulted/intimidated; **das lasse ich mir nicht gefallen** I'm not standing for that; **alles mit sich geschehen** ~**:** put up with anything and everything; Ⓒ (*zugestehen, be*~) **lass den Kindern den Spaß** let the children enjoy themselves; **jmdn. in Frieden** ~**:** leave sb. in peace; **lass ihn in seinem Glauben** don't disillusion him; **nichts unversucht** ~**:** try everything; **etw. ungesagt** ~**:** leave sth. unsaid; **jmdn. kalt/unbeeindruckt** ~**:** leave sb. cold/unimpressed; **das muss man ihm/ihr** ~**:** one must grant *or* give him/her that; Ⓓ (*hinein*~/*heraus*~) let *or* allow (**in** + *Akk.* into, **aus** out of); **jmdn. in die Wohnung** ~**:** let *or* allow sb. into the flat (*Brit.*) *or* (*Amer.*) apartment; Ⓔ (*unter*~) stop; (*Begonnenes*) put aside; **lass das!** stop that *or* it!; **etw. nicht** ~ **können** be unable to stop sth.; **es nicht** ~ **können, etw. zu tun** be unable to stop doing sth.; **tu, was du nicht** ~ **kannst** go ahead and do what you want to do; **die Arbeit Arbeit sein** ~ (*ugs.*) forget about work (*coll.*); **lass das Grübeln!** stop brooding!; Ⓕ (*zurücklassen; bleiben* ~) leave; **jmdn. allein** ~**:** leave sb. alone *or* on his/her own; Ⓖ (*über*~) **jmdm. etw.** ~**:** let sb. have sth.; **jmdm. etw. als** *od.* **zum Pfand** ~**:** leave sb. sth. as security; **jmdm. etw. billig/für 10 Mark** ~**:** let sb. have sth. cheaply/for ten marks; Ⓗ (*als Aufforderung*) **lass/lasst uns gehen/fahren!** let's go!; Ⓘ (*verlieren*) lose; (*ausgeben*) spend; **sein Leben für eine Idee** ~**:** lay down one's life for an idea; **er hat zwei Söhne im Krieg** ~ **müssen** he lost two sons in the war; **er hat im Kasino viel Geld ge**~**:** he lost/(*langfristig*) has lost a lot of money at the casino; Ⓙ (*abwarten, bis ...*) **lass sie nur erst einmal erwachsen sein** wait till she's grown up.
❷ *unr. refl. V.* Ⓐ **die Tür lässt sich leicht öffnen** the door opens easily; **dieses Material lässt sich gut verarbeiten** this material is easy to work with; **das lässt sich nicht beweisen** it can't be proved; **das lässt sich machen** that can be done; ⇒ *auch* **hören** 1 B, C; Ⓑ (*unpers.*) **es lässt sich nicht leugnen/verschweigen, dass ...** it cannot be denied *or* there's no denying that .../we/you *etc.* cannot hide the fact that ...; **hier lässt es sich leben/wohl sein** it's a good life here.
❸ *unr. itr. V.* Ⓐ (*ugs.*) **Lass mal. Ich mache das schon** Leave it. I'll do it; **Lass doch! Du kannst mir das Geld später zurückgeben** That's all right. You can pay me back later; Ⓑ (*veran*~) **ich lasse bitten** would you ask him/her/them to come in; **einspannen** ~**:** have the horses harnessed; **ich habe mir sagen** ~, **dass ...** I've been told *or* informed that ...; Ⓒ (*veralt.: aufgeben*) **von jmdm./etw.** ~**:** part from sb./sth.; **vom Alkohol nicht** ~ **können** be unable to give up alcohol

**lässig** /ˈlɛsɪç/ ❶ *Adj.* casual. ❷ *adv.* Ⓐ (*ungezwungen*) casually; Ⓑ (*ugs.: leicht*) easily; effortlessly

**Lässigkeit** *die;* ~ Ⓐ casualness; Ⓑ (*ugs.: Leichtigkeit*) effortlessness

**lässlich,** ***läßlich** /ˈlɛslɪç/ *Adj.* (*kath. Kirche, auch fig.*) venial, pardonable ‹sin›

**Lasso** /ˈlaso/ *das od. der;* ~**s,** ~**s** lasso

**lässt,** ***läßt** /lɛst/ *3. Pers. Sg. Präsens v.* **lassen**

**Last** /last/ *die;* ~, ~**en** Ⓐ load; (*Trag*~) load; burden; Ⓑ (*belastendes Gewicht*) weight; Ⓒ (*Bürde*) burden; **die** ~ **des Amtes/der Verantwortung** the burden of office/responsibility; **die** ~ **auf andere abwälzen** shift the burden on to others; **jmdm. zur** ~ **fallen/werden** be/become a burden on sb.; **jmdm. etw. zur** ~ **legen** charge sb. with sth.; accuse sb. of sth.; Ⓓ *Pl.* (*Abgaben*) charges; (*Kosten*) costs; **die steuerlichen** ~**en** the tax burden *sing.;* Ⓔ **zu** ~**en** ⇒ **zulasten**

**Last-:** ~**arm** *der* (*Physik*) load arm; weight arm; ~**auto** *das* ⇒ ~**kraftwagen**

**lasten** *itr. V.* Ⓐ be a burden; **auf jmdm./etw.** ~**:** weigh heavily [up]on sb./sth.; **das Amt lastet auf seinen Schultern** (*fig.*) the burden of office rests on his shoulders; **auf seinen Schultern lastet die ganze Arbeit** (*fig.*) all the work falls on his shoulders; **eine** ~**de Stille/Hitze** (*fig.*) an oppressive silence/heat; Ⓑ (*belastet sein mit*) **auf dem Haus** ~ **zwei Hypotheken** the house is encumbered with two mortgages

**Lasten-:** ~**auf·zug** *der* goods lift (*Brit.*); freight elevator (*Amer.*); ~**ausgleich** *der* (*Bundesrepublik Deutschland*): *compensation paid to individuals for damage and losses during and immediately after the Second World War*

**Laster**[1] *der;* ~**s,** ~ (*ugs.: Lkw*) truck; lorry (*Brit.*)

**Laster**[2] *das;* ~**s,** ~**:** vice; **ein langes** ~ (*fig. ugs.*) a beanpole

**Lästerer** *der;* ~**s,** ~ Ⓐ **ein** ~ **sein** have a malicious tongue; be constantly making malicious remarks; Ⓑ (*veralt.: Gottes*~) blasphemer

**lasterhaft** *Adj.* (*abwertend*) depraved

**Lasterhaftigkeit** *die;* ~**:** depravity

**Laster·höhle** *die* (*ugs. abwertend*) den of vice *or* iniquity

**Lästerin** *die;* ~, ~**nen** ⇒ **Lästerer**

**Laster·leben** *das* (*oft scherzh.*) life of depravity

**lästerlich** ❶ *Adj.* malicious ‹remark›; malevolent ‹curse, oath›. ❷ *adv.* ‹curse› malevolently; ‹speak› maliciously

**Läster·maul** *das* (*abwertend salopp*) **ein** ~ **sein/haben** have a malicious tongue; be constantly making malicious remarks; **halt dein** ~**!** keep your malicious remarks to yourself!

**lästern** /ˈlɛstɐn/ ❶ *itr. V.* (*abwertend*) **über jmdn./etw.** ~**:** make malicious remarks about sb./sth. ❷ *tr. V.* (*veralt.: schmähen*) blaspheme against ‹God, God's law, etc.›

**Lästerung** *die;* ~, ~**en** malicious remark; (*gegen Gott*) blasphemy

**Last·esel** *der* pack donkey

**Lastex** Ⓦⓩ /ˈlastɛks/ *das;* ~**:** Lastex ®; stretch fabric

**Lastex·hose** *die* stretch trousers *or* pants *pl.*

**lästig** /ˈlɛstɪç/ *Adj.* tiresome ‹person›; tiresome, irksome ‹task, duty, etc.›; troublesome ‹illness, cough, etc.›; **jmdm.** ~ **sein** *od.* **fallen/werden** be/become a nuisance to sb.

**Last-:** ~**kahn** *der* [cargo] barge; ~**kraftwagen** *der* (*bes. Amtsspr.*) heavy goods (*Brit.*) *or* (*Amer.*) freight vehicle; ~**pferd** *das* pack horse; ~**schiff** *das* cargo ship; ˙freighter; ~**schrift** *die* Ⓐ (*Betrag*) debit; Ⓑ (*Bescheinigung*) debit advice; Ⓒ (*Vorgang*) debiting; Ⓓ (*Verkehr*) direct debit; ~**tier** *das* pack animal; ~**träger** *der,* ~**trägerin** *die* porter; bearer; ~**wagen** *der* truck; lorry (*Brit.*); ~**wagen·fahrer** *der,* ~**wagen·fahrerin** *die* ▶ 159 truck driver; lorry driver (*Brit.*); ~**zug** *der* truck *or* (*Brit.*) lorry and trailer/trailers

**Lasur** /laˈzu:ɐ̯/ *die;* ~, ~**en** varnish; (*farbig*) glaze

**lasziv** /lasˈtsi:f/ *Adj.* lascivious

**Laszivität** /lastsiviˈtɛ:t/ *die;* ~**:** lasciviousness

**Latein** /laˈtain/ *das;* ~**s** ▶ 696 Latin; **mit seinem** ~ **am Ende sein** be at one's wit's end; ⇒ *auch* **Deutsch**

**Latein-:** ~**amerika** (*das*) Latin America; ~**amerikaner** *der,* ~**amerikanerin** *die* Latin American; ~**amerikanisch** *Adj.* Latin American

**Lateiner** /laˈtainɐ/ *der;* ~**s,** ~, **Lateinerin** *die;* ~, ~**nen** Latin scholar; Latinist; (*Schüler*) Latin pupil

**lateinisch** *Adj.* ▶ 696 Latin; ⇒ *auch* **deutsch; Deutsche**[2]

**Latein-:** ~**schule** *die* (*hist.*) grammar school; ~**unterricht** *der* latin teaching; ⇒ *auch* **Englischunterricht**

**latent** /laˈtɛnt/ ❶ *Adj.* latent. ❷ *adv.* ~ **vorhanden sein** be latent

**Latenz** /laˈtɛnts/ *die* (*geh.*) latency

**Latenz·periode** *die* (*Psych.*) latency period

**Laterna magica** /laˈtɛrna ˈma:gika/ *die;* ~, **Laternae magicae** /-nɛ -tsɛ/ magic lantern

**Laterne** /laˈtɛrnə/ *die;* ~, ~**n** Ⓐ (*Leuchte*) lamp; lantern (*Naut.*); **gute Handwerker/so ein Auto kann man mit der** ~ **suchen** (*fig.*) good craftsmen/cars like that are few and far between; Ⓑ (*Straßen*~) street light; street lamp; Ⓒ **die rote** ~ **übernehmen/an eine andere Elf abgeben** (*Sport Jargon*) drop to/move off the bottom of the table; Ⓓ (*Bauw.*) lantern

**Laternen-:** ~**licht** *das* light of the street lamp/lamps; ~**parker** *der;* ~~**s,** ~~, ~**parkerin** *die;* ~~, ~~**nen** (*scherzh.*) driver who regularly parks in the road; ~**pfahl** *der* lamppost

**Latex** /ˈla:tɛks/ *der;* ~, **Latizes** /ˈla:titse:s/ latex

**Latifundium** /latiˈfʊndiʊm/ *das;* ~**s, Latifundien** (*hist.*) latifundium

**latinisieren** /latiniˈzi:rən/ *tr. V.* latinize

**Latinismus** *der;* ~, **Latinismen** (*Sprachw.*) Latinism

**Latinist** *der;* ~**en,** ~**en, Latinistin** *die;* ~, ~**nen** Latinist; Latin scholar

**Latinum** /laˈti:nʊm/ *das;* ~**s: das kleine/große** ~**:** ≈ GCSE/'A' level Latin [examination]

**Latizes** ⇒ **Latex**

**Latrine** /laˈtri:nə/ *die;* ~, ~**n** latrine

**Latrinen·parole** *die* (*ugs. abwertend*) empty rumour

**Latsche**[1] /ˈlatʃə/ *die;* ~, ~**n** (*variety of*) [Swiss] mountain pine

**Latsche**[2] /ˈla:tʃə/ *die;* ~, ~**n** ⇒ **Latschen**

**latschen** /ˈla:tʃn̩/ *itr. V.; mit sein* (*salopp*) trudge; (*schlurfend*) slouch

**Latschen** *der;* ~**s,** ~ (*ugs.*) old worn-out shoe; (*Hausschuh*) old worn-out slipper; **wenn ich nicht bald etwas zu essen kriege, kippe ich noch aus den** ~ (*salopp*) if I don't get something to eat soon, I

*old spelling (see note on page 1707)

shall keel over; **er ist bald aus den ~ gekippt, als er hörte, dass ich im Lotto gewonnen hatte** (*salopp*) he was flabbergasted when he heard I'd got a prize in the lottery

**Latschen·kiefer** *die:* ⇒ **Latsche[1]**

**Latte** /'latə/ *die;* ~, ~**n** Ⓐ lath; slat; (*Zaun*~) pale; **eine lange ~** (*ugs.*) a beanpole; Ⓑ (*Sport: Quer~ des Tores*) [cross]bar; Ⓒ (*Leichtathletik*) bar; Ⓓ *in* **eine [lange] ~ von Schulden/Vorstrafen** (*ugs.*) a [large] pile of debts/a [long] list *or* string of previous convictions

**Latten-:** ~**kiste** *die* crate; ~**kreuz** *das* (*Fuß-, Handball*) angle of the [cross]bar and the post; **im ~kreuz** in the top corner of the net; ~**rost** *der* (*auf dem Boden*) duckboards *pl.;* (*eines Bettes*) slatted frame; ~**schuss**, *~**schuß** *der* (*Ballspiele*) **es war nur ein ~schuss** the shot only hit the [cross]bar; ~**zaun** *der* paling fence

**Lattich** /'latıç/ *der;* ~**s**, ~**e** lettuce

**Latüchte** /la'tʏçtə/ *die;* ~, ~**n** (*ugs. scherzh.*) lamp; **geh mir aus der ~!** (*salopp*) get out of the light!

**Latwerge** /lat'vɛrgə/ *die;* ~, ~**n** Ⓐ (*Med. veralt.*) confection; Ⓑ (*bes. südwestd.: Mus*) [fruit] purée

**Latz** /lats/ *der;* ~**es**, **Lätze** /'lɛtsə/ Ⓐ bib; **jmdm. eine[n] vor den ~ knallen** *od.* **ballern** (*salopp*) sock (*sl.*) *or* thump sb.; Ⓑ ⇒ **Hosenlatz**

**Lätzchen** /'lɛtsçən/ *das;* ~**s**, ~: bib

**Latz-:** ~**hose** *die* bib and brace; (*für Kinder*) dungarees *pl.;* ~**rock** *der* bib-top pinafore dress

**lau** /lau/ *Adj.* Ⓐ (*mäßig warm*) tepid, lukewarm ‹water etc.›; (*nicht mehr kalt*) warm ‹beer etc.›; Ⓑ (*mild*) mild ‹wind, air, evening, etc.›; mild and gentle ‹rain›; Ⓒ (*unentschlossen*) lukewarm; half-hearted

**Laub** /laup/ *das;* ~**[e]s** leaves *pl.;* **dichtes/neues ~:** thick/new foliage; **~ tragende Bäume** trees bearing [broad] leaves

**Laub-:** ~**baum** *der* broad-leaved tree; ~**blatt** *das* [broad] leaf; ~**dach** *das* (*dicht.*) leafy canopy (*poet.*); canopy of leaves

**Laube** *die;* ~, ~**n** Ⓐ summer house; (*überdeckter Sitzplatz*) bower; arbour; ⇒ *auch* **fertig**; Ⓑ (*Archit.*) porch

**Lauben-:** ~**kolonie** *die* group of allotment gardens; ~**pieper** *der;* ~~**s**, ~~, ~**pieperin** *die;* ~~, ~~**nen** (*berlin. scherzh.*) allotment gardener

**Laub-:** ~**frosch** *der* tree frog; ~**hölzer** *Pl.* broad-leaved trees and shrubs; ~**hüttenfest** *das* (*jüd. Rel.*) Feast of Tabernacles; Succoth; ~**krone** *die* Ⓐ (*geh.: Wipfel*) treetop; Ⓑ (*Krone*) crest coronet

**Laub·säge** *die* fretsaw

**Laubsäge·arbeit** *die* fretsaw work; **eine ~:** a piece of fretsaw work

**laub-, Laub-:** ~**sänger** *der* (*Zool.*) leaf warbler; *~**tragend** ⇒ **Laub**; ~**wald** *der* deciduous wood/forest; ~**werk** *das* Ⓐ (*Archit., Kunst*) foliage; Ⓑ (*geh.*) ⇒ **Belaubung B**

**Lauch** /laux/ *der;* ~**[e]s**, ~**e** (*Bot.*) allium; (*Porree*) leek

**Laudatio** /lau'da:tsio/ *die;* ~, ~**nes** /-'tsio:ne:s/ *od.* ~**nen** /-'tsio:nən/ eulogy; encomium

**Laue[ne]** /'lauə(nə)/ *die;* ~, ~**n** (*schweiz.*) ⇒ **Lawine**

**Lauer** /'lauɐ/ *die;* ~ *in* **auf der ~ liegen** *od.* **sein** (*ugs.*) (*jmdm. auflauern*) lie in wait; (*etw. erfahren wollen*) be on the lookout; (*um zu hören*) be listening out; **sich auf die ~ legen** settle down to lie in wait

**lauern** *itr. V.* Ⓐ (*auch fig.*) lurk; **auf jmdn./etw. ~:** lie in wait for sb./sth.; **er wartete ~d auf unsere Antwort** he slyly awaited our reply; **ein ~der Blick** a sly look; Ⓑ (*ugs.: ungeduldig warten*) **auf jmdn./etw. ~:** wait [impatiently] for sb./sth.

**Lauf** /lauf/ *der;* ~**[e]s**, **Läufe** /'lɔyfə/ Ⓐ running; Ⓑ (*Sport: Wettrennen*) heat; Ⓒ (*Ver~, Entwicklung*) course; **im ~[e] der Zeit** in the course of time; **im ~[e] der Jahre** over the years; as the years go/went by; **im ~[e] des Tages** during the day; **[irgendwann] im ~[e] des Sommers** [some time] during the summer; **im ~[e] seines Lebens** in the course of *or* during his life; **einer Sache** (*Dat.*) **ihren** *od.* **freien ~ lassen** give free rein to sth.; **seinem Zorn freien ~ lassen** give vent to one's anger; **seiner Fantasie freien ~ lassen** give free rein to one's imagination; (*zu sehr*) indulge in flights of fancy; **lass doch den Dingen ihren ~!** let matters *or* things take their course; **der ~ der Geschichte/Welt** the course of history/the way of the world; **seinen ~ nehmen** take its course; Ⓓ (*von Schusswaffen*) barrel; **etw. vor den ~ bekommen** get a shot at sth.; Ⓔ (*eines Flusses, einer Straße*) course; **der obere/untere ~ eines Flusses** the upper/lower reaches *pl.* of a river; **der ~ der Straße** the route followed by the road; **dem ~ der Straße/Bahnschienen folgen** follow the road/railway lines; Ⓕ (*Musik*) run; Ⓖ (*Jägerspr.*) leg; Ⓗ (*von Maschinen*) running

**Lauf-:** ~**bahn** *die* Ⓐ (*Werdegang*) career; **eine wissenschaftliche/künstlerische ~bahn einschlagen** take up a career in the sciences/as an artist; Ⓑ (*Leichtathletik*) running track; ~**buchse** *die* (*Technik*) cylinder liner; ~**bursche** *der* errand boy; messenger boy

**laufen** ❶ *unr. itr. V.;* *mit sein* Ⓐ run; **ge~ kommen** come running up; **er lief, was er konnte** (*ugs.*) he ran as fast as he could; **jmdn. ~ lassen** (*ugs.*) let sb. go; Ⓑ (*gehen*) go; (*zu Fuß gehen*) walk; **auf und ab/hin und her ~:** walk up and down/back and forth; **wir sind im Urlaub viel ge~:** we did a lot of walking while on holiday; **es sind noch/nur fünf Minuten zu ~:** it's another/only five minutes' walk; **das Kind lernt ~:** the child is learning to walk; Ⓒ (*stoßen*) **in** (*Akk.*)**/gegen etw. ~:** walk into sth.; Ⓓ (*ugs.: ständig hingehen*) **dauernd zum Arzt/ins Kino/in die Kirche ~:** keep running to the doctor/be always going to the cinema (*Brit.*) *or* (*Amer.*) the movies/to church; **in jede Veranstaltung der Partei ~:** go to every event organized by the party; Ⓔ (*in einem Wettkampf*) run; (*beim Eislauf*) skate; (*beim Ski~*) ski; **ein Pferd ~ lassen** run a horse; Ⓕ (*im Gang sein*) ‹machine› be running; ‹radio, television, etc.› be on; (*funktionieren*) ‹machine› run; ‹radio, television, etc.› work; **ruhig/auf Hochtouren ~:** be running quietly/at full speed; Ⓖ (*sich bewegen, [aus]fließen; auch fig.*) **auf Schienen/über Rollen ~:** run on rails/over pulleys; **von den Fließbändern ~:** come off the conveyor belts; **es lief mir eiskalt über den Rücken** a chill ran down my spine; **ihm lief der Schweiß über das Gesicht** the sweat ran down his face; **Wasser in die Wanne ~ lassen** run the bathwater; **deine Nase läuft** your nose is running; you've got a runny nose; **der Käse läuft** the cheese has gone runny (*coll.*); Ⓗ (*gelten*) ‹contract, agreement, engagement, etc.› run; **der Vertrag läuft noch bis ...** the contract runs until ...; Ⓘ (*gespielt werden*) ‹programme, play› be on; ‹film› be on *or* showing; ‹show› be on *or* playing; **im dritten Programm ~:** be on the regional programme; **der Hauptfilm läuft schon** the main film has already started; Ⓙ (*fahren*) run; **auf Grund ~:** run aground; Ⓚ (*vonstatten gehen*) **parallel mit etw. ~:** run in parallel with sth.; **ich möchte wissen, wie der Prozess ge~ ist** I'd like to know the outcome of the trial; **der Laden läuft/die Geschäfte ~ gut/schlecht** (*ugs.*) the shop is doing well/badly/business is good/bad; **wie geplant/nach Wunsch ~:** go as planned *or* according to plan; **die Sache ist ge~** (*ugs.: daran ist nichts mehr zu ändern*) it's too late now; **schief ~** (*ugs.*) go wrong; Ⓛ (*eingeleitet sein*) ‹negotiations, investigations› be in progress *or* under way; ‹application› be under consideration; Ⓜ (*registriert sein*) **auf jmds. Namen** (*Akk.*) **~:** be in sb.'s name; Ⓝ (*ugs.: gut verkäuflich sein*) go *or* sell well; Ⓞ (*ver~*) run.

❷ *unr. tr. u. itr. V.* Ⓐ *mit sein* (*zurücklegen*) (*zu Fuß gehen*) walk; (*rennen*) run; **die 800 m/einige Runden/sechs Rennen ~** (*Sport*) run the 800 m./a few laps/[in] six races; Ⓑ *mit sein* (*erzielen*) **einen Rekord ~:** set up a record; **über die 100 m 9,9 Sekunden ~:** run the 100 m. in 9.9 seconds; Ⓒ *mit haben od. sein* **Ski/Schlittschuh/Rollschuh ~:** ski/skate/roller skate; Ⓓ **sich** (*Dat.*) **die Füße wund ~:** get sore feet from running/walking; **sich** (*Dat.*) **ein Loch in die Schuhsohle ~:** wear a hole in one's shoe *or* sole.

❸ *unr. refl. V.* Ⓐ **sich warm ~:** warm up; ⇒ *auch* **müde**; Ⓑ (*unpers.*) **in diesen Schuhen läuft es sich sehr bequem** these shoes are very comfortable for running/walking in *or* to run/walk in; **auf dem steinigen Weg lief es sich nicht gut** the stony path was not good for walking/running on

**laufend** ❶ *Adj.* Ⓐ (*ständig*) regular ‹interest, income›; recurring ‹costs›; **die ~en Arbeiten/Geschäfte** the day-to-day *or* routine work *sing.* /business *sing.;* Ⓑ (*gegenwärtig*) current ‹issue, year, month, etc.›; Ⓒ (*aufeinander folgend*) **zehn Mark der ~e Meter** ten marks a *or* per metre; Ⓓ **auf dem Laufenden sein/bleiben** be/keep *or* stay up-to-date *or* fully informed; **jmdn. auf dem Laufenden halten** keep sb. up-to-date *or* informed; **mit etw. auf dem Laufenden sein** be up-to-date with sth.

❷ *adv.* constantly; continually; ‹increase› steadily

***laufen|lassen** ⇒ **laufen 1 A**

**Läufer** /'lɔyfɐ/ *der;* ~**s**, ~ Ⓐ (*Sport*) runner; (*Handball*) halfback; Ⓑ (*Fußball veralt.*) halfback; Ⓒ (*Teppich*) (*long narrow*) carpet; Ⓓ (*Schach*) bishop; Ⓔ (*Landw.: junges Schwein*) young pig; Ⓕ (*Bauw.: Mauerstein*) stretcher

**Lauferei** *die;* ~, ~**en** (*ugs.*) running around *no pl.;* **die ~ zu den Ärzten kostet viel Zeit** it takes a lot of time to go the rounds of all the doctors

**Läuferin** *die;* ~, ~**nen** runner

**läuferisch** ❶ *Adj.* athletic; (*beim Eislaufen*) skating *attrib.* ❷ *adv.* as regards the skating

**Läufer·reihe** *die* (*Fußball veralt.*) halfback line

**Lauf-:** ~**feuer** *das* brush fire; **wie ein ~feuer** like wildfire; ~**fläche** *die* (*am Reifen*) tread; (*am Ski*) sole [of the ski]; ~**gewicht** *das* sliding weight; ~**graben** *der* (*Milit.*) communications trench

**läufig** /'lɔyfıç/ *Adj.* on heat *postpos.;* in season *postpos.*

**Lauf-:** ~**junge** *der:* ⇒ ~**bursche**; ~**katze** *die* (*Technik*) crab; ~**kran** *der* (*Technik*) travelling crane; ~**kundschaft** *die* passing trade; ~**kundschaft haben** have a passing trade; ~**masche** *die* ladder; ~**pass**, *~**paß** *der:* **der Präsident gab seinem Berater den ~pass** (*ugs.*) the president gave his adviser his marching orders (*coll.*); **er hat seiner Freundin den ~pass gegeben** (*ugs.*) he finished with his girlfriend (*coll.*); ~**pensum** *das* (*Sport*) **der Verteidiger bewältigte** *od.* **absolvierte ein ungeheures ~pensum** the defender never stopped running; ~**planke** *die* gangplank; gangway; ~**rad** *das* (*Technik*) Ⓐ (*des Fahrrads*) wheel; Ⓑ (*an Turbinen*) runner; ~**rolle** *die* (*Technik*) (*von Toren, Türen*) roller; (*von Panzern*) road wheel; (*von Möbeln*) castor; ~**schiene** *die* (*Technik*) track; rail; ~**schrift** *die* newscaster; ~**schritt** *der* Ⓐ **wir haben die ganze Strecke im ~schritt zurückgelegt** we ran all the way; **im ~schritt, marsch, marsch!** at the double, quick march!; Ⓑ (*Leichtathletik*) running step

**läufst** /lɔyfst/ *2. Pers. Sg. Präsens v.* **laufen**

**Lauf-:** ~**stall** *der* playpen; ~**steg** *der* catwalk

**läuft** /lɔyft/ *3. Pers. Sg. Präsens v.* **laufen**

**Lauf-:** ~**vogel** *der* (*Zool.*) ratite (*Zool.*); flightless bird; ~**werk** *das* (*Technik*) Ⓐ mechanism; Ⓑ (*Uhrwerk*) clockwork; mechanism; Ⓒ (*Eisenb.*) running gear; Ⓓ (*DV*) drive; ~**zeit** *die* Ⓐ term; **der Vertrag hatte eine ~zeit von zwei Jahren** the agreement ran for two years; **ein Kredit mit**

befristeter **~zeit** a limited-term loan; **B** (*Film, Theater*) run; **C** (*Sport*) time; **~zettel** *der* (*Bürow., Verwaltung*) **A** (*Rundschreiben*) circular; **B** (*Empfangsbestätigung*) distribution slip; circulation slip; **C** (*Passierschein*) pass; permit; **D** (*an Werkstücken*) work progress slip; control tag

**Lauge** /ˈlaugə/ *die;* ~, **~n** **A** soapy water; soapsuds; **B** (*Chemie*) alkaline solution

**Laugen·brezel** *die* (*südd.*) pretzel

**Lauheit** *die;* **~:** half-heartedness

**Lau·mann** *der* (*ugs. abwertend*) shilly-shallyer

**Laune** /ˈlaunə/ *die;* ~, **~n** **A** (*momentane Stimmung*) mood; **schlechte/gute ~ haben** be in a bad/good mood *or* temper; **[nicht] in** *od.* **bei ~ sein** [not] be in a good mood; **jmdn. bei guter ~ halten** keep sb. in a good mood; keep sb. happy (*coll.*); **bringt gute ~ mit!** come ready to enjoy yourselves; **B** (*wechselnde Stimmung*) mood; **sie hat nur selten ~n** she is rarely moody; **die ~n des Wetters/Zufalls** (*fig.*) the vagaries of the weather/of chance; **C** (*spontane Idee*) whim; **aus einer ~ heraus** on a whim; on the spur of the moment

**launenhaft** *Adj.* temperamental; (*unberechenbar*) capricious

**Launenhaftigkeit** *die;* **~:** moodiness; (*Unberechenbarkeit*) capriciousness

**launig** **1** *Adj.* witty. **2** *adv.* wittily

**launisch** *Adj.:* ⇒ **launenhaft**

**Laus** /laus/ *die;* ~, **Läuse** /ˈlɔyzə/ louse; **ihm ist eine ~ über die Leber gelaufen** (*ugs.*) he has got out of bed on the wrong side; **was ist ihm für eine ~ über die Leber gelaufen?** (*ugs.*) what's eating him? (*coll.*); **jmdm./sich eine ~ in den Pelz setzen** (*ugs.*) let sb./oneself in for something

**Laus·bub** *der* little rascal *or* devil; scamp

**Lausbuben·streich** *der* prank

**laus·bübisch** **1** *Adj.* impish. **2** *adv.* impishly

**Lausch·aktion** *die,* **Lausch·angriff** bugging operation (*coll.*)

**lauschen** /ˈlauʃn̩/ *itr. V.* **A** (*horchen*) listen (*so as to overhear sth.*); **an der Tür ~:** eavesdrop at the door; **B** (*zuhören*) listen [attentively]; **jmds. Worten** *usw.* **~:** listen [attentively] to sb.'s words *etc.*

**Lauscher** *der;* **~s,** ~ **A** eavesdropper; **der ~ an der Wand hört seine eigene Schand** (*Spr.*) eavesdroppers never hear any good of themselves; **B** (*Jägerspr.: Ohr*) ear

**Lauscherin** *die;* ~, **~nen** ⇒ **Lauscher** A

**lauschig** *Adj.* cosy, snug ‹corner›; **ein ~es Plätzchen im Grünen** a quiet *or* secluded spot in the country

**Lause-:** **~bengel,** **~junge,** **~lümmel** *der* (*salopp*) little rascal *or* devil; scamp

**lausen** *tr. V.* delouse; **ich denk, mich laust der Affe!** (*salopp*) well, I'll be damned *or* blowed!

**Lauser** *der;* **~s,** ~ (*landsch. ugs.*) little rascal *or* devil; scamp

**lausig** **1** *Adj.* (*ugs.*) **A** (*abwertend: unangenehm, schäbig*) lousy (*coll.*); rotten (*coll.*); **~e Zeiten** hard times; **B** (*sehr groß*) perishing (*Brit. sl.*), freezing ‹cold›; terrible (*coll.*), awful ‹heat›. **2** *adv.* terribly (*coll.*); awfully; **draußen ist es ~ kalt** it's perishing cold outside (*Brit. sl.*)

**laut**[1] /laut/ **1** *Adj.* **A** loud; (*fig.*) loud, garish ‹colour›; garish ‹advertisement›; **der Motor ist zu ~:** the engine is too noisy; **spreche ich jetzt ~ genug?** can you hear me now?; **er wusste sich ohne ein ~es Wort Respekt zu verschaffen** he was able to gain respect without raising his voice; **werden Sie bitte nicht ~!** there's no need to shout; **~ werden** (*fig.: bekannt werden*) be made known; **es sind Zweifel an der Gültigkeit dieser Aussage ~ geworden** doubts have been raised *or* expressed *or* voiced as to the validity of this statement; **B** (*geräuschvoll*) noisy.
**2** *adv.* **A** loudly; **~er sprechen** speak louder; speak up; **~ lachen** laugh out loud; **etw. nicht ~ sagen dürfen** not be allowed to say sth. out loud; **~ denken** think aloud; **das kannst du aber ~ sagen** (*ugs.*) you can say 'that again; **B** (*geräuschvoll*) noisily; **geht es hier immer so ~ zu?** is it always this noisy here?

**laut**[2] *Präp.* + *Gen. od. Dat.* (*Amtsspr.*) according to; (*gemäß*) in accordance with; **~ Vertrag** according to/in accordance with the contract

**Laut** *der;* **~[e]s, ~e** **A** (*Geräusch*) sound; **keinen ~ von sich geben** not make a sound; **~ geben** ‹dog, hound› give tongue; **B** (*sprachliche Einheit*) sound; **fremde/heimatliche ~e** sounds of a foreign/familiar tongue

**Laut·bildung** *die* (*Sprachw.*) articulation; formation of sounds

**Laute** *die;* ~, **~n** lute

**lauten** **1** *itr. V.* ‹answer, instruction, slogan› be, run; ‹letter, passage, etc.› read, go; ‹law› state; **die Anklage/das Urteil lautet auf ...** the charge/sentence is ...; **auf jmds. Namen** (*Akk.*) **~:** be in sb.'s name. **2** *tr. V.* (*Sprachw.: aussprechen*) pronounce

**läuten** /ˈlɔytn̩/ **1** *tr., itr. V.* ring; ‹alarm clock› go off; **12 Uhr/Mittag ~:** strike 12 o'clock/midday; **Feuer/Sturm ~** (*hist.*) ring the fire bell/storm bell; **ich habe davon ~ gehört** *od.* **hören, dass ...** I have heard rumours that ... **2** *itr. V.* (*bes. südd.: klingeln*) ring; **nach jmdm. ~:** ring for sb.; **es läutete** the bell rang *or* went (**zu** for)

**Lautenist** /lautəˈnɪst/ *der;* **~en, ~en, Lautenistin** *die;* ~, **~nen** ▶ **159** lutenist

**Lauten·spieler** *der,* **Lauten·spielerin** *die* lute player

**lauter**[1] *Adj.* (*geh.*) **A** honourable ‹person, intentions, etc.›; honest ‹truth›; **B** (*rein*) pure ‹gold, silver, etc.›; clear ‹water›

**lauter**[2] *indekl. Adj.* nothing but; sheer, pure ‹nonsense, joy, etc.›; **das sind ~ Lügen** that's nothing but lies; that's a pack of lies; **das sind ~ Kunden unserer Firma** they are all customers of our firm; **aus ~ kleinen Quadraten zusammengesetzt** made up entirely of little squares; **vor ~ Arbeit komme ich nicht ins Theater** I can't go to the theatre because of all the work I've got

**Lauterkeit** *die;* **~:** honourableness

**läutern** /ˈlɔytɐn/ *tr. V.* (*geh.*) **A** reform ‹character›; purify ‹soul›; **B** (*reinigen*) purify (**von** of)

**Läuterung** *die;* ~, **~en** (*geh.*) **A** (*des Charakters*) reformation; (*der Seele*) purification; **B** (*Reinigung*) purification

**laut-, Laut-:** **~gesetz** *das* (*Sprachw.*) phonetic law; **~getreu** **1** *Adj.* phonetically accurate; **2** *adv.* with phonetic accuracy; **~hals** *Adv.* ‹sing, shout, etc.› at the top of one's voice; **~hals lachen** roar with laughter

**Laut·lehre** *die* (*Sprachw.*) phonetics and phonology *no art.*

**lautlich** **1** *Adj.* phonetic. **2** *adv.* phonetically

**laut-, Laut-:** **~los** **1** *Adj.* silent; soundless; (*wortlos*) silent; **~lose Stille** utter *or* complete silence; **2** *adv.* silently; soundlessly; **~losigkeit** *die;* **~~:** silence; soundlessness; (*Wortlosigkeit*) silence; **~malend** *Adj.* (*Sprachw.*) onomatopoeic; **~schrift** *die* (*Phon.*) phonetic alphabet; (*Umschrift*) phonetic transcription

**Laut·sprecher** *der* loudspeaker; loud hailer (*esp. Naut.*); (*einer Stereoanlage usw.*) speaker; **über ~:** over the loudspeaker[s]

**Lautsprecher-:** **~an·lage** *die* public address *or* PA system; loudspeaker system; **~box** *die* speaker cabinet; **~wagen** *der* loudspeaker car/van

**laut-, Laut-:** **~stark** **1** *Adj.* loud; vociferous, loud ‹protest›; **2** *adv.* loudly; ‹protest› vociferously, loudly; **~stärke** *die* **A** volume; **in/bei voller ~stärke** at full volume; **das Radio auf volle ~stärke drehen** turn the radio right up; **B** (*Lärm*) **die ~stärke in diesem Raum** the volume of noise in this room; **~stärke·regler** *der* volume control

**Lautung** *die;* ~, **~en** (*Sprachw.*) pronunciation

**Laut-:** **~verschiebung** *die* (*Sprachw.*) sound shift; **die erste** *od.* **germanische/zweite** *od.* **hochdeutsche ~verschiebung** the first *or* Germanic/second *or* High German sound shift; **~wandel** *der* (*Sprachw.*) sound change

**Läut·werk** *das* **A** (*Eisenb.*) bell; **B** (*des Weckers*) alarm

**lau·warm** *Adj.* lukewarm ‹food›; lukewarm, tepid ‹drink›; (*nicht mehr kalt*) warm ‹beer etc.›

**Lava** /ˈla:va/ *die;* ~, **Laven** (*Geol.*) lava

**Lavabo** /laˈva:bo/ *das;* **~[s], ~s** (*schweiz.*) ⇒ **Waschbecken**

**Lava·strom** *der* lava stream; (*ausströmende Lava*) lava flow

**Lavendel** /laˈvɛndl̩/ *der;* **~s, ~:** lavender

**Lavendel·öl** *das* lavender oil

**lavieren**[1] /laˈvi:rən/ *tr. V., itr. V.* manœuvre

**lavieren**[2] *tr. V.* (*bild. Kunst*) wash; **eine lavierte Zeichnung** a wash drawing

**Lavoir** /laˈvo̯a:ɐ̯/ *das;* **~s, ~s** (*österr.*) ⇒ **Waschbecken**

**Lawine** /laˈvi:nə/ *die;* ~, **~n** (*auch fig.*) avalanche; **eine ~ von Protesten** (*fig.*) a storm of protest

**lawinen-, Lawinen-:** **~artig** *Adv.* like an avalanche; **~artig anschwellen** ‹political etc. movement, number of accidents etc.› snowball; **~gefahr** *die* danger of avalanches; **~[such-]hund** *der* avalanche dog

**lax** /laks/ **1** *Adj.* lax. **2** *adv.* laxly

**Laxativ** /laksaˈti:f/ *das;* **~s, ~e** (*Med.*) laxative

**Laxheit** *die;* **~:** laxness; laxity

**Lay-out** /leɪˈaʊt/ *das;* **~s, ~s** (*Druckw., Elektronik*) layout

**Layouter** /ˈle:|autɐ/ *der;* **~s,** ~, **Layouterin** *die;* ~, **~nen** layout artist

**Lazarett** /latsaˈrɛt/ *das;* **~[e]s** military hospital

**Lazarett·schiff** *das* hospital ship

**leasen** /ˈli:zn̩/ *tr. V.* rent; (*für längere Zeit mieten*) lease ‹car etc.›

**Leasing** /ˈli:zɪŋ/ *das;* **~s, ~s** (*Wirtsch.*) leasing

**Lebe-:** **~dame** *die* (*abwertend*) good-time girl; **~hoch** /--ˈ-/ *das* cheer; **ein dreifaches ~hoch** three cheers *pl.;* **~mann** *der* playboy

**leben** /ˈle:bn̩/ **1** *itr. V.* live; (*~dig sein*) be alive; **anständig/sorgenfrei ~:** live a respectable/carefree life; **auf dem Land/im Wasser ~de Tiere** animals which live on land/in water; **für jmdn./etw. ~** *od.* (*geh.*) **jmdm./einer Sache ~:** live for sb./sth.; **leb[e] wohl!** farewell!; **so [et]was lebt, und Schiller musste sterben!** (*scherzh.*) why do we have to put up with people like that?; **nicht mehr ~ wollen** not want to go on living; have lost the will to live; **er wird nicht mehr lange zu ~ haben** he will not live much longer; **lebst du noch?** (*ugs. scherzh.*) are you still in the land of the living? (*joc.*); **lang lebe der König!** long live the king!; **von seiner Rente/seinem Gehalt ~:** live on one's pension/salary; **von seiner Hände Arbeit ~:** live by the work of one's hands; **Wie geht es dir? — Man lebt!** (*ugs.*) How are you? — Oh, surviving (*coll.*); **~ und ~ lassen** live and let live; **davon kann ich/sie/er** *usw.* **nicht ~ und nicht sterben** it's hardly enough to keep body and soul together; **fleischlos ~:** not eat meat; **von Kartoffeln ~:** live on potatoes; **er lebt in seinen Werken** he lives on in his works; ⇒ *auch* **Brot**; **Diät**.
**2** *tr. V.* live; **ein glückliches Leben ~:** live a happy life

**Leben** *das;* **~s,** ~ **A** life; **das ~:** life; **jmdm. das ~ retten** save sb.'s life; **sein ~ für etw. wagen/** (*geh.*) **hingeben** risk/give one's life for sth.; **sich** (*Dat.*) **das ~ nehmen,** (*geh.*) **[freiwillig] aus dem ~ scheiden** take one's [own] life; **am ~ sein/bleiben** be/stay alive; **seines ~s nicht [mehr] sicher sein** not be safe [any more]; **um sein ~ rennen** run for one's life; **ums ~ kommen** lose one's life; **das nackte ~ retten** barely escape with one's life; **sein ~**

*old spelling (see note on page 1707)

**teuer verkaufen** sell one's life dearly; **seinem ~ ein Ende setzen** *od.* **machen** (*verhüll.*) take one's [own] life; **auf Tod und ~ kämpfen** be engaged in a life-and-death struggle; **etw. für sein ~ gern tun** love doing sth.; **etw. für sein ~ gern essen** love sth.; **etw. ins ~ rufen** bring sth. into being; **mit dem ~ davonkommen** escape with one's life; **jmdm. nach dem ~ trachten** try to kill sb.; **wie das blühende ~ aussehen** (*ugs.*) look the picture of health; **ein/sein [ganzes] ~ lang** one's whole life long; **zeit seines ~s** all his life; **noch nie im ~/zum ersten Mal im ~:** never in/for the first time in one's life; **jmdm. das ~ sauer machen** make sb.'s life a misery; **sich durchs ~ schlagen** struggle through life; **mit beiden Beinen** *od.* **Füßen im ~ stehen** have one's feet firmly on the ground; **nie im ~, im ~ nicht!** (*ugs.*) not on your life! (*coll.*); never in your life! (*coll.*); **ein ~ in Wohlstand/Armut** a life of affluence/poverty; **das süße ~:** la dolce vita; **wie das ~ so spielt** it's funny the way things turn out; **im öffentlichen ~ stehen** be in public life; **so ist das ~:** such is life; that's the way things go; **die Musik ist ihr ~:** music is her [whole] life; **B** (*Betriebsamkeit*) **auf dem Markt herrschte ein reges ~:** the market was bustling with activity; **das ~ auf der Straße** the comings and goings in the street; **~ ins Haus bringen** bring some life into the house

**lebend** *Adj.* living; live ‹animal›; **~e Sprachen** living languages; **tot oder ~:** dead or alive; **nicht mehr unter den Lebenden weilen** (*geh.*) have passed away

***lebend·gebärend** *Adj.* (*Zool.*) viviparous

**Lebend·gewicht** *das* **A** live weight; **B** (*scherzh.: Gewicht eines Menschen*) **100 kg ~ auf die Waage bringen** turn the scales at 100 kg

**lebendig** /le'bɛndɪç/ **1** *Adj.* **A** (*lebend*) living; **jmdn. ~** *od.* **bei ~em Leibe verbrennen** burn sb. alive; **man fühlt sich hier wie ~ begraben** being stuck here is like being buried alive (*coll.*); **ich kann ihn nicht wieder ~ machen** I can't bring him back to life [again]; **mehr tot als ~:** more dead than alive; **es von den Lebendigen nehmen** be unduly grasping; **B** (*wirksam*) living ‹tradition etc.›; **die Erinnerung daran wurde in ihm wieder ~:** the memory of it came back to him vividly; **C** (*lebhaft*) lively ‹account, imagination, child, etc.›; gay, bright ‹colours›; **auf der Straße wurde es allmählich ~:** the street began to fill with life.
**2** *adv.* (*lebhaft*) in a lively fashion *or* way; **etw. ~ schildern** give a lively description of sth.

**Lebendigkeit** *die;* **~:** liveliness

**lebens-, Lebens-: ~abend** *der* (*geh.*) evening *or* autumn of one's life (*literary*); **~abschnitt** *der* stage of *or* chapter in one's life; **~ader** *die* vital line of communication; **~alter** *das* age; **ein hohes ~alter erreichen** live to a considerable age *or* (*coll.*) a ripe old age; **~angst** *die* unwillingness to face life's problems; (*Angst um die Existenz*) worry about one's ability to survive; **~art** *die* **A** way of life; **B** (*Umgangsformen*) manners *pl.*; **keine ~art haben** have no manners; be ill-mannered; **~aufgabe** *die* life's work; **sich** (*Dat.*) **etw. zur ~aufgabe machen** make sth. one's life's work; **~baum** *der* **A** arbor vitae; **B** (*Rel., Kunstwiss.*) tree of life; **~bedingungen** *Pl.* conditions of life; **~bejahend** *Adj.* ‹person› with a positive attitude *or* approach to life; **~bejahung** *die* positive attitude *or* approach to life; affirmation of life; **~bereich** *der* area of life; **~beschreibung** *die* biography; (*Buch*) biography; life; **~dauer** *die* **A** lifespan; **B** (*von Maschinen*) [useful] life; **~echt** **1** *Adj.* true-to-life; **2** *adv.* in a true-to-life way; **~elixier** *das* (*Volksk.; auch fig.*) elixir of life; **~ende** *das* end [of one's life]; **bis an sein** *od.* **bis ans ~ende** to the end of one's life *or* days; **~erfahrung** *die* experience *no indef. art.* of life; **~erinnerungen** *Pl.* memories of one's life; (*aufgezeichnet*) memoirs; **~erwartung** *die* life expectancy; **~fähig** *Adj.* (*auch fig.*) viable; **~fähigkeit** *die* viability; **~form** *die* **A** (*Biol.*) life form; **B** (*~weise*) way of life; **~frage** *die* vital matter *or* question; **~fremd** *Adj.* out of touch with *or* remote from everyday life *postpos.*; **~freude** *die* zest for life; joie de vivre; **~froh** *Adj.* full of zest for life *or* joie de vivre *postpos.*; **~führung** *die* lifestyle; **eine moralisch einwandfreie ~führung** a completely blameless life; **~gefahr** *die* mortal danger; **für jmdn. besteht [keine] ~gefahr** sb.'s life is [not] in danger; **„Achtung, ~gefahr!"** 'danger'; **sie schwebt in ~gefahr** she is in danger of dying; (*von einer Kranken*) her condition is critical; **außer ~gefahr sein** be out of danger; **etw. unter ~gefahr** (*Dat.*) **tun** risk one's life to do sth.; **~gefährlich** **1** *Adj.* highly *or* extremely dangerous; critical ‹injury›; **2** *adv.* critically ‹injured, ill›; **jmdn. ~gefährlich verletzen** cause sb. critical injuries; **~gefährte** *der*, **~gefährtin** *die* (*geh.*) companion through life (*literary*); **~gefühl** *das* awareness of life; **~geister** *Pl.* **jmds. ~geister [wieder] wecken** put new life into sb.; **~gemeinschaft** *die* **A** (*von Menschen*) long-term relationship; **B** (*Biol.: von Tieren, Pflanzen*) biocoenosis; **~geschichte** *die* life story; **~groß** *Adj.* life-size; **~größe** *die:* **eine Statue in ~größe** a life-size statue; **ein Porträt von jmdm. in ~größe malen** paint a life-size portrait of sb.

**Lebens·haltung** *die* **A** (*~skosten*) cost of living; **die ~ ist teurer geworden** the cost of living has risen; **B** (*Lebensführung*) lifestyle

**Lebenshaltungs-: ~index** *der* (*Wirtsch.*) cost-of-living index; **~kosten** *Pl.* cost of living *sing.*

**lebens-, Lebens-: ~hilfe** *die* counselling; **~hunger** *der* desire to live life to the full; **~hungrig** *Adj.* ‹person› who is eager to live life to the full; **~inhalt** *der* purpose in life; **die Musik/ihre Familie ist ihr ~inhalt** music/her family is her whole life; **~jahr** *das* year of [one's] life; **die letzten ~jahre** the last years of one's life; one's last years; **in seinem 12. ~jahr** in his twelfth year; **mit dem vollendeten 18. ~jahr** on reaching the age of eighteen; **~kampf** *der* struggle for existence *or* life; **~kraft** *die* vitality; vital energy; **~kreis** *der:* **in jmds. ~kreis** (*Akk.*) **treten** come into *or* enter sb.'s life; **~künstler** *der*, **~künstlerin** *die:* **ein [echter/wahrer] ~künstler** a person who always knows how to make the best of things; **~lage** *die* situation [in life]; **in allen ~lagen** in any situation; **~lang** **1** *Adj.* lifelong; **2** *adv.* all one's life; **~länglich** **1** *Adj.* **~länglicher Freiheitsentzug** life imprisonment; **„~länglich" bekommen** *od.* (*ugs.*) **kriegen** get life imprisonment *or* (*coll.*) life; **2** *adv.* **jmdn. ~länglich gefangen halten** keep sb. imprisoned for life; **~längliche** *der/die; adj. Dekl.* (*salopp*) lifer (*coll.*); **~lauf** *der* **A** curriculum vitae; c.v.; **B** (*Verlauf eines ~*) life; **~licht** *das; Pl.* **~~er** (*geh.*) flame of life (*literary*); **jmdm. das ~licht ausblasen** *od.* **auspusten** (*ugs.*) send sb. to kingdom come (*coll.*); **~linie** *die* life line; **~lüge** *die* lifelong illusion; **~lust** *die* ⇒ **~freude**; **~lustig** *Adj.* ‹person› full of the joys of life; **~mitte** *die* middle years *pl.* of one's life; **die Krise in der ~mitte** midlife crisis

**Lebens·mittel** *das* food[stuff]; **~** *Pl.* food *sing.*; foods (*formal*); foodstuffs (*formal*); (*als Ware*) food *sing.*

**Lebensmittel-: ~abteilung** *die* food department; **~chemie** *die* food chemistry *no art.*; **~geschäft** *das* food shop; **~karte** *die* food ration card; **~vergiftung** *die* ▶ 474 (*Med.*) food poisoning

**lebens-, Lebens-: ~müde** *Adj.* weary of life *pred.*; **du bist wohl ~müde?** (*scherzh.*) you must be tired of living; **~müdigkeit** *die* weariness of life; **~mut** *der* courage to go on living; **~nah** **1** *Adj.* true-to-life ‹film, description, etc.›; **~naher Unterricht** teaching that is closely related to life; **2** *adv.* **etw. ~nah schildern** describe sth. in a true-to-life way; **~nerv** *der:* **eine Industrie/Firma in ihrem ~nerv treffen** hit a vital nerve of an industry/a firm; **~notwendig** *Adj.* essential; vital; vital ‹organ›; essential ‹foodstuff›

***leben·spendend** ⇒ **spenden B**

**lebens-, Lebens-: ~plan** *der* life plan; **so etwas wie einen ~plan hat sie nie gehabt** she has never planned her life; **~philosophie** *die* philosophy of life; (*Lehre*) life philosophy *no art.*; Lebensphilosophie *no art.*; **~qualität** *die* quality of life; **~raum** *der* **A** (*Umkreis*) lebensraum; **B** (*Biol.*) ⇒ **Biotop**; **~regel** *die* rule [of life]; maxim; **sich** (*Dat.*) **etw. zur ~regel machen** make sth. a rule [in life] *or* a maxim; **~retter** *der*, **~retterin** *die* rescuer; **sein ~retter** the person who saved his life; **du bist meine ~retterin** you saved my life; **~rhythmus** *der* rhythm of life; **sein ~rhythmus** the rhythm of his life; **~standard** *der* standard of living; **~stellung** *die* permanent position *or* job; job for life; **~stil** *der* lifestyle; **~tüchtig** *Adj.* able to cope with life *postpos.*; **~überdruss**, ***~überdruß** *der* weariness of life; world-weariness; **~umstände** *Pl.* circumstances; **~unfähig** *Adj.* non-viable; **~unterhalt** *der:* **seinen ~unterhalt verdienen/bestreiten** earn one's living/support oneself; **für jmds. ~unterhalt sorgen** support sb.; **~untüchtig** *Adj.* unable to cope with life *postpos.*; **~versicherung** *die* life insurance; life assurance; **eine ~versicherung abschließen** take out a life insurance *or* assurance policy; **~wandel** *der* way of life; **einen zweifelhaften/einwandfreien ~wandel führen** lead a dubious/an irreproachable life; **~weg** *der* [journey through] life; **jmdm. etw. mit auf den ~weg geben** give sb. sth. to take with him/her on his/her journey through life; **alles Gute für den weiteren ~weg** all the best for the future; **~weise** *die* way of life; **die sitzende ~weise** the sedentary life; **~weisheit** *die* **A** (*Erfahrung*) wisdom; **B** (*weiser Ausspruch*) wise saying *or* maxim; **~werk** *das* life's work; **~wert** *Adj.* **ein ~wertes Leben** a life worth living; **das ist kein ~wertes Dasein mehr** that's no kind of life any more; **das Leben ist ~wert** life is worth living; **~wert** *der* basic human value; **~wichtig** ⇒ **~notwendig**; **~wille** *der* will to live; **~zeichen** *das* sign of life; **kein ~zeichen [von sich] geben** show no sign of life; **kein ~zeichen von jmdm. bekommen** (*fig.*) have no sign of life from sb.; **~zeit** *die* life[span]; **auf ~zeit** for life; **ein Beamter auf ~zeit** an established civil servant; **~ziel** *das* aim in life; **~zweck** *der* purpose in life

**Leber** /'le:bɐ/ *die;* **~, ~n** ▶ 471 liver; **es an der ~ haben** (*ugs.*) have [got] liver trouble; **frisch** *od.* **frei von der ~ weg sprechen** *od.* **reden** (*ugs.*) speak one's mind; **sich** (*Dat.*) **etw. von der ~ reden** (*ugs.*) get sth. off one's chest (*coll.*); ⇒ *auch* Laus

**leber-, Leber-: ~blümchen** *das* liverwort; **~entzündung** *die* ▶ 474 inflammation of the liver; hepatitis (*Med.*); **~fleck** *der* liver spot; **~haken** *der* (*Boxen*) hook to the liver; **~käse** *der: meat loaf made with mincemeat, [minced liver,] eggs, and spices;* **~knödel** *der* (*südd., österr.*) *meat ball made from minced liver, onions, eggs, and flour;* **~krank** *Adj.* ‹patient etc.› suffering from a liver complaint *or* disorder; **~krank sein** have a liver complaint *or* disorder; **~krebs** *der* ▶ 474 (*Med.*) cancer of the liver; **~leiden** *das* ▶ 474 (*Med.*) liver complaint *or* disorder; **~pastete** *die* (*Kochk.*) liver pâté; **~schaden** *der* liver damage; damage to the liver; **~schrumpfung** *die;* **~~, ~~en** ⇒ **~zirrhose**; **~tran** *der* fish-liver oil; (*des Kabeljaus*) cod-liver oil; **~wurst** *die* liver sausage; **die gekränkte** *od.* **beleidigte ~wurst spielen** (*ugs.*) get all huffy (*coll.*); **~zirrhose** *die* ▶ 474 (*Med.*) cirrhosis of the liver

**Lebe-: ~welt** *die* playboy set; **~wesen** *das* living being *or* thing *or* creature; **einzellige ~wesen** single-celled creatures; unicellular organisms (*Biol.*); **~wohl** /--'-/ *das;* **~~[e]s, ~~** *od.* **~~e** (*geh.*) farewell; **jmdm. ~wohl sagen** bid sb. farewell

**lebhaft** ❶ *Adj.* Ⓐ (*lebendig*) lively ‹person, gesture, imagination, bustle, etc.›; lively, animated ‹conversation, discussion›; lively, brisk ‹activity›; busy ‹traffic›; brisk ‹business›; Ⓑ (*deutlich*) vivid ‹idea, picture, etc.›; **etw. in ~er Erinnerung haben** remember sth. vividly; Ⓒ (*kräftig*) lively ‹interest›; lively, gay ‹pattern›; bright, gay ‹colour›; vigorous ‹applause, opposition›. ❷ *adv.* Ⓐ (*lebendig*) in a lively way *or* fashion; **sich ~ unterhalten/~ diskutieren** have a lively *or* animated conversation/discussion; Ⓑ (*deutlich*) vividly; **sich ~ an etw.** (*Akk.*) **erinnern können** be able to remember sth. vividly; **sich** (*Dat.*) **etw. ~ vorstellen können** have a vivid picture of sth.; Ⓒ (*kräftig*) brightly, gaily ‹coloured›; gaily ‹patterned›; **etw. ~ bedauern** deeply regret sth.; **sich ~ für etw. interessieren** take a lively *or* keen interest in sth.

**Lebhaftigkeit** *die;* ~ Ⓐ (*reges Wesen*) liveliness; (*einer Unterhaltung, Diskussion*) liveliness; animation; Ⓑ (*Intensität*) liveliness; (*eines Musters*) liveliness; gaiety; (*von Farben*) brightness; gaiety

**Leb·kuchen** *der* ≈ gingerbread

**leb-, Leb-:** **~los** *Adj.* lifeless ‹body, eyes›; [**wie**] **~los daliegen** lie there as if dead; **~losigkeit** *die;* **~~:** lifelessness; **~tag** *der:* *in* [**all**] **mein/dein** *usw.* **~tag** (*ugs.*) all my/your *etc.* life; **so was habe ich mein ~tag nicht erlebt** (*ugs.*) I've never seen anything like it in all my life *or* in all my born days; **~zeiten** *Pl.: in* **bei** *od.* **zu ~zeiten** while still alive; **bei** *od.* **zu jmds. ~zeiten** while sb. is/was still alive; during sb.'s lifetime

**lechzen** /ˈlɛçtsn̩/ *itr. V.* (*geh.*) **nach einem Trunk/nach Kühlung ~:** long for a drink/to be able to cool off; **nach Rache/Macht** *usw.* **~:** thirst for revenge/power *etc.*

**Lecithin** /letsiˈtiːn/ ⇒ **Lezithin**

**leck** /lɛk/ *Adj.* leaky; **~ sein** leak

**Leck** *das;* **~[e]s, ~s** leak

**Lecke** /ˈlɛkə/ ⇒ **Salzlecke**

**lecken¹** ❶ *tr. V.* lick; **sich** (*Dat.*) **die Wunden/Lippen** *usw.* **~:** lick one's wounds/lips *etc.*; **jmdm. die Hand** *usw.* **~:** lick sb.'s hand *etc.*; **sich** (*Dat.*) **etw. von etw. ~:** lick sth. off sth.; **leck mich [doch]!** (*derb*) [why don't you] piss off! (*sl.*); ⇒ *auch* **Arsch** A; **Finger** B. ❷ *itr. V.* **an etw.** (*Dat.*) **~:** lick sth.

**lecken²** *itr. V.* (*leck sein*) leak

**lecker** *Adj.* tasty ‹meal›; delicious ‹cake etc.›; good ‹smell, taste›; (*fig.: ansprechend*) lovely ‹girl›; **hier riecht es aber ~:** there's a delicious smell around here

**Lecker·bissen** *der* delicacy; **ein musikalischer ~** (*fig.*) a musical treat

**Leckerei** *die;* **~, ~en** (*ugs.*) dainty; (*Süßigkeit*) sweet [meat]

**Lecker-:** **~maul** *das,* **~mäulchen** *das;* **~~s, ~~:** **ein ~maul** *od.* **~mäulchen sein** have a sweet tooth

**leck|schlagen** *unr. itr. V.; mit sein* (*Seemannsspr.*) be holed

**led.** *Abk.* **ledig**

**Leder** /ˈleːdɐ/ *das;* **~s, ~** Ⓐ leather; **in ~ [gebunden]** leather-bound; **ein Gürtel aus ~:** a leather belt; **zäh wie ~ sein** be as tough as leather; ‹person› be as hard as nails; **jmdm. ans ~ gehen/wollen** (*ugs.*) go for sb./be out to get sb.; **gegen jmdn./etw. vom ~ ziehen** (*ugs.*) speak one's mind about sb./sth.; Ⓑ (*Fenster~*) leather; chamois *or* chammy [leather]; Ⓒ (*Fußballjargon: Ball*) ball; leather (*dated sl.*)

**leder-, Leder-:** **~artig** *Adj.* leathery; leather-like ‹material›; **~band** *der* leather-bound volume; **~fetischist** *der,* **~fetischistin** *die* leather fetishist; **~garnitur** *die* leather-upholstered suite; **~handschuh** *der* leather glove; **~haut** *die* ▶471 (*Anat., Zool.*) dermis; **~hose** *die* leather shorts *pl.;* lederhosen *pl.;* (*lang*) leather trousers; **~jacke** *die* leather jacket; **~mantel** *der* leather [over]coat

**ledern¹** *tr. V.* leather

**ledern²** *Adj.* Ⓐ (*aus Leder*) leather; Ⓑ (*wie Leder*) leathery

*old spelling (see note on page 1707)

**Leder-:** **~nacken** *der* leatherneck (*sl.*); **~riemen** *der* [leather] strap; **~schuh** *der* leather shoe; **~schurz** *der* leather apron; **~sessel** *der* leather[-upholstered] armchair; **~sohle** *die* leather sole; **~waren** *Pl.* leather goods

**ledig** /ˈleːdɪç/ *Adj.* Ⓐ (*nicht verheiratet*) unmarried; single; **eine ~e Mutter** an unmarried mother; Ⓑ *in* **einer Sache** (*Gen.*) **~ sein** (*geh.*) be free of sth.

**Ledige** *der/die; adj. Dekl.* single person

**lediglich** *Adv.* only; merely; simply

**Lee** /leː/ *die od. das;* **~** (*Seemannsspr.*) **nach ~ drehen** turn to leeward; **in ~ liegen** lie to leeward

**leer** /leːɐ̯/ *Adj.* Ⓐ empty; blank, clean ‹sheet of paper›; **die Kasse ist ~** (*ugs.*) there's no money left; **sein Glas ~ trinken** empty *or* drain one's glass; **seinen Teller ~ essen** clear one's plate; **die Schachtel ~ machen** (*ugs.*) finish the box; **den Laden/die Regale ~ kaufen** strip every shelf in the shop/strip the shelves bare; **die Warnungen gingen ins Leere** the warnings fell on deaf ears; **~ ausgehen** come away empty-handed; **~ laufen** ‹machine› idle; ‹business› be at a standstill; ‹barrel etc.› run dry; **die Badewanne läuft ~:** the bathwater is running out: **der Tank lief ~:** the oil/wine *etc.* was running *or* draining out of the tank; **jmdn. ~ laufen lassen** (*Ballspiele*) send sb. the wrong way; sell sb. a dummy (*coll.*); Ⓑ (*menschenleer*) empty; empty, deserted ‹streets›; **vor ~en Bänken spielen** play to an empty house/empty houses; **die Wohnung steht ~:** the house is standing empty *or* is unoccupied; **~ stehend** empty, unoccupied ‹house, flat›; [**wie**] **~ gefegt** deserted; Ⓒ (*abwertend: oberflächlich*) empty ‹words, promise, talk, display›; vacant ‹expression›; **mit ~en Augen/~em Blick starren** stare vacantly

**Leere** *die;* **~** (*auch fig.*) emptiness; **eine gähnende ~:** a gaping void; **im Restaurant/Theatersaal herrschte ~:** the restaurant/theatre was completely empty; **eine innere ~** (*fig.*) a feeling of emptiness inside

**leeren** ❶ *tr. V.* Ⓐ empty; empty, clear ‹postbox›; Ⓑ (*österr.: gießen*) pour ‹water, milk, etc.›; empty ‹bucket›. ❷ *refl. V.* ‹hall, theatre, etc.› empty

**leer-, Leer-:** **~formel** *die* (*geh.*) empty formula; ***~gefegt** ⇒ **leer** B; **~gewicht** *das* unladen weight; **~gut** *das* empties *pl.;* **~lauf** *der* Ⓐ **im ~lauf den Berg hinunterfahren** ‹driver› coast down the hill in neutral; ‹cyclist› freewheel *or* coast down the hill; **eine Maschine auf ~lauf stellen** let a machine idle; Ⓑ (*fig.*) **es gab [viel] ~lauf im Büro** there were [long] slack periods in the office; **zwischen den Hauptdarbietungen gab es viel ~lauf** between the main acts there were long periods when nothing happened; ***~|laufen** ⇒ **leer** A; **~packung** *die* dummy; display package; ***~stehend** ⇒ **leer** B; **~taste** *die* space bar

**Leerung** *die;* **~, ~en** emptying; **die ~ der Mülltonnen erfolgt einmal wöchentlich** the dustbins are emptied once a week; **nächste ~ um 12 Uhr** (*auf Briefkästen*) next collection at 12.00

**Lefze** /ˈlɛftsə/ *die;* **~, ~n** lip; **die ~n eines Jagdhundes** the flews of a hound

**legal** /leˈgaːl/ ❶ *Adj.* legal; **auf ~em Wege** by legal means; legally. ❷ *adv.* legally

**legalisieren** *tr. V.* legalize

**Legalität** /legaliˈtɛːt/ *die;* **~:** legality; **außerhalb der ~:** outside the law; **am Rande der ~:** just within the bounds of legality

**Legalitäts·prinzip** *das* (*Rechtsw.*): *principle that all complaints must be investigated and that, where an offence appears to have been committed, a charge must be brought*

**Legasthenie** /legasteˈniː/ *die;* **~, ~n** (*Psych., Med.*) difficulty in learning to read and write

**Legastheniker** /legasˈteːnikɐ/ *der;* **~s, ~,** **Legasthenikerin** *die;* **~, ~nen** (*Psych., Med.*) one who has difficulty with reading and writing

**Legat¹** /leˈgaːt/ *der;* **~en, ~en** (*kath. Kirche*) legate

**Legat²** *das;* **~[e]s, ~e** (*Rechtsw.*) legacy

**Legations·rat** /legaˈtsi̯oːns-/ *der,* **Legations·rätin** *die* counsellor

**legato** /leˈgaːto/ *Adv.* (*Musik*) legato

**Lege-:** **~batterie** *die* laying battery; **~henne** *die* laying hen

**Legel** /ˈleːgl̩/ *der od. das;* **~s, ~** (*Seemannsspr.*) Ⓐ (*aus Tauwerk*) cringle; Ⓑ (*aus Holz*) mast hoop

**legen** /ˈleːgn̩/ ❶ *tr. V.* Ⓐ lay [down]; **jmdn. auf den Rücken ~:** lay sb. on his/her back; **einen Gegenspieler ~** (*Sportjargon*) bring down an opposing player; **etw. auf den Tisch/Boden ~:** lay sth. on the table/floor; **etw. aus der Hand ~:** put sth. down; **etw. in Spiritus ~:** preserve sth. in alcohol; **etw. beiseite ~:** put sth. aside *or* down; **das Fleisch in den Kühlschrank ~:** put the meat in the refrigerator; **die Hand an die Mütze ~:** raise one's hand to one's cap; **die Füße auf den Tisch ~:** put one's feet on the table; **etw. auf den Abend ~:** arrange sth. for the evening; Ⓑ (*ver~*) lay ‹pipe, cable, railway track, carpet, tiles, etc.›; plant ‹potatoes›; ⇒ *auch* **Fundament** A; **Grundstein**; **Karte** G; Ⓒ (*in eine bestimmte Form bringen*) **etw. in Falten ~:** fold sth.; **sich** (*Dat.*) **die Haare ~ lassen** have one's hair set; ⇒ *auch* **Falte** C; Ⓓ (*schräg hinstellen*) lean; **etw. an etw.** (*Akk.*) **~:** lean sth. [up] against sth.

❷ *tr., itr. V.* ‹hen› lay; **die Hühner ~ fleißig/schlecht** the hens are laying/not laying well.

❸ *refl. V.* Ⓐ lie down; **sich auf etw.** (*Akk.*) **~:** lie down on sth.; **sich in die Sonne ~:** lie in the sun; **das Schiff/Flugzeug legte sich auf die Seite** the ship keeled over/the aircraft banked steeply; **sich in die Kurve ~:** lean into the bend; ⇒ *auch* **Bett** A; **Ohr** B; Ⓑ (*nachlassen*) ‹wind, storm› die down, abate, subside; ‹noise› die down, abate; ‹enthusiasm› wear off, subside, fade; ‹anger› abate, subside; ‹excitement› die down, subside; Ⓒ (*sich herabsenken*) **sich auf** *od.* **über etw.** (*Akk.*) **~** ‹mist, fog› descend *or* settle on sth., [come down and] blanket sth.

**legendär** /legɛnˈdɛːɐ̯/ *Adj.* legendary

**Legende** /leˈgɛndə/ *die;* **~, ~n** Ⓐ legend; **zur ~ werden** (*fig.*) ‹event, incident, etc.› become legendary; **[schon zu Lebzeiten] zur ~ werden** (*fig.*) ‹person› become a legend [in one's own lifetime]; Ⓑ (*Zeichenerklärung*) legend; key

**legenden·umwoben** *Adj.* ‹person, figure, etc.› surrounded by legends

**leger** /leˈʒeːɐ̯/ ❶ *Adj.* Ⓐ (*ungezwungen*) casual; relaxed; (*oberflächlich*) casual; Ⓑ (*bequem*) casual ‹jacket etc.›. ❷ *adv.* Ⓐ (*ungezwungen*) casually; in a casual *or* relaxed manner; (*oberflächlich*) casually; Ⓑ (*bequem*) ‹dress› casually

**Leg·henne** /ˈleːk-/ *die* ⇒ **Legehenne**

**legieren** /leˈgiːrən/ *tr. V.* Ⓐ alloy; **Kupfer mit Zinn ~:** alloy copper and tin; Ⓑ (*Kochk.*) thicken

**Legierung** *die;* **~, ~en** alloy

**Legion** /leˈgi̯oːn/ *die;* **~, ~en** Ⓐ (*Milit.*) legion; (*Fremden~*) Legion; Ⓑ (*Menge*) horde (**von** of); **~ sein** (*geh.*) be legion

**Legionär** /legi̯oˈnɛːɐ̯/ *der;* **~s, ~e** legionary

**Legionärs·krankheit** *die* ▶474 (*Med.*) legionnaire's disease

**legislativ** /legɪslaˈtiːf/ ❶ *Adj.* (*Politik*) legislative. ❷ *adv.* by legislation

**Legislative** /legɪslaˈtiːvə/ *die;* **~, ~n** (*Politik*) legislature

**Legislatur** /legɪslaˈtuːɐ̯/ *die;* **~, ~en** Ⓐ legislature; Ⓑ ⇒ **Legislaturperiode**

**Legislatur·periode** *die* (*Politik*) parliamentary term; legislative period; (*Amtsdauer einer Regierung*) term of office

**legitim** /legiˈtiːm/ ❶ *Adj.* legitimate. ❷ *adv.* legitimately

**Legitimation** /legitimaˈtsi̯oːn/ *die;* **~, ~en** Ⓐ (*auch Rechtsw.: Ehelicherklärung*) legitimation; Ⓑ (*Ausweis*) proof of identity; (*Bevollmächtigung*) authorization

**legitimieren** ❶ *tr. V.* Ⓐ (*rechtfertigen*) justify; Ⓑ (*bevollmächtigen*) authorize; Ⓒ (*für *legitim erklären*) legitimize ‹child, relationship›. **❷** *refl. V.* show proof of one's identity

**Legitimität** /legitimi'tɛ:t/ *die;* **~:** legitimacy; (*Rechtfertigung*) justification

**Leguan** /le'gu̯a:n/ *der;* **~s, ~e** (*Zool.*) iguana

**Lehen** /'le:ən/ *das;* **~s, ~** (*hist.*) fief; **jmdm. etw. zu ~ geben** grant sb. sth. in fee

**Lehm** /le:m/ *der;* **~s** loam; (*Ton*) clay

**lehm-, Lehm-: ~bau** *der; Pl.* **~~ten** clay *or* mud building; **~bau·weise** *die* building with clay; (**~***flechtwerk*) wattle and daub construction; **~boden** *der* loamy soil; (*Tonerde*) clay soil; **~farben, ~farbig** *Adj.* clay-coloured; **~grube** *die* clay pit; **~haltig** *Adj.* loamy; (*tonartig*) clayey; **~hütte** *die* mud hut

**lehmig** *Adj.* loamy ‹soil, earth›; (*tonartig*) clayey ‹soil, shoes, etc.›

**Lehm·ziegel** *der* clay brick

**Lehn** /le:n/ ⇒ **Lehen**

**Lehn-:~bedeutung** *die* loan-meaning; **~bildung** *die* loan-formation

**Lehne** /'le:nə/ *die;* **~, ~n** **A** (*Rücken~*) back; (*Arm~*) arm; **B** (*südd., österr., schweiz.: Abhang*) slope

**lehnen** **❶** *tr. V.* lean (**an** + *Akk.*, **gegen** against); **den Kopf/Arm an etw.** (*Akk.*) **~:** lean one's head/arm on sth. **❷** *refl. V.* lean (**an** + *Akk.*, **gegen** against; **über** + *Akk.* over); **sich aus dem Fenster ~:** lean out of the window; **sich zu weit aus dem Fenster ~** (*fig.*) stick one's neck out (*coll.*); go too far. **❸** *itr. V.* be leaning (**an** + *Dat.* against)

**Lehns·dienst** *der* (*hist.*) feudal service *no pl.*, *no art.*

**Lehn·sessel** *der* armchair

**Lehns-:~frau** *die* vassal; **~herr** *der* feudal lord; **~herrin** *die* feudal lady; **~mann** *der; Pl.* **~männer** *od.* **~leute** vassal; **~pflicht** *die* feudal duty

**Lehn·stuhl** *der* armchair

**Lehns·wesen** *das* (*hist.*) system of feudal tenure; feudal system

**Lehn-: ~übersetzung** *die* loan translation; **~wort** *das; Pl.* **~wörter** loanword

**Lehr-: ~amt** *das* (*Schulw.*) teaching post; (*Beruf*) **das ~amt** the teaching profession; **das höhere ~amt** *teaching at Gymnasien or vocational schools;* **~amts·anwärter** *der,* **~amts·anwärterin** *die* (*Schulw.*) trainee primary-school teacher; **~amts·kandidat** *der,* **~amts·kandidatin** *die* trainee grammar-school teacher/vocational school teacher; **~anstalt** *die* (*Amtsspr.*) educational establishment; **höhere ~anstalt** (*veralt.*) secondary education establishment; **~auftrag** *der* lectureship (*not giving full status as member of a department or as a permanent civil servant*); **~beauftragte** *der/die* lecturer (*not having full status as member of a department or as a permanent civil servant*); **~befähigung** *die* (*Amtsspr.*) teaching qualification; **~behelf** *der* (*österr.*) ⇒ **~mittel**; **~berechtigung** *die* teaching qualification; **~beruf** *der* **A** ⇒ **Ausbildungsberuf**; **B** (*Lehrerberuf*) **der ~beruf** the teaching profession; **den ~beruf ausüben** teach; be a teacher/teachers; **~betrieb** *der* teaching programme; **~bub** *der* (*südd., österr., schweiz.*) ⇒ **~junge**; **~buch** *das* textbook; **~dichtung** *die* (*Literaturw.*) **A** didactic poetry; **B** (*Gedicht*) didactic poem

**Lehre**[1] /'le:rə/ *die;* **~, ~n** **A** (*Berufsausbildung*) apprenticeship; **eine ~ machen** serve an apprenticeship (**als** as); **bei einem Handwerker in die ~ gehen** be apprenticed to a craftsman; **bei jmdm. in die ~ gegangen sein** (*fig.*) have learnt a lot from sb.; **B** (*Weltanschauung*) doctrine; **die christliche ~:** Christian doctrine; **die ~ Kants/Hegels/Buddhas** the teachings *pl.* of Kant/Hegel/Buddha; **C** (*Theorie, Wissenschaft*) theory; **die ~ vom Schall** the science of sound *or* acoustics; **D** (*Erfahrung*) lesson; **lass dir das eine ~ sein!** let that be a lesson to you; **jmdm. eine [heilsame] ~ erteilen** teach sb. a [salutary] lesson; **aus etw. seine ~ ziehen** learn one's lesson from sth.; **E** (*Verhaltensregel*) precept

**Lehre**[2] *die;* **~, ~n** (*Bauw., Technik*) gauge

**lehren** *tr., itr. V.* teach; **jmdn. lesen/schreiben ~:** teach sb. to read/write; **ich bin das gelehrt worden** I was taught that; **ich werde dich ~, so bockig zu sein!** (*ugs.*) I'll teach you to be so contrary (*coll.*); **die Geschichte lehrt, dass ...** history teaches *or* shows us that ...; **erst die Zukunft wird uns ~, ...** time alone will tell ...

**Lehrende** *der/die; adj. Dekl.* (*Hochschulw.*) **~ und Lernende** teaching staff and students

**Lehrer** *der;* **~s, ~** ▶ **159** **A** (*auch fig.*) teacher; **er ist ~ für Geschichte** he teaches history; he is a history teacher; **B** (*Ausbilder*) instructor

**-lehrer** *der;* **~s, ~: Türkisch~/Ski~:** teacher of Turkish/skiing instructor; **unser Französisch~:** our French teacher

**lehrer-, Lehrer-: ~aus·bildung** *die* teacher training *no art.;* **~haft** *Adj.* (*abwertend*) schoolmasterly; (*von Frauen*) schoolmarmish (*coll.*)

**Lehrerin** *die;* **~, ~nen** ▶ **159** teacher; ⇒ *auch* **-in**; **Lehrer**; **-lehrer**

**Lehrer-: ~kollegium** *das* teaching staff; faculty (*Amer.*); **~mangel** *der* shortage of teachers

**Lehrerschaft** *die;* **~, ~en** teachers *pl.;* (*einer Schule*) teaching staff; faculty (*Amer.*)

**Lehrer-: ~schwemme** *die* (*ugs.*) glut of teachers; **~zimmer** *das* staffroom

**Lehr-: ~fach** *das* **A** subject; **B** (*Beruf des Lehrens*) teaching profession; **im ~fach tätig sein** be a teacher; be in teaching; **~film** *der* educational film; **~freiheit** *die* academic freedom *no art.;* **~gang** *der* course (**für, in** + *Dat.* in); **einen ~gang machen, an einem ~gang teilnehmen** take a course; **~gebäude** *das* (*geh.*) **das hegelsche ~gebäude** the edifice of Hegelian teachings; **~gegenstand** *der* (*österr.*) ⇒ **~fach** A; **~geld** *das* **A** (*hist.*) apprenticeship premium; **B** (*fig.*) **du kannst dir dein ~geld zurückgeben lassen!** your education was wasted on you; **~geld geben** *od.* **[be]zahlen [müssen]** learn the hard way

**lehrhaft** *Adj.* (*belehrend*) instructive; didactic ‹intention›

**Lehr-: ~herr** *der* (*geh. veralt.*) (master *of an apprentice*); **~jahr** *das* year as an apprentice; **sie ist im zweiten ~jahr** she is in the second year of her apprenticeship; **~jahre sind keine Herrenjahre** (*Spr.*) we all have to start at the bottom of the ladder; **~junge** *der* apprentice; **~kanzel** *die* (*österr.*) ⇒ **~stuhl**; **~körper** *der* (*Amtsspr.*) teaching staff; faculty (*Amer.*); **~kraft** *die* teacher

**Lehrling** /'le:ɐ̯lɪŋ/ *der;* **~s, ~e** ▶ **159** apprentice; (*in kaufmännischen Berufen*) trainee

**Lehrlings-: ~aus·bildung** *die* training of apprentices; **~heim** *das* apprentices' hostel

**lehr-, Lehr-: ~mädchen** *das* [girl] apprentice; (*in kaufmännischen Berufen*) [girl] trainee; **~meinung** *die* (*geh.*) [expert] opinion; **~meister** *der,* **~meisterin** *die* teacher; (*Vorbild*) mentor; **~methode** *die* teaching method; **~mittel** *das* (*Schulw.*) teaching aid; **~mittel** *Pl.* teaching materials; **~mittel·freiheit** *die* (*Schulw.*) free provision of teaching materials; **~pfad** *der* trail; (*Naturpfad*) nature trail; **~plan** *der* (*Schulw.*) syllabus; (*Gesamtlehrgang*) curriculum; **~probe** *die* (*Schulw.*) teaching practice; **eine ~probe geben** *od.* **machen** do a teaching practice; **~reich** *Adj.* instructive, informative ‹book, film, etc.›; **es war eine ~reiche Erfahrung für ihn** the experience taught him a lot; **~satz** *der* proposition; (*in der Geometrie, Logik*) theorem; **die euklidischen ~sätze** the propositions of Euclid; **~schwimmbecken** *das* learners' [swimming] pool; **~stelle** *die* apprenticeship; (*in kaufmännischen Berufen*) trainee post; **~stoff** *der* (*Schulw.*) syllabus; **~stück** *das* (*Literaturw.*) didactic play; **~stuhl** *der* (*Hochschulw.*) chair (**für** of); **~stuhl·inhaber** *der,* **~stuhl·inhaberin** *die* holder of a/the chair; **~veranstaltung** *die* (*Hochschulw.*) class; (*Vorlesung*) lecture; **~vertrag** *der* indentures *pl.;* **~werk** *das* course; (*Buch*) textbook; **~werkstatt** *die* apprentices' *or* training workshop; **~zeit** *die* [period of] apprenticeship

**Leib** /laip/ *der;* **~[e]s, ~er** (*geh.*) **A** body; **ich hatte keinen trockenen Faden mehr am ~[e]** I was wet through *or* soaked to the skin; **am ganzen ~ zittern** shiver all over; **bleib mir vom ~[e]!** keep away from me!; keep your distance!; **der ~ Christi/des Herrn** (*christl. Rel.*) the Body of Christ; **etw. am eigenen ~ erfahren** *od.* **erleben** experience sth. for oneself; **er hat sich mit ~ und Seele der Musik verschrieben** he dedicated himself heart and soul to music; **mit ~ und Seele Arzt/Krankenschwester** *usw.* **sein** be a dedicated doctor/nurse *etc.;* **mit ~ und Seele dabei sein** put one's whole heart into it; **jmdm. auf den ~** *od.* **zu ~e rücken** (*ugs.*) chivvy sb.; (*mit Kritik*) get at sb. (*coll.*); **jmdm. so zu ~e rücken, dass ...** go on at sb. until ...(*coll.*); **sich** (*Dat.*) **jmdn. vom ~e halten** (*ugs.*) keep sb. at arm's length; **jmdm. mit einer Sache vom ~e bleiben** (*ugs.*) not pester sb. with sth.; **einer Sache** (*Dat.*) **zu ~e gehen** *od.* **rücken** tackle sth.; set about sth.; **jmdm. auf den ~ geschnitten sein** be tailor-made for sb.; suit sb. down to the ground; **die Rolle ist ihm [wie] auf den ~ geschrieben** the part could have been written for him; (*fig.*) the role fits him like a glove; **was hast du für einen Ton am ~?** (*salopp*) what a way to talk!; ⇒ *auch* **lebendig** 1 A; **B** (*geh., fachspr.: Bauch*) belly; (*Magen*) stomach; **gesegneten ~es sein** (*veralt.*) be with child (*dated*); **C** (*veralt.*) **~ und Gut wagen/hingeben** risk/give one's all; **eine Gefahr für ~ und Leben** a danger to life and limb; **~ und Leben opfern** sacrifice one's life

**Leib-: ~arzt** *der,* **~ärztin** *die* personal physician; **~binde** *die* [warm] body belt

**Leibchen** /'laipçən/ *das;* **~s, ~** **A** (*Trachten~*) bodice; **B** (*landsch.: Unterhemd*) vest (*Brit.*); undershirt (*Amer.*)

**leib-, Leib-: ~diener** *der* valet; **~dienerin** *die* personal servant; **~eigen** *Adj.* (*hist.*) in serfdom *postpos.;* **~eigene** *der/die; adj. Dekl.* (*hist.*) serf; (*fig.*) slave; **~eigenschaft** *die* (*hist.*) serfdom *no def. art.*

**leiben** *itr. V. in* **wie er/sie** *usw.* **leibt und lebt** to a T

**Leibes-: ~ertüchtigung** *die* (*veralt.*) keeping fit *or* in trim *no art.;* physical training *no art.;* **~erziehung** *die* (*Schulw.*) physical education; PE; **~frucht** *die* (*Med.*) embryo; (*nach 8 Wochen*) foetus; (*Rechtsspr.*) unborn child; **~fülle** *die* (*geh.*) corpulence; (*Umfang*) girth; **~kräfte** *Pl. in* **aus** *od.* **nach ~kräften** with all one's might; **aus ~kräften schreien** shout for all one is worth; **~übungen** *Pl.* (*Schulw.*) physical education *sing.;* PE; **~visitation** /-vizitatsi̯o:n/ *die;* **~~, ~~en** body search

**Leib-: ~garde** *die* bodyguard; **die ~garde der Königin** (*in Großbritannien*) the Queen's Life Guards *pl.;* **~gardist** *der* [member of the/a] bodyguard; (*der britischen Monarchen*) Life Guard; **~gericht** *das* favourite dish

**leibhaftig** /laip'haftɪç/ **❶** *Adj.* **A** (*persönlich*) in person *postpos.;* **da stand er ~ vor uns** there he was, as large as life; **der ~e Beweis dafür, dass ...** the living proof that ...; **B** (*echt*) real; **ein ~er Herzog** a real live duke; **der ~e Teufel,** (*scherzh.*) **der Leibhaftige** the devil incarnate. **❷** *adv.* (*ugs.*) actually; believe it or not

**leiblich** *Adj.* **A** physical ‹well-being›; **B** (*blutsverwandt*) real ‹mother, parents, etc.›; **er liebte ihn wie seinen ~en Sohn** he loved him like his own son

**Leib-: ~rente** *die* life annuity; **~riemen** *der* (*veralt.*) belt; **~schmerzen** *Pl.* abdominal pain *sing.;* **~speise** *die* ⇒ **~gericht**; **~wache** *die* bodyguard; **~wächter** *der,* **~wächterin** *die* bodyguard; **~wäsche** *die* underwear; underclothes *pl.*

**Leiche** /ˈlaiçə/ *die;* ~, ~**n** A [dead] body; (*bes. eines Unbekannten*) corpse; **er sieht aus wie eine lebende** *od.* **wandelnde** ~ (*salopp*) he looks like death warmed up (*coll.*); **nur über meine** ~! over my dead body!; **über** ~**n gehen** (*abwertend*) be utterly ruthless *or* unscrupulous; **um seine Interessen durchzusetzen, geht er über** ~**n** he will stick at nothing to attain his own ends; **eine** ~ **im Keller haben** (*fig. ugs.*) have a skeleton in the cupboard; B (*landsch. veralt.: Begräbnis*) funeral; C (*Druckw.*) out (*Printing*); omission

**leichen-, Leichen-:** ~**begängnis** *das;* ~~**ses**, ~~**se** (*geh.*) funeral; ~**beschauer** *der,* ~**beschauerin** *die* ▶159 *doctor who performs a postmortem;* autopsist (*Amer.*); ~**bestatter** *der,* ~**bestatterin** *die* ▶159 undertaker; mortician (*Amer.*); ~**bitter·miene** *die* (*iron.*) doleful expression; ~**blass**, *~**blaß** *Adj.* deathly pale; white as a sheet *postpos.;* ~**fledderei** *die;* ~~, ~~**en** (*Rechtsw.*) *robbery of a dead or unconscious person;* ~**fledderer** *der;* ~~**s**, ~~, ~**fledderin** *die;* ~~, ~~**nen** (*Rechtsw.*) *one who robs a dead or unconscious person;* ~**frau** *die* layer-out; ~**halle** *die* mortuary; ~**hemd** *das* burial garment; ~**öffnung** *die* postmortem *or* autopsy (*with dissection*); ~**rede** *die* (*geh.*) funeral oration; ~**schänder** *der;* ~~**s**, ~~, ~**schänderin** *die;* ~~, ~~**nen** desecrator of a/the corpse; (*sexuell*) necrophiliac; ~**schändung** *die* desecration of a corpse; (*sexuell*) necrophilia *no art.;* **der zweite Schlag ist** ~**schändung** (*salopp, scherzh.*) these fists are lethal weapons (*joc.*); ~**schau** *die* postmortem; autopsy; ~**schau·haus** *das* morgue; ~**schmaus** *der* (*scherzh.*) funeral meal; ~**starre** *die* rigor mortis; ~**tuch** *das; Pl.* ~**tücher** (*veralt.*) winding sheet; shroud; ~**verbrennung** *die* cremation; ~**wagen** *der* hearse; ~**wäscher** *der;* ~~**s**, ~~, ~**wäscherin** *die: person who washes corpses for burial;* ~**zug** *der* (*geh.*) cortège; funeral procession

**Leichnam** /ˈlaiçna:m/ *der;* ~**s**, ~**e** (*geh.*) body; **jmds.** ~: sb.'s body *or* mortal remains *pl.*

**leicht** /laiçt/ 1 *Adj.* A light; lightweight ‹suit, material›; ~**e Waffen** small-calibre arms; ~**e Kleidung** thin clothes; (*luftig*) light *or* cool clothes; **gewogen und zu** ~ **befunden** tried and found wanting; **jmdn. um etw.** ~**er machen** (*ugs.*) relieve sb. of sth.; **mit** ~**er Hand** with ease; **etw. auf die** ~**e Schulter** *od.* **Achsel nehmen** (*ugs.*) take sth. casually; make light of sth.; B (*einfach*) easy ‹task, question, job, etc.›; (*nicht anstrengend*) light ‹work, duties, etc.›; **ein** ~**es Leben haben** have an easy life; **es** ~/**nicht** ~ **haben** have/not have it easy *or* an easy time of it; **nichts** ~**er als das** nothing could be simpler *or* easier; **du machst dir die Sache zu** ~: you're making it too easy for yourself *or* not taking it seriously enough; **es wäre ihm ein Leichtez zu helfen** it would be an easy *or* simple matter for him to help; **keinen** ~**en Stand haben** not have an easy time of it; **mit jmdm. [kein]** ~**es Spiel haben** find sb. is [not] easy meat; **man hats nicht** ~, **aber leicht hats einen** (*salopp*) it's a hard *or* tough life; ~ **fallen** be easy; **das fällt mir** ~: it is easy for me; I find it easy; **jmdm./sich etw.** ~ **machen** make sth. easy for sb./oneself; **es sich** (*Dat.*) *od.* **sich** (*Dat.*) **die Sache zu** ~ **machen** make it *or* things easy for oneself; **etw.** ~ **nehmen** make light of sth.; **seine Aufgabe nicht** ~ **nehmen** take one's task seriously; **nimms** ~: don't worry about it; **sich mit etw.** ~/**nicht** ~ **tun** manage sth. easily/have a hard time with sth.; C (*schwach*) slight ‹accent, illness, wound, doubt, etc.›; light ‹wind, rain, sleep, perfume›; **ein** ~**er Stoß [in die Rippen]** a gentle nudge [in the ribs]; **eine** ~**e Grippe** a mild attack of flu (*coll.*); D (*bekömmlich*) light ‹food, wine›; mild ‹cigar, cigarette›; E (*heiter*) light-hearted; **ihr wurde** ~ **ums Herz** (*geh.*) a weight was lifted from her heart; **ihr wurde es etwas/viel** ~**er** she felt somewhat/much easier *or* relieved; F (*unterhaltend*) light ‹music, reading, etc.›; G (*veralt. abwertend*) **ein** ~**es Mädchen** a loose-living girl.

2 *adv.* A lightly ‹built›; ~ **bewaffnet** lightly armed; ~ **geschürzt** scantily clad; ~ **bekleidet** lightly *or* thinly dressed; (*fast nackt*) scantily clad; B (*einfach, schnell, spielend*) easily; ~ **verdaulich** [easily] digestible; ~ **verkäuflich** fast-selling; ~ **verständlich** *od.* **zu verstehen sein** be easy to understand; be easily understood; ~ **zerbrechlich** very fragile; ~ **entzündlich** highly inflammable; **sie hat** ~ **reden** it's easy *or* all very well for her to talk; **das ist** ~**er gesagt als getan** that's easier said than done; **jemanden wie ihn werden Sie nicht so** ~ **wieder finden** you won't find someone like him again in a hurry (*coll.*); **sie wird** ~ **böse** she has a quick temper; **das ist** ~ **möglich** that is perfectly possible; **ihr wird** ~ **schlecht** the slightest thing makes her sick; C (*geringfügig*) slightly; ~ **gewürzt** lightly seasoned; **es regnete** ~: there was a light rain falling; **es hat** ~ **gefroren** there was a slight frost; ~ **verletzt/verwundet** slightly injured/wounded; D (*bekömmlich*) ~ **essen** eat light food

**leicht-, Leicht-:** ~**athlet** *der* [track/field] athlete; ~**athletik** *die* [track and field] athletics *sing.;* ~**athletin** *die* ⇒ ~**athlet**; ~**bau·platte** *die* (*Bauw.*) lightweight building board; ~**bau·weise** *die* lightweight construction; **etw. in** ~**bauweise herstellen** *od.* **produzieren** make sth. with lightweight materials; *~**bekleidet** ⇒ **leicht** 2A; ~**benzin** *das* benzine; ~**beschwingt** *Adj.* carefree; ‹music› with a gay lilt; *~**bewaffnet** ⇒ **leicht** 2A; ~**blütig** *Adj.* (*geh.*) happy-go-lucky; (~*sinnig*) frivolous; *~**entzündlich** ⇒ **leicht** 2B

**Leichter** *der;* ~**s**, ~ (*Seew.*) lighter

**leicht-, Leicht-:** *~|**fallen** ⇒ **leicht** 1B; ~**fertig** 1 *Adj.* A careless ‹behaviour, person›; rash ‹promise›; ill-considered, slapdash ‹plan›; B (*veralt.: moralisch bedenkenlos*) promiscuous; loose ‹woman›; 2 *adv.* carelessly; ~**fertigkeit** *die* carelessness; ~**fuß** *der* (*abwertend*) Casanova; ladykiller; ~**füßig** (*geh.*) 1 *Adj.* nimble; 2 *adv.* with light *or* nimble steps; ~**füßigkeit** *die;* ~~: lightness *or* nimbleness of foot; *~**geschürzt** ⇒ **leicht** 2A; ~**gewicht** *das* (*Schwerathletik*) A lightweight; ⇒ *auch* **Fliegengewicht**; B ⇒ ~**gewichtler**; C (*ugs. scherzh.*) (*Mädchen*) sylph; (*Mann*) featherweight; ~**gewichtler** /-gəvıçtlɐ/ *der;* ~~**s**, ~~ (*Schwerathletik*) lightweight; ~**gläubig** *Adj.* gullible; credulous; ~**gläubigkeit** *die* gullibility; credulity; ~**hin** *Adv.* A (*ohne Überlegung*) without [really] thinking; (*lässig*) casually; **etw.** ~**hin sagen** say sth. casually *or* unthinkingly; B (*nebenbei*) in an offhand *or* casual manner

**Leichtigkeit** /ˈlaiçtıçkait/ *die;* ~ A (*geringes Gewicht, Schwerelosigkeit*) lightness; B (*Mühelosigkeit*) ease; **es ist eine** ~ **[für ihn], das zu tun** it is a simple matter [for him] to do it; **mit** ~: with ease; easily

**leicht-, Leicht-:** ~**industrie** *die* light industry; ~**lebig** *Adj.* happy-go-lucky; ~**lebigkeit** *die;* ~~: happy-go-lucky attitude; ~**lohn·gruppe** *die* (*verhüll.*) low-wage group; *~|**machen** ⇒ **leicht** 1B; ~**matrose** *der* ordinary seaman; ~**metall** *das* light metal; (*Legierung*) [light] alloy; *~|**nehmen** ⇒ **leicht** 1B; ~**öl** *das* light oil; ~**schwer·gewicht** *das* (*Schwerathletik*) light heavyweight; **Weltmeister im** ~**schwergewicht** world light heavyweight champion; ~**sinn** *der* carelessness *no indef. art.;* (*mit Gefahr verbunden*) recklessness *no indef. art.;* (*Fahrlässigkeit*) negligence *no indef. art.;* **das sagst du so in deinem jugendlichen** ~**sinn** (*ugs.*) that's easier said than done; ~**sinnig** 1 *Adj.* careless; (*sich, andere gefährdend*) reckless; (*fahrlässig*) negligent; 2 *adv.* carelessly; (*gefährlich*) recklessly; ‹promise› rashly; ~**sinnig mit seinem Geld umgehen** be careless with one's money; ~**sinnigerweise** *Adv.* carelessly; (*gefährlicherweise*) recklessly; ‹promise› rashly; ~**sinnigkeit** *die;* ~~: ⇒ **Leichtsinn**; *~|**tun** ⇒ **leicht** 1B; *~**verdaulich** ⇒ **leicht** 2B; *~**verkäuflich** ⇒ **leicht** 2B; *~**verletzt** ⇒ **leicht** 2C; ~**verletzte** *der/die* slightly injured man/woman/person; **200** ~**verletzte** two hundred slightly injured; *~**verwundet** ⇒ **leicht** 2C; ~**verwundete** *der/die* slightly wounded man/woman/person; **die** ~**verwundeten** those with slight wounds

**leid** /lait/ *Adj.* **etw./jmdn.** ~ **sein/werden** (*ugs.*) be/get fed up with (*coll.*) *or* tired of sth./sb.; **wird sie es nie** ~, **das zu tun?** will she never tire of doing this?; **jmdm.** ~ **sein/werden** (*veralt.*) be/become wearisome to sb.; **die Arbeit ist ihm längst** ~: he wearied of the work long ago; ⇒ *auch* **Leid**[2]

**Leid**[1] *das;* ~**[e]s** A (*Schmerz*) suffering; (*Kummer*) grief; sorrow; **großes** *od.* **schweres** ~ **erfahren** suffer greatly; (*Kummer*) suffer great sorrow; **geteiltes** ~ **ist halbes** ~ (*Spr.*) a sorrow shared is a sorrow halved; **jmdm. sein** ~ **klagen** tell sb. all one's woes; B (*Unrecht*) wrong; (*Böses*) harm; **jmdm. ein** ~ **zufügen** wrong/harm sb.; do sb. wrong/harm; **ihm soll kein** ~ *od.* (*veralt.*) ~**s geschehen** he shall come to no harm; **sich** (*Dat.*) **ein** ~**s antun** (*ugs. veralt.*) take one's own life

**Leid**[2] ▶268 *in* **es tut mir** ~**[, dass...]** I'm sorry [that...]; **das braucht dir nicht** ~ **zu tun** you needn't feel sorry *or* (*coll.*) bad about that; **so** ~ **es mir tut, aber...** I'm very sorry, but...; **er tut mir** ~: I feel sorry for him; **es tut mir** ~ **darum/um ihn** I feel sorry *or* (*coll.*) bad about it/sorry for him

**Leide·form** *die* (*Sprachw.*) ⇒ **Passiv**

**leiden** ▶474 1 *unr. itr. V.* A suffer **(an, unter** + *Dat.* from); **unter jmdm.** ~: suffer because of sb.; B (*Schaden nehmen*) suffer **(durch, unter** + *Dat.* from); **durch den Frost** ~: suffer from *or* be harmed by the frost. 2 *unr. tr. V.* A **jmdn. [gut]** ~ **können** *od.* **mögen** like sb.; **ich kann sie/das nicht** ~: I can't stand her/it; B (*geh.: ertragen müssen*) suffer ‹hunger, thirst, want, torment, etc.›; C (*dulden*) tolerate; **sie ist überall/bei ihren Vorgesetzten wohl gelitten** (*geh.*) she is liked by everybody/by her superiors; D (*veralt.: aushalten*) **sie litt es nicht mehr zu Hause** she could endure it no longer at home

**Leiden** *das;* ~**s**, ~ A ▶474 (*Krankheit*) illness; (*Gebrechen*) complaint; **nach langem, schwerem** ~ **sterben** die after a long and painful illness; **[es ist] immer das alte** ~: [it's] the same old story; B (*Qual*) suffering; **Freud[en] und** ~**[en]** joy[s] and sorrow[s]; **das** *od.* **die** ~ **Christi** Christ's Passion; C **ein langes** ~ **[von Sohn]** (*ugs. scherzh.*) a beanpole [of a son]

**-leiden** *das;* ~**s**, ~: **ein Asthma**~/**Herz**~ **haben** have an asthmatic condition/a heart condition

**leidend** *Adj.* A (*krank*) ailing; in poor health *postpos.;* ~ **aussehen** look sickly *or* poorly; B (*schmerzvoll*) strained ‹voice›; martyred ‹expression›; ‹look› full of suffering

**Leidenschaft** *die;* ~, ~**en** passion **(zu, für** for); **mit** ~: fervently; passionately; **Reiten ist seine [ganze]** ~: riding is his great love; **seine** ~ **für etw. entdecken** realize one's great love for sth.; **er ist Sammler aus** ~: he is a dedicated collector; **ein Thema frei von jeder** ~ **diskutieren** discuss a subject dispassionately

**leidenschaftlich** 1 *Adj.* passionate; ardent, passionate ‹lover›; passionate[ly keen] ‹skier, collector, etc.›; violent, passionate ‹hatred, quarrel›; vehement ‹protest›. 2 *adv.* A passionately; (*eifrig*) dedicatedly; ~ **diskutiert werden** be discussed heatedly; **etw.** ~ **ablehnen/verneinen** reject/deny sth. vehemently; **er treibt** ~ **Sport/sammelt** ~ **Briefmarken** he is a passionately keen sportsman/stamp collector; B (*intensivierend*) **etw.** ~ **gern tun** adore doing sth.; **sie isst** ~ **gerne Schokolade** she adores *or* has a passion for chocolate

*old spelling (see note on page 1707)

**Leidenschaftlichkeit** *die;* ~ **A** passion; (*in der Liebe*) ardour; (*bei einer Diskussion*) heat; (*bei der Darlegung eines Standpunkts*) vehemence; **B** (*Begeisterung*) passionate dedication; **mit ungeheurer ~:** with tremendous enthusiasm

**leidenschaftslos** ❶ *Adj.* dispassionate; detached. ❷ *adv.* dispassionately; in a detached way

**Leidenschaftslosigkeit** *die;* ~: detachment; **mit völliger ~:** in an entirely detached manner; (*ohne Nachdruck*) without any expression

**leidens-, Leidens-: ~druck** *der* (*Psych.*) strain imposed by suffering; psychological strain (+ *Gen.* on); **~fähig** *Adj.* with a great capacity for suffering *postpos., not pred.*; **~fähigkeit** *die* capacity for suffering; **~gefährte** *der,* **~gefährtin** *die;* **~genosse** *der,* **~genossin** *die* fellow sufferer; **~geschichte** *die* (*christl. Rel.*) **die ~geschichte Christi** Christ's Passion; **seine ~geschichte** (*fig.*) his tale of woe; **~miene** *die* woeful *or* martyred expression; **~weg** *der* (*geh.*) life of suffering *or* hardship

**leider** *Adv.* ▶268 unfortunately; **ich habe ~ keine Zeit** unfortunately *or* I'm afraid I haven't any time; **~ ja/nein** I'm afraid so/afraid not; **~ Gottes ist es nun einmal so** (*ugs.*) that's how it is, I'm afraid *or* worse luck; (*in förmlichen Briefen*) **wir müssen Ihnen ~ mitteilen ...** we regret to inform you ...

**leid-: ~erfüllt** *Adj.* full of suffering *postpos.;* wretched; ‹look› of suffering; **~geprüft** *Adj.* sorely tried; long-suffering

**leidig** *Adj.* tiresome; wretched; **das ist ein ~er Trost** that's not much comfort

**leidlich** ❶ *Adj.* reasonable; passable. ❷ *adv.* reasonably; fairly; **es geht mir [ganz] ~** (*ugs.*) I'm quite well *or* not too bad; **sie kann ~ Klavier spielen** she can play the piano reasonably well

**leid-, Leid-: ~tragende** *der/die; adj. Dekl.* victim; **der** *od.* **die ~tragende/die ~tragenden [dabei] sein** be the one/ones to suffer [in this]; **~voll** *Adj.* (*geh.*) ‹life, youth, look› full of suffering; painful ‹experience›; **in der langen, ~vollen Geschichte Afrikas** in the long history of Africa with all its suffering; **~wesen** *das:* *in* **zu jmds. ~wesen** to sb.'s regret; **ja, sehr zu meinem ~wesen** yes, much to my regret

**Leier** /'laiɐ/ *die;* ~, **~n** lyre; **[es ist] immer die alte/dieselbe ~** (*ugs. abwertend*) [it's] always the same old story

**Leier·kasten** *der* (*ugs.*) barrel organ; hurdy-gurdy (*coll.*)

**Leierkasten·mann** *der* organ-grinder; hurdy-gurdy man (*coll.*)

**leiern** (*ugs.*) ❶ *tr. V.* **A** (*kurbeln*) wind; ⇒ *auch* **Kreuz** E; **B** (*auf der Drehorgel spielen*) grind out ‹tune›; **C** (*monoton aufsagen*) drone through; (*schnell*) reel *or* rattle off. ❷ *itr. V.* **A an etw.** (*Dat.*) **~:** wind away at sth.; **B** (*monoton sprechen*) drone [on]

**Leih-: ~arbeit** *die* (*Wirtsch.*) subcontracted labour; **~arbeiter** *der,* **~arbeiterin** *die* subcontracted worker; **~bibliothek** *die,* **~bücherei** *die* lending library

**leihen** /'laiən/ *unr. tr. V.* **A jmdm. etw. ~:** lend sb. sth.; lend sth. to sb.; **leihst du es mir?** will you lend it to me?; **B** (*ent~*) borrow; **[sich** (*Dat.*)**] [von** *od.* **bei jmdm.] etw. ~:** borrow sth. [from sb.]; **ein geliehener Wagen** a borrowed car; **C** (*geh.: gewähren*) lend, give ‹support›; give ‹attention›

**Leih-: ~frist** *die* loan period; (*bei Wagen, Frack usw.*) hire period; rental period (*Amer.*); **~gabe** *die* loan (*Gen.* from); **~gebühr** *die* hire *or* (*Amer.*) rental charge; (*bei Büchern*) lending charge; borrowing fee; **~haus** *das* pawnbroker's; pawnshop; **im ~haus sein** ‹possession› be at the pawnbroker's; be pawned; **~mutter** *die; Pl.* **~mütter** surrogate mother; **~mutterschaft** *die* surrogate motherhood; **~schein** *der* **A** (*im ~haus*) pawn ticket; **B** (*in der Bibliothek*) borrowing slip; **~verkehr** *der* [inter-library] loan service; **~wagen** *der* hire *or* (*Amer.*) rental car; **[sich** (*Dat.*)**] einen ~wagen nehmen** hire *or* (*Amer.*) rent a car; **~weise** ❶ *Adv.* on loan; **das hat er mir ~weise überlassen** he has lent it to me; **hier hast du das Buch, aber nur ~weise** I'll give you the book, but only to borrow; ❷ *adj.* **„~weise Überlassung durch die Nationalgalerie"** 'on loan from the National Gallery'

**Leim** /laim/ *der;* **~[e]s** glue; **aus dem ~ gehen** (*ugs.*) (*entzweigehen*) come apart; ‹marriage, friendship› break up; (*dick werden*) put on a lot of weight; ‹woman› lose one's figure; **jmdm. auf den ~ gehen** *od.* **kriechen** (*ugs.*) be taken in by sb.; fall for sb.'s trick/tricks; **jmdn. auf den ~ führen** (*ugs.*) take sb. in

**leimen** *tr. V.* **A** glue (**an** + *Akk.* to); (*zusammen~*) glue [together]; **B** (*ugs.: hereinlegen*) **jmdn. ~:** take sb. in

**Leim·farbe** *die* distemper

**leimig** *Adj.* gluey; (*noch nicht trocken*) tacky

**Leim·rute** *die* [bird]lime twig

**Lein** /lain/ *der;* **~[e]s, ~e** (*Bot.*) flax

**-lein** *das;* **-~s, -~:** little ...; **sein schwarzes Büch~:** his little black book

**Leine** /'lainə/ *die;* ~, **~n** **A** rope; (*Zelt~*) guy rope; **die ~n losmachen** (*Seemannsspr.*) cast off; **~ ziehen** (*ugs.*) clear off; **B** (*Wäsche~, Angel~*) line; **einen Fisch an die ~ kriegen** hook a fish; **C** (*Hunde~*) lead (*esp. Brit.*); leash; **den Hund an die ~ nehmen** put the dog on the lead/leash; **„Hunde sind an der ~ zu führen"** 'dogs must be kept on a lead/leash'; **jmdm. ~/mehr ~ lassen** (*ugs.*) give sb. plenty of/more leeway; **jmdn. an der [kurzen] ~ haben** *od.* **halten** (*ugs.*) keep sb. on a tight rein; **jmdn. an die ~ legen** (*ugs.*) get sb. under one's thumb

**leinen** *Adj.* linen ‹tablecloth, sheet, etc.›; cloth [-covered] ‹cushion etc.›; **~es Verdeck** canvas [car] hood

**Leinen** *das;* **~s** **A** (*Gewebe*) linen; **B** (*Buchw.*) cloth; **Ausgabe in ~:** cloth edition

**Leinen-: ~band** *der* cloth-bound volume; **~einband** *der* cloth binding; **~kleid** *das* linen dress; **~tuch** *das; Pl.* **~tücher** linen sheet; (*Tischtuch*) linen [table]cloth; **~zeug** *das* linen

**Leine·weber** *der,* **Leine·weberin** *die* linen weaver

**Lein-: ~kraut** *das* toadflax; **~öl** *das* linseed oil; **~pfad** *der* towpath; **~samen** *der* linseed

**Lein·wand** *die* **A** linen; (*grob*) canvas; **B** (*des Malers*) canvas; **C** (*für Filme und Dias*) screen; **einen Roman** *usw.* **auf die ~ bringen** (*fig.*) film a novel *etc.*; **jmdn. von der ~ kennen** (*fig.*) know sb. from films

**Leinwand-: ~bindung** *die* (*Textilind.*) plain weave; **~größe** *die* (*scherzh.*) famous film star; film great; **~held** *der* (*iron.*) hero of the silver screen

**Lein·zeug** *das* ⇒ **Leinenzeug**

**leis** ⇒ **leise**

**leise** /'laizə/ ❶ *Adj.* **A** quiet; soft ‹steps, music, etc.›; faint ‹noise›; **sei ~!** be quiet!; **könnt ihr nicht ~r sein?** can't you make less noise?; **das Radio/die Musik ~[r] stellen** turn the radio/music down; **B** (*leicht; kaum merklich*) faint; slight; slight, gentle ‹touch›; light ‹rain›; **ich habe ~ Bedenken** I have my doubts; **eine ~ Andeutung machen** give a gentle hint; **nicht die ~ste Ahnung haben, nicht im Leisesten ahnen** not have the faintest *or* slightest idea; **ich zweifle nicht im Leisesten daran, dass ...** I haven't the slightest doubt that ....
❷ *adv.* **A** quietly; **sprich doch etwas ~r** lower your voice; **~ weinend** crying softly; **B** (*leicht; kaum merklich*) slightly; ‹touch, rain› gently; **~ kochen** simmer gently; **~ zweifeln/hoffen/ahnen** have a slight doubt/hope/suspicion

**Leise-: ~treter** *der* (*abwertend*) pussyfooter; **~treterei** *die;* ~ (*abwertend*) pussyfooting; **~treterin** *die;* **~~,** **~~nen** ⇒ **~treter**

**Leiste** /'laistə/ *die;* ~, **~n** **A** strip; (*Holz~*) batten; (*profiliert*) moulding; (*halbrund*) beading; (*am Auto*) trim; (*Tapeten~*) [picture] rail; picture moulding (*Amer.*); (*eines Bilderrahmens*) frame wood; **eine ~:** a piece *or* strip of moulding/beading/trim/frame wood; (*Holz~*) a batten; **B** (*Knopf~*) facing; **C** ▶471 (*Anat.*) groin; **D** (*Weberei*) selvage

**leisten** ❶ *tr. V.* **A** do ‹work›; (*schaffen*) achieve ‹a lot, nothing›; **gute** *od.* **ganze Arbeit ~:** do good work *or* a good job; (*gründlich arbeiten*) do a thorough job; **der Motor leistet 80 PS** the engine develops *or* produces 80 b.h.p.; **der Wagen leistet 220 km/h** the car will do 220 k.p.h.; **die Produktionsstraße leistet 30 Einheiten pro Stunde** the production line has an output of 30 units per hour; **B** (*verblasst od. als Funktionsverb*) **jmdm. Hilfe ~:** help sb.; **einen Eid ~:** swear *or* take an oath; ⇒ *auch* **Abbitte; Beistand** A; **Beitrag** A; **Folge** C; **Gehorsam; Gewähr; Widerstand** A *usw.*
❷ *refl. V.* (*ugs.*) **A sich** (*Dat.*) **etw. ~:** treat oneself to sth.; **wer leistet sich** (*Dat.*) **denn heute noch diesen Luxus?** who nowadays is prepared to spend the money on such a luxury?; **B** (*mit „können"*) **sich** (*Dat.*) **etw. [nicht] ~ können** [not] be able to afford sth.; **er kann es sich** (*Dat.*) **~, das zu tun** he can afford to do it; (*etw. Riskantes*) he can get away with doing it; **C** (*wagen*) **sich** (*Dat.*) **etw. ~:** get up to sth.; **was der sich** (*Dat.*) **leistet!** the things he gets away with!; **sich** (*Dat.*) **einen groben Schnitzer ~:** make a great blunder; **wer hat sich** (*Dat.*) **diese Frechheit geleistet?** who was it who had the cheek to do/say *etc.* that?; **ich habe mir heute vielleicht was [Schönes] geleistet** (*ugs.*) I really excelled myself today (*iron.*); I did something really brilliant today (*iron.*)

**Leisten** *der;* **~s, ~:** last; **alles/alle über einen ~ schlagen** (*ugs.*) lump everybody/everything together

**Leisten-: ~bruch** *der* rupture; **~gegend** *die* ▶471 (*Anat.*) [area of the] groin

**Leistung** *die;* ~, **~en** **A** (*Qualität bzw. Quantität der Arbeit*) performance; **Bezahlung nach ~:** payment according to performance *or* results; (*in der Industrie*) payment according to productivity; **B** (*Errungenschaft*) achievement; (*im Sport*) performance; **reife ~!** (*Jugendspr.*) not bad!; **gute/hervorragende/außergewöhnliche ~en vollbringen** achieve good/outstanding/exceptional results; **eine große sportliche/technische ~:** a great sporting/technical feat; **die schulischen ~en** results at school; **C** (*Leistungsvermögen, Physik: Arbeits~*) power; (*Ausstoß*) output; **die ~ einer Fabrik** the output *or* [production] capacity of a factory; **D** (*Zahlung, Zuwendung*) payment; (*Versicherungsw.*) benefit; **die sozialen ~en der Firma** the firm's fringe benefits; **E** (*Dienst~*) service; **F** (*das Leisten*) carrying out; (*Eides~*) swearing; **jmdn. auf ~ verklagen** (*Rechtsspr.*) sue sb. for specific performance

**leistungs-, Leistungs-: ~berechtigt** *Adj.* (*Amtsspr.*) entitled to benefits *postpos.;* **~bilanz** *die* (*Wirtsch.*) balance of trade; **~druck** *der* (*bei Arbeitnehmern*) pressure to work harder; (*bei Sportlern, Schülern*) pressure to achieve *or* to do well; **~fähig** *Adj.* **A** capable ‹person›; (*körperlich*) able-bodied; (*gute Arbeit leistend*) efficient ‹worker, factory, industry, etc.›; powerful ‹engine, computer, etc.›; (*konkurrenzfähig*) competitive ‹firm, industry›; **B** (*zahlungsfähig*) capable of paying *postpos.;* solvent; **~fähigkeit** *die* (*eines Menschen*) capability; (*bei guter Arbeitsleistung*) efficiency; (*eines Betriebs, der Industrie*) productivity; (*Wirtschaftlichkeit*) efficiency; (*eines Motors, eines Computers usw.*) power; performance; **die Grenze seiner ~fähigkeit erreicht haben** have reached the limit of what one can do; **~gerecht** ❶ *Adj.* ‹salary, income› based on performance *or* results; (*in der Industrie*) based on productivity; ❷ *adv.* **~gerecht bezahlt werden** receive a performance-related salary; **~gesellschaft** *die* [highly] competitive society; performance-oriented society; ~**grenze** *die* maximum potential; (*eines Sportlers*) performance limit; (*von Maschinen, Fabriken*) maximum output; **seine ~grenze erreichen** reach the limit of one's/its capacity; ~**klage** *die* (*Rechtsw.*) action for specific performance; ~**kontrolle** *die* (*Schulw.*) **A der ~kontrolle dienen** be used as a check on the standard reached; **B** (*Test*) [performance] test; ~**kraft** *die* ⇒ ~**fähigkeit**; ~**kurs** *der* (*Schulw.*) extension course (*going beyond the basic course, based on a university form of study*); ~**kurve** *die* performance curve; (*eines Motors*) power curve; ~**lohn** *der* pay based on productivity; ~**motivation** *die* (*Psych.*) achievement motivation; ~**nachweis** *der* evidence of [academic] achievement; ~**niveau** *das* (*Schulw.*) level of achievement; (*Sport*) standard of performance; ~**orientiert** *Adj.* **A** achievement-oriented; [highly] competitive ‹society›; **B** ⇒ ~**gerecht**; ~**prämie** *die* (*Arbeitswelt*) productivity bonus; ~**prinzip** *das* achievement principle; competitive principle; ~**prüfung** *die* **A** (*Schulw.*) achievement test; **B** (*Sport*) trial; test [of performance]; ~**schau** *die* (*Wirtsch., Landw.*) [product] exhibition; ~**schwach** *Adj.* not performing well *pred.*; low-achieving *attrib.* ‹worker, pupil›; (*minderbegabt*) less able, lower-ability *attrib.* ‹pupil›; weak ‹team›; low-powered ‹engine›; ~**schwächer** lower-achieving *attrib.* ‹worker, pupil›; lower-ability *attrib.* ‹pupil›; less powerful ‹engine›; ~**schwäche** *die* poor performance; (*Schulw.*) low achievement; (*eines Motors*) low power; ~**sport** *der* competitive sport *no art.*; ~**sportler** *der* competitive sportsman; ~**sportlerin** *die* competitive sportswoman; ~**stand** *der* level of performance; (*Schulw.*) standard of work; (*Ausstoß*) level of output; ~**stark** *Adj.* high-performing *attrib.* ‹athlete›; able ‹pupil, athlete, etc.›; high-performance *attrib.*, powerful ‹engine, car›; highly efficient ‹business, power station›; (*sehr konkurrenzfähig*) highly competitive ‹business, athlete›; ~**stärke** *die* level of performance; (*Schulw.*) standard of work; (*Ausstoß*) level of output; ~**steigerung** *die* improvement in performance; (*eines Schülers*) improvement [in his/her work]; (*eines Unternehmens*) improvement in efficiency; (*in der Produktion*) improvement in output; ~**test** *der* (*bei Motoren, Maschinen*) performance test; (*bei Schülern*) achievement test; ~**vergleich** *der* competition; ~**vermögen** *das* ⇒ ~**fähigkeit**; ~**verweigerung** *die* (*bes. Soziol., Päd.*) refusal to work; (*allgemein*) refusal to be part of competitive society; ~**wettbewerb** *der* (*Wirtsch.*) competition [for high output and efficiency]; ~**zentrum** *das* (*Sport*) intensive training centre; ~**zulage** *die*, ~**zuschlag** *der* bonus (*for additional work, responsibility, etc.*); ~**zwang** *der* (*Soziol.*) (*bei Arbeitnehmern*) compulsion to work hard; (*bei Sportlern/Schülern*) compulsion to achieve *or* to do well

**Leit-:** ~**antrag** *der* (*Politik*) motion put forward by the party leadership; ~**artikel** *der* (*Zeitungsw.*) leading article; leader; ~**artikler** *der;* ~~**s**, ~~, ~**artiklerin** *die;* ~~, ~~**nen** (*Zeitungsw.*) leader writer; ~**bild** *das* model; ~**bilder der Mode** leaders of fashion

**leiten** /ˈlai̯tn̩/ *tr. V.* **A** (*anführen*) lead, head ‹expedition, team, discussion, etc.›; be head of ‹school›; (*verantwortlich sein für*) be in charge of ‹project, expedition, etc.›; manage ‹factory, enterprise›; (*den Vorsitz führen bei*) chair ‹meeting, discussion, etc.›; (*Musik: dirigieren*) conduct ‹orchestra, choir›; direct ‹small orchestra etc.›; (*Sport: als Schiedsrichter*) referee ‹game, match›; ~**der Angestellter** executive; manager; ~**de Angestellte** senior *or* managerial staff; ~**der Beamte** senior civil servant; **eine ~de Position** a position in [senior] management; a managerial position; **B** (*beg~, führen*) lead; **jmdn. auf die richtige Spur ~:** put sb. on the right track; **sich von etw. ~ lassen** [let oneself] be guided by sth.; **er lässt sich nur von seinen Gefühlen ~:** he is governed solely by his feelings; **sich schwer/leicht ~ lassen** be hard/easy to manage; **die ~de Hand/der ~de Gedanke** the guiding hand/principle; **C** (*lenken*) direct; route ‹traffic›; (*um~*) divert ‹traffic, stream›; **Erdöl durch Rohre ~:** pipe oil; **den Verkehr über eine Umgehungsstraße ~:** route/divert traffic along a bypass; **etw. an die zuständige Stelle ~:** pass on *or* forward sth. to the competent authority; **D** *auch itr.* (*Physik*) conduct ‹heat, current, sound›; **etw. leitet gut/schlecht** sth. is a good/bad conductor; **nicht ~de Materialien** non-conducting materials

**Leiter**[1] *der;* ~**s**, ~ **A** (*einer Delegation, Gruppe*) leader; head; (*einer Abteilung*) head; manager; (*eines Instituts*) director; (*einer Schule*) head teacher; headmaster (*Brit.*); principal (*esp. Amer.*); (*einer Diskussion*) leader; (*Vorsitz*) chair[man]; (*eines Chors*) choirmaster; (*Dirigent*) conductor; **kaufmännischer ~:** marketing manager; (*Verkaufs~*) sales manager; **technischer/künstlerischer ~:** technical/artistic director; **B** (*Physik*) conductor

**Leiter**[2] *die;* ~, ~**n** ladder; (*Steh~*) stepladder; **die ~ des Erfolgs** (*fig.*) the ladder of success

**Leiterin** *die;* ~, ~**nen** ⇒ **Leiter**[1]; (*einer Schule*) head teacher; headmistress (*Brit.*); principal (*esp. Amer.*); (*eines Chors*) choirmistress

**Leiter-:** ~**sprosse** *die* rung [of a/the ladder]; ~**wagen** *der* open-frame wooden handcart

**leit-, Leit-:** ~**faden** *der* **A** [basic] textbook; ~**faden der Physik** basic course in physics; introduction to physics; **B** (~*gedanke*) main idea *or* theme; **das durchzieht sein Werk wie ein ~faden** it runs through his works like a connecting thread; ~**fähig** *Adj.* (*Physik*) conductive; ~**fähigkeit** *die* (*Physik*) conductivity; ~**feuer** *das* (*Schifffahrt*) leading light; ~**fossil** *das* (*Geol.*) index fossil; ~**gedanke** *der* dominant *or* central theme; ~**hammel** *der* **A** bellwether; **B** (*abwertend: Führer*) leader [of the herd]; boss-figure; ~**linie** *die* **A** (*Richtlinie*) guideline; **B** (*Verkehrsw.*) lane marking; **C** (*Geom.*) directrix; ~**motiv** *das* (*Musik, Literaturw., fig.*) **A** leitmotiv; **B** (~*gedanke*) dominant *or* central theme; ~**planke** *die* crash barrier; guardrail (*Amer.*); ~**satz** *der* guiding principle; ~**spruch** *der* motto; ~**stelle** *die* control room; (*Büro*) central office; ~**stern** *der* (*auch fig. geh.*) lodestar; ~**strahl** *der* **A** (*Flugw., Milit.*) radio guidance beam; **B** (*Geom.*) radius vector; ~**tier** *das* (*Zool.*) leader [of the herd]; ~**ton** *der; Pl.* ~**töne** (*Musik*) leading note

**Leitung** *die;* ~, ~**en A** ⇒ **leiten** A: leading; heading; being in charge; management; chairing; (*Schulw.*) working as a/the head; (*Musik*) conducting; directing; (*Sport*) refereeing; **B** (*einer Expedition usw.*) leadership; (*Verantwortung*) responsibility (*Gen.* for); (*eines Betriebes, Unternehmens*) management; (*einer Sitzung, Diskussion*) chairmanship; (*Schulw.*) headship; (*Musik*) conductorship; (*Sport*) [task of] refereeing; **unter der ~ eines Managers stehen** be headed by a manager; **unter jmds. ~** (*Dat.*) **arbeiten** work under sb. *or* under sb.'s direction; (*Musik*) **unter der ~ von X/des Komponisten** conducted by X/the composer; **die ~ hatte Otto Klemperer** the conductor was Otto Klemperer; **die ~ der Sendung/Diskussion hat X** the programme is presented/the discussion is chaired by X; **bei einem Spiel die ~ haben** referee a match; **C** (*leitende Personen*) management; (*einer Schule*) head and senior staff; **D** (*Rohr~*) pipe; (*Haupt~*) main; **Wasser aus der ~ trinken** drink tap water; **E** (*Draht, Kabel*) cable; (*für ein Gerät*) lead; (*einzelne od. ohne Isolierung*) wire; **die ~en [im Haus/Auto usw.]** the wiring *sing.* [of the house/car *etc.*]; **F** (*Telefon~*) line; **es ist jemand in der ~** (*ugs.*) there's somebody on the line; **gehen Sie aus der ~!** get off the line!; **auf einer anderen ~ sprechen** be [talking] on another line; **eine lange ~ haben** (*ugs.*) be slow on the uptake; **er steht** *od.* **sitzt auf der ~** (*salopp*) he's not really with it (*coll.*)

**Leitungs-:** ~**draht** *der* [electrical] wire; (*größer*) [electrical] cable; ~**gremium** *das* [executive] committee; ~**mast** *der* (*für Strom*) pylon; (*Telefonmast*) telegraph pole; ~**netz** *das* **A** (*für Wasser, Gas*) mains network; mains *pl.*; (*für Fernwärme usw.*) network of pipes; **B** (*Elektrizität*) mains network *or* grid; **C** (*Telefonnetz*) telephone network; ~**rohr** *das* [water/gas] pipe; (*Hauptleitungsrohr*) main; ~**wasser** *das* tap water

**Leit-:** ~**währung** *die* (*Wirtsch.*) base *or* key currency; ~**werk** *das* **A** (*Flugw., Waffent.*) control surfaces *pl.*; (*am Heck*) tail unit; **B** (*Seew.*) approach pier; **C** (*DV*) control unit; ~**wert** (*Physik, Elektrot.*) conductance; ~**wort** *das* **A** *Pl.* ~**wörter** catchword; motto; **B** *Pl.* ~~**e** ⇒ **Leitspruch**; ~**zahl** *die* (*Fot.*) guide number; ~**zins[satz]** *der* (*Finanzw.*) **A** (*Diskontsatz*) discount rate; ≈ base rate; **B** ⇒ **Eckzins**

**Lektion** /lɛkˈtsi̯oːn/ *die;* ~, ~**en** lesson; **jmdm. eine ~ erteilen** (*fig.*) teach sb. a lesson

**Lektor** /ˈlɛktɔr/ *der;* ~**s**, ~**en** /lɛkˈtoːrən/ **A** ▶ **159** (*Hochschulw.*) *junior university teacher in charge of practical or supplementary classes etc.*; **B** ▶ **159** (*Verlags~*) [publisher's] editor

**Lektorat** /lɛktoˈraːt/ *das;* ~**[e]s**, ~**e A** (*Hochschulw.*) post of 'Lektor'; **B** (*im Verlag*) editorial department

**Lektorin** *die;* ~, ~**nen** ⇒ **Lektor**

**Lektüre** /lɛkˈtyːrə/ *die;* ~, ~**n A** reading; **bei der ~ des Romans** when reading the novel; **B** (*Lesestoff*) reading [matter]; **etw. als ~/als leichte ~ empfehlen** recommend sth. as a good read/as light reading; **nicht die richtige ~ für den Urlaub** not the right thing to read while on holiday; **das ist keine passende ~ für dich** that is not suitable reading for you

**Lemma** /ˈlɛma/ *das;* ~**s**, ~**ta** (*Sprachw.*) lemma; headword

**Lemming** /ˈlɛmɪŋ/ *der;* ~**s**, ~**e** (*Zool.*) lemming

**Lemure** /leˈmuːrə/ *der;* ~**n**, ~**n A** (*Myth.*) **die ~n** the lemures; **B** (*Zool.*) lemur

**Lende** /ˈlɛndə/ *die;* ~, ~**n** ▶ **471** loin

**lenden-, Lenden-:** ~**braten** *der* (*Kochk.*) roast loin; (*vom Rind*) sirloin steak; ~**gegend** *die* ▶ **471** loins *pl.*; lumbar region (*Anat.*); ~**lahm** *Adj.* **A** (*kreuzlahm*) **[furchtbar] ~lahm sein** be bent double with backache; **B** (*fig.*) crippled; feeble, lame ‹excuse›; ~**schurz** *der* loincloth; ~**stück** *das* (*Kochk.*) piece of loin; ~**wirbel** *der* ▶ **471** (*Anat.*) lumbar vertebra

**Leninismus** /leniˈnɪsmʊs/ *der;* ~**:** Leninism *no art.*

**Leninist** *der;* ~**en**, ~**en**, **Leninistin** *die;* ~, ~**nen** Leninist

**leninistisch** *Adj.* Leninist

**Lenkachse** *die* (*Eisenb.*) pivot axle

**lenkbar** *Adj.* **A** (*Technik*) **leicht/schwer ~ sein** be easy/difficult to steer; (*kontrollierbar*) be easy/difficult to control; **B** (*von Menschen*) acquiescent; obedient; manageable, controllable ‹child›

**lenken** /ˈlɛŋkn̩/ *tr. V.* **A** *auch itr.* steer ‹car, bicycle, etc.›; be at the controls of ‹aircraft›; guide ‹missile›; (*fahren*) drive ‹car etc.›; **wenn du geschickt lenkst** if you do some crafty steering; **B** direct, guide ‹thoughts etc.› (**auf** + *Akk.* to); turn ‹attention› (**auf** + *Akk.* to); steer ‹conversation›; **die Diskussion auf etw./jmdn. ~:** steer *or* bring the discussion round to sth./sb.; **den Verdacht auf jmdn. ~:** throw suspicion on sb.; **seine Blicke auf jmdn. ~:** turn one's gaze on sb.; **seine Schritte gen Bahnhof/heimwärts ~** (*geh., scherzh.*) direct one's steps towards the station/wend one's way homewards; **C** (*kontrollieren*) control ‹person, press, economy›; rule, govern ‹state›; **die ~de Hand** the guiding hand; **eine gelenkte Wirtschaft** a planned economy

*old spelling (see note on page 1707)

**Lenker** *der;* **~s, ~** Ⓐ *(Lenkstange)* handlebars *pl.; (Lenkrad)* steering wheel; **sich** *(Dat.)* **den goldenen ~ verdienen** *(ugs. spött.)* win the prize for bootlicking; Ⓑ *(Fahrer)* driver; Ⓒ *(fig. geh.)* director; controller; *(eines Staates)* captain

**Lenker-: ~band** *das* handlebar tape; **~hörnchen** *das* bar end

**Lenkerin** *die;* **~, ~nen** ⇒ **Lenker** B, C

**Lenker·vorbau** *der* stem

**Lenk-: ~flug·körper** *der (Waffent.)* guided missile; **~rad** *das* steering wheel; **jmdm. ins ~rad greifen** grab the steering wheel from sb.; **~rad·schaltung** *die (Kfz-W.)* steering column gear change *(Brit.) or (Amer.)* gearshift; ***~rad·schloss**, ***~rad·schloß** *das (Kfz-W.)* steering [wheel] lock; **~säule** *die (Kfz-W.)* steering column; **~stange** *die* handlebars *pl.*

**Lenkung** *die;* **~, ~en** Ⓐ *(Leitung)* control; *(eines Staates)* ruling *no indef. art.;* governing *no indef. art.;* Ⓑ *(Kfz-W.)* steering

**Lenz** /lɛnts/ *der;* **~es, ~e** *(dichter. veralt.)* spring; **der ~ ist da!** spring is here!; **der ~ des Lebens** *(fig.)* the springtime of life; **einen sonnigen** *od.* **ruhigen** *od.* **faulen ~ haben** *od.* **schieben** *(salopp)* have an easy time of it; *(eine leichte Arbeit haben)* have a cushy job *(coll.)*; **sich** *(Dat.)* **einen schönen ~ machen** *(salopp)* take it easy; **sie zählt erst 15 ~e** she is a girl of only 15 summers *(literary)*

**lenzen** *(Seemannsspr.)* ❶ *tr. V.* bail out ‹boat, water›; *(mit Pumpe)* pump out ‹water, bilge›. ❷ *itr. V.* scud [under light sail]

**Lenz·pumpe** *die (Seemannsspr.)* bilge pump

**Leopard** /leo'part/ *der;* **~en, ~en** leopard

**Lepra** /'le:pra/ *die;* **~:** leprosy *no art.*

**Lepra·kranke** *der/die* leper

**leprös** /le'prø:s/ *Adj.* leprous

**leptosom** /lɛpto'zo:m/ *Adj. (Med., Anthrop.)* leptosome; leptosomatic

**Lerche** /'lɛrçə/ *die;* **~, ~n** lark

**lernbar** *Adj.* learnable; **das ist [für jeden] ~:** that can be learnt [by anybody]; **leicht ~:** easy to learn *pred.*

**lern-, Lern-: ~begier** *die*, **~begierde** *die* eagerness to learn; **~begierig** *Adj.* eager to learn *postpos.;* **~behindert** *Adj. (Päd.)* educationally subnormal; with learning difficulties *postpos., not pred.;* **~behinderte** *der/die* slow learner; child with learning difficulties; **~eifer** *der* eagerness to learn

**lernen** /'lɛrnən/ ❶ *itr. V.* study; *(als Berufsausbildung)* train; **gut/schlecht ~:** be a good/poor learner *or* pupil; *(fleißig/nicht fleißig sein)* work hard/not work hard [at school]; **leicht ~:** find it easy to learn; find school work easy; **mit jmdm. ~** *(ugs.)* help sb. with his/her [school] work; **auf etw.** *(Akk.)* **~** *(ugs.)* train to be sth.
❷ *tr. V.* Ⓐ learn **(aus** from); **schwimmen/sprechen ~:** learn to swim/talk; **Trompete/Klavier ~:** learn to play the trumpet/piano; **er/mancher lernt es nie** *(ugs.)* he/some people [will] never learn; **von ihm kann man noch was ~:** you can learn a thing or two from him; **das will gelernt sein** that is something one has to learn; **gelernt ist gelernt** once learnt, never forgotten; **das Fürchten ~:** find out what it is to be afraid; Ⓑ **einen Beruf ~:** learn a trade; **Maurer/Bäcker** *usw.* **~:** train to be *or* as a bricklayer/baker *etc.;* **sie hat Friseuse gelernt** she trained as a hairdresser

**Lernende** *der/die; adj. Dekl.* ⇒ **Lehrende**

**Lerner** *der;* **~s, ~, Lernerin** *die;* **~, ~nen** *(Sprachw.)* learner

**lern-, Lern-: ~fabrik** *die (abwertend)* swotting factory *(Brit.)*; cramming mill *(Amer.)*; **~fähig** *Adj.* able to learn *pred.;* capable of learning *pred.;* **~hilfe** *die* aid to learning; **~mittel** *das* learning aid; *(Lehrmittel)* teaching aid; **~mittel** *Pl.* teaching materials; **~mittel·freiheit** *die* free provision of teaching materials; **~prozess**, ***~prozeß** *der* learning process; **~psychologie** *die* psychology of learning; **~schwester** *die* student nurse; **~ziel** *das* [educational] aim

**Les·art** /'le:s-/ *die* Ⓐ *(Fassung)* variant; Ⓑ *(Deutung)* interpretation; reading

**lesbar** *Adj.* Ⓐ legible; Ⓑ *(klar)* lucid ‹style›; *(verständlich)* comprehensible; **gut ~:** easy to read; very readable

**Lesbe** /'lɛsbə/ *die;* **~, ~n** *(ugs.)* Lesbian; dike *(sl.)*

**Lesben·bewegung** *die* gay women's movement

**Lesbierin** /'lɛsbi̯ərɪn/ *die;* **~, ~nen** Lesbian

**lesbisch** *Adj.* Lesbian; **~ sein** be a Lesbian/Lesbians

**Lese** /'le:zə/ *die;* **~, ~n** Ⓐ *(Weinernte)* grape harvest; Ⓑ *(geh.: Auswahl)* selection

**Lese-:** reading ...

**Lese-: ~abend** *der* [evening] reading; **einen ~abend geben** read from one's works; **~automat** *der* ⇒ **~gerät**; **~brille** *die* reading glasses *pl.;* **~buch** *das* reader; **~exemplar** *das* reading copy; *(noch ungebunden)* proof copy; **~gerät** *das (DV)* reader; **~hunger** *der* appetite for reading matter; **~lampe** *die* reading lamp; **~maschine** *die* ⇒ **~gerät**

**lesen**[1] ❶ *unr. tr., itr. V.* Ⓐ read; **sie las in der Zeitung/in einem Buch** she was reading the paper/a book; **er hat wochenlang an dem Buch ge~:** he has been reading the book for weeks; **er liest aus seinem neuesten Werk** he is reading from his latest work; **ein Gesetz [zum ersten Mal] ~** *(Parl.)* give a bill a [first] reading; **die/eine Messe ~:** say Mass/a Mass; **hier ist zu ~, dass ...** it says here that ...; **der Text ist so zu ~, dass ...** the text is to be taken as meaning that ...; ⇒ *auch* **Leviten**; Ⓑ *(entnehmen)* tell **(in** + *Dat.*, **aus** from); **in seiner Miene war Verbitterung zu ~:** there were signs of bitterness in his expression; **aus den Zeilen konnte man gewisse Zweifel ~:** reading between the lines, one could make out certain doubts; **Gedanken ~ können** be a mind-reader; **jmds. Gedanken ~:** read sb.'s mind *or* thoughts; **aus der Hand ~:** read palms; **sich** *(Dat.)* **aus der Hand ~ lassen** have one's palm *or* hand read; Ⓒ *(Hochschulw.)* lecture **(über** + *Akk.* on); **er liest neue Geschichte/Völkerrecht** he lectures on modern history/international law.
❷ *unr. refl. V.* read; **es liest sich leicht/schnell** it is easy/quick to read; **es liest sich sehr unterhaltsam** it's a very entertaining read

**lesen**[2] *unr. tr. V.* Ⓐ *(sammeln, pflücken)* pick ‹grapes, berries, fruit›; gather ‹firewood›; **Ähren ~:** glean [ears of corn]; Ⓑ *(aussondern)* pick over

**lesens·wert** *Adj.* worth reading *postpos.*

**Leser** *der;* **~s, ~:** reader

**Leser·analyse** *die* readership survey

**Lese·ratte** *die (ugs. scherzh.)* bookworm; voracious reader

**Leser·brief** *der* reader's letter; **~e** readers' letters; **„~e"** *(Zeitungsrubrik)* 'Letters to the editor'

**Leserin** *die;* **~, ~nen** ⇒ **Leser**

**Leser·kreis** *der* readership

**leserlich** ❶ *Adj.* legible. ❷ *adv.* legibly

**Leserschaft** *die;* **~:** readership

**Leser-: ~wunsch** *der* reader's request; **~wünsche** readers' requests; **~zahl** *die* circulation; **(~kreis)** readership; **~zuschrift** *die* reader's letter; **~zuschriften** readers' letters **(zu** in response to)

**Lese-: ~saal** *der* reading room; **~stoff** *der* reading matter; **~wut** *die* craving to read; **~zeichen** *das (auch DV)* bookmark; **~zirkel** *der: commercial enterprise which supplies a selection of magazines on a regular loan basis to subscribers*

**Lesung** *die;* **~, ~en** Ⓐ *(auch Parl.)* reading; Ⓑ *(christl. Kirche)* lesson

**Lethargie** /letar'gi:/ *die;* **~:** lethargy

**lethargisch** ❶ *Adj.* lethargic. ❷ *adv.* lethargically

**Lette** /'lɛtə/ *der;* **~n, ~n** Latvian; Lett

**Letter** *die;* **~, ~n** Ⓐ letter; Ⓑ *(Druckw.)* character; sort *(as tech. term)*

**Lettin** *die;* **~, ~nen** ⇒ **Lette**

**lettisch** *Adj.* ▶ **696** Latvian; Lettish ‹language›

**Lettland** *(das);* **~s** Latvia

**Lettner** /'lɛtnɐ/ *der;* **~s, ~** *(Archit.)* choir screen

**Letzt** /'lɛtst/ *in* **zu guter ~:** in the end; *(endlich)* at long last

**letzt...** *Adj.* ▶ **207**, ▶ **833** Ⓐ last; **die ~e Reihe** the back row; **auf dem ~en Platz sein** be [placed] last; *(während des Rennens)* be in last place; *(in einer Tabelle)* be in bottom place; **er war** *od.* **wurde Letzter, er ging als Letzter durchs Ziel** he came last; **~er Mann** *(bes. Fußball)* back; **der/die Letzte sein** be the last; **als Letzter aussteigen** be the last [one] to get off; **er ist der Letzte, dem ich das sagen würde** he's the last person I would tell [about it]; **am Letzten [des Monats]** on the last day of the month; **im ~en Moment** at the last moment; **die Letzten werden die Ersten sein** *(Spr.)* the last shall be first; **das ist mein ~es Wort/Angebot** that is my last word [on the subject]/my final offer; **mein ~es Geld** the last of my money; **ist das dein ~es Geld?** is that all the money you have left?; **mit ~er Kraft** gathering all his/her remaining strength; **~en Endes** in the end; when all is said and done; **jmds./die ~e Rettung sein** *(fig.)* be sb.'s/the last hope; ⇒ *auch* **Ölung**; **Wille**; Ⓑ *(äußerst...)* ultimate; **jmdm. das Letzte an ...** *(Dat.)* **abverlangen** demand of sb. the utmost *or* maximum ...; **das Letzte hergeben** give one's all; **bis aufs Letzte** totally; *(finanziell)* down to the last penny; **bis ins Letzte** down to the last detail; **bis zum Letzten** to the utmost; Ⓒ *(gerade vergangen)* last; *(neuest...)* latest ‹news›; **in den ~en Wochen/Jahren** in the last few weeks/in recent years; **in der ~en Zeit** recently; ⇒ *auch* **Schrei**; Ⓓ *(ugs. abwertend) (schlechtest...)* worst; *(entsetzlichst...)* most dreadful; **er ist der ~e Mensch** he is the lowest of the low; **die Show war das Letzte** *(ugs.)* the show was the end *(coll.) or* the pits *(coll.)*; **das ist doch das Letzte!** *(ugs.)* that really is the limit!; ⇒ *auch* **Dreck** B

***letzte·mal** ⇒ **Mal**[1]

**letzt·endlich** *Adv.* in the end; *(schließlich doch)* ultimately

***letzten·mal** ⇒ **Mal**[1]

**letztens** /'lɛtstn̩s/ *Adv.* Ⓐ *(kürzlich)* recently; Ⓑ **drittens/viertens und ~:** thirdly/fourthly and lastly

**letzter...** *Adj.* latter; **Letzteres** *od.* **das Letztere trifft hier zu** the latter is the case here

**letzt·genannt** *Adj.* last-mentioned; last-named ‹person›

**letzt·hin** *Adv.* Ⓐ *(kürzlich)* recently; Ⓑ *(schließlich doch)* ultimately

**letztlich** *Adv.* ultimately; in the end

**letzt-: ~mals** *Adv.* the last time; **er hat ~mals vor fünf Jahren teilgenommen** the last time he took part was five years ago; **~möglich** *Adj.* latest possible; **~willig** ❶ *Adj.* in his/her/the will *postpos.;* **~willige Verfügung** last will and testament; ❷ *adv.* in his/her/the will

**Leu** /lɔy/ *der;* **~en, ~en** *(dichter. veralt.)* lion

**Leucht-: ~boje** *die (Seew.)* light buoy; **~bombe** *die* parachute flare; **~buchstabe** *der* neon-sign letter; **~diode** *die* light-emitting diode; LED

**Leuchte** /'lɔyçtə/ *die;* **~, ~n** Ⓐ light; **hast du eine ~?** have you got a torch?; Ⓑ *(fig. ugs.)* **[in Mathe** *usw.***] eine ~ sein** be brilliant *or* shine [at maths *etc.*]; **er ist eine ~ auf diesem Gebiet** he is a leading light in this field

**leuchten** *itr. V.* Ⓐ ‹moon, sun, star, etc.› be shining; ‹fire, face› glow; **grell ~:** give a glaring light; glare; **in der Sonne ~** ‹hair, sea, snow› gleam in the sun; ‹mountains etc.› glow in the sun; **golden ~:** have a golden glow; **seine Augen leuchteten vor Freude** *(fig.)* his eyes were shining *or* sparkling with joy; Ⓑ shine a/the light; **jmdm. ~:** light the way for sb.; **mit etw. in etw.** *(Akk.)* **~:** shine sth. into sth.; **jmdm. mit etw. ins Gesicht ~:** shine sth. into sb.'s face

**leuchtend** *Adj.* Ⓐ shining ‹eyes›; brilliant, luminous ‹colours›; bright ‹blue, red, etc.›; **grell ~:** glaring; **sanft ~:** softly glowing; **etw. in den ~sten Farben schildern** (*fig.*) paint sth. in glowing colours; Ⓑ (*großartig*) shining ‹example›

**Leuchter** *der;* **~s, ~:** candelabrum; (*für eine Kerze*) candlestick; (*Kron~*) chandelier

**Leucht-: ~farbe** *die* luminous paint; **~feuer** *das* (*Seew.*) beacon; light; (*Flugw.*) runway light; **~gas** *das* ⇨ **Stadtgas**; **~geschoss, *~geschoß** *das* ⇨ **~kugel**; **~käfer** *der* firefly; (*Glühwürmchen*) glowworm; **~kraft** *die* Ⓐ brilliance; Ⓑ (*Astron.*) luminosity; **~kugel** *die* flare; **~pistole** *die* flare pistol; **~rakete** *die* rocket flare; **~reklame** *die* neon [advertising] sign; **~röhre** *die* neon tube; **~schrift** *die* neon letters *pl.*; (*Schild*) neon sign; **~spur·geschoss, *~spur·geschoß** *das* tracer bullet; **~stoff** *der* (*Physik*) fluorescent substance; (*nachleuchtend*) luminous substance; **~stoff·lampe** *die* fluorescent light *or* lamp; **~stoff·röhre** *die* fluorescent tube; (*für ~reklame*) neon tube; **~tonne** *die* light buoy; **~turm** *der* lighthouse; **~turm·wärter** *der*, **~turm·wärterin** *die* lighthouse keeper; **~zeiger** *der* luminous hand; **~ziffer** *die* luminous numeral; **~ziffer·blatt** *das* luminous dial

**leugnen** /ˈlɔygnən/ ❶ *tr. V.* deny; **er leugnete die Tat/das Verbrechen** he denied doing the deed/committing the crime; **er leugnet, daran beteiligt zu sein** *od.* **dass er daran beteiligt ist** he denies being involved *or* that he is involved in it; **es ist nicht zu ~:** it is undeniable. ❷ *itr. V.* deny it; (*alles ~*) deny everything; **er leugnet noch** he still denies doing it *or* that he did it

**Leugnung** *die;* **~, ~en** denial

**Leukämie** /lɔykɛˈmi:/ *die;* **~, ~n** ▶ 474 (*Med.*) leukaemia

**leukämisch** *Adj.* (*Med.*) leukaemic; ‹symptoms› of leukaemia

**Leukoplast** Ⓦ /lɔykoˈplast/ *das* sticking plaster (*containing zinc oxide*)

**Leukozyt** /lɔykoˈtsy:t/ *der;* **~en, ~en** ▶ 471 (*Anat.*) leucocyte

**Leumund** /ˈlɔymʊnt/ *der;* **~[e]s** (*geh.*) reputation; **den guten ~ verlieren** lose one's good name; **jmdm. einen guten ~ bescheinigen** vouch for sb.'s good character

**Leumunds·zeugnis** *das* Ⓐ (*geh.*) character reference (**über** + *Akk.* for); Ⓑ (*schweiz. Rechtsspr.*) ⇨ **Führungszeugnis**

**Leutchen** /ˈlɔytçən/ *Pl.* (*ugs.*) people; ⇨ *auch* **Leute B**

**Leute** /ˈlɔytə/ *Pl.* Ⓐ people; **die reichen/alten ~:** the rich/the old; **wir sind hier bei feinen ~n** we are in a respectable household; **die kleinen ~:** the ordinary people; the man *sing.* in the street; **was werden die ~ sagen?** (*ugs.*) what will people say?; **wir sind geschiedene ~:** our ways have parted; we have parted company; (*in Zukunft*) I will have no more to do with you/him *etc.*; **unter ~ gehen** mix with people; **vor allen ~n** in front of everybody; **hier ist es ja nicht wie bei armen ~n** (*scherzh.*) we're not in the poorhouse *or* (*Amer.*) on the breadline yet; **unter die ~ bringen** (*ugs.*) spread ‹rumour›; tell everybody about ‹suspicions etc.›; ⇨ *auch* **Kind**; Ⓑ (*ugs.: als Anrede*) **auf, [ihr] ~!** come on, everybody! (*coll.*); c'mon, folks! (*Amer.*); **~, ~!** oh dear!; Ⓒ (*ugs.: Arbeiter*) people; (*Milit.: Soldaten*) men; **die Hälfte der ~:** half the staff; Ⓓ (*landsch. ugs.: Familie*) **meine ~:** my family *sing. or* (*coll.*) folks; Ⓔ (*veralt.: Gesinde*) servants

**Leute·schinder** *der*, **Leute·schinderin** *die* (*abwertend*) slave driver

**Leutnant** /ˈlɔytnant/ *der;* **~s, ~s** *od. selten:* **~e** ▶ 91 second lieutenant (*Milit.*); **~ zur See** sub lieutenant (*Brit.*); lieutenant junior grade (*Amer.*)

*old spelling (see note on page 1707)

**leut·selig** ❶ *Adj.* affable. ❷ *adv.* affably

**Leut·seligkeit** *die* affability

**Levante** /leˈvantə/ *die;* **~** (*geh.*) the Levant

**Leviat[h]an** /leˈvi̯a:tan/ *der;* **~s, ~e** (*Myth.*) leviathan

**Leviten** /leˈvi:tn̩/ *Pl.* **in jmdm. die ~ lesen** (*ugs.*) read sb. the Riot Act (*coll.*)

**Levkoje** /lɛfˈkɔ̯ːə/ *die;* **~, ~n** (*Bot.*) stock

**Lex** /lɛks/ *die;* **~, Leges** /ˈle:ge:s/ (*Parl.*) **die ~ Heinze** the Heinze Act

**Lexem** /lɛˈkse:m/ *das;* **~s, ~e** (*Sprachw.*) lexeme

**Lexik** /ˈlɛksɪk/ *die;* **~** (*Sprachw.*) lexicon

**lexikalisch** /lɛksiˈka:lɪʃ/ (*auch Sprachw.*) ❶ *Adj.* lexical. ❷ *adv.* lexically

**lexikalisieren** *tr. V.* (*Sprachw.*) lexicalize

**Lexikograph** /lɛksikoˈgra:f/ *der;* **~en, ~en** ▶ 159 lexicographer

**Lexikographie** /lɛksikograˈfi:/ *die;* **~:** lexicography *no art.*

**Lexikographin** *die;* **~, ~nen** ▶ 159 lexicographer; ⇨ *auch* **-in**

**lexikographisch** ❶ *Adj.* lexicographical. ❷ *adv.* lexicographically; **~ gesehen** looked at from a lexicographical point of view; **~ arbeiten** work as a lexicographer

**Lexikologie** /lɛksikoloˈgi:/ *die;* **~:** lexicology *no art.*

**Lexikon** /ˈlɛksikɔn/ *das;* **~s, Lexika** *od.* **Lexiken** Ⓐ encyclopaedia (+ *Gen.*, **für** of); **ein wandelndes ~ sein** (*ugs. scherzh.*) be a walking encyclopaedia; Ⓑ (*veralt.: Wörterbuch*) dictionary; Ⓒ (*Sprachw.*) lexicon

**Lezithin**, (*fachspr.:*) **Lecithin** /letsiˈti:n/ *das;* **~s, ~e** (*Chemie, Biol.*) lecithin

**lfd.** *Abk.* **laufend**

**Lfg.** *Abk.* **Lieferung**

**Liaison** /li̯ɛˈzõ:/ *die;* **~, ~s** (*geh.*) liaison; (*fig.: zwischen Staaten, Firmen*) link; tie-up; **eine ~ eingehen** enter into a liaison

**Liane** /ˈli̯a:nə/ *die;* **~, ~n** (*Bot.*) liana

**Libanese** /libaˈne:zə/ *der;* **~n, ~n** Lebanese; **roter ~** (*Drogenjargon*) Lebanese red

**Libanesin** *die;* **~, ~nen** Lebanese; ⇨ *auch* **-in**

**libanesisch** *Adj.* Lebanese

**Libanon**[1] /ˈli:banɔn/ (*das*) *od.* *der;* **~s** Lebanon

**Libanon**[2] *der;* **~s** (*Gebirge*) Lebanon Mountains *pl.*

**Libelle** /liˈbɛlə/ *die;* **~, ~n** Ⓐ dragonfly; Ⓑ (*Haarspange*) winged hairslide; Ⓒ (*an Messinstrumenten*) bubble tube; (*Wasserwaage*) spirit level

**liberal** /libeˈra:l/ ❶ *Adj.* liberal; **~ wählen** vote liberal. ❷ *adv.* liberally; **jmdn. ~ erziehen** give sb. a liberal education; **~ ausgerichtet** following liberal principles *postpos., not pred.*

**Liberale** *der/die; adj. Dekl.* liberal

**liberalisieren** *tr. V.* liberalize; relax ‹import controls›

**Liberalisierung** *die;* **~, ~en** liberalization; (*von Kontrollen*) relaxation

**Liberalismus** /liberaˈlɪsmʊs/ *der;* **~:** liberalism

**Liberalität** /liberaliˈtɛ:t/ *die;* **~** Ⓐ liberalism; liberality; Ⓑ (*Großzügigkeit*) liberality

**Liberia** /li:ˈbe:ria/ (*das*)*;* **~s** Liberia

**Liberianer** *der;* **~s, ~, Liberianerin** *die;* **~, ~nen** Liberian; ⇨ *auch* **-in**

**liberianisch** *Adj.* Liberian

**Libero** /ˈli:bəro/ *der;* **~s, ~s** (*Fußball*) sweeper

**libidinös** /libidiˈnø:s/ *Adj.* (*Psych.*) libidinal

**Libido** /ˈli:bido/ *die;* **~** (*Psych.*) libido

**Librettist** /librɛˈtɪst/ *der;* **~en, ~en, Librettistin** *die;* **~, ~nen** librettist; ⇨ *auch* **-in**

**Libretto** /liˈbrɛto/ *das;* **~s, ~s** *od.* **Libretti** libretto

**Libyen** /ˈli:by̆ən/ (*das*)*;* **~s** Libya

**Libyer** /ˈli:by̆ɐ/ *der;* **~s, ~, Libyerin** *die;* **~, ~nen** Libyan

**libysch** /ˈli:bʏʃ/ *Adj.* Libyan

**licht** /lɪçt/ *Adj.* Ⓐ (*geh.*) light; light, pale ‹colour›; **es war ~er Tag** it was broad daylight; **einen ~en Moment** *od.* **Augenblick/~e Momente haben** (*fig.*) have a lucid moment/lucid moments; (*scherzh.*) have a bright moment/bright moments; Ⓑ (*dünn bewachsen*) sparse; thin; **~es Haar haben** be thin on top; **die Reihen der alten Kameraden/der Zuschauer werden ~er** (*fig.*) the ranks of old comrades are dwindling/the rows of spectators are emptying; Ⓒ (*bes. Technik*) **die ~e Höhe/Weite** the [overall] internal height/width; **die ~e Höhe/Weite einer Brücke** the headroom/span of a bridge

**Licht** *das;* **~[e]s, ~er/~e** Ⓐ light; **das ~ des Tages** the light of day; **etw. gegen das ~ halten** hold sth. up to the light; **etw. bei ~ sehen** see sth. in daylight; **bei ~ besehen** (*fig.*) seen in the light of day; **jmdm. das [ganze] ~ [weg]nehmen** take [all] sb.'s light; **jmdm. im ~ stehen** stand in sb.'s light; **das ~ der Welt erblicken** (*geh.*) see the light of day; **ein zweifelhaftes/ungünstiges ~ auf jmdn. werfen** (*fig.*) throw a dubious/unfavourable light on sb.; **~ in etw.** (*Akk.*) **bringen** (*fig.*) shed some light on sth.; **jmdn. hinters ~ führen** (*fig.*) fool sb.; pull the wool over sb.'s eyes; **jmdn./etw./sich ins rechte ~ rücken** *od.* **setzen** *od.* **stellen** (*fig.*) show sb./sth. in the correct light/appear in the correct light; **in einem guten** *od.* **günstigen/schlechten ~ erscheinen** (*fig.*) appear in a good *or* a favourable/a bad *or* an unfavourable light; **etw. in einem besseren ~ erscheinen lassen** (*fig.*) put a better complexion on sth.; **etw. in einem milderen ~ sehen** (*fig.*) take a more lenient view of sth.; **in ein falsches ~ geraten** (*fig.*) give the wrong impression; **das ~ scheuen** (*fig.*) shun the light; **ans ~ kommen** (*fig.*) come to light; be revealed; Ⓑ *Pl.* **~er** (*elektrisches ~*) light; **das ~ anmachen/ausmachen** switch *or* turn the light on/off; **mach doch ~!** turn the light on[, will you]!; Ⓒ *Pl.* **~er**, *auch* **~e** (*Kerze*) candle; **kein** *od.* **nicht gerade ein großes ~ sein** (*ugs.*) be no genius; be not exactly brilliant; **mir ging ein ~ auf** (*ugs.*) it dawned on me; I realized what was going on; **sein ~ [nicht] unter den Scheffel stellen** [not] hide one's light under a bushel; **jmdm. ein ~ aufstecken** (*ugs.*) enlighten sb.; put sb. wise; Ⓓ (*ugs.: Strom*) electricity; Ⓔ *Pl.* **~er** (*Jägerspr.*) eye

**licht-, Licht-: ~an·lage** *die* lighting installation; **~behandlung** *die* (*Med.*) phototherapy; (*mit Sonnen~*) sunlight treatment; **~beständig** *Adj.* light-fast; **~bild** *das* Ⓐ [small] photograph (*for passport etc.*; Ⓑ (*veralt.*) (*Diapositiv*) slide; (*Fotografie*) photograph; **~bilder·vortrag** *der* slide lecture; **~blick** *der* bright spot; **~bogen** *der* (*Elektrot.*) arc; **~brechung** *die* (*Optik*) refraction of light; **~bündel** *das* beam [of light]; **~druck** *der; Pl.* **~~e** (*Druckw.*) Ⓐ collotype; Ⓑ (*Bild*) collotype [print]; **~durchflutet** *Adj.* (*geh.*) flooded with light *postpos.*; **~durchlässig** *Adj.* translucent; **~echt** *Adj.* light-fast; **~echtheit** *die* lightfastness; **~effekt** *der* light effect; **~einwirkung** *die* effects *pl.* of light; **~elektrisch** *Adj.* (*Physik*) photoelectric; **~empfindlich** *Adj.* sensitive to light; (*Chemie*) photosensitive ‹film, solution, etc.›; **~empfindlichkeit** *die* sensitivity to light; (*Chemie*) photosensitivity

**lichten**[1] ❶ *tr. V.* thin out ‹trees etc.›; (*fig.*) reduce ‹number›. ❷ *refl. V.* Ⓐ ‹trees› thin out; ‹hair› grow thin; ‹fog, mist› clear, lift; **die Reihen ~ sich** (*fig.*) the numbers are dwindling; (*im Theater usw.*) the rows are emptying; Ⓑ (*geh.*) (*heller werden*) become lighter; lighten; (*fig.*) ‹mystery etc.› be cleared up

**lichten**[2] *tr. V.* (*Seemannsspr.*) **den/die Anker ~:** weigh anchor

**Lichter-: ~baum** *der* Christmas tree; **~fest** *das* (*jüd. Rel.*) Hanukkah; Festival of Lights; **~glanz** *der* blaze of lights; ⇨ *auch* **erstrahlen**; **~kette** *die* chain of lights

**lichterloh** /ˈlɪçtɐˈlo:/ ❶ *Adj.* blazing ‹fire›; fierce, leaping ‹flames›. ❷ *adv.* **~ brennen** be blazing fiercely; (*fig.*) ‹heart› be aflame

**Lichter-:** **~meer** *das* sea of lights; **das ~meer der Stadt** the sea of lights formed by the city; **~stadt** *die* city of light

**licht-, Licht-:** **~filter** *der od. das* light filter; **~geschwindigkeit** *die* speed of light; **~hof** *der* A *(Bauw.)* light well; B *(Fot.)* halation; **~hupe** *die* headlight flasher; **die ~hupe betätigen** flash [one's lights]; **~jahr** *das (Astron.)* light year; **~kegel** *der* beam; *(Physik)* cone of light; **~leitung** *die (ugs.)* lighting wire; **die ~leitungen** the wiring for the lights; **~los** *Adj.* dark; poorly lit; **~mangel** *der* lack of light; **~maschine** *die (Kfz-W.) (mit Gleichstrom)* dynamo; *(mit Wechselstrom)* alternator; generator *(esp. Amer.)*; **~mast** *der* lamp standard; **~mess**, ***~meß** *(das)*; **~~** *(kath. Kirche)* Candlemas; **[das Fest] Mariä ~mess** [the Feast of the] Purification of the Virgin Mary; **~nelke** *die* campion; **~orgel** *die* colour organ; clavilux; **~pause** *die* photostat *(Brit.* ®) *(of transparent original)*; **~punkt** *der* spot of light; **~quant** *das (Physik)* light quantum; **~quelle** *die* light source; **~reklame** *die* neon [advertising] sign; **~satz** *der (Druckw.)* filmsetting; **~schacht** *der* light shaft; **~schalter** *der* light switch; **~schein** *der* gleam [of light]; *(~strahl)* beam of light; **~scheu** *Adj.* A shadeloving ‹plant›; ‹animal› that shuns the light; B *(fig.)* shady ‹riff-raff›; **~schranke** *die* photoelectric beam; **~schutz·faktor** *der* protection factor *(against sunburn)*; **~seite** *die* bright *or* good side; **alles hat seine ~- und Schattenseiten** everything has its good and bad sides; **~setz·maschine** *die (Druckw.)* filmsetting machine; **~spiel·haus** *das*, **~spiel·theater** *das (geh.)* cinema; picture theatre *(dated)*; movie house *(Amer.)*; **~stark** *Adj. (Fot.)* fast ‹lens›; **~stärke** *die* A *(Physik)* luminous intensity; B *(Fot.)* speed *(of a lens)*; **~strahl** *der* beam [of light]; **~undurchlässig** *Adj.* lightproof

**Lichtung** *die;* **~, ~en** clearing; **auf dieser ~:** in this clearing

**Licht-:** **~verhältnisse** *Pl.* light conditions; **~wechsel** *der (Astron.)* light-variation; **~zeichen** *das* light signal

**Lid** /li:t/ *das;* **~[e]s, ~er** ▶ 471 eyelid

**Lid-:** **~schatten** *der* eyeshadow; **~strich** *der* line drawn with eyeliner pencil; eyelining *no indef. art.*

**lieb** /li:p/ ❶ *Adj.* A *(~evoll)* kind ‹words, gesture›; **viele ~e Grüße [an ... (*Akk.*)]** much love [to ...] *(coll.)*; **sei so ~ und hilf mir beim Aufräumen** be a dear and help me clear up; **das ist ~ von dir** it's sweet of you; B *(~enswert)* likeable; nice; *(stärker)* lovable, sweet ‹child, girl, pet›; **seine Frau/ihr Mann ist sehr ~:** his wife/her husband is a dear; **sie hat ein ~es Gesicht** she has a sweet *or* charming face; **~ aussehen** look sweet *or (Amer.)* cute; C *(artig)* good, nice ‹child, dog›; **die Kinder könnten etwas ~er sein** the children could be a little better behaved; **sei schön ~!** be a good girl/boy!; **sich bei jmdm. ~ Kind machen** *(ugs. abwertend)* get on the right side of sb.; **bei jmdm. ~ Kind sein** *(ugs. abwertend)* be sb.'s pet *or* favourite; D *(geschätzt)* dear; **sein ~stes Spielzeug** his favourite toy; **~er Hans/~e Else/~e Oma!** *(am Briefanfang)* dear Hans/Else/Grandma; **~e Karola, ~er Ernst!** *(am Briefanfang)* dear Karola and Ernst; **~er Gott** dear God; **der ~e Gott** the Good Lord; **die ~e Verwandtschaft** *(iron.)* my/our/your/their *etc.* dear relations *(iron.)*; **sie ist mir ~ und teuer** *od.* **wert** she is very dear to me; **wenn dir dein Leben ~ ist, ...** if you value your life ...; **eine ~ gewordene Gewohnheit ablegen** give up a habit of which one has grown very fond; **ein ~ gewordener Gegenstand** a much loved object; **das ~e Geld** *(iron.)* the wretched money; **den ~en langen Tag** *(ugs.)* all the livelong day; **so manches ~e Mal, so manch ~es Mal** *(veralt.)* many a time; **meine Lieben** *(Familie)* my people; my nearest and dearest *(joc.)*; *(als Anrede)* [you] good people; *(an Familie usw.)* my dears; **meine Liebe** my dear; *(herablassend)* my dear woman/girl; **mein Lieber** *(Mann an Mann)* my dear fellow; *(Frau/Mann an Jungen)* my dear boy; *(Frau an Mann)* my dear man; *(als Publikumsanrede)* **~e Mitbürgerinnen und Mitbürger** fellow citizens; **~e Kinder/Freunde/Genossen!** children/friends/comrades; **~e Hörerinnen und Hörer/~e Zuschauer!** *Anreden dieser Art sind im Englischen ungebräuchlich und werden deshalb nicht übersetzt;* **~e Gemeinde, ~e Schwestern und Brüder!** *(christl. Kirche)* dearly beloved; **[ach] du ~e Güte** *od.* **~e Zeit** *od.* **~er Himmel** *od.* **~es Lieschen** *od.* **~es bisschen** *(ugs.) (erstaunt)* good grief!; good heavens!; [good] gracious!; *(entsetzt)* good grief!; heavens above!; **mit jmdm./etw. seine ~e Not haben** have no end of trouble with sb./sth.; E *(angenehm)* welcome; **er ist uns (*Dat.*) ein ~er Gast** he is a welcome visitor [with us]; **unser Besuch war ihr nicht ~:** our visit was unwelcome [to her]; **es wäre mir ~/~er, wenn ...** I should be glad *or* should like it/should prefer it if ...; **am ~sten wäre mir, ich könnte heute noch abreisen** I should like it best if I could leave today; **wir hatten mehr Schnee, als mir ~ war** we had too much snow for my liking; **das wirst du noch früher erfahren, als dir ~ ist** you'll hear about it sooner than you've bargained for; F **jmdn. ~ haben** love sb.; *(jmdn. gern haben)* be fond of sb.; **jmdn./etw. ~ gewinnen** grow fond of sb./sth.; **jmdn. ~ behalten** [continue to] be fond of sb.; *(jmdn. weiter lieben)* go on loving sb.
❷ *adv.* A *(liebenswert)* kindly; **das hast du aber ~ gesagt** you 'did put that nicely; **sie hat sich sehr ~ um die alten Leute gekümmert** it was very sweet the way she looked after the old people; B *(artig)* nicely; **er ist ganz ~ ins Bett gegangen** he went off to bed as good as gold

**lieb·äugeln** *itr. V.* A **mit etw. ~:** have one's eye on sth.; fancy sth.; **er liebäugelt mit dem Gedanken, das zu tun** he's toying *or* flirting with the idea of doing it; B *(geh.: flirten)* **mit jmdm. ~:** make eyes at sb.

***lieb|behalten** ⇒ **lieb** 1F

**Liebchen** /'li:pçən/ *das;* **~s, ~** *(veralt.)* A **[mein] ~:** my darling; my sweet[heart]; B *(abwertend)* lady-love

**Liebe** /'li:bə/ *die;* **~, ~n** A love **(zu** for); **~ zu Gott** love of God; **aus ~ zu jmdm.** for love of sb.; **aus ~ heiraten** marry for love; **was macht die ~?** how's your love life?; **bei aller ~, aber das geht zu weit** much as I sympathize, that's going too far; **bei aller ~, aber ich kann das nicht** much as I'd like to, I can't do it; *(Briefschluss)* **in ~ dein Egon** [with] all my love, yours, Egon; **~ geht durch den Magen** *(scherzh.)* the way to a man's heart is through his stomach; **~ macht blind** *(Spr.)* love is blind *(prov.)*; **wo die ~ hinfällt!** *(ugs.)* the ways of love are strange indeed; **~ auf den ersten Blick** love at first sight; B **~ zu etw.** love of sth.; **seine ganze ~ gehört dem Meer** he adores the sea; **mit ~:** lovingly; with loving care; C *(ugs.: geliebter Mensch)* love; **seine große ~:** his great love; the [great] love of his life; D *(Gefälligkeit)* favour; **tu mir die ~ und warte noch** do me a favour and wait a while

**liebe-, Liebe-:** **~bedürftig** *Adj.* in need of love *or* affection *postpos.;* **~dienerei** /-di:nə'rai/ *die (abwertend)* toadying; sycophancy; **~dienern** *itr. V.* toady **(bei, vor** + *Dat.* to)

**Liebelei** /li:bə'lai/ *die;* **~, ~en** *(abwertend)* flirtation

**liebeln** *itr. V. (veralt.)* flirt

**lieben** ❶ *tr. V.* A **jmdn. ~:** love sb.; *(verliebt sein)* be in love with *or* love sb.; *(sexuell)* make love to sb.; **sich ~:** be in love; *(sexuell)* make love; **was sich liebt, das neckt sich** *(Spr.)* lovers always tease each other; B **etw. ~:** be fond of sth.; like sth.; *(stärker)* love sth.; **es ~, etw. zu tun** like *or* enjoy doing sth.; *(stärker)* love doing sth.; **diese Pflanzen ~ Schatten** these plants like shade; C **jmdn./etw. ~ lernen** learn to love sb./sth. ❷ *itr. V.* be in love; *(sexuell)* make love; **er ist unfähig zu ~:** he is incapable of love

**liebend** ❶ *Adj.* loving; **der/die Liebende** the lover; **eine Liebende** a woman in love; **Liebende** *pl.* lovers. ❷ *adv.* **etw. ~ gerne tun** [simply] love doing sth.

***lieben|lernen** ⇒ **lieben** 1C

**liebens-, Liebens-:** **~wert** *Adj.* likeable ‹person›; *(stärker)* loveable ‹person›; attractive, endearing ‹trait›; **~würdig** *Adj.* kind; charming ‹smile›; **seien Sie doch so ~würdig und öffnen Sie das Fenster** would you be so kind as to open the window?; **~würdigerweise** *Adv.* kindly; **~würdigkeit** *die;* **~~, ~~en** A kindness; **würden Sie die ~würdigkeit haben, das Fenster zu schließen?** would you be so kind as to shut the window?; B *(Handlung, Äußerung)* kindness; **jmdm. einige ~würdigkeiten sagen** *(iron.)* say a few choice words to sb. *(iron.)*

**lieber** ❶ *Adj.:* ⇒ **lieb**. ❷ *Adv.:* ⇒ **gern**

**liebes-, Liebes-:** **~abenteuer** *das* amorous adventure; **~affäre** *die* love affair; amour; **~akt** *der (geh.)* act of love; **ein Paar beim ~akt** a couple engaged in sexual intercourse; **~bande** *Pl. (dichter. veralt.)* bonds of love; **~bedürfnis** *das* need for love; **~beweis** *der* proof *or* token of love; **~beziehung** *die* [love] affair **(zu, mit** with); **~brief** *der* love letter; **~dichtung** *die* love poetry; **~dienerin** *die (verhüll. scherzh.)* lady of pleasure; **~dienst** *der* [act of] kindness; favour; **jmdm. einen ~dienst erweisen** do sb. a kindness *or* favour; **~entzug** *der (Psych.)* withdrawal of love; **~erklärung** *die* declaration of love; **~fähig** *Adj.* capable of love *postpos.;* **~fähigkeit** *die* capacity for love; **~film** *der* romantic film; **~gabe** *die* charitable gift; *(Spende)* donation; **~gedicht** *das* love poem; **~geschichte** *die* A love story; B *(~affäre)* [love] affair; **~gott** *der* god of love; **~göttin** *die* goddess of love; **~heirat** *die* love match; **~knochen** *der (landsch.)* eclair; **~kummer** *der* lovesickness; **~kummer haben** be lovesick; be unhappily in love; **sich aus ~kummer umbringen** kill oneself for love; **~kunst** *die* art of love; **~laube** *die (scherzh.)* love nest; **~leben** *das* love life; **~lied** *das* love song; **~müh[e]** *die: in* **das ist vergebliche** *od.* **verlorene ~müh[e]** that is a waste of effort; **~nacht** *die* night of love; **~nest** *das* love nest; **~paar** *das* courting couple; [pair of] lovers; **~perlen** *Pl.* hundreds and thousands; **~roman** *der* romantic novel; **~spiel** *das* love play; **~szene** *die* love scene; **~toll** *Adj.* love-crazed; **~töter** *Pl. (ugs. scherzh.)* passion killers *(sl. joc.)*; **~trank** *der;* **~~[e]s, ~tränke** love potion; **~trunken** *Adj. (dichter.)* intoxicated with love *postpos.;* **~verhältnis** *das* [love] affair; **~verlust** *der (Psych.)* loss of love

**liebe·voll** ❶ *Adj.* loving *attrib.* ‹care›; affectionate ‹embrace, gesture, person›. ❷ *adv.* A lovingly; affectionately; B *(mit Sorgfalt)* lovingly; with loving care; **sehr ~ dekoriert** decorated with much loving care

***lieb|gewinnen** ⇒ **lieb** 1F

***lieb·geworden** ⇒ **lieb** 1D

***lieb|haben** ⇒ **lieb** 1F

**Liebhaber** /'li:pha:bɐ/ *der;* **~s, ~** A lover; B *(Interessierter, Anhänger)* enthusiast (+ *Gen.* for); *(Sammler)* collector; **ein ~ von schönen Teppichen/Oldtimern** a lover of beautiful carpets/a vintage-car enthusiast; **ein Stück für ~:** a collector's item

**Liebhaber·ausgabe** *die* collector's edition; bibliophile edition

**Liebhaberei** *die;* **~, ~en** hobby

**Liebhaberin** *die;* **~, ~nen** ⇒ **Liebhaber**

**Liebhaber-:** **~preis** *der* collector's price; **~stück** *das* collector's item; **~wert** *die* **~wert haben** be valuable as a collector's item/collectors' items

**lieb·kosen** *tr. V. (geh.)* caress

**Liebkosung** *die;* **~, ~en** *(geh.)* caress

**lieblich** ❶ *Adj.* A charming; appealing; *(friedlich)* peaceful; gentle ‹landscape›; B *(angenehm)* sweet ‹scent, sound›; fragrant ‹flower›; melodious ‹sound›; mellow ‹red wine›; [medium] sweet ‹white wine›; **C** (*ugs. iron: unangenehm*) **das kann ja ~ werden** this is going to be just great (*coll. iron.*). **2** *adv.* **A** charmingly; sweetly; **B** (*angenehm*) pleasingly; **eine ~ klingende Stimme** a sweet and melodious voice

**Lieblichkeit** *die;* ~ **A** charm; sweetness; (*einer Landschaft*) gentleness; **B** (*angenehme Wirkung*) sweetness; (*des Klangs*) melodiousness; (*des Dufts*) fragrance; (*des Rotweins*) mellowness; **C** (*Karnevalsprinzessin*) **Ihre ~:** *title given to carnival queen*

**Liebling** *der;* **~s, ~e A** (*geliebte Person; bes. als Anrede*) darling; **B** (*bevorzugte Person*) favourite; (*des Publikums*) darling; **der ~ des Lehrers** teacher's pet; **der ~ der Nation** the nation's favourite; **ein ~ der Götter** (*fig.*) a darling of the gods

**Lieblings-** favourite

**lieb·los 1** *Adj.* loveless; (*grausam*) heartless, unfeeling ‹treatment, behaviour›. **2** *adv.* **A** without affection; **~ von jmdm. sprechen** speak unkindly of sb.; **B** (*ohne Sorgfalt*) carelessly; without proper care

**Lieblosigkeit** *die;* **~, ~en A** (*Handlung/Äußerung*) unkind *or* unfeeling act/word; **B** (*lieblose Art*) unkindness; lack of feeling; (*Mangel an Sorgfalt*) lack of care

**Lieb·reiz** *der* (*geh.*) beguiling charm

**Liebschaft** *die;* **~, ~en** [casual] affair; (*Flirt*) flirtation

**liebst...** /li:pst.../ **1** *Adj.:* ⇒ **lieb. 2** *Adv.* **am ~en** ⇒ **gern**

**Liebste** *der/die; adj. Dekl.* (*veralt.*) loved one; sweetheart; **meine ~:** my dearest

**Liebstöckel** /'li:p-ʃtœkl̩/ *das od. der;* **~s, ~** (*Bot.*) lovage

**Liechtenstein** (*das*); **~s** Liechtenstein; ⇒ *auch* **Fürstentum**

**Lied** /li:t/ *das;* **~[e]s, ~er** song; (*Kirchen~*) hymn; (*deutsches Kunst~*) lied; **und das Ende vom ~ ist dann, dass ...** (*ugs.*) and the upshot *or* net result is that; **es ist immer das alte** *od.* **gleiche** *od.* **dasselbe ~** (*ugs.*) it's always the same old story; **davon kann ich ein ~ singen** I can tell you a thing or two about that; **das Hohe ~** *od.* **~ der ~er** (*bibl.*) the Song of Songs

**Lieder-: ~abend** *der* [evening] song recital; (*mit deutschen Kunstliedern*) [evening] lieder recital; **~buch** *das* songbook; **~handschrift** *die* [medieval] song manuscript

**Liederjan** /'li:dɐja:n/ *der;* **~[e]s, ~e** (*ugs.*) messy devil

**liederlich** /'li:dɐlɪç/ **1** *Adj.* **A** (*schlampig*) slovenly; messy ‹hairstyle, person›; slipshod, slovenly ‹work›; **B** (*verwerflich*) dissolute; **ein ~es Weibsstück** (*salopp abwertend*) a floozie (*coll.*). **2** *adv.* sloppily; messily; **~ angezogen sein** be slovenly dressed; **~ geschrieben** written in a slipshod manner

**Liederlichkeit** *die;* ~ **A** (*Schlampigkeit*) slovenliness; **B** (*Verwerflichkeit*) dissoluteness

**Lieder-: ~macher** *der,* **~macherin** *die* singer-songwriter (*writing satirical songs mainly on topical/political subjects*); **~zyklus** *der* song cycle

**lief** /li:f/ *1. u. 3. Pers. Sg. Prät. v.* **laufen**

**Lieferant** /lifə'rant/ *der;* **~en, ~en** (*Firma*) supplier; (*Auslieferer*) delivery man; **~en werden gebeten, den Eingang im Hof zu benutzen** all deliveries via the entrance in the yard

**Lieferanten·eingang** *der* goods entrance; (*bei Wohnhäusern*) tradesmen's entrance

**Lieferantin** *die;* **~, ~nen** ⇒ **Lieferant**: supplier; delivery woman

**lieferbar** *Adj.* available; (*vorrätig*) in stock; **sofort ~:** available for immediate delivery; **~ zum 1.10.89** for delivery by 1.10.89

**Liefer-: ~bedingungen** *Pl.* terms of delivery; **~betrieb** *der,* **~firma** *die* supplier; **~frist** *die* delivery time; **bei Möbeln besteht eine ~frist von 6 bis 8 Wochen** there is 6-8 weeks delivery on furniture

*old spelling (see note on page 1707)

**liefern** /'li:fɐn/ *tr. V.* **A** (*bringen*) deliver (**an** + *Akk.* to); (*zur Verfügung stellen*) supply; **wir ~ auch ins Ausland** we also supply our goods abroad *or* deliver to foreign destinations; **wir ~ nicht an Privat** we do not supply private individuals; **jmdm. etw. ~:** supply sb. with sth.; deliver sth. to sb.; **B** (*hervorbringen*) produce; (*geben*) provide ‹eggs, honey, examples, raw material, etc.›; **den Nachweis** *od.* **Beweis für etw. ~:** provide proof of sth.; **C** (*austragen*) **sich** (*Dat.*) **eine Schlacht ~:** fight a battle [with each other]; **jmdm. ein gutes Spiel ~:** give sb. a good game *or* match; **D** (*ugs.:*) **geliefert sein** be sunk (*coll.*); have had it (*coll.*)

**Liefer-: ~schein** *der* acknowledgement of delivery; delivery note; **~termin** *der* delivery date **~umfang** *der* (*Kaufmannspr.*) scope of supply; **die Batterien gehören zum ~umfang** batteries are included [in the price]

**Lieferung** *die;* **~, ~en A** (*das Liefern*) delivery; **Zahlung bei ~:** payment on delivery; **B** (*Ware*) consignment [of goods]; delivery; **C** (*Buchw.*) instalment; (*eines Wörterbuchs usw.*) fascicle

**Liefer-: ~vertrag** *der* supply contract; **~wagen** *der* [delivery] van; (*offen*) pick-up; **~zeit** *die* delivery time

**Liege** /'li:gə/ *die;* **~, ~n** daybed; (*zum Ausklappen*) bed settee; sofa bed; (*als Gartenmöbel*) sunlounger

**Liege·geld** *das* (*Schifffahrt*) demurrage

**liegen** *unr. itr. V.;* (*südd., österr., schweiz. mit sein*) **A** lie; ‹person› be lying down; (*sich hinlegen*) lie down; **~ bleiben** ‹person› stay [lying]; **[im Bett] ~ bleiben** stay in bed; **bewusstlos/bewegungslos ~ bleiben** lie unconscious/motionless; **verletzt ~ bleiben** end up lying on the ground injured; **während der Krankheit musste er ~:** while he was ill he had to lie down all the time; **Weinflaschen sollen ~:** wine bottles should lie flat *or* on their sides; **die Beine sollen höher ~ als der Kopf** your legs should be [placed] higher than your head; **auf dem Boden ~:** lie on the floor; ‹carpet› be on the floor; **im Bett ~:** lie in bed; (*das Bett hüten*) be *or* stay in bed; **auf den Knien ~:** be prostrate on one's knees; **im Krankenhaus/auf Station 6 ~:** be in hospital/in ward 6; **krank im Bett ~:** be ill in bed; **der Wagen liegt gut auf der Straße** the car holds the road well; **richtig ~:** be in the right position; ‹hair› stay in place; **die Säge liegt gut/fest in der Hand** the saw rests comfortably/firmly in the hand; **B** (*vorhanden sein*) lie; **es liegt Schnee auf den Bergen** there is snow [lying] on the hills; **der Schnee liegt meterhoch** the snow is more than a metre deep; **der Schnee bleibt ~:** the snow lies; **der Stoff liegt 80 cm breit** the material is 80 cm wide; **C** (*sich befinden*) be; ‹object› be [lying]; ‹town, house, etc.› be [situated]; **etw. im Keller** *usw.* **~ haben** have sth. [lying] in the cellar *etc.;* **die Preise ~ höher** prices are higher; **die Verhältnisse ~/die Sache liegt anders** circumstances are/the situation is different; **wie die Dinge ~:** as things are or stand [at the moment]; **die Stadt liegt an der Küste** the town is *or* lies on the coast; **das Dorf liegt sehr hoch** the village is very high up; **das liegt an meinem Weg** it is on my way; **schön ~:** be beautifully situated; **ein einsam ~der Hof** an isolated farm; **verkehrsgünstig ~:** be well placed for transport; ‹town, city› have good communications; **etw. rechts/links ~ lassen** leave sth. on one's right/left; **das Fenster liegt nach vorn/nach Süden/zum Garten** the window is at the front/faces south/faces the garden; **es liegt nicht in meiner Absicht, das zu tun** it is not my intention to do that; **nichts liegt uns ferner, als ...** nothing could be further from our intentions than ...; **die Betonung liegt auf der ersten Silbe** the stress is on the first syllable; **das Essen lag mir schwer im Magen** the food/meal lay heavy on my stomach; **auf ihm liegt eine große Verantwortung** a heavy responsibility rests on his shoulders; **D** (*zeitlich*) be; **das liegt noch vor mir/schon hinter mir** I still have that to come/that's all behind me now; **die Stunden, die zwischen den Prüfungen lagen** the hours between the examinations; **das liegt so weit** *od.* **lange zurück** it is so long ago; **E das liegt an ihm** *od.* **bei ihm** it is up to him; (*ist seine Schuld*) it is his fault; **die Verantwortung/Schuld liegt bei ihm** it is his responsibility/fault; **an mir soll es nicht ~:** don't let me stop you; I won't stand in your way; (*ich werde mich beteiligen*) I'm easy (*coll.*); **es liegt daran, dass ...** it is because ...; **ich weiß nicht, woran es liegt** I don't know what the reason is; **woran mag es nur ~, dass ...?** why ever is it that ...?; **F** (*gemäß sein*) **es liegt mir nicht** it doesn't suit me; it isn't right for me; (*es spricht mich nicht an*) it doesn't appeal to me; (*ich mag es nicht*) I don't like it *or* care for it; **Physik liegt ihr sehr** physics is right up her street (*coll.*); **solche Tätigkeiten ~ ihm [sehr]** this kind of activity suits him [down to the ground]; **es liegt ihm nicht, das zu tun** he does not like doing that; (*so etwas tut er nicht*) it is not his way to do that; **mit Kindern umzugehen scheint ihr nicht zu ~:** handling children doesn't seem to be her cup of tea (*coll.*); **G daran liegt ihm viel/wenig/nichts** he sets great/little/no store by that; it means a lot/little/nothing to him; **ihr liegt [einiges] daran, anerkannt zu werden** it is of [some] importance to her to be recognized; **an ihm liegt mir schon etwas** I do care about him [a bit]; **H** (*bedeckt sein*) **der Tisch liegt voller Bücher** the desk is covered with books; **I** (*bes. Milit.: verweilen*) be; ‹troops› be stationed; ‹ship› lie; **vor Verdun ~:** be stationed *or* positioned outside Verdun; **irgendwo [in Quartier] ~:** be quartered *or* billeted somewhere; **J ~ bleiben** ‹thing› stay, be left; (*vergessen werden*) be left behind; (*nicht verkauft werden*) remain unsold; (*nicht erledigt werden*) be left undone; **diese Briefe können bis morgen ~ bleiben** these letters can wait until tomorrow; **etw. ~ lassen** leave sth.; (*vergessen*) leave sth. [behind]; (*unerledigt lassen*) leave sth. undone; **er ließ die Papiere auf dem Tisch ~:** he left the papers [lying] on the desk; **sie hat die Briefe ~ lassen** she left the letters unopened/unposted *etc.;* **alles stehen und ~ lassen** drop everything; **K ~ bleiben** (*eine Panne haben*) break down; ⇒ *auch* **Straße**

***liegen|bleiben** ⇒ **liegen** A, B, J, K

**liegend** reclining, recumbent ‹figure, posture›; prone ‹position›; horizontal ‹position, engine›; **etw. ~ aufbewahren** store sth. flat/on its side

***liegen|lassen** ⇒ **liegen** J

**Liegenschaft** *die;* **~, ~en** (*bes. Rechtsspr.*) land holding; (*Gebäude*) property

**Liege-: ~platz** *der* mooring; **~rad** *das* recumbent bicycle; **~sitz** *der* reclining seat; **~statt** *die* (*geh.*) resting place; (*Bett*) bed; **~stuhl** *der* (*einfach, mit Holzgestell*) deckchair; (*Luxusausstattung, mit Metallgestell*) lounger; **~stütz** *der;* **~~es, ~~e** press-up; **~stütz machen** do press-ups; **in den ~stütz gehen** get into a press-up position; **~wagen** *der* couchette car; **wollen Sie Schlafwagen oder ~wagen?** do you want a sleeper or a couchette?; **der ~wagen ist hinten** the couchettes are at the back of the train; **~wiese** *die* sunbathing lawn

**lieh** /li:/ *1. u. 3. Pers. Sg. Prät. v.* **leihen**

**lies** /li:s/ *Imperativ Sg. v.* **lesen**

**Lieschen** /'li:sçən/ **~ Müller** (*ugs.*) the average girl/woman (*coll.*); **Fleißiges ~** (*Bot.*) busy Lizzie; ⇒ *auch* **lieb** D

**Liese** *die;* **~, ~n** (*ugs. abwertend*) **eine dumme ~:** a stupid cow (*sl.*); **eine liederliche ~:** a slovenly Sue; a messy Jessie

**ließ** /li:s/ *1. u. 3. Pers. Sg. Prät. v.* **lassen**

**liest** /li:st/ *3. Pers. Sg. Präsens v.* **lesen**

**Lift** /lɪft/ *der;* **~[e]s, ~e** *od.* **~s A** lift (*Brit.*); elevator (*Amer.*); **B** *Pl.:* **~e** (*Ski~, Sessel~*) lift

**Lift·boy** *der* lift boy (*Brit.*); elevator boy (*Amer.*)

**liften**[1] /'lɪftn̩/ *itr. V.; mit sein* take the [ski] lift

**liften**[2] *tr. V.* **die Gesichtshaut ~:** tighten the skin of the face; **sich ~ lassen** (*ugs.*) have a facelift

**Liga** /'li:ga/ *die; ~,* **Ligen** league; (*Sport*) division; **~ für Menschenrechte** League of Human Rights

**Ligament** /liga'mɛnt/ *das; ~[e], ~e* ▶471 (*Anat.*) ligament

**Ligatur** /liga'tu:ɐ̯/ *die; ~, ~en* (*Druckw., Musik, Med.*) ligature; (*Musik: in der modernen Notenschrift*) ligature; tie

**Liguster** /li'gʊstɐ/ *der; ~s, ~* (*Bot.*) privet

**liieren** /li'i:rən/ ❶ *refl. V.* Ⓐ **sich mit jmdm. ~:** start an affair with sb.; **mit jmdm. liiert sein** be having an affair with sb.; Ⓑ (*bes. Wirtsch., Politik*) ‹firm› form links (**mit** with); **sich [miteinander] ~** ‹firms, countries› form links; **mit einer Firma liiert sein** have links with a firm. ❷ *tr. V.* (*bes. Wirtsch.*) **zwei Betriebe miteinander ~:** establish links between two businesses

**Likör** /li'kø:ɐ̯/ *der; ~s, ~e* liqueur

**lila** /'li:la/ *indekl. Adj.* mauve; (*dunkel~*) purple

**Lila** *das; ~s od.* (*ugs.*) **~s** mauve; (*Dunkel~*) purple

**Lilie** /'li:li̯ə/ *die; ~, ~n* Ⓐ lily; Ⓑ (*Her.*) fleur-de-lis

**Liliput-** /'li:lipʊt-/ miniature ‹railway, format›; tiny ‹house, country›

**Liliputaner** /lilipu'ta:nɐ/ *der; ~s, ~,* **Liliputanerin** *die; ~, ~nen* dwarf; midget

**Limburger** /'lɪmbʊrgɐ/ *der; ~s, ~,* **Limburger Käse** *der* Limburger [cheese]

**Limerick** /'lɪmərɪk/ *der; ~[s], ~s* limerick

**Limes** /'li:mɛs/ *der; ~, ~* Ⓐ (*hist.*) limes; Ⓑ (*Math.*) limit

**Limit** /'lɪmɪt/ *das; ~s, ~s* limit; **das äußerste ~:** the top limit; (*Termin*) the latest possible date; **das ~ überschreiten** exceed the limit; (*fig.*) go too far; **dieses ~ kann nicht unterschritten werden** one cannot go below this minimum; **jmdm. ein ~ [bis Ende der Woche** *usw.*] **setzen** set sb. a limit [of the end of the week *etc.*]

**limitieren** *tr. V.* limit; restrict

**Limo** /'lɪmo/ *die, auch: das; ~, ~[s]* (*ugs.*) fizzy drink; **die Kinder kriegen ~:** the children can have pop (*coll.*)

**Limonade** /limo'na:də/ *die; ~, ~n* fizzy drink; mineral; (*Zitronen~*) lemonade

**Limone** /li'mo:nə/ *die; ~, ~n* lime

**Limousine** /limu'zi:nə/ *die; ~, ~n* [large] saloon (*Brit.*) *or* (*Amer.*) sedan; (*mit Trennwand*) limousine

**lind** /lɪnt/ *Adj.* (*dichter.*) Ⓐ (*mild*) balmy ‹night, air›; Ⓑ (*sanft*) gentle ‹wind, voice›

**Linde** /'lɪndə/ *die; ~, ~n* Ⓐ (*Baum*) lime [tree]; Ⓑ (*Holz*) limewood

**Linden-: ~baum** *der* lime tree; **~blüten·honig** *der* lime-blossom honey; **~blüten·tee** *der* lime-blossom tea

**lindern** /'lɪndɐn/ *tr. V.* alleviate, relieve ‹suffering›; ease, relieve ‹pain›; quench, slake ‹thirst›

**Linderung** *die; ~* (*der Not*) relief; alleviation; (*des Schmerzes*) relief; **jmdm. [vorübergehend/sofort] ~ bringen** bring sb. [temporary/immediate] relief

**lind·grün** *Adj.* lime green

**Lind·wurm** /'lɪnt-/ *der* (*Myth.*) lindworm

**Lineal** /line'a:l/ *das; ~s, ~e* ruler; **Striche mit einem ~ ziehen** rule lines; **er ging, als ob er ein ~ verschluckt hätte** he walked as stiff as a poker

**linear** /line'a:ɐ̯/ ❶ *Adj.* Ⓐ (*Math., Physik; auch geh.: geradlinig*) linear; Ⓑ (*Arbeitswelt*) **~e Lohnerhöhung** phased pay rise in a series of equal steps; **~e Abschreibung** straight-line depreciation. ❷ *adv.* Ⓐ (*Phys., geh.*) linearly; in a linear manner; Ⓑ (*Arbeitswelt*) **die Gehälter ~ erhöhen/eine Lohnerhöhung ~ vornehmen** increase salaries/implement a pay increase in a series of equal steps

**Linguist** /lɪŋ'gʊɪst/ *der; ~en, ~en* linguist

**Linguistik** *die; ~:* linguistics *sing., no art.*

**Linguistin** *die; ~, ~nen* linguist

**linguistisch** ❶ *Adj.* linguistic. ❷ *adv.* linguistically

**Linie** /'li:ni̯ə/ *die; ~, ~n* Ⓐ line; **ein Kleid in modischer/strenger ~:** a dress in a fashionable/severe style *or* with fashionable/severe lines; **auf die [schlanke] ~ achten** (*ugs. scherzh.*) watch one's figure; **in einer ~ stehen/sich in einer ~ aufstellen** stand in line/line up; **die feindliche[n] ~[n]** (*Milit.*) [the] enemy lines *pl.*; **in der vordersten** *od.* **in vorderster ~ kämpfen** (*Milit.*) fight in the front line; **in vorderster ~ stehen** (*fig.*) be in the front line; **in ~ antreten** (*Milit.*) fall in; (*Sport*) line up; Ⓑ ▶818 (*Verkehrsstrecke*) route; (*Eisenbahn~, Straßenbahn~*) line; route; **die ~ Frankfurt-London** the Frankfurt-London route; **eine ~ stilllegen** stop a service; Ⓒ (*Verkehrsmittel*) **fahren Sie mit der ~ 4** take a *or* the number 4; **die ~ 12** the number 12; Ⓓ (*allgemeine Richtung*) line; policy; **eine ~ vertreten** take a line; **die große ~ wahren** stick to the broad principle; **eine/keine klare ~ erkennen lassen** reveal a/no clear policy; **sich auf der gleichen ~ bewegen** be on *or* along the same lines *pl.*; Ⓔ (*Verwandtschaftszweig*) line; **in direkter ~ von jmdm. abstammen** be directly descended from *or* a direct descendant of sb.; Ⓕ *in* **in erster ~ geht es darum, dass das Projekt beschleunigt wird** the first priority is to speed up the project; **in erster ~ kommt sein Stellvertreter infrage** his deputy is first in line; **wir müssen in erster ~ darauf bedacht sein, dass ...** our prime concern must be that ...; **Geld spielt in dieser Sache erst in zweiter ~ eine Rolle** money is only of secondary importance *or* plays only a secondary role in this matter; **auf der ganzen ~:** all along the line; Ⓖ (*Seemannsspr.: Äquator*) **die ~ passieren** *od.* **kreuzen** cross the line

**linien-, Linien-: ~blatt** *das* line guide; guide sheet; **~bus** *der* regular bus; **~dienst** *der* regular service; (*Flugw.*) scheduled *or* regular service; **im ~dienst fahren/fliegen** ‹bus, coach/aircraft› be used on regular routes; **~flug** *der* scheduled flight; **~flugzeug** *das* scheduled plane *or* aircraft; **~führung** *die* Ⓐ (*Art des Zeichnens*) linework; Ⓑ (*Gestaltung der Umriss~*) lines *pl.*; **~maschine** *die* ⇒ **~flugzeug**; **~netz** *das* route network; **~papier** *das* ruled *or* lined paper; **~richter** *der* (*Fußball usw.*) linesman; (*Tennis*) line judge; (*Rugby*) touch judge; **~richterin** *die* (*Fußball usw.*) lineswoman; (*Tennis*) line judge; (*Rugby*) touch judge; **~schiff** *das* Ⓐ liner; Ⓑ (*hist.*) ship of the line; **~treu** (*abwertend*) ❶ *Adj.* loyal to the party line *postpos.*; ❷ *adv.* ‹act› in accordance with the party line; **~verkehr** *der* regular services *pl.*; (*Flugw.*) scheduled *or* regular services *pl.*; **im ~verkehr fahren/fliegen** ‹aircraft› be used on regular *or* scheduled routes

**linieren** /li'ni:rən/, **liniieren** /lini'i:rən/ *tr. V.* rule; rule lines on; **lini[i]ertes Papier** ruled *or* lined paper

**Linierung, Liniierung** *die; ~, ~en* Ⓐ (*Vorgang*) ruling; Ⓑ (*Linien*) [ruled] lines *pl.*

**link** /lɪŋk/ (*salopp*) ❶ *Adj.* underhand; shady, underhand ‹deal›; **ein ~er Vogel** a shady customer (*coll.*) *or* character; **komm mir bloß nicht auf die ~e Tour!** just don't try and pull a fast one on me (*coll.*). ❷ *adv.* in an underhand way

**Link** *der; ~s, ~s* (*DV*) link

**link...** *Adj.* Ⓐ left; left[-hand] ‹edge›; **die ~e Spur** the left-hand lane; **~er Hand, zur ~en Hand** on the left-hand side; on the left; **auf der ~en Seite** on the left-hand side; **auf der ~en Seite gehen** walk on the left; **der ~e Außenstürmer/Verteidiger** (*Ballspiele*) the outside left/the left back; **mit dem ~en Fuß** *od.* **Bein zuerst aufgestanden sein** (*fig. ugs.*) have got out of bed on the wrong side; ⇒ *auch* **Ehe**; Ⓑ (*außen, sichtbar*) wrong, reverse ‹side›; **~e Maschen** (*Handarb.*) purl stitches; **eine ~e Masche stricken** purl one; Ⓒ (*in der Politik*) left-wing; leftist (*derog.*); **der ~e Flügel einer Partei** the left wing of a party

**Linke**[1] *der/die; adj. Dekl.* left-winger; leftist (*derog.*); **von den ~n organisiert sein** be organized by the left

**Linke**[2] *die; ~n, ~n* Ⓐ (*Hand*) left hand; **seine ~ einsetzen** (*Boxen*) use one's left; **zur ~n des Königs** on *or* to the left of the king; on the king's left; **jmdm. zur ~n** on sb.'s left; to the left of sb.; **zur ~n** on the left; Ⓑ (*Politik*) left

**linker·seits** *Adv.* on the left[-hand side]

**linkisch** ❶ *Adj.* awkward. ❷ *adv.* awkwardly

**links** /lɪŋks/ ❶ *Adv.* Ⓐ ▶818 (*auf der linken Seite*) on the left; (*Theater*) stage right; **die zweite Straße ~:** the second street *or* turning on the left; **~ von jmdm/etw.** on sb.'s left *or* to the left of sb./on *or* to the left of sth.; **von ~ kommen** come from the left; **nach ~ gehen/sich nach ~ wenden** go/turn to the left; **er wandte sich nach ~:** he turned to his *or* the left; **sich ~ halten** keep to the left; **weder nach ~ noch nach rechts schauend verließ sie den Saal** looking neither [to the] left nor [to the] right she walked out of the room; **er blickte weder nach ~ noch nach rechts, sondern rannte einfach über die Straße** he didn't look left or right, but just ran straight across the road; **sich ~ einordnen** move *or* get into the left-hand lane; **~ außen** (*Ballspiele*) ‹run, break through› down the left wing; **[den Ball] nach ~ außen spielen** play the ball out to the left wing; **jmdn./etw. ~ liegen lassen** (*fig.*) ignore sb./sth.; **ich weiß/sie wissen** *usw.* **nicht [mehr], was ~ und [was] rechts ist** (*fig.*) I don't know 'where I am/they don't know 'where they are *etc.*; Ⓑ (*Politik*) on the left wing; **~ stehen** *od.* **sein** be left-wing *or* on the left; **~ eingestellt sein** have left-wing leanings; **weit ~ stehen** be on the far left; **ganz ~ außen stehen** be on the extreme left [wing]; **nach ~ außen** to the extreme left; **~ stehend** left-wing; Ⓒ (*ugs.: ~händig*) left-handed; **mit ~** (*fig.*) easily; with no trouble; Ⓓ (*Handarb.*) **zwei ~, zwei rechts** two purl, two plain; purl two, knit two; **ein ~ gestrickter Pullover** a purl[-knit] pullover; Ⓔ (*~seitig*) **etw. von ~ bügeln** iron sth. on the wrong side *or* reverse side; **nach ~ wenden** turn ‹dress, skirt, etc.› inside out.
❷ ▶818 *Präp. mit Gen.* **~ des Rheins/der Straße** on the left side *or* bank of the Rhine/on the left-hand side of the road *or* to the left of the road

**links-, Links-: ~abbieger** *der*, **~abbiegerin** *die* (*Verkehrsw.*) motorist/cyclist/car *etc.* turning left; **die ~abbieger** the traffic *sing.* turning left; **als ~abbieger musste er ...** since he was turning left he had to ...; **~abbieger·spur** *die* (*Verkehrsw.*) left-hand turn lane; **~abweichler** *der*, **~abweichlerin** *die* (*Politik*) left deviationist; *~**außen** ⇒ **links** 1A, B; **~außen** *der; ~~s, ~~* Ⓐ (*Ballspiele*) left wing; outside left; Ⓑ (*Politik ugs.*) extreme left-winger; **~drall** *der* Ⓐ pull to the left; **der Tennisspieler gab dem Ball einen ~drall** the tennis player swerved the ball to the left; Ⓑ (*Waffent.*) left-handed twist; Ⓒ (*Politik ugs.*) tendency to the left; left-wing tendency; **~drehend** *Adj.* Ⓐ (*bes. Technik*) left-hand ‹thread›; Ⓑ (*Chemie, Physik*) laevorotatory; **~drehung** *die* (*Chemie, Physik*) laevorotation; **~extremismus** *der* (*Politik*) left-wing extremism; **~extremist** *der*, **~extremistin** *die* (*Politik*) left-wing extremist; **~gängig** *Adj.* ⇒ **~drehend** A; **~gerichtet** *Adj.* (*Politik*) left-wing orientated; **~gewinde** *das* (*Technik*) left-hand thread; **~händer** /-hɛndɐ/ *der; ~~s, ~~,* **~händerin** *die; ~~, ~~nen* left-hander; **~händer[in] sein** be left-handed; **~händig** ❶ *Adj.* left-handed; ❷ *adv.* with one's left hand; **~händigkeit** *die; ~~:* left-handedness; **~herum** *Adv.* [round] to the left;

l

etw. **~herum drehen** turn sth. anticlockwise *or* [round] to the left; **~intellektuelle** *der/die* left-wing intellectual; **~kurve** *die* left-hand bend; **~lastig** *Adj.* **A** ‹ship› listing to the left; ‹car› down at the left, leaning to the left; **~lastig sein** ‹ship› list to the left, have a list to the left; ‹car› be down at the left, lean to the left; **B** (*Politik ugs.*) leftist; **~läufig** *Adj.* running from right to left *postpos., not pred.;* **~liberal** *Adj.* left-wing liberal; **~liberale** *der/die* left-wing liberal; **~partei** *die* (*Politik*) left-wing party; **~radikal** (*Politik*) **1** *Adj.* radical left-wing; **2** *adv.* **eine ~radikal orientierte Gruppe** a group with a radical left-wing orientation; **~radikale** *der/die* left-wing radical; **~radikalismus** *der* left-wing radicalism; **~rheinisch** **1** *Adj.* on *or* to the left of the Rhine *postpos.;* **auf der ~rheinischen Seite** on the left side of the Rhine; **2** *adv.* on *or* to the left of the Rhine; **~ruck** *der* (*Politik ugs.*) shift to the left; **~rum** *Adv.* (*ugs.*) ⇒ **~herum**; **~seitig** **1** *Adj.* ‹paralysis› of the left side; **2** *adv.* on the left [side]; **~seitig gelähmt sein** be paralysed on *or* down the *or* one's left side; ***~stehend** ⇒ **links 1B**; **~steuerung** *die* left-hand drive; **~um** /*auch:* -'-/ *Adv.* (*bes. Milit.*) to the left; **~um kehrt!** to the left about turn!; **~um machen** do a left turn; **~verkehr** *der* driving *no art.* on the left

**linnen** /'lɪnən/ *Adj.* (*veralt.*) linen

**Linnen** *das;* **~s, ~** (*veralt.*) linen

**Linoleum** /li'no:leʊm/ *das;* **~s** linoleum; lino

**Linol·schnitt** *der* linocut

**Linse** /'lɪnzə/ *die;* **~, ~n** **A** (*Bot., Kochk.*) lentil; **B** (*Med., Optik*) lens; **C** (*ugs.: Objektiv*) lens; **jmdn. vor die ~ bekommen** get sb. in front of the camera

**linsen** *itr. V.* (*ugs.*) peep; peek

**Linsen-: ~gericht** *das* lentil dish; **für ein ~gericht** (*geh.*) for a mess of pottage; **~suppe** *die* lentil soup

**Lippe** /'lɪpə/ *die;* **~, ~n** ▶ **471** lip; **jmdm. nicht über die ~n kommen, nicht über jmds. ~n** (*Akk.*) **kommen** not pass sb.'s lips; **sie brachte es nicht über die ~n** she couldn't bring herself to say it; **jmdm. glatt von den ~n gehen** come easily to sb.'s lips; **ein fröhliches Lied auf den ~n** singing merrily; **an jmds. ~n** (*Dat.*) **hängen** hang on sb.'s every word; **eine [dicke** *od.* **große] ~ riskieren** (*salopp*) shoot one's mouth off (*sl.*)

**Lippen-: ~bekenntnis** *das* (*abwertend*) empty talk *no pl.;* **~bekenntnisse für etw. ablegen** pay lip service to sth.; **~blütler** *der;* **~~s, ~~** (*Bot.*) labiate; **~laut** *der* (*Phon.*) labial; **~stift** *der* lipstick

**liquid** /li'kvi:t/ *Adj.* (*Wirtsch.*) liquid ‹funds, resources›; solvent ‹business›; **ich bin zur Zeit nicht ~:** I'm out of funds at the moment

**Liquida** /'li:kvida/ *die;* **~, Liquidä** *od.* **Liquiden** (*Phon.*) liquid

**Liquidation** /likvida'tsjo:n/ *die;* **~, ~en** **A** (*verhüll.: Tötung*) liquidation; **B** (*Wirtsch.*) liquidation *no indef. art.;* **C** (*Rechnung*) account; **D** (*geh.: Tilgung*) elimination; (*eines Systems*) abolition

**liquide** ⇒ **liquid**

**liquidieren** /likvi'di:rən/ **1** *tr. V.* **A** (*verhüll.: töten*) liquidate; **B** (*Wirtsch.*) liquidate; **C** (*Rechnung ausstellen*) charge; **D** (*geh.: tilgen*) eliminate; abolish ‹system of government›. **2** *itr. V.* (*Wirtsch.*) go into liquidation

**Liquidierung** *die;* **~, ~en** ⇒ **Liquidation**

**Liquidität** /likvidi'tɛ:t/ *die;* **~, ~en** (*Wirtsch.*) liquidity; solvency; (*flüssige Mittel*) liquid assets *pl.*

**Liquiditäts·schwierigkeiten** *Pl.* **in ~ sein** (*Wirtsch.*) have liquidity problems

**lispeln** /'lɪspl̩n/ *itr. V.* **A** lisp; **er hat schon immer gelispelt** he's always had a lisp; **B** *auch tr.* (*flüstern*) whisper

**Lissabon** /'lɪsabɔn/ (*das*); **~s** ▶ **700** Lisbon

**Lissabonner** /'lɪsabɔnɐ/ ▶ **700** **1** *indekl. Adj.* Lisbon; ⇒ *auch* **Kölner 1**. **2** *der;* **~s, ~:** inhabitant/native of Lisbon; ⇒ *auch* **Kölner 2**

**Lissabonnerin** *die;* **~, ~nen** ⇒ **Lissabonner 2**

**List** /lɪst/ *die;* **~, ~en** **A** [cunning] trick *or* ruse; **zu einer ~ greifen** resort to a [cunning] trick *or* ruse; use a little cunning; **B** (*listige Art*) cunning; **mit ~ und Tücke** (*ugs.*) by cunning and trickery

**Liste** *die;* **~, ~n** list; **eine ~ über etw.** (*Akk.*) **anlegen/führen** draw up/keep a list of sth.; **jmdn./etw. auf eine ~ setzen** put sb./sth. on a list; **jmdn./etw. von einer ~ streichen** take *or* cross sb./sth. off a list; **eine schwarze ~:** a blacklist

**Listen-: ~platz** *der* (*Politik*) place on the [party] list; **~preis** *der* list price; **~wahl** *die* (*Parl.*) list system

**listig** **1** *Adj.* cunning; crafty. **2** *adv.* cunningly; craftily; **jmdn. ~ ansehen/angrinsen** look/grin at sb. slyly.

**Litanei** /lita'nai/ *die;* **~, ~en** (*Rel., auch fig. abwertend*) litany; **eine ~ beten/**(*abwertend*) **herbeten** recite a litany

**Litauen** /'li:tauən/ (*das*); **~s** Lithuania

**Litauer** *der;* **~s, ~, Litauerin** *die;* **~, ~nen** Lithuanian

**litauisch** *Adj.* ▶ **696** Lithuanian

**Liter** /'li:tɐ/ *der, auch: das;* **~s, ~** ▶ **611** litre

**literar·historisch** ⇒ **literaturgeschichtlich**

**literarisch** /lɪtə'ra:rɪʃ/ **1** *Adj.* literary. **2** *adv.* **~ hervortreten** emerge as a writer; **sich ~ betätigen** write; do some writing; **~ interessiert/gebildet sein** be interested in literature/be well-read

**Literat** /lɪtə'ra:t/ *der;* **~en, ~en, Literatin** *die;* **~, ~nen** writer; literary figure

**Literatur** /lɪtəra'tu:ɐ/ *die;* **~, ~en** literature; **belletristische ~:** belles-lettres *pl.;* **in die ~ eingehen** find one's place in literature

**literatur-, Literatur-: ~an·gabe** *die* [bibliographical] reference; **~denkmal** *das* literary monument; **~gattung** *die* literary genre; **~geschichte** *die* literary history; history of literature; **~geschichtlich** **1** *Adj.* literary-historical; **2** *adv.* **~geschichtlich interessiert/beschlagen sein** interested/versed in literary history; **~geschichtlich gesehen** from the point of view of literary history; **~hinweis** *der* reference to further reading; **~historiker** *der,* **~historikerin** *die* literary historian; **~kritik** *die* literary criticism; **~kritiker** *der,* **~kritikerin** *die* literary critic; **~papst** *der* (*iron.*) leading literary pundit; **~preis** *der* prize for literature; literary prize; **~verzeichnis** *das* list of references; **~wissenschaft** *die* literary studies *pl., no art.;* study of literature; **vergleichende ~wissenschaft** comparative literature; **~zeitschrift** *die* literary magazine; (*Fachzeitschrift*) literary journal

**Liter·flasche** *die* litre bottle

**liter·weise** *Adv.* by the litre; in litres

**Litfaß·säule** /'lɪtfas-/ *die* advertising column *or* pillar

**Lithograph** /lito'gra:f/ *der;* **~en, ~en** lithographer

**Lithographie** /litogra'fi:/ *die;* **~, ~n** **A** (*Verfahren*) lithography *no art.;* **B** (*Druck*) lithograph

**Lithographin** *die;* **~, ~nen** ⇒ **Lithograph**

**lithographisch** *Adj.* lithographic

**litt** /lɪt/ *1. u. 3. Pers. Sg. Prät. v.* **leiden**

**Liturgie** /litʊr'gi:/ *die;* **~, ~n** (*christl. Kirche*) liturgy

**liturgisch** **1** *Adj.* liturgical. **2** *adv.* liturgically

**Litze** /'lɪtsə/ *die;* **~, ~n** **A** braid; **B** (*Elektrot.*) flex (*Brit.*); cord (*Amer.*)

**live** /laif/ (*Rundf., Ferns.*) **1** *Adj.* live. **2** *adv.* live; **in dieser Sendung wird nur ~ gesungen** in this programme all the singing is live

**Live-: ~sendung, *~-Sendung** *die* (*Rundf., Ferns.*) live programme; (*Übertragung*) live broadcast; **~show, *~-Show** *die* live show; **~übertragung** *die* (*Rundf., Ferns.*) live broadcast

**Livius** /'li:vius/ (*der*) Livy

**Livree** /li'vre:/ *die;* **~, ~n** livery; **ein Diener in ~:** a liveried servant

**livriert** *Adj.* liveried

**Lizentiat, Lizentiatin** ⇒ **Lizenziat[1,2], Lizenziatin**

**Lizenz** /li'tsɛnts/ *die;* **~, ~en** licence; **etw. in ~ herstellen** manufacture sth. under licence

**Lizenz-: ~aus·gabe** *die* (*Buchw.*) licensed edition; **~gebühr** *die* licence fee; (*Verlagsw.*) royalty

**Lizenziat[1]** /litsɛn'tsia:t/ *der;* **~en, ~en** (*schweiz.*) licentiate

**Lizenziat[2]** *das;* **~s, ~e** (*schweiz.*) licentiate

**Lizenziatin** *die;* **~, ~nen** ⇒ **Lizenziat[1]**

**lizenzieren** /litsɛn'tsi:rən/ *tr. V.* license

**Lizenz-: ~spieler** *der,* **~spielerin** *die* (*Sport*) licensed professional; **~träger** *der,* **~trägerin** *die* licensee; **~vertrag** *der* licence agreement

**Lkw, LKW** *Abk.* **Lastkraftwagen** truck; lorry (*Brit.*)

**Lkw-Fahrer** *der,* **Lkw-Fahrerin** *die* truck *or* (*Brit.*) lorry driver; trucker (*Amer.*)

**Lob[1]** /lo:p/ *das;* **~[e]s, ~e** praise *no indef. art.;* **ein ~ bekommen** receive praise; come in for praise; **[ein] ~ für etw. verdienen** deserve praise for sth.; **jmdm. ~ spenden** (*geh.*) bestow praise on sb.; **über jedes ~ erhaben sein** be beyond praise; **voll des ~es** *od.* **des ~es voll über jmdn./etw. sein** (*geh.*) be full of praise for sb./sth.; **Gott sei ~ und Dank!** (*geh.*) praise and thanks be to God; **ein ~ dem Küchenchef/der Hausfrau** my compliments to the chef/the hostess

**Lob[2]** /lɔp/ *der;* **~s, ~s** (*Tennis*) lob

**Lobby** /'lɔbi/ *die;* **~, ~s** lobby

**Lobbyismus** *der;* **~:** lobbyism *no art.*

**Lobbyist** *der;* **~en, ~en, Lobbyistin** *die;* **~, ~nen** lobbyist

**loben** *tr., auch itr. V.* praise; **jmdn. für** *od.* **wegen etw. ~:** praise sb. for sth.; **jmdn./etw. ~d erwähnen** commend sb./sth.; **da lob ich mir ...** give me ... any day; what I like is ...; **das lob ich mir** good for you/him *etc.* (*coll.*); **„Bravo", lobte er [seinen Sohn]** 'Bravo', he said approvingly [to his son]; **er lobt gern** he is generous with his praise

**lobens·wert** **1** *Adj.* praiseworthy; laudable; commendable. **2** *adv.* laudably; commendably

**lobesam** *Adj.* (*veralt.*) **Kaiser Rotbart ~:** the good Emperor Redbeard *or* Barbarossa

**Lobes·hymne** *die* (*oft iron.*) hymn of praise; **~n auf jmdn./etw. singen** *od.* **anstimmen** (*fig.*) sing sb.'s praises/the praises of sth.; praise sb./sth. to the skies

**Lob-: ~gesang** *der* song *or* hymn of praise; **~hudelei** *die* (*abwertend*) extravagant praise *no pl.* (**auf** + *Akk.* of)

**löblich** /'lø:plɪç/ *Adj.* (*oft iron.*) laudable; commendable

**lob-, Lob-: ~lied** *das* song of praise; **ein ~lied auf jmdn./etw. anstimmen** (*fig.*) sing sb.'s praises/the praises of sth.; **~preisen** *unr. od. regelm. tr. V.* (*dichter.*) praise; **~preisung** *die;* **~, ~~en** (*dichter.*) praise; **zur ~preisung Gottes** in praise of God; **~rede** *die* eulogy; panegyric; **eine ~rede auf jmdn. halten** make a speech in praise of sb.; eulogize sb.

**Loch** /lɔx/ *das;* **~[e]s, Löcher** /'lœçɐ/ **A** ▶ **411** hole; **ein ~ im Zahn/Kopf haben** have a hole *or* cavity in one's tooth/gash on one's *or* the head; **sich** (*Dat.*) **ein ~ in den Kopf** *usw.* **stoßen** gash one's head *etc.;* **das ~ in etw.** (*Dat.*) **stopfen** (*fig.*) plug the gap in sth.; **ein großes ~ in jmds. Geldbeutel reißen** (*fig.*) make a big hole in sb.'s pocket; **jmdm. ein ~** *od.* **Löcher in den Bauch fragen** (*salopp*) drive sb. up the wall with [all] one's questions (*coll.*); **Löcher in die Luft gucken** *od.* **starren** (*ugs.*) gaze into space; **ein ~** *od.* **Löcher in die Luft schießen** (*ugs.*) shoot wide; miss completely; **auf** *od.* **aus dem letzten ~ pfeifen** be on one's/

*old spelling (see note on page 1707)

its last legs; ⇒ *auch* **saufen** 1 B; Ⓑ(*salopp abwertend: Wohnraum*) hole; Ⓒ(*salopp: Gefängnis*) nick (*sl.*); clink (*sl.*); **ins ~ kommen/im ~ sitzen** be put in/be in the nick *or* clink; Ⓓ(*derb: Vagina*) cunt (*coarse*); hole (*coarse*); Ⓔ(*ugs.: im Billardtisch*) pocket

**Loch-: ~beitel** *der* mortise chisel; **~billard** *das* pocket billiards; pool; **~eisen** *das* punch

**lochen** *tr. V.* Ⓐ punch holes/a hole in; punch, clip ‹ticket›; punch [holes in] ‹invoice, copy, bill› (*for filing*); (*perforieren*) perforate; Ⓑ(*DV*) punch

**Locher** *der;* **~s, ~** Ⓐ(*auch DV*) punch; Ⓑ(*Beruf*) keypunch operator

**löcherig** *Adj.* holey; full of holes *pred.;* **die Abwehr war ~** (*fig.*) the defence was full of gaps *or* was wide open; **sein Alibi/seine Argumentation war recht ~** (*fig.*) his alibi/argument was full of holes

**Locherin** *die;* **~, ~nen** keypunch operator

**löchern** *tr. V.* (*ugs.*) **jmdn. ~:** pester sb. to death; **jmdn. ~, etw. zu tun** pester sb. to do sth.

**Loch-: ~kamera** *die* pinhole camera; **~karte** *die* (*Technik, DV*) punch[ed] card

**Loch·karten·verfahren** *das* punch[ed]-card system

**löchrig** *Adj.* ⇒ **löcherig**

**Loch-: ~säge** *die* compass saw; keyhole saw; **~stickerei** *die* broderie anglaise; **~streifen** *der* (*Technik, DV*) punch[ed] tape; **~zange** *die* [ticket] punch; **~ziegel** *der* (*Bauw.*) perforated brick

**Locke** /ˈlɔkə/ *die;* **~, ~n** curl; **~n haben** have curly hair

**locken**[1] *tr. V.* Ⓐ lure; (*fig.*) entice (**aus** out of, **in** + *Akk.* into); **die Henne lockte die Küken** the hen called her chicks; **ein Tier aus dem Bau/in den Käfig ~:** lure an animal out of its hole/into its cage; **jmdn. in einen Hinterhalt/auf eine falsche Fährte ~:** lure sb. into an ambush/put sb. on the wrong track; Ⓑ(*reizen*) tempt; **es lockt mich sehr** I am very tempted; **ein ~des Angebot/Abenteuer** a tempting offer/alluring adventure

**locken**[2] ❶ *tr. V.* curl; **jmdm. das Haar ~:** curl sb.'s hair; **gelocktes Haar** curly hair. ❷ *refl. V.* ‹hair› curl

**löcken** /ˈlœkn̩/ *itr. V.* **wider** *od.* **gegen den Stachel ~** (*geh.*) kick against the pricks

**Locken-: ~haar** *das* curly hair; **~kopf** *der* Ⓐ curly hair; Ⓑ(*Mensch*) curly head; **~köpfig** *Adj.* curly haired; **~pracht** *die* (*scherzh.*) magnificent head of curls; **~wickler** *der;* **~~s, ~~:** [hair] curler *or* roller; **sich** (*Dat.*) **~wickler ins Haar drehen** put one's hair in curlers

**locker** ❶ *Adj.* Ⓐ loose ‹tooth, nail, chair leg, etc.›; **etw. ~ machen** loosen sth.; ⇒ *auch* **Schraube**; Ⓑ(*durchlässig, leicht*) loose ‹soil, snow, fabric›; light ‹mixture, cake›; Ⓒ(*entspannt*) relaxed ‹position, muscles›; slack ‹rope, rein›; (*fig.: unverbindlich*) loose ‹relationship, connection, etc.›; **das Seil/die Zügel ~ lassen** slacken the rope [off]/slacken the reins; **~ werden** ‹person› loosen up; Ⓓ(*leichtfertig*) loose ‹morals, life›; frivolous ‹jokes, remarks›; **sein ~es Mundwerk** (*salopp*) his big mouth (*coll.*); **ein ~er Vogel** (*ugs.*) a bit of a lad (*coll.*); ⇒ *auch* **Hand** F.

❷ *adv.* Ⓐ **~ sitzen** ‹tooth, screw, nail› be loose; **ein ~ sitzender Zahn** a loose tooth; **bei ihm sitzt das Geld ~ [in der Tasche]** (*fig.*) money burns a hole in his pocket; Ⓑ(*durchlässig*) loosely; ‹bake› lightly; Ⓒ(*entspannt, ungezwungen*) loosely; **etw. ganz ~ machen** (*ugs.*) do sth. without any trouble; **sich ~ geben** be relaxed; **~ vom Hocker** (*ugs.*) coolly; **dieses Gesetz wird ~ gehandhabt** this law is not strictly enforced

**locker-: ~|lassen** *unr. itr. V.* (*ugs.*) **nicht ~lassen** not give *or* let up; **~|machen** *tr. V.* (*ugs.*) fork up *or* out (*coll.*); shell out (*coll.*); **bei jmdm. etw. ~machen** get sb. to fork up *or* fork out sth.

**lockern** ❶ *tr. V.* Ⓐ loosen ‹screw, tie, collar, etc.›; slacken [off] ‹rope, dog leash, etc.›; (*fig.*) relax ‹regulation, law, etc.›; **seinen Griff ~:** loosen *or* relax one's grip; Ⓑ(*entspannen*) loosen up, relax ‹muscles, limbs›; (*fig.*) relax ‹attitude›; Ⓒ(*auf~*) loosen, break up ‹soil›. ❷ *refl. V.* Ⓐ ‹brick, tooth, etc.› work itself loose; **bei mir hat sich ein Zahn gelockert** one of my teeth has worked itself loose; **sein Griff lockerte sich** his grip loosened; Ⓑ(*entspannen*) ‹person› loosen up; (*vor Spielbeginn*) loosen *or* limber up; (*fig.*) ‹tenseness, tension› ease; **die Sitten haben sich gelockert** (*fig.*) morals have become *or* grown lax

**Lockerung** *die;* **~, ~en** Ⓐ loosening; (*fig.: von Bestimmung, Gesetz usw.*) relaxation; Ⓑ(*Entspannung*) loosening up; relaxation

**Lockerungs·übung** *die* loosening-up *or* limbering-up exercise

**lockig** *Adj.* curly

**Lock-: ~mittel** *das* enticement; **~ruf** *der* call; **~speise** *die* (*geh.*) bait; **~spitzel** *der* (*abwertend*) agent provocateur

**Lockung** *die;* **~, ~en** (*geh.*) temptation; **die ~ der Ferne** the lure of distant lands; **jmds. ~en** (*Dat.*) **widerstehen** resist sb.'s enticements

**Lock·vogel** *der* decoy; (*fig.*) lure; decoy

**Loden** /ˈloːdn̩/ *der;* **~s, ~:** loden

**Loden·mantel** *der* loden coat

**lodern** *itr. V.* (*geh., auch fig.*) blaze; **die Flammen loderten zum Himmel** the flames leapt up to the sky; **ihre Augen loderten vor Zorn** (*fig.*) her eyes blazed with anger

**Löffel** /ˈlœfl̩/ *der;* **~s, ~** Ⓐ spoon; (*als Maßangabe*) spoonful; **ein ~ Zucker** a spoonful of sugar; **den ~ abgeben** (*fig. salopp*) kick the bucket (*coll.*); **mit einem goldenen** *od.* **silbernen ~ im Mund geboren sein** (*fig. ugs.*) be born with a silver spoon in one's mouth; **jmdn. über den ~ barbieren** *od.* **balbieren** (*fig. ugs.*) do (*sl.*) *or* swindle sb.; Ⓑ(*Jägerspr.*) ear; (*fig.*) **sperr doch die ~ auf!** (*ugs.*) pin your lugholes (*Brit.*) *or* ears back! (*coll.*); **jmdm. eins** *od.* **ein paar hinter die ~ geben** (*ugs.*) give sb. a clout round the ear; **sich** (*Dat.*) **etw. hinter die ~ schreiben** (*ugs.*) get sth. into one's head

**Löffel·bagger** *der* mechanical shovel; excavator

**löffeln** *tr. V.* spoon [up]; **sie löffelte Suppe aus der Terrine** she ladled soup from the tureen

**Löffel·stiel** *der* [spoon] handle

**löffel·weise** *Adv.* by the spoonful

**log** /loːk/ *1. u. 3. Pers. Sg. Prät. v.* **lügen**

**Log** /lɔk/ *das;* **~s, ~e** (*Seew.*) log

**Logarithmen·tafel** *die* (*Math.*) log[arithmic] table

**logarithmieren** (*Math.*) ❶ *tr. V.* find the log[arithm] of. ❷ *itr. V.* do logs *or* logarithms

**logarithmisch** *Adj.* (*Math.*) logarithmic

**Logarithmus** /logaˈrɪtmʊs/ *der;* **~, Logarithmen** (*Math.*) logarithm; log

**Log·buch** *das* (*Seew.*) log [book]

**Loge** /ˈloːʒə/ *die;* **~, ~n** Ⓐ(*Theater*) box; Ⓑ(*Freimaurer~, Pförtner~*) lodge

**Logen-: ~bruder** *der* brother mason; **~platz** *der* (*Theater*) seat in a box; **~schließer** *der,* **~schließerin** *die* box attendant

**Logger** /ˈlɔgɐ/ *der;* **~s, ~** (*Seew.*) lugger

**Loggia** /ˈlɔdʒia/ *die;* **~, Loggien** Ⓐ(*Balkon*) balcony; Ⓑ(*Archit.*) loggia

**Logier·besuch** *der* (*veralt.*) house guest/guests

**logieren** (*veralt.*) ❶ *itr. V.* stay. ❷ *tr. V.* (*schweiz.*) **jmdn. bei sich ~:** put sb. up [at one's house/flat (*Brit.*) *or* (*Amer.*) apartment *etc.*]

**Logier·gast** *der* (*veralt.*) house guest

**Logik** /ˈloːgɪk/ *die;* **~:** logic; **in der ~:** in logic

**Logiker** /ˈloːgikɐ/ *der;* **~s, ~, Logikerin** *die;* **~, ~nen** Ⓐ(*Philos.*) logician; Ⓑ(*logisch Denkende/Denkender*) logical thinker

**Logis** /loˈʒiː/ *das;* **~** /loˈʒiː(s)/, **~** /loˈʒiːs/ Ⓐ lodgings *pl.;* room/rooms *pl.;* ⇒ *auch* **Kost**; Ⓑ /*auch:* ˈloːgɪs/ (*Seemannsspr.*) **das ~ [der Matrosen]** the crew's quarters *pl.*

**logisch** /ˈloːgɪʃ/ ❶ *Adj.* logical; **in keinem ~en Zusammenhang stehen** have no logical connection; **[ist doch] ~** (*ugs.*) yes, of course. ❷ *adv.* logically

**logischerweise** *Adv.* logically; (*selbstverständlich*) naturally

**Logistik** *die;* **~** Ⓐ(*Math.*) mathematical *or* symbolic logic *no art.;* Ⓑ(*Milit., Wirtsch.*) logistics *pl.;* (*als Fachbereich*) logistics *sing.*

**logistisch** (*Milit., Wirtsch.*) ❶ *Adj.* logistic[al]. ❷ *adv.* logistically

**Log·leine** *die* (*Seew.*) log line

**logo** /ˈloːgo/ *Adj.* (*salopp*) **[ist doch] ~!** you bet! (*coll.*); of course!

**Logo** *der od. das;* **~s, ~s** logo

**Logopäde** /logoˈpɛːdə/ *der;* **~n, ~n** speech therapist

**Logopädie** /logopɛˈdiː/ *die;* **~:** speech therapy *no art.*

**Logopädin** *die;* **~, ~nen** speech therapist

**Lohe**[1] /ˈloːə/ *die;* **~, ~n** (*dichter.: Flamme*) blaze; **die ~n** the raging flames

**Lohe**[2] *die;* **~, ~n** tan [bark]

**lohen**[1] *itr. V.* (*dichter.*) blaze

**lohen**[2] *tr. V.* tan ‹hides etc.› [with tanbark]

**Loh-: ~gerber** *der* [vegetable] tanner; **~gerberei** *die* Ⓐ(*Betrieb*) [vegetable] tannery; Ⓑ(*~gerbung*) [vegetable] tanning; **~gerberin** *die* ⇒ **~gerber**

**Lohn** /loːn/ *der;* **~[e]s, Löhne** /ˈløːnə/ Ⓐ wage[s *pl.*]; pay *no indef. art., no pl.;* **die Löhne drücken/einfrieren** (*ugs.*) lower/freeze wages; **bei jmdm./einer Firma in ~ und Brot stehen** be employed by sb./a firm; work for sb./a firm; **jmdn. um ~ und Brot bringen** deprive sb. of his/her livelihood; Ⓑ(*Belohnung, auch fig.*) reward; **als** *od.* **zum ~ für ...** as a reward for ...; **der Verbrecher hat seinen ~ bekommen** (*fig.*) the criminal got his deserts *pl.*

**lohn-, Lohn-: ~abbau** *der* reduction in wages; **~abhängig** *Adj.* wage-earning *attrib.;* **~abhängig sein** be a wage earner; **~abhängige** *der/die* wage earner; **~abrechnung** *die* wage slip; payslip; **~arbeit** *die* (*Soziol.*) wage labour; **~ausfall** *der* loss of earnings; **~ausgleich** *der* making-up of wages; **[eine] kürzere Arbeitszeit bei vollem ~ausgleich** shorter working hours with no loss of pay; **~buchhalter** *der,* **~buchhalterin** *die* payroll clerk; **~buchhaltung** *die* Ⓐ payroll accounting; Ⓑ(*Abteilung*) payroll office; **~büro** *das* payroll office; **~empfänger** *der,* **~empfängerin** *die* wage earner

**lohnen** ❶ *refl., itr. V.* be worth it; be worthwhile; **die Anstrengung hat sich gelohnt** it was worth the effort; **das lohnt [sich] nicht** it's not worth it; **es lohnt [sich], den Versuch zu machen** it's worth making the attempt; **das lohnt sich nicht für mich** it's not worth my while; **die Mühe hat [sich] gelohnt** it was worth the trouble *or* effort; **lohnt [sich] das?** is it worth it?; **der Film lohnt sich sehr** the film is well worth seeing.

❷ *tr. V.* Ⓐ(*rechtfertigen*) be worth; **die Ausstellung lohnt einen Besuch** the exhibition is worth a visit *or* is worth visiting; **das lohnt die Mühe nicht** it is not worth the trouble; Ⓑ **jmdm. etw. ~:** reward sb. for sth.; (*vergelten*) repay sb. for sth.; **Gott wird dir deine Hilfe ~** (*geh.*) God will reward you for your help

**löhnen** *tr., itr. V.* Ⓐ(*Lohn auszahlen*) pay; Ⓑ(*salopp: bezahlen*) pay; fork out *or* up (*coll.*)

**lohnend** *Adj.* rewarding ‹task›; worthwhile, rewarding ‹occupation›; worthwhile ‹aim›; (*einträglich*) financially rewarding; lucrative; **das Studium dieses Buches ist wirklich ~:** this book is really worth studying; it is really worth studying this book; **die Ausstellung ist wirklich ~:** the exhibition is really worth seeing

**lohnens·wert** *Adj.* worthwhile *attrib.;* worth while *pred.*

**lohn-, Lohn-: ~erhöhung** *die* wage *or* pay increase *or* (*Brit.*) rise; **~forderung** *die* wage demand *or* claim; **~fort·zahlung** *die* continued payment of wages; **~gruppe** *die* wage group; **~intensiv** *Adj.* (*Wirtsch.*) wage-intensive; **~kampf** *der* wage dispute; **~kosten** *Pl.* wage costs; **~kürzung** *die* wage cut *or* reduction; **~liste** *die* payroll; **~neben·kosten** *Pl.* non-wage [labour] costs *pl.*; **~pause** *die* pay pause; **~pfändung** *die* garnishment [of wages]; **~politik** *die* (*Politik, Wirtsch.*) pay policy; policy on wages; **~-Preis-Spirale** *die* wage-price spiral; **~raub** *der* (*abwertend*) wage exploitation; **~runde** *die* wage *or* pay round; **~skala** *die* wage *or* pay scale

**Lohn·steuer** *die* income tax

**Lohnsteuer-: ~jahres·ausgleich** *der* annual adjustment of income tax; **~karte** *die* income-tax card

**Lohn-: ~stopp** *der* wage *or* pay freeze; **~streifen** *der* payslip; **~tarif** *der* wage rate; **~tüte** *die* pay packet (*Brit.*); wage packet

**Löhnung** *die;* ~, **~en** Ⓐ (*Auszahlung*) payment of wages; Ⓑ (*Lohn*) pay

**Lohn-: ~zettel** *der* payslip; **~zuwachs** *der* pay increase

**Loipe** /ˈlɔypə/ *die;* ~, **~n** (*Skisport*) [cross-country] course

**Lok** /lɔk/ *die;* ~, **~s** engine; locomotive

**lokal** /loˈka:l/ ❶ *Adj.* Ⓐ (*örtlich*) local; **Lokales** (*Zeitungsw.*) local news *sing.*; Ⓑ (*Gram.*) of place *postpos.* ❷ *adv.* **jmdn. ~ betäuben** give sb. a local anaesthetic

**Lokal** *das;* **~s, ~e** pub (*Brit.*); bar (*Amer.*); (*Speise~*) restaurant

**Lokal-: ~anästhesie** *die* (*Med.*) local anaesthesia; **~augen·schein** *der* (*österr.*) ⇒ **Lokaltermin**; **~blatt** *das* (*Zeitungsw.*) local paper

**lokalisieren** *tr. V.* locate; (*eingrenzen, Med.*) localize; limit, contain ‹fire›

**Lokalisierung** *die;* ~, **~en** location; (*Eingrenzung, Med.*) localization

**Lokalität** /lokaliˈtɛ:t/ *die;* ~, **~en** locality; **die ~en kennen** know the locality *or* district *or* area; **wo sind hier die ~en?** (*verhüll.*) where is the cloakroom? (*Brit. euphem.*); where's the restroom? (*esp. Amer. euphem.*)

**Lokal-: ~kolorit** *das* local colour; **~matador** *der*, **~matadorin** *die* (*bes. Sport*) local hero *or* favourite; **~patriotismus** *der* local patriotism; **~politik** *die* local politics *sing.*, *no art.*; **~politiker** *der*, **~politikerin** *die* local politician; **~presse** *die* local press; **~redakteur** *der*, **~redakteurin** *die* (*Zeitungsw.*) local-news editor; editor of the local[-news] section; **~redaktion** *die* (*Rundf., Ferns., Zeitungsw.*) local-news section; **~runde** *die* round for everyone [in the pub (*Brit.*) *or* (*Amer.*) bar]; **eine ~runde ausgeben** *od.* (*salopp*) **schmeißen** buy a round *or* drink for everyone in the pub (*Brit.*) *or* (*Amer.*) bar; **~seite** *die* (*Zeitungsw.*) local page; **~teil** *der* (*Zeitungsw.*) local section; **~termin** *der* (*Rechtsspr.*) visit to the scene [of the crime]; **~verbot** *das:* **[in einer Gaststätte] ~verbot haben/bekommen** be/get banned [from a pub (*Brit.*) *or* (*Amer.*) bar]; **jmdm. ~verbot erteilen** ban sb. [from the/a pub (*Brit.*) *or* (*Amer.*) bar]; **~zeitung** *die* local [news]paper

**Lok·führer** *der*, **Lok·führerin** *die* ▶ 159 ⇒ **Lokomotivführer**

**Lokomotive** /lokomoˈti:və/ *die;* ~, **~n** locomotive; [railway] engine

**Lokomotiv·führer** *der*, **Lokomotiv·führerin** *die* ▶ 159 engine driver (*Brit.*); engineer (*Amer.*)

**Lokus** /ˈlo:kʊs/ *der;* ~ *od.* **~ses**, ~ *od.* **~se** (*salopp*) loo (*Brit. coll.*); john (*Amer. coll.*)

**Lokus·papier** *das* (*salopp*) loo paper (*Brit. coll.*); toilet paper

**Lombardei** /lɔmbarˈdai/ *die;* **~:** Lombardy

**lombardisch** *Adj.* Lombardic

**Lombard·satz** *der* (*Bankw.*) Lombard rate

**London** /ˈlɔndɔn/ (*das*); **~s** ▶ 700 London

**Londoner** ▶ 700 ❶ *indekl. Adj.* London. ❷ *der;* **~s, ~:** Londoner; ⇒ *auch* **Kölner**

**Londonerin** *die;* ~, **~nen** ⇒ **Londoner** 2

**Long·drink** /ˈlɔŋdrɪŋk/ *der* long drink

**Longe** /ˈlõ:ʒə/ *die;* ~, **~n** Ⓐ (*Reiten*) lunge; Ⓑ (*Turnen, Schwimmen*) harness

**Look** /lʊk/ *der;* **~s, ~s** look

**Looping** /ˈlu:pɪŋ/ *der;* **~s, ~s** (*Fliegerspr.*) loop; **einen ~ drehen** loop the loop

**Lorbeer** /ˈlɔrbe:ɐ̯/ *der;* **~s, ~en** Ⓐ (*Baum*) laurel; Ⓑ (*Gewürz*) bayleaf; Ⓒ (*~kranz*) laurel wreath; **mit etw. keine ~en ernten können** (*fig.*) get no credit for sth.; **[sich] auf seinen ~en ausruhen** (*fig. ugs.*) rest on one's laurels

**Lorbeer-: ~baum** *der* laurel [tree]; **~blatt** *das* bayleaf; **~kranz** *der* laurel wreath

**Lord** /lɔrt/ *der;* **~s, ~s** lord

**Lord·kanzler** *der* Lord Chancellor

**Lordschaft** *die:* **Eure ~:** Your Lordship

**Lord·siegel·bewahrer** *der;* **~s, ~:** Lord Privy Seal

**Lore** /ˈlo:rə/ *die;* ~, **~n** car; (*kleiner*) tub

**Lorenz** /ˈlo:rɛnts/ (*der*) Lawrence; Laurence

**Lorgnette** /lɔrnˈjɛtə/ *die;* ~, **~n** lorgnette

**Lorgnon** /lɔenˈjõ:/ *das;* **~s, ~s** lorgnon

**los** /lo:s/ ❶ *Adj.* Ⓐ (*abgetrennt*) **der Knopf ist ~:** the button has come off; **der Hund ist [von der Leine] ~:** the dog is off the leash; **jmdn./etw. ~ sein** (*befreit sein von*) be rid *or* (*coll.*) shot of sb./sth.; (*verloren haben*) have lost sth.; **einer Sache** (*Gen.*) **~ und ledig sein** (*geh.*) be totally free *or* well and truly rid of sth.; Ⓑ **es ist etwas ~:** something is *or* there is something going on; **hier ist viel/wenig/immer etw. ~:** there is a lot/not much/always sth. going on here; **was ist hier ~?** (*was geschieht?*) what's going on here?; (*was ist nicht in Ordnung?*) what's the matter here?; what's up here? (*coll.*); **mit jmdm./etw. ist nichts/nicht viel ~** (*ugs.*) sb./sth. isn't up to much (*coll.*); **was ist denn mit dir ~?** what's up *or* wrong *or* the matter with you?
❷ *Adv.* Ⓐ come on!; (*geh schon!*) go on!; **auf die Plätze** *od.* **Achtung, fertig, ~!** on your marks, get set, go; **~ doch!** go on!; **nun aber ~!** [come on,] let's get moving *or* going!; **nichts wie ~!** (*ugs.*) let's scarper (*Brit. coll.*); let's beat it (*coll.*); Ⓑ (*ugs.: ~gehen, ~fahren usw.*); **er ist mit dem Wagen ~:** he's gone off in the car; ⇒ *auch* **losmüssen**; **lossollen**; **loswollen**; Ⓒ (*ugs.: gelöst*) **ich habe die Schraube/das Brett/das Rad ~:** I have got the screw out/the board/wheel off; ⇒ *auch* **loshaben**; **loskriegen** *usw.*

**Los** *das;* **~es, ~e** Ⓐ lot; **etw. durch [das] ~ entscheiden** decide sth. by drawing lots; **das ~ soll entscheiden** it shall be decided by drawing lots; **das ~ hat mich getroffen** it has fallen to my lot; Ⓑ (*Lotterie~*) ticket; **ein halbes/ganzes ~:** a half ticket/full ticket; **das große ~:** [the] first prize; **mit jmdm./etw. das große ~ ziehen** (*fig.*) hit the jackpot with sb./sth.; Ⓒ (*geh.: Schicksal*) lot; **ihm war ein schweres ~ beschieden** his was a hard lot; Ⓓ (*Wirtsch.: Maßeinheit*) batch; lot; (*bei Versteigerungen*) lot; Ⓔ (*Bau~*) section

**-los** *Adj.* -less

**los|ballern** *itr. V.* (*salopp*) start blazing away

**lösbar** *Adj.* Ⓐ soluble, solvable ‹problem, equation, etc.›; Ⓑ (*löslich*) soluble ‹substance, gas›

**los-: ~|bekommen** *unr. tr. V.* get ‹string, tape, ribbon, etc.› off; get ‹screw, nail, etc.› out; **die Hände ~bekommen** get one's hands free; **~|binden** *unr. tr. V.* untie; **~|brechen** ❶ *unr. itr. V.; mit sein* Ⓐ (*beginnen*) ‹storm› break; ‹cheering, laughter, etc.› break out; Ⓑ (*abbrechen*) break off. ❷ *unr. tr. V.* break off

**Lösch-: ~arbeit** *die* firefighting operations *pl.*; **wir halfen bei den ~arbeiten** we helped to fight *or* to put out the fire; **~blatt** *das* piece of blotting paper; **~boot** *das* fire boat; **~eimer** *der* fire bucket

**löschen**[1] /ˈlœʃn̩/ *tr. V.* Ⓐ (*aus~*) put out, extinguish ‹fire, candle, flames, etc.›; **seinen Durst ~** (*fig.*) quench one's thirst; Ⓑ (*tilgen*) close ‹bank account›; delete, strike out ‹entry›; extinguish, wipe out, pay off ‹debt›; erase, wipe out ‹recording, memory, etc.›; **die Schrift auf der Tafel ~:** clean *or* (*Amer.*) erase the blackboard; **im Register gelöscht werden** ‹firm, name, etc.› be removed from the register; Ⓒ (*geh.: ausschalten*) switch off *or* turn off *or* out ‹light, lamp›; Ⓓ (*trocknen*) blot ‹ink etc.›; Ⓔ (*vermischen*) slake ‹lime›

**löschen**[2] *tr. V.* (*Seemannsspr.*) unload

**Löscher** *der;* **~s, ~** Ⓐ (*Tinten~*) blotter; Ⓑ (*Feuer~*) [fire] extinguisher

**Lösch-: ~fahrzeug** *das* fire engine; **~kalk** *der* slaked lime; **~kopf** *der* (*Elektronik*) erase head; **~mannschaft** *die* firefighting team; **~papier** *das* blotting paper; **~taste** *die* erase button; **~trupp** *der* ⇒ **~mannschaft**

**Löschung**[1] *die;* ~, **~en** (*eines Kontos*) closing; (*einer Eintragung*) deletion; striking out; (*einer Schuld*) extinguishing; wiping out; paying off

**Löschung**[2] (*Seemannsspr.*) *die;* **~:** unloading

**Lösch·zug** *der* set of firefighting appliances

**los|donnern** (*ugs.*) ❶ *itr. V.; mit sein* roar off. ❷ *tr. V.* „...", **donnerte er los** '...', he bellowed

**lose** ❶ *Adj.* Ⓐ (*nicht fest, auch fig.*) loose; **zwischen ihnen besteht nur eine ~ Bekanntschaft** (*fig.*) they are not closely acquainted; Ⓑ (*nicht verpackt*) loose ‹sugar, cigarettes, sweets, sheets of paper, nails, etc.›; unbottled ‹drink›; **etw. ~ verkaufen** sell sth. loose/unbottled; Ⓒ (*locker*) loose[-fitting] ‹clothes›; Ⓓ (*ugs.: leichtfertig*) **ein ~s Mädchen** (*veralt.*) a loose woman; **er ist ein ~er Vogel** he is a bit of a lad; Ⓔ (*ugs.: vorlaut, frech*) cheeky; impudent; **einen ~n Mund haben** be a cheeky *or* impudent so-and-so (*coll.*); **~e Reden führen** be cheeky; Ⓕ (*geh.: aufgelockert*) loose ‹group, line, etc.›.
❷ *adv.* Ⓐ (*nicht fest, auch fig.*) loosely; **~ herunterhängen** hang down loosely *or* loose; Ⓑ (*locker*) ‹hang, drape, etc.› loosely

**Loseblatt·sammlung** *die:* **als ~** *od.* **in Form einer ~ herauskommen** be published in loose-leaf form

**Löse·geld** *das* ransom; **1 Million Pfund ~:** a ransom of one million pounds; **das ~ wurde in einer Telefonzelle hinterlegt** the ransom money was left in a telephone kiosk

**los|eisen** *tr. V.* (*ugs.*) **jmdn./etw. von jmdm./etw. ~:** prise *or* get sb./sth. away from sb./sth.; **sich von jmdm./etw. ~:** get away from sb./sth.; **etw. bei jmdm. ~:** get sth. out of sb.

**losen** *itr. V.* draws lots (**um** for); **~, wer anfangen soll** draw lots to decide who will start

**lösen** /ˈlø:zn̩/ ❶ *tr. V.* Ⓐ remove, take *or* get off ‹stamp, wallpaper›; **etw. von etw. ~:** remove sth. from sth.; **das Fleisch von den Knochen ~:** take the meat off the bones; **den Blick von etw. nicht ~ können** (*fig.*) not be able to take one's eyes off sth.; Ⓑ (*lockern*) take *or* let ‹handbrake› off; release ‹handbrake›; undo ‹screw, belt, tie›; let ‹hair› down; remove, untie ‹string, rope, knot, bonds›; loosen ‹phlegm›; ease ‹cramp›; (*fig.*) ease, relieve ‹[mental] pain, tension, etc.›; remove ‹inhibitions›; **jmds. Zunge ~** (*fig.*) loosen sb.'s tongue; Ⓒ (*klären*) solve ‹problem, puzzle, equation, etc.›; resolve ‹contradiction, conflict›; solve, resolve ‹difficulty›; Ⓓ (*annullieren*) break off ‹engagement›; cancel ‹contract›; sever ‹connection, relationship›; **sein Arbeitsverhältnis ~:** terminate one's employment (*formal*); Ⓔ (*zergehen lassen*) **etw. in etw.** (*Dat.*) **~:** dissolve sth. in sth.; Ⓕ (*kaufen*) buy; obtain ‹ticket›.
❷ *refl. V.* Ⓐ (*lose werden*) come off; ‹avalanche› start; **sich von etw. ~:** come off sth.; Ⓑ (*sich trennen*) **sich aus etw. ~:** free oneself from sth.; **das Flugzeug löste sich vom Boden** the plane left the ground; **ein Läufer hat sich vom Feld gelöst** a runner broke away from the field; **sich von seinem Elternhaus ~** (*fig.*) break away from one's parental home; **sich aus einer Verpflichtung ~:** free *or* rid oneself of an obligation; Ⓒ (*sich lockern*) ‹wallpaper, plaster› come off *or* away; ‹packing, screw› come loose *or* undone; ‹paint, book cover› come off; ‹phlegm, cough›

*old spelling (see note on page 1707)

get looser; ‹cramp› ease; ‹muscle› loosen up; **D** (*sich klären, entwirren*) ‹puzzle, problem› be solved; **sich von selbst ~** ‹problem› solve *or* resolve itself; **E** (*zergehen*) **sich in etw.** (*Dat.*) **~:** dissolve in sth.; **F aus seiner Pistole löste sich ein Schuss** (*geh.*) his pistol went off

**Los·entscheid** *der:* **durch ~:** by drawing lots; (*bei einem Preisausschreiben*) by [making *or* having] a draw

**los-: ~|fahren** *unr. itr. V.; mit sein* **A** (*starten*) set off; (*wegfahren*) move off; **B** (*zufahren*) **auf jmdn./etw. ~fahren** drive/ride towards sb./sth.; **direkt auf jmdn./etw. ~fahren** drive/ride straight at sb./sth.; **~|gehen** *unr. itr. V.; mit sein* **A** (*aufbrechen*) set off; **auf ein Ziel ~gehen** (*fig.*) go straight for a goal; **~ gehts** let's be off; **B** (*ugs.: beginnen*) start; **es geht ~:** it's starting; (*fangen wir an*) let's go; **~ geht's** let's get started; **gleich geht es wieder ~ mit dem Lärm** the noise will soon start up again; **ich glaube, es geht ~!** (*salopp*) you/he, *etc.* must be kidding (*coll.*); **C** (*ugs.: abgehen*) ‹button, handle, etc.› come off; **D** (*angreifen*) **auf jmdn. ~gehen** go for sb.; **E** (*abgefeuert werden*) ‹gun, mine, firework, etc.› go off; **~|haben** *unr. tr. V.* (*ugs.*) **in seinem Beruf hat er was ~:** he's very good at his job; **~|heulen** *itr. V.* (*ugs.*) burst out crying; burst into tears; **~|kaufen** *tr. V.* **jmdn. ~kaufen** buy sb.'s freedom *or* release; **~|kommen** *unr. itr. V.; mit sein* (*ugs.*) **A** (*fortkommen*) get away; **B** (*freikommen*) get free; free oneself; (*freigelassen werden*) be freed; **von jmdm./etw. ~kommen** (*fig.*) get away from sb./get rid of sth.; **vom Alkohol ~kommen** (*fig.*) get off *or* give up alcohol; **er kam von dem Gedanken nicht ~:** he couldn't get the thought out of his mind; **~|kriegen** *tr. V.* (*ugs.*) **A** (*lösen können*) get ‹screw, nail, etc.› out; get ‹lid› off; **B** (*~werden*) get rid *or* (*coll.*) shot of; **C** (*verkaufen können*) get rid of; **~|lachen** *itr. V.* burst out laughing; **~|lassen** *unr. tr. V.* **A** (*nicht festhalten*) let go of; **der Gedanke/das Bild ließ sie nicht mehr ~** (*fig.*) she could not get the thought/image out of her mind; **B** (*freilassen*) let ‹person, animal› go; **C** (*ugs. abwertend: hetzen*) **jmdn. auf jmdn./etw. ~lassen** let sb. loose on sb./sth.; **D** (*ugs.: äußern*) come out with ‹remark, joke, etc.›; let out ‹curse›; **E** (*abschicken*) send off ‹letter, telegram, etc.›; **~|laufen** *unr. itr. V.; mit sein* (*weglaufen*) run off; (*anfangen zu laufen*) start running; **lauf schnell ~ und hol Brot** run out and get some bread; **~|legen** *itr. V.* (*ugs.*) **A** (*sich stürmisch äußern*) let rip; **mit Fragen ~legen** start firing questions; **wenn er ~legt** (*zu reden anfängt*) when *or* once he gets going *or* started; **B** (*anfangen*) get going *or* started; **mit der Arbeit ~legen** get down to work

**löslich** *Adj.* soluble; **leicht/schwer ~:** readily/not readily *or* only slightly soluble

**Löslichkeit** *die;* **~:** solubility

**los-: ~|lösen** **1** *tr. V.* remove; take off; **2** *refl. V.* ‹wallpaper› come off; ‹trailer› become uncoupled *or* detached; **~|machen** **1** *tr. V.* (*ugs.*) let ‹animal› loose; untie, undo ‹string, line, rope›; take out ‹plank›; unhitch ‹trailer›; **das Boot ~machen** cast off; **2** *refl. V.* (*ugs.: sich befreien, auch fig.*) free oneself (**von** from); **3** *itr. V.* **A** (*Seemannsspr.: ablegen*) cast off; **B** (*ugs.: sich beeilen*) get a move on (*coll.*); **nun mach ~, dass du fertig wirst** hurry up and get ready; **~|müssen** *unr. itr. V.* (*ugs.*) have to be off; have to go; **ich muss ~:** I must be off

**Los·nummer** *die* [lottery-]ticket number

**los-: ~|platzen** *itr. V.; mit sein* (*ugs.*) **A** burst out; **sofort platzte sie damit ~:** she blurted it out immediately; **B** (*plötzlich lachen*) burst out laughing; **~|rasen** *itr. V.; mit sein* race *or* tear off; **auf etw.** (*Akk.*) **~rasen** race towards sth.; **~|reißen** **1** *unr. tr. V.* tear off; (*schneller, gewaltsamer*) rip off; pull ‹plank› off; ‹wind› rip ‹tile› off; **er konnte seine Augen nicht von der Statue ~reißen** (*fig.*) he couldn't take his eyes off the statue; **2** *unr. refl. V.* break free *or* loose; **sich von etw.** (*Dat.*) **~reißen** break free *or* loose from sth.; (*fig.*) tear oneself away from sth.

**Löss, *Löß** /lœs/ *der;* **Lösses, Lösse** (*Geol.*) loess

**los-, Los-: ~|sagen** *refl. V.* **sich von jmdm./etw. ~sagen** renounce sb./sth.; break with sb./sth.; **~sagung** *die;* **~~,** **~~en** renunciation (**von** of); break (**von** with)

**Löss·boden, *Löß·boden** *der* loess soil; loessial soil

**los-: ~|schicken** *tr. V.* (*ugs.*) send off ‹letter, telegram, etc.›; **jmdn. ~schicken, um etw. zu holen** send sb. out to get sth.; **~|schießen** *unr. itr. V.* (*ugs.*) **A** start shooting; **B** *mit sein* (*sich schnell bewegen*) shoot *or* race off; **auf jmdn./etw. ~schießen** race towards sb./sth.; (*direkt*) race up to sb./sth.; **~|schlagen** **1** *unr. tr. V.* **A** (*abschlagen*) knock off; knock ‹board, plank› out; **den Verputz von der Wand ~schlagen** knock the rendering off the wall; **B** (*ugs.: verkaufen*) get rid of; flog (*Brit. sl.*); **2** *unr. itr. V.* **A** (*einschlagen*) **auf jmdn. ~schlagen** let fly at sb.; **B** (*bes. Milit.*) attack; launch one's attack; **~|schnallen** *tr. V.* unfasten; **~|sollen** *unr. itr. V.* **wann sollen wir ~?** what time should we be off?; **~|sprechen** *unr. tr. V.* (*bes. Rel.*) absolve (**von** from); **jmdn. von aller Schuld ~sprechen** absolve sb. of all guilt; **~|steuern** *itr. V.; mit sein* **auf etw.** (*Akk.*) **~steuern** head *or* make for sth.; **auf ein Ziel ~steuern** (*fig.*) aim for a goal; **~|tigern** *itr. V.; mit sein* (*ugs.*) march off; **~|trennen** *tr. V.* undo; unpick ‹seam, hem›

**Los·trommel** *die* [lottery] drum

**Losung**[1] *die;* **~, ~en** **A** (*Wahlspruch*) slogan; **B** (*Milit.: Kennwort*) password; **die ~ nennen** give the password

**Losung**[2] *die;* **~, ~en** (*Jägerspr.*) droppings *pl.*

**Lösung** *die;* **~, ~en** **A** (*Bewältigung*) solution (*Gen.* to); (*eines Konflikts, Widerspruchs*) resolution; (*einer Aufgabe, eines Problems, usw.*) solution (*Gen.*, **für** to); **des Rätsels ~:** the answer to the mystery; **das also ist des Rätsels ~:** so 'that's it *or* the answer; **B** (*Annullierung*) (*einer Verlobung*) breaking off; (*eines Vertrags*) cancellation; (*einer Verbindung, eines Verhältnisses*) severing; (*eines Arbeitsverhältnisses*) termination; **C** (*Physik, Chemie*) (*Flüssigkeit*) solution; (*das Auflösen*) dissolution; dissolving

**Lösungs-: ~mittel** *das* (*Physik, Chemie*) solvent; **~vorschlag** *der* proposed solution (**für** to); **ich hätte einen ~vorschlag für euer Problem** I think I might have a solution to your problem; I've got a suggestion as to how you might solve your problem

**Losungs·wort** *das; Pl.* **~e** *od.* **Losungs·wörter** password

**Los·verkäufer** *der,* **Los·verkäuferin** *die* [lottery-]ticket seller

**los-: ~|werden** *unr. tr. V.; mit sein* **A** (*sich befreien können von*) get rid of; **ich werde den Gedanken/Verdacht nicht ~, dass ...** I can't get the thought/suspicion/impression out of my mind that ...; **B** (*ugs.: aussprechen, mitteilen*) tell; **er wollte etwas ~werden** he wanted to tell me/us *etc.* something; **... konnte ich endlich meine Frage ~werden** ... I finally got the chance to put my question; **C** (*ugs.: verkaufen*) get rid of; flog (*Brit. sl.*); **D** (*ugs.: verlieren*) lose; **~|wollen** *unr. itr. V.* (*ugs.*) want to be off; **~|ziehen** *unr. itr. V.; mit sein* (*ugs.*) **A** (*~gehen*) set off; **B** (*abwertend: herziehen*) **über jmdn. ~ziehen** pull sb. to pieces

**Los·ziehung** *die* draw

**Lot** /lo:t/ *das;* **~[e]s, ~e** **A** (*Bauw.*) plumb [bob]; **B** (*Bauw.: Senkrechte*) **im ~ stehen** be plumb; **nicht im ~ sein, außer ~ sein** be out of plumb; **nicht im ~ sein** (*fig.*) not be straightened *or* sorted out; **[wieder] ins ~ kommen** (*fig.*) be all right [again]; **C** (*Seew.*) sounding line; lead line; **D** (*Geom.*) perpendicular; **das ~ fällen** drop a perpendicular; **E** (*veralt.: Maßeinheit*) *measure varying between 15.5 g and 16.6 g*

**loten** *tr. V.* **A** (*Bauw.*) plumb; **B** (*Seew.*) sound; take soundings of; plumb

**löten** /'lø:tn̩/ *tr. V.* (*Technik*) solder

**Lothringen** /'lo:trɪŋən/ (*das*); **~s** Lorraine

**Lothringer** *indekl. Adj.* **1** Lorraine *attrib.;* **das ~ Kreuz** the Cross of Lorraine. **2** *der;* **~s, ~:** Lorrainer

**Lothringerin** *die;* **~, ~nen** Lorrainer

**lothringisch** *Adj.* Lorraine *attrib.;* Lorrainese

**Lotion** /lo'tsi̯o:n/ *die;* **~, ~en** *od.* **~s** lotion

**Löt-: ~kolben** *der* soldering iron; **~lampe** *die* blowlamp

**Lot·leine** *die* (*Seew.*) sounding line; lead line

**Löt·mittel** *das* [soldering] flux

**Lotos** /'lo:tɔs/ *der;* **~, ~:** lotus

**Lotos-: ~blume** *die* lotus flower; **~sitz** *der* (*Yoga*) lotus position

**lot·recht** **1** *Adj.* perpendicular; vertical. **2** *adv.* perpendicularly; vertically

**Lot·rechte** *die; adj. Dekl.* perpendicular; vertical

**Lotse** /'lo:tsə/ *der;* **~n, ~n** ▶ **159** (*Seew.*) pilot; (*fig.*) guide; **ich mache den ~n** (*fig.*) I'll guide you; I'll show you the way

**lotsen** *tr. V.* **A** (*Seew.*) pilot; (*Flugw.*) guide; **B** (*leiten*) guide; **C** (*ugs.: führen, leiten*) drag

**Lotsen-: ~boot** *das* pilot boat; **~dienst** *der* **A** pilot service; **B** (*Verkehrsw.*) driver-guide service; **~zwang** *der* compulsory pilotage *no art.*

**Lotsin** *die;* **~, ~nen** ⇒ **Lotse**

**Löt·stelle** *die* soldered joint

**Lotterie** /lɔtə'ri:/ *die;* **~, ~n** lottery; **[in der] ~ spielen** take part in *or* do the lottery

**Lotterie-: ~einnehmer** *der;* **~~s, ~~, ~einnehmerin** *die;* **~~, ~~nen** lottery-ticket seller; **~gewinn** *der* win in the lottery; (*gewonnenes Geld*) lottery winnings *pl.;* **~los** *das* lottery ticket; **~spiel** *das* (*auch fig.*) lottery

**lotterig** /'lɔtərɪç/ *Adj.* (*ugs. abwertend*) slovenly, sloppy ‹work›; scruffy ‹appearance, house, clothes, etc.›

**Lotter·leben** *das* (*abwertend*) dissolute life

**Lotter·wirtschaft** *die* (*abwertend*) [slovenly] mess *or* muddle; shambles (*coll.*)

**Lotto** /'lɔto/ *das;* **~s, ~s** **A** national lottery; **4 Richtige im ~ haben** have four correct numbers in the national lottery; **~ spielen** do the [national] lottery; **B** (*Gesellschaftsspiel*) lotto

**Lotto-: ~annahmestelle** *die* acceptance point for national-lottery coupons; (*Stand*) national-lottery kiosk; **~gewinn** *der* win in the national lottery; (*gewonnenes Geld*) winnings *pl.* in the national lottery; **~schein** *der* national-lottery coupon; **~zahlen** *Pl.* winning national-lottery numbers

**Lotung** *die;* **~, ~en** **A** (*Bauw.*) plumbing; **B** (*Seew.*) sounding; plumbing; **die ~ der Wassertiefe** sounding *or* plumbing the depth of the water

**Lotus** /'lo:tʊs/ *der;* **~, ~:** lotus

**Löt·zinn** *der* [tin-lead] solder

**Louis** /'lu:i/ *der;* **~** /'lu:i(:s)/, **~** /'lu:i:s/ (*ugs.*) pimp

**Louisdor** /lu̯i'do:ɐ̯/ *der;* **~s, ~e** louis-d'or

**Lover** /'lavɐ/ *der;* **~s, ~** (*ugs.*) boyfriend

**Löwe** /'lø:və/ *der;* **~n, ~n** **A** lion; **B** (*Astrol.*) Leo; the Lion; ⇒ *auch* **Fisch**

**Löwen-: ~anteil** *der* lion's share; **sich den ~anteil [von etw.** (*Dat.*)**] sichern** get the lion's share [of sth.]; **~bändiger** *der;* **~~s, ~~, ~bändigerin** *die;* **~~, ~~nen** (*veralt.*) lion tamer; **~jagd** *die* lion hunting; (*Veranstaltung*) lion hunt; **~mähne** *die* **A** lion's mane; **B** (*ugs.: fülliges Haar*) [flowing] mane; **~maul, ~mäulchen** *das;* **~~s, ~~** (*Bot.*) snapdragon; antirrhinum; **~mut** *der* courage of a lion; **~zahn** *der* (*Bot.*) dandelion; (*Herbstlöwenzahn*) hawkbit

**Löwin** /'lø:vɪn/ *die;* **~, ~nen** lioness

**loyal** /lo̯a'ja:l/ **1** *Adj.* loyal (**gegenüber** to). **2** *adv.* loyally; **einen Vertrag ~ erfüllen/einhalten** faithfully fulfil/keep to an agreement

**Loyalität** /lo̯ajali'tɛ:t/ *die;* ~: loyalty (gegenüber to)

**LP** *Abk.* **Langspielplatte** LP

**LPG** *Abk.* (*DDR*) **Landwirtschaftliche Produktionsgenossenschaft;** ⇒ Produktionsgenossenschaft

**LSD** /ɛl|ɛs'de:/ *das;* ~[s] LSD

**lt.** *Abk.* **laut²**

**Luchs** /lʊks/ *der;* ~es, ~e (*auch* ~*fell*) lynx; **wie ein ~ aufpassen** watch like a hawk

**Luchs·auge** *das* (*fig.*) eagle eye; **den ~n meiner Wirtin entgeht nichts** my lynx-eyed landlady misses nothing

**Lücke** /'lʏkə/ *die;* ~, ~n Ⓐ gap; (*Park~, auf einem Formular, in einem Text*) space; **eine ~ füllen/schließen** fill/close a gap; Ⓑ (*Mangel*) gap; (*in der Versorgung*) break; (*im Gesetz*) loophole

**Lücken·büßer** *der,* **Lücken·büßerin** *die* (*ugs.*) stopgap; **den Lückenbüßer spielen** act as a stopgap

**lückenhaft** ❶ *Adj.* ‹teeth› full of gaps; gappy ‹teeth›; sketchy ‹knowledge›; sketchy, vague ‹memory›; incomplete, sketchy ‹report, account, etc.›; incomplete ‹statement›; ‹alibi› full of holes; **sein Wissen/seine Erinnerung ist ~:** there are gaps in his knowledge/memory. ❷ *adv.* ‹remember› vaguely, sketchily; **einen Fragebogen [sehr] ~ ausfüllen** fill in a questionnaire leaving [many] gaps

**Lückenhaftigkeit** *die;* ~ (*von Wissen, Kenntnissen*) sketchiness; (*eines Berichts*) incompleteness; sketchiness

**lücken-, Lücken-:** ~**los** ❶ *Adj.* unbroken ‹line, row, etc.›; complete ‹account, report, curriculum vitae›; solid, cast-iron ‹alibi›; comprehensive, perfect ‹knowledge›; **sie hat ein strahlend weißes, ~loses Gebiss** she has gleaming white teeth without any gaps; **eine ~lose Beweiskette** a solid chain of evidence. ❷ *adv.* without any gaps; **ein ~los nachgewiesenes Alibi** a cast-iron alibi; ~**losigkeit** *die;* ~~ (*einer Darstellung*) completeness; (*eines Alibis*) solidness

**lud** /lu:t/ *1. u. 3. Pers. Sg. Prät. v.* **laden**

**Lude** /'lu:də/ *der;* ~n, ~n (*salopp*) pimp; ponce

**Luder** *das;* ~s, ~ (*salopp*) so-and-so (*coll.*); **ein armes/freches ~:** a poor/cheeky so-and-so (*coll.*)

**Luft** /lʊft/ *die;* ~, **Lüfte** /'lʏftə/ Ⓐ air; **an die frische ~ gehen/in der frischen ~ sein** get out in[to]/be out in the fresh air; **jmdn. an die [frische] ~ setzen** *od.* **befördern** (*ugs.*) (*hinauswerfen*) show sb. the door; (*entlassen*) give sb. the sack (*coll.*) *or* (*coll.*) push; **etw. mit ~ kühlen** air-cool sth.; **die ~ anhalten** hold one's breath; **halt die ~ an!** (*ugs.*) (*hör auf zu reden!*) pipe down (*coll.*); put a sock in it (*Brit. sl.*); (*übertreib nicht so!*) come off it! (*coll.*); **tief ~ holen** take a deep breath; **~ schnappen** (*ugs.*) get some fresh air; **nach ~ schnappen** (*fig. ugs.*) struggle to keep one's head above water (*fig.*); **er kriegte keine/kaum ~:** he couldn't breathe/could hardly breathe; **die ~ ist rein** (*fig.*) the coast is clear; **hier/im Büro ist dicke ~** (*fig. ugs.*) there's a bad atmosphere here/in the office (*fig.*); **aus der Sache ist die ~ raus** (*fig. ugs.*) it's/the whole thing has gone flat; **sich in ~ auflösen** (*ugs.*) vanish into thin air; ‹plans› go up in smoke (*fig.*); **er ist ~ für mich** (*ugs.*) I ignore him completely; **jmdn. wie ~ behandeln** (*ugs.*) treat sb. as if he/she didn't exist; **die ~ aus jmds. Glas lassen** (*ugs. scherzh.*) fill sb. up; **da bleibt einem die ~ weg** (*ugs.*) it takes your breath away; **ihm/der Firma geht die ~ aus** (*fig. ugs.*) he's/the firm's going broke (*coll.*); **von ~ und Liebe kann man nicht leben** (*ugs.*) you can't live on nothing at all; Ⓑ (*Himmelsraum*) air; **Aufnahmen aus der ~ machen** take pictures from the air; **in die ~ ragen** soar *or* rise up into the sky; **sich in die Lüfte schwingen** (*geh.*) soar into the air; **etw. in die ~ sprengen** *od.* **jagen** (*ugs.*) blow sth. up; **aus der ~ gegriffen sein** (*fig.*) ‹story, accusation, etc.› be pure invention; **in der ~ liegen** (*fig.*) ‹crisis, ideas, etc.› be in the air; **in der ~ hängen** *od.* **schweben** (*fig. ugs.*) ‹plans, etc.› be up in the air; ‹person› be left dangling (*fig.*); **in die ~ gehen** (*fig. ugs.*) blow one's top (*coll.*); **etw. in der ~ zerreißen** (*fig. ugs.*) tear sth. to pieces; **ich könnte ihn in der ~ zerreißen** (*ugs.*) I could murder him (*coll.*); Ⓒ (*fig.: Spielraum*) space; room; **~ schaffen** *od.* **machen** create *or* make space *or* room; **sich** (*Dat.*) **~ [ver]schaffen** take the pressure off oneself; **deine 300 Mark haben mir erst mal ~ verschafft** your 300 marks have given me a breathing space; **in den Preisen ist noch ~ [drin]** (*ugs.*) there's some leeway in the prices; **sich** (*Dat.*) *od.* **seinem Herzen ~ machen** get it off one's chest (*coll.*); **ich hatte eine solche Wut, ich musste mir einmal ~ machen** I was so angry I had to give vent to my feelings; **seinem Zorn/Ärger** *usw.* **~ machen** (*ugs.*) give vent to one's anger; Ⓓ (*Brise*) breeze; **sich** (*Dat.*) **~ zufächeln** fan oneself

**Luft-:** ~**abwehr** *die* (*Milit.*) air defence; anti-aircraft defence; ~**akrobat** *der,* ~**akrobatin** *die* trapeze artist; ~**angriff** *der* (*Milit.*) air raid; ~**armee** *die* (*DDR*) air force unit; ~**aufklärung** *die* (*Milit.*) air reconnaissance; aerial reconnaissance; ~**aufnahme** *die* aerial photograph; ~**ballon** *der* balloon; ~**befeuchter** *der;* ~~s, ~~: humidifier; ~**bild** *das* aerial photograph; ~**blase** *die* air bubble; ~**-Boden-Rakete** *die* air-to-ground missile; ~**brücke** *die* airlift

**Lüftchen** /'lʏftçən/ *das;* ~s, ~: breeze; **kein ~ regte sich** there was not the slightest breath of wind

**luft-, Luft-:** ~**dicht** *Adj.* airtight; **etw. ~dicht abpacken/abschließen** pack sth. in an airtight container/put an airtight seal around sth.; ~**dichte** *die* (*Physik., Met.*) air density; ~**druck** *der; Pl.* ~**drücke** Ⓐ (*Physik*) air pressure; atmospheric pressure; Ⓑ (*Druckwelle*) blast; ~**druck·messer** *der;* ~~s, ~~: barometer; ~**durchlässig** *Adj.* pervious *or* permeable to air *postpos.;* well-ventilated ‹shoes›; ~**durchlässigkeit** *die* perviousness *or* permeability to air

**lüften** ❶ *tr. V.* Ⓐ air; (*ständig; mit Klimaanlage usw.*) ventilate; **das L~:** airing/ventilation; Ⓑ (*aus~*) air ‹clothes, bed. etc.›; Ⓒ (*hochheben*) raise, lift ‹hat, lid, veil, etc.›; Ⓓ (*enthüllen*) reveal; disclose ‹secret›; **jmds. Inkognito ~:** reveal sb.'s identity. ❷ *itr. V.* air the room/house/flat (*Brit.*) *or* (*Amer.*) apartment *etc.;* **wir müssen hier mal ~:** we must let some [fresh] air in here

**Lüfter** *der;* ~s, ~: fan

**Luft·fahrt** *die* aeronautics *sing., no art.;* (*mit Flugzeugen*) aviation *no art.*

**Luftfahrt·gesellschaft** *die* airline

**luft-, Luft-:** ~**fahrzeug** *das* aircraft; ~**feuchte,** ~**feuchtigkeit** *die* [atmospheric] humidity; ~**filter** *der od. das* (*Technik*) air filter; ~**flotte** *die* (*Milit.*) air fleet; ~**fracht** *die* air freight; ~**geist** *der* (*Myth.*) spirit of the air; ~**gekühlt** *Adj.* air-cooled; ~**getrocknet** *Adj.* air-dried; ~**gewehr** *das* air rifle; airgun; ~**hauch** *der* (*geh.*) breath of air; ~**herrschaft** *die* (*Milit.*) air supremacy; ~**hoheit** *die* air sovereignty; ~**hülle** *die* atmosphere

**luftig** ❶ *Adj.* airy ‹room, building, etc.›; well ventilated ‹cellar, store›; light, cool ‹clothes›; **auf der Terrasse ist es etwas ~er** there's more air out on the terrace. ❷ *adv.* **~/zu ~ angezogen sein** be lightly/not warmly enough dressed

**Luftikus** /'lʊftikʊs/ *der;* ~[ses], ~se (*ugs. abwertend*) careless and unreliable sort (*coll.*)

**Luft-:** ~**kampf** *der* air battle; aerial battle; ~**kissen** *das* (*Technik*) air cushion

**Luftkissen-:** ~**boot** *das* hovercraft; ~**fahrzeug** *das* hovercraft; air cushion vehicle

**luft-, Luft-:** ~**klappe** *die* ventilation flap; ~**korridor** *der* (*Flugw.*) air corridor; ~**krieg** *der* air warfare *no art.;* aerial warfare *no art.;* ~**kühlung** *die* (*Technik*) air cooling; **ein Motor mit ~kühlung** an air-cooled engine; ~**kur·ort** *der* climatic health resort; ~**lande·truppe** *die* (*Milit.*) airborne troops *pl.;* ~**leer** *Adj.* **ein ~leerer Raum** a vacuum; **im ~leeren Raum** (*fig.*) in a vacuum; ~**linie** *die:* **1 000 km ~linie** 1,000 km as the crow flies; ~**loch** *das* Ⓐ (*Öffnung*) air hole; Ⓑ (*ugs.: Windbö*) air pocket; ~**-~-Rakete** *die* (*Milit.*) air-to-air missile; ~**mangel** *der* Ⓐ lack of air; Ⓑ (*Atembeschwerden*) shortness of breath; ~**masche** *die* (*Handarb.*) chain stitch; ~**massen** *Pl.* (*Met.*) air masses; ~**matratze** *die* airbed; air mattress; Lilo ®; ~**mine** *die* aerial mine; air mine; ~**pirat** *der,* ~**piratin** *die* [aircraft] hijacker

**Luft·post** *die* airmail; **etw. per** *od.* **mit ~ schicken** send sth. [by] airmail

**Luftpost-:** ~**brief** *der* airmail letter; ~**leicht·brief** *der* aerogramme; ~**papier** *das* airmail paper

**Luft-:** ~**pumpe** *die* air pump; (*für Fahrrad*) [bicycle] pump; ~**raum** *der* airspace; ~**röhre** *die* ▶ 471 (*Anat.*) windpipe; trachea (*Anat.*); ~**sack** *der* Ⓐ (*Kfz-W.*) airbag; Ⓑ (*Zool.*) air sac; ~**schacht** *der* ventilation shaft; (*einer Klimaanlage*) ventilation duct; ~**schadstoff** *der* air pollutant; atmospheric pollutant; ~**schaukel** *die* swingboat; ~**schiff** *das* airship; *~**schiffahrt,** ~**schifffahrt** *die* airship travel; ~**schlacht** *die* air battle; aerial battle; **die ~schlacht um England** the Battle of Britain; ~**schlag** *der* air strike; ~**schlange** *die* [paper] streamer; ~**schleuse** *die* (*Technik*) airlock; ~**schloss,** *~**schloß** *das* castle in the air; ~**schlösser bauen** build castles in the air; ~**schraube** *die* (*Technik*) airscrew; propeller

**Luft·schutz** *der* air-raid protection *no art.*

**Luftschutz-:** ~**bunker,** ~**keller,** ~**raum** *der* air-raid shelter; ~**sirene** *die* air-raid siren; ~**übung** *die* air-raid drill; ~**wart** *der* (*hist.*) air-raid warden

**luft-, Luft-:** ~**sieg** *der* air victory; ~**spiegelung** *die* mirage; ~**sprung** *der* jump in the air; **vor Freude ~sprünge/einen ~sprung machen** *od.* **vollführen** jump for joy; ~**streitkräfte** *Pl.* (*Milit.*) air force *sing.;* ~**strom** *der* stream of air; ~**strömung** *die* (*Met.*) airstream; air current; ~**stützpunkt** *der* (*Milit.*) air base; ~**taxe** *die,* ~**taxi** *das* air taxi; ~**temperatur** *die* (*Met.*) air temperature; ~**überlegenheit** *die* (*Milit.*) air superiority; ~**-und-Raumfahrt-** aerospace

**Lüftung** *die;* ~, ~en Ⓐ (*das Lüften*) ventilation; Ⓑ (*Anlage*) ventilation system

**Lüftungs-:** ~**an·lage** *die* ventilation system; ~**klappe** *die* ventilation flap

**Luft-:** ~**veränderung** *die* change of air; ~**verflüssigung** *die* (*Physik*) liquefaction of air; ~**verkehr** *der* air traffic; ~**verpestung** *die* (*abwertend*), ~**verschmutzung** *die* air pollution; ~**verteidigung** *die* (*Milit.*) air defence; ~**waffe** *die* air force; **bei der ~waffe** in the air force; ~**weg** *der* Ⓐ **etw. auf dem ~weg verschicken/befördern** send/transport sth. by air; **auf dem ~weg reisen** travel by air; Ⓑ *Pl.* ▶ 471 (*Anat.: Atemwege*) airways; air passages; respiratory tract *sing.;* ~**widerstand** *der* (*Physik*) air resistance; ~**wurzel** *die* (*Bot.*) aerial root; ~**zufuhr** *die* air supply; ~**zug** *der* [gentle] breeze; (*in Zimmern, Gebäuden*) draught

**Lug** /lu:k/ *in* **~ und Trug** lies *pl.* and deception

**Luganer See,** (*schweiz.*) **Luganersee** *der;* ~s Lake Lugano

**Lüge** /'ly:gə/ *die;* ~, ~n lie; **eine barmherzige ~:** a compassionate falsehood; **jmdn. der ~ bezichtigen** accuse sb. of lying; call sb. a liar; **jmdm. ~n auftischen** (*ugs.*) serve sb. up a lot *or* load of lies (*coll.*); **~n haben kurze Beine** (*Spr.*) [the] truth will out; **jmdn./etw. ~n strafen** prove sb. a liar/give the lie to sth.; ⇒ *auch* **fromm** 1 C

**lugen** *itr. V.* (*südwestd.*) (*auch fig.*) peep; (*hervorgucken*) **aus etw. ~:** poke out of sth.

*old spelling (see note on page 1707)

**lügen** ❶ *itr. V.* lie; **hier wird nur gelogen und betrogen** there's nothing but lies and deception here; **~ wie gedruckt** lie like mad (*coll.*); be a terrible liar (*coll.*); **ich müsste ~, wenn ...** I should be lying if ...; **das Lügen** lying; **die Sterne ~ nicht** (*fig.*) the stars never lie; **wer einmal lügt, dem glaubt man nicht, und wenn er auch die Wahrheit spricht** (*Spr.*) a liar is never believed, even when he's telling the truth; ⇒ *auch* **Tasche**. ❷ *tr. V.* **er hat das alles gelogen** that was all a lie *or* all lies; **das ist gelogen!** that's a lie!

**Lügen-: ~bold** /-bolt/ *der;* **~~[e]s, ~~e** liar; **~detektor** *der* lie detector; **~gebäude** *das* tissue of lies; **~gespinst** *das* (*geh.*) web *or* tissue of lies

**lügenhaft** (*abwertend*) ❶ *Adj.* untruthful, mendacious ‹statement, account, report, etc.› ❷ *adv.* untruthfully; mendaciously

**Lügen-: ~kampagne** *die* campaign of lies; **~märchen** *das* tall story; cock and bull story; **~maul** *das* (*derb*) filthy liar

**Lügner** *der;* **~s, ~, Lügnerin** *die;* **~, ~nen** liar

**lügnerisch** *Adj.* untruthful; mendacious; lying *attrib.* ‹scoundrel›

**Lukas**[1] /ˈluːkas/ (*der*) (*Evangelist*) Luke

**Lukas**[2] *der;* **~, ~** (*Maschine*) try-your-strength machine; **hau den ~!** try your strength!

**Lukas·evangelium** *das* St Luke's Gospel; Gospel according to St Luke

**Luke** /ˈluːkə/ *die;* **~, ~n** Ⓐ (*Dach~*) skylight; Ⓑ (*bei Schiffen*) hatch; (*Keller~*) trapdoor

**lukrativ** /lukraˈtiːf/ ❶ *Adj.* lucrative. ❷ *adv.* lucratively

**lukullisch** /luˈkʊlɪʃ/ (*geh.*) ❶ *Adj.* Lucullan; epicurean. ❷ *adv.* **~ essen** *od.* **speisen** eat *or* have a Lucullan *or* an epicurean meal/meals

**Lulatsch** /ˈluːla(ː)tʃ/ *der;* **~[e]s, ~e** (*ugs.*) [long] lanky fellow; **ein langer ~:** a beanpole

**Lulle** /ˈlʊlə/ *die;* **~, ~n** (*ugs.*) cig (*coll.*); fag (*Brit. coll.*)

**lullen** *tr. V.* lull; **ein Kind in den Schlaf ~:** lull a child to sleep

**Lumme** /ˈlʊmə/ *die;* **~, ~n** (*Zool.*) guillemot

**Lümmel** /ˈlʏml̩/ *der;* **~s, ~** Ⓐ (*abwertend: Flegel*) lout; Ⓑ (*ugs., fam.: Bengel*) rascal; Ⓒ (*salopp: Penis*) willy (*coll.*)

**Lümmelei** *die;* **~, ~en** (*abwertend*) ⇒ **Flegelei**

**lümmelhaft** (*abwertend*) ⇒ **flegelhaft**

**lümmeln** *refl. V.* (*ugs. abwertend*) ⇒ **flegeln**

**Lump** /lʊmp/ *der;* **~en, ~en** scoundrel; rogue

**lumpen** (*ugs.*) ❶ *tr. V.* *in* **sich nicht ~ lassen** splash out (*coll.*). ❷ *itr. V.* be out on the tiles (*coll.*)

**Lumpen** *der;* **~s, ~** (*auch fig. abwertend*) rag

**Lumpen-: ~gesindel** *das* (*abwertend*) rabble; riff-raff; **~händler** *der* rag-and-bone man; **~händlerin** *die* rag-and-bone woman; **~hund, ~kerl** *der* (*abwertend*) scoundrel; bastard (*coll.*); **~pack** *das* (*abwertend*) ⇒ **~gesindel**; **~proletariat** *das* (*Soziol.*) lumpenproletariat; **~sammler** *der* Ⓐ rag-and-bone man; Ⓑ (*scherzh.: letztes Verkehrsmittel*) last bus/tram (*Brit.*) *or* (*Amer.*) streetcar/train; **~sammlerin** *die* rag-and-bone woman

**Lumperei** *die;* **~, ~en** (*abwertend*) dirty *or* mean trick; **eine große ~:** a very dirty *or* mean trick

**lumpig** (*abwertend*) ❶ *Adj.* Ⓐ (*kümmerlich*) paltry, miserable ‹pay, wages, etc.›; Ⓑ (*niederträchtig*) mean, shabby ‹behaviour, attitude›; mean ‹person›. ❷ *adv.* ‹act, behave› shabbily

**lunar** /luˈnaːɐ̯/ *Adj.* lunar

**Lunch** /lanʃ/ *der;* **~[e]s** *od.* **~[e]s** *od.* **~, ~[e]s** *od.* **~e** lunch; luncheon (*formal*)

**lunchen** /ˈlanʃn̩/ *itr. V.* have lunch *or* (*formal*) luncheon; lunch

**Lüneburger Heide** /ˈlyːnəbʊrɡə/ *die;* **~:** Lüneburg Heath

**Lunge** /ˈlʊŋə/ *die;* **~, ~n** ▶471 lungs *pl.;* (*~nflügel*) lung; **er hat es auf der ~** (*ugs.*) he has got lung trouble (*coll.*); **auf ~** *od.* **über die ~ rauchen** inhale; **die grüne ~ einer Großstadt** (*fig.*) the lungs *pl.* of a city; **sich** (*Dat.*) **die ~ aus dem Hals** *od.* **Leib schreien** (*ugs.*) yell one's head off (*coll.*)

**lungen-, Lungen-: ~bläschen** *das* ▶471 (*Anat.*) pulmonary alveolus; **~braten** *der* (*österr.*) ⇒ **Lendenbraten**; **~embolie** *die* ▶474 (*Med.*) pulmonary embolism; **~entzündung** *die* ▶474 pneumonia *no indef. art.;* **~flügel** *der* ▶471 lung; **~haschee** *das* (*Kochk.*) chopped lights *pl.* in sauce; **~krank** *Adj.* suffering from a lung disease *postpos.;* (*an Tuberkulose leidend*) suffering from tuberculosis *postpos.;* **~kranke** *der/die* person with *or* suffering from a lung disease; (*an Tuberkulose leidend*) tuberculosis sufferer; **~krebs** *der* ▶474 lung cancer; **~tuberkulose** *die* tuberculosis [of the lung]; pulmonary tuberculosis; **~zug** *der* inhalation; **einen tiefen ~zug machen** inhale deeply

**lungern** *itr. V.* ⇒ **herumlungern**

**Lunte** /ˈlʊntə/ *die;* **~, ~n** Ⓐ (*veralt.: Zündschnur*) fuse; match; **~ riechen** (*ugs.*) smell a rat; Ⓑ (*Jägerspr.: Schwanz*) brush

**Lupe** /ˈluːpə/ *die;* **~, ~n** magnifying glass; **jmdn./etw. unter die ~ nehmen** (*ugs.*) examine sb./sth. closely; take a close look at sb./sth.; **so etwas/solche Leute kann man mit der ~ suchen** (*ugs.*) things/people like that are very hard to find *or* are few and far between

**lupenrein** *Adj.* Ⓐ flawless ‹diamond, stone, etc.›; ‹diamond› of the first water; Ⓑ (*musterhaft*) genuine ‹amateur›; unimpeachable ‹record, reputation›; perfect ‹forgery, gentleman›

**lupfen** /ˈlʊpfn̩/ (*südd., schweiz., österr.*), **lüpfen** /ˈlʏpfn̩/ *tr. V.* raise; lift

**Lupine** /luˈpiːnə/ *die;* **~, ~n** (*Bot.*) lupin

**Lurch** /lʊrç/ *der;* **~[e]s, ~e** amphibian

**Lure** /ˈluːrə/ *die;* **~, ~n** (*hist.*) lur

**Lusche** /ˈlʊʃə/ *die;* **~, ~n** (*ugs.*) low card

**Lust** /lʊst/ *die;* **~, Lüste** /ˈlʏstə/ Ⓐ (*Bedürfnis*) **~ haben** *od.* **verspüren, etw. zu tun** feel like doing sth.; **große/keine ~ haben, etw. zu tun** really/not feel like doing sth.; **wir hatten nicht die geringste ~, das zu tun** we didn't feel in the least *or* slightest like doing it; **plötzlich ~ bekommen, etw. zu tun** suddenly feel like doing sth.; **auf etw.** (*Akk.*) **~ haben** fancy sth.; **ich hätte große ~ auf ...** (*Akk.*) I could really fancy ...; **ich habe jetzt keine ~:** I'm not in the mood at the moment; **das kannst du machen, wie du ~ hast** you can do it however you like *or* whatever way you like; **mir ist die ~ dazu vergangen** I've lost [all] enthusiasm for it; **ich mache das nach ~ und Laune** I do it when I feel like it; **ich hätte ~ dazu** I'd like to; Ⓑ (*Vergnügen*) pleasure; joy; **~ an etw.** (*Dat.*) **haben** take great pleasure in *or* really enjoy sth.; **die ~ an etw.** (*Dat.*) **verlieren** lose interest in *or* stop enjoying sth.; **aus purer ~ am Töten** out of sheer pleasure in killing; **er hat an allem die ~ verloren** he no longer takes pleasure in anything; **etw. mit ~ und Liebe tun** love doing sth.; Ⓒ (*Begierde*) desire; (*geschlechtlich*) desire; lust (*usu. derog.*); **die ~ des Fleisches** (*geh.*) the desires *pl.* *or* lusts *pl.* of the flesh

**Lustbarkeit** *die;* **~, ~en** (*geh. veralt.*) entertainment; festivity

**lust·betont** *Adj.* pleasure-orientated ‹behaviour›; fun-loving, pleasure-loving ‹person›; **~es Spielen** fun-orientated play

**Luster** /ˈlʊstɐ/ *der;* **~s, ~** (*österr.*) ⇒ **Lüster** A

**Lüster** /ˈlʏstɐ/ *der;* **~s, ~** Ⓐ (*veralt.: Kronleuchter*) chandelier; Ⓑ (*Überzug*) lustre

**lüstern** ❶ *Adj.* Ⓐ lecherous; lascivious; **nach jmdm. ~ sein** lust after sb.; Ⓑ (*begierig*) **mit ~en Augen/Blicken** with greedy eyes. ❷ *adv.* Ⓐ lecherously; lasciviously; Ⓑ (*begierig*) greedily

**Lust-: ~fahrt** *die* (*veralt.*) excursion; **~garten** *der* (*hist.*) pleasance (*arch.*); pleasure ground; **~gefühl** *das* feeling of pleasure; **~gewinn** *der* pleasure; **~greis** *der* (*abwertend*) [old] lecher; **~haus** *das* (*hist.*) summer house

**lustig** ❶ *Adj.* Ⓐ (*vergnügt*) merry; jolly; merry, jolly, jovial ‹person›; happy, enjoyable ‹time›; **dort war es immer sehr ~:** it was always a lot of fun there; **das kann ja ~ werden!** (*ugs. iron.*) this/that is going to be fun! **sich über jmdn./etw. ~ machen** make fun of sb./sth.; Ⓑ (*komisch*) funny; amusing; **etw. Lustiges** sth. funny; Ⓒ (*ugs.*) *in* **wie du ~ bist** (*ugs.*) however you fancy; whatever way you fancy; **solange du ~ bist** (*ugs.*) for as long as you like. ❷ *adv.* Ⓐ (*vergnügt*) ‹laugh, play› merrily, happily; **bei euch scheint es sehr ~ zuzugehen** you seem to be really enjoying yourselves *or* having a lot of fun; **~ brennen/flattern** (*fig.*) burn/flutter merrily; Ⓑ (*komisch*) funnily; amusingly; **sie kann so ~ erzählen** she can tell such funny *or* amusing stories; Ⓒ (*unbekümmert*) gaily

**-lustig** /ˈlʊstɪç/ *adj.* **[sehr] tanz~/sanges~/lese~ sein** be very fond of *or* keen on dancing/singing/reading; **der wanderlustige Urlauber** the holidaymaker who is keen on hiking

**Lustigkeit** *die;* **~** Ⓐ (*Fröhlichkeit*) merriness; jolliness; (*Frohsinn auch*) joviality; Ⓑ (*Komik*) funniness

**Lust·knabe** *der* (*veralt., scherzh.*) catamite

**Lüstling** /ˈlʏstlɪŋ/ *der;* **~s, ~e** (*veralt. abwertend, scherzh.*) lecher

**lust-, Lust-: ~los** ❶ *Adj.* Ⓐ (*unlustig*) listless; (*ohne Begeisterung*) unenthusiastic [and uninterested]; Ⓑ (*Börsenw.*) slack; dull; ❷ *adv.* listlessly; (*ohne Begeisterung*) without enthusiasm [or interest]; **sie stocherte ~los in ihrem Essen herum** she picked at her food with no real [interest or] enthusiasm; **~losigkeit** *die;* **~~:** Ⓐ (*Un~*) listlessness; (*mangelnde Begeisterung*) lack of [interest and] enthusiasm; Ⓑ (*Börsenw.*) slackness; dullness; **~molch** *der* (*ugs. scherzh.*) sex maniac; **ein alter ~molch** an old lecher; **~mord** *der* sex murder; **~mörder** *der* sex killer; **~objekt** *das* sex object; **~prinzip** *das* (*Psych.*) pleasure principle; **~schloss, *~schloß** *das* summer residence; **~schrei** *der* cry of pleasure; **~seuche** *die* Ⓐ (*veralt.: Syphilis*) syphilis *no art.;* Ⓑ (*geh.: Geschlechtskrankheit*) sexual scourge; **~spiel** *das* comedy; **~spiel·dichter** *der*, **~spiel·dichterin** *die* comic dramatist; **~wandeln** *itr. V.; mit sein od. haben* (*geh. veralt.*) stroll; take a stroll

**Lutheraner** /lʊtəˈraːnɐ/ *der;* **~s, ~, Lutheranerin** *die;* **~, ~nen** Lutheran

**Luther·bibel** *die* Luther's Bible; Lutheran Bible

**lutherisch, *Lutherisch** ❶ *Adj.* Lutheran; **das berühmte ~e Wort** Luther's famous words *pl.* ❷ *adv.* ‹think etc.› as a Lutheran; **jmdn. ~ erziehen** bring sb. up in the Lutheran religion

**luthersch, *Luthersch** /ˈlʊtɐʃ/ *Adj.* Luther's; **das berühmete ~e Wort** Luther's famous words *pl.*

**Luthertum** *das;* **~s** Lutheranism *no art.*

**lutschen** /ˈlʊtʃn̩/ ❶ *tr. V.* suck. ❷ *itr. V.* suck **an etw.** (*Dat.*) **~:** suck sth.; **am Daumen ~:** suck one's thumb

**Lutscher** *der;* **~s, ~** Ⓐ lollipop; Ⓑ (*Schnuller*) dummy (*Brit.*); pacifier (*Amer.*)

**Lüttich** /ˈlʏtɪç/ (*das*); **~s** Liège

**Luv** /luːf/ *die, auch das;* **~** (*Seemannsspr.*) *in* **in/nach ~:** to windward

**luven** /ˈluːvn̩/ *itr. V.* (*Seemannsspr.*) luff

**Lux** /lʊks/ *das;* **~, ~** (*Physik*) lux

**Luxation** /lʊksaˈtsi̯oːn/ *die;* **~, ~en** ▶474 (*Med.*) luxation (*Med.*); dislocation

**Luxemburg** /ˈlʊksm̩bʊrk/ (*das*); **~s** ▶700 Luxembourg; ⇒ *auch* **Großherzogtum**

**Luxemburger** ▶700 ❶ *indekl. Adj.* Luxembourg; **die ~ EG-Behörden** the EEC authorities in Luxembourg. ❷ *der;* **~s, ~:** Luxembourger; ⇒ *auch* **Kölner**

**Luxemburgerin** *die;* **~, ~nen** Luxembourger; ⇒ *auch* **-in**

**luxemburgisch** *Adj.* Luxembourgian

**luxuriös** /lʊksu'ri̯øːs/ ❶ *Adj.* luxurious; **ein ~es Leben führen** lead a life of luxury. ❷ *adv.* luxuriously; **[sehr] ~ leben/wohnen** live in [great] luxury

**Luxus** /'lʊksʊs/ *der;* **~** (*auch fig.*) luxury; **etw. ist reiner ~:** sth. is sheer extravagance; **den ~ lieben** love luxury; **im ~ leben** live in [the lap of] luxury; **sich (Dat.) den ~ leisten, etw. zu tun** (*fig.*) allow oneself the luxury of doing sth.

**Luxus-: ~artikel** *der* luxury article; **dieses Geschäft führt nur ~artikel** this shop sells only luxury goods; **~aus·führung** *die* de luxe version; **~ausgabe** *die* de luxe edition; **~dampfer** *der* luxury cruiser; **~hotel** *das* luxury hotel; **~jacht** *die* luxury yacht; **~kabine** *die* luxury cabin; **~klasse** *die* luxury class; **Automobile der ~klasse** luxury cars; **~limousine** *die* luxury limousine; **~schlitten** *der* (*ugs.*) classy car *or* job (*sl.*); **~weibchen** *das* (*abwertend*) woman who expects to live in luxury

**Luzern** /lu'tsɛrn/ (*das*); **~s** ▶ 700 Lucerne

**Luzerne** /lu'tsɛrnə/ *die;* **~, ~n** (*Bot.*) alfalfa; lucerne (*Brit.*)

**luzid** /lu'tsiːt/ *Adj.* lucid

**Luzidität** /lutsidi'tɛːt/ *die;* **~:** lucidity

**Luzifer** /'luːtsifɐ/ (*der*) Lucifer

**luziferisch** *Adj.* (*geh.*) diabolical; vicious ‹sarcasm›

**LW** *Abk.* **Langwelle** LW

**Lymph·drüse** *die* (*veralt.*) ⇨ **Lymphknoten**

**Lymphe** /'lʏmfə/ *die;* **~, ~n** lymph

**Lymph·knoten** *der* lymph node *or* gland

**lynchen** /'lʏnçn/ *tr. V.* lynch; (*scherzh.*) lynch; kill

**Lynch-: ~justiz** *die* lynch law; **~mord** *der* lynching

**Lyoner [Wurst]** /'li̯oːnɐ-/ *die;* **~, Lyoner [Würste]** bologna [sausage]

**Lyra** /'lyːra/ *die;* **~, Lyren** Ⓐ (*Mus.*) lyre; Ⓑ (*Astron.*) Lyra; the lyre

**Lyrik** /'lyːrɪk/ *die;* **~:** lyric poetry

**Lyriker** *der;* **~s, ~, Lyrikerin** *die;* **~, ~nen** lyric poet; lyricist

**lyrisch** ❶ *Adj.* Ⓐ lyric ‹poem, poetry, epic, drama›; lyrical ‹passage, style, description, etc.›; Ⓑ (*gefühlvoll*) lyrical; Ⓒ (*Mus.*) lyric. ❷ *adv.* lyrically

**Lyzeum** /ly'tseːʊm/ *das;* **~s, Lyzeen** /ly'tseːən/ girls' high school

l

# Mm

**m, M** /ɛm/ *das;* ~, ~: m/M; ⇒ *auch* **a, A**
**m** *Abk.* ▶489 **Meter** m
**M** *Abk.* (*DDR*) **¹Mark**
**MA** *Abk.* **Mittelalter**
**Mäander** /mɛ'andɐ/ *der;* ~s, ~ (*Geogr., Kunstwiss.*) meander
**Maar** /ma:ɐ̯/ *das;* ~[e]s, ~e (*Geogr.*) maar; (*See*) crater lake
**Maas** /ma:s/ *die;* ~: Meuse
**Maat** /ma:t/ *der;* ~[e]s, ~e[n] ▶91 **A** (*Seemannsspr.*) [ship's] mate; **B** (*Dienstgrad*) petty officer
**Mach** /max/ *das;* ~[s], ~ (*Physik*) Mach
**Machandel** /ma'xandl̩/ *der;* ~s, ~ (*nordd.*) ⇒ **Wacholder**
**Mạch·art** *die* style; (*Schnitt*) cut
**mạchbar** *Adj.* feasible
**Mạche** *die;* ~ (*ugs.*) **A** (*abwertend*) sham; **das ist reine** *od.* **nichts als ~:** it's pure sham; it's all put on; **B etw. in der ~ haben** have sth. on the stocks; be working on sth.; **jmdn. in der ~ haben/in die ~ nehmen** (*salopp*) (*jmdm. zusetzen*) be working/work on sb.; (*jmdn. verprügeln*) be working/work sb. over (*coll.*)
**machen** /'maxn̩/ ❶ *tr. V.* **A** (*herstellen*) make; **aus Plastik/Holz** *usw.* **gemacht** made of plastic/wood *etc.*; **aus diesen Äpfeln ~ wir Saft** we will make juice from these apples; **aus diesem Zimmer ~ wir gerade ein Büro** we are making *or* turning this room into an office; **sich** (*Dat.*) **etw. ~ lassen** have sth. made; **Geld/ein Vermögen/einen Gewinn ~:** make money/a fortune/a profit; **dafür ist er wie gemacht/nicht gemacht** (*fig.*) that's just his line/that's not his line; **etw. aus jmdm. ~:** make sb. into sth.; (*verwandeln*) turn sb. into sth.; **jmdn. zum Präsidenten** *usw.* **~:** make sb. president *etc.*; **er machte sie zu seiner Frau** (*geh. veralt.*) he made her his wife; **B** (*geben*) **jmdm. einen Kostenvoranschlag ~:** let sb. have *or* give sb. an estimate; **jmdm. einen guten Preis ~** (*ugs.*) (*beim Kauf*) make sb. a good offer; (*beim Verkauf*) name a good price; **C** (*zubereiten*) get, prepare ‹meal›; **den Salat ~** (*ugs.*) do the salad (*coll.*); **was machst du heute zum Abendessen?** what are you getting/doing for supper tonight?; **jmdm./sich [einen] Kaffee ~:** make [some] coffee for sb./oneself; **jmdm. einen Cocktail ~:** get *or* mix sb. a cocktail; **D** (*verursachen*) **jmdm. Arbeit ~:** cause *or* make [extra] work for sb.; **jmdm. Sorgen ~:** cause sb. anxiety; worry sb.; **jmdm. Mut/Hoffnung ~:** give sb. courage/hope; **das macht Durst/Hunger** *od.* **Appetit** this makes one thirsty/hungry; this gives one a thirst/an appetite; **das macht das Wetter** that's [because of] the weather; **das macht das viele Rauchen** that comes from smoking a lot; **mach, dass er gesund wird!** make him get well!; **mach, dass du nach Hause kommst!** (*ugs.*) off home with you!; **ich muss ~, dass ich zum Bahnhof komme** (*ugs.*) I must see that I get to the station; **E** (*ausführen*) do ‹job, repair, etc.›; **seine Hausaufgaben ~:** do one's homework; **ein Foto** *od.* **eine Aufnahme ~:** take a photograph; **ein Examen ~:** take an exam; **einen Spaziergang ~:** go for *or* take a walk; **eine Reise ~:** go on a journey *or* trip; **einen Besuch [bei jmdm.] ~:** pay [sb.] a visit; **wie mans macht, macht mans falsch** *od.* **verkehrt** (*ugs.*) [however you do it,] there's always something wrong; (*jmdm. ist nichts recht*) there's no pleasing some people; **er macht es nicht unter 100 DM** he won't do it for under *or* less than 100 marks; **F** (+ *Adj. od. V.: Zustand verändern*) **jmdn. glücklich/eifersüchtig** *usw.* **~:** make sb. happy/jealous *etc.*; **etw. größer/länger/kürzer ~:** make sth. bigger/longer/shorter; **mach es dir gemütlich** *od.* **bequem!** make yourself comfortable *or* at home; **das Kleid macht sie älter** the dress makes her look older; **jmdn. lachen/weinen/leiden ~** (*geh.*) make sb. laugh/cry/suffer; **G** (*tun*) do; **was machst du da?** what are you doing?; **musst du noch viel ~?** do you still have a lot to do?; **mach doch etwas!** 'do something!'; **mach ich, wird gemacht!** (*ugs.*) will do!; **was ~ Sie [beruflich]?** what do you do [for a living]?; **da ist nichts zu ~, dagegen kann man nichts ~:** there's nothing one can do [about it]; **was soll ich nur ~?** what am I to do?; **was macht der Fußball in der Küche?** what is the football doing in the kitchen?; **was hat er nur wieder gemacht [, dass alle so wütend sind]?** what has he been up to this time [to make everyone so angry]?; **so etwas macht man nicht** that [just] isn't done; **mach was dran!** (*ugs.*) what can you do?; **mit mir könnt ihr es ja ~** (*ugs.*) you can get away with it with me; **sie lässt alles mit sich ~:** she is very long-suffering; **H was macht ...?** (*wie ist um ... bestellt?*) how is ...?; **was macht die Arbeit?** how is the job [getting on]?; how are things at work?; **was macht die Gesundheit?** how are you keeping?; **I** (*ergeben*) (*beim Rechnen*) be; (*bei Geldbeträgen*) come to; **zwei mal zwei macht vier** two times two is four; **was** *od.* **wie viel macht das [alles zusammen]?** how much does that come to?; **das macht 12 DM** that is *or* costs 12 marks; (*Endsumme*) that comes to 12 marks; **J** (*schaden*) **was macht das schon?** what does it matter?; **macht das was?** does it matter?; do you mind?; **macht nichts!** (*ugs.*) never mind!; it doesn't matter; **K** (*teilnehmen an*) **einen Kursus** *od.* **Lehrgang ~:** take a course; **ein Seminar ~** (*ugs.*) take part in a seminar; **L** (*ugs.: veranstalten*) organize, (*coll.*) do ‹trips, meals, bookings, etc.›; **ein Fest ~:** give a party; **M machs gut!** (*ugs.*) look after yourself!; (*auf Wiedersehen*) so long!; **er macht es nicht mehr lange** (*ugs.*) he won't last much longer; **N** (*ugs.: ordnen, sauber ~, renovieren*); do ‹room, stairs, washing, etc.›; **das Bett ~:** make the bed; **die Haare/Fingernägel ~:** do one's hair/nails; **den Garten ~:** do the garden (*coll.*); **O** (*ugs. verhüll.: seine Notdurft verrichten*) **sein Geschäft ~:** relieve oneself; **groß/klein ~:** do big jobs/small jobs (*child language*); **P** (*ugs.: spielen, sein*) play, act ‹part, the clown, etc.›; **wer macht hier den Vorarbeiter?** who is the foreman here?; **Q es [mit jmdm.] ~** (*ugs. verhüll.*) have it off [with sb.] (*sl.*); **es jmdm. ~** (*derb*) give it to sb. (*sl.*).
❷ *refl. V.* **A** *mit Adj.* **sich ... ~:** make oneself ...; **sich hübsch ~:** smarten [oneself] up; **sich schmutzig ~:** get [oneself] dirty; **sich verständlich ~:** make oneself clear; **das macht sich bezahlt!** it's worth it!; **sie macht sich besser, als sie ist** she pretends to be better than she is; **B** (*beginnen*) **sich an etw.** (*Akk.*) **~:** get down to sth.; **mach dich ans Werk/an die Arbeit** get down to work; get on with it; **C** (*ugs.: sich entwickeln*) do well; get on; **du hast dich aber gemacht!** you've made great strides!; **D** (*passen*) **das macht sich gut hier** this fits in well; this looks good here; **E mach dir nichts daraus!** (*ugs.*) don't let it bother you; **ich mache mir nichts daraus** it doesn't bother me; **sich** (*Dat.*) **nichts/wenig aus jmdm./etw. ~** (*ugs.*) not care at all/much for sb./sth.; **F** (*gestalten*) **wir wollen uns** (*Dat.*) **einen schönen Abend ~:** we want to have an enjoyable evening; **macht euch ein paar schöne Stunden** enjoy yourselves for a few hours; **G sich** (*Dat.*) **Feinde ~:** make enemies; **sich** (*Dat.*) **jmdn. zum Freund/Feind ~:** make a friend/an enemy of sb.; **sich** (*Dat.*) **etw. zum Grundsatz/zur Aufgabe ~:** make sth. a principle/one's task; **H das macht sich von selbst** it takes care of itself; **wenn es sich [irgendwie] ~ lässt** if it can [somehow] be done; if it is [at all] possible.
❸ *itr. V.* **A** (*ugs.: sich beeilen*) **mach schon!** get a move on! (*coll.*); look snappy! (*coll.*); **mach schneller!** hurry up!; **B das macht müde** it makes you tired; it is tiring; **das macht hungrig** it makes you hungry; **das macht durstig** it makes you thirsty; **das Kleid macht dick** the dress makes one look fat; **C** (*tun*) **lass mich nur ~** (*ugs.*) leave it to me; **D** (*ugs. verhüll.*) ‹child, pet› perform (*coll.*); **ins Bett/in die Hose ~:** wet one's bed/pants; **E** (*salopp: tätig sein*) **er macht in Lederwaren** he is in leather goods; **der Konzern macht auch in Versicherungen** the group also does insurance; **F** (*salopp abwertend: mimen*) **auf naiv** *usw.* **~:** pretend to be naïve *etc.*; act naïve *etc.*; **auf feine Dame/großen Geschäftsmann ~:** act the fine lady/big business man; **auf vornehm ~:** give oneself airs; **G** *mit sein* (*landsch. ugs.: sich begeben*) go; **in den Westen ~:** go to the west
**Mạchenschaften** *Pl.* (*abwertend*) machinations; wheeling and dealing *sing.*
**Mạcher** *der;* ~s, ~, **Mạcherin** *die;* ~, ~nen (*ugs.*) doer; **der Typ des Machers** the dynamic type who just gets on with things
**-macher** *der;* ~s, ~, **-macherin** *die;* ~, ~nen ...-maker; **Filme~/Besen~/Bücher~:** film-maker/broom-maker/maker of books
**Mạcher·lohn** *der* (*Schneiderei*) making-up charge
**Machete** /ma'xe:tə/ *die;* ~, ~n machete
**Machiavellismus** /makiavɛ 'lɪsmʊs/ *der;* ~ (*Philos., Politik*) machiavellianism *no art.*
**machiavellịstisch** *Adj.* (*Philos., Politik*) machiavellian
**Machismo** /ma'tʃɪsmo/ *der;* ~[s] (*abwertend*) machismo
**Macho** /'matʃo/ *der;* ~s, ~s (*abwertend*) macho
**Macht** /maxt/ *die;* ~, **Mächte** /'mɛçtə/ **A** (*Kraft, Einfluss*) power; (*Stärke*) strength; (*Befugnis*) authority; power; **mit aller ~:** with all one's might; **alles, was in seiner ~ steht, tun** do everything in one's power; **seine ~ ausspielen** use one's authority *or* power; **das liegt nicht in ihrer ~:** that is not within her power; that is outside her authority; **~ über jmdn. haben** have a hold over sb.; **eine unwiderstehliche ~ auf** *od.* **über jmdn. ausüben** exert an irresistible influence over sb.; **die ~ der Gewohnheit/der Verhältnisse** the force of habit/circumstances; **der Frühling kommt mit ~:** spring is coming with a vengeance; **B** (*Herrschaft*) power *no art.*; **die ~ ergreifen** *od.* **an sich reißen** seize power; **an die ~ kommen** come to power; **C** (*Staat*) power; **D** (*Machtgruppe; geheimnisvolle Kraft*) power; force; **die Mächte der Reaktion** the forces of reaction; **die Mächte der Finsternis** the

powers of darkness; **böse Mächte** evil forces; **E** (*geh., veralt.: Heer*) forces *pl.*; **mit großer ~:** with a large force *or* army

**Macht-: ~anspruch** *der* claim *or* pretension to power; **~apparat** *der* power structure; **~ausübung** *die* exercise of power (*Gen.* by); **~befugnis** *die* authority *no pl., no art.*; power *no art.*; **~bereich** *der* sphere of influence; **~block** *der; Pl.* **~blöcke** power bloc

**Mächte·gruppierung** *die* (*Politik*) power grouping

**macht-, Macht-: ~entfaltung** *die* expansion of power; **~ergreifung** *die* (*Politik*) seizure of power (*Gen.* by); **~gier** *die* (*abwertend*) craving for power; **~gierig** *Adj.* with a craving for power *postpos., not pred.*; **~gierig sein** crave power; **~haber** /-ha:bɐ/ *der;* **~s, ~~, ~haberin** *die;* **~~, ~~nen** ruler; **die gegenwärtigen ~haber** those at present in power; **~hunger** *der* hunger for power; **~hungrig** *Adj.* power-hungry

**mächtig** /ˈmɛçtɪç/ **1** *Adj.* **A** powerful; **die Mächtigen dieser Welt** the high and mighty; the wielders of power; **B seiner Sinne od seiner selbst** (*Gen.*) **[nicht] ~ sein** [not] be in control of oneself; **einer Sprache** (*Gen.*) **/des Lesens und Schreibens ~ sein** (*geh.*) have a command of a language/be capable of reading and writing; **C** (*beeindruckend groß*) mighty; powerful, mighty ‹voice, blow›; tremendous, powerful ‹effect›; (*ugs.*) terrific (*coll.*) ‹luck›; terrible (*coll.*) ‹fright›; **~en Hunger/~e Angst haben** be terribly hungry/afraid; **D** (*landsch.: schwer*) heavy ‹food›; (*sättigend*) filling ‹food›.
**2** *adv.* (*ugs.*) terribly (*coll.*); extremely; **~ viel** an awful lot (*coll.*); **~ groß** tremendously large (*coll.*); **er ist ~ gewachsen** he has grown a lot; **ihr müsst euch ~ beeilen** you'll really have to step on it (*coll.*)

**Mächtigkeit** *die;* **~ A** (*Einfluss*) power; **B** (*Größe*) massive size; (*Gewalt*) force

**macht-, Macht-: ~instrument** *das* (*Politik*) instrument of power; **~kampf** *der* (*bes. Politik*) power struggle; **~los** *Adj.* powerless; impotent; **gegen etw. ~los sein, einer Sache** (*Dat.*) **~los gegenüberstehen** be powerless in the face of sth.; **gegenüber jmdm. ~los sein** be powerless against sb.; **gegen so viel Frechheit/Dummheit bin ich/ist man einfach ~los** there is nothing one can do in the face of such impudence/stupidity; **~losigkeit** *die;* **~~:** impotence (**gegen, gegenüber** in the face of); **~missbrauch, *~mißbrauch** *der* abuse of power; **~mittel** *das* instrument of power; **~politik** *die* power politics *sing., no art.*; **~position** *die* (*bes. Politik*) position of power; **~probe** *die* trial of strength; **~stellung** *die* ⇨ **~position**; **~streben** *das* ambition for power; **~übernahme** *die* (*Politik*) takeover [of power] (*Gen.* by); **~verhältnisse** *Pl.* balance of power *sing.*; (*innerhalb einer Organisation*) power structure *sing.*; **~voll 1** *Adj.* powerful; (*imponierend*) impressive ‹demonstration, appearance›; **2** *adv.* powerfully; (*imponierend*) impressively; **~vollkommenheit** *die* absolute power; **aus eigener ~vollkommenheit** on one's own authority *or* initiative; **~wechsel** *der* (*Politik*) change of government; **~wort** *das;* **~~e** word of command; decree; **ein ~wort sprechen** put one's foot down; lay down the law

**Mach·werk** *das* (*abwertend*) shoddy effort

**Macke** /ˈmakə/ *die;* **~, ~n A** (*salopp: Tick*) fad; **'ne ~ haben** have a fad; (*verrückt sein*) be off one's rocker (*coll.*); **B** (*ugs.: Defekt*) defect; (*optisch*) mark; blemish

**Macker** *der;* **~s, ~ A** (*Jugendspr.: Freund, Kerl*) guy (*coll.*); bloke (*Brit. sl.*); **B** (*abwertend*) macho

**MAD** *Abk.* **Militärischer Abschirmdienst** Military Counter Intelligence [Service]

**Madagaskar** /madaˈgaskar/ (*das*); **~s** Madagascar

**Madagasse** /madaˈgasə/ *der;* **~n, ~n, Madagassin** *die;* **~, ~nen** Madagascan; Madagasy

**madagassisch** *Adj.* Madagascan; Madagasy

**Madam** /maˈdam/ *die;* **~, ~s A** (*ugs. scherzh.*) [portly] matron; **B** (*landsch. scherzh.: Ehefrau*) better half (*joc.*)

**Mädchen** /ˈmɛːtçən/ *das;* **~s, ~ A** girl; (*ugs. veralt.: Freundin*) girl[friend]; **für kleine ~ müssen** (*fam. scherzh. verhüll.*) need to spend a penny (*Brit. coll.*); **B** (*Haus~*) maid; **~ für alles** (*ugs.*) maid of all work; (*im Büro usw.*) girl Friday; (*Mann*) man Friday

**Mädchen·alter** *das* girlhood years *pl.*; **im [zarten] ~alter** when still a [young] girl

**mädchenhaft 1** *Adj.* girlish; **~ aussehen** ‹boy› have a girlish look; look like a girl; ‹girl› look childlike. **2** *adv.* **sich ~ kleiden** dress in a girlish manner; ‹older woman› wear young clothes, dress like a young girl

**Mädchen-: ~handel** *der* white-slave traffic; **~händler** *der,* **~händlerin** *die* white-slave trader; **~klasse** *die* girls' class; **~kleidung** *die* girls' clothes *pl.*; **~name** *der* **A** (*Vorname*) girl's name; **B** (*Name vor der Ehe*) maiden name; **~pensionat** *das* girls' boarding school; **~schule** *die* girls' school; school for girls; **~zimmer** *das* **A** (*für ein ~zimmer*) girl's room; (*für mehrere*) girls' room; **B** (*für Hausmädchen*) maid's room

**Made** /ˈmaːdə/ *die;* **~, ~n** maggot; (*Larve*) larva; **leben wie die ~ im Speck** be living in the lap of luxury *or* off the fat of the land

**Madeira** /maˈdeːra/ *der;* **~s, ~s, Madeira·wein** *der* Madeira

**Madel** /ˈmaːdl̩/ *das;* **~s, ~n,** (*südd., österr. mundartl.*), **Mädel** /ˈmɛːdl̩/ *das;* **Mädels, Mädel,** *od. nordd.:* **Mädels** ⇨ **Mädchen A**

**Maderl, Mäderl** /ˈmɛːdɐl /,/ *das;* **~s, ~n** (*österr. ugs.*) ⇨ **Mädchen A**

**madig** *Adj.* maggoty; **jmdm. etw./ein Vergnügen ~ machen** (*ugs.*) spoil sb.'s pleasure in sth./spoil a pleasure for sb.; **jmdn./etw. ~ machen** (*ugs.*) run sb./sth. down

**Madonna** /maˈdɔna/ *die;* **~, Madonnen A** (*christl. Rel.*) **die ~:** Our Lady; the Virgin Mary; **B** (*Kunst*) madonna

**madonnen-, Madonnen-: ~gesicht** *das* madonna-like features *pl.*; **~haft 1** *Adj.* madonna-like; **2** *adv.* in a madonna-like manner; **~scheitel** *der* centre parting

**Madrigal** /madriˈgaːl/ *das;* **~s, ~e** (*Literaturw., Musik*) madrigal

**Maestro** /maˈɛstro/ *der;* **~s, ~s** *od.* **Maestri** maestro

**Maf[f]ia** /ˈmafi̯a/ *die;* **~, ~s A** Mafia; **B** (*fig.*) mafia

**Mafioso** /maˈfi̯oːzo/ *der;* **~s, Mafiosi** mafioso

**mag** /maːk/ *1. u. 3. Pers. Sg. Präsens v.* **mögen**

**Magazin** /magaˈtsiːn/ *das;* **~s, ~e A** (*Lager*) store; (*für Waren*) stockroom; (*für Waffen u. Munition*) magazine; (*in der Bibliothek*) stack [room]; stacks *pl.*; **B** (*für Patronen, Dias, Film usw.*) magazine; (*an Werkzeugmaschinen*) feeder; **C** (*Zeitschrift*) magazine; (*Rundf., Ferns.*) magazine programme

**Magazineur** /magatsiˈnøːɐ̯/ *der;* **~s, ~e** (*österr.*) storekeeper; stores supervisor

**magazinieren** *tr. V.* [put in] store; put ‹explosives, weapons› in a/the magazine

**Magd** /maːkt/ *die;* **~, Mägde** /ˈmɛːkdə/ **A** (*veralt.*) (*Landarbeiterin*) [female] farmhand; (*Vieh~*) milkmaid; (*Dienst~*) maidservant; **B** (*dichter. veralt.: Jungfrau*) maid; damsel; **Maria, die reine ~** (*christl. Rel.*) Mary, the pure Virgin

**Mägdelein** /ˈmɛːkdəlai̯n/ *das;* **~s, ~, Mägdlein** /ˈmɛːktlai̯n/ *das;* **~s, ~** (*dichter. veralt.*) maiden

**Magellan·straße** /mageˈlaːn-/ *die* Straits *pl.* of Magellan

**Magen** /ˈmaːgn̩/ *der;* **~s, Mägen** /ˈmɛːgn̩/ *od.* **~** ▶ 471 stomach; **mir knurrt der ~** (*ugs.*) my tummy is rumbling (*coll.*); **sich** (*Dat.*) **den ~ verderben** get an upset stomach; **etw. auf nüchternen** *od.* **leeren ~ essen/trinken** eat/drink sth. on an empty stomach; **etwas/nichts im ~ haben** have had something/nothing to eat; **jmdm. auf den ~ schlagen** upset sb.'s stomach; **jmdm. schwer im ~ liegen** lie heavy on sb.'s stomach; **diese Sache liegt mir schwer auf dem** *od.* **im ~** (*fig. ugs.*) this business is preying on my mind; **mit leerem ~:** with an empty stomach; **da dreht sich einem/mir der ~ um** (*ugs.*) it's enough to make *or* it makes one's/my stomach turn; (*fig.*) it makes you/me sick; ⇨ *auch* **Liebe A**

**magen-, Magen-: ~ausheberung** *die;* **~~, ~~en** (*Med.*) pumping-out of the stomach; **~beschwerden** *Pl.* stomach trouble *sing.*; **~bitter** *der;* **~~s,** bitters *pl.*; **~blutung** *die* gastric haemorrhage; **~-Darm-Kanal** *der* ▶ 471 (*Anat.*) gastro-intestinal tract; **~-Darm-Katarr[h]** *der* ▶ 474 (*Med.*) gastro-enteritis; **~drücken** *das;* **~~s** feeling of pressure in the stomach; (**~schmerzen**) stomach ache; **~durchbruch** *der* ▶ 474 (*Med.*) ⇨ **~perforation**; **~fahrplan** *der* (*ugs. scherzh.*) menu; eating schedule; **~freundlich** *adj.* kind to the stomach *pred.*; **~gegend** *die* region of the stomach; **ein unangenehmes Gefühl in der ~gegend** an unpleasant feeling in the [pit of the] stomach; **~geschwür** *das* ▶ 474 stomach ulcer; **~grube** *die* pit of the stomach; **~inhalt** *der* contents *pl.* of the stomach; **~katarr[h]** *der* ▶ 474 (*Med.*) gastritis; **~knurren** *das;* **~~s** (*ugs.*) tummy rumbles *pl.* (*coll.*); **~krampf** *der* stomach cramp; **~krämpfe** stomach spasms; **~krank** *Adj.* ‹person› suffering from a stomach disorder *or* complaint; **~krank sein/werden** have/get a stomach disorder *or* complaint; **~krankheit** *die* stomach complaint; **~krebs** *der* ▶ 474 cancer of the stomach; **~leiden** *das* ▶ 474 ⇨ **~krankheit**; **~leidend** *Adj.*: ⇨ **~krank**; **~mittel** *das* medicine for the stomach; stomachic (*Pharm.*); **~perforation** *die* ▶ 474 (*Med.*) perforation of the stomach; **~saft** *der* gastric juice; **~säure** *die* gastric acid; **~schleimhaut** *die* ▶ 471 lining of the stomach; **~schleimhaut·entzündung** *die* gastritis; **~schmerzen** *Pl.* ▶ 474 stomach ache *sing.*; **~spiegelung** *die* (*Med.*) gastroscopy; **~spülung** *die* (*Med.*) gastric irrigation; **~verstimmung** *die* stomach upset

**mager** /ˈmaːgɐ/ **1** *Adj.* **A** (*dünn*) thin; **B** (*fettarm*) low-fat; low in fat *pred.*; lean ‹meat›; **ein ~es Benzingemisch** (*Kfz-W.*) a lean mixture; **C** (*nicht ertragreich*) poor ‹soil, harvest›; infertile ‹field›; lean ‹years›; (*fig.: dürftig*) meagre ‹profit, increase, success, report, etc.›; thin ‹programme›; **D** (*Druckw.*) light-face ‹type, characters›. **2** *adv.* **~ essen** follow a low-fat diet; eat low-fat foods

**Mager·käse** *der* low-fat cheese

**Magerkeit** *die;* **~ A** thinness; **B** (*Ertragsarmut*) poorness; (*fig.: Dürftigkeit*) meagreness

**Mager-: ~milch** *die* skim[med] milk; **~quark** *der* low-fat curd cheese; **~sucht** *die* ▶ 474 (*Med.*) wasting disease; (*Anorexie*) anorexia

**Magie** /maˈgiː/ *die;* **~:** magic; **schwarze/weiße ~:** black/white magic

**Magier** /ˈmaːgi̯ɐ/ *der;* **~s, ~, Magierin** *die* (*auch fig.*) magician; **die drei Magier** (*bibl.*); the Three Magi

**magisch 1** *Adj.* **A** magic ‹powers›; **~es Quadrat** magic square; **B** (*geheimnisvoll*) magical ‹attraction, light, force, etc.›; (*unwirklich*) eerie ‹light, half-light›. **2** *adv.* (*durch Zauber*) by magic; (*wie durch Zauber*) as if by magic; magically; (*unwirklich*) eerily; **~ beleuchtet** with magical/eerie lighting *postpos., not pred.*

**Magister** /maˈgɪstɐ/ *der;* **~s, ~ A** ≈ Master's degree (*first degree at a German university*); **den ~ haben/machen** have/work for an MA *or* (*Amer.*) a Master's; **~ Artium** /- ˈartsi̯ʊm/ Master of Arts; **B** (*Inhaber des Titels*) ≈ person holding a Master's degree; **~ sein** ≈ have a Master's degree

**Magistrat**[1] /magɪsˈtraːt/ *der;* **~[e]s, ~e** City Council

*old spelling (see note on page 1707)

**Magistrat²** *der;* **∼en, ∼en** (*schweiz.*) Federal Councillor

**Magma** /'magma/ *das;* **∼s, Magmen** (*Geol.*) magma

**Magna Charta** /'magna 'karta/ *die;* **∼** (*hist.*) Magna Carta

**magna cum laude** /'magna kʊm 'laudə/ (*Hochschulw.*) with great distinction; *second of four grades of successful doctoral examination*

**Magnat** /ma'gna:t/ *der;* **∼en, ∼en** Ⓐ magnate; Ⓑ (*hist.*) great nobleman

**Magnesia** /ma'gne:zi̯a/ *die;* **∼** Ⓐ (*Chemie, Med.*) magnesia; Ⓑ (*Turnen*) chalk

**Magnesium** /ma'gne:zi̯ʊm/ *das;* **∼s** (*Chemie*) magnesium

**Magnet** /ma'gne:t/ *der;* **∼en** *od.* **∼[e]s, ∼e** (*auch fig.*) magnet

**Magnet-: ∼auf·zeichnung** *die* [magnetic] tape recording; **∼band** *das Pl.* **∼bänder** magnetic tape; **∼berg** *der* Magnetic Mountain; **∼bild·verfahren** *das* (*Technik*) videotape technique; **∼eisen·stein** *der* (*Mineral.*) magnetite; **∼feld** *das* (*Physik*) magnetic field

**magnetisch** ❶ *Adj.* (*auch fig.*) magnetic. ❷ *adv.* magnetically; **∼ gespeichert/aufgezeichnet** stored/recorded on magnetic tape; **jmdn. ∼ anziehen** (*fig.*) have a magnetic attraction for sb.

**Magnetiseur** /magneti'sø:ɐ̯/ *der;* **∼s, ∼e** mesmerist

**magnetisieren** *tr. V.* Ⓐ (*Physik*) magnetize; Ⓑ (*Psych. veralt.*) treat ‹patient› by mesmerism

**Magnetisierung** *die;* **∼, ∼en** (*Physik*) magnetization

**Magnetismus** *der;* **∼** Ⓐ (*Physik*) magnetism; Ⓑ (*Psych. veralt.*) mesmerism *no art.*

**Magnet-: ∼kern** *der* (*Physik*) core [of a/the magnet]; **∼kompass, *∼kompaß** *der* magnetic compass; **∼nadel** *die* [compass] needle

**Magneton** /'magnetɔn/ *das;* **∼s, ∼[s]** (*Kernphysik*) magneton

**Magnetophon** Ⓦⓩ /magneto'fo:n/ *das;* **∼s, ∼e** tape recorder

**Magnetosphäre** *die;* **∼:** magnetosphere

**Magnetron** /'magnetrɔn/ *das;* **∼s, ∼e** /-'tro:nə/ (*Physik*) magnetron

**Magnet-: ∼schalter** *der* (*Kfz-W.*) solenoid switch; (*im Spannungsregler*) [magnetic] cut-out; **∼spule** *die* Ⓐ coil [of an/the electromagnet]; Ⓑ (*Solenoid*) solenoid; **∼zündung** *die* (*Kfz-W.*) magneto ignition

**Magnifikat** /ma'gni:fikat/ *das;* **∼s** (*kath. Kirche*) magnificat

**Magnifizenz** /magnifi'tsɛnts/ *die;* **∼, ∼en** (*Hochschulw.*) **Seine/Eure ∼:** His/Your Magnificence (*mode of address or title of German university rector*); **die ∼en** the rectors

**Magnolie** /ma'gno:li̯ə/ *die;* **∼, ∼n** magnolia

**mäh** /mɛ:/ *Interj.* baa

**Mahagoni** /maha'go:ni/ *das;* **∼s** mahogany

**Maharadscha** /maha'ratʃa/ *der;* **∼s, ∼s** maharaja

**Maharani** /maha'ra:ni/ *die;* **∼, ∼s** maharanee

**Mäh·binder** *der* harvester[-binder]

**Mahd¹** /ma:t/ *die;* **∼, ∼en** (*landsch.*) Ⓐ (*Mähen*) mowing; Ⓑ (*das Gemähte*) mown grass; (*Heu*) [new-mown] hay

**Mahd²** *das;* **∼[e]s, Mähder** /'mɛ:dɐ/ (*österr., schweiz.*) high pasture

**Mäh·drescher** *der* combine harvester

**mähen¹** /'mɛ:ən/ ❶ *tr. V.* mow ‹grass, lawn, meadow›; cut, reap ‹corn›. ❷ *itr. V.* mow; (*Getreide ernten*) reap

**mähen²** *itr. V.* ‹sheep› bleat

**Mäher** *der;* **∼s, ∼** Ⓐ mower; (*von Getreide*) reaper; Ⓑ (*ugs.*) ⇒ **Mähmaschine**

**Mäherin** *die;* **∼, ∼nen** ⇒ **Mäher** A

**Mahl** /ma:l/ *das;* **∼[e]s, Mähler** /mɛ:lɐ/ (*geh.*) meal; repast (*formal*); **beim ∼ sitzen** sit at table

**mahlen** *unr. tr., itr. V.* grind; **etw. fein/grob ∼:** grind sth. fine/coarsely; **wer zuerst kommt, mahlt zuerst** (*Spr.*) the early bird catches the worm (*prov.*)

**Mahl-: ∼gang** *der* (*Technik*) grinding-machine; (*∼steine*) set of millstones; **∼gut** *das* grist

**mählich** /'mɛ:lɪç/ (*geh. veralt.*) ❶ *Adj.* gradual. ❷ *adv.* gradually

**Mahl-: ∼stein** *der* Ⓐ grinding stone; Ⓑ (*Mühlstein*) millstone; **∼strom** *der* (*geh.*) maelstrom; **∼zahn** *der* molar; **∼zeit** meal; **sich an die ∼en halten** eat meals at regular times; **∼zeit!** (*ugs.*) have a good lunch; bon appetit; **[na dann] prost ∼zeit!** (*ugs.*) what a delightful prospect! (*iron.*); (*an einen anderen*) [in that case] the best of British! (*Brit. coll.*)

**Mäh·maschine** *die* [power] mower; (*für Getreide*) reaper

**Mahn-: ∼bescheid** *der* writ for payment; **∼brief** *der* ⇒ **∼schreiben**

**Mähne** /'mɛ:nə/ *die;* **∼, ∼n** mane; (*scherzh.: Haarschopf*) mane [of hair]

**mahnen** /'ma:nən/ ❶ *tr., itr. V.* Ⓐ (*auffordern*) urge; **zur Eile/Vorsicht ∼:** urge haste/caution; **jmdn. zur Eile/Vorsicht ∼:** urge sb. to hurry/to be careful; **jmdn. eindringlich ∼:** give sb. an urgent warning; **jmdn. ∼d ansehen** look admonishingly at sb.; Ⓑ (*erinnern*) remind (**an** + *Akk.* of); **einen Schuldner [schriftlich] ∼:** send a debtor a [written] demand for payment *or* a reminder. ❷ *itr. V.* (*geh.*) **an etw.** (*Akk.*) **∼:** be reminiscent of sth.

**Mahner** *der;* **∼s, ∼, Mahnerin** *die;* **∼, ∼nen** (*geh.*) admonisher; (*Unheilsprophet*) Cassandra

**Mahn-: ∼gebühr** *die* reminder fee; **∼mal** *das; Pl.* **∼∼e** *od.* **∼mäler** memorial (*erected as a warning to future generations*); **∼ruf** *der* (*geh.*) warning cry; admonition; **∼schreiben** *das* reminder (+ *Gen.* from); (*an einen Schuldner*) demand [for payment]; reminder

**Mahnung** *die;* **∼, ∼en** Ⓐ (*Aufforderung*) exhortation; (*Warnung*) admonition; Ⓑ (*Erinnerung*) reminder; Ⓒ ⇒ **Mahnschreiben**

**Mahn·verfahren** *das* summary proceedings *pl.* [for the payment of a debt]

**Mähre** /'mɛ:rə/ *die;* **∼, ∼n** (*veralt. abwertend*) jade (*dated*)

**Mähren** (*das*)**; ∼s** Moravia

**mährisch** *Adj.* Moravian

**Mai** /mai̯/ *der;* **∼[e]s** *od.* **∼,** *dichter.:* **∼en, ∼e** ▶ 207 May; **der Erste ∼:** the first of May; May Day; **Kundgebungen zum Ersten ∼:** May Day rallies; **im ∼ des Lebens** (*geh.*) in the springtime of life; **wie einst im ∼:** as in the days of my/their *etc.* youth

**Mai-: ∼andacht** *die* (*kath. Kirche*) May devotion; **∼baum** *der* Ⓐ maypole; Ⓑ (*Birkenbäumchen*) *small birch tree traditionally tied to doorpost for May festival;* **∼blume** *die* Ⓐ mayflower; Ⓑ (*∼glöckchen*) lily of the valley; **∼bowle** *die: cup made of white wine and champagne with fresh woodruff*

**Maid** /mai̯t/ *die;* **∼, ∼en** (*veralt.*) maiden

**Mai·demonstration** *die* May Day demonstration

**Maie** *die;* **∼, ∼n** (*veralt.*): *young birch tree or birch leaves traditionally tied to doorpost for May celebrations*

**Maien·nacht** *die* (*dichter. veralt.*) May night

**Mai-: ∼feier** *die* May Day celebration; **∼feier·tag** *der* May Day *no def. art.;* **∼glöckchen** *das* lily of the valley; **∼käfer** *der* May bug; **∼königin** *die* (*Volksk.*) Queen of the May; **∼kundgebung** *die* May Day rally

**Mailand** (*das*)**; ∼s** ▶ 700 Milan

**Mailänder** /'mai̯lɛndɐ/ ▶ 700 ❶ *indekl. Adj.* Milan; Milanese ‹climate, spring, etc.› **die ∼ Scala** La Scala, Milan. ❷ *der;* **∼s, ∼:** Milanese; ⇒ *auch* **Kölner**

**Mailänderin** *die;* **∼, ∼nen** Milanese

**mailändisch** *Adj.* Milanese

**mailen** /meilən/ *tr. V.* e-mail

**Mai·parade** *die* May Day parade

**Mais** /mai̯s/ *der;* **∼es** maize; corn (*esp. Amer.*); (*als Gericht*) sweetcorn

**Mais-: ∼birne** *die* (*Sport*) [suspended] punchball (*Brit.*) *or* (*Amer.*) punching bag; **∼brei** *der* maize *or* (*Amer.*) corn [meal] porridge; **∼brot** *das* corn bread

**Maische** /'mai̯ʃə/ *die;* **∼, ∼n** (*bei Bier, Spiritus*) mash; (*bei Wein*) must

**maischen** *tr. V.* mash ‹malt›; crush ‹grapes›

**Mais-: ∼kolben** *der* corn cob; (*als Gericht*) corn on the cob; **∼korn** *das* grain of maize *or* (*Amer.*) corn; **∼mehl** *das* maize *or* (*Amer.*) corn flour

**Maison[n]ette** /mɛzɔ'nɛt/ *die;* **∼, ∼s, Maison[n]ette·wohnung** *die* maisonette

**Mais·stärke** *die* cornflour (*Brit.*); cornstarch (*esp. Amer.*)

**Maître de Plaisir** /mɛtrə de plɛ'zi:r/ *der;* **∼ ∼ ∼, ∼s** /mɛtrə-/ **∼ ∼** (*veralt., noch scherzh.*) Master of Ceremonies

**Majestät** /majɛs'tɛ:t/ *die;* **∼, ∼en** Ⓐ ▶ 91 (*Titel*) Majesty; **Seine/Ihre/Eure** *od.* **Euer ∼:** His/Her/Your Majesty; Ⓑ (*geh.: Erhabenheit*) majesty

**majestätisch** ❶ *Adj.* majestic. ❷ *adv.* majestically

**Majestäts·beleidigung** *die* lèse-majesté

**Majolika** /ma'jo:lika/ *die;* **∼, Majoliken** majolica; **Majoliken** pieces of majolica

**Majonäse** /majo'nɛ:zə/ *die;* **∼, ∼n** mayonnaise

**Major** /ma'jo:ɐ̯/ *der;* **∼s, ∼e** ▶ 91 (*Milit.*) major; (*der Luftwaffe*) squadron leader (*Brit.*); major (*Amer.*)

**Majoran** /'ma:joran/ *der;* **∼s, ∼e** marjoram

**Majorette** /majɔ'rɛt/ *die;* **∼, ∼s** *od.* **∼n** majorette

**Majorin** *die;* **∼, ∼nen** Ⓐ (*in der Heilsarmee*) major; Ⓑ (*veralt.*) major's wife

**majorisieren** *tr. V.* (*geh.*) outvote

**Majorität** /majori'tɛ:t/ *die;* **∼, ∼en** majority; **die ∼ haben** have a majority

**Majoritäts-: ∼beschluss, *∼beschluß** *der* majority decision; **∼prinzip** *das* principle of a majority vote; majority principle

**Majuskel** /ma'jʊskl̩/ *die;* **∼, ∼n** (*Druckw.*) capital [letter]

**makaber** /ma'ka:bɐ/ *Adj.* macabre

**Makedonien** /make'do:ni̯ən/ (*das*)**; ∼s** Macedonia

**Makedonier** *der;* **∼s, ∼, Makedonierin** *die;* **∼, ∼nen** Macedonian

**makedonisch** *Adj.* Macedonian

**Makel** /'ma:kl̩/ *der;* **∼s, ∼** (*geh.*) Ⓐ (*Schmach*) stigma; taint; **an ihm haftet ein ∼:** a stain *or* taint clings to him; Ⓑ (*Fehler*) blemish; flaw; **ohne ∼:** without a [single] flaw

**Mäkelei** *die;* **∼** (*abwertend*) carping

**mäkelig** *Adj.* (*abwertend*) carping; (*beim Essen*) fussy; particular

**makel·los** ❶ *Adj.* flawless, perfect ‹skin, teeth, figure, stone›; spotless, immaculate ‹white, cleanness, clothes›; impeccable ‹accent›; (*fig.*) spotless, unblemished ‹reputation, character›. ❷ *adv.* immaculately; spotlessly ‹clean›; (*fehlerfrei*) flawlessly

**Makellosigkeit** *die;* **∼** ⇒ **makellos**: flawlessness; perfection; spotlessness; immaculateness; impeccability; (*fig.*) spotlessness

**makeln** *tr. V.* (*ugs.*) be a broker for ‹stocks, shares›; be an agent for ‹houses, building sites, etc.›

**mäkeln** /'mɛ:kl̩n/ *itr. V.* (*abwertend*) carp; **an etw.** (*Dat.*) *od.* **über etw.** (*Akk.*) **∼:** carp at *or* find fault with sth.

**Make-up** /me:k'|ap/ *das;* **∼s, ∼s** Ⓐ make-up; Ⓑ (*Präparate*) make-up; **die ∼s** the make-up products; Ⓒ (*Tönungscreme*) liquid make-up; foundation

**Makkaroni** /maka'ro:ni/ *Pl.* macaroni *sing.*

**Makkaroni·fresser** *der,* **Makkaroni·fresserin** *die* (*derb abwertend*) Eyetie (*sl. derog.*); wop (*sl. derog.*)

**Makler** /'ma:klɐ/ *der;* **∼s, ∼** Ⓐ ▶ 159 (*Häuser∼*) estate agent (*Brit.*); realtor (*Amer.*); Ⓑ ▶ 159 (*Börsen∼*) broker

**Makler-: ~firma** *die* estate agents *pl.* (*Brit.*); (*Amer.*) realtors *pl.*; **~gebühr** *die* ⇒ **Maklerprovision**; **Maklerin** *die*; ~, **~nen** ⇒ **Makler**; **~provision** *die* agent's fee *or* commission; (*eines Börsenmaklers*) brokerage charges *pl.*

**Mako** /'mako/ *die*; ~, **~s** *od. der od. das*; **~[s]**, **~s** Egyptian cotton

**Makramee** /makra'me:/ *das*; **~[s]** macramé

**Makrele** /ma'kre:lə/ *die*; ~, **~n** mackerel

**Makro** *der od. das*; **~s**, **~s** (*DV*) macro

**makro-, Makro-** /makro-/: **~biotik** /-'bio:tɪk/ *die*; **~~**: macrobiotics *sing.*, *no art.*; **~biotisch** ❶ *Adj.* macrobiotic; ❷ *adv.* on macrobiotic principles; **~klima** *das* (*Met.*) macroclimate; **~kosmos** *der* macrocosm; **~molekül** *das* macromolecule

**Makrone** /ma'kro:nə/ *die*; ~, **~n** macaroon

**Makulatur** /makula'tu:ɐ̯/ *die*; ~, **~en** Ⓐ (*Druckw.*) spoilt sheets *pl.*; spoilage *no pl.*; Ⓑ (*Altpapier*) waste paper; **~ reden** (*ugs. abwertend*) talk rubbish

**mal** /ma:l/ ▶ **841** ❶ *Adv.* (*Math.*) times; (*bei Flächen*) by; **zwei ~ zwei** twice two; two times two; **der Raum ist 5 ~ 6 Meter groß** the room is five metres by six. ❷ *Partikel* (*ugs.*) **komm ~ her!** come here!; **hör ~ zu!** listen!; ⇒ *auch* **einmal** 2

**Mal**[1] *das*; **~[e]s**, **~e** *od.* (*nach Zahlwörtern*) **~**: time; **ein anderes ~**: another time; **nur dies eine ~**: just this once; **kein einziges ~**: not once; not a single time; **jedes ~**: every time; **das achte/dritte** *usw.* **~**: the eighth/third *etc.* time; (*zum achten/dritten usw. Mal*) for the eighth/third *etc.* time; **beim achten/dritten** *usw.* **~**: the eighth/third *etc.* time; **zum achten/dritten** *usw.* **~**: for the eighth/third *etc.* time; **das letzte ~** (*beim letzten Mal*) last time; (*zum letzten Mal*) for the last time; **das x-te ~**: the umpteenth time; (*zum x-ten Mal*) for the umpteenth time; **mit einem ~[e]** all at once; all of a sudden; **von ~ zu ~ heftiger werden** become more and more violent [each time]; **beide ~[e]** both times; **einige ~[e]** a few times; on a few occasions; **etliche ~[e]** several times; a number of times; **unzählige ~[e]** countless times; over and over again; **verschiedene ~[e]** on various occasions; **Dutzende** *od.* **dutzende/Millionen ~[e]** dozens/millions of times; **ein/ein halbes/zwei/viel Dutzend ~**: a/half a/two/many dozen times; **eine Million/acht Millionen ~**: a/eight million times

**Mal**[2] *das*; **~[e]s**, **~e** *od.* **Mäler** /'mɛ:lɐ/ Ⓐ mark; (*Mutter~*) birthmark; (*braun*) mole; Ⓑ (*geh.*: *Denk~*, *Mahn~*) memorial; Ⓒ (*Baseball*) base; Ⓓ (*Rugby*) goal; (*~feld*) in-goal

**Malachit** /mala'xi:t/ *der*; **~s**, **~e** malachite

**malad[e]** /ma'la:d(ə)/ *Adj.* (*veralt.*, *landsch.*) ill; sick (*esp. Amer.*)

**Malaga** /'malaga/ *der*; **~s**, **~s**, **Malagawein** *der* Malaga [wine]

**Malaie** /ma'laiə/ *der*; **~n**, **~n**, **Malaiin** *die*; ~, **~nen** ▶ **553** Malay

**malaiisch** *Adj.* ▶ **553**, ▶ **696** Malayan

**Malaise** /ma'lɛ:zə/ *die*; ~, **~n**, *schweiz.*: *das*; **~s**, **~s** Ⓐ malaise; sense of unease; Ⓑ (*Misere*) unhappy situation

**Malaria** /ma'la:ria/ *die*; ~ ▶ **474** malaria

**malaria·krank** *Adj.* suffering from malaria *postpos.*

**Malaria·mücke** *die* malaria mosquito

**Malawi** /ma'la:vi/ (*das*); **~s** Malawi

**Malawier** *der*; **~s**, ~, **Malawierin** *die*; ~, **~nen** Malawian

**malawisch** *Adj.* Malawian

**Malaysia** /ma'laizia/ (*das*); **~s** Malaysia

**malaysisch** *Adj.* Malaysian

**Mal·buch** *das* colouring book

**malen** ❶ *tr.*, *itr. V.* Ⓐ paint ‹picture, portrait, person, etc.›; (*mit Farbstiften*) draw with crayons; (*aus~*) colour; **sich ~ lassen** have one's portrait painted; **etw. in düsteren Farben ~** (*fig.*) paint *or* portray sth. in gloomy colours; **etw. allzu rosig/schwarz ~** (*fig.*) paint far too rosy/black a picture of sth.; Ⓑ (*sauber schreiben*) write carefully; Ⓒ (*anstreichen*) paint ‹door, window, etc.›; decorate ‹flat, room, walls›. ❷ *refl. V.* Ⓐ paint one's self-portrait; Ⓑ (*geh.*) **auf seinem Gesicht malte sich Erstaunen/Entsetzen** astonishment/horror was mirrored in his face

**Maler** /'ma:lɐ/ *der*; **~s**, ~ ▶ **159** painter

**Maler·arbeit** *die* painting and decorating *no pl.*

**Malerei** *die*; ~, **~en** Ⓐ painting *no art.*; Ⓑ (*Gemälde*) painting

**Malerin** *die*; ~, **~nen** ▶ **159** [woman] painter

**malerisch** ❶ *Adj.* Ⓐ picturesque ‹village, house, etc.›; **einen ~en Anblick bieten** look as pretty as a picture; Ⓑ (*zur Malerei gehörend*) artistic ‹skill, talent›; ‹skill, talent› as a painter; ‹motif, subject› for painters; **sein ~es Werk** his paintings *pl.* ❷ *adv.* Ⓐ picturesquely ‹situated›; Ⓑ ‹train› as a painter; **ihr ~ geschultes Auge** her trained artist's eye

**Maler-: ~lein·wand** *die* [artist's] canvas; **~meister** *der*, **~meisterin** *die* master painter [and decorator]

**Malesche** /ma'lɛʃə/ *die*; ~, **~n** (*nordd. ugs.*) mess; **in der ~ sitzen/in ~n kommen** be/land in the soup (*coll.*)

**Mal·feld** *das* (*Rugby*) in-goal

**Malheur** /ma'lø:ɐ̯/ *das*; **~s**, **~e** *od.* **~s** mishap; **das ist doch kein ~!** it's not the end of the world!

**Mali** /'ma:li/ (*das*); **~s** Mali

**maligne** /ma'lɪgnə/ *Adj.* (*Med.*) malignant

**maliziös** /mali'tsiø:s/ (*geh.*) ❶ *Adj.* malicious. ❷ *adv.* maliciously

**Mal·kasten** *der* paintbox

**mall** /mal/ *Adj.* (*ugs.*, *bes. nordd.*) barmy (*Brit. coll.*); crazy

**Mallorca** /ma'lɔrka/ (*das*); **~s** Majorca

**mallorquinisch** /malɔr'ki:nɪʃ/ *Adj.* Majorcan

**mal|nehmen** *unr. tr.*, *itr. V.* multiply (**mit** by); **das Malnehmen:** multiplication

**Maloche** /ma'lo:xə/ *die*; ~ (*salopp*) drudgery *no indef. art.*; slog; **auf ~ sein** be at work; (*schwer arbeiten*) slog away

**malochen** *itr. V.* (*salopp*) slog *or* slave [away]

**Mal-: ~pinsel** *der* paintbrush; **~stift** *der* crayon; **~strom** *der* ⇒ **Mahlstrom**

**Malta** /malta/ (*das*); **~s** Malta

**Mal·technik** *die* painting technique

**Malteser** /mal'te:zɐ/ ❶ *indekl. Adj.* Maltese. ❷ *der*; **~s**, ~ Ⓐ Maltese; ⇒ *auch* **Kölner** 2; Ⓑ ⇒ **Malteserritter**

**Malteser-: ~hilfsdienst** *der* ≈ St John Ambulance Brigade; **~kreuz** *das* (*auch Technik*) Maltese cross; **~orden** *der* Order of the Knights of St John; **~ritter** *der* Knight of St John

**maltesisch** *Adj.* ▶ **696** Maltese

**Maltesisch** *das*; ~ ▶ **696** (*Sprachw.*) Maltese

**Maltose** /mal'to:zə/ *die*; ~ (*Biochemie*) maltose

**malträtieren** /maltrɛ'ti:rən/ *tr. V.* maltreat; ill-treat

**Malus** /'ma:lʊs/ *der*; ~ *od.* **~ses**, ~ *od.* **~se** Ⓐ (*Versicherungsw.*) supplementary premium (*imposed after a number of claims*); Ⓑ (*Schulw.*) negative weighting; handicap; **einen ~ von ... bekommen** be marked down by ...

**Mal·utensilien** *Pl.* painting equipment *sing.* *or* (*coll.*) things

**Malve** /'malvə/ *die*; ~, **~n** mallow

**malven-: ~farben**, **~farbig** *Adj.* [pale] mauve

**Malwinen** /mal'vi:nən/ *Pl.* **die ~**: the Falkland Islands

**Malz** /malts/ *das*; **~es** malt

**Malz-: ~bier** *das* malt beer; **~bonbon** *das* malted cough lozenge

**Mal·zeichen** *das* multiplication sign

**mälzen** /'mɛltsn̩/ *tr.*, *itr. V.* (*Brauereiwesen*) malt

**Mälzerei** *die*; ~, **~en** (*Brauereiwesen*) Ⓐ (*Gebäude*) malthouse; malting; Ⓑ (*Malzbereitung*) malting

**Malz-: ~extrakt** *der* malt extract; **~kaffee** *der*: *coffee substitute made from germinated, dried, and roasted barley*; **~zucker** *der* (*Biochemie*) maltose

**Mama** /'mama, *geh. veralt.*: ma'ma:/ *die*; ~, **~s** (*fam.*) mamma

**Mama-: ~puppe** *die* talking doll (*saying 'Mama'*); **~söhnchen** *das* (*abwertend*) mummy's boy (*coll.*)

**Mameluck** /mamə'lʊk/ *der*; **~en**, **~en** (*hist.*) Mameluke

**Mami** /'mami/ *die*; ~, **~s** (*fam.*) mummy (*Brit. coll.*); mommy (*Amer. coll.*)

**Mammographie** /mamogra'fi:/ *die*; ~, **~n** (*Med.*) mammography *no art.*

**Mammon** /'mamɔn/ *der*; **~s** (*abwertend*) Mammon; **dem ~ nachjagen** devote oneself to the pursuit of Mammon *or* of riches; **der schnöde ~**: filthy lucre

**Mammut** /'mamʊt/ *das*; **~s**, **~e** *od.* **~s** mammoth

**Mammut-** mammoth; (*sehr lange dauernd*) marathon

**Mammut-: ~baum** *der* mammoth tree; sequoia; **~film** *der* mammoth [screen] epic; blockbuster; **~konzern** *der* mammoth concern; **~prozess**, ***~prozeß** *der* marathon trial; **~sitzung** *die* marathon session

**mampfen** /'mampfn̩/ *tr.*, *itr. V.* (*salopp*) munch; nosh (*coll.*)

**Mamsell** /mam'zɛl/ *die*; ~, **~en** *od.* **~s** (*veralt.*: *Hauswirtschafterin*) housekeeper

**man**[1] /man/ *Indefinitpron. im Nom.* Ⓐ one; you; **~ hat von dort eine herrliche Aussicht** one has *or* there is a magnificent view from there; **~ kann nie wissen** one *or* you never can tell; **dagegen muss ~ etwas unternehmen** something has to be done about it; **~ nehme 250 g Butter** take 250 grams of butter; **für weitere Auskünfte wende ~ sich an ...** for further information apply to ...; Ⓑ (*irgendjemand*) somebody; (*die Behörden; die Leute dort*) they; **~ hat mir gesagt ...** I was told ...; they told me ...; **hat ~ dir das nicht mitgeteilt?** didn't anybody/they tell you that?; **~ vermutet/hat herausgefunden, dass ...** it is thought/has been discovered that ...; they think/have discovered that ...; Ⓒ (*die Menschen im Allgemeinen*) people *pl.*; **das trägt ~ heute** that's what people wear *or* what is worn nowadays; **so etwas tut ~ [einfach] nicht** that's [just] not done; Ⓓ (*ich*) one; **~ versteht sein eigenes Wort nicht** you can't hear yourself speak

**man**[2] *Adv.* (*bes. nordd.*) **lass ~ gut sein!** forget it!; **na, denn ~ los** let's be off then

**Management** /'mænɪdʒmənt/ *das*; **~s**, **~s** management

**Management-Buy-out** *das* (*Wirtsch.*) management buyout

**managen** /'mɛnɪdʒn̩/ *tr. V.* Ⓐ (*ugs.*) fix; organize; **ich manage das schon** I'll fix it; (*durch Tricks*) I'll fiddle it (*coll.*); Ⓑ (*betreuen*) manage, act as manager for ‹singer, artist, player›; **von seiner Frau gemanagt werden** have one's wife as one's manager

**Manager** /'mɛnɪdʒɐ/ *der*; **~s**, ~, **Managerin** *die*; ~, **~nen** ▶ **159** manager; (*eines Fußballvereins*) club secretary

**Manager·krankheit** *die* ▶ **474** (*volkst.*) stress disease *no def. art.*

**manch** /manç/ *Indefinitpron.* Ⓐ many a; **[so] ~er Beamte**, **~ ein Beamter** many an official; **in [so] ~er Beziehung** in many respects; **[so] ~ schöne[n] Stunden** many a happy hour; **~ einer** *od.* **~er** many a person/man; **~ eine** *od.* **~e** many a woman; Ⓑ *substantivisch* **~e** some; (*viele*) many; **[so] ~er musste das erleben** many people had to go through this; **[so] ~es** a number of things; (*allerhand Verschiedenes*) all kinds of things; **[so] ~es von dem, was wir lernten** much of what we learnt

**manchenorts** ⇒ **mancherorts**

**mancherlei** *unbest. Gattungsz.*; *indekl.* Ⓐ various; a number of; **~ Käse** various kinds

*old spelling (see note on page 1707)

of cheese; **B** (*Verschiedenes*) various things; a number of things

**mancherorten, mancherorts** *Adv.* (*geh.*) in some places; (*an verschiedenen Orten*) in various places

**Manchester** /ˈmɛntʃɛstɐ/ *der;* **~s** [heavy] corduroy

**manch·mal** *Adv.* sometimes

**Mandant** /manˈdant/ *der;* **~en, ~en, Mandantin** *die;* **~, ~nen** (*Rechtsw.*) client

**Mandarin** /mandaˈriːn/ *der;* **~s, ~e** (*hist.*) mandarin

**Mandarine** /mandaˈriːnə/ *die;* **~, ~n** mandarin [orange]; tangerine

**Mandat** /manˈdaːt/ *das;* **~[e]s, ~e** **A** (*Parlamentssitz*) [parliamentary] seat; **sein ~ niederlegen** resign one's seat; **B** (*Auftrag*) (*eines Abgeordneten*) mandate; (*eines Anwalts*) brief; **das politische ~ der Studentenausschüsse** the right of student committees to make political statements on behalf of members; **C** (*Treuhandgebiet*) mandate; mandated territory

**Mandatar** /mandaˈtaːɐ̯/ *der;* **~s, ~e, Mandatarin** *die;* **~, ~nen** **A** mandatary; **B** (*österr.: Abgeordneter*) member [of parliament]; deputy

**Mandats-: ~gebiet** *das* mandated territory; mandate; **~träger** *der,* **~trägerin** *die* (*Politik*) member of parliament; deputy

**Mandel** /ˈmandl̩/ *die;* **~, ~n** **A** almond; **B** ▶ 471 (*Anat.*) tonsil

**mandel-, Mandel-: ~augen** *Pl.* (*geh.*) almond eyes; **~äugig** *Adj.* (*geh.*) almond-eyed; **~baum** *der* almond [tree]; **~entzündung** *die* ▶ 474 tonsillitis *no indef. art.*; **~förmig** *Adj.* almond-shaped; **~operation** *die* tonsillectomy

**Mandoline** /mandoˈliːnə/ *die;* **~, ~n** mandolin

**Mandrill** /manˈdrɪl/ *der;* **~s, ~e** (*Zool.*) mandrill

**Mandschure** /manˈdʒuːrə/ *der;* **~n, ~n** Manchu; Manchurian

**Mandschurei** *die;* **~:** Manchuria *no art.*

**Mandschurin** *die;* **~, ~nen** ⇒ **Mandschure**

**mandschurisch** *Adj.* Manchurian

**Manege** /maˈneːʒə/ *die;* **~, ~n** (*im Zirkus*) ring; (*in der Reitschule*) arena

**mang** /maŋ(k)/ *Präp. mit Dat. od. Akk.* (*nordd., berlin.*) among

**Mangan** /maŋˈgaːn/ *das;* **~s** (*Chemie*) manganese

**Mangan-: ~erz** *das* manganese ore; **~säure** *die* manganic acid

**Mangel**[1] /ˈmaŋl̩/ *der;* **~s, Mängel** /ˈmɛŋl̩/ **A** (*Fehlen*) lack (**an** + *Dat.* of); (*Knappheit*) shortage, lack (**an** + *Dat.* of); **es herrscht** *od.* **besteht ~ an etw.** (*Dat.*) there is a lack *or* shortage of sth.; sth. is in short supply; **~ an Vitaminen** vitamin deficiency; **aus ~** *od.* **wegen ~s an Beweisen** for lack of evidence; **aus ~ an Erfahrung** from *or* owing to lack of experience; **keinen ~ leiden** not go short [of anything]; not want for anything; **B** (*Fehler*) defect; **geringfügige Mängel** minor flaws *or* imperfections; **die Mängel eines Nachschlagewerkes/Drehbuchs** the shortcomings *or* deficiences of a reference work/film script

**Mangel**[2] *die;* **~, ~n** (*Wäsche~*) [large] mangle; **jmdn. durch die ~ drehen** *od.* **in die ~ nehmen** *od.* **in der ~ haben** (*fig. salopp*) put sb. through the hoop

**Mängel·bericht** *der* (*Technik*) defect report (+ *Gen.* on); list of faults

**Mangel-: ~beruf** *der* understaffed profession; **~erscheinung** *die* ▶ 474 (*Med.*) deficiency symptom

**mangelhaft** **1** *Adj.* (*fehlerhaft*) defective ‹goods, memory›; faulty ‹goods, German, English, etc.›; (*schlecht*) poor ‹memory, lighting›; bad ‹road conditions, German›; (*unzulänglich*) inadequate ‹knowledge, lighting›; incomplete ‹reports›; (*Schulw.*) **die Note „~"** the mark 'unsatisfactory'; (*bei Prüfungen*) the fail mark. **2** *adv.* (*fehlerhaft*) defectively; faultily; (*schlecht*) poorly; (*unzulänglich*) inadequately; **~ befestigte Straßen** badly made roads; **Französisch beherrsche ich nur ~:** I have only an imperfect command of French

**Mängel·haftung** *die* (*Rechtsw.*) liability for defects

**Mangel·krankheit** *die* ▶ 474 (*Med.*) deficiency disease

**mangeln**[1] *itr. V.* **es mangelt an etw.** (*Dat.*) (*ist nicht vorhanden*) there is a lack of sth.; (*ist unzureichend vorhanden*) there is a shortage of sth.; sth. is in short supply; **jmdm./einer Sache mangelt etw.** *od.* **es an etw.** (*Dat.*) sb./sth. lacks sth.; **es mangelt mir an Platz** I am short of space; **seine ~de Menschenkenntnis** his inadequate understanding of people; **die ~de Kompromissbereitschaft** the unwillingness to compromise

**mangeln**[2] **1** *tr. V.* mangle. **2** *itr. V.* do the mangling

**Mängel·rüge** *die* (*Rechtsw.*) complaint (*about quality, service, etc.*)

**mangels** /ˈmaŋls/ *Präp. mit Gen.* in the absence of; **~ eines eigenen Büros** having no office of his *etc.* own; **~ Beweisen** (*Dat.*) owing to lack of evidence

**Mangel·ware** *die:* **~ sein** be scarce *or* in short supply; ‹article› be a scarce commodity; **erfahrene Fachkräfte sind ~** (*fig. ugs.*) experienced skilled workers are thin on the ground (*coll.*)

**Mangel·wäsche** *die* [laundry for] mangling

**Mango** /ˈmaŋgo/ *die;* **~, ~s** mango

**Mangold** /ˈmaŋgɔlt/ *der;* **~[e]s** [Swiss] chard

**Mangrove** /maŋˈgroːvə/ *die;* **~, ~n** mangrove forest

**Mangrove[n]-: ~baum** *der* mangrove [tree]; **~küste** *die* mangrove coastline

**Manichäismus** /manɪçɛˈɪsmʊs/ *der;* **~:** Manichaeism *no art.*

**Manie** /maˈniː/ *die;* **~, ~n** mania; **bei jmdm. zur ~ werden** become an obsession with sb.

**Manier** /maˈniːɐ̯/ *die;* **~, ~en** **A** manner; **in gewohnter ~:** in his/her usual way *or* manner; **auf eine bravouröse ~:** brilliantly; in a masterly fashion; **in der ~ Dalís** in Dali's manner *or* style; in the manner of Dali; **B** *Pl.* (*Umgangsformen*) manners; **keine ~en haben** have no manners; **ich werde dir ~en beibringen!** I'll teach you some manners!; **C** (*veralt.*) **das ist doch keine ~!** that's no way to behave

**manieriert** /maniˈriːɐ̯t/ (*geh.*) **1** *Adj.* mannered. **2** *adv.* in a mannered fashion

**Manieriertheit** *die;* **~, ~en** (*geh.*) mannerism

**Manierismus** *der;* **~** (*Kunstwiss., Literaturw.*) mannerism

**manierlich** **1** *Adj.* **A** (*fam.*) well-mannered; well-behaved ‹child›; **B** (*ugs.: einigermaßen gut*) reasonable; decent. **2** *adv.* **A** (*fam.*) properly; nicely; **B** (*ugs.: einigermaßen gut*) **ganz/recht ~:** quite/really nicely *or* decently

**manifest** /maniˈfɛst/ *Adj.* (*geh.*) manifest; **es wird an diesem Beispiel ~:** it is made manifest by this example

**Manifest** *das;* **~[e]s, ~e** manifesto

**Manifestant** /manifɛsˈtant/ *der;* **~en, ~en** (*schweiz.*) demonstrator

**Manifestation** /manifɛstaˈtsi̯oːn/ *die;* **~, ~en** **A** (*Med., Psych. usw.*) manifestation; **B** (*schweiz.: Kundgebung*) demonstration

**manifestieren** (*geh.*) **1** *refl. V.* be manifested; manifest itself. **2** *tr. V.* demonstrate. **3** *itr. V.* (*veralt.*) demonstrate

**Maniküre** /maniˈkyːrə/ *die;* **~, ~n** **A** manicure; **~ machen** manicure oneself; **B** (*Person*) manicurist

**Maniküre·etui** *das* manicure set

**maniküren** *tr. V.* manicure

**Manila·faser** /maˈniːla-/ *die,* **Manilahanf** *der* Manila [hemp]

**Maniok** /maˈni̯ɔk/ *der;* **~s, ~s** manioc; cassava

**Manipulant** /manipuˈlant/ *der;* **~en, ~en, Manipulantin** *die;* **~, ~nen** (*geh.*) manipulator

**Manipulation** /manipulaˈtsi̯oːn/ *die;* **~, ~en** (*geh.*) manipulation

**manipulativ** /manipulaˈtiːf/ (*geh.*) **1** *Adj.* manipulative. **2** *adv.* by manipulation

**Manipulator** /manipuˈlaːtɔr/ *der;* **~s, ~en** /-toːren/ **A** (*Person, Gerät*) manipulator; **B** (*Zauberkünstler*) sleight-of-hand performer; (*Jongleur*) conjuror

**Manipulatorin** *die;* **~, ~nen** ⇒ **Manipulator**

**manipulierbar** *Adj.* (*geh.*) manipulable; susceptible to manipulation *postpos.*; **leicht ~:** easy to manipulate

**Manipulierbarkeit** *die;* **~** (*geh.*) manipulability; susceptibility to manipulation; **die ~ der öffentlichen Meinung** the extent to which public opinion can be manipulated

**manipulieren** /manipuˈliːrən/ *tr. V.* manipulate; rig ‹election result, composition of a committee›

**Manipulierung** *die;* **~, ~en** manipulation

**manisch** /ˈmaːnɪʃ/ (*geh., Psych.*) **1** *Adj.* manic. **2** *adv.* maniacally

**manisch-depressiv** *Adj.* (*Psych.; Med.*) manic-depressive; **~es Irresein** (*veralt.*) manic depression

**Manitu** /ˈmaːnitu/ *der;* **~s** manitou

**Manko** /ˈmaŋko/ *das;* **~s, ~s** **A** (*Mangel*) shortcoming; deficiency; (*Nachteil*) handicap; **B** (*Fehlbetrag*) deficit; **ein ~ von 1 200 DM haben** be 1,200 marks short

**Mann** /man/ *der;* **~[e]s, Männer** /ˈmɛnɐ/; ⇒ *auch* **Mannen** **A** man; **alle erwachsenen Männer wurden festgenommen** all adult males were arrested; **ein ~, ein Wort** a man's word is his bond; **ein ~ der Tat** a man of action; **ein ~ des Todes** (*geh.*) a doomed man; **ein ~ der Feder/der Wissenschaft** (*geh.*) a man of letters/of science; **ein ~ aus dem Volk** a man of humble origins; **ein ~ des Volkes** a man of the people; **der ~ am Klavier** the pianist; the man at the piano; **der geeignete** *od.* **richtige ~ sein** be the right man; **der böse** *od.* **schwarze ~:** the bogy man; **der ~ des Tages/Jahres** the man of the moment/year; **der ~ auf der Straße** the man in the street; **auf den ~ dressiert sein** ‹dog› be trained to attack people; **der ~ im Mond** the man in the moon; ; **[mein lieber] ~!** (*ugs.*) (*überrascht, bewundernd*) my goodness!; (*verärgert*) for goodness sake!; **~ [Gottes]!** (*ugs.*) my God!; **wie ein ~:** to a man; with one voice; **der Geschäftsleitung wie ein ~ entgegentreten** approach the management like one man *or* with a united front; **[nicht] ~s genug sein, etw. zu tun** [not] be man enough to do sth.; **[nicht] der ~ sein, etw. zu tun** [not] be the right man to do sth.; **er ist nicht der ~, der kurz entschlossen eine Entscheidung treffen kann** he is not the sort who can make a decision at the drop of a hat; **seinen ~ stehen** (*seine Pflicht tun*) do one's duty; (*selbstständig sein*) stand on one's own two feet; (*sich durchsetzen*) stand up for oneself; **seinen ~ gefunden haben** have met one's match; **dieser Beruf ernährt seinen ~:** you can make a good living in that job; **du hast wohl einen kleinen ~ im Ohr** (*salopp*) you must be out of your tiny mind (*sl.*); **etw. an den ~ bringen** (*ugs.*) (*verkaufen*) flog sth. (*Brit. coll.*); push sth. (*Amer.*); find a taker/takers for sth.; **seine Ansicht/seine Witze an den ~ bringen** (*ugs.*) find an audience for one's view/one's jokes; **seine Tochter an den ~ bringen** (*ugs. scherzh.*) find a taker for *or* marry off one's daughter; **~ für ~:** one by one; **Kämpfe** *od.* **der Kampf ~ gegen ~:** hand-to-hand fighting; **von ~ zu ~:** [from] man to man; **lass dir mal von ~ zu ~ sagen, ...** let me tell you straight, ...; ⇒ *auch* **Welt** A; **B** (*Besatzungsmitglied*) man; **mit 1 000 ~ Besatzung** with a crew of 1,000 [men]; **an Bord des Düsenjägers waren 4 ~:** there were four men on board the jet fighter; **bis zum letzten ~:** to the last man; **alle ~ an Deck!** (*Seemannsspr.*) all hands

m

on deck!; ~ **über Bord!** (*Seemannsspr.*) man overboard!; **mit ~ und Maus untergehen** (*Seemannsspr.*) go down with all on board; **C** (*Teilnehmer*) **pro ~** (*ugs.*) per person; per head; **alle ~ [hoch]** (*ugs.*) in force; all together; **wir gingen noch alle ~ [hoch] in eine Kneipe** (*ugs.*) afterwards the whole lot of us went into a pub (*Brit*) *or* (*Amer.*) bar; **uns fehlt der dritte/vierte ~ zum Skatspielen** we need a third/fourth person *or* player for a game of skat; **~ decken** mark [an/one's opponent]; **an** *od.* **in den ~ gehen** (*bes. Fußball*) go in hard; ⇒ *auch* **frei** 1 O; **Gott** A; **letzt...** A; **Not** F; **D** (*Ehemann*) husband; **als** *od.* **wie ~ und Frau leben** (*geh.*) live as man and wife; **~ und Frau werden** (*geh.*) become man and wife

**Manna** /'mana/ *das;* **~[s]**, *auch: die;* **~** (*bibl.*) manna

**mannbar** *Adj.* (*geh. veralt.*) **A** marriageable ‹daughter, girl›; **~ werden** become of marriageable age; **B** (*geschlechtsreif*) sexually mature ‹youth›; **das ~e Alter** sexual maturity

**Männchen** /'mɛnçən/ *das;* **~s, ~** **A** little man; **ein altes, verhutzeltes ~:** a little wizened old man; **~ malen** draw matchstick men; **B** (*Tier~*) male; (*Vogel~*) male; cock; **~ machen** ‹animal› sit up and beg; (*fig. ugs.: salutieren*) ‹soldier› salute smartly

**Mann·deckung** *die* (*Ballspiele*) man-to-man marking

**Männe** /'mɛnə/ *der;* **~, ~s** (*ugs.*) hubby (*coll.*)

**Männeken** /'mɛnəkn̩/ *das;* **~s, ~s** (*niederd., bes. berlin.*) little chap; **kleines ~:** tiny fellow

**Mannen** *Pl.* (*dichter. veralt.*) vassals; **der Trainer und seine ~** (*scherzh.*) the manager and his troops

**Mannequin** /'manəkɛ̃/ *das;* **~s, ~s** mannequin; [fashion] model

**männer-, Männer-:** **~arbeit** *die* a man's work; work for a man; **~bekanntschaft** *die* male *or* gentleman friend; **von ~bekanntschaften leben** earn one's living from prostitution; **~beruf** *der* all-male profession; (*überwiegend von ~n ausgeübt*) male-dominated profession; **~bund** *der* male society; **~chor** *der* male voice choir; **~fang** *der: in* **auf ~fang gehen/aus sein** (*ugs.*) go/be after the men; **~feindlich** ❶ *Adj.* anti-male; ❷ *adv.* in an anti-male way; **~freundschaft** *die* the friendship between men; **~gesangverein** *der* male choral society; **~gesellschaft** *die* male-dominated society; **~geschichten** *Pl.* (*ugs.*) affairs with men; **~haus** *das* (*Völkerk.*) men's house; **~herz** *das* man's heart; **~herzen** men's hearts; **~kleider** *Pl.* men's clothes; **~mordend** *Adj.* (*ugs. scherzh.*) man-eating (*fig.*); **~sache** *die: in* **das ist ~sache** that's men's business; **~station** *die* men's ward; **~stimme** *die* man's voice; male voice; **~treu** *die;* **~~, ~~** (*Bot.*) (*Veronica*) speedwell; veronica; (*Eryngium*) eryngo; sea holly; **~überschuss,** ***~überschuß** *der* surplus of men; **~welt** *die* (*scherzh.*) men *pl.;* **~wirtschaft** *die* (*scherzh.*) male housekeeping *no art.;* **~wohnheim** *das* men's hostel

**Mannes-:** **~alter** *das* manhood *no art.;* **im besten ~alter sein** be in the prime of life *or* in one's prime; **~jahre** *Pl.* [years of] manhood *sing.;* **~kraft** *die* (*geh.*) virility; **~tugend** *die* (*geh. veralt.*) manly virtue; **~wort** *das; Pl.* **~~e** (*geh.*) word as a gentleman; **~würde** *die* (*geh.*) honour as a gentleman; **~zucht** *die* (*geh. veralt.*) manly self-control *or* discipline

**mannhaft** ❶ *Adj.* manful; (*tapfer*) courageous ‹decision etc.›; (*entschlossen*) resolute ‹behaviour›; stout ‹resistance›. ❷ *adv.* manfully; (*tapfer*) courageously; (*entschlossen*) resolutely; **~ Widerstand leisten** offer stout resistance

**Mannhaftigkeit** *die;* **~:** manfulness; (*Mut*) [manly] courage

**mannig·fach** ❶ *Adj.* multifarious; manifold (*literary*). ❷ *adv.* in a whole variety of ways; **etw. ~ gestalten** give sth. many different forms

**mannig·faltig** (*geh.*) ❶ *Adj.* multifarious; manifold (*literary*); (*verschiedener Art*) diverse. ❷ *adv.* in a large variety of different ways; **das ~ gestaltete Programm** the programme with its diversity of different items

**Mannig·faltigkeit** *die;* **~:** [great] diversity

**Männin** /'mɛnɪn/ *die;* **~** (*bibl., dichter.*) woman; (*Gefährtin*) spouse

**Männlein** /'mɛnlain/ *das;* **~s, ~** **A** [**kleines**] **~:** little man; **B** (*ugs. scherzh.*) **~ und/oder Weiblein** men and/or women; (*bei jüngeren*) boys and/or girls

**männlich** ❶ *Adj.* **A** male ‹sex, line, descendant, flower, etc.›; **~er Vorname** boy's *or* man's name; **das ~e Tier** the male [animal]; **B** (*für den Mann typisch*) masculine ‹behaviour, characteristic, etc.›; male ‹vanity›; **ausgesprochen ~ wirken** have a decidedly masculine appearance; **eine ~e Haltung** a manly attitude; **~e Stärke/Energie** the strength/energy of a man; **C** (*Sprachw.*) masculine; (*Verslehre*) male ‹rhyme›. ❷ *adv.* in a masculine way

**Männlichkeit** *die;* **~** **A** masculinity; manliness; **B** (*Potenz*) virility; **C** (*scherzh.: Geschlechtsteile*) privates *pl.;* private parts *pl.*

**Männlichkeits·wahn** *der* obsession with masculinity

**Mann·loch** *das* (*Technik*) manhole

**Mannomann** /'mano'man/ *Interj.* (*salopp*) boy, oh boy!

**Manns·bild** *das* (*ugs., bes. südd., österr.*) man

**Mannschaft** *die;* **~, ~en** **A** (*Sport, auch fig.*) team; **die erste/zweite ~** (*Fußball*) the first/second eleven; **B** (*Schiffs-, Flugzeugbesatzung*) crew; **C** (*Milit.: Einheit*) unit; **vor versammelter ~:** in front of all the men; (*fig.*) in front of everybody; **D** *Pl.* (*Milit.: einfache Soldaten*) other ranks

**mannschaftlich** (*Sport*) ❶ *Adj.* as a team *postpos.;* **das ~e Zusammenwirken** the teamwork. ❷ *adv.* as a team

**Mannschafts-:** **~auf·stellung** *die* (*Sport*) **A** [composition of the] team; team line-up; **B** (*das Aufstellen*) selection of the team; **~dienst·grad** *der* (*Milit.*) [lower] non-commissioned rank; **~führer** *der,* **~führerin** *die* (*Sport*) team captain; **~geist** *der* (*Sport*) team spirit; **~kampf** *der* (*Sport*) team contest *or* event; **~kapitän** *der,* **~kapitänin** *die* (*Sport*) team captain; **~meisterschaft** *die* (*Sport*) team championship; **~raum** *der* (*Seew.*) crew's quarters *pl.;* **~spiel** *das* (*Sport*) **A** team game; **B** (*Zusammenspiel*) team play; teamwork; **~sport** *der* team sport; **~stärke** *die* **A** (*Sport*) team strength; **B** (*Milit.*) personnel; **~wagen** *der* personnel carrier; **~wertung** *die* (*Sport*) team placings *pl. or* classification

**manns-, Manns-:** **~hoch** *Adj.* as tall as a man *postpos.;* six-foot-high; **~leute** *Pl.* (*veralt.*) menfolk; **~person** *die* (*veralt.*) male personage; **~toll** *Adj.* (*ugs. abwertend*) man-mad (*coll.*); nymphomaniac; **~tollheit** *die* (*ugs. abwertend*) nymphomania *no art.;* **~volk** *das* (*veralt.*) menfolk *pl.*

**Mann·weib** *das* (*abwertend*) amazon

**Manometer** /mano'me:tɐ/ *das;* **~s, ~** **A** (*Physik*) manometer; pressure gauge; **B** *Interj.* (*salopp*) **~!** boy, oh boy!

**Manöver** /ma'nø:vɐ/ *das;* **~s, ~** **A** (*Milit.*) exercise; **~** *Pl.* manœuvres; **ins ~ gehen** *od.* **ziehen** go on manœuvres; **B** (*Bewegung; fig. abwertend: Trick*) manœuvre

**Manöver-:** **~gelände** *das* manœuvre area; **~gelände der amerikanischen Truppen** area used for manœuvres by the American troops; **~kritik** *die* (*Milit.*) exercise evaluation; (*fig.*) postmortem (*coll.*); **~kritik üben** (*fig.*) hold a postmortem; **~schaden** *der* damage *no pl.* caused by manœuvres/an exercise

**manövrieren** ❶ *itr. V.* manœuvre; **politisch klug/unklug ~** (*fig.*) perform clever/imprudent political manœuvres. ❷ *tr. V.* manœuvre ‹vehicle›; **jmdn. in eine einflussreiche Position ~** (*fig.*) wangle sb. into an influential position (*sl.*)

**manövrier-, Manövrier-:** **~fähig** *Adj.* manœuvrable; **~fähigkeit** *die* manœuvrability; **~unfähig** *Adj.* unmanœuvrable

**Mansarde** /man'zardə/ *die;* **~, ~n** attic; (*Zimmer*) attic room

**Mansarden-:** **~dach** *das* mansard roof; **~fenster** *das* mansard dormer window; **~wohnung** *die* attic flat (*Brit.*) *or* (*Amer.*) apartment

**Mansch** /manʃ/ *der;* **~[e]s** (*ugs.*) sloshy mess (*coll.*); (*Schneematsch*) slush

**manschen** *itr. V.* (*ugs.*) slosh about (*coll.*)

**Manschette** /man'ʃɛtə/ *die;* **~, ~n** **A** cuff; [**vor etw.** (*Dat.*)] **~n haben** (*fig. ugs.*) have got the willies (*coll.*) *or* have got the wind up (*Brit. coll.*) [about sth.]; **jetzt, wo es ernst wird, hat sie ~n** (*fig. ugs.*) now it's serious she's got cold feet; **sag bloß, du hast ~n vor ihm!** (*fig. ugs.*) don't say you're scared of him!; **B** (*Umhüllung*) paper frill; **C** (*Ringen: Würgegriff*) stranglehold; **D** (*Technik: Dichtungsring*) sealing ring; ring seal

**Manschetten·knopf** *der* cuff link

**Mantel** /'mantl̩/ *der;* **~s, Mäntel** /'mɛntl̩/ **A** coat; (*schwerer*) overcoat; **der ~ des Schweigens/Vergessens** (*fig.*) the cloak *or* mantle of silence/oblivion; **den ~ des Schweigens über etw.** (*Akk.*) **breiten** *od.* **decken** (*fig.*) observe a strict silence about sth.; **B** (*Technik*) (*Isolier~, Kühl~*) jacket; (*Ofen~*) casing; (*Rohr~*) sleeve; (*Kabel~*) sheath; (*Geschoss~*) [bullet] casing; (*einer Granate*) [shell] case; (*Glocken~*) cope; (*Reifen~*) [outer] cover; casing; **C** (*Geom.: Zylinder~, Kegel~*) curved surface; **D** (*Finanzw.*) share *or* (*Amer.*) stock certificate; **E** (*Arbeitswelt ugs.*) ⇒ **~tarifvertrag**

**Mäntelchen** /'mɛntl̩çən/ *das;* **~s, ~:** little coat; (*für Kinder*) [child's] coat; **einer Sache** (*Dat.*) **ein ~ umhängen** cover up sth.; (*etw. beschönigen*) gloss over sth.; ⇒ *auch* **Wind**

**Mantel-:** **~futter** *das* [over]coat lining; **~kleid** *das* coat dress; **~pavian** *der* hamadryas baboon; **~sack** *der* (*veralt.*) saddlebag; **~tarif** *der* (*Arbeitswelt*) terms of the **Manteltarifvertrag**; **~tarifvertrag** *der* (*Wirtsch.*) framework collective agreement [on working conditions]; **~tiere** *Pl.* (*Zool.*) tunicates

**Mantisse** /man'tɪsə/ *die;* **~, ~n** (*Math.*) mantissa

**Mantsch** /mantʃ/ *der;* **~[e]s** ⇒ **Mansch**

**mantschen** *itr. V.* ⇒ **manschen**

**Manual** /ma'nua:l/ *das;* **~s, ~e, Manuale** *das;* **~e[s], ~e[n]** (*Musik*) keyboard; manual

**manuell** /ma'nuɛl/ ❶ *Adj.* manual. ❷ *adv.* manually; by hand

**Manufaktur** /manufak'tu:ɐ/ *die;* **~, ~en** **A** [small] factory (*where goods are produced largely by hand*); **B** (*veralt.: handgearbeitete Ware*) hand-made *or* handcrafted article

**Manus** /'ma:nʊs/ *das;* **~, ~** (*österr., schweiz.*), **Manuskript** /manu'skrɪpt/ *das;* **~[e]s, ~e** **A** (*auch hist.*) manuscript; (*Typoskript*) typescript; (*zu einem Film/Fernsehspiel/Hörspiel*) script; **als ~ gedruckt** printed for private circulation; **B** (*Notizen eines Redners usw.*) notes *pl.*

**Maoismus** /mao'ɪsmʊs/ *der;* **~:** Maoism *no art.*

**Maoist** *der;* **~en, ~en, Maoistin** *die;* **~, ~nen** Maoist

**maoistisch** ❶ *Adj.* Maoist. ❷ *adv.* on Maoist lines

**Mäppchen** /'mɛpçən/ *das;* **~s, ~:** pencil case

**Mappe** /'mapə/ *die;* **~, ~n** **A** folder; (*größer, für Zeichnungen usw.*) portfolio; **B** (*Aktentasche*) briefcase; (*Schul~*) schoolbag

**Mär** /mɛ:ɐ/ *die;* **~, ~en** (*dichter.*) fable; (*fig.*) myth

**Marabu** /'ma:rabu/ *der;* **~s, ~s** (*Zool.*) marabou

**Marathon-** /'ma(:)ratɔn/**:** **~lauf** *der* marathon; **~läufer** *der,* **~läuferin** *die* marathon runner; **~sitzung** *die* marathon session

*old spelling (see note on page 1707)

**-marathon** *das;* **-~s, -~s** (*ugs.*) **Verhandlungs~/Sitzungs~:** marathon negotiations *pl.* /session

**Märchen** /ˈmɛːɐ̯çən/ *das;* **~s, ~** Ⓐ fairy story; fairy tale; Ⓑ (*ugs.: Lüge*) [tall] story (*coll.*); **erzähl doch keine ~!** don't give me that story! (*coll.*)

**Märchen-: ~buch** *das* book of fairy stories; **~dichtung** *die* fairy tale literature; **~erzähler** *der,* **~erzählerin** *die* teller of fairy stories; **~figur** *die* fairy tale figure; **~film** *der* film of a fairy story

**märchenhaft** ❶ *Adj.* Ⓐ fairy-story *attrib.;* (*wie ein Märchen*) fairy-story-like; as in a fairy story *postpos.;* Ⓑ (*zauberhaft*) magical; (*feenhaft*) fairy-like; **~ sein** be sheer magic; be like a dream; Ⓒ (*ugs.*) (*großartig*) fabulous; (*sehr groß*) fantastic (*coll.*), incredible (*coll.*) ‹speed, wealth›. ❷ *adv. s. Adj.:* Ⓐ as in a fairy story; **~ gestaltet** in the form of a fairy story; Ⓑ magically; **~ schön** be witchingly beautiful; Ⓒ (*ugs.*) fantastically (*coll.*); incredibly (*coll.*); **~ spielen** play like a dream *or* fabulously

**Märchen-: ~land** *das:* **das ~land** the world of fairy tale; fairyland; **~onkel** *der* (*fam.*) story-hour presenter; **~prinz** *der* fairy tale prince; (*fig.*) Prince Charming; **~prinzessin** *die* fairy tale princess; **~schloss,** ***~schloß** *das* fairy tale castle; **~stunde** *die* [children's] story hour; **~tante** *die* (*fam.*) [female] story-hour presenter

**Marder** /ˈmardɐ/ *der;* **~s, ~:** marten

**Mare** /ˈmaːrə/ *das;* **~, ~** *od.* **Maria** (*Astron.*) mare

**Margarete** /margaˈreːtə/ (*die*) Margaret

**Margarine** /margaˈriːnə/ *die;* **~:** margarine

**Marge** /ˈmarʒə/ *die;* **~, ~n** (*Wirtsch.*) margin; (*Preisdifferenz*) difference in price; (*bei Aktien*) increase in price (*over issue price*)

**Margerite** /margəˈriːtə/ *die;* **~, ~n** ox-eye daisy; (*als Zierpflanze*) marguerite

**marginal** /margiˈnaːl/ (*geh.*) ❶ *Adj.* marginal. ❷ *adv.* marginally

**Marginalie** /margiˈnaːli̯ə/ *die;* **~, ~n** marginal note; **~n** marginalia

**Maria** /maˈriːa/ (*die*); **~s** *od.* **Mariens** *od.* (*Rel.*) **Mariä** Mary; **Mariä Empfängnis/Geburt** Conception/Nativity of the Blessed Virgin Mary; **Mariä Himmelfahrt** Assumption

**marianisch** /maˈri̯aːnɪʃ/ *Adj.* (*kath. Kirche*) Marian

**Marianne** /maˈri̯anə/ (*die*) Marianne; (*fig.: Frankreich*) France; the French *pl.*

**Marie** /maˈriː/ *die;* **~** (*salopp: Geld*) dough (*coll.*); lolly (*Brit. coll.*)

**Marien-: ~altar** *der* Lady altar; **~bild** *das* madonna; **~dichtung** *die* (*Literaturw.*) Marian literature; **~käfer** *der* ladybird; **~kult** *der* Marian cult; Mariolatry; **~leben** *das* (*Literaturw., Kunstw.*) life of our Lady; **~legende** *die* legend of the Virgin Mary; Marian legend; **~verehrung** *die* worship of the Virgin Mary; Mariolatry

**Marihuana** /mariˈhu̯aːna/ *das;* **~s** marijuana

**Marille** /maˈrɪlə/ *die;* **~, ~n** (*bes. österr.*) apricot

**marin** /maˈriːn/ *Adj.* marine

**Marinade** /mariˈnaːdə/ *die;* **~, ~n** Ⓐ (*Beize*) marinade; Ⓑ (*Salatsauce*) [marinade] dressing; Ⓒ (*Fischkonserve*) marinaded fish

**Marine** /maˈriːnə/ *die;* **~, ~n** Ⓐ (*Flotte*) fleet; Ⓑ (*Kriegs~*) navy

**marine-, Marine-: ~blau** *Adj.* navy [blue]; **~flieger** *der* naval airman; **~infanterie** *die* marines *pl.;* **~infanterist** *der* marine; **~luft·waffe** *die* Fleet Air Arm (*Brit.*); Navy Air Force (*Amer.*); **~maler** *der,* **~malerin** *die* (*Kunst*) marine painter

**Mariner** *der;* **~s, ~** (*ugs.*) sailor

**Marine-: ~schule** *die* naval academy; **~soldat** *der,* **~soldatin** *die* marine; **~stütz·punkt** *der* naval base; **~truppen** *Pl.* marines; **~uniform** *die* naval uniform

**marinieren** *tr. V.* marinade; **marinierte Heringe** soused herrings

**Marionette** /mari̯oˈnɛtə/ *die;* **~, ~n** puppet; marionette; (*fig. abwertend*) puppet

**Marionetten-: ~regierung** *die* (*abwertend*) puppet government; **~spieler** *der* puppet master; puppeteer; **~spielerin** *die* puppeteer; **~theater** *das* puppet theatre

**maritim** /mariˈtiːm/ *Adj.* maritime

**Mark**[1] /mark/ *die;* **~, ~** *od.* (*ugs. scherzh.:*) **Märker** /ˈmɛrkɐ/ ▶ 337 mark; **Deutsche ~:** Deutschmark; German mark; **~ der DDR** GDR *or* East German mark; **zwei ~ fünfzig** two marks fifty; **die paar Märker** (*ugs.*) those few measly marks (*sl.*); **keine müde ~** (*ugs.*) not a penny; not a cent (*Amer.*); ⇒ *auch* **umdrehen** 1

**Mark**[2] *das;* **~[e]s** Ⓐ (*Knochen~*) marrow; medulla (*Anat.*); **jmdm. das ~ aus den Knochen saugen** (*fig. ugs.*) (*finanziell*) bleed sb. white; (*arbeitsmäßig*) work sb. to death; **das ging mir durch ~ und Bein** *od.* (*scherzh.*) **durch ~ und Pfennig** (*fig.*) it put my teeth on edge; it went right through me; **jmdn. bis ins ~ treffen** (*fig.*) cut *or* sting sb. to the quick; Ⓑ (*Bot.*) (*Frucht~*) pulp; (*inneres Gewebe*) medulla (*as tech. term*); pith

**Mark**[3] *die;* **~, ~en** (*hist.*) march; **die ~ Brandenburg** the Mark [of] Brandenburg

**markant** /marˈkant/ *Adj.* striking; distinctive; prominent ‹figure, nose, chin›; clear-cut, distinctive ‹features, profile›; **ein ~er Punkt in der Stadt** a landmark in the town

**mark·durch·dringend** ❶ *Adj.* spine-chilling; blood-curdling. ❷ *adv.* **~ schreien** utter a spine-chilling scream

**Marke** *die;* **~, ~n** Ⓐ (*Waren~*) brand; (*Fabrikat*) make; **Tabak der ~ Erinmore** the Erinmore brand of tobacco; Ⓑ (*Brief~, Rabatt~, Beitrags~*) stamp; **zehn ~n zu 60 Pfennig** ten 60-pfennig stamps; Ⓒ (*Garderoben~*) [cloakroom *or* (*Amer.*) checkroom] counter *or* tag; (*Zettel*) [cloakroom *or* (*Amer.*) checkroom] ticket; (*Essen~*) meal ticket; Ⓓ (*Erkennungs~*) [identification] disc; (*Dienst~*) [police] identification badge; ≈ warrant card (*Brit.*) *or* (*Amer.*) ID card; Ⓔ (*Lebensmittel~*) coupon; **auf ~n verkauft werden** be on coupons; Ⓕ (*Markierung*) mark; (*Sport: Rekord*) record [height/distance]; Ⓖ (*salopp*) **du bist mir vielleicht eine ~!** you are a fine one! (*iron.*)

**Märke** /ˈmɛrkə/ *die;* **~, ~n** (*österr.*) monogram

**Marken-: ~artikel** *der* proprietary *or* (*Brit.*) branded article; **~artikel** *Pl.* proprietary *or* (*Brit.*) branded goods; **~butter** *die* best butter (*legally defined first grade of butter*); **~erzeugnis** *das,* **~fabrikat** *das* proprietary *or* (*Brit.*) branded product; **~name** *der* brand name; **~schutz** *der* protection of trade marks; **~zeichen** *das* trade mark

**mark·erschütternd** ❶ *Adj.* heart-rending. ❷ *adv.* heart-rendingly

**Marketender** /markəˈtɛndɐ/ *der;* **~s, ~, Marketenderin** *die;* **~, ~nen** (*hist.*) sutler

**Marketender·ware** *die* troops' personal supplies *pl.;* ≈ NAAFI (*Brit.*) *or* (*Amer.*) PX goods *pl.*

**Marketing** /ˈmarkətɪŋ/ *das;* **~s** (*Wirtsch.*) marketing

**mark-, Mark-: ~graf** *der* margrave; **~gräfin** *die* margravine; **~gräflich** *Adj.* margrave's; of the margrave *postpos.*

**markieren** ❶ *tr. V.* Ⓐ (*auch fig.*) mark; (*Sport*) mark out ‹course›; Ⓑ (*ugs.*) sham ‹illness, breakdown, etc.›; **den Dummen ~:** act stupid; Ⓒ (*Sport*) mark ‹player›. ❷ *itr. V.* (*ugs.*) sham; put it on (*coll.*)

**Markierung** *die;* **~, ~en** Ⓐ (*Zeichen*) marking; **ein Flugzeug mit fremder ~:** an aircraft with foreign markings *pl.;* Ⓑ marking [out]

**Markierungs-: ~fähnchen** *das* course marker; marker flag; **~linie** *die* line

**markig** ❶ *Adj.* (*kernig*) pithy ‹saying, style›; (*kraftvoll*) vigorous, breezy ‹commands, manner›; powerful ‹voice›; **~e Worte** strong words; (*iron.: große Reden*) big words. ❷ *adv.* pithily

**märkisch** *Adj.* of the Mark [of] Brandenburg *postpos.;* ‹food, produce, etc.› from the Mark [of] Brandenburg; ⇒ *auch* **badisch**

**Markise** /marˈkiːzə/ *die;* **~, ~n** awning

**mark-, Mark-: ~klößchen** *das;* **~~s, ~~** (*Kochk.*) bone-marrow dumpling; **~knochen** *der* marrowbone; **~scheide** *die* (*Bergmannsspr.*) boundary (*of a mining area*); **~stein** *der* (*fig.*) milestone; **~stück** *das* ▶ 337 one-mark piece; **~stück·groß** *Adj.* the size of a one-mark piece *postpos.*

**Markt** /markt/ *der;* **~[e]s, Märkte** /ˈmɛrktə/ Ⓐ market; **heute/freitags ist ~:** today/Friday is market day; **zum** *od.* **auf den ~ gehen** go to the market; **auf dem ~:** at the market; Ⓑ ⇒ **~platz;** Ⓒ (*Super~*) supermarket; Ⓓ (*Warenverkehr, Absatzgebiet*) market; **der ~ für Gebrauchtwagen** the used-car market; **eine Ware auf den ~ bringen** *od.* **werfen** market a product; (*mit viel Werbung*) launch a product; **auf dem** *od.* **am ~ sein** ‹firm› be in the market; ‹article› be on the market; ⇒ *auch* **gemeinsam** 1 A; **grau** C; **schwarz** 1 C

**markt-, Markt-: ~absprache** *die* (*Wirtsch.*) marketing agreement; **~analyse** *die* (*Wirtsch.*) market analysis; **~anteil** *der* share of the market; **~anteile zurückgewinnen** regain parts of the market; **~beherrschend** *Adj.* market-dominating *attrib.;* **~beherrschend sein** have a dominant position in the market; **~bewusst,** ***~bewußt** ❶ *Adj.* aware of products and prices *postpos.;* ❷ *adv.* with a knowledge of products and prices; **~fähig** *Adj.* (*Wirtsch.*) marketable; **~fähig werden** become a marketable proposition; **~flecken** *der* (*veralt.*) small market town; **~forschung** *die* market research *no def. art.;* **~frau** *die* market woman; **~gängig** *Adj.* (*Wirtsch.*) with a ready sale *postpos., not pred.;* (*fig.: üblich*) customary; usual; **~gerecht** ❶ *Adj.* ‹product› geared to market requirements; ‹price› in line with market conditions; ❷ *adv.* in accordance with market conditions; **~halle** *die* covered market; **~lage** *die* market situation; state of the market; **~leiter** *der,* **~leiterin** *die* supermarket manager; **~lücke** *die* gap in the market; **in eine ~lücke [vor]stoßen** fill a gap in the market; **~ordnung** *die* Ⓐ (*Wirtsch.*) [Common] Market regulations *pl.;* Ⓑ (*bei Wochenmärkten*) market regulations *pl.;* **~platz** *der* market place *or* square; **~recht** *das* (*hist.*) right to hold a market; market right; **~schreier** *der,* **~schreierin** *die* barker; stallholder who cries his wares; (*fig. abwertend*) vociferous propagandist; **~schreierisch** (*abwertend, auch fig.*) ❶ *Adj.* vociferous; ❷ *adv.* vociferously; **~stand** *der* market stall; **~tag** *der* market day; **~üblich** *Adj.* customary [in the market] *postpos.;* **~übliche Zinsen** customary market rates; **~weib** *das* (*salopp*) market woman; **wie ein ~weib** like a fishwife; **~wert** *der* market value; **~wirtschaft** *die:* **[freie] ~wirtschaft** [free] market economy; **die soziale ~wirtschaft** the social market economy (*with State intervention safeguarding social justice and free competition*); **~wirtschaftlich** ❶ *Adj.* market economy; free market; ❷ *adv.* on market economy lines

**Markus·evangelium** /ˈmarkʊs-/ *das* St Mark's Gospel; Gospel according to St Mark

**Marmara·meer** /ˈmarmara-/ *das* Sea of Marmara

**Marmelade** /marməˈlaːdə/ *die;* **~, ~n** jam; (*Orangen~*) marmalade

**Marmelade[n]-: ~brot** [piece of] bread and jam; (*zugeklappt*) jam sandwich; **~glas** *das* jam jar

**Marmor** /ˈmarmɔr/ *der;* **~s** marble

**Marmor-: ~bild** *das* (*veralt.*) marble statue; **~block** *der; Pl.* **~blöcke** block of marble; marble block; **~bruch** *der* marble quarry; **~büste** *die* marble bust

**marmorieren** *tr. V.* **etw. ~:** give sth. a marbled effect; marble sth.; **eine marmorierte Platte** a marbled slab

**Marmorierung** *die;* **~, ~en** marbling; marbled effect

**Marmor·kuchen** *der* marble cake

**marmorn** *Adj.* marble; (*fig.*) pale as marble *postpos.;* ashen ‹pallor›

m

**marode** *Adj.* (*ugs. abwertend*) clapped-out (*Brit. sl.*)

**Marodeur** /maro'dø:ɐ̯/ *der;* **~s, ~e** (*Soldatenspr.*) looter

**Marokkaner** /marɔ'ka:nɐ/ *der;* **~s, ~, Marokkanerin** *die;* **~, ~nen** Moroccan

**marokkanisch** *Adj.* Moroccan

**Marokko** /ma'rɔko/ (*das*); **~s** Morocco

**Marone** /ma'ro:nə/ *die;* **~, ~n** **A** [sweet] chestnut; **B** ⇒ **Maronenpilz**

**Maronen·pilz** *der* chestnut boletus

**Maronit** /maro'ni:t/ *der;* **~en, ~en, Maronitin** *die;* **~, ~nen** (*Rel.*) Maronite

**Marotte** /ma'rɔtə/ *die;* **~, ~n** fad

**Marquis** /mar'ki:/ *der;* **~** /mar'ki:(s) /,/ **~** /mar'ki:s/ marquis

**Marquise** /mar'ki:zə/ *die;* **~, ~n** marquise

**Mars**[1] /mars/ *der;* **~** (*Astron.*), **Mars**[2] (*der*) (*Myth.*) Mars *no def. art.*

**Mars**[3] *der;* **~, ~e** *od. die;* **~, ~en** (*Seemannsspr.*) crow's nest

**Marsala** /mar'za:la/ *der;* **~s, ~s, Marsalawein** *der* Marsala

**Mars·bewohner** *der,* **Mars·bewohnerin** *die* Martian

**marsch** /marʃ/ *Interj.* **A** (*Milit.*) [forward] march; **kehrt — ~!** about turn *or* (*Amer.*) face! forward march!; ⇒ *auch* **Gleichschritt**; **B** (*ugs.*) **~ ~!** off with you!; (*beeil dich!*) move it! (*coll.*); look snappy! (*coll.*); **~ ins Bett!** off to bed [with you]!; **~ an die Arbeit!** get down to work!

**Marsch**[1] *der;* **~[e]s, Märsche** /'mɛrʃə/ **A** (*Milit.*) march; (*Wanderung*) [long] walk; hike; **ein ~ von einer Stunde** an hour's march/walk; **einen ~ [von einer Stunde] machen** go for *or* take a long walk [lasting an hour]; **jmdn. in ~ setzen** (*Milit.*) march sb. off; (*fig.*) mobilize sb.; **sich in ~ setzen** make a move; get moving; (*Milit.*) march off; **B** (*Musikstück*) march; **jmdm. [gehörig] den ~ blasen** (*fig. salopp*) give sb. a real rocket (*Brit. coll.*) *or* (*coll.*) bawling out

**Marsch**[2] *die;* **~, ~en** fertile marshland

**Marschall** /'marʃal/ *der;* **~s, Marschälle** /'marʃɛlə/ (*hist.*) marshal

**Marschall[s]·stab** *der* marshal's baton; **den ~ im Tornister tragen** (*fig.*) have what it takes to achieve high rank

**marsch-, Marsch-: ~befehl** *der* (*Milit.*) marching orders *pl.*; **der ~befehl** one's marching orders; **~bereit** *Adj.* (*Milit.*) ready to march *or* move *pred.*; (*ugs.*) ready to go *pred.*; **~boden** *der* [fertile] marshy soil; **~flug·körper** *der* cruise missile; **~gepäck** *das* (*Milit.*) marching pack; **unser ~gepäck** our marching packs *pl.*

**marschieren** *itr. V.*; *mit sein* **A** march; **B** (*ugs.: mit großen Schritten gehen*) march; stalk; (*wandern*) walk; hike; **C** (*ugs.: vorankommen*) **[richtig] ~:** progress smoothly; **der Fortschritt marschiert** the march of progress is inexorable

**Marsch-: ~kolonne** *die* (*Milit.*) marching column; **~land** *das* [fertile] marshland; **~lied** *das* marching song; **~musik** *die* march music; **~ordnung** *die* (*Milit.*) marching order; **~pause** *die* halt [on the march]; **eine ~pause einlegen** make a halt; **~richtung** *die* (*Milit.*) direction of march; **~route** *die* (*Milit.*) route; (*fig.*) line [of approach]; **die ~route für die Verhandlungen** (*fig.*) the line to be taken in the negotiations; **~säule** *die* column of marchers; **~tempo** *das* marching pace; (*Musik*) march tempo; **im ~tempo** at a quick march; (*Musik*) in march tempo; **~verpflegung** *die* (*Milit.*) marching rations *pl.*; (*fig. ugs.*) rations *pl.* [for the journey]

**Marseillaise** /marzɛ'jɛ:zə/ *die;* **~:** Marseillaise

**Marseille** /mar'zɛ:j/ (*das*); **~s** Marseilles

**Marshall·plan** /'marʃal-/ *der* (*hist.*) Marshall Plan

**Mars-: ~mensch** *der* Martian; **~segel** *das* (*Seemannsspr.*) main topsail; **~sonde** *die* (*Raumfahrt*) Mars probe

*old spelling (see note on page 1707)

**Mar·stall** /'mar-/ *der* (*hist.*) [royal *or* princely] stables *pl.*

**Marter** /'martɐ/ *die;* **~, ~n** (*geh.*) (*Folter*) torture; (*fig.: seelisch*) torment; **jmdm. ~n bereiten** *od.* **zufügen** (*körperlich*) subject sb. to torture; (*seelisch*) inflict torment on sb.

**Marter·instrument** *das* instrument of torture

**Marterl** /'martɐl/ *das;* **~s, ~n** (*bayr., österr.*) wayside shrine

**martern** *tr. V.* (*geh.*) torture; (*fig.: seelisch*) torment; **jmdn. zu Tode ~:** torture sb. to death

**Marter-: ~pfahl** *der* stake; **~tod** *der* (*geh.*) death by torture; (*Märtyrertod*) death of a martyr

**Marterung** *die;* **~, ~en** (*geh.*) torture; (*seelisch*) torment

**martialisch** /mar'tsi̯a:lɪʃ/ (*geh.*) ❶ *Adj.* warlike ‹appearance, figure, etc.›; martial ‹music›. ❷ *adv.* in a warlike manner; (*drohend*) threateningly; aggressively

**Martin-Horn** Ⓦⓩ *das* ⇒ **Martinshorn**

**Martini** /mar'ti:ni/ (*das*); *indekl.* **zu ~:** on St Martin's Day; at Martinmas

**Martins-: ~gans** *die* Martinmas goose; **~horn** *das* (*volkstümlich*) siren (*of emergency vehicle*); **mit ~horn** sounding its siren; **~tag** *der* St Martin's Day

**Märtyrer** /'mɛrtyrɐ/ *der;* **~s, ~, Märtyrerin** *die;* **~, ~nen** martyr

**Märtyrer-: ~krone** *die* martyr's crown; **die ~krone tragen** be a martyr/martyrs; **~tod** *der* death of a martyr; **den ~tod sterben** die a martyr's death

**Märtyrin** /'mɛrtyrɪn/ *die;* **~, ~nen** ⇒ **Märtyrerin**

**Martyrium** /mar'ty:ri̯ʊm/ *das;* **~s, Martyrien** martyrdom; **das war ein ~** (*fig.*) it was sheer martyrdom

**Marxismus** /mar'ksɪsmʊs/ *der;* **~:** Marxism *no art.*

**Marxismus-Leninismus** *der* Marxism-Leninism *no art.*

**Marxist** *der;* **~en, ~en, Marxistin** *die;* **~, ~nen** Marxist

**marxistisch** ❶ *Adj.* Marxist. ❷ *adv.* ‹view, interpret› from a Marxist point of view; ‹think, act› in line with Marxism

**marxistisch-leninistisch** ❶ *Adj.* Marxist-Leninist. ❷ *adv.* ‹view, interpret› from a Marxist-Leninist point of view; ‹think, act› in line with Marxism-Leninism

**März** /mɛrts/ *der;* **~[es],** *dichter.:* **~en** ▶ 207 March; ⇒ *auch* **April**

**März[en]-: ~becher** *der* **A** Spring Snowflake; **B** (*volkstümlich: Narzisse*) daffodil; **~bier** *das: kind of dark bock beer*

**Marzipan** /martsi'pa:n, *österr.* '---/ *das;* **~s,** *österr.: der;* **~s** marzipan

**Marzipan-: ~kartoffel** *die* marzipan ball; **~schwein** *das* marzipan pig

**Mascara** /mas'ka:ra/ *der;* **~, ~s** mascara brush/pencil

**Masche** /'maʃə/ *die;* **~, ~n** **A** stitch; (*Lauf~*) run; ladder (*Brit.*); (*beim Netz*) mesh; **die ~n eines Netzes** the mesh *sing.* of a net; **durch die ~n des Gesetzes schlüpfen** (*fig.*) slip through a loophole in the law; **B** (*ugs.: Trick*) trick; **das ist die ~:** that's the way *or* trick; **C** (*ugs.: Mode, Gag*) **die neueste ~:** the latest fad *or* craze; **D** (*österr.: Schleife*) bow

**Maschen-: ~draht** *der* wire netting; **~draht·zaun** *der* wire-netting fence; **~probe** *die* (*Handarb.*) tension check

**Maschine** /ma'ʃi:nə/ *die;* **~, ~n** **A** machine; (*Näh~/Wasch~*) [sewing/washing] machine; **ich bin doch keine ~:** I'm not a machine; **B** (*ugs.: Automotor*) engine; **C** (*Flugzeug*) [aero]plane; **die erste ~ nach Zürich** the first plane *or* flight to Zurich; **D** (*ugs.: Motorrad*) machine; **E** (*Schreib~*) typewriter; **einen Brief in die ~ diktieren** dictate a letter straight on to the typewriter; **~ schreiben** type; **F** (*ugs. abwertend: dicke Frau*) great hulk of a woman

**maschine·geschrieben** *Adj.* typed; typewritten

**maschinell** /maʃi'nɛl/ ❶ *Adj.* **A** machine *attrib.*; by machine *postpos.*; **~e Herstellung** machine production; **B** (*wie eine Maschine*) mechanical. ❷ *adv.* **A** by machine; **~ hergestellt** machine-made; **B** (*wie eine Maschine*) mechanically

**maschinen-, Maschinen-: ~bau** *der* **A** machine construction *no art.*; mechanical engineering *no art.*; **B** (*Lehrfach*) mechanical engineering *no art.*; **~bauer** *der;* **~~s, ~~, ~bauerin** *die;* **~~, ~~nen** ▶ 159 machine builder; **~bau·ingenieur** *der,* **~bau·ingenieurin** *die* mechanical engineer; **~fabrik** *die* engineering works *sing. or pl.*; **~geschrieben** *Adj.* ⇒ **maschinegeschrieben** 2; **~gewehr** *das* machine gun; **~halle** *die* machine shop; **~haus** *das* power house; (*auf Schiffen*) engine room; **~kraft** *die* mechanical power; engine power; **mit ~kraft** by mechanical *or* engine power; **~lesbar** ❶ *Adj.* machine-readable; ❷ *adv.* in machine-readable form; **~park** *der* plant; **~pistole** *die* sub-machine gun; **~raum** *der* engine room; **~satz** *der* (*Druckw.*) machine composition; **~schaden** *der* engine trouble *no indef. art.*; **~schlosser** *der,* **~schlosserin** *die* ▶ 159 fitter; **~schreiben** *das* typing; **das ~schreiben lernen** learn to type; **~schreiber** *der,* **~schreiberin** *die* typist; **~schrift** *die* typing; (*Schriftart*) typeface; type; **in ~schrift** typed; **~schriftlich** *Adj.* typewritten; typed; **~stürmer** *der* (*hist.*) machine breaker; machine wrecker; **~stürmerei** *die;* **~~:** machine breaking; machine wrecking; **~stürmerin** *die* ⇒ **~stürmer**; **~zeitalter** *das* machine age

**Maschinerie** /maʃinə'ri:/ *die;* **~, ~n** machinery; **die gnadenlose ~ der Justiz** (*fig. geh.*) the merciless wheels *pl.* of justice

***maschine·schreiben** ⇒ **Maschine E**

**Maschinist** *der;* **~en, ~en, Maschinistin** *die;* **~, ~nen** **A** machinist; **B** (*Schiffs~*) engineer

**Maser** /'ma:zɐ/ *die;* **~, ~n** figure

**maserig** *Adj.* figured

**masern** *tr. V.* grain ‹wood›

**Masern** *Pl.* ▶ 474 measles *sing. or pl.*

**Maserung** *die;* **~, ~en** (*in Holz, Leder*) [wavy] grain; (*in Marmor*) vein; (*in Fell*) patterning

**Maske** /'maskə/ *die;* **~, ~n** **A** (*auch fig.*) mask; **ihr Gesicht erstarrte zur ~:** her features froze into a mask; **die ~ fallen lassen** *od.* **abwerfen** (*fig.*) drop one's mask; **jmdm. die ~ vom Gesicht reißen** (*fig.*) unmask sb.; **B** (*Theater*) make-up; **~ machen** make up; **C** (*Mensch*) masker

**Masken-: ~ball** *der* masked ball; masquerade; **~bildner** *der;* **~~s, ~~, ~bildnerin** *die;* **~~, ~~nen** ▶ 159 make-up artist

**maskenhaft** ❶ *Adj.* mask-like. ❷ *adv.* like a mask; **ein ~ starres Gesicht** a face frozen into a mask

**Maskerade** /maskə'ra:də/ *die;* **~, ~n** **A** [fancy-dress] costume; **~ sein** (*fig.*) be a masquerade; **B** (*veralt.: Maskenball*) masquerade; (*Kostümfest*) fancy-dress ball

**maskieren** ❶ *tr. V.* **A** mask; **B** (*verkleiden*) dress up. ❷ *refl. V.* **A** put on a mask/masks; **B** (*sich verkleiden*) dress up

**Maskierung** *die;* **~, ~en** **A** (*das Verkleiden*) dressing up; **B** (*Verkleidung*) disguise; (*beim Kostümball*) [fancy-dress] costume; **C** (*Tarnung*) masking; disguising

**Maskottchen** /mas'kɔtçən/ *das;* **~s, ~:** [lucky] mascot

**maskulin** /masku'li:n, *auch* '---/ ❶ *Adj.* (*auch Sprachw.*) masculine. ❷ *adv.* in a masculine way

**Maskulinum** /'maskuli:nʊm/ *das;* **~s, Maskulina** (*Sprachw.*) masculine noun

**Masochismus** /mazɔ'xɪsmʊs/ *der;* **~** (*Psych.*) masochism *no art.*

**Masochist** /mazɔ'xɪst/ *der;* **~en, ~en, Masochistin** *die;* **~, ~nen** (*Psych.*) masochist

**masochistisch** (*Psych.*) ❶ *Adj.* masochistic. ❷ *adv.* masochistically; **~ veranlagt sein** have masochistic tendencies

**maß** *1. u. 3. Pers. Sg. Prät. v.* **messen**

**Maß¹** /ma:s/ *das;* **~es, ~e** Ⓐ measure (**für** of); **~e und Gewichte** weights and measures; Ⓑ (*fig.*) **ein gerüttelt ~ [an** (*Dat.*) *od.* **von etw.]** (*geh.*) a good measure [of sth.]; **das ~ ist voll** enough is enough; **das ~ voll machen** go too far; **mit zweierlei ~ messen** apply different [sets of] standards; Ⓒ (*Größe*) measurement; (*von Räumen, Möbeln*) dimension; measurement; **ihre ~e sind ...** her measurements *or* vital statistics are ...; **[bei] jmdm. ~ nehmen** take sb.'s measurements; measure sb. [up]; Ⓓ (*Grad*) measure, degree (**an** + *Dat.* of); **in solchem ~e** *od.* **in einem ~e, dass ...** to such an extent that ...; **in großem/gewissem ~e** to a great/certain extent; **im höchsten ~[e]** extremely; exceedingly; **in vollem ~e** fully; **im gleichen ~[e]** to the same extent; Ⓔ (*Mäßigung*) **weder ~ noch Ziel kennen** know no restraint; **ohne ~ und Ziel** immoderately; **in** *od.* **mit ~en** in moderation; **über die** *od.* **alle ~en** (*geh.*) beyond [all] measure; Ⓕ **~ halten** exercise moderation

**Maß²** *die;* **~, ~[e]** (*bayr., österr.*) litre [of beer]; **zwei ~ Bier** two litres of beer

**Massage** /ma'sa:ʒə/ *die;* **~, ~n** massage; **zur ~ gehen** go for a massage

**Massage-: ~gerät** *das* massager; **~institut** *das* (*auch verhüll.*) massage parlour; **~öl** *das* massage oil; **~salon** *der* (*verhüll.*) massage parlour (*euphem.*); **~stab** *der* vibrator

**Massaker** /ma'sa:kɐ/ *das;* **~s, ~:** massacre

**massakrieren** *tr. V.* massacre

**Maß-: ~analyse** *die* (*Chemie*) volumetric analysis; **~an·gabe** *die* stated dimensions *pl. or* measurements *pl.;* (*bei Hohlmaßen*) stated capacity; **~an·zug** *der* made-to-measure suit; tailor-made suit; **~arbeit** *die* Ⓐ custom-made item; (*Kleidungsstück*) made-to-measure item; **[eine] ~arbeit sein** be custom-made/made-to-measure; Ⓑ (*genaue Arbeit*) neat work

**Masse** /'masə/ *die;* **~, ~n** Ⓐ mass; (*Kochk.*) mixture; Ⓑ (*Menge*) mass; **~n an** (*Dat.*) *od.* **von Autos** masses of cars; **riesige ~n Papier** huge piles *or* heaps of paper; **die ~ der Befragten** the bulk of those questioned; **die ~ machts** (*ugs.*) it's quantity that's important; **sie kamen in ~n** they came in their masses *or* in droves; **das ist eine ganze ~:** that's a lot (*coll.*) *or* a great deal; Ⓒ (*Menschen~*) **eine große ~ [an] Menschen** (*Dat.*) a great mass of people; **die namenlose ~:** the anonymous masses *pl.;* **die breite ~:** the bulk *or* broad mass of the population; **die [werktätigen] ~n** the [working] masses; Ⓓ (*Physik*) mass; Ⓔ (*Wirtsch.*) assets *pl.;* (*Erb~*) estate; **mangels ~:** for lack of assets

**Maß-: ~einheit** *die* unit of measurement; **~einteilung** *die* calibrations *pl.*

**Massel** /'masl̩/ *der;* **~s** (*ugs.*) **~ haben** be dead lucky (*coll.*)

**Massen-: ~ab·fertigung** *die* (*oft abwertend*) mass processing *no indef. art.;* **~absatz** *der* mass sale; **für den ~absatz gefertigt** produced for mass sale; **~andrang** *der* crush; **~anziehung** *die* (*Physik*) gravitation; **~arbeitslosigkeit** *die* mass unemployment; **~artikel** *der* mass-produced article; **~aufgebot** *das* large body *or* contingent; **~bedarf** *der* mass demand; **~bedarfs·artikel** *der* mass consumer commodity; **~bewegung** *die* mass movement; **~blatt** *das* mass-circulation paper; **~demonstration** *die* mass demonstration; **~entlassungen** *Pl.* mass redundancies *pl.;* **~fabrikation** *die* mass production; **~gesellschaft** *die* (*Soziol.*) mass society; **~grab** *das* mass grave; **~güter** *Pl.* Ⓐ mass-produced goods; Ⓑ (*Frachtgut*) bulk goods

**massenhaft** ❶ *Adj.* in huge numbers *postpos.;* **das ~e Auftreten dieser Schädlinge** the appearance of huge numbers of these pests. ❷ *adv.* on a huge *or* massive scale; **~ kommen** come in vast *or* huge numbers; **~ Geld haben** (*ugs.*) have pots of money (*coll.*); **~ Schulden haben** have a pile of debts (*coll.*)

**massen-, Massen-: ~herstellung** *die* ⇨ **~produktion**; **~hinrichtung** *die* mass execution; **~hysterie** *die* mass hysteria; **~karambolage** *die* multiple crash; [multiple] pile-up; **~kommunikationsmittel** *das* medium of mass communication; mass medium; **~kundgebung** *die* mass rally; **~medium** *das* mass medium; **~mord** *der* mass murder; **~mörder** *der,* **~mörderin** *die* mass murderer; **~organisation** *die* mass organisation; **~produktion** *die* mass production; **etw. in ~produktion herstellen** mass-produce sth.; **~psychologie** *die* mass psychology *no art.;* **~psychose** *die* mass psychosis *no indef. art.;* **~quartier** *das* (*abwertend*) mass accommodation *no indef. art.;* **~schlägerei** *die* [grand] free-for-all; pitched battle (*fig.*); **~sport** *der* mass sport; **~sterben** *das;* **~~s, ~~: das ~sterben von ...** the death of huge numbers of ...; **ein ~sterben begann** people/animals *etc.* began to die in huge numbers; **~szene** *die* crowd scene; **~tourismus** *der* mass tourism *no art.;* **~verhaftung** *die* mass arrest; **~verkehrsmittel** *das* means *sing.* of mass transportation; **~vernichtung** *die* mass extermination; **~vernichtungs·waffen** *Pl.* weapons of mass destruction; **~wahn** *der* mass hysteria; **~ware** *die* mass-produced goods *pl.*; **~waren** mass-produced goods; **~weise** *Adv.* in huge numbers *or* quantities; **~wirksam** *Adj.* with mass impact *postpos., not pred.;* **~wirksam sein** have mass impact; **~wirkung** *die* mass impact

**Masseur** /ma'sø:ɐ̯/ *der;* **~s, ~e** ▶ 159 masseur

**Masseurin** *die;* **~, ~nen** ▶ 159 masseuse

**Masseuse** /ma'sø:zə/ *die;* **~, ~n** ▶ 159 (*auch verhüll.*) masseuse

**Maß·gabe** *die: in* **nach ~** (+ *Gen.*) (*geh.*) in accordance with; **mit der ~, etw. zu tun** with instructions to do sth.

**maß·gearbeitet** *Adj.* custom-made; made-to-measure ‹clothes›

**maß·gebend, maß·geblich** ❶ *Adj.* authoritative ‹book, expert, opinion›; definitive ‹text›; important, influential ‹person, circles, etc.›; decisive ‹factor, influence, etc.›; (*zuständig*) competent ‹authority, person, etc.›; **sein Urteil ist nicht ~:** his opinion carries no weight. ❷ *adv.* ‹influence› considerably, to a considerable extent; (*entscheidend*) decisively; **~ an etw.** (*Dat.*) **beteiligt sein** play a leading role in sth.

**maß-, Maß-: ~gerecht** ❶ accurate; **genau ~gerecht für etw. sein** be just the right size for sth.; ❷ *adv.* accurately; **~gerecht zugeschnittene Regalbretter** shelves cut to size; **~geschneidert** *Adj.* made-to-measure; (*fig.*) tailor-made; **~halte·appell** *der* call *or* appeal for moderation; ***~|halten** ⇨ **Maß¹** F

**massieren¹** ❶ *tr. V.* massage. ❷ *itr. V.* **gut ~ können** be a good masseur/masseuse

**massieren²** ❶ *tr. V.* mass ‹troops etc.›. ❷ *refl. V.* ‹troops etc.› mass

**massig** ❶ *Adj.* massive; bulky, massive ‹figure›. ❷ *adv.* (*ugs.*) **~ Geld verdienen** earn pots of money (*coll.*); **~ zu tun haben** have loads *or* tons to do (*coll.*)

**mäßig** /'mɛ:sɪç/ ❶ *Adj.* Ⓐ moderate; **im Essen ~ sein** eat in moderation; be a moderate eater; Ⓑ (*gering*) moderate, modest ‹interest, income, talent, attendance›; Ⓒ (*mittel~*) mediocre; indifferent; indifferent ‹health›; **seine Leistungen sind mehr als ~:** his performance is worse than mediocre. ❷ *adv.* Ⓐ in moderation; **~, aber regelmäßig** (*scherzh.*) in moderation but regularly; Ⓑ (*gering*) moderately ‹gifted, talented›; **nur ~ verkauft worden sein** have had only a modest sale; Ⓒ (*mittel~*) indifferently

**mäßigen** (*geh.*) ❶ *tr. V.* moderate ‹language, demands›; curb, check ‹anger, impatience›; slacken, reduce ‹speed›. ❷ *refl. V.* Ⓐ practise *or* exercise moderation (**bei** in); (*sich beherrschen*) control *or* restrain oneself; Ⓑ (*nachlassen*) ‹storm› abate; ‹heat› grow less intense

**Mäßigkeit** *die;* **~** Ⓐ moderation; **jmdm. ~ empfehlen** advise sb. to exercise moderation; Ⓑ (*Mittel~*) mediocrity

**Mäßigung** *die;* **~:** moderation; restraint; **jmdn. zur ~ mahnen** urge sb. to control *or* restrain himself/herself

**massiv** /ma'si:f/ ❶ *Adj.* Ⓐ solid; **~ bauen** build solidly; Ⓑ (*heftig*) massive ‹demand›; crude ‹accusation, threat›; heavy, strong ‹attack, criticism, pressure›; **~ werden** (*ugs.*) get tough. ❷ *adv.* ‹attack› heavily, strongly; ‹accuse, threaten› crudely

**Massiv** *das;* **~s, ~e** massif

**Massiv-: ~bau** *der,* **~bau·weise** *die* massive construction; **in ~bauweise errichtet sein** be of massive construction

**Massivität** /masivi'tɛ:t/ *die;* **~** ⇨ **massiv** B: massiveness; crudeness; heaviness; strength

**Maß·krug** *der* (*südd., österr.*) litre tankard *or* beer mug; (*aus Steingut*) stein

**Maß·liebchen** *das* daisy

**maß·los** ❶ *Adj.* (*äußerst*) extreme; (*übermäßig*) inordinate; gross ‹exaggeration, insult›; excessive ‹demand, claim›; (*grenzenlos*) boundless ‹ambition, greed, sorrow, joy›; extravagant ‹spendthrift›; **~ im Essen/Trinken sein** eat/drink to excess; **~ in seinen Ansprüchen sein** be excessive in one's demands. ❷ *adv.* (*äußerst*) extremely; (*übermäßig*) inordinately; ‹exaggerate› grossly; **sie ist ~ ehrgeizig** her ambition knows no bounds

**Maßlosigkeit** *die;* **~** ⇨ **maßlos:** extremeness; inordinateness; grossness; excessiveness; boundlessness

**Maßnahme** *die;* **~, ~n** measure; **~n gegen etw. einleiten/treffen** introduce/take measures against sth.; **~n zur Verhütung von Unfällen treffen** take measures *or* steps to prevent accidents; **eine abschreckende ~:** a deterrent

**Maß·regel** *die* regulation; (*Maßnahme*) measure

**maßregeln** *tr. V.* (*zurechtweisen*) reprimand; (*bestrafen*) discipline

**Maß·reg[e]lung** *die* (*Zurechtweisung*) reprimand; (*Bestrafung*) disciplinary measure

**Maß·schneider** *der,* **Maß·schneiderin** *die* bespoke tailor (*Brit.*); custom tailor (*Amer.*)

**Maß·stab** *der* Ⓐ standard; **einen hohen ~ anlegen/setzen** apply/set a high standard; **sich** (*Dat.*) **jmdn./etw. zum ~ nehmen** take sb./sth. as one's model; Ⓑ (*Geogr.*) scale; **diese Karte hat einen großen/kleinen ~:** this is a large-/small-scale map; **den ~ 1:150 000 haben** be drawn to a scale of 1: 150,000; **im ~ 1:100** to a scale of 1:100; Ⓒ (*Zollstock*) rule; (*Lineal*) ruler

**maßstäblich** /'-ʃtɛ:plɪç/, **maßstab[s]gerecht, maßstab[s]·getreu** ❶ *Adj.* scale *attrib.* ‹model, drawing, etc.›; [true] to scale *pred.;* ❷ *adv.* to scale

**maß-, Maß-: ~system** *das* system of measuring units; **~voll** ❶ *Adj.* moderate; ❷ *adv.* in moderation; **~voll urteilen** be moderate in one's judgements; **~vorlage** *die* (*Fußballjargon*) accurate pass; **~werk** *das* (*Archit.*) tracery

**Mast¹** /mast/ *der;* **~[e]s, ~en,** *auch:* **~e** (*Schiffs~, Antennen~*) mast; (*Stange, Fahnen~*) pole; (*Hochspannungs~*) pylon

**Mast²** *die;* **~, ~en** (*Landw.*) fattening; **für die ~ geeignet** suitable for fattening

**Mast-: ~baum** *der* mast; **~bulle** *der* (*gemästet*) fattened bull; (*für die ~ vorgesehen*) fattening bull; **~darm** *der* ▶ 471 (*Anat.*) rectum

**mästen** /'mɛstn̩/ *tr. V.* fatten; (*fig. ugs.*) overfeed; **sich ~** (*ugs.*) fatten oneself up

**Mast·futter** *das* fattening feed[stuff]

**Mastiff** /'mastɪf/ *der;* **~s, ~s** (*Zool.*) mastiff

**Mast-: ~korb** *der* crow's-nest; **~schwein** *das* (*gemästet*) fattened pig; (*für die ~ vorgesehen*) fattening pig

**Mästung** *die;* **~:** fattening

**Masturbation** /masturba'tsi̯o:n/ *die;* **~, ~en** masturbation

**masturbieren** /mastur'bi:rən/ *itr., tr. V.* masturbate

m

**Matador** /mata'do:ɐ̯/ *der;* **~s**, **~e**, **Matadorin** *die;* **~**, **~nen** (A) matador; (B) (*fig.*) star

**Match** /mɛtʃ/ *das od. der;* **~[e]s**, **~s** *od.* **~e** match

**Match-: ~ball** *der* ([*Tisch*]*tennis*) match point; **~beutel** *der*, **~sack** *der* duffle bag

**Mate** /'ma:tə/ *der;* **~**, **Mate·tee** *der* maté

**Mater** /'ma:tɐ/ *die;* **~**, **~n** (*Druckw.*) ⇒ **Matrize**

**material** *Adj.* (*Philos.*) material

**Material** /mate'ri̯a:l/ *das;* **~s**, **~ien** (A) material; (*Bau~*) materials *pl.*; (B) (*Hilfsmittel, Utensilien*) materials *pl.*; (*für den Bau*) equipment; **das rollende ~** (*Eisenb.*) the rolling stock; (C) (*Beweis~*) evidence

**Material-: ~aus·gabe** *die* (A) issue of materials; (B) (*Raum*) stores *pl.*; storeroom; **~beschaffung** *die* obtaining of materials; (*Kauf*) purchasing of materials; **~fehler** *der* material defect

**Materialisation** /materializa'tsi̯o:n/ *die;* **~**, **~en** (*Parapsych.*, *Physik*) materialization

**materialisieren** *tr.*, *refl. V.* (*Parapsych.*, *Physik*) materialize

**Materialismus** *der;* **~** (*auch abwertend*) materialism

**Materialist** *der;* **~en**, **~en**, **Materialistin** *die;* **~**, **~nen** (*auch abwertend*) materialist

**materialistisch** (*auch abwertend*) ❶ *Adj.* materialistic. ❷ *adv.* materialistically

**Materialität** /materi̯ali'tɛ:t/ *die;* **~** (*Philos.*) materiality

**Material-: ~kosten** *Pl.* cost *sing.* of materials; **~prüfung** *die* materials testing; **~prüfungen** tests on materials; **~sammlung** *die* collection *or* gathering of material; **~schlacht** *die* (*Milit.*) battle of matériel

**Materie** /ma'te:ri̯ə/ *die;* **~**, **~n** (A) (*geh.*) subject; (B) (*Physik, Philos.*) matter

**materiell** /mate'ri̯ɛl/ ❶ *Adj.* (A) (*stofflich*) material; physical; (B) (*wirtschaftlich*) material ‹value, damage›; (*finanziell*) financial; (C) (*abwertend: materialistisch*) materialistic. ❷ *adv.* (A) (*wirtschaftlich*) materially; (*finanziell*) financially; (B) (*abwertend*) materialistically; **~ eingestellt sein** be materialistic

**Mate·tee** *der* ⇒ **Mate**

**Mathe** /'matə/ *die;* **~** (*ugs.*) maths *sing.* (*Brit. coll.*); math (*Amer. coll.*)

**Mathe·arbeit** *die* (*ugs.*) maths test (*coll.*)

**Mathematik** /matəma'ti:k/ *die;* **~**: mathematics *sing.*, *no art.*

**Mathematiker** *der;* **~s**, **~**, **Mathematikerin** *die;* **~**, **~nen** ▶ **159** mathematician

**Mathematik·unterricht** *der* mathematics teaching/lesson; ⇒ *auch* **Englischunterricht**

**mathematisch** ❶ *Adj.* mathematical. ❷ *adv.* mathematically

**Matinee** /mati'ne:/ *die;* **~**, **~n** morning performance

**Matjes** /'matjəs/ *der;* **~**, **~**: matie [herring]

**Matjes-: ~filet** *das* filleted matie [herring]; **~hering** *der* salted matie [herring]

**Matratze** /ma'tratsə/ *die;* **~**, **~n** mattress; **er horcht an der ~** (*fig. scherzh.*) he's [in bed] having a kip (*Brit. coll.*) *or* (*coll.*) snooze

**Matratzen·lager** *das* mattress/mattresses on the floor

**Mätresse** /mɛ'trɛsə/ *die;* **~**, **~n** (*geh. veralt.*) mistress

**matriarchalisch** /matriar'ça:lɪʃ/ *Adj.* matriarchal

**Matriarchat** /matriar'ça:t/ *das;* **~[e]s**, **~e** matriarchy

**Matrikel** /ma'tri:kl̩/ *die;* **~**, **~n** (A) (*Hochschulw.*) student register; (B) (*österr.: Personenstandsregister*) register of births, deaths, and marriages

**Matrix** /'ma:trɪks/ *die;* **~**, **Matrizes** /ma'tri:tse:s/ (*Biol.*, *Math.*, *Sprachw.*) matrix

**Matrize** /ma'tri:tsə/ *die;* **~**, **~n** (*Druckw.*) (A) matrix; (B) (*Folie*) stencil; **einen Text auf ~** (*Akk.*) **schreiben** make a stencil of a text

**Matrone** /ma'tro:nə/ *die;* **~**, **~n** matron

**matronenhaft** (*abwertend*) ❶ *Adj.* matronly. ❷ *adv.* in a matronly manner *or* fashion

**Matrose** /ma'tro:zə/ *der;* **~n**, **~n** ▶ **159** (A) sailor; seaman; (B) (*Dienstgrad*) ordinary seaman

**Matrosen-: ~an·zug** *der* sailor suit; **~mütze** *die* sailor's cap

**Matsch** *der;* **~[e]s** (*ugs.*), **Matsche** /'matʃə/ *die;* **~e** (*nordd.*) (A) (*aufgeweichter Boden*) mud; (*breiiger Schmutz*) sludge; (*Schnee~*) slush; (B) (*Brei*) mush

**matschen** *itr. V.* (*ugs.*) **in etw.** (*Dat.*) **~**: splash about in sth.; **im Essen ~**: mess about with one's food

**matschig** *Adj.* (*ugs.*) (A) muddy; slushy ‹snow›; (B) (*weich*) mushy; squashy ‹fruit›

**Matsch·wetter** *das* (*ugs.*) **bei diesem ~**: when it's muddy like this; (*bei Schneematsch*) when it's slushy like this; **dieses widerliche ~**: this revolting weather, when there's mud/slush everywhere

**matt** /mat/ ❶ *Adj.* (A) weak; weary ‹limbs, spirit, etc.›; weak, faint ‹voice, smile, pulse›; feeble ‹applause, reaction›; limp, feeble ‹handshake›; faint ‹echo›; **vor Hunger/Durst ~ sein** be faint *or* weak with hunger/thirst; **sich ~ fühlen** feel weak and listless; **ein ~es Echo finden** find a lukewarm response; (B) (*glanzlos*) matt ‹paper, polish, etc.›; dull ‹metal, mirror, etc.›; dull, lustreless ‹eyes, look›; (C) (*undurchsichtig*) frosted ‹glass›; pearl ‹lightbulb›; (D) (*gedämpft*) soft, subdued ‹light›; soft, pale ‹colour›; (E) (*unbeherzt, nicht überzeugend*) feeble; weak; feeble, lame ‹excuse, joke›; (F) (*beim Schachspiel*) **[Schach und] ~!** checkmate!; **~ sein** be checkmated; **jmdn. ~ setzen** (*auch fig.*) checkmate sb.
❷ *adv.* (A) (*kraftlos*) weakly; ‹smile› weakly, faintly; ‹applaud, react› feebly; (B) (*gedämpft*) softly ‹lit›; **der Mond schien ~ durch die Bäume** the moon shone wanly through the trees; (C) (*mäßig*) ‹protest, contradict› feebly, weakly

**Matt** *das;* **~s** (*Schach*) [check]mate

**matt·blau** *Adj.* pale blue

**Matte**[1] /'matə/ *die;* **~**, **~n** (*auch Sport*) mat; **um 7 Uhr hier/dort auf der ~ stehen** (*fig. ugs.*) be here/there at 7 o'clock; **bei jmdm. auf der ~ stehen** (*fig. ugs.*) turn up on sb.'s doorstep

**Matte**[2] *die;* **~**, **~n** (*schweiz.*, *dichter. veralt.*) meadow

**Matt-: ~glas** *das* frosted glass; (*Fot.*) ground glass; **~gold** *das* dull gold

**Matthäi** /ma'tɛ:i/ *in* **bei ihm ist ~ am Letzten** (*ugs.*) it's all up with him; (*finanziell*) he hasn't got a penny to his name

**Matthäus** /ma'tɛ:ʊs/ (*der*); **Matthäus'** Matthew

**Matthäus·evangelium** *das* St Matthew's Gospel; the Gospel according to St Matthew

**mattieren** *tr. V.* give a matt finish to; matt; frost ‹glass›

**Mattigkeit** *die;* **~** (*Schwäche*) weakness; (*Erschöpfung*) weariness

**Matt-: ~lack** *der* matt varnish; **~scheibe** *die* (A) (*ugs.*) telly (*Brit. coll.*); box (*coll.*); (B) (*Fot.*) matt screen; ground-glass screen; **ich habe ~scheibe** (*fig. ugs.*) I'm not with it (*coll.*)

**Matur** /ma'tu:ɐ̯/ *die;* **~** (*schweiz.*), **Matura** *die;* **~a** (*österr.*, *schweiz.*) ⇒ **Abitur**

**Maturand** /matu'rant/ *der;* **~en**, **~en**, **Maturandin** *die;* **~**, **~nen** (*schweiz.*) ⇒ **Abiturient, Abiturientin**

**Maturant** /matu'rant/ *der;* **~en**, **~en**, **Maturantin** *die;* **~**, **~nen** (*österr.*) ⇒ **Abiturient, Abiturientin**

**Maturität** /maturi'tɛ:t/ *die;* **~** (A) (*veralt.: Reife*) maturity; (B) (*schweiz.*) ⇒ **Abitur**

**Matz** /mats/ *der;* **~es**, **~e** *od.* **Mätze** /'mɛtsə/ (*fam.*) **kleiner ~**: little man

**Mätzchen** /'mɛtsçən/ *das;* **~s**, **~** (*ugs.*) (*Posse*) antic; (*Kniff*) trick; **lasst die ~**: stop fooling about *or* around; stop your antics; **~ machen** fool about *or* around; **Hände hoch, und keine ~!** (*salopp*) stick 'em up, and no tricks! (*coll.*)

**Matze** /'matsə/ *die;* **~**, **~n**, **Matzen** /'matsn̩/ *der;* **~s**, **~**: matzo

**mau** /mau̯/ (*ugs.*) ❶ *Adj.* (*flau*) queasy; (*unwohl*) poorly. ❷ *adv.* badly; **die Geschäfte gehen ~**: business is bad

**mauen** *itr. V.* (*südwestd.*, *schweiz.*) miaow

**Mauer** /'mau̯ɐ/ *die;* **~**, **~n** (*auch Sport*) wall; **in den ~n einer Stadt** (*geh.*) in a town/city; **die [Berliner] ~** (*hist.*) the [Berlin] Wall; **die Chinesische ~**: the Great Wall of China; **eine ~ des Schweigens** (*fig.*) a wall of silence

**Mauer-: ~absatz** *der* offset; **~arbeit** *die* ⇒ **Maurerarbeit**; **~bau** *der* construction *or* building of the wall/walls; (*Bau der Berliner Mauer*) building of the Wall; **~blümchen** *das* (*ugs.*) (*beim Tanz*) wallflower (*coll.*); (*unscheinbares Mädchen, auch fig.*) Cinderella; **~brecher** *der* (*hist.*) battering ram; **~kelle** *die* ⇒ **Maurerkelle**; **~krone** *die* coping [of a/the wall]

**mauern** ❶ *tr. V.* build; **ein gemauerter Schornstein** a brick chimney. ❷ *itr. V.* (A) lay bricks; (B) (*Sportjargon*) (*Ballspiele*) play defensively; (*Kricket, fig.*) stonewall; (C) (*Kartenspiele*) hold back one's good cards

**Mauer-: ~schwalbe** *die*, **~segler** *der* swift; **~stein** *der* building brick; **~verband** *der* (*Bauw.*) masonry bond; **~vorsprung** *der* projecting section of a/the wall; **~werk** *das* (A) (*aus Stein*) stonework; masonry; (*aus Ziegeln*) brickwork; (B) (*~n*) walls *pl.*; **~ziegel** *der* [building] brick

**Mauke** /'maukə/ *die;* **~**, **~n** (*Tiermed.*) mallenders *pl.*

**Mauken** *Pl.* (*berlin. salopp*) hooves (*coll.*); feet

**Maul** /maul/ *das;* **~[e]s**, **Mäuler** /'mɔylɐ/ (A) (*von Tieren*) mouth; (B) (*derb: Mund*) gob (*sl.*); **ein freches** *od.* **loses ~ haben** have a cheeky tongue; **ein gottloses ~ haben** have an insolent tongue; **jmdn. aufs ~ hauen** smack sb. in the gob (*sl.*); **er hat fünf hungrige Mäuler zu stopfen** (*fig.*) he's got five hungry mouths to feed; **das** *od.* **sein ~ aufmachen** (*fig.*) say something; **dein/sein** *usw.* **ungewaschenes ~** (*fig.*) your/his *etc.* filthy trap (*sl.*) *or* mouth; **das ~ aufreißen** *od.* **voll nehmen, ein großes ~ haben** (*fig.*) shoot one's mouth off (*fig. sl.*); **sich** (*Dat.*) **das ~ [über jmdn.] zerreißen** (*fig.*) gossip maliciously [about sb.]; **ein schiefes ~ ziehen** (*fig.*) pull a long face; **das ~ halten** keep one's trap shut (*sl.*); **halts** *od.* **halt dein ~**: shut your trap (*sl.*); shut up (*coll.*); **das** *od.* **sein ~ nicht aufkriegen** (*fig.*) not dare [to] open one's mouth; **jmdm. übers ~ fahren** (*fig.*) cut sb. short; ⇒ *auch* **stopfen** 1 D; **verbrennen** 2 B

**Maul-: ~affe** *der* (A) *in* **~n feilhalten** (*abwertend*) stand gaping *or* (*coll.*) gawping; (B) (*veralt.*) gaping fool; **~beer·baum** *der* mulberry tree; **~beere** *die* mulberry

**maulen** *itr. V.* (*salopp*) grouse (*coll.*); moan; grumble

**maul-**, **Maul-: ~esel** *der* mule; (*Zool.*) hinny; **~faul** *Adj.* (*ugs. abwertend*) uncommunicative; taciturn; **sei doch nicht so ~faul!** come on, haven't you got any more to say for yourself than that?; **~held** *der* (*ugs. abwertend*) loudmouth; braggart

**Maul·korb** *der* (*auch fig.*) muzzle; **einem Hund/**(*fig.*) **jmdm. einen ~ anlegen** muzzle a dog/sb.; **einen ~ tragen** (*auch fig.*) be muzzled

**Maulkorb·erlass**, ***Maulkorb·erlaß** *der* (*ugs.*) decree muzzling freedom of speech

**Maul-: ~schelle** *die* (*ugs. veralt.*) slap round the face; **~schlüssel** *der* open-ended spanner; **~sperre** *die* (*salopp*) **die ~sperre kriegen** *od.* **bekommen** (*fig.*) gape in surprise; **~tasche** *die* (*Kochk.*) *filled pasta case served in soup*; **~tier** *das* mule; **~trommel** *die* Jew's harp; **~- und Klauen·seuche** *die* (*Tiermed.*) foot-and-mouth disease

**Maul·wurf** *der* mole

**Maulwurfs-: ~haufen** *der*, **~hügel** *der* molehill

**Mau-Mau** /mau̯'mau̯/ *das;* **~[s]** (*Kartenspiele*) Mau-Mau

*old spelling (see note on page 1707)

**maunzen** /'mauntsn̩/ *itr. V.* (*ugs.*) ‹cat› miaow plaintively; ‹baby› mewl
**Maure** /'maurə/ *der;* ~**n**, ~**n** Moor
**Maurer** /'maurɐ/ *der;* ~**s**, ~ ▶ 159 bricklayer; **pünktlich wie die** ~ (*ugs. scherzh.*) bang on time (*coll.*)
**Maurer-:** ~**arbeit** *die* bricklaying [work] *no pl.;* ~**geselle** *der* journeyman bricklayer; ~**handwerk** *das* bricklaying [trade]
**Maurerin** *die;* ~, ~**nen** ▶ 159 ⇒ **Maurer**
**Maurer-:** ~**kelle** *die* brick/layer's/ trowel; ~**kolonne** *die* bricklaying gang; ~**meister** *der* master bricklayer; ~**polier** *der* foreman bricklayer
**Mauretanien** /maure'ta:ni̯ən/ (*das*); ~**s** Mauritania
**Mauretanier** /maure'ta:ni̯ɐ/ *der;* ~**s**, ~, **Mauretanierin** *die;* ~, ~**nen** Mauritanian
**Maurin** *die;* ~, ~**nen** ⇒ **Maure**
**Mauritius** /mau'ri:tsi̯ʊs/ (*das*); **Mauritius'** Mauritius
**Maus** /maus/ *die;* ~, **Mäuse** /'mɔyzə/ **A** mouse; **da beißt die** ~ **keinen Faden ab** (*ugs.*) there's nothing to be done about it; **die weißen Mäuse** (*fig. ugs. scherzh.*) the traffic police; **weiße Mäuse sehen** (*fig. ugs.*) see pink elephants; **eine graue** ~ (*fig. ugs. abwertend*) a colourless nondescript sort of [a] person; ⇒ *auch* **Katze**; **B** *Pl.* (*salopp: Geld*) bread *sing.* (*coll.*); dough *sing.* (*coll.*); **ein paar Mäuse** a few marks/quid (*Brit. coll.*)/ bucks (*Amer. sl.*) *etc.*
**Mauschelei** *die;* ~, ~**en** (*ugs. abwertend*) shady wheeling and dealing *no indef. art.*
**mauscheln** /'mauʃl̩n/ *itr. V.* (*ugs. abwertend*) engage in shady wheeling and dealing; **da wird viel gemauschelt** a lot of shady wheeling and dealing goes on there
**Mauscheln** *das;* ~**s** *card game similar to four-card loo*
**Mäuschen** /'mɔysçən/ *das;* ~**s**, ~ **A** little mouse; ~ **sein** *od.* **spielen** (*fig. ugs.*) be a fly on the wall (*coll.*); **B** (*fig. ugs.*) **mein** ~**:** my sweet
**mäuschen·still** **1** *Adj.* ~ **sein** ‹person› be as quiet as a mouse; **es war** ~**:** it was so quiet you could have heard a pin drop. **2** *adv.* ~ **dort sitzen bleiben/sich** ~ **verhalten** sit there/keep as quiet as a mouse
**Mäuse·bussard** *der* (*Zool.*) [common] buzzard
**Mause-:** ~**falle** *die* mousetrap; (*fig.*) trap; ~**loch** *das* mousehole; **ich hätte mich am liebsten in ein** ~**loch verkrochen** (*ugs.*) I wished the ground would open and swallow me up
**Mäuse·melken** *das: in* **es ist zum** ~ (*ugs.*) it's enough to send *or* drive you up the wall (*coll.*)
**mausen** **1** *tr. V.* (*ugs. veralt.*) pinch (*coll.*). **2** *itr. V.* (*veralt.: Mäuse fangen*) catch mice; mouse
**Mauser** *die;* ~**:** moult; **in der** ~ **sein** be moulting
**Mäuserich** /'mɔyzərɪç/ *der;* ~**s**, ~**e** (*ugs.*) [male] mouse
**mausern** *refl. V.* moult; **sich zur Dame** ~ (*fig. ugs.*) blossom into a lady
**Mauser·pistole** *die* Mauser [pistol]
**mause·tot** *Adj.* (*ugs.*) [as] dead as a doornail *pred.;* stone dead
**Mause·zähnchen** *Pl.* (*Handarb.*) picot edging *sing.*
**maus·grau** *Adj.* mouse-grey
**mausig** *Adj. in* **sich** ~ **machen** (*salopp*) be cheeky and make a nuisance of oneself
**Mausklick** *der;* ~**s**, ~**s** (*DV*) mouse click
**Mäuslein** /'mɔyslain/ *das;* ~**s**, ~ ⇒ **Mäuschen**
**Mausoleum** /mauzo'le:ʊm/ *das;* ~**s**, **Mausoleen** mausoleum
**Maus:** ~**taste** *die* (*DV*) mouse button; **m**~**tot** *Adj.* (*österr.*) ⇒ **mausetot**; ~**zeiger** *der* (*DV*) mouse pointer
**Maut** /maut/ *die;* ~, ~**en** toll; ~ **bezahlen/ erheben** pay/levy a toll
**Maut-:** ~**gebühr** *die* toll; ~**straße** *die* toll road

**m.a.W.** *Abk.* **mit anderen Worten** in other words
**Max** /maks/ *in* **strammer** ~ (*Kochk.*) fried egg on ham and bread
**Maxi** *das;* ~**s**, ~**s** (*Mode*) maxi (*coll.*); **im** ~**:** in a maxi (*coll.*); **ein Rock in** ~**:** a maxi-length skirt; ~ **tragen** wear a maxi (*coll.*)
**maximal** /maksi'ma:l/ **1** *Adj.* maximum. **2** *adv.* ~ **zulässige Geschwindigkeit** maximum permitted speed; **bis zu** ~ **85 °C/ 20 t** up to a maximum of 85 °C/20 t; **dieses Boot ist für** ~ **vier Personen zugelassen** this boat is licensed to carry a maximum of four people
**Maximal-:** ~**forderung** *die* maximum demand; ~**wert** *der* maximum value
**Maxime** /ma'ksi:mə/ *die;* ~, ~**n** maxim
**maximieren** *tr. V.* maximize
**Maximierung** *die;* ~, ~**en** maximization
**Maximum** /'maksimʊm/ *das;* ~**s**, **Maxima** maximum (**an** + *Dat.* of)
**Maxi·single** *die* maxi-single
**Mayonnaise** /majɔ'nɛ:zə/ *die;* ~, ~**n** mayonnaise
**MAZ** /mats/ *die;* ~ (*Ferns.*) VTR
**Mazedonien** /matse'do:ni̯ən/ ⇒ **Makedonien**
**Mäzen** /mɛ'tse:n/ *der;* ~**s**, ~**e** (*geh.*) patron
**Mäzenatentum** /mɛtse'na:tn̩tu:m/ *das;* ~**s** (*geh.*) patronage
**Mäzenin** *die;* ~, ~**nen** (*geh.*) patron[ess]
**Mazurka** /ma'zʊrka/ *die;* ~, **Mazurken** *u.* ~**s** mazurka
**MdB, M.d.B.** *Abk.* **Mitglied des Bundestages** Member of the Bundestag
**MdL, M.d.L.** *Abk.* **Mitglied des Landtages** Member of the Landtag
**MdNR** *Abk.* **Mitglied des Nationalrates** (*Österr.*) Member of the Nationalrat
**MdV, M.d.V.** *Abk.* **Mitglied der Volkskammer** (*DDR*) Member of the Volkskammer
**m.E.** *Abk.* **meines Erachtens**
**Mechanik** /me'ça:nɪk/ *die;* ~ **A** (*Physik*) mechanics *sing., no art.;* **B** (*Bauelement*) mechanism; (*eines Klaviers*) action; **C** (*Funktion*) mechanics *sing. or pl.*
**Mechaniker** *der;* ~**s**, ~, **Mechanikerin** *die;* ~, ~**nen** ▶ 159 mechanic
**mechanisch** **1** *Adj.* mechanical; power *attrib.* ‹loom, press›. **2** *adv.* mechanically
**mechanisieren** *tr. V.* mechanize
**Mechanisierung** *die;* ~**:** mechanization
**Mechanismus** *der;* ~, **Mechanismen** (*auch fig.*) mechanism; (*fig.: einer Organisation, Bürokratie*) machinery
**meck** /mɛk/ (*Interj.*) me-e-eh (*of goat*)
**Mecker·ecke** *die* (*ugs.*) grumbles section (*Brit. coll.*); complaints column
**Meckerei** *die;* ~, ~**en** (*ugs. abwertend*) moaning; grousing (*sl.*); grumbling
**Meckerer** *der;* ~**s**, ~ (*ugs. abwertend*) moaner; grouser (*sl.*); grumbler
**Mecker·fritze** *der* (*salopp abwertend*) grouser (*sl.*); moaner; grumbler
**Meckerin** *die;* ~, ~**nen** ⇒ **Meckerer**
**Mecker·liese** *die* (*salopp abwertend*) moaning Minnie (*Brit. coll.*); grouser (*sl.*); grouch (*coll.*)
**meckern** /'mɛkɐn/ *itr. V.* **A** (*auch fig.*) bleat; **B** (*ugs. abwertend: nörgeln*) grumble; moan; grouse (*sl.*); **etw. zu** ~ **haben** have sth. to grumble *etc.* about
**Mecklenburg** /'me:klənbʊrk/ (*das*); ~**s** Mecklenburg
**mecklenburgisch** *Adj.* Mecklenburg *attrib.;* ⇒ *auch* **badisch**
**Mecklenburg-Vorpommer** *der;* ~**n**, ~**n**, **Mecklenburg-Vorpommerin** Mecklenburg-West Pomeranian
**mecklenburg-vorpommerisch** *Adj.* Mecklenburg-West Pomeranian
**Mecklenburg-Vorpommern** (*das*); ~**s** Mecklenburg-West Pomerania
**med.** *Abk.* **medizinisch** med.
**Medaille** /me'daljə/ *die;* ~, ~**n** medal; ⇒ *auch* **Kehrseite A**

**Medaillen-:** ~**gewinner** *der,* ~**gewinnerin** *die* medallist; medal winner; ~**spiegel** *der* medal table
**Medaillon** /medal'jõ:/ *das;* ~**s**, ~**s** **A** locket; **B** (*Kochk., bild. Kunst*) medallion
**Media-** /'mɛ:di̯a-/ (*Werbespr.*) ⇒ **Medien-**
**medial** /me'di̯a:l/ *Adj.* (*Parapsych.*) mediumistic
**Mediävist** /medi̯ɛ'vɪst/ *der;* ~**en**, ~**en** medievalist
**Mediävistik** *die;* ~**:** medieval studies *pl., no art.*
**Mediävistin** *die;* ~, ~**nen** medievalist
**medien-, Medien-:** ~**fachfrau** *die,* ~**fachmann** *der* media expert; ~**forschung** *die* media research; ~**konzern** *der* media concern; ~**landschaft** *die* media scene; ~**politik** *die* media policy; ~**politisch** *Adj.* media-policy *attrib.* ‹spokesman, measure, etc.›; ~ **präsenz** *die* media presence; ~**verbund** *der* **A** (*für den Unterricht*) multimedia system; **im** ~**verbund** using the multimedia system; **B** (*kommerziell*) media syndicate; (*Ergebnis einer Fusion*) media group
**Medikament** /medika'mɛnt/ *das;* ~**[e]s**, ~**e** medicine; (*Droge*) drug; **ein** ~ **gegen Kopfschmerzen** a remedy for headaches
**Medikamenten·schrank** *der* medicine cabinet
**medikamentös** /medikamɛn'tø:s/ **1** *Adj.* ‹treatment› with drugs. **2** *adv.* ‹treat, cure› with drugs
**Medikus** /'me:dikʊs/ *der;* ~, **Medizi** /'me:ditsi/ (*scherzh.*) doctor; doc (*coll.*)
**medioker** /me'di̯o:kɐ/ *Adj.* (*geh.*) mediocre
**Mediothek** /medi̯o'te:k/ *die;* ~, ~**en** audio-visual library
**Meditation** /medita'tsi̯o:n/ *die;* ~, ~**en** meditation
**Meditations·übung** *die* meditation exercise
**meditativ** /medita'ti:f/ (*geh.*) **1** *Adj.* meditative. **2** *adv.* through meditation
**mediterran** /meditɛ'ra:n/ *Adj.* Mediterranean
**meditieren** /medi'ti:rən/ *itr. V.* meditate (**über** + *Akk.* [up]on)
**Medium** /'me:di̯ʊm/ *das;* ~**s**, **Medien** medium; **das** ~ **Presse** the medium of the press
**Medizin** /medi'tsi:n/ *die;* ~, ~**en** **A** medicine *no art.;* **B** (*Heilmittel*) medicine (**gegen** for); **eine bittere** ~ **für jmdn. sein** (*fig.*) be a bitter pill for sb. to swallow
**Medizinal-** /meditsi'na:l-/**:** ~**assistent** *der* house officer (*Brit.*); houseman (*Brit.*); intern (*Amer.*); ~**assistentin** *die* house officer (*Brit.*); intern (*Amer.*); ~**rat** *der,* ~**rätin** *die* ≈ medical officer
**Medizin·ball** *der* (*Sport*) medicine ball
**Mediziner** /medi'tsi:nɐ/ *der;* ~**s**, ~, **Medizinerin** *die;* ~, ~**nen** ▶ 159 doctor; (*Student*) medical student; **seine Brüder sind alle** ~**:** his brothers are all medical men
**medizinisch** **1** *Adj.* **A** medical ‹journal, problem, etc.›; ~**e Fakultät** faculty of medicine; **B** (*heilend*) medicinal ‹bath etc.›; medicated ‹toothpaste, soap, etc.›. **2** *adv.* medically
**medizinisch-technisch** *Adj.* ~**e Assistentin** medical laboratory assistant
**Medizin-:** ~**mann** *der* medicine man; ~**schränkchen** *das* medicine cabinet; ~**student** *der,* ~**studentin** *die* medical student
**Meduse** /me'du:zə/ *die;* ~, ~**n** **A** (*Myth.*) Medusa; **B** (*Zool.*) medusa (*Zool.*); jellyfish
**Medusen·haupt** *das* **A** (*geh.*) head of Medusa; **B** ▶ 474 (*Med.*) caput medusae; cirsomphalos
**Meer** /me:ɐ̯/ *das;* ~**[e]s**, ~**e** **A** (*auch fig.*) sea; (*Weltmeer*) ocean; **die sieben** ~**e** the seven seas; **ans** ~ **fahren** go to the seaside; **am** ~**:** by the sea; **im** ~**:** in the sea; **aufs** ~ **hinausfahren** go out to sea; **übers** ~ **fahren** cross the sea; **1000 m über dem** ~**:** 1000 m above sealevel
**Meer-:** ~**busen** *der* gulf; **der Finnische/ Bottnische** ~**busen** the Gulf of Finland/ Bothnia; ~**enge** *die* straits *pl.;* strait

m

**Meeres-:** ~**algen** *Pl.* marine algae; ~**biologie** *die* marine biology *no art.;* ~**boden** *der* sea bed *or* bottom *or* floor; ~**bucht** *die* bay; ~**fauna** *die* marine fauna; ~**flora** *die* marine flora; ~**forschung** *die* marine research; ~**früchte** *Pl.* (*Kochk.*) seafood *sing.;* **ein Salat mit ~früchten** a seafood salad; ~**grund** *der* ⇨ ~**boden**; ~**klima** *das* maritime climate; ~**kunde** *die* oceanography *no art.;* ~**luft** *die* (*Met.*) maritime air; ~**oberfläche** *die* surface of the sea; ~**rauschen** *das;* ~~**s** sound of the sea; ~**spiegel** *der* sealevel; **200 m über/unter dem ~spiegel** 200 m above/below sealevel; ~**strand** *der* (*geh., dichter.*) seashore; strand (*poet.*); ~**straße** *die* straits *pl.;* strait; ~**strömung** *die* current; (*im Weltmeer*) ocean current; ~**tiefe** *die* depth of the sea; (*im Weltmeer*) depth of the ocean; ~**ufer** *das* shore

**meer-, Meer-:** ~**forelle** *die* salmon *or* sea trout; ~**gott** *der* sea god; ~**göttin** *die* sea goddess; ~**grün** *Adj.* sea-green; ~**jungfrau** *die* mermaid; ~**katze** *die* guenon; ~**rettich** *der* horseradish; ~**salz** *das* sea salt; ~**schaum** *der* meerschaum; ~**schaumpfeife** *die* meerschaum [pipe]; ~**schweinchen** *das* guinea pig; ~**ungeheuer** *das* (*Myth.*) sea monster; ~**wasser** *das* sea water

**Meeting** /'mi:tɪŋ/ *das;* ~**s**, ~**s** meeting

**mega-, Mega-** /mɛga-/ mega-

**Mega·hertz** *das* (*Phys.*) megahertz

**Megalith** /mɛga'li:t/ *der;* ~**s** *od.* ~**en**, ~**e[n]** megalith

**Megalith·grab** *das* megalithic tomb

**megaloman** /megalo'ma:n/ *Adj.* (*Psych.*) megalomaniac[al]; ~ **sein** be a megalomaniac

**Megalomanie** *die* (*Psych.*) megalomania *no art.*

**Megaphon** *das;* ~**s**, ~**e** megaphone; loud hailer

**Megäre** /me'gɛ:rə/ *die;* ~, ~**n** (*geh.*) fury

**Mega-:** ~**tonne** *die* megaton[ne]; ~**tote** *der* (*milit. Jargon*) mega death; ~**watt** *das* (*Physik*) megawatt

**Mehl** /me:l/ *das;* ~**[e]s** **A** flour; (*gröber*) meal; **B** (*Pulver*) powder; (*Knochen*~, *Fisch*~) meal

**Mehl-:** ~**beere** *die* whitebeam; ~**brei** *der* flour [and water/milk] paste

**mehlig** *Adj.* **A** floury; **B** (*wie Mehl*) powdery ‹sand etc.›; **C** (*nicht saftig*) mealy ‹potato, apple, etc.›

**Mehl-:** ~**sack** *der* (*Sack für* ~) flour sack; (*Sack voll* ~) sack of flour; **wie ein ~sack hinfallen** fall like a sack of potatoes; ~**schwalbe** *die* house martin; ~**schwitze** *die* (*Kochk.*) roux; ~**speise** *die* **A** *dish with flour as the main ingredient;* **B** (*österr.*) sweet; dessert; (*Kuchen*) cake; ~**tau** *der* mildew; ~**wurm** *der* mealworm

**mehr** /me:ɐ̯/ **1** *Indefinitpron.* more; ~ **als genug** more than enough; ~ **als die Hälfte** more than half; **ein Grund ~, es zu tun** one more *or* an additional reason for doing it; **das war ~ als unverschämt** that was impertinent, to say the very least; **das schmeckt nach ~** (*ugs.*) it's very moreish (*coll.*); ~ **nicht?** is that all?; ~ **und ~:** more and more; ~ **oder minder** *od.* **weniger** more or less.
**2** *adv.* **A** (*in größerem Maße*) more; **das sagt ihr ~ zu** it appeals to her more; she likes it better; **B** (*eher*) ~ **tot als lebendig** more dead than alive; ~ **schlecht als recht** after a fashion; **er ist ~ Künstler als Gelehrter** he is more of an artist than a scholar; **C** (+ *Negation*) **es war niemand ~ da** there was no one left; **es hat sich keiner ~ gemeldet** there was not another word from anyone; **ich erinnere mich nicht ~:** I no longer remember; **nicht ~ über etw.** (*Akk.*) **sprechen** not discuss sth. any more *or* further; **das wird nie ~ vorkommen** it will never happen again; **davon will ich nichts ~ hören** I don't want to hear any more about it; **da ist nichts ~ zu machen** there is nothing more to be done; **ich habe keine Lust/kein Interesse ~:** I have lost all desire/interest; **du bist doch kein Kind ~:** you're no longer a child; you're not a child any more; **er musste nicht ~ an die Front** he never had to go to the front; **sie hat ihren Großvater nicht ~ gekannt** she never had the chance to know her grandfather; **D** (*südd.*) **nur ~ 5 Mark** only 5 marks

**Mehr** *das;* ~**s** increase (**an** + *Dat.* in); **mit einem ~ an Zeit** with more time

**mehr-, Mehr-:** ~**arbeit** *die* extra *or* additional work; (*Überstunden*) overtime; **das bedeutet ~arbeit für mich** that means more *or* extra work for me; ~**aufwand** *der* additional expenditure *no pl.;* ~**ausgabe** *die* additional expenditure *no pl.;* ~**bändig** *Adj.* in several volumes *postpos.;* ~**bedarf** *der* (*Wirtsch.*) increased demand (**an** + *Dat.* for); ~**belastung** *die* extra *or* additional burden (*Gen.* on); ~**bereichs·öl** *das* (*Technik*) multi-purpose oil; ~**betrag** *der* extra *or* additional amount; (*Überschuss*) surplus; ~**deutig** **1** *Adj.* ambiguous; **2** *adv.* ambiguously; ~**deutigkeit** *die;* ~~, ~~**en** ambiguity; ~**dimensional** *Adj.* multidimensional; ~**einnahme** *die* additional revenue

**mehren** (*geh.*) **1** *tr. V.* increase. **2** *refl. V.* **A** increase; **diese Vorfälle ~ sich** these incidents are increasing in number; **B** (*veralt.*) **seid fruchtbar und mehret euch** (*bibl.*) be fruitful and multiply

**mehrer...** *Indefinitpron.* **A** *attr.* several; a number of; (*verschieden*) various; several; ~**e hundert/Hundert Bücher** several hundred[s of] books; **B** *allein stehend* ~**e** several people; ~**es** several things *pl.;* **sie kamen zu ~en** several of them came

**mehrerlei** *indekl. unbest. Gattungsz.* (*ugs.*) several [different]; various; *allein stehend* several *or* various things

**Mehr-:** ~**erlös** *der* extra *or* additional proceeds *pl.;* ~**ertrag** *der* additional profit

**mehr·fach** **1** *Adj.* multiple; (*wiederholt*) repeated; **ein Bericht in ~er Ausfertigung** several copies *pl.* of a report; **der ~e deutsche Meister** the player/sprinter *etc.* who has been German champion several times; **ein ~er Millionär** a multimillionaire; **er verdient ein Mehrfaches von dem, was ich bekomme** he earns several times as much as I do. **2** *adv.* several times; (*wiederholt*) repeatedly; ~ **vorbestraft sein** have several previous convictions

**Mehrfach-:** ~**impf·stoff** *der* polyvalent *or* mixed vaccine; ~**spreng·kopf** *der* multiple warhead

**mehr-, Mehr-:** ~**familien·haus** *das* multiple dwelling (*formal*); large house with several flats (*Brit.*) *or* (*Amer.*) apartments; ~**farben·druck** *der* [multi]colour printing; ~**farbig** *Adj.* multicoloured; [multi]colour *attrib.;* ~**gebot** *das* higher bid; ~**geschossig** *Adj.* ⇨ ~**stöckig**; ~**gewicht** *das* additional weight; (*Übergewicht*) excess weight

**Mehrheit** *die;* ~, ~**en** majority; **in der ~ sein** be in the majority; **die ~ haben/erringen** have/win a majority; **die ~ verlieren** lose one's majority; **er wurde mit großer ~ gewählt** he was elected by a large majority; **die ~ der Stimmen auf sich vereinigen** secure a majority of votes; **die/eine absolute ~** (*Politik*) an absolute majority; **die einfache/relative ~** (*Politik*) a simple/relative majority; **eine qualifizierte ~** (*Politik*) a qualified majority

**mehrheitlich** **1** *Adj.* majority; of the majority *postpos.* **2** *adv.* by a majority

**mehrheits-, Mehrheits-:** ~**beschluss**, *~**beschluß** *der*, ~**entscheidung** *die* majority decision; ~**fähig** *Adj.* ~**fähig sein** ‹law› be capable of securing a majority; ‹party› be capable of forming a majority; ~**partei** *die* majority party; ~**prinzip** *das* principle of majority rule; ~**wahlrecht** *das* first-past-the-post electoral system

**mehr-, Mehr-:** ~**jährig** *Adj.* **A** lasting several years *postpos.;* **eine ~jährige Erfahrung** several years' experience; several years of experience; **eine ~jährige Freundschaft** a friendship of several years' standing; **B** (*Bot.*) perennial; ~**kampf** *der* (*Sport*) multi-discipline event; ~**klassig** *Adj.* (*Schulw.*) ‹school› with several classes; ~**kosten** *Pl.* additional *or* extra costs; ~**malig** *Adj.* repeated; ~**mals** *Adv.* several times; (*wiederholt*) repeatedly; ~**parteiensystem** *das* multi-party system; ~**produktion** *die* increased production; (*Überproduktion*) surplus *or* excess production; ~**seitig** *Adj.* consisting of several pages *postpos., not pred.;* several pages long *postpos.;* ~**silbig** *Adj.* polysyllabic; ~**sprachig** *Adj.* multilingual; ~**sprachig aufwachsen** grow up speaking several languages; ~**sprachigkeit** *die;* ~~: multilingualism; ~**stimmig** (*Musik*) **1** *Adj.* for several voices *postpos.;* **ein ~stimmiges Lied** a part-song; **2** *adv.* ~**stimmig singen** sing in harmony; **etwas ~stimmig singen** sing sth. as a part-song; ~**stöckig** **1** *Adj.* several storeys high *postpos.;* (*vielstöckig*) multi-storey; **2** *adv.* ~**stöckig bauen** erect multi-storey buildings/a multi-storey building; ~**stufig** *Adj.* consisting of several steps *postpos., not pred.;* multi-stage ‹rocket›; ~**stündig** *Adj.* lasting several hours *postpos., not pred.;* ‹delay› of several hours; ~**stündige Verhandlungen** several hours of negotiations; ~**tägig** *Adj.* lasting several days *postpos., not pred.;* ~**teiler** *der* serial; (*Dokumentarfilm etc.*) series; ~**teilig** *Adj.* in several parts *postpos.*

**Mehrung** *die;* ~ (*geh.*) increase

**Mehrweg-:** ~**flasche** *die* returnable *or* reusable bottle; ~**verpackung** *die* reusable packaging

**mehr-, Mehr-:** ~**wert** *der* (*Wirtsch.*) surplus value; ~**wert·steuer** *die* ▶ 337 (*Wirtsch.*) value added tax (*Brit.*); VAT (*Brit.*); sales tax (*Amer.*); ~**wöchig** *Adj.* lasting several weeks *postpos., not pred.;* ‹absence› of several weeks; ~**zahl** *die* **A** (*Sprachw.*) plural; **B** (~*heit*) majority; ~**zeilig** *Adj.* of several lines *postpos.*

**Mehr·zweck-:** multi-purpose ...

**meiden** /'maidn̩/ *unr. tr. V.* (*geh.*) avoid

**Meierei** *die;* ~, ~**en** **A** (*hist.*) feudal estate; **B** (*Molkerei*) dairy

**Meile** /'mailə/ *die;* ~, ~**n** ▶ 265, ▶ 348 mile; **das riecht man drei ~n gegen den Wind** (*abwertend*) you can smell it a mile off; (*fig.*) you can tell that a mile off; it stands out a mile

**Meilen·stein** *der* (*auch fig.*) milestone

**meilen·weit** **1** *Adj.* ‹distance› of many miles. **2** *adv.* for miles; ~ **entfernt** (*auch fig.*) miles away (**von** from)

**Meiler** *der;* ~**s**, ~ **A** (*Kohlen*~) charcoal kiln; **B** (*Atom*~) [atomic] pile

**mein**[1] /main/ *Possessivpron.* my; **ich trinke so ~e acht Tassen Kaffee am Tag** I drink my eight cups of coffee a day; ~**e Damen und Herren** ladies and gentlemen; **das Buch dort, ist das ~[e]s?** that book over there, is it mine?; **das ist nicht ihr Vater, sondern ~er** that's not her father but mine; **was Mein ist, ist auch Dein** what's mine is yours; **das ist nicht sein Auto, sondern das ~e** that's not his car but mine; **der/die Meine** (*geh.*) my husband/wife; **die Meinen** (*geh.*) my family *sing.;* **das Meine** (*geh.: Eigentum*) my possessions *pl. or* property; **ich habe das Meine getan** (*was ich konnte*) I have done what I could; (*meinen Teil*) I have done my share; **sie kann Mein und Dein nicht unterscheiden** (*scherzh.*) she doesn't understand that some things don't belong to her

**mein**[2] *Gen. des Personalpronomens* **ich** (*dichter. veralt.*) ⇨ **meiner**

**Mein·eid** *der* perjury *no indef. art.;* **einen ~ schwören** perjure oneself; commit perjury

**meineidig** *Adj.* perjured; ~ **werden** perjure oneself; commit perjury

**Meineidige** *der/die; adj. Dekl.* perjurer

**meinen** **1** *itr. V.* think; **[ganz] wie Sie ~!** whatever you think; (*wie Sie möchten*) [just] as you wish; ~ **Sie?** do you think so?; **wie ~ Sie?** I beg your pardon?; **wie ~?**

*old spelling (see note on page 1707)

m

(*scherzh.*) beg your pardon?; **ich meine ja nur [so]** (*ugs.*) it was just an idea *or* a thought. ❷ *tr. V.* Ⓐ (*denken, glauben*) think; **meinst du, das weiß ich nicht?** do you think I don't know that?; **man könnte ~, ...** one might [almost] think ...; **man sollte ~, ...** one would think *or* would have thought ...; **das meine ich auch** I think so too; Ⓑ (*sagen wollen, im Sinn haben*) mean; **was meint er damit?** what does he mean by that?; **das habe ich nicht gemeint** that's not what I meant; **was ~ Sie?** what do you mean?; Ⓒ (*beabsichtigen*) mean; intend; **er meint es gut/ehrlich** he means well *or* his intentions are good/his intentions are honest; **es gut mit jmdm. ~:** mean well by sb.; **etw. wörtlich/ironisch ~:** mean sth. literally/ironically; **es war nicht böse gemeint** no harm was meant *or* intended; **er hat es nicht so gemeint** (*ugs.*) he didn't mean it like that; **das Wetter/die Sonne meint es gut mit uns** (*fig. ugs.*) the weather is [being] kind to us/the sun is certainly doing its best for us; Ⓓ (*sagen*) say; Ⓔ (*geh.*) **sie meinte zu träumen** she thought she was dreaming

**meiner** *Gen. des Personalpronomens* **ich** (*geh.*) **gedenke ~:** remember me; **erbarme dich ~:** have mercy upon me

**meinerseits** *Adv.* for my part; **ganz ~:** the pleasure is [all] mine

**meinesgleichen** *indekl. Pron.* people *pl.* like me *or* myself; (*abwertend*) the likes *pl.* of me; my sort *or* kind

**meinesteils** *Adv.* for my part

**meinethalben** *Adv.* (*veralt.*), **meinetwegen** *Adv.* Ⓐ because of me; (*für mich*) on my behalf; (*mir zuliebe*) for my sake; (*um mich*) about me; Ⓑ /*auch* --'--/ (*ugs.*) as far as I'm concerned; **meinetwegen!** if you like; **meinetwegen soll er sich den Hals brechen** he can break his neck for all I care; **also gut, meinetwegen!** fair enough!; **Darf ich heute Abend ausgehen? — Meinetwegen!** May I go out tonight? — It's all right with me; Ⓒ (*zum Beispiel*) for instance

**meinetwillen** *Adv. in* **um ~:** for my sake

**meinige** /'mainɪgə/ *Possessivpron.; adj. Dekl.* (*geh. veralt.*) **der/die/das ~:** mine; **ich habe das ~** *od.* **Meinige getan** (*was ich konnte*) I have done what I could; (*meinen Teil getan*) I have done my share; **die ~n** *od.* **Meinigen** my family *sing.*

**Meinung** *die;* ~, **~en** opinion; (*Ansicht, Auffassung*) opinion; view; **eine vorgefasste/gegenteilige ~ haben** have preconceived ideas *pl.*/hold an opposite opinion; **eine ~ zu etw./über jmdn./etw. haben** have an opinion on/about sb./sth.; **was ist deine** *od.* **was hast du für eine ~?** what is your opinion?; **die ~en sind geteilt** *od.* **gehen auseinander** opinions are divided; **anderer/geteilter ~ sein** be of a different opinion/differing opinions *pl.;* hold a different view/differing views *pl.;* **seine ~ ändern** change one's opinion *or* mind; **er ist der ~, dass ...** he is of the opinion *or* takes the view that ...; **nach meiner ~, meiner ~ nach** in my opinion *or* view; **ganz meine ~:** I agree entirely; **einer ~ sein** be of *or* share the same opinion; **eine hohe ~ von jmdm. haben** have a high opinion of sb.; think highly of sb.; **die öffentliche ~:** public opinion; **jmdm. [gehörig] die ~ sagen** give sb. a [good] piece of one's mind

**meinungs-, Meinungs-: ~äußerung** *die* [expression of] opinion; **das Recht auf freie ~äußerung** the right of free speech; **~austausch** *der* exchange of views; **in einem ~austausch mit jmdm. stehen** exchange views with sb.; **~bildend** *Adj.* opinion-forming; **~bildung** *die:* **die öffentliche ~bildung** the shaping of public opinion; **der Prozess der ~bildung ist bei uns noch im Gange** we have not yet formed an opinion; **~forscher** *der,* **~forscherin** *die* opinion pollster *or* researcher; **~forschung** *die* opinion research; **~forschungs·institut** *das* opinion research institute; **~freiheit** *die* freedom to form and express one's own opinions; (*Redefreiheit*) freedom of speech; **~mache** *die* (*abwertend*) attempted manipulation of people's opinions; **~macher** *der,* **~macherin** *die* opinion-maker; **~monopol** *das* (*abwertend*) monopolizing influence over public opinion; **~umfrage** *die* [public] opinion poll; **~umschwung** *der* swing of opinion; **~verschiedenheit** *die* (*auch verhüll.: Streit*) difference of opinion

**Meise** /'maizə/ *die;* ~, **~n** tit[mouse]; **eine ~ haben** (*salopp*) be nuts (*coll.*); be off one's head (*coll.*)

**Meißel** /'maisl̩/ *der;* **~s, ~:** chisel

**meißeln** ❶ *tr. V.* chisel; carve ‹statue, sculpture› with a chisel. ❷ *itr. V.* chisel; work with a chisel; carve; **an einer Statue ~:** be working on *or* carving a statue with a chisel

**Meiß[e]ner** /'maisənɐ/ *Adj.* **~ Porzellan** Meissen china *or* porcelain

**meist** /maist/ *Adv.* mostly; usually; (*zum größten Teil*) mostly; for the most part; **er hat ~ keine Zeit** he doesn't usually have any time; **er ist ~ betrunken** he's drunk most of the time

**meist...** *Indefinitpron. u. unbest. Zahlw.* most; **das ~e Geld haben** have [the] most money; **die ~e Angst haben** be [the] most afraid; **seine ~e Zeit** most of his time; **am ~en arbeiten** work [the] most; **die ~en Leute haben ...** most people have; **die ~en Leute, die da waren** most of the people who were there; **darüber habe ich mich am ~en gefreut** that pleased me [the] most; **die ~e Zeit des Jahres** most of the year; **die ~en meiner Kollegen** most of my colleagues; **er hat das ~e vergessen** he has forgotten most of it; **die am ~en befahrene Straße** the most used road; **das am ~en verkaufte Buch** the best-selling book

**meist·bietend** ❶ *Adj.* highest-bidding; **der ~bietende Käufer** the highest bidder. ❷ *adv.* **etw. ~bietend versteigern/verkaufen** *usw.* auction sth. off/sell sth. *etc.* to the highest bidder

**Meist·bietende** *der/die; adj. Dekl.* highest bidder

**meistens** /'maistn̩s/ *Adv.* ⇒ **meist**

**meistenteils** *Adv.* for the most part

**Meister** /'maistɐ/ *der;* **~s, ~** Ⓐ master craftsman; **~ im Kürschnerhandwerk sein** be a master furrier; **seinen ~ machen** (*ugs.*) get one's master craftsman's diploma *or* certificate; Ⓑ (*Vorgesetzter*) (*in der Fabrik, auf der Baustelle*) foreman; (*in anderen Betrieben*) boss (*coll.*); **in Ordnung, ~!** OK, chief *or* boss (*coll.*); Ⓒ (*geh.: Könner*) master; **es ist noch kein ~ vom Himmel gefallen** (*Spr.*) you can't always expect to get it right first time; **früh übt sich, was ein ~ werden will** (*Spr.*) there's nothing like starting young; **[in jmdm.] seinen ~ gefunden haben** have met one's match [in sb.]; Ⓓ (*Künstler, geh.: Lehrer*) master; **die alten ~:** the old masters; Ⓔ (*Sport*) champion; (*Mannschaft*) champions *pl.;* Ⓕ (*salopp: Anrede*) chief (*coll.*); guv (*Brit. coll.*); Ⓖ (*in Märchen*) **~ Lampe** Master Hare; **~ Petz** Bruin the Bear; (*Anrede*) Master Bruin; **~ Grimbart** Brock the Badger; (*Anrede*) Master Brock; **~ Urian** Old Nick

**Meister-: ~brief** *der* master craftsman's diploma *or* certificate; **~dieb** *der,* **~diebin** *die* master thief; **~elf** *die* (*Fußball*) **die ~elf aus München/die Münchner ~elf** the champions Munich; **~gesang** *der* Meistergesang; art and music of the Meistersingers

**meisterhaft** ❶ *Adj.* masterly. ❷ *adv.* in a masterly manner; **es ~ verstehen, etw. zu tun** be a [past] master *or* an expert at doing sth.; **die Gitarre ~ beherrschen** be a masterly guitar player

**Meister·hand** *die* master hand; **von ~:** by a master hand

**Meisterin** *die;* ~, **~nen** Ⓐ master craftswoman; Ⓑ (*geh.: Könnerin*) master; **im Erfinden von Ausreden ist sie eine ~:** she is a [past] master *or* an expert at inventing excuses; Ⓒ (*Sport*) [women's] champion

**Meister-: ~klasse** *die* Ⓐ (*Sport*) championship class; Ⓑ (*Musik, Kunst*) master class; **~leistung** *die* masterly performance; (*~stück*) masterpiece; (*geniale Tat*) master stroke

**meisterlich** (*geh. veralt.*) ⇒ **meisterhaft**

**Meister-: ~macher** *der,* **~macherin** *die* (*Sportjargon*) champion maker; **~mannschaft** *die* champions *pl.;* title-holders *pl.*

**meistern** *tr. V.* master; master, overcome ‹problem, difficulty›; control ‹anger, excitement, etc.›; **sein Schicksal/Leben ~:** cope with one's fate/with life

**Meister·prüfung** *die* examination for the/one's master craftsman's diploma *or* certificate

**Meisterschaft** *die;* ~, **~en** Ⓐ mastery; Ⓑ (*Sport*) championship; (*Veranstaltung*) championships *pl.;* **die ~ erringen** take the championship

**Meisterschafts-: ~kampf** *der* (*Sport*) championship; **~spiel** *das* (*Sport*) championship match *or* game

**Meister-: ~schüler** *der,* **~schülerin** *die* (*Musik, Kunst*) master-class student; **~singer** *der;* **~~s, ~~:** Meistersinger; mastersinger; **~stück** *das* Ⓐ *piece of work executed to qualify as a master craftsman;* Ⓑ (*~leistung*) masterpiece (**an** + *Dat.* of); (*geniale Tat*) master stroke; **~titel** *der* Ⓐ (*Sport*) championship [title]; Ⓑ (*im Handwerksberuf*) title of master craftsman

**Meisterung** *die;* **~:** mastering

**Meister-: ~werk** *das* masterpiece (**an** + *Dat.* of); **~würde** *die* title of master craftsman

**Meist·gebot** *das* highest bid

**Mekka** /'mɛka/ *(das);* **~s** ▶700 Mecca; (*fig.*) Mecca (+ *Gen.* for)

**Melamin·harz** /mela'mi:n-/ *das* melamine resin

**Melancholie** /melaŋko:'li:/ *die;* ~, (*Psych.:*) **~n** (*Gemütszustand*) melancholy; (*Psych.*) melancholia

**Melancholiker** /melaŋ'ko:likɐ/ *der;* **~s, ~, Melancholikerin** *die;* ~, **~nen** melancholic

**melancholisch** ❶ *Adj.* melancholy; melancholy, melancholic ‹person, temperament›. ❷ *adv.* melancholically

**Melanesien** /mela'ne:zi̯ən/ *(das);* **~s** Melanesia

**Melange** /me'lã:ʒ(ə)/ *die;* ~, **~n** Ⓐ (*österr.*) ⇒ **Milchkaffee;** Ⓑ (*Gemisch*) blend

**Melanom** /mela'no:m/ *das;* **~s, ~e** ▶474 (*Med.*) melanoma

**Melasse** /me'lasə/ *die;* **~:** molasses *sing.*

**Melde-: ~amt** *das* registration office (*for registering with the authorities on changing one's place of residence*); **~fahrer** *der* (*Milit.*) dispatch rider; **~frist** *die* (*bei der Anmeldung, Abmeldung*) registration period; (*Versicherungsw.*) notification period; **~gänger** *der;* **~~s, ~~** (*Milit.*) runner; messenger

**melden** /'mɛldn̩/ ❶ *tr. V.* Ⓐ report; (*registrieren lassen*) register ‹birth, death, etc.› (*Dat.* with); **wie soeben gemeldet wird** (*Fernseh., Rundf.*) according to reports just coming in; **etw. den Behörden ~:** report sth. to the authorities; **jmdn. als vermisst ~:** report sb. missing; **melde gehorsamst, ...** (*Milit. veralt.*) beg to report ...; **nichts/nicht viel zu ~ haben** (*ugs.*) have no/little say; Ⓑ (*ankündigen*) announce; **wen darf ich ~?** what name shall I say?; who shall I say is here?; Ⓒ (*Schülerspr.*) **jmdn. ~:** tell on sb; **das wird gemeldet!** I'll tell!
❷ *refl. V.* Ⓐ report; **sich polizeilich ~:** register with the police; **sich auf dem Polizeipräsidium ~:** report to police headquarters; **sich zum Militär ~:** enlist [in the armed forces]; **sich freiwillig ~:** volunteer (**zu** for); **sich auf eine Anzeige ~:** reply to *or* answer an advertisement; **sich zu einem Lehrgang ~:** sign on *or* enrol for a course; **sich zu einer Prüfung ~:** enter for an examination; **sich zum Dienst ~:** report for duty; ⇒ *auch* **krank** A; Ⓑ (*am Telefon*) answer; **der Teilnehmer meldet sich nicht/es meldet sich niemand** there is no answer *or* reply; Ⓒ (*ums Wort bitten*) put

m

one's hand up; **D** (*von sich hören lassen*) get in touch (**bei** with); **wenn du etwas brauchst, melde dich** if you need anything let me/us know; **Otto 2, bitte ~!** Otto 2, come in please!; **E** (*sich ankündigen*) ‹old age, rheumatism, etc.› make itself *or* its presence felt. **3** *itr. V.* ‹dog› start barking

**Melde·pflicht** *die* **A** (*Gesundheitsw.*) obligation (*on doctor*) to notify the authorities; **Thypus unterliegt der ~:** cases of typhoid must be notified to the authorities; **B** (*Verwaltung*) obligation to register with the authorities; **polizeiliche ~:** obligation to register with the police

**melde·pflichtig** *Adj.* **A** (*Gesundheitsw.*) notifiable ‹disease›; **B** (*Verwaltung*) ‹accident› which must be reported

**Melder** *der;* **~s, ~** (*Milit.*) runner; messenger

**Melde-: ~schluss, *~schluß** *der* closing date; **~wesen** *das* system of registration; **~zettel** *der* registration form

**Meldung** *die;* **~, ~en A** report; (*Nachricht*) piece of news; (*Ankündigung*) announcement; **~en aus dem Ausland** news from abroad; **~en vom Sport** sports news *sing.;* **~en in Kürze** news headlines; **B ~ machen** *od.* **erstatten** (*Milit.*) report; make a report; **C** (*Anzeige*) report; **über etw.** (*Akk.*) **~ machen** report sth.; **D** (*An~*) (*bei einem Wettbewerb, Examen*) entry; (*bei einem Kurs*) enrolment; **wir bitten um freiwillige ~en** we are asking *or* calling for volunteers; **seine ~ [zu etw.] zurückziehen** withdraw [from sth.]; **E** (*Wort~*) request to speak; **gibt es noch weitere ~en?** does anyone else wish to speak?

**meliert** /meˈliːɐt/ *Adj.* mottled; **grün/braun ~:** mottled green/brown; **[grau] ~es Haar** hair streaked with grey

**Melioration** /melioraˈtsioːn/ *die;* **~, ~en** (*Landw.*) melioration; land improvement

**Melisse** /meˈlɪsə/ *die;* **~, ~n** melissa; balm

**Melk-: ~an·lage** *die* (*Landw.*) milking equipment *no indef. art.;* **~eimer** *der* (*Landw.*) milking pail

**melken** /ˈmɛlkn̩/ **1** *regelm.* (*auch unr.*) *tr. V.* (*auch fig. salopp*) milk. **2** *regelm.* (*auch unr.*) *itr. V.* (*veralt.: Milch geben*) give milk; **eine ~de Kuh** a cow in milk; a milch cow

**Melker** *der;* **~s, ~** ▶ 159 milker

**Melkerin** *die;* **~, ~nen** milkmaid

**Melk-: ~maschine** *die* milking machine; **~schemel** *der* milking stool

**Melodei** /meloˈdai/ *die;* **~, ~en** (*dichter. veralt.*) ⇒ **Melodie** A

**Melodie** /meloˈdiː/ *die;* **~, ~n A** melody; (*Weise*) tune; melody; **nach einer ~:** to a melody/tune; **B** (*Satz~*) intonation

**Melodien-: ~folge** *die,* **~reigen** *der* medley [of tunes]; musical medley

**Melodik** /meˈloːdɪk/ *die;* **~** (*Musik*) **A** (*Lehre*) theory of melody; **B** (*melodische Merkmale*) melodic characteristics *pl.*

**melodiös** /meloˈdiøːs/ **1** *Adj.* melodious. **2** *adv.* melodiously

**melodisch 1** *Adj.* melodic; melodious. **2** *adv.* melodically; melodiously; **~ sprechen** speak in a melodic *or* melodious voice

**Melodram** /meloˈdraːm/ *das;* **~s, Melodramen, Melodrama** *das;* **~as, Melodramen** melodrama

**melodramatisch 1** *Adj.* melodramatic. **2** *adv.* melodramatically

**Melone** /meˈloːnə/ *die;* **~, ~n A** melon; **B** (*ugs. scherzh.*) bowler [hat]

**Membran** /mɛmˈbraːn/ *die;* **~, ~en, Membrane** *die;* **~, ~n A** (*Technik*) diaphragm; **B** (*Biol., Chemie*) membrane

**Memento** /meˈmɛnto/ *das;* **~s, ~s A** (*kath. Rel.*) Memento; **B** (*geh.: Mahnung*) warning reminder

**Memme** /ˈmɛmə/ *die;* **~, ~n** (*veralt. abwertend*) [craven] coward

**Memoiren** /meˈmo̯aːrən/ *Pl.* memoirs

**Memorandum** /memoˈrandʊm/ *das;* **~s, Memoranden** *od.* **Memoranda** memorandum

**Memorial** /memoˈri̯aːl/ *das;* **~s, ~s** (*geh.*) memorial event; (*Rennen*) memorial race

**memorieren** /memoˈriːrən/ *tr. V.* (*geh. veralt.*) memorize

**Menage** /meˈnaːʒə/ *die;* **~, ~n** cruet [stand]

**Menagerie** /menaʒəˈriː/ *die;* **~, ~n** (*veralt.*) menagerie

**menagieren** /menaˈʒiːrən/ *itr. V.* (*österr. Milit.*) draw rations

**mendeln** /ˈmɛndl̩n/ *itr. V.* (*Biol.*) Mendelize

**mendelsche Gesetze** /ˈmɛndl̩ʃə-/ *Pl.* (*Biol.*) Mendel's laws

**Menetekel** /meneˈteːkl̩/ *das;* **~s, ~** (*geh.*) warning sign *or* portent

**Menge** /ˈmɛŋə/ *die;* **~, ~n A** (*Quantum*) quantity; amount; **die dreifache ~:** three times *or* triple the amount; three times as much; **in ausreichender ~:** in sufficient quantities *pl.;* **in ~n zu ...** in quantities of ...; **B** (*große Anzahl*) large number; lot (*coll.*); **eine ~ Leute** a lot *or* lots *pl.* of people (*coll.*); **eine ~** (*ugs.*) a lot *or* lots [of it/them] (*coll.*); **eine ~ Zeit** (*ugs.*) a lot *or* lots of time; plenty of time; **Kuchen/Blumen in ~n** cakes/flowers in abundance; lots of cakes/flowers (*coll.*); **er weiß eine [ganze] ~** (*ugs.*) he knows [quite] a lot (*coll.*) *or* a great deal; **sie bildet sich eine ~ ein** (*ugs.*) she is very conceited (**auf** + *Akk.* about); **eine ~ trinken/essen** (*ugs.*) drink/eat a hell of a lot (*coll.*); **jede ~ Arbeit/Alkohol** *usw.* (*ugs.*) masses *pl. or* loads *pl.* of work/alcohol *etc.* (*coll.*); ⇒ *auch* **rau** 1 H; **C** (*Menschen~*) crowd; throng; **D** (*Math.*) set

**mengen** (*veralt.*) **1** *tr. V.* mix; **Rosinen unter den Teig ~:** mix raisins into the dough. **2** *refl. V.* (*ugs.*) mingle (**unter** + *Akk.* with)

**mengen-, Mengen-: ~an·gabe** *die* indication of quantity/quantities; **~lehre** *die* (*Math., Logik*) set theory *no art.;* **~mäßig 1** *Adj.* quantitative; **2** *adv.* quantitatively; as far as quantity is/was concerned; **~rabatt** *der* (*Wirtsch.*) bulk discount

**Menhir** /ˈmɛnhɪr/ *der;* **~s, ~e** menhir

**Meningitis** /menɪŋˈgiːtɪs/ *die;* **~, Meningitiden** ▶ 474 (*Med.*) meningitis

**Meniskus** /meˈnɪskʊs/ *der;* **~, Menisken** ▶ 471 (*Anat., Optik*) meniscus

**Meniskus·riss, *Meniskus·riß** *der* ▶ 474 (*Med.*) torn meniscus

**Menkenke** /mɛŋˈkɛŋkə/ *die;* **~** (*md. ugs.*) fuss; **mach keine ~:** don't make a fuss

**Mennige** /ˈmɛnɪgə/ *die;* **~:** red lead

**Menopause** /menoˈpau̯zə/ *die;* **~, ~n** (*Physiol.*) menopause

**Menora** /mɛnoˈraː/ *die;* **~, ~:** menorah

**Mensa** /ˈmɛnza/ *die;* **~, ~s** *od.* **Mensen** refectory, canteen (*of university, college*)

**Mensa·essen** *das* refectory *or* canteen food

**Mensch**[1] /mɛnʃ/ *der;* **~en, ~en A** (*Gattung*) **der ~:** man; **die ~en** man *sing.;* human beings; **das Gute im ~en** the good in man; **das sind starrköpfige ~en** they are stubborn people; **alle ~en müssen sterben** we are all mortal; **der ~ lebt nicht vom Brot allein** (*Spr.*) man does not live by bread alone (*prov.*); **ich bin auch nur ein ~:** I'm only human; **der ~ denkt, Gott lenkt** (*Spr.*) man proposes, God disposes (*prov.*); **das sind doch keine ~en mehr!** they are a pack of animals; **nur noch ein halber ~ sein** be just about all in; **wieder ein ~ sein** (*ugs.*) feel like a human being again; **~en fressend** man-eating; **B** (*Person*) person; man/woman; **~en** people; **kein ~:** no one; **es war kein ~ da** there was no one *or* not a soul there; **unter die ~en gehen** mix with people; **des ~en Wille ist sein Himmelreich** you/he *etc.* must do whatever makes you/him *etc.* happy; **wie der erste ~/die ersten ~en** extremely awkwardly; **ein neuer ~ werden** become a new man/woman; **von ~ zu ~:** man to man/woman to woman; **~, ärgere dich nicht** (*Gesellschaftsspiel*) ludo; **C** *Pl.* (*~heit*) mankind *sing., no art.;* man *sing., no art.;* **D** (*salopp: Anrede*) (*bewundernd*) wow; (*erstaunt*) wow; good grief; (*vorwurfsvoll*) for heaven's sake; **~, war das ein Glück!** boy, that was a piece of luck!; **~, hast du dich verändert!** good Lord, haven't you changed!; **~, das habe ich ganz vergessen!** damn *or* (*Brit.*) blast, I completely forgot!; **~ Meier!** good grief!

**Mensch**[2] *das;* **~[e]s, ~er** (*abwertend: Frau*) slut; trollop

**menschen-, Menschen-: ~affe** *der* anthropoid [ape]; **~ähnlich** *Adj.* manlike; like a human being/human beings *postpos.;* **~alter** *das* lifetime; **~ansammlung** *die* gathering [of people]; (*~menge*) crowd [of people]; **~arm** *Adj.* sparsely populated; **~auflauf** *der* crowd [of people]; **~bild** *das* conception of man; **~feind** *der,* **~feindin** *die* misanthropist; **~feindlich 1** *Adj.* **A** misanthropic; **B** (*unmenschlich*) inhuman ‹system, policy etc.›; ‹environment› hostile to man; **2** *adv.* **A** misanthropically; **B** (*unmenschlich*) inhumanly; **~feindlich konzipierte Trabantenstädte** satellite towns designed in a way that creates an environment hostile to man; **~feindlichkeit** *die* ⇒ **menschenfeindlich** 1: misanthropy; inhumanity; hostility to man; **~fleisch** *das* human flesh; ***~fressend** ⇒ **Mensch** A; **~fresser** *der,* **~fresserin** *die* (*ugs.*) cannibal; (*Mythol.*) maneater; **er ist doch kein ~fresser** (*scherzh.*) he won't eat *or* bite you; **~freund** *der,* **~freundin** *die* philanthropist; **~freundlich 1** *Adj.* **A** philanthropic; **B** (*human*) ‹environment› catering for human needs; ‹architecture› designed with [the needs of] people in mind; **2** *adv.* **A** philanthropically; **B ~freundlich gestaltet/konstruiert** designed with [the needs of] people in mind; **~freundlichkeit** *die* philanthropy; **aus reiner ~freundlichkeit** out of the sheer goodness of one's heart; **~führung** *die* leadership; **~gedenken** *das:* **das wird seit ~gedenken so gemacht** it has been done that way for as long as anyone can remember; **der heißeste Sommer seit ~gedenken** the hottest summer in living memory; **~geschlecht** *das* (*geh.*) human race; **~gestalt** *die* human form; **ein Engel/Teufel** *od.* **Satan in ~gestalt sein** be an angel in human form/the devil incarnate; **~gewühl** *das* milling crowd; **~haar** *das* human hair; **~hand** *die* (*geh.*) hand of man; human hand; **von ~hand geschaffen** created by the hand of man *or* by human hand; **~handel** *der* trade *or* traffic in human beings; (*Sklavenhandel*) slave trade; **~händler** *der,* **~händlerin** *die* trafficker [in human beings]; (*Sklavenhändler*) slave trader; **~hass, *~haß** *der* misanthropy; **~hasser** *der;* **~~s, ~~, ~hasserin** *die;* **~~, ~~nen** ⇒ **~feind**; **~jagd** *die* (*abwertend*) manhunting; manhunts *pl.;* (*Verfolgung*) persecution; **eine ~jagd** a manhunt; **~kenner** *der,* **~kennerin** *die* judge of character *or* human nature; **~kenntnis** *die* ability to judge character *or* human nature; **~kette** *die* human chain; **~kind** *das* creature; soul; **~leben** *das* life; **ein ~leben lang währen** (*geh.*) last a whole lifetime; **der Unfall forderte vier ~leben** (*geh.*) the accident claimed four lives; **~leben waren nicht zu beklagen** (*geh.*) there was no loss of life; **~leer** *Adj.* deserted; **~liebe** *die* philanthropy; love of humanity *or* mankind; **~masse** *die* crowd [of people]; **~material** *das* (*Militärjargon*) [human] material; **~menge** *die* crowd [of people]; **~möglich** *Adj.* humanly possible; **das ist doch nicht ~möglich!** but that's impossible!; **alles Menschenmögliche tun** do all that is/was humanly possible; **~opfer** *das* **A** human sacrifice; **B** (*~leben*) **es waren Hunderte von ~opfern zu beklagen** hundreds of lives were lost; **~raub** *der* kidnapping; abduction; **~recht** *das* human right; **~rechts·konvention** *die* Human Rights Convention; **~rechts·verletzung** *die* human rights violation; **~scheu** *Adj.* afraid

*old spelling (see note on page 1707)

of people; (*ungesellig*) unsociable; **~scheu** *die* fear of people; **~schinder** *der*, **~schinderin** *die* (*abwertend*) cruel and ruthless slave driver; **~schlag** *der* race *or* breed [of people]; **~seele** *die* human soul; **keine ~seele** not a [living] soul

**Menschens·kind** *Interj.* (*salopp*) (*erstaunt*) good heavens; good grief; (*vorwurfsvoll*) for heaven's sake

**Menschen·sohn** *der* (*christl. Rel.*) Son of Man

**menschen-, Menschen-: ~unwürdig** ❶ *Adj.* degrading and inhumane ‹treatment›; ‹accommodation› unfit for human habitation; ‹conditions› unfit for human beings; ‹behaviour› unworthy of a human being; ❷ *adv.* ‹treat› in a degrading and inhumane way; ‹live, be housed› in conditions unfit for human beings; **~verächter** *der* despiser of humanity *or* mankind; **~verachtung** *die* contempt for humanity *or* mankind; **~verstand** *der* human intelligence *or* intellect; ⇒ *auch* **gesund**; **~werk** *das* (*geh.*) work of man; **alles ~werk ist vergänglich** the works *pl.* of men are ephemeral; **~würde** *die* human dignity *no art.*; **~würdig** ❶ *Adj.* humane ‹treatment›; ‹accommodation› fit for human habitation; ‹conditions› fit for human beings; ‹behaviour› worthy of a human being; ❷ *adv.* ‹treat› humanely; ‹live, be housed› in conditions fit for human beings

**Menschewik** /mɛnʃe'vɪk/ *der;* **~en, ~en** *u.* **~i, Menschewikin** *die;* **~, ~nen** (*hist.*) Menshevik

**Menschheit** *die;* **~:** mankind *no art.*; humanity *no art.*; human race

**Menschheits-: ~entwicklung** *die* evolution of man; **~geschichte** *die* history of mankind *or* of the human race; **~traum** *der* dream of mankind

**menschlich** ❶ *Adj.* Ⓐ human; **~es Versagen** human error; **das ~e Leben** human life; ⇒ *auch* **irren** A; Ⓑ (*annehmbar*) civilized; **wieder ganz ~ aussehen** (*ugs.*) look quite presentable again; Ⓒ (*human*) humane ‹person, treatment, etc.›; human ‹trait, emotion, etc.›; **sich von der ~en Seite zeigen** show one's human side. ❷ *adv.* Ⓐ **er ist ~ sympathisch** I like him as a person; **sich ~ näher kommen** get on closer [personal] terms [with one another]; Ⓑ (*human*) humanely; in a humane manner

**Menschliche** *das; adj. Dekl.* **nichts ~s war ihr fremd** she was familiar with every aspect of human experience; **er hat nichts ~s an sich** he shows no human traits; there's nothing human about him

**Menschlichkeit** *die* humanity *no art.*; **etw. aus reiner ~ tun** do sth. for purely humanitarian reasons

**Mensch·werdung** /-ve:ɐ̯dʊŋ/ *die;* **~** (*christl. Rel.*) incarnation

**Mensen** ⇒ **Mensa**

**Menstruation** /mɛnstrua'tsi̯o:n/ *die;* **~, ~en** (*Physiol.*) menstruation; (*Periode*) [menstrual] period

**menstruieren** *itr. V.* (*Physiol.*) menstruate

**Mensur** /mɛn'zu:ɐ̯/ *die;* **~, ~en** Ⓐ students' duel; **eine ~ schlagen** fight a duel; Ⓑ (*Fechten*) [fencing] measure *or* distance

**mental** /mɛn'ta:l/ (*geh.*) ❶ *Adj.* mental. ❷ *adv.* mentally

**Mentalität** /mɛntali'tɛ:t/ *die;* **~, ~en** mentality

**Menthol** /mɛn'to:l/ *das;* **~s** menthol

**Mentor** /'mɛntɔr/ *der;* **~s, ~en** /-'to:rən/, **Mentorin** *die;* **~, ~nen** Ⓐ (*geh.*) mentor; Ⓑ (*veralt.: Lehrer[in]*) tutor; Ⓒ (*Schulw.*) supervisor

**Menu** /me'ny/ *das;* **~s, ~s** (*schweiz.*), **Menü** /me'ny:/ *das;* **~s, ~s** (*auch DV*) menu; (*im Restaurant*) set meal *or* menu

**Menuett** /me'nu̯ɛt/ *das;* **~s, ~e** *od.* **~s** minuet

**Menü·leiste** *die* (*DV*) menu bar

**mephistophelisch** /mefɪsto'fe:lɪʃ/ (*geh.*) Mephistophelian

**Mercator·projektion** /mɛr'ka:tɔr-/ *die* (*Geogr.*) Mercator's projection

**Mergel** /'mɛrgl̩/ *der;* **~s** (*Geol.*) marl

**Meridian** /meri'di̯a:n/ *der;* **~s, ~e** (*Geogr., Astron.*) meridian

**Meridian·kreis** *der* (*Astron.*) meridian circle

**Meringe** /me'rɪŋə/ *die;* **~, ~n** meringue

**Merino** /me'ri:no/ *der;* **~s, ~s** Ⓐ (*Schaf*) merino [sheep]; Ⓑ (*Stoff*) merino

**Merino-: ~schaf** *das* merino [sheep]; **~wolle** *die* merino wool

**Meriten** /me'ri:tn̩/ *Pl.* (*geh. veralt.*) merits

**merkantil** /mɛrkan'ti:l/ *Adj.* (*geh.*) mercantile

**Merkantilismus** *der;* **~** (*hist.*) mercantilism *no art.*

**merkantilistisch** *Adj.* (*hist.*) mercantilist

**merkbar** ❶ *Adj.* Ⓐ perceptible; noticeable; (*deutlich*) noticeable; Ⓑ (*leicht zu behalten*) **eine gut** *od.* **leicht ~e Nummer** an easily remembered number; **leicht/schwer ~ sein** be easy/difficult to remember. ❷ *adv.* perceptibly; noticeably; (*deutlich*) noticeably

**Merk-: ~blatt** leaflet; (*mit Anweisungen*) instruction leaflet; **~buch** *das* notebook

**merken** /'mɛrkn̩/ ❶ *tr. V.* notice; **deutlich zu ~ sein** be plain to see; be obvious; **er hat [davon] nichts gemerkt** he didn't notice anything [of that]; **davon merkt man nicht viel** it's hardly noticeable; **an seinem Benehmen merkt man, dass ...** you can tell by his behaviour that ...; **das merkt doch jeder/keiner** everybody/nobody will notice; **jmdn. etw. ~ lassen** let sb. see sth.; **du merkst aber auch alles!** (*ugs. iron.*) how very observant of you!; **merkst du was?** (*ugs.*) have you noticed something?. ❷ *refl. V.* **sich** (*Dat.*) **etw. ~:** remember sth.; **hast du dir die Adresse gemerkt?** have you made a mental note of the address?; **diesen Mann muss man sich** (*Dat.*) **~:** this is a man to take note of; **ich werd mirs** *od.* **werds mir ~** (*ugs.*) I won't forget that; I'll remember that; **merk dir das** just remember that

**Merk-: ~heft** *das* notebook; **~hilfe** *die* mnemonic; memory aid

**merklich** ❶ *Adj.* perceptible; noticeable; (*deutlich*) noticeable. ❷ *adv.* perceptibly; noticeably; (*deutlich*) noticeably

**Merkmal** *das;* **~s, ~e** feature; characteristic; **besondere ~e** distinguishing features *or* marks

**Merk-: ~satz** *der* mnemonic sentence/phrase; mnemonic; **~spruch** *der* Ⓐ pithy maxim *or* saying; Ⓑ (**~hilfe**) mnemonic verse/sentence/phrase mnemonic

**Merkur**[1] /mɛr'ku:ɐ̯/ *der;* **~s** (*Astron.*), **Merkur**[2] (*der*) (*Myth.*) Mercury

**merkwürdig** ❶ *Adj.* strange; odd; peculiar. ❷ *adv.* strangely; oddly; peculiarly

**merkwürdiger·weise** *Adv.* strangely *or* oddly *or* curiously enough

**Merkwürdigkeit** *die;* **~, ~en** Ⓐ strangeness; oddness; peculiarity; Ⓑ (*Erscheinung*) curiosity

**Merk-: ~zeichen** *das* mark; marker; **~zettel** *der* note; (*Liste*) list

**Merowinger** *der;* **~s, ~, Merowingerin** *die;* **~, ~nen** (*hist.*) Merovingian

**merzerisieren** /mɛrtsəri'zi:rən/ *tr. V.* (*Textilind.*) mercerize

**Mesalliance** /meza'li̯ã:s/ *die;* **~, ~n** (*geh.*) mésalliance

**meschugge** /me'ʃʊgə/ *Adj.; nicht attrib.* (*salopp*) barmy (*Brit. coll.*); nuts *pred.* (*coll.*); off one's rocker *pred.* (*coll.*)

**Meskalin** /mɛska'li:n/ *das;* **~s** mescaline

**Mesmerismus** /mɛsmə'rɪsmʊs/ *der;* **~** *Mesmer's theory of biomagnetic effects*

**Mesner** /'mɛsnɐ/ *der;* **~s, ~, Mesnerin** *die;* **~, ~nen** sexton

**Mesolithikum** /mezo'li:tikʊm/ *das;* **~s** (*Geol.*) mesolithic period

**mesolithisch** *Adj.* (*Geol.*) mesolithic

**Mesopotamien** /mezopo'ta:mi̯ən/ (*das*)*;* **~s** Mesopotamia

**Mesozoikum** /mezo'tso:ikʊm/ *das;* **~s** (*Geol.*) Mesozoic era

**mesozoisch** *Adj.* (*Geol.*) Mesozoic

**Mess·band, *Meß·band** *das; Pl.* **Messbänder** measuring tape

**messbar, *meßbar** /'mɛsba:ɐ̯/ *Adj.* measurable; **schwer ~:** difficult to measure

**Mess-, *Meß-: ~becher** *der* measuring jug; **~bild** *das* (*Kartographie*) photogrammetric photograph; **~buch** *das* missal; mass book; **~diener** *der*, **~dienerin** *die* (*kath. Kirche*) server

**Messe**[1] /'mɛsə/ *die;* **~, ~n** (*Gottesdienst, Musik*) mass; **die ~ halten** *od.* (*geh.*) **zelebrieren** say *or* celebrate mass; **für jmdn. eine ~ lesen** say a mass for sb.

**Messe**[2] *die;* **~, ~n** Ⓐ (*Ausstellung*) [trade] fair; **auf der ~:** at the [trade] fair; Ⓑ (*landsch.: Jahrmarkt, Volksfest*) fair

**Messe**[3] *die;* **~, ~n** (*Seew., Milit.*) mess; (*Raum*) mess room

**Messe-: ~besucher** *der*, **~besucherin** *die* visitor to a/the [trade] fair; **~gelände** *das* site of a/the [trade] fair; (*mit festen* **~hallen**) exhibition centre; **~halle** *die* exhibition hall

**messen** ❶ *unr. tr. V.* Ⓐ measure; **[jmdm.] den** *od.* **jmds. Blutdruck/Puls ~:** take sb.'s blood pressure/pulse; **jmds. Temperatur ~:** take sb.'s temperature; **die Zeit eines Sprinters ~:** time a sprinter; **am Morgen wurden schon 20° ge~:** the temperature was already 20° in the morning; **etw. nach Litern/Metern ~:** measure sth. in litres/metres; ⇒ *auch* **Fieber**; Ⓑ (*beurteilen*) judge (**nach** by); **etw. an etw.** (*Dat.*) **~:** judge sth. by sth.; **jmdn. an jmdm. ~:** judge sb. by comparison with sb.; compare sb. with sb.; **ge~ an** (+ *Dat.*) having regard to; Ⓒ (*geh.*) **jmdn. mit den Augen** *od.* **Blicken ~:** look sb. up and down. ❷ *unr. itr. V.* measure; **er misst 1,85 m** he's 1.85 m [tall]; **genau ~:** make an exact measurement/exact measurements. ❸ *unr. refl. V.* (*geh.*) compete (**mit** with); **sich mit jmdm./etw. [in etw.** (*Dat.*)**] [nicht] ~ können** [not] be as good as sb./sth. [in sth.]

**Messer** *das;* **~s, ~** Ⓐ knife; (*Hack~*) chopper; (*Rasier~*) [cut-throat] razor; **mit ~ und Gabel essen** eat with a knife and fork; **jmdm. das ~ an die Kehle setzen** (*fig. ugs.*) hold sb. at gunpoint; **auf des ~s Schneide stehen** (*fig.*) hang in the balance; be balanced on a knife-edge; **es steht auf des ~s Schneide, ob ...** it's touch and go whether ...; **jmdn. ans ~ liefern** (*fig. ugs.*) inform on sb.; **bis aufs ~** (*fig. ugs.*) ‹fight etc.› to the bitter end; **jmdm. ins [offene] ~ laufen** (*fig. ugs.*) play right into sb.'s hands; **da geht mir das ~ in der Tasche auf** (*fig. ugs.*) I see red; Ⓑ (*ugs.: Skalpell*) **jmdn. unter dem ~ haben** have sb. under the knife (*coll.*); **unters ~ müssen** have to go under the knife (*coll.*); Ⓒ (*Technik*) cutter; (*Klinge*) blade

**messer-, Messer-: ~bänkchen** *das* (*individual eater's*) knife rest; **~griff** *der*, **~heft** *das* knife handle; handle of a/the knife; **~held** *der* (*abwertend*) thug with a knife; **~klinge** *die* knife blade; blade of a/the knife; **~rücken** *der* back of a/the knife; **~scharf** ❶ *Adj.* razor-sharp; (*fig.*) trenchant ‹criticism›; incisive ‹logic›; razor-sharp ‹wit, intellect›; ❷ *adv.* (*fig. ugs.*) ‹think› with penetrating insight; ‹argue› incisively; **~schmied** *der*, **~schmiedin** *die* ▶ 159 *maker of saws, knives, and other cutting tools;* **~spitze** *die* Ⓐ point of a/the knife; Ⓑ (*Mengenangabe*) **eine ~spitze** just a trace; **eine ~spitze Salz** a large pinch of salt; **~stecher** *der;* **~~s, ~~:** knifeman; **~stecherei** /-ʃtɛçə'rai̯/ *die;* **~~, ~~en** knife fight; fight with knives; **~stecherin** *die;* **~~, ~~nen:** knifewoman; **~stich** *der* knife thrust; (*Wunde*) knife wound; stab wound; **~werfer** *der*, **~werferin** *die* knife-thrower

**Messe-: ~stadt** *die* town well known for its trade fairs; **die ~stadt Leipzig** Leipzig with its trade fairs; **~stand** *der* stand [at a/the trade fair]

m

**Mess-**, ***Meß-:** **~fühler** *der* (*Technik*) sensor; **~gerät** *das* measuring device *or* instrument; (*Zähler*) meter; **~glas** *das* measuring glass; graduated measure; **~gewand** *das* chasuble

**messianisch** /mɛ'si̯a:nɪʃ/ *Adj.* Messianic

**Messianismus** *der;* ~: Messianism *no art.*

**Messias** /mɛ'si:as/ *der;* ~: Messiah

**Messing** /'mɛsɪŋ/ *das;* ~s brass; **mit ~ beschlagen sein** have brass fittings *pl.*

**messingen** *Adj.* brass

**Messing·waren** *Pl.* brassware *sing.*

**Mess-**, ***Meß-:** **~instrument** *das* measuring instrument; **~latte** *die* surveyor's wooden rod *or* staff

**Messner, Messnerin** ⇨ **Mesner, Mesnerin**

**Mess-**, ***Meß-:** **~opfer** *das* (*kath. Kirche*) sacrifice of the mass; **~stab** *der* measuring rod; **~technik** *die* technology of measurement; **~tisch** *der* plane table; **~tisch·blatt** *das* large-scale map (*1:25,000*); **~uhr** *die* dial flowmeter

**Messung** *die;* ~, ~en (*das Messen, Messergebnis*) measurement; (*das Ablesen, Ableseergebnis*) reading

**Mess-**, ***Meß-:** **~wein** *der* (*kath. Kirche*) Communion wine; altar wine; **~wert** *der* measured value; (*Ableseergebnis*) reading; **~zylinder** *der* measuring cylinder

**Mestize** /mɛs'ti:tsə/ *der;* ~n, ~n mestizo

**Met** /me:t/ *der;* ~[e]s mead

**Metabolismus** /metabo'lɪsmʊs/ *der* (*Physiol.*) metabolism

**Metall** /me'tal/ *das;* ~s, ~e metal; **die ~ verarbeitende Industrie** the metalworking industry

**Metall-:** **~arbeiter** *der*, **~arbeiterin** *die* metalworker; **~bearbeitung** *die* metalworking

**metallen** ❶ *Adj.* Ⓐ (*aus Metall*) metal; Ⓑ (*geh.: metallisch*) metallic. ❷ *adv.* (*geh.*) **ihr Haar glänzte/die Becken klirrten ~:** her hair gleamed/the cymbals sounded metallically

**Metaller** *der;* ~s, ~, **Metallerin** *die;* ~, ~nen (*ugs.*) metalworker

**Metall·geld** *das* metal money; specie (*as tech. term*)

**metall·haltig** *Adj.* metalliferous

**metallic** /me'talɪk/ *indekl. Adj.* metallic [grey/blue/*etc.*]

**Metallic·lackierung** *die* metallic finish

**Metall·industrie** *die* metal-processing and metal-working industries *pl.*

**metallisch** ❶ *Adj.* metallic; metal *attrib.*, metallic ‹conductor, coating›. ❷ *adv.* metallically

**metallisieren** *tr. V.* (*Technik*) metallize

**Metall-:** **~kunde** *die* [physical] metallurgy *no art.*; **~säge** *die* hacksaw; **~überzug** *der* metal *or* metallic coating

**Metallurg** /meta'lʊrk/ *der;* ~en, ~en, **Metallurge** *der;* ~en, ~en, **Metallurgin** *die;* ~, ~nen ▶ 159 metallurgist

**Metallurgie** /metalʊr'gi:/ *die;* ~: [extractive] metallurgy *no art.*

**metallurgisch** *Adj.* metallurgical

***metall·verarbeitend** ⇨ **Metall**

**Metall·waren** *Pl.* metalware *sing.*

**Metamorphose** /metamɔr'fo:zə/ *die;* ~, ~n metamorphosis

**Metapher** /me'tafɐ/ *die;* ~, ~n (*Stilk.*) metaphor; **Gebrauch von ~n** use of metaphor

**Metaphorik** /meta'fo:rɪk/ *die;* ~ (*Stilk.*) Ⓐ (*Gebrauch von Metaphern*) use of metaphor; Ⓑ (*Metaphern*) imagery; metaphors *pl.*

**metaphorisch** (*Stilk.*) ❶ *Adj.* metaphorical. ❷ *adv.* metaphorically

**meta-**, **Meta-:** **~physik** *die;* ~~, ~~en Ⓐ metaphysics *sing.*, *no art.*; Ⓑ (*darstellendes Werk*) metaphysical work; **~physiker** *der*, **~physikerin** *die* metaphysicist; **~physisch** ❶ *Adj.* metaphysical; ❷ *adv.* metaphysically; **~physisch denken** think in metaphysical terms; **~sprache** *die* (*Sprachw., Math.*) metalanguage; **~stase** /-'sta:zə/ *die;* ~~, ~~n ▶ 474 (*Med.*) metastasis

**Meteor** /mete'o:ɐ̯/ *der;* ~s, ~e (*Astron.*) meteor

**Meteorit** /meteo'ri:t/ *der;* ~en *od.* ~s, ~e[n] (*Astron.*) meteorite

**Meteorologe** /meteoro'lo:gə/ *der;* ~n, ~n ▶ 159 meteorologist; (*im Fernsehen*) weatherman

**Meteorologie** *die;* ~: meteorology *no art.*

**Meteorologin** *die;* ~, ~nen ▶ 159 meteorologist; (*im Fernsehen*) weather lady

**meteorologisch** ❶ *Adj.* meteorological. ❷ *adv.* meteorologically

**Meter** /'me:tɐ/ *der od. das;* ~s, ~ ▶ 265, ▶ 411, ▶ 489 metre; **drei ~ hoch/breit/tief/lang** three metres high/wide/deep/long; **[ungefähr] in 100 ~ Höhe/Entfernung** at a height/distance of [about] 100 metres; **nach ~n** by the metre; **auf den letzten ~n** in the last few metres; ⇨ *auch* **laufend** 1 C

**meter-**, **Meter-:** **~dick** *Adj.* a metre thick *postpos.*; (*sehr dick*) metres thick *postpos.*; **~hoch** *Adj.* a metre high *postpos.*; (*sehr hoch*) metres high *postpos.*; ‹snow› a metre/metres deep; **der Schnee lag ~hoch** the snow was a metre/metres deep; **~lang** *Adj.* a metre long *postpos.*; (*sehr lang*) metres long *postpos.*; **~maß** *das* tape measure; (*Stab*) [metre] rule; **~ware** *die* fabric/material *etc.* sold by the metre; **etw. als ~ware kaufen/verkaufen** buy/sell sth. by the metre; **~weise** *Adv.* by the metre; **ich habe den Stoff gleich ~weise gekauft** I bought yards of the material straight away; **~weit** ❶ *Adj.* (*in der Länge*) a metre long *postpos.*; (*sehr lang*) metres long *postpos.*; (*in der Breite*) a metre wide *postpos.*; (*sehr breit*) metres wide *postpos.*; ❷ *adv.* **das Ziel ~weit verfehlen** be yards off [the] target; **einen Baumstamm ~weit schleudern** hurl a tree trunk several yards

**Methan** /me'ta:n/ *das;* ~s methane

**Methan·gas** *das* methane gas

**Methanol** /meta'no:l/ *das;* ~s (*Chemie*) methanol

**Methode** /me'to:də/ *die;* ~, ~n method; **~ haben** be quite deliberate

**Methoden·lehre** *die* ⇨ **Methodologie**

**Methodik** /me'to:dɪk/ *die;* ~, ~en methodology; **~ zeigen** be methodical

**methodisch** ❶ *Adj.* methodological; (*nach einer Methode vorgehend*) methodical. ❷ *adv.* methodologically; (*nach einer Methode*) methodically; **~ vorgehen** proceed methodically

**Methodist** /meto'dɪst/ *der;* ~en, ~en Methodist

**Methodisten·kirche** *die* Methodist church

**Methodistin** *die;* ~, ~nen Methodist

**methodistisch** *Adj.* Methodist

**Methodologie** /metodolo'gi:/ *die;* ~, ~n methodology

**methodologisch** *Adj.* methodological

**Methusalem** /me'tu:zalɛm/ *der;* ~s, ~s Methuselah; **[so] alt wie ~ sein** be as old as Methuselah; **als ~:** when a very old man

**Methyl·alkohol** *der* methyl alcohol

**Methylen** /metʏ'le:n/ *das;* ~s (*Chemie*) methylene

**Metier** /me'ti̯e:/ *das;* ~s, ~s profession; **sein ~ beherrschen, sich auf sein ~ verstehen** know one's job; **Langstreckenlauf war sein ~:** long-distance running was his métier

**Metonymie** /metonʏ'mi:/ *die;* ~, ~n (*Rhet., Stilk.*) metonymy

**Metren** ⇨ **Metrum**

**Metrik** /'me:trɪk/ *die;* ~, ~en Ⓐ (*Verslehre*) metrics; Ⓑ (*Musik*) study of rhythm and tempo *or* of metre

**metrisch** ❶ *Adj.* Ⓐ (*Verslehre, Musik*) metrical; Ⓑ (*auf den Meter bezogen*) metric. ❷ *adv.* metrically

**Metro** /'me:tro/ *die;* ~, ~s Metro

**Metronom** /metro'no:m/ *das;* ~s, ~e (*Musik*) metronome

**Metropole** /metro'po:lə/ *die;* ~, ~n (*größte Stadt*) metropolis; (*Zentrum für etw.*) capital; metropolis

**-metropole** *die* capital; metropolis; **die deutsche Bier~:** the German beer capital; **die Schwarzwald~:** the chief city of the Black Forest

**Metropolit** /metropo'li:t/ *der;* ~en, ~en (*kath. u. orthodoxe Kirche*) metropolitan

**Metrum** /'me:trʊm/ *das;* ~s, **Metren** (*Verslehre, Musik*) metre

**Mett** /mɛt/ *das;* ~[e]s (*landsch.*) minced meat, mince (*pork*)

**Mettage** /mɛ'ta:ʒə/ *die;* ~, ~n (*Zeitungsw.*) page make-up

**Mette** /'mɛtə/ *die;* ~, ~n (*kath. u. ev. Kirche*) midnight mass; (*am frühen Morgen*) early [morning] mass

**Metteur** /mɛ'tø:ɐ̯/ *der;* ~s, ~e, **Metteurin** *die;* ~, ~nen (*Zeitungsw.*) make-up arranger

**Mett·wurst** *die: soft smoked sausage made of minced pork and beef*

**Metze** /'mɛtsə/ *die;* ~, ~n (*veralt.*) strumpet (*arch.*); whore

**Metzelei** /mɛtsə'lai̯/ *die;* ~, ~en (*abwertend*) slaughter; butchery

**metzeln** *tr. V.* ⇨ **niedermetzeln**

**Metzger** /'mɛtsgɐ/ *der;* ~s, ~ ▶ 159 (*bes. westmd., südd., schweiz.*) butcher; (*im Schlachthof*) slaughterman; ⇨ *auch* **Bäcker**

**Metzger-** ⇨ **Fleischer-**

**Metzgerei** *die;* ~, ~en (*bes. westmd., südd., schweiz.*) butcher's [shop]

**Meuchel-** /'mɔyçl̩-/: **~mord** *der* (*abwertend*) [cowardly/treacherous] murder; **~mörder** *der*, **~mörderin** *die* (*abwertend*) [cowardly/treacherous] murderer

**meucheln** *tr. V.* (*geh. abwertend*) murder [in a cowardly/treacherous manner]; assassinate ‹king, ruler, etc.›

**meuchlerisch** (*abwertend*) ❶ *Adj.* cowardly; (*heimtückisch*) treacherous. ❷ *adv.* in a cowardly/treacherous manner

**meuchlings** /'mɔyçlɪŋs/ *Adv.* (*geh. abwertend*) treacherously

**Meute** /'mɔytə/ *die;* ~, ~n Ⓐ (*Jägerspr.*) pack; Ⓑ (*ugs. abwertend: Menschengruppe*) mob

**Meuterei** /mɔytə'rai̯/ *die;* ~, ~en mutiny; (*fig.*) revolt; mutiny

**Meuterer** /'mɔytərɐ/ *der;* ~s, ~, **Meuterin** *die;* ~, ~nen mutineer; (*fig.*) rebel

**meutern** *itr. V.* Ⓐ mutiny (**gegen** against); ‹prisoners› riot; Ⓑ (*ugs.: Unwillen äußern*) moan (**gegen** about)

**Mexikaner** /mɛksi'ka:nɐ/ *der;* ~s, ~, **Mexikanerin** *die;* ~, ~nen ▶ 553 Mexican

**mexikanisch** *Adj.* ▶ 553 Mexican

**Mexiko** /'mɛxiko/ (*das*); ~s ▶ 700 Mexico

**MEZ** *Abk.* **mitteleuropäische Zeit** CET

**Mezzo·sopran** /'mɛtso-/ *der*, **Mezzo·sopranistin** (*Musik*) mezzo-soprano

**Mfg.** *Abk.* **Mitfahrgelegenheit**

**MfS** *Abk.* (*DDR*) **Ministerium für Staatssicherheit**

**mg** *Abk.* ▶ 353 **Milligramm** mg

**MG** *Abk.* **Maschinengewehr**

**mhd.** *Abk.* **mittelhochdeutsch** MHG

**MHz** *Abk.* (*Physik*) **Megahertz** MHz

**Mi.** *Abk.* **Mittwoch** Wed.

**Mia.** *Abk.* **Milliarde[n]** bn.

**miau** /mi'au̯/ *Interj.* miaow

**miauen** *itr. V.* miaow

**mich** /mɪç/ ❶ *Akk. des Personalpron.* **ich** me. ❷ *Akk. des Reflexivpron. der 1. Pers.* myself; **Was tust du im Badezimmer? — Ich wasche ~:** What are you doing in the bathroom? — I'm washing [myself]; **ich möchte ~ entschuldigen** I'd like to apologize

**Michael** /'mɪçae:l/ (*der*) Michael

**Michaeli[s]** (*das*); ~, **Michael[i]stag** *der* Michaelmas

**Michel** /'mɪçl̩/ *der;* ~s, ~ *in* **der deutsche ~:** *proverbial figure representing the blinkered, simple-minded German, uninterested in politics and the world at large*

*old spelling (see note on page 1707)

**Michigan·see** /mɪʃɪgən-/ *der;* **~s** Lake Michigan

**mick[e]rig** /'mɪk(ə)rɪç/ *Adj.* (*ugs.*) miserable; measly (*sl.*); miserable, paltry, (*sl.*) measly ‹amount›; puny ‹person›; puny, stunted ‹plant, tree›

**Mickymaus** /'mɪki-/ *die;* **~:** Mickey Mouse *no art.*

**Midi** /'mi:di/ *das;* **~s, ~s** (*Mode*) midi (*coll.*); **im ~:** in a midi; **~ tragen/gehen** wear a midi[-skirt/dress/coat]

**Midlife·krise** /'mɪtlaif-/ *die* midlife crisis

**mied** /mi:t/ *1. u. 3. Pers. Sg. Prät. v.* **meiden**

**Mieder** /'mi:dɐ/ *das;* **~s, ~** **A** (*Korsage*) girdle; **B** (*Leibchen*) bodice

**Mieder-: ~hose** *die* pantie-girdle; **~waren** *Pl.* corsetry *sing.*

**Mief** /mi:f/ *der;* **~[e]s** (*salopp abwertend*) fug (*coll.*); **der ~ der Kleinstadt** (*fig.*) the claustrophobic small-town atmosphere

**miefen** *itr. V.* (*ugs. abwertend*) pong (*coll.*); stink

**Miene** /'mi:nə/ *die;* **~, ~n** expression; face; **mit unbewegter ~:** with an impassive expression; impassively; **keine ~ verziehen** not turn a hair; **er schluckte die Medizin, ohne eine ~ zu verziehen** he swallowed the medicine without turning a hair; **~ machen, etw. zu tun** make as if to do sth.; **gute ~ zum bösen Spiel machen** grin and bear it

**Mienen·spiel** *das* facial expressions *pl.*

**mies** /mi:s/ (*ugs.*) **1** *Adj.* (*abwertend*) terrible (*coll.*); lousy (*coll.*); rotten (*coll.*); lousy (*coll.*), foul ‹mood›; **jmdn./etw. ~ machen** (*ugs.*) run sb./sth. down; **jmdm. etw. ~ machen** spoil sth. for sb. **2** *adv.* **A** (*abwertend: schlecht*) terribly badly (*coll.*); lousily (*coll.*); rottenly (*coll.*); **das ist aber ~ gearbeitet** the workmanship on this is terrible (*coll.*) *or* lousy (*coll.*) *or* rotten (*coll.*); **B** (*unwohl*) **ihm geht es ~:** he's in a terrible state (*coll.*)

**Miese** /'mi:zə/ *Pl.; adj. Dekl.* (*salopp*) **2 000 ~ auf dem Konto haben** be 2,000 marks in the red at the bank; **in den ~n sein** be in the red; (*beim Kartenspiel*) be down on points

**Miese·peter** *der;* **~s, ~** (*ugs. abwertend*) misery guts (*coll.*)

**miesepet[e]rig** *Adj.* (*ugs. abwertend*) grumpy

**mies-, Mies-: *~|machen** ⇒ **mies** 1; **~macher** *der,* **~macherin** *die* (*ugs. abwertend*) carping critic; (*Spielverderber*) killjoy; **~muschel** *die* [common] mussel

**Miet·ausfall** *der* loss of rent

**Miete**[1] /'mi:tə/ *die;* **~, ~n** **A** rent; (*für ein Auto, Boot*) hire charge; (*für Fernsehgeräte usw.*) rental; **das ist schon die halbe ~** (*fig. ugs.*) I'm/you're *etc.* halfway there; **B** (*das Mieten*) renting; **zur ~ wohnen** live in rented accommodation; rent a house/flat (*Brit.*) *or* (*Amer.*) apartment/room/rooms; **bei jmdm. zur ~ wohnen** lodge with sb.

**Miete**[2] *die;* **~, ~n** (*Landw.*) pit

**Miet·einnahmen** *Pl.* income *sing.* from rents

**mieten** *tr. V.* **A** rent; (*für kürzere Zeit*) hire; **B** (*veralt.: in Dienst nehmen*) hire ‹servant›

**Mieter** /'mi:tɐ/ *der;* **~s, ~:** tenant

**Miet·erhöhung** *die* rent increase

**Mieterin** *die;* **~, ~nen** tenant

**Mieter·schutz** *der* protection of tenants; tenants' protection

**miet·frei** *Adj., adv.* rent-free

**Miet·kauf** *der* (*Wirtsch.*) ≈ hire purchase (*Brit.*) *or* (*Amer.*) installment plan (*with option to buy outright or terminate the agreement at a specified date*)

**Mietling** /'mi:tlɪŋ/ *der;* **~s, ~e** (*veralt. abwertend*) hireling

**Miet-: ~partei** *die* tenant; **~preis** *der* rent; (*für ein Auto, Boot*) hire charge; (*für Fernsehgeräte usw.*) rental; **~recht** *das* law of landlord and tenant

**Miets-: ~haus** *das* block of rented flats (*Brit.*) *or* (*Amer.*) apartments; **~kaserne** *die* (*abwertend*) tenement block

**Miet-: ~verhältnis** *das* (*Amtsspr.*) tenancy; **~vertrag** *der* tenancy agreement; **~wagen** *der* hire car; **~wohnung** *die* rented flat (*Brit.*) *or* (*Amer.*) apartment; **~wucher** *der* charging of exorbitant rents; **~zahlung** *die:* **mit seiner ~zahlung im Rückstand sein** be behind with the rent; **~zins** *der; Pl.* **~e** (*südd., österr., schweiz., Amtsspr.*) rent; **~zuschuss, *~zuschuß** *der* assistance with the rent

**Mieze** /'mi:tsə/ *die;* **~, ~n** **A** (*fam.: Katze*) puss; pussy (*child lang.*); **B** (*salopp: Mädchen*) chick (*sl.*); (*als Anrede*) sweetie

**Mieze·katze** *die* (*fam.*) puss; pussy cat (*child lang.*)

**Migräne** /mi'grɛ:nə/ *die;* **~, ~n** ▶ 474 migraine

**Migräne·anfall** *der* attack of migraine

**Migrant** *der;* **~en, ~en, Migrantin** *die;* **~, ~nen** migrant

**Mikado** /mi'ka:do/ *das;* **~s** spillikins *sing.;* jackstraws *sing.*

**mikro-, Mikro-** micro-

**Mikro** /'mi:kro/ *das;* **~s, ~s** (*ugs.*) mike (*coll.*)

**Mikrobe** /mi'kro:bə/ *die;* **~, ~n** microbe

**Mikro-: ~elektronik** *die* microelectronics *sing., no art.;* **~faser** *die* microfibre; **~fiche** /-fi:ʃ/ *das od. der;* **~~s, ~~s** microfiche; **~film** *der* microfilm; **~klima** *das* microclimate; **~kosmos** *der* (*Philos.*) microcosm; **~meter** *der od. das* micron

**Mikronesien** /mikro'ne:zi̯ən/ (*das*); **~s** Micronesia

**mikro-, Mikro-: ~organismus** *der* (*Biol.*) micro-organism; **~phon** /--'-/ *das;* **~~s, ~~e** microphone; **~prozessor** /-pro'tsɛsɔr/ *der* microprocessor; **~skop** /-'sko:p/ *das;* **~~s, ~~e** microscope; **~skopie** /-sko'pi:/ *die;* **~~:** microscopy *no art.;* **~skopisch** **1** *Adj.* microscopic; **2** *adv.* microscopically; **etw. ~skopisch untersuchen** examine sth. under the microscope; **~welle** *die* (*ugs.*) microwave [oven]; **~wellen** *Pl.* microwaves; **~wellen·herd** *der* microwave oven

**Milan** /'mi:lan/ *der;* **~s, ~e** (*Zool.*) kite

**Milbe** /'mɪlbə/ *die;* **~, ~n** mite; (*Zecke*) tick

**Milch** /mɪlç/ *die;* **~** **A** milk; **~ geben** give *or* yield milk; **aussehen wie ~ und Blut** have a lilies-and-roses complexion; **das Land, wo ~ und Honig fließt** (*bibl.*) the land flowing with milk and honey; **B** (*Fischsamen*) milt; soft roe

**Milch-: ~bar** *die* milk bar; **~bart** *der* (*abwertend*) callow youth; **~becher** *der* milk mug; **~brötchen** *das* milk roll; **~drüse** *die* ▶ 471 mammary gland; **~eiweiß** *das* (*Biol.*) milk protein; **~flasche** *die* **A** (*für Säuglinge*) feeding bottle; baby's bottle; **B** (*Flasche für ~*) milk bottle; **~frau** *die* (*ugs.*) dairywoman; **~gebiss, *~gebiß** *das* ▶ 471 milk teeth *pl.;* **~geschäft** *das* dairy; **~gesicht** *das* (*abwertend*) callow youth; **~glas** *das* **A** milk glass; (*aufgeraut*) frosted glass; **B** (*Trinkglas*) milk glass

**milchig** **1** *Adj.* milky. **2** *adv.* **~ weiß** milky-white; **die ~-trübe Färbung des Wassers** the milky cloudiness of the water

**Milch-: ~kaffee** *der* coffee with plenty of milk; **~kännchen** *das* milk jug; **~kanne** *die* milk can; (*zum Transportieren von Milch*) [milk] churn; **~kuh** *die* dairy *or* milk *or* milch cow; **~mädchen** *das* dairymaid; **~mädchen·rechnung** *die* (*ugs.*) naïve miscalculation; **~mann** *der* ▶ 159 (*ugs.*) milkman; **~mix·getränk** *das* milk shake

**Milchner** /'mɪlçnɐ/ *der;* **~s, ~** (*Zool.*) milter

**Milch-: ~pumpe** *die* breast pump; **~reis** *der* rice pudding; **~säure** *die* (*Chemie*) lactic acid; **~schokolade** *die* milk chocolate; **~schorf** *der* ▶ 474 milk crust; crusta lactea (*Med.*); **~straße** *die* Milky Way; Galaxy; (*System*) Galaxy; **~straßen·system** *das* (*Astron.*) galaxy; **~suppe** *die* milk soup; **~vieh** *das* dairy cattle; **~wirtschaft** *die* dairying *no art.;* **~zahn** *der* milk tooth; **~zucker** *der* (*Chemie*) lactose

**mild** /mɪlt/, **milde** **1** *Adj.* **A** (*gütig*) lenient ‹judge, judgement›; benevolent ‹ruler›; mild, lenient, light ‹punishment›; mild ‹words, accusation›; mild, gentle ‹reproach›; gentle ‹smile, voice›; **jmdn. ~[e] stimmen** induce sb. to take a lenient attitude; **B** (*nicht rau*) mild ‹climate, air, winter, etc.›; **C** (*gedämpft*) soft ‹light, glow›; **D** (*nicht scharf*) mild ‹spice, coffee, tobacco, cheese, etc.›; smooth ‹brandy›; **~ schmecken** be mild/smooth; **E** (*schonend*) mild ‹soap, shampoo, detergent›; **F** (*veralt.: mildtätig*) charitable; **eine ~e Gabe** alms *pl.* **2** *adv.* **A** (*gütig*) leniently; ‹smile, say› gently; **B** (*nicht rau*) **der Wind wehte/die Sonne schien ~:** the wind blew gently/a gentle sun shone down; **C** (*sanft*) **~ schimmern/leuchten** shimmer softly/shine gently; **D** (*gelinde*) mildly; **~e ausgedrückt** to put it mildly; putting it mildly

**Milde** *die;* **~** **A** (*Gnade, Güte*) leniency; **[jmdm. gegenüber] ~ walten lassen** be lenient [with sb.]; **väterliche/christliche ~:** fatherly/Christian kindness; **B** (*des Klimas usw.*) mildness; **C** (*milder Geschmack*) (*von Tabak, Gewürzen usw.*) mildness; (*von Weinbrand*) smoothness; **D** (*Gedämpftheit*) softness; **E** (*veralt.: Wohltätigkeit*) charity

**mildern** **1** *tr. V.* **A** (*herabmindern*) moderate ‹criticism, judgement›; mitigate ‹punishment›; **~de Umstände** mitigating circumstances; **B** (*dämpfen*) moderate ‹language›; soothe ‹anger›; lessen ‹agitation›; **C** (*abschwächen*) reduce ‹intensity, strength, effect›; modify ‹impression›; ease, soothe, relieve ‹pain›; alleviate ‹poverty, need›; ease ‹sorrow›. **2** *refl. V.* **A** (*geringer werden*) ‹anger, rage, agitation› abate; **B** (*abschwächen*) ‹effect› be reduced; ‹impression› be modified; **C** (*wärmer werden*) ‹weather› become milder

**Milderung** *die;* **~** **A** (*eines Tadels, Urteils*) moderation; (*einer Strafe*) mitigation; **B** (*Linderung*) (*von Schmerz*) easing; soothing; relief; (*von Armut, Not*) alleviation

**Milderungs·grund** *der* mitigating circumstance

**mild·tätig** **1** *Adj.* charitable; **für ~tätige Zwecke sammeln** collect for charity. **2** *adv.* **~ wirken** perform charitable acts

**Mild·tätigkeit** *die* charity

**Milieu** /mi'li̯ø:/ *das;* **~s, ~s** **A** (*soziales Umfeld*) milieu; environment; (*fig.: Prostitution usw.*) world of pimps and prostitutes; **das ~ der Berliner Kneipen** the world of Berlin pubs (*Brit.*) *or* (*Amer.*) bars; **er stammt aus kleinbürgerlichem ~:** his background is petit bourgeois; **B** (*Biol.: Lebensraum*) environment

**milieu-, Milieu-: ~geschädigt** *Adj.* (*Psych.*) maladjusted (*as a result of adverse environmental influences*); **~schilderung** *die* description of the physical and social environment; **~studie** *die* study of an environment; **~theorie** *die* (*Psych.*) environmentalism *no art.*

**militant** /mili'tant/ *Adj.* militant

**Militanz** *die;* **~:** militancy

**Militär**[1] /mili'tɛ:ɐ̯/ *das;* **~s** **A** armed forces *pl.;* military; **beim ~ sein/vom ~ entlassen werden** be in/be discharged from the forces; **zum ~ müssen** have to join the forces; **zum ~ einberufen werden** be called up; **B** (*Soldaten*) soldiers *pl.;* army; **~ gegen jmdn. einsetzen** use the army against sb.

**Militär**[2] *der;* **~s, ~s** [high-ranking military] officer

**Militär-: ~akademie** *die* military academy; **~arzt** *der* medical officer; **~attaché** *der* military attaché; **~basis** *die* military base; **~block** *der; Pl.* **~blöcke** military [alliance-]bloc; **~dienst** *der* military service; **seinen ~dienst ableisten** do one's military *or* national service; **~diktatur** *die* military dictatorship; **~fahrzeug** *das* military vehicle; **~flugplatz** *der* military airfield; **~flugzeug** *das* military aircraft; **~geistliche** *der* army chaplain; **~gericht** *das* military court; court martial; **vor ein ~gericht gestellt werden** be brought before *or* tried by a military court; be court-martialled;

m

**~gerichtsbarkeit** *die* military jurisdiction *no art.;* **~hilfe** *die* military aid *no art.;* **~hubschrauber** *der* military helicopter

**Militaria** /mili'ta:ri̯a/ *Pl.* military objects; militaria

**militärisch** ❶ *Adj.* military; **jmdm. ~e Ehren erweisen** award *or* give sb. military honours; **mit allen ~en Ehren** with full military honours. ❷ *adv.* **gegen jmdn. ~ vorgehen** take military action against sb.; **jmdn. ~ grüßen** salute sb.; **~ strammstehen** stand to attention

**militarisieren** /militari'zi:rən/ *tr. V.* militarize

**Militarisierung** *die;* **~:** militarization

**Militarismus** *der;* **~** (*abwertend*) militarism

**Militarist** *der;* **~en, ~en, Militaristin** *die;* **~, ~nen** (*abwertend*) militarist

**militaristisch** *Adj.* (*abwertend*) militarist; militaristic

**Militär-: ~junta** *die* military junta; **~kapelle** *die* (*Musik*) military band; **~marsch** *der* military march; **~musik** *die* military music; **~parade** *die* military parade; **~polizei** *die* military police; **~putsch** *der* military putsch; **~regierung** *die* military government; **~seelsorge** *die* pastoral care of military personnel; **in der ~seelsorge tätig sein** look after the spiritual welfare of military personnel; **~streife** *die* military patrol; **~stützpunkt** *der* military base; **~wesen** *das* military affairs *pl., no art.;* **~wissenschaft** *die* military science

**Military** /'mɪlɪtərɪ/ *die;* **~, ~s** (*Reiten*) three-day event

**Militär·zeit** *die* time in the forces *or* services

**Miliz** /mi'li:ts/ *die;* **~, ~en** militia; (*Polizei*) police

**Milizionär** /militsi̯o'nɛ:ɐ̯/ *der;* **~s, ~e** (A) militiaman; (B) (*Polizist*) policeman

**milk** /mɪlk/, **milkst, milkt** (*veralt.*) *Imperativ Sg., 2. u. 3. Pers. Sg. Präsens v.* **melken**

**Mill.** *Abk.* **Million** m.

**Mille** /'mɪlə/ *die;* **~, ~** (*salopp*) grand (*coll.*); thousand marks/pounds *etc.;* **zwei ~:** two grand (*coll.*)

**Millennium** /mɪ'lɛni̯ʊm/ *das;* **~s, Millennien** millennium

**milli-** /'mɪli-/, **Milli-** milli-

**Milliardär** /mɪli̯ar'dɛ:ɐ̯/ *der;* **~s, ~e, Milliardärin** *die;* **~, ~nen** multi-millionaire (*possessing at least a thousand million marks etc.*); billionaire (*Amer.*); ⇒ *auch* **Millionär**

**Milliarde** /mɪ'li̯ardə/ *die;* **~, ~n** ▶841 thousand million; billion; **mehrere ~n Mark/Einwohner** several thousand million *or* several billion marks/inhabitants; ⇒ *auch* **Million**

**Milliarden-: ~höhe** *die:* **in ~höhe** of the order of a thousand million *or* a billion; **~kredit** *der* credit of the order of a thousand million *or* a billion; ⇒ *auch* **millionen-, Millionen-**

**milliardst...** *Ordinalz.* ▶841 thousand millionth; billionth; ⇒ *auch* **hundertst...**

**milliardstel** *Bruchz.* thousand millionth; billionth; ⇒ *auch* **hundertstel**

**Milliardstel** *das, schweiz. der;* **~s, ~:** part in a billion *or* thousand million; ⇒ *auch* **Hundertstel**

**Milli-: ~bar** *das* (*Met.*) millibar; **~gramm** *das* ▶353 milligram; **~liter** *der od. das* ▶611 millilitre

**Milli·meter** *der od. das* ▶489 millimetre

**Millimeter-: ~arbeit** *die* (*ugs.*) (*am Steuer*) delicate piece of manœuvring; (*bei Ballspielen*) [neat] piece of precision play; **~papier** *das* [graph] paper ruled in millimetre squares

**Million** /mɪ'li̯o:n/ *die;* **~, ~en** ▶841 (A) million; **eine ~ Menschen war** *od.* **waren ...** a million people were ...; **zwei ~en [Einwohner]** two million [inhabitants]; (B) *Pl.* (*unbestimmte Anzahl od. Summe*) millions; **~en von Menschen** millions of people; **in die ~en gehen** run into millions

**Millionär** /mɪli̯o'nɛ:ɐ̯/ *der;* **~s, ~e, Millionärin** *die;* **~, ~nen** millionaire

*old spelling (see note on page 1707)

**millionen-, Millionen-: ~auf·lage** *die* (*Buchw.*) **dieses Buch erschien in ~auflage** *od.* **erlebte eine ~auflage** [over] a million copies of this book were printed; **~auftrag** *der* contract worth a million/worth millions; **~fach** ❶ *Adj.* millionfold ‹increase etc.›; **in ~fachen Tests** in a million tests; **~fache Zustimmung finden** meet with the approval of millions of people; **es kam zu ~fachen Protesten** there were millions of protests; ❷ *adv.* a million times; **~geschäft** *das* deal worth a million/worth millions; **~gewinn** *der* (A) (*Ertrag*) profit of a million/of millions; **~gewinne** profits running into millions; (B) (*Lotteriegewinn*) prize of a million/of millions; **~heer** *das* millions *pl.;* **~höhe** *die:* **in ~höhe** of the order of a million; **~kredit** *der* credit of the order of a million; ***~mal** ⇒ **Mal**[1]; **~schaden** *der* damage *no pl., no indef. art.* running into millions; **~schwer** *Adj.* (*ugs.*) worth millions *pred.;* **~stadt** *die* town with over a million inhabitants; **~vermögen** *das* fortune of millions

**millionst...** *Ordinalz.* ▶841 millionth; ⇒ *auch* **hundertst...**

**million[s]tel** *Bruchz.* ▶841 millionth; ⇒ *auch* **hundertstel**

**Million[s]tel** *das od.* (*schweiz.*) *der;* **~s, ~** ▶841 millionth; (*Teilmenge*) part in a million; ppm

**Milz** /mɪlts/ *die;* **~** ▶471 (*Anat.*) spleen

**Milz·brand** *der* ▶474 (*Tiermed.*) anthrax

**Mime** /'mi:mə/ *der;* **~n, ~n** (*geh.*) Thespian

**mimen** ❶ *tr. V.* (A) (*ugs. abwertend*) put on a show of ‹admiration, efficiency›; **Trauer/Besorgnis ~:** act sad/concerned (*coll.*); **den Kranken/Unschuldigen ~:** pretend to be ill/act the innocent; **den starken Mann ~:** act tough; (B) (*darstellen*) play; act; **den Tell ~:** play Tell. ❷ *itr. V.* (*ugs. abwertend*) **auf Millionär/krank** *usw.* **~:** pretend to be a millionaire/to be ill *etc.*

**Mimesis** /'mi:mezɪs/ *die;* **~, Mimesen** (*Liter., Philos.*) mimesis; imitation

**Mimik** /'mi:mɪk/ *die;* **~:** gestures and facial expressions *pl.*

**Mimikry** /'mɪmikri/ *die;* **~** (*Zool.*) mimicry; (*fig.*) camouflage

**Mimin** *die;* **~, ~nen** ⇒ **Mime**

**mimisch** ❶ *Adj.* mimic; **seine ~e Ausdruckskraft** the expressive power of his gestures and facial movements; **eine ~e Begabung** a gift for mimic expression. ❷ *adv.* ‹show› by means of gestures and facial expressions; **~ begabt sein** have a gift for mimic expression

**Mimose** /mi'mo:zə/ *die;* **~, ~n** (A) mimosa; (*volkst.: Akazie*) silver wattle; (B) (*empfindsamer Mensch*) oversensitive person; **die reinste ~ sein** be extraordinarily sensitive

**mimosenhaft** ❶ *Adj.* oversensitive. ❷ *adv.* oversensitively

**Min.** *Abk.* **Minute[n]** min.

**Minarett** /mina'rɛt/ *das;* **~s, ~e** *od.* **~s** minaret

**mind.** *Abk.* **mindestens**

**minder** /'mɪndɐ/ *Adv.* (*geh.*) less; **[nicht] ~ angenehm sein** be [no] less pleasant; ⇒ *auch* **mehr**

**minder...** *Adj.* inferior ‹goods, brand›; **von ~er Bedeutung/Qualität sein** be of less importance/inferior *or* lower quality

**minder-, Minder-: ~begabt** *Adj.* less gifted *or* able; **~begütert** *Adj.* less well-off; **~bemittelt** *Adj.* without much money *postpos., not pred.;* **~bemittelt sein** not have much money; **er ist doch geistig ~bemittelt** (*fig. salopp abwertend*) he isn't all that bright (*coll.*); **~bemittelte** *der/die; adj. Dekl.* needy person; **~einnahme** *die* decrease in revenue; (*geringere Einnahme, als kalkuliert*) shortfall in revenue

**Minderheit** *die;* **~, ~en** minority

**Minderheiten·recht** *das* right of a/the minority

**Minderheits·regierung** *die* minority government

**minder-, Minder-: ~jährig** *Adj.* (*Rechtsw.*) ‹child etc.› who is/was a minor *or* under age; **~jährig sein** be a minor *or* under age; **~jährige** *der/die; adj. Dekl.* (*Rechtsw.*) minor; person under age; **~jährigkeit** *die;* **~~** (*Rechtsw.*) minority; **bis zum Ende der ~jährigkeit** until he/she comes/came of age

**mindern** (*geh.*) ❶ *tr. V.* reduce ‹income, price, number of staff, tension, etc.›; impair ‹performance, abilities›; diminish, reduce ‹value, quality, dignity, pleasure, influence›; detract from ‹reputation›. ❷ *refl. V.* diminish; ‹vehemence› lessen

**Minderung** *die;* **~, ~en** ⇒ **mindern** 1: reduction (*Gen.* in); impairment (*Gen.* of); diminution (*Gen.* of); detraction (*Gen.* from)

**minder·wertig** *Adj.* (*abwertend*) inferior, low-quality ‹goods, material›; low-quality, low-grade ‹meat›; (*fig.*) inferior; **ein moralisch ~wertiger Mensch** (*abwertend*) a person of questionable character

**Minder·wertigkeit** *die* ⇒ **minderwertig**: inferiority; low quality; low grade; (*fig.*) inferiority

**Minderwertigkeits-: ~gefühl** *das* (*Psych.*) feeling of inferiority; **~komplex** *der* (*Psych.*) inferiority complex

**Minder·zahl** *die* minority

**mindest...** /'mɪndəst.../ *Adj.* slightest; least; **ohne die ~e Angst** without the slightest *or* least trace of fear; **ich habe nicht die ~e Ahnung** I haven't the slightest idea; **das ist das Mindeste, was du tun kannst** it is the least you can do; **sie versteht nicht das Mindeste vom Kochen** she doesn't know the slightest *or* first thing about cooking; **nicht im Mindesten** *od.* **~en** not in the least; **zum Mindesten** *od.* **~en** at least

**Mindest-: ~alter** *das* minimum age; **~anforderung** *die* minimum requirement; **~betrag** *der* minimum amount

**mindestens** /'mɪndəstn̩s/ *Adv.* at least

**Mindest-: ~gebot** *das* reserve price; **~geschwindigkeit** *die* minimum speed; **~größe** *die* minimum size; **~haltbarkeits·datum** *das* best-before date; **~lohn** *der* minimum wage; **~maß** *das* minimum (**an** + *Dat.*, **von** of); **~preis** *der* minimum [legal] price; **~strafe** *die* (*Rechtsw.*) minimum penalty; **~urlaub** *der* minimum holiday entitlement; **~zahl** *die* minimum

**Mine** /'mi:nə/ *die;* **~, ~n** (A) (*Erzbergwerk*) mine; (B) (*Sprengkörper*) mine; **auf eine ~ laufen** strike a mine; (C) (*Bleistift~*) lead; (*Kugelschreiber~, Filzschreibe~*) refill

**Minen-: ~feld** *das* minefield; **~leger** *der;* **~~s, ~~** (*Milit.*) minelayer; **~such·boot** *das* (*Milit.*) minesweeper; **~such·gerät** *das* (*Milit.*) mine-detector; **~werfer** *der* (*Milit. Hist.*) trench mortar

**Mineral** /mine'ra:l/ *das;* **~s, ~e** *od.* **Mineralien** mineral

**Mineral-: ~bad** *das* spa; **~brunnen** *der* ⇒ **~quelle**; **~dünger** *der* inorganic fertilizer

**Mineraloge** /mɪnera'lo:gə/ *der;* **~n, ~n** mineralogist

**Mineralogie** *die;* **~:** mineralogy *no art.*

**Mineralogin** *die;* **~, ~nen** ⇒ **Mineraloge**

**mineralogisch** *Adj.* mineralogical

**Mineral·öl** *das* mineral oil

**Mineralöl-: ~gesellschaft** *die* oil company; **~industrie** *die* oil industry; **~steuer** *die* tax on oil

**Mineral-: ~quelle** *die* mineral spring; **~salz** *das,* **~stoff** *der* mineral salt; **~wasser** *das; Pl.* **~wässer** mineral water

**mini-, Mini-** mini-

**Mini** *das;* **~s, ~s** (*Mode*) mini (*coll.*); **im ~:** in a mini (*coll.*); **diese Kleider sind alle in ~:** all these dresses are mini-length *or* (*coll.*) minis *pl.;* **~ tragen** wear a mini (*coll.*)

**Miniatur** /mini̯a'tu:ɐ̯/ *die;* **~, ~en** miniature

**Miniatur-: ~ausgabe** *die* (*Buchw.*) abridged edition; **~maler** *der* miniaturist; **~malerei** *die* miniature painting; **~malerin** *die* ⇒ **~maler**

**Mini·golf** *das* minigolf; crazy golf

**minimal** /mini'ma:l/ ❶ *Adj.* minimal; marginal ‹advantage, lead›; very slight ‹benefit, profit›.

**2** *adv.* minimally; **sie unterscheiden sich nur ~:** the differences between them are minimal

**Minimal-: ~forderung** *die* minimum demand; **~gewicht** *das* minimum weight; **~wert** *der* minimum value

**minimieren** *tr. V.* (*bes. Math.*) minimize

**Minimierung** *die;* ~, **~en** (*bes. Math.*) minimization

**Minimum** /ˈmiːnimʊm/ *das;* **~s, Minima** minimum (**an** + *Dat.* of); **ein ~ an Vertrauen** a certain minimum degree of trust; **etw. unter dem ~ verkaufen** sell sth. below the minimum [legal] price

**Mini-: ~rock** *der* miniskirt; **~spion** *der* miniaturized listening *or* (*coll.*) bugging device

**Minister** /miˈnɪstɐ/ *der;* **~s, ~** ▶ 91, ▶ 159 minister (**für** for); (*eines britischen Hauptministeriums*) Secretary of State (**für** for); (*eines amerikanischen Hauptministeriums*) Secretary (**für** of)

**Minister-: ~amt** *das* ministerial office; **~ebene** *die: in* **auf ~ebene** at ministerial level

**Ministerial-: ~beamte** *der,* **~beamtin** *die* ministry official; **~direktor** *der,* **~direktorin** *die* head of a ministry department; **~dirigent** *der,* **~dirigentin** *die* head of a section within a ministry department

**Ministeriale** /minɪsteˈri̯aːlə/ *der/die; adj. Dekl.* ⇒ **Ministerialbeamte**

**Ministerial·rat** *der,* **Ministerial·rätin** *die* ⇒ **Ministerialdirigent**

**ministeriell** /minɪsteˈri̯ɛl/ **1** *Adj.* ministerial. **2** *adv.* by the minister

**Ministerin** *die;* ~, **~nen** ▶ 91, ▶ 159 ⇒ **Minister**

**Ministerium** /minɪsˈteːri̯ʊm/ *das;* **~s, Ministerien** Ministry; Department (*Amer.*)

**Minister-: ~präsident** *der,* **~präsidentin** *die* **A** (*eines deutschen Bundeslandes*) minister-president; prime minister (*Brit.*); governor (*Amer.*); **B** (*Premierminister[in]*) Prime Minister; **~rat** *der* Council of Ministers; **~sessel** *der* (*ugs.*) ministerial post

**ministrabel** /minɪsˈtraːbl̩/ *Adj.* capable of holding ministerial office *pred.*

**Ministrant** /minɪsˈtrant/ *der;* **~en, ~en, Ministrantin** *die* (*kath. Kirche*) server

**ministrieren** *itr. V.* (*kath. Kirche*) serve [at the altar]; act as server

**Minna** /ˈmɪna/ *die;* **~, ~s** (*ugs. veralt.*) maid; **jmdn. zur ~ machen** (*ugs.*) tear sb. off a strip (*Brit. coll.*); bawl out (*coll.*); **eine grüne ~** (*ugs.*) a Black Maria; a patrol wagon (*Amer.*)

**Minne** /ˈmɪnə/ *die;* **~** (*MA.*) courtly love

**Minne-: ~dienst** *der* (*MA.*) knight's homage to his lady; **~sang** *der* (*Literaturw.*) Minnesong; **~sänger** *der,* **~singer** *der;* **~~s, ~~** (*MA.*) Minnesinger

**Minorität** /minoriˈtɛːt/ *die;* **~, ~en** ⇒ **Minderheit**

**Minuend** /miˈnu̯ɛnt/ *der;* **~en, ~en** minuend

**minus** /ˈmiːnʊs/ **1** *Konj.* ▶ 841 (*Math.*) minus. **2** *Adv.* **A** ▶ 728 (*bes. Math.*) minus; **~ fünf Grad, fünf Grad ~:** minus five degrees; five degrees below [zero]; **B** (*Elektrot.*) negative. **3** *Präp. mit Gen.* (*Kaufmannsspr.*) less; minus

**Minus** *das;* **~** **A** (*Fehlbetrag*) deficit; (*auf einem Konto*) overdraft; **~ machen** make a loss; **im ~ sein** be in debit; be in the red; **B** (*Nachteil*) minus; drawback; (*im Beruf*) disadvantage

**Minus·betrag** *der* deficit

**Minuskel** /miˈnʊskl̩/ *die;* **~, ~n** (*Druckw.*) minuscule

**Minus-: ~pol** *der* (*Physik*) negative pole; (*einer Batterie*) negative terminal; **~punkt** *der* **A** minus *or* penalty point; **B** (*Nachteil*) disadvantage; **~zeichen** *das* minus sign

**Minute** /miˈnuːtə/ *die;* **~, ~n** **A** ▶ 265, ▶ 752 minute; **6 ~n nach/vor zwei** six minutes to/past two; **es ist neun Uhr [und] sieben ~n** it is seven minutes past nine *or* nine seven; **~ um ~ verging** *od.* **verstrich** minutes went by *or* passed; **B** (*Moment*) minute; moment; **hast du ein paar ~n Zeit für mich?** can you spare me a few minutes *or* moments?; **in letzter ~:** at the last minute *or* moment; **auf die ~ pünktlich sein** *od.* **kommen** be punctual to the minute

**minuten·lang** **1** *Adj.* ‹applause, silence, etc.› lasting [for] several minutes; **sein ~es Schweigen** his silence, which lasted for several minutes. **2** *adv.* for several minutes

**Minuten·zeiger** *der* minute hand

**-minütig** *Adj.* **ein fünf~er Heulton** a wail lasting five minutes; **eine fünfzehn~e Verspätung** a fifteen-minute delay; a delay of fifteen minutes

**minütlich** /miˈnyːtlɪç/ **1** *Adj.* **in ~en Abständen** at intervals of a minute. **2** *adv.* every minute

**minuziös** /minuˈtsi̯øːs/ (*geh.*) **1** *Adj.* minutely *or* meticulously precise *or* detailed ‹account, description›; minute ‹detail›; ‹manœuvre› requiring minute precision. **2** *adv.* meticulously

**Minze** /ˈmɪntsə/ *die;* **~, ~n** mint

**Mio.** *Abk.* **Million[en]** m.

**mir** /miːɐ̯/ **1** *Dat. Sg. des Personalpron.* **ich** **A** to me; (*nach Präpositionen*) me; **gib es ~:** give it to me; give me it; **gib ~ das Buch** give me the book; **Freunde von ~:** friends of mine; **gehen wir zu ~:** let's got to my place; **~ nichts, dir nichts** (*ugs.*) just like that; without so much as a 'by your leave'; **von ~ aus** as far as I'm concerned; **Kann ich das Radio abstellen? — Von ~ aus** Can I turn the radio off? — As far as I'm concerned you can; **B** (*Dativus ethicus*) **geht ~ nicht an meinen Schreibtisch!** keep away from my desk!; **und grüß ~ alle Verwandten!** and give my regards to all the relatives; **du bist ~ vielleicht einer!** (*ugs.*) a fine one you are!; **wie du ~, so ich dir** tit for tat; (*drohend*) I'll get my own back. **2** *Dat. des Reflexivpron. der 1. Pers. Sg.* myself; **ich habe ~ deine Vorschläge genau überlegt** I have given careful thought to your suggestions; **ich habe ~ gedacht, dass ...** I thought that ...; **ich will ~ ein neues Kleid kaufen** I want to buy myself a new dress; **ich nehme ~ noch von dem Braten** I'll help myself to some more roast

**Mirabelle** /miraˈbɛlə/ *die;* **~, ~n** mirabelle

**Mirakel** /miˈraːkl̩/ *das;* **~s, ~** (*geh. veralt.*) miracle

**Misanthrop** /mizanˈtroːp/ *der;* **~en, ~en, Misanthropin** *die;* **~, ~nen** (*geh.*) misanthrope

**Misch-: ~batterie** *die* mixer tap; mixing faucet (*Amer.*); **~blut** *das* (*geh.*) ⇒ **Mischling** A; **~brot** *das* bread made from wheat and rye flour; **~ehe** *die* mixed marriage

**mischen** /ˈmɪʃn̩/ **1** *tr. V.* mix; **etw. in etw.** (*Akk.*) **~:** put sth. into sth.; **Wasser und Wein ~:** mix water with wine; **[sich** (*Dat.*)**] Tees/Tabake ~:** blend [one's own] teas/tobaccos; **die Karten ~:** shuffle the cards. **2** *refl. V.* **A** (*sich ver~*) mix (**mit** with); ‹smell, scent› blend (**mit** with); **in meine Freude mischte sich Angst** my joy was mingled with fear; **B** (*sich ein~*) **sich in etw.** (*Akk.*) **~:** interfere *or* meddle in sth.; **sich in das Gespräch ~:** butt into the conversation; **C** (*sich begeben*) **sich unters Publikum** *usw.* **~:** mingle with the audience *etc.* **3** *itr. V.* **A** (*Kartenspiel*) shuffle; **wer muss ~?** whose shuffle is it?; **B** (*Film, Rundf., Ferns.*) mix; ⇒ *auch* **gemischt**

**Mischer** *der;* **~s, ~** (*Bauw.*) [cement] mixer

**Misch-: ~farbe** *die* non-primary colour; **~form** *die* mixture; (*Kunstform*) fusion; **~futter** *das* mixed feed; **~gewebe** *das* mixture; **~kultur** *die* **A** (*Landw.*) mixed cultivation; **B** (*Soziol.*) mixed culture

**Mischling** /ˈmɪʃlɪŋ/ *der;* **~s, ~e** **A** half-caste; half-breed; **B** (*Biol.*) hybrid

**Mischmasch** /ˈmɪʃmaʃ/ *der;* **~[e]s, ~e** (*ugs., meist abwertend*) hotchpotch; mishmash; (*Essen*) concoction

**Misch·maschine** *die* (*Bauw.*) cement mixer

**Mischpoke** /mɪʃˈpoːkə/ *die;* **~** (*salopp abwertend*) **A** (*Verwandtschaft*) tribe (*derog.*); **B** (*Gesellschaft*) mob (*coll.*); shower (*Brit. coll.*)

**Misch-: ~pult** *das* (*Film, Rundf., Ferns.*) mixing desk *or* console; **~sprache** *die* hybrid language; **~trommel** *die* mixing drum

**Mischung** *die;* **~, ~en** **A** (*Gemisch, auch fig.*) mixture; (*Tee~, Kaffee~, Tabak~*) blend; (*Pralinen~*) assortment; **B** (*das Mischen*) mixing; (*von Tee, Kaffee, Tabak*) blending

**Mischungs·verhältnis** *das* proportion in the mixture

**Misch·wald** *der* mixed [deciduous and coniferous] forest

**miserabel** /mizəˈraːbl̩/ (*ugs.*) **1** *Adj.* **A** (*schlecht*) dreadful (*coll.*), atrocious ‹film, wine, food›; pathetic, miserable ‹achievement›; miserable, dreadful (*coll.*), atrocious ‹weather›; **B** (*elend*) miserable; wretched; **mir ist ~ zumute, ich fühle mich ~:** I feel dreadful; **C** (*niederträchtig*) abominable ‹behaviour›. **2** *adv.* **A** (*schlecht*) dreadfully (*coll.*); atrociously; ‹sleep› dreadfully badly (*coll.*); **~ bezahlt werden** be very badly *or* poorly paid; **B** (*elend*) **ihm geht es gesundheitlich ~:** he's in a bad way; **C** (*niederträchtig*) **sich ~ benehmen** *od.* **verhalten** behave abominably

**Misere** /miˈzeːrə/ *die;* **~, ~n** (*geh.*) wretched *or* dreadful state; (*Elend*) misery; (*Not*) distress; **seine finanzielle ~:** his wretched *or* dreadful financial state

**Miserere** /mizeˈreːrə/ *das;* **~s** (*bibl.*) miserere

**Mispel** /ˈmɪspl̩/ *die;* **~, ~n** medlar

**miss, *miß** /mɪs/ *Imperativ Sg. v.* **messen**

**Miss, *Miß** /mɪs/ *die;* **~, ~es** /ˈmɪsɪz/ Miss

**miss·achten, *miß·achten** *tr. V.* **A** (*ignorieren*) disregard; ignore; **B** (*gering schätzen*) disdain; be contemptuous of; **sich missachtet fühlen** feel scorned

**Miss·achtung, *Miß·achtung** *die* **A** (*Nichtbeachtung*) disregard (+ *Gen.* of, for); **die ~ der Vorschriften/meines Rates** disregarding *or* ignoring the regulations/my advice; **B** (*Verachtung*) disdain, contempt (+ *Gen.* for)

**Miss·behagen, *Miß·behagen** *das* [feeling of] unease; uncomfortable feeling; **bei dem Gedanken daran befiel sie ein tiefes ~:** she did not at all like the thought of it

**Miss·bildung, *Miß·bildung** *die* deformity

**miss·billigen, *miß·billigen** *tr. V.* disapprove of

**Miss·billigung, *Miß·billigung** *die* disapproval

**Miss·brauch, *Miß·brauch** *der* **A** (*das ~en*) abuse; misuse; (*falsche Anwendung*) misuse; (*von Feuerlöscher, Notbremse*) improper use; **mit seiner Stellung/Macht ~ treiben** abuse *or* misuse one's position/power; **unter ~ seines Amtes** by misusing his position; **B** (*übermäßiger Gebrauch*) misuse; **C** (*geh.: Vergewaltigung*) rape

**miss·brauchen, *miß·brauchen** *tr. V.* **A** abuse; misuse; abuse ‹trust›; **jmdn. für** *od.* **zu etw. ~:** use sb. for sth.; **B** (*übermäßig gebrauchen*) misuse ‹drugs, medicines›; **C** (*geh.: vergewaltigen*) rape

**missbräuchlich, *mißbräuchlich** /-brɔyçlɪç/ **1** *Adj.* **~e Verwendung/Anwendung** misuse. **2** *adv.* **etw. ~ verwenden/handhaben** misuse sth.

**miss·deuten, *miß·deuten** *tr. V.* misinterpret

**Miss·deutung, *Miß·deutung** *die* misinterpretation

**missen** *tr. V.* (*geh.*) **A** (*entbehren*) do *or* go without; do without ‹person›; **jmdn./etw. nicht ~ können/mögen** be unable to do without/not want to be without sb./sth.; **B** (*selten*) ⇒ **vermissen** 1

**Miss·erfolg, *Miß·erfolg** *der* failure

**Miss·ernte, *Miß·ernte** *die* crop failure

**Misse·tat** /ˈmɪsə-/ *die* (*geh. veralt.*) misdeed

**Misse·täter** *der,* **Misse·täterin** *die* (*geh. veralt.*) malefactor

m

**miss·fallen**, ***miß·fallen** *unr. itr. V.* **etw. missfällt jmdm.** sb. dislikes *or* does not like sth.; **es missfiel mir, wie unfreundlich sie ...** I disliked *or* did not like the unkind way she ...

**Missfallen**, ***Mißfallen** *das;* **~s** displeasure (**über** + *Akk.* at); (*Missbilligung*) disapproval (**über** + *Akk.* of); **~ erregen** arouse displeasure/disapproval; **jmds. ~ erregen** incur sb.'s displeasure/disapproval

**Missfallens·äußerung**, ***Mißfallens·äußerung** *die* expression of displeasure/disapproval

**miss·fällig**, ***miß·fällig** (*veralt.*) ❶ *Adj.* disapproving. ❷ *adv.* disapprovingly

**miss·gebildet**, ***miß·gebildet** *Adj.* deformed

**Miss·geburt**, ***Miß·geburt** *die* (*Med.*) monster; monstrosity; **diese ~ von [einem] Krämer!** (*fig. abwertend*) that misbegotten scoundrel of a shopkeeper

**miss·gelaunt**, ***miß·gelaunt** (*geh.*) ❶ *Adj.* ill-humoured. ❷ *adv.* ill-humouredly

**Miss·geschick**, ***Miß·geschick** *das* (*ärgerlicher Vorfall*) mishap; (*Pech*) bad luck; (*Unglück*) misfortune; **jmdm. passiert** *od.* **widerfährt ein ~:** sb. has a mishap/a piece *or* stroke of bad luck/a misfortune; **vom ~ verfolgt sein** be dogged by bad luck/misfortune

**Missgestalt**, ***Mißgestalt** *die* (*geh.*) misshapen figure

**miss·gestaltet**, ***miß·gestaltet** *Adj.* misshapen; deformed ‹person, child›

**miss·gestimmt**, ***miß·gestimmt** ❶ *Adj.* (*geh.*) ill-humoured; **~ sein** be in a bad mood. ❷ *adv.* ill-humouredly

**miss·glücken**, ***miß·glücken** *itr. V.; mit sein* fail; be unsuccessful; **der Kuchen/Plan ist mir missglückt** the cake I made turned out a failure/my plan failed *or* was a failure; **ein missglückter Versuch** a failed *or* unsuccessful attempt

**miss·gönnen**, ***miß·gönnen** *tr. V.* **jmdm. etw. ~:** begrudge sb. sth.; **er missgönnte ihr, dass sie ...** he begrudged the fact that she ...

**Miss·griff**, ***Miß·griff** *der* error of judgement; **einen ~ tun** *od.* **machen** make an error of judgement

**Miss·gunst**, ***Miß·gunst** *die* [envy and] resentment (**gegenüber** of); (*fig.: des Schicksals*) malevolence

**miss·günstig**, ***miß·günstig** ❶ *Adj.* resentful; (*fig.*) malevolent ‹fate›. ❷ *adv.* resentfully; (*fig.*) malevolently

**miss·handeln**, ***miß·handeln** *tr. V.* maltreat; ill-treat; **misshandelte Frauen/Kinder** battered wives/children

**Miss·handlung**, ***Miß·handlung** *die* maltreatment; ill-treatment; **~en** maltreatment *sing.;* ill-treatment *sing.*

**Miss·helligkeiten**, ***Miß·helligkeiten** *Pl.* (*geh.*) differences

**missingsch** /ˈmɪsɪŋʃ/ *Adv.* **~ sprechen** speak Missingsch

**Missingsch** *das;* **~:** Missingsch (*Hamburg dialect made up of High German and some Low German elements*)

**Mission** /mɪˈsi̯oːn/ *die;* **~, ~en** Ⓐ (*geh.: Auftrag*) mission; **in geheimer ~:** on a secret mission; Ⓑ (*geh.: Personengruppe*) mission; (*Delegation*) delegation; Ⓒ (*Rel.*) mission; **in der [äußeren/inneren] ~ tätig sein** do missionary work [abroad/in one's own country]; Ⓓ (*geh.: diplomatische Vertretung*) mission

**Missionar** /mɪsi̯oˈnaːɐ̯/ *der;* **~s, ~e,** (*österr.*) **Missionär** /mɪsi̯oˈnɛːɐ̯/ *der;* **~s, ~e, Missionarin** *die;* **~, ~nen,** (*österr.*) **Missionärin** *die;* **~, ~nen ▶ 159** missionary

**missionarisch** ❶ *Adj.* missionary. ❷ *adv.* **~ tätig sein** do missionary work

**Missionar·stellung** *die* (*ugs.*) missionary position

*old spelling (see note on page 1707)

**missionieren** ❶ *itr. V.* do missionary work. ❷ *tr. V.* convert by missionary work; (*fig.*) convert to one's own ideas

**Missionierung** *die;* **~: die ~ eines Landes/eines Volkes** missionary work in a country/among a people; (*als Ergebnis*) the conversion of a country/people [by missionary work]

**Missions-: ~chef** *der,* **~chefin** *die* (*Politik*) head of a/the mission; **~gesellschaft** *die* missionary society; **~station** *die* mission station; **~wissenschaft** *die* missiology *no art.;* study of the Christian mission

**Miss·klang**, ***Miß·klang** *der* discord; dissonance; (*fig.*) discord; **mit einem ~ enden** (*fig.*) end on a note of discord; **es gab einige Missklänge** (*fig.*) there was a certain amount of discord

**Miss·kredit**, ***Miß·kredit** *der: in* **jmdn./etw. in ~ bringen** bring sb./sth. into discredit; bring discredit on sb./sth.; **bei jmdm. in ~ geraten** get a bad name with sb.

**misslang**, ***mißlang** *1. u. 3. Pers. Sg. Prät. v.* **misslingen**

**miss·launig**, ***miß·launig** *Adj.* (*geh.*) ⇒ **missgelaunt**

**misslich**, ***mißlich** *Adj.* (*geh.*) awkward, difficult ‹situation›; difficult ‹conditions›; unfortunate ‹consequences, incident›; **es steht ~ um die [Finanzkraft der] Firma** the firm is not doing very well [financially]

**Misslichkeit**, ***Mißlichkeit** *die;* **~, ~en** (*geh.*) (*missliche Situation*) awkward *or* difficult situation; (*misslicher Vorfall*) unfortunate incident

**missliebig**, ***mißliebig** /ˈmɪsliːbɪç/ *Adj.* unpopular; **~e Ausländer** unwanted foreigners; **sich ~ machen** make oneself persona non grata (**bei** with)

**misslingen**, ***mißlingen** /mɪsˈlɪŋən/ *unr. itr. V.; mit sein* fail; be unsuccessful; be a failure; **ein misslungener Kuchen** an unsuccessful attempt at a cake; **ein misslungener Versuch** a failed *or* unsuccessful attempt

**Misslingen**, ***Mißlingen** *das;* **~s** failure

**misslungen**, ***mißlungen** /mɪsˈlʊŋən/ *2. Part. v.* **misslingen**

**Miss·mut**, ***Miß·mut** *der* ill humour *no indef. art.;* **mit leichtem ~:** somewhat in a bad temper; **jmds. ~** (*Akk.*) **erregen** put sb. in a bad mood

**miss·mutig**, ***miß·mutig** ❶ *Adj.* bad-tempered; sullen ‹face›; **warum bist du heute so ~?** why are you in such a bad mood today? ❷ *adv.* bad-temperedly

**miss·raten**, ***miß·raten** *unr. itr. V.; mit sein* ‹cake, photo, etc.› turn out badly; **gänzlich ~:** be a complete failure; **das Bild/der Kuchen ist ihr ~/nicht ~:** her picture/cake turned out badly/well; **ein ~es Kind** a child who has turned out badly

**Miss·stand**, ***Miß·stand** *der:* **die vorhandenen Missstände** the serious shortcomings that exist; **das ist ein ~:** it is deplorable; **Missstände in der Verwaltung** serious irregularities in the administration; **soziale Missstände** social evils; **einen ~ beseitigen** put an end to a deplorable state of affairs

**Miss·stimmung**, ***Miß·stimmung** *die* (*gedrückte Stimmung*) ill humour *no indef. art.;* (*gereizte Stimmung*) discord *no indef. art.*

**misst**, ***mißt** *2. u. 3. Pers. Sg. Präsens v.* **messen**

**Miss·ton**, ***Miß·ton** *der; Pl.* **Miss·töne** discordant note; (*fig.*) note of discord; discordant note; **mit einem ~ enden** (*fig.*) end on a note of discord

**misstönend**, ***mißtönend**, **misstönig**, ***mißtönig** ❶ *Adj.* discordant. ❷ *adv.* discordantly

**miss·trauen**, ***miß·trauen** *itr. V.* **jmdm./einer Sache ~:** mistrust *or* distrust sb./sth.; **sich** (*Dat.*) **selbst ~:** have no confidence in oneself

**Misstrauen**, ***Mißtrauen** *das;* **~s** mistrust, distrust (**gegen** of); **voll[er] ~:** extremely mistrustful *or* distrustful (**gegen** of); **~ gegen jmdn./etw. haben, jmdm./einer Sache ~ entgegenbringen** mistrust *or* distrust sb./sth.

**Misstrauens-**, ***Mißtrauens-: ~antrag** *der* motion of no confidence; **~votum** *das* vote of no confidence (**gegen[über]** in)

**misstrauisch**, ***mißtrauisch** /ˈmɪstrau̯ɪʃ/ ❶ *Adj.* mistrustful; distrustful; (*argwöhnisch*) suspicious. ❷ *adv.* mistrustfully; distrustfully; (*argwöhnisch*) suspiciously

**Miss·vergnügen**, ***Miß·vergnügen** *das* (*geh.*) (*Ärger*) annoyance; (*Unzufriedenheit*) discontentment; **jmdm. ~ bereiten** make sb. annoyed/discontented

**miss·vergnügt**, ***miß·vergnügt** (*geh.*) ❶ *Adj.* (*verärgert*) annoyed; (*unzufrieden*) discontented; (*verdrießlich*) ill-humoured. ❷ *adv. s. Adj.:* in an annoyed way; discontentedly; ill-humouredly

**Miss·verhältnis**, ***Miß·verhältnis** *das* disparity; (*an Größe*) disproportion

**miss·verständlich**, ***miß·verständlich** ❶ *Adj.* unclear; ‹formulation, concept, etc.› that could be misunderstood; **~ sein** be liable to be misunderstood. ❷ *adv.* ‹express oneself, describe› in a way that could be misunderstood

**Miss·verständnis**, ***Miß·verständnis** *das* Ⓐ misunderstanding; Ⓑ (*Meinungsverschiedenheit*) misunderstanding; disagreement

**miss·verstehen**, ***miß·verstehen** *unr. tr. V.;* **ich missverstehe, missverstanden, misszuverstehen** misunderstand

**Miss·wahl**, ***Miß·wahl** *die: contest for the title of 'Miss Europe', 'Miss World' etc.*

**Miss·weisung**, ***Miß·weisung** *die* (*Physik*) declination

**Miss·wirtschaft**, ***Miß·wirtschaft** *die* mismanagement

**Mist** /mɪst/ *der;* **~[e]s** Ⓐ dung; (*Dünger*) manure; (*mit Stroh usw. gemischt*) muck; **das ist nicht auf ihrem ~ gewachsen** (*fig. ugs.*) that didn't come out of her own head; Ⓑ (**~haufen**) dung/manure/muck heap; Ⓒ (*ugs. abwertend*) (*Schund*) rubbish, junk, trash *all no indef. art.;* (*Unsinn*) rubbish, nonsense, (*coll.*) rot *all no indef. art.;* (*lästige, dumme Angelegenheit*) nonsense; **mach deinen ~ doch alleine!** bloody (*Brit. sl.*) *or* damn well do it yourself!; **~ bauen** make a mess of things; mess things up; **mach bloß keinen ~!** just don't do anything stupid!; **so ein ~!** what a damned *or* blasted nuisance!; damn *or* blast it!

**Mist·beet** *das* hotbed; forcing bed

**Mistel** /ˈmɪstl̩/ *die;* **~, ~n** mistletoe

**Mistel·zweig** *der* piece of mistletoe

**misten** ❶ *tr. V.* Ⓐ (*düngen*) manure; Ⓑ ⇒ **ausmisten.** ❷ *itr. V.* (*Landw.*) dung

**Mist-: ~fink** *der* (*derb*) dirty *or* (*coll.*) mucky so-and-so; **~forke** *die* (*nordd.*), **~gabel** *die* dung fork; **~haufen** *der* dung/manure/muck heap

**mistig** (*salopp*) ❶ *Adj.* rotten (*coll.*). ❷ *adv.* in a rotten way (*coll.*)

**Mist·käfer** *der* dung beetle

**Mistral** /mɪsˈtraːl/ *der;* **~s** mistral

**Mist-: ~stück** *das* (*derb*) lousy good-for-nothing bastard (*sl.*); (*Frau*) lousy good-for-nothing bitch (*sl.*); **~vieh** *das* (*derb*) Ⓐ (*Tier*) bloody (*Brit. sl.*) *or* damn animal; **dieses ~vieh von Katze** that bloody (*Brit. sl.*) *or* damn cat; Ⓑ ⇒ **~stück; ~wagen** *der* dung cart; **~wetter** *das* (*salopp*) lousy weather (*coll.*); **bei so einem ~wetter** in lousy weather like this (*coll.*)

**Miszellen** /mɪsˈtsɛlən/ *Pl.* (*geh.*) miscellany *sing.*

**mit** /mɪt/ ❶ *Präp. mit Dat.* Ⓐ (*Gemeinsamkeit, Beteiligung*) with; **~ jmdm. spielen/essen/streiten** play/eat/quarrel with sb.; **ein Fest ~ Damen** a celebration at which ladies are/were present; **Verkehrsunfälle ~ Kindern** traffic accidents involving children; Ⓑ (*Zugehörigkeit*) with; **ein Haus ~ Garten** a house with a garden; **Herr Müller ~ Frau** Herr Müller and his wife; Ⓒ (*einschließlich*) with; including; **ein Zimmer ~ Frühstück** a room with breakfast included;

**~ mir waren ...** including me *or* myself there were ...; **~ mir nicht!** (*ugs.*) count me out! (*coll.*); **D** (*Inhalt*) **ein Sack ~ Kartoffeln/Glas ~ Marmelade** a sack of potatoes/pot of jam; **E** (*Begleitumstände*) with; **etw. ~ Absicht tun/~ Nachdruck fordern** do sth. deliberately/demand sth. forcefully; **~ 50 [km/h] fahren** drive at 50 [k.p.h]; **~ dem Auftrag, etw. zu tun** with the task of doing sth.; **F** (*Hilfsmittel*) with; **~ Maschine geschrieben sein** be typed; **~ der Bahn/dem Auto fahren** go by train/car; **~ der Fähre/„Hamburg"** on the ferry/the 'Hamburg'; **G** (*allgemeiner Bezug*) with; **~ der Arbeit ging es recht langsam voran** the work went very slowly; **~ Zustimmung seiner Eltern** with the consent of his parents; **~ einer Tätigkeit beginnen/aufhören** take up/give up an occupation; **was ist ~ ihm?** (*ugs.*) what's up with him? (*coll.*); **raus/fort ~ dir!** out/off you go!; **H** (*zeitlich*) **~ Einbruch der Dunkelheit/Nacht** when darkness/night falls/fell; **~ dem Einsetzen des Nachtfrostes** when we/they *etc.* start/started to get frosts at night; **~ 20 [Jahren]** at [the age of] twenty; **~ dem heutigen Tag bist du volljährig** today you have reached your majority; **~ der Zeit/den Jahren** in time/as the years go/went by; **I** (*gleiche Richtung*) with; **~ dem Strom/Wind** with the tide/wind.
**2** *Adv.* **A** (*auch*) too; as well; **~ dabei sein** be there too; **er ist beim letzten Ausflug nicht ~ gewesen** he didn't come [with us] on our last trip; **waren eure Kinder im Urlaub ~?** did your children go on holiday with you?; **warst du auch ~ im Konzert?** were you at the concert too?; ⇒ *auch* **Partie** F; **B** (*neben anderen*) also; too; as well; **es lag ~ an ihm** it was partly his doing; **das musst du ~ berücksichtigen** you must also take that into account; you must take that into account too *or* as well; **C** (**~** *Sup.*) (*ugs.*) **dieses ist ~ das wichtigste der Bücher** this is one of the most important of the books; **seine Arbeit war ~ am besten** his work was among the best; **~ der Beste** one of the best; **D** (*vorübergehende Beteiligung*) **er ist bereit, heute ~ zu helfen** he's willing to help [just for] today; **ihr könntet ruhig einmal ~ anfassen** it wouldn't hurt you to lend a hand just for once; **E** ⇒ *auch* **damit** 1 C; **womit** B

**Mit·angeklagte** *der/die* co-defendant; (*mit geringerer Strafandrohung*) defendant to a lesser charge

**Mit·arbeit** *die* **A** (*das Tätigsein*) collaboration (**bei, an** + *Dat.* on); **die ~ in der Praxis ihres Mannes** working in her husband's practice; **unter ~ (*Dat.*) von** in collaboration with; **B** (*Mithilfe*) assistance (**bei, in** + *Dat.* in); **seine zwanzigjährige ~ in der Organisation** his twenty years of service to the organization; **unter ~ von** with the assistance of; **C** (*Beteiligung*) participation (**in** + *Dat.* in)

**mit|arbeiten** *itr. V.* **A** (*mithelfen*) **bei einem Projekt/an einem Buch ~:** collaborate on a project/book; **im elterlichen Geschäft ~:** work in one's parents' shop; **ich arbeite bei einem Projekt mit, das ...** I'm working [with others] on a project that ...; **B** (*sich beteiligen*) participate (**in** + *Dat.* in); **im Unterricht besser ~:** take a more active part in lessons; **C** (*ugs.: auch arbeiten*) **seine Frau arbeitet mit** his wife works too

**Mit·arbeiter** *der*, **Mit·arbeiterin** *die* **A** (*Betriebsangehörige[r]*) employee; **B** (*bei einem Projekt, an einem Buch*) collaborator; **ein freier Mitarbeiter** a freelance; a freelance worker; **ein freier/ständiger Mitarbeiter bei einer Zeitung** a freelance contributor to a newspaper/a writer on the permanent staff of a newspaper

**Mitarbeiter·stab** *der* staff; **zu jmds. engstem ~ gehören** be one of sb.'s closest assistants

**Mit·begründer** *der*, **Mit·begründerin** *die* co-founder

**mit|bekommen** *unr. tr. V.* **A** **etw. ~:** be given *or* get sth. to take with one; (*fig.*) inherit sth.; **etw. bei der Heirat ~:** be given sth. on marriage; **B** (*wahrnehmen*) be aware of; (*durch Hören, Sehen*) hear/see; **es war so laut, dass ich nur die Hälfte mitbekam** it was so noisy that I only caught half of it; **hast du das ~?** (*ugs.*) did you know?; **C** (*miterleben*) **etw. ~:** manage to hear/see sth.; **etwas von etw. ~:** hear/see something of sth.; **nicht viel/nichts von etw. ~:** not be able to hear/see much/anything of sth.; **D** (*verstehen*) **ich war so müde, dass ich nicht viel ~ habe** I was so tired that I did not grasp very much; **ich habe gar nicht ~, wie er das meinte** I did not realize at all how he meant it

**mit|benutzen**, (*bes. südd.*) **mit|benützen** *tr. V.* share; have the use of

**Mit·benutzung**, (*südd.*) **Mit·benützung** *die* use

**Mit·besitz** *der* share [of the ownership]; **an etw. (*Dat.*) [einen] ~ haben** have a share in sth.

**Mit·besitzer** *der*, **Mit·besitzerin** *die* joint owner; co-owner

**mit|bestimmen** **1** *itr. V.* have a say (**in** + *Dat.* in); **mehr ~ können** *od* **dürfen** have a greater say. **2** *tr. V.* have an influence on; **etw. maßgeblich ~:** have a determining influence on

**Mit·bestimmung** *die* participation (**bei** in); (*der Arbeitnehmer*) co-determination; **betriebliche ~, ~ am Arbeitsplatz** involvement of employees in management decisions

**Mit·bestimmungs-:** **~gesetz** *das* law of co-determination; **~recht** *das* right of co-determination

**Mit·bewerber** *der*, **Mit·bewerberin** *die* competitor; **ich hatte nur einen Mitbewerber für** *od.* **um diese Stelle** there was only one other applicant for the job [besides me]; **alle Mitbewerber hatten bessere Qualifikationen** all the other applicants had better qualifications; **seine Mitbewerber** the other competitors/applicants

**Mit·bewohner** *der*, **Mit·bewohnerin** *die* other occupant; **seine Mitbewohner** his fellow occupants; the other occupants

**mit|bringen** *unr. tr. V.* **A** **etw. ~:** bring sth. with one; **etw. aus der Stadt/dem Urlaub/von dem Markt/der Reise ~:** bring sth. back from town/holiday/the market/one's trip; **jmdm./sich etw. ~:** bring sth. with one for sb./bring sth. back for oneself; **Gäste ~:** bring guests home; **eine Grippe/großen Hunger ~** (*fig.*) come back with influenza/feeling very hungry; **B** (*einbringen*) have, possess ‹ability, gift, etc.› (**für** for); **genügend Zeit ~:** come with enough time at one's disposal

**Mitbringsel** /-brɪŋzl/ *das;* **~s, ~:** [small] present; (*Andenken*) [small] souvenir

**Mit·bürger** *der*, **Mit·bürgerin** *die* fellow citizen; **ältere Mitbürger** (*Amtsspr.*) senior citizens

**mit|denken** *unr. itr. V.* follow [the argument/explanation/what is being said *etc.*]; **ein Schüler, der mitdenkt** a pupil who follows the lesson; **die Fähigkeit zum M~:** the ability to think for oneself

**mit|dürfen** *unr. itr. V.* (*ugs.*) (*mitkommen dürfen*) be allowed to come along *or* too; (*mitgehen, mitfahren dürfen*) be allowed to go along *or* too

**Mit·eigentum** *das* ⇒ **Mitbesitz**

**Mit·eigentümer** *der*, **Mit·eigentümerin** *die* ⇒ **Mitbesitzer**

**mit·einander** *Adv.* **A** with each other *or* one another; **~ sprechen/kämpfen** talk to each other *or* one another/fight with each other *or* one another; **B** (*gemeinsam*) together; **~ gegen jmdn. kämpfen** fight together against sb.; **alle ~:** all together; **ihr seid Gauner, alle ~!** you are all a pack of rogues!; you're all rogues, the lot of you!

**Mit·einander** *das;* **~[s]** living and working together *no art.;* **im ~:** by mutual cooperation

**mit|empfinden** **1** *unr. tr. V.* **jmds. Schmerz/Leid ~:** know the pain/sorrow sb. is/was feeling. **2** *unr. itr. V.* **mit jmdm. ~:** sympathize with sb.

**Mit·empfinden** *das* sympathy

**Mit·erbe** *der*, **Mit·erbin** *die* (*Rechtsw.*) joint heir; co-heir

**mit|erleben** *tr. V.* **A** (*dabei sein bei*) witness ‹events etc.›; **sie hat das Unglück miterlebt** she was involved in the accident; **eine Premiere ~:** be present at a première; **B** (*mitmachen*) be alive during

**mit|essen** **1** *unr. tr. V.* eat ‹skin etc.› as well; **bei dem Apfel habe ich einen Wurm mitgegessen** I've swallowed a grub along with the apple. **2** *unr. itr. V.* **jmdn. einladen mitzuessen** invite sb. to eat with one *or* have a meal; **bei jmdm. ~:** eat *or* have a meal with sb.

**Mit·esser** *der* **A** blackhead; **B** (*ugs. scherzh.*) **einen [zusätzlichen] ~ haben** have one more to dinner/lunch/*etc.*

**Mit·esserin** *die* ⇒ **Mitesser** B

**mit|fahren** *unr. itr. V.; mit sein* **bei jmdm. [im Auto] ~:** go with sb. [in his/her car]; (*auf einer Reise*) travel with sb. [in his/her car]; (*mitgenommen werden*) get *or* have a lift with sb. [in his/her car]; **jmdn. ~ lassen** let sb. go; (*jmdn. mitnehmen*) give sb. a lift

**Mit·fahrer** *der*, **Mit·fahrerin** *die* fellow passenger; (*vom Fahrer aus gesehen*) passenger

**Mitfahrer·zentrale** *die: office for putting those wanting lifts in touch with those who can offer them*

**Mitfahr·gelegenheit** *die* lift

**mit|fühlen** *tr., itr. V.* ⇒ **mitempfinden**

**mit·fühlend** **1** *Adj.* sympathetic. **2** *adv.* sympathetically

**mit|führen** *tr. V.* **A** (*Amtsspr.: bei sich tragen*) **etw. ~:** carry sth. [with one]; **führen Sie zollpflichtige Waren mit?** have you anything to declare?; **B** (*transportieren*) ‹river, stream› carry along

**mit|geben** *unr. tr. V.* **jmdm. etw. ~:** give sb. sth. to take with him/her; **er gab mir einen Brief an seine Eltern mit** he gave me a letter for *or* to give to his parents; **ich werde Ihnen eine Begleitung ~:** I'll get somebody to accompany you; **jmdm. eine gute Erziehung/Ausbildung ~** (*fig.*) provide sb. with a good training/education

**Mit·gefangene** *der/die* fellow prisoner

**Mit·gefühl** *das* sympathy

**mit|gehen** *unr. itr. V.; mit sein* **A** (*mitkommen*) go too; **mit jmdm. ~:** go with sb.; **sie ist bis zur Bushaltestelle mitgegangen** she went with him/her *etc.* to the bus stop; **etw. ~ lassen** (*fig. ugs.*) walk off with sth. (*coll.*); pinch sth. (*coll.*); **B** (*sich mitreißen lassen*) **begeistert/enthusiastisch ~:** respond enthusiastically (**bei, mit** to); **C** (*weggerissen werden*) be carried away

**mit·genommen** *Adj.* **1** ⇒ **mitnehmen**. **2** (*beschädigt*) worn-out ‹furniture, carpet›; **~ sein/aussehen** ‹book etc.› be/look to be in a sorry state; (*fig.*) ‹person› be/look worn out

**Mit·gift** *die;* **~, ~en** (*veralt.*) dowry

**Mitgift·jäger** *der* (*veralt. abwertend*) dowry hunter

**Mit·glied** *das* member (+ *Gen.*, **in** + *Dat.* of); **~ im Finanzausschuss sein** be a member of *or* sit on the finance committee; **„Zutritt nur für ~er"** 'members only'

**Mitglieder-:** **~liste** *die* list of members; **~versammlung** *die* general meeting; **~zahl** *die* number of members; membership

**Mitglieds-:** **~ausweis** *der* membership card; **~beitrag** *der* membership subscription

**Mitgliedschaft** *die;* **~:** membership (+ *Gen.*, **in** + *Dat.*) of

**Mitglied[s]·staat** *der* member state *or* country

**mit|haben** *unr. tr. V.* (*ugs.*) **etw./jmdn. ~:** have got sth./sb. with one

**mit|halten** *unr. itr. V.* **A** (*Schritt halten*) keep up (**bei** in, **mit** with); **keiner konnte [mit ihm] ~** (*in einer Diskussion, auf einem*

m

*Fachgebiet usw.*) nobody could touch him; Ⓑ (*beim Essen, Trinken*) eat/drink one's share

**mit|helfen** *unr. itr. V.* help (**bei, in** + *Dat.* with); **ein bisschen ~:** lend a hand for a bit; **bei dem Bau der Garage ~:** help to build the garage

**Mit·helfer** *der,* **Mit·helferin** *die* (*abwertend*) accomplice

**Mit·herausgeber** *der,* **Mit·herausgeberin** *die* joint editor; co-editor; (*Verlag*) co-publisher

**mit·hilfe** ❶ *Präp. mit Gen.* with the help *or* aid of.
❷ *Adv.* **~ von** with the help *or* aid of

**Mit·hilfe** *die* help; assistance

**mit·hin** *Adv.* therefore

**mit|hören** ❶ *tr. V.* listen to; (*zufällig*) overhear ‹conversation, argument, etc.›; (*abhören*) listen in on. ❷ *itr. V.* listen; (*zufällig*) overhear; **fürchten, dass mitgehört wird** be afraid that somebody is listening in; ⇒ *auch* **Feind**

**Mit·inhaber** *der,* **Mit·inhaberin** *die* joint owner; co-owner; (*einer Firma, eines Restaurants auch*) joint proprietor

**mit|kämpfen** *itr. V.* take part in the fighting

**Mit·kämpfer** *der,* **Mit·kämpferin** *die* comrade-in-arms; (*Sport*) teammate

**mit|klingen** *unr. itr. V.:* ⇒ **mitschwingen**

**mit|kommen** *unr. itr. V.; mit sein* Ⓐ come too; **kommst du mit?** are you coming [with me/us]?; **ich kann nicht ~:** I can't come; **bis zur Tür ~:** come with sb. to the door; Ⓑ (*Schritt halten*) keep up; **in der Schule/im Unterricht gut/schlecht ~:** get on well/badly at school/with one's lessons; **da komme ich nicht mehr mit!** (*fig. ugs.*) I can't understand it at all!

**mit|können** *unr. itr. V.* (*ugs.*) **er kann mit** he can come too; (*darf mitgehen, mitfahren*) he can go too

**mit|kriegen** *tr. V.* (*ugs.*) ⇒ **mitbekommen**

**mit|laufen** ❶ *unr. itr. V.; mit sein* Ⓐ **mit jmdm. ~:** run with sb.; Ⓑ (*Sport*) **beim 100-m-Lauf** *usw.* **~:** run in the 100 m. *etc.*; Ⓒ **ein Tonband ~ lassen** have a tape recorder running; Ⓓ (*ugs.: nebenbei erledigt werden*) **die Reparaturen müssen nebenher ~:** the repairs have to be fitted in along with everything else *or* as we go along. ❷ *unr. tr. V.; mit sein* **ein Rennen ~:** run in a race

**Mit·läufer** *der,* **Mit·läuferin** *die* (*abwertend*) [mere] supporter; (*Schmarotzer*) hanger-on

**Mit·laut** *der* consonant

**Mit·leid** *das* pity, compassion (**mit** for); (*Mitgefühl*) sympathy (**mit** for); **mit jmdm. ~ haben** *od.* **empfinden** feel pity *or* compassion/have *or* feel sympathy for sb.; **jmds. ~ erregen** arouse sb.'s sympathy; **ein Sympathie und ~ erregendes Schicksal** a fate arousing compassion and sympathy

**Mit·leidenschaft** *die:* *in* **jmdn./etw. in ~ ziehen** affect sb./sth.

**mitleid·erregend** *Adj.* pitiful

**mit·leidig** ❶ *Adj.* compassionate; (*mitfühlend*) sympathetic. ❷ *adv.* compassionately; (*mitfühlend*) sympathetically; (*iron.*) pityingly

**mitleid[s]-:** **~los** ❶ *Adj.* pitiless; (*herzlos*) unfeeling; ❷ *adv.* without pity; (*herzlos*) unfeelingly; **~voll** ❶ *Adj.* compassionate; ❷ *adv.* compassionately

**mit|lesen** *unr. tr. V.* Ⓐ (*zur Kenntnis nehmen*) **etw. ~:** read sth. (*as well as sth. else*); Ⓑ (*zugleich lesen*) **etw. [mit jmdm.] ~:** read sth. at the same time as sb.; **mein Gegenüber las meine Zeitung mit** the person opposite me was also reading my newspaper

**mit|machen** ❶ *tr. V.* Ⓐ (*teilnehmen an*) go on ‹trip›; join in ‹joke›; follow ‹fashion›; fight in ‹war›; do ‹course, seminar›; Ⓑ (*ugs.: billigen*) **das mache ich nicht mit** I can't go along with it; **ich mache das nicht länger mit!** I'm not standing for it any longer!; Ⓒ (*ugs.: zusätzlich erledigen*) **jmds. Arbeit ~:** do sb.'s work as well as one's own; Ⓓ (*ugs.: erleiden*) **zwei Weltkriege/viele Bombenangriffe mitgemacht haben** have been through two world wars/many bomb attacks; **er hat viel mitgemacht** he has been through a great deal.
❷ *itr. V.* Ⓐ (*sich beteiligen*) join in; **bei einem Wettbewerb/einer Aktion ~:** take part in a competition/take part in *or* join in a campaign; **willst du ~?** do you want to join in?; **da[bei] mache ich nicht mit** I'm not joining in; you can count me out (*coll.*); Ⓑ (*ugs.: funktionieren*) **meine Beine machen nicht mehr mit** my legs are giving up on me (*coll.*); **mein Herz/Kreislauf macht nicht mit** my heart/circulation can't take it

**Mit·mensch** *der* fellow man; fellow human being; **urteile nicht so hart über deine ~en** don't be so harsh in your judgements of other people

**mit·menschlich** *Adj.* human, interpersonal ‹relations, relationships›; interpersonal ‹contacts, communication›

**mit|mischen** *itr. V.* (*ugs.*) Ⓐ (*sich einmischen*) interfere (**bei** in); (*sich beteiligen*) get involved (**bei** in); Ⓑ (*Sportjargon*) (*mit vollem Einsatz kämpfen*) give everything one's got; (*dem Gegner Paroli bieten*) give as good as one gets

**mit|müssen** *unr. itr. V.* (*mitkommen müssen*) have [got] to come with sb.; (*mitgehen, -fahren müssen*) have [got] to go with sb.

**Mitnahme** *die; ~, ~n* (*Amtsspr.*) **die ~ von Taschen in das Museum ist nicht erlaubt** it is forbidden *or* visitors are not allowed to take bags into the museum; **die Diebe verschwanden unter ~ des gesamten Schmucks** the thieves vanished with all the jewelry *or* vanished, taking all the jewelry with them

**Mitnahme-:** **~markt** *der* (*retail*) cash and carrry [store]; **~preis** *der* (*Kaufmannsspr.*) take-away price

**mit|nehmen** *unr. tr. V.* Ⓐ **jmdn. ~:** take sb. with one; **etw. ~:** take sth. with one; (*verhüll.: stehlen*) walk off with sth. (*coll.*); (*kaufen*) take sth.; **etw. wieder ~:** take sth. away [with one] again; **das Frachtschiff nimmt auch Passagiere mit** the cargo ship also carries passengers; **Essen/Getränke zum M~:** food/drinks to take away *or* (*Amer.*) to go; **könntest du einen Brief für mich ~?** could you take a letter for me?; **jmdn. im Auto ~:** give sb. a lift [in one's car]; Ⓑ (*ugs.: streifen*) **der LKW hat die Hecke mitgenommen** the truck *or* (*Brit.*) lorry took the hedge with it; Ⓒ (*ugs.: wahrnehmen*) do (*coll.*) ‹sights etc.›; **auch Soho ~:** take in Soho as well; **sie nimmt alles mit, was sich ihr bietet** she makes the most of everything life has to offer her; Ⓓ (*in Mitleidenschaft ziehen*) **jmdn. ~:** take it out of sb.; **von etw. mitgenommen sein** be worn out by sth.; (*traurig gemacht*) be grieved by sth.; Ⓔ (*lernen*) **etw. aus einem Vortrag/einer Predigt ~:** get sth. out of *or* from a lecture/sermon

**Mitnehm·preis** *der* ⇒ **Mitnahmepreis**

**mitnichten** *Adv.* (*veralt.*) in no way; not at all; by no means; **er gehorchte ~:** he wouldn't obey at all

**Mitra** /ˈmiːtra/ *die; ~,* **Mitren** (*kath. Kirche*) mitre

**mit|rauchen** ❶ *tr. V.* **eine [Zigarette] ~:** have a cigarette with sb. ❷ *itr. V.* inhale other people's tobacco smoke

**mit|rechnen** ❶ *itr. V.* work the sum out at the same time; **ich habe bei deiner Addition mitgerechnet** I did the addition at the same time as you. ❷ *tr. V.* **etw. ~:** include sth. [in the calculation]

**mit|reden** *itr. V.* Ⓐ (*Sinnvolles beisteuern*) join in the conversation; **die einzige Kunstart, bei der sie ~ kann** the only art form she knows enough about to hold a conversation; Ⓑ (*mitbestimmen*) have a say

**mit|reisen** *itr. V.* **[mit jmdm.] ~:** travel with sb.

**Mit·reisende** *der/die* fellow passenger; **einer der ~n** one of the other passengers

**mit|reißen** *unr. tr. V.* Ⓐ (*wegreißen*) ‹avalanche, flood› sweep away; **der Abstürzende hat die ganze Seilschaft mitgerissen** the falling climber dragged the whole of the roped party down with him; Ⓑ (*begeistern*) **die Begeisterung/seine Rede hat alle Zuhörer mitgerissen** the audience was carried away with enthusiasm/by his speech; **nicht gerade ~d** not exactly thrilling; **sein ~des Spiel** his exciting playing; **die ~de Musik** the rousing music

**mitsammen** /mɪtˈzamən/ *Adv.* (*österr.*) together

**mit·samt** *Präp. mit Dat.* together with; **die ganze Familie ~ Hund und Katze** the whole family, complete with cat and dog

**mit|schicken** *tr. V.* **ich schicke dir [im Brief] sein Foto mit** I'll send you his photo [with the letter]; **jmdm. einen Führer ~:** send a guide [along] with sb.

**mit|schleifen** *tr. V.* (*auch fig. ugs.*) **jmdn./etw. ~:** drag sb./sth. along

**mit|schleppen** *tr. V.* (*ugs.*) Ⓐ (*tragen*) **etw. ~:** lug *or* (*coll.*) cart sth. with one; Ⓑ ⇒ **mitschleifen**

**mit|schneiden** *unr. tr. V.* (*Rundf., Ferns.*) record [live]

**Mit·schnitt** *der* (*Rundf., Ferns.*) [live] recording

**mit|schreiben** ❶ *unr. tr. V.* **etw. ~:** take sth. down. ❷ *unr. itr. V.* write *or* take down what is/was said; (*in Vorlesungen usw.*) take notes

**Mit·schuld** *die* share of the blame *or* responsibility (**an** + *Dat.* for); (*an Verbrechen*) complicity (**an** + *Dat.* in)

**mit·schuldig** *Adj.* **an etw.** (*Dat.*) **~ sein/werden** be/become partly to blame *or* partly responsible for sth.; (*an Verbrechen*) be/become guilty of complicity in sth.; **sich ~ machen** put oneself in the position of being partly to blame *or* partly responsible for sth.; (*an Verbrechen*) become guilty of complicity as a result of one's own actions

**Mit·schuldige** *der/die* one who is/was partly to blame *or* partly responsible (**an** + *Dat.* for); (*an Verbrechen*) accomplice (**an** + *Dat.* in)

**Mit·schüler** *der,* **Mit·schülerin** *die* schoolfellow

**mit|schwingen** *unr. itr. V.* **in seinen Worten/seiner Stimme schwang Triumph/Freude mit** there was a note of triumph/joy in his words/voice

***mit|sein** ⇒ **mit** 2 A

**mit|singen** ❶ *unr. tr. V.* join in ‹song etc.›. ❷ *unr. itr. V.* join in [the singing]; sing along; **im Chor ~:** be a member of the choir

**mit|sollen** *itr. V.* (*ugs.*) **soll der Koffer auch mit?** is this case to go too?; **wenn ich mitsoll, musst du es nur sagen** just say if you want me to go with you

**mit|spielen** *itr. V.* Ⓐ (*sich beteiligen*) join in the game; **wenn das Wetter mitspielt** (*fig.*) if the weather is kind; Ⓑ (*mitwirken*) **in einem Film/bei einem Theaterstück ~:** be *or* act in a film/play; **in einem Orchester/in** *od.* **bei einem Fußballverein ~:** play in an orchestra/for a football club; Ⓒ (*sich auswirken*) play a part (**bei** in); **viele Gründe haben bei der Entscheidung mitgespielt** there were many reasons for this decision; Ⓓ (*zusetzen*) **jmdm. übel** *od.* **böse ~** ‹authorities› treat sb. badly; ‹opponent› give sb. a rough time

**Mit·spieler** *der,* **Mit·spielerin** *die* player; (*in derselben Mannschaft*) teammate; **seine ~** (*Sport*) his teammates; (*bei Kartenspielen usw.*) the other players

**Mit·sprache** *die* say; **ein Recht auf ~:** the right to a share in decisions

**Mitsprache·recht** *das:* **ein/kein ~ bei etw. haben** have a say/no say in sth.; **ein ~ bekommen** gain the right to a share in decisions

**mit|sprechen** ❶ *unr. tr. V.* (*gemeinsam sprechen*) join in [saying]. ❷ *unr. itr. V.:* ⇒ **mitreden**

**Mit·streiter** *der,* **Mit·streiterin** *die* (*geh.*) comrade-in-arms; **er fand viele Mitstreiter**

m

*old spelling (see note on page 1707)

(*fig.*) he found many people who were willing to join his campaign

**Mitt-: ~achtziger** *der* man in his mid-eighties; **~achtzigerin** *die* woman in her mid-eighties

***mittag** /ˈmɪta:k/ ⇨ **Mittag¹** A

**Mittag¹** *der;* **~s, ~e** (A) midday *no art.;* **gegen ~:** around midday *or* noon; **jeden/diesen ~:** every day at lunchtime/at lunchtime today; **heute/morgen/gestern ~:** at midday *or* lunchtime today/tomorrow/yesterday; **über ~:** at midday *or* lunchtime; **zu ~ essen** have lunch; **was essen wir zu ~?** what is there for lunch?; **was gibts zu ~?** what's for lunch?; **was gibt es heute ~ zu essen?** what's for lunch today?; (B) (*ugs.:* *~spause*) lunch hour; lunch break; **~ machen** (*ugs.*) take one's lunch hour *or* lunch break; (C) (*dichter. veralt.:* *Süden*) south

**Mittag²** *das;* **~s** (*ugs.*) lunch; **~ essen** have lunch

**Mittag-: ~brot** *das* (*landsch.*), **~essen** *das* lunch; midday meal; **beim ~essen sitzen** be having [one's] lunch *or* one's midday meal; **nach dem ~essen** after lunch

**mittäglich** /ˈmɪtɛ:klɪç/ (1) *Adj.* midday; lunchtime ‹invitation›. (2) *adv.* at midday *or* lunchtime; **es war ~ heiß auf der Straße** the street was baking in the noonday heat

**mittags** /ˈmɪta:ks/ *Adv.* ▶ 752 at midday *or* lunchtime; **bis ~:** until midday *or* lunchtime; **12 Uhr ~:** 12 noon; 12 o'clock midday; **dienstags ~:** Tuesday lunchtime; **von morgens bis ~:** in the morning until midday

**Mittags-: ~glut** *die,* **~hitze** *die* midday *or* noonday heat; heat of midday; **~linie** *die* (*Astron.*) meridian; **~mahl** *das* (*geh.*) luncheon; **~pause** *die* lunch hour; lunch break; **~pause haben** have one's lunch hour *or* lunch break; **nach der ~pause** after lunch; **in der ~pause sein** (*ugs.*) have gone to lunch; **~ruhe** *die* period of quiet after lunch; **~ruhe halten** have one's after-lunch rest; **~schlaf** *der* after-lunch sleep; **[seinen] ~schlaf halten** have an after-lunch sleep; **~schläfchen** *das* (*ugs.*) after-lunch nap; **[s]ein ~schläfchen halten** have an after-lunch nap; **~sonne** *die* midday *or* noonday sun; **~sonne haben** get the midday sun; **~stunde** *die* midday; **um die ~stunde** at midday; **~tisch** *der* (A) lunch table; **der ~tisch ist gedeckt** the table is laid for lunch; **am ~tisch sitzen** be sitting at the table having lunch; (B) (*veralt.:* *im Restaurant*) lunch; midday meal; **einen ~tisch für Studenten anbieten** do student lunches; **~zeit** *die* (A) (*Zeit gegen 12 Uhr*) lunchtime *no art.;* midday *no art.;* **in der ~zeit** at lunchtime; **um die ~zeit** at lunchtime; around midday; (B) (*~pause*) lunch hour; lunch break

**Mit·täter** *der,* **Mit·täterin** *die* accomplice

**Mit·täterschaft** *die* complicity; **jmdn. der ~ (*Gen.*) bei etw. anklagen** accuse sb. of complicity in sth.

**Mitte** /ˈmɪtə/ *die;* **~, ~n** (A) (*Teil*) middle; (*Punkt*) middle; centre; (*eines Kreises, einer Kugel, Stadt*) centre; **bis zur ~ gekommen sein** (*beim Lesen*) be halfway through; **wir nahmen sie in die ~:** we had her between us; **eine Politik der ~** (*fig.*) a middle-of-the-road policy; **die goldene ~** (*fig.*) the golden mean; **ab durch die ~!** (*fig. ugs.*) off you go; (B) ▶ 76, ▶ 207 (*Zeitpunkt*) middle; **~ des Monats/Jahres** in the middle of the month/year; **~ Februar** in mid-February; in the middle of February; **er ist ~ dreißig** he's in his mid-thirties; (C) (*Politik*) (*Gruppierung*) centre; **eine Partei der ~:** a centrist party; (D) (*Kreis von Menschen*) **wir haben sie wieder in unserer ~ begrüßt** we welcomed her back into our midst *or* amongst us; **der Tod hat ihn aus unserer ~ gerissen** (*geh.*) death has taken him from our midst; (E) (*veralt.:* *Taille*) middle; waist

**mit|teilen** (1) *tr. V.* **jmdm. etw. ~:** tell sb. sth.; (*informieren*) inform sb. of *or* about sth.; communicate sth. to sb. (*formal*); (*amtlich*) notify *or* inform sb. of sth.; **er teilte mit, dass ...** he announced that ...; **teile ihr die schlechte Nachricht schonend mit** break the news to her gently. (2) *refl. V.* (*geh.*) (A) (*sich anvertrauen*) **sich jmdm. ~:** confide in sb.; (B) (*sich übertragen auf*) **sich jmdm. ~:** communicate itself to sb.

**mitteilsam** *Adj.* communicative; (*gesprächig*) talkative

**Mitteilsamkeit** *die;* **~:** communicativeness; (*Gesprächigkeit*) talkativeness

**Mit·teilung** *die* communication; (*Bekanntgabe*) announcement; **jmdm. eine vertrauliche ~ machen** give sb. confidential information; **ich muss dir eine traurige ~ machen** I have some sad news for you; **zweckdienliche ~en** useful information *sing.*

**Mitteilungs·bedürfnis** *das* need to talk [to others]

**Mittel** /ˈmɪtl̩/ *das;* **~s, ~** (A) means *sing.;* (*Methode*) way; method; (*Werbe~, Propaganda~, zur Verkehrskontrolle*) device (+ *Gen.* for); **mit allen ~n versuchen, etw. zu tun** try by every means to do sth.; **kein ~ unversucht lassen** try every means; **zum letzten** *od.* **äußersten ~ greifen, und das Kind in ein Erziehungsheim bringen** as a last resort put the child in a community home; **[nur] ~ zum Zweck sein** be [just] a means to an end; **~ und Wege suchen/finden** look for/find ways and means; (B) (*Arznei*) **ein ~ gegen Grippe/Husten/Schuppen** *usw.* a remedy *or* cure for influenza/coughs *pl.*/dandruff *sing. etc.;* **ein ~ gegen Schmerzen** a pain-reliever; **ein ~ zum Einreiben** a cream/ointment *etc.* to be rubbed in; ⇨ *auch* **schmerzstillend**; (C) (*Substanz*) **ein ~ gegen Ungeziefer/Insekten** a pesticide/an insect repellent; **ein ~ zur Reinigung von Teppichböden/zum Entfernen von Flecken** a cleaning agent for carpets/a stain remover; (D) *Pl.* (*Geld~*) funds; [financial] resources; (*Privat~*) means; resources; **mit** *od.* **aus öffentlichen ~n** from public funds; **von seinen bescheidenen ~n** with his modest means; **meine ~ sind erschöpft** my funds are exhausted; **etw. aus eigenen ~n bezahlen** pay for sth. out of one's own resources; (E) (*Durchschnittswert*) average; **im ~:** on [the] average; **das arithmetische/geometrische ~** (*Math.*) the arithmetic/geometric mean

**mittel-, Mittel-: ~achse** *die* central axis; **~alter** *das* Middle Ages *pl.;* **das finstere ~alter** the Dark Ages *pl.;* **das sind Zustände wie im ~alter** (*ugs.*) it's positively medieval; **~alterlich** *Adj.* medieval; **~amerika** (*das*) Central America [and the West Indies]

**mittelbar** (1) *Adj.* indirect. (2) *adv.* indirectly

**mittel-, Mittel-: ~bau** *der; Pl.* **~~ten** (A) (*Gebäudeteil*) central *or* main part [of a/the building]; (B) (*Hochschulw.*) non-professorial teaching staff; **~deck** *das* (*Schiffbau*) middle deck; **~deutsch** *Adj.* (A) (*Geogr.*) of central Germany *postpos., not pred.;* (B) (*Sprachw.*) middle German; (C) (*Politik veralt.*) East German; **~deutschland** (*das*) (A) (*Geogr.*) central Germany; (B) (*Politik veralt.*) East Germany; **~ding** *das:* **ein ~ding sein** be something in between; **ein ~ding zwischen Moped und Fahrrad** something between a moped and a bicycle; **~europa** (*das*) Central Europe; **~europäer** *der,* **~europäerin** *die* Central European; **~europäisch** *Adj.* Central European; **~fein** (1) *Adj.* medium-fine ‹thread›; medium-grade ‹peas, sandpaper›; medium-ground ‹coffee›; ‹paper› containing 40-50% mechanical wood; (2) *adv.* **~fein gemahlen** medium ground; **~feld** *das* (A) (*Fußball: Spielfeldteil, Spieler*) midfield; (B) (*Sport: im Wettbewerb*) **im ~feld sein** be in the pack; (*in der Tabelle*) be in mid-table; **~feld·spieler** *der,* **~feld·spielerin** *die* (*Fußball*) midfield player; **~finger** *der* middle finger; **~fristig** /-frɪstɪç/ (*Finanzw.*) (1) *Adj.* medium-term ‹solution, financial planning›; (2) *adv.* **[etw.] ~fristig planen** plan [sth.] on a medium-term basis; **~fuß** *der* (*Anat., Zool.*) metatarsus; **~gang** *der* (*eines Eisenbahnwagens, Schiffes*) central gangway; (*einer Kirche, eines Flugzeugs*) central *or* centre aisle; **~gebirge** *das* low-mountain region; low mountains *pl.;* **~gewicht** *das* (*Schwerathletik*) (A) middleweight; ⇨ *auch* **Fliegengewicht**; (B) (*Sportler*) ⇨ **~gewichtler**; **~gewichtler** /-gəvɪçtlɐ/ *der;* **~~s, ~~:** middleweight; **~groß** *Adj.* medium-sized; ‹person› of medium height; **~hand** *die* (*Anat.*) metacarpus; **~hand·knochen** *der* (*Anat.*) metacarpal [bone]; **~hochdeutsch** *Adj.* Middle High German; **~hochdeutsch** *das* Middle High German; **~klasse** *die* (A) (*Güteklasse*) middle range; (*Größenklasse*) middle [size-]range; **ein Wagen der ~klasse** a car in the middle range/a medium-sized car; (B) (*~schicht*) middle class; **~klasse·wagen** *der* car in the middle range; (*hinsichtlich der Größe*) medium-sized car; **~kreis** *der* (*Ballspiele*) centre circle; **~latein** *das* medieval Latin; **~lateinisch** *Adj.* medieval Latin; **~linie** *die* centre line; (*Fußball*) halfway line; **~los** *Adj.* without means *postpos.;* penniless; (*arm*) poor; (*verarmt*) impoverished; **~los dastehen** be left without means; **~losigkeit** *die;* **~~:** lack of means; (*Armut*) poverty; **~maß** *das:* **gutes ~maß sein** be a good average; **das gesunde ~maß** the happy medium; **~mäßig** (*oft abwertend*) (1) *Adj.* mediocre; indifferent; indifferent ‹weather›; (2) *adv.* indifferently; **~mäßigkeit** *die* (*oft abwertend*) mediocrity; **~meer** *das* Mediterranean [Sea]; **~meerisch** *Adj.* Mediterranean

**Mittelmeer-: ~länder** *Pl.* Mediterranean countries; **~raum** *der* Mediterranean [area]

**mittel-, Mittel-: ~ohr** *das* (*Anat.*) middle ear; **~ohr·entzündung** *die* ▶ 474 (*Med.*) inflammation of the middle ear; **~prächtig** (*ugs. scherzh.*) (1) *Adj.* **[nur] ~prächtig** not particularly marvellous; (2) *adv.* **Wie gehts? — ~prächtig** How are you? — Fair to middling (*coll.*); **~punkt** *der* (A) (*Geom.*) centre; (*einer Strecke*) midpoint; (B) (*Mensch/Sache im Zentrum*) centre *or* focus of attention; **ein kultureller ~punkt** a cultural centre; **im ~punkt stehen** be the centre *or* focus of attention; **im ~punkt der Diskussion stehen** be the main topic of the discussion; **etw. in den ~punkt [seiner Rede] stellen** focus on sth. [in one's speech]; **~punkt·schule** *die: school centrally situated in a wide rural catchment area*

**mittels** *Präp. mit Gen.* (*Papierdt.*) by means of

**mittel-, Mittel-: ~scheitel** *der* centre parting; **~schicht** *die* (*Soziol.*) ⇨ **~klasse** B; **~schiff** *das* (*Archit.*) nave; **~schule** *die* (A) ⇨ **Realschule**; (B) (*österr. veralt., schweiz.*) secondary school; high school (*Amer.*); **~schul·lehrer** *der,* **~schul·lehrerin** *die* (A) ⇨ **Realschullehrer**; (B) (*österr. veralt., schweiz.*) secondary school *or* (*Amer.*) high school teacher; **~schwer** *Adj.* ‹climb, problem, etc.› of medium *or* moderate difficulty; moderately difficult ‹climb, problem, etc.›; moderately heavy ‹suitcase etc.›

**Mittels-: ~mann** *der Pl.* **~männer** *od.* **~leute**, **~person** *die* intermediary; go-between

**mittel-, Mittel-: ~stadt** *die* medium-sized town; **~stand** *der* middle class; **~ständisch** *Adj.* middle-class; medium-sized ‹firm› (*in private ownership*); **~ständler** /-ʃtɛntlɐ/ *der;* **~~s, ~~, ~ständlerin** *die;* **~~, ~~nen** (*ugs.*) middle-class person; member of the middle class; **~steinzeit** *die* mesolithic period; **~stellung** *die* intermediate *or* midway position; **etw. nimmt eine ~stellung zwischen A und B ein** sth. is intermediate between A and B; **~stimme** *die* (*Musik*) middle part *or* voice

**Mittel·strecke** *die* (A) medium haul *or* distance; **auf ~n** over medium distances; (B) (*Sport*) middle distance; **auf [den] ~n** in middle-distance running

**Mittelstrecken-: ~flug** *der* medium-haul flight; **~lauf** *der* (*Sport*) middle-distance race; (*Disziplin*) middle-distance running *no art.;* **~läufer** *der,* **~läuferin** *die* (*Sport*) middle-distance runner; **~rakete** *die* medium-range missile

m

**Mittel-: ~streifen** *der* central reservation; median strip (*Amer.*); **~stufe** *die* (*Schulw.*) middle school; **~stürmer** *der*, **~stürmerin** *die* (*Sport*) centre forward; **~teil** *der od. das* middle section; (*eines Buches*) middle [part]; **~weg** *der* middle course; **der goldene ~weg** the happy medium; **~welle** *die* (*Physik, Rundf.*) medium wave; **auf** *od.* **über ~welle** on [the] medium wave; **~wert** *der* mean [value]; **~wort** *das; Pl.* **~wörter** participle

**mitten** *Adv.* **~ an/auf etw.** (*Akk. od. Dat.*) in the middle of sth.; **der Teller brach ~ durch** the plate broke in half; **~ in etw.** (*Akk./Dat.*) into/in the middle of sth.; **~ durch die Stadt** right through the town; **~ durch die Menge** through the middle of the crowd; **~ aus etw.** from the middle of sth.; **~ darin** ⇒ **~drin; mitten unter uns** (*Dat.*) in our midst; **der Schuss traf ihn ~ ins Herz** the shot hit him right in the heart; **~ in der Luft/im Pazifik** in mid-air/mid-Pacific; **~ in der Aufregung** in the midst of the excitement

**mitten-: ~drin** *Adv.* **A** (*zwischen anderen*) [right] in the middle; **B** (*gerade dabei*) **~drin sein, etw. zu tun** be [right] in the middle of doing sth.; **~durch** *Adv.* [right] through the middle; **sie schnitt den Kuchen ~durch** she cut the cake in half *or* into two equal pieces; **~mang** *Adv.* (*nordd., berlin.*) [right] in/into the middle of it/them

**Mitter·nacht** /ˈmɪtɐ-/ *die* ▶ **752** midnight *no art.*

**mitter·nächtlich** *Adj.* midnight; **zu ~er Stunde** at midnight; at the midnight hour (*literary*)

**Mitternachts-: ~sonne** *die* midnight sun; **~stunde** *die* midnight hour; **zur/bis zur ~stunde** at/by around midnight

**mittig** (*Technik*) **1** *Adj.* aligned. **2** *adv.* ‹arranged› in line; ‹divided› centrally

**mittler...** /ˈmɪtlər.../ *Adj.* **A** (*zwischen anderen befindlich*) middle; **der/die/das ~e** the middle one; **die ~e Reife** (*Schulw.*) *standard of achievement for school-leaving certificate at a Realschule or for entry to the sixth form in a Gymnasium;* ⇒ *auch* **Osten** c; **B** (*einen Mittelwert darstellend*) average ‹temperature›; moderate ‹speed›; medium-sized ‹company, town›; medium ‹quality, size›; **ein Mann ~en Alters** a middle-aged man

**Mittler** /ˈmɪtlɐ/ *der;* **~s, ~:** mediator

**Mittler·amt** *das* role of mediator

**Mittlerin** *die;* **~, ~nen** mediator

**Mittler·rolle** *die* mediating role

**mittler·weile** /ˈmɪtlɐˈvailə/ *Adv.* **A** (*seitdem, allmählich*) since then; (*bis jetzt*) by now; **B** (*unterdessen*) in the mean time

**mit|tragen** *unr. tr. V.* bear part of, share ‹responsibility, cost›; take part of, share ‹blame›; give one's support to ‹aims, proposal›

**mit|trinken 1** *unr. tr. V.* **etw. ~:** drink sth. with me/us *etc.;* **trinkst du einen mit?** are you going to have a drink with me/us *etc.?* **2** *unr. itr. V.* **mit jmdm. ~:** have a drink with sb.

**mitt-, Mitt-: ~schiffs** *Adv.* (*Seemannsspr.*) amidships; **~sommer** *der* midsummer; **~sommer·nacht** *die* midsummer's night; (*Nacht der Sommersonnenwende*) Midsummer Night

**mit|tun** *unr. itr. V.* (*landsch.*) join in

**Mittwoch** /ˈmɪtvɔx/ *der;* **~[e]s, ~e** ▶ **207**, ▶ **833** Wednesday; ⇒ *auch* **Dienstag; Dienstag-**

**mittwochs** *Adv.* ▶ **833** on Wednesday[s]; ⇒ *auch* **dienstags**

**mit·unter** *Adv.* now and then; from time to time; sometimes

**mit·verantwortlich** *Adj.* partly responsible *pred.;* (*beide/alle zusammen*) jointly responsible *pred.*

**Mit·verantwortung** *die* share of the responsibility; **~ übernehmen** take one's share of the responsibility

*old spelling (see note on page 1707)

**mit|verdienen** *itr. V.* go out to work as well; **der ältere Sohn verdient jetzt mit** the eldest son is earning now too

**Mit·verfasser** *der*, **Mit·verfasserin** *die* co-author; joint author

**Mit·verschulden** *das:* **ihn trifft ein ~ an seinem Unfall** he was partly to blame for his accident

**mit|versichern** *tr. V.* include in one's insurance

**Mit·welt** *die* fellow men *pl.;* **die ~:** sb.'s fellow men

**mit·wirken** *itr. V.* **A** (*tätig sein*) **an etw.** (*Dat.*)**/bei etw. ~:** collaborate on/be involved in sth.; **an der Aufklärung eines Verbrechens ~:** help to solve a crime; **ohne jmds. M~:** without sb.'s help *or* assistance; **B** (*mitspielen*) **in einem Orchester/Theaterstück ~wirken** play in an orchestra/act *or* appear in a play; **C** (*Bedeutung haben*) **[bei etw.] ~:** play a role [in sth.]

**Mitwirkende** *der/die; adj. Dekl.* (*an einer Sendung*) participant; (*in einer Show*) performer; (*in einem Theaterstück*) actor; **die ~n** (*in einem Theaterstück*) the cast *sing.*

**Mit·wirkung** *die* **jmds. ~ an etw.** (*Dat.*)**/bei etw.** sb.'s collaboration on/involvement in sth.; **unter ~ vieler Fachwissenschaftler** in collaboration with many experts; **die Veranstaltung findet unter ~ bekannter Künstler statt** some famous artists are taking part in the event

**Mit·wisser** *der;* **~s, ~, Mit·wisserin** *die;* **~, ~nen: ~ einer Sache** (*Gen.*) **sein** know about sth.; (*einer Straftat*) be an accessory to sth.; **er hatte zu viele Mitwisser** there were too many people who knew about what he'd done; **zum Mitwisser gemacht werden** be told about it; (*bei einer Straftat*) be made an accessory

**Mitwisserschaft** *die;* **~:** knowledge of the matter/crime; **seine ~ leugnen** deny all knowledge [of the matter]

**mit|wollen** *unr. itr. V.* (*ugs.*) (*mitkommen wollen*) want to come with sb.; (*mitgehen, mitfahren wollen*) want to go with sb.

**mit|zählen 1** *itr. V.* **A** count; **die Sonntage zählen bei den Urlaubstagen nicht mit** Sundays don't count as holidays; **B** (*gelten*) ‹objection› be valid; ‹factor› be relevant. **2** *tr. V.* count in; include

**mit|ziehen** *unr. itr. V.; mit sein* **A** (*mitgehen*) go with him/them *etc.;* **mit der Kapelle ~:** march along with the band; **mit dem Zirkus ~:** travel round with the circus; **B** (*ugs.: mitmachen*) go along with it; (*bei einer Klage, Initiative*) give it one's backing; **C** (*Sport*) go with him/her *etc.*

**Mix·becher** /ˈmɪks-/ *der* [cocktail] shaker

**Mixed** /mɪkst/ *das;* **~[s], ~[s]** (*Sport*) mixed doubles

**Mixedpickles** /mɪkstˈpɪkl̩s/ *Pl.* mixed pickles

**mixen** /ˈmɪksn̩/ *tr. V.* (*auch Rundf., Ferns., Film*) mix; **sich** (*Dat.*) **einen Drink ~:** fix oneself a drink; **etw. unter etw.** (*Akk.*) **~** (*Kochk.*) mix sth. into sth.

**Mixer** *der;* **~s, ~ A** (*Bar~*) barman; bartender (*Amer.*); **B** (*Gerät*) blender and liquidizer

**Mixerin** *die;* **~, ~nen** barmaid

**Mix·getränk** *das* mixed drink; cocktail

**Mixtur** /mɪksˈtuːɐ̯/ *die;* **~, ~en A** (*Pharm., fig.*) mixture; **B** (*Musik*) mixture [stop]

**mm** *Abk.* ▶ **489** **Millimeter** mm.

**Mnemo·technik** /mnemo-/ *die* (*Psych.*) mnemonics *sing., no art.*

**Mo.** *Abk.* **Montag** Mon.

**Mob** /mɔp/ *der;* **~s** (*abwertend*) mob

**mobben** /ˈmɔbn̩/ *tr. V.* (*ugs.*) hassle and bully

**Mobbing** /ˈmɔbɪŋ/ *das;* **~s** (*ugs.*) hassling and bullying

**Möbel** /ˈmøːbl̩/ *das;* **~s, ~:** piece of furniture; **neue ~:** new furniture *sing.*

**Möbel-: ~geschäft** *das* furniture shop; **~haus** *das* furniture store; **~industrie** *die* furniture industry; **~lager** *das* furniture warehouse; (*zur Einlagerung*) furniture repository; **~packer** *der* removal man; **~politur** *die* furniture polish; **~schreiner** *der*, **~schreinerin** *die* ⇒ **Möbeltischler; ~spedition** *die* furniture-removal firm; **~stück** *das* piece of furniture; **~tischler** *der*, **~tischlerin** *die* cabinetmaker; **~wagen** *der* furniture van; removal van

**mobil** /moˈbiːl/ *Adj.* **A** (*auch Milit.*) mobile; (*einsatzbereit*) mobilized; **~ machen** mobilize; rope in (*coll.*) ‹person›; **B** (*ugs.*) (*lebendig*) lively; (*rüstig*) sprightly; **C** (*Rechtsw., Wirtsch.*) movable ‹property›; floating ‹capital›

**Mobile** /ˈmoːbilə/ *das;* **~s, ~s** mobile

**Mobil·funk** *der* mobile telephony

**Mobiliar** /mobiˈli̯aːɐ̯/ *das;* **~s** furnishings *pl.*

**Mobilisation** /mobilizaˈt͜si̯oːn/ *die;* **~, ~en** (*Milit., Politik*) mobilization

**mobilisieren** *tr. V.* **A** (*Milit., fig.*) mobilize; **die Massen ~** (*fig.*) stir the masses into action; **B** (*aktivieren*) activate ‹circulation etc.›; summon up ‹energy etc.›; **C** (*Wirtsch.*) make ‹capital› available; realize ‹capital›

**Mobilisierung** *die;* **~, ~en A** (*Milit., fig.*) mobilization; **B** (*Aktivierung*) (*des Kreislaufs*) activation; (*von Energie*) summoning up; **C** (*Wirtsch.: von Kapital*) realization

**Mobilität** /mobiliˈtɛːt/ *die;* **~** (*Soziol.*) mobility; **geistige ~** (*fig.*) mental agility

**Mobilmachung** *die;* **~, ~en** mobilization; **die allgemeine ~ ausrufen** order a general mobilization

**Mobil·telefon** *das* cellular phone

**möbl.** *Abk.* **möbliert** furn.

**möblieren** *tr. V.* furnish; **ein möbliertes Zimmer** a furnished room; **möbliert wohnen** live in furnished accommodation; **ein möblierter Herr** (*ugs. veralt.*) a lodger

**Möblierung** *die;* **~, ~en A** (*das Möblieren*) furnishing; **B** (*Einrichtung*) furnishings and furniture (+ *Gen.* in)

**Moçambique** /mosamˈbiːk/ (*das*)*;* **~s** ⇒ **Mosambik**

**Mocca** /ˈmɔka/ ⇒ **Mokka**

**mochte** /ˈmɔxtə/ *1. u. 3. Pers. Sg. Prät. v.* **mögen**

**möchte** /ˈmœçtə/ *1. u. 3. Pers. Sg. Konjunktiv II v.* **mögen**

**Möchte·gern-: ~dichter/~casanova/~politiker** would-be poet/Casanova/politician

**modal** /moˈdaːl/ *Adj.* (*Sprachw.*) modal

**Modalität** /modaliˈtɛːt/ *die;* **~, ~en A** (*geh.*) (*Bedingung*) provision; condition; (*Umstand*) circumstance; **B** (*Sprachw., Philos.*) modality

**Modal-: ~satz** *der* (*Sprachw.*) modal sentence/phrase; **~verb** *das* (*Sprachw.*) modal verb

**Modder** /ˈmɔdɐ/ *der;* **~s** (*nordd. ugs.*) mud

**modd[e]rig** /ˈmɔd(ə)rɪç/ *Adj.* (*nordd. ugs.*) muddy

**Mode** /ˈmoːdə/ *die;* **~, ~n A** fashion; **die ~ verlangt, dass ...** fashion dictates that ...; **jede ~ mitmachen** follow fashion's every whim; **mit der ~ gehen** follow the fashion; **etw. ist [in] ~:** sth. is in *or* the fashion; **[ganz] groß in ~** *od.* **große ~ sein** be all the rage *or* very fashionable; **nach der neuesten ~:** in the latest style; **in ~/aus der ~ kommen** come into/go out of fashion; **neue ~n** (*abwertend*) newfangled ideas; **was sind denn das für neue ~n?** (*ugs.*) what do you think you're/does he think he's *etc.* doing?; **B** *Pl.* (*~kleidung*) fashions

**mode-, Mode-: ~artikel** *der* **A** (*modisches Zubehör*) [fashion] accessory; **B** (*viel gekaufter Artikel*) fashionable novelty; in thing; **~arzt** *der*, **~ärztin** *die* (*ugs.*) fashionable doctor; **~ausdruck** *der; Pl.* **~ausdrücke** vogue word; 'in' expression (*coll.*); **~beruf** *der* fashionable occupation; **~bewusst, *~bewußt 1** *Adj.* fashion-conscious; **2** *adv.* fashionably; **~branche** *die* fashion *or* (*Brit. coll.*) rag trade; **~designer** *der*, **~designerin** *die* fashion designer; **~farbe** *die* fashionable colour; **~geschäft** *das* fashion store; (*kleiner*) boutique; **~haus** *das* **A** fashion house; **B** (*Geschäft*) fashion store;

**~journal** *das* fashion magazine; **~krankheit** *die* fashionable disease *or* complaint

**Modell** /mo'dɛl/ *das;* **~s, ~e** (*auch fig.*) model; (*Technik: Entwurf*) [design] model; pattern; (*in Originalgröße*) mock-up; **jmdm. ~ sitzen** *od.* **stehen** model *or* sit for sb.

**Modell-:** **~bauer** *der;* **~~s, ~~, ~bauerin** *die;* **~~, ~~nen** model-maker; **~charakter** *der:* **etw. hat ~charakter** sth. can act as a model; **etw. hat ~charakter für etw.** sth. acts as *or* provides a model for sth.; **~eisen·bahn** *die* model railway

**Modelleur** /modɛ'lø:ɐ̯/ *der;* **~s, ~e** modeller

**Modell-:** **~fall** *der* **A** model; perfect example; **B** (*klassisches Beispiel*) textbook case; **~flugzeug** *das* model aircraft

**modellhaft** *Adj.* exemplary; model *attrib.;* pilot ‹scheme›; **etw. hat ~en Charakter** sth. can act as a model

**modellieren** **1** *tr. V.* **A** model, mould ‹figures, objects›; mould ‹clay, wax›; **jmdn./etw. in Ton ~:** model sb./sth. in clay; **etw. nach etw. ~** (*fig.*) model sth. on sth.; **B** (*gestalten*) design ‹clothes›; **C** (*Wissensch.*) model ‹processes›. **2** *itr. V.* model (*esp. in clay or wax*)

**Modellier·masse** *die* modelling material (*esp. clay or wax*)

**Modell-:** **~kleid** *das* model dress; **~pflege** *die* (*Kfz-W.*) improving the specification; **~projekt** *das* pilot scheme; **~reihe** *die* (*Wirtsch.*) range [of models]; **~versuch** *der* pilot scheme; **~zeichnung** *die* drawing [of a model/mock-up]

**modeln** /'mo:dl̩n/ *tr. V.* **etw. nach dem Vorbild von etw. ~:** model sth. on sth.

**Modem** /'mo:dem/ *der od. das;* **~s, ~s** (*DV*) modem

**Moden-:** **~schau** *die* fashion show *or* parade; **~zeit·schrift** *die* ⇒ Modezeitschrift

**Mode-:** **~püppchen** *das,* **~puppe** *die* fashion-crazy bird (*Brit. sl.*) *or* (*Amer. coll.*) dame

**Moder** /'mo:dɐ/ *der;* **~s** **A** mould; (*~geruch*) mustiness; (*Verwesung, auch fig.*) decay; **es riecht nach ~:** there is a musty smell; **B** ⇒ **Modder**

**moderat** /mode'ra:t/ *Adj.* moderate

**Moderation** /modera'tsi̯o:n/ *die;* **~, ~en** (*Rundf., Ferns.*) presentation; **die ~ haben** be the presenter

**Moderator** /mode'ra:tɔr/ *der;* **~s, ~en** /-'to:rən/, **Moderatorin** *die;* **~, ~nen** ▶ 159 (*Rundf., Ferns.*) presenter

**moderieren** /mode'ri:rən/ **1** *tr. V.* (*Rundf., Ferns.*) present ‹programme›. **2** *itr. V.* be the presenter

**moderig** *Adj.* musty

**modern**[1] /'mo:dɐn/ *itr. V.; auch mit sein* go mouldy; (*verwesen*) decay; **~de Gebeine** mouldering skeletons

**modern**[2] /mo'dɛrn/ **1** *Adj.* modern; (*modisch*) fashionable. **2** *adv.* in a modern manner *or* style; (*modisch*) fashionably; (*aufgeschlossen*) progressively; **~ denken** have modern/progressive ideas; **~ eingestellt** *od.* **denkend** with modern/progressive ideas *postpos., not pred.*

**Moderne** *die;* **~** **A** **die ~, das Zeitalter der ~:** the modern age; modern times; **B** (*Kunstrichtung*) **die ~:** modern arts *pl.;* **typisch für die ~:** typical of modern writing/painting/music *etc.*

**modernisieren** **1** *tr. V.* modernize; (*modisch gestalten*) bring ‹clothes› in line with the current fashion. **2** *itr. V.* introduce modern methods

**Modernisierung** *die;* **~, ~en** modernization

**Modernismus** *der;* **~, Modernismen** **A** modernism; **B** (*Stilelement*) modernism; modernistic element

**modernistisch** (*abwertend*) **1** *Adj.* modernistic. **2** *adv.* in a modernistic style *or* manner

**Modernität** *die;* **~:** modernity

**Mode-:** **~sache** *die: in* [eine] **~sache sein** be a [passing] fashion; **~salon** *der* [smart] fashion boutique; **~schau** *die* ⇒ **Modenschau**; **~schmuck** *der* costume jewellery; **~schöpfer** *der* ▶ 159 couturier; **~schöpferin** *die* ▶ 159 couturière; **~schriftsteller** *der,* **~schriftstellerin** *die* fashionable author; **~tanz** *der* dance [briefly] in vogue; **~torheit** *die* crazy fashion; **~trend** *der* fashion trend; **~wort** *das; Pl.* **~wörter** vogue word; 'in' expression (*coll.*); **~zar** *der,* **~zarin** *die* (*ugs.*) fashion mogul; **~zeichner** *der* (*veralt.*), **~zeichnerin** *die* (*veralt.*) dress designer; **~zeitschrift** *die* fashion magazine

**Modi** ⇒ **Modus**

**Modifikation** /modifika'tsi̯o:n/ *die;* **~, ~en** modification

**modifizierbar** *Adj.* modifiable

**modifizieren** /modifi'tsi:rən/ *tr. V.* (*geh.*) modify

**Modifizierung** *die;* **~, ~en** (*geh.*) modification

**modisch** /'mo:dɪʃ/ **1** *Adj.* fashionable; trendy (*coll. derog.*). **2** *adv.* fashionably; trendily (*coll. derog.*)

**Modistin** /mo'dɪstɪn/ *die;* **~, ~nen** milliner

**Modul**[1] /'mo:dʊl/ *der;* **~s, ~n** (*Math.*) modulus

**Modul**[2] /mo'du:l/ *das;* **~s, ~e** (*DV, Elektronik*) module

**Modulation** /modula'tsi̯o:n/ (*auch Musik, Technik*) *die;* **~, ~en** modulation

**modulieren** *tr., itr. V.* (*auch Musik, Technik*) modulate

**Modus** /'mɔdʊs/ *der;* **~, Modi** **A** (*geh.*) procedure (+ *Gen.* for); method; **nach diesem ~:** by this method; **B** (*Sprachw.*) mood

**Modus Vivendi** /- vi'vɛndi/ *der;* **~ ~, Modi Vivendi** (*geh.*) modus vivendi

**Mofa** /'mo:fa/ *das;* **~s, ~s** [low-powered] moped

**Mofa·fahrer** *der,* **Mofa·fahrerin** *die* moped rider

**Mogelei** *die;* **~, ~en** (*ugs.*) cheating *no pl.*

**mogeln** (*ugs.*) **1** *itr. V.* cheat; (*lügen*) fib; **beim Kartenspiel/bei der Klassenarbeit ~:** cheat at cards/in the class test. **2** *tr. V.* **etw. in etw.** (*Akk.*) **~:** slip sth. into sth. **3** *refl. V.* **sich in/zwischen etw.** (*Akk.*) **~** ‹error› slip into/in among sth.

**Mogel·packung** *die* (*abwertend*) deceptive packaging

**mögen** /'mø:gn̩/ **1** *unr. Modalverb; 2. Part.* **~:** **A** (*wollen*) want to; **das hätte ich sehen ~:** I would have liked to see that; **sie mochte nicht länger bleiben** she didn't want to stay any longer; **B** (*geh.: sollen*) **das mag genügen** that should be *or* ought to be enough; **bitte ihn** *od.* **sag ihm, er möge kommen** (*veralt.*) ask/tell him to come; **C** (*geh.: Wunschform*) **möge er bald kommen!** I do hope he'll come soon!; **möge es so bleiben** may it stay like that; **das möge der Himmel verhüten!** Heaven forbid!; **D** (*Vermutung, Möglichkeit*) **sie mag/mochte vierzig sein** she must be/must have been [about] forty; **wie alt sie wohl sein mag?** I wonder how old she is; **Meier, Müller, Koch — und wie sie alle heißen ~:** Meier, Müller, Koch and [the rest,] whatever they're called; **wie viele Personen ~ das sein?** how many people would you say there are?; **was mag sie damit gemeint haben?** what can she have meant by that?; **[das] mag sein** maybe; **es mag sein, dass ...** it may be *or* it is possible that ...; **E** (*geh.: Einräumung*) **er mag tun, was er will** no matter what he does; **es mag kommen, was will** come what may; **mag er nur warten** let him wait; he can wait; **wer er auch sein mag** whoever he may be; **wie dem auch sein mag** be that as it may; **mag das Wetter auch noch so schlecht sein, ...** however bad the weather may be, ...; ⇒ *auch* **hingehen** D; **F** *Konjunktiv II + Inf.* (*den Wunsch haben*) **ich/sie möchte gern wissen ...** I would *or* should/she would like to know ...; **ich möchte ihn [gerne] sprechen** I should like to speak to him; **möchten Sie etwas essen/trinken?** would you like something to eat/drink?; **ich möchte nicht stören, aber ...** I don't want to interrupt, but ...; **ich möchte zu gerne wissen** I'd love to know ...; **ich möchte sagen, ...** (*in zögernder Aussage*) I'd say ...; **man möchte meinen, er sei der Chef** one would [really] think he was the boss.
**2** *unr. tr. V.* **[gern] ~:** like; **sie mag keine Rosen** she does not like roses; **er mag mich nicht** he does not like me; **sie mag ihn sehr [gern]** she likes him very much; (*hat ihn sehr gern*) she is very fond of him; **sie ~ sich** they're fond of one another; **möchten Sie ein Glas Wein?** would you like a glass of wine?; **ich mag lieber/am liebsten Bier** I like beer better/best [of all]; **ich möchte lieber Tee** I would prefer tea *or* rather have tea; **ich möchte nicht, dass er heute kommt** I would not like him to come today.
**3** *unr. itr. V.* **A** (*es wollen*) like to; **ich mag nicht** I don't want to; **magst du?** do you want to?; (*bei einem Angebot*) would you like one/some?; **magst du noch?** do you want any more?; **ich möchte schon, aber ...** I should like to, but ...; **B** (*fahren, gehen usw. wollen*) **ich möchte nach Hause/in die Stadt/auf die Schaukel** I want *or* I'd like to go home/into town/on the swing; **er möchte zu Herrn A** he would like to see Mr A

**Mogler** /'mo:glɐ/ *der;* **~s, ~, Moglerin** *die;* **~, ~nen** (*ugs.*) cheat

**möglich** /'mø:klɪç/ *Adj.* possible; **es war ihm nicht ~ [zu kommen]** he was unable [to come]; it was not possible for him [to come]; **sobald/so gut es mir ~ ist** as soon/as well as I can; **das ist schon eher ~:** that is more likely [to be possible]; **[jmdm.] etw. ~ machen** ‹thing› make sth. possible [for sb.]; ‹person› arrange sth. [for sb.]; **das** *od.* **alles Mögliche tun** do everything possible; do one's utmost; **dort kann man alles Mögliche kaufen** (*ugs.*) you can get all sorts of things there; **sie hatte alles Mögliche zu kritisieren** she criticized everything; **alle ~en Entschuldigungen** (*ugs.*) every excuse you can think of; **alle ~en Leute** (*ugs.*) all sorts of people; **das ist gut/leicht/durchaus ~:** that is very/wholly/entirely possible; **bei ihm ist alles ~:** he is capable of anything; **man sollte es nicht für ~ halten** one would not believe it possible; **[das ist doch] nicht ~!** impossible!; I don't believe it!; **ist das ~!** [that's] incredible!; whatever next!

**möglicherweise** *Adv.* possibly; **~ hat er Glück/Glück gehabt** he may be/may have been lucky; **wir werden ~ versetzt** we may [possibly] be transferred; **~ hast du es nur geträumt** it's possible that you just dreamt it

**Möglichkeit** *die;* **~, ~en** **A** (*möglicher Weg*) possibility; (*Methode*) way; **nach ~:** if possible; **B** (*Möglichsein*) possibility; **es besteht die ~, dass ...** there is a chance *or* possibility that ...; **es besteht die ~, eine Zusatzversicherung abzuschließen** it is possible to arrange additional insurance; **ist es die** *od.* **ist [denn] das die ~!** (*ugs.*) well, I'll be damned! (*coll.*); whatever next!; **C** (*Gelegenheit*) opportunity; chance; **die ~ haben, etw. zu tun** have an opportunity of doing sth. *or* to do sth.; **D** *Pl.* (*Mittel*) [*esp.* financial] means *or* resources; **künstlerische ~en** artistic resources *or* potential *sing.*

**Möglichkeits·form** *die* (*Sprachw.*) subjunctive

**möglichst** **1** *Adv.* **A** (*so weit wie möglich*) as much *or* far as possible; **sich ~ zurückhalten** restrain oneself as far as possible; **B** (*wenn möglich*) if [at all] possible; **macht ~ keinen Lärm** don't make any noise if you can possibly help it; **C** (*so ... wie möglich*) **~ groß/schnell/oft** as big/fast/often as possible; **mit ~ großer Sorgfalt** with the greatest possible care. **2** *adj.* **in sein Möglichstes tun** do one's utmost; do everything possible

**Mogul** /'mo:gʊl/ *der;* **~s, ~n** (*hist.*) Mogul

**Mohair** /mo'hɛ:ɐ̯/ *der;* **~s** mohair

**Mohammed** /'mo:hamɛt/ (*der*) Muhammad

**Mohammedaner** *der;* **~s, ~, Mohammedanerin,** *die;* **~, ~nen** Muslim; Muhammadan

m

**mohammedanisch** ❶ *Adj.* Muslim, Muhammadan. ❷ *adv.* ~ **geprägt** imbued with Muslim *or* Muhammadan characteristics *postpos.*

**Mohikaner** /mohi'ka:nɐ/ *der;* ~**s**, ~, **Mohikanerin** *die;* ~, ~**nen** Mohican; **der letzte Mohikaner, der Letzte der Mohikaner** (*ugs. scherzh.*) the last one; the last survivor (*joc.*)

**Mohn** /mo:n/ *der;* ~**s** Ⓐ (*Pflanze*) poppy; Ⓑ (*Samen*) poppy seed; (*auf Brot, Kuchen*) poppy seeds *pl.*

**Mohn-:** ~**blume** *die* poppy; ~**brötchen** *das* poppy-seed roll; ~**feld** *das* field of poppies; ~**kuchen** *der* poppy-seed cake

**Mohr** /mo:ɐ̯/ *der;* ~**en**, ~**en** (*veralt.*) Moor; **schwarz wie ein** ~**:** as black as the ace of spades; **der ~ hat seine Schuldigkeit getan, der ~ kann gehen** (*fig.*) when one has served one's purpose one is simply discarded

**Möhre** /'mø:rə/ *die;* ~, ~**n** carrot

**Mohren·kopf** *der* Ⓐ chocolate marshmallow; Ⓑ (*Gebäck*) *small cream-filled spherical sponge cake covered with chocolate*

**Möhren·saft** *der* carrot juice

**Mohren·wäsche** *die* [attempt at] whitewashing (*fig.*)

**Mohrin** *die;* ~, ~**nen** ⇒ **Mohr**

**Mohr·rübe** *die* carrot

**Moiré** /mọa're:/ *der;* ~**s**, ~**s** moiré

**mokant** /mo'kant/ (*geh.*) ❶ *Adj.* mocking. ❷ *adv.* mockingly

**Mokassin** /moka'si:n/ *der;* ~**s**, ~**s** moccasin

**Mokick** /'mo:kɪk/ *das;* ~**s**, ~**s** light motorcycle (*with kick-starter*)

**mokieren** /mo'ki:rən/ *refl. V.* (*geh.*) **sich über etw.** (*Akk.*) ~**:** mock *or* scoff at sth.; **sich über jmdn.** ~**:** mock sb.

**Mokka** /'mɔka/ *der;* ~**s** Ⓐ (*Bohnen*) mocha [coffee]; Ⓑ (*Getränk*) strong black coffee

**Mokka-:** ~**löffel** *der* [small] coffee spoon; ~**tasse** *die* small coffee cup

**Mol** /mo:l/ *das;* ~**s**, ~**e** (*Chemie*) mole

**Molar** /mo'la:ɐ̯/ *der;* ~**s**, ~**en**, **Molar·zahn** *der* molar

**Molch** /mɔlç/ *der;* ~**[e]s**, ~**e** newt

**Moldau**[1] /'mɔldau/ *die;* ~**:** [river] Vltava

**Moldau**[2] *die;* ~ (*Sowjetrepublik*) Moldavia

**Mole** /'mo:lə/ *die;* ~, ~**n** [harbour] mole

**Molekül** /mole'ky:l/ *das;* ~**s**, ~**e** (*Chemie*) molecule

**molekular** /moleku'la:ɐ̯/ *Adj.* molecular

**Molekular-:** molecular

**Molesten** /mo'lɛstn̩/ *Pl.* (*veralt.*) minor ailments

**molk** /mɔlk/ *1. u. 3. Pers. Sg. Prät. v.* **melken**

**Molke** *die;* ~**:** whey

**Molkerei** *die;* ~, ~**en** dairy

**Molkerei-:** ~**butter** *die* dairy butter; ~**genossenschaft** *die* cooperative dairy; ~**produkt** *das* dairy product

**Moll** /mɔl/ *das;* ~ (*Musik*) minor [key]; **in ~ enden** finish in a minor key

**Moll-:** ~**akkord** *der* (*Musik*) minor chord; ~**drei·klang** *der* minor triad

**Molle** *die;* ~, ~**n** (*berlin.*) [glass of] beer; **eine ~ zischen** have a jar (*coll.*)

**Mollen·friedhof** *der* (*berlin. scherzh.*) beer belly (*coll.*)

**Molli** /'mɔli/ *der;* ~**s**, ~**s** (*salopp*) Molotov cocktail

**mollig** /'mɔlɪç/ ❶ *Adj.* Ⓐ (*rundlich*) plump; Ⓑ (*warm*) cosy; snug; **ein ~er Wintermantel** a warm and cosy winter coat. ❷ *adv.* cosily; snugly; ~ **warm** warm and cosy

**Moll-:** ~**ton·art** *die* (*Musik*) minor key; ~**ton·leiter** *die* (*Musik*) minor scale

**Molluske** /mɔ'lʊskə/ *die;* ~, ~**n** (*Biol.*) mollusc

**Moloch** /'mo:lɔx/ *der;* ~**s**, ~**e** (*geh.*) Moloch; voracious giant

**Molotow·cocktail** /'mɔlotɔf-/ *der* Molotov cocktail

**Molybdän** /molʏp'dɛ:n/ *das;* ~**s** (*Chemie*) molybdenum

**Moment**[1] /mo'mɛnt/ *der;* ~**[e]s**, ~**e** moment; **einen ~ zögern** hesitate [for] a moment; **einen ~ bitte!** just a moment, please!; ~ **[mal]!** [hey!] just a moment!; wait a mo! (*coll.*); **im nächsten/gleichen ~:** the next/at the same moment; **jeden ~** (*ugs.*) [at] any moment; **im ~:** at the moment; ⇒ *auch* **licht A**

**Moment**[2] *das;* ~**[e]s**, ~**e** Ⓐ (*Umstand*) factor, element (**für** in); **das auslösende ~ für etw. sein** be the trigger for sth.; Ⓑ (*Physik*) moment

**momentan** /momɛn'ta:n/ ❶ *Adj.* Ⓐ present; current; Ⓑ (*vorübergehend*) temporary; (*flüchtig*) momentary; **eine ~e Besserung** a short-lived improvement. ❷ *adv.* Ⓐ at the moment; at present; Ⓑ (*vorübergehend*) temporarily; (*flüchtig*) momentarily; for a moment

**Moment·aufnahme** *die* (*Fot.*) snapshot

**Monaco** /'mo:nako/ (*das*); ~**s** Monaco

**Monade** /mo'na:də/ *die;* ~, ~**n** (*Philos.*) monad

**Monarch** /mo'narç/ *der;* ~**en**, ~**en** monarch

**Monarchie** *die;* ~, ~**n** monarchy

**Monarchin** *die;* ~, ~**nen** monarch

**monarchisch** ❶ *Adj.* monarchical. ❷ *adv.* monarchically; ~ **regiert** ruled by a monarch/monarchs

**Monarchismus** *der;* ~**:** monarchism *no art.*

**Monarchist** *der;* ~**en**, ~**en**, **Monarchistin** *die;* ~, ~**nen** monarchist

**monarchistisch** ❶ *Adj.* monarchist ‹party, group›; monarchistic ‹tendency, views›. ❷ *adv.* monarchistically

**Monat** /'mo:nat/ *der;* ~**s**, ~**e** month; **letzten ~:** last month; **im ~ April** in the month of April; **am 10. dieses ~s** on the tenth [of this month]; **Ihr Schreiben vom 22. dieses ~s** your letter of the 22nd [inst.]; **sie ist im vierten ~ [schwanger]** she is four months pregnant; **er war drei ~e [lang] hier** he was here for three months; **er ist seit drei ~en hier** he has been here for three months; **was verdienst du im ~?** how much do you earn per month?; **ich bezahle 250 DM im ~:** I pay 250 marks a month *or* per month; ⇒ *auch* **hinaus**

**monatelang** ❶ *Adj.* lasting for months *postpos., not pred.;* **die ~en Verhandlungen** the negotiations, which lasted for several months; **nach ~er Krankheit** after months of illness; **mit ~er Verspätung** months late. ❷ *adv.* for months [on end]

**-monatig** Ⓐ (... *Monate alt*) ...-month-old; **ein achtmonatiges Kind** an eight-month-old baby; Ⓑ (... *Monate dauernd*) ... month's/months'; ...-month; **eine viermonatige Kur** a four-month course of treatment; **mit dreimonatiger Verspätung** three months late

**monatlich** ❶ *Adj.* monthly. ❷ *adv.* monthly; every month; (*im Monat*) per month; **etw. ~ überweisen** pay sth. monthly; **sich ~ treffen** meet every month

**-monatlich** ❶ *Adj.* ...-monthly; **acht~/drei~:** eight-monthly/three-monthly. ❷ *adv.* every ... months

**Monats-:** ~**abrechnung** *die* monthly accounts *pl.;* (*Abrechnungsblatt*) monthly [statement of] account; ~**anfang** *der,* ~**beginn** *der* beginning of the month; **zu/am ~anfang** *od.* ~**beginn** at the beginning of the month; ~**beitrag** *der* monthly subscription; ~**binde** *die* sanitary towel (*Brit.*); sanitary napkin (*Amer.*); ~**blutung** *die* [monthly] period; ~**einkommen** *das* monthly income; ~**ende** *das* end of the month; ~**erste** *der; adj. Dekl.* first [day] of the month; ~**frist** *die:* **in** *od.* **innerhalb** *od.* **binnen ~frist** within [a period of] a *or* one month; **nach ~frist** after [a period of] a *or* one month; **vor ~frist** in less than a month; within [a period of] a *or* one month; (*vor einem Monat*) a month ago; ~**gehalt** *das* month's salary; **vier ~gehälter** four months' salary *sing.;* **ein dreizehntes ~gehalt** an extra month's salary; **ein ~gehalt von 3 000 DM** a monthly salary of 3,000 marks; ~**hälfte** *die* half of the month; ~**karte** *die* monthly season ticket; ~**letzte** *der; adj. Dekl.* last day of the month; ~**lohn** *der* month's wages; **vier ~löhne** four months' wages *pl.;* **ein ~lohn von 2 000 DM** a monthly wage of 2,000 marks; ~**miete** *die* month's rent; **zwei ~mieten** two months' rent; **eine ~miete von 1 000 DM** a monthly rent of 1,000 marks; ~**mitte** *die* middle of the month; ~**rate** *die* monthly instalment; ~**wechsel** *der* (*veralt.*) monthly allowance (*esp. for a student*)

**monat[s]weise** *Adv.* by the month

**Mönch** /mœnç/ *der;* ~**[e]s**, ~**e** monk

**mönchisch** *Adj.* monkish; of a monk *postpos., not pred.*

**Mönchs-:** ~**kloster** *das* monastery; ~**kutte** *die* monk's habit *or* cowl; ~**latein** *das* monkish Latin; dog Latin (*derog.*); ~**leben** *das* monastic life; life of a monk; ~**orden** *der* monastic order

**Mönch[s]tum** *das;* ~**s** Ⓐ monasticism; Ⓑ (*das Mönchsein*) monkhood

**Mönchs·zelle** *die* monk's cell

**Mond** /mo:nt/ *der;* ~**[e]s**, ~**e** Ⓐ moon; **den ~ anbellen** (*fig. ugs.*) talk to a brick wall; **ich könnte** *od.* **möchte ihn auf den** *od.* **zum ~ schießen** (*salopp*) I wish he'd get lost (*coll.*); **auf** *od.* **hinter dem ~ leben** (*fig. ugs.*) be a bit behind the times *or* not quite with it (*coll.*); **lebst du auf dem ~?** (*ugs.*) where have you been?; **wir leben auch nicht hinter dem ~** (*ugs.*) we're not fuddy-duddies (*sl.*); we do have some idea of what's going on; **in den ~ gucken** (*fig. ugs.*) be left empty-handed *or* (*coll.*) out in the cold; **etw. in den ~ schreiben** (*ugs.*) write sth. off; **nach dem ~ gehen** (*ugs.*) ‹clock, watch› be hopelessly wrong; Ⓑ (*dichter. veralt.*) month; **viele ~e waren ins Land gegangen** many moons had passed

**Mondamin** Ⓦⓩ /mɔnda'mi:n/ *das;* ~**s** (*a proprietary brand of*) cornflour

**mondän** /mɔn'dɛ:n/ ❶ *Adj.* [highly] fashionable; smart; **die ~e Welt** the smart set. ❷ *adv.* fashionably; in a fashionable style

**mond-, Mond-:** ~**aufgang** *der* moonrise; ~**auto** *das* (*Raumf.*) moon buggy; ~**bahn** *die* orbit of a satellite; (*des Erdmondes*) lunar orbit; ~**beschienen** *Adj.* moonlit

**Monden·schein** *der* (*dichter.*) moonlight

**Mondes·finsternis** *die* (*österr.*) ⇒ **Mondfinsternis**

**mond-, Mond-:** ~**fähre** *die* (*Raumf.*) lunar module; ~**finsternis** *die* (*Astron.*) lunar eclipse; eclipse of the moon; ~**flug** *der* lunar expedition; ~**gebirge** *das* lunar mountain range *or* mountains *pl.;* ~**gesicht** *das* moon face; ~**gestein** *das* moon rock; ~**hell** *Adj.* (*geh.*) moonlit; ~**jahr** *das* lunar year; ~**kalb** *das* (*salopp*) dimwit (*coll.*); dope (*coll.*); ~**krater** *der* lunar crater; ~**lande·fähre** *die* (*Raumf.*) lunar module; ~**landschaft** *die* (*auch fig.*) lunar landscape; ~**landung** *die* moon landing; ~**licht** *das* moonlight; ~**los** *Adj.* moonless; ~**oberfläche** *die* lunar surface; ~**phase** *die* moon's phase; ~**preis** *der* (*Wirtsch. Jargon*) artificially high price (*from which the actual asking price is 'reduced'*); (*Wucherpreis*) exorbitant price; ~**rakete** *die* moon rocket; ~**schein** *der* moonlight; **der kann mir mal im ~schein begegnen** (*salopp*) he can get lost (*coll.*); ~**sichel** *die* crescent moon; ~**sonde** *die* lunar probe; ~**stein** *der* moonstone; ~**süchtig** *Adj.* sleepwalking *attrib.* (*esp. by moonlight*); ~**süchtig sein** be a sleepwalker; ~**süchtigkeit** *die;* ~~**:** sleepwalking (*esp. by moonlight*); ~**umkreisung** *die* orbiting of the moon; ~**umlaufbahn** *die* lunar orbit; ~**untergang** *der* moonset; ~**wechsel** *der* change of the moon

**Monegasse** /mone'gasə/ *der;* ~**n**, ~**n**, **Monegassin** *die;* ~, ~**nen** Monégasque

**monegassisch** *Adj.* Monégasque

**monetär** /mone'tɛ:ɐ̯/ ❶ *Adj.* monetary. ❷ *adv.* on a monetary basis

**Monetarismus** /moneta'rɪsmʊs/ *der;* ~ (*Wirtsch.*) monetarism *no art.*

m

*old spelling (see note on page 1707)

**Moneten** /mo'ne:tn̩/ *Pl. (ugs.)* cash *sing.;* dough *sing. (coll.)*

**Mongole** /mɔŋ'go:lə/ *der;* **~n, ~n** (A) Mongol; (B) *(Bewohner der Mongolei)* Mongolian

**Mongolei** /mɔŋgo'lai/ *die;* **~:** Mongolia; **in der Inneren/Äußeren ~:** in Inner/Outer Mongolia

**Mongolen-: ~falte** *die (Anthrop.)* Mongolian fold; **~fleck** *der (Anthrop.)* Mongolian spot

**mongolid** /mɔŋgo'li:t/ *Adj. (Anthrop.)* Mongoloid

**Mongolide** *der/die; adj. Dekl. (Anthrop.)* Mongoloid

**Mongolin** *die;* **~, ~nen** (A) Mongol; (B) *(Bewohnerin der Mongolei)* Mongolian

**mongolisch** *Adj.* ▶ 696 Mongolian

**Mongolismus** *der;* **~** ▶ 474 *(Med.)* mongolism *no art.*

**mongoloid** *Adj. (Med.)* mongoloid

**Mongoloide** *der/die; adj. Dekl. (Med.)* Mongoloid

**monieren** /mo'ni:rən/ *tr. V.* criticize; *(beanstanden)* find fault with

**Monismus** /mo'nɪsmʊs/ *der;* **~** *(Philos.)* monism *no art.*

**Monitor** /'mo:nitɔr/ *der;* **~s, ~en** /-'to:rən/ *(Ferns., Technik, Physik)* monitor

**mono** /'mo:no/ *Adv. (ugs.)* ‹hear, play, etc.› in mono *(coll.)*

**mono-, Mono-:** mono-

**monochrom** /mono'kro:m/ *Adj. (Malerei, Fot.)* monochrome; monochromatic ‹light›

**monocolor** /monoko'lo:ɐ̯/ *Adj. (österr. Politik)* one-party

**monogam** /mono'ga:m/ ❶ *Adj.* monogamous. ❷ *adv.* monogamously

**Monogamie** *die;* **~:** monogamy

**Mono·gramm** *das;* **~s, ~e** monogram

**Monographie** /monogra'fi:/ *die;* **~, ~n** monograph

**Monokel** /mo'nɔkl̩/ *das;* **~s, ~:** monocle

**Mono·kultur** *die (Landw.)* monoculture

**Monolith** /mono'li:t/ *der;* **~s** *od.* **~en, ~en** monolith

**Monolog** /mono'lo:k/ *der;* **~s, ~e** monologue; **einen ~ halten** hold a monologue

**monologisch** ❶ *Adj.* monologic[al]; ‹form› of a monologue; ‹statement› in the form of a monologue. ❷ *adv.* in monologue

**monologisieren** *itr. V.* talk in monologue

**monoman** /mono'ma:n/ *(Psych.)* ❶ *Adj.* monomaniacal. ❷ *adv.* monomaniacally

**Monomanie** /monoma'ni:/ *die;* **~, ~n** *(Psych.)* monomania

**Monophthong** /mono'ftɔŋ/ *der;* **~s, ~e** *(Sprachw.)* monophthong

**Monopol** /mono'po:l/ *das;* **~s, ~e** monopoly **(auf** + *Akk.*, **für** in, of)

**monopolisieren** *tr. V.* monopolize

**Monopolisierung** *die;* **~, ~en** monopolization

**Monopolist** *der;* **~en, ~en, Monopolistin** *die;* **~, ~nen** monopolist

**monopol-, Monopol-: ~kapital** *das* monopoly capital; **~kapitalismus** *der* monopoly capitalism; **~kapitalistisch** ❶ *Adj.* monopoly capitalist; ❷ *adv.* ‹structured, organized› on the principles of monopoly capitalism; **~stellung** *die* [position of] monopoly

**Monopoly** (Wz) /mo'no:poli/ *das;* **~:** Monopoly ® *(game)*

**Monotheismus** /monote'ɪsmʊs/ *der;* **~** *(Rel.)* monotheism

**monotheistisch** *(Rel.)* ❶ *Adj.* monotheistic. ❷ *adv.* monotheistically

**monoton** /mono'to:n/ ❶ *Adj.* monotonous. ❷ *adv.* monotonously

**Monotonie** *die;* **~, ~n** monotony

**Monotype** (Wz) /'mɔnotaip/ *die;* **~, ~s** *(Druckw.)* Monotype ® [composing machine]

**Mon·oxid, Mon·oxyd** *das (Chemie)* monoxide

**Mono·zelle** *die (Elektrot.)* [single-cell] battery

**Monster** /'mɔnstɐ/ *das;* **~s, ~:** monster; *(hässlich)* [hideous] brute

**Monster-** mammoth; *(sehr lange dauernd)* marathon

**Monster-: ~film** *der* (A) *(ugs.)* mammoth [screen] epic; blockbuster *(sl.)*; (B) *(Film mit ~n)* horror film [with a monster/monsters]; **~prozess, *~prozeß** *der* marathon trial; **~veranstaltung** *die* giant spectacular; *(sehr lange dauernd)* marathon [event]

**Monstranz** /mɔn'strants/ *die;* **~, ~en** *(kath. Kirche)* monstrance

**Monstren** ⇒ **Monstrum**

**monströs** /mɔn'strø:s/ *(geh.)* ❶ *Adj.* (A) *(auch fig.)* monstrous; [huge and] hideous; (B) *(gigantisch)* massive, overpowering ‹building, monument›. ❷ *adv.* monstrously

**Monstrosität** /mɔnstrozi'tɛ:t/ *die;* **~, ~en** monstrosity; *(fig.: monströse Tat)* monstrous action; atrocity

**Monstrum** /'mɔnstrʊm/ *das;* **~s, Monstren** (A) *(auch fig.: Mensch)* monster; (B) *(Ungetüm)* hulking great thing *(coll.)*; **das/ein ~ von ...** the/a giant [of a] ...

**Monsun** /mɔn'zu:n/ *der;* **~s, ~e** *(Geogr.)* monsoon

**Monsun-: ~regen** *der (Geog.)* monsoon rains *pl.;* **~wald** *der (Geog.)* monsoon forest

**Montag** /'mo:nta:k/ *der* ▶ 207, ▶ 833 Monday; ⇒ *auch* **blau; Dienstag; Dienstag-**

**Montag-** Monday; ⇒ *auch* **Dienstag-**

**Montage** /mɔn'ta:ʒə/ *die;* **~, ~n** (A) *(Bauw., Technik) (Zusammenbau)* assembly; *(Einbau)* installation; *(Aufstellen)* erection; *(Anbringen)* fitting **(an** + *Akk. od. Dat.* to); mounting **(auf** + *Akk. od. Dat.* on); **auf ~** *(ugs.)* away on a job; (B) *(Film, bild. Kunst, Literaturw.)* montage; (C) *(Druckw.)* make-up

**Montage-: ~band** *das; Pl.* **~bänder** assembly line; **~halle** *die* assembly shop

**montags** *Adv.* ▶ 833 on Monday[s]; ⇒ *auch* **dienstags**

**Montags·wagen** *der (ugs.)* Friday car

**Montan-: ~industrie** *die* coal and steel industry; **~union** *die* European Coal and Steel Community

**Monteur** /mɔn'tø:ɐ̯/ *der;* **~s, ~e** ▶ 159 mechanic; *(Installateur)* fitter; *(Elektro~)* electrician

**Monteur·anzug** *der* [mechanic's] overalls *pl.*

**Monteurin** *die;* **~, ~nen** ▶ 159 ⇒ **Monteur**

**montieren** /mɔn'ti:rən/ *tr. V.* (A) *(zusammenbauen)* assemble **(aus** from); erect ‹building›; (B) *(anbringen)* fit **(an** + *Akk. od. Dat.* to; **auf** + *Akk. od. Dat.* on); *(einbauen)* install **(in** + *Akk.* in); *(befestigen)* fix **(an** + *Akk. od. Dat.* to); **eine Lampe an die** *od.* **der Decke ~:** put up *or* fix a light on the ceiling; **eine Antenne auf das** *od.* **dem Dach ~:** put up *or* mount an aerial on the roof; (C) *(Film, bild. Kunst)* put together; *(Druckw.)* make up

**Montierer** *der;* **~s, ~, Montiererin** *die;* **~, ~nen** assembly worker

**Montur** /mɔn'tu:ɐ̯/ *die;* **~, ~en** (A) *(ugs.)* outfit *(coll.)*; gear *no pl. (coll.)*; (B) *(veralt.: Uniform)* uniform

**Monument** /monu'mɛnt/ *das;* **~[e]s, ~e** *(auch fig.)* monument

**monumental** ❶ *Adj. (auch fig.)* monumental; *(massiv)* massive. ❷ *adv.* in a monumental style; *(überdimensional)* on a monumental scale

**Monumental-:** monumental

**Moor** /mo:ɐ̯/ *das;* **~[e]s, ~e** bog; *(Bruch)* marsh; *(Flach~)* fen; *(Hoch~)* high moor

**Moor-: ~bad** *das* mudbath; **~boden** *der* bog soil; *(Torfboden)* peaty soil

**moorig** *Adj.* boggy

**Moor-: ~kultur** *die* bogland/fenland [reclamation and] cultivation; **~leiche** *die* [well-preserved] body found in a bog

**Moos** /mo:s/ *das;* **~es, ~e** (A) moss; **~ ansetzen** gather moss; *(fig. ugs.)* become old hat *(coll.)*; (B) *(salopp)* cash; dough *(coll.)*; (C) *Pl. auch:* **Möser** *(südd., österr., schweiz.)* bog; *(Bruch)* marsh

**moos-: ~bedeckt, ~bewachsen** *Adj.* moss-covered; **~grün** *Adj.* moss-green

**moosig** *Adj.* (A) mossy; *(moosbedeckt)* moss-covered; (B) *(südd., österr., schweiz.: sumpfig)* marshy

**Moos-: ~rose** *die,* **~röschen** *das* moss rose

***Mop** ⇒ **Mopp**

**Moped** /'mo:pɛt/ *das;* **~s, ~s** moped

**Moped·fahrer** *der,* **Moped·fahrerin** *die* moped rider

**Mopp** /mɔp/ *der;* **~s, ~s** mop

**Moppel** /'mɔpl̩/ *der;* **~s, ~** *(fam. scherzh.)* podge *(coll.)*

**moppen** /'mɔpn̩/ *tr., itr. V.* mop; mop the floor in ‹room›

**Mops** /mɔps/ *der;* **~es, Möpse** /'mœpsə/ (A) *(Hund)* pug [dog]; (B) *(salopp: dicke Person)* podge *(coll.)*; fatty *(derog.)*; (C) *Pl. (salopp: Geld)* bread *(sl.)*; lolly *(Brit. coll.)*; **die paar Möpse** such a piffling sum *(coll.)*; such peanuts *(sl.)*

**mopsen** ❶ *tr. V. (fam.)* pinch *(coll.)*. ❷ *refl. V. (ugs.)* be bored

**mops·fidel** *Adj. (ugs.)* very jolly *or* cheerful

**mopsig** *Adj. (ugs.)* (A) podgy; tubby; (B) **sich ~ machen, ~ werden** get fresh

**Moral** /mo'ra:l/ *die;* **~** (A) *(Norm)* morality; **gegen die ~ verstoßen** offend against morality *or* the code of conduct; **die herrschende ~:** [currently] accepted standards *pl.;* (B) *(Sittlichkeit)* morals *pl.;* **keine ~ haben** have no sense of morals; **[eine] doppelte ~:** double standards *pl.;* **[jmdm.] ~ predigen** *(abwertend)* moralize [to sb.]; (C) *(Selbstvertrauen)* morale; **die ~ ist gut/schlecht** morale is high/low; (D) *(Lehre)* moral; (E) *(Philos.)* ethics *sing.*

**Moral-: ~apostel** *der (abwertend)* upholder of moral standards; **~begriff** *der* [personal] moral code; sense of morals

**Moralin** *das;* **~s** *(abwertend, scherzh.)* [hypocritical] moral indignation; *(rechthaberisch)* [priggish] self-righteousness

**moralin·sauer** *(abwertend, scherzh.)* ❶ *Adj.* [priggishly] indignant; *(rechthaberisch)* [priggishly] self-righteous; holier-than-thou *(coll.)*. ❷ *adv.* with [priggish] indignation

**moralisch** /mo'ra:lɪʃ/ ❶ *Adj.* (A) moral; **das war [für ihn] eine ~e Ohrfeige** that was a slap in the face [for him]; **[s]einen Moralischen haben** *(ugs.) (Gewissensbisse haben)* have a fit of remorse; *(niedergeschlagen sein)* be down in the dumps *(coll.) (as the result of a failure)*; (B) *(sittlich einwandfrei)* moral; morally upright; *(tugendhaft)* virtuous; (C) *(diszipliniert)* **eine gute ~e Verfassung** good morale; **~er Zusammenbruch** breakdown of *or* in morale.
❷ *adv.* (A) morally; **ein ~ hoch stehender Mensch** a person of unimpeachable morals *or* high moral standing; (B) *(tugendhaft)* morally; virtuously; **jmdm. ~ kommen** *(ugs.)* adopt a high moral tone with sb.

**moralisieren** *itr. V. (geh.)* moralize

**Moralismus** *der;* **~** (A) *(Moralität)* sense of morality; (B) *(abwertend: das Moralisieren)* moralizing

**Moralist** *der;* **~en, ~en, Moralistin** *die;* **~, ~nen** moralist

**moralistisch** ❶ *Adj.* moralistic. ❷ *adv.* moralistically; from a moralistic viewpoint

**Moralität** *die;* **~, ~en** (A) *(geh.)* morality; (B) *(Literaturw.)* morality [play]

**Moral-: ~kodex** *der* moral code; **~philosophie** *die* moral philosophy; **~prediger** *der,* **~predigerin** *die (abwertend)* moralizing prig; **~predigt** *die (abwertend)* [moralizing] lecture; homily; **[jmdm.] eine ~predigt halten** deliver a homily [to sb.]; **~theologie** *die* moral theology *no art.;* **~vorstellung** *die* ideas *pl.* on *or* attitude to morality

**Moräne** /mo'rɛ:nə/ *die;* **~, ~n** *(Geol.)* moraine

**Morast** /mo'rast/ *der;* **~[e]s, ~e** *od.* **Moräste** /mo'rɛstə/ (A) bog; swamp; (B) *(Schlamm)* mud; *(auch fig.)* mire; **im ~ versinken** sink into the mire

**morastig** *Adj.* muddy

**Moratorium** /mora'to:ri̯ʊm/ *das;* **~s, Moratorien** *(Wirtsch., Politik)* moratorium **(für** on)

m

**morbid** /mɔr'bi:t/ *Adj.* (*geh.*) (*kränklich*) sickly; (*todgeweiht*) deathly pale; (*fig.*) moribund, degenerate ‹society, institution, etc.›

**Morbidität** /mɔrbidi'tɛ:t/ *die;* ~ **A** (*geh.*) sickliness; (*fig.*) moribund *or* degenerate state; **B** (*Med.*) morbidity

**Morchel** /'mɔrçl̩/ *die;* ~, ~**n** morel

**Mord** /mɔrt/ *der;* ~**[e]s**, ~**e** murder (**an** + *Dat.* of); (*durch ein Attentat*) assassination; **einen ~ begehen** commit murder; **einen ~ an jmdm. begehen** murder sb.; **ein versuchter ~:** an attempted murder; **wegen ~es angeklagt/verurteilt** accused of *or* charged with murder/condemned for murder; (*in Schlagzeilen*) **~ aus Eifersucht** jealousy killing; **~ an Außenminister** foreign minister murdered/assassinated; **dann gibt es ~ und Totschlag** (*fig. ugs.*) all hell is/will be let loose; **das ist [glatter** *od.* **der reinste] ~** (*fig. ugs.*) it's sheer murder; (*unverantwortlich*) it's sheer lunacy

**Mord-:** ~**anklage** *die* charge of murder; **unter ~anklage stehen** be charged with murder; ~**anschlag** *der* attempted murder (**auf** + *Akk.* of); (*Attentat*) assassination attempt (**auf** + *Akk.* on); **einen ~anschlag auf jmdn. verüben** make an attempt on sb.'s life; **einem ~anschlag zum Opfer fallen** be murdered/assassinated; ~**brenner** *der,* ~**brennerin** *die;* ~~, ~~**nen** murdering fire-raiser; ~**bube** *der* (*veralt.*) murdering thug; ~**drohung** *die* murder threat

**morden** *tr., itr. V.* murder; **das sinnlose Morden:** the senseless killing

**Mörder** /'mœrdɐ/ *der;* ~**s**, ~**:** murderer (*esp. Law*); killer; (*politischer* ~) assassin; **vierfacher ~ sein** have committed four murders

**Mörder-:** ~**bande** *die* gang of murderers *or* killers; ~**grube** *die* ⇒ **Herz** B; ~**hand** *in* **durch** *od.* **von ~hand sterben** (*geh.*) die at the hand of a murderer

**Mörderin** *die;* ~, ~**nen** murderer; murderess; (*politische* ~) assassin

**mörderisch** **1** *Adj.* **A** (*ugs.: furchtbar, mächtig*) murderous; fiendish ‹cold›; dreadful (*coll.*) ‹crowd, clamour, weather, storm›; cutthroat ‹competition›; **B** (*todbringend*) murderous. **2** *adv.* **A** (*ugs.*) dreadfully (*coll.*); frightfully (*coll.*); ~ **fluchen/toben** curse/rage like blazes (*sl.*); **B** (*todbringend*) murderously

**mord-, Mord-:** ~**fall** *der* murder case; **der ~fall Dr. Crippen** [the case of] the Dr Crippen murders; ~**gierig** *Adj.* intent on murder *postpos.*; (*blutgierig*) bloodthirsty; ~**instrument** *das* **A** murder weapon; **B** (*fig. scherzh.*) murderous[-looking] weapon *or* device

**Mordio** /'mɔrdi̯o/ ⇒ **Zeter**

**Mord-:** ~**kommission** *die* murder *or* (*Amer.*) homicide squad; ~**prozess**, *~**prozeß** *der* murder trial; ~**sache** *die* murder case; **die ~sache Müller** the Müller murder [case]

**mords-, Mords-** (*ugs.*) terrific (*coll.*); tremendous (*coll.*)

**mords-, Mords-:** ~**arbeit** *die* (*ugs.*) **eine ~arbeit** a hell of a job (*coll.*); **sich** (*Dat.*) **eine ~arbeit machen** take a tremendous amount of trouble (*coll.*) (**mit** over); ~**ding** *das; Pl.* ~~**er** (*ugs.*) whopper (*coll.*); ~**dusel** *der* (*ugs.*) ⇒ ~**glück**; ~**gaudi** *die* (*bayr., österr. ugs.*) ⇒ ~**spaß**; ~**geschrei** *das* (*ugs.*) terrific hubbub (*coll.*); (*Lärm*) frightful racket (*coll.*); (*furchtbares Theater*) terrible fuss (*coll.*) (**um** over); ~**glück** *das* (*ugs.*) **ein ~glück** incredible luck (*coll.*); **ein ~glück haben** be incredibly lucky (*coll.*); ~**hunger** *der* (*ugs.*) terrific hunger (*coll.*); **einen ~hunger haben** be ravenous *or* famished; ~**kerl** *der* (*ugs.*) **A** (*Riese*) enormous bloke (*Brit. coll.*); huge guy (*coll.*); **B** (*tüchtiger Kerl*) really good sort (*coll.*); great guy (*Amer.*); (*Kamerad*) real pal (*coll.*); ~**krach** *der* (*ugs.*) **A** terrible din *or* racket (*coll.*); **B** (*Streit*) terrific row (*coll.*); ~**mäßig** (*ugs.*) **1** *Adj.* terrific (*coll.*); tremendous (*coll.*); (*entsetzlich*) terrible (*coll.*); infernal (*coll.*) ‹din, racket›; ~**mäßiges Glück** incredible luck (*coll.*); **2** *adv.* tremendously (*coll.*); incredibly (*coll.*); (*entsetzlich*) terribly (*coll.*); ~**schreck**, ~**schrecken** *der* (*ugs.*) hell of a fright (*coll.*); terrible fright (*coll.*); ~**spaß** *der* (*ugs.*) **ein ~spaß** tremendous fun (*coll.*); **einen ~spaß haben** have a whale of a time (*coll.*); ~**stimmung** *die* (*ugs.*) terrific atmosphere (*coll.*); ~**wut** *die* (*ugs.*) towering rage; **eine ~wut [im Bauch] haben** be fuming with rage

*old spelling (see note on page 1707)

**Mord-:** ~**tat** *die* (*geh.*) murder; ~**verdacht** *der* suspicion of murder; ~**versuch** *der* attempted murder; (*Attentat*) assassination attempt; ~**waffe** *die* murder weapon

**Mores** /'mo:re:s/ *Pl. in* **jmdn. ~ lehren** (*ugs.*) tell sb. what's what *or* where he/she gets off (*coll.*); **dich werde ich ~ lehren!** I'll give you a piece of my mind!

**morganatisch** /mɔrga'na:tɪʃ/ *Adj. in* ~**e Ehe** (*hist.*) morganatic marriage

**morgen** /'mɔrgn̩/ *Adv.* ▶ **833** tomorrow; ~ **früh/Mittag/Abend** tomorrow morning/lunchtime/evening; ~ **in einer Woche/in vierzehn Tagen** tomorrow week/fortnight; a week/fortnight tomorrow; ~ **um diese** *od.* **die gleiche Zeit** this time tomorrow; **bis ~!** until tomorrow!; see you tomorrow!; ~ **ist auch [noch] ein Tag** tomorrow is another day; ~, ~, **nur nicht heute, sagen alle faulen Leute** (*Spr.*) ≈ never put off till tomorrow what you can do today; **die Mode/Technik von ~** (*fig.*) tomorrow's fashions *pl.*/technology; ⇒ *auch* **Morgen²** A

**Morgen¹** *das;* ~**: das ~:** the future

**Morgen²** *der;* ~**s**, ~ **A** ▶ **369** morning; **am ~**, (*geh.*) **des ~s** in the morning; **am folgenden** *od.* **nächsten ~:** next *or* the following morning; **heute/gestern ~:** this/yesterday morning; **früh am ~, am frühen ~:** early in the morning; **am ~ seiner Abreise** on the morning of his departure; **eines [schönen] ~s** one [fine] morning; **bis in den [frühen] ~ feiern/arbeiten** celebrate/work until the early hours; **gegen ~:** towards morning; ~ **für ~:** every single morning; morning after morning; **es wird ~:** day *or* dawn is breaking; **sie gingen erst, als es bereits ~ wurde** they didn't go until it was already becoming daylight; **den ganzen ~:** all morning; **guten ~!** good morning!; ~! (*ugs.*) morning! (*coll.*); **[jmdm.] guten ~ sagen** *od.* **wünschen** say good morning [to sb.]; wish [sb.] good morning; (*grüßen*) say hello [to sb.]; **schön** *od.* **frisch wie der junge ~** (*scherzh.*) fresh as a daisy; **B** (*fig. geh.*) **der ~ des Lebens** the springtide of life (*literary*); **der ~ der Freiheit/eines neuen Zeitalters** the dawn of liberty/of a new age; **C** (*geh. veralt.*) east; **gen ~:** towards the east; **D** ▶ **301** (*veralt.: Feldmaß*) ≈ acre; **fünf ~ Land** five acres of land

**Morgen-:** ~**andacht** *die* morning service; ~**ausgabe** *die* morning edition; ~**dämmerung** *die* dawn; daybreak; **in der ~dämmerung** at daybreak

**morgendlich** *Adj.* morning; **die ~e Kühle/Stille** the cool/peace of [early] morning; **der ~e Sturm aufs Badezimmer** (*scherzh.*) the fight for the bathroom every morning

**morgen-, Morgen-:** ~**frühe** *die* early morning; ~**gabe** *die* (*hist.*) *husband's present to wife on morning after wedding night;* ~**gebet** *das* morning prayer; ~**grauen** *das* daybreak; **im** *od.* **beim ~grauen** in the first light of day; ~**gymnastik** *die* morning exercises *pl.*; daily dozen (*coll.*); ~**kaffee** *der* **A** (*Mahlzeit*) light breakfast with coffee; **B** (*Kaffee*) breakfast coffee;

**Morgenland** *das;* ~**[e]s** (*veralt.*) East; Orient

**morgenländisch** (*veralt.*) **1** *Adj.* oriental; eastern. **2** *adv.* in an oriental style *or* fashion

**Morgen-:** ~**licht** *das* morning light; **beim ersten ~licht** in the first light of day; ~**luft** *die* morning air; ~**luft wittern** (*fig. scherzh.*) see one's chance; ~**mantel** *der* dressing gown; ~**muffel** *der* (*ugs.*) **ein ~muffel sein** be grumpy in the mornings; ~**nebel** *der* morning fog; (*weniger dicht*) morning mist; ~**post** *die* morning post; ~**rock** *der* dressing gown; ~**rot** *das,* ~**röte** *die* (*geh.*) rosy dawn; (*tiefer*) red dawn; (*fig.*) dawn

**morgens** *Adv.* ▶ **752** in the morning; (*jeden Morgen*) every morning; ~ **um 7 Uhr, um 7 Uhr ~:** at 7 in the morning/every morning; **Dienstag** *od.* **dienstags ~:** on Tuesday morning[s]; **von ~ bis abends** all day long; from morning to evening

**Morgen-:** ~**sonne** *die* morning sun; ~**sonne haben** get the morning sun; ~**spaziergang** *der* (*esp. early*) morning walk; ~**stern** *der* **A** morning star; **B** (*hist.*) spiked mace; (*mit Kette*) nail-studded flail; ~**stunde** *die* hour of the morning; **die frühen ~stunden** the early *or* small hours [of the morning]; ~**stunde hat Gold im Munde** (*Spr.*) the early bird catches the worm (*prov.*); ~**zeitung** *die* morning paper

**morgig** *Adj.* tomorrow's; **der ~e Tag** tomorrow

**moribund** /mori'bʊnt/ *Adj.* (*Med., auch fig.*) moribund

**Moritat** /'mo:rita:t/ *die;* ~, ~**en** (*usually gruesome*) street ballad

**Moritz** /'mo:rɪts/ *in* **wie sich der kleine ~ das vorstellt** (*ugs. scherzh.*) as some Simple Simon might imagine it

**Mormone** /mɔr'mo:nə/ *der;* ~**n**, ~**n**, **Mormonin** *die;* ~, ~**nen** Mormon

**Morph** /mɔrf/ *das;* ~**s**, ~**e** (*Sprachw.*) morph

**Morphem** /mɔr'fe:m/ *das;* ~**s**, ~**e** (*Sprachw.*) morpheme

**Morpheus** /'mɔrfɔys/ (*der*) (*Myth.*) Morpheus

**Morphin** /mɔr'fi:n/ *das;* ~**s** (*Chemie, Med.*) ⇒ **Morphium**

**Morphing** /'mɔrfɪŋ/ *das;* ~**s** morphing

**Morphinismus** *der;* ~ (*Med.*) morphinism *no art.*; morphine addiction *no art.*

**Morphinist** *der;* ~**en**, ~**en**, **Morphinistin** *die;* ~, ~**nen** morphine addict

**Morphium** /'mɔrfi̯ʊm/ *das;* ~**s** morphine

**Morphium·sucht** *die* ⇒ **Morphinismus**

**morphium·süchtig** *Adj.* addicted to morphine *pred.*

**Morphologie** /mɔrfolo'gi:/ *die;* ~ (*Biol., Sprachw.*) morphology

**morphologisch** (*Biol., Sprachw.*) **1** *Adj.* morphological. **2** *adv.* morphologically

**morsch** /mɔrʃ/ *Adj.* (*auch fig.*) rotten; brittle ‹bones›; crumbling ‹rock, masonry›

**Morse-:** ~**alphabet** *das* Morse code *or* alphabet; ~**apparat** *der* Morse telegraph

**morsen** /'mɔrzn̩/ **1** *itr. V.* send a message/messages in Morse. **2** *tr. V.* send ‹signal, message› in Morse

**Mörser** /'mœrzɐ/ *der;* ~**s**, ~ (*auch Milit.*) mortar

**Morse·zeichen** *das* Morse symbol

**Mortadella** /mɔrta'dɛla/ *die;* ~, ~**s** mortadella

**Mortalität** /mɔrtali'tɛ:t/ *die;* ~**:** mortality [rate]

**Mörtel** /'mœrtl̩/ *der;* ~**s** mortar

**Mosaik** /moza'i:k/ *das;* ~**s**, ~**en** *od.* ~**e** (*auch fig.*) mosaic; **mit ~en ausgelegt** covered in mosaics

**Mosaik-:** ~**[fuß]boden** *der* mosaic floor; ~**stein** *der* tessera; (*fig.*) piece of a jigsaw

**mosaisch** /mo'za:ɪʃ/ (*Rel.*) **1** *Adj.* Mosaic ‹Law›; Jewish ‹faith›. **2** *adv.* in the Jewish faith

**Mosambik** /mozam'bi:k/ (*das*); ~**s** Mozambique

**Moschee** /mɔ'ʃe:/ *die;* ~, ~**n** mosque

**Moschus** /'mɔʃʊs/ *der;* ~**:** musk

**Moschus·ochse** *der* musk ox

**Mose** /'mo:zə/ (*der*); ~**[s]** (*Rel.*) Moses; **die fünf Bücher ~:** the Pentateuch

**Möse** /'mø:zə/ *die;* ~, ~**n** (*vulg.*) cunt (*coarse*)

**Mosel** /'mo:zl̩/ *die;* ~ ▶ **306** Moselle

**Möser** /'mø:zɐ/ ⇒ **Moos** C

**mosern** /'mo:zɐn/ *itr. V.* (*ugs.*) gripe (*coll.*) (**über** + *Akk.* about); **du findest aber auch an allem etwas zu ~:** you always manage to find something to complain about (*coll.*)

**Moses**[1] *der;* ~, ~ (*Seemannsspr.*) ship's boy

**Moses**[2] (*der*) Moses; **die fünf Bücher Mosis** (*Rel.*) the Pentateuch

**Moskau** /ˈmɔskau/ (*das*); ~**s** ▶ 700 Moscow

**Moskauer** ▶ 700 ❶ *indekl. Adj.* Moscow *attrib.* ❷ *der;* ~**s**, ~: Muscovite; ⇒ *auch* **Kölner**

**Moskauerin** *die;* ~, ~**en** Muscovite

**Moskito** /mɔsˈkiːto/ *der;* ~**s**, ~**s** mosquito

**Moskito·netz** *das* mosquito net

**Moskowiter** /mɔskoˈviːtɐ/ *der;* ~**s**, ~, **Moskowiterin** *die;* ~, ~**nen** (*veralt.*) Muscovite

**moskowitisch** /mɔskoˈviːtɪʃ/ *Adj.* (*veralt.*) Muscovite

**Moslem** /ˈmɔslɛm/ *der;* ~**s**, ~**s** ⇒ **Muslim**

**moslemisch** ⇒ **muslimisch**

**Most** /mɔst/ *der;* ~[**e**]**s**, ~**e** Ⓐ (*südd.: junger Wein*) new wine; Ⓑ (*Weinbasis*) must; Ⓒ (*südd.: Obstsaft*) [cloudy fermented] fruit juice; Ⓓ (*südd., schweiz., österr.: Obstwein*) fruit wine; (*Apfel*~) [rough] cider

**Most·apfel** *der* [sour] cider apple

**Mostert** /ˈmɔstɐt/ *der;* ~**s** (*nordwestd.*), **Mostrich** /ˈmɔstrɪç/ *der;* ~**s** (*nordostd.*) mustard

**Motel** /ˈmoːtl̩/ *das;* ~**s**, ~**s** motel

**Motette** /moˈtɛtə/ *die;* ~, ~**n** (*Musik*) motet

**Motion** /moˈtsi̯oːn/ *die;* ~, ~**en** Ⓐ (*schweiz.*) motion (*Gen.* by); Ⓑ (*Sprachw.*) change of form determined by gender

**Motiv** /moˈtiːf/ *das;* ~**s**, ~**e** Ⓐ motive; **das ~ einer Tat** the motive for an action; Ⓑ (*Literaturw., Musik usw.: Thema*) motif; theme; (*bild. Kunst: Gegenstand*) subject

**Motivation** /motivaˈtsi̯oːn/ *die;* ~, ~**en** (*Psych., Päd.*) motivation

**Motiv·forschung** *die* motivation research

**motivieren** *tr. V.* (*geh.*) Ⓐ (*begründen*) give a [sufficient] reason for; **eine Entscheidung/sein Verhalten ~:** account for a decision/one's behaviour; Ⓑ (*anregen*) motivate; [**hoch**] **motiviert** [highly] motivated

**Motivierung** *die;* ~, ~**en** (*geh.*) motivation

**Motocross** /motoˈkrɔs/ *das;* ~, ~**e** Ⓐ (*Sport*) motocross *no pl.;* Ⓑ (*Veranstaltung*) motocross event *or* meeting

**Motodrom** /motoˈdroːm/ *das;* ~**s**, ~**e** autodrome; speedway (*Amer.*)

**Motor** /ˈmoːtɔr/ *der;* ~**s**, ~**en** (*Verbrennungs*~) engine; (*Elektro*~) motor; (*fig.*) driving force (*Gen.* behind)

**Motor-:** ~**block** *der; Pl.* ~**blöcke** (*Kfz-W.*) engine block; cylinder block; ~**boot** *das* motor boat; (*im Gegensatz zum Segelboot*) power boat

**Motoren-:** ~**geräusch** *das* sound of the engine/engines; ~**lärm** *der* engine noise

**Motor-:** ~**fahrzeug** *das* motor vehicle; ~**flug** *der* [powered] flying (*as a sport*); ~**haube** *die* (*Kfz-W.*) bonnet (*Brit.*); hood (*Amer.*)

**-motorig** *adj.* -engined; **ein~/zwei~:** single-engined/twin-engined

**Motorik** /moˈtoːrɪk/ *die;* ~ Ⓐ (*bes. Med.*) motor functions *pl.;* Ⓑ (*Lehre*) study of motor functions

**motorisch** *Adj.* Ⓐ (*Psych.*) motor *attrib.;* Ⓑ (*Kfz-W.*) with regard to the engine *postpos., not pred.*

**motorisieren** ❶ *tr. V.* motorize; (*mit Maschinen ausrüsten*) mechanize; **ein Boot ~:** fit a boat with an engine; **motorisierte Besucher** visitors with cars; **sind Sie motorisiert?** (*ugs.*) have you got any wheels? (*coll.*). ❷ *refl. V.* get a car/motorcycle; get oneself wheels (*coll.*)

**Motorisierung** *die;* ~ ⇒ **motorisieren** 1: motorization; mechanization

**Motor-:** ~**jacht** *die* motor yacht; ~**leistung** *die* (*Kfz-W.*) engine performance; (*PS*) power output; ~**öl** *das* (*Kfz-W.*) engine oil; ~**rad** *das* motorcycle

**Motorrad-:** ~**brille** *die* motorcycling goggles; ~**fahrer** *der*, ~**fahrerin** *die* motorcyclist; ~**rennen** *das* motorcycle race; (*Sport*) motorcycle racing; ~**sport** motorcycling

**Motor-:** ~**raum** *der* (*Kfz-W.*) engine compartment; ~**roller** *der* motor scooter; ~**säge** *die* power saw; ~**schaden** *der* engine trouble *no indef. art.;* (*Panne*) mechanical breakdown; ~**schiff** *das* motor ship *or* vessel; ~**schlitten** *der* motor rized sledge; ~**sport** *der* motor sport *no art.;* ~**wäsche** *die* engine wash-down

**Motte** /ˈmɔtə/ *die;* ~, ~**n** Ⓐ moth; **von etw. angezogen werden wie die ~n vom Licht** be attracted by sth. as moths to the light; [**ach,**] **du kriegst die ~n!** (*ugs.*) my godfathers!; **die ~n haben** (*salopp veralt.*) have TB; Ⓑ (*salopp veralt.: Mädchen*) chick (*sl.*); **flotte** *od.* **tolle ~:** smasher (*sl.*); **kesse ~:** saucy *or* pert little miss (*coll.*)

**motten-, Motten-:** ~**echt**, ~**fest** *Adj.* mothproof; ~**fraß** *der* moth [damage]; ~**kiste** *die* Ⓐ (*veralt.*) mothproof chest; Ⓑ (*fig.*) **Filme/Geschichten/Gags aus der ~kiste** ancient films/stories/gags; ~**kugel** *die* mothball; ~**pulver** *das* moth powder; ~**zerfressen** *Adj.* moth-eaten

**Motto** /ˈmɔto/ *das;* ~**s**, ~**s** motto; (*Schlagwort*) slogan; **der Kirchentag stand unter dem ~: ...** the motto of the church assembly was ...; **nach dem ~: ... leben** live according to the maxim: ...

**motzen** /ˈmɔtsn̩/ *itr. V.* (*ugs.*) grouch (*coll.*), bellyache (*sl.*) (**über** + *Akk.* about); **was hast du schon wieder zu ~?** what are you bellyaching about now? (*sl.*)

**motzig** (*ugs.*) ❶ *Adj.* grouchy (*coll.*); grumpy. ❷ *adv.* grouchily (*coll.*); grumpily

**Mountain·bike** /ˈmaʊntɪnbaik/ *das* mountain bike

**Mousse** /mʊs/ *die;* ~, ~**s** (*Kochk.*) mousse

**moussieren** /mʊˈsiːrən/ *itr. V.* sparkle; (*als Eigenschaft*) be sparkling; ~**der Wein** sparkling wine

**Möwe** /ˈmøːvə/ *die;* ~, ~**n** gull

**Mozart·zopf** /ˈmoːtsart-/ *der* bag wig

**MPi** /ˈɛmˈpiː/*die;* ~, ~**s** sub-machine gun

**Mrd.** *Abk.* **Milliarde** bn.

**m.s., MS** *Abk.* **multiple Sklerose** MS

**Ms., MS** *Abk.* **Manuskript** MS

**MS** *Abk.* **Motorschiff** MV; MS (*Amer.*)

**MTA** *Abk.* **medizinisch-technische Assistentin** medical-laboratory assistant

**MTB** *Abk.* **Mountainbike** MTB

**mtl.** *Abk.* **monatlich** mthly.

**Mücke** /ˈmʏkə/ *die;* ~, ~**n** Ⓐ midge; gnat; (*größer*) mosquito; **aus einer ~ einen Elefanten machen** (*ugs.*) make a mountain out of a molehill; **die ~ machen** (*salopp*) push off (*coll.*); Ⓑ *Pl.* (*salopp: Geld*) bread (*sl.*); lolly (*Brit. coll.*)

**Muckefuck** /ˈmʊkəfʊk/ *der;* ~**s** (*ugs.*) coffee substitute

**mucken** /ˈmʊkn̩/ *itr. V.* (*ugs.*) grumble; mutter; **ohne zu ~:** without a murmur

**Mucken** *Pl.* (*ugs.*) whims; (*Eigenarten*) little ways *or* peculiarities; (*Launen*) moods; [**seine**] **~ haben** ‹person› have one's little ways/one's moods; ‹car, machine› be a little unpredictable *or* temperamental; **jmdm. seine ~ austreiben** sort sb. out (*coll.*)

**Mücken·stich** *der* midge/mosquito bite

**Mucker** *der;* ~**s**, ~ (*ugs. abwertend*) yes-man

**Muckerin** *die;* ~, ~**nen** (*ugs. abwertend*) yes-woman

**Muckertum** *das* (*ugs. abwertend*) being *no art.* a yes-man (*coll.*)

**Mucks** /mʊks/ *der;* ~**es**, ~**e** (*ugs.*) murmur [of protest]; slight[est] sound; **keinen ~ sagen** *od.* **von sich geben** not utter a [single] word *or* sound; **die Kinder gaben keinen ~ von sich** there was not the slightest sound/murmur out of the children

**mucksen** *refl. V.* (*ugs.*) Ⓐ (*meist negativ*) make a sound; (*sich rühren*) stir; budge; **sie wagten nicht, sich zu ~:** they didn't dare to budge [an inch]/make a sound; Ⓑ (*aufbegehren*) object; make noises (*coll.*)

**Muckser** *der;* ~**s**, ~ (*ugs.*) ⇒ **Mucks**

**mucks·mäuschen·still** (*ugs.*) ❶ *Adj.* utterly silent; ‹person› as quiet as a mouse *postpos.;* **es wurde ~:** you could have heard a pin drop. ❷ *adv.* in total silence; without making a sound

**Mud[d]** /mʊt/ *der;* ~**s** (*nordd.*) mud

**müde** /ˈmyːdə/ ❶ *Adj.* tired; (*ermattet*) weary; (*schläfrig*) sleepy; **mit ~n Schritten** with weary steps; **ich war zum Umfallen ~:** I was out on my feet; **Bier macht ~:** beer makes you feel sleepy; **sich ~ laufen/weinen** tire oneself out with walking/crying; **ein ~s Lächeln** (*auch fig.*) a weary smile; **jmdn./etw.** *od.* **jmds./einer Sache ~ sein** (*geh.*) be tired of sb./sth.; **jmds./einer Sache** (*Gen.*) **~ werden** (*geh.*) tire *or* grow tired of sb./sth.; **nicht ~ werden, etw. zu tun** never tire of doing sth.; (*bei unangenehmer Tätigkeit*) never stop doing sth.; ⇒ *auch* **Mark**[1]
❷ *adv.* wearily; (*schläfrig*) sleepily

**-müde** *adj.* tired of ...; **amts~/kino~/stadt~:** tired of [holding] office/[going to] the cinema/city life *postpos.*

**Müdigkeit** *die;* ~**:** tiredness; **~/eine tiefe ~ kam über ihn** he began to feel tired/a great weariness come over him; **von ~ übermannt werden** be overcome by fatigue; **ich könnte vor ~ umfallen** I'm so tired I can hardly stand; [**nur**] **keine ~ vorschützen!** (*ugs.*) it's no use saying you're tired!

**-müdigkeit** *die* weariness of ...; **Zivilisations~:** weariness of civilized living; culture fatigue; **Kriegs~:** war-weariness

**Müesli** /ˈmyːɛsli/ *das;* ~**s** (*schweiz.*) ⇒ **Müsli**

**Muff**[1] /mʊf/ *der;* ~[**e**]**s** (*nordd.*) musty smell; (*Gestank*) fug

**Muff**[2] *der;* ~[**e**]**s**, ~**e** muff

**Muffe** *die;* ~, ~**n** Ⓐ (*Technik*) sleeve; (*Verbindungsstück*) sleeve [coupling]; Ⓑ (*fig.*) **jmdm. geht die ~** (*salopp*) sb. is shaking in his shoes; **~ haben** (*salopp*) be in a funk (*coll.*) (**vor** + *Dat.* about)

**Muffel** /ˈmʊfl̩/ *der;* ~**s**, ~ (*ugs.*) Ⓐ sourpuss (*coll.*); grouch (*coll.*); Ⓑ (*desinteressierter Mensch*) **was ... betrifft, ist er ein [richtiger] ~:** as far as ... is concerned he's just not interested

**-muffel** *der;* ~**s**, ~ (*ugs.*) person indifferent to ...

**muffelig** (*ugs.*) ❶ *Adj.* grumpy; surly; **du bist aber ~ heute!** you 'are in a bad mood today! ❷ *adv.* grumpily

**muffeln**[1] (*ugs.*) ❶ *itr. V.* be grumpy *or* in a huff. ❷ *tr., itr. V.* mutter [grumpily]; grunt

**muffeln**[2] *itr. V.* (*südd., österr.: muffig riechen*) smell musty

**Muffen·sausen** *das* (*salopp*) **~ haben/kriegen** be/get in a funk (*coll.*) (**vor** + *Dat.* about)

**muffig**[1] *Adj.* (*modrig riechend*) musty; (*stickig; auch fig.*) stuffy

**muffig**[2] (*ugs.*) ⇒ **muffelig**

**Muffigkeit** *die;* ~ (*ugs.*) grumpiness; surliness

**Mufflon** /ˈmʊflɔn/ *der;* ~**s**, ~**s** (*Zool.*) mouflon

**Mufti** /ˈmʊfti/ *der;* ~**s**, ~**s** mufti

**Mugel** /ˈmuːgl̩/ *der;* ~**s**, ~[**n**] (*österr.*) hillock; (*auf der Skipiste*) mogul

**muh** /muː/ *Interj.* (*Kinderspr.*) moo

**Müh** /myː/ ⇒ **Mühe**

**Mühe** /ˈmyːə/ *die;* ~, ~**n** trouble; **alle ~ haben, etw. zu tun** be hard put to do sth.; **mit jmdm./etw. seine ~ haben** have a lot of trouble *or* a hard time with sb./sth.; **die ~ hat sich gelohnt** it was worth the trouble *or* effort; **keine ~ scheuen** spare no pains *or* effort; **sich** (*Dat.*) **viel ~ machen** go to *or* take a lot of trouble (**mit** over); **machen Sie sich** [**bitte**] **keine ~!** (*tun Sie es nicht*) [please] don't put yourself out!; [please] don't bother!; **wenn es dir keine ~ macht, ...** if it's no trouble *or* bother, ...; **es hat viel ~ gekostet** it took much time and effort; **die ~ kannst du dir sparen** you can save yourself the trouble; **sich** (*Dat.*) **~ geben[, etw. zu tun]** make an effort *or* take pains [to do sth.]; **sich** (*Dat.*) **mit jmdm./etw. ~ geben** take [great] pains *or* trouble over sb./sth.; **wenn du dir mehr ~ geben würdest** if you would take more trouble/try harder; **gib dir doch etwas ~!** do make some sort of an effort!; **gib dir keine ~!** you needn't bother;

m

**mit Müh und Not** with great difficulty; only just; **der** (*Gen.*) *od.* **die ~ wert sein** be worth the trouble *or* worth it; **wäre es der ~ wert, nach X zu fahren?** would it be worth [while] going to X?

**mühelos** ❶ *Adj.* effortless. ❷ *adv.* effortlessly; without the slightest difficulty

**Mühelosigkeit** *die;* **~:** effortlessness

**muhen** *itr. V.* moo

**mühen** *refl. V.* (*geh.*) strive; **sich mit etw. ~:** take pains over sth.; **sosehr er sich auch mühte** hard though he tried

**mühe·voll** *Adj.* laborious; painstaking ‹work›; **ein ~er Weg** an arduous path

**Mühewaltung** /-valtʊŋ/ *die;* **~** (*Papierdt.*) efforts *pl.;* (*im Brief*) **für Ihre ~ dankend** thanking you for your trouble

**Muh·kuh** *die* (*Kinderspr.*) moo-cow (*child lang.*)

**Mühl·bach** *der* millstream

**Mühle** /ˈmyːlə/ *die;* **~, ~n** Ⓐ mill; **in die ~ der Justiz geraten** (*fig.*) become enmeshed in the wheels *or* machinery of justice; **das ist Wasser auf seine ~** (*ugs.*) it's [all] grist to his mill; it just confirms what he has always thought; ⇒ *auch* **Gott**; Ⓑ (*Kaffee~*) [coffee] grinder; Ⓒ (*Spiel*) nine men's morris; Ⓓ (*Figur beim Mühlespiel*) mill; Ⓔ (*ugs. abwertend*) (*Auto, Motorrad*) heap (*coll.*); (*Auto, Flugzeug*) crate (*coll.*); (*Fahrrad*) rattletrap

**Mühle·spiel** *das* nine men's morris

**Mühl-: ~rad** *das* mill wheel; **~stein** *der* millstone

**Muhme** /ˈmuːmə/ *die;* **~, ~n** (*veralt.*) aunt

**Mühsal** /ˈmyːzaːl/ *die;* **~, ~e** (*geh.*) tribulation; (*Strapaze*) hardship; (*Arbeit*) toil *no pl.*

**mühsam** ❶ *Adj.* laborious; **ein ~es Lächeln** a forced smile. ❷ *adv.* laboriously; (*schwierig*) with difficulty; **~ verdientes Geld** hard-earned money

**müh·selig** (*geh.*) ❶ *Adj.* laborious; arduous ‹journey, life›; **... alle, die ihr ~ und beladen seid** (*bibl.*) ... all ye that labour and are heavy laden. ❷ *adv.* with [great] difficulty

**Müh·seligkeit** *die* (*geh.*) laboriousness; (*einer Reise, des Lebens*) arduousness

**Mulatte** /muˈlatə/ *der;* **~n, ~n, Mulattin** *die;* **~, ~nen** mulatto

**Mulde** /ˈmʊldə/ *die;* **~, ~n** Ⓐ hollow; Ⓑ (*Trog*) trough

**Muli** /ˈmuːli/ *das;* **~s, ~s** mule

**Mull**[1] /mʊl/ *der;* **~[e]s** (*Stoff*) mull; (*Verband~*) gauze

**Mull**[2] *der;* **~[e]s, ~e** (*nordd.: Humus*) mull

**Müll** /mʏl/ *der;* **~s** Ⓐ refuse; rubbish; garbage (*Amer.*); trash (*Amer.*); (*Industrie~*) [industrial] waste; **etw. in den ~ werfen** throw sth. in the dustbin (*Brit.*) *or* (*Amer.*) garbage can; **„~ abladen verboten"** 'no dumping'; 'no tipping' (*Brit.*); Ⓑ (*alte Sachen*) rubbish; junk

**Müll-: ~abfuhr** *die* Ⓐ refuse *or* (*Amer.*) garbage collection; Ⓑ (*Unternehmen*) refuse *or* (*Amer.*) garbage collection [service]; **~ablade·platz** *der* [refuse] dump *or* (*Brit.*) tip; **~auto** *das* ⇒ **~wagen**; **~beutel** *der* dustbin (*Brit.*) *or* (*Amer.*) garbage can liner

**Mull·binde** *die* gauze bandage

**Müll-: ~deponie** *die* (*Amtsspr.*) refuse disposal site; **~eimer** *der* rubbish *or* waste bin; **~entsorgung** *die* refuse disposal

**Müller** /ˈmʏlɐ/ *der;* **~s, ~** ▶ 159 miller

**Müller·bursche** *der* (*veralt.*) miller's lad

**Müllerin** *die;* **~, ~nen** (*veralt.*) miller's wife

**Müll-: ~fahrer** *der,* **~fahrerin** *die* ▶ 159 dustcart (*Brit.*) *or* (*Amer.*) garbage truck driver; **~halde** *die* refuse dump; **~haufen** *der* heap of rubbish *or* (*Amer.*) garbage; **~kippe** *die* ⇒ **Müllabladeplatz**; **~mann** *der* (*ugs.*) dustman (*Brit.*); garbage man (*Amer.*); **~sack** *der* refuse bag; **~schippe** *die* dustpan; **~schlucker** *der* rubbish *or* (*Amer.*) garbage chute; **~tonne** *die* dustbin (*Brit.*); garbage *or* trash can (*Amer.*); **~tüte** *die* bin bag; **~verbrennung** *die* refuse *or* (*Amer.*) garbage incineration; **~verbrennungs·anlage** *die* refuse *or* (*Amer.*) garbage incinerator; **~verwertung** *die* refuse *or* (*Amer.*) garbage recycling; **~wagen** *der* dustcart (*Brit.*); garbage truck (*Amer.*); **~werker** *der;* **~~s, ~~, ~werkerin** *die;* **~~, ~~nen** refuse *or* (*Amer.*) garbage operative

**Mull·windel** *die* muslin nappy (*Brit.*) *or* (*Amer.*) diaper

**mulmig** /ˈmʊlmɪç/ *Adj.* Ⓐ (*ugs.: bedenklich*) ticklish; tricky; (*unbehaglich*) uncomfortable; **als es ~ wurde** when things began to look nasty; Ⓑ (*ugs.: übel*) (*im Magen*) queasy; (*unbehaglich*) uneasy; **ein ~es Gefühl haben** feel queasy/uneasy; **mir war ganz ~ zumute** I felt quite weak at the knees; Ⓒ (*faulig*) rotten

**Multi** /ˈmʊlti/ *der;* **~s, ~s** (*ugs.*) multinational

**multi-, Multi-:** multi‹-lingual, -millionaire, -national›

**Multifunktions·taste** *die* multi-function button

**Multi·halle** *die* multi-purpose hall

**Multikulti** *das;* **~s** multicultural mix

**Multikulturalismus** *der;* **~:** multiculturalism

**multikulturell** *Adj.* multicultural

**multi·medial** ❶ *Adj.* multimedia *attrib.;* **~medialer Unterricht** teaching with multimedia material. ❷ *adv.* on a multimedia basis

**Multimedia-** /-ˈmeːdi̯a/**: ~show** *die* multimedia presentation; **~system** *das* (*Päd.*) multimedia method; **~technik** *die* (*DV*) multimedia technology

**multipel** /mʊlˈtiːpl̩/ *Adj.* (*bes. Fachspr.*) multiple; **multiple Sklerose** (*Med.*) multiple sclerosis

**Multiplechoice·verfahren** /ˈmʌltɪpl ˈtʃɔɪs.../ *das* (*Psych., Päd.*) multiple-choice method; **Prüfungen nach dem ~:** examinations using multiple-choice tests

**Multiplikand** /mʊltipliˈkant/ *der;* **~en, ~en** (*Math.*) multiplicand

**Multiplikation** /mʊltiplikaˈt͜si̯oːn/ *die;* **~, ~en** (*Math.*) multiplication

**Multiplikator** /mʊltipliˈkaːtɔr/ *der;* **~s, ~en** /-ˈtoːrən/ Ⓐ (*Math.*) muliplier; Ⓑ (*fig.*) disseminator (*of information, opinions*)

**multiplizieren** /mʊltipliˈt͜siːrən/ ❶ *tr. V.* (*Math., fig.*) multiply (**mit** by). ❷ *refl. V.* (*fig.*) multiply [several times]

**Mumie** /ˈmuːmi̯ə/ *die;* **~, ~n** mummy

**mumienhaft** ❶ *Adj.* mummy-like. ❷ *adv.* like a mummy; as though mummified

**Mumifikation** /mumifikaˈt͜si̯oːn/ *die;* **~, ~en** mummification

**mumifizieren** /mumifiˈt͜siːrən/ *tr. V.* mummify

**Mumifizierung** *die;* **~, ~en** mummification

**Mumm** /mʊm/ *der;* **~s** (*ugs.*) (*Mut*) guts *pl.* (*coll.*); spunk (*coll.*); (*Tatkraft*) drive; zap (*coll.*); (*Kraft*) muscle-power; ⇒ *auch* **Knochen** A

**Mummel·greis** /ˈmʊml̩-/ *der* (*ugs. abwertend*) old dodderer; doddery old man

**Mümmel·mann** /ˈmʏml̩-/ *der* (*fam. scherzh.*) hare

**mummeln**[1] *tr., refl. V.* (*fam.*) **jmdn./sich in eine Decke ~:** wrap sb./oneself [up] snugly in a blanket

**mummeln**[2] (*nordd.*), **mümmeln** *tr., itr. V.* (*fam.*) (*kauen*) chew; (*knabbern*) nibble

**Mummenschanz** /ˈmʊmənʃant͜s/ *der;* **~es** (*veralt.*) Ⓐ (*Fest*) fancy-dress party *or* ball; Ⓑ (*Verkleidung*) fancy dress

**Mumpf** /mʊmpf/ *der;* **~s** (*schweiz.*) mumps *sing.*

**Mumpitz** /ˈmʊmpɪt͜s/ *der;* **~es** (*ugs. abwertend*) rubbish; tripe (*coll.*)

**Mumps** /mʊmps/ *der od. die;* **~** ▶ 474 mumps *sing.*

**München** /ˈmʏnçn̩/ (*das*); **~s** ▶ 700 Munich

**Münch[e]ner** /ˈmʏnçnɐ/ ❶ *indekl. Adj.* Munich *attrib.* ❷ *der;* **~s, ~:** inhabitant/native of Munich; ⇒ *auch* **Kölner**

**Münch[e]nerin** *die;* **~, ~nen** inhabitant/native of Munich

**Mund** /mʊnt/ *der;* **~[e]s, Münder** /ˈmʏndɐ/ mouth; **seinen/den ~ verziehen** make a face; **seinen/den ~ spitzen** purse one's lips; **vor Staunen blieb ihm der ~ offen stehen** he gaped in astonishment; **er küsste ihren ~** *od.* **küsste sie auf den ~:** he kissed her on the lips; **den Finger auf den ~ legen** put one's finger to one's lips; **von ~ zu ~ beatmet werden** be given mouth-to-mouth resuscitation *or* the kiss of life; **aus dem ~ riechen** have bad breath; **mit vollem ~ sprechen** speak with one's mouth full; **etw. aus jmds. ~ hören** hear *or* have sth. from sb.'s [own] lips; **sein ~ steht nicht** *od.* **nie still** (*ugs.*) he never stops talking; **den ~ nicht aufbekommen** *od.* **aufkriegen** (*fig. ugs.*) not open one's mouth; have nothing to say for oneself; **den ~ aufmachen/nicht aufmachen** (*fig. ugs.*) say something/not say anything; **den ~ voll nehmen** (*fig. ugs.*) talk big (*coll.*); **nimm doch den ~ nicht so voll!** don't be such a bighead!; **~ und Augen** *od.* **Nase aufreißen** *od.* **aufsperren** (*ugs.*) gape in astonishment; **einen großen ~ haben** (*fig. ugs.*) talk big (*coll.*); **den** *od.* **seinen ~ halten** (*ugs.*) (*schweigen*) shut up (*coll.*); (*nichts sagen*) not say anything; (*nichts verraten*) keep quiet (**über** + *Akk.* about); **jmdm. den ~ verbieten** silence sb.; **jmdm. den ~ [ganz] wässrig machen** (*ugs.*) [really] make sb.'s mouth water; **er/sie ist nicht auf den ~ gefallen** (*fig. ugs.*) he's/she's never at a loss for words; **... ist in aller ~e** everybody's talking about ...; **etw./ein Wort in den ~ nehmen** utter sth./use a word; **jmdm. nach dem ~ reden** echo what sb. says; (*schmeichelnd*) butter sb. up; tell sb. what he/she wants to hear; **jmdm. über den ~ fahren** (*ugs.*) cut sb. short; **von ~ zu ~ gehen** be passed on from mouth to mouth; **sich** (*Dat.*) **etw. vom ~e absparen** scrimp and save for sth.; **ein ~ voll Wein** a mouthful of wine; ⇒ *auch* **berufen**[2] A; **fusselig; Hand** F; **stopfen** 1 B; **verbrennen** 2 B

**Mund·art** *die* dialect

**Mundart-: ~dichter** *der,* **~dichterin** *die* dialect author; (*Lyriker[in]*) dialect poet; **~dichtung** *die* Ⓐ dialect literature; Ⓑ (*Werk*) work [written] in dialect; **~forschung** *die* dialectology; dialect research

**mundartlich** ❶ *Adj.* dialectal ‹forms, expressions, words›; ‹texts, poems, etc.› in dialect. ❷ *adv.* in dialect; **stark ~ gefärbt** strongly coloured by dialect

**Mundart-: ~sprecher** *der,* **~sprecherin** *die* dialect speaker; **~wörterbuch** *das* dialect dictionary

**Mund·dusche** *die* water pick

**Mündel** /ˈmʏndl̩/ *das;* **~s, ~:** ward

**mündel·sicher** (*Bankw.*) ❶ *Adj.* gilt-edged; trustee *attrib.* (*Amer.*). ❷ *adv.* in gilt-edged *or* (*Amer.*) trustee securities

**munden** *itr. V.* (*geh.*) taste good; **es mundete ihm nicht** he did not enjoy it; he did not like the taste of it; **das wird dir ~:** this will tickle your palate

**münden** /ˈmʏndn̩/ *itr. V.; mit sein* ▶ 306 ‹river› flow (**in** + *Akk.* into); ‹corridor, street, road› lead (**in** + *Akk. od. Dat.*, **auf** + *Akk. od. Dat.* into); **in eine/einer Frage** *usw.* **~** (*fig.*) ‹discussion› lead to a question *etc.*

**mund-, Mund-: ~falte** *die* line at the corner of the mouth; **~faul** (*ugs.*) ❶ *Adj.* uncommunicative; ❷ *adv.* uncommunicatively; **~fäule** *die* ▶ 474 (*Med.*) ulcerative stomatitis; **~gerecht** ❶ *Adj.* bite-sized; (*fig.*) easily digestible ‹information›; ❷ *adv.* ‹serve› in bite-sized pieces; ‹divided› into small mouthfuls; (*fig.*) in an easily digestible form; **~geruch** *der* bad breath *no indef. art.;* **~harmonika** *die* mouth organ; **~höhle** *die* ▶ 471 oral cavity

**mündig** *Adj.* Ⓐ of age *pred.;* **drei ~e Töchter** three daughters who are of age; **~ werden** come of age; **jmdn. ~ sprechen** *od.* **für ~ erklären** declare sb. of age; Ⓑ (*urteilsfähig*) responsible adult *attrib.;* **~ werden** become capable of mature judgement

*old spelling (see note on page 1707)

***mündig|sprechen** ⇒ mündig A

**Mündig·sprechung** *die;* ~, ~en **jmds.** ~: the declaration that sb. is/was of age

**mündlich** ❶ *Adj.* oral; ~e **Zusage** verbal agreement; ~e **Verhandlung** (*Rechtsw.*) hearing. ❷ *adv.* orally; ‹agree› verbally; **alles Weitere** ~ (*im Brief*) I'll tell you the rest when we meet

**Mund-:** ~**öffnung** *die* (*Zool.*) oral aperture; ~**partie** *die* lower part of one's face; ~**pflege** *die* oral hygiene; ~**raub** *der* petty theft [of food/consumables]; ~**schenk** /-ʃɛŋk/ *der;* ~~en, ~~en (*hist.*) cupbearer; ~**schutz** *der* A (*Med.*) face mask; B (*Boxen*) gumshield

**M-und-S-Reifen** /'ɛm ʊnt 'ɛs-/ *der* snow tyre

**mund-, Mund-:** ~**stellung** *die* position of the mouth; ~**stück** *das* A (*bei Instrumenten, Pfeifen usw.*) mouthpiece; B (*bei Zigaretten*) tip; C (*beim Zaumzeug*) bit; ~**tot** *Adj.* **in jmdn./eine Organisation** ~**tot machen** silence sb./an organization; ~**tuch** *das; Pl.* ~**tücher** (*geh. veralt.*) [table] napkin

**Mündung** *die;* ~, ~en A ▶ 306 mouth; (*größer*) estuary; B (*bei Straßen*) end; C (*bei Feuerwaffen*) muzzle

**Mündungs·feuer** *das* muzzle flash

**Mund-:** ~**verkehr** *der* oral sex; *~**voll** *der;* ~~, ~~: mouthful; ~**vorrat** *der* (*veralt.*) victuals *pl.;* ~**wasser** *das; Pl.* ~**wässer** mouthwash; ~**werk** *das* (*ugs.*) **ein flinkes** ~**werk haben** talk nineteen to the dozen (*Brit.*); **ein loses** ~**werk [haben]** [have] a loose tongue; ~**winkel** *der* corner of one's mouth; ~**-zu-**~**-Beatmung** *die* mouth-to-mouth resuscitation; kiss of life; ~**-zu-Nase-Beatmung** *die* mouth-to-nose resuscitation

**Munition** /muni'tsi̯o:n/ *die;* ~ (*auch fig.*) ammunition; **seine** ~ **verschossen haben** (*auch fig.*) have run out of ammunition

**Munitions-:** ~**depot** *das* ammunition dump; ~**fabrik** *die* munitions factory; ~**lager** *das* ammunition dump

**Munkelei** *die;* ~, ~en (*ugs.*) A rumour-mongering; B (*Gerücht[e]*) rumour[s]

**munkeln** /'mʊŋkl̩n/ *tr., itr. V.* (*ugs.*) **man munkelt so allerlei, es wird so allerlei gemunkelt** there are all kinds of rumours [flying about]; **es wird gemunkelt** *od.* **man munkelt, dass ...** there is a rumour that ...

**Münster** /'mʏnstɐ/ *das;* ~s, ~: minster; (*Dom*) cathedral; **das Straßburger** ~: Strasbourg Cathedral

**munter** /'mʊntɐ/ ❶ *Adj.* A cheerful; merry; (*lebhaft*) lively ‹eyes, game›; ~ **werden** cheer up; liven up; **[gesund und]** ~ **sein** be as fit as a fiddle; ‹elderly person› be hale and hearty; B (*wach*) awake; ~ **werden** wake up; come round (*joc.*); **jmdn.** ~ **machen** wake sb. up. ❷ *adv.* A merrily; cheerfully; B (*unbekümmert*) gaily; cheerfully

**Munterkeit** *die;* ~: cheerfulness; gaiety

**Münz-:** ~**anstalt** *die* mint; ~**automat** *der* slot machine; (*Telefon*) payphone; pay station (*Amer.*)

**Münze** /'mʏntsə/ *die;* ~, ~n A ▶ 337 coin; **klingende** *od.* **bare** ~ (*geh.*) cash; **etw. für bare** ~ **nehmen** (*fig.*) take sth. literally; **jmdm. [etw.] in** *od.* **mit gleicher** ~ **heimzahlen** pay sb. back in the same coin [for sth.]; B (*Münzanstalt*) mint

**Münz·einwurf** *der* [coin] slot

**münzen** *tr. V.* coin; **auf jmdn./etw. gemünzt sein** (*fig.*) ‹remark etc.› be aimed at sb./sth.

**Münzen·sammlung** *die* coin collection

**Münz-:** ~**fälscher** *der,* ~**fälscherin** *die* counterfeiter [of coins]; ~**fälschung** *die* counterfeiting [of coins]; ~**fernsprecher** *der* coin-box telephone; payphone; pay station (*Amer.*); ~**fuß** *der* standard [for content] of coinage; ~**gewicht** *das* standard weight (*of a coin*); ~**hoheit** *die* coining prerogative (*of the State*); ~**kunde** *die* numismatics *sing.;* ~**recht** *das* A ⇒ ~hoheit; B (~*gesetze*) coinage laws *pl.;* ~**sammlung** *die* coin collection; ~**tankstelle** *die* coin-in-the-slot petrol (*Brit.*) *or* (*Amer.*) gas station; ~**wechsler** *der* change machine; ~**wesen** *das* coinage [system]; ~**zähler** *der* [slot] meter

**Muräne** /mu'rɛ:nə/ *die* moray eel

**mürb** /mʏrp/ (*südd., österr.*), **mürbe** /'mʏrbə/ *Adj.* A crumbly ‹biscuit, cake, etc.›; tender ‹meat›; soft ‹fruit›; mealy ‹apple›; **das Fleisch** ~**e machen** tenderize the meat; B (*brüchig*) crumbling; (*morsch*) rotten; ‹leather› worn soft; ~**e werden/sein** (*fig.: zermürbt*) get/be worn out; **jmdn.** ~**e machen** (*fig.*) wear sb. down

**Mürbe·teig,** (*südd., österr.*) **Mürb·teig** *der* short pastry

**Murks** /mʊrks/ *der;* ~es (*salopp abwertend*) botch; mess; **das ist doch** ~! this is a right botch-up!; ~ **machen** make a botch *or* mess [of it]

**murksen** *itr. V.* (*salopp abwertend*) mess about (**an** + *Dat.* with); **bei einer Arbeit** ~: make a botch *or* mess of a job

**Murmel** /'mʊrml̩/ *die;* ~, ~n marble; ~**n spielen** play [with] marbles

**murmeln**[1] *tr., itr. V.* A mumble; mutter; (*sehr leise*) murmur; **etw. vor sich hin** ~: mutter *or* mumble/murmur sth. to oneself; B (*dichter.*) ‹stream, fountain› murmur

**murmeln**[2] *itr. V.* (*M*~ *spielen*) play [with] marbles

**Murmel·tier** *das* marmot; ⇒ *auch* **schlafen** 1 A

**murren** /'mʊrən/ *itr. V.* grumble (**über** + *Akk.* about); **was hast du nun schon wieder zu** ~? what are you grumbling about now?; **ohne zu** ~: without a murmur

**mürrisch** /'mʏrɪʃ/ ❶ *Adj.* grumpy; (*wortkarg*) surly; surly, sullen ‹expression›. ❷ *adv.* grumpily; (*wortkarg*) sullenly

**Mus** /mu:s/ *das od. der;* ~es, ~e purée; **zu** ~ **kochen** cook to a pulp; **jmdn./etw. zu** ~ **machen** *od.* **schlagen** (*salopp*) beat sb./sth. to a pulp

**Muschel** /'mʊʃl̩/ *die;* ~, ~n A mussel; B (*Schale*) [mussel] shell; C (*am Telefon*) (*Hör*~) earpiece; (*Sprech*~) mouthpiece; D (*Ohr*~) [outer] ear

**Muschel-:** ~**bank** *die; Pl.* ~**bänke** mussel bed; ~**kalk** *der* (*Geol.*) Muschelkalk

**Muschi** /'mʊʃi/ *die;* ~, ~s A (*Kinderspr.: Katze*) pussy [cat]; B (*salopp: Vulva*) pussy (*coarse*)

**Muschkote** /mʊʃ'ko:tə/ *der;* ~n, ~n (*Soldatenspr. veralt., abwertend*) common soldier; squaddy (*Brit. sl.*)

**Muse** /'mu:zə/ *die;* ~, ~n muse; **die leichte** ~: light [musical] entertainment; **von der** ~ **geküsst werden** (*scherzh.*) get some inspiration

**museal** /muze'a:l/ (*geh.*) ❶ *Adj.* A museum *attrib.;* of the museum *postpos.;* B (*wie ein Museum, wie im Museum*) museum-like ‹building, appearance›. ❷ *adv.* like a museum; in the style of a museum

**Museen** ⇒ **Museum**

**Muselman** /'mu:zl̩man/ *der;* ~en, ~en, **Muselmanin** *die;* ~, ~nen, **Musel·mann** *der; Pl.* **Muselmänner** (*veralt., noch scherzh.*) Muslim

**Musen-:** ~**almanach** *der* (*hist.*): *18th/19th century annual anthology of mainly unpublished poetry;* ~**sohn** *der* (*veralt., noch scherzh.*) son of the Muses; ~**tempel** *der* (*veralt., noch scherzh.*) temple of the Muses

**Museum** /mu'ze:ʊm/ *das;* ~s, **Museen** museum; **ins** ~ **gehen** go to a/the museum

**museums-, Museums-:** ~**aufseher** *der,* ~**aufseherin** *die* ▶ 159 museum attendant; ~**führer** *der,* ~**führerin** *die* museum guide; ~**reif** *Adj.* (*ugs. iron.*) fit for a museum *postpos.;* **das ist wirklich** ~**reif** it's a real museum piece *or* positively antiquated; ~**stück** *das* (*auch fig. ugs. iron.*) museum piece; ~**wärter** *der,* ~**wärterin** *die* ▶ 159 museum attendant; ~**wert** *der:* ~**wert haben** (*ugs.*) be a valuable museum piece; (*abwertend*) be positively antiquated *or* a museum piece

**Musical** /'mju:zɪkl̩/ *das;* ~s, ~s musical

**Music·box** /'mju:zɪk-/ *die;* ~, ~en ⇒ **Musikbox**

**Musik** /mu'zi:k/ *die;* ~, ~en A music; **einen Text in** ~ **setzen** set a text to music; **die** ~ **lieben** like music; ~ **im Blut haben** have music in one's blood; ~ **in jmds. Ohren** (*Dat.*) **sein** (*fig. ugs.*) be music to sb.'s ears; **dahinter** *od.* **darin sitzt** *od.* **steckt** ~ (*fig. ugs.*) there is real power in it; B (*Werk*) *Pl.:* ~**en** piece [of music]; (*Partitur*) score (**zu** for); **die** ~ **zu diesem Stück** the [incidental] music for this play; C (*ugs.: Kapelle*) band; D (*Gastr.*) ⇒ **Handkäse**

**Musikalien** /muzi'ka:li̯ən/ *Pl.* sheet music *sing.*

**Musikalien·handlung** *die* music shop

**musikalisch** /muzi'ka:lɪʃ/ ❶ *Adj.* musical; **die** ~**e Leitung haben** be the musical director; (*als Dirigent*) be the conductor; ~**e Leitung: ...** conducted by ... ❷ *adv.* musically; **er ist** ~ **veranlagt** he is musical

**Musikalität** /muzikali'tɛ:t/ *die;* ~: musicality

**Musikant** /muzi'kant/ *der;* ~en, ~en musician

**Musikanten·knochen** *der* ▶ 471 funny bone

**Musikantin** *die;* ~, ~nen ⇒ **Musikant**

**musikantisch** (*ugs.*) ❶ *Adj.* full of brio *postpos.;* with a swing to it *postpos.* ❷ *adv.* with brio

**Musik-:** ~**automat** *der* A (*Spieluhr o. Ä.*) mechanical instrument; B ⇒ ~**box;** ~**box** *die* jukebox; ~**-CD** *die* audio CD; music CD; ~**direktor** *der,* ~**direktorin** *die;* ~~, ~~nen musical director; ~**drama** *das* music drama

**Musiker** *der;* ~s, ~, **Musikerin** *die;* ~, ~nen ▶ 159 musician; **die** ~ **stimmten ihre Instrumente** the players were tuning their instruments

**musik-, Musik-:** ~**erziehung** *die* musical education; ~**festspiele** *Pl.* music festival *sing.;* ~**freund** *der,* ~**freundin** *die* music lover; ~**geschichte** *die* history of music; **in die** ~**geschichte eingehen** find a place in musical history; ~**geschichtlich,** ~**historisch** ❶ *Adj.* musico-historical; ❷ *adv.* in terms of the history of music; from the point of view of musical history; ~**hochschule** *die* academy *or* college of music; ~**instrument** *das* musical instrument; ~**kapelle** *die* band; ~**korps** *das* military band (*forming a separate unit*); ~**kritik** *die* A music criticism; B (*Artikel*) music review; ~**kritiker** *der,* ~**kritikerin** *die* music critic; ~**leben** *das* musical life; ~**lehre** *die* A musical theory *no art.;* B (*Buch*) manual of musical theory; music textbook; ~**lehrer** *der,* ~**lehrerin** *die* music teacher; ~**lexikon** *das* musical encyclopaedia; encyclopaedia of music; ~**pädagogik** *die* [theory of] music teaching; ~**saal** *der* A (*in der Schule*) music room; B (*Konzertsaal*) concert hall; ~**schule** *die* school of music; ~**stück** *das* piece of music; **ein** ~**stück Chopins/von Chopin** a piece by Chopin; ~**stunde** *die* music lesson; ~**theater** *das* music theatre (*where text and production are as important as the music*); ~**theorie** *die* A (*theoretische Erfassung*) theory of music; B (*Lehrfach*) musical theory *no art.;* ~**therapie** *die* music therapy; ~**truhe** *die* radiogram (*in a large cabinet*); ~**unterricht** *der* A (*das Unterrichten*) music teaching; B (*Stunde*) music lesson; (*Stunden*) music lessons *pl.;* C (*als Schulfach*) music; ⇒ *auch* **Englischunterricht**

**Musikus** /'mu:zikʊs/ *der;* ~, **Musizi** /'mu:zitsi/ *od.* ~**se** (*scherzh.*) musician

**Musik-:** ~**verlag** *der* music publishers *pl.;* music publishing house; ~**video** *das* music video; ~**werk** *das* musical work; composition; ~**wissenschaft** *die* musicology; ~**wissenschaftler** *der,* ~**wissenschaftlerin** *die* ▶ 159 musicologist

**musisch** ❶ *Adj.* artistic ‹talent, person, family, etc.›; ‹talent› for the arts; ‹education› in the arts;

**die ~en Fächer** art and music; **ein ~es Gymnasium:** *a* **Gymnasium** *specializing in teaching art and music.* **2** *adv.* artistically; **~ veranlagt sein** have an artistic disposition

**musizieren** /muzi'tsi:rən/ *itr. V.* play music; (*bes. unter Laien*) make music; **früher wurde viel mehr musiziert** there used to be a lot more music-making

**Muskat** /mʊs'ka:t/ *der;* **~[e]s, ~e** nutmeg

**Muskateller** /mʊska'tɛlɐ/ *der;* **~s, ~:** muscatel [wine]

**Muskat·nuss, *Muskat·nuß** *die* nutmeg

**Muskel** /'mʊskl̩/ *der;* **~s, ~n** ▶471 muscle; **der hat vielleicht ~n!** (*ugs.*) he has quite some muscles (*coll.*); he's really muscular; **~n bekommen** develop muscles; **seine ~n spielen lassen** flex one's muscles

**Muskel-: ~atrophie** *die* ▶474 (*Med.*) muscular atrophy; **~faser** *die* ▶471 muscle fibre; **~kater** *der* stiff muscles *pl.*; **~kater haben** be stiff and aching; **~kater in den Waden haben** have stiff calves; be stiff in one's calves; **~kraft** *die* muscle-power; **~krampf** *der* cramp; **~krämpfe/einen ~krampf bekommen** get cramp; **~mann** *der* (*ugs.*) muscleman; **~paket** *das* (*ugs.*) **A** (**~n**) bulging muscles *pl.* **B** ⇒ **Muskelmann**; **~protz** *der* (*ugs.*) muscleman; Tarzan (*joc.*); **~riss, *~riß** *der* ▶474 torn muscle; **~schwund** *der* ▶474 (*Med.*) muscular atrophy; **~zerrung** *die* ▶474 (*Med.*) pulled muscle; **sich** (*Dat.*) **eine ~zerrung zuziehen** pull a muscle

**Muskete** /mʊs'ke:tə/ *die;* **~, ~n** (*hist.*) musket

**Musketier** /mʊske'ti:ɐ̯/ *der;* **~s, ~e** (*hist.*) musketeer

**Muskulatur** /mʊskula'tu:ɐ̯/ *die;* **~, ~en** ▶471 musculature; muscular system

**muskulös** /mʊsku'lø:s/ *Adj.* muscular

**Müsli** /'my:sli/ *das;* **~s, ~s** muesli

**Muslim** /'mʊslɪm/ *der;* **~s, ~e** *od.* **~s** Muslim

**Muslimin** *die;* **~, ~nen** Muslim [woman]

**muslimisch** **1** *Adj.* Muslim. **2** *adv.* on Muslim principles; **~ erzogen werden** be brought up in the Muslim faith

**muss, *muß** /mʊs/ *1. u. 3. Pers. Sg. Präsens v.* **müssen**

**Muss, *Muß** *das;* **~:** necessity; must (*coll.*); **es ist kein ~:** it's not essential

**Muss-Bestimmung, *Muß-Bestimmung** *die* absolute *or* fixed rule

**Muße** /'mu:sə/ *die;* **~:** leisure; **dazu fehlt mir die ~:** I have no time to spare for it; **etw. in** *od.* **mit ~ tun** do sth. at one's leisure; take one's time over sth.

**Muss·ehe, *Muß·ehe** *die* (*ugs.*) shotgun marriage

**Musselin** /mʊsə'li:n/ *der;* **~s, ~e** muslin

**müssen** /'mʏsn̩/ **1** *unr. Modalverb; 2. Part.* **~** **A** (*gezwungen, verpflichtet, notwendig sein*) have to; **er muss es tun** he must do it; he has to *or* (*coll.*) has got to do it; **er muss es nicht tun** he does not have to do it; he has not got to do it (*coll.*); **er musste es tun** *od.* **hat es tun ~:** he had to do it; **du musstest nicht kommen** you did not have to come; **muss er es tun?** must he do it?; does he have to *or* (*coll.*) has he got to do it?; **irgendwann muss es ja doch mal gemacht werden** after all, it's got to be done some time; **wir werden zurückkommen ~:** we shall have to come back; **heiraten ~** (*ugs.*) have to get married; **muss das jetzt sein?** does it have to be now?; **muss das sein?** it is really necessary?; (*Ärger über jmds. Verhalten ausdrückend*) do you have to?; **es muss nicht sein** it is not essential; **es muss ja nicht stimmen** it is not necessarily true; **so musste es ja kommen** it was inevitable that it should come to this; it had to happen; **warum muss das ausgerechnet mir passieren?** why does it have to happen to me, of all people? **das muss man gesehen haben!** you mustn't miss ist!; it's not to be missed!; (*iron.*) it's a sight not to be missed!; **wir ~ Ihnen leider mitteilen, dass ...** we regret to have to inform you that ...; **das muss man sich** (*Dat.*) **mal vorstellen!** just imagine!; **das muss 1980 gewesen sein** it must have been in 1980; **er muss gleich hier sein** he will be here *or* he is bound to be here at any moment; **B** *im 2. Konjunktiv* **es müsste doch möglich sein** it ought to be possible; **das müsstest du eigentlich schon wissen** you really ought to *or* should know that by now; **so müsste es immer sein** it ought to be like this all the time; this is how it should always be; **reich müsste man sein!** how nice it would be to be rich!; all one needs is [plenty of] money!; **man müsste nochmals zwanzig sein** oh to be twenty again!; **C** *verneint* (*nordd.: dürfen*) **du musst nicht alles glauben, was er sagt** you must not believe everything he says.

**2** *unr. itr. V.* **A** (*irgendwohin gehen ~*) have to go; **ich muss zur Arbeit/nach Hause** I have to *or* must go to work/go home; **der Brief muss zur Post** the letter needs posting *or* taking to the post; **muss der Antrag heute zum Amt?** does the application have to be taken to the office today?; **ich muss mal** (*fam.*) I've got to *or* need to spend a penny (*Brit. coll.*) *or* (*Amer. coll.*) go to the john; **B** (*gezwungen, verpflichtet sein*) **muss er?** does he have to?; has he got to? (*coll.*); **er muss nicht** he doesn't have to *or* (*coll.*) hasn't got to; **kein Mensch muss ~:** nobody 'has to do 'anything; **C** (*ugs.: an der Reihe sein*) **heute muss Peter** it's Peter's turn today

**Muße·stunde** *die* free hour; hour of leisure

**müßig** /'my:sɪç/ **1** *Adj.* **A** idle ‹person›; ‹hours, weeks, life› of leisure; **B** (*zwecklos*) pointless. **2** *adv.* idly

**Müßig-: ~gang** *der* leisure; (*Untätigkeit*) idleness; **~gang ist aller Laster Anfang** (*Spr.*) the devil finds work for idle hands; **~gänger** *der;* **~~s, ~~, ~gängerin** *die;* **~~, ~~nen** idler; **~gänger** *Pl.* people with time on their hands

**Müßigkeit** *die;* **~** (*geh.*) **A** idleness; **B** (*Zwecklosigkeit*) pointlessness

**musste, *mußte** /'mʊstə/ *1. u. 3. Pers. Sg. Prät. v.* **müssen**

**Mustang** /'mʊstaŋ/ *der;* **~s, ~s** mustang

**Muster** /'mʊstɐ/ *das;* **~s, ~** **A** (*Vorlage*) pattern; **nach einem ~ stricken** knit from a pattern; **das ausgefüllte Formular dient als ~ für den Antragsteller** the form that is filled in is intended as a specimen for the applicant to follow; **nach diesem ~ arbeiten** (*fig.*) operate on these lines *or* on this model; **B** (*Vorbild*) model (**an** + *Dat.* of); **er ist ein ~ an Fleiß** he is a model of industry; **er ist ein ~ von einem Ehemann** (*ugs.*) he is a model husband; **C** (*Verzierung*) pattern; **~ entwerfen** produce designs; **in welchem ~ strickst du die Jacke?** which stitch are you using to knit the jacket?; **D** (*Warenprobe*) sample; **unverkäufliches ~:** sample not for sale; (*veralt.: auf einer Warensendung*) **~ ohne Wert** sample with no commercial value

**muster-, Muster-: ~beispiel** *das* perfect example; (*Vorbild*) model; **ein ~beispiel dafür sein, wie ...** be a perfect example of how ...; **~betrieb** *der* model enterprise; (*Fabrik*) model factory; **~buch** *das* **A** (*Kunstwiss.: Motivsammlung*) pattern book; **B** (*mit Proben*) book of samples; pattern book; **~ehe** *die* perfect *or* ideal marriage; **~exemplar** *das* **A** (*oft iron.: Vorbild*) perfect specimen; **ein ~exemplar von [einem] Sohn** a model son; **B** (*Probeexemplar*) specimen copy; **~gültig** **1** *Adj.* exemplary; perfect, impeccable ‹order›; **2** *adv.* in an exemplary fashion

**musterhaft** **1** *Adj.* exemplary; perfect, impeccable ‹order, condition›; model ‹pupil›. **2** *adv.* in an exemplary fashion; **~ geführt** perfectly *or* impeccably run

**Muster-: ~haus** *das* show house; **~knabe** *der* (*oft abwertend*) model child; **~koffer** *der* case of samples; **~ländle** /-lɛndlə/ *das;* **~~s** (*scherzh.*): *Baden-Württemberg, the 'model state' of the FRG*

**mustern** *tr. V.* **A** (*betrachten*) eye; (*gründlich*) scrutinize; (*Milit.: inspizieren*) inspect ‹troops›; **jmdn. von Kopf bis Fuß** *od.* **von oben bis unten ~:** look sb. up and down; **B** (*Milit.: ärztlich untersuchen*) **einen Wehrpflichtigen/den Jahrgang 1962 ~:** give somebody liable for military service his medical/give those born in 1962 their medicals

**Muster-: ~prozess, *~prozeß** *der* test case; **~schüler** *der,* **~schülerin** *die* model pupil; **~sendung** *die* consignment of samples

**Musterung** *die;* **~, ~en** **A** (*das Betrachten*) scrutiny; (*Milit.: Inspektion*) inspection; **B** (*Milit.: von Wehrpflichtigen*) medical examination; medical; **C** (*Verzierung*) pattern

**Musterungs·bescheid** *der* summons to attend one's medical examination

**Mut** /mu:t/ *der;* **~[e]s** **A** courage; **es gehört viel ~ dazu** it takes a lot of courage [to do it]; **allen** *od.* **all seinen ~ zusammennehmen** take one's courage in both hands; screw up one's courage; **sich** (*Dat.*) **~ antrinken** give oneself Dutch courage; **mit dem ~ der Verzweiflung** with courage born of desperation; **jmdm. ~ zusprechen** [try to] bolster up sb.'s courage; **sich gegenseitig ~ machen** keep each other's spirits up; **das gab** *od.* **machte ihr neuen ~:** that gave her new heart; **den ~ [nicht] sinken lassen** *od.* **verlieren** [not] lose heart; **[neuen] ~ fassen** take [new] heart; **nur ~!** don't lose heart!; (*trau dich*) be brave!; **B** (*veralt.*) *in* **guten** *od.* **frohen ~es sein** be in good spirits; **mit frischem ~:** full of cheer (*dated*); with a cheerful countenance; **zu ~e** ⇒ **zumute**

**Mutation** /muta'tsi̯o:n/ *die;* **~, ~en** (*Biol.*) mutation

**Mütchen** /'my:tçən/ *in* **sein ~ [an jmdm.] kühlen** (*ugs.* [*scherzh.*]) vent one's wrath [on sb.]

**mutieren** *itr. V.* (*Biol.*) mutate

**mutig** **1** *Adj.* brave; courageous, brave ‹words, decision, speech›; **dem Mutigen gehört die Welt** fortune favours the brave. **2** *adv.* bravely; courageously

**mut·los** *Adj.* (*niedergeschlagen*) dejected; despondent; (*entmutigt*) disheartened; dispirited

**Mut·losigkeit** *die;* **~:** dejection; despondency

**mutmaßen** /'mu:tma:sn̩/ *tr., itr. V.* conjecture; **~, dass ...** suppose *or* surmise that ...; **darüber ist schon viel gemutmaßt worden** there has been much conjecture *or* speculation about that

**mutmaßlich** **1** *Adj.* supposed; presumed; suspected ‹terrorist etc.›. **2** *adv.* (*geh.*) **es wird sich ~ noch verschlechtern** it is presumed it will get worse; **sie sind ~ ertrunken** they are presumed drowned

**Mutmaßung** *die;* **~, ~en** conjecture

**Mut·probe** *die* test of courage

**Muttchen** /'mʊtçən/ *das;* **~s, ~** (*ugs.*) **A** (*Koseform*) mama; **B** **[altes] ~:** little old lady; **C** (*abwertend: biedere Frau*) good little housewife; (*mütterlicher Typ*) matronly sort (*coll.*); motherly soul

**Mutter**[1] /'mʊtɐ/ *die;* **~, Mütter** /'mʏtɐ/ **A** mother; **sie wird ~** (*ist schwanger*) she is expecting a baby; **eine werdende ~:** an expectant mother; **eine ~ von drei Kindern** a mother of three; **~ sein** be a mother; **grüßen Sie Ihre Frau ~!** remember me to your mother; **wie bei ~n** just like at home; ‹food› like mother makes/used to make; **die ~ Gottes** (*kath. Rel.*) the Mother of God; **~ Erde/Natur** (*dichter.*) Mother Earth/Nature; **bei ~ Grün schlafen** (*ugs.*) sleep out in the open; **die ~ der Kompanie** (*Soldatenspr.*) the company sergeant major; **B** (*Wirtsch.: ~gesellschaft*) parent company

**Mutter**[2] *die;* **~, ~n** (*Schrauben~*) nut

**Mütter·beratungs·stelle** *die* advisory centre for [pregnant or nursing] mothers

**Mutter-: ~bindung** *die* (*Psych.*) attachment to the/one's mother; **~boden** *der* topsoil; **~brust** *die* mother's breast

*old spelling (see note on page 1707)

**Mütterchen** /ˈmʏtɐçən/ *das;* **~s,** **~** Ⓐ (*Koseform*) mummy (*Brit. coll.*); mommy (*Amer. coll.*); Ⓑ **[altes] ~:** little old lady; Ⓒ *in* **~ Russland** Mother Russia

**Mutter-: ~erde** *die* ⇒ **~boden; ~freuden** *Pl. in* **~freuden entgegensehen** (*geh.*) be expecting a child

**Mütter·genesungs·heim** *das* convalescent home for mothers

**Mutter-: ~gesellschaft** *die* (*Wirtsch.*) parent company; **~glück** *das* joys *pl.* of motherhood; **~gottes** /--ˈ--/ *die;* **~~** (*kath. Rel.*) mother of God; (*Bild*) Madonna

**Mütter·heim** *das* [residential] home for [unmarried] mothers and their children

**Mutter-: ~herz** *das* mother's heart; (*scherzh. Anrede*) mother [dear]; **~instinkt** *der* maternal instinct; **~komplex** *der* (*Psych.*) Ⓐ (*~bindung*) mother fixation; Ⓑ (*~instinkt*) [excessive] maternal instinct; mothering instinct; **~korn** *das; Pl.* **~~e** (*Bot.*) ergot; **~kreuz** *das* (*ns.*) *medal awarded to prolific mothers* (*in the Nazi period*); **~kuchen** *der* (*Med.*) placenta; **~land** *das* Ⓐ (*Kolonialstaat*) mother country; Ⓑ (*Heimat*) original home; motherland; **~leib** *der* womb; (*Zool.*) uterus

**mütterlich** ❶ *Adj.* Ⓐ (*von der Mutter*) his/her *etc.* mother's; (*verallgemeinernd*) the mother's; (*einer Mutter*) maternal ‹line, love, instincts, etc.›; **die ~en Pflichten** the duties of a mother; Ⓑ (*fürsorglich*) motherly ‹woman, care›. ❷ *adv.* in a motherly way

**mütterlicher·seits** *Adv.* on the/his/her *etc.* mother's side; **sein Großvater ~:** his maternal grandfather; his grandfather on his mother's side

**Mütterlichkeit** *die;* **~:** motherliness; (*mütterliche Gefühle*) motherly feeling

**mutter-, Mutter-: ~liebe** *die* motherly love *no art.;* **~los** *Adj.* motherless; **~mal** *das; Pl.* **~~e** birthmark; **~milch** *die* mother's milk; **etw. mit der ~milch einsaugen** (*fig.*) imbibe sth. with one's mother's milk; **~mord** *der* matricide; **~mund** *der* ▶ 471 neck of the womb; cervix

**Mütter·pass, *Mütter·paß** *der: document carried by pregnant woman which gives details of her medical history, blood group, etc.*

**Mutter-: ~pflicht** *die* duty as a mother; maternal duty; **~schaf** *das* mother ewe

**Mutterschaft** *die;* **~:** motherhood

**Mutterschafts-: ~geld** *das* maternity benefit; **~urlaub** *der* maternity leave

**mutter-, Mutter-: ~schiff** *das* mother ship; (*im Weltraum*) parent ship; **~schutz** *der* Ⓐ (*Rechtsw.*) *laws pl. protecting working pregnant women and mothers of newborn babies;* Ⓑ (*ugs.: Urlaub*) maternity leave; **~schwein** *das* mother sow; **~seelen·allein** *Adj.* all alone; all on my *etc.* own; **~söhnchen** *das* (*abwertend*) mummy's *or* (*Amer.*) mama's boy; **~sprache** *die* native language; mother tongue; **~sprachler** /-ʃpraːxlɐ/ *der;* **~~s, ~~, ~sprachlerin** *die;* **~~, ~~nen** (*Sprachw.*) native speaker; **~stelle** *die:* **bei** *od.* **an jmdm. ~stelle vertreten** take the place of a mother to sb.

**Mütter·sterblichkeit** *die* childbirth mortality

**Mutter-: ~stute** *die* dam; **~tag** *der* Mother's Day *no def. art.;* **~tier** *das* Ⓐ (*Tier, das Junge hat*) mother [animal]; dam; Ⓑ (*Zuchttier*) brood animal; **~witz** *der* Ⓐ (*Humor*) natural wit; Ⓑ (*Schläue*) native cunning

**Mutti** /ˈmʊti/ *die;* **~, ~s** mummy (*Brit. coll.*); mum (*Brit. coll.*); mommy (*Amer. coll.*); mom (*Amer. coll.*)

**mut-, Mut-: ~wille** *der* wilfulness; (*Über~*) devilment; **aus [bloßem] ~willen** from [sheer] devilment; **~willig** ❶ *Adj.* wilful; wanton ‹destruction›; (*übermütig*) high-spirited; ❷ *adv.* wilfully; wantonly; (*aus Über~*) from devilment; **~willigkeit** *die;* **~~:** ⇒ **~wille**

**Mützchen** *das;* **~s, ~s** little cap

**Mütze** /ˈmʏtsə/ *die;* **~, ~n** cap; **etwas** *od.* **eins auf die ~ kriegen** (*fig. ugs.*) get told off; get a telling off; **eine ~ voll Schlaf** (*ugs.*) a nap; forty winks *pl.*

**Mützen·schirm** *der* peak of the/one's cap

**MW** *Abk.* Ⓐ (*Rundf.*) **Mittelwelle** MW; Ⓑ (*Physik*) **Megawatt** MW

**Mw.-St., MwSt.** *Abk.* ▶ 337 **Mehrwertsteuer** VAT

**mykenisch** /myˈkeːnɪʃ/ *Adj.* Mycenaean

**Mykologie** /mykoloˈgiː/ *die;* **~:** mycology *no art.*

**Mykose** /myˈkoːzə/ *die;* **~, ~n** mycosis

**Myom** /myˈoːm/ *das;* **~s, ~e** ▶ 474 (*Med.*) myoma

**Myriade** /myˈri̯aːdə/ *die;* **~, ~n** (*geh.*) myriad

**Myrrhe** /ˈmʏrə/ *die;* **~, ~n** myrrh

**Myrte** /ˈmʏrtə/ *die;* **~, ~n** myrtle

**Myrten·kranz** *der* myrtle wreath

**Mysterien·spiel** *das* miracle play

**mysteriös** /mʏsteˈri̯øːs/ ❶ *Adj.* mysterious. ❷ *adv.* mysteriously

**Mysterium** /mʏsˈteːri̯ʊm/ *das;* **~s, Mysterien** mystery

**Mystifikation** /mʏstifikaˈtsi̯oːn/ *die;* **~, ~en** shrouding *no indef. art.* in mystery

**mystifizieren** /mʏstifiˈtsiːrən/ *tr. V.* shroud in mystery; (*unklar machen*) obfuscate

**Mystifizierung** *die;* **~, ~en** ⇒ **Mystifikation**

**Mystik** /ˈmʏstɪk/ *die;* **~:** mysticism

**Mystiker** *der;* **~s, ~, Mystikerin** *die;* **~, ~nen** mystic

**mystisch** ❶ *Adj.* mystical. ❷ *adv.* mystically

**Mystizismus** /mʏstiˈtsɪsmʊs/ *der;* **~:** mysticism

**mythisch** /ˈmyːtɪʃ/ *Adj.* Ⓐ mythical; ‹heroes, traditions› of myth [and legend], of mythology; Ⓑ (*legendär*) legendary

**Mythologie** /mytoloˈgiː/ *die;* **~, ~n** mythology

**mythologisch** *Adj.* mythological

**mythologisieren** *tr. V.* mythologize

**Mythos** /ˈmyːtɔs/ *der;* **~, Mythen** Ⓐ (*Sage, auch fig.: Unwahrheit*) myth; Ⓑ (*glorifizierte Person od. Sache*) legend

m

# Nn

**n, N** /ɛn/ *das;* ~, ~: n/N; ⇨ *auch* **a, A**

**N** *Abk.* ▶ 400 **Nord[en]** N

**'n** ⇨ **ein; einen**

**na** /na/ *Interj.* (*ugs.*) **A** (*als Frage, Anrede, Aufforderung*) well; **na, wie gehts?** well, how are you?; **na, du?** oh, it's you?; **na los!** come on then!; **na, wirds bald?/wo bleibst du denn?** come on, aren't you ready yet?/ what's happened to you?; **na und?** (*wennschon*) so what?; **B** (*beschwichtigend*) **na, na, na!** now, now, come along; **C** ([*zögernd*] *zustimmend*) **na schön!, na gut!** oh, OK (*coll.*); well, all right; **na ja, wenn du meinst** well [all right], if you think so; **na, dann bis später** right, see you later then; **D** (*bekräftigend*) **na und ob!** and how! (*coll.*); I'll say! (*coll.*); **na, der wird schauen!** gosh, he'll get a surprise!; **na und wie!** and how! (*coll.*); **na eben!** exactly!; **na dann!** oh, in 'that case!; **na endlich!** at last!; **E** (*triumphierend*) **Na also! Ich hatte doch recht!** There you are! I was right!; **F** (*zweifelnd, besorgt*) **na, wenn das mal gut geht** *od.* **klappt** well, let's hope it'll be OK (*coll.*); **na, wenn das dein Vater merkt!** oh dear, what if your father notices?; **G** (*ablehnend*) **na, ich danke** you can keep it; **H** (*unsicher*) **na, ich weiß nicht** hmm, I'm not sure; (*staunend*) **na so [et]was!** well I never!; **I** (*konsterniert*) **na, was soll das denn?** now what's all this about?; **J** (*drohend*) **na warte!** just [you] wait!; (*auf einen nicht Anwesenden bezogen*) just let him wait!

**Nabe** /'na:bə/ *die;* ~, ~n hub

**Nabel** /'na:bl̩/ *der;* ~s, ~ ▶ 471 navel; **der ~ der Welt** (*geh.*) the hub of the universe

**Nabel-:** **~binde** *die* umbilical bandage; **~bruch** *der* ▶ 474 (*Med.*) umbilical hernia; **~frei** *Adj.* **ein ~freies Top** a crop top; **~frei gehen** wear a crop top; **~schau** *die* (*salopp*) **~schau halten** bare one's soul; **das Buch ist nichts als eine egozentrische ~schau** the book is nothing but a self-indulgent ego trip (*coll.*); **~schnur** *die Pl.* **~schnüre** umbilical cord

**Naben-:** **~dynamo** *der* hub dynamo; **~schaltung** *die* hub gear

**nach** /na:x/ ❶ *Präp. mit Dat.* **A** (*räumlich*) to; **~ Rom fahren** travel to Rome; **ist das der Zug ~ Köln?** is that the train for Cologne *or* the Cologne train?; **ja, der Zug fährt ~ Köln** yes, this train goes to Cologne; **~ Hause gehen** go home; **~ ... abreisen** leave for ...; **sich ~ vorn/hinten beugen** bend forwards/backwards; **stell den Schrank weiter ~ hinten** put the cupboard further back; **komm ganz ~ vorn** come right to the front; **~ links/rechts** to the left/right; **~ der Seite** to the side; **~ allen Richtungen** in all directions; **~ Osten [zu]** eastwards; [towards the] east; **~ ... zu** towards ...; **~ außen/innen** outwards/inwards; **ich bringe den Abfall ~ draußen** I am taking the rubbish outside; **ein Zimmer ~ der Straße** a room looking out on to *or* facing the street; **B** ▶ 752 (*zeitlich*) after; **~ fünf Minuten** after five minutes; five minutes later; **zehn [Minuten] ~ zwei** ten [minutes] past two; **wird man noch ~ 100 Jahren daran denken?** will anyone remember it in a hundred years' time?; **1500 Jahre ~ Christi Geburt** *od.* (*bes. DDR*) **~ unserer Zeitrechnung** in AD 1500; **vier Wochen ~ Erhalt der Rechnung** four weeks after receipt of *or* after receiving the invoice; **gleich ~ Erhalt der Rechnung** immediately upon *or* after receiving the invoice; **C** (*mit bestimmten Verben, bezeichnet das Ziel der Handlung*) for; **greifen/streben/schicken ~:** grasp/strive/ send for; **D** (*bezeichnet [räumliche und zeitliche] Reihenfolge*) after; **~ Ihnen/dir!** after you; **die Post kommt ~ dem Rathaus** the post office is after *or* past the town hall; **~ „für" steht der Akkusativ** after 'für' one has the accusative; 'für' takes the accusative; **der Bundestagspräsident kommt ~ dem Bundespräsidenten** (*im gesellschaftlichen Rang*) the president of the Federal Parliament is lower in rank than the Federal President; ⇨ *auch* **ander... B**; **E** (*gemäß*) according to; (*in Übereinstimmung mit*) in accordance with; **~ meiner Ansicht** *od.* **Meinung, meiner Ansicht** *od.* **Meinung ~:** in my view *or* opinion; **~ menschlichem Ermessen** as far as anyone can judge; **aller Wahrscheinlichkeit ~:** in all probability; **~ Lage der Dinge wird es kaum möglich sein** as matters stand it will hardly be possible; **je** *od.* **ganz ~ Wunsch** just as you/ they *etc.* wish; however you/they *etc.* like; **Variationen ~ einem Thema von Händel** variations on a theme of Handel; **[frei] ~ Goethe** [freely] adapted from Goethe; **~ einer Vorlage zeichnen** draw from an original; **eine Suppe ~ Art des Hauses** (*Kochk.*) a soup à la maison; **~ rheinischer Art** (*Kochk.*) in the Rhenish style; **~ altem Brauch** in accordance with *or* by ancient custom; **~ der neuesten Mode gekleidet** dressed in [accordance with] the latest fashion; **~ etw. schmecken/riechen** taste/ smell of sth.; **seinem Wesen ~:** by nature; **sie kommt eher ~ dem Vater** (*ugs.*) she takes more after her father; **~ dem [zu urteilen], was er gesagt hat** going *or* judging by what he said; from what he said; **jmdn. nur dem Namen ~ kennen** know sb. by name only; **~ jmdm. genannt werden** be named after sb.; **Dienst ~ Vorschrift** work to rule; **dem Gesetz ~:** in accordance with the law; by law; **~ Paragraph 5, Artikel 4** in accordance with *or* under paragraph 5, clause 4; **der Größe ~/~ dem Gewicht** according to *or* by size/weight; **~ Stunden/ Umsatz bezahlt werden** be paid by the hour/according to turnover; **15 Schillinge sind etwa 2 DM ~ unserem Geld** 15 schillings are about 2 marks in our money. ❷ *Adv.* **A** (*räumlich*) **[alle] mir ~!** [everybody] follow me!; **B** (*zeitlich*) **~ und ~:** little by little; gradually; **~ wie vor** still; as always

**nach|äffen** /-ɛfn̩/ *tr. V.* (*abwertend*) mimic

**Nachäfferei** *die;* ~ (*abwertend*) mimicry; mimicking

**nach|ahmen** /-a:mən/ *tr. V.* **A** (*kopieren*) imitate; **B** (*nacheifern*) emulate

**nachahmens·wert** *Adj.* worthy of imitation *postpos.*; exemplary; **nicht ~:** not to be imitated *postpos.*

**Nachahmer** *der;* ~s, ~, **Nachahmerin** *die;* ~, ~nen imitator

**Nachahmung** *die;* ~, ~en **A** imitation; **B** (*das Nacheifern*) emulation

**Nachahmungs·trieb** *der* (*Verhaltensf., Psych.*) imitative instinct

**nach|arbeiten** ❶ *tr. V.* **A** (*nachholen*) **eine Stunde ~:** work an extra hour to make up; **sie muss die versäumten Stunden ~:** she has to make up for the hours she missed; **B** (*überarbeiten*) go over, finish off ‹workpiece›; (*retuschieren*) retouch ‹picture›; **C** (*nachbilden*) copy (+ *Dat.* from). ❷ *itr. V.* do extra work to make up

**Nachbar** /'naxba:ɐ̯/ *der;* ~n *od. selten* ~s, ~n neighbour; **Herr ~:** neighbour; **die lieben ~n** (*iron.*) the nice people next door (*iron.*); **~s Hund** the neighbours'/neighbour's dog; **mein ~ im Kino** the man [sitting] next to me in the cinema

**Nachbar-:** **~dorf** *das* neighbouring village; **~haus** *das* house next door; **unser ~haus** the house next door to us

**Nachbarin** *die;* ~, ~nen neighbour; **meine ~ im Kino** the woman [sitting] next to me in the cinema

**Nachbar·land** *das* neighbouring country; **unser westliches ~:** our western neighbour

**nachbarlich** ❶ *Adj.* **A** (*dem Nachbarn/den Nachbarn gehörend*) neighbour's/neighbours'; (*benachbart*) neighbouring; next-door; **B** (*unter Nachbarn üblich*) neighbourly; **in gutem ~em Einvernehmen leben** be good neighbours. ❷ *adv.* (*freundschaftlich*) in a neighbourly way

**Nachbarschaft** *die;* ~ **A** (*die Nachbarn*) **die [ganze] ~:** all the neighbours *pl.;* the whole neighbourhood; **es hat sich in der ganzen ~ herumgesprochen** everybody in the neighbourhood has heard about it; **B** (*Beziehungen*) **gute ~:** good neighbourliness; **wir halten** *od.* **pflegen eine gute ~:** we try to be good neighbours; **C** (*Gegend*) neighbourhood; (*Nähe*) vicinity

**nachbarschaftlich** ❶ *Adj.* neighbourly. ❷ *adv.* ⇨ **nachbarlich 2**

**Nachbarschafts-:** **~haus** *das* (*Sozialwesen*) neighbourhood [social] centre; **~hilfe** *die* **A** (*gegenseitige Hilfe*) neighbourly help; **mit ~hilfe gebaut** built with the assistance of the neighbours; **B** (*Sozialwesen*) neighbourhood social welfare organization (*run by independent welfare organizations*)

**Nachbars-:** **~familie** *die* family next door; **~frau** *die* woman next door

**Nachbar-:** **~tisch** *der* next *or* neighbouring table; **~wissenschaft** *die* allied *or* related science

**Nach·beben** *das* aftershock

**nach|behandeln** *tr. V.* **A** (*nochmals behandeln*) treat again; **B** (*nach ärztlicher Behandlung*) **jmdn./etw. ~:** give sb./sth. follow-up treatment

**Nach·behandlung** *die* follow-up treatment; aftercare

**nach|bekommen** *unr. tr. V.* **A** (*mehr bekommen*) **[noch] etw. ~:** have some more of sth.; (*bei Tisch*) have seconds of sth.; **B** (*mehr kaufen können*) get more of

**nach|bereiten** *tr. V.* (*bes. Päd.*) **A** (*analysieren*) assess the effectiveness of ‹lesson›; **B** (*vertiefen*) go over [again] (*in order to internalize the material*)

**Nachbereitung** *die;* ~, ~en (*bes. Päd.*) **A** (*Analyse*) assessment; **B** (*Vertiefung*) further study (*for internalization*)

**nach|bessern** *tr. V.* repair; make good, put right ‹defects›

**nach|bestellen** *tr. V.* **[noch] etw. ~:** order more of sth.; ‹shop› order further stock of sth., reorder sth.; **die Teile des Geschirrs ~:** order more [parts] of the service

**Nach·bestellung** *die;* ~, ~en further order (+ *Gen.* for); (*vom Händler aufgegeben*) repeat order (+ *Gen.* for)

**nach|beten** *tr. V.* (*ugs. abwertend*) repeat parrot-fashion; regurgitate

n

*old spelling (see note on page 1707)

# nach

## *Wohin?* = to

***Ich fuhr mit dem Zug nach Wien***
= I went to Vienna by train, I took the train to Vienna

Aber:

***Der Zug nach Wien hält nicht in Wels***
= The train for *od.* to Vienna does not stop in Wels

***Passagiere nach Zürich***
= passengers [bound] for Zurich

***Das Schiff ist unterwegs*** od. ***auf dem Wege nach Bombay***
= The ship is on its way to *od.* is bound for Bombay

***Sie sind nach Australien abgereist***
= They have left for Australia

***Die Maschine flog nach Osten***
= The aircraft flew east[wards] *od.* towards the east

***nach dem Meer zu***
= towards the sea

***nach allen Richtungen***
= in all directions

## *Wann?* = after

***Nach dem Rennen gab er ein Interview***
= He gave an interview after the race

***nach Erhalt der Rechnung***
after receiving the invoice

***Nach fünf Minuten trafen die ersten Läufer ein***
= After five minutes *od.* Five minutes later the first runners arrived

***Nach 22.00 Uhr verkehren die Züge stündlich***
= After 10 p.m. trains run every hour

Aber bei Uhrzeitangaben:

***um Viertel/fünfundzwanzig nach sieben***
= at a quarter/twenty-five past seven

Auch in der Reihenfolge:

***Nach Ihnen!***
= After you

***eins nach dem andern***
= one thing after another

***Nach „für" steht der Akkusativ***
= 'Für' is followed by the accusative

***B kommt nach A in der Weltrangliste***
= B comes after *od.* below A in the world rankings

## *Gemäß* = according to, in accordance with

***Diesem Bericht nach soll sie ein Kind erwarten***
= According to this report she is expecting a child

***nach deutschem Recht***
= in accordance with German law

***nach der neuesten Mode gekleidet***
= dressed in [accordance with] the latest fashion

***nach italienischer Art***
= in the Italian manner

***meiner Ansicht*** od. ***Meinung nach***
= in my opinion

***aller Wahrscheinlichkeit nach***
= in all probability

***nach etwas urteilen***
= to judge by sth.

***Seiner Sprache nach ist er Norddeutscher***
= Going *od.* Judging by the way he speaks, he's North German

**nach|bezahlen** ⇨ nachzahlen

**nach|bilden** *tr. V.* reproduce, copy (+ *Dat.* from); **einem ägyptischen Original nachgebildet sein** be a reproduction *or* copy of an Egyptian original

**Nach·bildung** *die* **A** (*das Nachbilden*) copying; **B** (*Gegenstand*) copy; replica

**nach|bleiben** *unr. tr. V.; mit sein* (*landsch.*) be left (*from an injury etc.*); **wenn da bloß nichts nachbleibt!** let's hope there's no lasting damage *or* after-effects!

**nach|blicken** *tr. V.* (*geh.*) **jmdm./einer Sache ~:** look *or* gaze after sb./sth.

**Nach·blutung** *die* secondary haemorrhage

**nach|bringen** *unr. tr. V.* bring along ‹sth. left behind›; **sie hat ihm den Schirm nachgebracht** she brought the umbrella he left behind

**nach·christlich** *Adj.:* **im ersten ~en Jahrhundert** in the first century AD

**nach|datieren** *tr. V.* backdate

**nach·dem** *Konj.* **A** (*zeitlich*) after; **ich ging erst, ~ ich mich vergewissert hatte** I only left when I had made sure; I did not leave until I had made sure; **~ ich das Buch gelesen hatte** after *or* when I had read the book; **B** (*südd.: kausal*) since; **C** ⇨ **je**[1] 3 B

**nach|denken** *unr. itr. V.* think (**über** + *Akk.* about); (*lange u. erwägend*) reflect (**über** + *Akk.* on); **darüber darf man gar nicht ~!** it doesn't bear thinking about; **denk mal [gut** *od.* **scharf] nach** have a [good] think; think carefully; **er dachte darüber nach, wie er sich entscheiden sollte** he considered how he should decide; **ohne nachzudenken** without stopping to think

**Nach·denken** *das* thought; **Zeit zum ~:** time to think; **nach langem ~:** after thinking about it for a long time; after mature consideration (*formal*); **in tiefes ~ versunken** sunk in thought

**nachdenklich** **1** *Adj.* thoughtful; pensive; **jmdn. [sehr] ~ machen** *od.* **stimmen** [really] make sb. think; give sb. [much] cause for thought. **2** *adv.* thoughtfully; pensively

**Nach·dichtung** *die* adaptation/recreation (*in another language*)

**nach|drängen** *itr. V.; mit sein* (*nach vorn schieben*) push forwards; (*von hinten*) push from behind; **einige liefen auf das Spielfeld, andere drängten nach** some ran on to the pitch and others crowded after them

**Nach·druck** *der; Pl.* **~e** **A** **mit ~:** emphatically; **etw. mit ~/mit größtem ~ fordern** demand sth. vigorously *or* forcefully/with the utmost vigour; **seinen Worten ~ verleihen** give one's words emphasis; **auf etw.** (*Akk.*) **[besonderen] ~ legen** place [particular] emphasis on sth.; stress sth. [particularly]; **B** (*Druckw.*) reprint; (*beim Copyrightvermerk*) **~[, auch auszugsweise,] verboten** not to be reproduced [in part or in whole]

**nach|drucken** *tr. V.* reprint ‹book›; print more ‹invoices, letterheads, etc.›

**nachdrücklich** **1** *Adj.* emphatic ‹warning, confirmation, advice›; insistent ‹demand›; urgent ‹request, appeal›. **2** *adv.* emphatically; **ich muss Sie ~ bitten, zu ...** I must urgently request you to ...; **etw. ~ verlangen** demand sth. vigorously; **~ darauf hinweisen, dass ...** emphasize that ...:

**Nachdrücklichkeit** *die;* **~** ⇨ **nachdrücklich**: emphatic nature; insistent nature; urgency

**nach|dunkeln** *itr. V.; mit sein* get darker

**Nach·durst** *der* morning-after thirst

**nach|eifern** *itr. V.* **jmdm. ~:** emulate sb.

**nach|eilen** *itr. V.; mit sein* **jmdm. ~:** hurry after sb.

**nach·einander** *Adv.* **A** (*räumlich, zeitlich*) one after the other; **kurz/unmittelbar ~:** one shortly/immediately after the other; **fünfmal/drei Tage ~:** five times/three days in a row; **B** *in Verbindung mit best. Verben* **~ sehen** keep an eye on each other; **sich ~ richten** coordinate with one another; **sich ~ sehnen** long for one another

**nach|empfinden** *unr. tr. V.* **A** (*nachfühlen*) empathize with ‹feeling›; share ‹delight, sorrow›; **ich kann [dir] deinen Ärger gut ~:** I can well understand *or* appreciate your feeling of anger; **B** (*nachmachen*) recreate ‹expression, atmosphere, event›; take ‹work of art› as a model; **einer Sache** (*Dat.*) **nachempfunden sein** take its inspiration from sth.; be modelled on sth.

**Nachen** /ˈnaxn̩/ *der;* **~s, ~** (*dichter.*) shallop

**nach|erzählen** *tr. V.* retell

**Nach·erzählung** *die* retelling [of a story]; (*Schulw.*) reproduction

**Nachfahr** /-faːɐ̯/ *der;* **~en** *od. selten* **~s, ~en** (*geh.*) descendant; (*fig.: Nachfolger*) successor

**nach|fahren** *unr. itr. V.; mit sein* follow [on]; **jmdm. ~:** follow sb.

**Nachfahrin** *die;* **~, ~nen** (*geh.*) descendant; (*fig.: Nachfolgerin*) successor

**nach|fassen** **1** *itr. V.* **A** (*noch einmal zufassen*) change one's grip (**an** + *Dat.* on); (*beim Fangen des Balls*) make a second attempt to gather the ball; **B** (*ugs.: nachfragen*) ask a supplementary question; **C** (*bes. Soldatenspr.*) **[noch einmal** *od.* **noch mal] ~:** have seconds. **2** *tr. V.* (*bes. Soldatenspr.*) have seconds of ‹soup etc.›

**Nach·feier** *die* belated celebration

**nach|feiern** **1** *tr. V.* celebrate ‹birthday, Christmas› at a later date. **2** *itr. V.* have a belated celebration

**Nach·folge** *die* succession; **die ~ B.s regeln** settle who is to be B's successor; **jmds. ~ antreten** succeed sb.; **die ~ Christi** the discipleship of Christ

**nach|folgen** *itr. V.; mit sein* follow; **jmdm./einer Sache ~:** follow sb./sth.; **jmdm. im Amt ~:** succeed sb. in office

n

**nach·folgend** *Adj.* following; subsequent ‹chapter, issue›; **im Nachfolgenden** below; in the text that follows

**Nachfolge·organisation** *die* successor organization (*Gen.* to)

**Nachfolger** *der;* **~s, ~, Nachfolgerin** *die;* **~, ~nen** successor

**Nachfolge·staat** *der* succession *or* successor state

**nach|fordern** *tr. V.* **[noch] 500 DM ~:** demand an additional 500 marks

**Nach·forderung** *die* additional demand (*Gen.*, **von** for)

**nach|forschen** *itr. V.* make inquiries; investigate [the matter]; **~, ob .../wer .../welcher ...** try to find out *or* investigate whether .../who .../which ...; **einer Sache** (*Dat.*) **~** (*geh.*) investigate a matter

**Nach·forschung** *die* investigation; inquiry; **~en [nach etw.] anstellen** make inquiries [into sth.]; **die ~en, wohin ...** the inquiries as to where ...

**Nach·frage** *die* [A] (*Kaufmannsspr.*) demand (**nach** for); **es herrscht keine ~ mehr danach** there is no longer any demand for it; ⇒ *auch* **Angebot**; [B] (*veralt.: Frage*) inquiry; question; **danke der [gütigen] ~/für die [gütige] ~** (*meist scherzh.*) how kind of you to inquire

**nach|fragen** *itr. V.* ask; inquire; **bei jmdm. ~:** ask sb.; **ob ich mal ~ soll?** should I ask about it *or* make inquiries?; **um etw. ~:** ask for *or* request sth.

**Nach·frist** *die* (*Rechtsw.*): *additional time given for performance of a contract*

**nach|fühlen** *tr. V.* empathize with; **jmdm. seine Wut ~:** understand sb.'s anger; **das kann ich dir ~!** I know how you feel!

**nach|füllen** *tr. V.* refill ‹glass, vessel, etc.›; (*wenn nicht leer*) fill up; top up; **jmdm. das Glas** *od.* **jmds. Glas ~:** refill/fill up sb.'s glass; **Salz/Wein ~:** put [some] more salt/wine in

**Nach·gang** *in* **im ~** (*Amtsspr.*) subsequently

**nach|geben** ❶ *unr. itr. V.* [A] give way; (*aus Schwäche*) give in; **jmdm. zu viel ~:** give in to sb. *or* let sb. have his/her way too often; **seiner Verzweiflung/Müdigkeit ~:** give in to one's despair/tiredness; [B] (*sich dehnen*) stretch; **das Material gibt ein wenig nach** there is some give in the material; [C] (*Bankw., Wirtsch.: sinken*) ‹prices, currency› weaken. ❷ *unr. tr. V.* [A] (*mehr geben*) **jmdm. [etwas] Fleisch/Suppe** *usw.* **~:** give sb. [some] more meat/soup *etc.*; [B] *in* **jmdm. nichts/nicht viel** *od.* **wenig ~:** be sb.'s equal/almost sb.'s equal (**an** + *Dat.* in)

**nach·geboren** *Adj.* [A] posthumous ‹son, daughter›; [B] (*viel jünger*) much younger; born much later *postpos.*

**Nach·gebühr** *die* excess postage

**Nach·geburt** *die* [A] (*Vorgang*) expulsion of the afterbirth; [B] (*Gewebe*) afterbirth

**nach|gehen** *unr. itr. V.; mit sein* [A] (*folgen*) **jmdm./einer Sache ~:** follow sb./sth.; **gehen Sie der Musik nach** follow the sound of the music; **einer Sache/einer Frage/einem Problem** *usw.* **~** (*fig.*) look into a matter/question/problem *etc.*; [B] (*nicht aus dem Kopf gehen*) **jmdm. ~:** remain on sb.'s mind; occupy sb.'s thoughts; [C] **seinen Geschäften** *od.* **Beschäftigungen/seinem Tagewerk ~:** go about one's business/daily work; **seinen Interessen/seinem Studium ~:** pursue one's interests/one's studies; **einem Beruf ~:** practise a profession; [D] ‹clock, watch› be slow; **[um] eine Stunde ~:** be an hour slow; **eine Stunde am Tag ~:** lose an hour a day

**nach·gelassen** ❶ *2. Part. v.* **nachlassen.** ❷ *Adj.*; unpublished (*at the author's/composer's death*); **die ~en Schriften des Autors** the unpublished writings left by the author

**nach·gemacht** ❶ *2. Part. v.* **nachmachen.** ❷ *Adj.* imitation ‹leather, gold›; **~ aussehen** look like an imitation

**nach·geordnet** *Adj.* (*Amtsspr.*) inferior ‹authority›; ‹person› subordinate

**nach·gerade** *Adv.* [A] (*allmählich*) in time; by and by; [B] (*geradezu*) positively; **das ist ~ eine Unverschämtheit** it's an absolute cheek

**nach|geraten** *unr. itr. V.; mit sein* **jmdm. ~:** take after sb.

**Nach·geschmack** *der* aftertaste; **einen üblen** *od.* **unguten ~ hinterlassen** (*fig.*) leave a nasty taste in the mouth

**nach·gewiesener·maßen** *Adv.* as has been proved

**nach·giebig** /-gi:bɪç/ *Adj.* [A] (*nicht streng*) indulgent; yielding; **seinen Kindern gegenüber zu ~ sein** be too indulgent to *or* (*coll.*) soft with one's children; [B] (*weich*) soft; yielding

**Nachgiebigkeit** *die;* **~** [A] (*gütige Art*) indulgence; [B] (*Weichheit*) softness

**nach|gießen** ❶ *unr. tr. V.* pour [in] some more; **darf ich Ihnen [noch] Wein ~?** may I top up your wine? ❷ *unr. itr. V.* (*die Gläser nachfüllen*) top up the drinks; **jmdm. ~:** pour sb. some more; top sb. up (*coll.*)

**nach|grübeln** *itr. V.* ponder (**über** + *Akk.* over)

**nach|gucken** (*ugs.*) ⇒ **nachsehen** 1 A, B, C, 2 A, B

**nach|haken** *itr. V.* [A] (*ugs.: noch einmal fragen*) raise another question; **an einem Punkt muss ich ~:** I must come back on one point; [B] (*ugs.: nachgehen*) make further inquiries; [C] (*Fußball*) tackle from behind

**Nach·hall** *der;* **~[e]s, ~e** reverberation; (*fig. geh.: Nachwirkung*) reverberations *pl.*; (*in der Literatur o. Ä.*) lingering echo

**nach|hallen** *itr. V.* reverberate; **seine Schritte hallten in dem leeren Haus nach** his footsteps echoed in the empty house

**Nachhall·zeit** *die* (*Physik*) reverberation period

**nach·haltig** ❶ *Adj.* [A] lasting; **jmdm. einen ~en Schreck versetzen** give sb. a fright that he/she will not forget [for a long time]. [B] (*Ökologie*) sustainable. ❷ *adv.* [A] (*auf längere Zeit*) for a long time; (*nachdrücklich*) persistently; **jmdn. ~ prägen** have a lasting effect on sb.; **~ geschädigt werden** sustain lasting damage [B] (*Ökologie*) sustainably

**nach|hängen** *unr. itr. V.* [A] (*in Gedanken*) dwell on; **seinen Gedanken ~:** lose oneself in one's thoughts; give oneself up to one's thoughts; [B] (*anhaften*) **jmdm. ~:** stick to sb.; [C] (*ugs.: in der Schule zurück sein*) lag behind

**nach·hause** *Adv.* (*österr., schweiz.*) home

**Nach·hause·weg** *der* way home

**nach|helfen** *unr. itr. V.* help; **jmdm. ~:** help sb. along; lend sb. a hand; **der Schönheit ~:** improve on Mother Nature; **dem Glück ~:** assist one's chances

**nach·her** /*auch:* '--/ *Adv.* [A] afterwards; (*später*) later [on]; **bis ~!** see you later!; **ich kann mich erst ~ darum kümmern** I can't deal with it until after that *or* later; [B] (*ugs.: womöglich*) then perhaps; (*sonst*) otherwise; **erzählen Sie die Geschichte nicht weiter, ~ ist sie nicht wahr** don't tell this story to anyone — it might turn out to be untrue

**Nach·hilfe** *die* coaching

**Nachhilfe-: ~lehrer** *der*, **~lehrerin** *die* coach; **~schüler** *der:* **mein ~schüler** the boy I am coaching; **sie hat drei ~schüler** she is coaching three boys; **~schülerin** *die:* **meine ~schülerin** the girl I am coaching; **sie hat drei ~schülerinnen** she is coaching three girls; **~stunde** *die* private lesson; **~unterricht** *der* coaching

***nach·hinein, Nachhinein** *in* **im ~** (*nachträglich*) afterwards; later; (*zurückblickend*) with hindsight; **im ~ ist man immer klüger** one is always wiser after the event

**Nach·hol·bedarf** *der* need to catch up; **ein ~ an etw.** (*Dat.*) a need to make up for the shortage of sth.

**nach|holen** *tr. V.* [A] (*nachträglich erledigen*) catch up on ‹work, sleep›; make up for ‹working hours missed›; **er hat viel/einiges nachzuholen** he has a lot of/some catching up to do; **den Schulabschluss ~:** take one's final school examination as a mature student; **ich habe ihr nicht gratuliert — ich muss es morgen ~:** I didn't congratulate her — I shall have to do it tomorrow instead; [B] (*zu sich holen*) fetch; **seine Familie ~:** bring one's family to join one

**Nach·hut** *die;* **~, ~en** (*Milit.; auch fig.*) rearguard

**Nach·impfung** *die* booster injection

**nach|jagen** *itr. V.; mit sein* **jmdm./einer Sache ~:** chase after sb./sth.; **dem Erfolg/Geld ~** (*fig.*) devote oneself to the pursuit of success/money

**Nach·klang** *der* reverberation

**nach|klingen** *unr. itr. V.; mit sein* go on sounding; **in jmdm. ~** (*fig. geh.*) linger on in sb.'s mind; stay with sb.

**Nachkomme** *der;* **~n, ~n** descendant; (*eines Tieres*) offspring; **ohne ~n sterben** die without issue

**nach|kommen** *unr. itr. V.; mit sein* [A] follow [later]; come [on] later; **seine Familie wird [später] ~:** his family will join him later; **da kann noch etwas ~** (*ugs.*) something could still turn up; **die ~den Truppen** the cars/troops following behind; [B] **seinen Pflichten ~:** fulfil one's duties; **seinen Verpflichtungen ~:** meet one's commitments; **einem Wunsch/Befehl/einer Bitte ~:** comply with a wish/an order/grant a request; [C] (*Schritt halten können*) be able to keep up; **ich komme mit dem Abtrocknen nicht nach** I can't dry [the dishes] fast enough

**Nachkommenschaft** *die;* **~:** descendants *pl.*; (*eines Tieres*) offspring

**Nachkömmling** /-kœmlɪŋ/ *der;* **~s, ~e** much younger child (*than the rest*); afterthought (*joc.*); **Christoph, unser ~:** Christoph, much the youngest child in our family

**Nach·kriegs-: ~generation** *die* post-war generation; **~zeit** *die* post-war period; **in der [ersten] ~zeit** [immediately] after the war

**Nach·kur** *die* [period of] convalescence (*after a health cure*)

**nach|laden** *unr. itr. V.* reload

**Nach·lass, *Nach·laß** *der;* **Nachlasses, Nachlasse** *od.* **Nachlässe** [A] estate; (*hinterlassene Gegenstände*) personal effects *pl.* (*left by the deceased*); **literarischer/künstlerischer ~:** unpublished/unexhibited works *pl.* (*left by a writer/an artist*); **aus dem ~ veröffentlichen** publish posthumously; [B] (*Kaufmannsspr.: Rabatt*) discount; reduction; **ein hoher ~:** a high discount *or* big reduction

**nach|lassen** ❶ *unr. itr. V.* [A] (*schwächer/weniger werden*) let up; ‹rain, wind› ease, let up; ‹storm, heat› abate, die down; ‹anger› subside, die down; ‹pain, stress, pressure› ease, lessen; ‹noise› lessen; ‹fever› go down; ‹speed, demand› decrease, drop; ‹effect› wear off; ‹interest, enthusiasm, strength, courage› flag, wane; ‹resistance› weaken; (*schlechter werden*) ‹health, hearing, memory› get worse, deteriorate; ‹reactions› become slower; ‹performance› deteriorate, fall off; ‹business› drop off, fall off; **meine Augen haben stark nachgelassen** my eyesight has deteriorated considerably; [B] (*landsch.: aufhören*) **mit etw. nicht ~:** keep on with sth.; **du sollst damit jetzt ~!** stop that at once!; ⇒ *auch* **Schreck**.
❷ *unr. tr. V.* [A] (*Kaufmannsspr.*) give *or* allow a discount of; **man hat mir 30% des Preises nachgelassen** they gave me 30% off [the price] *or* a discount of 30%; [B] (*erlassen*) **jmdm. seine Schulden ~:** let sb. off his/her debts; [C] (*lockern*) slacken ‹rope›

**Nachlass·gericht, *Nachlaß·gericht** *das* (*Rechtsw.*) ≈ probate court

**nach·lässig** ❶ *Adj.* [A] (*unordentlich*) careless; untidy ‹dress›; negligent ‹staff›; lax, casual ‹behaviour, way of talking›; [B] (*unbeteiligt*) indifferent; apathetic. ❷ *adv.* [A] (*unordentlich*) carelessly; untidily ‹dressed›; [B] (*unbeteiligt*) indifferently; apathetically

*old spelling (see note on page 1707)

**nachlässigerweise** *Adv.* carelessly

**Nach·lässigkeit** *die;* ~, ~en Ⓐ ⇒ **nachlässig** 1 A: carelessness; untidiness; negligence; laxness; casualness; Ⓑ (*Fehler*) careless mistake; **die kleinste ~:** the slightest mistake

**Nachlass-, *Nachlaß-: ~pfleger** *der,* **~pflegerin,** *die* (*Rechtsw.*) administrator [of an/the estate] (*appointed by the court until the estate is settled*); **~verwalter** *der,* **~verwalterin,** *die* (*Rechtsw.*) executor

**Nach·lauf** *der* (*Kfz-W.*) castor angle

**nach|laufen** *unr. itr. V.; mit sein* **jmdm./einer Sache ~:** run *or* chase after sb./sth.; **einem Mädchen ~** (*ugs.*) chase a girl; **einer Illusion** (*Dat.*) **~** (*fig.*) chase after *or* pursue an illusion; **diese Kleider laufen sich nach** (*fig. ugs.*) these dresses are everywhere

**nach|legen** *tr., itr. V.* **[Holz/Kohlen] ~:** put some more wood/coal on

**Nach·lese** *die* Ⓐ gleaning; (*Ertrag*) gleanings *pl.;* Ⓑ (*geh.: Auswahl*) further selection

**nach|lesen** *unr. tr. V.* look up; (*überprüfen*) check; **in den Statistiken ist nachzulesen, dass ...** the statistics show that ...

**nach|liefern** *tr. V.* (*später liefern*) supply later; (*zusätzlich liefern*) supply additionally; **der Rest wird nächste Woche nachgeliefert** the rest of the delivery will follow next week

**Nach·lieferung** *die* Ⓐ (*das Nachliefern*) [subsequent] delivery; Ⓑ (*Ware*) further consignment

**nach|lösen** ❶ *tr. V.* **eine Fahrkarte ~:** buy a ticket [on the train/tram (*Brit.*) *or* (*Amer.*) streetcar]. ❷ *itr. V.* pay the excess [fare]; (*für die 1. Klasse*) pay the extra [fare]

**nachm.** *Abk.* **nachmittags** p.m.

**nach|machen** *tr. V.* Ⓐ (*auch tun*) copy; (*imitieren*) imitate; do an impersonation of ‹politician etc.›; (*genauso herstellen*) reproduce ‹period furniture etc.›; forge ‹signature›; forge, counterfeit ‹money›; **jmdm. alles ~:** copy everything sb. does; **das soll mir einer ~!** follow that!; **das macht ihm so schnell keiner nach** nobody is going to equal that in a hurry; ⇒ *auch* **nachgemacht**; Ⓑ (*ugs.: später machen*) do later; take ‹exam› later; **Hausaufgaben ~:** catch up on one's homework

**nach|malen** *tr. V.* go over [with fresh paint]

**nach·malig** *Adj.* (*veralt.*) future; **X, der ~e US-Präsident** X, who was to become President of the USA

**nach|messen** ❶ *unr. tr. V.* check the measurements of; check ‹distance, length, etc.›. ❷ *itr. V.* check the measurements

**Nach·mieter** *der,* **Nach·mieterin** *die* next tenant; **einen Nachmieter stellen** find a tenant to take over the lease

***nach·mittag** ⇒ **Nachmittag** A

**Nach·mittag** *der* Ⓐ afternoon; **zwei ~e in der Woche arbeiten** work two afternoons a week; **den ganzen ~:** all afternoon; **am ~,** (*geh.*) **des ~s** in the afternoon; (*heute*) this afternoon; **am frühen/späten ~:** early/late in the afternoon; **am selben ~:** the same afternoon; **am ~ des 8. März** on the afternoon of 8 March; **an einem sonnigen ~ im Juli** one sunny afternoon in July; **heute/morgen/gestern ~:** this/tomorrow/yesterday afternoon; Ⓑ (*Veranstaltung*) social afternoon

**nachmittäglich** /-mɪtɛːklɪç/ *Adj.* afternoon ‹walk, nap›

**nach·mittags** *Adv.* ▶ 752 in the afternoon; (*heute*) this afternoon; **dienstags ~:** on Tuesday afternoons; **um vier Uhr ~:** at four in the afternoon; at 4 p.m.

**Nach·mittags-: ~kaffee** *der* afternoon coffee [and cakes]; **~vor·stellung** *die* afternoon performance; [afternoon] matinée

**Nachnahme** *die;* ~, ~n Ⓐ **per ~:** cash on delivery; COD; Ⓑ (*Sendung*) COD parcel

**Nachnahme-: ~gebühr** *die* (*Postw.*) cash on delivery fee; **~sendung** *die* (*Postw.*) COD parcel

**Nach·name** *der* surname; **wie heißt du mit ~n?** what is your surname?

**nach|nutzen** *tr. V.* (*DDR*) take over ‹sb. else's innovation/method›; make use of ‹sb. else's experience›

**nach|plappern** *tr. V.* (*oft abwertend*) repeat parrot-fashion; **jmdm. alles ~:** repeat everything sb. says

**Nach·porto** *das* excess postage

**nach|prägen** *tr. V.* Ⓐ mint more, re-mint ‹coins, medals›; **[noch] 100 Stück wurden nachgeprägt** another 100 copies were minted; Ⓑ (*fälschen*) forge; counterfeit

**Nach·prägung** *die* Ⓐ (*Vorgang*) re-minting; Ⓑ (*Münze*) copy; (*Fälschung*) forgery; counterfeit [coin]

**nachprüfbar** *Adj.* verifiable

**Nachprüfbarkeit** *die;* ~: verifiability

**nach|prüfen** ❶ *tr. V.* Ⓐ check ‹document, statement, weight, alibi›; verify ‹correctness›; Ⓑ (*später prüfen*) examine ‹candidate› later; (*bei der Fahrprüfung*) test ‹learner driver› later. ❷ *itr. V.* check

**Nach·prüfung** *die* Ⓐ checking; Ⓑ (*spätere Prüfung*) postponed examination

**nach|rechnen** ❶ *tr. V.* check ‹figures›. ❷ *itr. V.* Ⓐ (*zur Kontrolle*) check [the figures]; Ⓑ (*zurückverfolgen*) [think back and] work it out

**Nach·rede** *die:* **üble ~:** malicious gossip; (*Rechtsw.*) defamation [of character]

**nach|reden** *tr. V.* Ⓐ (*wiederholen*) repeat; Ⓑ ⇒ **nachsagen** B

**nach|reichen** *tr. V.* hand in subsequently

**nach|reifen** *itr. V.; mit sein* ripen further (*after picking*)

**nach|reisen** *itr. V.; mit sein* **jmdm. ~:** travel after sb.; (*losfahren*) set off after sb.

**nach|rennen** *unr. itr. V.:* ⇒ **nachlaufen**

**Nachricht** /ˈnaːxrɪçt/ *die;* ~, ~en Ⓐ (*Mitteilung*) news *no pl.;* **das ist eine gute ~:** that is [a piece of] good news; **gute/schlechte ~en** good/bad news; **eine ~ hinterlassen** leave a message; **ich habe keine ~ von ihm** (*Brief usw.*) I haven't heard *or* had any word from him; **wir warten auf ~** *od.* **sind noch ohne ~** (*Bestätigung*) we are waiting to hear *or* have not heard yet; **jmdm. ~ geben** inform sb.; Ⓑ *Pl.* (*Ferns., Rundf.*) news *sing.;* **~en hören** listen to the news; **Sie hören ~en** here is the news; **das kam in den ~en** it was on the news

**Nachrichten-: ~agentur** *die* news agency; **~dienst** *der* Ⓐ (*Geheimdienst*) intelligence service; Ⓑ ⇒ **~agentur**; **~magazin** *das* news magazine; **~satellit** *der* communications satellite; **~sendung** *die* news broadcast; **~sperre** *die* news embargo *or* blackout; **~sprecher** *der,* **~sprecherin** *die* ▶ 159 newsreader; **~technik** *die* telecommunications [technology] *no art.;* **~übermittlung** *die* news transmission *no art.*

**nach|rücken** *itr. V.; mit sein* (*aufrücken*) move up; **[auf den Posten] ~:** be promoted [to the post]; take over [the post]; **dem Feind ~** (*Mil.*) move up behind the enemy

**Nach·ruf** *der;* ~[e]s, ~e obituary (**auf** + *Akk.* of)

**nach|rufen** *unr. tr., itr. V.* **jmdm. [etw.] ~:** call [sth.] after sb.

**Nach·ruhm** *der;* ~[e]s posthumous reputation

**nach|rühmen** *tr. V.* **jmdm. etw. ~:** credit sb. with sth.; **ihm rühmt man nach, dass er ...** he is famous for the fact that he ...

**nach|rüsten** ❶ *itr. V.* counter-arm. ❷ *tr. V.* (*Technik: zusätzlich ausstatten*) **mit etw. ~:** equip additionally with sth.; upgrade ‹television, hi-fi, etc.› with sth.

**Nach·rüstung** *die;* ~ Ⓐ (*Waffen*) counter-arming; Ⓑ (*Technik*) [additional] equipment; (*von Stereoanlagen usw.*) upgrading

**Nachrüstungs·beschluss, *Nachrüstungs·beschluß** *der* (*Politik*) decision to counter-arm

**nach|sagen** *tr. V.* Ⓐ (*wiederholen*) repeat; **sag mir Folgendes nach** repeat the following after me; Ⓑ (*über jmdn. sagen*) **jmdm. Schlechtes ~:** speak ill of sb.; **man sagt ihm nach, er verstehe etwas davon** he is said to know something about it; **du darfst dir nicht ~ lassen, dass ...** you mustn't let it be said of you that ...; **wir wollen uns doch nichts ~ lassen!** we don't want anything said against us!; we don't want to get a bad reputation!

**Nach·saison** *die* late season

**nach|salzen** *unr.* (*auch regelm.*) *tr., itr. V.* **[etw.] ~:** put more salt in/on [sth.]

**Nach·satz** *der* Ⓐ (*letzte Bemerkung*) postscript; (*gesprochen*) final remark; Ⓑ (*Sprachw.*) postponed clause

**Nach·schau** *in:* **~ halten** (*geh.*) investigate; look into it

**nach|schauen** (*bes. südd., österr., schweiz.*) ⇒ **nachsehen** 1 A, B, C, 2 A, B

**nach|schenken** *tr., itr. V.* top up one's/sb.'s glass; **jmdm. [Wein] ~:** top up sb.'s glass [with wine]

**nach|schicken** *tr. V.* Ⓐ (*durch die Post o. Ä.*) forward; send on; Ⓑ (*folgen lassen*) **jmdm. jmdn. ~:** send sb. after sb.

**Nach·schlag** *der* Ⓐ (*ugs.: zusätzliche Portion*) second helping; seconds *pl.;* Ⓑ (*Musik: verzierender Ton*) grace note (*after another note*); (*Abschluss eines Trillers*) two-note termination (*of a trill*)

**nach|schlagen** ❶ *unr. tr. V.* look up ‹word, reference, text›; (*ugs.*) consult, look at ‹dictionary, book›; **schlag mal nach, was X heißt** look up to see what X means. ❷ *unr. itr. V.* Ⓐ **im Lexikon/Wörterbuch ~:** consult the encyclopaedia/dictionary; Ⓑ *mit sein* (*geh.: ähnlich werden*) **jmdm. ~:** take after sb.

**Nachschlage·werk** *das* work of reference

**nach|schleichen** *unr. itr. V.; mit sein* **jmdm. ~:** creep *or* steal after sb.

**nach|schleifen**[1] *unr. tr. V.* resharpen ‹knife, blade›; repolish ‹lens›

**nach|schleifen**[2] *tr. V.* (*ugs.*) drag [along] behind one/it

**Nach·schlüssel** *der* duplicate key

**nach|schmeißen** *unr. tr. V.* (*ugs.*) Ⓐ (*billig o. ä. geben*) give away; **man bekommt sie nachgeschmissen** you get them for next to nothing; **sie haben ihm das Abitur nachgeschmissen** his school-leaving exam was handed to him on a plate (*coll.*); Ⓑ ⇒ **nachwerfen** A

**Nach·schrift** *die* Ⓐ notes *pl.* (+ *Gen.* on); Ⓑ (*Postskriptum*) postscript (+ *Gen.* to)

**Nach·schub** *der* (*Milit.*) Ⓐ supply (**an** + *Dat.* of); (*fig.*) [provision of] further *or* fresh supplies *pl.* (**an** + *Dat.* of); **der ~ ist schlecht organisiert** the supply services *or* supplies are badly organized; Ⓑ (*~material*) supplies *pl.* (**an** + *Dat.* of); (*fig.*) further supplies *pl.*

**Nachschub·weg** *der* (*Milit.*) supply line

**Nach·schuss, *Nach·schuß** *der* Ⓐ (*Wirtsch.*) contribution in excess of one's original share; further call; Ⓑ (*Ballspiele*) shot on the rebound

**nach|schütten** *tr. V.* put on more ‹coal, coke, etc.›; pour in more ‹water›

**nach|schwatzen,** (*bes. südd., österr.*) **nach|schwätzen** *tr. V.* (*abwertend*) repeat [parrot-fashion]

**nach|sehen** ❶ *unr. itr. V.* Ⓐ (*hintersehen*) **jmdm./einer Sache ~:** look *or* gaze after sb./sth.; Ⓑ (*kontrollieren*) check *or* have a look [to see]; **~, wer da ist** go and see *or* have a look who's there; Ⓒ (*nachschlagen*) look it up; have a look. ❷ *unr. tr. V.* Ⓐ (*nachlesen*) look up ‹word, passage›; Ⓑ (*überprüfen*) check [over]; look over; Ⓒ ▶ 268 (*nicht verübeln*) overlook, let pass ‹remark›; **jmdm. etw./zu viel ~:** let sb. get away with sth./too much

**Nach·sehen** *das: in* **das ~ haben** not get a look-in; (*nichts abbekommen*) be left with nothing; **jmdm. bleibt das ~:** sb. does not get a look-in; (*bekommt nichts ab*) sb. is left with nothing

**nach|senden** *unr. od. regelm. tr. V.:* ⇒ **nachschicken**

n

**Nach·sendung** *die (Postw.)* forwarding
**nach|setzen** *itr. V.* **jmdm./einem Tier ~:** pursue sb./an animal
**Nach·sicht** *die* leniency; forbearance; **mit jmdm. ~ haben** *od.* **üben** be lenient with sb.; make allowances for sb.; **ich muss um ~ bitten, dass ich so spät komme** please forgive me *or* I must apologize for coming so late; **keine ~ kennen** make no allowances; *(bei Strafen)* show no mercy
**nachsichtig** ❶ *Adj.* lenient, forbearing **(gegen, mit** towards); *(verständnisvoll)* understanding. ❷ *adv.* leniently; *(verständnisvoll)* understandingly
**Nachsichtigkeit** *die;* **~:** leniency; forbearance
**nachsichts·voll** ⇨ **nachsichtig**
**Nach·silbe** *die (Sprachw.)* suffix
**nach|sinnen** *unr. itr. V. (geh.)* ponder; **einer Sache** *(Dat.)* **~:** think back to sth.
**nach|sitzen** *unr. itr. V.* be in detention; **[eine Stunde] ~ müssen** have [an hour's] detention
**Nach·sommer** *der* Indian summer
**Nach·sorge** *die (Med.)* aftercare *no indef. art.*
**Nach·spann** *der;* **~[e]s, ~e** *(Film, Ferns.)* [final] credits *pl.*
**Nach·speise** *die* dessert; sweet
**Nach·spiel** *das* Ⓐ **die Sache wird noch ein ~ haben!** this affair will have repercussions; **ein gerichtliches ~ haben** result in court proceedings; Ⓑ *(Theater o. Ä.)* epilogue; *(Musik)* postlude; Ⓒ *(beim Geschlechtsverkehr)* afterplay
**nach|spielen** ❶ *tr. V.* Ⓐ *(Kartenspiel)* **den Buben** *usw.* **~:** follow up with the jack *etc.;* Ⓑ *(auch spielen)* **er hat es mir vorgespielt, ich musste es ~:** he played it over to me, and I then had to play it myself; Ⓒ *(nachahmen)* imitate, mimic ‹person›; re-enact ‹scene›; Ⓓ *(anderswo aufführen)* take up, put on ‹new play etc.›. ❷ *itr. V. (Ballspiele, bes. Fußball)* **[einige Minuten] ~:** play [a few minutes of] time added on; **der Schiedsrichter lässt ~:** the referee has added on time [for stoppages]
**nach|spionieren** *itr. V.* **jmdm. ~:** spy on sb.
**nach|sprechen** *unr. tr. V.* **[jmdm.] etw. ~:** repeat sth. [after sb.]
**nach|spülen** ❶ *tr. V.* rewash; wash again; *(mit klarem Wasser)* rinse. ❷ *itr. V.* Ⓐ *(ausspülen)* give it/them a rinse; **mit viel Wasser ~:** rinse out with plenty of water; Ⓑ *(ugs.: trinken)* **mit einem Bierchen ~:** have a beer as a chaser *(coll.)* *or* to wash it down
**nach|spüren** *itr. V.* **jmdm./einer Bande ~:** track down sb./a gang; **einer Sache** *(Dat.)* **~** *(fig.)* follow up *or* investigate sth.
**nächst** /nɛ:çst/ *Präp. mit Dat. (geh.)* next to
**nächst...** ❶ *Sup. zu* **nahe.** ❷ *Adj.* Ⓐ **▸818**, **▸833** **der ~e Weg zum Bahnhof** the shortest way to the station; **in ~er Nähe** very near; Ⓑ **▸818** *(unmittelbar danach)* next; **die ~e Straße links** the next street on the left; **beim ~en Bäcker** at the next baker's we come to; ⇨ *auch* **best...** B; Ⓒ **▸207** *(zeitlich)* next; **am ~en Tag** the next day; **am ~en Ersten** on the first of next month; **bei ~er Gelegenheit** at the next opportunity; **in ~er Zukunft** in the very near future; **in den ~en Tagen/Jahren** in the next few days/years; **beim ~en Mal, das ~e Mal** the next time; **der Nächste, bitte!** next [one], please; **wer kommt als Nächster dran?** whose turn is it next?; **als Nächstes räume ich den Boden auf** the next thing I do *or* my next job will be to tidy the loft
**nächst·beste** *Adj.* ⇨ **erstbeste**
**Nächst·beste** *der/die/das; adj. Dekl.* the first one [to turn up]; **das ~, was ich finde** the first thing I find
**Nächste** *der;* **~n, ~n** *(geh.)* neighbour; **jeder ist sich selbst der ~:** one has to look after one's own interests

**nach|stehen** *unr. itr. V.* **jmdm. an etw.** *(Dat.)* **nicht ~:** be sb.'s match in sth.; **jmdm./einer Sache in nichts ~:** be in no way inferior to sb./sth.
**nach·stehend** ❶ *Adj.* following. ❷ *adv.* below
**nach|steigen** *unr. itr. V.; mit sein (ugs.)* **einem Mädchen ~:** try to get off with *(Brit. coll.)* *or* *(Amer. coll.)* make it with a girl
**nach|stellen** ❶ *tr. V.* Ⓐ *(Sprachw.)* **A wird B** *(Dat.)* **nachgestellt** A is placed after B; **nachgestellte Präposition** postpositive preposition; **nachgestellter Satz** postponed clause; Ⓑ *(zurückstellen)* put back ‹clock, watch›; Ⓒ *(neu/genauer einstellen)* [re]adjust; take up the adjustment on ‹brakes, clutch›; Ⓓ *(darstellen)* portray; represent. ❷ *itr. V. (geh.)* **einem Tier/einem Flüchtling ~:** hunt an animal/hunt *or* pursue a fugitive; **Hühnern** *usw.* **~** ‹dog› chase chickens *etc.;* **einem Mädchen ~** *(ugs.)* chase a girl
**Nach·stellung** *die* Ⓐ *(Sprachw.)* postposition; Ⓑ *Pl.* *(Verfolgung)* pursuit *sing.;* *(ugs.: Umwerbung)* advances
**Nächsten·liebe** *die* charity [to one's neighbour]; brotherly love
**nächstens** /'nɛ:çstn̩s/ *Adv.* Ⓐ *(demnächst)* shortly; in the near future; **passen Sie ~ besser auf!** be more careful next time; Ⓑ *(ugs.: wenn es so weitergeht)* if it goes on like this
**nächst-:** **~folgend** *Adj.* next; **~gelegen** *Adj.* nearest; **~höher** *Adj.* next higher; **die ~höhere Klasse** the next class [up]; **~jährig** *Adj.* next year's; **~liegend** *Adj.* first, immediate ‹problem›; [most] obvious ‹explanation etc.›; **das Nächstliegende** the [most] obvious thing; **~möglich** *Adj.* earliest possible
**nach|stoßen** *unr. itr. V.* Ⓐ *mit sein (Milit.: vordringen)* move up *or* advance [behind them]; Ⓑ *(im Gespräch)* follow up [with another thrust]
**nach|suchen** *itr. V.* Ⓐ *(geh.: bitten)* **um etw. ~:** request sth.; *(bes. schriftlich)* apply for sth.; Ⓑ *(intensiv suchen)* search
***nacht** /naxt/ ⇨ **Nacht**
**Nacht** *die;* **~, Nächte** /'nɛçtə/ night; **es wird/ist ~:** it is getting dark/it is dark; night is falling/has fallen; **die ~ brach herein** night fell; **bei ~, in der ~,** *(geh.)* **des ~s** at night[-time]; **eines ~s** one night; **~ für ~:** night after night; **letzte ~:** last night; **die halbe ~:** half the night; **die ganze ~ [hindurch]** all night long; **diese ~:** tonight; **mitten in der ~:** in the middle of the night; **bis tief in die ~ hinein, bis spät in der ~:** until late at night; *(bis in die Morgenstunden)* into the small hours; **in der ~ vom 12. auf den 13. Mai** on the night of 12 May; **in der ~ auf Montag** on Sunday night; **über ~ bleiben** stay overnight; **über ~ berühmt werden** *(fig.)* become famous overnight; **zu[r] ~ essen** *(südd., österr.)* have one's evening meal; **gute ~!** good night!; **[na,] dann gute ~!** *(iron.)* [well,] that's that!; **die ~ zum Tage machen, sich** *(Dat.)* **die ~ um die Ohren schlagen** *(ugs.)* stay up all night; **bei ~ und Nebel** under cover of darkness; *(heimlich)* furtively; like a thief in the night; **~ der langen Messer** *(salopp)* night of the long knives; **die ~ des Wahnsinns/Krieges/der Tyrannei** *(dichter.)* the dark night of madness/war/tyranny; **gestern/morgen ~:** last/tomorrow night; **heute ~:** tonight; *(letzte Nacht)* last night; ⇨ *auch* **hässlich** 1 A; **heilig** B; **schwarz** 1 A
**nacht·aktiv** *Adj. (Zool.)* nocturnal
**nach|tanken** *tr., itr. V.* fill up; ‹aircraft› refuel; **20 Liter ~:** put in another 20 litres
**nacht-, Nacht-:** **~arbeit** *die* night work *no art.;* **~aufnahme** *die* night photograph *or* shot; **~bar** *die* night spot *(coll.);* **~blau** *Adj.* *(geh., dichter.)* midnight blue; **~blind** *Adj.* night-blind; **~blindheit** *die* night blindness; **~creme** *die* night cream; **~dienst** *der* night duty; **~dienst haben** be on night duty; ‹chemist's shop› be open late
**Nach·teil** *der* disadvantage; **der ~, allein zu reisen** the disadvantage *or* drawback of travelling alone; **aus etw. entsteht** *od.* **erwächst jmdm. ein ~:** sth. puts sb. at a disadvantage; **im ~ sein, sich im ~ befinden** be at a disadvantage; **ich hatte nur ~e davon** I had nothing but disadvantages as a result; **der Prozess ging zu seinem ~ aus** the trial went against him; **sich zu seinem ~ verändern** change for the worse; **jmdm. zum ~ gereichen, zu jmds. ~ gereichen** *(geh.)* be to sb.'s detriment
**nachteilig** ❶ *Adj.* detrimental; harmful; **über sie ist nichts Nachteiliges bekannt** nothing to her disadvantage is known about her. ❷ *adv.* detrimentally; harmfully; **sich ~ auswirken** have a detrimental *or* harmful effect
**nächte·lang** ❶ *Adj.;* lasting several nights *postpos.;* *(ganze Nächte dauernd)* all-night. ❷ *adv.* night after night
**nachten** /'naxtn̩/ *itr. V. (unpers.) (schweiz., sonst dichter.)* **es nachtet** night *or* darkness is falling
**Nacht-:** **~essen** *das (bes. südd., schweiz.)* evening meal; supper; *(formell)* dinner; **~eule** *die (ugs. scherzh.)* night owl *(coll.);* **~falter** *der* moth; **~flug** *der* night flight; **~frost** *der* night frost; **~gebet** *das* bedtime prayer; **~geschirr** *das* chamber pot; **~gespenst** *das* [nocturnal] ghost; **~gewand** *das (geh.)* nightdress; **~hemd** *das* nightshirt; **~himmel** *der* night sky
**Nachtigall** /'naxtɪgal/ *die;* **~, ~en** nightingale; **~, ich hör dir trapsen** *(salopp)* I can see which way the wind blows *or* what he/she's after
**Nachtigallen·schlag** *der* song of the nightingale
**nächtigen** /'nɛçtɪgn̩/ *(österr., sonst geh.)* spend the night
**Nach·tisch** *der* dessert; sweet; **zum** *od.* **als ~:** as a *or* for dessert; **was gibts zum ~?** what's for pudding *or* *(coll.)* afters?
**Nacht-:** **~kästchen** *das (südd., österr.)* bedside table; **~klub** *der* nightclub; **~lager** *das* Ⓐ *(geh.: Schlafstätte)* resting place for the night; Ⓑ *(Biwak)* bivouac; **~leben** *das* nightlife
**nächtlich** /'nɛçtlɪç/ *Adj.* nocturnal; night ‹sky›; ‹darkness, stillness› of the night; **durch den ~en Wald gehen** go through the dark woods [at night-time]; **~e Ruhestörung** *(Rechtsspr.) causing a disturbance at night*
**Nacht-:** **~lokal** *das* night spot *(coll.);* **~luft** *die* night air; **~mahl** *das (österr., auch südd.)* evening meal; supper; *(formell)* dinner; **~mahr** /-ma:ɐ/ *der;* **~~[e]s, ~~e** Ⓐ *(Gespenst)* [nocturnal] ghost *or* spectre; Ⓑ *(Albtraum)* nightmare; **~mensch** *der* night owl *(coll.);* **~mütze** *die* nightcap; **~portier** *der* night porter; **~quartier** *das* accommodation *no indef. art.* for the night
**Nachtrag** /-tra:k/ *der;* **~[e]s, Nachträge** /-trɛ:gə/ appendix; *(als weiteres Buch/Heft)* supplement
**nach|tragen** *unr. tr. V.* Ⓐ *(hinterhertragen)* **jmdm. etw. ~:** follow sb. carrying sth.; Ⓑ *(schriftlich ergänzen)* insert, add; *(noch sagen)* add; **nachzutragen wäre noch, dass ...** I should add that ...; it should be added that ...; Ⓒ *(übel nehmen)* **jmdm. etw. ~:** hold sth. against sb.
**nach·tragend** *Adj.* unforgiving; *(rachsüchtig)* vindictive; **ich bin nicht ~:** I don't bear grudges
**nachträglich** /-trɛ:klɪç/ ❶ *Adj.* later; subsequent ‹apology›; *(verspätet)* belated ‹greetings, apology›; *(zusätzlich)* additional; **eine ~e Gratifikation** a retrospective bonus. ❷ *adv.* afterwards; subsequently; *(verspätet)* belatedly; **~ feiern** have a belated celebration
**Nachtrags·haushalt** *der* supplementary budget
**nach|trauern** *itr. V.* **jmdm./einer Sache ~:** bemoan *or* lament the passing of sb./sth.; *(sich sehnen nach)* pine for sb./sth.
**Nacht·ruhe** *die* night's sleep; **angenehme ~!** sleep well!; **er wünschte ihnen eine angenehme ~:** he [said he] hoped they would sleep well

n

*old spelling (see note on page 1707)

**nachts** *Adv.* ▶ 752 at night; **montag~** *od.* **montags ~:** on Monday nights; **um 3 Uhr ~, ~ um 3 [Uhr]** at 3 o'clock in the morning

**nacht-, Nacht-: ~schatten·gewächs** *das (Bot.)* plant of the Solanaceae family; **~schattengewächse** Solanaceae; **~schicht** *die* night shift; **~schicht haben** be on night shift; work nights; **~schlafend** *Adj. in* **bei/zu ~schlafender Zeit** *od.* **Stunde** *(ugs.)* at a time when all good people are in their beds; **~schwärmer** *der (scherzh.)* nocturnal reveller; **~schwarz** *Adj. (geh.)* jet-black; **~schwester** *die* night nurse; **~speicher·ofen** *der* night storage heater; **~strom** *der* off-peak electricity; **~stuhl** *der* commode

**nachts·über** *Adv.* overnight; during the night

**Nacht-: ~tarif** *der* night rate; *(für Strom)* off-peak rate; **~tisch** *der* bedside table; **~tisch·lampe** *die* bedside light; **~topf** *der* chamber pot; **auf den ~topf gehen** use the chamber pot; **~tresor** *der* night safe

**nach|tun** *unr. tr. V. (ugs.)* copy; **es jmdm. ~:** copy sb.

**Nacht-und-Nebel-Aktion** *die* hush-hush [*esp.* night-time] operation

**nacht-, Nacht-: ~vorstellung** *die* late-night show; **~wache** *die* **A** *(Wachdienst)* night watch; *(im Krankenhaus)* night duty; *(eines Soldaten)* night guard-duty; **bei einem Kranken ~wache halten** sit up [at night] with a sick person; **B** *(Person)* night guard; *(für Fabrik, Büro o. Ä.)* nightwatchman; **~wächter** *der* ▶ 159 **A** nightwatchman; **B** *(salopp: Dummkopf)* dimwit *(coll.)*; thickhead *(coll.)*; **~wächter·staat** *der* laissez-faire state providing for security only; **~wandeln** *itr. V.; auch mit sein* sleepwalk; **~wanderung** *die* nocturnal ramble; **~wandler** /-vandlɐ/ *der;* **~~s, ~~, ~wandlerin** *die;* **~~, ~~nen** sleepwalker; somnambulist *(formal)*; **~wandlerisch** *Adj. in* **mit ~wandlerischer Sicherheit** with the sureness of a sleepwalker; with instinctive sureness; **~zeit** *die: in* **zu später** *od.* **vorgerückter ~zeit** at a late hour [of the night]; **~zeug** *das (ugs.)* overnight things *pl. (coll.)*; **~zug** *der* night train; **~zu·schlag** *der* night work supplement

**nach|untersuchen** *tr. V.* **jmdn./etw. ~:** give sb. a follow-up examination/check sth.

**Nach·untersuchung** *die* follow-up examination; check-up

**Nach·versicherung** *die* **A** *(Rentenversicherung)* retrospective state pension contributions *pl. (for previously uninsured employee)*; **B** *(von Sachwerten o. Ä.)* additional insurance cover

**nachvollziehbar** *Adj.* comprehensible; **leicht/schwer ~:** easy/difficult to comprehend; **das ist für mich nicht ~:** I find this impossible to understand *or* comprehend

**nach|vollziehen** *unr. tr. V.* reconstruct ‹train of thought›; *(begreifen)* comprehend

**nach|wachsen** *unr. itr. V.; mit sein* **[wieder] ~:** grow again

**Nach·wahl** *die (Politik)* postponed election; *(nach dem Tod o. Ä. eines Abgeordneten)* by-election

**Nach·wehen** *Pl. (Med.)* afterpains; *(fig. geh.)* unpleasant after-effects

**nach|weinen** *itr. V.* **jmdm./einer Sache ~:** bemoan the loss of sb./sth.; **einer Sache** *(Dat.)* **nicht ~:** have no regrets about sth.; ⇒ *auch* **Träne**

**Nachweis** /-vais/ *der;* **~es, ~e** proof *no indef. art. (Gen.,* **über** + *Akk.* of); *(Zeugnis)* certificate **(über** + *Akk.* of); **den ~ für etw. erbringen** *od.* **führen** produce *or* furnish proof of sth.; **als** *od.* **zum ~:** as proof; **es gelang ihm der ~, dass ...** he managed to prove that ...

**nachweisbar** **1** *Adj.* demonstrable ‹fact, truth, error, defect, guilt›; provable ‹fact, guilt›; detectable ‹substance, chemical›; **die Siedlung ist bis ins 7. Jahrhundert ~:** the settlement can be shown to have existed up to the 7th century. **2** *adv.* demonstrably

**nach|weisen** *unr. tr. V.* **A** prove; **jmdm. einen Fehler/Diebstahl ~:** prove sb. made a mistake/committed a theft; **man konnte ihm nichts ~:** they could not prove anything against him; **im Körper wurden Spuren des Giftes nachgewiesen** traces of the poison were detected in the body; **B** *(Amtsspr.) (vermitteln)* arrange ‹hotel room›; *(informieren über)* provide information on ‹hotel room, job›

**nachweislich** **1** *Adj.* demonstrable; **eine ~e Falschmeldung** a demonstrably wrong report. **2** *adv.* demonstrably; as can be proved

**Nach·welt** *die* posterity *no art.;* future generations *pl., no art.*

**nach|werfen** *unr. tr. V.* **A jmdm. etw. ~:** throw sth. after sb.; **jmdm. einen wütenden Blick ~** *(fig.)* cast a furious glance in sb.'s direction; **eine Münze ~:** put in another coin; **B** ⇒ **nachschmeißen A**

**nach|winken** *itr. V.* **jmdm./einer Sache ~:** wave after sb./sth.

**nach|wirken** *itr. V.* have a lasting effect **(bei** on); ‹medicine› continue to have an effect; ‹literary work› continue to have an influence

**Nach·wirkung** *die* after-effect; *(fig.: Einfluss)* influence

**nach|wollen** *itr. V. (ugs.)* **jmdm. ~:** want to follow sb.

**Nach·wort** *das; Pl.* **~e** afterword, postface **(zu** to)

**Nach·wuchs** *der; o. Pl* **A** *(fam.: Kind[er])* offspring; **sie erwartet ~:** she's expecting [a baby]; **B** *(junge Kräfte)* new blood; *(für eine Branche usw.)* new recruits *pl.; (in der Ausbildung)* trainees *pl.;* **der musikalische ~:** the rising generation of musicians

**Nachwuchs-: ~autor** *der,* **~autorin** *die* up-and-coming author; **~kraft** *die* new recruit; *(in der Ausbildung)* trainee; **~kräfte** junior staff; **~mangel** *der* lack of new blood *or* new recruits; **~sorgen** *Pl.* recruitment problems; **~spieler** *der,* **~spielerin** *die (Sport)* up-and-coming player

**nach|zahlen** *tr., itr. V.* **A** pay later; pay ‹salary› in arrears; **1 000 DM Steuern ~:** pay 1,000 marks back tax; **B** *(zusätzlich zahlen)* **25 DM ~:** pay another 25 marks

**nach|zählen** *tr., itr. V.* [re]count; check

**Nach·zahlung** *die* additional payment; *(spätere Zahlung)* deferred payment; *(Steuerzahlung)* back tax

**nach|zeichnen** *tr. V.* copy ‹picture›; draw ‹tree, horse›; *(mit Pauspapier o. Ä.)* trace ‹picture, tree, horse›; *(fig.: schildern)* portray

**Nach·zeitigkeit** *die;* **~** *(Sprachw.)* future sense of the subordinate clause

**nach|ziehen** **1** *unr. itr. V.* **A** *(ugs.: ebenso handeln)* do likewise; follow suit; **B** *mit sein (hinterhergehen)* **jmdm./einer Sache ~:** follow sb./sth.; **C** *mit sein (nachträglich übersiedeln)* **jmdm. ~:** [go to] join sb. **2** *unr. tr. V.* **A** *(hinter sich herziehen)* drag ‹foot, leg›; **B** *(verstärkend)* retrace, go over ‹line›; pencil ‹eyebrows›; **die Lippen ~:** put on more lipstick; **C** *(festziehen)* tighten [up] ‹nut, bolt›

**Nach·zug** *der (Eisenb.)* relief train

**Nachzügler** /-tsy:klɐ/ *der;* **~s, ~:** straggler; *(spät Ankommender)* latecomer

**Nackedei** /'nakədai/ *der;* **~s, ~s** **A** *(fam. scherzh.: Kind)* **[kleiner] ~:** naked little thing *or* monkey; little bare-bum *(Brit. coll.)*; **B** *(ugs. scherzh.: Person)* person in the buff; *(im Bild, Film usw.)* nude

**Nacken** /'nakn̩/ *der;* **~s, ~** ▶ 471 back *or* nape of the neck; *(Hals)* neck; **den Hut in den ~ schieben** push one's hat right back; **den Kopf in den ~ werfen** throw one's head right back; **das Haar fiel ihm bis in den ~:** his hair hung down the back of his neck; **die Arme im ~ verschränken** fold one's arms behind one's neck; **den ~ steif halten** *(fig. ugs.)* keep one's chin up; **jmdm. im ~ sitzen** *(fig.)* be breathing down sb.'s neck; **die Furcht/Angst sitzt ihm im ~:** he is gripped by fear

**nackend** *(veralt., noch landsch.)* ⇒ **nackt A**

**Nacken-: ~haar** *das* hair on the back of one's neck; neck hair; **~rolle** *die* bolster; **~schutz** *der* neck guard

**nackert** /'nakɐt/ *(südd., österr. ugs.)*, **nackig** *(bes. md.)* ⇒ **nackt A**

**nackt** /nakt/ *Adj.* **A** *(unbekleidet)* naked; bare ‹feet, legs, arms, skin, fists›; **mit ~em Oberkörper** stripped to the waist; **~ und bloß** completely naked; **sich ~ ausziehen** strip naked; strip off completely; **~ baden** bathe in the nude; **B** *(kahl)* bald ‹head›; hairless ‹chin›; featherless ‹bird›; bare ‹rocks, island, tree, branch, walls, bulb›; **auf dem ~en Boden schlafen** sleep on the bare floor; **C** *(unverhüllt)* stark ‹poverty, misery, horror›; naked ‹greed›; plain ‹fact, words›; plain, unvarnished ‹truth›; **~e Angst** sheer *or* stark terror; **D** bare ‹existence›; **das ~e Leben retten** barely manage to escape with one's life; save one's skin [and nothing more]

**Nackt-: ~arsch** *der (salopp scherzh.)* bare-bum *(Brit. coll.)*; bare-bottom; **~baden** *das;* **~~s** nude bathing; **~bade·strand** *der* nudist beach

**Nackte** *der/die; adj. Dekl.* naked man/woman; *(im Bild, Film usw.)* nude; **die ~n am Strand** the naked people *or* people in the nude on the beach

**Nackt-: ~foto** *das* nude photo; **~frosch** *der (fam. scherzh.)* **[kleiner] ~frosch** naked little thing *or* monkey; litte bare-bum *(Brit. coll.)*

**Nacktheit** *die;* **~:** nakedness; nudity; *(fig.: der Landschaft usw.)* bareness

**Nackt-: ~kultur** *die; (ugs.)* nudism *no art.;* **~samer** /-za:mɐ/ *der;* **~~s, ~~** *(Bot.)* gymnosperm; **~tänzerin** *die* nude dancer

**Nadel** /'na:dl̩/ *die;* **~, ~n** needle; *(Steck~, Hut~, Haar~)* pin; *(Häkel~)* hook; *(für Tonabnehmer)* stylus; **etw. mit heißer/mit der heißen ~ nähen** *(fig. ugs.)* sew sth. in a great hurry; **an der ~ hängen** *(fig. ugs.)* be on the needle *(sl.)*; **man konnte eine ~ fallen hören** you could have heard a pin drop

**nadel-, Nadel-: ~baum** *der* conifer; coniferous tree; **~drucker** *der (DV)* dot-matrix printer; **~förmig** *Adj.* needle-shaped; needle-like ‹point etc.›; **~geld** *das (veralt.)* pin money *no indef. art.;* **~holz** *das* **A** softwood; pinewood; **B** *(Baum)* conifer; **~kissen** *das* pincushion

**nadeln** *itr. V.* ‹tree› shed its needles

**Nadel-: ~öhr** *das* eye of a/the needle; **~spitze** *die* point of a/the needle; **~stärke** *die* needle size; size of needle; **~stich** *der* **A** *(Stich)* needle prick; *(einer Stecknadel usw.)* pinprick; *(fig.: Bosheit)* barbed *or (coll.)* snide remark; **jmdm. ~stiche versetzen** aim barbed *or (coll.)* snide remarks at sb.; **B** *(Nähstich)* stitch; **~streifen** *der* pinstripe; **~streifen·anzug** *der* pinstripe suit; **~wald** *der* coniferous forest

**Nadir** /na'di:ɐ̯/ *der;* **~s** *(Astron.)* nadir

**Nagel** /'na:gl̩/ *der;* **~s, Nägel** /'nɛ:gl̩/ **A** nail; *(Med.: für Bruchstellen)* pin; **B** *(fig.)* **ein ~ zu jmds. Sarg sein** *(salopp)* be a nail in sb.'s coffin; **den ~ auf den Kopf treffen** *(ugs.)* hit the nail on the head *(coll.)*; **Nägel mit Köpfen machen** *(ugs.)* do things properly; make a real job of it; **den Sport** *usw.*/**den Beruf an den ~ hängen** *(ugs.)* give up sport *etc./(coll.)* chuck in one's job; **seine Boxhandschuhe an den ~ hängen** *(ugs.)* hang up one's boxing gloves; **C** ▶ 471 *(Finger~, Zehen~)* nail; **das brennt mir auf** *od.* **unter den Nägeln** *(fig. ugs.)* it's so urgent I just have to get on with it *or* it just won't wait; **sich** *(Dat.)* **etw. unter den ~ reißen** *(fig. salopp)* make off with sth.; ⇒ *auch* **Schwarze**[3] **B**

**nagel-, Nagel-: ~bett** *das* ▶ 471 nail bed; **~brett** *das* bed of nails; **~bürste** *die* nail-brush; **~feile** *die* nail file; **~fest** ⇒ **niet- und nagelfest**; **~haut** *die* ▶ 471 cuticle; **~hautentferner** *der;* **~~s, ~~:** cuticle remover

n

**Nägel·kauen** *das;* **~s** nail-biting *no art.*

**Nagel-: ~kopf** *der* nail head; **~lack** *der* nail varnish (*Brit.*); nail polish; **~lackentferner** *der;* **~~s, ~~:** nail-varnish (*Brit.*) *or* nail-polish remover

**nageln** *tr. V.* nail (**an** + *Akk.* to, **auf** + *Akk.* on); (*Med.*) pin ‹bone, leg, etc.›; **aus Brettern Kisten ~:** nail planks together to make crates

**nagel-, Nagel-: ~neu** *Adj.* (*ugs.*) brand-new; **~pflege** *die* care of the nails; nail care; **~probe** *die* (*fig.*) acid test (**auf** + *Akk.* of); **die ~probe machen** try the acid test; **~reiniger** *der;* **~~s, ~~:** nail-cleaner; **~schere** *die* nail scissors *pl.;* **~schuh** *der* hobnailed boot; **~zange** *die* nail clippers *pl.*

**nagen** /ˈnaːɡn̩/ ❶ *itr. V.* gnaw; **an etw.** (*Dat.*) **~:** gnaw [at] sth.; **an der Unterlippe ~:** chew one's lower lip; **an jmdm. ~** (*fig.*) prey on sb.; **an jmds. Gesundheit ~** (*fig.*) undermine sb.'s health. ❷ *tr. V.* gnaw off; **ein Loch ins Holz ~:** gnaw a hole in the wood. ❸ *refl. V.* **sich durch etw. ~:** gnaw through sth.

**nagend** *Adj.* gnawing ‹pain, hunger, fear›; nagging ‹pain, doubts, uncertainty, etc.›

**Nage·tier** *das* rodent

**nah** /naː/ ⇨ **nahe**

**Näh·arbeit** *die* [piece of] sewing; **~en** sewing jobs; sewing *sing.*

**Nah-: ~aufnahme** *die* (*Fot.*) close-up [photograph]; **~bereich** *der* Ⓐ (*Fot.*) foreground; Ⓑ (*nähere Umgebung*) [immediate] surrounding area; locality; (*Fernspr.*) local area

**nah[e]** /ˈnaː(ə)/ ❶ *Adj.* **näher** /ˈnɛːɐ/, **nächst...** /nɛːçst.../ Ⓐ ▶265 (*räumlich*) near *pred.;* close *pred.;* nearby *attrib.;* **es ist ganz nah bis zum Bahnhof** it's not far to the station; **ich bin dir in Gedanken ~** (*geh.*) I am close to you *or* with you in my thoughts; **in der näheren Umgebung** in the neighbourhood; around here/there; **in der nächsten Umgebung von Köln** in the immediate neighbourhood of Cologne; ⇨ *auch* **Osten** C; Ⓑ (*zeitlich*) imminent; near *pred.;* **in ~r Zukunft** in the near future; **Weihnachten ist/die Ferien sind ~:** Christmas is/the holidays are nearly here; **die Rettung ist ~:** help is imminent *or* at hand; **das nahe Wochenende** the fast approaching weekend; Ⓒ (*eng*) close ‹relationship, relative, friend›; **seine nähere/nächste Verwandtschaft** his close/closest relatives *pl.* ❷ *adv.* **näher, am nächsten** Ⓐ ▶265 (*räumlich*) **~ an** (+ *Dat./Akk.*), **~ bei** close to; **~ gelegen** nearby; **komm mir nicht zu ~!** don't come too close!; keep your distance!; **~ beieinander** close together; **von nahem** from close up; at close quarters; **aus** *od.* **von nah und fern** (*geh.*) from near and far; (*fig.*) **jmdm. zu nahe treten** offend sb.; **jmdm. die moderne Kunst** *usw.* **nahe bringen** make modern art *etc.* accessible to sb.; (*lebendig machen*) bring modern art *etc.* to life for sb.; **jmdm. etw. näher bringen** make sth. more real *or* more accessible to sb.; **das brachte sie einander nahe** that brought them closer together; **jmdm. nahe gehen** affect sb. deeply; **einer Sache** (*Dat.*) **nahe kommen** come close to sth.; **jmdm. [menschlich] nahe kommen** get to know sb. well; **jmdm. [menschlich] näher kommen** get on closer terms with sb.; **sich** (*Dat.*) **näher kommen** become closer; **nahe legen** + *Akk.* suggest; give rise to ‹suspicion, supposition, thought›; **jmdm. etw. nahe legen** suggest sth. to sb.; **jmdm. den Rücktritt nahe legen, jmdm. nahe legen zurückzutreten** put it to sb. that he/she should resign; **nahe liegen** ‹thought› suggest itself; ‹suspicion, question› arise; **näher liegen** be more obvious; **was liegt da näher, als ...** what can be more obvious *or* natural than ...; **nahe liegend** ‹question, idea› which [immediately] suggests itself; natural ‹suspicion›; obvious ‹reason, solution›; **das nahe Liegende** the obvious thing [to do]; **jmdm. nahe stehen** be on close *or* intimate terms with sb.; **jmdm. näher stehen** be closer to sb.; **einer Partei nahe stehen** sympathize with a party; **eine der Witwe nahe stehende Cousine** a cousin who is/was on close terms with the widow; **die ihm nahe Stehenden** those close to him; Ⓑ (*zeitlich*) **~ an Mittag** nearly midday; **~ an die achtzig** (*ugs.*) pushing eighty (*coll.*); **~ bevorstehen** be in the offing; be fast approaching; **~ daran sein, etw. zu tun** be on the point of doing sth.; Ⓒ (*eng*) closely; **nah befreundet sein** be close friends; ⇨ *auch* **näher**. ❸ *Präp. mit Dat.* (*geh.*) near; close to; **den Tränen/dem Wahnsinn ~ sein** be on the brink of tears/on the verge of madness; **dem Tode ~ sein** be close to death

**Nähe** /ˈnɛːə/ *die;* **~** ▶818 Ⓐ closeness; proximity; (*Nachbarschaft*) vicinity; **in der ~ der Stadt** near the town; **in nächster** *od.* **unmittelbarer ~ des Sees** right next to the lake; **in meiner ~:** near me; (*um mich herum*) around me; (*in der Nachbarschaft*) in my neighbourhood; near where I live; **ich traue mich nicht in seine ~:** I dare not go anywhere near him; **seine ~ stört mich** having him around puts me off; **jmds. ~ suchen** seek sb.'s company; **menschliche Wärme und ~ spüren** feel the warmth of human friendship around one; **er wohnt in der ~/ganz in der ~:** he lives in the vicinity *or* nearby/very near; **irgendwo hier/dort [ganz] in der ~:** somewhere [very] near here/there; **bleibt in der ~!** stay nearby; don't go too far away; **etw. aus der ~ betrachten** take a closer look at sth.; **aus der ~ betrachtet** (*auch fig.*) viewed more closely; **in unmittelbare ~ rücken** ‹events› become imminent; **die zeitliche ~ zu den Ereignissen erlaubt noch keine distanzierte Analyse** the closeness *or* recentness of the events does not yet permit a detached analysis; ⇨ *auch* **greifbar** 1 A

**nahe-: ~bei** *Adv.* nearby; close by; ***~|bringen** ⇨ **nah[e]** 2 A; ***~|gehen** ⇨ **nah[e]** 2 A

**Nah·einstellung** *die* (*Fot.*) close focusing

**nahe-: *~|kommen** ⇨ **nah[e]** 2 A; ***~|legen** ⇨ **nah[e]** 2 A; ***~|liegen** ⇨ **nah[e]** 2 A; **~liegend** *Adj.* ‹question, idea› which [immediately] suggests itself; natural ‹suspicion›; obvious ‹reason, solution›; **das Naheliegende** the obvious thing [to do]; **~ sein** ‹thought› suggest itself; ‹suspicion, question› arise

**nahen** (*geh.*) ❶ *refl. V.; mit sein* (*veralt.: sich nähern*) approach; draw near *or* (*arch.*) nigh; **sich jmdm. ~:** approach sb. ❷ *itr. V.; mit sein* draw near; **sein/ihr Ende nahte** the end was near; **eine ~de Katastrophe** imminent disaster

**nähen** ❶ *itr. V.* sew; (*Kleider machen*) make clothes; **an einem Mantel ~:** work on [the sewing of] a coat. ❷ *tr. V.* Ⓐ sew ‹seam, hem›; (*mit der Maschine*) machine ‹seam, hem›; (*herstellen*) make ‹dress, coat, curtains, etc.›; **etw. an** *od.* **auf etw.** (*Akk.*) **~:** sew sth. on to sth.; Ⓑ (*Med.*) stitch ‹wound etc.›; **der Patient musste genäht werden** (*ugs.*) the patient had to have stitches; ⇨ *auch* **doppelt** 2 A

**näher** ❶ *Komp. zu* **nahe.** ❷ *Adj.* Ⓐ ▶265 (*kürzer*) shorter ‹way, road›; Ⓑ (*genauer*) further, more precise ‹information›; closer ‹investigation, inspection›; **die ~en Umstände** the precise circumstances; **bei ~em Hinsehen** on closer examination; **wissen Sie Näheres [darüber]?** do you know any more [about it]?; do you know any details?; **Näheres hierzu siehe unten** for further information on this see below; **des ~en** (*geh.*) in detail. ❸ *adv.* Ⓐ **bitte treten Sie ~!** please come in/nearer/this way; **es bringt uns unserem Ziel nicht ~:** it does not bring us any closer to our goal; Ⓑ (*genauer*) more closely; (*im Einzelnen*) in [more] detail; **etw. ~ ansehen** have a closer look at sth.; examine sth. more closely; **~ auf etw.** (*Akk.*) **eingehen, sich ~ mit etw. befassen** go into sth. in [more] detail; **jmdn./etw. ~ kennen lernen** get to know sb./sth. better; **ich kenne ihn nicht ~:** I don't know him well; **allmählich kommen wir der Sache ~:** we're gradually getting to the point

***näher|bringen** ⇨ **nah[e]** 2 A

**Nah·erholungs·gebiet** *das* nearby recreational area

**Näherin** *die;* **~, ~nen** needlewoman; (*hist.*) seamstress

**näher-: *~|kommen** ⇨ **nah[e]** 2 A; ***~|liegen** ⇨ **nah[e]** 2 A

**nähern** ❶ *refl. V.* Ⓐ (*herankommen*) approach; **die Tiere näherten sich bis auf wenige Meter** the animals came up to within a few metres; **sich jmdm./einer Sache** (*Dat.*) **~:** approach sb./sth.; draw nearer to sb./sth.; **sich dem Ende ~** ‹stay, summer› near its end, draw to an end; **sich dem Ziel der Reise ~:** near one's destination; Ⓑ (*Kontakt aufnehmen*) **sich jmdm. ~:** approach sb.; Ⓒ (*sich angleichen*) **sich einem Ideal ~:** come close to an ideal; approximate to an ideal. ❷ *tr. V.* (*heranbringen*) **etw. einer Sache** (*Dat.*) **~:** bring sth. closer to sth.

***näher|stehen** ⇨ **nah[e]** 2 A

**Näherung** *die;* **~, ~en** approximation

**Näherungs·wert** *der* (*Math.*) approximate value

**nahe-: *~|stehen** ⇨ **nah[e]** 2 A; ***~stehend** ⇨ **nah[e]** 2 A; **~zu** *Adv.* (*mit Adjektiven*) almost; nearly; well-nigh ‹impossible, superhuman›; all but ‹exhausted, impossible›; (*mit Zahlenangabe*) close on

**Näh-: ~faden** *der* sewing thread; **~garn** *das* [sewing] cotton

**Nah·kampf** *der* Ⓐ (*Milit.*) close combat; Ⓑ (*Boxen*) infighting

**Näh-: ~kästchen** *das* Ⓐ ⇨ **~kasten**; Ⓑ **aus dem ~kästchen plaudern** (*ugs. scherzh.*) tell all; (*als Kenner, Fachmann*) tell the inside story; **~kasten** *der* sewing box; workbox; **~korb** *der* sewing basket

**nahm** /naːm/ *1. u. 3. Pers. Sg. Prät. v.* **nehmen**

**Näh-: ~maschine** *die* sewing machine; **~nadel** *die* sewing needle

**Nah·ost** *in* **in/aus** *usw.* **~:** in/from *etc.* the Middle East

**nah·östlich** *Adj.* Middle Eastern

**Nähr-: ~boden** *der* culture medium; (*fig.*) breeding ground; **~creme** *die* skin food

**nähren** /ˈnɛːrən/ ❶ *tr. V.* Ⓐ (*ernähren*) feed ‹animal, child› (**mit** on); **gut/schlecht genährt** well-fed/underfed; Ⓑ (*geh.: entstehen lassen*) nurture ‹hope, suspicion, hatred›; cherish ‹desire, hope›; foster ‹plan, hatred›; Ⓒ (*geh.: Lebensunterhalt geben*) provide a [good] living for; **dieser Beruf nährt seinen Mann** you can make a good living in this job. ❷ *itr. V.* (*nahrhaft sein*) be nourishing. ❸ *refl. V.* (*geh.*) **sich von etw. ~:** live on sth.; ‹animal› feed on sth.

**nahrhaft** *Adj.* nourishing; nutritious; **ein ~es Essen** *od.* (*geh.*) **Mahl** a square meal

**Nähr-: ~lösung** *die* Ⓐ fluid culture medium; Ⓑ (*für Hydrokultur, künstliche Ernährung*) nutrient solution; **~salze** *Pl.* nutrient salts; **~stoffe** *Pl.* nutrients

**Nahrung** /ˈnaːrʊŋ/ *die;* **~:** food; **flüssige/feste ~:** liquids *pl.*/solids *pl.;* **die ~ verweigern** refuse food; **geistige ~** (*fig.*) intellectual nourishment; **dem Verdacht/den Gerüchten** *usw.* **~ geben** *od.* **bieten** (*fig.*) help to nurture *or* foster the suspicion/the rumours *etc.;* **es gab seinem Zorn neue ~** (*fig.*) it gave fresh fuel to his anger; it rekindled his anger

**Nahrungs-: ~aufnahme** *die* intake of food; **die ~aufnahme verweigern** refuse food; **~mittel** *das* food [item]; **~mittel** *Pl.* foodstuffs; **~mittel·chemie** *die* food chemistry *no art.;* **~mittel·industrie** *die* food *or* foodstuffs industry; **~quelle** *die* source of food; **~suche** *die* search for food; **auf ~suche gehen** search for food; (*jagen*) hunt for food

**Nähr·wert** *der* nutritional value; **keinen [sittlichen** *od.* **geistigen] ~ haben** (*fig. salopp*) be completely and utterly pointless

**Näh·seide** *die* sewing silk

**Naht** /naːt/ *die;* **~, Nähte** /ˈnɛːtə/ Ⓐ seam; **aus den** *od.* **allen Nähten platzen** (*fig. ugs.*) ‹person, fig.: institution etc.› be bursting at the seams; Ⓑ (*Med., Anat.*) suture

*old spelling (see note on page 1707)

**Näh·tisch** *der* sewing table

**naht·los** ❶ *Adj.* seamless; (*fig.*) perfectly smooth ‹transition›. ❷ *adv.* **Studium und Beruf gehen nicht ~ ineinander über** there is not a perfectly smooth transition from study to work

**Naht·stelle** *die* Ⓐ (*Schweißnaht*) seam; Ⓑ (*Berührungsstelle*) point of contact, interface (**von** between); (*Grenzlinie*) borderline

**Nah-: ~verkehr** *der* local traffic; **nur im ~verkehr eingesetzt werden** be used only for local services; **~verkehrs·mittel** *das* form of local transport; **~verkehrs·zug** *der* local train

**Näh·zeug** *das* sewing things *pl.*

**Nah·ziel** *das* short-term *or* immediate aim

**naiv** /na'i:f/ ❶ *Adj.* naïve; ingenuous ‹look, child›; unaffected ‹pleasure›; **ein ~er Zugang zur Musik** an unsophisticated approach to music; **die Naive/den Naiven spielen** act naïve. ❷ *adv.* naïvely; **sich ~ an etw.** (*Dat.*) **freuen** take an unaffected pleasure in sth.

**Naive** *die; adj. Dekl.* (*Theater*) ingénue

**Naivität** /naivi'tɛ:t/ *die;* **~:** naïvety; (*eines Blickes, Kindes*) ingenuousness; (*von Vergnügen*) unaffectedness

**Naivling** *der;* **~s, ~e** (*ugs. abwertend*) [naïve] simpleton

**Name** /'na:mə/ *der;* **~ns, ~n,** (*seltener*) **Namen** /'na:mən/ *der;* **~s, ~:** name; **wie ist der ~ dieser Tiere/Leute?** what are these animals/people called?; **die Dinge/das Unrecht beim ~n nennen** call a spade a spade/acknowledge injustice as such; **[gestatten,] mein ~ ist Maier** [allow me to introduce myself,] my name is Maier; **wie war gleich Ihr ~?** what was your name again?; **ich kenne ihn/es nur dem ~n nach** I know him/it only by name; **der Hund hört auf den ~n Fifi** the dog answers to the name of Fifi; **unter jmds. ~n** (*Dat.*) under sb.'s name; **das Konto läuft auf meinen ~n/das Auto ist auf meinen ~n gemeldet** the account is in/the car is registered in my name; **ein Mann mit ~n Emil** a man by the name of Emil; **er rief mich bei** *od.* **mit meinem ~n** he called me by my name; **in jmds./einer Sache ~n, im ~n von jmdm./etw.** on behalf of sb./sth.; **im eigenen ~n handeln** act on one's own account; **im ~n des Volkes/Gesetzes** (*Rechtsspr.*) in the name of the people/the law; **in Gottes ~n!** (*ugs.*) for God's sake; **sich** (*Dat.*) **einen ~n machen** make a name for oneself; ⇒ *auch* **daher** B; **Hase** A; **hergeben** A; **Kind** A

**namen-, Namen-: ~forschung** *die* ⇒ **~kunde**; **~gebung** *die;* **~~, ~~en** (*allgemein*) giving of names; (*in einem bes. Fall*) choice of name; **~gedächtnis** *das* memory for names; **~kunde** *die* onomastics *sing., no art.;* **~liste** *die* list of names; **~los** ❶ *Adj.* Ⓐ nameless; (*unbekannt*) unknown; anonymous ‹author, poet›; Ⓑ (*geh.: unbeschreiblich*) unspeakable, indescribable ‹misery›; inexpressible ‹joy›; ❷ *adv.* (*geh.*) unspeakably; unutterably; **~register** *das* ⇒ **~liste**

**namens** ❶ *Adv.* by the name of; called. ❷ *Präp. mit Gen.* (*Amtsspr.*) on behalf of

**Namens-: ~änderung** *die* change of name; **~gebung** *die;* **~~, ~~en** ⇒ **Namengebung**; **~nennung** *die* mention of a name/of names; (*Nennung des eigenen Namens*) giving of one's name; **~patron** *der,* **~patronin,** *die* patron saint; **~schild** *das* Ⓐ (*an Türen usw.*) nameplate; Ⓑ (*zum Anstecken*) name badge; **~tag** *der* name day; **sie hat am … ~tag** it is her name day on the …; **~vetter** *der* namesake; **~zug** *der* Ⓐ (*Unterschrift*) signature; Ⓑ (*veralt.: Monogramm*) monogram

**namentlich** /'na:məntlɪç/ ❶ *Adj.* by name *postpos.;* **eine ~e Liste** a list of names; **eine ~e Abstimmung** a roll-call vote. ❷ *Adv.* Ⓐ (*mit Namen*) by name; **jmdn. ~ nennen** mention sb. by name; name sb.; Ⓑ (*besonders*) particularly; especially

**namhaft** ❶ *Adj.* Ⓐ (*berühmt*) noted; of note *postpos.;* Ⓑ (*ansehnlich*) noteworthy ‹sum, difference›; notable ‹contribution, opportunity›; Ⓒ *in* **jmdn./etw. ~ machen** (*Papierdt.*) name sb./sth. ❷ *adv.* (*beträchtlich*) considerably

**Namibia** /na'mi:bi̯a/ (*das*)**;** **~s** Namibia

**Namibier** *der;* **~s, ~,** **Namibierin** *die;* **~, ~nen** Namibian

**nämlich** /'nɛ:mlɪç/ ❶ *Adv.* Ⓐ **er kann nicht kommen, er ist ~ krank** he cannot come, as he is ill; he can't come — he's ill[, you see] (*coll.*); Ⓑ (*und zwar*) namely; (*als Füllwort*) **das war ~ ganz anders** it was quite different in fact *or* actually. ❷ *Adj.* (*geh. veralt.*) same; (*steigernd*) selfsame

**nannte** /'nantə/ *1. u. 3. Pers. Sg. Prät. v.* **nennen**

**Nano·technologie** /'nano…/ *die* nanotechnology

**nanu** /na'nu:/ *Interj.* **~, was machst du denn hier?** hello, what are you doing here?; **~, wo ist denn der ganze Käse geblieben?** that's funny, what's happened to all that cheese?; **~, Sie gehen schon?** what, you're going already?

**Napalm** /'na:palm/ *das;* **~s** napalm

**Napalm·bombe** *die* napalm bomb

**Napf** /napf/ *der;* **~[e]s, Näpfe** /'nɛpfə/ bowl (*esp. for animal's food*)

**Napf·kuchen** *der* gugelhupf; ring cake

**Naphthalin** /nafta'li:n/ *das;* **~s** naphthalene

**Nappa** /'napa/ *das;* **~[s], ~s, Nappa·leder** *das* nappa [leather]

**Narbe** /'narbə/ *die;* **~, ~n** Ⓐ scar; **von dieser Verletzung werden ~n zurückbleiben** this wound will leave scars; **tiefe ~n bei jmdm. hinterlassen** (*fig.*) leave sb. deeply scarred; Ⓑ (*Bot.*) stigma

**Narben-: ~bildung** *die* scar formation; **~leder** *das* (*Gerberei*) grained leather; **~seite** *die* (*Gerberei*) hair *or* grain side

**narbig** *Adj.* scarred; (*von Pocken o. Ä.*) pitted; pockmarked

**Narbung** *die;* **~, ~en** (*Gerberei*) grain[ing]

**Narkose** /nar'ko:zə/ *die;* **~, ~n** (*Med.*) narcosis; **mit** *od.* **in/ohne ~:** under anaesthesia/without an anaesthetic; **dem Patienten eine ~ geben** give the patient a general anaesthetic; **aus der ~ aufwachen** come round from the anaesthetic; **jmdn. aus der ~ holen** awaken sb. from the anaesthetic

**Narkose-: ~arzt** *der,* **~ärztin** *die* anaesthetist; **~gewehr** *das* tranquillizer gun; **~mittel** *das* anaesthetic

**Narkotikum** /nar'ko:tikʊm/ *das;* **~s, Narkotika** (*Med.*) narcotic

**narkotisch** ❶ *Adj.* (*Med., auch fig.*) narcotic; overpowering ‹scent›. ❷ *adv.* **auf jmdn. ~ wirken** have a narcotic effect on sb.

**narkotisieren** *tr. V.* (*Med.*) anaesthetize ‹patient›; put ‹patient› under a general anaesthetic

**Narr** /nar/ *der;* **~en, ~en** fool; (*Hof~*) jester; fool; (*Fastnachts~*) carnival jester *or* reveller; **sich zum ~en machen** let oneself be fooled; **jmdn. zum ~en haben** *od.* **halten** play tricks on sb.; (*täuschen*) pull the wool over sb.'s eyes; **einen ~en an jmdm. gefressen haben** (*ugs.*) be dotty about sb. (*coll.*)

**narren** /'narən/ *tr. V.* (*geh.*) **jmdn. ~:** make a fool of sb.; (*täuschen*) deceive sb.

**narren-, Narren-: ~freiheit** *die* freedom to do as one pleases; **jmdm. ~freiheit gewähren** let sb. do as he/she pleases; **~hände** *Pl. in* **~hände beschmieren Tisch und Wände** (*Spr.*) little vandals scribble on everything; **~kappe** *die* (*hist.*) jester's cap and bells; **~possen** *Pl.* (*geh. veralt.*) tomfoolery *sing.;* **~sicher** (*ugs.*) ❶ *Adj.* foolproof; ❷ *adv.* in a foolproof way; **~zepter** *das* jester's sceptre *or* bauble

**Narretei** /narə'tai̯/ *die;* **~, ~en** (*geh.*) Ⓐ (*Scherz*) prank; **~en** fooling about *sing.;* Ⓑ (*Torheit*) folly; stupidity

**Narrheit** *die;* **~, ~en** Ⓐ (*Art*) foolishness; Ⓑ (*Handlung*) foolish prank

**Närrin** /'nɛrɪn/ *die;* **~, ~nen** fool; **liebe ~nen und Narren!** my dear she-asses and jackasses! (*form of address used by speakers at carnival time*)

**narrisch** (*südd.*) ⇒ **närrisch** 1 A, B, 2 A, B

**närrisch** /'nɛrɪʃ/ ❶ *Adj.* Ⓐ (*verrückt*) crazy; (*wirr im Kopf*) scatterbrained; dotty (*coll.*); **[ein] ~es Zeug reden** talk gibberish; **halb/ganz ~ [vor Glück]** be almost/quite beside oneself [with joy]; **auf etw.** (*Akk.*) *od.* **nach etw. ganz ~ sein** be mad keen on sth. (*coll.*); Ⓑ (*ugs.: sehr viel, groß*) terrific (*coll.*); **ein ~es Geld** a fantastic amount of money (*coll.*); Ⓒ (*karnevalistisch*) carnival-crazy ‹season›; **das ~e Treiben [beim Karneval** *od.* **Fasching]** the mad *or* crazy carnival antics *pl.*
❷ *adv.* Ⓐ (*verrückt*) crazily; **sich ~ benehmen** carry on like a madman/madwoman; act crazy; Ⓑ (*ugs.: sehr*) terrifically (*coll.*); **~ verliebt sein** be madly in love (*coll.*)

**Narziss, *Narziß** /nar'tsɪs/ *der;* **~** *od.* **Narzisses, Narzisse** Narcissus

**Narzisse** /nar'tsɪsə/ *die;* **~, ~n** narcissus; **gelbe ~:** daffodil

**Narzissmus, *Narzißmus** *der;* **~** (*Psych.*) narcissism

**narzisstisch, *narzißtisch** *Adj.* (*Psych.*) narcissistic

**nasal** /na'za:l/ ❶ *Adj.* nasal. ❷ *adv.* nasally

**Nasal** *der;* **~s, ~e** (*Sprachw.*) nasal

**nasalieren** *tr. V.* (*Sprachw.*) nasalize

**Nasal·laut** *der* (*Sprachw.*) nasal

**naschen** /'naʃn̩/ ❶ *itr. V.* Ⓐ (*Süßes essen*) eat sweet things; (*Bonbons essen*) eat sweets (*Brit.*) *or* (*Amer.*) candy; **[so] gern ~:** have [such] a sweet tooth; Ⓑ (*heimlich essen*) have a nibble; **er hat vom Pudding genascht** he's been at the pudding. ❷ *tr. V.* Ⓐ (*essen*) eat ‹sweets, chocolate, etc.›; Ⓑ (*heimlich essen*) **er/sie hat Milch genascht** he/she has been at the milk

**Näschen** /'nɛ:sçən/ *das;* **~s, ~:** little nose

**Nascherei** *die;* **~, ~en** Ⓐ [continually] eating sweet things; **hör auf mit der ~!** don't keep eating sweet things all the time!; Ⓑ (*Süßigkeit*) **~en** sweets

**naschhaft** *Adj.* fond of sweet things *postpos.;* sweet-toothed; **[so] ~ sein** have [such] a sweet tooth

**Naschhaftigkeit** *die;* **~:** fondness for sweet things; **ihre ~ kostet viel Geld** her sweet tooth comes expensive

**Nasch-: ~katze** *die* (*fam.*) compulsive nibbler; (*Süßigkeiten naschend*) compulsive sweet (*Brit.*) *or* (*Amer.*) candy eater; **~sucht** *die* addiction to sweet things; **~werk** *das* (*veralt.*) sweet titbits

**Nase** /'na:zə/ *die;* **~, ~n** Ⓐ ▶ 471 nose; **mir blutet die ~:** my nose is bleeding; I've got a nosebleed; **mir läuft die ~, meine ~ läuft** I've got a runny nose; Ⓑ (*fig.*) **direkt vor deiner ~** (*ugs.*) right under your nose; **der Bus ist mir vor der ~ weggefahren** (*ugs.*) I missed the bus by a whisker; **jmdm. die Tür vor der ~ zuschlagen** (*ugs.*) shut the door in sb.'s face; **jmdm. etw. vor der ~ wegschnappen** (*ugs.*) snatch sth. from under sb.'s nose; **man hat ihm einen jungen Manager vor die ~ gesetzt** (*ugs.*) they have appointed a young manager over his head; **die ~ voll haben** (*ugs.*) have had enough; **von jmdm./etw. die ~ [gestrichen] voll haben** (*ugs.*) be sick [to death] of sb./sth.; **seine ~ in etw./alles stecken** (*ugs.*) stick one's nose into sth./everything (*coll.*); **nicht weiter sehen als seine ~** (*ugs.*) see no further than the end of one's nose; **ihm passt** *od.* **gefällt deine ~ nicht** (*ugs.*) he doesn't like your face; **sich** (*Dat.*) **die ~ begießen** (*ugs.*) have a drink or two; **die** *od.* **seine ~ in die Bücher stecken** (*ugs.*) get down to one's studies; **jmdm. eine lange ~ machen** *od.* **eine ~ drehen** (*ugs.*) cock a snook at sb.; **immer der ~ nach** (*ugs.*) just follow your nose; **fass dich an die eigene ~!** (*ugs.*) you're a fine one to talk!; **jmdn. an der ~ herumführen** (*ugs.*) pull the wool over sb.'s eyes; **auf der ~ liegen** (*ugs.*) be laid up; **auf die ~ fallen** (*ugs.*) come a cropper (*sl.*); **jmdm. etw. auf die ~ binden** (*ugs.*) let sb. in on sth.; **jmdm. auf der ~ herumtanzen** (*ugs.*) play sb. up; **jmdm. eins** *od.* **was auf die ~**

**geben** (*ugs.*) put sb. in his/her place; **jmdm. etw. aus der ~ ziehen** (*ugs.*) worm sth. out of sb.; **das sticht mir schon lange in die ~** (*ugs.*) I've had my eye on that for a long time; **jmdn. mit der ~ auf etw.** (*Akk.*) **stoßen** (*ugs.*) spell sth. out to sb.; **pro ~** (*ugs.*) per head; **jmdm. unter die ~ reiben, dass ...** (*ugs.*) rub it in that ...; **das brauchst du mir nicht unter die ~ zu reiben** (*ugs.*) you don't have to rub my nose in it; ⇒ *auch* **Mund**; **rümpfen**; **C** (*Geruchssinn, Gespür*) nose; **eine gute ~ für etw. haben** have a good nose for sth.; (*etw. intuitiv wissen*) have a sixth sense for sth.; **D** (*geh.: Bug*) bow; (*eines Flugzeugs*) nose; **E** (*Felsvorsprung*) spur; **F** (*ugs.: Farbtropfen*) run

**nase·lang** ⇒ **nasenlang**

**näseln** /ˈnɛːzl̩n/ *itr. V.* talk through one's nose

**näselnd** **1** *Adj.* nasal. **2** *adv.* nasally; **~ sprechen** speak in a nasal tone

**nasen-, Nasen-:** **~bär** *der* coati; **~bein** *das* ▶ 471 nasal bone; **~bluten** *das;* **~~s** bleeding from the nose; **~bluten haben/bekommen** have/get a nosebleed; **~flügel** *der* ▶ 471 side of the nose; (*einschl. ~loch*) nostril; **~höhle** *die* ▶ 471 (*Anat.*) nasal cavity; **~lang** *in* **alle ~lang** constantly; all the time; **~länge** *die:* **mit einer ~länge** (*Pferdesport*), **um eine ~länge** (*fig.*) by a head; **er war mir um eine ~länge voraus** he was fractionally ahead of me; **~loch** *das* ▶ 471 nostril; **~pflaster** *das* nose plaster; **~ring** *der* nosering; **~rücken** *der* ▶ 471 ridge of the/one's nose; **~scheide·wand** *die* ▶ 471 nasal septum; **~schleim** *der* nasal mucus; **~schleim·haut** *die* ▶ 471 nasal mucous membrane; **~spitze** *die* ▶ 471 tip of the/one's nose; **nicht weiter sehen, als die ~spitze reicht** (*fig. ugs.*) not be able to see further than the end of one's nose; **jmdm. etw. an der ~spitze ansehen** (*fig. ugs.*) tell sth. by sb.'s face; **~spray** *der od. das* nasal spray; **~stüber** *der;* **~~s, ~~:** swat on the nose; **~tropfen** *Pl.* nose drops; **~wurzel** *die* ▶ 471 root of the nose

**nase-, Nase-:** **~rümpfen** *das;* **~~s:** **mit ~rümpfen** with a look of disgust *or* disdain; **dafür hat sie nur ein ~rümpfen übrig** she only turns up her nose at that; **~rümpfend** **1** *Adj.* disapproving; **2** *adv.* disdainfully; **~weis** **1** *Adj.* precocious; pert ‹remark, reply›; **sei nicht so ~weis!** don't be such a little know-all!; **2** *adv.* precociously; **~weis** *der;* **~~es, ~~e** (*fam.*) [little] know-all; [little] clever Dick (*coll.*)

**nas-, Nas-:** **~führen** *tr. V.* lead up the garden path; **sich genasführt fühlen** feel one has been led up the garden path; **~horn** *das* rhinoceros; **~lang** ⇒ **nasenlang**

**-nasig** *adj.* -nosed

**nass, *naß** /nas/, **nasser** *od.* **nässer** /ˈnɛsɐ/, **nassest...** *od.* **nässest...** /ˈnɛsəst.../ **1** *Adj.* **A** wet; **~ machen** + *Akk.* make wet; sprinkle ‹washing›; **sich/das Bett ~ machen** wet oneself/one's bed; **mit nassen Augen** with tears in one's eyes; **durch und durch** *od.* **bis auf die Haut ~:** wet through; soaked to the skin; **~ geschwitzt** soaked in sweat *postpos.;* **wie ein nasser Sack** (*ugs.*) as limp as a wet sack; **ein nasses Grab** (*dichter.*) a watery grave; **mach dich bloß nicht ~!** (*fig. salopp*) don't overdo it! (*iron.*); **jmdn. ~ machen** (*Sportjargon*) trounce sb.; beat sb. hollow (*coll.*); **B** **für ~** (*bes. berlin. u. ostmd.*) for free; for nothing.

**2** *adv.* **sich ~ rasieren** have a wet shave; (*immer*) use a razor and shaving cream

**Nass, *Naß** *das;* **Nasses** (*dichter. od. scherzh.*) **A** (*Wasser*) water; (*Regen*) wetness (*esp. joc.*); **hinein ins kühle ~!** in[to the water] we go!; **B** (*Getränk*) **das edle** *od.* **kostbare ~:** the precious liquid

**Nassauer** /ˈnasauɐ/ *der;* **~s, ~, Nassauerin** *die;* **~, ~nen** (*ugs. abwertend*) sponger; (*Schnorrer[in]*) scrounger (*coll.*)

**nassauern** (*ugs. abwertend*) **1** *tr. V.* **etw. bei jmdm. ~:** scrounge sth. from sb. (*coll.*). **2** *itr. V.* scrounge (*coll.*)

**Nässe** /ˈnɛsə/ *die;* **~:** wetness; (*an Wänden usw.*) dampness; **bei ~:** in the wet; in wet weather; **„vor ~ schützen"** 'protect from damp'

**nässen** **1** *itr. V.* ‹wound, eczema› suppurate. **2** *tr. V.* (*geh.*) make wet; wet ‹bed, feet, etc.›

**nass, *naß-, Nass, *Naß-:** **~forsch** **1** *Adj.* brash. **2** *adv.* brashly; ***~geschwitzt** ⇒ **nass** 1 A; **~kalt** *Adj.* cold and wet; raw; **~rasur** *die* wet shaving *no art.;* **zur ~rasur braucht man ...** for a wet shave one needs ...; **~wäsche** *die: washing not dried by the laundry;* wet washing

**Nas·tuch** *das; Pl.* **Nastücher** (*schweiz.*) handkerchief

**Nation** /naˈtsi̯oːn/ *die;* **~, ~en** nation; **die Vereinten ~en** the United Nations *sing.;* **der Liebling der ~ sein** (*ugs.*) be a national hero

**national** /natsi̯oˈnaːl/ **1** *Adj.* **A** national; **~e und internationale Märkte** domestic and international markets; **B** (*patriotisch*) nationalist. **2** *adv.* **A** (*innerstaatlich*) at a national level; nationally; **B** (*patriotisch*) ‹think, feel› nationalistically

**national-, National-:** **~bewusst, *~bewußt** *Adj.* nationally conscious; **~bewusst sein** be conscious of one's nationality; have a sense of national identity; **~bewusst·sein, *~bewußt·sein** *das* [sense of] national consciousness; sense of national identity; **~charakter** *der* national character; **~china** (*das*) (*veralt.*) Nationalist China

**Nationale** *das;* **~s, ~** (*österr.*) **A** personal details *or* particulars *pl.;* **B** (*Fragebogen*) form *or* questionnaire asking for personal details

**National-:** **~elf** *die* (*Fußball*) national team *or* side; **~epos** *das* national epic; **~farben** *Pl.* national colours; **~feier·tag** *der* national holiday; **~flagge** *die* national flag; **~gefühl** *das* national feeling; feeling for one's country; **~gericht** *das* national dish; **~getränk** *das* national drink; **~held** *der* national hero; **~heldin** *die* national heroine; **~hymne** *die* national anthem

**nationalisieren** *tr. V.* nationalize

**Nationalisierung** *die;* **~, ~en** nationalization

**Nationalismus** *der;* **~:** nationalism *usu. no art.*

**Nationalist** *der;* **~en, ~en, Nationalistin** *die;* **~, ~nen** nationalist

**nationalistisch** **1** *Adj.* nationalist; nationalistic. **2** *adv.* nationalistically

**Nationalität** /natsi̯onaliˈtɛːt/ *die;* **~, ~en** ▶ 553 nationality; **welcher ~ sind Sie?** what nationality are you?

**Nationalitäten-:** **~frage** *die* problem of different nationalities within one state; **~staat** *der* multinational state

**national-, National-:** **~literatur** *die* national literature; **~mannschaft** *die* national team; **~ökonomie** *die* political economy *no art.;* **~park** *der* national park; **~preis** *der:* (*DDR*) *annual award for achievement in science, technology, and the arts;* **~rat** *der* **A** (*österr., schweiz.*) National Council; **B** (*Mitglied*) member of the National Council; **C** (*DDR*) *highest governing body of the 'Nationale Front';* **~rätin** *die* ⇒ **~rat** B; **~sozialismus** *der* National Socialism; **~sozialist** *der,* **~sozialistin** *die* National Socialist; **~sozialistisch** **1** *Adj.* National Socialist; **2** *adv.* **eindeutig ~sozialistisch geprägt sein** bear all the marks of National Socialism; **~spieler** *der,* **~spielerin** *die* (*Sport*) national player; international; **~sprache** *die* national language; **~staat** *der* nation state; **~staatlich** *Adj.* **~staatliche Bestrebungen** efforts towards the creation of a nation state; **~staatliches Denken** thinking in nationalistic terms; **~stolz** *der* national pride; **~straße** *die* (*schweiz.*) national highway; **~tracht** *die* national costume; **~versammlung** *die* National Assembly

**nativ** *Adj.* virgin ‹olive oil›

**NATO, Nato** /ˈnaːto/ *die;* **~:** NATO; Nato *no art.*

**nato·grün** *Adj.* dark olive green

**NATO-Staat** *der* NATO state *or* country

**Natrium** /ˈnaːtri̯ʊm/ *das;* **~s** (*Chemie*) sodium

**Natron** /ˈnaːtrɔn/ *das;* **~s; [doppeltkohlensaures] ~:** sodium bicarbonate; bicarbonate of soda; bicarb (*coll.*); **[kohlensaures] ~:** sodium carbonate; soda

**Natron·lauge** *die* caustic soda [solution]

**Natter** /ˈnatɐ/ *die;* **~, ~n** colubrid; **eine ~ am Busen nähren** (*fig. geh.*) nurture a viper in one's bosom (*literary*)

**Nattern·gezücht** *das* (*veralt. abwertend*) nest of vipers

**Natur** /naˈtuːɐ̯/ *die;* **~, ~en** **A** nature *no art.;* **die Wunder der ~:** the wonders of nature; **wider die ~:** unnatural; **zurück zur ~:** back to nature; **die unberührte ~:** unspoilt nature; **die freie ~:** [the] open countryside; **Tiere in freier ~ sehen** see animals in the wild; **nach der ~ zeichnen/malen** draw/paint from nature; **B** (*Art, Eigentümlichkeit*) nature; **eine gesunde/eiserne/labile ~ haben** (*ugs.*) have a healthy/cast-iron/delicate constitution; **das widerspricht ihrer ~:** it is not in her nature; **jmdm. gegen** *od.* **wider die ~ gehen** go against sb.'s nature; **jmdm. zur zweiten ~ werden** become second nature to sb.; **die Verletzung war nur leichter ~:** the injury was only slight; **in der ~ der Sache/der Dinge liegen** be in the nature of things; **C** (*Mensch*) sort *or* type of person; sort (*coll.*); type (*coll.*); **D** (*natürlicher Zustand*) **Möbel in Kiefer ~:** natural pine furniture; **sie ist von ~ aus blond/ein gutmütiger Mensch** she is naturally fair/good-natured; **Hat sie eine Dauerwelle? — Nein, das ist alles ~:** Is her hair permed? — No, it's naturally curly

**Natural·abgaben** *Pl.* taxes [paid] in kind

**Naturalien** /natuˈraːli̯ən/ *Pl.* natural produce *sing.* (*used as payment*); **in ~** (*Dat.*) **bezahlen** pay in kind

**Naturalien·kabinett** *das* (*veralt.*) natural-history collection

**naturalisieren** *tr. V.* (*auch Biol.*) naturalize; **sich ~:** become naturalized

**Naturalisierung** *die;* **~, ~en** (*auch Biol.*) naturalization

**Naturalismus** *der;* **~:** naturalism

**Naturalist** *der;* **~en, ~en, Naturalistin** *die;* **~, ~nen** naturalist

**naturalistisch** **1** *Adj.* **A** naturalistic; **B** (*den Naturalismus betreffend*) naturalist. **2** *adv.* **A** ‹paint, describe› naturalistically; **B** (*den Naturalismus betreffend*) naturalistically; ‹influenced› by naturalism

**Natural-:** **~lohn** *der* wages *pl.* [paid] in kind; **~wirtschaft** *die* barter economy

**natur-, Natur-:** **~apostel** *der* (*iron.*) back-to-nature freak (*coll.*); **~belassen** *Adj.* natural ‹oils, foods, etc.›; **~beobachtung** *die* observation of nature; **~beschreibung** *die* description of nature; **~blond** *Adj.* naturally fair *or* blond; **~bursche** *der* child of nature; **~darm** *der* natural [animal] intestine (*used as sausage-casing*); **~denkmal** *das* natural monument; **~dünger** *der* natural fertilizer

**nature** /naˈtyːɐ̯/ *indekl. Adj.* (*Gastr.*) ‹steak, escalope, etc.› au naturel

**Naturell** *das;* **~s, ~e** disposition; temperament; **das widerspricht seinem ~:** it's not in his nature

**natur-, Natur-:** **~ereignis** *das* natural phenomenon; (*Versicherungsw.*) act of God; **~erscheinung** *die* natural phenomenon; **~erzeugnis** *das* ⇒ **~produkt**; **~farbe** *die* **A** natural colour; **B** (*Farbstoff*) natural dye; **~farben** *Adj.* natural-coloured ‹leather, wool, wood, etc.›; **~faser** *die* natural fibre; **~film** *der* nature film; **~forscher** *der,* **~forscherin** *die* naturalist; **~forschung** *die* natural-history research; **~freund** *der,* **~freundin** *die* nature lover; **~gegeben** *Adj.* natural and inevitable ‹state of affairs›; **etw. als ~gegeben ansehen** regard sth. as part of the natural order [of things]; **~gemäß** **1** *Adv.* naturally; **2** *adj.* **A** natural; ‹forest

*old spelling (see note on page 1707)

n

# Nationalität

## 1. Adjektive

Alle Nationalitätsbezeichnungen im Englischen werden groß geschrieben:

***die italienische Sprache***
= the Italian language

***ein indischer Brauch***
= an Indian custom

***Diese Haltung ist typisch deutsch***
= This attitude is typically German

Wenn man bloß die Nationalität einer Person angeben will, verwendet man im Englischen oft das prädikative Adjektiv, wo man im Deutschen das Substantiv verwendet:

***Seine Frau ist Schottin***
= His wife is Scottish

***Der Lehrer ist Franzose***
= The teacher is French

Diese Adjektive werden von den Ländernamen abgeleitet. Bei Ländernamen, die auf **-a** enden, werden sie durch Hinzufügen eines **-n** gebildet, und bei denen, die auf **-y** enden, wird das **-y** durch **-ian** ersetzt. (Ausnahmen: China→Chinese; Germany→German; Canada→Canadian).

America→American
Australia→Australian
Roumania→Roumanian
Italy→Italian
Austria→Austrian
Russia→Russian
India→Indian
Burgundy→Burgundian usw.

Andere Ableitungen sind nicht regelmäßig gebildet. Mehrere enden auf **-ish**, den deutschen Formen entsprechend:

England→English
Scotland→Scottish
Turkey→Turkish
Finland→Finnish
Britain→British
Spain→Spanish
Denmark→Danish

Sonstige Beispiele:

France→French
Iceland→Icelandic
Greece→Greek

## 2. Substantive

Die Bezeichnungen der Einwohner haben die gleiche Form wie das Adjektiv, sofern dieses auf **-an** oder **-ese** endet. Die substantivierte Einwohnerbezeichnung erfordert im Singular einen Artikel:

***ein reicher Amerikaner***
= a rich American

***die Inder***
= the Indians

***Sie heiratet einen Italiener***
= She is marrying an Italian

***Als Japanerin fühlt sie sich benachteiligt***
= As a Japanese she feels disadvantaged

Die Substantive, die auf **-ese** und **-ss** enden, lauten im Singular und Plural gleich:

***die Chinesen***
= the Chinese

***die Schweizer***
= the Swiss

In den Fällen, wo das entsprechende Adjektiv auf **-[i]sh** oder **-ch** endet, wird oft **-man** bzw. **-woman** angefügt (im Plural **-men** bzw. **-women**). Nur wenn das Volk gemeint ist, verwendet man oft die Form des Adjektivs. Andere Formen sind unregelmäßig, aber meist ihren deutschen Entsprechungen sehr ähnlich:

English→Englishman/Englishwoman→Englishmen/Englishwomen; the English

Scottish, Scots→Scot, Scotsman/Scotswoman→Scotsmen/Scotswomen; the Scots

Welsh→Welshman/Welshwoman→Welshmen/Welshwomen; the Welsh

Irish→Irishman/Irishwoman→Irishmen/Irishwomen; the Irish

French→Frenchman/Frenchwoman→Frenchmen/Frenchwomen; the French

Dutch→Dutchman/Dutchwoman→Dutchmen/Dutchwomen; the Dutch

British→Briton→Britons; the British

Swedish→Swede→Swedes; the Swedish

Finnish→Finn→Finns; the Finnish

Danish→Dane→Danes; the Danish

Spanish→Spaniard→Spaniards; the Spanish

Polish→Pole→Poles; the Polish

Turkish→Turk→Turks; the Turkish

***eine Britin/Schwedin/Finnin/Dänin/Spanierin/Polin/Türkin*** kann nur als 'a British/Swedish/Finnish/Danish/Spanish/Polish/Turkish woman/girl' übersetzt werden.

## Sonstige Ausdrücke

***Sie ist von Geburt Spanierin***
= She is Spanish by birth

***Er ist deutscher Abstammung***
= He is of German extraction

***Ich stamme aus Norddeutschland***
= I come from North Germany

***Er ist belgischer Staatsbürger***
= He is a Belgian national

***ein eingebürgerter Schweizer***
= a naturalized Swiss [citizen]

n

‹management› in keeping with the natural environment; **~geschichte** *die* (A) natural history; (B) (*veralt.*) ⇒ **~kunde**; **~geschichtlich** ❶ *Adj.* natural history; ‹teaching› of natural history; **die ~geschichtliche Entwicklung des Menschen** the natural history of mankind; ❷ *adv.* from the point of view of natural history; **~gesetz** *das* law of nature; **~getreu** ❶ *Adj.;* lifelike ‹portrait, imitation›; faithful ‹reproduction›; ❷ *adv.* ‹draw› true to life; ‹reproduce› faithfully; **etw. ~getreu darstellen** portray sth. in a true-to-life way; **~gewalt** *die* force of nature; **~gottheit** *die* (*Rel.*) nature deity; **~haft** *Adj.* (*geh.*) natural; **~heil·kunde** *die* naturopathy *no art.;* **~heil·verfahren** *das* naturopathic treatment; **~identisch** *Adj.* nature-identical; **~katastrophe** *die* natural disaster; **~kind** *das* child of nature; **~kraft** *die* force of nature; **~krause** *die* naturally frizzy hair *no indef. art.;* **~kunde** *die* (*veralt.*) nature study *no art.;* **~kundlich** *Adj.* natural-history ‹museum, field trip, etc.›; **~landschaft** *die* natural *or* unspoilt landscape; **~lehr·pfad** *der* nature trail

**natürlich** /na'ty:ɐ̯lɪç/ ❶ *Adj.* natural; **eines ~en Todes sterben** die a natural death; die of natural causes; **ein Bild in ~er Größe** a life-size portrait; **das ist die ~ste Sache der Welt** it is the most natural thing in the world; ⇒ *auch* **Person**. ❷ *adv.* ‹laugh, behave› naturally. ❸ *Adv.* (A) (*selbstverständlich, wie erwartet*) naturally; of course; (B) (*zwar*) of course; **er wird natürlich zustimmen, aber ...** of course he is bound to agree, but ...

**natürlicher·weise** *Adv.* naturally; of course

**Natürlichkeit** *die;* **~:** naturalness

**natur-, Natur-: ~locken** *Pl.* natural curls; **~nah[e]** *Adj.* ‹life, existence› close to nature; semi-natural; **~notwendigkeit** *die* objective necessity; **~park** *der* ≈ national park; **~philosophie** *die* philosophy of nature; **~produkt** *das* natural product; **~produkte** natural produce *sing.;* **~recht** *das* natural law; **~rein** *Adj.* pure ‹honey, jam, fruit, juice, etc.›; ‹wine› free of additives; **~religion** *die* nature religion; **~schauspiel** *das* natural spectacle; **~schönheit** *die* site of natural beauty; **~schutz** *der* [nature] conservation; **unter ~schutz** (*Dat.*) **stehen** be protected by law; be a protected species/variety/area *etc.;* **etw. unter ~schutz** (*Akk.*) **stellen** protect sth. by law; **~schutz·gebiet** *das* nature reserve; **~seide** *die* real *or* natural silk; **~stein** *der* natural stone; **~stoff** *der* natural substance; **~talent** *das* [great] natural talent *or* gift; (*begabter Mensch*) naturally talented *or* gifted person; **ein ~talent sein** have a [great] natural gift *or* talent; **~ton** *der; Pl.* **~töne** (*Musik*) natural note; **~trieb** *der* (*veralt.*) [natural] instinct; **~trüb** *Adj.* unfiltered, naturally cloudy ‹fruit juice›; **~verbunden** *Adj.* ‹person› in tune with nature; **~volk** *das* primitive people; **~widrig** *Adj.* unnatural; against nature *postpos.;* **~wissenschaft** *die* natural science *no art.;* **die ~wissenschaften** the [natural] sciences; **~wissenschaftler** *der*, **~wissenschaftlerin** *die* [natural] scientist;

**~wissenschaftlich** ❶ *Adj.* scientific; ❷ *adv.* scientifically; **~wüchsig** (*Philos.*) ❶ *Adj.* natural; organic; ❷ *adv.* naturally; organically; **~wunder** *das* miracle *or* wonder of nature

**nauf** /nauf/ (*südd.*) ⇒ **hinauf**

**naus** /naus/ (*südd.*) ⇒ **hinaus**

**Nautik** /'nautɪk/ *die;* ~ Ⓐ nautical science *no art.;* Ⓑ (*Navigation*) navigation *no art.*

**nautisch** /'nautɪʃ/ *Adj.* (*Seew.*) naval ‹officer›; navigational ‹instrument, calculation›

**Navel·orange** /'na:vl̩-/ *die* navel orange

**Navigation** /naviga'tsjo:n/ *die;* ~ (*Seew., Flugw.*) navigation *no art.*

**Navigations-:** **~fehler** *der* (*Seew., Flugw.*) navigational error; **~instrument** *das* (*Seew., Flugw.*) navigational instrument; **~karte** *die* (*Seew., Flugw.*) navigational chart; **~offizier** *der* (*Seew., Flugw.*) navigating officer

**Navigator** /naviga'to̯r/ *der;* **~s, ~en, Navigatorin** *die;* **~, ~nen** (*Seew., Flugw.*) navigator

**navigieren** *tr., itr. V.* navigate

**Nazarener** /natsa're:nɐ/ *der;* **~s,** ~, **Nazarenerin** *die;* **~, ~nen** Nazarene

**Nazareth** /'na:tsarɛt/ (*das*); **~s** Nazareth

**Nazi** /'na:tsi/ *der;* **~s, ~s** Nazi

**Nazi·deutschland** (*das*) Nazi Germany

**Nazismus** *der;* **~:** Nazi[i]sm *no art.*

**nazistisch** *Adj.* Nazi

**Nazi-:** **~vergangenheit** *die* Nazi past; **~zeit** *die* Nazi period

**NB, N.B.** *Abk.* **notabene** NB

**n.Br.** *Abk.* **nördliche[r] Breite; 60° n.Br.** lat. 60°N

**n.Chr.** *Abk.* ▶ 207 **nach Christus** AD

**NDR** *Abk.* **Norddeutscher Rundfunk** North German Radio

**ne** /nə/ (*ugs.*) ⇒ **nicht** C

**'ne** /nə/ (*ugs.*) ⇒ **eine**

**Neandertaler** /ne'andɐta:lɐ/ *der;* **~s,** ~ (*Anthrop.*) Neanderthal man; **[die] Neandertaler lebten in ...** Neanderthal man *sing.* lived in ...

**Neapel** /ne'a:pl̩/ (*das*); **~s** ▶ 700 Naples

**Neapolitaner** /neapoli'ta:nɐ/ *der;* **~s,** ~ Ⓐ Neapolitan; Ⓑ (*österr.: Gebäck*) wafer biscuit with chocolate cream filling

**Neapolitanerin** *die;* **~, ~nen** ⇒ **Neapolitaner** A

**nebbich** /'nɛbɪç/ *Interj.* (*salopp*) so what!

**Nebel** /'ne:bl̩/ *der;* **~s,** ~ Ⓐ fog; (*weniger dicht*) mist; **bei ~:** in fog/mist; when it is foggy/misty; **im ~ der Vergessenheit versinken** (*fig.*) sink into the mists *pl.* of oblivion; **ein ~ von Tabakrauch** a thick haze of tobacco smoke; **ausfallen wegen ~[s]** (*ugs. scherzh.*) be cancelled; ⇒ *auch* **Nacht;** Ⓑ (*Astron.*) nebula

**Nebel-:** **~bank** *die; Pl.:* **~bänke** (*über dem Meer*) fog bank; (*über dem Land*) large patch of fog; **~bildung** *die* formation of fog; **stellenweise ~bildung** local mist or fog patches; **~feld** *das* mist/fog patch; patch of mist/fog

**nebelhaft** *Adj.* hazy ‹idea, recollection, etc.›; **das liegt in ~er Ferne** that's in the distant future

**Nebel·horn** *das* foghorn

**nebelig** ⇒ **neblig**

**Nebel-:** **~kammer** *die* (*Atomphysik*) cloud chamber; **~krähe** *die* hooded crow

**nebeln** ❶ *itr. V.* (*unpers.*) (*geh.*) **es nebelt** it is foggy; (*weniger dicht*) it is misty; **es begann zu ~:** it began to grow foggy/misty. ❷ *tr. V.* spray ‹pesticide, insecticide›

**nebel-, Nebel-:** **~schein·werfer** *der* fog lamp; **~schleier** *der* (*geh. dichter.*) veil of mist; **~schluss·leuchte, *~schluß·leuchte** *die* rear fog lamp; **~schwaden** *Pl.* swathes of mist; **~verhangen** *Adj.* (*geh.*) shrouded in mist *postpos.;* **~wand** *die* wall of fog; **~werfer** *der* (*Milit.*) six-barrelled rocket mortar; nebelwerfer

**neben** /'ne:bn̩/ ❶ *Präp. mit Dat.* Ⓐ (*Lage*) next to; beside; **sie fuhren ~ dem Zug her** they kept pace with the train; **dicht ~ jmdm./etw. sitzen** sit close *or* right beside sb./sth.; **er duldet keinen Konkurrenten ~ sich** (*fig.*) he brooks no competition; **ihr sollt keine anderen Götter ~ mir haben!** (*bibl.*) thou shalt have no other gods before me; Ⓑ (*außer*) apart from; aside from (*Amer.*); **wir brauchen ~ Schere und Papier auch Leim** as well as scissors and paper we need glue.
❷ *Präp. mit Akk.* Ⓐ (*Richtung*) next to; beside; **sich dicht ~ jmdn./etw. setzen** sit down close *or* right beside sb./sth.; Ⓑ (*verglichen mit*) beside; compared to *or* with

**neben-, Neben-:** **~absicht** *die* secondary aim; **~akzent** *der* (*Phon.*) secondary accent *or* stress; **~amtlich** ❶ *Adj.* ‹activity› relating to a secondary office/occupation; ❷ *adv.* **etw. ~amtlich amtlich machen** do sth. as a secondary office/occupation

**neben·an** *Adv.* next door; **die Kinder von ~** (*ugs.*) the children from next door; **nach ~ gehen** go next door

**Neben-:** **~an·schluss, *~an·schluß** *der* extension; **~arbeit** *die* Ⓐ second job; Ⓑ (*unwichtige Arbeit*) less important job; **~arbeiten** less important work *sing. or* jobs; **~arm** *der* branch; **~aus·gabe** *die* additional expense; **[eventuelle] ~ausgaben** incidental expenses; **~aus·gang** *der* side exit; **~bedeutung** *die* secondary meaning

**neben·bei** *Adv.* Ⓐ ‹work› on the side, as a sideline; (*zusätzlich*) as well; in addition; **sie versorgt ihren Haushalt und hilft ~ im Geschäft** she looks after the house and helps in the shop as well; **für Geologie interessiert er sich nur ~:** his interest in geology is only secondary; Ⓑ (*beiläufig*) ‹remark› incidentally, by the way; ‹ask› by the way; ‹inform› by the by; ‹mention› in passing; **~ gesagt** *od.* **bemerkt** incidentally; by the way; **dies nur ~:** that is only by the way

**neben-, Neben-:** **~bemerkung** *die* incidental remark; **~beruf** *der* second job; sideline; **er ist im ~beruf Fotograf** he has a second job *or* sideline as a photographer; **~beruflich** ❶ *Adj.* **eine ~berufliche Tätigkeit** a second job; **er musste ~berufliche Tätigkeiten annehmen** he had to take on extra work *sing. or* jobs; ❷ *adv.* on the side; **er arbeitet ~beruflich als Übersetzer** he translates as a sideline; **~beschäftigung** *die* second job; sideline; **seine zahlreichen ~beschäftigungen** his many sidelines; **~buhler** *der;* **~buhlerin** *die* rival; **~effekt** *der* side effect

**neben·ein·ander** *Adv.* Ⓐ next to one another *or* each other; ‹be sitting, standing› next to one another, side by side; (*fig.: zusammen*) ‹live, exist› side by side; **~ wohnen** live next door to one another *or* each other; **~ legen** + *Akk.* lay *or* place ‹objects› next to each other *or* side by side; **~ schalten** + *Akk.* (*Elektrot.*) connect *or* wire ‹devices, lamps, etc.› in parallel; **sich zu zweit ~ aufstellen** line up two abreast; Ⓑ (*gleichzeitig*) together

**Nebeneinander** *das;* **~s** juxtaposition

**nebeneinander·her** *Adv.* alongside each other *or* one another; ‹walk› side by side

***nebeneinander|legen** *usw.* ⇒ **nebeneinander** A

**Neben-:** **~ein·gang** *der* side entrance; **~einkünfte** *Pl.* additional *or* supplementary income *sing.;* **~einnahme** *die:* **~einnahme[n]** additional *or* supplementary income; **~erwerb** *der* second job; secondary occupation; **~erwerbs·betrieb** *der:* (*Landw.*) *smallholding, market stall, etc. run to supplement a person's main income;* **~fach** *das* subsidiary subject; minor (*Amer.*); **etw. im ~fach studieren** study sth. as a subsidiary subject; minor in sth. (*Amer.*); **~fluss, *~fluß** *der* ▶ 306 tributary; **~form** *die* variant; **~frage** *die* side issue; secondary issue; **~frau** *die* concubine; **~gebäude** *das* Ⓐ annexe; outbuilding; Ⓑ (*Nachbargebäude*) adjacent *or* neighbouring building; **~geordnet** *Adj.* (*Sprachw.*) coordinate ‹clause›; **~geräusch** *das* background noise; **~geräusche** (*Funkw., Fernspr.*) interference *sing.;* noise *sing.;* (*bei Tonband, Plattenspieler*) [background] noise *sing.;* **~gleis** *das* (*Eisenb.*) siding; **jmdn. auf ein ~gleis [ab]schieben** (*fig.*) put sb. out of harm's way; **~handlung** *die* subplot; **~haus** *das* house next door; neighbouring house

**neben·her** *Adv.* ⇒ **nebenbei**

**nebenher-:** **~|fahren** *unr. itr. V.; mit sein* drive alongside; (*mit dem Rad, Motorrad*) ride alongside; **~|gehen** *unr. itr. V.; mit sein* walk alongside; **~|laufen** *unr. itr. V.; mit sein* Ⓐ run alongside; Ⓑ (*zugleich ablaufen*) proceed at the same time

**neben·hin** *Adv.* ‹ask› by the way; ‹mention, say› in passing

**neben-, Neben-:** **~höhle** *die* ▶ 471 (*Anat.*) paranasal sinus; **~kläger** *der,* **~klägerin** *die* (*Rechtsw.*) accessory prosecutor; **~kosten** *Pl.* Ⓐ additional costs; Ⓑ (*bei Mieten*) heating, lighting, and services; **~kriegs·schau·platz** *der* secondary theatre of war; (*fig.*) secondary area of conflict; **~linie** *die* Ⓐ (*Eisenb.*) ⇒ **~strecke;** Ⓑ (*Genealogie*) collateral branch; **~mann** *der; Pl.:* **~männer** *od.* **~leute** neighbour; **sein ~mann** the person sitting/standing/walking next to him; his neighbour; **~niere** *die* ▶ 471 (*Anat.*) adrenal *or* suprarenal gland; **~nieren·rinde** *die* ▶ 471 (*Anat.*) adrenal *or* suprarenal cortex; **~ordnend** *Adj.* (*Sprachw.*) coordinating ‹conjunction›; **~produkt** *das* (*auch fig.*) by-product; **~raum** *der* next *or* adjoining room; room next door; (*kleiner, unwichtiger*) side room; **~rolle** *die* supporting role; **eine ~rolle [in etw. (*Dat.*)] spielen** (*fig.*) play a secondary *or* minor role [in sth.]; **~sache** *die* minor *or* inessential matter; **~sachen** inessentials; minor *or* inessential matters; **das ist ~sache** (*ugs.*) that's beside the point; **~sächlich** *Adj.* of minor importance *postpos.;* unimportant; minor, trivial ‹detail›; **etw. als ~sächlich abtun** reject sth. as irrelevant *or* beside the point; **sich über ~sächliche Dinge aufregen** get worked up about trivial things *or* matters; **~sächlichkeit** *die;* **~, ~en** Ⓐ unimportance; (*fehlender Bezug zur Sache*) irrelevance; Ⓑ (*Unwichtiges*) matter of minor importance; unimportant matter; (*nicht zur Sache Gehörendes*) irrelevancy; **~satz** *der* (*Sprachw.*) ⇒ **Gliedsatz;** **~stehend** *Adj.* accompanying ‹text, illustration, table, etc.›; (*auf der Seite gegenüber*) ‹text, illustration, table, etc.› opposite; **~stelle** *die* Ⓐ extension; Ⓑ (*Filiale*) branch; **~straße** *die* side street; (*außerhalb der Stadt*) minor road; **~strecke** *die* Ⓐ (*Eisenb.*) branch *or* local line; Ⓑ (*Entlastungsstraße*) minor road running parallel to the main road; **~tätigkeit** *die* second job; sideline; **~tisch** *der* next *or* neighbouring table; **~tür** *die* Ⓐ side door; Ⓑ (*benachbarte Tür*) next *or* neighbouring door; **~verdienst** *der* additional earnings *pl. or* income; **~winkel** *der* (*Geom.*) adjacent angle; **~wirkung** *die* side effect; **~zimmer** *das* next room; **sie gingen in ein ~zimmer** they went into an adjoining room; **~zweck** *der* secondary aim

**neblig** *Adj.* foggy; (*weniger dicht*) misty

**nebst** /ne:pst/ *Präp. mit Dat.* (*veralt.*) together with; plus; (*zusätzlich zu*) in addition to

**nebst·bei** (*österr.*) ⇒ **nebenbei**

**nebst·dem** (*schweiz.*) ⇒ **außerdem**

**nebulos** /nebu'lo:s/, **nebulös** /nebu'lø:s/ (*geh.*) ❶ *Adj.* nebulous ‹idea, concept›; obscure, vague ‹hint›. ❷ *adv.* ‹talk, hint› vaguely

**Necessaire** /nesɛ'sɛ:ɐ̯/ *das;* **~s, ~s** Ⓐ sponge bag (*Brit.*); toilet bag (*Amer.*); Ⓑ (*Behälter für Nähzeug*) sewing bag

**necken** /'nɛkn̩/ *tr. V.* tease; **jmdn. mit jmdm./etw. ~:** tease sb. about sb./sth.; **sich ~:** tease each other *or* one another; ⇒ *auch* **lieben**

**Neckerei** *die;* **~:** teasing

**neckisch** ❶ *Adj.* Ⓐ teasing; (*verspielt*) playful; (*schelmisch*) mischievous; Ⓑ (*kess*) jaunty, saucy ‹cap›; saucy, provocative ‹dress, blouse, etc.›. ❷ *adv.* ‹smile, say› saucily, cheekily

*old spelling (see note on page 1707)

**nee** /neː/ (*ugs.*) no; nope (*Amer. coll.*)

**Neer** /neːɐ̯/ *die;* ~, ~**en** (*nordd.*) eddy

**Neffe** /ˈnɛfə/ *der;* ~**n**, ~**n** nephew

**neg.** *Abk.* **negativ** neg.

**Negation** /negaˈtsi̯oːn/ *die;* ~, ~**en** negation

**negativ** /ˈneːgatiːf/ ❶ *Adj.* negative; ~**e Zahlen** (*Math.*) negative *or* minus numbers. ❷ *adv.* ‹answer› in the negative; **einen Antrag ~ bescheiden** reject an application; **einer Sache** (*Dat.*) **~ gegenüberstehen** take a negative view of a matter; **etw. ~ beeinflussen** have a negative influence on sth.; **etw. ~ bewerten** judge sth. unfavourably; **sich ~ äußern** comment negatively (**zu** on); **der Test/die Testbohrung verlief ~:** the test proved unsuccessful/the test well yielded nothing; **~ geladen** (*Physik*) negatively charged

**Negativ** *das;* ~**s**, ~**e** (*Fot.*) negative

**Negativ-:** ~**beispiel** *das* negative example; **das ~beispiel Stalin** the negative example of Stalin; ~**bilanz** *die* generally negative picture; (*Ergebnis*) generally negative outcome; ~**bild** *das* (*Fot.*) negative image; ~**film** *der* negative film

**Negativität** /negativiˈtɛːt/ *die;* ~**:** negativity; negativeness

**Negativum** /ˈneːgativʊm/ *das;* ~**s**, **Negativa** (*Faktor*) negative factor; (*Eigenschaft*) negative characteristic

**neger** (*österr. ugs.*) *in:* **~ sein** be broke (*coll.*)

**Neger** /ˈneːgɐ/ *der;* ~**s**, ~ Ⓐ Negro ; Ⓑ (*Fernsehen: schwarze Tafel*) gobo; (*Texttafel*) cue card

**Negerin** *die;* ~, ~**nen** Negress

**Neger-:** ~**krause** *die* (*ugs. veralt.*) frizzy hair *no art.;* ~**kuss**, *~**kuß** *der* ⇒ **Mohrenkopf** A

**Negerlein** *das;* ~**s**, ~**:** little Negro

**Neger·sklave** *der* Negro slave

**negieren** *tr. V.* Ⓐ deny ‹fact, assertion, guilt, etc.›; Ⓑ (*ablehnen*) reject ‹opinion, suggestion›; Ⓒ (*Sprachw.*) negate

**Negligee**, **Negligé** /negliˈʒeː/ *das;* ~**s**, ~**s** négligé; negligee

**negrid** /neˈgriːt/ *Adj.* (*Anthrop.*) Negrid

**negroid** /negroˈiːt/ *Adj.* (*Anthrop.*) Negroid

**nehmen** /ˈneːmən/ *unr. tr. V.* Ⓐ (*ergreifen, an sich bringen, an~, als Beispiel ~*) take; **etw. in die Hand/unter den Arm ~:** take sth. in one's hand/take *or* put sth. under one's arm; **etw. an sich** (*Akk.*) **~:** pick sth. up; (*und aufbewahren*) take charge of sth.; **sich** (*Dat.*) **etw. ~:** take sth.; (*sich bedienen*) help oneself to sth.; **sich** (*Dat.*) **einen Mann/eine Frau ~:** take a husband/wife; **woher ~ und nicht stehlen?** (*scherzh.*) where on earth am I going to get hold of that/them *etc.?*; **zu sich ~:** take in ‹orphan›; **sie nahm ihren Vater zu sich** she had her father come and live with her; **Gott hat ihn zu sich genommen** (*geh.*) God has taken him unto Himself ; **auf sich** (*Akk.*) **~:** take on ‹responsibility, burden›; take ‹blame›; **es auf sich** (*Akk.*) **~, etw. zu tun** take on the responsibility of doing sth.; **die Dinge ~, wie sie kommen** take things as they come; **jmdn. ~, wie er ist** take sb. as he is; **nimm doch mal den Fall, dass man dir einen Vertrag anböte** let's assume [that] they offered you a contract; Ⓑ (*weg~*) **jmdm./einer Sache etw. ~:** deprive sb./sth. of sth.; **jmdm. die Sicht/den Ausblick ~:** block sb.'s view; **jmdm. den Glauben/alle Illusionen ~** (*fig.*) deprive *or* rob sb. of his/her belief/all his/her illusions; **die Angst/die Sorgen von jmdm. ~:** relieve sb. of his/her fear/worries; **es sich** (*Dat.*) **nicht ~ lassen, etw. zu tun** not let anything stop one from doing sth.; **das nimmt der Sache den ganzen Reiz** it takes all the fun out of it ; Ⓒ (*benutzen*) use ‹ingredients, washing powder, wool, brush, knitting needles, etc.›; **man nehme ...** (*in Rezepten*) take ...; **den Zug/das Auto/ein Taxi** *usw.* **~:** take the train/the car/a taxi *etc.;* **[sich** (*Dat.*)**] einen Anwalt/Privatlehrer** *usw.* **~:** get a lawyer/private tutor *etc.;* Ⓓ (*aussuchen*) take; **ich nehme die Pastete/die broschierte Ausgabe** I'll have the pâté/the paperback; Ⓔ (*in Anspruch ~*) take ‹lessons, holiday, etc.›; **einen Tag frei ~:** take a day off; Ⓕ (*verlangen*) charge; **was ~ Sie dafür?** what *or* how much do you charge for it?; Ⓖ (*ein~, essen*) take ‹medicines, tablets, etc.›; **etwas [Richtiges] zu sich ~:** have something [decent] to eat; **sie nimmt die Pille** she's taking *or* she's on the pill (*coll.*); **das Frühstück/einen Imbiss ~** (*geh.*) take breakfast/a snack; **den Kaffee ~** (*geh.*) have [one's] coffee; Ⓗ (*auffassen*) take (**als** as); **etw. ernst/leicht ~:** take sth. seriously/lightly; **jmdn. ernst ~:** take sb. seriously; **gleichgültig/je nachdem, wie mans nimmt** (*ugs.*) however you look at it/depending on how you look at it; **jmdn. nicht für voll ~** (*ugs.*) not take sb. seriously; Ⓘ (*behandeln*) treat ‹person›; **wissen, wie man jmdn. zu ~ hat** know how to treat sb.; Ⓙ (*überwinden, militärisch ein~*) take ‹obstacle, bend, incline, village, bridgehead, etc.›; (*fig.*) take ‹woman›; Ⓚ (*auf~*) **etw. auf Videokassette/Band ~:** record sth. on video cassette/record *or* tape sth.; Ⓛ (*Sport*) take ‹ball, punch›; **einen Spieler hart ~:** foul a player blatantly

**Nehrung** /ˈneːrʊŋ/ *die;* ~, ~**en** sand bar

**Neid** /nait/ *der;* ~**[e]s** envy; jealousy; **aus ~:** out of envy; **von ~ erfüllt [sein]** [be] filled with envy; **vor ~ platzen** (*ugs.*) die of envy (*coll.*); **gelb** *od.* **grün vor ~ werden, vor ~ erblassen** turn *or* go green with envy; **das muss der ~ ihr lassen** (*ugs.*) you've got to give her that; you've got to say that much for her; **das ist der ~ der Besitzlosen** (*ugs.*) that's just sour grapes; **nur kein ~!** don't be envious

**neiden** *tr. V.* (*geh.*) **jmdm. etw. ~:** envy sb. [for] sth.

**Neider** *der;* ~**s**, ~**:** envious person; **seine ~:** those who are/were envious of him; **erfolgreiche Leute haben immer viele ~:** successful people are always much *or* greatly envied

**neid·erfüllt** *Adj.* filled with *or* full of envy *postpos.*

**Neiderin** *die;* ~, ~**nen** ⇒ **Neider**

**Neid·hammel** *der* (*salopp abwertend*) envious sod (*sl.*)

**neidisch** ❶ *Adj.* envious; **auf jmdn./etw. ~ sein** be envious of sb./sth. ❷ *adv.* enviously

**neid-:** ~**los** ❶ *Adj.* ungrudging ‹admiration›; ‹joy› without envy; ❷ *adv.* ‹acknowledge, admire› without envy; ~**voll** ❶ *Adj.* envious ‹glance›; ‹person› filled with *or* full of envy; ‹admiration› mixed with envy; ❷ *adv.* ‹watch› full of envy

**Neige** /ˈnaigə/ *die;* ~ (*geh.*) dregs *pl.;* lees *pl.;* **ein Glas bis zur ~ leeren** drain a glass to the dregs; **etw. bis zur ~ auskosten** (*fig.*) enjoy sth. to the full; **etw. bis zur bitteren ~ durchstehen** (*fig.*) see sth. through to the bitter end; **zur ~ gehen** (*aufgebraucht sein*) ‹money, supplies, etc.› run low; (*zu Ende gehen*) ‹year, day, holiday› draw to its close

**neigen** ❶ *tr. V.* tip, tilt ‹bottle, glass, barrel, etc.›; incline ‹head, upper part of body›; **den Kopf zum Gruß ~:** incline one's head in greeting. ❷ *refl. V.* Ⓐ ‹person› lean, bend; ‹ship› heel over, list; ‹scales› tip; ‹sun› sink; ‹branches› bow down; **sich nach vorne/zur Seite ~:** bend *or* lean over *or* forward/lean to one side; Ⓑ (*schräg abfallen*) ‹meadows› slope down; **eine geneigte Fläche** a sloping surface; Ⓒ (*geh.: zu Ende gehen*) ‹day, year, holiday› draw to its close. ❸ *itr. V.* Ⓐ **zu Erkältungen/Krankheiten ~:** be susceptible *or* prone to colds/illnesses; **zur** *od.* **zu Korpulenz/Schwermut ~:** have a tendency to put on weight/tend to be melancholy; **ein zum** *od.* **zu Jähzorn ~der Mensch** a person who is prone to violent outbursts of temper; Ⓑ (*tendieren*) tend; **zu der Ansicht** *od.* **der Auffassung ~, dass ...** tend towards the view or opinion that ...; ⇒ *auch* **geneigt** 2

**Neigung** *die;* ~, ~**en** Ⓐ (*des Kopfes*) nod; Ⓑ (*Geneigtsein*) inclination; (*eines Geländes*) slope; **die Straße weist eine leichte ~ auf** the street has a slight incline *or* gradient; Ⓒ (*Vorliebe*) inclination; **seine politischen/künstlerischen ~en** his political/artistic leanings; **eine ~ für etw.** a penchant *or* fondness for sth.; Ⓓ (*Anfälligsein*) tendency; **eine ~ zur Korpulenz/zum Faulsein haben** have a tendency to put on weight/to be lazy; Ⓔ (*Lust*) inclination; Ⓕ (*Liebe*) affection; fondness; liking; **jmds. ~ gewinnen/erwidern** win/return sb.'s affection

**Neigungs-:** ~**ehe** *die* love match; ~**messer** *der;* ~~**s**, ~~**:** clinometer; inclinometer; ~**winkel** *der* angle of inclination

**nein** /nain/ *Partikel* no; **~ danke** no, thank you; **sie kann nicht Nein sagen** she can't say no; **da sage ich nicht Nein** I wouldn't say no; **man muss auch Nein sagen können** one must be able to say no; **~, nicht!** no, don't!; **~, so was!** well I never!; **~ und abermals ~!** no, and that's final!; **aber ~!** good heavens no!; **du gehst doch jetzt noch nicht, ~?** you're not going now, are you?; **das wird dir doch nicht zu viel, ~?** that's not too much for you, is it?; **~, dass ich das noch erleben durfte!** simply wonderful, that I should live to see this!; **~, wie schön Sie das gesagt haben!** gosh, you really put that beautifully! (*coll.*)

**'nein** (*südd.*) ⇒ **hinein**

**Nein** *das;* ~**[s]**, ~**[s]** no; **bei seinem ~ bleiben** stick by one's refusal; **mit ~ stimmen** vote no

**Nein-:** ~**sager** *der;* ~~**s**, ~~, ~**sagerin** *die;* ~~, ~~**nen** (*abwertend*) person who always says no *or* who says no to everything; ~**stimme** *die* no-vote; vote against

**Nekrolog** /nekroˈloːk/ *der;* ~**[e]s**, ~**e** (*geh.*) obituary; necrology (*rare*)

**Nekrophilie** /nekrofiˈliː/ *die;* ~**:** necrophilia *no art.*

**Nektar** /ˈnɛktar/ *der;* ~**s**, ~**e** Ⓐ (*Bot., Myth.*) nectar; Ⓑ (*Getränk*) *drink made from crushed fruit, sugar, and water*

**Nektarine** /nektaˈriːnə/ *die;* ~, ~**n** nectarine

**Nelke** /ˈnɛlkə/ *die;* ~, ~**n** Ⓐ pink; (*Dianthus caryophyllus*) carnation; Ⓑ (*Gewürz*) clove

**Nelken·öl** *das* oil of cloves

**Nelson** /ˈnɛlzɔn/ *der;* ~**[s]**, ~**s** (*Ringen*) nelson

**Nemesis** /ˈneːmezɪs/ *die;* ~**:** nemesis

**'nen** /nən/ ⇒ **einen**

**nennbar** *Adj.* specifiable ‹change, problem›; nameable ‹feeling›; **nicht ~:** unspecifiable/unnameable

**Nenn·betrag** *der* ⇒ **Nennwert**

**nennen** /ˈnɛnən/ ❶ *unr. tr. V.* Ⓐ call; **jmdn. nach jmdm. ~:** call *or* name sb. after sb.; **sie nannten das Kind Günther** they called *or* named the child Günther; **jmdn. beim Vornamen ~:** call sb. by his/her first *or* Christian name; **jmdn. einen Lügner ~:** call sb. a liar; **wenn du es so ~ willst** if you want to call it that; **das nenne ich Mut/eine Überraschung** that's what I call courage/well, that 'is a surprise; **Max Müller, genannt „der weiße Würger"** Max Müller, known as the 'White Strangler'; Ⓑ (*mitteilen*) give ‹name, date of birth address, reason, price, etc.›; **jmdm. ein gutes Hotel/einen Arzt ~:** give sb. the name of a good hotel/a doctor; Ⓒ (*anführen*) give, cite ‹example›; (*erwähnen*) mention ‹person, name›; **das oben Genannte** the item[s] mentioned above; **die im folgenden genannten Punkte** the points mentioned below.
❷ *unr. refl. V.* ‹person, thing› be called; **er nennt sich Maler/Dichter** *usw.* (*behauptet Maler/Dichter usw. zu sein*) he calls himself a painter/poet *etc.;* **und so was nennt sich nun ein Freund/tolerant** (*ugs.*) and he/she has the nerve to call himself/herself a friend/tolerant; **und das nennt sich ein gutes Hotel** and that's supposed to be a good hotel

**nennens·wert** *Adj.* considerable ‹influence, changes, delays, damage›; **kaum ~e Veränderungen** changes scarcely worth mentioning; **es ist nichts Nennenswertes passiert** nothing worth mentioning *or* nothing of note has happened

**Nenner** *der;* ~s, ~ (*Math.*) denominator; **der gemeinsame ~:** the common denominator; **etw. auf einen [gemeinsamen] ~ bringen** (*fig.*) reduce sth. to a common denominator

**Nenn-:** **~fall** *der* ⇒ **Nominativ**; **~form** *die* ⇒ **Infinitiv**; **~leistung** *die* (*Technik*) rated output; (*Elektrot.*) rated power; (*eines Motors*) rated horsepower; **~onkel** *der* uncle only in name; **er ist nicht mein richtiger Onkel, sondern nur ein ~onkel** he's not my real uncle, I just call him that; **~tante** *die* aunt only in name; ⇒ *auch* **~onkel**

**Nennung** *die;* ~, ~en **A** ⇒ **nennen** 1 B, C: giving; citing; mentioning; **B** (*Sport*) entry (**zu, für** for)

**Nenn-:** **~wert** *der* (*Wirtsch.*) nominal *or* face value; (*von Aktien*) par *or* nominal *or* face value; **~wort** *das; Pl.* **~wörter** ⇒ **Substantiv**

**neo-, Neo-:** neo-

**Neolithikum** /neo'li:tikʊm/ *das;* ~s (*Archäol.*) neolithic period

**Neologismus** /neolo'gɪsmʊs/ *der;* ~, **Neologismen** (*Sprachw.*) neologism

**Neon** /'ne:ɔn/ *das;* ~s (*Chemie*) neon

**Neon-:** **~licht** *das; Pl.* **~~er** neon light; **~reklame** *die* neon sign; **~röhre** *die* neon tube; [neon] strip light

**Nepal** /'ne:pal/ (*das*); ~s Nepal

**Nepalese** /nepa'le:zə/ *der;* ~n, ~n, **Nepalesin** *die;* ~, ~nen Nepali; Nepalese

**Nepotismus** /nepo'tɪsmʊs/ *der;* ~: nepotism *no art.*

**Nepp** /nɛp/ *der;* ~s (*ugs. abwertend*) daylight robbery *no art.;* rip-off (*coll.*)

**neppen** *tr. V.* (*ugs. abwertend*) rook; rip ‹tourist, customer, etc.› off (*sl.*)

**Nepper** *der;* ~s, ~, **Nepperin** *die;* ~, ~nen (*ugs. abwertend*) shark; rip-off merchant (*coll.*)

**Nepp·lokal** *das* (*ugs. abwertend*) clip joint (*coll. derog.*)

**Neptun**[1] /nɛp'tu:n/ *der;* ~s (*Astron.*), **Neptun**[2] (*der*); ~s (*Myth.*) Neptune

**Nerv** /nɛrf/ *der;* ~s, ~en **A** ▶ 471 nerve; **an den ~ der Sache rühren** (*fig.*) get to the heart of the matter; **das Buch trifft den ~ der Zeit** (*fig.*) the book taps the pulse of the age; **den ~ haben, etw. zu tun** (*fig. ugs.*) have the nerve to do sth.; **jmdm. den ~ töten** (*fig. ugs.*) drive sb. up the wall (*coll.*); **B** *Pl.* (*nervliche Konstitution*) nerves; **gute/schwache ~en haben** have strong/bad nerves; **meine ~en halten das nicht aus** my nerves won't stand it; **die ~en [dazu] haben, etw. zu tun** have the nerve to do sth.; **die ~en bewahren** *od.* **behalten** keep calm; **die ~en verlieren** lose control [of oneself]; lose one's cool (*sl.*); **ich bin mit den ~en fertig** *od.* **am Ende** my nerves cannot take any more; **du hast vielleicht ~en!** (*ugs.*) you've got a nerve!; **~en haben wie Drahtseile** *od.* **Stricke** (*ugs.*) have nerves of steel; **jmdm. auf die ~en gehen** *od.* **fallen** get on sb.'s nerves; **C** (*in Blättern, Insektenflügeln*) vein; nerve

**nerven** (*salopp*) **1** *tr. V.* **jmdn. ~:** get on sb.'s nerves. **2** *itr. V.* be wearing on the nerves

**nerven-, Nerven-:** **~an·spannung** *die* nervous strain; nervous tension *no indef. art.;* **~arzt** *der,* **~ärztin** *die* neurologist; **~aufreibend** *Adj.* nerve-racking; **~belastung** *die* strain on the nerves; **~beruhigend** *Adj.* sedative ‹effect, drug›; **~beruhigend wirken** have a calming effect on the nerves; ‹drug› act as a sedative/tranquillizer; **~beruhigungs·mittel** *das* sedative; (*gegen Depressionen, Angstzustände*) tranquillizer; **~bündel** *das* **A** (*ugs.*) bundle of nerves (*coll.*); **B** ▶ 471 (*Anat.*) bundle of nerve fibres; **~entzündung** *die* ▶ 474 (*Med.*) neuritis; **~faser** *die* ▶ 471 (*Anat.*) nerve fibre; **~gas** *das* nerve gas; **~gift** *das* neurotoxin; **~heil·anstalt** *die* (*veralt.*) mental *or* psychiatric hospital; **~kitzel** *der* (*ugs.*) kick (*coll.*); **~klinik** *die* **A** clinic for nervous diseases; **B** (*ugs.*) mental *or* psychiatric hospital; **~kostüm** *das* (*ugs. scherzh.*) nerves *pl.;* **ein schwaches ~kostüm haben** have bad nerves; **~kraft** *die* nervous strength; **~krank** *Adj.* **A** ‹person› suffering from a nervous disease *or* disorder; **B** (*psychisch krank*) mentally ill; **~kranke** *der/die* **A** person suffering from a nervous disease *or* disorder; **B** (*psychisch Kranke*) mentally ill person; **~kranke sind ...** the mentally ill are ...; **~krankheit** *die* ▶ 474 **A** nervous disease *or* disorder; **B** (*psychische Krankheit*) mental illness; **~krieg** *der* (*ugs.*) war of nerves; **~leiden** *das* ▶ 474 nervous complaint *or* disorder; **~nahrung** *die:* **~nahrung sein** be good for the *or* one's nerves; **~probe** *die* mental trial; **~sache** *die: in* **das ist reine ~sache** (*ugs.*) it's a matter *or* question of nerves; **~säge** *die* (*salopp*) pain in the neck (*coll.*); **~schmerz** *der* ▶ 474 (*Med.*) neuralgia; **~schock** *der* nervous *or* psychic shock; **~schwach** *Adj.* ‹person› with bad nerves *not pred.;* neurasthenic ‹person› (*Med.*); **~schwäche** *die* ▶ 474 **A** neurasthenia (*Med.*); **B** (*psychische Schwäche*) bad nerves *pl.;* **~stärkend** *Adj.* nerve-strengthening; **ein ~stärkendes Mittel** a nerve tonic; **~strang** *der* ⇒ **~bündel** B; **~system** *das* ▶ 471 (*Anat.*) nervous system; **~zelle** *die* ▶ 471 (*Anat.*) nerve cell; **~zusammen·bruch** *der* ▶ 474 nervous breakdown

**nervig** *Adj.* (*auch fig.*) sinewy

**nervlich** **1** *Adj.* nervous ‹strain›; **eine ~e Belastung für jmdn. sein** be a strain on sb.'s nerves. **2** *adv.* **dieser ständigen Spannung war er ~ nicht gewachsen** his nerves were not up to this constant tension

**nervös** /nɛr'vø:s/ **1** *Adj.* **A** nervy, jittery ‹person›; nervous ‹haste, movement›; **~ sein** be jittery (*coll.*) *or* on edge; **das macht mich ganz ~:** it really gets on my nerves; (*das beunruhigt mich*) it makes me really nervous; **B** (*Med.*) nervous ‹twitch, gastric disorder, etc.›. **2** *adv.* **A** nervously; **B** (*Med.*) **~ bedingt sein** be caused by nerves

**Nervosität** /nɛrvozi'tɛ:t/ *die;* ~: nervousness; **voller ~:** nervously

**nerv·tötend** *Adj.* nerve-racking ‹wait›; nerve-shattering ‹sound, noise›; soul-destroying ‹activity, work›

**Nerz** /nɛrts/ *der;* ~es, ~e mink

**Nerz·mantel** *der* mink coat

**Nessel**[1] /'nɛsl/ *die;* ~, ~n nettle; **sich in die ~n setzen** (*fig. ugs.*) get [oneself] into hot water (*coll.*)

**Nessel**[2] *der;* ~s, ~ (*Stoff*) coarse, untreated cotton cloth

**Nessel-:** **~fieber** *das* nettle rash accompanied by fever; **~sucht** *die* nettle rash; hives

**Nest** /nɛst/ *das;* ~[e]s, ~er **A** nest; **sich** (*Dat.*) **gemeinsam ein ~ einrichten** (*fig.*) set up home together; **das eigene** *od.* **sein eigenes ~ beschmutzen** (*fig.*) foul one's own nest; **er hat sich ins warme** *od.* **gemachte ~ gesetzt** (*fig. ugs.*) he had his future made for him; **B** (*fam.: Bett*) bed; **raus aus dem ~!** show a leg! (*coll.*); **C** (*ugs. abwertend: kleiner Ort*) little place; **ein winziges ~:** a tiny little place; **ein gottverlassenes/armseliges ~:** a godforsaken/miserable hole; **D** (*Schlupfwinkel*) hideout; den; **E** (*Haartracht*) plaited bun

**Nest-:** **~bau** *der* nest-building *no art.;* **~beschmutzer** *der;* ~~s, ~~, **~beschmutzerin** *die;* ~~, ~~nen (*abwertend*) person who is/was guilty of fouling his/her own nest

**nesteln** /'nɛstl̩n/ *itr. V.* fiddle, (*ungeschickt*) fumble (**an** + *Dat.* with)

**nest-, Nest-:** **~flüchter** *der;* ~~s, ~~ (*Zool.*) (*bird*) precocial *or* nidifugous bird; (*animal*) precocial animal; **~häkchen** *das* (*fam.*) [spoilt] baby of the family; **~hocker** *der* (*Zool.*) nidicolous bird/animal; **~warm** *Adj.* ‹eggs› warm from the nest; **~wärme** *die* warmth of a [happy] family upbringing *or* of [happy] family life

**nett** /nɛt/ **1** *Adj.* **A** nice; (*freundlich*) nice; kind; **sei so ~ und hilf mir!** would you be so good *or* kind as to help me?; **sie war so ~, uns einen Kaffee anzubieten** she very kindly offered us a coffee; **das war [nicht] ~ von dir** that was[n't very] nice of you; **~, dass du anrufst** it's nice *or* kind of you to ring; **etwas Nettes erleben/sagen** have a pleasant experience/say something nice; **B** (*hübsch*) pretty ‹girl, town, dress, etc.›; nice, pleasant ‹pub, house, town, etc.›; **C** (*ugs.: beträchtlich*) nice little (*coll.*) ‹profit, extra earnings, income›; **sie hat eine ganz ~e Oberweite** she's very well endowed (*coll.*); **eine ~e Summe/eine ~e Stange Geld** a tidy sum (*coll.*); **D** (*ugs. iron.: unerfreulich*) nice (*coll.*) ‹affair›; nice (*coll.*), fine ‹state of affairs, mess›; **das sind ja ~e Aussichten** that's a nice *or* charming prospect (*coll.*); **das kann ja ~ werden!** that'll be fun (*coll.*).
**2** *adv.* (*angenehm*) nicely; (*freundlich*) nicely; kindly; **sich ~ mit jmdm. unterhalten** have a pleasant conversation with sb.; **hier sitzt man sehr ~:** it's very nice *or* pleasant sitting here

**netter·weise** *Adv.* (*ugs.*) kindly; **würden Sie mir ~ diesen Platz überlassen?** would you be so kind as to let me have your seat?

**Nettigkeit** *die;* ~, ~en **A** kindness; goodness; **B** (*Äußerung*) **jmdm. ein paar ~en sagen** say a few nice *or* kind things to sb.; (*iron.*) say a few choice words to sb.

**netto** /'nɛto/ *Adv.* ▶ 353 ‹weigh, earn, etc.› net

**Netto-:** **~einkommen** *das* net income; **~ertrag** *der* net return; **~gehalt** *das* net salary; **~gewicht** *das* net weight; **~preis** *der* net price; **~raum·zahl** *die* net register tonnage; **~register·tonne** *die* (*Seew.*) net register ton; **~sozial·produkt** *das* (*Wirtsch.*) net national product

**Netz** /nɛts/ *das;* ~es, ~e **A** (*auch Fischer~, Tennis~, Ballspiele*) net; (*Haar~*) [hair] net; (*Einkaufs~*) string bag; (*Gepäck~*) [luggage] rack; (*Sicherheits~*) safety net; **sich in einem ~ von Lügen verstricken** (*fig.*) become entangled in a web of lies; **jmdm. ins ~ gehen** (*fig.*) fall into sb.'s trap; **jmdm. durchs ~ gehen** (*fig.*) slip through sb.'s net; **seine ~e überall auswerfen** (*fig.*) put out feelers in all directions; **ans ~ gehen** (*Tennis*) go to the net; **B** (*Spinnen~*) web; **C** (*Verteiler~, Verkehrs~, System von Einrichtungen DV, Fernspr.*) network; (*für Strom, Wasser, Gas*) mains *pl.;* **ans ~ gehen** ‹power station› go on stream; **das soziale ~:** the social security system; **D** (*Math.*) net

**netz-, Netz-:** **~anbieter** *der* (*DV, Fernspr.*) network provider; **~anschluss**, ***~anschluß** *der* mains connection; **~artig** *Adj.* netlike ‹material, pattern, etc.›; **~auge** *das* (*Zool.*) compound eye; **~ball** *der* (*Tennis, Volleyball*) net ball

**netzen** *tr. V.* (*geh.*) moisten ‹soil, plant, one's lips›; wet ‹hair, cheeks›

**Netz-:** **~frequenz** *die* (*Elektrot.*) mains frequency; **~gerät** *das* (*Elektrot.*) power pack; **~gewölbe** *das* (*Kunstwiss.*) net vault; **~haut** *die* ▶ 471 (*Anat.*) retina

**Netzhaut-:** **~ab·lösung** *die* (*Med.*) detachment of the retina; retinal detachment; **~entzündung** *die* (*Med.*) retinitis

**Netz-:** **~hemd** *das* string vest; **~karte** *die* area season ticket; (*Eisenb.*) unlimited travel ticket; **~magen** *der* (*Zool.*) reticulum; honeycomb stomach; **~roller** *der* (*Tennis*) net cord [stroke]; **~spannung** *die* (*Elektrot.*) mains voltage; **~stecker** *der* mains plug; **~strumpf** *der* net stocking; **~werk** *das* (*auch Elektrot.*) network

**neu** /nɔy/ **1** *Adj.* **A** ▶ 369 new; **ein ganz ~es Fahrrad** a brand new bicycle; **die Neue Welt** the New World; **das Neue Testament** the New Testament; **die ~este Mode/die ~esten Schlager/der ~este Witz** the latest fashion/hits/joke; **die ~e Literatur/Physik** modern literature/physics; **die ~esten Nachrichten/Ereignisse** the latest news/most recent events; **viel Glück im ~en Jahr** best wishes for the New Year; Happy New Year; **er brachte eine ~e Flasche** he fetched another bottle; **das sieht aus wie ~:** that looks like new *or* as good as

n

*old spelling (see note on page 1707)

new; **das ist mir ~:** that is news to me; **ich bin ~ in dieser Gegend/in diesem Beruf** I am new to this area/job; **das Neue daran ist ...** what's new about it is ...; **den Reiz des Neuen haben** have novelty value; **das Neueste auf dem Markt** the latest thing on the market; **der/die Neue** the new man/woman/boy/girl; **etw./nichts Neues wissen/berichten** know/report something/nothing new; **was gibt es Neues?** what's new?; **weißt du schon das Neueste?** (*ugs.*) have you heard the latest?; **etw. Neues unternehmen/anfangen** do/start something new *or* different; **eine ~e Flasche aufmachen** open another bottle; **eine ~e Seite/Zeile beginnen** start a new *or* fresh page/line; **aufs Neue** anew; afresh; again; **auf ein Neues!** let's try again!; **von ~em** all over again; (*noch einmal*) [once] again; **von ~em beginnen** start *or* begin all over again; make a fresh start; **seit ~estem werden dort keine Kreditkarten mehr akzeptiert** just recently they've started refusing to accept credit cards; **in ~erer/~ester Zeit** quite/just *or* very recently; **das ist ~eren Datums** that is of a more recent date; **die ~en** *od.* **~eren Sprachen** modern languages; B (*kürzlich geerntet*) new ‹wine, potatoes›; C (*sauber*) clean ‹shirt, socks, underwear, etc.›.

❷ *adv.* A **~ tapeziert/gespritzt/gestrichen/möbliert/eröffnet** repapered/resprayed/repainted/refurnished/reopened; **einen Sessel ~ beziehen** re-cover an armchair; **ein Geschäft ~ eröffnen** reopen a shop; **sich ~ einkleiden/einrichten** provide oneself with a new set of clothes/refurnish one's home; **noch einmal ~ beginnen** start again from scratch; **sich ~ formieren** ‹party, organization, etc.› re-form; **~ bearbeitet** [newly] revised ‹edition›; newly adapted ‹version›; B (*gerade erst*) **diese Ware ist ~ eingetroffen** this item has just come in *or* arrived; **das Geschäft ist ~ eröffnet** the shop has only just been opened; **ein ~ eröffneter Laden** a newly-opened shop; **~ erschienene Bücher** newly published books; books that have just come out *or* appeared; **3 000 Wörter sind ~ hinzugekommen** 3,000 new words have been added; **~ vermählt** newly wed *or* married; **die neu Vermählten** the newly-weds

**neu-, Neu-: ~an·fertigung** *die* A making; (*serienweise*) manufacture; B (*Angefertigtes*) **eine ~anfertigung sein** be new; **~ankömmling** *der* new arrival; **~anschaffung** *die* A **die ~anschaffung von Produktionsanlagen** the acquisition of new production plant; **~anschaffungen machen** buy new items; B (*Artikel, Gegenstand*) new acquisition; **~apostolisch** *Adj.* (*christl. Rel.*) New Apostolic; **die ~apostolische Gemeinde** the New Apostolic Church

**neu·artig** *Adj.* new; **ein ~er Staubsauger** a new type of vacuum cleaner; **das Neuartige an diesem Gerät** the novel feature of this device

**Neuartigkeit** *die;* **~:** novelty

**Neu-: ~auf·lage** *die* reprint [with alterations]; (*mit umfangreichen Veränderungen*) new edition; **eine ~auflage des vorjährigen Endspiels** (*fig.*) a repeat of last years's final; **~aus·gabe** *die* new edition

**Neu·bau** *der; Pl.* **~ten** A new house/building; B (*Wiedererrichtung*) rebuilding

**Neubau-: ~viertel** *das* new district; **~wohnung** *die* flat (*Brit.*) *or* (*Amer.*) apartment in a new block/house; new flat (*Brit.*) *or* (*Amer.*) apartment

**neu-, Neu-: *~bearbeitet** ⇒ **neu** 2A; **~bearbeitung** *die* A (*eines Buches, Textes*) revision; (*eines Theaterstücks*) adaptation; B (*~e Fassung*) new version; **~bedeutung** *die* (*Sprachw.*) new meaning; **~beginn** *der* new beginning; **~besetzung** *die:* **die ~besetzung einer Stelle** the refilling of a post; **eine ~besetzung ihrer Rolle wurde notwendig** it became necessary to cast someone else in her part; **~bildung** *die* A **die ~bildung der Regierung/des Kabinetts** the formation of a new government/cabinet; B (*von Gewebe*) regeneration; (*~ Gebildetes*) new growth; **die ~bildung von Geschwülsten** the growth of new tumours; (*wiederholt*) the regrowth of tumours; C (*eines Wortes*) coining; (*~es Wort*) neologism; **~bürger** *der,* **~bürgerin** *die* new citizen

**Neu-Delhi** /nɔy'de:li/ (*das*)*;* **~s** ▶ 700 New Delhi

**neu-, Neu-: ~deutsch** *Adj.* (*meist abwertend*) modern West German ‹society›; typical West German ‹arrogance, smugness, customs›; **~druck** *der; Pl.* **~~e** reprint [with corrections]; **~ein·stellung** *die:* **eine ~einstellung vornehmen** take on a new employee; (*von Angestellten*) make a new appointment; **~einstellungen notwendig machen** make it necessary to take on new staff; **~einstudierung** *die* (*Theater*) new production

**Neu·england** (*das*) New England

**neu·englisch** *Adj.* modern English

**Neu-: ~entdeckung** *die* A (*auch fig.*) new discovery; B (*Wiederentdeckung*) rediscovery; **~entwicklung** *die* A **die ~entwicklung von Heilmitteln/Maschinen** the development of new medicines/machines; B (*neu Entwickeltes*) new development

**neuerdings** /'nɔyɐ'dɪŋs/ *Adv.* A recently; **Fahrkarten gibt es ~ nur noch am Automaten** as of a short while ago one can only get tickets from a machine; **~ kann man direkt dorthin fliegen** it has recently become possible to fly there direct; **er trägt ~ eine Perücke** he has recently started wearing a wig; B (*südd., österr., schweiz.: erneut*) again

**Neuerer** *der;* **~s, ~, Neuerin** *die;* **~, ~nen** innovator

**neuerlich** ❶ *Adj.* further. ❷ *adv.* again

**neu-, Neu-: *~eröffnet** ⇒ **neu** 2 A, B; **~eröffnung** *die* A opening; B (*Wiedereröffnung*) reopening; **~erscheinung** *die* new publication; (*Schallplatte*) new release

**Neuerung** *die;* **~, ~en** innovation

**Neu·erwerbung** *die* A **die ~ von Büchern/Möbeln** *usw.* the acquisition of new books/furniture *etc.;* B (*Gegenstand*) new acquisition; C (*Sport*) new signing

**neuestens** /'nɔyəstṇs/ *Adv.* ⇒ **neuerdings** A

**Neu·fassung** *die* revised version; (*eines Films*) remake

**Neufundland** (*das*)*;* **~s** Newfoundland

**Neufundländer** *der;* **~s, ~** (*Hunderasse*) Newfoundland [dog]

**neu-, Neu-: ~geboren** *Adj.* newborn; **sich wie ~geboren fühlen** feel a new man/woman; **~geborene** *das; adj. Dekl.* newborn child; **~geburt** *die* (*geh.*) rebirth; **~gestaltung** *die* (*einer Gemeinschaft, Gesellschaft*) reorganization; reshaping; (*der Politik, eines Programms*) reshaping; (*einer Titelseite, einer Einrichtung*) redesigning; (*eines Stadtviertels, einer Parkanlage*) replanning; **~gewürz** *das* (*österr.*) allspice; pimento

**Neu·gier, Neugierde** /-gi:ɐ̯də/ *die;* **~:** curiosity; (*Wissbegierde*) inquisitiveness; **aus [reiner] ~:** out of [sheer] curiosity; **vor ~ platzen** be bursting with curiosity

**neu·gierig** ❶ *Adj.* curious; inquisitive; prying (*derog.*), nosy (*coll. derog.*) ‹person›; **sei nicht so ~!** don't be so inquisitive *or* (*coll. derog.*) nosy!; **da bin ich aber ~!** (*iron.*) I'll believe it when I see it; I can hardly wait! (*iron.*); **auf etw.** (*Akk.*) **~ sein** be curious about sth.; **viele Neugierige** many inquisitive people *or* spectators; **ich bin ~, was er dazu sagt** I'm curious to know what he'll say about it; **ich bin ~, ob er kommt** I wonder whether he'll come; **er war ~ [zu hören], was passiert war** he was curious to know what had happened.

❷ *adv.* ‹ask› inquisitively; ‹peer› nosily (*coll. derog.*); **jmdn. ~ mustern** eye sb. curiously; **~ lehnten die Nachbarn aus dem Fenster** the neighbours leaned out of the window full of curiosity

**neu-, Neu-: ~gliederung** *die* reorganization; restructuring; **~gotik** *die* Gothic Revival; **~gotisch** *Adj.* neo-Gothic; **~gründung** *die* A **die ~gründung eines Vereins/einer Partei/Universität** *usw.* the founding *or* establishment of a new club/party/university *etc.;* B (*~ Gegründetes*) **eine ~gründung sein** have recently been founded *or* established; C (*erneute Gründung*) refoundation; re-establishment

**Neu·guinea** (*das*) New Guinea

**Neuheit** *die;* **~, ~en** A novelty; **den Reiz der ~ haben** have novelty value; B (*Neues*) new product/gadget/article *etc.*

**neu·hoch·deutsch** *adj.* New High German

**Neu·hoch·deutsch** *das* New High German

**Neuigkeit** *die;* **~, ~en** piece of news; **~en** news *sing.*

**Neu·inszenierung** *die* (*Theater*) new production

**Neu·jahr** *das* ▶ 369 New Year's Day; **~ feiern** celebrate New Year; ⇒ *auch* **prosit**

**Neujahrs-: ~abend** *der* New Year's Eve; **~an·sprache** *die* New Year address; **~fest** *das* New Year's Day; (*Feier*) New Year celebration; **das jüdische/chinesische ~fest** the Jewish/Chinese New Year; **das ~fest begehen** celebrate New Year; **~gruß** *der* New Year greetings *pl.;* **~karte** *die* New Year card; **~konzert** *das* New Year concert; **~nacht** *die* New Year's night; **~tag** *der* New Year's Day

**neu-, Neu-: ~land** *das* A newly reclaimed *or* new land; B (*unerforschtes Land*) new *or* virgin territory; **wissenschaftliches/medizinisches ~land betreten** (*fig.*) break new ground in science/medicine; **~latein** *das* New Latin; Neo-Latin; **~lateinisch** *Adj.* Neo-Latin

**neulich** *Adv.* recently; the other day; **~ morgens/abends** the other morning/evening; **der Mann von ~, der in unserem Zugabteil saß** (*ugs.*) the man who was sitting in our compartment on the train the other day

**Neuling** /'nɔylɪŋ/ *der;* **~s, ~e** newcomer (**in** + *Dat.* to); new man/woman/girl/boy; (*auf einem Gebiet*) novice

**neu·modisch** (*abwertend*) ❶ *Adj.* newfangled (*derog.*). ❷ *adv.* ‹dress› in a newfangled way

**Neu·mond** *der* new moon; **heute ist/haben wir ~:** there's a new moon today; **zwei Tage nach ~:** two days after the new moon

**neun** /nɔyn/ *Kardinalz.* ▶ 76, ▶ 841 nine; **alle ~[e]** (*Kegeln*) a floorer; ⇒ *auch* **acht**

**Neun** *die;* **~, ~en** nine; **ach, du grüne ~e** (*ugs.*) oh, my goodness!; good grief!; ⇒ *auch* **Acht**[1] A, B, D, E, G

**neun-, Neun-** (⇒ *auch* **acht-, Acht-**)**: ~eck** *das* nonagon; **~eckig** *Adj.* nonagonal; ⇒ *auch* **achteckig**; **~einhalb** *Bruchz.* nine and a half

**Neuner** *der;* **~s, ~** (*ugs.*) nine ⇒ *auch* **Acht**[1] A, B, E; **Achter** D

**neunerlei** *indekl. Gattungsz.* A *attr.* nine kinds *or* sorts of; nine different ‹sorts, kinds, sizes, possibilities›; B *subst.* nine [different] things

**Neuner·probe** *die* (*Math.*) casting out nines [check]

**neun-, Neun-** (⇒ *auch* **acht-, Acht-**)**: ~fach** *Vervielfältigungsz.* ninefold; ⇒ *auch* **achtfach**; **~fache** *das; adj. Dekl.* **das ~fache von 4 ist 36** nine fours are *or* nine times four makes thirty-six; ⇒ *auch* **Achtfache**; **~hundert** *Kardinalz.* ▶ 841 nine hundred; **~jährig** *Adj.* (*9 Jahre alt*) nine-year-old *attrib.;* (*9 Jahre dauernd*) nine-year *attrib.;* ⇒ *auch* **achtjährig**; **~köpfig** *Adj.* nine-headed ‹monster›; ‹family, committee› of nine; **~mal** *Adv.* nine times; ⇒ *auch* **achtmal**; **~mal·gescheit, ~mal·klug** (*spöttisch*) ❶ *Adj.* smart-aleck *attrib.* (*coll.*); **du bist immer so ~malgescheit** *od.* **~malklug** you're such a smart aleck (*coll.*); **ein ~malgescheiter** *od.* **~malkluger** a smart aleck (*coll.*); ❷ *adv.* in a smart-aleck way (*coll.*); **~schwänzig** /-ʃvɛntsɪç/ *Adj.* in **~schwänzige Katze** (*Seemannsspr.*) cat-o'-nine-tails; **~stellig** *Adj.* nine-figure *attrib.;* ⇒ *auch* **achtstellig**; **~stöckig** *Adj.* nine-storey *attrib.;* ⇒ *auch* **achtstöckig**; **~stündig** *Adj.* nine-hour *attrib.*; lasting nine hours *postpos.*, *not pred.*; ⇒ *auch* **achtstündig**

**neunt** /nɔynt/ *in* **wir waren zu ~:** there were nine of us; ⇒ *auch* **acht²**

**neunt...** *Ordinalz.* ▶207, ▶841 ninth; ⇒ *auch* **acht...**

**neun-** (⇒ *auch* **acht-, Acht-**): **~tägig** *Adj.* (*9 Tage alt*) nine-day-old *attrib.*; (*9 Tage dauernd*) nine-day-long *attrib.*; ⇒ *auch* **achttägig**; **~tausend** *Kardinalz.* ▶841 nine thousand

**Neuntel** *das* (*schweiz. meist der*); **~s, ~:** ▶841 ninth

***neunte·mal, *neunten·mal** ⇒ **Mal¹**

**neuntens** *Adv.* ninthly

**Neun·töter** *der* (*Zool.*) red-backed shrike

**neun·zehn** *Kardinalz.* ▶76, ▶752, ▶841 nineteen; ⇒ *auch* **achtzehn**

**neunzehnt...** *Ordinalz.* ▶207 nineteenth; ⇒ *auch* **acht...**

**neunzig** /ˈnɔyntsɪç/ *Kardinalz.* ▶76, ▶841 ninety; ⇒ *auch* **achtzig**

**neunzig-, Neunzig-:** ⇒ *auch* **achtzig-, Achtzig-**

**Neunzig** *die*; **~, ~en** ninety; ⇒ *auch* **Achtzig**

**neunziger** *indekl. Adj.* **die ~ Jahre** the nineties; ⇒ *auch* **achtziger**

**Neunziger·jahre** *Pl.* ▶76, ▶207 nineties *pl.*

**neunzigst...** /ˈnɔyntsɪçst.../ *Ordinalz.* ▶841 ninetieth; ⇒ *auch* **acht..., achtzigst...**

**Neu-:** **~ordnung** *die* reorganization; **~orientierung** *die* reorientation; **~philologe** *der* modern linguist; **~philologie** *die* modern languages [and literature] *sing.*; *no art.*; **~philologin** *die* ⇒ **~philologe**; **~prägung** *die* **A** (*Münzk.*) new minting; **die ~prägung von Münzen** the minting of new coins; **B** (*Sprachw.*) new coinage; neologism; **die ~prägung von Wörtern/Wendungen** *usw.* the coining of new words/expressions *etc.*

**Neuralgie** /nɔyralˈgiː/ *die*; **~, ~n** ▶474 (*Med.*) neuralgia

**neuralgisch** ❶ *Adj.* **A** (*Med.*) neuralgic; **B** (*empfindlich*) **das ist mein ~er Punkt** it's a sore *or* touchy point with me. ❷ *adv.* (*empfindlich*) ‹react› touchily

**neu-, Neu-:** **~reg[e]lung** *die* **A** **die ~regelung der Arbeitszeit/der Zulassung zu den Universitäten** *usw.* the revision of regulations governing working hours/admission to university *etc.*; **B** (*Bestimmung*) new regulation; **~reich** *Adj.* (*abwertend*) nouveau riche; **Familie ~reich** (*ugs.*) the typical nouveau riche family; **~reiche** *der/die* nouveau riche; **die ~reichen** the nouveaux riches; the new rich

**Neuritis** /nɔyˈriːtɪs/ *die*; **~, Neuritiden** (*Med.*) neuritis

**Neuro·chirurgie** *die*; **~** (*Med.*) neurosurgery

**Neurodermitis** *die*; **~, Neurodermitiden** ▶474 (*Med.*) neurodermatitis

**Neurologe** *der*; **~n, ~n** ▶159 neurologist

**Neurologie** *die*; **~** **A** neurology; **B** (*Abteilung*) neurology department; (*Station*) neurology ward; (*ugs.*: *Klinik*) neurology clinic

**Neurologin** *die*; **~, ~nen** ▶159 neurologist

**neurologisch** *Adj.* neurological

**Neuron** /ˈnɔyrɔn/ *das*; **~s, ~e** *od.* **~en** ▶471 (*Anat.*) neuron

**Neurose** /nɔyˈroːzə/ *die*; **~, ~n** ▶474 (*Med.*, *Psych.*) neurosis

**Neurotiker** /nɔyˈroːtikɐ/ *der*; **~s, ~, Neurotikerin** *die*; **~, ~nen** (*Med.*, *Psych.*, *auch ugs.*) neurotic

**neurotisch** *Adj.* (*Med.*, *Psych.*, *auch ugs.*) neurotic

**Neu-:** **~satz** *der* (*Druckw.*) new setting; **~schnee** *der* fresh snow

**Neuseeland** (*das*); **~s** New Zealand

**Neuseeländer** *der*; **~s, ~:** New Zealander

**Neuseeländerin** *die*; **~, ~nen** New Zealander; New Zealand lady/woman/girl; ⇒ *auch* **-in**

**neuseeländisch** *Adj.* New Zealand

**neu-, Neu-:** **~silber** *das* German silver; nickel silver; **~sprachler** /-ʃpraːxlɐ/ *der*; **~~s, ~~, ~sprachlerin** *die*; **~~, ~~nen** modern linguist; **~sprachlich** *Adj.* modern languages *attrib.* ‹teaching›; **der ~sprachliche Zweig** (*Schulw.*) the modern languages side; **ein ~sprachliches Gymnasium** a grammar school with emphasis on modern languages

**neustens** /ˈnɔystn̩s/ ⇒ **neuerdings** A

**neutestamentlich** *Adj.* New Testament *attrib.*

**neutral** /nɔyˈtraːl/ ❶ *Adj.* **A** (*auch Völkerr.*, *Phys.*, *Chem.*) neutral; **B** (*Sprachw.*) neuter. ❷ *adv.* **sich ~ verhalten** remain neutral; **ich kann das nicht ~ entscheiden/beurteilen** I cannot give an impartial decision/judgement

**-neutral** *adj.* **kosten~/erfolgs~:** not affecting costs/profits *postpos.*, *not pred.*; **geschmacks~/geruchs~:** neutral-tasting/neutral-smelling

**Neutralisation** /nɔytralizaˈtsi̯oːn/ *die*; **~, ~en** (*auch Chemie*) neutralization

**neutralisieren** *tr. V.* (*auch Völkerr.*, *Chem.*, *Elektrot.*) neutralize; (*Rennsport*) stop ‹race›

**Neutralisierung** *die*; **~, ~en** (*auch Völkerr.*, *Chem.*, *Elektrot.*) neutralization; (*Rennsport*) stopping

**Neutralität** /nɔytraliˈtɛːt/ *die*; **~, ~en** (*auch Völkerr.*, *Chem.*, *Elektrot.*) neutrality

**Neutralitäts-:** **~abkommen** *das* (*Völkerr.*) treaty of neutrality; **~verletzung** *die* (*Völkerr.*) violation of neutrality

**Neutron** /ˈnɔytrɔn/ *das*; **~s, ~en** /-ˈtroːnən/ (*Kernphysik*) neutron

**Neutronen-:** **~bombe** *die* neutron bomb; **~waffe** *die* neutron weapon; **~zahl** *die* (*Kernphysik*) neutron number

**Neutrum** /ˈnɔytrʊm/ *das*; **~s, Neutra** (*österr. nur so*) *od.* **Neutren** **A** (*Sprachw.*) neuter; **B** (*abwertend: Mensch ohne erotische Ausstrahlung*) sexless individual

**neu-, Neu-:** ***~vermählt** ⇒ **neu** 2 B; **~vermählte** *Pl.*; *adj. Dekl.* (*geh.*) newly-weds; **~wagen** *der* new car; **~wahl** *die* new election; **die ~wahl des Bundespräsidenten** the election of a new Federal President; **~wahlen ansetzen/ausschreiben** call new elections; **~wert** *der* **A** value when new; original value; (*Versicherungsw.*) replacement value; **B** (*marx.*: **~ geschaffener Wert**) new value; **~wertig** *Adj.* as new; **~wertiger Kühlschrank für 150 DM zu verkaufen** for sale, refrigerator, as new — 150 DM; **~wort** *das*; *Pl.* **~wörter** (*Sprachw.*) new word; neologism; **~zeit** *die* (*Zeit nach 1500*) modern era *or* age; (*Gegenwart*) modern times *pl.*; modern age; **~zeitlich** ❶ *Adj.* modern; since the Middle Ages *postpos.*, *not pred.*; (*modern*) modern ‹device, equipment, methods, etc.›; ❷ *adv.* (*modern*) ‹equip, fit› with all modern conveniences; **~zu·gang** *der* (*im Krankenhaus*) new admission; (*im Gefängnis*) new inmate; (*bei Militär, bei einer Firma, einem Verein*) new recruit; (*Buch für eine Bibliothek*) new accession; **~zulassung** *die* (*Amtsspr.*) **A** **die ~zulassung von Kraftfahrzeugen** the registration of new vehicles; **B** (*Fahrzeug*) new registration

**Nexus** /ˈnɛksʊs/ *der*; **~, ~:** nexus

**Niagara·fall** /ni̯aˈgaːra-/ *der*, **Niagarafälle** *Pl.* Niagara Falls

**Nibelungen·treue** /ˈniːbəlʊŋən-/ *die*; **~** (*oft abwertend*) unquestioning loyalty [unto death]

**Nicaragua** /nikaˈraːgu̯a/ (*das*); **~s** Nicaragua

**Nicaraguaner** *der*; **~s, ~, Nicaraguanerin** *die*; **~, ~nen** Nicaraguan; ⇒ *auch* **-in**

**nicaraguanisch** *Adj.* Nicaraguan

**nicht** /nɪçt/ *Adv.* **A** not; **sie raucht ~** (*im Moment*) she is not smoking; (*gewöhnlich*) she does not *or* doesn't smoke; **alle klatschten, nur sie ~:** they all applauded except for her; **Wer hat das getan? — Sie ~!** Who did that? — It wasn't her; **Gehst du hin? — Nein, ich gehe ~!** Are you going? — No, I'm not; **Ich mag ihn ~. — Ich auch ~:** I don't like him. — Neither do I; **ich kann das ~ mehr** *od.* **länger sehen** I can't stand the sight of it any more *or* longer; **~ einmal** *od.* (*ugs.*) **mal** not even; **~ mehr als** no more than; **~ ihn kenne ich, sondern sie** I don't know him, but I know her; **~ einer** not one; **~ dass ich ~ wollte, ich habe bloß keine Zeit** [it's] not that I don't want to, I just don't have the time; **das ist wirklich/absolut/gewiss/gar ~ schlimm!** it's not as bad as all that!; **B** (*Bitte, Verbot o. Ä. ausdrückend*) **~!** [no,] don't!; „**~ hinauslehnen!**" (*im Zug*) 'do not lean out of the window'; **bitte ~!** please don't!; **~ doch!** not at all!; (*bitte aufhören*) stop that!; **~ doch, ärgere dich doch ~!** come, come *or* come on, there's no need to get so worked up; **nur das ~!** anything but that!; **ärgere dich doch ~, das ist die Sache gar ~ wert** don't get so angry, it just isn't worth it; **C** (*Zustimmung erwartend*) **er ist dein Bruder, ~?** he's your brother, isn't he?; **du magst das, ~ [wahr]?** you like that, don't you?; **kommst du [etwa] ~?** aren't you coming[, then]?; **willst du ~ mitkommen?** won't you come too?; **ist es ~ herrlich hier?** isn't it glorious here?; **D** (*verwundert*) **was du ~ sagst!** you don't say!; **was ich mir ~ alles bieten lassen muss!** the things I have to put up with!; **E** (*[bedingte] Anerkennung ausdrückend*) **~ übel!** not bad!; **sie ist ~ dumm!** she's not stupid

**nicht-, Nicht-:** non-; **~beteiligung/~demokratisch/~akademiker** non-participation/non-democratic/non-graduate

**nicht-, Nicht-:** **~achtung** *die* **A** *in* **jmdn. mit ~achtung strafen** punish sb. by ignoring him/her; send sb. to Coventry; **B** (*Geringschätzung*) lack of regard *or* respect; **~achtung des Gerichts** contempt of court; **~amtlich** *Adj.* unofficial; **~anerkennung** *die* non-recognition; **~angriffs·pakt** *der* non-aggression pact; **~beachtung** *die* non-observance; **~beachtung einer roten Ampel** failure to observe a red light; **~befolgung** *die*: **~befolgung der Anweisungen/eines Befehls** failure to follow the instructions/to obey an order; **~befolgung der Bestimmungen/Vorschriften** non-compliance *or* failure to comply with the instructions/regulations; **~berufstätig** *Adj.* non-employed ‹housewives›

**Nichte** *die*; **~, ~n** niece

**nicht-, Nicht-:** **~ehelich** (*bes. Rechtsspr.*) ❶ *Adj.* illegitimate ‹child, birth›; **aus ~ehelichen Beziehungen geborene Kinder** children born out of wedlock; ❷ *adv.* ‹born› out of wedlock; **~einhaltung** *die* non-compliance, failure to comply (*Gen.* with); non-observance; **~ein·mischung** *die* (*Politik*) non-intervention; non-interference; **~eisen·metall** *das* non-ferrous metal; **~erfüllung** *die* non-fulfilment; **~erscheinen** *das*; **~~s** non-appearance; failure to appear; **~fach·mann** *der* non-expert; layman; **~flektierbar** *Adj.* (*Sprachw.*) non-inflected; **~gefallen** *das*: *in* **bei ~gefallen** (*Kaufmannsspr.*) if not satisfied

**nichtig** *Adj.* **A** (*geh.*: *wertlos, belanglos*) vain ‹things, pleasures, etc.›; paltry ‹desire›; trivial ‹reason›; petty ‹quarrel›; idle ‹chatter, thoughts›; empty ‹pretext›; **B** (*Rechtsspr.*: *ungültig*) invalid, void ‹contract, will, marriage, etc.›; **für ~ erklären** (*Rechtsspr.*) declare ‹contract, will, etc.› invalid *or* void; annul ‹marriage›; ⇒ *auch* **null**

**Nichtigkeit** *die*; **~, ~en** **A** (*geh.*) ⇒ **nichtig** A: vanity; paltriness; pettiness, triviality; idleness; emptiness; **B** (*geh.*: *belanglose Sache*) trifle; **C** (*Rechtsspr.*) invalidity; voidness; (*einer Ehe*) nullity

**Nichtigkeits·klage** *die* (*Rechtsw.*) nullity suit

**nicht-, Nicht-:** **~in·anspruch·nahme** *die* (*Amtsspr.*) failure to take advantage; **~kapitalistisch** *Adj.* non-capitalist ‹country, state›; ***~leitend** ⇒ **leiten** D; **~leiter** *der* (*Physik*) non-conductor; **~metall** *das* non-metal; **~mitglied** *das* non-member; **~öffentlich**

*old spelling (see note on page 1707)

*Adj.* not open to the public *pred.;* closed, private ‹meeting›; **die ~ öffentliche Beweisaufnahme** the hearing of the evidence in camera; ***~organisiert** ⇒ **organisiert**; **~raucher** *der* non-smoker; **ich bin ~raucher** I don't smoke; I'm a non-smoker; **„~raucher"** 'no smoking'; **~raucher·abteil** *das* non-smoking *or* no-smoking compartment; **~raucherin** *die* ⇒ **~raucher**; ***~rostend** ⇒ **rosten**

**nichts** /nɪçts/ *Indefinitpron.* nothing; **er sieht ~:** he sees nothing; he doesn't see anything; **hast du ~ gegessen?** haven't you eaten anything?; **ich möchte ~:** I don't want anything; **das ist ~ für mich** it's not for me; it isn't my cup of tea (*coll.*); **für ~ und wieder ~** (*ugs.*) for nothing at all; **sich in ~ von jmdm./etw. unterscheiden** be no different from sb./sth.; **~ zu machen!** (*ugs.*) nothing doing (*coll.*); **er ist durch ~ zu überzeugen** nothing will convince him; **von mir bekommst du ~ mehr** you'll get nothing more from me; you won't get anything more from me; **ich will ~ mehr davon hören** I don't want to hear any more about it; **die Ärzte konnten ~ mehr für ihn tun** the doctors could do nothing more *or* could not do any more for him; **~ anderes** nothing else; **jetzt interessiert er sich für ~ anderes mehr** he's now no longer interested in anything else; **haben Sie ~ anderes als Hamburger?** haven't you got anything else besides hamburgers?; **~ als** nothing but; **das/er ist zu ~ zu gebrauchen** it's/he's no use; it's/he's useless; **das war wohl ~** (*salopp*) that wasn't exactly brilliant; **wir wissen ~ Näheres/Genaues** we don't know any more/any details; **~ wie ins Bett/weg!** quick into bed/let's go!; **~ wie hinterher!** put your skates on, after him/her/them! (*sl.*); **~ weiter** nothing else; **von ~ kommt ~:** you don't get anything without effort; **~ da!** (*ugs.*) nothing doing! (*coll.*); **wie ~:** in a trice *or* flash; **die Angelegenheit ist ~ weniger als schön** it's not at all a nice business; ⇒ *auch* **danken** 2 A

**Nichts** *das;* **~, ~e** Ⓐ (*Philos.: das Nichtsein*) nothingness *no art.;* Ⓑ (*leerer Raum*) void; **er war wie aus dem ~ aufgetaucht** he appeared from nowhere; Ⓒ (*wenig von etw.*) **er hat die Fabrik aus dem ~ aufgebaut** he built the factory up from nothing; **vor dem ~ stehen** be left with nothing; be faced with ruin; **ein ~ von einem Bikini** *usw.* **[sein]** [be] a scrap of a bikini *etc.;* Ⓓ (*abwertend: Mensch*) nobody; nonentity

**nichts·ahnend** *Adj.* unsuspecting

**Nicht-:** **~schwimmer** *der* non-swimmer; **er war ~schwimmer** he could not swim; **~schwimmer·becken** *das* non-swimmers' *or* learners' pool **~schwimmerin** *die* ⇒ **~schwimmer**

**nichts-:** **~desto·minder**, **~desto·trotz** (*ugs. scherzh.*), **~desto·weniger** *Adv.* nevertheless; none the less

**Nicht-:** **~sein** *das* (*Philos.*) non-existence *no art.;* non-being *no art.;* **~sesshafte**, ***~seßhafte** *der/die; adj. Dekl.* (*Amtsspr.*) person of no fixed abode (*Admin. Lang.*)

**nichts-**, **Nichts-:** **~könner** *der*, **~könnerin** *die* (*abwertend*) incompetent; bungler; **~nutz** *der;* **~~es, ~~e** (*veralt. abwertend*) good-for-nothing; **mein ~nutz von Bruder** my good-for-nothing [of a] brother; **~nutzig** *Adj.* (*veralt. abwertend*) good-for-nothing *attrib.;* worthless ‹existence›; **~sagend** ❶ *Adj.* meaningless, empty ‹talk, phrases, etc.›; (*fig.: ausdruckslos*) vacant ‹smile›; expressionless ‹face›; **ein ~sagender Typ** a nonentity; ❷ *adv.* meaninglessly ‹formulated›; ‹smile› vacantly; **~tuer** /-tu:ɐ/ *der;* **~~s, ~~** (*abwertend*) layabout; loafer; **die reichen ~tuer** the idle rich; **~tuerei** /---'-/ *die;* **~~** (*abwertend*) idle loafing; **~tuerin** *die;* **~~, ~~nen** ⇒ **~tuer**; **~tun** *das* Ⓐ (*Untätigkeit*) inactivity; doing nothing *no art.;* Ⓑ (*Müßiggang*) idleness *no art.;* lazing about *no art.;* **das süße ~tun** being gloriously idle; **~würdig** (*geh. abwertend*) ❶ *Adj.* worthless, despicable ‹person›; base, unworthy, despicable ‹deed›; **~würdiger!** worthless *or* despicable wretch!; ❷ *adv.* ‹betray, deceive› basely; ‹act› unworthily; **~würdigkeit** *die;* **~~** (*geh. veralt.*) ⇒ **~würdig**: worthlessness; despicableness; baseness; unworthiness

**nicht-**, **Nicht-:** **~tänzer** *der*, **~tänzerin** *die* non-dancer; **ich bin ~tänzer[in]** I don't dance; **~zielend** *Adj.* (*Sprachw.*) intransitive; **~zustandekommen** *das;* **~~s** (*eines Vertrags*) non-conclusion; **das ~zustandekommen der Konferenz** the failure of the conference to take place; **~zutreffende** *das; adj. Dekl.* **~zutreffendes streichen** delete as applicable

**Nickel**[1] /'nɪkl/ *das;* **~s** nickel

**Nickel**[2] *der;* **~s, ~** (*ugs. veralt.: Münze*) 10-pfennig piece

**Nickel-:** **~brille** *die* metal-rimmed glasses *or* spectacles; **~legierung** *die* nickel alloy

**nicken** /'nɪkn/ ❶ *itr. V.* Ⓐ nod; **befriedigt/zustimmend ~:** nod one's satisfaction/agreement; **mit dem Kopf ~:** nod one's head; Ⓑ (*fam.: schlafen*) doze; snooze (*coll.*). ❷ *tr. V.* (*geh.:* **~d** *ausdrücken*) nod; **Zustimmung/Beifall ~:** nod one's agreement/approval

**Nickerchen** *das;* **~s, ~** (*fam.*) nap; snooze (*coll.*); **ein ~ halten** *od.* **machen** take *or* have forty winks *or* a nap

**Nicki** /'nɪki/ *der;* **~[s], ~s** velour pullover *or* sweater

**Nicotin** ⇒ **Nikotin**

**nie** /ni:/ *Adv.* never; **mich besucht ~ jemand** nobody ever visits me; **fast ~:** hardly ever; **~ mehr!** never again!; **[einmal und] ~ wieder** [only once and] never again; **~ und nimmer!** never!; **~ im Leben!** not on your life!; **das werde ich ~ im Leben vergessen** I shall never forget it as long as I live

**nieder** /'ni:dɐ/ ❶ *Adj.* Ⓐ (*von minderem Rang*) lower ‹class, intelligence›; petty, minor ‹official›; lowly ‹family, origins, birth›; menial ‹task›; **das ~e Volk** the common people; **der ~e Klerus/Adel** the lower clergy/aristocracy; Ⓑ (*bes. südd.*) ⇒ **niedrig** A; Ⓒ (*Biol.: nicht hoch entwickelt*) lower ‹plant, animal, organism›; ⇒ *auch* **Jagd** A. ❷ *Adv.* (*hinunter*) down; **die Waffen ~!** lay down your arms!; **~ mit dem Militarismus!** down with militarism!

**nieder-**, **Nieder-:** **~|beugen** (*geh.*) ❶ *tr. V.* bend ‹knee› downwards; bow ‹head›; ❷ *refl. V.* bend down; **~|brennen** ❶ *unr. itr. V.;* *mit sein* (*herunterbrennen*) ‹fire› burn low; ‹building› burn down; ❷ *unr. tr. V.* burn down ‹building, village, etc.›; **~|brüllen** *tr. V.* (*ugs.*) **jmdn. ~brüllen** shout sb. down; **~deutsch** *Adj.* Low German ‹dialect›; North German ‹custom, farmhouse, landscape›; **~|donnern** *itr. V.;* *mit sein* ‹avalanche› thunder down; ‹roof› come crashing down; **~druck** *der; Pl.* **~drücke** (*Technik*) low pressure; **~|drücken** *tr. V.* Ⓐ (*herunterdrücken*) press down; press *or* push down, (*formal*) depress ‹handle, lever›; Ⓑ (*bedrücken*) depress; ‹memory› weigh on, oppress ‹person›; ⇒ *auch* **niedergedrückt**; **~|fallen** *unr. itr. V.;* *mit sein* (*geh.*) ‹snow› fall; **vor jmdm. ~fallen** fall down [on one's knees] before sb.; **~frequenz** *die* (*Physik*) low frequency; **~gang** *der* Ⓐ (*Verfall*) fall; decline; Ⓑ (*Seemannsspr.: Treppe*) companionway; companion ladder; **~gedrückt** ❶ *2. Part. v.* **~drücken;** ❷ *Adj.* depressed; dejected; **~|gehen** *unr. itr. V.;* *mit sein* Ⓐ (*landen*) ‹plane, spacecraft, balloonist› come down; ‹parachutist› drop; ‹birds, flock› land; Ⓑ (*fallen*) ‹rain, satellite, avalanche› come down; ‹meteor› come to earth; Ⓒ (*Boxen: zu Boden fallen*) go down; Ⓓ (*sich senken*) ‹theatre curtain› fall; Ⓔ (*untergehen*) ‹sun, moon› go down; ‹epoch› decline; **~geschlagen** ❶ *2. Part. v.* **~schlagen;** ❷ *Adj.* despondent; dejected; **~geschlagenheit** *die;* **~geschlagenheit** despondency; dejection; **~|halten** *unr. tr. V.* Ⓐ (*unterdrücken*) oppress ‹nation, people, class›; keep ‹nation, people, class› in subjection; keep ‹person› down; Ⓑ (*kontrollieren*) keep down ‹resistance›; Ⓒ (*unten halten*) hold down; **~|holen** *tr. V.* haul down, lower ‹sail, flag›; **~|kämpfen** *tr. V.* Ⓐ (*besiegen*) overcome ‹enemy, opponent›; Ⓑ (*zurückhalten*) suppress ‹rage, excitement›; fight back ‹tears›; fight ‹tiredness›; **~|knien** *itr. V.* (*auch mit sein*), *refl. V.* kneel down; (*unterwürfig, demütig*) go down on one's knees; **~|knüppeln** *tr. V.* **jmdn. ~knüppeln** beat *or* club sb. to the ground with a truncheon; **~|kommen** *unr. itr. V.;* *mit sein* (*geh. veralt.*) be delivered (**mit** of); give birth (**mit** to); **~kunft** /-kʊnft/ *die;* **~~, ~künfte** /-kʏnftə/ (*geh. veralt.*) confinement; **~lage** *die* Ⓐ (*das Besiegtwerden*) defeat; **eine ~lage einstecken müssen** suffer a defeat; **jmdm. eine ~lage beibringen** inflict a defeat on sb.; Ⓑ (*Zweiggeschäft*) branch; (*Lager*) warehouse; depot

**Nieder·lande** *Pl.:* **die ~:** the Netherlands

**Niederländer** *der;* **~s, ~** ▶ **553** Dutchman; Netherlander; **die ~:** the Dutch

**Niederländerin** *die;* **~, ~nen** ▶ **553** Dutchwoman; Netherlander; ⇒ *auch* **-in**

**niederländisch** *Adj.* ▶ **553**, ▶ **696** Dutch; Netherlands *attrib.* ‹government, embassy, etc.›; **das Niederländische** Dutch

**nieder-**, **Nieder-:** **~|lassen** ❶ *unr. refl. V.* Ⓐ (*ein Geschäft, eine Praxis eröffnen*) set up *or* establish oneself in business; ‹doctor, lawyer› set up a practice *or* in practice; **sich als Fotograf ~lassen** set up as a photographer; **~gelassene Ärzte** *registered doctors/specialists having their own independent practices;* Ⓑ (*seinen Wohnsitz nehmen*) settle; Ⓒ (*geh.: sich setzen*) sit down; seat oneself; ‹bird› settle, alight; ❷ *unr. tr. V.* lower ‹theatre curtain, blind, etc.›; **~lassung** *die;* **~~, ~~en** Ⓐ ⇒ **~lassen** A: setting up in business; setting up of a practice *or* in practice; Ⓑ (*Ort*) settlement; Ⓒ (*Wirtsch.: Zweigstelle*) branch; **~|legen** *tr. V.* Ⓐ (*geh.: hinlegen*) lay *or* put *or* set down; lay ‹wreath›; **die Waffen ~legen** lay down one's arms; Ⓑ (*nicht weitermachen*) lay down, resign [from] ‹office›; relinquish ‹command›; discontinue ‹course of treatment›; **das Mandat ~legen** ‹member of parliament› resign one's seat; ‹lawyer› give up the brief; ⇒ *auch* **Arbeit** A; Ⓒ (*geh.: aufschreiben*) set down; **~legung** *die;* **~~, ~~en** Ⓐ (*geh.: eines Kranzes*) laying; Ⓑ (*eines Amtes*) resignation (+ *Gen.* from); (*eines Kommandos*) relinquishing; **die ~legung der Arbeit** stopping work; Ⓒ (*geh.:* **~schrift**) setting down; **~|machen** *tr. V.* (*ugs.*) butcher; **~|mähen** *tr. V.* mow down ‹prisoners, soldiers, etc.›; **~|metzeln** *tr. V.* butcher

**Nieder·österreich** (*das*) Lower Austria

**nieder-:** **~|prasseln** *itr. V.;* *mit sein* ‹rain, hail› beat down; ‹blows, rebukes, questions, etc.› rain down; **~|reißen** *unr. tr. V.* Ⓐ (*abreißen*) pull down ‹building, wall›; Ⓑ (*zu Boden reißen*) **jmdn. ~reißen** knock sb. over; **~rheinisch** *Adj.* in the Lower Rhine valley *postpos.*

**Nieder·sachse** *der* inhabitant of Lower Saxony; (*von Geburt*) native of Lower Saxony; ⇒ *auch* **Kölner** 2

**Nieder·sachsen** (*das*) Lower Saxony

**Nieder·sächsin** *die* ⇒ **Niedersachse**

**niedersächsisch** *Adj.* Lower Saxon

**nieder-**, **Nieder-:** **~|schießen** ❶ *unr. tr. V.* gun down; **der ~geschossene** the victim of the shooting; ❷ *unr. itr. V.;* *mit sein* (*herabfliegen*) ‹bird› stoop, swoop down; ‹aircraft› hurtle down; **~schlag** *der* Ⓐ (*Met.*) precipitation; **es sind zeitweise ~schläge, teils Regen, teils Schnee, zu erwarten** occasional showers can be expected, some falling as snow; Ⓑ (*Boxen*) knock-down; Ⓒ (*Ausdruck*) expression; **[seinen] ~schlag in etw.** (*Dat.*) **finden** find expression in sth.; Ⓓ (*Chemie*) precipitate; Ⓔ **radioaktiver ~schlag** [radioactive] fallout; **~|schlagen** ❶ *unr. tr. V.* Ⓐ (*zu Boden schlagen*) **jmdn. ~schlagen** knock sb. down; Ⓑ (*umschlagen*) turn down ‹hat brim, collar›; Ⓒ (*beenden*) suppress, put down ‹revolt, uprising, etc.›; put an end to ‹strike›; Ⓓ (*senken*) lower ‹eyes, eyelids›; **den Blick ~schlagen** lower one's eyes; Ⓔ (*Rechtsspr.: einstellen*) abandon ‹proceedings›; dismiss ‹claim›; **ein Verfahren ~schlagen** dismiss a case; Ⓕ (*Rechtsspr.: erlassen*) waive ‹costs›; remit ‹punishment›; ⇒

*auch* **niedergeschlagen**; ❷ *unr. refl. V.* [A] **sich in etw.** (*Dat.*) **∼schlagen** ‹experience, emotion› find expression in sth.; ‹performance, hard work› be reflected in sth.; [B] ‹steam› condense; **∼schlags·arm** *Adj.* ‹climate, area, period› with low precipitation *not pred.*; **∼schlags·frei** *Adj.* ‹period› without [any] precipitation *not pred.*; **die Aussichten: heiter bis wolkig und ∼schlagsfrei** the outlook: dry with variable amounts of cloud; **∼schlagung** *die*; **∼∼, ∼∼en** [A] (*einer Revolte, eines Aufstands*) suppression; putting down; [B] (*Rechtsspr.*) ⇒ **∼schlagen** 1 E, F: abandonment; dismissal; waiving; remission; **∼|schmettern** *tr. V.* [A] (*∼schlagen*) **jmdn. ∼schmettern** send sb. crashing to the ground/floor; [B] (*erschüttern*) ‹bad news› shatter; ‹rejection, result› devastate; **∼schmetternd** *Adj.* shattering ‹experience, news›; devastating ‹result, review›; **∼|schreiben** *unr. tr. V.* write down; write ‹essay, novel›; **∼|schreien** *unr. tr. V.* **jmdn. ∼schreien** shout sb. down; **∼schrift** *die* [A] (*das Schreiben*) writing down; **etw. zur ∼schrift erklären** (*Rechtsspr.*) dictate a statement on sth.; [B] (*Schriftstück*) document; (*Protokoll*) minutes *pl.*; **∼|setzen** ❶ *refl. V.* sit down; ❷ *tr. V.* put *or* set down; **∼|sinken** *unr. itr. V.*; *mit sein* sink down; **ohnmächtig ∼sinken** sink unconscious to the ground/floor; **∼spannung** *die* (*Elektrot.*) low voltage *or* tension; **∼|stechen** *unr. tr. V.* stab; (*erstechen*) stab to death; **∼|stimmen** *tr. V.* vote ‹proposal, person, etc.› down; **∼|stoßen** ❶ *unr. tr. V.* (*geh.: zu Boden stoßen*) **jmdn. ∼stoßen** knock sb. down; ❷ *unr. itr. V.*; *mit sein* ‹hawk, etc.› stoop, swoop down; ‹aircraft› hurtle down; **∼|strecken** (*geh.*) ❶ *tr. V.* **jmdn. ∼strecken** knock sb. down; (*mit einem Schuss*) shoot sb. down; **einen Tiger/Hirsch ∼strecken** bring down a tiger/stag; ❷ *refl. V.* (*sich hinlegen*) lie down; **auf das** *od.* **dem Sofa ∼gestreckt** stretched out on the sofa; **∼|stürzen** *itr. V.*; *mit sein* (*geh.*) [A] (*zu Boden fallen*) fall down; **ohnmächtig ∼stürzen** fall unconscious to the ground/floor; [B] (*herabfallen*) ‹rocks› fall; ‹avalanche› sweep down; **∼tourig** /-tu:rɪç/ (*Technik*) ❶ *Adj.* **im ∼tourigen Bereich** at low revs (*coll.*); ❷ *adv.* at low revs (*coll.*); **∼tracht** *die*; **∼tracht** (*geh.*) malice; (*als Charaktereigenschaft*) vileness; despicableness; **etw. aus ∼tracht tun** do sth. out of malice; **∼trächtig** ❶ *Adj.* malicious ‹person, slander, lie, etc.›; (*verachtenswert*) vile, despicable ‹person›; base, vile ‹misrepresentation, slander, lie›; ❷ *adv.* ‹betray, lie, treat› in a vile *or* despicable way; ‹smile› maliciously; **∼trächtigkeit** *die* [A] ⇒ **∼trächtig** 1: maliciousness; vileness; despicableness; baseness; [B] (*gemeine Handlung*) vile *or* despicable act; **∼|trampeln** *tr. V.* (*ugs.*), **∼|treten** *unr. tr. V.* tread ‹grass, flowers, carpet pile, etc.›; (*fig.*) trample ‹person› underfoot

**Niederung** *die*; **∼, ∼en** low-lying area; (*an Flussläufen, Küsten*) flats *pl.*; (*Tal*) valley; **sumpfige ∼en** marshes; **die ∼en des [alltäglichen] Lebens** (*fig.*) the lowly spheres of everyday life

**nieder-, Nieder-: ∼|walzen** *tr. V.* flatten; **jmdn. mit Argumenten ∼walzen** (*fig.*) overwhelm sb. with arguments; **∼|werfen** ❶ *unr. tr. V.* [A] (*geh.: besiegen*) overcome, defeat ‹enemy, rebels, etc.›; [B] (*geh.: beenden*) ⇒ **∼schlagen** 1 C; [C] (*geh.: schwächen*) ‹illness, fever› lay ‹person› low; [D] (*geh.: erschüttern*) ‹bad news› shake ‹person› profoundly; **der Tod seiner Frau hat ihn ∼geworfen** he took the death of his wife very badly; ❷ *unr. refl. V.* throw oneself down; **sich vor jmdm. ∼werfen** prostrate oneself before sb.; **∼werfung** *die*; **∼∼, ∼∼en** (*geh.*) (*von Feinden, Aufständischen*) overthrow; defeat; (*einer Revolte, eines Aufstands*) suppression; putting down; **∼wild** *das* (*Jägerspr.*) *smaller game animals, e.g. roe-deer, hare, fox, badger*; **∼|zwingen** *unr. tr. V.* (*geh.*) force ‹opponent› to the ground *or* down; (*fig.*) suppress ‹anger, excitement›

**niedlich** /ˈni:tlɪç/ ❶ *Adj.* sweet; cute (*Amer. coll.*); sweet little *attrib.*; dear little *attrib.* ❷ *adv.* ‹dance, nibble› sweetly, prettily; ‹babble, play› sweetly, cutely (*Amer. coll.*); **auf dem Foto guckt die Kleine so ∼:** in the photo the little girl has such a sweet expression

**niedrig** ❶ *Adj.* [A] ▶ 411 (*von geringer Höhe*) low; short ‹grass›; [B] (*von geringem Rang*) lowly ‹origins, birth›; low ‹rank, status, intellectual level›; [C] (*sittlich tief stehend*) base ‹instinct, desire, emotion, person›; vile ‹motive›; **von ∼er Gesinnung** low-minded. ❷ *adv.* ‹hang, fly› low

**Niedrigenergie·haus** *das* low-energy house

**Niedrigkeit** *die*; **∼, ∼en** [A] (*geringe Höhe*) lowness; [B] (*niedrige Gesinnung*) baseness; [C] (*gemeine Tat*) base deed

**Niedrig-: ∼lohn** *der* low wages *pl.*; **∼lohn·land** *das* country with a low-wage economy; **etw. im ∼lohnland Taiwan produzieren** produce sth. in Taiwan, with its low wages *or* low-wage economy; **∼preis** *der* low price; **∼wasser** *das* [A] (*von Seen/Flüssen*) **bei ∼wasser** when the [level of the] lake/river is low; [B] (*bei Ebbe*) low tide; low water; **bei ∼wasser** at low tide *or* low water

**niemals** /ˈni:ma:ls/ *Adv.* never

**niemand** /ˈni:mant/ *Indefinitpron.* nobody; no one; **∼ war im Büro** there was nobody *or* no one in the office; there wasn't anybody *or* any one in the office; **wir haben ∼[en] gesehen** we saw nobody *or* no one; we didn't see anybody *or* any one; **∼ anders** *od.* **anderer** nobody *or* no one else; **es kann ∼ anders** *od.* **anderer als du gewesen sein** it can't have been anybody *or* any one [else] but you; **das war ∼ anders als der Kaiser** it was none other than the emperor himself; **er hat mit ∼[em] von uns reden wollen** he didn't want to talk to any of us; **das darfst du ∼[em] sagen!** you mustn't tell anybody that!; **∼ Bekanntes** nobody I know/he knows *etc.*; (*keine prominenten Leute*) nobody famous; **lass ∼ Fremdes herein** don't let anybody *or* anyone in you don't know; don't let any strangers in; **er ist ∼[e]s Feind** he has no enemies; **ein N∼ sein** be a nobody

**Niemands·land** *das* [A] (*auch fig.*) no man's land; [B] (*unerforschtes Gebiet, auch fig.*) unknown *or* unexplored territory

**Niere** /ˈni:rə/ *die*; **∼, ∼n** ▶ 471 kidney; **künstliche ∼:** kidney machine; artificial kidney; **jmdm. an die ∼n gehen** (*fig. ugs.*) get to sb. (*coll.*)

**nieren-, Nieren-: ∼becken·entzündung** *die* pyelitis; **∼entzündung** *die* nephritis; **∼förmig** *Adj.* kidney-shaped; **∼kolik** *die* renal colic; **∼leiden** *das* ▶ 474 kidney disease; **∼stein** *der* ▶ 474 kidney stone; renal calculus (*Med.*); **∼tisch** *der* kidney-shaped table

**nieseln** /ˈni:zl̩n/ *unpers. V.* drizzle

**Niesel-: ∼priem** *der* (*veralt. scherzh.*) misery [guts] (*coll.*); **∼regen** *der* drizzle

**niesen** /ˈni:zn̩/ *itr. V.* sneeze

**Nies-: ∼pulver** *das* sneezing powder; **∼reiz** *der* urge to sneeze

**Nieß·brauch** /ˈni:sbraux/ *der* (*Rechtsw.*) usufruct

**Nies·wurz** *die* (*Bot.*) hellebore

**Niet** /ni:t/ *der*, (*auch:*) *das*; **∼[e]s, ∼e** (*fachspr.*) ⇒ **Niete**[2]

**Niete**[1] /ˈni:tə/ *die*; **∼, ∼n** [A] (*Los*) blank; **eine ∼ ziehen** draw a blank; [B] (*ugs.: Mensch*) dead loss (*coll.*) (**in** + *Dat.* at)

**Niete**[2] *die*; **∼, ∼n** rivet

**nieten** /ˈni:tn̩/ *tr. V.* rivet

**Nieten·hose** *die* [pair of] studded jeans

**niet- und nagelfest** *in* **[alles] was nicht ∼ ist** (*ugs.*) [everything] that's not nailed *or* screwed down

**nigel·nagel·neu** *Adj.* (*schweiz. ugs.*) brand-new

**Niger**[1] /ˈni:gɐ/ *(das)*; **∼s** (*Staat*) Niger

**Niger**[2] *der*; **∼[s]** ▶ 306 (*Fluss*) Niger

**Nigeria** /niˈge:ri̯a/ *(das)*; **∼s** Nigeria

**Nigerianer** *der*; **∼s, ∼, Nigerianerin** *die*; **∼, ∼nen** Nigerian; ⇒ *auch* **-in**

**nigerianisch** *Adj.* Nigerian

**Nigger** /ˈnɪgɐ/ *der*; **∼s, ∼** (*abwertend, oft als Schimpfwort*) nigger (*derog.*)

**Nihilismus** /nihiˈlɪsmʊs/ *der*; **∼:** nihilism

**Nihilist** *der*; **∼en, ∼en, Nihilistin** *die*; **∼, ∼nen** nihilist

**nihilistisch** *Adj.* nihilistic

**Nikolaus**[1] /ˈnɪkolaus/ *der*; **∼, ∼e** [A] St Nicholas; [B] (*Tag*) St Nicholas' Day

**Nikolaus**[2] (*der*) (*hist. Name*) Nicholas

**Nikolaus·tag** *der* St Nicholas' Day

**Nikotin** /nikoˈti:n/ *das*; **∼s** nicotine

**nikotin-, Nikotin-: ∼arm** *Adj.* low-nicotine *attrib.*; low in nicotine *pred.*; **∼frei** *Adj.* nicotine-free; **∼gehalt** *der* nicotine content; **∼haltig** *Adj.* containing nicotine *postpos.*, *not pred.*; **∼haltig sein** contain nicotine; **∼vergiftung** *die* nicotine poisoning

**Nil** /ni:l/ *der*; **∼[s]** ▶ 306 Nile

**Nil·pferd** *das* hippopotamus; hippo (*coll.*)

**Nimbus** /ˈnɪmbʊs/ *der*; **∼, ∼se** [A] (*geh.: Ruhm*) aura; **sein ∼ als großer Dichter** his reputation as a great poet; [B] (*Kunstwiss.*) nimbus

**nimm** /nɪm/ *Imperativ Sg. v.* **nehmen**

**nimmer** /ˈnɪmɐ/ *Adv.* [A] (*geh. veralt.: niemals*) never; [B] (*südd., österr.*) never again; **das kann ich ∼ aushalten** I can't endure it any longer; ⇒ *auch* **nie**

**Nimmerleinstag** /ˈnɪmɐlainsta:k/ *in* **am ∼** (*ugs. scherzh.*) never; **etw. auf den** *od.* **bis zum ∼ verschieben** (*ugs. scherzh.*) put sth. off indefinitely

**nimmer-, Nimmer-: ∼mehr** *Adv.* [A] (*veralt.: nie*) never; [B] (*südd., österr.: nie wieder*) never again; **∼müde** (*geh.*) ❶ *Adj.* tireless, untiring ‹helper, worker, etc.›; **in ∼müder Arbeit** working tirelessly *or* untiringly; ❷ *adv.* tirelessy; untiringly; **∼satt** *Adj.* (*fam.*) insatiable; **∼satt** *der*; **∼∼[e]s, ∼∼e** (*fam.*) gannet (*coll.*); **∼wieder·sehen** *in* **auf ∼wiedersehen verschwinden** (*ugs.*, *oft scherzh.*) vanish never to be seen again

**Nimrod** /ˈnɪmrɔt/ *der*; **∼s, ∼e** (*geh.*, *oft scherzh.*) Nimrod

**Nippel** /ˈnɪpl̩/ *der*; **∼s, ∼** [A] (*Technik; ugs.: Brustwarze*) nipple; [B] (*am Wasserball*) valve

**nippen** /ˈnɪpn̩/ *itr. V.* (*trinken*) sip; take a sip/sips; (*essen*) nibble (**von** at); **vom Wein ∼:** sip [at] the wine; take a sip/sips of the wine; **am Glas ∼:** sip from *or* take a sip/sips from the glass

**Nippes** /ˈnɪpəs/, **Nipp·sachen** *Pl.* [porcelain] knick-knacks; small [porcelain] ornaments

**Nipp·tide** *die* neap tide

**nirgend-: ∼her** *Adv.* ⇒ **nirgendwoher**; **∼hin** *Adv.* ⇒ **nirgendwohin**

**nirgends** /ˈnɪrgn̩ts/ *Adv.* nowhere; **er war ∼ zu finden** he was nowhere *or* wasn't anywhere to be found; **ich fühle mich ∼ so wohl wie hier** there is nowhere *or* isn't anywhere I feel as happy as here; **sonst ∼:** nowhere else; **er hält es ∼ lange aus** he doesn't stay anywhere for long

**nirgend-: ∼wo** *Adv.* ⇒ **nirgends**; **∼woher** *Adv.* from nowhere; **sie konnten die Medikamente ∼woher bekommen** they couldn't get the medicines from anywhere; **∼wohin** *Adv.* **der Weg führt ∼wohin** the path doesn't go anywhere; **wir gehen ∼wohin** we're not going anywhere

**Nirwana** /nɪrˈva:na/ *das*; **∼[s]** nirvana

**Nische** /ˈni:ʃə/ *die*; **∼, ∼n** [A] (*Einbuchtung*) niche; [B] (*Erweiterung eines Raumes*) recess

**Niss, *Niß** /nɪs/ *die*; **∼, Nisse** (*veralt.*), **Nisse** /ˈnɪsə/ *die*; **∼, ∼n** nit

**nisten** /ˈnɪstn̩/ *itr. V.* nest; **eine tiefe Traurigkeit nistete in ihrem Herzen** (*fig. geh.*) a deep sadness dwelt in her heart

**Nist-: ∼kasten** *der* nest box; nesting box; **∼platz** *der* nesting site; **∼zeit** *die* nesting time *or* season

**Nitrat** /niˈtra:t/ *das*; **∼[e]s, ∼e** (*Chemie*) nitrate

**Nitrid** /niˈtri:t/ *das*; **∼s, ∼e** (*Chemie*) nitride

**nitrieren** *tr. V.* [A] (*Chemie*) nitrate; [B] (*Technik*) nitride ‹steel›

*old spelling (see note on page 1707)

**Nitrit** /ni'tri:t/ *das;* **∼s, ∼e** (*Chemie*) nitrite

**Nitro·glyzerin** /ni:tro-/ *das* nitroglycerine

**Niveau** /ni'vo:/ *das;* **∼s, ∼s** **A** level; **auf dem geistigen ∼ eines Fünfjährigen stehen** have the mental age of a five-year-old; **überhaupt kein ∼ haben** ‹programme, article, etc.› be totally undistinguished, lack any distinction whatever; **eine Zeitung mit ∼:** a quality newspaper; **er hat wenig ∼:** he is not very cultured *or* knowledgeable; **der Unterricht dieses Lehrers hat ein sehr hohes ∼:** this teacher's lessons are intellectually very demanding; **B** (*Qualitäts∼*) standard

**niveau-, Niveau-: ∼los** *Adj.* intellectually undemanding ‹lesson›; mediocre ‹performance, programme, exhibition›; [intellectually] dull ‹person›; **∼unterschied** *der* ⇒ **Niveau A, B:** difference in level/standard; **∼voll** *Adj.* intellectually demanding ‹lecture›; cultured and intelligent ‹person›; ‹entertainment, programme› of quality *postpos., not pred.;* [high-]quality ‹goods›

**nivellieren** /nivɛ'li:rən/ *tr. V.* **A** (*ausgleichen*) level *or* even out ‹difference›; (*nach unten*) level down; **B** (*Vermessungsw.*) level

**Nivellier·instrument** *das;* **∼[e]s, ∼en** [surveyor's] level

**Nivellierung** *die;* **∼, ∼en** levelling out; evening out; (*nach unten*) levelling down

**nix** /nɪks/ *Indefinitpron.* (*ugs.*) ⇒ **nichts**

**Nix** *der;* **∼es, ∼e** (*germ. Myth.*) nix; (*mit Fischschwanz*) merman

**Nixe** *die;* **∼, ∼n** (*germ. Myth.*) nixie; (*mit Fischschwanz*) mermaid

**Nizza** /'nɪtsa/ (*das*)*;* **∼s** Nice

**N.N.** *Abk.* **nomen nescio** n.n.; (*vorläufig unbekannt*) A. N. Other

**NN** *Abk.* **Normallnull[punkt]; unter/über NN** below/above sea level

**NNO** *Abk.* ▶ **400** **Nordnordost[en]** NNE

**NNW** *Abk.* ▶ **400** **Nordnordwest[en]** NNW

**NO** *Abk.* ▶ **400** **Nordost[en]** NE

**nobel** /'no:bl̩/ ❶ *Adj.* **A** (*geh.: edel*) noble; noble[-minded] ‹person›; **B** (*oft spött.: luxuriös*) elegant, (*coll.*) posh ‹boutique, house, hotel›; fine ‹cigar›; **∼, ∼!** very posh (*coll.*); **∼ geht die Welt zugrunde** (*iron.*) one has to make a splash even if it's the last one (*coll.*); **C** (*ugs.: freigebig*) lavish, generous ‹tip, present›; generous ‹person›. ❷ *adv.* **A** (*geh.: edel*) nobly; **B** (*oft spött.: luxuriös*) ‹dress, live, eat› in the grand style

**Nobel-: ∼marke** luxury brand; **∼hotel/∼restaurant/∼boutique** posh hotel/restaurant/boutique (*coll.*); **∼herberge/∼kutsche** (*salopp*) posh *or* swish hotel/car (*coll.*)

**Nobel-** /nɔ'bɛl-/**: ∼preis** *der* Nobel prize; **∼preis·träger** *der,* **∼preis·trägerin** *die* Nobel prizewinner

**Noblesse** /no'blɛsə/ *die;* **∼** (*geh.*) **A** (*edle Art*) nobility; noble-mindedness; **B** (*Eleganz*) elegance

**noch** /nɔx/ ❶ *Adv.* **A** ([*wie*] *bisher, derzeit*) still; **∼ nicht** not yet; **∼ regnet es nicht** it's not raining yet; it hasn't started raining yet; **sie sind immer ∼ nicht da** they're still not here; **ich sehe ihn kaum ∼:** I hardly ever see him any more; **ich habe ∼ nie Pizza gegessen** I've never eaten a pizza before; **ich bleibe ∼ ein Weilchen** I'll stay a little bit longer; **∼ nach Jahren** even years later; **er hat [bis jetzt] ∼ immer/nie gewonnen** he's won every time up until now/never won yet; **B** (*als Rest einer Menge*) **ich habe [nur] ∼ zehn Mark** I've [only] ten marks left; **es dauert ∼ fünf Minuten** it'll be another five minutes; **Beuteltiere gibt es ∼/nur ∼ in Australien** marsupials still exist/now only exist in Australia; **es sind ∼ 10 km bis zur Grenze** it's another 10 km. to the border; **es fehlt [mir/dir** *usw.***] ∼ eine Mark** I/you *etc.* need another mark; **C** (*bevor etw. anderes geschieht*) just; **ich will ∼ [schnell] duschen** I just want to have a [quick] shower; **ich mache das [jetzt/dann] ∼ fertig** I'll just get this finished; **D** (*irgendwann einmal*) some time; one day; **du wirst ihn [schon] ∼ kennen lernen** you'll get to know him yet; **er wird ∼ anrufen/kommen** he will still call/come; **E** (*womöglich*) if you're/he's *etc.* not careful; **du kommst ∼ zu spät!** you'll be late if you're not careful; **er endet ∼ im Gefängnis** he'll land up in prison if he doesn't watch out *or* isn't careful; **F** (*drückt eine geringe zeitliche Distanz aus*) only; **gestern habe ich ihn ∼ gesehen/∼ mit ihm gesprochen** I saw him only yesterday/I was speaking to him only yesterday; **∼ Ende des 19. Jahrhunderts** as late as the end of the 19th century; **sie war eben** *od.* **gerade ∼ hier** she was here only a moment ago; **es ist ∼ keine Woche her, dass ...** it was less than a week ago that ...; **G** (*nicht später als*) **das muss ∼ diese Woche/vor Monatsende geschehen** that's got to happen this week/by the end of the month; **∼ am selben Abend** the [very] same evening; **∼ ehe er antworten konnte, legte sie auf** even before he could reply she hung up; **er wurde ∼ am Unfallort operiert** he was operated on at the scene of the accident; **H** (*drückt aus, dass etw. unwiederholbar ist*) **ich habe Großvater ∼ gekannt** I'm old enough to have known grandfather; **dass er das ∼ erleben durfte!** and to think that he lived long enough to experience that!; **I** (*drückt aus, dass sich etw. im Rahmen hält*) **das lasse ich mir gerade ∼ gefallen** I'll put up with it; **Er hat ∼ Glück gehabt. Es hätte weit schlimmer kommen können** He was lucky. It could have been much worse; **das ist [im Vergleich] ∼ billig** that's [still] cheap in comparison; **es ist immer ∼ teuer genug** it's still expensive enough; **der Koffer geht ∼ zu** the case will still close; **das geht ∼:** that's [still] all right *or* (*coll.*) OK; **das ist ∼ lange kein Grund** that still isn't any sort of reason; **wenn er sich [wenigstens] ∼ entschuldigt hätte** if he had apologized at least; **das ist ja ∼ [ein]mal gut gegangen** (*ugs.*) it was just about all right; **J** (*außerdem, zusätzlich*) **wer war ∼ da?** who else was there?; **er hat [auch/außerdem] ∼ ein Fahrrad** he has a bicycle as well; **∼ etwas Kaffee?** [would you like] some more coffee?; **wenn man alt ist und [dann auch] ∼ allein** when you're old and [also] on your own; **hinzu kommt ∼, dass ...** on top of that there's the fact that ...; **∼ ein/zwei Bier, bitte!** another beer/two more beers, please!; **und ∼ eins** *od.* **etwas** and another thing; **ich habe das ∼ einmal/∼ einige Male gemacht** I did it again/several times more; **da möchte ich ∼ einmal/einige Male hin** (*ugs.*) I'd like to go there again; **∼ einmal so lang** as long again; **Spanien? Und ∼ dazu im Juli?** Spain, and in July too?; **er ist frech und ∼ dazu dumm** *od.* **dumm dazu** he's cheeky and stupid with it; **und es schneite ∼ dazu** *od.* **auch ∼:** and what's more, it was snowing; **Geld/Kleider** *usw.* **∼ und ∼** *od.* (*ugs. scherzh.*) **∼ und nöcher** heaps and heaps of money/clothes *etc.* (*coll.*); **K** (*bei Vergleichen*) **er ist ∼ größer [als Karl]** he is even taller [than Karl]; **das ist ∼ viel wichtiger** that's far *or* much more important still; **er will ∼ mehr haben** he wants even *or* still more; **das ist ∼ besser** that's even better *or* better still; **es war ∼ anders** it was different again; **darüber hat er sich ∼ mehr gefreut** he was even more pleased about that; **jeder ∼ so dumme Mensch versteht das** anyone, however stupid, can understand that; **und wenn er auch ∼ so bittet** however much he pleads; **du kannst ∼ so sehr bitten** you can plead as much as you like; **L** (*nach etw. Vergessenem fragend*) **wie heißt/hieß sie [doch] ∼?** [now] what's/what was her name again?
❷ *Partikel* **das ist ∼ Qualität!** that's what I call quality; **auf ihn kann man sich wenigstens ∼ verlassen** one can rely on 'him at least; **du wirst es ∼ bereuen!** you'll regret it!; **der wird sich ∼ wundern** (*ugs.*) he's in for a surprise; **das dauert ∼ keine zehn Minuten** it won't even take ten minutes; **er kann ∼ nicht einmal lesen** he can't even read; **∼ in der größten Hitze trägt er seinen Pullover** however hot it is he still wears his pullover.
❸ *Konj.* (*und auch nicht*) nor; **weder ... ∼:** neither ... nor; **weder er ∼ die Mutter ∼ der Vater** neither he nor his mother nor his father; **er hat keine Verwandten** *od.* **nicht Verwandte ∼ Freunde** he has no relatives or friends

**nochmalig** /'nɔxma:lɪç/ *Adj.* further

**noch·mals** *Adv.* again; (*einige Minuten später*) after another few minutes; **∼: wo waren Sie zwischen ...?** once again: where were you between ...?

**Nocken** /'nɔkn̩/ *der;* **∼s, ∼** (*Technik*) cam

**Nocken·welle** *die* (*Technik*) camshaft

**Nockerl** /'nɔkɐl/ *das;* **∼s, ∼n** (*österr., bayr. Kochk.*) [semolina] dumpling; **Salzburger ∼n** Salzburg dumpling soufflé *sing.*

**NOK** *Abk.* **Nationales Olympisches Komitee** NOC

**nölen** /'nø:lən/ *itr. V.* (*bes. nordd. abwertend*) **A** (*trödeln*) dawdle; **B** (*sprechen*) speak in a slow drawl

**Nom.** *Abk.* **Nominativ** Nom.

**Nomade** /no'ma:də/ *der;* **∼n, ∼n** nomad

**nomadenhaft** *Adj.* (*auch fig.*) nomadic

**Nomadentum** *das;* **∼s** (*Völkerk.*) nomadism

**Nomadin** *die;* **∼, ∼nen** nomad

**nomadisieren** *itr. V.* lead a nomadic existence; **∼de Stämme** nomadic tribes

**Nomen** /'no:mən/ *das;* **∼s, Nomina** **A** (*Substantiv*) noun; substantive; **B** (*deklinierbares Wort*) declinable word (*including nouns, adjectives, and numerals*)

**nomen est omen** /'no:mən 'ɛst 'o:mən/ (*geh.*) true to his/its *etc.* name

**Nomenklatur** /nomɛnkla'tu:ɐ̯/ *die;* **∼, ∼en** (*Wissensch.*) nomenclature

**Nomina** ⇒ **Nomen**

**nominal** /nomi'na:l/ *Adj.* (*Sprachw., Wirtsch.*) nominal

**Nominal-: ∼einkommen** *das* (*Wirtsch.*) nominal income; **∼lohn** *der* (*Wirtsch.*) nominal wages *pl.;* **∼stil** *der* (*Sprachw.*) style in which there is a preponderance of nominal constructions; **∼wert** *der* (*Wirtsch.*) ⇒ **Nennwert**

**Nominativ** /'no:minati:f/ *der;* **∼s, ∼e** (*Sprachw.*) nominative [case]; (*Wort im ∼*) nominative [form]; **im ∼ stehen** be in the nominative [case]

**nominell** /nomi'nɛl/ ❶ *Adj.* nominal ‹member, leader›; ‹Christian› in name only. ❷ *adv.* **er ist nur ∼ Präsident** he is President in name only; **∼ ist er nur Berater des Präsidenten** nominally he is just an adviser to the President

**nominieren** /nomi'ni:rən/ *tr. V.* **A** (*zur Wahl vorschlagen*) nominate; **B** (*Sport: aufstellen*) name ‹player, team›

**Nominierung** *die;* **∼, ∼en** **A** (*für eine Wahl*) nomination; **B** (*Sport: Aufstellung*) selection

**Nonchalance** /nõʃa'lã:s/ *die;* **∼:** nonchalance

**nonchalant** /nõʃa'lã:/ ❶ *Adj.* nonchalant. ❷ *adv.* nonchalantly

**None** /'no:nə/ *die;* **∼, ∼n** **A** (*kath. Kirche*) nones; **B** (*Musik*) ninth

**Nonius** /'no:ni̯ʊs/ *der;* **∼, Nonien** /...i̯ən/ (*Technik*) vernier

**Nonkonformismus** /nɔnkɔnfɔr'mɪsmʊs/ *der;* **∼:** nonconformism

**nonkonformistisch** ❶ *Adj.* nonconformist; unconventional ‹dress›. ❷ *adv.* ‹think, behave, argue, etc.› in an unconventional way

**Nonne** /'nɔnə/ *die;* **∼, ∼n** **A** nun; **B** (*Zool.*) nun [moth]

**Nonnen-: ∼kloster** *das* convent; nunnery; **∼schule** *die* (*ugs.*) convent school

**Non·plus·ultra** /nɔnplʊs'ʊltra/ *das;* **∼** (*geh., oft scherzh.*) ultimate (**an** + *Dat.* in); non plus-ultra; **das/ein ∼ an Handlichkeit** *usw.* the ultimate in handiness *etc.*

**Nonsens** /'nɔnzɛns/ *der;* **∼[es]** nonsense

**nonstop** /nɔn'stɔp/ *adv.* non-stop

**Nonstop-: ∼flug** *der* non-stop flight; **∼kino** *das* 24-hour cinema

**Noppe** /ˈnɔpə/ *die;* ~, ~**n** Ⓐ (*in einem Faden, Gewebe*) knop; nub; Ⓑ (*auf einer Oberfläche*) bump; (*auf einem Tischtennisschläger*) pimple

**Nord**[1] /nɔrt/ ▶400 Ⓐ (*Seemannsspr., Met.: Richtung*) north; **nach** ~: northwards; **aus** *od.* **von** ~: from the north; Ⓑ (*nördliches Gebiet, Politik*) North; ~ **und Süd** North and South; **aus** ~ **und Süd** from the North and [from] the South; **zwischen** ~ **und Süd** between [the] North and [the] South; Ⓒ *einem Subst. nachgestellt* (*nördlicher Teil, nördliche Lage*) **Autobahnkreuz Köln** ~: motorway intersection Cologne North; **Europa** ~ (*Milit.*) Northern Europe

**Nord**[2] *der;* ~**[e]s**, ~**e** (*Seemannsspr.*) northerly; (*dichter.*) north wind

**nord-, Nord-:** ~**afrika** (*das*) North Africa; ~**amerika** (*das*) North America; ~**amerikaner** *der,* ~**amerikanerin** *die* North American; ~**amerikanisch** *Adj.* North American; ~**atlantik·pakt** *der* North Atlantic alliance; ~**deutsch** ❶ *Adj.* North German; ❷ *adv.* **etw.** ~**deutsch aussprechen** pronounce sth. with a North German accent; ~**deutschland** (*das*) North Germany

**norden** *tr. V.* ▶400 **etw.** ~: orient sth. to the north

**Norden** *der;* ~**s** Ⓐ (*Richtung*) north; **im** ~: in the north; **aus dem** *od.* **von** ~: from the north; **nach** ~: northwards; **die Grenze nach** ~: the northern border; **gegen** *od.* (*geh.*) **gen** ~: northwards; Ⓑ (*Gegend*) northern part; **aus dem** ~: from the north; Ⓒ (*Geogr.*) North; **der hohe/höchste** ~: the far North

**nord-, Nord-:** ~**england** (*das*) the North of England; ~**europa** (*das*) Northern Europe; ~**europäisch** *Adj.* Northern European; ~**flanke** *die* (*Milit., Geogr.*) northern flank; (*Met.*) northern edge; ~**hang** *der* northern slope; ~**insel** *die* North Island; ~**irland** (*das*) Northern Ireland

**nordisch** *Adj.* (*auch Völkerk.*) Nordic; ~**e Kombination** (*Skisport*) Nordic combined

**Nordistik** /nɔrˈdɪstɪk/ *die;* ~: Scandinavian Studies *pl.*, *no art.*

**Nord-:** ~**kap** *das* North Cape; ~**korea** (*das*) North Korea; ~**küste** *die* north *or* northern coast; ~**länder** *der;* ~~**s**, ~~, ~**länderin** *die;* ~~, ~~**nen** native/inhabitant of [a country of] the North (*esp. Scandinavia*)

**nördlich** /ˈnœrtlɪç/ ▶400 ❶ *Adj.* Ⓐ (*im Norden gelegen*) northern; **15° ~er Breite** 15 degrees north; **das** ~**e Frankreich** northern France; **der** ~**ste Punkt** the most northerly point; ⇨ *auch* **Eismeer**; **Polarkreis**; **Wendekreis** A; Ⓑ (*nach, aus dem Norden*) northerly; Ⓒ (*aus dem Norden kommend, für den Norden typisch*) Northern. ❷ *adv.* northwards; ~ **von ...** [to the] north of ...; **sehr [weit]** ~ **sein** be a long way north. ❸ *Präp. mit Gen.* [to the] north of

**nord-, Nord-:** ~**licht** /ˈ--/ *das; Pl.* ~~**er** Ⓐ northern lights *pl.*; aurora borealis; **ein** ~**licht/**~**lichter** the northern lights; Ⓑ (*scherzh.*) Northerner; ~**nord·ost**[1] (*Seemannsspr., Met.*) north-north-east; ⇨ *auch* ~[1] A; ~**nord·ost**[2] *der* (*Seemannsspr.*) north-north-easter[ly]; ~**nord·osten** *der* ▶400 north-north-east; ⇨ *auch* ~**en** A; ~**nord·west**[1] (*Seemannsspr., Met.*) north-north-west; ⇨ *auch* ~[1] A; ~**nord·west**[2] *der* (*Seemannsspr.*) north-north-wester[ly]; ~**nord·westen** *der* north-north-west; ⇨ *auch* ~**en** A; ~**ost**[1] (*Seemannsspr., Met.*) north-east; **nach** ~**ost** north-eastwards; **aus** *od.* **von** ~**ost** from the north-east; ~**ost**[2] *der* (*Seemannsspr.*) north-easter[ly]; (*dichter.*) north-east[erly] wind; ~**osten** *der* Ⓐ (*Richtung, Gegend*) north-east; ⇨ *auch* ~**en** A; ~**östlich** ▶400 ❶ *Adj.* Ⓐ (*im* ~*osten gelegen*) north-eastern; ⇨ *auch* **nördlich** 1 A; Ⓑ (*nach* ~*osten gerichtet, aus* ~*osten kommend*) north-easterly; ❷ *adv.* north-eastwards; ~**östlich von ...** [to the] north-east of ...; ⇨ *auch* **nördlich** 2; ❸ *Präp. mit Gen.* [to the] north-east of; ~**-Ostsee-Kanal** *der* Kiel Canal; ~**ost·wind** *der* north-east[erly] wind; ~**pol** /ˈ--/ *der* Ⓐ North Pole; Ⓑ (*eines Magneten*) north pole

**Nordpolar-:** ~**gebiet** *das* North Polar Region; ~**meer** *das* Arctic Ocean

**Nord-:** ~**pol·expedition** *die* expedition to the North Pole; ~**rand** *der* northern edge

**Nordrhein-Westfale** *der;* ~**n**, ~**n** North Rhine-Westphalian

**Nord·rhein-Westfalen** (*das*) North Rhine-Westphalia

**nordrhein-westfälisch** *Adj.* North Rhine-Westphalian

**Nord·see** *die* North Sea

**nord-, Nord-:** ~**seite** /ˈ---/ *die* northern side; (*eines Gebäudes, Geländes*) north side; ~**stern** /ˈ--/ *der* North Star; Polaris; ~**-Süd-Dialog** *der* (*Politik*) North-South dialogue; ~**-Süd-Gefälle** *das* (*Politik*) North-South gap; ~**südlich** ▶400 ❶ *Adj.* **in** ~**südlicher Richtung** from north to south; ❷ *adv.* ~**südlich verlaufen** run from north to south; ~**wand** /ˈ--/ *die* (*Felswand*) north face; ~**wärts** /ˈ--/ *Adv.* ▶400 Ⓐ (*nach* ~*en*) northwards; Ⓑ (*im* ~*en*) to the north; ~**west**[1] Ⓐ (*Seemannsspr., Met.*) north-west; **nach** ~**west** north-westwards; **aus** *od.* **von** ~**west** from the north-west; Ⓑ *einem Subst. nachgestellt* **Autobahnkreuz Frankfurt-**~**west** motorway intersection Frankfurt North-West; ~**west**[2] *der* (*Seemannsspr.*) north-wester[ly]; (*dichter.*) north-west[erly] wind; ~**westen** *der* ▶400 Ⓐ (*Richtung, Gegend*) north-west; ⇨ *auch* ~**en** A; ~**westlich** ▶400 ❶ *Adj.* Ⓐ (*im* ~*westen gelegen*) north-western; ⇨ *auch* **nördlich** 1 A; Ⓑ (*nach* ~*westen gerichtet, aus* ~*westen kommend*) north-westerly; ❷ *adv.* (*nach* ~*westen*) north-westwards; ~**westlich von ...** [to the] north-west of ...; ⇨ *auch* **nördlich** 2; ❸ *Präp. mit Gen.* [to the] north-west of; ~**west·wind** *der* north-west[erly] wind; ~**wind** /ˈ--/ *der* north *or* northerly wind

**Nörgelei** *die;* ~, ~**en** (*abwertend*) Ⓐ (*das Nörgeln*) moaning; grumbling; (*das Kritteln*) carping; Ⓑ (*Äußerung*) moan; grumble; **deine ewigen** ~**en** your constant moaning *sing. or* grumbling *sing.*

**nörgelig** *Adj.* (*abwertend*) moaning *attrib.*; grumbling *attrib.*; grumbly (*coll.*); **ein** ~**er Kerl** a moaner *or* grumbler; **müde und** ~: tired and niggly

**nörgeln** /ˈnœrgl̩n/ *itr. V.* (*abwertend*) moan, grumble (**an** + *Dat.* about); (*kritteln*) carp (**an** + *Dat.* about)

**Nörgler** *der;* ~**s**, ~, **Nörglerin** *die;* ~, ~**nen** (*abwertend*) moaner; grumbler; (*Krittler*) carper; fault-finder

**nörglerisch** *Adj.* (*abwertend*) moaning *attrib.*; grumbling *attrib.*; grumbly (*coll.*); (*krittelig*) carping *attrib.*

**nörglig** ⇨ **nörgelig**

**Norm** /nɔrm/ *die;* ~, ~**en** Ⓐ norm; **zur** ~ **werden/als** ~ **gelten** become the norm/count as the norm; Ⓑ (*geforderte Arbeitsleistung*) quota; target; **die** ~ **erfüllen** fulfil one's/its quota; meet *or* achieve one's/its target; Ⓒ (*Sport*) qualifying standard; Ⓓ (*technische, industrielle* ~) standard; standard specifications *pl.*; **der** ~ **entsprechen** conform to the standard; Ⓔ (*Buchw.*) signature (*at foot of page*)

**normal** /nɔrˈmaːl/ ❶ *Adj.* Ⓐ normal; **du bist doch nicht** ~! (*ugs.*) there must be something wrong with you!; Ⓑ (*ugs.: gewöhnlich*) ordinary. ❷ *adv.* Ⓐ normally; Ⓑ (*ugs.: gewöhnlich*) in the normal *or* ordinary way; Ⓒ (*ugs.:* ~*erweise*) normally; usually

**Normal** *das;* ~**s** (*ugs.*) ≈ two star (*Brit.*); regular (*Amer.*); **für 50 Mark** ~, **bitte!** 50 marks' worth of two-star, please!

**Normal·benzin** *das* ≈ two-star petrol (*Brit.*); regular (*Amer.*)

**Normale** *die;* ~**[n]**, ~**n** (*Math.*) normal

**normalerweise** *Adv.* normally; usually

**Normal-:** ~**fall** *der* normal case; **im** ~**fall** normally, usually; ~**form** *die* Ⓐ (*Math.*) standard *or* normal form; Ⓑ (*Sport*) usual form; ~**gewicht** *das* normal weight

**normalisieren** ❶ *tr. V.* normalize. ❷ *refl. V.* return to normal

**Normalisierung** *die;* ~, ~**en** normalization

**Normalität** /nɔrmaliˈtɛːt/ *die;* ~: normality *no def. art.*

**Normal-:** ~**maß** *das* Ⓐ (*normales Maß*) normal size; (*normales Niveau*) normal level; ~**maße haben** be [of] a normal size; Ⓑ (*Messwesen*) standard measure; ~**null** *das;* ~~**s** (*Geodäsie*) national datum level; ~**spur** *die* (*Eisenb.*) standard gauge; ~**ton** *der; Pl.* ~**töne** Ⓐ (*Akustik*) reference tone; Ⓑ (*Musik*) standard pitch; ~**uhr** *die* Ⓐ (*genau gehende Uhr*) regulator; Ⓑ (*öffentliche Uhr*) public clock; ~**verbraucher** *der,* ~**verbraucherin** *die* Ⓐ ordinary *or* average consumer; Ⓑ (*ugs.: Durchschnittsmensch*) average punter (*coll.*); **Otto** ~**verbraucher** (*scherzh.*) the average punter (*coll.*); ~**zeit** *die* standard time; ~**zu·stand** *der* Ⓐ normal state; **im** ~**zustand** in its/his normal state; Ⓑ ⇨ **Normzustand**

**Normandie** /nɔrmanˈdiː/ *die;* ~: Normandy; **in/aus der** ~: in/from Normandy

**Normanne** /nɔrˈmanə/ *der;* ~**n**, ~**n**, **Normannin** *die;* ~, ~**nen** Norman

**normannisch** *Adj.* Norman

**normativ** /nɔrmaˈtiːf/ *Adj.* normative

**Norm·blatt** *das* list of standard specifications

**normen** *tr. V.* standardize

**Normen-:** ~**aus·schuss**, *~**aus·schuß** *der* standards committee; ~**kontroll·verfahren** *das:* (*Rechtsw.*) *suit brought before the constitutional court relating to the constitutionality of a law*

**Norm·erhöhung** *die* raising of production targets

**normieren** *tr. V.* standardize

**Normierung** *die;* ~, ~**en**, **Normung** *die;* **Normung**, **Normungen** standardization

**Norm·zustand** *der* (*Physik, Technik*) standard state

**Norne** /ˈnɔrnə/ *die;* ~, ~**n** (*nord. Myth.*) Norn

**Norwegen** /ˈnɔrveːgn̩/ (*das*); ~**s** Norway

**Norweger** *der;* ~**s**, ~, **Norwegerin** *die;* ~, ~**nen** ▶553 Norwegian; ⇨ *auch* **-in**

**Norweger·muster** *das* (*Handarb.*) ≈ Fair Isle design

**norwegisch** *Adj.* ▶553, ▶696 Norwegian; ⇨ *auch* **deutsch**; **Deutsch**; **Deutsche**[2]

**Nostalgie** /nɔstalˈgiː/ *die;* ~: nostalgia

**nostalgisch** ❶ *Adj.* nostalgic. ❷ *adv.* nostalgically; ~ **gestimmt** in a nostalgic mood

***not** ⇨ **Not** E

**Not** /noːt/ *die;* ~, **Nöte** /ˈnøːtə/ Ⓐ (*Bedrohung, Gefahr*) **in seiner** ~: at that perilous juncture; **jmdm. in der Stunde der** ~ **helfen** help sb. in his/her hour of need; **in höchster** *od.* **äußerster** ~: in extremis; **Rettung in** *od.* **aus höchster** ~: rescue from extreme difficulties; **in** ~ **sein** be in desperate straits; ~ **bricht Eisen** desperation gives you strength; ~ **lehrt beten** adversity teaches you to pray; **in** ~ **und Tod** (*geh.*) through thick and thin; Ⓑ (*Mangel, Armut*) need; poverty [and hardship]; ~ **leiden** suffer poverty *or* want [and hardship]; ~ **leidende Menschen** needy *or* impoverished people; **etw. aus** ~ **tun** do sth. from sheer need; **in** ~ **geraten/sein** encounter hard times/be suffering want [and deprivation]; **in diesem Land herrscht große** ~: there is great poverty and hardship in this country; **er kennt keine** ~: he's doing all right for himself; ~ **macht erfinderisch** necessity is the mother of invention (*prov.*); ~ **kennt kein Gebot** [when] needs must; **in der** ~ **frisst der Teufel Fliegen** beggars can't be choosers (*prov.*); Ⓒ (*Verzweiflung*) anguish; distress; Ⓓ (*Sorge, Mühe*) trouble; **in Nöten sein** have many troubles; **seine [liebe]** ~ **haben, etw. zu tun** have great difficulty in doing sth.; **seine [liebe]** ~ **mit jmdm./etw. haben** have a lot of trouble *or* a lot of problems with sb./sth.; **mit knapper** ~: by the skin of one's teeth; Ⓔ (*veralt.: Notwendigkeit*) necessity; **ohne** ~ (*geh.*) without pressing cause; **zur** ~: if need be; if necessary; **wenn** ~ **am Mann ist** when the need arises; **aus der** ~ **eine Tugend machen**

*old spelling (see note on page 1707)

n

make a virtue of necessity; ~ **tun** *od.* **sein** (*geh., landsch.*) be necessary

**Notabeln** /no'ta:bl̩n/ *Pl.* (*hist.*) Notables

**notabene** /nota'be:nə/ *Adv.* (*geh. veralt.*) nota bene (*arch. literary*); please note

**Not-: ~abitur** *das: early* **Abitur** *taken in wartime by students about to be conscripted;* **~anker** *der* (*Seew., auch fig.*) sheet anchor

**Notar** /no'ta:ɐ̯/ *der;* **~s, ~e** notary

**Notariat** /notar'i̯a:t/ *das;* **~[e]s, ~e** Ⓐ (*Amt*) notaryship; Ⓑ (*Kanzlei*) notary's office

**notariell** /nota'ri̯ɛl/ ❶ *Adj.* notarial. ❷ *adv.* **~ beglaubigt** attested by a notary

**Notarin** *die;* **~, ~nen** notary

**Not-: ~arzt** *der,* **~ärztin** *die* doctor on [emergency] call; emergency doctor; **~arzt·wagen** *der* doctor's car for emergency calls

**Notation** /nota'tsi̯o:n/ *die;* **~, ~en** (*Musik, Schach*) notation

**Not-: ~aufnahme** *die* (*Gesundheitswesen*) casualty department; casualty *no art.;* **~aus·gabe** *die* (*Zeitungsw.*) emergency edition; **~aus·gang** *der* emergency exit; **~behelf** *der* makeshift; **~beleuchtung** *die* emergency lighting *no indef. art.;* **~bremse** *die* emergency brake; **die ~bremse ziehen** pull the emergency brake; pull the communication cord (*Brit. Railw.*); (*Sportjargon*) bring the attacker down; **~brücke** *die* temporary bridge; **~dienst** *der* ⇒ **Bereitschaftsdienst**

**Notdurft** /-dʊrft/ *die;* ~ Ⓐ (*geh.*) **seine [große/kleine] ~ verrichten** relieve oneself; Ⓑ (*geh. veralt.: das Nötige*) need; **mehr als seine knappe ~ verdienen** earn more than one needs to buy the bare necessities of life

**not·dürftig** ❶ *Adj.* meagre ‹payment, pension›; rough and ready, makeshift ‹shelter, repair›; scanty ‹cover, clothing›. ❷ *adv.* scantily ‹clothed›; **etw. ~ reparieren** repair sth. in a rough and ready *or* makeshift way; **sich ~ verständigen** manage to communicate after a fashion

**Note** /'no:tə/ *die;* **~, ~n** Ⓐ (*Zeichen*) note; **eine ganze/halbe ~:** a crotchet/quaver (*Brit.*); a whole note/half note (*Amer.*); **etw. in ~n setzen** (*veralt.*) set sth. to music; Ⓑ *Pl.* (*Text*) music *sing.;* **nach/ohne ~n spielen** play from/without music; Ⓒ (*Schul~*) mark; Ⓓ (*Eislauf, Turnen*) score; Ⓔ (*Dipl.*) note; Ⓕ (*Flair*) touch; **einer Sache eine persönliche ~ geben** give sth. a personal touch; Ⓖ **▶ 337** (*Bank~*) note

**Notebook** /'noʊtbʊk/ *das;* **~s, ~s** (*DV*) notebook [computer]

**Noten-: ~aus·tausch** *der* (*Dipl.*) exchange of notes; **~bank** *die; Pl.* **~~en** bank of issue; **~blatt** *das* sheet of music; **~druck** *der* Ⓐ (*Druck von Banknoten*) printing of [bank]notes; Ⓑ (*Druck von Musikalien*) music printing; printing of music; Ⓒ (*Leistungsdruck*) pressure to achieve high marks; **~durch·schnitt** *der* average mark; **~heft** *das* Ⓐ (*Publikation*) book of music; Ⓑ (*Heft mit ~papier*) manuscript book; **~linie** *die* (*Musik*) line [of the staff]; **~papier** *das* music paper; **~pult** *das* music rest; music stand; **~schlüssel** *der* clef; **~schrift** *die* [musical] notation; **~ständer** *der* music stand

**not-, Not-: ~fall** *der* Ⓐ (*Gefahr*) emergency; **im ~fall** in an emergency; **für den ~fall** in case of emergency; **in** *od.* **bei ~fällen** in emergencies; Ⓑ (*Schwierigkeiten*) case of need; **im ~fall** if need be; **für den ~fall habe ich immer einen Reservekanister im Kofferraum** I always have a spare can of petrol (*Brit.*) *or* (*Amer.*) gasoline in the boot (*Brit.*) *or* (*Amer.*) trunk, just in case; **~falls** *Adv.* if need be; if necessary; **~gedrungen** *Adv.* of necessity; **ich habe ~gedrungen eine neue gekauft** I had no choice but to *or* I was forced to buy a new one; **~geld** *das* (*Finanzw.*) necessity money; emergency money; **~gemeinschaft** *die* Ⓐ (*Interessengemeinschaft*) emergency action organization; Ⓑ (*durch gemeinsame ~lage Verbundene*) union born of necessity; **~groschen** *der* nest egg; **die 500 DM lege ich als ~groschen zurück** I'll put that 500 marks away for a rainy day; **~hilfe** *die* (*Rechtsw.*) assistance in an emergency (*as required by law*); **in ~hilfe schießen** shoot in defence of a third person

**notieren** /no'ti:rən/ ❶ *tr. V.* Ⓐ **[sich** (*Dat.*)**] etw. ~:** note sth. down; make a note of sth.; **die Polizei hat den Fahrer notiert** the police took [down] the driver's particulars; **jmdn. für etw. ~:** put sb.'s name down for sth.; **~ Sie bitte: ...** please note that down: ...; **ein Musikstück ~:** write a piece of music down [in musical notation]; Ⓑ (*Börsenw., Wirtsch.*) quote (**mit** at). ❷ *itr. V.* (*Börsenw., Wirtsch.*) be quoted (**mit** at); **die meisten Rohstoffe ~ unverändert** most commodity prices are unchanged

**Notierung** *die;* **~, ~en** Ⓐ ⇒ **Notation;** Ⓑ (*Börsenw., Wirtsch.*) quotation; (*Preis*) quoted [price] (**für** of); (*von Devisen*) rate (**für** for)

**nötig** /'nø:tɪç/ ❶ *Adj.* necessary; **dafür** *od.* **dazu fehlt mir die ~e Geduld/das ~e Geld** I don't have the patience/money necessary *or* needed for that; **es ist nicht ~, dass du dabei bist** there's no need for you to be there; you don't have to be there; **etw./jmdn. ~ haben** need sth./sb.; **Hilfe dringend ~ haben** be in urgent need of help; need help urgently; **es ~ haben, etw. zu tun** need to do sth.; **er hat es manchmal ~, dass man ihn zurechtweist** he sometimes needs reprimanding; **das habe ich nicht ~** (*das lasse ich mir nicht gefallen*) I won't have that; **sich zu entschuldigen, hat er natürlich nicht ~** (*iron.*) of course he does not feel the need to apologize; **du hast/er hat** *usw.* **es gerade ~** (*ugs.*) you're/he's a fine one to talk (*coll.*); **das wäre [doch] nicht ~ gewesen!** (*ugs.*) you shouldn't have!; **das Nötige veranlassen** do all that is necessary; **das Nötigste** the bare essentials *pl.*
❷ *adv.* **er braucht ~ Hilfe** he is in urgent need of *or* urgently needs help; **was er am ~sten braucht, ist ...** what he most urgently needs is ...; **ich muss ~ aufs Klo** (*ugs.*) I'm dying to go to the loo (*Brit. coll.*) *or* (*Amer. coll.*) the john

**nötigen** ❶ *tr. V.* Ⓐ (*zwingen*) compel; force; (*Rechtsspr.*) intimidate; coerce; **jmdn. zur Unterschrift ~:** compel *or* force sb. to sign; **sich genötigt sehen, etw. zu tun** feel compelled to do sth.; Ⓑ (*geh.: auffordern*) press; urge; **lass dich nicht [lange] ~:** don't wait to be asked. ❷ *itr. V.* (*geh.*) **zur Wachsamkeit/zu einer vorsichtigen Fahrweise ~:** compel one to be vigilant/drive carefully

**nötigenfalls** *Adv.* if necessary; if need be

**Nötigung** *die;* **~, ~en** Ⓐ (*bes. Rechtsspr.*) intimidation; coercion; Ⓑ (*geh.: Notwendigkeit*) necessity; Ⓒ (*geh.: das Nötigen*) urging

**Notiz** /no'ti:ts/ *die;* **~, ~en** Ⓐ note; **sich** (*Dat.*) **eine ~ machen** make a note; Ⓑ (*Zeitungs~*) **eine [kurze] ~:** a brief report; Ⓒ **in von jmdm./etw. [keine] ~ nehmen** take [no] notice of sb./sth.; Ⓓ (*Börsenw.*) ⇒ **Notierung** B

**Notiz-: ~block** *der; Pl.* **~~s** *od.* **~blöcke** notepad; **~buch** *das* notebook; **~zettel** *der* note; **etw. als ~zettel benutzen** use sth. to write a note/notes on

**not-, Not-: ~lage** *die* serious difficulties *pl.;* **jmds. ~lage ausnutzen** exploit sb.'s plight; **~lager** *das* makeshift bed; **~landen: ich ~lande, ~gelandet, ~zulanden** ❶ *itr. V.; mit sein* do an emergency landing; ❷ *tr. V.* **er konnte/musste die Maschine ~landen** he was able to do/had to do an emergency landing; **~landung** *die* emergency landing; ***~leidend** *Adj.* needy; impoverished; (*fig.*) ailing ‹industry›; (*Finanzw.*) ‹loan› in default; unsecured ‹credit›; **die ~leidenden** the [poor and] needy; **~lösung** *die* stopgap; **~lüge** *die* evasive lie; (*aus Rücksichtnahme*) white lie; **um der Bestrafung zu entgehen, griff er zu einer ~lüge** he resorted to a lie to avoid punishment; **~maßnahme** *die* emergency measure; **~opfer** *das* (*Steuerw.*) emergency levy

**notorisch** /no'to:rɪʃ/ ❶ *Adj.* notorious. ❷ *adv.* notoriously; **~ lügen** be a notorious liar

**not-, Not-: ~pfennig** *der* ⇒ **~groschen;** **~ruf** *der* Ⓐ (*Hilferuf*) emergency call; (*eines Schiffes*) Mayday call; distress call; Ⓑ (*Nummer*) emergency number; Ⓒ (*eines Tieres*) alarm call; **~ruf·nummer** *die* emergency number; **~ruf·säule** *die* emergency telephone (*mounted in a piller*); **~schlachten** *tr., itr. V.;* **ich ~schlachte, ~geschlachtet, ~zuschlachten** slaughter ‹sick or injured animal›; **~schlachtung** *die* slaughtering (*of sick or injured animal*); **~schrei** *der* Ⓐ (*geh. veralt.*) cry of distress; Ⓑ ⇒ **~ruf** C; **~situation** *die* emergency; **~sitz** *der* extra seat; (*ausklappbar*) tip-up seat; fold-away seat; **~stand** *der* Ⓐ (*Krise, Übelstand*) crisis; Ⓑ (*Staatsrecht*) state of emergency; **den ~stand erklären** *od.* **verkünden** *od.* **ausrufen** declare a state of emergency; **äußerer ~stand** threat of attack; **innerer/ziviler ~stand** internal/civil emergency; Ⓒ (*bes. Rechtsw.*) necessity; **rechtfertigender ~stand** *necessity which justifies a normally illegal act;* **~stands·gebiet** *das* Ⓐ (*auch fig.*) disaster area; Ⓑ (*Wirtsch.*) depressed area; **~stands·gesetz** *das* emergency law; **~stands·gesetzgebung** *die* emergency legislation; **~taufe** *die* emergency baptism (*by a layman*); **~unterkunft** *die* emergency accommodation *no pl., no indef. art.;* **~unterkünfte** emergency accommodation *sing.;* **~verband** *der* emergency dressing; **~verordnung** *die* emergency decree; **~vorrat** *der* emergency supply; **~wassern** *itr. V.; mit sein, tr. V.;* **ich ~wassere, ~gewassert, ~zuwassern** ditch; **~wehr** *die* (*Rechtsw.*) self-defence; **in** *od.* **aus ~wehr** in self-defence

**not·wendig** ❶ *Adj.* Ⓐ necessary; **es ist ~, dass wir etwas tun** we must do something; **das Notwendigste** the bare essentials *pl.;* Ⓑ (*zwangsläufig*) necessary; (*unvermeidlich*) inevitable; ⇒ *auch* **Übel.** ❷ *adv.* Ⓐ ⇒ **nötig** 2; Ⓑ (*zwangsläufig, unbedingt*) necessarily

**notwendiger·weise** *Adv.* necessarily

**Notwendigkeit** *die;* **~, ~en** necessity

**not-, Not-: ~zeichen** *das* distress signal; **~zeit** *die* time of emergency; (*Zeit des Mangels*) time of need; **~zucht** *die* (*Rechtsw. veralt.*) rape; **~zucht [an jmdm.] begehen** *od.* **verüben** commit rape [on sb.]; **~züchtigen** *tr. V.;* **ich ~züchtige, genotzüchtigt, ~zuzüchtigen** (*Rechtsw. veralt.*) rape; **~zucht·verbrechen** *das* (*Rechtsw. veralt.*) rape

**Nougat** /'nu:gat/ *der; auch das;* **~s** nougat

**Nov.** *Abk.* **November** Nov.

**Nova** ⇒ **Novum**

**Novelle** /no'vɛlə/ *die;* **~, ~n** Ⓐ (*Literaturw.*) novella; Ⓑ (*Gesetzes~*) amendment

**novellieren** *tr. V.* (*Politik, Rechtsw.*) amend

**Novellierung** *die;* **~, ~en** (*Politik, Rechtsw.*) amendment

**novellistisch** ❶ *Adj.* **die ~e Literatur** literature in novella form; the novella; **das ~e Werk Kellers** Keller's novellas. ❷ *adv.* **etw. ~ gestalten/bearbeiten** put sth. into/treat sth. in novella form

**November** /no'vɛmbɐ/ *der;* **~[s], ~ ▶ 207** November; ⇒ *auch* **April**

**novemberlich** ❶ *Adj.* Novemberish. ❷ *adv.* **~ unfreundlich/trüb sein** be as dreary/grey as in November

**Novität** /novi'tɛ:t/ *die;* **~, ~en** Ⓐ novelty; (*neue Erfindung*) innovation; (*neue Schallplatte*) new release; (*neues Buch*) new publication; Ⓑ (*veralt.: Nachricht*) piece of news; **~en** news *sing.*

**Novize** /no'vi:tsə/ *der;* **~n, ~n, Novize** *die;* **~, ~n** novice

**Noviziat** /novi'tsi̯a:t/ *das;* **~[e]s, ~e** noviciate

**Novizin** *die;* **~, ~nen** novice

**Novum** /'no:vʊm/ *das;* **~s, Nova** novelty; (*neue Erfindung*) innovation; **ein ~ in der Geschichte der Partei** an unprecedented event in the history of the party

n

**NPD** *Abk.* **Nationaldemokratische Partei Deutschlands** National Democratic Party of Germany

**Nr.** *Abk.* **Nummer** No

**NRW** *Abk.* **Nordrhein-Westfalen**

**NSDAP** *Abk.* **Nationalsozialistische Deutsche Arbeiterpartei** National Socialist German Workers' Party

**N.T.** *Abk.* **Neues Testament** NT

**nu** /nu:/ *Adv.* (*bes. nordd.*) ⇨ **nun**

**Nu** *der: in* **im Nu, in einem Nu** in no time

**Nuance** /'nỹã:sə/ *die;* ~, ~**n** Ⓐ (*Unterschied, Feinheit*) nuance; Ⓑ (*Grad*) shade; **[um] eine ~ dunkler/schneller** a shade darker/faster

**nuancenreich** ❶ *Adj.* full of nuances *postpos.*; finely *or* subtly nuanced. ❷ *adv.* with subtlety of nuance

**nuancieren** *tr., itr. V.* **etw. ~:** give sth. subtle nuances; **farblich stärker ~:** give more definite nuances of colour

**nuanciert** ❶ *Adj.* finely *or* subtly nuanced. ❷ *adv.* **[sehr] ~:** with [great] subtlety of nuance

**'nüber** /'nʏ:bɐ/ *Adv.* (*südd.*) ⇨ **hinüber**

**nüchtern** /'nʏçtɐn/ ❶ *Adj.* Ⓐ (*nicht betrunken*) sober; **mit ~em Kopf** with a clear head; **wieder ~ werden** sober up; Ⓑ (*mit leerem Magen*) **der Patient muss ~ sein** the patient's stomach must be empty; **auf ~en Magen rauchen** smoke on an empty stomach; **das war ein Schreck auf ~en Magen** (*scherzh.*) that's just what I needed at that time of the morning (*iron.*); Ⓒ (*realistisch*) sober; sober, matter-of-fact ‹account, assessment, question, etc.›; bare ‹figures›; Ⓓ (*schmucklos, streng*) austere; bare ‹room›; unadorned, bare ‹walls›; (*ungeschminkt*) bare, plain ‹fact›; Ⓔ (*bes. nordostd.: ungewürzt, ungesalzen*) bland; (*fade*) insipid.
❷ *adv.* Ⓐ (*realistisch*) soberly; **wir sollten einmal ganz ~ darüber sprechen** we ought to have a down-to-earth talk about this sometime; Ⓑ (*schmucklos, streng*) austerely

**Nüchternheit** *die;* ~ Ⓐ sobriety; Ⓑ (*Realitätsbezogenheit*) sobriety; soberness; Ⓒ (*Schmucklosigkeit*) austerity

**Nuckel** /'nʊkl̩/ *der;* ~**s**, ~ (*ugs.*) ⇨ **Schnuller**

**nuckeln** (*ugs.*) ❶ *itr. V.* suck (**an** + *Dat.* at); **am Daumen/Schnuller ~:** suck one's thumb/a *or* one's dummy. ❷ *tr. V.* suck

**Nuckel·pinne** *die* (*salopp*) old banger (*Brit. coll.*) *or* (*coll.*) crate

**Nudel** /'nu:dl̩/ *die;* ~, ~**n** Ⓐ piece of spaghetti/vermicelli/tortellini *etc.*; (*als Suppeneinlage*) noodle; ~**n** (*Teigwaren*) pasta *sing.*; (*als Suppeneinlage, Reisnudeln*) noodles; **Spaghetti und andere ~n** spaghetti and other types of pasta; Ⓑ (*ugs.*) **eine dicke ~:** a fatty (*coll.*); **eine giftige ~:** a nasty piece of work (*coll.*); **eine komische ~:** a real character

**Nudel-:** ~**brett** *das* board (*for rolling out pasta dough*); pastry board; ~**holz** *das* rolling pin

**nudeln** *tr. V.* cram ‹geese›; (*fig. ugs.*) stuff

**Nudel-:** ~**salat** *der* pasta salad; ~**suppe** *die* soup with noodles; ~**teig** *der* pasta dough

**Nudismus** /nu'dɪsmʊs/ *der;* ~**:** nudism *no art.*; naturism *no art.*

**Nudist** /nu'dɪst/ *der;* ~**en**, ~**en**, **Nudistin** *die;* ~, ~**nen** nudist; naturist

**Nugat** ⇨ **Nougat**

**nuklear** /nukle'a:ɐ̯/ ❶ *Adj.* nuclear. ❷ *adv.* **~ angetrieben** nuclear-powered; **~ bewaffnet** possessing nuclear weapons *postpos.*

**Nuklear-:** ~**krieg** *der* nuclear war; ~**macht** *die* nuclear power; ~**medizin** *die* nuclear medicine *no art.*; ~**physik** *die* nuclear physics *sing.*, *no art.*; ~**waffe** *die* nuclear weapon

**Nukleus** /'nu:kleʊs/ *der;* ~, **Nuklei** [...ei] (*Biol., Anat., Sprachw.*) nucleus

**null** /nʊl/ ▶ **841** ❶ *Kardinalz.* ▶ **728**, ▶ **752** nought; **~ Komma sechs** [nought] point six; **sieben, ~, ~, sechs, ~, vier** (*Fernspr.*) seven double-O, six O four (*Brit.*); seven zero zero, six zero four (*Amer.*); **~ Grad Celsius** nought *or* zero degrees Celsius; **bei ~ Fehlern** if there are no mistakes; **fünf zu ~ Tore** five goals to nil; **fünf zu ~:** five-nil; **das Spiel endete ~ zu ~:** the game was a goalless draw; **fünfzehn ~** (*Tennis*) fifteen-love; **gegen ~ Uhr** around twelve midnight; **es ist ~ Uhr dreißig** it is twelve-thirty a.m.; **elf Uhr, ~ Minuten und fünfzehn Sekunden** eleven, no minutes, and fifteen seconds; **etw. für ~ und nichtig erklären** declare sth. null and void; **in ~ Komma nichts** (*ugs.*) in less than no time; **gleich ~ sein** (*fig.*) be practically zero; **auf ~ stehen** ‹indicator, needle, etc.› be at zero; **fünf Grad unter/über ~:** five degrees below/above zero *or* freezing; **die Augen auf ~ gestellt haben** (*salopp*) have snuffed it (*sl.*); **jmdn. auf ~ bringen** (*salopp*) destroy sb. (*fig.*).
❷ *indekl. Adj.* (*ugs.*) **~ Ahnung/Interesse** no idea/interest at all; **auf etw.** (*Akk.*) **~ Bock haben** not fancy sth. at all

**Null**[1] *die;* ~, ~**en** Ⓐ (*Ziffer*) nought; zero; **eine schwarze ~ schreiben** make *or* show a small profit; Ⓑ (*abwertend*) (*Versager*) failure; dead loss (*coll.*); (*unbedeutender Mensch*) nonentity

**Null**[2] *der* (*auch: das*); ~**[s]**, ~**s** (*Skat*) null; **~ Hand** null from hand

**Null-** zero

**null·acht·fünfzehn, null·acht·fuffzehn** (*ugs. abwertend*) ❶ *indekl. Adj.* run-of-the-mill; **das Essen war eher ~:** the meal really wasn't anything to write home about. ❷ *adv.* **~ gekleidet/eingerichtet** dressed/furnished in a run-of-the-mill way

**Null·acht·fünfzehn-, Null·acht·fuffzehn-** (*ugs. abwertend*) run-of-the-mill

**Null-:** ~**-Bock-Generation** *die* (*ugs.*) switched-off generation; ~**diät** *die* absolute diet

***Nulleiter** ⇨ **Nullleiter**

**Null-:** ~**leiter** *der* (*Elektrot.*) neutral conductor; ~**lösung** *die* (*Politik*) zero option; ~**menge** *die* (*Math.*) empty set; ~**meridian** *der* (*Geogr.*) Greenwich meridian; ~**nummer** *die: free first issue* (*of magazine etc.*)

***Nullösung** ⇨ **Nulllösung**

**Null ouvert** /nʊl|u'vɛ:ɐ̯/ *der;* (*auch:*) *das;* ~**[s]**, ~**s** (*Skat*) open null

**Null-:** ~**punkt** *der* zero; **die Temperatur ist auf den ~punkt abgesunken** the temperature has dropped to zero *or* to freezing point; **die Stimmung war auf dem ~punkt angelangt** *od.* **hatte den ~punkt erreicht** (*fig.*) we/they were in very low spirits; ~**spiel** *das* (*Skat*) null; **beim ~spiel** when playing null *or* a null game; ~**tarif** *der:* **die Rentner haben ~tarif im Nahverkehr/Schwimmbad** *usw.* pensioners can use local public transport/the swimming pool *etc.* free of charge; **zum ~tarif** free of charge; **zum ~tarif einkaufen/fernsehen** (*scherzh.*) go shoplifting/watch television without a licence; ~**wachstum** *das* zero growth

**Nulpe** /'nʊlpə/ *die;* ~, ~**n** (*ugs. abwertend*) drip (*coll.*)

**Numerale** /nʊmə'ra:lə/ *das;* ~**s**, **Numeralien** *od.* **Numeralia** (*Sprachw.*) ⇨ numeral

**Numeri** ⇨ **Numerus**

***numerieren** ⇨ **nummerieren**

***Numerierung** ⇨ **Nummerierung**

**numerisch** /nu'me:rɪʃ/ ❶ *Adj.* numerical. ❷ *adv.* numerically; **~ überlegen sein** be superior in numbers

**Numero** /'nʊmərо/ *in Verbindung mit einer Zahl* (*veralt.*) number

**Numerus** /'nʊmərʊs/ *der;* ~, **Numeri** Ⓐ (*Sprachw.*) number; Ⓑ (*Math.*) antilogarithm; antilog (*coll.*)

**Numerus clausus** /- 'klaʊzʊs/ *der;* ~ *fixed number of students admissible to a university to study a particular subject;* numerus clausus

**Numismatik** /nʊmɪs'ma:tɪk/ *die;* ~**:** numismatics *sing.*, *no art.*

**Nummer** /'nʊmɐ/ *die;* ~, ~**n** Ⓐ number; **ein Wagen mit [einer] Münchner ~:** a car with a Munich registration; **ich bin unter der ~ 242679 zu erreichen** I can be reached on 242679; **bloß eine ~ sein** (*fig.*) be just a *or* nothing but a number; **[die] ~ eins** [the] number one; **Thema ~ eins sein** be the number-one topic of conversation; **ich muss auf ~ null** (*ugs. verhüll.*) I must go to the loo (*Brit. coll.*) *or* (*Amer. coll.*) the john; **er sitzt auf ~ sicher** (*ugs.*) he's doing time (*coll.*); **auf ~ sicher gehen** (*ugs.*) play safe; not take any chances; **bei jmdm. eine gute** *od.* **große** *od.* **dicke ~ haben** (*ugs.*) be well in with sb. (*coll.*); Ⓑ (*Ausgabe*) number; issue; Ⓒ (*Größe*) size; **diese Sache ist eine ~/ein paar ~n zu groß für dich** (*ugs.*) this business is in a different league from anything you could cope with; Ⓓ (*Darbietung*) turn; Ⓔ (*ugs.: Musikstück*) number; Ⓕ (*ugs.: Person*) character; **er ist eine ~ [für sich]** he is a real character *or* quite a character; **er ist eine große ~ im Verkaufen** he's quite a *or* (*coll.*) some salesman; Ⓖ (*derb: Koitus*) screw (*coarse*)

**nummerieren** /nʊmə'ri:rən/ *tr. V.* number

**Nummerierung** *die;* ~, ~**nen** numbering

**Nummern-:** ~**konto** *das* (*Bankw.*) numbered account; ~**oper** *die* (*Musik*) number opera; ~**scheibe** *die* dial; ~**schild** *das* Ⓐ (*eines Fahrzeugs*) number plate; license plate (*Amer.*); Ⓑ (*an Häusern, Straßen*) number; ~**schlüssel** *der* (*DV*) numerical code

**nun** /nu:n/ ❶ *Adv.* now; **von ~ an** from now on; **~, wo sie krank ist** now [that] she's ill; **~ erst, erst ~:** only now; **gestern ist er ~ endlich wiedergekommen** he finally came back yesterday.
❷ *Partikel* now; **so wichtig ist es ~ auch wieder nicht** it's not all 'that important; **~ ist es in der Tat zutreffend, dass ...** now it is indeed quite correct that ...; **und bei dem Lärm soll man ~ schlafen können!** and people are supposed to sleep with that noise going on; **und so was nennt sich ~ Diplomübersetzer** and he calls himself a qualified translator; **das hast du ~ davon!** it serves you right!; **hat sich das ~ gelohnt?** was it really worth it?; **~ gib schon her!** now hand it over!; **~ mach dir deswegen mal keine Sorgen!** now don't you worry; **kommst du ~ mit oder nicht?** now are you coming or not?; **er muss es tun, ob er ~ will oder nicht** he has to do it, whether he wants to or not; **so ist das ~ [einmal/mal]** that's just the way it is *or* things are; **er braucht ~ einmal viel Schlaf** he happens to need a lot of sleep; **~ gut** *od.* **schön** [well,] all right; **~, ~!** now, come on; **ja ~!** oh, well!; nun? well?; **Das Brett ist etwas zu lang — Nun, das lässt sich ändern** The board is a bit too long — Well, that can be altered; **~ ja ...** well, yes ...; **~ denn!** (*also gut*) well, all right!; (*also los*) well then;
❸ *Konj.* (*veralt. geh.*) now that

**nun·mehr** *Adv.* (*geh.*) Ⓐ now; **er ist ~ seit zehn Jahren Kanzler** he has been Chancellor now for ten years; **seine ~ 80-jährige Mutter** his mother, [who is] now 80 years old; Ⓑ (*von ~ an*) from now on; henceforth

**'nunter** /'nʊntɐ/ *Adv.* (*südd.*) ⇨ **hinunter**

**Nuntius** /'nʊntsi̯ʊs/ *der;* ~, **Nuntien** nuncio; ⇨ *auch* **apostolisch**

**nur** /nu:ɐ̯/ ❶ *Adv.* Ⓐ (*nicht mehr als*) only; just; **ich habe ~ eine Stunde Zeit/zehn Mark** I only have an hour/ten marks; **ich habe es für ~ fünf Mark gekauft** I bought it for just five marks; **er hat ~ einen einzigen Fehler gemacht** he made just a single mistake; **um eines ~ möchte ich dich bitten** I'd ask just one thing of you; **er tat es ~ ungern** he did it only reluctantly; **das ist ~ recht und billig** it is only right and proper; **ohne auch ~ zu lächeln** without so much as smiling; **eine ~ mittelmäßige Leistung** only a mediocre performance; Ⓑ (*ausschließlich*) only; **~ er darf das** only he is allowed to do that; **alle durften mitfahren, ~ ich nicht** everyone was allowed to

*old spelling (see note on page 1707)

n

go, all except me; **er will dir doch ~ helfen!** he only wants to help you; **~ darauf will ich mich beschränken** I want to restrict myself to just this; **ich frage mich ~, warum** I just want to know why; **er tut das mit Absicht, ~ um dich zu provozieren** he does it deliberately, just to provoke you; **nicht ~ ..., sondern auch ...** not only ..., but also ...; **ich tue es nicht nur wegen des Geldes, sondern auch, weil ...** I'm not doing it just for the money, but also because ...; **nicht ~, dass ...** it's not just that ...; **[alles,] ~ das nicht** anything but that; **~ gut, dass ...** it's a good thing that ...; **~ schade, dass ...** it's just a pity that ...; **ich male ~ so zum Spaß** I paint just for fun; **Warum fragst du? — Ach, ~ so** Why do you ask? — Oh, no particular reason; **das hat er ~ so gesagt[, ohne sich dabei etwas zu denken]** he just said it without thinking; **~ dass ...** except that ...; **das weiß ich ~ zu gut** I know that only too well; **das ist ~ zu wahr!** it's only too true!

❷ *Partikel* Ⓐ *(in Wünschen)* **wenn das ~ gut geht!** let's [just] hope it goes well; **dass ihm ~ nichts zustößt!** let's [just] hope nothing happens to him; **wenn er ~ käme/hier wäre** if only he would come/he were here; Ⓑ *(ermunternd, tadelnd)* **sag ihm ~ deine Meinung** just tell him what you think; **~ keine Hemmungen!** don't be inhibited!; **Lass ~! Ich schaffe das schon allein** Don't bother! I can do it by myself; **wehr dich ~!** stand up for yourself!; **~ her damit!** hand it over!; **~ weiter!** keep going; **~ zu!** go ahead; **sieh ~, was du gemacht hast!** just look what you've done; Ⓒ *(warnend)* **lass dich ~ nicht erwischen** just don't let me/him/her/them catch you; **er soll es ~ wagen** just let him try; **glaub ~ nicht, dass ich das nicht merke** don't think I don't notice; **~ vorsichtig/langsam** just be careful/take it easy; **~ Geduld** just be patient; **~ nicht!** don't, for goodness' sake!; Ⓓ *(fragend)* just; **wie soll ich ihm das ~ erklären?** just how am I supposed to explain it to him?; **was sollen wir ~ tun?** what on earth are we going to do?; **was hat er ~?** whatever's the matter with him?; **wie kann ich das ~ wieder gutmachen?** however can I make amends?; Ⓔ *(verallgemeinernd)* just; **er lief, so schnell er ~ konnte** he ran just as fast as he could; **alles, was man sich ~ vorstellen kann** everything one could imagine; Ⓕ *(sogar)* only; just; **davon werden die Schmerzen ~ [noch] schlimmer** that only *or* just makes the pain [even] worse; Ⓖ **es wimmelte ~ so von Insekten** it was just teeming with insects; **er schlug auf den Tisch, dass es ~ so krachte** he crashed his fist [down] on the table.

❸ *Konj.* but; **ich kann dir das Buch leihen, ~ nicht heute** I can lend you the book, but *or* only not today; **das Wetter ist schön, ~ noch etwas kalt** the weather is fine, though still somewhat cold

**Nur·haus·frau** *die* full-time housewife; **sie ist ~:** she is only *or* just a housewife

**Nürnberg** /ˈnʏrnbɛrk/ *(das)*; **~s** ▶ 700 Nuremberg

**Nürnberger** *indekl. Adj.* Nuremberg *attrib.*; **bei ihm hilft nur der ~ Trichter** you really have to drum things into him; ⇨ *auch* **Kölner**

**nuscheln** /ˈnʊʃl̩n/ *tr., itr. V. (ugs.)* mumble

**Nuss, *Nuß** /nʊs/ *die;* **~, Nüsse** /ˈnʏsə/ Ⓐ nut; **eine taube ~** *(fig.)* a useless article *or* item *(coll.)*; **eine harte ~ [für jmdn.]** *(fig.)* a hard *or* tough nut [for sb. to crack]; Ⓑ *(salopp abwertend: Mensch)* so-and-so *(coll.)*; Ⓒ *(Kochk.: Fleischstück)* eye; Ⓓ *(Technik)* socket; Ⓔ *in* **jmdm. eins** *od.* **eine auf/vor die ~ geben** *(ugs.)* belt sb. [one] in the head/face *(coll.)*

**Nuss·baum, *Nuß·baum** *der* Ⓐ walnut tree; Ⓑ *(Holz)* walnut

**nuss·braun, *nuß·braun** *Adj.* nut-brown

**Nüsschen, *Nüßchen** /ˈnʏsçən/ *das;* **~s, ~:** Ⓐ little nut; Ⓑ *(Kochk.)* eye

**Nuss-, *Nuß-: ~kern** *der* [nut] kernel; **~knacker** *der* nutcrackers *pl.*; **~schale** *die* nutshell; *(fig.: Boot)* cockleshell; **das Boot wurde wie eine ~schale umhergeworfen** the boat was tossed about like a cork; **~schokolade** *die* nut chocolate

**Nüster** /ˈnʏstɐ/ *die;* **~, ~n** nostril

**Nut** /nuːt/ *die;* **~, ~en, Nute** /ˈnuːtə/ *die;* **~e, ~en** *(Technik)* groove

**nuten** *(Technik)* ❶ *tr. V.* groove. ❷ *itr. V.* cut grooves

**Nutria¹** /ˈnuːtria/ *die;* **~, ~s** *(Tier)* coypu

**Nutria²** *der;* **~s, ~s** *(Pelz)* nutria [fur]; coypu fur

**Nutsche** /ˈnuːtʃə/ *die;* **~, ~n** *(Technik)* vacuum filter

**Nutte** /ˈnʊtə/ *die;* **~, ~n** *(derb abwertend)* tart *(sl.)*; pro *(Brit. coll.)*; hooker *(Amer. sl.)*

**nutz** /nʊts/ *(südd., österr.)* ⇨ **nütze**

**Nutz** *in* **jmdm. zu** *od.* **zu jmds. ~ und Frommen [dienen]** *(veralt.)* [be] for the benefit of sb.; **zu ~e** ⇨ **zunutze**

**nutz-, Nutz-: ~an·wendung** *die* Ⓐ practical application; Ⓑ *(praktische Lehre)* moral; practical lesson; **~bar** *Adj.* usable; exploitable, utilizable ‹mineral resources, invention›; cultivatable ‹land, soil›; **etw. praktisch ~bar machen** turn sth. to practical use; **landwirtschaftlich ~bar** usable for agriculture *postpos.*; **die Sonnenenergie ~bar machen** harness solar energy **(für** for)

**Nutzbarkeit** *die;* **~:** usability; *(von Bodenschätzen)* exploitability; utilizability

**Nutzbarmachung** /-maxʊŋ/ *die;* **~, ~en** utilization; *(von Bodenschätzen)* exploitation; utilization; *(von Forschungsergebnissen)* application

**nutz·bringend** ❶ *Adj.* *(nützlich)* useful; *(gewinnbringend)* profitable. ❷ *adv.* profitably; **die Reserven so ~ wie möglich einsetzen** use the reserves to maximum advantage

**nütze** /ˈnʏtsə/ *in* **zu etw. ~ sein** be good for sth.; **[jmdm.] zu nichts ~ sein** be no use *or* good [to sb.]; **du bist zu gar nichts ~:** you're totally useless; **wozu ist das ~?** what's the good of that?

**Nutz·effekt** *der* Ⓐ useful effect; Ⓑ *(Technik)* ⇨ **Wirkungsgrad**

**nutzen** /ˈnʊtsn̩/ ❶ *tr. V.* Ⓐ use; exploit, utilize ‹natural resources›; cultivate ‹land, soil›; use, harness ‹energy source›; exploit ‹advantage›; **eine Fläche landwirtschaftlich ~:** use an area for agriculture; **eine Erfindung industriell ~:** give an invention an industrial application; Ⓑ *(be~, aus~)* use; make use of; **wir müssen das herrliche Wetter ~:** we must take advantage of the marvellous weather; **eine Gelegenheit ~, etw. zu tun** take [advantage of] an opportunity to do sth.; **seine Chance ~:** take one's chance; **~ wir die Zeit!** let's make the most of the time.

❷ *itr. V.* ⇨ **nützen 1**

**nützen** /ˈnʏtsn̩/ ❶ *itr. V.* be of use (+ *Dat.* to); **nichts ~:** be useless *or* no use; **seine Bitten nützten nichts** his pleas were to no avail *or* were in vain; **jmdm. sehr ~:** be very useful *or* of great use to sb.; **wem soll das ~?** who is supposed to gain from that?; **was hat ihm das genützt?** what good did it do him?; **wozu nützt das alles jetzt noch?** what's the point of all that now?; **es würde nichts/wenig ~:** it wouldn't be any/much use *or* wouldn't do any/much good; **dein Leugnen nützt jetzt auch nichts mehr** and it's no use your denying it any longer; **da nützt alles nichts** there's nothing to be done; **es nützt alles nichts, wir müssen jetzt anfangen** *(ugs.)* it's no good, we've got to start now.

❷ *tr. V.* ⇨ **nutzen 1**

**Nutzen** *der;* **~s** Ⓐ benefit; **der ~ des Kanals für die Schifffahrt** the usefulness *or* benefits *pl.* of the canal to shipping; **die Maßnahme hat großen/wenig/keinen ~:** the measure is very useful/of little/no use; **den ~ [von etw.] haben** benefit *or* gain [from sth.]; **~ aus etw. ziehen** benefit from sth.; exploit sth.; **er hätte dem Land großen ~ gebracht** he would have been of great service to the country; **ich habe das Buch mit großem ~ gelesen** I profited greatly from reading the book; **[jmdm.] von ~ sein** be of use [to sb.]; Ⓑ *(Profit)* profit; **etw. mit ~ verkaufen** sell sth. at a profit

**Nutzer** *der;* **~s, ~** *(Amtsspr.)* user

**Nutz-: ~fahrzeug** *das* *(Lastwagen, Lieferwagen usw.)* commercial vehicle; goods vehicle; *(Bus, Straßenbahn usw.)* public-service vehicle; **~fläche** *die* Ⓐ *(von Gebäuden)* usable floor space; Ⓑ *(Landw.)* **landwirtschaftliche ~flächen** land *sing.* available for agriculture; **~garten** *der* kitchen garden; **~holz** *das* timber; **~land** *das* ⇨ **~fläche B**; **~last** *die (Kfz-W.)* maximum permitted load; **~leistung** *die (Technik)* effective *or* useful output *or* power

**nützlich** /ˈnʏtslɪç/ ❶ *Adj.* useful; **jmdm. ~ sein** be useful *or* of use to sb.; **kann ich Ihnen ~ sein?** can I do anything for you?; **sich ~ machen** make oneself useful; ⇨ *auch* **angenehm 1**. ❷ *adv.* usefully

**Nützlichkeit** *die;* **~:** usefulness

**Nützlichkeits·denken** *das* utilitarian thinking

**nutzlos** ❶ *Adj.* useless; *(vergeblich)* futile; vain *attrib.*; in vain *pred.*; **es wäre ~, das zu tun** it would be useless *or* pointless *or* futile doing that; **all sein Flehen war ~:** all his pleading was in vain *or* of no avail. ❷ *adv.* uselessly; *(vergeblich)* futilely; in vain; **er hat das Geld ~ vergeudet** he squandered the money on useless items

**Nutz·losigkeit** *die;* **~:** uselessness; *(Vergeblichkeit)* futility; vainness

**nutznießen** /-niːsn̩/ *itr. V. (geh.)* **von etw. ~:** benefit *or* profit from sth.

**Nutznießer** *der;* **~s, ~, Nutznießerin** *die;* **~, ~nen** Ⓐ beneficiary; Ⓑ *(Rechtsw.)* usufructuary

**Nutz·pflanze** *die* economically useful plant

**Nutz·tier** *das* economically useful animal

**Nutzung** *die;* **~, ~en** use; *(des Landes, des Bodens)* cultivation; *(von Bodenschätzen)* exploitation; utilization; *(einer Energiequelle)* use; harnessing; **die wirtschaftliche/landwirtschaftliche ~ einer Fläche** the use of an area for financial benefit/for agriculture; **jmdm. etw. zur ~ überlassen** give sb. the use of sth.

**Nutzungs·recht** *das (Rechtsw.)* right of use; **das ~ an etw.** *(Dat.)* the right to use sth.

**NVA** *Abk.* **Nationale Volksarmee** *(DDR)* National People's Army

**NW** *Abk.* ▶ 400 **Nordwest[en]** NW

**Nylon** Ⓦⓩ /ˈnailɔn/ *das;* **~s** nylon

**Nylon·strumpf** *der* nylon stocking

**Nymphe** /ˈnʏmfə/ *die;* **~, ~n** *(Myth., Zool.)* nymph

**nymphoman** /nʏmfoˈmaːn/ *Adj.* *(Psych.)* nymphomaniac; **~ sein** be a nymphomaniac

**Nymphomanie** *die;* **~** *(Psych.)* nymphomania *no art.*

**Nymphomanin** *die;* **~, ~nen** *(Psych.)* nymphomaniac

**nymphomanisch** *Adj.* *(Psych.)* ⇨ **nymphoman**

n

# Oo

**o, O** /oː/ *das;* ~, (*ugs.:*) **~s**, ~, (*ugs.:*) **~s** o/O; ⇒ *auch* **a, A**

**o** /oː/ *Interj.* oh; ⇒ *auch* **oh**

**O** *Abk.* **Ost[en]** E

**ö, Ö**/øː/ *das;* ~, (*ugs.:*) **~s**, ~, (*ugs.:*) **~s** o/O umlaut; ⇒ *auch* **a, A**

**o.ä.** *Abk.* **oder ähnlich...** or similar

**o.Ä** *Abk.* **oder Ähnliches**

**ÖAMTC** *Abk.* **Österreichischer Automobil-, Motorrad- und Touring Club** Austrian Automobile, Motorcycle, and Touring Club

**Oase** /oˈaːzə/ *die;* ~, **~n** (*auch fig.*) oasis

**ob**[1] /ɔp/ *Konj.* (A) whether; **ob du ihn anrufst?** would you give him a ring?; **ob wir es schaffen?** will we manage it?; **ob ich doch lieber zu Hause bleibe?** hadn't I better stay at home?; **ob ... oder ...** whether ... or ...; **ob er will oder nicht** whether he wants to or not; **ob arm, ob reich** whether rich or poor; (B) (*veralt.*) *in* **ob ... auch** *od.* **gleich** even though; (C) *in* **und ob!** of course!; you bet! (*coll.*); **Hast du keinen Hunger mehr? — Und ob!** Don't you want any more? — You bet I do! (*coll.*); ⇒ *auch* **als**

**ob**[2] *Präp.* (A) *mit Gen., selten Dativ* (*veralt. geh.: wegen*) on account of; (B) *mit Dativ* (*schweiz., veralt.: über*) above

**o.B.** *Abk.* **ohne Befund**

**OB** *Abk.* **Oberbürgermeister[in]**

**Obacht** /ˈoːbaxt/ *die;* ~ (*bes. südd.*) caution; **~, da kommt ein Auto!** watch out! *or* look out! *or* careful!, there's a car coming; **~ auf jmdn./etw. geben** look after *or* take care of sb./sth.; (*aufmerksam sein*) pay attention to sb./sth.; **~ geben, dass ...** take care that ...

**ÖBB** *Abk.* **Österreichische Bundesbahnen** Austrian Federal Railways

**Obdach** /ˈɔpdax/ *das;* **~[e]s** (*geh.*) shelter; **kein ~ haben** be without shelter

**obdach·los** *Adj.* homeless; **~ werden** be made homeless

**Obdachlose** *der/die; adj. Dekl.* homeless person/man/woman; **die ~n** the homeless

**Obdachlosen·asyl** *das,* **Obdachlosen·heim** *das* hostel for the homeless

**Obdachlosigkeit** *die;* **~:** homelessness

**Obduktion** /ɔpdukˈtsi̯oːn/ *die;* ~, **~en** (*Med., Rechtsw.*) postmortem [examination]; autopsy

**Obduktions·befund** *der* (*Med., Rechtsw.*) findings *pl. or* results *pl.* of a/the postmortem [examination] *or* autopsy

**obduzieren** /ɔpduˈtsiːrən/ ❶ *tr. V.* carry out *or* perform a/the postmortem [examination] *or* autopsy on. ❷ *itr. V.* carry out *or* perform a postmortem examination *or* autopsy

**O-Beine** *Pl.* bandy legs; bow legs

**o-beinig, O-beinig** *Adj.* bandy-legged; bow-legged

**Obelisk** /obeˈlɪsk/ *der;* **~en, ~en** obelisk

**oben** /ˈoːbn̩/ *Adv.* (A) (*an hoch/höher gelegenem Ort*) **hier/dort ~:** up here/there; **[hoch] ~ am Himmel** [high] up in the sky; **~ bleiben** stay up; **weiter ~:** further up; **nach ~:** upwards; **der Weg nach ~:** the way up; **warme Luft steigt nach ~:** warm air rises; **das Auto blieb mit den Rädern nach ~ liegen** the car came to rest upside down; **~ auf dem Dach** up on the roof; **Wo ist er? — Da ~.** Where is he? — Up there; **[im Bett] ~ schlafen** sleep in the upper bunk; **von ~:** from above; **von ~ herab** (*fig.*) condescendingly; (B) (*im Gebäude*) upstairs; **du bleibst heute besser ~** (*in der Wohnung*) you had better stay at home today; **nach ~:** upstairs; **ich komme gerade von ~:** I have just come down; **der Aufzug fährt nach ~/kommt von ~:** the lift (*Brit.*) *or* (*Amer.*) elevator is going up/coming down; **hier ~:** up here; (C) (*am oberen Ende, zum oberen Ende hin*) at the top; **~ im Schrank** at the top of the cupboard; **ein ~ offener Zylinder** a cylinder open at the top; **nach ~ [hin]** towards the top; **weiter ~ [im Tal/am Berg]** further *or* higher up [the valley/mountain]; **von ~:** from the top; **~ links/rechts** at the top on the left/right; **~ rechts in der Ecke** in the top right-hand corner; **~ [rechts] auf der Seite** on the top [right] of the page; **~ [links/rechts]** (*in Bildunterschriften*) above [left/right]; **auf Seite 25 ~:** at the top of page 25; **die fünfte Zeile von ~:** the fifth line from the top; the fifth line down; **~ auf dem Bücherschrank** up on top of the bookcase; **der Weisheitszahn ~ links** the upper left wisdom tooth; **nach ~ kommen** (*an die Oberfläche*) come up; **Fett schwimmt ~:** fat floats on the top *or* the surface; (*fig.*) there are always some people who do all right; **„~"** 'this side up'; **wo** *od.* **was ist [bei dem Bild] ~:** which is the right way up [on the picture]?; which is the top [of the picture]?; **bis ~ hin** (*ugs.*) up to the top; **bis ~ hin voll sein** (*ugs.*) be full to the top; **der Keller steht bis ~ hin unter Wasser** (*ugs.*) the cellar is full up with water; **von ~ bis unten** from top to bottom; **er musterte sie von ~ bis unten** he looked her up and down; **er ist ~ nicht ganz richtig** (*ugs.*) he's not quite right in the head (*coll.*) *or* up top (*coll.*); **~ ohne** topless; **hier wird ~ ohne bedient** there are topless waitresses here; **~ herum** (*im Bereich der Brust*) round the top; **es steht mir bis hier ~** (*ugs.*) I'm fed up to the back teeth with it (*coll.*); **~ an der Tafel** at the head of the table; **er saß weiter ~ als ich** (*fig.*) he sat further up the table than me; (D) (*an der Oberseite*) on top; (E) (*in einer Hierarchie, Rangfolge*) at the top; **weit/ganz ~:** near the top/right at the top; **der Befehl kam von ~:** the order came from above; **etw. nach ~ weitergeben** pass sth. on up; **die da ~** (*ugs.*) the high-ups (*coll.*); **der Weg nach ~:** the road to the top; **er wollte nach ~:** he wanted to get to *or* make it to the top; **sich ~ halten** stay at the top; **die Band ist jetzt ganz ~:** the group is now riding high [in the charts]; (F) ([*weiter*] *vorn im Text*) above; **~ erwähnt** *od.* **genannt** *od.* **stehend** above-mentioned; **von dem Obengenannten ...** of the above-mentioned ...; **das Obenstehende** the above; **der ~ [schon] erwähnte Fall** the case [already] referred to above; (G) (*im Norden*) up north; **hier/dort ~:** up here/there [in the north]; **~ in Dänemark/im Norden** up in Denmark/up [in the] north; **weiter ~:** further up [north]

**oben-, Oben-: ~an** *Adv.* at the top; **diese Frage steht für mich immer ~an** this question will always have top priority for me; **~auf** *Adv.* (A) (*zuoberst*) on [the] top; (B) (*guter Dinge*) on top of the world; (C) (*gesund*) fit and well; **~drauf** *Adv.* (*ugs.*) on top; **~drein** *Adv.* (*ugs.*) on top of that; **~drüber** *Adv.* (*ugs.*) above it/them; (*darauf*) on it/them; ***~erwähnt, *~genannt** ⇒ **oben** F; **~hinaus** *in* **~hinaus wollen** (*ugs.*) be aiming at big things; ***~stehend** ⇒ **oben** F; **~stehende** *das; adj. Dekl.* **das ~stehende:** the above

**ober** /ˈoːbɐ/ *Adj.* (A) upper *attrib.;* top *attrib.;* (*ganz oben liegend*) top *attrib.;* **die ~e rechte Ecke** the top right-hand corner; **am ~en Ende der Tafel/der Straße** at the top [end] of the table/street; **das Oberste zuunterst kehren** turn everything upside down; **das ~ste Stockwerk/die ~ste Stufe** the top[most] storey/step; (B) (*der Quelle näher gelegen*) upper; (C) (*in der Rangfolge o. Ä.*) higher ‹authority›; upper ‹[social] class, storey, floor›; **die ~en Klassen der Schule** the senior classes *or* forms of the school; **das ~ste Gericht des Landes** the highest court in the land; **der Oberste Sowjet** the Supreme Soviet; **das Oberste Gericht** (*DDR*) the Supreme Court; ⇒ *auch* **Obere; zehntausend**

**Ober** *der;* **~s,** ~ (A) waiter; **Herr ~!** waiter!; (B) (*Spielkarte*) ≈ queen

**ober-, Ober-: ~arm** *der* ▶ 471 upper arm; **~arzt** *der,* **~ärztin** *die* (*Vertreter[in] des Chefarztes*) assistant medical director; (*Leiter[in] einer Spezialabteilung*) consultant; **~auf·seher** *der,* **~aufseherin** *die* senior supervisor; **~auf·sicht** *die* overall supervision; **die ~aufsicht über etw.** (*Akk.*) **haben** have overall supervisory responsibility for sth.; **~bau** *der; Pl.* **~~ten** (A) (*eines Gebäudes*) superstructure; (B) (*Straßenbau*) pavement; (C) (*Eisenb.*) permanent way; superstructure and roadbed; **~bauch** *der* ▶ 471 (*Anat.*) upper abdomen; **~bayern** (*das*) Upper Bavaria; **~befehl** *der* (*Milit.*) supreme command *no art.;* **den ~befehl über etw.** (*Akk.*) **haben** be in supreme command of sth.; **~befehlshaber** *der* (*Milit.*) supreme commander; commander-in-chief; **~begriff** *der* generic term; **~bekleidung** *die* outer clothing; **~bett** *das* duvet (*Brit.*); continental quilt (*Brit.*); stuffed quilt (*Amer.*); **~bürgermeister** *der* ▶ 91 mayor; (*von bestimmten englischen/schottischen Großstädten*) Lord Mayor/Provost; **~bürgermeisterin** *die* mayor[ess]; **~deck** *der* upper deck; (*eines Busses*) upper *or* top deck; **~deutsch** ❶ *Adj.* Upper German; ❷ *adv.* **etw. ~deutsch aussprechen** pronounce sth. with an Upper German accent

**Obere** *der; adj. Dekl.* (A) (*geh.*) **die ~n [des Landes]** those in high places [in the country]; **seine ~n** his superiors; (B) (*eines Klosters o. Ä.*) superior

**ober-, Ober-: ~faul** *Adj.* (*ugs.*) very fishy (*coll.*); **~feldwebel** *der* (*beim Heer*) staff sergeant (*Brit.*); sergeant first class (*Amer.*); platoon sergeant (*Amer.*); (*bei der Luftwaffe*) flight sergeant (*Brit.*); master sergeant (*Amer.*); **~fläche** *die* surface; (*Flächeninhalt*) surface area; **an die ~fläche kommen** come to the surface; surface; **wieder an die ~fläche kommen** resurface; **die Diskussion blieb zu sehr an der ~fläche** (*fig.*) the discussion remained far too superficial; **~flächen·struktur** *die* (*auch Sprachw.*) surface structure

**oberflächlich** ❶ *Adj.* superficial; **eine ~e Düngung des Bodens kann ...** top-dressing the soil can ...; **eine erste, ~ Berechnung/Schätzung** a first, rough calculation/estimate. ❷ *adv.* superficially; **etw. nur ~ kennen** have only a superficial knowledge of sth.; **etw. ~ lesen** read sth. cursorily; **er arbeitet zu ~:** he is too superficial in the way he works

**Oberflächlichkeit** *die;* **~:** superficiality

**ober-, Ober-: ~förster** *der* (*veralt.*) *senior forestry official;* **~gärig** /-ɡɛːrɪç/ *Adj.* top-fermented ‹beer›; top-fermenting ‹yeast›; **~gefreite** *der* (*beim Heer*) lance corporal (*Brit.*); private first class (*Amer.*); (*bei der Luftwaffe*) leading aircraftman (*Brit.*); airman first class (*Amer.*); (*bei der Marine*) able rating (*Brit.*);

*old spelling (see note on page 1707)

O

seaman (*Amer.*); **~geschoss, *~geschoß** *das* upper storey; **das Haus hat zwei ~geschosse** the house has three storeys; **er wohnt im fünften ~geschoss** he lives on the fifth floor (*Brit.*) *or* (*Amer.*) the sixth floor; **~grenze** *die* upper limit

**ober·halb** ❶ *Adv.* above; **weiter ~:** further up; **~ von** above. ❷ *Präp. mit Gen.* above

**Ober-: ~hand** *die: in* **die ~hand [über jmdn./etw.] haben** have the upper hand [over sb./sth.]; **die ~hand [über jmdn./etw.] gewinnen/bekommen** gain *or* get the upper hand [over sb./sth.]; **~haupt** *das* head; (*einer Verschwörung*) leader; **~haus** *das* (*Parl.*) upper house *or* chamber; (*in Großbritannien*) House of Lords; Upper House; **~hemd** *das* shirt; **~herrschaft** *die* sovereignty; supreme power; **~hirte** *der* (*geh.*) spiritual leader *or* head; **~hoheit** *die* sovereignty; supreme power

**Oberin** *die;* **~, ~nen** Ⓐ (*christliche Kirche*) Mother Superior; Ⓑ ⇒ **Oberschwester**

**ober-, Ober-: ~inspektor** *der,* **~inspektorin** *die* senior inspector; (*bei der Polizei*) detective chief inspector; **~irdisch** ❶ *Adj.* surface *attrib.* ‹pipes, cables›; ‹pipes, cables› laid above ground; **~irdische Lagerung** above-ground storage; storage above ground; **~irdische Pflanzenteile** parts of a/the plant above the ground; ❷ *adv.* **die U-Bahn fährt hier ~irdisch** the underground [system] runs above ground here; **~italien** (*das*) Northern Italy; **~kante** *die* top edge; **es steht mir bis ~kante Unterlippe** (*salopp*) I'm sick to death of it (*coll.*); **~kellner** *der* head waiter; **~kiefer** *der* upper jaw; **~kirchenrat** *der* Ⓐ (*Gremium*) *highest administrative body of some evangelical Land churches;* Ⓑ (*Person*) *member of an Oberkirchenrat a;* **~kirchenrätin** *die* ⇒ **~kirchenrat** B; **~klasse** *die* Ⓐ (*Soziol.*) upper class; Ⓑ (*Schulw.*) senior class *or* form; Ⓒ (*bei Autos*) luxury class; **ein Wagen der ~klasse** a large luxury car; **~kommandierende** *der; adj. Dekl.* (*Milit.*) supreme commander; commander-in-chief; **~kommando** *das* supreme command (**über** + *Akk.* of); **jmds. ~kommando** (*Dat.*) **unterstehen** be under the supreme command of sb.; **~körper** *der* upper part of the body; **mit nacktem ~körper** stripped to the waist; **den ~körper frei machen** strip to the waist; **~land** *das* uplands *pl.;* **das Berner ~land** the Bernese Oberland; **~landes·gericht** *das* Higher Regional Court; ≈ *high court and court of appeal of a Land;* **~länge** *die* ascender; **~lastig** *Adj.* (*Seemannsspr.*) top-heavy; **~lauf** *der* ▶ **306** upper reaches *pl.;* **~leder** *das* upper; **~lehrer** *der* (*fig.*) schoolmaster; **~lehrerhaft** *Adj.* (*abwertend*) schoolmasterish; **~lehrerin** *die* (*fig.*) schoolmistress; **~leitung** *die* Ⓐ (*elektrische Leitung*) overhead cable; Ⓑ (*Kontrolle*) overall control; **~leitungs·bus** *der* trolley bus (*Brit.*); **~leutnant** *der* ▶ **91** (*beim Heer*) lieutenant (*Brit.*); first lieutenant (*Amer.*); (*bei der Luftwaffe*) flying officer (*Brit.*); first lieutenant (*Amer.*); **~leutnant zur See** sub lieutenant (*Brit.*); lieutenant junior grade (*Amer.*); **~licht** *das; Pl.* **~~er** Ⓐ light from above; Ⓑ (*Deckenlampe*) ceiling light; overhead light; Ⓒ high window; (*über einer Tür*) fanlight; (*Klappfenster*) transom; **~lid** *das* upper [eye] lid; **~liga** *die* (*Sport*) Ⓐ second division; Ⓑ (*DDR*) first division; **~lippe** *die* ▶ **471** upper lip; **~lippen·bart** *der* moustache; **~maat** *der* (*Marine*) petty officer; **~material** *das:* **„~material Leder"** 'leather uppers'; **~österreich** (*das*) Upper Austria; **~post·direktion** *die: regional postal administration;* **~prima** *die* (*Schulw. veralt.*) top form (*of a Gymnasium*); ≈ upper sixth [form] (*Brit.*); **~primaner** *der,* **~primanerin** *die* (*Schulw. veralt.*) pupil in the top form (*of a Gymnasium*); **~regierungs·rat** *der,* **~regierungsrätin** *die: senior civil servant;* **~rheinisch** *Adj.* in the Upper Rhine valley *postpos.;* **Oberrheinische Tiefebene** Upper Rhine valley

**Obers** /'o:bɐs/ *das;* **~** (*österr.*) ⇒ **Sahne**

**ober-, Ober-: ~schenkel** *der* ▶ **471** thigh; **~schenkel·hals·bruch** *der* ▶ **474** (*Med.*) fracture of the neck of the femur; **~schicht** *die* (*Soziol.*) upper class; **der ~schicht angehören** be a member of the upper classes *pl.;* **~schlesien** (*das*) Upper Silesia; **~schule** *die* Ⓐ secondary school; Ⓑ (*DDR*) unified comprehensive school; **[allgemeinbildende] polytechnische ~schule** *unified comprehensive school for children aged 7-17;* **erweiterte ~schule** *unified comprehensive school providing a further two years' preparation for university entrance qualification;* **~schulrat** *der,* **~schulrätin** *die* local education officer; **~schwester** *die* senior nursing officer; (*Stationsschwester*) ward sister; matron; **~seite** *die* top[side]; upper side; (*eines Stoffes*) right side; **~sekunda** *die* (*Schulw. veralt.*) seventh year (*of a Gymnasium*); **~sekundaner** *der,* **~sekundanerin** *die* (*Schulw. veralt.*) pupil in the seventh year (*of a Gymnasium*); **~seminar** *das* (*Hochschulw.*) graduate class

**oberst...** ⇒ **ober...**

**Oberst** *der;* **~en** *od.* **~s, ~en** *od.* **~e** ▶ **91** (*beim Heer*) colonel; (*bei der Luftwaffe*) group captain (*Brit.*); colonel (*Amer.*)

**Ober-: ~staatsanwalt** *der,* **~staatsanwältin** *die* ▶ **91** (*senior public prosecutor at a regional court*); **~stadt** *die* upper part of the town; upper town; **~stadtdirektor** *der,* **~stadtdirektorin** *die* chief executive [of a/the town council]; **~steiger** *der* (*Bergbau*) undermanager; **~stimme** *die* (*Musik*) treble; (*Sopran*) soprano; (*Diskant*) descant

**Oberst·leutnant** *der* ▶ **91** (*beim Heer*) lieutenant colonel; (*bei der Luftwaffe*) wing commander; lieutenant colonel (*Amer.*)

**Ober-: ~stübchen** *das* ⇒ **richtig** 1 B; **~studiendirektor** *der* ▶ **91** headmaster (*Brit.*); principal; **~studiendirektorin** *die* ▶ **91** headmistress (*Brit.*); principal; **~studienrat** *der,* **~studienrätin** *die* ▶ **91** senior teacher; **~stufe** *die* (*Schulw.*) upper school; **~teil** *das od. der* top [part]; (*eines Bikinis, Anzugs, Kleids usw.*) top [half]; **~tertia** *die* (*Schulw. veralt.*) fifth year (*of a Gymnasium*); **~tertianer** *der,* **~tertianerin** *die* (*Schulw. veralt.*) pupil in the fifth year (*of a Gymnasium*); **~ton** *der; Pl.* **~töne** (*Musik, Physik*) overtone

**Ober-: ~wasser** *das* headwater; (*fig.*) **~wasser haben** feel in a strong position; **~wasser bekommen/kriegen** have one's hand strengthened; **~weite** *die* bust measurement; **sie hat ~weite 91** she has a 36-inch bust; **eine beachtliche ~weite haben** (*ugs.*) be well-endowed (*joc.*)

**Ob·frau** *die* ⇒ **Obmännin**

**ob·gleich** *Konj.* ⇒ **obwohl**

**Ob·hut** *die;* **~** (*geh.*) care; **jmdn./etw. in seine ~ nehmen** take sb./sth. into one's care; **jmdn./etw. jmds. ~** (*Dat.*) **anvertrauen** entrust sb./sth. to sb.'s care; **unter jmds. ~** (*Dat.*) **stehen** be in sb.'s care

**obig** /'o:bɪç/ *Adj.* above; **die ~e Tabelle** the above table; the table above

**Objekt** /ɔp'jɛkt/ *das;* **~s, ~e** Ⓐ (*auch Sprachw., Kunstwiss.*) object; (*Fot., bei einem Experiment*) subject; Ⓑ (*Kaufmannsspr.: Immobilie*) property; Ⓒ (*bes. DDR: Projekt*) project; Ⓓ (*österr. Amtsspr.: Gebäude*) building; Ⓔ (*DDR: staatliche Einrichtung*) (*Fabrik*) factory; (*Gaststätte, Verkaufsstelle*) establishment

**objektiv** /ɔpjɛk'ti:f/ ❶ *Adj.* objective; real, actual ‹cause, danger›. ❷ *adv.* objectively; **er hat uns ~ geschadet** he did in fact do us harm

**Objektiv** *das;* **~s, ~e** Ⓐ (*Optik*) objective; Ⓑ (*Fot.*) lens

**objektivieren** *tr. V.* objectify; objectivize

**Objektivismus** *der;* **~** (*Philos.*) objectivism *no def. art.*

**Objektivität** /ɔpjɛktivi'tɛ:t/ *die;* **~:** objectivity

**Objekt-: ~satz** *der* (*Sprachw.*) object clause; **~schutz** *der* (*Amtsspr.*) protection of property; **für etw. ~schutz beantragen** apply to have sth. protected; **~träger** *der* (*Optik*) [specimen] slide

**Oblate** /o'bla:tə/ *die;* **~, ~n** wafer

**Ob·leute** *Pl.* ⇒ **Obmann**

**ob|liegen, ob·liegen** *unr. itr. V.* (*geh.*) **etw. liegt jmdm. ob** *od.* **obliegt jmdm.** sth. is sb.'s responsibility

**Obliegenheit** *die;* **~, ~en** (*geh.*) duty; **seine dienstlichen ~en erfüllen** carry out one's duties; **zu jmds. ~en gehören** be one of sb.'s duties

**obligat** /obli'ga:t/ *Adj.* Ⓐ (*geh.*) ⇒ **obligatorisch** 1 A; Ⓑ (*iron.: unvermeidlich*) obligatory; Ⓒ (*Musik*) obbligato

**Obligation** /obliga'tsi̯o:n/ *die;* **~, ~en** (*Wirtsch.*) bond; debenture

**obligatorisch** /obliga'to:rɪʃ/ ❶ *Adj.* Ⓐ obligatory; compulsory ‹subject, lecture, etc.›; necessary ‹qualification›; Ⓑ ⇒ **obligat** B. ❷ *adv.* obligatorily; compulsorily

**Obligatorium** /obliga'to:ri̯ʊm/ *das;* **~s, Obligatorien** (*schweiz.*) (*Verpflichtung*) compulsory duty; (*Beitrag*) compulsory contribution

**Obligo** /'o:bligo/ *das;* **~s, ~s** (*Wirtsch.*) liability; **ohne ~:** without recourse

**Ob·mann** *der;* **~[e]s, Obmänner** *od.* **Obleute, Obmännin** /'ɔpmɛnɪn/ *die;* **~, ~nen** (*bes. österr.*) chairman; (*einer Delegation*) head; (*einer Gruppe*) representative

**Oboe** /o'bo:ə/ *die;* **~, ~en** oboe

**Oboist** /obo'ɪst/ *der;* **~en, ~en, Oboistin** *die;* **~, ~nen** ▶ **159** oboist; oboe player

**Obolus** /'o:bolʊs/ *der;* **~, ~** *od.* **~se** (*geh. scherzh.*) small sum; (*Spende*) small contribution

**Obrigkeit** /'o:brɪçkait/ *die;* **~, ~en** authorities *pl.*

**obrigkeitlich** *Adj.* Ⓐ official ‹decree, approval, etc.›; Ⓑ (*autoritär*) authoritarian

**Obrigkeits-: ~denken** *das* (*abwertend*) attitude of obedience to authority; **~staat** *der* authoritarian state

**Obrist** /o'brɪst/ *der;* **~en, ~en** (*veralt., noch abwertend*) colonel

**ob·schon** *Konj.* (*geh.*) although; though

**Observanz** /ɔpzɛr'vants/ *die;* **~, ~en** Ⓐ kind; type; Ⓑ (*Rel.*) observance

**Observation** /ɔpzɛrva'tsi̯o:n/ *die;* **~, ~en** Ⓐ (*Überwachung*) surveillance *no pl.;* **~en** surveillance operations; Ⓑ (*wissenschaftlich*) observation

**Observatorium** /ɔpzɛrva'to:ri̯ʊm/ *das;* **~s, Observatorien** observatory

**observieren** *tr. V.* Ⓐ **jmdn./etw. ~:** keep sb./sth. under surveillance; Ⓑ (*wissenschaftlich*) observe; **einen Patienten ~:** keep a patient under observation

**Obsession** /ɔpzɛ'si̯o:n/ *die;* **~, ~en** (*Psych., geh.*) obsession

**ob·siegen,** *auch:* **ob|siegen** *itr. V.* (*geh. veralt.*) be victorious

**obskur** /ɔps'ku:ɐ̯/ *Adj.* (*geh.*) Ⓐ (*unbekannt, unklar*) obscure; Ⓑ (*dubios*) dubious

**Obskurantismus** /ɔpskuran'tɪsmʊs/ *der;* **~** (*geh.*) obscurantism

**obsolet** /ɔpzo'le:t/ *Adj.* (*geh.*) obsolete

**Obst** /o:pst/ *das;* **~[e]s** fruit

**Obst-: ~anbau,** *der,* **~bau** *der* fruit-growing; **~anbau betreiben** grow fruit; **~baum** *der* fruit tree; **~garten** *der* orchard; **~händler** *der,* **~händlerin** *die* ▶ **159** fruiterer

**obstinat** /ɔpsti'na:t/ (*geh.*) ❶ *Adj.* obstinate. ❷ *adv.* obstinately

**Obst·kuchen** *der* fruit flan

**Obstler** /'o:pstlɐ/ *der;* **~s, ~** (*bes. südd.*) fruit brandy

**Obst·messer** *das* fruit knife

**Obstruktion** /ɔpstrʊk'tsi̯o:n/ *die;* **~, ~en** (*auch Parl., Med.*) obstruction; (*Pol.: durch Dauerreden*) filibustering

**Obstruktions·politik** *die* (*Parl.*) policy of obstruction; (*durch Dauerreden*) filibustering policy

**Obst-: ~saft** *der* fruit juice; **~salat** *der* fruit salad; **~tag** *der* day for eating only fruit;

**~torte** *die* fruit flan; **~wasser** *das; Pl.* **~wässer** fruit brandy; **~wein** *der* fruit wine

**obszön** /ɔps'tsø:n/ ❶ *Adj.* obscene. ❷ *adv.* obscenely

**Obszönität** /ɔpstsøni'tɛ:t/ *die;* ~, **~en** obscenity

**O·bus** *der* trolley bus (*Brit.*)

**ob|walten, ob·walten** *itr. V.* (*geh. veralt.*) prevail

**ob·wohl** ❶ *Konj.* although; though. ❷ *Adv.* (*ugs.*) although

**ob·zwar** *Konj.* (*geh.*) ~ **[dass]** although

**Occasion** (*österr., schweiz.*) ⇨ **Okkasion**

**och** /ɔx/ *Interj.* (*ugs.*) oh

**Ochs** /ɔks/ *der;* **~en, ~en** (*südd., österr., schweiz., ugs.*), **Ochse** /'ɔksə/ *der;* **~en, ~en** Ⓐ ox; bullock; **~ am Spieß** roast ox; **du sollst dem ~en, der da drischt, nicht das Maul verbinden** you shouldn't be too strict with those who have to work hard; ⇨ *auch* **dastehen** A; Ⓑ (*salopp*) numskull (*coll.*); **ich ~e!** what a numskull I am!

**ochsen** *tr., itr. V.* ⇨ **büffeln**

**Ochsen-: ~brust** *die* (*Kochk.*) brisket of beef; **~frosch** *der* bullfrog; **~gespann** *das* Ⓐ team *or* span of oxen; Ⓑ (*Wagen*) ox cart; **~maul·salat** *der* (*Kochk.*) ox-cheek salad; **~schwanz·suppe** *die* (*Kochk.*) oxtail soup; **~tour** *die* (*ugs. scherzh.*) Ⓐ long, hard climb; Ⓑ (*Schinderei*) hard slog; **~ziemer** *der* [bull's] pizzle; **~zunge** *die* (*Kochk.*) ox-tongue

**Öchsle·grad** *der* degree Öchsle

**ocker** /'ɔkɐ/ *indekl. Adj.* ochre

**Ocker** *das;* **~s, ~:** ochre

**ocker-: ~braun** *Adj.* ochre-brown; **~gelb** *Adj.* ochre-yellow

**öd** /ø:t/ (*geh.*) ⇨ **öde**

**od.** *Abk.* **oder**

**Ode** /'o:də/ *die;* ~, **~n** ode (**an** + *Akk.* to, **auf** + *Akk.* on)

**öde** /'ø:də/ *Adj.* Ⓐ (*verlassen*) deserted ‹beach, village, house, street, etc.›; (*unbewohnt*) desolate ‹area, landscape›; Ⓑ (*unfruchtbar*) barren; Ⓒ (*langweilig*) tedious; dreary; dreary ‹life, time›; barren, tedious, dreary ‹existence›

**Öde** *die;* ~, **~n** Ⓐ ⇨ **öde** A-C: desertedness; desolateness; barrenness; Ⓑ (*öde Gegend*) wasteland; waste; Ⓒ (*Langeweile*) tediousness; dreariness

**Odem** /'o:dəm/ *der;* **~s** (*dichter. veralt.*) breath

**Ödem** /ø'de:m/ *das;* **~s, ~e** ▶ **474** (*Med.*) oedema

**oder** /'o:dɐ/ *Konj.* Ⓐ or; ~ **auch** or; ~ **aber** or else; ⇨ *auch* **entweder**; Ⓑ (*in Fragen*) **du kommst doch mit, ~?** you will come, won't you?; **er ist doch hier, ~?** he is here, isn't he? (*zweifelnd*) he is here — or isn't he?; **das ist doch erlaubt, ~ [nicht** *od.* **etwa nicht]?** that is allowed, isn't it?; **das ist doch nicht erlaubt, ~ [doch** *od.* **etwa doch]?** that isn't allowed, is it?; **das hört sich gut an, ~?** it sounds good, don't you think *or* agree?

**Odermennig** /'o:dɐmɛnɪç/ *der;* **~[e]s, ~e** (*Bot.*) agrimony

**Oder-Neiße-[Friedens]grenze** (*DDR*), **Oder-Neiße-Linie** *die* Oder-Neisse Line

**Ödipus·komplex** /'ø:dipʊs-/ *der* (*Psych.*) Oedipus complex

**Odium** /'o:diʊm/ *das;* **~s** (*geh.*) odium

**Öd·land** *das* uncultivated land (*and land exploited for raw materials, e. g. gravel pits*); **Ödländer** uncultivated land *sing. or* areas

**Ödnis** *die;* ~ (*geh.*) ⇨ **Öde**

**Odyssee** /ody'se:/ *die;* ~, **~n** odyssey; **Homers ~:** Homer's Odyssey

**Odysseus** /o'dysɔʏs/ (*der*)**; ~:** Odysseus

**Œuvre** /'ø:vrə/ *das;* ~, **~s** (*geh.*) œuvre

**OEZ** *Abk.* **osteuropäische Zeit** EET

**Öfchen** /'ø:fçən/ *das;* **~s, ~:** small stove *etc.;* ⇨ **Ofen** A-D

**Ofen** /'o:fn̩/ *der;* **~s, Öfen** Ⓐ heater; (*Kohle~*) stove; (*Ölöfen, Petroleum~*) stove; heater; (*elektrischer ~*) heater; fire; **wenn sie uns erwischen, ist der ~ aus** (*ugs.*) if they catch us, it's all over; **jetzt ist bei mir der ~ aus** (*ugs.: jetzt habe ich aber genug*) that does it!; Ⓑ (*Back~*) oven; Ⓒ (*Industrie~*) furnace; (*Brenn~, Trocken~*) kiln; Ⓓ (*landsch.: Herd*) cooker; Ⓔ **in heißer ~** (*salopp*) fast set of wheels (*coll.*)

**ofen-, Ofen-: ~bank** *die; Pl.* **~bänke** bench round a/the stove; **~frisch** *Adj.* oven-fresh; freshly baked; **~heizung** *die* heating *no art.* by stoves; **das Haus hat ~heizung** the house is heated by stoves; **~klappe** *die* Ⓐ damper; Ⓑ (**~tür**) stove door; **~rohr** *das* [stove] flue; **~schirm** *der* fire screen; **~setzer** *der,* **~setzerin** *die* (*der/die Öfen baut*) stove builder; (*der/die Öfen instand setzt*) stove fitter; **~warm** *Adj.* oven-hot

**Off** *das;* **~s** (*Film*) **aus dem ~:** from off camera

**offen** /'ɔfn̩/ ❶ *Adj.* Ⓐ open; **mit ~em Mund/~en Augen** with one's mouth/eyes open; **der Knopf/Schlitz/Schuh ist ~:** the button is/one's flies/shoelaces are undone; **ein ~es Hemd** a shirt with the collar unfastened; **sie trägt ihr Haar ~:** she wears her hair loose; **ein ~es Haus führen** *od.* **haben** keep open house; **eine ~e Anstalt** an open prison; **~ bleiben** remain *or* stay open; **etw. ~ halten/lassen** keep/have sth. open; **~ stehen** be open; **der Mund stand ihm vor Staunen ~:** his mouth hung open in astonishment; **~ haben** *od.* **sein** be open; **ein ~er Umschlag** an unsealed envelope; **ein ~er Brief** an open letter; **Tag der ~en Tür** open day; **~e Beine** ulcerated legs; **die Tür ist ~** (*nicht abgeschlossen*) the door is unlocked; **mit ~en Karten spielen** play with the cards face up on the table; (*fig.*) put one's cards on the table; **~es Licht/Feuer** a naked light/an open fire; **eine ~e Bauweise** an open layout; **das ~e Meer, die ~e See** the open sea; **~es Gelände** open terrain; **die Jagd ist ~:** it's open season; **Beifall auf ~er Szene** spontaneous applause; **unter ~em Himmel** in the open; **~e Türen einrennen** (*fig.*) fight a battle that's/battles that are already won; **bei ihm rennst du ~e Türen ein** (*fig.*) you're preaching to the converted with him; **mit ~en Augen** *od.* **Sinnen durch die Welt** *od.* **durchs Leben gehen** go about/go through life with one's eyes open; **mit ~en Augen in sein Verderben/Unglück rennen** be heading for disaster with one's eyes open; **ein ~es Geheimnis** an open secret; **für neue Ideen** *od.* **gegenüber neuen Ideen ~ sein** be receptive *or* open to new ideas; **etw. ~ legen** reveal sth.; (*bekannt geben*) disclose sth.; **jmdm. ~ stehen** be open to sb.; **es steht dir ~ teilzunehmen** you are free to attend; ⇨ *auch* **Arm** A; **Handelsgesellschaft**; **Karte** G; **Ohr** B; **Straße** A; **Strecke** B; **Visier** A; Ⓑ (*lose*) loose ‹sugar, flour, oats, etc.›; **~er Wein** wine on tap *or* draught; **ein Glas von dem ~en Rotwein** a glass of the draught red wine; Ⓒ (*frei*) vacant ‹job, post›; **~e Stellen** vacancies; (*als Rubrik*) 'Situations Vacant'; **lassen Sie die Zeile ~:** leave the line blank; Ⓓ (*ungewiss, ungeklärt*) open, unsettled ‹question›; uncertain ‹result›; **~ bleiben** remain open; ‹decision› be left open **~ lassen, ob ...:** leave it open whether ...; **der Ausgang des Spiels ist noch völlig ~:** the result of the match is still wide open; **wann es stattfindet, ist immer noch ~:** it's not yet been decided when it will take place; Ⓔ (*noch nicht bezahlt*) outstanding ‹bill›; **der ~e Betrag** the amount outstanding; **~ stehen** be outstanding; **~ stehende Rechnungen** outstanding bills; Ⓕ (*freimütig, aufrichtig*) frank [and open] ‹person›; frank, candid ‹look, opinion, reply›; open, frank ‹confession, manner›; frank ‹talk›; honest ‹character, face›; **~ zu jmdm. sein** be open *or* frank with sb.; Ⓖ (*unverhohlen*) open ‹threat, mutiny, hostility, opponent, etc.›; **in ~em Kampf** in an open fight; Ⓗ (*Sprachw.*) open ‹vowel, syllable›. ❷ *adv.* Ⓐ (*frei zugänglich, sichtbar, unverhohlen*) openly; ⇨ *auch* **zutage**; Ⓑ (*freimütig, aufrichtig*) openly; frankly; **~ gesagt** frankly; to be frank *or* honest; **~ gestanden** to tell you the truth; **darf ich ~ reden?** can I be frank?; can I speak frankly?; Ⓒ (*Sprachw.*); **das e ~ aussprechen** pronounce 'e' as an open vowel

**offen·bar** ❶ *Adj.* obvious; **seine Absicht war allen ~:** his intention was obvious *or* apparent to all. ❷ *adv.* Ⓐ (*offensichtlich*) obviously; clearly; Ⓑ (*anscheinend*) evidently

**offenbaren** (*geh.*) ❶ *tr. V.* reveal. ❷ *refl. V.* Ⓐ (*sich erweisen*) **sich als etw. ~** ‹person› show *or* reveal oneself to be sth.; **seine Worte offenbarten sich als Lüge** his words were revealed as a lie *or* to be a lie; Ⓑ (*sich mitteilen*) **sich jmdm. ~:** confide in sb.

**Offenbarung** *die;* ~, **~en** Ⓐ revelation; Ⓑ (*Rel.*) revelation; **die ~ [des Johannes]** [the Book of] Revelations

**Offenbarungs·eid** *der* (*Rechtsw.*) oath of disclosure

**offen-: *~|bleiben** ⇨ **offen** 1 A, D; ***~|halten** ⇨ **offen** 1 A

**Offen·heit** *die;* ~ ⇨ **offen** F: frankness [and openness]; candidness; candour; openness; honesty; **~ gegenüber den Problemen anderer zeigen** be responsive to other people's problems

**offen-, Offen-: ~herzig** ❶ *Adj.* Ⓐ frank, candid ‹conversation, remark›; frank and open ‹person›; Ⓑ (*iron.: dekolletiert*) revealing, low-cut ‹dress›; ❷ *adv.* frankly; openly; **~herzigkeit** *die;* **~~:** frankness; candidness; candour; **~kundig** ❶ *Adj.* obvious, evident (**für** to); obvious, patent, manifest ‹lie, betrayal, misuse›; **~kundig werden** become apparent; ❷ *adv.* obviously; clearly; ***~|lassen** ⇨ **offen** 1 A, D; ***~|legen** ⇨ **offen** 1 A; **~sichtlich** ❶ *Adj.* obvious; evident; ❷ *adv.* obviously; evidently; (*anscheinend*) evidently

**offensiv** /ɔfən'zi:f/ ❶ *Adj.* Ⓐ offensive; aggressive ‹marketing strategy›; Ⓑ (*Sport*) attacking. ❷ *adv.* Ⓐ offensively; ‹speak, argue, behave› aggressively; Ⓑ (*Sport*) **~ spielen** play an attacking game

**Offensive** *die;* ~, **~n** (*auch Sport*) offensive; **in der ~:** on the offensive; **die ~ ergreifen, in die ~ gehen** go on to the offensive

**Offensiv-: ~krieg** *der* offensive war; **~spiel** *das* (*Sport*) attacking game

***offen|stehen** ⇨ **offen** 1 A, E

**öffentlich** /'œfn̩tlɪç/ ❶ *Adj.* public; state *attrib.*, [state-]maintained ‹school›; **alle Teilnehmer am ~en Straßenverkehr** all road users; **etw. in ~er Sitzung beraten** debate sth. in open session; **die ~e Ordnung/Sicherheit** public order/security; **Erregung ~en Ärgernisses** (*Rechtsw.*) creating a public nuisance; **~es Ärgernis erregen** create a public nuisance; **die ~e Meinung** public opinion; **das ~e Recht** (*Rechtsw.*) public law; **Anstalt des ~en Rechts** institution incorporated under public law; **Körperschaft des ~en Rechts** public corporation; **der ~e Dienst** the civil service; **die Ausgaben der ~en Hand** public spending *sing.;* **von der ~en Hand finanziert** financed out of public funds; **die ~en Hände** local authorities and the state; **ein ~es Haus** (*veralt. verhüll.*) a house of ill repute; **ein ~es Geheimnis** an open secret; **eine Persönlichkeit des ~en Lebens** a public figure.
❷ *adv.* Ⓐ publicly; ‹perform, appear› in public; **~ tagen** meet in open session; **~ auftreten** appear in public; **etw. ~ versteigern** sell sth. by public auction; Ⓑ (*vom Staat usw.*) publicly ‹funded etc.›

**Öffentlichkeit** *die;* ~ Ⓐ public; **unter Ausschluss der ~:** in private *or* secret; (*Rechtsw.*) in camera; **etw. an die ~ bringen** bring sth. to public attention; make sth. public; **mit etw. an die ~ gehen** make sth. public; **vor die ~ treten** appear in public; **in aller ~:** [quite openly] in public; ⇨ *auch* **Flucht**[1] B; Ⓑ (*das Öffentlichsein*) **das Prinzip der ~ in der Rechtsprechung** the principle that justice be administered in open court; **die ~ einer Versammlung herstellen** throw a meeting open to the public

*old spelling (see note on page 1707)

**Öffentlichkeits·arbeit** *die* public relations work *no art.*

**öffentlich-rechtlich** *Adj.* under public law *postpos., not pred.;* **~es Fernsehen** state-owned television; **~e Körperschaften** bodies incorporated under public law

**offerieren** /ɔfəˈriːrən/ *tr. V.* (*bes. Kaufmannsspr.*) offer

**Offerte** /ɔˈfɛrtə/ *die;* ~, **~n** (*Kaufmannsspr.*) offer

**Offizial·verteidiger** /ɔfiˈtsi̯aːl-/ *der,* **Offizial·verteidigerin** *die* (*Rechtsw.*) ⇒ **Pflichtverteidiger**

**offiziell** /ɔfiˈtsi̯ɛl/ ❶ *Adj.* Ⓐ official; Ⓑ (*förmlich*) formal. ❷ *adv.* Ⓐ officially; Ⓑ (*förmlich*) **bei der Feier ging es furchtbar ~ zu** the celebration was terribly formal

**Offizier** /ɔfiˈtsiːɐ̯/ *der;* **~s, ~e** Ⓐ ▶ 159 officer; **~ werden** become an officer; gain a commission; Ⓑ (*Schach*) piece (*other than a pawn*)

**Offizierin** *die;* ~, **~nen** ▶ 159 ⇒ **Offizier** A

**Offiziers-: ~an·wärter** *der,* **~an·wärterin** *die* officer cadet; **~kasino** *das* officers' mess; **~korps** *das* officer corps; **~lauf·bahn** *die* officer's career; **~messe** *die* (*Seemannsspr.*) wardroom; **~rang** *der* officer's rank

**Offizin** /ɔfiˈtsiːn/ *die;* ~, **~en** Ⓐ (*Pharm.*) dispensary; Ⓑ (*veralt.: Apotheke*) chemist's [shop] (*Brit.*); drugstore (*Amer.*); Ⓒ (*veralt.: Druckerei*) printing works *sing. or pl.*

**offiziös** /ɔfiˈtsi̯øːs/ ❶ *Adj.* semi-official. ❷ *adv.* semi-officially; **wie ~ verlautet wurde** according to semi-official sources

**Offizium** /ɔˈfiːtsi̯ʊm/ *das;* **~s, Offizien** (*kath. Kirche*) Ⓐ ⇒ **Chorgebet**; Ⓑ (*hist.*) **das Heilige ~:** the Holy Office

**offline** /ˈɔflai̯n/ *Adv.* (*DV*) off-line

**öffnen** /ˈœfnən/ ❶ *tr.* (*auch itr.*) *V.* open; turn on ‹tap›; undo ‹coat, blouse, button, zip›; **die Grenzen ~:** open [up] the borders; **die Bank ist** *od.* **hat über Mittag geöffnet** the bank is open at lunchtime; **der Zoo wird um 9 Uhr geöffnet** the zoo opens at 9 a.m.; **sich** (*Dat.*) **die Pulsadern ~:** slash one's wrists; **„hier ~"** 'open here'; **jmdm. den Blick für etw. ~:** open sb.'s eyes to sth.; **mit geöffnetem Mund atmen** breathe with one's mouth open *or* through one's mouth; **eine Leiche ~:** carry out a post-mortem *or* an autopsy on a body; ⇒ *auch* **Auge**.
❷ *itr. V.* Ⓐ **[jmdm.] ~:** open the door [to sb.]; **wenn es klingelt, musst du ~:** if there's a ring at the door, you must go and answer it; Ⓑ (*geöffnet werden*) ‹shop, bank, etc.› open; Ⓒ (*sich* ~) ‹door› open.
❸ *refl. V.* Ⓐ open; **die Erde öffnete sich** the ground opened up; Ⓑ (*sich erweitern*) ‹valley, lane, forest, etc.› open out (**auf** + *Akk.*, **zu** on to); ‹view› open up; Ⓒ (*sich aufschließen*) **sich einer Sache** (*Dat.*) **~:** become receptive to sth.; Ⓓ (*sich ergeben*) ‹opportunity etc.› open up; Ⓔ (*seine Verschlossenheit aufgeben*) open up (+ *Dat.* to); Ⓕ (*offen sein*) ‹plain, clearing, etc.› open up; **sich nach Süden/Norden ~** ‹room etc.› be open to the south/north

**Öffner** *der;* **~s, ~:** opener

**Öffnung** *die;* ~, **~en** Ⓐ (*offene Stelle*) opening; (*Fot., Optik*) aperture; Ⓑ (*das Öffnen*) opening; **die ~ der Grenzen** the opening [up] of the borders; **eine ~ der Leiche** a post-mortem on the body; Ⓒ (*das Aufgeschlossensein*) openness (**für** to); **eine ~ nach links anstreben** (*Pol.*) strive to open the party up to left-wing ideas

**Öffnungs·zeit** *die;* **~en** *pl.* (*eines Geschäfts, einer Bank*) opening times; hours of business; (*eines Museums, Zoos usw.*) opening times

**Offset·druck** /ˈɔfsɛt-/ *der; Pl.* **~e** Ⓐ offset printing; Ⓑ (*Produkt*) offset print

**Off·sprecher** *der,* **Off·sprecherin** *die* (*Film*) off-screen narrator

**Off·stimme** *die* (*Film*) off-screen voice

**o-förmig, O-förmig** *Adj.* circular

**oft** /ɔft/ *Adv.* **öfter** /ˈœftɐ/; (*selten*) **öftest** /ˈœftəst/ often; **wie oft fährt der Bus?** how often does the bus go *or* run?; **wie ~ soll ich dir noch sagen, dass ...?** how many [more] times do I have to tell you that ...?

**öfter** /ˈœftɐ/ *Adv.* now and then; [every] once in a while; **des Öfteren** (*geh.*) on many occasions

**öfters** /ˈœftɐs/ *Adv.* (*österr. ugs.*) ⇒ **öfter**

**oftmals** *Adv.* often; frequently

**o.g.** *Abk.* **oben genannt**

**o.G.** *Abk.* **ohne Gewähr**

**OG** *Abk.* **Obergeschoss**

**ÖGB** *Abk.* **Österreichischer Gewerkschaftsbund** Austrian Trade Union Federation

**ogottogott** /ˈoɡɔtoɡɔt/ *Interj.* goodness me; oh dear, oh dear

**oh** /oː/ *Interj.* oh

**Oheim** /ˈoːhai̯m/ *der;* **~s, ~e** (*veralt.*) uncle

**OHG** *Abk.* **Offene Handelsgesellschaft** general partnership

**Ohm** /oːm/ *das;* **~[s], ~** (*Physik*) ohm

**ohmsch** /oːmʃ/ *Adj.* (*Physik*) **das ~e Gesetz** Ohm's Law; **der ~e Widerstand** ohmic resistance

**ohne** /ˈoːnə/ ❶ *Präp. mit Akk.* Ⓐ without; **~ mich!** [you can] count me out!; **der Versuch blieb ~ Erfolg** the attempt was unsuccessful; **sie ist ~ Jacke gekommen** she came without a jacket; **~ Appetit sein** have no appetite; **ein Mann ~ jeglichen Humor** a man totally lacking in humour *or* without any sense of humour; Ⓑ (*mit Auslassung des Akkusativs*) **ich rauche nur ~:** I only smoke untipped *or* filterless cigarettes; **wir baden am liebsten ~:** we prefer to bathe in the nude; **wenn du keinen Zucker hast, trinke ich den Tee auch ~:** if you haven't got any sugar, I can have my tea without; **du brauchst ein Visum, ~ lassen sie dich nicht einreisen** you need a visa, they won't let you in without one; **er/sie ist [gar] nicht [so] ~** (*ugs.*) he's/she's quite something; **der Vorschlag ist [gar] nicht [so] ~** (*ugs.*) it's not such a bad *or* daft suggestion; ⇒ *auch* **oben** C; Ⓒ **~ weiteres** (*leicht, einfach*) easily; (~ *Einwand*) readily; **das würde ich nicht so ~ weiteres glauben** I wouldn't believe it just like that; **die Genehmigung kriegst du ~ weiteres** you won't have any problem *or* difficulty getting approval; **das traue ich ihm ~ weiteres zu** I can quite *or* easily believe he's capable of that; Ⓓ excluding; **~ mich sind es 10 Teilnehmer** there are ten participants excluding *or* not counting *or* not including me.
❷ *Konj.* **er nahm Platz, ~ dass er gefragt hätte** he sat down without asking; **~ zu zögern** without hesitating; without hesitation

**ohne-: ~dies** *Adv.* (*geh.*) in any case; **die, die ~dies schon [am meisten] Geld haben** those who already have [the most] money in any case; **~einander** *Adv.* without each other; **~gleichen** *Adv., nachgestellt* **mit einer Hartnäckigkeit ~gleichen** with unparalleled obstinacy; **ein Skandal/eine Frechheit ~gleichen** an unprecedented scandal/impertinence; **das ist ein Unsinn ~gleichen** I've never heard such nonsense; **~hin** *Adv.* anyway; **er war ~hin schon überlastet** he was already overburdened as it was; **das hat ~hin keinen Zweck** there is really no point in it

**Ohnmacht** /ˈoːnmaxt/ *die;* ~, **~en** Ⓐ faint; swoon (*literary*); **in ~ fallen** *od.* (*geh.*) **sinken** faint *or* pass out/swoon; **sich einer ~ nahe fühlen** feel faint; **aus der** *od.* **seiner ~ erwachen** come to; **von** *od.* **aus einer ~ in die andere fallen** (*ugs. scherzh.*) constantly be having fits (*coll.*); Ⓑ (*Machtlosigkeit*) powerlessness; impotence

**ohnmächtig** ❶ *Adj.* Ⓐ unconscious; **~ werden** faint; pass out; **~ sein** have fainted *or* passed out; be in a dead faint; **~ zusammenbrechen** collapse unconscious; **halb ~:** half fainting; Ⓑ (*machtlos*) powerless; impotent; impotent, helpless ‹fury, rage›; helpless ‹bitterness, despair›.
❷ *adv.* impotently; **~ zusehen** watch powerless *or* helplessly

**Ohnmachts·anfall** *der* fainting fit

**oho** /oˈhoː/ ❶ *Interj.* oho; (*protestierend*) oh no. ❷ ⇒ **klein** 1 A

**Öhr** /øːɐ̯/ *das;* **~[e]s, ~e** eye

**Ohr** /oːɐ̯/ *das;* **~[e]s, ~en** Ⓐ ▶ 471 ear; **auf dem linken ~ taub sein** be deaf in one's left ear; **jmdm. etw. ins ~ flüstern** whisper sth. in sb.'s ear; **gute/schlechte ~en haben** have good/poor hearing *sing.;* **er hört nur auf einem ~:** he only has one good ear; **ein geschultes ~:** a trained ear; **mit den ~en wackeln** wiggle one's/its ears; **das war nicht für deine/fremde ~en [bestimmt]** that wasn't for your/everbody's ears; **ich habe seine Worte/die Melodie noch im ~:** his words are still ringing in my ears/the tune is still going around my head; **die Melodie geht einem gleich/leicht ins ~:** the tune is very catchy; Ⓑ (*fig.*) **wo hast du bloß deine ~en?** (*ugs.*), **du sitzt wohl auf den** *od.* **deinen ~en!** (*ugs.*) are you deaf or something? (*coll.*); **wasch dir mal die ~en!** (*ugs.*) get your ears seen to! (*coll.*); **die ~en aufmachen** *od.* **aufsperren** (*ugs.*) pin back one's ears; **tauben ~en predigen** (*geh.*) preach to deaf ears; **ich bin ganz ~:** I'm all ears; **mir klingen die ~en** my ears are burning; **die Wände haben ~en** the walls have ears; **ein offenes ~ für jmdn./etw. haben** be ready to listen to sb./be open to *or* ready to listen to sth.; **jmdm. sein ~ leihen** lend sb. one's ear[s]; **bei jmdm. ein offenes ~ finden** (*geh.*) find a sympathetic *or* ready listener in sb.; **[vor jmdm./etw.] die ~en verschließen** (*geh.*) close one's ears to sb./sth.; **die ~en spitzen** (*ugs.*) prick up one's ears; **spitz mal die ~en!** (*ugs.*) pin back your ears (*coll.*); **jmdm. die ~en lang ziehen** (*ugs.*) take sb. by the ear and give him/her a good talking-to (*coll.*); **halt die ~en steif!** (*ugs.*) keep smiling!; **die ~en hängen lassen** (*ugs.*) lose heart; get downhearted; **sich** (*Dat.*) **[fast] die ~en brechen** (*salopp scherzh.*) bite off [almost] more than one can chew; **auf dem** *od.* **diesem ~ hört er schlecht/nicht** (*ugs.*) he doesn't want to hear anything about that; **sich aufs ~ legen** *od.* (*ugs.*) **hauen** get one's head down (*coll.*); **noch feucht/nicht [ganz] trocken hinter den ~en sein** (*ugs.*) be still wet behind the ears; **schreib dir das mal hinter die ~en!** (*ugs.*) just you remember that!; **eine** *od.* **eins/ein paar hinter die ~en kriegen** (*ugs.*) get a thick ear (*coll.*); **jmdm. [mit etw.] in den ~en liegen** (*ugs.*) pester sb. the whole time [with sth.]; **mit den ~en schlackern** (*ugs.*) be staggered; **da kannst du/kann man nur mit den ~en schlackern** it's just staggering; **bis über beide ~en verliebt [in jmdn.]** (*ugs.*) head over heels in love [with sb.]; **bis über beide** *od.* **die ~en in etw. stecken** (*ugs.*) be up to one's ears in sth. (*coll.*); **jmdn. übers ~ hauen** (*ugs.*) take sb. for a ride (*coll.*); put one over on sb. (*coll.*); **viel** *od.* **eine Menge um die ~en haben** (*ugs.*) have a lot on one's plate (*coll.*); **jmdm. etw. um die ~en hauen** *od.* **schlagen** (*ugs.*) throw sth. back at sb.; **jmdm. um die ~en fliegen** (*ugs.*) blow up in sb.'s face; **von einem ~ zum anderen strahlen** (*ugs.*) grin from ear to ear; **etw. kommt jmdm. zu den ~en heraus** (*ugs.*) sb. has got sth. coming out of his/her ears; **zum einen ~ rein- und zum anderen wieder rausgehen** (*ugs.*) go in one ear and out the other (*coll.*); ⇒ *auch* **Durchzug** A; **faustdick** 2; **Fell** A; **Floh** A; **Mann** A; **Nacht**

**ohren-, Ohren-: ~arzt** *der,* **~ärztin** *die* otologist; ear specialist; **~beichte** *die* (*kath. Rel.*) auricular confession; **~betäubend** ❶ *Adj.* ear-splitting; deafening; deafening ‹applause›; ❷ *adv.* deafeningly; **~betäubend lärmen** make a deafening noise; **~klappe** *die* ear flap; **~leiden** *das* ear complaint; **~sausen** *das;* **~~s** ▶ 474 ringing in the *or* one's ears; tinnitus (*Med.*); **~schmalz** *das* earwax; **~schmaus** *der* (*ugs.*) **ein ~schmaus sein** be a joy to hear; **~schmerz** *der* earache; **~schmerzen haben** have [an] earache *sing.;* **~schützer** *der;* **~~s, ~~:** earmuff; **~sessel** *der* wing chair; **~zeuge** *der,* **~zeugin** *die:* **ich wurde ~ des Gesprächs** I heard the conversation myself

O

**ohr-, Ohr-:** **~feige** *die* box on the ears; **~feigen bekommen** *od.* (*ugs.*) **einstecken** get one's ears boxed; **jmdm. eine ~feige geben** *od.* (*ugs.*) **verpassen** box sb.'s ears; give sb. a box on the ears; **~feigen** /-faign/ *tr. V.* **jmdn. ~feigen** box sb.'s ears; **ich könnte mich [selbst] ~feigen!** (*ugs.*) I could kick myself!; **~feigen·gesicht** *das* (*salopp abwertend*) **er hat ein richtiges ~feigengesicht** he's got the sort of face you'd like to clout; **~klipp** /-klɪp/ *der;* **~~s, ~~s** ear clip; **~läppchen** *das;* **~~s, ~~** ▶ 471 earlobe; **~muschel** *die* ▶ 471 external ear; auricle; **~ring** *der* earring; **~stecker** *der* ear stud; **~wurm** der Ⓐ earwig; Ⓑ (*ugs.: Melodie*) catchy tune; **ein ~wurm sein** be really catchy

**o.J.** *Abk.* **ohne Jahr** n.d.

**oje** /o'je:/ *Interj.* (*veralt.*), **ojemine** /o'je:mine/, **ojerum** /o'je:rʊm/ *Interj.* (*veralt.*) oh dear; dear me

**Okarina** /oka'ri:na/ *die;* **~, ~s** *od.* **Okarinen** ocarina

**okay** /o'ke/ *Interj., Adj., adv.* (*ugs.*) OK (*coll.*); okay (*coll.*); **das geht ~:** that's OK *or* okay

**Okay** *das;* **~[s], ~s** (*ugs.*) OK (*coll.*); okay (*coll.*)

**Okkasion** /ɔka'zi̯o:n/ *die;* **~, ~en** (*veralt.*) opportunity

**okkult** /ɔ'kʊlt/ *Adj.* occult

**Okkultismus** *der;* **~:** occultism *no art.*

**Okkupant** /ɔku'pant/ *der;* **~en, ~en, Okkupantin** *die;* **~, ~nen** (*abwertend*) occupier

**Okkupation** /ɔkupa'tsi̯o:n/ *die;* **~, ~en** (*abwertend*) occupation

**okkupieren** *tr. V.* Ⓐ (*abwertend*) occupy; Ⓑ (*sich aneignen*) **jmds. Stuhl ~:** occupy sb.'s chair

**öko-, Öko-** /øko-/ eco-

**Ökoaudit** /'ø:ko:ɔ:dɪt/ *das;* **~s, ~s** eco-audit; environmental audit

**Ökologe** /øko'lo:gə/ *der;* **~n, ~n** ecologist

**Ökologie** *die;* **~:** ecology

**Ökologin** *die;* **~, ~nen** ecologist

**ökologisch** ❶ *Adj.* ecological. ❷ *adv.* ecologically

**Ökonom** /øko'no:m/ *der;* **~en, ~en** economist

**Ökonomie** *die;* **~, ~n** Ⓐ economics *sing.*; **politische ~:** political economy; Ⓑ (*Wirtschaft, Wirtschaftlichkeit*) economy

**Ökonomik** *die;* **~:** economics *pl.*

**Ökonomin** *die;* **~, ~nen** economist

**ökonomisch** ❶ *Adj.* Ⓐ economic; **eine ~e Abhandlung** a treatise on economics; Ⓑ (*sparsam*) economical. ❷ *adv.* economically

**Öko·steuer** *die;* **~, ~n** eco-tax

**Öko·system** *das* ecosystem

**Ökotrophologie** /økotrofolo'gi:/ *die;* **~:** home economics *sing., no art.*

**Okt.** *Abk.* **Oktober** Oct.

**Oktaeder** /ɔkta'|e:dɐ/ *das;* **~s, ~** (*Math.*) octahedron

**Oktan·zahl** /ɔk'ta:n-/ *die* octane rating *or* number

**Oktav** /ɔk'ta:f/ *das;* **~s** octavo

**Oktav-:** **~band** *der* octavo volume; **~heft** *das* octavo notebook

**Oktave** /ɔk'ta:və/ *die;* **~, ~n** octave

**Oktett** /ɔk'tɛt/ *das;* **~[e]s, ~e** octet

**Oktober** /ɔk'to:bɐ/ *der;* **~[s], ~** ▶ 207 October; ⇒ *auch* **April**

**Oktober-:** **~fest** *das* Munich October festival; **~revolution** *die* (*hist.*) October Revolution

**oktroyieren** /ɔktro̯a'ji:rən/ *tr. V.* (*geh.*) impose; force; **jmdm. etw. ~:** impose *or* force sth. on sb.

**Okular** /oku'la:ɐ̯/ *das;* **~s, ~e** eyepiece

**okulieren** *tr. V.* (*Gartenbau*) bud

**Ökumene** /øku'me:nə/ *die;* **~** (*christl. Rel.*) Ⓐ ecumenical Christianity; Ⓑ (*Bewegung*) ecumenical movement

*old spelling (see note on page 1707)

**ökumenisch** ❶ *Adj.* (*christl. Rel.*) ecumenical; **Ökumenischer Rat der Kirchen** World Council of Churches. ❷ *adv.* ecumenically

**Okzident** /'ɔktsidɛnt/ *der;* **~s** (*veralt., geh.*) Occident

**Öl** /ø:l/ *das;* **~[e]s, ~e** oil; **auf ~ stoßen** strike oil; **~ exportierende Länder** oil-exporting countries; **in ~ malen** paint in oils; **eine Landschaft in ~:** a landscape in oils; **~ auf die Wogen gießen** (*fig.*) pour oil on troubled waters; **~ ins Feuer gießen** (*fig.*) add fuel to the flames; **das ging ihm runter wie ~** (*fig. ugs.*) he lapped it up

**Öl-:** **~baum** *der* olive tree; **~berg** *der* Mount of Olives; **~bild** *das* oil painting; **~bohrung** *die* drilling *no art.* for oil; **eine ~bohrung/~bohrungen durchführen** drill for oil; **~druck** *der; Pl.* **~drücke** (*Technik*) oil pressure; **~druck·bremse** *die* hydraulic brake

**Oldtimer** /'oʊldtaɪmə/ *der;* **~s, ~:** vintage car; (*vor 1905 gebaut*) veteran car

**Oleander** /ole'andɐ/ *der;* **~s, ~** (*Bot.*) oleander

**ölen** *tr. V.* oil; oil, lubricate ‹shaft, engine, etc.›; **wie geölt** (*fig. ugs.*) like clockwork; ⇒ *auch* **Blitz** A

**öl-, Öl-:** ***~exportierend** ⇒ **Öl**; **~farbe** *die* Ⓐ oil-based paint; Ⓑ (*zum Malen*) oil paint; **mit ~farben malen** paint in oils; **~feld** *das* oilfield; **~film** *der* film of oil

**OLG** *Abk.* **Oberlandesgericht**

**öl-, Öl-:** **~gemälde** *das* oil painting; **~götze** *der: in* **wie ein ~götze/wie die ~götzen** (*ugs.*) like a zombie/zombies; **~hahn** *der: in* **den ~hahn zudrehen** (*fig.*) stop the supply of oil; **~haltig** *Adj.* containing oil *postpos., not pred.*; oil-bearing ‹rock, shale, etc.›; **~heizung** *die* oil-fired heating *no indef. art.*

**ölig** ❶ *Adj.* (*auch fig. abwertend*) oily. ❷ *adv.* Ⓐ **~ glänzen** have an oily sheen; Ⓑ (*fig. abwertend*) in an oily way

**Oligarchie** /oligar'çi:/ *die;* **~, ~n** oligarchy

**oliv** /o'li:f/ *Adj.* olive[-green]

**Oliv** *das;* **~s, ~** *od.* **~s** olive[-green]

**Olive** /o'li:və/ *die;* **~, ~n** olive

**Oliven-:** **~baum** *der* olive tree; **~öl** *das* olive oil

**oliv·grün** *Adj.* olive-green

**Öl-:** **~kanister** *der* oilcan; **~jacke** *die* oilskin jacket; **~kanne** *die* oilcan; **~krise** *die* oil crisis; **~kuchen** *der* (*Landw.*) oilcake

**oll** /ɔl/ *Adj.* (*ugs., bes. nordd.*) old; **je ~er, je doller** (*ugs. scherzh.*) the older they get, the more they want to live it up

**Öl·lampe** *die* oil lamp

**Olle**[1] *der; adj. Dekl.* (*ugs., bes. nordd.*) Ⓐ (*alter Mann*) old boy (*coll.*); Ⓑ (*Vater, Ehemann*) old man (*coll.*); **meine ~n** my old man and old lady (*coll.*); Ⓒ (*Chef*) old man (*coll.*); boss (*coll.*)

**Olle**[2] *die; adj. Dekl.* (*ugs., bes. nordd.*) Ⓐ (*alte Frau*) old dear (*coll.*); Ⓑ (*Mutter, Ehefrau*) old lady (*coll.*); Ⓒ (*Chefin*) boss (*coll.*)

**Öl-:** **~leitung** *die* oil pipe; (*größer*) oil pipeline; **~malerei** *die* oil painting *no art.*; **~messstab, *~meßstab** *der* (*bes. Kfz-W.*) dipstick; **~mühle** *die* oil mill; **~multi** *der* oil multinational; **~ofen** *der* oil heater; **~papier** *das* oiled paper; **~pest** *die* oil pollution *no indef. art.*; **~preis** *der* oil price; **~pumpe** *die* oil pump; **~quelle** *die* oil well; **~raffinerie** *die* oil refinery; **~sardine** *die* sardine in oil; **eine Dose ~n** a tin of sardines; **~scheich** *der* (*ugs.*) oil sheikh; **~schiefer** *der* oil shale; **~schinken** *der* (*ugs. abwertend*) large pretentious oil painting; **~spur** *die* trail of oil; **~stand** *der* oil level; **~tank** *der* oil tank; **~tanker** *der* oil tanker; **~teppich** *der* oil slick

**Ölung** *die;* **~, ~en** oiling; lubrication; **Letzte ~** (*kath. u. orthodoxe Kirche*) extreme unction

**Öl-:** **~wanne** *die* (*bes. Kfz-W.*) sump; **~wechsel** *der* (*bes. Kfz-W.*) oil change

**Olymp** /o'lʏmp/ *der;* **~s** Ⓐ Mount Olympus; Ⓑ (*ugs. scherzh.: im Theater*) **der ~:** the gods *pl.*; **auf dem ~:** [up] in the gods

**Olympia**[1] /o'lʏmpi̯a/ (*das*); **~s** (*Geogr.*) Olympia

**Olympia**[2] *das;* **~[s]** ⇒ **Olympiade** A

**Olympiade** /olʏm'pi̯a:də/ *die;* **~, ~n** Ⓐ Olympic Games *pl.*; Olympics *pl.*; **die ~ 1980** the 1980 Olympic Games *or* Olympics; Ⓑ (*Wettbewerb*) Olympiad; Ⓒ (*Zeitraum*) Olympiad

**olympia-, Olympia-:** **~dorf** *das* Olympic village; **~mannschaft** *die* Olympic team *or* squad; **~sieger** *der,* **~siegerin** *die;* Olympic champion; **~stadion** *das* Olympic stadium; **~teilnehmer** *der,* **~teilnehmerin** *die* Olympic competitor; **~verdächtig** *Adj.* (*ugs.*) Olympic-standard; **~verdächtig sein** be of Olympic standard

**Olympier** /o'lʏmpi̯ɐ/ *der;* **~s, ~** (*geh. veralt.*) Olympian

**Olympionike** /olʏmpi̯o'ni:kə/ *der;* **~n, ~n, Olympionikin** *die;* **~, ~nen** (*geh.*) Ⓐ (*Sieger[in]*) Olympic champion; Ⓑ (*Teilnehmer[in]*) Olympic competitor

**olympisch** *Adj.* Ⓐ Olympic; **die Olympischen Spiele** the Olympic Games; the Olympics; Ⓑ (*zum Olymp gehörend, auch fig. geh.*) Olympian

**Öl-:** **~zeug** *das* oilskins *pl.*; **~zweig** *der* olive branch

**Oma** /'o:ma/ *die;* **~, ~s** (*fam.*) gran[ny] (*coll./child lang.*); grandma (*coll./child lang.*)

**Ombuds-** /'ɔmbʊts-/: **~frau** *die* ombudswoman; **~mann** *der; Pl.* **~männer** *od.* **~leute** ombudsman

**Omega** /'o:mega/ *das;* **~[s], ~s** omega

**Omelett** *das;* **~[e]s, ~e** *od.* **~s,** (*österr., schweiz.*) **Omelette** /ɔm(ə)'lɛt/ *die;* **~, ~en** (*Kochk.*) omelette

**Omen** /'o:mən/ *das;* **~s, ~** *od.* **Omina** /'o:mina/ omen

**Omi** /'o:mi/ *die;* **~, ~s** (*fam.*) granny (*coll./child lang.*)

**Omikron** /'o:mikrɔn/ *das;* **~[s], ~s** omicron

**ominös** /omi'nø:s/ ❶ *Adj.* Ⓐ ominous; Ⓑ (*bedenklich, zweifelhaft*) sinister; (*berüchtigt*) unsavoury. ❷ *adv.* ominously

**Omnibus** /'ɔmnibʊs/ *der;* **~ses, ~se** omnibus (*formal*); (*Privat- und Reisebus auch*) coach

**Omnibus-** ⇒ **Bus-**

**omnipotent** /ɔmnipo'tɛnt/ *Adj.* (*geh.*) omnipotent

**Omnipotenz** /ɔmnipo'tɛnts/ *die;* **~** (*geh.*) omnipotence

**Onanie** /ona'ni:/ *die;* **~:** onanism *no art.*; masturbation *no art.*

**onanieren** *itr. V.* masturbate

**Ondit** /õ'di:/ *das;* **~[s], ~s** (*geh.*) on dit; rumour

**ondulieren** /ɔndu'li:rən/ *tr. V.* (*veralt.*) crimp; wave

**Onkel**[1] /'ɔŋkl̩/ *der;* **~s, ~** *od.* (*ugs.*) **~s** Ⓐ uncle; Ⓑ (*Kinderspr.: Mann*) **der ~ dort** that man there; **sag dem ~ guten Tag!** say hello to the nice man; **der ~ Doktor** the nice doctor; Ⓒ (*ugs. abwertend*) bloke (*Brit. coll.*); guy (*coll.*)

**Onkel**[2] *der;* **~s, ~s** *in* **großer** *od.* **dicker ~:** big toe; **über den großen ~ gehen** walk pigeon-toed

**Onkel·ehe** *die* (*ugs.*): *cohabitation of a widow with a man who* (*in order to retain benefits due to her from the first marriage*) *is not married to her*

**onkel·haft** ❶ *Adj.* avuncular. ❷ *adv.* in an avuncular manner

**online** /'ɔnlaɪn/ ❶ *Adj.* online; **~ gehen** go online. ❷ *Adv.* online

**Online-:** **~betrieb** *der* (*DV*) online operation; **~dienst** *der* (*DV*) online service; **~zeit** *die* (*DV*) connection *or* usage time

**ONO** *Abk.* ▶ 400 **Ostnordost[en]** ENE

**onomato·poetisch** *Adj.* (*Sprachw.*) onomatopoeic; onomatopoetic

**ontisch** /'ɔntɪʃ/ (*Philos.*) ❶ *Adj.* ontic. ❷ *adv.* ontically

**Onto·genese** /ɔnto-/ *die (Biol.)* ontogeny; ontogenesis

**onto·genetisch** *(Biol.)* ❶ *Adj.* ontogenetic. ❷ *adv.* ontogenetically

**onto·logisch** *(Philos.)* ❶ *Adv.* ontological. ❷ *adv.* ontologically

**Onyx** /'o:nyks/ *der;* **~[e]s, ~e** *(Mineral., Med.)* onyx

**o.O.** *Abk.* **ohne Ort** n.p.

**OP** /o:'pe:/ *der;* **~[s], ~[s]** *Abk.* **Operationssaal**

**Op.** *Abk.* **Opus** op.

**Opa** /'o:pa/ *der;* **~s, ~s** *(fam.)* grandad *(coll./child lang.)*; grandpa *(coll./child lang.)*

**opak** /o'pa:k/ *Adj.* opaque

**Opal** /o'pa:l/ *der;* **~s, ~e** opal

**opalisieren** *itr. V.* opalesce; **~d** opalescent

**Op-Art** /'ɔp|a:ɐ̯t/ *die;* **~:** op art

**OPEC** /'o:pɛk/ *die;* **~** *Abk.* OPEC

**Oper** /'o:pɐ/ *die;* **~, ~n** opera; *(Institution, Ensemble)* Opera; *(~nhaus)* Opera; opera house; **in die ~ gehen** go to the opera; **an die/zur ~ gehen** *(als Sänger)* become an opera singer; **quatsch keine ~n!** *(salopp)* don't talk rot! *(coll.)*

**Opera** ⇒ **Opus**

**Operateur** /opəra'tø:ɐ̯/ *der;* **~s, ~e** Ⓐ *(Arzt)* [operating] surgeon; Ⓑ *(Filmvorführer)* projectionist

**Operation** /opəra'tsi̯o:n/ *die;* **~, ~en** ▶ 474 operation; **~ gelungen, Patient tot** *(ugs.)* [it was] a brilliant idea, but it hasn't done the trick *(coll.)*

**operationalisieren** /opəratsi̯onali'zi:rən/ *tr. V. (Wissensch., Päd.)* operationalize

**Operations-: ~basis** *die (bes. Milit.)* base of operations; **~gebiet** *das (Milit., auch fig.)* area of operations; **~narbe** *die* operation scar; **~saal** *der* operating theatre *(Brit.) or* -room; **~schwester** *die* theatre sister *(Brit.)*; operating-room nurse *(Amer.)*; **~tisch** *der* operating table

**operativ** /opəra'ti:f/ ❶ *Adj.* Ⓐ *(Med.)* operative; Ⓑ *(Milit.)* operational. ❷ *adv.* Ⓐ *(Med.)* by operative surgery; **etw. ~ entfernen** operate to remove sth.; Ⓑ *(Milit.)* operationally

**Operator** /opə'ra:tɔr/ *der;* **~s, ~en, Operatorin** *die;* **~, ~nen** *(DV)* [computer] operator

**Operette** /opə'rɛtə/ *die;* **~, ~n** operetta

**operettenhaft** ❶ *Adj.* reminiscent of operetta *postpos.* ❷ *adv.* in a way reminiscent of operetta

**Operetten·staat** *der (abwertend)* little tinpot state *(derog.)*

**operieren** ❶ ▶ 474 *tr. V.* operate on ‹patient›; **jmdn. am Magen ~:** operate on sb.'s stomach; **sich ~ lassen** have an operation. ❷ *itr. V.* operate; **vorsichtig ~** *(vorgehen)* proceed carefully

**Opern-: ~arie** *die* [operatic] aria; **~bühne** *die* opera house; **~führer** *der* opera guide; **~glas** *das* opera glass[es *pl.*]; **~haus** *das* opera house; **~sänger** *der*, **~sängerin** *die* ▶ 159 opera singer

**Opfer** /'ɔpfɐ/ *das;* **~s, ~** Ⓐ *(Verzicht)* sacrifice; **ein ~ [für etw.] bringen** make a sacrifice [for sth.]; **kein ~ scheuen** consider no sacrifice too great; **unter großen ~n** by making great sacrifices; **manches ~ auf sich** *(Akk.)* **nehmen** make quite a few sacrifices; Ⓑ *(Geschädigter)* victim; **das Haus wurde ein ~ der Flammen** *(geh.)* the house fell victim to the flames; **jmdm./einer Sache zum ~ fallen** fall victim to sb./sth.; be the victim of sb./sth.; Ⓒ *(~gabe)* sacrifice; **jmdm./einer Sache etw. zum ~ bringen** sacrifice sth. to sb./sth.

**opfer-, Opfer-: ~bereit** *Adj.* ‹person› who is ready *or* willing to make sacrifices; **~bereitschaft** *die* readiness *or* willingness to make sacrifices; **~gabe** *die* [sacrificial] offering; **~gang** *der* Ⓐ *(kath. Kirche)* offertory procession; Ⓑ *(geh.)* **seinen ~gang antreten** sacrifice oneself; **~lamm** *das* sacrificial lamb; **wie ein ~lamm** *(fig. ugs.)* like a lamb to the slaughter; **~mut** *der (geh.)* readiness *or* willingness to make sacrifices

**opfern** ❶ *tr. V.* Ⓐ *(darbringen)* sacrifice; make a sacrifice of; offer up ‹fruit, produce, etc.›; Ⓑ *(fig.: hingeben)* sacrifice, give up ‹time, holiday, money, life›. ❷ *itr. V.* **[den Göttern] ~:** offer sacrifice [to the gods]. ❸ *refl. V.* Ⓐ **sich für jmdn./etw. ~:** sacrifice oneself for sb./sth.; Ⓑ *(ugs. scherzh.)* be the martyr; **wer opfert sich denn und isst den Nachtisch auf?** who's going to volunteer to finish off the dessert?

**Opfer-: ~stock** *der; Pl.* **~stöcke** offertory box; **~tier** *das* sacrificial animal; **~tod** *der (geh.)* **den ~tod sterben** sacrifice one's life

**Opferung** *die;* **~, ~en** Ⓐ sacrifice; Ⓑ *(kath. Kirche)* offertory

**Opfer·wille** *der* ⇒ **Opfermut**

**opfer·willig** *Adj.* ⇒ **opferbereit**

**Opiat** /o'pi̯a:t/ *das;* **~[e]s, ~e** opiate

**Opium** /'o:pi̯ʊm/ *das;* **~s** *(auch fig.)* opium

**Opium-: ~höhle** *die (ugs.)* opium den; **~krieg** *der (hist.)* Opium War; **~raucher** *der*, **~raucherin** *die* opium smoker; **~rausch** *der* opium dream; **~sucht** *die* opium addiction

**ÖPNV** *Abk.* **öffentlicher Personennahverkehr** local public transport

**Opossum** /o'pɔsʊm/ *das;* **~s, ~s** opossum

**Opponent** /ɔpo'nɛnt/ *der;* **~en, ~en, Opponentin** *die;* **~, ~nen** opponent

**opponieren** *itr. V.* take the opposite side; **gegen jmdn./etw. ~:** oppose sb./sth.

**opportun** /ɔpɔr'tu:n/ *Adj. (geh.)* appropriate; *(günstig)* advantageous

**Opportunismus** *der;* **~:** opportunism

**Opportunist** *der;* **~en, ~en, Opportunistin** *die;* **~, ~nen** opportunist

**opportunistisch** ❶ *Adj.* opportunist; opportunistic. ❷ *adv.* opportunistically; **~ handeln** be opportunistic; *(im Einzelfall)* act in an opportunistic fashion

**Opportunität** /ɔpɔrtuni'tɛ:t/ *die;* **~, ~en** *(geh.)* appropriateness

**Opportunitäts·prinzip** *das: (Rechtsw.) principle that the public prosecutor has the power to decide whether or not to institute proceedings*

**Opposition** /ɔpozi'tsi̯o:n/ *die;* **~, ~en** *(auch Politik, Sprachw., Astron., Schach, Fechten)* opposition; **etw. aus [reiner** *od.* **lauter] ~ tun** do sth. just to be contrary; **~ gegen jmdn./etw. machen** *(ugs.)* oppose sb./sth.; **in die ~ gehen** *(Politik)* go into opposition; **Jupiter und Mars stehen in ~:** Jupiter and Mars are in opposition

**oppositionell** /ɔpozitsi̯o'nɛl/ ❶ *Adj.* opposition *attrib.* ‹group, movement, circle, etc.›; ‹newspaper, writer, artist, etc.› opposed to the government; ‹feelings› of opposition; ‹attempts› at opposition; opposing ‹trend, tendency›; **~es Verhalten** opposition; **die seit 1982 ~e SPD** the SPD, in opposition since 1982. ❷ *adv.* **~ eingestellt sein** hold opposing views

**Oppositionelle** *der/die; adj. Dekl.* member of the opposition; *(Regimekritiker)* dissident

**Oppositions-: ~führer** *der*, **~führerin** *die* opposition leader; *(in Großbritannien)* Leader of the Opposition; **~partei** *die* opposition party

**Optativ** /'ɔptati:f/ *der;* **~s, ~e** *(Sprachw.)* optative

**optieren** /ɔp'ti:rən/ *itr. V.* Ⓐ *(Völkerr.)* opt; **für Polen ~:** opt for Polish citizenship; Ⓑ *(Rechtsw.)* **auf etw.** *(Akk.)* **~:** take an option on sth.

**Optik** *die;* **~, ~en** Ⓐ *(Wissenschaft)* optics *sing., no art.*; Ⓑ *(Fot. ugs.) (Linse)* lens; *(Linsen)* optics *pl.*; lens system; **das ist eine Frage der ~** *(fig.)* it depends on your point of view; Ⓒ *(Erscheinungsbild)* appearance; **der ~ wegen** for visual effect

**Optiker** *der;* **~s, ~, Optikerin** *die;* **~, ~nen** ▶ 159 optician

**Optima** ⇒ **Optimum**

**optimal** /ɔpti'ma:l/ ❶ *Adj.* optimal; optimum *attrib.* ❷ *adv.* **jmdn. ~ beraten** give sb. the best possible advice; **ein Problem ~ lösen** find the optimal *or* optimum solution to a problem

**optimieren** *tr. V.* optimize

**Optimierung** *die;* **~, ~en** optimization

**Optimismus** *der;* **~:** optimism

**Optimist** *der;* **~en, ~en, Optimistin** *die;* **~, ~nen** optimist; **~ sein** be an optimist

**optimistisch** ❶ *Adj.* optimistic. ❷ *adv.* optimistically

**Optimum** /'ɔptimʊm/ *das;* **~s, Optima** *(auch Biol.)* optimum

**Option** /ɔp'tsi̯o:n/ *die;* **~, ~en** Ⓐ *(Völkerr.)* opting; Ⓑ *(Rechtsw.)* option (**auf** + *Akk.* on)

**optisch** ❶ *Adj.* optical; visual ‹impression›; **eine ~e Täuschung** an optical illusion; **aus ~en Gründen** for [the sake of] optical *or* visual effect; *(fig.)* for [the sake of] effect. ❷ *adv.* optically; visually ‹impressive, successful, effective›; **~ wahrnehmbar sein** be perceivable with the eye

**opulent** /opu'lɛnt/ ❶ *Adj.* Ⓐ sumptuous ‹meal, banquet, etc.›; Ⓑ *(aufwendig [gestaltet])* opulent; lavish ‹theatrical production›. ❷ *adv.* opulently ‹dressed›; **~ essen** eat a sumptuous meal

**Opus** /'o:pʊs/ *das;* **~, Opera** /'o:pəra/ opus; *(Gesamtwerk)* œuvre

**Orakel** /o'ra:kl̩/ *das;* **~s, ~** *(auch fig.)* oracle; **in ~n reden** *od.* **sprechen** *(fig.)* talk *or* speak in riddles

**orakel·haft** *Adj.* oracular

**orakeln** ❶ *tr. V.* **~, dass ...** make mysterious prophecies that ... ❷ *itr. V.* make mysterious prophecies

**oral** /o'ra:l/ ❶ *Adj.* oral. ❷ *adv.* orally; **~ verkehren** have oral intercourse *or* sex

**orange** /o'rã:ʒ(ə)/ *indekl. Adj.* orange

**Orange**[1] *das;* **~s, ~** *od. (ugs.)* **~s** orange

**Orange**[2] *die;* **~, ~n** *(bes. südd., österr., schweiz.: Apfelsine)* orange

**Orangeade** /orã'ʒa:də/ *die;* **~, ~n** orangeade

**Orangeat** /orã'ʒa:t/ *das;* **~s, ~e** candied orange peel

**orange·farben, orange·farbig** *Adj.* orange[-coloured]

**orangen** /o'rã:ʒn̩/ *Adj.* orange

**orangen-, Orangen-: ~baum** orange tree; **~farben, ~farbig** *Adj.* ⇒ **orangefarben**; **~marmelade** *die* orange marmalade; **~saft** *der* orange juice; **~schale** *die* orange peel *no pl.*

**Orangerie** /orãʒə'ri:/ *die;* **~, ~n** orangery

**Orang-Utan** /'o:raŋ'|u:tan/ *der;* **~s, ~s** orang-utan

**Oranien** /o'ra:ni̯ən/ *(das);* **~s** Orange; **Wilhelm von ~:** William of Orange

**Oranier** *der;* **~s, ~, Oranierin** *die;* **~, ~nen** member of the House of Orange

**Oratorium** /ora'to:ri̯ʊm/ *das;* **~s, Oratorien** oratorio

**Orchester** /ɔr'kɛstɐ/ *das;* **~s, ~:** orchestra; *(~graben)* orchestra [pit]

**Orchester-: ~begleitung** *die* orchestral accompaniment; **~graben** *der* orchestra pit; **~musiker** *der*, **~musikerin** *die* orchestral musician

**orchestral** /ɔrkɛs'tra:l/ ❶ *Adj.* orchestral. ❷ *adv.* **~ begleitet** accompanied by an orchestra

**orchestrieren** *tr. V. (Musik, auch fig.)* orchestrate

**Orchestrierung** *die;* **~, ~en** *(Musik, auch fig.)* orchestration

**Orchidee** /ɔrçi'de:(ə)/ *die;* **~, ~n** orchid

**Orden** /'ɔrdn̩/ *der;* **~s, ~** Ⓐ *(Gemeinschaft)* order; **in einen ~ eintreten, einem ~ beitreten** join an order; become a member of an order; Ⓑ *(Ehrenzeichen)* decoration; *(Milit.)* decoration; *(in runder Form)* medal; **jmdm. einen ~ [für etw.] verleihen** decorate sb. [for sth.]; **ihm wurde der ~ pour le Mérite verliehen** he was given the Ordre pour le Mérite; **einen ~ bekommen** receive a decoration/medal

**orden·geschmückt** *Adj.* bemedalled and beribboned

**Ordens-: ~band** *das; Pl.* **~bänder** ribbon; **~bruder** *der* brother [of an/the order]; monk; **~regel** *die* rule [of an/the order];

O

**~schwester** *die* sister [of an/the order]; nun; **~tracht** *die* habit [of an/the order]; **~verleihung** *die* awarding of a/the decoration; **die jährliche ~verleihung** the annual award of decorations

**ordentlich** /ˈɔrdn̩tlɪç/ ❶ *Adj.* **A** (*ordnungsliebend*) [neat and] tidy; (*methodisch*) orderly; **B** (*geordnet*) [neat and] tidy ‹room, house, desk, etc.›; neat ‹handwriting, clothes›; **C** (*anständig*) respectable; proper ‹manners›; **etwas Ordentliches lernen** learn a proper trade; **D** (*planmäßig*) regular, ordinary ‹meeting›; **~es Mitglied** full member; **~es Gericht** court exercising civil and criminal jurisdiction; ⇒ *auch* **Professor** A; **E** (*ugs.: richtig*) proper; real; **etwas Ordentliches essen** have some proper food; **eine ~e Tracht Prügel** a real good hiding (*coll.*); **F** (*ugs.: tüchtig*) **ein ~es Stück Kuchen** a nice big piece of cake; **ein ~es Stück Arbeit/Weg** a fair old bit of work (*coll.*) /a fair old way (*coll.*); **die haben ja ~e Preise** their prices are steep (*coll.*); **G** (*ugs.: recht gut*) decent ‹wine, flat, marks, etc.›; **ganz ~**: pretty good.
❷ *adv.* (*geordnet*) **A** tidily; neatly; ‹write› neatly; **~ aufgeräumt** neatly tidied; **B** (*anständig*) properly; **C** (*ugs.: gehörig*) **~ feiern** have a real good celebration (*coll.*); **~ einen heben** (*ugs.*) have a fair few drinks (*coll.*); **greift ~ zu!** tuck in!; **sich ~ ausschlafen** have a really good sleep; **letzte Nacht hat es ~ geschneit** it really snowed last night; **es jmdm. ~ geben** give sb. a piece of one's mind; **D** (*ugs.: recht gut*) ‹ski, speak, etc.› really well; **ganz ~ verdienen** earn a pretty good wage

**Ordentlichkeit** *die;* **~**: [neatness and] tidiness; (*der Schrift, Kleidung*) neatness; (*methodische Veranlagung*) orderliness

**Order** /ˈɔrdɐ/ *die;* **~**, **~s** *od.* **~n** **A** (*Befehl*) order; **~ haben, etw. zu tun** have orders to do sth.; **sich an seine ~ halten** obey one's orders; **B** *Pl.* **~s** (*Kaufmannsspr.: Auftrag*) order; **einer Firma eine ~ erteilen** place an order with a firm

**ordern** *tr., itr. V.* (*Kaufmannsspr.*) order

**Order·papier** *das* (*Bankw.*) instrument made out to order (*and transferable by endorsement*)

**Ordinal·zahl** *die* ordinal [number]

**ordinär** /ɔrdiˈnɛːɐ̯/ ❶ *Adj.* **A** (*abwertend*) vulgar; common; vulgar ‹joke, song, expression, language›; cheap and obtrusive ‹perfume›; **B** (*alltäglich*) ordinary. ❷ *adv.* vulgarly; in a vulgar manner

**Ordinariat** /ɔrdinaˈri̯aːt/ *das;* **~[e]s**, **~e** **A** (*kath. Kirche*) ordinariate; **B** (*Hochschulw.*) chair

**Ordinarius** /ɔrdiˈnaːri̯ʊs/ *der;* **~**, **Ordinarien** **A** (*Professor*) [full] professor (*holding a chair*) (**für** of); **B** (*kath. Kirche*) ordinary

**Ordinate** /ɔrdiˈnaːtə/ *die;* **~**, **~n** (*Math.*) ordinate

**Ordinaten·achse** *die* (*Math.*) axis of ordinates

**Ordination** /ɔrdinaˈt͜si̯oːn/ *die;* **~**, **~en** **A** (*ev., kath. Kirche*) ordination; **B** (*Med.: Verordnung*) prescription; **C** (*Med. veralt.: Sprechstunde*) surgery

**ordinieren** *tr. V.* **A** (*ev., kath. Kirche*) ordain; **B** (*Med.*) prescribe

**ordnen** /ˈɔrdnən/ ❶ *tr. V.* **A** arrange; (*systematisieren*) arrange, organize ‹ideas, thoughts, material, etc.›; **B** (*regeln*) regulate ‹traffic›; **sein Leben/seine Finanzen ~**: straighten out one's life/put one's finances in order; **seine Angelegenheiten ~**: settle one's affairs; ⇒ *auch* **geordnet**. ❷ *refl. V.* form up; **ihre Gedanken ordneten sich** (*fig.*) her thoughts became more collected

**Ordner** *der;* **~s**, **~** **A** (*Hefter*) file; **B** (*Aufsichtsperson*) steward; (*bei Demonstrationen*) marshal; steward

**Ordnerin** *die;* **~**, **~nen** ⇒ **Ordner** B

**Ordnung** *die;* **~**, **~en** **A** (*ordentlicher Zustand*) order; tidiness; **~ halten** keep things tidy; **durch sie kam etwas mehr ~ ins Haus** she made the house a little tidier; **~ in die Papiere bringen** put the papers into order; **hier herrscht ~**: everything is neat and tidy here; **hier herrscht ja eine schöne ~!** (*iron.*) a nice mess we've got here!; **der ~ halber** *od.* **wegen** (*weil es sich so gehört*) for the sake of form; **~ schaffen, für ~ sorgen** sort things out; **sehr auf ~ halten** set great store by tidiness; **~ ist das halbe Leben** (*Spr.*) muddle makes trouble; **etw. in ~ bringen** sort sth. out; **in ~ kommen** sort itself out; **in ~ sein** (*ugs.*) be OK (*coll.*) *or* all right; **ist dein Pass in ~?** is your passport in order?; **das Fleisch ist nicht ganz in ~**: the meat has started to go bad; **hier ist etw. nicht in ~**: there's something wrong here; **mit ihr ist etwas nicht in ~, sie ist nicht in ~** (*ugs.*) there's something wrong *or* the matter with her; **jetzt bin ich wieder in ~** (*ugs.*) I'm better *or* all right now; **sie ist in ~** (*ugs.: ist nett, verlässlich o. ä.*) she's OK (*coll.*); **alles [ist] in schönster** *od.* **bester ~**: everything's [just] fine; [things] couldn't be better; **[das] geht [schon] in ~** (*ugs.*) that'll be OK (*coll.*) *or* all right; **ich finde es nicht in ~, dass ...** I don't think it's right that ...; **sie scheint es ganz in [der] ~ zu finden, wenn ...** she doesn't seem to mind at all if ...; **in ~!** (*ugs.*) OK! (*coll.*); all right!; **B** (*geregelter Ablauf*) routine; **hier muss alles seine ~ haben** we/they *etc.* like to keep to a routine here; **C** (*System von Normen*) order; **die ~ einer Gemeinschaft** the rules *pl.* of a community; ⇒ *auch* **öffentlich** 1; **D** (*Disziplin*) order; **hier/da herrscht ~**: we have some discipline here/they have some discipline there; **sich an ~ gewöhnen** get used to discipline; **~ halten** ‹teacher etc.› keep order; **sehr auf ~ halten** be a great disciplinarian; **E** (*System*) order; (*Struktur*) structure; **F** (*Formation*) formation; **G** (*Biol.*) order; **H** (*Rang*) **eine Straße zweiter ~**: a second-class road; **ein Stern vierter ~**: a fourth-magnitude star; **ein Reinfall/Fehlschlag** *usw.* **erster ~** (*fig. ugs.*) a disaster/failure *etc.* of the first order *or* water; **I** (*Math.*) order; **J** (*Mengenlehre*) ordered set; **K** (*Gesellschafts~*) order

**ordnungs-, Ordnungs-:** **~amt** *das:* [*offices of*] *municipal authority responsible for registering residents, regulating public events such as demonstrations and galas, supervising trading standards, and licensing street traders, street musicians, etc.;* **~gemäß** ❶ *Adj.* ‹conduct etc.› in accordance with the regulations; **alles ging seinen ~gemäßen Gang** everything took its proper course; ❷ *adv.* in accordance with the regulations; **~halber** *Adv.* as a matter of form; **~hüter** *der* (*scherzh.*) custodian of the law (*joc.*); **~liebe** *die* liking for neatness and tidiness; **~liebend** *Adj.* ‹person› who likes to see things neat and tidy; **~ruf** *der* call to order; **jmdm. einen ~ruf erteilen** call sb. to order; **~sinn** *der* liking for neatness and tidiness; **~strafe** *die* (*Rechtsw.*) penalty for contempt of court; **~widrig** (*Rechtsw.*) ❶ *Adj.* ‹actions, behaviour, etc.› contravening the regulations; illegal ‹parking›; **~widriges Verhalten im Verkehr** an infringement of traffic regulations; ❷ *adv.* **~widrig parken** park illegally; **~widrig handeln** act in contravention of the regulations; contravene *or* infringe the regulations; **~widrigkeit** *die* (*Rechtsw.*) infringement of the regulations; **~zahl** *die* ordinal [number]; (*Physik*) atomic number

**Ordonnanz** /ɔrdɔˈnant͜s/ *die;* **~**, **~en** (*Milit.*) orderly

**Ordonnanz·offizier** *der* (*Milit.*) aide[-de-camp]

**Oregano** /oˈreːgano/ *der;* **~**: oregano

**ORF** *Abk.* **Österreichischer Rundfunk** Austrian Radio

**Organ** /ɔrˈgaːn/ *das;* **~s**, **~e** **A** ▸ **471** (*Anat., Biol.*) organ; **ein/kein ~ für etw. haben** (*fig.*) have a feeling/no feeling for sth.; **B** (*ugs.: Stimme*) voice; **er hat ein furchtbar lautes ~**: his voice is awfully loud; **C** (*Zeitung*) organ (*formal*); **D** (*Institution*) organ; (*Mensch*) agent; **die Polizei ist nur ausführendes ~**: the police act only as an executive agency; **staatliche ~e** organs of state; **bewaffnete ~e der DDR** armed defensive forces of the GDR

**Organ·bank** *die; Pl.* **~en** (*Med.*) organ bank

**Organdy** /ɔrˈgandi/ *der;* **~s** organdy

**Organ·empfänger** *der,* **Organ·empfängerin** *die* (*Med.*) organ recipient; recipient of an/the organ

**Organisation** /ɔrganizaˈt͜si̯oːn/ *die;* **~**, **~en** organization

**Organisations-:** **~büro** *das* organizational headquarters *sing. or pl.;* **~grad** *der* level of (*trade union etc.*) membership; **gewerkschaftlicher ~grad** degree of unionization; **~talent** *das* **A** (*Fähigkeit*) talent for organization; **B** (*Mensch*) person with a talent for organization; **ein [ausgesprochenes] ~talent sein** have a [marked] talent for organization

**Organisator** /ɔrganiˈzaːtɔr/ *der;* **~s**, **~en** /-ˈtoːrən/. **Organisatorin** *die;* **~**, **~nen** organizer

**organisatorisch** ❶ *Adj.* organizational. ❷ *adv.* organizationally; **~ begabt sein** have a talent for organization

**organisch** ❶ *Adj.* **A** (*auch Chemie*) organic; **~e Chemie** organic chemistry; **B** (*Med.*) organic; physical. ❷ *adv.* **A** organically; **sich ~ in etw.** (*Akk.*) **einfügen** form an organic part of sth.; **B** (*Med.*) organically; physically

**organisierbar** *Adj.* organizable; **etw. ist ~**: sth. can be organized

**organisieren** ❶ *tr. V.* **A** (*vorbereiten, aufbauen*) organize; **B** (*ugs.: beschaffen*) get [hold of]. ❷ *itr. V.* **gut ~ können** be a good organizer. ❸ *refl. V.* organize (**zu** into); **er will sich ~**: he wants to join the union *etc.*

**organisiert** *Adj.* organized ‹system etc.›; **gewerkschaftlich ~e/nicht ~e Arbeiter** unionized/non-unionized workers; **sind Sie politisch/gewerkschaftlich ~?** are you a member of a political party/trade union?

**Organismus** *der;* **Organismen** organism

**Organist** *der;* **~en**, **~en**, **Organistin** *die;* **~**, **~nen** ▸ **159** organist; ⇒ *auch* **-in**

**Organ-:** **~spender** *der,* **~spenderin** *die* organ donor; **~transplantation** *die,* **~verpflanzung** *die* organ transplantation

**Organza** /ɔrˈgant͜sa/ *der;* **~s** organza

**Orgasmus** /ɔrˈgasmʊs/ *der;* **~**, **Orgasmen** orgasm

**orgastisch** *Adj.* orgastic; orgasmic

**Orgel** /ˈɔrgl̩/ *die;* **~**, **~n** organ; **~ spielen** play the organ

**Orgel-:** **~bauer** *der;* **~~s**, **~~**, **~bauerin** *die;* **~~**, **~~nen** organ builder; **~konzert** *das* organ concerto; (*Solo*) organ recital; **~musik** *die* organ music

**orgeln** *itr. V.* **A** (*Drehorgel spielen*) grind the organ; **B** (*ugs.: tönen*) ‹barrel organ, song› grind on; **C** (*Jägerspr.: schreien*) bell

**Orgel-:** **~pfeife** *die* organ pipe; **[dastehen] wie die ~pfeifen** (*scherzh.*) [stand in a row] from the tallest to the shortest; **~punkt** *der* (*Musik*) pedal *or* organ point; **~werk** *das* work for the organ

**orgiastisch** ❶ *Adj.* orgiastic. ❷ *adv.* orgiastically

**Orgie** /ˈɔrgi̯ə/ *die;* **~**, **~n** (*auch fig.*) orgy; **eine ~ feiern** have an orgy

**Orient** /ˈoːri̯ɛnt/ *der;* **~s** **A** (*Vorder- u. Mittelasien*) Middle East and south-western Asia (*including Afghanistan and Nepal*); **der Vordere ~**: the Middle East; **B** (*veralt.: Osten*) Orient

**Orientale** /ori̯ɛnˈtaːlə/ *der;* **~n**, **~n** ⇒ **Orient** A: *man from the Middle East* [*or south-western Asia*]

**Orientalin** *die;* **~**, **~nen** ⇒ **Orient** A: *woman from the Middle East* [*or south-western Asia*]; ⇒ *auch* **-in**

**orientalisch** *Adj.* oriental

**Orientalist** *der;* **~en**, **~en**, **Orientalistin** *die;* **~**, **~nen** orientalist; ⇒ *auch* **-in**

**Orientalistik** *die;* **~**: [Middle Eastern and] oriental studies

*old spelling (see note on page 1707)

**orientieren** ❶ *refl. V.* [A] (*sich zurechtfinden*) get one's bearings; **ich muss mich zuerst ~, wo ich eigentlich bin** first I must get my bearings [and find out where I am]; **sich an etw.** (*Dat.*)/**nach einer Karte ~:** get one's bearings by sth./using a map; [B] **sich über etw.** (*Akk.*) **~:** inform oneself about sth.; [C] **sich an etw.** (*Dat.*) **~:** be oriented towards sth.; ‹policy, advertising› be geared towards sth.; **politisch links/rechts orientiert sein** lean towards the left/right politically; **sich an bestimmten Leitbildern ~:** follow certain models; [D] **sich auf jmdn./etw. ~:** concentrate [one's attention] on sb./sth.
❷ *tr. V.* [A] (*unterrichten*) inform (**über** + *Akk.* about); **die Gespräche haben nur ~den Charakter** the talks are only for the purposes of exchanging information; [B] **sein Ziel nach etw. ~:** base one's aims on sth.; **gewerkschaftlich orientierte Interessen** interests centred on the trade unions; [C] **jmdn. auf etw.** (*Akk.*) **~:** direct sb.'s attention to sth.; **alle Kräfte auf eine Politik des Friedens ~:** concentrate every effort on a policy of promoting peace.
❸ *itr. V.* [A] **über etw.** (*Akk.*) **~:** report on sth.; [B] **auf etw.** (*Akk.*) **~:** concentrate [one's/its attention] on sth.

**-orientiert** *adj.* orientated towards …

**Orientierung** *die;* ~ [A] (*das Sichorientieren*) **hier ist die ~ schwer** it's difficult to get your bearings here; **die ~ verlieren** lose one's bearings; [B] (*Unterrichtung*) **zu Ihrer ~:** for your information; **die ~ der Bevölkerung** informing the population (**über** + *Akk.* about); [C] (*das Sichausrichten*) orientation (**auf** + *Akk.* towards, **an** + *Dat.* according to); [D] (*Konzentration, Hinwendung*) **die ~ auf etw.** (*Akk.*) concentration on sth.; **jmdm. die ~ auf etw.** (*Akk.*) **geben** direct sb.'s attention to sth.

**orientierungs-, Orientierungs-: ~hilfe** *die* aid to orientation; **als ~hilfe legen wir Ihnen eine Karte bei** we enclose a map to help you find your way; **~lauf** *der* orienteering event; (*Disziplin*) orienteering *no art.*; **~los** *Adj.* (*auch fig.*) disoriented; **~los umherirren** wander around in a state of disorientation; **~punkt** *der* landmark by which one can/could find one's bearings; (*fig.*) point of reference; **~sinn** *der* sense of direction; **~stufe** *die* (*Schulw.*) ⇒ **Förderstufe**

**Orient-** /ˈoːri̯ɛnt-/: **~tabak** *der* Oriental tobacco; **~teppich** *der* oriental carpet; (*Läufer*) oriental rug

**orig.** *Abk.* **original** genuine

**Origano** /oˈriːgano/ *der;* **~:** oregano

**original** /origiˈnaːl/ ❶ *Adj.* original; (*echt*) genuine; authentic. ❷ *adv.* **~ indische Seide** genuine Indian silk; **etw. ~ übertragen** broadcast sth. live

**Original** *das;* **~s, ~e** [A] (*Urschrift o. Ä.*) original; [B] (*eigenwilliger Mensch*) character

**original-, Original-: ~aus·gabe** *die* original *or* first edition; **~fassung** *die* original version; **in der spanischen ~fassung** in the original Spanish version; **~getreu** ❶ *Adj.* faithful *or* true [to the original] *postpos.;* ❷ *adv.* in a manner faithful *or* true to the original

**Originalität** /originaliˈtɛːt/ *die;* ~ [A] (*Echtheit*) genuineness; authenticity; [B] (*Einmaligkeit*) originality

**Original-: ~titel** *der* original-language title; **~ton** *der; Pl.* **~töne** (*Film, Ferns.*) direct sound; original sound; **Reportageausschnitte im ~ton von 1936** excerpts from news reports with the original 1936 soundtrack; **„~ton DDR-Fernsehen"** 'GDR television commentary'

**originär** /origiˈnɛːɐ̯/ *Adj.*; *adv.* original

**originell** /origiˈnɛl/ ❶ *Adj.* (*ursprünglich*) original; (*neu*) novel; (*ugs.: witzig*) witty, funny, comical ‹story›; comical, funny ‹costume›; **ein ~er Kopf sein** have an original mind. ❷ *adv.* (*ursprünglich*) ‹write, argue› with originality; (*ugs.: witzig*) ‹write, argue› wittily

**Orkan** /ɔrˈkaːn/ *der;* **~[e]s, ~e** hurricane; (*fig.*) thunderous storm; **der Sturm schwoll zum ~ an** the storm rose to hurricane force

**orkan·artig** *Adj.* ‹winds, gusts› of almost hurricane force; **~er Beifall** (*fig.*) thunderous applause

**Orkney·inseln** /ˈɔːknɪ-/ *Pl.* Orkney Islands; Orkneys

**Orkus** /ˈɔrkʊs/ *der;* ~ (*geh.*) Orcus; Hades

**Ornament** /ɔrnaˈmɛnt/ *das;* **~[e]s, ~e** (*Kunstw.*) ornament

**ornamental** /ɔrnamɛnˈtaːl/ *Adj.* (*Kunstw.*) ornamental; decorative

**Ornat** /ɔrˈnaːt/ *der;* **~[e]s, ~e** (*eines Priesters*) vestments *pl.;* (*eines Hochschullehrers*) academic dress; (*eines Richters*) official robes *pl.;* **in vollem ~** (*ugs. scherzh.*) dressed [up] to the nines

**Ornithologe** /ɔrnitoˈloːgə/ *der;* **~n, ~n** ornithologist

**Ornithologie** *die;* **~:** ornithology *no art.*

**Ornithologin** *die;* **~, ~nen** ornithologist

**ornithologisch** *Adj.* ornithological

**Ort**[1] /ɔrt/ *der;* **~[e]s, ~e** [A] (*Platz*) place; **an öffentlichen ~en** in public places; **etw. an seinem ~ lassen** leave sth. where it is/was; **ein ~ des Schreckens/der Stille** a place of terror/quiet; **~ der Handlung: …** the scene of the action is …; **an den ~ des Verbrechens zurückkehren** return to the scene of the crime; **an ~ und Stelle** there and then; **an ~ und Stelle sein/ankommen** (*an der gewünschten Stelle*) be/arrive there; **höheren ~[e]s** higher up; **am angegebenen ~** (*Schrift u. Druckw.*) in the same work; **der gewisse** *od.* **stille** *od.* **bewusste ~** (*ugs. verhüll.*) the smallest room (*coll. euphem.*); ⇒ *auch* **Örtchen**; [B] (*~schaft*) (*Dorf*) village; (*Stadt*) town; **am ~ wohnen** live in the village/town; **von ~ zu ~:** from place to place; **das beste Hotel am ~:** the best hotel in the place

**Ort**[2] *in* **vor ~:** on the spot; (*Bergmannsspr.*) at the [coal]face

**Örtchen** /ˈœrtçən/ *das;* **~s, ~** (*ugs. verhüll.*) **das ~:** the smallest room (*coll. euphem.*); **aufs ~ müssen** have to pay a visit (*coll. euphem.*)

**orten** *tr. V.* (*bes. Flugw., Seew.*) find the position of

**orthodox** /ɔrtoˈdɔks/ *Adj.* [A] (*Rel.*) orthodox; **die ~en Kirchen** the Orthodox Churches; [B] (*starr*) rigid; [C] (*strenggläubig*) strict; [D] (*fig.: traditionell*) orthodox

**Orthodoxie** /ɔrtodɔˈksiː/ *die;* ~ (*Rel.*) orthodoxy

**Orthographie** *die;* **~, ~n** orthography

**orthographisch** ❶ *Adj.* orthographic; **~e Fehler** spelling mistakes. ❷ *adv.* orthographically; **~ richtig schreiben** spell correctly

**Orthopäde** /ɔrtoˈpɛːdə/ *der;* **~n, ~n** ▶ 159 orthopaedist; orthopaedic specialist

**Orthopädie** /ɔrtopɛˈdiː/ *die;* **~, ~n** [A] orthopaedics *sing.*, *no art.;* **Facharzt für ~** ⇒ **Orthopäde**; [B] (*ugs.: Abteilung*) orthopaedic department; **auf/in der ~ liegen** be a patient in the orthopaedic department

**Orthopädin** *die;* **~, ~nen** ▶ 159 ⇒ **Orthopäde**

**orthopädisch** ❶ *Adj.* orthopaedic. ❷ *adv.* orthopaedically

**örtlich** /ˈœrtlɪç/ ❶ *Adj.* [A] (*Med.*) local ‹anaesthetic etc.›; [B] (*begrenzt*) local. ❷ *adv.* [A] (*Med.*) locally; **~ betäubt werden** be given a local anaesthetic; [B] (*begrenzt*) **~ begrenzte Kampfhandlungen** [limited] local encounters; **~ verschieden sein** vary from place to place

**Örtlichkeit** *die;* **~, ~en** [A] (*Gebiet*) locality; **sich mit den ~en vertraut machen** get to know the area; [B] (*Stelle*) place; [C] ⇒ **Örtchen**

**orts-, Orts-: ~an·gabe** *die* indication of place; **~ansässig** *Adj.* local; **seine Familie ist schon lange ~ansässig** his family has lived locally for a long time; **die ~ansässigen** the local residents; **~aus·gang** *der* end of the village/town; **~bestimmung** *die* (*Geogr.*) determination of the latitude and longitude of a place

**Ortschaft** *die;* **~, ~en** (*Dorf*) village; (*Stadt*) town; **geschlossene ~:** built-up area

**orts-, Orts-: ~ein·gang** *der* entrance to the village/town; **~fremd** *Adj.* [A] (*nicht ~ansässig*) **~fremde Personen** visitors to the village/town; **die ~fremden Besucher** visitors from outside the village/town; [B] (*nicht ~kundig*) **~fremd sein** be a stranger [to the village/town]; **~fremde** *Pl.* strangers [to the village/town]; **~gebunden** *Adj.* tied to the locality *postpos.;* **~gespräch** *das* (*Fernspr.*) local call; **~gruppe** *die* local branch; **~kenntnis** *die* knowledge of the place; **[gute] ~kenntnisse haben** know the place [well]; **~kranken·kasse** *die* compulsory medical *or* health insurance scheme (*organized at district level*); **~kundig** *Adj.* **ein ~kundiger Führer** a guide who knows the place well; **ein ~kundiger** someone who knows the place well; **~name** *der* place name; **~netz** *das* [A] (*Fernspr.*) local exchange network; [B] (*Energiewirtsch.*) local distribution network; **~netz·kennzahl** *die* (*Fernspr.*) dialling code; area code (*Amer.*); **~schild** *das* place name sign; **~sinn** *der* sense of direction; **~tarif** *der* local rate; **~teil** *der* area [of the village/town]; **~üblich** *Adj.* local ‹customs, practices›; **die ~übliche Miete** the rents *pl.* here/there; **~verkehr** *der* [A] (*Straßenverkehr*) local traffic; [B] (*Post*) local postal service; [C] (*Telefon*) local telephone service; **~wechsel** *der* change of locality; **ein ~wechsel wird dir gut tun** a change of environment will do you good; **~zeit** *die* local time; **~zu·lage** *die*, **~zuschlag** *der: salary weighting allowance for employees in the public services*

**Ortung** *die;* **~, ~en** (*bes. Flugw., Seew.*) **die ~ von feindlichen Schiffen/Flugzeugen** finding the position of enemy ships/aircraft

**Öse** /ˈøːzə/ *die;* **~, ~n** eye; (*an Schuh, Stiefel*) eyelet

**osmanisch** /ɔsˈmaːnɪʃ/ *Adj.* (*hist.*) **das Osmanische Reich** the Ottoman Empire

**Osmose** /ɔsˈmoːzə/ *die;* **~, ~n** (*chem., Bot.*) osmosis

**OSO** *Abk.* ▶ 400 **Ostsüdost[en]** ESE

**Ossi**[1] /ˈɔsi/ *der;* **~s, ~s** (*ugs.*) Easterner; East German

**Ossi**[2] *die;* **~, ~s** (*ugs.*) Easterner; East German [woman]

**Ost**[1] /ɔst/ ▶ 400 [A] (*bes. Seemannsspr., Met.: Richtung*) east; **nach ~:** eastwards; **aus** *od.* **von ~:** from the east; [B] (*östliches Gebiet, Politik*) East; **in ~ und West** in the East and [in] the West; **aus ~ und West** from East and West; **~ und West** the East and the West; **zwischen ~ und West** between [the] East and [the] West; [C] *einem Substantiv nachgestellt* East; **Berlin (~)** East Berlin

**Ost**[2] *der;* **~[e]s, ~e** (*Seemannsspr.*) easterly; (*dichter.*) east wind

**ost-, Ost-: ~afrika** (*das*) East Africa; **~asien** (*das*) East *or* Eastern Asia; **~asiatisch** *Adj.* East Asian

**Ost·berlin** (*das*) East Berlin

**Ost·berliner** ❶ *der* East Berliner. ❷ *indekl. Adj.* East Berlin

**Ost·berlinerin** *die* ⇒ **Ostberliner**

**ost-, Ost-: ~besuch** *der* (*ugs.*) visitor/visitors from East Germany; **~block** *der* Eastern bloc; **~block·staat** *der* Eastern-bloc state; **~deutsch** ❶ *Adj.* [A] Eastern German; [B] (*politisch*) East German; ❷ *adv.* in an Eastern German manner; **~deutsche** *der/die* [A] (*Politik*) East German; [B] (*Geogr.*) Eastern German; **~deutschland** (*das*) [A] (*Politik*) East Germany; [B] (*Geogr.*) Eastern Germany; **~elbisch** *Adj.* from east of the Elbe *postpos.* (*usu. referring to the conservative landowners in 19th-century Prussia*)

**Osten** *der;* **~s** ▶ 400 [A] (*Richtung*) east; **nach ~:** eastwards; **aus** *od.* **von ~:** from the east; ⇒ *auch* **Norden** A; [B] (*Gegend*) eastern part; **aus dem ~:** from the east; [C] (*Geogr.*) **der ~:** the East; **der Ferne ~:** the Far East; **der Mittlere ~:** south-western Asia (*including Afghanistan and Nepal*); **der**

**Nahe ~:** the Middle East; **D** (*Politik*) **der ~** (*der Ostblock*) the East; (*die DDR, Ostdeutschland*) the East; East Germany

**Ost·ende** /ɔst'|ɛndə/ (*das*); **~s** ▶ **700** Ostend

**ostentativ** /ɔstɛnta'ti:f/ (*geh.*) **1** *Adj.* pointed ‹absence, silence›; overt ‹hostility›; exaggerated ‹heartiness›; studied ‹calm, casualness›; ostentatious ‹gesture›. **2** *adv.* pointedly; ‹embrace› ostentatiously

**Oster-: ~ei** *das* Easter egg; **~feier·tag** *der:* *in* **über die ~feiertage** over Easter; on Easter Sunday and [Easter] Monday; **der erste/zweite ~feiertag** Easter Sunday/Monday; **~fest** *das* Easter [holiday]; **~glocke** *die* daffodil; **~hase** *der* Easter hare (*said to bring children their Easter Eggs*); **~insel** *die* Easter Island; **~kerze** *die* (*kath. Rel.*) paschal *or* Easter candle; **~lamm** *das* Paschal lamb

**österlich** /'ø:stɐlɪç/ **1** *Adj.* Easter *attrib.* **2** *adv.* **~ geschmückt** decorated for Easter

**Oster-: ~marsch** *der* Easter march (*against war and nuclear weapons*); **~montag** *der* Easter Monday *no def. art.*; ⇒ *auch* **Dienstag**

**Ostern** /'o:stɐn/ *das;* **~, ~** ▶ **369** Easter; **Frohe** *od.* **Fröhliche ~:** Happy Easter!; **diese/letzte/nächste ~:** this/last/next Easter; **zu** *od.* (*bes. südd.*) **an ~:** at Easter; **[zu/über] ~ Besuch bekommen** have people to stay at/over Easter; **zu ~ einen Kuchen backen** bake a cake for Easter; **wenn ~ und Pfingsten** *od.* **Weihnachten zusammenfallen** *od.* **auf einen Tag fallen** (*ugs.*) not this side of doomsday (*coll.*)

**Österreich** /'ø:stəraiç/ (*das*); **~s** Austria; **~-Ungarn** (*hist.*) Austria-Hungary

**Österreicher** *der;* **~s, ~, Österreicherin** *die;* **~, ~nen** Austrian; **er/sie ist ~/~in** he/she is Austrian; ⇒ *auch* **-in**

**österreichisch** *Adj.* Austrian; **das Österreichische** what is Austrian; (*Sprache*) Austrian German; **~-ungarisch** (*hist.*) Austro-Hungarian; ⇒ *auch* **deutsch**; **Deutsch**

**Oster-: ~sonntag** *der* Easter Sunday *no def. art.*; ⇒ *auch* **Dienstag**; **~spiel** *das* Easter play

**Ost·erweiterung** *die* (*Politik*) Eastward expansion

**Oster: ~woche** *die* week before Easter; **~zeit** *die:* **in der ~zeit** at Easter time

**ost-, Ost-: ~europa** (*das*) Eastern Europe; **~europäisch** *Adj.* East[ern] European; **~europäische Zeit** Eastern European Time; **~flanke** *die* (*Milit., Geogr.*) eastern flank; (*Met.*) eastern edge

**Ost·friesische Inseln** *Pl.* East Frisian Islands

**Ost·friesland** (*das*); **~s** East Friesland; Ostfriesland

**Ost-: ~gebiet** *das* **A** (**~en**) eastern part; **B** *Pl. former German territories east of the Oder-Neisse line;* **~geld** *das* (*ugs.*) East German money; **~germanisch** *Adj.* East Germanic; **~gote** *der,* **~gotin** *die* Ostrogoth; **~hang** *der* eastern slope; **~jude** *der,* **~jüdin** *die* East[ern] European Jew; **~kirche** *die* Eastern Church; **~kolonisation** *die* (*hist.*) *German colonization of Eastern Europe in the Middle Ages;* **~küste** *die* east[ern] coast

**Ostler** /'ɔstlɐ/ *der;* **~s, ~, Ostlerin** *die;* **~, ~nen** (*ugs.*) East German

**östlich** /'œstlɪç/ **1** *Adj.* ▶ **400** **A** (*im Osten*) eastern; **15 Grad ~er Länge** 15 degrees east [longitude]; **~st** easternmost; **das ~e Ufer** the east bank; **der ~ste Punkt** the most easterly point; **B** (*nach, aus dem Osten*) easterly; **C** (*aus dem Osten kommend, für den Osten typisch*) Eastern; **D** (*politisch*) Eastern; ‹delegates, spies, etc.› from the East; ‹infiltration› by the East; ‹influence, policies› of the East. **2** *adv.* eastwards; **~ von ...** [to the] east of ... **3** *Präp. mit Gen.* [to the] east of

**ost-, Ost-: ~mark¹** *die; Pl.* **~~** (*ugs.*) East German mark; **~mark²** *die* (*hist.*) East March; **~nord·ost¹** /--'-/ (*Seemannsspr., Met.*) east-north-east; ⇒ *auch* **Nord¹** A; **~nord·ost²** /--'-/ *der* (*Seemannsspr.*) east-north-easter[ly]; **~nord·osten** /--'--/ *der* east-north-east; ⇒ *auch* **Norden** A; **~politik** *die* Ostpolitik (*West German policy towards Eastern Europe, and towards East Germany in particular*); **~preuße** *der* East Prussian; **~preußen** (*das*) East Prussia; **~preußisch** *Adj.* East Prussian

**Östrogen** /œstro'ge:n/ *das;* **~s, ~e** (*Physiol.*) oestrogen

**Ost·see** *die* Baltic [Sea]

**Ostsee-** Baltic

**ost-, Ost-: ~seite** *die* eastern side; **~süd·ost¹** /--'-/ (*Seemannsspr., Met.*) east-south-east; ⇒ *auch* **Nord¹** A; **~süd·ost²** /--'-/ *der* (*Seemannsspr.*) east-south-easter[ly]; **~süd·osten** /--'--/ *der* east-south-east; ⇒ *auch* **Norden** A; **~teil** *der* eastern part; **~verträge** *Pl.* (*Politik*) treaties with the Eastern bloc; **~wärts** *Adv.* ▶ **400** **A** (*nach ~en*) eastwards; **B** (*im ~en*) to the east; **~-West-Dialog** *der* (*Politik*) East-West dialogue; **~-West-Konflikt** *der* (*Politik*) East-West conflict; **~westlich** **1** *Adj.* east-west *attrib.*; from east to west *postpos.*; **2** *adv.* east-west; [from] east to west; **~wind** *der* east[erly] wind; **~zone** *die* Eastern zone; **die ~zone** (*ugs.: die DDR*) the East

**Oszillation** /ɔstsɪla'tsio:n/ *die;* **~, ~en** (*Physik, auch fig.*) oscillation

**oszillieren** /ɔstsɪ'li:rən/ *itr. V.* (*Physik, auch fig.*) oscillate

**Oszillograph** *der;* **~en, ~en** (*Physik*) oscillograph

**O-Ton** *der; Pl.* **O-Töne** ⇒ **Originalton**

**Otter¹** /'ɔtɐ/ *der;* **~s, ~** (*Fisch~*) otter

**Otter²** *die;* **~, ~n** (*Viper*) adder; viper

**Ottern·gezücht** *das* (*veralt. abwertend*) brood of vipers

**Otto** /'ɔto/ *der;* **~s, ~s** (*salopp*) whopper (*coll.*); ⇒ *auch* **flott**; **Normalverbraucher**

**Ottomane** /ɔto'ma:nə/ *die;* **~, ~n** (*veralt.*) ottoman

**Otto·motor** *der* Otto engine

**Ottone** /ɔ'to:nə/ *der;* **~n, ~n** (*hist.*) Ottonian (*Saxon emperor, esp. Otto I, II, or III*)

**ÖTV** *Abk.* **Gewerkschaft öffentliche Dienste, Transport und Verkehr** union of transport and public-service workers

**out** /aut/ *Adj.* **~ sein** (*ugs.*) be out

**outen** /'autn̩/ *tr. V.* (*ugs.*) out (*coll.*)

**Output** /'autput/ *der od. das;* **~s, ~s** output

**Ouvertüre** /uvɛr'ty:rə/ *die;* **~, ~n** (*auch fig.*) overture (+ *Gen.* to)

**oval** /o'va:l/ *Adj.* oval

**Oval** *das;* **~s, ~e** oval

**Ovation** /ova'tsio:n/ *die;* **~, ~en** ovation; **jmdm. ~en darbringen** give sb. an ovation

**Overall** /'ouvərɔ:l/ *der;* **~s, ~s** overalls *pl.*

**Ovid** /o'vi:t/ (*der*) Ovid

**ÖVP** *Abk.* **Österreichische Volkspartei** Austrian People's Party

**Ovulation** /ovula'tsio:n/ *die;* **~, ~en** (*Zool., Physiol.*) ovulation

**Ovulations·hemmer** *der;* **~s, ~** (*Med.*) anovulant

**Oxid** /ɔ'ksi:t/ *das;* **~[e]s, ~e** (*Chemie*) oxide

**Oxidation** /ɔksida'tsio:n/ *die;* **~, ~en** (*Chemie*) oxidation

**oxidieren** (*Chemie*) **1** *itr. V.*; *auch mit sein* oxidize. **2** *tr. V.* oxidize

**Oxyd** *usw.* ⇒ **Oxid** *usw.*

**Ozean** /'o:tsea:n/ *der;* **~s, ~e** (*auch fig.*) ocean

**Ozean·dampfer** *der* ocean-going steamer; (*für Passagiere*) ocean liner

**Ozeanien** /otse'a:njən/ (*das*); **~s** Oceania

**ozeanisch** *Adj.* oceanic; (*Ozeanien betreffend*) Oceanic

**Ozeanographie** /otseanogra'fi:/ *die;* **~:** oceanography *no art.*

**Ozeanologe** *der;* **~n, ~n** oceanologist

**Ozeanologie** *die;* **~:** oceanology

**Ozeanologin** *die;* **~, ~nen** oceanologist

**ozeanologisch** **1** *Adj.* oceanological. **2** *adv.* **~ interessiert sein** be interested in oceanology

**Ozelot** /'o:tselɔt/ *der;* **~s, ~e** *od.* **~s** (*Tier, Fell*) ocelot

**Ozon** /o'tso:n/ *der od. das;* **~s** ozone; **lieber warmer Mief als kalter ~!** (*ugs. scherzh.*) I'd rather be breathing a warm fug than cold fresh air

**Ozon-: ~alarm** *der* ozone alert; **bei ~alarm** when there is/was an ozone alert; **~alarm geben** issue an ozone alert; **~konzentration** *die;* ozone concentration; **~loch** *das* hole in the ozone layer; **~schicht** *die* ozone layer; **~wert** *der* ozone value

O

# Pp

**p, P** /pe/ *das;* ~, ~**:** p/P; ⇒ *auch* **a, A**
**p.A.** *Abk.* (*österr.*) **per Adresse** c/o
**Pa** /pa/ *der;* ~**s**, ~**s** (*fam. veralt.*) dad (*coll.*)
**paar** /paːɐ̯/ *indekl. Indefinitpron.* **ein ~ ...** a few ...; (*zwei od. drei*) a couple of ...; a few ...; **ein ~ Hundert Bücher** *usw.* a few hundred/a couple of hundred books *etc.*; **ein ~ waren dagegen** a few [people]/a couple [of people] were against [it]; **in ein ~ Tagen** in a few/a couple of days[' time]; **ein ~ Mal[e]** a few times/a couple of times; **deine ~ Mark** the few marks/couple of marks you've got; **die ~ Mal[e], die ich dort war** the few times I've been there; **alle ~ Minuten** every few minutes/every couple of minutes; **du kriegst gleich ein ~ [gelangt]** (*ugs.*) I'll stick one on you (*coll.*); ⇒ *auch* **Zeile A**
**Paar** *das;* ~**[e]s**, ~**e** Ⓐ pair; (*Mann und Frau, Tanz~*) couple; **sich in** *od.* **zu ~en aufstellen** line up in pairs; Ⓑ (*Tiere, Dinge*) pair; **ein ~ Würstchen** two sausages; a couple of sausages; **ein ~ Schuhe** a pair of shoes; **zwei ~ Socken** two pairs of socks; **ein ~ Hosen** (*ugs.*) a pair of trousers
**paaren** ❶ *refl. V.* Ⓐ (*sich begatten*) ‹animals› mate; ‹people› couple, copulate; Ⓑ (*sich verbinden*) **sich mit etw. ~:** be combined with sth. ❷ *tr. V.* Ⓐ (*kreuzen*) mate; Ⓑ (*zusammenstellen*) pair; Ⓒ (*verbinden*) combine (**mit** with)
**Paarhufer** *der;* ~**s**, ~ (*Zool.*) even-toed ungulate (*Zool.*); cloven-hoofed animal
**paarig** (*bes. Biol., Anat.*) ❶ *Adj.* paired *attrib.*; ~ **sein** occur in pairs. ❷ *adv.* ~ **angeordnet** arranged in pairs *postpos.*
**paar-, Paar-:** ~**lauf** *der,* ~**laufen** *das;* ~~**s** pairs skating; pairs *pl.*; *~**mal** ⇒ **paar**; ~**reim** *der* (*Verslehre*) rhyming couplets *pl.*
**Paarung** *die;* ~, ~**en** Ⓐ (*Zool.*) mating; Ⓑ (*das Zusammenstellen*) pairing; **die ~ der Mannschaften für das Endturnier** deciding which teams will/would play each other in the finals; Ⓒ (*das Verbinden*) combination
**Paarungs-:** ~**verhalten** *das* (*Zool.*) mating behaviour; ~**zeit** *die* (*Zool.*) mating season
**paar·weise** ❶ *Adv.* in pairs. ❷ *adj.* ‹arrangement etc.› in pairs
**Paar·zeher** *der;* ~**s**, ~ (*Zool.*) ⇒ **Paarhufer**
**Pacht** /paxt/ *die;* ~, ~**en** Ⓐ (*Nutzung*) **etw. in ~ nehmen** lease sth.; take sth. on lease; **etw. in ~ haben** have sth. on lease; **etw. in ~ geben** lease sth.; let sth. on lease; Ⓑ (*Vertrag*) lease; Ⓒ (*Miete*) rent
**Pacht·brief** *der* lease
**pachten** *tr. V.* lease; take a lease on; **jmdn./etw. [für sich] gepachtet haben** (*fig. ugs.*) have got a monopoly on sb./sth. (*coll.*)
**Pächter** /ˈpɛçtɐ/ *der;* ~**s**, ~, **Pächterin** *die;* ~, ~**nen** leaseholder; lessee; (*eines Hofes*) tenant
**Pacht·geld** *das* rent
**Pachtung** *die;* ~, ~**en** leasing
**Pacht-:** ~**vertrag** *der* lease; ~**zins** *der; Pl.* ~~**e** rent
**Pack**[1] /pak/ *der;* ~**[e]s**, ~**e** *od.* **Päcke** /ˈpɛkə/ pile; (*zusammengeschnürt*) bundle; (*Packung*) pack; (*Kartenspiel*) pack (*Brit.*); deck (*Amer.*)
**Pack**[2] *das;* ~**[e]s** (*ugs. abwertend*) rabble; riff-raff; ~ **schlägt sich, ~ verträgt sich** (*ugs.*) rabble *or* riff-raff like that are at each other's throats one minute and the best of friends [again] the next
**Päckchen** /ˈpɛkçən/ *das;* ~**s**, ~ Ⓐ (*kleines Paket*) package; small parcel; (*Bündel*) packet; bundle; (*Postw.*) small parcel (*below a specified weight*); **sein ~ zu tragen haben** (*fig. ugs.*) have one's troubles; Ⓑ ⇒ **Packung A**
**Pack·eis** *das* pack ice
**packeln** /ˈpakl̩n/ *itr. V.* (*österr. abwertend*) make *or* do a deal/deals
**packen** ❶ *tr. V.* Ⓐ pack; **etw. in einen Koffer/ein Paket ~:** pack *or* put sth. in[to] a suitcase/put sth. in[to] a parcel; **etw. aus etw. ~:** unpack sth. from sth.; **sich/jmdn. ins Bett ~** (*ugs.*) go to bed/put sb. to bed; **der Bus war gepackt voll** (*fig. ugs.*) the bus was jam-packed (*coll.*); Ⓑ (*fassen*) grab [hold of]; seize; **jmdn. am** *od.* **beim Kragen ~:** grab [hold of] *or* seize sb. by the collar; **eine Windbö packte das Auto** a gust of wind caught the car; ⇒ *auch* **Ehre**; Ⓒ (*überkommen*) **Furcht/Angst** *usw.* **packte ihn/er wurde von Furcht/Angst** *usw.* **gepackt** he was seized with fear *etc.*; **es hat ihn gepackt** (*ugs.*) he's got it bad (*coll.*); Ⓓ (*fesseln*) enthral; ‹thriller, crime story, etc.› grip; **ein ~des Rennen** a thrilling race; Ⓔ (*ugs.: schaffen*) **ein Examen ~:** manage to get through an exam (*coll.*); **es ~:** make a go of it; ~ **wir's noch?** are we going to make it?; **einen Gegner ~** (*Sportjargon: besiegen*) get the better of an opponent; Ⓕ (*ugs.: begreifen*) get (*coll.*); Ⓖ (*salopp: weggehen*) ~ **wir's?** shall we push off? (*coll.*).
❷ *itr. V.* (*Koffer usw. ~*) pack.
❸ *refl. V.* (*ugs. veralt.*) beat it (*coll.*); clear off (*coll.*)
**Packen** *der;* ~**s**, ~**:** pile; (*von Büchern, Zeitungen*) pile; stack; (*zusammengeschnürt*) bundle; (*von Geldscheinen*) wad
**Packer** *der;* ~**s**, ~**:** packer; (*Möbel~*) [packer and] removal man (*Brit.*) *or* (*Amer.*) moving man
**Packerei** *die;* ~, ~**en** Ⓐ (*ugs. abwertend*) packing and unpacking; Ⓑ (*eines Betriebs*) packing department
**Packerin** *die;* ~, ~**nen** packer
**Pack-:** ~**esel** *der* (*ugs.*) pack donkey; (*fig.*) packhorse; ~**papier** *das* [stout] wrapping paper; ~**pferd** *das* packhorse; ~**tisch** *der* packing table
**Packung** *die;* ~, ~**en** Ⓐ packet; pack (*esp. Amer.*); **eine ~ Zigaretten** a packet *or* (*Amer.*) pack of cigarettes; **eine ~ Pralinen** a box of chocolates; Ⓑ (*Med., Kosmetik*) pack; Ⓒ (*Technik*) packing
**Pack-:** ~**wagen** *der* Ⓐ luggage van (*Brit.*); baggage car (*Amer.*); Ⓑ (*hist.: Fuhrwerk*) baggage wagon; ~**zettel** *der* packing slip
**Pädagoge** /pɛdaˈgoːgə/ *der;* ~**n**, ~**n** ▶ **159** Ⓐ (*Erzieher, Lehrer*) teacher; Ⓑ (*Wissenschaftler*) educationalist; educational theorist
**Pädagogik** *die;* ~**:** [theory and methodology of] education
**Pädagogin** *die;* ~, ~**nen** ▶ **159** ⇒ **Pädagoge**
**pädagogisch** ❶ *Adj.* Ⓐ (*erzieherisch*) educational; **seine ~en Fähigkeiten** his teaching ability *sing.*; Ⓑ (*die Pädagogik betreffend*) ‹lecture, dissertation, etc.› on education; **Pädagogische Hochschule** College of Education; **eine ~e Ausbildung** a training in education. ❷ *adv.* Ⓐ (*erzieherisch*) educationally ‹sound, wrong›; ~ **wirken** have an educational effect; Ⓑ (*die Pädagogik betreffend*) ~ **nicht auf dem neuesten Stand sein** not be up with the latest developments in educational theory [and methodology]
**pädagogisieren** *tr. V.* (*oft abwertend*) **etw. ~:** look at sth. through the eyes of an educational theorist
**Paddel** /ˈpadl̩/ *das;* ~**s**, ~**:** paddle
**Paddel·boot** *das* canoe
**paddeln** *itr. V.*; *mit sein; ohne Richtungsangabe auch mit haben* Ⓐ (*Paddelboot fahren*) paddle; canoe; (*als Sport*) canoe; Ⓑ (*ugs.: schlecht schwimmen*) dog-paddle
**Paddel·sport** *der* canoeing *no art.*
**Paddler** *der;* ~**s**, ~, **Paddlerin** *die;* ~, ~**nen** canoeist
**Päderast** /pedeˈrast/ *der;* ~**en**, ~**en** pederast
**Päderastie** /pɛderasˈtiː/ *die;* ~**:** pederasty *no art.*
**Pädiater** /pɛˈdi̯aːtɐ/ *der;* ~**s**, ~, **Pädiaterin** *die;* ~, ~**nen** (*Med.*) paediatrician
**Pädiatrie** /pɛdi̯aˈtriː/ *die;* ~ (*Med.*) paediatrics *sing.*, *no art.*
**pädiatrisch** *Adj.* (*Med.*) paediatric
**paff** /paf/ *Interj.* bang
**paffen** ❶ *tr. V.* puff at ‹pipe etc.›; puff out ‹smoke›; **vierzig Zigaretten am Tag ~:** puff one's way through forty cigarettes a day. ❷ *itr. V.* puff away; **er pafft nur** he's just puffing at it
**Page** /ˈpaːʒə/ *der;* ~**n**, ~**n** ▶ **159** Ⓐ (*Hotel~*) page; bellboy; Ⓑ (*hist.*) page
**Pagen·kopf** *der* pageboy cut *or* style
**Pager** /ˈpeɪdʒɐ/ *der;* ~**s**, ~**:** pager
**paginieren** /pagiˈniːrən/ *tr. V.* (*Schrift- und Buchw.*) paginate
**Pagode** /paˈgoːdə/ *die;* ~, ~**n** Ⓐ (*Gebäude*) pagoda; Ⓑ (*österr., sonst veralt.: Figur*) mandarin
**pah** /paː/ *Interj.* bah; huh (*Amer.*)
**Paillette** /pai̯ˈjɛtə/ *die;* ~, ~**n** (*Mode*) paillette; sequin; spangle
**Pak** /pak/ *die;* ~, ~ *od.* ~**s** (*Milit.*) Ⓐ (*Panzerabwehrkanone*) anti-tank gun; Ⓑ (*Artillerie*) anti-tank force
**Paket** /paˈkeːt/ *das;* ~**[e]s**, ~**e** Ⓐ pile; (*zusammengeschnürt*) bundle; (*Eingepacktes, Post~, Schachtel*) parcel; (*Packung*) packet; pack (*esp. Amer.*); Ⓑ (*fig.: Gesamtheit*) package
**Paket-:** ~**annahme** *die* Ⓐ acceptance of parcels; Ⓑ (*Stelle*) parcels office; (*Schalter*) parcels counter; ~**ausgabe** *die* Ⓐ issue of parcels; Ⓑ ⇒ ~**annahme B**; ~**boot** *das* (*veralt.*) packet [boat]; ~**dienst** *der* parcel service; ~**karte** *die* parcel dispatch form; ~**post** *die* Ⓐ (*Beförderung*) parcel post; Ⓑ (*Fahrzeug*) parcel *or* post office delivery van; ~**schalter** *der* parcels counter; ~**sendung** *die* parcel
**Pakistan** /ˈpaːkɪstaːn/ (*das*); ~**s** Pakistan
**Pakistaner** *der;* ~**s**, ~, **Pakistanerin** *die;* ~, ~**nen**, **Pakistani** /pakɪsˈtaːni/ *der;* ~**[s]**, ~**[s]**/*die;* ~, ~**[s]** ▶ **553** Pakistani
**pakistanisch** *Adj.* ▶ **553** Pakistani
**Pakt** /pakt/ *der;* ~**[e]s**, ~**e** pact; **einen ~ [ab]schließen** make *or* conclude a pact
**paktieren** *itr. V.* (*oft abwertend*) make *or* do a deal/deals (**mit** with)
**Paladin** /palaˈdiːn/ *der;* ~**s**, ~**e** Ⓐ (*Myth.*) paladin; Ⓑ (*Gefolgsmann*) henchman
**Palais** /paˈlɛː/ *das;* ~ /...ɛː(s)/, ~ /...ɛːs/ palace
**Paläolithikum** /paleoˈliːtikʊm/ *das;* ~**s** Palaeolithic
**Paläontologie** /paleɔntoloˈgiː/ *die;* ~**:** palaeontology *no art.*
**Paläozän** /paleoˈtsɛːn/ *das;* ~**s** (*Geol.*) Palaeocene
**Paläozoikum** /paleoˈtsoːikʊm/ *das;* ~**s** palaeozoic era

p

**Palast** /pa'last/ *der;* **~[e]s, Paläste** /pa'lɛstə/ palace
**palast·artig** *Adj.* palatial
**Palästina** /palɛ'sti:na/ *(das);* **~s** Palestine
**Palästinenser** *der;* **~s, ~, Palästinenserin** *die;* **~, ~nen** ▶ 553 Palestinian
**palästinensisch** *Adj.* ▶ 553 Palestinian
**Palast·revolution** *die (Politik, auch fig.)* palace revolution
**Palatschinke** /pala'tʃɪŋkə/ *die;* **~, ~n** *(österr.)* pancake with sweet filling
**Palaver** /pa'la:vɐ/ *das;* **~s, ~** *(ugs. abwertend)* palaver; **ein ~ abhalten** palaver
**palavern** *itr. V. (ugs. abwertend)* palaver
**Paletot** /'paləto/ *der;* **~s, ~s** *(man's double-breasted)* overcoat [*with high velvet collar*]
**Palette** /pa'lɛtə/ *die;* **~, ~n** Ⓐ *(Malerei)* palette; Ⓑ *(bes. Werbespr.: Vielfalt)* diverse range; **die ganze ~:** the whole range; Ⓒ *(Technik, Wirtsch.: Untersatz)* pallet
**paletti** *Adj.: in* **alles ~** *(ugs.)* everything's OK *(coll.) or* all right
**Palimpsest** /palɪm'psɛst/ *der od. das;* **~[e]s, ~e** palimpsest
**Palindrom** /palɪn'dro:m/ *das;* **~s, ~e** palindrome
**Palisade** /pali'za:də/ *die;* **~, ~n** Ⓐ *(Pfahl)* pale; stake; Ⓑ *(Anlage)* palisade
**Palisander** /pali'zandɐ/ *der;* **~s, ~, Palisander·holz** *das (Dalbergia nigra)* Brazilian rosewood; *(Dalbergia latifolia)* blackwood
**Palme** /'palmə/ *die;* **~, ~n** palm [tree]; **jmdn. auf die ~ bringen** *(ugs.)* ‹person› rile sb. *(coll.)*; ‹situation› make sb. wild; **auf die ~ gehen** *(ugs.)* go off the deep end *(coll.)*; **die ~ [des Sieges]** *(fig. geh.)* the palm [of victory]
**Palmen-:** ⇒ **Palm-**
**Palm-: ~kätzchen** *das* [willow] catkin; **~öl** *das* palm oil; **~sonntag** */auch:* -'--/ *der (christl. Kirche)* Palm Sunday; ⇒ *auch* **Dienstag**; **~wedel** *der* palm frond; **~zweig** *der* Ⓐ palm branch; Ⓑ *(christl. Kirche)* palm; **~wein** *der* palm wine
**Pamp** /pamp/ *der;* **~s** *(nordd., ostd.)* mush
**Pampa** /'pampa/ *die;* **~, ~s** pampa *usu. in pl.*; **[mitten] in der ~** *(Jugendspr.)* out in the wilds *(coll.)*
**Pampe** /'pampə/ *die;* **~** *(bes. nordd. u. md.)* Ⓐ *(Matsch)* mud; mire; Ⓑ *(Brei)* mush
**Pampelmuse** /'pampl̩mu:zə/ *die;* **~, ~n** grapefruit
**Pampf** /pampf/ *der;* **~s** *(südd.)* mush
**Pamphlet** /pam'fle:t/ *das;* **~[e]s, ~e** *(Streitschrift)* polemical pamphlet; *(Schmähschrift)* defamatory pamphlet
**pampig** ❶ *Adj.* Ⓐ *(ugs. abwertend: frech)* insolent; Ⓑ *(bes. nordd., ostd.: breiig)* mushy. ❷ *adv. (ugs. abwertend: frech)* insolently
**Pamps** ⇒ **Pamp**
**pan-, Pan-** /pan-/: *in Zus.* pan-
**Panade** /pa'na:də/ *die;* **~, ~n** *(Kochk.)* breadcrumb coating
**Panama**[1] /'panama/ *(das)* Panama
**Panama**[2] *der;* **~s, ~s** Ⓐ *(Textilind.)* Panama fabric; Ⓑ *(Hut)* panama [hat]
**Panamaer** *der;* **~s, ~, Panamaerin** *die;* **~, ~nen** Panamanian
**panamaisch** *Adj.* Panamanian
**Panamakanal** *der;* **~s** Panama Canal
**Panda** /'panda/ *der;* **~s, ~s** panda
**Pandekten** /pan'dɛktn̩/ *Pl.* pandects; *(fig.)* jurisprudence *sing.*
**Pandschab** /pan'dʒa:p/ *das;* **~s** Punjab
**Paneel** /pa'ne:l/ *das;* **~s, ~e** Ⓐ *(einzelnes Feld)* panel; Ⓑ *(Täfelung)* panelling
**paneelieren** *tr. V.* panel
**Pan·flöte** *die* pan pipes *pl.*
**pan·germanisch** *Adj.* pan-German
**pan·hellenisch** *Adj.* pan-Hellenic
**Panier**[1] /pa'ni:ɐ̯/ *das;* **~s, ~e** *(veralt.)* banner; *(Motto)* motto
**Panier**[2] *die;* **~** *(österr. Kochk.)* ⇒ **Panade**
**panieren** *tr. V. (Kochk.)* **etw. ~:** bread sth.; coat sth. with breadcrumbs

**Panier·mehl** *das* breadcrumbs *pl.*
**Panik** /'pa:nɪk/ *die;* **~, ~en** panic; **[eine] ~ brach aus** panic broke out; **jmdn. in ~** *(Akk.)* **versetzen** throw sb. into a state of panic; **von ~ ergriffen** panic-stricken; **nur keine ~!** don't panic!
**Panik-: ~mache** *die (abwertend)* panic-mongering; **~macher** *der,* **~macherin** *die (abwertend)* panicmonger
**panisch** ❶ *Adj.* panic *attrib.* ‹fear, terror›; panic-stricken ‹voice, flight›; **~e Angst vor etw.** *(Dat.)* **haben** have a panic fear of sth. ❷ *adv.* **sich ~ vor etw.** *(Dat.)* **fürchten** have a panic fear of sth.
**Panje·wagen** /'panjə-/ *der: small wooden cart drawn by a horse (in Eastern Europe)*
**Pankreas** /'pankreas/ *das;* **~, Pankreaten** ▶ 471 *(Anat.)* pancreas
**Panne** /'panə/ *die;* **~, ~n** Ⓐ *(Auto~)* breakdown; *(Reifen~)* puncture; flat [tyre]; **ich hatte eine ~** *(mit dem Auto)* my car broke down/my car *or* I had a puncture; *(mit dem Fahrrad)* I had some trouble with my bicycle/my bicycle *or* I had a puncture; Ⓑ *(Betriebsstörung)* breakdown; Ⓒ *(Missgeschick)* slip-up; mishap; **mit unserem Urlaub haben wir eine ganz schöne ~ erlebt** our holiday this year was a real disaster; **bei der Organisation gab es viele ~n** there were many organizational hitches
**Pannen·dienst** *der* breakdown service
**Panoptikum** /pa'nɔptikʊm/ *das;* **~s, Panoptiken** Ⓐ *(Kuriositätenkabinett)* collection of curios; Ⓑ *(Wachsfiguren)* waxworks *sing. or pl.*
**Panorama** /pano'ra:ma/ *das;* **~s, Panoramen** panorama
**Panorama-: ~aufnahme** *die* panorama; **~bus** *der* coach with panoramic windows; **~scheibe** *die* panoramic window; *(an Autos)* wraparound windscreen; **~spiegel** *der (Kfz-W.)* panoramic mirror
**panschen** /'panʃn̩/ ❶ *tr. V. (ugs. abwertend)* water down; adulterate; **Whisky mit Wasser ~:** adulterate whisky with water. ❷ *itr. V.* Ⓐ *(ugs. abwertend: mischen)* water down *or* adulterate the wine/beer *etc.*; Ⓑ *(ugs.: planschen)* splash about
**Panscher** *der;* **~s, ~** *(ugs.)* adulterator
**Panscherei** *die;* **~, ~en** Ⓐ *(ugs. abwertend: das Mischen)* watering-down; adulteration; Ⓑ *(ugs.: das Planschen)* splashing [about]
**Panscherin** *die;* **~, ~nen** ⇒ **Panscher**
**Pansen** /'panzn̩/ *der;* **~s, ~** Ⓐ *(Magen der Wiederkäuer)* rumen; Ⓑ *(nordd.: Magen)* stomach; belly
**Panter** ⇒ **Panther**
**Pan·theismus** *der* pantheism *no art.*
**pan·theistisch** *Adj.* pantheistic
**Panther** /'pantɐ/ *der;* **~s, ~:** panther
**Pantine** /pan'ti:nə/ *die;* **~, ~n** *(nordd.)* clog; ⇒ *auch* **Latschen**
**Pantoffel** /pan'tɔfl̩/ *der;* **~s, ~n** Ⓐ backless slipper; Ⓑ *(mit Absatz)* mule; Ⓒ *(fig.)* **unterm ~ stehen** *(ugs.)* be henpecked
**Pantoffel-: ~held** *der (ugs. abwertend)* henpecked husband; **~kino** *das (ugs.)* telly *(coll.)*; **~tierchen** *das (Biol.)* slipper animalcule
**Panto·graph** /panto-/ *der;* **~en, ~en** pantograph
**Pantolette** /panto'lɛtə/ *die;* **~, ~en** backless slipper
**Pantomime**[1] /panto'mi:mə/ *die;* **~, ~n** mime
**Pantomime**[2] *der;* **~n, ~n** mime
**Panto·mimik** *die* mime
**panto·mimisch** ❶ *Adj.* ‹presentation, depiction› in mime. ❷ *adv.* **etw. ~ darstellen/zeigen** present/show sth. in mime; mime sth.
**pantschen** *usw.* /'pantʃn̩/ ⇒ **panschen** *usw.*
**Panzer** /'pantsɐ/ *der;* **~s, ~** Ⓐ *(Milit.)* tank; **die schwedischen ~:** the Swedish tanks *or* armour *sing.*; Ⓑ *(Zool.)* armour *no indef. art.*; *(von Schildkröten, Krebsen)* shell; Ⓒ *(hist.: Rüstung)* armour *no indef. art.*; **ein ~:** a suit of armour; **ein ~ der Gleichgültigkeit** *(fig.)* a defensive barrier of indifference; Ⓓ *(Panzerung)* armour-plating *or* -plate *no indef. art.*; *(eines Reaktors)* shielding
**Panzer-: ~ab·wehr** *die (Milit.)* Ⓐ *(Verteidigung)* anti-tank defence; Ⓑ *(Truppe)* anti-tank force; **~abwehr·kanone** *die (Milit.)* anti-tank gun; **~abwehr·rakete** *die (Milit.)* anti-tank rocket; **~division** *die (Milit.)* tank division; armoured division; **~faust** *die (Milit.)* anti-tank rocket launcher; bazooka; **~glas** *das* bulletproof glass; **~grenadier** *der (Milit.)* soldier in the armoured infantry; **~hemd** *das (hist.)* coat of [chain] mail; **~kette** *die* tank track; **~kreuzer** *der (Marine hist.)* armoured cruiser; **„~kreuzer Potemkin"** 'The Battleship Potemkin'; **~mine** *die* anti-tank mine
**panzern** ❶ *tr. V.* armour[-plate]. ❷ *refl. V. (hist.)* put on one's armour
**Panzer-: ~platte** *die* armour-plate; **~schlacht** *die (Milit.)* tank battle; **~schrank** *der* safe; **~späh·wagen** *der (Milit.)* armoured scout car; **~sperre** *die (Milit.)* anti-tank obstacle; **~truppe** *die (Milit.)* tank force
**Panzer·wagen** *der (Milit.)* Ⓐ ⇒ **Panzer** A; Ⓑ *(Waggon)* armoured wagon
**Papa** /'papa, *geh., veralt.* pa'pa:/ *der;* **~s, ~s** *(ugs.)* daddy *(coll.)*; **der Herr ~** /-'-/ your/my/his *etc.* [dear] father
**Papagallo** /papa'galo/ *der;* **~[s], ~s** *od.* **Papagalli** Latin Romeo
**Papagei** /papa'gai̯/ *der;* **~en** *od.* **~s, ~e[n]** parrot; **alles wie ein ~ nachplappern** repeat everything parrot-fashion
**Papageien·krankheit** *die* ▶ 474 *(Med.)* parrot disease; psittacosis *no art.*
**Paparazzo** *der;* **~s, Paparazzi** paparazzo
**Paper** /'peɪpə/ *das;* **~s, ~s** paper
**Paperback** /'peɪpəbæk/ *das;* **~s, ~s** paperback
**Papeterie** /papɛtə'ri:/ *die;* **~, ~n** *(schweiz.)* stationer's
**Papi** /'papi/ *der;* **~s, ~s** *(ugs.)* daddy *(coll.)*
**Papier** /pa'pi:ɐ̯/ *das;* **~s, ~e** Ⓐ paper; **ein Blatt/Fetzen/eine Rolle ~:** a sheet/scrap/roll of paper; **[nur] auf dem ~** *(fig.)* [only] on paper; **etw. aufs ~ werfen** *(fig. geh.)* jot sth. down; **etw. zu ~ bringen** get *or* put sth. down on paper; **~ ist geduldig** *(Spr.)* what's written down in black and white isn't necessarily true; **die ~ verarbeitende Industrie** the paper-processing industry; Ⓑ *Pl. (Ausweis[e])* [identity] papers; **dann können Sie sich Ihre ~e holen** *(ugs.)* then you might as well collect your cards on the way out; Ⓒ *(Finanzw.: Wert~)* security
**Papier-: ~blume** *die* paper flower; **~deutsch** *das (abwertend)* officialese
**papieren** ❶ *Adj.* Ⓐ *(aus Papier)* paper; Ⓑ *(fig.)* wooden ‹style etc.›; Ⓒ *(wie Papier)* papery. ❷ *adv. (fig.)* ‹speak› woodenly; ‹write› in a wooden style
**Papier-: ~fabrik** *die* paper mill; **~fähnchen** *das* paper pennant; **~fetzen** *der* scrap of [torn] paper; **~format** *das* paper size; **~geld** *das* paper money; **~geschäft** *das* stationer's; **~hand·tuch** *das* paper towel; **~korb** *der* waste-paper basket; *(öffentlicher)* litter bin; **~kram** *der (ugs. abwertend)* [tedious] paperwork; **~krieg** *der (ugs. abwertend)* tedious form-filling; *(Korrespondenz)* tiresome exchange of letters
**Papiermaché** /papi̯ema'ʃe/ *das;* **~s, ~s** papier mâché
**papier-, Papier-: ~mühle** *die* Ⓐ *(Maschine)* [paper-pulp] beater; Ⓑ *(Fabrik)* paper mill; **~rolle** *die* roll of paper; *(in Registrierkassen)* paper roll; **~schere** *die* paper scissors *pl.*; **~schlange** *die* [paper] streamer; **~schnitzel** *der od. das* bit *or* scrap of paper; **~serviette** *die* paper serviette *or* napkin; **~taschen·tuch** *das* paper handkerchief; **~tiger** *der* paper tiger; ***~verarbeitend** ⇒ **Papier** A; **~währung** *die* paper currency; **~waren** *Pl.* stationery *sing.*; **~waren·handlung** *die* stationer's
**Papist** /pa'pɪst/ *der;* **~en, ~en, Papistin** *die;* **~, ~nen** *(abwertend)* papist

*old spelling (see note on page 1707)

**papistisch** *Adj.* (*abwertend*) papist

**papp** /pap/ *in* **ich kann nicht mehr ~ sagen** (*ugs.*) I'm full to bursting point (*coll.*)

**Papp** *der;* **~s, ~s** (*bes. südd.*) mush

**Papp-: ~band** *der* book bound in boards; **~becher** *der* paper cup; **~deckel** *der* cardboard; **ein ~deckel** a piece of cardboard

**Pappe** /'papə/ *die;* **~, ~n** Ⓐ (*Karton*) cardboard; **eine ~:** a piece of cardboard; Ⓑ (*ugs.: Brei*) mush; **er ist nicht von** *od.* **aus ~** (*ugs.*) he's not to be trifled with; **5 000 Mark sind nicht von** *od.* **aus ~** (*ugs.*) 5,000 marks isn't chicken feed (*coll.*)

**Pappel** /'papl̩/ *die;* **~, ~n** poplar

**Pappel·allee** *die* avenue of poplars

**päppeln** /'pɛpl̩n/ *tr. V.* feed up; **eine Industrie ~** (*fig. ugs.*) featherbed an industry

**pappen** (*ugs.*) ❶ *tr. V.* stick (**an, auf** + *Akk.* on). ❷ *itr. V.* (*haften bleiben*) stick (**an** + *Dat.* to); (*klebrig sein*) be sticky

**Pappen-: ~deckel** *der* (*bes. südd.*) ⇒ **Pappdeckel**; **~heimer** /-haimɐ/ *Pl.*: *in* **ich kenne meine/wir kennen unsere ~heimer** (*ugs.*) I/we know them well (*coll.*); **~stiel** *der: in* **das ist kein ~stiel** (*ugs.*) it's not chicken feed (*coll.*); **etw. für einen ~stiel kaufen/kriegen** (*ugs.*) buy/get sth. for a song *or* for next to nothing

**papperlapapp** /papəla'pap/ *Interj.* rubbish

**pappig** *Adj.* Ⓐ sticky; Ⓑ doughy ‹bread etc.›; Ⓒ (*breiig*) mushy

**Papp-: ~kamerad** *der* (*ugs., auch fig.*) cardboard figure; **~karton** *der* cardboard box; **~maschee** /-ma'ʃeː/ *das;* **~~s, ~~s** papier mâché; **~nase** *die* false nose (*made of cardboard*); **~schnee** *der* sticky snow; **~teller** *der* paper *or* cardboard plate

**Paprika** /'paprika/ *der;* **~s, ~[s]** Ⓐ pepper; Ⓑ (*Gewürz*) paprika

**Paprika-: ~schnitzel** *das* cutlet with paprika sauce; **~schote** *die* pepper; **gefüllte ~schoten** stuffed peppers

**Paps** /paps/ *der;* **~** (*ugs.*) dad (*coll.*)

**Papst** /paːpst/ *der;* **~[e]s, Päpste** /'pɛːpstə/ pope; (*fig. iron.*) high priest

**-papst** *der* (*fig. iron.*) high priest of ...

**Päpstin** *die;* **~, ~nen** pope; (*fig. iron.*) high priestess

**-päpstin** *die* (*fig. iron.*) high priestess of...

**päpstlich** /'pɛːpstlɪç/ *Adj.* papal; (*fig. abwertend*) pontifical; **~er Gesandter** nuncio; **nicht ~er sein als der Papst** (*fig.*) not be a stickler for the regulations

**Papsttum** *das;* **~s** papacy

**Papua-Neu·guinea** /'paːpu̯a-/ (*das*); **~s** Papua New Guinea

**Papyrus** /pa'pʏrʊs/ *der;* **~, Papyri** papyrus

**Papyrus·rolle** *die* papyrus scroll

**para-, Para-** /'paːra/ para-

**Parabel** /pa'raːbl̩/ *die;* **~, ~n** Ⓐ (*bes. Literaturw.*) parable; Ⓑ (*Math.*) parabola

**Parabol·antenne** *die* parabolic antenna

**parabolisch** /para'boːlɪʃ/ *Adj.* parabolic

**Parabol·spiegel** *der* (*Technik*) parabolic mirror

**Parade** /pa'raːdə/ *die;* **~, ~n** Ⓐ (*Milit.*) parade; **eine ~ abnehmen** take the salute at a parade; Ⓑ (*Ballspiele*) save; **jmdm. in die ~ fahren** (*fig. ugs.*) cut sb. short; Ⓒ (*Fechten*) parry; Ⓓ (*Pferdesport*) **ganze ~:** halt; **halbe ~:** half-halt; **in ~** (*Dat.*) **stehen** halt

**Parade-: ~bei·spiel** *das* perfect example; **~bett** *das* (*veralt.*) large imposing bed

**Paradeiser** /para'daizɐ/ *der;* **~s, ~** (*österr.*) tomato

**Parade-: ~kissen** *das* (*veralt.*) decorative pillow; **~marsch** *der* (*Milit.*) marching in parade step; (*Stechschritt*) goose-stepping; **~pferd** *das* Ⓐ (*Pferd*) parade horse; Ⓑ (*ugs.: Musterexemplar*) showpiece; (*Person*) star; **~platz** *der* (*hist.*) parade ground; **~schritt** *der* (*Milit.*) parade step; (*Stechschritt*) goose step; **~stück** *das* showpiece; **~uniform** *die* (*Milit.*) full-dress uniform

**paradieren** *itr. V.* (*Milit.*) parade

**Paradies** /para'diːs/ *das;* **~es, ~e** (*auch fig.*) paradise; **die Vertreibung aus dem ~:** the expulsion from paradise; **das ~ auf Erden** heaven on earth

**paradiesisch** ❶ *Adj.* Ⓐ (*Rel.*) paradisical; Ⓑ (*herrlich*) heavenly; magnificent ‹view›. ❷ *adv.* (*herrlich*) **~ ruhig gelegen** in a wonderfully peaceful situation; **dort ist es ~ schön** it's beautiful there, a real paradise

**Paradies·vogel** *der* bird of paradise; (*fig.*) strange and beautiful creature

**Paradigma** /para'dɪgma/ *das;* **~s, Paradigmen** *od.* **Paradigmata** (*bes. Sprachw.*) paradigm

**paradigmatisch** (*bes. Sprachw.*) ❶ *Adj.* paradigmatic. ❷ *adv.* paradigmatically

**paradox** /para'dɔks/ *Adj.* Ⓐ paradoxical; Ⓑ (*ugs.: merkwürdig*) odd; strange

**Paradox** *das;* **~es, ~e** (*bes. Philos., Rhet.*) paradox

**paradoxer·weise** *Adv.* Ⓐ paradoxically; Ⓑ (*ugs.: merkwürdigerweise*) strangely *or* oddly enough

**Paradoxie** /paradɔ'ksiː/ *die;* **~, ~n** Ⓐ paradox; Ⓑ (*Eigenschaft*) paradoxicalness

**Paradoxon** /pa'raːdɔksɔn/ *das;* **~s, Paradoxa** (*Philos., Rhet.*) paradox

**Paraffin** /para'fiːn/ *das;* **~s, ~e** (*Chemie*) paraffin; (*für Kerzen*) paraffin wax

**Paragraph** /para'graːf/ *der;* **~en, ~en** section; (*im Vertrag*) clause

**Paragraphen-: ~dickicht** *das,* **~gestrüpp** *das* (*abwertend*) jungle of regulations; **~hengst** *der* (*salopp abwertend*) lawyer; **~reiter** *der,* **~reiterin** *die* (*abwertend*) Ⓐ (*Jurist[in]*) lawyer; Ⓑ (*Pedant[in]*) stickler for the rules

**Paraguay** /'paragvai/ (*das*); **~s** Paraguay

**Paraguayer** *der;* **~s, ~, Paraguayerin** *die;* **~, ~nen** Paraguayan

**paraguayisch** *Adj.* Paraguayan

**Parallaxe** /para'laksə/ *die;* **~, ~n** (*Physik, Astron.*) parallax

**parallel** /para'leːl/ ❶ *Adj.* (*auch fig.*) parallel. ❷ *adv.* **~ verlaufen** (*auch fig.*) run parallel (**mit, zu** to); **~ zu etw.** (*fig.*) in parallel with sth.

**Parallele** *die;* **~, ~n** Ⓐ (*Math.*) parallel [line]; **eine ~ zu etw. ziehen** draw a line parallel to sth.; Ⓑ (*fig.*) parallel; **jmdn./etw. mit jmdm./etw. in ~ setzen** *od.* **stellen** draw a parallel between sb./sth. and sb./sth.

**Parallel·fall** *der* parallel case

**Parallelität** /paraleli'tɛːt/ *die;* **~, ~en** (*auch Math.*) parallelism

**Parallel·klasse** *die* (*Schulw.*) parallel class

**Parallelogramm** /paralelo'gram/ *das;* **~s, ~e** (*Math.*) parallelogram

**Parallel-: ~schaltung** *die* (*Elektrot.*) parallel connection; **~schwung** *der* (*Skisport*) parallel swing; **~straße** *die* street running parallel (**von** to); **~ton·art** *die* (*Musik*) relative key

**Paralyse** /para'lyːzə/ *die;* **~, ~n** ▶ 474 (*Med., fig.*) paralysis

**paralysieren** *tr. V.* (*Med., fig.*) paralyse

**Paralytiker** *der;* **~s, ~, Paralytikerin** *die;* **~, ~nen** paralytic

**paralytisch** *Adj.* (*Med.*) paralytic

**Parameter** /pa'raːmetɐ/ *der;* **~s, ~** Ⓐ (*Wirtsch., Technik, Math.*) parameter; (*beim Kegelschnitt*) principal parameter

**para·militärisch** ❶ *Adj.* paramilitary. ❷ *adv.* ‹operate, be organized› along paramilitary lines

**Paranoia** /para'nɔya/ *die;* **~** ▶ 474 (*Med.*) paranoia

**paranoid** /parano'iːt/ *Adj.* (*Med.*) paranoid

**Paranoiker** /para'noːikɐ/ *der;* **~s, ~, Paranoikerin** *die;* **~, ~nen** (*Med.*) paranoiac

**paranoisch** *Adj.* (*Med.*) paranoiac

**Para·nuss, *Para·nuß** *die* Brazil nut

**Paraphe** /pa'raːfə/ *die;* **~, ~n** Ⓐ (*geh.: Namenszug*) signature; Ⓑ (*Dipl.*) initials *pl.*

**paraphieren** *tr. V.* (*Dipl.*) initial

**Paraphierung** *die;* **~, ~en** initialling

**Para·phrase** *die* (*Sprachw., Musik*) paraphrase

**paraphrasieren** *tr. V.* Ⓐ (*Sprachw.*) paraphrase; Ⓑ (*Musik*) compose a paraphrase on

**Para·psychologie** *die* parapsychology *no art.*

**Parasit** /para'ziːt/ *der;* **~en, ~en** (*Biol., fig. abwertend*) parasite

**parasitär** /parazi'tɛːɐ̯/, **parasitisch** (*Biol., fig. abwertend*) ❶ *Adj.* parasitic. ❷ *adv.* parasitically; **~** *od.* **parasitisch leben** (*Biol.*) be parasitic; (*fig.*) be a parasite

**Parasol** /para'zoːl/ *der;* **~s, ~e** *od.* **~s, Parasol·pilz** *der* parasol mushroom

**Parasympathikus** /parazʏm'paːtikʊs/ *der;* **~** ▶ 471 (*Anat., Physiol.*) parasympathetic nervous system

**parat** /pa'raːt/ *Adj.* ready; **eine Ausrede/Antwort ~ haben** be ready with an excuse/answer; **ich habe kein passendes Beispiel ~:** I can't think of a suitable example

**Para·typhus** *der* ▶ 474 (*Med.*) paratyphoid [fever]

**Paravent** /para'vãː/ *der od. das;* **~s, ~s** (*österr., sonst veralt.*) screen

**Pärchen** /'pɛːɐ̯çən/ *das;* **~s, ~:** pair; (*Liebespaar*) couple

**pärchen·weise** *Adv.* in pairs

**Parcours** /par'kuːɐ̯/ *der;* **~** /...ɐ̯(s)/, **~** /...ɐ̯s/ (*Pferdesport*) course

**Pardon** /par'dõː/ *der od. das;* **~s** pardon; **jmdn. um ~ bitten** (*veralt.*) ask sb.'s pardon; **jmdm. ~ gewähren** (*veralt.*) pardon sb.; **kein[en] ~ kennen** be completely ruthless; **~!** I beg your pardon

**Parenthese** /parɛn'teːzə/ *die;* **~, ~n** (*Sprachw.*) Ⓐ (*Satzteil*) parenthesis; Ⓑ (*Klammern o. Ä.*) parenthesis; parentheses *pl.*; **in ~:** in parenthesis

**par excellence** /parɛksɛ'lãːs/ *Adj.; nachgestellt* par exellence; **ein Gentleman ~:** an outstanding example of a gentleman

**Parforce-** /par'fɔrs-/: **~jagd** *die* (*Jagdw. veralt.*) hunt with horses and hounds; (*Art des Jagens*) riding to hounds; **~ritt** *der* (*geh.*) feat of concentrated effort

**Parfum** /par'fœ̃ː/ *das;* **~s, ~s, Parfüm** /par'fyːm/ *das;* **~s, ~s** perfume; scent

**Parfümerie** /parfymə'riː/ *die;* **~, ~en** perfumery

**Parfüm-: ~fläschchen** *das,* **~flasche** *die* perfume bottle; scent bottle

**parfümieren** *tr. V.* perfume; scent; **sich [viel zu stark] ~:** put [too much] perfume *or* scent on

**Parfüm-: ~wolke** *die* cloud of perfume *or* scent; **~zerstäuber** *der* perfume spray; perfume atomizer

**pari** /'paːri/ Ⓐ *in* **zu/über/unter ~** (*Börsenw.*) at/above/below par; Ⓑ *in* **die/ihre Chancen stehen ~:** the odds are even/they have the same *or* an equal chance

**Paria** /'paːri̯a/ *der;* **~s, ~s** (*auch fig.*) pariah

**parieren**[1] /pa'riːrən/ *itr. V.* (*ugs.*) do what one is told; **jmdm. ~:** do what sb. tells one; **aufs Wort ~:** jump to it (*coll.*)

**parieren**[2] *tr. V.* Ⓐ (*Fechten, Boxen, fig.*) parry; Ⓑ (*Fußball*) save ‹shot›; parry ‹attack›; Ⓒ (*Pferdesport*) hold ‹horse› at half-halt; (*zum Stehen bringen*) halt

**Pari·kurs** *der* (*Wirtsch.*) par value; (*bei Devisen*) par rate of exchange

**Pariser** /pa'riːzɐ/ ❶ *indekl. Adj.* ▶ 700 Parisian; Paris *attrib.*; **die ~ Metro** the Paris Metro; ❷ *der;* **~s, ~** Ⓐ (*Einwohner*) ▶ 700 Parisian; Ⓑ (*ugs.: Kondom*) French letter (*coll.*)

**Pariserin** *die;* **~, ~nen** Parisian

**pariserisch** *Adj.* Parisian

**Parität** /pari'tɛːt/ *die;* **~, ~en** Ⓐ (*Gleichheit*) parity; equality; Ⓑ (*Wirtsch.*) parity

**paritätisch** ❶ *Adj.* equal; **~e Mitbestimmung** co-determination based on equal representation. ❷ *adv.* equally; **Ausschüsse müssen ~ besetzt werden** there must be equal representation on committees

**Park** /park/ *der;* **~s, ~s** park; (*Schloss~ usw.*) grounds *pl.*

**Parka** *der;* **~s, ~s** parka

**Park-: ~an·lage** *die* park; (*bei Schlössern usw.*) grounds *pl.*; **~bahn** *die* (*Raumf.*) parking orbit; **~bank** *die; Pl.* **~bänke** park bench

**parken ❶** *tr. V.* park. **❷** *itr. V.* **A** park; **„P~ verboten!"** 'No Parking'; **B** (*stehen*) be parked; **ein ~des Auto** a parked car

**Parkett** /par'kɛt/ *das;* **~[e]s, ~e A** (*Bodenbelag*) parquet floor; **~ legen** lay parquet flooring; **sich auf jedem ~ bewegen können** (*fig.*) be able to move in any circles; **B** (*Theater*) [front] stalls *pl.*; parquet (*Amer.*); **das ~ applaudierte** there was applause from the stalls; **C** *in* **etw. aufs ~ legen** (*ugs.*) dance sth.; ⇒ *auch* **Sohle A**

**Parkett·[fuß]boden** *der* parquet floor; **~ haben** have parquet flooring

**parkettieren** *tr. V.* lay parquet flooring; parquet

**Parkett·platz** *der* seat in the [front] stalls

**Park-: ~gebühr** *die* parking fee; **~haus** *das* multi-storey car park

**parkieren** (*schweiz.*) ⇒ **parken**

**Parkinson·krankheit** /'parkɪnzɔn'--/ *die* Parkinson's disease

**Park-: ~kralle** *die* wheel clamp; **~landschaft** *die* parkland; **~leit·system** *das* (*Verkehrsw.*) *traffic-control system providing information on the location of available parking spaces*; **~leuchte** *die*, **~licht** *das* parking light; **~lücke** *die* parking space; **~platz** *der* **A** car park; parking lot (*Amer.*); **B** (*für ein einzelnes Fahrzeug*) parking space; place to park; **~platz·not** *die* lack of parking space[s]; **~scheibe** *die* parking disc; **~schein** *der* car park ticket; **~uhr** *die* parking meter; **~verbot** *das* ban on parking; **hier ist ~verbot** you are not allowed to park here; **im ~verbot stehen** be parked illegally; **aus dem ~verbot wegfahren** move one's car from where it is/was parked illegally; **~verbots·schild** *das* no-parking sign

**Parlament** /parla'mɛnt/ *das;* **~[e]s, ~e** parliament; (*eines bestimmten Landes*) Parliament *no def. art.*

**Parlamentär** /parlamɛn'tɛ:ɐ̯/ *der;* **~s, ~e, Parlamentärin** *die;* **~, ~nen** peace negotiator

**Parlamentarier** /parlamɛn'ta:ri̯ɐ/ *der;* **~s, ~, Parlamentarierin** *die;* **~, ~nen** member of parliament; (*in Großbritannien*) Member of Parliament; MP; (*in den Vereinigten Staaten*) Congressman/Congresswoman; **die Bonner ~:** the members of the Bonn Parliament; **die dem Europarat angehörenden ~:** the MPs *or* deputies in the Council of Europe

**parlamentarisch ❶** *Adj.* parliamentary; **~er Staatssekretär [im Bundesministerium für ...]** parliamentary secretary [to the Federal Ministry of ...]. **❷** *adv.* **etw. ~ diskutieren** discuss sth. in parliament

**Parlamentarismus** *der;* **~:** parliamentarianism *no art.*; parliamentary system

**Parlaments-: ~aus·schuss, *~aus·schuß** *der* parliamentary committee; **~ferien** *Pl.* [parliamentary] recess *sing.*; **~gebäude** *das* parliament building[s *pl.*]; **die ~gebäude** (*in London*) the Houses of Parliament; **~mitglied** *das* member of parliament; (*in Großbritannien*) Member of Parliament; MP; (*in den Vereinigten Staaten*) member of Congress; **~reform** *die* parliamentary reform; **~sitzung** *die* sitting [of parliament]; **~wahl** *die* parliamentary election

**parlieren** /par'li:rən/ *itr. V.* (*geh.; oft iron.*) make conversation; (*plaudern*) chat (**über** + *Akk.* about); (*reden*) talk ‹French etc.›

**Parmesan** /parme'za:n/ *der;* **~[s]** Parmesan

**Parnass, *Parnaß** /par'nas/ *der;* **~** *od.* **Parnasses** (*dichter.*) Parnassus *no def. art.* (*poet.*)

**Parodie** /paro'di:/ *die;* **~, ~n** parody; **eine ~ auf etw./jmdn.** a parody of sth./take-off of sb.

*old spelling (see note on page 1707)

**parodieren** *tr. V.* parody ‹literary work, manner›; take off ‹person›; satirize ‹event›

**Parodist** *der;* **~en, ~en, Parodistin** *die;* **~, ~nen** parodist

**parodistisch** *Adj.* parodistic; ‹ability› as a parodist

**Parodontose** /parodɔn'to:zə/ *die;* **~, ~n** periodontosis *no art.* (*Dent.*); receding gums *pl., no art.*

**Parole** /pa'ro:lə/ *die;* **~, ~n A** (*Wahlspruch*) motto; (*Schlagwort*) slogan; **B** (*bes. Milit.: Kennwort*) password; **C** (*Gerücht*) rumour

**Paroli** /pa'ro:li/ *in* **jmdm./einer Sache ~ bieten** give sb. as good as one gets/pit oneself against sth.

**Part** /part/ *der;* **~s, ~s** *od.* **~e A** (*Musik: Stimme, Partie*) part; **B** (*Theater, Film: Rolle*) part; role; **einen/den [entscheidenden] ~ in** *od.* **bei etw.** (*Dat.*) **spielen** (*auch fig.*) play a/the [crucial] part *or* role in sth.

**Parte** /'partə/ *die;* **~, ~n** (*österr.: Todesanzeige*) death announcement

**Partei** /par'tai̯/ *die;* **~, ~en A** (*Politik*) party; **in** *od.* **bei der ~ sein** be a party member; **die ~ wechseln** change parties; **B** (*Rechtsw.*) party; **C** (*Gruppe, Mannschaft*) side; **es mit beiden ~en halten** run with the hare and hunt with the hounds (*fig.*); **~ sein** be an interested party; **jmds.** *od.* **für jmdn./für etw. ~ ergreifen** *od.* **nehmen** side with sb./take a stand for sth.; **gegen jmdn./etw. ~ nehmen** *od.* **ergreifen** side against sb./take a stand against sth.; **über den ~en stehen** be impartial; **D** (*Miets~*) tenant; (*mehrere Personen*) tenants *pl.*

**partei-, Partei-: ~ab·zeichen** *das* party badge; **~amtlich** *Adj.* official party ‹regulations etc.›; **~apparat** *der* party machine *or* organization; **~bonze** *der* (*abwertend*) party bigwig (*coll.*); **~buch** *das* party membership book; **das falsche/richtige ~buch haben** belong to the wrong/right party; **~chef** *der*, **~chefin** *die* party leader; **~chinesisch** *das* (*ugs. scherzh.*) party gobbledegook; **~disziplin** *die* party discipline

**Parteien-: ~landschaft** *die* party political scene *or* set-up; **~verkehr** *der* (*österr.*) **„~verkehr von 9 bis 14 Uhr"** 'open to the public from 9 till 2'

**partei-, Partei-: ~freund** *der*, **~freundin** *die* fellow party member; party colleague; **~führer** *der*, **~führerin** *die* party leader; **~führung** *die* party leadership; **der ~führung angehören** be one of the party leaders *pl. or* executive; **~gänger** *der;* **~~s, ~~, ~gängerin** *die;* **~~, ~~nen** (*oft abwertend*) [loyal] party supporter; **Mussolini und seine ~gänger** Mussolini and his party faithful; **~genosse** *der*, **~genossin** *die* (*hist.: Mitglied der NSDAP*) party member; (*einer Arbeiter~*) **~genosse X** Comrade X; **~intern ❶** *Adj.* internal [party] ‹conflict, matters, material, etc.›; **❷** *adv.* within the party

**parteiisch ❶** *Adj.* biased. **❷** *adv.* in a biased manner

**Partei·leitung** *die* ⇒ **~führung**

**parteilich ❶** *Adj.* **A** (*eine Partei betreffend*) party ‹matter, work, principles, etc.›; **B** (*parteiisch*) biased ‹judgement, view, etc.›; **C** (*der Parteilinie folgend*) in accordance with the party line *postpos.* **❷** *adv.* **A** (*von der Partei*) by the party; **B** (*parteiisch*) in a biased manner; **C** (*der Parteilinie folgend*) ‹think, behave, act› in accordance with the party line

**Parteilichkeit** *die;* **~ A** (*Linientreue*) adherence to the party line; **B** (*einseitige Parteinahme*) bias, partiality (**für** towards)

**partei-, Partei-: ~linie** *die* party line; **~los** *Adj.* (*Politik*) independent ‹MP›; **er ist ~los** he is not attached to *or* aligned with any party; **~lose** *der/die; adj. Dekl.* (*Politik*) independent; person not attached to a party; **~losigkeit** *die;* **~~** (*Politik*) independence; **~mitglied** *das* party member; **~nahme** *die;* **~~, ~~n** partisanship; taking sides *no art.*; **~organ** *das* **A** party representative; (*Gruppe*) group of persons representing a party; **B** (*Zeitung*) party organ; **~politik** *die* party politics *sing.*; **~politisch ❶** *Adj.* party political; **❷** *adv.* from a party political point of view; **~programm** *das* party manifesto *or* programme; **~tag** *der* party conference *or* (*Amer.*) convention

**Parteiung** *die;* **~, ~en** ‹political, religious› group

**Partei-: ~verfahren** *das: proceedings instituted by the party against a member;* **~vorsitzende** *der/die* party leader; **~vorstand** *der* party executive; **~zugehörigkeit** *die* party membership

**parterre** /par'tɛr/ *Adv.* on the ground *or* (*Amer.*) first floor

**Parterre** /par'tɛr/ *das* **~s, ~s A** (*Erdgeschoss*) ground floor; first floor (*Amer.*); **im ~:** on the ground *or* (*Amer.*) first floor; **B** (*Theater veralt.*) stalls *pl.* (*Brit.*); parterre (*Amer.*); parquet (*Amer.*)

**Parterre·wohnung** *die* ground-floor flat (*Brit.*); first-floor apartment (*Amer.*)

**Partie** /par'ti:/ *die;* **~, ~n A** (*Teil*) part; **B** (*Spiel, Sport: Runde*) game; (*Golf*) round; **eine ~ Schach spielen** play a game of chess; **C** (*Musik*) part; **D** (*Ehepartner*) **eine gute ~ [für jmdn.] sein** be a good match [for sb.]; **sie hat eine gute/glänzende ~ gemacht** she has married well/extremely well; **E** (*veralt.: Ausflug*) **eine ~ aufs Land machen** go on *or* for an outing *or* a trip into the country; **F mit von der ~ sein** join in; (*bei einer Reise usw.*) go along too; **da bin ich mit von der ~!** count me in!; **G** (*Kaufmannsspr.*) batch; **H** (*österr.: Gruppe von Arbeitern*) gang

**Partie-: ~führer** *der* (*österr.: Vorarbeiter*) foreman; **~führerin** (*österr.: Vorarbeiterin*) forewoman

**partiell** /par'tsi̯ɛl/ **❶** *Adj.* partial. **❷** *adv.* partially

**Partikel**[1] /par'ti:kl̩/ *die;* **~, ~n** (*Sprachw.*) particle

**Partikel**[2] *das;* **~s, ~** *od. die;* **~, ~n** (*bes. Physik, Chemie, Technik*) particle

**partikular** /partiku'la:ɐ̯/, **partikulär** /partiku'lɛ:ɐ̯:/ *Adj.* (*geh.*) minority *attrib.* ‹interest, viewpoint›

**Partikularismus** *der;* **~** (*meist abwertend*) particularism *no art.*

**partikularistisch** *Adj.* (*meist abwertend*) particularistic

**Partisan** /parti'za:n/ *der;* **~s** *od.* **~en, ~en** guerrilla; (*gegen Besatzungstruppen im Krieg*) partisan

**Partisanen·krieg** *der* guerilla war; (*Kriegführung*) guerilla warfare

**Partisanin** *die;* **~, ~nen** ⇒ **Partisan**

**Partita** /par'ti:ta/ *die;* **~, Partiten** (*Musik*) partita

**Partitur** /parti'tu:ɐ̯/ *die;* **~, ~en** (*Musik*) score

**Partizip** /parti'tsi:p/ *das;* **~s, ~ien** /-'tsi:pi̯ən/ (*Sprachw.*) participle; **das 1. ~** *od.* **~ Präsens/das 2. ~** *od.* **~ Perfekt** the present/past participle

**Partizipation** /partitsipa'tsi̯o:n/ *die;* **~, ~en** participation (**an** + *Dat.* in)

**Partizipations·geschäft** *das* (*Wirtsch.*) joint venture

**Partizipial-** (*Sprachw.*) participial

**partizipieren** *itr. V.* **an etw.** (*Dat.*) **~:** have a share in sth.

**Partner** /'partnɐ/ *der;* **~s, ~, Partnerin** *die;* **~, ~nen** partner; (*Bündnis~*) ally; (*im Film/Theater*) co-star

**Partner·look** *der* coordinated fashion (*in which man and woman wear matching clothes*); **~ tragen** wear matching his-and-hers outfits

**Partnerschaft** *die;* **~, ~en** partnership

**partnerschaftlich ❶** *Adj.* ‹cooperation etc.› on a partnership basis; **wir haben ein ~es Verhältnis** ours is a relationship between equal partners; **sein Führungsstil ist [sehr] ~:** his style of leadership involves treating people [very much] as equal partners. **❷** *adv.* in a spirit of partnership; (*als Partnerschaft*) as a partnership; **sich jmdm. gegenüber** *od.* **zu jmdm. ~ verhalten** treat sb. as an equal [partner]

**Partner-: ~stadt** *die* twin town (*Brit.*); sister city *or* town (*Amer.*); **~tausch** *der* partner-swapping (*coll.*); **~wahl** *die* choice of mate *or* partner

**partout** /par'tu:/ *Adv.* (*ugs.*) at all costs; **er will es ~ nicht einsehen** but he absolutely refuses to see it

**Party** /'pa:ɐ̯ti/ *die;* **~, ~s** *od.* **Parties** party; **eine ~ [zu ihrem bestandenen Examen/zu seinem Geburtstag] geben** give a party [to celebrate her passing the exam/for his birthday]; **auf** *od.* **bei ~s** at parties; **auf eine** *od.* **zu einer ~ gehen** go to a party

**Party-: ~keller** *der: basement room equipped for parties;* **~löwe** *der* [male] partygoer (*who is the centre of attraction*); social lion

**Parvenü** /parve'nY:/ *der;* **~s, ~s** (*österr.:*) **Parvenu** /parve'nY:/ *der;* **~s, ~s** (*geh.*) parvenu

**Parze** /'partsə/ *die;* **~, ~n** (*röm. Myth.*) **die drei ~n** the Three Fates

**Parzelle** /par'tsɛlə/ *die;* **~, ~n** [small] plot [of land]

**parzellieren** *tr. V.* divide into [small] plots

**Pascal** /pas'kal/ *das;* **~s, ~:** pascal

**Pasch** /paʃ/ *der;* **~[e]s, ~e** *u.* **Päsche** Ⓐ (*beim Würfelspiel*) **einen ~ werfen** (*bei zwei Würfeln*) throw doubles *pl.;* (*bei drei Würfeln*) throw triplets; Ⓑ (*beim Domino*) double

**Pascha** /'paʃa/ *der;* **~s, ~s** Ⓐ (*hist.*) pasha; Ⓑ (*fig. abwertend*) male chauvinist; **den ~ spielen** act the lord and master

**Paspel** /'paspl̩/ *die;* **~, ~n** *od. der;* **~s, ~:** piping *no pl.*

**paspelieren** *tr. V.* pipe ‹pocket, collar, hem, seam›

**Pass, *Paß** /pas/ *der;* **Passes, Pässe** /'pɛsə/ Ⓐ (*Reise~*) passport; **der diplomatischen Vertretung die Pässe zustellen** break off diplomatic relations; Ⓑ (*Gebirgs~*) pass; Ⓒ (*Ballspiele*) pass

**passabel** /pa'sa:bl̩/ ❶ *Adj.* reasonable; tolerable; fair ‹report›; presentable ‹appearance›. ❷ *adv.* reasonably *or* tolerably well

**Passage** /pa'sa:ʒə/ *die;* **~, ~n** Ⓐ (*Ladenstraße*) [shopping] arcade; Ⓑ (*Abschnitt*) (*im Text*) passage; (*im Film*) sequence; (*beim Eistanz, bei Turnübungen*) routine; (*Musik*) [virtuoso] passage; Ⓒ (*Stelle zum Passieren, Schiffs~, Reiten*) passage

**Passagier** /pasa'ʒi:ɐ̯/ *der;* **~s, ~e** passenger; **~e der Lufthansa nach London** Lufthansa passengers [bound] for London; **blinder ~:** stowaway

**Passagier-: ~dampfer** *der* passenger steamer; **~flugzeug** *das* passenger aircraft

**Passagierin** *die;* **~, ~nen** ⇒ **Passagier**

**Passagier-: ~liste** *die* passenger list; **~schiff** *das* passenger ship

**Passah** /'pasa/ *das;* **~s** (*jüd. Rel.*) Passover

**Passah·fest** *das* (*jüd. Rel.*) Feast of the Passover

**Pass·amt, *Paß·amt** *das* passport office

**Passant** /pa'sant/ *der;* **~en, ~en, Passantin** *die;* **~, ~nen** Ⓐ (*Fußgänger[in]*) passer-by; Ⓑ (*schweiz.: Durchreisende[r]*) traveller [passing through]

**Passat** /pa'sa:t/ *der;* **~[e]s, ~e, Passatwind** *der* trade wind

**Pass·bild, *Paß·bild** *das* passport photograph

**passé** /pa'se:/ *indekl. Adj.* (*ugs.*) (*überholt*) passé; out of date; (*vorüber*) over [and done with]; **er ist als Politiker ~:** as a politician he has had his day

**Passe** /'pasə/ *die;* **~, ~n** (*Schneiderei*) yoke

**Pässe** /'pɛsə/ ⇒ **Pass**

**passee** ⇒ **passé**

**passen** ❶ *itr. V.* Ⓐ (*die richtige Größe/Form haben*) fit; **etw. passt [jmdm.] gut/nicht** sth. fits [sb.] well/does not fit [sb.]; **etw. passt [nicht] in/auf/unter etw.** (*Akk.*)**/zwischen zwei Sachen** sth. fits/does not fit into/on [to]/underneath sth./between two things; **der Schlüssel passt nicht ins Schloss** the key does not fit the lock; **das Buch passt nicht in den Karton** the book won't go in the box; **ein Kleidungsstück ~d machen** make an article of clothing fit; Ⓑ (*geeignet sein*) be suitable, be appropriate (**auf** + *Akk.*, **zu** for); (*harmonieren*) ‹colour etc.› match; **dieses Bild passt besser in die Diele** this picture goes better in the hall; **zu etw./jmdm. ~:** go well with sth./be well suited to sb.; **zueinander ~** ‹things› go well together; ‹two people› be suited to each other; **das** *od.* **dieses Benehmen passt zu ihm/passt nicht zu ihm** (*ugs.*) that's just like him (*coll.*)/that's not like him; **diese Beschreibung passt [genau] auf sie/[absolut] nicht auf sie** this description fits her [exactly]/does not fit her [at all]; **sie passt nicht hierher/nach X** she does not fit in here/in X; **nicht in die Welt ~:** be unsuited to this life; **sie passt nicht zu uns** *od.* **in unseren Kreis** she is out of place in our circle; ⇒ *auch* **Faust**; **Konzept**; **Kram**; **passend**; Ⓒ (*genehm sein*) **jmdm. ~** ‹time› be convenient for sb., suit sb.; **jmdm. passt etw. nicht** sth. is inconvenient for sb.; (*jmd. mag etw. nicht*) sb. does not like sth.; **das könnte dir so ~!** (*ugs.*) you'd just love that, wouldn't you?; Ⓓ (*Kartenspiel*) pass; **bei dieser Frage muss ich ~** (*fig.*) I'll have to pass on that question; Ⓔ (*österr.: warten, lauern*) wait (**auf** + *Akk.* for).
❷ *tr. V.* Ⓐ (*auch itr.*) *V.* (*Ballspiele*) pass ‹ball›; Ⓑ (*passgerecht einfügen*) **etw. in etw.** (*Akk.*) **~:** fit sth. into sth.
❸ *refl. V.* (*ugs.: sich schicken*) be proper *or* (*coll.*) done; **das/es passt sich einfach nicht** it simply isn't done *or* the done thing (*coll.*)

**passend** *Adj.* Ⓐ (*geeignet*) suitable ‹dress, present, etc.›; appropriate, right ‹words, expression›; right ‹moment›; **bei einer ~en Gelegenheit** at an opportune moment; **haben Sie es ~?** (*ugs.*) have you got the right money?; Ⓑ (*harmonierend*) matching ‹shoes etc.›; **die zum Kleid ~en Schuhe** the shoes to go with *or* match the dress

**Passepartout** /paspar'tu/ *das;* (*schweiz.:*) *der;* **~s, ~s** Ⓐ (*Umrahmung*) mount; Ⓑ (*bes. schweiz.*) ⇒ **Hauptschlüssel**

**pass-, *paß-, Pass-, *Paß-: ~form** *die* fit; **eine gute ~form haben** be a good fit; **~foto** *das* ⇒ **~bild**; **~gang** *der* amble; **im ~gang gehen** amble; **~genau, ~gerecht** *Adj.* that fits/fit exactly *or* perfectly *postpos., not pred.;* **die Schuhe sind ~genau** *od.* **~gerecht** the shoes fit exactly *or* are a perfect fit

**passierbar** *Adj.* passable ‹road›; navigable ‹river›; negotiable ‹path›

**passieren** ❶ *tr. V.* Ⓐ pass; **die Grenze ~:** cross the border; **eine Brücke/einen Tunnel ~:** pass over a bridge/through a tunnel; **die Zensur ~** (*fig.*) be passed by the censor; get past the censor; ⇒ *auch* **Revue** D; Ⓑ pass through a sieve; strain ‹curd cheese etc.›. ❷ *itr. V.;* *mit sein* happen; ‹murder, event› take place; **es ist ein Unglück/etwas Schreckliches passiert** there has been an accident/something dreadful has happened; **gib es ihm sofort zurück, sonst passiert was!** give it back to him straight away, or there'll be trouble!; **jmdm. ist etwas/nichts passiert** something/nothing happened to sb.; (*jmd. ist verletzt/nicht verletzt*) sb. was/was not hurt; **mir ist eine Panne/ein Versehen passiert** I [have] had a breakdown/made a mistake; **das kann doch jedem mal ~!** that can happen to anybody!

**Passier-: ~schein** *der* pass; permit; **~schlag** *der* (*Tennis*) passing shot

**Passion** /pa'si̯o:n/ *die;* **~, ~en** Ⓐ passion; Ⓑ (*christl. Rel., Kunst, Musik*) Passion

**passioniert** *Adj.* ardent, passionate ‹collector, card player, huntsman›

**Passions-: ~spiel** *das* Passion play; **~zeit** *die* (*christl. Rel.*) Passiontide

**passiv** /'pasi:f/ ❶ *Adj.* passive; non-active ‹member›; **~e Handelsbilanz** balance of trade deficit; **das ~e Wahlrecht** eligibility [for political office]; **das ~e Wahlrecht haben** be eligible to stand as a candidate; ⇒ *auch* **Bestechung**. ❷ *adv.* passively; **sich [bei** *od.* **in etw.** (*Dat.*)**] ~ verhalten** take a passive stance [in sth.]; take no active part [in sth.]

**Passiv** *das;* **~s, ~e** (*Sprachw.*) passive; **im ~ stehen** be in the passive

**Passiva** /pa'si:va/ *Pl.* (*Wirtsch.*) liabilities

**Passiv·bildung** *die* (*Sprachw.*) formation of the passive

**Passiven** ⇒ **Passiva**

**passivisch** (*Sprachw.*) ❶ *Adj.* passive. ❷ *adv.* passively; in the passive form

**Passivität** /pasivi'tɛ:t/ *die;* **~:** passivity

**Passiv-: ~posten** *der* (*Kaufmannsspr.*) liability; **~saldo** *der* (*Kaufmannsspr.*) debit balance; **~seite** *die* (*Kaufmannsspr.*) liabilities side

**Pass-, *Paß-: ~kontrolle** *die* Ⓐ (*das Kontrollieren*) passport inspection *or* check; Ⓑ (*Stelle*) passport control; **~stelle** *die* ⇒ **~amt**; **~straße** *die* [mountain] pass road

**Passung** *die;* **~, ~en** (*Technik*) fit; tolerance [for mating parts]

**Passus** /'pasʊs/ *der;* **~, ~** /'pa'su:s/ passage

**Pass-, *Paß-: ~wort** *das* (*DV*) password; **~zwang** *der* obligation to carry a passport

**Paste** /'pastə/ *die;* **~, ~n** (*auch Pharm.*) paste

**Pastell** /pas'tɛl/ *das;* **~[e]s, ~e** Ⓐ (*Farbton*) pastel shade; Ⓑ (*Maltechnik*) pastel *no art.;* **in ~:** in pastel; Ⓒ (*Bild*) pastel [drawing]

**pastell-, Pastell-: ~farbe** *die* pastel colour; **~farben** *Adj.* pastel-coloured; **~malerei** *die* pastel drawing; **~ton** *der* pastel shade

**Pastetchen** *das;* **~s, ~:** [small] vol-au-vent; (*Hülle*) [small] vol-au-vent case

**Pastete** /pas'te:tə/ *die;* **~, ~n** Ⓐ (*gefüllte ~*) vol-au-vent; (*Hülle*) vol-au-vent case; Ⓑ (*in einer Schüssel o. Ä. gegart*) pâté; (*in einer Hülle aus Teig gebacken*) pie

**pasteurisieren** /pastøri'zi:rən/ *tr. V.* pasteurize

**Pasteurisierung** *die;* **~, ~en** pasteurization

**Pastille** /pas'tɪlə/ *die;* **~, ~n** pastille

**Pastinake** /pasti'na:kə/ *die;* **~, ~n** parsnip

**Past·milch** *die* (*schweiz.*) pasteurized milk

**Pastor** /'pastɔr/ *der;* **~s, ~en** ▶ 91 pastor; ⇒ *auch* **Pfarrer**

**pastoral** /pasto'ra:l/ *Adj.* Ⓐ (*seelsorgerlich*) pastoral; Ⓑ (*salbungsvoll*) unctuous; Ⓒ (*idyllisch*) pastoral ‹literature›

**Pastorale** *das;* **~s, ~s** *od. die;* **~, ~n** Ⓐ (*Musik*) pastorale; Ⓑ (*Literaturw., Kunst*) pastoral

**Pastorin** *die;* **~, ~nen** ▶ 91 pastor

**Pate** /'pa:tə/ *der;* **~n, ~n** (*Taufzeuge*) godparent; (*Patenonkel; in der Mafia*) godfather; (*DDR*) sponsor (*responsible for the child's socialist upbringing*); **bei etw. ~ stehen** (*fig.*) be [the influence/influences] behind sth.; (*als Vorbild dienen*) act as the model for sth.

**Patene** /pa'te:nə/ *die;* **~, ~n** (*christl. Kirche*) paten

**Paten-: ~kind** *das* godchild; (*DDR*) sponsored child; **~onkel** *der* godfather; (*DDR*) [male] sponsor

**Patenschaft** *die;* **~, ~en** (*christl. Rel.*) godparenthood; (*DDR, fig.*) sponsorship (**für, über** + *Akk.* of)

**Paten-: ~sohn** *der* godson; (*DDR*) sponsored boy; **~stadt** *die* twin town (*Brit.*); sister city *or* town (*Amer.*)

**patent** /pa'tɛnt/ (*ugs.*) ❶ *Adj.* Ⓐ (*tüchtig*) capable; **ein ~er Kerl** a great guy (*coll.*); Ⓑ (*zweckmäßig*) ingenious ‹device, method, idea›; clever ‹slogan etc.›. ❷ *adv.* ingeniously; cleverly; neatly ‹solved›

**Patent** *das;* **~[e]s, ~e** Ⓐ (*Schutz*) patent; **ein ~ auf etw.** (*Akk.*) **haben** have a patent for sth.; **etw. zum** *od.* **als ~ anmelden, auf** *od.* **für etw. ein ~ anmelden** apply for a patent for sth.; **„als ~ angemeldet"** 'patent pending'; 'patent applied for'; Ⓑ (*Erfindung*) [patented] invention; (*fig.: Konstruktion/Verfahren*) [patent] design/method; Ⓒ (*Ernennungsurkunde*) certificate [of appointment]; (*eines Kapitäns*) master's certificate; (*eines Offiziers*) commission

P

**Patent-:** **~amt** *das* Patent Office; **~an·mel·dung** *die* patent application

**Paten·tante** *die* godmother; (*DDR*) [female] sponsor

**patent-, Patent-:** **~anwalt** *der*, **~anwäl·tin** *die* ▸ 159 patent agent *or* (*Amer.*) attorney; **~fähig** *Adj.* patentable; **~gesetz** *das* Patents Act

**patentieren** *tr. V.* patent; **jmdm. etw. ~:** grant sb. a patent for sth.; **sich** (*Dat.*) **eine Erfindung ~ lassen** have an invention patented

**Patent-:** **~inhaber** *der*, **~inhaberin** *die* patentee; **~lösung** *die* patent remedy (**für**, **zu** for)

**Paten·tochter** *die* god-daughter; (*DDR*) sponsored girl

**Patent-:** **~recht** *das* Ⓐ (*Rechtsnormen*) patent law *no art.*; Ⓑ (*berechtigter Anspruch*) patent rights *pl.*; **~register** *das* (*österr.*, *schweiz.*) ⇒ **~rolle**; **~rezept** *das* patent remedy (**gegen**, **für** for); **kein ~rezept dafür haben, wie man etw. tut** have no magic recipe for doing sth.; **~rolle** *die* ≈ Register of Patents (*Brit.*); **~schrift** *die* patent specification; **~schutz** *der* patent protection

**Pater** /'pa:tɐ/ *der;* **~s**, **~** *od.* **Patres** /'pa:tre:s/ (*kath. Kirche*) Father

**Paternoster**[1] /pa:tɐ'nɔstɐ/ *der;* **~s**, **~** (*Aufzug*) paternoster [lift]

**Paternoster**[2] *das;* **~s**, **~** (*Gebet*) Lord's Prayer

**pathetisch** /pa'te:tɪʃ/ ❶ *Adj.* emotional, impassioned ‹speech, manner›; melodramatic ‹gesture›; emotive ‹style›; pompous ‹voice›. ❷ *adv.* emotionally; with much emotion; (*dramatisch*) [melo]dramatically

**Pathologe** /pato'lo:gə/ *der;* **~n**, **~n** ▸ 159 pathologist

**Pathologie** /patolo'gi:/ *die;* **~**, **~n** Ⓐ (*Gebiet*) pathology *no art.*; Ⓑ (*Abteilung/Institut*) pathology department/institute

**Pathologin** *die;* **~**, **~nen** ▸ 159 pathologist

**pathologisch** ❶ *Adj.* (*Med.; auch fig.*) pathological. ❷ *adv.* pathologically

**Pathos** /'pa:tɔs/ *das;* **~:** emotionalism; **ein unechtes/hohles ~:** false/empty pathos; **eine Rede voller ~:** a speech full of emotion; **etw. mit ~ vortragen** recite sth. with much feeling

**Patience** /pa'sjã:s/ *die;* **~**, **~n** [game of] patience; **~n/eine ~ legen** play patience/a game of patience

**Patient** /pa'tsi̯ɛnt/ *der;* **~en**, **~en**, **Patientin** *die;* **~**, **~nen** ▸ 474 patient; **~ von** *od.* **bei Dr. X sein** be a patient of Dr X

**Patin** *die;* **~**, **~nen** (*Taufzeugin*) godmother; (*DDR*) sponsor (*responsible for the child's socialist upbringing*); ⇒ *auch* **Pate**

**Patina** /'pa:tina/ *die;* **~:** patina; **~ ansetzen** become covered with a patina; (*fig.*) begin to show its age; become dated

**patinieren** *tr. V.* patinate

**Patisserie** /patɪsə'ri:/ *die;* **~**, **~n** (*schweiz.*) patisserie

**Patres** ⇒ **Pater**

**Patriarch** /patri'arç/ *der;* **~en**, **~en** patriarch

**patriarchalisch** ❶ *Adj.* patriarchal; (*fig.: autoritär*) authoritarian. ❷ *adv.* in a patriarchal *or* (*fig.*) authoritarian manner

**Patriarchat** *das;* **~[e]s**, **~e** Ⓐ (*Gesellschaftsordnung*) patriarchy; Ⓑ (*kath. u. orthodoxe Kirche*) patriarchate

**Patriot** /patri'o:t/ *der;* **~en**, **~en**, **Patriotin** *die;* **~**, **~nen** patriot

**patriotisch** ❶ *Adj.* patriotic. ❷ *adv.* patriotically; **~ erzogen werden** be brought up to be a patriot

**Patriotismus** *der;* **~:** patriotism *usu. no def. art.*

**Patrize** /pa'tri:tsə/ *die;* **~**, **~n** (*Druckw.*) steel punch *or* die

**Patriziat** /patri'tsi̯a:t/ *das;* **~[e]s**, **~e** (*hist.*) patriciate

**Patrizier** /pa'tri:tsi̯ɐ/ *der;* **~s**, **~**, **Patrizierin** *die;* **~**, **~nen** (*hist.*) patrician

**Patron** /pa'tro:n/ *der;* **~s**, **~e** Ⓐ (*Schutzheiliger*) patron saint; Ⓑ (*Stifter einer Kirche*) patron; founder; Ⓒ (*ugs. abwertend: Kerl*) type (*coll.*); **ein übler ~:** a nasty piece of work (*coll.*); Ⓓ (*hist.: Schutzherr; veralt.: Gönner*) patron

**Patronage** /patro'na:ʒə/ *die;* **~**, **~n** favouritism *no art.*; (*im Staatsapparat*) patronage *no art.*

**Patronat** /patro'na:t/ *das;* **~[e]s**, **~e** Ⓐ (*hist.; Würde, Amt*) patronate; Ⓑ (*Schirmherrschaft; Kirchenrecht: Rechtstellung*) patronage

**Patrone** /pa'tro:nə/ *die;* **~**, **~n** Ⓐ (*für das Gewehr, den Füller*) cartridge; (*für die Kleinbildkamera*) cassette; Ⓑ (*Textilind.*) point paper plan; draft

**Patronen-:** **~gurt** *der*, **~gürtel** *der* cartridge belt; (*über der Schulter getragen*) bandoleer; **~hülse** *die* cartridge case; **~tasche** *die* cartridge pouch

**Patronin** *die;* **~**, **~nen** Ⓐ (*Schutzheilige*) patron saint; Ⓑ (*veralt.: Gönnerin*) patroness

**Patrouille** /pa'trʊljə/ *die;* **~**, **~n** patrol

**Patrouillen-:** **~boot** *das* patrol boat; **~gang** *der* patrol

**patrouillieren** /patrʊl'ji:rən/ *itr. V.; auch mit sein* be on patrol; **durch die Straßen ~:** patrol the streets

**patsch** /patʃ/ *Interj.* splat; slap; (*auf Wasser usw.*) splash

**Patsche** *die;* **~**, **~n** Ⓐ (*ugs.*) ⇒ **Klemme** B; Ⓑ (*ugs.: Hand*) paw (*coll.*); **kleine ~n** (*eines Kindes*) little hands; Ⓒ (*Feuer~*) fire beater

**patschen** *itr. V.* (*ugs.*) Ⓐ (*klatschen*) slap; **sich** (*Dat.*) **auf die Schenkel ~:** slap one's thighs; **das Kind patschte in die Hände** the child clapped its hands; Ⓑ *mit sein* (*~d gehen/fallen*) splash; **über die Fliesen ~** (*mit nassen Stiefeln usw.*) go flip-flop over the tiles; (*unbeholfen*) lollop over the tiles; **durch die Pfützen ~:** splash *or* go splashing through the puddles; Ⓒ (*~des Geräusch hervorbringen*) ‹slush, wet shoes› squelch

**patsch-, Patsch-:** **~hand** *die*, **~händchen** *das* (*fam.*) [little] hand; handy-pandy (*child lang.*); **~nass**, ***~naß** *Adj.* (*ugs.*) sopping wet; **~nass geschwitzt** soaked in sweat

**patt** /pat/ (*Schach*) **~ sein** be stalemated

**Patt** *das;* **~s**, **~s** (*Schach; auch fig.*) stalemate; **mit einem ~ enden** *od.* **ausgehen** end in stalemate

**Patte** *die;* **~**, **~n** [pocket] flap

**Patt·situation** *die* [position of] stalemate

**patzen** /'patsn̩/ *itr. V.* Ⓐ (*ugs.: Fehler machen*) slip up (*coll.*); boob (*coll.*); **der Pianist hat ziemlich/erheblich gepatzt** the pianist came rather/well and truly unstuck (*coll.*); Ⓑ (*österr.: klecksen*) make a blot/blots

**Patzer** *der;* **~s**, **~** (*ugs.*) slip (*coll.*); boob (*coll.*); **ein dicker ~:** a real howler (*coll.*)

**patzig** (*ugs. abwertend*) ❶ *Adj.* snotty (*coll.*); (*frech*) cheeky. ❷ *adv.* snottily (*coll.*); (*frech*) cheekily

**Paukant** /pau̯'kant/ *der;* **~en**, **~en** (*Studentenspr.*) duellist

**Pauke** /'pau̯kə/ *die;* **~**, **~n** kettledrum; **~n** (*im Orchester*) timpani; **die ~ schlagen** beat the drum/drums; **auf die ~ hauen** (*ugs.*) (*feiern*) paint the town red (*coll.*); (*großtun*) blow one's own trumpet; (*sich lautstark äußern*) come right out with it; **mit ~n und Trompeten durchfallen** (*ugs.*) ‹candidate› fail resoundingly; ‹broadcast, film, etc.› be a resounding failure; **jmdn. mit ~n und Trompeten empfangen** (*fig.*) give sb. the red-carpet treatment

**pauken** ❶ *tr. V.* (*ugs.*) swot up (*Brit. sl.*), bone up on (*Amer. coll.*) ‹facts, figures, etc.›; **Latein/Mathe ~:** swot up one's Latin/maths. ❷ *itr. V.* Ⓐ (*ugs.: lernen*) swot (*Brit. sl.*); (*fürs Examen*) cram (*coll.*); Ⓑ (*Musik*) (*in einer Band o. Ä.*) play the big drum[s]; (*im Orchester*) play the timpani; Ⓒ (*Studentenspr.*) duel

**Pauken-:** **~schlag** *der* Ⓐ drumbeat; **Haydns Sinfonie mit dem ~schlag** Haydn's Surprise Symphony; Ⓑ (*fig. Eklat*) sensation; bombshell; **~schlägel**, ***~schlegel** *der* drumstick

**Pauker** *der;* **~s**, **~** Ⓐ (*Musik*) (*im Orchester*) timpanist; (*in einer Band*) big-drum player; Ⓑ (*Schülerspr.: Lehrer*) teacher; teach (*school sl.*)

**Paukerei** *die;* **~** (*ugs. abwertend*) swotting (*Brit. sl.*); boning up (*Amer. coll.*); (*fürs Examen*) cramming

**Paukerin** *die;* **~**, **~nen** ⇒ **Pauker**

**Paukist** *der;* **~en**, **~en**, **Paukistin** *die;* **~**, **~nen** ▸ 159 ⇒ **Pauker** A

**Paulus** /'pau̯lʊs/ (*der*); **~'** Paul

**Pauperismus** /pau̯pə'rɪsmʊs/ *der;* **~** (*Soziol.*) pauperism *usu. no art.*

**Paus·backen** *Pl.* (*fam.*) chubby cheeks

**pausbäckig** /'pau̯sbɛkɪç/ *Adj.* chubby-cheeked; chubby-faced; chubby ‹face›

**pauschal** /pau̯'ʃa:l/ ❶ *Adj.* Ⓐ (*rund gerechnet*) all-inclusive ‹price, settlement›; **eine ~e Summe/Bezahlung** a lump sum/payment; Ⓑ (*verallgemeinernd*) sweeping ‹judgement, criticism, statement›; indiscriminate ‹prejudice›; wholesale ‹discrimination›. ❷ *adv.* Ⓐ (*alles zusammengenommen*) ‹cost› overall, all in all; ‹pay› in a lump sum; **das Angebot gilt ~ für 10 Tage** the offer covers all costs *or* is inclusive for 10 days; **eine Frage ~ beantworten** answer a question in general terms; Ⓑ (*ohne zu differenzieren*) wholesale

**Pauschale** *die;* **~**, **~n** *od. das;* **~s**, **Pauschalien** /-'ʃa:li̯ən/ flat-rate payment; (*Pauschalsumme*) lump sum; **monatliche ~:** flat monthly rate

**Pauschal·gebühr** *die* flat-rate [charge]

**Pauschal-:** **~preis** *der* (*Einheitspreis*) flat rate; (*Inklusivpreis*) inclusive *or* all-in price; **~reise** *die* package holiday; (*mit mehreren Reisezielen*) package tour; **~summe** *die* lump sum; **~urteil** *das* (*abwertend*) sweeping judgement *or* statement

**Pausch·betrag** /'pau̯ʃ-/ *der* lump sum

**Pause**[1] /'pau̯zə/ *die;* **~**, **~n** Ⓐ (*Unterbrechung*) break; (*Ruhe~*) rest; (*Theater*) interval (*Brit.*); intermission (*Amer.*); (*Kino*) intermission; (*Sport*) half-time interval; **kleine/große ~** (*Schule*) short/[long] break; (*Theater*) short/main interval (*Brit.*) *or* (*Amer.*) intermission; **in** *od.* **während der ~** (*Schule*) in *or* during break; (*Theater*) in *or* during the interval (*Brit.*) *or* (*Amer.*) intermission; (*Sport*) at half-time; **wann haben wir [große] ~?** (*Schule*) when is [the long] break?; **es klingelt zur ~** (*Schule*) the bell is ringing for break; **[eine] ~ machen** take *or* have a break; (*zum Ausruhen*) have a rest; **wir machen kurz/eine Viertelstunde ~:** we'll take a short break/a quarter of an hour's break; **eine ~ einlegen** *od.* **einschieben** have a rest; **mach mal ~!** take a break!; Ⓑ (*in der Unterhaltung o. Ä.*) pause; (*verlegenes Schweigen*) silence; Ⓒ (*Musik*) rest; **eine ganze/halbe ~:** a semibreve/minim rest; a whole [note]/half [note] rest (*Amer.*)

**Pause**[2] *die;* **~**, **~n** (*Kopie*) tracing; (*Licht~*) Photostat (*Brit.* ®)

**pausen** *tr. V.* trace; (*eine Lichtpause machen*) Photostat (*Brit.* ®)

**Pausen-:** **~brot** *das* sandwich (*eaten during break*); **~füller** *der* (*ugs.*) interval material *no art.*; **~hof** *der* school yard

**pausen·los** ❶ *Adj.* incessant ‹noise, moaning, questioning›; continous, uninterrupted ‹work, operation›. ❷ *adv.* incessantly; ceaselessly; ‹work› non-stop

**Pausen·zeichen** *das* Ⓐ (*Musik*) rest; Ⓑ (*Rundfunk, Ferns.*) interval signal

**pausieren** *itr. V.* Ⓐ (*innehalten*) pause; Ⓑ (*aussetzen*) have *or* take a rest; **acht Wochen ~ müssen** (*Sport*) ‹player› be out of the game for eight weeks

**Paus·papier** *das* (*durchsichtig*) tracing paper; (*Kohlepapier*) carbon paper

*old spelling (see note on page 1707)

**Pavian** /ˈpaːvi̯aːn/ *der;* **~s, ~e** baboon
**Pavillon** /ˈpavɪljɔn/ *der;* **~s, ~s** (*Archit.*) pavilion; (*einer Schule o. Ä.*) annexe
**Paycard** /ˈpeɪkɑːd/ *die;* **~, ~s** [charge] card
**Pazifik** /paˈtsiːfɪk/ *der;* **~s** Pacific
**pazifisch** *Adj.* Pacific ‹area›; **der Pazifische Ozean** the Pacific Ocean
**Pazifismus** *der;* **~:** pacifism *no art.*
**Pazifist** *der;* **~en, ~en, Pazifistin** *die;* **~, ~nen** pacifist
**pazifistisch** ❶ *Adj.* pacifist. ❷ *adv.* in a pacifist way
**PC** *der;* **~[s], ~[s]** (*DV*) PC
**PDS** *Abk.* **Partei des Demokratischen Sozialismus** Party of Democratic Socialism
**Pech** /pɛç/ *das;* **~[e]s, ~e** Ⓐ pitch; **schwarz wie ~ sein** be pitch-black; ‹hair› be jet-black; **zusammenhalten wie ~ und Schwefel** (*ugs.*) be inseparable; ‹friends› be as thick as thieves (*coll.*); Ⓑ (*Missgeschick*) bad luck; **großes/unerhörtes ~:** rotten (*coll.*)/ (*coll.*) terrible luck; **bei** *od.* **mit etw./mit jmdm. ~ haben** have bad luck with sth./ sb.; be unlucky with sth./sb.; **im Leben/in der Liebe/bei den Frauen/beim Examen ~ haben** have no luck in life/in love/ with women/in the exam; **~ gehabt!** (*ugs.*) tough luck! (*coll.*); **dein ~, wenn du nicht aufpasst** (*ugs.*) that's just your hard luck if you don't pay attention; **sein ~!** (*ugs.*) that's his lookout; **~ für dich** (*ugs.*) that's just too bad (*coll.*); **vom ~ verfolgt sein** be dogged by bad luck
**pech-, Pech-: ~blende** *die* (*Mineral.*) pitchblende; **~[raben]schwarz** *Adj.* (*ugs.*) pitch-black ‹night, darkness›; jet-black ‹eyes›; raven[-black] ‹hair›; **~strähne** *die* run of bad luck; **~vogel** *der* unlucky devil (*coll.*); (*Opfer vieler Unfälle*) walking disaster area (*coll.*)
**Pedal** /peˈdaːl/ *das;* **~s, ~e** pedal; (*bei der Orgel*) pedals *pl.*; **mit/ohne ~ spielen** (*beim Klavier*) use/not use pedal; **[kräftig] in die ~e treten** (*beim Fahrrad*) pedal [really] hard
**Pedale** *die;* **~, ~n** (*landsch.*) ⇒ **Pedal**
**pedant** (*österr.*) ⇒ **pedantisch**
**Pedant** /peˈdant/ *der;* **~en, ~en** pedant
**Pedanterie** /pedantəˈriː/ *die;* **~, ~n** pedantry; **seine ~n** his pedantic ways
**Pedantin** *die;* **~, ~nen** ⇒ **Pedant**
**pedantisch** ❶ *Adj.* pedantic. ❷ *adv.* pedantically
**Peddig·rohr** /ˈpɛdɪç-/ *das* rattan [cane]
**Pedell** /peˈdɛl/ *der;* **~s, ~e,** (*österr. meist:*) **~en, ~en** (*veralt.*) caretaker (*Brit.*); janitor (*esp. Amer.*)
**Pediküre** /pediˈkyːrə/ *die;* **~, ~n** Ⓐ ⇒ **Fußpflege;** Ⓑ (*Fußpflegerin*) chiropodist
**pediküren** *tr. V.* pedicure ‹feet, nails›
**Peep·show** /ˈpiːp-/ *die;* **~, ~s** peep show
**Peergroup** /ˈpiːɐ̯gruːp/ *die;* **~, ~s** (*Soziol.*) peer group
**Pegel** /ˈpeːgl̩/ *der;* **~s, ~** Ⓐ (*Gerät*) water level indicator; (*für die Gezeiten am Meer*) tide gauge; Ⓑ (*Wasserstand*) water level; (*Technik, Physik; auch fig.*) level (*of noise, alcohol consumption, etc.*)
**Pegel·stand** *der* water level
**Peil·antenne** *die* (*Funkw., Seew.*) direction-finding antenna
**peilen** /ˈpai̯lən/ ❶ *tr. V.* Ⓐ take a bearing on ‹transmitter, fixed point›; ⇒ *auch* **Daumen; Lage** C; Ⓑ (*Wassertiefe messen*) sound ‹depth›; take soundings in ‹bay etc.›. ❷ *itr. V.* Ⓐ take one's bearings; get a fix; Ⓑ (*Wassertiefe messen*) take a sounding/soundings; Ⓒ (*ugs.: spähen*) peek
**Peilung** *die;* **~, ~en** (*Seew.*) Ⓐ (*das Peilen*) taking a bearing; (*des eigenen Standorts*) plotting one's position; (*Resultat*) fix; bearing; Ⓑ (*der Wassertiefe*) sounding
**Pein** /pai̯n/ *die;* **~** (*geh.*) torment; **körperliche/seelische ~:** physical/mental anguish; **jmdm. [viel** *od.* **große] ~ bereiten** cause sb. [much] anguish
**peinigen** /ˈpai̯nɪgn̩/ *tr. V.* (*geh.*) torment; (*foltern*) torture; **von Durst/Kälte gepeinigt werden** suffer agonies from thirst/cold; **von Schmerzen gepeinigt werden** be tormented by *or* racked with pain; ⇒ *auch* **Blut**
**Peiniger** *der;* **~s, ~, Peinigerin** *die;* **~, ~nen** (*geh.*) tormentor; (*Folterer*) torturer
**Peinigung** *die;* **~, ~en** (*geh.*) torment; (*Folterung*) torture
**peinlich** ❶ *Adj.* Ⓐ embarrassing; awkward ‹question, position, pause›; **es ist mir sehr ~:** I feel very bad (*coll.*) *or* embarrassed about it; **es ist mir sehr ~, Ihnen das mitteilen zu müssen** I feel terrible about having to tell you this (*coll.*); **es ist mir sehr ~, aber ich wollte Sie fragen, …** I don't know quite how to put this, but I wanted to ask you …; Ⓑ (*äußerst genau*) meticulous; scrupulous; **er hielt sich mit ~ster Genauigkeit an diese Vorschrift** he was most punctilious in observing this regulation; Ⓒ (*Rechtsspr. veralt.*) **das ~e Gericht** the criminal *or* penal court; **ein ~es Verhör** an interrogation under torture.
❷ *adv.* Ⓐ unpleasantly ‹surprised›; **[von etw.] ~ berührt** *od.* **betroffen sein** be painfully embarrassed [by sth.]; Ⓑ (*überaus [genau]*) scrupulously; meticulously; **er vermied es ~[st], dieses heikle Thema zu berühren** he took [the utmost] pains to avoid touching on this delicate subject; **~ genau registriert** listed down to the last detail
**Peinlichkeit** *die;* **~, ~en** Ⓐ embarrassment; **die ~ der Situation** the awkwardness of the situation; Ⓑ (*Genauigkeit*) scrupulousness; meticulousness; Ⓒ (*peinliche Situation*) embarrassing situation; (*heikle Situation*) awkward situation; (*Fehler*) embarrassing blunder
**peinsam** *Adj.* (*meist scherzh.*) ⇒ **peinlich** 1 A
**pein·voll** *Adj.* (*geh.*) painful; agonizing ‹uncertainty›; ‹period› full of anguish
**Peitsche** /ˈpai̯tʃə/ *die;* **~, ~n** whip; **er knallte mit der ~:** he cracked the whip; ⇒ *auch* **Zuckerbrot**
**peitschen** ❶ *tr. V.* whip; (*fig.*) ‹storm, waves, rain› lash. ❷ *itr. V.*; *mit sein* ‹rain› lash (**an,** **gegen** + *Akk.* against, **in** + *Akk.* into); ‹shot› ring out
**Peitschen-: ~hieb** *der* lash [of the whip]; **wie ein ~hieb** like a whiplash; **~knall** *der* crack of the whip; **~lampe** *die* street lamp (*hanging over the street from a curved standard*); **~stiel** *der* whip handle; whipstock
**pejorativ** /pejoraˈtiːf/ (*Sprachw.*) ❶ *Adj.* pejorative. ❷ *adv.* perjoratively
**Pekinese** /pekiˈneːzə/ *der;* **~n, ~n** Pekinese
**Peking·mensch** /ˈpeːkɪŋ-/ *der* Peking Man
**Pektin** /pɛkˈtiːn/ *das;* **~s, ~e** (*Biol.*) pectin
**pekuniär** /pekuˈni̯ɛːɐ̯/ ❶ *Adj.* pecuniary; financial. ❷ *adv.* financially
**Pelerine** /peləˈriːnə/ *die;* **~, ~n** cape
**Pelikan** /ˈpeːlikaːn/ *der;* **~s, ~e** pelican
**Pelle** /ˈpɛlə/ *die;* **~, ~n** (*bes. nordd.*) skin; (*abgeschält*) peel; **Kartoffeln in** *od.* **mit der ~ kochen** boil potatoes in their skins; **sie hocken sich** (*Dat.*) **[dauernd] auf der ~** (*salopp*) they never leave each other alone; **jmdm. nicht von der ~ gehen** (*salopp*) refuse to leave sb. alone *or* in peace; ⇒ *auch* **rücken** 2 A; **sitzen** A
**pellen** (*bes. nordd.*) ❶ *tr. V.* peel ‹potato, egg, etc.›; **sie pellte sich/das Kind aus dem warmen Winterzeug** (*fig.*) she peeled off her/the child's warm winter things; ⇒ *auch* **Ei** A. ❷ *refl. V.* ‹person, skin› peel
**Pell·kartoffel** *die* potato boiled in its skin
**Pelz** /pɛlts/ *der;* **~es, ~e** Ⓐ fur; coat; (*des toten Tieres*) skin; pelt; **einen weichen ~ haben** have a soft coat; have soft fur; **einem Tier den ~ abziehen** skin an animal; Ⓑ (*gegerbt; als Material*) fur; **aus ~:** made of fur; **mit ~ gefüttert** fur-lined; Ⓒ fur; (*~mantel*) fur coat; (*~jacke*) fur jacket; Ⓓ (*ugs.: Haut*) **sich** (*Dat.*) **die Sonne auf den ~ brennen** *od.* **scheinen lassen** soak up the sun; **jmdm./einem Tier eins auf den ~ brennen** take a potshot at sb./an animal; ⇒ *auch* **Laus; rücken** 2 A; **sitzen** A
**pelz-, Pelz-: ~besatz** *der* fur trimming; **~besetzt** *Adj.* fur-trimmed; **~futter** *das* fur lining; **~gefüttert** *Adj.* fur-lined; **~händler** *der,* **~händlerin** *die* furrier; **~hand·schuh** *der* fur glove; (*~gefüttert*) fur-lined glove
**pelzig** *Adj.* Ⓐ (*wie Pelz, mit Flaum*) furry; downy ‹peach›; Ⓑ (*bes. westd.: mehlig*) mealy ‹apple›; (*holzig*) woody ‹radish›; Ⓒ (*belegt*) furred, coated ‹tongue, mouth›
**Pelz-: ~imitation** *die* imitation fur; **~jacke** *die* fur jacket; **~kragen** *der* fur collar; **~mantel** *der* fur coat; **~mütze** *die* fur hat; **~stiefel** *der* fur boot; (*pelzgefüttert*) fur-lined boot; **~tier** *das* animal prized for its fur; **~tier·farm** *die* fur farm; **~tier·jäger** *der,* **~tier·jägerin** *die* fur-hunter; trapper; **~tier·zucht** *die* fur farming *no def. art.*; **~waren** *Pl.* furs; fur goods; **~werk** *das* fur
**Pence** /ˈpɛns/ *Pl. von* **Penny**
**Pendant** /pãˈdãː/ *das;* **~s, ~s** (*Gegenstück*) counterpart (**zu** of); (*ein Stück von einem Paar*) companion piece (**zu** of); (*Entsprechung*) equivalent (**zu** of)
**Pendel** /ˈpɛndl̩/ *das;* **~s, ~:** pendulum
**pendeln** *itr. V.* Ⓐ (*hin- u. herschwingen*) swing [to and fro] (**an** + *Dat.* by); (*mit weniger Bewegung*) dangle; Ⓑ *mit sein* (*hin- u. herfahren*) **zwischen X und Y ~** ‹bus, ferry, etc.› operate a shuttle service between X and Y; ‹person› commute between X and Y; Ⓒ (*Boxen*) weave
**Pendel-: ~tür** *die* swing door; **~uhr** *die* pendulum clock; **~verkehr** *der* Ⓐ (*Berufsverkehr*) commuter traffic; Ⓑ (*mit ~zug o. Ä.*) shuttle service; **~zug** *der* shuttle[-service] train
**Pendler** *der;* **~s, ~, Pendlerin** *die;* **~, ~nen** commuter
**Penes** ⇒ **Penis**
**penetrant** /peneˈtrant/ (*abwertend*) ❶ *Adj.* Ⓐ (*durchdringend*) penetrating, pungent ‹smell, taste›; overpowering ‹stink, perfume›; Ⓑ (*aufdringlich*) pushing, (*coll.*) pushy ‹person›; overbearing ‹tone, manner›; aggressive, pointed ‹question›. ❷ *adv.* Ⓐ (*durchdringend*) overpoweringly; **es riecht/schmeckt ~ nach …** there is an overpowering smell/an overpowering *or* pungent taste of …; Ⓑ (*aufdringlich*) overbearingly; in an overbearing manner
**Penetranz** /peneˈtrants/ *die;* **~** Ⓐ (*von Geruch, Geschmack*) overpowering nature; Ⓑ (*Aufdringlichkeit*) overbearing nature
**Penetration** /penetraˈtsi̯oːn/ *die;* **~, ~en** Ⓐ (*Technik*) penetration; (*Wirtsch.*) penetration [of the market]; Ⓑ (*Med.*) perforation
**penetrieren** *tr. V.* (*geh.*) penetrate
**peng** /pɛŋ/ *Interj.* bang
**penibel** /peˈniːbl̩/ ❶ *Adj.* over-meticulous ‹person›; (*pedantisch*) pedantic; **penible Kleinarbeit** painstakingly detailed work. ❷ *adv.* painstakingly; over-meticulously ‹dressed›
**Penicillin** ⇒ **Penizillin**
**Penis** /ˈpeːnɪs/ *der;* **~, ~se** *od.* **Penes** /ˈpeːneːs/ ▶ 471 penis
**Penis·neid** *der* (*Psych.*) penis envy
**Penizillin** /penitsɪˈliːn/ *das;* **~s, ~e** penicillin
**Pennäler** /pɛˈnɛːlɐ/ *der;* **~s, ~** (*ugs.*) [secondary] schoolboy
**Pennälerin** *die;* **~, ~nen** (*ugs.*) [secondary] schoolgirl
**Penn·bruder** *der* (*ugs. abwertend*) tramp (*Brit.*); hobo (*Amer.*)
**Penne** /ˈpɛnə/ *die;* **~, ~n** Ⓐ (*Schülerspr.: Schule*) [secondary] school; swot-shop (*Brit. sl.*); Ⓑ (*ugs. abwertend: Nachtquartier*) doss-house (*Brit. coll.*); flophouse (*sl.*)
**pennen** *itr. V.* (*salopp*) Ⓐ (*schlafen*) kip (*coll.*); **auf einer Bank ~:** doss down on a bench (*sl.*); Ⓑ (*fig.: nicht aufpassen*) be half asleep; **du hast im Unterricht wohl mal wieder gepennt?** (*fig.*) I suppose you were dreaming again during the lesson?; Ⓒ (*koitieren*) **mit jmdm. ~:** sleep with sb.
**Penner** *der;* **~s, ~, Pennerin** *die;* **~, ~nen** (*salopp abwertend*) Ⓐ (*Stadtstreicher*) tramp (*Brit.*); hobo (*Amer.*); Ⓑ (*jmd., der viel schläft*) sleepyhead

P

**Penny** /ˈpɛni/ *der;* ~**s**, ~**s** ▶337 penny; **20 Pence** 20 pence

**Pensa, Pensen** ⇨ **Pensum**

**Pension** /pãˈzi̯o:n/ *die;* ~, ~**en** Ⓐ *(Ruhestand)* **[vorzeitig] in** ~ **gehen** retire [early]; **in** ~ **sein** be retired *or* in retirement; **einen Beamten in** ~ *(Akk.)* **schicken** retire a civil servant; Ⓑ *(Ruhegehalt)* [retirement] pension; Ⓒ *(Haus für [Ferien]gäste)* guest house; *(auf dem Kontinent)* pension; Ⓓ *(Unterkunft u. Verpflegung)* board; **[die] halbe/volle** ~: half/full board; **bei jmdm. in** ~ **sein** board with sb.

**Pensionär** /pãzi̯oˈnɛ:ɐ̯/ *der;* ~**s**, ~**e**, **Pensionärin** *die;* ~, ~**nen** Ⓐ *(Beamter in Ruhestand)* retired civil servant; *(ugs.: Rentner)* [old-age] pensioner; ~ **sein** be retired *or* in retirement; Ⓑ *(schweiz., sonst veralt.: Bewohner einer Pension)* boarder; [paying] guest

**Pensionat** /pãzi̯oˈna:t/ *das;* ~**[e]s**, ~**e** *(veralt.)* boarding school *(esp. for girls)*

**pensionieren** *tr. V.* pension off; retire; **sich [vorzeitig]** ~ **lassen** retire [early]; take [early] retirement

**Pensionierung** *die;* ~, ~**en** retirement; **bis zur** ~: up to [his, her, *etc.*] retirement

**Pensionist**, *der;* ~**en**, ~**en**, **Pensionistin** *die;* ~, ~**nen** *(südd., österr., schweiz.)* ⇨ **Pensionär** A

**pensions-, Pensions-:** ~**alter** *das* retirement age; ~**an·spruch** *der* pension entitlement; ~**ansprüche** pension rights; ~**berechtigt** *Adj.* entitled to a pension *postpos.;* ~**berechtigung** *die* pension entitlement; ~**gast** *der* patron [of a/the guest house]; ~**kasse** *die (Versicherungsw.)* [staff] pension fund; ~**reif** *Adj. (ugs.)* ripe for retirement *pred.;* ~**rückstellungen** *Pl. (Wirtsch.)* pension reserves

**Pensum** /ˈpɛnzʊm/ *das;* ~**s**, **Pensen** *od.* **Pensa** Ⓐ *(Arbeit)* amount of work; work quota; **sein tägliches** ~ **[an Arbeit] erledigen** do one's daily stint [of work]; Ⓑ *(Päd. veralt.: Lehrstoff)* syllabus

**Pentagon** /pɛntaˈgo:n/ *das;* ~**s**, ~**e** Ⓐ *(Geom.)* pentagon; Ⓑ *(amerikan. Verteidigungsministerium)* Pentagon

**Penta-:** ~**gramm** *das* pentagram; ~**meter** /-ˈ---/ *der (Verslehre)* pentameter

**Pentatonik** /pɛntaˈto:nɪk/ *die;* ~ *(Musik)* pentatonic scale

**Pent·haus** /ˈpɛnt-/ *das,* **Penthouse** /ˈpɛnthaʊs/ *das;* ~, ~**s** penthouse

**Penunse** /peˈnʊnzə/ *die;* ~, ~**n**, **Penunze** /peˈnʊntsə/ *die;* ~, ~**n** *(ugs.)* ~**[n]** cash; dough *(coll.)*

**Pep** /pɛp/ *der;* ~**[s]** *(ugs.)* pep *(sl.)*; zip; ~ **haben** be dynamic *or* full of zip

**Peperoni** /pepeˈro:ni/ *die;* ~, ~: chilli

**Pepita** /peˈpi:ta/ *der od. das;* ~**s**, ~**s** shepherd's check

**Pepsin** /pɛˈpsi:n/ *das;* ~**s**, ~**e** *(Med.)* pepsin

**per** /pɛr/ *Präp. mit Akk.* Ⓐ *(mittels)* by; ~ **Post** by post; ~ **Adresse X** care of X; c/o X; ⇨ *auch* **Anhalter**; **du**; **Eilbote**; **Einschreiben**; **Nachnahme**; Ⓑ *(Kaufmannsspr.: [bis] zum)* by; *(am)* on; ~ **Jahresende** by the end of the year; ~ **sofort** immediately; as of now; Ⓒ *(Kaufmannsspr.: pro)* per; **etw.** ~ **Kilo/Stück verkaufen** sell sth. by the kilo/by the piece *or* separately

**per definitionem** /- definiˈtsi̯o:nɛm/ *Adv. (geh.)* by definition

**perennierend** /pɛrɛˈni:rənt/ *Adj. (Biol., Geogr., fig.)* perennial

**Perf.** *Abk.* **Perfekt** perf.

**perfekt** /pɛrˈfɛkt/ ❶ *Adj.* Ⓐ *(hervorragend)* outstanding; first-rate; *(vollkommen)* perfect ‹crime, host›; faultless ‹English, French, etc.›; **eine** ~**e Sekretärin** a fully accomplished secretary; Ⓑ *(ugs.: endgültig, abgeschlossen)* finalized; concluded; ~ **sein/werden** ‹contract, deal› be concluded *or* finalized; ‹scandal, defeat› be complete; ~ **machen** finalize ‹contract, date, booking, deal›; complete ‹disaster›. ❷ *adv.* Ⓐ *(hervorragend)* outstandingly well; *(vollkommen)* ‹fit, work, etc.› perfectly; ~ **beherrschen** have a complete mastery of ‹language, material›; play ‹game› with complete mastery; **er spricht** ~ **Englisch** he speaks faultless *or* perfect English; Ⓑ *(ugs.: vollständig)* good and proper *(coll.)*; **er hat sich** ~ **blamiert** he made a complete fool of himself

**Perfekt** /ˈpɛrfɛkt/ *das;* ~**s**, ~**e** *(Sprachw.)* perfect [tense]

**Perfektion** /pɛrfɛkˈtsi̯o:n/ *die;* ~: perfection; **handwerkliche/technische** ~: mastery of a craft/technical mastery; **etw. mit [großer]** ~ **ausführen/spielen** do/play sth. to perfection; do/play sth. with great mastery; **Reitkunst in höchster** *od.* **absoluter** ~: the art of riding at its most perfect

**perfektionieren** *tr. V.* perfect

**Perfektionismus** *der;* ~: perfectionism

**Perfektionist** *der;* ~**en**, ~**en**, **Perfektionistin** *die;* ~, ~**nen** perfectionist

**perfektionistisch** ❶ *Adj.* perfectionist ‹standards etc.›. ❷ *adv.* in a perfectionist manner

**perfektiv** /ˈpɛrfɛkti:f/ *Adj. (Sprachw.)* perfective

**perfid** /pɛrˈfi:t/, **perfide** *(geh.)* ❶ *Adj.* perfidious. ❷ *adv.* perfidiously

**Perfidie** /pɛrfiˈdi:/ *die;* ~, ~**n** *(geh.)* perfidy

**Perforation** /pɛrforaˈtsi̯o:n/ *die;* ~, ~**en** *(Technik, Med.)* perforation

**perforieren** *tr. V. (Technik, Med.)* perforate

**Pergament** /pɛrgaˈmɛnt/ *das;* ~**[e]s**, ~**e** parchment; *(bes. für Bucheinbände)* vellum

**Pergament·band** *der* vellum-bound volume

**pergamenten** *Adj.* Ⓐ parchment; vellum ‹binding›; vellum-bound ‹book›; Ⓑ *(wie aus Pergament)* ‹skin, face› like parchment

**Pergament·papier** *das* greaseproof paper

**Pergola** /ˈpɛrgola/ *die;* ~, **Pergolen** pergola

**Periode** /peˈri̯o:də/ *die;* ~, ~**n** Ⓐ *(auch Chemie, Physik, Technik, Astron., Met., Sprachw., Musik)* period; *(Geol.)* era; **sie hat ihre** ~ **nicht bekommen** she didn't get *or* have her period; Ⓑ *(Math.)* repetend; period; **3,3** ~: 3.3 recurring

**Perioden·system** *das (Chemie)* periodic system; *(grafische Darstellung)* periodic table

**Periodikum** /peˈri̯o:dikʊm/ *das;* ~**s**, **Periodika** periodical

**periodisch** ❶ *Adj.* Ⓐ *(regelmäßig)* regular; ‹meeting, statement of account› at regular intervals; *(Chemie)* periodic ‹system›; **eine** ~**e Dezimalzahl** *(Math.)* a recurring decimal; Ⓑ *(zeitweilig)* sporadic ‹moods etc.›. ❷ *adv.* Ⓐ *(regelmäßig)* regularly; at regular intervals; Ⓑ *(zeitweilig)* periodically; from time to time

**peripher** /periˈfe:ɐ̯/ ❶ *Adj. (auch Anat., fig.)* peripheral; ~**e Stadtteile** districts on the outskirts of the town. ❷ *adv. (auch Anat., fig.)* peripherally; **die Siedlung liegt** ~: the estate is on the outskirts; **ein Thema nur** ~ **behandeln** just touch on a subject

**Peripherie** /perifeˈri:/ *die;* ~, ~**n** Ⓐ periphery; *(einer Stadt)* outskirts *pl.*; fringe; *(Geom.: Begrenzungslinie)* circumference; **die** ~ **des Körpers** the peripheral areas of the body; Ⓑ *(Datenverarb.: periphere Geräte)* peripherals *pl.*

**Peripherie·gerät** *das (DV)* peripheral device; peripheral

**Periskop** /periˈsko:p/ *das;* ~**s**, ~**e** periscope

**Peristaltik** /periˈstaltɪk/ *die;* ~ *(Physiol.)* peristalsis

**Perkussion** *die;* ~, ~**nen** percussion

**Perkussionist** *der;* ~**en**, ~**en**, **Perkussionistin** *die;* ~, ~**nen** percussionist

**perkutan** /pɛrkuˈta:n/ *Adj. (Med.)* percutaneous

**Perle** /ˈpɛrlə/ *die;* ~, ~**n** Ⓐ *(auch fig.)* pearl; ~**n vor die Säue werfen** *(fig. ugs.)* cast pearls before swine; ⇨ *auch* **Krone** A; Ⓑ *(aus Holz, Glas o. Ä.)* bead; *(Tröpfchen)* drop; *(Bläschen beim Sekt usw.)* bubble; Ⓒ *(ugs. scherzh.: Hausgehilfin)* [invaluable] home help

**perlen** *itr. V.* Ⓐ *auch mit sein* **auf etw.** *(Dat.)* ~: form pearls on sth.; ‹dew› form droplets on sth.; **der Schweiß perlte ihm auf der Stirn** beads of perspiration stood out on his brow; Ⓑ *mit sein* **von etw.** ~ ‹dew, sweat› trickle *or* drip from sth.; **Tränen perlten über ihre Wangen** tears trickled *or* rolled down her cheeks; Ⓒ *(Bläschen bilden)* ‹champagne etc.› sparkle, bubble; Ⓓ *(melodisch ertönen)* ‹laughter, music› ripple

**perlen-, Perlen-:** ~**bestickt** *Adj.* embroidered *or* decorated with pearls *postpos.;* ~**fischer** *der* pearl fisher; ~**fischerei** *die* pearl fishing; ~**fischerin** *die* ⇨ ~**fischer**; ~**kette** *die* string of pearls; pearl necklace; *(mit Holz~ usw.)* string of beads; bead necklace; ~**kollier** *das* pearl necklace; ~**schnur** *die* string of pearls; *(mit Holz~ usw.)* string of beads; ~**stickerei** *die* pearl embroidery; *(mit Holz~ usw.)* bead embroidery; ~**taucher** *der,* ~**taucherin** *die* pearl diver

**perl-, Perl-:** ~**garn** *das* pearl cotton; ~**grau** *Adj.* pearl-grey; ~**huhn** *das* guineafowl; ~**muschel** *die* pearl oyster; ~**muster** *das* moss stitch; ~**mutt** /-mʊt/ *das;* ~~**s**, ~**mutter** *die;* ~~ *od. das;* ~~**s** mother-of-pearl; ~**muttern** *Adj.* mother-of-pearl; *(fig.: wie Perlmutter)* like mother-of-pearl *postpos.*

**Perlon** Ⓦⓩ *das;* ~**s** ≈ nylon

**Perlon·strumpf** *der* ≈ nylon stocking

**Perl-:** ~**schrift** *die* elite; ~**wein** *der* sparkling wine; ~**zwiebel** *die* pearl *or* cocktail onion

**permanent** /pɛrmaˈnɛnt/ ❶ *Adj.* permanent ‹institution, deficit, crisis›; constant ‹danger, threat, squabble›. ❷ *adv.* constantly

**Permanenz** /pɛrmaˈnɛnts/ *die;* ~: permanence; **in** ~: permanently; **in** ~ **tagen** sit continuously; be in permanent session

**permissiv** /pɛrmɪˈsi:f/ *Adj. (Soziol., Psych.)* permissive

**per pedes** *Adv. (ugs.)* on Shank's pony

**Perpendikel** /pɛrpɛnˈdi:kl/ *der od. das;* ~**s**, ~ Ⓐ *(veralt.: einer Uhr)* pendulum; Ⓑ *(Schiffbau)* perpendicular

**perpetuieren** /pɛrpetuˈi:rən/ *tr. V. (geh.)* perpetuate

**Perpetuum mobile** /pɛrˈpɛ:tuʊm ˈmo:bilə/ *das;* ~~**[s]**, ~~**[s]** *od.* **Perpetua mobilia** Ⓐ *(utopische Maschine)* perpetual-motion machine; Ⓑ *(Musik)* perpetuum mobile

**perplex** /pɛrˈplɛks/ *(ugs.)* ❶ *Adj.* *(verblüfft)* baffled, puzzled (**über** + *Akk.* by); *(verwirrt)* bewildered. ❷ *adv.* ~ **dreinschauen** look baffled/bewildered

**Perron** /pɛˈrõ:/ *der;* ~**s**, ~**s** *(österr., schweiz.)* platform

**per saldo** /-ˈsaldo/ *(Kaufmannsspr.)* net; *(fig.: im Endeffekt)* on balance; ~ **rund 4 Millionen Verlust/Gewinn** a net loss/gain of about four million

**Persenning** /pɛrˈzɛnɪŋ/ *die;* ~, ~**e[n]** *od.* ~**s** Ⓐ *(bes. Seemannsspr.: Bezug)* tarpaulin; Ⓑ *(Textilind.: Segeltuch)* [waterproof] canvas

**Perser** /ˈpɛrzɐ/ *der;* ~**s**, ~ ▶553 Ⓐ Persian; Ⓑ ⇨ **Perserteppich**

**Perserin** *die;* ~, ~**nen** ▶553 Persian

**Perser-:** ~**katze** *die* Persian [cat]; ~**teppich** *der* Persian carpet; *(kleiner)* Persian rug

**Persianer** /pɛrˈzi̯a:nɐ/ *der;* ~**s**, ~: Persian lamb; *(*~*mantel)* Persian lamb coat

**Persianer·mantel** *der* Persian lamb coat

**Persien** /ˈpɛrzi̯ən/ *(das);* ~**s** Persia

**Persiflage** /pɛrziˈfla:ʒə/ *die;* ~, ~**n** [gentle] mocking *no indef. art.;* **eine** ~ **auf jmdn./etw.** a [gentle] satire of sb./sth.

**persiflieren** *tr. V.* satirize

**Persil·schein** /pɛrˈzi:l-/ *der (ugs. scherzh.)* certificate of blamelessness

**persisch** *Adj.* ▶553, ▶696 Persian; ⇨ *auch* **deutsch**; **Deutsch**; **Deutsche**[2]

**Person** /pɛrˈzo:n/ *die;* ~, ~**en** Ⓐ person; **eine männliche/weibliche** ~: a male/female; ~**en** *(als Gruppe)* people; **die Familie besteht aus fünf** ~**en** it is a family of five; ~**en sind bei dem Brand nicht umgekommen** there was no loss of life in the fire; **pro** ~: per person; **seine** *od.* **die eigene** ~ **zu wichtig nehmen** take oneself too seriously; **deine** ~**/die** ~ **des Kanzlers soll**

*old spelling (see note on page 1707)

**nicht erwähnt werden** you are/the Chancellor is not to be mentioned in person; **ich für meine ~ ...** I for my part ...; **sich in der ~ irren** get the wrong person; **der Minister in [eigener] ~:** the minister in person; **sie ist die Güte/Geduld in ~:** she is kindness/patience personified *or* itself; **Politiker und Lyriker in einer ~ sein** be a politician and a lyric poet rolled into one; **Fragen zur ~:** questions to sb. on his/her identity; **Angaben zur ~ machen** give one's personal details; **jmdn. zur ~ vernehmen** *od.* **befragen** (*Rechtsw.*) examine *or* question sb. concerning his/her identity; **eine natürliche/juristische ~** (*Rechtsw.*) a natural/juristic person; ⇨ *auch* **Ansehen** B; **B** (*in der Dichtung, im Film*) character; **die ~en der Handlung** the characters [in the action]; (*im Theater*) the dramatis personae; **komische** *od.* **lustige ~** (*Literaturw.*) [stock] comic figure; **C** (*emotional: Frau*) female (*derog./joc.*); **D** (*Sprachw.*) person; **in der dritten ~ Singular/Plural** in the third person singular/plural

**Personal** /pɛrzo'na:l/ *das;* **~s** **A** (*in einem Betrieb o. Ä.*) staff; (*hinsichtlich der Verwaltung*) personnel; **ungenügend/ausreichend mit ~ versehen** inadequately/adequately staffed; **das fliegende ~:** the flight personnel; the aircrews *pl.;* **B** (*im Haushalt*) servants *pl.;* [domestic] staff *pl.*

**Personal-:** **~ab·bau** *der* reduction in staff; (*in mehreren Abteilungen/Betrieben*) staff cuts *pl.;* **~ab·teilung** *die* personnel department; **~akte** *die* personal file *or* dossier; **~angaben** *Pl.* personal details *or* particulars; **~ausweis** *der* identity card; **~bedarf** *der* staffing requirements *pl.;* **~bestand** *der* number of staff *or* employees (+ *Gen.* in); **~büro** *das* personnel office; **~chef** *der,* **~chefin** *die* ▶159 personnel manager; **~einsparung** *die* saving in staff

**Personalien** /pɛrzo'na:li̯ən/ *Pl.* personal details *or* particulars; **die ~ angeben** give one's [personal] particulars

**personalisieren** *tr. V.* personalize; reduce ‹quarrel, relations, etc.› to a personal level

**Personal-:** **~kosten** *Pl.* (*Wirtsch., Verwaltung*) staff costs; **~mangel** *der* staff shortage; **~planung** *die* (*bes. Wirtsch.*) personnel planning; **~politik** *die* staff *or* personnel policy; (*bei der Einstellung von ~politik*) staffing policy; **~pronomen** *das* (*Sprachw.*) personal pronoun; **~rat** *der* **A** (*Ausschuss*) staff council (*for civil servants*); **B** (*einzelnes Mitglied*) staff council representative; **~rätin** *die* ⇨ **~rat** B; **~union** *die* **A** (*im Staatsrecht*) personal union; **B** (*Vereinigung von Ämtern*) combination of the functions (**zwischen** + *Dat.* of)

**Persönchen** /pɛr'zø:nçən/ *das;* **~s, ~:** little lady

**personell** /pɛrzo'nɛl/ **1** *Adj.* staff ‹changes, difficulties›; ‹savings› in staff; ‹questions, decisions› regarding staff *or* personnel. **2** *adv.* with regard to staff *or* personnel

**Personen-:** **~auf·zug** *der* passenger lift (*Brit.*) *or* (*Amer.*) elevator; **~beförderung** *die* (*Verkehrsw.*) passenger transport *no art.;* **~beförderung mit der Bahn** carrying passengers by rail; **~beschreibung** *die* personal description; **~gedächtnis** *das* memory for faces; **~gesellschaft** *die* (*Wirtsch.*) general partnership; **~kraftwagen** *der* (*bes. Amtsspr.*) private car *or* (*Amer.*) automobile; **~kreis** *der* group [of people]; **~kult** *der* (*abwertend*) personality cult; **~nah·verkehr** *der* local public transport; **~name** *der* personal name; **~register** *das* index of names; **~schaden** *der* (*Versicherungsw.*) physical *or* personal injury; **bei dem Unfall entstand kein ~schaden** nobody was injured in the accident; **Unfälle mit ~schaden** accidents in which injuries are/were sustained; **~stands·register** *das* register of births, marriages, and deaths; **~verkehr** *der* (*Verkehrsw.*) passenger transport *no art.;* **~verzeichnis** *das* **A** (**~register**) index of names; **B** (*im Drama*) list of characters; **~waage** *die* scales *pl.;* **~wagen** *der* **A** (*Auto*) [private] car; automobile (*Amer.*); (*im Unterschied zum Lastwagen*) passenger car *or* (*Amer.*) automobile; **B** (*bei Zügen*) passenger coach; **~zug** *der* slow *or* stopping train; (*im Unterschied zum Güterzug*) passenger train

**Personifikation** /pɛrzonifika'ts̯i̯o:n/ *die;* **~, ~en** personification

**personifizieren** /pɛrzonifi'ts̯i:rən/ *tr. V.* personify; **das personifizierte schlechte Gewissen** the very picture *or* personification of a guilty conscience

**Personifizierung** *die;* **~, ~en** personification

**persönlich** /pɛr'zø:nlıç/ **1** *Adj.* personal; **er findet für jeden ein ~es Wort** he has a friendly word for everyone; **etw. steht jmdm. zur ~en Verfügung** sth. is available to sb. for his/her own *or* personal use; **eine ~e Bemerkung** an observation from one's personal point of view; **eine ~e Frage/Bemerkung** (*zur anderen Person*) a personal question/observation; **~ werden** get personal; **~es Fürwort** (*Sprachw.*) personal pronoun. **2** *adv.* personally; (*auf Briefen*) 'private [and confidential]'; **sich um alles ~ kümmern** see to everything personally *or* oneself; **~ erscheinen/gehen/kommen** appear/go/come in person; **nimm doch nicht gleich alles [so] ~!** don't take everything so personally!

**Persönlichkeit** *die;* **~, ~en** **A** (*Wesensart*) personality; **B** (*Mensch*) person of character; **eine/keine ~ sein** have a strong personality/lack personality; **C** (*herausragende Person*) personality; **~en des öffentlichen Lebens** public figures

**Persönlichkeits-:** **~recht** *das* (*Rechtsw.*) right to live one's own life; **~spaltung** *die* (*Psych.*) split personality; **~wahl** *die* (*Politik*) **A** *electoral system in which votes are cast for a candidate rather than a party;* **B** (*Wahl mit starken Persönlichkeiten*) personality contest; **diese Wahl war eine reine ~wahl** this election was fought purely on the basis of personalities

**Perspektiv** /pɛrspɛk'ti:f/ *das;* **~s, ~e** [handheld] telescope

**Perspektive** /pɛrspɛk'ti:və/ *die;* **~, ~n** (*Optik, bild. Kunst, auch fig.*) perspective; (*Blickwinkel*) angle; viewpoint; (*Zukunftsaussicht*) prospect; **aus soziologischer ~/aus der ~ des Soziologen** (*fig.*) from a sociological viewpoint/the viewpoint of a sociologist; **aus dieser ~ [gesehen]** (*fig.*) [seen] from this point of view; **eine neue ~ gewinnen** (*fig.*) gain a new perspective *or* aspect

**perspektivisch** **1** *Adj.* ‹drawing etc.› in perspective; ‹effect, narrowing, etc.› of perspective; **~e Verkürzung** foreshortening. **2** *adv.* in perspective; **~ verkürzen** foreshorten

**Peru** /pe'ru:/ *(das);* **~s** Peru

**Peruaner** /pe'ru̯a:nɐ/ *der;* **~s, ~, Peruanerin** *die;* **~, ~nen** Peruvian

**peruanisch** *Adj.* Peruvian

**Perücke** /pɛ'rʏkə/ *die;* **~, ~n** wig

**pervers** /pɛr'vɛrs/ (*abwertend*) **1** *Adj.* **A** (*bes. in sexueller Hinsicht*) perverted; (*fig.: gegen jede Vernunft*) perverse; **ein ~er Mensch** a pervert; **B** (*ugs.: empörend, schändlich*) outrageous; scandalous. **2** *adv.* in a perverted manner; **~ veranlagt sein** be of a perverted disposition

**Perversion** /pɛrvɛr'zi̯o:n/ *die;* **~, ~en** perversion

**Perversität** /pɛrvɛrzi'tɛ:t/ *die;* **~, ~en** **A** (*Eigenschaft*) perversion; **B** (*Handlung*) perversity; (*sexuell*) perverted act

**pervertieren** /pɛrvɛr'ti:rən/ **1** *tr. V.* pervert; (*verderben*) corrupt. **2** *itr. V.; mit sein* become perverted (**zu** into)

**perzentuell** /pɛrts̯ɛn'tu̯ɛl/ (*österr.*) ⇨ **prozentual**

**Perzeption** /pɛrts̯ɛp'ts̯i̯o:n/ *die;* **~, ~en** (*Philos., Psych., Physiol.*) perception

**perzeptiv** /pɛrts̯ɛp'ti:f/ *Adj.* (*Philos., Psych., Physiol.*) perceptive

**pesen** /'pe:zn̩/ *itr. V.; mit sein* (*ugs.*) dash; (*mit Fahrzeug*) race

**Pessar** /pɛ'sa:ɐ̯/ *das;* **~s, ~e** pessary

**Pessimismus** /pɛsi'mısmʊs/ *der;* **~:** pessimism

**Pessimist** *der;* **~en, ~en, Pessimistin** *die;* **~, ~nen** pessimist

**pessimistisch** **1** *Adj.* pessimistic. **2** *adv.* pessimistically; **etw. ~ sehen** *od.* **betrachten** take a pessimistic view of sth.; **sich zu etw. ~ äußern** express a pessimistic view on sth.

**Pest** /pɛst/ *die;* **~** ▶474 plague; (*fig.: Mensch, Ungeziefer*) pest; menace; **ich hasse ihn/es wie die ~** (*ugs.*) I hate his guts/can't stand it (*coll.*); **wie die ~ stinken** (*salopp*) stink to high heaven (*coll.*)

**Pest-:** **~beule** *die* [pestilential] bubo; **~gestank** *der* (*abwertend*) foul stench; **~hauch** *der* (*geh.*) miasma

**Pestilenz** /pɛsti'lɛnts̯/ *die;* **~, ~en** (*veralt.*) pestilence (*arch.*); plague (*lit. or fig.*)

**Pestizid** /pɛsti'ts̯i:t/ *das;* **~s, ~e** pesticide

**Pest·kranke** *der/die* person stricken with the plague

**Peter**[1] /'pɛ:tɐ/ *(der)* Peter

**Peter**[2] *der;* **~s, ~** (*ugs.*) fellow; **ein vergesslicher/dummer ~:** a forgetful/silly old thing (*coll.*); **Schwarzer ~** (*Kartenspiel*) ≈ old maid (*with a black cat card instead of an old maid*); **jmdm. den Schwarzen ~ zuschieben** *od.* **zuspielen** (*fig.*) pass the buck to sb. (*coll.*)

**Petersilie** /petɐ'zi:li̯ə/ *die;* **~:** parsley; **ihm ist die ~ verhagelt** (*ugs.*) he's down in the dumps

**Peters·kirche** *die:* **die ~:** St Peter's

**Peter·wagen** *der* (*ugs.*) [police] patrol car; panda car (*Brit.*)

**Petition** /peti'ts̯i̯o:n/ *die;* **~, ~en** (*Amtsspr.*) petition

**Petitions-:** **~aus·schuss,** ***~aus·schuß** *der* petitions committee (*in W. German parliaments*); **~recht** *das* right of petition

**Petrarca** /pe'trarka/ *(der)* Petrarch

**Petri Heil** /'pe:tri-/ (*Gruß der Angler*) good fishing!; make a good catch!

**Petri·jünger** *der,* **Petri·jüngerin** *die* (*ugs. scherzh.*) angling buff (*coll.*)

**Petro-** /'petro:-/: **~chemie** *die* **A** (*Wissenschaft*) petrochemistry; **B** (*Erdölindustrie*) petrochemicals industry; **~dollar** *der* (*Wirtsch.*) petrodollar

**Petrol** /pe'tro:l/ *das;* **~s** (*schweiz.*), **Petroleum** /pe'tro:leʊm/ *das;* **~s** **A** paraffin (*Brit.*); kerosene (*Amer.*); **B** (*veralt.*) ⇨ **Erdöl**

**Petroleum-:** **~kocher** *der* paraffin (*Brit.*) *or* (*Amer.*) kerosene stove; **~lampe** *die* paraffin (*Brit.*) *or* (*Amer.*) kerosene lamp

**Petrus** /'pe:trʊs/ *(der);* **Petrus** *od.* **Petri** **A** (*christl. Rel.: Apostel*) St Peter; **B** (*Patron des Wetters*) the clerk of the weather; **wenn ~ mitspielt** if [the clerk of] the weather doesn't let us down

**Petschaft** /'pɛtʃaft/ *das;* **~s, ~e** seal; (*zur Beglaubigung od. als Unterschrift*) signet

**Petticoat** /'pɛtıkoʊt/ *der;* **~s, ~s** [stiffened] petticoat

**Petting** /'pɛtıŋ/ *das;* **~[s], ~s** petting; **[mit jmdm.] ~ machen** have a petting session [with sb.]

**Petunie** /pe'tu:ni̯ə/ *die;* **~, ~n** (*Bot.*) petunia

**Petze** *die;* **~, ~n** (*Schülerspr. abwertend*) telltale; sneak (*Brit. school coll.*)

**petzen** (*Schülerspr.*) **1** *itr. V.* tell tales; sneak (*Brit. school coll.*). **2** *tr. V.* **~, dass ...** tell teacher/sb.'s parents that ...

**Petzer** *der;* **~s, ~** (*Schülerspr. abwertend*) telltale; sneak (*Brit. school coll.*); tattletale (*Amer. school sl.*)

**Petz·liese** *die* (*Schülerspr. abwertend*) [girl who is a] telltale

**peu à peu** /pøa'pø/ *Adv.* bit by bit

**Pf** *Abk.* **Pfennig**

**Pfad** /pfa:t/ *der;* **~[e]s, ~e** **A** path; **krumme ~e** *od.* **auf krummen ~en wandeln** (*fig. geh.*) deviate from the straight and narrow; **vom ~ der Tugend abweichen**

P

(*fig. geh.*) stray from the path of virtue; ⇒ *auch* **austreten** 1 B **B** (*DV*) path

**Pfad-: ~finder** *der* Scout; **er ist bei den ~n** he is in the Scouts; **~finderin** *die* Guide (*Brit.*); girl scout (*Amer.*); **sie ist bei den ~nen** she is in the Guides (*Brit.*) *or* (*Amer.*) girl scouts

**Pfaffe** /ˈpfafə/ *der;* **~n, ~n** (*abwertend*) cleric; Holy Joe (*coll. derog.*)

**pfäffisch** /ˈpfɛfɪʃ/ *Adj.* (*abwertend*) priestly; (*frömmelnd*) sanctimonious

**Pfahl** /pfa:l/ *der;* **~[e]s, Pfähle** /ˈpfɛ:lə/ post; stake; (*Bauw.: Stütze für Gebäude*) pile; **[jmdm.] ein ~ im Fleisch[e] sein** be a thorn in sb.'s flesh

**Pfahl-: ~bau** *der; Pl.* **~~ten** pile dwelling; **~dorf** *das* pile-village

**pfählen** /ˈpfɛ:lən/ *tr. V.* **A** (*Landw.*) stake ‹trees etc.›; **B** (*hist.: hinrichten*) impale

**Pfahl-: ~werk** *das* pilework; piling; **~wurzel** *die* (*Bot.*) taproot

**Pfalz** /pfalts/ *die;* **~, ~en A** (*Gebiet*) **die ~:** the Palatinate; **B** (*hist.: Palast*) [imperial *or* royal] palace

**Pfälzer** /ˈpfɛltsɐ/ ❶ *der;* **~s, ~ A** (*Person*) inhabitant/native of the Palatinate; **B** (*Wein*) wine from the Palatinate. ❷ *indekl. Adj.* ‹wine etc.› from the Palatinate

**Pfälzerin** *die;* **~, ~nen** ⇒ **Pfälzer** 1

**Pfalz·graf** *der* (*hist.*) Count Palatine

**Pfand** /pfant/ *das;* **~[e]s, Pfänder** /ˈpfɛndɐ/ **A** security; pledge (*esp. fig.*); **etw. auf ~ leihen** lend sth. against a security; **etw. als** *od.* **in ~ nehmen/etw. als** *od.* **zum** *od.* **in ~ geben** take/give sth. as [a] security; **ich gebe** *od.* **setze meine Ehre/mein Leben dafür zum ~, dass ...** (*fig. geh.*) I pledge my honour/stake my life on it that ...; **als ~ seiner Liebe** (*geh.*) as a token of his love; **B** (*für leere Flaschen usw.*) deposit (**auf** + *Dat.* on); **[ein] ~ für etw. bezahlen** pay a deposit on sth.; **kostet die Flasche ~?** is there a deposit on the bottle?; **C** (*beim Pfänderspiel*) forfeit

**pfändbar** *Adj.* distrainable (*Law*) ‹goods, chattels›; attachable (*Law*) ‹wages etc.›

**Pfand·brief** *der* (*Wirtsch., Bankw.*) mortgage bond

**pfänden** /ˈpfɛndn̩/ *tr.* (*auch itr.*) *V.* impound, seize [under distress] (*Law*) ‹goods, chattels›; attach ‹wages etc.› (*Law*); **bei ihm wurde gepfändet, er ist gepfändet worden** the bailiffs have been on to him; execution was levied against him (*Law*)

**Pfänder** ⇒ **Pfand**

**Pfänder·spiel** *das* [game of] forfeits

**Pfand-: ~flasche** *die* returnable bottle (*on which a deposit is payable*); **~haus** *das* (*veralt.*), **~leihe** *die;* **~~, ~~n** pawnshop; pawnbroker's; **etw. auf die** *od.* **in die** *od.* **zur ~leihe bringen** take sth. to the pawnbroker's; **~leiher** *der;* **~~s, ~~, ~leiherin** *die;* **~~, ~~nen** ▶ 159 pawnbroker; **~recht** *das* (*Rechtsw.*) [right of] lien (**an** + *Dat.* on, upon); **~schein** *der* pawn ticket

**Pfändung** *die;* **~, ~en** seizure; distraint (*Law*); (*von Geldsummen, Vermögensrechten*) attachment (*Law*); **der Gerichtsvollzieher kam zur ~:** the bailiff came to seize *or* impound possessions

**Pfändungs·verfügung** *die* (*Rechtsw.*) garnishee *or* attachment order (*Law*)

**Pfand·verkauf** *der* sale of property put up as security; distress sale (*Law*)

**Pfanne** /ˈpfanə/ *die;* **~, ~n A** (*zum Braten, Backen*) [frying] pan; **sich** (*Dat.*) **ein paar Eier in die ~ schlagen** fry [up] some eggs; **jmdn. in die ~ hauen** (*ugs.*) (*kritisieren*) take sb. to pieces; (*ruinieren*) land sb. in trouble; (*vernichtend schlagen*) beat sb. hollow (*coll.*); **B** (*hist.: Zünd~*) [priming] pan; **etw. auf der ~ haben** (*ugs. fig.*) have sth. at the ready; **C** (*Geogr.: Senke*) pan; (*Salz~*) salt pan; **D** (*Hüttenw.*) [foundry] ladle; **E** (*Bett~*) bedpan; **F** (*Bauw.: Dach~*) pantile; **G** (*Anat.: Gelenk~*) socket

*old spelling (see note on page 1707)

**Pfannen·gericht** *das* (*Kochk.*) fried dish

**Pfann·kuchen** *der* **A** (*bes. südd.: Eierkuchen*) pancake; **B** (*Berliner ~*) doughnut; **aufgehen wie ein ~** (*ugs.*) turn into a real dumpling

**Pfarr-: ~amt** *das* **A** parish office; **B** (*Stellung*) pastorate; **~bezirk** *der* parish

**Pfarre** /ˈpfarə/ *die;* **~, ~n** (*veralt.*), **Pfarrei** /pfaˈrai/ *die;* **~, ~en A** (*Bezirk*) parish; **B** (*Dienststelle*) parish office; **C** ⇒ **Pfarrhaus**

**Pfarrer** /ˈpfarɐ/ *der;* **~s, ~** ▶ 91, ▶ 159 (*katholisch*) parish priest; (*evangelisch*) pastor; (*anglikanisch*) vicar; (*von Freikirchen*) minister; (*Militär~*) chaplain; padre; (*in der Anschrift*) **Herrn ~ Meyer** [the] Revd. Meyer; **Frau ~ Meyer** (*~in*) [the] Revd. Meyer; (*~sfrau*) Mrs Meyer

**Pfarrerin** *die;* **~, ~nen** [woman] pastor; (*in Freikirchen*) [woman] minister; **Frau ~ Schmidt** Pastor *or* [the] Revd. Schmidt

**Pfarrers·frau** *die* the pastor's wife; (*in Freikirchen*) minister's wife; (*anglikanisch*) vicar's wife

**Pfarr-: ~haus** *das* vicarage; (*katholisch*) presbytery; (*in Schottland*) manse; **~kirche** *die* parish church

**Pfau** /pfau/ *der;* **~[e]s, ~en** (*österr. auch:*) **~en, ~e** peacock; **er ist eben ein [eitler] ~** (*fig.*) he is as vain as a peacock

**Pfauen-: ~auge** *das* peacock butterfly; (*Nachtpfauenauge*) peacock moth; **~feder** *die* peacock feather

**Pfd.** *Abk.* **Pfund** lb.

**Pfeffer** /ˈpfɛfɐ/ *der;* **~s, ~ A** pepper; **roter ~:** cayenne [pepper]; red pepper; **spanischer ~:** paprika; **hingehen** *od.* **bleiben, wo der ~ wächst** (*ugs.*) go to hell (*coll.*); get lost (*coll.*); ⇒ *auch* **Hase** A; **Hintern**; **B** (*Textilw.*) **~ und Salz** pepper-and-salt; **C** (*ugs.: Schwung*) punch (*coll.*); zap (*coll.*); **dahinter steckt ~:** it's got plenty of zap (*coll.*) *or* (*coll.*) zing

**Pfeffer-: ~fresser** *der* (*Zool.*) toucan; **~gurke** *die* pickled gherkin; **~korn** *das* peppercorn; **~kuchen** *der* ≈ gingerbread

**Pfefferminz·bonbon** *der od. das* peppermint [sweet]

**Pfeffer·minze** *die* peppermint [plant]

**Pfefferminz-: ~likör** *der* peppermint liqueur; **~plätzchen** *das* peppermint drop; (*weich*) peppermint cream; **~tee** *der* peppermint tea

**Pfeffer·mühle** *die* pepper mill

**pfeffern** *tr. V.* **A** (*würzen*) season with pepper; **stark gepfeffert** very peppery; **B** (*ugs.: werfen*) chuck (*coll.*); (*mit Wucht*) fling; hurl; **jmdm. eine ~** (*salopp*) sock *or* biff sb. one (*coll.*); **eine gepfeffert kriegen** (*salopp*) get a clout *or* (*coll.*) biff; ⇒ *auch* **gepfeffert**

**Pfeffer-: ~nuss, *~nuß** *die* [small round] gingerbread biscuit; **~steak** *das* steak au poivre; pepper steak; **~strauch** *der* pepper plant; **~streuer** *der;* **~~s, ~~:** pepper pot; **~-und-Salz-Muster** *das* pepper-and-salt pattern

**pfeffrig** /ˈpfɛfrɪç/ *Adj.* peppery

**Pfeifchen** /ˈpfaifçən/ *das;* **~s, ~** (*fam.: Tabakpfeife*) pipe

**Pfeife** /ˈpfaifə/ *die;* **~, ~n A** (*Tabak~*) pipe; **~ rauchen** smoke a pipe; be a pipe smoker; **eine ~ rauchen** smoke *or* have a pipe; **B** (*Musikinstrument*) pipe; (*aus Zinn*) penny whistle; tin whistle; (*der Militärkapelle*) fife; (*Triller~, an einer Maschine usw.*) whistle; (*Orgel~*) [organ] pipe; **nach jmds. ~ tanzen** (*fig.*) dance to sb.'s tune; **C** (*salopp abwertend: Versager*) washout (*sl.*)

**pfeifen** ❶ *unr. itr. V.* **A** whistle; ‹bird› sing; pipe; ‹mouse› squeak; **dreimal kurz ~:** give three short whistles; **er pfiff vor Bewunderung** he gave a whistle of admiration; he whistled in admiration; **sie pfiff [nach] ihrem Hund/einem Taxi** she whistled her dog/for a taxi; **von den Rängen wurde laut gepfiffen und gebuht** there were loud catcalls and boos from the auditorium; **etwas** *od.* **es pfiff in der Leitung** there was a whistle *or* a whistling noise on the telephone line; **seine Lungen ~/es pfeift in seiner Brust** he wheezes in his lungs/chest; **~der Atem** wheezing [breath]; ⇒ *auch* **Loch** A; **B** *mit sein* **die Kugeln pfiffen ihm um die Ohren** the bullets whistled around him; **C** (*auf einer Trillerpfeife o. Ä.*) ‹policeman, referee, etc.› blow one's whistle; (*Sport: als Schiedsrichter fungieren*) act as referee; **er pfeift beim Endspiel** he is refereeing the final; **D** (*salopp*) **auf jmdn./etw. ~:** not give a damn about sb./sth.; **ich pfeife auf dein Geld** you can keep your money (*coll.*); **E** (*salopp: geständig sein*) squeal (*sl.*).
❷ *unr. tr. V.* **A** whistle ‹tune etc.›; ‹bird› pipe, sing ‹song›; (*auf einer Pfeife*) pipe, play ‹tune etc.›; (*auf einer Trillerpfeife o. Ä.*) blow ‹signal etc.› on one's whistle; **einen Elfmeter ~** (*Sport*) blow [the whistle] for a penalty; **sich** (*Dat.*) **eins ~** (*ugs.*) whistle [nonchalantly] to oneself; (*fig.: sich nichts daraus machen*) shrug one's shoulders; **ich pfeif dir was** (*salopp spött.*) go and get knotted (*coll.*); **B** (*Sport: als Schiedsrichter leiten*) referee ‹match›; **C** (*salopp: verraten*) let out ‹secret›; **wer hat dir das gepfiffen?** who let on to you about that? (*coll.*); **D** (*salopp: trinken*) **einen ~:** knock one back (*sl.*)

**Pfeifen-: ~deckel** *der* [pipe-]bowl lid; **~deckel!** (*ugs.*) no way! (*coll.*); **~kopf** *der* pipe bowl; **~raucher** *der*, **~raucherin** *die* pipe smoker; **~reiniger** *der;* **~~s, ~~:** pipe-cleaner; **~ständer** *der* pipe rack; **~stopfer** *der;* **~~s, ~~:** tobacco-stopper; **~tabak** *der* pipe tobacco; **~werk** *das* (*Musik*) [organ] pipes *pl.*; pipework

**Pfeifer** *der;* **~s, ~ A** (*Musik*) (*bes. hist.*) piper; (*in einer Militärkapelle*) fife player; **B** (*jmd., der pfeift*) whistler

**Pfeiferei** *die;* **~, ~en** (*abwertend*) whistling

**Pfeiferin** *die;* **~, ~nen** ⇒ **Pfeifer**

**Pfeif-: ~kessel** *der* whistling kettle; **~konzert** *das* chorus of catcalls; **~ton** *der; Pl.* **~töne** whistling sound

**Pfeil** /pfail/ *der;* **~[e]s, ~e** arrow; (*Wurfpfeil*) dart; **~ und Bogen** bow and arrow; **wie ein ~ davonschießen** be off like a shot *or* like lightning; **schnell wie ein ~:** as quick as lightning; **alle [seine] ~e verschossen haben** (*fig.*) have run out of arguments; ⇒ *auch* **Amor**

**Pfeiler** *der;* **~s, ~** (*Bauw., Bergbau* auch fig.) pillar; (*Brücken~*) pier

**pfeil-, Pfeil-: ~flügel** *der* (*Flugzeugtechnik*) swept-back wing; **~förmig** ❶ *Adj.* arrow-shaped; sagittate ‹leaf›; ❷ *adv.* **~förmig angeordnet** arranged in the shape of an arrow *postpos.*; **~gerade** ❶ *Adj.* [as] straight as an arrow *postpos.*; dead straight; ❷ *adv.* [as] straight as an arrow; **~gift** *das* arrow poison; **~richtung** *die:* **in ~richtung** in the direction of the arrow; **~schnell** ❶ *Adj.* lightning-swift; ❷ *adv.* like a shot; **~spitze** *die* arrowhead

**Pfennig** /ˈpfɛnɪç/ *der;* **~s, ~e** ▶ 337 pfennig; **es kostet 20 ~:** it costs 20 pfennig[s]; **hast du ein paar einzelne ~e?** have you any single pfennig pieces?; **eine Briefmarke zu 60 ~:** a 60-pfennig stamp; **er hat keinen ~ [Geld]** he hasn't a penny *or* (*Amer.*) cent; **es ist keinen ~ wert** (*ugs.*) it isn't worth a penny *or* (*Amer.*) a [red] cent; **bis auf den letzten ~:** down to the last penny *or* (*Amer.*) cent; **auf den ~ genau** correct to the last penny *or* (*Amer.*) cent; **auf den ~ sehen** (*ugs.*) watch *or* count every penny *or* (*Amer.*) cent; **nicht für fünf ~ Anstand/Verstand/Geschmack/Humor** *usw.* **haben** (*ugs.*) have not an ounce of respectability/common sense/have no taste/sense of humour whatsoever; **das interessiert mich nicht für fünf ~** (*ugs.*) that doesn't interest me in the slightest; **wer den ~ nicht ehrt, ist des Talers nicht wert** (*Spr.*) take care of the pennies and the pounds will look after themselves (*prov.*); ⇒ *auch* **Heller**; **Mark²** A; **umdrehen** 1

**pfennig-, Pfennig-: ~ab·satz** *der* stiletto heel; **~betrag** *der* amount of less than a mark; (*kleiner Betrag*) tiny amount; **~fuchser** /-fʊksɐ/ *der;* **~~s, ~~, ~fuchserin** *die;* **~~, ~~nen** (*ugs.*) penny-pincher;

**~groß** *Adj.* ≈ the size of a 1 p piece (*Brit.*) or (*Amer.*) a cent *postpos.*

**Pferch** /pfɛrç/ *der;* **~[e]s, ~e** pen

**pferchen** *tr. V.* cram; pack

**Pferd** /pfeːɐ̯t/ *das;* **~[e]s, ~e** Ⓐ horse; **zu ~[e]** on horseback; **aufs/vom ~ steigen** mount/dismount; **zu ~:** by horse; on horseback; **das hält ja kein ~ aus** (*ugs.*) that's more than flesh and blood can stand; **ich denk, mich tritt ein ~** (*salopp*) I'm absolutely flabbergasted; **man hat schon ~e kotzen sehen** (*salopp*) [you never know,] anything can happen; **immer sachte mit den jungen ~en** (*fig. ugs.*) not so fast! (*coll.*); **er ist das beste ~ im Stall** (*ugs.*) he is their/our number one man; **wie ein ~ arbeiten** (*ugs.*) work like a Trojan; **keine zehn ~e bringen mich dahin/dazu, es zu tun** (*ugs.*) wild horses would not drag me there/make me do it; **ihm gehen die ~e durch** (*ugs.*) he flies off the handle (*coll.*); **auf das falsche ~ setzen** (*fig.*) back the wrong horse; **die ~e scheu machen** (*ugs.*) put people off; **das ~ am** *od.* **beim Schwanze aufzäumen** (*ugs.*) put the cart before the horse; **mit ihr kann man ~e stehlen** (*ugs.*) she's game for anything; ⇒ *auch* **trojanisch**; Ⓑ (*Turngerät*) horse; Ⓒ (*Schachfigur*) knight

**Pferdchen** *das;* **~s, ~** Ⓐ (*kleines Pferd*) little horse; Ⓑ (*salopp: Prostituierte*) tart (*sl.*); hooker (*Amer. sl.*) (*working for a pimp*)

**Pferde-: ~anhänger** *der* ⇒ **~transportwagen**; **~apfel** *der* (*ugs.*) piece of horse dung; **~äpfel** horse droppings; horse dung; **~bremse** *die* (*Zool.*) horsefly; **~decke** *die* horse blanket; **~fleisch** *das* horsemeat; **~fuhrwerk** *das* horse and cart; **~fuhrwerke** horse-drawn carts; **~fuß** *der* Ⓐ (*fig.: Mangel, Nachteil*) snag; drawback; Ⓑ (*eines ~s*) horse's foot; (*des Teufels*) cloven hoof; **~gebiss**, ***~gebiß** *das* Ⓐ (*fig. ugs.*) **er hat ein ~gebiss** he has teeth *pl.* like a horse; Ⓑ (*eines ~s*) horse's teeth *pl.*; **~gesicht** *das* (*ugs.*) horsy face; **er hat ein ~gesicht** he has a face like a horse; **~händler** *der*, **~händlerin** *die* horse dealer; **~knecht** *der* (*veralt.*) groom; **~kopf** *der* horse's head; **~koppel** *die* paddock; **~länge** *die* length; **mit zwei ~längen Vorsprung siegen** win by two lengths (**vor** + *Dat.* from); **~metzger** *der* (*landsch.*) ⇒ **~schlachter**; **~mist** *der* horse manure; **~pfleger** *der*, **~pflegerin** *die* groom; **~rasse** *die* breed of horse; **~renn·bahn** *die* racecourse; **~rennen** *das* horse race; (*Sportart*) horseracing; **beim ~rennen sein** be at the races *pl.*; **~schlachter, ~schlächter** *der* (*bes. nordd.*) horse butcher; **~schlitten** *der* horse[-drawn] sleigh; **~schwanz** *der* horse's tail; (*fig.: Frisur*) ponytail; **~sport** *der* equestrian sport *no art.*; (*~rennen*) horseracing *no art.*; **~stall** *der* stable; **~stärke** *die* horsepower; **~transport·wagen** *der* horsebox; **~wagen** *der* (*für Güter*) cart; (*für Personen*) carriage; (*der amerikanischen Pioniere usw.*) wagon; **~wirt** *der*, **~wirtin** *die* fully qualified groom (*with veterinary training*); **~zucht** *die* horse breeding *no art.*

**pfiff** /pfɪf/ *1. u. 3. Pers. Sg. Prät. v.* **pfeifen**

**Pfiff** *der;* **~[e]s, ~e** Ⓐ whistle; Ⓑ (*ugs.: besonderer Reiz*) style; **mit ~:** stylish; with style; (*adv.*) stylishly; ‹cook› with flair; **der letzte** *od.* **richtige ~:** the finishing touch; that extra something; Ⓒ (*ugs.*) ⇒ **Dreh** A

**Pfifferling** /ˈpfɪfɐlɪŋ/ *der;* **~s, ~e** chanterelle; **keinen** *od.* **nicht einen ~ wert sein** (*ugs.*) be not worth a bean (*coll.*)

**pfiffig** ❶ *Adj.* smart; bright, clever ‹idea›; artful, knowing ‹smile, expression›. ❷ *adv.* artfully; cleverly; **jmdn. ~ ansehen/anlächeln** look/smile knowingly *or* artfully at sb.

**Pfiffikus** /ˈpfɪfikʊs/ *der;* **~[ses], ~se** (*ugs.*) smart lad

**Pfingsten** /ˈpfɪŋstn̩/ *das;* **~, ~:** Whitsun; **zu** *od.* (*bes. südd.*) **an ~:** at Whitsun; **habt ihr schöne ~ gehabt?** did you have a nice Whitsun?; ⇒ *auch* **Ostern**

**Pfingst-: ~feier·tag** *der:* **über die ~feiertage** over Whitsun; **an den ~feiertagen** on Whit Sunday and Whit Monday; **der erste/zweite ~feiertag** Whit Sunday/Monday; **~fest** *das* Whitsun [holiday]; (*Rel.*) Whitsun festival

**pfingstlich** ❶ *Adj.* Whitsuntide *attrib.*; (*Rel.*) pentecostal ‹miracle›. ❷ *adv.* **~ geschmückt** decorated for Whitsun *postpos.*

**Pfingst-: ~montag** *der* Whit Monday *no def. art.*; **~ochse** *der:* *in* **er sah aus/hatte sich herausgeputzt wie ein ~ochse** (*ugs.*) he looked like/was dressed up like a dog's dinner (*coll.*); **~rose** *die* peony; **~sonntag** *der* Whit Sunday *no def. art.*; **~woche** *die* week before Whitsun

**Pfirsich** /ˈpfɪrzɪç/ *der;* **~s, ~e** peach

**Pfirsich-: ~baum** *der* peach tree; **~blüte** *die* peach blossom; **~haut** *die* Ⓐ peach skin; Ⓑ (*fig.: Gesichtshaut*) peaches-and-cream complexion

**Pflänzchen** /ˈpflɛntsçən/ *das;* **~s, ~** Ⓐ little plant; Ⓑ (*fig.: Mensch*) **ein [zartes] ~:** a delicate creature

**Pflanze** /ˈpflantsə/ *die;* **~, ~n** Ⓐ plant; **~n fressend** (*Biol.*) herbivorous; Ⓑ (*ugs.: Mensch*) **du bist mir vielleicht eine ~!** you're a right one! (*coll.*); **eine echte Berliner ~** (*veralt.*) a genuine Berlin type

**pflanzen** ❶ *tr. V.* plant (**in** + *Akk.* in); (*fig.*) plant, stick ‹flag›. ❷ *refl. V.* (*ugs.*) plant oneself

**pflanzen-, Pflanzen-: ~farb·stoff** *der* Ⓐ (*pflanzlicher Farbstoff*) vegetable dye; Ⓑ (*Bot.: Pigment*) plant *or* vegetable pigment; **~fett** *das* vegetable fat; ***~fressend** ⇒ **Pflanze** A; **~fresser** *der* herbivore; **~kunde** *die* botany *no def. art.*; **~öl** *das* vegetable oil; **~reich** *das* plant kingdom; **~schutz·mittel** *das* [crop] pesticide; (*für den Garten*) garden pesticide; **~welt** *die* flora

**Pflanzer** *der;* **~s, ~, Pflanzerin** *die;* **~, ~nen** planter; plantation owner

**Pflanz-: ~gut** *das* seed stock; **~holz** *das* dibble; **~kartoffel** *die* seed potato

**pflanzlich** *Adj.* plant *attrib.* ‹life, motif›; vegetable ‹dye, fat›; (*vegetarisch*) vegetarian

**Pflänzling** /ˈpflɛntslɪŋ/ *der;* **~s, ~e** seedling

**Pflanzung** *die;* **~, ~en** Ⓐ plantation; Ⓑ (*das Pflanzen*) planting

**Pflaster** /ˈpflastɐ/ *das;* **~s, ~** Ⓐ (*Straßen~*) road surface; (*auf dem Gehsteig*) pavement; **~ treten** (*ugs.*) trail through the streets; Ⓑ (*ugs.: Ort*) **ein teures/gefährliches** *od.* **heißes ~:** an expensive/dangerous place *or* spot to be; **mir wird das ~ hier zu heiß** this place is getting too hot for me; Ⓒ (*Wund~*) sticking plaster

**Pflaster·maler** *der*, **Pflaster·malerin** *die* pavement artist

**pflastern** *tr.* (*auch itr.*) *V.* surface ‹road, path›; (*mit Kopfsteinpflaster, Steinplatten*) pave ‹street, path›; ⇒ *auch* **Vorsatz**

**Pflaster·stein** *der* paving stone; (*Kopfstein*) cobblestone

**Pflaume** /ˈpflaumə/ *die;* **~, ~n** Ⓐ plum; **getrocknete ~n** [dried] prunes; Ⓑ (*ugs. abwertend: Versager*) dead loss (*coll.*); (*Feigling*) baby; Ⓒ (*derb: Vulva*) pussy (*coarse*)

**pflaumen-, Pflaumen-: ~baum** *der* plum tree; **~kuchen** *der* plum flan; **~mus** *das* plum purée; **~saft** *der* plum juice; **~schnaps** *der* plum brandy; **~weich** *Adj.* (*ugs. abwertend*) weak-kneed; spineless

**Pflege** /ˈpfleːgə/ *die;* **~:** care; (*Maschinenpflege, Fahrzeugpflege*) maintenance; (*fig.: von Beziehungen, Kunst, Sprache*) cultivation; fostering; **die ~ des Körpers** personal hygiene; **die Blumen brauchen viel/kaum ~:** the flowers need a lot of/hardly any attention; **jmdn./etw. in ~** (*Akk.*) **nehmen** look after sb./sth.; **jmdm. etw.** *od.* **etw. bei jmdm. in ~** (*Akk.*) **geben** give sb. sth. to look after; entrust sth. to sb.'s care; **ein Kind in ~** (*Akk.*) **nehmen** look after a child; (*als ~eltern*) foster a child; **jmdm. ein Kind** *od.* **ein Kind bei jmdm. in ~** (*Akk.*) **geben** give sb. a child to look after; (*bei ~eltern*) have a child fostered by sb.; **bei jmdm. in ~** (*Dat.*) **sein** be looked after by sb.

**pflege-, Pflege-: ~bedürftig** *Adj.* needing care *or* attention *postpos.*; ‹person› in need of care; **~bedürftig sein** need looking after; need attention; **~eltern** *Pl.* foster-parents; **~fall** *der* person in [permanent] need of nursing; **ein ~fall sein/zum ~fall werden** be/become in [permanent] need of nursing; **~heim** *das* nursing home (*esp. Brit.*); **~kind** *das* foster-child; **~leicht** *Adj.* easy-care *attrib.* ‹textiles, flooring›; minimum-care *attrib.* ‹plant, pan›; **~leicht sein** require little attention *or* care; ‹cloth, clothing› be made of easy-care material; **~mutter** *die; Pl.* **~mütter** foster-mother

**pflegen** ❶ *tr. V.* look after; care for; care for, nurse ‹sick person›; care for, take care of ‹skin, teeth, floor›; look after, maintain ‹bicycle, car, machine›; look after, tend ‹garden, plants›; cultivate ‹relations, arts, interests›; foster ‹contacts, co-operation›; keep up, pursue ‹hobby›; **jmdn./ein Tier gesund ~:** nurse sb./an animal back to health; **Kontakt/den Umgang mit jmdm. ~:** keep in touch with/associate with sb. ❷ *itr. V.*; *mit Inf.* + *zu* **etw. zu tun ~:** be in the habit of doing sth.; usually do sth.; **..., wie er zu sagen pflegt/pflegte** ..., as he is wont to say/as he used to say; **er pflegte jeden Morgen um sieben Uhr aufzustehen** he used to get up every morning at seven. ❸ *refl. V.* take care of oneself; (*gesundheitlich*) look after oneself; **sie sollte sich mehr ~:** she should take more care of herself. ❹ *regelm.* (*veralt. auch unr.*) *itr. V.* (*geh.*) **einer Sache** (*Gen.*) **~:** indulge in sth.; **der Ruhe ~:** rest; take one's ease; ⇒ *auch* **gepflegt**

**Pflege·notstand** *der* health-care crisis

**Pfleger** *der;* **~s, ~** Ⓐ ▶ 159 (*Kranken~*) [male] nurse; Ⓑ ▶ 159 (*Tier~*) keeper

**Pflegerin** *die;* **~, ~nen** Ⓐ ▶ 159 (*Kranken~*) nurse; Ⓑ ▶ 159 (*Tier~*) keeper

**pflegerisch** *Adj.* nursing *attrib.*

**Pflege-: ~satz** *der* hospital [daily] rate; charge for a hospital bed [per day]; **~sohn** *der* foster-son; **~tochter** *die* foster-daughter; **~vater** *der* foster-father; **~versicherung** *die* [long-term] care insurance

**pfleglich** ❶ *Adj.* careful. ❷ *adv.* with care

**Pflegling** /ˈpfleːklɪŋ/ *der;* **~s, ~e** charge; (*Pflegekind*) foster-child; **unsere ~e** the children/animals in our care

**Pflegschaft** *die;* **~, ~en** (*Rechtsw.*) (*durch Pflegeeltern*) foster care; (*eines Vermögens*) trusteeship

**Pflicht** /pflɪçt/ *die;* **~, ~en** Ⓐ duty; **seine alltäglichen [kleinen] ~en** his everyday chores; **die ~ ruft** duty calls; **~ sein** be obligatory; **es ist seine [(*salopp*) verdammte** *od.* **verfluchte] ~ und Schuldigkeit** [damn it all,] it's his bounden duty; **jmdn. in die ~ nehmen** (*geh.*) make sb. discharge his/her duties; Ⓑ (*Sport*) compulsory exercises *pl.*

**pflicht-, Pflicht-: ~bewusst**, ***~bewußt** ❶ *Adj.* conscientious; **~bewusst sein** have a sense of duty; ❷ *adv.* conscientiously; with a sense of duty; **~bewusstsein**, ***~bewußtsein** *das* sense of duty; **~eifer** *der* zeal; **~eifrig** ❶ *Adj.* zealous; ❷ *adv.* zealously; full of zeal; **~erfüllung** *die* performance of one's duty; **in treuer/gewissenhafter ~erfüllung** faithfully/conscientiously following the path of duty; **~exemplar** *das* (*Verlagsw.*) deposit copy; **~fach** *das* compulsory subject; **es ist ~fach** it is a compulsory subject; **~gefühl** *das* sense of duty; **aus [bloßem] ~gefühl** [simply] from a sense of duty; **~gemäß** ❶ *Adj.* in accordance with one's duty *postpos.*; ❷ *adv.* in accordance with one's duty; **ich teile Ihnen ~gemäß mit, dass ...** it is my duty to inform you that ...

**-pflichtig** *Adj.* subject to ...; **beitrags~e Beschäftigung** occupation entailing the payment of insurance contributions; ⇒ *auch* **abgaben~**; **zuschlags~**

**pflicht-, Pflicht-: ~lektüre** *die* required reading; (*Schulw.*) set books *pl.*; **zur ~lektüre gehören, ~lektüre sein** be required reading; (*in der Schule*) be a set book/be set

P

books; **~schuldig** ❶ *Adj.* dutiful; (*höflich*) polite; ❷ *adv.* dutifully; (*höflich*) politely; **~teil** *der od. das:* (*Rechtsw.*) *portion of an estate that must go to the closest relation regardless of testator's dispositions;* legitimate portion; **jmdn. auf den** *od.* **das ~teil setzen** leave sb. nothing but the legal minimum; **~übung** *die* Ⓐ (*Sport*) compulsory exercise; Ⓑ (*fig.*) ritual exercise; (*Buch, Film usw.*) obligatory effort; **~um·tausch** *der* compulsory exchange of currency; **~vergessen** ❶ *Adj.* neglectful of one's duty *postpos.*; negligent ‹behaviour›; ❷ *adv.* negligently; **~verletzung** *die* breach of duty; **~versichert** *Adj.* compulsorily insured; **~versicherung** *die* compulsory insurance; **~verteidiger** *der*, **~verteidigerin** *die:* (*Rechtsw.*) *defense counsel appointed by the court;* assigned counsel; **~widrig** *Adj., adv.* in breach of one's duty *postpos.*

**Pflock** /pflɔk/ *der;* **~[e]s, Pflöcke** /'pflœkə/ peg; (*für Tiere*) stake

**pflog** /pflo:k/ (*veralt.*) *1. u. 3. Pers. Sg. Prät. v.* **pflegen** 4

**pflücken** /'pflʏkn̩/ *tr. V.* pick ‹flowers, fruit, hops›; **Kirschen in einen Korb ~:** pick cherries and put them in a basket

**Pflücker** *der;* **~s, ~, Pflückerin** *die;* **~, ~nen** ▶ 159 picker

**Pflück·maschine** *die* [mechanical] picker

**Pflug** /pflu:k/ *der;* **~[e]s, Pflüge** /'pfly:gə/ plough; **Land unter den ~ nehmen** (*geh.*) put land to the plough

**pflügen** /'pfly:gn̩/ *tr., itr. V.* plough; (*fig. geh.*) ‹ship› plough *or* carve a way through ‹waves, sea›

**Pflug·schar** *die* ploughshare

**Pforte** /'pfɔrtə/ *die;* **~, ~n** Ⓐ (*Tor*) gate; (*Tür*) door; (*Eingang*) entrance; **seine ~n öffnen/schließen** (*fig. geh.*) open/close its doors; **Pforzheim, die ~ zum Schwarzwald** (*fig.*) Pforzheim, the gateway to the Black Forest; Ⓑ (*Geogr.*) **die Westfälische ~:** the Minden Gap; the Porta Westfalica; **die Burgundische ~:** the Belfort Gap

**Pförtner** /'pfœrtnɐ/ *der;* **~s, ~** ▶ 159 Ⓐ porter; (*eines Wohnblocks, Büros*) doorkeeper; (*am Tor*) gatekeeper; Ⓑ ▶ 471 (*Anat.*) pylorus

**Pförtner·haus** *das* gatehouse; porter's lodge

**Pförtnerin** *die;* **~, ~nen** ▶ 159 ⇒ **Pförtner** A

**Pförtner·loge** *die* porter's lodge

**Pfosten** /'pfɔstn̩/ *der;* **~s, ~** Ⓐ post; (*Tür~*) jamb; Ⓑ (*Sport: Tor~*) [goal]post

**Pfosten·schuss, *Pfosten·schuß** *der* (*Ballspiele*) shot hitting the [goal]post

**Pfötchen** /'pfø:tçən/ *das;* **~s, ~:** [little] paw; **~ geben** hold out a paw; **[gib] ~!** [give us a] paw!

**Pfote** /'pfo:tə/ *die;* **~, ~n** Ⓐ paw; **die ~ geben** hold out a paw; **[gib die] ~!** [give us a] paw!; Ⓑ (*ugs.: Hand*) paw (*coll.*); mitt (*sl.*); **sich** (*Dat.*) **die ~n verbrennen** (*fig.*) burn one's fingers (*fig.*); **seine ~n in etw.** (*Dat.*)/**überall [drin] haben** (*fig. salopp*) have a hand in sth./everything; be mixed up in sth./everything; Ⓒ (*salopp abwertend: Schrift*) ⇒ **Klaue** D

**Pfriem** /pfri:m/ *der;* **~[e]s, ~e** awl

**Pfropf** /pfrɔpf/ *der;* **~[e]s, ~e** blockage; (*in der Vene*) clot; **ein ~ aus Haaren** a plug *or* (*Brit. coll.*) wodge of hair

**pfropfen**[1] *tr. V.* (*ugs.*) cram; stuff; **gepfropft voll** crammed [full]; packed

**pfropfen**[2] *tr. V.* (*Gartenbau*) graft ‹scion› (**auf** + *Akk.* on); improve ‹tree, vine› by grafting

**Pfropfen** *der* (*für Flaschen*) stopper; (*Korken*) cork; (*für Fässer*) bung

**Pfröpfling** /'pfrœpflɪŋ/ *der;* **~s, ~e** scion

**Pfropf-: ~messer** *das* grafting knife; **~reis** *das* scion

**Pfründe** /'pfrʏndə/ *die;* **~, ~n** Ⓐ (*kath. Kirche*) living; benefice; **auf einer ~ sitzen** hold a living; Ⓑ (*fig.*) sinecure

**Pfuhl** /pfu:l/ *der;* **~[e]s, Pfühle** /'pfy:lə/ muddy pool; (*fig.*) murky waters *pl.*; **ein ~ der Sünde** *od.* **Sittenlosigkeit** (*fig.*) a sink of iniquity

**pfui** /pfʊɪ/ *Interj.* Ⓐ (*Ekel ausdrückend*) ugh; yuck (*sl.*); (*zu Kindern, Hunden*) [ugh,] you mucky pup; (*hör auf*) stop that; **~ Teufel** *od.* **Deibel** *od.* **Spinne!** (*ugs.*) ugh *or* (*sl.*) yuck, how disgusting!; **das ist ~:** that's yucky (*sl.*) *or* disgusting; Ⓑ (*Missbilligung, Empörung ausdrückend*) ugh; really; (*Ruf*) boo; **~, schäm dich!** shame on you!; **Pfui** *od.* **~ rufen** boo

**Pfui·ruf** *der* boo

**Pfund** /pfʊnt/ *das;* **~[e]s, ~e** (*bei Maßangaben ungebeugt*) Ⓐ ▶ 353 (*Gewicht*) pound (*= 500 grams in German-speaking countries*); **zwei ~ Kartoffeln** two pounds of potatoes; **überflüssige ~e loswerden** ‹person› get rid of unwanted pounds; Ⓑ ▶ 337 (*Währungseinheit*) pound; **100 ~:** £100; one hundred pounds; **wie viel ist das in ~ [Sterling]?** how much is that in pounds [sterling]?; **mit seinem ~[e] wuchern** (*geh.*) make the most of one's capabilities

**pfundig** (*ugs.*) ❶ *Adj.* great (*coll.*); fantastic (*coll.*). ❷ *adv.* fantastically (*coll.*)

**Pfunds-: ~kerl** *der* (*ugs.*) great bloke (*Brit. coll.*); great guy (*coll.*); **~stimmung** *die* (*ugs.*) terrific atmosphere (*coll.*)

**pfund·weise** *Adv.* by the pound; **die könnte ich ~ essen** I could eat pounds of them

**Pfund·zeichen** *das* pound sign

**Pfusch** /pfʊʃ/ *der;* **~[e]s** Ⓐ (*ugs. abwertend*) **das ist ~:** it's a botch-up; **[großen] ~ machen** botch it [in a big way]; Ⓑ (*österr.: Schwarzarbeit*) work done on the side (*and not declared for tax*); (*nach Feierabend*) moonlighting (*coll.*); **etw. im ~ machen** do sth. on the side

**Pfusch·arbeit** *die* (*ugs. abwertend*) botch; botched-up job

**pfuschen** *itr. V.* Ⓐ (*ugs. abwertend*) botch it; do a botched-up job; Ⓑ (*österr.: schwarzarbeiten*) do work on the side (*not declared for tax*); (*nach Feierabend*) moonlight (*coll.*)

**Pfuscher** *der;* **~s, ~** Ⓐ (*ugs. abwertend*) botcher; bungler; Ⓑ (*österr.: Schwarzarbeiter*) person doing work on the side; (*nach Feierabend*) moonlighter (*coll.*)

**Pfuscherei** *die;* **~, ~en** botching *no pl.*; (*Pfuscharbeit*) botched-up job

**Pfuscherin** *die;* **~, ~nen** ⇒ **Pfuscher**

**Pfütze** /'pfʏtsə/ *die;* **~, ~n** puddle

**PH** *Abk.* **Pädagogische Hochschule**

**Phalanx** /'fa:laŋks/ *die;* **~, Phalangen** (*hist., fig.*) phalanx

**phallisch** /'falɪʃ/ (*geh.*) ❶ *Adj.* phallic. ❷ *adv.* like a phallus

**Phallus** /'falʊs/ *der;* **~, Phalli** *od.* **Phallen,** (*auch:*) **~se** (*geh.*) phallus

**Phallus-: ~kult** *der* phallic cult; **~symbol** *das* phallic symbol

**Phänomen** /fɛno'me:n/ *das;* **~s, ~e** phenomenon; **er ist ein ~** (*ugs.*) he is phenomenal

**phänomenal** /fɛnome'na:l/ ❶ *Adj.* phenomenal. ❷ *adv.* phenomenally

**Phänomenologie** *die* (*Philos.*) phenomenology

**Phantasie** *usw.* ⇒ **Fantasie** *usw.*

**Phantast** *usw.* ⇒ **Fantast** *usw.*

**Phantom** /fan'to:m/ *das;* **~s, ~e** phantom; illusion; **einem ~ nachjagen** (*fig.*) chase [after] an illusion *or* a shadow

**Phantom-: ~bild** *das* Ⓐ (*Kriminalistik*) Identikit [picture] ®; (*aus Fotos*) photofit picture; Ⓑ (*Fot.*) see-through *or* cut-away picture; **~schmerz** *der* phantom limb [pain]

**Pharao** /'fa:rao/ *der;* **~s, ~nen** /fara'o:nən/ Pharaoh

**Pharisäer** /fari'zɛ:ɐ/ *der;* **~s, ~** (*auch fig.*) Pharisee

**pharisäerhaft** *Adj.* (*geh.*) holier-than-thou

**Pharisäerin** *die;* **~, ~nen** pharisee

**Pharisäertum** *das;* **~s** (*geh.*) Pharisaism; hypocrisy

**Pharma-: ~berater** *der*, **~beraterin** *die* ⇒ **~referent**; **~industrie** *die* pharmaceutical industry

**Pharmakologe** /farmako'lo:gə/ *der;* **~n, ~n** pharmacologist

**Pharmakologie** /farmakolo'gi:/ *die;* **~:** pharmacology *no art.*

**Pharmakologin** *die;* **~, ~nen** pharmacologist

**pharmakologisch** ❶ *Adj.* pharmacological. ❷ *adv.* pharmacologically; **~ ausgebildet** trained in pharmacology *postpos.*

**Pharma·referent** *der*, **Pharma·referentin** *die* pharmaceutical representative

**Pharmazeut** /farma'tsɔyt/ *der;* **~en, ~en** pharmacist

**Pharmazeutik** /farma'tsɔytɪk/ *die;* **~** ⇒ **Pharmazie**

**Pharmazeutin** *die;* **~, ~nen** pharmacist

**pharmazeutisch** ❶ *Adj.* pharmaceutical. ❷ *adv.* pharmaceutically; **~ ausgebildet** with pharmaceutical training *postpos.*

**Pharmazie** /farma'tsi:/ *die;* **~:** pharmaceutics *sing., no art.*; pharmaceutical chemistry *no art.*

**Phase** /'fa:zə/ *die;* **~, ~n** phase

**Phasen·verschiebung** *die* (*Physik*) phase difference

**-phasig** *Adj.* -phase

**Phenacetin** /fenatse'ti:n/ *das;* **~s** (*Pharm.*) phenacetin

**Philanthrop** /filan'tro:p/ *der;* **~en, ~en, Philanthropin** *die;* **~, ~nen** (*geh.*) philanthropist

**philanthropisch** (*geh.*) ❶ *Adj.* philanthropic. ❷ *adv.* philanthropically

**Philatelie** /filate'li:/ *die;* **~:** philately *no art.*

**Philatelist** *der;* **~en, ~en, Philatelistin** *die;* **~, ~nen** philatelist

**Philharmonie** /fɪlharmo'ni:/ *die;* **~, ~n** Ⓐ (*Orchester*) philharmonic [orchestra]; Ⓑ (*Gebäude, Saal*) philharmonic hall

**Philharmoniker** /fɪlhar'mo:nikɐ/ *der;* **~s, ~, Philharmonikerin** *die;* **~, ~nen** member of a/the philharmonic orchestra; **die Wiener Philharmoniker** the Vienna Philharmonic Orchestra

**philharmonisch** *Adj.* philharmonic

**Philipp** /'fi:lɪp/ (*der*) Philip

**Philippika** /fi'lɪpika/ *die;* **~, Philippiken** (*geh.*) philippic; diatribe

**Philippinen** /fɪlɪ'pi:nən/ *Pl.* Philippines

**Philister** /fi'lɪstɐ/ *der;* **~s, ~, Philisterin** *die;* **~, ~nen** (*geh.*) Philistine

**philister·haft, philiströs** (*geh.*) ❶ *Adj.* Philistine. ❷ *adv.* in a Philistine manner

**Philologe** /filo'lo:gə/ *der;* **~n, ~n** teacher/student of language and literature; philologist (*Amer.*)

**Philologie** *die;* **~, ~n** study of language and literature; philology *no art.* (*Amer.*)

**Philologin** *die;* **~, ~nen** ⇒ **Philologe**

**philologisch** ❶ *Adj.* literary and linguistic; philological (*Amer.*). ❷ *adv.* from a literary and linguistic viewpoint; philologically (*Amer.*)

**Philo·semit** *der*, **Philo·semitin** *die* [keen] supporter of the Jewish/Israeli cause

**Philosoph** /filo'zo:f/ *der;* **~en, ~en** ▶ 159 philosopher

**Philosophie** *die;* **~, ~n** philosophy

**philosophieren** *itr.* (*auch tr.*) *V.* philosophize

**Philosophin** *die;* **~, ~nen** ▶ 159 philosopher

**philosophisch** ❶ *Adj.* philosophical; ‹dictionary, principles› of philosophy; **~e Fakultät** (*Hochschulw.*) ≈ arts faculty. ❷ *adv.* philosophically

**Phiole** /'fio:lə/ *die;* **~, ~n** pear-shaped flask (*with long neck*)

**Phlegma** /'flɛgma/ *das;* **~s** *od.* (*österr. meist:*) **~:** phlegmatic disposition; (*Trägheit*) lethargy; (*Apathie*) apathy

**Phlegmatiker** /flɛ'gma:tikɐ/ *der;* **~s, ~:** phlegmatic person; (*träger Mensch*) lethargic person

**phlegmatisch** ❶ *Adj.* phlegmatic; (*träge*) lethargic; (*apathisch*) apathetic. ❷ *adv.* ⇒ **1:** phlegmatically; lethargically; apathetically

*old spelling (see note on page 1707)

P

**Phobie** /fo'bi:/ *die;* ~, ~**n** (*Psych.*) phobia

**Phon** /fo:n/ *das;* ~**s**, ~**s** phon; **50** ~**:** 50 phons

**Phonem** /fo'ne:m/ *das;* ~**s**, ~**e** (*Sprachw.*) phoneme

**Phonetik** /fo'ne:tɪk/ *die;* ~**:** phonetics *sing.*

**phonetisch** ❶ *Adj.* phonetic. ❷ *adv.* phonetically

**Phönix** /'fø:nɪks/ *der;* ~**[es]**, ~**e** phoenix; **wie ein ~ aus der Asche** like a phoenix from the ashes

**Phönizier** /fø'ni:tsi̯ɐ/ *der;* ~**s**, ~, **Phönizierin** *die;* ~, ~**nen** (*hist.*) Phoenician

**Phono-** /'fo:no-/ phono ‹socket, input›; ~**geschäft**/~**abteilung** audio and record store/department

**Phono·gerät** *das* record player

**Phono·graph** *der* (*veralt.*) [cylinder] phonograph

**Phono·koffer** *der* portable record player

**Phonologie** *die;* ~ (*Sprachw.*) phonology

**phonologisch** (*Sprachw.*) ❶ *Adj.* phonological. ❷ *adv.* phonologically

**Phono·typistin** /-ty'pɪstɪn/ *die;* ~, ~**nen** audio typist

**phon·stark** *Adj.* loud; noisy; high-volume ‹reproduction›

**Phon·zahl** *die* phon count; ≈ decibel level

**Phosphat** /fɔs'fa:t/ *das;* ~**[e]s**, ~**e** (*Chemie*) phosphate

**Phosphor** /'fɔsfɔr/ *der;* ~**s** phosphorus

**Phosphor·bombe** *die* phosphorus [incendiary] bomb

**Phosphoreszenz** /fɔsforɛs'tsɛnts/ *die;* ~**:** phosphorescence

**phosphoreszieren** *itr. V.* phosphoresce; be phosphorescent; ~**d** phosphorescent

**phosphor·haltig** *Adj.* containing phosphorus *postpos.*, *not pred.*; **stark ~:** with a high phosphorus content; **[stark] ~ sein** contain [a high level of] phosphorus

**Phosphor·säure** *die* phosphoric acid

**photo-, Photo-** ⇒ *auch* **foto-, Foto-**

**Photo** /'fo:to/ *das;* ~**s**, ~**s** ⇒ **Foto**

**Photo-:** ~**chemie** *die* photochemistry *no art.*; ~**element** *das* (*Elektrot.*) photoelement; photovoltaic cell; ~**metrie** *die;* ~~ (*Physik*) photometry *no art.*

**Photon** /'fo:tɔn/ *das;* ~**s**, ~**en** /fo'to:nən/ (*Physik*) photon

**Photo-:** ~**synthese** *die* photosynthesis; ~**voltaik** /...vɔlta:ɪk/ *die;* ~~**:** photovoltaics *sing.*, *no art.*; ~**voltaik·anlage** *die* photovoltaic array; ~**zelle** *die* photo[-electric] cell

**Phrase** /'fra:zə/ *die;* ~, ~**n** Ⓐ (*abwertend*) [empty] phrase; cliché; **leere ~n** empty phrases; waffle *sing.*; ~**n dreschen** (*ugs.*) spout clichés; dole out catchphrases; Ⓑ (*Musik*, *Sprachw.*) phrase

**phrasen-, Phrasen-:** ~**drescher** *der* (*ugs. abwertend*) phrase-monger; cliché-monger; ~**drescherei** /-drɛʃə'rai̯/ *die;* ~~, ~~**en** (*ugs. abwertend*) phrase-mongering; cliché-mongering; ~**drescherin** *die* ⇒ ~**drescher**; ~**haft** (*abwertend*) ❶ *Adj.* empty; trite; (*voller Klischees*) cliché-ridden; ❷ *adv.* in an empty *or* trite manner

**Phraseologie** /frazeolo'gi:/ *die;* ~, ~**n** (*Sprachw.*) idiomatic usage *no art.*; (*Buch*) dictionary of idioms

**phraseologisch** *Adj.* (*Sprachw.*) idiomatic; phrasal ‹unit›; ~**es Wörterbuch** dictionary of idioms

**phrasieren** *itr.*, *tr. V.* (*Musik*) phrase

**Phrasierung** *die;* ~, ~**en** (*Musik*) phrasing

**pH-Wert** /pe:'ha:-/ *der* (*Chemie*) pH [value]

**Physik** /fy'zi:k/ *die;* ~**:** physics *sing.*, *no art.*; **ein Lehrbuch der ~:** a physics textbook

**physikalisch** /fyzi'ka:lɪʃ/ ❶ *Adj.* physics *attrib.* ‹experiment, formula, research, institute›; physical ‹map, chemistry, therapy, process›; ~**e Gesetze** laws of physics; physical laws. ❷ *adv.* in terms of physics

**Physiker** *der;* ~**s**, ~, **Physikerin** *die;* ~, ~**nen** ▶ 159 physicist

**Physik·saal** *der* (*Schulw.*) physics laboratory

**Physikum** /'fy:zikʊm/ *das;* ~**s**, **Physika** (*Hochschulw.*) *examination ending the preclinical stage*

**Physiognomie** /fyzi̯ogno'mi:/ *die;* ~, ~**n** physiognomy

**Physiologe** /fyzi̯o'lo:gə/ *der;* ~**n**, ~**n** ▶ 159 physiologist

**Physiologie** /fyzi̯olo'gi:/ *die;* ~**:** physiology

**Physiologin** *die;* ~, ~**nen** ▶ 159 physiologist

**physiologisch** ❶ *Adj.* physiological. ❷ *adv.* physiologically

**Physio·therapeut** *der*, **Physio·therapeutin** *die* ▶ 159 physiotherapist

**Physio·therapie** /fyzi̯o-/ *die* physiotherapy

**physisch** ❶ *Adj.* physical. ❷ *adv.* physically

**Pi** /pi:/ *das;* ~**[s]**, ~**s** pi

**Pianist** /pi̯a'nɪst/ *der;* ~**en**, ~**en**, **Pianistin** *die;* ~, ~**nen** ▶ 159 pianist

**Piano** /'pi̯a:no/ *das;* ~**s**, ~**s** piano

**Pianoforte** /pi̯ano'fɔrtə/ *das;* ~**s**, ~**s** (*veralt.*) pianoforte (*formal/arch.*)

**picheln** /'pɪçl̩n/ (*ugs.*) ❶ *itr. V.* booze (*coll.*). ❷ *tr. V.* **einen ~ gehen** go out for a jar (*Brit. coll.*)

**Pickel** /'pɪkl̩/ *der;* ~**s**, ~ Ⓐ (*auf der Haut*) pimple; Ⓑ (*Spitzhacke*) pickaxe; (*Eis*~) ice axe

**Pickel·haube** *die* spiked helmet

**pickelig** *Adj.* pimply; ~ **[im Gesicht] sein** have a spotty *or* pimply face

**picken** /'pɪkn̩/ ❶ *itr. V.* peck (**nach** at; **an** + *Akk.*, **gegen** on, against). ❷ *tr. V.* Ⓐ ‹bird› peck; (*ugs.*) ‹person› pick; (*aufheben*) pick up; Ⓑ (*österr. ugs.: kleben*) stick

**picklig** ⇒ **pickelig**

**Picknick** /'pɪknɪk/ *das;* ~**s**, ~**e** *od.* ~**s** picnic; ~ **machen** *od.* **halten** have a picnic

**picknicken** *itr. V.* picnic

**picobello** /'pi:ko'bɛlo/ (*ugs.*) ❶ *indekl. Adj.* super-duper (*sl.*); (*makellos*) immaculate. ❷ *adv.* immaculately; ~ **in Ordnung** in immaculate order; spick and span

**Pidgin·englisch** /'pɪdʒɪn-/ *das* pidgin English

**Piefke** /'pi:fkə/ *der;* ~**s**, ~**s** Ⓐ (*bes. nordd. abwertend*) bumptious lout; Ⓑ (*österr. abwertend: Deutscher*) bloody (*Brit. sl.*) *or* damn German

**pieken** ⇒ **piken**

**piek·fein** /'pi:k'fai̯n/ (*ugs.*) ❶ *Adj.* posh (*coll.*). ❷ *adv.* poshly (*coll.*); ~ **angezogen** wearing posh clothes (*coll.*); dressed to the nines

**piep** /pi:p/ *Interj.* ~, ~! cheep, cheep!; **nicht ~ sagen** (*ugs.*) not say a word; **er kann nicht mehr ~ sagen** (*ugs.*) he's been silenced

**Piep** *der;* ~**s**, ~**e** (*ugs.*) Ⓐ (*Ton*) peep; **keinen ~ [davon] sagen** not say a thing [about it]; Ⓑ *in* **einen [kleinen] ~ haben** have a [bit of a] screw loose (*coll.*)

**piepe** /'pi:pə/, **piep·egal** *Adj.: in* **[jmdm.] ~ sein** (*ugs.*) not matter at all [to sb.]; **es ist mir ~!** (*ugs.*) I don't give a damn

**piepen** *itr. V.* (*ugs.*) squeak; ‹small bird› cheep; chirp; ‹paging device› bleep; **bei dir piepts wohl!** (*salopp*) you must be off your rocker (*coll.*); **zum P~ sein** (*ugs.*) be a hoot *or* a scream (*coll.*)

**Piepen** *Pl.* (*salopp: Geld*) dough *sing.* (*coll.*); **50 ~:** 50 marks/francs *etc.*

**Piep-:** ~**hahn** *der; Pl.* ~**hähne** (*Kinderspr.*) willy (*coll.*); ~**matz** *der* (*Kinderspr.*) dicky bird (*coll.*)

**pieps** /pi:ps/ ⇒ **piep**

**Pieps** *der;* ~**es**, ~**e** (*ugs.*) ⇒ **Piep** A

**piepsen** (*ugs.*) ❶ *itr. V.* ⇒ **piepen**. ❷ *itr.*, *tr. V.* (*mit hoher Stimme sprechen*) pipe; (*aufgeregt*) squeal

**Piepser** *der;* ~**s**, ~ (*ugs.*) Ⓐ (*Piepsen*) chirp; tweet; Ⓑ (*kleiner Empfänger*) bleeper

**piepsig** *Adj.* (*ugs.*) squeaky

**Pier** /pi:ɐ̯/ *der;* ~**s**, ~**e** *od.* ~**s** *od.* (*Seemannsspr.*) *die;* ~, ~**s** jetty

**Piercing** /'pi:ɐ̯sɪŋ/ *das;* ~**s** [body] piercing

**piesacken** /'pi:zakn̩/ *tr. V.* (*ugs.*) pester; **hör endlich auf, mich damit zu ~!** stop pestering me about that!

**pieseln** /'pi:zl̩n/ *itr.* (*auch tr.*) *V.* (*salopp*) ⇒ **pinkeln**

**Pietät** /pi̯e'tɛ:t/ *die;* ~, ~**en** Ⓐ respect; (*Ehrfurcht*) reverence; Ⓑ (*Bestattungsinstitut*) [firm of] funeral directors *or* (*Amer.*) morticians

**pietät-, Pietät-:** ~**los** ❶ *Adj.* irreverent; (*gefühllos*) unfeeling; (*respektlos*) disrespectful; lacking in respect *postpos.*; ❷ *adv.* irreverently; ~**losigkeit** *die;* ~~, ~~**en** irreverence; (*Gefühllosigkeit*) lack of feeling; (*Respektlosigkeit*) lack of respect; (*Handlung*) act of irreverence; ~**voll** ❶ *Adj.* respectful; (*ehrfurchtsvoll*) reverent; ❷ *adv.* respectfully; (*ehrfurchtsvoll*) reverently

**Pietismus** /pi̯e'tɪsmʊs/ *der;* ~**:** pietism *no art.*

**Pietist** *der;* ~**en**, ~**en**, **Pietistin** *die;* ~, ~**nen** pietist

**pietistisch** ❶ *Adj.* pietistic. ❷ *adv.* in a pietistic manner

**piff, paff** /'pɪf 'paf/ *Interj.* (*Kinderspr.*) bang, bang

**Pigment** /pɪ'gmɛnt/ *das;* ~**[e]s**, ~**e** pigment

**Pigmentation** /pɪgmɛnta'tsi̯o:n/ *die;* ~, ~**en** pigmentation

**Pigment·fleck** *der* pigmentation mark

**Pik**[1] /pi:k/ *der: in* **einen ~ auf jmdn. haben** (*ugs.*) have it in for sb.

**Pik**[2] *das;* ~**[s]**, ~**[s]**, *österr. auch die;* ~, ~ (*Kartenspiel*) Ⓐ (*Farbe*) spades *pl.*; **von ~ habe ich nur noch die Sieben** the only spade I have left is the seven; ~ **ziehen/ausspielen** draw/play spades; Ⓑ (*Karte*) spade

**pikant** /pi'kant/ ❶ *Adj.* Ⓐ piquant; (*würzig*) spicy; well-seasoned; (*appetitanregend*) appetizing; **ich möchte lieber etwas Pikantes** I'd rather have something savoury; Ⓑ (*fig.: witzig*) piquant; ironical; Ⓒ (*verhüll.: schlüpfrig*) racy ‹joke, story›; titillating ‹pictures›. ❷ *adv.* spicily; **etw. ~ zubereiten** season sth. well; ~ **gewürzt** piquantly *or* appetizingly seasoned

**Pikanterie** /pikantə'ri:/ *die;* ~, ~**n** Ⓐ (*fig.*) piquancy; (*Witzigkeit*) irony; Ⓑ (*verhüll.: schlüpfrige Geschichte*) racy story

**pikanter·weise** *Adv.* (*geh.*) ironically [enough]

**Pik-:** *~**as**, ~**ass** *das* ace of spades; ~**bube** *der* jack of spades; ~**dame** *die* queen of spades

**Pike** /'pi:kə/ *die;* ~, ~**n** pike; **etw. von der ~ auf [er]lernen** learn sth. by working one's way up from the bottom

**Pikee** /pi'ke:/ *der; österr. auch das;* ~**s**, ~**s** (*Textilw.*) piqué

**piken** *tr.*, *itr. V.* (*ugs.*) prick; **etw. in etw.** (*Akk.*) **~:** poke sth. into sth.; **jmdm. eine Nadel in den Arm ~:** poke a needle into sb.'s arm

**pikieren** *tr. V.* (*Gartenbau*) prick out ‹seedlings›

**pikiert** /pi'ki:ɐ̯t/ ❶ *Adj.* piqued; nettled; **ein ~es Gesicht machen** look aggrieved. ❷ *adv.* ‹reply, say› in an aggrieved tone *or* voice

**Pikkolo**[1] /'pɪkolo/ *der;* ~**s**, ~**s** [trainee] waiter

**Pikkolo**[2] *das;* ~**s**, ~**s** (*Flöte*) piccolo

**Pikkolo**[3] *die;* ~, ~**[s]** (*Fläschchen*) miniature bottle of champagne (*for one person*)

**Pikkolo·flöte** *die* piccolo

**Pik·könig** *der* king of spades

**piksen** /'pi:ksn̩/ *tr.*, *itr. V.* (*ugs.*) ⇒ **piken**

**Pik·sieben** *die* (*Kartenspiel*) seven of spades; **dastehen wie ~** (*ugs.*) stand there looking stupid

**Pilger** /'pɪlgɐ/ *der;* ~**s**, ~**:** pilgrim

**Pilger·fahrt** *die* pilgrimage

**-pilger** *der:* **Mekka~/Rom~:** pilgrim on his/her way to Rome/Mecca

**Pilgerin** *die;* ~, ~**nen** pilgrim

**pilgern** *itr. V.* Ⓐ (*auch fig.*) go on *or* make a pilgrimage; Ⓑ (*ugs.: gehen*) traipse (*coll.*)

P

**Pilgerschaft** *die;* ~, ~**en** pilgrimage
**Pilger-:** ~**stab** *der* pilgrim's staff; ~**väter** *Pl.* (*hist.*) Pilgrim Fathers
**Pille** /'pɪlə/ *die;* ~, ~**n** pill; **sie nimmt schon seit Jahren die** ~: she's been on the pill for years (*coll.*); **eine bittere** ~ **[für jmdn.] sein** (*fig.*) be a bitter pill [for sb.] to swallow; **jmdm. die bittere** ~ **versüßen** *od.* **verzuckern** (*fig.*) sugar the pill for sb.; (*es jmdm. erleichtern*) make it easier for sb.
**Pillen-:** ~**dreher** *der* Ⓐ (*Käfer*) scarab [beetle]; Ⓑ (*ugs. scherzh.: Apotheker*) pill peddler (*coll.*); ~**dreherin** *die* ⇒ ~**dreher** B; ~**knick** *der;* ~~**[e]s** decline in the birth rate [due to the pill]
**Pilot** /pi'lo:t/ *der;* ~**en**, ~**en**, **Pilotin** *die;* ~, ~**nen** Ⓐ ▶ 159 pilot; Ⓑ (*Motorsport*) [racing] driver
**Pilot-:** ~**projekt** *das* pilot project; ~**studie** *die* pilot study
**Pils** /pɪls/ *das;* ~, ~: Pils; Pils[e]ner [beer]
**Pilz** /pɪlts/ *der;* ~**es**, ~**e** Ⓐ fungus; (*Speise*~, *auch fig.*) mushroom; **essbare, giftige und ungenießbare** ~**e** mushrooms, poisonous and inedible fungi; **in die** ~**e gehen** (*ugs.*) go mushrooming; **wie** ~**e aus dem Boden** *od.* **der Erde schießen** be springing up like mushrooms; Ⓑ (*ugs.:* ~*infektion*) fungus [infection]
**pilz-, Pilz-:** ~**förmig** *Adj.* mushroom-shaped; ~**krankheit** *die* ▶ 474 Ⓐ (*Mykose*) mycosis; Ⓑ (*bei Pflanzen*) fungus [disease]; ~**kultur** *die* fungus culture; ~**kunde** *die* mycology
**Pilzling** /'pɪltslɪŋ/ *der;* ~**s**, ~**e** (*österr.*) ⇒ **Steinpilz**
**Pilz·vergiftung** *die* ▶ 474 fungus poisoning *no art.*; (*durch verdorbene Pilze*) mushroom poisoning *no art.*
**Piment** /pi'mɛnt/ *der od. das;* ~**[e]s**, ~**e** pimento; allspice
**Pimmel** /'pɪml/ *der;* ~**s**, ~ (*salopp*) willy (*coll.*)
**pimpern** /'pɪmpɐn/ (*salopp*) ❶ *itr. V.* have it off (*sl.*). ❷ *tr. V.* have it off with (*sl.*)
**Pimpf** /pɪmpf/ *der;* ~**[e]s**, ~**e** Ⓐ (*ugs.: Junge*) kid (*coll.*); Ⓑ (*ns.*) *member of the* **Jungvolk**
**pingelig** /'pɪŋəlɪç/ (*ugs.*) ❶ finicky; pernickety (*coll.*); (*wählerisch*) fussy; choosy (*coll.*). ❷ *adv.* in a pernickety way (*coll.*); (*pedantisch*) pedantically
**Pingpong** /'pɪŋpɔŋ/ *das;* ~**s** (*ugs.*) ping-pong
**Pinguin** /'pɪŋgui:n/ *der;* ~**s**, ~**e** penguin
**Pinie** /'pi:niə/ *die;* ~, ~**n** [stone *or* umbrella] pine
**Pinke** /'pɪŋkə/ *die;* ~ (*ugs. veralt.*) dough (*coll.*); lolly (*Brit. coll.*)
**Pinkel** /'pɪŋkl/ *der;* ~**s**, ~ (*ugs. abwertend*) **ein [feiner]** ~: a stuck-up prig
**pinkeln** *itr.* (*auch tr.*) *V.* (*salopp*) Ⓐ pee (*coll.*); ‹esp. child› wee (*sl.*); ~ **[gehen]** [go and] have a pee (*coll.*); Ⓑ (*unpers.: regnen*) **es pinkelt** it's spitting
**Pinkel·pause** *die* (*ugs.*) stop for a pee (*coll.*); rest stop (*Amer.*)
**Pinke·pinke** ⇒ **Pinke**
**pink·farben** /'pɪŋk-/ *Adj.* [shocking] pink
**Pinne** /'pɪnə/ *die;* ~, ~**n** (*Seemannsspr.*) tiller
**pinnen** *tr. V.* (*ugs.*) pin (**auf, an** + *Akk.* on)
**Pinn·wand** *die* pinboard
**Pinscher** /'pɪnʃɐ/ *der;* ~**s**, ~ Ⓐ pinscher; Ⓑ (*ugs. abwertend: Mensch*) pipsqueak (*coll.*)
**Pinsel** /'pɪnzl/ *der;* ~**s**, ~ Ⓐ brush; (*Mal*~) paintbrush; **mit leichtem/kühnem** ~: with light/bold brush strokes; Ⓑ (*ugs. abwertend: Dummkopf*) nitwit (*coll.*); idiot (*coll.*)
**Pinsel·führung** *die* brushwork *no indef. art.*
**pinseln** *tr. V.* Ⓐ (*ugs.: anstreichen*) paint ‹room, house, etc.›; Ⓑ (*malen*) paint ‹landscape, picture›; daub ‹slogans›; Ⓒ (*ugs.: schreiben*) write ‹letters, homework› in one's best writing; Ⓓ (*streichen*) brush [on] ‹paint›, put on ‹paint› with a brush; apply ‹liquid› [with a brush] (**auf** + *Akk.* to); Ⓔ (*Med.: ein*~) paint ‹wound, gums, throat, etc.›
**Pinsel·strich** *der* Ⓐ brush stroke; Ⓑ (*Pinselführung*) brushwork *no indef. art.*
**Pinte** /'pɪntə/ *die;* ~, ~**n** Ⓐ (*ugs.*) ⇒ **Kneipe** A; Ⓑ (*hist.: Hohlmaß*) [*former*] *measure of capacity for liquids*
**Pin-up-Girl** /pɪn'|ap-/ *das;* ~**s**, ~**s** pin-up girl
**Pinzette** /pɪn'tsɛtə/ *die;* ~, ~**n** tweezers *pl.*; **chirurgische** ~: surgical forceps *pl.*
**Pionier** /pio'ni:ɐ/ *der;* ~**s**, ~**e** Ⓐ (*Milit.*) sapper; engineer; Ⓑ (*fig.: Wegbereiter*) pioneer; Ⓒ (*DDR*) **[Junger]** ~: [Young] Pioneer
**Pionier·arbeit** *die* pioneering work
**Pionierin** *die;* ~, ~**nen** pioneer
**Pionier·truppe** *die* (*Milit.*) corps of engineers
**Pipapo** /pipa'po:/ *das;* ~**s** (*salopp*) **das ganze** ~: all the frills; **mit allem** ~: with all the frills
**Pipeline** /'paiplain/ *die;* ~, ~**s** pipeline
**Pipette** /pi'pɛtə/ *die;* ~, ~**n** (*Chemie*) pipette
**Pipi** /pi'pi:/ *das;* ~**s** (*Kinderspr.*) ~ **machen** do wee-wees (*sl.*); ~ **müssen** have to do wee-wees *or* have a wee (*sl.*)
**Pipifax** /'pipifaks/ *der;* ~ (*salopp*) piffling trifles *pl.* (*sl.*)
**Piranha** /pi'ranja/ *der;* ~**[s]**, ~**s** piranha
**Pirat** /pi'ra:t/ *der;* ~**en**, ~**en** pirate
**Piraten-:** ~**schiff** *das* pirate ship; ~**sender** *der* pirate radio station
**Piraterie** /piratə'ri:/ *die;* ~, ~**n** piracy *no art.*
**Piratin** *die;* ~, ~**nen** ⇒ **Pirat**
**Pirol** /pi'ro:l/ *der;* ~**s**, ~**e** oriole
**Pirouette** /pi'ruɛtə/ *die;* ~, ~**n** pirouette
**Pirsch** /pɪrʃ/ *die;* ~ (*Jägerspr.*) [deer-]stalking; **auf die** ~ **gehen** go [deer-]stalking
**pirschen** ❶ *itr. V.* Ⓐ (*Jägerspr.*) stalk; go stalking; **auf Rehwild** (*Akk.*) ~: stalk roe deer; Ⓑ (*ugs.: schleichen*) creep [silently]; steal. ❷ *refl. V.* (*ugs.*) creep [silently]; steal
**Pisse** /'pɪsə/ *die;* ~ (*derb*) piss (*coarse*)
**pissen** *itr.* (*auch tr.*) *V.* (*derb*) Ⓐ piss (*coarse*); **ich muss** ~ **[gehen]** I must have a piss; Ⓑ (*unpers.: regnen*) piss down (*sl.*)
**Pissoir** /pɪ'soa:ɐ/ *das;* ~**s**, ~**e** *od.* ~**s** [public] urinal
**Piss·pott**, ***Piß·pott** *der* (*salopp*) piss-pot (*coarse*)
**Pistazie** /pɪs'ta:tsiə/ *die;* ~, ~**n** pistachio
**Piste** /'pɪstə/ *die;* ~, ~**n** Ⓐ (*Skisport*) piste; ski run; (*Renn*~) course; Ⓑ (*Rennstrecke*) track; Ⓒ (*Flugw.*) runway; **auf der** ~ **aufsetzen** touch down; Ⓓ (*Straße*) dirt road
**Pistole** /pɪs'to:lə/ *die;* ~, ~**n** pistol; **wie aus der** ~ **geschossen** like a shot *or* a flash; **jmdm. die** ~ **auf die Brust setzen** (*fig.*) hold a pistol to sb.'s head
**Pistolen-:** ~**schuss**, *~**schuß** *der* pistol shot; ~**tasche** *die* holster
**pitsch·nass**, ***pitsch·naß** /'pɪtʃ'nas/ *Adj.* (*ugs.*) dripping wet; wet through
**pittoresk** /pɪto'rɛsk/ (*geh.*) ❶ *Adj.* picturesque. ❷ *adv.* picturesquely
**Pizza** /'pɪtsa/ *die;* ~, ~**s** *od.* **Pizzen** pizza
**Pizza·bäcker** *der*, **Pizza·bäckerin** *die* pizza cook
**Pizzeria** /pɪtse'ri:a/ *die;* ~, ~**s** *od.* **Pizzerien** pizzeria
**Pkw, PKW** *Abk.* **Personenkraftwagen** [private] car; automobile (*Amer.*)
***placieren** ⇒ **platzieren**
**placken** /'plakn/ *refl. V.* (*ugs.*) slave away
**Plackerei** *die;* ~, ~**en** (*ugs.*) drudgery *no indef. art.*; [hard] grind
**pladdern** /'pladɐn/ *itr. V.* (*unpers.*) **es pladdert** (*nordd.*) it's pouring [down]
**plädieren** /plɛ'di:rən/ *itr. V.* (*Rechtsw.*) plead (**auf** + *Akk.*, **für** for); (*das Plädoyer halten*) ‹counsel› make one's final speech, sum up; (*fig.*) argue (**für** for, in favour of); **auf Freispruch/auf schuldig** ~: plead for acquittal/for a verdict of guilty; **er plädiert dafür, dass ...** he argues *or* advocates that ...
**Plädoyer** /plɛdoa'je:/ *das;* ~**s**, ~**s** (*Rechtsw.*) final speech, summing up (*for the defence/prosecution*); (*fig.*) plea; **sein** ~ **halten** make one's final speech; sum up
**Plafond** /pla'fõ:/ *der;* ~**s**, ~**s** (*südd., österr., auch fig.*) ceiling
**Plage** /'pla:gə/ *die;* ~, ~**n** Ⓐ [cursed *or* (*coll.*) pestilential] nuisance; **das macht ihm das Leben zur** ~: it makes his life a misery; **die ägyptischen** ~**n** (*bibl.*) the plagues of Egypt; Ⓑ (*ugs.: Mühe*) bother; trouble; **seine** ~ **mit jmdm./etw. haben** find sb./sth. a real handful
**Plage·geist** *der* (*fam.*) pest
**plagen** ❶ *tr. V.* Ⓐ torment; plague; **Zweifel** ~ **ihn** he is plagued *or* beset with doubts; **von Kopfschmerzen/Träumen geplagt** plagued with headaches/dreams; **er ist ein geplagter Mensch** he has a hard time of it; Ⓑ (*ugs.: bedrängen*) harass; (*mit Bitten, Fragen*) pester. ❷ *refl. V.* Ⓐ (*sich abmühen*) slave away; **sie musste sich** ~, **um die Arbeit zu bewältigen** she had to struggle to get through all the work; Ⓑ (*leiden*) **sich mit etw.** ~: be troubled *or* bothered by sth.
**Plagiat** /pla'gia:t/ *das;* ~**[e]s**, ~**e** plagiarism *no art.*; **ein [eindeutiges]** ~: a [clear] case of plagiarism
**Plagiator** /pla'gia:tɔr/ *der;* ~**s**, ~**en**, **Plagiatorin** *die;* ~, ~**nen** (*geh.*) plagiarist
**plagiieren** /plagi'i:rən/ *tr.* (*auch itr.*) *V.* (*geh.*) plagiarize
**Plaid** /ple:t/ *das od. der;* ~**s**, ~**s** Ⓐ (*Decke*) tartan [travelling] rug (*Brit.*) *or* (*Amer.*) lap robe; Ⓑ (*Tuch*) plaid
**Plakat** /pla'ka:t/ *das;* ~**[e]s**, ~**e** poster; (*zum Tragen*) placard; „~**e ankleben verboten**" 'post no bills'
**plakatieren** ❶ *tr. V.* announce by poster. ❷ *itr. V.* put up posters
**plakativ** /plaka'ti:f/ ❶ *Adj.* bold and simple, eye-catching ‹design, representation›; bold ‹colours›. ❷ *adv.* eye-catchingly; in a bold and simple style
**Plakat-:** ~**kunst** *die* poster art *no art.*; ~**maler** *der*, ~**malerin** *die* poster artist; ~**wand** *die* [poster] hoarding; billboard
**Plakette** /pla'kɛtə/ *die;* ~, ~**n** Ⓐ (*Schildchen*) badge; (*Scheibe*) disc; Ⓑ (*an einem Gebäude*) plaque
**plan** /pla:n/ *Adj.* (*Technik*) flat; plane ‹surface›; ~ **liegen** lie flat
**Plan**[1] *der;* ~**[e]s**, **Pläne** /'plɛ:nə/ Ⓐ plan; **nach** ~ **verlaufen** go according to plan; **auf dem** ~ **stehen** be on the agenda; be planned; **wir sind im** ~ (*Zeit*~) we are on schedule; Ⓑ (*Karte*) map; plan; (*Stadt*~) [street] plan
**Plan**[2] *der: in* **auf den** ~ **treten, auf dem** ~ **erscheinen** (*geh.*) appear on the scene; **auf den** ~ **rufen** (*geh.*) bring ‹person› on to the scene; bring ‹opponent› into the arena; arouse ‹curiosity›
**Plane** *die;* ~, ~**n** tarpaulin
**planen** *tr., itr. V.* plan
**Planer** *der;* ~**s**, ~, **Planerin** *die;* ~, ~**nen** planner
**Plan·erfüllung** *die* (*bes. DDR*) attainment of the planned [production] target
**planerisch** *Adj.* planning ‹measures, genius, ability›; **eine** ~**e Meisterleistung** a masterpiece of planning
**Pläne·schmieden** *das;* ~**s** planning; making plans
**Planet** /pla'ne:t/ *der;* ~**en**, ~**en** planet
**Planetarium** /plane'ta:rium/ *das;* ~**s**, **Planetarien** planetarium
**Planeten-:** ~**bahn** *die* planetary orbit; ~**system** *das* planetary system
**Planetoid** *der;* ~**en**, ~**en** asteroid, planetoid
**planieren** *tr. V.* level; grade (*as tech. term*)
**Planier·raupe** *die* bulldozer
**Plan·jahr** *das* (*bes. DDR*) planning year
**Planke** /'plaŋkə/ *die;* ~, ~**n** Ⓐ plank; board; Ⓑ (*Zaun*) [close-boarded] wooden fence

*old spelling (see note on page 1707)

P

**Plänkelei** *die;* ~, ~**en** ⇒ **Geplänkel** A

**plänkeln** /ˈplɛŋkl̩n/ *itr. V.* have a rough and tumble; fight playfully

**Plankton** /ˈplaŋktɔn/ *das;* ~**s** (*Biol.*) plankton

**plan-**, **Plan-:** ~**los** ❶ *Adj.* aimless; (*ohne System*) unsystematic; ❷ *adv.* ⇒ **1**: aimlessly; unsystematically; ~**losigkeit** *die;* ~~: aimlessness; (*Mangel an System*) lack of system; ~**mäßig** ❶ *Adj.* Ⓐ regular, scheduled ‹service, steamer›; ~**mäßige Ankunft/Abfahrt** scheduled time of arrival/departure; Ⓑ (*systematisch*) systematic; ❷ *adv.* Ⓐ (*wie geplant*) according to plan; as planned; (*pünktlich*) on schedule; Ⓑ (*systematisch*) systematically; ~**mäßigkeit** *die;* ~: methodicalness; (*Vorgehen*) systematic procedure; ~**quadrat** *das* grid square

**Plansch·becken** /ˈplanʃ-/ *das* paddling pool

**planschen** *itr. V.* splash [about]

**Plan-:** ~**soll** *das* planned [production] target; ~**spiel** *das* simulation; (*Kriegsspiel*) war game; ~**stelle** *die* established post

**Plantage** /planˈtaːʒə/ *die;* ~, ~**n** plantation

**Planung** *die;* ~, ~**en** Ⓐ (*das Planen*) planning; **in** (*Dat.*) ~ **sein** be planned; **bei der** ~: at the planning stage; Ⓑ (*Plan*) plan

**Planungs·stadium** *das* planning stage; **im** ~: at the planning stage

**plan-**, **Plan-:** ~**voll** ❶ *Adj.* methodical; systematic; ❷ methodically; systematically; ~**wagen** *der* covered wagon; ~**wirtschaft** *die* planned economy

**Plapperei** *die;* ~, ~**en** (*ugs. abwertend*) chatter

**Plapper·maul** *das* (*ugs. abwertend*) chatterbox

**plappern** /ˈplapɐn/ (*ugs.*) ❶ *itr. V.* Ⓐ (*schwätzen*) chatter; Ⓑ (*ausplaudern*) blab. ❷ *tr. V.* babble ‹nonsense›

**plärren** /ˈplɛrən/ ❶ *tr. V.* bawl [out] ‹song›; ‹radio etc.› blare out. ❷ *itr. V.* Ⓐ bawl; yell; ‹radio etc.› blare; Ⓑ (*ugs.: weinen*) wail; (*sehr laut*) howl

**Pläsier** /plɛˈziːɐ̯/ *das;* ~**s**, ~**e** (*veralt.*) pleasure (**an** + *Dat.* in); **lass ihm doch sein** ~: let him have his fun

**Plasma** /ˈplasma/ *das;* ~**s**, **Plasmen** (*Med.*, *Physik*) plasma; (*Proto*~) protoplasm

**Plast** /plast/ *der;* ~[**e**]**s**, ~**e** (*regional*) plastic

**Plaste** /ˈplastə/ *die;* ~, ~**n** (*regional ugs.*) plastic

**Plastik**[1] /ˈplastɪk/ *die;* ~, ~**en** Ⓐ (*Werk, Kunst*) sculpture; Ⓑ (*Med.*) plastic surgery operation; **jmdm. eine** ~ **machen** perform plastic surgery on sb.

**Plastik**[2] *das;* ~**s** (*ugs.*) plastic

**Plastik-:** ~**beutel** *der* plastic bag; ~**bombe** *die* plastic bomb; ~**folie** *die* plastic film; ~**geld** *das* (*ugs.*) plastic money (*coll.*); ~**tüte** *die* plastic bag

**Plastilin** /plastiˈliːn/ *das;* ~**s** ≈ Plasticine ®

**plastisch** ❶ *Adj.* Ⓐ (*knetbar*) plastic; workable; Ⓑ (*bildhauerisch*) sculptural; ‹ability› as a sculptor; Ⓒ (*dreidimensional*) three-dimensional ‹effect, formation, vision›; sculptural ‹decoration›; Ⓓ (*fig.: anschaulich*) vivid ‹description, picture›; Ⓔ (*Med.*) plastic ‹surgery, surgeon›. ❷ *adv.* Ⓐ (*bildhauerisch*) sculpturally; **etw.** ~ **ausarbeiten** *od.* **gestalten** sculpture sth.; Ⓑ (*dreidimensional*) three-dimensionally; Ⓒ (*fig.: anschaulich*) vividly; **sich** (*Dat.*) **etw.** ~ **vorstellen können** have a clear picture of sth. [in one's mind]

**Plastizität** /plastitsiˈtɛːt/ *die;* ~ Ⓐ plasticity; Ⓑ (*fig.: Anschaulichkeit*) vividness; (*von Prosa usw.*) graphic quality; (*eines Bildes*) three-dimensional quality

**Platane** /plaˈtaːnə/ *die;* ~, ~**n** plane tree

**Plateau** /plaˈtoː/ *das;* ~**s**, ~**s** plateau

**Plateau·sohle** *die* platform sole

**Platin** /ˈplaːtiːn/ *das;* ~**s** platinum

**platin·blond** *Adj.* platinum blonde

***Platitüde** ⇒ **Plattitüde**

**Platon** /ˈplaːtɔn/ (*der*) Plato

**platonisch** /plaˈtoːnɪʃ/ ❶ *Adj.* Ⓐ Platonic ‹philosophy, state›; Ⓑ (*nicht sinnlich*) platonic ‹love, relationship›. ❷ *adv.* platonically

**platsch** /platʃ/ *Interj.* splash

**platschen** *itr. V.* Ⓐ splash; Ⓑ *mit sein* (~*d schlagen*) splash (**an** + *Akk.*, **gegen** against); Ⓒ (*planschen*) splash about

**plätschern** /ˈplɛtʃɐn/ *itr. V.* Ⓐ splash; ‹rain› patter; ‹stream› burble; (*fig.*) ~**de Unterhaltung** casual *or* desultory conversation; Ⓑ (*planschen*) splash about; Ⓒ *mit sein* ‹stream› burble along

**platsch·nass**, ***platsch·naß** *Adj.* (*ugs.*) ⇒ **klatschnass**

**platt** /plat/ ❶ *Adj.* Ⓐ (*flach*) flat; **sich** (*Dat.*) **die Nase** ~ **drücken** flatten one's nose; **ein Platter** (*ugs.*) a flat (*coll.*); a flat tyre; (*mit Loch*) a puncture; **etw.** ~ **machen** (*salopp abwertend*) close sth. down; **das** ~**e Land** (*ugs.*) the countryside; the rural areas *pl.*; **sie ist** ~ **wie ein [Bügel]brett** (*salopp*) she is flat-chested; Ⓑ (*geistlos*) dull, vapid ‹conversation, book›; vacuous, feeble ‹poem, joke›; shallow, empty ‹materialism, argument, imitation›; Ⓒ (*ausgesprochen*) downright ‹lie, swindle, slander›; sheer ‹cynicism›; Ⓓ (*ugs., bes. nordd.: erstaunt*) dumbfounded; flabbergasted.
❷ *adv.* Ⓐ (*flach*) **sich** ~ **legen** lie down flat; Ⓑ (*geistlos*) feebly.
❸ *Adv.* ~ **sprechen** talk Low German dialect

**Platt** *das;* ~[**s**] Ⓐ [local] Low German dialect; (*allgemein: Niederdeutsch*) Low German; Ⓑ (*ugs.: Dialekt*) patois

**Plätt·brett** *das* (*nordd., md.*) ⇒ **Bügelbrett**

**Plättchen** /ˈplɛtçən/ *das;* ~**s**, ~: small plate *or* disc

**platt·deutsch** *Adj.*: ⇒ **niederdeutsch**

**Platte** *die;* ~, ~**n** Ⓐ (*Stein*~) slab; (*Metall*~) plate; sheet; (*Mikroskopie usw.: Glas*~) slide; (*Elektronik*) board; (*Paneel*) panel; (*Span*~, *Hartfaser*~ *usw.*) board; (*Styropor*~ *usw.*) sheet; (*Tisch*~) [table] top; (*Grab*~) [memorial] slab; (*fotografische* ~) [photographic] plate; (*Druck*~) [pressure] plate; (*Kachel, Fliese*) tile; (*zum Pflastern*) flagstone; paving stone; **etw./jmdn. auf die** ~ **bannen** (*scherzh.*) immortalize sb./sth. [in a photograph] (*joc.*); Ⓑ (*Koch*~) hotplate; Ⓒ (*Schall*~) [gramophone] record; **eine** ~ **mit Gitarrenmusik** a record of guitar music; **etw. auf** ~ (*Akk.*) **aufnehmen** make a record of sth.; **die** ~ **kenne ich [schon]** (*fig. ugs.*) I've heard that one before; **leg [doch endlich mal] 'ne neue/andere** ~ **auf!** (*fig. ugs.*) can't you talk about sth. else for a change?; **immer dieselbe** ~! (*fig. ugs.*) always the same old tune; Ⓓ (*Teller*) plate; (*zum Servieren, aus Metall*) dish; Ⓔ (*Speise*) dish; **kalte** ~: selection of cold meats [and cheese]; Ⓕ (*ugs.: Glatze*) bald pate; Ⓖ (*Gaumen*~) [dental] plate; Ⓗ **die** ~ **putzen** (*salopp*) make oneself scarce (*coll.*); ~ **machen** (*salopp*) doss *or* kip down (*Brit. coll.*); bed down; Ⓘ (*österr. ugs.: Bande*) gang

**Plätte** /ˈplɛtə/ *die;* ~, ~**n** (*österr.*) flat-bottomed barge (*with pointed prow*)

**Plätt·eisen** /ˈplɛt-/ *das* (*nordd., md.*) iron; (*hist.*) flat iron

**plätten** *tr., itr. V.* (*nordd., md.*) iron

**Platten-:** ~**album** *das* record album; ~**cover** *das* record sleeve; ~**firma** *die* record company; ~**hülle** *die* record sleeve; ~**sammlung** *die* record collection

**Plattensee** *der;* ~**s** (*Geogr.*) Lake Balaton

**Platten-:** ~**spieler** *der* (*als Baustein*) record deck; (*komplettes Gerät*) record player; ~**teller** *der* turntable; ~**wechsler** *der* record changer

**platter·dings** *Adv.* (*ugs.*) absolutely

**platt-**, **Platt-:** ~**fisch** *der* flatfish; ~**form** *die* Ⓐ platform; Ⓑ (*fig.: Basis*) basic programme; (*Wahlplattform*) platform; [election] programme; **eine gemeinsame** ~**form** common ground; (*bei Wahlen*) a common platform; ~**fuß** *der* Ⓐ flat foot; Ⓑ (*ugs.: Reifenpanne*) flat (*coll.*); flat tyre; ~**füßig** *Adj.* flat-footed

**Plattheit** *die;* ~, ~**en** Ⓐ flatness; Ⓑ (*fig.*) dullness; Ⓒ (*Plattitüde*) platitude

**Plattitüde** /platiˈtyːdə/ *die;* ~, ~**n** (*geh.*) platitude

**Plätt·wäsche** *die* (*nordd., md.*) laundry to be ironed; ironing

**Platz** /plats/ *der;* ~**es**, **Plätze** /ˈplɛtsə/ Ⓐ (*freie Fläche*) space; area; (*Bau*~, *Ausstellungsgelände usw.*) site; (*umbaute Fläche*) square; **ein freier** ~: an open space; Ⓑ (*Park*~) car park; [parking] lot (*Amer.*); (*Camping*~) [camp]site; [camp]ground (*Amer.*); (*Schrott*~, *Lager*~) yard; Ⓒ (*Sport*~) (*ganze Anlage*) ground; (*Spielfeld*) field; (*Tennis*~, *Volleyball*~ *usw.*) court; (*Golf*~) course; **der** ~ **ist nicht bespielbar** the ground is not playable; **einen Spieler vom** ~ **stellen/tragen** send/carry a player off [the field]; **auf eigenem/gegnerischem** ~ **spielen** play at home/away; Ⓓ (*Stelle*) place; spot; (*Position*) location; position; (*wo jmd., etw. hingehört*) place; **ein** ~ **an der Sonne** (*fig.*) a place in the sun; **auf die Plätze, fertig, los!** on your marks, get set, go!; **sich** (*Dat.*) **einen festen** ~ **in der Literatur erobern** become firmly established in literature; **am** *od.* **an seinem** ~: in its/his place; **nicht** *od.* **fehl am** ~[**e**] **sein** (*fig.*) be out of place; be inappropriate; **am** ~[**e**] **sein** (*fig.*) be appropriate; be called for; Ⓔ (*Sitz*~) seat; (*am Tisch, Steh*~ *usw.; fig.: im Kurs, Krankenhaus, Kindergarten usw.*) place; **der Bus/Saal hat 60 Plätze** the bus/hall will take 60 *or* has room for 60; **erster/zweiter** ~ (*im Kino usw.*) seat at the front/back; ~ **nehmen** sit down; **nehmen Sie** ~! take a seat; ~ **behalten** (*geh.*) remain seated; Ⓕ (*bes. Sport: Platzierung*) place; **auf** ~ **drei** *od.* **dem dritten** ~: in third place; **den dritten** ~ **belegen** come third; **der Song ist auf** ~ **eins/neun der Hitparade** the song is number one/nine in the hit parade; Ⓖ (*Ort*) place; locality; **am** ~: in the town/village; **das größte Hotel am** ~: the largest hotel in the place; **die Bedeutung des** ~**es Frankfurt** (*bes. Wirtsch.*) the importance of Frankfurt as a location; Ⓗ (*Raum*) space; room; **im Kofferraum ist kein** ~ **mehr** there is no room left in the boot (*Brit.*) *or* (*Amer.*) trunk; **er/es hat [noch]** ~/**keinen** ~: there is enough space *or* room [left] for him/it/no room for him/it; **es nimmt viel** ~ **weg** it takes up a lot of space; **drei Familien/500 Autos** (*Dat.*) ~ **bieten** have room for three families/500 cars; **der Saal bietet** ~ *od.* **hat** ~ **für 3 000 Personen** the hall takes *or* holds 3,000 people; **im Viktoriasee hätte ganz Irland** ~: the whole of Ireland could fit into Lake Victoria; **[jmdm./einer Sache]** ~ **machen** make room [for sb./sth.]; **macht doch mal ein bisschen** ~: clear a bit of space; (*aufrücken*) move up a bit; **einem neuen System** ~ **machen** give way to a new system; ~ **da!** make way!; out of the way!; ~ **greifen** (*fig.*) spread

**Platz-:** ~**angst** *die* Ⓐ (*volkst.: Klaustrophobie*) claustrophobia; Ⓑ (*Med.*) agoraphobia; ~**anweiser** *der;* ~~**s**, ~~: ▶ 159 usher; ~**anweiserin** *die;* ~~, ~~**nen** ▶ 159 usherette

**Plätzchen** /ˈplɛtsçən/ *das;* ~**s**, ~ Ⓐ little place *or* spot; (*kleiner Raum*) little space; Ⓑ (*Keks*) biscuit (*Brit.*); cookie (*Amer.*); (*Schokoladen*~) [chocolate] pastille

**platzen** *itr. V.*; *mit sein* Ⓐ burst; (*explodieren*) explode; **dem Boxer war eine Augenbraue geplatzt** one of the boxer's eyebrows had split open; **vor Wut/Spannung** (*Dat.*) ~ (*fig.*) be bursting with rage/excitement; **er ist vor Lachen fast geplatzt** he nearly died with laughter; ⇒ *auch* **Neid**; Ⓑ (*ugs.: scheitern*) fall through; **geplatzt sein** ‹concert, meeting, performance, holiday, engagement› be off; **der Wechsel ist geplatzt** the bill has bounced (*sl.*); **etw.** ~ **lassen** put the kibosh on sth. (*coll.*); **der Betrug platzte** (*ugs.*) the plot collapsed; **einen Spionagering/eine Bande** ~ **lassen** bust a spy ring/a gang (*coll.*); Ⓒ (*ugs.: hinein*~) **in eine Versammlung** ~: burst into a meeting

**Platz·hirsch** *der* (*Jägerspr.*) dominant stag; (*fig. ugs.: beherrschende Figur*) boss-type (*coll.*); **er ist hier der** ~: he's the big noise around here (*coll.*)

P

**platzieren** /pla'tsi:rən/ ❶ *tr. V.* [A] place; position ‹loudspeakers›; **Polizisten an den Ausgängen ~:** post policemen by the exits; [B] (*Sport: gezielt werfen, schlagen usw.*) place ‹shot, ball›; (*Boxen, Fechten*) land ‹blow, hit›; **ein platzierter Schuss** a well-aimed shot; [C] (*Wirtsch.: unterbringen, anlegen*) place ‹money›. ❷ *refl. V.* [A] (*sich setzen*) place *or* seat oneself (**auf** + *Akk. od. Dat.* on); (*sich stellen*) take up position (**an** + *Akk. od. Dat.* at, by); [B] (*Sport*) be placed; **er konnte sich nicht ~:** he was unplaced

**Platzierung** *die; ~, ~en* [A] (*das Platzieren*) placing; (*auf Sitzplätze*) seating; (*das Aufstellen*) positioning; (*von Polizisten usw.*) posting; [B] (*Sport*) placing; place; **eine gute ~/gute ~en erreichen** be well placed

**platz-, Platz-: ~karte** *die* reserved-seat ticket; **sich** (*Dat.*) **eine ~karte bestellen** reserve a seat; **~konzert** *das* open-air concert (*by a military or brass band*); **~mangel** *der* lack of space; **~miete** *die* [A] (*auf Märkten, Messen usw.*) pitch rent; [B] (*Theater*) [cost of a] season ticket (*for a particular seat*); [C] (*Sport*) ground hire charge; (*Tennis*) court hire charge; court fees *pl.*; **~patrone** *die* blank [cartridge]; **~raubend** *Adj.* wasting space *postpos., not pred.*; bulky; **~raubend sein** take up a lot of space; **~regen** *der* downpour; cloudburst; **~sparend** ❶ *Adj.* space-saving; **möglichst ~sparend** saving as much space as possible *postpos., not pred.*; ❷ *adv.* economically; in a space-saving manner; **~verweis** *der* (*Sport*) sending-off; **einen ~verweis gegen jmdn. verhängen** order sb. off the field; **~vorteil** *der* (*Sport*) home advantage; **~wart** *der; ~~[e]s, ~~e* (*Sport*) groundsman; **~wartin** *die; ~~, ~~nen* groundswoman; **~wunde** *die* lacerated wound

**Plauderei** *die; ~, ~en* chat

**Plauderer** *der; ~s, ~,* **Plauderin** *die; ~, ~nen* talker; conversationalist

**plaudern** /'plaudɐn/ *itr. V.* [A] chat (**über** + *Akk.*, **von** about); **nett ~:** have a nice chat; [B] (*etw. aus~*) let on (*coll.*); **er plaudert** he doesn't keep his mouth shut (*sl.*)

**Plauder·ton** *der* conversational *or* chatty tone; **im ~:** in a conversational tone

**Plausch** /plauʃ/ *der; ~[e]s, ~e* (*bes. südd., österr.*) cosy chat

**plauschen** *itr. V.* (*bes. südd., österr.*) chat; **miteinander ~:** have a chat

**plausibel** /plau'zi:bl̩/ ❶ *Adj.* plausible; **jmdm. etw. ~ machen** make sth. seem convincing to sb. ❷ *adv.* plausibly

**Plauze** /'plautsə/ *die; ~, ~n* (*salopp, bes. ostmd.*) [A] (*Lunge*) lung; [B] (*Bauch*) belly; **auf der ~ liegen** (*fig.*) be laid up

**Playback** /'pleɪbæk/ *das; ~s, ~s* (*Tontechnik*) [A] (*Aufnahme*) pre-recorded version; recording; (*Begleitung*) [pre-recorded] backing; [B] (*Verfahren*) (*beim Fernsehen*) miming to a recording; (*bei Schallplatten*) double-tracking

**Play·boy** /'pleɪbɔɪ/ *der* playboy

**Plazenta** /pla'tsɛnta/ *die; ~, ~s od.* **Plazenten** ▶ 471 (*Med.*) placenta

**Plazet** /'pla:tsɛt/ *das; ~s, ~s* (*geh.*) approval

***plazieren** *usw.* ⇨ **platzieren** *usw.*

**Plebejer** /ple'be:jɐ/ *der; ~s, ~,* **Plebejerin** *die; ~, ~nen* [A] (*hist.*) plebeian; [B] (*abwertend*) common type

**plebejisch** ❶ *Adj.* [A] (*hist.*) plebeian; [B] (*abwertend*) common. ❷ *adv.* (*abwertend*) in a common manner

**Plebiszit** /plebɪs'tsi:t/ *das; ~[e]s, ~e* plebiscite

**plebiszitär** /plebɪstsi'tɛ:ɐ̯/ ❶ *Adj.* plebiscitary; ‹decision, legislation, election› by plebiscite. ❷ *adv.* by plebiscite

**Plebs¹** /plɛps/ *die; ~* (*hist.*) plebs *pl.* (*of ancient Rome*)

**Plebs²** *der; ~es od. österr.: die; ~* (*abwertend*) **der ~:** common herd; the masses *pl.*

*old spelling (see note on page 1707)

**pleite** /'plaitə/ (*ugs.*) *in* **~ sein** ‹person› be broke (*coll.*); ‹company› have gone bust (*coll.*); ⇨ *auch* **Pleite** A

**Pleite** *die; ~, ~n* (*ugs.*) [A] (*Bankrott*) bankruptcy *no def. art.*; **vor der ~ stehen** be faced with bankruptcy; **~ machen** *od.* **gehen** go bust (*coll.*); [B] (*Misserfolg*) flop (*sl.*); washout (*coll.*)

**Pleite·geier** *der* (*ugs.*) spectre of bankruptcy; **den ~ vertreiben** chase the wolf from the door

**Plejaden** /ple'ja:dn̩/ *Pl.* (*Astron.*) Pleiades

**Plektron** /'plɛktrɔn/ *das; ~s,* **Plektren, Plektrum** /'plɛktrʊm/ *das; ~s,* **Plektren** plectrum

**plempern** /'plɛmpɐn/ (*ugs.*) ❶ *tr. V.* sprinkle; spatter. ❷ *itr. V.* potter

**plemplem** /plɛm'plɛm/ *in* **~ sein** (*ugs.*) be nuts (*coll.*) *or* cuckoo (*sl.*); **ich bin doch nicht ~:** I'm not crazy

**Plenar-** /ple'na:ɐ̯-/: **~saal** *der* plenary chamber; **~sitzung** *die* plenary session

**Plenum** /'ple:nʊm/ *das; ~s* (*Versammlung*) plenary meeting; (*Sitzung*) plenary session

**Pleonasmus** /pleo'nasmʊs/ *der; ~,* **Pleonasmen** (*Stilk.*) pleonasm

**pleonastisch** /pleo'nastɪʃ/ (*Stilk.*) ❶ *Adj.* pleonastic. ❷ *adv.* pleonastically

**Pleuel·stange** /'plɔy̯əl-/ *die* (*Technik*) connecting rod

**Plexi·glas** ⓌⓏ /'plɛksigla:s/ *das* ≈ Perspex ®

**plieren** /'pli:rən/ *itr. V.* (*nordd.*) squint

**plinkern** /'plɪŋkɐn/ *itr. V.* (*nordd.*) blink

**Plissee** /plɪ'se:/ *das; ~s, ~s* [A] (*Falten*) accordion pleats *pl.*; [B] (*Stoff*) accordion-pleated material

**Plissee·rock** *der* accordion-pleated skirt

**plissieren** *tr. V.* pleat

**PLO** *Abk.* **Palästinensische Befreiungsorganisation** PLO

**Plombe** /'plɔmbə/ *die; ~, ~n* [A] (*Siegel*) [lead] seal; [B] (*veralt.: Zahnfüllung*) filling

**plombieren** *tr. V.* [A] (*versiegeln*) seal; [B] (*veralt.*) fill ‹tooth›

**Plombierung** *die; ~, ~en* [A] (*Versiegelung*) sealing; [B] (*veralt.: das Füllen*) filling

**Plörre** /'plœrə/ *die; ~, ~n* (*nordd. abwertend*) dishwater (*coll.*)

**Plot** /plɔt/ *der; ~s, ~s* (*Literaturw.*) plot

**plötzlich** /'plœtslɪç/ ❶ *Adj.* sudden. ❷ *adv.* suddenly; **~ aufragen** rise up abruptly; **..., aber etwas** *od.* **ein bisschen ~** (*salopp*) ..., and jump to it; ..., and make it snappy (*coll.*)

**Plötzlichkeit** *die; ~:* suddenness

**Pluder·hose** /'plu:dɐ-/ *die* pantaloons *pl.*; (*orientalischer Art*) Turkish trousers *pl.*; (*hist.*) slops *pl.*

**Plumeau** /ply'mo:/ *das; ~s, ~s* duvet

**plump** /plʊmp/ ❶ *Adj.* [A] (*dick*) plump; podgy; massive ‹stone, lump›; (*unförmig*) ungainly, clumsy ‹shape›; (*rundlich*) bulbous; [B] (*schwerfällig*) awkward, clumsy ‹movements, style›; [C] (*abwertend: dreist*) crude, blatant ‹lie, deception, trick›; (*leicht durchschaubar*) blatantly obvious; (*unbeholfen*) clumsy ‹excuse, advances›; crude ‹joke, forgery›; **~e Vertraulichkeit** embarrassing overfamiliarity. ❷ *adv.* [A] (*schwerfällig*) clumsily; awkwardly; [B] (*abwertend: dreist*) in a blatantly obvious manner; **~ gefälscht** crudely *or* clumsily forged

**Plumpheit** *die; ~, ~en* [A] (*Dicke*) plumpness; podginess; (*Unförmigkeit*) ungainliness; clumsiness; (*Rundlichkeit*) bulbousness; [B] (*Schwerfälligkeit*) clumsiness; awkwardness; (*eines dicken Menschen*) ponderousness; [C] (*abwertend: Dreistigkeit*) blatant nature; (*primitive Art*) crudity; clumsiness

**plumps** *Interj.* bump; thud; (*ins Wasser*) splash; **~ machen** go bump

**Plumps** *der; ~es, ~e* (*ugs.*) bump; thud; (*ins Wasser*) splash

**plumpsen** [A] *itr. V.* fall with a bump; thud; (*ins Wasser*) splash; [B] *unpers.* **es plumpste** there was a thud *or* bump; (*ins Wasser*) there was a splash

**Plumps·klo[sett]** *das* (*ugs.*) earth closet

**plump·vertraulich, *plump-vertraulich** ❶ *Adj.* overfamiliar; (*bei Männern*) hail-fellow-well-met. ❷ *adv.* with excessive familiarity

**Plunder** /'plʊndɐ/ *der; ~s* (*ugs. abwertend*) junk; rubbish

**Plünderei** *die; ~, ~en* ⇨ **Plünderung**

**Plünderer** *der; ~s, ~,* **Plünderin** *die; ~, ~nen* looter

**plündern** /'plʏndɐn/ *itr., tr. V.* [A] loot; plunder, pillage ‹town›; [B] (*scherzh.: [fast] leeren*) raid ‹larder, fridge, account›; ‹bird, animal› strip ‹tree, border›

**Plünderung** *die; ~, ~en* looting; (*einer Stadt*) plundering; **~en** cases of looting/plundering

**Plünnen** *Pl.* (*bes. nordd. ugs.: Kleider*) gear *sing.* (*coll.*)

**Plural** /'plu:ra:l/ *der; ~s, ~e* [A] plural; **„Atlanten" ist [der] ~ von** *od.* **zu „Atlas"** 'Atlanten' is the plural of 'Atlas'; [B] (*Wort*) word in the plural; plural form; **im ~ stehen** be [in the] plural

**Pluraletantum** /plurale'tantʊm/ *das; ~s,* **Pluraliatantum** /pluralia'tantʊm/ plural-only noun

**pluralisch** (*Sprachw.*) ❶ *Adj.* plural ‹form, ending›; ‹word, clause› in the plural. ❷ *adv.* in the plural

**Pluralismus** *der; ~:* pluralism

**pluralistisch** ❶ *Adj.* pluralistic. ❷ *adv.* pluralistically; along pluralistic lines

**plus** /plʊs/ ▶ 841 ❶ *Konj.* (*Math.*) plus. ❷ *Adv.* [A] ▶ 728 (*bes. Math.*) plus; [B] (*Elektrot.*) positive. ❸ *Präp. mit Dat.* (*Kaufmannsspr.*) plus

**Plus** *das; ~* [A] (*Überschuss*) surplus; (*auf einem Konto*) credit balance; **~ machen** make a profit; **im ~ sein** be in credit; [B] (*Vorteil*) advantage; [extra] asset; **das ist ein ~ für dich** it's a point in your favour

**Plüsch** /ply:ʃ/ *der; ~[e]s, ~e* plush

**Plüsch-: ~sessel** *der* plush chair; **~sofa** *das* plush sofa; **~tier** *das* cuddly toy

**Plus-: ~pol** *der* (*Physik*) positive pole; (*einer Batterie*) positive terminal; **~punkt** *der* [A] [plus] point; [B] ⇨ **Plus** B; **~punkte sammeln** strengthen one's/its position; (*sich beliebt machen*) gain brownie points

**Plusquam·perfekt** /'plʊskvampɛrfɛkt/ *das* pluperfect [tense]

**plustern** /'plu:stɐn/ ❶ *tr. V.* ruffle [up] ‹feathers›. ❷ *refl. V.* ‹bird› ruffle [up] its feathers

**Plus·zeichen** *das* plus sign

**Pluto¹** /'plu:to/ *der; ~* (*Astron.*), **Pluto²** (*der*) (*Myth.*) Pluto

**Plutokrat** /pluto'kra:t/ *der; ~en, ~en* (*geh. abwertend*) plutocrat

**Plutokratie** /plutokra'ti:/ *die; ~, ~n* (*geh. abwertend*) plutocracy

**Plutokratin** *die; ~, ~nen* ⇨ **Plutokrat**

**Plutonium** /plu'to:ni̯ʊm/ *das; ~s* (*Physik*) plutonium

**PLZ** *Abk.* **Postleitzahl**

**Pneu** /pnɔy̯/ *der; ~s, ~s* (*bes. österr., schweiz.*) tyre

**Pneumatik¹** /pnɔy̯'ma:tɪk/ *die; ~, ~en* [A] pneumatics *sing., no art.*; [B] (*Anlage*) pneumatic system

**Pneumatik²** *der; ~s, ~s,* (*österr.:*) *die; ~, ~en* (*österr., schweiz., veralt.*) tyre

**pneumatisch** (*Technik*) ❶ *Adj.* pneumatic. ❷ *adv.* pneumatically

**Po** /po:/ *der; ~s, ~s* (*ugs.*) bottom

**Pöbel** /'pø:bl̩/ *der; ~s* (*abwertend*) rabble

**pöbelhaft** (*abwertend*) ❶ *Adj.* loutish; uncouth. ❷ *adv.* in a loutish manner

**Pöbel·herrschaft** *die* mob rule

**pöbeln** *itr. V.* make rude *or* coarse remarks

**pochen** /'pɔxn̩/ *itr. V.* [A] (*meist geh.: klopfen*) knock (**gegen** at, on); (*kräftig*) rap; thump; **an die Tür ~:** knock at *or* on the door; **es pocht** somebody is knocking at *or* on the door; [B] (*geh.: sich berufen*) **auf etw.** (*Akk.*) **~:** insist on sth.; [C] (*geh.: pulsieren*) ‹heart› pound, thump; ‹blood› pound, throb

**pochieren** /pɔˈʃi:rən/ *tr. V. (Kochk.)* poach

**Pocke** /ˈpɔkə/ *die;* ~, ~**n** pock

**Pocken** *Pl.* ▶474 smallpox *sing.*

**pocken-, Pocken-:** ~**narbe** *die* pockmark; ~**narbig** *Adj.* pockmarked; ~**schutz·impfung** *die* smallpox vaccination

**pockig** *Adj.* pockmarked ‹face, surface›; pimpled ‹leather›

**Podest** /poˈdɛst/ *das od. der;* ~**[e]s**, ~**e** Ⓐ rostrum; Ⓑ *(bes. nordd.: Treppenabsatz)* landing

**Podex** *der;* ~**[es]**, ~**e** *(fam.)* bottom; behind

**Podium** /ˈpo:di̯ʊm/ *das;* ~**s**, **Podien** Ⓐ *(Plattform)* platform; *(Bühne)* stage; Ⓑ *(trittartige Erhöhung)* rostrum; podium

**Podiums·diskussion** *die,* **Podiums·gespräch** *das* panel discussion

**Po·ebene** *die (Geogr.)* plain of the River Po

**Poem** /poˈe:m/ *das;* ~**s**, ~**e** *(veralt.)* poem

**Poesie** /poeˈzi:/ *die;* ~, ~**n** Ⓐ poetry; **ein Abend voller** ~: an evening full of magic; Ⓑ *(Gedicht)* poem

**Poesie·album** *das* autograph album *(with verses or sayings contributed by friends)*

**Poet** /poˈe:t/ *der;* ~**en**, ~**en** *(veralt.)* poet; bard *(literary)*

**Poetik** /poˈe:tɪk/ *die;* ~, ~**en** Ⓐ poetics *sing.;* Ⓑ *(Lehrbuch)* treatise on poetry

**Poetin** *die;* ~, ~**nen** poetess; poet; bard *(literary)*

**poetisch** ❶ *Adj.* poetic[al]. ❷ *adv.* poetically

**pofen** /ˈpo:fn̩/ *itr. V. (nordd. salopp)* kip *(Brit. coll.)*; snooze *(coll.)*

**Pogrom** /poˈgro:m/ *das od. der;* ~**s**, ~**e** pogrom

**Pogrom-:** ~**hetze** *die* hate campaign *(leading up to a pogrom)*; ~**stimmung** *die* bloodthirsty mood

**Pointe** /ˈpo̯ɛ̃:tə/ *die;* ~, ~**n** *(eines Witzes)* punch line; *(einer Geschichte)* point; *(eines Sketches)* curtain line; **die** ~ **verderben** spoil the effect of the story/joke; **eine überraschende** ~: a surprising twist

**pointiert** /po̯ɛ̃ˈti:ɐ̯t/ ❶ *Adj.* pointed ‹remark›. ❷ *adv.* pointedly

**Pokal** /poˈka:l/ *der;* ~**s**, ~**e** Ⓐ *(Trinkgefäß)* goblet; Ⓑ *(Siegestrophäe,* ~*wettbewerb)* cup

**Pokal-:** ~**sieger** *der,* ~**siegerin** *die (Sport)* cup winners *pl.;* ~**spiel** *das (Sport)* cup tie; ~**wettbewerb** *der (Sport)* cup competition

**Pökel-:** ~**fleisch** *das* salt meat; ~**hering** *der* salt herring

**pökeln** /ˈpø:kl̩n/ *tr. V.* salt

**Poker** /ˈpo:kɐ/ *das od. der;* ~**s** poker; *(fig.)* manoeuvrings *pl.*

**Poker-:** ~**gesicht** *das* poker face; **ein** ~**gesicht machen** put on a poker-faced expression; ~**miene** *die* poker face

**pokern** *itr. V.* Ⓐ *(Poker spielen)* play poker; Ⓑ *(fig.)* **um etw.** ~: bid for sth.

**Pol** /po:l/ *der;* ~**s**, ~**e** pole; **der ruhende** ~ *(fig.)* the calming influence

**Polack** /pɔˈlak/ *der;* ~**en**, ~**en**, **Polacke** *der;* ~**n**, ~**n** *(ugs. abwertend)* [dirty *(derog.)*] Pole

**polar** /poˈla:ɐ̯/ *Adj.* Ⓐ polar; Ⓑ *(gegensätzlich)* diametrically opposed; ~**e Gegensätze** complete *or* polar opposites

**Polar-:** ~**eis** *das* polar ice; ~**expedition** *die* polar expedition; ~**front** *die (Met.)* polar front; ~**fuchs** *der* Arctic fox

**Polarisation** /polarizaˈtsi̯o:n/ *die;* ~, ~**en** polarization

**polarisieren** ❶ *tr. V. (Chemie, Physik)* polarize. ❷ *refl. V. (in Gegensätzen hervortreten)* become polarized

**Polarisierung** *die;* ~, ~**en** *(auch Chemie, Physik)* polarization

**Polarität** *die;* ~, ~**en** *(auch Geogr., Astron., Physik)* polarity

**Polar-:** ~**kreis** *der* polar circle; **nördlicher/südlicher** ~**kreis** Arctic/Antarctic Circle; ~**licht** *das; Pl.* ~**er** aurora; polar lights *pl.*

**Polaroid·kamera** Ⓦ /polaroˈi:t-/ *die* Polaroid camera ®

**Polar-:** ~**station** *die* polar [research] station; ~**stern** *der* polar star; pole star; ~**zone** *die* frigid zone; polar region

**Polder** *der;* ~**s**, ~: polder

**Pole** *der;* ~**n**, ~**n** ▶553 Pole

**Polemik** /poˈle:mɪk/ *die;* ~, ~**en** polemic; **ein Pamphlet voller** ~: a pamphlet full of polemics

**polemisch** ❶ *Adj.* polemic[al]. ❷ *adv.* polemically

**polemisieren** *itr. V.* polemize

**polen** *tr. V. (Physik, Elektrot.)* connect; **auf diesem Sektor sind Paris und Bonn nicht gleich gepolt** *(fig.)* in this area Paris and Bonn hold different views

**Polen** *(das);* ~**s** Poland; **noch ist** ~ **nicht verloren** *(fig.)* all is not [yet] lost; **da/dann ist** ~ **offen** *(fig.)* all hell is/will be let loose

**Polente** /poˈlɛntə/ *die;* ~ *(salopp)* cops *pl. (coll.)*

**Poleposition, *Pole-position** /ˈpoʊlpəzɪʃən/ *die;* ~: pole position

**Police** /poˈli:sə/ *die;* ~, ~**n** *(Versicherungsw.)* policy

**Polier** /poˈli:ɐ̯/ *der;* ~**s**, ~**e** [site] foreman

**polieren** *tr. V.* polish; *(fig.)* polish up; **jmdm. die Fresse** ~ *(derb)* smash sb.'s face in

**Polier-:** ~**mittel** *das* polish; ~**tuch** *das; Pl.* ~**tücher** polishing cloth

**-polig** /ˈpo:lɪç/ *adj.* **ein**~/**drei**~/**mehr**~: single-/three-/multi-pin

**Poli·klinik** *die* outpatients' department *or* clinic

**Polin** *die;* ~, ~**nen** Pole; ⇒ *auch* **-in**

**Polio** /ˈpo:li̯o/ *die;* ~: polio

**Polit-** political; ~**blatt** politically oriented publication

**Polit·büro** *das* politburo

**Politesse** /poliˈtɛsə/ *die;* ~, ~**n** [woman] traffic warden

**Politik** /poliˈti:k/ *die;* ~, ~**en** Ⓐ politics *sing., no art.;* **eine gemeinsame/neue** ~: a common/new policy; Ⓑ *(eine spezielle* ~*)* policy; **eine** ~ **der kleinen Schritte** a gradualist policy; Ⓒ *(Taktik)* tactics *pl.*

**-politik** *die ...* policy; **die unterschiedliche Schul**~ **der einzelnen Länder** the different education policies of the different States

**Politika** ⇒ **Politikum**

**Politiker** /poˈli:tikɐ/ *der;* ~**s**, ~, **Politikerin** *die;* ~, ~**nen** ▶159 politician

**Politikum** /poˈli:tikʊm/ *das;* ~**s**, **Politika** political issue; *(Ereignis)* political event

**Politik·wissenschaft** *die* political science *no art.*

**politisch** ❶ *Adj.* Ⓐ political; Ⓑ *(klug u. berechnend)* politic. ❷ *adv.* Ⓐ politically; Ⓑ *(klug u. berechnend)* politicly; judiciously

**-politisch** *adj., adv.* concerning ... policy

**Politische** *der/die; adj. Dekl. (ugs.)* political prisoner

**politisieren** ❶ *itr. V.* talk politics; politicize; **es wurde viel politisiert** there was a great deal of political discussion. ❷ *tr. V.* Ⓐ *(politisch aktivieren)* make politically active; Ⓑ *(politisch behandeln)* politicize

**Politisierung** *die;* ~: politicization

**Politologe** /politoˈlo:gə/ *der;* ~**n**, ~**n** political scientist

**Politologie** *die;* ~: political science *no art.*

**Politologin** *die;* ~, ~**nen** political scientist

**politologisch** *Adj.* ‹analysis› in terms of political science; ‹sense› of political science; ~**es Studium** political studies *pl.*

**Politur** /poliˈtu:ɐ̯/ *die;* ~, ~**en** polish

**Polizei** /poliˈtsai̯/ *die;* ~, ~**en** Ⓐ police *pl.;* **er ist od. arbeitet bei der** ~: he is in the police force; Ⓑ *(Dienststelle)* police station

**Polizei-:** ~**apparat** *der* police force; ~**auf·gebot** *das* police contingent; **trotz überdurchschnittlichen** ~**aufgebots** despite the larger than average police presence; ~**auto** *das* police car; ~**beamte** *der,* ~**beamtin** *die* ▶159 police officer; ~**behörde** *die* police authority; ~**chef** *der,* ~**chefin** *die* chief of police; chief constable *(Brit.)*; ~**direktion** *die* police authority; ~**ein·satz** *der* police operation; ~**eskorte** *die* police escort; ~**funk** *der* police radio; ~**gewahrsam** *der* [police] custody; ~**gewalt** *die* Ⓐ *(Machtbefugnis)* police powers *pl.;* Ⓑ *(ausgeübte Gewalt)* use of force by the police; ~**gewerkschaft** *die* police trade union; ~**griff** *der* [police] arm hold *or* lock; **er wurde im** ~**griff abgeführt** he was frogmarched away; ~**hund** *der* police dog; ~**knüppel** *der* [policeman's] truncheon; ~**kommissar,** *(südd., österr., schweiz.)* ~**kommissär** *der,* ~**kommissarin,** *(südd., österr., schweiz.)* ~**kommissärin** *die* ≈ [police] superintendent; ~**kontrolle** *die* police check; *(Kontrollpunkt)* police checkpoint; ~**kräfte** *Pl.* police *pl.*

**polizeilich** ❶ *Adj.* police; ~**e Meldepflicht** obligation to register with the police. ❷ *adv.* by the police; ~ **verboten** prohibited by order of the police

**polizei-, Polizei-:** ~**methoden** *Pl. (abwertend)* **das sind ja** ~**methoden!** that is sheer brutality *sing.;* ~**präsident** *der,* ~**präsidentin** *die* chief of police; chief constable *(Brit.)*; ~**präsidium** *das* police headquarters *sing. or pl.;* ~**revier** *das* Ⓐ *(*~*dienststelle)* police station; **sich auf dem** ~**revier melden** report to the police; Ⓑ *(Bezirk)* police district; ~**schutz** *der* police protection; ~**sirene** *die* [police car] siren; ~**spitzel** *der* police informer; ~**staat** *der* police state; ~**streife** *die* police patrol; ~**stunde** *die* closing time; **die** ~**stunde verlängern** extend the opening hours *pl.;* **die** ~**stunde aufheben** waive the restrictions on opening hours *pl.;* ~**verordnung** *die* police regulation; ~**wache** *die* police station; ~**widrig** ❶ *Adj.* against police regulations *postpos.;* illegal; ❷ *adv.* against police regulations; illegally

**Polizist** /poliˈtsɪst/ *der;* ~**en**, ~**en** ▶159 policeman

**Polizistin** *die;* ~, ~**nen** ▶159 policewoman

**Polka** /ˈpɔlka/ *die;* ~, ~**s** polka

**Pollen** /ˈpɔlən/ *der;* ~**s**, ~ *(Bot.)* pollen

**Poller** *der;* ~**s**, ~: bollard

**Pollution** /pɔluˈtsi̯o:n/ *die;* ~, ~**en** *(Med.)* [nocturnal] emission

**polnisch** /ˈpɔlnɪʃ/ *Adj.* ▶553, ▶696 Polish; **eine** ~**e Wirtschaft** *(ugs. abwertend)* a shambles; ⇒ *auch* **deutsch; Deutsch; Deutsche**[2]

**Polo** /ˈpo:lo/ *das;* ~**s** polo

**Polo·hemd** *das* short-sleeved shirt

**Polonaise, Polonäse** /poloˈnɛ:zə/ *die;* ~, ~**n** polonaise

**Polster** /ˈpɔlstɐ/ *das od. (österr.) der;* ~**s**, ~ *od. (österr.)* **Pölster** /ˈpœlstɐ/ Ⓐ *(*~*ung)* upholstery *no pl., no indef. art.;* Ⓑ *(Schulterpolster)* [shoulder] pad; Ⓒ *(Rücklage)* reserves *pl.;* Ⓓ *(Bot.)* cushion; Ⓔ *(österr.: Kissen)* cushion; *(Kopfkissen)* pillow

**Pölsterchen** *das;* ~**s**, ~: bulge of fat

**Polsterer** *der;* ~**s**, ~ ▶159 upholsterer

**Polster·garnitur** *die* suite

**Polsterin** *die;* ~, ~**nen** ⇒ **Polsterer**

**Polster·möbel** *das* piece of upholsterd furniture; **teure** ~: expensive upholstered furniture *sing.*

**polstern** *tr. V.* upholster ‹furniture›; pad ‹door›; **sie ist gut gepolstert** *(fig. ugs. scherzh.)* she is well-upholstered *(joc.)*; **finanziell gut gepolstert sein** *(fig. ugs. scherzh.)* be comfortably off

**Polster-:** ~**sessel** *der* [upholstered] armchair; easy chair; ~**stuhl** *der* upholstered chair; ~**tür** *die* padded door

**Polsterung** *die;* ~, ~**en** Ⓐ *(Polster)* upholstery *no pl.; no indef. art.;* Ⓑ *(das Polstern)* upholstering

**Polter·abend** *der; party on the eve of a wedding (at which crockery is smashed to bring good luck)*

**Polter·geist** *der* poltergeist

**poltern** /ˈpɔltɐn/ ❶ *itr. V.* Ⓐ *(lärmen)* crash *or* thump about; **es poltert** there is a bang *or* crash; **ein** ~**der Lärm** a din *or* racket; Ⓑ

*mit sein* (*sich laut bewegen*) **der Karren polterte über das Pflaster** the cart clattered over the cobblestones; **er kam ins Zimmer gepoltert** he came clumping into the room; **C** (*schimpfen*) rant [and rave]; **D** (*ugs.: Polterabend feiern*) hold a **Polterabend**. **2** *tr. V.* **„Ruhe!" polterte er** 'Be quiet!' he bawled

**poly-, Poly-** /poly-/ poly-

**poly-, Poly-: ~eder** /-'|e:dɐ/ *das;* **~~s, ~~** (*Geom.*) polyhedron; **~ester** /-'|ɛstɐ/ *der* (*Chemie*) polyester; **~gam** /-'ga:m/ **1** *Adj.* polygamous; **2** *adv.* polygamously; **~gamie** /-ga'mi:/ *die;* **~~:** polygamy; **~glott** /-'glɔt/ *Adj.* polyglot

**Polynesien** /poly'ne:zi̯ən/ (*das*); **~s** Polynesia

**polynesisch** *Adj.* Polynesian

**Polyp** /po'ly:p/ *der;* **~en, ~en** **A ▶ 474** (*Zool., Med.*) polyp; **B** (*salopp: Polizist*) cop (*coll.*); copper (*Brit. coll.*); **C** (*veralt.: Krake*) octopus

**poly-, Poly-: ~phonie** /-fo'ni:/ *die;* **~~** (*Musik*) polyphony; **~technik** *die* (*DDR*), **~technikum** *das* polytechnic; **~technisch** **1** *Adj.* polytechnic; **2** *adv.* **er war ~technisch ausgebildet** he had a polytechnic training

**Pomade** /po'ma:də/ *die;* **~, ~n** pomade; hair cream

**pomadig** **1** *Adj.* **A** pomaded; greased down; (*fig.*) over-slick; **B** (*bes. nordd.: blasiert*) blasé; **C** (*ugs.: langsam*) sluggish. **2** *adv.* **A** (*bes. nordd.: blasiert*) in a blasé way; **B** (*ugs.: langsam*) sluggishly

**Pomeranze** /pomə'rantsə/ *die;* **~, ~n** Seville *or* sour *or* bitter orange

**Pommer** *der;* **~n, ~n, Pommerin** *die;* **~, ~nen** Pomeranian

**Pommern** (*das*); **~s** Pomerania

**Pommes frites** /pɔm'frit/ *Pl.* chips *pl.* (*Brit.*); French fries *pl.* (*Amer.*)

**Pomp** /pɔmp/ *der;* **~[e]s** pomp

**Pompeji** /pɔm'pe:ji/ (*das*); **~s ▶ 700** Pompeii

**pomphaft, pompös** /pɔm'pø:s/ **1** *Adj.* grandiose; ostentatious. **2** *adv.* grandiosely; ostentatiously

**Poncho** /'pɔntʃo/ *der;* **~s, ~s** poncho

**Pond** /pɔnt/ *das;* **~s, ~** (*Physik*) gram-force

**Pontifikal-** /pɔntifi'ka:l-/: **~amt** *das,* **~messe** *die* (*kath. Kirche*) Pontifical Mass

**Pontifikat** /pɔntifi'ka:t/ *das od. der;* **~[e]s, ~e** (*kath. Kirche*) pontificate

**Pontius** /'pɔntsi̯ʊs/ *in* **von ~ zu Pilatus laufen** (*ugs.*) rush from pillar to post

**Ponton** /põ'tõ:/ *der;* **~s, ~s** pontoon

**Pony**[1] /'pɔni/ *das;* **~s, ~s** pony

**Pony**[2] *der;* **~s, ~s** (*Frisur*) fringe

**Pony·frisur** *die* [hairstyle with a] fringe

**Pool** /pu:l/ *der;* **~s, ~s** (*Wirtsch.*) pool

**Pool·billard** *das* pool

**Pop** /pɔp/ *der;* **~[s]** pop

**Popanz** *der;* **~es, ~e** **A** (*abwertend*) bogey; bugbear; (*willenloser Mensch*) puppet; **B** (*veralt.: Schreckgestalt*) scarecrow

**Pop-Art** /'pɔp|a:ɐ̯t/ *die;* **~:** pop art

**Popcorn** /'pɔpkɔrn/ *das;* **~s** popcorn

**Pope** *der;* **~n, ~n** (*abwertend*) cleric

**Popel** /'po:pl̩/ *der;* **~s, ~** (*ugs.*) **A** bogy (*sl.*); **B** (*abwertend: Mensch*) nobody

**popelig** (*ugs. abwertend*) **1** *Adj.* crummy (*coll.*); lousy (*coll.*); (*durchschnittlich*) second-rate. **2** *adv.* crummily (*sl.*)

**Popelin** /popə'li:n/ *der;* **~s, ~e, Popeline** *der;* **~s, ~** *od. die;* **~, ~** poplin

**Popeline·mantel** *der* poplin coat

**popeln** *itr. V.* (*ugs.*) **[in der Nase] ~:** pick one's nose

**Pop-: ~farbe** *die* brilliant colour; **~festival** *das* pop festival; **~gruppe** *die* pop group; **~konzert** *das* pop concert

**poplig** ⇒ **popelig**

**Pop·musik** *die* pop music

**Popo** /po'po:/ *der;* **~s, ~s** (*fam.*) bottom

**Popo·scheitel** *der* (*ugs. scherzh.*) straight middle *or* centre parting

**Popper** /'pɔpɐ/ *der;* **~s, ~, Popperin** *die;* **~, ~nen** *fashion-conscious, apolitical young person*

**poppig** /'pɔpɪç/ **1** *Adj.* trendy. **2** *adv.* trendily

**Pop·star** *der* pop star

**populär** /popu'lɛ:ɐ̯/ **1** *Adj.* popular (**bei** with); **in ~em Deutsch** in German which is comprehensible to the layman. **2** *adv.* popularly; **etw. ~ ausdrücken** express sth. in layman's language

**popularisieren** *tr. V.* popularize

**Popularisierung** *die;* **~, ~en** popularization

**Popularität** *die;* **~:** popularity

**populär·wissenschaftlich** **1** *Adj.* popular science *attrib.*; **zu ~ sein** be too much on the popular-science level. **2** *adv.* in a popular scientific way

**Population** *die;* **~, ~en** population

**Populismus** *der;* **~:** populism *no art.*

**Populist** *der;* **~en, ~en, Populistin** *die;* **~, ~nen** populist

**Pore** /'po:rə/ *die;* **~, ~n** pore

**poren·tief** (*Werbespr.*) **1** *Adj.* deep-down. **2** *adv.* pore-deep

**porig** *Adj.* porous

**Porno** /'pɔrno/ *der;* **~s, ~s** (*ugs.*) **A** (**~grafie**) porn[o] (*coll.*); **B** (**~film, ~heft** *usw.*) porn[o] film/magazine *etc.*

**porno-, Porno-: ~film** *der* (*ugs.*) porn[o] film (*coll.*); **~graphie** /--'-/ *die* pornography; **~graphisch** /-'--/ **1** *Adj.* pornographic; **2** *adv.* pornographically

**porös** /po'rø:s/ porous

**Porosität** /porozi'tɛ:t/ *die;* **~:** porousness

**Porphyr** /'pɔrfy:ɐ̯/ *der;* **~s, ~e** /pɔr'fy:rə/ (*Geol.*) porphyry

**Porree** /'pɔre/ *der;* **~s, ~s** leek; **ich mag ~:** I like leeks

**Portal** /pɔr'ta:l/ *das;* **~s, ~e** portal

**Portefeuille** /pɔrt(ə)'fø:j/ *das;* **~s, ~s** (*geh. veralt.*) wallet

**Portemonnaie** /pɔrtmɔ'ne:/ *das;* **~s, ~s** purse

**Porti** *Pl.* ⇒ **Porto**

**Portier** /pɔr'ti̯e:/ *der;* **~s, ~s,** *österr.:* /pɔr'ti:ɐ̯/ *der;* **~s, ~e ▶ 159** **A** (*Pförtner*) porter. **B** (*veralt.: Hausmeister*) caretaker; **stiller ~** (*bes. berlin.*) list of tenants' names

**portieren** *tr. V.* (*schweiz.*) put up; nominate

**Portiers·frau** *die* **A** (*woman*) porter; **B** (*Frau des Portiers*) porter's wife

**Portier[s]·loge** *die* porter's lodge

**Portion** /pɔr'tsi̯o:n/ *die;* **~, ~en** **A** (*beim Essen*) portion; helping; **eine halbe ~** (*fig. ugs. spött.*) a feeble little titch (*coll.*); **eine ~ Eis** one ice cream; **eine zweite ~:** a second helping; **B** (*ugs.: Anteil*) amount; **eine große ~ Geduld** a fair amount of patience

**portionieren** *tr. V.* divide into portions

**portions·weise** *Adv.* in portions

**Porto** /'pɔrto/ *das;* **~s, ~s** *od.* **Porti** postage (**für** on, for); **„~ zahlt Empfänger"** 'postage will be paid by licensee'

**porto-, Porto-: ~frei** *Adj.* post-free; **~kasse** *die* (*Wirtsch.*) cash box (*for postal expenses*); **~pflichtig** *Adj.* liable *or* subject to postage *postpos.*

**Porträt** /pɔr'trɛ:/ *das;* **~s, ~s** portrait; **jmdm. ~ sitzen** sit for sb. [for a portrait]

**Porträt·aufnahme** *die* portrait [photograph]

**porträtieren** /pɔrtrɛ'ti:rən/ *tr. V.* paint a portrait of/take a portrait [photograph] of; (*fig.*) portray

**Porträtist** *der;* **~en, ~en, Porträtistin** *die;* **~, ~nen** portrait painter/portrait photographer; portraitist

**Portugal** /'pɔrtugal/ (*das*); **~s** Portugal

**Portugiese** /pɔrtu'gi:zə/ *der;* **~n, ~n, Portugiesin** *die;* **~, ~nen ▶ 553** Portuguese; ⇒ *auch* **-in**

**portugiesisch** *Adj.* **▶ 553, ▶ 696** Portuguese; ⇒ *auch* **deutsch; Deutsch; Deutsche**[2]

**Portwein** /'pɔrtvai̯n/ *der* port

**Porzellan** /pɔrtsɛ'la:n/ *das;* **~s, ~e** **A** porcelain; china; **~ zerschlagen** (*fig. ugs.*) cause a lot of harm *or* trouble; **B** (*Gegenstand aus ~*) piece of porcelain *or* china

**Porzellan-: ~erde** *die* china clay; kaolin; **~geschirr** *das* china [crockery]; **~laden** *der; Pl.* **~läden** china shop; ⇒ *auch* **Elefant**

**pos.** *Abk.* **positiv** pos.

**Posaune** /po'zau̯nə/ *die;* **~, ~n** trombone

**posaunen** **1** *itr. V.* (*musizieren*) play the trombone. **2** *tr. V.* (*ugs. abwertend*) **A** (*hinaus~*) **etw. in die** *od.* **alle Welt ~:** tell the whole world about sth.; **B** (*laut sprechen*) bellow; bawl

**Posaunen-: ~chor** *der* brass ensemble; **~engel** *der* **A** (*Kunst*) angel with a trumpet; **B** (*ugs. scherzh.*) chubby-cheeks *sing.*

**Posaunist** *der;* **~en, ~en, Posaunistin** *die;* **~, ~nen ▶ 159** trombonist

**Pose** /'po:zə/ *die;* **~, ~n** pose

**Posemuckel** /po:zə'mʊkl̩/ (*das*); **~s** (*salopp abwertend*) the back of beyond

**posieren** *itr. V.* pose

**Position** /pozi'tsi̯o:n/ *die;* **~, ~en** **A** position; **in gesicherter ~ sein** have a secure position; **B** (*Wirtsch.: einzelner Posten*) item

**Positions-: ~lampe** *die,* **~licht** *das* (*Seew., Flugw.*) navigation light; **~wechsel** *der* change of position *or* attitude

**positiv** /'po:ziti:f/ **1** *Adj.* positive; **~e Zahlen** (*Math.*) positive *or* plus numbers; **ist es schon ~, dass ...?** (*ugs.*) is it definite *or* certain that ...? **2** *adv.* positively; **einen Antrag ~ bescheiden** accept an application; **einer Sache** (*Dat.*) **~ gegenüberstehen** take a positive view of a matter; **etw. ~ beeinflussen** have a positive influence on sth.; **etw. ~ bewerten** judge sth. favourably; **der Test verlief ~:** the test proved successful; **ich weiß das ~** (*ugs.*) I know that for certain *or* for sure; **sich ~ verändern** change for the better

**Positiv**[1] *der;* **~s, ~e** (*Sprachw.*) positive

**Positiv**[2] *das;* **~s, ~e** **A** (*Fot.*) positive; **B** (*kleine Orgel*) positive organ

**Positiva** ⇒ **Positivum**

**Positivismus** *der;* **~:** positivism *no art.*

**positivistisch** *Adj.* positivist[ic]

**Positivum** /'po:ziti:vʊm/ *das;* **~s, Positiva** (*geh.*) positive aspect

**Positron** /'po:zitrɔn/ *das;* **~s, Positronen** (*Physik*) positron

**Positur** /pozi'tu:ɐ̯/ *die;* **~, ~en** **A** pose; posture; **sich in ~ setzen** *od.* **stellen** *od.* **werfen** (*ugs. leicht spött.*) strike a pose; take up a posture; **B** (*Sport*) stance; **in ~ gehen/sein** take up/have taken up one's stance

**Posse** /'pɔsə/ *die;* **~, ~n** farce

**Possen** *der;* **~s, ~** (*veralt.*) **A** *Pl.* pranks; tricks; **~ reißen** play tricks; **B** **jmdm. einen ~ spielen** play a prank *or* trick on sb.

**Possen·reißer** *der,* **Possen·reißerin** *die;* **~, ~nen** clown; buffoon

**possessiv** /'pɔsɛsi:f/ *Adj.* (*Sprachw.*) possessive

**Possessiv** *das;* **~s, ~e, Possessiv·pronomen** *das,* **Possessivum** /pɔsɛ'si:vʊm/ *das;* **~s, Possessiva** (*Sprachw.*) possessive pronoun

**possierlich** /pɔ'si:ɐ̯lɪç/ **1** *Adj.* sweet; cute (*Amer.*). **2** *adv.* sweetly; cutely (*Amer.*)

**Post** /pɔst/ *die;* **~, ~en** **A** post (*Brit.*); mail; **er ist** *od.* **arbeitet bei der ~:** he works for the Post Office; **etw. mit der** *od.* **per ~ schicken** send sth. by post *or* mail; **ist ~ für mich da?** is there any post *or* mail for me?; **sonntags kommt** *od.* **gibt es keine ~:** there is no post *or* delivery on Sundays; **mit gleicher ~:** by the same post; **mit getrennter ~:** under separate cover; **auf [die] ~ warten** (*ugs.*) wait for [the] post; ⇒ *auch* **ab** 2 B; **B** (**~amt**) post office; **auf die** *od.* **zur ~ gehen** go to the post office; **C** (*veralt.: ~kutsche*) mail [coach]; **D** (**~bus**) post [office] bus; **E** (*veralt.: Botschaft*) news *sing.*

**postalisch** /pɔs'ta:lɪʃ/ *Adj.* postal; **auf ~em Wege** by post

**Postament** /pɔsta'mɛnt/ *das;* **~[e]s, ~e** pedestal

*old spelling (see note on page 1707)

P

**Post-: ~amt** *das* post office; **~an·schrift** *die* postal address; **~an·weisung** *die* **A** *(Geldsendung) remittance paid in at a post office and delivered to the addressee by a postman;* **B** *(Formular)* postal remittance form; **~auto** *das* post office *or* mail van; **~beamte** *der*, **~beamtin** *die* ▶ 159 post office official; **~bote** *der (ugs.)* postman *(Brit.)*; mailman *(Amer.)*; **~botin** *die (ugs.)* postwoman *(Brit.)*; mailwoman *(Amer.)*; **~bus** *der* post [office] bus

**Pöstchen** /'pœstçən/ *das*; **~s**, **~** *(abwertend)* little job *or* number *(coll.)*

**Post·dienst** *der* **A** post office; **ein Beamter im ~:** a post office official; **B** *(die Post)* postal service; **C** *(Service der Post)* postal service

**Posten** /'pɔstn̩/ *der*; **~s**, **~** **A** *(bes. Milit.: Wach~)* post; **auf dem ~ sein** *(ugs.) (in guter körperlicher Verfassung sein)* be in good form; *(wachsam sein)* be on one's guard; **sich nicht [ganz] auf dem ~ fühlen** *(ugs.)* be a bit under the weather *(coll.)*; **auf verlorenem ~ stehen** *od.* **kämpfen** be fighting a losing battle; **B** *(bes. Milit.: Wachmann)* sentry; guard; **~ stehen** *od. (Soldatenspr.:)* **schieben** stand guard *or* sentry; **C** *(Anstellung)* post; position; job; **D** *(Funktion)* position; **E** *(bes. Kaufmannsspr.: Rechnungs~)* item; **F** *(bes. Kaufmannsspr.: Waren~)* quantity

**Posten-: ~dienst** *der (bes. Milit.)* guard duty; **~jäger** *der*, **~jägerin** *die (salopp)* careerist

**Poster** /'po:stɐ/ *das od. der*; **~s**, **~[s]** poster

**post-, Post-: ~fach** *das* **A** ▶ 187 *(im ~amt)* post office *or* PO box; **B** *(im Büro, Hotel o. Ä.)* pigeon-hole; **~flugzeug** *das* mail plane; **~frisch** *Adj. (Philat.)* in mint condition **~pos.**; **~gebühr** *die* [postal] charge *or* rate; **~geheimnis** *das* secrecy of the post; **~gewerkschaft** *die* post office workers' union; **~giro·amt** *das* post office giro office; ≈ national giro[bank] centre *(Brit.)*; **~giro·konto** *das* post office giro account; ≈ national giro[bank] account *(Brit.)*; **~horn** *das* post horn

**posthum** /pɔst'hu:m/ ⇒ **postum**

**postieren** *tr. V.* **A** *(aufstellen)* post; station; **sich ~:** station *or* position oneself; **B** *(stellen)* position

**Postille** /pɔs'tɪlə/ *die*; **~**, **~n** *(spött. abwertend) (Zeitschrift)* mag *(coll.)*; *(Zeitung)* rag *(derog.)*

**Postillion** /pɔstɪl'jo:n/ *der*; **~s**, **~e** *(veralt.)* mail coach driver

**Postillon d'Amour** /pɔstijõda'mu:r/ *der*; **~ ~**, **~s ~** *(scherzh.)* go-between

**post-, Post-: ~karte** *die* postcard; **~karten·größe** *die* postcard size; **in ~kartengröße** postcard-sized; **~kasten** *der (bes. nordd.)* postbox; mail box *(Amer.)*; pillar box *(Brit.)*; **~kunde** *der*, **~kundin** *die* post office user; **~kutsche** *die* mail coach; **~lagernd** *Adj., adv.* poste restante; general delivery *(Amer.)*; **~leit·zahl** *die* ▶ 187 postcode; postal code; Zip code *(Amer.)*; **~minister** *der*, **~ministerin** *die* Postmaster General; **~modern** **1** *Adj.* postmodern[ist] ‹architecture, style›; **2** *adv.* **etw. ~modern stylen/bauen** design/build sth. in the postmodern[ist] style; **~moderne** *die* **A** *(Stil)* postmodernism; **B** *(Epoche)* postmodern age; **~paket** *das* parcel; **per ~paket** [by] parcel post; **~sache** *die (Amtsspr.)* item of post office mail; **~schalter** *der* post office counter; **~scheck** *der* post office giro cheque; ≈ national giro[bank] cheque *(Brit.)*; **~scheck·amt** *das (veralt.)* ⇒ **~giroamt**; **~scheck·konto** *das (veralt.)* ⇒ **~girokonto**; **~sendung** *die* postal item

**Post·skriptum** /-'skrɪptʊm/ *das*; **~s**, **Post·skripta** postscript

**Post-: ~spar·buch** *das* post office savings book *(Brit.)*; **~spar·kasse** *die* post office savings bank *(Brit.)*; **~stelle** *die* **A** *(kleines ~amt)* sub-post office; **B** *(in einem Betrieb)* post room; **~stempel** *der* **A** *(Gerät)* stamp [for cancelling mail]; **B** *(Abdruck)* postmark

**Postulat** /pɔstu'la:t/ *das*; **~[e]s**, **~e** **A** *(Forderung)* demand; **B** *(Gebot)* decree

**postulieren** *tr. V.* **A** *(fordern)* postulate; demand; **B** *(behaupten)* assert

**postum** /pɔs'tu:m/ **1** *Adj.* posthumous. **2** *adv.* posthumously

**post-, Post-: ~wagen** *der (Eisenb.)* mail van *(Brit.)*; mail car *(Amer.)*; **~weg** *der*: **auf dem ~weg** by post *or* mail; **~wendend** *Adv.* by return [of post]; *(fig.)* immediately; **~wert·zeichen** *das (Amtsspr.)* postage stamp; **~wesen** *das* postal operations *pl.*; **~wurf·sendung** *die* direct-mail item; **~zug** *der* mail train; **~zustellung** *die* postal delivery *no def. art.*

**Pot** /pɔt/ *das*; **~s** *(Drogenjargon)* pot *(sl.)*

**potemkinsch** /po'tɛmki:nʃ/ *Adj.* in **~e Dörfer** façade *sing.*; sham *sing.*

**potent** /po'tɛnt/ *Adj.* **A** *(zeugungsfähig)* potent; **B** *(finanzstark)* [financially] strong; **C** *(fähig)* capable; able

**Potentat** /potɛn'ta:t/ *der*; **~en**, **~en**, **Potentatin** *die*; **~**, **~nen** *(abwertend)* potentate

**Potential** *usw.* ⇒ **Potenzial** *usw.*

**Potenz** /po'tɛnts/ *die*; **~**, **~en** **A** potency; **B** *(Stärke)* power; **C** ▶ 841 *(Math.)* power; **mit ~en rechnen** do calculations involving powers; **eine Zahl in die sechste ~ erheben** raise a number to the power [of] six; **das ist Blödsinn in [höchster] ~** *(fig.)* that is complete *or* utter nonsense; **D** *(Med.: Grad der Verdünnung)* potency

**Potenz·angst** *die* impotence anxiety

**Potenzial** /potɛn'tsi̯a:l/ *das*; **~s**, **~e** **A** *(Mittel, Möglichkeit)* potential; **das ~ an Energie/Aggression** energy resources *pl.*/ aggressive capacity; **B** *(Physik)* potential

**potenziell** /potɛn'tsi̯ɛl/ **1** *Adj.* potential. **2** *adv.* potentially

**potenzieren** **1** *tr. V.* **A** *(verstärken)* increase; **B** *(Math.)* **mit 5 ~:** raise to the power [of] 5; **mit diesem Rechner kann man auch ~:** you can calculate *or* work out powers on this calculator. **2** *refl. V. (sich steigern)* increase

**potenz·steigernd** *Adj.* potency *attrib.*; to increase potency *postpos.*

**Potpourri** /'pɔtpʊri/ *das*; **~s**, **~s** *od. österr.: die*; **~**, **~s** *(auch fig.)* potpourri, medley **(aus, von** of)

**Pott** /pɔt/ *der*; **~[e]s**, **Pötte** /'pœtə/ *(ugs., bes. nordd.)* **A** *(Topf)* pot; **B** *(Nachttopf)* chamber pot; po *(coll.)*; potty *(coll.)*; **zu ~[e] kommen** *(fig.)* get the job over and done with; **C** *(Schiff)* tub *(derog./joc.)*

**pott-, Pott-: ~asche** *die* potash; **~hässlich**, ***~häßlich** *Adj. (ugs.)* dead ugly *(coll.)*; ‹person, face› [as] ugly as sin *(coll.)*; **~wal** *der* physeterid *(Zool.)*; *(Spermwal)* sperm whale

**potz·tausend** *Interj. (veralt.)* **A** *(überrascht)* upon my soul *(dated)*; **B** *(unwillig)* damn it [all]

**poussieren** /pu'si:rən/ **1** *itr. V. (ugs. veralt.: flirten)* flirt. **2** *tr. V. (veralt.: umwerben)* curry favour with

**power** /'po:vɐ/ *Adj. (veralt.)* miserable; **eine ~e Gegend** a poor area

**Powidl** /'pɔvidl̩/ *der*; **~s** *(österr.)* ⇒ **Pflaumenmus**

**PR** *Abk.* **Public Relations** PR

**Prä** /prɛ:/ *das*; **~s**: **[das] ~ haben** have priority

**Präambel** /prɛ'ambl̩/ *die*; **~**, **~n** preamble

**Pracht** /praxt/ *die*; **~:** splendour; magnificence; **eine [wahre] ~ sein** *(ugs.)* be [really] marvellous *or (coll.)* great; **in voller ~:** in all its/their splendour

**Pracht-: ~aus·gabe** *die* de luxe edition; **~bau** *der*; *Pl.* **~~ten** splendid *or* magnificent building; **~exemplar** *das (ugs.)* magnificent specimen; beauty

**prächtig** /'prɛçtɪç/ **1** *Adj.* **A** *(prunkvoll)* splendid; magnificent; **B** *(großartig)* splendid; marvellous; **ein ~er Muskelriss** *(iron.)* a terrific example of a torn muscle *(coll.)*. **2** *adv.* **A** *(prunkvoll)* splendidly; magnificently; **B** *(großartig)* splendidly; marvellously

**pracht-, Pracht-: ~kerl** *der (ugs.)* great chap *or (Brit. coll.)* bloke *or (coll.)* guy; **ein ~kerl [von einem Kind]** a great kid *(sl.)*; **~straße** *die* boulevard; **~stück** *das (ugs.)* magnificent specimen; beauty; **ein ~stück von [einem] Karpfen** a beautiful specimen of a carp; **sie/er ist ein ~stück** *(Kind)* she/he is a really splendid girl/boy; *(Frau)* she is a magnificent *or* splendid woman; *(Mann)* he is a great chap *or (Brit. coll.)* bloke *or (coll.)* guy; **~voll** *Adj., adv.* ⇒ **prächtig**; **~weib** *das (ugs.)* magnificent *or* splendid woman; *(gut aussehend)* gorgeous female *(coll.)*

**Prädestination** /prɛdɛstina'tsi̯o:n/ *die*; **~:** predestination

**prädestinieren** *tr. V.* predestine

**prädestiniert** *Adj.* predestined; **etw. ist für ein Ziel ~:** sth. is just right for a purpose; **er ist für diese Rolle einfach ~:** he is just the man for this part

**Prädikat** /prɛdi'ka:t/ *das*; **~[e]s**, **~e** **A** *(Auszeichnung)* rating; **das ~ „gut"** the rating of 'good'; **Qualitätswein mit ~:** *wine made from selected grapes of specified maturity;* **B** *(Sprachw.)* predicate

**prädikativ** /prɛdika'ti:f/ *(Sprachw.)* **1** *Adj.* predicative. **2** *adv.* predicatively

**Prädikativ** *das*; **~s**, **~e** ⇒ **Prädikatsnomen**

**Prädikativ·satz** *der (Sprachw.)* predicate *or* predicative clause

**Prädikats·nomen** *das (Sprachw.)* predicate nominative *or* complement

**prä·disponieren** *tr. V. (Med.)* predispose **(für** to)

**Präferenz** /prɛfe'rɛnts/ *die*; **~**, **~en** preference

**Präferenz-: ~liste** *die* priority list; **~stellung** *die (Wirtsch.)* privileged status

**Präfix** /prɛ'fɪks/ *das*; **~es**, **~e** *(Sprachw.)* prefix

**Prag** /pra:k/ *(das)*; **~s** ▶ 700 Prague

**Präge** *die*; **~**, **~n** mint

**Präge-: ~druck** *der* embossing; **~form** *die (Münzwesen)* coining die

**prägen** /'prɛ:gn̩/ *tr. V.* **A** emboss ‹metal, paper, leather›; **B** *(herstellen)* mint, strike ‹coin›; **C** *(auf~) (vertieft)* impress; *(erhaben)* emboss; **D** *(fig.: beeinflussen)* shape; mould; **Tempo und Wagemut ~ seinen Stil** his style is characterized by speed and daring; **eine männlich geprägte Arbeitswelt** a male-oriented work environment; **E** *(fig.: erfinden)* coin ‹word, expression, concept›

**Präge-: ~stempel** *der (Druckw.)* die; **~stock** *der (Druckw.)* punch

**Pragmatik** /pra'gma:tɪk/ *die*; **~** **A** pragmatism; **B** *(Sprachw.)* pragmatics *sing.*, *no art.*

**Pragmatiker** *der*; **~s**, **~**, **Pragmatikerin** *die*; **~**, **~nen** pragmatist

**pragmatisch** **1** *Adj.* pragmatic. **2** *adv.* pragmatically

**Pragmatismus** *der*; **~:** pragmatism

**prägnant** /prɛ'gnant/ **1** *Adj.* concise; succinct. **2** *adv.* concisely; succinctly

**Prägnanz** /prɛ'gnants/ *die*; **~:** conciseness; succinctness

**Prägung** *die*; **~**, **~en** **A** *(von Papier, Leder, Metall)* embossing; *(von Münzen)* minting; striking; **B** *(auf Metall, Papier) (vertieft)* impression; *(erhaben)* embossing; **C** *(Eigenart)* character; **D** *(eines sprachlichen Ausdrucks)* coining; **E** *(geprägter Ausdruck)* coinage

**prä·historisch** *Adj.* prehistoric

**prahlen** /'pra:lən/ *itr. V.* boast, brag **(mit** about)

**Prahler** *der*; **~s**, **~:** boaster; braggart

**Prahlerei** *die*; **~**, **~en** *(abwertend)* boasting; bragging; **~en** boasts

**Prahlerin** *die*; **~**, **~nen** boaster; braggart

**Prahl·hans** *der*; **~es**, **Prahlhänse** /-hɛnzə/ *(ugs.)* show-off

**Prahm** /pra:m/ *der*; **~[e]s**, **~e** *od.* **Prähme** /'prɛ:mə/ pra[a]m

P

**Präjudiz** /prɛju'di:ts/ *das;* **~es, ~e** (*Rechtsw., Politik*) precedent

**präjudizieren** *tr. V.* (*Rechtsw., Politik*) prejudge

**Praktik** /'praktɪk/ *die;* **~, ~en** practice

**Praktika** ⇒ **Praktikum**

**praktikabel** /prakti'ka:bl̩/ *Adj.* practicable; practical

**Praktikant** /prakti'kant/ *der;* **~en, ~en, Praktikantin** *die;* **~, ~nen** Ⓐ (*in einem Betrieb*) student trainee; trainee student; Ⓑ (*an der Hochschule*) physics/chemistry student (*doing a period of practical training*)

**Praktiker** *der;* **~s, ~, Praktikerin** *die;* **~, ~nen** Ⓐ practical person; Ⓑ (*ugs.: Arzt/Ärztin*) general practitioner; GP

**Praktikum** /'praktikʊm/ *das;* **~s, Praktika** period of practical instruction *or* training

**praktisch** /'praktɪʃ/ ❶ *Adj.* Ⓐ (*auf die Praxis bezogen*) practical; **~es Jahr** year of practical training; **~er Arzt** general practitioner; Ⓑ (*wirklich*) practical ‹result, problem, matter, etc.›; concrete ‹example›; Ⓒ (*nützlich*) practical ‹furniture, clothes, etc.›; useful ‹present›; Ⓓ (*geschickt, realistisch*) practical; **er hat einen ~en Verstand** he is practically minded. ❷ *adv.* Ⓐ (*auf die Praxis bezogen*) in practice; **~ experimentieren/arbeiten** do practical experiments/work; Ⓑ (*wirklich*) in practice; Ⓒ (*nützlich*) practically; Ⓓ (*geschickt, realistisch*) practically; **~ veranlagt** practically minded; practical; Ⓔ (*ugs.: so gut wie*) practically; virtually

**praktizieren** /prakti'tsi:rən/ ❶ *tr. V.* Ⓐ (*anwenden*) practise; **~de Katholiken** practising Catholics; Ⓑ (*ugs.: irgendwohin bringen*) conjure; **jmdm. etw. in die Tasche/ins Essen ~:** slip sth. into sb.'s pocket/food. ❷ *itr. V.* (*als Arzt*) practise

**Prälat** /prɛ'la:t/ *der;* **~en, ~en, Prälatin** *die;* **~, ~nen** (*Kirche*) prelate

**Präliminarien** /prɛlimi'na:ri̯ən/ *Pl.* preliminaries

**Praline** /pra'li:nə/ *die;* **~, ~n, Praliné, Pralinee** (*österr., schweiz., sonst veralt.*) /prali'ne:/ *das;* **~s, ~s** [filled] chocolate

**prall** /pral/ ❶ *Adj.* Ⓐ (*fest und straff*) hard ‹ball›; firm ‹tomato, grape›; bulging ‹sack, wallet, bag›; big strong *attrib.* ‹thighs, muscles, calves›; well-rounded ‹buttocks›; full, well-rounded ‹breasts›; full, swollen ‹udder›; full, chubby ‹cheeks›; taut, full ‹sail›; firm ‹pillow, bed›; (*fig.*) intense ‹life›; vivid ‹picture›; full, rich ‹laughter›; fully inflated ‹balloon›; Ⓑ (*intensiv*) blazing ‹sun›; strong ‹light›. ❷ *adv.* Ⓐ (*fest und straff*) fully ‹inflated›; **ein ~ gestopfter Rucksack** a rucksack filled to bursting; **eine ~ gefüllte Brieftasche** a wallet bulging with banknotes; Ⓑ (*intensiv*) **die Sonne scheint ~:** the sun is blazing [down]

**prallen** *itr. V.* Ⓐ *mit sein* (*hart auftreffen*) crash (**gegen/auf/an** + *Akk.* into); collide (**gegen/auf/an** + *Akk.* with); **der Ball prallte an den Pfosten** the ball hit the post; Ⓑ (*scheinen*) blaze

**prall·voll** *Adj.* (*ugs.*) ‹suitcase, rucksack› full to bursting; packed ‹room›; bulging ‹wallet›; very full ‹diary›

**Präludium** /prɛ'lu:di̯ʊm/ *das;* **~s, Präludien** /...i̯ən/ prelude

**Prämie** /'prɛ:mi̯ə/ *die;* **~, ~n** Ⓐ (*Leistungs~; Wirtschaft: ~ zum Grundlohn*) bonus; (*Belohnung*) reward; (*Spar~, Versicherungs~*) premium; Ⓑ (*einer Lotterie*) [extra] prize

**prämien-, Prämien-: ~begünstigt** ❶ *Adj.* ≈ premium[-account] *attrib.*; **~begünstigtes Bausparen** ≈ saving with a building society premium account; ❷ *adv.* **~begünstigt sparen** ≈ save with a premium account; **~los** *das* ≈ Premium [Savings] Bond (*Brit.*); **~sparen** *das;* **~~s** ≈ Premium Bond saving (*Brit.*)

**prämieren** /prɛ'mi:rən/, **prämiieren** /prɛmi'i:rən/ *tr. V.* award a prize to ‹person, film›; give an award for ‹best essay etc.›

**Prämierung, Prämiierung** *die;* **~, ~en** Ⓐ (*Auszeichnung*) **er/der Film wurde zur ~ vorgeschlagen** it was proposed that he should be given a prize/that a prize should be given for the film; Ⓑ (*Preisverleihung*) **die ~ der besten Schüler/Filme** the presentation of prizes to the best pupils/for the best films

**Prämisse** /prɛ'mɪsə/ *die;* **~, ~n** Ⓐ (*auch Philos.*) premiss; **unter der ~, dass ...** on the premiss that ...

**pränatal** /prɛna'ta:l/ *Adj.* (*Med.*) pre-natal

**prangen** /'praŋən/ *itr. V.* Ⓐ be prominently displayed; **auf dem Sofa prangte ein großes Kissen** a large cushion was placed eye-catchingly on the sofa; Ⓑ (*geh.: auffallen*) be resplendent; **Sterne ~ am Himmel** stars are glittering in the sky

**Pranger** *der;* **~s, ~** (*hist.*) pillory; **jmdn./etw. an den ~ stellen** (*fig.*) pillory sb./sth.

**Pranke** /'praŋkə/ *die;* **~, ~n** Ⓐ (*Pfote*) paw; Ⓑ (*salopp: große Hand*) paw (*coll.*)

**Präparat** /prɛpa'ra:t/ *das;* **~[e]s, ~e** Ⓐ (*Mittel, Substanz*) preparation; Ⓑ (*Biol., Med.: präpariertes Objekt*) specimen

**Präparation** /prɛpara'tsi̯o:n/ *die;* **~, ~en** preparation

**präparieren** ❶ *tr. V.* Ⓐ (*Biol., Med.: konservieren*) preserve; Ⓑ (*Biol., Anat.: zerlegen*) dissect; Ⓒ (*vorbereitend bearbeiten, geh.: vorbereiten*) prepare. ❷ *refl. V.* (*geh.: sich vorbereiten*) prepare oneself

**Präposition** /prɛpozi'tsi̯o:n/ *die;* **~, ~en** (*Sprachw.*) preposition

**präpositional** /prɛpozitsi̯o'na:l/ *Adj.* (*Sprachw.*) prepositional

**Präpositional-** (*Sprachw.*) prepositional

**präpotent** /prɛpo'tɛnt/ *Adj.* (*österr.*) officiously impertinent

**Prärie** /prɛ'ri:/ *die;* **~, ~n** prairie

**Prärie·wolf** *der* prairie wolf; coyote

**Präsens** /'prɛ:zɛns/ *das;* **~, Präsentia** /prɛ'zɛntsi̯a/ *od.* **Präsenzien** /prɛ'zɛntsi̯ən/ (*Sprachw.*) present [tense]

**präsent** /prɛ'zɛnt/ *Adj.* present; **Forderungen/Fragen ~ haben** have one's demands/questions ready; **ich habe den Vorfall** *od.* **der Vorfall ist mir im Augenblick nicht ~:** I do not recall the incident at the moment

**Präsent** *das;* **~[e]s, ~e** (*geh.*) present; **jmdm. ein ~ machen** give sb. a present

**präsentabel** /prɛzɛn'ta:bl̩/ (*veralt.*) presentable

**Präsentation** /prɛzɛnta'tsi̯o:n/ *die;* **~, ~en** Ⓐ (*Vorstellung*) presentation; Ⓑ (*Wirtsch.*) presentment

**präsentieren** ❶ *tr. V.* Ⓐ (*anbieten; überreichen*) offer; Ⓑ (*vorlegen*) present; **jmdm. die Rechnung [für etw.] ~:** present sb. with the bill [for sth.]; Ⓒ (*Milit.*) **präsentiert das Gewehr!** present arms! ❷ *refl. V.* (*sich zeigen*) present oneself; appear. ❸ *itr. V.* (*Milit.*) present arms

**Präsentier·teller** *der:* **auf dem ~ sitzen** (*ugs. abwertend*) be on show *or* display

**Präsent·korb** *der* gift hamper

**Präsenz** /prɛ'zɛnts/ *die;* **~:** presence

**Präsenz-: ~bibliothek** *die* reference library; **~liste** *die* [attendance] register; **~pflicht** *die* duty to attend

**Präser** /'prɛze/ *der;* **~s, ~** (*salopp*), **Präservativ** /prɛzɛrva'ti:f/ *das;* **~s, ~e** condom

**Präses** /'prɛ:zɛs/ *der;* **~, Präsides** /'prɛ:zide:s/ Ⓐ (*kath. Kirche*) chairman; Ⓑ (*ev. Kirche*) president (*of a synod*)

**Präsident** /prɛzi'dɛnt/ *der;* **~en, ~en** ▶ 91 president

**Präsidenten·wahl** *die* presidential election

**Präsidentin** *die;* **~, ~nen** ▶ 91 president

**Präsidentschaft** *die;* **~, ~en** presidency

**Präsidentschafts·kandidat** *der,* **Präsidentschafts·kandidatin** *die* candidate for the presidency

**präsidial** /prɛzi'di̯a:l/ *Adj.* (*Politik*) presidential

**Präsidial·demokratie** *die* presidential democracy

**Präsidien** *Pl.* ⇒ **Präsidium**

**präsidieren** ❶ *itr. V.* preside. ❷ *tr. V.* (*schweiz.*) **einen Verein** *usw.* **~:** be president of a society *etc.*

**Präsidium** /prɛ'zi:di̯ʊm/ *das;* **~s, Präsidien** Ⓐ (*Führungsgruppe*) committee; **im ~ sitzen** be on the committee; Ⓑ (*Vorsitz*) chairmanship; Ⓒ (*Polizei~*) police headquarters *sing. or pl.*

**prasseln** /'prasl̩n/ *itr. V.* ‹rain, hail› pelt down; ‹shots› clatter; ‹fire› crackle; **Kies prasselte gegen das Auto** gravel rattled against the car; **~der Beifall** thunderous applause

**prassen** /'prasn̩/ *itr. V.* live extravagantly; (*schlemmen*) feast

**Prasser** *der;* **~s, ~:** spendthrift; extravagant person; (*Schlemmer*) glutton

**Prasserei** *die;* **~, ~en** Ⓐ extravagant living *no pl.*; Ⓑ (*das Schlemmen*) gluttony *no pl.*; (*Gelage*) feasting *no pl.*

**Prasserin** *die;* **~, ~nen** ⇒ **Prasser**

**präsumtiv** /prɛzʊm'ti:f/ *Adj.* Ⓐ prospective; Ⓑ (*Rechtsw.*) presumptive

**Prätendent** /prɛtɛn'dɛnt/ *der;* **~en, ~en, Prätendentin** *die;* **~, ~nen** pretender

**prätentiös** /prɛtɛn'tsi̯ø:s/ *Adj.* pretentious

**Präteritum** /prɛ'te:ritʊm/ *das;* **~s, Präterita** (*Sprachw.*) preterite [tense]

**Pratze** /'pratsə/ *die;* **~, ~n** (*bes. südd.*) ⇒ **Pranke**

**präventiv** /prɛvɛn'ti:f/ ❶ *Adj.* preventive. ❷ *adv.* preventively; **~ vorgehen** take preventive measures

**Präventiv-: ~krieg** *der* preventive war; **~maßnahme** *die* preventive measure

**Praxis** /'praksɪs/ *die;* **~, Praxen** Ⓐ (*im Unterschied zur Theorie*) practice *no art.*; **in der ~:** in practice; **etw. in die ~ umsetzen** put sth. into practice; **Beispiele aus der ~:** practical examples; **er ist ein Mann der ~:** he is a practical man; Ⓑ (*Erfahrung*) [practical] experience; Ⓒ (*eines Arztes, Anwalts, Psychologen, Therapeuten usw.*) practice; Ⓓ (*~räume*) (*eines Arztes*) surgery (*Brit.*); office (*Amer.*); (*eines Anwalts, Psychologen, Therapeuten usw.*) office; Ⓔ (*Handhabung*) procedure

**praxis-: ~bezogen** ❶ *Adj.* practical ‹experience, training›; ‹project› based on practical work; ❷ *adv.* practically; **~nah, ~orientiert** ❶ *Adj.* practical; ❷ *adv.* practically

**Präzedenz·fall** /prɛtse'dɛnts-/ *der* precedent

**präzis** (*österr.*), **präzise** /prɛ'tsi:zə/ ❶ *Adj.* precise ‹definition, answer›; specific ‹wishes, suspicion›. ❷ *adv.* precisely

**präzisieren** *tr. V.* make more precise; state more precisely; **ein Angebot näher ~:** give more precise details of an offer; **seine Wünsche ~:** specify one's wishes

**Präzision** /prɛtsi'zi̯o:n/ *die;* **~:** precision

**Präzisions-: ~arbeit** *die* precision work; (*genau nach Zeitplan*) precise timing; **~instrument** *das* precision instrument; **~uhr** *die* precision [stop]watch/clock

**predigen** /'pre:dɪgn̩/ ❶ *itr. V.* (*Predigt halten*) deliver *or* give a/the sermon; **gegen etw. ~:** preach against sth. ❷ *tr. V.* Ⓐ (*verkündigen*) preach; Ⓑ (*ugs.: auffordern zu*) preach; Ⓒ (*ugs.: belehrend sagen*) **wie oft habe ich dir das schon gepredigt!** how often have I told you that!

**Prediger** *der;* **~s, ~, Predigerin** *die;* **~, ~nen** preacher; **ein ~ in der Wüste** (*fig.*) a voice [crying] in the wilderness

**Predigt** /'pre:dɪçt/ *die;* **~, ~en** Ⓐ sermon; **eine ~ halten** deliver *or* give a sermon; Ⓑ (*ugs.: Ermahnung*) lecture; **jmdm. eine ~ halten** lecture sb.; **ich bin deine endlosen ~en leid** I am tired of your endless lecturing

**Predigt·text** *der* text (*for a sermon*)

**Preis** /prais/ *der;* **~es, ~e** Ⓐ ▶ 337 (*Kauf~*) price (**für** of); **das hat seinen ~** it costs money; (*fig.*) there is a price to be paid for it; **im ~ steigen** rise in price; **jeden ~ für etw. zahlen** pay any price for sth.; **jmdm. einen guten ~ machen** give sb. a good price; **nach dem ~ fragen** ask the price; **eine Ware unter[m] ~ verkaufen**

*old spelling (see note on page 1707)

sell an article at a reduced *or* cut price; **etw. zum halben ~ erwerben** buy sth. at half-price; **hoch/gut im ~ stehen** fetch a high/good price; **diese Ausstellung möchte ich um jeden ~ besuchen** (*fig.*) I should like to go to this exhibition at all costs; **diese Einladung möchte ich um keinen ~ annehmen** (*fig.*) I wouldn't accept this invitation at any price; **B** (*Belohnung*) prize; **einen ~ auf jmds. Kopf aussetzen** put a price on sb.'s head; **der Große ~ von Frankreich** (*Rennsport*) the French Grand Prix; **der ~ der Nationen** (*Reitsport*) Prix des Nations; **C** (*geh.: Lob*) praise; **ein Gedicht zum ~e der Natur** a poem in praise of nature

**-preis** *der* price of ...

**preis-, Preis-: ~ab·schlag** *der* (*Kaufmannsspr.*) ⇒ **~nachlass**; **~ab·sprache** *die* (*Wirtsch.*) price-fixing agreement; **~änderung** *die* price change *or* variation; **~angabe** *die* (*displayed or listed*) price; **~anstieg** *der* rise *or* increase in prices; **~auf·gabe** *die* [prize] competition; **eine ~aufgabe lösen** solve a puzzle (*in a prize competition*); **~auf·schlag** *der* (*Kaufmannsspr.*) additional *or* extra charge; **~auf·trieb** *der* (*Wirtsch.*) rise *or* increase in prices; **~aus·schreiben** *das* [prize] competition; **~aus·zeichnung** *die* labelling with a price/prices; **~bewegung** *die* movement of prices; **~bewusst**, ***~bewußt** **1** *Adj.* price-conscious; **2** *adv.* price-consciously; **~bewusst tanken** be conscious of petrol (*Brit.*) *or* (*Amer.*) gasoline prices [when filling up]; **~bindung** *die* (*Wirtsch.*) price-fixing; **~bindung der zweiten Hand** resale price maintenance; **~boxer** *der* (*ugs. veralt.*) prizefighter; **~brecher** *der*, **~brecherin** *die* cut-price operator; **~einbruch** *der* (*Wirtsch.*) [massive] drop in prices

**Preisel·beere** /ˈpraizl̩beːrə/ *die* cowberry; cranberry (*Gastr.*)

**Preis·empfehlung** *die* (*Kaufmannsspr.*) recommended price

**preisen** *unr. tr. V.* (*geh.*) praise; **man pries ihn als den besten Kenner auf diesem Gebiet** he was acclaimed as the leading authority in this field; **sich glücklich ~ [können]** [be able to] count *or* consider oneself lucky

**Preis-: ~entwicklung** *die* price trend; **~erhöhung** *die* price increase *or* rise

**-preis·erhöhung** *die* increase in the price of ...

**preis-, Preis-: ~ermäßigung** *die* price reduction; **~explosion** *die* snowballing prices *pl.*; **~frage** *die* **A** (*bei einem ~ausschreiben*) [prize] question; (*fig.*) big question; sixty-four thousand dollar question; **B** (*Geldfrage*) question of price; **~gabe** *die* (*geh.*) **A** (*Verzicht*) abandonment; **B** (*von Geheimnissen*) revelation; giving away; **~|geben** *unr. tr. V.* (*geh.*) **A** (*ausliefern*) **jmdn. einer Sache** (*Dat.*) **~geben** expose sb. to *or* leave sb. to be the victim of sth.; **die Bauten waren dem Verfall ~gegeben** the buildings were left to fall into ruin; **B** (*aufgeben*) relinquish ‹ideal, independence›; surrender ‹territory›; **C** (*verraten*) betray; give away; **~gebunden** *Adj.* (*Wirtsch.*) subject to price maintenance *postpos.*; **~gefälle** *das* difference *or* variation in prices; **~gefüge** *das* (*Wirtsch.*) price structure; **~gekrönt** *Adj.* prize *or* awardwinning; **er/sein Werk ist ~gekrönt** he has been given/his work has won a prize *or* an award; **~gericht** *das* jury; panel of judges; **~gestaltung** *die* pricing; **~grenze** *die* price limit; **obere/untere ~grenze** ceiling *or* maximum/floor *or* minimum price; **~günstig** **1** *Adj.* ‹goods› available at unusually low prices; ‹purchases› at favourable prices; inexpensive ‹holiday›; **das ~günstigste Angebot** the best bargain *or* value; **das ist [sehr] ~günstig** that is [very] good value; **2** *adv.* **etw. ~günstig herstellen/verkaufen/bekommen** produce/sell/get sth. at a low price; **hier kann man ~günstig einkaufen** their prices are very reasonable here; **~index** *der* (*Wirtsch.*) price index; **~klasse** *die* price range; **~kontrolle** *die* price control; **~lage** *die* price range; **in jeder ~lage** at prices to suit every pocket; **~lawine** *die* (*ugs.*) snowballing prices *pl.*

**preislich** *Adj.* price; in price *postpos.*; **in ~er Hinsicht** as regards price

**preis-, Preis-: ~liste** *die* price list; **~nachlass**, ***~nachlaß** *der* price reduction; discount; **mit erheblichem ~nachlass** at a greatly reduced price; **~niveau** *das* (*Wirtsch.*) price level; **~politik** *die* policy on prices; **~rätsel** *das* [prize] competition; **~richter** *der*, **~richterin** *die* judge; **~schießen** *das*; **~~s**, **~~:** shooting competition *or* contest; **~schild** *das* price tag; **~schlager** *der* (*ugs.*) bargain [offer]; **~schlager der Saison** best bargain of the season; **~schraube** *die* (*Wirtschaftsjargon*) **an der ~schraube drehen** put [one's] prices up; **~schwankung** *die* price fluctuation; **~senkung** *die* price reduction *or* cut; **~skat** *der* skat competition; **~steigerung** *die* rise *or* increase in prices; **~steigerungs·rate** *die* (*Wirtsch.*) rate of increase in prices; **~stopp** *der* price freeze; **~sturz** *der* sharp drop *or* fall in prices; **~träger** *der*, **~trägerin** *die* prizewinner; **~treiber** *der* (*abwertend*) person who/company which forces prices up; **dieses Reiseunternehmen gilt als ~treiber** this tour operator is known for forcing prices up; **~treiberei** *die*; **~~** (*abwertend*) forcing up of prices; **~treiberin** *die* ⇒ **~treiber**; **~vergleich** *der* price comparison; **~vergleiche anstellen** compare prices; **~verleihung** *die* presentation [of prizes/awards]; award ceremony; **~vor·teil** *der* price benefit; **~wert** **1** *Adj.* good value *pred.*; **ein ~wertes Angebot** a bargain [offer]; **haben Sie ~wertere Schuhe?** do you have any shoes which are less expensive?; **2** *adv.* **sie hat ~wert eingekauft** she bought things at reasonable prices; **dort kann man ~wert einkaufen** you get good value for money there; **hier kann man ~wert essen** you can eat at a reasonable price here; **~würdig** *Adj.* (*geh.*) praiseworthy

**prekär** /preˈkɛːɐ̯/ *Adj.* precarious

**Prell-: ~ball** *der: (Sport) game similar to volleyball;* **~bock** *der* (*Eisenb.*) buffer

**prellen** /ˈprɛlən/ **1** *tr. V.* **A** (*betrügen*) cheat (**um** out of); **die Zeche ~:** avoid paying the bill; **B** (*verletzen*) bash; bruise; **C** (*Ballsport*) bounce. **2** *refl. V.* (*sich verletzen*) bruise oneself; **ich habe mich an der Schulter geprellt** I have bruised *or* bashed my shoulder

**Prellung** *die*; **~, ~en** bruise

**Premier** /prəˈmi̯eː/ *der*; **~s, ~s** premier

**Premiere** /prəˈmi̯eːrə/ *die*; **~, ~n** opening night; first night; (*Uraufführung*) première; (*fig.*) first appearance; **das Stück hat morgen ~:** the play has its opening night/première tomorrow

**Premieren-: ~abend** *der* opening night; first night; (*eines neuen Stückes*) première; **~publikum** *das* audience at a/the première/opening *or* first night

**Premier-** /prəˈmi̯eː-/: **~minister** *der*, **~ministerin** *die* prime minister

**Presbyter** /ˈprɛsbytɐ/ *der*; **~s, ~, Presbyterin**, *die*; **~, ~nen** (*ev. Kirche*) presbyter; elder

**Presbyterianer** /prɛsbyteˈri̯aːnɐ/ *der*; **~s, ~, Presbyterianerin** *die*; **~, ~nen** Presbyterian

**presbyterianisch** *Adj.* Presbyterian

**preschen** /ˈprɛʃn̩/ *itr. V.*; *mit sein* tear; **sie kam ins Zimmer geprescht** she came dashing into the room

**Presse** /ˈprɛsə/ *die*; **~, ~n** **A** (*zum Zusammenpressen*) press; **B** (*zum Auspressen*) (*von Obst, Knoblauch*) press; (*von Zitronen*) squeezer; **C** (*Zeitungen*) press; **D** (*Druckw. veralt.: Druckmaschine*) press; **E** (*ugs., abwertend: Schule*) crammer

**Presse-: ~agentur** *die* press agency; news agency; **~amt** *das* press office; **~ausweis** *der* press card; **~ball** *der: celebrity dance held by a national or provincial journalists' association;* **~bericht** *der* press report; **~chef** *der*, **~chefin** *die* [chief] press officer; **~dienst** *der* regular press release; **~empfang** *der* press reception; **~erklärung** *die* press statement; **~fotograf** *der*, **~fotografin** *die* press photographer; **~freiheit** *die* freedom of the press; **~gesetz** *das* press law; **~kampagne** *die* press campaign; **~karte** *die* press ticket; **~kommentar** *der* press commentary; **~konferenz** *die* press conference; **~konzentration** *die* concentration of the press; **~meldung** *die* press report

**pressen** *tr. V.* **A** (*zusammendrücken*) press; **B** (*aus~*) press ‹fruit, garlic›; squeeze ‹lemon›; **C** (*drücken*) press; **Kleider in einen Koffer ~:** squash *or* squeeze clothes into a suitcase; **jmdm. die Hand auf den Mund ~:** press one's hand over sb.'s mouth; **mit gepresster Stimme** (*fig.*) in a strained voice; **D** (*herstellen*) press ‹record›; mould ‹plastic object›; **E** (*zwingen*) force; **F** (*veralt.: unterdrücken*) oppress

**Presse-: ~notiz** *die* news item; **etw. in einer kurzen ~notiz erwähnen** give sth. a mention in the press; **~organ** *das* (*Zeitung*) newspaper; (*Zeitschrift*) journal; magazine; **die ~organe** the press; **~recht** *das* press legislation; **~referent** *der*, **~referentin** *die* press officer; **~sprecher** *der*, **~sprecherin** *die* ▶ 159 spokesman; press officer; **~stelle** *die* press office; **~stimmen** *Pl.* press commentaries *or* reviews; **~tribüne** *die* press box; **auf der ~tribüne** in the press box; **~vertreter** *der*, **~vertreterin** *die* representative of the press; **~zentrum** *das* press centre

**Press-, *Preß-: ~glas** *das* pressed glass; **~holz** *das* compressed wood

**pressieren** *itr. V.* (*bes. südd.*) ‹matter› be urgent; **er ist sehr pressiert/mir pressierts sehr** he is/I am in a great hurry

**Pression** /prɛˈsi̯oːn/ *die*; **~, ~en** pressure

**Press-, *Preß-: ~kohle** *die* compressed coal *no pl.*; **~kopf** *der* brawn; head cheese (*Amer.*); **~luft** *die* compressed air

**Press·luft-, *Preß·luft-: ~bohrer** *der* pneumatic drill; **~hammer** *der* (*Bauw.*) pneumatic *or* air hammer

**Press·sack, *Preß·sack** *der* ⇒ **Presskopf**

**Pressung** *die*; **~, ~en** (*das Pressen*) pressure; (*das Gepresstwerden*) compression

**Press·wehe, *Preß·wehe** *die* (*Med.*) contraction (*in second stage of labour*)

**Prestige** /prɛsˈtiːʒə/ *das*; **~s** prestige

**Prestige-: ~denken** *das* desire to establish one's prestige; **~frage** *die* question *or* matter of prestige; **~verlust** *der* loss of prestige

**pretiös** ⇒ **preziös**

**Pretiosen** ⇒ **Preziosen**

**Preuße** /ˈprɔysə/ *der*; **~n, ~n** Prussian; **so schnell schießen die ~n nicht** (*fig.*) these things take time

**Preußen** (*das*); **~s** Prussia

**Preußentum** *das*; **~s** **A** (*preußische Wesensart*) Prussian character; **B** (*Volkszugehörigkeit*) Prussianness; **C** (*die Preußen*) Prussian people *pl.*; Prussians *pl.*

**Preußin** *die*; **~, ~nen** ⇒ **Preuße**

**preußisch** /ˈprɔysɪʃ/ *Adj.* Prussian; ⇒ *auch* **deutsch**; **Deutsch**; **Deutsche**[2]

**preußisch·blau** *Adj.*, **Preußisch·blau** *das* Prussian blue

**preziös** /preˈtsi̯øːs/ *Adj.* (*geh.*) precious

**Preziosen** /preˈtsi̯oːzn̩/ *Pl.* valuables

**Pricke** /ˈprɪkə/ *die*; **~, ~n** (*Seew.*) perch

**prickelig** *Adj.* tingling

**prickeln** /ˈprɪkl̩n/ *itr. V.* **A** (*kribbeln, kitzeln*) tingle; **es prickelte ihm in den Fingerspitzen** his fingertips were tingling; **B** (*perlen*) sparkle; **C** (*reizen*) **eine ~de Spannung** a tingling atmosphere; **der ~de Reiz des Unbekannten** the thrill of the unknown

**pricklig** *Adj.* ⇒ **prickelig**

**Priel** /priːl/ *der*; **~[e]s, ~e** narrow channel (*in mudflats*)

**Priem** /priːm/ *der*; **~[e]s, ~e** **A** (*Kautabak*) chewing tobacco; **~ kauen** chew tobacco; **B** (*Stück Kautabak*) quid [of tobacco]

P

**priemen** *itr. V.* chew tobacco

**pries** /pri:s/ *1. u. 3. Pers. Sg. Prät. v.* **preisen**

**Priester** /'pri:stɐ/ *der;* **~s, ~:** priest; **Hoher ~** (*bibl.*) high priest

**Priester·amt** *das* priesthood

**Priesterin** *die;* **~, ~nen** priestess

**priesterlich** *Adj.* priestly ‹function›; clerical ‹robe, collar›; priest's ‹blessing›

**Priester·rock** *der* cassock

**Priesterschaft** *die;* **~:** priests *pl.*

**Priester·seminar** *das* seminary

**Priestertum** *das;* **~s** priesthood

**Priester·weihe** *die* ordination [to the priesthood]

**prima** /'pri:ma/ ❶ *indekl. Adj.* [A] (*ugs.*) great (*coll.*); fantastic (*coll.*); [B] (*Kaufmannsspr. veralt.*) first-class; top-quality. ❷ *adv.* (*ugs.*) ‹taste› great (*coll.*), fantastic (*coll.*); ‹sleep› fantastically (*coll.*) *or* really well; **es geht mir ~:** I feel great (*coll.*); **es lief alles ~:** everything went really well; **das finde ich ~:** that's fantastic *or* great (*coll.*); **das hast du ~ gemacht** well done indeed

**Prima** *die;* **~, Primen** (*Schulw.*) [A] (*veralt.*) eighth and ninth years (*of a Gymnasium*); [B] (*österr.*) first year (*of a Gymnasium*)

**Prima-: ~ballerina** *die* (*Theater*) prima ballerina; **~donna** /-'dɔna/ *die;* **~~, ~donnen** prima donna

**Primaner** /pri'ma:nɐ/ *der;* **~s, ~** (*Schulw.*) [A] (*veralt.*) pupil in the eighth and ninth years (*of a Gymnasium*); **wie ein ~** (*fig.*) like a schoolboy; [B] (*österr.*) pupil in the first year (*of a Gymnasium*)

**primanerhaft** ❶ *Adj.* schoolboyish/schoolgirlish. ❷ *adv.* like a schoolboy/schoolgirl

**Primanerin** *die;* **~, ~nen** ⇒ **Primaner**

**primär** /pri'mɛ:ɐ̯/ ❶ *Adj.* primary. ❷ *adv.* primarily

**Primar·lehrer** /pri'ma:ɐ̯-/ *der,* **Primar·lehrerin** *die* (*schweiz.*) primary school teacher

**Primär·literatur** *die* primary literature

**Primar-: ~schule** *die* (*schweiz.*) primary school; **~stufe** *die* primary stage (*of education*)

**Primas** /'pri:mas/ *der;* **~, ~se** *od.* **Primaten** [A] (*kath. Kirche*) primate; [B] *Pl. nur* **~se** (*Geiger*) leading fiddle player

**Primat**[1] /pri'ma:t/ *der od. das;* **~[e]s, ~e** [A] (*Vorrang*) primacy, priority (**vor** + *Dat.*, **über** + *Akk.* over); [B] (*kath. Kirche*) primacy

**Primat**[2] *der;* **~en, ~en** (*Zool.*) primate

**Prime** /'pri:mə/ *die;* **~, ~n** (*Musik*) [A] (*Einklang*) unison; [B] (*Ton*) keynote; tone

**Primel** /'pri:ml̩/ *die;* **~, ~n** primula; primrose; (*Schlüsselblume*) cowslip; **eingehen wie eine ~** (*salopp*) go completely to pot (*coll.*)

**Primi** *Pl.* ⇒ **Primus**

**primitiv** /primi'ti:f/ ❶ *Adj.* [A] (*einfach, schlicht*) simple; crude (*derog.*); **die ~sten Regeln des Anstands** the most basic rules of behaviour; [B] (*oft abwertend: dürftig*) primitive; [C] (*abwertend: niveaulos, ungebildet*) primitive ‹person, behaviour›; crude ‹expression, view, idea, speech›; [D] (*urtümlich, ursprünglich, naiv*) primitive. ❷ *adv.* [A] (*einfach, schlicht*) in a simple manner; crudely (*derog.*); [B] (*oft abwertend: dürftig*) primitively; [C] (*abwertend: niveaulos, ungebildet*) ‹argue› primitively; ‹talk› crudely; [D] (*urtümlich*) primitively

**Primitivität** /primitivi'tɛ:t/ *die;* **~** ⇒ **primitiv** 1 B-D: primitiveness; crudeness

**Primitivling** *der;* **~s, ~e** (*abwertend*) peasant (*fig.*)

**Primus** /'pri:mʊs/ *der;* **~, Primi** *od.* **~se** (*veralt.*) top of the class

**Prim·zahl** *die* (*Math.*) prime [number]

**Printe** /'prɪntə/ *die;* **~, ~n** *kind of oblong sweet spiced cake*

**Prinz** /prɪnts/ *der;* **~en, ~en** prince

**Prinzessin** *die;* **~, ~nen** princess

**Prinz·gemahl** *der* prince consort

**Prinzip** /prɪn'tsi:p/ *das;* **~s, ~ien** /-'tsi:pi̯ən/ principle; **aus ~:** on principle; **er hat es aus ~ getan** he did it as a matter of principle; **im ~:** in principle; **ein Mensch von ~ien sein** be a man/woman of principle

**Prinzipal** /prɪntsi'pa:l/ *der;* **~s, ~e** (*veralt.*) [A] (*eines Theaters*) [theatre] manager; (*einer Theatergruppe*) leader; [B] (*Leiter eines Privatbetriebs*) proprietor; (*Lehrherr*) master

**Prinzipalin** *die;* **~, ~nen** (*veralt.*) [A] (*eines Theaters*) [theatre] manager[ess]; (*einer Theatergruppe*) leader; [B] (*Leiterin eines Privatbetriebs*) proprietress; (*Lehrherrin*) mistress

**prinzipiell** /prɪntsi'pi̯ɛl/ ❶ *Adj.* in principle *postpos., not pred.;* ‹rejection› on principle; **eine ~e Frage/Frage von ~er Bedeutung** a question of principle/of fundamental importance. ❷ *adv.* [A] (*im Prinzip*) in principle; [B] (*aus Prinzip*) on principle; as a matter of principle

**prinzipien-, Prinzipien-: ~los** *Adj.* unprincipled; **~losigkeit** *die;* **~:** lack of principles; **~reiter** *der* (*abwertend*) person who sticks rigidly to his/her principles; **~reiterei** *die* (*abwertend*) rigid adherence to principles; **~reiterin** *die* ⇒ **~reiter**

**prinzlich** *Adj.* prince's

**Prinz·regent** *der* Prince Regent

**Prion** *das;* **~s, ~en** (*Biol.*) prion

**Prior** /'pri:ɔr/ *der;* **~s, ~en** /pri'o:rən/ (*kath. Kirche*) prior

**Priorin** *die;* **~, ~nen** (*kath. Kirche*) prioress

**Priorität** /priori'tɛ:t/ *die;* **~, ~en** [A] (*Vorrang*) priority; precedence; **~ vor etw.** (*Dat.*) **haben** have *or* take precedence over sth.; [B] *Pl.* (*Rangfolge*) priorities; **~en setzen** establish priorities; **die richtigen ~en setzen** get one's priorities right

**Prise** /'pri:zə/ *die;* **~, ~n** [A] pinch; **eine ~ Salz** a pinch of salt; **eine ~ Sarkasmus/Ironie** (*fig.*) a hint *or* touch of sarcasm/irony; [B] (*Seew.*) prize; **eine ~ machen** take a prize

**Prisma** /'prɪsma/ *das;* **~s, Prismen** (*Math., Optik*) prism

**prismatisch** /prɪs'ma:tɪʃ/ ❶ *Adj.* prismatic. ❷ *adv.* prismatically

**Prismen** ⇒ **Prisma**

**Pritsche** /'prɪtʃə/ *die;* **~, ~n** [A] (*Liegestatt*) plank bed; [B] (*Ladefläche*) platform; [C] (*Narren~*) slapstick

**Pritschen·wagen** *der* platform truck

**privat** /pri'va:t/ ❶ *Adj.* private; personal ‹opinion, happiness, etc.›; **eine Feier im ~en Kreis** a celebration restricted to one's intimate circle; **an/von ~:** to/from private individuals *pl.* ❷ *adv.* privately; **~ ist er ganz anders** he's completely different in private; **jmdn. ~ sprechen** speak to sb. in private *or* privately; **der Patient liegt ~:** the patient is in a/the private ward; **~ versichert** privately insured; covered by private insurance (*postpos.*)

**Privat-: ~adresse** *die* private *or* home address; **~an·gelegenheit** *die* private affair *or* matter; **das ist seine ~angelegenheit** that's his own business *or* his own private affair; **~audienz** *die* private audience; **~besitz** *der* private property; **das Gemälde befindet sich im ~besitz** the painting is privately owned *or* in private ownership; **~detektiv** *der,* **~detektivin** *die* ▶ 159 private detective *or* investigator; **~dozent** *der,* **~dozentin** *die: lecturer who is not a member of the salaried university staff;* **~druck** *der; Pl.* **~~e** privately published edition; **als ~druck erscheinen** be published privately; **~eigentum** *das* private property; **das ~eigentum an den Produktionsmitteln** private ownership of the means of production; **~fernsehen** *das* privately operated television; ≈ commercial television; **~frau** *die* ⇒ **~person; ~gelehrte** *der/die* (*veralt.*) scholar [working] on his/her own account; **~gespräch** *das* private conversation; (*Telefongespräch*) private call

**Privatier** /priva'ti̯e:/ *der;* **~s, ~s** (*veralt.*) man of private *or* independent means

**privatim** /pri'va:tɪm/ *adv.* (*geh.*) privately

**Privat-: ~initiative** *die* private initiative; **~interesse** *das* private interest

**privatisieren** ❶ *tr. V.* (*Wirtsch.*) privatize; transfer into private ownership. ❷ *itr. V.* (*geh.: als Privatier leben*) live on a private income

**Privatisierung** *die;* **~, ~en** (*Wirtsch.*) privatization; transfer into private ownership

**privat-, Privat-: ~klage** *die* (*Rechtsw.*) private action *or* prosecution; **~kläger** *der,* **~klägerin** *die* (*Rechtsw.*) plaintiff [in a/the private action]; **~klinik** *die* private clinic *or* hospital; **~leben** *das* private life; **sich ins ~leben zurückziehen** return to private life; **~lehrer** *der,* **~lehrerin** *die* private tutor; **~mann** *der; Pl.* **~leute** ⇒ **~person; ~patient** *der,* **~patientin** *die* private patient; **~person** *die* private individual; **als ~person auftreten** appear in a private capacity; **~quartier** *das* private accommodation *no pl.;* **zahlreiche ~quartiere** plentiful private accommodation *sing.;* **~recht** *das* (*Rechtsw.*) private *or* civil law; **~rechtlich** (*Rechtsw.*) ❶ *Adj.* civil-law *attrib.;* under private *or* civil law *postpos.;* ❷ *adv.* in private *or* civil law; **~sache** *die* ⇒ **~angelegenheit; ~sammlung** *die* private collection; **~schule** *die* private school; (*Eliteschule in Großbritannien*) public school; **~sekretär** *der,* **~sekretärin** *die* private secretary (**von,** *Gen.* to); **~sphäre** *die* privacy; (**~leben**) private life; **~station** *die* private ward; **~stunde** *die* private lesson; **~unternehmen** *das* private concern *or* enterprise; **~unterricht** *der* private tuition; private lessons *pl.;* **~vergnügen** *das* (*ugs.*) **eine Dienstreise ist kein ~vergnügen** you don't go on business trips for your own enjoyment; **das ist doch mein ~vergnügen** that's my own business *or* affair; **~vermögen** *das* private fortune; **~vermögen/kein ~vermögen haben** have a/no private fortune; ***~versichert** ⇒ **privat** 2; **~versicherung** *die* private insurance; **in einer ~versicherung sein** be privately insured; be in a private insurance scheme; **~weg** *der* private way; **~wirtschaft** *die* private sector; **~wirtschaftlich** ❶ *Adj.* private-sector *attrib.;* ‹enterprise, company, firm› in the private sector; **auf ~wirtschaftlicher Basis** on a private-enterprise basis; ❷ *adv.* **~wirtschaftlich orientiert/gesehen** orientated towards/from the point of view of the private sector; **~wirtschaftlich geführt** run as a private enterprise; **~wohnung** *die* private flat (*Brit.*) *or* (*Amer.*) apartment

**Privileg** /privi'le:k/ *das;* **~[e]s, ~ien** /-'le:gi̯ən/ privilege

**privilegieren** *tr. V.* grant privileges to

**privilegiert** *Adj.* privileged

**pro** /pro:/ *Präp. mit Akk.* per; **~ Jahr/Monat** per year *or* annum/month; **~ Person** per person; **~ Kopf** per head; **~ Stück** each; apiece; **~ Nase** (*ugs.*) each; a head

**pro-: pro-; ~westlich/~kommunistisch** pro-western/pro-communist

**Pro** *das; in* **[das] ~ und [das] Kontra** the pros and cons *pl.*

**Proband** /pro'bant/ *der;* **~en, ~en, Probandin** *die;* **~, ~nen** [A] (*Psych., Med.: Testperson*) subject; [B] (*Strafentlassener*) offender on probation

**probat** /pro'ba:t/ *Adj.* tried and tested; (*wirksam*) effective

**Probe** /'pro:bə/ *die;* **~, ~n** [A] (*Prüfung*) test; **die ~ aufs Exempel machen** put it to the test; **auf ~ sein** be on probation; **ein Beamter/eine Ehe auf ~:** a probationary civil servant/a trial marriage; **jmdn./etw. auf die ~ stellen** put sb./sth. to the test; **jmds. Geduld/Liebe/Freundschaft auf eine harte ~ stellen** sorely try *or* test sb.'s patience/sorely test sb.'s love/friendship; **jmdn. auf ~ einstellen** employ sb. on a trial basis; **~ laufen** test-run; **etw. ~ laufen lassen** test-run sth.; **ein Auto ~ fahren** test-drive a car; **ein Boot ~ fahren** test a boat out on the water; [B] (*Muster, Teststück*) sample; **eine ~ seines Könnens zeigen** *od.* **geben** (*fig.*) show what one can do; [C] (*Theater~, Orchester~*) rehearsal

**probe-, Probe-: ~ab·zug** *der* (*Druckw., Fot.*) proof; **~alarm** *der* practice alarm;

*old spelling (see note on page 1707)

(*Feueralarm*) fire drill *or* -practice; **~aufnahme** *die* [A] test take; [B] (*bei der Auswahl von Filmschauspielern*) screen test; **mit jmdm. ~aufnahmen machen** screen-test sb.; **~bohrung** *die* test drilling *no indef. art.*, *no pl.*; **~bohrungen/eine ~bohrung durchführen** drill test wells/a test well; **~druck** *der; Pl.* **~~e** (*Druckw.*) proof; **~exemplar** *das* specimen copy; ***~|fahren** ⇒ Probe; **~fahrt** *die* trial run; (*vor dem Kauf, nach einer Reparatur*) test drive; **eine ~fahrt machen** go for a trial run/test drive *or* test run; **hast du mit deinem neuen Boot schon eine ~fahrt gemacht?** have you tried out your new boat yet?; **~flug** *der* test flight; **~halber** *adv.* as a test; **jmdn. ~halber beschäftigen** employ sb. on a trial basis; **~jahr** *das* probationary year; **~lauf** *der* (*Technik*) test run

**proben** *tr., itr. V.* rehearse

**Proben·arbeit** *die* rehearsals *pl.* (**zu** for)

**probe-, Probe-: ~nummer** *die* specimen copy; **~weise** ❶ *Adv.* ‹employ› on a trial basis; **den Motor ~weise laufen lassen** test[-run] the engine; ❷ *adj.* trial; **~zeit** *die* [A] probationary *or* trial period; [B] (*schweiz. Rechtsspr.: Bewährungsfrist*) period of probation; **eine ~zeit von drei Jahren** three years' probation

**probieren** ❶ *tr. V.* [A] (*versuchen*) try; have a go *or* try at; **~, ob der Schlüssel passt** try the key to see whether it fits; [B] (*kosten*) taste; try; sample; [C] (*aus~*) try out; (*an~*) try on ‹clothes, shoes›; [D] (*Theaterjargon: proben*) rehearse. ❷ *itr. V.* [A] (*versuchen*) try; have a go *or* try; **P~ geht über Studieren** the proof of the pudding is in the eating (*prov.*); [B] (*kosten*) have a taste; **willst du ~?** do you want a taste?; **probier mal!** have a taste!; try some!; [C] (*Theaterjargon*) rehearse

**Problem** /pro'ble:m/ *das;* **~s, ~e** problem; **vor einem ~ stehen** be faced *or* confronted with a problem

**Problem-** problem; **ihr Kind war eine ~geburt** she had a difficult time with the birth of her child

**Problematik** /proble'ma:tɪk/ *die;* **~** (*Schwierigkeit*) problematic nature; (*Probleme*) problems *pl.*

**problematisch** *Adj.* problematic[al]

**problematisieren** *tr. V.* **etw. ~:** expound the problems of sth.

**problem-, Problem-: ~bewusstsein**, ***~bewußtsein** *das* awareness of the problem/problems (**für** of); **~film** *der* serious film; **~kind** *das* problem child; **~los** ❶ *Adj.* problem-free; ❷ *adv.* without any problems; **~stellung** *die* way of looking at *or* posing a problem/problems; (*zu erörterndes Thema*) problem; **~stück** *das* problem play

**Produkt** /pro'dʊkt/ *das;* **~[e]s, ~e** (*auch Math., fig.*) product; **~e der Landwirtschaft** agricultural produce *sing. or* products; **das ~ aus fünf mal zwei** the product of five times two

**Produkten-: ~börse** *die* (*Wirtsch.*) ⇒ **Warenbörse**; **~handel** *der* (*Kaufmannsspr.*) trade in agricultural commodities

**Produktion** /prodʊk'tsio:n/ *die;* **~, ~en** production; **die ~ steigern/stoppen** increase/stop production

**Produktions-: ~ablauf** *der* production process; **~abteilung** *die* production department; **~anlage** *die* production unit; **~anlagen** production plant *sing.*; **~ausfall** *der* loss of production; **~genossenschaft** *die* (*DDR*) cooperative; **eine landwirtschaftliche ~genossenschaft** a collective farm; **~güter** *Pl.* (*Wirtsch.*) producer goods; **~kosten** *Pl.* production costs; **~leistung** *die* output; **~leiter** *der*, **~leiterin** *die* production manager; **~mittel** *Pl.* (*marx.*) means of production; **~prozess**, ***~prozeß** *der* production process; **~verfahren** *das* production process; **~verhältnisse** *Pl.* (*marx.*) relations of production; **~weise** *die* production methods *pl.*; **~ziffern** *Pl.* production figures; **~zweig** *der* branch of production

**produktiv** /prodʊk'ti:f/ ❶ *Adj.* productive; prolific ‹writer, artist, etc.›. ❷ *adv.* ‹work, cooperate› productively

**Produktivität** /prodʊktivi'tɛ:t/ *die;* **~:** productivity

**Produktiv·kraft** *die* (*marx.*) productive force; force of production

**Produzent** /produ'tsɛnt/ *der;* **~en, ~en**, **Produzentin** *die;* **~, ~nen** ▶159 producer

**produzieren** ❶ *tr. V.* [A] *auch itr.* (*herstellen*) produce; [B] (*ugs.: hervorbringen*) make ‹bow, noise›; come up with ‹excuse, report›. ❷ *refl. V.* (*ugs.: großtun*) show off

**Prof.** *Abk.* **Professor** Prof.

**profan** /pro'fa:n/ ❶ *Adj.* [A] (*weltlich*) profane; secular; secular ‹building›; [B] (*alltäglich*) mundane. ❷ *adv.* (*alltäglich*) mundanely; in a mundane way

**Profan·bau** *der; Pl.* **~ten** (*Archit., Kunstwiss.*) secular building

**profanieren** *tr. V.* (*geh.*) [A] (*entweihen*) profane; [B] (*säkularisieren*) secularize

**Profession** /profɛ'sio:n/ *die;* **~, ~en** (*österr., sonst veralt.*) occupation; (*akademische, wissenschaftliche, medizinische ~*) profession; (*handwerkliche ~*) trade

**Professionalismus** /profɛsiona'lɪsmʊs/ *der;* **~:** professionalism

**professionell** /profɛsio'nɛl/ ❶ *Adj.* professional. ❷ *adv.* professionally

**Professor** /pro'fɛsɔr/ *der;* **~s, ~en** /-'so:rən/ ▶91, ▶159 [A] (*Hochschul~*) professor; **ordentlicher ~:** [full] professor (*holding a chair*); **außerordentlicher ~:** extraordinary professor (*not holding a chair*); **außerplanmäßiger ~:** supernumerary professor; ⇒ *auch* **zerstreut** 1; [B] (*österr., sonst veralt.: Gymnasial~*) [grammar school] teacher; **Herr ~!** sir!

**-professor** *der;* **~s, ~en** [A] professor of ‹history, mathematics, etc.›; [B] (*österr., sonst veralt.: -lehrer*) ‹history, mathematics, etc.› teacher (*at a Gymnasium*)

**professoral** /profɛso'ra:l/ *Adj.* (*auch abwertend*) professorial

**Professorenschaft** *die;* **~:** professoriate

**Professorin** /profɛ'so:rɪn/ *die;* **~, ~nen** ▶91 [A] (*Hochschul~*) professor; ⇒ *auch* **-in**; [B] (*österr.: Studienrätin*) mistress

**Professur** /profɛ'su:ɐ̯/ *die;* **~, ~en** professorship, chair (**für** in)

**Profi** *der;* **~s, ~s** (*ugs.*) pro (*coll.*)

**Profi·fußball** *der* professional football

**profihaft** ❶ *Adj.* professional. ❷ *adv.* professionally

**Profil** /pro'fi:l/ *das;* **~s, ~e** [A] (*Seitenansicht*) profile; **im ~:** in profile; [B] (*von Reifen, Schuhsohlen*) tread; [C] (*ausgeprägte Eigenart*) image; **kein ~ haben** *od.* **besitzen** lack a distinctive image; [D] (*Geol.*) profile

**Profi·lager** *das* (*Sportjargon*) **ins ~ überwechseln** turn professional

**profilieren** ❶ *refl. V.* make one's name *or* mark; (*sich unterscheiden*) give oneself a clearer image. ❷ *tr. V.* profile ‹moulding, frame, etc.›; put a tread on ‹tyre, shoe›

**profiliert** *Adj.* [A] (*markant, bedeutend*) prominent; [B] **eine grob ~e Gummisohle** a rubber sole with a heavy tread

**Profilierung** *die;* **~, ~en** [A] ⇒ **Profil** A; [B] (*Unterscheidung*) image; **die politische ~ einer Gruppe** the political complexion of a group

**profil-, Profil-: ~los** *Adj.* ‹politican, writer› lacking any distinctive image; **~neurose** *die* neurosis about one's image; **~sohle** *die* treaded sole; **~stahl** *der* (*Technik*) sectional steel; **~träger** *der* (*Technik*) sectional beam

**Profi-: ~spieler** *der*, **~spielerin** *die* professional player; **~sport** *der* professional sport

**Profit** /pro'fi:t/ *der;* **~[e]s, ~e** profit; **etw. mit ~ verkaufen** sell sth. at a profit; **aus etw. ~ ziehen** *od.* **herausschlagen** turn sth. to one's profit *or* advantage; **~ machen** make a profit; **mit/ohne ~ arbeiten** run/not run at a profit

**profitabel** /profi'ta:bl̩/ ❶ *Adj.* profitable. ❷ *adv.* profitably

**profit-, Profit-: ~bringend** ⇒ **profitabel**; **~gier** *die* (*abwertend*) greed for profit; **~gierig** *Adj.* (*abwertend*) greedy for profit *postpos.*; profit-seeking

**profitieren** ❶ *itr. V.* profit (**von, bei** by); (*fig.*) profit, gain (**von, bei, an** + *Dat.* from, by); **ich kann dabei nur ~:** I can't lose. ❷ *tr. V.* **er hat bei diesem Geschäft nichts/wenig profitiert** he did not make a profit/much of a profit on the deal

**Profit-: ~jäger** *der*, **~jägerin** *die* profiteer; **~maximierung** *die* maximization of profits; **~rate** *die* (*Wirtsch., marx.*) rate of profit; **~streben** *das* (*abwertend*) profit-seeking

**pro forma** /pro: 'fɔrma/ *Adv.* [A] (*der Form halber*) as a matter of form; [B] (*zum Schein*) for the sake of appearances

**profund** /pro'fʊnt/ *Adj.* (*geh.*) profound; deep

**Prognose** /pro'gno:zə/ *die;* **~, ~n** (*auch Med.*) prognosis; (*Wetter~, Wirtschafts~*) forecast; **eine ~ stellen** make a prognosis/give *or* make a forecast

**prognostizieren** /prognɔsti'tsi:rən/ *tr. V.* (*geh.*) forecast; predict

**Programm** /pro'gram/ *das;* **~s, ~e** [A] programme; program (*Amer., Computing*); (*Theater~ auch*) bill; (*bei Pferderennen*) card; (*Verlags~*) list; (*Ferns.: Sender*) channel; **das ~ für die kommende Woche** (*Ferns., Rundfunk*) the programmes *pl.* for the coming week; **etw. passt jmdm. nicht ins** *od.* **in sein ~:** sth. doesn't fit in with sb.'s plans; **nach ~** (*fig.*) according to plan; **auf jmds./dem ~ stehen** (*fig.*) be on sb.'s/the programme *or* agenda; **auf dem ~ stehen** (*bei einer Sitzung, Versammlung*) be on the agenda; [B] (*Kaufmannsspr.: Sortiment*) range

**-programm** *das;* **~s, ~e** programme; program (*Amer., Computing*); **Besuchs~:** programme of visits

**Programm·änderung** *die* change of programme

**Programmatik** /progra'ma:tɪk/ *die;* **~, ~en** (*Politik*) [political] objectives *pl.*

**programmatisch** ❶ *Adj.* programmatic ‹speech, statement›; **die ~en Ziele/Absichten der Regierung** the aims of the government's programme. ❷ *adv.* **die ~ festgelegten Ziele der Partei** the aims laid down in the party's programme

**programm-, Programm-: ~direktor** *der*, **~direktorin** *die* (*Ferns.*) director of programmes; **~folge** *die* (*Ferns.*) order of programmes; (*einer Show*) order of acts; running order; **~gemäß** ❶ *Adj.* **die ~gemäße Abfolge der Darbietungen** the order of acts as stated in the programme; ❷ *adv.* according to programme *or* plan; **~gestaltung** *die* programme planning; **~heft** *das* programme; **~hinweis** *der* programme announcement

**programmieren** *tr. V.* [A] (*DV*) program; [B] (*auf etw. festlegen*) programme; condition; **auf Erfolg programmiert sein** be geared to achieving success; [C] (*nach einem Programm ansetzen*) schedule

**Programmierer** *der;* **~s, ~**, **Programmiererin** *die;* **~, ~nen** ▶159 (*DV*) programmer

**Programmier·sprache** *die* (*DV*) programming language

**Programmierung** *die;* **~, ~en** ⇒ **programmieren** A-C: programming; conditioning; scheduling

**Programm-: ~musik** *die* programme music; **~punkt** *der* item on the programme; (*bei einer Sitzung*) item on the agenda

***Programmusik** ⇒ **Programmmusik**

**Programm-: ~vor·schau** *die* (*im Fernsehen*) preview [of the week's/evening's *etc.* viewing]; (*im Kino*) trailers *pl.*; **~zeitschrift** *die* radio and television magazine; **~zettel** *der* programme

**Progression** /progrɛ'sio:n/ *die;* **~, ~en** (*Steuerw.*) progressive tax system; **in die ~ kommen** move into a higher tax bracket

**progressiv** /progrɛ'si:f/ ❶ *Adj.* progressive. ❷ *adv.* progressively; **er schreibt sehr ~:**

he's a very progressive writer; **sie erziehen ihre Kinder sehr ~:** they are giving their children a very modern upbringing

**Progressiv·steuer** *die (Steuerw.)* progressive tax

**Prohibition** /prohibi'tsio:n/ *die;* **~:** prohibition

**Projekt** /pro'jɛkt/ *das;* **~[e]s, ~e** project

**Projekt·gruppe** *die* project team *or* group

**projektieren** *tr. V. (entwerfen)* draw up the plans for; plan; *(planen)* project; plan

**Projektil** /projɛk'ti:l/ *das;* **~s, ~e** projectile

**Projektion** /projɛk'tsio:n/ *die;* **~, ~en** *(Optik, Math., Geogr., Psych.)* projection

**Projektions-: ~apparat** *der* projector; **~ebene** *die (Math.)* plane of projection; **~wand** *die* projection screen

**Projekt·leiter** *der,* **Projekt·leiterin** *die* project leader

**Projektor** /pro'jɛktɔr/ *der;* **~s, ~en** /-'to:rən/ projector

**Projekt·planung** *die* project planning

**projizieren** /proji'tsi:rən/ *tr. V. (Optik, Math., Psych.)* project

**Proklamation** /proklama'tsio:n/ *die;* **~, ~en** proclamation

**proklamieren** *tr. V.* proclaim

**Pro-Kopf-** per head *or* capita *postpos.*

**Prokura** /pro'ku:ra/ *die;* **~, Prokuren** *(Kaufmannsspr.)* [full] power of attorney; procuration *(formal)*

**Prokurist** /proku'rɪst/ *der;* **~en, ~en, Prokuristin** *die;* **~, ~nen** ≈ authorized signatory; **~ bei einer Firma sein** ≈ have [full] signing powers in a firm

**Prolet** /pro'le:t/ *der;* **~en, ~en** Ⓐ *(abwertend: ungebildeter Mensch)* peasant; boor; Ⓑ *(ugs. veralt.: Proletarier)* prole *(coll.)*

**Proletariat** /proleta'ria:t/ *das;* **~[e]s** proletariat

**Proletarier** /prole'ta:riɐ/ *der;* **~s, ~, Proletarierin** *die;* **~, ~nen** proletarian

**proletarisch** ❶ *Adj.* proletarian. ❷ *adv.* ‹think, behave› like a proletarian

**proletarisieren** *tr. V.* proletarianize

**proletenhaft** *(abwertend)* ❶ *Adj.* boorish. ❷ *adv.* boorishly

**Proletin** *die;* **~, ~nen** ⇒ **Prolet**

**Prolog** /pro'lo:k/ *der;* **~[e]s, ~e** *(auch Radsport)* prologue

**Prolongation** /prolɔŋga'tsio:n/ *die;* **~, ~en** Ⓐ *(Wirtsch.)* renewal; Ⓑ *(bes. österr.)* prolonging; *(eines Vertrages)* extension

**prolongieren** *tr. V.* Ⓐ *(Wirtsch.: stunden)* renew; Ⓑ *(bes. österr.: verlängern)* extend ‹contract, engagement›

**Promenade** /promə'na:də/ *die;* **~, ~n** promenade

**Promenaden-: ~deck** *das* promenade deck; **~konzert** *das* promenade concert; **~mischung** *die (scherzh.)* mongrel

**promenieren** *itr. V.; auch mit sein (geh.)* promenade

**Promi**[1] *der;* **~s, ~s** *(ugs. scherzh.)* celebrity

**Promi**[2] *die;* **~, ~s** *(ugs. scherzh.)* celebrity

**Promille** /pro'mɪlə/ *das;* **~s, ~** Ⓐ *(Tausendstel)* **ein Blutalkoholgehalt von zwei ~:** a blood alcohol level of two parts per thousand; **bei 0,4/unter einem ~ liegen** be 0.4/ less than one in a *or* per thousand; Ⓑ *(ugs.: Blutalkohol)* alcohol level; **Ich fahre! Du hast zu viel ~:** I'll drive. You're over the limit; **er fährt nur ohne ~:** he never drinks and drives

**Promille·grenze** *die* legal [alcohol] limit

**prominent** /promi'nɛnt/ *Adj.* prominent

**Prominente** *der/die; adj. Dekl.* prominent figure

**Prominenz** /promi'nɛnts/ *die;* **~:** prominent figures *pl.*; *(das Prominentsein)* prominence; **er gehört zur politischen ~:** he is a prominent political figure

**Promiskuität** /promiskui'tɛ:t/ *die;* **~:** promiscuity

*old spelling (see note on page 1707)

**Promotion**[1] /promo'tsio:n/ *die;* **~, ~en** Ⓐ *(Erlangung der Doktorwürde)* gaining of a/ one's doctorate; **er schloss sein Studium mit der ~ ab** he completed his studies by gaining *or* obtaining his doctorate; **jmds. ~ [zum Doktor der Philosophie] feiern** celebrate the award of a doctorate *or* Ph.D. to sb.; Ⓑ *(österr.: offizielle Feier)* [doctoral] degree ceremony; **seine ~ zum Doktor der Philosophie** his Ph.D. ceremony

**Promotion**[2] /prə'moʊʃən/ *die;* **~** *(Wirtsch.)* promotion; **für etw. ~ machen** promote sth.

**promovieren** /promo'vi:rən/ ❶ *itr. V.* Ⓐ *(die Doktorwürde erlangen)* gain *or* obtain a/ one's doctorate; Ⓑ *(eine Dissertation schreiben)* do a doctorate (**über** + *Akk.* on). ❷ *tr. V.* confer a doctorate *or* the degree of doctor on

**prompt** /prɔmpt/ ❶ *Adj.* prompt. ❷ *adv.* Ⓐ *(umgehend)* promptly; Ⓑ *(ugs., meist iron.: wie erwartet)* [and] sure enough; **er ist auf den Trick ~ hereingefallen** and sure enough he fell for the trick; **„Gleich fällt er", dachte ich, und ~ fiel er** 'He's going to fall,' I thought and sure enough he did; **er wird ~ in die Falle hineinlaufen** as sure as fate he'll fall into the trap

**Promptheit** *die;* **~:** promptness

**Pronomen** /pro'no:mən/ *das;* **~s, ~** *od.* **Pronomina** /pro'no:mina/ *(Sprachw.)* pronoun

**pronominal** /pronomi'na:l/ *(Sprachw.)* ❶ *Adj.* pronominal. ❷ *adv.* pronominally

**Pronominal-** *(Sprachw.)* pronominal

**prononciert** /pronõ'si:ɐt/ *(geh.)* ❶ *Adj.* pronounced, definite, decided ‹opinion, views›; staunch, determined ‹supporter, advocate, etc.›. ❷ *adv. (entschieden)* clearly; **sich ~ über etw.** *(Akk.)* **äußern** express a definite opinion on sth.

**Propädeutik** /propɛ'dɔytɪk/ *die;* **~, ~en** *(Wissensch.)* Ⓐ preparatory instruction *no indef. art.*; **die philosophische ~:** philosophical propaedeutics *pl.*; Ⓑ *(Lehrbuch)* introductory textbook (**zu** on)

**propädeutisch** *Adj.* *(Wissensch.)* propaedeutic

**Propaganda** /propa'ganda/ *die;* **~** Ⓐ *(auch fig. ugs.)* propaganda; Ⓑ *(Reklame)* publicity

**Propaganda-: ~apparat** *der* propaganda machine; **~feld·zug** *der* propaganda campaign; **~minister** *der,* **~ministerin** *die* minister of propaganda; **~sender** *der (abwertend) (Rundf.)* propaganda station; *(Ferns.)* propaganda channel

**Propagandist** *der;* **~en, ~en, Propagandistin** *die;* **~, ~nen** Ⓐ propagandist; Ⓑ *(Wirtsch.: Werbefachmann/-frau)* demonstrator; *(Vertreter)* representative

**propagandistisch** ❶ *Adj.* propagandist; propaganda *attrib.* ‹purposes, measures, success, effort›. ❷ *adv.* ‹use, distort, etc.› for propaganda purposes

**propagieren** *tr. V. (geh.)* propagate ‹idea, view, belief, etc.›; **ein vereinigtes Europa ~:** propagate the idea of a united Europe

**Propan** /pro'pa:n/ *das;* **~s, Propan·gas** *das* propane

**Propeller** /pro'pɛlɐ/ *der;* **~s, ~** Ⓐ propeller; airscrew; prop *(coll.)*; Ⓑ *(Seew.: Schiffsschraube)* propeller; screw

**Propeller-: ~an·trieb** *der* propeller drive; **mit ~antrieb** propeller-driven; **~flugzeug** *das* propeller-driven aircraft

**proper** /'prɔpɐ/ ❶ *Adj.* Ⓐ *(adrett)* smart; Ⓑ *(ordentlich und sauber)* neat and tidy; Ⓒ *(sorgfältig, genau)* meticulous. ❷ *adv.* Ⓐ *(ordentlich und sauber)* neatly and tidily; Ⓑ *(sorgfältig, genau)* meticulously

**Prophet** /pro'fe:t/ *der;* **~en, ~en** prophet; **ich bin doch kein ~!** *(ugs.)* I can't see into the future!; **der ~ gilt nichts in seinem Vaterland[e]** *(Spr.)* a prophet is without honour in his own country; ⇒ *auch* **Bart** A; **Berg** A

**Prophetin** *die;* **~, ~nen** prophetess

**prophetisch** ❶ *Adj.* prophetic. ❷ *adv.* prophetically

**prophezeien** /profe'tsaiən/ *tr. V.* prophesy *(Dat.* for); predict ‹result, weather›; **das kann ich dir ~!** I can promise you that!

**Prophezeiung** *die;* **~, ~en** ⇒ **prophezeien:** prophecy; prediction

**prophylaktisch** /profy'laktɪʃ/ *(Med.)* ❶ *Adj.* prophylactic. ❷ *adv.* prophylactically; as a prophylactic measure

**Prophylaxe** /profy'laksə/ *die;* **~, ~n** *(Med.)* prophylaxis

**Proportion** /propɔr'tsio:n/ *die;* **~, ~en** *(auch Math., Musik)* proportion

**proportional** /propɔrtsio'na:l/ *(auch Math.)* ❶ *Adj.* proportional; **umgekehrt ~ zu ...** in inverse proportion to ...; *(Math. auch)* inversely proportional to ... ❷ *adv.* proportionally; in proportion; **~ [zu** *od.* **mit] einer Sache** *(Dat.)* in proportion to sth.

**proportioniert** /propɔrtsio'ni:ɐt/ *Adj.* proportioned

**Proporz** /pro'pɔrts/ *der;* **~es, ~e** *(Politik)* proportional representation *no art.*; **Ämter im** *od.* **nach dem ~ besetzen** fill posts in proportion to the number of votes received

**Proporz·wahl** *die (bes. österr. u. schweiz.)* ⇒ **Verhältniswahl**

**Proppen** /'prɔpn̩/ *der;* **~s, ~** Ⓐ *(nordd.)* ⇒ **Pfropfen;** Ⓑ *(ugs.: Kind)* podge *(coll.)*

**proppen·voll** *Adj. (ugs.)* jam-packed *(coll.)*

**Propst** /pro:pst/ *der;* **~[e]s, Pröpste** /prø:pstə/, **Pröpstin** *die;* **~, ~nen** *(kath., ev. Kirche)* provost

**Pro·rektor** *der,* **Pro·rektorin** *die (Hochschulw.)* ≈ pro-vice-chancellor

**Prosa** /'pro:za/ *die;* **~:** prose

**prosaisch** ❶ *Adj.* Ⓐ *(geh., oft abwertend: nüchtern)* prosaic; plain ‹building›; Ⓑ *(veralt.: in Prosa abgefasst)* prose *attrib.* ❷ *adv. (geh., oft abwertend)* prosaically

**Prosaist** *der;* **~en, ~en, Prosaistin** *die;* **~, ~nen** prose writer

**Proselyt** /proze'ly:t/ *der;* **~en, ~en, Proselytin** *die;* **~, ~nen** proselyte; **Proselyten machen** *(geh. abwertend)* proselytize

**Pro·seminar** *das (Hochschulw.)* introductory seminar course *(for students in their first and second year)*

**prosit** /'pro:zɪt/ *Interj.* ▶ 369 your [very good] health; **~ Neujahr!** happy New Year!

**Prosit** *das;* **~s, ~s** ▶ 369 toast; **ein ~ dem Geburtstagskind!** here's to the birthday boy/girl!

**Prosodie** /prozo'di:/ *die;* **~, ~n** *(Verslehre)* prosody

**Prospekt** /pro'spɛkt/ *der od. (bes. österr.) das;* **~[e]s, ~e** Ⓐ *(Werbeschrift)* brochure; *(Werbezettel)* leaflet; *(Verlags~)* illustrated catalogue; *(nur mit Neuerscheinungen)* seasonal list; Ⓑ *(Theater: Bühnenbild)* backdrop; backcloth; Ⓒ *(bild. Kunst: Ansicht)* perspective view; Ⓓ *(Wirtsch.)* prospectus

**prospektiv** /prospɛk'ti:f/ *Adj.* prospective

**prosperieren** /prospe'ri:rən/ *itr. V. (geh.)* prosper; ‹art, science› prosper, flourish

**Prosperität** /prosperi'tɛ:t/ *die;* **~** *(geh.)* prosperity

**prost** /pro:st/ *Interj. (ugs.)* cheers *(Brit. coll.)*; **na denn** *od.* **dann ~!** *(ugs. iron.)* that's brilliant! *(coll. iron.)*; ⇒ *auch* **Mahlzeit**

**Prost** *das;* **~[e]s, ~e** *(ugs.)* ⇒ **Prosit**

**Prostata** /'prɔstata/ *die;* **~, ~e** /'prɔstatɛ/ ▶ 471 *(Anat.)* prostate [gland]

**prosten** *itr. V.* say cheers *(Brit. coll.)*

**Prösterchen** /'prø:stɐçən/ *Interj. (fam.)* cheers *(Brit. coll.)*

**prostituieren** /prostitu'i:rən/ ❶ *tr. V. (geh.)* prostitute. ❷ *refl. V. (auch fig., geh.)* prostitute oneself; **sich als Künstler ~** *(fig. geh.)* prostitute one's artistic talent

**Prostituierte** *die/der; adj. Dekl.* ▶ 159 prostitute

**Prostitution** /prostitu'tsio:n/ *die;* **~** *(auch fig. geh.)* prostitution *no art.*

**Proszenium** /pro'stse:nium/ *das;* **~s, Proszenien** *(Theater)* proscenium

**Protagonist** /protago'nɪst/ *der;* **~en, ~en, Protagonistin** *die;* **~, ~nen** *(geh.)* protagonist

**Protegé** /prote'ʒe:/ *der;* **~s, ~s** (*geh.*) protégé

**protegieren** /prote'ʒi:rən/ *tr. V.* (*geh.*) sponsor; patronize ‹artist, composer, etc.›

**Protein** /prote'i:n/ *das;* **~s, ~e** (*Biochemie*) protein

**Protektion** /protɛk'tsio:n/ *die;* **~, ~en** (*geh.*) patronage *no indef. art.*

**Protektionismus** *der;* **~** (*Wirtsch.*) protectionism *no art.*

**Protektorat** /protɛkto'ra:t/ *das;* **~[e]s, ~e** Ⓐ(*geh.: Schirmherrschaft*) patronage; Ⓑ(*Völkerr.: Schutzherrschaft, Schutzgebiet*) protectorate

**Protest** /pro'tɛst/ *der;* **~[e]s, ~e** Ⓐprotest; **[bei jmdm.] ~ gegen jmdn./etw. erheben** *od.* **einlegen** make a protest [to sb.] against sb./sth.; **etw. aus ~ tun** do sth. as a *or* in protest; **unter [lautem] ~:** protesting [loudly]; Ⓑ(*Finanzw.*) protest; **der Wechsel ist zu ~ gegangen** the bill has been protested; Ⓒ(*DDR Rechtsw.*) protest

**Protest·aktion** *die* protest campaign

**Protestant** /protɛs'tant/ *der;* **~en, ~en, Protestantin** *die;* **~, ~nen** Protestant

**protestantisch** ❶*Adj.* Protestant. ❷*adv.* **[streng] ~ erzogen sein** have had a [strict] Protestant upbringing

**Protestantismus** *der;* **~:** Protestantism *no art.*

**Protest-:** **~bewegung** *die* protest movement; **~demonstration** *die* protest demonstration

**protestieren** ❶*itr. V.* protest, make a protest (**gegen** against, about). ❷*tr. V.* (*Finanzw.*) protest

**Protest-:** **~kundgebung** *die* protest rally; **~marsch** *der* protest march; **~note** *die* (*Dipl.*) protest note; **~ruf** *der* shout of protest; **~sänger** *der*, **~sängerin** *die* protest singer; **~song** *der* protest song; **~streik** *der* protest strike; **~sturm** *der* storm of protest; **~versammlung** *die* protest meeting; **~welle** *die* wave of protest

**Prothese** /pro'te:zə/ *die;* **~, ~n** Ⓐartificial limb; prosthesis (*Med.*); Ⓑ(*Zahn~*) set of dentures; dentures *pl.;* prosthesis (*Med.*)

**Protokoll** /proto'kɔl/ *das;* **~s, ~e** Ⓐ(*wörtlich mitgeschrieben*) transcript; (*Ergebnis~*) minutes *pl.;* (*bei Gericht*) record; records *pl.;* (*einer Verhandlung auf diplomatischer Ebene*) protocol; **[das] ~ führen** make a transcript [of the proceedings]; (*bei einer Sitzung Notizen machen*) take *or* keep the minutes; **etw. zu ~ geben/zu ~ geben, dass ...** make a statement about sth./to the effect that ...; **zu ~ nehmen** take down ‹statement etc.›; (*bei Gericht*) enter ‹objection, statement› in the record; Ⓑ(*diplomatisches Zeremoniell*) protocol; Ⓒ(*Strafzettel*) ticket

**Protokollant** /protokɔ'lant/ *der;* **~en, ~en, Protokollantin** *die;* **~, ~nen** transcript writer; (*eines Ergebnisprotokolls*) keeper of the minutes; (*bei Gericht*) court reporter

**protokollarisch** /protokɔ'la:rɪʃ/ ❶*Adj.* Ⓐ(*in Form, aufgrund eines Protokolls*) on record *postpos.;* (*bei einer Sitzung*) minuted; Ⓑ(*das diplomatische Zeremoniell betreffend*) **die ~en Vorschriften** the rules of protocol. ❷*adv.* Ⓐ(*in Form, aufgrund eines Protokolls*) **etw. ~ niederschreiben** (*bei einer Sitzung*) take sth. down in the minutes; (*bei Gericht*) enter sth. in the *or* place sth. on record; Ⓑ(*das diplomatische Zeremoniell betreffend*) from the point of view of protocol

**Protokoll-:** **~chef** *der*, **~chefin** *die* Chief of Protocol; **~führer** *der*, **~führerin** *die* ⇒ **Protokollant**

**protokollieren** ❶*tr. V.* take down; minute, take the minutes of ‹meeting›; minute, record in the minutes ‹remark›. ❷*itr. V.* (*bei einer Sitzung*) take *or* keep the minutes; (*bei Gericht*) keep the record; (*bei polizeilicher Vernehmung*) keep a record

**Proton** /'pro:tɔn/ *das;* **~s, ~en** /-'to:nən/ (*Physik*) proton

**Proto·plasma** /proto'plasma/ *das* (*Biol.*) protoplasm

**Proto·typ** /'pro:toty:p/ *der* Ⓐ(*geh.: Inbegriff*) archetype; epitome; Ⓑ(*Urform, erste Ausführung, Motorsport*) prototype

**Protozoon** /proto'tso:ɔn/ *das;* **~s, zoen** (*Biol.*) protozoan

**Protz** /prɔts/ *der;* **~es** *od.* **~en, ~e** *od.* **~en** (*ugs.*) Ⓐ(*Angeber*) swank[pot] (*coll.*); show-off; Ⓑ(*Prunk*) swank (*coll.*); show

**-protz** *der;* **~es** *od.* **~en, ~e** *od.* **~en** (*ugs.*) **Bildungs~/Sex[ual]~** *usw.* swank[pot] (*coll.*) when it comes to education/sex *etc.;* **Muskel~:** muscleman

**protzen** *itr. V.* (*ugs.*) swank (*coll.*); show off; **mit etw. ~:** show sth. off

**Protzerei** *die;* **~, ~en** (*ugs.*) Ⓐ(*das Protzen*) swanking (*coll.*); showing off; Ⓑ(*protzige Äußerung*) swanky remark (*coll.*)

**protzig** (*ugs. abwertend*) ❶*Adj.* swanky (*coll.*); showy. ❷*adv.* swankily (*coll.*)

**Provenienz** /prove'niɛnts/ *die;* **~, ~en** (*geh.*) provenance

**provenzalisch** /provɛn'tsa:lɪʃ/ *Adj.* Provençal

**Proviant** /pro'viant/ *der;* **~s, ~e** provisions *pl.;* **~ [für die Reise] mitnehmen** take some food for the journey

**Provider** /prɔ'vaidɐ/ *der;* **~s, ~** (*DV*) [service] provider

**Provinz** /pro'vɪnts/ *die;* **~, ~en** Ⓐ(*Verwaltungsbezirk*) province; Ⓑ(*oft abwertend: kulturell rückständige Gegend*) **aus der ~ kommen/in der ~ leben** come from/live in the provinces *pl.;* **finsterste** *od.* **hinterste ~ sein** be terribly provincial

**Provinz-:** **~bewohner** *der*, **~bewohnerin** *die* (*oft abwertend*) provincial; **~blatt** *das* (*abwertend*) provincial [news]paper; local rag (*derog.*)

**Provinzialismus** /provɪntsia'lɪsmʊs/ *der;* **~, Provinzialismen** Ⓐ(*Sprachw.*) provincialism; Ⓑ(*abwertend*) provincialism

**provinziell** /provɪn'tsiɛl/ (*meist abwertend*) ❶*Adj.* provincial; parochial ‹views›. ❷*adv.* provincially

**Provinzler** /pro'vɪntslɐ/ *der;* **~s, ~, Provinzlerin** *die;* **~, ~nen** (*ugs. abwertend*) [narrow-minded] provincial

**Provinz-:** **~nest** *das* (*ugs. abwertend*) [tiny] provincial backwater; **~stadt** *die* provincial town

**Provision** /provi'zio:n/ *die;* **~, ~en** (*Kaufmannsspr.*) commission; **auf** *od.* **gegen ~ arbeiten** work on a commission basis

**provisorisch** /provi'zo:rɪʃ/ ❶*Adj.* temporary ‹accommodation, filling, bridge, etc.›; provisional ‹status, capital, etc.›; provisional, caretaker *attrib.* ‹government›; provisional, temporary ‹measure, regulation, etc.›; **bei uns ist alles noch sehr ~:** everything's still very makeshift in our house/flat *etc.* ❷*adv.* temporarily; **etw. ~ reparieren** do *or* effect a temporary repair on sth.

**Provisorium** /provi'zo:riʊm/ *das;* **~s, Provisorien** (*geh.*) temporary measure

**provokant** /provo'kant/ (*geh.*) ⇒ **provokativ**

**Provokateur** /provoka'tøːɐ̯/ *der;* **~s, ~e, Provokateurin** *die;* **~, ~nen** agent provocateur; agitator

**Provokation** /provoka'tsio:n/ *die;* **~, ~en** provocation

**provokativ** /provoka'ti:f/, **provokatorisch** /provoka'to:rɪʃ/ (*geh.*) ❶*Adj.* provocative. ❷*adv.* provocatively

**provozieren** /provo'tsi:rən/ ❶*tr. V.* Ⓐ(*herausfordern*) provoke; Ⓑ(*auslösen*) provoke; cause ‹accident, fight›. ❷*itr. V.* be provocative; **zum Nachdenken [über etw.** (*Akk.*)**] ~:** provoke people into thinking [about sth.]

**Prozedur** /protse'du:ɐ̯/ *die;* **~, ~en** (*auch DV*) procedure

**Prozent** /pro'tsɛnt/ *das;* **~[e]s, ~e** Ⓐ*nach Zahlenangaben Pl. ungebeugt* (*Hundertstel*) per cent *sing.;* **fünf ~:** five per cent; **ich bin mir zu 90 ~ sicher** I'm 90 per cent certain; **der Plan wurde zu 90 ~ erfüllt** 90 per cent of the plan was fulfilled; **etw. in ~en ausdrücken** express sth. as a percentage; **60 ~ Alkohol enthalten** contain 60 per cent alcohol by volume; be 105 per cent proof; Ⓑ*Pl.* (*ugs.: Gewinnanteil*) share *sing.* of the profits; (*Rabatt*) discount *sing.;* **auf etw.** (*Akk.*) **~e bekommen** get a discount on sth.

**-prozentig** *adj.* -per-cent

**Prozent-:** **~punkt** *der* percentage point; **~rechnung** *die* percentage calculation; **~satz** *der* percentage; **zu einem beträchtlichen ~satz** be to a considerable extent

**prozentual** /protsɛn'tua:l/ ❶*Adj.* percentage; **der ~e Anteil der Autobesitzer an der Bevölkerung** the percentage of car owners in the population. ❷*adv.* **~ am Gewinn beteiligt sein** have a percentage share in the profits

**Prozess, *Prozeß** /pro'tsɛs/ *der;* **~es, ~e** Ⓐtrial; (*Fall*) [court] case; **jmdm. den ~ machen** take sb. to court; **es wurde ihm wegen der Ermordung von X der ~ gemacht** he stood trial charged with the murder of X; **der ~ Meyer gegen Schulze** the case of Meyer versus Schulze; **einen ~ gewinnen/verlieren** win/lose a case *or* lawsuit; ⇒ *auch* **anstrengen** 2 C; **führen** 1 C; Ⓑ(*Entwicklung, Ablauf*) process; Ⓒ(*fig.*) **mit jmdm./etw. kurzen ~ machen** (*ugs.*) make short work of sb./sth.; **jetzt wird kurzer ~ gemacht** (*ugs.*) we're going to sort this out once and for all

**prozess-, *prozeß-, Prozess-, *Prozeß-:** **~bevollmächtigte** *der/die* (*Rechtsspr.*) person with power of attorney in legal proceedings; **~führend** *Adj.* (*Rechtsspr.*) **die ~führenden Parteien** the litigants; **~gegner** *der*, **~gegnerin** *die* (*Rechtsspr.*) opposing party

**prozessieren** *itr. V.* go to court; **mit jmdm. um etw.** *od.* **wegen etw. ~:** be engaged in a court action *or* lawsuit with sb. about sth.; **gegen jmdn. ~:** bring an action *or* a lawsuit against sb.; (*seit längerer Zeit*) be engaged in an action *or* a lawsuit against sb.

**Prozession** /protsɛ'sio:n/ *die;* **~, ~en** procession

**Prozess·kosten, *Prozeß·kosten** *Pl.* legal costs

**Prozessor** /pro'tsɛsɔr/ *der;* **~s, ~en** /-'so:rən/ (*DV*) [central] processor

**Prozess-, *Prozeß-:** **~ordnung** *die* (*Rechtsw.*) code of procedure; **~rechner** *der* (*DV*) process-control computer; **~recht** *das* (*Rechtsw.*) procedural law; **~vollmacht** *die* (*Rechtsw.*) power of attorney in legal proceedings; **~wärme** *die* (*Kerntechnik*) process heat

**prüde** /'pry:də/ (*abwertend*) ❶*Adj.* prudish. ❷prudishly; **~ erzogen worden sein** have had a prudish upbringing

**Prüderie** /pry:də'ri:/ *die;* **~** (*abwertend*) prudery; prudishness

**prüfen** /'pry:fn/ ❶*tr. V.* Ⓐ*auch itr.* test ‹pupil› (**in** + *Dat.* in); (*beim Examen*) examine ‹pupil, student, etc.› (**in** + *Dat.* in); **ein geprüfter Elektrotechniker** a qualified electrician; **mündlich/schriftlich geprüft werden** have an oral/a written test/examination; **Latein/Anatomie ~:** be the examiner for Latin/Anatomy; **jmds. Kenntnisse ~:** test sb.'s knowledge; Ⓑ(*untersuchen*) examine (**auf** + *Akk.* for); check, examine ‹device, machine, calculation› (**auf** + *Akk.* for); investigate, look into ‹complaint›; (*testen*) test (**auf** + *Akk.* for); test, inspect ‹goods, materials, food›; test, check ‹temperature›; **einen Fall nochmals ~:** re-examine a case; Ⓒ(*kontrollieren*) check ‹papers, passport, application, calculation, information, correctness, etc.›; audit, check, examine ‹accounts, books›; Ⓓ(*vor einer Entscheidung*) check ‹price›; examine ‹offer›; consider ‹application›; **drum prüfe, wer sich ewig bindet** (*Spr.*) marry in haste, repent at leisure (*prov.*); Ⓔ(*forschend ansehen*) scrutinize; **jmdn. ~d** *od.* **mit ~den Blicken ansehen** scrutinize sb.; Ⓕ(*geh.: großen Belastungen aussetzen*) try; **sie ist vom Leben schwer geprüft worden** her life has been a hard trial; Ⓖ(*Sport: stark fordern*) test. ❷*refl. V.* search one's heart

**Prüfer** *der;* **~s, ~, Prüferin** *die;* **~, ~nen** Ⓐtester; inspector; (*Buch~*) auditor; Ⓑ(*im Examen*) examiner

**Prüf·gerät** *das* (*Technik*) piece of test equipment; test instrument

**Prüfling** /'pry:flɪŋ/ *der;* **~s, ~e** examinee; [examination] candidate

**Prüf-: ~stand** *der* (*Technik*) test bed; test stand; **auf dem ~stand** (*fig.*) under the microscope (*fig.*); **~stein** *der* touchstone (**für** for, of); measure (**für** of); **~stück** *das* testpiece; [test] specimen

**Prüfung** *die;* **~, ~en** A ▶ 369 (*Examen*) examination; exam (*coll.*); **eine ~ machen** *od.* **ablegen** take *or* do an examination; B (*das [Über]prüfen*) ⇒ **prüfen** B-D: examination; investigation; inspection; (*Kontrolle*) check; (*das Kontrollieren*) checking *no indef. art.;* (*Test*) test; (*das Testen*) testing *no indef. art.;* **klinische ~en** clinical trials; **nach/bei ~ Ihrer Beschwerde** after/on examining *or* investigating your complaint; **nach nochmaliger ~ Ihres Antrags** on reconsidering your application; C (*geh.: schicksalhafte Belastung*) trial

**Prüfungs-: ~angst** *die* examination phobia; (*im Einzelfall*) examination nerves *pl.;* **~arbeit** *die* examination; exam (*coll.*); **~auf·gabe** *die* problem set in an/the examination; **~aus·schuss, *~aus·schuß** *der* board of examiners; **~ergebnis** *das* examination result; **~kandidat** *der,* **~kandidatin** *die* [examination] candidate; **~ordnung** *die* examination regulations *pl.;* **~termin** *der* date of an/the examination; **~unterlagen** *Pl.* documents required on entering for an/the examination

**Prüf·verfahren** *das* test procedure

**Prügel** /'pry:gl̩/ *der;* **~s, ~** A (*Knüppel*) stick; cudgel; B *Pl.* (*Schläge*) beating *sing.;* (*als Strafe für Kinder*) hiding (*coll.*); **~ bekommen** *od.* **beziehen** get a hiding (*coll.*) *or* beating

**Prügelei** *die;* **~, ~en** (*ugs.*) punch-up (*coll.*); fight

**Prügel·knabe** *der* whipping boy

**prügeln** ❶ *tr.* (*auch itr.*) *V.* beat; **musst du immer gleich ~?** do you have to resort to beatings straight away? ❷ *refl. V.* **sich ~:** fight; **sich mit jmdm. [um etw.] ~:** fight sb. [over *or* for sth.]

**Prügel-: ~strafe** *die* corporal punishment *no art.;* **~szene** *die* A (*im Film, Theaterstück*) fight scene; B (*Prügelei*) fight

**Prunk** /prʊŋk/ *der;* **~[e]s** splendour; magnificence; (*einer Ausstattung, eines Saales usw. auch*) sumptuousness; (*eines Gebäudes, einer Architektur usw.*) magnificence; grandeur; (*einer Zeremonie*) splendour; pageantry; **~ entfalten** put on a display of splendour

**Prunk·bau** *der; Pl.* **~ten** magnificent building

**prunken** *itr. V.* A be resplendent; **~d** magnificent; B (*prahlen, sich hervortun*) show off; **mit etw. ~:** flaunt *or* make a great show of sth.

**prunk-, Prunk-: ~stück** *das* showpiece; **~süchtig** *Adj.* ‹person› with a passion for splendour [and grandeur]; **~voll** ❶ *Adj.* magnificent; splendid; ❷ *adv.* magnificently; splendidly; magnificently, splendidly, sumptuously ‹furnished, decorated›

**prusten** /'pru:stn̩/ *itr. V.* (*ugs.*) (*schnauben*) snort; (*keuchen*) puff and blow; **vor Lachen ~:** snort with laughter

**PS** *Abk.* A **Pferdestärke** h.p.; B **Postskript[um]** PS

**Psalm** /psalm/ *der;* **~s, ~en** psalm

**Psalmist** *der;* **~en, ~en** (*Rel.*) psalmist

**Psalter** /'psaltɐ/ *der;* **~s, ~** A (*Musik*) psaltery; B (*Rel.*) psalter

**PSchA** *Abk.* **Postscheckamt**

**pscht** /pʃt/ ⇒ **pst**

**pseudo-, Pseudo-** /psɔydo-/ (*abwertend*) pseudo-

**Pseudonym** /psɔydo'ny:m/ *das;* **~s, ~e** pseudonym; (*eines Schriftstellers*) pseudonym; nom de plume; pen name

*old spelling (see note on page 1707)

**pst** /pst/ *Interj.* sh; hush

**Psyche** /'psy:çə/ *die;* **~, ~n** A psyche; B (*österr.: Frisiertoilette*) dressing table

**psychedelisch** /psyçe'de:lɪʃ/ ❶ *Adj.* psychedelic. ❷ *adv.* psychedelically

**Psychiater** /psy'çi̯a:tɐ/ *der;* **~s, ~, Psychiaterin** *die;* **~, ~nen** ▶ 159 psychiatrist

**Psychiatrie** /psyçi̯a'tri:/ *die;* **~, ~n** A psychiatry *no art.;* B (*ugs.*) (*Abteilung*) psychiatric department; (*Klinik*) psychiatric clinic

**psychiatrisch** ❶ *Adj.* psychiatric. ❷ *adv.* **jmdn. ~ untersuchen/behandeln** give sb. a psychiatric examination/psychiatric treatment

**psychisch** ❶ *Adj.* psychological; psychological, mental ‹strain, disturbance, process›; mental ‹illness›. ❷ *adv.* psychologically; **~ gesund/krank sein** be mentally fit/ill; **ein ~ bedingtes Leiden** an illness of psychological origin

**psycho-, Psycho-** /psy:ço-/: **~analyse** *die* psychoanalysis *no art.;* **~analytiker** *der,* **~analytikerin** *die* ▶ 159 psychoanalyst; **~analytisch** ❶ *Adj.* psychoanalytical; ❷ *adv.* psychoanalytically; **~diagnostik** *die* psychodiagnostics *sing., no art.;* **~drama** *das* A (*Literaturw.*) psychological drama; B (*Psych.*) psychodrama; **~gen** /-'ge:n/ *Adj.* (*Med., Psych.*) psychogenic; **~gramm** *das* (*Psych.*) psychograph; **~krimi** /'----/ *der* (*ugs.*) psychological thriller; **~loge** /-'lo:gə/ *der;* **~~n, ~~n** ▶ 159 psychologist; **~logie** /-lo'gi:/ *die;* **~~:** psychology; **~login** *die;* **~~, ~~nen** ▶ 159 psychologist; **~logisch** ❶ *Adj.* A psychological; B (*ugs.: ~logisch geschickt*) **das war nicht sehr ~logisch von dir** that wasn't very good psychology on your part; ❷ *adv.* psychologically; **~logisch geschult** trained in psychology; **~logisieren** *itr.* (*auch tr.*) *V.* (*abwertend*) psychologize; **~path** /-'pa:t/ *der;* **~~en, ~~en, ~pathin** *die;* **~~, ~~nen** psychopath; **~pathie** /-pa'ti:/ *die;* **~~, ~~n** psychopathy *no art.;* **~pathisch** ❶ *Adj.* psychopathic; ❷ *adv.* psychopathically; **~pathologie** *die* psychopathology *no art.;* **~pharmakon** /-'farmakɔn/ *das;* **~~s, ~pharmaka** psychotropic drug

**Psychose** /psy'ço:zə/ *die;* **~, ~n** psychosis

**psycho-, Psycho-: ~somatisch** (*Med.*) ❶ *Adj.* psychosomatic; ❷ *adv.* **~somatisch bedingt** of psychosomatic origin *postpos.;* **~terror** /'----/ *der* psychological intimidation; **~therapeut** *der,* **~therapeutin** *die* ▶ 159 psychotherapist; **~therapeutisch** ❶ *Adj.* psychotherapeutic; ❷ *adv.* **jmdn. ~therapeutisch behandeln** give sb. psychotherapeutic treatment; **~therapie** *die* psychotherapy *no art.;* **~thriller** /'----/ *der* psychological thriller

**Psychotiker** /psy'ço:tikɐ/ *der;* **~s, ~, Psychotikerin** *die;* **~, ~nen** psychotic

**psychotisch** *Adj.* psychotic

**PTA** *Abk.* **pharmazeutisch-technische Assistentin** pharmaceutical-laboratory assistant

**ptolemäisch** /ptole'mɛ:ɪʃ/ *Adj.* Ptolemaic

**Ptolemäus** /ptole'mɛ:ʊs/ (*der*) Ptolemy

**PTT** *Abk.* **Schweizerische Post-, Telefon- und Telegrafenbetriebe** *Swiss postal, telephone, and telegraph services*

**pubertär** /pubɛr'tɛ:ɐ̯/ ❶ *Adj.* pubertal; **sein Benehmen ist typisch ~:** his behaviour is typical for the age of puberty. ❷ *adv.* **~ bedingt** caused by puberty *postpos.*

**Pubertät** /pubɛr'tɛ:t/ *die;* **~:** puberty; **in die ~ kommen** reach puberty

**pubertieren** *itr. V.* reach puberty; **~d** pubescent

**Publicity** /pʌ'blɪsɪtɪ/ *die;* **~:** publicity

**publicity·scheu** *Adj.* publicity-shunning *attrib.;* **~ sein** shun publicity

**Publicrelations, Public Relations** /'pʌblɪk rɪ'leɪʃənz/ *Pl.* public relations

**publik** /pu'bli:k/ *Adj.; in* **~ sein/werden** be/become public knowledge; **die Sache ist längst ~:** that's long been common knowledge; **etw. ~ machen** make sth. public

**Publikation** /publika'tsi̯o:n/ *die;* **~, ~en** publication

**Publikum** /'pu:blikʊm/ *das;* **~s** A (*Zuschauer, Zuhörer*) audience; (*bei Sportveranstaltungen*) crowd; B (*Kreis von Interessierten*) public; (*eines Schriftstellers*) readership; C (*Besucher*) clientele

**publikums-, Publikums-: ~erfolg** *der* success with the public; **~liebling** *der* idol of the public; **~verkehr** *der:* **„heute kein ~verkehr!"** 'closed to the public [today]'; **~wirksam** *Adj.* with public appeal *postpos., not pred.;* punchy ‹headline›; ‹headline› with a strong appeal; effective, compelling ‹broadcast›; **~wirksam sein** have public appeal

**publizieren** /publi'tsi:rən/ *tr.* (*auch itr.*) *V.* publish; **in verschiedenen Fachzeitschriften ~:** have articles *or* work published in various journals

**Publizist** *der;* **~en, ~en** commentator on politics and current affairs; publicist

**Publizistik** *die;* **~:** mass communications *pl., no art.;* (*Journalismus*) journalism *no art.*

**Publizistin** *die;* **~, ~nen** ⇒ **Publizist**

**publizistisch** ❶ *Adj.* **seine ~e Aktivität** his journalistic activities *pl.;* **die Reise war ein ~er Misserfolg** the trip failed to get the media's attention. ❷ *adv.* **etw. ~ verbreiten** disseminate sth. via the media; **~ tätig sein** work in mass communications/as a journalist

**Publizität** /publitsi'tɛ:t/ *die;* **~:** publicity

**Puck** /pʊk/ *der;* **~s, ~s** (*Eishockey*) puck

**puckern** /'pʊkɐn/ *itr. V.* (*ugs.*) throb

**Pudding** /'pʊdɪŋ/ *der;* **~s, ~e** *od.* **~s** *thick, usually flavoured, milk-based dessert;* ≈ blancmange; ⇒ *auch* **hauen** 2 C

**Pudding·pulver** *das* ≈ blancmange powder

**Pudel** /'pu:dl̩/ *der;* **~s, ~** A (*Hund*) poodle; **das war also des ~s Kern** (*fig.*) so 'that's what was behind it; **wie ein begossener ~ dastehen** (*ugs.*) stand there crestfallen; (*nach einer Zurechtweisung*) stand there sheepishly; B (*ugs.: beim Kegeln*) miss; **einen ~ werfen** *od.* **schießen** miss

**pudel-, Pudel-: ~mütze** *die* bobble *or* pompom hat; **~nass, *~naß** *Adj.* (*ugs.*) drenched; soaked to the skin; **~wohl** *Adv.* (*ugs.*) **sich ~wohl fühlen** feel on top of the world

**Puder** /'pu:dɐ/ *der;* **~s, ~:** powder

**Puder·dose** *die* powder compact

**pudern** *tr. V.* powder; **sich** (*Dat.*) **die Nase ~:** powder one's nose

**Puder-: ~quaste** *die* powder puff; **~zucker** *der* icing sugar (*Brit.*); confectioners' sugar (*Amer.*)

**Puertoricaner** /pu̯ɛrtori'ka:nɐ/ *der;* **~s, ~, Puertoricanerin** *die;* **~, ~nen** Puerto Rican; ⇒ *auch* **-in**

**puertoricanisch** *Adj.* Puerto Rican

**puff** /pʊf/ *Interj.* bang

**Puff**[1] *der;* **~[e]s, Püffe** /'pʏfə/ (*ugs.*) A (*Stoß*) thump; (*leichter/kräftiger Stoß mit dem Ellenbogen*) nudge/dig; **einen ~** *od.* **einige Püffe vertragen [können]** (*fig.*) be able to take a few knocks; B (*Knall*) bang

**Puff**[2] *der od. das;* **~s, ~s** (*salopp: Bordell*) knocking shop (*Brit. sl.*); brothel

**Puff**[3] *der;* **~[e]s, ~e** *od.* **~s** A (*Wäsche~*) linen basket; B (*Sitzkissen*) pouffe; C (*veralt.: Bausch*) puff

**Puff·ärmel** *der* puff *or* puffed sleeve

**puffen** (*ugs.*) ❶ *tr.* (*auch itr.*) *V.* A (*stoßen*) thump; (*mit dem Ellenbogen*) nudge; dig; **~ und schubsen** push and shove; B (*irgendwohin befördern*) push; shove; (*mit dem Ellenbogen*) elbow; **jmdn. zur Seite ~:** push *or* shove/elbow sb. aside. ❷ *itr. V.* ‹locomotive› puff

**Puffer** *der;* **~s, ~** A (*Vorrichtung*) buffer; B ⇒ **Kartoffel~**

**Puffer-: ~staat** *der* buffer state; **~zone** *die* buffer zone

**Puff-: ~mutter** *die; Pl.* **~mütter** (*salopp*) madam; **~reis** *der* puffed rice

**puh** /pu:/ *Interj.* ugh; (*erleichtert*) phew

**pulen** /ˈpu:lən/ (*nordd. ugs.*) ❶ *itr. V.* pick (**an** + *Dat.* at); **[sich (*Dat.*)] in der Nase ~:** pick one's nose. ❷ *tr. V.* pick (**aus** out of); **etw. von etw. ~:** pick sth. off sth.

**Pulk** /pʊlk/ *der;* **~[e]s, ~s** *od.* **~e** Ⓐ (*Milit.: Verband*) group; Ⓑ (*Menge*) crowd; (*Sport: Hauptfeld*) pack; bunch

**Pulle** /ˈpʊlə/ *die;* **~, ~n** (*salopp*) bottle; **volle ~** (*fig. salopp*) flat out

**pullen** ❶ *itr. V.* (*Seemannsspr.*) row. ❷ *itr. V.* (*Pferdesport*) pull

**pullern** /ˈpʊlɐn/ *itr. V.* (*fam., bes. ostmd.*) pee (*coll.*)

**Pulli** /ˈpʊli/ *der;* **~s, ~s** (*ugs.*), **Pullover** /pʊˈlo:vɐ/ *der;* **~s, ~:** pullover; sweater

**Pullunder** /pʊˈlʊndɐ/ *der;* **~s, ~:** slipover

**Puls** /pʊls/ *der;* **~es, ~e** Ⓐ pulse; **jmds. ~ fühlen/messen** feel/take sb.'s pulse; Ⓑ (*Elektrot., Nachrichtent.*) pulse

**Puls·ader** *die* artery; **sich** (*Dat.*) **die ~n aufschneiden** slash one's wrists

**pulsen** *itr. V.* (*auch fig.*) pulse

**pulsieren** *itr. V.* (*auch fig.*) pulsate; ‹blood› pulse

**Puls-: ~schlag** *der* (*auch fig.*) pulse; (*einzelner ~schlag*) beat; **~wärmer** *der;* **~~s, ~~:** wristlet; **~zahl** *die* (*Med.*) pulse rate

**Pult** /pʊlt/ *das;* **~[e]s, ~e** Ⓐ desk; (*Lese~*) lectern; desk; Ⓑ (*Schalt~*) control desk; console

**Pulver** /ˈpʊlfɐ/ *das;* **~s, ~** Ⓐ powder; Ⓑ (*Schieß~*) [gun]powder; **das ~ hat er [auch] nicht [gerade] erfunden** (*ugs.*) he'll never set the world *or* (*Brit.*) the Thames on fire; **sein ~ verschossen haben** (*fig. ugs.*) have shot one's bolt; Ⓒ (*salopp: Geld*) dough (*coll.*)

**Pülverchen** /ˈpʏlfɐçən/ *das;* **~s, ~** (*spött.*) [medicinal] powder

**Pulver-: ~dampf** *der* gun smoke; **~fass,** ***~faß** *das* barrel of gunpowder; (*kleiner*) powder keg; **auf einem** *od.* **dem ~fass sitzen** (*fig.*) be sitting on a powder keg *or* on top of a volcano; **~form** *die:* *in* **in ~form** in powder form

**pulverisieren** *tr. V.* pulverize; powder

**Pulver-: ~kaffee** *der* instant coffee; **~kammer** *die* Ⓐ (*Schiffbau*) powder magazine; Ⓑ (*Milit. veralt.*) chamber

**pulvern** *tr. V.* **zu viel Geld in die Rüstung ~:** throw money away on arms

**Pulver·schnee** *der* powder snow

**Puma** /ˈpu:ma/ *der;* **~s, ~s** puma

**Pummel** /ˈpʊml̩/ *der;* **~s, ~** (*ugs.*), **Pummelchen** *das;* **~s, ~** (*ugs.*) podge

**pumm[e]lig** /ˈpʊm(ə)lɪç/ *Adj.* (*ugs.*) chubby

**Pump** /pʊmp/ *der;* **~s** (*salopp*) **auf ~:** on tick (*coll.*)

**Pumpe** /ˈpʊmpə/ *die;* **~, ~n** Ⓐ pump; Ⓑ (*salopp: Herz*) ticker (*joc.*)

**pumpen** *tr., itr. V.* Ⓐ (*auch fig.*) pump; Ⓑ (*salopp: verleihen*) lend; **jmdm. etw. ~:** lend sb. sth.; Ⓒ (*entleihen*) borrow; **sich** (*Dat.*) **[bei** *od.* **von jmdm.] etw. ~:** borrow sth. from *or* (*coll.*) off sb.

**Pumpen·schwengel** *der* pump handle

**pumpern** /ˈpʊmpɐn/ *itr. V.* (*südd., österr. ugs.*) thump; ‹heart› thump, pound; ‹heavy artillery› thud

**Pumper·nickel** *der* pumpernickel

**Pump·hose** *die* harem trousers *pl.*; (*veralt.: Knickerbocker*) knickerbockers *pl.*

**Pumps** /pœmps/ *der;* **~, ~:** court shoe

**Pump·station** *die* pumping station

**Punier** /ˈpu:ni̯ɐ/ *der;* **~s, ~, Punierin** *die;* **~, ~nen** Phoenician

**punisch** *Adj.* Punic

**Punk** /paŋk/ *der;* **~[s], ~s** punk

**Punker** /ˈpaŋkɐ/ *der;* **~s, ~, Punkerin** *die;* **~, ~nen** Ⓐ (*Musiker[in]*) punk rocker; Ⓑ (*Anhänger[in]*) punk

**Punk·rock** *der* punk rock

**Punkt** /pʊŋkt/ *der;* **~[e]s, ~e** Ⓐ (*Tupfen*) dot; (*größer*) spot; **ein Stoff mit blauen ~en** a fabric with blue spots; **das ist [nicht] der springende ~** (*fig.*) that's [not] the point; **ein dunkler ~ [in jmds. Vergangenheit]** a dark chapter [in sb.'s past]; Ⓑ (*Satzzeichen*) full stop; period; **drei ~e bedeuten eine Auslassung im Zitat** three dots mean an omission in the quotation; **einen ~ machen** *od.* **setzen** put a full stop; **nun mach [aber] mal einen ~!** (*fig. ugs.*) come off it! (*coll.*); **ohne ~ und Komma reden** (*ugs.*) talk nineteen to the dozen (*Brit.*); rabbit (*Brit. coll.*) *or* talk on and on; Ⓒ (*i-~*) dot; **den ~ auf dem i vergessen** forget to dot the i; **etw. auf den ~ genau wissen** know sth. quite precisely; ⇒ *auch* **i, I;** Ⓓ (*Stelle*) point; **an einem ~ sein, wo ...** (*fig.*) have reached the point *or* stage where ...; **ein schwacher/wunder/neuralgischer ~** (*fig.*) a weak/sore/vulnerable *or* sensitive point; **die Unterhaltung war/die Verhandlungen waren an einem toten ~ angelangt** the conversation had come to a dead stop/the talks had reached deadlock *or* an impasse; **ein starker Kaffee half ihm über den toten ~ hinweg** a strong coffee helped him to get his second wind; **nachmittags um zwei Uhr habe ich meinen toten ~:** I'm at my lowest ebb at two o'clock in the afternoon; Ⓔ (*Gegenstand, Thema, Abschnitt*) point; (*einer Tagesordnung*) item; point; **in diesem/über diesen ~:** on this point; **sich in allen ~en einig sein** agree on all points; **~ für ~:** point by point; **etw. auf den ~ bringen** sum sth. up; put sth. in a nutshell; **jmdn. in allen ~en der Anklage freisprechen** acquit sb. on all counts; Ⓕ (*Bewertungs~*) point; (*bei einer Prüfung*) mark; **nach ~en siegen** win on points; **~e sammeln** (*fig.*) score points (**bei** with); Ⓖ (*Musik*) dot; Ⓗ (*Math.*) point; Ⓘ **▶ 752** (*Zeit~*) point; **jetzt ist der ~ gekommen, wo ich ...** the moment *or* time has now arrived when I ...; **~ 12 Uhr** at 12 o'clock on the dot; Ⓙ *nach Zahlenangaben ungebeugt* (*Druckw.*) point

**Pünktchen** /ˈpʏŋktçən/ *das;* **~s, ~:** little dot *or* spot; **rote ~:** little red dots *or* spots

**punkten** *itr. V.* (*bes. Boxen*) pick up points; score [points]

**punkt-, Punkt-: ~feuer** *das* (*Milit.*) precision fire; **~förmig** *Adj.* **eine ~förmige Lichtquelle** a point source of light; **~gewinn** *der* (*Sport, bes. Ballspiele*) **sie blieben im Turnier ohne ~gewinn** they failed to win any points in the competition; **~gleich** *Adj.* (*Sport*) level on points *pred.*; **~gleich stehen** be level on points; **die ~gleichen Teams** the teams on equal points; **~gleichheit** *die* (*Sport*) **bei ~gleichheit** if the same number of points have been scored

**punktieren** *tr. V.* Ⓐ (*mit Punkten darstellen*) dot; Ⓑ (*Med.*) puncture; Ⓒ (*Musik*) **eine Rolle ~:** transpose individual notes in a vocal part; Ⓓ *auch itr.* (*Musik: verlängern*) dot ‹note›

**Punktion** /pʊŋkˈtsi̯o:n/ *die;* **~, ~en** (*Med.*) puncture

**pünktlich** /ˈpʏŋktlɪç/ ❶ *Adj.* Ⓐ punctual; **er ist immer ~:** he's always punctual *or* on time; **der Zug ist ~/nicht ~:** the train is on time/is late; Ⓑ (*veralt.: gewissenhaft genau*) meticulous. ❷ *adv.* Ⓐ punctually; on time; **das Konzert beginnt ~ um 20 Uhr** the concert will begin at 8 o'clock sharp; **~ auf die Minute** punctually to the minute; Ⓑ (*veralt.: gewissenhaft, genau*) meticulously

**Pünktlichkeit** *die;* **~:** punctuality

**punkt-, Punkt-: ~nieder·lage** *die* (*Sport*) defeat on points; points defeat; **~richter** *der,* **~richterin** *die* (*Sport*) judge; **~schweißen** *tr., itr. V.; nur Inf. u. 2. Part. gebr.* spot weld; **~sieg** *der* (*Sport*) win on points; points win; **~spiel** *das* (*Mannschaftssport*) league game

**punktuell** /pʊŋkˈtu̯ɛl/ ❶ *Adj.* isolated ‹interventions, checks, approaches, initiatives, etc.›; **einige ~e Verbesserungen** improvements in a few matters of detail. ❷ *adv.* **sich nur mit einem Thema nur ~ befassen** deal only with certain *or* particular points relating to a topic; **Kontrollen wurden nur ~ durchgeführt** only spot checks were carried out

**Punktum** *Interj.* (*veralt.*) *in* **[und damit] ~:** and that's that; and that's final *or* flat

**Punkt-: ~wertung** *die* points system; **~zahl** *die* score; number of points; (*beim Eiskunstlauf*) score; [number of] marks

**Punsch** /pʊnʃ/ *der;* **~[e]s, ~e** *od.* **Pünsche** /ˈpʏnʃə/ punch

**Punze** /ˈpʊnt͡sə/ *die;* **~, ~n** Ⓐ (*Werkzeug*) punch; (*zum Gravieren*) burin; Ⓑ (*Gütezeichen*) hallmark

**Pupille** /puˈpɪlə/ *die;* **~, ~n** pupil

**Püppchen** /ˈpʏpçən/ *das;* **~s, ~** Ⓐ ([*kleine*] *Puppe*) little doll *or* (*child lang.*) dolly; Ⓑ (*Kosewort*) pet; (*niedliches Mädchen*) little sweetie (*coll.*); (*hübsches, aber nichts sagendes Mädchen*) dolly bird (*Brit. sl.*)

**Puppe** /ˈpʊpə/ *die;* **~, ~n** Ⓐ doll[y]; Ⓑ (*Marionette*) puppet; marionette; (*fig.*) puppet; **die ~n tanzen lassen** (*fig. ugs.*) pull the strings; (*es hoch hergehen lassen*) paint the town red (*coll.*); Ⓒ (*salopp: Mädchen*) bird (*sl.*); (*als Anrede*) sweetie (*coll.*); Ⓓ (*Zool.*) pupa; Ⓔ (*ostmd.: aus Getreidegarben*) stook; shock; Ⓕ *in* **bis in die ~n** (*ugs.*) till all hours

**Puppen-: ~doktor** *der* (*ugs.*) doll repairer; **etw. zum ~doktor bringen** take sth. to the dolls' hospital; **~gesicht** *das* baby-doll face; **~haus** *das* doll's house; dollhouse (*Amer.*); **~spiel** *das* Ⓐ puppet theatre; Ⓑ (*Stück*) puppet show; **~spieler** *der,* **~spielerin** *die* puppeteer; **~stube** *die* doll's house; dollhouse (*Amer.*); **~theater** *das* puppet theatre; **~wagen** *der* doll's pram

**puppig** *Adj.* (*ugs.*) Ⓐ ⇒ **niedlich**; Ⓑ (*kinderleicht*) dead easy

**pur** /pu:ɐ̯/ *Adj.* Ⓐ (*rein*) pure; Ⓑ (*unvermischt*) neat; straight; **bitte einen Whisky ~!** a neat whisky, please; Ⓒ (*bloß*) sheer; pure; **das ist ~er Wahnsinn** that's sheer *or* pure *or* absolute madness

**Püree** /pyˈre:/ *das;* **~s, ~s** Ⓐ purée; Ⓑ ⇒ **Kartoffelbrei**

**pürieren** /pyˈri:rən/ *tr. V.* (*Kochk.*) purée ‹potatoes, apples, etc.›; (*zerstampfen*) mash

**Purismus** *der;* **~** (*Sprachw., Kunstw.*) purism

**Purist** *der;* **~en, ~en, Puristin** *die;* **~, ~nen** purist

**puristisch** ❶ *Adj.* purist; puristic. ❷ *adv.* puristically

**Puritaner** /puriˈta:nɐ/ *der;* **~s, ~, Puritanerin** *die;* **~, ~nen** Ⓐ Puritan; Ⓑ (*fig.*) puritan

**puritanisch** *Adj.* Ⓐ Puritan; Ⓑ (*fig.*) puritanical

**Puritanismus** *der;* **~:** Puritanism *no art.*

**Purpur** /ˈpʊrpʊr/ *der;* **~s** Ⓐ (*Farbton*) crimson; Ⓑ (*Gewand*) purple

**purpur-, Purpur-: ~farben, ~farbig** *Adj.* crimson; **~mantel** *der* crimson *or* purple robe

**purpurn, purpur·rot** *Adj.* crimson

**Purzel·baum** *der* (*ugs.*) somersault; **einen ~ machen** *od.* **schlagen** do *or* turn a somersault

**purzeln** /ˈpʊrt͡sl̩n/ *itr. V.; mit sein* (*fam.*) tumble; **auf dem Eis ~:** fall over on the ice

**puschen** *usw.* ⇒ **pushen** *usw.*

**Puschen** /ˈpu:ʃn̩/ *der;* **~s, ~** (*nordd.*) slipper

**pushen** /ˈpʊʃn̩/ ❶ *tr. V.* Ⓐ (*Drogenjargon*) push; Ⓑ (*Journalistenjargon*) push. ❷ *itr. V.* (*Drogenjargon*) be a pusher

**Pusher** *der;* **~s, ~, Pusherin** *die;* **~, ~nen** (*Drogenjargon*) pusher

**pusselig** *Adj.* (*ugs., bes. nordd.*) Ⓐ (*Geduld fordernd*) fiddly ‹work, task›; Ⓑ (*übergenau*) pernickety (*coll.*); (*umständlich*) fussy

**pusseln** /ˈpʊsl̩n/ *itr. V.* (*ugs.*) potter about; mess about (**an** + *Dat.* with)

**Puszta,** ***Pußta** /ˈpʊsta/ *die;* **~, Pussten** puszta; *steppeland in Hungary*

**Puste** /ˈpu:stə/ *die;* **~** (*salopp*) puff; breath; **ganz aus der** *od.* **außer ~ sein** be out of puff; be puffed [out]; ⇒ *auch* **ausgehen** 1 B

**Puste-: ~blume** *die* (*ugs.*) dandelion clock; **~kuchen** *in* **[ja** *od.* **aber] ~kuchen** (*ugs.*) (*es ist/war nicht der Fall*) not a bit of it!; (*es hat nicht geklappt*) nothing doing!

**Pustel** /ˈpʊstl/ *die;* ~, ~**n** ▶ 474 pimple; spot; pustule (*Med.*)

**pusten** (*ugs.*) ❶ *itr. V.* Ⓐ (*blasen*) ‹person, wind› blow; **es pustet draußen ganz schön** (*ugs.*) there's a fair old wind blowing out there (*coll.*); ~ **müssen** (*ugs.: bei einer Verkehrskontrolle*) have to blow into the bag; Ⓑ (*keuchen*) puff [and pant *or* blow]. ❷ *tr. V.* (*blasen*) blow; **jmdm. was** *od.* **eins** ~ (*salopp*) tell sb. where to get off (*coll.*)

**Puste·rohr** *das* (*ugs.*) pea-shooter

**putativ** /putaˈtiːf/ *Adj.* (*Rechtsspr.*) putative

**Putativ·notwehr** *die* (*Rechtsw.*) **in** ~ **handeln** act in the mistaken belief that one is being attacked

**Pute** /ˈpuːtə/ *die;* ~, ~**n** Ⓐ (*Truthenne*) turkey hen; (*als Braten*) turkey; Ⓑ (*salopp abwertend: Mädchen, Frau*) **eine dumme/extravagante** ~: a silly goose *or* creature/an extravagant creature; **eine eingebildete** ~: a stuck-up little madam

**Puter** *der;* ~**s**, ~: turkeycock; (*als Braten*) turkey

**puter·rot** *Adj.* scarlet; bright red

**Putsch** /pʊtʃ/ *der;* ~**[e]s**, ~**e** putsch; coup [d'état]

**putschen** *itr. V.* organize a putsch *or* coup

**Putschist** *der;* ~**en**, ~**en**, **Putschistin** *die;* ~, ~**nen** putschist; rebel

**Putsch·versuch** *der* attempted putsch *or* coup

**Pütt** /pʏt/ *der;* ~**s**, ~**e** *od.* ~**s** (*rhein., westfäl. Bergmannsspr.*) pit; mine; **auf dem** ~ **sein** work in the mine

**Putte** /ˈpʊtə/ *die;* ~, ~**n** (*Kunstwiss.*) putto

**Putz** /pʊts/ *der;* ~**es** Ⓐ (*Baumaterial*) plaster; (*für Außenmauern*) rendering; (*Rau*~) roughcast; **eine Wand mit** ~ **bewerfen** *od.* **verkleiden** plaster/render/roughcast a wall; **die Rohre liegen über** ~: the pipes are exposed; **auf den** ~ **hauen** (*fig. salopp*) (*angeben*) boast; brag; (*ausgelassen feiern*) have a rave-up (*Brit. coll.*); Ⓑ (*salopp: Streit*) row (*coll.*); **wenn er spät nach Hause kommt, kriegt er** ~ **mit seiner Frau** when he gets home late, his wife starts rowing with him; ~ **machen** (*salopp*) cause aggro (*Brit. sl.*); Ⓒ (*veralt.: Kleidung*) finery

**Putze** *die;* ~, ~**n** (*salopp*) char (*Brit. coll.*); cleaner

**putzen** *tr. V.* Ⓐ (*blank reiben*) polish; clean; **Schuhe/die Fenster** ~: polish *or* clean one's shoes/clean the windows; **den Teller blank** ~ (*fig.*) clear one's plate; ⇒ *auch* **Klinke** A; Ⓑ (*säubern*) clean; groom ‹horse›; **[sich (*Dat.*)] die Zähne/die Nase** ~: clean *or* brush one's teeth/blow one's nose; **er putzte seinem Kind die Nase** he wiped his child's nose; **sich** ~ ‹cat› wash itself; ‹bird› preen itself; Ⓒ *auch itr.* (*bes. rhein., südd., schweiz.: sauber machen*) clean ‹room, shop, etc.›; ~ **gehen** work as a cleaner *or* (*Brit.*) char[woman]; Ⓓ (*zum Essen, Kochen vorbereiten*) wash and prepare ‹vegetables›; Ⓔ (*Sportjargon: besiegen*) beat; Ⓕ (*beschneiden*) trim ‹wick, lamp, candle›; Ⓖ (*österr.: chemisch reinigen*) [dry-]clean; **etw.** ~ **lassen** take sth. to the [dry-]cleaners; Ⓗ (*veralt.: schmücken*) dress ‹person› up; decorate ‹Christmas tree etc.›; **sich** ~: dress [oneself] up; Ⓘ *auch itr.* (*veralt.: zieren*) decorate; adorn; **deine Schleife putzt aber ungemein!** your ribbon makes you look really pretty!

**Putzerei** *die;* ~, ~**en** Ⓐ (*ugs. abwertend: das Putzen*) [obsessive] cleaning; Ⓑ (*österr.: Reinigungsanstalt*) dry-cleaner's

**Putz-:** ~**fimmel** *der* (*ugs. abwertend*) mania for cleaning; ~**frau** *die* ▶ 159 cleaner; char[lady] (*Brit.*)

**putzig** (*ugs.*) ❶ *Adj.* Ⓐ (*entzückend*) sweet; cute (*Amer.*); (*possierlich*) funny; comical; Ⓑ (*seltsam*) funny; peculiar. ❷ *adv.* Ⓐ (*entzückend*) sweetly; cutely (*Amer.*); (*possierlich*) comically; Ⓑ (*seltsam*) peculiarly

**putz-, Putz-:** ~**lappen** *der* [cleaning] rag; cloth; ~**leute** *Pl.* cleaners; ~**macherin** *die* ▶ 159 milliner; ~**mann** *der;* ▶ 159 cleaner; ~**mittel** *das* cleaning agent; ~**munter** (*ugs.*) ❶ *Adj.* chirpy (*coll.*); perky; ~**munter sein** be as bright as a button; ❷ *adv.* chirpily (*coll.*); perkily; ~**tuch** *das; Pl.* ~**tücher** cloth; (*Lappen*) [cleaning] rag; ~**wolle** *die* cotton waste

**puzzeln** /ˈpazl̩n/ *itr. V.* do jigsaw puzzles/a jigsaw [puzzle]

**Puzzle** /ˈpazl̩/ *das;* ~**s**, ~**s**, **Puzzle·spiel** *das* jigsaw [puzzle]

**PVC** *Abk.* **Polyvinylchlorid** PVC

**Pygmäe** /pʏˈgmɛːə/ *der;* ~**n**, ~**n** pygmy

**pygmäenhaft** *Adj.* pygmy-like

**Pyjama** /pʏˈdʒaːma/ *der* (*österr., schweiz. auch: das*); ~**s**, ~**s** pyjamas *pl.*

**Pyjama·hose** *die* pyjama trousers *pl.*

**Pykniker** /ˈpʏknikɐ/ *der;* ~**s**, ~, **Pyknikerin** *die;* ~, ~**nen** (*Med., Anthrop.*) stocky person; pyknic *as tech. term*

**pyknisch** *Adj.* (*Med., Anthrop.*) stocky; pyknic *as tech. term*

**Pylon** /pʏˈloːn/ *der;* ~**en**, ~**en**, **Pylone** *die;* ~, ~**n** Ⓐ (*Tempeleingang*) pylon; Ⓑ (*bei Brücken*) [suspension-bridge] tower; Ⓒ (*Straßenmarkierung*) traffic cone

**Pyramide** /pʏraˈmiːdə/ *die;* ~, ~**n** pyramid

**pyramiden·förmig** *Adj.* pyramidal; pyramid-shaped

**Pyrenäen** /pyreˈnɛːən/ *Pl.* Pyrenees

**Pyrenäen·halb·insel** *die* Iberian Peninsula

**pyro-, Pyro-** /pʏro-/: ~**mane** /-ˈmaːnə/ *der;* ~~**n**, ~~**n** (*Med., Psych.*) pyromaniac; ~**manie** *die* (*Med., Psych.*) pyromania; ~**manin** *die;* ~~, ~~**nen** ⇒ ~**mane**; ~**techniker** *der*, ~**technikerin** *die* fireworks expert; pyrotechnist

**Pyrrhus·sieg** /ˈpʏrʊs-/ *der* (*geh.*) Pyrrhic victory

**pythagoräisch** /pʏtagoˈrɛːɪʃ/ ⇒ **pythagoreisch**

**Pythagoras** /pʏˈtaːgoras/ (*der*) Pythagoras

**pythagoreisch** /pʏtagoˈreːɪʃ/ *Adj.* Pythagorean; **der** ~**e Lehrsatz** (*Geom.*) Pythagoras' theorem

**Python** /ˈpyːtɔn/ *der;* ~**s**, ~**s** *od.* ~**en** /pyˈtoːnən/, **Python·schlange** *die* python

P

# Qq

**q, Q** /ku:/ *das;* ~, ~: q, Q; **das Gütezeichen Q** (*DDR*) the grade A marking; ⇒ *auch* **a,** A

**qm** *Abk.* ▶ 301 **Quadratmeter** sq. m.

**qua** /kva/ (*geh.*) ❶ *Präp., meist mit ungebeugtem Substantiv* Ⓐ *auch mit Gen.* (*mittels*) by means of; Ⓑ (*gemäß*) in accordance with; (*kraft*) by virtue of; ~ **Herkunft** by virtue of its/their *etc.* origins. ❷ *Konj.* (*als*) ~ **Beamter** [in his function] as an official

**quabbelig** /ˈkvabəlɪç/, **quabblig** *Adj.* (*nordd.*) jelly-like ‹frogspawn›; (*weich und dick*) flabby, podgy ‹face›

**quackeln** /ˈkvakl̩n/ (*bes. nordd. ugs.*) ❶ *itr. V.* chatter; (*dauernd*) natter on (*Brit. coll.*). ❷ *tr. V.* **dummes Zeug** ~: talk drivel

**Quacksalber** /ˈkvakzalbɐ/ *der;* ~s, ~ (*abwertend*) quack [doctor]

**Quacksalberei** *die;* ~, ~en (*abwertend*) quackery

**Quacksalberin** *die;* ~, ~nen ⇒ **Quacksalber**

**Quaddel** /ˈkvadl̩/ *die;* ~, ~n [irritating] spot

**Quader** /ˈkva:dɐ/ *der;* ~s, ~ *od.* (*österr.:*) ~n Ⓐ (*Steinblock*) ashlar block; [rectangular] block of stone; Ⓑ (*Geom.*) rectangular parallelepiped; cuboid

**Quader·stein** *der* ⇒ **Quader** A

**Quadrant** /kvaˈdrant/ *der;* ~en, ~en (*Geom., Geogr., Astron., Math.*) quadrant

**quadrat-, Quadrat-** ▶ 301 square ‹kilometre etc.›

**Quadrat**[1] /kvaˈdra:t/ *das;* ~[e]s, ~e Ⓐ (*Geom.*) square; **6 cm im** ~: 6 cm. square; Ⓑ (*Math.: zweite Potenz*) square; **eine Zahl ins** ~ **erheben** square a number; **drei im** *od.* **zum** ~: three squared; **Pech/Glück im** ~ (*ugs.*) terrible [bad] luck/terrific luck (*coll.*); Ⓒ (*bebaute Fläche*) block [of houses]; **ums** ~ **gehen** walk round the block

**Quadrat**[2] *das;* ~[e]s, ~en (*Druckw.*) quadrat

**quadratisch** *Adj.* Ⓐ square; Ⓑ (*Math.*) quadratic

**Quadrat-:** ~**latschen** *der* (*salopp*) Ⓐ (*Schuh*) dirty great shoe (*sl.*); Ⓑ (*Pl.: Füße*) dirty great feet (*sl.*); ~**meter** *der od. das* ▶ 301 square metre; **unsere Wohnung hat 92** ~**meter** our flat (*Brit.*) *or* (*Amer.*) apartment has 92 square metres of floor space; ~**schädel** *der* Ⓐ (*ugs.: Kopf*) dirty great nut (*sl.*); Ⓑ (*ugs. abwertend: sturer Mensch*) mule; pigheaded type

**Quadratur** /kvadraˈtu:ɐ̯/ *die;* ~, ~en (*Math., Astron.*) quadrature; **die** ~ **des Zirkels** (*geh.*) the achievement of the impossible

**Quadrat-:** ~**wurzel** *die* (*Math.*) square root (**aus** of); ~**zahl** *die* square number

**quadrieren** (*Math.*) ❶ *tr. V.* square. ❷ *itr. V.* square numbers

**Quadriga** /kvaˈdri:ga/ *die;* ~, **Quadrigen** quadriga

**Quadrille** /kaˈdrɪljə/ *die;* ~, ~n (*Tanz, Musik*) quadrille

**Quadrillion** /kvadrɪˈli̯o:n/ *die;* ~, ~en quadrillion (*Brit.*); septillion (*esp. Amer.*)

**quadro-, Quadro-** /ˈkva:dro-/ quadraphonic ‹system, effect, sound, etc.›

**quadro·phon** (*Akustik*) ❶ quadraphonic. ❷ *adv.* in quad[raphony]

**Quadro·phonie** *die;* ~ (*Akustik*) quadraphony

**Quai** /ke/ *der od. das;* ~s, ~s (*schweiz.*) Ⓐ ⇒ **Kai**; Ⓑ (*Uferstraße*) embankment [road]

**quak** *Interj.* ~! (*von Enten*) quack!; (*von Fröschen*) croak!

**quaken** /ˈkva:kn̩/ *itr. V.* ‹duck› quack; ‹frog› croak; (*fig. abwertend*) ‹person, radio› squawk

**quäken** /ˈkvɛ:kn̩/ ❶ *tr. V.* squawk; bawl out ‹song›. ❷ *itr. V.* Ⓐ (*unangenehm tönen*) ‹voice› squawk; (*kreischen*) screech; ‹radio› blare; Ⓑ (*klagen*) ‹child› whine, whinge

**Quäker** /ˈkvɛ:kɐ/ *der;* ~s, ~, **Quäkerin** *die;* ~, ~nen Quaker

**Qual** /kva:l/ *die;* ~, ~en Ⓐ torment; agony *no indef. art.;* **[für jmdn.] eine** ~**/eine einzige** ~ **sein** be agony *or* torment/one long torment for sb.; **er macht uns** (*Dat.*) **das Leben/den Aufenthalt zur** ~: he's making our lives *pl.*/our stay a misery; **er hat die** ~ **der Wahl** (*scherzh.*) he is spoilt for choice; Ⓑ (*Schmerzen*) agony; ~**en** pain *sing.;* agony *sing.;* (*seelisch*) torment *sing.;* **jmds.** ~**en lindern** ease sb.'s pain *or* suffering; **jmdn. von seinen** ~**en erlösen** put sb. out of his/her agony; **unter [schlimmsten]** ~**en sterben** die in [the most terrible] agony; **jmdm. [große]** ~**en bereiten** cause sb. [great] pain; torment sb.; **er konnte sein letztes Werk nur unter** ~**en vollenden** he could only complete his last work in great pain *or* suffering

**quälen** /ˈkvɛ:lən/ ❶ *tr. V.* Ⓐ (*körperlich, seelisch*) torment ‹person, animal›; maltreat, be cruel to ‹animal›; (*foltern*) torture; ~**de Schmerzen** agonizing *or* excruciating pain *sing.;* **ihn quälte der Gedanke[, dass ...]** he was tormented by the thought [that ...]; ~**de Ungewissheit** agonizing uncertainty; Ⓑ (*plagen*) ‹cough etc.› plague; (*belästigen*) pester; ⇒ *auch* **gequält**. ❷ *refl. V.* Ⓐ (*leiden*) suffer; **sich sehr** ~: suffer greatly; suffer agonies; Ⓑ (*sich abmühen*) struggle; **sich durch ein Buch** ~: struggle through a book

**Quälerei** *die;* ~, ~en Ⓐ torment; (*Folter*) torture; (*Grausamkeit*) cruelty; **Tierversuche sind [eine] reine** ~: animal experiments are simply cruel; Ⓑ (*das Belästigen*) pestering; Ⓒ (*ugs.: große Anstrengung*) **das Treppensteigen ist eine** ~ **für ihn** climbing stairs is a terrible struggle for him

**quälerisch** *Adj.* (*geh.*) agonizing

**Quäl·geist** *der; Pl.* ~er (*fam.*) pest

**Qualifikation** /kvalifikaˈtsi̯o:n/ *die;* ~, ~en Ⓐ ⇒ **Qualifizierung** A; Ⓑ (*Befähigung*) capability; Ⓒ (*Sport*) qualification; (*Wettkampf zur* ~) qualifier; qualifying round; **sie schafften die** ~ **für die Endrunde** they managed to qualify for the final round

**Qualifikations-:** ~**runde** *die* (*Sport*) qualifying round; ~**spiel** *das* (*Sport*) qualifier, qualifying match (**zu, für** for)

**qualifizieren** /kvalifiˈtsi:rən/ ❶ *refl. V.* Ⓐ (*sich bilden*) gain qualifications; **sich für einen Posten/zum Facharbeiter** ~: gain the qualifications needed for a post/to be a skilled worker; Ⓑ (*Sport*) qualify. ❷ *tr. V.* Ⓐ (*ausbilden*) **jmdn. [zu etw.]** ~: train sb. [to be sth.]; (*weiterbilden*) give sb. further training [for sth.]; Ⓑ (*befähigen*) qualify; **seine Berufserfahrung qualifiziert ihn zum** *od.* **als Abteilungsleiter** his experience gives him the necessary qualifications for the post of departmental manager

**qualifiziert** ❶ *2. Part. v.* **qualifizieren**. ❷ *Adj.* Ⓐ ‹work, post› requiring particular qualifications; Ⓑ (*sachkundig*) competent; skilled ‹work›; **hoch** ~: highly qualified; Ⓒ ~**e Mitbestimmung** (*Wirtsch.*) full participation by employees in decision-making; ~**e Straftat** (*Rechtsw.*) aggravated offence; ⇒ *auch* **Mehrheit**. ❸ *adv.* (*sachkundig*) competently

**Qualifizierung** *die;* ~, ~en Ⓐ (*Ausbildung*) training; (*erworbene Qualifikation*) qualifications *pl.;* Ⓑ (*Weiterbildung*) further training

**Qualität** /kvaliˈtɛ:t/ *die;* ~, ~en Ⓐ quality; **Waren guter/schlechter/erster** ~: goods of high/low/prime quality; ~ **kaufen** buy quality goods; Ⓑ (*Textilw.*) material *no pl.;* **schwere** ~**en** heavy fabrics; Ⓒ (*Schach*) **die** ~ **gewinnen** win the exchange

**qualitativ** /kvalitaˈti:f/ ❶ *Adj.* qualitative; ‹difference, change› in quality. ❷ *adv.* with regard to quality; ~ **gut** good-quality; of good quality *postpos.;* ~ **besser werden** improve in quality

**qualitäts-, Qualitäts-:** ~**arbeit** *die* high-quality workmanship; ~**bewusst**, *~**bewußt** *Adj.* quality-conscious; ~**erzeugnis** *das* quality product; ~**kontrolle** *die* quality control; ~**unterschied** *der* difference in quality; ~**ware** *die* quality goods *pl.;* ~**waren** quality goods; ~**wein** *der* [high-]quality wine (*from a recognized growing area, and made with a permitted type of grape*)

**Qualle** /ˈkvalə/ *die;* ~, ~n jellyfish; ~n jellyfish

**quallig** *Adj.* ⇒ **quabbelig**

**Qualm** /kvalm/ *der;* ~[e]s Ⓐ [thick] smoke; (~*wolken*) clouds of [thick] smoke; Ⓑ (*bes. nordd.: Dampf*) steam

**qualmen** ❶ *itr. V.* Ⓐ give off clouds of [thick] smoke; **aus dem Kamin qualmt es** clouds of [thick] smoke are coming from the fireplace; ~**de Schornsteine** chimneys belching [thick] smoke; Ⓑ (*ugs.: rauchen*) puff away. ❷ *tr. V.* (*ugs.: rauchen*) puff away at ‹cigarette etc.›

**qualmig** *Adj.* (*ugs.*) thick with smoke *postpos.;* smoke-filled

**qual·voll** ❶ *Adj.* agonizing; **einen** ~**en Tod sterben** die in great pain. ❷ *adv.* agonizingly; ~ **sterben** die in great pain

**Quant** /kvant/ *das;* ~s, ~en (*Physik*) quantum

**Quäntchen** /ˈkvɛntçən/ *das;* ~s, ~ (*veralt.*) scrap; **ein** ~ **Salz** a pinch of salt; **kein** ~: not an iota; **ein** ~ **Glück** (*fig. geh.*) a little bit of luck; **dieses** ~ **Hoffnung** (*fig. geh.*) this glimmer of hope

**quanteln** /ˈkvantl̩n/ *tr. V.* (*Physik*) quantize

**Quanten**[1] ⇒ **Quant, Quantum**

**Quanten**[2] *Pl.* (*salopp*) dirty great feet (*sl.*)

**Quanten-:** ~**mechanik** *die* (*Physik*) quantum mechanics *sing., no art.;* ~**sprung** *der* (*Physik, fig.*) quantum leap; ~**theorie** *die* (*Physik*) quantum theory *no art.*

**quantifizierbar** *Adj.* quantifiable

**quantifizieren** /kvantifiˈtsi:rən/ quantify

**Quantität** /kvantiˈtɛ:t/ *die;* ~, ~en quantity; (*Zahl*) number

**quantitativ** /kvantitaˈti:f/ ❶ *Adj.* quantitative. ❷ *adv.* quantitatively

**Quantum** /ˈkvantʊm/ *das;* ~s, **Quanten** quota (**an** + *Dat.* of); (*Dosis*) dose; **mein tägliches** ~ **Kaffee** my daily quota *or* (*joc.*) dose of coffee; **ein gehöriges** ~ **Glück** (*fig.*) a good helping *or* big slice of luck

**Quappe** /ˈkvapə/ *die;* ~, ~n Ⓐ (*Fisch*) burbot; Ⓑ (*Kaul*~) tadpole

**Quarantäne** /karanˈtɛ:nə/ *die;* ~, ~n quarantine; **über jmdn./etw.** ~ **verhängen** put sb./sth. under quarantine; **unter** ~ **stellen** put into quarantine; **unter** ~ **stehen** be in quarantine

**Quarantäne·station** *die* isolation ward

**Quargel** /ˈkvargl̩/ *der od. das;* **~s,** ~ *(österr.)* *soft, smelly sour-milk cheese*

**Quark[1]** /kvark/ *der;* **~s** Ⓐ quark; [sour skim milk] curd cheese; Ⓑ *(ugs. abwertend: Quatsch)* twaddle; piffle *(sl.)*; **so ein ~!** what a load of rubbish!; **sich über jeden ~ aufregen** make a fuss about every tiny *or (sl.)* piffling detail; **seine Nase in jeden ~ stecken** poke one's nose in everywhere

**Quark[2]** /kwɑːk/ *das;* **~s, ~s** *(Physik)* quark

**Quark·speise** *die* quark dish

**Quart[1]** /kvart/ *die;* ~, **~en** Ⓐ *(Musik)* ⇒ **Quarte**; Ⓑ *(Fechten)* quart

**Quart[2]** *das;* **~s, ~e** Ⓐ *(hist.: Hohlmaß)* *(in Preußen)* quart; *(in Bayern)* ≈ half-pint; Ⓑ *(Buchw.)* quarto

**Quarta** /ˈkvarta/ *die;* ~, **Quarten** *(Schulw.)* Ⓐ *(veralt.)* third year *(of a Gymnasium)*; Ⓑ *(österr.)* fourth year *(of a Gymnasium)*

**Quartal** /kvarˈtaːl/ *das;* **~s, ~e** quarter [of the year]; **in diesem/im nächsten ~:** this quarter/next quarter

**quartal[s]-, Quartal[s]-: ~ende** *das* end of a/the quarter; **~säufer** *der,* **~säuferin** *die* *(ugs.)* periodic boozer *(coll.)*; **~weise** *Adv.* quarterly

**Quartaner** /kvarˈtaːnɐ/ *der;* **~s,** ~, **Quartanerin** *die;* ~, **~nen** *(Schulw.)* Ⓐ *(veralt.)* pupil in the third year *(of a Gymnasium)*; Ⓑ *(österr.)* pupil in the fourth year *(of a Gymnasium)*

**Quartär** /kvarˈtɛːɐ̯/ *das;* **~s** *(Geol.)* Quaternary [Period]

**Quart·band** *der* quarto volume

**Quarte** *die;* ~, **~n** *(Musik)* fourth

**Quarten** ⇒ **Quart[1]**, **Quarta**, **Quarte**

**Quartett** /kvarˈtɛt/ *das;* **~[e]s, ~e** Ⓐ quartet; **ein kriminelles ~:** a quartet of criminals; [a gang of] four criminals; Ⓑ *(Spiel)* *card game in which one tries to get sets of four;* ≈ Happy Families; Ⓒ *(Spielkarten)* pack *(Brit.)* *or (Amer.)* deck of cards for ~; *(Satz von vier Spielkarten)* set of four *Quartett* cards; Ⓓ *(Verslehre)* quatrain

**Quart·format** *das* *(Buchw.)* quarto

**Quartier** /kvarˈtiːɐ̯/ *das;* **~s, ~e** Ⓐ *(Unterkunft)* accommodation *no indef. art.;* accommodations *pl.* *(Amer.)*; place to stay; *(Mil.)* quarters *pl.;* **die ~e der Truppen/der Athleten** the troops'/athletes' quarters; **ein billiges ~:** somewhere cheap to stay; **bei jmdm. ~ beziehen** put up *or* move in with sb.; **in einer Schule in ~ liegen** *(Milit. veralt.)* be quartered *or* billeted in a school; Ⓑ *(bes. schweiz., österr.: Stadtviertel)* quarter; district

**Quartier·macher** *der* *(Milit. veralt.)* billeting officer

**Quart·sext·akkord** *der* *(Musik)* six-four chord

**Quarz** /kvaːɐ̯ts/ *der;* **~es, ~e** Ⓐ *(Mineral)* quartz; Ⓑ *(~kristall)* quartz crystal

**quarz·gesteuert** *Adj.* quartz ‹clock, watch›; crystal-controlled ‹transmitter›

**Quarz·glas** *das* quartz glass

**Quarzit** /kvarˈtsiːt/ *der;* **~s, ~e** *(Geol., Mineral.)* quartzite

**Quarz-: ~kristall** *der* quartz crystal; **~lampe** *die* quartz lamp; **~steuerung** *die* *(Elektrot.)* [quartz-]crystal control; **~uhr** *die* quartz clock; *(Armbanduhr)* quartz watch

**Quasar** /kvaˈzaːɐ̯/ *der;* **~s, ~e** *(Astron.)* quasar

**quasi** /ˈkvaːzi/ *Adv.* **[so] ~:** more or less; *(so gut wie)* as good as; *(fast)* almost

**quasi-, Quasi-** quasi-‹military, religious, philosopher›; *(fast)* semi-‹automatic, official›

**Quasselei** *die;* ~, **~en** *(ugs.)* [constant] prattling *or* jabbering

**quasseln** /ˈkvasl̩n/ *(ugs.)* ❶ *itr. V.* chatter; rabbit on *(Brit. sl.)* **(von** about). ❷ *tr. V.* spout, babble ‹nonsense›; **hör nicht auf sein Quasseln:** don't listen to his blather *or* waffle

**Quassel·strippe** *die* Ⓐ *(ugs. scherzh.: Telefon)* blower *(Brit. coll.)*; Ⓑ *(ugs. abwertend: Schwätzer)* chatterbox

**Quaste** *die;* ~, **~n** Ⓐ *(Troddel; auch fig.)* tassel; Ⓑ *(nordd.)* ⇒ **Quast** A

**Quästur** /kvɛsˈtuːɐ̯/ *die;* ~, **~en** *(bes. Hochschulw.)* bursar's office

**Quatsch** /kvatʃ/ *der;* **~[e]s** Ⓐ *(ugs. abwertend: dumme Äußerung)* rubbish; **~ mit Soße** *(salopp)* absolute rubbish; stuff and nonsense *(coll.)*; **so ein ~!** what rubbish!; Ⓑ *(ugs. abwertend: dumme Handlung)* nonsense; *(ugs.: Unfug)* messing about; **lass den ~:** stop that nonsense; stop messing about; **mach keinen ~:** don't do anything stupid; Ⓒ *(ugs.: Jux)* lark *(coll.)*; **die Kinder haben nur ~ gemacht** the children were just larking about *(coll.)* *or* fooling around; **das habe ich aus ~ gesagt** I said it for a laugh; Ⓓ *(ugs.: wertloser Gegenstand)* trashy thing; *(wertloses Zeug)* trash *no indef. art.*

**quatschen** ❶ *itr. V.* Ⓐ *(ugs.: dumm reden)* rabbit on *(Brit. coll.)*; blather; *(viel reden)* chatter; natter *(Brit. coll.)*; **im Unterricht ~:** chatter in class; Ⓑ *(ugs.: klatschen)* gossip; **es wird so viel gequatscht** there is so much gossip; Ⓒ *(ugs.: klatschen, berichten)* blab; open one's mouth; Ⓓ *(ugs.: sich unterhalten)* [have a] chat *or (coll.)* natter **(mit** with); *(ugs.: reden)* talk **(mit** to); **lass ihn erst mal ~:** let him say his bit *(coll.)*; Ⓔ *(landsch.: ein klatschendes Geräusch verursachen)* squelch.
❷ *tr. V.* Ⓐ *(ugs.: äußern)* spout ‹nonsense, rubbish›; **was hast du da wieder gequatscht?** what sort of rubbish have you been talking?; Ⓑ *(salopp)* **jmdn. dämlich ~:** talk sb.'s head off

**Quatsch·kopf** *der* *(salopp)* stupid chatterbox; *(Schwätzer, Schwafler)* windbag

**quatsch·nass, *quatsch·naß** *Adj.* *(ugs.)* sopping wet

**Queck·silber** /ˈkvɛk-/ *das* mercury; *(fig.)* quicksilver; **~ im Leib** *od.* **im Hintern haben** *(fig. ugs.)* have ants in one's pants *(coll.)*

**quecksilber-, Quecksilber-: ~haltig** *Adj.* containing mercury *postpos., not pred.;* **~haltig sein** contain mercury; **~säule** *die* [column of] mercury; **~vergiftung** *die* mercury poisoning

**queck·silbrig** *Adj.* Ⓐ silvery; Ⓑ *(fig.: unruhig)* fidgety

**Quell** /kvɛl/ *der;* **~[e]s, ~e** *(geh.)* spring; *(fig.: Ursprung)* source; fount *(poet.)*

**Quell·bewölkung** *die* *(Met.)* cumulus clouds *pl.*

**Quelle** /ˈkvɛlə/ *die;* ~, **~n** Ⓐ spring; *(eines Baches, eines Flusses)* source; Ⓑ *(fig.)* source; **die ~ der Weisheit** the fount of wisdom *(poet.)*; **eine Mitteilung aus zuverlässiger ~:** a piece of information from a reliable source; **an der ~ sitzen** *(ugs.)* *(für Informationen)* have access to inside information; *(für günstigen Erwerb)* be at the source of supply

**quellen[1]** *unr. itr. V.; mit sein* Ⓐ *(hervordringen)* ‹liquid› gush, stream; *(aus der Erde)* well up; ‹smoke› billow; ‹crowd› stream, pour; *(fig.)* ‹tears› well up; Ⓑ *(sich wölben)* bulge; **die Augen quollen ihm [fast] aus dem Kopf** his eyes nearly popped out [of his head]; Ⓒ *(sich ausdehnen)* swell [up]

**quellen[2]** *tr. V.* (~ *lassen*) soak ‹peas, beans›; steep ‹barley›

**Quellen-: ~an·gabe** *die* reference; **~forschung** *die* source research; **~nachweis** *der* ⇒ **~angabe**; **~sammlung** *die* collection of source materials; **~steuer** *die* *(Finanzw.)* tax deducted at source; **~studium** *das* study of [the] sources; **~verzeichnis** *das* list of references

**Quell-: ~fluss, *~fluß** *der* *(Geogr.)* headstream; **~gebiet** *das* *(Geogr.)* headwater region; **~wasser** *das; Pl.* **~~** *od.* **~wässer** spring water

**Quengelei** *die;* ~ *(ugs.)* nagging; pestering

**quengelig** *(ugs.)* ❶ *Adj.* whining; fretful; **~ werden** start whining *or (coll.)* grizzling. ❷ *adv.* in a whining voice; fretfully

**quengeln** /ˈkvɛŋl̩n/ *itr. (auch tr.) V.* *(ugs.)* Ⓐ *(weinen)* ‹baby› whimper, *(coll.)* grizzle; Ⓑ *(drängen)* nag; Ⓒ *(nörgeln)* carp

***Quentchen** ⇒ **Quäntchen**

**quer** /kveːɐ̯/ *Adv.* sideways; crosswise; *(schräg)* diagonally; at an angle; **~ zu etw.** at an angle to sth.; *(rechtwinklig)* at right angles to sth.; **der Wagen steht ~ auf der** *od.* **zur Fahrbahn** the car is standing sideways across the road; **das Blatt/den Stoff ~ legen** lay the sheet/material crosswise; **die Streifen verlaufen ~:** the stripes are diagonal/*(horizontal)* horizontal; **~ auf dem Bett liegen** lie across the bed; **~ durch/über** (+ *Akk.*) straight through/across; **~ über die Straße gehen** go straight across the road; *(schräg)* cross the road at an angle; **~ durch Amerika fahren** travel right across America; **~ durch die Parteien** *(fig.)* across all party boundaries; **sich ~ legen** *(fig. ugs.)* make difficulties; *(hartnäckig)* dig in one's heels; **~ schießen** *(fig. ugs.)* put a spanner in the works *(coll.)*

**quer-, Quer-: ~achse** *die* transverse axis; **~balken** *der* Ⓐ cross-beam; *(kleiner)* crosspiece; Ⓑ *(Musik)* stroke; **~beet** *Adv. ugs.* *(~feldein)* across country; *(ohne Ziel)* at random; *(fig.: überall)* everywhere and anywhere; **~denker** *der,* **~denkerin** *die* lateral thinker; **~durch** /-ˈ-/ *Adv.* straight through [the middle of] it/them

**Quere** *die: in* **jmdm./sich in die ~ kommen** *od.* **geraten** *(jmdm./sich begegnen)* bump into sb./one another *(coll.)*; **jmdm. in die ~ kommen** *od.* **geraten** *(fig.: jmdn. behindern)* get in sb.'s way *(coll.)*; **jmdm./einem Auto/einem Flugzeug in die ~ geraten** cross sb.'s path/the path of a car/an aircraft

**Querele** /kveˈreːlə/ *die;* ~, **~n** *(geh.)* squabble, wrangle **(um** about, over)

**queren** *tr. V.* *(geh.)* cross

**quer·feld·ein** *Adv.* across country

**Querfeldein-: ~lauf** *der* *(Wettbewerb)* cross-country [race]; *(Sportart)* cross-country running; **~rennen** *das* *(Wettbewerb)* cross-country [cycle] race; *(Sportart)* cyclo-cross *no def. art.*

**quer-, Quer-: ~flöte** *die* transverse flute; **~format** *das* landscape format; *(Bild/Buch)* picture/book in landscape format; ***~gestreift** ⇒ **gestreift** 2; **~kopf** *der* *(ugs.)* awkward cuss *(coll.)*; *(komischer Kauz)* oddball *(coll.)*; **~köpfig** *Adj.* awkward; perverse; **~lage** *die* *(Med.)* transverse presentation; **~latte** *die* horizontal slat; *(Fuß-, Handball)* crossbar; ***~|legen** ⇒ **quer**; **~pass,** ***~paß** *der* *(Fuß-, Handball)* crossfield pass; cross; lateral pass *(Amer.)*; **~richtung** *die* transverse direction; **in [der] ~richtung** transversely; crosswise; *(schräg)* diagonally; **~ruder** *das* *(Flugw.)* aileron; ***~|schießen** ⇒ **quer**; **~schiff** *das* *(Archit.)* transept; **~schläger** *der* *(Geschoss)* deflected shot; ricochet; **~schnitt** *der* Ⓐ cross section; **im ~schnitt** in cross section; Ⓑ *(Auswahl)* selection **(durch** from); **ein repräsentativer ~schnitt der Wähler** a representative cross section of voters; **~schnitt[s]·gelähmt** *Adj.* *(Med.)* paraplegic; **~schnitt[s]·gelähmte** *der/die* ▶ 474 *(Med.)* paraplegic; **~schnitt[s]·lähmung** *die* ▶ 474 *(Med.)* paraplegia *no indef. art.;* paraplegic condition; **~schuss,** ***~schuß** *der* *(ugs.)* spanner in the works *(coll.)*; **~schüsse gegen jmds. Politik** attempts at obstructing sb.'s policies; **~straße** *die* *(Abzweigung)* turning; *(Nebenstraße)* side street; **die zweite ~straße links** the second turning on the left; **~streifen** *der* diagonal stripe; *(horizontal)* horizontal stripe; **~summe** *die* *(Math.)* sum of the digits **(von, aus** of); **eine Zahl, deren ~summe 19 ergibt** a number the sum of whose digits is 19; **~treiber** *der,* **~treiberin** *die* *(ugs. abwertend)* troublemaker

*old spelling (see note on page ??)

q

**Querulant** /kveru'lant/ *der;* **~en, ~en, Querulantin** *die;* **~, ~nen** (*abwertend*) malcontent

**Quer-: ~verbindung** *die* connection, link (**zu** with); (*Verkehrsw.*) cross-country route; (*direkte Verbindung*) direct connection; **~verweis** *der* (*Buchw.*) cross reference

**Quetsche[1]** /'kvɛtʃə/ *die;* **~, ~n** (*bes. südd., westmd.*) ⇒ **Zwetsche**

**Quetsche[2]** *die;* **~, ~n** Ⓐ (*bes. nordd.*) potato crusher; Ⓑ (*ugs. abwertend: Ort, Betrieb*) miserable hole

**quetschen** ❶ *tr. V.* Ⓐ crush ‹person, limb, thorax›; **sich** (*Dat.*) **den Arm/die Hand ~:** get one's arm/hand caught; **sich** (*Dat.*) **den Finger/die Zehe ~:** pinch one's finger/toe; Ⓑ (*drücken, pressen*) squeeze, squash (**gegen, an** + *Akk.* against, **in** + *Akk.* into); (*bes. nordd.: auspressen*) squeeze ‹juice› (**aus** out of); **ein paar Zeilen an den Rand ~** (*ugs.*) squeeze a few lines into the margin; Ⓒ (*bes. nordd.: zerdrücken*) mash ‹potatoes›. ❷ *refl. V.* **sich in/durch etw.** (*Akk.*) **~:** squeeze [one's way] into/through sth.

**Quetsch-: ~kartoffeln** *Pl.* (*bes. berlin.*) mashed potatoes; **~kommode** *die* (*salopp scherzh.: Akkordeon*) squeeze box (*sl.*)

**Quetschung** *die;* **~, ~en** ▶ 474 bruise; contusion (*Med.*)

**Quetsch·wunde** *die* ▶ 474 (*Med.*) contusion

**Queue** /kø:/ *das od.* (*österr.*) *der;* **~s, ~s** cue

**quick** /kvɪk/ (*bes. nordd.*) ❶ *Adj.* lively. ❷ *adv.* in a lively way; animatedly

**quick·lebendig** ❶ *Adj.* [very] lively; active; (*bes. im Alter*) sprightly; spry; vivacious ‹personality›; frisky ‹small animal›; **~ sein** be full of [the joys of] life; be bright as a button; ‹child› be full of beans (*coll.*). ❷ *adv.* bright as a button; ‹talk› animatedly

**quiek[s]en** /'kvi:k(s)n̩/ ❶ *itr. V.* squeak; ‹piglet, fig.: person› squeal (**vor** with); **zum Quiek[s]en sein** be a hoot (*coll.*). ❷ *tr. V.* squawk

**Quietismus** /kvie'tɪsmʊs/ *der;* **~:** quietism *no def. art.*

**quietschen** /'kvi:tʃn̩/ *itr. V.* ‹thing› squeak; ‹brakes, tyres, crane› squeal, screech; (*ugs.*) ‹person› squeal, shriek (**vor** + *Dat.* with)

**quietsch-, Quietsch-: ~fidel** (*ugs.*) ❶ *Adj.* [really] chirpy (*coll.*) *or* (*esp. Amer.*) chipper; (*gesund und munter*) bright-eyed and bushy-tailed *pred.* (*coll.*); ❷ *adv.* [really] chirpy (*coll.*); **~lebendig** *Adj.* (*ugs.*) bright-eyed and bushy-tailed *pred.* (*coll.*); (*sehr aktiv*) full of beans *pred.* (*coll.*); (*hellwach*) wide awake; **~ton** *der; Pl.* **~töne** (*ugs.*) screeching noise; (*bes. durch Reibung*) squeal; **~vergnügt** (*ugs.*) ❶ *Adj.* [really] chirpy (*coll.*) *or* (*esp. Amer.*) chipper; ❷ *adv.* as happily *or* (*coll.*) chirpily as could be

**Quinta** /'kvɪnta/ *die;* **~, Quinten** (*Schulw.*) Ⓐ (*veralt.*) second year (*of a Gymnasium*); Ⓑ (*österr.*) fifth year (*of a Gymnasium*)

**Quintaner** /kvɪn'ta:nɐ/ *der;* **~s, ~, Quintanerin** *die;* **~, ~nen** (*Schulw.*) Ⓐ (*veralt.*) pupil in the second year (*of a Gymnasium*); Ⓑ (*österr.*) pupil in the fifth year (*of a Gymnasium*)

**Quinte** /'kvɪntə/ *die;* **~, ~n** (*Musik*) fifth

**Quinten·zirkel** *der* (*Musik*) circle of fifths

**Quint·essenz** *die* (*geh.*) substance; (*wesentlicher Punkt*) essential point; (*Schlussfolgerung*) conclusion; **als ~ bleibt festzuhalten, dass …** the essential point *or* conclusion to be drawn is that …

**Quintett** /kvɪn'tɛt/ *das;* **~[e]s, ~e** (*Musik*) quintet

**Quint·sext·akkord** *der* (*Musik*) six-five chord

**Quirl** /kvɪrl/ *der;* **~[e]s, ~e** Ⓐ (*Küchengerät*) *long-handled blender with a star-shaped head;* Ⓑ (*Mensch*) live wire

**quirlen** ❶ *tr. V.* ≈ whisk. ❷ *itr. V.* swirl [about]

**quirlig** *Adj.* lively; (*flink*) nimble

**quitt** /kvɪt/ *Adj.* (*ugs.*) quits; **mit jmdm. ~ sein** be quits with sb.; **damit sind wir ~:** that makes us quits

**Quitte** /'kvɪtə/ *die;* **~, ~n** quince

**quitte[n]·gelb** *Adj.* pale greenish-yellow

**quittieren** *tr. V.* Ⓐ *auch itr.* (*bescheinigen*) acknowledge, confirm ‹receipt, condition›; receipt, give a receipt for ‹sum, invoice›; **würden Sie bitte auf der Rückseite der Rechnung ~?** could you please receipt the bill on the back?; Ⓑ (*reagieren auf*) **etw. mit etw. ~:** react *or* respond to sth. with sth.; **ein Urteil mit Pfiffen ~:** greet a decision with catcalls; Ⓒ **den Dienst ~** (*veralt.*) resign one's position; ‹officer› resign one's commission

**Quittung** *die;* **~, ~en** Ⓐ receipt (**für, über** + *Akk.* for); Ⓑ (*fig.*) come-uppance (*coll.*); deserts *pl.*; **nun hast du die ~ für deine Faulheit** you've got what you deserve for being lazy

**Quittungs·block** *der; Pl.* **~s** *od.* **Quittungsblöcke** receipt pad

**Quivive** /ki'vi:f/ *das: in* **auf dem ~ sein** (*ugs.*) be on the alert *or* (*coll.*) watch it

**Quiz** /kvɪs/ *das;* **~, ~:** quiz

**Quiz·sendung** *die* quiz programme

**quoll** /kvɔl/ *1. u. 3. Pers. Sg. Prät. v.* **quellen**

**Quorum** /'kvo:rʊm/ *das;* **~s** (*bes. Politik*) quorum

**Quote** /'kvo:tə/ *die;* **~, ~n** (*Anteil*) proportion; (*Zahl*) number

**Quoten·regelung** *die: requirement that women should be adequately represented*

**Quotient** /kvo'tsiɛnt/ *der;* **~en, ~en** (*Math.*) quotient (**aus** of)

**quotieren** *tr., itr. V.* (*Börsenw.*) quote

q

# Rr

**r, R** /ɛr/ *das;* ~, ~: r, R; **er rollt das R** he rolls his r's; ⇒ *auch* **a, A**

**R** *Abk.* (*Physik*) **Reaumur** Réaum.

**Rabatt** /ra'bat/ *der;* ~**[e]s**, ~**e** discount; ~ **gewähren** give a discount

**Rabatte** /ra'batə/ *die;* ~, ~**n** border

**rabattieren** *tr. V.* (*Kaufmannsspr.*) **[jmdm.] einen Auftrag mit 30 Prozent** ~**:** give [sb.] a discount of 30 per cent on an order

**Rabatt·marke** *die* trading stamp

**Rabatz** /ra'bats/ *der;* ~**es** (*ugs.*) **A** (*Lärm*) racket; din; **B** (*Protest*) ~ **machen** kick up a fuss, (*coll.*) raise a stink (**bei** with)

**Rabauke** /ra'baukə/ *der;* ~**n**, ~**n** (*ugs.*) roughneck (*coll.*); (*Rowdy*) hooligan

**Rabbi** /'rabi/ *der;* ~**[s]**, ~**nen** /ra'bi:nən/ *od.* ~**s** ▶ 91 **A** (*Titel*) Rabbi; **B** (*Person*) rabbi

**Rabbinat** *das* rabbinate

**Rabbiner** /ra'bi:nɐ/ *der;* ~**s**, ~**:** rabbi

**rabbinisch** *Adj.* rabbinical

**Rabe** /'ra:bə/ *der;* ~**n**, ~**n** raven; **ein weißer** ~ (*fig.*) a great rarity; **schwarz wie ein** ~/**wie die** ~**n** (*ugs.*) as black as pitch; (*schmutzig*) as black as soot; **stehlen** *od.* (*salopp*) **klauen wie ein** ~/**wie die** ~**n** (*ugs.*) pinch everything one can lay one's hands on (*coll.*)

**raben-, Raben-:** ~**aas** *das* (*salopp abwertend*) beast; wretch; ~**eltern** *Pl.* (*abwertend*) uncaring [brutes of] parents; ~**krähe** *die* carrion crow; ~**mutter** *die; Pl.* ~**mütter** (*abwertend*) uncaring [brute of a] mother; ~**schwarz** *Adj.* **A** jet-black; raven-black ‹beard, hair›; coal-black ‹man, woman›; pitch-black ‹night›; **B** (*unheilvoll*) black ‹thoughts, soul, day›; disastrous ‹day, year›

**rabiat** /ra'bja:t/ **1** *Adj.* **A** (*gewalttätig*) violent; brutal; savage ‹kick›; ruthless ‹methods›; **B** (*wütend*) furious; blistering, savage ‹attack›; rabid ‹opponent›. **2** *adv.* **A** (*gewalttätig*) violently; brutally; **B** (*wütend*) furiously

**Rabulist** /rabu'lɪst/ *der;* ~**en**, ~**en** (*geh.*) sophist; quibbler

**Rabulistik** *die;* ~ (*geh.*) sophistry

**Rabulistin** *die;* ~, ~**nen** ⇒ **Rabulist**

**rabulistisch** (*geh.*) **1** *Adj.* sophistical. **2** *adv.* sophistically

**Rache** /'raxə/ *die;* ~**:** revenge; **[an jmdm.]** ~ **nehmen** take revenge [on sb.]; ~ **üben** take revenge; wreak vengeance (*literary*); **aus** ~**:** in revenge; ~ **ist süß** *od.* (*ugs. scherzh.*) **Blutwurst** revenge is sweet; **das ist die** ~ **des kleinen Mannes** (*ugs., oft scherzh.*) that's how ordinary mortals get their own back [on the powers that be] (*coll.*); **die** ~ **ist mein** (*bibl.*) vengeance is mine

**Rache-:** ~**akt** *der* (*geh.*) act of revenge, reprisal (*Gen.* by, on the part of); ~**durst** *der* (*geh.*) thirst for revenge *or* (*literary*) vengeance; ~**engel** *der* avenging angel; ~**gefühl** *das* desire *no pl.* for revenge

**rächen** /'rɛçn̩/ **1** *tr. V.* avenge ‹person, crime›; take revenge for ‹insult, crime›; **jmds. Mord an jmdm.** ~**:** take revenge on sb. for sb.'s murder. **2** *refl. V.* **A** take one's revenge; **sich an jmdm. [für etw.]** ~**:** take one's revenge on sb. [for sth.]; get even with sb. [for sth.]; **B** (*sich übel auswirken*) ‹mistake[s], bad behaviour› take its/their toll; **dein Leichtsinn wird sich noch** ~/**es wird sich noch** ~**, dass du das tust** you will have to pay [the penalty] for your recklessness/for doing that

**Rachen** /'raxn̩/ *der;* ~**s**, ~ **A** ▶ 471 (*Schlund*) pharynx (*Anat.*); **jmdm. den** ~ **pinseln** paint sb.'s throat; **B** (*Maul*) mouth; maw (*literary*); (*fig.*) jaws *pl.*; **jmdm. den** ~ **stopfen** (*salopp*) shut sb. up (*coll.*); **jmdm. etwas in den** ~ **werfen** *od.* **schmeißen** (*salopp*) give sb. sth. to keep him/her happy

**Rachen-:** ~**höhle** *die* ▶ 471 (*Anat.*) pharyngeal cavity; ~**mandel** *die* ▶ 471 (*Anat.*) [pharyngeal] tonsil

**Rache·plan** *der* plan for revenge

**Rächer** *der;* ~**s**, ~, **Rächerin** *die;* ~, ~**nen** (*geh.*) avenger

**Rache·schwur** *der* (*geh.*) oath of revenge

**Rach·gier** *die* lust for revenge

**rach·gierig** (*geh.*) ⇒ **rachsüchtig**

**Rachitis** /ra'xi:tɪs/ *die;* ~ ▶ 474 (*Med.*) rickets *sing.*

**rachitisch** *Adj.* with rickets *postpos., not pred.*; rachitic (*Med.*)

**Rach·sucht** *die* (*geh.*) lust for revenge

**rach·süchtig** (*geh.*) **1** *Adj.* vengeful; ~ **sein** ‹person› be out for revenge. **2** *adv.* vengefully; seeking to exact revenge

**Racker** *der;* ~**s**, ~ (*fam.*) rogue; rascal

**rackern** /'rakɐn/ *itr. V.* (*ugs.*) drudge; toil

**Racket** /'rɛkət/ *das;* ~**s**, ~**s** (*Tennis*) racket

**Raclette** /'raklɛt/ *die;* ~, ~**s** *od. das;* ~**s**, ~**s** (*Kochk.*) raclette

**Rad**[1] /ra:t/ *das;* ~**es**, **Räder** /'rɛ:dɐ/ **A** wheel; (*Zahn*~) gear; (*kleines Zahn*~) cog; (*einer Uhr*) [toothed] wheel; (*für Riemen*) pulley; **das** ~ **der Zeit/der Geschichte lässt sich nicht anhalten** (*fig.*) the march of time/of history cannot be halted; **fünftes** *od.* **das fünfte** ~ **am Wagen sein** (*fig. ugs.*) be superfluous; (*die Harmonie stören*) be in the way; **er kam unter die Räder des Lkws** he was run over by the lorry (*Brit.*) *or* truck; **unter die Räder kommen** (*fig. ugs.*) fall into bad ways; (*total verkommen*) go to the dogs (*coll.*); **nur** *od.* **bloß ein** ~ **im Getriebe sein** be just a small cog in the machine; **B** (*Fahr*~) bicycle; bike (*coll.*); **mit dem** ~ **fahren** go by bicycle *or* (*coll.*) bike; ~ **fahren** cycle; ride a bicycle *or* (*coll.*) bike; (*fig. ugs. abwertend: unterwürfig sein*) suck up to people (*coll.*); **er fährt gern** ~**:** he likes cycling; **C** (*Turnen*) cartwheel; **ein** ~ **schlagen** *od.* **ausführen** do *or* perform a cartwheel; ~ **schlagen** do a cartwheel; (*mehrmals*) do cartwheels; **D** (*hist.: Foltergerät*) wheel; **jmdn. aufs** ~ **flechten** break sb. on the wheel; **E** (*bei Vögeln: Schwanzfedern*) fan; **ein** ~ **schlagen** ‹peacock› fan out its tail

**Rad**[2] *das;* ~**[s]**, ~ (*Physik*) rad

**Rad·achse** *die* (*Technik*) axle

**Radar** /ra'da:ɐ̯/ *der od. das;* ~**s** (*Technik*) radar

**Radar-:** ~**an·lage** *die* radar installation; ~**astronomie** *die* radar astronomy *no art.*; ~**falle** *die* (*ugs.*) [radar] speed trap; ~**gerät** *das* radar [system]; ~**geräte** radar [equipment] *sing.*; ~**kontrolle** *die* (*Verkehrsw.*) [radar] speed check; ~**schirm** *der* radar screen

**Radau** /ra'dau/ *der;* ~**s** (*ugs.*) row (*coll.*); racket

**Radau·bruder** *der* (*ugs. abwertend*) rowdy

**Rad·aufhängung** *die* (*Kfz-W.*) suspension

**Rädchen** /'rɛ:tçən/ *das;* ~**s**, ~ **A** [little] wheel; (*Zahnrad*) [small] cog; ⇒ *auch* **Rad** A; **B** (*Fahrrad*) [little] bicycle *or* (*coll.*) bike; **C** (*für Schnittmuster*) tracing wheel; (*für Gebäckteig*) pastry wheel

**Rad·dampfer** *der* paddle steamer

**radebrechen** **1** *tr. V.* **Französisch/Deutsch** *usw.* ~**:** speak broken French/German *etc.* **2** *itr. V.* speak pidgin

**radeln** /'ra:dl̩n/ *itr.* (*auch tr.*) *V.*; *mit sein* (*ugs., bes. südd.*) cycle; **irgendwohin** ~**:** go somewhere by bike (*coll.*); bike it somewhere (*coll.*); **50 km** ~**:** cycle 50 km

**Rädels·führer** /'rɛ:dls-/ *der*, **Rädels·führerin** *die* (*abwertend*) ringleader

**-räderig** ⇒ **-rädrig**

**rädern** /'rɛ:dɐn/ *tr. V.* **jmdn.** ~ (*hist.*) break sb. on the wheel; ⇒ *auch* **gerädert**

**Räder·werk** *das* (*Mechanik*) mechanism; works *pl.*; (*Räder*) wheels *pl.*; (*Zahnräder*) gears *pl.*; cogs *pl.*; **das** ~ **der Justiz** (*fig.*) the wheels *pl. or* machinery of justice

**rad-, Rad-:** *~|**fahren** ⇒ **Rad** B; ~**fahrer** *der*, ~**fahrerin** *die* **A** cyclist; **B** (*ugs. abwertend: Schmeichler*) toady; crawler (*coll.*); ~**fahr·weg** *der* cycle path *or* -track

**Radi** /'ra:di/ *der;* ~**s**, ~ (*bayr., österr. ugs.*) [large white] radish

**radial** /ra'dja:l/ **1** *Adj.* radial. **2** *adv.* radially; ~ **verlaufend** radiating

**Radiator** /ra'dja:tɔr/ *der;* ~**s**, ~**en** /-'to:rən/ [central-heating] radiator

**Radicchio** /ra'dɪkjo/ *der;* ~**s** radicchio

**Radien** ⇒ **Radius**

**radieren** /ra'di:rən/ *tr.* (*auch itr.*) *V.* **A** (*tilgen*) erase; **B** (*Grafik*) etch

**Radierer** *der;* ~**s**, ~ **A** (*ugs.*) ⇒ **Radiergummi**; **B** (*Künstler*) etcher

**Radiererin** *die;* ~, ~**nen** ⇒ **Radierer** B

**Radier-:** ~**gummi** *der* rubber [eraser]; ~**kunst** *die* etching; ~**nadel** *die* (*Grafik*) [dry-point] etching needle

**Radierung** *die;* ~, ~**en** (*Grafik*) etching

**Radieschen** /ra'di:sçən/ *das;* ~**s**, ~**:** radish; **sich** (*Dat.*) **die** ~ **von unten betrachten** (*salopp*) be pushing up the daisies (*sl.*)

**radikal** /radi'ka:l/ **1** *Adj.* radical; drastic ‹measure, method, cure›; (*rücksichtslos*) ruthless ‹measure, method, hardness›; **ein** ~**er Bruch mit der Vergangenheit** a complete break with the past. **2** *adv.* radically; (*rücksichtslos*) ruthlessly; (*vollständig*) ‹abolish, eradicate› totally, completely; ~ **gegen jmdn. vorgehen** adopt drastic *or* ruthless methods against sb.; ~ **[links/rechts] denken/eingestellt sein** have radical [left-wing/right-wing] views

**Radikal** *das;* ~**s**, ~**e** **A** (*Chemie*) [free] radical; **B** (*Math., Sprachw.*) radical

**Radikale** *der/die; adj. Dekl.* radical

**Radikalen·erlass**, ***Radikalen·erlaß** *der: decree excluding members of extremist organizations from civil-service employment*

**radikalisieren** **1** *tr. V.* make [more] radical. **2** *refl. V.* become more radical (**durch** owing to, as a result of)

**Radikalisierung** *die;* ~, ~**en** radicalization; (*das Radikalwerden*) growing radicalism, trend to radicalism (*Gen.* among)

**Radikalismus** *der;* ~, **Radikalismen** radicalism; (*Haltung*) radical attitude; (*Unnachgiebigkeit*) rigid attitude

**Radikalität** /radikali'tɛ:t/ *die;* ~**:** radicalness; radical nature; (*Härte*) ruthlessness; (*Vollständigkeit*) completeness

**Radikal·kur** *die* (*auch fig.*) drastic remedy (**gegen** for)

**Radio** /'ra:djo/ *das* (*südd., schweiz. auch: der*); ~**s**, ~**s** radio; **sie haben nicht einmal** ~**:** they don't even have a radio; **im** ~**:** on the radio; ~ **hören** listen to the radio

*old spelling (see note on page 1707)

**radio-, Radio-:** **~aktiv** ❶ *Adj.* radioactive; ❷ *adv.* radioactively; **~aktiv verseucht** contaminated by radioactivity *postpos.;* **~aktivität** *die* radioactivity; **~apparat** /'----/ *der* radio set; **~astronomie** *die* radio astronomy *no art.;* **~biologie** *die* ⇒ **Strahlenbiologie;** **~gerät** /'----/ *das* radio set; **~isotop** *das* (*Physik*) radioisotope; **~loge** /-'lo:gə/ *der;* **~~n, ~~n** ▶ 159 radiologist; **~logie** *die;* **~~:** radiology *no art.;* **~login** *die;* **~~, ~~nen** ▶ 159 radiologist; **~musik** /'----/ *die* music on the radio; **~sender** /'----/ *der* radio station; **~therapie** *die* (*Med.*) radiotherapy; **~wecker** /'----/ *der* radio alarm clock; **~welle** /'----/ *die* (*Technik, Physik*) radio wave

**Radium** /'ra:di̯ʊm/ *das;* **~s** radium

**Radius** /'ra:di̯ʊs/ *der;* **~, Radien** /'ra:di̯ən/ (*Math.*) radius

**Rad-:** **~kappe** *die* hubcap; **~kranz** *der* (*Technik*) Ⓐ (*beim Fahrrad*) wheel rim; Ⓑ (*beim Zahnrad*) toothed rim; **~lager** *das* wheel bearing

**Radler** *der;* **~s, ~** Ⓐ cyclist; Ⓑ (*bes. südd.: Getränk*) shandy

**Radler·hose** *die* cycle shorts *pl.*

**Radlerin** *die;* **~, ~nen** cyclist

**Rad·nabe** *die* [wheel] hub

**Radon** /'ra:dɔn/ *das;* **~s** (*Chemie*) radon

**Rad-:** **~renn·bahn** *die* cycle racing track; (*Stadion*) velodrome; **~rennen** *das* cycle race; (*Sport*) cycle racing; **~rennfahrer** *der,* **~rennfahrerin** *die* racing cyclist

**-rädrig** /-rɛ:drɪç/ *Adj.* -wheeled; **drei/vier~:** three-/four-wheeled

**rad-, Rad-:** ***~|schlagen** ⇒ **Rad** c; **~sport** *der* cycling *no def. art.;* **~stand** *der* wheelbase; **~tour** *die* bicycle ride; (*länger*) cycling tour; **eine ~tour machen** go for a bicycle ride/on a cycling tour; **~wanderung** *die* cycling tour; **~wechsel** *der* wheel change; **~weg** *der* cycle path *or* -track

**RAF** *Abk.* **Rote-Armee-Fraktion** Red Army Faction

**raffen** /'rafn̩/ *tr. V.* Ⓐ (*an sich reißen*) snatch; grab; rake in (*coll.*) ‹money›; (*abwertend: in seinen Besitz bringen*) **etw. [an sich] ~:** seize sth.; (*eilig*) snatch *or* grab sth.; Ⓑ (*zusammenhalten*) gather ‹material, curtain›; Ⓒ (*gekürzt wiedergeben*) condense ‹text›; (*kürzen*) shorten ‹text, play, film›

**Raff·gier** *die* rapacity; acquisitive greed

**raff·gierig** ❶ *Adj.* greedy. ❷ *adv.* greedily

**Raffinement** /rafinə'mã:/ *das;* **~s, ~s** (*geh.*) Ⓐ (*Feinheit*) refinement; Ⓑ ⇒ **Raffinesse** A

**Raffinerie** /rafinə'ri:/ *die;* **~, ~n** refinery

**Raffinesse** /rafi'nɛsə/ *die;* **~, ~n** Ⓐ (*Schlauheit*) guile; ingenuity; Ⓑ (*Finesse*) refinement

**raffinieren** /rafi'ni:rən/ *tr. V.* (*bes. Chemie, Geol.*) refine

**raffiniert** ❶ *Adj.* Ⓐ ingenious ‹plan, design›; (*verfeinert*) refined, subtle ‹colour, scheme, effect›; sophisticated ‹dish, cut (of clothes)›; Ⓑ (*gerissen*) cunning, artful ‹person, trick›. ❷ *adv.* Ⓐ ingeniously; cleverly; (*verfeinert*) with great refinement/sophistication; **eine ~ geschnittene Bluse** a blouse with a sophisticated cut; Ⓑ (*gerissen*) cunningly; artfully

**Raffiniertheit** *die;* **~** Ⓐ (*Klugheit*) ingenuity; (*Verfeinerung*) refinement; sophistication; (*der Kleidung*) stylishness; (*von Speisen*) subtle flavour; Ⓑ (*Gerissenheit*) cunning; artfulness

**Raffke** /'rafkə/ *der;* **~s, ~s** (*ugs. abwertend*) money-grubber

**Rage** /'ra:ʒə/ *die;* **~** (*ugs.*) fury; rage; **in [blinder] ~:** in a [blind] fury; **in ~ sein** be livid (*Brit. coll.*) *or* furious; **jmdn. in ~ bringen** make sb. hopping mad (*coll.*) *or* absolutely furious; **in ~ kommen** *od.* **geraten** fly into a rage; **immer mehr in ~ kommen** become more and more furious

**ragen** /'ra:gn̩/ *itr. V.* Ⓐ (*vertikal*) rise [up]; ‹mountains› tower up; **aus dem Wasser ~:** stick *or* jut right out of the water; **in die Höhe** *od.* **in den Himmel ~:** tower *or* soar into the sky; **er ragte aus der Menge** he towered above the rest of the crowd; Ⓑ (*horizontal*) project, stick out (**in** + *Akk.* into; **über** + *Akk.* over)

**Raglan·ärmel** /'raglan-/ *der* raglan sleeve

**Ragout** /ra'gu:/ *das;* **~s, ~s** (*Kochk.*) ragout

**Ragtime** /'rægtaɪm/ *der;* **~** (*Musik*) Ⓐ (*Stil, Musik*) ragtime *no art.;* Ⓑ (*Musikstück*) rag

**Rah[e]** /'ra:(ə)/ *die;* **~, Rahen** (*Seemannsspr.*) yard

**Rahm** /ra:m/ *der;* **~[e]s** (*bes. südd., österr., schweiz.*) cream; ⇒ *auch* **abschöpfen**

**rahmen**[1] *tr. V.* frame

**rahmen**[2] *tr. V.* (*bes. südd., österr., schweiz.*) skim ‹milk›

**Rahmen** *der;* **~s, ~** Ⓐ frame; (*Kfz-W.: Fahrgestell*) chassis; Ⓑ (*fig.: Bereich, Literaturw.: ~erzählung*) framework; (*szenischer Hintergrund*) setting; (*Zusammenhang*) context; (*Grenzen*) bounds *pl.;* limits *pl.;* **in großem/bescheidenem ~ feiern** celebrate on a grand/modest scale; **aus dem ~ fallen** be out of place; stick out; ‹behaviour› be unsuited to the occasion; **im ~ einer Sache** (*Gen.*) (*in den Grenzen*) within the bounds of sth.; (*im Zusammenhang*) within the context of sth.; (*im Verlauf*) in the course of sth.; **im ~ des Möglichen** within the bounds of possibility; **im ~ der Wiener Festwochen** as part of the Vienna Festival; **im ~ bleiben** stay within reasonable bounds; ‹person› not overdo it, not go too far; ‹prices› not be too high; **den ~ sprengen** be out of proportion; **den ~ einer Sache** (*Gen.*) **sprengen** go beyond the scope of sth.

**Rahmen-:** **~abkommen** *das* basic agreement; **~antenne** *die* (*Funkw.*) frame aerial *or* (*Amer.*) antenna; **~bedingung** *die* prevailing condition *or* circumstance; (*Soziol.*) structural condition; **~erzählung** *die* (*Literaturw.*) framework story; **~gesetz** *das* (*Rechtsw.*) *law providing framework for more specific legislation;* **~gesetze** *Pl.* outline legislation *sing.;* **~handlung** *die* (*Literaturw.*) framework plot; subplot (*framing the main plot*); **~programm** *das* supporting programme; **~richtlinie** *die* overall guideline

**rahmig** *Adj.* (*bes. südd., österr., schweiz.*) creamy

**Rahm-:** **~käse** *der* cream cheese; **~soße** *die* (*bes. südd., österr., schweiz.*) cream sauce

**Rah·segel** *das* (*Seemannsspr.*) square sail

**Rain** /rain/ *der;* **~[e]s, ~e** Ⓐ (*geh.: Ackergrenze*) margin of a/the field; Ⓑ (*südd., schweiz.: Abhang*) slope

**räkeln** /'rɛ:kl̩n/ ⇒ **rekeln**

**Rakete** /ra'ke:tə/ *die;* **~, ~n** rocket; (*Milit.*) missile

**raketen-, Raketen-:** **~abschussbasis,** ***~abschußbasis** *die* missile [launching] base; **~antrieb** *der* rocket propulsion; **~basis** *die* ⇒ **~abschussbasis;** **~flugzeug** *das* rocket plane; **~getrieben** *Adj.* rocket-propelled; **~schlitten** *der* (*Technik*) rocket sled; **~startrampe** *die* rocket launching pad; **~stufe** *die* (*Technik*) rocket stage; **~träger** *der* missile-carrier; **~triebwerk** *das* (*Technik*) rocket engine; **~werfer** *der* (*Milit.*) rocket launcher

**Raki** /'ra:ki/ *der;* **~[s], ~s** raki

**Ralle** /'ralə/ *die;* **~, ~n** (*Zool.*) rail

**Rallye** /'rali/ *die;* **~, ~s** *od. schweiz. das;* **~s, ~s** (*Motorsport*) rally; **die ~ Monte Carlo** the Monte Carlo Rally; **eine ~ fahren** take part in a rally

**ramm-, Ramm-:** **~bär** *der* (*Bauw.*) [piledriver] ram; **~bock** *der* Ⓐ (*hist.*) battering ram; Ⓑ ⇒ **~bär;** Ⓒ ⇒ **Ramme;** **~dösig** *Adj.* (*salopp*) Ⓐ (*benommen*) dizzy; Ⓑ (*dumm*) dopey (*coll.*)

**Ramme** /'ramə/ *die;* **~, ~n** (*Bauw.*) (*Pfahl~*) piledriver; (*für Erde, Steine*) rammer

**rammeln** /'raml̩n/ ❶ *itr. V.* Ⓐ (*Jägerspr.*) mate; Ⓑ (*derb: koitieren*) have a screw (*coarse*). ❷ *tr. V.* Ⓐ (*Jägerspr.*) serve; mount; Ⓑ (*derb: koitieren mit*) screw (*coarse*)

**rammen** ❶ *tr. V.* ram; **etw. in etw.** (*Akk.*) **~:** ram *or* jam sth. into sth. ❷ *itr. V.* (*stoßen*) ram, crash (**gegen, auf** + *Akk.* into)

**Rammler** *der;* **~s, ~** (*Jägerspr.*) buck [rabbit]

**Rampe** /'rampə/ *die;* **~, ~n** Ⓐ (*waagrechte Fläche*) [loading] platform; Ⓑ (*schiefe Fläche*) ramp; (*Auffahrt*) [sloping] drive; (*Bergsteigen*) sloping slab of rock; Ⓒ ⇒ **Startrampe;** Ⓓ (*Theater*) apron; forestage; **an** *od.* **vor die ~ treten** come to the front of the stage; **[nicht] über die ~ kommen** (*Theaterjargon*) [not] come across

**Rampen·licht** *das; Pl.* **~er** (*Theater*) Ⓐ (*Licht*) [light *sing.* from the] footlights *pl.;* **im ~ [der Öffentlichkeit] stehen** be in the limelight; Ⓑ (*Lichtquelle*) footlight

**ramponieren** /rampo'ni:rən/ *tr. V.* (*ugs.*) batter; **ramponiert** battered, knocked-about ‹furniture, phone-box›; run-down, down-at-heel ‹dwelling, room›; shabby ‹suit›; dented ‹confidence›

**Ramsch**[1] /ramʃ/ *der;* **~[e]s, ~e** (*ugs. abwertend*) Ⓐ (*Ware*) trashy goods *pl.;* Ⓑ (*Kram*) junk

**Ramsch**[2] *der;* **~[e]s, ~e** (*Kartenspiel*) ramsch

**ramschen** *tr., auch itr. V.* (*ugs.*) grab; **[Sachen] beim Schlussverkauf ~:** get masses of things cheap in a sale/the sales

**Ramsch-:** **~laden** *der; Pl.* **~läden** (*ugs. abwertend*) shop selling trashy goods; **~ware** *die* (*ugs. abwertend*) trashy goods *pl.;* **~waren** trashy goods

**ran** /ran/ *Adv.* (*ugs.*) Ⓐ ⇒ **heran;** Ⓑ (*fang an*) off you go; get going; (*fangen wir an*) let's go; **los, ~ an die Arbeit!** come on, get down to work!; Ⓒ (*greif[t] an*) go at him/them!; (*beim Boxen*) let him/them have it!; ⇒ *auch* **rangehen; ranhalten; rankommen** *usw.*

**Ranch** /rɛntʃ/ *die;* **~, ~[e]s** ranch

**Rancher** /'rɛntʃɐ/ *der;* **~s, ~:** rancher

**Rand** /rant/ *der;* **~[e]s, Ränder** /'rɛndɐ/ Ⓐ edge; (*Einfassung*) border; (*Hut~*) brim; (*Brillen~, Gefäß~, Krater~*) rim; (*eines Abgrunds*) brink; (*auf einem Schriftstück*) margin; (*Weg~*) verge; (*Stadt~*) edge; outskirts *pl.;* **voll bis zum ~:** full to the brim; **etwas an den ~ schreiben** write sth. in the margin; (*fig.*) **etw. am ~e erwähnen** mention sth. in passing; **am ~e liegen** ‹problem etc.› be of marginal importance; **außer ~ und Band geraten/sein** (*ugs.*) go/be wild (**vor** with); (*rasen*) go/be berserk (**vor** with); **das versteht sich am ~e** it goes without saying; **am ~e der Pleite sein** be on the verge of bankruptcy; **jmdn. an den ~ des Wahnsinns/Ruins bringen** bring sb. to the verge *or* brink of insanity/ruin; **zu ~e** ⇒ **zurande;** ⇒ *auch* **Grab;** Ⓑ (*Schmutz~*) mark; (*rund*) ring; (*in der Wanne*) tidemark (*coll.*); **dunkle Ränder unter den/um die Augen haben** have dark lines under/dark rings round one's eyes; Ⓒ (*salopp: Mund*) gob (*sl.*); trap (*sl.*)

**Randale** /ran'da:lə/ *die* (*salopp*) riot; **~ machen/beginnen** riot/start to riot

**randalieren** *itr. V.* riot; rampage; (*Radau machen*) create an uproar; **~de Halbstarke** young hooligans on the rampage

**Randalierer** *der;* **~s, ~,** **Randaliererin** *die;* **~, ~nen** hooligan

**Rand·bemerkung** *die* marginal note *or* comment; (*mündlich*) incidental remark; aside

**Rande** /'randə/ *die;* **~, ~n** (*schweiz.*) beetroot

**Rändel** /'rɛndl̩/ *das;* **~s, ~** (*Mech.*) knurl

**rändeln** *tr. V.* (*Mech.*) knurl; mill ‹coins›

**Ränder** ⇒ **Rand**

**rand-, Rand-:** **~erscheinung** *die* peripheral phenomenon; **~figur** *die* minor figure; (*Nebenrolle*) minor part; **~gebiet** *das* outlying district; (*Grenzgebiet*) frontier area *or* district; **die ~gebiete einer Stadt** the outskirts of a town; **ein ~gebiet der Medizin** a fringe area of medicine; **~gruppe** *die* (*Soziol.*) fringe *or* marginal group; **~los** *Adj.* rimless ‹spectacles›; brimless ‹hat›; ‹paper› with no margin; **~notiz** *die* marginal note; **~problem** *das* secondary problem; **~ständig** *Adj.* (*Soziol.*) marginal; **~stein** *der* kerb;

r

**~streifen** *der* verge; (*auf Autobahnen*) hard shoulder

**rand·voll** ❶ *Adj.* ‹glass etc.› full to the brim (**mit** with); brim-full ‹glass, cup, bowl› (**mit** of); **~ mit Notizen** crammed full of notes. ❷ *adv.* **~ gefüllt** jam-packed (*coll.*); chock-full; (*mit Flüssigkeit*) full to the brim

**Rand·zone** *die* outlying area; (*einer Stadt*) outskirts *pl.*; (*fig.*) fringe area

**rang** /raŋ/ *1. u. 3. Pers. Sg. Prät. v.* **ringen**

**Rang** *der;* **~[e]s, Ränge** /ˈrɛŋə/ **A** (*Stellung, Stufe*) rank; (*in der Gesellschaft*) status; (*in Bezug auf Bedeutung, Qualität*) standing; **im ~ eines Generals stehen** hold the rank of general; **jmdm. den ~ streitig machen** try to step [up] into sb.'s shoes; **jmdm./einer Sache den ~ ablaufen** leave sb./sth. far behind; **alles, was ~ und Namen hat** everybody who is anybody; **ein Physiker von ~:** an eminent physicist; **einen außerordentlichen künstlerischen ~ haben** be of exceptional artistic importance; **ersten ~es** of the greatest significance; (*qualitätsmäßig*) of the first order; **B** (*im Theater*) circle; **erster ~:** dress circle; **zweiter ~:** upper circle; **dritter ~:** gallery; **die Zuschauer auf den Rängen** the audience in the circle [and gallery] seats; **vor überfüllten/fast leeren Rängen spielen** play to a packed/a nearly empty house; **C** (*Sport*) ⇒ **Platz F**; **D** (*Gewinnklasse in Lotterien*) prize category

**Rang-: ~ab·zeichen** *das* insignia [of rank]; **~älteste** *der/die; adj. Dekl.* senior officer (*holding a particular rank*)

**Range** /ˈraŋə/ *die;* **~, ~n** (*bes. md.*) [young] tearaway; **freche** *od.* **kesse ~n** cheeky brats

**ran|gehen** *unr. itr. V.* (*ugs.*) **A** ⇒ **herangehen**; **B** (*erotisch*) **bei den Mädchen ~:** be a fast worker with the girls (*coll.*)

**Rangelei** *die;* **~, ~en** (*ugs.*) ⇒ **Gerangel**

**rangeln** /ˈraŋl̩n/ *itr. V.* (*ugs.*) wrestle; struggle; (*kämpfen*) ‹children› scrap; **um etw. ~:** scramble *or* tussle for sth.; (*fig.: argumentieren*) wrangle over sth.

**Rang-: ~folge** *die* order of precedence; (*finanziell*) order of merit; **~höchste** *der/die; adj. Dekl.* most senior person; (*Tier*) dominant animal

**Rangier·bahn·hof** *der* marshalling yard

**rangieren** /raŋˈʒiːrən/ ❶ *tr. V.* shunt ‹trucks, coaches›; switch ‹cars› (*Amer.*). ❷ *itr. V.* be placed; **an letzter Stelle/auf Platz zwei ~:** be placed last/second; **hinter/vor jmdm. ~** (*bei der Arbeit usw.*) be junior/senior to sb.

**Rangierer** *der;* **~s, ~:** shunter (*Brit.*); switchman (*Amer.*)

**Rangiererin** *die;* **~, ~nen** shunter (*Brit.*)

**Rangier-: ~lok** *die* (*ugs.*), **~lokomotive** *die* shunting *or* (*Amer.*) switch engine

**rang-, Rang-: ~liste** *die* **A** (*Sport*) ranking list; **Nummer eins der internationalen ~liste** number one in the world rankings; **B** (*von Offizieren, Beamten*) army/navy/civilservice list; **~mäßig** ❶ *Adj.* according to rank *postpos.*; ‹equality etc.› with regard to rank; **~mäßige Unterschiede** differences of rank; ❷ *adv.* according to *or* with regard to rank; **~ordnung** *die* order of precedence; (*Verhaltensf.*) pecking order; **der ~ordnung nach unter/über jmdm. stehen** be below/above sb. in the pecking order *or* hierarchy; **~unterschied** *der* difference in [social] status; (*Milit.*) difference in rank

**ran|halten** *unr. refl. V.* (*ugs.*) get a move on (*coll.*); (*bei der Arbeit*) get stuck in (*coll.*)

**rank** *Adj.* (*geh.*) lissom; **~ und schlank** lithe and lissom

**Ranke** /ˈraŋkə/ *die;* **~, ~n** (*Bot.*) tendril

**Ränke** /ˈrɛŋkə/ *Pl.* (*geh. veralt.*) intrigues; **~ schmieden** (*geh.*) scheme; hatch plots

**ranken** ❶ *refl. V.* climb, grow (**an** + *Dat.* up, **über** + *Akk.* over); **sich um etw. ~:** entwine itself around sth.; (*fig. geh.*) ‹legends, mysteries› be woven around sth. ❷ *itr. V.* **A** *mit sein* ⇒ **ranken 1**; **B** (*Ranken treiben*) put out tendrils

**Ranken-: ~gewächs** *das* creeper; **~werk** *das* mass of entwined tendrils

**ran-: ~|klotzen** *itr. V.* (*salopp*) get stuck in (*coll.*); pull one's finger out (*coll.*); (*auf Dauer*) keep hard at it; **~|kommen** *unr. itr. V.*; *mit sein* (*ugs.*) ⇒ **herankommen A, C**; **~|können** *unr. itr. V.* (*ugs.*) **an etw.** (*Akk.*) **nicht ~können** be unable to get at sth.; **ich kann nicht ~können** I can't get at it/them

**Rankune** /raŋˈkyːnə/ *die;* **~** (*geh. veralt.*) [sense of] rancour; acrimony

**ran-: ~|lassen** *unr. tr. V.* **A** (*ugs.: herankommen lassen*) **jmdn. ~lassen** let sb. get up close; (*salopp: sexuell*) **sie lässt ihn nicht ~:** she won't let him do it (*coll.*); **sie lässt jeden ~:** she's anybody's; **jmdn. an etw.** (*Akk.*) **nicht ~lassen** not let sb. anywhere near sth.; **B** (*ugs.: tätig werden lassen*) **jmdn. an etw.** (*Akk.*) **~lassen** let sb. have a go at sth.; **lass mich mal ~!** let me have a go!; **~|machen** *refl. V.* (*ugs.*) ⇒ **heranmachen A, B**; **~|müssen** *unr. itr. V.* (*ugs.: arbeiten müssen*) have to get stuck in (*coll.*)

**rann** /ran/ *1. u. 3. Pers. Sg. Prät. v.* **rinnen**

**rannte** /ˈrantə/ *1. u. 3. Pers. Sg. Prät. v.* **rennen**

**ran-: ~|schmeißen** *unr. refl. V.* **sich an jmdn. ~schmeißen** (*ugs.*) throw oneself at sb.; **~|wollen** *unr. itr. V.* (*ugs.*) want to get down to work; **an etw.** (*Akk.*) **nicht ~wollen** not feel like getting on with sth.

**Ranzen** /ˈrantsn̩/ *der;* **~s, ~** **A** (*Schul~*) satchel; (*veralt.: Rucksack*) rucksack; **B** (*salopp: Bauch*) [fat] belly

**ranzig** *Adj.* rancid

**Rap** /ræp/ *der;* **~[s], ~s** rap

**rapid** /raˈpiːt/ (*südd., österr., schweiz.*), **rapide** ❶ *Adj.* rapid. ❷ *adv.* rapidly

**Rappe** /ˈrapə/ *der;* **~n, ~n** black horse

**Rappel** /ˈrapl̩/ *der;* **~s, ~** (*ugs.*) crazy turn (*coll.*); **du hast wohl einen ~?** are you crazy?

**rappelig** *Adj.* (*ugs.*) nervy; **das macht mich ganz ~:** it really irritates me

**rappeln** *itr. V.* **A** (*ugs.: klappern, rütteln*) rattle (**an** + *Dat.* at); ‹alarm, telephone› jangle; **es rappelt an der Tür** there's a rattling at the door; **bei ihm rappelts** (*salopp*) he's got one of his crazy turns (*coll.*); **B** *mit sein* (*ugs.: sich fortbewegen*) clatter [along]; **C** (*österr. ugs.: verrückt sein*) be a bit crackers (*Brit. coll.*)

**rappen** /ˈræpn̩/ *itr. V.* rap

**Rappen** *der;* **~s, ~:** [Swiss] centime

**Rappen·spalter** *der;* **~s, ~**, **Rappen·spalterin** *die;* **~, ~nen** (*schweiz. ugs.*) penny-pincher

**Rapper** /ˈræpɐ/ *der;* **~s, ~**, **Rapperin** *die;* **~, ~nen** rapper

**rapplig** *Adj.* ⇒ **rappelig**

**Rapport** /raˈpɔrt/ *der;* **~s, ~e** **A** (*veralt.*) report; **jmdm. ~ erstatten** report to sb.; **sich zum ~ melden** report; **jmdn. zum ~ bestellen** ask sb. to give a report; **B** (*Psych.*) rapport

**Raps** /raps/ *der;* **~es** (*Bot., Landwirtsch.*) rape

**Raps·öl** *das* rape oil

**Rapunzel** /raˈpʊntsl̩/ *die;* **~, ~n** **A** (*Märchengestalt*) Rapunzel; **B** ⇒ **Feldsalat**

**rar** /raːɐ̯/ *Adj.* (*knapp*) scarce; (*selten vorkommend; begehrt*) rare ‹case, opportunity, stamp, etc.›; **sich ~ machen** (*ugs.*) not be around much (*coll.*); (*selten erscheinen*) make only rare appearances; **sie machten sich ~, als wir ihre Hilfe brauchten** they made themselves scarce when we needed their help; **du hast dich in letzter Zeit bei uns ~ gemacht** we haven't seen much of you at our place recently

**Rarität** /rariˈtɛːt/ *die;* **~, ~en** rarity

**Raritäten-: ~kabinett** *das: room housing a display of rare specimens;* **~sammlung** *die* collection of rare specimens

**rasant** /raˈzant/ ❶ *Adj.* **A** (*ugs.*) (*sehr schnell*) tremendously fast (*coll.*) ‹car, horse, runner, etc.›; tremendous (*coll.*), lightning *attrib.* ‹speed, acceleration›; meteoric, lightning *attrib.* ‹development, progress, growth›; hairy (*coll.*) ‹driving›; (*schnittig*) racy ‹car, styling›; **in ~em Tempo, in ~er Fahrt** at a terrific speed (*coll.*); **B** (*ugs.*) (*schwungvoll*) dynamic, lively ‹show›; action-packed, exciting ‹film, story›; (*fabelhaft*) terrific (*coll.*) ‹film, show, dress, song, etc.›; (*rassig*) classy (*sl.*) ‹woman›; dashing ‹style, dress›; **eine ~e Kür laufen** skate an exciting programme; **C** (*Ballistik: flach*) flat ‹trajectory›.
❷ *adv.* **A** (*ugs.*) (*sehr schnell*) at terrific speed (*coll.*); ‹increase› by leaps and bounds; **~ beschleunigen** ‹car› have terrific acceleration (*coll.*); ‹car, driver› accelerate like a mad thing (*coll.*); **~ gestylt** *od.* **geschnitten** (*schnittig*) racily styled; with racy lines; **B** (*ugs.*) (*schwungvoll*) dashingly; (*rassig*) stylishly; **C** (*Ballistik: flach*) **~ verlaufen** ‹trajectory› be flat

**Rasanz** /raˈzants/ *die;* **~** **A** (*ugs.: Schnelligkeit*) terrific speed (*coll.*); **die ~ der Beschleunigung** the terrific [rate of] acceleration (*coll.*); **B** (*ugs.: Dynamik*) verve; excitement

**rasch** /raʃ/ ❶ *Adj.* quick; quick, rapid ‹step, progress, decision, action›; speedy, swift ‹end, action, decision, progress›; fast, quick ‹service, work, pace, tempo, progress›; **ein ~es Tempo** a fast pace; (*eines Fahrzeugs*) a high speed; **in ~er Folge** in rapid *or* swift succession. ❷ *adv.* quickly; ‹drive, act› quickly, fast; ‹decide, end, proceed› swiftly, rapidly; **das geht mir zu ~:** that's too quick for me; **notieren Sie das ~!** make a quick note of that!

**rascheln** /ˈraʃl̩n/ *itr. V.* rustle; **die Maus raschelte** the mouse made a rustling noise; **es raschelte im Stroh** there was a rustling in the straw; **mit der Zeitung ~:** rustle the newspaper

**rasen** /ˈraːzn̩/ *itr. V.* **A** *mit sein* (*ugs.: eilen*) dash *or* rush [along]; (*fahren*) tear *or* race along; (*fig.*) ‹pulse› race; **gegen einen Baum ~:** crash [at full speed] into a tree; **ein Auto kam um die Ecke gerast** a car came tearing *or* racing round the corner; **die Zeit raste** (*fig.*) the time simply flew past; **B** (*toben*) ‹person› rage; (*wie wahnsinnig*) rave; (*fig.*) ‹storm, sea, war› rage; **[vor Begeisterung] ~:** go wild [with enthusiasm]

**Rasen** *der;* **~s, ~:** grass *no indef. art.*; (*gepflegte ~fläche*) lawn; (*eines Spielfeldes usw.*, *Grassode*) turf; **in unserem Garten ist hauptsächlich ~:** our garden is mainly grass *or* lawn; **ihn deckt der kühle** *od.* **grüne ~** (*geh. verhüll.*) he has been laid to rest; **er musste den ~ verlassen** (*Sportjargon*) he was sent off [the field *or* (*coll.*) park]

**rasend** ❶ *Adj.* **A** (*sehr schnell*) **in ~er Fahrt, mit ~er Geschwindigkeit** at breakneck speed; **B** (*tobend*) raging; (*wie wahnsinnig*) raving; (*verrückt*) mad; **[vor Wut** *usw.*] **~ werden** be beside oneself [with rage *etc.*]; **die Schmerzen machen mich ~:** the pain is driving me mad; **C** (*heftig*) violent ‹jealousy, rage›; violent, excruciating ‹pain›; tumultuous ‹applause›; **~e Kopfschmerzen haben** have a splitting headache. ❷ *adv.* (*ugs.*) incredibly (*coll.*) ‹fast, funny, expensive›; madly (*coll.*) ‹in love›; insanely ‹jealous›; **ich täte es ~ gern** I'd really love to do it

**Rasen-: ~fläche** *die* lawn; (*kleiner*) patch of grass; **~mäher** /-mɛːɐ/ *der;* **~s, ~:** lawnmower; **~platz** **A** ⇒ **~fläche**; **B** (*Fußball usw.*) pitch; (*Tennis*) grass court; **~schere** *die* grass shears *pl.*; **~sprenger** *der;* **~~s, ~~:** lawn sprinkler; **~stück** *das* area of lawn

**Raser** *der;* **~s, ~** (*ugs. abwertend*) speed merchant (*coll.*); (*rücksichtslos*) road hog

**Raserei** *die;* **~, ~en** **A** (*ugs.: schnelles Fahren*) tearing along *no art.*; **B** (*das Toben*) [insane] frenzy; (*Wut*) rage; **jmdn. zur ~ bringen** drive sb. mad *or* to distraction

**Raserin** *die;* **~, ~nen** ⇒ **Raser**

**Rasier-: ~apparat** *der* [safety] razor; (*elektrisch*) electric shaver *or* razor; **~creme** *die* shaving cream

**rasieren** /raˈziːrən/ *tr. V.* **A** shave; **sich ~:** shave; **sich nass/trocken/elektrisch ~:** have a wet/dry shave/use an electric shaver; **sich** (*Dat.*)**/jmdm. die Beine** *usw.* **~:**

*old spelling (see note on page 1707)

shave one's/sb.'s legs; (*ab~*) **sich** (*Dat.*)/ **jmdm. die Haare/den Bart ~:** shave off one's/sb.'s hair/beard; **B** (*zerstören*) raze to the ground

**Rasierer** *der;* **~s,** **~** (*ugs.*) [electric] shaver

**Rasier-: ~klinge** *die* razor blade; **~messer** *das* cutthroat razor; **~pinsel** *der* shaving brush; **~schaum** *der* **A** (*in der Sprühdose*) shaving foam; **B** (*der ~seife*) shaving lather; **~seife** *die* shaving soap; **~wasser** *das; Pl.* **~wässer** (*nach der Rasur*) aftershave; (*vor der Rasur*) pre-shave lotion; **~zeug** *das* shaving things *pl.*

**Räson** /rɛ'zɔŋ/ *die: in* **zur ~ kommen,** (*veralt.*) **~ annehmen** come to one's senses; **jmdn. zur ~ bringen** make sb. see reason

**räsonieren** /rɛzo'ni:rən/ *itr. V.* (*veralt. abwertend*) **A** (*sich wortreich äußern*) reason [at length]; expatiate; **B** (*nörgeln*) grumble (**über** + *Akk.* about)

**Raspel** /'raspḷ/ *die;* **~, ~n** **A** (*grobe Feile*) rasp; **B** (*Küchengerät*) grater

**raspeln** *tr. V.* **A** *auch itr.* (*mit einer Feile*) rasp; **an etw.** (*Dat.*) **~:** work away at sth. with a rasp; **B** (*Kochk.*) grate

**rass, *raß** /ra:s/, **räss, *räß** /rɛ:s/ *Adj.* (*südd., österr., schweiz.*) highly-seasoned; hot ‹curry, goulash›

**Rasse** /'rasə/ *die;* **~, ~n** **A** (*Biol.*) breed; **ein Pferd von edler ~:** a horse of noble pedigree; **B** (*Anthrop.: Menschen~*) race; **C** **~ haben** *od.* **sein** (*ugs.*) be terrific (*coll.*); (*Temperament haben*) have plenty of spirit *or* mettle; **von** *od.* **mit ~** (*ugs.*) terrific (*coll.*); (*temperamentvoll*) [high-]spirited

**Rasse·hund** *der* pedigree dog

**Rassel** /'rasḷ/ *die;* **~, ~n** **A** (*Musikinstrument*) rattle, *esp.* maraca; **B** (*Spielzeug*) rattle

**Rassel·bande** *die* (*ugs. scherzh.*) [gang of] little rascals *pl.*

**rasseln** *itr. V.* **A** rattle; **mit seinen Ketten/ seinem Schlüsselbund ~:** rattle one's chains/jangle one's bunch of keys; **der Wecker rasselt** the alarm goes off with a jangling sound; **~d atmen** (*fig.*) breathe stertorously; **seine Lunge rasselt** (*fig.*) he has a rattle in his lung; ⇒ *auch* **Säbel**; **B** *mit sein* (*sich ~d fortbewegen*) clatter; **gegen einen Baum ~** (*ugs.*) go smash into a tree (*coll.*); **C** *mit sein* (*salopp: durchfallen*) **durch eine Prüfung ~:** come unstuck in *or* (*Amer.*) flunk an exam (*coll.*)

**Rassen-: ~diskriminierung** *die* racial discrimination *no art.;* **~frage** *die* race issue; race question; **~gesetze** *Pl.* race laws; **~hass, *~haß** *der* racial hatred *no art.;* **~konflikt** *der* racial conflict; **~krawall** *der* race riot; **~problem** *das* racial problem; **das ~problem** the race problem; **~schranke** *die* racial barrier; **~trennung** *die* racial segregation *no art.;* **~unruhen** *Pl.* racial unrest; **~vorurteil** *das* racial prejudice

**Rasse·pferd** *das* thoroughbred [horse]

**rasse·rein** *Adj.* ⇒ **reinrassig**

**rassig** *Adj.* spirited, mettlesome ‹horse›; spirited, vivacious ‹woman›; sporty ‹car›; tangy ‹wine, perfume›; (*markant*) striking ‹face, features, beauty›

**rassisch** **1** *Adj.* racial; **aus ~en Gründen** for reasons of race. **2** *adv.* racially

**Rassismus** *der;* **~:** racism; racialism

**Rassist** *der;* **~en, ~en, Rassistin** *die;* **~, ~nen** racist; racialist

**rassistisch** **1** *Adj.* racist; racialist. **2** *adv.* racialistically; **~ begründet** for racialist reasons *postpos.;* ‹policy› based on race; **~ gefärbt** with a racialist slant

**Rast** /rast/ *die;* **~, ~en** rest; **~ machen** stop for a break; **ohne ~ und Ruh** (*geh.*) without respite

**Raste** *die;* **~, ~n** (*Technik*) notch

**rasten** *itr. V.* rest; take a rest *or* break; **eine Stunde ~:** have an hour's rest; **wer rastet, der rostet** (*Spr.*) if you don't keep at it, you get rusty; ⇒ *auch* **ruhen** D

**Raster** *der;* **~s, ~** **A** (*Druckw.*) (*Platte, Linien*) screen; **B** (*fig.*) [conceptual] framework; set pattern

**Raster-: ~ätzung** *die* (*Druckw.*) half-tone engraving; **~fahndung** *die* (*Kriminologie*) *pinpointing of suspects by means of computer analysis of data on many people*

**rastern** *tr. V.* screen; (*Ferns.*) scan

**Raster·punkt** *der* (*Druckw.*) half-tone dot

**Raster·schaltung** *die* ⇒ **Indexschaltung**

**Rasterung** *die;* **~, ~en** **A** (*das Rastern*) screening; (*Ferns.*) scanning; **B** (*Struktur*) screen

**rast-, Rast-: ~haus** *das* roadside café; (*mit Hotelbetrieb*) roadside hotel; motel; (*an der Autobahn*) motorway restaurant; **~hof** *der* [motorway] motel [and service area]; **~los** **1** *Adj.* restless ‹person, spirit›; restless, unsettled ‹life›; (*ununterbrochen*) unremitting, ceaseless ‹work, search›; (*unermüdlich*) tireless, unflagging ‹work, enthusiasm›; **2** *adv. s. Adj.:* restlessly; unremittingly; ceaselessly; tirelessly; unflaggingly; **~losigkeit** *die;* **~~:** restlessness; **~platz** *der* **A** place to rest; **B** (*an Autobahnen*) parking place (*with benches and WCs*); picnic area; **~stätte** *die* service area

**Rasur** /ra'zu:ɐ̯/ *die;* **~, ~en** **A** (*das Rasieren*) shave; **nach der ~:** after shaving; **B** (*ausradierte Stelle*) erasure

**rät** /rɛ:t/ *3. Pers. Sg. Präsens v.* raten

**Rat** /ra:t/ *der;* **~[e]s, Räte** /'rɛ:tə/ **A** (*Empfehlung*) advice; **ein ~:** a piece *or* word of advice; **gib mir einen ~, was ich tun soll!** please tell me what I should do; **ich gab ihm den ~ zu ...** I advised him to ...; **jmds. ~ einholen, sich** (*Dat.*) **bei jmdm. ~ holen** take advice from sb.; **bei jmdm. ~ suchen** seek sb.'s advice; **da ist guter ~ teuer** I/we *etc.* hardly know which way to turn; **jmdm. mit ~ und Tat zur Seite stehen** *od.* **beistehen** stand by sb. with moral and practical support; **mit sich zu ~[e] gehen** give the matter a lot of thought; **jmdn./etw. zu ~[e] ziehen** consult sb./sth.; **B** (*Ausweg*) way out; solution; **[sich** (*Dat.*)**] keinen ~ wissen** not know what to do; **ich wusste [mir] keinen ~ mehr** I was at my wit's end *or* completely at a loss; **weiß jemand ~?** has anybody any ideas?; **C** (*Gremium*) council; (*Sowjet*) soviet; **der ~ der Stadt** the town council; **~ für Gegenseitige Wirtschaftshilfe** Council for Mutual Economic Aid; COMECON; **D** (*Ratsmitglied*) councillor; council member; **E** (*Titel*) Councillor

**Rate** /'ra:tə/ *die;* **~, ~n** **A** (*Teilbetrag*) instalment; **etw. auf ~n kaufen** buy sth. by instalments *or* (*Brit.*) on hire purchase *or* (*Amer.*) on the installment plan; **B** (*Statistik: Verhältnis*) rate

**Räte·demokratie** *die* government by soviets *no art.;* sovietism *no art.*

**raten** **1** *unr. itr. V.* **A** (*einen Rat, Ratschläge geben*) **jmdm. ~:** advise sb.; **lass dir von einem Freund ~:** take the advice of a friend; **er lässt sich von niemandem ~:** he won't listen to anybody; **wem nicht zu ~ ist, dem ist [auch] nicht zu helfen** (*Spr.*) you can't help some people — they just won't listen; ≈ you can take a horse to the water, but you can't make him drink (*prov.*); **sich** (*Dat.*) **nicht zu ~ wissen** be quite at a loss; **wozu rätst du mir?** what do you advise me to do?; **ich würde zu diesem Bewerber ~:** my advice would be to choose this applicant; **B** (*schätzen*) guess; **richtig/ falsch ~:** guess right/wrong; **dreimal darfst du ~** (*ugs. iron.*) I'll give you three guesses.
**2** *tr. V.* **A** (*an~*) **jmdm. ~, etw. zu tun** advise sb. to do sth.; **was rätst du mir?** what do you advise [me to do]?; **lass dir das ge~ sein!** you better had [do that]!; (*tu das nicht*) don't you dare do that!; **das möchte ich dir auch ge~ haben!** I should hope so!; **B** (*er~*) guess

**Raten-: ~kauf** *der* purchase by instalments *or* (*Amer.*) on the installment plan; **~zahlung** *die* **A** payment by instalments; **B** (*das Zahlen des Teilbetrags*) hire purchase (*Brit.*) *or* (*Amer.*) installment plan payment; **die dritte ~zahlung ist fällig** the third instalment is due

**Räte·republik** *die* (*hist.*) soviet republic

**Rate·spiel** *das* guessing-game

**Rat-: ~geber** *der* adviser; (*Buch*) guide; **~geberin** *die* adviser; **~haus** *das* town hall; **jmdn. ins ~haus wählen** elect sb. to the town council; **die FDP ist wieder ins ~haus eingezogen** the FDP is again represented on the town council; **~haus·saal** *der* town-hall council chamber

**Ratifikation** /ratifika'tsi̯o:n/ *die;* **~, ~en** ratification

**ratifizieren** /ratifi'tsi:rən/ *tr. V.* ratify

**Ratifizierung** *die;* **~, ~en** ratification

**Rätin** /'rɛ:tɪn/ *die;* **~, ~nen** councillor

**Ratio** /'ra:tsi̯o/ *die;* **~** (*geh.*) [pure] reason *no art.;* rational logic *no art.*

**Ration** /ra'tsi̯o:n/ *die;* **~, ~en** ration; **jmdn. auf halbe/doppelte ~ setzen** (*ugs.*) put sb. on half/double rations; ⇒ *auch* **eisern** 1 D

**rational** /ratsi̯o'na:l/ **1** *Adj.* rational; **~e Zahlen** rational numbers. **2** *adv.* rationally

**rationalisieren** *tr., itr. V.* rationalize

**Rationalisierung** *die;* **~, ~en** rationalization; **~en** rationalization measures

**Rationalisierungs·maßnahme** *die* rationalization measure

**Rationalismus** *der;* **~:** rationalism *no art.*

**Rationalist** *der;* **~en, ~en, Rationalistin** *die;* **~, ~nen** rationalist

**rationalistisch** **1** *Adj.* rationalistic; rationalist ‹principles›; **das ~e Zeitalter** the age of reason. **2** *adv.* rationalistically

**Rationalität** /ratsi̯onali'tɛ:t/ *die;* **~:** rationality

**rationell** /ratsi̯o'nɛl/ **1** *Adj.* efficient; (*wirtschaftlich*) economic. **2** *adv.* efficiently; (*wirtschaftlich, kräftesparend*) economically

**rationieren** *tr. V.* ration

**Rationierung** *die;* **~, ~en** rationing *no indef. art.;* **~en vornehmen** introduce rationing [measures]

**rat·los** **1** *Adj.* baffled; at a loss *pred.;* helpless ‹look›; **einer Sache** (*Dat.*) **~ gegenüberstehen** not know what to do about sth. **2** *adv.* helplessly; in a baffled way

**Rat·losigkeit** *die;* **~:** perplexity; helplessness; **in meiner ~:** not knowing what to do

**Rätoromanisch** /rɛtoro'ma:nɪʃ/ *das;* **~[s]** Rhaeto-Romanic; Rhaeto-Romance

**ratsam** /'ra:tza:m/ *Adj.* advisable; (*weise*) prudent

**ratsch** /ratʃ/ *Interj.* zip; (*beim Zerreißen*) rip; **es machte ~:** there was a ripping sound; ⇒ *auch* **ritsch**

**Ratsche** /'ra:tʃə/ *die;* **~, ~n** (*bes. südd., österr.*), **Rätsche** /'rɛ:tʃə/ *die;* **Rätsche, Rätschen** (*südd.*) **A** (*Geräuschinstrument*) [football fan's] rattle; **B** (*Technik: Sperre*) ratchet

**ratschen**[1] (*ugs.*) **1** *itr. V.* (*Geräusch erzeugen*) rip. **2** *refl. V.* (*landsch.: kratzen*) scratch oneself

**ratschen**[2] (*bes. südd., österr.*), **rätschen** (*südd.*) *itr. V.* **A** (*Ratsche drehen*) swing a/ one's rattle; (*fig.*) make a rasping noise; **B** (*ugs.: schwatzen*) gossip

**Rat-: ~schlag** *der* [piece of] advice; (*Hinweis*) tip; **auf meinen ~schlag hin** acting on my advice; **~schläge** advice/tips; **kluge ~schläge** (*iron.*) brilliant advice *sing.* (*iron.*); **~schluss, *~schluß** *der* (*geh.*) counsel (*formal*); **nach Gottes unerforschlichem ~schluss** in accordance with the unfathomable will of God

**Rätsel** /'rɛ:tsḷ/ *das;* **~s, ~** **A** (*Denkaufgabe*) riddle; (*Bilder~, Kreuzwort~ usw.*) puzzle; **das ist des ~s Lösung** (*fig.*) [so] that is the explanation; **jmdm. ~/ein ~ aufgeben** ask *or* set sb. riddles/a riddle; (*fig.: vor Probleme stellen*) puzzle *or* baffle sb.; **B** (*Geheimnis*) mystery; enigma; **jmdm.** *od.* **für jmdn. ein ~ sein/bleiben** be/remain a mystery to sb.; **vor einem ~ stehen** be baffled

r

**Rätsel·ecke** *die* (*ugs.*) puzzle corner (*in a magazine/newspaper*)

**rätselhaft** ❶ *Adj.* mysterious; (*unergründlich*) enigmatic ‹smile, expression, person›; baffling ‹problem›; **es blieb/es ist [mir] ~, warum ...** it remained/is a mystery [to me] why ... ❷ *adv.* mysteriously; (*unergründlich*) enigmatically

**Rätselhaftigkeit** *die;* **~:** enigmatic nature; mysteriousness

**Rätsel·heft** *das* puzzle magazine

**rätseln** *itr. V.* puzzle, rack one's brains (**über** + *Akk.* over); **~, wer .../ob ...** try to work out who .../whether ...

**Rätsel·raten** *das* [A] ⇒ **Rätsel** A: solving puzzles/riddles *no art.;* [B] (*das Rätseln*) puzzling; (*das Raten*) guessing; **das ~, wer sein Nachfolger werden soll** the guessing game as to who is to be his successor

**rätsel·voll** ❶ *Adj.* mysterious; enigmatic ‹person›. ❷ *adv.* mysteriously; ‹smile› enigmatically

**Rats-:** **~herr** *der,* **~herrin** *die* [town/city] councillor; **~keller** *der* [restaurant in the] town-hall cellar; **~stube** *die* (*veralt.*) [town hall] council-chamber

**Rattan** /'ratan/ *das;* **~s** rattan [cane]

**Ratte** /'ratə/ *die;* **~, ~n** (*auch fig.*) rat; **die ~n verlassen das sinkende Schiff** the rats are leaving the sinking ship

**Ratten-:** **~bekämpfung** *die* rat control; **~fänger** *der,* **~fängerin** *die* [A] ratcatcher; **der ~fänger von Hameln** (*Lit.*) the Pied Piper of Hamelin; [B] (*abwertend: Volksverführer*) pied piper; **~gift** *das* rat poison; **~schwanz** *der* [A] (*fig.: große Anzahl*) **ein ~schwanz von Änderungen/Gerüchten** a whole welter *or* string of changes/rumours; [B] (*scherzh.: Zopf*) pigtail; [C] (*Schwanz der Ratte*) rat's tail

**rattern** /'ratɐn/ *itr. V.* [A] (*knattern*) clatter; ‹sewing machine, machine gun› chatter; ‹engine› rattle; [B] *mit sein* (*sich ~d fortbewegen*) clatter [along]

**Ratz** /rats/ *der;* **~es, ~e** [A] (*südd., österr., schweiz.*) rat; [B] (*volkst.: Siebenschläfer*) [edible] dormouse; **schlafen wie ein ~:** sleep like a log

**ratze·kahl** *Adv.* (*ugs.*) totally; completely

**ratzen** *itr. V.* (*ugs.*) [have a] kip (*Brit. coll.*)

**rau** /rau/ ❶ *Adj.* [A] (*nicht glatt*) rough; **in einer ~en Schale steckt oft ein weicher Kern** (*Spr.*) behind a rough exterior there often beats a heart of gold; [B] (*nicht mild*) harsh, raw ‹climate, winter›; raw ‹wind›; [C] (*unwirtlich*) bleak, inhospitable ‹region, mountains, etc.›; rough ‹weather›; [D] (*kratzig*) husky, hoarse ‹voice›; [E] (*entzündet*) sore ‹throat›; [F] (*grob, nicht feinfühlig*) rough; harsh ‹words, tone›; **er ist ~, aber herzlich** he is a rough diamond; [G] (*Ballspiele*) rough ‹play›; [H] (*ugs.*) **in ~en Mengen** in huge *or* vast quantities.
❷ *adv.* [A] (*kratzig*) ‹speak etc.› huskily, hoarsely; [B] (*grob, nicht feinfühlig*) roughly; [C] (*Ballspiele*) roughly; **~ spielen** play rough

**Raub** /raup/ *der;* **~[e]s** [A] robbery; (*Entführung*) kidnapping; **jmdn. wegen ~es anklagen/verurteilen** accuse/convict sb. of robbery *or* (*jur.*) larceny [from the person]; **der ~ der Sabinerinnen** (*Myth.*) the rape of the Sabine women; [B] (*Beute*) [robber's] loot; stolen goods *pl.;* **ein ~ der Flammen werden** (*geh.*) be consumed by the flames (*literary*)

**rau-, Rau-:** **~bauz** /-bauts/ *der;* **~~es, ~~e** (*ugs.*) ⇒ **~bein**; **~bauzig** *Adj.* (*ugs.*) ⇒ **~beinig**; **~bein** *das* (*ugs.*) rough diamond; **~beinig** *Adj.* (*ugs.*) gruff; rough and ready

**Raub·bau** *der* overexploitation (**an** + *Dat.* of); (*beim Fischfang*) overfishing; (*beim Bergbau*) overworking; **~ an etw.** (*Dat.*) **treiben** over-exploit sth.; **~ mit seiner Gesundheit treiben** (*fig.*) ruin one's health by overdoing things; **~ an seinen Kräften** (*fig.*) overtaxing one's strength

*old spelling (see note on page 1707)

**Raub·druck** *der; Pl.* **~e** pirated edition

**rauben** ❶ *tr. V.* steal; kidnap ‹person›; **jmdm. etw. ~:** rob sb. of sth.; (*geh.: wegnehmen*) deprive sb. of sth.; **jmdm. den Atem/die Sprache ~:** take sb.'s breath away/render sb. speechless; **er hat ihr die Unschuld geraubt** (*veralt.*) he deprived her of her virginity; he deflowered her (*dated*). ❷ *itr. V.* rob; (*plündern*) plunder

**Räuber** /'rɔybɐ/ *der;* **~s, ~** [A] robber; (*Entführer*) kidnapper; (*fig. scherzh.*) rascal; **~ und Gendarm** cops and robbers; **anscheinend bin ich unter die ~ gefallen** (*ugs.*) it seems I'm being fleeced (*coll.*); [B] (*Zool.: Tier*) predator

**Räuber-:** **~bande** *die* (*veralt.*) band of robbers; **~geschichte** *die* [A] story about robbers; [B] (*ugs.: erlogene Geschichte*) tall story; **~hauptmann** *der* (*veralt.*) robber chief; **~höhle** *die* (*veralt.*) robber's den; **hier sieht es aus wie in einer ~höhle** it's a frightful mess in here (*coll.*)

**Räuberin** *die;* **~, ~nen** ⇒ **Räuber** A

**räuberisch** ❶ *Adj.* [A] rapacious, predatory ‹gang, horde, etc.›; **~e Erpressung** (*Rechtsw.*) extortion by means of force *or* under threat of force; [B] (*Zool.*) predatory ‹animal, fish, etc.›. ❷ *adv.* (*Zool.*) **~ lebend** living as a predator/as predators; predatory

**räubern** *itr. V.* go robbing; (*plündern*) loot

**Räuber-:** **~pistole** *die* (*ugs. scherzh.*) tall story; **~zivil** *das* (*ugs. scherzh.*) scruffy clothes *pl.*

**raub-, Raub-:** **~fisch** *der* predatory fish; **~gier** *die* rapacity; **~gierig** *Adj.* rapacious; **~katze** *die* wild cat; **~kopie** *die* pirated copy; **~mord** *der* (*Rechtsw.*) murder (**an** + *Dat.* of) in the course of a robbery *or* with robbery as motive; **~mörder** *der,* **~mörderin** *die* robber and murderer; **~ritter** *der* (*hist.*) robber baron; **~tier** *das* predator; beast of prey; **~tier·käfig** *der* predators' cage; (*für Löwen und Tiger*) lions' and tigers' cage; **~überfall** *der* robbery (**auf** + *Akk.* of); (*von einer Bande auf eine Bank od. dergl.*) raid (**auf** + *Akk.* on); **~vogel** *der* bird of prey; **~wild** *das* (*Jägerspr.*) predators *pl.* (*hunted as game*); **~zug** *der* plundering raid

**Rauch** /raux/ *der;* **~[e]s** smoke; **kein ~ ohne Flammen** (*Spr.*) there's no smoke without fire (*prov.*); **in ~ [und Flammen] aufgehen** go up in smoke *or* flames; **sich in ~ auflösen, in ~ aufgehen** (*fig.*) go up in smoke

**Rauch-:** **~ab·zug** *der* smoke outlet; (*Rohr, Schacht*) flue; **~bombe** *die* smoke bomb

**rauchen** ❶ *itr. V.* smoke; **es rauchte in der Küche** there was smoke in the kitchen; **sonst raucht es!** (*ugs.*) or there'll be trouble. ❷ *tr.* (*auch itr.*) *V.* smoke ‹cigarette, pipe, etc.›; **~ Sie?** do you smoke?; **eine ~:** have a smoke; **stark** *od.* **viel ~:** be a heavy smoker; **„Rauchen verboten"** 'No smoking'

**Rauch·entwicklung** *die* build-up of smoke

**Raucher** *der;* **~s, ~:** smoker; **möchten Sie ~ oder Nichtraucher [fliegen]?** would you like smoking or no smoking?

**Räucher·aal** *der* smoked eel

**Raucher-:** **~ab·teil** *das* smoking compartment; smoker; **~bein** *das* ▶ 474 (*Med.*) *narrowing of the arteries of the leg as a result of heavy smoking*

**Räucher·hering** *der* smoked herring

**Raucher·husten** *der* smoker's cough

**Raucherin** *die;* **~, ~nen** smoker

**Räucher-:** **~kammer** *die* smokehouse; **~lachs** *der* smoked salmon

**Raucher·lunge** *die* (*volkst.*) smoker's lung

**räuchern** /'rɔyçɐn/ ❶ *tr. V.* smoke ‹meat, fish›. ❷ *itr. V.* burn incense/joss sticks *etc.*

**Räucher-:** **~schinken** *der* smoked ham; **~speck** *der* smoked [streaky] bacon; **~stäbchen** *das* joss stick

**rauch-, Rauch-:** **~fahne** *die* plume of smoke; **~fang** *der* [A] (*~abzug*) chimney hood; [B] (*österr.: Schornstein*) chimney; **~fang·kehrer** *der,* **~fang·kehrerin** *die* (*österr.*) chimney sweep; **~farben, ~farbig** *Adj.* smoke-coloured; smoke-grey; **~fass**

***~faß** *das* (*kath. Kirche*) censer; **~gas** *das* flue gas; **~gasentschwefelung** *die;* **~~:** flue gas desulphurization; **~geschwängert** *Adj.* smoke-filled; **die Luft war ~geschwängert** the air was heavy with smoke; **~geschwärzt** *Adj.* smoke-blackened; **~glas** *das* smoked glass

**rauchig** *Adj.* smoky; husky ‹voice›

**rauch-, Rauch-:** **~los** *Adj.* smokeless; **~melder** *der* smoke detector; **~pilz** *der* mushroom cloud; **~salon** *der* smoking room; **~säule** *die* column *or* pillar of smoke; **~schwaden** *der* cloud of smoke; **~signal** *das* smoke signal; **~tisch** *der* smoker's table; **~verbot** *das* ban on smoking; **aus Sicherheitsgründen herrscht ~verbot** smoking is prohibited for safety reasons; **~vergiftung** *die* poisoning *no art.* by smoke inhalation; **~verzehrer** *der;* **~~s, ~~:** air cleaner [and freshener]; **~waren** *Pl.* (*fachspr.*) ⇒ **Pelzwaren**; **~wolke** *die* cloud of smoke; **~zeichen** *das* smoke signal

**Räude** /'rɔydə/ *die;* **~, ~n** mange *no art.*

**räudig** *Adj.* mangy; **ein ~es Schaf** (*fig.*) a bad apple (*fig.*); **du ~er Hund!** (*derb*) you dirty rat! (*sl.*)

**rauf** /rauf/ *Adv.* (*ugs.*) up; **~ mit euch!** up you go!; ⇒ *auch* **herauf**; **hinauf**

**rauf-** (*ugs.*) up; **~brüllen/~klettern** shout/climb

**Rau·faser·tapete** *die* woodchip wallpaper

**Raufbold** /-bɔlt/ *der;* **~[e]s, ~e** (*veralt.*) ruffian

**rauf|bringen** *unr. tr. V.* (*ugs.*) (*her*) bring up; (*hin*) take up

**Raufe** *die;* **~, ~n** hay rack

**raufen** ❶ *itr., refl. V.* fight; **[sich] wegen** *od.* **um etw. ~:** fight [each other] over sth. ❷ *tr. V.* pull up ‹weeds, plants, etc.›; pull ‹flax›; **sich** (*Dat.*) **die Haare/den Bart ~:** tear one's hair/at one's beard

**Rauferei** *die;* **~, ~en** fight

**rauf|gehen** *unr. itr. V.; mit sein* (*ugs.*) go up

**Rauf·handel** *der;* **~s, Raufhändel** (*veralt.*) brawl; fight

**rauf-:** **~|holen** *tr. V.* (*ugs.*) fetch *or* bring up; **~|kommen** *unr. itr. V.; mit sein* (*ugs.*) come up

**rauf·lustig** *Adj.* (*veralt.*) pugnacious; **er ist ein ~er Bursche** he is always spoiling for a fight

**Rau·frost** *der* rime

***rauh** *usw.* ⇒ **rau** *usw.*

**Rau·haar·dackel** *der* wire-haired dachshund

**Rauheit** *die;* **~, ~en** ⇒ **rau** A-D: roughness; harshness; rawness; bleakness; inhospitableness; huskiness; hoarseness

***Rauh·faser·tapete** *usw.* ⇒ **Raufasertapete** *usw.*

**raum** /raum/ *Adj.* (*Seemannsspr.*) [A] (*weit*) open ‹sea›; [B] (*von hinten*) quartering, following ‹sea, current, wind›

**Raum** *der;* **~[e]s, Räume** /'rɔymə/ [A] (*Wohn~, Nutz~*) room; **im ~ stehen** (*fig.*) be in the air; ‹threat› be hanging in the air; **etw. im ~ stehen lassen** (*fig.*) leave sth. hanging in the air; **eine Anschuldigung im ~ stehen lassen** leave an accusation unanswered; [B] (*nicht fest eingegrenztes Gebiet*) expanse; **~ und Zeit** (*Philos.*) space and time; [C] (*Platz*) room; space; **5 m ~:** a space of 5 m; **auf engstem ~ leben** live in a very confined space; **einen zu breiten ~ einnehmen** (*fig.*) be given too much attention; [D] (*Welt~*) space *no art.;* [E] (*Gebiet*) area; region; **im ~ Hamburg** in the Hamburg area *or* region; [F] (*Wirkungsfeld*) sphere; [G] (*Math.*) space

**Raum-:** **~akustik** *die* (*Physik*) room acoustics *sing., no art.;* **~angabe** *die* (*Sprachw.*) adverbial expression of place; **~anzug** *der* spacesuit; **~ausstatter** *der;* **~~s, ~~:** [A] (*Beruf*) interior decorator; [B] (*Geschäft*) [firm of] interior decorators *pl.;* **~ausstatterin** *die;* **~~, ~~nen** ⇒ **~ausstatter** A; **~bild** *das* (*Optik*) stereoscopic picture; 3-D picture; **~deckung** *die* (*Ballspiele*) zonal defence

# Rauminhalt

## Raummaße

| | | |
|---|---|---|
| ***1 Kubikzentimeter*** | = one cubic centimetre (cc) | = 0.06 cubic inch (cu. in.) |
| ***1 Kubikmeter*** | = one cubic metre (cu. m) | = 35.714 cubic feet (cu. ft) *od.* 1.307 cubic yards (cu. yds) |

## Hohlmaße

| | | |
|---|---|---|
| ***1 Zentiliter*** | = one centilitre (cl) | = 0.0176 pints (*brit.*), 0.021 pints (*amerik.*) |
| ***1 Liter*** | = one litre (l) | = 1.76 pints (*brit.*), 2.1 pints (*amerik.*) *od.* 0.22 gallons (*brit.*), 0.264 gallons (*amerik.*) |

***Wie viel*** od. ***Welches Volumen hat es?***
= What is its volume?

***Es hat ein Volumen von 6 m³***
= Its volume is 6 cubic metres, ≈ the volume is 200 cubic feet

***Wie viel fasst der Tank?***
= How much does the tank hold?, What is the capacity of the tank?

***Der Tank fasst 45 Liter***
= The tank holds 45 litres, ≈ the tank holds 10 gallons (*brit.*)/ 12 gallons (*amerik.*)

***Die beiden Tanks haben das gleiche Fassungsvermögen***
= The two tanks have the same capacity *od.* hold the same amount

***Mein Wagen verbraucht 10 Liter auf 100 Kilometer***
≈ My car does 28 (*UK*) *od.* 23 (*USA*) miles per gallon (m.p.g.).

[Um Liter auf 100 Kilometer in miles per gallon umzurechnen (oder auch umgekehrt), dividiert man 280 (bei britischen *gallons*) bzw. 230 (bei *US gallons*) durch die Literzahl (bzw. Meilenzahl) Zahl].

***Benzin wird literweise verkauft***
= Petrol is sold by the litre

Der Hubraum eines Motors wird im britischen Einflussbereich in Kubikzentimeter (cc) bzw. Liter angegeben, dagegen in den USA und Kanada in cubic inches (cu. in.):

***Wie viel Hubraum hat der Motor?***
= What is the capacity of the engine *od.* (*amerik.*) motor?

***Der Motor hat 1 600 cm³*** od. ***1,6 Liter Hubraum***
= It's a 1600 cc *od.* 1.6 litre engine (*brit.*) *od.* a 96 cu. in. motor (*amerik.*)

**räumen** /ˈrɔymən/ ❶ *tr. V.* Ⓐ (*entfernen*) clear [away]; clear ‹snow›; **Minen ~:** clear mines; (*auf See*) sweep *or* clear mines; **etw. vom Tisch ~:** clear sth. off the table; **etw. aus dem Weg ~:** clear sth. out [of] the way; Ⓑ (*an einen Ort*) clear; move; **seine Sachen auf die Seite ~:** clear *or* move one's things to one side; **etw. in Schubfächer** (*Akk.*) **~:** put sth. away in drawers; Ⓒ (*frei machen*) clear ‹street, building, warehouse, stocks, etc.›; Ⓓ (*verlassen*) vacate ‹hotel room›; vacate, clear ‹hall, cinema, etc.›; vacate, move out of ‹house, flat›; evacuate, vacate ‹military position, area›; Ⓔ (*durch die Polizei usw. frei machen*) clear ‹room, hall, street, etc.›.
❷ *itr. V.* clear up

**Raum-: ~ersparnis** *die* saving of space; **~fähre** *die* space shuttle; **~fahrer** *der,* **~fahrerin** *die* astronaut; (*Kosmonaut*) cosmonaut; **~fahrt** *die* Ⓐ space flight; space travel; Ⓑ (*~flug*) space flight

**Raumfahrt-: ~behörde** *die* space agency; **~medizin** *die* space medicine *no art.;* **~technik** *die* space technology *no art.*

**Raum·fahrzeug** *das* spacecraft

**Räum·fahrzeug** *das* bulldozer; (*für Schnee*) snowplough

**raum-, Raum-: ~flug** *der* space flight; **~forschung** *die* space research *no art.;* **~gestalter** *der,* **~gestalterin** *die* interior designer; **~gleiter** *der;* **~s, ~** (*Raumf.*) space shuttle; **~greifend** *Adj.* (*Sport*) long ‹pass, stride, etc.›; **~inhalt** *der* ▶ 611 (*Math.*) volume; **~kapsel** *die* space capsule; **~klang** *der* stereophonic sound

**räumlich** ❶ *Adj.* Ⓐ (*den Raum betreffend*) spatial; **aus ~en Gründen** for reasons of space; **wir sind ~ sehr beschränkt** we are cramped for space; **~e Nähe** physical proximity; Ⓑ (*dreidimensional*) three-dimensional; stereophonic ‹sound›; stereoscopic ‹vision›; **~ wirken** have a three-dimensional effect; **~es Vorstellungsvermögen** ability to visualize things in three dimensions.
❷ *adv.* Ⓐ spatially; **in zeitlich und ~ enger Nachbarschaft** in close temporal and spatial proximity; Ⓑ (*dreidimensional*) three-dimensionally

**Räumlichkeit** *die;* **~, ~en** Ⓐ *Pl.* rooms; **uns** (*Dat.*) **fehlen die ~en** we don't have enough space; **die ~en des Museums** the museum's premises; Ⓑ (*räumliche Wirkung*) three-dimensionality

**raum-, Raum-: ~maß** *das* ▶ 611 measure of capacity; **~meter** *der od. das* cubic metre (*of stacked wood, logs*); **~not** *die* shortage *or* lack of space (*Gen.* in); **~ordnung** *die* (*Amtsspr.*) regional planning; **~ordnungs·plan** *der* (*Amtsspr.*) regional development plan; **~pfleger** *der* cleaner; **~pflegerin** *die* cleaning lady; cleaner; **~schiff** *das* spaceship; **~sonde** *die* space probe; **~sparend** *Adj.* ⇒ **platzsparend**; **~station** *die* space station; **~teiler** *der* room divider; **~transporter** *der* space shuttle

**Räumung** *die;* **~, ~en** Ⓐ clearing; Ⓑ (*einer Wohnung, eines Hotelzimmers*) vacation; vacating; Ⓒ (*wegen Gefahr*) evacuation; Ⓓ (*von Vorräten, eines Geschäfts*) clearance

**Räumungs-: ~klage** *die* (*Rechtsw.*) action for eviction; **~klage erheben** ≈ apply for an eviction order; **~verkauf** *der* (*Kaufmannsspr.*) clearance sale

**raunen** /ˈraunən/ *tr., itr. V.* (*geh.*) whisper; **ein Raunen ging durch die Reihen** a murmur went through the ranks

**raunzen** /ˈrauntsn̩/ *itr. V.* (*bes. südd., österr.*) grumble; grouse (*coll.*)

**Raupe** /ˈraupə/ *die;* **~, ~n** Ⓐ (*Larve*) caterpillar; Ⓑ ⇒ **Planierraupe**; Ⓒ ⇒ **~nkette**

**Raupen-: ~fahrzeug** *das* Caterpillar vehicle; Caterpillar ®; **~kette** *die* Caterpillar track; **~schlepper** *der* Caterpillar tractor

**Rau-: ~putz** *der* roughcast; **~reif** *der* hoar frost

**raus** /raus/ *Adv.* (*ugs.*) out; **~ mit euch!** out you go!; **Nazis ~!** Nazis out!; ⇒ *auch* **heraus; hinaus** A

**Rausch** /rauʃ/ *der;* **~[e]s, Räusche** /ˈrɔyʃə/ Ⓐ (*durch Alkohol*) state of drunkenness; **sich** (*Dat.*) **einen ~ antrinken** get drunk; **einen [leichten/schweren] ~ haben** be [slightly/very] drunk; **seinen ~ ausschlafen** sleep off the effects of drink; sleep it off (*coll.*); **etw. im ~ tun** do sth. while drunk; Ⓑ (*durch Drogen*) drugged state; **einen ~ haben** be drugged; be high (*coll.*) [on drugs]; **etw. im ~ tun** do sth. while drugged; Ⓒ (*starkes Gefühl*) transport; **der ~ des Erfolgs/Sieges** the exhilaration *or* intoxication of success/victory; **ein wilder/blinder ~:** a wild/blind frenzy; **der ~ der Geschwindigkeit** the exhilaration *or* thrill of speed

**rausch·arm** ❶ *Adj.* low-noise. ❷ *adv.* with a low noise level

**Rausche·bart** *der* (*scherzh.*) Ⓐ full beard; Ⓑ (*Mann*) bearded [old] gentleman

**rauschen** *itr. V.* Ⓐ ‹water, wind, torrent› rush; ‹trees, leaves› rustle; ‹skirt, curtains, silk› swish; ‹waterfall, strong wind› roar; ‹rain› pour down; **ich hörte das Wasser ~:** I heard the sound of rushing water; **es rauscht im Radio** there's a hiss coming from the radio; **das Rauschen der Brandung/des Meeres** the roar of the surf/sea; **~der Beifall** (*fig.*) resounding applause; **~de Feste** (*fig.*) glittering parties; Ⓑ *mit sein* (*sich bewegen*) ‹water, river, etc.› rush; ‹bird, bullet, etc.› whoosh; **der Ball rauschte ins Tor** (*Sport ugs.*) the ball slammed into the back of the net; **sie rauschte aus dem Zimmer** she swept out of the room

**Rausch·gift** *das* drug; narcotic; **~ nehmen** take drugs; be on drugs

**rausch·gift-, Rausch·gift-: ~handel** *der* drug trafficking; **~händler** *der,* **~händlerin** *die* drug trafficker; **~süchtig** *Adj.* drug-addicted; addicted to drugs *postpos.;* **sie war ~süchtig** she was addicted to drugs *or* a drug addict; **~süchtige Jugendliche** young drug addicts; **~süchtige** *der/die* drug addict; **~tote** *der/die* person who dies/died as a result of drug abuse; **im vergangenen Jahr gab es 400 ~tote** last year 400 people died as a result of drug abuse

**Rausch·gold** *das* Dutch metal

**Rauschgold·engel** *der* angel (*made of Dutch metal*)

**rausch·haft** *Adj.* ecstatic

**Rausch·mittel** *das* ⇒ **Rauschgift**

**raus-: ~|dürfen** *unr. itr. V.* (*ugs.*) ⇒ **heraus-, hinausdürfen**; **~|ekeln** *tr. V.* (*ugs.*) ⇒ **hinausekeln**; **~|fahren** *unr. tr. V.; mit sein* (*ugs.*) ⇒ **heraus-, hinausfahren**; **~|feuern** *tr. V.* (*ugs.*) chuck out (*coll.*); **~|fliegen** *unr. itr. V.; mit sein* (*ugs.*) ⇒ **heraus-, hinausfliegen**; **~|gehen** *unr. itr. V.; mit sein* (*ugs.*) ⇒ **heraus-, hinausgehen**; **~|kommen** *unr. itr. V.; mit sein* (*ugs.*) ⇒ **heraus-, hinauskommen**; **~|können** *unr. itr. V.* (*ugs.*) be able to go/come out; (*sich befreien können*) be able to get out; **~|kriegen** *tr. V. (ugs.)* get out (**aus** of); **ich habe das Rätsel/die Aufgabe nicht ~gekriegt** I couldn't do the puzzle/exercise; **~|müssen** *unr. itr. V. (ugs.)* have got to go/come out; **wir müssen aus unserer Wohnung ~:** we have got to get out of our flat (*Brit.*) *or* (*Amer.*) apartment; **~|nehmen** *unr. tr. V. (ugs.)* ⇒ **heraus-, hinausnehmen**; **~|pauken** *tr. V. (ugs.)* **jmdn. ~pauken** get sb. off the hook (*coll.*)

**räuspern** /ˈrɔyspɐn/ *refl. V.* clear one's throat

**raus-, Raus-: ~|schmeißen** *unr. tr. V. (ugs.)* chuck (*coll.*) *or* sling (*coll.*) ‹objects› out *or* away; give ‹employee› the push (*coll.*) *or* sack (*coll.*) *or* boot (*sl.*); chuck (*coll.*) *or* throw ‹customer, drunk, tenant› out (**aus** of); **das ist ~geschmissenes Geld** that's money down the drain (*coll.*); **~schmeißer** *der;* **~~s, ~~** *(ugs.)* Ⓐ *(Person)* chucker-out (*coll.*); bouncer (*coll.*); Ⓑ *(Tanz)* last dance; **~schmeißerin** *die;* **~~, ~~nen** ⇒ **~schmeißer** A; **~schmiss, *~schmiß** *der (ugs.)* ⇒ **~schmeißen**: chucking out (*coll.*); slinging out (*coll.*); sacking (*coll.*); chucking out (*coll.*); throwing out; **nach dem ~schmiss des Angetrunkenen ...** after the drunk had been chucked out; **nach unserem ~schmiss aus der Wohnung** after we were chucked (*coll.*) *or* thrown out of our flat; **~|sollen** *itr. V. (ugs.)* **der Zahn/Blinddarm soll ~:** the tooth/appendix is to come out; **wir sollen zum Jahresende aus unserer Wohnung ~:** we're to be out of our flat by the end of the year; **~|wollen** *unr. itr. V. (ugs.)* want to go/come out; **ich will ~!** I want to get out!

**Raute** /ˈrautə/ *die;* **~, ~n** Ⓐ *(Pflanze)* rue; Ⓑ *(Geom.)* rhombus

**rauten·förmig** *Adj.* rhombic; diamond-shaped

**rautiert** /rauˈtiːɐt/ *Adj.* squared ‹paper›

**Rave** /reɪv/ *der;* **~s, ~s** rave

**raven** /ˈreɪvn̩/ *itr. V.* rave

**Raver** /ˈreɪvɐ/ *der;* **~s, ~:** raver

**Ravioli** /raˈvi̯oːli/ *Pl. (Kochk.)* ravioli *sing.*

**Rayon** /rɛˈjõː/ *der;* **~s, ~s** *od. (österr.)* **~e** Ⓐ *(Warenhausabteilung)* department; Ⓑ *(österr., schweiz.: Bezirk)* district

**Rayons·inspektor** *der*, **Rayons·inspektorin** *die (österr. schweiz.)* district inspector

**Razzia** /ˈratsi̯a/ *die;* **~, Razzien** raid; **in dieser Kneipe führte die Polizei oft Razzien durch** the police has often raided this bar

**Re** *das;* **~s, ~s** *(Skat)* redouble

**Reagens** *das;* **~, Reagenzien** /reaˈgɛntsi̯ən/, **Reagenz** /reaˈgɛnts/ *das;* **Reagenzes, Reagenzien** *(Chemie)* reagent

**Reagenz-: ~glas** *das* test tube; **~papier** *das* test paper

**reagieren** *itr. V.* Ⓐ react (**auf** + *Akk.* to); Ⓑ *(Chemie)* react; **miteinander ~:** react together

**Reaktanz** /reakˈtants/ *die;* **~, ~en** *(Elektrot.)* reactance

**Reaktion** /reakˈtsi̯oːn/ *die;* **~, ~en** *(auch Politik abwertend, Chemie)* reaction (**auf** + *Akk.* to)

**reaktionär** /reaktsi̯oˈnɛːr/ *Adj. (Politik abwertend)* reactionary

**Reaktionär** *der;* **~s, ~e**, **Reaktionärin** *die;* **~, ~nen** *(Politik abwertend)* reactionary

**reaktions-, Reaktions-: ~fähig** *Adj.* Ⓐ capable of reacting *postpos.*; **durch den Alkoholgenuss war er nicht mehr voll ~fähig** his alcohol intake had impaired his reactions; Ⓑ *(Chemie)* reactive; **~fähigkeit** *die* Ⓐ ability to react; **jmds. ~fähigkeit überprüfen** test sb.'s reactions; Ⓑ *(Chemie)* reactivity; **~geschwindigkeit** *die (Chemie)* reaction rate; **~schnell** ❶ *Adj.* ‹person› with quick reactions; **~schnell sein** have quick reactions; **durch sein ~schnelles Abbremsen** through his quick reaction in braking; ❷ *adv.* **sie schrieb ~schnell die Autonummer auf** she reacted quickly and wrote down the car's number; **~schnelligkeit** *die* speed of reaction; **~vermögen** *das* ⇒ **~fähigkeit**; **~wärme** *die (Chemie)* heat of reaction; **~weg** *der* reaction distance; **~zeit** *die (Physiol.)* reaction time

**reaktiv** /reakˈtiːf/ ❶ *Adj.* reactive. ❷ *adv.* reactively

**reaktivieren** *tr. V.* Ⓐ *(wieder anstellen)* recall [to duty]; Ⓑ *(wieder in Gebrauch nehmen)* bring ‹vehicle, machine, etc.› back into service; *(fig.)* brush *or* polish up ‹knowledge, skill, etc.›; Ⓒ *(Chemie)* reactivate ‹catalyst, serum›

**Reaktivierung** *die* Ⓐ *(Wiedereinstellung)* recalling [to duty]; Ⓑ *(Wiederinbetriebnahme)* **die ~ einer Sache** *(Gen.)* **beschließen** decide to bring sth. back into service; Ⓒ *(Chemie)* reactivation

**Reaktor** /reˈaktɔr/ *der;* **~s, ~en** /-ˈtoːrən/ reactor

**real** /reˈaːl/ ❶ *Adj.* Ⓐ real; Ⓑ *(wirklichkeitsbezogen)* realistic. ❷ *adv.* Ⓐ actually; Ⓑ *(wirklichkeitsbezogen)* realistically; Ⓒ *(Wirtsch.)* in real terms

**Real-: ~einkommen** *das* real income; **~enzyklopädie** *die (veralt.)* ⇒ **~lexikon**

**Realien** /reˈaːli̯ən/ *Pl.* Ⓐ *(Tatsachen)* realities *pl.*; facts *pl.*; Ⓑ *(veralt.: Naturwissenschaften)* natural sciences

**Real·injurie** *die (Rechtsw.)* assault and battery

**Realisation** /realizaˈtsi̯oːn/ *die;* **~, ~en** Ⓐ ⇒ **realisieren** A: realization; implementation; Ⓑ *(Film, Ferns.)* production

**realisierbar** *Adj.* ⇒ **realisieren** A, C: realizable; implementable; sellable

**Realisierbarkeit** *die;* **~:** practicability; feasibility

**realisieren** /realiˈziːrən/ *tr. V.* Ⓐ *(geh.: verwirklichen)* realize ‹plan, idea, proposals, aim, project, wish›; implement ‹plan, programme, decision›; Ⓑ *(geh.: verstehen)* realize; Ⓒ *(Wirtsch.)* realize ‹profit, assets, etc.›; sell ‹property›

**Realisierung** *die;* **~, ~en** ⇒ **realisieren** A, C: realization; implementation; selling

**Realismus** *der;* **~, Realismen** realism

**Realist** *der;* **~en, ~en** realist

**Realistik** *die;* **~:** realism

**Realistin** *die;* **~, ~nen** realist

**realistisch** ❶ *Adj.* realistic. ❷ *adv.* realistically

**Realität** *die;* **~, ~en** Ⓐ reality; Ⓑ *Pl. (österr.)* ⇒ **Immobilien**

**Realitäten-: ~händler** *der*, **~händlerin** *die*, **~vermittler** *der*, **~vermittlerin** *die (österr.)* estate agent (*Brit.*); real estate agent (*Amer.*)

**realitäts-, Realitäts-: ~bezogen** *Adj., adv.* ⇒ **~nah**; **~fern** ❶ *Adj.* unrealistic; ❷ *adv.* unrealistically; **~nah** ❶ *Adj.* realistic; ❷ *adv.* realistically; **~sinn** *der* sense of reality

**realiter** /reˈaːlitɐ/ *Adv. (geh.)* in reality

**Real-: ~kanzlei** *die (österr.)* estate agency (*Brit.*); real estate office (*Amer.*); **~katalog** *der (Bibliothekswesen)* subject catalogue; **~konkurrenz** *die (Rechtsw.)* accumulation of offences *(dealt with at the same trial)*; **~lexikon** *das* specialist encyclopaedia; **~lohn** *der (Wirtsch.)* real wages *pl.*; **~politik** *die* realpolitik; practical politics *sing.*; **~politiker** *der*, **~politikerin** *die* practical politician; **~schule** *die* ≈ secondary modern school (*Brit. Hist.*); **~schüler** *der*, **~schülerin** *die* ≈ secondary modern school pupil (*Brit. Hist.*); **~schul·lehrer** *der*, **~schul·lehrerin** *die* ≈ secondary modern school teacher (*Brit. Hist.*)

**Reanimation** *die (Med.)* resuscitation

**reanimieren** *tr. V. (Med.)* resuscitate

**Reaumur** /ˈreːomyːɐ/ Réaumur; ⇒ *auch* **Grad** C

**Rebbe** /ˈrɛbə/ *der;* **~[s], ~s** *(jidd.)* ⇒ **Rabbi**

**Rebe** /ˈreːbə/ *die;* **~, ~n** Ⓐ *(Wein~)* vine shoot; Ⓑ *(geh.: Weinstock)* [grape] vine

**Rebell** /reˈbɛl/ *der;* **~en, ~en** rebel; *(Aufständischer)* rebel; insurgent

**rebellieren** *itr. V.* rebel (**gegen** against)

**Rebellin** *die;* **~, ~nen** ⇒ **Rebell**

**Rebellion** /rebɛˈli̯oːn/ *die;* **~, ~en** rebellion; *(Aufstand)* rebellion; insurrection

**rebellisch** ❶ *Adj.* rebellious. ❷ *adv.* rebelliously

**Reben·saft** *der (geh.)* juice of the grape

**Reb-: ~huhn** *das* partridge; **~laus** *die* phylloxera; **~sorte** *die* type of grape; **~stock** *der* vine

**Rechaud** /reˈʃoː/ *der od. das;* **~s, ~s** Ⓐ *(Gastr.)* food/tea/coffee warmer; réchaud; Ⓑ *(südd., österr., schweiz.)* gas cooker

**rechen** /ˈrɛçn̩/ *tr. V. (bes. südd.)* rake

**Rechen** *der;* **~s, ~** Ⓐ *(bes. südd.: Harke)* rake; Ⓑ *(Gitter an Gewässern)* grating

**Rechen-: ~an·lage** *die* computer; **~art** *die* type of arithmetical operation; **~aufgabe** *die* arithmetical problem; **~automat** *der* calculator; **~brett** *das* abacus; **~buch** *das (veralt.)* arithmetic book; **~exempel** *das:* **das ist doch ein ganz einfaches ~exempel** that's a matter of simple arithmetic; **~fehler** *der* arithmetical error; **~heft** *das* arithmetic book; **~künstler** *der*, **~künstlerin** *die* mathematical genius *or* wizard; **~lehrer** *der*, **~lehrerin** *die (veralt.)* arithmetic teacher; **~maschine** *die* calculator; **~operation** *die* arithmetical operation; **~papier** *das* arithmetic paper

**Rechenschaft** *die;* **~:** account; **jmdm. über etw.** *(Akk.)* **~ geben** *od.* **ablegen** account to sb. for sth.; **von jmdm. ~ über etw.** *(Akk.)* **verlangen** demand an explanation *or* account from sb. about sth.; **jmdm. über etw.** *(Akk.)* **~ schuldig sein** *od.* **schulden** have to account to sb. for sth.; **ich bin Ihnen keine ~ schuldig** I am not answerable to you; I owe you no explanation; **jmdn. für etw. zur ~ ziehen** call *or* bring sb. to account for sth.

**Rechenschafts-: ~bericht** *der* report; **~legung** *die;* **~~, ~~en** report; **zur öffentlichen ~legung verpflichtet sein** be obliged to render public account

**Rechen-: ~schieber** *der*, **~stab** *der* slide rule; **~stunde** *die* arithmetic lesson; **~unterricht** *der* teaching of arithmetic; *(Fach)* arithmetic *no art.*; **~zentrum** *das* computer centre

**Recherche** /reˈʃɛrʃə/ *die;* **~, ~n** Ⓐ *(geh.)* investigation; enquiry; **~n über jmdn./etw. anstellen** make investigations *or* enquiries about sb./into sth.; Ⓑ *(DV)* search

**recherchieren** *(geh.)* ❶ *itr. V.* investigate; make investigations *or* enquiries. ❷ *tr. V.* investigate

**rechnen** /ˈrɛçnən/ ❶ *tr. V.* Ⓐ **eine Aufgabe ~:** work out a problem; Ⓑ *(veranschlagen)* reckon; estimate; **wir ~ pro Person drei Flaschen Bier** we are reckoning on three bottles of beer per person; **wir müssen zwei Stunden ~:** we must reckon on two hours; **alles in allem gerechnet** all in all; altogether; **gut/rund gerechnet** at a generous/rough estimate; **das ist zu hoch/niedrig gerechnet** that's an overestimate/underestimate; Ⓒ *(berücksichtigen)* take into account; **ich rechne es mir zur Ehre** *(geh.)* I consider it *or* count it an honour; Ⓓ *(einbeziehen)* count; **jmdn. zu seinen Freunden ~:** count sb. among *or* as one of one's friends; **jmdn. zu den Fachleuten ~:** rate sb. as an expert.
❷ *itr. V.* Ⓐ *(addieren)* do *or* make a calculation/calculations; **an einer Aufgabe/auf der Tafel ~:** do *or* make calculations on a problem/the blackboard; **der Lehrer rechnet mit den Kindern** the teacher is doing arithmetic with the children; **gut/schlecht ~ können** be good/bad at figures *or* arithmetic; Ⓑ *(zählen)* reckon; **vom 1. April an gerechnet** reckoning from 1 April; **in Schillingen/nach Lichtjahren ~:** reckon in shillings/light years; Ⓒ *(ugs.: be~)* calculate; estimate; **das ist zu viel gerechnet** that's too high an estimate; **er ist ein klug ~der Kopf** he is a shrewdly calculating person; Ⓓ *(wirtschaften)* budget carefully; **mit**

*old spelling (see note on page 1707)

r

jeder Mark od. jedem Pfennig ~ müssen have to count or watch every penny; Ⓔ (sich verlassen) auf jmdn./etw. od. mit jmdm./etw. ~: reckon or count on sb./sth.; Ⓕ (etw. einkalkulieren) mit etw. ~: reckon with sth.; mit einer Antwort ~: expect an answer; wir haben mit mehr Besuchern gerechnet we reckoned on or expected more visitors; man muss mit allem/mit dem Schlimmsten ~: one has to be prepared for anything/for the worst. ❸ refl. V. (sich rentieren) das rechnet sich nicht it doesn't pay

**Rechnen** das; ~s arithmetic

**Rechner** der; ~s, ~ Ⓐ (Mensch) ein guter/schlechter ~ sein be good/bad at figures or arithmetic; ein nüchterner ~ sein (fig.) be shrewdly calculating; Ⓑ (Gerät) calculator; (Computer) computer

**Rechner·architektur** die (DV) computer architecture

**Rechnerei** die; ~, ~en (ugs.) Ⓐ (das Rechnen) das war eine komplizierte ~: that was a complicated piece of figurework; dazu war eine ewige ~ nötig it involved [some] endless calculations; Ⓑ (Rechnung) calculation

**rechner·gesteuert** Adj. (Elektronik) computer-controlled

**Rechnerin** die ⇒ Rechner A

**rechnerisch** ❶ Adj. arithmetical; ‹value› in figures; die ~e Ermittlung des Schadens calculating the damage in figures. ❷ adv. ‹determine› by calculation, mathematically; diese Ergebnisse sind ~ falsch the figurework in these results is wrong

**rechner·unterstützt** Adj. computer-aided

**Rechnung** die; ~, ~en Ⓐ (Aus~) calculation; [jmdm.] eine ~ aufmachen work it out [for sb.]; seine ~ geht [nicht] auf (fig.) his plans [do not] work out; Ⓑ (schriftliche Kosten~) bill; invoice (Commerc.); eine hohe/niedrige ~: a large/small bill; eine ~ über 500 Mark a bill for 500 marks; die ~ beträgt od. macht ... the bill is for ...; die ~ ist überfällig the account is overdue; etw. [mit] auf die ~ setzen put sth. on or add sth. to the bill; das geht auf meine ~: I'm paying for that; diese Runde od. Lage geht auf meine ~: this round's on me; this is my round; etw. auf ~ bestellen/kaufen order/buy sth. on account; er hatte aber die ~ ohne den Wirt gemacht (fig.) there was one thing he hadn't reckoned with; [mit jmdm.] eine [alte] ~ begleichen (fig.) settle a[n old] score [with sb.]; auf seine od. (schweiz.) die ~ kommen get one's money's worth; auf eigene ~: on one's own account; (auf eigenes Risiko) at one's own risk; [jmdm.] etw. in ~ stellen charge [sb.] for sth.; Ⓒ (Be~, Überlegung) calculation; nach meiner ~: according to my calculations; einer Sache (Dat.) ~ tragen, etw. in ~ stellen od. setzen take sth. into account; ⇒ auch begleichen

**Rechnungs-:** ~art die type of calculation; ~betrag der amount of a/the bill/invoice; ~block der; Pl. ~~s od. ~blöcke receipt pad; ~buch das Ⓐ accounts book or ledger; Ⓑ (schweiz.) ⇒ Rechenbuch; ~einheit die (Geldw.) unit of account; ~fehler der (schweiz.) ⇒ Rechenfehler; ~führung die ⇒ Buchführung; ~hof der audit office; ~jahr das financial or fiscal year; ~prüfer der, ~prüferin die auditor; ~prüfung die (Wirtsch., Politik) audit; ~wesen das (Wirtsch.) accountancy no art.

**recht** /rɛçt/ ❶ Adj. Ⓐ (geeignet) right; Ⓑ (richtig) right; ganz ~! quite right!; das ist ~, so ist es ~, (ugs.) ~ so that's fine; bin ich hier ~? am I in the right place?; Ⓒ (gesetzmäßig, anständig) right; proper; was dem einen ~ ist, ist dem anderen billig (Spr.) what's sauce for the goose is sauce for the gander (prov.); ~ und billig right and proper; alles, was ~ ist (das kann man nicht leugnen) you've got to give him/it etc. his/its etc. due; (das geht zu weit) there is a limit; Ⓓ (wunschgemäß) jmdm. ~ sein be all right with sb.; es war ihr nicht ~, dass ... she was not pleased that ...; wenn es dir ~ ist if it's all right with you; Ⓔ (wirklich, echt) real; keine ~e Lust haben, etw. zu tun not particularly or really feel like doing sth.; Ⓕ (ziemlich) er hat sich ~e Mühe gegeben he made quite an effort; er ist noch ein ~es Kind (veralt.) he is still a child.
❷ adv. Ⓐ (geeignet) du kommst gerade ~, um zu ... you are just in time or you've come just at the right time to ...; du kommst mir gerade ~ (auch iron.) you're just the person I needed; Ⓑ (richtig) correctly; wenn ich es mir ~ überlege, dann ... if I really stop and think about it; verstehen Sie mich bitte ~: please don't misunderstand me; habe ich ~ gehört? did I hear right or correctly?; ich denke, ich höre nicht ~ (ugs.) I think I must be hearing things; gehe ich ~ in der Annahme, dass ...? am I right in assuming that ...?; Ⓒ (gesetzmäßig, anständig) ~ handeln/leben act/live properly; tue ~ und scheue niemand (Spr.) do what's right and fear no one; ⇒ auch Recht D; geschehen C; Ⓓ (wunschgemäß) man kann ihm nichts ~ machen there's no pleasing him; man kann es nicht allen ~ machen you can't please everyone; Ⓔ (wirklich, echt) really; rightly; er kann sich nicht ~ entscheiden he cannot really or rightly decide; die Wunde will nicht ~ heilen the wound is not healing properly; ⇒ auch erst 2; Ⓕ (ziemlich) quite; rather; „~ herzliche Grüße, Dein Peter" 'best wishes, Peter'

**recht...** Adj. Ⓐ right; right[-hand] ‹edge›; die ~e Spur the right-hand lane; ~er Hand, zur ~en Hand, auf der ~en Seite on the right-hand side; auf der ~en Seite gehen walk on the right; der ~e Außenstürmer/Verteidiger (Ballspiele) the outside right/the right back; Ⓑ (außen, sichtbar) right ‹side›; ~e Maschen (Handarb.) knit stitches; eine ~e Masche stricken knit one; Ⓒ (in der Politik) right-wing; rightist (derog.); der ~e Flügel einer Partei the right wing of a party; Ⓓ (Geom.) ein ~er Winkel a right angle

**Recht** das; ~[e]s, ~e Ⓐ (~sordnung) law; das ~ brechen/beugen break/bend the law; ~ sprechen administer the law; administer justice; von ~s wegen by law; (ugs.: eigentlich) by rights; gegen ~ und Gesetz verstoßen infringe or violate the law; Ⓑ (~sanspruch) right; das ~ haben, etw. zu tun have the right to do sth.; das ~ des Stärkeren the law of the jungle; das ist sein gutes ~: that is his right; alle ~e vorbehalten all rights reserved; mit welchem ~ hat er das getan? by what right did he do that?; gleiche ~e, gleiche Pflichten (Spr.) equal rights mean equal obligations; sein ~ fordern od. verlangen demand one's rights; der Körper verlangt sein ~: the body demands its due; zu seinem ~ kommen (fig.) be given due attention; auf sein ~ pochen insist or stand on one's rights; Ⓒ (Berechtigung) right (auf + Akk. to); gleiches ~ für alle! equal rights for all!; das ~ war auf seiner Seite he had right on his side; etw. mit [gutem] ~ tun be [quite] right to do sth.; das Gericht hat für ~ erkannt, dass ... the court has decided or has reached the verdict that ...; im ~ sein be in the right; zu ~: rightly; with justification; Ⓓ ~ haben be right; ~ behalten be proved right; jmdm. ~ geben concede or admit that sb. is right; ~ bekommen win one's case; Ⓔ Pl. (veralt.: Jura) jurisprudence; Doktor beider ~e Doctor of Laws

**Rechte**[1] der/die; adj. Dekl. right-winger; rightist (derog.); die ~n the right sing.

**Rechte**[2] die; adj. Dekl. Ⓐ (Hand) right hand; seine ~ einsetzen (Boxen) use one's right; zur ~n des Königs on or to the right of the king; jmdm. zur ~n to the right of sb.; zur ~n on the right; Ⓑ (Politik) right

**Recht·eck** das rectangle

**recht·eckig** Adj. rectangular

**Rechte·hand·regel** die (Physik) right-hand rule

**rechten** itr. V. (geh.) argue; dispute

**rechtens**, ***Rechtens**[1] Adv. (von Rechts wegen) legally; by law; (zu od. mit Recht) rightly

**Rechtens**[2] in ~ sein be legal

**rechter·seits** Adv. on the right[-hand side]

**recht·fertigen** ❶ tr. V. justify; sein Handeln ist durch nichts zu ~: nothing can justify his behaviour; etw. vor jmdm. ~: justify sth. to sb.; er hat sich bemüht, das in ihn gesetzte Vertrauen zu ~: he tried to live up to the trust placed in him. ❷ refl. V. justify oneself (vor + Dat. to)

**Recht·fertigung** die justification; er konnte nichts zu seiner ~ vorbringen he could not say anything to justify himself

**Rechtfertigungs·grund** der justification

**recht-, Recht-:** ~gläubig Adj. orthodox; ~gläubigkeit die orthodoxy; ~haber der; ~~s, ~~ (abwertend) self-opinionated person; er ist ein ~haber he's self-opinionated; he always thinks he's right; ~haberei die; ~~ (abwertend) self-opinionatedness; ~haberin die; ~~, ~~nen ⇒ ~haber; ~haberisch (abwertend) ❶ Adj. self-opinionated; ❷ adv. in a self-opinionated manner

**rechtlich** ❶ Adj. Ⓐ legal; Ⓑ (veralt.: rechtschaffen) upright; honest. ❷ adv. Ⓐ legally; ~ nicht zulässig not permissible in law; illegal; etw. ~ verankern establish sth. in law; Ⓑ (veralt.: rechtschaffen) uprightly; honestly; ein ~ denkender Mensch an honest-minded person

**Rechtlichkeit** die; ~ ⇒ Rechtmäßigkeit

**recht·los** Adj. without rights postpos.; jmdn. ~ machen deprive sb. of his/her etc. rights; die ~e Stellung der Sklaven the slaves' position without rights

**Rechtlosigkeit** die; ~: lack of rights

**rechtmäßig** ❶ Adj. lawful; rightful; legitimate ‹claim›. ❷ adv. lawfully; rightfully; das steht ihm ~ zu that is his by right or rightfully his; etw. ~ beanspruchen have a legal or rightful claim to sth.

**Rechtmäßigkeit** die; ~: legality; lawfulness; (eines Anspruchs) legitimacy

**rechts** ❶ Adv. Ⓐ ▶ 818 (auf der rechten Seite) on the right; (Theater) stage left; die zweite Straße ~: the second street or turning on the right; ~ von jmdm./etw. on sb.'s right or the right of sb./on or to the right of sth.; von ~ kommen come from the right; nach ~ gehen/sich nach ~ wenden go/turn to the right; sich ~ halten keep to the right; sich ~ einordnen move or get into the right-hand lane; ~ außen (Ballspiele) ‹run, break through› down the right wing; [den Ball] nach ~ außen spielen play the ball out to the right wing; ⇒ auch links A; Ⓑ (Politik) on the right wing; ~ stehen od. sein be right-wing or on the right; ~ eingestellt sein have right-wing leanings; weit ~ stehen be on the far right; ganz ~ außen stehen be on the extreme right [wing]; nach ~ außen to the extreme right; ~ stehend right-wing; Ⓒ (ugs.: ~händig) right-handed; alles mit ~ machen do everything right-handed or with the right hand; Ⓓ (Handarb.) ein glatt ~ gestrickter Pullover a pullover in stocking stitch; ⇒ auch links 1 D; Ⓔ (~seitig) on the right [side]; etw. von ~ bügeln iron sth. on the right side; nach ~ wenden turn ‹dress, skirt, etc.› right side out.
❷ ▶ 818 Präp. mit Gen. ~ des Rheins/der Straße on the right side or bank of the Rhine/on the right-hand side of the road or to the right of the road

**Rechts-:** ~abbieger der, ~abbiegerin die (Verkehrsw.) motorist/cyclist/car etc. turning right; die ~abbieger the traffic sing. turning right; ⇒ auch Linksabbieger; ~abbieger·spur die (Verkehrsw.) right-turn lane; ~ab·teilung die legal department; ~abweichler der, ~abweichlerin die (Politik) right deviationist; ~angelegenheit die legal matter; ~anspruch der legal right or entitlement; einen ~anspruch auf etw.

(*Akk.*) **haben** have a legal right to *or* be legally entitled to sth.; **~anwalt** *der*, **~anwältin** *die* ▶ 159 lawyer; solicitor (*Brit.*); attorney (*Amer.*); (*vor Gericht*) barrister (*Brit.*); attorney[-at-law] (*Amer.*); advocate (*Scot.*); **sich** (*Dat.*) **einen ~anwalt nehmen** get a lawyer *or* (*Amer.*) an attorney

**Rechtsanwalts-: ~büro** *das*, **~kanzlei** *die* ⇒ Anwaltsbüro

**rechts-, Rechts-: ~auffassung** *die* (*Rechtsw.*) conception of legality; **~aufsicht** *die: state supervision of the legality of administrative acts;* **~auskunft** *die* piece of legal advice; **~auskünfte** legal advice *sing.*; ***~außen** ⇒ rechts 1A, B; **~außen** *der; ~~, ~~* Ⓐ (*Ballspiele*) right wing; outside right; Ⓑ (*Politik ugs.*) extreme right-winger; **~beistand** *der* ▶ 159 legal adviser; **~beratung** *die* legal advice; **~beugung** *die* (*Rechtsw.*) perversion of justice *or* the law; **~bewusst·sein** ***~bewußt·sein** *das*, sense of [what is] right and wrong; **~brecher** *der*, **~brecherin** *die; ~~, ~~nen* lawbreaker

**recht-, Recht-: ~schaffen** ❶ *Adj.* honest; upright; honest, decent ‹work›; ❷ *adv.* Ⓐ (*ehrlich, redlich*) honestly; uprightly; **~schaffen leben** live an honest[, decent] life; Ⓑ (*intensivierend*) really ‹tired, full, etc.›; **~schaffenheit** *die; ~:* honesty, uprightness; **~schreib[e]·buch** *das* spelling book; speller; (*Wörterbuch*) spelling dictionary; **~schreiben** *itr. V.; nur im Inf. gebr.* spell; **sie ist im ~schreiben schwach** she's poor at spelling; **~schreibfehler** *der* spelling mistake; **~schreibung** *die* orthography; **~schreib·wörter·buch** *das* spelling dictionary

**rechts-, Rechts-: ~drall** *der* Ⓐ pull to the right; **der Wagen hatte einen ~drall** the car was pulling to the right; **der Tennisspieler gab dem Ball einen ~drall** the tennis player swerved the ball to the right; Ⓑ (*Waffent.*) right-handed twist; Ⓒ (*Politik ugs.*) tendency to the right; right-wing tendency; **~drehend** *Adj.* Ⓐ (*bes. Technik*) right-hand ‹thread›; Ⓑ (*Chemie, Physik*) dextrorotatory; **~drehung** *die* (*Chemie, Physik*) dextrorotation; **~empfinden** *das* sense of [what is] right and wrong; **~extremismus** *der* (*Politik*) right-wing extremism; **~extremist** *der*, **~extremistin** *die* (*Politik*) right-wing extremist; **~fähig** *Adj.* (*Rechtsw.*) having legal capacity *postpos., not pred.*; **~fähigkeit** *die* legal capacity; **~fall** *der* (*Rechtsw.*) legal case; court case; **~findung** *die; ~~* (*Rechtsw.*) legal finding; **~frage** *die* (*Rechtsw.*) legal question *or* issue; **~gängig** *Adj.* ⇒ **~drehend** A; **~gefühl** *das* sense of [what is] right and wrong; **~gelehrte** *der/die* jurist; **~gerichtet** *Adj.* (*Politik*) right-wing orientated; **~geschäft** *das* legal transaction; **~geschichte** *die* legal history; **~gewinde** *das* (*Technik*) right-hand thread; **~grund** *der* (*Rechtsw.*) cause in law; **~grund·satz** *der* (*Rechtsw.*) legal principle; **~gültig** (*Rechtsw.*) ❶ *Adj.* legally valid; ❷ *adv.* **etw. ~gültig abschließen** conclude sth. in legally valid form; **~gut** *das* (*Rechtsw.*) object/interest protected by law; **~handel** *der; Pl.* **~händel** (*geh.*) lawsuit; court case; **~händer** /-hɛndɐ/ *der; ~~s, ~~,* **~händerin** *die; ~~, ~~nen* right-hander; **~händer[in] sein** be right-handed; **~händig** ❶ *Adj.* right-handed; ❷ *adv.* right-handed; with one's right hand; **~händigkeit** *die; ~~:* righthandedness; **~handlung** *die* (*Rechtsw.*) legal act; **~hängigkeit** *die; ~~* (*Rechtsw.*) pendency; **~herum** *Adv.* [round] to the right; **etw. ~herum drehen** turn sth. clockwise *or* [round] to the right; **~hilfe** *die* (*Rechtsw.*) [official] assistance between courts; **~kraft** *die* (*Rechtsw.*) legal force; **einer Sache** (*Dat.*) **~kraft verleihen** make sth. law; give legal effect to sth.; **~kräfte** *Pl.* (*Politik*) right-wing forces; **~kräftig** (*Rechtsw.*) ❶ *Adj.* final [and absolute] ‹decision, verdict, etc.›; **~kräftig sein/werden** ‹contract, agreement› be in/come into force; ❷ *adv.* **jmdn. ~kräftig verurteilen** pass a final sentence on sb.; **die Ehe wurde ~kräftig geschieden** the divorce became absolute; **~kundig** *Adj.* versed in the law *postpos.*; **~kurve** *die* right-hand bend; **~lage** *die* (*Rechtsw.*) legal situation; **~lastig** *Adj.* Ⓐ ‹ship› listing to the right; ‹car› down at the right, leaning to the right; Ⓑ (*Politik ugs.*) rightist; **~läufig** *Adj.* (*bes. Technik*) running from left to right; **~lehre** *die* ⇒ **~wissenschaft**; **~liberal** *Adj.* right-wing liberal; **~liberale** *der/die* right-wing liberal; **~missbrauch**, ***~mißbrauch** *der* (*Rechtsw.*) abuse of a/one's right; **~mittel** *das* (*Rechtsw.*) appeal; **es ist kein ~mittel zulässig** there is no right of appeal; **~mittel einlegen** lodge an appeal; appeal; **~mittelbelehrung** *die* (*Rechtsw.*) information *no pl., no indef. art.* on one's right to appeal; **~nachfolge** *die* Ⓐ (*Rechtsw.*) succession [to rights and obligations]; Ⓑ (*Staatensukzession*) succession; **~norm** *die* (*Rechtsw.*) legal norm; **~ordnung** *die* legal system; **~partei** *die* (*Politik*) right-wing party; **~pflege** *die* (*Rechtsw.*) administration of justice; **~pfleger** *der*, **~pflegerin** *die: official with certain administrative and judicial powers;* **~philosophie** *die* philosophy of law

**Rechtsprechung** *die; ~, ~en* administration of justice; (*eines Gerichts*) jurisdiction

**rechts-, Rechts-: ~radikal** (*Politik*) ❶ *Adj.* radical right-wing; ❷ *adv.* **eine ~radikal orientierte Gruppe** a group with a radical right-wing orientation; **~radikale** *der/die* right-wing radical; **~radikalismus** *der* right-wing radicalism; **~rheinisch** ❶ *Adj.* on *or* to the right of the Rhine *postpos.*; **auf der ~rheinischen Seite** on the right side of the Rhine; ❷ *adv.* on *or* to the right of the Rhine; **~ruck** *der* (*Politik ugs.*) shift to the right; **~rum** *Adv.* (*ugs.*) ⇒ **~herum**; **~sache** *die* (*Rechtsw.*) legal matter; (*Streitsache*) case; **~schutz** *der* (*Rechtsw.*) legal protection; **~schutz·versicherung** *die* insurance for legal costs; **~seitig** ❶ *Adj.* ‹paralysis› of the right side; **die ~seitige Uferbefestigung** the reinforcement of the right bank; ❷ *adv.* on the right [side]; **~seitig gelähmt sein** be paralysed on *or* down the *or* one's right side; **~sicherheit** *die* (*Rechtsw.*) certainty of the law; **~sprache** *die* (*Sprachw.*) legal terminology; **~spruch** *der* judgement; **~staat** *der* [constitutional] state founded on the rule of law; **~staatlich** ❶ *Adj.* founded on the rule of law *postpos.*; ❷ *adv.* **~staatlich orientiert** oriented towards maintaining and promoting the rule of law *postpos.*; **~staatlich einwandfrei** legally correct; **~staatlichkeit** *die; ~~:* rule of law; ***~stehend** ⇒ rechts 1B; **~steuerung** *die* right-hand drive; **~streit** *der* lawsuit; **~titel** *der* (*Rechtsw.*) legal title; **~um** *Adv.* (*bes. Milit.*) to the right; **~um kehrt!** to the right about turn!; **~um machen** do a right turn; **~unsicherheit** *die* (*Rechtsw.*) uncertainty regarding the law; **~verbindlich** *Adj.* (*Rechtsw.*) legally binding; **~verdreher** *der; ~~s, ~~,* **~verdreherin** *die; ~~, ~~nen* Ⓐ (*abwertend*) person who twists the law; shyster (*Amer. sl.*); Ⓑ (*ugs. scherzh.: ~anwalt*) legal eagle (*coll.*); **~verkehr** *der* driving *no art.* on the right; **in Frankreich ist ~verkehr** they drive on the right in France; **~verletzung** *die* (*Rechtsw.*) infringement *or* violation of the law; **~verordnung** *die* (*Rechtsw.*) statutory instrument; **~vertreter** *der*, **~vertreterin** *die* (*Rechtsw.*) legal representative; **~weg** *der* (*Rechtsw.*) recourse to legal action *or* the courts *or* the law; **den ~weg beschreiten** (*geh.*) take legal proceedings *or* action; go to the courts *or* to court; **unter Ausschluss des ~wegs** without the possibility of recourse to legal action *or* the courts *or* the law; **~wesen** *das* legal system; **~widrig** ❶ *Adj.* unlawful; illegal; ❷ *adv.* unlawfully; illegally; **~widrigkeit** *die* Ⓐ unlawfulness; illegality; Ⓑ (*Handlung*) unlawful act; **~wirksam** *Adj.* ⇒ **~gültig**; **~wissenschaft** *die* jurisprudence; **Professor für ~wissenschaft** Professor of Law; **~wissenschaftler** *der*, **~wissenschaftlerin** *die* ▶ 159 jurist

**recht-: ~wink[e]lig** *Adj.* right-angled; **~zeitig** ❶ *Adj.* (*früh genug*) timely; (*pünktlich*) punctual; **wir bitten um ~zeitige Lieferung** please deliver in good time; ❷ *adv.* (*früh genug*) in time; (*pünktlich*) on time; **~zeitig zu/zum/zur** in [good] time for; **sagen Sie mir bitte ~zeitig Bescheid** please let me know in good time; **~zeitig zu Bett gehen** go to bed early

**Reck** /rɛk/ *das; ~[e]s, ~e od. ~s* horizontal bar; high bar

**Recke** /ˈrɛkə/ *der; ~n, ~n* (*geh.*) warrior

**recken** ❶ *tr. V.* Ⓐ stretch; **den Hals/Kopf ~:** crane one's neck; **die Faust ~:** raise one's fist; Ⓑ (*bes. nordd.: in Form ziehen*) **etw ~:** pull sth. back into shape. ❷ *refl. V.* stretch oneself; **sich ~ und strecken** have a good stretch

**Reck-: ~stange** *die* horizontal *or* high bar; **~turnen** *das* horizontal-bar exercises *pl.*

**Recorder** /reˈkɔrdɐ/ *der; ~s, ~:* recorder

**recyceln** /riˈsai̯kl̩n/ *tr. V.; 2. Part.* **recycelt** recycle

**Recycling** /riˈsai̯klɪŋ/ *das; ~s* recycling

**Redakteur** /redakˈtøːɐ̯/ *der; ~s, ~e,* **Redakteurin** *die; ~, ~nen* ▶ 159 editor; **~ für Politik/Wirtschaft** political/economics editor; **~ vom Dienst** duty editor

**Redaktion** /redakˈt͜si̯oːn/ *die; ~, ~en* Ⓐ (*Redakteure*) editorial staff; Ⓑ (*Büro*) editorial department *or* office/offices *pl.*; Ⓒ (*Fach~*) editorial department; Ⓓ (*das Redigieren*) editing

**redaktionell** /redakt͜si̯oˈnɛl/ ❶ *Adj.* editorial; **die ~e Verantwortung tragen** be responsible for the editing. ❷ *adv.* editorially; **etw. ~ bearbeiten** edit sth.

**Redaktions·schluss**, ***Redaktions·schluß** *der* time of going to press; **nach ~:** after going to press

**Redaktor** /reˈdaktɔr/ *der; ~s, ~en* /-ˈtoːrən/, **Redaktorin** *die; ~, ~nen* (*bes. schweiz.*) editor

**Rede** /ˈreːdə/ *die; ~, ~n* Ⓐ speech; (*Ansprache*) address; speech; **eine ~ halten** give *or* make a speech; **die ~ des Betriebsleiters** the manager's speech; ⇒ *auch* **schwingen**; Ⓑ (*Vortrag*) rhetoric; **die Kunst/Gabe der ~:** the art/gift of rhetoric; **etw. in freier ~ vortragen** make a speech *or* speak about sth. without notes; Ⓒ (*Äußerung, Ansicht*) **~ und Gegenrede** dialogue; **„…", das war seine stehende od. ständige ~:** '…' was one of his favourite sayings; **der langen ~ kurzer Sinn ist, dass …** the long and the short of it is that …; **das war schon immer meine ~** (*ugs.*) that is what I've always said; **lockere/kluge ~n** loose/clever talk *sing.*; **dumme ~n führen** talk nonsense; **die ~ auf ein anderes Thema bringen** turn the conversation to another subject; **von jmdm./etw. ist die ~:** there is some talk about sb./sth.; **es ist die ~ davon, dass …** it is being said *or* people are saying that …; **davon kann keine ~ sein** it's out of the question; **nicht der ~ wert sein** be not worth mentioning; **jmdm. ~ und Antwort stehen** give a full explanation [of one's actions] to sb.; **jmdn. zur ~ stellen** make someone explain himself/herself; **die in ~ stehende Person/der in ~ stehende Fall** (*Papierdt.*) the person/case in question; Ⓓ (*Gerücht*) **es geht die ~, dass …** (*geh.*) there is a rumour *or* it is rumoured that …; Ⓔ (*Sprachw.*) **[direkte od. wörtliche/indirekte] ~:** [direct/indirect] speech; **gebundene/ungebundene ~:** verse/prose

**rede-, Rede-: ~duell** *das* duel of words; **~figur** *die* (*Rhet., Stilk.*) figure of speech; **~fluss**, ***~fluß** *der* (*abwertend*) flow of words; **~freiheit** *die* freedom of speech; **~gewandt** *Adj.* eloquent; **~gewandtheit** *die* eloquence; **~kunst** *die* rhetoric

**reden** ❶ *tr. V.* Ⓐ (*sagen*) say; speak; **kein Wort ~:** not say *or* speak a word; Ⓑ (*sprechen*) talk; **Unsinn/viel ~:** talk nonsense/(*coll.*) a lot; **es wird immer viel geredet** there is always a lot of talk (*coll.*); **es kann**

*old spelling (see note on page 1707)

r

**dir doch egal sein, was über dich geredet wird** it should not matter to you what people say about you; **etw. zu ~ haben** have sth. to talk about; **C** **jmdn. besoffen ~** (*salopp*) drive sb. round the bend with one's nattering (*Brit. coll.*) *or* chattering. **2** *itr. V.* **A** (*sprechen*) talk; speak; **viel/wenig ~:** talk a lot (*coll.*)/not talk much; **er redete vor sich hin** he was talking to himself; **darüber ließe sich ~:** that's a possibility; **B** (*sich äußern, eine Rede halten*) speak; **er lässt mich nicht zu Ende ~:** he doesn't let me finish what I'm saying; **wer redet heute Abend?** who is to speak this evening?; **gut ~ können** be a good speaker; ⇒ *auch* **gut** 2 B; **C** (*sich unterhalten*) talk; **mit jmdm./über jmdn. ~:** talk to/about sb.; **darüber wird noch zu ~ sein** we shall have to come back to that; **miteinander ~:** have a talk [with one another]; **mit ihm kann man nicht ~:** you just can't talk to him; **sie ~ nicht mehr miteinander** they are no longer on speaking terms; **so lasse ich nicht mit mir ~:** I won't be spoken to like that; **~ wir nicht mehr darüber!** let's not talk about it any more; **was gibt es da groß zu ~?** so what?; **nicht zu ~ von ...** not to mention ...; **mit sich ~ lassen** (*bei Geschäften*) be open to offers; (*bei Meinungsverschiedenheiten*) be willing to discuss the matter; **von sich ~ machen** make a name for oneself.
**3** *refl. V.* **sich heiser/in Wut ~:** talk oneself hoarse/into a rage

**Redens·art** *die* **A** expression; (*Sprichwort*) saying; **B** *Pl.* (*Phrase*) empty *or* meaningless words; **allgemeine ~en** empty generalizations; **jmdn. mit ~en abspeisen** put sb. off with [fine] words

**Reden·schreiber** *der*, **Reden·schreiberin** *die* speechwriter

**Rederei** *die; ~, ~en* **A** talking; talk; **B** (*Pl.: Gerücht*) **die ~en über seine Vergangenheit** the gossip *sing.* about his past

**Rede-: ~schwall** *der* (*abwertend*) torrent of words; **~strom** *der* ⇒ **~fluss**; **~verbot** *das* ban on speaking; **~verbot haben/erhalten** be banned from speaking; **~weise** *die* manner of speaking; **~wendung** *die* **A** (*Sprachw.*) idiom; idiomatic expression; **B** (*Floskel*) expression; phrase; **~zeit** *die:* **die ~zeit auf zehn Minuten begrenzen** restrict speakers to ten minutes; **er musste aufhören, seine ~zeit war abgelaufen** he had to stop speaking because he had run out of time

**redigieren** /redi'gi:rən/ *tr. V.* edit

**redlich** **1** *Adj.* **A** (*rechtschaffen, aufrichtig*) honest; honest, upright ‹person›; **B** (*intensivierend*) real ‹effort›. **2** *adv.* **A** (*rechtschaffen, aufrichtig*) honestly; **sich ~ durchs Leben schlagen** make an honest living; **bleibe im Lande und nähre dich ~** (*Spr.*) stay here where you can earn a decent living; **B** (*intensivierend*) really

**Redlichkeit** *die; ~:* honesty

**Redner** *der; ~s, ~* **A** (*Vortragender*) speaker; **B** (*Rhetoriker*) orator; **er ist kein ~:** he is no orator; he is not a good speaker

**Redner·bühne** *die* [speaker's] platform *or* rostrum

**Rednerin** *die; ~, ~nen* ⇒ **Redner**

**rednerisch** **1** *Adj.* oratorical; **eine ~e Glanzleistung** a masterpiece of oratory. **2** *adv.* oratorically

**Redner-: ~liste** *die* list of speakers; **~pult** *das* lectern

**Redoute** /re'du:tə/ *die; ~, ~n* **A** (*veralt.: Festsaal*) ballroom; **B** (*österr.*) ⇒ **Maskenball**

**red·selig** *Adj.* talkative

**Red·seligkeit** *die* talkativeness

**Reduktion** /reduk'tsio:n/ *die; ~, ~en* reduction

**redundant** /redun'dant/ *Adj.* (*Sprachw., Kommunikationsf.*) redundant

**Redundanz** /redun'dants/ *die; ~, ~en* (*Sprachw., Kommunikationsf.*) redundancy

**reduzieren** /redu'tsi:rən/ **1** *tr. V.* (*auch Chemie, Physik*) reduce (**auf** + *Akk.* to). **2** *refl. V.* decrease; diminish

**Reduzierung** *die; ~, ~en* ⇒ **Reduktion**

**Reede** /'re:də/ *die; ~, ~n* (*Seew.*) roads *pl.*; roadstead; **das Schiff liegt auf der ~:** the ship is [lying] in the roads

**Reeder** *der; ~s, ~:* shipowner

**Reederei** *die; ~, ~en* shipping firm *or* company

**Reederei·flagge** *die* house flag

**Reederin** *die; ~, ~nen* ⇒ **Reeder**

**reell** /re'ɛl/ **1** *Adj.* **A** (*anständig*) honest, straight ‹person, deal, etc.›; sound, solid ‹business, firm, etc.›; straight ‹offer›; **B** (*wirklich*) real; **C** (*ugs.: den Erwartungen entsprechend*) decent; realistic ‹price›; **ein ~es Mittagessen** a solid *or* decent lunch. **2** *adv.* **A** (*anständig*) honestly; **B** (*wirklich*) actually; really; **C** (*ugs.: den Erwartungen entsprechend*) **der Wirt hat ~ eingeschenkt** the landlord poured [out] a decent measure/decent measures

**Reep** /re:p/ *das; ~[e]s, ~e* (*Seemannsspr.*) rope

**Reet** /re:t/ *das; ~s* (*nordd.*) reeds *pl.*

**Reet·dach** *das* thatched roof (*with reeds*)

**reet·gedeckt** *adj.* thatched

**REFA** /'re:fa/ *der; ~s Abk.* **Reichsausschuss für Arbeitszeitermittlung** (*heute:* **Verband für Arbeitsstudien**) work-study organization

**REFA-Fachfrau** *die*, **REFA-Fachmann** *der* work-study expert

**Refektorium** /refɛk'to:rium/ *das; ~s,* **Refektorien** refectory

**Referat** /refe'ra:t/ *das; ~[e]s, ~e* **A** (*umfangreichere Abhandlung*) paper; **ein ~ halten** give *or* present a paper; **B** (*kurzer schriftlicher Bericht*) report (+ *Gen.* on); **C** (*Abteilung, Fachgebiet*) department

**Referendar** /referɛn'da:ɐ̯/ *der; ~s, ~e,* **Referendarin** *die; ~, ~nen* *candidate for a higher civil-service post who has passed the first state examination and is undergoing in-service training*

**Referendum** /refe'rɛndum/ *das; ~s,* **Referenden** *od.* **Referenda** referendum

**Referent** /refe'rɛnt/ *der; ~en, ~en* **A** (*Vortragender*) person presenting a/the paper; (*Redner*) speaker; **B** (*Gutachter*) examiner; **C** (*Sachbearbeiter*) expert (**für** on); (*eines Ministers*) adviser (**für** on)

**Referentin** *die; ~, ~nen* ⇒ **Referent**

**Referenz** /refe'rɛnts/ *die; ~, ~en* **A** (*Empfehlung*) reference; **B** (*Person, Stelle*) referee; **jmdn. als ~ angeben** give sb.'s name *or* give sb. as a reference

**referieren** /refe'ri:rən/ **1** *itr. V.* **über etw.** (*Akk.*) **~:** give *or* present a paper on sth.; (*zusammenfassend*) give a report on sth. **2** *tr. V.* **etw. ~:** give *or* present a paper on sth.; (*zusammenfassend*) give a report on sth.

**Reff**[1] /rɛf/ *das; ~s, ~s* (*Seemannsspr.*) reef

**Reff**[2] *das; ~[e]s, ~e* (*ugs. abwertend*) old hag

**reffen** *tr.* (*auch itr.*) *V.* (*Seemannsspr.*) reef ‹sail›; **wir müssen ~:** we must reef sail

**Refinanzierung** *die* (*Geldw.*) procurement of funds to provide credit

**reflektieren** /reflɛk'ti:rən/ **1** *tr. V.* (*zurückstrahlen*) reflect. **2** *itr. V.* **A** (*nachdenken*) reflect, ponder (**über** + *Akk.* [up]on); **B** (*ugs.: streben nach*) **auf etw.** (*Akk.*) **~:** have [got] one's eye on sth. **3** *tr. V.* (*nachdenken über*) reflect [up]on; ponder

**reflektiert** **1** *Adj.* reflective. **2** *adv.* reflectively; in a reflective manner

**Reflektor** /re'flɛktɔr/ *der; ~s, ~en* /-'to:rən/ reflector

**reflektorisch** *Adj.* (*Physiol.*) reflex *attrib.*

**Reflex** /re'flɛks/ *der; ~es, ~e* **A** (*Physiol.*) reflex; **B** (*Licht~*) reflection

**Reflex-: ~bewegung** *die* reflex movement; **~handlung** *die* reflex action

**Reflexion** /reflɛ'ksio:n/ *die; ~, ~en* reflection

**Reflexions·winkel** *der* (*Physik*) angle of reflection

**reflexiv** /reflɛ'ksi:f/ **1** *Adj.* **A** (*Sprachw.*) reflexive; **B** (*geh.: reflektiert*) reflective. **2** *adv.* **A** (*Sprachw.*) reflexively; **B** (*geh.: reflektiert*) through reflection

**Reflexiv** *das; ~s, ~e,* **Reflexiv·pronomen** *das* (*Sprachw.*) reflexive pronoun

**Reform** /re'fɔrm/ *die; ~, ~en* reform

**Reformation** *die; ~* (*hist.*) Reformation

**Reformations·fest** *das* Reformation Day

**Reformator** /refɔr'ma:tɔr/ *der; ~s, ~en* /-ma'to:rən/ **A** reformer; **B** (*hist.*) Reformer

**reformatorisch** *Adj.* reformational; reformatory, reformative ‹zeal, attempts›

**reform-, Reform-: ~bedürftig** *Adj.* in need of reform *postpos.*; **~bestrebungen** *Pl.* efforts towards reform; **~bewegung** *die* reform movement

**Reformer** *der; ~s, ~,* **Reformerin** *die; ~, ~nen* reformer

**reformerisch** *Adj.* reforming *attrib.* ‹government›; ‹idea, policy, party, etc.› of reform; ‹efforts› towards reform

**reform·freudig** *Adj.* ‹person› eager for reform

**Reform·haus** *das* health food shop

**reformieren** *tr. V.* reform; **die reformierte Kirche** the Reformed Church

**Reformierte** *der/die; adj. Dekl.* member of the Reformed Church

**Reformismus** *der; ~* (*bes. Politik*) reformism

**Reformist** *der; ~en, ~en,* **Reformistin** *die; ~, ~nen* (*bes. Politik*) reformist

**reformistisch** *Adj.* (*Politik*) reformist

**Reform-: ~kost** *die* health food; **~kurs** *der* policy of reform; **auf ~kurs** (*Akk.*) **gehen** embark on a policy of reform; **~politik** *die* policy of reform

**Refrain** /rə'frɛ̃:/ *der; ~s, ~s* (*eines Lieds*) chorus; refrain; (*eines Gedichts*) refrain

**Refraktor** /re'fraktɔr/ *der; ~s, ~en* /-'to:rən/ (*Astron.*) refractor

**Refugium** /re'fu:gium/ *das; ~s,* **Refugien** (*geh.*) refuge

**Regal**[1] /re'ga:l/ *das; ~s, ~e* [set *sing.* of] shelves *pl.*; **ein Buch aus dem ~ nehmen/ins ~ zurückstellen** take a book from/put a book back on the shelf

**Regal**[2] *das; ~s, ~e* (*Musik*) regal

**Regal**[3] *das; ~s, ~ien* /...liən/ (*hist.*) [royal] prerogative

**Regal·brett** *das* shelf

**Regatta** /re'gata/ *die; ~,* **Regatten** (*Sport*) regatta

**Reg.-Bez.** *Abk.* **Regierungsbezirk**

**rege** /'re:gə/ **1** *Adj.* **A** (*betriebsam*) busy ‹traffic›; brisk ‹demand, trade, business, etc.›; **[ein] ~s Treiben** bustling activity; hustle and bustle; **~ Beteiligung** *od.* **Teilnahme** good participation *or* attendance; **~r Briefwechsel** lively correspondence; **B** (*lebhaft*) lively; lively, animated ‹discussion, conversation›; keen ‹interest›; **geistig noch sehr ~ sein** be still mentally alert *or* active; **eine ~ Fantasie** a lively *or* vivid imagination. **2** *adv.* **A** (*betriebsam*) actively; **~ an etw.** (*Akk.*) **teilnehmen** take an active part in sth.; **B** (*lebhaft*) actively; **für sein Alter bewegt er sich noch sehr ~:** he is still very active for his age; **~ plaudern** chat animatedly

**Regel** /'re:gl̩/ *die; ~, ~n* **A** (*Vorschrift*) rule; **die ~n eines Spiels/der Rechtschreibung** the rules of a game/of spelling; **die ~n des Anstands** the rules of decency; **die ~n des Verkehrs** traffic regulations; **nach allen ~n der Kunst** (*fig.*) well and truly; **B** (*Gewohnheit*) rule; custom; **die ~ sein** be the rule; **das ist bei ihm die ~:** that is his rule *or* custom; **sich** (*Dat.*) **etw. zur ~ machen** make a habit *or* rule of sth.; **[bei jmdm.] zur ~ werden** become a rule *or* habit [with sb.]; **in der** *od.* **aller ~:** as a rule; **C** (*Menstruation*) period; **die** *od.* **ihre ~ haben/bekommen** have a *or* her period; **sie hat mit 13 ihre ~ bekommen** her periods started when she was 13

r

**regelbar** *Adj.* adjustable

**regel-, Regel-: ~fall** *der* rule; **im ~fall** as a rule; **~los** ❶ *Adj.* disorderly; (*ungeregelt*) irregular; **ein ~loses Durcheinander** a confused muddle; **sie stürmten in ~loser Flucht davon** they fled pell-mell; ❷ *adv.* in a disorderly manner; (*ungeregelt*) irregularly; **~losigkeit** *die; ~~, ~~en* disorderliness; irregularity; **~mäßig** ❶ *Adj.* regular; ❷ *adv.* regularly; **sie schreibt ~mäßig** she has even *or* regular handwriting; **~mäßigkeit** *die* regularity

**regeln** ❶ *tr. V.* [A] (*festsetzen, einrichten*) settle ‹matter, question, etc.›; put ‹finances, affairs, etc.› in order; **etw. durch Gesetz ~:** regulate sth. by law; **wir haben die Sache so geregelt, dass ...** we've arranged things so that ...; **er wird die Sache schon ~** *od.* (*nordd. ugs.*) **geregelt kriegen** he will see to it; **kriegst du das geregelt?** (*nordd. ugs.*) can you manage it/that?; [B] (*einstellen, regulieren*) regulate; (*steuern*) control. ❷ *refl. V.* take care of itself; **die Sache hat sich [von selbst] geregelt** the matter has sorted itself out *or* resolved itself

**regel-, Regel-: ~recht** ❶ *Adj.* [A] (*ugs.: richtiggehend*) proper (*coll.*); real; real ‹shock›; real, absolute ‹scandal›; complete, utter ‹flop, disaster›; real, downright ‹impertinence, insult›; **eine ~rechte Schlägerei** a regular fight *or* brawl (*coll.*); **ich hatte ~rechte Angst** I was really afraid; [B] (*ordnungsgemäß*) proper; ❷ *adv.* (*ugs.: richtiggehend*) really; **ich habe mich ~recht mit ihm angefreundet** I became quite friendly with him; **jmdn. ~recht hinauswerfen** throw sb. out good and proper (*coll.*); **~studien·zeit** *die* (*Hochschulw.*) *period within which a course must be completed;* **~technik** *die* control engineering

**Regelung** *die; ~, ~en* [A] ⇒ **regeln 1 A, B:** settlement; putting in order; regulation; control; [B] (*Vorschrift*) regulation

**Regelungs·technik** *die* control engineering

**regel·widrig** ❶ *Adj.* that is against the rules *postpos.;* (*gegen die Vorschriften*) that is against the regulations *postpos.;* (*Ballspiele*) improperly taken ‹penalty kick, throw-in, etc.›; **~ sein** be against the rules/regulations; **~es Verhalten im Verkehr** breaking traffic regulations. ❷ *adv.* **sich [im Verkehr] ~ verhalten** break [traffic] regulations; **den Stürmer ~ attackieren** (*Ballspiele*) foul the forward

**Regel·widrigkeit** *die* breach of the rules/regulations

**regen** /ˈreːgn/ ❶ *tr. V.* (*geh.*) move. ❷ *refl. V.* [A] (*sich bewegen*) move; **kein Lüftchen/kein Blatt regte sich** not a breath of air/not a leaf stirred; [B] (*geh.: sich bemerkbar machen*) ‹hope, doubt, desire, conscience› stir

**Regen** *der; ~s, ~* [A] rain; **bei strömendem ~:** in pouring rain; **bei ~ wird in der Halle gespielt** if it's raining the match will be played inside; **es wird ~ geben** it will rain; it is going to rain; **es sieht nach ~ aus** it looks like rain; **auf ~ folgt Sonnenschein** (*Spr.*) good times always follow bad; **ein warmer ~** (*fig.*) a windfall; **vom** *od.* **aus dem ~ in die Traufe kommen** (*fig.*) jump out of the frying pan into the fire; **jmdn. im ~ stehen lassen** *od.* **in den ~ stellen** (*fig. ugs.*) leave sb. in the lurch; [B] (*fig.*) shower; **ein ~ von Schimpfwörtern ging auf ihn nieder** curses rained down upon him

**regen·arm** *Adj.* ‹period, region, etc.› with little rain[fall], with low rainfall; **der letzte Sommer war so ~, dass ...** there was so little rain last summer that ...

**Regen·bogen** *der* rainbow

**regen·bogen-, Regen·bogen-: ~farben, ~farbig** *Adj.* rainbow-coloured; **~haut** *die* ▸ **471** (*Anat.*) iris; **~presse** *die* (*abwertend*) gossip magazines *pl.;* **~trikot** *das* (*Radsport*) rainbow jersey

**regen-, Regen-: ~cape** *das* rain cape; **~dach** *das* rain canopy; **~dicht** *Adj.* rainproof

**Regeneration** *die* [A] regeneration; [B] (*Technik: Rückgewinnung*) reclamation

**regenerations·fähig** *Adj.* (*Biol., Med.*) capable of regeneration *postpos.*

**Regenerator** *der* (*Technik*) regenerator

**regenerieren** /regeneˈriːrən/ ❶ *refl. V.* (*Biol., Med.*) regenerate. ❷ *tr. V.* [A] (*erneuern*) regenerate; **sich ~** ‹person› recuperate; ‹group, organization, etc.› regenerate itself; [B] (*Technik: wiedergewinnen*) reclaim

**regen-, Regen-: ~fall** *der* fall of rain; **heftige/anhaltende ~fälle** heavy rains *or* heavy [falls *pl.* of] rain *sing.*/continuous rain *sing.;* **~frei** *Adj.* without rain *postpos.;* rainless; **~guss, *~guß** *der* downpour; **~haut** *die* [light] plastic mackintosh *or* (*coll.*) mac; **~macher** *der,* **~macherin** *die* rainmaker; rain doctor; **~mantel** *der* raincoat; mackintosh; mac (*coll.*); **~nass, *~naß** *Adj.* that is/are wet from the rain *postpos., not pred.;* **~nass sein** be wet from the rain; **~pfeifer** *der* (*Zool.*) plover; **~pfütze** *die* [rain] puddle; **~reich** *Adj.* ‹period, region, etc.› with high rainfall; **der letzte Frühling war so ~reich, dass ...** there was so much rain last spring that ...; **~rinne** *die* gutter; **~schauer** *der* shower [of rain]; rain shower; **~schirm** *der* umbrella

**Regent** /reˈgɛnt/ *der;* **~en, ~en** [A] (*Herrscher*) ruler; (*Monarch*) monarch; [B] (*Stellvertreter*) regent

**Regen·tag** *der* rainy day

**Regentin** *die; ~, ~nen* ⇒ **Regent**

**Regen·tonne** *die* water butt

**Regentschaft** *die; ~, ~en* regency

**Regen-: ~um·hang** *der* rain cape; **~wald** *der* (*Geogr.*) rainforest; **~wasser** *das* rainwater; **~wetter** *das* rainy *or* wet weather; **er macht ein Gesicht wie drei Tage ~wetter** (*ugs.*) he looks as miserable as sin; **~wolke** *die* rain cloud; **~wurm** *der* earthworm; **~zeit** *die* rainy season

**Reggae** /ˈrɛgeɪ/ *der;* **~[s]** reggae

**Regie** /reˈʒiː/ *die;* **~** [A] (*Theater, Film, Ferns., Rundf.*) direction; **die ~ bei etw. haben** *od.* **führen** direct sth.; **unter der ~ von ...** directed by ...; [B] (*Leitung, Verwaltung*) management; **etw. in eigene ~ bekommen** *od.* **nehmen** take over control of sth.; **unter staatlicher ~:** under state control; **etw. in eigener ~ tun** (*ugs.*) do sth. oneself

**Regie-: ~an·weisung** *die* stage direction; **~assistent** *der,* **~assistentin** *die* assistant director; **~fehler** *der* (*fig. scherzh.*) slip-up

**regieren** /reˈgiːrən/ ❶ *itr. V.* rule (**über** + *Akk.* over); ‹monarch› reign, rule (**über** + *Akk.* over); ‹party, administration› govern; (*fig.*) ‹peace, corruption, terror, etc.› reign; **der Regierende Bürgermeister von Berlin** the Governing Mayor of Berlin. ❷ *tr. V.* [A] rule; govern; ‹monarch› reign over, rule; **ein demokratisch regierter Staat** a democratically governed state; [B] (*Sprachw.*) govern, take ‹case›

**Regierung** *die; ~, ~en* [A] (*Herrschaft*) rule; (*eines Monarchen*) reign; **die ~ übernehmen** *od.* **antreten** take over; come to power; [B] (*eines Staates*) government

**regierungs-, Regierungs-: ~antritt** *der:* **bei ~antritt der Sozialisten** when the Socialists come/came to power; (*nach der Wahl auch*) when the Socialists take/took office; **~bank** *die; Pl.* **~bänke** government bench; **~beamte** *der,* **~beamtin** *die* government official; **~bezirk** *der: largest administrative division of a Land;* **~bildung** *die* formation of a/the government; **mit der ~bildung betraut werden** be asked to form a government; **~chef** *der,* **~chefin** *die* head of government; **~erklärung** *die* government statement; (*in Großbritannien*) Queen's/King's Speech; **~feindlich** *Adj.* anti-government; **~form** *die* form of government; **~freundlich** *Adj.* pro-government; **~gebäude** *das* government building; **~gewalt** *die* government power *no art.;* **~kreise** *Pl.* government circles; **~krise** *die* government crisis; **~partei** *die* ruling *or* governing party; party in power; **~präsident** *der,* **~präsidentin** *die: head of a Regierungsbezirk;* **~rat** *der* [A] (*Amtstitel*) senior civil servant; [B] (*schweiz.: Kantonsregierung*) canton government; **~rätin** *die* ⇒ **~rat A;** **~sitz** *der* seat of government; **~sprecher** *der* government spokesman; **~sprecherin** *die* government spokeswoman; **~treu** *Adj.* loyal to the government *postpos.;* **~truppe** *die* government troops *pl.;* **~umbildung** *die* government reshuffle; **~vorlage** *die* government bill; **~wechsel** *der* change of government; **~zeit** *die* rule; (*eines Monarchen*) reign; (*einer Regierung, eines Regierungschefs*) period *or* term of office; **nach 12-jähriger ~zeit** after 12 years in power *or* in office

**Regie·stuhl** *der* director's chair

**Regime** /reˈʒiːm/ *das;* **~s, ~** /reˈʒiːmə/ (*abwertend*) regime

**Regime-: ~gegner** *der,* **~gegnerin** *die* opponent of a/the regime; **~kritiker** *der,* **~kritikerin** *die* critic of a/the regime; dissident

**Regiment** /regiˈmɛnt/ *das;* **~[e]s, ~e** *od.* **~er** [A] *Pl.* **~e** (*Herrschaft*) rule; **das ~ antreten/an sich reißen** come to/seize power; **das ~ führen** (*fig.*) give the orders; **ein strenges/straffes ~ führen** (*fig.*) be strict/run a tight ship (*coll.*); [B] *Pl.* **~er** (*Milit.*) regiment

**Regiments·kommandeur** *der* regimental commander

**Region** /reˈgi̯oːn/ *die;* **~, ~en** [A] region; [B] (*geh.: Bereich, Sphäre*) sphere; **in höheren ~en schweben** have one's head in the clouds

**regional** /regi̯oˈnaːl/ ❶ *Adj.* regional. ❷ *adv.* regionally; **~ verschieden sein** differ from region to region

**Regional·aus·gabe** *die* regional edition

**Regionalismus** *der;* **~:** regionalism *no art.*

**Regional-: ~liga** *die* regional league; **~programm** *das* regional programme

**Regisseur** /reʒɪˈsøːɐ̯/ *der;* **~s, ~e, Regisseurin** *die;* **~, ~nen** (*Theater, Film*) director; (*Ferns., Rundf.*) director; producer

**Register** /reˈgɪstɐ/ *das;* **~s, ~** [A] index; [B] (*Daumen~*) thumb index; [C] (*amtliche Liste*) register; [D] (*Musik*) (*bei Instrumenten*) register; (*Orgel~*) stop; (*Tonbereich*) register; **alle ~ ziehen** (*fig.*) pull out all the stops; [E] (*hist.: Urkundensammlung*) file; [F] (*Druckw.*) register; **~ halten** be in register

**Register·tonne** *die* register tonne

**Registrator** /regɪsˈtraːtɔr/ *der;* **~s, ~en** /-straˈtoːrən/ (*veralt.*) registrar

**Registratur** /regɪstraˈtuːɐ̯/ *die;* **~, ~en** [A] (*das Registrieren*) registration; [B] (*Büro*) filing room; [C] (*Schrank, Regal*) filing cabinet; [D] (*Musik: Orgel~*) stop mechanism

**registrieren** /regɪsˈtriːrən/ *tr. V.* [A] (*eintragen, verzeichnen*) register; [B] (*aufzeichnen*) register; [C] (*bemerken*) note; register; [D] (*feststellen*) note; **alle Zeitungen registrierten den Fall** all the papers mentioned the case; **es wurde sehr wohl registriert, dass er häufig unpünktlich war** it did not pass unnoticed that he often arrived late

**Registrier·kasse** *die* cash register

**Registrierung** *die;* **~, ~en** [A] (*Eintragung, Aufzeichnung*) registration; [B] (*Feststellung*) **sich auf die ~ der Tatsachen beschränken** restrict oneself/itself to noting the facts

**Reglement** /regləˈmãː, *schweiz.:* regləˈmɛnt/ *das;* **~s, ~s** *od.* (*schweiz.*) **~e** rules *pl.*

**reglementieren** *tr. V.* regulate; regiment ‹people, life›

**Reglementierung** *die;* **~, ~en** regulation; (*Bevormundung*) regimentation

**Regler** *der;* **~s, ~** (*Technik*) regulator; (*Kybernetik*) control

**Reglette** /reˈglɛtə/ *die;* **~, ~n** (*Druckw.*) lead; reglet

**reg·los** *Adj.* ⇒ **regungslos**

**Reglosigkeit** *die;* **~** ⇒ **Regungslosigkeit**

**regnen** /ˈreːgnən/ ❶ *itr., tr. V.* (*unpers.*) rain; **es regnet** it is raining; **es regnet/regnete jeden Tag** it rains/rained every day; ⇒ *auch*

*old spelling (see note on page 1707)

r

Strom A. ❷ *itr. V.; mit sein (fig.)* rain down; **es regnete Steine** *(fig.)* stones rained down; **es regnete Briefe/Anfragen** *usw. (fig.)* there was a flood *or* deluge of letters/enquiries *etc.*

**Regner** *der;* **~s, ~:** sprinkler

**regnerisch** *Adj.* rainy; **~-trüb** dull and rainy *or* wet

**regredieren** /regre'di:rən/ *itr. V. (Psych.)* regress

**Regress, *Regreß** /re'grɛs/ *der;* **~es, ~e** Ⓐ *(Rechtsw.)* recourse; **~ auf jmdn. nehmen** have recourse against sb.; Ⓑ *(Philos.)* regress

**Regress-, *Regreß-: ~anspruch** *der (Rechtsw.)* right to compensation; **~forderung** *die (Rechtsw.)* demand *or* claim for compensation; **~forderungen stellen** demand *or* claim compensation

**Regression** /regrɛ'si̯o:n/ *die;* **~, ~en** Ⓐ **wirtschaftliche ~:** economic recession; Ⓑ *(Psych., Geol., Statistik, Biol.)* regression

**regressiv** /regrɛ'si:f/ *Adj. (Psych., Geol., Statistik, Biol.)* regressive

**regress·pflichtig, *regreß·pflichtig** *Adj.* liable for compensation *postpos.*

**regsam** *Adj. (geh.)* lively; active; **geistig ~ sein** have a lively *or* active mind

**Regsamkeit** *die;* **~** *(geh.)* liveliness; activeness

**regulär** /regu'lɛ:ɐ̯/ *Adj.* Ⓐ *(vorschriftsmäßig)* in accordance with the regulations *postpos.*; *(richtig, gesetzlich)* proper; regular ‹troops›; normal, regular ‹working hours›; **die ~e Spielzeit** *(Sport)* normal time; Ⓑ *(normal, üblich)* normal; regular ‹flight›; Ⓒ *(ugs.: regelrecht)* proper *(coll.)*; regular *(coll.)*

**Regularität** /regulari'tɛ:t/ *die;* **~, ~en** *(auch Sprachw.)* regularity

**Regulation** /regula'tsi̯o:n/ *die;* **~, ~en** Ⓐ ⇒ **Regulierung**; Ⓑ *(Biol., Med.)* regulation

**Regulativ** /regula'ti:f/ *das;* **~s, ~e** Ⓐ *(regulierendes Element)* regulative; regulator; **Angebot und Nachfrage sind ~e des Marktes** supply and demand have a regulating effect on the market; Ⓑ *(regelnde Vorschrift)* regulation

**Regulator** /regu'la:tɔr/ *der;* **~s, ~en** /-la'to:rən/ Ⓐ *(regulierende Kraft, Technik)* regulator; Ⓑ *(veralt.: Pendeluhr)* pendulum clock

**regulierbar** *Adj.* regulable; adjustable ‹backrest›

**regulieren** /regu'li:rən/ ❶ *tr. V.* regulate; *(einstellen)* adjust; regulate; set ‹clock, watch›; **automatisch regulierte Türen** automatically controlled doors. ❷ *refl. V.* regulate itself; **sich selbst ~d** self-regulating

**Regulierung** *die;* **~, ~en** ⇒ **regulieren**: regulation; adjustment; setting

**Regung** *die;* **~, ~en** *(geh.)* Ⓐ *(Bewegung)* movement; Ⓑ *(Gefühl)* stirring; **seine erste ~ war Unmut** his first emotion was displeasure; **sie folgte einer ~ ihres Herzens** she followed the promptings of her heart; Ⓒ *(Bestrebung)* striving

**regungs·los** *Adj.* motionless

**Regungslosigkeit** *die;* **~:** motionlessness; **in voller ~ verharren** stay completely motionless

**Reh** /re:/ *das;* **~[e]s, ~e** roe deer

**Rehabilitand** *der;* **~en, ~en, Rehabilitandin** *die;* **~, ~nen** *(Med.)* person undergoing rehabilitation

**Rehabilitation** *die;* **~, ~en** rehabilitation

**Rehabilitations·zentrum** *das* rehabilitation centre

**rehabilitieren** *tr. V.* rehabilitate

**Rehabilitierung** *die* rehabilitation

**reh-, Reh-: ~bock** *der* roebuck; **~braten** *der (Kochk.)* roast venison; **~braun** *Adj.* light reddish brown; **~keule** *die (Kochk.)* haunch of venison; **~kitz** *das* fawn *or* kid [of a/the roe deer]; **~rücken** *der (Kochk.)* saddle of venison; **~wild** *das (Jägerspr.)* roe deer *pl.*

**Reibach** /'raibax/ *der;* **~s** *(ugs.)* profits *pl.*; **einen [kräftigen] ~ machen** make a killing *(coll.)*

**Reib·ahle** *die (Technik)* reamer

**Reibe** /'raibə/ *die;* **~, ~n** grater

**Reib·eisen** *das* grater; **rau wie ein ~:** as rough as sandpaper; **eine Stimme wie ein ~:** a voice like a rasp

**Reibe-: ~kuchen** *der (Kochk.) grated raw potatoes fried into a pancake;* **~laut** *der (Sprachw.)* fricative

**reiben** ❶ *unr. tr. V.* Ⓐ rub; **jmdm./sich die Backen ~:** rub sb.'s/one's cheeks; **das Pferd rieb sich an der Mauer** the horse rubbed itself against the wall; **etw. sauber ~:** rub sth. clean; **etw. blank ~:** rub sth. until it shines; **einen Fleck aus einem Kleid ~:** rub a mark off a dress; **sich** *(Dat.)* **den Schlaf aus den Augen ~:** rub the sleep from one's eyes; **sich** *(Dat.)* **die Haut/die Hand wund ~:** chafe one's skin/hand; Ⓑ *(zerkleinern)* grate. ❷ *unr. itr. V.* Ⓐ rub; **mit einem Tuch über die Schuhe ~:** rub one's/sb.'s shoes with a cloth; Ⓑ *(scheuern)* ‹collar, shoes, etc.› rub (**an** + *Dat.* on). ❸ *unr. refl. V.* **sich an einem Problem ~:** come up against a problem; **sich mit jmdm. ~:** be at loggerheads with sb.; **sich [aneinander] ~:** rub each other up the wrong way

**Reiberei** *die;* **~, ~en** friction *no pl.*; **er hatte ständig ~en mit seinen Eltern** there was constant friction between him and his parents

**Reib·fläche** *die* striking surface *(of matchbox)*

**Reibung** *die;* **~, ~en** Ⓐ *(das Reiben)* rubbing; Ⓑ ⇒ **Reiberei**; Ⓒ *(Physik)* friction

**reibungs-, Reibungs-: ~elektrizität** *die (Physik)* frictional electricity; **~fläche** *die (fig.)* source of friction; **~los** ❶ *Adj.* smooth; ❷ *adv.* smoothly; **~wärme** *die (Physik)* frictional heat; **~wider·stand** *der (Physik)* frictional resistance

**reich** /raiç/ ❶ *Adj.* Ⓐ *(vermögend)* rich; **~ heiraten** marry [into] money; Ⓑ *(prächtig)* costly ‹goods, gifts›; rich ‹décor, ornamentation, finery, furnishings›; Ⓒ *(üppig)* rich; rich, abundant ‹harvest›; lavish, sumptuous ‹meal›; abundant ‹mineral resources›; productive ‹oil well›; **~ an etw.** *(Dat.)* **sein** be rich in sth.; **in ~em Maße** *(geh.)* in abundance; Ⓓ *(vielfältig)* rich ‹collection, possibilities, field of activity›; wide, large, extensive ‹selection, choice›; wide ‹knowledge, experience›; full ‹life›.
❷ *adv.* richly; **~ geschmückt** richly decorated; richly adorned ‹façade, building›; **~ verziert** highly ornate

**-reich** rich in ...; **variations~/kontrast~:** rich in variation/contrast; **wasser~ sein** have abundant water

**Reich** *das;* **~[e]s, ~e** Ⓐ empire; *(König~)* kingdom; realm; **das [Deutsche] ~** *(hist.)* the German Reich *or* Empire; **das Russische ~** *(hist.)* the Russian Empire; **das Dritte ~** *(hist.)* the Third Reich; Ⓑ *(fig.)* realm; **ins ~ der Fabel gehören** belong to the realm[s] of fantasy; **das ~ der Pflanzen/Tiere** the plant/animal kingdom; **Dein ~ komme** *(bibl.)* thy Kingdom come

**Reiche** *der/die; adj. Dekl.* rich man/woman; **die ~n** the rich

**reichen** ❶ *itr. V.* Ⓐ *(aus~)* be enough; **das Geld reicht nicht** I/we *etc.* haven't got enough money; **der Stoff reicht für ein** *od.* **zu einem Kostüm** there's enough material to make a suit; **das Brot muss noch bis Montag ~:** the bread must last till Monday; **die Farbe hat gerade gereicht** there was just enough paint; **das Seil reicht nicht** the rope's not long enough; **jetzt reichts mir aber!** now I've had enough!; **danke, es reicht** that's enough, thank you; ⇒ *auch* **langen**; Ⓑ *(sich erstrecken)* reach; ‹forest, fields, etc.› extend; **bis zu etw. ~:** extend as far as sth.; **er reicht mit dem Kopf bis zur Decke** his head touches the ceiling; **bis zum Horizont ~:** extend *or* stretch to the horizon; **sein Einfluss reicht sehr weit** his influence extends a long way; **soweit das Auge reicht** *(geh.)* as far as the eye can see; **jmdm. bis an die Schultern ~:** come up to sb.'s shoulder; **an die Grenze des Pathologischen ~:** verge on the pathological; Ⓒ **mit dem Geld/Brot** *usw.* **[nicht] ~:** [not] have enough money/bread *etc.*; **damit müssen wir ~:** we'll have to make it last.
❷ *tr. V.* Ⓐ *(geh.: entgegenhalten)* hand; *(herüber~, hinüber~)* pass; hand; **jmdm. die Hand ~:** hold out one's hand to sb.; **das Abendmahl ~:** administer *or* give Communion; **sich** *(Dat.)* **die Hand ~:** shake hands; **jmdm. Feuer ~:** give sb. a light; Ⓑ *(servieren)* serve ‹food, drink›

**reich-, Reich-: *~geschmückt** ⇒ **reich** 2; **~haltig** *Adj.* extensive; wide, large, extensive ‹range, selection›; varied ‹programme›; substantial ‹meal›; **~haltigkeit** *die;* **~~:** extensiveness; *(eines Programms)* varied content; *(einer Mahlzeit)* substantialness; **die ~haltigkeit des Materials** the wealth of material

**reichlich** ❶ *Adj.* large; substantial; ample ‹space, time, reward›; plenty of ‹time, space›; good ‹hour, year›; generous ‹tip›; **~e Niederschläge** heavy rain/hail/snow; **der Mantel ist ein bisschen ~** *(ugs.)* the coat is a bit on the large side.
❷ *adv.* amply; **~ Trinkgeld geben** tip generously; **Fleisch ist noch ~ vorhanden** there is still plenty of meat left; **~ Zeit/Platz/Gelegenheit haben** have plenty of *or* ample time/room/opportunity; **das ist ~ gerechnet** that's a generous estimate; **~ spenden** give *or* donate generously; **~ zu leben haben** live well.
❸ *Adv.* Ⓐ *(mehr als)* over; more than; **nach ~ einer Stunde** a good hour later; **~ vier Wochen** a good month; **~ 5 000 Mark** a good 5,000 marks; Ⓑ *(ugs.: ziemlich, sehr)* **~ frech/teuer/spät** a bit too cheeky/dear/late

**reichs-, Reichs-: ~acht** *die (hist.)* imperial ban; **~adel** *der (hist.)* nobility of the Empire; **~adler** *der (hist.)* Imperial Eagle; **~apfel** *der (hist.)* imperial orb; **~arbeitsdienst** *der (ns.)* Reich Labour Service; **~bahn** *die* Ⓐ *(DDR)* **Deutsche ~bahn** [East German] State Railway; Ⓑ *(hist.)* German National Railway; Ⓒ **die schwedische/japanische ~bahn** the Swedish/Japanese National Railway; **~deutsch** *Adj.* within the German Reich *postpos.*; **~deutsche** *der/die* German citizen living within the German Reich; **~grenze** *die* frontier of the Empire; **~insignien** *Pl. (hist.)* imperial insignia *pl.*; **~kanzler** *der* Ⓐ *(1871-1918)* Imperial Chancellor; Ⓑ *(Weimarer Republik)* Chancellor of the Republic; Ⓒ *(Drittes Reich)* Reich Chancellor; **~mark** *die; Pl.* **~~** *(hist.)* Reichsmark; **~präsident** *der (hist.)* President of Germany; **~regierung** *die* government of a/the nation *(under a monarch)*; **~stadt** *die (hist.)* free city *or* town of the [Holy Roman] Empire; **~stände** *Pl. (hist.)* estates of the Empire; **~tag** *der* Ⓐ *(in Schweden)* Riksdag; [Swedish] Diet; *(in Finnland)* Parliament; *(in Japan)* [Imperial *or* Japanese] Diet; Ⓑ *(hist.: bis 1806)* Imperial Diet; Diet of the Holy Roman Empire; Ⓒ *(1871-1945 in Deutschland)* Reichstag; **~tags·brand** *der (hist.)* Reichstag Fire; **~unmittel·bar** *Adj. (hist.)* subordinate directly to the Kaiser *or* Emperor *postpos.*; **~verweser** *der;* **~~s, ~~** *(hist.)* Regent of the Empire; **~wehr** *die (hist.)* German *or* Imperial Army *(1919-35)*; Reichswehr

**Reichtum** *der;* **~s, Reichtümer** /'raiçty:mɐ/ Ⓐ *(Vermögen, Besitz)* wealth (**an** + *Dat.* of); **sein seelischer/innerer ~** *(fig.)* the richness of his spirit/inner life; Ⓑ *Pl. (Vermögenswerte)* riches; **die Reichtümer der Erde** the riches of the earth; **damit kann man keine Reichtümer erwerben** one cannot get rich that way; Ⓒ *(Reichhaltigkeit)* wealth (**an** + *Dat.* of); **der ~ an Singvögeln** the abundance of songbirds; **der ~ seiner Kompositionen** the richness of his compositions

***reich·verziert** ⇒ **reich** 2

**Reich·weite** *die* Ⓐ reach; *(eines Geschützes, Senders, Flugzeugs)* range ; **sich außer ~ halten** keep out of reach/range; **in ~ sein/**

r

**kommen** be/come within reach/range; **Geschütze mit großer ~:** long-range guns; **B** (*Physik: Strahlungsweite*) range

**reif** /raif/ *Adj.* **A** (*voll entwickelt*) ripe ‹fruit, grain, cheese›; mature ‹brandy, cheese›; **das Geschwür ist ~:** the boil has come to a head; **~ für etw. sein** (*ugs.*) be ready for sth.; **er ist ~ fürs Irrenhaus** (*ugs.*) he belongs in the loony bin (*sl.*); **er brauchte nur die ~e Frucht zu pflücken** (*fig.*) it just fell into his lap; **B** (*erwachsen, erfahren*) mature; **in [den] ~eren Jahren, im ~eren Alter** in one's mature years; **die ~eren Jahrgänge** those of mature age; **C** (*ausgewogen, durchdacht*) mature; **eine ~e Leistung** (*ugs.*) a solid achievement; **~ für die** *od.* **zur Veröffentlichung sein** be ready for publication; **die Zeit ist noch nicht ~:** the time is not yet ripe

**-reif** ready for ...; **kino-/test-/olympia~:** ready for the cinema/for testing/for the Olympics; **aufführungs~:** ready to be performed

**Reif**[1] *der;* **~[e]s** hoar frost

**Reif**[2] *der;* **~[e]s, ~e** (*geh.*) (*Fingerring*) ring; (*Arm~*) bracelet; (*Diadem*) circlet

**Reife** *die;* **~ A** (*das Reifsein*) ripeness; (*das Reifen*) ripening; **während der ~:** during ripening; **zur ~ kommen** ripen; **B** (*von Menschen*) maturity; **Zeugnis der ~:** Abitur certificate; **C** (*von Gedanken, Produkten*) maturity; **mittlere ~** (*Schulw.*) *school-leaving certificate usually taken after the fifth year of secondary school*

**Reife·grad** *der* degree of ripeness

**reifen**[1] ❶ *itr. V.* **A** *mit sein* (*reif werden*) ‹fruit, cereal, cheese› ripen; ‹ovum, embryo, cheese› mature; **B** *mit sein* (*geh.: älter, reifer werden*) mature (**zu** into); **diese Erfahrungen haben ihn [zum Manne] ~ lassen** (*geh.*) these experiences made a man of him; **ein gereifter Mann** (*geh.*) a mature man; **C** *mit sein* ‹idea, plan, decision› mature; ‹resistance› develop, grow; **zur Gewissheit ~** (*geh.*) grow *or* harden into certainty. ❷ *tr. V.* (*geh.*) ripen ‹fruit, cereal›; mature ‹person›

**reifen**[2] *itr. V.* **es hat gereift** there is/was a hoar frost

**Reifen** *der;* **~s, ~ A** (*Metallband, Sportgerät*) hoop; **B** (*Gummi~*) tyre; **C** (*Schmuckstück*) (*Fingerring*) ring; (*Arm~*) bracelet; (*Diadem*) circlet

**Reifen-: ~druck** *der; Pl.* **~drücke** tyre pressure; **~panne** *die* flat tyre; puncture; **~profil** *das* [tyre] tread; **~schaden** *der* tyre defect; faulty tyre; **~wechsel** *der* tyre change

**Reife-: ~prüfung** *die: school-leaving examination for university entrance qualification;* **~zeugnis** *das* Abitur certificate

**Reif·glätte** *die* ice on the roads

**reiflich** ❶ *Adj.* [very] careful; **bei/nach ~er Überlegung** on mature consideration/after [very] careful consideration. ❷ *adv.* [very] carefully; **über etw.** (*Akk.*) **~ nachdenken** give [very] careful thought *or* consideration to sth.; consider sth. [very] carefully

**Reif·rock** *der* (*hist.*) hooped skirt

**Reifung** *die;* **~** ⇒ **reifen**[1] 1: ripening; maturing; maturation

**Reifungs·prozess,** ***Reifungs·prozeß** *der* ⇒ **reifen**[1] 1: process of ripening *or* maturing; (*eines Menschen*) stage of becoming mature

**Reigen** /ˈraign̩/ *der;* **~s, ~ A** round dance; **den ~ eröffnen/anführen** lead off [in the round dance]; **B** (*fig.*) **den ~ eröffnen** start off; **den ~ der Gratulanten eröffnen** be the first to offer congratulations; **den ~ schließen** close; finish off; **ein bunter ~ von Melodien** a medley of tunes

**Reihe** /ˈraiə/ *die;* **~, ~n A** row; **Geräte in ~ schalten** (*Elektrot.*) connect pieces of equipment in series; **in ~n** (*Dat.*) **antreten** line up; (*Milit.*) fall in; **sich in fünf ~n aufstellen** line up in five rows; form five lines; **die ~n der älteren Generation lichten sich** (*fig.*) the ranks of the older generation are thinning out; **in Reih und Glied** (*Milit.*) in rank and file; **aus der ~ tanzen** (*fig. ugs.*) be different; **nicht in der ~ sein** (*fig. ugs.*) be feeling below par; **etw. in die ~ bringen** (*fig. ugs.*) put sth. straight *or* in order; **[wieder] in die ~ kommen** (*fig. ugs.*) get [back] on one's feet; **B** (*Reihenfolge*) series; **die ~ ist an ihm/ihr** *usw.*, **er/sie** *usw.* **ist an der ~:** it's his/her *etc.* turn; **wer ist an der ~?** (*ugs.*) whose turn is it?; **Punkt drei der Tagesordnung ist jetzt an der ~:** we now come to the third item on the agenda; **du kommst jetzt an die ~** (*ugs.*) it's your turn now; **der ~ nach, nach der ~:** in turn; one after the other; **C** (*größere Anzahl*) number; **eine ganze ~ Frauen** a whole lot of women (*coll.*); **D** (*Gruppe*) ranks *pl.;* **die ~n schließen** close ranks; **aus den eigenen ~n** from one's/its own ranks; **E** (*bes. Fußball*) **aus der zweiten ~ schießen** take a long shot/long shots [at goal]; **F** (*Math.*) series; **G** (*Schach*) rank; **H** (*Musik*) series

**reihen**[1] (*geh.*) ❶ *tr. V.* (*auf~*) string; thread; **Perlen auf eine Schnur ~:** string pearls [on a thread]; **um etw. gereiht sein** be ranged around sth.; **Zahl an Zahl ~:** string numbers together. ❷ *refl. V.* (*sich an~, ein~*) follow; **sich um jmdn. ~:** gather round sb.

**reihen**[2] *tr. V.* (*heften*) tack; baste

**Reihen** *der;* **~s, ~** (*veralt.*) ⇒ **Reigen**

**reihen-, Reihen-: ~dorf** *das* ⇒ **Straßendorf**; **~folge** *die* order; **die ~folge einhalten** keep in order *or* sequence; **in kurzer ~folge** in quick succession; **~haus** *das* terraced house; **~schaltung** *die* (*Elektrot.*) series connection; **~untersuchung** *die* (*Med.*) mass screening; **~weise** *Adv.* **A** (*ugs.: in großer Zahl*) by the dozen; **B** (*in ~*) in rows *or* lines

**Reiher** *der;* **~s, ~:** heron

**Reiher·feder** *die* heron feather

**reihern** *itr. V.* (*salopp*) puke (*coarse*)

**Reih·garn** *das* tacking *or* basting thread

**reih·um** *Adv.* **etw. ~ gehen lassen** pass sth. round; **die Flasche ging ~:** the bottle went *or* was passed round; **etw. ~ tun** do sth. in turn

**Reihung** *die;* **~, ~en** ⇒ **reihen**[1] 1: stringing; threading; ranging

**Reim** /raim/ *der;* **~[e]s, ~e** rhyme; **einen ~ auf ein Wort suchen** try to find something to rhyme with a word; **sich** (*Dat.*) **keinen ~ auf etw.** (*Akk.*) **machen [können]** (*fig.*) not [be able] to see rhyme or reason in sth.

**reimen** ❶ *itr. V.* make up rhymes. ❷ *tr. V.* rhyme; **ein Wort auf ein anderes ~:** rhyme one word with another; **eine gereimte Fabel** a fable in rhyme. ❸ *refl. V.* rhyme (**auf** + *Akk.* with); **das reimt sich nicht** (*fig.*) that makes no sense

**Reimerei** *die;* **~, ~en** (*abwertend*) **eine ~:** a piece of doggerel; **~en** doggerel *sing.*

**Reime·schmied** *der* (*abwertend*) rhymester

**reim-, Reim-: ~lexikon** *das* rhyming dictionary; **~los** *Adj.* unrhymed; rhymeless; **~paar** *das* (*Verslehre*) rhyming couplet

**Reimport** *der* (*Wirtsch.*) reimport

**Reim-: ~wort** *das; Pl.* **~wörter** rhyme word; **~wörter·buch** *das* rhyming dictionary

**rein**[1] /rain/ (*ugs.*) **~ mit dir!** in you go/come!

**rein**[2] ❶ *Adj.* **A** (*unvermischt*) pure; **~es Hochdeutsch sprechen** speak faultless *or* perfect German; **B** (*nichts anderes als*) pure; sheer; **etw. aus ~em Trotz tun** do sth. out of sheer *or* pure contrariness; **~e Theorie/Mathematik** pure theory/mathematics; **die ~e Wahrheit sagen** tell the plain *or* unvarnished truth; **C** (*ohne Ausnahme*) **es war ~e Männersache** it was exclusively a men's affair; **eine ~e Arbeitergegend** a purely *or* entirely working-class district; **D** (*ugs.: intensivierend*) pure; sheer; **das ist der ~ste Quatsch** that's pure *or* sheer *or* absolute nonsense; **Sie sind der ~ste Dichter** you are a real poet; **dein Zimmer ist der ~ste Saustall** (*derb*) your room is a real pigsty; **E** (*meist geh.: frisch, sauber*) clean; fresh ‹clothes, sheet of paper, etc.›; pure, clean ‹water, air›; clear, fresh ‹complexion›; (*fig.*) **ein ~es Gewissen haben** have a clear conscience; **sein Gewissen ~waschen** (*ugs.*) apease one's consciense; **jmdn./jmds. Namen/sich ~waschen** (*ugs.*) clear sb./sb.'s name/oneself; **~ klingen** make *or* have a pure sound; **etw. ins Reine schreiben** make a fair copy of sth.; **etw. ins Reine bringen** clear sth. up; put sth. straight; **mit jmdm./etw. ins Reine kommen** get things straightened out with sb./get sth. sorted *or* straightened out; **mit sich [selbst] ins Reine kommen** sort things out in one's own mind; **mit etw. im Reinen sein** have got sth. sorted out; **mit jmdm. im Reinen sein** have got things straightened out with sb. ❷ *Adv.* **A** (*ausschließlich*) purely; **B** (*vor allem, besonders*) purely; **~ zufällig/unmöglich** purely *or* quite by chance/quite impossible; **~ zeitlich** purely from the point of view of time; **C** (*ugs.: intensivierend*) **~ gar nichts** absolutely nothing

**rein-: ~|beißen** *unr. itr. V.* (*ugs.*) take a bite; **in etw.** (*Akk.*) **~beißen** take a bite of sth.; **zum Reinbeißen sein** *od.* **aussehen** (*ugs.*) ‹cake etc.› look tempting; (*fig.*) ‹girl› look good enough to eat; **~|dürfen** *unr. itr. V.* be allowed in

**Reineclaude** /rɛːnəˈkloːdə/ ⇒ **Reneklode**

**Reineke** /ˈrainəkə/ *der;* **~s, ~s** Reynard *no art.;* **Meister ~, ~ Fuchs** Reynard the Fox

**Reine·mache·frau** *die* cleaning lady; cleaner

**Reine·machen** *das;* **~s** (*bes. nordd.*) cleaning session; **beim ~ sein** be doing the cleaning; **eine Frau kommt zum ~:** a woman comes to do the cleaning

**rein-, Rein-: ~erbig** *Adj.* (*Biol.*) homozygous; **~erlös** *der,* **~ertrag** *der* net profits *pl. or* proceeds *pl.*

**Reinette** /rɛˈnɛtə/ ⇒ **Renette**

**reine·weg** *Adv.* (*ugs.*) really; (*ganz u. gar*) absolutely; **das ist ~ zum Verzweifeln** it's enough to drive you to despair

**Rein·fall** *der* (*ugs.*) let-down; **das Stück war ein böser ~:** the play was a complete flop (*coll.*); **mit unserem letzten Auto haben wir einen großen ~ erlebt** our last car was a complete disaster

**rein|fallen** *unr. itr. V.; mit sein* (*ugs.*) ⇒ **hereinfallen A, hineinfallen**

**Reinfektion** *die* (*Med.*) reinfection

**rein|gehen** *unr. itr. V.; mit sein* (*ugs.*) ⇒ **hineingehen**

**Reingeschmeckte** /-gəʃmɛktə/ *der/die; adj. Dekl.* (*scherzh.*) outsider

**Rein-: ~gewicht** *das* net weight; **~gewinn** *der* net profit

**Rein·haltung** *die:* **die ~ der Seen/der Luft** keeping the lakes/air clean *or* pure; **die ~ der Sprache** keeping the language pure

**rein|hauen** *unr. tr. V.* (*salopp*) **A** (*schlagen*) bash; **in die Tasten ~:** pound *or* thump the keys; **Kokain haut viel mehr rein** (*fig.*) cocaine gives you much more of a kick (*coll.*); **jmdm. eine ~:** thump sb. [one] (*coll.*); **B** (*essen*) tuck in (*coll.*)

**Reinheit** *die;* **~ A** (*Klarheit*) purity; **B** (*Sauberkeit*) cleanness; (*des Wassers, der Luft*) purity; (*der Haut*) clearness

**Reinheits-: ~gebot** *das* beer purity regulations *pl.;* **~grad** *der* degree of purity

**reinigen** /ˈrainɪgn̩/ *tr. V.* clean; clean, cleanse ‹wound, skin›; purify ‹effluents, air, water, etc.›; **Kleider [chemisch] ~ lassen** have clothes [dry-]cleaned; **das Gewitter hat die Luft gereinigt** the storm has cleared the air; **ein ~des Gewitter** (*fig.*) an argument that clears the air; **die Atmosphäre ~** (*fig.*) clear the air

**Reinigung** *die;* **~, ~en A** ⇒ **reinigen**: cleaning; cleansing; purification; dry-cleaning; **B** (*Betrieb*) [dry-]cleaner's

**Reinigungs-: ~creme** *die* cleansing cream; **~milch** *die* cleansing milk; **~mittel** *das* cleaning agent; (*für die Haut*) cleanser; cleansing product

**Reinkarnation** *die;* **~, ~en** reincarnation

**rein-, Rein-: ~|knien** *refl. V.* (*ugs.*) ⇒ **hineinknien**; **~|kommen** *unr. itr. V.; mit sein*

*old spelling (see note on page 1707)

(*ugs.*) ⇒ **herein-, hineinkommen**; **~|können** *unr. itr. V.* be able to go/come in; **~|kriechen** *unr. itr. V.; mit sein (ugs.)* crawl in; **in etw.** (*Akk.*) **~kriechen** crawl into sth.; **jmdm. hinten ~kriechen** (*derb*) lick sb.'s arse (*coarse*); **~|kriegen** *tr. V.* (*ugs.*) ⇒ **hereinbekommen**; **hineinbekommen**; **~kultur** *die* **A** (*Landw.*) monoculture; **B** (*Biol.*) pure culture; **Kitsch/Konservatismus in ~kultur** (*fig.*) pure *or* unadulterated kitsch/pure *or* sheer Conservatism; **~|legen** *tr. V.* (*ugs.*) ⇒ **hereinlegen**; **~leinen** *Adj.* pure linen

**reinlich** ❶ *Adj.* **A** (*~keitsliebend*) cleanly; **B** (*sauber*) clean; neat ‹dress›; **C** (*gründlich*) clear[-cut] ‹division, distinction, etc.›. ❷ *adv.* **A** (*sauber*) cleanly; neatly ‹dressed, folded›; **B** (*gründlich*) clearly

**Reinlichkeit** *die;* ~ ⇒ **reinlich**: cleanliness; neatness; clearness

**rein-, Rein-: ~mache·frau** *die* ⇒ **Reinemachefrau**; **~|müssen** *unr. itr. V.* have to go/come in; **~rassig** *Adj.* pure-bred, thoroughbred ‹animal›; **~rassigkeit** *die* purity of breeding; **~|reißen** *unr. tr. V.* (*ugs.*) **jmdn. ~reißen** drag sb. in (*fig.*); **~|reiten** *unr. tr. V.* (*ugs.*) **jmdn. ~reiten** drag sb. in (*fig.*); **~|riechen** *unr. itr. V.* (*ugs.*) **in die Exportabteilung ~riechen** get a taste of work in the export department; **~|schauen** *itr. V.* (*ugs.*) look in; **~schiff** (*das*) (*Seemannsspr.*) *in* **~schiff machen** clean the decks [thoroughly]; **~|schlagen** *unr. tr. V.* **A** (*ugs.*) knock in; **etw. in etw.** (*Akk.*) **~schlagen** knock sth. into sth.; **B jmdm. eine ~schlagen** (*salopp*) thump sb. [one] (*coll.*); **~schrift** *die* fair copy; **~schriftlich** *Adj.* **eine ~schriftliche Fassung** a fair copy; **~seiden** *Adj.* pure silk; **~|sollen** *itr. V.* be supposed to go/come in; **~|stecken** *itr. V.* put in; **~|steigern** *refl. V.* (*ugs.*) work oneself up; become worked up; **~|treten** (*ugs.*) ❶ *unr. itr. V.; mit sein (hineintreten)* **in etw.** (*Akk.*) **~treten** step in[to] sth.; ❷ *unr. tr., itr. V.* **jmdm.** *od.* **jmdn. hinten ~treten** kick sb. up the backside; ***~|waschen** ⇒ **rein²** E; **~weg** *Adv.* ⇒ **reineweg**; **~wollen¹** *Adj.* pure wool; **~|wollen²** *unr. itr. V.* (*ugs.*) want to come/go in; **seltsam, dass so viele Leute ins Kino ~wollten** it's odd that so many people wanted to get into the cinema; **~|würgen** *tr. V.* **A** (*ugs.*) **sich** (*Dat.*) **~würgen** force ‹food, medicine, etc.› down; **etw. in sich** (*Akk.*) **~würgen** force sth. down; **B jmdm. eine** *od.* **eins ~würgen** come down on sb. like a ton of bricks (*coll.*); **er hat einen ~gewürgt gekriegt** he/she/they *etc.* came down on him like a ton of bricks (*coll.*) **~|ziehen** *tr. V.* **A** ⇒ **hineinziehen** 1; **B sich** (*Dat.*) **etw. ~ziehen** (*salopp*) take ‹drug›; watch ‹film, show, video›

**Reis¹** /rais/ *der;* **~es** rice

**Reis²** *das;* **~es, ~er A** (*geh.: Zweig*) twig; **~er** (*~ig*) brushwood *sing.;* **B** (*geh.: Spross*) shoot; **C** (*Pfropfreis*) scion

**Reis-: ~auf·lauf** *der* (*Kochk.*) baked rice dish; (*süß*) *baked pudding of rice with layers of fruit etc.;* **~bauer** *der;* **~~n, ~~n, ~bäuerin** *die;* **~~, ~~nen** rice grower; **~brei** *der* rice pudding

**Reise** /ˈraizə/ *die;* **~, ~n A** journey; (*kürzere Fahrt, Geschäfts~*) trip; (*Ausflug*) outing; excursion; trip; (*Schiffs~*) voyage; (*ins Weltall*) voyage; flight; (*im Flugzeug*) flight; (*Kreuzfahrt*) cruise; (*Überfahrt*) crossing; **eine ~ mit dem Auto/der Eisenbahn** a journey by car/train; a car/train journey; **eine ~ zur See** a sea voyage; (*Kreuzfahrt*) a cruise; **eine dienstliche ~:** a business trip; **eine ~ um die Welt** a journey round the world; **auf meinen ~n** on my travels; **eine ~ machen** make a journey/go on a trip/an outing; **auf ~n sein** travel; (*nicht zu Hause sein*) be away; **viel auf ~n sein** *od.* **gehen** travel a lot; do a lot of travelling; **jeden Sommer gehen wir auf die ~** *od.* **auf ~n** we travel every summer; **auf der ~ gabs viel zu sehen** there was a lot to see during *or* on the journey/trip; **wohin soll diesmal die ~ gehen?** where will you/shall we go this time?; **glückliche** *od.* **gute ~!** have a good journey; **wenn einer eine ~ tut, dann kann er was erzählen** (*Spr.*) travelling is always eventful; **die** *od.* **seine letzte ~ antreten** (*geh. verhüll.*) go to meet one's Maker; **B** (*Drogenjargon*) trip (*coll.*)

**-reise** *die;* **~, ~n** ... journey/trip; **Schweiz~/Afrika~:** journey/trip to Switzerland/Africa; **Bus~:** bus trip *or* journey

**reise-, Reise-: ~andenken** *das* souvenir; **~apotheke** *die* [traveller's] first aid kit; **~bedarf** *der* travel requisites *pl.;* **~begleiter** *der,* **~begleiterin** *die* travelling companion; (*~leiter[in]*) courier; (*für Kinder*) chaperon; **~bekanntschaft** *die* acquaintance made on a/the journey; **ich habe eine interessante ~bekanntschaft gemacht** I met somebody interesting on the journey; **~bericht** *der* (*privat*) account of one's journey; (*offiziell*) report of one's journey; (*Buch*) travel book; (*Film*) travelogue; travel film; (*Artikel*) travel story; **~beschreibung** *die* account of a journey/one's travels; (*Buch*) travel book; **~büro** *das* travel agent's; travel agency; **~bus** *der* coach; **~decke** *die* travelling rug; **~fähig** *Adj.* **~fähig sein** be able to travel; **ein ~fähiger Patient** a patient able to travel; **~fertig** *Adj.* **~fertig sein** be ready to leave; **~fieber** *das* (*ugs.*) nervous excitement about the journey; **~fieber haben** be nervous and excited about the journey; **~führer** *der* **A** (*~leiter*) courier; **B** (*Buch*) guidebook; **~führerin** *die* courier; **~geld** *das* **A** (*Geld für die ~*) money for the journey; **B** ⇒ **~spesen**; **~gepäck** *das* luggage (*Brit.*); baggage (*Amer.*); (*am Flughafen*) baggage; **~gepäck·versicherung** *die* luggage/baggage insurance; **~geschwindigkeit** *die* average speed for a/the journey; **~gesellschaft** *die* **A** (*~gruppe*) party of tourists; **eine deutsche ~gesellschaft** a party of German tourists; **B** (*ugs.: ~veranstalter*) travel firm; tour operator; **~gruppe** *die* ⇒ **~gesellschaft** A; **~kasse** *die* holiday fund; **~koffer** *der* suitcase; **~kosten** *Pl.* travel expenses; **~kosten·abrechnung** *die* travel expenses claim; **~krankheit** *die* travel sickness *no pl.;* **~land** *das:* **ein beliebtes/teures ~land sein** be a popular country with/an expensive country for tourists; **Spanien ist ~land Nr. 1 für die Deutschen** Spain is the most popular holiday destination for the Germans; **~leiter** *der,* **~leiterin** *die* ▶ 159 courier; **~leitung** *die* **A** (*das Leiten*) **er hat die ~leitung übernommen** he has taken on the job of courier; **~leitung durch erfahrene Mitarbeiter** only experienced couriers are used; **B** (*Person*) courier/couriers; **~lektüre** *die* reading matter for the journey; **etw. als ~lektüre kaufen** buy sth. to read on the journey; **~lustig** *Adj.* **~lustig sein** (*häufig ~n unternehmend*) be a keen traveller; (*zum Reisen aufgelegt sein*) be keen to travel

**reisen** *itr. V.; mit sein* **A** travel; **viel gereist sein** be well-travelled; **er reist für einige Tage nach Paris** he's going to Paris for a few days; **in Unterwäsche/Hundefutter** *usw.* **~** (*ugs.*) travel in underwear/dog food *etc.;* **B** (*ab~*) leave; set off

**Reisende** *der/die; adj. Dekl.* **A** traveller; (*Fahrgast*) passenger; **B** (*Vertreter*) [travelling] sales representative; [commercial] traveller

**Reise-: ~necessaire** *das* sponge bag (*Brit.*); toiletries bag (*Amer.*); **~pass**, ***~paß** *der* passport; **~pläne** *Pl.* travel plans; **~prospekt** *der* travel brochure; **~rad** *das* touring bicycle; tourer; **~route** *die* route; **~ruf** *der* SOS message for travellers; **~scheck** *der* **A** ▶ 337 traveller's cheque; **B** (*DDR*) *coupon of entitlement to a holiday at a specified place;* **~schreibmaschine** *die* portable typewriter; **~spesen** *Pl.* travelling expenses; **~tag** *der* **A** (*Abreisetag*) departure day; **B am dritten ~tag erreichten sie Athen** on the third day after setting out they reached Athens; **~tasche** *die* holdall; **~verkehr** *der* holiday traffic; **~wecker** *der* travel alarm; **~welle** *die* surge of holiday traffic; **~wetter** *das* weather for travelling; **das ist ideales/kein ~wetter** that's ideal/no weather for travelling; **~wetterbericht** *der* holiday weather forecast; **~zeit** *die* **A** (*Zeit der An-, Abreise*) travelling time; **B** (*günstige Zeit*) time to travel; **C** (*Urlaubszeit*) holiday time *or* season; **~ziel** *das* destination; **unser ~ziel für diesen Sommer ist Mallorca** we're going on holiday to Mallorca this summer; **Paris ist ein beliebtes ~ziel** Paris is a popular holiday destination; **~zug** *der* (*Eisenb.*) holiday train

**Reis·feld** *das* paddy field

**Reisig** *das;* **~s** brushwood

**Reisig-: ~besen** *der* besom; **~bündel** *das* bundle of brushwood

**Reis-: ~korn** *das* grain of rice; **~mehl** *das* rice flour; **~papier** *das* rice paper

**reiß-, Reiß-: ~ahle** *die* scriber; **~aus** *der: in* **~aus nehmen** (*ugs.*) scram (*coll.*); scarper (*Brit. coll.*); **~brett** *das* drawing board; **~brett·stift** *der* ⇒ **~zwecke**

**reißen** /ˈraisn̩/ ❶ *unr. tr. V.* **A** (*zer~*) tear; (*in Stücke*) tear up; **ein Loch in die Hose ~:** tear *or* rip a hole in one's trousers; **B** (*ab~, weg~*) tear; **eine Pflanze aus dem Boden ~:** tear a plant out of the ground; **jmdm. etw. aus den Händen/Armen ~:** snatch *or* tear sth. from sb.'s hands/arms; **der Sturm riss die Ziegel von den Dächern** the gale ripped *or* tore the tiles off the roofs; **sich** (*Dat.*) **die Kleider vom Leibe ~:** tear one's clothes off; **jmdn. aus seinen Gedanken ~** (*fig.*) awaken sb. rudely from his/her thoughts; **etw. aus dem Zusammenhang ~:** take sth. out of context; **C** (*ziehen an*) pull; (*heftig*) yank (*coll.*); **D** (*werfen, ziehen*) **eine Welle riss ihn zu Boden** a wave knocked him to the ground; **er riss den Wagen zur Seite** he wrenched the [steering] wheel over; **jmdn. in die Tiefe ~:** drag sb. down into the depths; **der Fluss hat die Brücke mit sich gerissen** the river swept *or* carried the bridge away; **das Boot wurde in den Strudel gerissen** the boat was sucked into the whirlpool; **er riss sie in seine Arme** he pulled her into his arms; **[innerlich] hin und her gerissen sein** *od.* **werden** (*fig.*) be torn [two ways]; **von Zweifeln hin und her gerissen werden** (*fig.*) be torn by doubt; **E** (*töten*) ‹wolf, lion, etc.› kill, take ‹prey›; **F** (*sich einer Sache bemächtigen*) **an sich ~:** seize ‹object, power, control, advantage, etc.›; **er will immer das Gespräch an sich ~:** he always wants to monopolize the conversation; **G** (*ugs.: machen*) crack ‹joke›; make ‹remark›; **H** (*Leichtathletik*) **die Latte/eine Hürde ~:** knock the bar down/knock a hurdle over; **I** *unpers.* (*schmerzen*) **es reißt mich in den Waden** my calves are aching; **J** (*veralt.: zeichnen*) draw; **K** *in* **jmdm. eine ~** (*österr. salopp*) stick one on sb. (*sl.*).
❷ *unr. itr. V.* **A** *mit sein* ‹paper, fabric› tear, rip; ‹rope, thread› break, snap; ‹film› break; ‹muscle› tear; **wenn alle Stricke** *od.* **Stränge ~** (*fig.*) if all else fails; **B** (*ziehen*) **an etw.** (*Dat.*) **~:** pull at sth.; **der Hund riss an der Leine** the dog strained at the leash; **C** (*Leichtathletik*) bring the bar down/knock the hurdle over; **D** (*Schwerathletik*) snatch.
❸ *unr. refl. V.* **A** (*sich los~*) tear oneself/itself (**aus, von** from); **sich aus seinen Träumen ~:** jerk oneself out of one's reveries; **B** (*ugs.: sich bemühen um*) **ich reiße mich nicht um diese Arbeit** I'm not all that keen on this work (*coll.*); **sie ~ sich um die Eintrittskarten** they are scrambling to *or* fighting each other to get tickets; **sie ~ sich alle darum, mitzuspielen** they are all after the chance to play; **C** (*sich verletzen*) scratch oneself; **D** (*sich beibringen*) **sich eine Wunde ~:** cut oneself

**Reißen** *das;* **~s** (*ugs.*) **ich habe ein ~ in allen Gliedern** all my limbs are aching; **das ~ haben** have got rheumatism

**reißend** *Adj.* rapacious ‹animal›; stabbing ‹pain›; **~en Absatz finden** sell like hot cakes; **ein ~er Fluss** a raging torrent

**Reißer** *der;* **~s, ~ A** (*ugs., oft abwertend*) thriller; **B** (*ugs.: Verkaufserfolg*) big seller

**reißerisch** *(abwertend)* ❶ *Adj.* sensational; lurid ‹headline›; garish, lurid ‹colour›. ❷ *adv.* sensationally

**reiß-, Reiß-:** **~feder** *die* ruling pen; **~fest** *Adj.* unbreakable; non-tear ‹fabric›; **~festigkeit** *die* breaking strength; **~leine** *die* *(Flugw.)* ripcord; **~nadel** *die* scriber; **~nagel** *der* ⇒ **~zwecke**; **~schiene** *die* T-square; **~stift** *der* ⇒ **~zwecke**

**Reis·stroh** *das* rice grass

**Reiß-:** **~verschluss**, ***~verschluß** *der* zip [fastener]; **den ~verschluss an etw.** *(Dat.)* **aufmachen/zumachen** undo/do up the zip on sth.; unzip/zip up sth.; **jmdm. den ~verschluss aufmachen** undo sb.'s zip; **~wolf** *der* shredder; *(Textilw.)* devil; **~wolle** *die* shoddy; **~zahn** *der (Zool.)* carnassial [tooth]; **~zeug** *das* drawing instruments *pl.;* **~zwecke** *die* drawing pin *(Brit.)*; thumbtack *(Amer.)*

**Reis-:** **~tafel** *die (Kochk.)* rijsttafel; **~wein** *der* rice wine

**Reit·bahn** *die* riding arena

**reiten** /'raitn̩/ ❶ *unr. itr. V.; meist mit sein* ride; **auf etw.** *(Dat.)* **~:** ride [on] sth.; **im Schritt/Trab/Galopp ~:** ride at a walk/trot/gallop. ❷ *unr. tr. V.; auch mit sein* [A] ride; **Schritt/Trab/Galopp ~:** ride at a walk/trot/gallop; **ein Pferd müde ~:** ride a horse until it is tired; **ein Turnier/einen Wettbewerb ~:** ride in a tournament/competition; **ein scharfes Tempo ~:** ride at a furious pace; **ich habe mir die Knie steif geritten** I rode until my knees were stiff; **was reitet denn den?** *(fig. ugs.)* what's eating him? *(coll.)*; [B] *(begatten)* ride; mount. ❸ *unr. refl. V.* **im Regen reitet es sich schwerer** riding is more difficult in the rain

**Reiten** *das;* **~s** riding *no art.*

**Reiter** *der;* **~s, ~** [A] rider; **ich bin kein guter ~:** I'm not a good rider *or* horseman; ⇒ *auch* **apokalyptisch**; [B] *(Milit.: Absperrung)* barrier; **spanischer ~:** barbed wire barricade; [C] *(österr.: Heu~)* rickstand; [D] *(an der Waage)* rider; [E] *(Kartei~)* tab

**Reiterei** *die;* **~, ~en** [A] *(Kavallerie)* cavalry; [B] *(ugs.: das Reiten)* riding *no art.*

**Reiterin** *die;* **~, ~nen** rider; **sie ist eine gute ~:** she is a good rider *or* horsewoman

**Reiter·regiment** *das (Milit.)* cavalry regiment

**Reiters·mann** *der; Pl.* **~männer** *od.* **~leute** *(veralt.)* horseman

**Reiter·stand·bild** *das* equestrian statue

**Reit-:** **~gerte** *die* riding whip; **~hose** *die* riding breeches *pl.;* **~knecht** *der (veralt.)* groom; **~kunst** *die* riding skills *pl.;* equestrian skills *pl.;* **~peitsche** *die* riding whip; **~pferd** *das* saddle horse; **~schule** *die* riding school; **~sitz** *der* [A] *(auf Pferd)* **im ~sitz auf etw.** *(Dat.)* **sitzen** sit astride sth.; [B] *(Turnen)* straddle seat; **~sport** *der* [horse] riding; **~stall** *der* riding stable; **~stiefel** *der* riding boot; **~stunde** *die* riding lesson; **~tier** *das* mount; **das ist ein ~tier** this animal is used for riding; **~turnier** *das* riding event; **~weg** *der* bridle path; bridleway

**Reiz** /raits/ *der;* **~es, ~e** [A] *(Physiol.)* stimulus; [B] *(Anziehungskraft)* attraction; appeal *no pl.;* *(des Verbotenen, Fremdartigen, der Ferne usw.)* lure; **etw. übt einen großen ~ auf jmdn. aus** sth. holds *or* has great attraction *or* appeal for sb.; **in dieser Aufgabe liegt für mich ein besonderer ~:** this task has a particular attraction *or* appeal for me; **ich kann dieser Sache** *(Dat.)* **keinen ~ abgewinnen** this has no appeal for me; **die neue Aufgabe hat gewiss ihre ~e** the new job certainly has its attractions; **an ~ verlieren** lose some of its attraction *or* appeal; [C] *(Zauber)* charm; **weibliche ~e** female charms; **sie ließ alle ihre ~e spielen** she used all her charms

**reizbar** *Adj.* [A] *(leicht zu verärgern)* irritable; **leicht ~ sein** be very irritable; [B] *(empfindlich)* sensitive

*old spelling (see note on page 1707)

**Reizbarkeit** *die;* **~** [A] *(Erregbarkeit)* irritability; [B] *(Empfindlichkeit)* sensitivity

**reizen** ❶ *tr. V.* [A] annoy; tease ‹animal›; *(herausfordern, provozieren)* provoke; *(zum Zorn treiben)* anger; **jmds. Zorn ~, jmdn. zum Zorn ~:** provoke sb. to anger; **jmdn. bis aufs Blut ~:** make sb.'s blood boil; ⇒ *auch* **gereizt**; [B] *(anziehen)* attract; **jmds. Verlangen ~:** rouse sb.'s desire; [C] *(Physiol.)* irritate; **seine Nerven waren zu sehr gereizt** his nerves were too much on edge; [D] *(Interesse erregen bei)* **jmdn. ~:** attract sb.; appeal to sb.; **jmds. Hass/Widerspruch ~:** arouse sb.'s hatred/make sb. want to contradict; **es würde mich sehr ~, das zu tun** I'd love to do that; **das Angebot reizt mich** I find the offer tempting; [E] *(Kartenspiele)* bid.
❷ *itr. V.* [A] *(Physiol.)* irritate; **der Qualm reizt zum Husten** the smoke makes you cough; [B] *(anregen)* **das reizt zum Lachen** it makes people laugh; **eine solche Ansicht reizt zum Widerspruch** such an opinion invites contradiction; [C] *(Kartenspiele)* bid; **hoch ~** *(fig.)* play for high stakes

**reizend** ❶ *Adj.* charming; delightful, lovely ‹child›; **das ist ja ~** *(iron.)* [that's] charming! *(iron.)*. ❷ *adv.* charmingly; **wir haben uns ~ unterhalten** we had a delightful chat

**Reiz-:** **~gas** *das* irritant gas; **~husten** *der* ▶ 474 *(Med.)* dry cough

**Reizker** /'raitskɐ/ *der;* **~s, ~** *(Bot.)* Lactarius; **Echter ~:** saffron milk cap

**reiz-, Reiz-:** **~klima** *das (Med., Met.)* bracing climate; **~los** ❶ *Adj.* unattractive ‹person, face, task, etc.›; ‹landscape, scenery› lacking in charm; bland ‹food, diet›; ❷ *adv.* unattractively; **~losigkeit** *die;* **~~:** ⇒ **~los**: unattractiveness; lack of charm; blandness; **~mittel** *das (Med.)* stimulant; **~schwelle** *die (Med., Psych.)* stimulus threshold; absolute threshold; **~stoff** *der* irritant; **~thema** *das* emotive issue; **~überflutung** *die;* **~en** *(Psych.)* overstimulation

**Reizung** *die;* **~, ~en** [A] annoyance; *(Herausforderung)* provocation; *(eines Tieres)* teasing; [B] ▶ 474 *(Physiol., Med.)* irritation

**reiz-, Reiz-:** **~voll** ❶ *Adj.* [A] *(hübsch)* charming; delightful; [B] *(interessant)* attractive; **das ist wenig ~voll für ihn** it doesn't appeal to him much; **es wäre ~voll, mit ihm darüber zu sprechen** it would be interesting to talk to him about it; **die Aussicht ist nicht gerade ~voll** the prospect isn't exactly enticing. ❷ *adv.* *(hübsch)* charmingly; delightfully; **~wäsche** *die* *(ugs.)* sexy underwear; **~wort** *das; Pl.* **~wörter** [A] *(Emotionen hervorrufend)* emotive word; [B] *(Psych.)* stimulus word

**Rekapitulation** *die (auch Biol.)* recapitulation

**rekapitulieren** *tr. V.* recapitulate

**rekeln** /'re:kl̩n/ *refl. V. (ugs.)* stretch; **sich in der Sonne/im Liegestuhl ~:** stretch out in the sun/in the deckchair

**Reklamation** /reklama'tsi̯o:n/ *die;* **~, ~en** complaint **(wegen** about); **spätere ~[en] ausgeschlossen!** money cannot be refunded after purchase

**Reklame** /re'kla:mə/ *die;* **~, ~n** [A] *(Werbung)* advertising *no indef. art.;* *(Ergebnis)* publicity *no indef. art;* **schlechte ~:** poor advertising/publicity; **~ für jmdn./etw. machen** promote sb./advertise *or* promote sth.; [B] *(ugs.: Werbemittel)* advert *(Brit. coll.)*; ad *(coll.)*; advertisement; *(im Fernsehen, Radio auch)* commercial; **nichts als ~:** nothing but adverts/commercials; **die BBC bringt keine ~:** there are no adverts *etc.*/commercials on BBC

**Reklame-:** **~rummel** *der (ugs. abwertend)* [publicity] ballyhoo, hype *(coll.)* **(um** surrounding); **~sendung** *die* ⇒ **Werbesendung**; **~schild** *das* advertising sign; **~trommel** *die: in* **für jmdn./etw. die ~trommel rühren** *(ugs.)* promote sb./advertise *or* promote sth. in a big way; **~zettel** *der* advertising leaflet

**reklamieren** ❶ *itr. V. (sich beschweren)* complain; make a complaint. ❷ *tr. V.* [A] *(beanstanden)* complain about, make a complaint about **(bei** to, **wegen** on account of); **reklamierte Güter** goods about which there has been a complaint; [B] *(beanspruchen)* claim; **jmdn. für sich ~:** monopolize sb.; **etw. für sich ~:** claim sth. for oneself

**rekognoszieren** /rekɔgnɔs'tsi:rən/ *tr. V. (österr., schweiz., Milit.)* reconnoitre

**Rekommandation** /rekɔmanda'tsi̯o:n/ *die;* **~, ~en** [A] *(österr.)* recommendation; [B] *(österr. Postw.)* registered letter

**rekommandieren** *tr. V. (österr. Postw.)* register

**rekonstruierbar** *Adj.* reconstructible; **leicht/schwer ~ sein** be easy/difficult to reconstruct

**rekonstruieren** *tr. V.* [A] reconstruct; [B] *(regional: modernisieren)* modernize; renovate ‹building›

**Rekonstruktion** *die* [A] reconstruction; [B] *(regional: Modernisierung)* modernization/renovation

**Rekonvaleszent** /rekɔnvalɛs'tsɛnt/ *der;* **~en, ~en, Rekonvaleszentin** *die;* **~, ~nen** convalescent

**Rekonvaleszenz** /rekɔnvalɛs'tsɛnts/ *die* ▶ 474 *(Med.)* convalescence *no art.*

**Rekord** /re'kɔrt/ *der;* **~[e]s, ~e** record; **einen ~ aufstellen/innehaben** set up/hold a record

**Rekord-** record ‹harvest, temperature, fee›

**Rekorder** ⇒ **Recorder**

**Rekord-:** **~halter** *der,* **~halterin** *die,* **~inhaber** *der,* **~inhaberin** *die* record holder; **~lauf** *der* record-breaking run; **~leistung** *die* record

**Rekordler** /re'kɔrtlɐ/ *der;* **~s, ~, Rekordlerin** *die;* **~, ~nen** record holder

**Rekord-:** **~marke** *die* record; **~versuch** *der* attempt at a/the record; **~zeit** *die* record time

**Rekrut** /re'kru:t/ *der;* **~en, ~en** *(Milit.)* recruit

**rekrutieren** ❶ *refl. V.* **sich aus einem bestimmten Kreis ~:** be drawn from a particular sphere; **sich aus Beamten/Selbstständigen ~:** consist *or* be composed of civil servants/self-employed people; ❷ *tr. V. (Milit. veralt., auch fig.)* recruit **(aus** from)

**Rekrutierung** *die;* **~, ~en** recruitment; recruiting

**Rekrutin** *die;* **~, ~nen** ⇒ **Rekrut**

**Rekta** ⇒ **Rektum**

**rektal** /rɛk'ta:l/ *(Med.)* ❶ *Adj.* rectal. ❷ *adv.* rectally

**Rektion** /rɛk'tsi̯o:n/ *die;* **~, ~en** *(Grammatik)* **die ~ einer Präposition** the case governed by a preposition; **nur bei einigen Präpositionen schwankt die ~:** only a few prepositions can take more than one case

**Rektor** /'rɛktɔr/ *der;* **~s, ~en** /-'to:rən/ [A] *(Schulleiter)* head[master]; [B] *(Universitäts~)* Rector; ≈ Vice-Chancellor *(Brit.)*; *(einer Fachhochschule)* principal

**Rektorat** /rɛkto'ra:t/ *das;* **~[e]s, ~e** [A] *(Amt, Amtszeit)* headship; *(an der Universität)* Rectorship; ≈ Vice-Chancellorship *(Brit.)*; [B] *(Amtszimmer)* head[master]'s room *or* office; *(an der Universität)* Rector's office; ≈ Vice-Chancellor's office *(Brit.)*

**Rektorin** *die;* **~, ~nen** [A] *(Schulleiterin)* head[mistress]; [B] ⇒ **Rektor** B

**Rektoskop** /rɛkto'sko:p/ *das;* **~s, ~e** *(Med.)* proctoscope; rectoscope

**Rektoskopie** /rɛktosko'pi:/ *die;* **~, ~n** *(Med.)* proctoscopy

**Rektum** /'rɛktʊm/ *das;* **~s, Rekta** /'rɛkta/ *(Anat.)* ▶ 471 rectum

**rekultivieren** *tr. V. (Landw.)* recultivate

**rekurrieren** /reku'ri:rən/ *itr. V.* [A] *(geh.: Bezug nehmen)* **auf etw.** *(Akk.)* **~:** refer back to sth.; [B] *(österr. Rechtsspr.)* **gegen etw. ~:** appeal against sth.

**Rekurs** *der* [A] *(geh.: Bezug)* reference **(auf +** *Akk.* to); **auf etw.** *(Akk.)* **~ nehmen** refer back to sth.; [B] *(Rechtsspr.)* appeal; **~ einlegen** lodge an appeal

**Relais** /rəˈlɛː/ *das;* ~ /rəˈlɛː(s)/, ~ /rəˈlɛːs/ (*Elektrot.*) relay

**Relais-:** **~schaltung** *die* (*Elektrot.*) relay circuit; **~station** *die* (*Elektrot.*) relay station

**Relation** /relaˈtsi̯oːn/ *die;* ~, **~en** (*auch Math.*) relation; **in einer/keiner ~ zu etw. stehen** bear a/no relation to sth.

**relativ** /relaˈtiːf/ ❶ *Adj.* relative; ⇒ *auch* Mehrheit; Gehör. ❷ *adv.* Ⓐ (*ziemlich*) relatively; Ⓑ (*vergleichsweise*) **~ zu** relative to

**relativieren** *tr. V.* relativize

**Relativierung** *die;* ~, **~en** relativization

**Relativismus** *der;* ~ (*Philos.*) relativism

**relativistisch** *Adj.* (*auch Philos., Physik*) relativistic

**Relativität** /relativiˈtɛːt/ *die;* ~, **~en** relativity

**Relativitäts·theorie** *die* (*Physik*) theory of relativity

**Relativ-:** **~pronomen** *das* (*Sprachw.*) relative pronoun; **~satz** *der* (*Sprachw.*) relative clause

**Relaxans** /reˈlaksans/ *das;* ~, **Relaxantien** (*Med.*) relaxant

**relaxed** /riˈlɛkst/ *Adj.* (*salopp*) laid-back (*coll.*)

**Relegation** /relegaˈtsi̯oːn/ *die;* ~, **~en** expulsion

**relegieren** /releˈgiːrən/ *tr. V.* expel

**relevant** /releˈvant/ *Adj.* relevant (**für** to)

**Relevanz** *die;* **~:** relevance (**für** to)

**Relief** /reˈli̯ɛf/ *das;* **~s**, **~s** *od.* **~e** (*bild. Kunst; Geogr.*) relief

**relief-, Relief-:** **~artig** ❶ *Adj.* raised in relief *postpos.;* ❷ *adv.* **~artig erhoben** raised in relief *postpos.;* **~druck** *der; Pl.* **~~e** Ⓐ (*Verfahren*) relief printing; Ⓑ (*Erzeugnis*) relief print; **~karte** *die* relief map

**Religion** /reliˈgi̯oːn/ *die;* ~, **~en** Ⓐ (*auch fig.*) religion; Ⓑ (*Unterrichtsfach*) religious instruction *or* education; RI; RE

**religions-, Religions-:** **~ausübung** *die* practice of religion; **freie ~ausübung** freedom to practise one's religion; **~bekenntnis** *die* religion; denomination; [religious] confession; **~freiheit** *die* religious freedom; **~friede** *der* religious peace; **~gemeinschaft** *die* denomination; **~geschichte** *die* history of religion; **~krieg** *der* religious war; **~lehre** *die* ⇒ Religion B; **~lehrer** *der*, **~lehrerin** *die* religious instruction *or* education teacher; RI *or* RE teacher; **~los** *Adj.* Ⓐ ‹person› who has no religious beliefs; **ich bin ~los** I'm not religious; Ⓑ (*gottlos*) irreligious; **~philosophie** *die* philosophy of religion; **~stifter** *der*, **~stifterin** *die* founder of a/the religion; **~streit** *der* religious dispute; **~stunde** *die* religious instruction *or* education lesson; RI *or* RE lesson; **~unterricht** *der* ⇒ Religion B; ⇒ *auch* Englischunterricht; **~wissenschaft** *die* religious studies *pl., no art.;* **vergleichende ~wissenschaft** comparative religion; **~wissenschaftler** *der*, **~wissenschaftlerin** *die* religious scholar; **~zugehörigkeit** *die* religion; religious confession; **~zwang** *der: compulsion to belong to a particular denomination*

**religiös** /reliˈgi̯øːs/ ❶ *Adj.* religious. ❷ *adv.* in a religious manner; **~ erzogen werden** have *or* receive a religious upbringing; **~ leben** live a religious life

**Religiosität** /religi̯oziˈtɛːt/ *die;* **~:** religiousness

**Relikt** /reˈlɪkt/ *das;* **~[e]**, **~e** Ⓐ (*auch Sprachw.*) relic; Ⓑ (*Biol.*) relict; relic

**Reling** /ˈreːlɪŋ/ *die;* ~, **~s** *od.* **~e** (*Seew.*) [deck] rail

**Reliquie** /reˈliːkvi̯ə/ *die;* ~, **~n** (*Rel., bes. kath. Kirche*) relic

**Reliquien·schrein** *der* reliquary

**Rembours·geschäft** /rãˈbuːɐ̯-/ *das* (*Finanzw.*) documentary credit trading; **ein ~:** a documentary credit transaction

**Remigrant** /rɛmiˈgrant/ *der;* **~en**, **~en**, **Remigrantin** *die;* ~, **~nen** returning emigrant; (*nach der Rückkehr*) returned emigrant; **türkische ~en** returning/returned Turkish emigrants

**remilitarisieren** *tr. V.* remilitarize

**Remilitarisierung** *die* remilitarization

**Reminiszenz** /reminɪsˈtsɛnts/ *die;* ~, **~en** (*geh.*) reminiscence (**an** + *Akk.* of)

**remis** /rəˈmiː/ *indekl. Adj.* (*bes. Schach*) drawn; **~ enden/ausgehen** end in a draw; **sie trennten sich ~:** they held each other to a draw; **~ spielen** draw

**Remis** *das;* ~ /rəˈmiː(s)/, ~ /rəˈmiːs/ *od.* **~en** (*bes. Schach*) draw; **~ anbieten** offer a draw

**Remise** /reˈmiːzə/ *die;* ~, **~n** Ⓐ (*veralt.*) coach house; (*Geräteschuppen*) shed; Ⓑ (*Schach*) ⇒ Remis

**Remission** *die* Ⓐ (*Buchw.*) return; Ⓑ (*Med.*) remission

**Remittende** /remɪˈtɛndə/ *die;* ~, **~n** (*Buchw.*) return

**Remittent** /remɪˈtɛnt/ *der;* **~en**, **~en**, **Remittentin** *die;* ~, **~nen** (*Finanzw.*) payee

**remittieren** /remɪˈtiːrən/ ❶ *tr. V.* (*Buchw.*) return. ❷ *itr. V.* (*Med.*) remit

**Remmidemmi** /rɛmiˈdɛmi/ *das;* ~ (*ugs.*) row (*coll.*); racket; **~ machen** make a row (*coll.*) *or* racket

**Remoulade** /remuˈlaːdə/ *die;* ~, **~n**, **Remouladen·soße** *die* remoulade

**Rempelei** *die;* ~, **~en** (*ugs.*) pushing and shoving; jostling; (*Sport*) pushing; **hören Sie doch mit der ~ auf!** stop pushing and shoving!

**rempeln** /ˈrɛmpl̩n/ (*ugs.*) push; shove; jostle; (*Sport*) push

**Rempler** *der;* **~s**, ~ (*ugs.*) **jmdm. einen ~ geben** push against sb.

**Remuneration** /remuneraˈtsi̯oːn/ *die;* ~, **~en** (*österr., sonst veralt.*) compensation

**Ren** /rɛn/ *das;* **~s**, **~s** *od.* **~e** reindeer

**Renaissance** /rənɛˈsãːs/ *die;* ~, **~n** Ⓐ Renaissance; Ⓑ (*Wiederaufleben*) revival; **eine ~ erleben** enjoy a renaissance

**Renaissance·musik** *die* Renaissance music

**Rendezvous** /rãdeˈvuː/ *das;* ~ /...ˈvuː(s)/, ~ /ˈrãdeˈvuːs/ rendezvous

**Rendezvous·manöver** *das* (*Raumf.*) rendezvous manœuvre

**Rendite** /rɛnˈdiːtə/ *die;* ~, **~n** (*Wirtsch.*) [annual] yield *or* return

**Rendite·objekt** *das* investment property

**Renegat** /reneˈgaːt/ *der;* **~en**, **~en** (*abwertend*) renegade

**Renegatentum** *das;* **~s** (*abwertend*) apostasy; **jmdm. ~ vorwerfen** accuse sb. of being a renegade

**Renegatin** *die;* ~, **~nen** ⇒ Renegat

**Reneklode** /reːnəˈkloːdə/ *die;* ~, **~n** greengage

**Renette** /reˈnɛtə/ *die;* ~, **~n** rennet

**renitent** /reniˈtɛnt/ ❶ *Adj.* refractory. ❷ *adv.* refractorily

**Renitenz** /reniˈtɛnts/ *die;* **~:** refractoriness

**Renn-:** **~auto** *das* racing car; **~bahn** *die* (*Sport*) racetrack; (*für Pferde*) racecourse; racetrack; **~boot** *das* (*Motorboot*) power boat; (*Segelboot*) racing yacht; (*Ruderboot*) racing shell

**rennen** /ˈrɛnən/ ❶ *unr. itr. V.; mit sein* Ⓐ run; **um die Wette ~:** have a race; race each other; **wütend aus dem Zimmer ~:** storm out of the room; **in sein Verderben/den Tod ~** (*fig.*) rush headlong to one's doom/hasten to one's death; **meine Uhr rennt wieder** (*fig. ugs.*) my watch is fast again; Ⓑ (*ugs. abwertend: hingehen*) run [off]; **dauernd ins Kino/zur Polizei ~:** be always going to the cinema/running to the police; Ⓒ (*stoßen an*) **an/gegen jmdn./etw. ~:** run *or* bang into sb./sth.; **mit dem Kopf an** *od.* **gegen etw.** (*Akk.*) **~:** bang one's head against *or* on sth.

❷ *unr. tr. V.* Ⓐ (*sich zuziehen*) **sich** (*Dat.*) **an etw.** (*Dat.*) **ein Loch in den Kopf/ins Knie ~:** run *or* bang into sth. and hurt one's head/knee; Ⓑ (*ugs.: stoßen*) **jmdm. etw. in das Bein/die Rippen ~:** run sth. into sb.'s leg/ribs

**Rennen** *das;* **~s**, **~:** running; (*Pferde~, Auto~*) racing; (*einzelner Wettbewerb*) race; **zum ~ gehen** (*Pferde~*) go to the races; (*Auto~*) go to the racing; **gut im ~ liegen** be well placed; (*fig.*) be one of the front runners; **das ~ ist gelaufen** the race is over *or* has been run; (*fig.*) it's all over; **ein totes ~** (*Sport*) a dead heat; **das ~ machen** (*ugs.*) win; **das ~ aufgeben** give up

**Renner** *der;* **~s**, ~ Ⓐ (*ugs.: Verkaufserfolg*) big seller; Ⓑ (*Pferd*) racer

**Rennerei** *die;* ~, **~en** (*ugs.*) running around; **du glaubst nicht, was das für eine ~ war** you wouldn't believe how much running *or* chasing around it involved; **die ~ mit den Weihnachtsgeschenken** running around getting the Christmas presents; **das Schlimmste ist die ewige ~ zum Klo** the worst thing is having to run to the loo (*Brit. coll.*) *or* (*Amer. coll.*) john all the time

**Renn-:** **~fahrer** *der*, **~fahrerin** *die* ▶ 159 racing driver; (*Radsport*) racing cyclist; (*Motorradsport*) racing motorcyclist; **~jacht** *die* racing yacht; **~leitung** *die* Ⓐ (*das Leiten*) race organization; Ⓑ (*Personen*) race organizers *pl.;* **~lenker** *der* drop[ped] handlebars *pl.;* **~maschine** *die* (*Jargon*) racing bike; **~pferd** *das* racehorse; **~platz** *der* ⇒ **~bahn**; **~rad** *das* racing cycle; **~sport** *der* racing *no art.;* **~stall** *der* Ⓐ racing stable; (*die Pferde allein*) string; Ⓑ (*Mannschaft*) team; **~strecke** *die* (**~bahn**) racetrack; (*Distanz*) race distance; **~wagen** *der* racing car

**Renommee** /renɔˈmeː/ *das;* **~s**, **~s** (*geh.*) reputation

**renommieren** /renɔˈmiːrən/ *itr. V.* show off; **mit etw. ~:** brag about sth.; **mit seinem Titel/Wissen ~:** flaunt one's title/show off *or* flaunt one's knowledge

**Renommier-:** **~stück** *das:* **das ~stück des Museums** the museum's showpiece [exhibit]; **ihr ~stück, das dreireihige Perlen hat** her finest piece of jewelry with its three rows of pearls; **~sucht** *die* (*abwertend*) urge to show off

**renommiert** *Adj.* renowned (**wegen** for)

**renovieren** /renoˈviːrən/ *tr. V.* renovate; redecorate ‹room, flat›

**Renovierung** *die;* ~, **~en** renovation; (*eines Zimmers, einer Wohnung*) redecoration

**rentabel** /rɛnˈtaːbl̩/ ❶ *Adj.* profitable; **~ sein** be profitable; ‹equipment, machinery› pay its way. ❷ *adv.* profitably

**Rentabilität** /rɛntabiliˈtɛːt/ *die;* ~ (*bes. Wirtsch.*) profitability; (*von Geräten usw.*) cost-effectiveness

**Rentabilitäts·prüfung** *die* (*Wirtsch.*) profitability analysis

**Rente** /ˈrɛntə/ *die;* ~, **~n** Ⓐ pension; **auf** *od.* **in ~ gehen** (*ugs.*) retire; **auf** *od.* **in ~ sein** (*ugs.*) be retired; **jmdn. auf ~ setzen** (*ugs.*) pension sb. off; Ⓑ (*Kapitalertrag*) annuity

**renten-, Renten-:** **~alter** *das* pensionable age *no art.;* **im ~alter sein** *od.* **stehen** be of pensionable age; **~anpassung** *die* index-linking of pensions (*to the average national wage*); **~an·spruch** *der* pension entitlement; **~berechtigt** *Adj.* entitled to a pension *postpos.;* **~empfänger** *der*, **~empfängerin** *die* pensioner; **~erhöhung** *die* pension increase; **~markt** *der* (*Börsenw.*) fixed securities market; **~papier** *das* (*Finanzw.*) fixed interest security; **~pflichtig** *Adj.* responsible for providing a pension *postpos.;* **~versicherung** *die* Ⓐ (*Versicherung*) pension scheme; **eine private ~versicherung abschließen** join a private pension scheme; Ⓑ (*Behörde*) *state pension authority*

**Ren·tier**[1] *das* reindeer

**Rentier**[2] /rɛnˈti̯eː/ *der;* **~s**, **~s** Ⓐ (*veralt.: mit Vermögen*) man with a private income; Ⓑ (*selten: Rentner*) pensioner

**rentieren** /rɛnˈtiːrən/ *refl. V.* be profitable; ‹equipment, machinery› pay its way; ‹effort, visit, etc.› be worth while; **eine Geschirrspülmaschine rentiert sich für uns nicht** it's not worth our having *or* not worth our while to have a dishwasher

r

**Rentner** /ˈrɛntnɐ/ *der;* **∼s**, **∼**, **Rentnerin** *die;* **∼**, **∼nen** pensioner

**Reorganisation** *die* reorganization

**reorganisieren** *tr. V.* reorganize

**Reorganisierung** *die* reorganization

**reparabel** /repaˈraːbl̩/ *Adj.* repairable; **nicht mehr ∼ sein** be no longer repairable; be beyond repair; **die Ehe ist nicht mehr ∼** (*fig.*) the marriage has failed irretrievably

**Reparationen** /reparaˈt͜si̯oːnən/ *Pl.* (*Politik*) reparations; **∼ leisten** *od.* **zahlen** make *or* pay reparations

**Reparations·zahlung** *die* reparation payment

**Reparatur** /reparaˈtuːɐ̯/ *die;* **∼**, **∼en** repair (**an** + *Dat.* to); **in ∼ sein** be being repaired; **etw. in ∼ geben** take sth. in to have it repaired

**reparatur-, Reparatur-: ∼anfällig** *Adj.* prone to break down *postpos.;* **∼arbeit** *die* repair work; **∼en** repair work *sing.;* repairs; **∼bedürftig** *Adj.* ‹device, appliance, vehicle, etc.› [which is] in need of repair; **∼bedürftig sein** be in need of repair; need repairing; **∼kosten** *Pl.* repair costs; **die ∼kosten für das Auto** the cost of repairing the car; **∼werkstatt** *die* repair [work]shop; (*für Autos*) garage

**reparieren** /repaˈriːrən/ *tr. V.* repair; mend; (*bei komplexeren Geräten, größeren Schäden*) repair; **einen Fehler ∼** (*fig.*) put right an error

**repatriieren** /repatriˈiːrən/ *tr. V.* (*Politik, Rechtsw.*) Ⓐ (*wieder einbürgern*) **jmdn. ∼:** restore sb.'s citizenship; Ⓑ (*wieder heimführen*) repatriate

**Repatriierung** *die;* **∼**, **∼en** Ⓐ (*Wiedereinbürgerung*) **jmds. ∼:** the restoration of sb.'s citizenship; Ⓑ (*Heimführung*) repatriation

**Repertoire** /repɛrˈto̯aːɐ̯/ *das;* **∼s**, **∼s** (*auch fig.*) repertoire

**Repertoire·stück** *das* stock play

**Repertorium** /repɛrˈtoːri̯ʊm/ *das;* **∼s**, **Repertorien** reference work

**repetieren** /repeˈtiːrən/ *tr. V.* Ⓐ (*einüben*) learn by repetition; Ⓑ (*veralt.: wiederholen*) repeat ‹year›

**Repetier-: ∼gewehr** *das* repeating rifle; repeater; **∼uhr** *die* repeating watch; repeater

**Repetitor** /repeˈtiːtɔr/ *der;* **∼s**, **∼en** /-tiˈtoːrən/, **Repetitorin** *die;* **∼**, **∼nen** Ⓐ (*für Studenten*) *private tutor who coaches (esp. law) students for examinations;* Ⓑ (*Musik*) répétiteur

**Replik** /reˈpliːk/ *die;* **∼**, **∼en** Ⓐ (*geh.: Erwiderung*) reply; rejoinder; Ⓑ (*Rechtsw.*) reply; replication; Ⓒ (*Kunst*) replica

**Replikat** /repliˈkaːt/ *das;* **∼[e]s**, **∼e** (*Kunst*) replica

**Report** /reˈpɔrt/ *der;* **∼[e]s**, **∼e** Ⓐ (*Bericht*) report; Ⓑ (*Finanzw.*) premium

**Reportage** /repɔrˈtaːʒə/ *die;* **∼**, **∼n** report

**Reporter** /reˈpɔrtɐ/ *der;* **∼s**, **∼**, **Reporterin** *die;* **∼**, **∼nen** ▶ 159 reporter; ⇒ *auch* **-in**

**repräsentabel** /reprɛzɛnˈtaːbl̩/ ❶ *Adj.* imposing. ❷ *adv.* imposingly

**Repräsentant** /reprɛzɛnˈtant/ *der;* **∼en**, **∼en** representative

**Repräsentanten·haus** *das* House of Representatives

**Repräsentantin** *die;* **∼**, **∼nen** representative; ⇒ *auch* **-in**

**Repräsentanz** /reprɛzɛnˈtant͜s/ *die;* **∼**, **∼en** Ⓐ (*Interessenvertretung*) representation; Ⓑ (*Wirtsch.*) branch

**Repräsentation** *die;* **∼**, **∼en** Ⓐ (*bes. Politik*) representation; Ⓑ (*das Typischsein*) representativeness; Ⓒ (*Vertretung in der Öffentlichkeit*) **die Rolle des Präsidenten besteht vorwiegend in der ∼:** the role of the President is primarily that of official figurehead; **die wichtigste Pflicht einer Diplomatenfrau ist die ∼:** the most important duty of a diplomat's wife is attending official and social functions; Ⓓ (*aufwendiger Lebensstil*) **etw. dient nur der ∼:** sth. is for prestige purposes only

**repräsentativ** /reprɛzɛntaˈtiːf/ ❶ *Adj.* Ⓐ (*auch Politik*) representative; **für etw. ∼ sein** be representative of sth.; Ⓑ (*ansehnlich*) imposing; (*mit hohem Prestigewert*) prestigious; **eine ∼e Erscheinung** a man/woman of distinguished *or* imposing appearance. ❷ *adv.* Ⓐ (*bes. Politik*) representatively; **ein ∼ strukturiertes politisches System** a political system with a representative structure; Ⓑ (*luxuriös*) imposingly

**Repräsentativ·umfrage** *die* (*Statistik*) representative survey

**repräsentieren** /reprɛzɛnˈtiːrən/ ❶ *tr. V.* represent. ❷ *itr. V.* (*Repräsentation betreiben*) attend official and social functions

**Repressalie** /reprɛˈsaːli̯ə/ *die;* **∼**, **∼n** repressive measure; (*Vergeltungsmaßnahme*) reprisal; **∼n anwenden** *od.* **ergreifen** resort to repressive measures/take reprisals

**Repression** /reprɛˈsi̯oːn/ *die;* **∼**, **∼en** repression

**repressions·frei** ❶ *Adj.* free of repression *postpos.* ❷ *adv.* **∼ erzogen werden** have an upbringing that is/was free of repression

**repressiv** /reprɛˈsiːf/ ❶ *Adj.* repressive. ❷ *adv.* repressively

**Reprint** /reˈprɪnt/ *der;* **∼s**, **∼s** (*Buchw.*) reprint

**Reprise** *die* Ⓐ (*Theater*) revival; (*Film*) rerun; Ⓑ (*einer Schallplatte*) re-issue; Ⓒ (*Musik*) reprise; Ⓓ (*Börsenw.*) recovery

**reprivatisieren** *tr. V.* (*Wirtsch., Politik*) reprivatize

**Reprivatisierung** *die* (*Wirtsch., Politik*) reprivatization

**Repro** /ˈreːpro/ *die;* **∼**, **∼s** (*Druckw.*) repro

**Reproduktion** *die* reproduction

**Reproduktions-: ∼bedingungen** *Pl.* (*polit. Ökonomie*) conditions of reproduction; **∼kamera** *die* (*Druckw.*) process camera; **∼kosten** *Pl.* (*Wirtsch.*) reproduction costs; **∼prozess**, ***∼prozeß** *der* (*polit. Ökonomie*) reproduction process; **∼verfahren** *das* (*Druckw.*) reproduction process

**reproduzieren** *tr. V.* (*auch Druckw., polit. Ökonomie*) reproduce

**Repro-: ∼graphie** *die* (*Druckw.*) Ⓐ (*Verfahren*) reprography *no art.;* Ⓑ (*Erzeugnis*) reproduction; **∼technik** /ˈ----/ *die* reproduction technology *no art.*

**Reps** /rɛps/ *Pl.* (*ugs.*) Republicans

**Reptil** /rɛpˈtiːl/ *das;* **∼s**, **∼ien** /rɛpˈtiːli̯ən/ reptile

**Reptilien·fonds** *der* (*Politik*) slush fund

**Republik** /repuˈbliːk/ *die;* **∼**, **∼en** republic

**Republikaner** /republiˈkaːnɐ/ *der;* **∼s**, **∼**, **Republikanerin** *die;* **∼**, **∼nen** Ⓐ republican; Ⓑ (*Angehörige[r] der republikanischen Partei*) Republican

**republikanisch** ❶ *Adj.* Ⓐ republican; Ⓑ (*eine ∼e Partei betreffend*) Republican. ❷ *adv.* Ⓐ **ein ∼ aufgebauter Staat** a state with a republican structure; Ⓑ **∼ wählen** vote Republican

**Republik-: ∼flucht** *die* (*DDR*) illegal emigration; **∼flüchtling** *der* (*DDR*) illegal emigrant

**Repulsions·motor** /repʊlˈzi̯oːns-/ *der* (*Technik*) repulsion motor

**repulsiv** /repʊlˈziːf/ *Adj.* (*Physik*) repulsive

**Repunze** /reˈpʊnt͜sə/ *die;* **∼**, **∼n** hallmark

**Reputation** /reputaˈt͜si̯oːn/ *die;* **∼**, **∼en** reputation; standing

**reputierlich** *Adj.* (*veralt.*) upright; decent

**Requiem** /ˈreːkvi̯ɛm/ *das;* **∼**, **∼s** requiem

**requirieren** /rekviˈriːrən/ *tr. V.* (*veralt.*) requisition

**Requisit** /rekviˈziːt/ *das;* **∼[e]s**, **∼en** Ⓐ (*Theater*) prop (*coll.*); property; Ⓑ (*fig.*) requisite

**Requisiten·kammer** *die* (*Theater*) prop store *or* room (*coll.*); property store *or* room

**Requisiteur** /rekviziˈtøːɐ̯/ *der;* **∼s**, **∼e** (*Theater*) prop man (*coll.*); property man

**Requisiteurin** *die;* **∼**, **∼nen** (*Theater*) prop woman (*coll.*); property woman

**Requisition** *die;* **∼**, **∼en** (*veralt.*) requisition

**resch** /rɛʃ/ *Adj.* (*bayr., österr.*) Ⓐ (*knusprig*) crusty ‹rolls, bread›; crisp ‹fried potatoes, batter›; Ⓑ (*ugs.: lebhaft*) vivacious

**Reseda** /reˈzeːda/ *die;* **∼**, **∼s**, **Resede** *die;* **Resede**, **Reseden** Reseda; (*Garten∼*) mignonette

**Reservat** /rezɛrˈvaːt/ *das;* **∼[e]s**, **∼e** Ⓐ (*Tier∼*) reserve; Ⓑ (*für Volksstämme*) reservation

**Reserve** /reˈzɛrvə/ *die;* **∼**, **∼n** Ⓐ (*Vorrat*) reserve (**an** + *Dat.* of); **etw. in ∼ haben** have sth. in reserve; **etw. in ∼ halten** keep *or* hold sth. in reserve; ⇒ *auch* **eisern** 1 D; **still** 1 F; Ⓑ (*Milit.*) reserves *pl.;* **Offizier der ∼:** reserve officer; Ⓒ (*Sport*) reserves *pl.;* Ⓓ (*Zurückhaltung*) reserve; **jmdn. aus der ∼ [heraus]locken** (*ugs.*) bring sb. out of his/her shell; Ⓔ (*Bedenken*) reservation

**Reserve-: ∼bank** *die; Pl.* **∼bänke** (*Sport*) substitutes' bench; **∼fonds** *der* (*Wirtsch.*) reserve [fund]; **∼frau** *die* ⇒ **∼mann**; **∼kanister** *der* spare [petrol (*Brit.*) *or* (*Amer.*) gasoline] can; **∼mann** *der; Pl.* **∼männer** *od.* **∼leute** replacement; (*Sport*) substitute; reserve; **∼offizier** *der* reserve officer; **∼rad** *das* spare wheel; **∼reifen** *der* spare tyre; **∼spieler** *der*, **∼spielerin** *die* (*Sport*) substitute; reserve; **∼tank** *der* reserve [fuel] tank; **∼truppe** *die* (*Milit.*) reserve troops *pl.;* **∼übung** *die* (*Milit.*) reservists' exercise

**reservieren** *tr. V.* reserve

**reserviert** ❶ *Adj.* reserved. ❷ *adv.* in a reserved way

**Reserviertheit** *die;* **∼:** reserve

**Reservierung** *die;* **∼**, **∼en** reservation

**Reservist** *der;* **∼en**, **∼en** (*Milit.*) reservist; (*Sportjargon*) substitute; reserve

**Reservisten·übung** *die* (*Milit.*) reservists' exercise

**Reservoir** /rezɛrˈvo̯aːɐ̯/ *das;* **∼s**, **∼e** (*auch fig.*) reservoir (**an** + *Dat.* of)

**Residenz** /reziˈdɛnt͜s/ *die;* **∼**, **∼en** Ⓐ (*Wohnsitz*) residence; Ⓑ (*Hauptstadt*) [royal] capital

**Residenz-: ∼pflicht** *die* Ⓐ (*von Beamten*) obligation to live within a reasonable distance of one's place of work; Ⓑ (*ev. u. kath. Kirche*) obligation [on a clergyman] to live in the accommodation provided with the post; **∼stadt** *die* ⇒ **Residenz** B

**residieren** /reziˈdiːrən/ *itr. V.* reside

**Resignation** /rezɪgnaˈt͜si̯oːn/ *die;* **∼**, **∼en** resignation; **in ∼ versinken** become resigned

**resignativ** /rezɪgnaˈtiːf/ *Adj.* ‹mood, atmosphere› of resignation

**resignieren** /rezɪˈgniːrən/ *itr. V.* give up

**resigniert** ❶ *Adj.* resigned. ❷ *adv.* resignedly

**Resistance** /rezisˈtãːs/ *die;* **∼** (*hist.*) Resistance

**resistent** /rezɪsˈtɛnt/ *Adj.* (*Biol., Med.*) resistant (**gegen** to)

**Resistenz** /rezɪsˈtɛnt͜s/ *die;* **∼**, **∼en** (*auch Biol., Med.*) resistance (**gegen** to)

**resolut** /rezoˈluːt/ ❶ *Adj.* resolute. ❷ *adv.* resolutely

**Resolutheit** *die;* **∼:** resoluteness

**Resolution** /rezoluˈt͜si̯oːn/ *die;* **∼**, **∼en** resolution

**Resonanz** /rezoˈnant͜s/ *die;* **∼**, **∼en** Ⓐ (*Physik, Musik*) resonance; Ⓑ (*Reaktion*) response (**auf** + *Akk.* to); **∼/keine ∼ finden, auf ∼/auf keine ∼ stoßen** meet with a/no response

**Resonanz-: ∼boden** *der* (*Musik*) sounding board; soundboard; **∼körper** *der* (*Musik*) soundbox

**Resopal** Ⓦⓩ /rezoˈpaːl/ *das;* **∼s** ≈ melamine

**resorbieren** /rezɔrˈbiːrən/ *tr. V.* (*Biol., Med.*) absorb

**Resorption** /rezɔrpˈt͜si̯oːn/ *die;* **∼**, **∼en** (*Biol., Med.*) absorption

**resozialisierbar** *Adj.* (*bes. Rechtsspr.*) able to be reintegrated into society *postpos.*

---

*old spelling (see note on page 1707)

**resozialisieren** *tr. V.* (*bes. Rechtsspr.*) reintegrate into society

**Resozialisierung** *die;* ~, ~en (*bes. Rechtsspr.*) reintegration into society

**Respekt** /re'spɛkt/ *der;* ~[e]s [A] (*Achtung*) respect; **~ vor jmdm./etw. haben** have respect for sb./sth.; **jmdm. ~ einflößen** *od.* **abnötigen** command sb.'s respect; **bei allem ~:** with all due respect (**vor** + *Dat.* to); **allen ~!, ~, ~!** good for you!; well done!; [B] (*Furcht*) **jmdm. ~ einflößen** intimidate sb.; **vor jmdm./etw. [größten] ~ haben** be [much] in awe of sb./sth.; **sich** (*Dat.*) **den nötigen ~ verschaffen** command proper respect; [C] (*Schrift- u. Buchw., Kunstwiss.*) margin

**respektabel** /respɛk'ta:bl̩/ ❶ *Adj.* respectable. ❷ *adv.* respectably

**respekt·einflößend** *Adj.* impressive; fearsome ‹claws, teeth›

**respektieren** *tr. V.* [A] respect; [B] (*Finanzw.*) honour ‹bill of exchange etc.›

**respektierlich** *Adj.* (*veralt.*) respectable

**respektive** /rɛspɛk'ti:və/ *Konj.* (*geh.*) [A] (*oder*) or; [B] (*oder vielmehr*) or rather; (*oder genauer gesagt*) or more precisely; [C] (*und im anderen Fall*) **grün ~ blau** green and blue respectively

**respekt·los** ❶ *Adj.* disrespectful. ❷ *adv.* disrespectfully

**Respektlosigkeit** *die;* ~, ~en [A] (*Haltung*) disrespectfulness; lack of respect; [B] (*Äußerung*) disrespectful remark; (*Handlung*) impertinence

**Respekts·person** *die* person who commands/commanded respect

**respekt·voll** ❶ *Adj.* respectful. ❷ *adv.* respectfully

**Respiration** /respira'tsi̯o:n/ *die;* ~ (*Med.*) respiration

**Respirator** /rɛspi'ra:tɔr/ *der;* ~s, ~en /-ra'to:rən/ (*Med.*) respirator

**respirieren** /rɛspi'ri:rən/ *itr. V.* (*Med.*) respire

**Ressentiment** /rɛsãti'mã:/ *das;* ~s, ~s [A] (*geh.: Abneigung*) antipathy (**gegen** towards); [B] (*Psych.*) resentment

**Ressort** /rɛ'so:ɐ̯/ *das;* ~s, ~s area of responsibility; (*Abteilung*) department; **in jmds. ~ fallen** come within sb.'s area of responsibility; **das Abwaschen ist mein ~** (*scherzh.*) the washing-up is my department

**Ressort-: ~chef** *der,* **~chefin** *die,* **~leiter** *der,* **~leiterin** *die* head of department; **~minister** *der,* **~ministerin** *die* departmental minister

**Ressource** /rɛ'sʊrsə/ *die;* ~, ~n [A] resource; [B] *Pl.* (*Ersparnisse*) resources

**Rest** /rɛst/ *der;* ~[e]s, ~e [A] rest; (~*betrag*) rest; balance; ~e (*historische ~e, Ruinen, Leiche*) remains; (*einer Kultur*) relics; **jmdm./einer Sache den ~ geben** (*ugs.*) finish sb./sth. off; **das ist der ~ von meinem Vermögen** this is all that's left of my fortune; **ein ~ von Farbe/Leim/Käse/Wein ist noch da** there's still a little bit of paint/glue/cheese/a little bit *or* a drop of wine left; **bis auf einen ~ ist es alles verbraucht** it's all been used up apart from a little bit; **der letzte ~:** the last bit; **ein trauriger ~ von Käse/Kuchen** a few pathetic scraps *pl.* of cheese/cake; **morgen gibt es ~e** tomorrow we're having leftovers; **~ machen** (*nordd.*) finish up what's left; **machen Sie doch ~ mit dem Fleisch** (*nordd.*) do finish up the meat; **das ist der ~ vom Schützenfest** (*ugs.*) that's all there is left; **hast du den letzten ~ von Verstand verloren?** have you lost all the sense you had left?; **der ~ ist Schweigen** (*man schweigt besser darüber*) the less said, the better; (*das Weitere ist unbekannt*) the rest is a mystery; [B] (*Endstück*) remnant; [C] (*Math.*) remainder; **20 durch 6 ist 3, ~ 2** 20 divided by 6 is 3 with *or* and 2 left over

**Rest-: ~alkohol** *der* residual alcohol; **~auf·lage** *die* remaindered stock

**Restaurant** /rɛsto'rã:/ *das;* ~s, ~s restaurant

**Restauration** /restaura'tsi̯o:n/ *die;* ~, ~en [A] (*auch Politik*) restoration; [B] (*hist.*) Restoration; [C] (*österr., sonst veralt.*) restaurant

**Restaurations-: ~arbeit** *die* restoration work; **~arbeiten** restoration work *sing.;* **~betrieb** *der* restaurant; **~zeit** *die* restoration; (*hist.*) Restoration

**restaurativ** /restaura'ti:f/ ❶ *Adj.* [A] (*Geschichte, Politik*) ‹efforts› to restore the old order; ‹phase, time› in which the old order is/was restored; ‹policies› aimed at restoring the old order; [B] (*das Restaurieren betreffend*) restorative; **eine ~e Meisterleistung** a masterpiece of restoration. ❷ *adv.* (*das Restaurieren betreffend*) **etw. ~ aufarbeiten** restore sth.; **etw. ~ retten** save sth. by restoration

**Restaurator** /restau̯'ra:tɔr/ *der;* ~s, ~en /-ra'to:rən/, **Restauratorin** *die;* ~, ~nen restorer

**restaurieren** /restau'ri:rən/ ❶ *tr. V.* restore. ❷ *refl. V.* (*ugs. scherzh.: sein Äußeres herrichten*) make oneself presentable

**Restaurierung** *die;* ~, ~en restoration

**Rest-: ~bestand** *der* remaining stock; (*an Büchern*) remaindered stock; **~betrag** *der* balance; amount *or* sum remaining

**Reste-: ~essen** *das* (*fam.*) leftovers *pl.;* **~verkauf** *der* remnants sale; **~verwertung** *die* making use of leftovers

**restituieren** /restitu'i:rən/ *tr. V.* (*bes. Rechtsw.*) [A] (*aufheben*) set aside ‹judgement, decision›; [B] (*erstatten*) **etw. ~:** make restitution for sth.

**Restitution** /restitu'tsi̯o:n/ *die;* ~, ~en [A] (*bes. Rechtsw.: Wiederherstellung*) restitution; [B] (*Rechtsw.: Aufhebung*) setting aside; [C] (*Biol.*) regeneration

**Restitutions·klage** *die* (*Rechtsw.*) action for a retrial

**restlich** *Adj.* remaining; **die ~en** the rest

**rest·los** ❶ *Adj.* complete; total. ❷ *adv.* completely; totally; **~ verzweifelt sein** be in complete *or* total despair; **alles ~ aufessen** eat every last morsel; **~ ausverkauft sein** be completely sold out

**Rest-: ~müll** *der* general waste; non-recyclable waste; **~posten** *der* (*Kaufmannsspr*) remaining stock *no indef. art.*

**Restriktion** /restrɪk'tsi̯o:n/ *die;* ~, ~en (*auch Sprachw.*) restriction

**restriktiv** /restrɪk'ti:f/ ❶ *Adj.* (*auch Sprachw.*) restrictive. ❷ *adv.* restrictively; **sich ~ auf etw.** (*Akk.*) **auswirken** have a restrictive effect on sth.

**restringieren** /restrɪŋ'gi:rən/ *tr. V.* (*Sprachw.*) **restringierter Kode** restricted code

**Rest-: ~strafe** *die* the remainder of a/the/one's sentence; **~summe** *die* amount remaining; (*von Geld*) balance; **~zahlung** *die* payment of the balance; **eine ~zahlung von 500 Mark leisten** pay off the balance of 500 marks

**Resultante** /rezʊl'tantə/ *die;* ~, ~n (*Physik*) resultant

**Resultat** /rezʊl'ta:t/ *das;* ~[e]s, ~e result; **zum ~ kommen, dass ...** come to the conclusion that ...

**resultieren** /rezʊl'ti:rən/ *itr. V.* result (**aus** from); **daraus resultiert, dass ...** the result *or* upshot of this is that ...

**Resultierende** *die; adj: Dekl.* (*Physik*) resultant

**Resümee** /rezʏ'me:/ *das;* ~s, ~s résumé

**resümieren** /rezʏ'mi:rən/ ❶ *tr. V.* **etw. ~:** summarize sth. ❷ *itr. V.* sum up

**retardieren** /retar'di:rən/ *tr. V.* retard; **~des Moment** (*Literaturw.*) retardation

**retirieren** /reti'ri:rən/ *itr. V.* (*Milit.*) retreat; (*geh.: sich zurückziehen*) retire

**Retorte** /re'tɔrtə/ *die;* ~, ~n (*Chemie*) retort; **aus der ~** (*ugs., oft abwertend*) artificial; **ein Baby aus der ~:** a test tube baby

**Retorten·baby** *das* (*ugs.*) test tube baby

**retour** /re'tu:ɐ̯/ *Adv.* (*bes. südd., österr., schweiz.*) back; **1,50 DM ~:** you get 1.50 marks back

**Retour-: ~fahr·karte** *die* (*österr.*) return ticket; **~gang** *der* (*österr.*) reverse gear; **~kutsche** *die* (*ugs.*) tit-for-tat response

**retournieren** /retʊr'ni:rən/ ❶ *tr. V.* return. ❷ *itr. V.* (*Sport, bes. Tennis*) make a return; return the ball

**retrograd** /retro'gra:t/ *Adj.* (*Med.*) **~e Amnesie** retroactive *or* retrograde amnesia

**Retrospektive** /retrospɛk'ti:və/ *die;* ~, ~n [A] (*Rückblick*) retrospective view; **in der ~:** in retrospect; [B] (*Ausstellung*) retrospective

**retten** /'rɛtn̩/ ❶ *tr. V.* save; (*vor Gefahr*) save; rescue; (*befreien*) rescue; **jmdm. das Leben ~:** save sb.'s life; **jmdn. aus der Gefahr ~:** save sb. from danger; **jmdn. vor jmdm./etw. ~:** save sb. from sb./sth.; **jmdm. kommt die ~de Idee** sb. sees the perfect answer; **das ~de Ufer erreichen** reach the safety of the shore; **versuchen zu ~, was zu ~ ist** try to save what can be saved; **ist er noch zu ~?** (*ugs. fig.*) has he gone [completely] round the bend? (*coll.*); **das alte Haus/der Patient ist nicht mehr zu ~:** the old house is past saving/the patient is beyond help; **nicht mehr zu ~ sein** (*ugs.*) be a hopeless case; **seine Habe über den Krieg ~:** manage to keep one's possessions through the war.

❷ *refl. V.* (*fliehen*) escape (**aus** from); **sich vor etw.** (*Dat.*) **~:** escape [from] sth.; **sich ans Ufer ~:** manage to reach the bank; **der Pilot rettete sich mit dem Schleudersitz** the pilot saved himself by using the ejector seat; **rette sich, wer kann!** [it's] every man for himself!; **sich vor jmdm./etw. nicht [mehr]** *od.* **kaum [noch] ~ können** be besieged by sb./be swamped with sth.; **sich ins Ziel ~** (*Sport*) just hold on to cross the line first.

❸ *itr. V.* (*Ballspiele*) save

**Retter** *der;* ~s, ~, **Retterin** *die;* ~, ~nen rescuer; (*eines Landes, einer Bewegung o. Ä.*) saviour; **der/ein ~ in der Not** the/a helper in my/our *etc.* hour of need; **Christ der ~:** Christ the Saviour

**Rettich** /'rɛtɪç/ *der;* ~s, ~e radish

**Rettung** *die* [A] rescue; (*Rel., eines Landes usw.*) salvation; (*vor Zerstörung*) saving; **jmdm. ~ bringen** rescue *or* save sb.; **die ~ kam in der letzten Minute** rescue came at the last moment *or* the eleventh hour; **er verdankt dem Medikament seine ~:** he owes his life to the medicine; **er dachte nur an seine eigene ~:** he thought only of saving himself *or* saving his own skin; **auf ~ warten/hoffen** wait for rescue/hope to be rescued; **für jmdn/etw. gibt es keine ~:** sb. is beyond help/sth. is past saving; **es war jmds. ~, dass ...** sb. was saved by the fact that ...; **das war meine letzte ~:** that was my last hope [of salvation]; (*es hat mich schließlich gerettet*) that was my salvation; [B] (*österr.: ~sdienst*) ambulance service; [C] (*österr.: ~swagen*) ambulance

**rettungs-, Rettungs-: ~aktion** *die* rescue operation; **~anker** *der* sheet anchor; **~boje** *die* (*Seew.*) lifebuoy; **~boot** *das* lifeboat; **~dienst** *der* ambulance service; (*Bergwacht, Seerettungsdienst, bei Katastrophen*) rescue service; **~flugzeug** *das* rescue aircraft *or* plane; **~gürtel** *der* lifebelt; **~hubschrauber** *der* rescue helicopter; **~insel** *die* (*Seew.*) [inflatable] life raft; **~kommando** *das* rescue team; **~los** ❶ *Adj.* hopeless; inevitable ‹disaster›; ❷ *adv.* hopelessly; **~mannschaft** *die* rescue team; **~medaille** *die* life-saving medal; **~ring** *der* [A] lifebelt; [B] (*ugs.: Fettwulst*) spare tyre (*coll.*); **~schuss, *~schuß** *der: in* **finaler ~schuss** fatal shot fired to save lives; **~schwimmen** *das* life-saving *no art.;* **~schwimmer** *der,* **~schwimmerin** *die* lifesaver; (*am Strand, im Schwimmbad*) lifeguard; **~trupp** *der* rescue team; **~versuch** *der* rescue attempt; **~wagen** *der* ambulance; (*der Bergwacht, bei Katastrophen*) rescue vehicle; **~weste** *die* (*Seew.*) life jacket

**Retusche** /re'tʊʃə/ *die;* ~, ~n (*bes. Fot., Druckw.*) retouching; (*Stelle*) retouch; **eine ~/~n vornehmen** retouch

**Retuscheur** /retʊ'ʃø:ɐ̯/ *der;* **~s, ~e, Retuscheurin** *die;* **~, ~nen** (*bes. Fot., Druckw.*) retoucher

**retuschieren** *tr. V.* (*bes. Fot., Druckw.*) retouch; (*fig.*) gloss over ‹statement, remark›

**Reue** /'rɔy̯ə/ *die;* **~:** remorse (**über** + *Akk.* for); (*Rel.*) repentance; ⇒ *auch* **tätig**

**Reue·gefühl** *das* (*geh.*) feeling of remorse; **~ überkam sie** she was overcome by [feelings of] remorse

**reuen** *tr. V.* (*meist geh.*) **etw. reut jmdn.** sb. regrets sth.; **das Geld reut mich** I regret having spent the money

**reue·voll** (*geh.*) ⇒ **reumütig**

**Reu·geld** *das* (*Rechtsw., Wirtsch., Pferderennen*) forfeit

**reuig** (*geh.*) ⇒ **reumütig**

**reu·mütig** ❶ *Adj.* remorseful; repentant, penitent ‹sinner›. ❷ *adv.* remorsefully; **~ gestand er seine Sünden** repentantly *or* penitently he confessed his sins; **du wirst ~ zurückkehren** you'll be back, saying you're sorry

**Reuse** /:rɔy̯zə/ *die;* **~, ~n** fish trap

**reüssieren** /re|ʏ'si:rən/ *itr. V.* be successful; succeed; achieve success

**Revalvation** /revalva'ts̯i̯o:n/ *die;* **~, ~en** (*Wirtsch.*) revaluation

**Revanche** /re'vã:ʃ(ə)/ *die;* **~, ~n** revenge; (*Sport: Rückkampf,* **~***spiel*) return match/fight/game; **jmdm. ~ geben** give sb. his/her revenge; **~ nehmen** *od.* **üben** get one's revenge; **~ fordern** (*Sport, Spiel*) demand a return match/fight/game

**Revanche-: ~kampf** *der* (*Sport*) return fight; **~partie** *die* (*bes. Schach*) return match; **~politik** *die* revanchist policy

**revanchieren** *refl. V.* Ⓐ get one's revenge, (*coll.*) get one's own back (**bei** on); Ⓑ (*ugs.: sich erkenntlich zeigen*) **sich bei jmdm. für eine Einladung/seine Gastfreundschaft ~:** return sb.'s invitation/repay sb.'s hospitality; **ich werde mich für eure Hilfe beim Umzug ~:** I'll return your favour of helping me move

**Revanchismus** *der;* **~** (*Politik*) revanchism *usu. no art.*

**Revanchist** *der;* **~en, ~en, Revanchistin** *die;* **~, ~nen** (*Politik*) revanchist

**revanchistisch** *Adj.* (*Politik*) revanchist

**Revenue** /rəvə'nʏ:/ *die;* **~, ~n** (*Wirtsch.*) revenue

**Reverenz** /reve'rɛnts̯/ *die;* **~, ~en** Ⓐ (*Hochachtung*) esteem, respect (**vor** + *Dat.* for); **jmdm. seine ~ erweisen** pay sb. one's respects; Ⓑ (*Verbeugung*) bow; **seine ~ vor jmdm. machen** bow to sb.

**Revers**[1] /rə've:ɐ̯/ *das od.* (*österr.*) *der;* **~** /rə'vɛ:ɐ̯(s)/, **~** /rə'vɛ:ɐ̯s/ lapel

**Revers**[2] /re'vɛrs/ *der;* **~es, ~e** (*Münzk.*) reverse

**Revers**[3] /re'vɛrs/ *der;* **~es, ~e** (*Rechtsw.*) [written] undertaking

**reversibel** /revɛr'zi:bl̩/ *Adj.* (*Technik, Med.*) reversible

**reversieren** *itr. V.* (*österr.*) reverse

**Reversion** /revɛr'zi̯o:n/ *die;* **~, ~en** (*Biol., Psych.*) reversion

**revidieren** /revi'di:rən/ *tr. V.* Ⓐ (*abändern*) revise; amend ‹law, contract›; Ⓑ (*kontrollieren*) check; (*Buchf.*) audit ‹accounts, books›

**Revier** /re'vi:ɐ̯/ *das;* **~s, ~e** Ⓐ (*Aufgabenbereich*) province; **der Weinkeller ist mein ~** (*scherzh.*) the wine cellar is my province *or* preserve; Ⓑ (*Zool.*) territory; Ⓒ (*Polizei***~**) (*Dienststelle*) [police] station; (*Bereich*) district; (*des einzelnen Polizisten*) beat; Ⓓ (*Forst***~**) district; Ⓔ (*Jagd***~**) preserve; shoot; Ⓕ (*Bergbau*) coalfield; **das ~:** the Ruhr/Saar coalfields *pl.;* Ⓖ (*Milit. veralt.: Unterkunft*) barracks *sing. or pl.;* Ⓗ (*Milit. veralt.: Kranken***~**) sickbay

**Revier-: ~förster** *der,* **~försterin** *die* forest warden; forester; **~stube** *die* (*Milit. veralt.*) sickbay

**Revirement** /revirə'mã:/ *das;* **~s, ~s** reshuffle

**Revision** /revi'zi̯o:n/ *die;* **~, ~en** Ⓐ (*das Ändern*) revision; (*eines Gesetzes, Vertrags*) amendment; Ⓑ (*Rechtsw.*) appeal [on a point/points of law]; **~ einlegen, in die ~ gehen** lodge an appeal [on a point/points of law]; Ⓒ (*Kontrolle*) inspection; (*Buchf.*) audit; Ⓓ (*Druckw.*) revision of the page proofs; **~ lesen** read the page proofs

**Revisionismus** *der;* **~** (*Politik*) revisionism *usu. no art.*

**Revisionist** *der;* **~en, ~en, Revisionistin** *die;* **~, ~nen** (*Politik*) revisionist

**revisionistisch** *Adj.* (*Politik*) revisionist

**Revisions-: ~bogen** *der* (*Druckw.*) final page proof; **~gericht** *das* (*Rechtsw.*) court of appeal [dealing with points of law]; **~verfahren** *das* (*Rechtsw.*) appeal proceedings *pl.* [on a point/points of law]; **~verhandlung** *die* (*Rechtsw.*) hearing of an/the appeal [on a point/points of law]

**Revisor** /re'vi:zɔr/ *der;* **~s, ~en** /revi'zo:rən/, **Revisorin** *die;* **~, ~nen** Ⓐ (*Buchf.*) auditor; Ⓑ (*Druckw.*) reader of the page proofs

**Revolte** /re'vɔltə/ *die;* **~, ~n** revolt

**revoltieren** *itr. V.* revolt, rebel (**gegen** against); (*fig.*) ‹stomach› rebel

**Revolution** /revolu'ts̯i̯o:n/ *die;* **~, ~en** Ⓐ (*auch fig.*) revolution; Ⓑ (*Skat*) revolution

**revolutionär** /revoluts̯i̯o'nɛ:ɐ̯/ ❶ *Adj.* revolutionary. ❷ *adv.* in a revolutionary way

**Revolutionär** *der;* **~s, ~e, Revolutionärin** *die;* **~, ~nen** revolutionary

**revolutionieren** *tr. V.* revolutionize; **eine ~de Entdeckung** a revolutionary discovery

**Revolutions-: ~rat** *der* (*Politik*) revolutionary council; **~regierung** *die* revolutionary government; **~tribunal** *das* (*hist.*) Revolutionary Tribunal

**Revoluzzer** /revo'lʊtsɐ/ *der;* **~s, ~, Revoluzzerin** *die;* **~, ~nen** (*abwertend*) phoney revolutionary

**Revoluzzertum** *das;* **~s** (*abwertend*) phoney revolutionary fervour

**Revolver** /re'vɔlvɐ/ *der;* **~s, ~** Ⓐ revolver; Ⓑ (*Technik*) turret

**Revolver-: ~blatt** *das* (*abwertend*) scandal rag; **~held** *der* (*abwertend*) gunslinger; **~kopf** *der* (*Technik*) turret; **~lauf** *der* revolver barrel; **~presse** *die* (*abwertend*) yellow press; scandal rags *pl.;* **~schnauze** *die* (*ugs. abwertend*) Ⓐ (*Mundwerk*) big trap (*sl.*) *or* mouth; Ⓑ (*Mensch*) loudmouth; **~tasche** *die* holster

**Revue** /re'vʏ/ *die;* **~, ~n** Ⓐ (*Theater*) revue; Ⓑ (*Truppe*) revue company; Ⓒ (*Zeitschrift*) review; Ⓓ (*Milit.*) review; **etw. ~ passieren lassen** (*fig.*) review sth.; **er ließ seine Freunde ~ passieren** (*fig.*) he brought back to mind *or* he recalled his friends

**Revue·theater** *das* revue theatre

**Rezensent** /rets̯ɛn'zɛnt/ *der;* **~en, ~en, Rezensentin** *die;* **~, ~nen** reviewer

**rezensieren** /rets̯ɛn'zi:rən/ ❶ *tr. V.* review. ❷ *itr. V.* write reviews

**Rezension** /rets̯ɛn'zi̯o:n/ *die;* **~, ~en** review

**Rezensions·exemplar** *das* review copy

**rezent** /re'ts̯ɛnt/ *Adj.* (*Geol.*) Recent

**Rezept** /re'ts̯ɛpt/ *das;* **~[e]s, ~e** Ⓐ (*Med.*) prescription; (*fig.*) remedy (**gegen** for); **nur auf ~:** only on prescription; Ⓑ (*Anleitung*) recipe; (*fig.*) formula

**Rezept·block** *der; Pl.* **~s** *od.* **Rezept·blöcke** prescription pad

**rezept·frei** ❶ *Adj.* **~e Mittel** medicines obtainable without a prescription. ❷ *adv.* **etw. ~ verkaufen/erhalten** sell/obtain sth. without a prescription *or* over the counter

**rezeptieren** *tr.* (*auch itr.*) *V.* prescribe

**Rezeption** /rets̯ɛp'ts̯i̯o:n/ *die;* **~, ~en** Ⓐ (*im Hotel*) reception *no art.;* Ⓑ (*Aufnahme*) reception

**rezeptiv** /rets̯ɛp'ti:f/ *Adj.* receptive (**für** to)

**rezept·pflichtig** *Adj.* ‹medicine, drug, etc.› obtainable only on prescription; **nicht ~ sein** be obtainable without a prescription *or* over the counter

**Rezeptur** /rets̯ɛp'tu:ɐ̯/ *die;* **~, ~en** Ⓐ (*das Rezeptieren*) prescription; Ⓑ (*für Nahrungsmittel*) recipe (*Gen.* for); (*für Arzneimittel, Farbe, Baustoff*) formula

**Rezession** /rets̯ɛ'si̯o:n/ *die;* **~, ~en** (*Wirtsch.*) recession

**rezessiv** /rets̯ɛ'si:f/ (*Biol.*) ❶ *Adj.* recessive. ❷ *adv.* recessively

**rezipieren** /rets̯i'pi:rən/ *tr. V.* receive; (*übernehmen*) adapt

**reziprok** /rets̯i'pro:k/ *Adj.* (*bes. Math., Sprachw.*) reciprocal

**Rezitation** /rets̯ita'ts̯i̯o:n/ *die;* **~, ~en** recitation

**Rezitations·abend** *der* [evening] recitation; (*mit Rezitation von Gedichten*) [evening] poetry-reading; poetry evening

**Rezitativ** /retsita'ti:f/ *das;* **~s, ~e** (*Musik*) recitative

**rezitieren** /rets̯i'ti:rən/ *tr.* (*auch itr.*) *V.* recite; **er rezitierte aus seinem Roman** he gave a reading *or* he read from his novel; **er rezitiert gern** he enjoys giving recitations

**R-Gespräch** /'ɛr-/ *das* (*Fernspr.*) reverse-charge call (*Brit.*); collect call (*Amer.*)

**RGW** *Abk.* **Rat für Gegenseitige Wirtschaftshilfe** COMECON

**rh** /ɛr'ha:/ *Abk.* (*Med.*) **Rhesusfaktor negativ** Rh negative

**Rh** /ɛr'ha:/ *Abk.* (*Med.*) **Rhesusfaktor positiv** Rh positive

**Rhabarber**[1] /ra'barbɐ/ *der;* **~s** rhubarb

**Rhabarber**[2] *das;* **~s** (*ugs.*) **sie murmelten „~, ~"** they mumbled 'rhubarb, rhubarb' (*coll.*)

**Rhapsode** /ra'pso:də/ *der;* **~n, ~n** (*Musik, Literaturw.*) rhapsodist; rhapsode; (*fig.*) rhapsodic composer

**Rhapsodie** /rapso'di:/ *die;* **~, ~n** (*Musik, Literaturw.*) rhapsody

**rhapsodisch** *Adj.* rhapsodic

**Rhein** /rai̯n/ *der;* **~[e]s** ▶ 306 Rhine

**Rhein·fall** *der* Rhine Falls

**rheinisch** *Adj.* Rhenish; **eine ~e Spezialität** a speciality of the Rhine region

**Rheinland** *das;* **~[e]s** Rhineland

**Rheinländer** *der;* **~s, ~, Rheinländerin** *die;* **~, ~nen** Rhinelander

**Rheinland-Pfalz** (*das*); **~'** the Rhineland-Palatinate; **in/aus ~:** in/from the Rhineland-Palatinate

**rheinland-pfälzisch** *Adj.* ‹capital, citizen, etc.› of the Rhineland-Palatinate

**Rhein·wein** *der* Rhine wine; Rhenish [wine]; (*Weißwein auch*) hock

**Rhesus-** /'re:zʊs/: **~affe** *der* rhesus monkey; **~faktor** *der* (*Med.*) rhesus factor; Rh factor

**Rhetorik** /re'to:rɪk/ *die;* **~, ~en** rhetoric

**Rhetoriker** *der;* **~s, ~, Rhetorikerin** *die;* **~, ~nen** rhetorician

**rhetorisch** ❶ *Adj.* rhetorical; **eine ~e Frage** a rhetorical question. ❷ *adv.* rhetorically

**Rheuma** /'rɔy̯ma/ *das;* **~s** ▶ 474 (*ugs.*) rheumatism; rheumatics *pl.* (*coll.*)

**Rheuma-: ~decke** *die* thermal blanket; **~mittel** *das* (*ugs.*) rheumatism pills *pl.*/cream *etc.;* **~wäsche** *die* thermal underwear

**Rheumatiker** /rɔy̯'ma:tikɐ/ *der;* **~s, ~, Rheumatikerin** *die;* **~, ~nen** (*Med.*) rheumatic; rheumatism sufferer

**rheumatisch** (*Med.*) ❶ *Adj.* rheumatic. ❷ *adv.* rheumatically

**Rheumatismus** /rɔy̯ma'tɪsmʊs/ *der;* **~, Rheumatismen** ▶ 474 (*Med.*) rheumatism

**Rhinozeros** /ri'no:ts̯erɔs/ *das;* **~[ses], ~se** Ⓐ (*Nashorn*) rhinoceros; rhino (*coll.*); Ⓑ (*ugs.: Trottel*) nitwit (*coll.*); fathead (*coll.*)

**Rhizom** /ri'ts̯o:m/ *das;* **~s, ~e** (*Bot.*) rhizome

**Rhododendron** /rodo'dɛndrɔn/ *der od. das;* **~s, Rhododendren** rhododendron

---

*old spelling (see note on page 1707)

r

**Rhodos** /ˈroːdɔs/ *(das);* ~' Rhodes

**Rhomben** ⇒ **Rhombus**

**rhombisch** *Adj.* *(bes. Math.)* rhombic

**Rhomboid** /rɔmboˈiːt/ *das;* ~**[e]s**, ~**e** *(Math.)* rhomboid

**Rhombus** /ˈrɔmbʊs/ *der;* ~, **Rhomben** /ˈrɔmbn̩/ rhombus

**Rhythmen** ⇒ **Rhythmus**

**Rhythmik** /ˈrʏtmɪk/ *die;* ~ **A** *(auch Musik)* rhythm; **B** *(Päd.)* rhythmics *sing., no art.*

**Rhythmiker** *der;* ~**s**, ~, **Rhythmikerin** *die;* ~, ~**nen** rhythmist

**rhythmisch** **1** *Adj.* rhythmical; rhythmic; ~**e Instrumente** rhythm instruments; ~**e Gymnastik** rhythmic gymnastics *sing.* **2** *adv.* rhythmically

**Rhythmus** /ˈrʏtmʊs/ *der;* ~, **Rhythmen** /ˈrʏtmən/ *(auch fig.)* rhythm; **aus dem ~ kommen** lose the rhythm

**Rhythmus-:** ~**gitarre** *die* rhythm guitar; ~**gruppe** *die* rhythm section; ~**instrument** *das* rhythm instrument

**RIAS, Rias** /ˈriːas/*der;* ~ *Abk.* *(hist.)* **Rundfunk im amerikanischen Sektor [Berlin]** RIAS; Radio in the American Sector [of Berlin]

**ribbeln** /ˈrɪbl̩n/ *tr. V.* *(landsch.)* rub

**Ribisel** /ˈriːbiːzl̩/ *die;* ~, ~**[n]** *(österr.)* ⇒ **Johannisbeere**

**Richt-:** ~**antenne** *die* directional aerial *or* *(Amer.)* antenna; ~**baum** *der: tree used for topping-out ceremony;* ~**beil** *das* *(hist.)* executioner's axe; ~**blei** *das* *(Bauw.)* plumb [bob]; ~**block** *der; Pl.* ~**blöcke** [execution] block

**richten** /ˈrɪçtn/ **1** *tr. V.* **A** *(lenken)* direct ‹gaze› **(auf** + *Akk.* at, towards); turn ‹eyes, gaze› **(auf** + *Akk.* towards); point ‹torch, telescope, gun› **(auf** + *Akk.* at); aim, train ‹gun, missile, telescope, searchlight› **(auf** + *Akk.* on); *(fig.)* direct ‹activity, attention› **(auf** + *Akk.* towards); **etw. nach jmdm./etw. ~:** arrange sth. to suit sb./sth.; **die Augen gen Himmel ~:** look heavenwards; **die Waffe gegen sich selbst ~:** turn the weapon on oneself; **das Schiff/den Kurs eines Schiffes nach Norden ~:** steer the ship on/steer a northerly course; **B** *(zukommen lassen)* address ‹letter, remarks, words› **(an** + *Akk.* to); direct, level ‹criticism› **(an** + *Akk.* at); send ‹letter of thanks, message of greeting› **(an** + *Akk.* to); **eine Bitte/Frage an jmdn. ~:** put a request/question to sb.; **ein Gesuch an jmdn. ~:** petition sb.; **eine Mahnung an jmdn. ~:** give sb. a warning; **das Wort an jmdn. ~** *(geh.)* address sb.; **C** *(gerade ~)* straighten; set ‹fracture›; **D** *(einstellen)* aim ‹cannon, missile›; direct ‹aerial›; **E** *(aburteilen)* judge; *(verurteilen)* condemn; **F** *(bes. südd., österr., schweiz.: instand setzen, in Ordnung bringen)* fix; repair ‹shoes›; *(einrichten)* arrange; fix; **[sich** *(Dat.)*] **die Haare/den Schlips ~:** do one's hair/adjust *or* straighten one's tie; **es wird sich schon alles ~:** everything will sort itself out; **das lässt sich schon ~:** it can be arranged; **G** *(bes. südd., österr., schweiz.: vorbereiten)* get ready; prepare; make ‹bed, nest›; get ‹food, meal›; **den Tisch/das Zimmer ~:** lay *or* set the table/get the room ready; **[jmdm.] ein Bad ~:** run a bath [for sb.]; **H** *(geh. veralt.: hin~)* execute; **sich selbst ~:** die by one's own hand **2** *refl. V.* **A** *(sich hinwenden)* **sich auf jmdn./etw. ~** *(auch fig.)* be directed towards sb./sth.; **ihre Augen richteten sich auf mich** her gaze was turned towards me; **B** *(sich wenden)* **sich an jmdn./etw. ~** ‹person› turn on sb./sth.; ‹appeal, explanation› be directed at sb./sth.; **C** *(kritisieren, schädigen)* **sich gegen jmdn./etw. ~** ‹person› criticize sb./sth.; ‹criticism, accusations, etc.› be aimed *or* levelled *or* directed at sb./sth.; **diese Lehre richtet sich gegen den Staat** this doctrine is directed against the state; **D** *(sich orientieren)* **sich nach jmdm./jmds. Wünschen ~:** fit in with sb./sb.'s wishes; **sich nach jmds. Anweisungen ~:** comply with sb.'s instructions; **sich nach den Vorschriften ~:** keep to *or* follow the rules; **sich nach den Wünschen seiner Kunden ~:** be guided by one's customers' wishes; **E** *(abhängen)* **sich nach jmdm./etw. ~:** depend on sb./sth.; **F** *(Milit.)* **richt't euch!** right dress! **3** *itr. V.* *(urteilen)* judge; pass judgement; **über jmdn. ~:** judge sb.; pass judgement on sb.; *(zu Gericht sitzen)* sit in judgement over sb.

**Richter** *der;* ~**s**, ~ ▶ **159** judge; **die ~** *(~schaft)* the judiciary *sing.*; **sich zum ~ über jmdn./etw. aufwerfen** presume to pass judgement *or* sit in judgement on sb./sth.; **jmdn. vor den ~ bringen** take sb. to court; **der himmlische/höchste ~:** the Heavenly/Supreme Judge; **vor dem höchsten ~ stehen** stand before the Judgement Seat *or* the Throne of Judgement

**Richter·amt** *das* office of judge

**Richterin** *die;* ~, ~**nen** ▶ **159** judge

**richterlich** **1** *Adj.* judicial. **2** *adv.* ‹examined, approved, etc.› by a judge

**Richterschaft** *die;* ~, ~**en** judiciary

**Richter-:** ~**skala** *die* Richter scale; ~**spruch** *der* judge's verdict; *(Verkündigung der Strafe)* sentence; ~**stuhl** *der* bench; **der ~stuhl Gottes** the Judgement Seat; the Throne of Judgement

**Richt-:** ~**fest** *das* topping-out ceremony; ~**funk** *der* *(Funkw.)* directional radio; ~**geschwindigkeit** *die* *(Verkehrsw.)* recommended maximum speed

**richtig** **1** *Adj.* **A** right; *(zutreffend)* right; correct; correct ‹realization›; accurate ‹prophecy, premonition›; **sehr ~!** quite right!; **bin ich hier ~ bei Schulzes?** is this the Schulzes' home?; **die ~e Haltung von Katzen** the right way to keep cats; **ich halte es für das Richtigste, wenn du mitkommst** I think the best thing would be for you to come [too]; **das ist genau das Richtige für mich** that's just right for me; **mit etw. ~ liegen** *(ugs.)* get it right with sth.; **ich habe ~ gelegen** *(ugs.)* I was right; **etw. ~ stellen** correct sth.; **B** *(ordentlich)* proper; **ein ~er Mann/Fachmann** a real man/expert; **er ist ~** *(ugs.)* he's OK *(coll.)* *or* all right; **nicht ganz ~ [im Kopf** *od.* *(ugs.)* **im Oberstübchen] sein** be not quite right in the head *(coll.)* *or* not quite all there *(coll.)*; **C** *(wirklich, echt)* real; *(regelrecht)* real; proper *(coll.)*; **du bist ein ~er Esel** you're a right *or* proper idiot *(coll.)*. **2** *adv.* **A** right; correctly; **sehe ich das ~?** *(fig.)* am I right?; **habe ich ~ gehört?** *(fig.)* do my ears deceive me?; **~ sitzen** *od.* **passen** ‹clothes› fit properly; **meine Uhr geht ~:** my watch is right; **eine ~ gehende Uhr** an accurate clock/watch; **das Radio funktioniert nicht mehr ~:** the radio doesn't work properly anymore; **etw. ~ anpacken** tackle sth. the right way; **~ wählen** make the right choice; **du kommst [mir] gerade ~!** you've come at just the right moment; *(ugs. iron.)* nothing doing!; **B** *(ordentlich)* properly; **~ ausschlafen/frühstücken** have a good sleep/breakfast; **C** *(~gehend)* really; **D** *(in der Tat)* yes; **ja ~!** yes, that's right!; **das habe ich doch ~ wieder versäumt** sure enough, I've missed it again

**Richtige**[1] *der/die; adj. Dekl.* right man/woman/person; **sie sucht noch den ~n** she's still looking for Mr Right; **an die ~/den ~n geraten** *(iron.)* choose the wrong person to try it on with *(Brit. coll.)*; **du bist mir der ~!** *(ugs.)* you're a right one!

**Richtige**[2] *der; adj. Dekl.* **drei/sechs ~ im Lotto** three/six right in the lottery

**Richtige**[3] *das; adj. Dekl.* right thing; **das ~ sein** be right; **hast du was ~s gegessen?** have you eaten properly?; have you had a proper meal?; **nichts ~s gefunden haben** not have found anything suitable; **nichts ~s gelernt haben** have had no proper education

**richtig·gehend** **1** *Adj.* real; proper *(coll.)*. **2** *adv.* really

**Richtigkeit** *die;* ~**:** correctness; *(einer Ahnung, Prophetie)* accuracy; **die ~ einer Abschrift bescheinigen** certify a copy as [being] accurate; **etw. hat seine ~,** **mit etw. hat es seine ~:** sth. is right; **das wird schon seine ~ haben** I'm sure it's all right *or* *(coll.)* OK

**richtig-, Richtig-:** *~|**liegen** ⇒ **richtig** 1A; *~|**stellen** ⇒ **richtig** 1A; ~**stellung** *die* correction

**Richt-:** ~**kranz** *der: wreath used in the topping-out ceremony;* ~**linie** *die* guideline; ~**mikrofon** *das* directional microphone; ~**platz** *der* place of execution; ~**preis** *der* recommended price; **unverbindlicher ~preis** manufacturer's recommended price; ~**scheit** *das* *(Bauw.)* straight edge; ~**schnur** *die; Pl.* ~**en** **A** *(fig.)* guiding principle; **B** *(Bauw.)* line; ~**schwert** *das* *(hist.)* executioner's sword; ~**spruch** *der* **A** *(beim Richtfest) verse address at the topping-out ceremony;* **B** *(veralt.: Urteilsspruch)* judgement; *(Verkündigung der Strafe)* sentence; ~**stätte** *die* *(geh.)* ⇒ **Richtplatz**; ~**strahler** *der* *(Funkt.)* directional aerial *or* *(Amer.)* antenna

**Richtung** *die;* ~, ~**en** **A** ▶ **400** direction; **die ~ ändern** *od.* **wechseln** change direction; **in ~ Osten** in an easterly direction; eastwards; *(auf der Autobahn)* on the eastbound carriageway; **in ~ Ulm** in the direction of Ulm; **nach/aus allen ~en** in/from all directions; **der Zug/die Autobahn ~ Ulm** the train to Ulm/the motorway in the direction of Ulm; **eine ~ einschlagen** head in a direction; **eine andere ~ einschlagen** change direction; ‹ship, aircraft› change course; **~ auf den Wald nehmen, die ~ zum** *od.* **nach dem Wald einschlagen** head in the direction of the wood; **[in] ~** *(Akk.)* **Bad verschwinden** *(ugs.)* disappear in the direction of the bathroom *(coll.)*; **aus welcher ~ kam der Schuss?** from what direction did the shot come?; **wir gehen in diese ~:** we're going this way *or* in this direction; **ihre Gedanken nahmen eine andere ~** *(fig.)* her thoughts took a different turn; **ein erster Schritt in ~ auf die Integration** *(fig.)* a first step towards *or* in the direction of integration; **der Pullover lag nicht so ganz in meiner ~** *od.* **war nicht so ganz meine ~** *(fig.)* the pullover wasn't quite [to] my taste; **er hat Angst, sich in irgendeine ~ festzulegen** *(fig.)* he's afraid to commit himself in any way; **der erste Versuch in dieser ~** *(fig.)* the first experiment of this kind; **die ~ stimmt** *(fig. ugs.)* it's/he's *etc.* on the right lines; **ich hätte jetzt Lust auf Fisch oder irgendetwas in dieser ~:** I could just fancy some fish or something in that line; **B** *(fig.: Tendenz)* movement; trend; *(die Vertreter einer ~)* *(in der Kunst, Literatur)* movement; *(in einer Partei)* faction; *(Denk~, Lehrmeinung)* school of thought; **die ganze ~ seiner Äußerungen** the whole tendency *or* drift of his remarks

**richtung·gebend** ⇒ **richtungsweisend**

**richtungs-, Richtungs-:** ~**änderung** *die* change in *or* of direction; *(eines Schiffs, Flugzeugs)* change of course; **die politische ~änderung XYs** *(fig.)* XY's change of political course; ~**gewerkschaft** *die: trade union linked to one party, ideology, etc.;* ~**kämpfe** *Pl.* factional struggles; ~**los** **1** *Adj.* lacking [a sense of] direction *postpos.;* **~los sein** lack [a sense of] direction; **2** *adv.* aimlessly; ~**losigkeit** *die;* ~~: lack of [a sense of] direction

**richtung·weisend** **1** *Adj.* ‹idea, resolution, paper, speech› that points the way ahead; *(in der Mode)* trend-setting; **für jmdn./etw. ~ sein** point the way ahead for sb./sth. **2** *adv.* **sie hat sich zu diesem Thema ~ geäußert** she set out ideas on this subject which point the way ahead; **Kunststoffe haben die heutige Technik ~ beeinflusst** plastics have had a determining influence on the direction in which today's technology has developed

**Richt·waage** *die* spirit level

**Ricke** /ˈrɪkə/ *die;* ~, ~**n** *(Jägerspr.)* doe *(of roe-deer)*

**rieb** /riːp/ *1. u. 3. Pers. Sg. Prät. v.* **reiben**

**riechen** /ˈriːçn̩/ **1** *unr. tr. V.* **A** smell; **ich rieche Tabak gern** I like the smell of tobacco; **ich rieche Gas** I [can] smell gas;

r

**jmdn./etw. nicht ~ können** (*fig. salopp*) not be able to stand sb./sth.; **B** (*wittern*) ‹dog etc.› scent, pick up the scent of ‹animal›; **er roch die Gefahr sofort** (*fig.*) he scented *or* sensed danger immediately; **ich konnte ja nicht ~, dass ...** (*fig.*) [I'm not psychic,] I couldn't know that ... **2** *unr. itr. V.* **A** (*Gerüche wahrnehmen*) smell; **Hunde können sehr gut ~:** dogs have a very good sense of smell; **an jmdm./etw. ~:** smell sb./sth.; **lass mich mal [daran] ~:** let me have a sniff; **B** (*einen Geruch haben*) smell (**nach** of); **gut/schlecht ~:** smell good/bad; **diese Blumen ~ nicht** these flowers have no smell *or* scent; **hier riecht es verbrannt/nach Krankenhaus** there is a burnt/hospital smell *or* smell of burning/hospital here; **er roch aus dem Mund** he had bad breath; his breath smelt; **das riecht nach Betrug** (*fig.*) that smells *or* smacks of deceit

**Riecher** *der;* **~s, ~** (*salopp*) **A** (*Nase*) conk (*coll.*); **B** (*fig.: Gespür*) nose; **einen guten ~ für etw. haben** have a sixth sense for sth.

**Riech-: ~fläschchen** *das* smelling bottle; **~kolben** *der* (*salopp scherzh.*) conk (*sl.*); **~organ** *das* olfactory organ; **~salz** *das* smelling salts *pl.*

**Ried**[1] /ri:t/ *das;* **~[e]s, ~e A** (*Schilf*) reeds *pl.*; **B** (*Gebiet*) reedy marsh

**Ried**[2] *die;* **~, ~en, Riede** *die;* **~e, ~en** (*österr.*) [patch of] vineyard

**Ried·gras** *das* (*Bot.*) sedge

**rief** /ri:f/ *1. u. 3. Pers. Sg. Prät. v.* **rufen**

**Riefe** *die;* **~, ~n** groove

**Riege** /ˈri:gə/ *die;* **~, ~n** (*Turnen*) squad; (*fig.*) team

**Riegel** /ˈri:gl̩/ *der;* **~s, ~ A** (*an der Tür usw.*) bolt; **einer Sache** (*Dat.*) **einen ~ vorschieben** (*fig.*) put a stop to sth.; (*etw. verhindern*) not let sth. happen; **B ein ~ Schokolade** a bar of chocolate; **C** (*bes. Fußball: Abwehr*) packed defence; **D** (*Milit.*) [defensive] wall; **E** (*Schneiderei*) (*Lasche*) loop; (*an Jacke, Mantel usw.*) half-belt

**Riegel·haus** *das* (*schweiz.*) half-timbered house

**Riemchen** *das;* **~s, ~:** [small] strap *or* belt

**Riemen** /ˈri:mən/ *der;* **~s, ~ A** (*Gurt*) strap; (*Treib~, Gürtel*) belt; **sich am ~ reißen** (*ugs.*) pull oneself together; get a grip on oneself; **den ~ enger schnallen** (*fig. ugs.*) tighten one's belt; **B** (*Schnürsenkel*) leather shoelace; **C** (*derb: Penis*) prick (*coarse*); **D** (*Ruder*) [long] oar; **sich [kräftig] in die ~ legen** (*auch fig.*) put one's back into it

**Riemen-: ~an·trieb** *der* belt drive; **~scheibe** *die* belt pulley

**Ries** /ri:s/ *das;* **~es, ~e** (*veraltet*) two reams; **vier ~ Papier** eight reams of paper

**Riese** /ˈri:zə/ *der;* **~n, ~n A** giant; **ein ~ von einem Menschen** a giant of a man/woman; ⇒ *auch* **abgebrochen** 2 B; **B** (*salopp: Tausender* [*Banknote*]) thousand-mark/dollar *etc.* note; **das kostet drei ~n** that costs three grand [in marks *etc.*] (*coll.*)

**-riese** *der;* **~n, ~n** giant; **Automobil~:** giant car manufacturer; **Chemie~:** giant chemical firm; **Branchen~:** giant of the industry

**Riesel·feld** *das* (*Landw.*) field irrigated with sewage

**rieseln** /ˈri:zl̩n/ *itr. V.; mit Richtungsangabe mit sein;* **A** (*rinnen*) trickle; **B** (*fallen*) ‹sand, lime› trickle [down]; ‹snow› fall gently *or* lightly; **der Kalk rieselte von den Wänden** lime was crumbling off the walls

**Riesen-** giant ‹building, tree, salamander, tortoise, etc.›; enormous ‹task, selection, profit, sum, portion›; tremendous (*coll.*) ‹effort, rejoicing, success, hit›; (*abwertend: schrecklich*) terrific (*coll.*), terrible (*coll.*) ‹stupidity, mess, scandal, fuss›; **ich habe einen ~hunger** I am tremendously *or* terribly hungry (*coll.*); **ein ~rindvieh** (*ugs.*) an almighty idiot (*coll.*); **ein ~spaß** (*ugs.*) tremendous *or* terrific fun (*coll.*)

**riesen-, Riesen-: ~baby** *das* (*ugs.*) **A** oversize baby (*joc.*); **B** (*abwertend*) ⇒ **Elefantenküken; ~bock·wurst** *die* giant bockwurst; **~groß** *Adj.* enormous; huge; gigantic; terrific (*coll.*) ‹surprise›; **eine ~große Dummheit** something terribly stupid (*coll.*); **~haft** *Adj.* enormous; huge; gigantic; **~rad** *das* big wheel; Ferris wheel; **~rad fahren** go on the big wheel *or* Ferris wheel; **~saurier** *der* giant dinosaur; **~schlange** *die* boa; **~schritt** *der* giant stride; **~slalom** *der* (*Skisport*) giant slalom; **~stern** *der* (*Astron.*) giant [star]; **~wuchs** *der* (*Biol.*) gigantism

**riesig 1** *Adj.* **A** (*sehr groß*) enormous; huge; gigantic; vast ‹country›; tremendous ‹joy, enthusiasm, effort, progress, strength›; terrific (*coll.*), terrible (*coll.*) ‹hunger, thirst›; **~e Ausmaße haben** be of enormous size; **ein ~er Spaß** terrific *or* tremendous fun (*coll.*); **B** (*ugs.: großartig*) fabulous (*coll.*), tremendous (*coll.*) ‹party, film, etc.›. **2** *adv.* (*ugs.*) tremendously (*coll.*); terribly (*coll.*)

**Riesin** *die;* **~, ~nen** giantess

**Riesling** /ˈri:slɪŋ/ *der;* **~s, ~e** Riesling

**riet** /ri:t/ *1. u. 3. Pers. Sg. Prät. v.* **raten**

**Riff**[1] /rɪf/ *das;* **~[e]s, ~e** reef

**Riff**[2] *der;* **~s, ~s** (*Jazz*) riff

**Riffel** /ˈrɪfl̩/ *die;* **~, ~n A** corrugation; (*Vertiefung*) groove; (*in einer Säule*) flute; (*Erhöhung*) rib; **B** (*Textilw.*) (*Maschine*) ripple [machine]; (*Kamm*) ripple

**riffeln** *tr. V.* **A** rib ‹glass›; ripple ‹lake›; ⇒ *auch* **geriffelt; B** (*Textilw.*) ripple ‹flax›

**Rififi** /ˈrɪfifi/ *das;* **~s** (*ugs.*) master crime

**Rigg** /rɪk/ *das;* **~s, ~s** (*Seemannsspr.*) rig

**rigid** /riˈgi:t/, **rigide 1** *Adj.* (*geh., Med.*) rigid. **2** *adv.* (*geh.*) rigidly

**Rigidität** /rigidiˈtɛ:t/ *die;* **~** (*geh., Med.*) rigidity

**Rigorismus** /rigoˈrɪsmʊs/ *der;* **~** (*geh.*) rigorism

**rigoros** /rigoˈro:s/ **1** *Adj.* rigorous. **2** *adv.* rigorously; **etw. ~ ablehnen** reject sth. categorically

**Rigorosität** *die;* **~** (*geh.*) rigorousness

**Rigorosum** /rigoˈro:zʊm/ *das;* **~s, Rigorosa** *od. bes. österr.* **Rigorosen** (*Hochschulw.*) oral part of the doctoral examination

**Rikscha** /ˈrɪkʃa/ *die;* **~, ~s** rickshaw

**Rille** /ˈrɪlə/ *die;* **~, ~n** groove; (*in einer Säule*) flute

**Rind** /rɪnt/ *das;* **~[e]s, ~er A** cow; (*Stier*) bull; **~er** cattle *pl.*; **20 ~er** twenty head of cattle; **ein gemästetes ~:** a fattened ox; **Hackfleisch/ein Steak vom ~:** minced *or* (*Amer.*) ground beef/a beef steak; **B** (*ugs.: ~fleisch*) beef; **C** (*Zool.*) bovine

**Rinde** *die;* **~, ~n A** (*Baum~*) bark; **B** (*Brot~*) crust; (*Käse~*) rind; **C** (*Hirn~*) cortex

**Rinder-: ~braten** *der* (*gebraten*) roast beef *no indef. art.*; (*roh*) roasting beef *no indef. art.*; **ein ~braten** a joint of roast beef; (*roh*) a joint of [roasting] beef; **~bremse** *die* horsefly; **~brust** *die* brisket of beef; **~filet** *das* fillet of beef; **~herde** *die* herd of [beef] cattle; **~leber** *die* ox liver; **~lende** *die* loin of beef; **~pest** *die* rinderpest; cattle plague; **~seuche** *die* cattle disease; **~talg** *der* (*zum Kochen*) beef suet; (*für Salbe usw.*) beef tallow; **~wahn·sinn** *der* ▶ 474 mad cow disease; **~zucht** *die* cattle breeding *or* -rearing *no art.*

**Rind-: ~fleisch** *das* beef; **~fleisch·brühe** *die* beef broth; **~fleisch·suppe** *die* beef soup

**rinds-, Rinds-: ~braten** *der* (*bes. südd., österr.*) ⇒ **Rinderbraten; ~fett** *das* (*südd., österr.*) clarified butter; **~leber** *die* (*bes. südd., österr.*) ⇒ **Rinderleber; ~leder** *das* cowhide; oxhide; **~ledern** *Adj.* cowhide; oxhide; **~lende** *die* (*bes. südd., österr.*) ⇒ **Rinderlende**

**Rind·vieh** *das; Pl.* **Rindviecher A** cattle *pl.*; **20 Stück ~:** twenty head of cattle; **B** (*ugs. abwertend*) ass; [stupid] fool; **ich ~!** what an idiot I am! (*coll.*)

**Ring** /rɪŋ/ *der;* **~[e]s, ~e A** ring; **die ~e tauschen** *od.* **wechseln** (*geh.*) exchange rings; **an den ~en turnen** perform *or* exercise on the rings; **10 ~e schießen** shoot *or* score a ten; **einen ~ bilden** ‹spectators etc.› form a ring *or* circle; ‹stones, road› form a ring; **B** (*~straße*) ring road; **den ~ fahren** take the ring road; **C** (*Box~*) ring; **~ frei zur zweiten Runde** seconds out for the second round; **D** (*Vereinigung*) **ein ~ für Theaterbesuche** a theatre-going circle; **ein ~ von Händlern** a ring of dealers; **E** (*Wurf~*) hoop

**Ring-: ~bahn** *die* circle line; **~buch** *das* ring binder

**Ringel** /ˈrɪŋl̩/ *der;* **~s, ~:** [small] ring; **die ~ ihrer Haare** the ringlets in her hair

**Ringel·blume** *die* marigold

**ringelig** *Adj.* curly; ‹hair› in ringlets

**Ringel·locke** *die* ringlet

**ringeln 1** *tr. V.* curl; coil ‹tail›; ⇒ *auch* **geringelt. 2** *refl. V.* curl

**Ringel-: ~natter** *die* ring snake; **~piez** /-pi:ts/ *der;* **~~[es], ~~e** (*ugs. scherzh.*) **~piez [mit Anfassen]** hop (*coll.*); hoedown (*Amer.*); **~reigen** *der,* **~reihen** *der;* **~~s, ~~:** ring-a-ring-o'-roses; **~reigen tanzen** *od.* **spielen** play ring-a-ring-o'-roses; **~schwanz** *der* curly tail; **~söckchen** *das,* **~socke** *die* [horizontally] striped sock; **~spiel** *das* (*österr.*) merry-go-round; **~taube** *die* wood pigeon; ring-dove; **~wurm** *der* (*Zool.*) annelid

**ringen 1** *unr. tr. V.* (*Sport, fig.*) wrestle; (*fig.: kämpfen*) struggle, fight (**um** for); **gegen jmdn.** *od.* **mit jmdm. ~** (*Sport*) wrestle with sb.; (*fig.*) **mit den Tränen ~:** fight back one's tears; **die Ärzte ~ um sein Leben** the doctors are struggling *or* fighting to save his life; **nach Atem** *od.* **Luft ~:** struggle for breath; **nach** *od.* **um Fassung ~:** fight to maintain one's composure; **er rang nach Worten** *od.* **um Worte** he struggled to find the right words; **ich habe lange mit mir gerungen, ob ...** I had a long struggle with my conscience to decide whether ...

**2** *unr. tr. V.* **A** (*bes. Sport*) **den Gegner zu Boden ~:** bring one's opponent down; **B** (*gewaltsam reißen*) **jmdm. etw. aus den Händen/der Hand ~:** wrest sth. from sb.'s hands/hand; **C** *in* **die Hände ~:** wring one's hands.

**3** *unr. refl. V.* (*geh.*) **ein Seufzer rang sich aus ihrer Brust** a sigh forced its way up from deep within her

**Ringen** *das;* **~s** (*Sport*) wrestling *no art.*

**Ringer** *der;* **~s, ~, Ringerin** *die;* **~, ~nen** wrestler

**ring-, Ring-: ~fahndung** *die* intensive manhunt [over a wide area]; **~finger** *der* ring finger; **~förmig 1** *Adj.* in the shape of a ring *postpos.*; circular; annular ‹eclipse›; **~förmige Verbindungen** (*Chem.*) ring *or* cyclic compounds; **2** *adv.* ‹arrange› in a ring *or* circle; ‹spread out› in rings *or* circles; **die Straße verläuft ~förmig um die ganze Stadt** the road rings the whole town; **~kampf** *der* **A** [stand-up] fight; **B** (*Sport*) (*Wettbewerb*) wrestling bout; (*Sportart*) ⇒ **Ringen; ~kämpfer** *der,* **~kämpferin** *die* wrestler

**Ringlein** *das;* **~s, ~:** [little] ring

**Ringlotte** /rɪŋˈglɔtə/ *die;* **~, ~n** (*bes. österr.*) greengage

**Ring-: ~mauer** *die* ringwall; **~muskel** *der* ▶ 471 (*Anat.*) sphincter; **~richter** *der,* **~richterin** *die* (*Boxen*) referee

**rings** /rɪŋs/ *Adv.* all around; **sich ~ im Kreise umsehen** look all around one; **~ von Bergen umgeben** completely surrounded by mountains

**Ring·schlüssel** *der* ring spanner

**rings·herum** *Adv.* all around [it/them *etc.*]; ⇒ *auch* **rings**

**Ring·straße** *die* ring road; (*um den Stadtkern*) inner ring road

**rings-: ~um, ~umher** *Adv.* all around; ⇒ *auch* **rings**

*old spelling (see note on page 1707)

**Ring-: ~tennis** *das* deck tennis; **~wall** *der* (*Archäol.*) ringwall

**Rinne** /'rɪnə/ *die;* ~, **~n** channel; (*Dach~, Rinnstein*) gutter; (*tiefer*) gully; (*Abfluss*) drainpipe; (*Rille*) groove; (*im Meeresboden*) trench

**rinnen** *unr. itr. V.* Ⓐ *mit sein* run; **das Geld rinnt ihm durch die Finger** money just slips through his fingers; Ⓑ (*südd.: undicht sein*) leak

**Rinnsal** /'rɪnza:l/ *das;* **~[e]s, ~e** (*geh.*) rivulet; **ein ~ von Blut/Öl** a trickle of blood/oil

**Rinn·stein** *der* gutter; **jmdn. aus dem ~ auflesen** (*fig.*) pick sb. out of the gutter; **im ~ enden** *od.* **landen** (*fig.*) end up in the gutter

**Riposte** /ri'pɔstə/ *die;* ~, **~n** (*Fechten*) riposte

**Rippchen** *das;* **~s,** ~ (*Kochk. südd.*) rib [of pork]

**Rippe** /'rɪpə/ *die;* ~, **~n** Ⓐ ▶ 471 (*Anat., Bot., Technik, Textilw., Bautechnik, fig.*) rib; (*Technik: Kühl~*) fin; **sie hat nichts auf den ~n** (*ugs.*) she is only skin and bone; **bei ihm kann man die ~n zählen** (*ugs.*) you can see his ribs sticking out; **dass er was auf die ~n kriegt** (*ugs.*) to put some flesh on his bones; **ich kann es mir nicht aus den ~n schneiden** (*ugs.*) I can't just produce it out of thin air; Ⓑ (*einer Zitrusfrucht*) segment; (*einer Tafel Schokolade*) strip

**Rippen-: ~bogen** *der* ▶ 471 (*Anat.*) costal arch; **~bruch** *der* ▶ 474 (*Med.*) rib fracture; **~fell** *das* ▶ 471 (*Anat.*) costal pleura; **~fell·entzündung** *die* ▶ 474 (*Med.*) pleurisy *no indef. art.*; **~speer** *der od. das;* **~~[e]s: [Kasseler] ~speer** cured rib of pork; **~stoß** *der* dig in the ribs; (*sanfter, auch fig.*) nudge; **~stück** *das* (*Kochk.*) piece of rib

**Ripp·samt** *der* corduroy

**Rips** /rɪps/ *der;* **~es, ~e** (*Textilw.*) rep[p]

**Risiko** /'ri:ziko/ *das;* **~s, Risiken** *od.* **~s** *od. österr.* **Risken** risk; **das ~ eingehen, dass etw. geschieht** run the risk of sth. happening; **ein/kein ~ eingehen** take a risk/not take any risks; **die Sache ist mit einem gewissen ~ verbunden** there is a certain amount of risk involved [in it]; **auf eigenes/dein/mein ~:** at one's/your/my own risk

**risiko-, Risiko-: ~faktor** *der* risk factor; **der ~faktor Alkohol** the risk factor represented by alcohol; **~frei** ⇒ **~los**; **~freudig** ❶ *Adj.* risky ‹driving›; ‹player, speculator› who likes taking risks; **er ist sehr ~freudig** he likes playing with fire *or* taking [a lot of] risks; ❷ *adv.* **er fährt/spielt sehr ~freudig** he likes to take [a lot of] risks when he drives/plays; **~geburt** *die* (*Med.*) difficult *or* complicated birth; **~gruppe** *die* risk group; **~los** ❶ *Adj.* safe; without risk *postpos.*; ❷ *adv.* safely; without taking risks; **~reich** *Adj.* very risky; **~schwangerschaft** *die* pregnancy involving some risk

**riskant** /rɪs'kant/ ❶ *Adj.* risky. ❷ *adv.* riskily; **er fährt zu ~:** he takes too many risks [in his driving]

**riskieren** /rɪs'ki:rən/ *tr. V.* risk; venture ‹smile, remark›; run the risk of ‹accident, thrashing, etc.›; (*gefährden*) put ‹reputation, job› at risk; risk ‹life, reputation›; **etwas/nichts ~:** take a risk/not take any risks; **einen verstohlenen Blick ~:** steal a furtive glance

**Rispe** /'rɪspə/ *die;* ~, **~n** (*Bot.*) panicle

**riss, *riß** /rɪs/ *1. u. 3. Pers. Sg. Prät. v.* **reißen**

**Riss, *Riß** /rɪs/ *der;* **Risses, Risse** Ⓐ (*im Stoff, Papier, Gewebe*) tear; (*im Tonband*) break; **die Hose hat einen ~/du hast einen ~ in der Hose** the trousers/your trousers are torn *or* have a tear; **einen ~ bekommen** tear; Ⓑ (*Spalt, Sprung*) crack; (*fig.: Kluft*) rift; split; **einen ~ bekommen** become cracked; (*fig.*) ‹friendship› begin to break up; Ⓒ (*Zeichnung*) plan; (*Entwurf*) sketch

**rissig** *Adj.* cracked; chapped ‹lips›

**Rist** /rɪst/ *der;* **~es, ~e** (*des Fußes*) instep; (*der Hand*) back [of the hand]

**Rist·griff** *der* (*Turnen*) overgrasp

**rite** /'ri:tə/ *Adv.* (*Hochschulw.*) **~ bestehen** get a pass (*in one's doctoral examination*); **mit „~" bewertet werden** be given a pass

**Riten** ⇒ **Ritus**

**ritsch** *Interj.* rip; zip; **~, ratsch** rip, rip

**ritt** *1. u. 3. Pers. Sg. Prät. v.* **reiten**

**Ritt** *der;* **~[e]s, ~e** ride; **einen weiten/scharfen ~ machen** go for a long/hard ride; **auf einen** *od.* **in einem ~** (*ugs.*) in one go (*coll.*)

**Rittberger** /'rɪtbɛrgɐ/ *der;* **~s,** ~ (*Sport*) loop jump; **einen ~ springen** do a loop jump

**Ritter** *der;* **~s,** ~ Ⓐ knight; **jmdn. zum ~ schlagen** (*hist.*) knight sb.; dub sb. [a] knight; **fahrender ~** (*hist.*) knight errant; **~ ohne Furcht und Tadel** chevalier sans peur et sans reproche; (*fig. geh., oft scherzh.*) knight in shining armour; Ⓑ (*Adelstitel*) (*als Teil eines Namens*) Ritter; (*Ordens~*) Knight; Ⓒ *in arme* **~** (*Kochk.*) French toast

**Ritter-: ~burg** *die* knight's castle; **~dichtung** *die* (*Literaturwiss.*) knightly poetry; **~gut** *das* (*hist.*) ≈ manor; feudal estate; **~kreuz** *das* (*ns.*) Knight's Cross

**ritterlich** ❶ *Adj.* Ⓐ chivalrous; Ⓑ (*zum Rittertum gehörend*) knightly ‹life, culture, virtues, ideals›. ❷ *adv.* chivalrously

**Ritterlichkeit** *die;* **~:** chivalrousness; chivalry

**Ritter-: ~orden** *der* order of knights; knightly order; **~roman** *der* romance of chivalry; knightly romance

**Ritterschaft** *die;* ~ (*hist.*) knighthood

**Ritter-: ~schlag** *der* (*hist.*) knightly accolade; **den ~schlag empfangen** be knighted; be dubbed [a] knight; **~sporn** *der;* **~~[e]s, ~~e** (*Bot.*) larkspur; (*Gartenrittersporn*) delphinium; **~stand** *der* (*hist.*) knighthood; **jmdn. in den ~stand aufnehmen** make sb. a knight

**Rittertum** *das;* **~s** (*hist.*) knighthood

**Ritter·zeit** *die* days *pl.* of the knights; (*Zeit der Ritterlichkeit*) Age of Chivalry

**rittlings** /'rɪtlɪŋs/ *Adv.* astride; **~ auf einem Stuhl sitzen** sit astride a chair

**Ritt·meister** *der* (*Milit. hist.*) cavalry captain

**Ritual** /ri'tu̯a:l/ *das;* **~s, ~e** *od.* **Ritualien** /-li̯ən/ (*Rel., fig.*) ritual

**ritualisieren** *tr. V.* (*geh.*) ritualize

**Ritual·mord** *der* ritual murder

**rituell** /ri'tu̯ɛl/ (*Rel., fig.*) ❶ *Adj.* ritual. ❷ *adv.* ritually

**Ritus** /'ri:tʊs/ *der;* ~, **Riten** (*Rel., fig.*) rite

**Ritz** /rɪts/ *der;* **~es, ~e** Ⓐ (*Kratzer*) scratch; Ⓑ ⇒ **Ritze**

**Ritze** *die;* ~, **~n** crack; [narrow] gap; **durch eine ~ spähen** peer through a crack *or* slit; **auf der ~ schlafen** (*ugs. scherzh.*) sleep on the join (*of a pair of* [*twin*] *beds*)

**Ritzel** /'rɪtsl̩/ *das;* **~s,** ~ (*Technik*) pinion

**ritzen** *tr. V.* Ⓐ scratch; (*tiefer*) cut; **sich** (*Dat.*) **das Kinn ~:** scratch/cut one's chin; Ⓑ (*ein~*) carve ‹name etc.› (**in** + *Akk.* in); (*in eine Metallplatte*) engrave ‹drawing etc.›

**Rivale** /ri'va:lə/ *der;* **~n, ~n, Rivalin** *die;* ~, **~nen** rival

**rivalisieren** *itr. V.* **mit jmdm. um etw. ~:** compete with sb. for sth.; **~de Gruppen** rival groups

**Rivalität** /rivali'tɛ:t/ *die;* ~, **~en** rivalry *no indef. art.*

**Riviera** /ri'vi̯e:ra/ *die;* **~:** Riviera

**Rizinus** /'ri:tsinʊs/ *der;* ~, ~ *od.* **~se** Ⓐ (*Pflanze*) castor-oil plant; Ⓑ (*~öl*) castor oil

**Roastbeef** /'ro:stbi:f/ *das;* **~s, ~s** Ⓐ (*roh*) sirloin (*Brit.*); Ⓑ (*gebraten*) roast [sirloin (*Brit.*) of] beef

**Robbe** /'rɔbə/ *die;* ~, **~n** seal

**robben** *itr. V.; meist, mit Richtungsangabe nur, mit sein* crawl

**Robben-: ~fang** *der* sealing; seal-hunting; **~schlag** *der* seal cull

**Robe** /'ro:bə/ *die;* ~, **~n** Ⓐ robe; (*schwarz*) gown; Ⓑ (*Abendkleid*) evening gown

**Robinie** /ro'bi:ni̯ə/ *die;* ~, **~n** (*Bot.*) robinia; false acacia

**Robinsonade** /robɪnzo'na:də/ *die;* ~, **~n** (*Roman/Abenteuer*) Robinson-Crusoe style novel/adventure

**roboten** /'rɔbɔtn̩/ *itr. V.* (*ugs.*) slave [away]

**Roboter** /'rɔbɔtɐ/ *der;* **~s, ~:** robot

**robust** /ro'bʊst/ *Adj.* robust

**Robustheit** *die;* **~:** robustness; (*Gesundheit*) robust constitution

**roch** /rɔx/ *1. u. 3. Pers. Sg. Prät. v.* **riechen**

**Rochade** /rɔ'xa:də/ *die;* ~, **~n** (*Schach*) castling; **kleine/große ~:** short/long castling; **die ~ ausführen** castle

**röcheln** /'rœçl̩n/ *itr. V.* breathe stertorously; ‹dying person› give the death rattle

**Rochen** /'rɔxn̩/ *der;* **~s,** ~ (*Zool.*) ray

**rochieren** /rɔ'xi:rən/ *itr. V.* Ⓐ (*Schach*) castle; Ⓑ *mit Richtungsangabe mit sein* (*Sport*) change over; switch positions

**Rock**[1] /rɔk/ *der;* **~[e]s, Röcke** /'rœkə/ Ⓐ skirt; (*Schotten~*) kilt; **hinter jedem ~ her sein** *od.* **herlaufen** (*ugs.*) be after *or* chase every bit of skirt (*sl.*); Ⓑ (*landsch.: Jacke*) jacket; **der grüne ~ [des Försters]** the [forester's] green coat; **den bunten ~ anziehen/ausziehen** (*fig. veralt.*) go for a soldier (*arch.*)/leave the army; **des Königs ~ tragen** (*fig. veralt.*) be a soldier of the King; **der letzte ~ hat keine Taschen** (*fig.*) you can't take it with you

**Rock**[2] *der;* **~[s]** (*Musik*) rock [music]

**Rock and Roll** /'rɔk ɛnt 'rɔl/ *der;* **~[s], ~[s]** rock and roll *no pl.*

**Rock·auf·schlag** *der* [jacket] lapel; **am ~:** in one's lapel

**Röckchen** /'rœkçən/ *das;* **~s, ~:** little skirt; (*kurz*) short skirt

**rocken** *itr. V.* rock

**Rocker** *der;* **~s, ~:** rocker

**rockig** *Adj.* rock ‹music›; rock-like ‹jazz etc.›

**Rock·musik** *die* rock music

**Rock-: ~oper** *die* rock opera; **~schoß** *der* coat-tail; ⇒ *auch* **~zipfel**; **~zipfel** *der: in* **an jmds.** *od.* **jmdm. am ~zipfel hängen** cling *or* hang on to sb.; (*fig.: unselbstständig sein*) lean on *or* be dependent on sb.; **jmdn. [gerade noch] am ~zipfel erwischen** just [manage to] catch sb.; ⇒ *auch* **Rock**[1] A

**Rodel** /'ro:dl̩/ *der;* **~s,** ~ (*südd.*) ⇒ **Rodelschlitten**

**Rodel·bahn** *die* toboggan run; (*bei sportlichen Veranstaltungen*) luge run

**rodeln** /'ro:dl̩n/ *itr. V.; meist, mit Richtungsangabe nur, mit sein* sledge; toboggan; (*als Sport*) luge

**rödeln** *itr. V.* beaver away

**Rodeln** *das;* **~s** sledging *no art.*; tobogganing *no art.*; (*Sport*) luge

**Rodel·schlitten** *der* sledge; toboggan; (*bei sportlichen Veranstaltungen*) luge

**roden** /'ro:dn̩/ ❶ *tr. V.* Ⓐ clear ‹wood, land›; (*ausgraben*) grub up ‹tree›; Ⓑ (*ernten*) lift ‹potatoes etc.›. ❷ *itr. V.* clear the land

**Rodeo** /ro'de:o/ *das od. der;* **~s, ~s** rodeo

**Rodler** /'ro:dlɐ/ *der;* **~s,** ~, **Rodlerin** *die;* ~, **~nen** tobogganer; (*bei sportlichen Veranstaltungen*) luger

**Rodung** *die;* ~, **~en** Ⓐ (*das Roden*) clearing; clearance; (*das Ausgraben*) grubbing up; Ⓑ (*gerodete Fläche*) clearance

**Rogen** /'ro:gn̩/ *der;* **~s, ~:** roe

**Roggen** /'rɔgn̩/ *der;* **~s** rye

**Roggen-: ~brot** *das* rye bread; **ein ~brot** a loaf of rye bread; **~brötchen** *das* rye-bread roll

**roh** /ro:/ ❶ *Adj.* Ⓐ raw ‹food›; unboiled ‹milk›; raw, uncooked ‹ham›; **jmdn./etw. wie ein ~es Ei behandeln** handle sb./sth. with kid gloves; Ⓑ (*nicht bearbeitet*) rough, unfinished ‹wood›; rough, uncut ‹diamond›; rough-hewn, undressed ‹stone›; crude ‹ore, metal›; unbleached ‹cloth›; untreated ‹skin›; raw ‹silk, sugar›; Ⓒ (*ungenau*) rough; Ⓓ (*brutal*) brutish ‹person, treatment, etc.›; (*grausam*) callous ‹person, treatment›; (*grob*) coarse, uncouth ‹manners, words, joke›; brute *attrib.* ‹force›.

r

**2** *adv.* **A** (*ungenau*) roughly; ~ **zusammengeschlagen** crudely knocked together; **B** (*brutal*) brutishly; (*grausam*) callously; (*grob*) coarsely; in an uncouth manner

**Roh-:** **~bau** *der; Pl.* **~~ten** shell [of a/the building]; **das Haus ist im ~bau fertig** the shell of the house is complete; **~diamant** *der* rough *or* uncut diamond; **~eisen** *das* pig iron

***Roheit** ⇒ **Rohheit**

**Roh-:** **~ertrag** *der* (*Wirtsch.*) gross return; **~erz** *das* crude ore; **~erzeugnis** *das* ⇒ **~produkt**; **~fassung** *die* unfinished version

**Rohheit** /'ro:hait/ *die;* ~, **~en** **A** (*Brutalität*) brutishness; (*Grausamkeit*) callousness; (*Grobheit*) coarseness; uncouthness; **B** (*Handlung*) brutish/callous deed; (*Äußerung*) callous remark

**Roh·kost** *die* raw fruit and vegetables *pl.*

**Rohköstler** /'ro:kœstlɐ/ *der;* **~s**, ~, **Rohköstlerin** *die;* ~, **~nen** *person who eats raw fruit and vegetables only*

**Rohling** /'ro:lɪŋ/ *der;* **~s**, **~e** **A** (*abwertend: Mensch*) brute; beast; **B** (*Technik*) blank

**Roh-:** **~material** *das* raw material; **~öl** *das* crude oil; **~produkt** *das* natural product [requiring further treatment]; (*~stoff*) raw material

**Rohr** /ro:ɐ̯/ *das;* **~[e]s**, **~e** **A** (*Leitungs~*) pipe; (*als Bauteil*) tube; (*Geschütz~*) barrel; **das Schiff feuerte aus allen ~en** the ship fired with all its guns; **B** (*Röhricht*) reeds *pl.*; **C** (*Schilf usw. als Werkstoff*) reed; (*Bambus, Zucker~ usw.*) cane; **ein aus ~ geflochtener Korb/Stuhl** a reed basket/chair; **ein Korb/Stuhl aus ~** (*aus Peddigrohr*) a cane basket/chair; **spanisches ~:** rattan cane; **D** (*Schilf-, Riedhalm*) reed; **E** (*südd., österr.: Backofen*) oven

**Rohr-:** **~ammer** *die* (*Zool.*) reed bunting; **~blatt** *das* reed; **~bruch** *der* burst pipe

**Röhrchen** /'rø:ɐ̯çən/ *das;* **~s**, **~:** small pipe; (*Behälter*) small tube; (*Reagenzglas*) test tube; **ins ~ blasen** take the breathalyser test

**Rohrdommel** /-dɔməl/ *die;* ~, **~n** (*Zool.*) bittern

**Röhre** /'rø:rə/ *die;* ~, **~n** **A** (*Rohr*) tube; (*Leitungs~*) pipe; (*Tunnel~*) bore; (*Jägerspr.: Gang eines Baus*) gallery; ⇒ *auch* **kommunizieren** A; **B** (*Leuchtstoff~*) [fluorescent] tube; (*Elektronen~*) valve (*Brit.*); tube (*Amer.*); (*ugs.: Bild~*) [picture] tube; **vor der ~ sitzen** sit in front of the box (*coll.*); **C** (*Behälter*) **eine ~ [mit] Tabletten** a tube of pills; **D** (*eines Ofens*) oven; **in die ~ sehen** *od.* **gucken** (*fig. ugs.*) be left out [in the cold]

**röhren** *itr. V.* ‹stag etc.› bell; (*fig.*) roar

**röhren-, Röhren-:** **~förmig** *Adj.* tubular; **~hose** *die* drainpipe trousers; **~knochen** *der* long bone; **~pilz** *der* boletus

**Rohr-:** **~flöte** *die* reed pipe; (*Panflöte*) pan pipes *pl.*; **~geflecht** *das* woven cane

**Röhricht** /'rø:rɪçt/ *das;* **~s**, **~e** reeds *pl.*

**Rohr-:** **~kolben** *der* reed mace; cat's-tail; **~krepierer** *der;* **~~s**, **~~:** barrel burst; **~leger** *der;* **~~s**, **~~**, **~legerin** *die;* **~~**, **~~nen** pipelayer; **~leitung** *die* pipe; (*über längere Entfernung*) pipeline

**Röhrling** /'rø:ɐ̯lɪŋ/ *der;* **~s**, **~e** boletus

**Rohr-:** **~post** *die* pneumatic dispatch; **etw. mit ~post befördern** convey sth. by pneumatic tube; **~sänger** *der* (*Zool.*) reed warbler; **~spatz** *der:* *in* **schimpfen wie ein ~spatz** (*ugs.*) really create (*coll.*); **~stock** *der* cane [walking stick]; **~zange** *die* footprint; **~zucker** *der* cane sugar

**Roh·seide** *die* raw silk

**roh·seiden** *Adj.* raw-silk *attrib.*

**Roh·stoff** *der* raw material

**Rohstoff-:** **~mangel** *der* lack of raw materials; **~preis** *der* raw material price; **~reserve** *die* reserve of raw materials

*old spelling (see note on page 1707)

**Roh-:** **~übersetzung** *die* rough translation; **~zucker** *der* raw *or* unrefined sugar; **~zustand** *der* raw state; **im ~zustand** in a raw state; (*von Gütern*) in an unfinished state; (*von einem Schriftstück usw.*) in a rough draft

**Rokoko** /'rɔkoko/ *das;* **~[s]** rococo; (*Zeit*) rococo period

**Rokoko·möbel** *das* piece of rococo furniture; **teure ~:** expensive rococo furniture *sing.*

***Rolladen** ⇒ **Rollladen**

**Roll·bahn** *die* (*Flugw.*) taxiway

**Röllchen** /'rœlçən/ *das;* **~s**, ~ **A** (*Spule*) little reel *or* spool; **B** (*etwas Zusammengerolltes*) little roll; **C** (*Walze*) little roller; **D** ⇒ **Rolle** D

**Rolle** /'rɔlə/ *die;* ~, **~n** **A** (*Spule*) reel; spool; **eine ~ Film** a spool of film; (*Schmalfilm*) a reel of film; **B** (*zylindrischer [Hohl]körper; Zusammengerolltes*) roll; (*zum Verschicken von Plakaten o. Ä.*) [cardboard] tube; (*von Papier zum Drucken*) reel; (*Schrift~*) scroll; **eine ~ Bindfaden/Drops/Markstücke/Kekse** a reel of string/tube of fruit drops/roll of one-mark pieces/[round] packet of biscuits; **C** (*Walze*) roller; (*Teig~*) rolling pin; **D** (*Rad*) [small] wheel; (*an Möbeln usw.*) castor; (*für Gardine, Schiebetür usw.*) runner; (*mit einer Rille für ein Seil o. Ä.*) pulley; **E** (*Turnen, Kunstflug*) roll; **eine ~ [vorwärts/rückwärts] machen** do a [forward/backward] roll; **F** (*Theater, Film usw., fig.*) role; part; (*Soziol.*) role; **sich in die ~ eines anderen versetzen** put oneself in sb. else's position; **[bei jmdm./einer Sache] eine entscheidende/überragende ~ spielen** be of crucial/overriding importance [to sb./for sth.]; **es spielt keine ~:** it is of no importance; (*es macht nichts aus*) it doesn't matter; (*es gehört nicht zur Sache*) it is irrelevant; **Geld spielt [bei ihm] keine ~:** money is no object [for him]; **solche Erwägungen dürfen dabei keine ~ spielen** such considerations must not be allowed to enter into it *or* influence things; **aus der ~ fallen** forget oneself; **G** (*Radsport*) roller (*on a pacing motorcycle*); (*fig. ugs.*) **von der ~ kommen** get left behind; lose ground

**rollen** **1** *tr. V.* **A** roll; (*im Rollstuhl*) wheel; **die Augen ~:** roll one's eyes; **das R ~:** roll one's r's; **sich (*Dat.*) eine Zigarette ~:** roll oneself a cigarette; **B** (*auf~, zusammen~, ein~*) roll up ‹blanket, carpet, map, etc.›; **jmdn./etw./sich in eine Decke ~:** roll sb./sth./oneself up in a blanket; **C** (*aus~*) roll out ‹dough›.
**2** *itr. V.* **A** *mit sein* ‹ball, wheel, etc.› roll; ‹vehicle› move; ‹aircraft› taxi; **mit den Augen ~:** roll one's eyes; **ins R~ kommen** start to move; get under way (*lit. or fig.*); (*unbeabsichtigt*) start to move; **es werden Köpfe ~** (*fig.*) heads will roll; **etw. ins R~ bringen** set sth. in motion; get sth. going (*lit. or fig.*); (*unbeabsichtigt*) set sth. moving; **B** (*Seemannsspr.: schlingern [und stampfen]*) ‹ship› roll [and pitch]; **C** (*donnern*) *mit Richtungsangabe mit sein* ‹thunder, guns, echo› rumble.
**3** *refl. V.* **A** (*sich ein~*) ‹paper, carpet› curl [up]; **B** (*sich wälzen*) roll; **er rollte sich in die Rückenlage** he rolled over on to his back

**rollen-, Rollen-:** **~fach** *das* (*Theater*) type of role; **das ~fach der Naiven** the ingénue type of role; **~förmig** *Adj.* cylindrical; **~konflikt** *der* (*Soziol.*) role conflict; **~lager** *das* (*Technik*) roller bearing; **~spiel** *das* (*Sozialpsych.*) role playing *no pl., no art.;* role play *no pl., no art.;* **~tausch** *der* exchange of roles; (*bei entgegengesetzten ~*) role reversal; **~verhalten** *das* role[-specific] behaviour; **~verteilung** *die* (*Sozialpsych.*) allocation of roles

**Roller** *der;* **~s**, ~ **A** scooter; **~ fahren** ride a/one's scooter; **B** (*Fußball*) half-hit shot along the ground; **C** (*Deo~*) roll-on [container]

**Rollerblade** Ⓦ /'roʊləbleɪd/ *der;* **~s**, **~s** Rollerblade ®

**rollern** *itr. V.; meist, mit Richtungsangabe nur, mit sein* ride a/one's scooter

**Rollerskate** /'roʊləskeɪt/ *der;* **~s**, **~s** roller skate

**Roll-:** **~feld** *das* [operational] airfield; landing field; **~film** *der* roll film; **~geld** *das* (*Eisenb.*) parcel freight [charge] (*for delivery to and collection from station or depot*); **~gut** *das* (*Eisenb.*) freight (*delivered to and collected from station or depot*); **~kommando** *das* party of bully boys; **~kragen** *der* polo neck; **~kragen·pullover** *der* polo neck[ed] sweater; **~kur** *die* (*Med.*) *treatment in which the patient takes medicine and then lies in different positions;* **~laden** *der; Pl.* **~läden**, *auch* **~~:** [roller] shutter; **~mops** *der* rollmops

***Rolladen** ⇒ **Rollladen**

**Rollo** /'rɔlo/ *das;* **~s**, **~s** [roller] blind

**Roll-:** **~schinken** *der* rolled smoked ham; **~schuh** *der* roller skate; **~schuh laufen** roller skate

**Rollschuh-:** **~bahn** *die* roller skating rink; **~laufen** *das;* **~~s** roller skating *no art.;* **~läufer** *der,* **~läuferin** *die* roller skater

**Roll-:** **~splitt** *der* loose chippings *pl.;* **~sprung** *der* (*Leichtathletik*) Western roll; **~stuhl** *der* wheelchair; **~stuhl·fahrer** *der,* **~stuhl·fahrerin** *die* person in a wheelchair; **~treppe** *die* escalator

**Rom**[1] /ro:m/ (*das*); ▶ **700** | **~s** Rome; **viele Wege führen nach ~** (*Spr.*) there is more than one way to skin a cat (*prov.*); **Zustände wie im alten ~** (*fig.*) everything in chaos; **~ ist auch nicht an einem Tag erbaut worden** (*Spr.*) Rome wasn't built in a day (*prov.*)

**Rom**[2] /rɔm/ *der;* **~s**, **~a** European gypsy

**Roman** /ro'ma:n/ *der;* **~s**, **~e** novel; **einen ganzen/langen ~ erzählen** (*fig.*) tell a very long story *or* (*derog.*) a long rigmarole; **erzähl keine ~e** (*fig.*) don't tell stories; (*fass dich kürzer*) we don't want any long rigmaroles

**Romancier** /romã'si̯e:/ *der;* **~s**, **~s** novelist

**Romane** /ro'ma:nə/ *der;* **~n**, **~n** speaker of a Romance language; Latin

**Roman-:** **~figur** *die* character from *or* in a novel; **eine ~figur bei Dickens** a character from *or* in a Dickens novel; **~form** *die* novel form; **in ~form** in the form of a novel; **~heft** *das* [paper-covered] novelette

**Romani** /'romani/ *das;* **~s** (*Sprachw.*) Romany

**Romanik** /ro'ma:nɪk/ *die;* **~:** Romanesque; (*Zeit*) Romanesque period

**Romanin** *die;* ~, **~nen** ⇒ **Romane**; ⇒ *auch* **-in**

**romanisch** ▶ **696** | **1** *Adj.* **A** Romance ‹language, literature›; Latin ‹people, country, charm›; ‹Department› of Romance Studies; **B** (*Kunstwiss.: der Romanik*) Romanesque. **2** *adv.* ‹build› in a Romanesque style

**romanisieren** *tr. V.* **A** (*romanisch machen*) give ‹town etc.› a Latin character; **B** (*hist.: römisch machen*) romanize ‹country etc.›

**Romanist** *der;* **~en**, **~en** Romance scholar; Romanist; (*Student*) student of Romance languages and literature

**Romanistik** /roma'nɪstɪk/ *die;* **~:** Romance studies *pl., no art.;* (*Sprache und Literatur*) Romance languages and literature *no art.*

**Romanistin** *die;* ~, **~nen** ⇒ **Romanist**

**romanistisch** *Adj.* Romance ‹studies›; ‹periodical› for Romance studies

**Romantik** /ro'mantɪk/ *die;* ~ **A** (*romantischer Charakter*) romanticism; romantic nature; **die ~ des Zigeunerlebens/der Straße** the romance of gypsy life/of the road; **B** (*Literaturw., Musik usw.*) (*Bewegung*) Romanticism *no art.;* Romantic movement; (*Epoche*) Romantic period; **die jüngere/ältere ~:** the younger/older Romantics *pl.*

**Romantiker** *der;* **~s**, ~, **Romantikerin** *die;* ~, **~nen** **A** (*Kunstwiss.*) Romantic; **B** (*romantischer Mensch*) romantic

**romantisch** **1** *Adj.* **A** romantic; **B** (*Literaturw., Musik usw.*) Romantic. **2** *adv.* romantically; **~ veranlagt sein** have a romantic disposition

**romantisieren** *tr. V.* romanticize
**Roman·werk** *das* Ⓐ (*Roman*) novel; Ⓑ (*Romane eines Autors*) novels *pl.*
**Romanze** /ro'mantsə/ *die;* ~, ~**n** (*Literaturw., Musik, fig.*) romance
**Römer** /'rø:mɐ/ *der;* ~**s**, ~ Ⓐ ▶553, ▶700 (*Person*) Roman; **die [alten]** ~**:** the [ancient] Romans; Ⓑ (*Weinglas*) rummer
**Römer·brief** *der* Epistle to the Romans
**Römerin** *die;* ~, ~**nen** ▶553 Roman; ⇒ *auch* **-in**
**Römer·topf** Ⓦⓩ *der* oval earthenware cooking pot; ≈ cooking brick
**römisch** ❶ *Adj.* ▶553, ▶700 Roman. ❷ *adv.* **das** ~ **besetzte Gallien** the part of Gaul occupied by the Romans
**römisch-katholisch** ❶ *Adj.* Roman Catholic. ❷ *adv.* ~ **getauft** baptized into the Roman Catholic church
**röm.-kath.** *Abk.* **römisch-katholisch** RC
**Rommé** /'rɔme/ *das;* ~**s**, ~**s** (*Kartenspiele*) rummy *no art.*
**Rondeau** /rõ'do/ *das;* ~**s**, ~**s** Ⓐ (*Literaturw.*) rondeau; Ⓑ (*österr.: Beet, Platz*) ⇒ **Rondell** A, B
**Rondell** /rɔn'dɛl/ *das;* ~**s**, ~**e** Ⓐ (*Beet*) circular flower bed; Ⓑ (*Platz*) circus; Ⓒ (*österr.: Weg*) circular path; Ⓓ (*Archit.: Turm*) round tower
**Rondo** /'rɔndo/ *das;* ~**s**, ~**s** Ⓐ (*Literaturw.*) rondeau; Ⓑ (*Musik*) rondo
**röntgen** /'rœntgn̩/ *tr. V.* X-ray; **sich** (*Akk.*)/ **sich** (*Dat.*) **den Magen** ~ **lassen** have an X-ray/have one's stomach X-rayed
**Röntgen-:** ~**aufnahme** *die,* ~**bild** *das* X-ray [image/photograph]; ~**gerät** *das* X-ray apparatus
**röntgenisieren** *tr. V.* (*österr.*) ⇒ **röntgen**
**Röntgenologe** /rœntgeno'lo:gə/ *der;* ~**n**, ~**n** ▶159 radiologist
**Röntgenologie** *die;* ~**:** radiology *no art.*
**Röntgenologin** *die;* ~, ~**nen** ▶159 radiologist
**Röntgen-:** ~**schirm** *der* X-ray screen; ~**strahlen** *Pl.* X-rays; ~**therapie** *die* X-ray treatment *no indef. art.;* **eine** ~**therapie** a course of X-ray treatment; ~**untersuchung** *die* X-ray examination
**Roquefort** /'rɔkfo:ɐ/ *der;* ~**s**, ~**s** Roquefort
**Ro-Ro-Schiff** /ro'ro:-/ *das* ro-ro *or* roll-on roll-off ship
**rosa** /'ro:za/ ❶ *indekl. Adj.* pink; ⇒ *auch* **Brille**. ❷ *adv.* pink
**Rosa** *das;* ~**s**, ~ *od.* ~**s** pink
**rosa-:** ~**farben**, ~**farbig** *Adj.* pink; ~**rot** *Adj.* [deep] pink; (*fig.*) rosy; ⇒ *auch* **Brille**
**rösch** /rø:ʃ/ *Adj.* (*südd.*) crisp
**Röschen** /'rø:sçən/ *das;* ~**s**, ~ Ⓐ (*kleine Rose*) [little] rose; Ⓑ (*Blumenkohl*~) [cauliflower] floweret; (*Rosenkohl*~) [Brussels] sprout
**rosé** /ro'ze:/ ❶ *indekl. Adj.* pale pink. ❷ *adv.* pale pink
**Rose** /'ro:zə/ *die;* ~, ~**n** Ⓐ rose; **sie sind nicht [gerade] auf** ~**n gebettet** their life is no bed of roses; **keine** ~ **ohne Dornen** (*Spr.*) no rose without a thorn; Ⓑ (*Fenster*~) rose window; Ⓒ (*Jägerspr.*) burr
**Rosé**[1] *das;* ~**s**, ~ *od.* ~**s** pale pink
**Rosé**[2] *der;* ~**s**, ~**s** rosé [wine]
**rosen-, Rosen-:** ~**beet** *das* rose bed; ~**blatt** *das* rose petal; (*Laubblatt*) rose leaf; ~**blüte** *die* Ⓐ rose [bloom]; Ⓑ (*das Blühen*) flowering period for roses; **die** ~**blüte hat begonnen** the roses have started to flower *or* bloom; ~**duft** *der* scent of roses; ~**garten** *der* rose garden; ~**gewächs** *das* (*Bot.*) rose; rosaceous plant; **die** ~**gewächse** the Rosaceae; ~**holz** *das* rosewood; ~**kohl** *der* [Brussels] sprouts *pl.;* ~**kranz** *der* (*kath. Kirche*) rosary; **einen** ~**kranz beten** say a rosary; ~**montag** *der* the day before Shrove Tuesday; ~**montags·zug** *der: carnival procession on the day before Shrove Tuesday;* ~**öl** *das* attar of roses; ~**quarz** *der* rose quartz; ~**rot** *Adj.* deep pink; ~**stock** *der* rose tree; standard rose; ~**strauß** *der; Pl.* ~**sträuße** bunch *or* bouquet of roses; ~**wasser** *das; Pl.* ~**wässer** rose water; ~**züchter** *der,* ~**züchterin** *die* rose grower
**Rosette** /ro'zɛtə/ *die;* ~, ~**n** Ⓐ (*Archit.*) rose window; Ⓑ (*Verzierung, Bot.*) rosette
**Rosé·wein** *der* rosé wine
**rosig** ❶ *Adj.* Ⓐ rosy ‹face, complexion, etc.›; pink ‹piglet etc.›; ~ **und gesund aussehen** be glowing with health; Ⓑ (*fig.*) rosy; optimistic ‹mood›; **etw. in den** ~**sten Farben schildern** paint sth. in the most glowing colours. ❷ *adv.* **ihm geht es nicht gerade** ~**:** things aren't too good with him
**Rosine** /ro'zi:nə/ *die;* ~, ~**n** raisin; (*Korinthe*) currant; **[große]** ~**n im Kopf haben** (*fig. ugs.*) have big ideas; **sich** (*Dat.*) **die** ~**n herauspicken** *od.* **aus dem Kuchen picken** (*fig. ugs.*) take the pick of the bunch [for oneself]
**Rosinen-:** ~**brot** *das* currant bread; (*Laib*) currant loaf; ~**kuchen** *der* currant cake
**Rosmarin** /'ro:smari:n/ *der;* ~**s** rosemary
**Ross, *Roß** /rɔs/ *das;* **Rosses, Rosse** *od.* **Rösser** /'rœsɐ/ Ⓐ (*geh.; südd., österr., schweiz. noch Normalspr.*) horse; steed (*poet./ joc.*); **hoch zu** ~**:** on horseback; (*scherzh.*) on one's [trusty] steed (*joc.*); **auf dem** *od.* **seinem hohen** ~ **sitzen** be on one's high horse; **von seinem** *od.* **vom hohen** ~ **herunterkommen** *od.* **-steigen** get down off one's high horse; ~ **und Reiter nennen** name names; Ⓑ *Pl.* **Rösser** (*ugs.: Trottel*) fool; idiot
**Ross-, *Roß-** ⇒ *auch* **Pferde-**
**Rössel** /'rœsl̩/ *das;* ~**s**, ~ Ⓐ (*landsch.*) small horse; Ⓑ (*Schach*) knight
**Rössel·sprung** *der: puzzle in which certain syllables make up a phrase or saying when taken in a sequence of knight's moves in a squared diagram*
**Ross-, *Roß-:** ~**haar** *das* horsehair; ~**kastanie** *die* horse chestnut; ~**kur** *die* (*ugs.*) drastic cure *or* remedy; ~**täuscher** *der* (*abwertend*) confidence trickster; con artist (*coll.*); con man (*coll.*); ~**täuscherei** *die;* ~~, ~~**en** (*abwertend*) confidence *or* (*coll.*) con trick; ~**täuscherin** *die* (*abwertend*) confidence trickster; con artist (*coll.*)
**Rost**[1] /rɔst/ *der;* ~**[e]s**, ~**e** Ⓐ (*Gitter*) grating; grid; (*eines Ofens, einer Feuerstelle*) grate; (*Brat*~) grill; (*im Freien*) barbecue; **vom** ~ (*Gastr.*) fresh from the grill; **auf dem** ~ **gegrillte Steaks** grilled steaks; (*im Freien*) barbecued steaks; Ⓑ (*Bett*~) base; frame
**Rost**[2] *der;* ~**[e]s** (*auch Bot.*) rust; ~ **ansetzen** begin to rust; go rusty
**rost-, Rost-:** ~**beständig** *Adj.* rust-resistant; (*absolut*) rustproof; ~**bildung** *die* rust-formation; rusting; ~**braten** *der* grilled steak; (*österr.: Entrecote*) entrecôte; rib steak; ~**brat·wurst** *die* grilled sausage; ~**braun** *Adj.* reddish-brown; russet; auburn ‹hair›
**Röst·brot** /'rœst-, 'rø:st-/ *das* toast
**Röste** /'rø:stə/ *die;* ~, ~**n** (*Hüttenw.*) roasting furnace
**rosten** *itr. V.; auch mit sein* rust; (*auch fig.*) get rusty; **alte Liebe rostet nicht** (*scherzh.*) old habits die hard; **eine nicht** ~**de Klinge** a non-rusting blade; **nicht** ~**der Stahl** stainless steel
**rösten** /'rœstn̩, 'rø:stn̩/ *tr. V.* Ⓐ roast ‹coffee, malt, chestnuts, etc.›; toast ‹bread›; **sich [in der Sonne]** ~ **lassen** roast oneself in the sun; Ⓑ (*bes. südd., österr., schweiz.: braten*) roast ‹meat›; (*auf dem Grill*) grill ‹meat›; (*in der Pfanne*) fry ‹meat, fish, egg, potatoes, etc.›; (*in der heißen Asche/Glut*) bake ‹potatoes›; Ⓒ (*Hüttenw.*) roast, calcine ‹ore›
**Röster** *der;* ~**s**, ~ Ⓐ (*Toaster*) toaster; Ⓑ (*österr.*) (*Zwetschgenmus*) plum purée; (*Holunderbeerenmus*) elderberry purée
**Rösterei** *die;* ~, ~**en** [coffee *etc.*] roasting establishment
**rost-, Rost-:** ~**farben**, ~**farbig** *Adj.* rust-coloured; russet; ~**fleck** *der* Ⓐ rust stain; Ⓑ (*rostige Stelle*) rust spot; (*größer*) patch of rust; ~**fraß** *der* rusting process; rusting *no art.;* ~**frei** *Adj.* Ⓐ (*nicht* ~*end*) stainless ‹steel›; Ⓑ (*ohne* ~) rust-free
**Rösti** /'rø:sti/ *die;* ~ (*schweiz. Kochk.*) thinly sliced fried potatoes *pl.*
**rostig** *Adj.* rusty
**Röst·kartoffeln** *Pl.* fried potatoes
**rost-, Rost-:** ~**laube** *die* (*ugs.*) picturesque old rust-heap; ~**rot** *Adj.* rust-coloured; russet; ~**schutz** *der* Ⓐ protection *no art.* against rust; rust protection *no art.;* Ⓑ (*Mittel*) rustproofing agent; ~**schutz·farbe** *die* anti-rust paint; ~**schutz·mittel** *das* ⇒ ~**schutz** B; ~**stelle** *die* patch of rust; (*kleiner*) rust spot
**rot** /ro:t/ ❶ *Adj.* red; **ein Roter** (*ugs.: Wein*) a red [wine]; **ein Roter/eine Rote** (*ugs.*) (*Mensch mit* ~*en Haaren*) a redhead; (*Sozialist*) a red (*coll.*); a leftie (*coll.*); **der Rote Platz** Red Square; **die Rote Armee** (*hist.*) the Red Army; **das Rote Meer** the Red Sea; **das Rote Kreuz** the Red Cross; **der Rote Halbmond/Löwe/Davidstern/die Rote Sonne** the Red Crescent/Lion/Star of David/ Sun; ~ **werden** turn red; ‹person› go red; blush; ‹traffic light› change to red; **er bekam einen** ~**en Kopf** he went red in the face; he blushed; **heute** ~, **morgen tot** (*Spr.*) here today, gone tomorrow; **lieber** ~ **als tot** (*ugs.*) better red than dead; ~ **geweinte Augen** eyes red from crying; ⇒ *auch* **Faden** A; **Zahl**.
❷ *adv.* red; ~ **gepunktet** with red dots *postpos., not pred.;* **etw.** ~ **schreiben/anstreichen** write/mark sth. in red; **[im Gesicht]** ~ **anlaufen** go red in the face; ~ **glühend** red-hot
**Rot** *das;* ~**s**, ~ *od.* ~**s** Ⓐ red; (*Schminke*) rouge; **die Ampel zeigt** ~**:** the traffic lights are red; **bei** ~ **über die Kreuzung fahren** cross the junction on the red; Ⓑ (*Spielkartenfarbe*) hearts *pl.;* ⇒ *auch* **Pik**[2]
**Rotarier** /ro'ta:ri̯ɐ/ *der;* ~**s**, ~, **Rotarierin** *die;* ~, ~**nen** Rotarian
**Rotarmist** /'ro:tarmɪst/ *der;* ~**en**, ~**en** (*hist.*) Red Army soldier
**Rotation** /rota'tsi̯o:n/ *die;* ~, ~**en** rotation
**Rotations-:** ~**achse** *die* axis [of rotation]; ~**druck** *der* rotary printing *no art.;* ~**fläche** *die* (*Math.*) surface of revolution; ~**körper** *der* (*Math.*) solid of revolution; ~**maschine** *die* (*Druckw.*) rotary press
**rot-, Rot-:** ~**auge** *das* (*Zool.*) roach; ~**backig**, ~**bäckig** *Adj.* rosy-cheeked ‹child, girl›; ruddy-cheeked ‹old man, farmer, etc.›; ~**barsch** *der* rosefish; ~**bart** *der* (*ugs.*) red-beard; red-bearded type (*coll.*); ~**blond** *Adj.* sandy ‹hair›; sandy-haired ‹person›; ~**braun** *Adj.* reddish-brown; russet; ~**buche** *die* [European] beech; ~**dorn** *der; Pl.* ~~**e** [pink] hawthorn
**Röte** /'rø:tə/ *die;* ~, ~**n** Ⓐ red[ness]; **eine** ~ **stieg ihm ins Gesicht** his face reddened; he blushed; Ⓑ (*Bot.*) madder
**Rötel** /'rø:tl̩/ *der;* ~**s**, ~**:** red chalk
**Röteln** /'rø:tl̩n/ *Pl.* **[die]** ~ ▶474 German measles *sing.*
**röten** ❶ *tr. V.* redden; make red; **Scham rötete ihr Gesicht** her face went red with embarrassment. ❷ *refl. V.* go *or* turn red
**rot-, Rot-:** ~**fuchs** *der* Ⓐ (*Tier, Pelz*) red fox; Ⓑ (*Pferd*) chestnut; (*heller*) sorrel; Ⓒ (*ugs.: Rothaariger*) redhead; ~**gardist** *der,* ~**gardistin** ~~, ~~**nen** *die* Red Guard; ~**gesichtig** *Adj.* red-faced; (*gesund, mit roten Backen*) ruddy-cheeked; *~**geweint** ⇒ **rot** 1; *~**glühend** ⇒ **rot** 2; ~**glut** *die* red heat; ~**gold** *das* red gold; ~**grün** *Adj.* (*Politik*) ‹coalition› of Greens and Socialists; red-green ‹coalition›; ~**grün·blindheit** /-'---/ *die* ▶474 (*Med.*) [red-green] colour-blindness; daltonism; ~**guss**, *~**guß** *der* red brass; ~**haarig** *Adj.* red-haired; **eine** ~**haarige/ein** ~**haariger** a redhead; ~**haut** *die* (*ugs. scherzh.*) redskin; ~**hirsch** *der* red deer
**rotieren** /ro'ti:rən/ *itr. V.* Ⓐ rotate; Ⓑ (*ugs.: hektisch sein*) flap (*coll.*); get into a flap (*coll.*); **er ist am R**~**:** he is in a flap (*coll.*)
**Rot-:** ~**käppchen** (*das*)*;* ~~**s** Little Red Riding Hood; ~**kehlchen** *das;* ~~**s**, ~~**:**

r

robin [redbreast]; **~kohl** *der,* (*bes. südd., österr.*) **~kraut** *das* red cabbage; **~kreuz·schwester** *die* Red Cross nurse; **~lauf** *der* (*Tiermed.*) swine erysipelas

**rötlich** /ˈrøːtlɪç/ ❶ *Adj.* reddish. ❷ *adv.* **~ braun** reddish-brown

***rötlich·braun** ⇒ rötlich 2

**rot-, Rot-: ~licht** *das; Pl.* **~lichter** red light; **bei ~licht** under a red light; **~liegende** *das; adj. Dekl.* (*Geol.*) Rothliegende; **~nasig** *Adj.* red-nosed

**Rotor** /ˈroːtɔr/ *der;* **~s, ~en** /roˈtoːrən/ (*Technik*) rotor

**rot-, Rot-: ~schwanz** *der,* **~schwänz·chen** *das* redstart; **~|sehen** *unr. itr. V.* (*ugs.*) see red; **~stichig** /-ʃtɪçɪç/ *Adj.* (*Fot.*) with a red cast *postpos., not pred.;* **~stichig sein** have a red cast; **~stift** *der* red pencil; (*Kugelschreiber*) red ballpoint; **dem ~stift zum Opfer fallen** (*aufgegeben werden*) be scrapped; (*gestrichen werden*) be deleted; **den ~stift ansetzen** (*fig.*) make economies; **~tanne** *die* common *or* Norway spruce

**Rotte** /ˈrɔtə/ *die;* **~, ~n** Ⓐ gang; mob; Ⓑ (*Milit.*) pair [operating together]; Ⓒ (*Jägerspr.*) (*von Wildschweinen*) herd; (*von Wölfen*) pack; Ⓓ (*Eisenb.*) gang

**rotten** *tr. V.* (*Textilw.*) ret ‹flax, hemp›

**Rotten·führer** *der* (*Eisenb.*) foreman

**Rottweiler** /ˈrɔtvailɐ/ *der;* **~s, ~** (*Hunderasse*) Rottweiler

**Rotunde** /roˈtʊndə/ *die;* **~, ~n** (*Archit.*) rotunda

**Rötung** *die;* **~, ~en** reddening

**rot·wangig** /-vaŋɪç/ *Adj.* (*geh.*) ⇒ **rotbackig**

**Rot·wein** *der* red wine

**Rotwein-: ~glas** *das* glass for red wine; **~fleck** *der* red wine stain

**Rotwelsch** *das;* **~[s]** thieves' cant *or* argot

**Rot-: ~wild** *das* (*Jägerspr.*) red deer; **~wurst** *die* blood sausage

**Rotz** /rɔts/ *der;* **~es** (*salopp*) Ⓐ snot (*sl.*); **frech wie ~** (*salopp*) cheeky as anything; **~ und Wasser heulen** (*salopp*) cry one's eyes out; **der ganze ~** (*salopp*) the whole bloody (*Brit. sl.*) *or* (*coll.*) damn lot; Ⓑ (*Tiermed.*) glanders *pl.*

**Rotz·bengel** *der* (*derb abwertend*) snotty brat (*sl.*)

**rotzen** (*derb*) ❶ *itr. V.* Ⓐ blow one's nose loudly; Ⓑ (*Schleim in den Mund ziehen*) sniff back one's snot (*sl.*); Ⓒ (*ausspucken*) gob (*sl.*). ❷ *tr. V.* spit

**Rotz·fahne** *die* (*derb*) snot rag (*sl.*)

**rotz·frech** (*salopp*) ❶ *Adj.* insolent; snotty (*sl.*); **ein ~er Bengel** a snotty little brat (*sl.*). ❷ *adv.* insolently; snottily (*sl.*)

**rotzig** ❶ *Adj.* Ⓐ (*derb*) snotty (*sl.*) ‹nose, handkerchief, child›; Ⓑ (*salopp: frech*) insolent; snotty (*sl.*). ❷ *adv.* (*salopp abwertend*) insolently; snottily (*sl.*)

**Rotz·nase** *die* Ⓐ (*derb*) snotty nose (*sl.*); Ⓑ (*salopp abwertend: Bengel*) snotty little brat (*sl.*)

**rotznäsig** /-nɛːzɪç/ (*derb abwertend*) ❶ *Adj.* Ⓐ snotty-nosed (*sl.*); Ⓑ (*ungezogen*) snotty (*sl.*). ❷ *adv.* snottily (*sl.*)

**Rouge** /ruːʒ/ *das;* **~s, ~s** rouge

**Roulade** /ruˈlaːdə/ *die;* **~, ~n** (*Kochk.*) [beef/veal/pork] olive

**Rouleau** /ruˈloː/ *das;* **~s, ~s** [roller] blind

**Roulett** /ruˈlɛt/ *das;* **~[e]s, ~e, Roulette** /ruˈlɛtə/ *das;* **~es, ~es** roulette

**Route** /ˈruːtə/ *die;* **~, ~n** route

**Routine** /ruˈtiːnə/ *die;* **~** Ⓐ (*Erfahrung*) experience; (*Übung*) practice; (*Fertigkeit*) proficiency; expertise; Ⓑ (*gewohnheitsmäßiger Ablauf*) routine *no def. art.;* **in ~ erstarrt sein** have got into a rut

**routine-, Routine-: ~angelegenheit** *die* routine matter; **~mäßig** ❶ *Adj.* routine; ❷ *adv.* as a matter of routine; **~sache** *die* ⇒ **~angelegenheit; ~untersuchung** *die* routine examination

**Routinier** /rutiˈni̯eː/ *der;* **~s, ~s** experienced man; (*Experte*) expert

**routiniert** /rutiˈniːɐ̯t/ ❶ *Adj.* (*gewandt*) expert; skilled; (*erfahren*) experienced; **ihr Auftreten ist mir zu ~:** her manner is too slick for my taste. ❷ *adv.* expertly; skilfully

**Rowdy** /ˈrau̯di/ *der;* **~s, ~s** (*abwertend*) hooligan

**Rowdytum** *das;* **~s** (*abwertend*) hooliganism

**Royalist** /rɔ̯ajaˈlɪst/ *der;* **~en, ~en, Royalistin** *die;* **~, ~nen** royalist

**royalistisch** ❶ *Adj.* royalist. ❷ *adv.* along royalist lines; **~ eingestellt sein** have royalist ideas

**Ruanda** /ˈru̯anda/ (*das*)**; ~s** Rwanda

**rubbeln** /ˈrʊbl̩n/ *tr., itr. V.* (*bes. nordd.*) rub [vigorously]

**Rübe** /ˈryːbə/ *die;* **~, ~n** Ⓐ turnip; (*Zucker~*) [sugar] beet; **rote ~:** beetroot; **gelbe ~** (*südd.*) carrot; Ⓑ (*salopp: Kopf*) nut (*coll.*); **eins auf die ~ kriegen** get a bonk *or* bash on the nut (*coll.*); **~ runter** *od.* **ab!** off with his/her head!

**Rubel** /ˈruːbl̩/ *der;* **~s, ~** ▶ 337 rouble; **der ~ rollt** (*fig. ugs.*) the money keeps rolling in

**Rüben-: ~kraut** *das* (*westdt.*) [sugar beet] syrup; **~zucker** *der* beet sugar

**rüber** /ˈrʏbɐ/ *Adv.* (*ugs.*) over

**rüber-: ~|dürfen** *unr. itr. V.* be allowed over; **über etw.** (*Akk.*) **~dürfen** be allowed to cross sth.; **~|faxen** *tr. V.* fax over; **jmdm. etw. ~faxen** fax sth. over to sb.; **~|gehen** *unr. itr. V.; mit sein* go over; **bei Rot ~gehen** cross over when the lights are red; **~|kommen** *unr. itr. V.; mit sein* Ⓐ come over; **komm doch einen Moment ~:** come over here a moment; Ⓑ (**~können**) manage to get over/across; **über die Straße/die Mauer nicht ~kommen** be unable to cross the road/get over the wall; Ⓒ (*salopp: verstanden werden*) come across; **~|können** *unr. itr. V.* be able to get over *or* across; **über etw.** (*Akk.*) **~können** be able to cross sth.; **~|müssen** *unr. itr. V.* have to get over *or* across; **über etw.** (*Akk.*) **~müssen** have to cross sth.; **er muss wieder ~ nach Amerika** he has to go back to America; **~|schicken** *tr. V.* send over; **~|sollen** *itr. V.* be supposed to go over; **soll der Schrank auch ~?** is the cupboard to go over there too?; **~|steigen** *unr. itr. V.; mit sein* **[über etw.** (*Akk.*)**] ~steigen** climb over [sth.]; **~|wollen** *unr. itr. V.* want to get over *or* across; **über etw.** (*Akk.*) **~wollen** want to cross sth.; **[in den Westen/Osten] ~wollen** want to cross over to the West/East

**Rübezahl** /ˈryːbətsaːl/ (*der*)**; ~s** Rübezahl (*spirit of the Sudeten Mountains*)

**Rubikon** /ˈruːbikɔn/ *der;* **~s** (*hist.*) *in:* **den ~ überschreiten** (*geh.*) cross the Rubicon

**Rubin** /ruˈbiːn/ *der;* **~s, ~e** ruby

**rubin·rot** *Adj.* ruby[-red]

**Rüb-** /ˈryːp-/: **~kohl** *der* (*schweiz.*) kohlrabi; **~öl** *das* rape oil

**Rubrik** /ruˈbriːk/ *die;* **~, ~en** (*Spalte*) column; (*Zeitungs~*) column; section; (*fig.: Kategorie*) category; **unter der ~ ...** under the heading [of] ...; (*in der Zeitung usw.*) in the ... section

**Rüb·samen** *der* oilseed rape

**Ruch** /ruːx/ *der;* **~[e]s** [bad] reputation; **im ~ der Korruption stehen** have the reputation of being corrupt

**ruch·bar** *Adj. in* **~ werden** (*geh.*) become known

**ruch·los** (*geh.*) ❶ *Adj.* dastardly; heinous ‹crime›. ❷ *adv.* in a dastardly fashion

**Ruchlosigkeit** *die;* **~:** dastardliness

**ruck, zuck** /rʊk ˈtsʊk/ *Interj.* in no time; **~, ~ gehen** only take a moment *or* second

**Ruck** /rʊk/ *der;* **~[e]s, ~e** jerk; **ein ~ nach links** (*Politik*) a sudden swing to the left; **in einem ~** (*fig. ugs.*) in one go; **sich** (*Dat.*) **einen ~ geben** (*fig.*) pull oneself together

**Rück·antwort** *die* reply; **um ~ wird gebeten** please reply

**ruck·artig** ❶ *Adj.* jerky. ❷ *adv.* (*mit einem Ruck*) with a jerk

**rück-, Rück-: ~besinnung** *die* recollection (**auf** + *Akk.* of); **eine ~besinnung auf bewährte Tugenden** a return to traditional virtues; **~bezüglich** (*Sprachw.*) ❶ *Adj.* reflexive; ❷ *adv.* reflexively; **~bildung** *die* Ⓐ (*Biol.*) atrophy; Ⓑ (*Med.*) regression; Ⓒ (*Sprachw.*) back-formation; **~blende** *die* flashback; **~blick** *der* look back (**auf** + *Akk.* at); retrospective view (**auf** + *Akk.* of); **im ~blick** in retrospect; **~blickend** ❶ *Adj.* retrospective; ❷ *adv.* retrospectively; in retrospect; **~datieren** *tr. V.; nur im Inf. u. 2. Part.* backdate

**ruckeln** /ˈrʊkl̩n/ *itr. V.* (*bes. nordd., mitteld.*) give a slight jolt

**rucken** ❶ *itr. V.* jerk; give a jerk; ‹car› jolt; give a jolt; ❷ *tr. V.* jerk

**rücken** /ˈrʏkn̩/ ❶ *tr. V.* move; **den Tisch an die Wand ~:** move *or* push the table against the wall; **es ließ sich nicht von der Stelle ~:** it was impossible to shift it; **etw. in ein völlig neues Licht ~** (*fig.*) show sth. in a completely new light.
❷ *itr. V.* Ⓐ *mit sein* move; **der Zeiger rückte auf 12** the hand moved up to 12; **mit seinem Stuhl näher an den Tisch ~:** move one's chair closer to the table; **jmdm. auf den Balg** *od.* **Pelz** *od.* **die Pelle ~** (*ugs.*) squeeze right up to sb; **die Polizei ist mir auf die Pelle** *od.* **den Pelz gerückt** (*fig.*) the police are breathing down my neck; **kannst du ein bisschen ~?** could you move up/over a bit?; **mit dem König ein Feld nach vorn ~** (*Schach*) move the king forwards one square; **ins Feld/ins Manöver ~** (*Milit.*) move into the field/go on manœuvres; **in weite Ferne ~** (*fig.*) recede into the distance; ‹project› become an increasingly remote possibility; Ⓑ **an etw.** (*Dat.*) **~** (*ziehen*) pull at sth.; (*schieben*) push at sth.; **an seiner Krawatte/Brille ~:** adjust one's tie/glasses; **hört auf, mit den Stühlen zu ~:** stop shifting your chairs

**Rücken** *der;* **~s, ~** Ⓐ ▶ 471 back; **ein Stück vom ~** (*Rindfleisch*) a piece of chine; (*Hammel, Reh*) a piece of saddle; **auf dem ~ liegen** lie on one's back; **legen Sie sich bitte auf den ~!** please lie [down] on your back; **jmdm. die Hände auf den ~ binden** tie sb.'s hands behind his/her back; **~ gegen** *od.* **an ~ stehen** stand back to back; **es lief mir [heiß und kalt] über den ~:** [hot and cold] shivers ran down my spine; **die Sonne/den Wind im ~ haben** have the sun/wind behind one; **verlängerter ~** (*scherzh.*) backside; posterior (*joc.*); **jmdm. den ~ zuwenden** turn one's back on sb.; **jmdm./einer Sache den ~ kehren** (*fig.*) turn one's back on sb./sth.; give sb./sth. up; **jmdm. den ~ stärken** *od.* **steifen** (*fig.*) give sb. moral support; **den ~ frei haben** (*fig.*) be free of any obligations; not be tied [down]; **sich** (*Dat.*) **den ~ freihalten** (*fig.*) not commit oneself; not enter into any obligations; **jmdm. den ~ freihalten** *od.* **decken** (*fig.*) ensure sb. is not troubled with other problems; **hinter jmds. ~** (*Dat.*) (*fig.*) behind sb.'s back; **im ~** (*fig.*) behind one; **er hat die Gewerkschaft im ~** (*fig.*) he has the backing of the union; **jmdm. in den ~ fallen** (*fig.*) stab sb. in the back; **mit dem ~ an der** *od.* **zur Wand** (*fig.*) with one's back to the wall; **mit dem ~ zur Wand stehen** (*fig.*) have one's back to the wall; Ⓑ (*Rückseite*) back; (*Buch~*) spine; (*der Nase*) bridge; (*des Berges*) ridge; Ⓒ ⇒ **~schwimmen**

**rücken-, Rücken-: ~aus·schnitt** *der* back neckline; **mit tiefem ~ausschnitt** with a low[-cut] back; **~deckung** *die* Ⓐ (*bes. Mittel*) rear cover; Ⓑ (*Unterstützung*) backing; **jmdm. ~deckung geben** give sb. one's backing; **~flosse** *die* dorsal fin; **~frei** *Adj.* backless ‹dress›; **~lage** *die* supine position; **in [der] ~lage** on one's back; **~lehne** *die* [chair/seat] back; **~mark** *das* ▶ 471 (*Anat.*) spinal marrow *or* cord

**Rücken·mark[s]-: ~entzündung** *die* ▶ 474 (*Med.*) myelitis *no indef. art.;* **~erweichung** *die* ▶ 474 (*Med.*) myelomalacia *no indef. art.;* **~punktion** *die* (*Med.*) spinal puncture

**Rücken-: ~muskulatur** *die* ▶ 471 back *or* (*Anat.*) dorsal muscles *pl.;* **~schild** *das*

*old spelling (see note on page 1707)

(*Bürow.*) spine label; **~schmerzen** *Pl.* backache *sing.*; **~schwimmen** *das* backstroke; **~stärkung** *die* [moral] support

**Rück·entwicklung** *die* ⇒ **Rückbildung** A, B

**Rücken-: ~wind** *der* tail *or* following wind; **~wind haben** have a tail *or* following wind; (*fig.*) be making good progress; **mit ~wind spielen** play with the wind behind one; **~wirbel** *der* ▶471 (*Anat.*) dorsal vertebra

**rück-, Rück-: ~erinnerung** *die* recollection; reminiscence; **~|erstatten** *tr. V.*; *nur im Inf. u. 2. Part.* repay; **jmdm. die Reisekosten ~erstatten** repay *or* reimburse sb. his/her travelling expenses; **~erstattung** *die* repayment; reimbursement; (*von Steuern*) rebate; **~fahr·karte** *die*; **~fahr·schein** *der* return [ticket]; **~fahr·scheinwerfer** *der* (*Kfz-W.*) reversing light; **~fahrt** *die* return journey; **auf der ~fahrt** on the return journey *or* way back; **~fall** *der* **A** (*Med., auch fig.*) relapse; **einen ~fall bekommen** *od.* **erleiden** have *or* suffer a relapse; **ein ~fall in alte Gewohnheiten/in die Barbarei** *usw.* (*fig.*) a relapse into *or* return to old habits/to barbarism *etc.*; **B** (*Rechtsspr.*) **Diebstahl/Einbruch im ~fall** subsequent *or* second offence of theft/burglary; **~fällig** *Adj.* **A** (*Med., auch fig.*) relapsed ‹patient, alcoholic, etc.›; **[wieder] ~fällig werden** have a relapse; ‹alcoholic etc.› go back to one's old ways; **B** (*Rechtsspr.*); **~fällig werden** commit a second offence; **~fall·täter** *der*, **~fall·täterin** *die* (*Rechtsspr.*) recidivist; subsequent *or* second offender; **~flug** *der* return flight; **~fluss**, ***~fluß** *der* reflux; return flow; **~frage** *die* query; **nach telefonischer ~frage** after checking up on the telephone; **~|fragen** *itr. V.*; *nur im Inf. u. 2. Part.* query it; **bei jmdm. ~fragen** raise a query with sb.; check with sb.; **~front** *die* back; rear; **~führung** *die* return; (*in die Heimat*) repatriation; **~gabe** *die* **A** return; **gegen ~gabe der Eintrittskarte** upon returning the [entrance] ticket; **B** (*Ballspiele*) back pass; **~gabe·recht** *das* right of return; **~gang** *der* drop, fall (+ *Gen.* in); (*qualitätsmäßig*) decline (+ *Gen.* in); **ein ~gang an Besuchern/Geburten** *usw.* a decrease in the number of visitors/births *etc.*

**-rückgang** *der* decrease in ...; **Preis-/Produktions~:** drop in price/fall in output

**rück-, Rück-: ~gängig** *Adj.* **A** **~gängig machen** cancel ‹agreement, decision, etc.›; break off ‹engagement›; **einen Kauf ~gängig machen** return what one has bought; **es lässt sich nicht mehr ~gängig machen** what's done cannot be undone; **B** (*im ~gang begriffen*) on the decline *postpos.*; **~gebildet** *Adj.* **A** (*Biol.*) atrophied; **B** (*Sprachw.*) produced by back-formation; **~gewinnung** *die* recovery (**aus** from); **die ~gewinnung von Rohstoffen aus Müll** the recovery *or* reclaiming of raw materials from waste products; **der Partei ist die ~gewinnung des Rathauses nicht gelungen** the party did not succeed in regaining control of the town council; **~grat** *das* ▶471 spine; (*bes. fig.*) backbone; **~grat haben/kein ~grat haben** have guts (*coll.*)/be spineless; **~grat zeigen** show [real] guts (*coll.*) *or* fight; **jmdm. das ~grat brechen** (*fig.*) break sb.'s resistance; **~grat[s]·verkrümmung** *die* ▶474 (*Med.*) spinal curvature; **~griff** *der* **A** recourse; **es bleibt immer noch der ~griff auf unsere Reserven** we can always have recourse to our reserves; **B** (*das Wiederaufgreifen*) return (**auf** + *Akk.* to); **~halt** *der* **A** support; backing; **er hat an seinen Freunden einen festen ~halt** he gets firm support *or* backing from his friends; **B** *in* **ohne ~halt** without reservation; unreservedly; **~halt·los** **1** *Adj.* unreserved, unqualified ‹criticism, support›; complete, absolute ‹frankness›; ‹fight› with no holds barred; **2** *adv.* unreservedly; without reservation; ‹trust› completely, absolutely; ‹confess› with complete frankness; ‹fight› with total commitment; **~hand** *die* (*Sport, bes. Tennis*) backhand; **einen Ball mit [der] ~hand schlagen/annehmen** hit/take the ball on one's backhand; **~kauf** *der* repurchase; (*einer Versicherung*) surrender; **~verkaufs·recht** *das* (*Rechtsw.*) right of repurchase

**Rückkehr** /ˈrʏkkeːɐ̯/ *die*; **~:** return; **jmdn. zur ~ [nach Litauen] bewegen** persuade sb. to return [to Lithuania]

**Rückkehrer** *der*; **~s, ~:** homecomer; **~ aus dem Urlaub** people returning from holiday

**rückkoppeln** *tr. V.*; *nur im Inf. u. 2. Part.* (*Elektrot.*) feed back; **A mit B ~** (*fig.*) [re]create links between A and B

**Rück·kopp[e]lung** *die* (*Elektrot.*) feedback; (*fig.*) [re]creation of links

**Rückkunft** /-kʊnft/ *die*; **~** (*geh.*) return

**rück-, Rück-: ~lage** *die* **A** (*Spargeld*) savings *pl.*; **eine kleine ~lage haben** have a small sum saved up; have a small nest egg; **B** (*Wirtsch.: Reserve*) reserves *pl.*; (*Sozialw.*) credit reserve; **~lauf** *der* **A** (*~fluss*) return flow; **B** (*~transport*) return; **C** (*bei Maschinen*) return travel; (*beim Tonbandgerät*) rewind; **~läufig** **1** *Adj.* **A** (*sinkend*) decreasing ‹number›; declining ‹economic growth etc.›; falling ‹rate, production, etc.›; **~e Entwicklung** downward trend; decline; **B** (*~wärts verlaufend*) reverse ‹process, dictionary›; reverse, retrograde ‹motion›; **~läufiges Wachstum** reversal of growth; **2** *adv.* in reverse order; **~licht** *das*; *Pl.* **~~er** rear *or* tail light

**rücklings** *Adv.* **A** (*auf dem Rücken*) on one's back; **B** (*mit dem Rücken nach vorn*) facing backwards

**Rück-: ~marsch** *der* march back; (*~zug*) retreat; **sich auf dem ~marsch befinden** ‹troops, tanks› be returning from the front/be retreating; **~nahme** /-naːmə/ *die*; **~~, ~~n** taking back; (*einer Behauptung, einer Anordnung, einer Klage usw.*) withdrawal; (*eines Verbotes*) cancellation; **die ~nahme von etw. verweigern** refuse to take sth. back; **~pass**, ***~paß** *der* (*Sport*) back pass; **~porto** *das* return postage; **~prall** *der*; **~~[e]s, ~~e** rebound; (*eines Geschosses*) ricochet; **~reise** *die* return journey; **~ruf** *der* **A** (*Fernspr.*) return call; **ich erwarte deinen ~ruf** I shall wait for you to phone back; **B** (*das Zurückbeordern*) recall

**Ruck·sack** *der* rucksack; (*Touren~*) backpack

**Rucksack·tourist** *der*, **Rucksack·touristin** *die* backpacker

**rück-, Rück-: ~schau** *die* review (**auf** + *Akk.* of); **~schau halten** look back; **~schau auf etw.** (*Akk.*) **halten** pass sth. in review; review sth.; **~schlag** *der* **A** setback; **in seinem Leben gab es immer wieder ~schläge** throughout his life he suffered repeated setbacks; **B** (*Tennis, Tischtennis usw.*) return; **~schlag·ventil** *das* (*Technik*) non-return valve; check valve; **~schluss**, ***~schluß** *der* conclusion (**auf** + *Akk.* about); **aus etw. ~schlüsse auf etw.** (*Akk.*) **ziehen** draw conclusions from sth. about sth.; **~schritt** *der* retrograde step; **das ist kein Fortschritt, sondern ein ~schritt** that's not a forward, but a backward step; **~schrittlich** **1** *Adj.* reactionary; retrograde ‹development›; **2** *adv.* **~schrittlich eingestellt sein** have reactionary ideas; **~schwung** *der* (*Turnen*) backward swing; **~seite** *die* back; (*eines Gebäudes usw.*) back; rear; (*einer Münze usw.*) reverse; (*des Mondes*) far side; **siehe ~seite** see over[leaf]; **auf der ~seite eines Tiefs** (*Met.*) in the rear of *or* behind a depression; **~seitig** **1** *Adj.* rear, back ‹entrance›; ‹explanation etc.› overleaf; **2** *adv.* **~seitig gelegen** situated at the back *or* rear; **~sendung** *die* return; **~sicht** *die* **A** consideration; **mit ~sicht auf etw.** (*Akk.*) taking sth. into consideration; in view of sth.; **~sicht auf jmdn. nehmen** show consideration for *or* towards sb.; (*Verständnis haben*) make allowances for sb.; **ohne ~sicht auf etw.** (*Akk.*) with no regard for *or* regardless of sth.; **ohne ~sicht auf Verluste** (*ugs.*) regardless; **keine ~sicht kennen** show no consideration; (*unbarmherzig sein*) be ruthless; **B** (*Erwägung, Grund*) **~en** considerations; **aus finanziellen ~sichten** for financial reasons; **C** (*Sicht nach hinten*) rear view; **~sicht·nahme** *die*; **~~:** consideration; **unter ~sichtnahme** (*Dat.*) **auf etw.** (*Akk.*) taking sth. into consideration/making allowances for sth.; **gegenseitige ~sichtnahme ist notwendig** it is essential that people show mutual consideration

**rücksichts-, Rücksichts-: ~los** **1** *Adj.* **A** inconsiderate; thoughtless; **ein ~loser Autofahrer** an inconsiderate driver; (*verantwortungslos*) a reckless driver; **B** (*schonungslos*) ruthless; **ein ~loser Kampf** a bitter struggle; a fight with no holds barred; **2** *adv.* **A** inconsiderately; thoughtlessly; (*verantwortungslos*) recklessly; **sich ~los durch die Menge schieben** shove one's way through the crowd regardless of anyone else; **B** (*schonungslos*) ruthlessly; **jmdm. ~los die Wahrheit sagen** tell sb. the truth regardless of his/her feelings; **~losigkeit** *die*; **~~, ~~en** **A** lack of consideration; thoughtlessness; (*Verantwortungslosigkeit*) recklessness; **so eine ~losigkeit!** how inconsiderate *or* thoughtless!; **B** (*Schonungslosigkeit*) ruthlessness; **~voll** **1** *Adj.* considerate; thoughtful; **2** *adv.* considerately; thoughtfully

**rück-, Rück-: ~sitz** *der* back seat; **auf dem ~sitz/den ~sitzen** in the back; in *or* on the back seat/seats; **~spiegel** *der* rear-view mirror; **~spiel** *das* (*Sport*) second *or* return leg; **~sprache** *die* consultation; **[mit jmdm.] ~sprache nehmen** *od.* **halten** (*Papierdt.*) consult [sb.]; **~stand** *der* **A** (*Übriggebliebenes, Rest*) residue; **radioaktive ~stände** traces of radioactivity; **B** (*offener Rechnungsbetrag*) **~stände/ein ~stand** arrears *pl.*; **~stände eintreiben** collect outstanding debts; **ein ~stand in der Miete** rent arrears *pl.*; **C** (*Zurückbleiben hinter dem gesetzten Ziel, Soll usw.*) backlog; (*bes. Sport: hinter dem Gegner*) deficit; **[mit den Zahlungen/mit der Arbeit** *usw.*] **im ~stand sein/in ~stand** (*Akk.*) **geraten** be/get behind [with one's payments/work *etc.*]; **seinen/einen ~stand aufholen** (*bei der Arbeit*) make up *or* catch up one's/a backlog; (*bei einem Spiel/Rennen/(fig.) bei der Rüstung usw.*) make up the deficit; close the gap; **die Mannschaft lag mit 0:3 im ~stand** (*Sport*) the team was trailing by three to nil; **mit 38 hundertstel Sekunden ~stand auf den zweiten Platz kommen** (*Sport*) take second place .38 of a second behind; **~ständig** *Adj.* **A** (*unterentwickelt*) underdeveloped; backward; **B** (*überholt*) outdated; antiquated; **~ständig sein** be behind the times; **C** (*schon länger fällig*) outstanding ‹payment, amount›; ‹wages› still owing; **~ständige Steuern** tax arrears; **~ständigkeit** *die*; **~~** **A** backwardness; **B** (*Überholtheit*) outdated nature; (*Ansichten*) old-fashioned *or* antiquated ideas *pl.*; **~stau** *der* (*von Wasser*) backing up; backwater; (*von Fahrzeugen*) tailback; **~stellung** *die* **A** (*das Zurückstellen*) postponement (**um** by); **eine ~stellung vom Wehrdienst** a temporary exemption from military service; **B** (*Wirtsch.*) reserve [fund]; **~stoß** *der* (*Physik*) reaction; (*einer Feuerwaffe*) recoil; **~strahler** *der* reflector; **~stufung** *die*; **~~, ~~en** downgrading; **~taste** *die* backspacer; backspace key; **~tausch** *der*: **beim ~tausch [von Devisen]** when changing currency back; **~tritt** *der* **A** (*von einem Amt*) resignation (**von** from); (*von einer Kandidatur, von einem Vertrag usw.*) withdrawal (**von** from); **B** ⇒ **~trittbremse**; **~tritt·bremse** *die* back-pedal brake

**Rücktritts-: ~drohung** *die* threat to resign; **~erklärung** *die* announcement of one's intention to resign; **~gesuch** *das* offer of resignation; **sein ~gesuch einreichen** hand in *or* tender one's resignation; **~recht** *das* right to withdraw [from a contract]

**rück-, Rück-: ~|übersetzen** *tr. V.*; *nur im Inf. u. 2. Part.* translate back; **~übersetzung** *die* back-translation; **~|vergüten** *tr. V.*; *nur im Inf. u. 2. Part.* refund; **~vergütung** *die* refund; **~|versichern** *refl. V.*; *nur im Inf. u. 2. Part.* **A** cover oneself [two ways];

r

hedge one's bets; **B** (*Versicherungsw.*) reinsure; **~versicherung** *die* **A** [double] insurance; (*Schutz*) safeguard; protection; **B** (*Versicherungsw.*) reinsurance; **~wand** *die* back wall; (*eines Regals usw.*) back; **~wanderer** *der*, **~wanderin** *die* repatriate

**rückwärtig** /-vɛrtɪç/ ❶ *Adj.* **A** back; rear; **die ~e Seite** the back *or* rear; **auf den ~en Verkehr achten** keep an eye on the traffic behind [one]; **B** (*Milit.*) rearward ‹lines of communication›. ❷ *adv.* **die ~ gelegene Tür** the door at the back

**rückwärts** /-vɛrts/ *Adv.* **A** backwards; **ein Blick [nach] ~:** a look back; a backward look; **ein Salto/eine Rolle ~:** a back somersault/backward roll; **~ fahren** reverse; **~ einparken** reverse *or* back into a parking space; **es ging ~** (*fig.*) it got worse; **mit dem Umsatz ist es immer mehr ~ gegangen** the turnover has gone down and down; **~ gewandt** turned backwards (*postpos.*); **B** (*südd., österr.: hinten*) behind; **[etwas] weiter ~:** [a little] further back; **~ einsteigen!** enter at the rear [of the vehicle]; **sich nach ~ fallen lassen/lehnen** fall/lean back

**rückwärts-, Rückwärts-: ~bewegung** *die* backward movement; **~drehung** *die* turn backwards; **durch ~drehung einer Sache** (*Gen.*) by turning sth. back; **~gang** *der* (*Kfz-W.*) reverse [gear]; **im ~gang** in reverse; **den ~gang einlegen** (*auch fig.*) go into reverse; ***~|gehen** ⇒ **rückwärts** A; ***~gewandt** ⇒ **rückwärts** A

**Rückweg** *der* return journey; **auf dem ~:** on the way back; **den ~ antreten, sich auf den ~ machen** set off *or* start on one's way back; **jmdm. den ~ abschneiden** cut off sb.'s line of retreat

**ruck·weise** ❶ *Adv.* (*mit einem Ruck*) with a jerk; (*mit mehreren*) in a series of jerks. ❷ *adj.* jerky

**rück-, Rück-: ~wendung** *die* reorientation; **~wirkend** ❶ *Adj.* retrospective; backdated ‹pay increase›; ❷ retrospectively; **~wirkend vom** *od.* **zum 1. April in Kraft treten** take effect [retrospectively] as from 1 April; **die Gehaltserhöhung erfolgt ~wirkend vom 1. Januar** the rise (*Brit.*) *or* (*Amer.*) raise is *or* has been backdated to 1 January; **~wirkung** *die* **A** (*zeitlich*) retrospective force; **mit ~wirkung vom ...** [retrospectively] as from ...; **B** (*Auswirkung*) repercussion (**auf** + *Akk.* on); **~zahlbar** *Adj.* repayable; **~zahlung** *die* repayment; **~zahlungs·bedingungen** *Pl.* repayment terms; **~zieher** *der* **A** (*Fußball*) overhead kick; **B** (*fig. ugs.*) (*von Behauptungen, Forderungen usw.*) climbdown; (*von einem Vorhaben*) backing out *no art.*; **einen ~zieher machen** climb down/back out; (*salopp: Coitus interruptus*) pull out (*coll.*)

**Rück·zug** *der* retreat; **auf dem ~ sein** be retreating; **jmdn. zum ~ zwingen** force sb. to retreat

**Rückzugs-: ~gebiet** *das* reserve (*for native inhabitants/wild animals*); **~gefecht** *das* (*Milit., fig.*) rearguard action

**rüde** /ˈryːdə/ ❶ *Adj.* uncouth; coarse ‹language›. ❷ *adv.* in an uncouth manner

**Rüde** *der;* **~n, ~n** **A** (*Hund*) [male] dog; (*Fuchs/Wolf*) [male] fox/wolf; **unser Hund ist ein ~:** our dog is a male; **B** (*Jägerspr.: Hetzhund*) hound; hunting dog

**Rudel** /ˈruːdl̩/ *das;* **~s, ~** (*von Hirschen, Gämsen*) herd; (*von Wölfen, Hunden*) pack; (*fig.: von Menschen*) horde

**Ruder** /ˈruːdɐ/ *das;* **~s, ~** **A** (*Riemen*) oar; **sich in die ~ legen** (*kräftig rudern*) row strongly *or* vigorously; (*fig. ugs.: etw. in Angriff nehmen*) put one's back into it; **B** (*Steuer~*) rudder; (*Steuerrad*) helm; **am ~ sein/bleiben** (*fig.*) be/stay at the helm; **das ~ fest in der Hand haben** (*fig.*) be firmly in control; **das ~ herumwerfen** (*fig.*) change course *or* tack; **ans ~ kommen** (*fig.*) take the helm; party, leader come to power; **aus dem ~ laufen** (*auch fig.*) go off course; **C** (*eines Flugzeugs*) (*Höhen~*) elevator; (*Quer~*) aileron; (*Seiten~*) rudder

**Ruder-: ~bank** *die; Pl.* **~bänke** thwart; (*einer Galeere*) oarsman's bench; **~blatt** *das* **A** (*eines Steuerruders*) rudder [blade]; **B** (*eines Riemens*) blade; **~boot** *das* rowboat; rowing boat (*Brit.*)

**Ruderer** *der;* **~s, ~:** oarsman; rower

**Ruder-: ~gänger** *der;* **~~s, ~~, ~gast** *der* (*Seemannsspr.*) helmsman; **~haus** *das* (*Seemannsspr.*) wheelhouse

**-ruderig** *Adj.* -oared

**Ruderin** *die;* **~, ~nen** oarswoman; rower

**rudern** ❶ *itr. V.* **A** *meist, mit Richtungsangabe nur, mit sein* row; **B** (*fig.*) **mit den Armen ~:** swing one's arms [about]; **C** *mit sein* ‹waterfowl› paddle. ❷ *tr. V.* row ‹boat, person, object›

**Ruder-: ~pinne** *die* tiller; **~regatta** *die* rowing regatta; **~sport** *der* rowing *no art.*

**Rudiment** /rudiˈmɛnt/ *das;* **~[e]s, ~e** **A** (*Biol., geh.*) vestige; **B** *Pl.* (*veralt.: Grundbegriffe*) rudiments

**rudimentär** /rudimɛnˈtɛːɐ̯/ (*Biol., geh.*) ❶ *Adj.* rudimentary. ❷ *adv.* in a rudimentary form

**Ruf** /ruːf/ *der;* **~[e]s, ~e** **A** call; (*Schrei*) shout; cry; (*Tierlaut*) call; **B** (*fig.: Aufforderung, Forderung*) call (**nach** for); **der ~ zu den Waffen** (*geh.*) the call to arms; **dem ~ des Herzens/Gewissens/der Natur folgen** *od.* **gehorchen** follow one's heart/listen to the voice of conscience/nature; **der ~ nach der Todesstrafe** the call for the death penalty; **C** (*Berufung*) **sie bekam einen ~ an die Universität Bremen** *od.* **nach Bremen** she was offered a chair *or* professorship at Bremen University; **D** (*Papierdt.: Telefonnummer*) telephone [number]; **~ 33700** tel. [no.] 33700; **E** (*Leumund*) reputation; **eine Firma von ~:** a firm of repute *or* with a good reputation; **ein Mann von gutem/schlechtem ~:** a man with a good/bad reputation; **jmdn./etw. in schlechten ~ bringen** give sb./sth. a bad name; **besser als sein ~ sein** be not as bad as one/it is made out to be; **ist der ~ erst ruiniert, lebt es sich ganz ungeniert** (*Spr.*) you needn't worry if you've no reputation to lose

**Rufe** /ˈruːfə/ *die;* **~, ~n, Rüfe** /ˈryːfə/ *die;* **~, ~n** (*schweiz.*) landslide

**rufen** ❶ *unr. itr. V.* **A** call (**nach** for); (*schreien*) shout (**nach** for); ‹animal› call; **hast du sein R~ nicht gehört?** didn't you hear him calling?; **jmdm. ~** (*südwestd., schweiz.*) call to sb.; **Mutter/der Gong ruft zum Essen** mother is calling [out] that lunch/dinner is ready/the gong is sounding for lunch/dinner; **die Glocke ruft zum Gottesdienst/Gebet** the bell is calling to worship/prayer; **die Pflicht/die Arbeit ruft** (*fig.*) duty calls; **B** (*schweiz.: hervor~*) **einer Sache** (*Dat.*) **~:** cause sth.; give rise to sth.

❷ *unr. tr. V.* **A** **etw. ~:** call sth.; (*schreien*) shout sth.; (*unpers.*) **aus dem Zimmer rief es: „Herein!"** from inside the room a voice called 'come in!'; **B** (*herbei-*) **jmdn. ~:** call sb.; **jmdn. zu Hilfe ~:** call to sb. to help; **dringende Geschäfte riefen ihn nach München** (*fig.*) he was called to Munich on urgent business; **jmdm./sich** (*Dat.*) **etw. ins Gedächtnis** *od.* **in Erinnerung ~:** remind sb. of sth./recall sth.; **[jmdm.] wie ge~ kommen** (*ugs.*) come at just the right moment; **du kommst/der Wind kommt mir wie ge~:** you're just the person I wanted/the wind is just what I wanted; **C** (*telefonisch*) call; **jmdn. [unter der Nummer 347106] ~:** call *or* ring sb. [on 347106]; **~ Sie 888666** ring 888666; (*über Funk*) **Teddybär ruft Zeppelin** Teddy Bear calling Zeppelin; **D** (*nennen*) **jmdn./** (*südwestd., schweiz.:*) **jmdm. etw. ~:** call sb. sth.; **E** (*geh., veralt.: anreden*) **jmdn. bei** *od.* **mit seinem Namen ~:** address sb. by name.

❸ *refl. V.* **sich heiser ~:** call until one is hoarse; (*schreien*) shout oneself hoarse

**Rufer** *der;* **~s, ~, Ruferin** *die;* **~, ~nen** person calling; **ein Rufer in der Wüste** (*fig, geh.*) a voice [crying] in the wilderness

**Rüffel** /ˈrʏfl̩/ *der;* **~s, ~** (*ugs.*) ticking-off (*coll.*)

**rüffeln** *tr. V.* (*ugs.*) **jmdn. ~:** tick sb. off (*coll.*)

**Ruf-: ~mord** *der* character assassination; **~mord·kampagne** *die* smear campaign; **~name** *der* first name (*by which one is generally known*); **~nummer** *die* telephone number; **~säule** *die* emergency telephone (*mounted in a pillar*); **~weite** *die:* **in/außer ~weite sein** be within/beyond hailing distance; **~zeichen** *das* **A** (*Fernspr.*) ringing tone; **B** (*österr.: Ausrufezeichen*) exclamation mark

**Rugby** /ˈrakbi/ *das;* **~[s]** rugby [football]

**Rüge** /ˈryːgə/ *die;* **~, ~n** reprimand; **jmdm. eine ~ wegen etw.** (*Gen.*) **erteilen** reprimand sb. for sth.; **eine ~ erhalten** be reprimanded

**rügen** *tr. V.* reprimand ‹person› (**wegen** for); (*mit Nachdruck kritisieren*) censure ‹carelessness etc.›; **Mängel ~:** complain about faults *or* defects

**Ruhe** /ˈruːə/ *die;* **~** **A** (*Stille*) silence; **im Saal herrschte absolute ~:** there was dead silence *or* a complete hush in the hall; **endlich war im Klassenzimmer ~ eingetreten** at last the classroom had become quiet; **die nächtliche ~ stören** disturb the nocturnal peace; **~ [bitte]!** quiet *or* silence [please]!; **[einen Moment] um ~ bitten** ask for [a moment's] silence; **jmdn. um ~ bitten** ask sb. to be quiet; **~ geben/halten** be/keep quiet; **jmdn. zur ~ ermahnen** tell sb. to be quiet; **B** (*Ungestörtheit*) peace; **in ~ [und Frieden]** in peace [and quiet]; **vor jmdm. ~ haben** not be bothered by sb.; **ich möchte mal meine ~ haben** I should like [to have] some peace [and quiet]; **er braucht ~ bei seiner Arbeit** he needs peace and quiet *or* must not be disturbed while he is working; **die [öffentliche] ~ wiederherstellen** restore [law and] order; **für ~ und Ordnung sorgen** uphold *or* preserve law and order; **jmdn. in ~ lassen** leave sb. in peace; **lass mich in ~!** leave me alone!; **jmdn. mit etw. in ~ lassen** stop bothering sb. with sth.; **jmdn. nicht zur ~ kommen lassen** give sb. no peace; **keine ~ geben** not stop pestering; (*nicht nachgeben*) not give up; (*weiter protestieren*) go on protesting; **hier hast du fünf Mark, aber nun gib auch ~!** here's five marks, but now stop bothering me/us!; **C** (*Unbewegtheit*) rest; **zur ~ kommen** come to rest; ‹weel› stop turning; **die ~ vor dem Sturm** the calm before the storm; **D** (*Erholung, das Sichausruhen*) rest *no def. art.*; **der ~ pflegen** (*geh.*) take it *or* things easy; seek repose (*literary*); **angenehme ~** (*geh.*) sleep well; **sich zur ~ begeben** (*geh.*) retire [to bed]; **die ewige ~** (*geh.*) eternal rest; **jmdn. zur letzten ~ betten** (*geh.*) lay sb. to rest; **E** (*~stand*) **sich zur ~ setzen** take one's retirement; retire (**in** + *Dat.* to); **F** (*Gelassenheit*) calm[ness]; composure; **er ist die ~ selbst** (*ugs.*) he is calmness itself; **[die] ~ bewahren/die ~ verlieren** keep calm/lose one's composure; keep/lose one's cool (*coll.*); **sich aus der ~ bringen lassen** let oneself get worked up; (*ängstlich werden*) let oneself get rattled (*coll.*); **in [aller] ~:** [really] calmly; **lesen Sie sich die Prüfungsaufgaben in [aller] ~ durch** read through the examination questions calmly and in your own time; **ich muss mir das in [aller] ~ überlegen** I must have a quiet think about it; **jmdm. keine ~ lassen** not give sb. any peace; **der Gedanke lässt ihm keine ~ mehr** he can't stop thinking about it; **die ~ weghaben** (*ugs.*) be completely unflappable (*coll.*); **~ ist die erste Bürgerpflicht** (*veralt.*) orderly behaviour is the first duty of the citizen; (*scherzh.*) the main thing is to keep calm; **immer mit der ~!** (*nur keine Panik*) don't panic!; (*nichts überstürzen*) one thing at a time; no need to rush

**ruhe-, Ruhe-: ~bank** *die; Pl.* **~bänke** bench; **~bedürfnis** *das* need of rest; **~bedürftig** *Adj.* in need of rest *postpos.*; **~gehalt** *das* [retirement] pension; **~geld** *das*

*old spelling (see note on page 1707)

r

[old-age] pension; **~genuss**, ***~genuß** *der (österr. Amtsspr.)* [retirement] pension; **~kissen** *das* cushion; *(Kopfkissen)* pillow; ⇒ *auch* **Gewissen**; **~lage** *die* **A** *(Körperlage)* [fully] relaxed position; **B** *(eines beweglichen Gegenstands)* neutral position; *(unbeweglich)* immobile position; **~los** **1** *Adj.* restless; **2** *adv.* restlessly; **~losigkeit** *die;* **~~:** restlessness

**ruhen** *itr. V.* **A** *(aus~)* rest; **hier lässt es sich gut ~:** it's very restful here; **nach dem Essen sollst du ~ oder tausend Schritte tun** *(Spr.)* after a meal one should take either a rest or a good walk; **B** *(geh.: schlafen)* sleep; **ich wünsche gut** *od.* **wohl zu ~:** I hope you sleep well; **C** **im Grabe ~:** lie in one's grave; **in fremder Erde ~:** be buried in foreign soil; **„Ruhe sanft** *od.* **in Frieden!"** 'Rest in Peace'; **„Hier ruht in Gott …"** 'Here lies …'; **D** *(stillstehen)* ‹work, business› have stopped; ‹production, firm› be at a standstill; ‹field› rest; ‹employment, insurance› be suspended; **der Verkehr ruht fast völlig** there is hardly any traffic; **die Waffen ~:** there is a ceasefire; **ihre Hände ~ nie** her hands are never still; **nicht ~ [und rasten]** *od.* **nicht ~ noch rasten** *od.* **weder ~ noch rasten, bis …** not rest until …; **E** *(liegen)* rest; **der Braten muss zehn Minuten ~:** the roast must be left to stand for ten minutes; **in sich** *(Dat.)* **[selbst] ~:** be a well-balanced [and harmonious] person; **F** **eine Angelegenheit ~ lassen** let a matter rest; *(vorläufig)* shelve a matter; **ein Problem ~ lassen** leave a problem [on one side]

**ruhend** *Adj.* *(unbeweglich)* stationary; *(liegend)* reclining ‹Venus etc.›; **~er Verkehr** parked vehicles *pl.*

***ruhen|lassen** ⇒ **ruhen** F

**ruhe-, Ruhe-:** **~pause** *die* break; **eine ~pause einlegen** take a break; **~punkt** *der* resting point; *(in einer Entwicklung)* restful *or* quiet point; **~stand** *der* retirement; **in den ~stand gehen/versetzt werden** go into retirement/be retired; **er ist im ~stand/Lehrer im ~stand** he is retired/a retired teacher; **seine Versetzung in den ~stand** his retirement; **~ständler** *der;* **~~s, ~~, ~ständlerin** *die;* **~~, ~~nen** retired person; **~statt** *die;* **~~, ~stätten, ~stätte** *die (fig. geh.)* [last] resting place; **~störend** *Adj.* **~störender Lärm** disturbance of the peace; **~störung** *die* disturbance; *(Rechtsw.)* disturbance of the peace; **jmdn. wegen ~störung anzeigen** report sb. [to the police] for disturbing the peace; **~strom** *der (Elektrot.)* closed-circuit current; **~tag** *der* **A** *(einer Gaststätte)* closing day; **[wir haben] dienstags** *od.* **Dienstag ~tag** [we are] closed on Tuesdays; **B** *(arbeitsfreier Tag)* day of rest; **~zeit** *die* rest period; time of rest; *(für Bäume usw.)* dormant period *or* season

**ruhig** /ˈruːɪç/ **1** *Adj.* **A** *(still, leise)* quiet; **seid doch mal ~!** do be quiet!; **um diese Angelegenheit/diesen Politiker ist es sehr ~ geworden** one does not hear much about this matter/politician any more; **B** *(friedlich, ungestört)* peaceful ‹times, life, scene, valley, etc.›; quiet ‹talk, reflection, life›; **wir suchten uns ein ~es Plätzchen** we looked for a quiet *or* peaceful spot; **überleg es dir mal in einer ~en Stunde** think about it when you have a quiet moment; **er hat keine ~e Minute** he doesn't have a moment's peace; **ein ~er Job** *od.* **Posten** *(ugs.)* a cushy job *or* number *(coll.)*; **einen ~en Verlauf nehmen** go smoothly; be uneventful; **C** *(unbewegt)* calm ‹sea, weather›; still ‹air›; *(fig.)* peaceful ‹melody›; quiet ‹pattern›; *(gleichmäßig)* steady ‹breathing, hand, flame, steps›; smooth ‹flight, crossing›; **eine Gliedmaße ~ stellen** immobilize a limb; **D** *(gelassen)* calm ‹voice etc.›; quiet, calm ‹person›; **er gab sich Mühe, ~ zu bleiben** he made an effort to keep calm *or (coll.)* keep his cool; **~en Gewissens** with an easy *or* a clear conscience; **sei ganz ~:** you needn't worry; **[nur immer] ~ Blut!** *(ugs.)* keep your hair on! *(coll.)*; **einen Patienten ~ stellen** *(verhüll.)* calm a patient.

**2** *adv.* **A** *(still, leise)* quietly; **wir wohnen sehr ~:** we live in a very quiet area; **sich ~ verhalten** keep quiet; **B** *(friedlich, ohne Störungen)* ‹sleep› peacefully; ‹go off› smoothly, peacefully; *(ohne Zwischenfälle)* uneventfully; ‹work, think› in peace; **hier geht es sehr ~ zu** it is very peaceful here; **ich kann nicht ~ schlafen** I can't sleep properly; **C** *(unbewegt)* ‹sit, lie, stand› still; *(gleichmäßig)* ‹burn, breathe› steadily; ‹run, fly› smoothly; **D** *(gelassen)* ‹speak, watch, sit› calmly; **sie sahen ~ zu, wie das Kind geschlagen wurde** they watched unmoved as the child was beaten.

**3** *Adv.* by all means; **du kannst ~ mitkommen** by all means come along; you're welcome to come along; **streichle ihn ~ mal** go ahead and stroke him; **man kann ihm das ~ ganz direkt sagen** there's no harm in telling him to his face; **du kannst es mir ~ glauben/sagen** it's OK, you can take my word for it/you can tell me; **du könntest dich ~ entschuldigen/ihm ~ etwas helfen** it wouldn't hurt you to apologize/to help him a bit; **lach mich ~ aus** all right *or* go ahead, laugh at me[, I don't care]; **soll er ~ meckern** *(ugs.)* let him moan[, I don't care]

***ruhig|stellen** ⇒ **ruhig** 1C, D

**Ruhm** /ruːm/ *der;* **~[e]s** fame; **diese Erfindung begründete seinen ~:** this invention made him famous *or* made his name; **sich mit ~ bedecken** *(geh.)* cover oneself with glory; **er hat sich nicht [gerade] mit ~ bekleckert** *(ugs. iron.)* he didn't exactly cover himself with glory *or* distinguish himself; **der zweifelhafte ~ dieser Erfindung** *(fig.)* the dubious reputation of this invention

**rühmen** /ˈryːmən/ **1** *tr. V.* praise. **2** *refl. V.* **sich einer Sache** *(Gen.)* **~:** boast about sth.; **wenige dürfen sich ~, ihn gesehen zu haben** only a few can claim to have seen him

**rühmens·wert** *Adj.* laudable; praiseworthy

**Ruhmes·blatt** *das:* **das war kein ~ für ihn/die Bundesrepublik** it did not reflect any credit on him/the Federal Republic; it did him/the Federal Republic no credit

**rühmlich** *Adj.* laudable, praiseworthy ‹behaviour, action, etc.›; notable ‹exception›; **er hat kein ~es Ende genommen** he came to a discreditable end

**ruhm·los** **1** *Adj.* inglorious. **2** *adv.* ingloriously

**ruhm·reich** **1** *Adj.* glorious ‹victory, history›; celebrated ‹general, army, victory›. **2** *adv.* **~ kämpfen** fight with great glory; **~ siegen** win a famous *or* glorious victory

**Ruhr** /ruːɐ̯/ *die;* **~, ~en** ▸ **474** dysentery *no art.*

**Rühr·ei** *das* scrambled egg[s *pl.*]

**rühren** /ˈryːrən/ **1** *tr. V.* **A** *(um~)* stir ‹sauce, dough, etc.›; *(ein~)* stir ‹egg, powder, etc.› **an, in** + *Akk.* into; **B** *(bewegen)* move ‹limb, fingers, etc.›; **ich konnte die Glieder nicht mehr ~:** I could no longer move; ⇒ *auch* **Finger** B; **C** *(erweichen)* move; touch; **jmdn. zu Tränen ~:** move sb. to tears; **es rührte ihn überhaupt nicht, dass …** it didn't bother him at all that …; ⇒ *auch* **gerührt**; **rührend**; **D** *(geh. veralt.)* **die Trommel/die Leier ~:** beat the drum/play the lyre.

**2** *itr. V.* **A** *(um~)* stir; **im Kaffee** *od.* **in der Kaffeetasse ~:** stir one's coffee; **B** *(Milit.)* stand at ease; **C** *(geh.: her~)* **das rührt daher, dass …** that stems from the fact that …; **D** *(geh.: vorsichtig anfassen)* **an etw.** *(Akk.)* **~:** touch sth.; *(fig.: im Gespräch be~)* touch on sth.; **wir wollen nicht [mehr] daran ~:** let's not go into that [any further].

**3** *refl. V.* **A** *(sich bewegen)* move; **er rührte sich nicht von der Stelle** he did not budge *or* stir; **niemand rührte sich** nobody moved *or* stirred; *(fig.: unternahm etwas)* nobody did anything; **kein Blatt/kein Lüftchen rührte sich** not a leaf stirred/there was not a breath of wind; **es rührte sich nichts** there was no sign of movement; *(nichts geschah)* nothing happened; **er hat sich seit zwei Monaten nicht gerührt** *(ugs.: nicht geschrieben)* he has given no sign of life for two months; **B** *(Milit.)* **rührt euch!** at ease!

**Rühren** *das;* **~s** **A** stirring *no art.*; **beim ~ des Teigs** when stirring the dough; **B** **ein menschliches ~ verspüren** *(scherzh.)* feel the call of nature

**rührend** **1** *Adj.* touching; **er sorgt in ~er Weise für seine Eltern** it is touching how he looks after his parents; **das ist ~ von Ihnen** that is terribly sweet *or* kind of you *(coll.)*; **das ist ja ~!** *(auch iron.)* that's really charming! **2** *adv.* touchingly; **er sorgt ~ für sie** it is touching the way he looks after her/them

**Ruhrgebiet** *das;* **~[e]s** Ruhr [district]

**rührig** **1** *Adj.* active; *(mit Unternehmungsgeist)* enterprising; go-ahead; *(emsig)* busy; industrious. **2** *adv.* actively; *(mit Unternehmungsgeist)* enterprisingly; *(emsig)* busily; industriously

**Rührigkeit** *die;* **~:** active nature; *(Unternehmungsgeist)* enterprise

**rühr-, Rühr-:** **~löffel** *der* mixing spoon; **~mich·nicht·an** *das;* **~~, ~~** *(Bot.)* touch-me-not; ⇒ *auch* **Kräutchen**; **~selig** **1** *Adj.* **A** emotional ‹person›; **B** *(allzu gefühlvoll)* over-sentimental ‹manner, mood, etc.›; maudlin, *(coll.)* tear-jerking ‹play, song, etc.›; **2** *adv.* in an over-sentimental manner; **der Film endete ~selig** the film had a tear-jerking *or* weepy ending *(coll.)*; **~seligkeit** *die* sentimentality; **~stück** *das (Literaturw.)* sentimental drama; melodrama; **~teig** *der* [cake] mixture

**Rührung** *die;* **~:** emotion; **von tiefer ~ ergriffen** deeply moved

**Ruin** /ruˈiːn/ *der;* **~s** ruin; **jmdn. an den Rand des ~s bringen** bring sb. to the brink of ruin; **du bist noch mein ~** *(ugs.)* you'll be the ruin *or* end of me

**Ruine** *die;* **~, ~n** ruin

**Ruinen·feld** *das* [expanse *sing.* of] ruins *pl.*

**ruinieren** *tr. V.* ruin; **sich finanziell ~:** ruin oneself [financially]; **du ruinierst meine Nerven** you are turning me into a nervous wreck; ⇒ *auch* **Ruf** E

**ruinös** /ruiˈnøːs/ *Adj.* ruinous

**Ruländer** /ˈruːlɛndɐ/ *der;* **~s, ~:** Ruländer [grape/wine]

**rülpsen** /ˈrʏlpsn̩/ *itr. V.* *(ugs.)* belch

**Rülpser** *der;* **~s, ~** *(ugs.)* belch

**rum** /rʊm/ *Adv.* *(ugs.)* ⇒ **herum**

**Rum** /rʊm/ *der;* **~s, ~s** rum

**Rumäne** /ruˈmɛːnə/ *der;* **~n, ~n** ▸ **553** Romanian

**Rumänien** *(das);* **~s** Romania

**Rumänin** *die;* **~, ~nen** ▸ **553** Romanian

**rumänisch** ▸ **553**, ▸ **696** **1** *Adj.* Romanian. **2** *adv.* Romanian; ⇒ *auch* **deutsch**; **Deutsch**; **Deutsche**[2]

**Rumba** /ˈrʊmba/ *die;* **~, ~s** *od. der;* **~s, ~s** rumba

**rum-:** **~|ballern** *itr. V.* *(ugs.)* blast away; **~|brüllen** *itr. V.* *(ugs.)* ⇒ **herumbrüllen**; **~|fliegen** *(ugs.)* **1** *unr. itr. V.;* *mit sein* **A** ⇒ **herumfliegen** 1 A; **B** *(herumliegen)* lie about *or* around; **im Zimmer ~fliegen** litter the room; **2** *unr. tr. V.* ⇒ **herumfliegen** 2; **~|fummeln** *itr. V.* *(ugs.)* ⇒ **herumfummeln**; **~|gammeln** *itr. V.* *(ugs.)* ⇒ **gammeln** B; **~|hampeln** *itr. V.* *(ugs.)* hop *or* jig about; **~|hängen** *unr. itr. V.* *(ugs.)* **A** *(sich ziellos aufhalten/untätig od. arbeitslos sein)* hang about *or* around; **B** ⇒ **herumhängen** A; **~|kriegen** *tr. V.* *(ugs.)* ⇒ **herumkriegen**; **~|labern** *itr. V.* *(salopp abwertend)* natter *(Brit. coll.) or* chatter away *(coll.)*; rabbit on *(Brit. sl.)*; **~|laufen** *unr. itr. V.;* *mit sein (ugs.)* ⇒ **herumlaufen**; **~|liegen** *unr. itr. V.* *(ugs.)* ⇒ **herumliegen**; **~|lungern** *itr. V.* *(salopp)* ⇒ **herumlungern**; **~|machen** *itr. V.* *(salopp)* **A** ⇒ **herummachen**; **B** ⇒ **herumfummeln** A; **C** *(sich [sexuell] einlassen)* play around; *(koitieren)* do it *(sl.)*; *(schmusen)* neck *(coll.)*

**Rummel** /ˈrʊml/ *der;* **~s** *(ugs.)* **A** *(laute Betriebsamkeit)* commotion; *(Aufhebens)* fuss,

r

to-do (**um** about); **der ganze ~:** the whole business; Ⓑ (*bes. nordd.: Jahrmarkt*) fair; **auf den ~ gehen** go to the fair

**Rummel·platz** *der* (*bes. nordd.*) fairground

**Rummy** /'rœmi/ *das;* **~s, ~s** (*österr.*) ⇒ **Rommé**

**rumoren** /ru'mo:rən/ *itr. V.* (*ugs.*) Ⓐ (*rumpeln*) make a noise; (*poltern*) ‹person› bang about; **es rumorte in seinem Bauch** (*fig.*) his stomach rumbled; Ⓑ (*aufbegehren*) protest; stage a protest/protests

**Rumpel·kammer** *die* (*ugs.*) boxroom (*Brit.*); junk room

**rumpeln** /'rʊmpl̩n/ *itr. V.* (*ugs.*) Ⓐ (*poltern*) bump and bang about; **es rumpelte** *unpers.* there was banging and bumping; (*im Magen*) there was a rumble *or* rumbling; Ⓑ *mit sein* (*sich* **~d** *fortbewegen*) rumble; bump and bang

**Rumpelstilzchen** /'rʊmpl̩ʃtɪltsçən/ (*das*); **~s** Rumpelstiltskin *no art.*

**Rumpf** /rʊmpf/ *der;* **~[e]s, Rümpfe** /'rʏmpfə/ Ⓐ (*bei Lebewesen*) trunk [of the body]; **den ~ drehen/beugen** turn one's body/bend from the hips; Ⓑ (*beim Schiff*) hull; Ⓒ (*beim Flugzeug*) fuselage

**Rumpf·beuge** *die* (*Gymnastik*) trunk-bend; bend from the hips; **~ rückwärts** arch

**rümpfen** /'rʏmpfn̩/ *tr. V.* **die Nase [bei etw.] ~:** wrinkle one's nose at sth.; **über jmdn./etw. die Nase ~** (*fig.*) look down one's nose at sb./turn up one's nose at sth.

**Rumpsteak** /'rʊmp-ste:k/ *das;* **~s, ~s** rump steak

**rums** /rʊms/ *Interj.* (*Geräusch*) bump; (*lauter, heller*) bang; (*beim Zusammenstoß*) crash

**rumsen** *itr. V.* (*ugs.*) Ⓐ *unpers.* **es rumst** there's a bump *or* bang; (*wiederholt*) there's bumping and banging; (*laut, beim Zusammenstoß*) there's a crash; Ⓑ *mit sein* (*auftreffen*) **gegen etw. ~:** bang into sth.

**rum-: ~|sitzen** *unr. itr. V.* (*ugs.*) ⇒ **herumsitzen**; **~|stehen** *unr. itr. V.* (*ugs.*) ⇒ **herumstehen**; **~|toben** *itr. V.* (*ugs.*) Ⓐ *auch mit sein* ‹child› charge *or* romp [noisily] about; ‹students etc.› rag; Ⓑ (*wüten*) rant and rave

**Rum·topf** *der: fruits preserved in rum and sugar*

**rum|treiben** *unr. refl. V.* (*ugs.*) ⇒ **herumtreiben**

**Rum·verschnitt** *der* rum blend (*with other spirits*)

**rum|ziehen** *unr. tr., itr. V.* (*ugs.*) ⇒ **herumziehen**

**Run** /rʌn/ *der;* **~s, ~s** [big] rush; **ein [starker] ~ auf etw.** (*Akk.*) a [big] run on sth.

**rund** /rʊnt/ ❶ *Adj.* Ⓐ (*kreis~*) round; **~e Augen machen** (*ugs.*) ‹child› gaze wide-eyed; **ein Gespräch am ~en Tisch** (*fig.*) a round-table conference; Ⓑ (*dicklich*) plump ‹arms etc.›; chubby ‹cheeks›; fat ‹stomach›; **er ist dick und ~ geworden** he has become rather rotund *or* stout; Ⓒ (*ugs.: ganz*) round ‹dozen, number, etc.›; **~e drei Jahre** three years or as near as makes no difference; Ⓓ (*abgerundet*) full, rounded ‹tone, sound, flavour›; **eine ~e Sache** a nice piece of work.
❷ *adv.* **~ laufen** (*Kfz-W.*) ‹engine› run smoothly; ⇒ *auch* **rundgehen**.
❸ *Adv.* Ⓐ (*ugs.: etwa*) about; approximately; Ⓑ **~ um jmdn./etw.** [all] around sb./sth.; **eine Sendung ~ um das Kind** a broadcast on all aspects of childhood; ⇒ *auch* **Uhr**

**Rund** *das;* **~[e]s, ~e** (*geh.*) Ⓐ (*runde Form*) round; (*Mond usw.*) orb (*literary*); Ⓑ (*runde Fläche*) circle

**Rund-: ~bau** *der; Pl.* **~~ten** circular building; rotunda; **~blick** *der* panorama; view in all directions; **~bogen** *der* (*Kunstwiss., Archit.*) round arch; **~brief** *der* circular [letter]

**Runde** /'rʊndə/ *die;* **~, ~n** Ⓐ (*Sport: runde Strecke*) lap; **die schnellste ~ fahren** do the fastest lap; **seine ~n ziehen** *od.* **drehen** do one's laps; Ⓑ (*Sport: Durchgang, Partie; Boxen: Abschnitt*) round; **eine ~ Golf/Skat** a round of golf/skat; **über die ~n kommen** (*fig. ugs.*) get by; manage; Ⓒ (*Personenkreis*) circle; (*Gesellschaft*) company; **in fröhlicher ~ beisammensitzen** sit together in a happy circle *or* group; Ⓓ (*Umkreis*) **in der ~:** round about; **in die ~ blicken** look all around one; Ⓔ (*Rundgang*) round; (*Spaziergang*) walk; **eine ~ durch die Kneipen machen** go on a pub crawl (*Brit. coll.*); go barhopping (*Amer.*); **die ~ machen** (*ugs.*) ‹drink, rumour› go the rounds *pl.*; circulate; Ⓕ **eine ~ Bier schmeißen** (*ugs.*) buy *or* stand a round of beer; **die ~ geht auf mich/auf den Wirt** this round is on me/on the house

**runden** ❶ *tr. V.* Ⓐ (*rund machen*) round; Ⓑ (*fig.: ab~*) round off, fill out ‹picture, impression›. ❷ *refl. V.* become round

**Runden·rekord** *der* (*Motorsport*) lap record

**rund-, Rund-: ~erneuern** *tr. V.* (*Kfz-W.*) remould; retread; **~erneuerte Reifen** remoulds; retreads; **~erneuerung** *die* (*Kfz-W.*) remoulding; retreading; **~fahrt** *die* (*auch Sport*) tour (**durch** of); **eine ~fahrt durch Amsterdam** a circular tour of *or* a trip round Amsterdam; **eine ~fahrt machen** go on a [circular] tour; **~flug** *der* [short] circular flight; circuit; **~frage** *die* survey (*using a questionnaire*); questionnaire

**Rund·funk** *der* Ⓐ radio; (*das Senden*) radio broadcasting *no art.*; **im ~:** on the radio; **~ hören** listen to the radio; Ⓑ (*Einrichtung, Gebäude*) radio station; **sie ist** *od.* **arbeitet beim ~:** she works in radio

**Rundfunk-: ~anstalt** *die* broadcasting corporation; (*Sender*) radio station; **~empfang** *der* radio reception *no indef. art.*; **~empfänger** *der* radio receiver; **~gebühren** *Pl.* radio licence fees; **~gerät** *das* radio set; **~hörer** *der*, **~hörerin** *die* [radio] listener; **~programm** *das* Ⓐ (*Sendefolge*) [schedule *sing.* of] radio programmes *pl.*; Ⓑ (*Programmheft*) radio programme guide; **~redakteur** *der*, **~redakteurin** *die* radio producer; **~reporter** *der*, **~reporterin** *die* radio reporter; **~sender** *der* radio station; (*technische Anlage*) radio transmitter; **~sendung** *die* radio programme; **~sprecher** *der*, **~sprecherin** *die* radio announcer; **~station** *die* radio station; **~techniker** *der*, **~technikerin** *die* radio engineer; **~teilnehmer** *der*, **~teilnehmerin** *die* radio licence holder; (*Hörer*) radio listener; **~übertragung** *die* radio broadcast

**rund-, Rund-: ~gang** *der* Ⓐ (*des Wachmanns, Chefarztes usw.*) round (**durch** of); **einen ~gang durch die Stadt machen** go for a walk round the town; Ⓑ (*Umgang*) gallery; **~|gehen** *unr. itr. V.*; *mit sein* Ⓐ *unpers.* (*ugs.*) **es geht ~** (*es ist viel Betrieb*) it's all go (*coll.*); (*es geht flott zu*) things are going with a swing; Ⓑ (*herumgereicht werden*) be passed round; (*fig.*) ‹story, rumours› go *or* do the rounds; **er ließ die Flasche ~gehen** he passed the bottle round; **~heraus** *Adv.* straight out; ‹say, ask› bluntly; ‹refuse› flatly; **~herum** *Adv.* Ⓐ (*ringsum*) all around; (*darum herum*) all round it; **~herum an der Wand** all round the walls; Ⓑ (*völlig*) completely; (*fig.*) entirely ‹satisfied, practical›; **~kurs** *der* (*bes. Motor-, Fahrradsport*) circuit

**rundlich** *Adj.* Ⓐ (*fast rund*) roundish; Ⓑ (*mollig*) plump; chubby

**rund-, Rund-: ~reise** *die* [circular] tour (**durch** of); **eine ~reise [mit dem Bus/Auto] durch den Schwarzwald machen** tour the Black Forest [by coach/car]; **~schädel** *der* (*Anthrop.*) round *or* (*as tech. term*) brachycephalic skull; **~schau** *die* Ⓐ (*geh.*) ⇒ **~blick**; Ⓑ (*in Zeitungstiteln*) review; **~schlag** *der* (*Boxen, Faustball, Eishockey*) swing; (*fig.*) [general] broadside; **~schreiben** *das* ⇒ **~brief**; **~sicht** *die* ⇒ **~blick**; **~spruch** *der* (*schweiz.*) ⇒ **Rundfunk**; **~strecke** *die* circuit; **~strick·nadel** *die* circular-knitting needle; **~stück** *das* (*nordd.*) [oval] roll; **~um** *Adv.* ⇒ **~herum**

**Rundung** *die;* **~, ~en** curve; (*hervortretend*) bulge

**rund·weg** *Adv.* ‹refuse, deny› flatly, point-blank

**Rund·weg** *der* circular path *or* walk

**Rune** /'ru:nə/ *die;* **~, ~n** rune

**Runen-: ~schrift** *die* runic alphabet; **~stein** *der* rune stone; **~zeichen** *das* runic character

**Runge** /'rʊŋə/ *die;* **~, ~n** [load-retaining] stanchion

**Runkel·rübe** /'rʊŋkl̩ry:bə/ *die* mangel-wurzel

**runter** /'rʊntɐ/ *Adv.* (*ugs.*) **~ [da, das ist mein Platz]!** get off [there, that's my seat]!; **~ mit den Klamotten** off with your clothes; get those clothes off; **~ mit den Füßen** take your feet [down] off the table; **Kopf ~!** head/heads down!; ⇒ *auch* **herunter**; **hinunter**

**runter-: ~|bringen** *unr. tr. V.* ⇒ **herunterbringen**; **~|dürfen** *unr. itr. V.* (*ugs.*) be allowed to come down; (*hinausgehen dürfen*) be allowed out; **~|fallen** *unr. itr. V.*; *mit sein* (*ugs.*) fall down; (*von der Leiter usw.*) fall off; **die Leiter/von der Leiter ~fallen** fall off the ladder; **die Kreide fiel ihm ~:** he dropped the chalk; **~|gehen** *unr. itr. V.*; *mit sein* (*ugs.*) Ⓐ (*nach unten gehen*) go down; Ⓑ (*niedriger werden*) ‹price, temperature, pressure, etc.› go down, drop; Ⓒ (*die Höhe senken*) go down (**auf** + *Akk.* to); (*langsamer fahren*) slow down (**auf** + *Akk.* to); **wir müssen mit den Preisen ~gehen** we must reduce our prices; ⇒ *auch* **heruntergehen** D, E; **hinuntergehen**; **~|hauen** *unr. tr. V.* **jmdm. eine/ein paar ~hauen** (*salopp*) give sb. a clip/a couple of clips round the ear; **~|holen** *tr. V.* (*ugs.*) Ⓐ fetch down; ⇒ *auch* **herunterholen** B; Ⓑ **sich/jmdm. einen ~holen** (*vulg.*) jerk off (*coarse*) *or* (*Brit. coarse*) wank/jerk (*coarse*) *or* (*Brit. coarse*) wank sb. off; **~|kommen** *unr. itr. V.*; *mit sein* (*ugs.*) come down; ⇒ *auch* **herunterkommen** B, C; **~|können** *unr. itr. V.* (*ugs.*) ⇒ **herunterkönnen**; **~|kriegen** *tr. V.* (*ugs.*) Ⓐ get down; **etw. ~kriegen [können]** manage to get sth. down; Ⓑ (*wegbekommen*) get off ‹dirt, sth. sticky›; **~|lassen** *unr. tr. V.* (*ugs.*) ⇒ **herunterlassen**; **hinunterlassen**; **~|machen** *tr. V.* (*salopp*) ⇒ **heruntermachen**; **~|müssen** *unr. itr. V.* (*ugs.*) have to go/come down; **ich muss von der Autobahn ~** (*fig.*) I'll have to get off the motorway; **~|reißen** *unr. tr. V.* (*ugs.*) ⇒ **herunterreißen**; **~|rutschen** *itr. V.*; *mit sein* (*ugs.*) ⇒ **herunterrutschen**; ⇒ *auch* **Buckel** A; **~|spülen** *tr. V.* (*ugs.*) ⇒ **hinunterspülen**

**Runzel** /'rʊntsl̩/ *die;* **~, ~n** wrinkle

**runzelig** *Adj.* wrinkled

**runzeln** ❶ *tr. V.* **die Stirn/die Brauen ~:** wrinkle one's brow/knit one's brows; (*ärgerlich*) frown; **mit gerunzelter Stirn** with wrinkled brow; (*ärgerlich*) frowning. ❷ *refl. V.* wrinkle

**runzlig** *Adj.* ⇒ **runzelig**

**Rüpel** /'ry:pl̩/ *der;* **~s, ~** (*abwertend*) lout

**Rüpelei** *die;* **~, ~en** (*abwertend*) Ⓐ (*Benehmen*) loutishness; loutish behaviour; Ⓑ (*Handlung*) piece of coarseness; **noch so eine ~ von dir, und wir gehen nach Hause** any more of that coarseness from you and we're going home; **~en** coarseness *sing.*

**rüpelhaft** (*abwertend*) ❶ *Adj.* loutish. ❷ *adv.* in a loutish manner

**rupfen** /'rʊpfn̩/ *tr. V.* Ⓐ pluck ‹goose, hen, etc.›; ⇒ *auch* **Hühnchen**; Ⓑ (*abreißen*) pull up ‹weeds, grass›; pull off ‹leaves etc.›; Ⓒ (*ugs.: übervorteilen*) fleece ‹person› [of his/her money]

**Rupfen** *der;* **~s** hessian

**Rupie** /'ru:pi̯ə/ *die;* **~, ~n** ▶ 337 rupee

**ruppig** /'rʊpɪç/ ❶ *Adj.* (*abwertend*) gruff ‹person, behaviour›; sharp ‹tone›; **er war ~ zu ihr** he was short with her; he snapped at her. ❷ *adv.* (*abwertend*) gruffly; **~ spielen** play rough *or* a rough game

**Ruppigkeit** *die;* **~, ~en** (*abwertend*) Ⓐ (*Benehmen*) gruffness; Ⓑ (*Handlung*) piece of uncouthness; **~en** rough *or* uncouth behaviour *sing.*

*old spelling (see note on page 1707)

**Ruprecht** ⇒ **Knecht** B
**Rüsche** /'ry:ʃə/ *die;* ~, ~**n** ruche; frill
**Ruß** /ru:s/ *der;* ~**es** soot
**Russe** /'rʊsə/ *der;* ~**n**, ~**n** ▶553 Russian; **der** ~ (*ugs.*) Russians *pl.*; (*die russische Regierung*) the Russians *pl.*
**Rüssel** /'rʏsl̩/ *der;* ~**s**, ~ **A** (*des Elefanten*) trunk; (*des Schweins*) snout; (*bei Insekten u. Ä.*) proboscis; **B** (*salopp: Nase*) conk (*coll.*)
**Rüssel·tier** *das* proboscidean
**rußen** ❶ *itr. V.* give off sooty smoke. ❷ *tr. V.* (*schwärzen*) blacken with soot
**Russen·bluse** *die*, **Russen·kittel** *der* Russian blouse
**Russen·mafia** *die* Russian Mafia
**Ruß·fleck** *der* soot mark
**ruß·geschwärzt** *Adj.* blackened with soot *postpos.*
**rußig** *Adj.* sooty
**Russin** *die;* ~, ~**nen** ▶553 Russian; ⇒ *auch* **-in**
**russisch** ▶553, ▶696 ❶ *Adj.* Russian; ~**es Roulett** Russian roulette; ⇒ *auch* **Ei** A. ❷ *adv.* **A** ~ **verwaltet/besetzt** administered/occupied by Russia; **B** (*auf Russisch*) in Russian; ⇒ *auch* **deutsch**; **Deutsche**[2]
**Russisch** *das;* ~[**s**] ▶696 Russian; ⇒ *auch* **Deutsch**
**Russisch·brot**, ***Russisch Brot** *das* alphabet biscuits *pl.* (*Brit.*) *or* (*Amer.*) cookies
**Russisch·grün** *das* Russian green
**Russland**, ***Rußland** (*das*); ~**s** Russia
**rüsten** /'rʏstn̩/ ❶ *itr. V.* (*sich bewaffnen*) arm; **zum Krieg** ~: arm for war. ❷ *itr., refl. V.* (*geh.: sich bereit machen, auch fig.*) get ready; prepare; **sich zur Reise** ~: get ready *or* prepare oneself for the journey
**Rüster** /'ry:stɐ/ *die;* ~, ~**n** **A** ⇒ **Ulme**; **B** ⇒ **Rüsternholz**
**Rüstern·holz** *das* elmwood
**rüstig** ❶ *Adj.* **A** (*leistungsfähig*) sprightly; active; **er ist noch** ~: he is still hale and hearty; **B** (*geh.: kraftvoll*) strong. ❷ *adv.* (*geh.: kraftvoll*) strongly; ~ **ausschreiten** stride out vigorously
**rustikal** /rʊsti'ka:l/ ❶ *Adj.* country-style ‹food, inn, clothes, etc.›; farmhouse *attrib.* ‹food›; rustic ‹pattern›; rustic, farmhouse *attrib.* ‹furniture›; (*als Nachahmung*) rustic-style ‹furniture etc.›; **ein Schrank aus Eiche** ~: a rustic-style oak cupboard. ❷ *adv.* in [a] country style; ~ **essen** eat farmhouse *or* country-style food; ‹furnish› in a rustic *or* farmhouse style
**Rüst-:** ~**kammer** *die* (*hist.*) armoury; ~**tag** *der* (*jüd. Rel.*) day of preparation
**Rüstung** *die;* ~, ~**en** **A** (*Bewaffnung*) armament *no art.*; (*Waffen*) arms *pl.*; weapons *pl.*; **B** (*hist.: Schutzbekleidung*) suit of armour; **in voller** ~: in full armour
**Rüstungs-:** ~**auftrag** *der* arms order; ~**aus·gaben** *Pl.* arms expenditure *sing.*; ~**begrenzung** *die* arms limitation; ~**betrieb** *der*, ~**fabrik** *die* armaments factory; ~**haus·halt** *der* armaments *or* arms budget; ~**industrie** *die* armaments *or* arms industry; ~**kontrolle** *die* arms control; ~**politik** *die* arms policy; ~**produktion** *die* arms production *no art.*; ~**stopp** *der* arms freeze; ~**wett·lauf** *der* arms race
**Rüst-:** ~**zeit** *die* **A** (*ev. Kirche*) period of reflection; retreat; **B** (*Arbeitswiss.*) set-up time; ~**zeug** *das* **A** (*Wissen*) requisite know-how; **B** (*Ausrüstung*) equipment [for the job *or* task]
**Rute** /'ru:tə/ *die;* ~, ~**n** **A** (*Stock*) switch; (*Birken*~, *Angel*~, *Wünschel*~) rod; (*zum Züchtigen*) cane; (*Bündel*) birch; **B** (*veralt.: Längenmaß*) rod; perch; **C** (*Jägerspr.: männliches Glied*) penis; (*derb: menschlicher Penis*) prick (*coarse*); **D** (*Jägerspr.: Schwanz*) tail
**Ruten-:** ~**bündel** *das* **A** bundle of [birch] rods; **B** (*altröm.: Faszes*) fasces *pl.*; ~**gänger** *der;* ~~**s**, ~~, ~**gängerin** *die;* ~~, ~~**nen** dowser; diviner
**Ruthenium** /ru'te:ni̯ʊm/ *das;* ~**s** (*Chemie*) ruthenium
**Rutsch** /rʊtʃ/ *der;* ~[**e**]**s**, ~**e** **A** (*das* ~*en*) slide; **in einem** *od.* **auf einen** ~ (*fig. ugs.*) in one go; **B** (*Erdmasse*) landslide; **C** (*ugs.: Ausflug*) trip; jaunt; **guten** ~ [**ins neue Jahr**]! happy New Year!
**Rutsch·bahn** *die* slide; (*auf dem Rummelplatz*) helter-skelter
**Rutsche** *die;* ~, ~**n** chute
**rutschen** *itr. V.; mit sein* **A** slide; ‹clutch, carpet› slip; (*aus*~) ‹person› slip; ‹car etc.› skid; (*nach unten*) slip [down]; **rutsch mal zur Seite!** (*ugs.*) move up a bit! (*coll.*); **ins R**~ **kommen** ‹person› [start to] slip; ‹car etc.› go into a skid; **auf seinem Platz hin und her** ~: slide *or* shift about on one's seat; **von/aus etw.** ~: slip *or* slide off/out of sth.; **die Brille/der Rock rutscht** the glasses keep/skirt keeps slipping [down]; **das trockene Brot rutscht schlecht/will nicht** ~ (*ugs.*) the dry bread doesn't go down easily/won't go down; **B** (*ugs.: kurz verreisen*) slip off
**rutsch·fest** *Adj.* **A** (*strapazierfähig*) hard-wearing; **B** (*nicht rutschig*) anti-skid ‹tyre›; skid-proof ‹road surface›; non-slip ‹mat, material›
**Rutsch·gefahr** *die* danger of skidding
**rutschig** *Adj.* slippery
**Rutsch·partie** *die* (*ugs.*) succession of slides; (*im Auto*) succession of skids
**rütteln** /'rʏtl̩n/ ❶ *tr. V.* **A** shake; **jmdn. aus dem Schlaf** ~: shake sb. out of his/her sleep; **jmdn. am Arm/an der Schulter** ~: shake sb. by the arm/shoulder; **B** (*Bauw.*) vibrate ‹concrete etc.›. ❷ *itr. V.* **A** shake; **an der Tür/den Fenstern** ~: shake the door/windows; (*sodass es klappert*) rattle at the door/windows; ‹wind› make the door/windows rattle; **an den Fundamenten von etw.** ~ (*fig.*) rock *or* shake the foundations of sth.; **daran ist nicht** *od.* **gibt es nichts zu** ~ (*fig.*) there's nothing you can do about that; **B** (*sich ruckartig hin u. her bewegen*) shake about; ‹engine› hunt; run unevenly
**Rüttler** /'rʏtlɐ/ *der;* ~**s**, ~ (*Bauw.*) vibrator

# S s

**s, S** /ɛs/ *das;* ~, ~: s, S; ⇒ *auch* **a, A**

**s** *Abk.* **Sekunde** sec.; s.

**S** *Abk.* [A] ▸ 400 | **Süden** S.; [B] (*österr.*) **Schilling** Sch.

**s.** *Abk.* **siehe**

**S.** *Abk.* **Seite** p.

**s. a.** *Abk.* **siehe auch**

**Sa.** *Abk.* **Samstag** Sat.

**SA** *Abk.* (*ns.*) **Sturmabteilung** SA

**Saal** /za:l/ *der;* **~[e]s, Säle** /ˈzɛ:lə/ [A] hall; (*Ball~*) ballroom; (*für Konzerte*) **der große/kleine ~:** the large/small auditorium; [B] (*Publikum*) audience

**Saal-:** **~ordner** *der,* **~ordnerin** *die* steward; **~schlacht** *die* [violent] brawl, rough-house (*between rival political factions*)

**Saarland** /ˈza:ɐ̯lant/ *das;* **~[e]s** Saarland; Saar (*esp. Hist.*); **das ~:** the Saarland; (*Hist.*) the Saar; **im/aus dem ~:** in/from the Saarland

**Saarländer** /-lɛndɐ/ *der;* **~s,** ~, **Saarländerin** *die;* ~, **~nen** Saarlander

**saarländisch** *Adj.* Saarland *attrib.* ‹government, population, etc.›; Saar *attrib.* ‹industry, miners, etc.›; ‹history› of the Saar

**Saat** /za:t/ *die;* ~, **~en** [A] (*Getreide usw.*) [young] crops *pl.;* (*fachspr.: Pflanzgut*) seedlings *pl.;* young plants *pl.;* **die ~ des Bösen ist aufgegangen** (*fig. geh.*) the seeds of evil have borne fruit; [B] (*das Säen*) sowing; **mit der ~ beginnen** start sowing; [C] (*Samenkörner*) seed[s *pl.*]

**Saat-:** **~gut** *das* seed[s *pl.*]; **~kartoffel** *die* seed potato; **~korn** *das* [A] (*zum Aussäen*) seedcorn; [B] (*Samenkorn*) grain; **~krähe** *die* rook

**Sabbat** /ˈzabat/ *der;* **~s, ~e** sabbath; **es ist ~:** it is the sabbath

**Sabbat·jahr** *das* (*jüd. Rel.*) sabbatical year

**Sabbel** /ˈzabl̩/ *der;* **~s,** ~ (*nordd. abwertend*) [A] (*Mund*) gob (*sl.*); **halt den ~:** shut your trap (*sl.*); [B] ⇒ **Sabber**

**sabbeln** (*nordd.*) ❶ *itr. V.* [A] (*abwertend: sprechen*) natter (*Brit. coll.*) *or* chatter [on]; rabbit on (*Brit. sl.*); [B] ⇒ **sabbern** 1 A. ❷ *tr. V.* (*abwertend*) jabber ‹nonsense, rubbish›

**Sabber** /ˈzabɐ/ *der;* **~s** (*ugs.*) slobber; (*eines Kindes*) dribble

**sabbern** ❶ *itr. V.* [A] ‹dog, person› slaver, slobber; ‹baby› dribble; [B] (*abwertend*) ⇒ **sabbeln** 1 A. ❷ *tr. V.* (*abwertend*) ⇒ **sabbeln** 2

**Säbel** /ˈzɛ:bl̩/ *der;* **~s, ~:** sabre; **mit dem ~ rasseln** (*fig. abwertend*) rattle the sabre

**Säbel-:** **~beine** *Pl.* (*ugs. scherzh.*) bandy *or* bow legs; **~fechten** *das* (*Fechten*) sabre fencing *no art.;* **Weltmeister im ~fechten** world champion at sabre; world sabre champion; **~gerassel** *das* (*abwertend*) sabre-rattling

**säbeln** *tr. V.* (*ugs.*) hack, saw ‹bread etc.›

**Säbel·rasseln** *das;* **~s** (*abwertend*) sabre-rattling

**säbel·rasselnd** *Adj.* (*abwertend*) sabre-rattling

**Sabotage** /zaboˈta:ʒə/ *die;* ~, **~n** sabotage *no art.;* **Versuch der ~:** attempted sabotage

**Sabotage·akt** *der* act of sabotage

**Saboteur** /zaboˈtø:ɐ̯/ *der;* **~s, ~e, Saboteurin** *die;* ~, **~nen** saboteur

**sabotieren** *tr. V.* sabotage; disobey ‹order›

**Saccharin** /zaxaˈri:n/ *das;* **~s** saccharin

**sach-, Sach-:** **~bearbeiter** *der,* **~bearbeiterin** *die* person responsible (**für** for); (*Experte*) specialist, expert (**für** on); **~bereich** *der* area; field; **der ~bereich Öffentlichkeitsarbeit** the field of public relations; all matters *pl.* concerning public relations; **~beschädigung** *die* (*Rechtsw.*) wilful damage to property; **~bezogen** ❶ *Adj.* relevant; pertinent ‹remark›; ❷ *adv.* to the point; **~bezüge** *Pl.* payment *sing.* in kind; **~buch** *das* [popular] non-fiction *or* informative book; **~bücher lesen** read non-fiction *sing.;* **~dienlich** *Adj.* (*Papierdt.*) useful; helpful

**Sache** /ˈzaxə/ *die;* ~, **~n** [A] thing; **scharfe ~n trinken** drink the hard stuff (*coll.*); **bewegliche/unbewegliche ~n** (*Rechtsspr., Wirtsch.*) movable/fixed assets; (*Rechtsw.: Eigentum*) movables *or* chattels/immovables *or* real estate *sing.;* [B] (*Angelegenheit*) matter; business (*esp. derog.*); **das ist eine andere ~/eine ~ für sich** that's a different/a separate matter; **eine ernste/schlimme/heikle/faule ~:** a serious/a bad/an awkward/a shady business; **es ist beschlossene ~[, dass ...]** it's [all] arranged *or* settled [that ...]; **es ist die einfachste ~ [von] der Welt** it's the simplest thing in the world; **das ist meine/seine ~:** that's my business/his own affair; **das ist so eine ~:** it's a bit tricky; **das ist nicht jedermanns ~:** it's not everyone's cup of tea; **du hast dir die ~ sehr leicht gemacht** you made it *or* things *pl.* very easy for yourself; **so kommen wir der ~ näher** we are getting warmer *or* coming to the point; **~n gibts[, die gibts gar nicht]!** (*ugs.*) would you believe *or* credit it!; **mach ~n!** you don't say!; **was sind denn das für ~n!** (*ugs.*) what's all this then!; what's going on!; **von dir hört man ja nette ~n!** (*iron.*) I've heard some things about you!; **[mit jmdm.] gemeinsame ~ machen** join forces [with sb.]; **sagen/jmdm. sagen, was ~ ist** (*ugs.*) come out with it/come clean with sb. (*coll.*); (*die Dinge beim Namen nennen*) say/tell sb. what's what; (*sagen, worum es geht*) say/tell sb. what gives (*coll.*); (*bestimmen*) say/tell sb. what goes (*coll.*); **[sich (*Dat.*)] seiner ~ sicher** *od.* **gewiss sein** be sure one is right; **bei der ~ sein/bleiben** concentrate/keep one's mind on it; (*im Gespräch usw.*) stick to the point; **nicht bei der ~ sein** let one's mind wander; **zur ~ kommen** come to the point; **das tut nichts zur ~:** that's irrelevant; that's got nothing to do with it; [C] (*Rechts~*) case; **die Verhandlung in ~n Maier gegen Schulze** the hearing in the case of Maier versus Schulze; **Fragen/Angaben zur ~:** questions/statements about the case; [D] (*Anliegen*) cause; **es dient der großen ~:** it's in a good cause; [E] *Pl.* (*ugs.: Stundenkilometer*) **100 ~n** 100 kilometres per hour; **wie viel ~n hat er draufgehabt?** how fast was he going?

**Sach·einlage** *die* (*Wirtsch.*) investment in kind

**Sächelchen** /ˈzɛçl̩çən/ *das;* **~s, ~:** [little] thing

**Sachen·recht** *das* (*Rechtsw.*) law of property

**Sacher·torte** /ˈzaxɐ-/ *die: rich iced chocolate cake;* Sachertorte

**sach-, Sach-:** **~frage** *die* question about the matter/issue itself (*as opposed to personalities, methods, etc.*); **~gebiet** *das* subject [area]; field; **das ~gebiet Ornithologie** the field of ornithology; **~gemäß, ~gerecht** ❶ *Adj.* proper; correct; ❷ *adv.* properly; correctly; **~katalog** *der* (*Buchw.*) subject catalogue; **~kenner** *der,* **~kennerin** *die* expert; **~kenntnis** *die* expertise; knowledge of the subject; **von keiner ~kenntnis getrübt** (*scherzh.*) without having the faintest idea [what it's all about]; **~kunde** *die* [A] ⇒ **~kenntnis;** [B] ≈ general subjects *pl.;* **~kundig** ❶ *Adj.* with a knowledge of the subject *postpos., not pred.;* **sich ~kundig machen** acquaint oneself with the subject; ❷ *adv.* expertly; **~lage** *die* situation; **~leistung** *die* (*Amtsspr., Versicherungsw.*) benefit in kind

**sachlich** ❶ *Adj.* [A] (*objektiv*) objective; (*nüchtern*) functional ‹building, style, etc.›; matter-of-fact, down-to-earth ‹letter etc.›; [B] (*sachbezogen*) factual ‹error›; actual, material ‹difference›; material ‹consideration›; **aus ~en Gründen** for practical reasons. ❷ *adv.* [A] (*objektiv*) objectively; ‹state› as a matter of fact; (*nüchtern*) ‹furnished› in a functional style; ‹written› in a matter-of-fact way; [B] (*sachbezogen*) factually ‹wrong›; actually ‹justified›

**sächlich** /ˈzɛçlɪç/ *Adj.* (*Sprachw.*) neuter

**Sachlichkeit** *die;* **~:** objectivity; (*Nüchternheit*) functionalism; **Neue ~** (*Kunstwiss.*) new objectivity

**Sach-:** **~mangel** *der* (*Rechtsw.*) material defect; **~register** *das* [subject] index; **~schaden** *der* damage [to property] *no indef. art.;* **ein ~schaden von 30 000 Mark** damage amounting to 30,000 marks

**Sachse** /ˈzaksə/ *der;* **~n, ~n** Saxon

**sächseln** /ˈzɛksl̩n/ *itr. V.* **er sächselt** he speaks in Saxon dialect

**Sachsen** (*das*); **~s** Saxony

**Sachsen-Anhalt** (*das*); **~s** Saxony-Anhalt

**Sachsen-Anhalter,** *der;* **~s,** ~, **Sachsen-Anhalterin** *die;* ~, **~nen, Sachsen-Anhaltiner** *der;* **~s,** ~, **Sachsen-Anhaltinerin** *die;* ~, **~nen** native of Saxony-Anhalt; (*Einwohner[in]*) inhabitant of Saxony-Anhalt

**sachsen-anhaltinisch, sachsen-anhaltisch** *Adj.* Saxony-Anhalt *attrib.*

**Sächsin** /ˈzɛksɪn/ *die;* ~, **~nen** ⇒ **Sachse**

**sächsisch** /ˈzɛksɪʃ/ ❶ *Adj.* Saxon; ‹capital, economy, etc.› of Saxony. ❷ *adv.* ‹speak, write› in Saxon dialect; ⇒ *auch* **badisch**

**Sach·spende** *die* gift *or* contribution in kind

**sacht** /zaxt/ ❶ *Adj.* [A] (*behutsam*) gentle; (*langsam*) smooth ‹take-off›; gentle, gradual ‹acceleration›; [B] (*leise*) quiet. ❷ *adv.* [A] gently; [B] (*leise*) quietly

**sachte** ❶ ⇒ **sacht.** ❷ *adv.* (*ugs.*) [A] (*Beschwichtigung*) **~[, ~]** take it easy; (*nicht so hastig*) not so fast; [B] **so [ganz] ~** (*allmählich*) gradually

**sach-, Sach-:** **~verhalt** *der;* **~~[e]s, ~~e** facts *pl.* [of the matter]; **~versicherung** *die* (*Versicherungsw.*) property insurance; **~verstand** *der* expertise; grasp of the subject; **~verständig** ❶ *Adj.* expert ‹opinion etc.›; knowledgeable ‹person›; ❷ *adv.* expertly; knowledgeably; **~verständige** *der/die; adj. Dekl.* expert; **~verständigen·ausschuss,** ***~verständigen·ausschuß** *der* committee of experts; **~verständigen·gutachten** *das* expert's report; (*von mehreren*) experts' report; **~walter** /-valtɐ/ *der;* **~~s, ~~, ~walterin** *die;* **~~, ~~nen** [A] (*geh.: Fürsprecher*) champion; [B] (*Rechtsw.: Interessenvertreter der Gläubiger*) trustee in bankruptcy; **~wert** *der* [A] intrinsic *or* real value; [B] (*Wertobjekt*) material asset; **~wissen** *das* specialist knowledge; **~wörterbuch** *das* specialist *or* subject dictionary; **ein ~wörterbuch der Literatur** a dictionary

*old spelling (see note on page 1707)

of literature; **~zwang** *der* [factual *or* material] constraint

**Sack** /zak/ *der;* **~[e]s, Säcke** /'zɛkə/ **A** *(Behältnis)* sack; *(aus Papier, Kunststoff)* bag; **ein ~ Zement** a bag of cement; **drei Säcke [voll] Kartoffeln** three sacks of potatoes; **einen ~ voll ...** *(fig.)* a [whole] load *or* mass of ... *(coll.)*; **den ~ schlägt man, den Esel meint man** *(Spr.)* he/she is being used as a scapegoat; **jmdn. im ~ haben** *(salopp)* have got round sb.; **etw. im ~ haben** *(salopp)* have sth. in the bag *(coll.)*; **jmdn. in den ~ stecken** *(ugs.)* put sb. in the shade; **mit ~ und Pack** with bag and baggage; ⇒ *auch* **nass** 1 A; **schlafen** 1 A; **B** *(Hautfalte)* **Säcke unter den Augen haben** have bags under one's eyes; **C** *(derb: Hoden~)* balls *pl.* *(coarse)*; **D** *(derb abwertend: Mensch)* sod *(Brit. sl.)*; **E** *(bes. südd., österr., schweiz.)* *(Hosentasche)* [trouser] pocket; *(Geldbeutel)* purse

**Sack·bahn·hof** *der* ⇒ **Kopfbahnhof**

**Säckchen** /'zɛkçən/ *das;* **~s, ~:** small sack; bag

**Säckel** /'zɛkl̩/ *der;* **~s, ~** *(bes. südd., österr.)* **A** *(veralt.: Geldbeutel)* money bag; purse; **B** *(Hosentasche)* [trouser] pocket; **C** ⇒ **Sack** D

**sacken** *itr. V.; mit sein* ‹person› slump; ‹ship etc.› sink; ‹plane› drop rapidly, plummet; **er sackte in die Knie** his knees gave way

**säcke·weise** *Adv.* ⇒ **sackweise** B

**sack-, Sack-: ~gasse** *die* cul-de-sac; *(fig.)* impasse; **~hüpfen** *das;* **~~s** sack race; **beim ~hüpfen** in the sack race; **~kleid** *das* sack; **~leinen** *das,* **~leinwand** *die* sacking; **~pfeife** *die* bagpipes *pl.;* **~tuch** *das; Pl.* **~tücher** *(südd., österr., schweiz.)* handkerchief; **~weise** *Adv.* **A** *(in Säcken)* in sacks; **B** *(massenhaft)* loads *or* masses of *(coll.)*

**Sadismus** /za'dɪsmʊs/ *der;* **~, Sadismen** **A** *(Veranlagung; abwertend: Quälerei)* sadism *no art.;* **B** *(Handlung)* act of sadism

**Sadist** *der;* **~en, ~en, Sadistin** *die;* **~, ~nen** sadist

**sadistisch** **1** *Adj.* sadistic. **2** *adv.* sadistically; **~ veranlagt sein** have sadistic tendencies

**Sado·masochismus** /zadomazɔ'xɪsmʊs/ *der* *(Med.)* sadomasochism *no art.*

**sado·masochistisch** *(Med.)* **1** *Adj.* sadomasochistic. **2** *adv.* sadomasochistically; **~ veranlagt sein** have sadomasochistic tendencies

**säen** /'zɛ:ən/ *tr. (auch itr.) V. (auch fig.)* sow; **dünn** *od.* **nicht gerade dicht gesät sein** *(fig.)* be thin on the ground

**Safari** /za'fa:ri/ *die;* **~, ~s** safari

**Safe** /seɪf/ *der od. das;* **~s, ~s** **A** safe; **B** *(Schließfach)* safe-deposit box

**Saffian** /'zafi̯an/ *der;* **~s, Saffian·leder** *das* morocco [leather]

**Safran** /'zafran/ *der;* **~s, ~e** saffron

**Saft** /zaft/ *der;* **~[e]s, Säfte** /'zɛftə/ **A** juice; **jmdn. im eigenen ~ schmoren lassen** *(fig. ugs.)* let sb. stew in his/her own juice; **B** *(in Pflanzen)* sap; **Blut ist ein ganz besonderer ~:** blood is thicker than water *(fig.)*; **ohne ~ und Kraft** *(abwertend)* weak and lifeless; *(adv.)* without any zest; **C** *(salopp: Elektrizität)* juice *(sl.)*; **D** *(veralt.: Körperflüssigkeit)* fluid; **E** *(österr.: Soße)* gravy

**saft·grün** *Adj.* lush green

**Saft·heini** *der (ugs.)* right twit *(Brit. coll.)*; jerk *(coll.)*

**saftig** **1** *Adj.* **A** *(voll Saft)* juicy; sappy ‹stem›; lush ‹meadow, green›; *(fig.: lebensvoll)* lusty; **B** *(ugs.: stark, intensiv)* hefty ‹slap, blow›; good ‹thrashing›; steep *(coll.)* ‹prices, bill›; terrific, big ‹surprise, punch-up›; crude, coarse ‹joke, song, etc.›; strongly-worded ‹letter etc.›; strong, juicy ‹curse›. **2** *adv.* **A eine ~ grüne Wiese** a lush green meadow; **B** *(ugs.: kräftig)* ‹curse, hit out› well and truly, good and proper

**Saftigkeit** *die;* **~, ~en** **A** juiciness; **die ~ der Wiesen** the lushness of the meadows; **B** *(Äußerung)* crude remark

**saft-, Saft-: ~kur** *die* juice diet; **~laden** *der; Pl.* **~läden** *(salopp abwertend)* lousy outfit *(coll.)*; **~los** *Adj.* **A** juiceless; **~los sein** have *or* contain no juice; **B** *(fig.)* feeble, anodyne ‹language›; **~- und kraftlos** feeble; wishy-washy; *(adv.)* without any zest; **~presse** *die* juice extractor; **~sack** *der* *(derb abwertend)* bastard *(coll.)*; **~tag** *der* juice[-diet] day

**Saga** /'za(:)ga/ *die;* **~, ~s** *(Literaturw.)* saga

**Sage** /'za:gə/ *die;* **~, ~n** legend; *(bes. nordische)* saga; *(fig.: Gerücht)* rumour

**Säge** /'zɛ:gə/ *die;* **~, ~n** **A** saw; **B** *(bayr., österr.: ~werk)* sawmill

**Säge-: ~blatt** *das* saw blade; **~bock** *der* sawhorse; **~fisch** *der* sawfish; **~mehl** *das* sawdust; **~mühle** *die* sawmill

**sagen** **1** *tr. V.* **A** *(äußern, behaupten)* say; **so etwas sagt man nicht** it's not done to say things like that; **das kann man nicht [so ohne weiteres] ~:** you can't really say *or* tell; **das kann jeder ~:** anybody can claim that; it's easy to talk; **das ist nicht zu viel gesagt** that's not overstating the case *or* no exaggeration; **man sagt [von ihm** *od.* **über ihn], dass ...** it is said [of him] that ...; **das sagst du so einfach!** that's easy to say *or* easily said; **da soll noch einer ~** *od.* **da sage noch einer, dass ...** never let it be said that ...; **na, wer sagts denn!** *(ugs.)* there you are[, I knew it]!; **sag das nicht!** *(ugs.)* don't [just] assume that!; not necessarily!; **das ist nicht gesagt** it's not necessarily the case; it's by no means certain; **dann will ich nichts gesagt haben** in that case forget I said anything; **was ich noch ~ wollte** [oh] by the way; before I forget; **unter uns gesagt** between you and me; **das oben Gesagte** what has been said above; the above remarks *pl.;* *(in einem Vortrag)* the foregoing [remarks]; **das musste einmal gesagt werden** it had to be said; **wie gesagt** as I've said *or* mentioned; **das ist leichter gesagt als getan** that's easier said than done; **das kann man wohl ~, das kann man** *od.* **kannst du laut ~** *(ugs.)* you can say 'that again; **gesagt, getan** no sooner said than done; **das kostet Tausende, [ach,] was sage ich, Millionen!** it costs thousands, what am I talking about, millions!; **~ wir einmal** *od.* *(ugs.)* **mal** let's say; **wir treffen uns, ~ wir, um 10 vor 8** let's meet at, say, ten to eight; **sage und schreibe** *(ugs.)* believe it or not; would you believe; **um nicht zu ~:** not to say; **sag bloß, du hast es vergessen!** *(ugs.)* don't say you've forgotten it!; **B** *(meinen)* say; **was ~ Sie dazu?** what do you think about that?; **was soll man dazu noch ~?** *(ugs.)* what 'can one say; **was sagst du nun?** *(ugs.)* now what do you say?; what do you say to that?; **C** ▸ 818 *(mitteilen)* **jmdm. etw. ~:** say sth. to sb.; *(zur Information)* tell sb. sth.; **[jmdm.] seinen Namen/seine Gründe ~:** give [sb.] one's name/reasons; **[jmdm.] die Wahrheit ~:** tell [sb.] the truth; **sag mal/~ Sie [mal], gibt es ...?** tell me, is there ...?; **ich habe mir ~ lassen, dass ...** I've been told that ...; **das sag ich dir** *(ugs.)* I'm telling *or* warning you; **ich habs [dir] ja gleich gesagt!** *(ugs.)* I told you so!; *(habe dich gewarnt)* I warned you!; **ich will dir mal was ~:** let me tell you something; **lass dir das gesagt sein** *(ugs.)* make a note of *or* remember what I'm saying; **das sag ich [deinen Eltern** *usw.*] *(Kinderspr.)* I'll tell on you [to your parents *etc.*]; **wem ~ Sie das!** *(ugs.)* you don't need to tell me [that]!; **das brauchst du mir nicht zu ~** *(ugs.)* you don't need to tell me that; I know that only too well; **was Sie nicht ~!** *(ugs., oft iron.)* you don't say!; **das kann ich dir ~!** *(ugs.)* you can be sure of that *or* bank on that; **wenn ich es [dir] sage!** *(ugs.)* I promise [you]; **jmdm. Grobheiten ~:** speak rudely to sb.; **und dann muss ich mir von ihm auch noch ~ lassen, dass ...** and then I have to put up with him telling me that ...; **er lässt sich** *(Dat.)* **nichts ~:** he won't be told; you can't tell him anything; **das ist zu viel gesagt** that's going too far; that's an exaggeration; **D** *(nennen)* **zu jmdm./etw. X ~:** call sb./sth. X; **du kannst du zu mir ~:** you can call me 'du' *or* say 'du' to me; **E** *(formulieren, ausdrücken)* say; **das hast du gut gesagt** you put that well; that was well said; **so kann man es auch ~:** you could put it like that; **etw. in aller Deutlichkeit ~:** make sth. perfectly clear; **das sagt er nur so** he doesn't mean it; **es ist nicht zu ~, wie ...** no words can express *or* say *or* there is no expressing how ...; **du sagst es!** very true!; **willst du damit ~, dass ...?** are you trying to say *or* do you mean [to say] that ...?; **das wollte ich damit nicht ~:** I didn't mean that; **will ~:** or rather; that is to say; **F** *(bedeuten)* mean; **damit ist viel/wenig/nichts gesagt** that's saying a lot/not saying much/that doesn't mean anything; **das will** *od.* **hat nichts zu ~:** that doesn't mean anything; that isn't important; **hat das etwas zu ~?** does that mean anything?; **G** *(anordnen, befehlen)* tell; **du hast mir gar nichts zu ~:** you've no right to order me about; **von ihm lasse ich mir nichts ~:** I'm not taking any orders from him; **sich** *(Dat.)* **etw. nicht zweimal ~ lassen** *(ugs.)* not need to be told *or* asked twice; **das lass/ließ ich mir nicht zweimal ~:** I'd love to/I jumped at it; **etwas/nichts zu ~ haben** ‹person› have a/no say; *(zuständig/nicht zuständig sein)* be in authority/have no authority.

**2** *refl. V.* **A sich** *(Dat.)* **etw. ~:** say sth. to oneself; **das hättest du dir damals schon ~ können** you should have realized [that] then; **B das sagt sich so einfach** *(ugs.)* that's easy to say *or* easily said.

**3** *itr. V.* **wie sagt man [da]?** what does one say?; what's the [right] word?; *(Aufforderung an ein Kind)* what do you say [now]?; **wenn ich so ~ darf** if I may put it this way; *(bei einem etwas gewagten Ausdruck)* if you will pardon the expression; **sag bloß!** *(ugs.)* you don't say!

**sägen** /'zɛ:gn̩/ **1** *itr. V.* **A** saw; *(fig.: auf einer Geige usw.)* saw away; **an jmds. Stuhl ~** *(fig.)* try to undermine sb.'s position; **B** *(ugs. scherzh.: schnarchen)* snore loudly. **2** *tr. V.* saw; *(zersägen)* saw up ‹tree etc.›

**Sagen-: ~buch** *das* book of legends; **~gestalt** *die* legendary figure

**sagenhaft** **1** *Adj.* **A** *(ugs.)* incredible *(coll.)* ‹wealth, mess, memory, etc.›; fabulous *(coll.)* ‹party, wealth›; **B** *(der Sage angehörend)* legendary. **2** *adv.* incredibly *(coll.)*

**sagen·umwoben** *Adj. (geh.)* ‹castle, place› steeped in legend; ‹historical figure› at the centre of many legends

**Sagen·welt** *die* legendary world

**Säge-: ~späne** *Pl.* wood shavings; **~werk** *das* sawmill; **~zahn** *der* sawtooth

**Sago** /'za:go/ *der od. das;* **~s** sago

**sah** /za:/ *1. u. 3. Pers. Sg. Prät. v.* **sehen**

**Sahelzone** /'za:hɛl- *od.* za'he:l-/ *die;* **~:** Sahel

**Sahne** /'za:nə/ *die;* **~:** cream

**Sahne-: ~bonbon** *der od. das* cream toffee; **~eis** *das* cream ice; **~quark** *der* creamy quark; quark with a high fat content; **~torte** *die* cream cake *or* gateau

**sahnig** *Adj.* creamy

**Saison** /zɛ'zõ:/ *die;* **~, ~s** season; **während/außerhalb der ~:** during the season/out of season *or* in the off-season; **~ haben** have one's busy time *or* season; ‹hotel› be open for the season; *(ugs.: sehr gefragt sein)* ‹goods› be much in demand

**saisonal** /zɛzo'na:l/ **1** *Adj.* seasonal. **2** *adv.* ‹fluctuate› according to the season

**saison-, Saison-: ~arbeit** *die* seasonal work; **~arbeiter** *der,* **~arbeiterin** *die* seasonal worker; **~ausverkauf** *der* end-of-season sale; **~bedingt** **1** *Adj.* seasonal; **2** *adv.* due to seasonal influences; **~zuschlag** *der* seasonal supplement

**Saite** /'zai̯tə/ *die;* **~, ~n** *(Musik, Sport)* string; **das/sie brachte in mir eine verwandte ~ zum Klingen** *(fig.)* it/she struck

S

a responsive chord in me; **andere** *od.* **strengere ~n aufziehen** (*fig.*) take stronger measures; get tough (*coll.*)

**Saiten-: ~halter** *der* (*Musik*) (*an der Geige*) tailpiece; (*an der Laute, Gitarre*) string holder; **~instrument** *das* stringed instrument; **~spiel** *das* (*geh.*) string playing; (*Musik*) string music

**-saitig** /-zaitıç/ -string[ed]

**Sakko** /'zako/ *der od. das;* **~s, ~s** jacket

**sakral** /za'kra:l/ *Adj.* religious; **~e Gewänder** priest's vestments; **~e Gesänge** sacred songs *or* chants

**Sakral·bau** *der; Pl.* **~ten** (*Archit., Kunstwiss.*) religious building

**Sakrament** /zakra'mɛnt/ *das;* **~[e]s, ~e** Ⓐ (*christl., bes. kath. Kirche*) sacrament; Ⓑ **~ [noch mal]!** for Heaven's sake

**sakramental** /zakramɛn'ta:l/ *Adj.* sacramental

**Sakramentalien** /zakramɛn'ta:li̯ən/ *Pl.* (*kath. Rel.*) sacramentals

**Sakrileg** /zakri'le:k/ *das;* **~s, ~e** act of sacrilege; **ist es ein ~?** is it sacrilege?

**Sakristan** /zakrıs'ta:n/ *der;* **~s, ~e, Sakristanin** *die;* **~, ~nen** sacristan

**Sakristei** /zakrıs'tai̯/ *die;* **~, ~en** sacristy

**sakrosankt** /zakro'zaŋkt/ *Adj.* sacrosanct

**säkular** /zɛku'la:ɐ̯/ *Adj.* Ⓐ (*geh.: weltlich; auch Astron., Geol.*) secular; Ⓑ (*geh.: herausragend*) outstanding

**säkularisieren** *tr. V.* secularize ‹property, art, etc.›; deconsecrate ‹church›

**Salamander** /zala'mandɐ/ *der;* **~s, ~:** salamander; **einen** *od.* **den ~ reiben** (*Studentenspr.*): *scrape one's glass three times on the table, empty it, and after brief drumming put it down with a bang (as a mark of honour)*

**Salami** /za'la:mi/ *die;* **~, ~[s]** salami

**Salami·taktik** *die* step-by-step policy

**Salär** /za'lɛ:ɐ̯/ *das;* **~s, ~e** (*bes. schweiz., auch südd., österr., sonst veralt.*) salary

**Salat** /za'la:t/ *der;* **~[e]s, ~e** Ⓐ salad; Ⓑ **[grüner] ~:** lettuce; **ein Kopf ~:** a [head of] lettuce; Ⓒ (*ugs.: Wirrwarr*) muddle; mess; **jetzt haben wir den ~!** (*ugs. iron.*) now we're in a right mess!

**Salat-: ~besteck** *das* salad servers *pl.;* **~blatt** *das* lettuce leaf; **~gurke** *die* cucumber; **~kartoffel** *die: potato suitable for potato salad;* **~kopf** *der* lettuce; **~öl** *das* salad oil; **~schüssel** *die* salad bowl; **~soße** *die* salad dressing

**salbadern** /zal'ba:dɐn/ *tr. V.* (*ugs. abwertend*) waffle [pretentiously]

**Salbe** /'zalbə/ *die;* **~, ~n** ointment; (*gegen Muskelkater usw.*) embrocation

**Salbei** /'zalbai̯/ *der od. die;* **~:** sage

**salben** *tr. V.* Ⓐ (*einreiben*) put ointment on ‹part of body›; Ⓑ (*kath. Kirche*) anoint ‹sick or dying person, (Hist.) king, emperor, etc.›; (*hist.*) **jmdn. zum Kaiser ~:** anoint sb. emperor

**Salbung** *die;* **~, ~en** (*Weihung*) anointing; (*kath. Kirche*) unction; **die letzte ~:** extreme unction

**salbungs·voll** (*abwertend*) ❶ *Adj.* unctuous. ❷ *adv.* unctuously

**saldieren** /zal'di:rən/ ❶ *tr. V.* Ⓐ (*Buchf., Finanzw.*) balance ‹credit and debit sides›; **einen Gewinn ~:** produce a profit balance; Ⓑ (*österr.: quittieren*) confirm payment of; give a receipt for. ❷ *itr. V.* Ⓐ (*Buchf., Finanzw.*) balance the books; Ⓑ (*österr.: quittieren*) confirm payment

**Saldo** /'zaldo/ *der;* **~s, ~s** *od.* **Saldi** *od.* **Salden** (*Buchf., Finanzw.*) balance; **im ~ sein/bleiben** be/remain in debt

**Saldo-: ~übertrag** *der,* **~vortrag** *der* (*Buchf.*) balance brought forward

**Säle** ⇒ **Saal**

**Salicylsäure** (*chem. fachspr.*) ⇒ **Salizylsäure**

**Salier** /'za:li̯ɐ/ *der;* **~s, ~, Salierin** *die;* **~, ~nen** (*hist.*) Salian

**Saline** /za'li:nə/ *die;* **~, ~n** salt works *sing. or pl.*

*old spelling (see note on page 1707)

**Salizyl·säure** /zali'tsy:l-/ *die* (*Chemie*) salicylic acid

**Salm** /zalm/ *der;* **~[e]s, ~e** (*bes. rhein.*) salmon

**Salmiak** /zal'mi̯ak/ *der od. das;* **~:** sal ammoniac

**Salmiak-: ~geist** *der* [liquid] ammonia; ammonia water; **~pastille** *die* sal ammoniac pastille

**Salmonelle** /zalmo'nɛlə/ *die;* **~, ~n** salmonella

**Salomon** /'za:lomɔn/ (*der*) Solomon

**Salomonen** /zalo'mo:nən/ *Pl.* Solomon Islands

**salomonisch** (*geh.*) ❶ *Adj.* Solomon-like; **ein ~es Urteil** a judgment of Solomon. ❷ *adv.* with the wisdom of Solomon

**Salon** /za'lõ:/ *der;* **~s, ~s** Ⓐ (*Raum*) drawing room; salon; Ⓑ (*Geschäft*) [hair *etc.*] salon; Ⓒ (*veralt.: Zirkel*) [literary] salon; Ⓓ (*Ausstellung*) Salon

**salon-, Salon-: ~fähig** ❶ *Adj.* socially acceptable; (*nach einem Bad o. Ä.*) **ich bin noch nicht ~fähig** I am not yet presentable; ❷ *adv.* in a socially acceptable manner; properly ‹dressed›; **~kommunist** *der,* **~kommunistin** *die* (*iron.*) parlour communist; **~löwe** *der* (*abwertend*) society man; **~musik** *die* salon music; **~wagen** *der* Pullman car *or* coach

**salopp** /za'lɔp/ ❶ *Adj.* casual ‹clothes›; free and easy, informal ‹behaviour, household, etc.›; very colloquial, slangy ‹saying, expression, etc.›. ❷ *adv.* ‹dress› casually; informally; **~ reden** use slangy *or* [very] colloquial language

**Salpeter** /zal'pe:tɐ/ *der;* **~s** saltpetre

**Salpeter·säure** *die* nitric acid

**salpetrig** *Adj.* **~e Säure** nitrous acid

**Salto** /'zalto/ *der;* **~s, ~s** *od.* **Salti** Ⓐ somersault; (*beim Turnen auch*) salto; **ein ~ vorwärts/rückwärts** a forward/backward somersault; **einen ~ springen** do *or* turn a somersault; Ⓑ (*Fliegerspr.*) ⇒ **Looping**

**Salto mortale** /- mɔr'ta:lə/ *der;* **~ ~, ~ ~** *od.* **Salti mortali** salto mortale

**Salut** /za'lu:t/ *der;* **~[e]s, ~e** (*Milit.*) salute; **~ schießen** fire a salute; **21 Schuss ~ abgeben** fire a twenty-one-gun salute

**salutieren** *itr. V.* (*bes. Milit.*) salute; **vor jmdm. ~:** salute sb.

**Salut·schuss, *Salut·schuß** *der* (*Milit.*) gun salute; **sieben Salutschüsse** a seven-gun salute

**Salvadorianer** /zalvado'ri̯a:nɐ/ *der;* **~s, ~, Salvadorianerin** *die;* **~, ~nen** Salvadoran

**Salve** /'zalvə/ *die;* **~, ~n** (*Milit.*) salvo; (*aus Gewehren*) volley; **eine ~ des Beifalls/von Gelächter** (*fig.*) a burst of applause/laughter

**Salz** /zalts/ *das;* **~es, ~e** salt; **das ~ der Ironie** (*fig.*) the spice of irony; **~ auf die** *od.* **in die Wunde streuen** (*fig.*) rub salt into the wound; **jmdm. nicht das ~ in der Suppe gönnen** (*ugs.*) begrudge sb. everything

**salz-, Salz-: ~arm** ❶ *Adj.* low in salt *postpos.;* low-salt; ❷ *adv.* **~arm kochen** use little salt in cooking; **~arm essen** eat food containing little salt; **~berg·werk** *das* salt mine; **~brezel** *die* [salted] pretzel

**salzen** *tr. V.* salt; **die Suppe ist stark/zu wenig/kaum gesalzen** the soup has a lot of/too little/hardly any salt in it

**salz-, Salz-: ~fässchen, *~fäßchen** *das* Ⓐ salt cellar; Ⓑ (*ugs. scherzh.: beim Menschen*) hollow between the collarbones; **~fleisch** *das* ⇒ **Pökelfleisch**; **~haltig** *Adj.* containing salt *postpos., not pred.;* salty; **sehr ~haltig sein** have a high salt content; **~hering** *der* salted herring

**salzig** *Adj.* salty

**salz-, Salz-: ~kartoffel** *die* boiled potato; **~korn** *das* grain of salt; **~lake** *die* brine; **~lecke** *die* (*Jägerspr.*) salt lick; **~los** ❶ *Adj.* salt-free; (*nicht gesalzen*) unsalted; ❷ *adv.* ‹cook› without any salt; **~los essen** eat unsalted food; **~lösung** *die* saline solution; **~mandel** *die* salted almond; **~napf** *der* salt cellar; **~säule** *die* pillar of salt; **zur ~säule erstarren** (*fig.*) be rooted to the spot *or* turned to stone; **~säure** *die* (*Chemie*) hydrochloric acid; **~see** *der* salt lake; (*ausgetrocknet*) salt flats *pl.;* **~sole** *die* brine; **~stange** *die* salt stick; **~streuer** *der;* **~~s, ~~:** salt sprinkler; salt shaker (*Amer.*); **~wasser** *das; Pl.* **~wässer** Ⓐ (*zum Kochen*) salted water; Ⓑ (*Meerwasser*) salt water; Ⓒ (*Lake*) brine; **~werk** *das* salt works *sing. or pl.;* **~wüste** *die* salt desert

**Sä·mann** *der* (*dichter.*) sower

**SA-Mann** /ɛs'|a:-/ *der; Pl.* **SA-Männer** *od.* **SA-Leute** (*ns.*) SA man; stormtrooper

**Samariter** /zama'ri:tɐ/ *der;* **~s, ~** Ⓐ **[barmherziger] ~:** good Samaritan; **bei jmdm. ~ spielen** play *or* act the good Samaritan to sb.; Ⓑ (*schweiz.*) ⇒ **Sanitäter**

**Samariter·dienst** *der* selfless act [of kindness]

**Samariterin** *die;* **~, ~nen** Ⓐ ⇒ **Samariter** A; Ⓑ (*schweiz.*) ⇒ **Sanitäterin**

**Sä·maschine** *die* seeder, (*esp.*) seed drill

**Samba** /'zamba/ *der;* **~s, ~s** *od. die;* **~, ~s** samba

**Sambesi** /zam'be:zi/ *der;* **~[s]** ▶ 306 Zambezi

**Sambia** /'zambi̯a/ (*das*)**; ~s** Zambia

**Sambier** /'zambi̯ɐ/ *der;* **~s, ~, Sambierin** *die;* **~, ~nen** Zambian

**Same**[1] /'za:mə/ *der;* **~n, ~n** ⇒ **Lappe**

**Same**[2] *der;* **~ns, ~n** (*geh.*) seed

**Samen** /'za:mən/ *der;* **~s, ~** Ⓐ (*~korn*) seed; Ⓑ (*~körner*) seed[s. *pl.*]; Ⓒ (*Sperma*) sperm; semen

**Samen-: ~anlage** *die* (*Bot.*) ovule; **~bank** *die; Pl.* **~~en** (*Med., Tiermed.*) sperm bank; **~erguss, *~erguß** *der* ejaculation; **~faden** *der* ⇒ **Spermium**; **~flüssigkeit** *die* seminal fluid; **~handlung** *die* seed merchant's [shop *or* (*Amer.*) store]; **~kapsel** *die* seed capsule; **~korn** *das* seed; **~leiter** *der* ▶ 471 (*Anat.*) sperm[atic] duct; **~strang** *der* ▶ 471 (*Anat.*) spermatic cord; **~zelle** *die* sperm cell

**Sämereien** /zɛ:mə'rai̯ən/ *Pl.* seeds

**sämig** /'zɛ:mıç/ *Adj.* thick ‹sauce, soup, etc.›; viscous ‹liquid›

**Samin** *die;* **~, ~nen** ⇒ **Samin**

**Sämisch·leder** *das* chamois leather

**Sämling** /'zɛ:mlıŋ/ *der;* **~s, ~e** seedling

**Sammel-: ~album** *das* [collector's] album; **~auftrag** *der* (*Postw.*) multiple *or* combined transfer; **~band** *der* anthology (**über** + *Akk.* of); **~becken** *das* collecting basin; reservoir; (*fig.*) gathering point *or* place; **~bestellung** *die* joint order; **~bezeichnung** *die* (*Sprachw.*) collective term; **~büchse** *die* collecting box; **~fahrschein** *der* group ticket; **~konto** *das* (*Buchf.*) collation account; **~lager** *das* assembly *or* transit camp; **~mappe** *die* folder; file

**sammeln** /'zamln/ ❶ *tr.* (*auch itr.*) *V.* Ⓐ collect; gather ‹honey, firewood, fig.: material, experiences, impressions, etc.›; gather, pick ‹berries, herbs, mushrooms, etc.›; **Kräfte ~:** summon up one's strength; **die gesammelten Werke Tolstois** Tolstoy's collected works; Ⓑ (*zusammenkommen lassen*) gather ‹people› [together]; assemble ‹people›; cause ‹light rays› to converge. ❷ *refl. V.* Ⓐ (*sich versammeln*) gather [together]; ‹light rays› converge; **sich um jmdn./etw. ~:** gather round sb./sth.; Ⓑ (*sich konzentrieren*) collect oneself; gather oneself together

**Sammel-: ~platz** *der* (*für Gegenstände*) collection *or* collecting point; (*für Menschen*) assembly point; **~punkt** *der* Ⓐ (*~platz*) assembly point; Ⓑ (*Brennpunkt*) focal point; **~stelle** *die* ⇒ **~platz**

**Sammelsurium** /zaml'zu:ri̯ʊm/ *das;* **~s, Sammelsurien** (*abwertend*) hotchpotch; **ein ~ von alten Gläsern und Flaschen** a jumble of old glasses and bottles

**Sammel-: ~tasse** *die* [collector's] ornamental cup and saucer; **~transport** *der* (*von Menschen, Vieh*) mass transport; (*von Gütern*) bulk shipment; **~visum** *das* collective *or* group visa; **~wut** *die* collecting mania

**Sammet** /'zamət/ *der;* ~**s**, ~**e** (*schweiz., sonst veralt.*) ⇒ **Samt**

**Sammler** /'zamlɐ/ *der;* ~**s**, ~ Ⓐ collector; (*von Pilzen, Kräutern, Beeren usw.*) gatherer; picker; Ⓑ (*Technik: Akkumulator*) accumulator; storage battery

**Sammler·fleiß** *der* keenness *or* dedication to collecting; **mit** ~: with the dedication of a true collector

**Sammlerin** *die;* ~, ~**nen** ⇒ **Sammler** A

**Sammler-:** ~**objekt** *das,* ~**stück** *das* collector's item; ~**wert** *der* value to collectors; ~**wert haben** be of value to collectors

**Sammlung** *die;* ~, ~**en** Ⓐ collection; Ⓑ **[innere]** ~: composure

**Sammlungs·bewegung** *die* movement combining disparate elements; all-embracing movement

**Samoa·inseln** /za'mo:a-/ *Pl.* **die** ~ (*als Ganzes*) Samoa *sing.;* (*als einzelne Inseln*) the Samoan Islands

**Samoaner** /zamo'a:nɐ/ *der;* ~**s**, ~, **Samoanerin** *die;* ~, ~**nen** Samoan

**samoanisch** *Adj.* Samoan

**Samowar** /zamo'va:ɐ̯/ *der;* ~**s**, ~**e** samovar

**sampeln** *tr. V.* sample

**Sampler** *der;* ~**s**, ~**s** sampler

**Samstag** /'zamsta:k/ *der;* ~**[e]s**, ~**e** ▶ 207, ▶ 833 Saturday; **langer** ~: Saturday on which the shops stay open late; ⇒ *auch* **Dienstag**; **Dienstag-**

**samstägig** /'zamstɛ:gɪç/ *Adj.* on Saturday *postpos.*

**samstäglich** ❶ *Adj.* [regular] Saturday. ❷ *adv.* on Saturdays

**samstags** *Adv.* ▶ 833 on Saturdays

**samt** /zamt/ ❶ *Präp. mit Dat.* together with. ❷ *Adv.* ~ **und sonders** one and all; without exception

**Samt** *der;* ~**[e]s**, ~**e** velvet; **eine Haut wie** ~: a velvety skin; **in** ~ **und Seide** (*veralt.*) in all one's finery

**samt·artig** ❶ *Adj.* velvety. ❷ *adv.* ‹soft etc.› as velvet

**Samt·band** *das; Pl.* ~**bänder** velvet ribbon; (*breit*) velvet band

**samten** *Adj.* Ⓐ (*aus Samt*) velvet; Ⓑ (*wie Samt*) velvety

**Samt·handschuh** *der* velvet glove; **jmdn. mit** ~**en anfassen** (*fig.*) handle sb. with kid gloves

**samtig** *Adj.* velvety

**Samt·kleid** *das* velvet dress

**sämtlich** /'zɛmtlɪç/ *Indefinitpron. u. unbest. Zahlwort* Ⓐ *attr.* all the; **die Kleidung** ~**er Gefangener** *od.* **Gefangenen** all the prisoners' clothes; **Goethes** ~**e Werke** the complete works of Goethe; Ⓑ *allein stehend* all

**Samt·pfötchen** *das* velvety paw; **wie auf** ~ **gehen** tread softly

**samt·weich** *Adj.* velvety[-soft]; soft as velvet *postpos.*

**Sanatorium** /zana'to:ri̯ʊm/ *das;* ~**s**, **Sanatorien** sanatorium

**Sand** /zant/ *der;* ~**[e]s**, ~**e** *od.* **Sände** /'zɛndə/ Ⓐ sand; **... gibt es wie** ~ **am Meer** (*ugs.*) there are countless ...; ... are pretty thick on the ground (*coll.*); **da ist** ~ **im Getriebe** (*fig. ugs.*) there's something gumming up the works (*coll.*); **jmdm.** ~ **ins Getriebe streuen** (*fig. ugs.*) put a spanner in sb.'s works; **jmdm.** ~ **in die Augen streuen** (*fig.*) pull the wool over sb.'s eyes; **da habe ich auf** ~ **gebaut** (*fig.*) I was on shaky ground; **im** ~**[e] verlaufen** (*fig. ugs.*) come to nothing; **etw. [total] in den** ~ **setzen** (*fig. ugs.*) make a [complete] mess of sth.; Ⓑ *Pl.* ~**e** (*bes. Geol.:* ~*art*) [type of] sand; Ⓒ (*Seemannsspr.*) sands *pl.;* sandbank; **auf [einen]** ~ **geraten** *od.* **laufen** run aground on a sandbank

**Sandale** /zan'da:lə/ *die;* ~, ~**n** sandal

**Sandalette** /zanda'lɛtə/ *die;* ~, ~**n** [high-heeled] sandal

**Sand-:** ~**bahn·rennen** *das* (*Motorradsport*) speedway racing; ~**bank** *die; Pl.* ~**bänke** sandbank; ~**boden** *der* sandy soil; ~**burg** *die* sandcastle; ~**dorn** *der; Pl.* ~~**e** (*Bot.*) hippophaë; **[Echter]** ~**dorn** sea buckthorn

**Sandel-** /'zandl̩-/: ~**holz** *das* sandalwood; ~**öl** *das* sandalwood oil

**sand-, Sand-:** ~**farben**, ~**farbig** *Adj.* sand-coloured; ~**förmchen** /-fœrmçən/ *das;* ~~**s**, ~~: sand mould; ~**haufen** *der* pile of sand; ~**hose** *die* sand spout

**sandig** *Adj.* sandy

**Sandinist** /zandi'nɪst/ *der;* ~**en**, ~**en**, **Sandinistin** *die;* ~, ~**nen** Sandinista

**Sand-:** ~**kasten** *der* Ⓐ [child's] sandpit; sandbox (*Amer.*); Ⓑ (*Milit.*) sand table; ~**kasten·spiel** *das* (*Milit.*) sand table exercise; ~**korn** *das* grain of sand; ~**kuchen** *der* Madeira cake; ~**mann** *der,* ~**männchen** *das* sandman; ~**papier** *das* sandpaper; ~**sack** *der* Ⓐ sandbag; Ⓑ (*Boxen*) punching bag; ~**stein** *der* Ⓐ sandstone; Ⓑ (*als Baustein*) sandstone block; ~**strahlen** *tr. V.* (*Technik*) sandblast; ~**strahl·gebläse** *das* (*Technik*) sandblaster; ~**strand** *der* sandy beach; ~**sturm** *der* sandstorm

**sandte** /'zantə/ *1. u. 3. Pers. Sg. Prät. v.* **senden**

**Sand·uhr** *die* sandglass

**Sandwich** /'zɛntvɪtʃ/ *der od. das;* ~**s**, ~**[e]s** sandwich

**Sandwich·bauweise** *die* sandwich construction

**Sand·wüste** *die* [sandy] desert

**sanforisieren** Ⓦⓩ /zanfori'zi:rən/ *tr. V.* Sanforize ®

**sanft** /zanft/ ❶ *Adj.* gentle; (*leise, nicht intensiv*) soft ‹music, colour, light›; (*friedlich*) peaceful; **kommen Sie mir bloß nicht auf die** ~**e [Tour]** (*ugs.*) it's no use trying to soft-soap me; **es auf die** ~**e Tour versuchen** (*ugs.*) try the gentle *or* diplomatic approach; (*bei Bitten*) try wheedling *or* cajolery. ❷ *adv.* gently; (*leise*) ‹speak, play› softly; (*friedlich*) peacefully; **ruhe** ~ (*auf Grabsteinen*) rest in peace; **es regnete** ~: a gentle rain was falling

**Sänfte** /'zɛnftə/ *die;* ~, ~**n** litter; (*geschlossen*) sedan chair

**Sanftheit** *die;* ~: gentleness; (*von Klängen, Licht, Farben*) softness

**Sanft·mut** *die;* ~: gentleness; **mit** ~: gently; (*nachsichtig*) leniently

**sanftmütig** /-my:tɪç/ ❶ *Adj.* gentle; docile ‹horse›. ❷ *adv.* gently

**Sanftmütigkeit** *die;* ~: gentleness; (*Fügsamkeit*) docility

**sang** /zaŋ/ *1. u. 3. Pers. Sg. Prät. v.* **singen**

**Sang** *der;* ~**[e]s** (*veralt.*) song; singing; **mit** ~ **und Klang** singing and playing [music]; **er ist mit** ~ **und Klang durchs Examen gefallen** (*ugs. iron.*) he failed the exam in style (*iron.*)

**Sänger** /'zɛŋɐ/ *der;* ~**s**, ~ ▶ 159 Ⓐ (*Singender*) singer; (*Vogel*) songbird; **darüber schweigt des** ~**s Höflichkeit** let's draw a veil over that; Ⓑ (*veralt.: Dichter*) bard; **ein fahrender** *od.* **wandernder** ~ (*hist.*) a wandering minstrel

**Sänger-:** ~**bund** *der* choral union; ~**fest** *das* choral *or* choir festival

**Sängerin** *die;* ~, ~**nen** singer; ⇒ *auch* **-in**

**Sänger·knabe** *der* ⇒ **Wiener**[2]

**Sanges·bruder** *der* (*geh., veralt.*) fellow choir-member

**sang·los** *Adv. in* **sang- und klanglos** (*ugs.*) (*ohne viel Aufhebens*) simply; without any ado *or* fuss; (*unbemerkt*) unnoticed

**Sanguiniker** /zaŋ'gu̯i:nikɐ/ *der;* ~**s**, ~, **Sanguinikerin** *die;* ~, ~**nen** sanguine person

**sanguinisch** ❶ *Adj.* sanguine. ❷ *adv.* sanguinely; ~ **veranlagt sein** have a sanguine disposition

**sanieren** /za'ni:rən/ ❶ *tr. V.* Ⓐ (*umgestalten*) redevelop ‹area›; rehabilitate ‹building›; (*renovieren*) renovate [and improve] ‹flat etc.›; Ⓑ (*Wirtsch.*) restore ‹firm› to profitability; (*rehabilitieren*) put ‹firm› back on its feet; rehabilitate ‹agriculture, coal mining, etc.›; Ⓒ (*Med.: heilen*) heal ‹wound, ulcer, etc.›; clear up the infection in, treat ‹tooth etc.›. ❷ *refl. V.* ‹company etc.› restore itself to profitability, get back on its feet again; ‹person› get oneself out of the red

**Sanierung** *die;* ~, ~**en** Ⓐ ⇒ **sanieren** A: redevelopment; rehabilitation; renovation; Ⓑ (*Wirtsch.*) restoration to profitability; Ⓒ (*Med.: Heilung*) healing; (*Behandlung*) treatment

**Sanierungs-:** ~**gebiet** *das* redevelopment area; ~**maßnahme** *die* Ⓐ (*bei einem Stadtteil usw.*) redevelopment measure; Ⓑ (*Wirtsch.*) [financial] rehabilitation measure

**sanitär** /zani'tɛ:ɐ̯/ *Adj.* sanitary; ~**e Anlagen** sanitary installations

**Sanitär-:** ~**bereich** *der* [field of] sanitation; ~**installation** *die* Ⓐ (*das Einbauen*) fitting of sanitation *no indef. art.;* Ⓑ (*Anlage*) sanitary installation

**Sanität** /zani'tɛ:t/ *die;* ~, ~**en** (*schweiz., österr.*) Ⓐ (*Milit.*) medical service; Ⓑ (*ugs.: Sanitätswagen*) ambulance

**Sanitäter** /zani'tɛ:tɐ/ *der;* ~**s**, ~ Ⓐ (*Krankenpfleger*) first-aid worker; first-aid man; (*im Krankenwagen*) ambulance man; Ⓑ (*Soldat*) medical orderly

**Sanitäterin** *die;* ~, ~**nen** Ⓐ (*Krankenpflegerin*) first-aid worker; (*im Krankenwagen*) ambulance worker; Ⓑ (*Soldatin*) medical orderly

**Sanitäts-:** ~**auto** *das* (*ugs.*) ambulance; ~**dienst** *der* Ⓐ first-aid duty; (*im Krankenwagen*) ambulance duty; Ⓑ (*Milit.*) medical service *or* corps; ~**kasten** *der* (*bes. Milit.*) first-aid box *or* kit; ~**offizier** *der* (*Milit.*) medical officer; ~**truppe** *die* (*Milit.*) medical corps; ~**wache** *die* first-aid post; ~**wagen** *der* ambulance; ~**wesen** *das* (*bes. Milit.*) medical service

**sank** /zaŋk/ *1. u. 3. Pers. Sg. Prät. v.* **sinken**

**Sanktion** /zaŋk'tsi̯o:n/ *die;* ~, ~**en** Ⓐ (*geh., Rechtsspr.: Billigung*) approval; sanction; Ⓑ (*Völkerr., Soziol.*) sanction; (*geh.: Bestrafung*) punitive measure *or* sanction; Ⓒ (*Rechtsw.*) (*Gesetzesklausel*) penalty [clause]; sanction

**sanktionieren** *tr. V.* sanction

**Sanktionierung** *die;* ~, ~**en** sanctioning *no indef. art.*

**Sankt-Lorenz-Strom** /zaŋkt'lo:rɛntsʃtro:m/ *der;* ~**[e]s** St Lawrence [river]

**Sankt-Nimmerleins-Tag** /zaŋkt'nɪmɐlai̯ns-/ *der* ⇒ **Nimmerleinstag**

**sann** /zan/ *1. u. 3. Pers. Sg. Prät. v.* **sinnen**

**Sansibar** /'zanziba:ɐ̯/ *(das);* ~**s** Zanzibar

**Sanskrit** /'zanskrɪt/ *das;* ~**s** ▶ 696 Sanskrit

**Saphir** /'za:fɪr/ *der;* ~**s**, ~**e** sapphire

**sapperlot** /zapɐ'lo:t/ *Interj.* (*veralt.*) upon my soul (*dated*)

**sapphisch** /'zapfɪʃ/ ❶ *Adj.* Ⓐ Sapphic; ~**e Strophe** sapphic verse *or* stanza; Ⓑ (*geh.: lesbisch*) sapphic; lesbian. ❷ *adv.* Ⓐ (*wie Sappho*) in the style of Sappho; Ⓑ (*geh.*) ~ **veranlagt** with sapphic *or* lesbian tendencies

**Sarabande** /zara'bandə/ *die;* ~, ~**n** (*Musik*) saraband

**Sarde** /'zardə/ *der;* ~**n**, ~**n** Sardinian

**Sardelle** /zar'dɛlə/ *die;* ~, ~**n** anchovy

**Sardellen·paste** *die* anchovy paste

**Sardin** *die;* ~, ~**nen** Sardinian

**Sardine** /zar'di:nə/ *die;* ~, ~**n** sardine

**Sardinen·büchse** *die* tin of sardines; (*leer*) sardine tin; **das Schiff war eine schwimmende** ~ (*fig.*) they were packed like sardines on the ship

**Sardinien** /zar'di:ni̯ən/ *(das);* ~**s** Sardinia

**sardisch** *Adj.* ▶ 696 Sardinian

**sardonisch** /zar'do:nɪʃ/ (*geh.*) ❶ *Adj.* sardonic. ❷ *adv.* sardonically

**Sarg** /zark/ *der;* ~**[e]s**, **Särge** /'zɛrgə/ coffin; ⇒ *auch* **Nagel** B

**Sarg-:** ~**deckel** *der* coffin lid; ~**nagel** *der* (*Nagel, ugs. scherzh.: Zigarette*) coffin nail (*lit., or fig. sl.*); ~**träger** *der,* ~**trägerin** *die* pallbearer

S

**Sari** /'za:ri/ *der;* ~[s], ~s sari

**Sarkasmus** /zar'kasmʊs/ A (*Spott*) sarcasm; B (*Äußerung*) sarcastic remark

**sarkastisch** ❶ *Adj.* sarcastic. ❷ *adv.* sarcastically

**Sarkophag** /zarko'fa:k/ *der;* ~s, ~e sarcophagus

**saß** /za:s/ *1. u. 3. Pers. Sg. Prät. v.* **sitzen**

**Satan** /'za:tan/ *der;* ~s, ~e A (*bibl.*) Satan *no def. art.;* ⇒ *auch* **Teufel**; B (*ugs. abwertend: Mensch*) fiend

**satanisch** ❶ *Adj.* satanic; fiendish. ❷ *adv.* satanically

**Satans·braten** *der* (*ugs.*) devil

**Satellit** /zatɛ'li:t/ *der;* ~en, ~en (*Raumf., Astron., auch fig.*) satellite

**Satelliten-:** ~**anlage** *die* (*ugs.*) satellite receiver; ~**bild** *das* ⇒ ~foto; ~**fernsehen** *das* satellite television; ~**foto** *das* (*bes. Met.*) satellite picture; ~**schüssel** *die* (*ugs.*) satellite dish; ~**staat** *der* (*abwertend*) satellite [state]; ~**übertragung** *die* (*Ferns.*) satellite transmission

**Satin** /za'tɛ̃:/ *der;* ~s, ~s satin

**Satire** /za'ti:rə/ *die;* ~, ~n satire

**Satiriker** *der;* ~s, ~, **Satirikerin** *die;* ~, ~nen A satirist; B (*Spötter*) lampooner; mocker

**satirisch** ❶ *Adj.* A satirical; B (*spöttisch*) mocking ‹remarks›. ❷ *adv.* A satirically; with a satirical touch; B (*spöttisch*) mockingly; in a satirical vein

**Satisfaktion** /zatɪsfak'tsi̯o:n/ *die;* ~, ~en (*geh. od. Studentenspr. veralt.*) satisfaction

**satisfaktions·fähig** *Adj.* (*veralt.*) able to give/demand satisfaction [in a duel] *pred.*

**satt** /zat/ ❶ *Adj.* A full [up] *pred.;* well-fed; ~ **sein** be full [up]; have had enough [to eat]; ~ **werden** have enough [to eat]; eat one's fill; **von so einem Salat werde ich nicht ~:** a salad like that is not enough for me *or* to fill me up; **sich ~ essen/trinken** eat/drink as much as one wants; eat/drink one's fill; **etw. macht ~:** sth. is filling; **ich kann mich an ihr/an der Akropolis nicht ~ sehen** (*fig.*) I can't take my eyes off her/I can gaze endlessly at the Acropolis; B (*selbstgefällig*) smug, self-satisfied ‹person, smile, expression, etc.›; C **jmdn./etw. ~ haben** (*ugs.*) be fed up with sb./sth. (*coll.*); **ich habe es ~, allein zu fahren** I'm fed up with travelling alone (*coll.*); **etw. ~ bekommen** *od.* **kriegen** (*ugs.*) get fed up with sth.; D (*intensiv*) rich, deep ‹colour›; rich, pure ‹sound›; E (*ugs.: beeindruckend*) tremendous (*coll.*) ‹price›; **ein ~er Schuss** a super shot (*coll.*); **~e 100 000 Mark** a cool 100,000 marks (*coll.*); **~e 180 km/h** an impressive 180 k.p.h.
❷ *adv.* A (*selbstgefällig*) smugly; complacently; B (*reichlich*) **nicht ~ zu essen haben** not have enough to eat; **Hummer ~:** as much lobster as one can eat; **Tennis ~** (*fig.*) as much tennis as one could possibly want; C (*schweiz.: straff*) tightly

**satt·blau** *Adj.* deep blue

**Sattel** /'zatl/ *der;* ~s, **Sättel** /'zɛtl/ A saddle; **ohne ~ reiten** ride bareback; **jmdm. in den ~ helfen, jmdn. in den ~ heben** help sb. into the saddle; (*fig.: fördern*) give sb. a leg up; (*fig.: an die Macht bringen*) put sb. in the driving seat; **jmdn. aus dem ~ heben** unseat sb.; (*fig.: jmdm. die Macht nehmen*) depose sb.; remove sb. from office; **fest im ~ sitzen** (*fig.*) be firmly in the saddle; **in allen Sätteln gerecht sein** (*fig.*) be able to turn one's hand to anything; B (*Berg~*) saddle; col; C (*Schneidern: Passe*) yoke; D (*bei Saiteninstrumenten*) nut; E (*Turnen: beim Seitpferd*) saddle

**sattel-, Sattel-:** ~**dach** *das* gable *or* saddle roof; ~**decke** *die* saddlecloth; ~**fest** *Adj.* experienced; **in etw.** (*Dat.*) **~fest sein** be au fait with sth.; be well up in sth.; **weniger ~feste Kandidaten** candidates less sure of their facts; ~**gurt** *der* girth

**satteln** ❶ *tr. V.* saddle. ❷ *itr. V.* saddle the/one's horse

*old spelling (see note on page 1707)

**Sattel-:** ~**nase** *die* saddle nose; ~**punkt** *der* (*Math.*) saddle point; ~**schlepper** *der* tractor [unit]; (*mit Anhänger*) articulated lorry (*Brit.*); semi[-trailer] (*Amer.*); ~**stütze** *die* seatpost; seat pillar; ~**tasche** *die* (*am Pferd, Fahrrad*) saddlebag; ~**zeug** *das* saddle equipment; saddlery; ~**zug** *der* articulated vehicle

**Sattheit** *die;* ~ A repleteness *no def. art.;* **die ~ der Konsumgesellschaft** the satiety of the consumer society; B (*Selbstgefälligkeit*) smugness; complacency; C (*Intensität*) richness; fullness

**sättigen** /'zɛtɪɡn̩/ ❶ *itr. V.* be filling. ❷ *tr. V.* A (*ausfüllen*) saturate ‹market, colour›; B (*erfüllen*) **gesättigt sein von etw.** be filled with *or* full of sth.; C (*geh.: satt machen*) fill ‹sb.›; satisfy ‹sb., fig.: curiosity, ambition, etc.›. ❸ *refl. V.* **sich mit** *od.* **an etw.** (*Dat.*) ~ (*geh.*) satisfy one's appetite with sth.

**sättigend** *Adj.* filling

**Sättigung** *die;* ~, ~en A (*bes. Chemie, Physik*) saturation; B (*das Sattsein*) repleteness *no def. art.;* (*das Sättigen*) satisfying; **die ~ der Hungernden** the feeding of the starving

**Sättigungs-:** ~**grad** *der* (*Wirtsch.*) [degree of] saturation; ~**punkt** *der* (*Chemie*) saturation point

**Sattler** /'zatlɐ/ *der;* ~s, ~ ▶ 159 saddler; (*allgemein: Hersteller von Lederwaren*) leather worker

**Sattlerei** *die;* ~, ~en A (*Handwerk*) saddlery; B (*Werkstatt*) saddler's workshop

**Sattlerin** *die;* ~, ~nen ▶ 159 ⇒ **Sattler**

**sattsam** *Adv.* ad nauseam; ~ **bekannt** only too well known; notorious

**saturiert** /zatu'ri:ɐ̯t/ *Adj.* (*geh.*) A (*zufrieden gestellt*) satisfied; B (*abwertend: selbstgefällig*) **~e Wohlstandsbürger** sated and self-satisfied members of the affluent society

**Saturn**[1] /za'tʊrn/ *der;* ~s (*Astron.*), **Saturn**[2] (*der*) (*Myth.*) Saturn *no def. art.*

**Satyr** /'za:tʏr/ *der;* ~s *od.* ~n, ~n satyr

**Satyr·spiel** *das* satyric drama

**Satz** /zats/ *der;* ~es, **Sätze** /'zɛtsə/ A (*sprachliche Einheit*) sentence; (*Teil~*) clause; **in** *od.* **mit einem ~:** in one sentence; briefly; B (*Teil eines Musikwerks*) movement; (*Periode*) period; C (*Musik: Kompositionsweise*) [method of] composition; **der vierstimmige/kontrapunktische ~:** four-part/contrapuntal writing; D (*Sport*) (*Tennis, Volleyball*) set; (*Tischtennis, Badminton*) game; E (*Sprung*) leap; jump; **einen ~ über etw.** (*Akk.*) **machen** *od.* **tun** jump *or* leap across sth.; **er war mit einem ~ an der Tür** in one bound he was at the door; **in** *od.* **mit wenigen Sätzen** in a few strides; F (*Amtsspr.: Tarif*) rate; G (*Set*) set; **ein ~ Reifen** a set of tyres; H (*Boden~*) sediment; (*von Kaffee*) grounds *pl.;* I (*Druckw.: das Setzen*) setting; (*Gesetztes*) type matter; **mit dem ~ beginnen** start setting; **das Manuskript ist in ~/geht in [den] ~:** the manuscript is being set/is being sent for setting; J (*DV*) record

**Satz-:** ~**an·weisung** *die* (*Druckw.*) setting instructions *pl.;* ~**aussage** *die* (*Sprachw.*) predicate; ~**ball** *der* (*Tennis, Volleyball*) set point; (*Tischtennis, Badminton*) game point; ~**bau** *der* sentence construction; ~**bauplan** *der* (*Sprachw.*) sentence pattern

**Sätzchen** /'zɛtsçən/ *das;* ~s, ~ A (*Sprung*) little jump; B (*Äußerung*) little sentence

**satz-, Satz-:** ~**ergänzung** *die* (*Sprachw.*) complement; ~**fehler** *der* (*Druckw.*) literal; printer's error; ~**fertig** *Adj.* (*Druckw.*) ready for setting *postpos.;* ~**gefüge** *das* (*Sprachw.*) complex sentence; ~**gegenstand** *der* (*Sprachw.*) subject [of a/the sentence]; ~**glied** *das* (*Sprachw.*) component part [of a/the sentence]; ~**konstruktion** *die* (*Sprachw.*) sentence construction; ~**lehre** *die* A (*Sprachw.*) syntax *no art.;* B (*Musik*) composition theory *no art.;* ~**rechner** *der* (*Druckw.*) composer; ~**reif** *Adj.* (*Druckw.*) ready for setting *postpos.;* ~**spiegel** *der* (*Druckw.*) type area; ~**technisch** (*Druckw.*) ❶ *Adj.* **aus ~technischen Gründen** for reasons of setting; ❷ *adv.* **~technisch gesehen** from the typographic point of view; ~**teil** *der* (*Sprachw.*) ⇒ ~**glied**

**Satzung** /'zatsʊŋ/ *die;* ~, ~en articles of association *pl.;* statutes *pl.*

**satzungs-:** ~**gemäß** *Adj., adv.* in accordance with the articles of association *or* the statutes; ~**widrig** *Adj., adv.* contrary to the articles of association *or* the statutes

**satz-, Satz-:** ~**weise** *Adv.* sentence by sentence; ~**wertig** *Adj.* (*Sprachw.*) forming a clause *postpos.;* **~wertiger Infinitiv/~wertiges Partizip** infinitive/participial clause; ~**zeichen** *das* (*Sprachw.*) punctuation mark; ~**zusammenhang** *der* (*Sprachw.*) sentence correlation

**sau-, Sau-** (*salopp*) bloody ... (*Brit. sl.*); damn ... (*coll.*); (*sehr schlecht*) lousy ... (*coll.*); ~**dreckig/~schwer** bloody (*Brit. sl.*) *or* (*coll.*) damn filthy/difficult

**Sau** /zau̯/ *die;* ~, **Säue** /'zɔy̯ə/ A (*weibliches Schwein*) sow; B (*bes. südd.: Schwein*) pig; **jmdn. zur ~ machen** (*derb*) tear a strip off sb. (*sl.*); **wie eine gesengte ~ fahren** (*derb*) drive like a madman; **unter aller ~** (*derb abwertend*) bloody awful (*Brit. sl.*); the pits (*coll.*); **keine ~** (*derb*) not a bloody (*Brit. sl.*) *or* (*coll.*) damn soul; C (*derb abwertend: schmutziger Mensch*) (*Mann*) dirty pig; (*Frau*) dirty cow (*sl.*); D (*derb abwertend: gemeiner Mensch*) swine E **die ~ rauslassen** (*fig. ugs.*) let one's hair down

**-sau** *die* (*derb*) ... pig *or* swine; pig *or* swine of a/an ...

**Sau-:** ~**arbeit** *die* (*salopp*) bloody awful job (*Brit. sl.*); hell of a job (*coll.*); ~**bande** *die* (*salopp*) wretched swine (*derog.*) *pl.;* (*mehr scherzh.*) bunch of good-for-nothings (*sl.*)

**sauber** /'zau̯bɐ/ ❶ *Adj.* A clean; **~e Flüsse/Wälder** unpolluted rivers/forests; **etw. ~ machen** clean sth.; **~ machen** (*putzen*) clean; do the cleaning; **bei jmdm. ~ machen** clean for sb.; **etw. ~ halten** keep sth. clean; **das Kind ist ~:** the child is toilet-trained; **ein Glas ~ ausspülen** rinse [out] a glass; **der ~e Bildschirm** (*fig.*) the unpolluted TV screen; **mein Tor bleibt ~** (*fig. Fußball*) I'll keep a clean sheet; B (*sorgfältig*) neat ‹handwriting, division, work, etc.›; C (*fehlerlos*) perfect, faultless ‹accent, technique, etc.›; D (*anständig*) upstanding ‹attitude, person›; upright ‹young man›; unsullied ‹character›; **er ist ~** (*ugs.*) he is straight; (*hat nichts Kriminelles gemacht*) he has a clean record; **~ bleiben** keep one's hands clean (*coll.*); **nicht [ganz] ~ sein** (*ugs.*) be a bit shady *or* dodgy (*coll.*); **also dann alles Gute, und bleib ~!** (*ugs. scherzh.*) all the best, and be good!; E (*gerecht*) fair ‹solution, description›; equitable ‹solution, plan›; F (*iron.: unanständig*) nice, fine (*iron.*); ⇒ *auch* **Früchtchen**; G (*ugs., bes. südd., österr., schweiz.: beachtlich*) fantastic (*coll.*); **ein ~es Sümmchen** a tidy little sum (*coll.*); H (*südd., österr., schweiz.: schmuck*) smart ‹girl etc.›.
❷ *adv.* A (*sorgfältig*) neatly ‹written, dressed, mended, etc.›; B (*fehlerlos*) **[sehr] ~:** [quite] perfectly *or* faultlessly; C (*anständig*) conscientiously; D (*gerecht*) ‹judge etc.› fairly; E (*iron.: unanständig*) nicely (*iron.*); **das hast du ~ hingekriegt** a nice *or* fine job you made of that

***sauber|halten** ⇒ **sauber** 1 A

**Sauberkeit** *die;* ~ A cleanness; (*bes. der Person*) cleanliness; **ihre Wohnung blitzt vor ~:** her flat (*Brit.*) *or* (*Amer.*) apartment is sparkling clean; B (*Sorgfältigkeit*) neatness; C (*Anständigkeit*) uprightness

**Sauberkeits·fimmel** *der* (*ugs. abwertend*) mania for cleanliness; **einen ~ haben** have a thing about cleanliness (*coll.*)

**säuberlich** /'zɔy̯bɐlɪç/ ❶ *Adj.* neat. ❷ *adv.* neatly; **fein ~ geordnet/verpackt** *usw.* neatly arranged/packed *etc.*

***sauber|machen** ⇒ **sauber** 1 A

**Sauber·mann** *der* (*iron.*) decent and upright fellow; nice guy (*coll.*); (*Moralapostel*) upholder of moral standards

**säubern** /ˈzɔybɐn/ *tr. V.* **A** (*sauber machen*) clean; **die Schuhe vom Lehm ~:** clean the mud off the shoes; **eine Wunde ~:** cleanse a wound; **das Wasser von Schadstoffen ~:** cleanse the water of pollutants; purify the water; **B** (*befreien*) clear, rid (**von** of); purge ‹party, government, etc.› (**von** of); **Bibliotheken von verbotenen Büchern ~:** rid libraries of banned books

**Säuberung** *die;* ~, ~**en** **A** (*das Saubermachen*) cleaning; **B** (*Entfernung*) purging; **einer ~ zum Opfer fallen** be the victim of a purge; **C** (*Politik:* ~*saktion*) purge; **ethnische ~** (*verhüll.*) ethnic cleansing

**Säuberungs·aktion** *die* purge; clean-up operation

**sau·blöd[e]** (*salopp abwertend*) **1** *Adj.* bloody silly *or* stupid. **2** *adv.* in a bloody silly *or* stupid manner (*sl.*); **frag doch nicht so ~:** don't ask such bloody silly *or* stupid questions (*sl.*)

**Sauce** ⇒ **Soße** A

**Saucier** /zoˈsi̯eː/ *der;* ~**s,** ~**s** sauce chef

**Sauciere** /zoˈsi̯ɛːrə/ *die;* ~, ~**n** sauceboat

**Saudi** /ˈzaudi/ *der;* ~**s,** ~**s, Saudi-Araber** *der,* **Saudi-Araberin** *die* ▶ 553 Saudi

**Saudi-Arabien** *(das);* ~**s** Saudi Arabia

**saudi-arabisch, saudisch** *Adj.* ▶ 553 Saudi Arabian; Saudi

**sau·dumm** ⇒ **saublöd**

**sauer** /ˈzauɐ/ **1** *Adj.* **A** sour; sour, tart ‹fruit›; sharp-tasting ‹bread, coffee, etc.›; pickled ‹herring, gherkin, etc.›; acid[ic] ‹wine, vinegar›; **saure Drops** acid drops (*Brit.*); **saure Nieren** (*Kochk.*) *dish of sliced kidneys with lemon-flavored sauce;* **saurer Regen** acid rain; ⇒ *auch* **Apfel** A; **Bier**; **B** (*ugs.: verärgert*) cross, annoyed (**auf** + *Akk.* with); (*verdrossen*) sour; **C** (*bes. Landw.*) acidic; **D** (*Chemie*) acid[ic]; **E** (*mühselig*) hard; difficult; **gib ihm Saures!** (*ugs.*) let him have it! (*coll.*). **2** *adv.* **A** (*in, mit Essig*) in vinegar; **B** (*ugs.: verärgert*) crossly; **~ [auf jmdn./etw.] reagieren** get annoyed *or* cross [with sb./sth.]; **C** (*Chemie*) **~ reagieren** react acidically; **D** (*mühsam*) with difficulty; **~ erspartes/verdientes Geld** hard-saved/hard-earned money; **jmdn. ~ ankommen** be hard for sb. to take *or* accept; **E ~ aufstoßen** belch (*with acid taste*); **das wird ihm noch einmal ~ aufstoßen** (*fig. ugs.*) he will live to regret that

**Sauer-:** ~**ampfer** /-ampfɐ/ *der* sorrel; ~**braten** *der: braised beef marinated in vinegar and herbs;* sauerbraten (*Amer.*); ~**brunnen** *der* **A** (*Quelle*) mineral spring containing carbon dioxide; **B** (*Wasser*) mineral water containing carbon dioxide

**Sauerei** *die;* ~, ~**en** (*salopp abwertend*) **A** (*Unflätigkeit*) obscenity; ~**en erzählen** tell filthy stories; **B** (*Gemeinheit*) bloody (*Brit. sl.*) *or* (*coll.*) damn scandal (*sl.*)

**Sauer-:** ~**kirsche** *die* sour cherry; ~**klee** *der* wood sorrel; ~**kohl** *der* (*bes. nordd.*); ~**kraut** *das* sauerkraut; pickled cabbage

**säuerlich** **1** *Adj.* **A** **[leicht] ~:** slightly sour; slightly sharp ‹sauce›; slightly sour *or* tart ‹fruit›; **ein leicht ~er Riesling** a Riesling with a touch of acidity; **B** (*verdorben*) sourish; slightly sour; **C** (*missvergnügt*) sourish; slightly sour. **2** *adv.* (*missvergnügt*) somewhat sourly

**Säuerling** *der;* ~**s,** ~**e** **A** (*Mineralwasser*) ⇒ **Sauerbrunnen** B; **B** (*ugs.: Wein*) acidy wine

**Sauer·milch** *die* sour milk

**säuern** /ˈzɔyɐn/ **1** *tr. V.* **A** (*gären lassen*) leaven ‹bread, dough, etc.›; pickle ‹cabbage, cucumber, etc.›; **B** (*Kochk.: würzen*) give zest *or* piquancy to. **2** *itr. V.; auch mit sein* (*gären*) turn sour; **der Kohl säuert in Fässern** the cabbage is pickling in vats

**Sauer-:** ~**rahm** *der* sour cream; ~**rahm·butter** *die* butter made from sour cream

**Sauer·stoff** *der* oxygen

**sauerstoff-, Sauerstoff-:** ~**apparat** *der* oxygen apparatus; ~**arm** *Adj.* low in oxygen *postpos.;* ~**flasche** *die* oxygen cylinder; ~**gerät** *das* oxygen apparatus; ~**haltig** *Adj.* containing oxygen *postpos., not pred.;* ~**haltig sein** contain oxygen; ~**mangel** *der* lack of oxygen; ~**mangel im Blut/Zellgewebe** oxygen deficiency in the blood/cell tissue; ~**maske** *die* oxygen mask; ~**zelt** *das* (*Med.*) oxygen tent; ~**zufuhr** *die* oxygen supply

**Sauer·teig** *der* leaven

**sauer·töpfisch** /-tœpfɪʃ/ *Adj.* (*ugs. abwertend*) sour ‹expression, look, etc.›; sour-faced ‹person›

**Säuerung** *die;* ~, ~**en** (*von Brot, Teig*) leavening; (*von Kohl, Kraut usw.*) pickling

**Saufbold** /-bɔlt/ *der;* ~**[e]s,** ~**e** (*veralt. abwertend*) drunkard; boozer (*coll.*)

**Sauf·bruder** *der* (*salopp, oft abwertend*) boozing companion (*coll.*)

**saufen** /ˈzaufn̩/ **1** *unr. itr. V.* **A** drink; **B** (*salopp*) (*trinken*) drink; swig (*coll.*); (*Alkohol trinken*) drink; booze (*coll.*); **~ wie ein Loch** drink like a fish; **C** (*salopp: alkoholabhängig sein*) drink. **2** *unr. tr. V.* **A** drink; **B** (*salopp: trinken*) drink; **er hat so viel [Schnaps] gesoffen, dass ...** he knocked back so much booze that ... (*coll.*); **einen ~ gehen** go for a drink. **3** *unr. refl. V.* (*salopp*) **sich dumm/zu Tode ~:** drink oneself stupid/to death; **sich arm ~:** drink one's last penny away; **sich (*Dat.*) die Jacke *od.* Hucke voll ~:** get tanked up (*sl.*)

**Säufer** /ˈzɔyfɐ/ *der;* ~**s,** ~ (*salopp, oft abwertend*) boozer (*coll.*); piss artist (*sl.*)

**Sauferei** *die;* ~, ~**en** (*salopp*) **A** (*Gelage*) booze-up (*coll.*); **B** (*das Saufen*) boozing *no def. art.* (*coll.*)

**Säuferin** *die;* ~, ~**nen** (*salopp, oft abwertend*) boozer (*coll.*); drunkard

**Säufer-:** ~**leber** *die* (*ugs.*) hobnail[ed] liver; ~**nase** *die* (*ugs.*) drinker's nose; ~**wahn** *der* ▶ 474 (*Med. veralt.*) delirium tremens

**Sauf-:** ~**gelage** *das* (*salopp*) booze-up (*coll.*); ~**kumpan** *der* (*salopp*) boozing companion (*coll.*)

**Sau·fraß** *der* (*salopp abwertend*) pigswill (*coll.*); rubbish

**säufst** /zɔyfst/ *2. Pers. Sg. Präsens v.* **saufen**

**säuft** /zɔyft/ *3. Pers. Sg. Präsens v.* **saufen**

**saugen** /ˈzaugn̩/ **1** *tr. V.* **A** *auch unr.* (*aufnehmen*) suck; ⇒ *auch* **Finger** B; **B** *auch itr.* (*mit dem Staubsauger*) vacuum; hoover (*coll.*); **C** (*entfernen*) suck up. **2** *regelm.* (*auch unr.*) *itr. V.* **an etw.** (*Dat.*) **~:** suck [at] sth.; **an einer Pfeife/Zigarette ~:** draw on a pipe/cigarette. **3** *unr.* (*auch regelm.*) *refl. V.* **A** (*eindringen*) soak (**in** + *Akk.* into); **B** (*aufnehmen*) **sich voll etw. ~:** become soaked with sth.

**säugen** /ˈzɔygn̩/ *tr. V.* suckle

**Sauger** *der;* ~**s,** ~ **A** (*auf Flaschen*) teat; **B** (*Saugheber*) siphon; **C** ⇒ **Schnuller**

**Säuger** /ˈzɔygɐ/ *der;* ~**s,** ~, **Säuge·tier** *das* (*Zool.*) mammal

**saug-, Saug-:** ~**fähig** *Adj.* absorbent; ~**fähigkeit** *die* absorbency; ~**glocke** *die* (*Med.*) suction cup; (*zur Geburtshilfe*) vacuum extractor; venteuse; ~**heber** *der* siphon; ~**kraft** *die* suction [strength]

**Säugling** /ˈzɔyklɪŋ/ *der;* ~**s,** ~**e** baby; infant

**Säuglings-:** ~**alter** *das* infancy; babyhood; **im ~alter** in *or* during infancy; ~**heim** *das* home for babies; ~**pflege** *die* baby care; ~**schwester** *die* infant *or* baby nurse; ~**station** *die* baby ward; ~**sterblichkeit** *die* infant mortality

**Saug-:** ~**napf** *der* (*Zool.*) sucker; ~**organ** *das* (*Biol.*) suctorial organ; ~**reflex** *der* sucking reflex; ~**rüssel** *der* (*Zool.*) proboscis; ~**wurm** *der* (*Zool.*) trematode

**Sau-:** ~**hatz** *die* (*Jägerspr.*) [wild] boar hunt; ~**haufen** *der* (*salopp abwertend*) bunch of layabouts (*sl.*); ~**hund** *der* (*derb abwertend*) bastard (*coll.*); bloody (*Brit. sl.*) *or* (*coll.*) damn swine

**säuisch** /ˈzɔyɪʃ/ (*salopp*) **1** *Adj.* **A** (*abwertend: unanständig*) obscene ‹phone call›; filthy, obscene ‹book, joke, behaviour›; **B** (*stark, groß*) hellish (*coll.*). **2** *adv.* (*sehr*) hellishly (*coll.*); **~ viel Glück haben** have a hell of a lot of luck (*coll.*)

**sau-, Sau-:** ~**kalt** *Adj.* (*salopp*) bloody cold (*Brit. sl.*); damn cold (*coll.*); ~**kälte** *die* (*salopp*) bloody cold (*Brit. sl.*) *or* (*coll.*) damn cold weather; **das ist eine ~kälte** it's bloody (*Brit. sl.*) *or* (*coll.*) damn cold *or* freezing; ~**kerl** *der* (*salopp abwertend*) bastard (*coll.*); ~**laden** *der; Pl.* ~**läden** (*salopp abwertend*) dump (*coll.*)

**Säule** /ˈzɔylə/ *die;* ~, ~**n** **A** column; (*nur als Stütze, auch fig.*) pillar; **B** (*Zapf*~) [petrol (*Brit.*) *or* (*Amer.*) gasoline] pump

**Säulen-:** ~**bau** *der; Pl.* ~**ten** building with columns; ~**fuß** *der* base [of a/the column/pillar]; ~**gang** *der* colonnade; ~**halle** *die* columned hall; ~**heilige** *der* stylite; **er ist ja kein ~heiliger** (*fig.*) he's no plaster saint; ~**kaktus** *der* cereus; ~**ordnung** *die* (*Archit.*) order [of columns]; **die dorische ~ordnung** the Doric order; ~**portal** *das* (*Archit.*) columned doorway

**Saum** /zaum/ *der;* ~**[e]s, Säume** /ˈzɔymə/ hem; (*fig. geh.*) edge

**Sau·magen** *der* (*Kochk.*) stuffed pig's stomach

**sau·mäßig** (*salopp*) **1** *Adj.* **A** (*sehr groß*) **das ist eine ~e Arbeit/Hitze** that's a hell of a job/temperature (*coll.*); **~es Glück haben** be damned lucky (*coll.*); **B** (*abwertend: schlecht*) lousy (*coll.*). **2** *adv.* **A** (*sehr*) damned (*coll.*); **~ viel verdienen** earn a hell of a lot (*coll.*); **es tat ~ weh** it hurt like hell; **B** (*abwertend: sehr schlecht*) lousily (*coll.*)

**säumen**[1] /ˈzɔymən/ *tr. V.* hem; (*fig. geh.*) line

**säumen**[2] *itr. V.* (*geh.: zögern*) tarry (*literary*)

**säumig** *Adj.* (*geh.*) tardy; dilatory

**Säumigkeit** *die;* ~ (*geh.*) tardiness; dilatoriness

**Säumnis** /ˈzɔymnɪs/ *die;* ~, ~**se** *od. das;* ~**ses,** ~**se** (*geh.*) **A** delay; **B** (*Unterlassung*) omission; failing

**saum-, Saum-:** ~**pfad** *der* mule track; ~**selig** (*geh.*) **1** *Adj.* dilatory; slow; **2** *adv.* in a dilatory manner; slowly; ~**seligkeit** *die* (*geh.*) dilatoriness; slowness

**Saum·tier** *das* pack animal

**Sauna** /ˈzauna/ *die;* ~, ~**s** *od.* **Saunen** sauna

**Sauna·bad** *das* sauna

**saunieren** /zauˈniːrən/ *itr. V.* have *or* take a sauna

**Säure** /ˈzɔyrə/ *die;* ~, ~**n** **A** (*von Früchten*) sourness; tartness; (*von Wein, Essig*) acidity; (*von Soßen*) sharpness; **B** (*Chemie*) acid

**säure-, Säure-:** ~**arm** *Adj.* low in acid *postpos.;* ~**beständig** *Adj.* acid-resistant; ~**fest** *Adj.* acid-proof; ~**frei** *Adj.* acid-free; ~**gehalt** *der* acid content

***Saure·gurken·zeit, Saure-Gurken-Zeit** *die* (*ugs.*) slack *or* dead season; (*in den Medien*) silly season (*Brit.*)

**säure·haltig** *Adj.* acid[ic]

**Saurier** /ˈzauri̯ɐ/ *der;* ~**s,** ~**:** large prehistoric reptile

**Saus** /zaus/ *in* **in ~ und Braus leben** live the high life

**Sause** *die;* ~, ~**n** (*ugs. veralt.*) **A** (*Gelage*) booze-up (*coll.*); **B** (*Zug durch die Kneipen*) pub crawl (*Brit. coll.*); **eine ~ machen** go on a pub crawl (*Brit. coll.*); go barhopping (*Amer.*)

**säuseln** /ˈzɔyzl̩n/ **1** *itr. V.* (*rascheln*) ‹leaves, branches, etc.› rustle; ‹wind› murmur. **2** *tr. V.* (*iron.: sagen*) whisper

**sausen** *itr. V.* **A** (*Geräusch machen*) ‹wind› whistle; ‹storm› roar; ‹head, ears› buzz; ‹propeller, engine, etc.› whirr, **das Blut sauste ihm in den Ohren** blood was pounding in his ears; **B** *mit sein* (*hinfahren, -gehen*) ‹person› rush; ‹vehicle› roar; **er sauste mit dem Fahrrad um die Ecke** he sped round the corner on his bike; **durchs Examen ~** (*fig.*) fail one's exam; **C** *mit sein* ‹whip, bullet, etc.› whistle; **D** **einen ~ lassen** (*salopp*) blow off (*sl.*); **E** (*salopp*) **ein Konzert ~ lassen** give a concert a miss; **eine Einladung ~ lassen** not take up an invitation;

S

**eine Stellung/ein Geschäft ~ lassen** let a job/a business deal go; **ein Vorhaben ~ lassen** not bother to follow up a plan; F **jmdn. ~ lassen** (*salopp*) drop sb.

***sausen|lassen** ⇒ **sausen** E, F

**Sauser** *der;* **~s, ~** (*bes. südwestd., österr., schweiz.*) new wine

**Sause-: ~schritt** *der: in* **im ~schritt** (*ugs.*) at breakneck speed; **~wind** *der* A (*Kinderspr.*) wind; B (*ugs.: Mensch*) live wire

**sau-, Sau-: ~stall** *der* A pigsty; B (*fig. salopp abwertend*) hole (*coll.*); dump (*coll.*); **~wetter** *das* (*salopp abwertend*) lousy weather (*coll.*); **~wohl** *Adj.*; *in* **sich ~wohl fühlen** (*salopp*) feel bloody (*Brit. sl.*) *or* (*coll.*) damn good *or* great; **~wut** *die* (*salopp*) **eine ~wut [auf jmdn.] haben** be bloody (*Brit. sl.*) *or* (*coll.*) damn mad [with sb.]

**Savanne** /za'vanə/ *die;* **~, ~n** savannah

**Savoyen** /za'vɔyən/ *(das)*; **~s** Savoy

**Sax** *das;* **~es, ~e** (*Musikerjargon*) sax (*coll.*)

**Saxer,** *der;* **~s, ~, Saxerin** *die;* **~, ~nen** (*Musikerjargon*) sax player (*coll.*)

**Saxophon** /zakso'fo:n/ *das;* **~s, ~e** saxophone

**Saxophonist** *der;* **~en, ~en, Saxophonistin** *die;* **~, ~nen** ▶ 159 saxophonist

**S-Bahn** /'ɛs-/ *die* city and suburban railway; S-bahn

**S-Bahn-: ~hof** *der,* **~-Station** *die* S-bahn station; **~-Zug** *der* city and suburban train; S-bahn train

**S-Bahn-Surfen** *das;* **~s** train surfing

**SBB** *Abk.* **Schweizerische Bundesbahn** Swiss Federal Railways

**SB-**/ɛs'be:-/**: ~-Laden** *der; Pl.* **~-Läden** self-service shop; **~-Tank·stelle** *die* self-service petrol (*Brit.*) *or* (*Amer.*) gasoline station

**SBZ** /ɛsbe:'tsɛt/*die;* **~** *Abk.* **Sowjetische Besatzungszone** Soviet occupied zone

**Scampi** /'skampi/ *Pl.* scampi

**Scanner** /'skænə/ *der;* **~s, ~** (*DV, Med., graf. Technik*) scanner

**Scene** /si:n/ *die;* **~, ~s** (*salopp*) scene

**sch** /ʃ/ *Interj.* A (*ruhig*) sh[h]; hush; B (*weg da*) shoo

**Schabe** /'ʃa:bə/ *die;* **~, ~n** A cockroach; B (*südd., schweiz.: Motte*) moth

**Schabe·fleisch** *das* minced beef

**Schab·eisen** *das* scraper

**schaben** ❶ *tr. V.* A (*schälen*) scrape ‹carrots, potatoes, etc.›; (*glätten*) shave ‹leather, hide, etc.›; plane ‹wood, surface, etc.›; **sich** (*Dat.*) **den Bart ~** (*ugs. scherzh.*) have a shave; shave; B (*scheuern*) rub; C (*entfernen*) scrape. ❷ *itr. V.* scrape; **an/auf etw.** (*Dat.*) **~:** scrape against sth./scrape sth.

**Schaber** *der;* **~s, ~:** scraper

**Schabernack** /'ʃa:bɐnak/ *der;* **~[e]s, ~e** A (*Streich*) prank; **jmdm. einen ~ spielen, mit jmdm. seinen ~ treiben** play a prank on sb.; B (*Scherz, Spaß*) **aus ~ etw. tun** do sth. for a joke; C (*scherzh.: Kind*) monkey; rascal

**schäbig** /'ʃɛ:bɪç/ ❶ *Adj.* A (*abgenutzt*) shabby; B (*jämmerlich, gering*) pathetic; miserable; **~e Gehälter** paltry wages; C (*gemein*) shabby; mean; D (*geizig*) stingy. ❷ *adv.* A (*abgenutzt*) shabbily; B (*jämmerlich*) miserably; **~ bezahlen** pay poorly; C (*gemein*) meanly

**Schäbigkeit** *die;* **~:** shabbiness; (*des Gehalts*) paltriness; (*Geiz*) stinginess

**Schablone** /ʃa'blo:nə/ *die;* **~, ~n** A pattern; B (*fig., meist abwertend*) **in ~n denken/sprechen** *od.* **reden** think in stereotypes/speak in clichés; **nach ~ arbeiten** work according to a set pattern *or* routine

**schablonen-, Schablonen-: ~denken** *das* stereotyped way of thinking; **~druck** *der* A (*Vervielfältigungsverfahren*) stencil printing; B (*Siebdruck*) screen printing; **~haft** ❶ *Adj.* stereotyped ‹thinking›; clichéd ‹remark, expression, etc.›; ❷ *adv.* ‹speak› in a clichéd manner; ‹think, act, argue, etc.› in a stereotyped manner

*old spelling (see note on page 1707)

**Schab·messer** *das* A (*Schabeisen*) scraper; scraping knife; B (*zur Holzbearbeitung*) spokeshave

**Schabracke** /ʃa'brakə/ *die;* **~, ~n** A (*Pferdedecke*) caparison; B (*an Fenstern*) pelmet

**Schabsel** /'ʃa:psl̩/ *das;* **~s, ~:** shavings *pl.*

**Schab·technik** *die* mezzotint technique

**Schach** /ʃax/ *das;* **~s, ~s** A (*Spiel*) chess; B (*Schachspiel: Stellung*) check; **~ [dem König]!** check; **[dem gegnerischen König/dem Gegner] ~ bieten** check the opponent's king/the opponent; **der Turm/der Gegner bietet ~:** the rook/the opponent gives check; **ewiges ~:** perpetual check; **im ~:** in check; **jmdn./etw. in ~ halten** (*ugs. fig.*) keep sb./sth. in check; ⇒ *auch* **matt** 1 F

**Schach-: ~aufgabe** *die* chess problem; **~brett** *das* chessboard; **~brett·muster** *das* chequerboard pattern; (*auf Stoff*) chequered pattern; **~ecke** *die* (*ugs.*) chess column

**Schacher** /'ʃaxɐ/ *der;* **~s** (*abwertend*) haggling (**um** over); (*bes. Politik*) horse-trading (**um** about)

**Schächer** /'ʃɛçɐ/ *der;* **~s, ~** (*bibl.*) thief

**schachern** *itr. V.* haggle (**um** over)

**schach-, Schach-: ~figur** *die* chess piece; chessman; **~matt** *Adj.* A (*Schachspiel*) **~matt!** checkmate!; **~matt sein** be checkmated; **jmdn. ~matt setzen** (*Schachspiel*) checkmate sb.; (*fig.: ausschalten*) render sb. powerless; B (*erschöpft*) exhausted; **~partie** *die* game of chess; **~spiel** *das* A (*Spiel*) chess; B (*das Spielen*) chess-playing; C (*Partie*) game of chess; D (*Brett und Figuren*) chess set; **~spieler** *der,* **~spielerin** *die* chess player

**Schacht** /ʃaxt/ *der;* **~[e]s, Schächte** /'ʃɛçtə/ shaft

**Schachtel** /'ʃaxtl̩/ *die;* **~, ~n** A box; **eine ~ Zigaretten** a packet *or* (*Amer.*) pack of cigarettes; **eine ~ Pralinen/Streichhölzer** a box of chocolates/matches; B *in* **alte ~** (*salopp abwertend*) old bag (*sl.*)

**Schächtelchen** /'ʃɛçtl̩çən/ *das;* **~s, ~:** [little] box

**Schachtel-: ~halm** *der* (*Bot.*) horsetail; **~satz** *der* (*Sprachw.*) involved sentence

**schächten** /'ʃɛçtn̩/ *tr., itr. V.* slaughter according to Jewish rites

**Schach-: ~turnier** *das* chess tournament; **~zug** *der* A (*Schachspiel*) move [in chess]; B (*fig.*) move

**schade** /'ʃa:də/ *Adj.* **[ach, wie] ~!** [what a] pity *or* shame; **es/das ist [sehr] ~!** it's/that's a [terrible] pity *or* shame; **[es ist zu] ~, dass ...** it's a [real] pity *or* shame that ...; **nur ~** *od.* **~ nur, dass ...** it's just a pity *or* shame that ...; **[es ist] ~ um jmdn./etw.** it's a pity or shame about sb./sth.; **~ drum!** what a pity *or* shame; **um die Vase ist es nicht weiter ~:** it doesn't matter about the vase; the vase is no great loss; **für jmdn./für** *od.* **zu etw. zu ~ sein** be too good for sb./sth.; **sich** (*Dat.*) **zu ~ für** *od.* **zu etw./für jmdn. sein** consider oneself too good for sth./sb.

**Schade** *in* **es soll dein ~ nicht sein** (*veralt.*) it will not be to your disadvantage

**Schädel** /'ʃɛ:dl̩/ *der;* **~s, ~** A ▶ 471 head; (*Skelett*) skull; **jmdm. eins auf** *od.* **über den ~ geben** (*ugs.*) hit *or* knock sb. over the head; **mir brummt der ~** (*ugs.*) my head is throbbing; **einen dicken** *od.* **harten ~ haben** (*fig.*) be stubborn *or* pigheaded; **sich** (*Dat.*) **[an etw.** (*Dat.*)**] den ~ einrennen** (*fig.*) beat *or* run one's head against a brick wall [with sth.]; B (*fig.: Verstand*) **streng deinen ~ mal an!** tax your brains a bit!; **es geht** *od.* **will nicht in seinen ~ [hinein], dass ...** (*ugs.*) he can't get it into his head that ...

**Schädel-: ~basis·bruch** *der* ▶ 474 (*Med.*) basal skull fracture; **~bruch** *der* ▶ 474 (*Med.*) skull fracture; **~decke** *die* ▶ 471 (*Anat.*) skullcap; calvaria; **~lage** *die* (*Med.*) cephalic *or* head presentation; **~naht** *die* ▶ 471 (*Anat.*) suture

**schaden** *itr. V.* **jmdm./einer Sache ~:** damage *or* harm sb./sth.; **Rauchen schadet Ihrer Gesundheit/Ihnen** smoking damages your health/is bad for you; **jmds. Ansehen [sehr] ~:** do [great] damage to sb.'s reputation; **das würde dir nichts ~** (*ugs.*) that wouldn't hurt you *or* do you any harm; **das schadet nichts** (*ugs.*) (*ist nicht schlimm*) that doesn't matter; (*ist ganz gut*) that won't do any harm; **es kann nichts ~, wenn ...** (*ugs.*) it would do no harm if ...

**Schaden** *der;* **~s, Schäden** /'ʃɛ:dn̩/ A (*Beschädigung*) damage *no pl., no indef. art.*; **ein kleiner/großer ~:** little/major damage; **jmdm. [einen] ~ zufügen** harm sb.; **~ leiden** (*geh.*) suffer; **wer den ~ hat, braucht für den Spott nicht zu sorgen** (*Spr.*) the laugh is always on the loser; **aus ~ wird man klug** (*Spr.*) once bitten, twice shy (*prov.*); **er hat an seiner Gesundheit ~ genommen** (*geh.*) his health has suffered; B (*Nachteil*) disadvantage; **es ist dein eigener** *od.* **zu deinem eigenen ~:** it is to your own disadvantage; **es soll Ihr ~ nicht sein** it will not be to your disadvantage; **zu ~ kommen** suffer; be adversely affected; C (*Defekt*) damage *no pl., no indef. art.*; **das Haus weist einige Schäden auf** the house has some defects; D (*Verletzung*) injury; **zu ~ kommen** be hurt *or* injured

**schaden-, Schaden-: ~ersatz** *der* (*Rechtsw.*) damages *pl.*; (*Versicherungsw.*) **~ersatz leisten** pay damages/compensation; **jmdn. auf ~ersatz verklagen** sue sb. for damages/compensation; **~ersatz·anspruch** *der,* **~ersatz·forderung** *die* (*Rechtsw.*) claim for damages; (*Versicherungsw.*) claim for compensation; **~freude** *die* malicious pleasure; **..., sagte er voller ~freude ...** he said gloatingly; **~froh** ❶ *Adj.* gloating; **~froh sein** gloat; ❷ *adv.* with malicious pleasure

**Schadens·fall** *der* (*Rechtsw., Versicherungsw.*) case of damage; (*Verlust*) case of loss; **im ~:** in the event of damage/loss

**schadhaft** /'ʃa:thaft/ *Adj.* defective

**Schadhaftigkeit** *die;* **~:** defectiveness

**schädigen** /'ʃɛ:dɪgn̩/ *tr. V.* damage ‹health, reputation, interests›; harm, hurt ‹person›; cause losses to ‹firm, industry, etc.›; **er hat den Betrieb um mehrere tausend Mark geschädigt** he caused losses of several thousand marks to the firm; **jmdn. gesundheitlich ~:** damage sb.'s health

**Schädigung** *die;* **~, ~en** damage *no pl., no indef. art.* (*Gen.* to); **materielle/gesundheitliche ~en** financial losses/damage to one's/your *etc.* health

**schädlich** /'ʃɛ:tlɪç/ *Adj.* harmful; **~ für die Gesundheit** damaging *or* injurious to the health; **~e Folgen/Wirkungen/Einflüsse** damaging or detrimental consequences/effects/influences

**Schädlichkeit** *die;* **~:** harmfulness

**Schädling** /'ʃɛ:tlɪŋ/ *der;* **~s, ~e** pest

**Schädlings-: ~bekämpfer** *der;* **~~s, ~~, ~bekämpferin** *die;* **~~, ~~nen** pest control expert; **~bekämpfung** *die* pest control; **~bekämpfungs·mittel** *das* pesticide

**schadlos** *Adj. in* **sich an jmdm./etw. ~ halten** take advantage of sb./sth.

**Schad·stoff** *der* harmful chemical

**schadstoff·arm** *Adj.* (*bes. Kfz-W.*) low in harmful substances *postpos.*; clean-exhaust ‹vehicle›; (*mit Katalysator*) ‹vehicle› with exhaust emission control

**Schaf** /ʃa:f/ *das;* **~[e]s, ~e** A sheep; ⇒ *auch* **Bock** A; **schwarz** B; B (*ugs.: Dummkopf*) twit (*Brit. coll.*); idiot (*coll.*)

**Schaf·bock** *der* ram

**Schäfchen** /'ʃɛ:fçən/ *das;* **~s, ~** A [little] sheep; (*Lamm*) lamb; **sein[e] ~ ins Trockene bringen** (*ugs.*) take care of number one (*coll.*); **sein[e] ~ im Trockenen haben** (*ugs.*) have taken care of number one (*coll.*); **~ zählen** (*zum Einschlafen*) count sheep; B *Pl.* (*ugs.: Schutzbefohlene*) flock *sing. or pl.*; C (*fam.: einfältiger Mensch*) silly thing

S

**Schäfchen·wolke** *die* fleecy cloud

**Schäfer** *der;* **~s,** **~** ▸ 159 shepherd

**Schäfer·dichtung** *die* (*Literaturw.*) pastoral *or* bucolic poetry

**Schäferei** *die;* **~, ~en** A sheep farming; sheep rearing; B (*Betrieb*) sheep farm

**Schäfer·hund** *der* A (*Rasse*) Alsatian (*Brit.*); German shepherd; **ein deutscher ~:** an Alsatian (*Brit.*); a German shepherd; B (*Hirtenhund*) sheepdog

**Schäferin** *die;* **~, ~nen** ▸ 159 shepherdess

**Schäfer-: ~spiel** *das* (*Literaturw.*) pastoral [play]; **~stündchen** *das* lovers' tryst

**Schaf·fell** *das* sheepskin

**schaffen** /ˈʃafn̩/ ❶ *unr. tr. V.* A (*schöpferisch gestalten*) create; **der ~de Mensch** creative man; **für jmdn./etw. od. zu jmdm./etw. wie ge~ sein** be made *or* perfect for sb./sth.; B *auch regelm.* (*herstellen*) create ‹conditions, jobs, situation, etc.›; make ‹room, space, fortune›; **klare Verhältnisse ~:** clear things up; straighten things out; ⇒ *auch* **Abhilfe; Ordnung** A.

❷ *tr. V.* A (*bewältigen*) **etw. ~:** manage to do sth.; **viel ~:** manage to do a great deal; **eine Arbeit ~:** get a job done; **wenn wir uns beeilen, ~ wir es vielleicht noch** we might still make it if we hurry; **das schafft er nie** he'll never manage it; **das hätten wir geschafft, das wäre geschafft** there, that's done; **er hat die Prüfung nicht geschafft** (*ugs.*) he didn't pass the exam; B (*ugs.: erschöpfen*) wear out; **die Hitze/Arbeit hat mich geschafft** the heat/work took it out of me; C (*befördern*) **etw. aus etw./in etw.** (*Akk.*) **~:** get sth. out of/into sth.; **die Kisten auf den Speicher/in den Keller ~:** take the boxes to the attic/cellar.

❸ *itr. V.* A (*südd.: arbeiten*) work; B **sich** (*Dat.*) **zu ~ machen** (*an etw. hantieren*) busy oneself; (*Tätigkeit vortäuschen*) fiddle *or* tinker about; **was machst du dir an meinem Schreibtisch zu ~?** what are you doing at my desk?; **mit ihm will ich nichts zu ~ haben** I don't want to have anything to do with him; **was habe ich mit dieser Angelegenheit zu ~?** what does this matter have to do with me?; **jmdm. zu ~ machen** cause sb. trouble

**Schaffen** *das;* **~s** work; **im Zenit seines ~s** at the peak of his creative work

**Schaffens-: ~drang** *der* energy; **~freude** *die* enthusiasm [for one's work]; (*eines Künstlers*) pleasure in creating things; **~kraft** *die* energy for work; (*eines Künstlers*) creativity; creative power

**Schaffer** *der;* **~s, ~** (*bes. südd.*) hard worker

**Schafferei** *die;* **~** (*bes. südd.*) hard work

**Schafferin** *die;* **~, ~nen** ⇒ **Schaffer**

**Schaf·fleisch** *das* mutton

**Schaffner** /ˈʃafnɐ/ *der;* **~s, ~** ▸ 159 (*im Bus*) conductor; (*im Zug*) guard (*Brit.*); conductor (*Amer.*); (*der Fahrausweise verkauft/kontrolliert*) inspector

**Schaffnerin** *die;* **~, ~nen** ▸ 159 (*im Bus*) conductress (*Brit.*); (*im Zug*) guard (*Brit.*); conductress (*Amer.*); (*die Fahrausweise verkauft/kontrolliert*) inspector

**schaffner·los** *Adj.* (*Verkehrsw.*) ‹bus, tram, etc.› without a conductor; ‹train› without a guard (*Brit.*) *or* (*Amer.*) conductor/an inspector *postpos.*

**Schaffung** *die;* **~:** creation

**Schaf-: ~garbe** *die* yarrow; **~herde** *die* flock of sheep; **~hirt** *der* shepherd; **~hirtin** *die* shepherdess; **~kälte** *die: spell of cold weather frequently occurring in mid-June;* **~kopf** ⇒ **Schafskopf**

**Schäflein** /ˈʃɛːflai̯n/ *das;* **~s, ~** ⇒ **Schäfchen** A, B

**Schafott** /ʃaˈfɔt/ *das;* **~[e]s, ~e** scaffold

**Schaf·schur** *die* sheep shearing

**Schafs-: ~käse** *der* sheep's milk cheese; **~kopf** der A (*Kartenspiel*) sheep's head; B (*ugs.: Trottel*) dope (*coll.*); idiot (*coll.*); **~pelz** *der* sheepskin

**Schaf·stall** *der* sheepfold

**Schaft** /ʃaft/ *der;* **~[e]s, Schäfte** /ˈʃɛftə/ A (*Griff; auch Archit.*) shaft; (*eines Messers, Beils, Meißels*) handle; (*eines Gewehrs usw.*) stock; B (*eines Baumes, einer Feder*) shaft; C (*am Schuh*) upper; D (*am Stiefel*) leg; E (*Bot.*) stem; stalk

**Schaft·stiefel** *der* high boot

**Schaf-: ~wolle** *die* sheep's wool; **~zucht** *die* A (*das Züchten*) sheep breeding *no art.;* B (*Betrieb*) sheep farm

**Schah** /ʃaː/ *der;* **~s, ~s** Shah

**Schakal** /ʃaˈkaːl/ *der;* **~s, ~e** jackal

**Schäker** /ˈʃɛːkɐ/ *der;* **~s, ~** (*veralt.*) A (*Witzbold*) joker; B (*jmd., der flirtet*) flirt

**schäkern** *itr. V.* (*veralt.*) A (*spaßen*) fool about; B (*flirten*) flirt

**schal** /ʃaːl/ *Adj.* stale ‹drink, taste, smell, joke›; empty ‹words, feeling›

**Schal** *der;* **~s, ~s** *od.* **~e** A (*Halstuch*) scarf; B (*Vorhang~*) curtain

**Schälchen** /ˈʃɛːlçən/ *das;* **~s, ~:** small bowl *or* dish

**Schale** /ˈʃaːlə/ *die;* **~, ~n** A (*Obstschale*) skin; (*abgeschälte ~*) peel *no pl.;* **Kartoffeln in der ~** (*Kochk.*) jacket potatoes; B (*Nuss~, Eier~*) shell; C (*tieferes Gefäß*) bowl; (*flacheres Gefäß*) dish; (*Waag~*) pan; scale; (*Sekt~*) champagne glass; D *in* **[groß] in ~ sein** (*ugs.*) be dressed up to the nines; **sich in ~ werfen** *od.* **schmeißen** (*ugs.*) get dressed [up] to the nines; E (*Zool.*) shell; F (*bes. österr.: Tasse*) [shallow] cup; G (*des BH*) cup

**schälen** /ˈʃɛːlən/ ❶ *tr. V.* peel ‹fruit, vegetable›; shell ‹egg, nut, pea›; skin ‹tomato, almond›; **einen Baumstamm ~:** remove the bark from a tree trunk; **den Knochen aus einem Schinken ~:** bone a ham; **etw. aus der Verpackung ~** (*fig.*) get sth. out of its wrappings; **sich aus den Kleidern ~** (*fig.*) get oneself out of one's clothes.

❷ *refl. V.* A (*sich ~ lassen*) peel; **Tomaten/Eier ~ sich leichter** tomatoes/eggs can be skinned/shelled more easily; B ‹person, skin, nose, etc.› peel; **du schälst dich am Rücken/auf der Nase/im Gesicht** your back/nose/face is peeling

**Schalen-: ~obst** *das* nuts *pl.;* **~sitz** *der* bucket seat; **~tier** *das* shell animal; **~wild** *das* (*Jägerspr.*) hoofed game

**Schalheit** *die;* **~** ⇒ **schal**: staleness; emptiness

**Schalk** /ʃalk/ *der;* **~[e]s, ~e** *od.* **Schälke** /ˈʃɛlkə/ rogue; prankster; **jmdm. sitzt der ~/jmd. hat den ~ im Nacken** (*fig.*) sb. is really roguish *or* mischievous; **jmdm. schaut der ~ aus den Augen** (*fig.*) sb. has a roguish *or* mischievous look in his eye

**schalkhaft** (*geh.*) ❶ *Adj.* roguish; mischievous. ❷ *adv.* roguishly; mischievously

**Schal·kragen** *der* shawl collar

**Schalks·narr** *der* (*veralt.*) A (*Hofnarr*) jester; fool; B (*Schalk*) rogue; prankster; wag

**Schall** /ʃal/ *der;* **~[e]s, ~e** *od.* **Schälle** /ˈʃɛlə/ A (*Klang*) sound; **mit lautem ~:** loudly; **leerer ~ sein** be meaningless *or* irrelevant; **~ und Rauch sein** not mean anything; **Name ist ~ und Rauch** names mean nothing; B (*Physik*) sound *no art.*

**schall-, Schall-: ~dämmend** *Adj.* sound-deadening; sound-absorbing; **~dämmung** *die* sound insulation; **~dämpfer** *der* A (*am Auto, für Feuerwaffen*) silencer; B (*Musik*) mute; **~dicht** *Adj.* soundproof

***Schallehre** ⇒ **Schalllehre**

**schallen** *regelm.* (*auch unr.*) *itr. V.* ring out; (*nachhallen*) resound; echo; **eine ~de Ohrfeige** a resounding slap; **~des Gelächter** ringing laughter; **~d lachen** roar with laughter

**Schall-: ~geschwindigkeit** *die* speed *or* velocity of sound; **~lehre** *die* acoustics *sing., no art.;* **~loch** *das* A (*Musik*) soundhole; B (*an einem Turm usw.*) belfry window; **~mauer** *die* sound *or* sonic barrier

***Schalloch** ⇒ **Schallloch**

**Schall·platte** *die* record

**Schallplatten-:** ⇒ **Platten-**

**schall-, Schall-: ~quelle** *die* sound source; **~schluckend** *Adj.* sound-absorbent; sound-deadening; **~trichter** *der* (*am Grammophon*) horn; (*am Blasinstrument*) bell; **~welle** *die* (*Physik*) sound wave; **~wort** *das Pl.* **~wörter** (*Sprachw.*) onomatopoeic word

**Schalmei** /ʃalˈmai̯/ *die;* **~, ~en** shawm

**Schalotte** /ʃaˈlɔtə/ *die;* **~, ~n** shallot

**schalt** /ʃalt/ *1. u. 3. Pers. Sg. Prät. v.* **schelten**

**Schalt·anlage** *die* (*Elektrot.*) switchgear

**schalten** /ˈʃaltn̩/ ❶ *tr. V.* A switch; **ein Gerät auf „aus" ~:** turn an appliance to 'off'; B (*Elektrot.: verbinden*) connect; **in Reihe/parallel ~:** connect in series/in parallel.

❷ *itr. V.* A (*Schalter betätigen*) switch, turn (**auf** + *Akk.* to); **du musst zweimal ~:** you have to operate the switch twice; **er schaltet immer gleich auf stur** (*fig. ugs.*) he immediately digs his heels in (*fig.*); B ‹machine› switch (**auf** + *Akk.* to); ‹traffic light› change (**auf** + *Akk.* to); C (*im Auto*) change [gear]; **in den 4. Gang ~:** change into fourth gear; D (*geh.: verfahren*) act; **er kann mit dem Geld frei ~:** he can do as he pleases with the money; he has a free hand with the money; **~ und walten** manage one's affairs; **sie kann ~ und walten, wie sie will** she can manage things as she pleases; E (*ugs.: begreifen*) twig (*coll.*); catch on (*coll.*).

❸ *refl. V.* (*sich ~ lassen*) **das Gerät schaltet sich leicht/schwer** the switch on this device is easy/difficult to operate; **der Wagen schaltet sich schlecht** it's difficult to change gear in this car

**Schalter** /ˈʃaltɐ/ *der;* **~s, ~** A (*Strom~*) switch; B (*Post~, Bank~, Fahrkarten~ usw.*) counter; (*mit Fenster auch*) window C (*am Fahrrad*) gear lever

**Schalter-: ~beamte** *der,* **~beamtin** *die* counter clerk; (*im Bahnhof*) ticket clerk; **~halle** *die* hall; (*im Bahnhof*) booking hall (*Brit.*); ticket office; **~raum** *der* counter room; (*im Bahnhof*) ticket office; **~schluss,** ***~schluß** *der* closing time; **~stunden** *Pl.* business hours; hours of business

**Schalt-: ~fläche** *die* (*DV*) button; **~getriebe** *das* (*Kfz-W.*) [manual] gearbox; **~hebel** *der* A (*am Schalter*) switch; **an den ~hebeln der Macht sitzen** (*fig.*) hold the reins of power; B (*einer Gangschaltung*) gear lever; gear shift (*Amer.*); **~jahr** *das* leap year; **alle ~jahre [ein]mal** (*ugs.*) once in a blue moon; **~knüppel** *der* [floor-mounted] gear lever; **~kreis** *der* (*Elektrot.*) circuit; **~pause** *die* (*Rundfunk*) pause [in transmission]; **~plan** *der* (*Elektrot.*) wiring *or* circuit diagram; **~pult** *das* control desk; (*kleiner*) control panel; **~satz** *der* (*Sprachw.*) parenthetic clause; **~stelle** *die* control centre; **~tafel** *die* (*Elektrot.*) control panel; **~tag** *der* leap day

**Schaltung** *die;* **~, ~en** A (*Rundfunk: Verbindung*) link-up; B (*Gangschaltung*) manual gear change; C (*Elektrot.*) circuit; wiring system; D ⇒ **~plan**

**Schaltwerk** *das* changer; derailleur

**Schalt·zentrale** *die* (*Technik*) control centre

**Schaltzug** *der* gear cable

**Schaluppe** /ʃaˈlʊpə/ *die;* **~, ~n** (*Frachtschiff*) sloop

**Scham** /ʃaːm/ *die;* **~** A shame; **ohne/ohne jede ~:** unashamedly/without the slightest shame; **ich hätte vor ~ in den Boden versinken können** I could have sunk through the floor with embarrassment *or* shame; **aus/vor ~ erröten** blush with shame; **nur keine falsche ~:** no need for any false modesty; B (*geh. verhüll.: ~gegend*) private parts *pl.*

**Schamane** /ʃaˈmaːnə/ *der;* **~n, ~n, Schamanin** *die;* **~, ~nen** (*Völkerk.*) shaman

**Scham·bein** *das* ▸ 471 (*Anat.*) pubic bone

**schämen** /ˈʃɛːmən/ *refl. V.* be ashamed; **sich einer Sache** (*Gen.*) *od.* **für etw. od. wegen etw. ~:** be ashamed of sth.; **sich für jmdn. ~:** be ashamed for sb.; **du solltest dich [was** (*ugs.*)**] ~!** you [really] should be ashamed of yourself; **schäm dich** shame on you

**Scham-: ~gefühl** *das* sense of shame; **~haar** *das* pubic hair

S

**schamhaft** ❶ *Adj.* bashful ‹person, look, etc.›; modest ‹clothing›. ❷ *adv.* ‹look, smile, etc.› bashfully; ‹dress, behave› modestly

**Schamhaftigkeit** *die;* ~: modesty

**scham-, Scham-:** ~**lippe** *die* ▶ 471 (*Anat.*) labium; **innere/äußere** ~**lippen** labia minora/majora; ~**los** ❶ *Adj.* **A** (*skrupellos, dreist*) shameless; barefaced, shameless ‹lie, slander›; **B** (*unanständig*) indecent ‹gesture, remark, dress, etc.›; shameless ‹person›; ❷ *adv.* **A** (*skrupellos, dreist*) shamelessly; **B** (*unanständig*) indecently; ~**losigkeit** *die;* ~~, ~~**en** (*Skrupellosigkeit, Dreistigkeit*) shamelessness; (*Unanständigkeit*) indecency; shamelessness; **ich kann solche** ~**losigkeiten nicht dulden** I cannot tolerate such shameless behaviour *sing.*

**Schamotte·stein** /ʃaˈmɔte-/ *der* firebrick

**Schampon** /ˈʃampɔn/ ⇒ **Shampoo**

**schamponieren** *tr. V.* shampoo

**Schampus** /ˈʃampʊs/ *der;* ~ (*ugs.*) bubbly (*coll.*); champers *sing.* (*Brit. coll.*)

**scham·rot** *Adj.* red with shame *postpos.;* ~ **werden** blush with shame

**Scham·röte** *die:* **ihm stieg die** ~ **ins Gesicht** he blushed with shame

**schandbar** ⇒ **schändlich**

**Schande** /ˈʃandə/ *die;* ~: disgrace; shame; **es ist eine [wahre]** ~: it is a[n absolute] disgrace; **es wäre doch eine** ~, **das wegzuwerfen** it would be a shame to throw it away; **zu meiner** ~ **muss ich sagen, dass ...** it must be said to my shame that ...; ~ **über dich!** shame on you!; **jmdm./einer Sache [keine]** ~ **machen** [not] disgrace sb./sth.; bring [no] disgrace *or* shame on sb./sth.; **etw. gereicht jmdm. zur** ~ (*geh.*) sth. is a disgrace to sb.; ***zu** ~**n** ⇒ **zuschanden**

**schänden** /ˈʃɛndn̩/ *tr. V.* **A** dishonour, discredit ‹name, reputation, etc.›; **B** (*beschädigen*) defile ‹memorial, work of art, etc.›; desecrate, defile ‹holy place, grave, relic›; violate ‹corpse›; **C** (*veralt.: vergewaltigen*) violate; ⇒ *auch* **Arbeit A**

**Schand·fleck** *der* blot; **ein** ~ **in der Landschaft sein** be a blot on the landscape; **er war schon immer der** ~ **[in] unserer Familie** he always 'was the disgrace of our family

**schändlich** ❶ *Adj.* **A** (*verwerflich*) shameful; disgraceful; **B** (*ugs.: scheußlich*) disgraceful; dreadful (*coll.*), terrible (*coll.*) ‹weather›. ❷ *adv.* **A** (*verwerflich*) shamefully; disgracefully; **B** (*ugs.: überaus*) dreadfully (*coll.*), terribly (*coll.*)

**Schändlichkeit** *die;* ~, ~**en** **A** (*Eigenschaft*) shamefulness; disgracefulness; **B** (*Handlung*) shameful action

**Schand-:** ~**mal** *das; Pl.* ~~**e**, *od.* ~**mäler** **A** mal (*hist.*) brand; **B** (*geh.: Schandfleck*) blemish; ~**tat** *die* disgraceful *or* abominable deed; **zu jeder** ~**tat** *od.* **zu allen** ~**taten bereit sein** (*ugs. scherzh.*) be game for anything

**Schändung** *die;* ~, ~**en** **A** ⇒ **schänden A, B**: dishonouring; discrediting; desecration; defilement; **B** (*veralt.: Vergewaltigung*) violation

**Schanker** /ˈʃaŋkɐ/ *der;* ~**s**, ~ ▶ 474 (*Med.*) chancre; **harter/weicher** ~: hard/soft chancre

**Schank-:** ~**erlaubnis** *die* licence [to sell alcohol]; ~**tisch** *der* bar; ~**wirtschaft** *die* public house (*Brit.*); bar (*Amer.*)

**Schanze** /ˈʃant͜sə/ *die;* ~, ~**n** **A** (*Milit. veralt.*) entrenchment; fieldwork; **B** (*Sprung*~) [ski] jump

**Schanzen·rekord** *der* (*Skispringen*) ski jump record

**Schar** /ʃaːɐ̯/ *die;* ~, ~**en** crowd; horde; (*von Vögeln*) flock; **in [großen** *od.* **hellen]** ~**en** in swarms *or* droves

**Scharade** /ʃaˈraːdə/ *die;* ~, ~**n** charade

**Schäre** /ˈʃɛːrə/ *die;* ~, ~**n** skerry

**scharen** ❶ *refl. V.* (*sich zusammenfinden*) gather. ❷ *tr. V.* **die Kinder/Klasse um sich** ~: gather the children/class around one[self]

**Schären·küste** *die* skerry coast

**scharen·weise** *Adv.* in swarms *or* hordes

**scharf** /ʃarf/; **schärfer** /ˈʃɛrfɐ/, **schärfst...** /ˈʃɛrfst.../ ❶ *Adj.* **A** sharp; **B** (*stark gewürzt, brennend, stechend*) hot; strong ‹drink, vinegar, etc.›; caustic ‹chemical›; pungent, acrid ‹smell›; **C** (*durchdringend*) shrill; (*hell*) harsh; (*kalt*) biting ‹cold, wind, air, etc.›; sharp ‹frost›; **D** (*deutlich wahrnehmend*) keen; sharp; **E** (*stark*) strong ‹spectacles›; powerful ‹lens, microscope, telescope, etc.›; **F** (*deutlich hervortretend*) sharp ‹contours, features, nose, photograph›; **G** (*schonungslos*) tough, fierce ‹resistance, competition, etc.›; sharp ‹criticism, remark, words, etc.›; strong, fierce ‹opponent, protest, etc.›; severe, harsh ‹sentence, law, measure, etc.›; strict, tough ‹examiner, teacher›; tough, rigorous ‹inquiry, interrogation›; bitter, fierce ‹fighting, argument, etc.›; fierce ‹dog›; **eine** ~**e Zunge haben** have a sharp tongue; **jmdn./etw. in** ~**er Form kritisieren** criticize sb./sth. in strong terms; **H** (*schnell*) fast; hard ‹ride, gallop, etc.›; **ein** ~**es Tempo fahren** drive at quite a speed; **I** (*explosiv*) live; (*Ballspiele*) powerful ‹shot›; ~**e Schüsse abgeben** fire live bullets; **J** (*Sprachw.*) pronounced; clear; **das** ~**e S** (*bes. österr.*) the German letter 'ß'; **K** (*ugs.: großartig*) great (*coll.*); **L** (*ugs. empörend*) outrageous; **M** (*ugs.: geil*) sexy ‹girl, clothes, pictures, etc.›; randy ‹fellow, thoughts, etc.›; **N** *in* ~ **auf jmdn./etw. sein** (*ugs.*) really fancy sb. (*coll.*)/be really keen on sth. ❷ *adv.* **A** ~ **würzen/abschmecken** season/flavour highly; ~ **riechen** smell pungent *or* strong; **B** (*durchdringend*) shrilly; (*hell*) harshly; (*kalt*) bitingly; **C** (*deutlich wahrnehmend*) ‹listen, watch, etc.› closely, intently; ‹think, consider, etc.› hard; ~ **aufpassen** pay close attention; **D** (*deutlich hervortretend*) sharply; **einen Sender** ~ **einstellen** tune in a radio station properly; **etw.** ~ **umreißen** (*fig.*) outline sth. clearly *or* precisely; **E** (*schonungslos*) ‹attack, criticize, etc.› sharply, strongly; ‹contradict, oppose, etc.› strongly, fiercely; ‹examine, investigate, etc.› rigorously; ‹watch, observe, etc.› closely; ‹fight, quarrel, etc.› fiercely, bitterly; ~ **durchgreifen** take vigorous *or* strong action; **F** (*schnell*) fast; ~ **bremsen** brake hard *or* sharply; **das Auto fuhr** ~ **rechts heran** the car pulled up well over to the right; **G** **das Gewehr ist** ~ **geladen** the rifle is loaded with live ammunition; ~ **schießen** shoot with live ammunition; **den Ball** ~ **ins Netz schießen** hammer the ball into the net (*coll.*); **H** (*akzentuiert*) clearly; **I** (*ugs.: großartig*) splendidly

**Scharf·blick** *der* perspicacity

**Schärfe** /ˈʃɛrfə/ *die;* ~, ~**n** **A** (*von Messer usw.*) sharpness; **B** (*von Geschmack*) hotness; (*von Chemikalien*) causticity; (*von Geruch*) pungency; **C** (*Intensität*) shrillness; (*von Licht, Farbe usw.*) harshness; (*des Windes*) bitterness; (*des Frostes*) sharpness; **D** (*Empfindlichkeit, analytische Fähigkeit*) sharpness; keenness; **E** (*Klarheit*) clarity; sharpness; **F** (*Härte*) ⇒ **scharf 1 G**: toughness; ferocity; sharpness; strength; severity; harshness; strictness; rigour; bitterness; **G** (*Heftigkeit*) harshness; **H** (*Ballspiele*) power

**schärfen** ❶ *tr. V.* (*auch fig.*) sharpen. ❷ *refl. V.* become sharper *or* keener

**Schärfen·tiefe** *die* (*Fot.*) depth of focus

**schärfer** ⇒ **scharf**

**scharf-, Scharf-:** ~**kantig** *Adj.* sharp-edged; ~|**machen** *tr. V.* (*ugs.*) stir up; **einen Hund** ~**machen** urge a dog on; ~**macher** *der* (*ugs.*) rabble-rouser; ~**macherei** /-maxəˈrai̯/ *die;* ~~, ~~**en** (*ugs.*) rabble-rousing; ~**macherin** *die* ⇒ ~**macher**; ~**richter** *der* hangman; executioner; ~**schütze** *der* (*Milit.*) marksman; (*auch fig. Ballspiele*) sharpshooter; ~**schützin** *die* (*Milit.*) markswoman; (*auch fig. Ballspiele*) sharpshooter; ~**sichtig** /-zɪçtɪç/ ❶ *Adj.* sharp-sighted; perspicacious; ❷ *adv.* with sharp-sightedness; ~**sinn** *der* astuteness; acumen; ~**sinnig** ❶ *Adj.* astute; ❷ *adv.* astutely

**schärfst...** ⇒ **scharf**

**Schärfung** *die;* ~, ~**en** sharpening

**scharfzüngig** /-t͜sʏŋɪç/ ❶ *Adj.* sharp-tongued. ❷ *adv.* sharply; in a sharp-tongued manner

**Scharlach** /ˈʃarlax/ *der;* ~**s** ▶ 474 (*Med.*) scarlet fever

**scharlach·rot** *Adj.* scarlet

**Scharlatan** /ˈʃarlatan/ *der;* ~**s**, ~**e** (*abwertend*) charlatan

**Scharlatanerie** *die;* ~, ~**n** **A** charlatanism; **B** (*einzelne Handlung*) charlatanry

**Scharmützel** /ʃarˈmʏt͜sl̩/ *das;* ~**s**, ~ (*Milit.*) skirmish

**Scharnier** /ʃarˈniːɐ̯/ *das;* ~**s**, ~**e** hinge

**Schärpe** /ˈʃɛrpə/ *die;* ~, ~**n** sash

**scharren** /ˈʃarən/ ❶ *itr. V.* **A** (*schaben, schleifen*) scrape; **die Pferde** ~ **ungeduldig** the horses are pawing at the ground impatiently; **der Hund scharrte an der Tür** the dog scratched *or* pawed at the door; **mit den Füßen** ~: scrape one's feet; **B** (*wühlen*) scratch. ❷ *tr. V.* **A** scrape ‹fallen leaves, twigs, sand, dirt›; **B** (*herstellen*) scrape, scratch out ‹hole, hollow, etc.›

**Scharte** /ˈʃartə/ *die;* ~, ~**n** **A** nick; **eine** ~ **auswetzen** (*fig.*) make good a/the mistake; **B** (*Gebirgs*~) wind gap; **C** (*Schieß*~) crenel

**Scharteke** /ʃarˈteːkə/ *die;* ~, ~**n** (*abwertend*) **A** (*Buch*) trashy old tome; **B** (*Frau*) [old] hag; [old] bag (*sl.*)

**schartig** *Adj.* nicked; jagged

**Schaschlik** /ˈʃaʃlɪk/ *der od. das;* ~**s**, ~**s** (*Kochk.*) shashlik

**schassen** /ˈʃasn̩/ *tr. V.* (*ugs.*) throw *or* (*coll.*) chuck out

**Schatten** /ˈʃatn̩/ *der;* ~**s**, ~ **A** shadow; **nur noch ein** ~ **seiner selbst sein** (*fig.*) be only a shadow of one's former self; **einen** *od.* **seinen** ~ **auf etw.** (*Akk.*) **werfen** (*fig. geh.*) cast a *or* its shadow over sth.; **das große Ereignis wirft schon seine** ~ **voraus** (*fig.*) the big event is already making itself felt; **jmd./man kann nicht über seinen [eigenen]** ~ **springen** a leopard cannot change its spots (*prov.*); **B** (*schattige Stelle*) shade; **40° im** ~: 40° in the shade; **das Tal lag im** ~: the valley lay in shadow; **in jmds.** ~ **stehen** (*fig.*) be in sb.'s shadow; **jmdn./etw. in den** ~ **stellen** (*fig.*) put sb./sth. in the shade; **C** (*dunkle Stelle, auch fig.*) shadow; **nicht der** ~ **eines Verdachts** not a shadow of suspicion; **D** (*Gestalt*) shadow; **E** **das Reich der** ~ (*Myth.*) the realm of shades; **F** (*Beobachter*) shadow

**Schatten-:** ~**bild** *das* **A** (*Schatten*) shadow; **B** (*Schattenriss*) silhouette; ~**boxen** *das;* ~~**s** shadow boxing; ~**dasein** *das: in* **ein** ~**dasein fristen** lead a shadowy existence; **aus dem** *od.* **seinem** ~**dasein heraustreten** emerge from its/one's shadowy existence

**schattenhaft** *Adj.* shadowy; **etw. ist nur** ~ **zu erkennen** sth. is only vaguely recognizable

**schatten-, Schatten-:** ~**kabinett** *das* (*Politik*) shadow cabinet; ~**los** *Adj.* shadeless; without shade *postpos.;* ~**morelle** /-morɛlə/ *die;* ~, ~**n** morello cherry; ~**reich** *das* (*Myth.*) realm of shades; ~**riss**, ***~riß** *der* silhouette; ~**seite** *die* **A** shady side; **die** ~**seiten des Lebens kennen lernen** (*fig.*) get to know the dark side of life; **B** (*Kehrseite*) disadvantage; negative aspect; ~**spender** *der* (*geh.*) source of shade; ~**spiel** *das* **A** (*Theater*) shadow theatre; **B** (*Stück*) shadow play; shadow show; **C** (*Kinderspiel*) ~**spiele machen** make shadow pictures; ~**wirtschaft** *die* ≈ black economy [and social security scrounging]

**schattieren** *tr. V.* shade

**Schattierung** *die;* ~, ~**en** **A** shading; **B** (*Variante, Nuance*) shade; **aller ideologischen/religiösen** ~**en** of every ideological/religious shade *or* (*Amer.*) stripe

**schattig** *Adj.* shady

**Schatt·seite** *die* (*österr., schweiz.*) ⇒ **Schattenseite**

*old spelling (see note on page 1707)

S

**Schatulle** /ʃa'tʊlə/ *die;* ~, ~**n** casket

**Schatz** /ʃats/ *der;* ~**es, Schätze** /'ʃɛtsə/ **A** treasure *no indef. art.;* **ein ~ von Erinnerungen/Erfahrungen** *(fig.)* a wealth of memories/experience; **B** *Pl. (Bodenschätze)* natural resources; **C** *(ugs.: Anrede)* love *(coll.)*; darling; **D** *(ugs.: hilfsbereiter Mensch)* treasure *(coll.)*; **sei ein ~ und räum schnell auf** be a dear and clear up quickly

**Schätzchen** /'ʃɛtsçən/ *das;* ~**s,** ~: darling

**schätzen** /'ʃɛtsn/ **1** *tr. V.* **A** *(ein~, bewerten)* estimate; **wie alt schätzt du ihn?** how old do you think he is?; **sich glücklich ~:** deem oneself lucky; **grob geschätzt** at a rough estimate; **ein Haus/einen Gebrauchtwagen ~:** value a house/a second-hand car; **B** *(ugs.: annehmen)* reckon; think; **C** *(würdigen, hoch achten)* **jmdn. ~:** hold sb. in high regard *or* esteem; **hoch geschätzt** highly esteemed *or* respected; **ein geschätzter Künstler** a highly regarded artist; **etw. zu ~ wissen** appreciate sth.; **ich weiß es zu ~, dass ...** I appreciate the fact that ...; **jmdn./etw. ~ lernen** come to appreciate *or* value sb./sth.
**2** *itr. V.* guess; **schätz mal** guess; have a guess

***schätzenlernen** ⇒ **schätzen 1 C**

**Schatz-:** ~**kammer** *die (hist.)* treasure chamber; ~**kanzler** *der,* ~**kanzlerin** *die* Chancellor of the Exchequer *(Brit.)*; ~**meister** *der,* ~**meisterin** *die* treasurer

**Schätzung** *die;* ~, ~**en** estimate; *(eines Gebäudes, Grundstückwerts usw.)* valuation; **nach grober/vorsichtiger ~:** at a rough/cautious estimate; **nach meiner ~:** according to my reckoning

**schätzungs·weise** *Adv.* roughly; approximately

**Schätz·wert** *der* estimated value

**Schau** /ʃau/ *die;* ~, ~**en** **A** *(Ausstellung)* exhibition; **B** *(Vorführung)* show; **es war eine reine ~:** it was all show; **die** *od.* **eine ~ sein** *(Jugendspr.)* be really something; be something else *(coll.)*; **eine ~ machen** *od.* **abziehen** *(ugs.) (sich in Szene setzen)* put on a show; *(sich aufspielen)* show off; *(sich lautstark ereifern)* make a scene *or* fuss; **jmdm. die ~ stehlen** steal the show from sb.; **C** **in zur ~ stellen** *(ausstellen)* exhibit; display; *(offen zeigen)* display; **seine Gefühle zur ~ tragen** make a show of one's emotions; **D** *(geh.: Betrachtung)* vision; **E** *(geh.: Blickwinkel)* perspective

**Schau-:** ~**bild** *das* **A** *(Diagramm)* chart; **B** *(Nachbildung)* diagram; ~**bude** *die* show booth; ~**bühne** *die (veralt.)* theatre

**Schauder** /'ʃaudɐ/ *der;* ~**s,** ~ *(vor Kälte, Angst)* shiver; *(vor Angst)* shudder; **mir lief ein ~ den Rücken hinunter** a shiver/shudder ran down my spine

**schauderbar** *(ugs. scherzh.)* ⇒ **schauderhaft**

**schauder·erregend** *Adj.* terrifying; horrifying

**schauderhaft** **1** *Adj.* **A** *(fürchterlich)* terrible; dreadful; awful; **B** *(schaudererregend)* ghastly; terrible; horrifying. **2** *adv.* **A** *(fürchterlich)* terribly; dreadfully; **B** *(überaus)* terribly *(coll.)*; dreadfully *(coll.)*

**schaudern** *itr. V.* **A** *(vor Kälte)* shiver; **B** *(vor Angst)* shudder; **C** *unpers.* **es schauderte ihn [vor Kälte]** he shivered [with cold]; **bei dem Gedanken schauderte [es] ihn** he shuddered at the thought

**schauen** **1** *itr. V. (bes. südd., österr., schweiz.)* **A** *(sehen)* look; **jmdm./einander [fest] in die Augen ~:** look [straight] into sb.'s/each other's eyes; **auf jmdn./etw. ~:** look at sb./sth.; *(fig.)* look to sb./sth.; **um sich ~:** look around [one]; **zu tief in den Becher** *od.* **ins Glas geschaut haben** have had a drop too much [to drink]; have had one too many; **B** *(dreinblicken)* look; **der hat vielleicht geschaut, als er uns sah** his eyes opened wide when he saw us; **seine Augen schauten vergnügt/spöttisch** amusement/mockery showed in his eyes; **C** **schau, schau!** well, well; what do you know; **da schau her!** *(Verwunderung ausdrückend)* well, well; how about that?; *(Empörung ausdrückend)* well, well, how about 'that?; **da schau her, was du ...** just look what you ...; **schau [mal], ich finde, du solltest ...** look, I think you should ...; **D** *(sich kümmern um)* **nach jmdm./etw. ~:** take *or* have a look at sb./sth.; **die Nachbarn haben nach den Blumen geschaut** the neighbours looked after the flowers; **E** *(Acht geben)* **auf etw.** *(Akk.)* ~: set store by sth.; **er schaut darauf, dass alle pünktlich sind** he sets store by everybody being punctual; **F** *(ugs.: sich bemühen)* **schau, dass du ...** see *or* mind that you ...; **G** *(nachsehen)* have a look.
**2** *tr. V.* **A** *(sich ansehen)* **Fernsehen ~:** watch television; **~ Sie, was ich gefunden habe** look what I've found; **B** *(geh.: erfassen)* behold

**Schauer** *der;* ~**s,** ~ **A** *(Met.)* shower; **B** *(geh.)* ⇒ **Schauder**

**schauer·artig** *Adj. (Met.)* ~**e Regenfälle** showers; ~**e Schneefälle** snow showers

**Schauer·geschichte** *die* horror story

**schauerlich** **1** *Adj.* **A** *(schauererregend)* horrifying; ghastly; **B** *(ugs.: fürchterlich)* terrible *(coll.)*; dreadful *(coll.)*. **2** *adv.* **A** *(ugs.: fürchterlich)* dreadfully *(coll.)*, terribly *(coll.)*; **ein ~ gemusterter Teppich** a hideously patterned carpet; **B** *(überaus)* terribly *(coll.)*; dreadfully *(coll.)*

**Schauer·roman** *der* Gothic novel

**Schaufel** /'ʃaufl/ *die;* ~, ~**n** **A** shovel; *(für Mehl usw.)* scoop; *(Kehrschaufel)* dustpan; *(vom ~rad, Mühlrad)* paddle; **zwei ~n Erde** two shovelfuls of soil; **B** *(Jägerspr.: vom Geweih)* palm

**schaufeln** /'ʃaufln/ *tr. V.* shovel; dig ‹hole, grave, trench, etc.›

**Schaufel-:** ~**rad** *das* paddle wheel; ~**rad·dampfer** *der* paddle steamer; ~**rad·bagger** *der* bucket excavator

**Schau·fenster** *das* shop window

**Schaufenster-:** ~**auslage** *die* window display; ~**bummel** *der* window shopping expedition; **einen ~bummel machen** go window shopping; ~**dekorateur** *der,* ~**dekorateurin** *die* ▶ 159 window dresser; ~**puppe** *die* mannequin

**Schau-:** ~**flug** *der* air display; *(von einem Flugzeug)* aerobatics demonstration; ~**geschäft** *das* show business *no art.;* ~**kampf** *der (Boxen)* exhibition fight; ~**kasten** *der* display case; showcase

**Schaukel** /'ʃaukl/ *die;* ~, ~**n** **A** swing; **B** *(bes. südd.: Wippe)* see-saw

**schaukeln** **1** *itr. V.* **A** swing; *(im Schaukelstuhl)* rock; **auf einem Stuhl ~:** rock one's chair backwards and forwards; **B** *(sich hin und her bewegen)* sway [to and fro]; *(sich auf und ab bewegen)* ‹ship, boat› pitch and toss; ‹vehicle› bump [up and down]; **C** *(unpers.)* **auf der Überfahrt/in dem klapprigen Bus hat es ganz schön geschaukelt** the boat pitched and tossed quite a bit during the crossing/it was a pretty bumpy ride in the rickety bus.
**2** *tr. V.* **A** rock; **ein Kind auf den Knien ~:** dandle a child on one's knee; **B** *(ugs.: fahren)* take; **jmdn. durch die Gegend ~:** drive sb. round the area; **C** *(ugs.: bewerkstelligen)* manage; **wir werden die Sache schon ~:** we'll manage it somehow

**Schaukel-:** ~**pferd** *das* rocking horse; ~**stuhl** *der* rocking chair

**schau-, Schau-:** ~**laufen** *das;* ~**s** *(Eislauf)* exhibition skating *no art.;* ~**lustig** *Adj.* curious; ~**lustige** *der/die; adj. Dekl.* curious onlooker

**Schaum** /ʃaum/ *der;* ~**s, Schäume** /'ʃɔymə/ **A** foam; *(von Seife usw.)* lather; *(von Getränken, Suppen usw.)* froth; **etw. zu ~ schlagen** *(Kochk.)* beat sth. until frothy; **den ~ von etw. abschöpfen** *(Kochk.)* skim sth.; **~ schlagen** *(fig. ugs.)* talk big; **B** *(Geifer)* foam; froth; **~ vor dem Mund haben** *(auch fig.)* foam *or* froth at the mouth

**Schaum·bad** *das* **A** *(Badezusatz)* bubble bath; **B** *(Wannenbad)* bubble *or* foam bath

**schäumen** /'ʃɔymən/ **1** *itr. V.* **A** *(Schaum bilden)* foam; froth; ‹soap etc.› lather; ‹beer, fizzy drink, etc.› froth [up]; **B** *(mit Wasser)* produce lather; **stark/schwach ~:** produce a large amount of/little lather; **eine stark ~de Zahnpasta** a very frothy toothpaste; **C** *(wütend sein)* fume; **vor Wut ~:** fume with anger. **2** *tr. V. (Technik)* foam ‹plastics, concrete, etc.›; **geschäumter Kunststoff** foamed plastic

**Schaum-:** ~**gebäck** *das* meringues *pl.;* ~**gummi** *der* foam rubber

**schaumig** *Adj.* frothy ‹drink, dessert, etc.›; sudsy, lathery ‹water›; **Butter und Zucker ~ rühren** beat butter and sugar until fluffy

**Schaum-:** ~**krone** *die* **A** *(auf Wellen)* white crest; **B** *(auf Bier)* head [of froth]; ~**schläger** *der* **A** *(abwertend)* boaster; **B** ⇒ **Schneebesen**; ~**schlägerei** *die (abwertend)* boasting; ~**schlägerin** *die* ⇒ ~**schläger A**; ~**stoff** *der* [plastic] foam; ~**wein** *der* sparkling wine

**Schau-:** ~**platz** *der* scene; **direkt vom ~platz berichten** give an on-the-spot report; ~**prozess,** *~**prozeß** *der* show trial

**schaurig** /'ʃaurɪç/ **1** *Adj.* **A** *(furchtbar)* dreadful; frightful; *(unheimlich)* eerie; **eine ~e Geschichte** a blood-curdling story; **B** *(ugs.: grässlich, geschmacklos)* hideous; dreadful *(coll.)*. **2** *adv.* **A** *(fürchterlich)* dreadfully; *(unheimlich)* eerily; **B** *(ugs.: grässlich, geschmacklos)* hideously; horribly *(coll.)*; **C** *(ugs.: überaus)* dreadfully *(coll.)*

**schau-, Schau-:** ~**spiel** *das* **A** *(Drama)* drama *no art.;* **B** *(ernstes Stück)* play; **C** *(geh.: Anblick)* spectacle; ~**spieler** *der* ▶ 159 *(auch fig.)* actor; ~**spielerei** *die* **A** *(Beruf)* acting *no art.;* **B** *(fig. ugs.: das Sichverstellen)* play-acting; ~**spielerin** *die (auch fig.)* ▶ 159 actress; ~**spielerisch** **1** *Adj.* acting ‹career›; **eine großartige ~spielerische Leistung** a great piece of acting; **eine ~spielerische Begabung** a gift of *or* talent for acting. **2** *adv.* **etw. ~spielerisch darstellen** act sth.; **sie ist ~spielerisch begabt** she has acting talent

**schauspielern** *itr. V. (ugs.)* **A** *(als Schauspieler)* act; **B** *(fig.)* play-act

**Schauspiel-:** ~**führer** *der* theatre goer's guide; ~**haus** *das* theatre; playhouse; ~**kunst** *die* dramatic art

**Schausteller** /-ʃtɛlɐ/ *der;* ~**s,** ~ ▶ 159 showman

**Schaustellerin** *die;* ~, ~**nen** ▶ 159 showwoman

**Schau-:** ~**tafel** *die* illustrated chart; ~**turnen** *das* gymnastic display

**Scheck** /ʃɛk/ *der;* ~**s,** ~**s** ▶ 337 cheque

**Scheck·buch** *das (veralt.)* chequebook

**Schecke**[1] /'ʃɛkə/ *der;* ~**n,** ~**n** *(Pferd)* piebald; *(Rind)* mottled bull

**Schecke**[2] *die;* ~, ~**n** *(Pferd)* piebald; *(Rind)* mottled cow

**Scheckheft** *das* chequebook

**scheckig** *Adj.* **A** ⇒ **gescheckt**; **B** *(voller Flecken)* blotchy ‹face, skin, etc.›; **sich ~ lachen** *(ugs.)* laugh oneself silly

**Scheck·karte** *die* ▶ 337 cheque card

**scheel** /ʃe:l/ *(ugs.)* **1** *Adj.* disapproving; *(misstrauisch)* suspicious; *(neidisch)* envious; jealous. **2** *adv.* disapprovingly; *(misstrauisch)* suspiciously; *(neidisch)* enviously; jealously

**Scheffel** /'ʃɛfl/ *der;* ~**s,** ~: bushel; ⇒ *auch* **Licht**

**scheffeln** *tr. V. (ugs.)* rake in *(coll.)* ‹money, profits, etc.›; pile up, accumulate ‹medals, awards, etc.›

**scheffel·weise** *Adv. (ugs.)* by the sackful; in large quantities; **~ Geld haben/verdienen** have/earn stacks of money *(coll.)*

**Scheibchen** /'ʃaipçən/ *das;* ~**s,** ~ *(von Fleisch, Brot usw.)* [small] slice; *(aus Kunststoff, Metall usw.)* [small] disc

**Scheibe** /'ʃaibə/ *die;* ~, ~**n** **A** *(flacher, runder Gegenstand)* disc; *(Sportjargon: Puck)* puck; *(Schieß~)* target; *(Wähl~)* dial; **B** *(abgeschnittene ~)* slice; **etw. in ~n schneiden** slice sth. up; cut sth. [up] into slices;

S

**sich** (*Dat.*) **von jmdm./etw. eine ~ abschneiden können** (*fig.*) be able to learn a thing or two from sb./sth.; **... in ~n** slices of *or* sliced ...; (C) (*Glas~*) pane [of glass]; (*Fenster~*) [window] pane; (*Windschutz~*) windscreen (*Brit.*); windshield (*Amer.*); (*Spiegel~*) glass; **die ~n des Wagens herunterdrehen** wind down the car windows; (D) (*ugs.: Schallplatte*) disc; record

**Scheiben-: ~bremse** *die* (*Technik*) disc brake; **~gardine** *die* net curtain; **~honig** *der* (A) comb honey; (B) ⇒ **~kleister**; **~kleister** *der* (*ugs. verhüll.*) **~kleister!** blast [it]! (*coll.*); damn it! (*coll.*); **so ein ~kleister!** what a blasted nuisance *or* mess!; **~rad** *das* disc wheel; **~schießen** *das*; **~~s** (*Milit.*, *Sport*) target-shooting; **~waschanlage** *die* (*Kfz-W.*) windscreen washer system *or* unit; **~wischer** *der* windscreen wiper

**Scheich** /ʃaiç/ *der*; **~[e]s**, **~s** *od.* **~e** (A) sheikh; (B) (*ugs.: Freund*) guy (*coll.*); bloke (*Brit. sl.*)

**Scheichtum** *das*; **~s**, **Scheichtümer** /-ty:mɐ/ sheikhdom

**Scheide** /ˈʃaidə/ *die*; **~**, **~n** (A) (*Waffen~*) sheath; (*des Schwerts, Säbels*) scabbard; sheath; (B) ▶ **471** (*Anat.*) vagina

**scheiden** ❶ *unr. tr. V.* (A) dissolve ‹marriage›; divorce ‹married couple›; **eine geschiedene Frau** a divorced woman; a divorcée; **sich [von jmdm.] ~ lassen** get divorced *or* get a divorce [from sb.]; **sie lässt sich nicht [von ihm] ~:** she won't give him a divorce; **ich bin [schuldig/unschuldig] geschieden** I am divorced [and I was the guilty/innocent party]; (B) (*geh.: trennen*) divide; separate; **von dem Moment an waren wir geschiedene Leute** from that moment on, we went our separate ways; **wir sind geschiedene Leute!** you and I must part; (C) (*geh.: unter~*) distinguish; (D) (*bes. Chemie*) separate; extract.

❷ *unr. itr. V.*; *mit sein* (*geh.*) (A) (*auseinander gehen*) part; (B) (*sich entfernen*) depart; leave; **von jmdm. ~:** part from sb.; **aus dem Dienst/Amt ~:** retire from service/one's post *or* office; **aus dem Leben ~:** depart this life.

❸ *unr. refl. V.* (*sich unter~*) diverge; differ; ⇒ *auch* **Geist** D

**Scheide·weg** *der*: *in* **am** *od.* **an einem ~ stehen** face a crucial decision

**Scheidung** *die*; **~**, **~en** (A) (*Ehe~*) divorce; **die ~ einreichen** file [a petition] for divorce; **die ~ aussprechen** grant the divorce; **in ~ leben** be in the process of getting a divorce; (B) (*Unter~*) distinction

**Scheidungs-: ~grund** *der* grounds *pl.* for divorce; **sie war der ~grund** they got divorced because of her; **~klage** *die* petition for divorce; **~urkunde** *die* divorce certificate

**Schein** /ʃain/ *der*; **~[e]s**, **~e** (A) (*Licht~*) light; **der ~ des brennenden Hauses/der sinkenden Sonne** the glow of the burning house/setting sun; (B) (*An~*) appearances *pl.*, *no art.*; (*Täuschung*) pretence; **den ~ wahren** keep up appearances; **der ~ spricht gegen ihn** appearances are against him; **der ~ trügt** appearances are deceptive; **~ und Wirklichkeit** *od.* **Sein** appearances and reality; **etw. nur zum ~ tun** [only] pretend to do sth.; make a show of doing sth.; (C) (*Bescheinigung*) receipt; (*vom Arzt*) doctor's certificate; (*Hochschulw.*) certificate; (D) ▶ **337** (*Geld~*) note

**Schein·argument** *das* spurious argument

**scheinbar** ❶ *Adj.* (*nicht wirklich*) apparent; seeming. ❷ *adv.* (A) (*nicht wirklich*) seemingly; (B) (*ugs.*) ⇒ **anscheinend**

**Schein·blüte** *die* (A) (*Bot.*) composite flower; (B) (*fig.*) illusory boom

**scheinen** *unr. itr. V.* (A) (*Helligkeit ausstrahlen*) shine; (B) (*den Eindruck erwecken*) seem; appear; **es scheint, dass .../als ob ...** it appears that .../as if ...; **mir scheint, [dass] ...** it seems *or* appears to me that ...; **wie es scheint ...** apparently; **er kommt scheints nicht mehr** (*ugs.*) it doesn't look as though he's coming now; **sie schienen es zufrieden zu sein** (*veralt.*) they seemed to be satisfied *or* happy with it

**schein-, Schein-: ~gefecht** *das* (*auch fig.*) mock fight *or* battle; **~heilig** ❶ *Adj.* (*heuchlerisch*) hypocritical; (*Nichtwissen vortäuschend*) innocent; ❷ *adv.* (*heuchlerisch*) hypocritically; (*Nichtwissen vortäuschend*) innocently; **~heiligkeit** *die* hypocrisy; **~schwangerschaft** *die* (*Med.*) false pregnancy; **~tod** *der* (*Med.*) apparent death; **~tot** *Adj.* (A) (*Med.*) apparently *or* seemingly dead; (B) (*salopp: alt*) with one foot in the grave *postpos.*; **~tot sein** have one foot in the grave; **~welt** *die* illusory *or* unreal world; **~werfer** *der* floodlight; (*am Auto*) headlight; (*im Theater, Museum usw.*) spotlight; (*Suchscheinwerfer*) searchlight; **~werfer·licht** *das* floodlight; (*des Autos*) headlights *pl.*; (*im Theater, Museum usw.*) spotlight [beam]; (*des Suchscheinwerfers*) searchlight [beam]; **im ~werferlicht [der Öffentlichkeit] stehen** be in the [public] spotlight

**scheiß-, Scheiß-** (*derb*) bloody (*Brit. sl.*)

**Scheiß** /ʃais/ *der*; **~** (*salopp*) shit *no indef. art.* (*coarse*); crap *no indef. art.* (*coarse*); **so ein ~!** oh, shit! (*coarse*); **~ machen** (*Fehler machen*) make a bloody mess (*Brit. sl.*); (*unklug handeln*) act in a bloody silly way (*Brit. sl.*)

**Scheiß·dreck** *der* (*derb*) (A) (*Kot*) shit (*coarse*); crap (*coarse*); (B) (*Blödsinn, Minderwertiges*) shit *no indef. art.* (*coarse*); crap *no indef. art.* (*coarse*); (*Angelegenheiten*) bloody (*Brit.*) *or* damned business (*sl.*); **red keinen ~!** don't talk carp! (*coarse*); **das geht dich einen ~ an** that's none of your bloody business (*Brit. sl.*); **einen ~ werde ich tun** like hell I will (*coll.*)

**Scheiße** /ˈʃaisə/ *die*; **~** (*derb*) (*auch fig.*) shit (*coarse*); crap (*coarse*); **[bis zum Hals] in der ~ sitzen** *od.* **stecken** (*fig.*) be in the shit (*coarse*); be up shit creek (*coarse*); **der Film ist große ~** (*fig.*) the film is a load of shit *or* crap (*coarse*); **verdammte/schöne ~!** shit (*coarse*); bloody hell (*Brit. sl.*)

**scheiß·egal** *Adj.*: *in* **~ sein** not matter a damn (*sl.*); **das ist mir ~:** I don't give a damn (*sl.*) *or* (*coarse*) shit; **das kann dir doch ~ sein** you needn't give a damn (*sl.*) *or* (*coarse*) shit about that

**scheißen** *unr. itr. V.* (*derb*) (A) (*den Darm entleeren*) [have *or* (*Amer.*) take a] shit (*coarse*); crap (*coarse*); have a crap (*coarse*); **in die Hose ~:** shit one's pants (*coarse*); **auf jmdn./etw. ~** (*fig.*) not give a shit (*coarse*) *or* (*sl.*) damn about sb./sth.; **wir ~ auf ihn/drauf** (*fig.*) to hell with him/with it/that (*coll.*); (B) **[einen] ~** (*eine Blähung entweichen lassen*) fart (*coarse*)

**Scheißer** *der*; **~s**, **~** (A) (*derb*) bastard (*coll.*); shithead (*coarse*); (B) (*salopp: unbedeutender Mensch*) arsehole (*Brit. coarse*); asshole (*Amer. coarse*); (C) (*fam.: Kosewort*) monkey

**scheiß-, Scheiß-: ~freundlich** *Adj.*, *adv.* (*derb*) as nice as pie; **~haufen** *der* (*derb*) pile of shit (*coarse*); **~haus** *das* (*derb*) bog (*sl.*); shithouse (*coarse*); **~kerl** *der* (*derb*) bastard (*coll.*); **~vornehm** *Adj.* (*derb*) bloody (*Brit. sl.*) *or* (*coll.*) damn posh

**Scheit** /ʃait/ *das* **~[e]s**, **~e** *od.* **~er** ⇒ **Holzscheit**

**Scheitel** /ˈʃaitl̩/ *der*; **~s**, **~** (A) parting; (*geh.: Haar*) hair; **einen ~ ziehen** make a parting; (B) (*oberste Stelle*) top of one's head; **vom ~ bis zur Sohle** from head to toe; (C) (*höchster Punkt*) vertex; (D) (*Math.: bei Winkel*) apex; vertex; (E) (*Math.: bei Kurve*) vertex

**scheiteln** *tr. V.* part ‹hair›

**Scheitel-: ~punkt** *der* vertex; **~winkel** *der* (*Math.*) vertically opposite angle

**Scheiter·haufen** *der*: **auf dem ~ sterben/verbrannt werden** die/be burned at the stake; **einen ~ für die Hexe errichten** build a pile of wood on which the witch is to be burnt

**scheitern** /ˈʃaitɐn/ *itr. V.*; *mit sein* fail; ‹talks, marriage› break down; ‹plan, project› fail, fall through; **an jmdm./etw. ~:** fall through *or* fail because of sb./sth.; **die Partei scheiterte an der Fünfprozentklausel** the party was defeated by the five-per-cent clause; **jmds. Pläne zum Scheitern bringen** thwart *or* frustrate sb.'s plans; **zum Scheitern verurteilt sein** be doomed to failure; **eine gescheiterte Existenz sein** be a failure

**Schekel** /ˈʃeːkl/ *der*; **~s**, **~** ▶ **337** shekel

**Schelde** /ˈʃɛldə/ *die*; **~:** Schelde [tributary]

**Schelf** /ʃɛlf/ *der od. das*; **~s**, **~e** (*Geogr.*) continental shelf

**Schellack** /ˈʃɛlak/ *der*; **~s**, **~e** shellac

**Schelle** /ˈʃɛlə/ *die*; **~**, **~n** (A) bell; (B) *Pl.* (*Spielkartenfarbe*) bell; ⇒ *auch* **Pik**[2]

**schellen** *itr. V.* (*westd.*) ring; **an der Tür dreimal ~:** ring the [door] bell three times; **nach jmdm. ~:** ring for sb.; **es schellt** the bell is ringing

**Schellen-: ~baum** *der* Turkish crescent; pavillon chinois; **~kranz** *der* tambourine (*without drumskin*); **~trommel** *die* tambourine

**Schell·fisch** *der* cod

**Schell·kraut** *das*: **[großes] ~:** [greater] celandine

**Schelm** /ʃɛlm/ *der*; **~[e]s**, **~e** rascal; rogue

**Schelmen-: ~roman** *der* (*Literaturw.*) picaresque novel; **~streich** *der*, **~stück** *das* roguish prank

**Schelmerei** *die*; **~**, **~en** (A) (*Eigenschaft*) roguishness; roguery; (B) roguish prank

**Schelmin** *die*; **~**, **~nen** rascal; rogue

**schelmisch** ❶ *Adj.* roguish; mischievous. ❷ *adv.* roguishly; mischievously

**Schelte** /ˈʃɛltə/ *die*; **~**, **~n** (*geh.*) scolding; **~ bekommen** be given *or* get a scolding; **sei pünktlich, sonst gibt es ~:** be punctual, otherwise you'll get a scolding

**schelten** (*bes. südd.*, *sonst geh.*) ❶ *unr. itr. V.* **auf** *od.* **über jmdn./etw. ~:** moan about sb./sth.; **[mit jmdm.] ~:** scold [sb.]. ❷ *unr. tr. V.* (A) (*tadeln*) scold; (B) (*geh.: nennen*) call

**Schelt·wort** *das*; *Pl.* **~~e** (*geh.*) oath

**Schema** /ˈʃeːma/ *das*; **~s**, **~s** *od.* **~ta** *od.* **Schemen** (A) (*Muster*) pattern; **sie lässt sich in kein ~ pressen** (*fig.*) she does not fit into any pattern *or* mould; ⇒ *auch* **F**; (B) (*Skizze*) diagram

**schematisch** ❶ *Adj.* (A) (*einem Schema folgend*) diagrammatic; (B) (*mechanisch*) mechanical. ❷ *adv.* (A) (*als Schema*) in diagram form; (B) (*mechanisch*) mechanically

**schematisieren** *tr. V.* (A) schematize; **etw. schematisiert darstellen** describe sth. by means of a simple formula; (B) (*vereinfachen*) simplify

**Schematisierung** *die*; **~**, **~en** (A) schematization; (B) (*Vereinfachung*) simplification

**Schemel** /ˈʃeːml/ *der*; **~s**, **~** (A) (*Hocker*) stool; (B) (*südd.: Fußbank*) footstool

**Schemen**[1] ⇒ **Schema**

**Schemen**[2] /ˈʃeːmən/ *der od. das*; **~s**, **~:** shadowy figure

**schemenhaft** ❶ *Adj.* shadowy. ❷ *adv.* **etw. ~ erkennen/sehen** make out/see only the outline *or* silhouette of sth.

**Schenke** /ˈʃɛŋkə/ *die*; **~**, **~n** pub (*Brit.*); bar (*Amer.*); (*bes. auf dem Lande*) inn

**Schenkel** /ˈʃɛŋkl/ *der*; **~s**, **~** (A) ▶ **471** (*Ober~*) thigh; **sich** (*Dat.*) **auf die ~ schlagen** slap one's thigh; **dem Pferd die ~ geben** press one's horse on; (B) (*Math.*) side; (C) (*von einer Zange, Schere*) shank; (*vom Zirkel*) leg

**Schenkel-: ~bruch** *der* ▶ **474** (*Med.*) fracture of the femur; **~druck** *der*; *Pl.* **~drücke**, **~hilfe** *die* (*Reiten*) knee pressure *no indef. art.*

**schenken** ❶ *tr. V.* (A) (*geben*) give; **jmdm. etw. [zum Geburtstag] ~:** give sb. sth. *or* sth. to sb. [as a birthday present *or* for his/her birthday]; **etw. geschenkt bekommen** be given sth. [as a present]; **sich gegenseitig etw. ~:** give each other presents; exchange

*old spelling (see note on page 1707)

S

presents; **den Rest des Geldes schenke ich dir** you can keep the rest of the money; **ich möchte nichts geschenkt haben** I don't want any presents; (*bevorzugt werden*) I don't want to be given special *or* preferential treatment; **das möchte ich nicht geschenkt haben, das wäre mir geschenkt zu teuer** (*ugs.*) I wouldn't want that if it was given to me; **das ist ja geschenkt!** (*ugs.*) it's a gift!; **geschenkt ist geschenkt** a gift is a gift; **sie schenkte ihm fünf Kinder** (*fig. geh.*) she bore him five children; ⇒ *auch* **Gaul**; **B** (*verleihen*) give; **C** (*ugs.: erlassen*) **jmdm./sich etw. ~:** spare sb./oneself sth.; **ihr ist im Leben nichts geschenkt worden** she has never had it easy in life; **D** **jmdm./einer Sache Beachtung/Aufmerksamkeit ~:** give sb./sth. one's attention; **jmdm. das Leben ~:** spare sb.'s life; **einem Kind das Leben ~** (*geh.*) give birth to a child; **E** (*geh. veralt.: eingießen*) pour. ❷ *refl. V.* (*ugs.: erlassen*) **sich** (*Dat.*) **etw. ~:** give sth. a miss; **deine Ausreden kannst du dir ~:** you can save your excuses. ❸ *itr. V.* give presents *or* gifts

**Schenker** *der;* **~s, ~, Schenkerin** *die;* **~, ~nen** **A** giver; **B** (*Rechtsspr.*) donator

**Schenkung** *die;* **~, ~en** (*Rechtsw.*) gift

**scheppern** /ˈʃɛpɐn/ *itr. V.* (*ugs.*) clank; ‹bell› clang; **es hat gescheppert** there was a clatter *or* clanking; (*beim Autounfall*) there was a smash *or* crash; (*es gab eine Ohrfeige*) he/she got a box on the ears

**Scherbe** /ˈʃɛrbə/ *die;* **~, ~n** fragment; (*archäologischer Fund*) [pot]sherd; **die ~n zusammenkehren** sweep up the [broken] pieces; **die ~n des Tellers/Spiegels** the fragments *or* [broken] pieces of the plate/mirror; **beim Spülen hat es ~n gegeben** something got broken during the washing-up; **es gab ~n** (*fig.*) sparks flew; **in tausend ~n zerspringen** be smashed to smithereens; **die ~n ihrer Ehe** (*fig.*) the shattered remains of their marriage; **~n bringen Glück** (*Spr.*) break a thing, mend your luck

**Scherben-: ~gericht** *das* ostracism *no art.*; **ein ~gericht über jmdn. veranstalten** (*fig.*) judge sb. with unnecessary harshness; **~haufen** *der* pile of broken fragments *or* pieces; (*fig.*) shattered remains

**Schere** /ˈʃeːrə/ *die;* **~, ~n** **A** (*Werkzeug*) scissors *pl.*; **eine ~:** a pair of scissors; **B** (*Zool.*) claw; **C** (*Turnen*) scissors

**scheren¹** *unr. tr. V.* **A** crop; (*von Haar befreien*) shear, clip ‹sheep›; clip ‹dog, horse, etc.›; **sich** (*Dat.*) **den Bart ~** (*veralt.*) trim one's beard; (*abrasieren*) shave one's beard; **B** (*Textilind.*) shear; **C** (*kürzen*) cut, mow ‹lawn›; clip, trim ‹hedge, bush, etc.›

**scheren²** *tr., refl. V.* **sich um jmdn./etw. nicht ~:** not care about sb./sth.; **es schert ihn [herzlich] wenig** *od.* **nicht im Geringsten** he could not care less *or* in the least

**scheren³** *refl. V.* **scher dich in dein Zimmer** go *or* get [off] to your room; **~ Sie sich an die Arbeit/in Ihr Büro** get to work/[off] to your office; **sich ins Bett ~:** get [off] to bed; ⇒ *auch* **Henker** B; **Teufel**

**Scheren-: ~gitter** *das* [folding] grille; **~griff** *der* (*Turnen*) scissors hold; **~schlag** *der* (*Fußball*) scissors kick; **~schleifer** *der*, **~schleiferin** *die* knife grinder; **~schnitt** *der* silhouette

**Schererei** *die;* **~, ~en** (*ugs.*) trouble *no pl.*

**Scherflein** /ˈʃɛrflain/ *das;* **~s, ~** (*geh.*) mite; **[s]ein ~ [zu etw.] beitragen** *od.* **beisteuern** make one's/a little contribution [to sth.]

**Scherge** /ˈʃɛrgə/ *der;* **~n, ~n** (*geh.*) henchman

**Scher-: ~messer** *das* [cutting] blade; **~sprung** *der* (*bes. Turnen*) scissors jump

**Scherung** *die;* **~, ~en** **A** (*Math.*) shearing; **B** (*Mechanik*) shear[ing]

**Scherz** /ʃɛrts/ *der;* **~es, ~e** joke; **seine ~e mit jmdm. treiben** play jokes on sb.; **er versteht keinen ~:** he can't take a joke; **mach keine ~e** you must be joking; **seine ~e über jmdn./etw. machen** make *or* crack jokes about sb./sth.; **etw. aus** *od.* **zum ~ sagen** say sth. as a joke *or* in jest; **... und solche** *od.* **ähnliche ~e** (*ugs.*) ... and what have you (*coll.*); **~ beiseite** joking aside *or* apart; **[ganz] ohne ~** (*ugs.*) no kidding (*coll.*)

**Scherz·artikel** *der* joke article

**scherzen** *itr. V.* joke; **mit etw.** *od.* **über etw.** (*Akk.*) **~:** joke about sth.; **Sie belieben zu ~** (*geh., oft iron.*) you jest; **ich scherze nicht** I'm not joking; **mit jmdm./etw. ist nicht zu ~:** sb./sth. is not to be trifled with

**Scherz-: ~frage** *die* riddle; **~gedicht** *das* humorous poem

**scherzhaft** ❶ *Adj.* jocular; joking *attrib.* ❷ *adv.* jocularly; jokingly; **etw. ~ sagen/meinen** say/mean sth. as a joke *or* in fun

**Scherzo** /ˈskɛrtso/ *das;* **~s, ~s** *od.* **Scherzi** (*Musik*) scherzo

**Scherz·wort** *das; Pl.* **~~e** joke; witticism

**schesen** /ˈʃeːzn̩/ *itr. V.; mit sein* (*bes. nordd.*) rush

**scheu** /ʃɔy/ ❶ *Adj.* (*schüchtern*) shy; timid ‹animal›; (*ehrfürchtig*) awed; **~ machen** frighten ‹animal›; ⇒ *auch* **Pferd**. ❷ *adv.* **A** (*schüchtern*) shyly; **B** (*von Tieren*) timidly

**Scheu** *die;* **~** **A** (*Schüchternheit*) shyness; (*Ehrfurcht*) awe; **voller ~ sein** be very shy *or* timid/be full of awe; **ohne jede ~:** without any inhibitions; **B** (*von Tieren*) timidity

**Scheuche** /ˈʃɔyçə/ *die;* **~, ~n** scarecrow

**scheuchen** *tr. V.* **A** (*treiben*) shoo; drive; **B** (*fig.*) force; **jmdn. zum Arzt/an die Arbeit ~:** make sb. go *or* urge sb. to go to the doctor/to work

**scheuen** ❶ *tr. V.* (*meiden*) shrink from; shun ‹people, light, company, etc.›; **weder Kosten noch Mühe ~:** spare neither expense nor effort; **Arbeit scheue ich nicht** I'm not afraid of work. ❷ *refl. V.* **sich vor etw.** (*Dat.*) **~:** be afraid of *or* shrink from sth. ❸ *itr. V.* ‹horse› shy (**vor** + *Dat.* at)

**Scheuer** *die;* **~, ~n** (*bes. südd.*) barn

**Scheuer-: ~bürste** *die* scrubbing brush; **~lappen** *der* cleaning cloth (*for wiping surfaces*); **~leiste** *die* **A** (*Fußleiste*) skirting [board] (*Brit.*); baseboard (*Amer.*); **B** (*Seew.*) rubbing strake; **~mittel** *das* scouring agent

**scheuern** ❶ *tr., itr. V.* **A** (*reinigen*) scour; scrub; **B** (*reiben*) rub; chafe. ❷ *tr. V.* **A** (*reiben an*) rub; **B** *in* **jmdm. eine ~** (*ugs.*) give sb. a clout; clout sb.; **eine gescheuert kriegen** (*ugs.*) get a clout round the ears (*coll.*). ❸ *refl. V.* (*reiben*) **sich** (*Akk.*) **wund ~:** rub oneself raw; chafe oneself; **sich** (*Dat.*) **das Knie [wund] ~:** rub one's knee raw; chafe one's knee

**Scheuer-: ~pulver** *das* scouring powder; **~sand** *der* scouring sand; **~tuch** *das; Pl.* **~tücher** scouring cloth

**Scheu·klappe** *die* blinker; **~n haben** *od.* **tragen** wear blinkers; be blinkered (*also fig.*)

**Scheune** /ˈʃɔynə/ *die;* **~, ~n** barn

**Scheunen-: ~drescher** *der: in* **wie ein ~drescher essen** *od.* **fressen** (*salopp*) eat like a horse (*coll.*); **~tor** *das* barn door; ⇒ *auch* **dastehen** A

**Scheusal** /ˈʃɔyzal/ *das;* **~s, ~e** *od.* (*ugs.*) **Scheusäler** /ˈʃɔyzɛlɐ/ (*abwertend*) monster

**scheußlich** /ˈʃɔyslɪç/ ❶ *Adj.* **A** dreadful; **B** (*ugs.: äußerst unangenehm*) terrible (*coll.*); dreadful (*coll.*); dreadful (*coll.*), ghastly (*coll.*) ‹weather, taste, smell›. ❷ *adv.* **A** dreadfully; **B** (*ugs.: sehr*) terribly (*coll.*); dreadfully (*coll.*); **sich ~ erkälten** catch a dreadful cold (*coll.*)

**Scheußlichkeit** *die;* **~, ~en** **A** dreadfulness; **B** (*etw. Scheußliches*) dreadful thing; (*Grausamkeit*) atrocity

**Schi** /ʃiː/ *usw.* ⇒ **Ski** *usw.*

**Schicht** /ʃɪçt/ *die;* **~, ~en** **A** (*Lage*) layer; (*Geol.*) stratum; (*von Farbe*) coat; (*sehr dünn*) film; **B** (*Gesellschafts~*) stratum; **breite ~en [der Bevölkerung]** broad sections of the population; **in allen ~en** at all levels of society; **die besitzenden ~en** the propertied classes; **C** (*Abschnitt eines Arbeitstages, Arbeitsgruppe*) shift; **~ haben**, **auf ~ sein** be working one's shift; **er geht morgens zur ~:** he's on the morning shift; **~ arbeiten** work shifts; be on shift work

**Schicht-: ~arbeit** *die* shift work; **~arbeiter** *der*, **~arbeiterin** *die* shift worker

**schichten** *tr. V.* stack; **die Bretter zu einem Stapel ~:** stack the boards [up]

**Schicht-: ~gestein** *das* (*Geol.*) ⇒ **Sedimentgestein**; **~käse** *der: low-fat quark containing a layer of higher-fat quark;* **~stufe** *die* (*Geol.*) cuesta

**Schichtung** *die;* **~, ~en** stacking; (*Geol., Met., Soziol.*) stratification

**schicht-, Schicht-: ~unterricht** *der* teaching *no art.* in shifts; **~wechsel** *der* change of shifts; **~wechsel ist um 6** we/they *etc.* change shifts at 6; **~weise** *Adv.* **A** in layers; layer by layer; (*bei Farben*) in coats; **B** (*in Gruppen*) in shifts

**schick** /ʃɪk/ ❶ *Adj.* **A** stylish; stylish, chic ‹clothes, fashions›; (*elegant*) smart ‹woman, girl, man›; **B** (*ugs.: großartig, toll*) great (*coll.*); fantastic (*coll.*). ❷ *adv.* **A** stylishly; stylishly, smartly ‹furnished, decorated›; **~ frisiert sein** have a fashionable hairstyle *or* (*coll.*) hairdo; **B** (*ugs.: großartig, toll*) **abends sind wir ~ ausgegangen** we had a great evening out (*coll.*)

**Schick** *der;* **~[e]s** **A** style; (*von Frauenmode, Frau*) chic; style; **B** (*oberd., niederd.*) **nun hat** *od.* **kriegt alles wieder seinen ~!** now everything's as it should be

**schicken** ❶ *tr. V.* send; **jmdm. etw. ~, etw. an jmdn. ~:** send sth. to sb.; send sb. sth.; **jmdm. etw. ins Haus ~:** send sth. to sb.'s home; **jmdn. nach Hause/auf** *od.* **in die** *od.* **zur Schule/ins** *od.* **zu Bett/in den Krieg ~:** send sb. home/to school/to bed/to war; **jmdn. einkaufen** *od.* **zum Einkaufen ~:** send sb. to do the shopping. ❷ *itr. V.* (*rufen, holen lassen*) **nach jmdm. ~:** send for sb. ❸ *refl. V.* **A** (*unpers. veralt.: sich ziemen*) be proper *or* fitting; **das schickt sich nicht für eine junge Dame** it does not befit *or* become a young lady; it is not proper for a young lady; **B** (*geduldig ertragen*) **sich in etw.** (*Akk.*) **~:** resign *or* reconcile oneself to sth.

**Schickeria** /ʃɪkəˈriːa/ *die;* **~** (*ugs.*) smart set

**Schicki[micki]** /ˈʃɪkɪ(ˈmɪkɪ)/ *der;* **~s, ~s** (*ugs.*) **A** (*Mensch*) trendy (*coll.*); **B** (*Modisches*) trendy (*coll.*) goods *pl.*/clothes *pl.*/architecture *etc.*

**schicklich** (*veralt.*) ❶ *Adj.* proper; fitting; (*dezent*) seemly. ❷ *adv.* fittingly; (*dezent*) in a seemly way

**Schicksal** /ˈʃɪkzaːl/ *das;* **~s, ~e** **A** (*Geschick, Los*) fate; destiny; (*schweres Los*) fate; **ich habe manche schwere ~e miterlebt** I've witnessed many a hard fate; **[das ist] ~** (*ugs.*) it's just fate; **er hat ein schweres ~ gehabt** fate has been unkind to him; **B** (*höhere Macht*) fate *no art.*; destiny *no art.*; **das ~ hat es mit ihm gut gemeint** fortune smiled on him; **~ spielen** play the role of fate *or* destiny

**-schicksal** *das:* **ein Emigranten~/Flüchtlings~/Behinderten~:** life *or* experiences as an emigré/a refugee/a handicapped person

**schicksalhaft** ❶ *Adj.* fateful. ❷ *adv.* **~ bedingt/verbunden** determined/linked by fate; **sie sind ~ aufeinander angewiesen** their fates are inextricably linked

**schicksals-, Schicksals-: ~drama** *das* (*Literaturw.*) fate drama; **~frage** *die* crucial question; (*Angelegenheit*) fundamental issue; **~gefährte** *der*, **~gefährtin** *die* companion in misfortune; **die drei waren ~gefährten** the three shared the same fate; **~gemeinschaft** *die:* **sie bildeten** *od.* **waren eine ~gemeinschaft** they shared a common fate; **~genosse** *der*, **~genossin** *die* ⇒ **~gefährte**; **~glaube** *der* fatalism; **~göttin** *die* goddess of fate; **die ~göttinnen** the Fates; **~schlag** *der* stroke of fate; **~schwer** *Adj.* momentous ‹day, decision›; **~tragödie** *die* (*Literaturw.*) ⇒ **~drama**

**Schickse** /ˈʃɪksə/ *die;* **~, ~n** (*salopp abwertend*) floozie (*coll.*)

**Schickung** *die;* ~, ~**en** (*geh.*) stroke of fate

**Schiebe-:** ~**dach** *das* sliding roof; sunroof; ~**fenster** *das* sliding window

**schieben** /ˈʃiːbn̩/ **1** *unr. tr. V.* **A** push; push, wheel ‹bicycle, pram, shopping trolley›; (*drängen*) push; shove; **die Lokomotive schob die Waggons auf ein Nebengleis** the locomotive shunted the wagons into a siding; **B** (*stecken*) put; (*gleiten lassen*) slip; **den Riegel vor die Tür** ~: slip the bolt across; **den Ball ins Tor** ~ (*Fußballjargon*) slip the ball into the net; **etw. von einem Tag auf den anderen** ~ (*fig.*) keep putting sth. off from one day to the next; **C** **etw. auf jmdn./etw.** ~: blame sb./sth. for sth.; **die Schuld/die Verantwortung auf jmdn.** ~: put the blame on sb. *or* lay the blame at sb.'s door/lay the responsibility at sb.'s door; **D** (*salopp: handeln mit*) traffic in; push ‹drugs›.
**2** *unr. refl. V.* **A** (*sich zwängen*) **sich durch die Menge** ~: push one's way through the crowd; **B** (*sich bewegen*) move; **ihr Rock schob sich nach oben** her skirt slid up; **sich an die Spitze** ~ (*Sportjargon*) move up to the front.
**3** *unr. itr. V.* **A** push; (*heftig*) push; shove; **B** *mit sein* (*salopp: gehen*) mooch (*coll.*); **C** (*ugs.: mit etw. handeln*) **mit etw.** ~: traffic in sth.; **D** (*Skat*) shove

**Schieber** *der;* ~**s**, ~ **A** (*an einer Tür*) bolt; (*am Ofen*) damper; (*an Rohrleitungen*) sluice valve; **B** (*ugs.: Schwarzhändler*) black marketeer; (*Drogen*~) pusher; (*Waffen*~) gunrunner; **C** (*ugs.: Tanz*) one-step

**Schieberin** *die;* ~, ~**nen** ⇒ **Schieber** B

**Schieber·mütze** *die* ⇒ **Schlägermütze**

**Schiebe-:** ~**tür** *die* sliding door; ~**wand** *die* sliding partition

**Schieb-:** ~**lade** *die* ⇒ **Schublade**; ~**lehre** *die* (*Technik*) vernier [calliper] gauge

**Schiebung** *die;* ~, ~**en** (*ugs.*) **A** (*betrügerisches Geschäft*) shady deal; **B** (*Begünstigung*) pulling strings; (*bei einer Wahl, einem Wettbewerb*) rigging; (*bei einem Wettlauf, -rennen*) fixing; **„[das ist ja]** ~**!", riefen die Zuschauer** the spectators shouted '[it's a] fix!'

**schied** /ʃiːt/ *1. u. 3. Pers. Sg. Prät. v.* **scheiden**

**schiedlich-friedlich** *Adv.* amicably

**Schieds-:** ~**frau** *die* arbitrator; ~**gericht** *das* **A** (*Rechtsw.*) arbitration tribunal; **B** (*Sport*) panel of judges; (*Fechten*) jury; ~**kommission** *die* (*Rechtsw.*) ⇒ ~**gericht** A; ~**mann** *der; Pl.* ~**leute** *od.* ~**männer** arbitrator; ~**richter** *der* ▶ **159** **A** (*Sport*) referee; (*Tennis, Tischtennis, Hockey, Kricket, Federball*) umpire; (*Eislauf, Ski, Schwimmen*) judge; **B** (*Rechtsw.*) arbitrator; ~**richter·ball** *der* (*Fußball*) drop ball; (*Basketball*) jump ball; (*Wasserball*) neutral throw; ~**richterin** *die* ▶ **159** ⇒ ~**richter**; ~**richterlich** *Adj.* **A** (*Sport*) ‹decision, permission, etc.› of the referee/umpire; **B** (*Rechtsw.*) **die** ~**richterliche Entscheidung** the decision of the arbitrator/arbitrators; ~**richtern** *itr., tr. V.* (*Sport*) referee; (*Tennis, Tischtennis, Hockey, Kricket, Federball*) umpire; ~**spruch** *der* (*Rechtsw.*) arbitration decision

**schief** /ʃiːf/ **1** *Adj.* **A** (*schräg*) leaning ‹wall, fence, post›; (*nicht parallel*) crooked; not straight *pred.;* crooked ‹nose›; sloping, inclined ‹surface›; worn[-down] ‹heels›; (*fig.*) wry ‹smile, look›; **eine** ~**e Schulter haben** have one shoulder higher than the other; **er hält den Kopf** ~: he holds his head to one side; **der Schiefe Turm von Pisa** the Leaning Tower of Pisa; **eine** ~**e Ebene** (*Math., Phys.*) an inclined plane; **sich die Absätze** ~ **laufen** *od.* **treten** wear down one's heels on one side; ⇒ *auch* **Bahn** A; **Gesicht** A; **B** (*fig.: verzerrt*) distorted ‹picture, presentation, view, impression›; false ‹comparison›.
**2** *adv.* **A** (*schräg*) **der Baum ist** ~ **gewachsen** the tree has grown crooked *or* hasn't grown straight; **das Bild hängt/der Teppich liegt** ~: the picture/carpet is crooked; **der Tisch steht** ~: the table isn't level; **sich** (*Dat.*) **die Mütze** ~ **aufsetzen** put one's cap on at an angle; **jmdn.** ~ **ansehen** (*ugs.*) look at sb. askance; ~ **gewickelt sein** (*ugs.*) be very much mistaken; ~ **liegen** (*ugs.*) be on the wrong track; ⇒ *auch* **Haussegen**; **B** (*fig.: verzerrt*) **etw.** ~ **darstellen** give a distorted account of sth.

**Schiefer** /ˈʃiːfɐ/ *der;* ~**s** **A** (*Gestein*) slate; **B** (*südd., österr.: Splitter*) splinter

**schiefer-, Schiefer-:** ~**dach** *das* slate roof; ~**grau** *Adj.* slate-grey; ~**tafel** *die* slate

**schief-:** *~**|gehen** ⇒ **gehen** I; *~**gewickelt** ⇒ **schief** 2 A; ~**|lachen** *refl. V.* (*ugs.*) kill oneself laughing (*coll.*); laugh one's head off; *~**|laufen** ⇒ **schief** 1 A, **laufen** 1 K; *~**|liegen** ⇒ **schief** 2 A; *~**|treten** ⇒ **schief** 1 A

**schielen** /ˈʃiːlən/ *itr. V.* **A** squint; have a squint; **leicht/stark** ~: have a slight/pronounced squint; **auf dem rechten Auge** ~: have a squint in one's right eye; **B** (*ugs.: blicken*) look out of the corner of one's eye; **nach etw.** ~: steal a glance at sth.; (*fig.*) have one's eye on sth.; **C** (*ugs.: spähen*) peep; **nach rechts und links** ~: glance right and left

**schien** /ʃiːn/ *1. u. 3. Pers. Sg. Prät. v.* **scheinen**

**Schien·bein** *das* ▶ **471** shinbone; **sich ans** *od.* **am** ~ **stoßen** bang one's shin; **jmdm.** *od.* **jmdn. vor das** ~ **treten** kick sb. on the shin

**Schiene** /ˈʃiːnə/ *die;* ~, ~**n** **A** rail; ~**n legen** lay track; **aus den** ~**n springen** come off the rails; **B** (*Gleit*~) runner; **in einer** ~ **laufen** move on a runner; **C** (*Med.: Stütze*) splint; **D** (*Reiß*~) T-square; **E** (*schmale Leiste*) right-angle moulding; (*in Korbwaren*) rib; **F** (*hist.: Teil der Rüstung*) splint

**-schiene** *die:* **Nord**~**/Süd**~**/Rhein**~: northern/southern/Rhine sector

**schienen** *tr. V.* **jmds. Arm/Bein** ~: put sb.'s arm/leg in a splint/splints; put a splint/splints on sb.'s arm/leg

**Schienen-:** ~**bus** *der* railbus; ~**fahrzeug** *das* track vehicle; ~**strang** *der* [railway] line *or* track; ~**verkehr** *der* rail traffic

**schier**[1] /ʃiːɐ̯/ *Adv.* (*veralt.: geradezu*) well-nigh; almost

**schier**[2] *Adj.* (*bes. nordd.*) pure; (*fig.*) sheer ‹malevolence, stupidity›

**Schierling** /ˈʃiːɐ̯lɪŋ/ *der;* ~**s**, ~**e** hemlock

**Schierlings·becher** *der* cup of hemlock

**Schieß-:** ~**befehl** *der* order to shoot; ~**bude** *die* shooting gallery; ~**buden·figur** *die* target [in a shooting gallery]; **du siehst aus wie eine** ~**budenfigur** (*ugs.*) you look a real clown; ~**eisen** *das* (*ugs.*) shooting iron (*coll.*)

**schießen** /ˈʃiːsn̩/ **1** *unr. itr. V.* **A** shoot; ‹pistol, rifle› shoot, fire; **auf jmdn./etw.** ~: shoot/fire at sb./sth.; **gut/schlecht** ~ ‹person› be a good/bad shot; **es wurde aus dem Fenster geschossen** a shot/shots came from the window; **sie schoss ihm/sich ins Bein** she shot him/herself in the leg; **mit Schrot/einem Pfeil** ~: fire shot/shoot an arrow; **B** (*Fußball*) shoot; **der Stürmer schoss hoch über das Tor** the forward's shot went high over the goal; **C** *mit sein* (*ugs.: schnellen*) shoot; **er schoss vom Stuhl in die Höhe** he shot up out of his chair; **ein Gedanke schoss ihr durch den Kopf** (*fig.*) a thought flashed through her mind; **zum Schießen sein** (*ugs.*) be a scream (*coll.*); **jmdn.** ~ **lassen** (*salopp*) drop sb.; **einen Plan** ~ **lassen** (*salopp*) ditch (*coll.*) *or* drop a plan; **D** *mit sein* (*fließen, heraus*~) gush; (*spritzen*) spurt; **ich spürte, wie mir das Blut in den Kopf schoss** I felt the blood rush to my head; **aus dem Dachstuhl schossen Flammen** flames were shooting from the attic; **E** *mit sein* (*schnell wachsen*) shoot up; (*fig.*) ‹building› spring up; **der Junge ist sehr in die Höhe geschossen** the boy has shot up a lot; **die Preise** ~ **in die Höhe** (*fig.*) prices are shooting up *or* rocketing; **F** (*Drogenjargon*) fix.
**2** *unr. tr. V.* **A** shoot; fire ‹bullet, missile, rocket›; **jmdn./etw. in den Weltraum** ~: launch sb./sth. into space; **an der Schießbude einen Preis** ~: win a prize at the shooting gallery; **jmdn. zum Krüppel** ~: shoot and maim sb.; **B** (*Fußball*) score ‹goal›; **den Ball ins Netz** ~: put the ball in the net; **er schoss seine Mannschaft in Führung** he scored the goal that put his team ahead; **das 3:2** ~: make it 3-2; **C** (*ugs.: fotografieren*) **einige Aufnahmen** ~: take a few snaps

*__schießen|lassen__ ⇒ **schießen** 1 C

**Schießerei** *die;* ~, ~**en** **A** shooting *no indef. art., no pl.;* **B** (*Schusswechsel*) gun battle; **die** ~ **am Ende des Films** the shoot-out at the end of the film

**Schieß-:** ~**gewehr** *das* (*Kinderspr.*) rifle; ~**hund** *der* (*Jägerspr., veralt.: Jagdhund*) gun dog; **aufpassen wie ein** ~**hund** (*ugs.*) be on one's toes; ~**platz** *der* firing range; ~**pulver** *das* gunpowder; **er hat das** ~**pulver [auch] nicht erfunden** (*ugs.*) he's not exactly a genius; ~**scharte** *die* crenel; ~**scheibe** *die* target; ~**sport** *der* shooting *no art.;* ~**stand** *der* **A** shooting range; **B** ⇒ ~**bude**; ~**übung** *die* target practice

**Schiff** /ʃɪf/ *das;* ~**[e]s**, ~**e** **A** ship; **mit dem** *od.* **per** *od.* **zu** ~: by ship *or* sea; ~ **voraus!** ship ahead!; **das** ~ **der Wüste** (*fig.*) the ship of the desert; **B** (*Archit.: Kirchen*~) (*Mittel*~) nave; (*Quer*~) transept; (*Seiten*~) aisle; **C** (*Druckw.*) galley

*__Schiffahrt__ *usw.* ⇒ **Schifffahrt** *usw.*

**schiffbar** *Adj.* ▶ **306** navigable

**Schiffbarmachung** *die;* ~: **seit der** ~ **dieses Flusses** since this river was made navigable

**schiff-, Schiff-:** ~**bau** *der;* shipbuilding *no art.;* ~**bauer** *der;* ~~**s**, ~~, ~**bauerin** *die;* ~~, ~~**nen** ▶ **159** shipbuilder; ~**bruch** *der* (*veralt.*) shipwreck; ~**bruch erleiden** ‹ship› be wrecked; ‹person› be shipwrecked; **[mit etw.]** ~**bruch erleiden** (*fig.*) fail [in sth.]; ~**brüchig** *Adj.* shipwrecked; ~**brüchige** *der/die; adj. Dekl.* shipwrecked man/woman; **die** ~**brüchigen** those shipwrecked

**Schiffchen** *das;* ~**s**, ~ **A** (*Spielzeug*) [little] boat; **B** (*ugs.: Kopfbedeckung*) forage cap; **C** (*Weberei, Handarbeit, Nähen*) shuttle

**schiffen** *itr. V.* **A** *mit sein* (*veralt.: mit dem Schiff fahren*) ship; travel by ship; **B** (*derb: urinieren*) piss (*coarse*); **C** (*unpers. salopp: regnen*) **es schifft** it's pissing down (*sl.*); it's chucking it down (*sl.*)

**Schiffer** *der;* ~**s**, ~, **Schifferin** *die;* ~, ~**nen** boatman/boatwoman; (*eines Lastkahns*) bargee; (*Kapitän[in]*) skipper

**Schiffer-:** ~**klavier** *das* accordion; ~**knoten** *der* seaman's knot; ~**mütze** *die* [peaked] sailor's cap

**Schiff·fahrt** *die* **A** (*Schiffsverkehr*) shipping *no indef. art.;* **die** ~ **einstellen** suspend all shipping movements; **B** (*Schifffahrtskunde*) navigation

**Schifffahrts-:** ~**gesellschaft** *die* shipping company; ~**linie** *die* shipping route; ~**straße** *die*, ~**weg** *der* [navigable] waterway

**Schiffs-:** ~**arzt** *der*, ~**ärztin** *die* ship's doctor; ~**ausrüster** *der;* ~~**s**, ~~, ~**ausrüsterin** *die;* ~~, ~~**nen** ship's chandler; ~**bau** *der;* ⇒ **Schiffbau**; ~**bauch** *der* (*ugs.*) belly of a/the ship; ~**brücke** *die* pontoon bridge

**Schiff·schaukel** *die* swingboat; ~ **fahren** go on a/the swingboat

**Schiffs-:** ~**eigner** *der*, ~**eignerin** *die* shipowner; ~**fahrt** *die* boat trip; (*länger*) cruise; ~**führer** *der*, ~**führerin** *die* ⇒ **Schiffer**; ~**glocke** *die* ship's bell; ~**junge** *der* ▶ **159** ship's boy; ~**ladung** *die* [ship's] cargo; **eine ganze** ~**ladung** an entire shipload; ~**laterne** *die* (*Seemannsspr.*) ship's lantern; ~**makler** *der*, ~**maklerin** *die* shipbroker; ~**modell** *das* model ship; ~**name** *der* ship's name; ~**papiere** *Pl.* ship's papers; ~**passage** *die* passage; ~**reise** *die* voyage; (*Vergnügungsreise*) cruise; ~**rumpf** *der* [ship's] hull; ~**schraube** *die* ship's propeller

*old spelling (see note on page 1707)

or screw; **~taufe** *die* naming of a/the ship; **~verkehr** *der* shipping traffic; **auf dem Fluss war lebhafter** *od.* **reger ~verkehr** the river was busy with traffic; **~zwieback** *der* hard tack; ship's biscuit

**Schiit** /ʃi'i:t/ *der;* **~en, ~en, Schiitin** *die;* **~, ~nen** Shiite

**schiitisch** *Adj.* Shiite

**Schikane** /ʃi'ka:nə/ *die;* **~, ~n** Ⓐ (*Bosheit*) harassment *no indef. art.;* **das ist eine ~:** that amounts to *or* is harassment; **aus reiner ~:** purely in order to harass him/her *etc.;* **Beschimpfungen und ~n** abuse and harassment; Ⓑ *in* **mit allen ~n** (*ugs.*) ‹kitchen, house› with all mod cons (*Brit. coll.*); ‹car, bicycle, stereo› with all the extras; Ⓒ (*Motorsport*) chicane

**schikanieren** *tr. V.* **jmdn. ~:** harass sb.; mess sb. about (*coll.*); **Rekruten/seine Ehefrau ~:** bully recruits/one's wife

**schikanös** /ʃika'nø:s/ ❶ *Adj.* harassing ‹action, measure›; bullying ‹husband, superior officer›; **~e Behandlung** harassment/bullying. ❷ *adv.* **jmdn. ~ behandeln** harass sb.

**Schild**[1] /ʃɪlt/ *der;* **~[e]s, ~e** Ⓐ shield; **jmdn. auf den ~ [er]heben** (*geh.*) (*als Anführer*) make sb. one's leader; (*als Leitbild*) make sb. one's figurehead; **etw./nichts im ~e führen** be up to something/not be up to anything; **etwas gegen jmdn./etw. im ~e führen** be plotting sth. against sb./sth.; Ⓑ (*Wappen~*) shield; escutcheon; Ⓒ ⇒ **Schirm** C

**Schild**[2] *das;* **~[e]s, ~er** (*Verkehrs~*) sign; (*Nummern~*) number plate; (*Namens~*) nameplate; (*Plakat*) placard; (*an einer Mütze*) badge; (*auf Denkmälern, Gebäuden, Gräbern*) plaque; (*Etikett*) label

**Schild-: ~bürger** *der* (*abwertend*) ≈ wise man of Gotham; Gothamite; fool; **~bürgerin** *die* (*abwertend*) Gothamite; fool; **~bürgerstreich** *der* (*abwertend*) act of monumental dim-wittedness; **~drüse** *die* ▶ **471** (*Med.*) thyroid [gland]

**Schilder-: ~brücke** *die* (*Verkehrsw.*) sign gantry; **~haus** *das,* **~häuschen** *das* sentry box

**schildern** /'ʃɪldɐn/ *tr. V.* describe; (*in einer Erzählung*) portray; describe; **die Gräuel dieses Krieges sind kaum zu ~:** the atrocities committed in this war beggar description; ⇒ *auch* **Farbe** B

**Schilderung** *die;* **~, ~en** description; (*von Ereignissen*) account; description; (*in einer Erzählung*) portrayal; description

**Schilder·wald** *der* (*Verkehrsw. abwertend*) maze of traffic signs

**Schild-: ~knappe** *der* (*hist.*) squire; shield-bearer; **~kröte** *die* tortoise; (*Seeschildkröte*) turtle; **~kröten·suppe** *die* turtle soup; **~laus** *die* scale insect; **~patt** *das* tortoiseshell; **~wache** *die* (*veralt.*) sentry; **~wache stehen** stand sentry

**Schilf** /ʃɪlf/ *das;* **~[e]s, ~e** Ⓐ (**~rohr**) reed; Ⓑ (*Röhricht*) reeds *pl.*

**Schilf-: ~dach** *das* roof thatched with reeds; **~gras** *das,* **~rohr** *das* ⇒ **Schilf** A; **~rohr·sänger** *der* sedge warbler

**Schiller-: ~kragen** *der* large open-necked collar; **~locke** *die* Ⓐ (*Gebäck*) cream horn; Ⓑ (*Räucherfisch*) strip of smoked fish (*esp. dogfish*)

**schillern** /'ʃɪlɐn/ *itr. V.* shimmer; **in allen Regenbogenfarben ~:** shimmer with all the colours of the rainbow; **ein ~der Charakter** (*fig.*) an ambivalent character; **ein ~der Begriff** (*fig.*) a shifting concept

**Schilling** /'ʃɪlɪŋ/ *der;* **~s, ~e** ▶ **337** schilling; **das kostet 30 ~:** that costs 30 schillings

**Schillum** /'ʃɪlʊm/ *das;* **~s, ~s** chillum

**schilpen** /'ʃɪlpn̩/ ⇒ **tschilpen**

**schilt** /ʃɪlt/ *3. Pers. Sg. Präsens v.* **schelten**

**Schimäre** /ʃi'mɛ:rə/ *die;* **~, ~n** chimera

**schimärisch** *Adj.* chimerical

**Schimmel** /'ʃɪml̩/ *der;* **~s, ~** Ⓐ (*Belag*) mould; (*auf Leder, Papier*) mildew; Ⓑ (*Pferd*) white horse

**schimmelig** *Adj.* mouldy; mildewy ‹paper, leather›; **~ werden** go mouldy/get covered with mildew

**schimmeln** *itr. V.; auch mit sein* go mouldy; ‹leather, paper› get covered with mildew

**Schimmel·pilz** *der* mould

**Schimmer** /'ʃɪmɐ/ *der;* **~s** Ⓐ (*Schein*) gleam; (*von Perlmutt*) lustre; shimmer; (*von Seide*) shimmer; sheen; (*von Haar*) sheen; (*von Kerzen*) [soft] glow; Ⓑ (*Anflug, Hauch*) glimmer; **noch einen ~ [von] Anstand haben** still have a scrap of decency; **keinen [blassen]** *od.* **nicht den leisesten ~ [von etw.] haben** (*ugs.*) not have the faintest *or* foggiest idea [about sth.] (*coll.*)

**schimmern** *itr. V.* Ⓐ (*matt glänzen*) gleam; ‹water, sea› glisten, shimmer; ‹teeth› glisten; ‹metal› glint, gleam; ‹silk, mother-of-pearl› shimmer; **der Stoff/die Seide schimmert rötlich** the material has a reddish tinge/the silk has a reddish sheen; Ⓑ (*durch~*) show (**durch** through)

**schimmlig** ⇒ **schimmelig**

**Schimpanse** /ʃɪm'panzə/ *der;* **~n, ~n** chimpanzee

**Schimpf** *der;* **~[e]s** (*geh.*) affront; **jmdm. einen ~ antun/zufügen** affront sb.; **mit ~ und Schande** in disgrace

**Schimpfe** *die;* **~** (*ugs.*) **~ bekommen** get an earful (*coll.*)

**schimpfen** ❶ *itr. V.* Ⓐ carry on (*coll.*) (**auf, über** + *Akk.* about); (*meckern*) grumble, moan (**auf, über** + *Akk.* at); Ⓑ (*zurechtweisen*) **mit jmdm. ~:** tell sb. off; scold sb. ❷ *tr. V.* Ⓐ (*bes. md.: aus~*) **jmdn. ~:** tell sb. off; scold sb.; Ⓑ **jmdn. dumm/faul ~:** call sb. stupid/lazy. ❸ *refl. V.* (*spött.: vorgeben zu sein*) **sich Professor/Dichter ~:** call oneself a professor/poet

**Schimpferei** *die;* **~, ~en** (*abwertend*) carrying on (*coll.*); (*Meckerei*) grumbling; moaning; (*das Zurechtweisen*) telling off, scolding (**mit** of)

**schimpflich** (*geh.*) ❶ *Adj.* shameful, disgraceful ‹behaviour, treatment›; dishonourable ‹occupation›; (*entwürdigend*) humiliating ‹defeat, terms, etc.›. ❷ *adv.* shamefully; disgracefully; (*entwürdigend*) humiliatingly

**Schimpf-: ~name** *der* [abusive] nickname; **jmdn. mit ~namen belegen** call sb. names; **~wort** *das; Pl.* **~wörter** (*Beleidigung*) insult; (*derbes Wort*) swear word

**Schindel** /'ʃɪndl̩/ *die;* **~, ~n** shingle

**Schindel·dach** *das* shingle roof

**schinden** /'ʃɪndn̩/ ❶ *unr. tr. V.* Ⓐ maltreat; ill-treat; (*ausbeuten*) slave-drive; **jmdn./ein Tier zu Tode ~:** work sb./an animal to death; Ⓑ (*ugs.: herausschlagen*) **Zeilen ~:** pad as much as possible; fill up space with as little as possible; **[bei jmdm.] Eindruck ~:** make an impression [on sb.]; **Applaus ~ wollen** fish for applause; **Zeit ~:** play for time. ❷ *unr. refl. V.* (*ugs.: sich abplagen*) slave away; **sich mit einer Arbeit ~:** slave away at a job

**Schinder** *der;* **~s, ~** Ⓐ slave driver; Ⓑ (*veralt.: Abdecker*) knacker (*Brit.*)

**Schinderei** *die;* **~, ~en** Ⓐ ill-treatment *no pl.;* (*Ausbeutung*) slave-driving *no pl.;* Ⓑ (*Strapaze, Qual*) struggle; (*Arbeit*) toil

**Schinderin** *die;* **~, ~nen** ⇒ **Schinder** A

**Schind-: ~luder** *das: in* **mit etw. ~luder treiben** (*ugs.*) (*ausbeuten*) take advantage of *or* abuse sth.; (*vergeuden*) squander sth.; **wir dürfen nicht länger mit der Natur ~luder treiben** we must stop this appalling waste of natural resources; **~mähre** *die* (*abwertend*) nag

**Schinken** /'ʃɪŋkn̩/ *der;* **~s, ~** Ⓐ ham; Ⓑ (*ugs.*) (*Buch*) great tome; (*Gemälde*) enormous painting; (*Film, Theaterstück*) epic

**Schinken-: ~brot** *das* slice of bread and ham; (*zugeklappt*) ham sandwich; **~speck** *der* bacon

**Schintoismus** /ʃɪnto'ɪsmʊs/ *der;* **~:** Shintoism *no art.*

**Schippe** /'ʃɪpə/ *die;* **~, ~n** Ⓐ (*nordd., md.: Schaufel*) shovel; **~ und Eimer** bucket and spade; **~ und Handfeger** dustpan and brush; **jmdn. auf die ~ nehmen** (*fam.*) kid sb. (*sl.*); pull sb.'s leg; **dem Tod von der ~ springen** (*ugs.*) escape death by a hair's breadth; Ⓑ (*Kartenspiel*) ⇒ **Pik**[2]; Ⓒ (*ugs.: Flunsch*) **eine ~ ziehen** *od.* **machen** pout

**schippen** *tr. V.* (*nordd., md.*) Ⓐ shovel; Ⓑ (*ausheben*) dig ‹ditch, grave, etc.›

**Schipper** *der;* **~s, ~** (*nordd.*) ⇒ **Schiffer**

**schippern** (*ugs.*) ❶ *itr. V.; mit sein* cruise. ❷ *tr. V.* ship ‹goods, materials›; skipper ‹ship›

**Schirm** /ʃɪrm/ *der;* **~[e]s, ~e** Ⓐ umbrella; brolly (*Brit. coll.*); (*Sonnen~*) sunshade; parasol; Ⓑ (*Lampen~*) shade; Ⓒ (*Mützen~*) peak; Ⓓ (*gegen Licht*) eyeshade; (*Ofen~, Kamin~*) guard; (*Strahlen~*) shield; (*beim Schweißen o. Ä.*) mask; visor; Ⓔ (*Bild~*) screen; Ⓕ (*Schutz*) shield

**Schirm-: ~bild** *das* (*Med.*) X-ray [picture]; **~bild·gerät** *das* (*Med.*) X-ray machine; **~herr** *der* patron; **~herrin** *die* patroness; **~herrschaft** *die* patronage; **die ~herrschaft über etw.** (*Akk.*) **übernehmen** become patron of sth.; **~mütze** *die* peaked cap; **~pilz** *der* parasol mushroom; **~ständer** *der* umbrella stand

**Schirokko** /ʃi'rɔko/ *der;* **~s, ~s** sirocco

**Schisma** /'ʃɪsma/ *das;* **~s, Schismen** *od.* **~ta** (*Kirche, Politik*) schism

**schiss, *schiß** /ʃɪs/ *1. u. 3. Pers. Sg. Prät. v.* **scheißen**

**Schiss, *Schiß** *der;* **Schisses** (*salopp: Angst*) **[vor etw.] ~ haben** be shit-scared [of sth.] (*coarse*); **~ kriegen** get the shits (*coarse*)

**schizoid** /ʃɪtso'i:t/ (*Med.*) ❶ *Adj.* schizoid. ❷ *adv.* **~ veranlagt sein** have schizoid tendencies

**schizophren** /ʃɪtso'fre:n/ (*Med., auch fig.*) ❶ *Adj.* schizophrenic. ❷ *adv.* schizophrenically

**Schizophrenie** *die;* **~, ~n** (*Med., auch fig.*) schizophrenia

**schlabberig** *Adj.* (*ugs.*) Ⓐ (*locker fallend*) baggy ‹clothes›; loose, limp ‹material›; Ⓑ (*abwertend: wässrig*) watery

**schlabbern** /'ʃlabɐn/ ❶ *tr. V.* (*ugs.*) (*schlürfen*) ‹person› slurp; ‹animal› lap up. ❷ *itr. V.* Ⓐ (*abwertend*) slobber; Ⓑ (*schlenkern*) ‹dress› flap; ‹trousers› be baggy

**schlabbrig** *Adj.* ⇒ **schlabberig**

**Schlacht** /ʃlaxt/ *die;* **~, ~en** battle; **die ~ bei** *od.* **von/um X** the battle of/for X; **in die ~ ziehen** go into battle; **sich eine ~ liefern** do battle; **sich eine erbitterte ~ liefern** (*fig.*) fight fiercely; **jmdm. eine ~ liefern** do battle with sb.; **eine ~ schlagen** fight a battle

**Schlacht·bank** *die; Pl.* **Schlachtbänke** slaughtering block; **sich wie ein Lamm zur ~ führen lassen** (*geh.*) let oneself be led like a lamb to the slaughter

**schlachten** *tr.* (*auch itr.*) *V.* slaughter; kill ‹rabbit, chicken, etc.›; **sein Sparschwein ~** (*scherzh.*) raid one's piggy bank

**Schlachtenbummler** /-bʊmlɐ/ *der,* **Schlachtenbummlerin** *die* (*Sportjargon*) away supporter; **die englischen ~:** the visiting English supporters

**Schlachter** *der;* **~s, ~, Schlächter** *der;* **~s, ~** (*nordd.*) ▶ **159** butcher

**Schlachterei** *die;* **~, ~en, Schlächterei** *die;* **~, ~en** Ⓐ (*nordd.: Fleischerei*) butcher's [shop]; Ⓑ (*abwertend: Gemetzel*) slaughter; butchery *no indef. art.*

**Schlacht-: ~feld** *das* battlefield; **auf dem ~feld bleiben** (*veralt. verhüll.*) fall in battle; **das Zimmer sah wie ein ~feld aus** the room looked as if a bomb had hit it; **~fest** *das: feast at which the meat of freshly slaughtered animals, esp. pork, is eaten;* **~haus** *das* slaughterhouse; **~hof** *der* slaughterhouse; abattoir; **~opfer** *das* (*Rel.*) animal sacrifice; **~ordnung** *die* (*Milit. hist.*) battle order; **~plan** *der* (*Milit.*) plan of battle; battle plan; (*fig.*) plan of action; **~platte** *die: dish with assorted cooked meats, sausages, and sauerkraut;* **~reif** *Adj.* ready for slaughtering *postpos.;* **~ross, *~roß** *das* (*veralt.*) warhorse; charger; **ein altes ~ross**

S

(*fig. scherzh.*) an old warhorse; **~schiff** *das* (*Milit.*) battleship; **~tier** *das* animal kept for meat; (*kurz vor der Schlachtung*) animal for slaughter

**Schlachtung** *die;* ~, **~en** slaughter[ing]

**Schlachtvieh** *das* animals *pl.* kept for meat; (*kurz vor der Schlachtung*) animals *pl.* for slaughter

**Schlacke** /ˈʃlakə/ *die;* ~, **~n** **A** cinders *pl.;* (*größere Stücke*) clinker; **B** *Pl.* (*Physiol.: Ballaststoffe*) roughage *sing.;* **C** (*Hochofen~*) slag; **D** (*Geol.: Lava*) slag; clinker

**schlackern** /ˈʃlakɐn/ *itr. V.* (*nordd., westmd.*) **A** (*schlenkern*) ‹dress› flap; ‹bag› dangle; ‹trousers› be baggy; **B** (*wackeln, zittern*) shake; tremble; **mit den Armen ~:** flap one's arms about; ⇒ *auch* **Ohr**

**Schlackwurst** *die* ⇒ **Zervelatwurst**

**Schlaf** /ʃlaːf/ *der;* **~[e]s** sleep; **einen leichten/festen/gesunden ~ haben** be a light/heavy/good sleeper; **keinen ~ finden** (*geh.*) be unable to sleep; **jmdn. um den** *od.* **seinen ~ bringen** ‹worry etc.› give sb. sleepless nights/a sleepless night; ‹noise› stop sb. from sleeping; **jmdn. in den ~ singen/wiegen** sing/rock sb. to sleep; **jmdn. aus dem ~ reißen** wake sb. up with a start; **den ~ des Gerechten schlafen** (*scherzh.*) sleep the sleep of the just; **das kann** *od.* **mache ich im ~** (*fig.*) I can do that with my eyes closed *or* shut; **halb im ~:** half asleep

**Schlaf-:** **~anzug** *der* pyjamas *pl.;* **ein ~anzug** a pair of pyjamas; **~bedürfnis** *das* need for sleep

**Schläfchen** /ˈʃlɛːfçən/ *das;* **~s, ~:** nap; snooze (*coll.*); **ein ~ halten** have a nap *or* (*coll.*) snooze

**Schlafcouch** *die* bed settee; sofa-bed

**Schläfe** /ˈʃlɛːfə/ *die;* ~, **~n** ▶ 471 temple; **er hat/bekommt graue ~n** his hair has gone/is going grey at the temples

**schlafen** ❶ *unr. itr. V.* **A** (*auch fig.*) sleep; **tief** *od.* **fest ~** (*zur Zeit*) be sound asleep; (*gewöhnlich*) sleep soundly; be a sound sleeper; **lange ~:** sleep for a long time; (*am Morgen*) sleep in; **~ gehen** go to bed; **sich ~ legen** lie down to sleep; (*ins Bett gehen*) go to bed; **im Hotel/bei Bekannten ~:** stay in a hotel/with friends; **schlaf gut!** sleep well!; **hast du gut ge~?** did you sleep well?; **schläft sie immer noch?** is she still asleep?; **er schläft noch halb** he's still half asleep; **darüber muss ich noch ~:** I'd like to sleep on it; **~ wie ein Murmeltier** *od.* **Bär** *od.* **Sack** *od.* **Stein** (*ugs.*) sleep like a log *or* top; **bei jmdm. ~:** sleep at sb.'s house/in sb.'s room *etc.;* **mit jmdm. ~** (*verhüll.*) sleep with sb. (*euphem.*); **B** (*ugs.: nicht aufpassen*) be asleep.
❷ *unr. refl. V.* (*unpers.*) **auf dem Sofa schläft es sich gut** the sofa's good to sleep on

**Schläfenbein** *das* ▶ 471 (*Anat.*) temporal bone

**Schlafengehen** *das;* **~s** going *no def. art.* to bed

**Schlafenszeit** *die* bedtime

**Schläfer** /ˈʃlɛːfɐ/ *der;* **~s, ~, Schläferin** *die;* **~, ~nen** sleeper

**schlaff** /ʃlaf/ ❶ *Adj.* **A** (*nicht straff, nicht fest*) slack ‹cable, rope, sail›; flaccid, limp ‹penis›; loose, slack ‹skin›; sagging ‹breasts›; flabby ‹stomach, muscles›; **die Fahne war ~:** the flag hung limply; **B** (*schlapp, matt*) limp ‹body, hand, handshake›; shaky ‹knees›; feeble ‹blow›; **C** (*abwertend: träge*) lethargic; **~e Nachfrage** (*fig.*) weak demand. ❷ *adv.* **A** (*locker, nicht straff*) slackly; **das Segel hing ~:** the sail hung limply; **ihre Brüste hingen ~:** her breasts sagged; **B** (*schlapp, matt*) limply; **er saß ~ herum** (*ugs.*) he sat around listlessly

**Schlaffheit** *die;* **~:** limpness; (*der Haut*) looseness, slackness; (*des Bauches, der Muskeln*) flabbiness

**Schlaf-:** **~gast** *der* overnight guest; **~gelegenheit** *die* place to sleep; **~gewohnheiten** *Pl.* sleeping habits

*old spelling (see note on page 1707)

**Schlafittchen** /ʃlaˈfɪtçən/ *das:* in **jmdn. am** *od.* **beim ~ kriegen** *od.* **fassen** (*ugs.*) collar *or* (*coll.*) nab sb.

**schlaf-, Schlaf-:** **~krankheit** *die* sleeping sickness; **~lied** *das* lullaby; **~los** *Adj.* sleepless ‹night›; **~los liegen** lie awake, unable to sleep; **~losigkeit** *die;* **~~:** sleeplessness; insomnia; **an ~losigkeit leiden** be an insomniac; suffer from insomnia; **~mittel** *das* sleep-inducing drug; soporific [drug]; **dieser Roman ist das reinste ~mittel** (*fig.*) this novel sends you [right off] to sleep; **~mütze** *die* **A** (*ugs.*) sleepyhead; (*jmd., der unaufmerksam ist*) daydreamer; **B** (*veralt.: Nachtmütze*) nightcap; **~mützig** *Adj.* (*ugs.*) dozy (*coll.*); **~raum** *der* bedroom; (*in Heim o. Ä.*) dormitory

**schläfrig** /ˈʃlɛːfrɪç/ ❶ *Adj.* sleepy; **~ sein/werden** ‹person› be/become sleepy *or* drowsy. ❷ *adv.* sleepily

**Schläfrigkeit** *die;* **~:** sleepiness; drowsiness

**Schlaf-:** **~rock** *der* (*veralt.*) nightgown; ⇒ *auch* **Apfel** A; **~saal** *der* dormitory; **~sack** sleeping bag

**schläfst** /ʃlɛːfst/ *2. Pers. Sg. Präsens v.* **schlafen**

**Schlaf-:** **~stadt** *die* dormitory town; **~stelle** *die* place to sleep; (*Bett*) bed; **~störungen** *Pl.* ▶ 474 (*Med.*) insomnia *sing.*

**schläft** /ʃlɛːft/ *3. Pers. Sg. Präsens v.* **schlafen**

**schlaf-, Schlaf-:** **~tablette** *die* sleeping pill *or* -tablet; **~trunk** *der* nightcap; **~trunken** ❶ *Adj.* (*geh.*) drowsy; ❷ *adv.* drowsily; [still] half asleep; **~wagen** *der* sleeping car; sleeper; **~wandeln** *itr. V.; auch mit sein* sleepwalk; **~wandler** *der;* **~~s, ~~, ~wandlerin** *die;* **~~, ~~nen** sleepwalker; **~wandlerisch** *Adj.* somnambulistic; **mit ~wandlerischer Sicherheit** with the sureness of a sleepwalker; with instinctive sureness; **~zimmer** *das* bedroom; (*Einrichtung*) bedroom suite; **~zimmerblick** *der* (*scherzh.*) bedroom eyes *pl.;* seductive eyes *pl.*

**Schlag** /ʃlaːk/ *der;* **~[e]s, Schläge** /ˈʃlɛːgə/ **A** blow; (*Faust~*) punch; blow; (*Klaps*) slap; (*leichter*) pat; (*als Strafe für ein Kind*) smack; (*Peitschenhieb*) lash; (*Tennis~, Golf~*) stroke; shot; **ein ~ auf den Kopf/ins Genick** a blow on the head/neck; **Schläge kriegen** (*ugs.*) get *or* be given a thrashing *or* beating; **~ auf ~** (*fig.*) in quick *or* rapid succession; **alles ging ~ auf ~:** everything went quickly; **die Fragen/Nachrichten kamen ~ auf ~:** the questions/news came thick and fast; **ein ~ ins Gesicht sein** (*fig.*) be a slap in the face; **das war ein ~ ins Kontor** (*ugs.*) that was a real blow (*coll.*); **ein ~ ins Wasser** a washout (*coll.*); **einen ~ [weg]haben** (*salopp*) be round the bend (*coll.*); be nuts (*coll.*); **keinen ~ tun** (*ugs.*) not do a stroke [of work]; **jmdm. einen ~ versetzen** deal sb. a blow; (*fig.*) be a blow to sb.; **einen vernichtenden ~ gegen jmdn. führen** (*fig.*) deal sb. a crushing blow; **auf einen ~** (*ugs.*) at one go; all at once; **mit einem ~[e]** (*ugs.*) suddenly; all at once; **mit einem ~ berühmt werden** become famous overnight; **zum entscheidenden ~ ausholen** (*fig.*) prepare to deal the decisive blow; ⇒ *auch* **Gürtellinie**; **B** (*Auf~, Aufprall*) bang; (*dumpf*) thud; (*Klopfen*) knock; **C** (*des Herzens, Pulses, der Wellen*) beating; (*eines Pendels*) swinging; **D** (*einzelne rhythmische Bewegung*) (*Herz~, Puls~, Takt~*) beat; (*eines Pendels*) swing; (*Ruder~, Kolben~*) stroke; **E** (*Töne*) (*einer Uhr*) striking; (*einer Glocke*) ringing; (*einer Trommel*) beating; (*eines Gongs*) clanging; **F** (*einzelner Ton*) (*Stunden~*) stroke; (*Glocken~*) ring; (*Trommel~*) beat; (*Gong~*) clang; **~** *od.* (*österr., schweiz.*) **schlag acht Uhr** on the dot *or* stroke of eight; **G** (*Vogelgesang*) song; **H** (*Blitz~*) flash [of lightning]; **I** (*Stromstoß*) shock; **J** (*ugs.: ~anfall*) stroke; **jmdn. trifft** *od.* **rührt der ~** (*ugs.*) sb. is flabbergasted; **ich dachte, mich trifft** *od.* **rührt der ~** (*ugs.*) I was flabbergasted; you could have knocked me down with a feather; **wie vom ~ getroffen** *od.* **gerührt** (*ugs.*) as if thunderstruck; **K** (*Schicksals~*) blow; **L** (*Tauben~*) cote; **M** (*ugs.: Portion*) helping; **[einen] ~ bei jmdm. haben** (*fig. ugs.*) be well in with sb. (*coll.*); **N** (*österr.: ~sahne*) whipped cream; **O** (*Wagen~, Kutschen~*) door; **P** (*Menschen~*) type; **ein Beamter vom alten ~:** a civil servant of the old school

**schlag-, Schlag-:** **~abtausch** *der* exchange of blows; (*fig.*) clash; **~ader** *die* ▶ 471 artery; **~anfall** *der* stroke; **einen ~anfall bekommen [haben]** have [had] a stroke; **~artig** ❶ *Adj.* very sudden; (*innerhalb kürzester Zeit geschehend*) instantaneous; ❷ *adv.* quite suddenly; (*innerhalb kürzester Zeit*) instantly; **~ball** *der* **A** (*Ballspiel*) *ball game similar to rounders;* **B** (*Ball*) *ball used in Schlagball;* **~bass, *~baß** *der* (*Musik*) plucked bass; **~baum** *der* barrier; **~bohrer** *der,* **~bohrmaschine** *die* percussion drill; hammer drill

**Schlägel** /ˈʃlɛːgl̩/ *der;* **~s, ~:** **A** (*Werkzeug*) mallet; **B** (*Trommelstock*) stick

**schlagen** ❶ *unr. tr. V.* **A** hit; beat; strike; (*mit der Faust*) punch; hit; (*mit der flachen Hand*) slap; (*mit der Peitsche*) lash; **ein Kind ~:** smack a child; (*aufs Hinterteil*) spank a child; **jmdn. bewusstlos/zu Boden ~:** beat sb. senseless/to the ground; (*mit einem Schlag*) knock sb. senseless/to the ground; **jmdn. zum Krüppel ~:** cripple sb. with a beating; **ich schlage dich zum Krüppel!** (*derb*) I'll beat you to a pulp (*coll.*); **etw. in Stücke ~:** smash sth. to pieces; **die Hände vors Gesicht ~:** cover one's face with one's hands; **jmdm. einen Schirm auf den Kopf ~:** hit sb. over the head with an umbrella; **sie schlug ihm das Buch aus der Hand** she knocked the book out of his hand; **ein Loch ins Eis ~:** break *or* smash a hole in the ice; **er hat ihr ein Loch in den Kopf ge~:** he hit her and cut her head open; ⇒ *auch* **grün** A; **B** (*mit Richtungsangabe*) hit ‹ball›; (*mit dem Fuß*) kick; **einen Nagel in etw.** (*Akk.*) **~:** knock a nail into sth.; **einen Pflock in den Boden ~:** knock a post into the ground; **die Eier in die Pfanne ~:** crack the eggs into the pan; **etw. durch ein Sieb ~:** press sth. through a sieve; **der Adler schlug die Fänge in seine Beute** the eagle sank its talons into its prey; **C** (*rühren*) beat ‹mixture›; whip ‹cream›; (*mit einem Schneebesen*) whisk; **die Sahne steif ~:** beat the cream till stiff; **D** (*läuten*) ‹clock› strike; ‹bell› ring; **die Uhr schlägt acht** the clock strikes eight; **eine geschlagene Stunde** (*ugs.*) a whole hour; **die Stunde der Rache/Wahrheit hat ge~** (*fig.*) the moment of revenge/truth has come; ⇒ *auch* **dreizehn**; **Stunde** A; **E** (*legen*) throw; **die Decke zur Seite ~:** throw aside the blanket; **ein Bein über das andere ~:** lay *or* put one leg over the other; cross one's legs; **F** (*einwickeln*) wrap (**in** + *Akk.* in); **G** (*besiegen, übertreffen*) beat; **jmdn. in etw.** (*Dat.*) **~:** beat sb. at sth.; **jmdn. um einige Meter ~:** beat sb. by a few metres; **eine Mannschaft [mit] 2 : 0 ~:** beat a team [by] 2-0; **sich ge~ geben** admit defeat; **H** *auch itr.* (*bes. Schach*) take ‹chessman›; **I** (*fällen*) fell ‹tree›; **J** ⇒ **Alarm** A; **Bogen** A; **Falte** A; **Haken** A; **Krach** C; **Kreis** A; **Kreuz** C; **Lärm**; **Rad[1]** C, E; **K** (*spielen*) beat ‹drum›; (*geh.*) play ‹lute, zither, harp›; **einen Wirbel auf der Trommel ~:** play a roll on the drum; **den Takt/Rhythmus ~:** beat time; **L** (*hinzufügen*) annex ‹territory›; **etw. in etw./auf etw.** (*Akk.*) **~:** add sth. to sth.; **M** (*befestigen*) (*mit Nägeln*) nail; (*mit Reißzwecken*) pin; (*mit Krampen*) staple; **N** (*prägen*) mint, strike ‹coin›; strike ‹medal›; **O** (*geh.*) **ein geschlagener Mann** a broken man; **das Schicksal hat ihn schwer ge~:** fate has treated him cruelly; **Gott hat ihn mit Blindheit ge~:** God struck him blind.
❷ *unr. itr. V.* **A** (*hauen*) **er schlug mit der Faust auf den Tisch/gegen die Tür** he beat the table/beat [on] the door with his fist; **jmdm. auf die Hand/ins Gesicht ~:** slap sb.'s hand/hit sb. in the face; **er hat nach mir ge~:** he hit *or* lashed out at me; **sie schlug wie wild um sich** she lashed *or* hit

out wildly all round her; **B** **mit den Flügeln ~** ‹bird› beat or flap its wings; **C** *mit sein (prallen)* bang; **mit dem Kopf auf etw.** (*Akk.*)/**gegen etw. ~:** bang one's head on/against sth.; **auf den Boden ~:** land with a thud on the floor; **die Wellen schlugen über den Deich** the waves broke over the dike; **D** *mit sein (schädigen)* **jmdm. auf den Magen ~:** affect sb.'s stomach; **E** (*pulsieren*) ‹heart, pulse› beat; (*heftig*) ‹heart› pound; ‹pulse› throb; **ihr schlug das Gewissen** (*fig.*) her conscience pricked her; **F** (*läuten*) ‹clock› strike; ‹bell› ring; ‹funeral bell› toll; **G** *auch mit sein (auftreffen)* **gegen/an etw.** (*Akk.*) ~ ‹rain, waves› beat against sth.; **das Segel schlug gegen den Mast** the sail flapped against the mast; **H** *meist mit sein (ein~)* **in etw.** (*Akk.*) ~ ‹lightning, bullet, etc.› strike *or* hit sth.; **I** *mit sein (ähnlich werden)* **nach dem Großvater/Onkel** *usw.* **~:** take after one's grandfather/uncle *etc.*; **J** (*sich hin und her bewegen*) bang; ‹sail, flag› flap; **K** *meist mit sein (sich irgendwohin bewegen)* ‹flames› shoot, leap; ‹smoke› billow; **L** *mit sein (irgendwohin dringen)* **der Lärm schlug an mein Ohr** the noise reached my ears; **die Röte/das Blut schlug ihr ins Gesicht** the colour/blood rushed to her face; **M** (*singen*) ‹nightingale, thrush, etc.› sing; **N** *auch mit sein (gehören)* **in jmds. Fach/Gebiet/Branche ~:** be sb.'s line.
❸ *unr. refl. V.* **A** (*sich prügeln*) fight; **sich mit jmdm. ~:** fight with sb.; **sich um etw. ~** (*auch fig.*) fight over sth.; **B** (*ugs.: sich behaupten*) hold one's own; **sich gut** *od.* **wacker** *od.* **tapfer ~:** hold one's own well; put up a good showing; **C** (*sich schädlich auswirken*) **sich/sich jmdm. auf das Gehirn/die Leber ~:** affect the/sb.'s brain/liver; **D** (*veralt.: sich duellieren*) **sich mit jmdm. ~:** fight a duel with sb.; ⇒ *auch* **Mensur** A; **E** (*sich begeben*) make one's way; **sich ins Gebüsch/Kornfeld ~:** slip away into the bushes/corn

**schlagend** ❶ *Adj.* cogent, compelling ‹argument, reason›; cogent ‹comparison›; conclusive ‹proof, evidence›; ⇒ *auch* **Verbindung** J; **Wetter**[2] C.
❷ *adv.* ‹prove, disprove› conclusively; ‹formulate› cogently

**Schlager** *der;* **~s, ~** **A** (*Lied*) pop song; (*Hit*) hit; **B** (*Erfolg*) (*Buch*) best seller; (*Ware*) best-selling line; (*Film, Stück*) hit

**Schläger** /ˈʃlɛːgɐ/ *der;* **~s, ~** **A** (*abwertend: Raufbold*) tough; thug; **B** (*Tennis~, Federball~, Squash~*) racket; (*Tischtennis~, Kricket~*) bat; (*[Eis]hockey~, Polo~*) stick; (*Golf~*) club; **C** (*Baseball, Schlagball: Spieler*) batter; **D** (*Fechten: Waffe*) straight-edged sabre

**Schlägerei** *die;* **~, ~en** brawl; fight

**Schlägerin** *die;* **~, ~nen** ⇒ **Schläger** A, C

**Schlager·musik** *die* popular music; pop music

**Schläger·mütze** *die: large soft peaked cap*

**Schlager-: ~sänger** *der,* **~sängerin** *die* pop singer; **~spiel** *das (Sportjargon)* big match; **~text** *der* pop [song] lyric; **~texter** *der,* **~texterin** *die* pop [song] lyricist

**Schläger·typ** *der (abwertend)* tough; thug

**schlag-, Schlag-: ~fertig** ❶ *Adj.* quick-witted ‹reply›; ‹person› who is quick at repartee; **er ist ~fertig** he is quick at repartee; ❷ *adv.* **~fertig antworten/parieren** give a quick-witted reply/riposte; **~fertigkeit** *die* quickness at repartee; **~fluss,** ***~fluß** *der (veralt.)* ⇒ **~anfall**; **~frau** *die (Rudern)* stroke; **~instrument** *das* percussion instrument; **~kraft** *die* **A** (*Kraft zum ~en*) weight of punch; **B** (*Milit.: Kampfkraft*) strike power; **C** (*fig.: Wirkungskraft*) effectiveness; (*von Argumenten*) compellingness; (*von Beispielen*) convincingness; **~kräftig** ❶ *Adj.* **A** (*Milit.: über große Kampfkraft verfügend*) powerful; **B** (*überzeugend*) compelling ‹argument›; convincing ‹example›; **C** (*effektiv*) strong, effective ‹support, back-up, team›; ❷ *adv.* (*überzeugend*) ‹argue› compellingly; **~licht** *das Pl.* **~~er** (*Kunst, Fot.*) shaft of light; **ein ~licht auf etw. werfen** highlight sth.; **~loch** *das* pothole; **~mann** *der* (*Rudern*) stroke; **~obers** /-|oːbɐs/ *das;* **~~** (*österr.*), **~rahm** *der (bes. südd., österr., schweiz.)* ⇒ **~sahne**; **~ring** *der* knuckle-duster; **~sahne** *die* whipping cream; (*geschlagen*) whipped cream; **~schatten** *der* [harsh] shadow; **~seite** *die* list; **[starke** *od.* **schwere] ~seite haben/bekommen** be listing [heavily] *or* have a [heavy] list/develop a [heavy] list; **~seite haben** (*ugs. scherzh.*) be rolling drunk; **~stock** *der* cudgel; (*für Polizei*) truncheon; **die Polizisten setzten ~stöcke ein** the police used their truncheons; **~werk** *das* striking mechanism; **~wetter** *Pl.* (*Bergbau*) firedamp *sing.*; **~wort** *das* **A** *Pl. meist* **~worte** (*Parole*) slogan; catchphrase; **B** *Pl. meist* **~worte** (*abwertend: Redensart*) cliché; **C** *Pl.* **~wörter** (*Buchw.: Stichwort*) headword; **nach ~wörtern und Verfassern katalogisieren** catalogue by subject and author; **~wort·katalog** *der (Buchw.)* subject catalogue; **~zeile** *die (Zeitungsw.)* headline; **~zeilen machen** (*fig.*) make headlines; **~zeug** *das* drums *pl.*; (*~instrumente*) percussion instruments *pl.*; **~zeuger** *der;* **~~s, ~~, ~zeugerin** *die;* **~~, ~~nen** ▶ **159** drummer; (*Perkusionist[in]*) percussionist

**schlaksig** /ˈʃlaːksɪç/ (*ugs.*) ❶ *Adj.* gangling; lanky.
❷ *adv.* lankily

**Schlamassel** /ʃlaˈmasl̩/ *der od. das;* **~s** (*ugs.*) mess; **da haben wir den ~!** a right *or* fine mess we're in now!

**Schlamm** /ʃlam/ *der;* **~[e]s, ~e** *od.* **Schlämme** /ˈʃlɛmə/ **A** (*aufgeweichte Erde*) mud; **B** (*Schlick*) sludge; silt

**Schlamm·bad** *das (Med.)* mudbath

**schlammig** *Adj.* **A** muddy; **B** (*schlickig*) sludgy; muddy

**Schlämm·kreide** /ˈʃlɛm-/ *die* whiting

**Schlamm·schlacht** *die (fig.)* mud-slinging *no indef. art.*

**Schlampe** *die;* **~, ~n** (*ugs. abwertend*) slut

**schlampen** *itr. V.* (*ugs. abwertend*) be sloppy; **bei etw. ~:** do sth. sloppily; **sie haben bei der Reparatur geschlampt** they made a sloppy job of the repair

**Schlamperei** *die;* **~, ~en** (*ugs. abwertend*) **A** (*Unordentlichkeit*) sloppiness; (*Nachlässigkeit*) slackness; **eine unerhörte ~!** an outrageous example of sloppiness/slackness; **B** (*Unordnung*) mess

**schlampert** /ˈʃlampɐt/ (*österr.*), **schlampig** (*ugs. abwertend*) ❶ *Adj.* **A** (*liederlich*) slovenly; **B** (*nachlässig*) sloppy, slipshod ‹work›.
❷ *adv.* **A** (*liederlich*) in a slovenly way; **B** (*nachlässig*) sloppily; in a sloppy *or* slipshod way

**Schlampigkeit** *die;* **~, ~en** (*ugs. abwertend*) **A** (*Liederlichkeit*) slovenliness; **B** (*Nachlässigkeit*) sloppiness

**schlang** /ʃlaŋ/ *1. u. 3. Pers. Sg. Prät. v.* **schlingen**

**schlänge** /ˈʃlɛŋə/ *1. u. 3. Pers. Sg. Konjunktiv II v.* **schlingen**

**Schlange** *die;* **~, ~n** **A** snake; ⇒ *auch* **Busen** A; **B** (*Menschen~*) queue; line (*Amer.*); **~ stehen** queue; stand in line (*Amer.*); **C** (*Auto~*) tailback (*Brit.*); backup (*Amer.*); **D** (*abwertend: Frau*) viper

**schlängeln** /ˈʃlɛŋl̩n/ *refl. V.* **A** ‹snake› wind [its way]; ‹road› wind, snake [its way]; **eine geschlängelte Linie** a wavy line; **B** (*sich irgendwo hindurch bewegen*) wind one's way

**Schlangen-: ~beschwörer** *der;* **~~s, ~~, ~beschwörerin** *die;* **~~, ~~nen** snake charmer; **~biss,** ***~biß** *der* snake-bite; **~brut** *die (geh. abwertend)* brood of vipers; **~fraß** *der (salopp abwertend)* muck (*coll.*); **~gift** *das* snake venom *or* poison; **~haut** *die* snake's skin; **~leder** *das* snake-skin; **~linie** *die* wavy line; **er fuhr mit seinem Moped ~linien** he weaved along on his moped; **~mensch** *der* contortionist

**schlank** /ʃlaŋk/ *Adj.* slim ‹person›; slim, slender ‹build, figure›; slender ‹column, tree, limbs›; **~ werden** get slimmer; slim down; **dieser Rock macht [dich] ~:** this skirt makes you look slim; **Joghurt macht ~:** yoghurt helps you slim; **sich ~ machen** (*fig.*) breathe in; ⇒ *auch* **Linie** A

**Schlankheit** *die;* **~** ⇒ **schlank**: slimness; slenderness

**Schlankheits·kur** *die* slimming diet; **eine ~ machen/beginnen** be/go on a slimming diet; (*in einer Klinik usw.*) have/start a course of slimming treatment

**schlank·weg** *Adv.* (*ugs.*) ‹refuse› flatly, point-blank; ‹accept› straight away; **jmdn. ~ einen Lügner nennen** come right out and call sb. a liar; **das ist alles ~ erfunden** that's all pure invention

**schlankwüchsig** /-vyːksɪç/ *Adj.* ‹person› of slender *or* slim build; slender ‹tree›

**schlapp** /ʃlap/ ❶ *Adj.* **A** worn out; tired out; (*wegen Schwüle*) listless; (*wegen Krankheit*) run-down; listless; **B** (*ugs.: ohne Schwung*) wet (*coll.*); feeble; **C** slack ‹rope, cable›; loose, slack ‹skin›; flabby ‹stomach, muscles›.
❷ *adv.* (*schlaff*) slackly; **das Segel hing ~:** the sail hung limply

**Schlappe** *die;* **~, ~n** setback; **eine [schwere] ~ einstecken [müssen]** *od.* **erleiden** suffer a [severe] setback

**schlappen** ❶ *itr. V.* **A** (*zu weit sein*) ‹shoe› be too wide; **B** *mit sein (schlurfend gehen)* shuffle.
❷ *tr. V.* (*schlabbern*) lap [up]

**Schlappen** *der;* **~s, ~** (*ugs.*) slipper

**Schlappheit** *die;* **~:** weariness; (*wegen Krankheit, Schwüle*) listlessness; (*ugs.: Schwunglosigkeit*) feebleness

**schlapp-, Schlapp-: ~hut** *der* slouch hat; **~|machen** *itr. V.* (*ugs.*) flag; (*zusammenbrechen*) flake out (*coll.*); (*aufgeben*) give up; **~ohr** *das* lop ear; **~schwanz** *der (salopp abwertend)* weed; wet (*coll.*)

**Schlaraffenland** /ʃlaˈrafn̩-/ *das;* **~[e]s** Cockaigne

**schlau** /ʃlau̯/ ❶ *Adj.* **A** shrewd; astute; (*gerissen*) wily; crafty; cunning; **sich** (*Dat.*) **ein ~es Leben machen** (*ugs.*) make life cushy for oneself (*coll.*); **das war besonders ~ [von dir]** (*iron.*) that was very clever *or* bright [of you] (*iron.*); **B** (*ugs.: gescheit*) clever; bright; smart; **aus etw. nicht ~ werden** (*ugs.*) not be able to make head or tail of sth.; **aus jmdm. nicht ~ werden** (*ugs.*) not be able to make sb. out; ⇒ *auch* **Buch** A.
❷ *adv.* shrewdly; astutely; (*gerissen*) craftily; cunningly

**Schlauberger** /ˈʃlau̯bɛrgɐ/ *der;* **~s, ~** (*ugs. scherzh.*) wily *or* crafty customer (*coll.*)

**Schlauch** /ʃlau̯x/ *der;* **~[e]s, Schläuche** /ˈʃlɔy̯çə/ **A** hose; **das war ein [ganz schöner] ~!** (*fig. ugs.*) it was a [real] slog; **B** (*Fahrrad~, Auto~*) tube; **C** (*für Wein usw.*) skin; **D** (*ugs.: schmaler Raum*) tunnel

**Schlauch·boot** *das* rubber dinghy; inflatable [dinghy]

**schlauchen** *tr. V.* (*ugs.*) **A** *auch itr.* (*anstrengen*) **jmdn. ~:** take it out of sb.; **geschlaucht sein** be whacked (*Brit. coll.*); be worn out; **B** (*scharf herannehmen*) **jmdn. ~:** put sb. through the mill

**schlauch·los** *Adj.* tubeless ‹tyre›

**Schläue** /ˈʃlɔy̯ə/ *die;* **~:** shrewdness; astuteness; (*Gerissenheit*) wiliness; craftiness; cunning

**Schlaufe** /ˈʃlau̯fə/ *die;* **~, ~n** (*zum Festhalten*) strap; (*Gürtel~, Verschluss*) loop

**Schlau-: ~kopf** *der (ugs.),* **~meier** *der (ugs. scherzh.)* ⇒ **Schlauberger**

**Schlawiner** /ʃlaˈviːnɐ/ *der;* **~s, ~** (*ugs.*) trickster; (*scherzh.: Schlingel*) rogue; rascal

**schlecht** /ʃlɛçt/ ❶ *Adj.* **A** bad; poor, bad ‹food, quality, style, harvest, health, circulation›; poor ‹salary, eater, appetite›; poor-quality ‹goods›; bad, weak ‹eyes›; **nicht ~!** not bad!; **in Mathematik ~ sein** be bad at mathematics; **[ein] ~es Englisch sprechen** speak poor English; **~ für die Gesundheit sein** be bad for one's health; **das wäre nicht ~/das Schlechteste** that wouldn't be a bad idea/a bad idea at all; **mit jmdm.** *od.* **um jmdn./mit etw. steht es ~:** sb./sth. is in a bad

way; (*jmd./etw. hat ~e Aussichten*) things look bad for sb./sth.; B (*böse*) bad; wicked; **das Schlechte im Menschen/in der Welt** the evil in man/the world; **ich hatte nur Schlechtes über ihn gehört** I had heard only bad things about him; **sie ist nicht die Schlechteste** she's not too bad; **jmdn. ~ machen** run sb. down; disparage sb.; ⇒ *auch* **Eltern**; C (*ungenießbar*) off; **die Milch/das Fleisch ist ~ geworden** the milk/meat has gone off; D (*unwohl, elend*) **jmdm. ist [es] ~:** sb. feels ill *or* unwell *or* poorly; **in ~er Verfassung sein** be in a bad way; **da kann einem ja ~ werden!** (*fig. ugs.*) it's enough to make you ill.
❷ *adv.* A badly; **er verdient ziemlich ~:** he is badly *or* poorly paid; **die Vorstellung war ~ besucht** the performance was poorly attended; **sie vertragen sich ~:** they don't get on well; **sie spricht ~ Englisch** she speaks poor English; **die Farben vertragen sich ~:** the colours don't go well together; **er sieht/hört ~:** his sight is poor/he has poor hearing; **sie waren nicht ~ beeindruckt** (*ugs.*) they weren't half impressed (*sl.*); **die Geschäfte gehen im Moment ~:** business is bad at the moment; **über jmdn.** *od.* **von jmdm. ~ sprechen** speak ill of sb.; **~ beraten** badly-advised; **~ bezahlt** badly *or* poorly paid; **~ sitzend** ill-fitting; B (*schwer*) **heute geht es ~:** today is difficult; **heute passt es mir ~:** it's not very convenient for me today; **das lässt sich ~ machen** that's difficult to manage; **das kann ich ~ sagen** I can't really say; **das wird sich ~ vermeiden lassen** it can hardly be avoided; **das kann er sich** (*Dat.*) **als Pfarrer ~ leisten** *od.* **erlauben** [in his position] as a vicar he really cannot afford to do that; C *in* **~ und recht, mehr ~ als recht** after a fashion; **sie hat sich ~ und recht durchs Leben geschlagen** she got by in life as best she could

***schlechtberaten, *schlechtbezahlt** ⇒ **schlecht** 2 A

**schlechter·dings** *Adv.* simply

**schlecht-: *~gehen** ⇒ **gehen** 1 K; ***~gelaunt** ⇒ **gelaunt**; **~hin** *Adv.* A *einem Subst. nachgestellt* **er war der Romantiker ~hin** he was the quintessential Romantic *or* the epitome of the Romantic; **das Prinzip des Privateigentums ~hin anfechten** attack the very principle of private property; B (*geradezu, ganz einfach*) quite simply

**Schlechtigkeit** *die; ~, ~en* A badness; wickedness; B (*böse Tat*) bad *or* wicked deed

**schlecht-, Schlecht-: *~|machen** ⇒ **schlecht** 1 B; ***~sitzend** ⇒ **schlecht** 2 A; **~weg** *Adv.:* ⇒ **~hin** B; **~wetter·geld** /-'---/ *das* bad weather allowance (*paid to building workers to make up for work lost due to bad weather*); **~wetter·periode** /-'-----/ *die* (*Met.*) period of bad weather

**schlecken** /'ʃlɛkn̩/ (*bes. südd., österr.*) ❶ *tr. V.* lap up.
❷ *itr. V.* A **an etw.** (*Dat.*) **~:** lick sth.; B ⇒ **naschen** 1 A

**Schleckerei** *die; ~, ~en* (*bes. südd., österr.*) A (*das Naschen*) ⇒ **Nascherei**; B (*Süßigkeit*) sweet

**Schlegel** /'ʃle:gl̩/ *der; ~s, ~* A (*Werkzeug*) mallet; B (*für Schlaginstrumente*) stick; C (*südd., österr.*) ⇒ **Keule** C

**Schleh·dorn** *der; Pl. ~e* blackthorn; sloe

**Schlehe** /'ʃle:ə/ *die; ~, ~n* sloe

**Schleiche** *die; ~, ~n* (*Zool.*) one of the Anguidae; **die ~n** the Anguidae

**schleichen** /'ʃlaiçn̩/ ❶ *unr. itr. V.; mit sein* creep; (*heimlich*) creep; steal; sneak; ‹cat› slink, creep; (*langsam fahren*) crawl along; **die Zeit schlich** time crept by.
❷ *unr. refl. V.* creep; steal; sneak; ‹cat› slink, creep; **Misstrauen schlich sich in ihr Herz** (*geh.*) distrust crept into her heart; **schleich dich!** (*ugs., bes. österr.*) get lost! (*coll.*); buzz off! (*sl.*)

**schleichend** *Adj.* insidious ‹disease›; slow[-acting], insidious ‹poison›; creeping ‹inflation›; gradual ‹crisis›

**Schleicher** *der; ~s, ~,* **Schleicherin** *die; ~, ~nen* (*abwertend*) toadying hypocrite

**Schleich-: ~handel** *der* black marketeering (**mit** in); **im ~handel** on the black market; **~katze** *die* viverrid (*Zool.*); **~weg** *der* secret path; **auf ~wegen, auf dem ~weg** (*fig.*) clandestinely; (*unrechtmäßig*) illicitly; by illicit means; **~werbung** *die* surreptitious advertising

**Schleie** /'ʃlaiə/ *die; ~, ~n* (*Zool.*) tench

**Schleier** /'ʃlaiɐ/ *der; ~s, ~* A (*durchsichtiges Gewebe*) veil; **den ~ nehmen** (*fig. geh.*) take the veil; **den ~ [des Geheimnisses] lüften** (*fig. geh.*) lift the veil of secrecy; **den ~ der Vergessenheit** *od.* **des Vergessens über etw.** (*Akk.*) **breiten** (*fig. geh.*) draw a veil over sth.; B (*Nebel~, Dunst~*) veil of mist/smoke; C (*Fot.: Farb~*) fog; **einen ~ haben** be fogged

**schleier-, Schleier-: ~eule** *die* barn owl; **~haft** *Adj.* **jmdm. [völlig** *od.* **vollkommen] ~haft sein/bleiben** be/remain a [total *or* complete] mystery to sb.; **~kraut** *das* (*Bot.*) baby's breath; **~schwanz** *der* (*Zool.*) fantail; **~tanz** *der* dance of the veils

**Schleife** /'ʃlaifə/ *die; ~, ~n* A bow; (*Fliege*) bow tie; B (*starke Biegung*) loop; (*eines Flusses*) loop; horseshoe bend; C (*Kranz~*) [inscribed] ribbon (*attached to a wreath*)

**schleifen**[1] *unr. tr. V.* A (*schärfen*) sharpen; grind, sharpen ‹axe›; B (*glätten*) grind; cut ‹diamond, glass›; (*mit Sand-/Schmirgelpapier*) sand; ⇒ *auch* **geschliffen**; C (*bes. Soldatenspr.: drillen*) **jmdn. ~:** drill sb. hard

**schleifen**[2] ❶ *tr. V.* A (*auch fig.*) drag; **jmdn. ins Kino ~** (*fig.*) drag sb. along to the cinema (*Brit.*) *or* (*Amer.*) movie; B (*niederreißen*) **etw. ~:** raze sth. [to the ground].
❷ *itr. V.; auch mit sein* drag; **die Kette schleift am Schutzblech** the chain scrapes the guard; **die Kupplung ~ lassen** (*Kfz-W.*) slip the clutch; **etw. ~ lassen** (*fig.*) let sth. slide; ⇒ *auch* **Zügel**

**Schleifer** *der; ~s, ~* A grinder; (*Diamanten~*) cutter; B (*Soldatenspr.*) slave driver; C (*Musik*) slur

**Schleiferei** *die; ~, ~en* A ⇒ **schleifen**[1] A, B: sharpening; grinding; cutting; sanding; B (*bes. Soldatenspr.: das Drillen*) hard drilling; C (*Betrieb*) grinding shop

**Schleiferin** *die; ~, ~nen* ⇒ **Schleifer** A

**Schleif-: ~lack·möbel** *das* piece of matt-lacquered furniture; **weiße ~~:** white matt-lacquered furniture *sing.*; **~spur** *die* drag mark; **~stein** *der* grindstone; **dasitzen wie ein Affe auf dem ~stein** (*ugs. scherzh.*) sit crouched there looking a proper charlie (*coll.*)

**Schleifung** *die; ~, ~en* razing [to the ground]

**Schleim** /ʃlaim/ *der; ~[e]s, ~e* A mucus; (*im Hals*) phlegm; (*von Schnecken, Aalen*) slime; (*Bot.*) mucilage; B (*sämiger Brei*) gruel

**Schleim-: ~beutel** *der* ▶ 471 (*Anat.*) synovial bursa; mucous bursa; **~haut** *die* ▶ 471 mucous membrane

**schleimig** ❶ *Adj.* A slimy; (*Physiol., Zool.*) mucous; B (*abwertend: heuchlerisch*) slimy.
❷ *adv.* (*abwertend*) slimily

**schleim-, Schleim-: ~lösend** *Adj.* expectorant; **~pilz** *der* slime mould *or* fungus; **~suppe** *die* (*Kochk.*) gruel

**schleißen** /'ʃlaisn̩/ *regelm.* (*auch unr.*) *tr. V.* A strip ‹feathers›; B (*bes. südd.: spalten*) split ‹wood›

**Schlemihl** /ʃle'mi:l/ *der; ~s, ~e* A (*Pechvogel*) unlucky devil; B (*ugs.: Schlitzohr*) crafty devil

**schlemmen** /'ʃlɛmən/ ❶ *itr. V.* (*prassen*) have a feast.
❷ *tr. V.* (*verzehren*) feast on

**Schlemmer** *der; ~s, ~:* gourmet

**Schlemmerei** *die; ~, ~en* (*oft abwertend*) A (*das Schlemmen*) feasting; gormandizing (*derog.*); B ⇒ **Schlemmermahl**

**Schlemmerin** *die; ~, ~nen* ⇒ **Schlemmer**

**Schlemmer-: ~lokal** *das* gourmet restaurant; **~mahl** *das* gourmet meal

**schlendern** /'ʃlɛndɐn/ *itr. V.; mit sein* stroll

**Schlendrian** /'ʃlɛndria:n/ *der; ~[e]s* (*ugs. abwertend*) slackness

**Schlenker** /'ʃlɛŋkɐ/ *der; ~s, ~* (*ugs.*) A (*Bogen*) swerve; **einen ~ machen** swerve; (*fig.*) dodge; B (*Umweg*) detour

**schlenkern** ❶ *itr. V.* A swing; dangle; **mit den Armen/mit den Beinen ~:** swing *or* dangle one's arms/legs; B ‹curtain, dress› flap; ‹car› swerve.
❷ *tr. V.* swing, dangle ‹arms, legs›

**schlenzen** /'ʃlɛntsn̩/ *tr. V.* flick ‹ball, puck›

**Schlepp** /ʃlɛp/ *der: in* **ein Fahrzeug in ~ nehmen** take a vehicle in tow

**Schlepp-: ~bügel** *der* (*Skisport*) T-bar; **~dampfer** *der* (*Seew.*) [steam-driven] tug

**Schleppe** *die; ~, ~n* A train; B (*Pferdesport, Jagdw.: künstliche Fährte*) drag

**schleppen** ❶ *tr. V.* A (*hinter sich herziehen*) tow ‹vehicle, ship›; B (*tragen*) carry; lug; C (*ugs.: mitnehmen*) drag; **jmdn. vor den Richter ~:** haul sb. up before the judge.
❷ *refl. V.* A drag *or* haul oneself; B (*sich hinziehen*) ‹trial, negotiations, etc.› drag on; C (*bes. nordostd.: sich abmühen*) **ich musste mich allein mit dem Kasten ~:** I had to lug the box around by myself.
❸ *itr. V.* (*schleifen*) drag

**schleppend** ❶ *Adj.* A (*schwerfällig*) shuffling, dragging ‹walk, steps›; B (*gedehnt*) dragging ‹speech›; slow ‹song, melody›; C (*nicht zügig*) slow ‹service›; **er beklagte sich über die ~e Bearbeitung seines Antrags** he complained about the delays in processing his application; **die Unterhaltung wurde immer ~er** the conversation dragged more and more.
❷ *adv.* A (*schwerfällig*) **~ gehen** shuffle along; B (*gedehnt*) ‹speak› in a dragging voice; ‹sing, play› slowly; C (*nicht zügig*) **die Unterhaltung kam nur ~ in Gang** conversation was slow to get going; **die Arbeiten gehen nur ~ voran** the work is progressing slowly

**Schlepper** *der; ~s, ~* A (*Schiff*) tug; B (*Traktor*) tractor; (*Sattel~*) tractor [unit]; C (*ugs.: jmd., der Kunden zuführt*) tout; D (*ugs.: Fluchthelfer*) *person who aids the entry of illegal immigrants or escape of illegal emigrants*

**Schlepperei** *die; ~, ~en* (*ugs. abwertend*) lugging around

**Schlepperin** *die; ~, ~nen* ⇒ **Schlepper** C, D

**Schlepp-: ~kahn** *der* dumb barge; **~lift** *der* T-bar [lift]; **~netz** *das* trawl [net]; **~seil** *das* ⇒ **~tau**; **~start** *der* (*Segelfliegen*) aerotow; **~tau** *das* towline; tow rope; (*aus Draht*) towline; tow cable; **etw. ins ~tau nehmen** take sth. in tow; **in jmds. ~tau** (*fig.*) in sb.'s wake; **~zug** *der* (*Schifffahrt*) train of barges

**Schlesien** /'ʃle:ziən/ (*das*); **~s** Silesia

**Schlesier** /'ʃle:ziɐ/ *der; ~s, ~,* **Schlesierin** *die; ~, ~nen* Silesian

**schlesisch** *Adj.* Silesian

**Schleswig-Holstein** (*das*); **~s** Schleswig-Holstein

**Schleswig-Holsteiner** ❶ *indekl. Adj.* Schleswig-Holstein. ❷ *der; ~s, ~:* native of Schleswig-Holstein; (*Einwohner*) inhabitant of Schleswig-Holstein

**schleswig-holsteinisch** *Adj.* Schleswig-Holstein *attrib.*

**Schleuder** /'ʃlɔydɐ/ *die; ~, ~n* A sling; (*mit Gummiband*) catapult (*Brit.*); slingshot (*Amer.*); B ⇒ **Wäscheschleuder**; C ⇒ **Zentrifuge**

**Schleuder-: ~ball** *der* A *team game played with a Schleuderball B*; B (*Ball*) *leather ball with a strap attached for throwing*; **~honig** *der* extracted honey

**schleudern** ❶ *tr. V.* A (*werfen*) hurl; fling; **der Wagen wurde aus der Kurve geschleudert** the car was sent skidding off the bend; **jmdm. Beleidigungen ins Gesicht**

*old spelling (see note on page 1707)

~ (*fig.*) hurl insults at sb.; **B** (*rotieren lassen*) centrifuge; spin ‹washing›.
**2** *itr. V.* **A** *mit sein* (*rutschen*) skid; **ins Schleudern geraten** *od.* **kommen** go into a skid; (*fig. ugs.*) run into trouble; **dein Argument hat ihn ins Schleudern gebracht** (*ugs.*) your argument completely threw him (*coll.*); **B** (*rotieren*) spin

**Schleuder-:** **~preis** *der* (*ugs.*) knock-down price; **~sitz** *der* ejector seat; **~ware** *die* (*ugs.*) cut-price item

**schleunig** /ˈʃlɔynɪç/ **1** *Adj.* **A** (*unverzüglich*) speedy; rapid; **B** (*eilig*) hurried.
**2** *adv.* **A** (*unverzüglich*) rapidly; speedily; **B** (*eilig*) hurriedly

**schleunigst** *Adv.* **A** (*auf der Stelle*) at once; immediately; straight away; **B** (*eilends*) hastily; with all haste

**Schleuse** /ˈʃlɔyzə/ *die;* ~, **~n** **A** sluice [gate]; **die ~n des Himmels öffneten sich** (*fig.*) the heavens opened; **B** (*Schiffs~*) lock; **C** (*Luft~*) airlock

**schleusen** *tr. V.* **A** **ein Schiff ~:** pass a ship through a/the lock; **B** (*geleiten*) shepherd; **C** (*schmuggeln*) smuggle ‹secrets›; infiltrate ‹spy, agent, etc.› (**in** + *Akk.* into)

**Schleusen-:** **~kammer** *die* lock chamber; **~tor** *das* lock gate; **~wärter** *der,* **~wärterin** *die* lock-keeper

**schlich** /ʃlɪç/ *1. u. 3. Pers. Sg. Prät. v.* **schleichen**

**Schlich** *der;* **~[e]s, ~e** trick; **alle ~e kennen** know all the tricks; **jmdm. auf die ~e** *od.* **hinter jmds. ~e kommen** get on to sb.

**schlicht** /ʃlɪçt/ **1** *Adj.* **A** simple; plain, simple ‹pattern, furniture›; (*geh.: glatt*) smooth ‹hair›; **in ~en Verhältnissen leben** live in modest circumstances; **B** (*unkompliziert*) simple, unsophisticated ‹person, view, etc.›; **C** (*bloß, rein*) simple; pure; **ein ~es Ja oder Nein** a simple yes or no.
**2** *adv.* simply; simply, plainly ‹dressed, furnished›; **wir haben ihn ~ Karl genannt** we gave him the plain, straightforward name Karl; **~ und einfach** (*ugs.*) quite *or* just simply; **er hat es ~ und ergreifend vergessen** (*ugs. scherzh.*) he just plain forgot

**schlichten** **1** *tr. V.* **A** settle ‹argument, difference of opinion›; settle ‹industrial dispute etc.› by mediation; **B** (*fachspr.*) smooth ‹wood, metal›; dress ‹stone, leather›; size ‹warp threads›.
**2** *itr. V.* mediate (**in** + *Dat.* in, **zwischen** between); **in einem Konflikt ~d eingreifen** intervene as mediator in a dispute

**Schlichter** *der;* **~s,** ~, **Schlichterin** *die;* ~, **~nen** mediator; (*durch Schiedsspruch*) arbitrator

**Schlichtheit** *die;* ~ ⇒ **schlicht** A, B: simplicity; plainness; unsophisticatedness

**Schlichtung** *die;* ~, **~en** settlement; (*in einem Arbeitskampf usw.*) mediation; (*durch Schiedsspruch*) arbitration

**Schlichtungs-:** **~ausschuss,** ***~ausschuß** *der* arbitration committee; **~verfahren** *das* arbitration process

**schlicht·weg** *Adv.* **er gab es ~ zu** he simply admitted it; **das ist ~ kriminell** that's just plain criminal

**Schlick** /ʃlɪk/ *der;* **~[e]s, ~e** silt

**schlief** /ʃliːf/ *1. u. 3. Pers. Sg. Prät. v.* **schlafen**

**Schliere** /ˈʃliːrə/ *die;* ~, **~n** (*Technik, Optik, Geol.*) schliere

**Schließe** /ˈʃliːsə/ *die;* ~, **~n** clasp; (*Schnalle*) buckle

**schließen** **1** *unr. tr. V.* **A** (*zumachen*) close; shut; put the top on ‹bottle›; turn off ‹tap›; fasten ‹belt, bracelet›; do up ‹button, zip›; close ‹street, route, electrical circuit›; close off ‹pipe›; (*fig.*) close ‹border›; fill, close ‹gap›; **mit geschlossenen Beinen** with one's legs together; **die Augen für immer geschlossen haben** (*geh. verhüll.*) have passed away; **B** (*unzugänglich machen*) close, shut ‹shop, factory›; (*außer Betrieb setzen*) close [down] ‹shop, school›; close *or* shut [down] ‹factory›; **C** (*ein~*) **etw./jmdn./sich in etw.** (*Akk.*) **~:** lock sth./sb./oneself in sth.; **D** (*beenden*) close ‹meeting, proceedings, debate›; end, conclude ‹letter, speech, lecture›; **die Rednerliste ist geschlossen** the list of speakers is closed; **E** (*befestigen*) **etw. an etw.** (*Akk.*) **~:** connect sth. to sth.; (*mit Schloss*) lock sth. to sth.; **F** (*eingehen, vereinbaren*) conclude ‹treaty, pact, ceasefire, agreement›; reach ‹settlement, compromise›; enter into ‹contract›; **wann wurde Ihre Ehe geschlossen?** when did you get married?; **Freundschaft/Bekanntschaft mit jmdm. ~:** make friends with/get to know sb.; ⇒ *auch* **Frieden**; **G** (*umfassen*) **jmdn. in die Arme ~:** take sb. in one's arms; embrace sb.; **etw. in seine Hand ~:** clasp sth. in one's hand; **etw. in sich ~** (*fig.*) contain sth.; **H** (*folgern*) **etw. aus etw. ~:** infer *or* conclude sth. from sth.; **aus etw. ~, dass ...** infer *or* conclude from sth. that ...
**2** *unr. itr. V.* **A** close; shut; **der Schlüssel/das Schloss schließt schlecht** the key won't turn properly/the lock doesn't work properly; **B** ‹shop› close, shut; ‹stock exchange› close; (*den Betrieb einstellen*) ‹shop› close [down]; ‹factory› close *or* shut [down]; **C** (*enden*) end; conclude; **D** (*urteilen*) **[aus etw.] auf etw.** (*Akk.*) **~:** infer *or* conclude sth. [from sth.]; **die Symptome lassen auf Hepatitis ~:** the symptoms indicate hepatitis; **etw. lässt darauf ~, dass ...** sth. indicates *or* suggests that ...; **vom Besonderen auf das Allgemeine ~:** proceed from the particular to the general; **von sich auf andere ~:** judge others by one's own standards.
**3** *unr. refl. V.* **A** ‹door, window› close, shut; ‹wound, circle› close; ‹flower› close [up]; **sich um etw. ~:** close around sth.; ⇒ *auch* **geschlossen**; **B** (*sich an~*) **an den Vortrag schloss sich eine Diskussion** the lecture was followed by a discussion

**Schließer** *der;* **~s,** ~ **A** (*Tür~*) doorkeeper; (*Vorrichtung*) [door-]closer; **B** (*im Gefängnis*) warder

**Schließerin** *die;* ~, **~nen** **A** doorkeeper; **B** (*im Gefängnis*) warder

**Schließ-:** **~fach** *das* locker; (*bei der Post*) post office box; PO box; (*bei der Bank*) safe-deposit box; **~frucht** *die* (*Bot.*) indehiscent fruit; **~korb** *der* hamper

**schließlich** *Adv.* **A** finally; in the end; (*bei Erwünschtem auch*) at last; **~ und endlich** (*ugs.*) in the end; finally; **B** (*bei einer Aufzählung*) **..., und ~ ...** ... and finally ...; **C** (*immerhin, doch*) after all; **er ist ~ mein Freund** he is my friend, after all; **er hat ~ nur seine Pflicht getan** after all, he was only doing his duty

**Schließ·muskel** *der* **▶471** (*Anat.*) sphincter

**Schließung** *die;* ~, **~en** **A** (*der Geschäfte, Büros usw.*) closing; shutting; (*Stilllegung, Einstellung*) closure; closing; (*fig.: einer Grenze*) closing; **zur ~ seiner Haushaltslücke** to fill the gap in his budget; **B** (*Beendigung*) **vor/nach ~ der Versammlung** before/after the meeting was closed; before/after the conclusion of the meeting; **die ~/einstweilige ~ der Debatte** the closure/adjournment of the debate; **C** ⇒ **schließen** 1 F: conclusion; reaching; **die ~ einer Ehe** the solemnization of a marriage

**schliff** /ʃlɪf/ *1. u. 3. Pers. Sg. Prät. v.* **schleifen**

**Schliff** *der;* **~[e]s, ~e** **A** (*das Schleifen*) cutting; (*von Messern, Sensen usw.*) sharpening; **B** (*Art, wie etw. geschliffen wird*) cut; (*von Messern, Scheren, Schneiden*) edge; **C** (*Lebensart*) refinement; polish; **D** (*Vollkommenheit*) **einem Brief/Text** *usw.* **den letzten ~ geben** put the finishing touches *pl.* to a letter/text *etc.*; **der Mannschaft den letzten ~ geben** put the finishing touches *pl.* to the team's training

**schlimm** /ʃlɪm/ **1** *Adj.* **A** (*schwerwiegend*) grave, serious ‹error, mistake, accusation, offence›; bad, serious ‹error, mistake›; **man hat ihm die ~sten Dinge nachgesagt** the most terrible things have been said about him; **das ist ~ für ihn** that's been serious for him; **B** (*übel*) bad; nasty, bad ‹experience›; **das war eine ~e Geschichte für ihn** that was a nasty business for him; **im ~sten Fall muss ich ...** if the worst comes to the worst I'll have to ...; **ist es ~, wenn wir erst morgen kommen?** does it matter if we don't come till tomorrow?; **[das ist alles] halb so ~:** it's not as bad as all that; **das Schlimmste ist, dass ...** the worst thing is *or* the worst of it is that ...; **es wurde immer ~er** it got worse and worse; **es ist nichts Schlimmes** it's nothing serious; **wenn es nichts Schlimmeres ist!** if it's nothing worse than that!; **ist nicht ~!** [it] doesn't matter; **es gibt Schlimmeres** there are worse things; **C** (*schlecht, böse*) wicked; (*ungezogen*) naughty ‹child›; **er ist ein ganz Schlimmer** (*scherzh.*) he's really wicked; **D** (*fam.: schmerzend, entzündet*) bad; sore; bad, nasty ‹wound›.
**2** *adv.* (*übel, arg*) **~ d[a]ran sein** (*körperlich, geistig*) be in a bad way; (*in einer ~en Situation*) be in dire straits; **es steht ~ um jmdn.** things look bad *or* serious for sb.; **es hätte ~er ausgehen können** things could have turned out worse

**schlimmsten·falls** *Adv.* if the worst comes to the worst; **~ kriegt man eine Verwarnung** at worst you'll get a caution

**Schlinge** /ˈʃlɪŋə/ *die;* ~, **~n** **A** (*Schlaufe*) loop; (*für den gebrochenen Arm o. Ä.*) sling; (*zum Aufhängen*) noose; **jmdm. die ~ um den Hals legen** put a noose round sb.'s neck; **die ~ zusammenziehen** (*fig.*) tighten the noose; ⇒ *auch* **Kopf** A; **B** (*Fanggerät*) snare; **~n legen** lay *or* set snares; **sich in der eigenen ~ fangen** (*fig.*) be hoist with one's own petard; **in jmds. ~ geraten** (*fig.*) fall into sb.'s trap

**Schlingel** /ˈʃlɪŋl/ *der;* **~s,** **~:** rascal; rogue

**schlingen** **1** *unr. tr. V.* **A** (*winden*) **etw. um etw. ~:** loop sth. round sth.; (*und zusammenbinden*) tie sth. round sth.; **sich** (*Dat.*) **einen Schal um den Hals ~:** wrap a scarf round one's neck; **die Arme um jmdn./etw. ~:** wrap one's arms round sb./sth.; **B** (*binden*) tie ‹knot›; **etw. zu einem Knoten ~:** tie sth. up in a knot; **C** (*flechten*) plait.
**2** *unr. refl. V.* (*sich winden*) **sich um etw. ~** ‹snake› wind *or* coil itself round sth.; ‹plant› wind *or* twine itself round sth.
**3** *unr. itr. V.* bolt one's food; wolf one's food [down]; **schling nicht so hastig!** don't bolt your food like that!

**Schlinger·bewegung** *die* (*Seew.*) rolling motion; **in ~en geraten** start to roll

**schlingern** /ˈʃlɪŋɐn/ *itr. V.; meist, mit Richtungsangabe nur, mit sein* ‹ship, boat› roll; ‹train, vehicle› lurch from side to side; **ins Schlingern kommen** (*fig. ugs.*) run into trouble

**Schling·pflanze** *die* creeper

**Schlips** /ʃlɪps/ *der;* **~es, ~e** tie; **jmdm. auf den ~ treten** (*fig. ugs.*) tread on sb.'s toes; **sich auf den ~ getreten fühlen** (*fig. ugs.*) feel *or* be put out; **mit ~ und Kragen** (*fig. ugs.*) wearing a collar and tie; with a collar and tie on

**Schlitten** /ˈʃlɪtn/ *der;* **~s,** ~ **A** sledge; sled; (*Pferde~*) sleigh; (*Rodel~*) toboggan; **~ fahren** go tobogganing; **die Kinder fuhren mit dem ~ den Hang hinunter** the children tobogganed down the slope; **mit jmdm. ~ fahren** (*fig. ugs.*) bawl sb. out (*coll.*); **ich werde mit ihm ~ fahren** (*fig. ugs.*) I'm going to give him hell (*coll.*); **B** (*salopp: Auto*) car; motor (*Brit.*); **ein alter ~:** an old banger (*Brit. sl.*); a jalopy; **C** (*Technik: Maschinenteil*) carriage

**Schlitten-:** **~fahrt** *die* sleigh ride; **~hund** *der* sled dog

**schlittern** /ˈʃlɪtɐn/ *itr. V.* **A** *auch mit sein* (*rutschen*) slide; **B** *mit sein* (*ins Rutschen kommen*) slip; slide; ‹vehicle› skid; ‹wheel› slip; **C** *mit sein* (*fig.*) **in die Pleite ~:** slide into bankruptcy; **in ein Abenteuer ~:** stumble into an adventure

**Schlitt-:** **~schuh** *der* [ice] skate; **~schuh laufen** *od.* **fahren** [ice-]skate; **~schuh·laufen** *das;* **~~s** [ice] skating *no art.*; **~schuh·läufer** *der,* **~schuh·läuferin** *die* [ice] skater

**Schlitz** /ʃlɪts/ *der;* **~es, ~e** **A** slit; (*Briefkasten~, Automaten~*) slot; **seine Augen wurden zu ~en** (*fig.*) his eyes narrowed to

S

slits; [B] (*Hosen~*) flies *pl.*; fly; (*Jacken~*) vent

**Schlitz·auge** *das* slit eye

**schlitzäugig** /-ɔygɪç/ *Adj.* slit-eyed

**schlitzen** *tr. V.* slit; (*auf~*) slit open

**Schlitz·ohr** *das* (*ugs.*) wily *or* crafty devil

**schlitzohrig** (*ugs.*) ❶ *Adj.* wily; crafty. ❷ *adv.* craftily

**schloh·weiß** /ˈʃloːˈvais/ *Adj.* snow-white ‹hair, head›; **er ist ~:** he has snow-white hair

**schloss, *schloß** /ʃlɔs/ *1. u. 3. Pers. Sg. Prät. v.* **schließen**

**Schloss, *Schloß** *das;* **Schlosses, Schlösser** /ˈʃlœsɐ/ [A] (*Tür~, Gewehr~*) lock; **die Tür fiel/fiel krachend ins ~:** the door clicked/slammed to *or* shut; [B] (*Vorhänge~*) padlock; **hinter ~ und Riegel** (*ugs.*) behind bars; [C] (*Verschluss*) clasp; [D] (*Wohngebäude*) castle; (*Palast*) palace; (*Herrschaftshaus*) mansion; (*in Frankreich*) château

**Schloss-, *Schloß-: ~anlage** *die* [A] castle buildings *pl.*; [B] *Pl.*; ⇒ **~park**; **~berg** *der* castle hill

**Schlösschen, *Schlößchen** /ˈʃlœsçən/ *das;* **~s, ~** ⇒ **Schloss** D: small castle *etc.*

**Schloße** /ˈʃloːsə/ *die;* **~, ~n;** (*bes. md.*) hailstone

**Schlosser** *der;* **~s, ~** ▶ 159 metalworker; (*Maschinen~*) fitter; (*für Schlösser*) locksmith; (*Auto~*) mechanic

**Schlosserei** *die;* **~, ~en** [A] (*Werkstatt*) metalworking shop; (*für Schlösser*) locksmith's workshop; [B] ⇒ **Schlosserhandwerk**

**Schlosser-: ~handwerk** *das;* ⇒ **Schlosser**: metalworking; fitter's trade; locksmithery; mechanic's trade; **das ~handwerk lernen** train to be a metalworker/fitter/locksmith/mechanic

**Schlosserin,** *die;* **~, ~nen** ⇒ **Schlosser**

**Schlosser·werkstatt,** *die* ⇒ **Schlosserei** A

**Schloss-, *Schloß-: ~garten** *der* castle *etc.* gardens *pl.*; **~herr** *der,* **~herrin** *die* owner of a/the castle *etc.*; **~hof** *der* castle *etc.* courtyard; **~hund** *der: in* **heulen wie ein ~hund** (*ugs.*) cry one's eyes out; **~kapelle** *die* castle *etc.* chapel; **~park** *der* castle *etc.* grounds *pl.*; **~ruine** *die* ruined castle *etc.*

**Schlot** /ʃloːt/ *der;* **~[e]s, ~e** *od.* **Schlöte** /ˈʃløːtə/ [A] (*bes. md.: Schornstein*) chimney [stack]; (*eines Schiffes*) funnel; **rauchen** *od.* **qualmen wie ein ~** (*ugs.*) smoke like a chimney; [B] (*Geol.: Eruptionsschacht*) chimney; vent; [C] (*ugs. abwertend: Nichtsnutz*) good-for-nothing

**Schlot·baron** *der* (*abwertend*) industrial baron *or* tycoon

**schlotterig** ⇒ **schlottrig**

**schlottern** /ˈʃlɔtɐn/ *itr. V.* [A] shake; tremble; **jmdm. ~ die Knie** sb.'s knees are shaking *or* trembling; **am ganzen Leibe ~:** shake *or* tremble all over; [B] ‹clothes› hang loose

**schlottrig** *Adj.* [A] trembling; shaking; [B] baggy ‹clothes›

**Schlucht** /ʃlʊxt/ *die;* **~, ~en** ravine; gorge

**schluchzen** /ˈʃlʊxtsn̩/ *itr. V.* sob; **unter Schluchzen** sobbing; **in heftiges Schluchzen ausbrechen** burst into heavy sobbing; **die ~den Klänge der Geigen** (*fig.*) the sobbing strains of the violins

**Schluchzer** *der;* **~s, ~:** sob

**Schluck** /ʃlʊk/ *der;* **~[e]s, ~e** *od.* **Schlücke** /ˈʃlʏkə/ [A] swallow; mouthful; (*großer ~*) gulp; (*kleiner ~*) sip; **einen tüchtigen ~ [Bier] trinken** take a good *or* long swig [of beer] (*coll.*); **sein Glas mit** *od.* **in einem** *od.* **auf einen ~ leeren** empty one's glass in one go *or* (*coll.*) swig; **hast du einen ~ zu trinken für uns?** have you got a drop of something for us to drink?; [B] (*ugs.: Getränk*) **ein guter ~:** a good drop [of stuff] (*coll.*); (*Wein*) a pleasant little number (*coll.*)

**Schluck·auf** *der;* **~s** hiccups *pl.*; hiccoughs *pl.*; **[den** *od.* **einen] ~ haben/bekommen** have/get [the] hiccups *or* hiccoughs

**Schlückchen** /ˈʃlʏkçən/ *das;* **~s, ~:** sip; **du nimmst doch noch ein ~?** you'll have another drop, won't you?; **ich geh zu Peter auf ein ~:** I'm off to Peter's for a drink

**schlucken** ❶ *tr. V.* [A] (*auch fig. ugs.*) swallow; **etw. hastig ~:** gulp sth. down; [B] (*ugs.: einatmen*) swallow ‹dust›; breathe in ‹gas›; [C] (*ugs. abwertend: in seinen Besitz bringen*) swallow [up]; [D] (*ugs.: verbrauchen*) swallow up; guzzle ‹petrol›.
❷ *itr. V.* (*auch fig.*) swallow; **Beschwerden beim S~ haben** have difficulty swallowing; **an etw.** (*Dat.*) **zu ~ haben** (*fig. ugs.*) find sth. hard to come to terms with

**Schlucken** *der;* **~s** ⇒ **Schluckauf**

**Schlucker** *der;* **~s, ~:** *in* **armer ~** (*ugs.*) poor devil *or* (*Brit. coll.*) blighter

**Schluck·impfung** *die* oral vaccination

**schlucksen** /ˈʃlʊksn̩/ *itr. V.* (*ugs.*) hiccup; hiccough

**schluck·weise** *Adv.* in sips

**Schluderei** *die;* **~, ~en** (*ugs. abwertend*) [A] sloppiness; slipshod work; [B] (*Fall von Nachlässigkeit*) slipshod piece of work; botched job; **~en** slipshod work *sing.*; botching *sing.*

**schluderig** ⇒ **schludrig**

**schludern** /ˈʃluːdɐn/ *itr. V.* (*ugs. abwertend*) work sloppily; **bei etw. ~:** make a botched job of sth.; (*etw. oberflächlich bearbeiten*) skimp sth.; **es wird zu viel geschludert** too much work is being botched

**schludrig** (*ugs. abwertend*) ❶ *Adj.* [A] (*nachlässig*) slipshod ‹work, examination›; botched ‹job›; slapdash ‹person, work›; **eine ~e Schrift** a messy scrawl; [B] (*schlampig [aussehend]*) scruffy.
❷ *adv.* [A] (*nachlässig*) in a slipshod *or* slapdash way; [B] (*schlampig [aussehend]*) scruffily

**Schludrigkeit** *die;* **~, ~en** (*ugs. abwertend*) [A] sloppiness; (*eines Menschen*) slapdash ways *pl.*; (*der Kleidung*) scruffiness; [B] (*Fall von Nachlässigkeit*) sloppiness; **diese ~en im Detail** this sloppiness when it comes to detail; this slipshod treatment of detail

**schlug** /ʃluːk/ *1. u. 3. Pers. Sg. Prät. v.* **schlagen**

**Schlummer** /ˈʃlʊmɐ/ *der;* **~s** (*geh.*) slumber (*poet./rhet.*); (*Nickerchen*) doze; **nach langem ~:** after a long slumber (*poet./rhet.*)

**Schlummer·lied** *das* (*geh.*) lullaby; cradle song

**schlummern** *itr. V.* [A] (*geh.: schlafen*) slumber (*poet./rhet.*); (*dösen*) doze; **tief ~d** in a deep slumber; [B] (*fig.: verborgen liegen*) **[in jmdm.] ~:** lie dormant [in sb.]; **~des Talent/~de Energie** latent talent/energy

**Schlummer·rolle** *die* bolster

**Schlumpf** /ʃlʊmpf/ *der;* **~s, Schlümpfe** /ˈʃlʏmpfə/ (*Comicfigur*) smurf

**Schlund** /ʃlʊnt/ *der;* **~[e]s, Schlünde** /ˈʃlʏndə/ [A] ▶ 471 (*Rachen*) [back of the] throat; pharynx (*Anat.*); (*eines Tieres*) maw; [B] (*geh.: gähnende Öffnung*) [gaping] mouth; (*Abgrund*) chasm; abyss

**Schlunze** /ˈʃlʊntsə/ *die;* **~, ~n** (*salopp abwertend, bes. nordd.*) slut

**schlüpfen** /ˈʃlʏpfn̩/ *itr. V.; mit sein* slip; **in ein/aus einem Kleid** *usw.* **~:** slip into *or* slip on/slip out of *or* slip off a dress *etc.*; **[aus dem Ei] ~** ‹chick› hatch out; **keiner kann aus seiner Haut ~** (*fig.*) nobody can completely change his/her identity

**Schlüpfer** *der;* **~s, ~** (*veralt.*) (*für Damen*) knickers *pl.* (*Brit.*); panties *pl.*; (*für Herren*) [under]pants *pl. or* trunks *pl.*; **ein ~:** a pair of knickers/underpants

**Schlupf·loch** /ˈʃlʊpf-/ *das* [A] (*Schlupfwinkel*) hiding place; [B] (*Durchschlupf*) hole; (*Lücke im Gesetz usw.*) loophole

**schlüpfrig** /ˈʃlʏpfrɪç/ *Adj.* [A] (*feucht u. glatt*) slippery; [B] (*abwertend: anstößig*) lewd

**Schlüpfrigkeit** *die;* **~, ~en** [A] (*feuchte Glätte*) slipperiness; [B] (*Anstößigkeit*) lewdness

**Schlupf-: ~wespe** *die* ichneumon fly; **~winkel** *der* hiding place; (*von Banditen, Flüchtlingen usw.*) hideout

**schlurfen** /ˈʃlʊrfn̩/ *itr. V.; mit sein* shuffle; (*ohne Richtungsangabe*) shuffle along

**schlürfen** /ˈʃlʏrfn̩/ ❶ *tr. V.* (*geräuschvoll*) slurp [up]; drink noisily; (*genussvoll*) savour; (*in kleinen Schlucken*) sip.
❷ *itr. V.* slurp; drink noisily

**Schluss, *Schluß** /ʃlʊs/ *der;* **Schlusses, Schlüsse** /ˈʃlʏsə/ [A] (*Endzeitpunkt*) end; (*eines Vortrags o. Ä.*) conclusion; (*Laden~*) closing time; (*Dienst~*) knocking-off time; **nach/gegen ~ der Aufführung** after/towards the end of the performance; **mit etw. ist ~:** sth. is at an end *or* over; (*ugs.: etw. ist ruiniert*) sth. has had it (*coll.*); **mit ihm ist ~** (*ugs.*) it's all up with him; (*das Verhältnis ist beendet*) it's all over with him; (*seine Karriere ist beendet*) he's past it; **mit dem Rauchen/Trinken ist jetzt ~:** there's to be no more smoking/drinking; you must stop smoking/drinking; (*auf sich bezogen*) I've given up smoking/drinking; **jetzt ist aber ~ [damit]!** that's enough of that; **~ jetzt!, ~ damit!** stop it!; that'll do!; **~ für heute!** that's it *or* that'll do for today; **am** *od.* **zum ~:** at the end; (*schließlich*) in the end; finally; **am** *od.* **zum ~ des Jahres** at the end of the year; **zum ~ möchte ich noch darauf hinweisen, dass ...** finally *or* in conclusion I should like to mention that ...; **kurz vor ~:** just before closing time; (*im Büro*) just before knocking-off time; **~ machen** (*ugs.*) stop; (*Feierabend machen*) knock off; (*seine Stellung aufgeben*) pack in one's job (*coll.*); (*eine Freundschaft usw. lösen*) break it off; (*sich das Leben nehmen*) end it all (*coll.*); **ich mache ~ für heute** I'm calling it a day; **ich muss jetzt ~ machen** (*am Telefon*) I'll have to go now; (*am Briefende*) I must stop now; **mit etw. ~ machen** stop sth.; **mit jmdm. ~ machen** finish with sb.; break it off with sb.; [B] (*letzter Abschnitt*) end; (*eines Zuges*) back; (*eines Buchs, Schauspiels usw.*) ending; [C] (*Folgerung*) conclusion (**auf** + *Akk.* regarding); (*Logik: Ableitung*) deduction; **Schlüsse aus etw. ziehen** draw conclusions from sth.; **ich werde meine Schlüsse daraus ziehen** I shall draw my own conclusions; [D] (*Technik, Bauw.*) **einen guten ~ haben** ‹piston› form a good seal; ‹door, window› be a good fit; [E] (*Reiten*) **diese Reiterin hat einen guten ~:** this rider keeps a good leg position; **mit den Knien ~ nehmen** grip with one's knees; [F] (*Musik*) cadence

**Schluss-, *Schluß-: ~abstimmung** *die* (*Parl.*) final vote; **~akkord** *der* (*Musik*) final chord; (*geh. fig.: Ausklang*) conclusion; finale; **~akte** *die* (*Dipl.*) final communiqué; **~bemerkung** *die* concluding remark; **~bilanz** *die* (*Kaufmannsspr.*) annual balance sheet; (*nach Abwicklung eines Unternehmens*) final balance [sheet]; **~drittel** *das* (*Eishockey*) third *or* final period

**Schlüssel** /ˈʃlʏsl̩/ *der;* **~s, ~** [A] key; **der ~ zur Wohnung/Wohnungstür** the key of the flat (*Brit.*) *or* (*Amer.*) apartment/the front door key; [B] (*Schrauben~*) spanner; [C] (*Lösungsweg, Lösungsheft*) key; (*Kode*) code; cipher; **der ~ zum Erfolg** (*fig.*) the key to *or* secret of succes; [D] (*Musik*) clef; [E] (*Aufgliederungsschema*) scheme *or* pattern [of distribution]

**schlüssel-, Schlüssel-: ~bart** *der* bit [of a/the key]; **~anhänger** *der* key fob; **~bein** *das* ▶ 471 (*Anat.*) collarbone; clavicle (*Anat.*); **~blume** *die* cowslip; (*Primel*) primula; **~brett** *das* keyboard; **~bund** *der od. das* bunch of keys; **~erlebnis** *das* (*Psych.*) crucial experience; **~fertig** *Adj.* ready to move into *postpos.*; **~figur** *die* key figure; **~industrie** *die* (*Wirtsch.*) key industry; **~kind** *das* (*ugs.*) latchkey child; **~loch** *das* keyhole; **~position** *die* ⇒ **~stellung**; **~ring** *der* key ring; **~roman** *der* (*Literaturw.*) roman à clef; **~stellung** *die* key position; **~wort** *das; Pl.* **~wörter** keyword; (*für ein Kombinationsschloss, fig.: verschlüsseltes Wort*) code word

*old spelling (see note on page 1707)

**schluss-, Schluss-, *schluß-, *Schluß-: ~endlich** *Adv.* (*bes. schweiz.*) finally; (*immerhin*) after all; **~folgern** *tr. V.* conclude (**aus** from); **~folgerung** *die* conclusion, inference (**aus** from); **~formel** *die* conventional ending; **~frau** *die* (*Ballspiele*) goalie (*coll.*)

**schlüssig** /ˈʃlʏsɪç/ ❶ *Adj.* Ⓐ conclusive ‹proof, evidence›; convincing, logical ‹argument, conclusion, statement›; Ⓑ **sich** (*Dat.*) **[darüber] ~ sein** have made up one's mind; **sich** (*Dat.*) **[darüber] ~ werden** make up one's mind. ❷ *adv.* conclusively

**Schlüssigkeit** *die;* **~:** conclusiveness

**Schluss-, *Schluß-: ~kapitel** *das* (*auch fig.*) final *or* closing chapter; **~leuchte** *die* ⇒ **~licht** A; **~licht** *das; Pl.* **~~er** Ⓐ (*an Fahrzeugen*) tail *or* rear light; Ⓑ (*ugs.: Letzter einer Kolonne*) **das ~licht machen** *od.* **bilden/sein** bring up the rear; Ⓒ (*ugs.: Letzter, Schlechtester*) **das ~licht der Bundesliga/Klasse sein** be bottom of the [national] league table/class; **~mann** *der;* (*Ballspiele*) goalie (*coll.*); **~pfiff** *der* (*Ballspiele*) final whistle; **~phase** *die* final phase; final stages *pl.*; **~punkt** *der* Ⓐ (*Satzzeichen*) full stop; Ⓑ (*Abschluss*) conclusion; (*einer Feier*) finale; **einen ~punkt unter etw.** (*Akk.*) **setzen** put an end to sth. once and for all; (*etw. beendet sein lassen*) declare sth. to be over and done with; **~runde** *die* (*Sport: eines Rennens*) final *or* last lap; (*Boxen, Ringen, fig.: des Wahlkampfes usw.*) final *or* last round; **~satz** *der* Ⓐ (*abschließender Satz*) last *or* concluding sentence; Ⓑ (*Musik*) last movement; finale; Ⓒ (*bes. Philos.*) conclusion; **~sprung** *der* (*Turnen*) jump with legs together; **~stein** *der* (*Archit.*) keystone; (*im Rippengewölbe*) boss; **~strich** *der* [bottom] line; **einen ~strich ziehen/unter etw.** (*Akk.*) **ziehen** (*fig.*) make a clean break/draw a line under sth.; **~verkauf** *der* [end-of-season] sale[s *pl.*]; **~wort** *das; Pl.* **~~e** final word[s]; **ein kurzes ~wort** a few closing remarks; **das ~wort haben** make the closing speech; (*in einer Debatte*) wind up

**Schmach** /ʃmaːx/ *die;* **~** (*geh.*) ignominy; shame; (*Demütigung*) humiliation; **etw. als ~ empfinden** consider sth. a disgrace; regard sth. as ignominious; **jmdm. [eine] ~ antun** *od.* **bereiten** bring shame/humiliation upon sb.; **[mit] ~ und Schande** [in] deep disgrace

**schmachten** /ˈʃmaxtn̩/ *itr. V.* (*geh.*) Ⓐ (*leiden*) languish; **in der Hitze ~:** fade away in the heat; **jmdn./einen Liebhaber ~ lassen** leave sb. to suffer *or* (*coll.*) stew/let a lover pine away; Ⓑ (*spött.: sich sehnen*) **nach jmdm./etw. ~:** pine *or* yearn for sb./sth.

**schmachtend** (*spött.*) ❶ *Adj.* soulful (*coll.*) ‹look, song›; languishing ‹tones›; schmaltzy (*coll.*) ‹song, music›. ❷ *adv.* soulfully (*coll.*)

**Schmacht·fetzen** *der* (*salopp abwertend*) tear jerker (*coll.*)

**schmächtig** *Adj.* slight; weedy (*coll. derog.*); **einen ~en Körper haben** be of slight build

**Schmacht·locke** *die* (*ugs. spött.*) kiss-curl

**schmach·voll** (*geh.*) ❶ *Adj.* ignominious; (*erniedrigend*) humiliating. ❷ *adv.* ignominiously; (*erniedrigend*) humiliatingly; **~ untergehen** come to an ignominious end

**schmackhaft** /ˈʃmakhaft/ ❶ *Adj.* tasty; **jmdm. etw. ~ machen** (*fig. ugs.*) make sth. palatable to sb. ❷ *adv.* in a tasty way; **etw. ~ zubereiten** make sth. tasty

**Schmäh** *der;* **~s, ~[s]** (*österr. ugs.*) Ⓐ [tall] story; (*Trick*) con (*coll.*); **einen ~ führen** entertain; tell jokes; Ⓑ (*Sarkasmus*) sarcasm; **Wiener ~:** Viennese snide humour (*coll.*)

**schmähen** /ˈʃmɛːən/ *tr. V.* (*geh.*) revile

**schmählich** ❶ *Adj.* shameful; (*verächtlich*) despicable. ❷ *adv.* shamefully; (*in verächtlicher Weise*) despicably

**Schmäh-: ~rede** *die* diatribe; **~schrift** *die* piece of invective; (*Pamphlet*) defamatory pamphlet

**Schmähung** *die;* **~, ~en** diatribe; **~en** abuse *sing.*; invective *sing.*; **jmdn. mit ~en überschütten** heap invective *or* abuse on sb.

**Schmäh·wort** *das; Pl.* **Schmäh·worte** term of abuse; **~e** abuse *sing.*

**schmal** /ʃmaːl/; **schmaler** *od.* **schmäler** /ˈʃmɛːlɐ/, **schmalst...** *od.* **schmälst...** ❶ *Adj.* Ⓐ narrow; slim, slender ‹hips, hands, figure, etc.›; thin ‹lips, face, nose, etc.›; **ein ~er Band, ein ~es Büchlein** a slim volume; **~er werden** ‹person, face› get thinner; Ⓑ (*geh.: knapp, karg*) meagre ‹income, profit, etc.›; meagre, scanty ‹food, selection›; **mit ~em Geldbeutel** of restricted means. ❷ *adv.* Ⓐ **eine ~ geschnittene Hose** slim-fit trousers; Ⓑ (*geh.: knapp, karg*) meagrely

**schmal·brüstig** /-brʏstɪç/ narrow-chested; (*fig.*) narrow ‹cupboard, views, etc.›

**schmäler** ⇒ **schmal**

**schmälern** *tr. V.* diminish; reduce; restrict, curtail ‹rights›; (*herabsetzen*) belittle

**Schmälerung** *die;* **~, ~en** reduction; (*Herabsetzung*) belittlement

**Schmal-: ~film** *der* 8 mm/16 mm cine film; **~film·kamera** *die* 8 mm/16 mm cine camera; **~hans** *in* **bei ihnen ist ~hans Küchenmeister** (*ugs. veralt.*) they are on short commons; **~seite** *die* short side; (*eines Korridors usw.*) end; **~spur** *die* (*Eisenb.*) narrow gauge

**Schmalspur-** (*ugs.*) small-time (*coll.*) ‹politician, academic›; (*dilettantisch*) lightweight ‹academic›; amateur ‹engineer›

**Schmalspur·bahn** *die* narrow-gauge railway

**schmälst...** ⇒ **schmal**

**schmal·wüchsig** *Adj.* slender ‹person, tree, etc.›; ‹person› of slender build

**Schmalz**[1] /ʃmalts/ *das;* **~es** (*Schweine~*) lard

**Schmalz**[2] *der;* **~es** (*ugs. abwertend*) Ⓐ (*Sentimentalität*) schmaltz (*coll.*); **mit viel ~:** with plenty of slushy *or* soppy sentimentality (*coll.*); Ⓑ (*Lied o. Ä.*) schmaltz *no indef. art.* (*coll.*)

**Schmalz·brot** *das* slice of bread and dripping

**schmalzig** (*abwertend*) ❶ *Adj.* schmaltzy (*coll.*); slushy[-sentimental]. ❷ *adv.* with schmaltzy (*coll.*) *or* slushy sentimentality; **~ sprechen** talk in a slushy-sentimental way; ‹lover› talk in a lovey-dovey tone (*coll.*)

**Schmalzler** /ˈʃmaltslɐ/ *der;* **~s** (*bayr.*) snuff (*containg a trace of animal fat*)

**Schmankerl** /ˈʃmaŋkɐl/ *das;* **~s, ~n** (*bayr., österr.*) delicacy; (*fig.*) treat

**schmarotzen** /ʃmaˈrɔtsn̩/ *itr. V.* Ⓐ (*abwertend*) sponge; freeload (*sl.*); **bei jmdm. ~:** sponge on sb.; Ⓑ (*Biol.*) live as a parasite (**in/auf** + *Dat.* in/on); **~d** parasitic

**Schmarotzer** *der;* **~s, ~** Ⓐ (*abwertend*) sponger; freeloader (*coll.*); Ⓑ (*Biol.*) parasite

**Schmarotzerin,** *die;* **~, ~nen** ⇒ **Schmarotzer** A

**Schmarotzer·pflanze** *die* parasitic plant

**Schmarotzertum** *das;* **~s** Ⓐ (*Biol.*) parasitism; Ⓑ (*abwertend*) sponging; freeloading (*sl.*)

**Schmarren** /ˈʃmarən/ *der;* **~s, ~** Ⓐ (*österr., auch südd.*) *pancake broken up with a fork after frying;* Ⓑ (*ugs. abwertend: Unsinn*) trash; rubbish; **das ist ein ~:** it's a load (*coll.*) of trash *or* rubbish; Ⓒ **einen ~** (*salopp: nichts*) not a thing; damn all (*Brit. coll.*); (*adverbiell*) not at all; no way; **das geht dich einen ~ an** it's none of your damn business (*coll.*)

**Schmatz** /ʃmats/ *der;* **~es, ~e** *od.* **Schmätze** /ˈʃmɛtsə/ (*ugs.*) loud kiss; smacker (*coll.*)

**schmatzen** *itr. V.* smack one's lips; (*geräuschvoll essen*) eat/drink noisily; (*fig.*) ‹mud, wet ground› squelch; **sie küssten sich, dass es schmatzte** they gave one another a resounding kiss *or* a (*coll.*) real smacker

**schmauchen** /ˈʃmauxn̩/ ❶ *tr. V.* puff away at ‹pipe, cigar, etc.›. ❷ *itr. V.* puff away

**Schmaus** /ʃmaus/ *der;* **~es, Schmäuse** /ˈʃmɔyzə/ (*veralt., noch scherzh.*) [good] spread (*coll.*); (*reichhaltig*) feast; **ein köstlicher ~:** a delicious repast (*formal/joc.*) *or* (*coll.*) spread

**schmausen** (*veralt.*) ❶ *itr. V.* eat with relish; **vergnügt ~:** tuck in contentedly (*coll.*). ❷ *tr. V.* eat ‹food› with relish

**schmecken** /ˈʃmɛkn̩/ ❶ *itr. V.* taste (**nach** of); **[gut] ~:** taste good; **das hat geschmeckt** that was good; (*war köstlich*) that was delicious; **nach nichts ~:** not taste of anything; be tasteless; **das schmeckt nach mehr** (*ugs.*) it tastes *or* it's moreish (*coll.*); **schmeckt es [dir]?** are you enjoying it *or* your meal?; [how] do you like it?; **wenn man krank ist, schmeckt es einem oft nicht [richtig]** when you're ill you're often off your food; **bei dir schmeckt es mir immer ausgezeichnet** your meals are always delicious; **lasst es euch ~!** enjoy your food!; tuck in (*coll.*)!; **wie schmeckt dir die Ehe?** (*fig.*) how do you like married life?; **diese Kritik schmeckte ihm gar nicht** (*fig.*) this criticism was not at all to his liking. ❷ *tr. V.* taste; (*kosten*) sample; **die Rute zu ~ bekommen** (*fig.*) get a taste of the rod

**Schmeichelei** *die;* **~, ~en** flattering remark; blandishment; **die ~en, die er ihr sagte** the flattering things he said to her

**schmeichelhaft** ❶ *Adj.* flattering; complimentary ‹words, speech›; **wenig ~:** not very flattering. ❷ *adv.* flatteringly

**schmeicheln** /ˈʃmaiçln/ *itr. V.* Ⓐ **jmdm. ~:** flatter sb.; **er schmeichelte ihr, sie sei ...** *od.* **dass sie ... sei** he flattered her by saying she was ...; **etw. in ~dem Ton sagen** say sth. in honeyed tones; **es schmeichelt ihm, dass ...** he finds it flattering that ...; **„Zwerg" ist noch geschmeichelt** 'dwarf' is putting it mildly; Ⓑ (*liebkosen*) be affectionate; **die Katze strich ~d um ihre Füße** the cat rubbed affectionately against her feet

**Schmeichel·wort** *das; Pl.* **~e;** blandishment; **~e** honeyed words; flattery *sing.*

**Schmeichler** /ˈʃmaiçlɐ/ *der;* **~s, ~, Schmeichlerin** *die;* **~, ~nen** flatterer

**schmeichlerisch** ❶ *Adj.* flattering; honeyed ‹words, tone›; (*sich anbiedernd*) cajoling ‹words, tone, glance›. ❷ *adv.* cajolingly; (*im ~en Ton*) in honeyed tones

**schmeißen** /ˈʃmaisn̩/ (*ugs.*) ❶ *unr. tr. V.* Ⓐ (*werfen*) chuck (*coll.*); sling (*coll.*); (*schleudern*) fling; hurl; **etw. nach jmdm. ~:** throw *or* (*coll.*) chuck sth. at sb.; **die Tür [ins Schloss] ~:** slam the door; **jmdn. aus dem Zimmer/der Schule ~:** chuck sb. out of the room/school (*coll.*); Ⓑ (*abbrechen, aufgeben*) chuck in (*coll.*) ‹job, studies, etc.›; Ⓒ (*spendieren*) stand ‹drink›; **eine Lage** *od.* **Runde [Bier] ~:** get *or* stand a round [of beer]; **[für jmdn.] eine Party ~:** throw a party [for sb.]; Ⓓ (*bewältigen*) handle; deal with; **wir werden den Laden schon ~:** we'll manage OK (*coll.*); Ⓔ (*Theater-, Fernsehjargon: misslingen lassen*) fluff (*coll.*) ‹scene, number›; make a mess of ‹performance›. ❷ *unr. refl. V.* Ⓐ (*sich werfen*) throw oneself; (*mit Wucht*) hurl oneself; **sich jmdm. an den Hals ~** ‹woman› throw oneself at sb.; ⇒ *auch* **Schale** D; Ⓑ **sich in seinen Smoking/in ein festliches Kleid** *usw.* **~:** get togged up (*coll.*) in one's dinner jacket/a party dress *etc.* ❸ *unr. itr. V.* **mit Steinen/Tomaten** *usw.* **[nach jmdm.] ~:** chuck stones/tomatoes *etc.* [at sb.] (*coll.*); **mit Geld um sich ~** (*fig.*) throw one's money around; lash out (*coll.*); **mit Geschenken um sich ~** (*fig.*) lash out (*coll.*) on masses of presents

**Schmeiß·fliege** *die* blowfly; (*blaue ~*) bluebottle

S

**Schmelz** *der;* ~**es,** ~**e** Ⓐ (*Glasur*) glaze; (*Email, Zahn*~) enamel; Ⓑ (*geh.: Lieblichkeit*) (*der Jugend*) bloom; (*von Farben*) lustre; soft gleam; (*Wohlklang*) mellifluousness

**Schmelze** *die;* ~, ~**n** Ⓐ (*das [Zer]schmelzen*) [process of] melting; Ⓑ (*Technik: verflüssigtes Material*) melt

**schmelzen** /ˈʃmɛltsn̩/ ❶ *unr. itr. V.; mit sein* Ⓐ melt; (*fig.*) ‹doubts, apprehension, etc.› dissolve, fade away; **sein Vermögen war geschmolzen** (*fig.*) his fortune had melted away; Ⓑ (*fig.: weich werden*) soften; **ihm schmolz das Herz** his heart melted.
❷ *unr. tr. V.* melt; smelt ‹ore›; render ‹fat›

**schmelzend** ❶ *Adj.* melting ‹glance, tones›; mellifluous, mellow ‹voice, tones, etc.›.
❷ *adv.* ~ **singen** sing in melting tones

**Schmelz-:** ~**hütte** *die* smelting works *sing. or pl.*; ~**käse** *der* processed cheese; ~**ofen** *der* (*Technik*) smelting furnace; ~**punkt** *der* melting point; ~**tiegel** *der* crucible; melting pot (*esp. fig.*); ~**wasser** *das; Pl.* ~**:** melted snow and ice; meltwater (*Geol.*)

**Schmerbauch** /ˈʃmeːɐ̯-/ *der* (*ugs.*) Ⓐ (*dicker Bauch*) potbelly; paunch; Ⓑ (*dickbäuchiger Mensch*) potbelly

**Schmerle** /ˈʃmɛrlə/ *die;* ~, ~**n** (*Zool.*) loach

**Schmerz** /ʃmɛrts/ *der;* ~**es,** ~**en** Ⓐ ▶ 474 (*physisch*) pain; (*dumpf u. anhaltend*) ache; **wo haben Sie** ~**en?** where does it hurt?; ~**en im Rücken/Arm** pain in one's back/arm; (*an verschiedenen Stellen*) pains in one's back/arm; ~**en haben** be in pain; **etw. mit** *od.* **unter** ~**en tun** do sth. in pain *or* agony; **vor** ~**[en] weinen/sich vor** ~**en winden** cry with/writhe in pain *or* agony; ~, **lass nach!** (*ugs. scherzh.*) oh no! it can't be!; that's the last straw!; Ⓑ ▶ 474 (*psychisch*) pain; (*Kummer*) grief; **ein seelischer** ~**:** mental anguish *or* suffering; **jmdm.** ~**en bereiten** cause sb. pain/grief; **der** ~ **um jmdn.** grief for sb.; **tiefen** ~ **über etw.** (*Akk.*) **empfinden** be deeply grieved by sth.; **etw. mit** ~**en erkennen** realize sth. with a sense of grief; **jmdn./etw. mit** ~**en erwarten** wait for sb./sth. in an agony of impatience; **hast du sonst noch** ~**en?** (*ugs. spött.*) is there anything else you want?

**schmerz·empfindlich** *Adj.* sensitive to pain *pred.*; ~ **sein** have a low pain threshold

**Schmerz·empfindlichkeit** *die;* ~**:** sensitivity to pain

**schmerzen** ▶ 474 ❶ *tr. V.* **jmdn.** ~**:** hurt sb.; (*Kummer bereiten*) grieve sb.; cause sb. sorrow; **es schmerzt mich, dass ...** it grieves *or* pains me that ...
❷ *itr. V.* hurt; **seine Wunde schmerzt** his wound is hurting *or* painful; **heftig** ~**:** be intensely painful

**Schmerzens-:** ~**geld** *das* (*Rechtsspr.*) compensation (*for pain and suffering caused*); exemplary damages (*Law*); ~**laut** *der* cry of pain; (*stöhnend*) moan; ~**mann** *der* (*Kunstwiss.*) Ecce Homo; ~**mutter** *die; Pl.* ~**mütter** (*Kunstwiss.*) Mater Dolorosa; ~**schrei** *der* cry of pain; (*laut*) scream [of pain]

**schmerz·frei** *Adj.* free of pain *pred.*; painless ‹operation›

**Schmerz·grenze** *die* (*fig.*) **jetzt/dann ist die** ~ **erreicht** this/that is the absolute limit

**schmerzhaft** *Adj.* painful; (*wund*) sore

**schmerzlich** ❶ *Adj.* painful; distressing; **die** ~**e Gewissheit haben, dass ...** be painfully aware that ...; **es ist mir eine** ~**e Pflicht, Ihnen mitteilen zu müssen, dass ...** it is my painful duty to inform you that ...
❷ *adv.* painfully

**schmerz-, Schmerz-:** ~**lindernd** ❶ *Adj.* pain-relieving; ~**linderndes Mittel** pain-relieving drug; palliative; ❷ *adv.* ~**lindernd wirken** relieve pain; ~**los** ❶ *Adj.* painless; ❷ *adv.* painlessly; ⇨ *auch* **kurz** 2 C; ~**schwelle** *die* (*Physiol.*) pain threshold; ~**stillend** ❶ *Adj.* pain-killing; analgesic (*Med.*); ~**stillendes Mittel** painkiller; analgesic; ❷ *adv.* ~**stillend wirken** have a pain-killing *or* analgesic effect; ~**tablette** *die* pain-killing *or* (*Med.*) analgesic tablet; ~**unempfindlich** *Adj.* insensitive to pain *pred.*; ~**verzerrt** *Adj.* ‹face, smile› distorted *or* twisted with pain; ~**voll** ❶ *Adj.* Ⓐ (*physisch*) [very] painful; Ⓑ (*psychisch*) painful; distressing; ❷ *adv.* painfully

**Schmetter·ball** *der* (*Tennis usw.*) smash

**Schmetterling** *der;* ~**s,** ~**e** Ⓐ butterfly; (*Nachtfalter*) moth; ~**e Europas** butterflies and moths of Europe; Ⓑ (*Schwimmen*) butterfly

**Schmetterlingsblütler** /-blyːtlɐ/ *der;* ~**s,** ~**:** papilionaceous plant

**Schmetterlings·stil** *der* (*Schwimmen*) butterfly [stroke]

**schmettern** /ˈʃmɛtɐn/ ❶ *tr. V.* Ⓐ (*schleudern*) hurl (**an** + *Akk.* at, **gegen** against); **jmdn./etw. zu Boden** ~**:** send sb./sth. crashing to the ground; **die Tür ins Schloss** ~**:** slam the door hard; Ⓑ (*laut spielen, singen usw.*) blare out ‹march, music›; ‹person› sing lustily ‹song›; bellow ‹order›; **einen Tusch** ~**:** unleash a loud flourish; Ⓒ (*Tennis usw.*) smash ‹ball›.
❷ *itr. V.* Ⓐ *mit sein* (*aufprallen*) crash; smash; Ⓑ (*schallen*) ‹trumpet, music, etc.› blare out; **ein** ~**der Klang** a blare

**Schmetter·schlag** *der* (*bes. Faustball, Volleyball*) smash

**Schmied** /ʃmiːt/ *der;* ~**[e]s,** ~**e** ▶ 159 blacksmith; ⇨ *auch* **Glück** B

**schmiedbar** *Adj.* malleable

**Schmiede** *die;* ~, ~**en** smithy; forge

**schmiede-, Schmiede-:** ~**arbeit** *die* piece of wrought-iron work; ~**arbeiten** [pieces *pl.* of] wrought-iron work *sing.*; ~**eisen** *das* wrought iron; (*schmiedbares Eisen*) forgeable iron; ~**eisern** *Adj.* wrought-iron; ~**hammer** *der* drop hammer; ~**kunst** *die* blacksmith's craft

**schmieden** *tr. V.* (*auch fig.*) forge (**zu** into, **aus** from, out of); **Pläne/ein Komplott** ~ (*fig.*) hatch plans/a plot; **Verse** *od.* **Reime** ~ (*spött.*) concoct verses; **an eine Mauer** *usw.* **geschmiedet werden** ‹prisoner› be fettered to a wall *etc.*

**Schmiedin** *die;* ~, ~**nen** ▶ 159 blacksmith

**schmiegen** /ˈʃmiːgn̩/ ❶ *refl. V.* snuggle, nestle (**in** + *Akk.* in); **sich an jmdn.** ~**:** snuggle [close] up to sb.; **sie schmiegte sich eng an seine Seite** she pressed *or* nestled close to his side; **sich an etw.** (*Akk.*) ~ (*fig.*) ‹road› hug sth.; ‹village› cling to sth.; **sich an jmds. Körper** ~ (*fig.*) ‹dress› hug sb.'s figure.
❷ *tr. V.* press (**an** + *Akk.* against)

**schmiegsam** *Adj.* supple ‹leather, material›

**Schmierage** /ʃmiˈraːʒə/ *die;* ~ (*ugs. scherzh.*) ⇨ **Schmiererei** A

**Schmiere**[1] *die;* ~, ~**n** Ⓐ (*Schmierfett*) grease; Ⓑ (*schwieriger Schmutz*) greasy *or* slimy mess; Ⓒ (*ugs. abwertend: Provinztheater*) fleapit (*coll.*) of a provincial theatre; (*veralt.: Wanderbühne*) troop of second-rate barnstormers

**Schmiere**[2] *die;* ~**:** *in* **[bei etw.]** ~ **stehen** (*ugs.*) act as lookout [while sth. takes place]; (*in der Schule*) keep cave (*Sch. sl.*) [while sth. is going on]

**schmieren** /ˈʃmiːrən/ ❶ *tr. V.* Ⓐ (*mit Schmiermitteln*) lubricate; (*mit Schmierfett*) grease; **[gehen** *od.* **laufen] wie geschmiert** (*ugs.*) [go] like clockwork *or* without a hitch; Ⓑ (*streichen, auftragen*) spread ‹butter, jam, etc.› (**auf** + *Akk.* on); **Salbe auf eine Wunde** ~**:** apply ointment to a wound; **sich** (*Dat.*) **Creme ins Gesicht/Pomade ins Haar** ~**:** rub cream into one's face/hair cream into one's hair; Ⓒ (*mit Aufstrich*) **Brote/Schmalzbrote** ~**:** spread slices of bread/bread and dripping; Ⓓ (*abwertend: unsauber schreiben*) scrawl ‹essay, school work›; (*schnell und nachlässig schreiben*) scribble, dash off ‹article, play, etc.›; **Parolen an Wände** *usw.* ~**:** scrawl *or* daub slogans on walls *etc.*; Ⓔ (*salopp: bestechen*) **jmdn.** ~**:** grease sb.'s palm; Ⓕ **jmdm. eine** ~ (*salopp*) give sb. a clout (*coll.*); **eine geschmiert kriegen** (*salopp*) get a clout (*coll.*); Ⓖ (*Kartenspiel, bes. Skatjargon*) play ‹high-counting card› to a trick won by one's partner.
❷ *itr. V.* Ⓐ ‹oil, grease› lubricate; Ⓑ (*ugs. unsauber schreiben*) ‹person› scrawl, scribble; ‹pen, ink› smudge, make smudges

**Schmieren-:** ~**komödiant** *der,* ~**komödiantin** *die* (*abwertend*) cheapjack play-actor; ~**komödie** *die,* ~**theater** *das* (*abwertend*) shoddy farce

**Schmiererei** *die;* ~, ~**en** (*ugs. abwertend*) Ⓐ (*unsauberes Schreiben*) scrawling; scribbling; **eine einzige** ~**:** one long scrawl; (*Kleckserei*) nothing but a smudgy mess; Ⓑ (*unsauber Geschriebenes*) scrawl; scribble

**Schmier-:** ~**fett** *das* grease; ~**film** *der* Ⓐ (*auf der Straße usw.*) greasy surface; Ⓑ (*Technik*) film of lubricant; ~**fink** *der* (*ugs. abwertend*) Ⓐ (*im Schreiben*) messy writer; (*jmd., der Wände beschmiert*) graffiti writer; (*jmd., der Diffamierendes schreibt*) muckraker; Ⓑ (*Kind, das sich/etw. schmutzig macht*) mucky pup (*coll.*); ~**geld** *das* (*ugs. abwertend*) slush money; ~**heft** *das* rough book

**schmierig** *Adj.* Ⓐ (*feucht-klebrig*) greasy ‹surface, clothes, hands, step, etc.›; slimy ‹earth, surface›; Ⓑ (*schmutzig*) mucky; (*dreckig*) filthy; Ⓒ (*abwertend: widerlich freundlich*) slimy, (*coll.*) smarmy ‹person›; Ⓓ (*abwertend: zweideutig*) dirty, smutty ‹joke etc.›

**Schmier-:** ~**käse** *der* (*bes. nordd.*) ⇨ **Streichkäse**; ~**mittel** *das* lubricant; ~**öl** *das* lubricating oil; ~**papier** *das* scrap paper; ~**seife** *die* soft soap

**schmilzt** /ʃmɪltst/ *2. u. 3. Pers. Sg. Präsens v.* **schmelzen**

**Schminke** /ˈʃmɪŋkə/ *die;* ~, ~**n** make-up

**schminken** ❶ *tr. V.* make up ‹face, eyes›; **die Lippen** ~**:** put lipstick on; **der Bericht ist stark geschminkt** (*fig.*) the report has been given a very favourable slant.
❷ *refl. V.* make oneself up; put on make-up; **sich leicht/stark** *od.* **kräftig** ~**:** put on a little/a lot of make-up

**Schmink-:** ~**stift** *der* stick of make-up *or* greasepaint; ~**tisch** *der* make-up table; ~**topf** *der* make-up jar

**Schmirgel** /ˈʃmɪrgl̩/ *der;* ~**s** emery

**schmirgeln** /ˈʃmɪrgl̩n/ *tr. V.* Ⓐ (*schleifen*) rub down; (*bes. mit Sandpapier*) sand; Ⓑ (*durch S*~ *entfernen*) remove ‹paint, rust› with emery paper/sandpaper

**Schmirgel·papier** *das* emery paper; (*Sandpapier*) sandpaper

**schmiss, *schmiß** /ʃmɪs/ *1. u. 3. Pers. Sg. Prät. v.* **schmeißen**

**Schmiss, *Schmiß** *der;* **Schmisses, Schmisse** Ⓐ (*Fechtwunde*) [sabre] cut; (*Narbe*) duelling scar; Ⓑ (*veralt.: Schwung, Elan*) punch; zip

**schmissig** (*veralt.*) ❶ *Adj.* rousing ‹march, song›; zippy ‹couplets etc.›.
❷ *adv.* rousingly; with a swing

**Schmock** /ʃmɔk/ *der;* ~**[e]s, Schmöcke** /ˈʃmœkə/ (*abwertend: Schreiberling*) hack writer

**Schmöker** /ˈʃmøːkɐ/ *der;* ~**s,** ~ (*ugs.*) lightweight adventure story/romance; **ein dicker** ~**:** a thick tome of light reading

**schmökern** (*ugs.*) ❶ *itr. V.* bury oneself in a book.
❷ *tr. V.* bury oneself in ‹book›

**schmollen** /ˈʃmɔlən/ *itr. V.* sulk; ‹lips, mouth› pout; **mit jmdm.** ~**:** be in a huff and refuse to speak to sb.

**Schmoll-:** ~**mund** *der* pouting mouth; **einen** ~**mund machen** *od.* **ziehen** pout; ~**winkel** *der: in* **sich in den** ~**winkel zurückziehen** (*ugs.*) go off into a corner to sulk; get a fit of the sulks; **im** ~**winkel sitzen** (*ugs.*) have [a fit of] the sulks

**schmolz** /ʃmɔlts/ *1. u. 3. Pers. Sg. Prät. v.* **schmelzen**

**Schmonzes** /ˈʃmɔntsəs/ *der;* ~ (*ugs. abwertend*) idle chatter; silly talk

**Schmonzette** /ʃmɔnˈtsɛtə/ *die;* ~, ~**n** (*ugs. abwertend*) trashy play; (*Film*) trashy film

**Schmor·braten** *der* pot roast; braised beef

**schmoren** /ˈʃmoːrən/ ❶ *tr. V.* braise; **jmdn. [im eigenen Saft]** ~ **lassen** (*ugs.*) leave sb.

*old spelling (see note on page 1707)

S

to stew in his/her own juice. **2** *itr. V.* **A** (*garen*) braise; **B** (*ugs.: schwitzen*) swelter; **in der Sonne ~:** roast in the sun

**Schmor·fleisch** *das* braising steak

**Schmu** /ʃmu:/ *der; ~s* (*ugs.*) little game; **erzähl mir keinen ~!** don't tell me any stories (*coll.*); **~ machen** cheat; work a fiddle (*coll.*)

**schmuck** /ʃmʊk/ (*veralt.*) **1** *Adj.* attractive; pretty; (*schick*) smart ‹clothes, house, ship, etc.›. **2** *adv.* attractively; smartly

**Schmuck** *der; ~[e]s* **A** (*~stücke*) jewelry; jewellery (*esp. Brit.*); **B** (*~stück*) piece of jewelry/jewellery; **C** (*Zierde*) decoration; **ornamentaler ~:** ornamentation; **die Stadt zeigte sich im ~ der Fahnen** (*geh.*) the town was decked with flags

**schmücken** /ˈʃmʏkn̩/ *tr. V.* decorate; embellish ‹writings, speech›; **sie schmückten sich mit Blumenkränzen** they adorned themselves with garlands; **~de Beiwörter/Zusätze** embellishments

**schmuck-, Schmuck-: ~kästchen** *das,* **~kasten** *der* jewelry *or* (*esp. Brit.*) jewellery box; **ihr Haus ist das reinste ~kästchen** her house is an absolute picture; **~los** *Adj.* plain; bare ‹room›; **ein ~loses Grab** an undecorated grave

**Schmucklosigkeit** *die; ~:* plainness; (*eines Zimmers*) bareness

**Schmuck-: ~sachen** *Pl.* jewelry *sing.;* jewellery *sing.* (*esp. Brit.*); **~stein** *der* attractive stone (*used in jewelry*); gemstone; **~stück** *das* piece of jewelry *or* (*esp. Brit.*) jewellery; **ein ~stück/das ~stück seiner Sammlung** (*fig.*) one of the jewels/the jewel of his collection; **~waren** *Pl.* jewelry *sing.;* jewellery *sing.* (*esp. Brit.*)

**Schmuddel** *der; ~s* (*ugs. abwertend*) muck (*coll.*); grime

**schmuddelig** *Adj.* (*ugs. abwertend*) grubby; mucky (*coll.*); (*schmutzig u. unordentlich*) messy; grotty (*Brit. coll.*)

**Schmuggel** /ˈʃmʊgl̩/ *der; ~s* smuggling *no art.;* **~ treiben** smuggle

**schmuggeln** *tr.* (*auch itr.*) *V.* smuggle (**in** + *Akk.* into; **aus** out of); **jmdm. einen Zettel in die Handtasche ~** (*fig.*) smuggle a note into sb.'s handbag

**Schmuggel·ware** *die* smuggled goods *pl.;* contraband *no pl.*

**Schmuggler** *der; ~s, ~,* **Schmugglerin** *die; ~, ~nen* smuggler

**schmunzeln** /ˈʃmʊntsl̩n/ *itr. V.* **[vor sich** (*Akk.*) **hin] ~:** smile [quietly] to oneself; **ein Schmunzeln unterdrücken** suppress a smile

**Schmus** /ʃmu:s/ *der; ~es* (*ugs.*) (*Angeberei*) big talk; (*Geschwafel*) waffle; (*Schmeicheleien*) soft soap; **so ein ~!** what a load of waffle/soft soap

**Schmuse·katze** *die* (*fam.*) cuddly sort (*coll.*); (*kleines Mädchen*) cuddly little thing (*coll.*); **eine ~ sein** be the cuddly sort (*coll.*)

**schmusen** /ˈʃmu:zn̩/ *itr. V.* (*ugs.*) **A** (*zärtlich sein*) cuddle; ‹couple› kiss and cuddle; (*knutschen*) neck (*coll.*); **mit jmdm. ~:** cuddle sb.; ‹lover› kiss and cuddle *or* (*coll.*) neck with sb.; **miteinander ~:** have a cuddle; ‹couple› have a kiss and a cuddle; **~de Pärchen** snogging (*Brit. coll.*) *or* (*coll.*) necking couples; **B** (*abwertend: schmeicheln*) softsoap

**Schmuser** *der; ~s, ~* (*ugs.*) affectionate type; cuddly sort (*coll.*); **er ist ein kleiner ~:** he's a cuddly little thing

**Schmuserin,** *die; ~, ~nen* (*ugs.*) affectionate type; cuddly sort (*coll.*); **sie ist eine kleine ~:** she's a cuddly little thing

**Schmutz** /ʃmʊts/ *der; ~es* **A** dirt; (*Schlamm*) mud; **der ~ von den Malern** the mess left by the painters; **etw. macht viel/keinen ~:** sth. makes a great deal of/leaves no mess; **durch den dicksten ~ laufen** walk through the worst bit of mud; **jmdn./etw. durch den ~ ziehen** *od.* **in den ~ treten** (*fig.*) drag sb./sth. through the mud (*fig.*); **B** (*abwertend: minderwertige, geschmacklose Literatur, Filme usw.*) filth; **~ und Schund** trash and filth; ⇒ *auch* **bewerfen** A

**schmutz·abweisend** *Adj.* dirt-resistant

**schmutzen** *itr. V.* get dirty

**Schmutz-: ~fänger** *der* **A** (*etw., das ~ anzieht*) dirt trap; **B** (*bei Fahrzeugen*) mudflap; **~fink** *der; ~en od. ~s, ~en* (*ugs.*) **A** (*unsauberer Mensch*) [dirty] pig (*coll.*); (*Kind*) dirty brat; **B** (*unmoralischer Mensch*) depraved type (*coll.*); **alter ~fink** dirty old man; **~fleck** *der* dirty mark (**in** + *Dat.* on); (*in der Landschaft usw.*) blot

**schmutzig** **1** *Adj.* **A** (*unsauber*) dirty; (*ungepflegt*) dirty, slovenly ‹person, restaurant, etc.›; **sich/sich** (*Dat.*) **die Finger ~ machen** get [oneself] dirty/get one's fingers dirty *or* grubby; ⇒ *auch* **Finger** A; **B** (*abwertend: unverschämt*) cocky ‹remarks›; **ein ~es Lächeln** a smirk; **C** (*abwertend: obszön*) smutty ‹joke, song, story›; dirty ‹thoughts›; **D** (*abwertend: unlauter*) dirty ‹business, war›; crooked, shady ‹practices, deal›; **eine ~e Gesinnung** a devious cast of mind. **2** *adv.* (*abwertend*) **~ grinsen** smirk

**Schmutzigkeit** *die; ~:* dirtiness

**Schmutz-: ~titel** *der* (*Druckw.*) half-title; **~wäsche** *die* dirty washing; **~wasser** *das; Pl.* **~wässer** dirty water; (*Abwasser*) sewage

**Schnabel** /ˈʃna:bl̩/ *der; ~s,* **Schnäbel** /ˈʃnɛ:bl̩/ **A** beak; **B** (*ugs.: Mund*) gob (*sl.*); **reden, wie einem der ~ gewachsen ist** say just what one thinks; **C** (*an einer Kanne*) spout; (*an einem Krug*) lip; **D** (*hist.: an Schiffen*) prow; **E** (*Musik: Mundstück*) mouthpiece

**Schnabel·hieb** *der* peck

**schnäbeln** /ˈʃnɛ:bl̩n/ *itr. V.* **A** ‹birds› bill; **B** (*ugs. scherzh.: sich küssen*) bill and coo

**Schnabel-: ~schuh** *der* (*hist.*) pointed shoe (*often with turned-up toe*); **~tier** *das* duck-billed platypus

**schnabulieren** /ʃnabuˈli:rən/ *tr., itr. V.* (*fam.*) eat with great enjoyment

**Schnack** /ʃnak/ *der; ~[e]s, ~s od.* **Schnäcke** /ˈʃnɛkə/ (*nordd.*) **A** (*Unterhaltung*) chat; **B** (*abwertend: Gerede*) [idle] chatter; gossip; **C** (*witziger Spruch*) witty saying; bon mot

**schnackeln** *itr. V.* (*ugs.*) **A** (*bes. bayr.: schnalzen*) **mit der Zunge/den Fingern ~:** click one's tongue/snap one's fingers; **B** (*unpers.*) **es hat geschnackelt** (*bes. südd.*) (*es ist geglückt*) it's come off; success [at last]!; (*jmd. hat begriffen*) it's clicked (*sl.*); **bei den beiden hats geschnackelt** those two have fallen for one another (*coll.*)

**schnacken** *itr. V.* (*nordd.*) chat; **platt ~:** talk in Low German dialect

**Schnake** /ˈʃna:kə/ *die; ~, ~n* **A** daddy-long-legs; crane fly; **B** (*bes. südd.: Stechmücke*) mosquito

**Schnaken·stich** *der* (*bes. südd.*) mosquito bite

**Schnalle** /ˈʃnalə/ *die; ~, ~n* **A** (*Gürtelschnalle*) buckle; **B** (*österr.: Türklinke*) door handle; **C** (*salopp: weibliche Person*) cow (*sl. derog.*); (*Prostituierte*) tart (*sl.*)

**schnallen** *tr. V.* **A** (*mit einer Schnalle festziehen*) buckle ‹shoe, belt›; fasten ‹strap›; **den Gürtel/Riemen enger/weiter ~:** tighten/loosen one's belt/the strap; **B** (*mit Riemen/Gurten befestigen*) strap (**auf** + *Akk.* on to); **C** (*los~*) **etw. von etw. ~:** unstrap sth. from sth.; **D** (*salopp: begreifen*) twig (*coll.*)

**Schnallen·schuh** *der* buckle shoe

**schnalzen** *itr. V.* **[mit der Zunge/den Fingern] ~:** click one's tongue/snap one's fingers; **mit der Peitsche ~:** crack the whip

**schnapp** *Interj.* click; (*beim Zufallen eines Deckels o. Ä.*) bang; (*beim Schneiden*) snip; **~ machen** go click/bang/snip

**Schnäppchen** /ˈʃnɛpçən/ *das; ~s, ~* (*ugs.*) snip (*Brit. coll.*); [real] bargain; **ein ~ machen** get a [real] bargain

**Schnäppchen·jäger** *der* (*ugs.*) bargain hunter

**schnappen** /ˈʃnapn̩/ **1** *itr. V.* **A** **nach jmdm./etw. ~** ‹animal› snap *or* take a snap at sb./sth.; **nach Luft ~** (*fig.*) gasp for breath *or* air; **B** *mit sein* (*schnellen*) **[in die Höhe] ~:** spring up [with a snap]; **ins Schloss ~** ‹door› click shut; ‹bolt› snap home; **C** (*leise knallen*) snap; ‹scissors› snip. **2** *tr. V.* **A** ‹dog, bird, etc.› snatch; **[sich** (*Dat.*)**] jmdn./etw. ~** (*ugs.*) ‹person› grab sb./sth.; (*mit raschem Zugriff*) snatch sb./sth.; ⇒ *auch* **Luft** A; **B** (*ugs.: festnehmen*) catch, (*coll.*) nab ‹thief etc.›

**Schnapper** *der; ~s, ~* (*Türfalle*) latch

**Schnapp-: ~messer** *das* **A** clasp knife; **B** (*Stichwaffe*) flick knife; **~schloss, *~schloß** *das* spring lock; **~schuss, *~schuß** *der* snapshot

**Schnaps** /ʃnaps/ *der; ~es,* **Schnäpse** /ˈʃnɛpsə/ **A** spirit; (*Klarer*) schnapps; **zwei Schnäpse** two glasses of spirit/schnapps; **B** (*Spirituosen*) spirits *pl.*

**Schnaps·brennerei** *die* distillery

**Schnaps·bruder** *der* (*ugs. abwertend*) boozer (*coll.*)

**Schnäpschen** /ˈʃnɛpsçən/ *das; ~s, ~* (*fam.*) small schnapps

**Schnaps·drossel** *die* (*scherzh.*) boozer (*coll.*)

**schnäpseln** /ˈʃnɛpsl̩n/ *itr. V.* (*ugs. scherzh.*) booze [the hard stuff] (*coll.*)

**Schnaps-: ~flasche** *die* spirits/schnapps bottle; **~glas** *das* schnapps glass; **~idee** *die* (*ugs.*) hare-brained idea; **~zahl** *die:* (*scherzh.*) *number in which all the digits are the same*

**schnarchen** /ˈʃnarçn̩/ *itr. V.* snore

**Schnarcher** *der; ~s, ~* (*ugs.*) **A** (*Mensch*) snorer; **B** (*Geräusch*) snore

**Schnarcherin,** *die; ~, ~nen* ⇒ **Schnarcher** A

**schnarren** /ˈʃnarən/ *itr. V.* ‹alarm clock, telephone, doorbell› buzz [shrilly]; **mit ~der Stimme** in a rasping voice

**schnattern** /ˈʃnatn̩/ *itr. V.* **A** ‹goose etc.› cackle, gaggle; **B** (*ugs.: eifrig schwatzen*) jabber [away]; chatter; **C** (*bes. nordd.: zittern*) **er schnatterte vor Kälte** his teeth were chattering with the cold

**schnauben** /ˈʃnaubn̩/ *regelm.* (*auch unr.*) *itr. V.* **A** ‹person, horse› snort (**vor** with); (*fig.*) ‹steam locomotive› puff, chuff; **heftig ~:** pant heavily; **wütend ~:** snort with fury; **B** (*bes. südd.: atmen*) breathe

**schnaufen** /ˈʃnaufn̩/ *itr. V.* puff, pant (**vor** with); (*fig.*) ‹steam locomotive› puff, chuff

**Schnaufer** *der; ~s, ~* (*ugs.*) breath; **einen ~ lang** for a second; **den letzten ~ tun** (*verhüll.*) breathe one's last

**Schnauferl** *das; ~s, ~,* (*österr.:*) **~n** (*ugs. scherzh.*) venerable old vehicle; oldie (*coll.*)

**Schnauz** /ʃnauts/ *der; ~es,* **Schnäuze** /ˈʃnɔytsə/ (*bes. schweiz.*) ⇒ **Schnauzbart** A

**Schnauz·bart** *der* **A** (*Bartform*) large moustache; mustachio (*arch.*); (*an den Seiten herabhängend*) walrus moustache; **B** (*ugs.: Bartträger*) heavily mustachioed fellow (*dated/literary*)

**schnauz·bärtig** *adj.* mustachioed (*dated/literary*)

**Schnäuzchen** /ˈʃnɔytsçən/ *das* **A** (*von Tieren*) little nose; (*der Maus usw.*) little snout; **B** (*von Menschen*) little mouth

**Schnauze** *die; ~, ~n* **A** (*von Tieren*) muzzle; (*der Maus usw.*) snout; (*Maul*) mouth; **eine kalte ~:** a cold nose; **B** (*derb: Mund, Mundwerk*) gob (*sl.*); **jmdm. in die ~ hauen** smack sb. in the gob (*sl.*); **die ~ voll haben** (*salopp*) be fed up to the back teeth (*coll.*); **eine große ~ haben** shoot one's mouth off (*sl.*); **eine freche/lose ~ haben** be a cheeky so-and-so (*coll.*)/have a loose tongue; **die ~ halten** keep one's trap shut (*sl.*); **[halt die] ~!** shut your trap! (*sl.*); **frei [nach] ~, nach ~** (*salopp*) as one thinks fit; as the mood takes one; ⇒ *auch* **verbrennen** 2 B; **C** (*ugs.*) ⇒ **Schnabel** C; **D** (*ugs.: Vorderteil*) (*eines Flugzeugs*) nose; (*eines Fahrzeugs*) front

S

**schnauzen** *tr., itr. V.* (*ugs.*) bark; (*ärgerlich*) snap; snarl

**schnäuzen** ⇒ **schnäuzen**

**Schnauzer** *der;* **~s,** **~** A (*Hund*) schnauzer; B (*ugs.*) ⇒ **Schnauzbart** A

**Schnecke** /ˈʃnɛkə/ *die* A (*Tier*) snail; (*Nackt~*) slug; **jmdn. [so] zur ~ machen** (*ugs.*) give sb. [such] a good carpeting (*coll.*); B (*ugs.: Gebäck*) Belgian bun; C (*Frisur*) coiled plait (*over the ear*); earphone; D (*Anat.: im Ohr*) cochlea; E (*bei Streichinstrumenten*) scroll; F (*Kunstwiss.*) ⇒ **Volute**

**Schnecken-:** **~frisur** *die* earphones *pl.;* **~gewinde** *das* (*Technik*) worm; **~haus** *das* snail shell; **~nudel** *die* (*bes. südd.*) ⇒ **Schnecke** B; **~post** *die* (*ugs.*) snail mail (*coll.*); **etw. mit der/per ~post schicken** send sth. by snail mail; **~tempo** *das* (*ugs.*) snail's pace; **im ~tempo** at a snail's pace

**Schnee** /ʃneː/ *der;* **~s** A snow; **in tiefem ~ liegen** lie under deep snow; **~ von gestern** (*ugs.*) things *pl.*/a thing of the past; ancient history (*fig.*); **anno ~, im Jahre ~** (*österr.*) in the year dot (*coll.*); B (*Eier~*) beaten egg white; **das Eiweiß zu ~ schlagen** beat the egg white until stiff; C (*Jargon: Kokain*) snow (*sl.*)

**Schnee·ball** *der* A snowball; B (*Strauch*) snowball tree; guelder rose

**Schneeball-:** **~schlacht** *die* snowball fight; **eine ~schlacht machen** have a snowball fight; **~system** *das* A (*Form des Warenabsatzes*) pyramid selling *no art.;* B (*Verbreitungsart*) cumulative [distribution] process; snowball; (*Fernspr.*) cascade system; (*von Briefen*) chain-letter system

**schnee-, Schnee-:** **~bedeckt** *Adj.* snow-covered; **~besen** *der* whisk; **~blind** *Adj.* snowblind; **~blindheit** *die* snow blindness; **~brett** *das* [stretch of] windslab; **~brille** *die* snow goggles *pl.;* **~decke** *die* blanket *or* covering of snow; **~fall** *der* snowfall; fall of snow; **dichter ~fall setzte ein** thick snow began to fall; **~flocke** *die* snowflake; **~fräse** *die* rotary [snow]plough; **~frau** *die* snow-woman; **~frei** *Adj.* free of snow *postpos.;* **~gestöber** *das* snow flurry; **~glatt** *Adj.* slippery with [packed] snow *postpos.;* **~glätte** *die* [slippery surface due to] packed snow; **bei ~glätte** when the roads are slippery because of packed snow; **~glöckchen** *das* snowdrop; **~grenze** *die* ▶ 411 snowline; (*beweglich*) snow limit; **~hase** *der* snow hare; **~huhn** *das* snow grouse; ptarmigan

**schneeig** *Adj.* snowy

**schnee-, Schnee-:** **~kette** *die* snow chain; **~könig** *der: in* **sich freuen wie ein ~könig** (*ugs.*) be as pleased as Punch; **~landschaft** *die* snowy *or* snow-covered landscape; **~mann** *der* snowman; **~matsch** *der* slush; **~pflug** *der* (*auch Ski*) snowplough; **~raupe** *die* snowmobile (*for preparing ski runs*); **~regen** *der* sleet; **~schauer** *der* snow shower; **~schmelze** *die* melting of the snow; thaw; **~schuh** *der* A (*veralt.*) ski; B (*Lauffläche*) snowshoe; **~sturm** *der* snowstorm; **~treiben** *das* driving snow; **~verhältnisse** *Pl.* snow conditions; **~verwehung** *die:* **~verwehung[en]** snowdrifts *pl.;* **eine ~verwehung** a mass of snowdrifts; ***~wächte, ~wechte** *die* cornice; **~wehe** *die* snowdrift; **~weiß** *Adj.* snow-white; as white as snow *postpos.*

**Schneewittchen** /-ˈvɪtçən/ (*das*)*;* **~s** Snow White

**Schneid** *der;* **~[e]s,** *südd., österr.: die;* **~** (*ugs.*) guts *pl.* (*coll.*); **ihm fehlt der ~:** he hasn't got the guts [to do it]; **dazu gehört ~:** that takes some nerve; **jmdm. den** *od.* **die ~ abkaufen** take the fight out of sb.

**Schneid·brenner** *der* (*Technik*) cutting torch; oxyacetylene cutter

**Schneide** /ˈʃnaidə/ *die;* **~, ~n** [cutting] edge; (*Klinge*) blade; **eine doppelte ~ haben** be two-edged

**schneiden** 1 *unr. itr. V.* A cut (**in** + *Akk.* into); B (*Medizinerjargon: operieren*) operate; C (*beim Fahren*) **bei Überholmanövern ~:** cut in after overtaking; D (*Schmerz verursachen*) ‹wind, cold› be biting; **~d** biting ‹wind, cold, voice, sarcasm›; **es schnitt ihm ins Herz** (*fig.*) it cut him to the quick.
2 *unr. tr. V.* A cut; cut, reap ‹corn etc.›; cut, mow ‹grass›; (*in Scheiben*) slice ‹bread, sausage, etc.›; (*klein ~*) cut up, chop ‹wood, vegetables›; (*zu~*) cut out ‹dress›; (*stutzen*) prune ‹tree, bush›; trim ‹beard›; **Kräuter in die Suppe/ Wurst unter die Kartoffeln ~:** cut up herbs/sausage and add them/it to the soup/ potatoes; **sich** (*Dat.*) **von jmdm. die Haare ~ lassen** have one's hair cut by sb.; **hier ist eine Luft zum Schneiden** (*fig.*) there's a terrible fug in here (*coll.*); **ein eng/weit/gut geschnittenes Kleid** a tight-fitting/loose-fitting/well-cut dress; **ein regelmäßig geschnittenes Gesicht** (*fig.*) a face with regular features; B (*Medizinerjargon: auf~*) operate on ‹patient›; cut [open] ‹tumour, ulcer, etc.›; lance ‹boil, abscess›; C (*Film, Rundf., Ferns.: cutten*) cut, edit ‹film, tape›; D (*beim Fahren*) **eine Kurve ~:** cut a corner; **jmdn./einen anderen Wagen ~:** cut in on sb./another car; E (*kreuzen*) ‹line, railway, etc.› intersect, cross; **die Linien/Straßen ~ sich** the lines/roads intersect; F (*Tennis usw.*) slice, put spin on ‹ball›; (*Fußball*) curve ‹ball, free kick›; (*Billard*) put side on ‹ball›; G **eine Grimasse ~:** grimace; H (*ignorieren*) **jmdn. ~:** cut sb. dead; send sb. to Coventry (*Brit.*).
3 *refl. V.* **ich habe mir** *od.* **mich in den Finger geschnitten** I've cut my finger; **wenn du das meinst, hast du dich geschnitten** (*fig.*) it you think that, you've made a big mistake

**Schneider** *der;* **~s, ~** A ▶ 159 tailor; (*Damen~*) dressmaker; **frieren wie ein ~** (*ugs.*) be frozen stiff; B (*ugs.: Schneidegerät*) cutter; (*für Scheiben*) slicer; C (*Skat: 30 Punkte*) schneider; **[im] ~ sein** have less than 30 points; be schneidered; **~ ansagen** declare schneider; **aus dem ~ sein** have made schneider; (*fig. ugs.: eine schwierige Situation überwunden haben*) be in the clear; be clear of trouble; D (*Tischtennis: unter 11 Punkte*) [score of] less than 11 points

**Schneiderei** *die;* **~, ~en** A tailor's shop; (*Damen~*) dressmaker's shop; B (*das Schneidern*) tailoring; (*von Damenkleidern*) dressmaking

**Schneiderin** *die;* **~, ~nen** ▶ 159 tailor; (*Damen~*) dressmaker

**Schneider-:** **~kostüm** *das* tailor-made *or* tailored suit; **~kreide** *die* tailor's chalk; French chalk; **~meister** *der,* **~meisterin** *die* master tailor; (*für Damenkleider*) master dressmaker

**schneidern** 1 *tr. V.* make ‹dress, clothes›; make, tailor ‹suit›; **sie schneidert ihre Sachen selbst** she makes her own clothes.
2 *itr. V.* make clothes/dresses; (*beruflich*) work as a tailor; (*als Schneiderin*) work as a dressmaker

**Schneider-:** **~puppe** *die* tailor's dummy; (*eines Damenschneiders*) dressmaker's dummy; **~sitz** *der* cross-legged position; **im ~sitz** cross-legged

**Schneide-:** **~tisch** *der* (*Film, Ferns.*) editing *or* cutting table; **~zahn** *der* ▶ 471 incisor

**schneidig** 1 *Adj.* A (*forsch, zackig*) dashing; (*waghalsig*) daring; bold; rousing, brisk ‹music›; B (*flott, sportlich*) dashing ‹appearance, fellow›; trim ‹figure›.
2 *adv.* briskly; **~ spielen** play in a rousing/ lively manner

**schneien** /ˈʃnaiən/ 1 *itr., tr. V.* (*unpers.*) **es schneit** it is snowing; **es schneit/schneite jeden Tag** it snows/snowed every day; **es schneit dicke Flocken** *od.* **in dicken Flocken** big flakes of snow are falling; **es schneit auf dem Bildschirm** (*fig.*) there's a snowstorm on the screen.
2 *itr. V.; mit sein* (*fig.*) ‹blossom, confetti, etc.› rain down, fall like snow

**Schneise** /ˈʃnaizə/ *die;* **~, ~n** A (*Wald~*) aisle; (*als Feuerschutz*) firebreak; B (*Flug~*) [air] corridor

**schnell** /ʃnɛl/ ▶ 348 1 *Adj.* quick ‹journey, decision, service, etc.›; fast ‹car, skis, road, track, etc.›; quick, rapid, swift ‹progress›; quick, swift ‹movement, blow, action›; **ein ~es Tempo** a high speed; a fast pace; **um ~e Erledigung der Angelegenheit bitten** request that the matter be handled speedily; **sie ist sehr ~ bei der Arbeit** she is a very quick worker; **~es Geld** (*ugs.*) money for jam (*coll.*); **die** *od.* **eine ~e Mark machen** (*salopp*) make a fast buck (*sl.*); **auf die Schnelle** (*ugs.*) in a trice; (*übereilt*) in [too much of] a hurry; in a rush; (*kurzfristig*) at short notice; quickly; **auf die Schnelle ein Bier/eins auf die Schnelle trinken** have a quick beer/a quick one.
2 *adv.* quickly; ‹drive, move, etc.› fast, quickly; ‹spread› quickly, rapidly; (*bald*) soon ‹sold, past, etc.›; **nicht so ~!** not so fast!; **mach ~!** (*ugs.*) move it! (*coll.*); **so ~ macht ihm das keiner nach** nobody is going to equal that in a hurry; **wie heißt er noch ~?** (*ugs.*) what's his name again?; **es ging ~er, als man dachte** it went quicker than expected; **das geht mir zu ~:** that's too quick for me

**Schnell-:** **~bahn** *die* (*Verkehrsw.*) municipal railway; **~boot** *das* high-speed patrol boat; (*Torpedoschnellboot*) motor torpedo boat; PT boat (*Amer.*); **~dienst** *der* express service

**Schnelle** *die;* **~, ~n** A (*Schnelligkeit*) rapidity; (*Tempo*) speed; B (*Geog.: Strom~*) rapids *pl.*

***schnellebig** ⇒ **schnelllebig**

**schnellen** 1 *itr. V.; mit sein* shoot (**aus** + *Dat.* out of; **in** + *Akk.* into); **in die Höhe ~** ‹person› leap to one's feet *or* up; ‹rocket, fig.: prices etc.› shoot up.
2 *tr. V.* send ‹ball, stone, etc.› flying; hurl ‹ball, stone, etc.›; whip ‹fishingline›; **sich mit dem Trampolin in die Höhe ~:** leap high into the air on a/the trampoline

**Schnell-:** **~feuer** *das* (*Milit.*) rapid fire; **~feuer·gewehr** *das* semi-automatic rifle; **~gaststätte** *die* fast-food restaurant; (*~imbiss*) snackbar; **~gericht** *das* convenience food; (*in Lokalen*) quick snack; **~hefter** *der* loose-leaf binder; quick-release file

**Schnelligkeit** *die;* **~, ~en** A (*Tempo*) speed; **die ~, mit der sie arbeitet** the speed at which she works; B (*das Schnellsein*) rapidity; speed

**schnell-, Schnell-:** **~imbiss,** ***~imbiß** *der* snackbar; **~kochplatte** *die* high-speed ring; **~kochtopf** *der* pressure cooker; **~kraft** *die* springiness; **~kurs** *der* crash course; **~lebig** /-leːbɪç/ *Adj.* A (*Biol.: kurzlebig*) short-lived ‹animal, insect›; B (*hektisch, betriebsam*) fast-moving ‹age›; **~paket** *das* (*Postw.*) express parcel; **~reinigung** *die* express cleaner's

**schnellstens** *Adv.* as quickly as possible; (*möglichst bald*) as soon as possible

**schnellst·möglich** 1 *Adj.* quickest possible; **auf ~e Erledigung der Arbeit drängen** press for the earliest possible completion of the work.
2 *adv.* ⇒ **schnellstens**

**Schnell-:** **~spanner** *der* quick-release; **~spann·nabe** *die* quick-release hub; **~straße** *die* expressway (*on which slow-moving vehicles are prohibited*); **~verfahren** *das* A (*bes. Technik*) high-speed process; **im ~verfahren** (*fig.*) at high speed; in a crash programme; B (*Rechtsw.*) summary trial; summary proceedings *pl.;* **im ~verfahren** in summary proceedings; **~verkehr** *der* (*Kfz-W.*) fast-moving traffic; (*~verkehrsnetz*) express services *pl.;* **~zug** *der* express [train]; **~zug·zuschlag** *der* express train supplement

**Schnepfe** /ˈʃnɛpfə/ *die;* **~, ~n** A (*Vogel*) snipe; (*Wald~*) woodcock; B (*salopp abwertend: weibliche Person*) **[blöde] ~:** [silly] cow (*sl. derog.*); C (*salopp abwertend: Prostituierte*) tart (*sl.*)

**schnetzeln** /ˈʃnɛts̩ln/ (*bes. südd.*) cut ‹meat› into thin strips

*old spelling (see note on page 1707)

**schneuzen** ⇒ **schnäuzen**

**Schnick·schnack** *der (ugs.; meist abwertend)* A *(wertloses Zeug)* trinkets *pl.*; *(Zierrat)* frills *pl. (fig.)*; **überflüssiger ~:** superfluous paraphernalia *sing.*; B *(Geschwätz)* waffle; *(Unsinn)* drivel; **~!** rubbish!

**schniefen** /ˈʃniːfn̩/ *itr. V.* sniffle; *(bes. beim Weinen)* snivel

**schniegeln** /ˈʃniːɡl̩n/ *refl. V.* spruce oneself up; ⇒ *auch* **geschniegelt**

**schnieke** /ˈʃniːkə/ ❶ *Adj. (berlin.)* A *(schick, elegant)* snazzy *(coll.)* ‹clothes, fashion, etc.›; B *(großartig)* super *(Brit. coll.)*.
❷ *adv.* snazzily *(coll.)*

**schnipp** *Interj.* snip; **~, schnapp!** snip, snip

**Schnippchen** *das; ~s* trick; **jmdm. ein ~ schlagen** *(ugs.)* outsmart sb. *(coll.)*; put one over on sb. *(sl.)*; **dem Tod/Schicksal ein ~ schlagen** *(ugs.)* cheat death/fate

**Schnippel** *der od. das; ~s, ~ (ugs.)* scrap; *(Papier~, Stoff~)* snippet; shred

**Schnippelchen** *das; ~s, ~:* tiny scrap; *(Papier~, Stoff~)* tiny snippet *or* shred

**schnippeln** *(ugs.)* ❶ *itr. V. (mit der Schere)* snip [away] **(an +** *Dat.* at); **an der Wurst ~** *(mit dem Messer)* cut little snippets of sausage.
❷ *tr. V.* A *(ausschneiden)* snip [out]; B *(zerkleinern)* shred ‹vegetables›; chop ‹beans etc.› [finely]

**schnippen** /ˈʃnɪpn̩/ ❶ *itr. V.* A *(mit der Schere)* snip; B *(mit den Fingern)* snap one's fingers **(nach** at); **mit Daumen und Mittelfinger ~:** snap one's thumb and middle finger together.
❷ *tr. V.* A *(wegschleudern)* flick **(von** off, from); **die Asche von der Zigarette ~:** flick the ash off one's cigarette; B *(herausschleudern)* tap ‹cigarette, card, etc.› **(aus** out of)

**schnippisch** *(abwertend)* ❶ *Adj.* pert ‹reply, tone, etc.›; *(anmaßend)* cocky ‹girl, tone, expression›.
❷ *adv.* pertly; *(anmaßend)* cockily

**Schnipsel** /ˈʃnɪpsl̩/ *der od. das; ~s, ~:* scrap; *(Papier~, Stoff~)* snippet; shred

**schnipseln** ⇒ **schnippeln**

**schnitt** /ʃnɪt/ *1. u. 3. Pers. Sg. Prät. v.* **schneiden**

**Schnitt** *der; ~[e]s, ~e* A cut; *(Operationsschnitt)* incision; cut; **etw. mit einem [schnellen] ~ durchtrennen** divide sth. by cutting it [quickly]; **sich** *(Dat.)* **einen ~ beibringen** cut oneself; B *(das Mähen) (von Gras)* mowing; cut; *(von Getreide)* harvest; **das Korn ist reif für den ~:** the corn is ready for reaping *or* harvesting; **einen** *od.* **seinen ~ [bei etw.] machen** *(fig. ugs.)* make a profit [from sth.]; C *(Form von Kleidung, Haar, Edelsteinen usw.)* cut; **eine Wohnung mit gutem ~** *(fig.)* a well-planned flat *(Brit.) or (Amer.)* apartment; **ihr Profil hat einen klassischen ~** *(fig.)* she has a classical profile; D *(Film, Ferns.)* editing; cutting; **ein harter/weicher ~:** editing with straight *or* sudden/gradual cuts; **~: Gisela Meyer;** edited by *or* editor Gisela Meyer; E *(Schnittmuster)* [dressmaking] pattern; F *(Längs-, Quer-, Schrägschnitt)* section; **etw. im ~ darstellen** show sth. in section; G *(ugs.: Durch~)* average; **er fährt einen ~ von 200 km/h** he is driving at *or* doing an average [speed] of 125 m.p.h.; **im ~:** on average; H *(Math.)* ⇒ **golden 1 c**; I *(Geom.: Schnittfläche)* intersection; J *(Ballspiele: Drall)* spin; **den Ball mit ~ spielen** *od.* **schlagen** put spin on the ball

**Schnitt-: ~blume** *die* cut flower; **~bohne** *die* French bean; **~brot** *das* cut *or* sliced bread

**Schnittchen** *das; ~s, ~:* canapé; [small] open sandwich

**Schnitte** *die; ~, ~n* A *(bes. nordd.: Scheibe)* slice; **eine ~ [Brot]** a slice of bread; **eine [belegte] ~:** an open sandwich; B *(österr.: Waffel)* wafer

**Schnitter** *der; ~s, ~,* **Schnitterin** *die; ~, ~nen (veralt.)* reaper

**schnitt-, Schnitt-: ~fest** *Adj.* firm ‹tomato, sausage, etc.›; **~fläche** *die* cut surface; **die ~fläche des Käses** the cut end of the cheese; **~holz** *das* cut timber

**schnittig** ❶ *Adj.* stylish, smart ‹suit, appearance, etc.›; *(sportlich)* racy ‹car, yacht, etc.›; *(stromlinienförmig)* streamlined ‹car, bow, etc.›.
❷ *adv.* stylishly; *(sportlich)* racily

**schnitt-, Schnitt-: ~käse** *der* cheese suitable for slicing; hard cheese; *(in Scheiben)* cheese slices *pl.*; **~lauch** *der* chives *pl.*; **~linie** *die* line of intersection; *(Linie, die eine andere kreuzt)* intersecting line; **~menge** *die (Math.)* **die ~menge A ∩ B** the intersection of the sets A and B; **~muster** *das* A [dressmaking] pattern; B *(ugs.)* ⇒ **~musterbogen**; **~muster·bogen** *der* pattern chart; **~punkt** *der* intersection; *(Geom.)* point of intersection; **~reif** *Adj.* ‹corn etc.› ready for reaping *or* harvesting; **~stelle** *die (DV)* interface; **~wunde** *die* cut; *(lang u. tief)* gash

**Schnitz·arbeit** *die* carving

**Schnitzel** /ˈʃnɪtsl̩/ *das; ~s, ~* A *(Fleisch)* [veal/pork] escalope; B *(Stückchen) (von Papier)* scrap; snippet; *(von Holz)* shaving; *(von Früchten usw.)* sliver

**Schnitzel·jagd** *die* paperchase

**schnitzeln** *tr. V.* chop up ‹vegetables etc.› [into small pieces]; shred ‹cabbage›

**schnitzen** ❶ *itr. V.* carve; **an etw.** *(Dat.)* **~:** carve away at sth.
❷ *tr. V.* carve

**Schnitzer** *der; ~s, ~* A *(Handwerker)* carver; B *(ugs.: Fehler)* boob *(Brit. coll.)*; goof *(coll.)*; **sich** *(Dat.)* **einen groben ~ leisten** make an awful boob *(Brit. coll.) or (coll.)* goof; *(mit einer Bemerkung)* drop an awful clanger *(coll.)*

**Schnitzerei** *die; ~, ~en* A *(Geschnitztes)* carving *(Gen.* by); B *(das Schnitzen)* carving *no art.*

**Schnitzerin,** *die; ~, ~nen* ⇒ **Schnitzer A**

**Schnitz-: ~messer** *das* wood carving knife; **~werk** *das* carving; *(mehrere Stücke)* carvings *pl.*

**schnob** /ʃnoːp/ *1. u. 3. Pers. Sg. Prät. v.* **schnauben**

**schnöd** /ʃnøːt/ *Adj. (bes. südd., österr.)* ⇒ **schnöde**

**schnodderig** /ˈʃnɔdərɪç/ *(ugs. abwertend)* ❶ *Adj.* brash; **ein ~es Mundwerk haben** have a big mouth.
❷ *adv.* brashly

**Schnodderigkeit** *die; ~, ~en (ugs.)* A *(Art, Wesen)* brashness; B *(Äußerung/Handlung)* brash remark/action

**schnoddrig** ⇒ **schnodderig**

**schnöde** *(geh. abwertend)* ❶ *Adj.* A *(verachtenswert)* despicable; contemptible; base ‹cowardice›; ⇒ *auch* **Mammon**; B *(gemein)* contemptuous, scornful ‹glance, reply, etc.›; harsh ‹reprimand›; **~r Undank** blatant ingratitude.
❷ *adv. (gemein)* contemptuously; ‹reprimand› harshly; ‹exploit, misuse› flagrantly, blatantly

**Schnorchel** /ˈʃnɔrçl̩/ *der; ~s, ~:* snorkel

**Schnörkel** /ˈʃnœrkl̩/ *der; ~s, ~:* scroll; curlicue; *(der Handschrift, in der Rede)* flourish

**schnorren** /ˈʃnɔrən/ *tr., itr. V. (ugs.)* scrounge *(coll.)*; **etw. bei** *od.* **von jmdm. ~:** scrounge *(coll.) or* cadge sth. off sb.

**Schnorrer** *der; ~s, ~,* **Schnorrerin** *die; ~, ~nen (ugs.)* scrounger *(coll.)*; sponger

**Schnösel** /ˈʃnøːzl̩/ *der; ~s, ~ (ugs. abwertend)* young whippersnapper

**schnöselig** *(ugs. abwertend)* ❶ *Adj.* cheeky; insolent.
❷ *adv.* cheekily; insolently

**Schnuckelchen** /ˈʃnʊkl̩çən/ *das; ~s, ~ (fam.)* sweetie[-pie] *(coll.)*; **mein kleines ~:** my little darling *or* pet

**schnuckelig** *Adj. (ugs.)* sweet; cute *(Amer. coll.)*

**Schnüffelei** *die; ~, ~en (ugs. abwertend)* A *(dauerndes Schnüffeln)* [constant] snooping *(coll.)*; B *(Vorfall von ~)* case of snooping *(coll.)*

**schnüffeln** /ˈʃnʏfl̩n/ ❶ *itr. V.* A *(riechen)* sniff; **an etw.** *(Dat.)* **~:** sniff sth.; B *(ugs. abwertend: heimlich suchen; spionieren)* snoop [about] *(coll.)*; **in etw.** *(Akk.)* **~:** pry into sth.; stick one's nose into sth. *(coll.)*; **in jmds. Papieren ~:** nose about in sb.'s papers; C *(Drogenjargon: Dämpfe ~)* sniff [glue/paint *etc.*]; D *(ugs.: die Nase hochziehen)* sniff.
❷ *tr. V. (Drogenjargon: zum S~ benutzen)* sniff ‹glue etc.›

**Schnüffler** *der; ~s, ~,* **Schnüfflerin** *die; ~, ~nen* A *(ugs. abwertend)* Nosey Parker; *(Spion)* snooper *(coll.)*; B *(Drogenjargon)* [glue-, paint-, *etc.*]sniffer

**Schnuller** /ˈʃnʊlɐ/ *der; ~s, ~:* dummy *(Brit.)*; pacifier *(Amer.)*

**Schnulze** /ˈʃnʊltsə/ *die; ~, ~n (ugs. abwertend)* *(Lied/Melodie)* slushy song/tune; *(Theaterstück, Film, Fernsehspiel)* tear jerker *(coll.)*; slushy play; **etw. als ~ singen** sing sth. in a slushy version

**schnupfen** /ˈʃnʊpfn̩/ ❶ *itr. V.* A *(Tabak ~)* take snuff; B *(bei Tränen, Nasenschleim)* sniff.
❷ *tr. V.* take a sniff of ‹cocaine etc.›; *(gewohnheitsmäßig)* sniff ‹cocaine etc.›; **Tabak ~:** take snuff

**Schnupfen** *der; ~s, ~:* [head] cold; **[den** *od.* **einen] ~ haben** have a [head] cold; **sich** *(Dat.)* **den ~ holen** catch a [head] cold

**Schnupfer** *der; ~s, ~,* **Schnupferin** *die; ~, ~nen* snuff-taker

**Schnupf-: ~tabak** *der* snuff; **~tabak[s]·dose** *die* snuff box

**schnuppe** /ˈʃnʊpə/ *in* **~ sein** *(ugs.)* be neither here nor there; **das/er ist mir ~/mir völlig ~** *(ugs.)* I don't care/I couldn't care less about it/him *(coll.)*

**schnuppern** /ˈʃnʊpɐn/ ❶ *itr. V.* sniff; **an etw.** *(Dat.)* **~:** sniff sth.
❷ *tr. V.* sniff; **Seeluft ~** *(fig.)* get some sea air

**Schnur** /ʃnuːɐ̯/ *die; ~,* **Schnüre** /ˈʃnyːrə/ *od.* **Schnuren** A *(Bindfaden)* piece of string; *(Kordel)* piece of cord; *(Zelt~)* guy [rope]; *(für Marionette, Drachen usw.)* string; **eine ~ um ein Paket binden** tie string round a parcel; **Perlen auf eine ~ aufziehen** string pearls; B *(Zierkordel)* piece of braid; **mit vielen Schnüren** with much braid[ing] *sing.*; C *(ugs.: Kabel)* flex *(Brit.)*; lead; cord *(Amer.)*

**Schnür·boden** *der* A *(Theater)* flies *pl.*; B *(Schiffbau)* mould loft

**Schnürchen** *das; ~s, ~ in* **wie am ~ [gehen** *od.* **klappen]** *(ugs.)* [go] like clockwork *or* without a hitch; **ein Gedicht wie am ~ aufsagen** *(ugs.)* say a poem off pat

**schnüren** /ˈʃnyːrən/ ❶ *tr. V.* A tie ‹bundle, string, sb.'s hands, etc.›; tie [up] ‹parcel, person›; tie, lace up ‹shoe, corset, etc.›; **etw. zu Bündeln/Paketen ~:** tie sth. up in bundles/parcels; **etw. um/auf etw.** *(Akk.)* **~:** tie sth. round/[on] to sth.; B **Angst schnürte ihm die Kehle/den Atem** *(fig.)* fear constricted his throat/almost stopped him from breathing.
❷ *refl. V. (sich hineindrücken)* **sich in das Fleisch** *usw.* **~:** cut into the flesh *etc.*
❸ *itr. V.* A *(zu eng sein)* be too tight; pinch; B *mit sein (Jägerspr.)* ‹fox, lynx, wolf› trot in a straight line; ‹fig.: person› trot

**schnur·gerade, schnur·grade** *(ugs.)* ❶ *Adj.* dead straight.
❷ *adv.* dead straight; **~ auf sein Ziel losgehen** *(fig.)* make straight for one's goal

**Schnur·keramik** *die (Archäol.)* corded ware

**schnurlos** *Adj.* cordless

**Schnürl-** /ˈʃnyːɐ̯l-/: **~regen** *der (österr.)* persistent rain; **~samt** *der (österr.)* corduroy

**Schnurr·bart** *der* moustache

**schnurr·bärtig** *Adj.* with a moustache *postpos.*; **~ sein** have a moustache

**Schnurre** *die; ~, ~n (veralt.)* anecdote

**schnurren** /ˈʃnʊrən/ *itr. V.* ‹cat› purr; ‹machine› hum; ‹camera, spinning wheel, etc.› whirr

**Schnurr·haar** *das (Zool.)* whiskers *pl.*

**Schnür·riemen** *der* A strap; B ⇒ **Schnürsenkel**

S

**schnurrig** *Adj.* (*veralt.*) droll; comic; funny; comic ‹old man etc.›

**Schnür-:** **~schuh** *der* lace-up shoe; **~senkel** *der* (*bes. nordd.*) [shoe]lace; (*für Stiefel*) bootlace; **sich** (*Dat.*) **die ~senkel binden** tie one's shoelaces

**schnur·springen** *unr. itr. V.; nur im Inf. und 2. Partizip; mit sein* (*österr.*) skip

**Schnür·stiefel** *der* lace-up boot

**schnur·stracks** *Adv.* (*ugs.*) straight; **der Weg geht ~ geradeaus** the way goes straight ahead; **~ auf jmdn./etw. zugehen** make a beeline for sb./sth.

**Schnürung** *die;* **~, ~en** lacing; (*Schnürsenkel*) laces *pl.*

**schnurz** /ʃnʊrts/ *Adj.* (*ugs.*) *in* **es ist [jmdm.] ~** (*salopp*) it doesn't matter a hoot [to sb.] (*sl.*); **ihm ist jmd./etw./alles ~ [und piepe]** he doesn't give a damn *or* couldn't care less about sb./sth./anything (*coll.*)

**Schnute** /ˈʃnu:tə/ *die;* **~, ~n** (*fam., bes. nordd.: Mund*) mouth; gob (*sl.*); **eine ~ ziehen** *od.* **machen** make *or* pull a [sulky] face

**schob** /ʃo:p/ *1. u. 3. Pers. Prät. v.* **schieben**

**Schober** /ˈʃo:bɐ/ *der;* **~s, ~** Ⓐ open-sided barn; Ⓑ (*Heuhaufen*) [hay]stack; [hay]rick

**Schock**[1] /ʃɔk/ *das;* **~[e]s, ~e** Ⓐ (*veralt.: 60 Stück*) **ein ~:** three score; five dozen; **7 bis 8 ~ Eier** 35-40 dozen eggs; Ⓑ (*ugs.: Menge*) [whole] load of (*coll.*)

**Schock**[2] *der;* **~[e]s, ~s** ▶ 474 (*auch Med.*) shock; **jmdm. einen [schweren/leichten] ~ versetzen** *od.* **geben** give sb. a [nasty/slight] shock *or* a [nasty/bit of a] fright; **unter ~ stehen** be in [a state of] shock; be suffering from shock

**Schock·behandlung** *die* shock treatment

**schocken** *tr. V.* (*ugs.: schockieren*) shock

**Schocker** *der;* **~s, ~** (*ugs.*) (*Roman/Film*) sensational book/film; shocker (*coll.*); (*Mensch*) sensationalist

**Schock·farbe** *die* (*ugs.*) violent colour

**schockieren** *tr. V.* shock; **über etw.** (*Akk.*) **schockiert sein** be shocked at sth.

**schock-, Schock-:** **~therapie** *die* (*auch fig.*) shock therapy *or* treatment; **~weise** *Adv.* Ⓐ (*in Schocks*) by the three score; five dozen at a time; Ⓑ (*ugs.: scharenweise*) in droves; **~wirkung** *die* shock effect; **unter ~wirkung stehen** be in a state of shock; be suffering from shock

**schofel** /ˈʃo:fl/, **schofelig** (*ugs. abwertend*) ❶ *Adj.* horrid (*coll.*); beastly (*coll.*); (*schändlich*) disgusting.
❷ *adv.* horridly

**Schöffe** /ˈʃœfə/ *der;* **~n, ~n** lay judge (*acting together with another lay judge and a professional judge*)

**Schöffen·gericht** *das: court presided over by a professional judge and two lay judges*

**Schöffin** *die;* **~, ~nen** ⇒ **Schöffe**

**Schokolade** /ʃokoˈla:də/ *die;* **~, ~n** Ⓐ (*Süßigkeit*) chocolate; Ⓑ (*Getränk*) [drinking] chocolate

**schokolade[n]-, Schokolade[n]-:** **~braun** *Adj.* chocolate[-brown]; **~eis** *das* chocolate ice cream; **~farben** *Adj.* chocolate-coloured; chocolate ‹brown›; **~guss, *~guß** *der* chocolate icing

**Schokoladen-:** **~pudding** *der* chocolate blancmange; **~raspel** *Pl.* chocolate flakes; grated chocolate *sing.;* **~seite** *die* (*ugs.*) best side; **~torte** *die* chocolate cake *or* gateau

**Scholar** /ʃoˈla:ɐ̯/ *der;* **~en, ~en** (*hist.*) [itinerant] scholar

**Scholastik** /ʃoˈlastɪk/ *die;* **~** (*Philosophie*) scholasticism

**Scholastiker** *der;* **~s, ~, Scholastikerin** *die;* **~, ~nen** scholastic

**scholastisch** *Adj.* scholastic

**scholl** /ʃɔl/ *1. u. 3. Pers. Sg. Prät. v.* **schallen**

**Scholle** /ˈʃɔlə/ *die;* **~, ~n** Ⓐ (*Erd~*) clod [of earth]; Ⓑ (*Eis~*) [ice] floe; Ⓒ (*Fisch*) (*Goldbutt*) flounder, *esp.* plaice; **die ~n** the plaice; (*als Familie*) the Pleuronectidae; Ⓓ (*Erdboden, Acker*) soil; **die heimatliche ~** (*fig.*) one's native soil; **auf eigener ~ sitzen** have a farm of one's own; Ⓔ (*Geol.*) massif

**Scholli** /ˈʃɔli/ *in* **mein lieber ~!** (*ugs.*) my goodness!; good heavens!

**Schöll·kraut** /ˈʃœl-/ *das* (*Bot.*) celandine

**schon** /ʃo:n/ ❶ *Adv.* Ⓐ (*bereits*) (*oft nicht übersetzt*) already; (*in Fragen*) yet; **er hat das ~ vergessen** he has already forgotten that; **hat Walter ~ angerufen?** has Walter telephoned yet?; **wollt ihr wirklich ~ gehen?** do you really mean to go already *or* so soon?; **er kommt ~ heute/ist ~ gestern gekommen** he's coming today/he came yesterday; **er ist ~ da/[an]gekommen** he is already here/has already arrived; **~ die Römer hatten gute Heizungen** even the Romans *or* the Romans already had good heating systems; **er ist ~ gestern angekommen** he arrived as early as yesterday; **ich bin ~ seit Mai/~ ein Jahr in Bremen** I've been here in Bremen since May/for a year; **wie lange bist du ~ hier?** how long have you been here?; **~ damals/jetzt** even at that time *or* in those days/even now; **~ [im Jahre] 1926** as early as 1926; back in 1926; **er war ~ immer faul** he always was lazy; **wie ~ gesagt ...** as I have already said, ...; as I said before, ...; **gestern kam er, wie ~ so oft, zu spät zur Arbeit** yesterday he was late for work, as so often before *or* as has so often been the case; Ⓑ (*fast gleichzeitig*) there and then; **er schwang sich auf das Fahrrad, und ~ war er weg** he jumped on the bicycle and was away [in a flash]; **kaum hatte er sich umgedreht, ~ ging der Krach los** he had scarcely turned his back when the row broke out; **in demselben Augenblick ~:** at that very *or* at the selfsame moment; ⇒ *auch* **kaum** E; Ⓒ (*jetzt*) **~ [mal]** now; (*inzwischen*) meanwhile; **wir treffen uns dann gleich, ihr könnt ja ~ mal vorgehen** we'll meet up in a minute, you can be going on ahead [meanwhile]; Ⓓ (*selbst, sogar*) even; (*nur*) only; **~ ein Tropfen von dem Gift kann tödlich sein** even a small amount *or* a mere drop of this poison can be fatal; **das weiß normalerweise ~ ein Zwölfjähriger** even a child of twelve would usually know that; **~ zwei Bier reichen aus, um ihn völlig betrunken zu machen** it only takes two beers to get him completely drunk; **das bekommt man ~ für 150 Mark** you can get it for as little as 150 marks; **für so ein Essen muss man ~ 30 Mark hinlegen** you have to pay as much as 30 marks for a meal like that; Ⓔ (*ohne Ergänzung, ohne weiteren Zusatz*) on its own; **das ist auch so ~ genug** that's [already] enough as it is; **[allein] ~ der Gedanke daran ist schrecklich** the mere thought *or* just the thought of it is dreadful; **~ der Name ist bezeichnend** the very name is significant; **~ darum** *od.* **aus diesem Grund** for this reason alone.
❷ *Partikel* Ⓐ (*verstärkend*) really; (*gewiss*) certainly; **du wirst ~ sehen!** you'll see!; **ich kann mir ~ denken, was du willst** I can well imagine what you want; **wenn wir ~ eine neue Maschine kaufen müssen, dann aber eine ordentliche** if we have to get a new machine, let's get a decent one; **wenn du ~ so früh gehen musst** if you really have to go so early; Ⓑ (*ugs. ungeduldig: endlich*) **nun sagen Sie [doch] ~!** come on, out with it; **nun komm ~!** come on!; hurry up!; **du hast meine Zigaretten geklaut, nun gibs ~ zu!** you've pinched my cigarettes, go on, admit it (*coll.*); **und wenn ~!** so what; what if he/she/it does/did/was *etc.;* Ⓒ (*beruhigend: wahrscheinlich*) all right; **es wird ~ gehen** *od.* **werden** it'll work out all right [in the end]; **er wird sich ~ wieder erholen** he'll recover all right; he's sure to recover; **doch, doch, das wird ~ stimmen** yes, yes, that must be right; Ⓓ (*zustimmend, aber etwas einschränkend*) **~ gut** OK (*coll.*); **ich glaube dir ~:** I believe you all right; fair enough, I believe you; **Lust hätte ich ~, nur keine Zeit** I'd certainly like to, but I've no time; **das ist ~ möglich, nur ...** that is quite possible, only ...; **er hat ~ recht, aber ...** he's right enough, but ...; Ⓔ (*andererseits*) **er ist nicht besonders intelligent, aber sein Bruder ~:** he's not particularly intelligent, but his brother is; **ob Willy kommt, weiß ich nicht, aber ich [komme] ~:** I don't know whether Willy's coming, but 'I'm coming *or* 'I am; Ⓕ (*einschränkend, abwertend*) **was weiß der ~!** what does 'he know [about it]!; **was ist** *od.* **bedeutet ~ Geld!** what does money matter?; what's the good of money [anyway]?; **wem nützt das ~?** what's the use of that [to anybody]?; **Ist was? — Nee, was soll ~ sein?** (*ugs.*) Is anything the matter? — No, should anything be [wrong]?; **was soll das ~ heißen?** what's 'that supposed to mean?

**schön** /ʃø:n/ ❶ *Adj.* Ⓐ (*anziehend, reizvoll*) beautiful; handsome ‹youth, man›; **das ~e Geschlecht** the fair sex; **die ~en Künste** the fine arts; **sie ist ~ von Gestalt** (*geh.*) she has a lovely figure; **das Schöne** beauty; (*~e Dinge*) beautiful things *pl.;* **~e Literatur** belles-lettres *pl.;* **~e Frau, was wünschen Sie?** (*scherzh.*) what is your wish, my pretty one?; **ich finde das Buch ~:** the book appeals to me; **bring mir etwas Schönes mit** bring me back something nice; Ⓑ (*angenehm, erfreulich*) pleasant, nice ‹day, holiday, dream, relaxation, etc.›; fine ‹weather›; (*nett*) nice; **das war eine ~e Zeit** those were wonderful days; **einen ~en Tod haben** die peacefully; **das war alles nicht ~ für sie** it was all rather unpleasant for her; **mach dir ein paar ~e Stunden** enjoy yourself for a few hours; **das ist ~ von dir** it's nice of you; **das ist ein ~er Zug an ihm** that is one of the good *or* nice things about him; **das Schöne daran/an ihm** the nice thing about it/him; **das ist zu ~, um wahr zu sein** that is too good to be true; **alles war in ~ster Ordnung** everything was in perfect order; **was hier vor sich geht, das ist nicht mehr ~** (*ugs.*) the goings-on here are beyond a joke; Ⓒ (*gut*) good ‹wine, beer, piece of work, etc.›; **~ schmecken/riechen** (*nordd. ugs.*) taste/smell really good *or* (*esp. Amer. coll.*) real good; Ⓓ (*in Höflichkeitsformeln*) **~e Grüße** best wishes; **[ich soll Ihnen einen] ~en Gruß von meiner Mutter [bestellen]** my mother sends you her kind regards; **recht ~en Dank für ...** thank you very much for ...; many thanks for ...; Ⓔ (*ugs.: einverstanden*) OK (*coll.*); all right; **also ~:** right then; **~ und gut** (*ugs.*) all well and good; **das ist alles ~ und gut, aber ...** (*ugs.*) that's all very well but ...; Ⓕ (*iron.: leer*) **eine ~e Floskel** a splendid platitude; **~e Worte** fine[-sounding] words; (*schmeichlerisch*) honeyed words; Ⓖ (*ugs.: beträchtlich*) handsome, (*coll.*) tidy ‹sum, fortune, profit›; considerable ‹quantity, distance›; pretty good ‹pension›; **das hat ein ganz ~es Gewicht** it's quite a weight; **ein ~es Alter erreichen** reach a fine old age; **einen ~en Schrecken davontragen** get a real *or* quite a fright; **eine ~e Leistung** no mean *or* quite an achievement; Ⓗ (*iron.: unerfreulich*) nice (*coll. iron.*); **das sind ja ~e Aussichten!** this is a fine lookout *sing.* (*iron.*); what a delightful prospect! *sing.* (*iron.*); **eine ~e Bescherung** a nice *or* fine mess (*coll. iron.*); **ein ~er Reinfall** a real disaster; **du machst [mir] ja ~e Geschichten!** you do get up to some fine tricks (*iron.*).
❷ *adv.* Ⓐ (*anziehend, reizvoll*) beautifully; **der Wein ist ~ klar** the wine is beautifully clear; **sie ist ~ eingerichtet** she has a lovely home; **sich ~ zurechtmachen** make oneself look nice; Ⓑ (*angenehm, erfreulich*) nicely; **~ warm/weich/langsam** nice and warm/soft/slow; **wir haben es ~ hier** we're very well off here; Ⓒ (*gut, ausgezeichnet*) well; **das habt ihr ~ gemacht** you did that well *or* nicely; you made a good job of that; Ⓓ (*in Höflichkeitsformeln*) **bitte ~, können Sie mir sagen, ...** excuse me, could you tell me ...; **grüß deine Mutter ~ von mir** give your mother my kind regards; Ⓔ (*iron.*) **wie es so ~ heißt, wie man so ~ sagt** as they say; Ⓕ (*ugs.: beträchtlich*) really; (*vor einem Adjektiv*) pretty; **ganz ~ arbeiten müssen** have to work jolly hard (*Brit. coll.*); **[ganz] ~ dämlich**

*old spelling (see note on page 1707)

S

damned stupid; **er sitzt [ganz] ~ in der Tinte** he's well and truly in the soup (*coll.*); **ganz ~ trinken/lügen** drink like a fish (*coll.*)/lie like anything (*coll.*).

❸ *Partikel* (*ugs. verstärkend*) **~ der Reihe nach!** one after the other in a nice orderly line; **~ ruhig bleiben/~ langsam fahren** be nice and quiet/drive nice and slowly; **bleib ~ liegen!** lie there and be good; **passt ~ auf!** pay careful attention; **jetzt gehst du ~ nach Hause** now go home like a good boy/girl; **sei ~ brav** be a good boy/girl

**Schöne** *die; adj. Dekl.* beauty; (*iron.: Frau*) member of the fair sex; **die ~n der Nacht** (*geh.*) the ladies of the night

**schonen** ❶ *tr. V.* treat ‹clothes, books, furniture, etc.› with care; (*schützen*) protect ‹hands, furniture›; (*nicht strapazieren*) spare ‹voice, eyes, etc.›; conserve ‹strength›; (*nachsichtig behandeln*) go easy on, spare ‹person›; **jmdm. eine Nachricht ~d beibringen** break news gently to sb.; **eine ~de Behandlung** gentle treatment.

❷ *refl. V.* take care of oneself; (*sich nicht überanstrengen*) take things easy; **sich mehr ~:** take things easier; **er schont sich nicht, wenn es um seine Patienten geht** he doesn't spare himself when it comes to his patients

**schönen** *tr. V.* brighten ‹colour›; clarify ‹wine›; (*mit Gelatine*) fine ‹wine›; touch up ‹picture›; enhance ‹picture, figure›; **[idealistisch] geschönt** (*fig.*) idealized; flattering

**Schoner** *der; ~s, ~* (*Seemannsspr.*) schooner

**Schön·färberei** *die; ~, ~en* embellishment; **frei von jeder** *od.* **ohne jede ~:** without any whitewashing

**Schon-: ~frist** *die* period of grace; (*nach einer Operation*) period of convalescence; **~gang** *der* Ⓐ (*Kfz-W.*) high gear; (*Overdrive*) overdrive; Ⓑ (*bei Waschmaschinen*) programme for delicate fabrics

**Schön·geist** *der* aesthete

**schön·geistig** *Adj.* aesthetic; **die ~e Literatur** belletristic literature

**Schönheit** *die; ~, ~en* beauty; **die ~en der Umgebung** the attractions of the area

**Schönheits-: ~chirurgie** *die* cosmetic surgery *no art.*; **~farm** *die* health farm; **~fehler** *der* blemish; (*fig.*) minor defect; (*Nachteil*) slight drawback; **~ideal** *das* ideal of beauty; **~königin** *die* beauty queen; **~konkurrenz** *die* beauty contest; **~pflästerchen** /-pflɛstɐçən/ *das; ~~s, ~~* (*Kosmetik*) beauty spot; **~pflege** *die* beauty care *no art.*; **~reparatur** *die* cosmetic repair; (*in einem Haus/einer Wohnung*) redecorating *no pl.*; **~sinn** *der* sense of beauty; aesthetic sense; **~wettbewerb** *der* beauty contest

**Schon-: ~klima** *das* benign climate; **~kost** *die* light food; **auf ~kost gesetzt werden** be put on a light diet

**schön|machen** (*ugs.*) ❶ *tr. V.* smarten ‹person, thing› up; make ‹person, thing› look nice; do up ‹building›.

❷ *refl. V.* smarten oneself up; make oneself look smart.

❸ *itr. V.* ‹dog› [sit up and] beg

**Schon·platz** *der* (*DDR*): *job given to someone temporarily incapacitated;* light job

**schön-, Schön-: ~|reden** *itr. V.* (*abwertend*) turn on the smooth talk; sweet-talk (*Amer.*); **das ~reden** smooth talking; sweet talk (*Amer.*); **~redner** *der* (*abwertend*) smooth *or* (*Amer.*) sweet talker; **~rednerei** *die; ~~, ~~en* (*abwertend*) smooth *or* (*Amer.*) sweet talk *no pl.*; **~en** blandishments; **~rednerin** *die* ⇒ **~redner**; **~|schreiben** *unr. itr.* (*auch tr.*) *V.* write neatly; (**~schrift schreiben**) do calligraphy; **~schreiben** (*als Unterrichtsfach*) handwriting *no art.*; **~schreibheft** *das* writing book; (*mit vorgedruckten Buchstaben*) copybook; **~schrift** *die* Ⓐ (*Zierschrift*) calligraphy; (*sorgfältige Schrift*) neat handwriting; **etw. in ~schrift abschreiben** copy sth. out neatly *or* in one's best handwriting; Ⓑ (*ugs.: Reinschrift*) neat *or* clean copy; **~|tun** *unr. itr. V.* (*ugs.*) **jmdm. ~tun** soft-soap sb.; butter sb. up

**Schonung** *die; ~, ~en* Ⓐ (*Nachsicht*) consideration; (*nachsichtige Behandlung*) considerate treatment; (*nach Krankheit/Operation*) [period of] rest; (*von Gegenständen*) careful treatment; **sein Zustand/Magen verlangt ~:** his condition/his stomach needs careful treatment; **sie braucht noch ~:** she still needs to be treated considerately; (*muss sich selbst schonen*) she must still take things easy; **er kannte ihr gegenüber keine ~:** he knew no mercy towards her; he did not spare her; Ⓑ (*Jungwald*) [young] plantation

**-schonung** *die* ‹fir, spruce, etc.› plantation

**schonungs-: ~bedürftig** *Adj.* in need of rest *postpos.*; **~bedürftig sein** need to take things carefully *or* easy; **~los** ❶ *Adj.* unsparing, ruthless ‹criticism etc.›; blunt ‹frankness›; **eine ~lose Aufklärung der Affäre** a rigorous elucidation of the affair; ❷ *adv.* unsparingly; ‹say› without mincing one's words

**Schonungslosigkeit** *die; ~:* ruthlessness; (*Strenge*) rigour

**Schön·wetter·periode** *die* spell of fine weather; fine spell

**Schon·zeit** *die* Ⓐ (*Jagdw.*) close season; Ⓑ (*Schonung*) period of rest; (*Erholungszeit*) period of convalescence; recovery period; (*fig.: Anfangszeit, in der man nachsichtig behandelt wird*) honeymoon period

**Schopf** /ʃɔpf/ *der; ~[e]s, Schöpfe* /ˈʃœpfə/ Ⓐ (*Haar~*) shock of hair; **die Gelegenheit beim ~[e] fassen** *od.* **nehmen** *od.* **packen** *od.* **ergreifen** (*ugs.*) seize *or* grasp the opportunity with both hands; Ⓑ (*Jägerspr.: Kopffedern*) crest

**schöpfen**[1] /ˈʃœpfn̩/ ❶ *tr. V.* Ⓐ scoop [up] ‹water, liquid›; (*mit einer Kelle*) ladle ‹soup›; **Wasser aus einem Brunnen ~:** draw water from a well; **Wasser aus dem Boot ~:** bale water out of the boat; Ⓑ (*geh.: einatmen*) draw, take ‹breath›; **frische Luft ~:** take a breath of fresh air; Ⓒ (*geh.: für sich gewinnen*) draw ‹wisdom, strength, knowledge› (**aus** from); **neuen Mut/neue Hoffnung ~:** take fresh heart/find fresh hope; **Argwohn** *od.* **Verdacht ~:** become suspicious.

❷ *itr. V.* **aus der Fantasie/jahrelanger Erfahrung** *usw.* **~:** draw on one's imagination/on years of experience *etc.*

**schöpfen**[2] *tr. V.* (*veralt.: schaffen*) create; coin ‹word›

**Schöpfer**[1] *der; ~s, ~:* creator; (*Gott*) Creator

**Schöpfer**[2] *der; ~s, ~* (*Kelle*) ladle

**Schöpferin** *die; ~, ~nen* creator

**schöpferisch** ❶ *Adj.* creative; constructive ‹criticism›; **der ~e Augenblick** the moment of inspiration; **eine ~e Pause** a pause for inspiration.

❷ *adv.* creatively; **~ tätig sein** be creative

**Schöpferkraft** *die* creative powers *pl.*; creativity

**Schöpf-: ~kelle** *die*, **~löffel** *der* ladle

**Schöpfung** *die; ~, ~en* Ⓐ (*geh.: Erschaffung*) creation; (*Erfindung*) invention; Ⓑ (*geh.: ~ der Welt*) **die ~:** the Creation; (*von Gott Erschaffenes*) Creation; Ⓒ (*geh.: Kunstwerk, ~ der Mode usw.*) creation; (*Werk*) work

**Schöpfungs-: ~geschichte** *die* Creation story; **~tag** *der* day of the Creation

**Schöppchen** /ˈʃœpçən/ *das; ~s, ~:* small glass of wine/beer

**Schoppen** /ˈʃɔpn̩/ *der; ~s, ~* Ⓐ [quarter-litre/half-litre] glass of wine/beer; Ⓑ (*veralt.: Hohlmaß*) **ein ~:** ≈ half a litre

**Schoppen·wein** *der* wine by the glass

**Schöps** /ʃœps/ *der; ~es, ~e* (*österr.*) ⇒ **Hammel** A, B

**Schöpserne** /ˈʃœpsɐnə/ *das; adj. Dekl.* (*österr.*) mutton

**schor** /ʃoːɐ̯/ *1. u. 3. Pers. Sg. Prät. v.* **scheren**

**Schorf** /ʃɔrf/ *der; ~[e]s, ~e* ▶ 474 Ⓐ (*Wund~*) scab; Ⓑ (*Pflanzenkrankheit*) scab *no art.*

**schorfig** *Adj.* scabby ‹wound›

**Schorle** /ˈʃɔrlə/ *die; ~, ~n* wine with mineral water; ≈ spritzer; (*mit Apfelsaft*) apple juice with mineral water

**Schorn·stein** /ˈʃɔrn-/ *der* chimney; (*Schiffs~, Lokomotiv~*) funnel; **der ~ raucht** (*fig.*) things are ticking over nicely; business is good; **Geld in den ~ schreiben** (*fig. ugs.*) write off money

**Schornstein·feger** *der; ~s, ~*, **Schornstein·fegerin** *die; ~, ~nen* ▶ 159 chimney sweep

**schoss, *schoß** /ʃɔs/ *1. u. 3. Pers. Sg. Prät. v.* **schießen**

**Schoß**[1] /ʃoːs/ *der; ~es, Schöße* /ˈʃøːsə/ Ⓐ lap; **ein Kind auf den ~ nehmen** take *or* sit a child on one's lap; **seine Frau saß bei ihm auf dem ~:** his wife sat on his knee; **die Hände in den ~ legen** (*fig.*) sit back and do nothing; **jmdm. in den ~ fallen** (*fig.*) just fall into sb.'s lap; **im ~ der Familie/der Kirche** (*fig.*) in the bosom of the family/of Mother Church; ⇒ *auch* **Abraham** B; **Hand** F; Ⓑ (*geh.: Mutterleib*) womb; **im ~ der Erde** (*fig.*) in the bowels of the earth; Ⓒ (*geh.: Vulva*) pudenda *pl.*; Ⓓ (*Rock~*) [coat-]tail

***Schoß**[2], **Schoss** *der;* **Schosses, Schosse** ⇒ **Schössling**

**Schoß·hund** *der*, **Schoß·hündchen** *das* lapdog

**Schössling, *Schößling** /ˈʃœslɪŋ/ *der; ~s, ~e* Ⓐ (*Trieb*) shoot; Ⓑ (*Ableger zum Pflanzen*) cutting

**Schot** /ʃoːt/ *die; ~, ~en* (*Seew.*) sheet

**Schote** /ˈʃoːtə/ *die; ~, ~n* Ⓐ pod; siliqua (*as tech. term*); **fünf ~n Paprika** five peppers; Ⓑ (*landsch.: Erbse*) **~n** peas

**Schott** /ʃɔt/ *das; ~[e]s, ~en* (*Seemannsspr.*) bulkhead; **die ~en dicht machen** (*fig. ugs.*) shut all the doors and windows

**Schotte** /ˈʃɔtə/ *der; ~n, ~n* ▶ 553 Scot; Scotsman; **er ist ~:** he's a Scot; he's Scottish; **die ~n** the Scots; the Scottish

**Schotten** *der; ~s, ~* (*Textilw.*) tartan [material]

**Schotten-: ~muster** *das* tartan pattern; **~rock** *der* tartan skirt; (*Kilt*) kilt; **~witz** *der* Scottish joke (*concerning thriftiness*)

**Schotter** /ˈʃɔtɐ/ *der; ~s, ~* Ⓐ (*für Straßen*) [road] metal; gravel; (*für Schienen*) ballast; Ⓑ (*Geol.*) gravel; Ⓒ (*salopp: Geld*) dough (*coll.*); lolly (*Brit. sl.*)

**Schotter-: ~decke** *die* [loose] gravel surface; **~straße** *die* road with [loose] gravel surface

**Schottin** *die; ~, ~nen* ▶ 553 Scot; Scotswoman

**schottisch** ▶ 553, ▶ 696 ❶ *Adj.* Scottish; Scots, Scottish ‹dialect, accent, voice, etc.›; **~er Whisky** Scotch whisky.

❷ *adv.* ‹speak› with a Scots *or* Scottish accent

**Schottland** (*das*); **~s** Scotland

**schraffieren** /ʃraˈfiːrən/ *tr. V.* hatch; (*feiner*) shade ‹drawing›

**Schraffierung** *die; ~, ~en*, **Schraffur** /ʃraˈfuːɐ̯/ *die; ~, ~en* hatching *no indef. art.*; (*feiner*) shading *no indef. art.*

**schräg** /ʃrɛːk/ ❶ *Adj.* Ⓐ diagonal ‹line, beam, cut, etc.›; sloping ‹surface, roof, wall, side, etc.›; slanting, slanted ‹writing, eyes, etc.›; tilted ‹position of the head etc., axis›; (*nicht genau diagonal*) oblique ‹line etc.›; **ein ~er Blick** (*fig. ugs.*) a sideways *or* sidelong glance; Ⓑ (*ugs.: unseriös*) offbeat; weird ‹ideas›; (*wild*) hot ‹music›; Ⓒ (*ugs.: zweifelhaft*) shady, (*coll.*) dodgy ‹type, firm, etc.›.

❷ *adv.* at an angle; (*diagonal*) diagonally; (*nicht genau diagonal*) obliquely; **den Kopf ~ halten** hold one's head to one side; tilt one's head; **~ stehende Augen** slanting eyes; **~ gegenüber** diagonally opposite; **~ links fahren/abbiegen** bear left; **die Sonnenstrahlen fallen ~ ein** the sun is slanting in; **er saß ~ vor/hinter mir** he was sitting in front of/behind me and to one side; **das Boot liegt ~:** the boat is listing *or* down at one side; **~ gedruckt** [printed] in italics *postpos.*; **jmdn. ~ angucken** (*fig. ugs.*) look askance at sb.

**Schräge** *die; ~, ~n* Ⓐ (*schräge Fläche*) sloping surface; (*Hang*) slope; **das Zimmer**

S

**hat eine ~:** the room has a sloping wall; Ⓑ (*Neigung*) slope; (*Dach~*) pitch; slope; **eine ~ von 10°** a 10° slope *or* incline

**Schräg-: ~heck** *das* (*Kfz-W.*) ⇒ **Fließheck**; **~lage** *die* angle; (*eines Schiffes*) list; (*eines Kindes bei der Geburt*) oblique position *or* presentation; (*eines Flugzeugs*) bank; **etw. in ~lage bringen** tilt *or* slant sth.; **das Schiff hat ~lage** the ship is listing *or* is at an angle; **~streifen** *der* diagonal stripe; **~strich** *der* oblique stroke

**schrak** /ʃraːk/ *1. u. 3. Pers. Sg. Prät. v.* **schrecken**

**Schramme** /ˈʃramə/ *die; ~, ~n* scratch

**Schrammel·musik** /ˈʃraml-/ *die: Viennese popular music played on violins, guitar, and accordion;* Schrammeln ensemble music

**Schrammeln** *Pl. quartet playing violins, guitar, and accordion;* Schrammeln ensemble *sing.*

**schrammen** *tr. V.* scratch (**an** + *Dat.* on)

**Schrank** /ʃraŋk/ *der; ~[e]s,* **Schränke** /ˈʃrɛŋkə/ Ⓐ cupboard; closet (*Amer.*); (*Glas~; kleiner Wand~*) cabinet; (*Kleider~*) wardrobe; (*Bücher~*) bookcase; (*im Schwimmbad, am Arbeitsplatz usw.*) locker; Ⓑ (*ugs.: großer Mann*) **ein [ganz schöner] ~:** a hulking great fellow (*coll.*)

**Schrank·bett** *das* foldaway bed

**Schränkchen** /ˈʃrɛŋkçən/ *das; ~s, ~:* cabinet

**Schranke** /ˈʃraŋkə/ *die; ~, ~n* Ⓐ (*auch fig.*) barrier; **jmdn. in die ~ fordern** (*geh.*) throw down the gauntlet to sb.; **vor den ~n des Gerichts** before a/the court; Ⓑ (*fig.: Grenze*) limit; **er kennt keine ~n** he knows no limits *or* bounds; **die ~n der Konvention durchbrechen** break the bounds of convention; **jmdn. in die** *od.* **seine ~n [ver]weisen** (*geh.*) put sb. in his/her place

**Schranken** *der; ~s, ~* (*österr.*) barrier

**schrankenlos** ❶ *Adj.* boundless, unbounded ‹admiration, confidence, loyalty, etc.›; unlimited, limitless ‹power, freedom, etc.›; unbridled, untrammelled ‹individualism, despotism›; unrestrained, unrestricted ‹exploitation›; unrestrained ‹brutality›; **sein Egoismus/seine Habgier war ~:** his egoism/greed knew no bounds.

❷ *adv.* boundlessly; ‹exploit› without restraint

**Schranken·wärter** *der,* **Schranken·wärterin** *die* level-crossing (*Brit.*) *or* (*Amer.*) grade-crossing attendant; crossing keeper

**Schränker** *der; ~s, ~,* **Schränkerin** *die; ~, ~nen* (*ugs.*) ⇒ **Geldschrankknacker**

**schrank-, Schrank-: ~fach** *das* [cupboard *or* (*Amer.*) closet] shelf; **~fertig** *Adj.* laundered; washed and ironed ‹laundry›; **~koffer** *der* wardrobe trunk; **~tür** *die* cupboard door; (*eines Kleiderschranks*) wardrobe door; **~wand** *die* shelf *or* wall unit

**Schranze** /ˈʃrantsə/ *die; ~, ~n* (*abwertend*) sycophantic courtier; (*fig.*) lackey

**Schrapnell** /ʃrapˈnɛl/ *das; ~s, ~e od. ~s* (*Milit.*) shrapnel [shell]

**Schrat** /ʃraːt/ *der; ~[e]s, ~e* forest goblin

**Schrat·segel** *das* (*Seew.*) fore-and-aft sail

**Schratt** /ʃrat/ *der; ~[e]s, ~e* ⇒ **Schrat**

**Schraub·deckel** *der* screw top

**Schraube** /ˈʃraubə/ *die; ~, ~n* Ⓐ (*Schlitz~*) screw; (*Sechskant~/Vierkant~*) bolt; **eine ~ ohne Ende** (*fig.*) a vicious *or* never-ending spiral; **bei ihm ist eine ~ locker** *od.* **los** (*fig. salopp*) he has [got] a screw loose (*coll.*); Ⓑ (*Schiffs~*) propeller; screw; Ⓒ (*Turnen*) twist; (*Kunstspringen*) twist dive; Ⓓ (*Kunstflug*) vertical spin

**schrauben** ❶ *tr. V.* Ⓐ (*befestigen*) screw (**an, auf** + *Akk.* on to); (*mit Sechskant-/Vierkant~*) bolt (**an, auf** + *Akk.* [on] to); (*entfernen*) unscrew/unbolt (**von** from); Ⓑ (*drehen*) screw ‹nut, hook, lightbulb, etc.› (**auf** + *Akk.* on to; **in** + *Akk.* into); (*lösen*) unscrew ‹cap etc.› (**von** from); **den Deckel vom Marmeladenglas ~:** twist the top off the jam jar; Ⓒ **etw. höher/niedriger ~:** screw sth. up/down; **die Preise/Erwartungen in die Höhe ~:** push prices up *or* make prices spiral/raise expectations.

❷ *refl. V.* **sich [in die Höhe] ~:** spiral upwards; ⇒ *auch* **geschraubt**

**Schrauben-: ~dreher** *der* (*Technik*) screwdriver; **~mutter** *die; Pl.* **~~n** nut; **~schlüssel** *der* spanner; **~zieher** *der* screwdriver

**Schrauber** *der* (*ugs.*) Ⓐ [power] screwdriver; Ⓑ (*salopp scherzh.*) mechanic

**Schraub-: ~glas** *das* screw top jar; **~stock** *der* vice; **~verschluss,** ***~verschluß** *der* screw top; **~zwinge** *die* screw clamp

**Schreber-** /ˈʃreːbɐ-/: **~garten** *der* ≈ allotment (*cultivated primarily as a garden*); **~gärtner** *der,* **~gärtnerin** *die* ≈ allotment holder

**Schreck** /ʃrɛk/ *der; ~[e]s, ~e* fright; scare; (*Schock*) shock; **jmdm. einen ~ einjagen** give sb. a fright *or* scare/shock; **vor ~:** with fright; ‹run away› in one's fright; **ein freudiger ~:** a thrill of joy; **ein heftiger ~ packte ihn** he was seized by a sudden terror; **auf den ~ [hin] muss ich einen trinken** (*ugs. scherzh.*) I must have a drink to get over the shock; **der ~ fuhr ihm in die Knochen** *od.* **Glieder** the fright/shock went right through him; **der ~ saß ihm noch in den Knochen** *od.* **Gliedern** he still hadn't recovered from the fright/shock; **krieg keinen ~!** (*ugs.*) don't be [too] shocked; **ach du ~!** (*ugs.*) oh my God!; **[oh] ~, lass nach!** (*scherzh.*) God help us!; oh no, not that!

**Schreck·bild** *das* terrible *or* frightening sight; (*Vorstellung*) terrible vision

**schrecken** ❶ *tr. V.* Ⓐ (*geh.*) frighten; scare; Ⓑ (*auf~*) startle (**aus** out of); make ‹person› jump; **du hast mich aus meinen Gedanken geschreckt** you startled me — I was thinking.

❷ *regelm.* (*auch unr.*) *itr. V.* start [up]; **aus dem Schlaf ~:** awake with a start; start from one's sleep

**Schrecken** *der; ~s, ~* Ⓐ (*Schreck*) fright; scare; (*Entsetzen*) horror; (*große Angst*) terror; **jmdm. einen ~ einjagen** give sb. a fright *or* scare; **ein jäher ~ durchfuhr ihn** (*geh.*) he was seized by a sudden terror; **jmdn. voll[er] ~ ansehen** look at sb. with fear *or* terror in one's eyes; **Angst und ~ verbreiten** spread fear and terror; **jmdn. in Angst und ~ versetzen** terrify sb.; **zu meinem [großen] ~:** to my [great] horror; **mit dem [bloßen] ~ davonkommen** escape with no more than a scare *or* fright; **lieber ein Ende mit ~ als ein ~ ohne Ende** it's better to make a painful break than draw out the agony; Ⓑ (*Schrecklichkeit, Schrecknis*) horror; **ein Bild des ~s** a terrible *or* terrifying picture; Ⓒ (*fig.: gefürchtete Sache, Person*) **der ~ des Volkes/** (*scherzh.*) **der Schule** *usw.* the terror of the nation/(*joc.*) the school *etc.*

**schrecken·erregend** ❶ *Adj.* terrifying.

❷ *adv.* terrifyingly

**schreckens-, Schreckens-: ~bleich** *Adj.* (*geh.*) pale with terror *postpos.;* as white as a sheet *postpos.;* **~herrschaft** *die* reign of terror; **~nachricht** *die* terrible piece of news; **die ~nachricht vom …** the terrible news of …; **~tat** *die* terrible deed *or* act; atrocity

**Schreck·gespenst** *das* Ⓐ spectre; (*gegenwärtig*) nightmare; **das ~ Aids** the spectre of Aids; Ⓑ (*ugs. abwertend: hässlicher Mensch*) (*Frau*) hideous hag; (*Mann*) ugly brute

**schreckhaft** ❶ *Adj.* Ⓐ (*leicht zu erschrecken*) easily scared; Ⓑ (*erschrocken*) frightened, scared ‹movement, reaction›.

❷ *adv.* ‹react› in a frightened *or* scared way; ‹start, gaze› in fright

**Schreckhaftigkeit** *die; ~:* easily scared nature; tendency to take fright

**schrecklich** ❶ *Adj.* Ⓐ terrible; **er war ~ in seinem Zorn** (*geh.*) he was terrible in his wrath; Ⓑ (*ugs.: unerträglich*) terrible (*coll.*); **es war mir ~, es zu tun** I felt terrible about doing it; Ⓒ (*ugs.: sehr groß*) **es hat ihm ~en Spaß gemacht** he found it terrific fun (*coll.*).

❷ *adv.* Ⓐ terribly; horribly; Ⓑ (*ugs. abwertend: unerträglich*) terribly (*coll.*); dreadfully (*coll.*); Ⓒ (*ugs.: sehr, äußerst*) terribly (*coll.*); **ich habe es ~ eilig** I'm in a terrible *or* terrific hurry (*coll.*)

**Schrecknis** *das; ~ses, ~se* (*geh.*) horror

**Schreck-: ~schraube** *die* (*ugs. abwertend*) battleaxe; **~schuss,** ***~schuß** *der* (*auch fig.*) warning shot; **~schuss·pistole,** ***~schuß·pistole** *die* blank [cartridge] gun *or* pistol; **~sekunde** *die* moment of terror/shock; (*Reaktionszeit*) reaction time; **eine ~sekunde lang** for one horrifying moment

**Schredder** *der; ~s, ~:* shredder

**Schredder-: ~anlage** *die* shredding plant; shredder; **~müll** *der* shredded waste

**schreddern** *tr. V.* shred

**Schrei** /ʃrai/ *der; ~[e]s, ~e* cry; (*lauter Ruf*) shout; (*durchdringend*) yell; (*gellend*) scream; (*kreischend*) shriek; (*des Hahns*) crow; **der ~ nach Gerechtigkeit** (*fig. geh.*) the cry for justice; **der letzte ~** (*fig. ugs.*) the latest thing; **nach dem letzten ~ gekleidet** (*fig. ugs.*) dressed in the latest style

**Schreib-: ~arbeit** *die:* **an einer ~arbeit sitzen** sit doing some writing; **~arbeiten** clerical work *sing.;* **~automat** *der* word processor; **~bedarf** *der* stationery; **~block** *der; Pl.* **~~s** *od.* **~blöcke** writing pad

**Schreibe** *die; ~* (*ugs.: Schreibstil*) style [of writing]

**schreiben** /ˈʃraibn̩/ ❶ *unr. itr. V.* write; ‹typewriter› type; **orthographisch richtig ~:** spell correctly; **auf** *od.* **mit der Maschine ~:** type; **mit der Hand/mit dem Bleistift/mit Tinte ~:** write in longhand/in pencil/in ink; **hast du mal was zum Schreiben?** have you got anything to write with?; **der Bleistift schreibt weich/hart** the pencil is soft/hard *or* has a soft/hard lead; **die Feder schreibt zu breit** the nib is too broad; **er hat großes Talent zum Schreiben:** he has great talent as a writer; **an einem Roman** *usw.* **~:** be writing a novel *etc.;* **jmdm.** *od.* **an jmdn. ~:** write to sb.

❷ *unr. tr. V.* Ⓐ write; **etw. mit der Hand/Maschine ~:** write sth. by hand *or* in longhand/type sth.; **wie schreibt man dieses Wort?** how is this word spelt?; **das Wort ist falsch/richtig/mit f geschrieben** the word is spelt wrongly *or* misspelt/spelt correctly/written *or* spelt with an f; **den Titel schreibt man groß** the title is written with capitals [at the beginning of each word]; **Noten ~:** write [out] music; **200 Anschläge pro Minute ~:** have a typing speed of 200 strokes *or* 40 words a minute; **wo steht das denn geschrieben?** (*fig.*) there's no law that says that, is there?; who says? (*coll.*); **die geschriebene Sprache/das geschriebene Wort** the written language/word; **er schreibt einen guten Stil** he has a good style [of writing]; **eine Klausur/Klassenarbeit ~:** do an exam/a class test; **die Zeitungen ~ viel Unsinn** the newspapers print a lot of nonsense; **was schreibt denn die NZZ darüber?** what does the NZZ have to say about it?; **Karl hat geschrieben. — So, was schreibt er denn?** I've had a letter from Karl. — Oh, what does he say?; **ich werde es ihm sofort ~/ihm ~, dass …** I'll write and tell him at once/write and tell him that …; **bitte ~ Sie mir den Betrag auf die Rechnung** please put the amount on my bill; Ⓑ (*veralt.*) **wir ~ heute den 21. September** today is 21 September; **man schreibt das Jahr 1925** the year is 1925; **den Wievielten ~ wir heute?** what is the date today *or* today's date?; Ⓒ (*erklären für*) ***jmdn. gesund/krank ~:** certify sb. as fit/give sb. a doctor's certificate; **er wollte sich vom Arzt arbeitsunfähig ~ lassen** he wanted the doctor to give him a certificate.

❸ *unr. refl. V.* Ⓐ (*richtig geschrieben werden*) be spelt; **schreibst du dich mit ei oder mit ey?** is your name spelt with ei or ey?; Ⓑ **sich mit jmdm. ~** (*ugs.*) correspond with sb.; Ⓒ **sich** (*Dat.*) **die Finger wund ~:** write until one's fingers are weary

*old spelling (see note on page 1707)

S

**Schreiben** *das;* **~s,** **~** Ⓐ writing *no def. art.;* Ⓑ (*Brief*) letter; **mit ~ vom ...** in a letter dated ...; **auf Ihr ~ vom ... teilen wir Ihnen mit, ...** in reply to your letter of the ... we inform you ...

**Schreiber** *der;* **~s,** **~** Ⓐ writer; (*Verfasser*) author; **er ist ein armseliger ~** (*abwertend*) he is a miserable hack [writer]; Ⓑ (*veralt.: Sekretär, Schriftführer*) secretary; clerk; Ⓒ (*ugs.: Schreibgerät*) **ich habe keinen ~ bei mir** I've got nothing to write with

**Schreiberin** *die;* **~, ~en** writer; (*Verfasserin*) authoress

**Schreiberling** /'ʃraibɐlɪŋ/ *der;* **~s, ~e** (*abwertend*) hack [writer]; scribbler

**schreib-, Schreib-: ~faul** *Adj.* lazy about [letter-]writing *postpos.;* **ich bin [sehr] ~faul** I'm a poor correspondent *or* not much of a letter writer; **~faulheit** *die* laziness about [letter-]writing; **~fehler** *der* spelling mistake; (*Versehen*) slip [of the pen]; **~gerät** *das* writing implement; **~heft** *das* (*usu. lined*) exercise book; (*im Gegensatz zum Rechenheft*) writing book; **~kraft** *die* ▶ 159 clerical assistant; ([*Steno*]*typistin*) [shorthand] typist; **~krampf** *der* writer's cramp; **einen ~krampf haben/bekommen** have/get writer's cramp; **~kundig** *Adj.* able to write *postpos.;* **~mappe** *die* writing case; **~maschine** *die* typewriter; **etw. mit [der]** *od.* **auf der ~maschine ~en** type sth.; **mit [der] ~maschine geschrieben** typewritten; typed; **sie kann gut ~maschine ~en** she is a good typist; **~maschinen·papier** *das* typing paper; **~papier** *das* writing paper; **~pult** *das* [writing] desk; **~schrift** *die* cursive writing; (*gedruckt*) [cursive] script; **~schutz** *der* (*DV*) write protection; **~stil** *der* written style; **~stube** *die* Ⓐ (*veralt.*) office (*for clerical staff*); (*hist.*) scriptorium; Ⓑ (*Milit.*) orderly room; **~tafel** *die* Ⓐ (*hist.*) [writing] tablet; Ⓑ (*für die Schule*) slate; **~tisch** *der* desk; **~tisch·täter** *der* mastermind behind the scenes; **~übung** *die* writing exercise

**Schreibung** *die;* **~, ~en** spelling; **eine falsche ~:** a misspelling; an incorrect spelling

**Schreib-: ~unter·lage** *die* desk pad; **~verbot** *das* writing ban; **ihm wurde ~verbot erteilt** he was banned from writing; **~waren** *Pl.* stationery *sing.;* writing materials; **~waren·geschäft** *das* stationer's; stationery shop *or* (*Amer.*) store; **~weise** *die* spelling; **~zeug** *das* writing things *pl.*

**schreien** ❶ *unr. itr. V.* ‹person› cry [out]; (*laut rufen/sprechen*) shout; (*durchdringend*) yell; (*gellend*) scream; ‹baby› yell, bawl; ‹animal› scream; ‹owl, gull, etc.› screech; ‹cock› crow; ‹donkey› bray; ‹crow› caw; ‹cat› howl; ‹monkey› shriek; **vor Lachen ~:** scream with laughter; **zum S~ sein** (*ugs.*) be a scream (*coll.*); **nach etw. ~:** yell for sth.; (*fig.*) cry out for sth.; (*fordern*) demand sth.; **die Kinder schrien nach der Mutter** the children were yelling *or* bawling for their mother.
❷ *unr. tr. V.* shout; **Hilfe ~:** shout for help.
❸ *unr. refl. V.* **sich heiser/müde ~:** shout *or* yell oneself hoarse/tire onself out with shouting *or* yelling

**schreiend** (*fig.*) ❶ *Adj.* Ⓐ (*grell*) garish ‹colour, poster, etc.›; loud ‹pattern›; Ⓑ (*empörend*) glaring, flagrant ‹injustice, anomaly›; blatant ‹wrong›.
❷ *adv.* Ⓐ (*grell*) garishly; **~ bunt** garishly coloured; Ⓑ (*empörend*) flagrantly; blatantly

**Schreier** *der;* **~s, ~, Schreierin** *die;* **~, ~nen** noisy person; bawler; **die größten Schreier** the noisiest people; those who make/made the most noise

**Schrei-: ~hals** *der* (*ugs.*) Ⓐ (*Kind*) bawler; Ⓑ (*abwertend: Randalierer*) rowdy; **~krampf** *der* screaming fit

**Schrein** /ʃrain/ *der;* **~[e]s, ~e** (*geh.*) shrine

**Schreiner** *der;* **~s, ~** ▶ 159 (*bes. südd.*) ⇒ **Tischler**

**Schreinerei** *die;* **~, ~en** (*bes. südd.*) ⇒ **Tischlerei**

**Schreinerin** *die;* **~, ~nen** ▶ 159 ⇒ **Schreiner**

**schreinern** (*bes. südd.*) ❶ *itr. V.* do joinery; **er kann gut ~:** he is good at joinery *or* woodworking.
❷ *tr. V.* make ‹furniture etc.›

**schreiten** /'ʃraitn̩/ *unr. itr. V.; mit sein* (*geh.*) Ⓐ walk; (*mit großen Schritten*) stride; (*marschieren*) march; **auf und ab ~:** pace up and down; **von Sieg zu Sieg ~** (*fig.*) march on from one victory to another; Ⓑ **zu etw. ~** (*fig.*) proceed to sth.; **zur Tat** *od.* **zum Werk ~:** go into action/get down to work

**schrickt** /ʃrɪkt/ *3. Pers. Sg. Präsens v.* **schrecken**

**schrie** /ʃri:/ *1. u. 3. Pers. Sg. Prät. v.* **schreien**

**schrieb** /ʃri:p/ *1. u. 3. Pers. Sg. Prät. v.* **schreiben**

**Schrieb** *der;* **~[e]s, ~e** (*ugs.*) missive (*coll.*)

**Schrift** /ʃrɪft/ *die;* **~, ~en** Ⓐ (*System*) script; (*Alphabet*) alphabet; **in kyrillischer/phonetischer ~:** in Cyrillic/phonetic script; in the Cyrillic/phonetic alphabet; Ⓑ (*Hand~*) [hand]writing; **er hat eine gute/unleserliche ~:** he has good/illegible handwriting; his writing is good/illegible; Ⓒ (*Druckw.: ~art*) [type]face; Ⓓ (*Text*) text; (*wissenschaftliche Abhandlung*) paper; (*Werk*) work; (*Bitt~*) petition; **Karl Hubers [frühe/gesammelte] ~en** Karl Hubers [early/collected] writings; **die [Heilige] ~:** the Scriptures *pl.;* Ⓔ *Pl.* (*schweiz.: Ausweispapiere*) [identity] papers

**schrift-, Schrift-: ~art** *die* (*Druckw.*) [type]face; **~bild** *das* (*bei Druck~*) [appearance of the] type; (*bei Hand~*) [appearance of one's] writing; **~deutsch** *Adj.* Ⓐ written German; Ⓑ ⇒ **hochdeutsch**; **~deutsch** *das* Ⓐ written German; **das schweizerische ~deutsch** written Swiss German; Ⓑ ⇒ **Hochdeutsch**

**Schriften·verzeichnis** *das* bibliography

**Schrift-: ~form** *die* (*Rechtsspr.*) written form; **... bedarf der ~form** ... must be drawn up in writing [and signed] by the party in question; **~führer** *der,* **~führerin** *die* secretary; **~gelehrte** *der* scribe (*Bibl.*); (*Islam*) mullah; **~grad** *der,* **~größe** *die* (*Druckw.*) type size; **~leiter** *der,* **~leiterin** *die* (*veralt.*) editor; **~leitung** *die* (*veralt.*) Ⓐ (*Funktion*) editorship; Ⓑ (*Abteilung*) editorial department

**schriftlich** ❶ *Adj.* written; **das Schriftliche** written work; (*ugs.: die ~e Prüfung*) the written exam; **ich habe [darüber] leider nichts Schriftliches** I'm afraid I haven't got anything in writing.
❷ *adv.* in writing; **soll ich es ~ machen?** should I put it in writing?; **jmdn. ~ einladen** send sb. a written invitation; **das lasse ich mir ~ geben** I'll get that in writing; **das kann ich dir ~ geben** (*fig. ugs.*) you can take that from me

**schrift-, Schrift-: ~probe** *die* Ⓐ (*einer Hand~*) sample *or* specimen of [one's] handwriting; Ⓑ (*Druckw.*) type specimen; **~rolle** *die* scroll; **~satz** *der* Ⓐ (*Druckw.*) type matter; Ⓑ (*Rechtsw.: Erklärung*) written statement; **~setzer** *der,* **~setzerin** *die* ▶ 159 typesetter; **~sprache** *die* written language; **die deutsche ~sprache** written German; **~sprachlich** ❶ *Adj.* used in the written language *postpos.;* ❷ *adv.* in the written language; **sich ~sprachlich ausdrücken** express oneself in language appropriate to a written style; **~steller** *der;* **~~s, ~~:** ▶ 159 writer; **die antiken ~steller** the authors of classical antiquity; **~stellerei** *die;* **~~:** writing *no def. art.;* **~stellerin** *die;* **~~, ~~nen** ▶ 159 writer; **~stellerisch** ❶ *Adj.* literary ‹work, activity›; ‹talent› as a writer; **die ~stellerische Tätigkeit** working as a writer; ❷ *adv.* **~stellerisch begabt/tätig sein** be talented as a writer/work as a writer; **~stellern** *itr. V.* work as a writer; do literary work; **~stück** *das* [official] document

**Schrifttum** *das;* **~s** literature; **das ~ zu diesem Thema** the literature on this subject

**Schrift-: ~verkehr** *der* correspondence; **mit jmdm. in regem ~verkehr stehen** have an active correspondence with sb.; **~wechsel** *der* correspondence; **~zeichen** *das* character; **~zug** *der* Ⓐ *Pl.* lettering *sing.;* (*Handschrift*) handwriting *sing.;* Ⓑ (*Namenszug*) lettering; (*als Firmenzeichen*) logo

**schrill** /ʃrɪl/ ❶ *Adj.* Ⓐ shrill; (*fig.*) strident ‹propaganda, colours, etc.›; Ⓑ (*Jugendspr.*) fab (*sl.*).
❷ *adv.* shrilly

**schrillen** *itr. V.* shrill; sound shrilly

**Schrippe** /'ʃrɪpə/ *die;* **~, ~n** (*bes. berlin.*) long [bread] roll

**schritt** /ʃrɪt/ *1. u. 3. Pers. Sg. Prät. v.* **schreiten**

**Schritt** *der;* **~[e]s, ~e** Ⓐ step; **mit großen/gemessenen ~en** with big/measured strides; **die ersten ~e machen** (*auch fig.*) take one's first steps; **er verlangsamte/beschleunigte seine ~e** he slowed/quickened his pace; **die Freude beflügelte meine ~e** (*geh.*) joy gave me wings; **einen ~ zur Seite/nach vorn machen** *od.* **tun** take a step sideways/forwards; **der Schnee knirschte unter unseren ~en** the snow crunched under our footsteps; **~ für ~, ~ um ~** (*auch fig.*) step by step; **den ersten ~ machen** *od.* **tun** (*fig.*) (*den Anfang machen*) take the first step; (*als Erster handeln*) make the first move; **in einem zweiten ~** (*fig.*) as a second stage; **den zweiten ~ vor dem ersten machen** *od.* **tun** (*fig.*) put the cart before the horse; **der erste ~ zur Diktatur** *usw.* the first step on the road to dictatorship *etc.;* **auf ~ und Tritt** wherever one goes; at every step; **er folgte ihr auf ~ und Tritt** he followed her wherever she went; Ⓑ *Pl.* (*Geräusch*) footsteps; Ⓒ (*als Längenmaß*) pace; **nur ein paar ~e von uns entfernt** only a few yards away from us; **in etwa 100 ~[en] Entfernung** at [a distance of] about 100 paces; **ein paar ~e gehen** take a little walk; **einen ~ weiter gehen** (*fig.*) go a step *or* stage further; **einen ~ zu weit gehen** (*fig.*) go too far; overstep the mark; **jmdn. einen großen** *od.* **guten ~ weiterbringen** (*fig.*) take sb. a lot further; **er ist der Konkurrenz immer ein paar ~e voraus** (*fig.*) he is always a few steps ahead of the competition; **sich** (*Dat.*) **jmdn. drei ~e vom Leibe halten** (*fig. ugs.*) keep sb. at arm's length; Ⓓ (*Gleich~*) **aus dem ~ kommen** *od.* **geraten** get out of step; **im ~ gehen** walk in step; Ⓔ (*des Pferdes*) walk; **im ~:** at a walk; Ⓕ (*Gangart*) walk; **jmdn. am ~ erkennen** recognize sb. by his/her walk *or* gait; **seinen ~ verlangsamen/beschleunigen** slow/quicken one's pace; **[mit jmdm./etw.] ~ halten** (*auch fig.*) keep up *or* keep pace [with sb./sth.]; Ⓖ (*~geschwindigkeit*) walking pace; **[im] ~ fahren** go at walking pace *or* a crawl; „**~ fahren**" 'dead slow'; Ⓗ (*fig.: Maßnahme*) step; measure; **~e unternehmen** *od.* **veranlassen** take steps; Ⓘ (*Teil der Hose, Genitalbereich*) crotch

***Schrittempo** ⇒ **Schritttempo**

**schritt-, Schritt-: ~geschwindigkeit** *die* walking pace; **[mit] ~geschwindigkeit fahren** go at walking pace *or* a crawl; **~macher** *der,* **~macherin** *die* pacemaker; **~tempo** *das* walking pace; **im ~tempo fahren** go at a walking pace *or* at a crawl; **~weise** ❶ *Adv.* step by step; gradually; ❷ *adj.* step by step; gradual

**schroff** /ʃrɔf/ ❶ *Adj.* Ⓐ precipitous, sheer ‹rock etc.›; Ⓑ (*plötzlich*) sudden, abrupt ‹transition, change›; (*krass*) stark ‹contrast›; **im ~en Widerspruch zu etw. stehen** be totally incompatible with sth.; Ⓒ (*barsch*) abrupt, curt ‹refusal, manner›; brusque ‹manner, behaviour, tone›.
❷ *adv.* Ⓐ ‹rise, drop› sheer; ‹fall away› precipitously; Ⓑ (*plötzlich, unvermittelt*) suddenly; abruptly; Ⓒ (*barsch*) curtly; ‹interrupt› abruptly; ‹treat› brusquely

**Schroffheit** *die;* **~, ~en** Ⓐ precipitousness; Ⓑ (*Plötzlichkeit*) suddenness; abruptness; (*Krassheit*) starkness; Ⓒ (*Barschheit*) curtness; abruptness; brusqueness; **mit**

S

**~:** curtly; **D** **seine ~en** his curt *or* brusque behaviour *sing.*; (*Bemerkungen*) his curt remarks

**schröpfen** /ˈʃrœpfn̩/ *tr. V.* **A** (*ugs.*) fleece; **B** (*Med.*) cup

**Schrot** /ʃroːt/ *der od. das;* **~[e]s, ~e** **A** coarse meal; (*aus Getreide*) whole meal (*Brit.*); whole grain; (*aus Malz*) grist; crushed malt; **B** (*aus Blei*) shot; **einem Hasen eine Ladung ~ aufbrennen** pepper a hare with shot; **C** *in* **ein Mann von echtem/bestem ~ und Korn** a man of sterling qualities; **ein Offizier/Kavalier** *usw.* **von altem ~ und Korn** an officer/a gentleman *etc.* of the old school

**schroten** *tr. V.* grind ‹grain etc.› [coarsely]; crush ‹malt› [coarsely]

**Schrot-: ~flinte** *die* shotgun; **~kugel** *die* pellet; **~ladung** *die* round of shot; small-shot charge

**Schrott** /ʃrɔt/ *der;* **~[e]s, ~e** **A** scrap [metal]; **das gehört auf den ~:** it belongs on the scrap heap; **ein Auto zu ~ fahren** (*ugs.*) write a car off; **B** (*salopp abwertend: minderwertiges Zeug*) rubbish; junk

**schrott-, Schrott-: ~händler** *der* ▶ 159 scrap dealer; scrap merchant; **~haufen** *der* scrap heap; (*ugs. fig.*) rusty heap; (*Unfallwagen*) heap of scrap; **~platz** *der* scrapyard; **~reif** *Adj.* ready for the scrap heap *postpos.*; fit for scrap *postpos.*; **ein Auto ~reif fahren** write a car off; **~wert** *der* scrap value

**schrubben** /ˈʃrʊbn̩/ *tr.* (*auch itr.*) *V.* scrub

**Schrubber** *der;* **~s, ~:** [long-handled] scrubbing brush

**Schrulle** /ˈʃrʊlə/ *die;* **~, ~n** **A** (*seltsame Idee*) cranky idea; (*Marotte*) quirk; **B** (*ugs. abwertend: Frau*) **[alte] ~:** old crone

**schrullen·haft, schrullig** *Adj.* cranky ‹person, idea›; zany (*coll.*) ‹story etc.›

**Schrulligkeit** *die;* **~:** crankiness; zaniness

**schrumpelig** *Adj.* (*ugs.*) wrinkly; wrinkled

**schrumpeln** /ˈʃrʊmpl̩n/ *itr. V.; mit sein* (*ugs.*) ‹skin› go wrinkled; ‹apple etc.› shrivel

**schrumpfen** /ˈʃrʊmpfn̩/ *itr. V.; mit sein* shrink; ‹metal, rock› contract; ‹apple etc.› shrivel; ‹skin› go wrinkled; (*abnehmen*) decrease; ‹supplies, capital, hopes› dwindle

**Schrumpf-: ~kopf** *der* (*Völkerk.*) shrunken head; **~leber** *die* cirrhotic liver; **eine ~leber haben/kriegen** have/get cirrhosis of the liver; **~niere** *die* cirrhotic kidney; **eine ~niere haben** have cirrhosis of the kidney

**schrumplig** ⇒ **schrumpelig**

**Schrunde** /ˈʃrʊndə/ *die;* **~, ~n** crack; (*von Kälte*) chap

**schrundig** *Adj.* cracked, chapped ‹skin, hands, etc.›

**Schub** /ʃuːp/ *der;* **~[e]s, Schübe** /ˈʃyːbə/ **A** (*Physik:* **~kraft**) thrust; (*eines Kolbenmotors*) pulling power; **B** ▶ 474 (*Med.: Phase*) phase; stage; **C** (*Gruppe, Anzahl*) batch; **~ auf** *od.* **um ~:** [in] one batch after another; **D** (*bes. ostmd.:* **~lade**) drawer

**Schuber** /ˈʃuːbɐ/ *der;* **~s, ~** **A** slip case; **B** (*österr.: Riegel*) bolt

**Schub·fach** *das* ⇒ **Schublade**

**Schub-: ~karre** *die*, **~karren** *der* wheelbarrow; **~kasten** *der* drawer; **~kraft** *die* thrust; **~lade** *die* drawer; (*fig.: Kategorie*) pigeon-hole; **in der ~lade liegen** (*fig.*) be ready for use

**schubladisieren** *tr. V.* (*schweiz.*) pigeon-hole

**Schubs** /ʃʊps/ *der;* **~es, ~e** (*ugs.*) shove; (*fig.: Ermunterung*) prod

**Schub·schiff** *das* push boat; pusher

**schubsen** *tr.* (*auch itr.*) *V.* (*ugs.*) push; shove

**schub·weise** **1** *Adv.* **A** in batches; **B** (*Med.*) in phases *or* stages.
**2** *adj.* **A** in batches *postpos.*; **B** (*Med.*) phased

**schüchtern** /ˈʃʏçtɐn/ **1** *Adj.* **A** shy ‹person, smile, etc.›; shy, timid ‹voice, knock, etc.›; **B** (*fig.: zaghaft*) tentative, cautious ‹attempt, beginnings, etc.›; cautious ‹hope›.
**2** *adv.* **A** shyly; ‹knock, ask, etc.› timidly; **er schwieg ~:** he was too shy to say anything; **B** (*fig.: zaghaft*) tentatively; cautiously

**Schüchternheit** *die;* **~:** shyness

**Schuft** /ʃʊft/ *der;* **~[e]s, ~e** (*abwertend*) scoundrel; swine

**schuften** (*ugs.*) **1** *itr. V.* slave *or* slog away; **er schuftet für zwei** he does the work of two [people].
**2** *refl. V.* **sich müde/krank** *usw.* **~:** tire oneself out/make oneself ill *etc.* with [over]work; **sich zu Tode ~:** work oneself to death

**Schufterei** *die;* **~** (*ugs.*) slaving away *no indef. art.*; slog

**schuftig** **1** *Adj.* mean; despicable.
**2** *adv.* meanly; despicably

**Schuftigkeit** *die;* **~, ~en** **A** meanness; **B** (*schuftige Handlung*) mean *or* despicable thing

**Schuh** /ʃuː/ *der;* **~[e]s, ~e** **A** shoe; (*hoher ~, Stiefel*) boot; **umgekehrt wird ein ~ draus** (*fig. ugs.*) the reverse *or* opposite is true; **wo drückt der ~?** (*fig. ugs.*) what's on your mind?; what's bugging you? (*sl.*); **wissen, wo jmdn. der ~ drückt** (*fig. ugs.*) know where sb.'s problems lie; **jmdm. etw. in die ~e schieben** (*fig. ugs.*) pin the blame for sth. on sb.

**Schuh-: ~anzieher** *der;* **~~s, ~~:** shoehorn; **~band** *das; Pl.* **~bänder** (*bes. südd.*) shoelace; **~bürste** *die* shoe brush

**Schuhchen, Schühchen** /ˈʃyːçən/ *das;* **~s, ~:** [little] shoe; (*Stiefelchen*) bootee

**Schuh-: ~creme** *die* shoe polish; **~größe** *die* shoe size; **welche ~größe hast du?** what size shoe[s] do you take?; **~löffel** *der* shoehorn; **~macher** *der* ▶ 159 shoemaker; ⇒ *auch* **Bäcker**; **~macherei** *die;* **~~, ~~en** **A** shoemaker's; **B** (*Handwerk*) shoemaking *no art.*; **~macherin** *die* ⇒ **~macher**; **~nummer** *die* shoe size; **~plattler** /-platlɐ/ *der;* **~~s, ~~:** *folk dance in Tirol, Bavaria and Carinthia, involving the slapping of the thighs, knees, and shoe soles;* **~putzer** *der;* **~~s, ~~** **A** shoeblack; shoe cleaner; **B** (*Gerät*) shoe-cleaning machine; **~putzerin** *die;* **~~, ~~nen** ⇒ **~putzer** A; **~riemen** *der* **A** sandal strap; **B** (*bes. westmd.: Schnürsenkel*) shoelace; **~sohle** *die* sole [of a/one's shoe]; **sich** (*Dat.*) **etw. an den ~sohlen abgelaufen haben** (*fig. ugs.*) have found sth. out ages ago; **~spanner** *der* shoe tree; **~werk** *das* footwear; shoes *pl.*; **~wichse** *die* (*veralt.*) shoe polish

**Schuko·stecker** Ⓦᶻ /ˈʃuːko-/ *der* two-pin earthed (*Brit.*) *or* (*Amer.*) grounded plug

**Schul-: ~abgänger** *der;* **~~s, ~~, ~abgängerin** *die;* **~~, ~~nen** school leaver; **~abschluss, *~abschluß** *der* school-leaving qualification; **~alter** *das* school age; **Kinder im ~alter** children of school age; **er kommt bald ins ~alter** he will soon be of school age; **~amt** *das* education authority; **~an·fang** *der* **A** (*Anfang des ~besuches*) first day at school; **etw. zum ~anfang bekommen** get sth. for starting school; **B** (*Anfang des ~tages*) **um 8 Uhr ist ~anfang** school starts at 8 o'clock; **~anfänger** *der*, **~anfängerin** *die* child [just] starting school; **~arbeit** *die* **A** ⇒ **~aufgabe**; **B** (*österr.: Klassenarbeit*) [written] class test; **C** (*Praxis des Unterrichts*) schoolwork *no art.*; **~atlas** *der* school atlas; **~aufgabe** *die* item of homework; **~aufgaben** homework *sing.*; **~aufsatz** *der* school essay; **~ausflug** *der* school outing; **~bank** *die; Pl.* **~bänke** [school] desk; **die ~bank drücken** (*ugs.*) go to *or* be at school; **~beginn** *der* ⇒ **~anfang**; **~beispiel** *das* textbook example (**für** of); **~besuch** *der* school attendance; **~bildung** *die* [school] education; schooling; **~brot** *das* sandwich (*eaten during break*); **~buch** *das* school book; **~bus** *der* school bus

**schuld** ⇒ /ʃʊlt/ *Adj.: in* **[an etw.** (*Dat.*)**] ~ sein** be to blame [for sth.]; **er ist nicht ~ daran** it is not his fault; he is not to blame [for this]; **sie ist an allem ~:** it's all her fault

**Schuld** *die;* **~, ~en** **A** (*das Schuldigsein*) guilt; **die Schwere einer ~:** the seriousness *or* degree of guilt; **er ist ohne [jede] ~:** he is [entirely] guiltless *or* blameless; **er ist sich** (*Dat.*) **keiner ~ bewusst** he is not conscious of having done any wrong; **~ und Sühne** crime and punishment; **... und vergib uns unsere ~** (*bibl.*) ... and forgive us our sins *or* trespasses; **B** (*Verantwortlichkeit*) blame; **es ist [nicht] seine ~:** it is [not] his fault; **ihn trifft keine ~:** no blame attaches to him; **er sucht die ~ immer zuerst bei anderen** he always tries to blame others first; **der Unfallgegner hat seine ~ anerkannt** the other party admitted liability for the accident; **er ist durch eigene ~ in diese Lage geraten** it was his own fault that he got into this situation; **jetzt hat er durch deine ~ seinen Zug verpasst** now he has missed his train because of you; **[an etw.** (*Dat.*)**] ~ haben** be to blame [for sth.]; **zu ~en** ⇒ **zuschulden**; **C** (*Verpflichtung zur Rückzahlung*) debt; (*Hypothek*) mortgage; **ich habe [bei der Bank] 5 000 Mark ~en** I have debts of 5,000 marks [with the bank]; I owe [the bank] 5,000 marks; **das Haus ist frei von ~en** the house is unmortgaged *or* free of mortgage; **in ~en geraten/sich in ~en stürzen** get into debt/into serious debt; **ich mache ungern ~en** I don't like getting into debt *or* running up debts; **er hat mehr ~en als Haare auf dem Kopf** (*ugs.*) he is up to his eyes *or* ears in debt; **D** *in* **[tief] in jmds. ~ stehen** *od.* **sein** (*geh.*) be [deeply] indebted to sb.

**Schuld·bekenntnis** *das* **A** confession [of guilt]; **B** (*Rechtsw.*) acknowledgement of indebtedness

**schuld·bewusst, *schuld·bewußt** **1** *Adj.* guilty ‹look, face, etc.›.
**2** *adv.* guiltily; **jmdn. ~ ansehen** give sb. a guilty look

**schulden** *tr. V.* owe ‹money, respect, explanation›; **was schulde ich Ihnen?** how much do I owe you?

**schulden-, Schulden-: ~berg** *der* (*ugs.*) pile of debts; **~frei** *Adj.* debt-free ‹person etc.›; unmortgaged ‹house etc.›; **ich bin/das Haus ist ~frei** I am free of debt/the house is free of mortgage; **~macher** *der*, **~macherin** *die* (*ugs. abwertend*) [habitual] debtor

**schuld-, Schuld-: ~frage** *die* question of guilt; **~gefühl** *das* feeling of guilt; guilty feeling; **~gefühle haben/bekommen** feel/start to feel guilty; **~haft** **1** *Adj.* culpable; **2** *adv.* culpably

**Schul·dienst** *der* [school]teaching *no art.*; **in den ~ gehen** go into teaching; **im ~ tätig sein** be in the teaching profession

**schuldig** *Adj.* **A** (*Schuld tragend*) guilty; **jmdn. ~ sprechen** *od.* **für ~ erklären** find sb. guilty; **er hat sich des Diebstahls ~ gemacht** he has been guilty of *or* committed theft; **er bekennt sich ~:** he admits his guilt; **er wurde/ist ~ geschieden** (*veralt.*) he was the guilty party in the divorce; **auf ~ plädieren** ‹public prosecutor› ask for a verdict of guilty; **das Gericht erkannte auf ~:** the court returned a verdict of guilty; **B** (*verantwortlich*) **der [an dem Unfall] ~e Autofahrer** the driver to blame *or* responsible [for the accident]; **C** **jmdm. etw. ~ sein/bleiben** owe sb. sth.; **was bin ich Ihnen ~?** what *or* how much do I owe you?; **jmdm. eine Erklärung/Dank** *usw.* **~ sein** owe sb. an explanation/a debt of gratitude *etc.*; **dafür bin ich dir keine Rechenschaft ~:** I don't have to account to you for that; **den Beweis bist du mir immer noch ~:** you have still not given *or* shown me any proof; **das bin ich ihm/der Partei ~:** I owe it to him/the party; **das ist er seiner gesellschaftlichen Stellung ~:** his social position requires it of him; **jmdm. die Antwort/Erklärung ~ bleiben** [still] owe sb. an answer/explanation; **er blieb ihnen die Antwort nicht ~:** he did not fail to give them an answer *or* leave them without an answer; **D** (*gebührend*) due; proper; **jmdm. den ~en Respekt erweisen** show sb. due respect *or* the respect due to him/her

*old spelling (see note on page 1707)

S

**Schuldige** *der/die; adj. Dekl.* guilty person; (*im Strafprozess*) guilty party; **der an dem Unfall ~:** the person responsible for *or* to blame for the accident; **einer muss ja der ~ sein** 'someone must have done it

**Schuldiger** *der;* **~s, ~** (*bibl.*) **wie wir vergeben unsern ~n** as we forgive those who sin *or* trespass against us

**Schuldigkeit** *die;* **~, ~en** duty; **meine [verdammte] Pflicht und ~:** my bounden duty; **seine ~ getan haben** (*fig.*) have served its/his purpose

**Schuld·komplex** *der* guilt complex

**schuld·los** *Adj.* innocent (**an** + *Dat.* of); **er wurde/ist ~ geschieden** he was the innocent party in the divorce

**Schuldner** *der;* **~s, ~, Schuldnerin** *die;* **~, ~nen** debtor

**Schuld-: ~schein** *der* IOU; promissory note (*Commerc.*); (*formell*) bond; **~spruch** *der* verdict of guilty; **~turm** *der* (*hist.*) debtors' prison; **~verschreibung** *die* (*Wirtsch.*) debenture bond; **~zuweisung** *die* recrimination

**Schule** /ˈʃuːlə/ *die;* **~, ~n** Ⓐ school; **die ~ wechseln** change schools; **zur** *od.* **in die ~ gehen, die ~ besuchen** go to school; **zur** *od.* **in die ~ kommen** come to school; (*als Schulanfänger*) start school; **von der ~ abgehen** leave school; **auf** *od.* **in der ~:** at school; **er ist an der ~:** he is a [school]-teacher; he teaches school (*Amer.*); **er ist durch eine harte ~ gegangen** (*fig.*) he has been through a hard school; **aus der ~ plaudern** (*fig.*) reveal [confidential] information; spill the beans (*coll.*); **~ machen** (*fig.*) become the accepted thing; form a precedent; **ein Diplomat** *usw.* **alter** *od.* **der alten ~:** a diplomat *etc.* of the old school; Ⓑ (*Ausbildung*) training; **[keine] ~ haben** ‹dog, singer, etc.› [not] be trained; **hohe ~** (*Reiten*) haute école; Ⓒ (*Lehr-, Übungsbuch*) manual; handbook; **eine ~ des Klavierspiels** a piano tutor; **eine ~ der Liebe** a handbook of *or* guide to love

**schulen** *tr. V.* train; **jmdn. politisch ~:** give sb. a political schooling; **er hat sich/seinen Stil an Adorno geschult** he modelled himself/his style on Adorno; **ein geschultes Auge** a practised *or* expert eye

**Schul-: ~englisch** *das* school English; **~entlassene** *der/die; adj. Dekl.* school leaver (*Brit.*); school graduate (*Amer.*)

**Schüler** /ˈʃyːlɐ/ *der;* **~s, ~** Ⓐ pupil; (*Schuljunge*) schoolboy; **~ und Studenten** schoolchildren and students; **die ~ der Grundschule** the primary school children *or* pupils; **ein ehemaliger ~ [der Schule]** a former pupil *or* an old boy [of the school]; **er ist noch ~:** he is still at school; **als ~ bekomme ich ...** as I am [still] at school, I receive ...; Ⓑ (*fig.: eines Meisters*) pupil; (*Jünger*) disciple

**schüler-, Schüler-: ~austausch** *der* school exchange; **~ausweis** *der* schoolchild's pass; **~brigade** *die* (*DDR*) work team of schoolchildren (*usu. working on a farm*); **~haft** ❶ *Adj.* (*wie ein Schuljunge*) schoolboyish; (*wie ein Schulmädchen*) schoolgirlish; ❷ *adv.* like a schoolboy/schoolgirl

**Schülerin** *die;* **~, ~nen** pupil; schoolgirl; **eine ehemalige ~ [der Schule]** a former pupil *or* an old girl [of the school]

**Schüler-: ~karte** *die* schoolchild's season ticket; **~lotse** *der,* **~lotsin** *die: pupil trained to help other schoolchildren to cross the road;* **~mit·verwaltung** *die* pupil participation *no art.* in school administration

**Schülerschaft** *die;* **~, ~en** pupils *pl.*

**Schüler-: ~sprache** *die* school slang; **~zeitung** *die* school magazine

**schul-, Schul-: ~fach** *das* school subject; **... ist ~fach** ... is taught in schools *or* is a school subject; **~ferien** *Pl.* school holidays *or* (*Amer.*) vacation *sing.*; **es sind noch ~ferien** the schools are still on holiday *or* (*Amer.*) vacation; **~fest** *das* school open day; **~frei** *Adj.* ‹day› off school; **morgen ist/haben wir ~frei** there is/we have no school tomorrow; **~frei bekommen** be let off school; **~freund** *der,* **~freundin** *die* school friend; **~funk** *der* schools broadcasting *no art.*; (*Sendungen*) [radio] programmes *pl.* for schools; **~gebäude** *das* school [building]; **~gebrauch** *der:* **für den ~gebrauch** for school use; for use in schools; **~gegenstand** *der* (*österr.*) ⇒ **~fach**; **~gelände** *das* school grounds *pl. or* premises *pl.*; **~geld** *das* school fees *pl.*; **lass dir dein ~geld wiedergeben!** (*ugs.*) they can't have taught you a thing at school; **~grammatik** *die* grammar [book] for schools; **~haus** *das* schoolhouse; **~heft** *das* exercise book; **~hof** *der* school yard

**schulisch** ❶ *Adj.* ‹conflicts, problems, etc.› at school; school ‹work etc.›; scholastic ‹questions etc.›; **seine ~en Leistungen** [the standard of] his school work *sing.*
❷ *adv.* at school

**schul-, Schul-: ~jahr** *das* Ⓐ school year; Ⓑ (*Klasse*) year; **ein zehntes ~jahr** a tenth-year class; **~jugend** *die* schoolchildren *pl.*; **~junge** *der* schoolboy; **~kamerad** *der,* **~kameradin** *die* (*veralt.*) schoolmate; **~kind** *das* schoolchild; **~klasse** *die* [school] class; **~landheim** *das* [school's] country hostel (*visited by school classes*); **~lehrer** *der,* **~lehrerin** *die* schoolteacher; **~leiter** *der* ▶159 headmaster; head teacher; **~leiterin** *die* ▶159 headmistress; head teacher; **~leitung** *die* Ⓐ [school] headship; Ⓑ (*Person*) head teacher; (*Personen*) school management; **~lektüre** *die* school reading [material]; (*einzelner Text*) school text; **~mädchen** *das* schoolgirl; **~mann** *der* (*veralt.*) schoolteacher; **~mappe** *die* schoolbag; **~medizin** *die* orthodox *or* traditional medicine *no art.*; **~meister** *der* Ⓐ (*veralt., scherzh.*) schoolmaster; Ⓑ (*abwertend: Krittler*) schoolmasterly type; pedagogue; **~meisterin** *die* Ⓐ (*veralt., scherzh.*) schoolmistress; Ⓑ schoolmistress type; pedagogue; **~meistern** *tr.* (*auch itr.*) *V.* (*abwertend*) lecture; **er ~meistert gern** he likes lecturing people; **~musik** *die* music *no art.* in schools; **~orchester** *das* school orchestra; **~ordnung** *die* school rules *pl.*; **~pflicht** *die* obligation to attend school; **die Einführung der [allgemeinen] ~pflicht** the introduction of compulsory school attendance [for all children]; **~pflichtig** *Adj.* required to attend school *postpos.*; **~pflichtig sein** have to attend school; **im ~pflichtigen Alter** of school age; **~praktikum** *das* teaching practice; **~ranzen** *der* [school] satchel; **~rat** *der,* **~rätin** *die* schools inspector; **~reif** *Adj.* ready for school *postpos.*; **~reife** *die* readiness for school; **~schiff** *das* training ship; **~schluss, *~schluß** *der* end of school; **nach ~schluss** after school; **~schwänzer** *der,* **~schwänzerin** *die* (*ugs.*) truant; **~speisung** *die* school meals *pl.*; **~sport** *der* sport *no art.* in schools; **~sprecher** *der* pupils' representative; ≈ head boy; **~sprecherin** *die* pupils' representative; ≈ head girl; **~stunde** *die* [school] period; lesson; **~system** *das* school system; **~tag** *der* school day; **der erste/letzte ~tag** the first/last day of school; **~tasche** *die* schoolbag; (*Ranzen*) [school] satchel

**Schulter** /ˈʃʊltɐ/ ▶471 *die;* **~, ~n** shoulder; **hängende ~n** drooping shoulders; (*als Merkmal*) round shoulders; **seine Frau reicht ihm gerade bis an die ~:** his wife only comes up to his shoulder; **er nahm das Kind auf die ~[n]** he lifted the child on to his shoulder[s]; **der Ringer zwang seinen Gegner auf die ~n** the wrestler forced his opponent on to his back; **~ an ~** (*auch fig.*) shoulder to shoulder; **mit den ~n** *od.* **die ~n zucken** shrug one's shoulders; **jmdn. über die ~ ansehen** (*fig.*) look down on sb.; look down one's nose at sb.; **jmdm. auf die ~ klopfen** pat sb. on the shoulder *or* (*fig.*) back; **sich** (*Dat.*) **selbst auf die ~ klopfen** (*fig.*) pat oneself on the back; **auf beiden ~n Wasser tragen** (*fig.*) have a foot in both camps; ⇒ *auch* **kalt** 1; **leicht** A

**schulter-, Schulter-: ~blatt** *das* ▶471 (*Anat.*) shoulder blade; **~frei** *Adj.* off-the-shoulder ‹dress›; **~halfter** *der* shoulder holster; **~höhe** *die* shoulder height; **~klappe** *die* shoulder strap; epaulette; **~lang** *Adj.* shoulder-length

**schultern** *tr. V.* shoulder; **das Gewehr ~:** shoulder arms; **etw. geschultert tragen** carry sth. on one's shoulder

**Schulter-: ~riemen** *der* shoulder strap; (*Milit.*) shoulder belt; **~schluss** *der,* ***~schluß** (*Solidarität*) solidarity; (*Zusammenarbeit*) collaboration; **~stand** *der* (*Turnen, Kunstfahren*) shoulder stand; **~stück** *das* Ⓐ (**~klappe**) shoulder strap; epaulette; Ⓑ (*Stück Fleisch*) piece of shoulder

**Schultheiß** /ˈʃʊltai̯s/ *der;* **~en, ~en** (*hist.*) sheriff; (*im Dorf*) mayor

**Schul·tüte** *die: cardboard cone of sweets given to a child on its first day at school*

**Schulung** *die;* **~, ~en** training; (*Veranstaltung*) training course; **politische ~:** political schooling

**Schulungs·kurs** *der* training course

**Schul-: ~unterricht** *der* school lessons *pl.*, *no art.*; **~weg** *der* way to school; **er hat einen ~weg von 10 km/Minuten** he lives 10 kilometres/minutes from his school; **~weisheit** *die* (*abwertend*) book learning; **~wesen** *das* school system

**Schulze** /ˈʃʊlt̮sə/ *der;* **~n, ~n** (*hist.*) ⇒ **Schultheiß**

**Schul-: ~zeit** *die* schooldays *pl.*; **~zentrum** *das* school complex; **~zeugnis** *das* school report; **~zimmer** *das* schoolroom

**Schummel** /ˈʃʊml̩/ *der;* **~s** (*ugs.*) cheating *no indef. art.*

**Schummelei** *die;* **~, ~en** (*ugs.*) ⇒ **Mogelei**

**schummeln** *itr., tr., refl. V.* (*ugs.*) ⇒ **mogeln**

**schummerig** /ˈʃʊmərɪç/ ❶ *Adj.* dim ‹light etc.›; dimly lit ‹room etc.›.
❷ *adv.* dimly

**Schummler** *der;* **~s, ~, Schummlerin** *die;* **~, ~nen** (*ugs.*) cheat

**schummrig** ⇒ **schummerig**

**Schund** *der;* **~[e]s** (*abwertend*) trash

**Schund-: ~literatur** *die* (*abwertend*) trashy literature; **~roman** *der* (*abwertend*) trashy novel

**schunkeln** /ˈʃʊŋkl̩n/ *itr. V.* rock to and fro together (*in time to music, with linked arms*)

**schupfen** /ˈʃʊpfn̩/ *tr. V.* (*österr., schweiz., südd.*) Ⓐ (*stoßen*) give sb. a shove *or* push; Ⓑ (*werfen*) throw; chuck (*coll.*)

**Schupfen** *der;* **~s, ~** (*österr., südd.*) shed; (*Wetterdach*) [wooden] shelter

**Schupo**[1] /ˈʃuːpo/ *die;* **~** *Abk.* **Schutzpolizei**

**Schupo**[2] *der;* **~s, ~s** (*veralt. ugs.*) cop (*coll.*)

**Schuppe** /ˈʃʊpə/ *die;* **~, ~n** Ⓐ scale; **es fiel ihm wie ~n von den Augen** he had a sudden, blinding realization; the scales fell from his eyes; Ⓑ *Pl.* (*auf dem Kopf*) dandruff *sing.*; (*auf der Haut*) flaking skin *sing.*

**schuppen** ❶ *tr. V.* scale ‹fish›.
❷ *refl. V.* ‹skin› flake; ‹person› have flaking skin

**Schuppen** *der;* **~s, ~** Ⓐ shed; Ⓑ (*ugs. abwertend*) (*hässliches Gebäude*) dump (*coll.*); (*kastenförmiger Bau*) box; Ⓒ (*ugs.: Lokal*) joint (*coll.*)

**schuppen·artig** ❶ *Adj.* scale-like.
❷ *adv.* like scales

**Schuppen·flechte** *die* ▶474 (*Med.*) psoriasis

**schuppig** *Adj.* Ⓐ scaly; Ⓑ (*mit Haut-, Kopfschuppen bedeckt*) flaky ‹skin›; dandruffy ‹hair›

**Schur** /ʃuːɐ̯/ *die;* **~, ~en** Ⓐ (*das Scheren*) shearing; Ⓑ (*Landw.: das Mähen, Schneiden*) cut

**Schür·eisen** *das* poker

**schüren** /ˈʃyːrən/ *tr. V.* Ⓐ poke ‹fire›; (*gründlich*) rake ‹fire, stove, etc.›; Ⓑ (*fig.*) stir up ‹hatred, envy, etc.›; fan the flames of ‹passion›; **jmds. Hoffnung ~:** raise sb.'s hopes

**schürfen** /ˈʃʏrfn̩/ ❶ *itr. V.* Ⓐ scrape; Ⓑ (*Bergbau*) dig [experimentally] (**nach** for); **nach Gold** *usw.* **~:** prospect for gold *etc.*; **tiefer ~** (*fig.*) dig deeper.

S

❷ *tr. V.* **A** **sich** (*Dat.*) **das Knie** *usw.* **[wund/blutig] ~:** graze one's knee *etc.* [and make it sore/bleed]; **B** (*Bergbau*) mine ‹ore etc.› open-cast *or* (*Amer.*) opencut.
❸ *refl. V.* graze oneself

**Schürf·wunde** *die* graze; abrasion

**Schür·haken** *der* poker (*with hooked end;*) (*für den Ofen*) rake

**schurigeln** /'ʃu:ri:gl̩n/ *tr. V.* (*ugs. abwertend*) **jmdn. ~:** make life unpleasant for sb.; (*schikanieren*) bully sb.

**Schurke** /'ʃʊrkə/ *der;* **~n, ~n, Schurkin** *die;* **~, ~nen** (*abwertend*) rogue; villain; **die Rolle des Schurken** the part of the villain *or* (*coll.*) baddy

**Schurkerei** *die;* **~, ~en** (*veralt. abwertend*) villainous deed

**schurkisch** (*veralt. abwertend*) ❶ *Adj.* villainous.
❷ *adv.* villainously

**Schur·wolle** *die:* **[reine] ~:** pure new wool

**Schurz** /ʃʊrts/ *der;* **~es, ~e** **A** apron; **B** (*Lenden~*) loincloth

**Schürze** /'ʃʏrtsə/ *die;* **~, ~n** apron; (*Frauen~, Latz~*) pinafore; **jmdm. an der ~ hängen** (*fig.*) be tied to sb.'s apron strings; **hinter jeder ~ her sein** *od.* **herlaufen** (*ugs.*) run *or* chase after anything in a skirt

**schürzen** *tr. V.* **A** gather up; **B** (*aufwerfen*) purse ‹lips, mouth›; **C** (*geh.: binden*) tie ‹knot›; knot ‹thread etc.›

**Schürzen-: ~band** *das; Pl.* **~bänder** ⇨ **Schürzenzipfel**; **~jäger** *der* (*ugs. abwertend*) skirt-chaser (*sl.*); **~zipfel** *der* apron string; **jmdm. am ~zipfel hängen** (*fig. ugs.*) be tied to sb.'s apron strings

**Schuss, *Schuß** /ʃʊs/ *der;* **Schusses, Schüsse** /'ʃʏsə/ **A** shot **(auf** + *Akk.* at); **21 ~ Salut** a 21-gun salute; **zum ~ kommen** get a chance of a shot; get a shot in; **weit** *od.* **weitab vom ~** (*fig. ugs.*) (*in sicherer Entfernung*) well away from the action; at a safe distance; (*abseits*) far off the beaten track; **der ~ kann nach hinten losgehen** (*fig. ugs.*) it could backfire *or* turn out to be an own goal; **ein ~ ins Schwarze** (*fig.*) a bull's eye; **ein ~ in den Ofen** (*fig.*) a complete waste of effort; **jmdm. einen ~ vor den Bug setzen** *od.* **geben** (*fig.*) fire a shot across sb.'s bows; **einen ~ haben** (*salopp*) be off one's rocker (*coll.*); **B** (*Menge Munition/Schießpulver*) round; **drei ~ Munition** three rounds of ammunition; **keinen ~ Pulver wert sein** (*fig. ugs.*) be worthless *or* not worth a thing; **C** (*~wunde*) gunshot wound; **D** (*mit einem Ball, Puck usw.*) shot **(auf** + *Akk.* at); **er ließ ihn nicht zum ~ kommen** he didn't let him get a shot in; **E** (*kleine Menge*) dash; **ein ~ Whisky** a dash *or* shot of whisky; **Cola** *usw.* **mit ~:** Coke ® *etc.* with something strong; brandy/rum *etc.* and Coke ® *etc.*; **eine Weiße mit ~** *a light top-fermented beer with a dash of fruit syrup, esp. raspberry-flavoured;* **F** (*Drogenjargon*) shot; fix (*sl.*); **jmdm./sich einen ~ setzen** give sb./oneself a fix; **der goldene ~:** the fatal shot; **G** (*Skisport*) schuss; **~ fahren** schuss; **im ~ abfahren** schuss down; **in ~ kommen** (*fig.*) get speed up; **H** (*ugs.*) **in ~ sein/kommen** be in/get into [good] shape; **etw. in ~ bringen** *od.* **kriegen/halten/haben** get sth. into/keep sth. in/have got sth. in [good] shape; **I** (*Weberei*) weft

**schuss·bereit, *schuß·bereit** *Adj.* ready to shoot *postpos.*

**Schussel** /'ʃʊsl̩/ *der;* **~s, ~** (*ugs.*) scatterbrain; wool-gatherer

**Schüssel** /'ʃʏsl̩/ *die;* **~, ~n** bowl; (*flacher*) dish; **vor leeren ~n sitzen** (*fig.*) go hungry; have nothing to eat

**schusselig** (*ugs.*) ❶ *Adj.* scatterbrained; (*fahrig*) dithery.
❷ *adv.* in a scatterbrained way

**Schusseligkeit** *die;* **~** (*ugs.*) wool-gathering; muddle-headedness; (*schusselige Art*) scatterbrained way

*old spelling (see note on page 1707)

**schusseln** *itr. V.* (*ugs.*) be scatterbrained; (*bei der Arbeit*) be careless; make careless *or* silly mistakes; **er hat mal wieder geschusselt** he's been wool-gathering again

**Schusser** *der;* **~s, ~** (*bes. südd.*) ⇨ **Murmel**

**schuss-, *schuß-, Schuss-, *Schuß-: ~faden** *der* (*Weberei*) weft thread; **~fahrt** *die* **A** (*Ski*) schuss; **B** (*fig.*) wild career; headlong rush; **~feld** *das* field of fire; **er hatte freies ~feld** he had a clear view of the target; (*Fußball usw.*) he had a clear shot [at goal]; **ins ~feld geraten** (*fig.*) come under fire; **~fest** *Adj.* bulletproof

**schusslig, *schußlig** /'ʃʊslɪç/ ⇨ **schusselig**

**Schuss-, *Schuß-: ~linie** *die* line of fire; **in die/jmds. ~linie geraten** *od.* **kommen** (*auch fig.*) come under fire/come under fire from sb.; **~verletzung** *die* gunshot wound; **~waffe** *die* weapon (*firing a projectile*); (*Gewehr usw.*) firearm; **~waffen·gebrauch** *der* use of firearms; **~wechsel** *der* exchange of shots; **~wunde** *die* gunshot wound

**Schuster** /'ʃu:stɐ/ *der;* **~s, ~** ▸ **159** (*ugs.*) shoemaker; (*Flick~*) shoe repairer; cobbler (*dated*); **auf ~s Rappen** (*scherzh.*) on Shanks's pony; **~, bleib bei deinem Leisten!** (*Spr.*) the cobbler should stick to his last (*prov.*); don't meddle with things you don't understand; ⇨ *auch* **Bäcker**

**Schuster-: ~ahle** *die* [shoemaker's] awl; **~draht** *der* waxed end; **~handwerk** *das* shoemaking *no art.*

**Schusterin** *die;* **~, ~nen** ▸ **159** ⇨ **Schuster**

**schustern** *tr., itr. V.* (*veralt.*) cobble (*dated*)

**Schuster-: ~palme** *die* (*volkst.*) aspidistra; **~werkstatt** *die* shoemaker's workshop; (*für Schuhreparaturen*) shoe repairer's workshop

**Schute** /'ʃu:tə/ *die;* **~, ~n** **A** (*Wasserfahrzeug*) barge; lighter; **B** (*Hut*) poke bonnet

**Schutt** /ʃʊt/ *der;* **~[e]s** **A** rubble; **„~ abladen verboten"** 'no tipping'; 'no dumping'; **in ~ und Asche liegen/sinken** (*geh.*) lie in ruins/be reduced to rubble; **B** (*Geol.*) debris; detritus

**Schutt·ablade·platz** *der* rubbish dump *or* (*Brit.*) tip; garbage dump (*Amer.*)

**Schütte** /'ʃʏtə/ *die;* **~, ~n** **A** (*Behälter*) [kitchen] drawer-container (*for flour etc.*); **B** (*Rutsche*) chute; **C** (*landsch.: Bündel*) sheaf

**Schüttel·frost** *der* ▸ **474** [violent] shivering fit; **~ haben** have violent shivers

**schütteln** /'ʃʏtl̩n/ ❶ *tr.* (*auch itr.*) *V.* **A** shake; **den Kopf [über etw.** (*Akk.*)**]/die Faust [gegen jmdn.] ~:** shake one's head [over sth.]/one's fist [at sb.]; **jmdm. die Hand ~:** shake sb.'s hand; shake sb. by the hand; **das Fieber/die Angst/das Grauen schüttelte ihn** he was shivering *or* shaking with fever/fear/gripped with horror; **von Angst/Ekel geschüttelt sein/werden** be gripped with fear/filled with revulsion; **das von Katastrophen und Krieg geschüttelte Land** the country [that was] torn by catastrophe and war; **B** (*unpers.*) **es schüttelte ihn [vor Kälte]** he was shaking [with *or* from cold].
❷ *refl. V.* shake oneself/itself; **sich im Fieber/vor Lachen ~:** be racked with fever/shake with laughter; **ich könnte mich [vor Ekel] ~:** I feel utterly revolted.
❸ *itr. V.* **mit dem Kopf ~:** shake one's head

**Schüttel·reim** *der: humorous rhyming couplet with two pairs of rhyming words having interchanging initial consonants*

**schütten** /'ʃʏtn̩/ ❶ *tr. V.* **A** pour ‹liquid, flour, grain, etc.›; (*unabsichtlich*) spill ‹liquid, flour, etc.›; tip ‹rubbish, coal, etc.›; **jmdm./sich Wein über den Anzug ~:** spill wine on sb.'s/one's suit; **B** **einen Eimer** *usw.* **voll Wasser** *usw.* (*Akk.*) **~** (*ugs.*) fill a bucket *etc.* with water *etc.*
❷ *itr. V.* (*unpers.*) (*ugs.: regnen*) pour [down]

**schütter** /'ʃʏtɐ/ *Adj.* sparse; thin

**Schütter** *der;* **~s, ~:** [coal] hod

**Schütt·gut** *das* bulk goods *pl.*

**Schutt-: ~halde** *die* pile *or* heap of rubble; **~haufen** *der* pile of rubble; (*Abfallhaufen*) rubbish heap; **~platz** *der* [rubbish] dump *or* (*Brit.*) tip; garbage dump (*Amer.*)

**Schutz** /ʃʊts/ *der;* **~es, ~e** **A** protection **(vor** + *Dat.*, **gegen** against); (*Feuer~*) cover; (*Zuflucht*) refuge; **im ~ der Dunkelheit/Nacht** under cover of darkness/night; **unter einem Baum ~ [vor dem Regen** *usw.***] suchen/finden** seek/find shelter *or* take refuge [from the rain *etc.*] under a tree; **jmdm. ~ gewähren** give *or* afford sb. protection; **jmdn. [vor jmdm.** *od.* **gegen jmdn./gegen etw.] in ~ nehmen** defend sb. *or* take sb.'s side [against sb./sth.]; ⇨ *auch* **Trutz**; **B** (*Vorrichtung*) guard

**schutz-, Schutz-: ~anstrich** *der* protective coating; **~bedürftig** *Adj.* in need of protection *postpos.*; **~befohlene** *der/die; adj. Dekl.* (*veralt.*) charge; **~behauptung** *die* (*bes. Rechtsw.*) attempt to justify one's behaviour; **~blech** *das* mudguard; **~brief** *der* (*Kfz-W.*) travel insurance; (*Dokument*) travel insurance certificate; **~brille** *die* [protective] goggles *pl.*; **~dach** *das* shelter; (*über der Haustür usw.*) canopy

**Schütze** /'ʃʏtsə/ *der;* **~n, ~n** **A** marksman; **ein guter/schlechter ~:** a good/poor shot *or* marksman; **der ~ konnte ermittelt werden** it was possible to establish who fired the shot/shots; **B** (*Fußball usw.: Torschütze*) scorer; **C** (*Mitglied eines ~nvereins*) **er ist ~** *od.* **bei den ~n** he is a member of a/the shooting *or* rifle club; **D** (*Milit.: einfacher Soldat*) private; **~ Arsch [im letzten** *od.* **dritten Glied]** (*derb*) the lowest of the low; **E** (*DDR Milit.*) soldier in the motorized arm; **F** (*Astrol., Astron.*) Sagittarius; **er/sie ist [ein] ~:** he/she is a Sagittarian

**schützen** ❶ *tr. V.* protect **(vor** + *Dat.* from, **gegen** against); (*vor Regen, Wind usw.*) ‹roof, wall› shelter **(vor** + *Dat.* from); ‹coat› protect **(gegen** against); (*absichern*) protect **(vor** + *Dat.* from); safeguard ‹interest, property, etc.› **(vor** + *Dat.* from); **sich ~d vor jmdn./etw. stellen** stand protectively in front of sb./sth.; **ein geschützter Platz** a sheltered spot; **geschützte Arten/Tiere/Pflanzen** protected species/animals/plants; **etw. patentrechtlich/urheberrechtlich/als Warenzeichen ~ lassen** patent sth./copyright sth./register sth. as a trade mark; **gesetzlich geschützt** registered [as a trade mark]; **„vor Wärme/Kälte/Licht ~"** 'keep away from heat/cold/light'; **„vor Nässe ~"** 'keep dry'.
❷ *itr. V.* provide *or* give protection **(vor** + *Dat.* from, **gegen** against); (*vor Wind, Regen*) provide *or* give shelter **(vor** + *Dat.* from)

**Schützen-: ~bruder** *der* fellow member of a/the shooting *or* rifle club; **~fest** *das: shooting competition with fair*

**Schutz·engel** *der* guardian angel

**Schützen-: ~graben** *der* (*Milit.*) trench; **~haus** *das* [shooting *or* rifle club] clubhouse; **~hilfe** *die* (*ugs.*) support; **~könig** *der* shooting champion; champion marksman; **~königin** *die* shooting champion; champion markswoman; **~panzer** *der* armoured personnel carrier; **~platz** *der: fairground where the Schützenfest takes place;* **~stand** *der* (*Milit.*) firing point (*in a foxhole*); **~verein** *der* shooting *or* rifle club

**Schutz-: ~film** *der* protective film; **~gebiet** *das* **A** [nature] reserve; **B** (*hist.: Kolonie*) protectorate; **~gebühr** *die* **A** token *or* nominal charge; **B** (*verhüll.: erpresste Zahlung*) protection money *no pl., no indef. art.*; **~gitter** *das* protective grid; **~gott** *der* tutelary *or* protective god; **~göttin** *die* tutelary *or* protective goddess; **~hafen** *der* port of refuge; **~haft** *die* preventive detention; **~heilige** *der/die* (*kath. Rel.*) patron saint; **~helm** *der* helmet; (*bei Renn-, Motorradfahrern*) crash helmet; (*bei Bauarbeitern usw.*) safety helmet; **~herrschaft** *die* (*Völkerr.*) protectorate; **~hülle** *die* [protective] cover; (*für Dokumente usw.*) folder; (*~umschlag*) dust jacket; **~hund** *der* guard dog; **~hütte** *die* **A** (*Unterstand*) shelter; **B** (*Berghütte*) mountain hut; **~impfung** *die* vaccination; inoculation

**Schützin** *die* **~, ~nen** **A** markswoman; ⇨ *auch* **Schütze A**; **B** (*Fußball usw.: Tor~*) scorer

S

**Schụtz-: ~kleidung** *die* protective clothing; **~kontakt** *der* (*Elektrot.*) earth contact; **~leute** ⇒ **~mann**

**Schützling** /ˈʃʏt͜slɪŋ/ *der;* **~s, ~e** protégé; (*Anvertrauter*) charge

**schụtz-, Schụtz-: ~los** *Adj.* defenceless; unprotected; **dem Gegner/Wind ~los ausgeliefert sein** be completely at the mercy of the enemy/the wind; **~mann** *der; Pl.* **~männer** *od.* **~leute** (*ugs. veralt.*) [police] constable; copper (*Brit. coll.*); **~marke** *die:* **[eingetragene] ~marke** registered trade mark; **~patron** *der* patron saint; **~polizei** *die* constabulary; police [force]; **~polizist** *der* (*veralt.*) police constable; **~raum** *der* shelter; **~schicht** *die* protective layer (**aus** of); (*flüssig aufgetragen*) protective coating; **~schild** *der* shield; (*der Polizei*) riot shield; **~suchend** *Adj.* seeking protection *postpos.;* **~truppe** *die* **A** peacekeeping force; **B** (*hist.: Kolonialtruppe*) colonial force *or* army; **~um·schlag** *der* dust jacket; (*für Papiere*) cover; **~verband** *der* protective bandage *or* dressing; **~vorrichtung** *die* safety device; (*Geländer, Gitter usw.*) safety measure; **~wall** *der* protective wall; (*fig.*) [protective] barrier; **der antifaschistische ~wall** (*DDR Amtsspr.*) the Berlin Wall; **~weg** *der* (*österr.*) pedestrian crossing; **~zoll** *der* protective tariff

**Schwa** /ʃva:/ *das;* **~[s], ~[s]** (*Sprachw.*) schwa

**schwabbelig** /ˈʃvabəlɪç/ *Adj.* flabby ‹stomach, person, etc.›; wobbly ‹jelly etc.›

**schwạbbeln** *itr. V.* (*ugs.*) wobble

**schwạbblig** ⇒ **schwabbelig**

**Schwabe** /ˈʃva:bə/ *der;* **~n, ~n** Swabian

**schwäbeln** /ˈʃvɛ:bl̩n/ *itr. V.* **er schwäbelt** he speaks in Swabian dialect

**Schwa̱ben** (*das*)*;* **~s** Swabia

**Schwa̱ben·streich** *der* (*scherzh.*) piece of folly

**Schwäbin** /ˈʃvɛ:bɪn/ *die;* **~, ~nen** Swabian

**schwä̱bisch** ❶ *Adj.* Swabian; **die Schwäbische Alb** the Swabian Mountains *pl.*
❷ *adv.* in Swabian dialect; (*mit ~em Akzent*) with a Swabian accent; ⇒ *auch* **badisch**; **deutsch**; **Deutsch**

**schwach** /ʃvax/; **schwächer** /ˈʃvɛçɐ/, **schwächst...** /ˈʃvɛçst.../ ❶ *Adj.* **A** (*kraftlos*) weak; weak, delicate ‹child, woman›; frail ‹invalid, old person›; low-powered ‹engine, car, bulb, amplifier, etc.›; weak, poor ‹eyesight, memory, etc.›; poor ‹hearing›; delicate ‹health, constitution›; **die Birne/die Brille ist ziemlich ~:** the lightbulb is of rather a low wattage/the glasses are not very strong; **auf ~en Beinen stehen** (*fig.*) ‹theory, evidence, argument, etc.› be shaky; **~ werden** grow weak; (*fig.: schwanken*) weaken; waver; (*nachgeben*) give in; **mir wird [ganz] ~:** I feel [quite] faint; **in einem ~en Moment, in einer ~en Stunde** in a weak moment; **er hat einen ~en Willen/Charakter** he is weak-willed/lacks strength of character; **B** (*nicht gut*) poor ‹pupil, player, runner, performance, result, effort, etc.›; weak ‹candidate, argument, opponent, play, film, etc.›; **sein schwächstes Buch/der schwächste Schüler** his worst book/the worst pupil; **er ist in Latein sehr ~:** he is very bad at Latin; **das ist aber ein ~es Bild!** (*fig. ugs.*) that's a poor show (*coll.*); **die Party war ~** (*ugs.*) the party wasn't up to much (*coll.*); **C** (*gering, niedrig, klein*) poor, low ‹attendance etc.›; sparse ‹population›; slight ‹effect, resistance, gradient, etc.›; light ‹wind, rain, current›; faint ‹groan, voice, pressure, hope, smile, smell›; weak, faint ‹pulse›; lukewarm ‹applause, praise›; faint, dim ‹light›; pale ‹colour›; low ‹fire, heat›; **die zahlenmäßig schwächere Gruppe** the group which is/was smaller in number; **die Nachfrage/das Geschäft ist zur Zeit ~:** demand/business is slack at the moment; **das ist nur ein ~er Trost** that is only a slight consolation; (*ugs.: hilft nur wenig*) that is little consolation *or* cold comfort; **das Licht wird schwächer** the light is fading; **D** (*wenig konzentriert*) weak ‹solution, acid, tea, coffee, beer, poison, etc.›; **Sherry ist schwächer als Whisky** sherry is not as strong as whisky; **E** (*Sprachw.*) weak ‹conjugation, verb, noun, etc.›.
❷ *adv.* **A** (*kraftlos*) weakly; **B** (*nicht gut*) poorly; **sehr ~ argumentieren** offer very weak arguments; **C** (*in geringem Maße*) poorly ‹attended, developed›; sparsely ‹populated›; slightly ‹poisonous, acid, alcoholic, sweetened, salted, inclined, etc.›; ‹rain› slightly; ‹remember, glow, smile, groan› faintly; lightly ‹accented›; ‹beat› weakly; **der Saal war nur ~ besetzt** there was only a small audience in the hall; **es war ~ windig** there was a light wind; **er wehrte sich nur ~:** he offered only faint resistance; **D** (*Sprachw.*) **~ gebeugt/konjugiert** weak

***schwachbesiedelt, *schwachbevölkert** ⇒ **schwach 2 B**

**Schwäche** /ˈʃvɛçə/ *die;* **~, ~n** **A** (*Kraftlosigkeit*) weakness; (*plötzlich auftretend*) [feeling of] faintness; **allgemeine ~:** general debility (*Med.*); **B** (*Mangel an Können*) weakness; **seine ~ in Mathematik** *usw.* his lack of ability in mathematics *etc.;* **C** (*Mangel*) weakness; failing; **D** (*Vorliebe*) weakness; **eine ~ für jmdn./etw. haben** have a soft spot for sb./a weakness for sth.

**Schwä̱che-: ~anfall** *der* sudden feeling of faintness; **~gefühl** *das* feeling of faintness

**schwächen** *tr. V.* weaken

**schwächer** ⇒ **schwach**

**Schwä̱che·zustand** *der* [state of] weakness; weak condition

**Schwạchheit** *die;* **~, ~en** **A** weakness; **die ~ des Greises/des Alters** the frailty of the old man/of old age; **B** (*Mangel, Fehler*) weakness; failing; **bilde dir nur keine ~en ein!** (*fig. ugs.*) don't kid yourself! (*sl.*)

**Schwạch·kopf** *der* (*salopp abwertend*) bonehead (*coll.*); dimwit (*coll.*)

**schwạ̈chlich** *Adj.* weakly, delicate ‹person›; frail ‹old person, constitution›; delicate ‹nerves, stomach, constitution›

**Schwạ̈chlichkeit** *die;* **~, ~en** weakness; (*der Nerven, der Konstitution*) delicateness

**Schwächling** /ˈʃvɛçlɪŋ/ *der;* **~s, ~e** weakling

**schwạch-, Schwạch-: ~punkt** *der* weak point; **~sichtig** *Adj.* (*Med.*) weak-sighted; **~sichtigkeit** *die;* **~~:** dimness of sight; amblyopia; **~sinn** *der* **A** ▶ **474** (*Med.*) mental deficiency; **B** (*ugs. abwertend: Unsinn*) [idiotic (*coll.*)] rubbish *or* nonsense; **~sinnig** ❶ *Adj.* **A** (*Med.*) mentally deficient; **B** (*ugs. abwertend: unsinnig*) idiotic (*coll.*), nonsensical ‹measure, policy, etc.›; rubbishy ‹film etc.›; ❷ *adv.* (*ugs. abwertend*) idiotically (*coll.*); stupidly

**schwächst...** ⇒ **schwach**

**Schwạch-: ~stelle** *die* weak spot *or* point; **~strom** *der* (*Elektrot.*) current of low amperage; (*mit niedriger Spannung*) low-voltage current

**Schwä̱chung** *die;* **~, ~en** weakening

**Schwaden** /ˈʃva:dn̩/ *der;* **~s, ~:** [thick] cloud

**Schwadron** /ʃvaˈdro:n/ *die;* **~, ~en** (*Milit. hist.*) squadron

**Schwadroneur** /ʃvadroˈnø:ɐ̯/ *der;* **~s, ~e** (*geh. abwertend*) windbag

**schwadroni̱eren** *itr. V.* (*abwertend*) bluster; **von etw. ~:** sound off about sth. (*coll.*)

**Schwafele̱i** *die;* **~, ~en** (*ugs. abwertend*) **A** rabbiting on (*Brit. sl.*); **B** (*Bemerkung*) rubbishy remark; **~en** blether *sing.*

**schwafeln** /ˈʃva:fl̩n/ (*ugs. abwertend*) ❶ *itr. V.* rabbit on (*Brit. sl.*), waffle (**von** about).
❷ *tr. V.* blether ‹nonsense›

**Schwager** /ˈʃva:gɐ/ *der;* **~s, Schwäger** /ˈʃvɛ:gɐ/ **A** brother-in-law; **B** (*veralt.: Postkutscher*) mail coach driver

**Schwägerin** /ˈʃvɛ:gərɪn/ *die;* **~, ~nen** sister-in-law

**Schwalbe** /ˈʃvalbə/ *die;* **~, ~n** **A** swallow; **eine ~ macht noch keinen Sommer** (*Spr.*) one swallow does not make a summer (*prov.*); **B** (*ugs.: Papierflieger*) paper aeroplane

**Schwạlben-: ~nest** *das* **A** swallow's nest; **B** (*Seemannsspr.*) cockpit locker; **~schwanz** *der* **A** swallow's tail; **B** (*Schmetterling*) swallowtail; **C** (*scherzh. veralt.: Frack*) [swallow]tails *pl.;* **D** (*Tischlerei*) dovetail [joint]

**Schwall** /ʃval/ *der;* **~[e]s, ~e** torrent; flood; **ein ~ Wasser/** (*fig.*) **von Lauten/Worten** a torrent of water/(*fig.*) sounds/words

**schwạllen** *tr., itr. V.* (*salopp*) ⇒ **schwafeln**

**schwamm** /ʃvam/ *1. u. 3. Pers. Sg. Prät. v.* **schwimmen**

**Schwạmm** *der;* **~[e]s, Schwämme** /ˈʃvɛmə/ **A** sponge; **~ drüber!** (*ugs.*) [let's] forget it; **B** (*südd., österr.: Pilz*) mushroom; **giftige Schwämme** poisonous fungi; **C** (*Pilzbefall*) dry rot *no art.*

**Schwammerl** /ˈʃvamɐl/ *das;* **~s, ~[n]** (*bayr., österr.*) mushroom; ⇒ *auch* **Pilz A**

**schwạmmig** ❶ *Adj.* **A** spongy; **B** (*abwertend: aufgedunsen*) flabby, bloated ‹face, body, etc.›; **C** (*abwertend: unpräzise*) woolly ‹concept, manner of expression, etc.›.
❷ *adv.* (*abwertend: unpräzise*) vaguely

**Schwạmmigkeit** *die;* **~** **A** sponginess; **B** (*abwertend: Aufgedunsenheit*) flabbiness; bloated appearence; **C** (*abwertend: Vagheit*) woolliness

**Schwan** /ʃva:n/ *der;* **~[e]s, Schwäne** /ˈʃvɛ:nə/ **A** swan; **mein lieber ~!** (*ugs.*) (*staunend*) my goodness!; good heavens!; (*warnend*) for heaven's sake!; **B** (*Sternbild*) **der ~:** Cygnus

**schwand** /ʃvant/ *1. u. 3. Pers. Sg. Prät. v.* **schwinden**

**schwa̱nen** *itr. V.* (*ugs.*) **jmdm. schwant etw.** sb. senses sth.; **ihm schwante nichts Gutes** he had a sense of foreboding

**Schwa̱nen-: ~gesang** *der* (*geh.*) swansong; **~hals** *der* **A** swan's neck; **B** (*oft scherzh.: langer Hals*) swanlike neck; **C** (*Technik*) swan neck

**schwang** /ʃvaŋ/ *1. u. 3. Pers. Sg. Prät. v.* **schwingen**

**Schwạng** *der: in* **im ~[e] sein** be in vogue; ‹rumour› be going the rounds; **in ~ kommen** come into vogue; ‹rumour› come into circulation

**schwanger** /ˈʃvaŋɐ/ *Adj.* pregnant (**von** by); **sie ist im vierten Monat ~:** she is in her fourth month [of pregnancy]; **mit etw. ~ gehen** (*fig.*) be big with sth. (*literary*); (*mit etw. erfüllt sein*) be full of sth.; (*scherzh.*) be mulling over sth.

**Schwạngere** *die; adj. Dekl.* expectant mother; pregnant woman

**schwängern** /ˈʃvɛŋɐn/ *tr. V.* make ‹woman› pregnant; **sich von jmdm. ~ lassen** get [oneself] pregnant by sb.; **von Duft geschwängert sein** (*fig. geh.*) ‹air› be heavy with scent

**Schwạngerschaft** *die;* **~, ~en** pregnancy

**Schwạngerschafts-: ~abbruch** *der* termination of pregnancy; abortion; **~streifen** *der* stretch mark

**schwạnk** *Adj. in* **wie ein ~es Rohr im Wind** (*geh.*) like a swaying reed

**Schwank** /ʃvaŋk/ *der;* **~[e]s, Schwänke** /ˈʃvɛŋkə/ **A** (*Literaturw.: Erzählung*) comic tale; (*auf der Bühne*) farce; **B** (*komische Episode*) comic event; **einen ~ aus seinem Leben erzählen** (*scherzh.*) tell the story of something funny that happened to one

**schwạnken** *itr. V.* (*mit Richtungsangabe mit sein*) **A** sway; ‹boat› rock; (*heftiger*) roll; ‹compass-needle etc.› swing [to and fro]; ‹ground, floor› shake; **mit ~den Schritten** with wavering steps; **B** (*fig.: unbeständig sein*) ‹prices, temperature, etc.› fluctuate; ‹number, usage, etc.› vary; **C** (*fig.: unentschieden sein*) waver; (*zögern*) hesitate; **zwischen zwei Möglichkeiten ~:** be unable to decide between two possibilities; **er schwankt noch, ob ...** he is still undecided [as to] whether ...; **~d werden, ins Schwanken kommen** *od.* **geraten** begin to waver *or* hesitate; become undecided; **jmdn. ~[d] machen** make sb. waver *or* uncertain

S

**Schwankung** *die;* ~, **~en** variation; (*der Kurse usw.*) fluctuation

**Schwanz** /ʃvants/ *der;* **~es, Schwänze** /ˈʃvɛntsə/ **A** tail; **ein Tier am** *od.* **beim ~ fassen** catch an animal by the tail; **den ~ des Festzugs bilden** (*fig.*) bring up the rear of the procession; **kein ~** (*fig. salopp*) not a bloody (*Brit. sl.*) *or* (*coll.*) damn soul; **den ~ einziehen** *od.* **einklemmen** *od.* **einkneifen** (*fig. salopp*) draw in one's horns; **jmdm. auf den ~ treten** (*fig. salopp*) tread *or* step on sb.'s toes; **da beißt sich die Katze in den ~** (*fig.*) that is a circular argument; **B** (*salopp: Penis*) prick (*coarse*); cock (*coarse*)

**Schwänzchen** *das;* **~s, ~** **A** [little] tail; **B** (*fam.: Penis*) willy (*coll.*)

**schwänzeln** /ˈʃvɛntsl̩n/ *itr. V.* **A** wag its tail/their tails; **B** *mit sein* (*~d laufen*) ‹dog etc.› run wagging its tail; **C** *mit Richtungsangabe mit sein* (*ugs. iron.: tänzeln*) mince; trip; (*ugs. abwertend: herumscharwenzeln*) **vor jmdm. ~:** crawl to sb.

**schwänzen** /ˈʃvɛntsn̩/ *tr., itr. V.* (*ugs.*) skip, cut ‹lesson etc.›; **[die Schule] ~:** play truant *or* (*Amer. coll.*) hookey; **den Dienst ~:** skive [off] (*Brit. coll.*)

**schwanz-, Schwanz-:** **~feder** *die* tail feather; **~flosse** *die* (*Zool., Flugw.*) tail fin; (*des Wals*) tail flukes *pl.*; **~lastig** *Adj.* tail-heavy; **~lurch** *der* (*Zool.*) caudate; **~wedelnd** *Adj.* tail-wagging *attrib.*; wagging its tail/their tails *postpos.*; **~wirbel** *der* ▶ 471 (*Anat., Zool.*) caudal vertebra

**schwappen** /ˈʃvapn̩/ ❶ *itr. V.* **A** **[hin und her] ~:** slosh [around]; **an die Bordwand ~:** splash *or* slap against the side of the boat; **B** *mit Richtungsangabe mit sein* splash, slosh (**über** + *Akk.* over, **aus** out of). ❷ *tr. V.* slosh ‹water, beer, etc.› (**auf** + *Akk.* on)

**Schwäre** /ˈʃvɛːrə/ *die;* **~, ~n** (*geh.*) [festering] ulcer

**schwären** *itr. V.* (*geh.*) fester; **eine ~de Wunde** (*auch fig.*) a festering wound *or* (*esp. fig.*) sore

**Schwarm** /ʃvarm/ *der;* **~[e]s, Schwärme** /ˈʃvɛrmə/ **A** swarm; **ein ~ Krähen/Heringe** a flock of crows/shoal of herrings; **B** (*fam.: Angebetete[r]*) idol; heart-throb; **sie hat einen neuen ~:** she's got a new flame; **C** (*Vorliebe*) **mein/sein** *usw.* **~** (*Tätigkeit*) my/his *etc.* passion; (*Gegenstand*) the apple of my/his *etc.* eye

**schwärmen** /ˈʃvɛrmən/ *itr. V.* **A** *mit Richtungsangabe mit sein* swarm; **B** (*begeistert sein*) **für jmdn./etw. ~:** be mad about *or* really keen on sb./sth.; **sie schwärmt für ihren Skilehrer** she has a crush on her skiing instructor (*coll.*); **von etw. ~:** go into raptures about sth.; **ins Schwärmen geraten** go into raptures

**Schwärmer** *der;* **~s, ~** **A** (*Fantast*) dreamer; (*Begeisterter*) [passionate] enthusiast; **B** (*Zool.: Schmetterling*) hawkmoth; **C** (*Feuerwerkskörper*) *firework emitting sparks and hopping short distances;* ≈ *jumping jack*

**Schwärmerei** *die;* **~, ~en** **A** (*Begeisterung*) [passionate *or* rapturous] enthusiasm; **eine ~ für jmdn./etw.** a passion for sb./sth.; **romantische ~:** romantic rapture *or* ecstasy; **B** (*schwärmerische Worte*) **[überschwängliche] ~[en]** rapturous hyperbole; (*Beschreibung*) rapturous description (**von** of); **C** (*Fantasterei*) fantasy

**Schwärmerin** *die;* **~, ~nen** ⇒ Schwärmer A

**schwärmerisch** ❶ *Adj.* rapturous ‹enthusiasm, admiration, letter, etc.›; effusive ‹person, language›; (*begeistert*) wildly enthusiastic. ❷ *adv.* rapturously; ‹speak› effusively

**Schwarm·geist** *der* **A** woolly-headed enthusiast; **B** (*hist.*) adventist

**Schwarte** /ˈʃvartə/ *die;* **~, ~n** **A** (*Speck~*) rind; (*Haut~*) skin; **B** (*ugs. abwertend: dickes Buch*) **[dicke] ~:** thick *or* weighty tome; **C** (*salopp: menschliche Haut*) skin; hide (*joc.*); **arbeiten, dass die ~ kracht** (*salopp*) work one's fingers to the bone; work until one drops; **D** (*Jägerspr.: Tierhaut*) skin; hide; **E** (*Brett mit Rinde*) slab

**Schwarten·magen** *der* (*Kochk.*) brawn

**schwarz** /ʃvarts/; **schwärzer** /ˈʃvɛrtsɐ/, **schwärzest...** /ˈʃvɛrtsəst.../ ❶ *Adj.* **A** black; Black ‹person›; filthy[-black] ‹hands, fingernails, etc.›; **~ wie die Nacht/wie Ebenholz** as black as pitch/jet-black; **mir wurde ~ vor den Augen** everything went black; **der Kaffee/Tee ist mir zu ~:** the coffee/tea is too strong for me; **der Kuchen ist schon ganz ~:** the cake is quite burnt; **B** (*fig.*) **der ~e Erdteil** *od.* **Kontinent** the Dark Continent; **die ~e Rasse** the Blacks *pl.*; **~e Blattern** *od.* **Pocken** smallpox *sing.*; **das ~e Schaf sein** be the black sheep; **~e Liste** blacklist; **~e Messe** Black Mass; **~e Gedanken** black *or* dismal thoughts; **das habe ich ~ auf weiß** I've got it in black and white *or* in writing; **das kann ich dir ~ auf weiß geben** you can take that from me; **er kann warten, bis er ~ wird** (*ugs.*) he can wait till the cows come home (*coll.*); **~ werden** (*Skat ugs.*) lose every trick; get whitewashed (*coll.*); **~ von Menschen** packed with people; **die ~e Kunst** [the art of] printing; (*Magie*) the black art; (*Kartenspiel*) **~er Peter** ≈ old maid (*with a black cat card instead of an old maid*); **etw. ~ malen** paint a black *or* gloomy picture of sth.; **vielleicht male ich zu ~:** perhaps I'm painting too black a picture; **~ sehen** look on the black side; be pessimistic; **für jmdn./etw. ~ sehen** be pessimistic about sb./sth.; **er sieht/malt alles ~ in ~:** he is deeply pessimistic about everything/paints a black picture of everything; **der ~e Tod** (*geh.*) the Black Death; **das Schwarze Meer** the Black Sea; ⇒ *auch* **Mann** A; **Schwarz**; **schwarzsehen**; **C** (*illegal*) illicit, shady ‹deal, exchange, etc.›; **eine ~e Kasse führen** run a separate account for underhand purposes; **der ~e Markt** the black market; **D** (*ugs.: katholisch*) Catholic; **E** (*ugs.: christdemokratisch*) Christian Democrat.
❷ *adv.* **A** ‹write, underline, etc.› in black; **~ gestreift/gemustert** with black stripes/a black pattern; **~ gerändert** black-edged; edged in black *postpos.*; dark-rimmed ‹eyes›; **B** (*illegal*) illegally; illicitly; **etw. ~ kaufen/verkaufen** buy/sell sth. illegally *or* on the black market; **~ Straßenbahn fahren** go on the tram (*Brit.*) *or* (*Amer.*) streetcar without paying; **die Arbeiten lassen wir ~ machen** we're going to get the work done by a moonlighter (*coll.*); **C** (*ugs.: christdemokratisch*) ‹vote› Christian Democrat; ‹ruled› by the Christian Democrats

**Schwarz** *das;* **~[es], ~:** black; **in ~ gehen, ~ tragen** wear black; **aus ~ Weiß machen [wollen]** (*ugs.*) [try to] argue that black is white

**schwarz-, Schwarz-:** **~afrika** (*das*) Black Africa; **~arbeit** *die* work done on the side (*and not declared for tax*); (*abends*) moonlighting (*coll.*); **~|arbeiten** *itr. V.* do work on the side (*not declared for tax*); (*abends*) moonlight (*coll.*); **~arbeiter** *der*, **~arbeiterin** *die* person who does work on the side; (*abends*) moonlighter (*coll.*); **~äugig** *Adj.* black-eyed; **~bär** *der* black bear; **~beere** *die* (*südd., österr.*) bilberry; **~braun** *Adj.* blackish-brown; **~brenner** *der*, **~brennerin** *die* illicit distiller; moonshiner (*Amer.*); **~brot** *das* black bread; **ein [Laib] ~brot** a loaf of black bread; **~bunt** *Adj.* (*Landw.*) black pied, Frisian ‹cattle›; **~drossel** *die* blackbird

**Schwarze**[1] *der; adj. Dekl.* **A** (*Neger*) Black; (*Dunkelhaariger*) dark-haired man/boy; **B** (*österr.: Kaffee*) black coffee; **C** (*ugs.: Konservativer*) Conservative

**Schwarze**[2] *die; adj. Dekl.* **A** (*Negerin*) Black [woman/girl]; (*Dunkelhaarige*) dark haired woman/girl; **B** (*ugs.: Konservative*) Conservative

**Schwarze**[3] *das; adj. Dekl.* **A** (*der Zielscheibe*) bull's eye; **ins ~ treffen** hit the bull's eye; (*fig.*) hit the nail on the head; **B** **er gönnt ihr nicht das ~ unter den Nägeln** (*ugs.*) he begrudges her everything; **C** **ihr kleines ~s** her plain black dress; her little black number (*coll.*)

**Schwärze** /ˈʃvɛrtsə/ *die;* **~, ~n** **A** (*Dunkelheit*) blackness; **B** (*Farbstoff*) black [dye]

**schwärzen** *tr. V.* blacken; black out ‹words›

**schwarz-, Schwarz-:** **~|fahren** *unr. itr. V.*; *mit sein* travel without a ticket *or* without paying; dodge paying the fare; **~fahrer** *der*, **~fahrerin** *die* fare dodger; **er ist ~fahrer** he's a fare dodger; ***~gerändert** ⇒ schwarz 2 A; **~haarig** *Adj.* black-haired; **~handel** *der* black market (**mit** in); (*Tätigkeit*) black marketeering (**mit** in); **~händler** *der*, **~händlerin** *die* black marketeer; (*mit Eintrittskarten*) tout; **~|hören** *itr. V.* (*Radio*) use a radio without [having] a licence; dodge paying one's radio licence fee; **~hörer** *der*, **~hörerin** *die* (*Radio*) radio user without a licence; radio licence dodger; **~kittel** *der* **A** (*scherzh.: Wildschwein*) wild boar; **B** (*abwertend: Geistlicher*) [Catholic] priest

**schwärzlich** *Adj.* blackish

**schwarz-, Schwarz-:** ***~|malen** ⇒ schwarz 1 B; **~malerei** *die* pessimism; gloominess; **hör auf mit dieser ewigen ~malerei!** stop always painting things so black!; **~markt** *der* black market; **~markt·preis** *der* black-market price; **~pulver** *das* black powder; **~rot·golden, ~-rot-golden** *Adj.* black, red, and gold; **~|schlachten** ❶ *itr. V.* slaughter animals illegally; ❷ *tr. V.* slaughter ‹animal› illegally; **~|sehen** *unr. itr. V.* (*Ferns.*) watch television without a licence; ⇒ *auch* schwarz 1 B; **~seher** *der*, **~seherin** *die* **A** (*ugs.*) pessimist; **B** (*Ferns.*) [television] licence dodger; **~sender** *der* pirate [radio] station; (*beim Amateurfunk*) pirate [radio] transmitter; **~specht** *der* black woodpecker; **~storch** *der* black stork

**Schwärzung** *die;* **~, ~en** blackening

**Schwarz·wald** *der;* **~[e]s** Black Forest

**Schwarzwälder** /-ˈvɛldɐ/ *die;* **~, ~** (*Torte*) Black Forest gateau

**schwarz·weiß, schwarz-weiß** *Adj.* black and white; **~ malen** (*fig.*) paint *or* put things in [crude] black-and-white terms

**schwarzweiß-, Schwarzweiß-:** **~aufnahme** *die* black and white photograph; **~fernseher** *der*, **~fernsehgerät** *das* black and white television [set]; **~film** *der* black and white film; **~foto** *das* black and white photo; ***~|malen** ⇒ **schwarzweiß, schwarz-weiß**; **~malerei** *die:* **der Bericht ist eine einzige ~malerei** the report paints *or* puts things in [crude] black-and-white terms; **~rot** *Adj.* black, white, and red; **~zeichnung** *die* black-and-white drawing

**Schwarz-:** **~wild** *das* (*Jägerspr.*) wild boars *pl.*; **~wurzel** *die* black salsify

**Schwatz** /ʃvats/ *der;* **~es, ~e** (*fam.*) chat; natter (*coll.*); **einen ~ halten** have a chat *or* (*coll.*) natter

**Schwätzchen** /ˈʃvɛtsçən/ *das;* **~s, ~** (*fam.*) [little] chat; [little] natter (*coll.*); ⇒ *auch* Schwatz

**schwatzen,** (*bes. südd.*) **schwätzen** /ˈʃvɛtsn̩/ ❶ *itr. V.* **A** (*sich unterhalten*) chat; **schwatzt nicht über Politik** don't talk about politics; **B** (*sich über belanglose Dinge auslassen*) chatter; natter (*coll.*); **C** (*etw. ausplaudern*) talk; blab; **D** (*in der Schule*) talk.
❷ *tr. V.* say; talk ‹nonsense, rubbish›

**Schwätzer** *der;* **~s, ~, Schwätzerin** *die;* **~, ~nen** (*abwertend*) chatterbox; (*geistloser Redner*) windbag; (*klatschhafter Mensch*) gossip

**schwatzhaft** *Adj.* (*abwertend*) talkative; garrulous; (*klatschhaft*) gossipy

**Schwatzhaftigkeit** *die;* **~** (*abwertend*) talkativeness; garrulousness; (*Klatschsucht*) gossipiness

**Schwebe** /ˈʃveːbə/ *die: in* **in der ~ bleiben, sich in der ~ halten** keep one's balance; ‹balloon› float in the air, hover; **in der ~ sein/bleiben** (*fig.*) be/remain in the balance; **eine Frage in der ~ lassen** (*fig.*) leave a question open *or* undecided

*old spelling (see note on page 1707)

**Schwebe-:** **~bahn** *die* (*Seilbahn*) cableway; (*Hängebahn*) [overhead] monorail; (*Magnetschwebebahn*) levitation railway; **~balken** *der* (*Turnen*) [balance] beam

**schweben** *itr. V.* **A** ‹bird, balloon, etc.› hover; ‹cloud, balloon, mist› hang; (*im Wasser*) float; **ihr war, als ob sie schwebte** she felt as if she were standing on air; **in Gefahr ~** (*fig.*) be in danger; **zwischen Leben und Tod ~** (*fig.*) hover between life and death; **was mir vor Augen schwebt, ist ...** (*fig.*) what I have in mind is ...; **B** *mit sein* (*durch die Luft*) float; (*herab~*) float [down]; (*mit dem Fahrstuhl*) glide; (*wie schwerelos gehen*) ‹dancer etc.› glide; **sich ~d fortbewegen** glide along; **C** (*unentschieden sein*) be in the balance; **das Verfahren schwebt noch** the trial is still pending; **alle ~den Fragen/Probleme** all outstanding questions/problems

**Schwebe·zustand** *der* state of uncertainty

**Schweb·stoff** *der* matter in suspension; suspended matter

**Schwede** /ˈʃveːdə/ *der;* **~n, ~n** **A** ▶ **553** Swede; **er ist ~:** he's a Swede; he's Swedish; **B** *in* **[du] alter ~!** (*ugs.*) old mate (*coll.*)

**Schweden** /ˈʃveːdn̩/ (*das*)*;* **~s** Sweden

**Schweden-:** **~bombe** *die* Ⓦⓩ (*österr.*) ⇒ Mohrenkopf A; **~platte** *die* (*Gastr.*) smorgasbord; **~punsch** *der* Swedish punch; arrack punch; **~stahl** *der* Swedish steel

**Schwedin** *die;* **~, ~nen** ▶ **553** Swede; ⇒ *auch* **-in**; Schwede A

**schwedisch** /ˈʃveːdɪʃ/ *Adj.* **A** ▶ **553**, ▶ **696** Swedish; ⇒ *auch* **deutsch**; **Deutsch**; **Deutsche**[2]; **B** *in* **hinter ~en Gardinen** (*ugs.*) behind bars (*coll.*)

**Schwefel** /ˈʃveːfl̩/ *der;* **~s** sulphur

**schwefel-, Schwefel-:** **~blume**, **~blüte** *die* (*Chemie*) flowers of sulphur *pl.;* **~dioxid**, **~dioxyd** *das* (*Chemie*) sulphur dioxide; **~gelb** *Adj.* sulphur-yellow; **~haltig** *Adj.* containing sulphur *postpos., not pred.;* sulphurous ‹Quelle, Boden›; **schwach ~haltig sein** have a low sulphur content; **~holz** *das* (*veralt.*) lucifer (*arch.*); match

**schwefelig** ⇒ **schweflig**

**schwefeln** *tr. V.* sulphurize

**Schwefel-:** **~säure** *die* (*Chemie*) sulphuric acid; **~wasser·stoff** *der* (*Chemie*) hydrogen sulphide

**schweflig** *Adj.* sulphurous ‹acid›

**Schweif** /ʃvaif/ *der;* **~[e]s, ~e** (*auch fig.: eines Kometen*) tail; (*eines Fuchses*) brush; (*fig.: von Anhängern, Fans o. Ä.*) retinue

**schweifen** **1** *itr. V.; mit sein* (*geh.: umher~; auch fig.*) wander; roam.
**2** *tr. V.* (*formen*) curve

**Schweif·säge** *die* turning saw

**Schweige-:** **~geld** *das* hush money; **er deckte die Geschäfte des Chefs und bekam dafür ~geld** he covered up his boss's deals and received a bribe to keep quiet; **~marsch** *der* silent [protest-]march; **~minute** *die* minute's silence

**schweigen** *unr. itr. V.* **A** (*nicht sprechen*) remain *or* stay *or* keep silent; say nothing; **kannst du ~?** can you keep a secret?; **~ Sie!** be silent *or* quiet! hold your tongue!; **auf etw.** (*Akk.*) *od.* **zu etw. ~:** say nothing in reply to sth.; **ganz zu ~ von ...** not to mention ...; let alone ...; **in ~der Andacht/Zustimmung** in silent worship/agreement; **die ~de Mehrheit** the silent majority; **B** (*aufhören zu tönen usw.*) ‹music, noise, etc.› stop; **der Sender schwieg ab ein Uhr nachts** the radio station stopped broadcasting at 1 a.m.; **die Geschütze ~** (*geh.*) the guns are silent

**Schweigen** *das;* **~s** silence; **das/sein ~ brechen** break the/one's silence; **..., da herrschte ~ im Lande** *od.* **Walde** ... [then] nobody said a word; **sich in ~ hüllen** maintain one's silence; **jmdn. zum ~ bringen** (*auch verhüll.*) silence sb.

**Schweige·pflicht** *die* (*eines Priesters*) obligation of secrecy; (*eines Arztes, Anwalts*) duty to maintain confidentiality

**schweigsam** *Adj.* silent; quiet; (*verschlossen*) taciturn; (*verschwiegen*) discreet

**Schweigsamkeit** *die;* **~:** silence; quietness; (*Verschlossenheit*) taciturnity; (*Verschwiegenheit*) discretion

**Schwein** /ʃvain/ *das;* **~[e]s, ~e** **A** pig; **Hackfleisch vom ~:** pork mince; **besoffen wie ein ~** (*derb*) pissed as a newt (*sl.*); **wie ein ~ bluten** (*derb*) bleed like a stuck pig; **sich benehmen wie ein ~/die ~e** (*derb*) behave like a pig/like pigs; **haben wir mal zusammen ~e gehütet?** (*spött.*) since when have we been on such familiar terms?; **B** (*Fleisch*) pork; **C** (*salopp abwertend*) (*gemeiner Mensch*) swine; (*Schmutzfink*) dirty *or* mucky devil (*coll.*); mucky pig (*coll.*); **D** (*salopp: Mensch*) **ein armes ~:** a poor devil; **kein ~ war da** there wasn't a bloody (*Brit. sl.*) *or* (*coll.*) damn soul there; **es macht kein ~ auf** nobody's opening the door; **E** (*ugs.: Glück*) **[großes] ~ haben** have a [big] stroke of luck; (*davonkommen*) get away with it; **hast du ein ~!** you're a lucky beggar!; **ich habe ~ gehabt** I was in luck

**-schwein** *das;* **~[e]s, ~e** (*derb abwertend*) pig; **Kapitalisten~/Kommunisten~:** capitalist pig/communist swine

**Schweinchen** *das;* **~s, ~:** piggy

**Schweine-** (*salopp*) **eine ~arbeit** a hell (*coll.*) *or* (*Brit. sl.*) sod of a job; **ein ~glück haben** be incredibly jammy (*Brit. coll.*) *or* (*coll.*) lucky; **heute ist wieder eine ~kälte** it's bloody (*Brit. sl.*) *or* (*coll.*) damn cold again today

**Schweine-:** **~bande** *die* (*derb*) pack of so-and-sos (*coll.*); (*stärker*) pack of bastards (*sl.*); **~bauch** *der* (*Kochk.*) belly pork; **~braten** *der* (*Kochk.*) roast pork *no indef. art.;* **ein ~braten** a joint of pork; **~filet** *das* (*Kochk.*) fillet of pork; **~fleisch** *das* pork; **~fraß** *der* (*derb abwertend*) pigswill (*coll.*); **~geld** *das* (*salopp*) **ein ~geld kosten/verdienen** cost/earn a packet (*coll.*) *or* a fortune; **~hund** *der* (*derb abwertend*) bastard (*sl.*); swine; **der innere ~hund** lack of will power; **~koben** *der* (*Stall*) pigsty; pigpen (*Amer.*); (*Verschlag*) pen (*in a sty*); **~kotelett** *das* (*Kochk.*) pork chop; (*vom Nacken*) pork cutlet; **~lende** *die* (*Kochk.*) loin of pork; **~mast** *die* fattening of pigs; pig-fattening; **~pest** *die* swine fever

**Schweinerei** *die;* **~, ~en** (*ugs. abwertend*) **A** (*Schmutz*) mess; **so eine ~!** what a mess!; **B** (*Gemeinheit*) mean *or* dirty trick; **es ist eine ~, dass das nicht erlaubt ist** it's disgusting that that's not allowed; **Er verdient mehr Geld als du? So eine ~!** He earns more money than you? Disgraceful!; **C** (*Zote*) dirty *or* smutty joke; (*Handlung*) obscene act

**schweinern** *Adj.* (*südd., österr.*) pork

**Schweinerne** *das; adj. Dekl.* (*südd., österr.*) pork

**Schweine-:** **~schmalz** *das* lard; (*zum Streichen*) dripping; **~schnitzel** *das* (*Kochk.*) escalope of pork; **~stall** *der* (*auch fig.*) pigsty; pigpen (*Amer.*); **ich halte es nicht länger aus in diesem ~stall** (*fig.*) I can't stand it any longer in this lousy joint (*coll.*); **~steak** *das* pork steak; **~zucht** *die* pig breeding *no art.;* **~zucht betreiben** breed pigs

**Schwein·igel** *der* (*ugs. abwertend*) **A** (*Schmutzfink*) dirty *or* mucky devil (*coll.*); mucky pig (*coll.*); **B** (*unanständiger Mensch*) dirty so-and-so (*coll.*)

**Schweinigelei** *die;* **~, ~en** (*ugs. abwertend*) **A** making *no art.* a [filthy] mess; (*Schmutz*) [filthy] mess; **B** (*Zote*) dirty *or* smutty story

**schweinigeln** *itr. V.* (*ugs. abwertend*) **A** (*Schmutz machen*) make a [filthy] mess; **B** (*Zoten reißen*) tell dirty *or* smutty stories

**schweinisch** (*ugs. abwertend*) **1** *Adj.* **A** (*schmutzig*) filthy; **B** (*unanständig*) dirty; smutty.
**2** *adv.* (*unanständig*) ‹behave› obscenely, disgustingly

**schweins-, Schweins-:** **~äuglein** *das* piggy eye; **~braten** *der* (*Kochk., bes. südd., österr., schweiz.*) ⇒ **Schweinebraten**; **~galopp** *die* **im ~galopp** (*scherzh.*) at a gallop; **im ~galopp angerannt kommen** come charging up [at a gallop]; **~hachse** *die*, (*bes. südd.*) **~haxe** *die* (*Kochk.*) knuckle of pork; **~kopf** *der* (*Kochk.*) pig's head; **~leder** *das* pigskin; **~ledern** *Adj.* pigskin; **~stelze** *die* (*österr.*) ⇒ **~hachse**

**Schweiß** /ʃvais/ *der;* **~es** **A** sweat; (*höflicher: Transpiration*) perspiration; **in ~ kommen** *od.* **geraten** start to sweat; **mir brach der ~ aus** I broke out in a sweat; **ihm brach der kalte ~ aus** he came out in a cold sweat; **in ~ gebadet sein** be bathed in sweat; **etw. im ~e seines Angesichts tun** (*geh.*) do sth. in *or* by the sweat of one's brow; **das hat viel ~ gekostet** that was a real sweat (*coll.*); **B** (*Jägerspr.: Blut*) blood

**schweiß-, Schweiß-:** **~ausbruch** *der* sweat; **einen ~ausbruch bekommen** start to sweat; **~band** *das; Pl.* **~bänder** sweat-band; **~bedeckt** *Adj.* covered in *or* with sweat *postpos.;* **~brenner** *der* (*Technik*) welding torch; **~draht** *der* (*Technik*) filler wire; welding wire; **~drüse** *die* ▶ **471** (*Anat.*) sweat gland

**schweißen** *tr., itr. V.* weld

**Schweißer** *der;* **~s, ~**, **Schweißerin** *die;* **~, ~nen** ▶ **159** welder

**schweiß-, Schweiß-:** **~fleck** *der* sweat stain; **~fuß** *der* sweaty foot; **~gebadet** *Adj.* bathed in sweat *postpos.;* **~geruch** *der* smell of sweat

**schweißig** *Adj.* sweaty

**schweiß- Schweiß-:** **~naht** *die* (*Technik*) weld; **~nass**, ***~naß** *Adj.* sweaty; damp with sweat *pred.;* **~perle** *die* bead of sweat; **~treibend** *Adj.* sudorific; diaphoretic; **Holzhacken ist eine ~treibende Arbeit** chopping wood makes you work up a sweat; **~tropfen** *der* drop of sweat; **~tuch** *das; Pl.* **~tücher** (*veralt.*) sudarium; **das ~tuch der Veronika** (*Bibl.*) the sudarium; the Veronica; Veronica's veil

**Schweiz** /ʃvaits/ *die;* **~:** Switzerland *no art.;* **in die ~ reisen** travel to Switzerland; **aus der ~ stammen** come from Switzerland

**Schweizer** **1** *indekl. Adj.* ▶ **553** Swiss.
**2** *der;* **~s, ~:** **A** (*Einwohner*) Swiss; **B** (*Landw.: Melker*) dairyman; **C** (*in der ~garde*) Swiss Guard; **D** (**~** *Käse*) Swiss cheese

**schweizer-, Schweizer-:** **~bürger** *der*, **~bürgerin** *die* Swiss citizen; **~deutsch** *Adj.* Swiss German; ⇒ *auch* **deutsch**; **Deutsch**; **Deutsche**[2]; **~garde** *die* Swiss Guard

**Schweizerin** *die;* **~, ~nen** ▶ **553** Swiss; ⇒ *auch* **-in**

**schweizerisch** *Adj.* ▶ **553** Swiss

**Schweizerland** *das;* **~[e]s** (*schweiz.*) ⇒ Schweiz

**Schweizer-:** **~psalm** *der* Swiss national anthem; **~volk** *das:* **das ~volk** the Swiss people

**Schwel·brand** *der* smouldering fire

**schwelen** /ˈʃveːlən/ **1** *itr. V.* (*auch fig.*) smoulder.
**2** *tr. V.* (*Technik*) carbonize ‹coal, peat, etc.› at low temperature

**schwelgen** /ˈʃvɛlgn̩/ *itr. V.* **A** (*essen u. trinken*) feast; **in etw.** (*Dat.*) **~:** feast on sth.; **B** **in Erinnerungen/Gefühlen** *usw.* **~:** wallow in memories/emotions *etc.;* **in Farben ~** (*geh.*) revel in colours

**schwelgerisch** **1** *Adj.* epicurean ‹person›; sumptuous, opulent ‹meal, grandeur›; rapturous ‹look, expression›; luxuriant ‹blossom›.
**2** *adv.* rapturously; with rapturous pleasure

**Schwelle** /ˈʃvɛlə/ *die;* **~, ~n** **A** (*auch Physiol., Psych., fig.*) threshold; **ich werde keinen Fuß mehr über seine ~ setzen** (*fig. geh.*) I shall not set foot in his house/flat *etc.* again; **jmdn. von der ~ weisen** (*fig. geh.*) turn sb. from one's door; **sich an der ~ des Todes befinden** (*fig. geh.*) be at death's door; **B** (*Eisenbahn~*) sleeper (*Brit.*);

S

[cross] tie (*Amer.*); **C** (*Geogr.*) swell; **D** (*Bauw.*) sill; sole plate; abutment piece (*Amer.*)

**schwellen¹** *unr. itr. V.; mit sein* swell; ‹limb, face, cheek, etc.› swell [up], become swollen; ‹river› become swollen, rise; **~d** full ‹lips›; ample ‹bosom›; thick ‹cushion, carpet›; bulging ‹wallet›; **der Sturm schwoll zum Orkan** the storm rose to a hurricane force; ⇨ *auch* **Kamm**

**schwellen²** *tr. V.* (*geh.*) belly, fill ‹sail, curtain›; **der Stolz schwellte ihm die Brust** (*fig.*) his breast swelled with pride

**Schwellen-: ~angst** *die* fear of entering a place; **~land** *das: country at the stage of economic take-off*

**Schweller** *der;* **~s,** **~** (*Musik*) swell

**Schwell·körper** (*Physiol.*) *der* corpus cavernosum

**Schwellung** *die;* **~,** **~en** (*Med.*) swelling

**Schwemme** /ˈʃvɛmə/ *die;* **~,** **~n** **A** (*Wirtsch.*) glut (**an** + *Dat.* of); **B** (*Kneipe*) bar; [basic] pub (*Brit.*); **C** (*für Tiere*) watering place; **D** (*österr.: im Warenhaus*) bargain basement

**-schwemme** *die;* **~,** **~n** glut; **Tomaten~/Milch~:** tomato/milk glut; **Lehrer~/Juristen~:** glut of teachers/lawyers

**schwemmen** *tr. V.* **A** (*treiben*) wash; **an Land geschwemmt werden** be washed ashore; **B** (*bes. österr.: spülen*) rinse

**Schwemm-: ~land** *das;* alluvial land; **~sand** *der* alluvial sand

**Schwengel** /ˈʃvɛŋl̩/ *der;* **~s,** **~** **A** (*Glocken~*) clapper; **B** (*Pumpen~*) handle; **C** (*salopp: Penis*) tool (*sl.*)

**Schwenk** /ʃvɛŋk/ *der;* **~s,** **~s** **A** (*Drehung*) swing; **die Kolonne machte einen ~ nach rechts** the column swung *or* wheeled to the right; **die Partei macht einen ~ nach links** (*fig.*) the party is swinging *or* shifting to the left; **B** (*Film, Ferns.*) pan; **die Kamera machte einen ~ auf den Helden** the camera panned to the hero

**Schwenk·arm** *der* swivel arm; swivelling arm

**schwenkbar** *Adj.* swivelling; **das Periskop ist ~:** the periscope can be swivelled round

**Schwenk·bereich** *der* working range; jib range

**schwenken** ❶ *tr. V.* **A** (*schwingen*) swing; wave ‹flag, handkerchief›; **B** (*spülen*) rinse; **C** (*drehen*) swing round; swivel; pan ‹camera›; swing, traverse ‹gun›; **D** (*Kochk.*) toss. ❷ *itr. V.; mit sein* ‹marching column› swing, wheel; ‹camera› pan; ‹path, road, car› swing; **er schwenkte in den Hof** he turned into the courtyard; **rechts schwenkt!** (*Milit.*) right wheel!

**Schwenker** *der;* **~s,** **~:** balloon glass

**Schwenk·kran** *der* swing-jib crane

**Schwenkung** *die;* **~,** **~en** ⇨ **Schwenk**

**schwer** /ʃveːɐ̯/ ❶ *Adj.* **A** heavy; heavy-[weight] ‹fabric›; (*massiv*) solid ‹gold›; **die Äste sind ~ von Früchten** the branches are heavy with fruit; **~es Geld kosten** (*fig. ugs.*) cost a packet (*coll.*) *or* a fortune; **mir wurden die Beine ~:** my legs grew heavy; **ihm wurde ~ ums Herz** (*geh.*) his heart grew heavy; **B** ▶ **353** (*bestimmtes Gewicht habend*) **2 Kilo ~ sein** weigh two kilos; **ein zwei Zentner ~er Sack** a two-centner sack; a sack weighing two centners; **wie ~ bist du?** how much do you weigh?; **eine mehrere Millionen ~e Frau** (*fig. ugs.*) a woman who's worth a few millions; **C** (*anstrengend, mühevoll*) heavy ‹work›; hard, tough ‹job›; hard ‹day›; difficult ‹birth›; troubled ‹dream›; **D** (*schwierig*) difficult; hard; **jmdm. fällt etw. ~:** sb. finds sth. difficult; **auch wenns ~ fällt** whether you like it or not; **es wird ~ halten, das zu tun** it will be difficult to do it *or* that; **es ~/nicht ~ haben** have it hard/easy; **sie hat es ~ mit ihrem Mann gehabt** she's had a hard time with her husband; **jmdm./sich etw. ~ machen** make sth. difficult for sb./oneself; **sich** (*Dat.*) **die Entscheidung ~ machen** find it hard to make a decision; find the decision a hard one; **etw. ~ nehmen** take sth. seriously; **sich** (*Akk. od. Dat.*) **mit** *od.* **bei etw. ~ tun** (*ugs.*) have trouble with sth; **sich** (*Akk. od. Dat.*) **mit jmdm. ~ tun** (*ugs.*) not get along with sb.; **Schweres durchmachen** go through hard times; **wir haben das Schwerste überstanden** we're over the worst; **E** (*schlimm*) severe ‹shock, disappointment, strain, storm›; serious, grave ‹wrong, injustice, error, illness, blow, reservation›; serious ‹accident, injury›; heavy ‹punishment, strain, loss, blow›; grave ‹suspicion›; **ein ~er Junge** (*ugs.*) a crook with a record (*coll.*); **F** (*~ verträglich*) heavy ‹food, wine›; **G** (*intensiv*) heavy ‹fragrance, perfume, etc.›; **H** (*anspruchsvoll*) heavy ‹book, music, etc.›; **I** (*Seemannsspr.*) heavy ‹sea, weather›; **J** (*schwül*) heavy; oppressive ‹air, atmosphere›.

❷ *adv.* **A** ▶ **353** heavily ‹built, armed›; **~ beladen** heavily laden *or* loaded ‹vehicle›; heavily laden ‹person, animal›; **~ wiegen** be heavy; (*fig.*) carry weight; **~ tragen** be carrying sth. heavy [with difficulty]; **~ heben** lift heavy weights; **~ zu tragen haben** have a heavy load to carry; **daran hat er ~ zu tragen** (*fig.*) it is a hard cross for him to bear; **~ auf jmdm./etw. liegen** *od.* **lasten** (*auch fig.*) weigh heavily on sb./sth.; **das Essen lag mir ~ im Magen** (*fig.*) the food lay heavily on my stomach; **B** (*anstrengend, mühevoll*) ‹work› hard; ‹breathe› heavily; **~ erkämpft sein** be hard won; **das habe ich mir ~ erkämpft** I gained it at great cost; **~ erkauft** dearly bought; bought at great cost *postpos.*; **er lernt nur ~:** he is a slow learner; **~ hören** be hard of hearing; **~ erziehbare Kinder** difficult children; **~ verdaulich sein** (*auch fig.*) be hard to digest; **~ verständlich** scarcely comprehensible; **C** (*schwierig*) with difficulty; **ein ~ zu lesender Text** a text that is hard *or* difficult to read; **D** (*sehr*) seriously ‹injured, wounded›; greatly, deeply ‹disappointed›; ‹punish› severely, heavily; **~ behindert** severely handicapped; (*körperlich auch*) severely disabled; **~ beschädigt** badly damaged; (*veralt.: ~ behindert*) severely disabled; **~ krank** seriously ill; **etw. ~ büßen** pay dearly for sth.; **~ aufpassen** (*ugs.*) take great care; **~ stürzen** fall heavily; have a heavy fall; **~ verunglücken** have a serious accident; **~ im Irrtum sein** (*ugs.*) be very much mistaken; **~ in Fahrt sein** (*ugs.*) be really worked up; **~ betroffen sein** be deeply affected; **~ beleidigt/betrunken sein** (*ugs.*) be deeply *or* very insulted/blind drunk; **sich ~ ärgern** (*ugs.*) get very annoyed; **sich ~ blamieren** (*ugs.*) make a proper fool of oneself; **das will ich ~ hoffen** (*ugs.*) I should jolly well think so (*Brit. coll.*); **er ist ~ in Ordnung** (*ugs.*) he's a good bloke (*Brit. coll.*) *or* (*coll.*) guy; **wir haben ~ einen draufgemacht** (*ugs.*) we really painted the town red (*coll.*); **E** (*unverträglich*) **~ essen** eat heavy food; **sie kocht zu ~:** the food she cooks is too heavy

**schwer-, Schwer-: ~arbeit** *die;* heavy work; **~arbeiter** *der,* **~arbeiterin** *die* worker engaged in heavy physical work; **~athlet** *der* weightlifter/wrestler/boxer/judoka/shot-putter/discus-thrower; **~athletik** *die* weightlifting *no art.*/combat sports *no art.*/shot-putting *no art.*/discus-throwing *no art.*; ***~behindert** ⇨ **schwer** 2 D; **~behinderte** *der/die* severely handicapped person; (*körperlich auch*) severely disabled person; **die ~behinderten** the severely handicapped/disabled; **~behinderten·ausweis** *der* disabled person's pass; ***~beladen** ⇨ **schwer** 2 A; ***~beschädigt** ⇨ **schwer** 2 D; **~beschädigte** *der/die; adj. Dekl.* severely disabled person; **die ~beschädigten** the severely disabled; ***~bewaffnet** ⇨ **schwer** 2 A; **~blütig** *Adj.* stolid; phlegmatic

**Schwere** *die;* **~** **A** weight; **eine ~ in den Gliedern** a heaviness in one's limbs; **B** (*Physik: Schwerkraft*) gravity; **C** ⇨ **schwer** 1 E: severity; seriousness; gravity; heaviness; **D** (*Schwierigkeitsgrad*) difficulty; **E** (*von Speisen, Parfums usw.*) heaviness

**Schwere·feld** *das* (*Geophysik*) gravitational field; field of gravity

**schwere·los** ❶ *Adj.* weightless. ❷ *adv.* weightlessly

**Schwerelosigkeit** *die;* **~:** weightlessness

**Schwerenöter** /ˈʃveːrənøːtɐ/ *der;* **~s,** **~** (*ugs. scherzh.*) ladykiller (*coll.*)

**schwer-, Schwer-: *~erziehbar** ⇨ **schwer** 2 B; ***~|fallen** ⇨ **schwer** 1 D; **~fällig** ❶ *Adj.* ponderous, slow-moving ‹animal›; ponderous, heavy ‹movement, steps›; (*auch geistig*) ponderous ‹person›; (*fig.*) cumbersome ‹bureaucracy, procedure›; ponderous ‹style, thinking›; ❷ *adv.* ponderously; **~fällig denken/antworten** think/answer slowly and ponderously; **~fälligkeit** *die* ⇨ **~fällig**: ponderousness; heaviness; (*fig.*) cumbersomeness; ponderousness; **~gewicht** *das* **A** heavyweight; **die Meisterschaften im ~gewicht** the heavyweight championships; **B** (*Sportler*) heavyweight; **C** (*Schwerpunkt*) main focus; emphasis; **sie studiert Russisch mit ~gewicht Sprachwissenschaft** she's studying Russian, specializing in linguistics; **D** (*ugs. scherzh.: dicker Mensch*) heavyweight; **~gewichtig** *Adj.* heavyweight *attrib.*; **~gewichtler** /ˈɡəvɪçtlɐ/ *der;* **~~s,** **~~** (*athletik*) heavyweight; ***~|halten** ⇨ **schwer** 1 D; **~hörig** *Adj.* hard of hearing *pred.*; **auf dem Ohr ist er ~hörig** (*fig.*) when it comes to that sort of thing, he doesn't want to know; **~hörige** *der/die; adj. Dekl.* person who is hard of hearing; **die ~n** the hard of hearing; **~hörigkeit** *die* hardness of hearing; **~industrie** *die* heavy industry; **~kraft** *die* (*Physik, Astron.*) gravity; ***~krank** ⇨ **schwer** 2 D; **~kranke** *der/die* seriously ill person; **die ~kranken** the seriously ill; **~kriegsbeschädigte** *der/die* severely war disabled person; **die ~kriegsbeschädigten** the severely war disabled

**schwerlich** *Adv.* hardly; **das wird dir ~ jemand glauben** it's hardly likely that anyone will believe you

**schwer-, Schwer-: *~|machen** ⇨ **schwer** 1 D; **~metall** *das* heavy metal; **~mut** *die* melancholy; **~mütig** ❶ *Adj.* melancholic; ❷ *adv.* melancholically; **er starrte ~mütig vor sich hin** he stared ahead full of melancholy; ***~|nehmen** ⇨ **schwer** 1 D; **~öl** *das* heavy oil; **~punkt** *der* (*Physik*) centre of gravity; (*fig.*) main focus; (*Hauptgewicht*) main stress; **der ~punkt seiner Tätigkeit liegt in** *od.* **auf der Forschung** his activity centres on research; **den ~punkt auf etw.** (*Akk.*) **legen** (*fig.*) put the main stress on sth.; focus mainly on sth.; **~punkt·mäßig** ❶ *Adj.* selective ‹strike, action›; ❷ *adv.* **im Lager und in der Packerei soll ~punktmäßig gestreikt werden** there are to be selective strikes in the warehouse and the packing department; **~punkt·programm** *das* programme of selective measures; **~reich** *Adj.* (*ugs.*) immensely rich (*coll.*)

**Schwerst-: ~arbeiter** *der,* **~arbeiterin** *die* worker engaged in very heavy work; **~behinderte** *der/die; adj. Dekl.* severely disabled person (*with a disablement of over 80%*); ⇨ *auch* **Schwerbehinderte**

**Schwert** /ʃveːɐ̯t/ *das;* **~[e]s,** **~er** **A** sword; **das ~ ziehen** *od.* **zücken** draw one's sword; **~er zu Pflugscharen** swords to ploughshares; ⇨ *auch* **zweischneidig**; **B** (*Schiffbau*) centreboard

**schwert-, Schwert-: ~fisch** *der* swordfish; **~leite** /ˈlaitə/ *die;* **~~,** **~~n** (*hist.*) accolade; dubbing ceremony; **~lilie** *die* iris; **~schlucker** *der,* **~schluckerin** *die;* **~~,** **~~nen** sword-swallower

***schwer|tun** ⇨ **schwer** 1 D

**Schwert·wal** *die* **[großer] ~:** killer whale; **[kleiner] ~:** false killer whale

**schwer-, Schwer-: ~verbrecher** *der,* **~verbrecherin** *die* serious offender; **ich lasse mich nicht wie ein ~verbrecher behandeln** I won't be treated like a common criminal; ***~verdaulich** ⇨ **schwer** 2 B; ***~verletzt** ⇨ **schwer** 2 D; **~verletzte** *der/die* seriously injured person; serious casualty; **die ~verletzten** the seriously injured;

*old spelling (see note on page 1707)

***~verständlich** ⇒ **schwer** 2 B; ***~verwundet** ⇒ **schwer** 2 D; **~verwundete** *der/die* seriously wounded person; **die ~verwundeten** the seriously wounded; **~wiegend** *Adj.* serious, grave ‹reservation, consequence, objection, accusation, etc.›; momentous ‹decision›; serious ‹case, problem›

**Schwester** /ˈʃvɛstɐ/ *die;* ~, ~n **A** sister; **B** (*Nonne*) nun; (*als Anrede*) Sister; **~ Petra** Sister Petra; **C** (*Kranken~*) nurse; (*als Anrede*) Nurse; (*zur Ober~*) Sister; **D** (*ugs.: ~firma*) associate firm

**Schwesterchen** *das;* **~s, ~:** little sister; **ein kleines ~:** a little sister

**Schwester-: ~firma** *die* associate firm *or* company; **~herz** *das* (*veralt., noch scherzh.*) dear sister; **hör mal, ~herz** listen, sister dear

**schwesterlich** ❶ *Adj.* sisterly.
❷ *adv.* **~ handeln** act in a sisterly way

**Schwester-: ~liebe** *die* sisterly love; **~mord** *der* sororicide; **~mörder** *der,* **~mörderin** *die* sororicide

**Schwestern·helferin** *die* ▶ 159 nursing auxiliary; auxiliary nurse

**Schwesternschaft** *die;* **~:** nurses *pl.;* nursing staff

**Schwestern-: ~schülerin** *die* probationer; **~wohn·heim** *das* nurses' home *or* hostel

**Schwester-: ~partei** *die* sister party; **~schiff** *das* sister ship

**Schwib·bogen** /ˈʃvɪp-/ *der* (*Archit.*) flying buttress

**schwieg** /ʃviːk/ *1. u. 3. Pers. Prät. v.* **schweigen**

**Schwieger-** /ˈʃviːgɐ-/: **~eltern** *Pl.* parents-in-law; **~mutter** *die; Pl.* **~mütter** mother-in-law; **~sohn** *der* son-in-law; **~tochter** *die* daughter-in-law; **~vater** *der* father-in-law

**Schwiele** /ˈʃviːlə/ *die;* **~, ~n** callus; **~n an den Händen** horny hands

**schwielig** *Adj.* callused; **~e Hände** horny hands

**schwierig** /ˈʃviːrɪç/ *Adj.* difficult

**Schwierigkeit** *die;* **~, ~en** difficulty; **in ~en** (*Akk.*) **geraten** get into difficulties; **jmdm. ~en machen** make difficulties for sb.; **Latein macht ihm ~en** he has difficulty *or* trouble with Latin; **mach keine ~en!** don't make difficulties!; don't be difficult *or* awkward!; **~en bekommen** have problems *or* trouble; **jmdn./sich in ~en** (*Akk.*) **bringen** get sb./oneself into trouble; **ohne ~en** without difficulty

**Schwierigkeits·grad** *der* degree of difficulty; (*von Lehrmaterial usw.*) level of difficulty

**Schwimm-: ~an·zug** *der* swimsuit; (*für Taucher*) wet suit; **~bad** *das* swimming baths *pl.* (*Brit.*); swimming pool; **~bagger** *der* dredger; **~becken** *das* swimming pool; **~blase** *die* swim bladder; air bladder; **~dock** *das* floating dock

***Schwimmeister** *usw.* ⇒ **Schwimmmeister**

**schwimmen** ❶ *unr. itr. V.* **A** *meist mit sein* swim; **~ gehen** go swimming; **B** *meist mit sein* (*treiben, nicht untergehen*) float; **die Kinder ließen ihre Schiffchen ~:** the children sailed their boats; **koreanische Schiffe ~ auf allen Meeren** Korean ships sail on all the seas of the world; **C** (*ugs.: unsicher sein*) be all at sea; **ins Schwimmen geraten** *od.* **kommen** start to flounder; **D** (*überschwemmt sein*) be awash; **E** *mit sein* (*triefen von*) **in etw.** (*Dat.*) **~:** be swimming in sth.; **im [eigenen] Blut ~:** be bathed in [one's own] blood; **in** *od.* **im Geld ~** (*fig.*) be rolling in money *or* in it (*coll.*); **F** *mit sein* (*ver~*) swim; **mir schwimmt es vor den Augen** everything is swimming in front of my eyes; **G** *in* **~des Fett** (*Kochk.*) deep fat; **etw. in ~dem Fett braten** deep-fry sth.; fry sth. in deep fat.
❷ *unr. tr. V.; auch mit sein* swim; **einen neuen Rekord ~:** swim a new record time

**Schwimmen** *das;* **~s** swimming *no art.*

**Schwimmer** *der;* **~s, ~ A** swimmer; **B** (*der Angel, Technik*) float

**Schwimmer·becken** *das* swimmers' pool

**Schwimmerin** *die;* **~, ~nen** swimmer

**schwimm-, Schwimm-: ~fähig** *Adj.* buoyant ‹material›; amphibious ‹vehicle›; **~flosse** *die* flipper; **~fuß** *der* webbed foot; **~gürtel** *der* swimming belt; **~halle** *die* indoor swimming pool; **bevor man in die ~halle kommt, muss man durch den Duschraum gehen** before entering the pool area, you have to go through the showers; **~haut** *die* web (*of bird's webbed foot*); **~kran** *der* floating crane; **~lehrer** *der,* **~lehrerin** *die* swimming instructor; **~meister** *der,* **~meisterin** *die* swimming supervisor [and instructor]; **~sport** *der* [competitive] swimming *no art.;* **~stadion** *das* swimming stadium; **~stil** *der* stroke; **~vogel** *der* web-footed bird; **~weste** *die* life jacket

**Schwindel** /ˈʃvɪndl̩/ *der;* **~s A** (*Gleichgewichtsstörung*) dizziness; giddiness; vertigo; **B** (*Anfall*) dizzy *or* giddy spell; attack of dizziness *or* giddiness *or* vertigo; **C** (*abwertend*) (*Betrug*) swindle; fraud; (*Lüge*) lie; **das ist alles ~, was er sagt** what he says is all lies; **den ~ kenne ich** (*ugs.*) that's an old trick; I know that trick; **er fällt auf jeden ~ rein** he'll fall for any trick; **D** *in* **der ganze ~** (*ugs. abwertend*) the whole lot (*coll.*) *or* (*sl.*) shoot

**Schwindel·anfall** *der* ⇒ **Schwindel** B

**Schwindelei** *die;* **~, ~en** (*ugs.*) **A** fibbing; **B** (*Lüge*) fib

**schwindel-, Schwindel-: ~erregend** *Adj.* vertiginous ‹height, speed, depths›; (*fig.*) meteoric ‹career, success›; **in ~erregender Höhe** at a dizzy height; **die Preise kletterten in ~erregende Höhe** (*fig.*) the prices rose sky high; **~frei** *Adj.* **~frei sein** have a head for heights; not suffer from vertigo; **~gefühl** *das* feeling of dizziness *or* giddiness *or* vertigo

**schwindelig** ⇒ **schwindlig**

**schwindeln** ❶ *itr. V.* **A** (*sich drehen*) **mich** *od.* **mir schwindelt** I feel dizzy *or* giddy; **in ~der Höhe** at a dizzy height; **ein ~der Abgrund** a vertiginous drop; **B** (*lügen*) tell fibs.
❷ *tr. V.* (*lügen*) **„…", schwindelte sie** '…,' she said, lying; **das ist alles geschwindelt** that's all lies.
❸ *refl. V.* **sich ins Kino/durch den Zoll ~:** trick *or* (*coll.*) wangle one's way in to the cinema/through the customs; **sich durchs Examen ~:** wangle one's way through the exam (*coll.*)

**schwinden** /ˈʃvɪndn̩/ *unr. itr. V.; mit sein* **A** (*geh.: abnehmen*) fade; ‹sound› die away, fade; ‹supplies, money› run out, dwindle; ‹effect› wear off; ‹interest› fade, wane, fall off; ‹fear, mistrust› lessen, diminish; ‹powers, influence› wane, decline; ‹courage, strength› fail; ‹years, time› pass by; ‹snow, illusion› disappear; **ihm schwand der Mut** his courage failed him; **im Schwinden [begriffen] sein** ‹effect› be wearing off; ‹interest, powers, influence› be on the wane; **B** (*fachspr.: Volumen verlieren*) shrink; ‹metal› contract, shrink

**Schwindler** *der;* **~s, ~** (*Lügner*) liar; (*Betrüger*) swindler; (*Hochstapler*) confidence trickster; con man (*coll.*); con artist (*coll.*)

**Schwindlerin** *die;* **~, ~nen** (*Lügnerin*) liar; (*Betrügerin*) swindler; (*Hochstaplerin*) confidence trickster; con artist (*coll.*)

**schwindlig** *Adj.* dizzy; giddy; **jmdm. wird es ~:** sb. gets dizzy *or* giddy; **da wird einem ja ~!** (*fig.*) it fairly makes your head spin

**Schwind·sucht** *die* (*veralt.*) consumption; tuberculosis; ⇒ *auch* **galoppieren**

**schwind·süchtig** *Adj.* (*veralt.*) consumptive; tubercular

**Schwinge** /ˈʃvɪŋə/ *die;* **~, ~n A** (*geh.; auch fig.*) wing; **B** (*bes. österr.: Korb*) shallow oval basket

**schwingen** ❶ *unr. itr. V.* **A** *mit sein* (*sich hin- u. herbewegen*) swing; **B** (*vibrieren*) vibrate; **etw. zum S~ bringen** cause sth. to vibrate; **C** (*Physik*) ‹wave› oscillate; **D** (*geh.: anklingen*) **in ihren Worten schwang Kritik** her words had a tone of criticism; **E** (*nachklingen*) linger; **F** *mit sein* (*Skilaufen*) swing; **G** (*schweiz.: ringen*) wrestle Swiss style (*with one's right hand on the belt of one's opponent's wrestling-suit and the left hand on his rolled-up right trouser leg*).
❷ *unr. tr. V.* **A** (*hin- u. herbewegen*) swing; wave ‹flag, wand›; (*fuchteln mit*) brandish ‹sword, axe, etc.›; **eine Rede ~** (*ugs.*) hold forth; **große Reden ~** (*ugs.*) talk big; ⇒ *auch* **geschwungen** 2; **Tanzbein**; **B** (*Landw.*) swingle ‹flax, hemp›.
❸ *unr. refl. V.* **A** (*sich schnell bewegen*) **sich über die Mauer ~:** swing oneself *or* vault over the wall; **sich aufs Pferd/Fahrrad ~:** swing oneself *or* leap on to one's horse/bicycle; **sich ins Auto/hinters Steuer ~** (*ugs.*) jump into one's car/get behind the wheel; **der Vogel schwang sich in die Luft** (*fig.*) the bird soared [up] into the air; **B** (*geh.: in einem Bogen verlaufen*) arch

**Schwinger** *der;* **~s, ~ A** (*Boxen*) swing; **B** (*schweiz.: Ringer*) [Swiss-style] wrestler; *see also* **schwingen** 1 G

**Schwing-: ~kreis** *der* (*Elektrot.*) oscillatory circuit; **~tür** *die* swing door

**Schwingung** *die;* **~, ~en A** swinging; (*Vibration*) vibration; **etw. in ~ versetzen** set sth. swinging/vibrating; **B** (*Physik*) oscillation

**Schwingungs·zahl** *die* (*Physik*) frequency of oscillation

**Schwipp-** /ʃvɪp-/: **~schwager** *der* (*ugs.*) husband's/wife's/brother's/sister's brother-in-law; **~schwägerin** *die* (*ugs.*) husband's/wife's/brother's/sister's sister-in-law

**Schwips** /ʃvɪps/ *der;* **~es, ~e** (*ugs.*) **einen [kleinen] ~ haben** be [a bit] tipsy *or* (*coll.*) merry

**schwirren** /ˈʃvɪrən/ *itr. V.* **A** (*tönen*) ‹insect› buzz; ‹bowstring› twang; **B** *mit sein* ‹arrow, bullet, etc.› whiz; ‹bird› whir; ‹insect› buzz; **allerlei schwirrte mir durch den Kopf** (*fig.*) all sorts of things buzzed through my head; **von den vielen Zahlen schwirrte mir der Kopf** (*fig.*) my head was buzzing *or* spinning from all the figures; **C** (*erfüllt sein von*) **die Stadt schwirrt von Gerüchten** the town is buzzing with rumours

**Schwitz·bad** *das* sweat bath

**Schwitze** *die;* **~, ~n** (*Kochk.*) roux

**schwitzen** ❶ *itr. V.* **A** (*auch fig.*) sweat; **ins S~ kommen** (*auch fig.*) start to sweat; **B** (*beschlagen*) steam up; **C** (*Harz absondern*) sweat.
❷ *refl. V.* **sich bei der Arbeit klatschnass ~:** get soaked with sweat from working; **sich halb tot ~** (*ugs.*) sweat like anything (*coll.*).
❸ *tr. V.* (*Kochk.: in heißem Fett*) sweat

**schwitzig** *Adj.* (*ugs.*) sweaty

**Schwitz-: ~kasten** *der* (*Ringen*) headlock; **jmdn. in den ~kasten nehmen** get sb. in a headlock; **~kur** *die* sweat cure

**schwofen** /ˈʃvoːfn̩/ *itr. V.* (*ugs.*) shake a leg (*coll.*); **~ gehen** go and shake a leg

**schwor** /ʃvoːɐ̯/ *1. u. 3. Pers. Sg. Prät. v.* **schwören**

**schwören** /ˈʃvøːrən/ ❶ *unr. tr., itr. V.* swear ‹fidelity, allegiance, friendship›; swear, take ‹oath›; **ich schwöre es[, so wahr mir Gott helfe]** I swear it[, so help me God]; **jmdm./sich etw. ~:** swear sth. to sb./oneself.
❷ *unr. itr. V.* swear an/the oath; **auf die Bibel/die Verfassung ~:** swear on the Bible/the Constitution; **ich könnte darauf ~** (*ugs.*) I could swear to it; **sie schwört auf ihren Kräutertee** she swears by her herbal tea

**Schwuchtel** /ˈʃvʊxtl̩/ *die;* **~, ~n** (*salopp*) queen (*sl.*)

**schwul** /ʃvuːl/ *Adj.* (*ugs.*) gay (*coll.*)

**schwül** /ʃvyːl/ *Adj.* **A** (*feuchtwarm*) sultry; close; **B** (*beklemmend*) oppressive; **C** (*sinnlich*) sensuous ‹perfume, fantasy, etc.›; steamy ‹eroticism›; sultry ‹look›; seductive ‹lighting, music›

**Schwule** *der; adj. Dekl.* (*ugs.*) gay (*coll.*); (*abwertend*) queer (*sl.*)

S

**Schwüle** *die;* ~: sultriness

**Schwulen-:** ~**bewegung** *die (ugs.)* gay rights movement; ~**lokal** *das (ugs.)* gay bar *(coll.)*

**Schwulität** /ʃvuli'tɛ:t/ *die;* ~, ~**en** *(ugs.)* **in** ~**en kommen** *od.* **geraten** get into a fix *or* jam *(coll.)*; **jmdn./sich in** ~**en bringen** get sb./oneself into a fix *or* jam *(coll.)*

**Schwulst** /ʃvʊlst/ *der;* ~**[e]s** *(abwertend)* bombast; pompousness; *(im Baustil)* over-ornateness; **dieser Film ist sentimentaler** ~: this film is full of sentimental affectation

**schwülstig** /'ʃvʏlstɪç/ ❶ *Adj.* bombastic, pompous ‹writing›; bombastic, pompous, grandiloquent ‹speech›; over-ornate ‹art, architecture›. ❷ *adv.* bombastically; pompously; ‹speak› bombastically, pompously, grandiloquently

**schwumm[e]rig** /'ʃvʊmərɪç/ *Adj. (ugs.)* Ⓐ *(unwohl)* queasy; funny *(coll.)*; **ihr wurde** ~: she started to feel queasy *or (coll.)* funny; Ⓑ *(bang)* jittery *(coll.)*; nervous; apprehensive; **mir wird schon** ~: I'm already starting to get the jitters *(coll.)*; I'm already getting butterflies [in my stomach]

**Schwund** /ʃvʊnt/ *der;* ~**[e]s** Ⓐ decrease, drop *(Gen.* in); *(an Interesse)* waning; falling off; **einen** ~ **an Wählerstimmen befürchten** ‹party› fear a decline in its share of the vote; Ⓑ *(Kaufmannsspr.)* shrinkage; Ⓒ *(Technik: Ausschuss)* wastage; Ⓓ *(Med.)* atrophy; Ⓔ *(Rundfunkt., Funkt.)* fading

**Schwung** /ʃvʊŋ/ *der;* ~**[e]s, Schwünge** /'ʃvʏŋə/ Ⓐ *(Bewegung)* swing; Ⓑ *(Linie)* sweep; **der elegante** ~ **ihrer Brauen/ihrer Nase** the elegant arch of her eyebrows/curve of her nose; **mit kühnem** ~ **überspannt die Brücke das Tal** the bridge crosses the valley in a bold arc; Ⓒ *(Geschwindigkeit)* momentum; ~ **holen** build *or* get up momentum; *(auf einer Schaukel usw.)* work up a swing; ~ **in etw.** *(Akk.)* **bringen, etw. in** ~ **bringen** *(fig. ugs.)* get sth. going; **jmdn. in** ~ **bringen, jmdm.** ~ **geben** *(fig. ugs.)* put some life into sb.; get sb. going; **in** ~ **sein** *(fig. ugs.)* *(in guter Stimmung)* have livened up; *(wütend)* be worked up; *(gut laufen)* ‹business, practice› do a lively trade; *(gut vorankommen)* be getting on well; be right in the swing [of it]; **in** ~ **kommen** *(fig. ugs.)* *(in gute Stimmung kommen)* get going; liven up; *(wütend werden)* get worked up; *(gut vorankommen)* get right in the swing [of it]; ‹business› pick up; **jmdn./einen Betrieb in** ~ **haben** *od.* **halten** *(ugs.)* keep sb. on his/her toes/keep a firm doing a flourishing *or* good trade; **in die Sache kommt** ~ *(ugs.)* things are picking up; Ⓓ *(Antrieb)* drive; energy; Ⓔ *(mitreißende Wirkung)* sparkle; vitality; Ⓕ *(ugs.: größere Menge)* stack *(coll.)*; *(von Menschen)* crowd; bunch *(sl.)*

**schwung·haft** ❶ *Adj.* thriving; brisk, flourishing ‹trade, business›. ❷ *adv.* **die Aktien werden** ~ **gehandelt** there's a brisk *or* flourishing trade in the shares; **das Geschäft entwickelt sich** ~: business is booming

**schwung-, Schwung-:** ~**kraft** *die (Physik)* centrifugal force; ~**los** ❶ *Adj.* Ⓐ *(antriebsschwach)* lacking in energy *or* drive *postpos.*; listless; Ⓑ *(langweilig)* lacklustre ‹speech, performance, etc.›; ❷ *adv.* ‹sing, dance, etc.› in a lacklustre way; ~**rad** *das (Technik)* flywheel; *(an einer Nähmaschine)* band wheel; ~**voll** ❶ *Adj.* Ⓐ *(mitreißend)* lively; spirited; spirited ‹words›; lively, *(coll.)* snappy ‹tune›; Ⓑ *(kraftvoll)* vigorous; **ein** ~**er Handel** a roaring trade; Ⓒ *(elegant)* sweeping ‹movement, gesture›; bold ‹handwriting, line, stroke›; ❷ *adv.* Ⓐ *(mitreißend)* spiritedly; with verve; ‹speak› spiritedly; Ⓑ *(kraftvoll)* with great vigour

**Schwur** /ʃvu:ɐ̯/ *der;* ~**[e]s, Schwüre** /'ʃvy:rə/ Ⓐ *(Gelöbnis)* vow; Ⓑ *(Eid)* oath; **die Hand zum** ~ **erheben** raise one's hand to take the oath

**Schwur·gericht** *das: court with a jury;* **vor das** ~ **kommen** be tried by a jury

**Schwyzerdütsch** /'ʃvi:tsədy:tʃ/, **Schwyzertütsch** /'ʃvi:tsəty:tʃ/ *das;* ~**[s]** *(schweiz.)* Swiss German

**Sciencefiction, *Science-fiction** /'saɪəns 'fɪkʃən/ *die;* ~: science fiction

**Scotch·terrier** /'skɔtʃ-/ *der* Scotch terrier

**Scylla** /'stsyla/ ⇒ **Szylla**

**SDR** *Abk.* **Süddeutscher Rundfunk** South German Radio

**SDS** *Abk.* **Sozialistischer Deutscher Studentenbund** Socialist German Students' Federation

**Séance** /ze'ã:s(ə)/ *die;* ~, ~**n** seance

**Seborrhö, Seborrhöe** /zebɔ'rø:/ *die;* ~, **Seborrhöen** ▸ 474 *(Med.)* seborrhoea

**sechs** /zɛks/ *Kardinalz.* ▸ 76, ▸ 752, ▸ 841 six; ⇒ *auch* **acht**

**Sechs** *die;* ~, ~**en** six; **eine** ~ **schreiben/bekommen** *(Schulw.)* get a 'fail' mark; ⇒ *auch* **Acht[1]** A, B, D, E, G; **Zwei** B

**sechs-, Sechs-:** ~**achtel·takt** *der* six-eight time; **im** ~**achteltakt** in six-eight time; ~**eck** *das* hexagon; ~**eckig** *Adj.* hexagonal; ⇒ *auch* **achteckig**

**Sechser** *der;* ~**s,** ~ Ⓐ *(ugs.)* *(Ziffer, beim Würfeln)* six; *(Bahn, Bus)* [number] six; *(im Lotto)* six winning numbers; Ⓑ *(berlin.: Fünfpfennigstück)* five-pfennig piece

**sechserlei** *Gattungsz.; indekl.* Ⓐ *attr.* six kinds *or* sorts of; six different ‹sorts, kinds, sizes, possibilities›; Ⓑ *subst.* six [different] things

**Sechser·pack** *der,* **Sechser·packung** *die* pack of six; *(bes. von Bier)* six-pack

**sechs-, Sechs-:** ~**fach** *Vervielfältigungsz.* sixfold; ⇒ *auch* **achtfach**; ~**fache** *das; adj. Dekl.* **etw. um ein** ~**faches/um das** ~**fache erhöhen** increase sth. by a factor of six; ⇒ *auch* **Achtfache**; ~**flach** *das;* ~~**[e]s,** ~~**e,** ~**flächner** /-flɛçnɐ/ *der;* ~~**s,** ~~: hexahedron; ~**hundert** *Kardinalz.* ▸ 841 six hundred; ~**jährig** *Adj.* *(6 Jahre alt)* six-year-old *attrib.;* six years old *postpos.;* *(6 Jahre dauernd)* six-year *attrib.;* ⇒ *auch* **achtjährig**; ~**kant·mutter** *die; Pl.* ~~**n** hexagon nut; ~**köpfig** *Adj.* six-headed ‹monster›; ‹family, committee› of six

**Sechsling** /'zɛkslɪŋ/ *der;* ~**s,** ~**e** sextuplet

**sechs-:** ~**mal** *Adv.* six times; ⇒ *auch* **achtmal**; ~**malig** *Adj.* **nach** ~**maliger Wiederholung konnte er es auswendig** after repeating it six times, he knew it by heart; ⇒ *auch* **achtmalig**; ~**seitig** *Adj.* six-sided; six-page *attrib.* ‹letter, article›; ~**stellig** *Adj.* six-figure; ⇒ *auch* **achtstellig**; ~**stöckig** *Adj.* six-storey *attrib.;* ⇒ *auch* **achtstöckig**

**sechst** /zɛkst/ *in* **wir waren zu** ~: there were six of us; ⇒ *auch* **acht[2]**

**sechst...** *Ordinalz.* ▸ 207, ▸ 841 sixth; ⇒ *auch* **acht...**

**sechs-, Sechs-:** ~**tage·rennen** *das (Radsport)* six-day race; ~**tage·woche** *die* six-day week; ~**tägig** *Adj.* *(6 Tage alt)* six-day-old *attrib.;* *(6 Tage dauernd)* six-day[-long] *attrib.;* ⇒ *auch* **achttägig**; ~**tausend** *Kardinalz.* ▸ 841 six thousand

**Sechste** *der/die; adj. Dekl.* sixth; ⇒ *auch* **Achte**

**sechs·teilig** *Adj.* six-piece ‹tool set etc.›; six-part ‹serial›; ⇒ *auch* **achtteilig**

**sechstel** *Bruchz.* ▸ 841 sixth

**Sechstel** *das, schweiz. meist der;* ~**s,** ~ ▸ 841 sixth; ⇒ *auch* **Achtel**

***sechste·mal, * sechsten·mal** ⇒ **Mal[1]**

**sechstens** *Adv.* sixthly

**Sechs-:** ~**tonner** *der;* ~~**s,** ~~: six-tonner; ~**und·sechzig** *das;* ~: sixty-six; ~**zylinder·motor** *der* six-cylinder engine

**sechzehn** /'zɛçtse:n/ *Kardinalz.* ▸ 76, ▸ 752, ▸ 841 sixteen; ⇒ *auch* **achtzehn**

**sechzehn-, Sechzehn-:** ~**jährig** *Adj.* *(16 Jahre alt)* sixteen-year-old *attrib.;* sixteen years old *pred.;* *(16 Jahre dauernd)* sixteen-year *attrib.;* ⇒ *auch* **achtjährig**; ~**meter·raum** *der (Fußball)* penalty area; ~**millimeter·film** *der* sixteen-millimetre film; 16-mm film

**sechzehnt...** *Ordinalz.* ▸ 207 sixteenth

**Sechzehntel** *das;* ~**s,** ~: sixteenth

**Sechzehntel·note** *die* sixteenth note

**sechzig** /'zɛçtsɪç/ *Kardinalz.* ▸ 76, ▸ 841 sixty; ⇒ *auch* **achtzig**

**sechziger** *indekl. Adj.* **die** ~ **Jahre** the sixties; **zwei** ~ **Briefmarken/Zigarren** two sixty-pfennig stamps/cigars; **eine** ~ **Glühbirne** a 60-watt bulb

**Sechziger[1]** *der;* ~**s,** ~ Ⓐ *(60-Jähriger)* sixty-year-old; sexagenarian; Ⓑ *(Bus, Bahn)* number sixty; Ⓒ *(Wein von 1960)* **der** ~: the '60 vintage

**Sechziger[2]** *die;* ~, ~ Ⓐ *(Briefmarke)* sixty-pfennig/schilling *etc.* stamp; Ⓑ *(Zigarre)* sixty-pfennig cigar; *(Glühbirne)* 60-watt bulb

**Sechziger[3]** *Pl.* sixties; **in den** ~**n sein** be in one's sixties

**Sechziger·jahre** *Pl.* ▸ 76, ▸ 207 sixties *pl.*

**sechzig·jährig** *Adj.* *(60 Jahre alt)* sixty-year-old *attrib.;* sixty years old *postpos.;* *(60 Jahre dauernd)* sixty-year *attrib.*

**Sechzig·jährige** *der/die; adj. Dekl.* sixty-year-old

**sechzigst...** /'zɛçtsɪçst/ *Ordinalz.* ▸ 841 sixtieth; ⇒ *auch* **achtzigst...**

**SED** *Abk.* **Sozialistische Einheitspartei Deutschlands** Socialist Unity Party of Germany *(state party of the former GDR)*

**Sedativum** /zeda'ti:vʊm/ *das;* ~**s, Sedativa** *(Med.)* sedative

**Sediment** /zedi'mɛnt/ *das;* ~**[e]s,** ~**e** *(Geol., Chemie, Med.)* sediment

**Sediment·gestein** *das (Geol.)* sedimentary rock

**See[1]** /ze:/ *der;* ~**s,** ~**n** lake; **der Genfer** ~: Lake Geneva; **der Obere** ~: Lake Superior

**See[2]** *die;* ~, ~**n** Ⓐ *(Meer)* sea; **an die** ~ **fahren** go to the seaside; **an der** ~: by the sea[side]; **auf** ~: at sea; **er ist auf** ~: he is away at sea; **auf** ~ **bleiben** *(geh. verhüll.)* be lost at sea; **auf hoher** ~: on the high seas; **in** ~ **gehen** *od.* **stechen** put to sea; **Leutnant/Kapitän zur** ~ *(Marine)* sub lieutenant/[naval] captain; **zur** ~ **fahren** be a seaman; **zur** ~ **gehen** *(ugs.)* go to sea; Ⓑ *(~mannsspr.: ~gang)* **ruhige/rauhe** *od.* **grobe** *od.* **schwere** ~: calm/rough or heavy sea; Ⓒ *(~mannsspr.: Woge)* sea

**see-, See-:** ~**aal** *der* flake; ~**adler** *der* sea eagle; white-tailed [sea] eagle; ~**anemone** *die* sea anemone; ~**bad** *das* seaside health resort; ~**bär** *der* Ⓐ *(Zool.)* fur seal; Ⓑ *(fam.: ~mann)* sea dog *(coll.)*; ~**beben** *das* seaquake; ~**bestattung** *die* burial at sea; ~**blockade** *die* naval blockade; ~**bühne** *die* lake stage; ~**elefant, *~-Elefant** *der* elephant seal; ~**fahrend** *Adj.* seafaring; ~**fahrer** *der (veralt.)* seafarer; **Sindbad der** ~**fahrer** Sindbad the Sailor; ~**fahrer·volk** *das* seafaring people; ~**fahrt** *die* Ⓐ seafaring *no art.;* sea travel *no art.;* *(~fahrtskunde)* navigation; ⇒ *auch* **christlich**; Ⓑ *(~reise)* voyage; *(Kreuzfahrt)* cruise; ~**fahrt[s]·buch** *das (~w.)* seaman's discharge book; ~**fahrt[s]·schule** *die* merchant navy college; ~**fest** *Adj.* Ⓐ ⇒ ~**tüchtig**; Ⓑ *(nicht leicht ~krank)* ~**fest sein** not suffer from seasickness; not get seasick; Ⓒ *(gesichert, fest angebracht)* secured [for sea]; ~**fisch** *der* sea fish; saltwater fish; ~**fracht** *die* sea freight; ~**funk** *der* maritime radio; ~**gang** *der:* **leichter/starker** *od.* **hoher** *od.* **schwerer** ~**gang** light/heavy *or* rough sea; **bei leichtem/schwerem** ~**gang** with a calm/heavy sea; ~**gefecht** *das* naval engagement; sea battle; naval battle; ~**gestützt** *Adj. (Milit.)* sea-based; ~**gras** *das* eel grass; *(als Polstermaterial)* sea grass; ~**hafen** *der* Ⓐ *(Hafenanlagen)* harbour; Ⓑ *(Stadt)* seaport; ~**handel** *der* maritime trade; ~**hase** *der (Zool.)* lumpsucker; ~**herrschaft** *die* maritime supremacy; ~**hund** *der* Ⓐ common seal; Ⓑ *(Pelz)* seal[skin]; ~**igel** *der* sea urchin; ~**jung·frau** *die (Myth.)* mermaid; ~**karte** *die* sea chart; ~**klar** *Adj. (Seemannsspr.)* ready to sail *pred.;* ~**klima** *das (Geogr.)* maritime climate; ~**krank** *Adj.* seasick;

*old spelling (see note on page 1707)

S

**~krankheit** *die* seasickness; **~krieg** *der* naval war; (*Kriegsführung*) naval warfare; **~lachs** *der* pollack

**Seelchen** /ˈzeːlçən/ *das;* **~s**, ~ (*spött.*) tender soul

**Seele** /ˈzeːlə/ *die;* ~, **~n** Ⓐ (*auch Rel., fig.*) soul; (*Psyche*) mind; **nun hat die liebe ~ Ruh** (*ugs.*) now he's *etc.* satisfied at last; **zwei ~n, ein Gedanke** two minds with but a single thought; **sich** (*Dat.*) **die ~ aus dem Leib schreien** (*ugs.*) shout/scream one's head off (*coll.*); **jmdm. auf der ~ lasten** *od.* **liegen** (*geh.*) weigh on sb.['s mind]; **jmdm. aus der ~ sprechen** *od.* **reden** (*ugs.*) take the words out of sb.'s mouth; **aus tiefster** *od.* **ganzer ~:** with all one's heart; ‹thank› from the bottom of one's heart; ‹sing› with all one's heart and soul; **jmdn. in tiefster ~ kränken/enttäuschen** cut sb. to the quick/profoundly *or* deeply disappoint sb.; **das tut mir in der ~ weh** it hurts me deeply; **mit ganzer ~:** heart and soul; **sich** (*Dat.*) **etw. von der ~ reden** unburden oneself about sth.; **die ~ einer Sache** *od.* **von etw. sein** be the heart of sth.; **eine arme ~:** a poor soul; ⇒ *auch* **aushauchen; Herz** B; **Leib** A; **Teufel;** Ⓑ (*Mensch*) soul; **eine ~ von Mensch** *od.* **von einem Menschen sein** be a good[-hearted] soul; Ⓒ (*Waffent.*) bore; Ⓓ (*Technik: eines Kabels usw.*) core

**seelen-, Seelen-: ~amt** *das* (*kath. Kirche*) requiem mass; **~arzt** *der,* **~ärztin** *die* psychoanalyst; **~friede[n]** *der* peace of mind; **~heil** *das* (*christl. Rel.*) salvation of one's/sb.'s soul; **ich mache das, wenn dein ~heil davon abhängt** (*iron.*) I'll do it, if it's a matter of life and death (*joc.*); **~leben** *das* (*geh.*) inner life; **~los** ❶ *Adj.* soulless; ❷ *adv.* soullessly; **~qual** *die* (*geh.*) mental anguish *or* torment *no pl.;* **~ruhe** *die* calmness; **in aller ~ruhe** calmly; **~ruhig** ❶ *Adj.* calm; unruffled; ❷ *adv.* calmly; **~vergnügt** ❶ *Adj.* cheerful; contented; ❷ *adv.* cheerfully; contentedly; **~verkäufer** *der* (*Seemannsspr. abwertend*) coffin ship; **~verwandtschaft** *die* **unsere/ihre ~verwandtschaft** the fact that we/they are kindred spirits; **~voll** ❶ *Adj.* soulful; ❷ *adv.* soulfully; **~wanderung** *die* (*bes. ind. Religionen*) transmigration of souls; **~zustand** *der* mental state; state of mind

**seelisch** ❶ *Adj.* psychological ‹cause, damage, tension›; mental ‹equilibrium, breakdown, illness, health›; mental [and emotional] ‹state, strain, low [point]›.
❷ *adv.* **~ bedingt sein** have psychological causes; **~ krank** mentally ill

**See·löwe** *der* sea lion

**Seel·sorge** *die* pastoral care

**Seelsorger** *der;* **~s**, ~, **Seelsorgerin** *die;* ~, **~nen** pastoral worker; (*Geistliche[r]*) pastor

**seelsorgerisch, seelsorg[er]lich** ❶ *Adj.* pastoral.
❷ *adv.* **eine Gemeinde ~ betreuen** provide pastoral care for a parish

**See-: ~luft** *die* sea air; **~macht** *die* maritime *or* naval power; sea power; **~mann** *der; Pl.* **~leute** ▶ 159 seaman; sailor

**seemännisch** /ˈzeːmɛnɪʃ/ *Adj.* nautical

**Seemanns-: ~braut** *die* sailor's lass; **~garn** *das* seaman's yarn; **~garn spinnen** spin yarns; **~grab** *das:* **ein ~grab finden** (*geh.*) go to a watery grave; **~heim** *das* sailors' home; **~lied** *das* sailors' song; **~sprache** *die* seaman's language; nautical language; **~tod** *der:* **den ~tod finden** *od.* **sterben** be drowned [at sea]

**See-: ~meile** *die* nautical mile; **~mine** *die* naval mine

**Seen-: ~gebiet** *das* lakeland [region]; **~kunde** *die* limnology *no art.*

**See·not** *die* distress [at sea]; **jmdn. aus ~ retten** rescue sb. in distress; **in ~ geraten** get into difficulties *pl.*

**Seen·platte** /ˈzeːən-/ *die* (*Geogr.*) lakeland area (*of glacial origin*)

**see-, See-: ~pferd[chen]** *das* sea horse; **~räuber** *der* pirate; **~räuberei** *die;* **~~:** piracy; **~recht** *das* maritime law; **~reise** *die* voyage; (*Kreuzfahrt*) cruise; **~rose** *die* Ⓐ (*Pflanze*) waterlily; Ⓑ (*Seeanemone*) sea anemone; **~sack** *der* kitbag; **~sand** *der* sea sand; **~schiff** *das* sea-going ship; ***~schiffahrt, ~schifffahrt** *die* maritime shipping *no art.;* sea shipping *no art.;* **~schlacht** *die* sea battle; naval battle; **~schwalbe** *die* tern; **~stern** *der* starfish; **~streitkräfte** *Pl.* naval forces; **~stück** *das* (*Kunstwiss.*) seascape; (*mit Schiffen usw.*) marine; **~tang** *der* seaweed; **~tüchtig** *Adj.* seaworthy; **~ufer** *das* lake shore; shore of a/the lake; **~vogel** *der* seabird; **~wärts** *Adv.* seawards; **~weg** *der* sea route; **auf dem ~weg** by sea; **~wind** *der* onshore wind; **~zeichen** *das* seamark; navigation mark; **~zunge** *die* sole

**Segel** /ˈzeːgl̩/ *das;* **~s**, **~:** sail; **mit vollen ~n** under full sail; (*fig.*) full speed ahead; **unter ~** (*Seemannsspr.*) under sail; **die ~ streichen** strike sail; (*fig.*) throw in the towel (**vor** + *Dat.* in the face of)

**segel-, Segel-: ~boot** *das* sailing boat; **~fahrt** *die* sailing trip; sail; (*länger*) sailing voyage; **~fliegen** *itr. V.; nur im Inf.* **~fliegen lernen** learn to fly a glider *or* to be a glider pilot; **man kann heute nicht ~fliegen** one can't go gliding today; **~fliegen** *das;* **~~s** gliding *no art.;* **~flieger** *der,* **~fliegerin** *die* glider pilot; **~flugzeug** *das* glider; **~jacht** *die* sailing yacht; **~macher** *der,* **~macherin** *die* ▶ 159 sailmaker

**segeln** ❶ *itr. V.* Ⓐ *mit sein, ohne Richtungsangabe auch mit haben* sail; **~ gehen** go sailing; go for a sail; Ⓑ *mit sein* (*ugs.: fallen*) fall; go flying; **durch die Prüfung ~** (*fig.*) fail *or* (*Amer. coll.*) flunk the examination; Ⓒ *mit sein* (*schweben*) ‹cloud, bird, leaf› sail.
❷ *tr. V.; auch mit sein* sail in ‹regatta›; **die Strecke in drei Stunden ~:** sail the course in three hours

**Segel-: ~regatta** *die* sailing regatta; **~schiff** *das* sailing ship; **~sport** *der* sailing *no art.;* **~törn** *der* (*Seemannsspr.*) sailing trip; **~tuch** *das; Pl.* **~~e** sailcloth

**Segen** /ˈzeːgn̩/ *der;* **~s**, ~ Ⓐ blessing; (*Gebet in der Messe*) benediction; **jmdm. den ~ erteilen** *od.* **spenden** ‹priest› pronounce the blessing on sb.; **über jmdn./etw. den ~ sprechen** bless sb./sth.; **[jmdm.] seinen ~ [zu etw.] geben** (*ugs.*) give [sb.] one's blessing [on sth.]; **meinen ~ hat er!** (*ugs.*) I have no objection [to his doing that]; (*iron.*) the best of luck to him!; Ⓑ (*Glück, Wohltat*) blessing; **ein wahrer ~:** a real blessing *or* boon; **darauf ruht kein ~** (*geh.*) no good will come of it; **etw. zum ~ der Menschheit nutzen** exploit sth. to the benefit of mankind; Ⓒ (*geh.: Ertrag*) yield; **der ganze ~** (*ugs.*) the whole lot (*coll.*); **reichen ~ tragen** (*fig. geh.*) have rich rewards

**segen·bringend** ❶ *Adj.* beneficent.
❷ *adv.* **sich auf etw.** (*Akk.*) **~ auswirken** have a beneficent effect on sth.

**segens·reich** *Adj.* Ⓐ prosperous ‹life, future›; Ⓑ ⇒ **segenbringend** 1

**Segens·wunsch** *der* Ⓐ (*Bitte*) blessing; Ⓑ *Pl.* (*geh.: Glückwünsche*) good wishes

**Segler** *der;* **~s**, ~ Ⓐ (*Schiff*) sailing ship *or* -vessel; Ⓑ (*Sportler*) yachtsman; Ⓒ (*Zool.*) swift

**Seglerin** *die;* ~, **~nen** yachtswoman

**Segment** /zɛˈgmɛnt/ *das;* **~[e]s**, **~e** segment

**segmentieren** *tr. V.* segment

**segnen** /ˈzeːgnən/ *tr. V.* Ⓐ bless; **er hob ~d die Hände** he raised his hands in blessing; Ⓑ (*ausstatten mit*) **mit jmdm./etw. gesegnet sein** (*auch iron.*) be blessed with sb./sth.; **im gesegneten Alter von 88 Jahren** at the venerable age of 88 years; **gesegneten Leibes sein** (*geh. veralt.*) be with child; **einen gesegneten Appetit/Schlaf haben** (*fam.*) have a healthy appetite/sleep like a log

**Segnung** *die;* ~, **~en** Ⓐ (*Wirkung*) blessing; (*iron.*) dubious blessing; Ⓑ (*das Segnen*) blessing

**seh·behindert** *Adj.* partially sighted; visually handicapped; **stark ~ sein** have severely impaired vision

**sehen** /ˈzeːən/ ❶ *unr. itr. V.* Ⓐ see; **schlecht/gut ~:** have bad *or* poor/good eyesight; **sehe ich recht?** am I seeing things?; **hast du ge~?** did you see?; **mal ~, wir wollen** *od.* **werden ~** (*ugs.*) we'll see; **siehste!** (*ugs.*), **siehst du wohl!** there, you see!; **lass mal ~:** let me *or* let's see; let me *or* let's have a look; **siehe oben/unten/Seite 80** see above/below/page 80; **wie ich sehe, haben Sie zu tun** I see you're busy; **da kann man** *od.* (*ugs.*) **kannste mal ~, ...** that just goes to show ...; Ⓑ (*hin~*) look; **auf etw.** (*Akk.*) **~:** look at sth.; **nach der Uhr ~:** look at one's watch; **jmdm. über die Schulter ~:** look over sb.'s shoulder; **sieh mal** *od.* **doch!** look!; **siehe da!** lo and behold!; **sieh einmal!** just look!; **alle Welt sieht auf Washington** (*fig.*) all eyes are turned on Washington; **in die Zukunft ~** (*fig.*) look into the future; Ⓒ (*zeigen, liegen*) **nach Süden/Norden ~:** face south/north; Ⓓ (*nach~*) have a look; see; **kannst du mal ~?** can you just have a look?; **nach der Post ~:** see whether there is any post; Ⓔ **nach jmdm. ~** (*betreuen*) keep an eye on sb.; (*besuchen*) drop by to see sb.; (*nach~*) look in on sb.; **nach etw. ~** (*betreuen*) keep an eye on sth.; (*nach~*) take a look at sth.; Ⓕ (*suchen*) **nach jmdm./etw. ~:** look for sb./sth.; Ⓖ (*achten*) **auf Sauberkeit/Ordnung ~:** be particular about cleanliness/tidiness; **er sieht nur auf seinen Vorteil/aufs Geld** he's only out for himself/he's only concerned about the money; **darauf ~, dass die Bestimmungen eingehalten werden** make sure that the regulations are adhered to; Ⓗ (*zu~, sich bemühen*) see; **wir müssen ~, dass wir pünktlich sind** we must see [to it] that we're on time; **man muss ~, wo man bleibt** (*ugs.*) you've got to take what chances you get; Ⓘ (*hervorragen*) show; **das Boot sah nur ein Stück aus dem Wasser** only a part of the boat showed above the water.
❷ *unr. tr. V.* Ⓐ (*erblicken*) see; **jmdn./etw. [nicht] zu ~ bekommen** [not] get to see sb./sth.; **sich am Fenster ~ lassen** show oneself at the window; **siehst du meine Brille?** can you see my glasses?; **von ihm/davon ist nichts zu ~:** he/it is nowhere to be seen; **hier gibt es nichts/etwas zu ~:** there's nothing/something to see here; **ich habe ihn kommen [ge]~:** I saw him coming; **das sieht man** you can see that; **sieht man das?** does it show?; **den möchte ich ~, der das gern tut** I'd like to meet the person who 'does enjoy doing it; **wenn ich das schon sehe, wird mir übel** just looking at it makes me feel sick; I feel sick just looking at it; **hat man so was schon ge~!** did you ever see anything like it!; **er hat schon bessere Zeiten ge~:** he has seen better days; **ich habe ihn selten so fröhlich ge~:** I've rarely seen him so happy; **[überall] gern ge~ sein** be welcome [everywhere]; **jmdn. vom Sehen kennen** know sb. by sight; **etw. gern ~:** approve of sth.; **er sieht es nicht gern, wenn seine Frau raucht** he doesn't like his wife to smoke; **jmdn./etw. nicht mehr ~ können** (*fig. ugs.*) not be able to stand the sight of sb./sth. any more; **kein Blut ~ können** (*ugs.*) not be able to stand the sight of blood; **er kann sich in dieser Gegend nicht mehr ~ lassen** he can't show his face around here any more; **mit ihm kann sie sich ~ lassen** she needn't be ashamed to be seen with him; **mit dieser Frisur kann ich mich nicht ~ lassen** I can't let people see me with my hair like this; **eine Leistung, die sich ~ lässt** an impressive *or* a considerable achievement; **du lässt dich ja überhaupt nicht mehr ~:** we never see anything of you any more; Ⓑ (*an~, betrachten*) watch ‹television, performance›; look at ‹photograph, object›; **hast du ihn gestern im Fernsehen ge~?** did you see him yesterday on television?; Ⓒ (*treffen*) see; **wann ~ wir uns?** when shall we see each other next?; **wir ~ uns morgen!** see you tomorrow!; **in letzter Zeit ~ wir Schulzes häufiger** we've seen more of the Schulzes [just] recently; Ⓓ (*sich vorstellen*) see; **er**

**sah sich schon als neuen Chef** he already saw himself as the new boss (*coll.*); **E** (*feststellen, erkennen*) see; **ich möchte doch einmal ~, ob er es wagt** I'd just like to see whether he dares [to]; **das sieht man an der Farbe** you can tell by the colour; **er sieht nur seinen Vorteil** he's only out for himself; **ich sehe schon, ich komme zu spät** I see I've come too late; **wir sahen, dass wir nicht mehr helfen konnten** we saw that we could not help any more; **etw. in jmdm. ~:** see sth. in sb.; **das wollen wir [doch] erst mal ~!** we'll 'see about that; **man wird ~ [müssen]** we'll [just have to] see; **das sehe ich noch nicht** (*ugs.*) I can't see that happening; **da sieht man es [mal] wieder** it's the same old story; **F** (*beurteilen*) see; **das sehe ich anders** I see it differently; **so sehe ich das nicht** that's not how I see it; **so darf man das nicht ~:** you mustn't look at it that way *or* like that; **das darfst du nicht so eng ~:** you mustn't take such a narrow view; **so ge~:** looked at that way *or* in that light; **dienstlich/menschlich/rechtlich ge~:** seen from a professional/human/legal point of view; **..., oder wie sehe ich das?** (*ugs.*) ..., am I right?; **ich werde ~, was ich für Sie tun kann** I'll see what I can do for you.
**3** *unr. refl. V.* **A** **er kann sich nicht satt ~:** he can't see enough (**an** + *Dat.* of); **ich habe mich müde ge~:** I've seen more than enough; **B** (*sich betrachten als*) **ich sehe mich getäuscht** I feel cheated; **sich genötigt/veranlasst ~, ... zu ...** feel compelled to ...; **sich in der Lage ~, ... zu ...** feel able to ...; think one is able to ...; **ich sehe mich außerstande, Ihnen zu helfen** I do not feel able to help you

**sehens-, Sehens-:** **~wert, ~würdig** *Adj.* worth seeing *postpos.*; **~würdigkeit** *die* sight; **die ~würdigkeiten [der Stadt] besichtigen** go sightseeing [in the town]; see the sights [of the town]

**Seher** *der;* **~s, ~:** seer; prophet

**Seher·blick** *der* prophetic *or* visionary powers *pl.*

**Seherin** *die;* **~, ~nen** seer; prophetess

**Seh-:** **~fehler** *der* sight defect; defect of vision; **~kraft** *die* sight

**Sehne** /ˈzeːnə/ *die;* **~, ~n** **A** ▶ 471 (*Anat.*) tendon; sinew; **B** (*Bogen~*) string; **C** (*Geom.*) chord

**sehnen** *refl. V.* **sich nach jmdm./etw. ~:** long *or* yearn for sb./sth.; **sich [danach] ~, etw. zu tun** long *or* yearn to do sth.; **er sehnt sich nach Hause** he longs to go home; **~des Verlangen** (*geh.*) longing; yearning

**Sehnen** *das;* **~s** (*geh.*) longing; yearning

**Sehnen·scheiden·entzündung** *die* ▶ 474 (*Med.*) tendosynovitis *no indef. art.*

**Seh·nerv** *der* ▶ 471 (*Anat.*) optic nerve

**sehnig** *Adj.* **A** stringy ‹meat›; **B** (*kräftig*) sinewy ‹figure, legs, arms, etc.›

**sehnlich** **1** *Adj.* **das ist mein ~stes Verlangen/mein ~ster Wunsch** that's what I long for most/that's my dearest wish.
**2** *adv.* **etw. ~[st] herbeiwünschen** look forward longingly to sth.; **sich** (*Dat.*) **etw. ~st wünschen** long *or* yearn for sth.; **jmdn. ~st erwarten** look forward eagerly to sb. coming

**Sehn·sucht** *die* longing; yearning; **~ nach jmdm. haben** long *or* yearn to see sb.; **die ~ nach der Ferne** the longing for faraway parts

**sehn·süchtig** **1** *Adj.* longing *attrib.*, yearning *attrib.* ‹desire, look, gaze, etc.›; ‹letter› full of longing *or* yearning; (*wehmütig verlangend*) wistful ‹gaze, sigh, etc.›; **~es Verlangen** longing; yearning.
**2** *adv.* longingly; (*wehmütig verlangend*) wistfully; **jmdn./etw. ~ erwarten** look forward longingly to seeing sb./to sth.; long for sb. to come/for sth.

**sehnsuchts·voll** (*geh.*) **1** *Adj.* longing *attrib.*, yearning *attrib.* ‹desire, look, gaze, etc.›; ‹letter, lines, song› full of longing *or* yearning; (*wehmütig*) wistful ‹gaze, sigh, tremolo, etc.›.
**2** *adv.* longingly; yearningly; (*wehmütig*) wistfully

**sehr** /zeːɐ̯/ *Adv.* **A** *mit Adj. u. Adv.* very; **~ viel** a great deal; **ich bin ~ dafür/dagegen** I'm very much in favour/against [it]; **~ zu meiner Überraschung** [very] much to my surprise; **ich bin Ihnen ~ dankbar** I'm most grateful to you; **ich bin Ihnen ~ verbunden** I'm [very] much obliged to you; **jmdn. ~ gern haben** like sb. a lot (*coll.*) *or* a great deal; **er wäre ~ wohl imstande gewesen, es zu tun** he would perfectly well have been able to do it; **B** *mit Verben* very much; greatly; **er hat ~ geweint** he cried a great deal *or* (*coll.*) a lot; **er hat sich darüber ~ geärgert** he was greatly *or* very annoyed about it; **das muss ich mir ~ überlegen** I'll have to give that a great deal of thought; I'll have to consider that very carefully; **du musst dich ~ vorsehen** you must be very careful; **es regnet ~:** it's raining hard; **danke ~!** thank you *or* thanks [very much]; **bitte ~, Ihr Schnitzel!** here's your steak, sir/madam; **Danke ~! — Bitte ~!** Thank you — You're welcome; **er hat sich so ~ geärgert/gefreut, dass ...** he was so annoyed/delighted that ...; **du glaubst nicht, wie ~ er sich gefreut hat** you wouldn't believe how delighted he was; **ja, ~!** yes, very much!; **nein, nicht ~!** no, not much!; **Langweilst du dich? — Sehr sogar!** Are you bored? — Yes, very!; **zu sehr:** too much; **Hat es ihr gefallen? — Nicht so ~!** Did she like it? — Not all that much!

**Seh-:** **~rohr** *das* periscope; **~schärfe** *die* visual acuity; **~schwäche** *die* weak vision *or* sight *no indef. art.*; **~störung** *die* sight defect; visual defect; **~störungen** impaired vision *sing.*; **~test** *der* eye test; **~vermögen** *das* sight

**sei** /zai̯/ *1. u. 3. Pers. Sg. Präsens Konjunktiv u. Imperativ Sg. v.* **sein**

**seibern** /ˈzai̯bɐn/ *itr. V.* dribble

**seichen** /ˈzai̯çn̩/ *itr. V.* (*bes. schwäb. salopp*) **A** pee (*coll.*); **ins Bett ~:** wet the bed; **B** (*dummes Zeug reden*) talk drivel

**seicht** /zai̯çt/ **1** *Adj.* ▶ 306, ▶ 411 shallow; (*fig.*) shallow; superficial.
**2** *adv.* (*fig.*) shallowly; superficially

**Seichtheit** *die;* **~** (*auch fig.*) shallowness

**seid** /zai̯t/ *2. Pers. Pl. Präsens u. Imperativ Pl. v.* **sein**

**Seide** /ˈzai̯də/ *die;* **~, ~n** silk

**Seidel** /ˈzai̯dl̩/ *das;* **~s, ~** (*half-litre*) beer mug

**Seidel·bast** *der* daphne

**seiden** **1** *Adj.* **A** (*aus Seide*) silk; **B** (*wie Seide*) silky.
**2** *adv.* silkily

**seiden-, Seiden-:** **~atlas** *der* silk satin; **~bau** *der* sericulture *no art.*; **~kleid** *das* silk dress; **~papier** *das* tissue paper; **~raupe** *die* silkworm; **~raupen·zucht** *die* sericulture *no art.*; **~spinner** *der* (*Zool.*) silk[worm] moth; **~straße** *die* (*hist.*) silk road; **~strumpf** *der* silk stocking; **~weich** *Adj.* silky-soft

**seidig** **1** *Adj.* silky.
**2** *adv.* silkily

**Seiende** /ˈzai̯əndə/ *das; adj. Dekl.* (*Philos.*) **das ~:** that which exists

**Seife** /ˈzai̯fə/ *die;* **~, ~n** **A** soap; **B** (*Geol.*) alluvial deposit; placer

**Seifen-:** **~blase** *die* soap bubble; (*fig.*) bubble; **~blasen machen** blow bubbles; **~kisten·rennen** *das* soapbox race; **~lauge** *die* [soap]suds *pl.*; **~oper** *die* (*ugs.*) soap opera; **~pulver** *das* soap powder; **~schale** *die* soap dish; **~schaum** *der* lather;

**seifig** *Adj.* soapy

**seihen** /ˈzai̯ən/ *tr. V.* strain

**Seil** /zai̯l/ *das;* **~s, ~e** rope; (*Draht~*) cable; **auf dem ~ tanzen** dance on the high wire; **in den ~en hängen** (*Boxen*) be on the ropes; (*fig. ugs.: müde sein*) be knackered (*Brit. coll.*) *or* shattered (*Brit. coll.*) *or* (*Amer. coll.*) tuckered

**Seil·bahn** *die* cableway

**Seiler** *der;* **~s, ~** ▶ 159 rope maker

**Seilerei** *die;* **~, ~en** **A** (*Herstellung*) rope making *no art.*; **B** (*Betrieb*) rope maker's

**Seilerin** *die;* **~, ~nen** ▶ 159 ⇒ **Seiler**

**seil·hüpfen** *itr. V.; nur im Inf. u. im 2. Part.; mit sein* ⇒ **seilspringen**

**Seilschaft** *die;* **~, ~en** (*Bergsteigen*) rope; (*fig.*) followers *pl.*

**seil-, Seil-:** **~springen** *unr. itr. V.; nur im Inf. u. im 2. Part.; mit sein* skip; **~tanz** *der* tightrope *or* high-wire act; **~tanzen** *itr. V.; nur im Inf. u. im 2. Part.* walk the tightrope *or* high wire; **~tänzer** *der*, **~tänzerin** *die* tightrope walker; **~winde** *die* cable winch

**Seim** /zai̯m/ *der;* **~[e]s, ~e** (*geh.*) glutinous *or* viscid mass; (*Honig~*) honey

**seimig** *Adj.* glutinous; viscid

**sein**[1] /zai̯n/ **1** *unr. itr. V.* **A** be; **wie ist der Wein?** how is the wine?; **wie ist das Wetter?** what is the weather like?; **wie wäre es mit einem Schnaps?** how about a schnaps?; **wie war das noch mit dem Scheck?** what was that again about a cheque?; **nun, wie ist es, gehst du mit oder nicht?** well, what about it? are you going too, or not?; **wie ist es mit dir, möchtest du ein Glas Glühwein?** how about you, would you like a glass of mulled wine?; **ist das kalt heute!** it's so cold today; **wie dem auch sei, sei es, wie es wolle** (*geh.*) be that as it may; **seien Sie bitte so freundlich und geben Sie mir ...** [would you] be so kind as to give me ...; **das Buch ist meins** *od.* (*ugs.*) **mir** the book is mine; **die Sache ist die: ...** it's like this: ...; **wenn ich du wäre ...** if I were you ...; **das wären neun Mark** that will be nine marks; **hier wären wir** here we are; **das wärs** that's that; (*beim Einkaufen*) that's all; that's it (*coll.*); **und das wäre?** and what might *or* would that be?; **er ist Schwede/Lehrer** he is Swedish *or* a Swede/a teacher; **was ist er [von Beruf]?** what does he do [for a living]?; **bist du es?** is that you?; **Karl wars** (*ist verantwortlich*) it was Karl [who did/said *etc.* it]; **keiner will es gewesen ~:** no one will admit it was him; **wer** (*ugs.*) *od.* **jemand ~:** be somebody; **nichts ~** (*ugs.*) be a nothing *or* a nonentity; **Everton ist Fußballmeister** Everton are football champions; **x sei 4** let x be 4; **B** (*unpers.*) **mir ist kalt/besser** I am *or* feel cold/better; **mir ist schlecht** I feel sick; **ist dir etwas?** are you all right?; is something the matter?; **jmdm. ist, als [ob] ...** sb. feels as if ...; (*jmd. hat den Eindruck* [*als*]) sb. has a feeling that ...; **jmdm. ist nach etw.** (*ugs.*) sb. feels like *or* fancies sth.; **mir ist nicht nach Scherzen** (*ugs.*) I'm not in a mood for joking; **C** (*ergeben*) be; make; **drei und vier ist** *od.* (*ugs.*) **sind sieben** three and four is *or* makes seven; **D** (*unpers.*) (*bei Zeitangabe*) be; **es ist drei Uhr/Mai/Winter** it is three o'clock/May/winter; **E** (*sich befinden*) be; **ist noch Bier im Haus?** is there any more beer in the house?; **morgen bin ich zu Hause** I shall be [at] home tomorrow; **wo warst du so lange?** where have you been all this time?; **bist du schon mal bei Eva gewesen?** have you ever been to Eva's?; **F** (*stammen*) be; come; **er ist aus Berlin** he is *or* comes from Berlin; **G** (*stattfinden*) be; (*sich ereignen*) be; happen; **es war an einem Sonntag im April** it was on a Sunday in April; **muss das ~?** is that really necessary?; **es hat nicht sollen ~** (*veralt., geh.*) it was not meant to be; **was darf es ~?** (*im Geschäft*) what can I get you?; **das kann schon ~:** that may well be; **das kann doch nicht ~!** that's just not possible!; **wenn etwas ist, ruf mich an** (*ugs.*) if anything comes up, give me a ring; **war etwas während meiner Abwesenheit?** did anything happen during my absence?; **es sei!** so be it; **was ~ muss, muss ~:** what must be, must be; **seis drum!** all right!; **sei es ..., sei es ...** (*geh.*) whether ... or ...; **H** (*existieren*) be; exist; **er ist nicht mehr** (*verhüll.*) he is no longer with us; **ist was?** (*ugs.*) is anything wrong *or* the matter?; **sie taten, als ob nichts wäre** they acted as

*old spelling (see note on page 1707)

S

if nothing had happened; **das war einmal** that's all past now; **es war einmal ein Prinz** once upon a time there was a prince; **es ist keine Hoffnung mehr** there is no hope [left]; **was nicht ist, kann noch werden** things can always change; **wenn du nicht gewesen wärest** if it hadn't been for you; **I** (*ugs.*) **etw. ~ lassen** stop sth.; **lassen wir die Idee/das Ganze lieber ~!** let's drop the idea/the whole thing; **jmdn./etw. ~ lassen** (*ugs.: in Ruhe lassen*) leave sb. alone *or* (*coll.*) be/leave sth. alone.
❷ *Hilfsverb* **A** (*... werden können*) **es ist niemand zu sehen** there's no one to be seen; **das war zu erwarten** that was to be expected; **die Schmerzen sind kaum zu ertragen** the pain is hardly bearable; **mit ihm ist zu reden** he's quite approachable; **es ist zu verkaufen** it is for sale; **B** (*... werden müssen*) **das Bemalen der Wände ist zu unterlassen** painting on the walls is prohibited; **die Richtlinien sind strengstens zu beachten** the guidelines are to be strictly followed; **C** (*zur Perfektumschreibung*) have; **er ist gestorben** he has died; **sie sind gerade mit dem Wagen in die Stadt** (*ugs.*) they've just driven off into town; **gestern bin ich gleich von der Arbeit nach Hause** (*ugs.*) I went straight home from work yesterday; **die Kinder sind spielen** (*ugs.*) the children have gone off to play; **D** (*zur Bildung des Zustandspassivs*) be; **wir waren gerettet** we were saved

**sein**[2] *Possessivpron.* (*bei Männern*) his; (*bei Mädchen*) her; (*bei Dingen, Abstrakta*) its; (*bei Tieren*) its; (*bei Männchen auch*) his; (*bei Weibchen auch*) her; (*bei Ländern*) its; her; (*bei Städten*) its; (*bei Schiffen*) her; its; (*nach man*) one's; his (*Amer.*); **jeder hat ~e Sorgen** everyone has his *or* (*coll.*) their troubles; **er trinkt am Tag ~e acht Tassen Kaffee** (*ugs.*) he regularly drinks eight cups of coffee a day; **das hat ~e zwei Millionen gekostet** (*ugs.*) it cost a good two million; **wenn man sich** (*Dat.*) **~er eigenen Unzulänglichkeit bewusst ist** when you're aware of your own inadequacy; when one is aware of one's own inadequacy; **dem Willi ~ Hund** (*salopp*) Willi's dog; his; **endlich war sie Sein** (*geh. veralt.*) at last she was his; **der/die/das ~e** (*geh.*) his; **die ~e** *od.* **Seine** (*veralt.*) his wife; **die ~en** *od.* **Seinen** (*geh.*) his family; **das ~e** *od.* **Seine** (*Eigentum*) what is his; **er hat das ~e** *od.* **Seine getan** (*was er konnte*) he has done what *or* all he could; (*~ Teil*) he has done his part *or* (*coll.*) bit; **jedem das ~e** *od.* **Seine** to each his own; (*jeder nach ~em Geschmack*) each to his own; **den ~en** *od.* **Seinen gibts der Herr im Schlaf** some people have all the luck

**sein**[3] *Gen. der Personalpronomen* **er, es** (*dichter. veralt.*) ⇒ **seiner**

**Sein** *das;* **~s** (*Philos.*) being; (*Dasein*) existence; **~ und Schein** appearance and reality

**seiner** (*geh.*) ❶ *Gen. des Personalpronomens* **er: sich ~ erbarmen** have pity on him; **~ gedenken** remember him. ❷ *Gen. des Personalpronomens* **es: das Tier lag dort, bis sich jemand ~ annahm** the animal lay there until somebody came and looked after it

**seiner-: ~seits** *Adv.* for his part; (*von ihm*) on his part; **er ~seits wollte nichts davon wissen** he for his part wanted nothing to do with it; **er unternimmt auch ~seits nichts** he doesn't do anything himself either; **~zeit** *Adv.* **A** (*damals*) at that time; in those days; **B** (*österr. veralt.: später*) later; **~zeitig** *Adj.* **der ~zeitige Präsident** the President at that time; the then President; **die ~zeitigen Verhältnisse** the conditions prevailing then *or* at that time

**seines·gleichen** *indekl. Pron.* **A** (*nach er*) his own kind; people *pl.* like himself; **er verkehrt am liebsten mit ~:** he prefers to associate with his own kind; **der König hat mich wie ~ behandelt** the King treated me as an equal; **B** (*nach man*) one's own kind; **C** (*nach es*) **das Kind soll mit ~ spielen** the child should play with others its own age; **das sucht** *od.* **hat nicht ~:** it is without equal *or* is unequalled

**seinet-: ~halben** (*veralt.*), **~wegen** *Adv.* **A** (*wegen seiner*) because of him; on his account; **das Kind ist schon lange weg: die Mutter macht sich ~wegen Sorgen** the child's been gone for a long time: the mother is worried for him/her; **B** (*ihm zuliebe, für ihn*) for his sake; for him; **C** (*von ihm aus*) **er sagte, ~wegen sollten wir ruhig gehen** he said as far as he was concerned we could go; **~willen** *Adv.* *in* **um ~willen** for his sake; for him

**seinige** /ˈzainɪgə/ *Possessivpron.* (*geh. veralt.*) **der/die/das ~:** his; **er hat das ~** *od.* **Seinige getan** (*was er konnte*) he had done what *or* all he could; (*sein Teil*) he has done his part; **die ~** *od.* **Seinige** his wife; **die ~n** *od.* **Seinigen** his family

***sein|lassen** ⇒ **sein**[1] 1 I

**seismisch** ❶ *Adj.* seismological; (*Erdbeben betreffend*) seismic. ❷ *adv.* seismologically

**Seismo-** /zaismo-/: **~gramm** *das* seismogram; **~graph** *der* seismograph; **~loge** *der;* **~~n, ~~n** seismologist; **~logie** *die;* **~~:** seismology *no art.;* **~login** *die;* **~~, ~~nen** seismologist

**seit** /zait/ ▶ **676** ❶ *Präp. mit Dat.* (*Zeitpunkt*) since; (*Zeitspanne*) for; **~ dem Zweiten Weltkrieg/1955/dem Unfall** since the Second World War/1955/the accident; **~ Wochen/Jahren/einiger Zeit** for weeks/years/some time [past]; **ich bin ~ zwei Wochen hier** I've been here [for] two weeks; **er geht ~ vier Wochen zur Schule** he has been going to school for four weeks; **~ damals, ~ der Zeit** since then; **~ wann hast du ihn nicht mehr gesehen?** when was the last time you saw him?.
❷ *Konj.* since; **~ du hier wohnst** since you have been living here; **~ er das gehört hat** since he heard that

**seit·dem** ❶ *Adv.* since then; **das Haus steht ~ leer** since then the house has stood empty. ❷ *Konj.* ⇒ **seit** 2

**Seite** /ˈzaitə/ *die;* **~, ~n** **A** side; **auf** *od.* **zu beiden ~n der Straße/des Tores** on both sides of the road/gate; **die hintere/vordere ~:** the back/front; **mit der ~ nach vorne** sideways [on]; **zur** *od.* **auf die ~ gehen** *od.* **treten** move aside *or* to one side; move out of the way; **zur ~!** make way!; **die ~n wechseln** (*Fußball*) change ends; **ein Auto auf die ~ winken** wave a car [over] to the side [of the road]; **jmdn. zur ~ nehmen** take sb. aside; **etw. zur ~ legen** *od.* **räumen** move *or* put sth. to one side *or* aside; **etw. auf die ~ schaffen** (*ugs.*) help oneself to sth.; **etw. auf die ~ legen** (*ugs.: sparen*) put sth. away *or* aside; **zur ~** (*Theater*) aside; **die eine/die andere ~ der Medaille** (*fig.*) the one/the other side of the coin; **alles** *od.* **jedes Ding hat seine zwei ~n** (*fig.*) there are two sides to everything; **ich schlafe auf der ~:** I sleep on my side; **er ist auf einer ~ gelähmt** he's paralysed down one side; **ich wünsche dir, dass du an seiner ~ glücklich wirst** (*geh.*) I hope you'll be happy with him; **halte dich an meiner ~:** stay beside me *or* by my side; **~ an ~:** side by side; **~ an ~ kämpfen** (*fig.*) stand shoulder to shoulder and fight; **jmdm. zur ~ stehen** stand by sb.; **jmdm. nicht von der ~ gehen** *od.* **weichen** not move from *or* leave sb.'s side; **setz dich an meine grüne ~!** (*scherzh.*) come and sit by me *or* by my side; **jmdn. von der ~ ansehen** look at sb. from the side; (*fig.*) look at sb. askance; **eine ~ Speck** a side of bacon; **B** (*Richtung*) side; **von allen ~n** (*auch fig.*) from all sides; **nach allen ~n** in all directions; (*fig.*) on all sides; **C** (*Buch~, Zeitungs~*) page; **die erste/letzte ~** (*eines Buchs*) the first/last page; (*einer Zeitung*) the front/back page; **~ wie viel?** (*ugs.*) what page?; **D** (*Eigenschaft, Aspekt*) side; **auf der einen ~, ... auf der anderen ~ ...** on the one hand ... on the other hand ...; **von der ~ kenne ich ihn noch nicht** I haven't seen that side of him yet; **etw. ist jmds. schwache ~** (*ugs.*) sth. is not exactly sb.'s forte; (*ist jmds. Schwäche*) sb. has a weakness for sth.; **jmds. starke ~ sein** (*ugs.*) be sb.'s forte *or* strong point; **sich von der besten ~ zeigen** show one's best side; **E** (*Partei*) side; **sich auf jmds. ~** (*Akk.*) **schlagen** take sb.'s side; **die ~n wechseln** (*fig.*) change sides; **auf jmds. ~ stehen** *od.* **sein** be on sb.'s side; **jmdn. auf seine ~ bringen** *od.* **ziehen** win sb. over; **auf/von ~n der Direktion** on/from the management side; **von anderer/offizieller ~ verlautete, dass ...** it was learned from other/official sources that ...; **ich werde von meiner ~ aus nichts unternehmen** I for my part will not do anything; **F** (*Familie*) side; **auf der väterlichen ~ stammt sie von ...** on her father's side she descends from ...

***seiten** *in* **auf/von ~** ⇒ **Seite** E; **aufseiten, vonseiten**

**seiten-, Seiten-: ~airbag** *der* (*Kfz.-W.*) side airbag; **~altar** *der* side altar; **~ansicht** *die* side view; (*Aufriss*) side elevation; **~arm** *der* arm; branch; **~ausgang** *der* side exit; **~blick** *der* sidelong look; (*kurzer Blick*) sidelong glance; **~eingang** *der* side entrance; **~flügel** *der* **A** (*eines Gebäudes*) wing; **B** (*eines Flügelaltars*) side panel; **~gebäude** *das* annex; (*eines Bauernhofs o. Ä.*) outbuilding; **~gewehr** *das* (*Milit.*) bayonet; **~halbierende** *die; adj. Dekl.* (*Math.*) median; **~hieb** *der* **A** (*fig.*) sideswipe (**auf** + *Akk.* at); **B** (*Fechten*) flank cut; **~lage** *die:* **in ~lage schlafen/schwimmen** sleep/swim on one's side; **den Verletzten in ~lage bringen** put the injured man on his side; **~lang** ❶ *Adj.* ‹letter› that goes on for pages; ❷ *adv.* **so geht es ~lang weiter!** it goes on like that for pages; **~leitwerk** *das* (*Flugw.*) vertical tail; **~linie** *die* **A** (*Geneal.*) offset; offshoot; **B** (*Fußball, Rugby*) touchline; (*Tennis, Hockey, Federball*) sideline; **~ruder** *das* (*Flugw.*) rudder

**seitens** *Präp. mit Gen.* (*Papierdt.*) on the part of; **~ der Arbeitgeber wird noch beraten** the employers are still discussing the matter

**seiten-, Seiten-: ~schiff** *das* [side] aisle; **~sprung** *der* infidelity; **einen ~sprung machen** have an affair; **~stechen** *das:* **~stechen haben/bekommen** have/get a stitch; **~straße** *die* side street; **eine ~straße der Schillerstraße** a side street off the Schillerstrasse; **~streifen** *der* verge; (*einer Autobahn*) hard shoulder; **„~streifen nicht befahrbar"** 'Soft Verges'; **~tal** *das* side valley; **~tasche** *die* side pocket; **~verkehrt** *Adj.* reversed; **~wand** *die* side wall; **~wechsel** *der* (*Ballspiele*) change of ends; **~wind** *der* side wind; crosswind; **~zahl** *die* **A** page number; **B** (*Anzahl der Seiten*) number of pages

**seit·her** *Adv.* since then; **~ habe ich ihn nicht gesprochen** I haven't spoken to him since [then]

**seitherig** *Adj.* **seine ~e Abwesenheit/Arbeit** his absence/work since then

**-seitig** *adj.* -page; **tausend~:** thousand-page *attrib.;* **ein mehrseitiger Brief/Bericht** a letter/report several pages long

**seitlich** ❶ *Adj.* **der Eingang ist ~:** the entrance is at the side; **ein ~er Wind** a side wind; a crosswind. ❷ *adv.* (*an der Seite*) at the side; (*von der Seite*) from the side; (*nach der Seite*) to the side; **~ von jmdm. stehen** stand to the side of sb.; **~ gegen etw. prallen** crash sideways into sth. ❸ *Präp. mit Gen.* beside; to the side of

**seitlings** /ˈzaitlɪŋs/ *Adv.* (*veralt.*) **~ reiten** ride side-saddle; **~ schlafen/liegen/fallen** sleep/lie/fall on one's side

**Seit·pferd** *das* (*Turnen*) side horse; pommel horse

**-seits** *adv.* **französischer~:** from the French side; **ärztlicher~:** from the medical angle

**seit·wärts** ❶ *Adv.* **A** (*zur Seite*) sideways; **B** (*an, auf der Seite*) to one side; **~ von etw.** to the side of sth. ❷ *Präp. mit Gen.* beside; to the side of

# seit

## 1. Als Präposition

■ **MIT EINEM ZEITPUNKT = SINCE**

***Wir wohnen seit 1995 hier***
= We have been living here since 1995

***Seit damals leidet er an Depressionen***
= Since then he has suffered from fits of depression

■ **MIT EINER ZEITSPANNE = FOR**

***Wir wohnen seit zwei Jahren hier***
= We have been living here for two years

***Er ist seit 20 Jahren bei der Firma***
= He has been with the firm for 20 years

***Ich kenne ihn schon seit einiger Zeit***
= I have known him for some time

Die Übersetzungen von *seit* sind also nicht problematisch, aber die Zeiten des Verbs sind in den beiden Sprachen meist unterschiedlich: im Deutschen steht durchweg das Präsens, während man im Englischen das Perfekt oder – bei einem ununterbrochenen Vorgang – vor allem seine Verlaufsform, das *Perfect Continuous*, verwendet (mit **know** und **love** z.B. kann man aber das *Perfect Continuous* nicht verwenden). Ähnlich wird ein Verb im Imperfekt durch ein Verb im Plusquamperfekt übersetzt:

***Ich wartete seit 8 Uhr/zwei Stunden***
= I had been waiting since 8 o'clock/for two hours

Negative und andere Beispiele, bei denen kein ununterbrochener Vorgang vorliegt, weisen aber in beiden Sprachen die gleichen Zeiten auf:

***Wir haben sie seit der Hochzeit nicht gesehen/nur einmal gesehen***
= We haven't seen her/have only seen her once since the wedding

***Ich war seit 1980 nicht dort gewesen***
= I hadn't been there since 1980

## 2. Als Konjunktion

Auch hier wird das englische *Perfect Continuous* bzw. das Perfekt bei einem ununterbrochenen Vorgang verwendet, wo im Deutschen das Präsens steht:

***Seit sie in Deutschland lebt, haben wir keinen Kontakt mehr***
Since she has been living in Germany we are no longer in touch

***Seit er dieses Mittel nimmt, hat er keine Schmerzen mehr***
= Since he has been taking this medication, he no longer has any pain

***Seit ich sie kenne, hat sie nie gelacht***
= Since I have known her, she has never laughed

Und in der Vergangenheit (etwa in der Erzählform):

***Seit sie in Deutschland lebte, hatten wir keinen Kontakt mehr***
= Since she had been living in Germany, we were no longer in touch

***Seit ich sie kannte, hatte sie nie gelacht***
= Since I had known her, she had never laughed

Aber bei einem Geschehen, das nicht andauert, wird das deutsche Perfekt mit dem englischen *Simple Past* übersetzt:

***Seit er das gehört hat, ist er wie verwandelt***
= Since he heard that, he's a changed man

**sek., Sek.** *Abk.* **Sekunde** sec.

**Sekante** /ze'kantə/ *die;* ~, ~**n** (*Math.*) secant

**sekkant** /zɛ'kant/ (*österr., sonst veralt.*) ❶ *Adj.* tiresome. ❷ *adv.* tiresomely

**sekkieren** *tr. V.* (*österr., sonst veralt.*) annoy; (*bedrängen*) pester

**Sekret** /ze'kre:t/ *das;* ~**[e]s**, ~**e** (*Med., Biol.*) secretion

**Sekretär** /zekre'tɛ:ɐ̯/ *der;* ~**s**, ~**e** Ⓐ ▶ 159 secretary; Ⓑ ▶ 159 (*Beamter*) middle-ranking civil servant; Ⓒ (*Schreibschrank*) secretaire; secretary; bureau (*Brit.*); Ⓓ (*Zool.*) secretarybird

**Sekretariat** /zekreta'ri̯a:t/ *das;* ~**[e]s**, ~**e** [secretary's/secretaries'] office

**Sekretärin** *die;* ~, ~**nen** ▶ 159 secretary

**Sekretion** /zekre'tsi̯o:n/ *die;* ~, ~**en** (*Med., Biol.*) secretion

**Sekt** /zɛkt/ *der;* ~**[e]s**, ~**e** high-quality sparkling wine; ≈ champagne

**Sekte** /'zɛktə/ *die;* ~, ~**n** sect

**Sekt·flasche** *die* champagne bottle

**Sektierer** *der;* ~**s**, ~, **Sektiererin** *die;* ~, ~**nen** sectarian; (*Politik: Abweichler*) deviationist

**sektiererisch** ❶ *Adj.* sectarian; (*Politik*) deviationist. ❷ *adv.* in a sectarian way; (*Politik*) in a deviationist way

**Sektierertum** *das;* ~**s** sectarianism; (*Politik*) deviationism

**Sektion** /zɛk'tsi̯o:n/ *die;* ~, ~**en** Ⓐ (*Abteilung*) section; (*im Ministerium*) department; Ⓑ (*DDR: an Hochschulen*) department; Ⓒ (*Med.*) autopsy; post mortem [examination] (+ *Gen.* on)

**Sektions·chef** *der*, **Sektions·chefin** *die* (*österr.*) *head of a ministry department*

**Sekt-:** ~**kellerei** *die* champagne producer's; (*Gebäude*) champagne cellars *pl.*; ~**kühler** *der* champagne cooler

**Sektor** /'zɛktɔr/ *der;* ~**s**, ~**en** /-'to:rən/ Ⓐ (*Fachgebiet*) field; sphere; **industrieller/wirtschaftlicher** ~: industrial/economic sector; Ⓑ (*Geom.; Besatzungszone*) sector

**Sektoren·grenze** *die* sector boundary

**Sekunda** /ze'kʊnda/ *die;* ~, **Sekunden** (*Schulw.*) Ⓐ (*veralt.*) sixth and seventh years (*of a Gymnasium*); Ⓑ (*österr.*) second year (*of a Gymnasium*)

**Sekundaner** *der;* ~**s**, ~, **Sekundanerin** *die;* ~, ~**nen** (*Schulw.*) Ⓐ (*veralt.*) (*Ober*~) pupil in the seventh year (*of a Gymnasium*); (*Unter*~) pupil in the sixth year (*of a Gymnasium*); Ⓑ (*österr.*) pupil in the second year (*of a Gymnasium*)

**Sekundant** /zekʊn'dant/ *der;* ~**en**, ~**en**, **Sekundantin** *die;* ~, ~**nen** second (*in a duel or match*)

**sekundär** /zekun'dɛ:ɐ̯/ ❶ *Adj.* secondary. ❷ *adv.* secondarily

**Sekundar·lehrer** *der*, **Sekundar·lehrerin** *die* (*schweiz.*) secondary-school teacher

**Sekundär·literatur** *die* secondary literature

**Sekundar-:** ~**schule** *die* (*schweiz.*) secondary school; ~**stufe** *die* secondary stage (*of education*)

**Sekunde** /ze'kʊndə/ *die;* ~, ~**n** Ⓐ ▶ 752 (*auch Math., Musik*) second; **es ist auf die** ~ **12 Uhr** it is twelve o'clock precisely; **meine Uhr geht auf die** ~ **genau** my watch keeps perfect time; Ⓑ (*ugs.: Augenblick*) second; moment

**sekundenlang** ❶ *Adj.* momentary. ❷ *adv.* for a moment; momentarily

**Sekunden-:** ~**schnelle** *die:* **in** ~**schnelle** in a matter of seconds; (*blitzschnell*) in a flash; ~**zeiger** *der* second hand

**sekundieren** *itr. V.* (*geh.*) **jmdm. [bei etw.]** ~: support sb., back sb. up [in sth.]; **jmdm. [bei einem Duell]** ~: act as sb.'s second [in a duel]

**Sekurit** Ⓦⓩ /zeku'ri:t/ *das;* ~**s** [toughened] safety glass

**selb...** /zɛlp.../ ⇒ **derselbe**

**selber** /'zɛlbɐ/ *indekl. Demonstrativpron.* ⇒ **selbst** 1

**Selber·machen** *das;* ~**s** (*ugs.*) do-it-yourself *no art.;* **Möbel zum** ~: furniture to make oneself *or* for the do-it-yourselfer

**selbig** *Demonstrativpron.* (*veralt.*) [the] same; **am** ~**en Tag** that same *or* very day

**selbst** /zɛlpst/ ❶ *indekl. Demonstrativpron.* **ich/du/er** ~: I myself/you yourself/he himself; **wir/ihr** ~: we ourselves/you yourselves; **sie** ~: she herself; (*Pl.*) they themselves; **Sie** ~: you yourself; (*Pl.*) you yourselves; **das Haus/der König** ~: the house itself/the king himself; **du hast es** ~ **gesagt** you said so yourself; (*stärker betont*) you yourself said so; **ich habe nicht** ~ **mit ihm gesprochen** I didn't speak to him myself; **sie backt/kocht** ~: she does the baking/cooking herself; ~ **gebacken** home-made; home-baked; ~ **gebraut** home-brewed; ~ **gemacht** home-made ‹jam, liqueur, sausages, basket, etc.›; self-made ‹dress, pullover, etc.; › ‹dress, pullover, etc.› one has made oneself; ~ **gestrickt** home-made, hand-knitted; (*fig. ugs.*) homespun ‹ideology etc.›; ~ **gedrehte Zigaretten** [one's own] rolled cigarettes; **mein erstes** ~ **verdientes Geld** the first money I earned myself; ~ **verfasste Gedichte/Lieder** poems/songs of one's own composition; **er denkt nur an sich** ~: he only thinks of himself; **Wie geht's dir? — Gut! Und** ~**?** (*ugs.*) How are you? — Fine! And how about you?; **von** ~: automatically; **etw. läuft ganz von** ~: sth. runs itself *or* requires no attention; **es versteht sich von** ~: it goes without saying; **die Ruhe/Bescheidenheit** ~ **sein** (*ugs.*) be calmness/modesty itself; ~ **ist der Mann** you have to get on and do things for yourself.
❷ *adv.* even; ~ **wenn er wollte** even if he wanted [to]

**Selbst** *das;* ~ (*geh.*) self; **das eigene** ~: one's own self

*old spelling (see note on page 1707)

**Selbst-: ~abholer** *der*, **~abholerin** *die* **A** (*Kaufmannsspr.*) *buyer who collects the goods himself/herself;* **ein Möbelmarkt für ~abholer** a cash-and-carry furniture store; **B** (*Postw.*) *person who collects his post himself;* **~abholer sein** collect the post oneself; **~achtung** *die* self-respect; self-esteem

**selb·ständig** ❶ ▶ 159 *Adj.* independent; **an ~es Arbeiten gewöhnt sein** be used to working on one's own *or* independently; **ein ~er Unternehmer** a self-employed business man; **sich ~ machen** set up on one's own; (*fig. scherzh.*) ‹pram, child, etc.› take off [on its/his/her own]. ❷ *adv.* independently; **~ arbeiten** work on one's own *or* independently; **~ denken** think for oneself

**Selbständige** *der/die; adj. Dekl.* ▶ 159 self-employed [business] person

**Selbständigkeit** *die;* **~:** independence

**selbst-, Selbst-: ~anzeige** *die* (*Rechtsw.*) self-denunciation; **~auf·opferung** *die* self-sacrifice *no art.;* **unter großer ~aufopferung** at the cost of considerable self-sacrifice; **~auslöser** *der* (*Fot.*) delayedaction shutter release; **~bedienung** *die* self-service *no art.;* **hier ist ~bedienung** it's self-service here; **~bedienungs·laden** *der; Pl.* **~bedienungsläden** self-service shop; **~befriedigung** *die* **A** masturbation *no art.;* **B** (*fig.*) **er tut das aus reiner ~befriedigung** he only does it for self-gratification; **~behauptung** *die* self-assertion *no art.;* **~beherrschung** *die* self-control *no art.;* **die ~beherrschung bewahren/verlieren** keep/lose one's self-control; **~beobachtung** *die* self-observation *no art.;* **~beschränkung** *die* self-restraint *no art.;* **in kluger ~beschränkung** wisely exercising self-restraint; **~besinnung** *die* (*geh.*) [inward] contemplation *no art.;* **~bestätigung** *die* (*Psych.*) self-affirmation *no art.;* **eine ~bestätigung** a boost to the ego; **~bestimmung** *die* self-determination *no art.;* **~bestimmungs·recht** *das* right of self-determination; **~beteiligung** *die* (*Versicherungsw.*) [personal] excess; **~betrug** *der* self-deception *no art.;* **~beweih·räucherung** *die* (*ugs.*) self-adulation *no art.;* **~bewusst**, ***~bewußt** ❶ *Adj.* **A** self-confident; self-possessed; **B** (*Philos.*) self-aware; ❷ *adv.* self-confidently; **~bewusst·sein**, ***~bewußt·sein** *das* **A** self-confidence *no art.;* (*einer sozialen Schicht o. Ä.*) self-assurance; **nationales ~bewusstsein** sense of national identity; **B** (*Philos.*) self-awareness *no art.;* **~bildnis** *das* self-portrait; **~disziplin** *die* self-discipline *no art.;* **~einschätzung** *die* self-assessment *no art.;* self-appraisal *no art.;* **~entfaltung** *die* blossoming of one's personality; **sie hatte keine Möglichkeit zur ~entfaltung** there was no opportunity for her to develop as an individual; **~entfremdung** *die* (*Soziol., Philos.*) self-alienation *no art.;* **~erfahrungs·gruppe** *die* (*Psych.*) sensitivity group; **~erhaltung** *die* self-preservation *no art.;* **~erhaltungs·trieb** *der* instinct for self-preservation; survival instinct; **~erkenntnis** *die* self-knowledge *no art.;* **~erkenntnis ist der erste Schritt zur Besserung** knowing your faults is the first step towards curing them; **~fahrer** *der* **A** *person who drives a car himself/herself;* **Autovermietung an ~fahrer** self-drive car hire; **B** (*Krankenfahrstuhl*) self-propelled wheelchair; **~fahrerin** *die* ⇒ **~fahrer** A; **~findung** *die;* **~~:** self-discovery *no art.;* ***~gebacken** ⇒ **selbst** 1; ***~gebraut** ⇒ **selbst** 1; ***~gedreht** ⇒ **selbst** 1; **~gefällig** (*abwertend*) ❶ *Adj.* self-satisfied; smug; ❷ *adv.* smugly; in a self-satisfied way; **~gefälligkeit** *die* self-satisfaction; smugness; ***~gemacht** ⇒ **selbst** 1; **~genügsam** ❶ *Adj.* modest [in one's demands]; ❷ *adv.* modestly; **~gerecht** (*abwertend*) ❶ *Adj.* self-righteous; ❷ *adv.* self-righteously; **~gespräch** *das* conversation with oneself; **~gespräche führen** talk to oneself; ***~gestrickt** ⇒ **selbst** 1; **~hass**, ***~haß** *der* self-hatred; **~herrlich** ❶ *Adj.* high-handed; autocratic ‹ruler, decision›; ❷ *adv.* high-handedly; in a highhanded manner; ‹decide, rule› autocratically; **~hilfe** *die* self-help *no art.;* **Hilfe zur ~hilfe leisten** help people to help themselves; **~hilfe·gruppe** *die* self-help group; **~ironie** *die* self-mockery; **~justiz** *die* self-administered justice; **~justiz üben** take the law into one's own hands; **~klebe·folie** *die* self-adhesive plastic sheeting; **~klebend** *Adj.* self-adhesive; **~kontrolle** *die* self-restraint; (*in den Medien*) self-regulation; **~kosten** *Pl.* (*Wirtsch.*) prime costs; **~kosten·preis** *der* (*Wirtsch.*) cost price; **zum [reinen] ~kostenpreis** at [no more than] cost; **etw. unter dem ~kostenpreis abgeben** sell sth. below cost *or* at less than cost; **~kritik** *die* self-criticism; **~kritisch** ❶ *Adj.* self-critical; ❷ *adv.* self-critically; **~laut** *der* vowel; **~los** ❶ *Adj.* selfless; ❷ *adv.* selflessly; unselfishly; **~mitleid** *das* self-pity; **~mord** *der* suicide *no art.;* **~mord begehen** *od.* **verüben** commit suicide; **mit ~mord drohen** threaten [to commit] suicide; **~mord mit Messer und Gabel** (*ugs. scherzh.*) suicide by unhealthy eating; eating one's way to an early grave; **~mörder** *der*, **~mörderin** *die* suicide; **~mörderisch** *Adj.* suicidal

**selbstmord-, Selbstmord-: ~gedanken** *Pl.* thoughts of suicide; **sich mit ~gedanken tragen** contemplate suicide; **~gefährdet** *Adj.* potentially suicidal; **~kandidat** *der*, **~kandidatin** *die* potential suicide; **~kommando** *das* suicide squad; **~versuch** *der* suicide attempt; **einen ~versuch unternehmen** attempt suicide

**selbst-, Selbst-: ~porträt** *das* self-portrait; **~redend** *Adv.* naturally; of course; ***~schuß**, **~schuss** *der* automatic firing device; **~schutz** *der* self-protection *no art.;* **~sicher** ❶ *Adj.* self-confident; ❷ *adv.* in a self-confident manner; full of self-confidence; **~sicherheit** *die* self-confidence; **~ständig** *usw.* ⇒ **selbständig** *usw.*; **~studium** *das* self-study; private study; **im ~studium** through self-study; by studying on one's own; **~sucht** *die* selfishness; self-interest; **~süchtig** ❶ *Adj.* selfish; ❷ *adv.* selfishly; **~tätig** ❶ *Adj.* automatic; ❷ *adv.* automatically; **~täuschung** *die* self-deception; delusion; **~tötung** *die* (*Amtsspr.*) suicide; **~überschätzung** *die* overestimation of one's abilities; **er leidet an ~überschätzung** (*ugs.*) he has an exaggerated opinion of himself; **~überwindung** *die* will power *no indef. art.;* **das kostete mich viel ~überwindung** I really had to force myself to do it; **~verachtung** *die* self-contempt; **~verbrennung** *die* self-immolation *no art.* [by burning]; ***~verdient** ⇒ **selbst** 1; ***~verfaßt** ⇒ **selbst** 1; **~vergessen** (*ugs.*) ❶ *Adj.* oblivious of all around one *postpos.;* lost to the world *postpos.;* ❷ *adv.* obliviously; **~verlag** *der* private publishing venture; **~verleugnung** *die* self-denial; **~vernichtung** *die* self-destruction; **~verschulden** *das* (*Amtsspr.*) **das war ~verschulden** it was his/their *etc.* own fault; **~verschuldet** *Adj.* **~verschuldete Unfälle** accidents for which people are themselves to blame; **deine Notlage ist ~verschuldet** you have brought your predicament on yourself; **~versorger** *der*, **~versorgerin** *die* self-sufficient person; (*im Urlaub*) self-caterer; **~verständlich** ❶ *Adj.* natural; **es war für ihn ~verständlich** it was completely natural *or* a matter of course for him; **etw. für ~verständlich halten, etw. als ~verständlich betrachten** regard sth. as a matter of course; (*für gegeben hinnehmen*) take sth. for granted; **das ist doch ~verständlich** that goes without saying; ❷ *adv.* naturally; of course; **~verständlich nicht!** of course not!; **~verständlichkeit** *die* matter of course; **ein Badezimmer ist heute eine ~verständlichkeit** a bathroom is no longer considered a luxury; **etw. mit der größten ~verständlichkeit tun** do sth. as if it were the most natural thing in the world; **~verständnis** *das* conception of oneself; **~verstümmelung** *die* self-mutilation; self-inflicted injury; **~verteidigung** *die* self-defence *no art.;* **~vertrauen** *das* self-confidence; **~verwaltung** *die* self-government *no art.;* **~verwirklichung** *die* self-realization *no art.;* **~wähl·fern·dienst** *der* (*Postw.*) direct dialling; STD; **~wert·gefühl** *das* (*Psych.*) [sense of] self-esteem; **~zerstörerisch** *Adj.* self-destructive; **~zerstörung** *die* self-destruction; **~zufrieden** (*oft abwertend*) ❶ *Adj.* self-satisfied; ❷ *adv.* in a self-satisfied manner; smugly; **~zweck** *der* end in itself; **~zweck sein/zum ~zweck werden** be/become an end in itself

**selchen** /ˈzɛlçn̩/ *tr. V.* (*bayr.*, *österr.*) smoke ‹meat, ham, etc.›

**selektieren** /zelɛkˈtiːrən/ ❶ *tr. V.* select; pick out. ❷ *itr. V.* make a choice; **~de Methoden** selective methods

**Selektion** *die;* **~, ~en** selection

**selektiv** ❶ *Adj.* selective. ❷ *adv.* selectively; on a selective basis

**Selen** /zeˈleːn/ *das;* **~s** (*Chemie*) selenium

**Selfmademan** /ˈzɛlfmeːtmɛn/ *der;* **~s, Selfmademen** self-made man

**selig** /ˈzeːlɪç/ ❶ *Adj.* **A** (*Rel.*) blessed; **jmdn. ~ preisen** declare sb. blessed; **bis an sein ~es Ende** until his dying day; **Gott hab ihn ~:** God rest his soul; ⇒ *auch* **Angedenken**; **geben** A; **glauben** B; **B** (*tot*) late [lamented]; **Schwester Modesta ~** (*veralt.*) Sister Modesta of blessed memory; **C** (*kath. Kirche*) **die ~e Dorothea** the blessed Dorothy; **jmdn. ~ sprechen** beatify sb.; **D** (*glücklich*) blissful ‹idleness, slumber, etc.›; blissfully happy ‹person›; **~ [über etw.** (*Akk.*)**] sein** be overjoyed *or* (*coll.*) over the moon [about sth.]; **werde ~ mit deinem Geld!** (*ugs.*) you can keep *or* (*sl.*) stuff your money; **jmdn./sich ~ preisen** (*geh.*) consider s.b./onself remarkably fortunate. ❷ *adv.* blissfully

**Selige** *der/die; adj. Dekl.* **A** (*veralt.*, *noch scherzh.*) **mein ~r/meine ~:** my late lamented *or* dear departed husband/wife; **B** *Pl.* **die ~n** (*die Toten*) the blessed spirits [of the departed]; **die Gefilde der ~n** the Elysian fields; **C** (*kath. Kirche: Seliggesprochene[r]*) beatified person

**Seligkeit** *die;* **~, ~en** **A** (*Rel.*) [state of] blessedness; beatitude; **die ewige ~:** eternal bliss; **von dieser Reise hängt doch nicht seine ~ ab** (*fig.*) he won't be heartbroken if he doesn't go on this trip; **B** (*Glücksgefühl*) bliss *no pl.;* [blissful] happiness *no pl.*

**selig-, Selig-:** ***~|preisen** ⇒ **selig** 1A, D; **~preisung** *die;* **~~, ~~en: die ~preisungen** (*bibl.*) the Beatitudes; **~|sprechen** ⇒ **selig** 1 C; **~sprechung** *die;* **~, ~en** (*kath. Kirche*) beatification

**Sellerie** /ˈzɛləri/ *der;* **~s, ~[s]** *od. die;* **~, ~** (*Stauden~*) celeriac; (*Stangen~*) celery

**selten** /ˈzɛltn̩/ ❶ *Adj.* rare; infrequent ‹visit, visitor›; **in den ~sten Fällen** very rarely; **seine Besuche sind ~ geworden** his visits have become few and far between; **ein ~er Vogel** (*fig. ugs.*) an odd character; a queer fish (*coll.*). ❷ *adv.* **A** rarely; **wir sehen uns nur noch ~:** we seldom *or* hardly ever see each other now; **ein Sommer wie ~ einer** a summer such as is only too rare; **~ so gelacht!** that was a good laugh!; (*iron.: gar nicht komisch*) very funny[, I don't think]; **B** (*sehr*) exceptionally; uncommonly

**Seltenheit** *die;* **~, ~en** rarity; **es ist eine ~, dass ...** it is rare that ...

**Seltenheits·wert** *der;* **~[es]** rarity value

**Selters·wasser** /ˈzɛltɐs-/ *das; Pl.* **Selterswässer** seltzer [water]

**seltsam** ❶ *Adj.* strange; peculiar; odd; **alt und ~ werden** become rather odd in one's old age. ❷ *adv.* strangely; peculiarly

**seltsamerweise** *Adv.* strangely enough

**Seltsamkeit** *die;* **~, ~en** **A** (*Art*) strangeness; oddness; **B** (*Ereignis, Merkmal*) peculiarity; oddity

**Semantik** /zeˈmantɪk/ *die;* **~** (*Sprachw.*) semantics *sing.*, *no art.*

**semantisch** (*Sprachw.*) ❶ *Adj.* semantic. ❷ *adv.* semantically

**Semasiologie** /zemazi̯oloˈgiː/ *die;* **~** (*Sprachw.*) semasiology *no art.*

S

**Semester** /ze'mɛstɐ/ *das;* **~s, ~** A semester; **er hat 14 ~ Jura studiert** he studied law for seven years; **Studenten des dritten ~s** students in their third semester; ≈ second-year students; B *(ugs.: Student)* **ein höheres ~:** a senior student; **die ersten ~:** the first-year students; **ein älteres ~** *(fig. scherzh.)* a member of the older generation

**Semesterferien** *Pl.* [university] vacation *sing.*

**semi-, Semi-** /zemi-/ semi-

**Semi·finale** *das (Sport)* semi-final

**Semikolon** /zemi'ko:lɔn/ *das;* **~s, ~s** *od.* **Semikola** semicolon

**Seminar** /zemi'na:ɐ̯/ *das;* **~s, ~e,** *österr., schweiz. auch* **~ien** /...i̯ən/ A *(Lehrveranstaltung)* seminar (**über** + *Akk.* on); B *(Institut)* department; **das juristische ~/~ für Alte Geschichte** the Law Department/Department of Ancient History; C *(Priester~)* seminary; D *(für Referendare) course for student teachers prior to their second state examination*

**Seminar·arbeit** *die* seminar paper

**Seminarist** *der;* **~en, ~en, Seminaristin** *die;* **~, ~nen** seminarist

**Seminar·schein** *der* certificate of attendance [at a seminar]

**Semiotik** /ze'mi̯o:tɪk/ *die;* **~** *(Philos., Sprachw.)* semiotics *sing., no art.*

**Semit** /ze'mi:t/ *der;* **~en, ~en, Semitin** *die;* **~, ~nen** Semite

**semitisch** *Adj.* Semitic

**Semmel** /'zɛml̩/ *die;* **~, ~n** *(bes. österr., bayr., ostmd.)* [bread] roll; **weggehen wie warme ~n** *(ugs.)* sell like hot cakes

**semmel-, Semmel-: ~blond** *Adj.* flaxen ‹hair›; flaxen-haired ‹person›; **~brösel** *der od. österr.: das* breadcrumb; **~knödel** *der (bayr., österr.)* bread dumpling

**sen.** *Abk.* **senior** sen.

**Senat** /ze'na:t/ *der;* **~[e]s, ~e** A *(Hist., Politik, Hochschulw.)* senate; **der US-~:** the US Senate; B *(an Gerichten)* panel of judges

**Senator** *der;* **~s, ~en, Senatorin** *die;* **~, ~nen** senator; **Herr Senator X** Senator X

**Senats·ausschuss, *Senats·ausschuß** *der* senate committee

**Send·bote** *der,* **Send·botin** *die (veralt.)* envoy; *(fig.)* ambassador

**Sende-** /'zɛndə-/: **~anlage** *die (Elektrot.)* transmitter; **~bereich** *der (Rundf., Ferns.)* transmitting area; **~folge** *die (Rundf., Ferns.)* A *(Reihenfolge)* sequence [of programmes]; B *(einer Geschichte)* episode; **~gebiet** *das (Rundf., Ferns.)* ⇒ **~bereich**; **~mast** *der* transmitter mast

**senden**[1] *unr. (auch regelm.) tr. V. (geh.)* send; **jmdm. etw. ~:** send sb. sth.; **etw. an jmdn. ~:** send sth. to sb.; **wir ~ Ihnen die Waren ins Haus** we will despatch the goods to you at your home address

**senden**[2] *regelm. (schweiz. unr.) tr., itr. V.* broadcast ‹programme, play, etc.›; transmit ‹concert, signals, Morse, etc.›; **Hilferufe ~:** send out distress signals

**Sende·pause** *die (Rundf., Ferns.)* intermission

**Sender** *der;* **~s, ~:** [broadcasting] station; *(Anlage)* transmitter

**Sende-: ~raum** *der (Rundf., Ferns.)* [broadcasting] studio; **~reihe** *die (Rundf., Ferns.)* series [of programmes]

**Sender·such·lauf** *der (Rundf., Ferns.)* [automatic] station search

**Sende-: ~saal** *der (Rundf., Ferns.)* [broadcasting] studio; **~schluss, *~schluß** *der (Rundf., Ferns.)* close-down; end of broadcasting; **zum ~schluss noch ein Krimi** now as our last programme, a thriller; **~station** *die (Funk, Rundf., Ferns.)* broadcasting station; *(Anlage)* transmitter; **~zeit** *die (Rundf., Ferns.)* broadcasting time; **die ~zeit um zehn Minuten überschreiten** overrun by ten minutes; **~zentrale** *die (Rundf., Ferns.)* main studio; **wir geben zurück in die ~zentrale** we return you to the studio

**Send·schreiben** *das (veralt.)* circular letter; *(des Papstes)* encyclical

**Sendung** *die;* **~, ~en** A consignment; B *(geh.: Aufgabe)* mission; C *(Rundf., Ferns.: Darbietung)* programme; broadcast; D *(Rundfunkt., Ferns.: Ausstrahlung)* transmission; broadcast[ing]; **auf ~ sein** be on the air

**Sendungs·bewusstsein, *Sendungs·bewußtsein** *das* sense of mission

**Senegal** /'ze:negal/ *(das);* **~s** *od. der;* **~[s] [der] ~:** Senegal

**Senegalese** /zenega'le:zə/ *der;* **~n, ~n, Senegalesin** *die;* **~, ~nen** Senegalese

**Seneschall** /'ze:nəʃal/ *der;* **~s, ~e** *(hist.)* seneschal

**Senf** /zɛnf/ *der;* **~[e]s, ~e** mustard; **seinen ~ dazugeben** *(fig. ugs.)* get one's word in *or* have one's say

**Senf-: ~gas** *das* mustard gas; **~gurke** *die: gherkin pickled with mustard seeds;* **~korn** *das* mustard seed; **~soße** *die* mustard sauce; **~topf** *der* mustard pot

**Senge** /'zɛŋə/ *Pl. (ostmd. ugs.)* ⇒ **Prügel** B

**sengen** ❶ *tr. V.* singe. ❷ *itr. V.* A *(brennen)* singe; B *(heiß sein)* be scorching; **eine ~de Hitze** a scorching heat; C **~ und brennen** *(veralt.)* burn and pillage

**senil** /ze'ni:l/ ❶ *Adj. (Med., auch abwertend)* senile. ❷ *adv.* in a senile manner

**Senilität** *die;* **~** *(Med., auch abwertend)* senility

**senior** /'ze:ni̯ɔr/ *indekl. Adj.; nach Personennamen* senior

**Senior** *der;* **~s, ~en** /ze'ni̯o:rən/ A *(Kaufmannsspr.)* senior partner; B *(Sport)* senior [player]; C *(Rentner)* senior citizen; D *(Ältester)* oldest member; E *(scherzh.: Vater)* old man *(coll.)*; F *(Werbesprache: älterer Mensch)* older person

**Senior·chef** *der,* **Senior·chefin** *die (Kaufmannsspr.)* boss *(coll.) (in a family firm)*

**Senioren-: ~heim** *das* home for the elderly; **~mannschaft** *die* senior team; **~meister** *der* A senior champion; B *(Mannschaft)* senior champions *pl.;* **~meisterin** *die* ⇒ **~meister** A

**Seniorin** /ze'ni̯o:rɪn/ *die;* **~, ~nen** ⇒ **Senior** A, B, D

**Senk·blei** *das (Bauw.)* plumb [bob]

**Senke** /'zɛŋkə/ *die;* **~, ~n** hollow

**Senkel** /'zɛŋkl̩/ *der;* **~s, ~** A *(Schnür~)* shoelace; B **jmdn. in den ~ stellen** *(ugs.)* put sb. in his/her place

**senken** ❶ *tr. V.* A lower; *(Bergbau)* sink ‹shaft›; lower ‹flag›; drop ‹starting flag›; **den Kopf ~:** bow one's head; **die Augen** *od.* **den Blick/die Stimme ~:** lower one's eyes *or* glance/voice; **mit gesenktem Blick** with [one's] eyes cast down; B *(herabsetzen)* reduce ‹fever, pressure, prices, etc.›; C *(Technik)* countersink ‹hole›. ❷ *refl. V.* ‹curtain, barrier, etc.› fall, come down; ‹ground, building, road› subside, sink; ‹water level› fall, sink; ‹lift cage› go down, descend; **sein Brustkorb hob und senkte sich** his chest rose and fell

**senk-, Senk-: ~fuß** *der (Anat.)* flat foot; **~grube** *die (Bauw.)* cesspit; **~kasten** *der (Technik)* caisson; **~lot** *das (Technik)* plumb [bob]; **~recht** ❶ *Adj.* vertical; **~rechte Linie** *(Geom.)* perpendicular line; perpendicular; **in ~rechter Stellung** in an upright position; **bleib** *od.* **halt dich ~recht!** *(ugs.)* stay upright *or (coll.)* on your two pins; **das ist das einzig Senkrechte** *(ugs.)* that's the only thing worth doing/eating/reading *etc.;* ❷ *adv.* vertically; **~recht aufeinander stehen** *(Geom.)* be perpendicular *or* at right angles to each other; **~recht von oben** from vertically above; **~rechte** *die; adj. Dekl.* A *(Geom.)* perpendicular; B vertical line; vertical; upright; **~recht·starter** *der* A *(Flugzeug)* vertical take-off aircraft; B *(ugs.) (Aufsteiger)* whizz-kid *(coll.)*; *(Sache)* instant success; **~recht·starterin** *die;* **~, ~nen** *(ugs.)* whizz-kid *(coll.)*

**Senkung** *die;* **~, ~en** A lowering; B *(Reduzierung)* reduction; lowering; **eine ~ des Preises um 5%** a reduction of the price by 5%; C *(Geol.)* [case of] subsidence; D *(Verslehre)* unstressed syllable

**Senk·waage** *die* hydrometer

**Senne** /'zɛnə/ *die;* **~, ~n** *(bayr., österr.)* Alpine pasture

**Senner** *der;* **~s, ~** *(bayr., österr.) Alpine herdsman and dairyman*

**Sennerin** *die;* **~, ~nen** *(bayr., österr.) Alpine herdswoman and dairywoman*

**Sennes·blätter** /'zɛnəs-/ *Pl.* senna leaves

**Senn·hütte** *die (bayr., österr.)* Alpine hut

**Sensation** /zɛnza'tsi̯o:n/ *die;* **~, ~en** sensation; *(Darbietung)* sensational performance; **~en sehen wollen** want to see something sensational *or* spectacular

**sensationell** ❶ *Adj.* sensational. ❷ *adv.* in a sensational manner; sensationally; **eine ~ aufgemachte Story** a sensationalized story

**Sensations-: ~gier** *die (abwertend)* craving for sensation; **~meldung** *die* sensational report *or* piece of news; **~prozess, *~prozeß** *der* sensational trial

**Sense** /'zɛnzə/ *die;* **~, ~n** A scythe; B *(salopp)* **jetzt ist ~:** this really is [the end of] it *(coll.)*

**Sensen·mann** *der (verhüll.)* Great Reaper

**sensibel** /zɛn'zi:bl̩/ ❶ *Adj.* sensitive. ❷ *adv.* sensitively

**sensibilisieren** *tr. V.* A *(geh.)* make ‹person› more sensitive (**für** to); B *(Physiol.)* sensitize

**Sensibilität** *die;* **~:** sensitivity

**sensitiv** /zɛnzi'ti:f/ *Adj.* sensitive

**Sensor** /'zɛnzɔr/ *der;* **~s, ~en** /-'zo:rən/ *(Technik)* A sensor; B ⇒ **~taste**

**sensorisch** *Adj. (Physiol.)* sensory

**Sensorium** /zɛn'zo:ri̯ʊm/ *das;* **~s, Sensorien** /...ri̯ən/ *(Physiol.)* sensorium

**Sensor·taste** *die (Technik)* touch panel; touch pad *(Computing)*

**Sensualismus** *der;* **~** *(Philos.)* sensationalism

**Sentenz** /zɛn'tɛnts/ *die;* **~, ~en** aphorism; maxim

**sentimental** /zɛntimɛn'ta:l/ ❶ *Adj.* sentimental. ❷ *adv.* sentimentally

**Sentimentalität** *die;* **~, ~en** sentimentality; **das sind bloße/überflüssige ~en** that is mere/unnecessary sentimentality

**separat** /zepa'ra:t/ ❶ *Adj.* separate; **~e Wohnung** self-contained flat *(Brit.) or (Amer.)* apartment. ❷ *adv.* separately; **er wohnt ~:** he has self-contained accommodation

**Separat·friede[n]** *der* separate peace [treaty]

**Separatismus** *der;* **~:** separatism *no art.*

**Separatist** *der;* **~en, ~en, Separatistin** *die;* **~, ~nen** separatist

**separatistisch** *Adj.* separatist

**Separee, Séparée**/zepa're:/ *das;* **~s, ~s** private room

**separieren** *tr. V.* separate

**Sepia** /'ze:pi̯a/ *die;* **~, Sepien** A *(Tier)* cuttlefish; B *(Farbstoff)* sepia

**Sepia·zeichnung** *die* sepia drawing

**Sepp[e]l·hose** /'zɛpl̩-/ *die (scherzh.)* lederhosen *pl.*

**Sepsis** /'zɛpsɪs/ *die;* **~, Sepsen** ▶ 474 *(Med.)* sepsis

**Sept.** *Abk.* **September** Sept.

**September** /zɛp'tɛmbɐ/ *der;* **~[s], ~** ▶ 207 September; ⇒ *auch* **April**

**Septett** /zɛp'tɛt/ *das;* **~[e]s, ~e** *(Musik)* septet

**Septime** /zɛp'ti:mə/ *die;* **~, ~n** *(Musik)* seventh

**septisch** *Adj. (Med.)* septic

**Septuaginta** /zɛptu̯a'gɪnta/ *die;* **~:** Septuagint

**Sequenz** /ze'kvɛnts/ *die;* **~, ~en** sequence

**sequestrieren** /zekvɛs'tri:rən/ *tr. V. (Rechtsw.)* sequestrate; sequester

*old spelling (see note on page 1707)

S

**Serail** /ze'ra:j/ *das;* **~s, ~s** seraglio

**Seraph** /'ze:raf/ *der;* **~s, ~e** *od.* **~im** (*Rel.*) seraph

**Serbe** /'zɛrbə/ *der;* **~n, ~n** Serb; Serbian; **~ sein** be a Serb *or* Serbian

**Serbien** /'zɛrbi̯ən/ *(das);* **~s** Serbia

**Serbin** *die;* **~, ~nen** ⇨ **Serbe**

**serbisch** *Adj.* ▶ **696** Serbian; ⇨ *auch* **deutsch; Deutsch; Deutsche**[2]

**serbo·kroatisch** /zɛrbokro'a:tɪʃ/ *Adj.* ▶ **696** Serbo-Croat; ⇨ *auch* **deutsch; Deutsch; Deutsche**[2]

**Serenade** /zere'na:də/ *die;* **~, ~n** (*Musik*) serenade

**Sergeant** /zɛr'ʒant/ *der;* **~en, ~en** *od.* (*bei engl. Ausspr.:*) /'sɑ:dʒənt/ **~s, ~s** (*Milit.*) sergeant

**Serie** /'ze:ri̯ə/ *die;* **~, ~n** series; **eine ~ Briefmarken** a set of stamps; **etw. in ~ herstellen** *od.* **fertigen** produce *or* manufacture sth. in series; **in ~ gehen** go into [series *or* full-scale] production

**seriell** *Adj.* (*Musik*) serial

**serien-, Serien-: ~fertigung** *die* series production; **~mäßig** ❶ *Adj.* standard ‹product, model, etc.›; (*immer eingebaut*) ‹feature, accessory› fitted as standard; ❷ *adv.* Ⓐ **~mäßig gefertigt** *od.* **gebaut** produced in series; Ⓑ (*nicht als Sonderausstattung*) ‹fitted, supplied, etc.› as standard; **~mäßig mit etw. ausgerüstet sein** have sth. as a standard fitting; **~mörder** *der* serial killer; **~produktion** *die* series production; **~reif** *Adj.* ready for [series] production *postpos.;* production ‹version, model›; **~weise** *Adv.* Ⓐ **~weise gebaut** *od.* **hergestellt werden** be in series production; Ⓑ (*ugs.: in großer Zahl*) en masse; wholesale

**Serigraphie** /zerigra'fi:/ *die;* **~, ~n** serigraphy *no art.*

**seriös** /ze'ri̯ø:s/ ❶ *Adj.* Ⓐ (*solide*) respectable ‹person, hotel, etc.›; (*vertrauenswürdig*) reliable, trustworthy ‹firm, partner, etc.›; Ⓑ (*ernst gemeint*) serious ‹offer, applicant, artist, etc.›. ❷ *adv.* Ⓐ (*solide*) respectably; (*vertrauenswürdig*) in a trustworthy manner; Ⓑ (*ernst gemeint*) seriously

**Seriosität** /zeri̯ozi'tɛ:t/ *die;* **~** (*geh.*) Ⓐ (*Solidität*) respectability; (*Vertrauenswürdigkeit*) reliability; trustworthiness; (*eines Geschäftsmanns, einer Firma*) probity; Ⓑ (*Ernsthaftigkeit*) seriousness

**Sermon** /zɛr'mo:n/ *der;* **~s, ~e** Ⓐ (*veralt.: Predigt*) sermon; Ⓑ (*abwertend: langatmige Rede*) [long] lecture

**serologisch** *Adj.* serological

**Serpentine** /zɛrpɛn'ti:nə/ *die;* **~, ~n** Ⓐ (*Weg*) zigzag mountain road (*with numerous hairpin bends*); Ⓑ (*Kehre*) hairpin bend

**Serum** /'ze:rʊm/ *das;* **~s, Seren** *od.* **Sera** (*Med., Physiol.*) serum

**Service**[1] /zɛr'vi:s/ *das;* **~, ~:** [dinner *etc.*] service

**Service**[2] /'zø:ɐ̯vɪs/ *der od. das;* **~, ~s** /'zø:ɐ̯vɪsɪs/ Ⓐ (*Bedienung, Kundendienst*) service; (*Kundendienstabteilung*) service department; Ⓑ (*Tennis: Aufschlag*) serve; service; **beim ~:** when serving

**servieren** /zɛr'vi:rən/ ❶ *tr. V.* Ⓐ (*auftragen*) serve ‹food, drink›; (*fig.*) serve up ‹information›; deliver ‹line, punchline, etc.›; **jmdm. etw. ~:** serve sb. sth.; Ⓑ (*Ballspiele*) **jmdm. den Ball ~:** feed/(*Tennis*) serve the ball to sb. ❷ *itr. V.* Ⓐ serve [at table]; **gleich wird serviert** dinner/lunch *etc.* is [about to be] served; Ⓑ (*Fußball*) pass; make a pass; (*Tennis*) serve

**Serviererin** *die;* **~, ~nen** ▶ **159** waitress

**Servier-: ~tochter** *die* (*schweiz.*) waitress; **~wagen** *der* [serving] trolley

**Serviette** /zɛr'vi̯ɛtə/ *die;* **~, ~n** napkin; serviette (*Brit.*)

**Servietten·ring** *der* napkin *or* (*Brit.*) serviette ring

**servil** /zɛr'vi:l/ (*geh. abwertend*) ❶ *Adj.* obsequious; servile. ❷ *adv.* obsequiously; in a servile manner

**Servilität** *die;* **~** (*geh. abwertend*) servility; obsequiousness

**Servo-** /'zɛrvo-/: **~bremse** *die* servo[-assisted] brake; **~lenkung** *die* power[-assisted] steering *no indef. art.*

**Servus** /'zɛrvʊs/ *Interj.* (*bes. südd., österr.*) (*beim Abschied*) goodbye; so long (*coll.*); (*zur Begrüßung*) hello

**Sesam** /'ze:zam/ *der;* **~s, ~s** Ⓐ (*Pflanze*) sesame; (*Samen*) sesame seeds *pl.;* Ⓑ **~, öffne dich!** open sesame!

**Sesam·brötchen** *das* sesame-seed roll

**Sessel** /'zɛsl̩/ *der;* **~s, ~** Ⓐ easy chair; (*mit Armlehne*) armchair; Ⓑ (*österr.: Stuhl*) chair

**Sessel-: ~lehne** *die* chair back; **~lift** *der* chairlift

**sesshaft, *seßhaft** /'zɛshaft/ *Adj.* settled ‹tribe, way of life›; **~ werden** settle [down]

**Sesshaftigkeit, *Seßhaftigkeit** *die;* **~:** settled way of life

**Session** /zɛ'si̯o:n/ *die;* **~, ~en** (*bes. Parl.*) [parliamentary *etc.*] session

**Set** /zɛt/ *das od. der;* **~[s], ~s** Ⓐ (*Satz*) set, combination (**aus** of); Ⓑ (*Deckchen*) table mat; place mat; Ⓒ (*Sozialpsych.*) set

**Setter** *der;* **~s, ~:** setter

**Setz·ei** *das* (*bes. nordostd.*) ⇨ **Spiegelei**

**setzen** /'zɛtsn̩/ ❶ *refl. V.* Ⓐ (*hin~*) sit [down]; **setz dich/setzt euch/~ Sie sich** sit down; take a seat; **sich aufs Sofa/in den Sessel/in den Schatten** *usw.* **~:** sit on the sofa/in the chair/in the shade *etc.;* **sich zu jmdm. ~:** [go and] sit with sb.; join sb.; **setz dich zu uns** come and sit with us; **der Vogel setzte sich auf seine Schulter** the bird landed *or* alighted on his shoulder; **sich an den Tisch** *od.* **zu Tisch ~:** sit [down] at the table; Ⓑ (*sinken*) ‹coffee, solution, froth, etc.› settle; ‹sediment› sink to the bottom; **das Erdreich setzt sich** there is some settlement *or* subsidence; Ⓒ (*in präp. Verbindungen*) **sich mit jmdm. ins Einvernehmen ~:** come to an agreement with sb.; ⇨ *auch* **Spitze** D, E; **Unrecht** B; **Verbindung** H; **Wehr;** Ⓓ (*dringen*) **der Staub/Geruch/Rauch setzt sich in die Kleider** the dust/smell/smoke gets into one's clothes.
❷ *tr. V.* Ⓐ (*platzieren*) put; **ein Kind jmdm. auf den Schoß ~:** put *or* sit a child on sb.'s lap; **ein Schiff auf Grund ~:** run a ship aground; **eine Figur/einen Stein ~:** move a piece/man; ⇨ *auch* **Fuß** A; Ⓑ (*einpflanzen*) plant ‹tomatoes, potatoes, etc.›; Ⓒ (*aufziehen*) hoist ‹flag etc.›; set ‹sails, navigation lights›; Ⓓ (*Druckw.*) set ‹manuscript etc.›; Ⓔ (*schreiben*) put ‹name, address, comma, etc.›; **seinen Namen unter etw.** (*Akk.*) **~:** put one's signature to sth.; sign sth.; **einen Punkt/ein Komma [falsch] ~:** put a full stop/comma [in the wrong place]; Ⓕ (*in präp. Verbindungen*) **jmdn. auf schmale Kost ~:** put sb. on short rations; **in/außer Betrieb ~:** start up/stop ‹machine etc.›; put ‹lift etc.› into operation/take ‹lift etc.› out of service; (*ein-/ausschalten*) switch on/off; **jmdn. in Erstaunen ~** (*geh.*) astonish sb.; ⇨ *auch* **Fuß** B; **Musik** A; **Stelle** A; **Szene** A; **Trab; Umlauf** B; **Werk** A; **Wort** B; **Zeitung;** Ⓖ (*aufstellen*) put up, build ‹stove›; stack ‹logs, bricks›; ⇨ *auch* **Denkmal;** Ⓗ **sein Geld auf etw.** (*Akk.*) **~:** put one's money on sth.; **seine Hoffnungen auf jmdn. ~:** place one's hopes in sb.; ⇨ *auch* **Vertrauen;** Ⓘ (*festlegen*) set ‹limit, deadline›; **einer Sache** (*Dat.*) **Grenzen** *od.* **Schranken ~:** keep sth. within limits; **sich** (*Dat.*) **ein Ziel ~:** set oneself a goal; ⇨ *auch* **Akzente; Ende; Priorität; Zeichen** B; Ⓙ (*ugs.*) **es setzt was** *od.* **Prügel** *od.* **Hiebe** he/she *etc.* gets a hiding (*coll.*) *or* thrashing; Ⓚ (*Jägerspr.: zur Welt bringen*) give birth to.
❸ *itr. V.* Ⓐ *meist mit sein* (*im Sprung*) leap, jump (**über** + *Akk.* over); **über einen Fluss ~** (*mit einer Fähre o. Ä.*) cross a river; Ⓑ (*beim Wetten*) bet; **auf ein Pferd/auf Rot ~:** back a horse/put one's money on red; Ⓒ (*Jägerspr.: Junges, Junge zur Welt bringen*) give birth

**Setzer** *der;* **~s, ~** (*Druckw.*) [type]setter

**Setzerei** *die;* **~, ~en** (*Druckw.*) composing room

**Setzerin** *die;* **~, ~nen** ⇨ **Setzer**

**Setz-: ~fehler** *der* (*Druckw.*) setting error; misprint; **~holz** *das* dibber; dibble; **~kasten** *der* Ⓐ (*Gartenbau*) seedling box; Ⓑ (*Druckw.*) [type] case

**Setzling** /'zɛtslɪŋ/ *der;* **~s, ~e** Ⓐ (*Pflanze*) seedling; Ⓑ (*Fisch*) young fish; **~e** fry *pl.*

**Setz·maschine** *die* (*Druckw.*) composing *or* typesetting machine

**Seuche** /'zɔyçə/ *die;* **~, ~n** epidemic; (*fig.*) scourge

**seuchen-, Seuchen-: ~artig** ❶ *Adj.* epidemic-like; ❷ *adv.* ‹spread› like an epidemic; **~bekämpfung** *die* epidemic control *no art.;* **~gefahr** *die* danger of an epidemic; **~herd** *der* source of the epidemic

**seufzen** /'zɔyftsn̩/ *itr., tr. V.* sigh; **schwer/erleichtert ~:** give *or* heave a deep sigh/a sigh of relief

**Seufzer** *der;* **~s, ~:** sigh; **seinen letzten ~ tun** (*verhüll.*) breathe one's last

**Seufzer·brücke** *die* Bridge of Sighs

**Sevilla** /ze'vɪlja/ *(das);* **~s** ▶ **700** Seville

**Sex** /zɛks/ *der;* **~[es]** sex *no art.;* (*Anziehungskraft*) sex appeal; sexiness

**Sex-: ~appeal, *~-Appeal** /- ə'pi:l/ *der;* **~s** sex appeal; **~bombe** *die* (*salopp*) sex bomb (*coll.*); sexpot (*coll.*); **~boutique** *die* sex shop; **~film** *der* sex film

**Sexismus** *der;* **~:** sexism *no art.*

**sexistisch** ❶ *Adj.* sexist. ❷ *adv.* ‹behave, think, etc.› in a sexist manner

**Sex·muffel** *der* (*scherzh.*) *person not interested in sex;* sexless wonder (*joc.*)

**Sexologie** *die;* **~:** sexology *no art.*

**Sex·shop** *der;* **~s, ~s** sex shop

**Sexta** /'zɛksta/ *die;* **~, Sexten** (*Schulw.*) Ⓐ (*veralt.*) first year (*of a Gymnasium*); Ⓑ (*österr.*) sixth year (*of a Gymnasium*)

**Sextaner** *der;* **~s, ~** (*Schulw.*) Ⓐ (*veralt.*) pupil in the first year (*of a Gymnasium*); Ⓑ (*österr.*) pupil in the sixth year (*of a Gymnasium*)

**Sextaner·blase** *die* (*ugs. scherzh.*) bladder of a five-year-old

**Sextanerin** *die;* **~, ~nen** ⇨ **Sextaner**

**Sextant** /zɛks'tant/ *der;* **~en, ~en** sextant

**Sexte** *die;* **~, ~n** (*Musik*) sixth

**Sextett** /zɛks'tɛt/ *das;* **~[e]s, ~e** (*Musik*) sextet

**Sexual-** /zɛ'ksu̯a:l-/: **~erziehung** *die* sex education; **~ethik** *die* sexual ethics *pl.;* **~hormon** *das* sex hormone

**Sexualität** /zɛksu̯ali'tɛ:t/ *die;* **~:** sexuality *no art.*

**Sexual-: ~kunde** *die* (*Schulw.*) sex education *no art.;* **~leben** *das* sex life; **~mord** *der* sex murder; **~mörder** *der* sex killer; **~objekt** *das* sex object; **~partner,** *der,* **~partnerin** *die* sexual partner; **~trieb** *der* sex[ual] drive *or* urge; **~verbrechen** *das* sex crime; **~verbrecher** *der* sex offender; **~wissenschaft** *die* sexology *no art.*

**sexuell** ❶ *Adj.* sexual. ❷ *adv.* sexually; **sich ~ befriedigen** get sexual satisfaction; (*masturbieren*) masturbate

**Sexus** /'zɛksu:s/ *der;* **~, ~** (*geh.*) sexuality *no art.*

**sexy** /'zɛksi/ (*ugs.*) ❶ *indekl. Adj.* sexy. ❷ *adv.* sexily

**Seychellen** /ze'ʃɛlən/ *Pl.* Seychelles

**Sezession** /zetsɛ'si̯o:n/ *die;* **~, ~en** secession

**Sezessionist** *der;* **~en, ~en, Sezessionistin** *die;* **~, ~nen** secessionist

**sezessionistisch** *Adj.* secessionist

**Sezessions·krieg** *der* [American] Civil War

**sezieren** /ze'tsi:rən/ ❶ *tr. V.* dissect ‹corpse›; (*fig.*) analyse ‹policy etc.›; dissect ‹language etc.›. ❷ *itr. V.* perform dissections/a dissection

**Sezier·messer** *das* dissecting knife

**SFB** *Abk.* **Sender Freies Berlin** Radio Free Berlin

**s-förmig, S-förmig** /'ɛs-/ *Adj.* S-shaped

**sfr.,** (*schweiz. nur:*) **sFr.** *Abk.* **Schweizer Franken**

**Sg.** *Abk.* **Singular** sing.

**SGB** *Abk.* **Schweizerischer Gewerkschaftsbund** Swiss Trades Union Federation

**Shampoo** /ʃam'pu:/ *das;* **~s, ~s, Shampoon** /ʃam'po:n/ *das;* **~ns, ~ns** shampoo

**shampoonieren** /ʃampo'ni:rən/ shampoo

**Sheriff** /'ʃɛrɪʃ/ *der;* **~s, ~s** sheriff

**Sheriff·stern** *der* sheriff's star

**Sherry** /'ʃɛrɪ/ *der;* **~s, ~s** sherry; ⇒ *auch* **Bier**

**Shetland-** /'ʃɛtlənd-/: **~inseln** *Pl.* Shetland Islands; Shetlands; **~pony** *das* Shetland pony; **~wolle** *die* Shetland wool

**Shooting·star** /'ʃu:tɪŋsta:/ *der;* **~s, ~s** whizz-kid (*coll.*)

**Shop** /ʃɔp/ *der;* **~s, ~s** shop

**Shorts** /ʃɔrts/ *Pl.* shorts

**Show** /ʃoʊ/ *die;* **~, ~s** show; ⇒ *auch* **Schau**

**Show·master** /'-ma:stə/ *der;* **~s, ~, Show·masterin** *die;* **~, ~nen** compère

**Siam** /zi:am/ *(das);* **~s** (*hist.*) Siam

**Siamese** /zia'me:zə/ *der;* **~n, ~n, Siamesin** *die;* **~, ~nen** Siamese

**siamesisch** *Adj.* Siamese

**Siam·katze** *die* Siamese cat

**Sibirien** /zi'bi:ri̯ən/ *(das);* **~s** Siberia

**sibirisch** *Adj.* Siberian; **~e Kälte** Arctic temperatures *pl.*

**Sibylle** /zi'bʏlə/ *die;* **~, ~n** sibyl; fortune teller

**sibyllinisch** (*geh.*) ❶ *Adj.* sibylline, mysterious ‹words, expression›. ❷ *adv.* in a sibylline manner; mysteriously

**sich** /zɪç/ *Reflexivpron. der 3. Pers. Sg. und Pl. Akk. und Dat.* ❶ *Akk.* [A] (*nach* **man** *od. Inf.*) oneself; (*3. Pers. Sg.*) himself/herself/itself; (*3. Pers. Pl.*) themselves; (*Höflichkeitsform Sg./Pl.*) yourself/yourselves; **er/sie hat ~ umgebracht** he killed himself/she killed herself; **sie versteckten ~:** they hid [themselves]; [B] (*bei reflexiven Verben*) **~ freuen/wundern/schämen/täuschen** be pleased/surprised/ashamed/mistaken.
❷ *Dat.* [A] (*nach* **man** *od. Inf.*) oneself; (*3. Pers. Sg.*) himself/herself/itself; (*3. Pers. Pl.*) themselves; (*Höflichkeitsform Sg./Pl.*) yourself/yourselves; [B] (*bei reflexiven Verben*) **~ etw. einbilden** imagine sth.; **~ etw. erhoffen** hope for sth. [for oneself]; **sie hat ~ den Fuß verstaucht/verrenkt** she sprained/twisted her ankle.
❸ *nach Präp.* (*nach* **man** *od. Inf.*) oneself; (*3. Pers. Sg.*) himself/herself/itself; (*3. Pers. Pl.*) themselves; (*Höflichkeitsform Sg./Pl.*) yourself/yourselves; **die Schuld auf ~ nehmen** take the blame upon oneself; **das ist eine Sache für ~:** that is a separate question; **das hat nichts auf ~:** that is of no consequence; **das hat etwas/viel für ~:** there is something/a great deal in that; **das Ding an ~** (*Philos.*) the thing in itself; **von ~ aus** on one's own initiative; without being told to; ⇒ *auch* **an** 2 B; **für** 1 A; **kommen** Q.
❹ (*in unpers. Ausdrucksweisen für* **man** *od. passivisch*) **auf dieser Straße fährt es ~ gut** this is a good road to drive on; **es lässt ~ nicht schneiden/öffnen** it cannot be cut/opened; it is impossible to cut/open it.
❺ (*einander*) one another; each other; **sie küssten ~:** they kissed [one another]; **sie sind ~ spinnefeind** they are at daggers drawn [with one another]; **sie sehen ~ ähnlich** they look alike

**Sichel** /'zɪçl̩/ *die;* **~, ~n** sickle

**sichel·förmig** ❶ *Adj.* crescent- *or* sickle-shaped. ❷ *adv.* in [the shape of] a crescent *postpos.*

**sicher** /'zɪçɐ/ ❶ *Adj.* [A] (*ungefährdet*) safe ‹road, procedure, etc.›; secure ‹job, investment, etc.›; **in ~em Abstand** at a safe distance; **vor jmdm./etw. ~ sein** be safe from sb./sth.; **~ ist ~:** it's better to be on the safe side; better safe than sorry; ⇒ *auch* **Nummer** A; [B] (*zuverlässig*) reliable ‹evidence, source›; secure ‹income›; certain, undeniable ‹proof›; (*vertrauenswürdig*) reliable, sure ‹judgment, taste, etc.›; **eine ~e Hand** a sure *or* steady hand; [C] (*selbstbewusst*) [self-]assured, [self-]confident ‹person, manner›; [D] (*gewiss*) certain; sure; **der ~e Sieg/Tod** certain victory/death; **er war sich** (*Dat.*) **seines Erfolges ~:** he was confident of success; **eine Strafe ist ihm ~:** he is certain *or* sure to be punished; **seiner** (*Gen.*) **selbst sehr ~ sein** be very sure of oneself.
❷ *adv.* [A] (*ungefährdet*) safely; **~ die Straße überqueren** cross the street in safety; **Geld ~ aufbewahren** keep money in a safe place; **um ganz ~ zu gehen** to be quite sure; [B] (*zuverlässig, vertrauenswürdig*) reliably; **~ [Auto] fahren** be a safe driver; **[nicht mehr] ~ auf den Beinen stehen** be [un]steady on one's legs; [C] (*selbstbewusst*) [self-]confidently; **~ auftreten** behave in a self-assured *or* self-confident manner.
❸ *Adv.* certainly; (*plädierend*) surely; **Kommst du? — Aber ~:** Are you coming? — Certainly; Of course; **du hast ~ schon gehört, dass ...** you are bound to *or* must have heard that ...; **~ kommt er bald** he is sure to come soon

**sicher|gehen** *unr. itr. V.; mit sein* play safe; **um sicherzugehen** to be on the safe side

**Sicherheit** *die;* **~, ~en** [A] safety; (*der Öffentlichkeit*) security; **die ~ der Arbeitsplätze** job security; **ein Gefühl der ~:** a sense of security; **in ~ sein** be safe; **jmdn./etw. in ~ [vor etw.** (*Dat.*)**] bringen** save *or* rescue sb./sth. [from sth.]; **sich vor etw.** (*Dat.*) **in ~ bringen** escape from sth.; **zur ~:** to be on the safe side; for safety's sake; **jmdn./sich in ~ wiegen** lull sb./[allow oneself to] be lulled into a [false] sense of security; ⇒ *auch* **öffentlich** 1; [B] (*Gewissheit*) certainty; **mit an ~** (*Akk.*) **grenzender Wahrscheinlichkeit** with almost complete certainty; almost certainly; **mit ~!** (*als Antwort*) certainly!; of course!; [C] (*Wirtsch.: Bürgschaft*) security; [D] (*Zuverlässigkeit, Vertrauenswürdigkeit*) reliability; soundness; [E] (*Selbstbewusstsein*) [self-] confidence; [self-]assurance; **~ im Auftreten/Benehmen** [self-]confidence of manner

**sicherheits-, Sicherheits-: ~abstand** *der* (*Verkehrsw.*) safe distance between vehicles; **einen zu geringen ~abstand einhalten** drive too close to the vehicle in front; **~beauftragte** *der/die* security officer; **~bindung** *die* (*Ski*) safety binding; **~glas** *das* safety glass; **~gurt** *der* [A] (*im Auto, Flugzeug*) seat belt; [B] (*für Bauarbeiter, Segler*) safety harness; **~halber** *Adv.* to be on the safe side; for safety's sake; **~kette** *die* safety *or* door chain; **~maßnahme** *die* safety measure; precaution; **~nadel** *die* safety pin; **~organe** *Pl.* security service *sing. or* services *pl.*; **~rat** *der* Security Council; **~risiko** *das* security risk; **~schloss**, ***~schloß** *das* safety lock; **~ventil** *das* (*Technik*) safety valve; **~verschluss**, ***~verschluß** *der* safety catch; **~vorkehrung** *die* [safety] precaution; safety measure; **~vorschrift** *die* safety regulation

**sicherlich** *Adv.* certainly; **er wird es ~ tun** he is certain *or* sure to do it

**sichern** ❶ *tr. V.* [A] make ‹door etc.› secure; (*garantieren*) safeguard ‹rights, peace›; (*schützen*) protect ‹rights etc.›; **etw./sich gegen etw.** *od.* **vor etw.** (*Dat.*) **~:** protect sth./oneself against sth.; **ein gesichertes Einkommen** a secure *or* guaranteed income; **eine Schusswaffe ~:** put the safety catch on a firearm; [B] (*verschaffen; polizeilich ermitteln*) secure ‹ticket, clue, etc.›; **[sich** (*Dat.*)**] etw. ~:** secure sth. ❷ *itr. V.* (*Jägerspr.*) scent; test the wind

**sicher|stellen** *tr. V.* [A] (*beschlagnahmen*) impound ‹goods, vehicle›; seize ‹stolen goods›; confiscate ‹licence etc.›; [B] (*gewährleisten*) guarantee ‹supply, freedom, etc.›; [C] (*beweisen*) establish [beyond doubt]

**Sicher·stellung** *die* [A] ⇒ **sicherstellen** A: impounding; seizure; confiscation; [B] (*Gewährleistung*) guarantee

**Sicherung** *die;* **~, ~en** [A] (*das Sichern*) safeguarding **(vor** + *Dat.*, **gegen** from, against); (*das Schützen*) protection **(vor** + *Dat.*, **gegen** from, against); [B] (*Elektrot.*) fuse; ⇒ *auch* **durchbrennen** A; [C] (*tech. Vorrichtung*) safety catch; [D] (*Schutz*) safeguard **(gegen** against)

**Sicherungs-: ~kasten** *der* fuse box; **~kopie** *die* (*DV*) back-up [copy]; **~verwahrung** *die* (*Rechtsw.*) preventive detention

**Sicht** /zɪçt/ *die;* **~, ~en** [A] (**~weite**) visibility *no art.*; (*Ausblick*) view **(auf** + *Akk.*, **in** + *Akk.* of); **gute** *od.* **klare/schlechte ~:** good/poor visibility; **die ~ beträgt nur fünfzig Meter** visibility is down to fifty metres; **in ~ kommen** come into sight; **außer ~ sein** be out of sight; **Land in ~!** land ahoy!; **auf ~ fliegen** fly by VFR; [B] (*Kaufmannsspr.*) **Wechsel auf ~:** bill payable on demand *or* at sight; [C] **auf lange/kurze ~:** in the long/short term; **auf lange** *od.* **weite ~ planen** plan on a long-term basis; [D] (*Betrachtungsweise*) point of view; **aus meiner ~/in der ~ des Historikers** as I see it/as the historian sees it; in my/the historian's view

**sichtbar** ❶ *Adj.* visible; (*fig.*) apparent ‹reason›; **für jedermann ~ sein** be obvious *or* evident to everyone; **sich** (*Dat.*) **~e Mühe geben** go to obvious *or* appreciable trouble; **etw. ~ machen** clarify sth. ❷ *adv.* visibly; **immer ~er zutage treten** (*fig.*) become increasingly obvious *or* apparent

**Sicht·blende** *die* screen; (*Jalousie*) blind

**sichten** *tr. V.* [A] (*erspähen*) sight; [B] (*durchsehen*) sift [through]; (*prüfen*) examine

**Sicht-: ~flug** *der* contact *or* VFR flying; **~gerät** *das* VDU; **~grenze** *die:* **die ~grenze liegt bei 30 Metern** [maximum] visibility is 30 metres; **~karte** *die* pass

**sichtlich** ❶ *Adj.* obvious; evident. ❷ *adv.* obviously; evidently; visibly ‹impressed›

**Sicht·linie** *die* (*Verkehrsw.*) sight line; **bis zur ~ vorfahren** drive up to a/the point where one can see what is coming

**Sichtung** *die;* **~, ~en** [A] sighting; [B] (*das Durchsehen*) sifting; (*das Prüfen*) examination; inspection

**Sicht-: ~verhältnisse** *Pl.* visibility *sing.*; **~vermerk** *der* visa; **~weite** *die* visibility *no art.*; **außer/in ~weite sein** be out of/in sight; **in ~weite kommen** come into sight

**sickern** /'zɪkɐn/ *itr. V.; mit sein* seep; (*spärlich fließen*) trickle; (*fig.*) ‹money› leak away

**Sicker·wasser** *das* [A] (*im Boden*) gravitational *or* drainage water; [B] (*aus einem Damm o. Ä.*) seepage (*from a dam etc.*)

**sie** /zi:/ ❶ *Personalpron.; 3. Pers. Sg. Nom. Fem.* (*bei weiblichen Personen und Tieren*) she; (*bei Dingen, Tieren*) it; (*bei Behörden*) they *pl.*; **Wer hat es gemacht? — Sie war es/Sie:** Who did it? — It was her/She did; **ich weiß mehr als ~:** I know more than she does; I know more than her (*coll.*); ⇒ *auch* **ihr**[1]; **ihrer** A.
❷ *Personalpron.; 3. Pers. Pl. Nom.* [A] they; **Wer hat es gemacht? — Sie waren es/Sie:** Who did it? — It was them/They did; **ich weiß mehr als ~:** I know more than they do; I know more than them (*coll.*); ⇒ *auch* **ihnen**; **ihrer** B; [B] (*ugs.: man*) **mir haben ~ mein Rad gestohlen** somebody's stolen my bike; **hier wollen ~ das neue Rathaus bauen** here's where they are going to build the new town hall; **den haben ~ verhaftet** he's been arrested.
❸ *Akk. des Personalpron.* **~** 1 (*bei weiblichen Personen und Tieren*) her; (*bei Dingen und Tieren*) it; (*bei Behörden*) them *pl.*
❹ *Akk. des Personalpron.* **~** 2 a them

**Sie**[1] *Personalpron.* [A] *Anrede an eine od. mehrere Personen* you; **jmdn. mit ~ anreden** address sb. as 'Sie'; use the polite form of address to sb.; **kommen ~ her!** come here!; [B] (*veralt.: Anrede an eine Untergebene*) you

**Sie**[2] *die;* **~, ~s** (*ugs.*) she

**Sieb** /zi:p/ *das;* **~[e]s, ~e** [A] sieve; (*Kaffee~, Tee~*) strainer; (*für Sand, Kies usw.*) riddle; (*Technik: Filter*) filter; **er hat ein Gedächtnis wie ein ~:** he's got a memory like a sieve; [B] (*Druckw.*) screen

*old spelling (see note on page 1707)

**Sieb·druck** *der; Pl.* **~e** (A) (*Verfahren*) [silk-]screen printing *no art.*; (B) (*Erzeugnis*) [silk-]screen print

**sieben¹** ❶ *tr. V.* (A) (*durch~*) sieve ‹flour etc.›; riddle ‹sand, gravel, etc.›; (B) (*auswählen*) screen ‹candidates, visitors, etc.›. ❷ *itr. V.* (A) use a sieve/strainer/riddle; (B) (*auswählen*) pick and choose; **bei der Prüfung haben sie [schwer] gesiebt** (*ugs.*) they weeded out [a lot of] people in the examination

**sieben²** *Kardinalz.* ▶76, ▶752, ▶841 seven; **die ~ fetten/mageren Jahre** the seven years of plenty/lean years; **die ~ Freien Künste** the liberal arts; ⇒ *auch* **acht**

**Sieben** *die;* **~, ~en** (A) (*Ziffer*) seven; (B) (*Spielkarte*) seven; (C) (*ugs.: Bus-, Bahnlinie*) number seven; ⇒ *auch* **Acht** A, G; **böse** 1 B

**sieben·armig** *Adj.* seven-armed; **~er Leuchter** (*jüd. Rel.*) seven-branched candelabrum; menorah

**Sieben·bürgen** *(das);* **~s** Transylvania

**Sieben·eck** *das* heptagon

**sieben·eckig** *Adj.* heptagonal

**Siebener** *der;* **~s, ~** (*ugs.*) (A) (*im Lotto usw.*) seven winning numbers *pl.*; (B) ⇒ **Sieben** A, B, C

**siebenerlei** *Gattungsz.; indekl.* (A) *attr.* seven kinds *or* sorts of; seven different ‹sorts, kinds, sizes, possibilities›; (B) *subst.* seven [different] things

**sieben-, Sieben-: ~fach** *Vervielfältigungsz.* sevenfold; ⇒ *auch* **achtfach**; **~fache** *das; adj. Dekl.* **das ~fache** seven times as much; ⇒ *auch* **Achtfache**; **~gestirn** *das;* **~~s** Pleiades *pl.*; **~hundert** *Kardinalz.* ▶841 seven hundred; **~jährig** *Adj.* (A) (*7 Jahre alt*) seven-year-old *attrib.*; seven years old *pred.*; (B) (*7 Jahre dauernd*) seven-year *attrib.*; **der ~jährige Krieg** the Seven Years War; ⇒ *auch* **achtjährig**; **~köpfig** *Adj.* seven-headed ‹monster›; ‹family, committee› of seven; **~mal** *Adj.* seven times; ⇒ *auch* **achtmal**; **~malig** *Adj.* **nach ~maligem Versuch** after the seventh attempt; ⇒ *auch* **achtmalig**; **~meilen·stiefel** *Pl.* (*scherzh.*) seven-league boots; **~meilenstiefel anhaben** (*ugs. scherzh.*) have got one's seven-league boots on; **mit ~meilenstiefeln** (*ugs. scherzh.*) with giant strides; **~meter** *der* (*Hockey*) penalty [shot]; (*Hallenhandball*) penalty [throw]; **~monats·kind** *das* child born two months prematurely; **~sachen** *Pl.* (*ugs.*) **meine/deine** *usw.* **~sachen** my/your *etc.* belongings *or* (*coll.*) bits and pieces; **~schläfer** *der* (A) (*Tier*) dormouse; (B) (*volkst.: Tag*) 27 June (*rain on which is supposed to foretell rain for seven weeks*); ≈ St. Swithin's Day; **~seitig** *Adj.* seven-sided ‹figure›; seven-page ‹letter, article, etc.›; **~stöckig** *Adj.* seven-storey ‹building›; ⇒ *auch* **achtstöckig**

**siebent** ⇒ **siebt**

**siebent...** *Ordinalz.* ▶841 ⇒ **siebt...**

**sieben·tausend** *Kardinalz.* ▶841 seven thousand

**Siebente** *der/die; adj. Dekl.* ⇒ **Siebte**

**sieben·teilig** *Adj.* seven-piece ‹tool set etc.›; seven-part ‹serial›; ⇒ *auch* **achtteilig**

**siebentel** /ˈziːbn̩tl̩/ ▶841 ⇒ **siebtel**

**Siebentel** *das;* **~s, ~** ▶841 ⇒ **Siebtel**

**siebentens** *Adv.* ⇒ **siebtens**

**sieben·zehn** (*veralt., zur Verdeutlichung*) ⇒ **siebzehn**

**siebt** /ziːpt/ *in* **wir waren zu ~:** there were seven of us; ⇒ *auch* **acht²**

**siebt...** /ziːpt.../ *Ordinalz.* ▶207, ▶841 seventh; ⇒ *auch* **acht...**

**Siebte** *der/die; adj. Dekl.* seventh; ⇒ *auch* **Achte**

**siebtel** /ˈziːptl̩/ *Bruchz.* ▶841 seventh

**Siebtel** *das* (*schweiz. meist* **der**); **~s, ~:** ▶841 seventh

***siebte·mal, *siebten·mal** ⇒ **Mal¹**

**siebtens** *Adv.* seventhly

**sieb-, Sieb-: ~zehn** *Kardinalz.* ▶76, ▶752, ▶841 seventeen; **~zehn·jährig** *Adj.* (*17 Jahre alt*) seventeen-year-old *attrib.*; seventeen years old *postpos.*; (*17 Jahre dauernd*) seventeen-year *attrib.*; ⇒ *auch* **achtjährig**; **~zehnt...** *Ordinalz.* ▶207 seventeenth; **~zehntel** *das* seventeenth; **~zehn·und·vier** *das;* **~~:** vingt-et-un

**siebzig** /ˈziːptsɪç/ *Kardinalz.* ▶76, ▶841 seventy; ⇒ *auch* **achtzig**

**Siebziger¹** *der;* **~s, ~** (A) (*70-Jähriger*) seventy-year-old; (B) (*ugs.: Autobus usw.*) number seventy; (C) (*Wein*) '70 vintage

**Siebziger²** *die;* **~, ~** (*ugs.*) (A) (*Briefmarke*) seventy-pfennig/centimes *etc.* stamp; (B) (*Zigarre*) seventy-pfennig cigar; (C) *Pl.* (*ugs.: 70er-Jahre*) seventies

**Siebziger·jahre** *Pl.* ▶76, ▶207 seventies *pl.*

**siebzig·jährig** *Adj.* (*70 Jahre alt*) seventy-year-old *attrib.*; seventy years old *pred.*; (*70 Jahre dauernd*) seventy-year *attrib.*; ⇒ *auch* **achtjährig**

**siebzigst...** *Ordinalz.* ▶841 seventieth

**siech** /ziːç/ *Adj.* (*geh.*) infirm; ailing

**Siechtum** *das;* **~s** (*geh.*) [long] infirmity

**siedeln** /ˈziːdl̩n/ *itr. V.* settle

**sieden** /ˈziːdn̩/ ❶ *unr. od.* (*fachspr. nur*) *regelm. itr. V.* (*bes. südd.*) boil; **~d heiß** boiling hot. ❷ *tr. V.* (A) *unr., auch regelm.* (*bes. südd.*) boil; (B) *unr. od. regelm.* (*veralt.*) obtain ‹salt, soap, etc.› by boiling

***siedend·heiß** ⇒ **sieden** 1

**Siede-: ~punkt** *der* ▶728 (*Physik; auch fig.*) boiling point; **auf den ~punkt steigen** (*fig.*) reach boiling point; **~wasser·reaktor** *der* (*Kerntechnik*) boiling-water reactor

**Siedler** *der;* **~s, ~, Siedlerin** *die;* **~, ~nen** settler

**Siedlung** *die;* **~, ~en** (A) (*Wohngebiet*) [housing] estate; (B) (*Niederlassung*) settlement

**Siedlungs·haus** *das* house on an estate; estate house

**Sieg** /ziːk/ *der;* **~[e]s, ~e** victory, (*bes. Sport*) win (**über** + *Akk.* over); **auf ~ spielen** go for a win; **den ~ davontragen** *od.* **erringen** (*geh.*) be victorious; (*Sport*) be the winner/winners; **ein ~ der Vernunft** (*fig.*) a victory for common sense

**Siegel** /ˈziːgl̩/ *das;* **~s, ~:** seal; (*von Behörden*) stamp; (*des Gerichtsvollziehers*) bailiff's seal; **unter dem ~ der Verschwiegenheit** (*fig.*) under the seal of secrecy

**Siegel·lack** *der* sealing wax

**siegeln** *tr. V.* seal

**Siegel·ring** *der* signet ring

**siegen** *itr. V.* win; **über jmdn. ~:** gain *or* win a victory over sb.; (*bes. Sport*) win against sb.; beat sb.; **mit 2 : 0 ~** (*Sport*) win 2-0 *or* by two goals to nil

**Sieger** *der;* **~s, ~:** winner; (*Mannschaft*) winners *pl.*; (*einer Schlacht*) victor; **als ~ hervorgehen** emerge victorious (**aus** from); **zweiter ~ sein** (*Sportjargon*) be runner-up/runners-up

**Sieger·ehrung** *die* presentation ceremony; awards ceremony

**Siegerin** *die;* **~, ~nen** ⇒ **Sieger**

**Sieger-: ~macht** *die* victorious power; **~podest** *das* winners' rostrum; **~urkunde** *die* winner's certificate

**sieges-, Sieges-: ~bewusst, *~bewußt** ❶ *Adj.* confident of victory *postpos.*; (*erfolgssicher*) confident of success *postpos.*; ❷ *adv.* confident of victory; confidently; **~gewiss, *~gewiß** (*geh.*) ⇒ **~sicher**; **~göttin** *die* (*Myth.*) goddess of victory; **~palme** *die* palm [of victory]; **die ~palme davontragen** (*fig.*) carry off the palm; **~säule** *die* victory column; **~sicher** ❶ *Adj.* certain *or* confident of victory *pred.*; (*erfolgssicher*) certain *or* confident of success *pred.*; ❷ *adv.* confident of victory; ‹say, smile› confidently; **~trunken** (*geh.*) ❶ *Adj.* intoxicated *or* drunk with victory *pred.*; ❷ *adv.* intoxicated *or* drunk with victory; **~zug** *der* (*auch fig.*) triumphant progress

**sieg-, Sieg-: ~gewohnt** *Adj.* ‹army› accustomed to victory; ‹team› used to winning; **~los** *Adj.* without a victory *postpos.*; (*Sport*) without a win *postpos.*; **~reich** *Adj.* victorious; winning ‹team›; successful ‹campaign›; **nach einer ~reichen Schlacht** after winning a battle; **~treffer** *der* (*bes. Fußball*) winning goal

**sieh** /ziː/, **siehe** *Imperativ Sg. v.* **sehen**

**siehst** /ziːst/ *2. Pers. Sg. Präsens v.* **sehen**

**sieht** /ziːt/ *3. Pers. Sg. Präsens v.* **sehen**

**Siel** /ziːl/ *der od. das;* **~[e]s, ~e** (*nordd.*) (A) (*Deichschleuse*) dike sluice *or* floodgate; (B) (*Abwasserkanal*) sewer

**Siele** *die;* **~, ~n** (*veralt.*) breast harness; **in den ~n sterben** (*fig.*) die in harness

**siena** /ˈzi̯eːna/ *indekl. Adj.* sienna

**siezen** /ˈziːtsn̩/ *tr. V.* call 'Sie' (*the polite form of address*); **sich ~:** call each other 'Sie'; **sich mit jmdm. ~:** call sb. 'Sie'

**Siff** *der;* **~s** (*ugs.*) filth; muck

**siffig** *Adj.* (*ugs.*) filthy

**Sigel** /ˈziːgl̩/ *das;* **~s, ~** (*Zeichen*) logogram; (*in der Stenografie*) grammalogue; (*Kürzel*) abbreviation

**Signal** /zɪˈgnaːl/ *das;* **~s, ~e** signal; **das ~ zum Angriff geben** give the signal to attack; **~e setzen** (*fig.*) set a new direction; **das ~ steht auf „Halt"** the signal is at 'stop'

**Signal-: ~an·lage** *die* (*Verkehrsw.*) signals *pl.*; **~brücke** *die* (*Eisenb.*) [signal] gantry

**Signalement** /zɪgnaləˈmɛnt/ *das;* **~s, ~e** (*schweiz.*) personal description *or* details *pl.*

**Signal-: ~flagge** *die* (*Seew.*) signal flag; **~horn** *das* horn; hooter (*Brit.*)

**signalisieren** *tr. V.* indicate ‹danger, change, etc.›; (*fig.: übermitteln*) signal ‹message, warning, order› (+ *Dat.* to)

**Signal-: ~lampe** *die* indicator light; **~mast** *der* (A) (*Seew.*) signalling mast; (B) (*Eisenb.*) signal post *or* mast; **~wirkung** *die* knock-on effect

**Signatar·macht** /zɪgnaˈtaːɐ̯-/ *die* (*Politik*) signatory power

**Signatur** /zɪgnaˈtuːɐ̯/ *die;* **~, ~en** (A) (*Namenszeichen*) initials *pl.*; (*Kürzel*) abbreviated signature; (*des Künstlers*) autograph; (B) (*veralt.: Unterschrift*) signature; (C) (*in einer Bibliothek*) shelf mark; (D) (*auf Landkarten*) [map] symbol

**Signet** /zɪnˈjeː/ *das;* **~s, ~s** (*Buchw.*) [publisher's] imprint

**signieren** ❶ *tr. V.* sign; autograph ‹one's own work›. ❷ *itr. V.* sign *or* autograph one's work

**signifikant** /zɪgnifiˈkant/ (*geh.*) ❶ *Adj.* (A) (*wesentlich*) significant; (B) (*typisch*) characteristic, typical (**für** of). ❷ *adv.* significantly

**Signifikanz** *die;* **~** (*geh.*) significance

**Sigrist** /ˈziːgrɪst/ *der;* **~en, ~en** (*schweiz.*) sexton

**Silbe** /ˈzɪlbə/ *die;* **~, ~n** syllable; **etw. mit keiner ~ erwähnen** not say a word about sth.

**Silben-: ~rätsel** *das: puzzle in which syllables must be combined to form words;* **~trennung** *die* word division (*by syllables*)

**Silber** /ˈzɪlbɐ/ *das;* **~s** (A) (*Edelmetall, Farbe*) silver; (B) (*silbernes Gerät*) silver[ware]; (C) (*Sport: ~medaille*) silver [medal]; **sie hat schon zweimal olympisches ~ geholt** she has already won two Olympic silver medals

**silber-, Silber-: ~ader** *die* vein of silver; **~arbeit** *die* silverwork; (*Gegenstand*) piece of silverwork; **~auf·lage** *die* silver plating *no indef. art.*; **~barren** *der* silver bar *or* ingot; **~blech** *das* rolled silver; **~besteck** *das* silver cutlery; **~blick** *der* (*ugs. scherzh.*) [slight] squint; **~blond** *Adj.* silver-blond; **~distel** *die* carline thistle; **~farben, ~farbig** *Adj.* silver; **~fischchen** *das;* **~~s, ~~:** silverfish; **~fuchs** *der* silver fox; **~führend** *Adj.* ⇒ **~haltig**; **~gehalt** *der* silver content; **~geld** *das* silver; **~geschirr** *das* silver plate; silverware; **~grau** *Adj.* silver-grey; **~haar** *das* (*geh.*) silvery hair; **~haltig** *Adj.* silver-bearing; argentiferous; **~hoch·zeit** *die* silver wedding; **~kette** *die* silver necklace; **~legierung** *die* silver alloy

**Silberling** *der;* **~s, ~e** (*veralt.*) piece of silver

S

**Silber-:** **~medaille** *die* silver medal; **~mine** *die* silver mine; **~möwe** *die* herring gull; **~münze** *die* silver coin

**silbern** ❶ *Adj.* Ⓐ (*aus Silber*) silver; Ⓑ (*silberfarben*) silver; silvery ‹moonlight, shade, gleam, etc.›. ❷ *adv.* Ⓐ (*mit Silber*) ‹ornament, coat, etc.› with silver; Ⓑ ‹shine, shimmer, etc.› with a silvery lustre; Ⓒ (*wohltönend*) ‹chime etc.› with a silvery sound

**silber-, Silber-:** **~papier** *das* silver paper; **~pappel** *die* white poplar; **~schmied** *der*, **~schmiedin** *die* ▶ 159 silversmith; **~streif** *der*, **~streifen** *der* silver line *or* strip; **ein ~streifen am Horizont** (*fig.*) a ray of hope on the horizon; **~weiß** *Adj.* silvery-white; **~zwiebel** *die* ⇒ **Perlzwiebel**

**-silbig** *Adj.* -syllable

**silbrig** *Adj.* (*geh.*) silvery

**Silhouette** /zi'lu̯ɛtə/ *die;* ~, **~n** Ⓐ silhouette; Ⓑ (*Mode*) line; **mit** *od.* **in modischer ~:** with a fashionable line *or* shape

**Silicat** (*fachspr.*) ⇒ **Silikat**

**Silicium** /zi'li:t͜si̯ʊm/ *das;* **~s** silicon

**Silicon** (*fachspr.*) ⇒ **Silikon**

**Silikat** /zili'ka:t/ *das;* **~[e]s**, **~e** (*Chemie*) silicate

**Silikon** /zili'ko:n/ *das;* **~s**, **~e** (*Chemie*) silicone

**Silikose** /zili'ko:zə/ *die;* ~, **~n** (*Med.*) silicosis

**Silizium** ⇒ **Silicium**

**Silo** /'zi:lo/ *der od. das;* **~s**, **~s** silo

**Silur** /zi'lu:ɐ̯/ *das;* **~s** (*Geol.*) Siluran

**Silvaner** /zɪl'va:nɐ/ *der;* **~s**, **~:** silvaner [wine]

**Silvester** /zɪl'vɛstɐ/ *der od. das;* **~s**, **~:** New Year's Eve; **~ feiern** see the New Year in

**Silvesternacht** *die* night of New Year's Eve

**Simbabwe** /zɪm'ba:bvə/ *(das);* **~s** Zimbabwe

**Simili·stein** /'zi:mili-/ *der* (*bes. Mineralogie*) imitation stone

**Simmer·ring** Ⓦⓩ /'zɪmɐ-/ *der* (*Technik*) ring type oil seal

**Simonie** /zimo'ni:/ *die;* ~, **~n** (*kath. Kirche*) simony

**simpel** /'zɪmpl̩/ ❶ *Adj.* Ⓐ (*einfach*) simple ‹question, task›; Ⓑ (*abwertend: beschränkt*) simple-minded ‹person›; simple ‹mind›; Ⓒ (*oft abwertend: schlicht*) basic ‹toy, dress, etc.›. ❷ *adv.* Ⓐ (*einfach*) simply; Ⓑ (*abwertend: beschränkt*) in a simple-minded manner; Ⓒ (*oft abwertend: schlicht*) simply; basically

**Simpel** *der;* **~s**, ~ (*bes. südd. ugs.*) simpleton; fool; **ich ~:** fool that I am/was

**Simplex** /'zɪmplɛks/ *das;* ~, **~e** *od.* **Simplizia** /zɪm'pli:t͜si̯a/ (*Sprachw.*) simplex

**simplifizieren** *tr., itr. V.* oversimplify

**Simplizität** *die;* **~:** simplicity

**Sims** /zɪms/ *der od. das;* **~es**, **~e** ledge; sill; (*Kamin~*) mantelpiece

**Simse** /'zɪmzə/ *die;* ~, **~n** (*Bot.*) bulrush

**Simson** /'zɪmzɔn/ *(der);* **~s** Samson

**Simulant** /zimu'lant/ *der;* **~en**, **~en**, **Simulantin** *die;* ~, **~nen** malingerer

**Simulation** *die;* ~, **~en** simulation

**Simulator** /zimu'la:tɔr/ *der;* **~s**, **~en** /-'to:rən/ (*Technik*) simulator

**simulieren** ❶ *tr. V.* feign, sham ‹illness, emotion, etc.›; simulate ‹situation, condition, etc.›. ❷ *itr. V.* feign illness; pretend to be ill; **er simuliert nur** he's just putting it on

**simultan** /zimʊl'ta:n/ ❶ *Adj.* simultaneous. ❷ *adv.* simultaneously

**Simultan-:** **~dolmetschen** *das;* **~~s** simultaneous interpreting *no art.*; **~dolmetscher** *der*, **~dolmetscherin** *die* simultaneous interpreter

**Sinai·halb·insel** /'zi:nai-/ *die* Sinai Peninsula

**sind** /zɪnt/ *1. u. 3. Pers. Pl. Präsens v.* **sein**

**sine tempore** /'zi:nə 'tɛmporə/ (*Hochschulw.*) at the time stated

**Sinfonie** /zɪnfo'ni:/ *die;* ~, **~n** (*auch fig.*) symphony

**Sinfonie-:** **~konzert** *das* symphony concert; **~orchester** *das* symphony orchestra

*old spelling (see note on page 1707)

**Sinfoniker** *Pl.* (*Orchester*) symphony orchestra *sing.*

**sinfonisch** (*Musik*) ❶ *Adj.* symphonic. ❷ *adv.* symphonically

**Singapur** /'zɪŋgapu:ɐ̯/ *(das);* **~s** ▶ 700 Singapore

**Sing·drossel** *die* song thrush

**singen** /'zɪŋən/ ❶ *unr. itr. V.* Ⓐ sing; **einen ~den Tonfall haben** have a lilting cadence; Ⓑ (*salopp: vor der Polizei aussagen*) squeal (*sl.*); **jmdn. zum S~ bringen** make sb. talk; Ⓒ (*dichter. veralt.*) **von etw. ~** ‹poet, poem› sing of sth. ❷ *unr. tr. V.* Ⓐ sing ‹song, aria, contralto, tenor, etc.›; **jmds. Lob/Ruhm ~** (*fig. geh.*) sing sb.'s praises; **das kannst du ~** (*fig. ugs.*) you can bet your life on that; Ⓑ **sich heiser/müde ~:** sing until one is hoarse/tired; **jmdn. in den Schlaf ~:** sing sb. to sleep

**Single**[1] /'zɪŋl̩/ *die;* ~, **~s** (*Schallplatte*) single

**Single**[2] *der;* **~[s]**, **~s** single person; **~s** single people *no art.*

**Single**[3] *das;* **~[s]**, **~[s]** (*Badminton, Tennis*) singles *sing. or pl.*

**Sing-:** **~sang** *der* Ⓐ (*das Singen*) singsong; Ⓑ (*Melodie*) simple tune; **~spiel** *das* (*Musik*) Singspiel; **~stimme** *die* voice

**singulär** (*geh.*) ❶ *Adj.* Ⓐ rare; Ⓑ (*einzigartig*) unique; singular. ❷ *adv.* rarely

**Singular** /'zɪŋgula:ɐ̯/ *der;* **~s**, **~e** singular; **Sinto ist der ~ von** *od.* **zu Sinti** 'Sinto' is the singular of 'Sinti'

**Singularetantum** /zɪŋgula:rə'tantʊm/ *das;* **~s**, **Singulariatantum** singular-only noun

**singularisch** (*Sprachw.*) ❶ *Adj.* singular ‹form, ending›. ❷ *adv.* in the singular

**Sing·vogel** *der* songbird

**sinken** /'zɪŋkn̩/ *unr. itr. V.; mit sein* Ⓐ ‹ship, sun› sink, go down; ‹plane, balloon› descend, go down; (*geh.*) ‹leaves, snowflakes› fall; **die ~de Sonne** the setting sun; **er ist tief gesunken** (*fig.*) he has sunk low; **er wäre am liebsten in den Boden gesunken** he wished the earth would [open and] swallow him up; **ins Bett/in einen Sessel ~** (*fig.*) fall into bed/sink into a chair; **in Ohnmacht ~** (*geh.*) swoon; fall into a faint; **in Schlaf ~** (*geh.*) sink into a sleep; Ⓑ (*nieder~*) fall; **jmdm. an die Brust ~:** fall upon sb.'s breast; **den Kopf ~ lassen** let one's head drop; **der Kopf sank ihm auf die Brust** his head dropped to his chest; **auf** *od.* (*geh.*) **in die Knie ~:** sink *or* fall to one's knees; **die Hände in den Schoß ~ lassen** let one's hands drop to one's lap; Ⓒ (*niedriger werden*) ‹temperature, level› fall, drop; **das Thermometer/Barometer sinkt** the temperature is falling/the barometer is going back; Ⓓ (*an Wert verlieren*) ‹price, value› fall, go down; **in jmds. Gunst/Achtung ~:** go down in sb.'s favour/estimation; Ⓔ (*nachlassen, abnehmen*) fall; go down; ‹excitement, interest› diminish, decline; **jmds. Mut/Vertrauen sinkt** sb. loses courage/confidence; **ihre gute Laune sank** her good mood gradually disappeared

**Sinn** /zɪn/ *der;* **~[e]s**, **~e** Ⓐ sense; **den** *od.* **einen sechsten ~ [für etw.] haben** have a sixth sense [for sth.]; **seine fünf ~e nicht beisammenhaben** (*ugs.*) be not quite right in the head; Ⓑ *Pl.* (*geh.: Bewusstsein*) senses; mind *sing.*; **ihm schwanden die ~e** he lost consciousness; **nicht bei ~en sein** be out of one's senses *or* mind; **bist du noch bei ~en?** have you gone out of your mind?; have you taken leave of your senses?; **wie von ~en** as if he/she had gone out of his/her mind; Ⓒ (*Gefühl, Verständnis*) feeling; **einen ~ für Schönheit/Stil/Gerechtigkeit/Humor** *usw.* **haben** have a sense of beauty/style/justice/humour *etc.*; **er hatte wenig ~ für Familienfeste** he didn't care much for family parties; Ⓓ (*geh.: Gedanken, Denken*) mind; **er hat ganz in meinem ~ gehandelt** he acted correctly to my mind *or* my way of thinking; **das ist nach meinem ~:** I like that; I agree with that; **mir steht der ~ [nicht] danach/nach etw.** I [don't] feel like it/sth.; **sich** (*Dat.*) **etw. aus dem ~ schlagen** put [all thoughts of] sth. out of one's mind; **etw. im ~ haben** have sth. in mind; **jmdm. in den ~ kommen** come to sb.'s mind; **das will mir nicht in den ~** (*veralt.*) I simply can't understand it; Ⓔ (*geh.: Denkungsart*) mind; way of thinking; Ⓕ (*~gehalt, Bedeutung*) meaning; **im strengen/wörtlichen ~:** in the strict/literal sense; **jmds. Rede dem ~e nach wiedergeben** convey the gist of sb.'s speech; Ⓖ (*Ziel u. Zweck*) point; **der ~ des Lebens** the meaning of life; **ohne ~ sein** be pointless *or* meaningless; **ohne ~ und Verstand** without thinking [about it/them]; Ⓗ *Pl.* (*sexuelles Verlangen*) desire *sing.*; desires

**Sinn·bild** *das* symbol

**sinn·bildlich** ❶ *Adj.* symbolic. ❷ *adv.* symbolically

**sinnen** *unr. itr. V.* (*geh.*) Ⓐ (*nachdenken*) think; ponder; **sie schaute ~d aus dem Fenster** she looked thoughtfully out of the window; Ⓑ (*planen*) **auf etw.** (*Akk.*) **~:** plan *or* plot sth.; **auf Rache ~:** be out for revenge

**sinnen-, Sinnen-:** **~freude** *die* (*geh.*) joie de vivre; zest for life; **~froh** *Adj.* (*geh.*) sensuous; **~lust** *die* sensuality; **~rausch** *der* (*geh.*) [sensual] passion

**sinn·entstellend** ❶ *Adj.* which distorts/distorted the meaning *postpos., not pred.* ❷ *adv.* ‹translate, shorten› so that the *or* its meaning is distorted

**Sinnes-:** **~art** *die* disposition; **~eindruck** *der* sense impression; sensation; **~organ** *das* sense organ; sensory organ; **~täuschung** *die* trick of the senses; **~wandel** *der* change of mind *or* heart

**sinn-, Sinn-:** **~fällig** ❶ *Adj.* obvious; visible ‹expression›; ❷ *adv.* **etw. ~fällig zum Ausdruck bringen** express sth. intelligibly *or* in an easily understood way; **~gebung** /-ge:bʊŋ/ *die;* **~~**, **~~en** (*geh.*) meaning; **~gedicht** *das* (*Literaturw.*) epigram; **~gehalt** *der* ⇒ **Sinn** F; **~gemäß** ❶ *Adj.* Ⓐ **eine ~gemäße Übersetzung** a translation which conveys the general sense; Ⓑ (*folgerichtig*) logical; ❷ *adv.* Ⓐ (*inhaltlich*) **etw. ~gemäß übersetzen/wiedergeben** translate the general sense of sth./give the gist of sth.; Ⓑ (*folgerichtig*) logically

**sinnieren** *itr. V.* ponder (**über** + *Akk.* over); muse (**über** + *Akk.* [up]on)

**sinnig** *Adj.* (*meist spött. od. iron.*) clever; sensible (*iron.*)

**sinnlich** ❶ *Adj.* Ⓐ sensory ‹impression, perception, stimulus›; Ⓑ (*sexuell*) sensual ‹love, mouth›; **~es Verlangen** sexual desire; Ⓒ (*sinnenfroh*) sensuous ‹pleasure, passion›. ❷ *adv.* Ⓐ ‹perceive, understand› through the senses; **die ~ wahrnehmbare Welt** the world perceived by the senses; Ⓑ (*sexuell*) sensually; **jmdn. ~ erregen** arouse sb. sexually

**Sinnlichkeit** *die;* ~ Ⓐ sensuality; Ⓑ (*sinnliche Wahrnehmbarkeit*) sensuousness

**sinn·los** ❶ *Adj.* Ⓐ (*unsinnig*) senseless; Ⓑ (*zwecklos*) pointless; Ⓒ (*abwertend: übermäßig*) mad; wild. ❷ *adv.* Ⓐ (*unsinnig*) senselessly; Ⓑ (*zwecklos*) pointlessly; Ⓒ (*abwertend: übermäßig*) like mad (*coll.*); **~ betrunken** blind drunk; **sich ~ besaufen** (*salopp*) get completely plastered (*sl.*)

**Sinnlosigkeit** *die* Ⓐ (*Wesen, Art*) senselessness; Ⓑ (*Zwecklosigkeit*) pointlessness

**sinn-, Sinn-:** **~reich** *Adj.* Ⓐ (*zweckmäßig*) useful; Ⓑ (*tiefsinnig*) profound; **~spruch** *der* saying; **~stiftung** *die:* **~stiftung durch Kunst** the endowment of life with meaning through art; **~verwandt** *Adj.* (*Sprachw.*) synonymous ‹words›; **~verwandte Wörter** synonyms; **~voll** ❶ *Adj.* Ⓐ (*vernünftig*) sensible; Ⓑ (*mit ~ erfüllt, einen ~ ergebend*) meaningful; **dieser Satz ist nur ~voll, wenn ...** this sentence only makes sense if ...; ❷ *adv.* Ⓐ (*vernünftig*) sensibly; Ⓑ (*mit ~ erfüllt, einen ~ ergebend*) meaningfully; **~widrig** *Adj.* (*geh.*) nonsensical; **~zusammenhang** *der* context

**Sinologe** /zino'lo:gə/ *der;* **~n**, **~n** sinologist; sinologue

**Sinologie** *die;* **~:** sinology *no art.*

**Sinologin** *die;* **~, ~nen** ⇒ **Sinologe**

**sinte·mal** /'zɪntə'ma:l/ *Konj.* (*veralt.*, *noch scherzh.*) because; since

**Sinter** /'zɪntɐ/ *der;* **~s, ~:** sinter

**sintern** *tr., itr. V.* (*Technik*) sinter

**Sint·flut** /'zɪnt-/ *die* Flood; Deluge; **nach mir/uns die ~:** I/we don't care what happens after I've/we've gone

**sintflut·artig** ❶ *Adj.* torrential. ❷ *adv.* in torrents

**Sinto** /'zɪnto/ *der;* **~, Sinti** Sinte

**Sinus** /'zi:nʊs/ *der;* **~, ~** *od.* **~se** Ⓐ (*Math.*) sine; Ⓑ ▶ 471 (*Anat.*) sinus

**Sinus·kurve** *die* sine curve

**Siphon** /'zi:fõ/ *der;* **~s, ~s** Ⓐ siphon; Ⓑ (*Geruchsverschluss*) [anti-siphon] trap; Ⓒ (*österr.: Sodawasser*) soda [water]

**Sippe** /'zɪpə/ *die;* **~, ~n** Ⓐ (*Völkerk.*) sib; Ⓑ (*meist scherzh. od. abwertend: Verwandtschaft*) clan; Ⓒ (*Biol.*) species

**Sippen·haft** *die: punishment of other members of a family or group for the crimes of one member*

**Sippschaft** *die;* **~, ~en** Ⓐ (*meist abwertend: Sippe*) clan; Ⓑ (*abwertend: Gesindel*) bunch (*coll.*); crowd (*coll.*)

**Sirene** /zi're:nə/ *die;* **~, ~n** Ⓐ siren; Ⓑ (*Zool.*) sirenian

**Sirenen·geheul** *das* wail of a/the siren/of sirens

**sirren** /'zɪrən/ *itr. V.* buzz

**Sirtaki** /zɪr'ta:ki/ *der;* **~, ~s** syrtos

**Sirup** /'zi:rʊp/ *der;* **~s, ~e** syrup; (*streichfähig auch*) treacle (*Brit.*); molasses *sing.* (*Amer.*)

**Sisal** /'zi:zal/ *der;* **~s** sisal

**sistieren** /zɪs'ti:rən/ *tr. V.* (*Rechtsw.*) detain

**Sistierung** *die;* **~, ~en** (*Rechtsw.*) detention

**Sisyphus·arbeit** /'zi:zyfʊs-/ *die* Sisyphean task; never-ending task

**Sitte** /'zɪtə/ *die;* **~, ~n** Ⓐ (*Brauch*) custom; tradition; **es ist in England [nicht] ~ ...** it is [not] the custom in England ...; **die ~n und Gebräuche eines Volkes** the customs and traditions of a people; **nach alter ~:** in the traditional way *or* manner; Ⓑ (*moralische Norm*) common decency; **gegen die guten ~n verstoßen** offend [against] common decency; Ⓒ *Pl.* (*Benehmen*) manners; **das sind ja feine ~n!** (*iron.*) that's a nice way to behave! (*iron.*); Ⓓ (*ugs.: Sittenpolizei*) vice squad

**sitten-, Sitten-:** **~dezernat** *das* vice squad; **~geschichte** *die* history of life and customs; **~lehre** *die* ethics *sing.*; moral philosophy; **~los** ❶ *Adj.* immoral; ❷ *adv.* immorally; **~polizei** *die* (*volkst.*) vice squad; **~richter** *der*, **~richterin** *die* (*oft abwertend*) moralist; moralizer; **sich zum ~richter erheben** sit in moral judgement [over sb.]; **~streng** *Adj.* (*veralt.*) morally strict; puritanical; **~strolch** *der* (*Pressejargon*) [sexual] molester; **~verfall** *der* moral decline; decline in moral standards; **~widrig** ❶ *Adj.* Ⓐ (*Rechtsw.*) illegal ‹methods, advertising, etc.›; Ⓑ (*unmoralisch*) immoral ‹behaviour›; ❷ *adv.* ⇒ **1:** illegally; immorally

**Sittich** /'zɪtɪç/ *der;* **~s, ~e** parakeet

**sittlich** ❶ *Adj.* moral; **ihm fehlt die ~e Reife** he is morally immature. ❷ *adv.* morally

**Sittlichkeit** *die* morality; morals *pl.*

**Sittlichkeits-:** **~verbrechen** *das* sexual crime; **~verbrecher** *der* sex offender

**sittsam** (*veralt.*) ❶ *Adj.* Ⓐ well-behaved ‹child etc.›; decorous ‹behaviour›; Ⓑ (*keusch*) demure. ❷ *adv.* Ⓐ in a well-behaved way; Ⓑ (*keusch*) demurely

**Situation** /zitu̯a'tsi̯o:n/ *die;* **~, ~en** situation

**Situations·komik** *die* comedy deriving from a/the situation

**situiert** *Adj.* **gut/schlechter ~ [sein]** [be] well off/worse off

**Sitz** /zɪts/ *der;* **~es, ~e** Ⓐ seat; **er hat sich einen Stein als ~ ausgesucht** he picked a rock to sit on; Ⓑ (*mit Stimmrecht*) seat; **~ und Stimme haben** have a seat and a vote; Ⓒ (*Regierungs~*) seat; (*Verwaltungs~*) headquarters *sing. or pl.*; (*einer Firma*) head office; headquarters *sing. or pl.*; Ⓓ (*sitzende Haltung*) sitting position; (*beim Reiten*) seat; Ⓔ (*von Kleidungsstücken*) fit; Ⓕ **auf einen ~** (*ugs.*) in *or* at one go

**Sitz-:** **~bad** *das* sitz-bath; hip bath; **~badewanne** *die* sitz-bath; hip bath; **~bank** *die; Pl.* **~bänke** bench; **~blockade** *die* sit-down blockade; **~ecke** *die* sitting area; (*Möbelstück*) corner seating unit

**sitzen** *unr. itr. V.; südd., österr., schweiz. mit sein* Ⓐ sit; **eine ~de Lebensweise** a sedentary life; **bleiben Sie bitte ~:** please don't get up; please remain seated; **er saß den ganzen Tag an der Schreibmaschine/in der Kneipe** he spent the whole day at the typewriter/in the pub (*Brit.*); **auf der Anklagebank ~:** be in the dock; **er sitzt noch bei Tisch** *od.* **beim Essen** he is still eating *or* having his meal; **ich habe stundenlang beim Friseur ~ müssen** I had to spend hours at the hairdresser's; **im Sattel ~:** be in the saddle; **er sitzt viel über den Büchern** he spends a lot of time sitting over his books; **auf etw.** (*Dat.*) **~** (*salopp: etw. nicht hergeben*) hang on to sth.; not let go of sth.; **jmdm. auf der Pelle** *od.* **dem Pelz ~** (*salopp*) keep bothering sb.; keep on at sb. (*coll.*); Ⓑ (*sein*) be; **die Firma sitzt in Berlin** the firm is based in Berlin; **die Tür sitzt schief in den Angeln** the door is not hanging straight; **der Schreck sitzt ihr noch in den Gliedern** she is still suffering from the shock; **einen ~ haben** (*salopp*) have had one too many; **etw. nicht auf sich** (*Dat.*) **~ lassen** not take sth.; not stand for sth.; Ⓒ ([*gut*] *passen*) fit; **die Krawatte sitzt nicht** the tie isn't straight; Ⓓ (*ugs.: gut eingeübt sein*) **Lektionen so oft wiederholen, bis sie ~:** keep on repeating lessons till they stick (*coll.*); **wir hatten so lange geübt, bis jede Schrittkombination wie im Schlafe saß** we had practised till we could do every step in our sleep; Ⓔ (*ugs.: wirksam treffen*) hit home; Ⓕ (*Mitglied sein*) be, sit (**in** + *Dat.* on); Ⓖ (*ugs.: eingesperrt sein*) be in prison *or* (*sl.*) inside; Ⓗ (*ugs.*) **~ bleiben** (*nicht versetzt werden*) stay down [a year]; have to repeat a year; (*abwertend: als Frau unverheiratet bleiben*) be left on the shelf; **auf etw.** (*Dat.*) **~ bleiben** (*etw. nicht verkaufen können*) be left *or* (*coll.*) stuck with sth.; **jmdn. ~ lassen** (*vergeblich warten lassen*) stand sb. up (*coll.*); (*im Stich lassen*) leave sb. in the lurch; (*nicht heiraten*) jilt sb.; **er hat Frau und Kinder ~ lassen** he left his wife and children

***sitzen|bleiben** ⇒ **sitzen** H

**Sitzenbleiber** *der;* **~s, ~, Sitzenbleiberin** *die;* **~, ~nen** (*ugs. abwertend*) pupil repeating a year; pupil who has to repeat a year

***sitzen|lassen** ⇒ **sitzen** B, H

**Sitz-:** **~erhöhung** *die* booster cushion; booster seat; **~fleisch** *das* (*ugs. scherzh.*) **kein ~fleisch haben** not have the staying power; not be able to stick at it; (*nicht stillsitzen können*) not be able to sit still; **~gelegenheit** *die* seat; **~gruppe** *die* group of seats; **~kissen** *das* (*im Sessel, Sofa*) [seat] cushion; (*auf dem Fußboden*) [floor] cushion; **~ordnung** *die* seating plan *or* arrangement; **~platz** *der* seat; **~riese** *der* (*ugs. scherzh.*): *person who looks tall when sitting down;* **~rohr** *das* seat tube; saddle tube; **~stange** *die* perch; **~streik** *der* sit-down strike

**Sitzung** *die;* **~, ~en** Ⓐ meeting; (*Parlaments~*) sitting; session; Ⓑ (*beim Zahnarzt*) visit; (*beim Psychotherapeuten*) session; (*ugs. scherzh.: Toilettenbesuch*) session; Ⓒ (*das Porträtsitzen*) sitting

**Sitzungs-:** **~bericht** *der* minutes *pl.*; **~periode** *die* session; **~saal** *der* conference hall; (*eines Gerichts*) courtroom; **~zimmer** *das* conference room

**sixtinisch** /zɪks'ti:nɪʃ/ *Adj.* Sistine

**Sizilianer** /zitsi'li̯a:nɐ/ *der;* **~s, ~, Sizilianerin** *die;* **~, ~nen** Sicilian; ⇒ *auch* **-in**

**sizilianisch** /zitsi'li̯a:nɪʃ/ *Adj.* Sicilian

**Sizilien** /zi'tsi:li̯ən/ (*das*); **~s** Sicily

**Skala** /'ska:la/ *die;* **~, Skalen** Ⓐ (*Maßeinteilung, Musik*) scale; Ⓑ (*Reihe*) range

**Skalar** *der;* **~s, ~s** (*Math., Physik*) scalar

**Skalde** /'skaldə/ *der;* **~n, ~n** skald

**Skalden·dichtung** *die* skaldic poetry

**Skalp** /skalp/ *der;* **~s, ~e** scalp

**Skalpell** /skal'pɛl/ *das;* **~s, ~e** scalpel

**skalpieren** *tr. V.* scalp

**Skandal** /skan'da:l/ *der;* **~s, ~e** Ⓐ scandal; Ⓑ (*bes. nordd.: Lärm*) row (*coll.*)

**Skandal-:** **~geschichte** *die* [piece of] scandal; **~nudel** *die* (*ugs.*) **sie ist eine ~nudel** she is always involved in some scandal or other

**skandalös** *Adj.* scandalous

**skandieren** /skan'di:rən/ *tr. V.* Ⓐ chant; Ⓑ (*Verslehre*) scan

**Skandinavien** /skandi'na:vi̯ən/ (*das*); **~s** Scandinavia

**Skandinavier** /skandi'na:vi̯ɐ/ *der;* **~s, ~, Skandinavierin** *die;* **~, ~nen** Scandinavian; ⇒ *auch* **-in**

**skandinavisch** *Adj.* Scandinavian

**Skarabäus** /skara'bɛ:ʊs/ *der;* **~, Skarabäen** scarab

**Skat** /ska:t/ *der;* **~[e]s, ~e** *od.* **~s** skat; **~ dreschen** *od.* **klopfen** (*salopp*) play skat

**Skat·blatt** *das* skat pack (*Brit.*) *or* (*Amer.*) deck

**Skateboard** /'skeɪtbɔ:d/ *das;* **~s, ~s** skateboard

**skateboarden** /'skeɪtbɔ:dn̩/ *itr. V.; mit sein* skateboard

**Skateboarder** /'skeɪtbɔ:dɐ/ *der;* **~s, ~:** skateboarder

**skaten** *itr. V.* Ⓐ (*ugs.*) play skat Ⓑ *mit sein* skate

**Skater** /'skeɪtɐ/ *der;* **~s, ~:** skater

**Skat·spieler** *der*, **Skat·spielerin** *die* skat player

**Skeet·schießen** /'ski:t-/ *das;* **~s** (*Sport*) skeet [shooting] *no art.*

**Skelett** /ske'lɛt/ *das;* **~[e]s, ~e** skeleton; **er ist nur noch ein ~** *od.* **das reinste ~:** he is little more than a skeleton

**Skelett·bauweise** *die* (*Bauw.*) skeleton construction

**Skepsis** /'skɛpsɪs/ *die;* **~:** scepticism

**Skeptiker** *der;* **~s, ~, Skeptikerin** *die;* **~, ~nen** sceptic

**skeptisch** ❶ *Adj.* sceptical. ❷ *adv.* sceptically

**Skeptizismus** *der;* **~:** scepticism

**Sketch** /skɛtʃ/ *der;* **~[es], ~e[s]** *od.* **~s** sketch

**Ski** /ʃi:/ *der;* **~s, ~er** *od.* **~:** ski; **~ laufen** *od.* **fahren** ski; **er läuft** *od.* **fährt gut ~:** he is a good skier; **~ Heil!** ski heil!; good skiing!

**Ski-:** **~bindung** *die* ski binding; **~bob** *der* ski-bob; **~fliegen** *das;* **~~s, ~flug** *der* ski flying *no art.*; **~haserl** *das;* **~~s, ~~n** (*südd., österr. scherzh.*) [girl] skier; **~lauf** *der*, **~laufen** *das;* **~~s** skiing *no art.*; **~läufer** *der*, **~läuferin** *die* skier; **~lehrer** *der*, **~lehrerin** *die* ski instructor; **~lift** *der* ski lift

**Skinhead** /'skɪnhɛd/ *der;* **~s, ~s** skinhead

**Ski-:** **~springen** *das;* **~~s** ski jumping *no art.*; **~springer** *der*, **~springerin** *die* ski jumper; **~stiefel** *der* ski boot; **~stock** *der* skistick; ski pole; **~zirkus** *der* (*Sportjargon*) ski circus

**Skizze** /'skɪtsə/ *die;* **~, ~n** Ⓐ (*Zeichnung*) sketch; Ⓑ (*Konzept*) outline; Ⓒ (*kurze Aufzeichnung*) [brief] account

**Skizzen·block** *der; Pl.* **~s** *od.* **Skizzen·blöcke** sketch pad; sketch block

**skizzen·haft** ❶ *Adj.* rough ‹drawing, outline›. ❷ *adv.* roughly

**skizzieren** *tr. V.* Ⓐ (*zeichnen*) sketch; Ⓑ (*aufzeichnen*) outline; Ⓒ (*entwerfen*) draft

**Sklave** /'skla:və/ *der;* **~n, ~n** slave; **jmdn. zum ~n machen** make a slave of sb.; **er ist der ~ seiner Gewohnheiten** (*fig. abwertend*) he is a slave to habit

S

**Sklaven-: ~arbeit** *die* **A** slavery *no art.*; work as slaves *no art.*; **B** *(abwertend: schwere Arbeit)* drudgery *no art.*; **~halter** *der*, **~halterin** *die* slave owner; **~halter·gesellschaft** *die (bes. marx.)* slave-owning society; **~händler** *der*, **~händlerin** *die (auch fig. abwertend)* slave trader

**Sklaverei** *die;* ~ **A** *(auch fig. abwertend)* slavery *no art.*; **B** *(oft abwertend: harte Arbeit)* drudgery *no art.*

**Sklavin** *die;* ~, **~nen** ⇒ **Sklave**; ⇒ *auch* **-in**

**sklavisch** /'skla:vɪʃ/ *(abwertend)* ❶ *Adj.* slavish. ❷ *adv.* slavishly

**Sklerose** /skle'ro:zə/ *die;* ~, **~n** ▶ 474 *(Med.)* sclerosis *no art.*

**skontieren** /skɔn'ti:rən/ *tr. V. (Kaufmannsspr.)* **eine Rechnung ~:** allow a [cash] discount on a bill

**Skonto** /'skɔnto/ *der od. das;* **~s**, **~s** *(Kaufmannsspr.)* [cash] discount; **bei Barzahlung binnen 10 Tagen gewähren wir 3% ~ auf den Rechnungsbetrag** we allow a 3% discount if payment is made in cash within ten days

**Skooter** /'sku:tɐ/ *der;* **~s**, **~:** dodgem; bumper car

**Skorbut** /skɔr'bu:t/ *der;* **~[e]s** ▶ 474 *(Med.)* scurvy *no art.*

**Skorpion** /skɔr'pio:n/ *der;* **~s**, **~e** **A** *(Tier)* scorpion; **B** *(Astrol.)* Scorpio; ⇒ *auch* **Fisch**

**Skribent** /skri'bɛnt/ *der;* **~en**, **~en**, **Skribentin** *die;* ~, **~nen** *(veralt. abwertend)* scribbler

**Skript** /skrɪpt/ *das;* **~[e]s**, **~en** *od.* **~s** script; *(Manuskript)* manuscript

**Skript·girl** *das* ▶ 159 *(Film)* script girl

**Skriptum** /'skrɪptʊm/ *das;* **~s**, **Skripten** *od.* **Skripta** *(österr., sonst veralt.)* manuscript

**Skrotum** /'skro:tʊm/ *das;* **~s**, **Skrota** ▶ 471 *(Anat.)* scrotum

**Skrupel** /'skru:pl̩/ *der;* **~s**, **~:** scruple; **~ haben** *od.* **kennen** have scruples

**skrupel·los** *(abwertend)* ❶ *Adj.* unscrupulous. ❷ *adv.* unscrupulously

**Skrupellosigkeit** *die;* ~ *(abwertend)* unscrupulousness

**skrupulös** /skrupu'lø:s/ *Adj. (veralt.)* scrupulous

**Skull** /skʊl/ *das;* **~s**, **~s** *(Seemannsspr., Rudersport)* scull

**skullen** *itr. V.; auch mit sein (Seemannsspr., Rudersport)* scull

**Skulptur** /skʊlp'tu:ɐ̯/ *die;* ~, **~en** sculpture

**skurril** /skʊ'ri:l/ ❶ *Adj.* absurd; droll ‹person›. ❷ *adv.* absurdly

**Skurrilität** *die;* ~, **~en** absurdity

**S-Kurve** /'ɛs-/ *die* S-bend; double bend

**Slalom** /'sla:lɔm/ *der;* **~s**, **~s** *(Ski-, Kanusport)* slalom; **im ~ fahren** *(fig.)* zigzag

**Slang** /slæŋ/ *der;* **~s** **A** *(oft abwertend: Umgangssprache)* slang; **B** *(Jargon)* jargon

**s-Laut**, ***S-Laut** /'ɛs-/ *der (stimmlos)* s-sound; *(stimmhaft)* z-sound

**Slawe** /'sla:və/ *der;* **~n**, **~n**, **Slawin** *die;* ~, **~nen** Slav; ⇒ *auch* **-in**

**slawisch** *Adj.* ▶ 696 Slav[ic]; Slavonic

**Slawist** *der;* **~en**, **~en** Slavicist; Slavist

**Slawistik** *die;* **~:** Slavonic studies *pl., no art.*

**Slawistin** *die;* ~, **~nen** ⇒ **Slawist**

**Slibowitz** /'sli:bovɪts/ *der;* **~[es]**, **~e** slivovitz

**Slip** /slɪp/ *der;* **~s**, **~s** briefs *pl.*

**Slipper** *der;* **~s**, **~[s]** slip-on [shoe]

**Slogan** /'slo:gn̩/ *der;* **~s**, **~s** slogan

**Slowake** /slo'va:kə/ *der;* **~n**, **~n** ▶ 553 Slovak

**Slowakei** *die;* **~:** Slovakia *no art.*

**Slowakin** *die;* ~, **~nen** ▶ 553 Slovak

**slowakisch** *Adj.* ▶ 553, ▶ 696 Slovak; Slovakian

**Slowene** /slo've:nə/ *der;* **~n**, **~n** Slovene; Slovenian

*old spelling (see note on page 1707)

**Slowenien** *(das);* **~s** Slovenia

**Slowenin** *die;* ~, **~nen** Slovene; Slovenian

**Slowenisch** *das;* **~en** ▶ 696 Slovene; Slovenian; ⇒ *auch* **Deutsch**

**Slow·fox** /'slo:fɔks/ *der* slow foxtrot

**Slum** /slam/ *der;* **~s**, **~s** slum

**Smaragd** /sma'rakt/ *der;* **~[e]s**, **~e** emerald

**Smaragd·eidechse** *die* green lizard

**smaragden** *Adj.* emerald

**smaragd·grün** *Adj.* emerald green

**smart** /sma:ɐ̯t/ *Adj.* smart

**Smog** /smɔk/ *der;* **~[s]**, **~s** smog

**Smog·alarm** *der* smog warning; **bei ~:** if there is a smog warning

**Smoking** /'smo:kɪŋ/ *der;* **~s**, **~s** dinner jacket *or (Amer.)* tuxedo and dark trousers

**Smutje** /'smʊtjə/ *der;* **~s**, **~s** *(Seemannsspr.)* ship's cook

**Snob** /snɔp/ *der;* **~s**, **~s** *(abwertend)* snob

**Snobismus** *der;* ~ *(abwertend)* snobbery; snobbishness

**snobistisch** *Adj. (abwertend)* snobbish

**Snowboard** /'snoʊbɔ:d/ *das;* **~s**, **~s** snowboard

**snowboarden** /'snoʊbɔ:dn̩/ *itr. V.; mit sein* snowboard

**Snowboarder** /'snoʊbɔ:dɐ/ *der;* **~s**, **~:** snowboarder

**so** /zo:/ ❶ *Adv.* **A** *(auf diese Weise; in, von dieser Art)* like this/that; this/that way; **schreibe den Brief so, wie ich es dir gesagt habe** write the letter as I told you; **er hat sich nicht so verhalten, wie allgemein erwartet wurde** he did not behave in the way that was generally expected; **ihr sollt alles so lassen, wie es ist** you are to leave everything the way it is; **wenn du es so nennen willst** if you want to call it that; **die so genannte Rechtschreibreform** the so-called spelling reform; **so ist sie nun einmal** that's the way she is; **ist das [wirklich] so?** is that [really] true?; **so?** really?; **wenn dem so ist** if that's the case; **sei doch nicht so** don't be like that; **ich will [mal] nicht so sein** I don't want to be awkward; **so ist das!** *(resigniert)* that's the way it goes!; that's how it goes!; **so ist es!** *(zustimmend)* that's correct *or* right!; **ach, so ist das!** *(begreifend)* oh, I 'see!; **so, so** *(meist iron.)* oh, I 'see! **recht so!, gut so!** right!; that's fine!; **mir ist so, als ob ...** I have a feeling that ...; **so kann es einem gehen, wenn ...** that's what can happen if ...; **und das kam so** and this is what happened; and it happened like this; **du musst dich entscheiden, so oder so** you must make up your mind one way or the other; **so oder so gerät der Minister unter Druck** either way the minister will come under pressure; **weiter so!** carry on in the same way!; **die Religion, so** *(so sagt/schreibt)* **Marx, ist ...** religion, according to Marx is ...; **„die Ausgaben", so** *(so sagte)* **der Minister, „..."** 'the expenditure', said the minister *or* the minister said, '...'; **B** *(in dem Maße, Grade; überaus)* so; **eine so große Frau** such a big woman; **er ist nicht so dumm, das zu tun** he is not so stupid as to do that; **er ist [nicht] so groß wie du** he is [not] as tall as you [are]; **so weiß wie Schnee** as white as snow; **so viel wie** *od.* **als** as much as; **das war so viel wie eine Zusage** that was tantamount to a commitment; **das ist so viel wie gar nichts** this is almost nothing; **nimm, so viel [wie] du willst** take as much as you like; **noch einmal so viel** the same again; **halb/doppelt so viel** half/twice as much; **so viel für heute** *(ugs.)* that's all *or* enough for today; **wo wenig wie** *od.* **als möglich** as little as possible; **ich kann es so wenig wie du** I can't do it any more than you can; **so weit** *(im großen Ganzen)* by and large; on the whole; *(bis jetzt)* up to now; **so weit wie** *od.* **als möglich** as far as possible; **so weit sein** *(ugs.)* be ready; **es ist so weit** the time has come; **so gut es geht** as best I/he *etc.* can; **so gut ich konnte** as best I could; **sei doch nicht so laut!** don't make such a noise!; **reg dich doch nicht so auf!** don't get so worked up!; **was schreist du so?** why are you yelling like that?; **so... [wie...]** as... [as...]; **so bald wie möglich** as soon as possible; **fast so groß wie...** almost as tall as...; **du weißt so gut wie ich, dass...** you know as well as I do that...; **er ist ja so nett!** he's so nice!; **C** *(ugs.: solch...)* such; **so ein Mann/so eine Frau/so ein Kind** such a man/woman/child; **ein so schönes Fest** such a lovely party; **so ein Pech/eine Frechheit!** what bad luck/a cheek!; **so ein Idiot!** what an idiot!; **hast du so etwas schon mal gesehen?** have you ever seen such a thing *or* anything like it?; **so etwas kann passieren** such things *pl.* can happen; **so etwas ist mir noch nie passiert** a thing like that has never *or* nothing like that has ever happened to me before; **so was von fett habe ich noch nie gesehen** I've never seen anyone so fat; **die Suppe war so was von ekelhaft** the soup was absolutely disgusting; **er ist so was von dämlich** he is so stupid; **so was von dämlich!** talk about stupidity! *(coll.)*; **ist sie nicht Kontoristin oder so was?** isn't she a clerk or something?; **[na** *od.* **nein** *od.* **also] so was!** *(überrascht/empört)* well, I never!; **so etwas Schönes** something as beautiful as that; such a beautiful thing; **und so was nennt** *od.* **schimpft sich Wissenschaft/Mutter** and they call that science/she calls herself a mother; **so einer/eine/eins** one like that; one of those; **mit so einer würde ich mich nicht einlassen** I wouldn't get mixed up with that sort of woman *or* a woman of that sort; **so einer** *od.* **jemand wie Schmidt** somebody like Schmidt; **Ein Grahambrötchen? — Nein, so eins** A granary roll? — No, one of those *or* one like that; **das ist so ein** *od.* **so'n kleiner Dicker** *(ugs.)* he's a little fat man; **so nennt man das also** so 'that's what it's called; **so einer bist du also!** so 'that's the sort of person you are!; **Banker und so** bankers and people like that; **heißt sie nicht Karobowski oder so [ähnlich]?** isn't her name Karobowski or something like that?; **ich spiele ein bisschen Tischtennis, Billard und so** I play a bit of table tennis, billiards and that sort of thing; **D** *(ugs.: ungefähr)* about; **so [um die** *od.* **an die** *od.* **etwa** *od.* **ungefähr] 50 Mark** about 50 marks; **E** *(ugs.: ohne etw. Bestimmtes)* **ich brauche keine Leiter, da komme ich auch so ran** I don't need a ladder, I can reach it [without one]; **geht es so, oder soll ich Ihnen eine Tüte geben?** can you manage, or shall I give you a bag?; **Nimmst du Zucker zum Kaffee? — Nein, ich trinke ihn so** do you take sugar in coffee? — no, without; **du kannst sie kochen oder einfach so essen** you can cook it or eat it raw *or* just as it is; **die können Sie so** *(ohne sie zu bezahlen)* **mitnehmen** you can take these — they're free; **kosten die was oder kriegt man die so?** do you have to pay for them, or are they free?; **Warum fragst du? — Ach nur so** *(ohne einen bestimmten Grund)* Why do you ask? — Oh, no particular reason.

❷ *Konj.* **A** **so dass** ⇒ **sodass**; **B** *(konzessiv)* however; **so sehr ich ihn auch immer unterstützt habe, dieses Mal kann ich ihm nicht helfen** however much I have always supported him, this time I can't help him ; **so Leid es mir tut, ich muss absagen** much as I regret it, I'll have to cry off; **C** *(geh.: wenn, falls)* **so Gott will** God willing.

❸ *Partikel* **A** **wie ich so ging, da sah ich ...** I was just walking along, when I saw ...; **ich weiß nicht so recht, ob ich gehen soll** I'm not really sure if I should go; **ach, das hab ich nur so gesagt** oh, I didn't mean anything by that; **das ist mir nur so rausgerutscht** *(ugs.)* it just slipped out; **wie ist der neue Chef denn so?** *(ugs.)* what's the new boss like, then? *(coll.)*; **er schlug die Tür zu, dass es nur so knallte** he slammed the door shut; **B** *(eine Zäsur ausdrückend)* right; OK; **so, und nun?** right, [and] now what?; **C** *(in Aufforderungen verstärkend)* **so halt doch endlich deinen Mund!** just hold your tongue, will you!; **so**

**komm doch** come on now; **so glaub mir doch** you must believe me

**So.** *Abk.* **Sonntag** Sun.

**s. o.** *Abk.* **siehe oben**

**SO** *Abk.* ▶ **400** **Südost[en]** SE

**sobald** *Konj.* as soon as

**Söckchen** /'zœkçən/ *das;* ~**s**, ~ (A) [little] sock; (B) *(Damen-, Kinderstrumpf)* [short] sock; ankle sock

**Socke** /'zɔkə/ *die;* ~, ~**n** sock; **sich auf die** ~**n machen** *(ugs.)* get going; **von den** ~**n sein** *(ugs.)* be flabbergasted

**Sockel** /'zɔkl/ *der;* ~**s**, ~ (A) *(einer Säule, Statue)* plinth; (B) *(unterer Teil eines Hauses, Schrankes)* base; (C) *(Elektrot.)* base

**Sockel·betrag** *der (Wirtsch.)* basic sum

**Socken** *der;* ~**s**, ~ *(südd., österr., schweiz.)* ⇒ **Socke**

**Socken·halter** *der* [sock] suspender

**Soda** /'zo:da/ *die;* ~ *od. das;* ~**s** soda

**so·dann** *Adv.* (A) *(danach)* then; thereupon; (B) *(außerdem)* and furthermore

**so·dass**, ***sodaß** *Konj.* so that; **er war krank,** ~ **er die Reise verschieben musste** he was sick, [and] so he had to postpone the trip

**Soda·wasser** *das; Pl.* **Sodawässer** soda; soda water

**Sod·brennen** *das;* ~**s** heartburn; pyrosis

**Sodom** /'zo:dɔm/ *das;* ~**:** Sodom; ~ **und Gomorrha** Sodom and Gomorrah

**Sodomie** *die;* ~**:** sodomy *no art.*

**sodomitisch** *Adj.* sodomitic[al]

**so·eben** *Adv.* just; **die Nachricht kam** ~**:** the news came just now

**Sofa** /'zo:fa/ *das;* ~**s**, ~**s** sofa; settee

**Sofa·kissen** *das* [sofa] cushion; scatter cushion

**so·fern** *Konj.* provided [that]

**soff** /zɔf/ *1. u. 3. Pers. Sg. Prät. v.* **saufen**

**so·fort** *Adv.* immediately; at once; **er war** ~ **tot** he died instantly; **komm** ~ **her!** come here this instant *or* at once!; **diese Regelung gilt ab** ~**:** this ruling has immediate effect *or* takes effect immediately; **Ingenieure ab** ~ **gesucht** engineers required, should be ready to start immediately; **ich bin** ~ **fertig** I'll be ready in a moment; *(mit einer Arbeit)* I'll be finished in a moment; **[ich] komme** ~**:** [I'm] just coming; *(Bedienung)* I'll be right with you

**Sofort·bild·kamera** *die (Fot.)* instant-picture camera

**Sofort·hilfe** *die* emergency relief *or* aid

**sofortig** *Adj. (unmittelbar)* immediate

**Sofort·maß·nahme** *die* immediate measure

**Soft·eis**, ***Soft-Eis** /'zɔft|ais/ *das* soft ice cream

**Softie** /'zɔfti/ *der;* ~**s**, ~**s** *(ugs.)* softy

**Software** /'zɔftvɛ:ɐ̯/ *die;* ~, ~**s** *(DV)* software

**sog** /zo:k/ *1. u. 3. Pers. Sg. Prät. v.* **saugen**

**Sog** *der;* ~**[e]s**, ~**e** (A) *(saugende Strömung)* suction; *(bei Schiffen)* wake; *(bei Fahr-, Flugzeugen)* slipstream; *(von Wasser, auch fig.)* current; (B) *(Meeresk.)* undertow

**sog.** *Abk.* **so genannt**

**so·gar** *Adv.* even; **sie ist krank,** ~ **schwer krank** she is ill, in fact *or* indeed seriously ill

***so·genannt** ⇒ **so** 1 A

**so·gleich** *Adv.* immediately; at once

**Sohle** /'zo:lə/ *die;* ~, ~**n** (A) *(Schuh~)* sole; **eine kesse** *od.* **heiße** ~ **aufs Parkett legen** *(ugs.)* put up a good show on the dance floor; **auf leisen** ~**n** softly; noiselessly; (B) *(Fuß~)* sole [of the foot]; **auf** *od.* **mit nackten** ~**n** barefoot; with bare feet; (C) *(Tal~)* bottom; *(eines Flusses)* bottom; bed; (D) *(Bergmannsspr.)* level; *(Gruben~)* floor; (E) *(Einlege~)* insole

**sohlen** *tr. V.* sole

**Sohn** /zo:n/ *der;* ~**es**, **Söhne** /'zø:nə/ (A) *(männlicher Nachkomme)* son; **der** ~ **Gottes** the Son of God; **der verlorene** ~**:** the prodigal son; (B) *(fam.: Anrede an einen Jüngeren)* son; boy

**Söhnchen** /'zø:nçən/ *das;* ~**s**, ~**:** little son; little boy

**Sohne·mann** *der (fam.)* son

**soigniert** /zo̯an'ji:ɐ̯t/ *Adj. (geh.)* soigné ‹man, appearance›; soignée ‹woman›

**Soiree** /zo̯a're:/ *die;* ~, ~**n** *(geh.)* soirée

**Soja-** /'zo:ja-/: ~**bohne** *die* soy[a] bean; ~**soße** *die* soy[a] sauce

**Sokrates** /'zo:kratɛs/ *(der);* **Sokrates'** Socrates

**Sokratiker** /zo'kra:tikɐ/ *der;* ~**s**, ~, **Sokratikerin** *die;* ~, ~**nen** Socratic

**sokratisch** *Adj.* Socratic

**Sol** *das;* ~**s**, ~**e** *(Chemie)* sol

**so·lang[e]** *Konj.* so *or* as long as; ~ **du nicht alles aufgegessen hast** unless *or* until you have eaten everything up

**solar** /zo'la:ɐ̯/ *Adj.* solar

**Solar-:** ~**batterie** *die (Elektrot.)* solar battery; ~**energie** *die (Physik)* solar energy

**Solarium** /zo'la:ri̯ʊm/ *das;* ~**s**, **Solarien** /...i̯ən/ solarium

**Solar-:** ~**kraftwerk** *das* ⇒ **Sonnenkraftwerk**; ~**plexus** /-plɛksʊs/ *der;* ~~, ~~ /-plɛksu:s/ ▶ **471** *(Anat.)* solar plexus; ~**technik** *die (Energietechnik)* solar technology *no art.*; ~**zelle** *die (Physik, Elektrot.)* solar cell

**Sol·bad** *das* (A) *(Kurort)* saltwater spa; (B) *(Bad)* saltwater bath; brine bath

**solch** /zɔlç/ *Demonstrativpron.* (A) *attr.* such; ~**e Leute** such people; people like that; **[ein]** ~**er Glaube** such a belief; **ich habe** ~**en Hunger** I am so hungry; **ich habe** ~**e Kopfschmerzen** I've got such a headache; **das macht** ~**en Spaß!** it's so much fun!; (B) *selbstständig* ~**e wie die** people like that; **sie ist keine** ~**e** she is not like that; **die Sache als** ~**e** the thing as such; **es gibt** ~**e und** ~**e** *(ugs.)* it takes all sorts *or* kinds [to make a world]; **Ärzte gibt es** ~**e und** ~**e** there are doctors and doctors; (C) *ungebeugt (geh.: so [ein])* such; **bei** ~ **einem herrlichen Wetter** when the weather is so beautiful

**solcher-:** ~**art** ❶ *indekl. Demonstrativpron.* such; ❷ *Adv.* thus; ~**gestalt** *Adv.* thus; in such a way

**solcherlei** *indekl. Adj.;* ⇒ **derlei**

**solcher·maßen** *Adv.* in such a way; in this way; *(in solchem Grade)* to such an extent

**Sold** /zɔlt/ *der;* ~**[e]s**, ~**e** (A) *(veralt.)* pay; **in jmds.** ~ **stehen** be in the pay of sb. *or* sb.'s pay; **im** ~**e des Kaisers stehen** be in the service of the emperor; (B) ⇒ **Wehrsold**

**Soldat** /zɔl'da:t/ *der;* ~**en**, ~**en** ▶ **159** soldier; ~ **auf Zeit** soldier serving for a fixed period

**Soldaten-:** ~**fried·hof** *der* military *or* war cemetery; ~**sprache** *die* army *or* soldiers' slang

**Soldatin** *die;* ~, ~**nen** ▶ **159** [female *or* woman] soldier; **sie ist** ~**:** she is a soldier

**soldatisch** ❶ *Adj.* military ‹discipline, expression, etc.›; soldierly ‹figure, virtue›. ❷ *adv.* in a military *or* soldierly manner

**Sold·buch** *das (hist.)* [military] pay-book

**Söldner** /'zœldnɐ/ *der;* ~**s**, ~**:** mercenary

**Söldner·heer** *das* mercenary army; army of mercenaries

**Söldnerin** *die;* ~, ~**nen** mercenary

**Söldner·truppe** *die* mercenary force; force of mercenaries

**Sole** /'zo:lə/ *die;* ~, ~**n** salt water; brine

**Sol·ei** *das* pickled egg

**solid** /zo'li:t/ ⇒ **solide**

**Solidar·gemeinschaft** *die* mutually supportive group; *(die Gesellschaft)* caring society

**solidarisch** ❶ *Adj.* ~**es Verhalten zeigen** show one's solidarity; **sich mit jmdm.** ~ **erklären** declare one's solidarity with sb. ❷ *adv.* ~ **handeln/sich** ~ **verhalten** act in/show solidarity

**solidarisieren** *refl. V.* show [one's] solidarity

**Solidarität** *die;* ~**:** solidarity

**Solidaritäts·streik** *der* solidarity strike

**solide** ❶ *Adj.* (A) *(massiv, gediegen)* solid ‹rock, wood, house›; sturdy ‹shoes, shed, material, fabric›; solid, sturdy ‹furniture›; [good-]quality ‹goods›; (B) *(gut fundiert)* sound ‹work, workmanship, education, knowledge›; solid ‹firm, business›; (C) *(anständig)* respectable ‹person, life, occupation, profession›. ❷ *adv.* (A) *(gediegen)* solidly ‹built›; sturdily ‹made›; (B) *(gut fundiert)* soundly ‹educated, constructed›; (C) *(anständig)* ‹live› respectably, steadily

**Solidität** *die;* ~ ⇒ **solide** 1 A-C: solidness; sturdiness; soundness; respectability

**Solipsismus** /zolɪ'psɪsmʊs/ *der;* ~ *(Philos.)* solipsism *no art.*

**Solist** /zo'lɪst/ *der;* ~**en**, ~**en**, **Solistin** *die;* ~, ~**nen** soloist

**solistisch** *Adj.* solo

**Solitär** /zoli'tɛ:ɐ̯/ *der;* ~**s**, ~**e** solitaire

**soll** *1. u. 3. Pers. Sg. Präsens v.* **sollen**

**Soll** /zɔl/ *das;* ~**[s]**, ~**[s]** (A) *(Kaufmannsspr., Bankw.: Schulden)* debit; ~ **und Haben** debit and credit; **im** ~**:** in debit; (B) *(Kaufmannsspr.: linke Buchführungsseite)* debit side; **etw. im** ~ **verbuchen** enter sth. on the debit side; (C) *(Wirtsch.: Arbeits~)* quota; **sein** ~ **erfüllen** *od.* **erreichen** achieve *or* meet one's target; (D) *(Wirtsch.: Plan~)* quota; target

**Soll·bruch·stelle**, ***Soll-Bruch·stelle** *die (Technik)* predetermined breaking point

**sollen** ❶ *unr. Modalverb; 2. Part.* ~ (A) *(bei Aufforderung, Anweisung, Auftrag)* **er soll sofort kommen** he is to come immediately; **solltest du nicht bei ihm anrufen?** were you not supposed to ring him?; **was soll ich als nächstes tun?** what shall I do next?; what do you want me to do next?; **du sollst Vater und Mutter ehren** *(bibl.)* honour thy father and thy mother; **du sollst das lassen!** stop that *or* it!; **soll ich dir mal erzählen, was mir gestern passiert ist?** shall I tell you what happened to me yesterday?; **du weißt, dass du das nicht tun sollst** you know that you shouldn't *or* are not supposed to do that; **sie sagte, dass das nicht mehr vorkommen soll** she said it wouldn't happen again; **[sagen Sie ihm,] er soll hereinkommen** tell him to come in; **der soll mir nur mal kommen, dem werde ichs schon zeigen!** *(ugs.)* just let him come and I'll show him what for! *(sl.)*; **und da soll man nicht böse werden/nicht lachen** and I'm not supposed to get angry/laugh; **ich soll dir schöne Grüße von Herrn Meier bestellen** Herr Meier asked me to give you *or* sends his best wishes; (B) *(bei Wunsch, Absicht, Vorhaben)* **es soll ihm nützen** may it be of use to him; **du sollst dich hier wie zu Hause fühlen** I/we should like you to feel at home here; **niemand soll sagen, dass ich meine Pflicht vernachlässigt hätte** let no one say *or* no one shall say [that] I neglected my duty; **das soll dich doch nicht stören** don't let it bother you; ~ **wir heute ein wenig früher gehen?** should we leave a little earlier today?; **du sollst alles haben, was du brauchst** you shall have everything you require; **der Schal soll zum Mantel passen** the scarf is to *or* should match the coat; **er hat alles für sich behalten; soll er doch!** *(ugs. abwertend)* he has kept everything to himself; well, let him, if he wants to!; **das sollte ein Witz sein** that was meant to be a joke; **was soll denn das heißen?** what is that supposed to mean?; **wozu soll denn das gut sein?** what's the good of that?; (C) *(bei Ratlosigkeit)* **was soll ich nur machen?** what am I to do?; **was soll nur aus ihm werden?** what is to become of him?; **er wusste nicht, wie er aus der Situation herauskommen sollte** he didn't know how to get out of the situation; (D) *(Notwendigkeit ausdrückend)* **man soll so etwas nicht unterschätzen** it's not to be taken *or* it shouldn't be taken so lightly; (E) *häufig im Konjunktiv II (Erwartung, Wünschenswertes ausdrückend)* **du solltest dich schämen** you ought to be ashamed of yourself; **das**

## sollen

### 1. Verpflichtung

■ **IM PRÄSENS:**

***soll, sollst, sollt, sollen***
= am/is/are to; (*vor allem bei Nichterfüllung*)
= am/is/are supposed to

***Er soll morgen zum Arzt***
= He is to go to the doctor tomorrow

***Er soll morgen zum Arzt, aber er hat keine Möglichkeit hinzukommen***
= He's supposed to go to the doctor tomorrow, but he has no way of getting there

Bei Dingen wird ausgesagt, wie etwas gewünscht wird:

***Die beiden Flächen sollen fluchten***
= The two surfaces are meant to be *od.* should be in alignment

Besonders in der 2. Person wirkt es oft als Befehl:

***Du sollst sofort damit aufhören!***
= You're to stop that at once!

***Sie sollen die Pillen jeden Tag einnehmen***
= You're to *od.* You must take the pills every day; (*wenn man es nicht tut*) You're supposed to take the pills every day

***Er soll hereinkommen***
= He is to come in; (*sagen Sie es ihm*) Tell him to come in

■ **IN DER VERGANGENHEIT:**

***Er sollte gestern zum Arzt***
= He was [supposed] to go to the doctor yesterday

***Sie sollte die Hauptrolle spielen***
= She was [meant] to play the lead

***Du solltest ihn anrufen*** od. ***hättest ihn anrufen sollen***
= You were meant to phone him *od.* should have phoned him

■ **IM KONJUNKTIV:**

***sollte, solltest, solltet, sollten***
= should, ought to

***Wir sollten früher aufstehen***
= We ought to *od.* should get up earlier

***Du solltest dich schämen!***
= You ought to be ashamed!

■ **IN DER VERGANGENHEIT:**

***hätte/hättest/hätten ... sollen***
= should have

***Das hätte er nicht tun/sagen sollen***
= He shouldn't have done/said that

***Du hättest dort hingehen sollen***
= You should have gone there

### 2. Zukunft

***soll, sollst, sollt, sollen***
= am/is/are to;

***sollte, solltest, solltet, sollten***
= was/were to

Hier wird vor allem das Geplante ausgedrückt:

***Ich soll die Abteilung übernehmen***
= I am to take over the department

***Er sagte mir, ich sollte die Abteilung übernehmen***
= He told me I was to take over the department

***Hier soll ein Bürogebäude gebaut werden***
= An office block is to be built here

***Du sollst dein Geld zurückbekommen***
= You shall get your money back

***Es soll nicht wieder vorkommen***
= It won't happen again

Vor allem in Fragen kommt Ratlosigkeit zum Ausdruck:

***Was soll man da machen?***
= What is one to do?, What shall I/we do?

***Ich weiß nicht, was ich machen soll***
= I don't know what I should do *od.* what to do

Die Vergangenheit *sollte, solltest, solltet, sollten* kann auch von einem Zeitpunkt in der Vergangenheit auf damals noch zukünftige Ereignisse bezogen sein:

***Sie sollten ihr Reiseziel nie erreichen***
= They were never to reach their destination

***Es sollte ganz anders kommen***
= Things were to turn out quite differently

### 3. Allgemein verbreitete Meinung, Bericht

***soll/sollte*** usw.
= is/was supposed to

***Er soll sehr reich sein*** (= *Es heißt, dass er sehr reich ist*)
= He is supposed *od.* is said to be very rich

***Sie soll geheiratet haben***
= They say *od.* I gather she has got married

***Seine Worte sollten als Warnung aufgefasst werden***
= His words were meant *od.* supposed to be taken as a warning

***Was soll dieses Bild darstellen?***
= What is this picture supposed *od.* meant to represent?

***Was soll das heißen?***
= What is that supposed to mean?

Die drei letzten Beispiele beziehen sich auf die Absicht des Sprechenden bzw. des Urhebers.

### 4. Konditional

***sollte*** usw. **in Bedingungssätzen**
= should

***Sollte er anrufen*** od. ***Falls er anrufen sollte, ...***
= Should he *od.* If he should telephone, ...

---

**hättest du besser nicht tun ~:** it would have been better if you hadn't done that; **mit deiner Erkältung solltest du besser zu Hause bleiben** with your cold you had better stay at home; **wie sollte ich das wissen?** how was I to know that?; **F** (*jmdm. beschieden sein*) **er sollte seine Heimat nicht wiedersehen** he was never to see his homeland again; **es hat nicht sein ~** *od.* **nicht ~ sein** it was not to be; **es sollte ganz anders kommen, als man erwartet hatte** things were to turn out quite differently than expected; **G** *im Konjunktiv II* (*eine Möglichkeit ausdrückend*) **sollte es regnen, [dann] bleiben wir zu Hause** if it should rain, we will stay at home; **sollte ich mich geirrt haben, tut es mir Leid** if I have made *or* should I have made a mistake, I'm sorry; **wenn du ihn sehen solltest, sage ihm bitte ...** if you should see him, please tell him ...; **ich versuche es, und sollte ich auch verlieren** (*geh.*) I'll try, even though I may lose; **H** *im Präsens* (*sich für die Wahrheit nicht verbürgend*) **das Restaurant soll sehr teuer sein** the restaurant is supposed *or* said to be very expensive; **wir ~ eine Gehaltserhöhung bekommen** we are supposed to be getting a pay rise; **das soll vorkommen** things like that can happen; **I** *im Konjunktiv II* (*Zweifel ausdrückend*) **sollte das sein Ernst sein?** is he really being serious?; **sollte das wirklich wahr sein?** is that really true?; **J** (*können*) **mir soll es gleich sein** it's all the same to me; it doesn't matter to me; **man sollte glauben, dass ...** you would think that ...; **so etwas soll es geben** it's not unheard of. **❷** *tr., itr. V.* **was soll das?** what's the idea?; **Was solls? Ich kann ja doch nichts ändern** So what? I can't change anything anyway; **Soll ich? — Ja, du sollst!** Should I? — Yes, you should!; **was soll ich dort?** what would I do there?; **was soll der Unsinn?** what's all this nonsense about?; **warum soll ich das?** why am I to do that?; why should I do that?; **was man nicht alles soll/sollte!** the things one has to do!/is supposed to do!

**Söller** /ˈzœlɐ/ *der;* **~s, ~** (*Archit.*) balcony

**Soll-: ~seite** *die* (*Kaufmannsspr., Bankw.*) debit side; **~zinsen** *Pl.* interest *sing.* on [one's] debit balance

**Solmisation** /zɔlmizaˈtsi̯o:n/ *die;* **~** (*Musik*) solmization

**solo** /ˈzo:lo/ *indekl. Adj.* **A** (*bes. Musik: als Solist*) solo; **B** (*ugs., oft scherzh.: ohne Begleitung*) on one's own *postpos.*

*old spelling (see note on page 1707)

S

**Solo** /ˈzoːlo/ *das;* **~s,** **~s** *od.* **Soli** /ˈzoːli/ Ⓐ (*bes. Musik*) solo; Ⓑ (*bes. Fußballjargon*) solo run

**Solo-:** **~gesang** *der* solo; **~tänzer** *der,* **~tänzerin** *die* soloist

**Sol·quelle** *die* salt water *or* brine spring

**solvent** /zɔlˈvɛnt/ *Adj.* (*bes. Wirtsch.*) solvent

**Solvenz** /zɔlˈvɛnts/ *die;* **~,** **~en** (*bes. Wirtsch.*) solvency

**Somalia** /zoˈmaːli̯a/ *(das);* **~s** Somalia

**Somalier** *der;* **~s,** **~,** **Somalierin** *die;* **~,** **~nen** Somali

**somatisch** /zoˈmaːtɪʃ/ *Adj.* (*Physiol.*) somatic

**Sombrero** /zɔmˈbreːro/ *der;* **~s,** **~s** sombrero

**so·mit** /*auch:* ˈ--/ *Adv.* consequently; therefore; **... und somit kommen wir zu Punkt 3** ... and so *or* thus we come to number 3

**Sommer** /ˈzɔmɐ/ *der;* **~s,** **~** ▶ 431 summer; ⇒ *auch* **Frühling**

**Sommer-:** **~abend** *der* summer['s] evening; **~anfang** *der* beginning of summer; **~anzug** *der* summer suit; **~fahrplan** *der* summer timetable; **~fell** *das* summer coat; **~ferien** *Pl.* summer holidays; **~frische** *die* (*veralt.*) Ⓐ (*Aufenthalt*) summer holiday; **~frische machen** be on one's summer holiday; Ⓑ (*Ort*) summer [holiday] resort; **~frischler** *der;* **~~s,** **~~,** **~frischlerin** *die;* **~~,** **~~nen** (*veralt.*) summer holidaymaker; **~gast** *der* summer visitor *or* holidaymaker; **~getreide** *das* (*Landw.*) summer cereal *or* corn; **~halbjahr** *das* summer season; **~haus** *das* [summer] holiday house; **~kleid** *das* summer dress; **~kleidung** *die* summer clothes *pl. or* clothing

**sommerlich** ▶ 431 ❶ *Adj.* summer; summery ‹warmth, weather›; summer's *attrib.* ‹day, evening›; **draußen ist es schon ganz ~:** it is already quite summery outside. ❷ *adv.* **es war oft schon ~ warm** it was often as warm as summer; **sich ~ kleiden** wear summer clothes

**Sommer-:** **~loch** *das* (*ugs.*) summer recess; **~mantel** *der* summer coat; **~mode** *die* summer fashions *pl.;* (*eines Modehauses*) summer collection; **~monat** *der* summer month; **~nacht** *die* summer['s] night; **~olympiade** *die* Summer Olympics *pl.;* **~pause** *die* summer break; (*im Parlament*) summer recess; **das Theater hat ~pause** the theatre is closed for the summer; **~reifen** *der* standard tyre; **~residenz** *die* summer residence

**sommers** *Adv.* in summer

**sommer-, Sommer-:** **~saison** *die* summer season; **~schlussverkauf,** ***~schlußverkauf** *der* summer sale/sales; **wann ist ~schlussverkauf?** when are the summer sales?; **~semester** *das* summer semester; **~smog** *der* summer smog; **~sonnenwende** *die* summer solstice; **~spiele** *Pl.* Ⓐ (*Theater*) summer festival *sing.;* Ⓑ (*Olympische ~spiele*) Summer Olympics; **~sprosse** *die* freckle; **~sprossig** *Adj.* freckled; **~tag** *der* summer['s] day; **~wetter** *das* summer weather; **~zeit** *die* Ⓐ (*Jahreszeit*) summertime; **zur ~zeit** in summertime; Ⓑ (*Uhrzeit*) summer time

**Somnambulismus** *der;* **~** ▶ 474 (*Med.*) somnambulism *no art.*

**son** /zoːn/ *Demonstrativpron.* (*salopp*) **~e nette Person/~ altes Haus** such a nice person/an old house; **~ Idiot!** what an idiot!

**so·nach** *Adv.* (*veralt.*) therefore; consequently

**Sonate** /zoˈnaːtə/ *die;* **~,** **~n** (*Musik*) sonata

**Sonatine** *die;* **~,** **~n** (*Musik*) sonatina

**Sonde** /ˈzɔndə/ *die;* **~,** **~n** Ⓐ (*Med.*) (*zur Untersuchung*) probe; (*zur Ernährung*) tube; Ⓑ (*Raum~*) [space] probe

**sonder** /ˈzɔndɐ/ *Präp. mit Akk.* (*veralt.*) without; **~ Zahl** innumerable

**Sonder-:** **~abschreibung** *die* (*Wirtsch., Steuerw.*) (*das Abschreiben*) special amortization; (*Betrag*) special depreciation provision; **~anfertigung** *die* special design; **das Auto ist eine ~anfertigung** the car has been custom-built *or* specially made; **~angebot** *das* special offer; **etw. im ~angebot anbieten** have a special offer on sth.; **~ausgabe** *die* Ⓐ special edition; Ⓑ (*Steuerw.: private Aufwendungen*) tax-deductible expenditure (*e.g. pensions, insurance contributions, interest payment*); Ⓒ (*Extraausgabe*) extra expense

**sonderbar** ❶ *Adj.* strange; odd. ❷ *adv.* strangely; oddly

**sonderbarer·weise** *Adv.* strangely *or* oddly enough

**Sonderbarkeit** *die;* **~:** strangeness; oddness

**Sonder-:** **~behandlung** *die* Ⓐ special treatment; Ⓑ (*ns. verhüll.: Liquidierung*) liquidation; **~botschafter** *der,* **~botschafterin** *die* ambassador extraordinary; **~druck** *der; Pl.* **~~e** offprint; **~fahrt** *die* special excursion; **~fall** *der* special case; exception; **~genehmigung** *die* special permit

**sonder·gleichen** *Adv., nachgestellt* **eine Frechheit/Unverschämtheit ~:** the height of cheek/impudence; **mit einer Hartnäckigkeit ~:** with unparalleled obstinacy

**Sonderheit** *in* **in ~** (*geh.*) particularly; in particular

**Sonder-:** **~kommando** *das* special unit; **~konto** *das* special account

**sonderlich** ❶ *Adj.* Ⓐ (*besonders groß, stark*) particular; [e]special; Ⓑ (*sonderbar*) strange; peculiar; odd. ❷ *adv.* Ⓐ (*besonders, sehr*) particularly; especially; **ihm geht es nicht ~:** he is not particularly *or* (*coll.*) all that well; Ⓑ (*sonderbar*) strangely

**Sonderling** *der;* **~s,** **~e** strange *or* odd person

**Sonder-:** **~marke** *die* special issue [stamp]; **~maschine** *die* special plane *or* aircraft; **~meldung** *die* (*Rundf., Ferns.*) news flash; **~müll** *der* hazardous waste

**sondern**[1] *tr. V.* (*geh.*) separate (**von** from)

**sondern**[2] *Konj.* but; **nicht er hat es getan, ~ sie** 'he didn't do it, 'she did; **nicht nur ..., ~ [auch] ...** not only ... but also ...; **Er ist kein Linguist. — Sondern?** He is not a linguist. — What is he then?; **es ist kein Original, ~ nur eine Reproduktion** it is not an original, but only a reproduction

**Sonder-:** **~nummer** *die* special edition *or* issue; **~preis** *der* special *or* reduced price; **~reg[e]lung** *die* special ruling

**sonders** ⇒ **samt** 2

**Sonder-:** **~schule** *die* special school; **~stempel** *der* special postmark; **~urlaub** *der* Ⓐ (*Milit.*) special leave; Ⓑ (*zusätzlicher Urlaub*) special *or* extra holiday; **~wunsch** *der* special request *or* wish; **~ziehungs·rechte** *Pl.* (*Wirtsch.*) special drawing rights; **~zug** *der* special train

**sondieren** /zɔnˈdiːrən/ *tr. V.* Ⓐ sound out; **das Terrain ~:** see *or* find out how the land lies; Ⓑ (*Med.*) probe

**Sondierungs·gespräch** *das* exploratory talks *pl.*

**sone** ⇒ **son**

**Sonett** /zoˈnɛt/ *das;* **~[e]s,** **~e** sonnet

**Song** /sɔŋ/ *der;* **~s,** **~s** song

**Sonn·abend** /ˈzɔn|aːbn̩t/ *der* ▶ 207, ▶ 833 (*bes. nordd.*) Saturday; **an ~en und Sonntagen** on Saturdays and Sundays; **der verkaufsoffene** *od.* **lange ~:** Saturday on which the shops are open all day; ⇒ *auch* **Dienstag; Dienstag-**

**sonn·abends** *Adv.* ▶ 833 on Saturday[s]; ⇒ *auch* **dienstags**

**Sonne** *die;* **~,** **~n** sun; (*Licht der ~*) sun[light]; **das Zimmer hat den ganzen Tag über ~:** the room gets sun[light] all day long

**sonnen** *refl. V.* sun oneself; **sich in etw.** (*Dat.*) **~** (*fig.*) bask in sth.

**sonnen-, Sonnen-:** **~anbeter** *der;* **~~s,** **~~,** **~anbeterin** *die;* **~~,** **~~nen** (*scherzh.*) sun worshipper; **~aufgang** *der* sunrise; **~bad** *das* sunbathing *no pl., no indef. art.;* **ein ~bad nehmen** sunbathe; **~baden** *itr. V.* sunbathe; **das ~baden** sunbathing *no art.;* **~bahn** *die* (*Astron.*) path of the sun; sun's path; **~bank** *die; Pl.* **~bänke** sunbed; **~beschienen** *Adj.* (*geh.*) sunny; **~bestrahlung** *die:* **bestimmte Pflanzen dürfen keiner direkten ~bestrahlung ausgesetzt werden** certain plants are not supposed to be put in direct sunlight; **~blende** *die* Ⓐ (*Fot.*) lens hood; Ⓑ (*im Auto*) sun visor; **~blume** *die* sunflower; **~blumen·kern** *der* sunflower seed; **~brand** *der* ▶ 474 sunburn *no indef. art.;* **~bräune** *die* suntan; **~brille** *die* sunglasses *pl.;* **~dach** *das* sun canopy; **~deck** *das* sun deck; **~durchflutet** *Adj.* (*geh.*) sunny; **~ein·strahlung** *die* (*Met.*) insolation; **~energie** *die* (*Physik*) solar energy; **~finsternis** *die* (*Astron.*) solar eclipse; eclipse of the sun; **~fleck** *der* (*Astron.*) sunspot; **~gebräunt** *Adj.* suntanned; **~geflecht** *das* ▶ 471 (*Anat.*) solar plexus; **~gott** *der* (*Rel.*) sun god; **~göttin** *die* (*Rel.*) sun goddess; **~hut** *der* sunhat; **~klar** *Adj.* (*ugs.*) crystal clear; **die Sache ist ~klar, er ist der Dieb** he is the thief — it's as clear as daylight; **~kollektor** *der* (*Energietechnik*) solar collector; **~kraftwerk** *das* solar power station; **~licht** *das* sunlight; **~öl** *das* suntan oil; sun oil; **~schein** *der* Ⓐ sunshine; **bei ~schein** in sunshine; **bei ~schein steigen die Temperaturen bis auf 24 °C** where the sun shines temperatures will rise to 24 °C; Ⓑ (*fam.: geliebtes Kind*) [little] ray of sunshine; **~schirm** *der* sunshade; (*zum Tragen*) parasol; sunshade; **~schutz·creme** *die* suntan lotion; **~segel** *das* Ⓐ (*Schutzdach*) awning; Ⓑ (*bei Raumflugkörpern*) solar sail; **~seite** *die* sunny side; **die ~seite des Lebens** (*fig.*) the bright side of life; **~stich** *der* ▶ 474 (*Med.*) sunstroke *no indef. art.;* **du hast wohl einen ~stich** (*fig. salopp*) you must be mad; **~strahl** *der* ray of sun[shine]; **~system** *das* (*Astron.*) solar system; **~tag** *der* Ⓐ sunny day; day of sunshine; Ⓑ (*Astron.*) solar day; **~tau** *der* (*Bot.*) sundew; **~uhr** *die* sundial; **~untergang** *der* sunset; **~wende** *die* solstice; **~wind** *der* (*Astron.*) solar wind; **~zelle** *die* (*Physik, Elektrot.*) solar cell

**sonnig** *Adj.* Ⓐ sunny; (*fig.*) happy ‹youth, childhood, time›; cheerful ‹sense of humour, ways›; Ⓑ (*iron.: naiv*) naive

**Sonn·tag** *der* ▶ 207, ▶ 833 Sunday; ⇒ *auch* **Dienstag; Dienstag-**

**sonn·täglich** ▶ 833 ❶ *Adj.* Sunday *attrib.* ❷ *adv.* **~ gekleidet sein** be dressed in one's Sunday best

**sonntags** *Adv.* ▶ 833 on Sunday[s]; ⇒ *auch* **dienstags**

**Sonntags-:** **~arbeit** *die* Sunday working *no art.;* **~ausflug** *der* Sunday outing; **~ausgabe** *die* Sunday issue *or* edition; **~beilage** *die* Sunday supplement; **~braten** *der* Sunday roast; **~dienst** *der* Sunday duty; **~fahrer** *der,* **~fahrerin** *die* (*abwertend*) Sunday driver; **~kind** *das* Ⓐ Sunday's child; Ⓑ (*Glückskind*) lucky person; **er ist ein ~kind** he was born lucky *or* under a lucky star; **~predigt** *die* Sunday sermon; **~reden** *Pl.* (*abwertend*) soapbox oratory *no pl., no art.;* **~schule** *die* Sunday school; **~staat** *der* (*scherzh.*) Sunday best; **im ~staat** in one's Sunday best; **~zeitung** *die* Sunday [news]paper

**Sonnwend·feier** *die* midsummer/midwinter festival *or* celebrations *pl.*

**Sonny·boy** /ˈsʌnɪ-/ *der;* **~s,** **~s** golden boy

**sonor** /zoˈnoːɐ̯/ *Adj.* sonorous

**sonst** /zɔnst/ *Adv.* Ⓐ **der ~ so freundliche Mann ...** the man, who is/was usually so friendly, ...; **er hat es wie ~ gemacht/besser als ~ gemacht** he did it as usual/better than usual; **alles war wie ~:** everything was [the same] as usual; **war das auch ~ so?** has it always been like that?; Ⓑ (*außerdem, im Übrigen*) otherwise; **~ war alles unverändert** otherwise nothing had changed; **wie gehts ~?** how are things otherwise?; **haben Sie ~ noch Fragen?** have you any other questions?; **kommt ~ noch jemand** *od.* **wer?** is anybody else coming?; **es wusste ~ niemand** nobody *or* no one else knew; **hat er ~ nichts erzählt?** [apart from that,] he didn't say anything else?; **er war ganz gut in Mathematik, aber ~?** he was quite good in mathematics, but apart from that?; **~ noch was?** (*ugs., auch iron.*) anything else?; **~ nichts, nichts ~:** nothing else; **und wer weiß wer ~ noch** and goodness knows who else; **[aber] ~ gehts dir gut** *od.* **~ tut dir nichts weh?** (*salopp iron.*) anything else [you'd want]? (*iron.*); **wer/was/wie/wo [denn] ~?** who/what/how/where else?; **~ jemand** *od.* **wer** (*ugs.*) somebody else; (*fragend, verneint*) anybody else; **da könnte ja ~ jemand kommen** (*ugs.*) anybody could *or* might come; **er meint, er ist ~ wer** (*ugs.*) he thinks he's really something *or* he's the bee's knees (*coll.*); **~ was** (*ugs.*) anything else; **er hat ~ was unternommen** (*ugs.*) he has tried all sorts of things; **man hätte annehmen können, die Kinder hätten ~ was angestellt** you would have thought the children had done something terrible; **~ wie** (*ugs.*) in some other way; (*fragend, verneint*) in any other way; **~ wo/wohin** (*ugs.*) somewhere else; (*fragend, verneint*) anywhere else; **~ woher** (*ugs.*) [from] somewhere else; (*fragend, verneint*) [from] anywhere else; **C** (*andernfalls*) otherwise; or

**sonstig...** *Adj.* other; further; **sein ~es Verhalten war gut** his behaviour was otherwise good; **„Sonstiges"** 'miscellaneous'

***sonst-: ~jemand, ~was** *usw.* ⇒ **sonst B**

**so·oft** *Konj.* whenever; **ich komme, ~ du es wünschst** I'll come as often as you wish

**Soor** /zo:ɐ̯/ *der;* **~[e]s, ~e** ▶ **474** (*Med.*) thrush *no art.*

**Sophismus** /zo'fɪsmʊs/ *der;* **~, Sophismen** (*Philos.*) sophism

**Sophisterei** *die;* **~, ~en** (*abwertend*) sophistry

**Sophistik** *die;* **~** (*Philos.*) sophistry

**sophistisch** **1** *Adj.* sophistic[al]. **2** *adv.* sophistically

**Sophokles** /'zo:foklɛs/ (*der*) Sophocles

**Sopran** /zo'pra:n/ *der;* **~s, ~e** (*Musik*) **A** (*Stimmlage*) soprano [voice]; **B** (*im Chor*) sopranos *pl.*; **C** (*Sängerin*) soprano

**Sopranist** *der;* **~en, ~en** sopranist

**Sopranistin** *die;* **~, ~nen** soprano

**Sorbe** /'zɔrbə/ *der;* **~n, ~n** Sorb

**Sorbet** /'zɔrbɛt/ *der od. das;* **~s, ~s** (*Gastr.*) sorbet

**Sorbin** *die;* **~, ~nen** ⇒ **Sorbe**

**Sore** /'zo:rə/ *die;* **~, ~n** (*Gaunerspr.*) loot

**Sorge** /'zɔrgə/ *die;* **~, ~n** **A** (*Unruhe, Angst*) worry; **keine ~:** don't [you] worry; **[keine] ~ haben, dass ...** [not] be worried that ...; **in ~ um jmdn./etw. sein** be worried about sb./sth.; **etw. erfüllt jmdn. mit ~:** sth. worries sb.; **B** (*sorgenvoller Gedanke*) worry; **ich mache mir ~n um dich/um deine Gesundheit** I am worried about you/about your health; **mach dir darum** *od.* **darüber** *od.* **deswegen keine ~:** don't worry about that; **der hat ~n!** (*ugs. iron.*) and he thinks 'he's got problems (*coll. iron.*); **lassen Sie das meine ~ sein** let 'me worry about that; **er ertränkte seine ~n im Alkohol** he drowned his sorrows in alcohol; **C** (*Mühe, Fürsorge*) care; **die ~ für die Familie** caring for the family; **die ~ um das tägliche Brot** the worry of providing one's daily bread; **für etw./** (*schweiz. auch:*) **einer Sache** (*Dat.*) **~ tragen** (*geh.*) take care of sth.; **ich werde dafür ~ tragen, dass ...** I will see to it *or* make sure that ...; **das lass nur meine ~ sein** let that be 'my concern *or* responsibility

**sorgen** **1** *refl. V.* worry, be worried (**um** about); **sie sorgt sich wegen jeder Kleinigkeit** she worries about every little detail. **2** *itr. V.* **A** **für jmdn./etw. ~:** take care of *or* look after sb./sth.; **für das Essen/Ruhe und Ordnung/gute Laune ~:** look after the food/make sure that law and order prevail/make sure that people are in a good mood; **für die Zukunft der Kinder ist gesorgt** the children's future is provided for; **B** (*verblasst: bewirken*) **für etw. ~:** cause sth.

**sorgen-, Sorgen-: ~frei** **1** *Adj.* carefree ‹person, future, existence, etc.›; **2** *adv.* **~frei leben** live in a carefree manner; **~kind** *das* (*auch fig.*) problem child; **~voll** **1** *Adj.* worried; anxious; **2** *adv.* worriedly; anxiously

**Sorge-: ~pflicht** *die:* **eine ~pflicht gegenüber seinen Kindern haben** have a duty to provide for one's children; **~recht** *das* (*Rechtsw.*) custody (**für** of)

**Sorg·falt** /'zɔrkfalt/ *die;* **~:** care; **große ~ auf etw.** (*Akk.*) **verwenden** *od.* **legen** take great *or* a great deal of care over sth.

**sorg·fältig** **1** *Adj.* careful; **eine ~e Arbeit** a job/piece of work done with care. **2** *adv.* carefully

**Sorgfältigkeit** *die;* **~:** carefulness

**Sorgfalts·pflicht** *die* duty of care

**sorg·los** **1** *Adj.* **A** (*ohne Sorgfalt*) careless; **B** (*unbekümmert*) carefree. **2** *adv.* **~ mit etw. umgehen** treat sth. carelessly

**Sorglosigkeit** *die;* **~** **A** (*Mangel an Sorgfalt*) carelessness; **B** (*Unbekümmertheit*) carefreeness

**sorgsam** **1** *Adj.* careful. **2** *adv.* carefully

**Sorte** /'zɔrtə/ *die;* **~, ~n** **A** sort; type; kind; (*Marke*) brand; **bitte ein Pfund von der besten ~:** a pound of the best quality, please; **B** *Pl.* (*Devisen*) foreign currency *sing.*

**Sorten·kurs** *der* (*Bankw.*) exchange rate

**sortieren** *tr. V.* sort [out] ‹pictures, letters, washing, etc.›; grade ‹goods etc.›; (*fig.*) arrange ‹thoughts›; **die Stücke werden nach der Größe sortiert** the pieces are sorted according to size

**Sortier·maschine** *die* sorter; sorting machine

**sortiert** *Adj.* **A** **ein gut/schlecht ~es Lager** a well-stocked/badly stocked warehouse; **dieses Geschäft ist sehr gut in französischen Rotweinen ~:** this shop has a good range of French red wines; **B** (*erlesen*) selected

**Sortiment** /zɔrti'mɛnt/ *das;* **~[e]s, ~e** **A** range (**an** + *Dat.* of); **B** (*Buchhandel*) retail book trade

**Sortimenter** *der;* **~s, ~, Sortimenterin** *die;* **~, ~nen** retail bookseller; book retailer

**Sortiments-: ~buchhandel** *der* retail book trade; **~buchhandlung** *die* retail bookshop

**SOS** /ɛs/o:'/ɛs/ *das;* **~:** SOS; **~ funken** send *or* put out an SOS

**so·sehr** *Konj.* however much

**so·so** **1** *Interj.* **A** (*ironisch, zweifelnd*) I see; **B** (*gleichgültig*) oh yes?; really? **2** *Adv.* (*ugs.*) so-so

**SOS-Ruf** /ɛs/o:'/ɛs-/ *der* SOS [call]

**Soße** /'zo:sə/ *die;* **~, ~n** **A** sauce; (*Braten~*) gravy; sauce; (*Salat~*) dressing; **B** (*salopp abwertend: schmutzige Flüssigkeit*) muck (*coll.*)

**Soßen-: ~löffel** *der* gravy *or* sauce ladle; **~schüssel** *die* gravy *or* sauce boat

**sott** /zɔt/ *1. u. 3. Pers. Sg. Prät. v.* **sieden**

**Soubrette** /zu'brɛtə/ *die;* **~, ~n** (*Musik, Theater*) soubrette

**Soufflé** /zu'fle:/ *das;* **~s, ~s** (*Gastr.*) soufflé

**Souffleur** /zu'flø:ɐ̯/ *der;* **~s, ~e** ▶ **159** (*Theater*) prompter

**Souffleur·kasten** *der* prompt box

**Souffleuse** /zu'flø:zə/ *die;* **~, ~n** ▶ **159** prompter

**soufflieren** /zu'fli:rən/ *tr. V.* prompt; **jmdm. etw. ~:** prompt sb. by whispering sth.

**Soul·musik** /'soul-/ *die* soul music

**Sound·karte** /'saund.../ *die* (*DV*) sound card

**so·und·so** **1** *Adv.*; *vorangestellt* **~ groß/breit/lang** [of] such-and-such a size/width/length; **~ viel kosten** cost such-and-such; cost so-and-so much. **2** *Adj.*; *nachgestellt* **Paragraph ~:** paragraph such-and-such *or* so-and-so; **Fanny ~:** Fanny something-or-other; **die Soundso:** what's-her-name

**Souper** /zu'pe:/ *das;* **~s, ~s** (*geh.*) dinner [party]

**soupieren** *itr. V.* (*geh.*) dine

**Soutane** /zu'ta:nə/ *die;* **~, ~n** soutane

**Souterrain** /'zu:tɛrɛ̃/ *das;* **~s, ~s** basement

**Souvenir** /zuvə'ni:ɐ̯/ *das;* **~s, ~s** souvenir

**souverän** /zuvə'rɛ:n/ **1** *Adj.* **A** (*unabhängig*) sovereign; **B** (*geh.: überlegen*) superior. **2** *adv.* **die Lage ~ meistern** be in total command of the situation; **er siegte ganz ~:** he won in a very impressive way

**Souverän** *der;* **~s, ~e** **A** (*Herrscher, Fürst*) sovereign; **B** (*schweiz.: die Stimmbürger*) electorate

**Souveränität** *die;* **~:** sovereignty

**so·viel** *Konj.* **A** (*nach dem, was*) as *or* so far as; **~ mir bekannt ist** so far as I know; **~ ich sehe** as far as I can see; **B** (*in wie großem Maße auch immer*) however much; ⇒ *auch* **so 1 B**

**Sowchose** /'zɔfço:zə/ *die;* **~, ~n** sovkhoz

**so·weit** *Konj.* **A** (*nach dem, was*) as *or* so far as; **~ mir bekannt ist** so far as I know; **~ ich sehe** as far as I can see; **B** (*in dem Maße, wie*) [in] so far as; **~ ich dazu in der Lage bin, will ich gerne helfen** [in] so far as I am in a position to do so *or* am able to, I should like to help; ⇒ *auch* **so 1 B**

**so·wenig** *Konj.* however little; ⇒ *auch* **so 1 B**

**so·wie** *Konj.* **A** (*und auch*) as well as; **B** (*sobald*) as soon as

**so·wie·so** *Adv.* anyway; **das ~!** (*ugs.*) that goes without saying!; of course!; **Herr S~:** Mr What's-his-name

**Sowjet** /zɔ'vjɛt/ *der;* **~s, ~s** **A** (*Behörde*) soviet; **der Oberste ~:** the Supreme Soviet; **B** *Pl.* (*Führung*) Soviets; Russians

**Sowjet-: ~armee** *die* Soviet army; **~bürger** *der,* **~bürgerin** *die* Soviet citizen

**sowjetisch** *Adj.* Soviet

**sowjetisieren** *tr. V.* sovietize

**Sowjet·mensch** *der* Soviet citizen

**Sowjetologie** *die;* **~:** sovietology *no art.*

**Sowjet-: ~republik** *die* **A** (*Gliedstaat*) Soviet republic; **Union der Sozialistischen ~republiken** Union of Soviet Socialist Republics; **B** (*hist.*) soviet republic; **~russe** *der,* **~russin** *die* Soviet Russian; **~stern** *der* Soviet star; star of the Soviets; **~union** *die* Soviet Union; **~zone** *die* (*hist.*) Soviet zone

**so·wohl** *Konj.* **~ ... als** *od.* **wie [auch] ...** both ... and ...; ... as well as ...

**Sozi** /'zo:tsi/ *der;* **~s, ~s** (*ugs., auch abwertend*) socialist

**sozial** /zo'tsia:l/ **1** *Adj.* social; **die ~e Frage** (*hist.*) the social question; **~e Einrichtungen** public amenities; **ich habe heute meinen ~en Tag** (*ugs.*) I'm feeling charitable *or* generous today; **dieses Verhalten ist nicht sehr ~:** this behaviour is not very public-spirited; **~e Marktwirtschaft** social market economy. **2** *adv.* socially; **~ denken** be socially minded; **~ handeln** act in a socially conscious *or* public-spirited way

**sozial-, Sozial-: ~abbau** *der* dismantling of the welfare state; **~abgaben** *Pl.* social welfare contributions; **~amt** *das* social welfare office; **~arbeit** *die* social work; **~arbeiter** *der,* **~arbeiterin** *die* ▶ **159** social worker; **~beruf** *der* social services profession; **in ~berufen arbeiten** work for *or* in the social services; **~demokrat** *der* Social Democrat; **~demokratie** *die* social democracy *no art.*; **~demokratin** *die* ⇒ **~demokrat**; **~demokratisch** *Adj.* social democratic; **~demokratische Partei [Deutschlands]** [German] Social Democratic Party; **~ethik** *die* social ethics *sing.*; **~fall** *der* hardship case; **~gericht** *das* social welfare court; **~geschichte** *die* social history; **~gesetzgebung** *die* social welfare legislation; **~hilfe** *die* social welfare; **~hygiene** *die* community medicine; **~imperialismus** *der* social imperialism

**Sozialisation** *die;* **~** (*Soziol., Psych.*) socialization

**sozialisieren** *tr. V.* **A** (*Wirtsch.: vergesellschaften*) nationalize; **B** (*Soziol., Psych.: zum Gemeinschaftsleben befähigen*) socialize

*old spelling (see note on page 1707)

**Sozialismus** *der;* ~: socialism *no art.*

**Sozialist** *der;* ~**en**, ~**en**, **Sozialistin** *die;* ~, ~**nen** socialist

**sozialistisch** ❶ *Adj.* socialist. ❷ ~ **regierte Länder** countries with socialist governments

**sozial-, Sozial-:** ~**kritisch** *Adj.* socially critical; critical of society *postpos.;* ~**kunde** *die* social studies *sing., no art.;* ~**leistungen** *Pl.* social welfare benefits; ~**liberal** *Adj.* Ⓐ (*sozial und liberal*) liberal socialist ‹politician etc.›; Ⓑ (*aus SPD und FDP*) liberal-social democrat ‹coalition etc.›; ~**pädagogik** *die* social education *no art.;* ~**partner** *der: die* ~**partner** employers and employees *or* trade unions; ~**plan** *der: written agreement between employer and works council which seeks to protect employees;* ~**politik** *die* social policy; ~**prestige** *das* social status; ~**produkt** *das* (*Wirtsch.*) national product; ~**psychologie** *die* social psychology *no art.;* ~**rente** *die* state pension; ~**rentner** *der,* ~**rentnerin** *die* old-age pensioner; ~**staat** *der* welfare state; ~**struktur** *die* social structure; ~**union** *die* unified social welfare system; ⇒ *auch* **Währungsunion**; ~**versicherung** *die* social security; ~**wissenschaft** *die* social science *no art.;* **die** ~**wissenschaften** the social sciences; ~**wohnung** *die* ≈ council flat (*Brit.*); municipal housing unit (*Amer.*)

**Sozietät** /zotsi̯eˈtɛːt/ *die;* ~, ~**en** Ⓐ (*Soziol.*) society *no art.;* Ⓑ (*Verhaltensf.*) society; social unit; Ⓒ (*gemeinsame Praxis*) joint practice

**sozio·kulturell** *Adj.* sociocultural

**Soziolekt** /zotsi̯oˈlɛkt/ *der;* ~[**e**]**s**, ~**e** (*Sprachw.*) sociolect; social dialect

**Sozio·linguistik** *die* sociolinguistics *sing.*

**Soziologe** /zotsi̯oˈloːgə/ *der;* ~**n**, ~**n** ▶ 159 sociologist

**Soziologie** *die;* ~: sociology; **die** ~ **lehrt uns, dass ...** sociology teaches us that ...

**Soziologin** *die;* ~, ~**nen** ▶ 159 sociologist

**soziologisch** ❶ *Adj.* sociological. ❷ *adv.* sociologically

**sozio·ökonomisch** *Adj.* socio-economic

**Sozius** /ˈzoːtsi̯ʊs/ *der;* ~, ~**se** Ⓐ *Pl. auch:* **Sozii** /ˈzoːtsii/ (*Wirtsch.: Teilhaber*) partner; Ⓑ (*beim Motorrad*) pillion

**Sozius·sitz** *der* pillion

**so·zu·sagen** *Adv.* so to speak; as it were; **es geschah** ~ **offiziell** it took place officially, so to speak *or* as it were

**Spachtel** /ˈʃpaxtl̩/ *der;* ~**s**, ~ *od. die;* ~, ~**n** Ⓐ (*für Kitt*) putty knife; (*zum Abkratzen von Farbe*) paint scraper; (*zum Malen*) palette knife; spatula; Ⓑ (~*masse*) filler

**Spachtel·masse** *die* filler

**spachteln** *tr. V.* Ⓐ stop, fill ‹hole, crack, etc.›; smooth over ‹wall, panel, surface, etc.›; smooth ‹filler, putty› (**in** + *Akk.* into); apply ‹paints› with a palette knife; Ⓑ (*ugs.: essen*) put away (*coll.*) ‹food, meal›

**Spagat**[1] /ʃpaˈgaːt/ *der od. das;* ~[**e**]**s**, ~**e** Ⓐ splits *pl.;* [**einen**] ~ **machen** do the splits; Ⓑ (*fig.*) **der** ~ **zwischen ... und ...:** the balancing act between ... and ...; **den** ~ **zwischen ... und ... schaffen/beherrschen** achieve the balancing act between ... and ...; succeed in bridging the gap between ... and ...

**Spagat**[2] *der;* ~[**e**]**s**, ~**e** (*südd., österr.*) string

**Spaghetti**[1] /ʃpaˈgɛti/ *Pl.* spaghetti *sing.*

**Spaghetti**[2] *der;* ~[**s**], ~**s** (*salopp abwertend*) ⇒ **Spaghettifresser**

**Spaghetti-:** ~**fresser** *der,* ~**fresserin** *die* (*salopp abwertend*) Eyetie (*sl. derog.*); wop (*sl. derog.*); ~**träger** *der* (*Mode*) spaghetti strap

**spähen** /ˈʃpɛːən/ *itr. V.* peer; (*durch ein Loch, eine Ritze usw.*) peep

**Späher** *der;* ~**s**, ~, **Späherin** *die;* ~, ~**nen** (*Milit.*) scout; (*Posten*) lookout; (*Spitzel*) informer

**Späh·trupp** *der* (*Milit.*) reconnaissance *or* scouting patrol *or* party

**Spalett** /ʃpaˈlɛt/ *das;* ~[**e**]**s**, ~**e** (*österr.*) [wooden] shutter

**Spalier** /ʃpaˈliːɐ̯/ *das;* ~**s**, ~**e** Ⓐ trellis; (*für Obstbäume*) espalier; Ⓑ (*aus Menschen*) double line; (*Ehren*~) guard of honour; ~ **stehen** line the route; ‹soldiers› form a guard of honour

**Spalier·obst** *das* Ⓐ (*Früchte*) espalier fruit; Ⓑ (*Pflanzen*) espalier

**Spalt** /ʃpalt/ *der;* ~[**e**]**s**, ~**e** opening; (*im Fels*) fissure; crevice; (*zwischen Vorhängen*) chink; gap; (*langer Riß*) crack; **die Tür einen** ~ [**weit**] **öffnen** open the door a crack *or* slightly; **einen** ~ [**weit**] **offen sein** ‹door› be open a crack, be *or* stand slightly ajar

**spalt-, Spalt-:** ~**bar** *Adj.* (*Physik*) fissionable ‹material, element, etc.›; ~**breit** *Adj.* narrow ‹opening›; ~**breit** *der;* ~~**s**, ~~: crack

**Spalte** *die;* ~, ~**n** Ⓐ crack; (*Fels*~) crevice; cleft; (*Gletscher*~) crevasse; crack; Ⓑ (*Druckw.: Druck*~) column; Ⓒ (*derb: Scham-, Gesäß*~) crack (*coarse*); Ⓓ (*österr.: Scheibe*) slice

**spalten** ❶ *unr.* (*auch regelm.*) *tr. V.* Ⓐ (*auch Physik, fig.*) split; **Holz** ~: chop wood; Ⓑ (*Chemie*) split; break down. ❷ *unr.* (*auch regelm.*) *refl. V.* Ⓐ (*auch Physik, fig.*) split; Ⓑ (*Chemie*) split; break down

**-spaltig** *adj.* (*Druckw.*) -column

**Spalt-:** ~**pilz** *der* Ⓐ (*Biol.*) bacterium; Ⓑ (*fig.*) divisive tendency; ~**produkt** *das* (*Physik*) fission product

**Spaltung** *die;* ~, ~**en** Ⓐ (*auch fig.*) splitting; (*fig.: durch eine Grenze*) division; Ⓑ (*fig.: das Gespaltensein*) split (*Gen.* in; **zwischen** + *Dat.* between); (*durch eine Grenze*) division; Ⓒ (*Physik*) fission; splitting; Ⓓ (*Chemie*) splitting; breaking down

**Span** /ʃpaːn/ *der;* ~[**e**]**s**, **Späne** /ˈʃpɛːnə/ (*Hobel*~) shaving; (*Feil*~) filing *usu. in pl.;* (*beim Bohren*) boring *usu. in pl.;* (*beim Drehen*) turning *usu. in pl.;* (*zum Feueranzünden*) splint; **feine** [**Metall**]**späne** swarf *sing.;* **wo gehobelt wird,** [**da**] **fallen Späne** (*Spr.*) you cannot make an omelette without breaking eggs (*prov.*)

**spänen** /ˈʃpɛːnən/ *tr. V.* (*Technik*) scour with steel wool

**Span·ferkel** *das* sucking pig

**Spange** /ˈʃpaŋə/ *die;* ~, ~**n** clasp; (*Haar*~) hairslide (*Brit.*); barrette (*Amer.*); (*Arm*~) bracelet; bangle

**Spangen·schuh** *der* strap shoe

**Spaniel** /ˈʃpaːni̯əl/ *der;* ~**s**, ~**s** spaniel

**Spanien** /ˈʃpaːni̯ən/ (*das*); ~**s** Spain

**Spanier** /ˈʃpaːni̯ɐ/ *der;* ~**s**, ~ ▶ 553 Spaniard; **die** ~: the Spanish *or* Spaniards; **seid ihr** ~? are you Spanish?; **stolz wie ein** ~ (*scherzh.*) as proud as a peacock

**Spanierin** *die;* ~, ~**nen** ▶ 553 ⇒ **Spanier**

**spanisch** ▶ 553, ▶ 696 ❶ *Adj.* Spanish; **das kommt mir/dir** *usw.* ~ **vor** (*ugs.*) that strikes me/you *etc.* as odd. ❷ *adv.* **sich** ~ **unterhalten** talk Spanish; ⇒ *auch* **deutsch**; **Deutsch; Reiter** A; **Rohr** C; **Wand** B

**Span·korb** *der* chip basket; chip

**spann** /ʃpan/ *1. u. 3. Pers. Sg. Prät. v.* **spinnen**

**Spann** *der;* ~[**e**]**s**, ~**e** instep

**Spann·beton** *der* (*Bauw.*) pre-stressed concrete

**Spanne** *die;* ~, ~**n** Ⓐ (*Zeit*~) span of time; **eine** ~ **von 12 Tagen/fünfzig Jahren** a period of twelve days/span *or* period of fifty years; Ⓑ (*veralt.: Längenmaß*) span; Ⓒ (*Handels*~) margin

**spannen** ❶ *tr. V.* Ⓐ tighten, tauten ‹violin string, violin bow, etc.›; draw ‹bow›; tension ‹spring, tennis net, drumhead, saw-blade›; stretch ‹fabric, shoe, etc.›; draw *or* pull ‹line› tight *or* taut; tense, flex ‹muscle›; cock ‹gun, camera shutter›; **eine Kamera** ~: cock the shutter on a camera; **seine Nerven waren zum Zerreißen gespannt** (*fig.*) his nerves were stretched to breaking point; Ⓑ (*befestigen*) put up ‹washing line›; stretch ‹net, wire, tarpaulin, etc.› (**über** + *Akk.* over); **einen Bogen Papier in die Schreibmaschine** ~: insert *or* put a sheet of paper in the typewriter; **etw. in einen Schraubstock** ~: clamp sth. in a vice; Ⓒ (*schirren*) hitch up, harness (**vor, an** + *Akk.* to); Ⓓ (*bes. südd., österr.: merken*) notice; ⇒ *auch* **Lage** C.
❷ *refl. V.* Ⓐ become *or* go taut; ‹muscles› tense; Ⓑ (*geh.: sich wölben*) **sich über etw.** (*Akk.*) ~ ‹bridge, rainbow› span sth.
❸ *itr. V.* Ⓐ (*zu eng sein*) ‹clothing› be [too] tight; ‹skin› be taut; Ⓑ **auf jmdn./etw.** ~ (*ugs.*) (*warten*) wait [impatiently] for sb./sth.; (*lauern*) lie in wait for sb./sth.

**spannend** ❶ *Adj.* exciting; (*stärker*) thrilling; **machs nicht so** ~! (*ugs.*) don't keep me/us in suspense. ❷ *adv.* excitingly; (*stärker*) thrillingly

**spannen·lang** *Adj.* (*veralt.*) a span tall/in length *postpos.*

**Spanner** *der;* ~**s**, ~ Ⓐ (*Schuh*~) shoe tree; (*Stiefel*~) boot tree; (*Hosen*~) [trouser] hanger; (*Gardinen*~) curtain-stretcher; (*für Tennisschläger*) [racket] press; Ⓑ (*Zool.*) geometer; Ⓒ (*ugs.: Voyeur*) peeping Tom

**Spann·kraft** *die* vigour

**Spannung** *die;* ~, ~**en** Ⓐ excitement; (*Neugier*) suspense; tension; **jmdn. mit** *od.* **voll** ~ **erwarten** await sb. eagerly; Ⓑ (*eines Romans, Films usw.*) suspense; Ⓒ (*Zwistigkeit, Nervosität*) tension; Ⓓ (*das Straffsein*) tension; tautness; Ⓔ (*elektrische* ~) tension; (*Voltzahl*) voltage; **unter** ~ **stehen** be live; Ⓕ (*Mechanik*) stress

**spannungs-, Spannungs-:** ~**gebiet** *das* (*Politik*) area of tension; ~**geladen** *Adj.* Ⓐ (*gespannt*) ‹atmosphere etc.› charged with tension; Ⓑ (*spannend*) ‹novel, film, etc.› full of suspense; ~**messer** *der;* ~~**s**, ~~ (*Elektrot.*) voltmeter; ~**verhältnis** *das* relationship of tension; ~**zu·stand** *der* Ⓐ (*Psych.*) state of tension; Ⓑ (*Mechanik*) condition of stress

**Spann·weite** *die* Ⓐ (*Zool.: Flügel*~) [wing]span; wingspread; (*eines Flugzeugs*) [wing]span; Ⓑ (*Bauw.*) span

**Span-:** ~**platte** *die* chipboard; ~**schachtel** *die* small box made of thin strips of wood (*for storing jewellery, letters, etc.*)

**Spant** /ʃpant/ *das od. der;* ~[**e**]**s**, ~**en** (*eines Schiffs*) rib; (*eines Flugzeugs*) frame; former

**Spar-:** ~**brief** *der* (*Bankw.*) savings certificate; ~**buch** *das* (*Bankw.*) savings book; passbook; (*bei der Bank auch*) bank book; ~**büchse** *die* money box; ~**einlage** *die* (*Bankw.*) savings deposit

**sparen** /ˈʃpaːrən/ ❶ *tr. V.* save; (*zurücklegen*) save, put away ‹money›; **die Mühe/den Ärger hätten wir uns** ~ **können** we could have saved *or* spared ourselves the effort/trouble; **du kannst dir jedes Wort** ~: you can save your breath; **deine Ratschläge kannst du dir** ~: you can keep your advice. ❷ *itr. V.* Ⓐ (*Geld zurücklegen*) save; **für** *od.* **auf etw.** (*Akk.*) ~: save up for sth.; **spare in der Zeit, so hast du in der Not** (*Spr.*) waste not, want not (*prov.*); Ⓑ (*sparsam wirtschaften*) economize (**mit** on); **er sparte nicht mit Lob** (*fig.*) he was unstinting *or* generous in his praise; **an etw.** (*Dat.*) ~ (*weniger nehmen*) be sparing with sth.; (*Billigeres nehmen*) economize on sth.; **am falschen Ort** *od.* **Ende** ~: make a false economy/false economies

**Sparer** *der;* ~**s**, ~, **Sparerin** *die;* ~, ~**nen** saver

**Spar·flamme** *die* low flame *or* heat; **auf** ~: on a low flame *or* heat

**Spargel** /ˈʃpargl̩/ *der;* ~**s**, ~, *schweiz. auch die;* ~, ~**n** asparagus *no pl., no indef. art.;* **ein** ~: an asparagus stalk

**Spargel-:** ~**creme·suppe** *die* cream of asparagus soup; ~**kraut** *das* asparagus fern; ~**spitze** *die* asparagus tip

**Spar-:** ~**groschen** *der* (*ugs.*) nest egg; savings *pl.;* ~**guthaben** *das* credit balance (*in a savings account*); **ein** ~**guthaben von 500 Mark haben** have 500 marks in one's savings *or* deposit account; ~**kasse** *die* savings bank; ~**kassen·buch** *das* savings book; passbook; ~**konto** *das* savings *or* deposit account

**spärlich** /ˈʃpɛːɐ̯lɪç/ ❶ *Adj.* sparse ‹vegetation, beard, growth›; thin ‹hair, applause›; scanty ‹leftovers, knowledge, news, evidence›; scanty, skimpy ‹clothing›; slack ‹demand›; scattered ‹remains, remnants›;

S

poor ‹lighting, harvest, result, source›; meagre ‹income, salary›; meagre, frugal ‹food, meal›. ❷ *adv.* sparsely, thinly ‹populated, covered›; poorly ‹lit, attended›; scantily, skimpily ‹dressed›; **die Nachrichten kamen/die Geldmittel flossen nur ~:** news/money was only coming in in dribs and drabs

**Spar-: ~maßnahme** *die* economy measure; **~paket** *das* austerity package; **~pfennig** *der* (*ugs.*) ⇨ **~groschen**; **~prämie** *die* savings premium; **~programm** *das* A (*bes. Politik*) programme of economy measures; B (*Technik*) economy programme

**Sparren** /ˈʃparən/ *der;* **~s, ~** A (*Dach~*) rafter; B (*Her.*) chevron; C (*ugs.: Spleen*) daft idea; **er hat einen ~ [zu viel** *od.* **zu wenig im Kopf]** (*ugs.*) he has a screw loose (*coll.*)

**Sparring** /ˈʃparɪŋ/ *das;* **~s** (*Boxen*) sparring *no art.*

**Sparrings·partner** *der,* **Sparrings·partnerin** *die* (*Boxen*) sparring partner

**sparsam** ❶ *Adj.* A thrifty ‹person›; (*wirtschaftlich*) economical; **durch ~en Umgang mit dem Material** by being economical *or* sparing with the material; **durch ~es Wirtschaften** by economizing; **mit etw. ~ sein** be economical with sth.; **er ist mit Worten/Lob immer sehr ~** (*fig.*) he is a man of few words/he is very sparing in his praise; B (*im Verbrauch*) economical; C (*fig.: gering, wenig, klein*) sparse ‹detail, decoration, interior, etc.›; economical ‹movement, manner of expression, etc.›; **er machte von dieser Möglichkeit nur ~en Gebrauch** he made little use of this opportunity; **die Wirkung ist schon bei ~ster Dosierung groß** even the most sparing dose has a strong effect.

❷ *adv.* A **~ mit der Butter/dem Papier umgehen** use butter/paper sparingly; economize on butter/paper; **~ leben** live frugally; **~ mit seinen Kräften umgehen** conserve one's energy; **~ wirtschaften** economize; budget carefully; B (*wirtschaftlich*) economically; C (*fig.: in geringem Maße*) ‹use› sparingly; sparsely ‹decorated, furnished›; **etw. ~ dosieren** use sth. in small doses

**Sparsamkeit** *die;* **~** A thrift[iness]; **das ist ~ am falschen Platze** that's a false economy; **aus ~:** for the sake of economizing; B (*Wirtschaftlichkeit*) economicalness; C (*fig.: geringes Maß*) economy

**Spar-: ~schwein** *das* piggy bank; **~strumpf** *der* stocking for keeping one's savings in

**Spartakiade** /ʃpartaˈki̯aːdə/ *die;* **~, ~n** Spartakiad

**Spartakist** /ʃpartaˈkɪst/ *der;* **~en, ~en, Spartakistin** *die;* **~, ~nen** Spartacist; Spartakist

**Spartaner** /ʃparˈtaːnɐ/ *der;* **~s, ~, Spartanerin** *die;* **~, ~nen** (*hist.*) Spartan

**spartanisch** ❶ *Adj.* (*auch fig.*). Spartan. ❷ *adv.* **~ leben** lead a Spartan life

**Sparte** /ˈʃpartə/ *die;* **~, ~n** A (*Teilbereich*) area; branch; (*eines Geschäfts*) line [of business]; (*des Wissens*) branch; field; speciality; (*des Sports, der Kunst*) discipline; B (*Rubrik*) section; (*Spalte*) column

**Sparten-: ~kanal** *der* special-interest channel; **~sender** *der* special-interest station

**Spar-: ~vertrag** *der* savings agreement; **~zins** *der; Pl.* **~en** interest *no pl.* on a savings account

**spasmisch** /ˈʃpasmɪʃ/ (*Med.*) ❶ *Adj.* spasmodic. ❷ *adv.* spasmodically

**Spasmus** /ˈʃpasmʊs/ *der;* **~, Spasmen** ▶ 474 (*Med.*) spasm

**Spaß** /ʃpaːs/ *der;* **~es, Späße** /ˈʃpɛːsə/ A (*Vergnügen*) fun; **wir hatten alle viel ~:** we all had a lot of fun *or* a really good time; we all really enjoyed ourselves; **~ an etw.** (*Dat.*) **haben** enjoy sth.; **verdirb ihm doch nicht seinen ~:** don't spoil his fun; **lass ihn doch, wenn er ~ dran hat!** let him, if it makes him happy; **meinetwegen, wenn du ~ daran hast** all right, if you want to; **~ an etw.** (*Dat.*) **finden** find sth. fun; **[jmdm.] ~/keinen ~ machen** be fun/no fun [for sb.]; **die Schule macht ihm großen/keinen/nicht viel ~:** he likes *or* enjoys school a great deal/doesn't like school/doesn't like school very much; **du machst mir [vielleicht] ~!** (*iron.*) you must be joking *or* (*sl.*) kidding; **sich** (*Dat.*) **einen ~ daraus machen, etw. zu tun** take great delight in doing sth.; **ein teurer ~** (*ugs.*) an expensive business; **was kostet der ~?** (*ugs.*) how much will that little lot cost? (*coll.*); **viel ~!** have a good time!; (*iron.*) have fun!; **das ist kein ~!** it's no fun; B (*Scherz*) joke; (*Streich*) prank; antic; **er macht nur ~:** he's only joking *or* (*sl.*) kidding; **~ beiseite!** joking aside *or* apart; **~ muss sein!** there's no harm in a joke; **da hört [für mich] der ~ auf** that's getting beyond a joke; **~/keinen ~ verstehen** be able/not be able to take a joke; have a/have no sense of humour; **in Gelddingen versteht er keinen ~:** he won't stand for any nonsense where money is concerned; **lass diese albernen Späße!** stop fooling around!; **er ist immer zu Späßen aufgelegt** he's always ready for a laugh; **im** *od.* **zum** *od.* **aus ~:** as a joke; for fun; **aus ~ an der Freude** (*scherzh.*) for the [sheer] fun of it; **sich** (*Dat.*) **einen ~ mit jmdm. machen** *od.* **erlauben** play a joke on sb.; **macht keine Späße!** surely you don't mean it; **aus [lauter] ~ und Tollerei** (*ugs.*) [just] for a laugh; just for the hell of it (*coll.*); **das ist kein ~ mehr!** that's gone beyond a joke; **seine Späße mit jmdm. treiben** get a laugh at sb.'s expense

**Späßchen** /ˈʃpɛːsçən/ *das;* **~s, ~:** little joke

**spaßen** /ˈʃpaːsn̩/ *itr. V.* A (*Spaß machen*) joke; kid (*coll.*); **Sie ~ wohl!** you must be joking *or* (*coll.*) kidding; B **er lässt nicht mit sich ~:** he won't stand for any nonsense; **mit ihm/damit ist nicht zu ~:** he/it is not to be trifled with; **mit so einer Entzündung ist nicht zu ~:** an inflammation like that shouldn't be shrugged off lightly

**spaßes·halber** *Adv.* for the fun of it; for fun

**spaßhaft** *Adj.* amusing; comical; funny

**spaßig** ❶ *Adj.* funny; comical; amusing. ❷ *adv.* in an amusing way

**Spaß-: ~macher** *der,* **~macherin** *die* joker; **~verderber** *der;* **~~s, ~~, ~verderberin** *die;* **~~, ~~nen** spoilsport; killjoy; wet blanket; **~vogel** *der* joker; **du bist vielleicht ein ~vogel!** you must be joking *or* (*coll.*) kidding

**spastisch** (*Med.*) ❶ *Adj.* spastic. ❷ *adv.* **~ gelähmt sein** suffer from spastic paralysis; **ein ~ Gelähmter** a spastic

**spät** /ʃpɛːt/ ❶ *Adj.* ▶ 752 late; belated ‹fame, repentance›; **am ~en Abend** in the late evening; **bis in die ~e Nacht** until late into the night; **die Werke des ~en Goethe** Goethe's late works; **wie ~ ist es?** what time is it?; **bei der Party ist es ziemlich ~ geworden** the party went on until quite late; **er kam zu ~er Stunde** (*geh.*) he came at a late hour; **ein ~es Mädchen** (*scherzh.*) an old maid; **ein ~es Glück** happiness late in life. ❷ *adv.* late; **~ am Abend** late in the evening; **du kommst aber ~!** you're very late; **wenn ich jetzt nicht losfahre, komme ich zu ~:** if I don't leave now I'll be late; **wir sind eine Station zu ~ ausgestiegen** we got out one station too far down the line; **wir sind [schon ziemlich] ~ dran** (*ugs.*) we're late [enough already]; **so ~ am Tage** so late in the day; **er hat erst ~ angefangen zu studieren** he began studying late in life; ⇨ *auch* **früh** 2

**Spat** /ʃpaːt/ *der;* **~[e]s, ~e** *od.* **Späte** /ˈʃpɛːtə/ (*Mineral*) spar

**spät-, Spät-: ~abends** *Adv.* /-ˈ-/ late in the evening; in the late evening; **~aussiedler** *der,* **~aussiedlerin** *die: person of German origin who emigrated from countries East of the Oder-Neisse border relatively late after 1945;* **~barock** *das od. der* (*Kunstwiss.*) late Baroque; **~dienst** *der* late duty; (*im Betrieb*) late shift; **~dienst haben** be on late shift

**Spatel** /ˈʃpaːtl̩/ *der;* **~s, ~** A spatula; B ⇨ **Spachtel** A

**Spaten** /ˈʃpaːtn̩/ *der;* **~s, ~:** spade

**Spaten·stich** *der* cut of the spade; **das Foto zeigt den Oberbürgermeister beim ersten ~:** the photo shows the mayor digging the first turf

**Spät·entwickler** *der,* **Spät·entwicklerin** *die;* **~, ~nen** late developer

**später** ❶ *Adj.* A (*nachfolgend, kommend*) later ‹years, generations, etc.›; B (*zukünftig*) future ‹owner, wife, etc.›. ❷ *Adv.* later; **er soll ~ [einmal] die Leitung der Firma übernehmen** he is to take over management of the firm at some future date; **was willst du denn ~ [einmal] werden?** what do you want to do when you grow up?; **jmdn. auf ~ vertrösten** put sb. off until later; **ich hebe es mir für ~ auf** I'll save it for later [on]; **[also dann] bis ~!** see you later!

**später·hin** *Adv.* (*geh.*) later [on]

**spätestens** *Adv.* at the latest; **~ gestern/[am] Freitag** yesterday/[on] Friday at the latest

**Spät-: ~folge** *die* long-term consequence; (*Med.*) late sequela; **~geburt** *die* post-term birth; **~gotik** *die* (*Kunstwiss.*) late Gothic; **~heimkehrer** *der* late returnee (*from a prisoner-of-war camp*); **~herbst** *der* late autumn *or* (*Amer.*) fall; **~lese** *die* late vintage; **~nachmittag** *der* late afternoon; **~schaden** *der* long-term damage *no pl., no indef. art.;* **~schalter** *der: counter that is open late;* **~schicht** *die* late shift; **~sommer** *der* late summer; **~vorstellung** *die* (*Film*) late showing; (*Theater*) late performance; **~werk** *das* late work

**Spatz** /ʃpats/ *der;* **~en, ~en** A sparrow; **er isst wie ein ~:** he eats like a bird; **besser ein ~ in der Hand als eine Taube auf dem Dach** (*Spr.*) a bird in the hand is worth two in the bush (*prov.*); **die ~en pfeifen es von den** *od.* **allen Dächern** it's common knowledge; B (*fam.: Liebling*) pet; C (*fam.: kleines Kind*) mite; tot (*coll.*)

**Spätzchen** /ˈʃpɛtsçən/ *das;* **~s, ~** A little sparrow; B ⇨ **Spatz** B, C

**Spätzeit** *die* end; **in der ~ der Renaissance** in the late Renaissance; **Dürers Bildnisse der ~:** Dürer's late portraits

**Spatzen·[ge]hirn** *das* (*salopp abwertend*) birdbrain (*coll.*); **sie hat ein ~:** she's birdbrained (*coll.*); she's a birdbrain (*coll.*)

**Spätzle** /ˈʃpɛtslə/ *Pl.* spaetzle; spätzle; *kind of noodles*

**Spät-: ~zug** *der* late train; **~zünder** *der* (*ugs. scherzh.*) **ein ~zünder sein** be slow on the uptake; **~zündung** *die* (*Technik*) retarded ignition

**spazieren** /ʃpaˈtsiːrən/ *itr. V.; mit sein* A stroll; **~ fahren** (*im Auto*) go for a drive *or* ride *or* spin; (*im Bus usw., mit dem Fahrrad od. Motorrad*) go for a ride; (*mit einem Schiff*) go for a [boat] trip; (*mit einem Ruderboot*) go for a row; (*mit einem Segelboot*) go for a sail; **jmdn. ~ fahren** (*im Auto*) take sb. for a drive *or* ride *or* spin; **ein Kind [im Kinderwagen] ~ fahren** take a baby for a walk [in a pram]; **die Kinder mit dem Schlitten/im Boot ~ fahren** take the children out on the sledge/on a boat trip; **~ gehen** go for a walk *or* stroll; **ein Stück ~ gehen** go for a little walk *or* stroll; **hier kann man schön ~ gehen** you can go for pleasant walks here; **eine schöne Gegend zum Spazierengehen** a pleasant area for walks; B (*veralt.: spazieren gehen*) go for a walk *or* stroll; **wir sind ~ gewesen** we went for a walk *or* stroll

***spazieren|fahren, *spazieren|gehen** ⇨ **spazieren** A

**Spazier-: ~fahrt** *die* (*mit dem Auto*) drive; ride; spin; (*mit dem Bus usw., mit dem Fahrrad od. Motorrad*) ride; (*mit einem Schiff*) [boat] trip; (*mit einem Ruderboot*) row; (*mit einem Segelboot*) sail; **~gang** *der* walk; stroll; **~gänger** *der;* **~~s, ~~, ~gängerin** *die;* **~~, ~~nen** person out for a walk *or* stroll; **~ritt** *der* ride; **~stock** *der; Pl.* **~stöcke** walking stick; **~weg** *der* footpath

**SPD** *Abk.* **Sozialdemokratische Partei Deutschlands** SPD

*old spelling (see note on page 1707)

**Specht** /ʃpɛçt/ *der;* **~[e]s, ~e** woodpecker

**Speck** /ʃpɛk/ *der;* **~[e]s, ~e** A bacon fat; (*Schinken~*) bacon; **durchwachsener ~:** streaky bacon; **fetter ~:** bacon fat; **ran an den ~!** (*ugs.*) get stuck in! (*coll.*); get to it! (*coll.*); **mit ~ fängt man Mäuse** (*Spr.*) if the bait is tempting enough, the fish will bite; B (*von Walen, Robben*) blubber; C (*ugs. scherzh.: Fettpolster*) fat; flab (*sl.*); **er hat ganz schön ~ auf den Rippen** he's well padded

**Speck·bauch** *der* (*ugs.*) potbelly; paunch

**speckig** *Adj.* greasy

**Speck-: ~nacken** *der* (*ugs.*) fat neck; **~scheibe** *die* rasher *or* slice of bacon; **~schwarte** *die* bacon rind; **~seite** *die* side of bacon; **~stein** *der* (*Mineral*) lard stone; soapstone; steatite

**Spediteur** /ʃpedi'tøːɐ̯/ *der;* **~s, ~e, Spediteurin** *die;* **~, ~nen** A (*Vermittler[in]*) forwarding agent; (*per Schiff*) shipping agent; (*per Flugzeug*) air freight agent; B (*Beförderer/Beförderin*) carrier; haulier; haulage contractor; (*per Schiff*) carrier; (*Möbelspediteur[in]*) furniture remover

**Spedition** /ʃpedi'tsi̯oːn/ *die;* **~, ~en** A (*Beförderung*) carriage; transport; B ⇒ **Speditionsfirma**

**Speditions-: ~firma** *die* forwarding agency; (*per Schiff*) shipping agency; (*Transportunternehmen*) haulage firm; firm of hauliers; (*per Schiff*) firm of carriers; (*Möbelspedition*) removal firm; **~kauffrau** *die,* **~kaufmann** *der* forwarding agent; shipping agent; (*für Möbelspedition*) furniture remover

**Speedway·rennen** /'spiːdweɪ-/ *das* (*Motorsport*) speedway racing; (*Veranstaltung*) speedway race

**Speer** /ʃpeːɐ̯/ *der;* **~[e]s, ~e** A spear; B (*Sportgerät*) javelin

**Speer-: ~spitze** *die* A (*auch fig.*) spearhead; B (*des Sportgeräts*) tip of a/the javelin; **~werfen** *das;* **~~s** ⇒ **~wurf** A; **~werfer** *der,* **~werferin** *die* (*Sport*) javelin-thrower; **~wurf** *der* A (*Disziplin*) javelin-throwing; B (*Wurf*) javelin-throw

**Speiche** /'ʃpai̯çə/ *die;* **~, ~n** A spoke; B ▶ 471 (*Anat.*) radius

**Speichel** /'ʃpai̯çl̩/ *der;* **~s** saliva; spittle

**Speichel-: ~drüse** *die* salivary gland; **~fluss,** ***~fluß** *der* A salivation *no art.;* B (*Med.: übermäßige Sekretion*) salivation *no art.;* ptyalism *no art.*

**speicheln** *itr. V.* salivate

**Speichen-: ~dynamo** *der* spoke dynamo; **~rad** *das* spoked wheel

**Speichen·reflektor** *der* wheel reflector

**Speicher** /'ʃpai̯çɐ/ *der;* **~s, ~** A storehouse; (*Lagerhaus*) warehouse; (*~becken*) reservoir; (*fig.*) store; B (*südd.: Dachboden*) loft; attic; **auf dem ~:** in the loft *or* attic; C (*Elektronik*) memory; store

**Speicher·kapazität** *die* storage capacity; (*DV*) memory *or* storage capacity

**speichern** *tr. V.* store

**Speicherung** *die;* **~, ~en** storing; storage

**speien** /'ʃpai̯ən/ *unr. tr., itr. V.* (*geh.*) A (*spucken*) spit; spew [forth] ‹lava, fire, etc.›; belch ‹smoke›; spout ‹water›; **der Drache spie Feuer** the dragon breathed fire; B (*erbrechen*) vomit

**Speise** /'ʃpai̯zə/ *die;* **~, ~n** A (*Gericht*) dish; **~n und Getränke** food and drink; „**kalte/warme ~n**" 'cold/hot dishes'; B (*geh.: Nahrung*) food; C (*nordd.: süße Nachspeise*) dessert; sweet (*Brit.*)

**Speise-: ~eis** *das* ice cream; **~fett** *das* edible fat; **~fisch** *der* food fish; **~gaststätte** *die* restaurant; **~kammer** *die* larder; pantry; **~karte** *die* menu; **~lokal** *das* restaurant

**speisen** **1** *itr. V.* (*geh.*) eat; (*dinieren*) dine; **haben Sie schon gespeist?** have you eaten yet?; **zu Mittag/Abend ~:** lunch *or* have lunch/dine *or* have dinner. **2** *tr. V.* A (*geh.: verzehren*) eat; (*dinieren*) dine on; **was wünschen Sie zu ~?** what do you wish to eat?; B (*geh.*) (*ernähren, auch fig.*) feed; (*bewirten*) dine; C (*Technik*) **etw. mit Strom/Wasser ~:** supply sth. with electricity/water; **ein von Batterien gespeister Elektromotor** an electric motor powered by batteries; **Strom in das öffentliche Netz ~:** feed electricity [in]to the national grid. **3** *refl. V.* be fed (**aus, von** by)

**Speisen-: ~auf·zug** *der* dumb waiter; **~folge** *die* (*geh.*) menu

**Speise-: ~öl** *das* edible oil; **~plan** *der* menu (*for the week etc.*); **~reste** *Pl.* leftovers; (*zwischen den Zähnen*) food particles; **~röhre** *die* ▶ 471 (*Anat.*) gullet; oesophagus (*Anat.*); **~saal** *der* dining hall; (*im Hotel, in einer Villa usw.*) dining room; (*auf Schiffen*) dining saloon; dining room; **~schrank** *der* food cupboard; **~wagen** *der* dining car; restaurant car (*Brit.*); **~würze** *die* seasoning additive; **~zettel** *der* menu; **auf dem ~zettel des Eichhörnchens stehen auch Vogeleier** (*fig.*) the squirrel's diet also includes birds' eggs; **~zimmer** *das* dining room

**Speisung** *die;* **~, ~en** A (*geh.*) feeding; B (*Technik*) supplying

**spei·übel** *Adj.* **mir ist ~:** I think I'm going to be violently sick

**Spektabilität** /ʃpɛktabili'tɛːt/ *die;* **~, ~en** (*Hochschulw.*) *title of the dean of a university;* **an seine ~ den Dekan der ... Fakultät** to the Dean of the Faculty of ...

**Spektakel**[1] /ʃpɛk'taːkl̩/ *der;* **~s, ~** (*ugs.*) A (*Lärm*) row (*coll.*); rumpus (*coll.*); racket; B (*laute Auseinandersetzung, Theater*) fuss; **einen ~ machen** kick up *or* make a fuss

**Spektakel**[2] *das;* **~s, ~** A (*veralt.*) spectacle; show; B (*fig.*) spectacle

**spektakulär** /ʃpɛktaku'lɛːɐ̯/ **1** *Adj.* spectacular; (*sensationell*) sensational. **2** *adv.* spectacularly; (*sensationell*) sensationally

**Spektral-: ~analyse** *die* (*Technik*) spectral analysis; **~farbe** *die* colour of the spectrum

**Spektren** ⇒ **Spektrum**

**Spektroskop** /ʃpɛktro'skoːp/ *das;* **~s, ~e** (*Technik*) spectroscope

**Spektrum** /'ʃpɛktrʊm/ *das;* **~s, Spektren** (*auch fig.*) spectrum

**Spekula** ⇒ **Spekulum**

**Spekulant** /ʃpeku'lant/ *der;* **~en, ~en, Spekulantin** *die;* **~, ~nen** speculator

**Spekulation** /ʃpekula'tsi̯oːn/ *die;* **~, ~en** A (*Mutmaßung, Erwartung; auch Philos.*) speculation; **das sind alles nur ~en** that is all merely speculation *sing. or* conjecture *sing.;* B (*Wirtsch.*) speculation (**mit** in); **die ~ mit Grundstücken** property speculation

**Spekulations-: ~geschäft** *das* (*Wirtsch.*) speculative deal; **~objekt** *das* object of speculative investment

**Spekulatius** /ʃpeku'laːtsi̯ʊs/ *der;* **~, ~:** *spiced biscuit in the shape of a human or other figure, eaten at Christmas*

**spekulativ** /ʃpekula'tiːf/ **1** *Adj.* speculative. **2** *adv.* speculatively

**spekulieren** /ʃpeku'liːrən/ *itr. V.* A (*ugs.*) **darauf ~, etw. tun zu können** count on being able to do sth.; **er spekuliert auf den Laden** he's counting on getting the shop; B (*mutmaßen*) speculate; C (*Wirtsch.*) speculate (**mit** in); ⇒ *auch* **Baisse**; **Hausse**

**Spekulum** /'ʃpeːkulʊm/ *das;* **~s, Spekula** (*Med.*) speculum

**Spelunke** /ʃpe'lʊŋkə/ *die;* **~, ~n** (*ugs. abwertend*) dive (*coll.*)

**Spelze** /'ʃpɛltsə/ *die;* **~, ~n** (*des Getreidekorns*) husk; (*der Grasblüte*) glume

**spelzig** *Adj.* full of husks *postpos.*

**spendabel** /ʃpɛn'daːbl̩/ *Adj.* generous; open-handed

**Spende** /'ʃpɛndə/ *die;* **~, ~n** donation; contribution; **eine kleine ~ bitte!** would you like to make a small donation?

**spenden** *tr., itr. V.* A donate; give; contribute; **[etw.] fürs Rote Kreuz ~:** contribute [sth.] to *or* for the Red Cross; **Blut/eine Niere ~:** give blood/donate a kidney; B (*fig. geh.*) give ‹light›; afford, give ‹shade›; give off ‹heat›; provide ‹water›; administer ‹communion, baptism›; give, bestow ‹blessing›; confer ‹holy orders›; **jmdm. Beifall/Trost ~:** give sb. applause/comfort; applaud/comfort sb.; **Leben ~d** life-giving

**Spenden-: ~aktion** *die* campaign for donations; **~auf·ruf** *der* appeal for donations; **~konto** *das* donations account

**Spender** *der;* **~s, ~** A donor; donator; contributor; (*Organ~, Blut~*) donor; **wer war der edle ~?** to whom am I indebted?; B (*Behälter*) dispenser

**Spenderherz** *das* donor heart

**Spenderin** *die;* **~, ~nen** ⇒ **Spender** A

**Spender-: ~niere** *die* donor kidney; **~organ** *das* donor organ

**spendieren** *tr. V.* (*ugs.*) get, buy ‹drink, meal, etc.›; stand ‹round›; **jmdm. ein Bier/eine Tafel Schokolade ~:** stand *or* get sb. a beer/buy *or* get sb. a bar of chocolate

**Spendier·hosen** *Pl.* *in* **die/seine ~ anhaben** be in a generous mood; be feeling generous

**Spengler** /'ʃpɛŋlɐ/ *der;* **~s, ~, Spenglerin** *die;* **~, ~nen** (*südd., österr., schweiz.*) ⇒ **Klempner**

**Spenzer** /'ʃpɛntsɐ/ *der;* **~s, ~** A (*Jacke*) spencer; B (*Unterhemd*) tight-fitting short-sleeved vest

**Sperber** /'ʃpɛrbɐ/ *der;* **~s, ~:** sparrowhawk

**Sperenzchen** /ʃpe'rɛntsçən/ *Pl.* (*ugs.*) **~ machen** give trouble; **mach keine ~!** don't be difficult!

**Sperling** /'ʃpɛrlɪŋ/ *der;* **~s, ~e** sparrow; **besser ein ~ in der Hand als eine Taube auf dem Dach** (*Spr.*) a bird in the hand is worth two in the bush (*prov.*)

**Sperma** /'ʃpɛrma/ *das;* **~s, Spermen** *od.* **Spermata** sperm; semen

**Spermium** /'ʃpɛrmi̯ʊm/ *das;* **~s, Spermien** (*Biol.*) spermatozoon; sperm

**sperr·angel·weit** *Adv.* (*ugs.*) **~ offen** *od.* **geöffnet** wide open

**Sperr·bezirk** *der* A restricted *or* prohibited area; B (*für Prostituierte*) *area in which prostitution is prohibited;* C (*Gesundheitswesen*) infected area

**Sperre** *die;* **~, ~n** A (*Barriere*) barrier; (*Straßen~*) roadblock; B (*Milit.*) obstacle; (*Draht~*) entanglement; C (*Eisenb.*) barrier; D (*fig.: Verbot, auch Sport*) ban; (*Handels~*) embargo; (*Import~, Export~*) blockade; (*Nachrichten~*) [news] blackout; E (*Psych.: Blockierung, Hemmung*) block; F (*Technik*) locking device

**sperren** **1** *tr. V.* A close ‹road, tunnel, bridge, entrance, border, etc.›; close off ‹area›; **etw. für jmdn./etw. ~:** close sth. to sb./sth.; B (*blockieren*) block ‹entrance, access, etc.›; C (*Technik*) lock ‹mechanism etc.›; D **jmdm. das Gehalt/den Urlaub ~:** stop sb.'s salary/leave; **einem Soldaten den Ausgang ~:** confine a soldier to barracks; E cut off, disconnect ‹water, gas, electricity, etc.›; **jmdm. den Strom/das Telefon ~:** cut off *or* disconnect sb.'s electricity/telephone; F (*Bankw.*) stop ‹cheque, overdraft facility›; freeze ‹bank account›; **jmdm. das Konto ~:** freeze sb.'s account; G (*ein~*) **ein Tier/jmdn. in etw.** (*Akk.*) **~:** shut *or* lock an animal/sb. in sth.; **jmdn. ins Gefängnis ~:** put sb. in prison; lock sb. up [in prison]; H (*Sport: behindern*) obstruct; I (*Sport: von der Teilnahme ausschließen*) ban; J (*Druckw.: spationieren*) print ‹word, text› with the letters spaced.
**2** *refl. V.* **sich [gegen etw.] ~:** balk *or* jib [at sth.].
**3** *itr. V.* (*Sport*) obstruct; **Sperren ohne Ball** obstruction off the ball

**Sperr-: ~feuer** *das* (*Milit.*) barrage; **~frist** *die* (*auch Rechtsspr.*) waiting period; **~gebiet** ⇒ **~bezirk**; **~gürtel** *der* cordon; **~holz** *das* plywood

**sperrig** *Adj.* unwieldy

**Sperr-: ~konto** *das* (*Bankw.*) blocked account; **~minorität** *die* (*Wirtsch., Politik*) blocking minority; **~müll** *der* bulky refuse (*for which there is a separate collection service*); **morgen ist ~müll** (*ugs.*) they're collecting bulky refuse tomorrow; **~sitz** *der* (*im Kino*) seat in the back stalls; (*im Zirkus*) front seat; (*im Theater*) seat in the front stalls; **wir saßen ~sitz** we sat in the back stalls/front seats/front stalls; **~stunde** *die* closing time

**Sperrung** *die;* ~, **~en** ⇒ **sperren** 1 A-F, I: closing; closing off; blocking; locking; stopping; cutting off; disconnection; freezing; banning

**Sperr·vermerk** *der* restriction note (*regarding sale of property, withdrawal of investment, disclosure of information, etc.*)

**Spesen** /ˈʃpe:zn̩/ *Pl.* expenses; **auf ~:** on expenses; **~ machen** incur expenses; **außer ~ nichts gewesen** (*scherzh.*) [it was] a waste of time and effort

**Spezerei** /ʃpe:tsəˈrai/ *die;* ~, **~en** (*veralt.*) spice

**Spezi** /ˈʃpe:tsi/ *der;* **~s, ~[s]** Ⓐ (*südd., österr., schweiz. ugs.*) [bosom] pal (*coll.*); chum (*coll.*); Ⓑ (*ugs.: Getränk*) lemonade and cola

**Spezial-: ~gebiet** *das* special *or* specialist field; **~geschäft** *das* specialist shop

**spezialisieren** *refl. V.* specialize (**auf** + *Akk.* in)

**Spezialist** *der;* **~en, ~en, Spezialistin** *die;* ~, **~nen** specialist

**Spezialität** /ʃpetsialiˈtɛ:t/ *die;* ~, **~en** speciality; specialty

**Spezialitäten·restaurant** *das* speciality restaurant

**Spezial·slalom** *der* (*Ski*) special slalom

**speziell** /ʃpeˈtsiɛl/ ❶ *Adj.* special; specific ‹question, problem, etc.›; specialized ‹book, knowledge, etc.›; **er ist mein ~er Freund** he's a special friend of mine; (*iron.*) we're the best of enemies (*joc.*); **auf dein Spezielles!** your very good health!. ❷ *Adv.* (*besonders, gerade*) especially; (*eigens*) specially; **~ du** you especially; you of all people

**Spezies** /ˈʃpe:tsiɛs/ *die;* ~, **~:** species; **eine besondere ~ [von] Mensch** a special type of person

**Spezifikation** /ʃpetsifikaˈtsio:n/ *die;* ~, **~en** specification

**Spezifikum** /ʃpeˈtsi:fikʊm/ *das;* **~s, Spezifika** Ⓐ (*Besonderheit*) specific characteristic; Ⓑ (*Pharm.*) specific

**spezifisch** ❶ *Adj.* specific; characteristic ‹smell, style›; **~es Gewicht/~e Wärme** (*Phys.*) specific gravity/heat. ❷ *adv.* specifically

**spezifizieren** *tr. V.* specify; (*einzeln aufführen*) itemize ‹bill, expenses, etc.›

**Spezifizierung** *die;* ~, **~en** specification; (*einer Rechnung, von Kosten*) itemization

**Sphäre** /ˈsfɛ:rə/ *die;* ~, **~n** (*auch fig.*) sphere; **in höheren ~n schweben** (*scherzh.*) have one's head in the clouds

**Sphären·harmonie** *die* (*Philos.*) harmony of the spheres

**sphärisch** *Adj.* Ⓐ spherical; Ⓑ (*fig.: himmlisch*) heavenly

**Sphäroid** /sfɛroˈi:t/ *das;* **~[e]s, ~e** (*Geom.*) spheroid

**Sphinx**[1] /sfɪŋks/ *die od. der;* ~, **~e** *od.* **Sphingen** /ˈsfɪŋən/ (*Ägyptologie, Kunstwiss.*) sphinx; **die ~ von Gise** the Sphinx at Giza

**Sphinx**[2] *die;* ~, **~e** *od.* **Sphingen** (*griech. Myth., Kunstwiss.*) Sphinx

**Spick·aal** *der* (*bes. nordd.*) smoked eel

**spicken** /ˈʃpɪkn̩/ ❶ *tr. V.* Ⓐ (*Kochk.*) lard; **jmdn. ~** (*fig. ugs.*) grease sb.'s palm; Ⓑ (*fig. ugs.: reichlich versehen*) **eine Rede mit Zitaten ~:** lard a speech with quotations; **das Diktat war mit Fehlern gespickt** the dictation was full of mistakes. ❷ *itr. V.* (*bes. südd. ugs.*) crib (*coll.*)

**Spick-: ~nadel** *die* larding needle; **~zettel** *der* (*bes. südd. ugs.*) crib (*coll.*); (*fig.: eines Redners*) notes *pl.*

**spie** /ʃpi:/ *1. u. 3. Pers. Sg. Prät. v.* **speien**

**Spiegel** /ˈʃpi:gl̩/ *der;* **~s,** ~ Ⓐ mirror; **in den ~ sehen** *od.* **schauen** look in the mirror; **im ~ der Presse** (*fig.*) as mirrored *or* reflected in the press; **dieser Roman ist ein ~ unserer Zeit** (*fig.*) this novel is a reflection of our time; **jmdm. den ~ vorhalten** (*fig.*) hold the mirror up to sb.; **das kannst du dir hinter den ~ stecken!** (*fig. ugs.*) you'll do well to remember that!; Ⓑ (*Wasserstand, Blutzucker~, Alkohol~ usw.*) level; (*Wasseroberfläche*) surface; Ⓒ (*am Frack, Smoking*) [silk] lapel; Ⓓ (*am Kragen*) tab; Ⓔ (*Jägerspr., Zool.*) (*bei Rehen, Hirschen usw.*) [white] rump patch; (*bei Vögeln*) speculum; Ⓕ (*fig.: Übersicht*) breakdown

**spiegel-, Spiegel-: ~bild** *das* (*auch fig., Math.*) reflection; **~bildlich** ❶ *Adj.* **eine ~bildliche Abbildung** a mirror image; ❷ *adv.* **~bildlich abgebildet** reproduced as a *or* in mirror image; **~blank** *Adj.* shining; **den Fußboden ~blank bohnern** polish the floor until it shines [like a mirror]; **~ei** *das* fried egg; **~fechterei** *die;* **~~, ~~en: das ist ~fechterei/sind ~fechtereien** that's all a sham; **~glas** *das* mirror glass; **~glatt** *Adj.* like glass *postpos.;* as smooth as glass *postpos.;* **die Straße war ~glatt gefroren** the road was like a sheet of glass; **~karpfen** *der* mirror carp

**spiegeln** ❶ *itr. V.* Ⓐ (*glänzen*) shine; gleam; Ⓑ (*als Spiegel wirken*) reflect the light; **nicht ~des Glas** non-reflective glass. ❷ *tr. V.* Ⓐ (*reflektieren*) reflect; mirror; Ⓑ (*Med.*) examine ‹body cavity› with a speculum. ❸ *refl. V.* (*auch fig.*) be mirrored *or* reflected; **in ihrem Gesicht spiegelte sich Freude** (*fig.*) her face shone with delight

**Spiegel-: ~reflex·kamera** *die* reflex camera; **~saal** *der* hall of mirrors; **~schrank** *der* wardrobe/cupboard/cabinet with mirror doors; **~schrift** *die* mirror writing; **~teleskop** *das* reflecting telescope; reflector

**Spiegelung** *die;* ~, **~en** Ⓐ (*auch fig., Math.*) reflection; Ⓑ (*Med.*) speculum examination

**spiegel·verkehrt** ❶ *Adj.* back-to-front ‹lettering›; **eine ~e Abbildung** a mirror image. ❷ *adv.* **etw. ~ abbilden** reproduce sth. as a *or* in mirror image

**Spiel** /ʃpi:l/ *das;* **~[e]s, ~e** Ⓐ (*das ~en, ~erei*) play; **er treibt ein ~ mit ihr** he's playing games *pl.* with her; **für ihn ist alles nur ein ~:** everything's just a game to him; **pass auf, dass du das ~ nicht zu weit treibst** be careful that you don't push your luck too far; **das ist doch ein ~ mit dem Leben** that's risking your/his *etc.* life; **wie im ~:** as if it were child's play; **ein ~ mit dem Feuer** (*fig.*) playing with fire; **ein [merkwürdiges] ~ des Zufalls/Schicksals** a whim of chance/fate; **ein seltsames ~ der Natur** a freak of nature; **freies ~ haben** be able to do what one wants *or* as one pleases; **genug des grausamen ~s!** (*scherzh.*) enough is enough!; Ⓑ (*Glücks~, Gesellschafts~*) game; (*Wett~*) game; match; **ein ~ spielen/gewinnen** play/win a game; **einen ~er aus dem ~ nehmen/ins ~ schicken** take a player off/send a player on; **dem ~ verfallen sein** be addicted to gambling *or* gaming; **sein Geld beim ~ verlieren** gamble one's money away; **machen Sie Ihr ~!** (*Roulette*) place your bets; faites vos jeux; **das ~ ist aus** the game is up; **gewonnenes ~ haben** be home and dry; **leichtes ~ [mit jmdm.] haben** have an easy job [with sb.]; **mit Frauen ihres Typs hat ein Casanova wie er leichtes ~:** women like her are easy game for a Casanova like him; **das ~ verloren geben** give the game up for lost; (*fig.*) throw in the towel *or* one's hand; **auf dem ~ stehen** be at stake; **etw. aufs ~ setzen** put sth. at stake; risk sth.; **ein falsches/doppeltes/unfaires ~ spielen** *od.* **treiben** play sb. false/double-cross sb./treat sb. unfairly; **jmdn./etw. aus dem ~ lassen** (*fig.*) leave sb./sth. out of it; **aus dem ~ bleiben** (*fig.*) ‹person› stay out of it; **jmdn./etw. ins ~ bringen** (*fig.*) bring sb./sth. into it; **ins ~ kommen** (*fig.*) ‹factor› come into play; ‹person, authorities, etc.› become involved; ‹matter, subject, etc.› come into it; **im ~ sein** (*fig.*) be involved; ⇒ *auch* **Hand** F; Ⓒ (*Utensilien*) game; **ein ~ Karten** a pack of cards; **das ~ ist nicht mehr vollständig** there's something missing from the set; **ein ~ Stricknadeln/Saiten** (*fig.*) a set of knitting needles/strings; Ⓓ (*eines Schauspielers*) performance; Ⓔ (*eines Musikers*) performance; playing; ⇒ *auch* **klingend** 2; Ⓕ (*Sport: ~weise*) game; Ⓖ (*Schau~*) play; Ⓗ (*Technik: Bewegungsfreiheit*) [free] play; Ⓘ (*fig.: Bewegung*) play

**Spiel-: ~alter** *das* playing stage; **~anzug** *der* playsuit; rompers *pl.;* **~art** *die* variety; **~automat** *der* gaming machine; (*Geschicklichkeitsspiel*) amusement machine; **~ball** *der* Ⓐ (*Sport*) (*Tennis*) game point; (*Volleyball*) match ball; Ⓑ (*Billard*) red [ball]; Ⓒ (*fig.*) plaything; **das Boot war ein ~ball der Wellen** the boat was at the mercy of *or* was tossed about by the waves; **sie ist der ~ball ihrer Leidenschaften** she allows herself to be torn hither and thither by her passions; Ⓓ (*Ball, mit dem gespielt wird*) match ball; **~bank** *die; Pl.* **~~en** casino; **~bein** *das* (*Sport*) free leg; (*Fußball*) striking leg; **~dose** *die* musical box (*Brit.*); music box (*Amer.*)

**spielen** ❶ *itr. V.* Ⓐ play; **~ gehen** go off to play; **der Wind spielte mit ihrem Haar** (*fig.*) the wind played in her hair; **um die Meisterschaft ~:** play for the championship; **sie haben 1:0/unentschieden gespielt** the match ended 1-0/in a draw; **er spielt in der Abwehr/als Libero** he plays in defence/as sweeper; **auf der Gitarre ~:** play the guitar; **er kann vom Blatt/nach Noten ~:** he can sight-read/play from music; **vierhändig ~:** play a [piano] duet/[piano] duets; **sie spielt nur mit ihm/seinen Gefühlen** she's only playing a game with him/playing with his feelings; **du darfst nicht mit deinem Leben ~:** you mustn't gamble with *or* risk your life; Ⓑ (*um Geld*) play; **er begann zu trinken und zu ~:** he began to drink and to gamble; **um Geld ~:** play for money; **mit hohem Einsatz ~:** play for high stakes; **an einem Spielautomaten ~:** play a fruit machine/(*Geschicklichkeitsspiel*) an amusement machine; ⇒ *auch* **Lotto**; Ⓒ (*als Schauspieler*) act; perform; Ⓓ (*sich ab~*) **der Roman/Film spielt im 17. Jahrhundert/in Berlin** the novel/film is set in the 17th century/in Berlin; Ⓔ (*fig.: sich bewegen*) ‹wind, water, etc.› play; **ein Lächeln spielte um ihre Lippen** (*fig.*) a smile played on her lips; **seine Muskeln ~ lassen** flex one's muscles; **seinen Charme/seine Beziehungen ~ lassen** (*fig.*) bring one's charm/connections to bear; **seine Fantasie ~ lassen** use one's imagination; Ⓕ (*fig.: übergehen*) **das Blau spielt ins Violette** the blue is tinged with purple; **ein ins Bräunliche ~des Rot** a red with a brownish tinge.
❷ *tr. V.* Ⓐ play; **Räuber und Gendarm ~:** play cops and robbers; **Cowboy ~:** play at being a cowboy; **er spielt hervorragend Schach/Tennis** he's an excellent chess/tennis player; **Geige/Akkordeon/Gitarre** *usw.* **~:** play the violin/accordion/guitar *etc.;* **er spielt hervorragend Gitarre** he's an outstanding guitarist; **Trumpf/Pik/ein As ~:** play a trump/spades/an ace; Ⓑ (*aufführen, vorführen*) put on ‹play›; show ‹film›; perform ‹piece of music›; play ‹record›; **spiel doch mal die Beatles** put the Beatles on; **das Radio spielte Jazz** there was jazz on the radio; **was wird hier gespielt?** (*fig. ugs.*) what's going on here?; Ⓒ (*schauspielerisch darstellen*) play ‹role›; **den Beleidigten/Unschuldigen ~** (*fig.*) act offended/play the innocent; **sie spielt gern die große Dame** (*fig.*) she likes playing *or* acting the grand lady; **[für jmdn.] den Chauffeur ~:** act as chauffeur for sb.; **[bei jmdm.] Babysitter ~** (*fig.*) be babysitter *or* do the babysitting [for sb.]; **sie reagierte mit gespielter Gleichgültigkeit** she reacted with feigned indifference; **sein Interesse war [nur] gespielt** he [only] pretended to be interested; his interest was [merely] feigned; **in gespieltem Ernst** with mock seriousness; Ⓓ (*Sport: werfen, treten, schlagen*) play; **einen Ball mit Rückhand/mit dem linken Fuß ~:** play a ball backhand/with the left foot; **den Ball ins Aus/vors Tor ~:** put the ball out/play the ball in towards the goal; **einen**

*old spelling (see note on page 1707)

S

**Ball mit dem Kopf ~:** head a ball. **❸** *refl. V.* **sich warm ~:** warm up; **sich hungrig/müde ~:** work up an appetite/tire oneself out playing

**spielend ❶** *Adj.* **mit ~er Leichtigkeit** with consummate *or* effortless ease. **❷** *adv.* easily; **etw. ~ beherrschen** master sth. effortlessly; **~ leicht** without the slightest effort

**Spieler** *der;* **~s, ~ Ⓐ** *(auch Sport, Musik)* player; **Ⓑ** *(Glücks~)* gambler; **Ⓒ** *(Schau~)* actor

**Spielerei** *die;* **~, ~en Ⓐ** playing *no art.; (im Glücksspiel)* gambling *no art.; (das Herumspielen)* playing *or* fiddling about *or* around **(an** + *Dat.* with); **Ⓑ** *(müßiges Tun, Spiel)* **eine ~ mit Worten/Zahlen** playing [around] with words/numbers; **eine mathematische ~:** a mathematical game; **für ihn ist das nur eine ~:** he's just playing about; **Ⓒ** *(Kinderspiel, Leichtigkeit)* child's play *no art.;* **das ist keine ~:** it has to be taken seriously; **Ⓓ** *(Tand)* gadget; **technische ~en** technical gadgetry *sing.*

**Spielerin** *die;* **~, ~nen Ⓐ ⇒ Spieler** A, B; **Ⓑ** *(Schau~)* actress

**spielerisch ❶** *Adj.* **Ⓐ** playful; **mit ~er Leichtigkeit** with consummate *or* effortless ease; **Ⓑ** *(Sport)* **sein ~es Können** his skill as a player; **~e Elemente** playing skills; **eine ausgezeichnete ~e Leistung** an outstanding [playing] performance; **Ⓒ** *(Musik)* **~es Können** playing ability. **❷** *adv.* **Ⓐ** playfully; **seine Hände glitten ~ über die Tasten** his hands glided lightly and easily over the keys; **Ⓑ** *(Sport)* in playing terms; **Ⓒ** *(Musik)* in terms of performance

**spiel-, Spiel-: ~feld** *das (Fußball, Hockey, Rugby usw.)* field; pitch *(Brit.); (Tennis, Squash, Federball, Volleyball usw.)* court; **~figur** *die* piece; **~film** *der* feature film; **~frei** *Adj.* **ein ~freier Tag** *(Theater)* a day when there is no performance/are no performances; *(Sport)* a day without a match; **~führer** *der,* **~führerin** *die (Sport)* [team] captain; **~gefährte** *der,* **~gefährtin** *die (geh.)* playmate; playfellow; **~geld** *das* play *or* toy money; **~hölle** *die (ugs. abwertend)* gambling den

**Spieliothek** /ʃpi:lio'te:k/ *die;* **~, ~en** games library

**Spiel-: ~kamerad** *der,* **~kameradin** *die* playmate; playfellow; **~karte** *die* playing card; **~kasino** *das* casino; **~leidenschaft** *die* passion for gambling; **~leiter** *der* **Ⓐ** *(im Fernsehen)* quizmaster; *(im Roulett)* tourneur; **Ⓑ ⇒ Regisseur; ~leiterin** *die* **Ⓐ** *(im Fernsehen)* quizmaster; *(im Roulett)* tourneuse; **Ⓑ ⇒ Regisseurin; ~macher** *der,* **~macherin** *die (Sportjargon)* key player; **~mann** *der; Pl.* **~leute Ⓐ** *(hist.: fahrender Sänger)* minstrel; **Ⓑ** *(Mitglied eines ~mannszuges)* bandsman; **~manns·zug** *der* marching band; **~marke** *die* chip; jetton; **~minute** *die (Sport)* minute [of play]

**Spielothek** /ʃpi:lo'te:k/ *die;* **~, ~en** games library

**Spiel-: ~phase** *die* stage of the game; **~plan** *der* **Ⓐ** *(Theater)* programme; **das Stück steht noch bis nächsten Monat auf dem ~plan** the play will continue running until next month; **Ⓑ** *(eines Brettspiels)* board; **~platz** *der* playground; **~raum** *der* **Ⓐ** room to move *(fig.)*; scope; latitude; *(bei Ausgaben, Budget)* leeway; **Ⓑ** *(Technik)* clearance; **~regel** *die (auch fig.)* rule of the game; **gegen die ~regeln verstoßen** *(auch fig.)* break the rules; **~runde** *die* round [of the game]; **~saal** *der* gambling room; **~sachen** *Pl.* toys; **~salon** *der* gaming room; **~schuld** *die* gambling debt; **~stand** *der:* **beim ~stand 1:1** with the score at 1-1; **bei diesem ~stand muss Schwarz gewinnen** as the game stands, Black must win; **~stärke** *die:* **der FC Sachsenfurt demonstrierte seine ~stärke** FC Sachsenfurt demonstrated the strength of its play; **~stein** *der* piece; *(beim Damespiel, Schach)* piece; man; **~straße** *die* play street; **~tag** *der* day of play; **~teufel** *der:* **dem ~teufel verfallen** *od.* **vom ~teufel besessen sein** have been bitten by the gambling bug *(coll.)*; **~tisch** *der* **Ⓐ** games table; *(für Glücksspiele)* gaming table; *(für Kartenspiele)* card table; **Ⓑ** *(der Orgel)* console; **~trieb** *der* play instinct; **~uhr** *die* **Ⓐ** musical clock; **Ⓑ** musical box *(Brit.)*; music box *(Amer.)*; **~verderber** *der;* **~~s, ~~, ~verderberin** *die;* **~~, ~~nen** spoilsport; **~verlauf** *der (Sport)* **der weitere ~verlauf** the rest of the game; **~waren** *Pl.* toys; **~waren·geschäft** *das* toyshop; **~wiese** *die* grass play area; *(fig.)* playground; **~zeit** *die* **Ⓐ** *(Theater: Saison)* season; **Ⓑ** *(Aufführungsdauer)* run; **Ⓒ** *(Sport)* playing time; **die normale ~zeit** normal time; **~zeug** *das* **Ⓐ** toy; *(fig.)* toy; plaything; **Ⓑ** *(~sachen, ~waren)* toys *pl.;* **~zeug·eisenbahn** *die* [toy] train set; **~zimmer** *das* playroom; **~zug** *der (Sport, in einem Brettspiel)* move

**Spieß** /ʃpi:s/ *der;* **~es, ~e Ⓐ** *(Waffe)* spear; **den ~ umdrehen** *od.* **umkehren** *(ugs.)* turn the tables; **wie am ~ schreien** *od.* **brüllen** *(ugs.)* scream one's head off; scream blue murder *(coll.)*; **Ⓑ** *(Brat~)* spit; *(Schaschlik~)* skewer; *(Cocktail~)* cocktail stick; **ein am ~ gebratener Ochse** an ox roasted on the spit; a spit-roasted ox; **Ⓒ** *(Fleisch~)* kebab; **Ⓓ** *(Soldatenspr.: Kompaniefeldwebel)* [company] sergeant major; **Ⓔ** *(Jägerspr.)* spike; pricket

**spieß-, Spieß-: ~bürger** *der,* **~bürgerin** *die (abwertend)* [petit] bourgeois; **~bürgerlich ⇒ spießig; ~bürgertum** *das (abwertend)* **Ⓐ** [petit] bourgeois existence; *(spießiges Wesen)* [petit] bourgeois conformism; **Ⓑ** *(die ~bürger)* [petite] bourgeoisie

**Spießchen** *das;* **~s, ~ Ⓐ** *(Cocktailspieß)* cocktail stick; **Ⓑ** *(Schaschlikspieß)* skewer; **Ⓒ** *(Fleischspieß)* kebab

**spießen** *tr. V.* **Ⓐ die Fleischstücke werden auf einen Schaschlikspieß gespießt** the pieces of meat are pushed on to a skewer; **ein Stück Käse/eine Olive auf einen Cocktailspieß ~:** spear a piece of cheese/an olive with a cocktail stick; **etw. in etw.** *(Akk.)* **~:** stick sth. in sth.

**Spießer** *der;* **~s, ~** *(abwertend)* [petit] bourgeois

**spießerhaft ⇒ spießig**

**Spießerin** *die;* **~, ~nen ⇒ Spießer**

**Spießertum** *das;* **~s** *(abwertend)* **⇒ Spießbürgertum**

**Spieß·geselle** *der,* **Spieß·gesellin** *die* **Ⓐ** *(abwertend: Komplize)* accomplice; **Ⓑ** *(veralt.: Kumpan)* companion

**spießig** *(abwertend)* **❶** *Adj.* [petit] bourgeois; **~e Kleinbürgerlichkeit** petit bourgeois narrow-mindedness. **❷** *adv.* ‹think, behave, etc.› in a [petit] bourgeois way; **eine ~ eingerichtete Wohnung** a flat *(Brit.)* or *(Amer.)* apartment furnished in a typically petit bourgeois style

**Spießigkeit** *die;* **~** *(abwertend)* [petit] bourgeois narrow-mindedness; *(einer Wohnungseinrichtung)* [petit] bourgeois style

**Spieß·rute** *die* **in ~n laufen** *(auch fig.)* run the gauntlet

**Spike** /ʃpaik/ *der;* **~s, ~s Ⓐ** spike; **Ⓑ** *Pl. (Schuhe)* spikes; **Ⓒ** *(eines Reifens)* stud; **Ⓓ** *Pl. (Reifen)* studded tyres

**Spike[s]·reifen** *der* studded tyre

**spillerig** /'ʃpɪlərɪç/ *Adj. (bes. nordd.)* spindly, skinny ‹limbs›; skinny ‹person›

**spinal** /ʃpi'na:l/ *(Anat.)* **❶** *Adj.* spinal; **~e Kinderlähmung** infantile paralysis; polio [myelitis]. **❷** *adv.* **~ gelähmt sein** suffer from spinal paralysis

**Spinat** /ʃpi'na:t/ *der;* **~[e]s, ~e** spinach

**Spinat·wachtel** *die (ugs. abwertend)* skinny old bag *(sl.)*

**Spind** /ʃpɪnt/ *der od. das;* **~[e]s, ~e** locker

**Spindel** /'ʃpɪndl̩/ *die;* **~, ~n Ⓐ** spindle; **Ⓑ** *(einer Treppe)* newel

**spindel·dürr** *Adj.* skinny ‹person›; spindly, skinny ‹limbs, finger›; **sie ist ~:** she's as thin as a rake

**Spinett** /ʃpi'nɛt/ *das;* **~[e]s, ~e** spinet

**Spinnaker** /'ʃpɪnakɐ/ *der;* **~s, ~** *(Seemannsspr.)* spinnaker

**Spinne** /'ʃpɪnə/ *die;* **~, ~n** spider

***spinne·feind, Spinne·feind** *(ugs.)* **in jmdm. ~ sein** hate sb.'s guts *(coll.)*

**spinnen** /'ʃpɪnən/ **❶** *unr. tr. V.* **Ⓐ** spin *(fig.)*; plot ‹intrigue›; think up ‹idea›; hatch ‹plot›; **ein Lügengewebe/Netz von Intrigen ~:** weave a tissue of lies/a web of intrigue; **Ⓑ** *(ugs.: lügen)* make up; **das spinnst du!** you're making it up!. **❷** *unr. itr. V.* **Ⓐ** spin; **an einer Intrige ~:** plot an intrigue; **Ⓑ** *(ugs.: verrückt sein)* be crazy *or (coll.)* nuts *or (sl.)* crackers; **Ich soll bezahlen? Du spinnst wohl!** [What,] me pay? You must be joking *or (sl.)* kidding; **ich glaube, ich spinne!** I don't believe it!; **du spinnst wohl [, das zu tun]** you must be crazy [to do it]; **Ⓒ** *(ugs.: Unsinn reden)* talk rubbish; **Ⓓ** *(ugs.: lügen)* make it up

**Spinnen-: ~gewebe** *das* **⇒ Spinngewebe; ~netz** *das* spider's web

**Spinner** *der;* **~s, ~ Ⓐ ▶159** *(Beruf)* spinner; **Ⓑ** *(ugs. abwertend)* nutcase *(coll.)*; idiot; **Ⓒ** *(Zool. veralt.)* silk moth; **Ⓓ** *(Angeln)* spinner

**Spinnerei** *die;* **~, ~en Ⓐ** spinning *no art.;* **Ⓑ** *(Werkstatt)* spinning mill; **Ⓒ** *(ugs. abwertend)* crazy idea

**Spinnerin** *die;* **~, ~nen Ⓐ ▶159** *(Beruf)* spinner; **Ⓑ** *(ugs. abwertend)* nutcase *(coll.)*; idiot

**spinnert** /'ʃpɪnɐt/ *Adj. (ugs., bes. südd.)* slightly potty *(coll.)*

**Spinn·gewebe** *das* cobweb

**spinnig** *Adj. (ugs.)* slightly potty *(coll.)*

**Spinn-: ~rad** *das* spinning wheel; **~rocken** *der* distaff; **~webe** *die;* **~~, ~~n** cobweb; **~wirtel** *der* whorl; wharve

**spintisieren** /ʃpɪnti'zi:rən/ *itr. V. (ugs.)* get weird *or* crazy ideas *(coll.)*

**Spintisiererei** *die;* **~, ~en** *(ugs.)* crazy fantasizing *no indef. art.*

**Spion** /ʃpi'o:n/ *der;* **~s, ~e Ⓐ** spy; **Ⓑ** *(Guckloch)* spyhole; **Ⓒ** *(Spiegel am Fenster)* telltale mirror

**Spionage** /ʃpio'na:ʒə/ *die;* **~:** spying; espionage; **~ treiben** spy; carry out espionage

**Spionage-: ~abwehr** *die* **Ⓐ** *(Tätigkeit)* counter-espionage; counter-intelligence; **Ⓑ** *(Dienst)* counter-espionage *or* counter-intelligence service; **er arbeitet in der ~abwehr** he works in counter-espionage *or* counter-intelligence; **~fall** *der* spy *or* espionage case; **~netz** *das* spy *or* espionage network; **~ring** *der* spy ring

**spionieren** *itr. V.* **Ⓐ** spy **(gegen** against); **Ⓑ** *(fig. abwertend)* spy; snoop [about] *(coll.)*

**Spioniererei** *die;* **~, ~en** *(fig. abwertend)* snooping [about] *no pl. (coll.)*

**Spionin** *die;* **~, ~nen** spy

**Spiral·bohrer** *der* twist drill *or* bit

**Spirale** /ʃpi'ra:lə/ *die;* **~, ~n Ⓐ** *(auch Geom., fig.)* spiral; *(Heiz~)* coil; **Ⓑ** *(zur Empfängnisverhütung)* coil

**Spiral·feder** *die* coil spring

**spiral·förmig ❶** *Adj.* spiral[-shaped]. **❷** *adv.* spirally

**spiralig ❶** *Adj.* spiral. **❷** *adv.* spirally

**Spiral·nebel** *der (Astron.)* spiral nebula

**Spirant** /spi'rant/ *der;* **~en, ~en** *(Sprachw.)* spirant

**Spiritismus** /ʃpiritɪsmʊs/ *der;* **~:** spiritualism; spiritism

**Spiritist** *der;* **~en, ~en, Spiritistin** *die;* **~, ~nen** spiritualist; spiritist

**spiritistisch ❶** *Adj.* spiritualist[ic]; spiritistic. **❷** *adv.* spiritualistically; spiritistically

**Spiritual** /'spɪrɪtjʊəl/ *das od. der;* **~s, ~s** [negro] spiritual

**spiritualisieren** *tr. V.* spiritualize

**Spiritualismus** /spiritu̯a'lɪsmʊs/ *der;* **~** *(Philos.)* spiritualism

**spiritualistisch ❶** *Adj.* spiritualist[ic]. **❷** *adv.* spiritualistically

**Spiritualität** /spiritu̯ali'tɛ:t/ *die;* ~**:** spirituality

**Spirituose** /spiri'tu̯o:zə/ *die;* ~, ~**n** spirit *usu. in pl.*

**Spiritus** /'ʃpi:ritʊs/ *der;* ~, ~**se** spirit; ethyl alcohol; **ein Organ in ~ konservieren** preserve an organ in alcohol; **mit ~ kochen** cook on a spirit stove

**Spiritus·kocher** *der* spirit stove

**Spital** /ʃpi'ta:l/ *das;* ~**s, Spitäler** /ʃpi'tɛ:lɐ/ (*bes. österr., schweiz.*) hospital; (*veralt.: Altersheim*) old people's home; (*veralt.: Armenhaus*) almshouse

**Spittel** /'ʃpɪtl̩/ *das,* (*schweiz.:*) *der;* ~**s,** ~ (*bes. schweiz. ugs.*) hospital

**spitz** /ʃpɪts/ ❶ *Adj.* **A** (*nicht stumpf*) pointed ‹tower, arch, shoes, nose, beard, etc.›; sharp ‹pencil, needle, stone, etc.›; fine ‹pen nib›; (*Geom.*) acute ‹angle›; **B** (*schrill*) shrill ‹cry etc.›; **C** (*ugs.: abgezehrt*) haggard; haggard, pinched ‹face›; **D** (*boshaft*) cutting ‹remark, etc.›; ~ **werden** get spiteful; **E** (*ugs.: geil*) randy; horny (*sl.*); ~ **auf jmdn. sein** really fancy sb. ❷ *adv.* **A** ~ **zulaufen** taper to a point; ~ **zulaufend** pointed; **B** (*boshaft*) cuttingly

**Spitz** *der;* ~**es,** ~**e** (*Hund*) spitz

**spitz-, Spitz-:** ~**ahorn** *der* Norway maple; ~**bart** *der* **A** goatee; pointed beard; **B** (*Mann*) man with a/the goatee *or* pointed beard; ~**bauch** *der* potbelly; ~**|bekommen** *unr. tr. V.* (*ugs.*) ⇒ ~**kriegen**; ~**bogen** *der* pointed arch; ~**bogen·fenster** *das* lancet window; ~**bube** *der* **A** (*veralt. abwertend: Gauner*) rogue; scoundrel; **B** (*scherzh.: Schlingel*) rascal; scallywag; scamp; **C** (*österr.: Plätzchen*) *sandwich of two or three biscuits stuck together with jam;* ~**büberei** /-byːbə'rai̯/ *die;* ~~, ~~**en** **A** piece of roguery; **B** roguery; ~**bübin** *die;* ~~, ~~**nen** ⇒ ~**bube** A, B; ~**bübisch** ❶ *Adj.* **A** (*verschmitzt*) roguish; mischievous; **B** (*veralt. abwertend: schurkisch*) villainous; ❷ *adv.* **A** (*verschmitzt*) roguishly; mischievously; **B** (*veralt. abwertend: schurkisch*) villainously

**spitze** *indekl. Adj.* (*ugs.*) ⇒ **klasse**

**Spitze** *die;* ~, ~**n** **A** (*Nadel~, Bleistift~ usw.*) point; (*Pfeil~, Horn~ usw.*) tip; **einer Sache** (*Dat.*) **die ~ nehmen** *od.* **abbrechen** (*fig.*) take the sting out of sth. (*fig.*); **B** (*Turm~, Baum~, Mast~ usw.*) top; (*eines Dreiecks, Kegels, einer Pyramide*) top; apex; vertex (*Math.*); (*eines Berges*) summit; top; **ein auf der ~ stehendes Dreieck** an inverted triangle; **C** (*Zigarren~, Haar~, Zweig~*) end; (*Schuh~*) toe; (*Finger~, Nasen~, Schwanz~, Flügel~, Spargel~*) tip; (*Lungen~*) apex; **die südliche ~ der Insel** the southern tip of the island; **D** (*vorderes Ende*) front; **an der ~ des Zuges/der Kolonne marschieren** march at the head of the procession/column; **an der ~ liegen** (*Sport*) be in the lead *or* in front; **sich an die ~ [des Feldes] setzen** (*Sport*) go into *or* take the lead; **E** (*führende Position*) top; **an der ~ [der Tabelle] stehen** *od.* **liegen** (*Sport*) be [at the] top [of the table]; **sich an die ~ [einer Bewegung] setzen** put oneself at the head [of a movement]; **die ~ halten/übernehmen** stay top/go to the top; **F** (*einer Firma, Organisation usw.*) head; (*einer Hierarchie*) top; (*leitende Gruppe*) management; **an der ~ des Unternehmens/der Partei stehen** be at the head of the company/party; **die ~n der Gesellschaft/der Partei** the leading figures of society/in the party; **G** ▸ 348 | (*Höchstwert*) maximum; peak; (*ugs.: ~nzeit*) peak period; **das Auto fährt 160 km ~:** the car has *or* does a top speed of 160 km. per hour; **wir wollen die Sache doch nicht auf die ~ treiben** we don't want to carry things too far; **H** **[absolute/einsame] ~ sein** (*ugs.*) be [absolutely] great (*coll.*); **I** (*fig.: Angriff*) dig **(gegen** at); ~**n austeilen** make pointed remarks; **J** (*Textilwesen*) lace; **K** (*Sport: Sturm~*) striker; **L** (*Zigaretten~, Zigarrenhalter*) [cigarette/cigar] holder; **M** (*Wirtsch.: Überschuss*) surplus

**Spitzel** *der;* ~**s,** ~ (*abwertend*) informer; **ein ~ der Polizei** a police informer; a copper's nark (*Brit. coll.*)

**Spitzel·dienste** *Pl.* (*abwertend*) **für jmdn. ~ leisten** act as an informer for sb.; **für ~ bin ich mir zu schade** I couldn't stoop to acting as *or* being an informer

**spitzeln** *itr. V.* (*abwertend*) act as an informer

**spitzen** ❶ *tr. V.* sharpen ‹pencil›; purse ‹lips, mouth›; **die Ohren ~** ‹dog› prick up its ears; (*fig.*) ‹person› prick up one's ears. ❷ *refl. V.* **sich auf etw.** (*Akk.*) ~ (*ugs.*) look forward [expectantly] to sth.; (*dringlich erhoffen*) have one's heart set on sth. ❸ (*landsch.: aufmerken*) prick up one's ears

**Spitzen-:** ~**bluse** *die* lace blouse; ~**deckchen** *das* lace mat; ~**erzeugnis** *das* top-quality product; ~**funktionär** *der,* ~**funktionärin** *die* top official; ~**gehalt** *das* top-level salary; ~**geschwindigkeit** *die* ▸ 348 | top speed; ~**kandidat** *der,* ~**kandidatin** *die* leading *or* top candidate; ~**klasse** *die* **A** top class; **ein Hotel der ~klasse** a top-class hotel; **zur ~klasse gehören** be top-class; **B** ~**klasse sein** (*ugs.*) be really great (*coll.*); ~**könner** *der,* ~**könnerin** *die* top-class talent; ~**kraft** *die* top-class *or* top-flight professional; ~**kragen** *der* lace collar; ~**leistung** *die* top-class performance; **eine ~leistung der Ingenieurskunst** a supreme achievement of engineering; ~**politiker** *der,* ~**politikerin** *die* top *or* leading politician; ~**position** *die* **A** (*Sport*) leading position; **B** (*leitende Position*) top position; ~**qualität** *die* top quality; **Erzeugnisse in ~qualität** top-quality products; ~**reiter** *der* **A** top rider; (*fig.*) leader; **B** (*Mannschaft*) top team; **C** (*Ware*) top *or* best seller; ~**reiterin** *die* ⇒ ~**reiter** A; ~**spiel** *das* (*Sport*) top match *or* game; ~**spieler** *der,* ~**spielerin** *die* top[-class] player; ~**sportler** *der* top sportsman; ~**sportlerin** *die* top sportswoman; ~**stellung** *die* top position; ~**tanz** *der* dancing *no art.* on points *or* on [full] point; ~**technologie** *die* state-of-the-art technology; ~**wert** *der* peak; maximum [value]; ~**zeit** *die* **A** peak time *or* period; **B** (*Sport*) (*beste Zeit*) best time; (*sehr gute Zeit*) outstanding *or* excellent time

**Spitzer** *der;* ~**s,** ~**:** [pencil] sharpener

**spitz-, Spitz-:** ~**findig** ❶ *Adj.;* hair-splitting, oversubtle; quibbling ‹distinction›; pettifogging ‹quibble›; **jetzt wirst du [zu] ~findig** now you're splitting hairs *or* being too subtle; ❷ *adv.* in an oversubtle way; **[zu] ~findig argumentieren** be oversubtle in one's arguments; split hairs; ~**findigkeit** *die;* ~~, ~~**en** **A** over subtlety; (*Haarspalterei*) hair-splitting; **B** (*etwas ~findiges*) nicety; (*Äußerung*) hair-splitting remark; ~**hacke** *die* pick; pickaxe

**spitzig** *Adj.* (*veralt.*) ⇒ **spitz** 1 A-D, 2

**spitz-, Spitz-:** ~**kehre** *die* **A** (*Haarnadelkurve*) hairpin bend; **B** (*Ski*) kick turn; ~**|kriegen** *tr. V.* (*ugs.*) tumble to (*coll.*); get wise to (*sl.*); **[es] ~kriegen, dass ...** tumble to *or* get wise to the fact that ...; ~**maus** *die* **A** shrew; **B** (*ugs. abwertend*) weasel-faced female (*derog.*); ~**name** *der* nickname; ~**wegerich** *der* (*Bot.*) ribwort; ~**winklig** ❶ *Adj.* acute-angled ‹triangle›; ❷ *adv.* at an acute angle; ~**züngig** ❶ *Adj.* sharp-tongued; ❷ *adv.* ‹reply› sharply

**Spleen** /ʃpli:n/ *der;* ~**s,** ~**e** *od.* ~**s** strange *or* peculiar habit; eccentricity; **du hast ja einen ~!** there must be something the matter with you!; you must be dotty (*coll.*); **die Lexikographen haben doch alle einen kleinen ~:** lexicographers are all a bit cracked (*coll.*)

**spleenig** *Adj.* eccentric; dotty (*coll.*)

**spleißen** /'ʃplai̯sn̩/ (*Seemannsspr.*) ❶ *unr. od. regelm. tr. V.* splice ‹rope›. ❷ *unr. od. regelm. itr. V.* make a splice/splices

**splendid** /ʃplɛn'di:t/ (*veralt.*) ❶ *Adj.* **A** generous; **B** (*kostbar*) sumptuous; magnificent. ❷ *adv.* **A** generously; **B** (*kostbar*) sumptuously; magnificently

**Splint** /ʃplɪnt/ *der;* ~**[e]s,** ~**e** (*Technik*) split pin

**Splint·holz** *das* sapwood; alburnum

**spliss, *spliß** /ʃplɪs/ *1. u. 3. Pers. Sg. Prät. v.* **spleißen**

**Splitt** /ʃplɪt/ *der;* ~**[e]s,** ~**e** [stone] chippings *pl.;* (*zum Streuen*) grit; (*in Beton*) aggregate

**splitten** *tr. V.* (*Wirtsch.*) **A** split ‹shares›; **B** (*Politik*) **die Stimmen ~:** *give one's first vote to a particular candidate and one's second to a party other than that of the chosen candidate*

**Splitter** *der;* ~**s,** ~**:** splinter; (*Granat~, Bomben~*) splinter; fragment; **du siehst den ~ im fremden Auge, aber nicht den Balken im eigenen** (*geh.*) you can see a mote in another's eye but not the beam that is in your own

**splitter-, Splitter-:** ~**bombe** *die* fragmentation bomb; ~**bruch** *der* ▸ 474 | (*Med.*) comminuted fracture; ~**faser·nackt** *Adj.* (*ugs.*) absolutely stark naked; completely starkers *pred.* (*Brit. coll.*); ~**frei** *Adj.* shatter-proof; ~**gruppe** *die* splinter group

**splitterig** *Adj.* **A** (*leicht splitternd*) ‹wood, plastic, etc.› that splinters easily; ~ **sein** splinter easily; **B** (*voller Splitter*) splintery

**splittern** *itr. V.* **A** (*Splitter bilden*) splinter; **B** *mit sein* (*in Splitter zerbrechen*) ‹glass, windscreen, etc.› shatter

**splitter·nackt** *Adj.* (*ugs.*) stark naked; starkers *pred.* (*Brit. coll.*)

**Splitter·partei** *die* splinter party

**Splitting** /'ʃplɪtɪŋ/ *das;* ~**s,** ~**s** **A** (*Steuerw.*) *taxation of husband and wife whereby each is taxed on half the total of their combined incomes;* **B** (*Wirtsch.*) splitting; **C** (*Politik*) *division of one's first and second votes between a particular candidate and a party other than that of the chosen candidate*

**Splitting·system** *das* (*Steuerw.*) *tax system in which husband and wife each pay income tax on half the total of their combined incomes*

**splittrig** ⇒ **splitterig**

**SPÖ** *Abk.* **Sozialistische Partei Österreichs** Austrian Socialist Party

**Spoiler** /'ʃpɔy̯lɐ/ *der;* ~**s,** ~ (*Kfz-W.*) spoiler

**Spökenkieker** /'ʃpø:kn̩ki:kɐ/ *der;* ~**s,** ~ **A** (*nordd.: Hellseher*) clairvoyant; person who has second sight; **B** (*ugs.: spintisierender Mensch*) crazy fantasist

**Spökenkiekerei** *die;* ~, ~**en** (*ugs.*) crazy fantasizing *no indef. art.*

**Spökenkiekerin** *die;* ~, ~**nen** ⇒ **Spökenkieker**

**Spondeus** /ʃpɔn'de:ʊs/ *der;* ~, **Spondeen** (*Verslehre*) spondee

**sponsern** /'ʃpɔnzɐn/ *tr. V.* sponsor

**Sponsor** /'ʃpɔnzɐ/ *der;* ~**s,** ~**en** /-'zo:rən/, **Sponsorin** *die;* ~, ~**nen** sponsor

**spontan** /ʃpɔn'ta:n/ ❶ *Adj.* spontaneous. ❷ *adv.* spontaneously

**Spontaneität** /ʃpɔntanei'tɛ:t/ *die;* ~ (*auch Psych., Med.*) spontaneity

**Sponti** /'ʃpɔnti/ *der;* ~**s,** ~**s** (*ugs.*) *member of an undogmatic leftist group*

**sporadisch** /ʃpo'ra:dɪʃ/ ❶ *Adj.* sporadic. ❷ *adv.* sporadically

**Spore** /'ʃpo:rə/ *die;* ~, ~**n** (*Biol.*) spore

**Sporen** ⇒ **Spore, Sporn**

**sporen-, Sporen-:** ~**klirrend** *Adv.* with a clatter of spurs; ~**pflanze** *die* (*Bot.*) cryptogam; ~**tierchen** *das* (*Zool.*) sporozoan

**Sporn** /ʃpɔrn/ *der;* ~**[e]s,** ~**e** *od.* **Sporen** /'ʃpo:rən/ **A** *Pl.* **Sporen** *od.* (*Zool.*) ~**e** spur; **einem Pferd die Sporen geben** spur a horse; **sich die [ersten] Sporen verdienen** (*fig.*) win one's spurs; **B** *Pl.* ~**e** (*hist.: am Schiff*) ram; **C** *Pl.* ~**e** (*eines Flugzeugs*) tail skid

**spornen** *tr. V.* spur ‹horse›

**sporn·streichs** *Adv.* (*veralt.*) straight away

**Sport** /ʃpɔrt/ *der;* ~**[e]s** **A** sport; (*als Unterrichtsfach*) sport; physical education; PE; ~ **treiben** do sport; **beim ~:** while doing sport; **und hier noch eine Meldung vom ~:** and finally an item of sports news; **B** (~*art*) sport; **C** (*Hobby, Zeitvertreib*) hobby;

*old spelling (see note on page 1707)

pastime; **sich** (*Dat.*) **einen ~ aus etw. machen** get a kick (*coll.*) out of sth.

**Sport-: ~abzeichen** *das* sports badge; **~angler** *der*, **~anglerin** *die* club angler; **~anlage** *die* sports complex; **~art** *die* [form of] sport; **~artikel** *der* piece of sports equipment; **~artikel** *Pl.* sports equipment *sing.*; **~arzt** *der*, **~ärztin** *die* sports doctor; **~bericht** *der* sports report; **~berichterstattung** *die* sports reporting; **~boot** *das* sports boat; **~coupé** *das* sports coupé; **~dress**, ***~dreß** *der* ⇒ **Dress** A

**Sport-: ~feld** *das* sports ground; (*Stadion*) sports stadium; **~fest** *das* sports festival; (*einer Schule*) sports day; **~fischen** *das*; **~~s** club fishing *no art. or* angling *no art.*; **~flieger** *der*, **~fliegerin** *die* sports pilot; **~flugzeug** *das* sports plane; **~freund** *der*, **~freundin** *die* **A** sports fan; **B** (*Kamerad[in]*) sporting friend; **~funktionär** *der*, **~funktionärin** *die* sports official; **~geist** *der* sportsmanship; sporting spirit; **~gerät** *das* piece of sports apparatus; **~geräte** (*als Gesamtheit*) sports apparatus *sing.*; **~hemd** *das* sports shirt; **~hochschule** *die* college of physical education

**sportiv** /spɔr'ti:f/ **1** *Adj.* sporty. **2** *adv.* sportily

**Sport-: ~journalist** *der*, **~journalistin** *die* sports journalist; **~kamerad** *der*, **~kameradin** *die* sporting friend; **~kleidung** *die* sportswear; sports clothes *pl.*; **~lehrer** *der*, **~lehrerin** *die* sports instructor; (*in einer Schule*) PE *or* physical education teacher; games teacher

**Sportler** /'ʃpɔrtlɐ/ *der;* **~s, ~:** sportsman

**Sportler·herz** *das* athletic heart

**Sportlerin** *die;* **~, ~nen** sportswoman

**sportlich 1** *Adj.* **A** sporting *attrib.* ‹success, performance, interests, etc.›; **~e Veranstaltungen** sports events; sporting events; **auf ~em Gebiet** in the field of sport; **B** (*fair*) sportsmanlike; sporting; **C** (*fig.: flott, rasant*) sporty ‹car, driving, etc.›; **D** (*zu ~er Leistung fähig*) sporty, athletic ‹person›; **E** (*jugendlich wirkend*) sporty, smart but casual ‹clothes›; smart but practical ‹hairstyle›. **2** *adv.* **A** as far as sport is concerned; **~ aktiv sein** be an active sportsman/sportswoman; **B** (*fair*) sportingly; **C** (*fig.: flott, rasant*) in a sporty manner

**sportlich-elegant 1** *Adj.* casually elegant. **2** *adv.* casually but elegantly ‹dressed›

**sport-, Sport-: ~maschine** *die* sports plane; **~medizin** *die* sports medicine *no art.*; **~medizinisch** *Adj.* **~medizinische Betreuung/Forschung** medical care of sportsmen/research into sports medicine; **~nachrichten** *Pl.* sports news *sing.*; **~platz** *der* sports field; (*einer Schule*) playing field/fields *pl.*; **~presse** *die* sports press; **~rad** *das* sports bike; **~schuh** *der* **A** sports shoe; **B** (*sportlicher Schuh*) casual shoe; **~sendung** *die* sports programme

**Sports-: ~freund** *der*, **~freundin** *die* sports enthusiast; **Hallo, ~freund! Wie gehts?** (*ugs.*) hello, mate (*coll.*), how are you?; **~kanone** *die* (*ugs.*) sporting ace; **~mann** *der; Pl.* **~männer** *od.* **~leute** sportsman

**Sport-: ~stadion** *das* [sports] stadium; **~student** *der*, **~studentin** *die* sports student; **~taucher** *der*, **~taucherin** *die* skin diver; **~unfall** *der* sporting *or* sports accident; **~verband** *der* sports association; **~verein** *der* sports club; **~verletzung** *die* sports injury; **~wagen** *der* **A** (*Auto*) sports car; **B** (*Kinderwagen*) pushchair (*Brit.*); stroller (*Amer.*); **~wissenschaft** *die* sports science *no art.*

**Spot** /spɔt/ *der;* **~s, ~s A** (*Werbe~*) commercial; advertisement; ad (*coll.*); **B** (*Leuchte*) spotlight; spotlamp; **C** (*Theat., Film, Fernsehen*) spot[light]

**Spot·markt** *der* (*Wirtsch.*) spot market

**Spott** /ʃpɔt/ *der;* **~[e]s** mockery; (*höhnischer*) ridicule; derision; **~ und Hohn** scorn and derision; **jmdn./etw. dem ~ preisgeben** hold sb./sth. up to ridicule; **seinen ~ mit jmdm./etw. treiben** make fun of sb./sth.

**spott-, Spott-: ~bild** *das* travesty; mockery; (*eines Menschen*) caricature; **~billig** (*ugs.*) **1** *Adj.* dirt cheap; **2** *adv.* **da kann man ~billig einkaufen** you can get *or* buy things dirt cheap there; **~drossel** *die* **A** mocking thrush; [**Eigentliche**] **~drossel** mockingbird; **B** (*fig.*) ⇒ **Spötter**

**Spöttelei** *die;* **~, ~en A** [gentle] mocking; [gentle] mockery; **B** (*spöttelnde Äußerung*) mocking remark

**spötteln** /'ʃpœtl̩n/ *itr. V.* mock [gently]; poke *or* make [gentle] fun; **über jmdn./etw. ~:** mock sb./sth. gently; poke gentle fun at *or* make [gentle] fun of sb./sth.

**spotten** /'ʃpɔtn̩/ *itr. V.* **A** mock; poke *or* make fun; (*höhnischer*) ridicule; be derisive; **über jmdn./etw. ~:** mock sb./sth.; make fun of sb./sth.; (*höhnischer*) ridicule sb./sth.; be derisive about sb./sth.; **du hast gut/leicht ~:** it's easy *or* all very well for you to mock *or* laugh; **jmds./einer Sache ~** (*geh.*) mock sb./sth.; **B** (*fig.*) be contemptuous of; scorn; **er spottete der Gefahr** (*Gen.*) (*geh.*) he was contemptuous of *or* scorned the danger; **das spottet jeder Beschreibung** (*ugs.*) it defies *or* beggars description

**Spötter** /'ʃpœtɐ/ *der;* **~s, ~:** mocker

**Spötterei** *die;* **~, ~en A** mockery; mocking; making fun; **B** (*spottende Äußerung*) mocking remark

**Spötterin** *die;* **~, ~nen** ⇒ **Spötter**

**Spott-: ~geburt** *die* (*geh. abwertend*) monstrosity; **~gedicht** *das* satirical poem, verse satire (**auf** + *Akk.* about); **~geld** *das* (*ugs.*) **etw. für** *od.* (*veralt.*) **um ein ~geld bekommen** get sth. dirt cheap

**spöttisch** /'ʃpœtɪʃ/ **1** *Adj.* mocking ‹smile, remark, speech, etc.›; (*höhnischer*) derisive, ridiculing ‹remark, speech, etc.›; **ein ~er Mensch** a person who likes poking fun. **2** *adv.* mockingly; **~ lächeln** give a mocking smile

**Spott-: ~lust** *die* love of *or* delight in mockery *or* poking fun; **~name** *der* [derisive] nickname; **~preis** *der* (*ugs.*) ridiculously low price; **etw. für einen** *od.* **zu einem ~preis bekommen** get sth. dirt cheap *or* for a song

**sprach** /ʃpra:x/ *1. u. 3. Pers. Sg. Prät. v.* **sprechen**

**Sprach-: ~barriere** *die* (*Soziol.*) language barrier; (*zwischen Gesellschaftsklassen*) linguistic barrier; **~bau** *der* (*Sprachw.*) linguistic structure; **~begabung** *die* talent *or* gift for languages; **~denkmal** *das* linguistic monument

**spräche** /'ʃprɛ:çə/ *1. u. 3. Pers. Sg. Konjunktiv II v.* **sprechen**

**Sprache** /'ʃpra:xə/ *die;* **~, ~n ▶ 696 A** language; **in englischer ~:** in English; **die ~ der Jäger/Mediziner** the language of the hunt/of medicine; hunting/medical language; **ihm blieb die ~ weg** (*ugs.*) he was speechless; he was at a loss for words; **es verschlug** *od.* **raubte mir die ~:** it took my breath away; **hast du die ~ verloren?** (*ugs.*) haven't you got a tongue in your head?; **B** (*Sprechweise*) way of speaking; speech; (*Stil*) style; **eine deutliche/unmissverständliche ~ [mit jmdm.] sprechen** speak bluntly [to sb.]; **C** (*Rede*) **die ~ auf jmdn./etw. bringen** bring the conversation round to sb./sth.; **etw. zur ~ bringen** bring sth. up; raise sth.; **zur ~ kommen** be brought up *or* raised; come up; **mit der ~ herausrücken/herauswollen** come out/want to come out with it; **heraus mit der ~!** come on, out with it!

**Sprachen-: ~schule** *die* language school; **~studium** *das* language studies *pl.*, *no art.*

**sprach-, Sprach-: ~entwicklung** *die* development of a/the language; **~erwerb** *der* (*Sprachw.*) language acquisition; **~familie** *die* language family; family of languages; **~fehler** *der* speech impediment *or* defect; **~forscher** *der*, **~forscherin** *die* linguistic researcher; **~führer** *der* phrase book; **~gebrauch** *der* [linguistic] usage; **im ~gebrauch der Nazis** in Nazi usage *or* language; in the language of the Nazis; **~gefühl** *das* feeling for language; **~genie** *das* linguistic genius; **~geographie** *die* linguistic geography *no art.*; **~geschichte** *die* **A** history of a/the language; (*Teilgebiet der ~Sprachwissenschaft*) historical linguistics *sing.*, *no art.*; **B** (*Buch*) history of a/the language; **~geschichtlich 1** *Adj.* historical-linguistic ‹studies, dissertation, etc.›; **2** *adv.* from the point of view of historical linguistics; **~gewaltig** *Adj.* powerfully eloquent; **~grenze** *die* language boundary; **~insel** *die* linguistic enclave *or* island; **~kenntnisse** *Pl.* knowledge *sing.* of a language/languages; **seine französischen ~kenntnisse** his knowledge of French; **~kompetenz** *die* linguistic competence; **~kritik** *die* critique of language; **~kultur** *die* level of compliance with linguistic norms; **~kundig** *Adj.* proficient in *or* conversant with the language *postpos.*; **~kurs** *der* language course; **~labor** *das* language laboratory *or* (*coll.*) lab; **~lehre** *die* **A** grammar; **B** (*Buch*) grammar [book]

**sprachlich 1** *Adj.* linguistic; **~e Feinheiten** subtleties of language. **2** *adv.* linguistically; **ein ~ hervorragender Aufsatz** an excellently written essay

**sprach-, Sprach-: ~los** *Adj.* speechless; dumbfounded; **~losigkeit** *die;* **~~:** speechlessness; dumbfoundedness; **~mittler** *der*, **~mittlerin** *die* mediator between languages; **~norm** *die* linguistic norm; **~pflege** *die* language cultivation; **~philosophie** *die* philosophy of language; **~raum** *der* language area; **~regelung** *die* instructions *pl.* as to the wording to be used; **nach der offiziellen ~regelung ist er „aus gesundheitlichen Gründen" zurückgetreten** according to the official version *or* as the official version has it, he resigned 'for reasons of health'; **~rohr** *das* (*Repräsentant*) spokesman; (*Propagandist*) mouthpiece; **~schöpfer** *der*, **~schöpferin** *die* linguistic innovator; **~schöpferisch** *Adj.* linguistically innovative *or* creative; **~silbe** *die* word element; element of word formation; **~spiel** *das* (*Sprachw.*) language game; **~spielerei** *die* game with words; **~störung** *die* (*Med., Psych.*) language disorder; (*Sprechstörung*) speech disorder; **~studium** *das* ⇒ **Sprachenstudium**; **~übung** *die* language exercise; linguistic exercise; **~unterricht** *der* language teaching *or* instruction; **~verwirrung** *die* linguistic confusion; **~wissenschaft** *die* linguistics *sing.*, *no art.*; **~wissenschaftler** *der*, **~wissenschaftlerin** *die* linguist; **~wissenschaftlich 1** *Adj.* linguistic; **eine ~wissenschaftliche Abhandlung** a linguistics dissertation; **2** *adv.* linguistically; **~wissenschaftlich interessierte Laien** laymen interested in linguistics

**sprang** /ʃpraŋ/ *1. u. 3. Pers. Sg. Prät. v.* **springen**

**spränge** /'ʃprɛŋə/ *1. u. 3. Pers. Sg. Konjunktiv II v.* **springen**

**Spray** /ʃpre:/ *das od. der;* **~s, ~s** spray

**Spray·dose** *die* aerosol [can]

**sprayen** *tr., itr. V.* spray

**Sprayer** /'spre:ɐ/ *der;* **~s, ~:** graffiti artist

**Sprech-: ~an·lage** *die* intercom (*coll.*); **~blase** *die* balloon (*coll.*); **~bühne** *die* theatre staging plays only; **~chor** *der* chorus; **im ~chor rufen** shout in chorus; chant ‹slogan›

**sprechen** /'ʃprɛçn̩/ **▶ 696 1** *unr. itr. V.* speak (**über** + *Akk.* about; **von** about, of); (*sich unterhalten, sich be~ auch*) talk (**über** + *Akk.*, **von** about); ‹parrot etc.› talk; **deutsch/flüsternd ~:** speak German/in a whisper *or* whispers; **er spricht wenig** he doesn't say *or* talk much; **Das war das Hörspiel „...". Es sprachen: ...** That was the play for radio '...'. Taking part were: ...; **es spricht Pfarrer N.** the speaker is the Revd. N.; **für/gegen etw. ~:** speak in favour of/against sth.; **das S~ fiel ihr noch schwer** she still found it difficult to speak; **mit jmdm. ~:** speak *or* talk with *or* to sb.; **seit dem Streit ~ sie nicht mehr miteinander** since the quarrel they are no longer on speaking terms

S

# Sprachen

Wie die Nationalitätsbezeichnungen, werden die englischen Bezeichnungen der Sprachen (auch die Adjektive) groß geschrieben:

***französische Verben***
= French verbs

***Das Buch ist deutsch geschrieben***
= The book is written in German

***In Finnland spricht man Finnisch***
= In Finland they speak Finnish

***Die Belgier sprechen meist entweder Flämisch oder Französisch***
= The Belgians mostly speak either Flemish or French

***Hindi, die Amtssprache Indiens, wird von den Hindus gesprochen***
= Hindi, India's official anguage, is spoken by the Hindus

**■ AUF/IN/ZU DEUTSCH USW.**

Die verschiedenen Kombinationen von Präposition und Sprache sowie in den meisten Fällen das deutsche Adverb werden durch **in** + Sprachbezeichnung übersetzt:

***Die Rede wurde auf Englisch gehalten*** od. ***englisch gehalten***
= The speech was given in English

***Sagen Sie es auf Deutsch***
= Say it in German

***Der Brief ist in Suaheli geschrieben***
= The letter is written in Swahili

***„Aquaplaning", zu Deutsch das Gleiten eines Fahrzeugs auf einer Wasserschicht***
'Aquaplaning', in plain English the skidding of a vehicle on a film of water

***Dort war ein Engländer, der italienisch sprach***
= There was an Englishman there who was speaking [in] Italian

**■ DAS SUBSTANTIVIERTE ADJEKTIV**

Das Englische, das Deutsche usw. = **English, German** usw., also ohne Artikel. Vergleichen Sie:

***Das Englische hat*** od. ***Im Englischen gibt es eine Verlaufsform***
= English has *od.* In English there is a continuous form

***Es wurde aus dem*** od. ***vom Italienischen ins Deutsche übersetzt***
= It was translated from Italian into German

**■ DAS SUBSTANTIV**

Das englische Substantiv zur Bezeichnung einer Sprache wird selten mit einem bestimmten Artikel verwendet, und zwar nur dann (wie im Deutschen), wenn es sich um eine näher bezeichnete Form der Sprache handelt:

***das Latein der Mönche des Mittelalters***
= the Latin of the medieval monks

Der unbestimmte Artikel **a, an** wird meist vermieden.

***Sie schreibt ein fehlerfreies/gepflegtes Englisch***
= She writes [a] faultless/cultivated English

***Er spricht ein fließendes, akzentfreies Spanisch***
= He speaks fluent Spanish without an accent

***Die Quäker sprachen ein altmodisches Englisch***
= The Quakers spoke an old-fashioned form of English

**■ DAS ADJEKTIV**

Das englische Adjektiv übersetzt auch den ersten Teil von Zusammensetzungen wie

***Deutschstunde, Französischunterricht, Englischlehrer***
= German lesson, French teaching, English teacher

Letzteres kann natürlich auch „englischer Lehrer" heißen, diese Bedeutung wird aber in der gesprochenen Sprache durch stärkere Betonung des Substantivs gekennzeichnet (English 'teacher), wohingegen, wenn ein Englischlehrer gemeint ist, das Adjektiv betont wird ('English teacher). Um Verwechslungen in der Schriftsprache zu vermeiden, kann man im letzteren Fall 'teacher of English' schreiben.

Die Adjektive, die mit **-sprachig** enden, haben zweierlei Bedeutungen (eine bestimmte Sprache sprechend oder in dieser Sprache verfasst bzw. gehalten) und Übersetzungen:

***Die deutschsprachige Bevölkerung***
= the German-speaking population

Aber:

***eine englischsprachige Zeitung***
= an English-language newspaper

***französischsprachiger Unterricht***
= teaching in French

S

*or* haven't been speaking to each other; **ich muss mit dir ~:** I must talk *or* speak with you; **er spricht mit sich selbst** he talks to himself; **wie sprichst du mit mir?** who do you think you're talking to?; **so spricht man nicht mit seiner Mutter** that's no way to talk *or* speak to one's mother; **sie spricht nicht mit jedem** she doesn't speak *or* talk to just anybody; **mit wem spreche ich?** who is speaking please?; to whom am I speaking, please?; **~ Sie noch?** (*am Telefon*) are you still there?; **er spricht gerade** (*telefoniert*) he's on the phone; **worüber habt ihr gesprochen?** what were you talking about?; **es wurde über alles Mögliche gesprochen** we/they *etc.* talked about all sorts of things; **darüber spricht er nicht gern** he doesn't like talking about that; **gut/schlecht von jmdm.** *od.* **über jmdn. ~:** speak well/ill of sb.; **für jmdn. ~:** speak for sb.; speak on *or* (*Amer.*) in behalf of sb.; **ich kann nur für mich ~:** I can only speak for myself; **vor einer Hörerschaft/der Betriebsversammlung ~:** speak in front of an audience/speak to *or* address a meeting of the workforce; **zu einem** *od.* **über ein Thema ~:** speak on *or* about a subject; **frei ~:** extemporize; speak without notes; **~ Sie!/bitte ~!** (*am Telefon*) you're through [now]; go ahead, please; **sprich!** (*geh.*) speak! (*literary*); **also sprach der Herr/Buddha/Zarathustra** (*dichter.*) thus spake the Lord/Buddha/Zarathustra (*Bibl./literary*); **lass Blumen ~!** say it with flowers!; **sein Herz ~ lassen** follow the dictates of one's heart; **aus seinen Worten/seinem Blick sprach Hass/Neid/Angst** *usw.* his words/the look in his eyes expressed hatred/envy/fear *etc.;* **auf jmdn./etw. zu ~ kommen** get to talking about sb./sth.; **auf jmdn. schlecht/nicht gut zu ~ sein** be ill-disposed towards sb.; **für/gegen jmdn./etw. ~** (*in günstigem/ungünstigem Licht erscheinen lassen*) be a point in sb.'s/sth.'s favour/against sb./sth.; **es scheint alles dafür/dagegen zu ~, dass die Regierung im Amt bleiben wird** it seems there is every reason to believe that the government will/won't stay in power; **was spricht denn dafür/dagegen?** what is there to be said for/against it?; **für sich [selbst] ~** (*fig.*) speak for itself/themselves. **❷** *unr. tr. V.* **Ⓐ** speak ‹language, dialect›; say ‹word, sentence›; **~ Sie Französisch?** do you speak French?; **„Hier spricht man Deutsch"** 'German spoken'; 'we speak German'; **Ⓑ** (*rezitieren*) say, recite ‹poem, text›; say ‹prayer›; recite ‹spell›; pronounce ‹blessing, oath›; **ein Schlusswort ~:** give *or* make a concluding speech; ⇒ *auch* **Recht** A; **Urteil**; **Ⓒ** **jmdn. ~:** speak to sb.; **Sie haben mich ~ wollen?** you wanted to see me *or* speak to me?; **ich bin heute für niemanden mehr zu ~:** I can't see anyone else today; **kann ich Sie mal einen Moment ~?** can I see you for a moment?; can I have a quick word?; **wir [beide] ~ uns noch!** you haven't heard the last of this; **Ⓓ** (*aus~*) pronounce ‹name, word, etc.›; **sprich ...** (*auszu~*) pronounced ...; (*das heißt*) that is to say ...; **Ⓔ** (*sagen*) say; **und Gott sprach: „Es werde Licht!"** and God said, 'Let there be light'; **die Wahrheit ~:** speak the truth; **was spricht denn die Uhr?** (*fig. scherzh.*) what's the time?

**sprechend** *Adj.* convincing ‹example, evidence›; expressive ‹face, eyes›; eloquent ‹facial expression, glance, portrayal›; descriptive ‹name›

**Sprecher** *der;* **~s, ~ Ⓐ** spokesman; **Ⓑ** (*Ansager*) announcer; (*Nachrichten~*) newscaster; newsreader; **Ⓒ** (*Kommentator, Erzähler*) narrator; **Ⓓ** (*Sprachw.: Sprachteilhaber, Sprechender*) speaker

**Sprecherin** *die;* **~, ~nen Ⓐ** spokeswoman; **Ⓑ** ⇒ **Sprecher** B, C, D

**sprech-, Sprech-: ~erziehung** *die* speech training; elocution; **~faul** *Adj.* uncommunicative; reluctant to talk *pred.;* **~funk** *der* radio-telephone system; **~funk·gerät** *das* radio-telephone; (*Walkie-Talkie*) walkie-talkie; **~gesang** *der* sprechgesang; **sein Vortrag war eine Art ~gesang** he delivered his speech in a kind of singsong; **~muschel**

*old spelling (see note on page 1707)

*die* mouthpiece; **~platte** *die* spoken-word record; **~rolle** *die* speaking part; **~silbe** *die* [phonological] syllable; **~stimme** *die* speaking voice; (*Mus.*) sprechstimme; **~stunde** *die* consultation hours *pl.*; (*eines Arztes*) surgery; consulting hours *pl.*; (*eines Rechtsanwalts usw.*) office hours *pl.*; **wann haben Sie ~stunde?** when are your consultation hours/when is your surgery *or* what are your surgery hours?; **zum Zahnarzt/zu einem Abgeordneten in die ~stunde gehen** go to the dentist's/MP's surgery; **~stunden·hilfe** *die* (*eines Arztes*) receptionist; (*eines Zahnarztes*) assistant; **~tag** *der: day on which authorities' offices are open to the public;* **heute ist kein ~tag** we/they are not open today; **~übung** *die* elocution *or* speech exercise; (*zu therapeutischen Zwecken*) speech exercise; **~weise** *die* manner of speaking; **~werkzeuge** *Pl.* speech organs; organs of speech; **~zeit** *die* visiting time; **~zelle** *die* telephone booth; **~zimmer** *das* consulting room

**Spree-Athen** (*das*) (*scherzh.*) Berlin

**Spreißel** /ˈʃprai̯sl̩/ *der*, (*österr.*) *das*; **~s, ~** **A** (*bes. südd.: Splitter*) splinter; **B** (*bes. österr.: Span*) splint

**Spreiz·dübel** *der* expanding anchor

**Spreize** /ˈʃprai̯tsə/ *die*; **~, ~n** **A** (*Bauw.*) horizontal stay *or* brace; **B** (*Turnen*) **in der ~ stehen** stand with one leg extended behind/forward/to the side

**spreizen** ❶ *tr. V.* spread ‹fingers, toes, etc.›; **die Flügel/den Schwanz ~** ‹bird› spread its wings/tail; **die Beine ~:** spread one's legs apart; open one's legs; **mit gespreizten Beinen stehen/sitzen** stand/sit with one's legs apart; **das rechte Bein vorwärts/seitwärts ~:** extend one's right leg in front/to the side. ❷ *refl. V.* (*geh.*) **A** (*sich zieren*) **sie spreizte sich erst dagegen, dann stimmte sie zu** she made a fuss at first, [but] then agreed; **B** (*sich aufspielen*) give oneself airs; put on airs; **sie spreizte sich vor ihren Bewunderern** she strutted about in front of her admirers

**Spreiz-:** **~fuß** *der* ▶ 474 (*Med.*) spread foot; **~hose** *die* ≈ Frejka pillow (*kind of romper incorporating a padded steel splint for keeping an infant's legs in the frog position*)

**Spreng·bombe** *die* high-explosive bomb

**Sprengel** /ˈʃprɛŋl̩/ *der*; **~s, ~** **A** (*Kirchen~*) parish; (*Diözese*) diocese; **B** (*österr.*) administrative district

**sprengen** /ˈʃprɛŋən/ ❶ *tr. V.* **A** blow up; blast ‹rock›; **etw. in die Luft ~:** blow sth. up; **B** (*gewaltsam öffnen, aufbrechen*) force [open] ‹door›; force ‹lock›; break open ‹burial chamber etc.›; burst, break ‹bonds, chains›; (*fig.*) break up ‹meeting, demonstration›; **Eis sprengt den Felsen** ice is breaking up the rock; **die Freude sprengte ihm fast die Brust** (*fig.*) his heart was bursting with joy; ⇒ *auch* **Bank²** B; **Rahmen** B; **C** (*be~*) water ‹flower bed, lawn›; sprinkle ‹street, washing› with water; (*verspritzen*) sprinkle; (*mit dem Schlauch*) spray. ❷ *itr. V.* **A** **im Steinbruch wird wieder gesprengt** they're blasting again in the quarry; **B** *mit sein* (*geh.*) ‹rider› thunder

**Spreng-:** **~kammer** *die* blast *or* charge chamber; **~kapsel** *die* blasting cap; **~kommando** *das* demolition squad; **~kopf** *der* warhead; **~kraft** *die* explosive power; **~ladung** *die* explosive charge; **~meister** *der*, **~meisterin** *die* (*im Steinbruch*) blaster; shot firer; (*bei Abbrucharbeiten*) demolition expert; **~satz** *der* explosive charge

**Sprengsel** /ˈʃprɛŋzl̩/ *der od. das*; **~s, ~** (*ugs.*) ⇒ **Sprenkel**

**Spreng-:** **~stoff** *der* explosive; **~stoff·anschlag** *der* bomb attack

**Sprengung** *die*; **~, ~en** **A** blowing-up; (*im Steinbruch*) blasting; **er drohte mit der ~ des Gebäudes** he threatened to blow up the building; **B** ⇒ **sprengen** 1B: forcing [open]; forcing; breaking open; bursting; breaking; (*fig.*) breaking up; **C** (*das Besprengen*) sprinkling; (*mit dem Schlauch*) spraying

**Spreng·wagen** *der* watering cart; [street] sprinkler

**Sprenkel** /ˈʃprɛŋkl̩/ *der*; **~s, ~:** spot; dot; speckle

**sprenkeln** *tr. V.* **A** (*mit Flecken versehen*) sprinkle spots of ‹colour›; **B** (*spritzen*) sprinkle ‹water›

**Spreu** /ʃprɔy̯/ *die*; **~:** chaff; **die ~ vom Weizen trennen** *od.* (*geh.*) **sondern** (*fig.*) separate the wheat from the chaff

**sprich** /ʃprɪç/ *Imperativ Sg. v.* **sprechen**

**sprichst** /ʃprɪçst/ *2. Pers. Sg. Präsens v.* **sprechen**

**spricht** /ʃprɪçt/ *3. Pers. Sg. Präsens v.* **sprechen**

**Sprich·wort** *das*; *Pl.* **Sprichwörter** proverb

**sprich·wörtlich** ❶ *Adj.* **A** proverbial; **B** (*fig.: notorisch*) proverbial. ❷ *adv.* **A** **..., so heißt es ~:** ..., as the proverb has it; **B** (*fig.: notorisch*) proverbially

**sprießen** /ˈʃpriːsn̩/ *unr. itr. V.*; *mit sein* ‹leaf, bud› shoot, sprout; ‹seedlings› come *or* spring up; ‹beard› sprout; (*fig.*) ‹mistrust, envy, etc.› well up; ‹club, organization, etc.› spring up

**Spriet** /ʃpriːt/ *das*; **~[e]s, ~e** (*Seemannsspr.*) sprit

**Spriet·segel** *das* (*Seemannsspr.*) spritsail

**Spring·brunnen** *der* fountain

**springen** /ˈʃprɪŋən/ ❶ *unr. itr. V.* **A** *mit sein* jump; (*mit Schwung*) leap; spring; jump; ‹frog, flea› hop, jump; **vom Fünfmeterbrett ~:** dive from the five-metre board; **mit Anlauf/aus dem Stand ~:** take a running/standing jump; **jmdm. an die Kehle ~:** leap at sb.'s throat; **auf die Beine** *od.* **Füße ~:** jump to one's feet; **B** *meist mit sein* (*Sport*) jump; (*beim Stabhochsprung, beim Kasten, Pferd*) vault; (*beim Turm~, Kunst~*) dive; **C** *mit sein* (*sich in Sprüngen fortbewegen*) bound; **wenn sie einen Wunsch hat, springt die ganze Familie** when she wants something the whole family jumps to it; **D** (*ugs.*) *in* **eine Runde Bier ~ lassen** stand a round of beer; **er könnte ruhig mal was ~ lassen** he could easily fork out something just once in a while (*sl.*); **E** *mit sein* (*fig.: schnellen, hüpfen, fliegen*) ‹pointer, milometer, etc.› jump (**auf** + *Akk.* to); ‹traffic lights› change (**auf** + *Akk.* to); ‹spark› leap; ‹ball› bounce; ‹cork› pop out (**aus** + *Dat.* of); ‹spring› jump out; **[von etw.] ~** ‹fan belt, bicycle-chain, button, tyre, etc.› come off [sth.]; **die Lokomotive ist aus dem Gleis gesprungen** the locomotive jumped the rails; **F** *mit sein* (*zer~, zerbrechen, zerreißen*) ‹string, glass, porcelain, etc.› break; **G** *mit sein* (*aufplatzen, bersten*) ‹seed-pod› burst [open]; **gesprungene Lippen** cracked *or* chapped lips; **H** *mit sein* (*Risse, Sprünge bekommen*) crack; **I** *mit sein* (*fig. geh.: spritzen, sprudeln*) ‹fountain, jet of water, blood, etc.› spurt; **J** *mit sein* (*südd.: laufen*) run; (*eilen*) hurry.
❷ *unr. tr. V.*; *auch mit sein* (*Sport*) perform ‹somersault, twist dive, etc.›; **5,20m/einen neuen Rekord ~:** jump 5.20m/make a record jump

**Springen** *das*; **~s, ~** (*Pferdesport*) jumping event

**Springer** *der*; **~s, ~** **A** (*Weit~, Hoch~, Ski~*) jumper; (*Stabhoch~*) [pole] vaulter; (*Kunst~, Turm~*) diver; (*Fallschirm~*) parachutist; **B** (*Schachfigur*) knight; **C** **junger ~** (*ugs.*) greenhorn; **D** (*Arbeiter*) worker who is moved from job to job as required

**Springerin** *die*; **~, ~nen** ⇒ **Springer** A, D

**spring-, Spring-:** **~flut** *die* spring tide; **~form** *die* spring form; **~ins·feld** *der*; **~~[e]s, ~~e** (*scherzh.*) (*leichtsinniger junger Mensch*) [young] madcap; (*lebhaftes Kind*) lively little nipper (*Brit. sl.*); **~kraut** *das* impatience; **~lebendig** *Adj.* extremely lively; full of beans *pred.* (*coll.*); **er ist trotz seines hohen Alters noch ~lebendig** he is still extremely sprightly despite his age; **~maus** *die* jerboa; **~messer** *das* flick knife; **~pferd** *das* jumper; **~quell** *der* (*dichter.*) fountain; **~reiten** *das* showjumping *no art.*; **~rollo** *das* roller blind; **~seil** *das* skipping rope (*Brit.*); jump rope (*Amer.*); **~turnier** *das* (*Reiten*) showjumping competition

**Sprinkler** /ˈʃprɪŋklɐ/ *der*; **~s, ~:** sprinkler

**Sprint** /ʃprɪnt/ *der*; **~s, ~s** (*auch Sport*) sprint; **die letzten 100 Meter im ~ zurücklegen** sprint the last 100 metres

**sprinten** *itr.* (*auch tr.*) *V.*; *meist, mit Richtungsangaben nur, mit sein* (*Sport; ugs.: schnell laufen*) sprint

**Sprinter** *der*; **~s, ~**, **Sprinterin** *die*; **~, ~nen** (*Sport*) sprinter

**Sprint·strecke** *die* sprint distance

**Sprit** /ʃprɪt/ *der*; **~[e]s, ~e** **A** (*ugs.: Treibstoff*) gas (*Amer. coll.*); juice (*sl.*); petrol (*Brit.*); **B** (*ugs.: Schnaps*) shorts *pl.*; **C** (*Äthylalkohol*) ethanol; ethyl alcohol

**Spritze** /ˈʃprɪtsə/ *die*; **~, ~n** **A** (*zum Vernichten von Ungeziefer*) spray; (*Teig~, Torten~, Injektions~*) syringe; **B** (*Injektion*) injection; jab (*coll.*); **eine ~ bekommen** have an injection *or* (*coll.*) jab; **an der ~ hängen** (*salopp*) be on the needle (*sl.*); **C** (*Feuer~*) hose; (*Löschfahrzeug*) fire engine

**spritzen** /ˈʃprɪtsn̩/ ❶ *tr. V.* **A** (*versprühen*) spray; (*ver~*) splash ‹water, ink, etc.›; spatter ‹ink etc.›; (*in Form eines Strahls*) spray, squirt ‹water, foam, etc.›; pipe ‹cream etc.›; **B** (*be~, besprühen*) water ‹lawn, tennis court›; water, spray ‹street, yard›; spray ‹plants, crops, etc.›; pump ‹concrete›; (*mit Lack*) spray ‹car etc.›; **jmdn. nass ~:** splash sb.; (*mit Wasserpistole, Schlauch*) spray sb.; **den Fußboden/die Wände nass ~:** splash/spray water over the floor/walls; **jmdn. ~** (*ugs.: nass~*) squirt sb.; **C** (*injizieren*) inject ‹drug etc.›; **D** (*~d herstellen*) create ‹ice rink› by spraying; pipe ‹cake decoration etc.›; produce ‹plastic article› by injection moulding; **E** (*ugs.: einer Injektion unterziehen*) **jmdn./sich ~:** give sb. an injection/inject oneself; **er hat sich mit einer Überdosis Heroin zu Tode gespritzt** he gave himself a fatal shot of heroin; **jmdm. ein Schmerzmittel ~:** give sb. a pain-killing injection; **F** (*verdünnen*) dilute ‹wine etc.› with soda water/lemonade *etc.*
❷ *itr. V.* **A** **die Kinder planschten und spritzten** the children splashed and threw water about; **in meinem Garten wird nicht gespritzt** chemical sprays aren't used in my garden; **B** *mit Richtungsangabe mit sein* ‹hot fat› spit; ‹mud etc.› spatter, splash; ‹blood, water› spurt; **das Wasser spritzte ihm ins Gesicht** the water splashed up into his face; **C** *mit sein* (*ugs.: rennen*) dash; (*diensteifrig*) dash *or* chase about; **D** (*ugs.: sich Rauschgift injizieren*) shoot (*sl.*); **E** (*derb: ejakulieren*) come [off] (*coll.*)

**Spritzen·haus** *das* (*veralt.*) fire station

**Spritzer** *der*; **~s, ~** (*kleiner Tropfen*) splash; (*von Farbe*) splash; spot; (*Schuss*) dash; splash; **ein paar ~ Spülmittel** a few squirts of washing-up liquid

**Spritz-:** **~flasche** *die* **A** spray bottle; **B** (*Chemie*) wash bottle; **~gebäck** *das*: *biscuit[s]/small cake[s] made by squeezing the dough through a piping bag;* **~guss**, ***~guß** *der* injection moulding *no art.*

**spritzig** ❶ *Adj.* **A** sparkling ‹wine›; tangy ‹fragrance, perfume›; **B** (*lebendig*) lively ‹show, music, article›; sparkling ‹production, performance›; racy ‹style›; **C** (*temperamentvoll*) nippy (*coll.*); zippy ‹car, engine›; **D** (*flink*) agile, nimble ‹person›. ❷ *adv.* sparklingly ‹produced, performed, etc.›; racily ‹written›; **die Mannschaft spielte sehr ~:** the team played with great speed and agility

**Spritz-:** **~lack** *der* spray paint; **~pistole** *die* spray gun; **~tour** *die* (*ugs.*) spin

**spröd, spröde** /ʃprøːt/ *Adj.* **A** brittle ‹glass, plastic, etc.›; dry ‹hair, lips, etc.›; (*rissig*) chapped ‹lips, skin›; (*rau*) rough ‹skin›; **B** (*fig.: rau klingend*) harsh, rough ‹voice›; **C** (*fig.: schwer handhabbar*) unwieldy ‹subject, problem›; refractory ‹material›; **D** (*fig.: abweisend*) aloof ‹person, manner, nature›; **eine Landschaft von spröder Schönheit** a landscape of forbidding beauty

**Sprödheit, Sprödigkeit** *die*; **~** **A** ⇒ **spröde** A: brittleness; dryness; roughness; **B** (*fig.: rauer Klang*) harshness; roughness; **C** ⇒ **spröde** C: unwieldiness; refractoriness; **D** (*fig.: abweisendes Wesen*) aloofness

S

**spross, *sproß** /ʃprɔs/ *1. u. 3. Pers. Sg. Prät. v.* **sprießen**

**Spross, *Sproß** *der;* **Sprosses, Sprosse** *od.* **Sprossen** Ⓐ *Pl.* **Sprosse** (*Bot.*) shoot; Ⓑ *Pl.* **Sprosse** (*geh.: Nachkomme*) scion; Ⓒ *Pl.* **Sprossen** (*Jägerspr.*) ⇒ **Sprosse** C

**Sprosse** *die;* ~, ~**n** Ⓐ (*auch fig.*) rung; Ⓑ (*eines Fensters*) glazing bar; sash bar; Ⓒ (*Jägerspr.*) point; tine

**sprossen** *itr. V.* ‹plant› shoot, put forth shoots

**Sprossen-:** ~**fenster** *das* window with glazing bars; ~**kohl** *der* (*österr.*) ⇒ **Rosenkohl**; ~**wand** *die* wall bars *pl.*

**Sprössling, *Sprößling** /ˈʃprœslɪŋ/ *der;* ~**s,** ~**e** (*ugs. scherzh.*) offspring; **seine** ~**e** his offspring *pl.*

**Spross·vokal, *Sproß·vokal** *der* (*Sprachw.*) svarabhakti

**Sprotte** /ˈʃprɔtə/ *die;* ~, ~**n** sprat; **Kieler** ~**n** smoked [Kiel] sprats

**Spruch** /ʃprʊx/ *der;* ~**[e]s, Sprüche** /ˈʃprʏçə/ Ⓐ (*Wahl~*) motto; (*Sinn~*) maxim; adage; (*Aus~*) saying; aphorism; (*Zitat*) quotation; quote; (*Parole*) slogan; (*Bibel~*) quotation; saying; Ⓑ *Pl.* (*ugs. abwertend: Phrase*) **das sind doch alles nur Sprüche** that's just talk *or* empty words *pl.*; **Sprüche machen** *od.* **klopfen** talk big (*coll.*); Ⓒ (*Gedicht, Lied*) medieval lyric poem; **das Buch der Sprüche** *od.* **die Sprüche Salomos** (*bibl.*) [the Book of] Proverbs; Ⓓ (*Richter~*) judgement; (*Schieds~*) ruling; (*Orakel~*) oracle

**Spruch-:** ~**band** *das; Pl.* ~**bänder** Ⓐ banner; Ⓑ (*auf einem Bild*) banderol[e]; ~**dichtung** *die* [medieval] didactic poetry

**Sprüche·klopfer** *der;* ~**s,** ~, **Sprüche·klopferin** *die;* ~, ~**nen** (*ugs. abwertend*) big mouth (*coll.*)

**Spruch·kammer** *die* (*Rechtsw. hist.*) denazification court

**Sprüchlein** /ˈʃprʏçlain/ *das;* ~**s,** ~ Ⓐ (*kleiner Spruch*) short maxim; Ⓑ (*vorgefertigter Text*) little piece

**spruch·reif** *Adj.* **das ist noch nicht** ~: that's not definite, so people mustn't start talking about it yet; **die Angelegenheit ist jetzt** ~: the matter can now be discussed/decided

**Spruch·weisheit** *die* wise saying

**Sprudel** /ˈʃpruːdl/ *der;* ~**s,** ~ Ⓐ (*Selterwasser*) sparkling mineral water; Ⓑ (*österr.: Erfrischungsgetränk*) fizzy drink

**sprudeln** ❶ *itr. V.* Ⓐ *mit sein* ‹spring, champagne, etc.› bubble (**aus** out of); Ⓑ (*beim Kochen*) bubble; Ⓒ (*beim Entweichen von Gas*) ‹lemonade, champagne, etc.› fizz, effervesce; **ein** ~**des Getränk** a fizzy drink; Ⓓ (*fig.: überschäumen*) ‹person› bubble [over] (**vor** + *Dat.* with); **ein** ~**des Temperament** a bubbly *or* an effervescent temperament. ❷ *tr. V.* (*österr.: quirlen*) whisk

**Sprudel·wasser** *das; Pl.* **Sprudelwässer** sparkling mineral water

**Sprudler** *der;* ~**s,** ~ (*österr.*) whisk

**Sprüh·dose** *die* aerosol [can]

**sprühen** /ˈʃpryːən/ ❶ *tr. V.* spray; **Wasser auf die Blätter** ~: spray the leaves with water; **ich sprühte mir etwas Spray aufs Haar** I put some spray on my hair; **seine Augen sprühten Feuer** *od.* **Funken/Hass** (*fig.*) his eyes flashed fire/hatred. ❷ *itr. V.* Ⓐ *mit Richtungsangabe mit sein* ‹sparks, spray› fly; ‹flames› spit; ‹waterfall› send out a fine spray; (*fig.*) ‹eyes› sparkle (**vor** + *Dat.* with); ‹intellect, wit› sparkle; **ein feiner Regen sprühte gegen die Scheibe** a fine rain drifted against the window pane; **aus seinen Augen sprühte Feuer/Zorn** (*fig.*) fire/anger flashed in his eyes; ~**der Witz** sparkling wit; **ein** ~**des Temperament** a bubbly *or* effervescent temperament; **von Ideen/vor Witz** (*Dat.*) ~ (*fig.*) bubble [over] with ideas/sparkle with wit; Ⓑ *unpers.* (*regnen*) **es sprüht** it is drizzling

**Sprüh-:** ~**flasche** *die* spray bottle; ~**pflaster** *das* spray dressing; ~**regen** *der* drizzle; fine rain

**Sprung** /ʃprʊŋ/ *der;* ~**[e]s, Sprünge** /ˈʃprʏŋə/ Ⓐ (*auch Sport*) jump; (*schwungvoll*) leap; (*Satz*) bound; (~ *über das Pferd*) vault; (*Wassersport*) dive; (*fig.*) leap; **zum** ~ **ansetzen** ‹tiger etc.› get ready to pounce; **sein Herz machte vor Freude einen** ~ (*fig.*) his heart leapt for joy; **ein [großer]** ~ **nach vorn** (*fig.*) a [great] leap forward; **sie hat den** ~ **zum Film nicht geschafft** (*fig.*) she didn't manage to move into films; **ein qualitativer** ~ (*Philos.*) a qualitative leap; ~ **auf, marsch, marsch!** (*Milit.*) on your feet, quick march!; **ein** ~ **ins kalte Wasser** (*fig.*) jumping in at the deep end; **keine großen Sprünge machen können** (*fig. ugs.*) not be able to afford many luxuries; **auf einen** ~ (*fig. ugs.*) for a few minutes; **auf dem** ~**[e] sein** (*fig. ugs.*) be in a rush; Ⓑ (*ugs.: kurze Entfernung*) stone's throw; (*mit dem Auto*) short drive; Ⓒ (*Riß*) crack; **einen** ~ **haben/bekommen** be cracked/crack; **einen** ~ **in der Schüssel haben** (*salopp*) be cracked (*coll.*); Ⓓ **in jmdm. auf die Sprünge helfen** (*ugs.*) help sb. on his/her way; **jmds. Gedächtnis auf die Sprünge helfen** jog sb.'s memory; **jmdm. auf** *od.* **hinter die Sprünge kommen** (*fig. ugs.*) get on to sb.; Ⓔ (*Jägerspr.: Gruppe von Rehen*) herd; Ⓕ (*Geol.*) fault

**sprung-, Sprung-:** ~**bein** *das* Ⓐ take-off leg; Ⓑ ▶ 471 (*Anat.*) ankle bone; ~**bereit** *Adj.* ready to jump *pred.*; ‹cat› ready to pounce *pred.*; ~**brett** *das* (*auch fig.*) springboard; ~**deckel** *der* spring lid; ~**feder** *die* [spiral] spring; ~**gelenk** *das* ▶ 471 (*Anat.*) ankle joint

**sprunghaft** ❶ *Adj.* Ⓐ (*unstet*) erratic ‹person, character, manner›; Ⓑ (*unzusammenhängend*) disjointed ‹conversation, thoughts›; Ⓒ (*unvermittelt*) sudden; abrupt; Ⓓ (*ruckartig*) rapid ‹change›; sharp ‹increase›. ❷ *adv.*; ⇒ 1 B-D: disjointedly; suddenly; abruptly; rapidly; sharply

**Sprunghaftigkeit** *die;* ~ ⇒ **sprunghaft** 1 A, B: erraticness; disjointedness

**Sprung-:** ~**höhe** *die* height; ~**lauf** *der* (*Ski*) ski jumping *no art.*; ~**rahmen** *der* spring bedframe; ~**schanze** *die* (*Ski*) ski jumping hill; ~**seil** *das* skipping rope (*Brit.*); jump rope (*Amer.*); ~**tuch** *das; Pl.* ~**tücher** safety blanket; ~**turm** *der* (*Sport*) diving platform

**Spucke** *die;* ~: spit; **mir blieb die** ~ **weg** (*ugs.*) it took my breath away; I was speechless; ⇒ *auch* **Geduld**

**spucken** /ˈʃpʊkn̩/ ❶ *itr. V.* Ⓐ spit; **in die Hände** ~ (*fig.: an die Arbeit gehen*) go to work with a will; Ⓑ (*ugs.: erbrechen*) throw up (*coll.*); be sick (*Brit.*); Ⓒ **auf etw.** (*Akk.*) ~ (*salopp*) not give a damn about sth. ❷ *tr. V.* spit; spit [up], cough up ‹blood, phlegm›; spew out ‹lava›; **Feuer** ~: breathe fire; ‹volcano› belch fire; ⇒ *auch* **Ton²** D

**Spuck·napf** *der* spittoon

**Spuk** /ʃpuːk/ *der;* ~**[e]s,** ~**e** Ⓐ [ghostly *or* supernatural] manifestation; Ⓑ (*abwertend: schreckliches Geschehen*) horrific episode

**spuken** *itr. V.* Ⓐ *auch unpers.* **in dem Haus spukt ein Geist** this house is haunted by a ghost; **hier/in dem Haus spukt es** this place/the house is haunted; **gestern hat es wieder gespukt** there was another manifestation *or* haunting yesterday; **dieser Aberglaube spukt noch immer in den Köpfen vieler Menschen** (*fig.*) this superstition still lurks in many people's minds; Ⓑ *mit sein* **durch die Gänge** ~: walk *or* haunt the corridors

**Spuk-:** ~**gestalt** *die* ghostly figure; ~**schloss, *~schloß** *das* haunted castle

**Spül-:** ~**becken** *das* Ⓐ sink; Ⓑ (*beim Zahnarzt usw.*) basin; ~**bürste** *die* washing-up brush

**Spule** /ˈʃpuːlə/ *die;* ~, ~**n** Ⓐ spool; bobbin; (*für Tonband, Film*) spool; reel; Ⓑ (*Elektrot.*) coil

**Spüle** *die;* ~, ~**n** sink unit; (*Becken*) sink

**spulen** *tr., itr. V.* spool; (*am Tonbandgerät*) wind; **etw. auf etw.** (*Akk.*) ~: wind sth. on to sth.

**spülen** /ˈʃpyːlən/ ❶ *tr. V.* Ⓐ rinse; bathe ‹wound›; Ⓑ (*landsch.: abwaschen*) wash up ‹dishes, glasses, etc.›; **Geschirr** ~: wash up; Ⓒ (*schwemmen*) wash. ❷ *itr. V.* Ⓐ (*beim WC*) flush [the toilet]; Ⓑ (*den Mund aus~*) rinse out [one's mouth]; Ⓒ (*landsch.*) ⇒ **abwaschen** 2

**Spül-:** ~**kasten** *der* cistern; ~**maschine** *die* dishwasher; ~**mittel** *das* washing-up liquid; ~**schwamm** *der* washing-up sponge; ~**tuch** *das; Pl.* ~**tücher** dish cloth

**Spülung** *die;* ~, ~**en** Ⓐ (*Med.*) irrigation; (*der Vagina*) douche; Ⓑ (*beim WC*) flush

**Spül·wasser** *das; Pl.* **Spülwässer** Ⓐ rinse water; Ⓑ (*Abwaschwasser*) dishwater

**Spul·wurm** *der* ascarid

**Spund** /ʃpʊnt/ *der;* ~**[e]s,** ~**e/Spünde** /ˈʃpʏndə/ Ⓐ *Pl.* **Spünde** (*Zapfen*) bung; Ⓑ *Pl.* ~**e** (*ugs.*) **[junger** *od.* **grüner]** ~: young greenhorn *or* tiro

**Spund-:** ~**loch** *das* bunghole; ~**wand** (*Bauw.*) sheet-pile wall

**Spur** /ʃpuːɐ̯/ *die;* ~, ~**en** Ⓐ (*Abdruck im Boden*) track; (*Folge von Abdrücken*) tracks *pl.*; (*Blut~, Schleim~ usw.*) trail; **von dem Vermissten fehlt jede** ~: there is no trace of the missing person; **eine heiße** ~ (*fig.*) a hot trail; **eine heiße** ~ **haben** (*fig.*) have a really good lead; **jmdm./einer Sache auf die** ~ **kommen** get on to the track of sb./sth.; **jmdm./einer Sache auf der** ~ **sein** be on the track *or* trail of sb./sth.; Ⓑ (*Anzeichen*) trace; (*eines Verbrechens*) clue (*Gen.* to); **die** ~**en des Krieges/häufigen Gebrauchs** the marks of war/frequent use; Ⓒ (*sehr kleine Menge; auch fig.*) trace; **da fehlt noch eine** ~ **Paprika** it needs just a touch of paprika; **er hat keine** ~ **[von] Ehrgefühl** he has not the slightest sense of honour; **von Reue/Mitgefühl keine** ~**/nicht die leiseste** ~: not a trace or sign/not the slightest trace *or* sign of penitence/sympathy; **keine** *od.* **nicht die** ~ (*ugs.: als Antwort*) not in the slightest; Ⓓ (*Verkehrsw.: Fahr~*) lane; **die** ~ **wechseln** change lanes; **in** *od.* **auf der rechten/linken** ~ **fahren** drive in the right-hand/left-hand lane; Ⓔ (*Fahrlinie*) **[die]** ~ **halten** stay on its line; **aus der** ~ **kommen** be thrown off its line; Ⓕ (*Technik*) ⇒ ~**weite**; Ⓖ (*Elektrot., DV*) track

**spürbar** ❶ *Adj.* noticeable; perceptible; distinct, perceptible ‹improvement›; evident ‹relief, embarrassment›. ❷ *adv.* noticeably; perceptibly; (*sichtlich*) clearly ‹relieved, on edge›; **die Temperatur ist** ~ **gesunken/gestiegen** there has been a noticeable drop/rise in temperature; ~ **besser/schlechter werden** distinctly improve/deteriorate

**Spur·breite** *die* ⇒ ~**weite**

**spuren** ❶ *itr. V.* (*ugs.*) toe the line (*coll.*); do as one's told. ❷ *tr. V.* (*Ski*) prepare ‹cross-country course›

**spüren** /ʃpyːrən/ ❶ *tr. V.* feel; (*instinktiv*) sense; (*merken*) notice; **nach der Anstrengung spürte ich alle Knochen** I could feel every bone in my body after the exertion; **ich spüre mein Kreuz/meinen Magen** I have a pain in my back/my stomach; **die Peitsche zu** ~ **bekommen** get a taste of the whip; **jmds. Hass zu** ~ **bekommen** suffer sb.'s hatred; **von Kameradschaft war nichts zu** ~: there wasn't a sign *or* trace of comradeship; **er ließ uns seine Verärgerung nicht** ~: he gave [us] no sign of his annoyance; **sie ließ ihn** ~, **dass sie ihn nicht mochte** she made it plain [to him] *or* let him see that she didn't like him. ❷ *itr. V.* (*Jägerspr.*) **[nach einem Tier]** ~: track [an animal]

**Spuren-:** ~**element** *das* (*Biochemie*) trace element; ~**sicherung** *die* (*Polizeiw.*) Ⓐ (*Vorgang*) collection of evidence; Ⓑ (*Abteilung*) scene-of-crime *or* forensic unit

**Spür·hund** *der* tracker dog; (*fig.: Spitzel*) bloodhound; snooper (*coll.*)

*old spelling (see note on page 1707)

S

**spur·los** ❶ *Adj.* total, complete ‹disappearance›. ❷ *adv.* ‹disappear› completely *or* without trace; **an jmdm. ~ vorübergehen** leave sb. untouched; have no effect on sb.; **es ist nicht ~ an ihm vorübergegangen** it has not failed to leave its mark on him

**Spür-: ~nase** *die* (*ugs.*) Ⓐ (*Geruchssinn, fig.*) nose; Ⓑ (*Person*) bloodhound; snooper (*coll.*); **~sinn** *der* (*feiner Instinkt*) intuition

**Spurt** /ʃpʊrt/ *der;* **~[e]s, ~s** *od.* **~e** Ⓐ spurt; Ⓑ (*Sport.: ~vermögen*) turn of speed

**spurten** *itr. V.* Ⓐ *mit Richtungsangabe mit sein* spurt; Ⓑ *mit sein* (*ugs.: schnell laufen*) sprint

**spurt·stark** *Adj.* (*bes. Sport*) capable of putting on a strong spurt *or* of sprinting strongly *postpos.;* nippy (*coll.*) ‹car›

**Spur-: ~wechsel** *der* change of lane; **~weite** *die* (*Kfz-W.*) track; (*Eisenb.*) gauge

**sputen** /ˈʃpuːtn̩/ *refl. V.* (*veralt.*) make haste

**Sputnik** /ˈʃpʊtnɪk/ *der;* **~s, ~s** sputnik

**Squash** /skvɔʃ/ *das;* **~** (*Sport*) squash *no art.*

**Squaw** /skwɔː/ *die;* **~, ~s** squaw

**SR** *Abk.* **Saarländischer Rundfunk** Saarland Radio

**SRG** *Abk.* **Schweizerische Radio- und Rundfunkgesellschaft** Swiss Broadcasting Company

**Sri Lanka** /ˈsriː ˈlaŋka/ (*das*)*;* **~s** Sri Lanka

***Srilanker, Sri-Lanker** *der;* **~s, ~, *Srilankerin, Sri-Lankerin** *die;* **~, ~nen** Sri Lankan

***srilankisch, sri-lankisch** *Adj.* Sri Lankan

**SS**[1] *Abk.* (*ns.*) **Schutzstaffel** SS

**SS**[2] *Abk.* **Sommersemester**

**SSD** (*DDR*) *Abk.* **Staatssicherheitsdienst**

**SS-Mann** *der; Pl.* **SS-Männer** *od.* **SS-Leute** SS man

**SSO** *Abk.* ▶ 400 **Südsüdost[en]** SSE

**SSV** *Abk.* **Sommerschlussverkauf**

**SSW** *Abk.* ▶ 400 **Südsüdwest[en]** SSW

**St.** *Abk.* Ⓐ **Sankt** St.; Ⓑ **Stück**

**s. t.** *Abk.* **sine tempore**

**Staat** /ˈʃtaːt/ *der;* **~[e]s, ~en** Ⓐ state; **die ~en** (*die USA*) the States; **von ~s wegen** on the part of the [state] authorities; **beim ~ [angestellt] sein** be a civil servant *or* in the civil service; **der schlanke ~:** the slimmed-down state; ⇨ *auch* **Vater** A; Ⓑ (*ugs.: Festkleidung, Pracht*) finery; **in vollem ~:** in all one's finery; **damit ist kein ~ zu machen** (*fig.*) it's not up to much (*coll.*); **mit diesem Mantel ist kein ~ mehr zu machen** (*fig. ugs.*) this coat is past it (*coll.*); Ⓒ (*Zool.: Insekten~*) colony; **~en bildend** social ‹insect›

**staaten-, Staaten-: *~bildend** ⇨ **Staat** C; **~bund** *der* confederation; **~los** *Adj.* stateless; **~lose** *der/die; adj. Dekl.* stateless person *or* subject

**staatlich** ❶ *Adj.* state *attrib.* ‹sovereignty, institutions, authorities, control, etc.›; ‹power, unity, etc.› of the state; state-owned ‹factory etc.›; **~e Mittel** government *or* public money *sing.* ❷ *adv.* by the state; **~ anerkannt/geprüft/gelenkt/finanziert** state-approved/-certified/-managed/-financed; **~ subventioniert werden** receive a state subsidy

**staats-, Staats-: ~affäre** *die:* **eine ~affäre aus etw. machen** (*ugs.*) make a song and dance about sth. (*coll.*); **~akt** *der* Ⓐ (*Festakt*) state ceremony; Ⓑ (*Rechtsvorgang*) act of state; **~aktion** *die:* **eine ~aktion aus etw. machen** (*ugs.*) make a song and dance about sth. (*coll.*); **~amateur** *der,* **~amateurin** *die* (*Sport*): *state-sponsored, nominally amateur, sportsman/sportswoman;* **~amt** *das* public office; **~angehörige** *der/die* national; **~angehörigkeit** *die;* **~~, ~~en** nationality; **~anleihe** *die* government bond; **~anwalt** *der,* **~anwältin** *die* ▶ 91, ▶ 159 public prosecutor; **~anwaltschaft** *die* public prosecutor's office; **~apparat** *der* state machine; **~ausgaben** *Pl.* public expenditure *sing.;* **~bank** *die; Pl.* **~~en** national bank; **~beamte** *der,* **~beamtin** *die* ▶ 159 civil servant; **~begräbnis** *das* state funeral; **~besuch** *der* state visit; **~bürger** *der,* **~bürgerin** *die* ▶ 553 citizen; **er ist deutscher ~bürger** he is a German citizen *or* national; ⇨ *auch* **Uniform**; **~bürger·kunde** *die* (*DDR*): *school subject involving ideological education of socialist citizens;* ≈ civics *sing. no art.;* **~bürgerlich** *Adj.* civil ‹rights›; civic ‹duties, loyalty›; ‹education, attitude› as a citizen; **~bürgerschaft** *die* ⇨ **~angehörigkeit**; **~chef** *der,* **~chefin** *die* head of state; **~diener** *der,* **~dienerin** *die* (*meist scherzh.*) public servant; **~dienst** *der* civil service; **~eigen** *Adj.* state-owned; **~eigentum** *das* state property; **~examen** *das: final university examination;* **~examen machen** ≈ take one's finals; **~feind** *der,* **~feindin** *die* enemy of the state; **~feindlich** *Adj.* anti-state; ‹organization, attitude› hostile to the state; **~finanzen** *Pl.* public finances; **~flagge** *die* state flag; (*Nationalflagge*) national flag; **~form** *die* type of state; state system; **~gebiet** *das* territory [of a/the state]; **~gefährdend** *Adj.* subversive; anti-state; **~gefährdung** *die* subversion [of the state]; **~geheimnis** *das* (*auch fig.*) state secret; **~geschäft** *das* affair of state; **~gewalt** *die* authority of the state; (*Exekutive*) executive power; **~grenze** *die* state frontier *or* border; **~haushalt** *der* national budget; **~hoheit** *die* sovereignty; **~hymne** *die* (*bes. DDR*) national anthem; **~kanzlei** *die* Minister-President's Office; (*Schweiz*) Cantonal Chancellery; **~karosse** *die* state coach; (*fig. scherzh.*) prestige limo (*Amer. coll.*) *or* limousine; **~kasse** *die* Ⓐ public purse; Ⓑ (*Fiskus*) treasury; **~kirche** *die* state *or* established church; **~kosten** *Pl.* **auf ~kosten** at public expense; **~kunst** *die* (*geh.*) statemanship; statecraft; **~macht** *die* power [of government]; **~mann** *der* statesman; **~männin** *die* stateswoman; **~männisch** /-mɛnɪʃ/ ❶ *Adj.* statesmanlike ‹wisdom, far-sightedness, etc.›; ‹abilities, skill› of a statesman; ❷ *adv.* in a statesmanlike manner; **~minister** *der,* **~ministerin** *die* minister of state; (*Minister[in] ohne Ressort*) minister without portfolio; (*Staatssekretär[in]*) secretary of state; **~oberhaupt** *das* head of state; **~oper** *die* State Opera; **~organ** *das* organ *or* instrument of state; **~partei** *die* [totalitarian] government party; **~politisch** ❶ *Adj.* ‹aims, tasks, etc.› of national policy; ❷ *adv.* from the point of view of national policy; **~polizei** *die* state police; **~präsident** *der,* **~präsidentin** *die* [state] president; **~prüfung** *die* state examination; **~raison** *die,* **~räson** *die* reasons *pl.* of State *no def. art.;* **aus [Gründen der] ~raison** for reasons of state; **~recht** *das* constitutional law; **~rechtler** /...rɛçtlɐ/ *der;* **~~s, ~~, ~rechtlerin** *die;* **~~, ~~nen** expert in constitutional law; **~regierung** *die* national government; **~religion** *die* state religion; **~säckel** *der* (*scherzh.*) state coffers *pl.;* **~schatz** *der* national *or* state reserves *pl.;* **~schiff** *das* (*geh.*) ship of state; **~schuld** *die* national debt; **~sekretär** *der,* **~sekretärin** *die* ▶ 159 permanent secretary; **~sicherheit** *die* Ⓐ state security; Ⓑ (*DDR ugs.*) ⇨ **~sicherheitsdienst**; **~sicherheits·dienst** *der* (*DDR*) State Security Service; **~streich** *der* coup d'état; **~theater** *das* state theatre; **~trauer** *die* national mourning *no indef. art.;* **~verbrechen** *das* crime against the state; **~verschuldung** *die* national debt; **~vertrag** *der* international treaty; (*zwischen Gliedstaaten*) interstate treaty *or* agreement; **der Österreichische ~vertrag** the Austrian State Treaty; **~wesen** *das* state [system]; **~wohl** *das* welfare *or* good of the state

**Stab** /ʃtaːp/ *der;* **~[e]s, Stäbe** /ˈʃtɛːbə/ Ⓐ rod; (*länger, für Stabhochsprung o. Ä.*) pole; (*eines Käfigs, Gitters, Geländers*) bar; (*Staffel~; geh.: Taktstock*) baton; (*Bischofs~*) crosier; (*Hirten~*) crook; **den ~ über jmdn./etw. brechen** (*geh.*) condemn sb./sth. out of hand; Ⓑ (*Milit.*) staff; Ⓒ (*Team*) team

**Stäbchen** /ˈʃtɛːpçən/ *das;* **~s, ~** Ⓐ (*kleiner Stab*) little rod; [small] stick; Ⓑ (*Ess~*) chopstick

**Stabelle** /ʃtaˈbɛlə/ *die;* **~, ~n** (*schweiz.*) stool

**Stab-: ~hochspringen** *das;* **~~s** pole-vaulting *no art.;* **~hochspringer** *der,* **~hochspringerin** *die* pole vaulter; **~hochsprung** *der* Ⓐ (*Disziplin*) pole-vaulting *no art.;* **im ~hochsprung** in the pole vault; Ⓑ (*Sprung*) pole vault

**stabil** /ʃtaˈbiːl/ ❶ *Adj.* Ⓐ (*solide, kräftig*) sturdy ‹chair, cupboard›; solid, sturdy ‹construction›; robust, sound ‹health, constitution›; Ⓑ (*beständig, dauerhaft*) stable ‹prices, government, economy, Chem.: solution, etc.›. ❷ *adv.* **~ gebaut** solidly built

**Stabilisator** /ʃtabiliˈzaːtɔr/ *der;* **~s, ~en** /-ˈtoːrən/ (*Technik, Chemie*) stabilizer; (*Kfz-W.*) anti-roll bar

**stabilisieren** ❶ *tr. V.* stabilize. ❷ *refl. V.* Ⓐ stabilize; become more stable; Ⓑ ‹health, circulation, etc.› become stronger

**Stabilisierung** *die;* **~, ~en** Ⓐ stabilization; Ⓑ (*Kräftigung*) strengthening

**Stabilität** /ʃtabiliˈtɛːt/ *die;* **~** Ⓐ (*einer Konstruktion*) sturdiness; (*von Gesundheit, Konstitution usw.*) robustness; soundness; Ⓑ (*das Beständigsein*) stability

**Stab-: ~lampe** *die* torch (*Brit.*); flashlight (*Amer.*); **~magnet** *der* bar magnet; **~reim** *der* (*Verslehre*) stave rhyme; head rhyme

**Stabs-: ~arzt** *der,* **~ärztin** *die* (*Milit.*) medical officer, MO (*with the rank of captain*); **~feldwebel** *der* (*Milit.*) warrant officer 2nd class; **~offizier** *der* (*Milit.*) staff officer

**Staccato** /staˈkaːto/ ⇨ **Stakkato**

**stach** /ʃtaːx/ *1. u. 3. Pers. Sg. Prät. v.* **stechen**

**Stachel** /ˈʃtaxl̩/ *der;* **~s, ~n** Ⓐ spine; (*Dorn*) thorn; Ⓑ (*Gift~*) sting; Ⓒ (*spitzes Metallstück*) spike; (*von ~draht*) barb; ⇨ *auch* **löcken**; Ⓓ (*geh.: etw. Quälendes*) barb; **der ~ der Eifersucht** the torment of jealousy; **einer Sache** (*Dat.*) **den ~ nehmen** take the sting out of sth.; **ein ~ im Fleisch** a thorn in the flesh; Ⓔ (*etw. Stimulierendes*) **der ~ des Ehrgeizes** the spur of ambition

**Stachel-: ~beere** *die* gooseberry; **~draht** *der* barbed wire; **~häuter** /-hɔytɐ/ *der;* **~~s, ~~** (*Zool.*) echinoderm

**stachelig** *Adj.* prickly

**stacheln** *itr. V.* prick; ‹beard› prickle

**Stachel·schwein** *das* porcupine

**stachlig** ⇨ **stachelig**

**Stadel** /ʃtaːdl/ *der;* **~s, ~** *od.* (*schweiz.*) **Städel** *od.* (*österr.*) **~n** (*südd., österr., schweiz.*) barn

**Stadion** /ˈʃtaːdi̯ɔn/ *das;* **~s, Stadien** stadium

**Stadium** /ˈʃtaːdi̯ʊm/ *das;* **~s, Stadien** stage

**Stadt** /ʃtat/ *die;* **~, Städte** /ˈʃtɛ(ː)tə/ Ⓐ town; (*Groß~*) city; **die ~ Basel** the city of Basel; **in die ~ gehen** go into town; go downtown (*Amer.*); **~ und Land** town and country; **in ~ und Land** throughout the country; Ⓑ (*Verwaltung*) town council; (*in der Großstadt*) city council; city hall *no art.* (*Amer.*); **bei der ~ [angestellt] sein/arbeiten** work for the council *or* (*Amer.*) for city hall

**stadt-, Stadt-: ~auswärts** *Adv.* out of town; **~autobahn** *die* urban motorway (*Brit.*) *or* (*Amer.*) freeway; **~bahn** *die* urban railway; **~bekannt** *Adj.* well known in the town/city *postpos.;* known all over the town/city *postpos.;* (*berüchtigt*) notorious throughout the town/city *postpos.;* **~bevölkerung** *die* urban population; (*einer bestimmten Stadt*) townspeople *pl.;* **~bewohner** *der,* **~bewohnerin** *die* town-/city-dweller; **~bibliothek** *die* municipal library; **~bild** *das* townscape; (*einer Großstadt*) cityscape; **~bücherei** *die* municipal [lending] library; **~bummel** *der* (*ugs.*) **einen ~bummel machen** take a stroll through the town/city centre

**Städtchen** /ˈʃtɛ(ː)tçən/ *das;* **~s, ~:** little town; **andere ~, andere Mädchen** move to a new town and you find a new girl

**Stadt·chronik** *die* history of the town/city

**Städte·bau** *der* urban building *or* development *no art.;* (*Planung*) town planning *no art.*

S

# Städte

Nur für wenige deutsche Städte gibt es besondere englische Namensformen: Am bekanntesten sind *Köln* = Cologne, *München* = Munich und *Hannover* = Hanover. In Österreich *Wien* = Vienna, in der Schweiz *Genf* = Geneva, *Basel* = Basle und *Luzern* = Lucerne. Unter den europäischen Hauptstädten fallen auf: *Brüssel* = Brussels, *Den Haag* = the Hague, *Rom* = Rome, *Athen* = Athens, *Prag* = Prague, *Warschau* = Warsaw und *Moskau* = Moscow. Überhaupt gibt es viele Unterschiede in der Transliteration von slawischen, griechischen, indischen und anderen fremdländischen Ortsnamen. Am besten schlägt man im Hauptteil dieses Wörterbuchs nach, der die wichtigsten geographischen Namen aufführt, oder auf einer englischsprachigen Landkarte.

**■ EINWOHNERBEZEICHNUNGEN UND ADJEKTIVE**

Die von den Städtenamen abgeleiteten Einwohnerbezeichnungen und Adjektive haben im Englischen verschiedene Formen, aber es gibt sie nur für bestimmte größere Städte. Einige Substantive haben die gleiche Form wie die deutschen, die auf **-er** enden (Londoner, New Yorker usw.).

Für britische Städte gibt es einige ganz ausgefallene Ableitungen:

Glasgow→Glaswegian Aberdeen→Aberdonian
Bath→Bathonian Liverpool→Liverpudlian
Manchester→Mancunian Oxford→Oxonian

Die Endung **-ian** kommt recht häufig vor (z.B. Bristol→Bristolian, Lancaster→Lancastrian), aber für die meisten britischen Städte gibt es keine Einwohnerbezeichnungen. Die hier angegebenen werden sowohl als Adjektive wie auch als Substantive verwendet; die Adjektive beziehen sich meist auf Charaktereigenschaften (*Liverpooler Humor* = Liverpudlian humour).

Weitere Beispiele im europäischen Ausland:

Paris→Parisian Rome→Roman
Vienna→Viennese Milan→Milanese
Venice→Venetian Athens→Athenian
Florence→Florentine Moscow→Muscovite

In Deutschland gibt es lediglich *Hannoveraner* = Hanoverian (das sich hauptsächlich auf das englische Königshaus und die Pferderasse bezieht). Man kann aber in vielen Fällen die deutsche Form mit der Endung auf **-er** verwenden (Berliner, Frankfurter usw.), die sich aber nur als Einwohnerbezeichnung eignet. Sonst muss man auf die Formel 'inhabitant of ...' bzw. bei einer Großstadt, die als 'city' gilt, 'citizen of ...' zurückgreifen:

***ein Dinkelsbühler/eine Dinkelsbühlerin***
= an inhabitant of Dinkelsbühl, a Dinkelsbühler

***die Münchener***
= the citizens *od.* people of Munich

Dasselbe gilt natürlich für Städte in anderen Ländern. Wenn man das Geschlecht hervorheben will, kann man 'a man/woman from ...' oder sogar den landessprachlichen Ausdruck verwenden:

***ein alter Bremer***
= an old man from Bremen, an old Bremen man

***eine schöne Madriderin***
= a beautiful woman/girl from Madrid, a beautiful madrileña

***eine junge Römerin***
= a young Roman girl

***viele Wiener/Wienerinnen***
= many Viennese men/women

Anstelle eines fehlenden abgeleiteten Adjektivs verwendet man einfach den Namen attributiv vor dem Substantiv (ohne Artikel bei Gebäuden und Einrichtungen) oder nachgestellt mit **of** bzw. **in**:

***der Aachener Dom***
= Aachen Cathedral

***der Ravensburger Stadtrat***
= Ravensburg Town Council, the Town Council of Ravensburg

***der Berliner Dialekt***
= Berlin dialect

***die New Yorker Gegend***
= the New York area

***die Pariser Straßen***
= the streets of Paris

***der Londoner Verkehr***
= the London traffic, the traffic in London

Der attributive Gebrauch von Städtenamen erstreckt sich auch auf Straßen:

***die Straße nach Portsmouth***
= the road to Portsmouth, the Portsmouth road

Die Adjektive, die auf **-isch** enden, werden auf ähnliche Weise übersetzt.

***hamburgischer Humor***
= Hamburg humour

***hannoverischer Gleichmut***
= Hanoverian equanimity

Die Dialekte, die auf **-erisch** enden, kann man nur als '... dialect' wiedergeben:

***Wienerisch***
= Viennese [dialect]

***Berlinerisch***
= Berlin dialect

S

**städte·baulich** ❶ *Adj.* ‹development› of urban building/town planning; town-planning ‹measure›. ❷ *adv.* from the point of view of town planning

**stadt·einwärts** *Adv.* into town; downtown (*Amer.*)

**Städte·partnerschaft** *die* twinning (*Brit.*) *or* (*Amer.*) sister-city arrangement (*between towns/cities*)

**Städter** *der;* **~s**, **~**, **Städterin** *die;* **~**, **~nen** Ⓐ town-dweller; (*Großstädter, -städterin*) city-dweller; Ⓑ (*Stadtmensch*) townie (*coll.*)

**Stadt-:** **~flucht** *die* migration from the city; **~führer** *der* town/city guidebook; **~gas** *das* town gas; **~gespräch** *das* Ⓐ (*Telefongespräch*) local call; Ⓑ *in* **~gespräch sein** be the talk of the town; **~guerilla**[1] *die* urban guerilla group; **~guerilla**[2] *der* urban guerrilla; **~halle** *die* civic *or* municipal hall; **~haus** *das* Ⓐ (*Verwaltungsgebäude*) council office building; Ⓑ (*Wohnhaus*) town house

**städtisch** ❶ *Adj.* Ⓐ (*kommunal*) municipal; **das Altersheim ist ~:** the old people's home is owned by the town/city; Ⓑ (*urban*) urban ‹life, way of life, etc.›; town ‹clothes›; ‹manners, clothes› of a town-dweller. ❷ *adv.* Ⓐ (*kommunal*) municipally; **~ verwaltet** run by the town/city council; Ⓑ (*urban*) **~/ausgesprochen ~ gekleidet** wearing town clothes/wearing clothes with a decidedly town style

**Stadt-:** **~kämmerer** *der*, **~kämmerin** *die* town/city treasurer; **~kasse** *die* Ⓐ (*Geldmittel*) municipal funds *pl., no art.;* Ⓑ (*Stelle*) town/city treasurer's office; **~kern** *der* ⇒ **~mitte**; **~kind** *das* Ⓐ town/city child; Ⓑ (*~mensch*) townie (*coll.*); **~kreis** *der* urban district; **~landschaft** *die* townscape; urban landscape; **~mauer** *die* town/city wall; **~mensch** *der* townie (*coll.*); **~mission** *die* town/city mission; **~mitte** *die* town centre; (*einer Großstadt*) city centre; downtown area (*Amer.*); **~park** *der* municipal park; **~parlament** *das* city council; **~plan** *der* [town/city] street plan *or* map; **~planer** *der*, **~planerin** *die* ▶ 159 | town planner; **~planung** *die* town planning *no art.;* **~rand** *der* outskirts *pl.* of the town/city; **am ~rand** on the outskirts of the town/city; **~rat** *der* Ⓐ town/city council; Ⓑ (*Mitglied*) town/city councillor; **~rätin** *die* ⇒ **~rat** B; **~recht** *das* town ordinances and privileges *pl.;* **~recht erhalten** receive its town charter; **~rundfahrt** *die* sightseeing tour round a/the town/city; **~sanierung** *die* town/city redevelopment; **~schreiber** *der*, **~schreiberin** *die* Ⓐ (*hist.*) town clerk; Ⓑ (*Schriftsteller*) writer-in-residence (*living in a town/city and writing about it*); **~staat** *der* city state; **~streicher** *der*, **~streicherin** *die* town/city tramp; **~teil** *der* district; part [of a/the town]; **~theater** *das* municipal theatre; **~tor** *das* town/city gate; **~väter** *Pl.* (*ugs. scherzh.*) city fathers; **~verkehr** *der* town/city traffic; **~verordnete** *der/die; adj. Dekl.* town/city councillor; **~verwaltung** *die* municipal authority; town/city council; **~viertel** *das* district; **~wappen** *das* town/city coat-of-arms; **~werke** *Pl.* municipal *or* council services; **~wohnung** *die* town/city flat (*Brit.*) *or* (*Amer.*) apartment; **~zentrum** *das* town/city centre; downtown area (*Amer.*)

**Stafette** /ʃtaˈfɛtə/ *die;* **~**, **~n** Ⓐ (*hist.: reitender Bote*) courier (*as one of a relay*); Ⓑ (*Gruppe von Kurieren*) relay; Ⓒ (*Formation als Begleitung*) formation of outriders

**Staffage** /ʃtaˈfaːʒə/ *die;* **~**, **~n**, Ⓐ (*Beiwerk*) accessories *pl.;* (*Dekoration*) decoration; Ⓑ (*bild. Kunst*) staffage

**Staffel** /ˈʃtafl/ *die;* **~**, **~n** Ⓐ (*Sport: Mannschaft*) team; (*für den ~lauf*) relay team; Ⓑ (*Sport: ~lauf*) relay race; Ⓒ (*Luftwaffe: Einheit*) flight; Ⓓ (*Formation von Schiffen, begleitenden Polizisten usw.*) escort formation

**Staffelei** *die;* **~**, **~en** easel

*old spelling (see note on page 1707)

**Staffel-:** ~**lauf** *der* (*Sport*) relay race; ~**läufer** *der*, ~**läuferin** *die* (*Sport*) relay runner/skier

**staffeln** *tr. V.* [A] (*aufstellen, formieren*) arrange in a stagger *or* in an echelon; **gestaffelte Abwehr** (*Fußball*) staggered defence [line-up]; [B] (*einteilen, abstufen*) grade <salaries, fees, prices>; stagger <times, arrivals, starting places>

**Staffelung** *die;* ~, ~**en** [A] (*Anordnung*) staggered arrangement; [B] (*Einteilung, Abstufung*) (*von Gebühren, Gehältern, Preisen*) grad[u]ation; (*von Vorgängen*) staggering

**Stag** /ʃta:k/ *das;* ~[e]s, ~e[n] (*Seew.*) stay

**Stagflation** /ʃtakfla'tsio:n/ *die;* ~, ~en (*Wirtsch.*) stagflation

**Stagnation** /ʃtagna'tsio:n/ *die;* ~, ~en stagnation

**stagnieren** *itr. V.* stagnate

**Stag·segel** *das* (*Seew.*) staysail

**stahl** /ʃta:l/ *1. u. 3. Pers. Sg. Prät. v.* **stehlen**

**Stahl** *der;* ~[e]s, **Stähle** /'ʃtɛ:lə/ *od.* ~e [A] steel; **die ~ verarbeitende Industrie** the steel-processing *or* steel industry; **Nerven wie** *od.* **aus ~ haben** have nerves of steel; [B] (*dichter.: Dolch, Schwert*) blade

**stahl-, Stahl-:** ~**arbeiter** *der* ▶ 159 steelworker; ~**bau** *der; Pl.* ~~ten [A] (*Bautechnik*) steel construction *no art.*; [B] (*Gebäude*) steel-frame building; ~**besen** *der* (*Musik*) wire brush; ~**beton** *der* (*Bauw.*) reinforced concrete; ferroconcrete; ~**beton·bau** *der* reinforced concrete construction; ~**blau** *Adj.* steel-blue; ~**blech** *das* sheet steel

**stählen** *tr. V.* (*geh.*) toughen; harden

**stählern** *Adj.* [A] (*aus Stahl*) steel; [B] (*fig. geh.*) <muscles, nerves> of steel; <will> of iron

**stahl-, Stahl-:** ~**grau** *Adj.* steel-grey; ~**hart** *Adj.* as hard as steel *postpos.*; ~**helm** *der* (*Milit.*) steel helmet; ~**kammer** *die* strongroom; ~**kocher** *der*, ~**kocherin** *die;* ~~, ~~**nen** (*ugs.*) steelworker; ~**mantel·geschoss**, *~**mantel·geschoß** *das* (*Milit.*) steel-jacketed bullet; ~**rohr** *das* steel tube; ~**rohr·möbel** *das* piece of tubular steel furniture; **moderne ~rohrmöbel** modern tubular steel furniture *sing.*; ~**ross**, *~**roß** *das* (*ugs. scherzh.*) bike (*coll.*); trusty steed (*coll. joc.*); ~**stich** *der* (*Grafik*) steel engraving; *~**verarbeitend** ⇒ **Stahl** A; ~**waren** *Pl.* steelware *sing.*; ~**wolle** *die* steel wool

**stak** /ʃta:k/ *1. u. 3. Pers. Sg. Prät. v.* **stecken**

**Stake** *die;* ~, ~n, **Staken** *der;* ~s, ~ (*nordd.*) pole

**staken** ❶ *tr. V.* punt <boat>. ❷ *itr. V.; mit sein* punt

**Staket** /ʃta'ke:t/ *das;* ~[e]s, ~e [A] (*Lattenzaun*) paling [fence]; [B] (*Latte*) pale

**Stakete** *die;* ~, ~n (*bes. österr.*) ⇒ **Staket** B

**Staketen·zaun** *der* paling fence

**Stakkato** /ʃta'ka:to/ *das;* ~s, ~s *od.* **Stakkati** (*Musik; auch fig.*) staccato

**staksen** /'ʃta:ksn̩/ *itr. V.; mit sein* (*ugs.*) stalk; (*taumelnd*) teeter

**staksig** (*ugs.*) ❶ *Adj.* spindly, shaky-legged <foal etc.>; teetering <steps>; **einen ~en Gang haben** walk as though on stilts. ❷ *adv.* **~ gehen** walk as though on stilts; (*unsicher*) walk with teetering steps

**Stalagmit** /ʃtalak'mi:t/ *der;* ~s *od.* ~en, ~e[n] (*Geol.*) stalagmite

**Stalaktit** /ʃtalak'ti:t/ *der;* ~s *od.* ~en, ~e[n] (*Geol.*) stalactite

**Stalinismus** /stalinɪsmʊs/ *der;* ~: Stalinism *no art.*

**Stalinist** *der;* ~en, ~en Stalinist

**stalinistisch** ❶ *Adj.* Stalinist. ❷ *adv.* in a Stalinist way; along Stalinist lines

**Stalin·orgel** *die* (*Soldatenspr.*) multiple rocket launcher

**Stall** /ʃtal/ *der;* ~[e]s, **Ställe** /'ʃtɛlə/ [A] (*Pferde~, Renn~*) stable; (*Kuh~*) cowshed; (*Hühner~*) [chicken] coop; (*Schweine~*) [pig]sty; (*für Kaninchen, Kleintiere*) hutch; (*für Schafe*) pen; **aus einem guten/demselben ~ kommen** (*fig. ugs. scherzh.*) have a good/the same background; **ein ganzer ~ voll Kinder** (*ugs.*) a whole horde of kids (*coll.*); ⇒ *auch* **Pferd** A; [B] (*Sportjargon: Rennfahrermannschaft*) [racing] team

***Stallaterne** *die* ⇒ **Stalllaterne**

**Stall·bursche** *der* ▶ 159 stable lad

**Ställchen** /'ʃtɛlçən/ *das;* ~s, ~ ⇒ **Stall** A: little stable/cowshed/coop/sty/hutch/pen

**Stall-:** ~**dung** *der* (*von Kühen/Schweinen/Schafen*) cow/pig/sheep dung; (*von Pferden*) horse manure; ~**hase** *der* (*ugs.*) domestic rabbit; ~**knecht** *der* ▶ 159 (*veralt.*) stable lad; (*für Kühe*) cowhand; ~**laterne** *die* stable lamp; ~**meister** *der*, ~**meisterin** *die* ▶ 159 head groom; ~**mist** *der* ⇒ ~**dung**

**Stallung** *die;* ~, ~en (*Pferdestall*) stable; (*Kuhstall*) cowshed; (*Schweinestall*) [pig]sty; **die ~en** the stables and other animal buildings

**Stallwache** *die* (*fig.*) caretakers *pl.*; **~ halten** keep an eye on things; hold the fort

**Stamm** /ʃtam/ *der;* ~[e]s, **Stämme** [A] (*Baum~*) trunk; **eine Hütte aus rohen Stämmen** a hut of rough-hewn boles; ⇒ *auch* **Apfel** A; [B] (*Volks~, Geschlecht*) tribe; **der ~ Davids** the house of David; **vom ~e Nimm sein** (*ugs. scherzh.*) be out for what one can get (*coll.*); [C] (*fester Bestand*) core; (*von Fachkräften, Personal*) permanent staff; **zum ~ gehören** be one of the regulars (*coll.*); (*der Belegschaft einer Firma*) be a permanent member of staff; **ein [fester] ~ von Kunden/Gästen** a number of regular customers/patrons; [D] (*Sprachw.*) stem; [E] (*Biol.: Kategorie*) phylum; (*Mikrobiol.: Bakterien~; Tierzucht*) strain

**Stamm-:** ~**aktie** *die* (*Wirtsch.*) ordinary share; ~**baum** *der* family tree; (*eines Tieres*) pedigree; (*Biol.*) phylogenetic tree; ~**buch** *das* [A] **jmdm. etw. ins ~buch schreiben** (*fig.*) make sb. take sth. to heart; [B] (*Familien~buch*) family album (*recording births, marriages, deaths, etc.*)

**stammeln** /'ʃtamln̩/ *tr., itr. V.* stammer

**Stamm·eltern** *Pl.* progenitors

**stammen** *itr. V.* ▶ 553 come (**aus, von** from); (*datieren*) date (**aus, von** from); **aus einem alten Geschlecht ~:** be descended from an ancient lineage; **der Schmuck stammt von meiner Mutter** the jewellery used to belong to my mother; **der Satz/die Idee stammt nicht von ihm** the saying/idea isn't his

**stammes-, Stammes-:** ~**fürst** *der*, ~**fürstin** *die* tribal chieftain; ~**geschichte** *die* (*Biol.*) phylogenesis *no art.*; ~**geschichtlich** ❶ *Adj.* phylogenetic; ❷ *adv.* phylogenetically; ~**häuptling** *der* tribal chief

**Stamm-:** ~**essen** *das* set meal; ~**form** *die* (*Sprachw.*) principal part; ~**gast** *der* (*im Lokal/Hotel*) regular customer/visitor; regular (*coll.*); ~**gericht** *das* set dish; ~**halter** *der* (*oft scherzh.*) son and heir (*esp. joc.*); ~**haus** *das* original building; ~**hirn** *das* (*Anat.*) ⇒ **Hirnstamm**; ~**holz** *das* (*Forstw.*) round timber

**stämmig** /'ʃtɛmɪç/ *Adj.* burly; sturdy <arms, legs>

**Stamm-:** ~**kapital** *das* (*Wirtsch.*) authorized *or* registered capital; ~**kneipe** *die* (*ugs.*) favourite *or* usual pub (*Brit.*) *or* (*Amer.*) bar; ~**kunde** *der* regular customer; ~**land** *das; Pl. geh. auch* ~e ancestral homeland; (*fig.*) home territory; ~**lokal** *das* favourite *or* usual restaurant/pub (*Brit.*) *or* bar (*Amer.*)/café; **dieses Café ist sein ~lokal** this café is his favourite haunt; ~**mutter** *die; Pl.* ~**mütter** progenetrix; ~**personal** *das* permanent staff; ~**platz** *der* (*auch fig.*) regular place; (*Sitz*) regular *or* usual seat; (*für Wohnwagen, Zelt usw.*) regular site; ~**schloss**, *~**schloß** *das* ancestral castle; ~**silbe** *die* (*Sprachw.*) stem syllable; ~**sitz** *der* [A] (*eines Adelsgeschlechts*) family seat; [B] **der ~sitz der Firma ist [in] X** the firm's head office is in X; ~**tafel** *die* genealogical table; ~**tisch** *der* [A] (*Tisch*) regulars' table (*coll.*); [B] (*~tischrunde*) group of regulars (*coll.*); [C] (*Treffen*) get-together with the regulars (*coll.*); ~**tisch·politik** *die* (*abwertend*) bar-room politics *pl.*; ~**tisch·runde** *die* group of regulars (*coll.*)

***Stammutter** ⇒ **Stammmutter**

**Stamm-:** ~**vater** *der* progenitor; ~**vokal** *der* (*Sprachw.*) stem vowel; ~**wähler** *der*, ~**wählerin** *die* committed *or* loyal voter; ~**würze** *die* (*Brauerei*) original wort; (*Gehalt*) original gravity

**Stamperl** /'ʃtampɐl/ *das;* ~s, ~n (*südd., österr. ugs.*) [small] schnaps glas; **trinken wir ein ~:** let's have a snifter (*coll.*)

**stampfen** /'ʃtampfn̩/ ❶ *itr. V.* [A] (*laut auftreten*) stamp; **mit den Füßen/dem Fuß/den Hufen ~:** stamp one's feet/foot/its hoofs; [B] *mit sein* (*sich fortbewegen*) tramp; (*mit schweren Schritten*) trudge; [C] (*mit wuchtigen Stößen sich bewegen*) <machine, engine, etc.> pound; [D] (*Seemannsspr.*) <ship> pitch. ❷ *tr. V.* [A] **mit den Füßen den Rhythmus ~:** tap the rhythm with one's feet; **etw. aus dem Boden** *od.* **der Erde ~** (*fig.*) produce sth. out of thin air; [B] (*fest~*) compress; (*rammen*) drive <pile> (**in** + *Akk.* into); [C] (*zerkleinern*) mash <potatoes>; pulp <fruit>; crush <sugar>; pound <millet, flour>

**Stampfer** *der;* ~s, ~ [A] (*für Erde usw.*) tamper; (*Stößel*) pestle; [B] (*Küchengerät*) masher

**Stampf·kartoffeln** *Pl.* (*nordd.*) mashed potatoes

**stand** /ʃtant/ *1. u. 3. Pers. Sg. Prät. v.* **stehen**

**Stand** *der;* ~[e]s, **Stände** /'ʃtɛndə/ [A] (*das Stehen*) standing position; **keinen guten/sicheren ~ haben** not have a good/secure footing; **aus dem ~** (*Sport*) from a standing position; **ein Sprung/Start aus dem ~:** a standing jump/start; **[bei jmdm.** *od.* **gegen jmdn.] einen schweren/keinen leichten ~ haben** (*fig.*) have a tough/not have an easy time [of it] [with sb.]; **etw. aus dem ~ [heraus] beantworten** (*ugs.*) answer sth. off the top of one's head (*coll.*); **die neue Partei schaffte aus dem ~ [heraus] fast 7%** starting from scratch, the new party managed to get almost 7% [of the vote]; [B] (*~ort*) position; [C] (*Verkaufs~; Box für ein Pferd*) stall; (*Messe~, Informations~*) stand; (*Zeitungs~*) [newspaper] kiosk; (*Taxi~*) rank (*Brit.*); stand; [D] (*erreichte Stufe; Zustand*) state; **jmdn. in den ~ setzen, etw. zu tun** put sb. in a position *or* enable sb. to do sth.; **der heutige ~ der Technik** the state of technological development today; **etw. auf den neu[e]sten ~ [der Wissenschaft] bringen** bring sth. up to date *or* update sth. [in line with the latest scientific research]; **ich werde Sie über den ~ der Dinge informieren** I'll keep you informed about how things stand; **bei dem jetzigen ~ der Dinge** as things stand *or* are now; **außer ~, außer ~e** ⇒ **außerstand, außerstande**; **im ~e** ⇒ **imstande**; **in ~** ⇒ **instand**; **zu ~e** ⇒ **zustande**; [E] (*des Wassers, Flusses*) level; (*des Thermometers, Zählers, Barometers*) reading; (*der Kasse, Finanzen*) state; (*eines Himmelskörpers*) position; **den ~ des Thermometers ablesen** take the thermometer reading; [F] (*Familien~*) status; **in den [heiligen] ~ der Ehe treten** (*geh., auch scherzh.*) enter the state of [holy] matrimony; [G] (*Gesellschaftsschicht*) class; (*Berufs~*) trade; (*Ärzte, Rechtsanwälte*) [professional] group; **der geistliche ~:** the clergy; **Leute von ~:** persons of rank; **der dritte ~** (*hist.*) the third estate; **die Stände** (*hist.*) the estates; [H] (*schweiz.: Kanton*) canton

**Standard** /'ʃtandart/ *der;* ~s, ~s standard

**Standard-:** standard <equipment, example, letter, form, solution, model, work, language>

**standardisieren** *tr. V.* standardize

**Standardisierung** *die;* ~, ~en standardization

**Standard·situation** *die* (*Sport*) set piece

**Standarte** /ʃtan'dartə/ *die;* ~, ~n [A] (*Feldzeichen, Fahne*) standard; [B] (*ns.: Verband*) [SA/SS] unit; [C] ⇒ **Lunte** B

**Stand-:** ~**bein** *das* (*bes. Sport*) support leg; (*Fechten*) rear leg; (*Basketball*) pivot leg; (*Eislauf*) tracing leg; ~**bild** *das* statue

**Ständchen** /'ʃtɛntçən/ *das;* ~s, ~: serenade; **jmdm. ein ~ bringen** serenade sb.

**Stände·ordnung** *die* (*hist.*) system of estates

**Stander** /ˈʃtandɐ/ *der;* **~s, ~:** pennant

**Ständer** /ˈʃtɛndɐ/ *der;* **~s,** ~ Ⓐ (*Gestell, Vorrichtung*) stand; (*Kleider~*) coat stand; (*Wäsche~*) clothes horse; (*Kerzen~*) candle holder; (*Pfeifen~, Platten~, Geschirr~*) rack; Ⓑ (*Elektrot.*) stator; Ⓒ (*salopp: erigierter Penis*) hard-on (*sl.*)

**Stände·rat** *der* (*schweiz.*) Ⓐ (*Vertretung*) upper chamber; Ⓑ (*Mitglied*) member of the upper chamber

**Stände·rätin** *die* ⇒ **Ständerat** B

**Ständer·pilz** *der* basidiomycete

**standes-, Standes-: ~amt** *das* registry office; **~amtlich** ❶ *Adj.* registry office ‹wedding, document›; ❷ *adv.* **sich ~amtlich trauen lassen, ~amtlich heiraten** get married in a registry office; **~beamte** *der,* **~beamtin** *die* registrar; **~bewusst,** ***~bewußt** *Adj.* conscious of one's social standing *or* rank *postpos.;* **~bewusstsein,** ***~bewußtsein** *das* consciousness of one's social standing *or* rank; **~dünkel** *der* (*abwertend*) snobbery; **~gemäß** ❶ *Adj.* befitting sb.'s station or social standing *postpos.;* **~gemäß sein** befit sb.'s station *or* social standing; ❷ *adv.* as befits one's station *or* social standing; **~organisation** *die* professional association; **~person** *die* (*veralt.*) person of rank; **~schranke** *die; meist Pl.* class barrier

**Stände·staat** *der* (*hist.*) corporative state

**Standes·unterschied** *der* difference of rank; class difference

**Stände·wesen** *das* corporative system

**stand-, Stand-: ~fest** *Adj.* Ⓐ (*fest stehend*) steady; stable; strong ‹stalk, stem›; **nicht mehr ganz ~fest sein** (*ugs. scherzh.*) be a bit wonky (*Brit. coll.*) *or* shaky on one's feet; Ⓑ (*~haft*) steadfast; **~festigkeit** *die* Ⓐ stability; (*eines Gebäudes*) structural strength; Ⓑ (*~haftigkeit*) steadfastness; **~foto** *das* (*Film*) still; **~gas** *das* (*Kfz-W.*) idling speed; **~geld** *das* stall fee; **~gericht** *das* drumhead court martial; **~haft** ❶ *Adj.* steadfast; ❷ *adv.* steadfastly; **~haftigkeit** *die;* **~~:** steadfastness; **~|halten** *unr. itr. V.* stand firm; **einer Sache** (*Dat.*) **~halten** withstand *or* stand up to sth.; **der Kritik ~halten** stand [up to] criticism; **einer näheren Überprüfung nicht ~halten** not stand [up to] *or* bear closer scrutiny

**ständig** ❶ *Adj.* Ⓐ (*andauernd*) constant ‹noise, worry, pressure, etc.›; **mit jmdm. in ~er Feindschaft leben** live in a permanent state of enmity with sb.; Ⓑ (*fest*) permanent ‹residence, correspondent, staff, member, etc.›; standing ‹committee›; regular ‹income›. ❷ *adv.* constantly; **musst du sie ~ unterbrechen?** do you have to keep [on] interrupting her?; **sie kommt ~ zu spät/ist ~ krank** she's forever coming late/[being] ill; **Macht er das oft? — S~:** Does he do that often? — All the time

**ständisch** ❶ *Adj.* corporative; **eine ~e Gesellschaftsordnung** a social order based on privilege. ❷ *adv.* corporatively

**stand-, Stand-: ~licht** *das; Pl.* **~~er** (*Kfz-W.*) (*Beleuchtung*) sidelights *pl.;* (*Leuchte, Lampe*) sidelight; **mit ~licht fahren** drive on sidelights; **~ort** *der* Ⓐ position; (*einer Firma, Fabrik usw.*) location; site; **von seinem ~ort aus konnte er nichts sehen** he couldn't see anything from where he was standing; **jmds. politischer ~ort** (*fig.*) sb.'s political stance *or* position; Ⓑ (*Milit.: Garnison*) garrison; base; Ⓒ (*Wirtsch.*) industrial location; **der ~ort Deutschland** Germany as an industrial location *or* as a place for industrial investment; **~ort·kommandant** *der* (*Milit.*) garrison commander; **~ort·vorteil** *der* (*Wirtsch.*) **um des ~ortvorteils willen ins Ausland gehen** move abroad for the better location; **sich** (*Dat.*) **einen ~ortvorteil verschaffen** move to a better location; **~pauke** *die* (*ugs.*) dressing down; **jmdm. eine [gehörige] ~pauke halten** give sb. a [good] dressing down; **~punkt** *der* (*fig.*) point of view; viewpoint; **den ~punkt vertreten/auf dem ~punkt stehen/sich auf den ~punkt stellen, dass ...** take the view that ...; **das ist doch kein ~punkt!** (*ugs.*) that's no attitude to take!; **~quartier** *das* base; **~rechtlich** ❶ *Adj.* summary ‹execution, shooting›; ❷ *adv.* **jmdn. ~rechtlich erschießen** shoot sb. summarily; **~spur** *die* (*Verkehrsw.*) hard shoulder; **~uhr** *die* grandfather clock; **~vogel** *der* (*Zool.*) sedentary bird

**Stange** /ˈʃtaŋə/ *die;* **~, ~n** Ⓐ (*aus Holz*) pole; (*aus Metall*) bar; (*dünner*) rod; (*Kleider~*) rail; (*Vogel~*) perch; **Kleider/Anzüge von der ~** (*ugs.*) off-the-peg-dresses/suits; **von der ~ kaufen** (*ugs.*) buy off the peg clothes; **jmdm. die ~ halten** (*ugs.*) stick up for sb. (*coll.*); **jmdn. bei der ~ halten** (*ugs.*) keep sb. at it (*coll.*); **bei der ~ bleiben** (*ugs.*) keep at it (*coll.*) ; **eine ~ Zimt/Vanille/Lakritze** *usw.* a stick of cinnamon/vanilla/liquorice *etc.;* **eine ~ Zigaretten** *a carton containing ten packets of cigarettes;* **eine [schöne] ~ Geld** (*ugs.*) a small fortune (*coll.*); Ⓑ (*bes. md.: zylindrisches Glas*) [straight] glass; Ⓒ (*Jägerspr.: Teil des Geweihs*) beam

**Stängel** /ˈʃtɛŋl̩/ *der;* **~s, ~:** stem; stalk

**Stangen-: ~bohne** *die* runner bean; **~brot** *das* French bread; **ein französisches ~brot** a baguette; **~spargel** *der* asparagus spears *pl. or* stalks *pl.*

**stank** /ʃtaŋk/ *1. u. 3. Pers. Sg. Prät. v.* **stinken**

**Stänkerer** *der;* **~s, ~, Stänkerin** *die;* **~, ~nen** (*ugs. abwertend*) grouser (*coll.*); stirrer

**stänkern** /ˈʃtɛŋkɐn/ *itr. V.* (*ugs. abwertend*) stir (*coll.*); **gegen jmdn./etw. ~:** go on about sb./sth.

**Stanniol** /ʃtaˈni̯o:l/ *das;* **~s, ~e** tin foil; (*Silberpapier*) silver paper

**Stanniol·papier** *das* silver paper

**stante pede** /ˈstantə ˈpe:də/ *Adv.* (*ugs. scherzh.*) posthaste; lickety-split (*coll.*)

**Stanze**[1] /ˈʃtant͜sə/ *die;* **~, ~n** (*Verslehre*) ottava rima (*with eleven-syllable lines*)

**Stanze**[2] *die;* **~, ~n** press; (*Prägestempel*) die; (*zum Lochen*) punch

**stanzen** *tr. V.* press; (*prägen*) stamp; (*aus~*) punch ‹holes, numbers, punchcards, discs, etc.›

**Stapel** /ˈʃta:pl̩/ *der;* **~s,** ~ Ⓐ pile; **ein ~ Holz** a pile *or* stack of wood; Ⓑ (*Schiffbau*) stocks *pl.;* **vom ~ laufen** be launched; **vom ~ lassen** launch ‹ship›; (*ugs. abwertend: von sich geben*) trot out (*coll. derog.*) ‹sayings, jokes, slogans, etc.›

**Stapel·lauf** *der* launch[ing]

**stapeln** ❶ *tr. V.* (*schichten*) pile up; stack; (*fig.: ansammeln*) accumulate. ❷ *refl. V.* pile up; (*gestapelt sein*) be piled up

**stapel·weise** *Adv.* **~ Briefe** piles *or* stacks of letters; **ich habe sie ~:** I have piles of them

**Stapfe** /ˈʃtapfə/ *die;* **~, ~n, Stapfen** *der;* **~s,** ~ footprint

**stapfen** *itr. V.; mit sein* tramp; **in jede Pfütze ~:** stamp in every puddle

**Stapler** /ˈʃta:plɐ/ *der;* **~s, ~:** ⇒ **Gabelstapler**

**Star**[1] /ʃta:ɐ̯/ *der;* **~[e]s, ~e** *od.* (*schweiz.*) **~en** (*Vogel*) starling

**Star**[2] *der;* **~s, ~s** (*berühmte Persönlichkeit*) star

**Star**[3] *der;* **~[e]s, ~e ▶ 474| der graue ~:** cataract; **der grüne ~:** glaucoma; **er ist am ~ operiert worden** he has been operated on for cataract/glaucoma

**Star-:** star ‹conductor, guest singer, etc.›; top ‹lawyer, model, agent›

**Star·allüren** *Pl.* prima donna behaviour *sing.;* **~ zeigen/haben** put on the airs of a star

**starb** /ʃtarp/ *1. u. 3. Pers. Sg. Prät. v.* **sterben**

**Star·besetzung** *die* all-star cast

**Staren·kasten** *der* starlings' nest box

**stark** /ʃtark/; **stärker** /ˈʃtɛrkɐ/, **stärkst...** /ˈʃtɛrkst.../ ❶ *Adj.* Ⓐ strong ‹man, current, structure, team, drink, verb, pressure, wind, etc.›; potent ‹drink, medicine, etc.›; powerful ‹engine, lens, voice, etc.›; (*ausgezeichnet*) excellent ‹runner, player, performance›; **den ~en Mann markieren** *od.* **mimen** (*ugs.*) put on a strongman act (*coll.*); **sein stärkstes Werk/Theaterstück** his best work/play; **jetzt heißt es ~ bleiben** we must not yield now; **sich für jmdn./etw. ~ machen** (*ugs.*) throw one's weight behind sb./sth.; ⇒ *auch* **Seite** D; **Stück** C; **Tobak;** Ⓑ (*dick*) thick; stout ‹rope, string›; (*verhüll.: korpulent*) well-built (*euphem.*); **Kleidung für stärkere Damen** clothes for the fuller figure; **eine 20 cm ~e Wand** a wall 20 cm thick; Ⓒ (*zahlenmäßig groß, umfangreich*) sizeable, large ‹army, police, presence, entourage›; big ‹demand›; **wir hoffen auf ~e Beteiligung** we hope a large number of people will take part; **eine 100 Mann ~e Truppe** a 100-strong unit; **das Kontingent ist 1 400 Mann ~:** the contingent is 1,400 strong; Ⓓ (*heftig, intensiv*) heavy ‹rain, snow, traffic, smoke, heat, cold, drinker, smoker, demand, pressure›; severe ‹heat, cold, frost, pain›; strong ‹impression, influence, current, resistance, sign, dislike›; grave ‹doubt, reservations›; great ‹heat, hunger, thirst, exaggeration, interest›; hearty ‹eater, appetite›; loud ‹applause›; **~es Fieber** high temperature; **unter ~er Anteilnahme der Bevölkerung** with large numbers of the population attending; **~er Widerhall** (*fig.*) a considerable response; **das ist [wirklich] ~** (*ugs.*) that [really] is a bit much! (*coll.*); Ⓔ (*Jugendspr.: großartig*) great (*coll.*); fantastic (*coll.*).
❷ *adv.* Ⓐ (*sehr, überaus, intensiv*) (*mit Adj.*) very; heavily ‹indebted, stressed›; greatly ‹increased, reduced, enlarged›; strongly ‹emphasized, characterized›; badly ‹damaged, worn, affected›; thickly, densely ‹populated›; (*mit Verb*) ‹rain, snow, drink, smoke, bleed› heavily; ‹exaggerate, impress› greatly; ‹enlarge, reduce, increase› considerably; ‹support, oppose, suspect› strongly; ‹remind› very much; **~ wirkend** with a powerful effect *postpos.;* **es erinnert ~ an ...** it is very reminiscent of ...; **~ riechen/duften** have a strong smell/scent; **~ gewürzt** strongly seasoned; **es ist ~/zu ~ gesalzen** it is very/too salty; **~ erkältet sein** have a heavy *or* bad cold; **er geht ~ auf die Sechzig zu** (*ugs.*) he's pushing sixty (*coll.*); Ⓑ (*Jugendspr.: großartig*) fantastically (*coll.*); Ⓒ (*Sprachw.*) **~ flektieren** *od.* **flektiert werden** be a strong noun/verb

**Stark·bier** *das* strong beer

**Stärke** /ˈʃtɛrkə/ *die;* **~, ~n** Ⓐ strength; (*eines Motors*) power; (*einer Glühbirne*) wattage; **eine Politik der ~:** power politics *sing.;* Ⓑ (*Dicke*) thickness; (*Technik*) gauge; Ⓒ (*zahlenmäßige Größe*) strength; size; **eine Truppe von 300 Mann ~:** a 300-strong unit; Ⓓ (*besondere Fähigkeit, Vorteil*) strength; **jmds. ~/nicht jmds. ~ sein** be sb.'s forte/not be sb.'s strong point; Ⓔ (*von Wind, Strömung, Eindruck, Einfluss, Nachfrage, Empfindung, Widerstand usw.*) strength; (*von Hitze, Kälte, Licht, Druck, Regenfall, Sturm, Schmerzen, Abneigung*) intensity; (*von Frost*) severity; (*von Lärm, Verkehr*) volume; (*von Appetit*) heartiness; Ⓕ (*organischer Stoff*) starch

**stärke·haltig** *Adj.* starchy

**Stärke·mehl** *das* cornflour (*Brit.*); cornstarch (*Amer.*)

**stärken** ❶ *tr. V.* Ⓐ (*kräftigen, festigen; auch fig.*) strengthen; boost ‹power, prestige›; ‹drink, food, etc.› fortify ‹person›; **die** *od.* **jmds. Gesundheit ~:** fortify *or* strengthen sb.'s constitution; **jmds. Selbstbewusstsein ~** (*fig.*) give sb.'s self-confidence a boost; **jmdn. in seinem Glauben ~:** reinforce sb.'s faith; ⇒ *auch* **Rücken** A; Ⓑ (*steif machen*) starch ‹washing etc.›. ❷ *refl. V.* (*sich erfrischen*) fortify *or* refresh oneself; **nun stärkt euch erst mal** have something to give you strength. ❸ *itr. V.* **ein ~des Mittel** a tonic

**stärker** ⇒ **stark**

**Stärke·zucker** *der* glucose

**stärkst...** ⇒ **stark**

**Stark-: ~strom** *der* (*Elektrot.*) heavy current; (*mit hoher Spannung*) high-voltage current; **~strom·leitung** *die* (*Elektrot.*) power line; **~ton** *der; Pl.* **~töne** (*Sprachw.*) stress

*old spelling (see note on page 1707)

S

**Star·kult** *der* (*abwertend*) star worship (**um** of)

**Stärkung** *die;* ~, ~**en** Ⓐ strengthening; **zur ~ trank er erst mal einen Whisky** he drank a whisky to fortify himself; **die ~ des Parlaments** the increase in the power *or* influence vested in parliament; Ⓑ (*Erfrischung*) refreshment

**Stärkungs·mittel** *das* tonic

**Starlet[t]** /'ʃta:lɛt/ *das;* ~**s**, ~**s** (*spött. abwertend*) starlet

**starr** /ʃtar/ ❶ *Adj.* Ⓐ rigid; (*steif*) stiff (**vor** + *Dat.* with); fixed ‹expression, smile, stare›; **~ vor Schreck** paralysed with terror; Ⓑ (*nicht abwandelbar*) inflexible, rigid ‹law, rule, principle›; Ⓒ (*unnachgiebig*) inflexible, obdurate ‹person, attitude, etc.›. ❷ *adv.* Ⓐ rigidly; (*steif*) stiffly; **jmdn. ~ ansehen/~ geradeaus schauen** look at sb./look straight in front of one with a fixed stare; Ⓑ (*unnachgiebig*) **~ bleibt er bei seiner Meinung** he sticks obdurately to his opinion

**Starre** *die;* ~ ⇒ **Starrheit**

**starren** *itr. V.* Ⓐ (*starr blicken*) stare (**in** + *Akk.* into, **auf, an, gegen** + *Akk.* at); **jmdm. ins Gesicht ~:** stare sb. in the face; Ⓑ (*ganz bedeckt sein mit*) **vor/von Schmutz** *od.* **Dreck ~:** be filthy; be covered in filth; **vor Perlen und Diamanten/Gold und Geschmeiden ~:** be covered in *or* laden with pearls and diamonds/gold and precious stones; **vor Waffen ~:** be bristling with weapons

**Starrheit** *die;* ~ ⇒ **starr** 1: Ⓐ rigidity; stiffness; fixity; Ⓑ inflexibility; rigidity; Ⓒ inflexibility; obduracy

**starr-, Starr-:** **~kopf** *der* (*abwertend*) pigheaded person; **ein ~kopf sein** be pigheaded; **~köpfig** *Adj.* (*abwertend*) pigheaded; **~krampf** *der* ⇒ **Wundstarrkrampf**; **~sinn** *der* pigheadedness; **~sinnig** *Adj.* (*abwertend*) pigheaded

**Start** /ʃtart/ *der;* ~**[e]s**, ~**s** Ⓐ (*Sport; auch fig.*) start; **einen guten/schlechten/langsamen ~ haben** get off to *or* make a good/bad/slow start; **den ~ freigeben** give clearance to start; **das Zeichen zum ~ geben** give the starting signal; Ⓑ (*Sport: ~platz*) start; **an den ~ gehen/am ~ sein** (*fig.: teilnehmen*) start; Ⓒ (*Sport: Teilnahme*) participation; **sein ~ ist infrage gestellt** it is uncertain whether he will start; Ⓓ (*eines Flugzeugs*) take-off; (*einer Rakete*) launch; **den ~ der Maschine freigeben** give the aircraft clearance for take-off; **zum** *od.* **an den ~ rollen** taxi to the runway for take-off

**start-, Start-:** **~automatik** *die* (*Kfz-W.*) automatic choke; **~bahn** *die* [take-off] runway; **~bereit** *Adj.* ready to start *postpos.;* ‹aircraft› ready for take-off; (*zum Aufbruch bereit*) ready to set off *postpos.;* **~block** *der; Pl.* **~blöcke** (*Leichtathletik, Schwimmen*) starting block

**starten** ❶ *itr. V.; mit sein* Ⓐ start; ‹aircraft› take off; ‹rocket› blast off, be launched; **zu früh ~** (*Sport*) jump the start; **gut/schnell ~** (*Sport*) make a good/quick start; get away well/quickly; Ⓑ (*an einem Wettkampf teilnehmen*) compete; (*bei einem Rennen*) start (**bei, in** + *Dat.* in); Ⓒ (*den Motor anlassen*) start the engine; Ⓓ (*aufbrechen*) set off; set out; **in den Urlaub ~:** set off on holiday; Ⓔ (*beginnen*) start; begin. ❷ *tr. V.* start ‹race, campaign, tour, production, etc.›; launch ‹missile, rocket, satellite, attack›; start [up] ‹engine, machine, car›

**Starter** *der;* ~**s**, ~ (*Sport, Kfz-W.*) starter

**Starterin** *die;* ~, ~**nen** (*Sport*) starter

**Starter·klappe** *die* (*Kfz-W.*) choke flap

**start-, Start-:** **~erlaubnis** *die* Ⓐ (*Sport*) authorization to compete; Ⓑ (*Flugw.*) clearance [for take-off]; **~geld** *das* (*Sport*) Ⓐ (*vom Teilnehmer bezahlt*) entry fee; Ⓑ (*vom Veranstalter bezahlt*) starting money; **~hilfe** *die* Ⓐ (*Unterstützung*) financial help, backing (*to get a project off the ground*); **jmdm. [finanzielle] ~hilfe geben** help sb. [financially] to get started; Ⓑ **ich brauche ~hilfe** I need help to get my car started; **~hilfe·kabel** *das* jump leads *pl.;* **~kapital** *das* starting capital; **~klar** *Adj.* ready to start *postpos.;* ‹aircraft› clear *or* ready for take-off; **~kommando** *das* (*Sport*) starter's order[s]; **~linie** *die* (*Sport*) starting line; **~loch** *das* (*Leichtathletik*) **in die ~löcher gehen** get on one's marks; **in den ~löchern kauern/hocken** (*fig.*) be waiting in the wings; **~nummer** *die* (*Sport*) [start] number; **~platz** *der* (*Sport*) starting position; **~rampe** *die* (*Raumflug; auch fig.*) launching pad; **~schuss**, ***~schuß** *der* (*Sport*) **der ~schuss fiel** the starter's gun went off; **den ~schuss zum 100-m-Lauf geben** fire the gun for the start of the 100 metres; **vor dem ~schuss loslaufen** jump the gun; **den ~schuss zu** *od.* **für etw. geben** (*fig.*) give sth. the go-ahead *or* the green light

**Stasi**[1] /'ʃta:zi/*die;* ~ *od. der;* ~**s** *Abk.* (*DDR ugs.*) **Staatssicherheit[sdienst]**

**Stasi**[2] *der;* ~**s**, ~**s** (*DDR ugs.*) state security man

**Statement** /'steɪtmənt/ *das;* ~**s**, ~**s** statement

**Statik** /'ʃta:tɪk/ *die;* ~ Ⓐ (*Physik*) statics *sing., no art.;* Ⓑ (*Bauw.*) static equilibrium; Ⓒ (*geh.: statischer Zustand*) stasis

**Statiker** *der;* ~**s**, ~, **Statikerin** *die* structural engineer [concerned with statics]

**Station** /ʃta'tsi̯o:n/ *die;* ~, ~**en** Ⓐ (*Haltestelle*) stop; Ⓑ (*Bahnhof, Sender, Forschungs~, Raum~*) station; Ⓒ (*Zwischen~, Aufenthalt*) stopover; **die ~en seiner Reise waren ...** the places where he stopped [off] on his journey were ...; **~ machen** stop over *or* off; make a stopover; Ⓓ (*Kranken~*) ward; **auf ~ sein** ‹doctor› be on ward duty; Ⓔ (*einer Entwicklung, Karriere usw.*) stage

**stationär** /ʃtatsi̯o'nɛ:ɐ̯/ ❶ *Adj.* Ⓐ (*Med.*) ‹admission, examination, treatment› in hospital, as an inpatient; **ein ~er Patient** an inpatient; Ⓑ (*ortsfest*) permanently stationed ‹troops, units›; Ⓒ (*Raumf.*) fixed ‹orbit›; **ein ~er Satellit** a satellite in a fixed orbit. ❷ *adv.* Ⓐ (*Med.*) in hospital; **jmdn. ~ behandeln/aufnehmen** treat/admit sb. as an inpatient; Ⓑ (*ortsfest*) in one place

**stationieren** *tr. V.* station ‹troops›; deploy ‹weapons, bombers, etc.›

**Stationierung** *die;* ~, ~**en** stationing; (*von Waffen, Raketen usw.*) deployment

**Stations-:** **~arzt** *der,* **~ärztin** *die* ward doctor; **~schwester** *die* ward sister; **~taste** *die* (*Rundf.*) preset [tuning] button; preset; **~vorsteher** *der,* **~vorsteherin** *die* (*Eisenb.*) station master

**statisch** /'ʃta:tɪʃ/ ❶ *Adj.* static; ‹laws› of statics; **~er Auftrieb** (*Physik*) static lift; **~e Berechnungen** (*Bauw.*) calculations relating to static equilibrium. ❷ *adv.* (*Bauw.*) with regard to static equilibrium

**Statist** /ʃta'tɪst/ *der;* ~**en**, ~**en** (*Theater, Film*) extra; (*fig.*) bystander; supernumerary; **zum ~en degradiert werden** (*fig.*) be demoted to the role of a mere accessory

**Statisten·rolle** *die* (*Theater, Film*) walk-on part

**Statistik** /ʃta'tɪstɪk/ *die;* ~, ~**en** Ⓐ (*Wissenschaft*) statistics *sing., no art.;* Ⓑ (*Zusammenstellung*) statistics *pl.;* **eine ~:** a set of statistics; **eine ~ über etw.** (*Akk.*) **erstellen** make a statistical study of sth.

**Statistiker** *der;* ~**s**, ~, **Statistikerin** *die;* ~, ~**nen** ▶ 159 statistician

**Statistin** *die;* ~, ~**nen** ⇒ **Statist**

**statistisch** ❶ *Adj.* statistical; **~es Amt/~e Behörde** office of statistics. ❷ *adv.* statistically

**Stativ** /ʃta'ti:f/ *das;* ~**s**, ~**e** tripod

**statt** /ʃtat/ ❶ *Konj.* ⇒ **anstatt** 1. ❷ *Präp. mit Gen.* instead of; **~ dessen** instead of this; (*relativisch*) instead of which

**Statt** *die;* ~, **Stätten** (*veralt., geh.*) abode (*arch.*); **an jmds./einer Sache ~:** in sb.'s place/in place of sth.; instead of sb./sth.; ⇒ *auch* **Eid**; **Kind** A

**statt·dessen** *Adv.* instead; ⇒ *auch* **statt** 2

**Stätte** /'ʃtɛtə/ *die;* ~, ~**n** (*geh.*) place; **eine heilige/historische ~:** a holy/historic site; **die ~ des Sieges/der Niederlage** the scene of the victory/defeat

**statt-, Statt-:** **~|finden** *unr. itr. V.* take place; ‹process, development› occur; **~|geben** *unr. itr. V.* (*Amtsspr.*) **einer Sache** (*Dat.*) **~geben** accede to sth.; **einer Klage ~geben** uphold a complaint; **~|haben** *unr. itr. V.* (*veralt.*) ⇒ **~finden**; **~haft** *Adj.* permissible; **~halter** *der* (*hist.*) governor; **~halterschaft** *die;* ~~, ~~**en** (*hist.*) governorship

**stattlich** ❶ *Adj.* Ⓐ well-built; strapping ‹lad›; (*beeindruckend*) imposing ‹figure, stature, building, etc.›; fine ‹farm, estate›; impressive ‹trousseau, collection›; **ein ~er Mann/eine ~e Frau** a fine figure of a man/woman; Ⓑ (*beträchtlich*) considerable; sizeable ‹part›; considerable, appreciable ‹sum, number›; **~e 8 000 Mark** an impressive 8,000 marks; all of 8,000 marks (*coll.*). ❷ *adv.* impressively; splendidly

**Stattlichkeit** *die;* ~**:** imposing nature; (*von Statur*) fine build *or* figure; **seine ~/die ~ seiner Erscheinung** his fine build *or* imposing stature

**Statue** /'ʃta:tu̯ə/ *die;* ~, ~**n** statue

**statuenhaft** ❶ *Adj.* statuesque. ❷ *adv.* like a statue; statuesquely

**Statuette** /ʃta'tu̯ɛtə/ *die;* ~, ~**n** statuette

**statuieren** *tr. V.* (*geh.*) establish ‹principle, purpose›; lay down ‹right, principle›; ⇒ *auch* **Exempel**

**Statur** /ʃta'tu:ɐ̯/ *die;* ~, ~**en** build; **kräftig von ~** *od.* **von kräftiger ~ sein** have a powerful build; **seine große/kleine/imponierende ~:** his tall/small/imposing stature

**Status** /'ʃta:tʊs/ *der;* ~, ~ /'ʃta:tu:s/ Ⓐ (*geh.: Stand, Zustand*) state; Ⓑ ([*rechtliche*] *Stellung*) status

**Status quo** /'sta:tʊs kvo:/ *der;* ~ (*geh.*) status quo

**Status·symbol** *das* status symbol

**Statut** /ʃta'tu:t/ *das;* ~**[e]s**, ~**en** statute

**Stau** *der;* ~**[e]s**, ~**s** *od.* ~**e** Ⓐ (*von Wasser, Blut usw.*) build-up; Ⓑ (*von Fahrzeugen*) tailback (*Brit.*); backup (*Amer.*); **3 km ~:** a tailback (*Brit.*) *or* backup (*Amer.*) *or* jam stretching for three kilometres; **im ~ stehen** sit *or* be stuck in a jam

**Staub** /ʃtau:p/ *der;* ~**[e]s** dust; **[im ganzen Haus] ~ wischen** dust [the whole house]; **[im Wohnzimmer] ~ saugen** vacuum *or* (*Brit. coll.*) hoover [the sitting room]; **[viel] ~ aufwirbeln** (*fig. ugs.*) stir things up [quite a bit] (*coll.*); cause [a lot of] aggro (*Brit. sl.*); **sich aus dem ~[e] machen** (*fig. ugs.*) make oneself scarce (*coll.*)

**Staub-:** **~beutel** *der* Ⓐ (*Bot.*) anther; Ⓑ (*eines ~saugers*) dust bag; **~blatt** *das* (*Bot.*) stamen

**Stäubchen** /'ʃtɔʏpçən/ *das;* ~**s**, ~**:** speck of dust

**Stau·becken** *das* reservoir

**stauben** *itr. V.* cause dust; ‹person› cause *or* raise dust; **es staubt sehr/mehr** there is a lot of dust/more dust; **er galoppierte davon, dass es nur so staubte** he galloped off raising clouds of dust

**stäuben** /'ʃtɔʏbn̩/ ❶ *tr. V.* **etw. auf/über etw.** (*Akk.*) **~:** sprinkle sth. on/over sth.; **dem Baby Puder auf die Haut ~:** dust the baby's skin with powder. ❷ *itr. V.* Ⓐ (*zerstieben*) scatter; ‹water› form spray, spray out; ‹sparks› fly; Ⓑ ⇒ **stauben**

**Staub-:** **~faden** *der* (*Bot.*) filament; **~fänger** *der* (*abwertend*) dust trap; **ein ~fänger sein** catch the dust; **~gefäß** *das* (*Bot.*) stamen

**staubig** *Adj.* dusty

**staub-, Staub-:** **~korn** *das* speck *or* particle of dust; **~lappen** *der* duster; **~lunge** *die:* ▶ 474 **eine ~lunge haben** have pneumoconiosis (*Med.*); **~saugen** ❶ *tr. V.* vacuum, (*Brit. coll.*) hoover ‹room, carpet, etc.›; ❷ *itr. V.* hoover (*Brit. coll.*); **~sauger** *der* vacuum cleaner; Hoover (*Brit.* ®); **~tuch** *das; Pl.* **~tücher** duster; **~wedel** *der* feather duster; **~wolke** *die* cloud of dust; **~zucker** *der* (*veralt., südd., österr.*) ⇒ **Puderzucker**

S

**stauchen** /ˈʃtau:xn̩/ *tr. V.* Ⓐ compress; (*Technik*) upset ‹metal›; Ⓑ (*stoßen*) thrust; jab ‹stick, arms, etc.›

**Stau·damm** *der* dam

**Staude** /ˈʃtau:də/ *die;* ~, ~**n** Ⓐ (*Bot.*) herbaceous perennial; Ⓑ (*bes. südd.: Strauch*) bush

**Stauden·gewächs** *das* (*Bot.*) herbaceous perennial

**stauen** /ˈʃtau:ən/ ❶ *tr. V.* Ⓐ dam [up] ‹stream, river›; staunch *or* stem flow of ‹blood›; Ⓑ (*Seemannsspr.: verladen*) stow. ❷ *refl. V.* ‹water, blood, etc.› accumulate, build up; ‹people› form a crowd; ‹traffic› form a tailback/tailbacks (*Brit.*) *or* (*Amer.*) backup/backups; (*fig.*) ‹anger› build up

**Stauer** *der;* ~**s**, ~, **Stauerin** *die* stevedore

**Staufer** /ˈʃtau:fɐ/ *der;* ~**s**, ~, **Stauferin** *die;* ~, ~**nen** (*hist.*) Hohenstaufen; **die Staufer** the Hohenstaufen dynasty *sing.*

**Stau·mauer** *die* dam [wall]

**staunen** /ˈʃtau:nən/ *itr. V.* be amazed *or* astonished (**über** + *Akk.* at); (*beeindruckt sein*) marvel (**über** + *Akk.* at); **er staunte nicht schlecht, als er das hörte/sah** (*ugs.*) he was flabbergasted when he heard it/saw it; **da staunst du, was?** (*ugs.*) quite a shock, isn't it?; shattered, eh? (*coll.*); **da kann man nur [noch]** ~**:** one can only marvel *or* wonder at it; ~**d** with *or* in amazement; **sie betrachtete ihn mit** ~**den Augen** she gazed at him wide-eyed with amazement; ⇒ *auch* **Bauklotz; hören** 2 C

**Staunen** *das;* ~**s** amazement, astonishment (**über** + *Akk.* at); (*staunende Bewunderung*) wonderment; **jmdn. in** ~ **[ver]setzen** astonish *or* amaze sb.; **er kam aus dem** ~ **nicht mehr heraus** he couldn't get over it

**Staupe** /ˈʃtau:pə/ *die;* ~, ~**n** distemper *no art.*

**Stau-:** ~**see** *der* reservoir; ~**stufe** *die* barrage

**Stauung** *die;* ~, ~**en** Ⓐ (*eines Bachs, Flusses*) damming; (*des Blutes, Wassers*) stemming the flow; (*das Sichstauen*) build-up; Ⓑ (*Verkehrsstau*) tailback (*Brit.*); backup (*Amer.*); jam

**Stau·werk** *das* barrage

**Std.** *Abk.* **Stunde** hr.

**Steak** /ste:k/ *das;* ~**s**, ~**s** steak

**Stearin** /ʃtea'ri:n/ *das;* ~**s**, ~**e** stearin

**Stech·apfel** *der* (*Bot.*) thorn apple; **[Gemeiner]** ~**:** jimson weed

**stechen** /ˈʃtɛçn̩/ ❶ *unr. itr. V.* Ⓐ ‹thorn, thistle, spine, needle› prick; ‹wasp, bee› sting; ‹mosquito› bite; ‹fig.: sun› be scorching; **das Insekt hat ihm ins Bein gestochen** the insect bit him in the leg; **sich** (*Dat.*) **in den Finger** ~**:** prick one's finger; Ⓑ (*hinein~*) **mit etw. in etw.** (*Akk.*) ~**:** stick *or* jab sth. into sth.; **jmdm. mit einer Nadel in den Hintern** ~**:** jab a needle into sb.'s behind; **nach jmdm.** ~**:** stab at sb.; try to stab sb.; Ⓒ (*die Stechuhr betätigen*) (*bei Arbeitsbeginn*) clock on; (*bei Arbeitsende*) clock off; Ⓓ (*Kartenspiel*) ‹suit› be trumps; Ⓔ (*Sport*) jump-off; Ⓕ ⇒ **See²** A.
❷ *unr. tr. V.* Ⓐ (*mit dem Messer, Schwert*) stab; (*mit der Nadel, mit einem Dorn usw.*) prick; ‹bee, wasp› sting; ‹mosquito› bite; (*Fischereiw.: fangen*) spear ‹eel, pike›; (*ab~*) stick ‹pig, calf›; **sich an etw.** (*Dat.*) ~**:** prick oneself on sth.; **sich in den Finger** ~**:** prick one's finger; Ⓑ (*hervorbringen*) make ‹hole, pattern›; **jmdm. Löcher in die Ohren** ~**:** pierce sb.'s ears; Ⓒ (*unpers.*) **es sticht mich in der Seite** I've got a stabbing pain in my side; Ⓓ (*herauslösen*) cut ‹peat, turf, asparagus, etc.›; pick ‹lettuce, mushrooms›; Ⓔ (*gravieren*) engrave ‹design etc.›; Ⓕ (*Kartenspiel*) take ‹card›

**Stechen** *das;* ~**s**, ~ (*Sport*) jump-off

**stechend** *Adj.* penetrating, pungent ‹smell›; penetrating ‹glance, eyes›

**Stech-:** ~**fliege** *die* stomoxyine fly; (*Wadenstecher*) stable fly; ~**ginster** *der* (*Bot.*) gorse; ~**kahn** *der* punt; ~**karte** *die* clocking-on card; ~**mücke** *die* mosquito; gnat; ~**palme** *die* holly; ~**schritt** *der* (*Milit.*) goose step; **im** ~**schritt marschieren** goose-step; ~**uhr** *die* time clock; ~**zirkel** *der* dividers *pl.*

**steck-, Steck-:** ~**brief** *der* description [of a/the wanted person]; (*Plakat*) 'wanted' poster; (*fig.: eines Menschen*) personal details *pl.*; (*fig.: eines Geräts*) [brief] specification; ~**brieflich** *Adv.* **der** ~**brieflich Gesuchte** the wanted man; **der Mörder wird** ~**brieflich gesucht** descriptions/'wanted' posters of the murderer have been circulated; ~**dose** *die* socket; power point

**stecken** /ˈʃtɛkn̩/ ❶ *tr. V.* Ⓐ put; **etw. in die Tasche** ~**:** put *or* (*coll.*) stick sth. in one's pocket; **steck dein Hemd in die Hose** tuck your shirt in[to your trousers]; **ein Kind ins Bett** ~**:** put a child to bed; **sein ganzes Vermögen in etw.** (*Akk.*) ~**:** put *or* invest all one's money in sth.; **sich hinter etw.** ~ (*ugs.*) set to work on sth. with a will; Ⓑ (*mit Nadeln*) pin ‹hem, lining, etc.›; pin [on] ‹badge›; pin up ‹hair›; Ⓒ (*pflanzen*) put in, plant ‹potatoes, onions, beans›; Ⓓ (*ugs.: mitteilen*) **etw. der Polizei** *usw.* ~**:** tip the police *etc.* off about sth.; **es jmdm.** ~ (*ugs.*) give sb. a piece of one's mind (*coll.*).
❷ *regelm.* (*geh. auch unr.*) *itr. V.* be; **der Schlüssel steckt [im Schloss]** the key is in the lock; **voller Ideen** ~**:** be full of ideas; **wo hast du denn so lange gesteckt?** (*ugs.*) where did you get to *or* have you been all this time?; **wo steckt meine Brille?** (*ugs.*) where have my glasses got to *or* gone?; **er steckt in Schwierigkeiten** (*ugs.*) he's having problems; **in den Anfängen** ~**:** be in the early stages; **ein Abzeichen steckte an seinem Revers** a badge was pinned to his lapel; **hinter etw.** (*Dat.*) ~ (*fig. ugs.*) be behind sth.; ~ **bleiben** get stuck; (*fig.*) ‹negotiations etc.› get bogged down; **die Kugel ist in der Lunge** ~ **geblieben** the bullet lodged in the lung; **es blieb in den Anfängen** ~ (*fig.*) it never got beyond the early stages; **das Wort blieb ihm vor Angst im Halse** *od.* **in der Kehle** ~**:** he was speechless with fear; **den Schlüssel [im Schloss]** ~ **lassen** leave the key in the lock; **lassen Sie** ~**!** (*ugs.: lassen Sie mich bezahlen*) put your money away!

**Stecken** *der;* ~**s**, ~ (*bes. südd.*) stick

**Stecken·pferd** *das* Ⓐ (*Spielzeug*) hobby horse; Ⓑ (*Liebhaberei*) hobby; **sein** ~ **reiten** go on about one's hobby horse; (*sich seinem Hobby widmen*) pursue one's [favourite] hobby

**Stecker** *der;* ~**s**, ~**:** plug

**Steck·kissen** *das* papoose carrier; carry-nest

**Steckling** /ˈʃtɛklɪŋ/ *der;* ~**s**, ~**e** cutting

**Steck-:** ~**nadel** *die* pin; **es ist so still, man könnte eine** ~**nadel fallen hören** it's so quiet you could hear a pin drop; **jmdn./etw. suchen wie eine** ~**nadel** (*ugs.*) search high and low for sb./sth.; **eine** ~**nadel im Heuhaufen suchen** (*ugs.*) look for a needle in a haystack; ~**nadel·kopf** *der* pinhead; ~**rübe** *die* (*bes. nordd.*) swede; ~**schloss**, *~**schloß** *das* safety lock (*inserted in main lock*); ~**schlüssel** *der* socket spanner; ~**schuss**, *~**schuß** *der: internal gunshot wound with bullet;* **er hat einen** ~**schuss in der Lunge** he has a bullet/pellet lodged in his lung; ~**tuch** *das;* ~**tücher** dress handkerchief

**Steg** /ʃte:k/ *der;* ~**[e]s**, ~**e** Ⓐ (*schmale Brücke*) [narrow] bridge; (*Fußgänger~*) footbridge; (*Laufbrett*) gangplank; (*Boots~*) landing stage; Ⓑ (*veralt.: Pfad*) path; Ⓒ (*bei Saiteninstrumenten, Brillen*) bridge

**Steg·reif** *der:* **aus dem** ~**:** impromptu; **er hielt aus dem** ~ **eine kleine Rede** he gave a short speech extempore *or* off the cuff; **etw. aus dem** ~ **beantworten** answer sth. off the top of one's head (*coll.*); **aus dem** ~ **spielen** improvise; ad lib

**Stegreif·rede** *die* impromptu *or* extempore speech

**Steh-:** ~**auf·männchen** *das* tumbling figure; tumbler; **er/sie ist ein [richtiges]** ~**aufmännchen** (*fig. ugs.*) nothing gets him/her down; ~**bier·halle** *die* stand-up beer hall; ~**empfang** *der* stand-up reception

**stehen** /ˈʃte:ən/ ❶ *unr. itr. V.; südd., österr., schweiz. mit sein* Ⓐ stand; **den ganzen Tag am Herd** ~**:** stand over the cooker all day; **er arbeitet** ~**d** *od.* **im Stehen** he works standing up; **jmdn.** ~ **lassen** walk off and leave sb. standing there; **sie steht zwischen ihnen** (*fig.*) she comes between them; **mit jmdm./etw.** ~ **und fallen** (*fig.*) stand or fall with sb./sth.; **das Haus steht noch/ist stehen geblieben** the house is still standing/was left standing; **er steht ihm** (*salopp*) he's got a hard-on (*sl.*); Ⓑ (*sich befinden*) be; ‹upright object, building› stand; ~ **bleiben** (*unverändert gelassen werden*) stay; be left; (*zurückgelassen werden*) be left behind; **etw.** ~ **lassen** leave sth.; (*vergessen*) leave sth. [behind]; **du kannst es nicht so** ~ **lassen** you can't leave it as it is; **lass die Vase** ~**!** leave the vase where it is; **den Teig eine Stunde** ~ **lassen** leave the dough to stand for an hour; **alles** ~ **und liegen lassen** drop everything; **sich** (*Dat.*) **einen Bart** ~ **lassen** grow a beard; **das Verb steht am Satzende** the verb comes at the end of the sentence; **wo steht dein Auto?** where is your car [parked]?; **sie haben dort einen Schrank** ~**:** they have a cupboard *or* (*Amer.*) closet [standing] there; **Schweißperlen standen auf seiner Stirn** beads of sweat stood out on his brow; **ich tue alles, was in meinen Kräften** *od.* **meiner Macht steht** I'll do everything in my power; **im Rentenalter** ~**:** be of pensionable age; **vor einer Entscheidung/dem Bankrott** ~**:** be faced with a decision/with bankruptcy; Ⓒ (*einen bestimmten Stand haben*) **auf etw.** (*Dat.*) ~ ‹needle, hand› point to sth.; **das Barometer steht hoch/tief/auf Regen** the barometer is reading high/low/indicating rain; **die Uhr steht auf 12** the clock shows 12; **die Ampel steht auf Rot** the traffic lights are [on] red; **es steht mir bis zum Hals[e]** *od.* **bis oben** *od.* **bis hier[hin]** I'm fed up to the back teeth with it (*coll.*); I'm sick to death of it (*coll.*); **der Wind steht günstig/nach Norden** (*Seemannsspr.*) the wind stands fair/is from the north; **das Spiel/es steht 1 : 1** (*Sport*) the score is one all; **wie steht es/das Spiel?** (*Sport*) what's the score?; **die Chancen** ~ **fifty-fifty** the chances are fifty-fifty; **die Sache steht gut/schlecht** things are going well/badly; **[wie gehts,] wie stehts?** how are things?; **wie steht es mit deinen Finanzen/mit deiner Gesundheit?** how are your finances/how is your health?; **wie steht es mit deinen Ferien?** what is happening about your holidays?; **der Weizen steht gut** the wheat is growing well; **in Blüte** ~**:** be in bloom; Ⓓ (*einen bestimmten Kurs, Wert haben*) ‹currency› stand (**bei** at); **wie steht das Pfund?** what is the rate for the pound?; how is the pound doing? (*coll.*); **der Schweizer Franken steht am besten** the Swiss franc is currently strongest; **die Aktie steht gut/schlecht** the share price is high/low; Ⓔ (*nicht in Bewegung sein*) be stationary; ‹machine etc.› be at a standstill; **meine Uhr steht** my watch has stopped; ~ **bleiben** (*anhalten*) stop; ‹time› stand still; ~ **bleiben!** (*Milit.*) halt!; **wo sind wir** ~ **geblieben?** (*fig.*) where had we got to?; where were we?; **das Kind ist in der Entwicklung** ~ **geblieben** the child is a case of arrested development; **ein** ~**der Zug** a stationary train; **etw./den Verkehr zum Stehen bringen** stop sth./bring traffic to a standstill; **zum Stehen kommen** come to a standstill; Ⓕ (*geschrieben, gedruckt sein*) be; **auf einer Liste** ~**:** be *or* appear on a list; **was steht in dem Brief?** what does it say in the letter?; **in der Zeitung steht, dass ...** it says in the paper that ...; **das Zitat steht bei Schiller** the quotation is from Schiller; Ⓖ (*Sprachw.: gebraucht werden*) ‹subjunctive etc.› occur; be found; **mit dem Dativ** ~**:** be followed by *or* take the dative; Ⓗ **zu jmdm./etw.** ~**:** stand by sb./sth.; **wie stehst du dazu?** what's your view on this?; **hinter jmdm./etw.** ~ (*jmdn. unterstützen*) be [right] behind sb./sth.; support sb./sth.; Ⓘ

*old spelling (see note on page 1707)

jmdm. [gut] ~ ‹dress etc.› suit sb. [well]; **Lächeln steht dir gut** (*fig.*) it suits you *or* you look nice when you smile; 🄹 (*sich verstehen*) **mit jmdm. gut/schlecht ~:** be on good/bad terms *or* get on well/badly with sb.; 🄺 **das** *od.* **die Entscheidung steht [ganz] bei Ihnen** that's [entirely] up to you; it's for you to decide; 🄻 **auf etw.** (*Akk.*) **steht Gefängnis** sth. is punishable by imprisonment; 🄼 (*ugs.: fertig-, zusammengestellt sein*) ‹plan, speech, team, programme, etc.› be finalized; 🄽 **für etw. ~** (*Gewähr bieten*) be a guarantee of sth.; (*stellvertretend*) stand for sth.; 🄾 **auf etw.** (*Akk.*) **~** (*ugs., bes. Jugendspr.: mögen*) be into sth. (*coll.*); **sie steht total auf ihn** she's nuts about him (*coll.*); ⇒ *auch* **Modell**; **Pate** A; **Posten** B; **Spalier** B; **Wache** A.
❷ *unr. refl. V.; südd., österr., schweiz. mit sein* (*ugs.*) 🄰 (*in bestimmten Verhältnissen leben*) **sich gut/schlecht/auf 3 000 Mark monatlich ~:** be comfortably/badly off/on 3,000 marks a month; 🄱 (*sich verstehen*) **sich gut/schlecht mit jmdm. ~:** be on good/bad terms *or* get on well/badly with sb.
❸ *tr. V.* (*Skisport, Eislauf*) **einen Sprung ~:** perform a jump without falling

**stehen-:** ***~|bleiben**, ***~|lassen** ⇒ **stehen** 1 A, B, E

**Steher** *der;* **~s, ~, Steherin** *die;* **~, ~nen** 🄰 (*Pferdesport*) stayer; 🄱 (*Radsport*) motor-paced racer

**Steher·rennen** *das* (*Radsport*) motor-paced race

**Steh-:** **~geiger** *der*, **~geigerin** *die* café violinist; **~kneipe** *die* stand-up bar; **~konvent** *der* (*scherzh. fig.*) [stand-up] chat; **einen ~konvent halten** *od.* **machen** stand around chatting *or* (*Brit. coll.*) having a good natter; **~kragen** *der* stand-up collar; (*für Herrenhemden*) choker; (*mit Ecken*) wing collar; **~lampe** *die* standard lamp (*Brit.*); floor lamp (*Amer.*); **~leiter** *die* stepladder

**stehlen** /ˈʃteːlən/ ❶ *unr. tr., itr. V.* steal; **jmdm. etw. ~:** steal sth. from sb.; **jmdm. das Portemonnaie ~:** steal sb.'s purse; **jmdm. die Zeit ~** (*fig.*) take up *or* waste sb.'s time; ⇒ *auch* **gestohlen** 2; **nehmen** A. ❷ *unr. refl. V.* steal; creep

**Steh-:** **~platz** *der* (*im Theater/Stadion*) standing place; (*im Bus*) space to stand; **40 ~plätze** standing room for 40; **es gab nur noch ~plätze** there was standing room only; **~pult** *das* high desk; **~vermögen** *das* stamina; staying power

**Steiermark** /ˈʃtaiɐmark/ *die;* **~:** Styria *no art.*

**steif** /ʃtaif/ ❶ *Adj.* 🄰 stiff; (*ugs.: erigiert*) erect ‹penis›; **~ vor Kälte** stiff with cold; **~ gefroren** frozen stiff; **die Sahne ~ schlagen** beat the cream until stiff; **der Pudding ist noch nicht ~:** the blancmange has not set yet; **~ wie ein Stock** as stiff as a ramrod; **er kam uns mit ~en Schritten entgegen** he walked towards us stiffly; **einen Steifen haben** (*salopp*) have a hard-on (*sl.*); 🄱 (*förmlich*) stiff, formal ‹person, greeting, style›; formal ‹reception›; 🄲 (*Seemannsspr.: stark*) stiff ‹wind, breeze›; 🄳 (*ugs.: stark*) strong ‹coffee›; stiff, strong ‹alcoholic drink›.
❷ *adv.* 🄰 stiffly; **bei ihnen geht es sehr ~ zu** things are very formal at their house; 🄱 (*Seemannsspr.: stark*) **der Wind steht** *od.* **weht ~ aus Südost** there's a stiff wind blowing from the south-east; 🄲 **~ und fest behaupten/glauben, dass ...** (*ugs.*) swear blind/be completely convinced that ...

***steif|halten** ⇒ **Nacken**; **Ohr** B

**Steifheit** *die;* **~:** stiffness; (*Förmlichkeit*) formality; stiffness

**Steif·leinen** *das* buckram

**Steig** *der;* **~[e]s, ~e** [mountain] path

**Steig-:** **~bügel** *der* ▶ 471 (*auch Anat.*) stirrup; **~bügel·halter** *der*, **~bügel·halterin** *die* (*abwertend*) backer; **die ~bügelhalter für Xs Karriere** those who advance/advanced X's career

**Steige** *die;* **~, ~n** 🄰 (*bes. südd., österr.: Steig*) [mountain] path; 🄱 (*bes. nordd.: Treppe*) steps *pl.*; (*Leiter*) ladder; 🄲 (*bes. südd., österr.: Lattenkiste*) open crate

**Steig·eisen** *das* (*in Schächten usw.*) step-iron; (*am Schuh anschnallbar*) climbing iron; (*Bergsteigen*) crampon

**steigen** /ˈʃtaign̩/ ❶ *unr. itr. V.; mit sein* 🄰 ‹person, animal, aircraft, etc.› climb; ‹mist, smoke, sun, object› rise; ‹balloon› climb, rise; **Drachen ~ lassen** fly kites; **ins Tal/in den Keller ~:** climb *or* go down into the valley/go down into the cellar; **auf einen Turm/eine Leiter ~:** climb a tower/ladder; **auf die Leiter ~:** get on to the ladder; **aus dem Wasser/Auto/Bett/aus der Wanne ~:** get out of the water/out of the car/out of bed/out of the bath; **ins Wasser/ins Auto/in die Wanne/ins Bett ~:** get into the water/car/bath/into bed; **in den/aus dem Bus/Zug ~:** board *or* get on/get off *or* out of the bus/train; **ins/aus dem Flugzeug ~:** board/leave the aircraft; **aufs/vom Fahrrad ~:** get on [to]/off one's bicycle; **aufs Pferd/aus dem Sattel** *od.* **vom Pferd ~:** mount *or* get on [to]/get off one's horse; **auf die Bremse/aufs Gas ~** (*ugs.*) step on the brakes/the gas (*coll.*); **in die Kleider ~** (*ugs.*) slip into one's clothes; **das Blut/eine Röte stieg ihm ins Gesicht** the blood rose into *or* rushed to his face/he blushed; **der Duft steigt mir in die Nase** the scent gets up my nose; ⇒ *auch* **Kopf** A; 🄱 (*an~, zunehmen*) rise (**auf** + *Akk.* to, **um** by) ‹price, cost, salary, output› increase, rise; ‹debts, tension› increase, mount; ‹chances› improve; **~de Preise** rising prices; **~de Ansprüche** growing *or* increasing demands; **in jmds. Achtung ~** (*fig.*) go up *or* rise in sb.'s estimation; 🄲 (*ugs.: stattfinden*) be on; **morgen soll ein Fest ~:** there's to be a party tomorrow; 🄳 (*Reitsport: sich aufbäumen*) ‹horse› rear.
❷ *unr. tr. V.; mit sein* climb ‹stairs, steps›

**Steiger** *der;* **~s, ~** ▶ 159 (*Bergbau*) overman

**steigern** ❶ *tr. V.* 🄰 increase ‹speed, value, sales, consumption, etc.› (**auf** + *Akk.* to); step up ‹demands, production, etc.›; raise ‹standards, requirements›; (*verstärken*) intensify ‹fear, tension›; heighten, intensify ‹effect›; exacerbate ‹anger›; **das Tempo ~:** step up the pace; **seine Leistung ~:** improve one's performance; 🄱 (*Sprachw.*) compare ‹adjective›. ❷ *refl. V.* 🄰 ‹confusion, speed, profit, etc.› increase; ‹pain, excitement, tension› become more intense; ‹excitement, tension› mount; ‹hate, anger› grow, become more intense; ‹costs› escalate; ‹effect› be heightened *or* intensified; **der Sturm steigerte sich zum Orkan** the gale increased to hurricane strength; **sich** *od.* **seine Leistung[en] ~:** improve one's performance; 🄱 (*hinein~*) **sich [mehr und mehr] in Wut/Zorn/einen Erregungszustand ~:** work oneself up into [more and more of] a fury/rage/state [of excitement]

**Steigerung** *die;* **~, ~en** 🄰 increase (+ *Gen.* in); (*Verstärkung*) intensification; (*einer Wirkung*) heightening; (*des Zorns*) exacerbation; (*Verbesserung*) improvement (+ *Gen.* in); (*bes. Sport: Leistungs~*) improvement [in performance]; **~ der Produktion/des Absatzes** increase in production/in sales; 🄱 (*Sprachw.*) comparison

**Steigerungs-:** **~form** *die* (*Sprachw.*) comparative [form]; **~stufe** *die* (*Sprachw.*) degree of comparison

**Steigung** *die;* **~, ~en** gradient; (*ansteigende Strecke*) gradient; climb; **in sanfter ~:** climbing gently

**Steigungs·winkel** *der* [angle of] gradient

**steil** /ʃtail/ ❶ *Adj.* 🄰 steep; upright, straight ‹handwriting, flame›; meteoric ‹career›; rapid ‹rise›; 🄱 (*Jugendspr. veralt.: beeindruckend*) fabulous (*coll.*); super (*coll.*); 🄲 (*Ballspiele*) deep ‹pass, ball›. ❷ *adv.* 🄰 steeply; **sie saß ~ aufgerichtet** she sat bolt upright; 🄱 (*Ballspiele*) **jmdn. ~ anspielen** play a deep ball to sb.; **er spielt [immer wieder] zu ~:** he's playing too many deep balls

**Steil·hang** *der* steep escarpment

**Steilheit** *die;* **~:** steepness

**Steil-:** **~küste** *die* (*Geogr.*) cliffs *pl.*; **~pass**, ***~paß** *der* (*Fußball*) deep [forward] pass; **~ufer** *das* steep bank; **~wand** *die* rock wall; **~wand·fahrer** *der*, **~wand·fahrerin** *die* wall-of-death rider; **~wand·zelt** *das* frame tent

**Stein** /ʃtain/ *der;* **~[e]s, ~e** 🄰 stone; (*Fels*) rock; **ihr Gesicht war zu ~ geworden** (*fig.*) her face had hardened; 🄱 (*losgelöstes Stück, Kern, Med., Edel~, Schmuck~*) stone; (*Kiesel~*) pebble; **der ~ der Weisen** (*geh.*) the philosophers' stone; **ein ~ des Anstoßes** (*geh.*) a bone of contention; **mir fällt ein ~ vom Herzen** that's a weight off my mind; **es friert ~ und Bein** (*ugs.*) it's freezing hard; **~ und Bein schwören** (*ugs.*) swear blind; **den ~ ins Rollen bringen** (*fig.*) set the ball rolling; **jmdm. [die** *od.* **alle] ~e aus dem Weg räumen** (*fig.*) smooth sb.'s path; make things easy for sb.; **jmdm. ~e in den Weg legen** (*fig.*) create obstacles *or* make things difficult for sb.; **eine Uhr mit 12 ~en** a 12-jewel watch; ⇒ *auch* **Krone** A; 🄲 (*Bau~*) [stone] block; (*Ziegel~*) brick; **keinen ~ auf dem anderen lassen** not leave one stone upon another; 🄳 (*Spiel~*) piece; (*rund, flach*) counter; **bei jmdm. einen ~ im Brett haben** (*fig.*) be in sb.'s good books; 🄴 (*Grab~*) gravestone

**stein-, Stein-:** **~adler** *der* golden eagle; **~alt** *Adj.* aged; ancient; **~alt werden** live to a great age; **~axt** *die* (*hist.*) stone axe; **~bau** *der; Pl.* **~~ten** stone building; **~block** *der; Pl.* **~blöcke** block of stone; **~bock** *der* 🄰 (*Tier*) ibex; 🄱 (*Astrol.*) Capricorn; the Goat; ⇒ *auch* **Fisch** C; **~boden** *der* stone floor; **~brech** /-brɛç/ *der;* **~~[e]s, ~~e** (*Bot.*) saxifrage; **~bruch** *der* quarry; **~butt** *der* turbot

**Steinchen** *das;* **~s, ~:** little stone; (*Kiesel~*) pebble

**Stein·druck** *der; Pl.* **~e** 🄰 (*Verfahren*) lithography *no art.*; 🄱 (*Grafik*) lithograph

**Stein·druckeiche** *die* holm oak

**steinern** *Adj.* 🄰 stone ‹floor, bench, etc.›; 🄱 (*wie versteinert*) stony ‹face, features›; **ein ~es Herz** a heart of stone

**stein-, Stein-:** **~erweichen** *das:* **zum ~erweichen** so as to make your heart bleed; heart-rendingly; **~frucht** *die* (*Bot.*) stone fruit; **~fuß·boden** *der* ⇒ **~boden**; **~garten** *der* rockery; rock garden; **~gut** *das* earthenware; **~hart** *Adj.* rock-hard

**steinig** *Adj.* stony

**steinigen** *tr. V.* stone ‹person›

**stein-, Stein-:** **~kauz** *der* little owl; **~kohle** *die* [hard] coal; **~krug** *der* earthenware jug; **~marder** *der* stone marten; **~metz** /-mɛts/ *der;* **~~en, ~~en**, **~metzin** *die;* **~~, ~~nen** ▶ 159 stonemason; **~obst** *das* stone fruit; **~pilz** *der* cep; **~reich** *Adj.* (*ugs.*) filthy rich; **~reich sein** be rolling [in money] (*coll.*); **~reich werden** make pots of money (*coll.*); **~salz** *das* rock salt; **~schlag** *der* (*Fachspr.*) rock fall; **„Achtung ~schlag"** 'beware falling rocks'; **~schleuder** *die* catapult (*Brit.*); slingshot (*Amer.*); **~topf** *der* earthenware pot; **~wurf** *der*: **jmdn. mit ~würfen wegjagen** chase sb. away by throwing stones [at him/her]; **[nur] einen ~wurf weit [entfernt]** (*fig.*) [only] a stone's throw away; **~wüste** *die* rocky desert; (*fig.: leere Stadt*) waste land of stone and concrete; **~zeit** *die* Stone Age; (*fig.*) stone age; **~zeitlich** *Adj.* Stone-Age *attrib.*; (*fig.: völlig veraltet*) antediluvian (*coll.*); **~zeug** *das* stoneware

**Steirer** /ˈʃtairɐ/ *der;* **~s, ~, Steierin** *die;* **Steierin, Steierinnen** Styrian

**steirisch** /ˈʃtairɪʃ/ *Adj.* Styrian

**Steiß** /ʃtais/ *der;* **~es, ~e** 🄰 (**~bein**) coccyx; 🄱 (*ugs.: Gesäß*) backside; behind (*coll.*)

**Steiß-:** **~bein** *das* ▶ 471 (*Anat.*) coccyx; **~lage** *die* (*Med.*) breech presentation

**Stellage** /ʃtɛˈlaːʒə/ *die;* **~, ~n** rack

**Stell·dich·ein** *das;* **~[s], ~[s]** (*veralt.*) rendezvous; tryst (*arch./literary*); **sich** (*Dat.*) **ein ~ geben** (*fig.*) gather; assemble

**Stelle** /ˈʃtɛlə/ *die;* **~, ~n** 🄰 place; **eine schöne ~ zum Campen** a nice spot for camping; **an dieser ~ ereignete sich der Unfall** this is the spot where the accident happened; **die Truhe ließ sich nicht von**

**der ~ rücken** the chest could not be shifted *or* would not budge; **sich nicht von der ~ rühren** not budge *or* move; **an jmds. ~ treten** take sb.'s place; **ich an deiner ~ würde das nicht machen** I wouldn't do it if I were you; **ich möchte nicht an deiner ~ sein** I shouldn't like to be in your place; **A an die ~ von B setzen** replace B with A; **an ~ +** *Gen.* instead of; **auf der ~:** immediately; **er war auf der ~ tot** he died instantly; **ich könnte auf der ~ einschlafen** I could go to sleep here and now; **auf der ~ treten** (*ugs.*), **nicht von der ~ kommen** (*fig.*) make no headway; not get anywhere; **zur ~ sein** be there *or* on the spot; **pünktlich zu ~ sein** arrive punctually; **Gefreiter Schulz meldet sich zur ~!** (*Milit.*) Lance Corporal Schulz reporting; **B** (*begrenzter Bereich*) patch; (*am Körper*) spot; **eine kahle ~:** a bare patch; (*am Kopf*) a bald patch; **seine empfindliche ~** (*fig.*) his sensitive *or* sore spot; **eine schwache ~ in der Argumentation** (*fig.*) a weak point in the argument; **C** (*Passage*) passage; **an anderer ~:** elsewhere; in another passage; **D** (*Punkt im Ablauf einer Rede usw.*) point; **an dieser/früherer ~:** at this point *or* here/earlier; **E** (*Platz in einer Rangordnung, Reihenfolge*) place; **an achter ~ liegen** be in eighth place; **er steht an führender ~:** he has a leading position; **etw. kommt an vorderster** *od.* **oberster ~:** sth. has top priority; **an erster ~ geht es hier um ...** here it is primarily a question of ...; **F** (*Math.*) figure; **die erste ~ hinter** *od.* **nach dem Komma** the first decimal place; **etw. bis auf zwei ~n hinter dem Komma ausrechnen** calculate sth. to two decimal places; **G** (*Arbeits~*) job; (*formeller*) position; (*bes. als Beamter*) post; **eine halbe/ganze ~:** a half-time/full-time job; **ohne ~ sein** be unemployed; **eine freie ~:** a vacancy; **H** (*Dienst~*) office; (*Behörde*) authority; **die zuständige ~:** the competent authority

**stellen** **1** *tr. V.* **A** put; (*mit Sorgfalt, ordentlich*) place; (*aufrecht hin~*) stand; **die Stühle um den Tisch ~:** place *or* put the chairs round the table; **wie sollen wir die Möbel ~?** how should we position the furniture?; **man soll die Flaschen ~, nicht legen** one should stand the bottles [up], not lay them down; **jmdn. wieder auf die Füße ~** (*fig.*) put sb. back on his/her feet; **jmdn. vor eine Entscheidung ~** (*fig.*) confront sb. with a decision; **auf sich [selbst] gestellt sein** (*fig.*) be thrown back on one's own resources; **etw. in den Mittelpunkt der Diskussion ~** (*fig.*) make sth. the focus of discussion; **B** (*ein~, regulieren*) set ‹points, clock, scales›; set ‹clock› to the right time; **den Wecker auf 6 Uhr ~:** set the alarm for 6 o'clock; **den Schalter auf null ~:** turn the switch to zero; set the switch at zero; **das Radio lauter/leiser ~:** turn the radio up/down; **die Heizung höher/niedriger ~:** turn the heating up/down; **C** (*bereit~*) provide; produce ‹witness›; **jmdm. etw. ~:** provide sb. with sth.; ⇒ *auch* **Verfügung** B; **D** **jmdn. besser ~** ‹firm› improve sb.'s pay; **gut/schlecht/besser gestellt** comfortably/badly/better off; **E** (*auf~*) set ‹trap›; lay ‹net›; **F** **kalt ~:** put ‹food, drink› in a cold place; leave ‹champagne etc.› to chill; **warm ~:** put ‹plant› in a warm place; keep ‹food› warm *or* hot; **G** (*fassen, festhalten*) catch ‹game›; apprehend ‹criminal›; **H** (*aufrichten*) ‹dog, horse, etc.› prick up ‹ears›; stick up ‹tail›; **I** (*er~*) prepare ‹horoscope, bill›; make ‹diagnosis, prognosis›; **J** *verblasst* put ‹question›; set ‹task, essay, topic, condition›; make ‹application, demand, request›; **jmdm. eine Frage/Aufgabe ~:** ask sb. a question/set sb. a task; **jmdn. unter Aufsicht/etw. unter Denkmalschutz ~:** place sb. under supervision/sth. under a conservation order; **jmdn. vor Gericht/unter Anklage ~:** take sb. to court/charge sb.; **K** (*bes. Theater, Film: arrangieren*) block in the moves for ‹scene›; **das Foto wirkt gestellt** the photo looks posed.

**2** *refl. V.* **A** place oneself; **sie stellte sich auf eine Leiter** she got on a ladder; **stell dich neben mich/ans Ende der Schlange/in die Reihe** come and stand by me/go to the back of the queue (*Brit.*) *or* (*Amer.*) line/get into line; **sich auf die Zehenspitzen ~:** stand on tiptoe; **ich stelle mich lieber** (*ugs.*) I'd rather stand; **sich gegen jmdn./etw. ~** (*fig.*) oppose sb./sth.; **sich hinter jmdn./etw. ~** (*fig.*) give sb./sth. one's backing; **sich vor jmdn. ~** (*fig.*) take sb.'s part; (*verteidigen*) defend sb.; ⇒ *auch* **Standpunkt**; **B** **sich schlafend/taub/tot** *usw.* **~:** feign sleep/deafness/death *etc.*; pretend to be asleep/deaf/dead *etc.*; ⇒ *auch* **dumm** 1 A; **C** (*sich ausliefern*) **sich [der Polizei] ~:** give oneself up [to the police]; **D** (*nicht ausweichen*) **sich einem Herausforderer/der Presse ~:** face a challenger/the press; **sich einer Diskussion ~:** consent to take part in a discussion; **er stellte sich der Kamera** he made himself available for photographs; **E** (*Stellung beziehen*) **sich positiv/negativ zu jmdm./etw. ~:** take a positive/negative view of sb./sth.; **sich mit jmdm. gut ~:** try to get on good terms with sb.

**stellen-, Stellen-:** **~angebot** *das* offer of a job; (*Inserat*) job advertisement; **„~angebote"** 'situations vacant'; **~anzeige** *die* job advertisement; **~gesuch** *das* 'situation wanted' advertisement; **„~gesuche"** 'situations wanted'; **~markt** *der* job market; **~suche** *die* job-hunting *no art.*; search for a job; **auf ~suche sein** be looking for a job; be job-hunting; **~weise** *Adv.* in places; **~weise Nebel/Schauer** fog patches/scattered showers; **~wert** *der* **A** (*Math.*) place value; **B** (*fig.: Bedeutung*) standing; status

**-stellig** -figure ‹number, salary›; -place ‹decimal›

**Stell-:** **~macher** *der*, **~macherin** *die* cartwright; **~platz** *der* space; (*auf einem Campingplatz*) pitch; site; **~probe** *die* (*Theater*) blocking rehearsal; **~schraube** *die* adjusting screw

**Stellung** *die;* **~, ~en** **A** position; **in gebückter/kniender ~:** in a bent/kneeling posture; **die ~ der Frau in der Gesellschaft** the position *or* standing of women in society; **in ~ gehen** (*Milit.*) take up [one's] position; **geh nur, ich halte in der Zwischenzeit die ~** (*fig.*) you can go while I hold the fort; **[zu/gegen etw.] ~ beziehen** (*fig.*) take a stand [on/against sth.]; **B** (*Posten*) job; (*formeller*) position; (*bes. als Beamter*) post; **C** (*Einstellung*) attitude (**zu** to, towards); **zu etw. ~ nehmen** express one's opinion *or* state one's view on sth.; **er hat zu dem Vorschlag offiziell ~ genommen** he made an official statement on the proposal

**Stellungnahme** *die;* **~, ~n** opinion; (*kurze Äußerung*) statement; **eine ~ zu etw. abgeben** give one's opinion *or* views on sth.; (*sich kurz zu etw. äußern*) make a statement on sth.

**stellungs-, Stellungs-:** **~befehl** *der* (*Milit.*) call-up papers *pl.*; draft card (*Amer.*); **~krieg** *der* positional warfare *no pl.*, *no indef. art.*; **~los** *Adj.* unemployed; jobless; **~spiel** *das* (*Fußball*) positioning; **~suche** *die* ⇒ **Stellensuche**; **~suchende** *der/die; adj. Dekl.* job-hunter; **~wechsel** *der* change of position; (*Wechsel der Arbeitsstelle*) change of job

**stell-, Stell-:** **~vertretend** **1** *Adj.* acting; (*von Amts wegen*) deputy ‹minister, director, etc.›; **2** *adv.* as a deputy; **~vertretend für jmdn.** deputizing for sb.; on sb.'s behalf; **~vertreter** *der*, **~vertreterin** *die* deputy; **jmdn. als seinen ~vertreter schicken** send sb. as one's representative; **der ~vertreter Christi** (*kath. Rel.*) the Vicar of Christ; **~vertreter·krieg** *der* proxy war; **~vertretung** *die* deputizing *no art.*; acting as deputy *no art.*; **die ~vertretung für jmdn.** *od.* **jmds. ~vertretung übernehmen** stand in *or* deputize for sb.; **~wand** *die* partition; **~werk** *das* (*Eisenb.*) signal box (*Brit.*); switch tower (*Amer.*); (*Anlage*) control gear for signals and points (*Brit.*) *or* (*Amer.*) switches

**Stelze** *die;* **~, ~n** **A** stilt; **B** (*ugs.: Bein*) leg; **der hat vielleicht ~n!** what long skinny legs *or* spindle-shanks he's got!

**stelzen** *itr. V.; mit sein* strut; stalk

**Stemm-:** **~bogen** *der* (*Skisport*) stem [turn]; **~eisen** *das* chisel

**stemmen** /ˈʃtɛmən/ **1** *tr. V.* **A** (*hoch~*) lift [above one's head]; (*Gewichtheben*) lift ‹weight›; **B** (*drücken*) brace ‹feet, knees› (**gegen** against); **die Arme in die Hüften/Seiten ~:** place one's arms akimbo; put one's hands on one's hips; **die Arme in die Hüften gestemmt** with arms akimbo; **C** (*meißeln*) chisel ‹hole etc.›.
**2** *refl. V.* **sich gegen etw. ~:** brace oneself against sth.; (*fig.: sich auflehnen*) resist sth.; **sich in die Höhe ~:** haul oneself to one's feet.
**3** *itr. V.* (*Skisport*) stem

**Stempel** /ˈʃtɛmpl/ *der;* **~s, ~** **A** stamp; (*Post~*) postmark; **jmdm./einer Sache seinen** *od.* **den ~ aufdrücken** (*fig.*) leave one's mark on sb./sth.; **den ~ einer Person/Sache tragen** (*fig.*) bear the stamp *or* imprint of sb./sth.; **B** (*Punze*) hallmark; **C** (*Bot.: Teil der Blüte*) pistil; **D** (*Technik*) (*zum Stanzen*) punch; (*zum Formen*) die; **E** (*Bauw., Bergbau: Stütze*) prop; **F** (*salopp: dicke Beine*) **[richtige] ~ haben** have legs like tree trunks

**Stempel-:** **~farbe** *die* stamp pad ink; **~geld** *das* (*ugs. veralt.*) dole [money] (*coll.*); **~kissen** *das* stamp pad; ink pad

**stempeln** **1** *tr. V.* **A** stamp ‹passport, form›; postmark ‹letter›; cancel ‹postage stamp›; **das Eingangsdatum auf die Briefe ~:** stamp the letters with the date of receipt; **B** hallmark ‹gold, silver, ring, brooch, etc.›; **C** (*brandmarken*) **jmdn. zum Verbrecher ~:** brand sb. [as] a criminal. **2** *itr. V.* (*ugs. veralt.*) be on the dole (*coll.*); **~ gehen** be on the dole (*coll.*); **er muss ~ gehen** he has to go on the dole

**stempelpflichtig** /-pflɪçtɪç/ *Adj.* (*österr.*) ⇒ **gebührenpflichtig**

***Stengel** ⇒ **Stängel**

**Steno**[1] /ˈʃteːno/ *die;* **~** (*ugs.*) shorthand; **kannst du ~?** do you know shorthand?

**Steno**[2] *das;* **~s, ~s** (*ugs.*) ⇒ **Stenogramm**

**steno-, Steno-:** **~block** /ˈ---/ *der; Pl.* **~~s** *od.* **~blöcke** ⇒ **~grammblock**; **~gramm** *das* shorthand text; **ein ~gramm aufnehmen** take a dictation in shorthand; **~gramm·block** *der; Pl.* **~blöcke** *od.* **~~s** shorthand pad; **~graf** *usw.* ⇒ **~graph** *usw.*; **~graph** *der* **▶ 159** stenographer; **~graphie** *die* stenography *no art.*; shorthand *no art.*; **~graphie lernen/können** learn shorthand/be able to do shorthand; **~graphieren** **1** *itr. V.* do shorthand; **sie kann gut ~graphieren** her shorthand is good; **2** *tr. V.* **etw. ~graphieren** take sth. down in shorthand; **~graphin** *die;* **~~, ~~nen** **▶ 159** ⇒ **~graph**; **~graphisch** **1** *Adj.* shorthand *attrib.*; stenographic ‹symbols›; **2** *adv.* **~grafisch abgefasste Notizen** shorthand notes; **~stift** /ˈ---/ *der* shorthand pencil; **~typistin** *die;* **~~, ~~nen** shorthand typist

**Stentor·stimme** /ˈʃtɛntɔr-/ *die* stentorian voice; **mit ~:** in a stentorian voice

**Stenz** /ʃtɛnts/ *der;* **~es, ~e** (*ugs. abwertend*) dandy; fop

***Step, Stepp** /ʃtɛp/ *der;* **~s, ~s** tap dance

**Stepp·decke** *die* quilt

**Steppe** /ˈʃtɛpə/ *die;* **~, ~n** steppe

**steppen**[1] *tr.* (*auch itr.*) *V.* (*nähen*) backstitch; **eine gesteppte Jacke** a quilted jacket

**steppen**[2] *itr. V.* (*tanzen*) tap dance

**Steppen-:** **~fuchs** *der* corsac; **~wolf** *der* ⇒ **Präriewolf**

**Stepperei** *die;* **~, ~en** backstitching *no pl.*

**Stepp-:** **~futter** *das* quilted lining; **~jacke** *die* quilted jacket

**Steppke** /ˈʃtɛpkə/ *der;* **~[s], ~s** (*ugs., bes. berlin.*) lad; nipper (*coll.*)

**Stepp-:** **~naht** *die* backstitched seam; **~stich** *der* backstitch

*old spelling (see note on page 1707)

S

**Stepp-, *Step-: ~tanz** *der* tap dance; **~tänzer** *der,* **~tänzerin** *die* tap dancer

**Sterbe-: ~bett** *das* deathbed; **auf dem ~bett liegen** be on one's deathbed; **~datum** *das* date of death; **~fall** *der* ⇒ **Todesfall**; **~geläut** *das* death knell; **~glocke** *die* funeral bell; **~hilfe** *die* ⇒ **Euthanasie**

**sterben** /'ʃtɛrbn̩/ ❶ *unr. itr. V.; mit sein* die; **eines sanften Todes ~** (*geh.*) die peacefully; **er starb als Christ** he died a Christian; **im Sterben liegen** lie dying; **und wenn sie nicht gestorben sind, dann leben sie noch heute** and they lived happily ever after; **davon stirbt man/stirbst du nicht gleich** (*ugs.*) it/they won't kill you; **zum Sterben langweilig/müde** deadly boring/dead tired; **er ist für mich gestorben** (*fig.*) he's finished *or* he doesn't exist as far as I'm concerned; **gestorben!** (*Film-, Fernsehjargon*) (*abgeschlossen*) [OK,] in the can!; (*abgebrochen*) cut!; **vor Angst/Scham/Neugier ~** (*ugs.*) die of fright/shame/be dying of curiosity.
❷ *unr. tr. V.; mit sein* **den Hungertod ~:** die of starvation; starve to death; **den Heldentod ~:** die a hero's death

**sterbens-, Sterbens-: ~angst** *die* terrible fear; **eine ~angst haben** be scared to death; be terribly afraid; be terrified; **~elend** *Adj.* wretched; **~krank** *Adj.* Ⓐ ⇒ **~elend**; Ⓑ (*sehr krank*) mortally ill; **~langweilig** *Adj.* deadly boring; **~wort, ~wörtchen** *das: in* **kein** *od.* **nicht ein ~wort** *od.* **~wörtchen** not a [single] word; **darüber haben wir kein ~wort** *od.* **~wörtchen gesagt** we didn't breathe a word [of it]

**Sterbe-: ~sakramente** *Pl.* (*kath. Kirche*) last rites; **~stunde** *die* ⇒ **Todesstunde**; **~urkunde** *die* death certificate; **~zimmer** *das:* **sein ~zimmer** the room in which he died

**sterblich** *Adj.* mortal; ⇒ *auch* **Hülle** A; **Überrest**

**Sterbliche** *der/die; adj. Dekl.* Ⓐ (*dichter.*) mortal; Ⓑ **ein gewöhnlicher ~r** an ordinary mortal *or* person

**Sterblichkeit** *die;* **~:** mortality

**stereo** /'ʃte:reo/ *Adv.* (*Akustik*) in stereo

**stereo-, Stereo-** stereo-

**Stereo** *das;* **~s** (*Akustik*) stereo

**stereo-, Stereo-: ~anlage** *die* stereo [system]; **~aufnahme** *die* stereo recording; **~empfang** *der* stereo reception; **~kamera** *die* stereocamera; stereoscopic camera; **~metrie** /-me'tri:/ *die;* **~~** (*Math.*) stereometry *no art.;* **~phon** /-'fo:n/ (*Akustik*) ❶ *Adj.* stereophonic; ❷ *adv.* stereophonically; **~phonie** /-fo'ni:/ *die;* **~~** (*Akustik*) stereophony *no art.;* **~skop** /-'sko:p/ *das;* **~~s, ~~e** stereoscope; **~skopie** /-sko'pi:/ *die;* **~~:** stereoscopy *no art.;* **~skopisch** *Adj.* stereoscopic; **~ton** *der; Pl.* **~töne** stereo sound; **~typ** /---'-/ ❶ *Adj.* Ⓐ stereotyped ‹discussion, pattern, etc.›; stereotyped, stock ‹question, reply, phrase, utterance›; mechanical ‹smile›; Ⓑ (*Druckw.*) stereotype; ❷ *adv.* Ⓐ in a stereotyped way; Ⓑ (*Druckw.*) in stereotype; **~typie** /-ty'pi:/ *die;* **~~** Ⓐ (*Druckw.*) stereotyping *no art.;* Ⓑ (*Psychiatrie, Med.*) stereotypy

**steril** /ʃte'ri:l/ ❶ *Adj.* (*auch fig. abwertend*) sterile; **etw. ~ machen** sterilize sth. ❷ *adv.* Ⓐ (*keimfrei*) **~ verpackt sein** be in a sterile pack/sterile packs; **etw. ~ auskochen** sterilize sth. by boiling; Ⓑ (*fig. abwertend: unschöpferisch, nüchtern*) sterilely

**Sterilisation** /ʃteriliza'tsi̯o:n/ *die;* **~, ~en** sterilization

**sterilisieren** *tr. V.* sterilize

**Sterilität** /ʃterili'tɛ:t/ *die;* **~** (*auch fig. abwertend*) sterility

**Sterling** /'stɛ:lɪŋ/ ▶ 337 *in* **1 Pfund ~:** £1 sterling; **einen Betrag in Pfund ~ tauschen** change a sum into sterling; **in ~ bezahlen** pay in sterling

**Sterling·silber** *das* sterling silver

**Stern** /ʃtɛrn/ *der;* **~[e]s, ~e** Ⓐ star; **~e sehen** (*ugs.*) see stars; **unter fremden ~en** (*geh.*) in foreign parts; **nach den ~en greifen** (*geh.*) reach for the moon; **in den ~en stehen** (*fig.*) be in the lap of the gods; **unter einem guten** *od.* **günstigen/ungünstigen ~ stehen** (*geh.*) have an auspicious start/be ill-starred; Ⓑ (*Orden, Auszeichnung*) star; **ein Hotel mit fünf ~en** a five-star hotel; Ⓒ (*bei Pferden, Rindern*) blaze; Ⓓ (*Jägerspr.*) iris

**Stern·bild** *das* constellation

**Sternchen** *das;* **~s, ~** Ⓐ [little] star; Ⓑ (*als Verweis*) asterisk; Ⓒ ⇒ **Starlet[t]**

**Stern-: ~deuter** /-dɔytɐ/ *der,* **~deuterin** *die* astrologer; **~deutung** *die* astrology *no art.*

**sternen-, Sternen-: ~banner** *das* Star-spangled Banner, Stars and Stripes *pl.;* **~himmel** *der* (*geh.*) starry sky; **~klar** *Adj.* starlit, starry ‹sky, night›; **~licht** *das* (*geh.*) starlight; **~zelt** *das* (*dichter.*) starry canopy

**stern-, Stern-: ~fahrt** *die* rally (*in which the participants converge from various starting points*); **eine ~fahrt nach X** a rally converging on X; **~förmig** *Adj.* star-shaped; stellate ‹leaf› (*Bot.*); **~globus** *der* (*Astron.*) celestial globe; **~gucker** *der;* **~~s, ~~, ~guckerin** *die;* **~~, ~~nen** (*ugs. scherzh.: Astronom*) stargazer; **~hagel·voll** *Adj.* (*salopp*) paralytic (*Brit. coll.*); blotto (*coll.*); **~haufen** *der* (*Astron.*) star cluster; **~hell** *Adj.* (*geh.*) starlit; starry; **~himmel** *der* starry sky; **~jahr** *das* sidereal year; **~karte** *die* ⇒ **Himmelskarte**; **~klar** *Adj.* starlit, starry ‹sky, night›; **~kunde** *die* astronomy *no art.;* **~kundig** *Adj.* **~kundig sein** have a knowledge of astronomy; **~los** *Adj.* starless; **~marsch** *der* [protest] march (*with marchers converging from various starting points*); **~miere** /-mi:rə/ *die;* **~~, ~~n** (*Bot.*) starwort; **~schnuppe** *die;* **~~, ~~n** shooting star; **~stunde** *die* (*geh.*) great moment; **seine ~stunde haben** have one's moment *or* hour of glory; **~tag** *der* (*Astron.*) sidereal day; **~warte** *die* observatory; **~zeichen** *das* ⇒ **Tierkreiszeichen**; **~zeit** *die* sidereal time

**Sterz**[1] /ʃtɛrts/ *der;* **~es, ~e** (*südd., österr.: Speise*) (*boiled or fried*) dumpling pieces *pl.*

**Sterz**[2] *der;* **~es, ~e** (*Bürzel*) rump

**stet** /ʃte:t/ *Adj.* (*geh.*) Ⓐ constant ‹goodwill, devotion, companion›; steady ‹rhythm›; Ⓑ (*ständig*) constant; continous

**Stethoskop** /ʃteto'sko:p/ *das;* **~s, ~e** (*Med.*) stethoscope

**stetig** /'ʃte:tɪç/ ❶ *Adj.* steady ‹growth, increase, decline›; constant, continuous ‹movement, vibration›. ❷ *adv.* ‹grow, increase, drop› steadily; ‹move, vibrate› constantly, continuously

**Stetigkeit** *die;* **~** ⇒ **stetig**: steadiness; constancy; continuousness

**stets** /ʃte:ts/ *Adv.* always

**Steuer**[1] /'ʃtɔyɐ/ *das;* **~s, ~** (*von Fahrzeugen*) [steering] wheel; (*von Schiffen*) helm; **ins ~ greifen** grab the [steering] wheel; **sich ans** *od.* **hinters ~ setzen** get behind the wheel; **das ~ herumreißen** pull the [steering] wheel over hard; **das ~ übernehmen** take over the wheel *or* the driving; (*bei Schiffen, fig.*) take over the helm; **Trunkenheit am ~:** drunken driving; being drunk at the wheel; **das ~ fest in der Hand haben** (*fig.*) have one's hand firmly on the helm

**Steuer**[2] *die;* **~, ~n** Ⓐ tax; **~n zahlen** (*Lohn-/Einkommensteuer*) pay tax; **etw. von der ~ absetzen** set sth. off against tax; **etw. mit einer ~ belegen** impose a tax on sth.; Ⓑ (*ugs.: Behörde*) tax authorities *pl.*

**steuer-, Steuer-: ~aufkommen** *das* (*Steuerw.*) tax revenue; **~bar** *Adj.* controllable; **~behörde** *die* tax authorities *pl.;* **~berater** *der,* **~beraterin** *die* ▶ 159 (*Steuerw.*) tax consultant *or* adviser; **~bescheid** *der* (*Steuerw.*) tax assessment; **~bevollmächtigte** *der/die; adj. Dekl.* (*Steuerw.*) tax consultant *or* adviser; **~bord** *das od.* (*österr.*) *der* (*Seew., Flugw.*) starboard; **nach ~bord gehen** turn to starboard; **~bord[s]** *Adv.* (*Seew., Flugw.*) to starboard; **~erhöhung** *die* (*Steuerw.*) tax increase; **~erklärung** *die* (*Steuerw.*) tax return; **~ermäßigung** *die* (*Steuerw.*) tax relief; **~erstattung** *die* (*Steuerw.*) tax refund; **~fahnder** *der;* **~~s, ~~, ~fahnderin** *die;* **~~, ~~nen** tax investigator; **~fahndung** *die* (*Steuerw.*) tax investigation; **~flucht** *die* (*Steuerw.*) tax evasion (*by transferring capital out of the country or living abroad*); **~frau** *die* (*Rudern*) cox; **~frei** *Adj.* (*Steuerw.*) tax-free; free of tax *pred.;* **~freibetrag** *der* (*Steuerw.*) tax allowance; **~gelder** *Pl.* (*Steuerw.*) taxes; **~gerät** *das* Ⓐ (*Rundfunkt.*) receiver; Ⓑ (*Elektrot.*) control device *or* unit; **~gesetz** *das* (*Steuerw.*) tax law; **~hinterziehung** *die* (*Steuerw.*) tax evasion; **~klasse** *die* (*Steuerw.*) tax category (*dependent on marital status [and number of children]*); **~knüppel** *der* control column; joystick (*coll.*)

**steuerlich** ❶ *Adj.* tax ‹advantages, benefits, etc.›. ❷ *adv.* **~ absetzbar** tax-deductible

**steuer-, Steuer-: ~los** *Adj.* out of control; **~mann** *der; Pl.* **~leute** *od.* **~männer** Ⓐ (*Seew. veralt.*) helmsman; steersman; Ⓑ (*Seew.*) ⇒ **Bootsmann** B; Ⓒ (*Rudern*) cox; **Vierer mit/ohne ~mann** coxed/coxless fours; **Einer mit ~mann** coxed single; Ⓓ (*Elektrot.*) controller; **~marke** *die* revenue stamp; (*für Hunde*) licence disc; **~moral** *die* tax-payer honesty; attitude to paying tax

**steuern** ❶ *tr. V.* Ⓐ (*fahren*) steer; (*fliegen*) pilot, fly ‹aircraft›; fly ‹course›; Ⓑ (*Technik*) control; Ⓒ (*beeinflussen*) control, regulate ‹process, activity, price, etc.›; steer ‹discussion etc.›; influence ‹opinion etc.›. ❷ *itr. V.* Ⓐ (*im Fahrzeug*) be at the wheel; (*auf dem Schiff*) be at the helm; Ⓑ *mit sein* (*Kurs nehmen, ugs.: sich hinbewegen; auch fig.*) head; Ⓒ (*geh.: entgegenwirken*) **jmdm./einer Sache ~:** curb sb./remedy sth.

**steuer-, Steuer-: ~oase** *die* (*ugs.*) tax haven; **~pflicht** *die* (*Steuerw.*) liability to [pay] tax; **~pflichtig** *Adj.* (*Steuerw.*) ‹person› liable to [pay] tax; taxable ‹goods, assets, income, profits, etc.›; **~pflichtige** *der/die; adj. Dekl.* (*Steuerw.*) person liable to [pay] tax; **~progression** *die* progressive taxation; **~prüfer** *der,* **~prüferin** *die* ⇒ **Wirtschaftsprüfer**; **~pult** *das* (*Elektrot.*) ⇒ **Schaltpult**; **~rad** *das* Ⓐ ⇒ **Lenkrad**; Ⓑ (*Seew.*) [ship's] wheel; helm; **~recht** *das* tax law; **~rechtlich** *Adj.* (*Steuerw.*) under the tax laws *postpos.;* **~ruder** *das* (*Seew.*) rudder; **~satz** *der* (*Steuerw.*) tax rate; rate of tax; **~schraube** *die: in* **die ~schraube anziehen/überdrehen** (*ugs.*) squeeze the taxpayer/squeeze the taxpayer too hard (*coll.*); **~schuld** *die* (*Steuerw.*) tax[es] owing *no indef. art.;* (*Verpflichtung*) tax liability; **~senkung** *die* (*Steuerw.*) tax cut; reduction in taxation; **~system** *das* (*Technik*) ⇒ **Steuerung** A; **~tabelle** *die* (*Steuerw.*) ≈ tax table

**Steuerung** *die;* **~, ~en** Ⓐ (*System*) controls *pl.;* **die automatische ~** (*Flugw.*) the automatic pilot; the autopilot; Ⓑ ⇒ **steuern** 1 A, C, D: steering; piloting; flying; control; regulation; steering; influencing; **die ~ übernehmen** (*Flugw.*) take over the controls; Ⓒ ⇒ **Steuergerät** B

**Steuer-: ~verkürzung** *die* (*Steuerw.*) tax evasion; **~vorteil** *der* (*Steuerw.*) tax advantage; **~zahler** *der;* **~~s, ~~, ~zahlerin** *die;* **~~, ~~nen** taxpayer

**Steven** /'ʃte:vn̩/ *der;* **~s, ~** (*Vorder~*) stem; (*Achter~*) sternpost

**Steward** /'stju:ɐt/ *der;* **~s, ~s** ▶ 159 steward

**Stewardess, *Stewardeß** /'stju:ɐdɛs/ *die;* **~, Stewardessen** ▶ 159 stewardess

**StGB** *Abk.* **Strafgesetzbuch**

**stibitzen** /ʃti'bɪtsn̩/ *tr. V.* (*fam.*) pinch (*coll.*); swipe (*coll.*)

**stich** /ʃtɪç/ *Imperativ Sg. v.* **stechen**

**Stich** *der;* **~[e]s, ~e** Ⓐ (*mit einer Waffe*) stab; (*fig.: böse Bemerkung*) dig; gibe; Ⓑ (*Dornen~, Nadel~*) prick; (*von Wespe, Biene, Skorpion usw.*) sting; (*Mücken~ usw.*) bite; Ⓒ (*~wunde*) stab wound; Ⓓ (*beim Nähen*) stitch; Ⓔ (*Schmerz*) stabbing *or* shooting *or* sharp pain; **es gab mir einen ~ [ins Herz]** (*fig.*) I was cut to the quick; Ⓕ (*Kartenspiel*) trick; Ⓖ **jmdn. im ~ lassen** leave sb. in the lurch; **mein Gedächtnis hat mich im ~ gelassen** my memory has

S

failed me; **etw. im ~ lassen** abandon sth.; **~ halten** ‹argument, alibi, etc.› hold water; **H** (*Fechten*) hit; **I** (*bild. Kunst*) engraving; **J** (*Farbschimmer*) tinge; **ein ~ ins Blaue** a tinge of blue; **sie hat einen ~ ins Ordinäre** (*fig.*) she is a touch vulgar; **K** **einen [leichten] ~ haben** (*ugs.*) ‹food, drink› be off, have gone off; (*salopp*) ‹person› be nuts (*coll.*); be round the bend (*coll.*); **L** (*Kochk. landsch.*) **ein ~ Butter** a knob of butter

**Stichel** *der;* **~s, ~:** graver; burin

**Stichelei** *die;* **~, ~en** (*ugs. abwertend*) **A** (*Bemerkung*) dig; gibe; **B** **hör auf mit deiner ~:** stop getting at me/him *etc.* (*coll.*)

**sticheln** *itr. V.* **A** (*Anspielungen machen*) make snide remarks (*coll.*) **(gegen** about); **B** (*nähen*) sew; (*sticken*) embroider

**stich-, Stich-: ~fest** ⇒ **hiebfest; ~flamme** *die* tongue *or* jet of flame; **~|halten** (*österr.*) ⇒ **~** G; **~haltig,** (*österr.*) **~hältig** ❶ *Adj.* sound, valid ‹argument, reason›; valid ‹assertion, reply›; conclusive ‹evidence›; **dieses Argument ist nicht ~haltig** this argument doesn't hold water; ❷ *adv.* **etw. ~haltig begründen** back sth. with sound *or* valid reasons; **~haltigkeit** *die;* **~~,** (*österr.*) **~hältigkeit** *die;* **~~:** ⇒ **~haltig**: soundness; validity; conclusiveness; **~kampf** *der* (*Sport*) play-off **(um** for)

**Stichling** /ˈʃtɪçlɪŋ/ *der;* **~s, ~e** stickleback

**Stich-: ~probe** *die* [random] sample; (*bei Kontrollen*) spot check; **~säge** *die* compass saw

**stichst** /ʃtɪçst/ *2. Pers. Sg. Präsens v.* **stechen**

**Stich·straße** *die* cul-de-sac

**sticht** /ʃtɪçt/ *3. Pers. Sg. Präsens v.* **stechen**

**Stich-: ~tag** *der* set date; (*letzter Termin*) deadline; **~waffe** *die* stabbing weapon; **~wahl** *die* final *or* deciding ballot; run-off; **~wort** *das* **A** *Pl.* **~wörter** headword; (*in Registern*) entry; **B** *Pl.* **~~e** (*Theater*) cue; **C** *Pl.* **~~e** (*Äußerung*) cue **(zu** for); **D** *Pl.* **~~e** (*Gedächtnisstütze*) keyword; (*Notiz*) note; **~wort·verzeichnis** *das* [subject] index; **~wunde** *die* stab wound

**Stick·arbeit** *die* (*Handarb.*) piece of embroidery

**sticken** /ˈʃtɪkn̩/ ❶ *itr. V.* do embroidery. ❷ *tr. V.* embroider

**Sticker**[1] *der;* **~s, ~:** embroiderer

**Sticker**[2] /ˈstɪkɐ/ *der;* **~s, ~** (*Aufkleber*) sticker

**Stickerei** *die;* **~, ~en** (*Handarb.*) **A** (*Verzierung*) embroidery *no pl.;* embroidered pattern; **~en** embroidery *sing.;* **B** (*gestickte Arbeit*) piece of embroidery

**Stickerin** *die;* **~, ~nen** embroiderer; embroideress

**Stick·garn** *das* embroidery thread

**stickig** *Adj.* stuffy; stale ‹air›

**stick-, Stick-: ~luft** *die* stale air; **~muster** *das* (*Handarb.*) embroidery pattern; **~oxid, ~oxyd** *das* nitrogen oxide; **~rahmen** *der* embroidery frame; **~stoff** *der* nitrogen; **~stoff·haltig** *Adj.* nitrogenous; containing nitrogen *postpos.;* **~stoff·oxid, ~stoff·oxid** *das* (*Chemie*) nitrogen oxide

**stieben** /ˈʃtiːbn̩/ *unr.* (*auch regelm.*) *itr. V.* (*geh., veralt.*) **A** *auch mit sein* (*auseinander wirbeln*) ‹dust, snow› be thrown up in a cloud; ‹sparks› fly; ‹water› spray; **sie rannten davon, dass es nur so stiebte** you couldn't see them for dust; **B** *mit sein* **Schnee stiebt durch die Ritzen** snow blows through the cracks; **C** *mit sein* (*davoneilen*) dash; **nach allen Seiten ~:** scatter in all directions

**Stief·bruder** /ˈʃtiːf-/ *der* stepbrother; (*ugs.: Halbbruder*) half-brother

**Stiefel** /ˈʃtiːfl/ *der;* **~s, ~** **A** boot; **das sind zwei Paar ~** (*fig.*) they are totally different things; **er kann einen [tüchtigen** *od.* **gehörigen] ~ vertragen** (*ugs.*) he can really put away the beer (*coll.*); **B** **einen ~ zusammenreden/-schreiben** (*ugs. abwertend*) talk/write a lot of nonsense *or* a load of rubbish; **seinen** *od.* **den [alten] ~ weitermachen** (*ugs.*) carry on in the same old way

**Stiefelette** /ʃtiːfəˈlɛtə/ *die;* **~, ~n** ankle boot

**Stiefel·knecht** *der* bootjack

**stiefeln** *itr. V.; mit sein* (*ugs.*) stride

**Stiefel·schaft** *der* boot leg; leg of a/the boot

**stief-, Stief-: ~eltern** *Pl.* step-parents; **~geschwister** *Pl.* **A** stepbrother[s] and [step]sister[s]; (*ugs.: Halbgeschwister*) half-brother[s] and -sister[s]; **~kind** *das* stepchild; (*fig.*) poor relation (*fig.*); **sie ist ein ~kind des Glücks** (*geh.*) she's always having bad luck; **~mutter** *die; Pl.* **~mütter** stepmother; **~mütterchen** *das* (*Bot.*) pansy; **~mütterlich** ❶ *Adj.* poor, shabby ‹treatment›; ❷ *adv.* **~mütterlich behandeln** treat ‹person› poorly *or* shabbily; neglect ‹pet, flowers, doll, problem›; **~schwester** die stepsister; (*ugs.: Halbschwester*) half-sister; **~sohn** *der* stepson; **~tochter** *die* stepdaughter; **~vater** *der* stepfather

**stieg** /ʃtiːk/ *1. u. 3. Pers. Sg. Prät. v.* **steigen**

**Stiege**[1] *die;* **~, ~n** **A** (*Holztreppe*) [wooden] staircase; [wooden] stairs *pl.;* **B** (*südd., österr.: Treppe*) stairs *pl.;* steps *pl.;* **C** (*Kiste für Gemüse, Obst*) [wooden] box; (*größer*) [wooden] crate

**Stiege**[2] *die;* **~, ~n** (*nordd. veralt.*) score

**Stiegen·haus** *das* (*südd., österr.*) ⇒ **Treppenhaus**

**Stieglitz** /ˈʃtiːglɪts/ *der;* **~es, ~e** goldfinch

**stiehl** /ʃtiːl/ *Imperativ Sg. v.* **stehlen**

**stiehlst** *2. Pers. Sg. Präsens v.* **stehlen**

**stiehlt** *3. Pers. Sg. Präsens v.* **stehlen**

**stiekum** /ˈʃtiːkʊm/ *Adv.* (*ugs.*) secretly; on the quiet

**Stiel** /ʃtiːl/ *der;* **~[e]s, ~e** **A** (*Griff*) handle; (*Besen~*) [broom]stick; (*für Süßigkeiten*) stick; **ein Eis am ~:** an ice lolly (*Brit.*); a Popsicle (*Amer.* ®); **B** (*bei Gläsern*) stem; **C** (*bei Blumen*) stem; stalk; (*an Obst, Obstblüten usw.*) stalk

**Stiel-: ~auge** *das* stalked eye; **er machte** *od.* **bekam ~augen** (*ugs. scherzh.*) (*erstaunt*) his eyes nearly popped out of his head; he stared goggle-eyed; (*begehrlich*) his eyes stood out on stalks; **~kamm** *der* tail comb; **~stich** *der* (*Handarb.*) stem stitch

**stier** ❶ *Adj.* vacant. ❷ *adv.* vacantly

**Stier** /ʃtiːɐ̯/ *der;* **~[e]s, ~e** **A** bull; **brüllen wie ein ~:** bellow like a bull; **den ~ bei den Hörnern fassen** *od.* **packen** take the bull by the horns; **B** (*Astrol.*) Taurus; the Bull; **er/sie ist [ein] ~:** he/she is a Taurus *or* Taurean

**stieren** *itr. V.* stare [vacantly] **(auf** + *Akk.* at); **in die Luft** *od.* **vor sich hin ~:** stare [vacantly] into space

**Stier-: ~kampf** *der* bullfight; **~kämpfer** *der* bullfighter; **~nacken** *der* (*fig.*) bull neck

**Stiesel** /ˈʃtiːzl/ *der;* **~s, ~** (*ugs.: abwertend*) boor; churl

**stieß** /ʃtiːs/ *1. u. 3. Pers. Sg. Prät. v.* **stoßen**

**Stift**[1] /ʃtɪft/ *der;* **~[e]s, ~e** **A** (*aus Metall*) pin; (*aus Holz*) peg; **B** (*Blei~, Bunt~, Zeichen~*) pencil; (*Mal~*) crayon; (*Schreib~*) pen; **C** (*ugs.: Lehrling*) apprentice

**Stift**[2] *das;* **~[e]s, ~e** **A** (*christl. Kirche: Institution*) foundation; **B** (*österr.: Kloster*) monastery; **C** (*Schule*) seminary; (*für Mädchen*) convent [school]; **D** (*Altenheim*) home for elderly gentlewomen

**stiften** ❶ *tr. V.* **A** found, establish ‹monastery, hospital, prize, etc.›; endow ‹prize, professorship, scholarship›; (*als Spende*) donate, give **(für** to); **B** (*herbeiführen*) cause, create ‹unrest, confusion, strife, etc.›; bring about ‹peace, order, etc.›; arrange ‹marriage›. ❷ *in* **~ gehen** (*ugs.*) disappear; hop it (*coll.*); do a bunk (*coll.*)

***stiften|gehen** ⇒ **stiften** 2

**Stifter** *der;* **~s, ~:** founder; (*Spender*) donor

**Stifter·figur** *die* (*bild. Kunst*) likeness of the founder/donor

**Stifterin** *die;* **~, ~nen** ⇒ **Stifter**

**Stifts-: ~hütte** *die* (*jüd. Rel.*) tabernacle; **~kirche** *die* collegiate church

**Stiftung** *die;* **~, ~en** **A** (*Rechtsspr.*) foundation; endowment; **B** (*Anstalt*) foundation; **C** (*Spende*) donation (*Gen.* by); **D** (*das Spenden*) donation (*Gen.*, **von** of)

**Stift·zahn** *der* (*Zahnmed.*) post crown

**Stigma** /ˈstɪgma/ *das;* **~s, Stigmen** *od.* **~ta** (*auch fig., kath. Kirche*) stigma

**Stigmatisation** /stɪgmatizaˈtsi̯oːn/ *die;* **~, ~en** stigmatization

**stigmatisieren** *tr. V.* stigmatize

**Stigmen** ⇒ **Stigma**

**Stil** /ʃtiːl/ *der;* **~[e]s, ~e** **A** style; **einen flüssigen ~ schreiben** write in a flowing style; **das ist schlechter politischer ~:** that is bad form politically; **in dem ~ ging es weiter** (*ugs.*) it went on in that vein; **im großen** *od.* **in großem ~:** on a grand scale; **B** **alten/neuen ~s** according to the old *or* Julian calendar/new *or* Gregorian calendar

**-stil** *der* style of …; **Schreib~:** style of writing

**stil-, Stil-: ~bildend** *Adj.* that influences *or* shapes style *postpos., not pred.;* **~bildend wirken** influence *or* shape style; **~blüte** *die* howler (*coll.*); **~bruch** *der* inconsistency of style; **~ebene** *die* style level; **~echt** ❶ *Adj.* period *attrib.* ‹furniture›; ❷ *adv.* true to style; **~element** *das* stylistic element

**Stilett** /ʃtiˈlɛt/ *das;* **~s, ~e** stiletto

**Stil·gefühl** *das* sense of *or* feeling for style

**stilisieren** *tr. V.* stylize

**Stilisierung** *die;* **~, ~en** stylization

**Stilist** *der;* **~en, ~en** stylist

**Stilistik** *die;* **~, ~en** **A** (*Lehre*) stylistics *sing., no art.;* **B** (*Buch*) book on stylistics

**Stilistin** *die;* **~, ~nen** stylist

**stilistisch** ❶ *Adj.* stylistic. ❷ *adv.* stylistically

**Stil·kunde** *die* ⇒ **Stilistik** A, B

**still** /ʃtɪl/ ❶ *Adj.* **A** (*ruhig, leise*) quiet; (*ganz ohne Geräusche*) silent; still; quiet, peaceful ‹valley, area, etc.›; **sei ~!** be quiet!; **im Saal wurde es ~:** the hall went quiet; **um ihn ist es ~ geworden** (*fig.*) you don't hear much about him any more; **in ~em Gedenken** in loving memory; **B** (*reglos*) still; **~es [Mineral-/Tafel-]wasser** still [mineral/table] water; **C** (*ohne Aufregung, Hektik*) quiet ‹day, life›; quiet, calm ‹manner›; **in einer ~en Stunde** in a quiet moment; **D** (*nicht gesprächig*) quiet; ⇒ *auch* **Wasser** B; **E** (*wortlos*) silent ‹reproach, grief, etc.›; **F** (*heimlich*) secret; **im Stillen** in secret; **~e Reserven** (*Wirtsch.*) secret *or* hidden reserves; (*ugs.*) [secret] savings; **G** **der Stille Ozean** the Pacific [Ocean].
❷ *adv.* **A** (*ruhig, leise*) quietly; (*geräuschlos*) silently; **B** (*zurückhaltend*) quietly; **C** (*wortlos*) in silence

**Still-BH** *der* nursing bra

**Stille** *die;* **~** **A** (*Ruhe*) quiet; (*Geräuschlosigkeit*) silence; stillness; **in der ~ der Nacht** in the still of the night; **tiefe ~:** deep silence; **gefräßige ~** (*scherzh.*) silence of people too busy eating to talk; **B** (*Regungslosigkeit*) (*des Meeres*) calm[ness]; (*der Luft*) stillness; **C** **in aller ~ heiraten** have a quiet wedding; **die Beerdigung fand in aller ~ statt** it was a quiet funeral

***Stilleben** ⇒ **Stillleben**

***stillegen** ⇒ **stilllegen**

***Stillegung** ⇒ **Stilllegung**

**stillen** ❶ *tr. V.* **A** **ein Kind ~:** breastfeed a baby; **ich muss das Baby jetzt ~:** I must feed the baby *or* give the baby a feed now; **B** (*befriedigen*) satisfy ‹hunger, desire, curiosity›; quench ‹thirst›; still (*literary*) ‹hunger, thirst, desire›; **C** (*eindämmen*) stop ‹bleeding, tears, pain›; stanch ‹blood›. ❷ *itr. V.* breastfeed; **~de Mütter** nursing mothers

**Still·halte·abkommen** *das* (*Polit., Finanzw.*) moratorium; standstill agreement

**still|halten** *unr. itr. V.* **A** (*sich nicht bewegen*) keep *or* stay still; **B** (*nicht reagieren*) keep quiet

**still-, Still-: ~leben** *das* (*bild. Kunst*) still life; **~|legen** *tr. V.* close *or* shut down; close ‹railway line›; lay up ‹ship, vehicle, fleet› **eine ~gelegte Bahn** a disused railway; **~legung** *die;* **~~, ~~en** closure; shut-down; (*von Schiff, Fahrzeug, Flotte*) laying up; (*einer Eisenbahnstrecke*) closure

*old spelling (see note on page 1707)

S

**stil·los** ❶ *Adj.* Ⓐ (*ohne Stil*) lacking *or* without any definite *or* recognizable style *postpos.;* Ⓑ (*gegen den Stil*) in bad *or* poor style *postpos.;* lacking in style *postpos.;* styleless; **Wein aus Biergläsern zu trinken ist ~:** drinking wine out of beer glasses shows a lack of style. ❷ *adv.* Ⓐ (*ohne Stil*) without any definite *or* recognizable style; Ⓑ (*gegen den Stil*) in bad *or* poor style; stylelessly

**Stillosigkeit** *die;* ~, **~en** Ⓐ lack of any definite *or* recognizable style; Ⓑ ⇒ **stillos** B: bad *or* poor style; lack of style; stylelessness; Ⓒ (*stilloses Verhalten*) [piece of] styleless behaviour

**still-, Still-: ~schweigen** *das* Ⓐ (*Schweigen*) silence; **mit ~schweigen** in silence; Ⓑ (*Diskretion*) **~schweigen bewahren** maintain silence; keep silent; **~schweigend** ❶ *Adj.* Ⓐ (*wortlos*) silent; Ⓑ (*ohne Abmachung*) tacit ‹assumption, agreement›; ❷ *adv.* Ⓐ (*wortlos*) in silence; Ⓑ (*ohne Abmachung*) tacitly; **das Projekt wurde ~schweigend eingestellt** the project was quietly shelved; **~|sitzen** *unr. itr. V.* sit still; **~stand** *der* standstill; **den Motor/die Entzündung/den Zug/den Verkehr zum ~stand bringen** stop the engine/inflammation/train/bring the traffic to a standstill; **die Blutung ist zum ~stand gekommen** the bleeding has stopped; **~|stehen** *unr. itr. V.* Ⓐ ‹factory, machine› be *or* stand idle; ‹traffic› be at a standstill; ‹heart etc.› stop; **ihr Mundwerk steht nie ~** (*ugs.*) she never stops talking; **die Zeit schien ~zustehen** time seemed to stand still; Ⓑ (*Milit.*) stand at *or* to attention; **~gestanden!** attention!

**Stillung** *die;* ~ ⇒ **stillen** 1 B, C: satisfying; quenching; stilling (*literary*); stopping; stanching; relieving

**still·vergnügt** ❶ *Adj.* inwardly contented. ❷ *adv.* ‹listen, smile, etc.› with inner contentment

**Still·zeit** *die* lactation period

**stil-, Stil-: ~mittel** *das* stylistic device; **~möbel** *das* piece of period furniture; **französische ~;** French period furniture *sing.;* **~richtung** *die* style; **~voll** ❶ *Adj.* stylish; ❷ *adv.* stylishly

**stimm-, Stimm-: ~abgabe** *die* voting *no art.;* **zur ~abgabe erscheinen** come to vote *or* to cast one's vote; **~band** *das; Pl.* **~bänder** vocal cord; **~berechtigt** *Adj.* entitled to vote *postpos.;* **~bruch** *der:* **er ist im ~bruch** his voice is breaking; **~bürger** *der* (*schweiz.*) voter; elector

**Stimmchen** *das;* **~s, ~:** little *or* small voice

**Stimme** /ˈʃtɪmə/ *die;* ~, **~n** Ⓐ voice; **die ~ des Blutes** (*fig.*) the call of the blood; **der ~ der Vernunft folgen** (*fig.*) listen to the voice of reason; **der ~ des Herzens/Gewissens folgen** (*fig. geh.*) follow [the dictates of] one's heart/conscience; **mit stockender ~:** in a faltering voice; **mit halber ~ singen** sing at half-power; **gut/nicht bei ~ sein** be in good/bad voice; Ⓑ (*Meinung*) voice; **die ~n in der Presse waren kritisch** press opinion was critical; Ⓒ (*bei Wahlen, auch Stimmrecht*) vote

**stimmen** ❶ *itr. V.* Ⓐ (*zutreffen*) be right *or* correct; **stimmt es, dass ...?** is it true that ...?; **das kann unmöglich ~:** that can't possibly be right; **stimmts, oder hab ich Recht?** (*ugs. scherzh.*) am I not right?; Ⓑ (*in Ordnung sein*) ‹bill, invoice, etc.› be right *or* correct; **stimmt so** that's all right; keep the change; **hier stimmt etwas nicht** there's something wrong here; **bei ihm stimmt es** *od.* **etwas nicht** (*salopp*) there must be something wrong with him; Ⓒ (*seine Stimme geben*) vote; **mit Ja ~:** vote yes *or* in favour. ❷ *tr. V.* Ⓐ (*in eine Stimmung versetzen*) make; **das stimmt mich traurig** that makes me [feel] sad; **sentimental gestimmt sein** be feeling sentimental; Ⓑ (*Musik*) tune ‹instrument›; **eine Gitarre höher/tiefer ~:** raise/lower the pitch of a guitar

**Stimmen-: ~fang** *der* vote-catching *no art.;* **er ist auf ~fang** he is out to catch votes; **~gewinn** *der* gain in votes; **~gewirr** *das* babble of voices; **~gleichheit** *die* tied vote; tie; **bei ~gleichheit** in the event of a tied vote *or* a tie; **~kauf** *der* vote-buying *no art.;* buying votes *no art.;* **~mehrheit** *die* majority [of votes]

**Stimm·enthaltung** *die* abstention; **~ üben** abstain; **bei vier ~en angenommen** accepted with four abstentions

**Stimmen·verlust** *der* loss of votes; **~e erleiden** lose votes

**Stimm·gabel** *die* (*Musik*) tuning fork

**stimm·gewaltig** ❶ *Adj.* ‹singer etc.› with a strong *or* powerful voice; strong, powerful ‹bass, contralto, etc.›. ❷ *adv.* ‹sing, speak› with *or* in a strong *or* powerful voice

**stimmhaft** (*Sprachw.*) ❶ *Adj.* voiced. ❷ *adv.* **~ gesprochen werden** be voiced

**stimmig** *Adj.* harmonious; **die Argumentation ist [in sich** (*Dat.*)**] ~:** the argument is consistent

**Stimm·lage** *die* Ⓐ voice; Ⓑ (*Musik*) voice; register

**stimmlich** ❶ *Adj.* vocal. ❷ *adv.* vocally

**stimm-, Stimm-: ~los** (*Sprachw.*) ❶ *Adj.* voiceless; unvoiced; ❷ *adv.* **~los ausgesprochen werden** not be voiced; **~recht** *das* right to vote; **~um·fang** *der* vocal range

**Stimmung** *die;* ~, **~en** Ⓐ mood; **er ist in gereizter ~:** he is in a very touchy mood; **in ~ sein** be in a good mood; **in ~ kommen** get in the mood; liven up; **jmdn. in ~ bringen** liven sb. up; **jmdm. die ~ verderben** spoil sb.'s [good] mood; **nicht in der [rechten] ~ sein, etw. zu tun** not be in the [right] mood to do sth.; **~en unterworfen sein** be moody; **für gute ~ sorgen** ensure a good atmosphere; Ⓑ (*Atmosphäre*) atmosphere; Ⓒ (*öffentliche Meinung*) opinion; **~ für/gegen jmdn./etw. machen** stir up [public] opinion in favour of/against sb./sth.; Ⓓ (*Musik*) pitch

**stimmungs-, Stimmungs-: ~barometer** *das: in* **das ~barometer steht auf null** (*ugs.*) the mood is bleak; **~bild** *das:* **ein ~bild von dem Ball geben** report on the atmosphere at the ball; **~kanone** *die* (*ugs. scherzh.*) entertainer who is always the life and soul of the party; **~umschwung** *der* change of mood; **~voll** ❶ *Adj.* atmospheric; ❷ *adv.* ‹describe, light› atmospherically; ‹sing, recite› with great feeling

**Stimm-: ~vieh** *das* (*abwertend*) **für ihn sind die Wähler doch nur ~vieh** he sees voters as nothing more than a means of getting to power; **~zettel** *der* ballot paper

**Stimulans** /ˈstiːmulans/ *das;* ~, **Stimulanzien** *od.* **Stimulantia** /stimuˈlant̮si̯a/ (*auch fig.*) stimulant

**Stimuli** ⇒ **Stimulus**

**stimulieren** *tr. V.* stimulate

**Stimulus** /ˈstiːmulʊs/ *der;* ~, **Stimuli** (*Psych., fig.*) stimulus (**für** to)

**stink-, Stink-** (*salopp*) stinking (*sl.*) ‹drunk, mood›; terribly (*coll.*) ‹bourgeois, posh›

**Stink·bombe** *die* stink bomb

**Stinke·finger** *der* (*ugs.*) *middle finger pointing up as a gesture of abuse, contenmpt, etc.;* **jmdm. den ~ zeigen** give sb. a one-finger salute (*coll.*)

**stinken** /ˈʃtɪŋkn̩/ *unr. itr. V.* Ⓐ (*abwertend*) stink; pong (*coll.*); **nach etw. ~:** stink *or* reek of sth.; **es stinkt nach Chemikalien/faulen Eiern** there's a stink *or* reek *or* stench of chemicals/bad eggs; **nach Geld ~** (*fig. ugs.*) be stinking rich (*coll.*); **vor Faulheit/Selbstgerechtigkeit ~** (*fig. ugs.*) be bone idle (*coll.*)/appallingly self-righteous; Ⓑ (*ugs.: Schlechtes vermuten lassen*) **die Sache/es stinkt** it smells; it's fishy (*coll.*); Ⓒ (*salopp: missfallen*) **die Hausarbeit stinkt mir** I'm fed up to the back teeth with housework (*coll.*); **mir stinkts** I'm fed up to the back teeth (*sl.*)

**stink·faul** *Adj.* (*salopp abwertend*) bone idle (*coll.*)

**stinkig** *Adj.* (*salopp abwertend*) Ⓐ (*stinkend*) stinking; smelly; Ⓑ (*widerwärtig*) vile (*coll.*), stinking (*coll.*) ‹mood›; **du bist heute so ~** (*fig.*) you're in such a vile *or* stinking mood today

**stink-, Stink-: ~langweilig** (*ugs.*) ❶ *Adj.* deadly boring; ❷ *adv.* in a deadly boring way; **~morchel** *die* (*Bot.*) stinkhorn; **~normal** (*salopp*) ❶ *Adj.* dead (*coll.*) *or* boringly ordinary; ❷ *adv.* in a dead ordinary way (*coll.*); **~reich** *Adj.* (*salopp*) stinking rich (*coll.*); **~tier** *das* skunk; **~vornehm** *Adj.* (*salopp*) terribly posh (*coll.*); **~wut** *die* (*salopp*) towering rage; **eine ~wut [auf jmdn.] haben** be livid (*Brit. coll.*) *or* furious [with sb.]

**Stint** /ʃtɪnt/ *der;* **~[e]s, ~e** Ⓐ (*Fisch*) smelt; Ⓑ (*nordd.: Junge*) boy; lad

**Stipendiat** /ʃtipɛnˈdi̯aːt/ *der;* **~en, ~en, Stipendiatin** *die;* ~, **~nen** person receiving a scholarship/grant

**Stipendium** /ʃtiˈpɛndi̯ʊm/ *das;* **~s, Stipendien** (*als Auszeichnung*) scholarship; (*als finanzielle Unterstützung*) grant

**Stippe** *die;* ~, **~n** (*bes. nordd.*) [thick] gravy

**stippen** /ˈʃtɪpn̩/ *tr. V.* (*bes. nordd.*) dunk

**Stipp·visite** *die* (*ugs.*) flying visit

**stipulieren** /stipuˈliːrən/ *tr. V.* establish; lay down; (*als Bedingung*) stipulate

**stirb** /ʃtɪrp/ *Imperativ Sg. v.* **sterben**

**stirbst** *2. Pers. Sg. Präsens v.* **sterben**

**stirbt** *3. Pers. Sg. Präsens v.* **sterben**

**Stirn** /ˈʃtɪrn/ *die;* ~, **~en** ▶ 471 forehead; brow; **sich** (*Dat.*) **die Haare aus der ~ kämmen** comb one's hair from one's forehead; **jmdm./einer Sache die ~ bieten** (*fig.*) stand *or* face up to sb./sth.; **die ~ haben, etw. zu tun** (*fig.*) have the nerve *or* gall to do sth.; **jmdm. an** *od.* **auf der ~ geschrieben stehen** (*geh.*) be written in *or* all over sb.'s face

**Stirn-: ~band** *das; Pl.* **~bänder** headband; **~bein** *das* ▶ 471 (*Anat.*) frontal bone

**Stirne** *die;* ~, **~n** ⇒ **Stirn**

**Stirn-: ~falte** *die* wrinkle [on one's forehead]; **~höhle** *die* ▶ 471 (*Anat.*) frontal sinus; **~höhlen·vereiterung** *die* suppurative *or* purulent frontal sinusitis; **~locke** *die* quiff (*Brit.*); cowlick; **~rad** *das* (*Technik*) spur wheel; spur gear; **~runzeln** *das;* **~~s** frown; **mit ~runzeln** with a frown; **~seite** *die* front [side]

**stob** /ʃtoːp/ *1. u. 3. Pers. Sg. Prät. v.* **stieben**

**stöbern** /ʃtøːbɐn/ *itr. V.* (*ugs.*) rummage

**Stochastik** *die* stochastic theory

**stochastisch** *Adj.* stochastic

**stochern** /ˈʃtɔxɐn/ *itr. V.* poke; **sich** (*Dat.*) **in den Zähnen ~:** pick one's teeth; **mit dem Feuerhaken im Feuer ~:** poke the fire; **im Essen ~:** pick at one's food

**Stock**[1] /ʃtɔk/ *der;* **~[e]s, Stöcke** /ˈʃtœkə/ Ⓐ (*Ast, Spazier~*) stick; (*Zeige~*) pointer; stick; (*Takt~*) baton; **steif wie ein ~:** as stiff as a poker; **den ~ gebrauchen/zu spüren bekommen** use/get the stick *or* cane; **am ~ gehen** walk with a stick; (*ugs.: erschöpft sein*) be whacked (*Brit. coll.*) *or* dead beat; (*ugs.: finanzielle Schwierigkeiten haben*) be [completely] broke (*coll.*); Ⓑ (*Ski~*) pole; stick; Ⓒ (*Pflanze*) (*Rosen~*) [rose] bush; (*Reb~*) vine; Ⓓ (*Eishockey, Hockey, Rollhockey*) stick; Ⓔ (*veralt.: Baumstumpf*) stump [and roots]; **über ~ und Stein** over hedge and ditch

**Stock**[2] *der;* **~[e]s, ~** (*Etage*) floor; storey; **das Haus hat vier ~:** the house is four storeys high; **in welchem ~?** on which floor?; **im fünften ~:** on the fifth (*Brit.*) *or* (*Amer.*) sixth floor

**stock-: ~besoffen** *Adj.* (*derb*) pissed as a newt/as newts *pred.* (*sl.*); blind drunk; **~blind** *Adj.* (*ugs.*) as blind as a bat *pred.* (*coll.*); totally blind

**Stöckchen** /ˈʃtœkçən/ *das;* **~s, ~:** little stick

**stock·dunkel** *Adj.* (*ugs.*) pitch-dark

**Stöckel·ab·satz** *der* high *or* stiletto heel

**stöckeln** /ˈʃtœkl̩n/ *itr. V.; mit sein* (*ugs.*) totter [on high heels]

**Stöckel·schuh** *der* high- *or* stiletto-heeled shoe; **~e** high heels; high- *or* stiletto-heeled shoes

**stocken** *itr. V.* Ⓐ (*aussetzen, stillstehen*) **ihm stockte das Herz/der Puls** his heart/

S

pulse missed *or* skipped a beat; **ihm stockte der Atem** he caught his breath; **das Blut stockte ihm in den Adern** (*fig.*) the blood froze in his veins; **B** (*unterbrochen sein*) ‹traffic› be held up, come to a halt; ‹conversation, production› stop; ‹business› slacken *or* drop off; ‹journey› be interrupted; **die Antwort kam ~d** he/she gave a hesitant reply; **ins Stocken geraten** ‹traffic› be held up, come to a halt; ‹conversation, production› stop; ‹talks, negotiations, etc.› grind to a halt; **C** (*innehalten*) falter; **er sprach ein wenig ~d** he faltered a little; **D** *auch mit sein* (*bes. südd., österr., schweiz.: gerinnen*) ‹milk› curdle

**stock-, Stock-: ~ente** *die* mallard; **~finster** *Adj.* (*ugs.*) pitch-dark; **~fisch** *der* **A** stockfish; **B** (*ugs. abwertend: Mensch*) boring *or* dull old stick; **~fleck** *der* mildew *or* mould spot; **~fleckig** *Adj.* mildewed; mouldy

**stockig** *Adj.* **A** (*muffig*) musty ‹clothes, smell, etc.›; **B** (*stockfleckig*) mildewed; mouldy

**-stöckig** /ˈʃtœkɪç/ -storey *attr.;* -storeyed

**stock-, Stock-: ~konservativ** *Adj.* (*ugs.*) arch-conservative; **~nüchtern** *Adj.* (*ugs.*) stone-cold sober; **~sauer** *Adj.* (*salopp*) pissed off (*Brit. sl.*) (**auf** + *Akk.* with); **~schirm** *der* walking-length umbrella; **~schnupfen** *der* heavy cold; **~steif** (*ugs.*) ❶ *Adj.* extremely stiff ‹gait›; ❷ *adv.* extremely stiffly; as stiff as a poker; **~taub** *Adj.* (*ugs.*) stone deaf; as deaf as a post

**Stockung** *die;* ~, **~en** **A** (*Unterbrechung*) hold-up (+ *Gen.* in); **B** (*des Pulses, der Atmung*) stoppage

**Stockwerk** *das* floor; storey; **im dritten ~:** on the third (*Brit.*) *or* (*Amer.*) fourth floor; **ein Haus mit fünf ~en** a five-storey[ed] house

**Stoff** /ʃtɔf/ *der;* **~[e]s, ~e** **A** (*für Textilien*) material; fabric; **B** (*Materie*) substance; **C** (*Philos.*) matter; **D** (*Thema*) subject [matter]; **~ für einen Roman sammeln** collect material for a novel; **einen ~ in der Schule durchnehmen** do a subject at school; **E** (*Gesprächsthema*) topic; **viel ~ zum Nachdenken** much food for thought; **F** (*salopp: Alkohol*) booze (*coll.*); **G** (*salopp: Rauschgift*) stuff (*sl.*); dope (*sl.*)

**Stoff·druck** *der* textile printing

**Stoffel** /ˈʃtɔfl̩/ *der;* **~s,** ~ (*ugs. abwertend*) boor; churl

**stoffelig** *Adj.* (*ugs. abwertend*) boorish; churlish

**stofflich** *Adj.* **A** (*materiell*) material; **B** (*thematisch*) thematic ‹effect etc.›; **die ~e Fülle des Buches** the richness *or* breadth of the book's subject matter

**Stofflichkeit** *die;* **~:** materiality

**Stoff-: ~muster** *das* **A** (*Zeichnung*) pattern; **B** (*kleines Stück*) swatch; sample of material; **~puppe** *die* rag doll; **~rest** *der* remnant; **~wechsel** *der* metabolism; **~wechsel·krankheit** *die* ▶ **474** metabolic disease; **~wechsel·produkt** *das* product of metabolism

**stöhnen** /ˈʃtøːnən/ *itr. V.* moan; (*vor Schmerz*) groan

**Stoiker** /ˈʃtoːikɐ/ *der;* **~s,** ~, **Stoikerin** *die;* ~, **~nen** (*Philos.*) Stoic; (*fig.*) stoic

**stoisch** ❶ *Adj.* (*Philos.*) Stoic; (*fig.*) stoic. ❷ *adv.* stoically

**Stoizismus** *der;* ~ (*Philos.*) Stoicism *no art.;* (*fig.*) stoicism

**Stola** /ˈʃtoːla/ *die;* ~, **Stolen** **A** shawl; (*Pelz~*) stole; **B** (*bes. kath. Kirche*) stole

**Stolle** *die;* ~, **~n** (*bes. nordd.*) stollen

**Stollen** /ˈʃtɔlən/ *der;* **~s,** ~ **A** (*Kuchen*) Stollen; **B** (*unterirdischer Gang*) gallery; tunnel; **C** (*Bergbau*) gallery; **D** (*bei Sportschuhen*) stud; **E** (*beim Hufeisen*) calk; **F** (*Verslehre*) stollen (*in Meistergesang*)

**stolpern** /ˈʃtɔlpɐn/ *itr. V.; mit sein* **A** stumble; trip; **ins Stolpern kommen** stumble; trip; (*fig.*) lose one's thread; **über jmdn. ~** (*fig. ugs.*) bump *or* run into sb.; **ich bin über dieses Wort/diesen Satz gestolpert** (*fig.*) I was puzzled by that word/sentence; **B** (*fig.: straucheln*) come to grief, (*coll.*) come unstuck (**über** + *Akk.* over)

**Stolper·stein** *der* stumbling block; **jmdm. ~e in den Weg legen** put obstacles in sb.'s way

**stolz** /ʃtɔlts/ ❶ *Adj.* **A** proud (**auf** + *Akk.* of); **B** (*überheblich*) proud[-hearted]; **warum so ~?** don't you know me any more?; **C** (*imposant*) proud ‹building, castle, ship, etc.›; **D** (*ugs.: beträchtlich*) steep (*coll.*), hefty (*coll.*) ‹price›; tidy (*coll.*) ‹sum›; **~ wie ein Spanier** as proud as can be; **~ wie ein Pfau** as proud as a peacock. ❷ *adv.* proudly

**Stolz** *der;* **~es** **A** pride; **sie setzte ihren ganzen ~ daran** she made it a point of pride; **B** (*Freude über etw.*) pride (**auf** + *Akk.* in); **die Rosen sind sein ganzer ~:** his roses are his pride and joy

**stolzgeschwellt** /-gəʃvɛlt/ *Adj.* **mit ~er Brust** his/her breast swelling with pride

**stolzieren** *itr. V.; mit sein* strut

**stop** /stɔp/ *Interj.* stop; (*Verkehrsw.*) halt

***Stop** ⇒ **Stopp**

**Stopf·ei** *das* darning egg

**stopfen** /ˈʃtɔpfn̩/ ❶ *tr. V.* **A** darn ‹socks, coat, etc., hole›; **B** (*hineintun*) stuff; **jmdm./sich etwas in den Mund ~:** stuff sth. into sb.'s/one's mouth; **die ganze Familie ins Auto ~** (*ugs.*) cram the whole family into the car; **C** (*füllen*) stuff ‹cushion, quilt, etc.›; fill ‹pipe›; **der Saal war gestopft voll** (*fig. südd.*) the hall was cram-full; **D** (*ausfüllen, verschließen*) plug, stop [up] ‹hole, leak›; **jmdm. das Maul ~** (*salopp*) shut sb. up; **er hat fünf hungrige Mäuler zu ~** (*fig. ugs.*) he has five hungry mouths to feed; **E** (*mästen*) stuff, cram ‹poultry›.

❷ *itr. V.* **A** (*den Stuhlgang hemmen*) cause constipation; **B** (*ugs.: sehr sättigen*) be very filling

**Stopfen** *der;* **~s,** ~ (*bes. westmd.*) stopper; (*Korken*) cork

**Stopf-: ~garn** *das* darning cotton *or* thread; **~nadel** *die* darning needle

**Stopp** *der;* **~s, ~s** **A** (*das Anhalten*) stop; **ohne ~:** without stopping; **die Fahrer mussten zum ~ an die Boxen** the drivers had to make a pit stop; **B** (*Einstellung*) freeze (*Gen.* on); **C** ⇒ **Stopp·ball**

**Stopp·ball** *der* (*Badminton,* [*Tisch*]*tennis*) drop shot

**Stoppel**[1] /ˈʃtɔpl̩/ *die;* ~, **~n** (*auch Bart~*) piece of stubble; **~n** *Pl.* stubble *sing.*

**Stoppel**[2] *der;* **~s, ~[n]** (*österr.*) stopper; (*Korken*) cork

**Stoppel-: ~bart** *der* (*ugs.*) stubble; **~feld** *das* stubble field

**stoppelig** *Adj.* stubbly

**stoppen** ❶ *tr. V.* **A** stop; **den Ball ~** (*Fußball*) trap *or* stop the ball; **er war nicht mehr zu ~** (*fig.*) there was no stopping him; **B** time ‹athlete, run›; **ich habe 11 Sekunden/103 km/h gestoppt** I made the time 11 seconds/the speed 103 k.p.h. ❷ *itr. V.* stop; **der Angriff stoppte** (*fig.*) the attack got no further *or* fizzled out

**Stopper** *der;* **~s,** ~, **Stopperin** *die;* ~, **~nen** (*Fußball*) centre half; stopper

**Stopp·licht** *das; Pl.* **~er** stop light

**stopplig** *Adj.* ⇒ **stoppelig**

**Stopp-: ~schild** *das* stop sign; **~signal** *das* stop signal; signal to stop; **~straße** *die* side road; road with a stop sign/stop signs; **~uhr** *die* stopwatch

**Stöpsel** /ˈʃtœpsl̩/ *der;* **~s,** ~ **A** plug; (*einer Karaffe usw.*) stopper; **B** (*Elektrot.*) [jack] plug

**stöpseln** (*Fernspr.*) ❶ *tr. V.* **jmdm. eine Verbindung ~:** put sb. through (**nach** to). ❷ *itr. V.* operate the plugs

**Stör** /ʃtøːɐ̯/ *der;* **~s, ~e** sturgeon

**stör·an·fällig** *Adj.* susceptible to faults *postpos.;* liable to break down *postpos.;* (*fig.*) liable to break down *postpos.*

**Storch** /ʃtɔrç/ *der;* **~[e]s, Störche** /ˈʃtœrçə/ stork; **wie ein ~ im Salat gehen** walk clumsily and stiff-leggedly; **da brat mir einer einen ~** (*ugs.*) well, I'll be damned (*coll.*)

**Storchen·nest** *das* stork's nest

**Storch·schnabel** *der* **A** (*Pflanze*) cranesbill; **B** (*Zeichenhilfe*) pantograph

**Store** /ʃtoːɐ̯/ *der;* **~s, ~s** net curtain

**stören** ❶ *tr. V.* **A** (*behindern*) disturb; disrupt ‹court proceedings, lecture, church service, etc.›; **bitte lassen Sie sich nicht ~:** please don't let me disturb you; **jmdn. in seiner Ordnung ~:** upset sb.'s routine; **B** (*stark beeinträchtigen*) disturb ‹relation, security, law and order, peaceful atmosphere, etc.›; interfere with ‹transmitter, reception›; (*absichtlich*) jam ‹transmitter›; **ein gutes Verhältnis ~:** spoil a good relationship; **hier ist der Empfang oft gestört** there is often interference [with reception] here; **C** (*missfallen*) bother; **das stört mich nicht** I don't mind; that doesn't bother me; **das stört mich an ihr** that's what I don't like about her; **stört es Sie, wenn ich das Fenster aufmache?** do you mind *or* will it bother you if I open the window?

❷ *itr. V.* **A** **darf ich reinkommen, oder störe ich?** may I come in, or am I disturbing you?; **entschuldigen Sie bitte, dass** *od.* **wenn ich störe** I'm sorry to bother you; **bitte nicht ~!** [please] do not disturb; **wenn ich störe, müsst ihr es mir sagen!** if I'm in the way, you must tell me; **sein Verhalten/seine Anwesenheit empfinde ich als ~d** I find his behaviour/presence irritating *or* annoying; **der Lärm machte sich sehr ~d bemerkbar** the noise was very intrusive; **B** (*als Mangel empfunden werden*) spoil the effect; **C** (*Unruhe stiften*) make *or* cause trouble.

❸ *refl. V.* **sich an jmdm./etw. ~:** take exception to sb./sth.

**Störenfried** /ˈʃtøːrənfriːt/ *der;* **~[e]s, ~e** (*abwertend*) troublemaker

**Störer** *der;* **~s,** ~, **Störerin** *die;* ~, **~nen** troublemaker

**Stör-: ~faktor** *der* disruptive factor *or* influence; **~fall** *der* (*Technik*) fault

**stornieren** *tr. V.* **A** (*Finanzw., Kaufmannsspr.*) reverse ‹wrong entry›; **B** (*Kaufmannsspr.*) cancel ‹order, contract›

**Storno** /ˈʃtɔrno/ *der od. das;* **~s, Storni** (*Finanzw., Kaufmannsspr.*) reversal

**störrisch** /ˈʃtœrɪʃ/ ❶ *Adj.* stubborn; obstinate; refractory ‹child, horse›; unmanageable ‹hair›; **~ wie ein Esel** as stubborn as a mule. ❷ *adv.* stubbornly; obstinately

**Stör·sender** *der* jammer

**Störung** *die;* ~, **~en** **A** disturbance; (*einer Gerichtsverhandlung, Vorlesung, eines Gottesdienstes*) disruption; **bitte entschuldigen Sie die ~, aber ...** I'm sorry to bother you, but ...; **B** (*Beeinträchtigung*) disturbance; disruption; **eine technische ~:** a technical fault; **eine nervöse ~:** a nervous disorder; **atmosphärische ~** (*Met.*) atmospheric disturbance; (*Rundf.*) atmospherics *pl.*

**Story** /ˈstɔrɪ/ *die;* ~, **~s** story

**Stoß** /ʃtoːs/ *der;* **~es, Stöße** /ˈʃtøːsə/ **A** (*mit der Faust*) punch; (*mit dem Fuß*) kick; (*mit dem Kopf, den Hörnern*) butt; (*mit dem Ellbogen*) dig; **jmdm. einen kleinen ~ mit dem Ellenbogen geben** nudge sb.; give sb. a nudge; **die Fahrgäste spürten einen leichten ~:** the passengers felt a slight bump; **jmdm. einen ~ versetzen** (*fig.*) give sb. a jolt; **B** (*mit einer Waffe*) (*Stich*) thrust; (*Schlag*) blow; **C** (*beim Schwimmen, Rudern*) stroke; **D** (*Stapel*) pile; stack; **E** (*beim Kugel~en*) put; throw; **F** (*stoßartige Bewegung*) thrust; (*Atem~*) gasp; **G** (*Erd~*) tremor; **H** (*Technik*) joint; **I** (*Jägerspr.*) tail [feathers]

**Stoß-: ~band** *das; Pl.* **~bänder** edging tape; **~dämpfer** *der* (*Kfz-W.*) shock absorber

**Stößel** /ˈʃtøːsl̩/ *der;* **~s, ~:** pestle

**stoß·empfindlich** *Adj.* sensitive to shock *postpos.;* **meine Uhr ist nicht ~:** my watch is shockproof

**stoßen** ❶ *unr. tr. V.* **A** *auch itr.* (*mit der Faust*) punch; (*mit dem Fuß*) kick; (*mit dem Kopf, den Hörnern*) butt; (*mit dem Ellbogen*) dig; **jmdn.** *od.* **jmdm. in die Seite ~:** dig

*old spelling (see note on page 1707)

sb. in the ribs; (*leicht*) nudge sb. in the ribs; Ⓑ (*hineintreiben*) plunge, thrust ‹dagger, knife›; push ‹stick, pole›; **jmdm. ein Messer in die Rippen ~:** plunge *or* thrust a knife into sb.'s ribs; Ⓒ (*~d hervorbringen*) knock, bang ‹hole›; Ⓓ (*schleudern*) push; **den Ball mit dem Kopf ~:** head the ball; **die Kugel ~** (*beim Kugel~*) put the shot; (*beim Billard*) strike the ball; **jmdn. von der Leiter/aus dem Zug ~:** push sb. off the ladder/out of the train; **man muss ihn immer erst darauf ~** (*fig.*) he always has to have things pointed out to him; Ⓔ (*zer~*) pound ‹sugar, cinnamon, pepper›; Ⓕ (*ugs.: hinweisen*) **jmdm. etw. ~:** hammer sth. home to sb.; hammer sth. into sb.'s head.
❷ *unr. itr. V.* Ⓐ *mit sein* (*auftreffen*) bump (**gegen** into); **mit dem Kopf gegen etw. ~:** bump one's head on sth.; Ⓑ *mit sein* (*begegnen*) **auf jmdn. ~:** bump *or* run into sb.; Ⓒ *mit sein* (*entdecken*) **auf etw.** (*Akk.*) **~:** come upon *or* across sth.; **auf Erdöl ~:** strike oil; **auf Ablehnung ~** (*fig.*) meet with disapproval; Ⓓ *mit sein* **zu jmdm. ~** (*jmdn. treffen*) meet up with sb.; (*sich jmdm. anschließen*) join sb.; Ⓔ *mit sein* (*zuführen*) **auf etw.** (*Akk.*) **~** ‹path, road› lead [in]to sth.; Ⓕ (*grenzen*) **an etw.** (*Akk.*) **~** ‹room, property, etc.› be [right] next to sth.; Ⓖ *mit sein* (*Jägerspr.*) **auf etw.** (*Akk.*) **~** ‹bird› swoop down on sth.; Ⓗ (*veralt.: blasen*) **in die Trompete/ins Horn** *usw.* **~:** blow *or* sound the trumpet/horn *etc.*
❸ *unr. refl. V.* bump *or* knock oneself; **ich habe mich am Kopf ge~:** I bumped *or* banged my head; **sich** (*Dat.*) **den Kopf blutig ~:** bang one's head and cut it; **sich an etw.** (*Dat.*) **~** (*fig.*) object to *or* take exception to sth.

**stoß-, Stoß-: ~fest** *Adj.* shockproof ‹watch, container, etc.›; hard-wearing ‹fabric, wallpaper, etc.›; **~gebet** *das* quick prayer; **~kraft** *die* Ⓐ force of the impact; Ⓑ (*vorwärts drängende Kraft*) force and momentum; (*Milit.*) strike power; (*Sport*) striking power; **~seufzer** *der* heartfelt groan; **~stange** *die* bumper

**stößt** /ʃtø:st/ *3. Pers. Sg. Präsens v.* **stoßen**

**stoß-, Stoß-: ~trupp** *der* (*Milit.*) unit of shock troops; **~verkehr** *der* rush hour traffic; **~waffe** *die* thrust weapon; **~weise** *Adv.* Ⓐ (*ruckartig*) spasmodically; ‹breathe› spasmodically, jerkily; Ⓑ (*in Stapeln*) by the pile; in piles; **~zahn** *der* tusk

**Stotterer** *der;* **~s, ~, Stotterin** *die;* **~, ~nen** stutterer; stammerer

**stottern** /ˈʃtɔtɐn/ ❶ *itr. V.* stutter; stammer; **sie stottert stark** she has a strong *or* bad stutter *or* stammer; **ins Stottern kommen** *od.* **geraten** start stuttering *or* stammering; **der Motor stottert** (*fig.*) the engine is spluttering. ❷ *tr. V.* stutter [out]; stammer [out]

**Stövchen** /ˈʃtø:fçən/ *das;* **~s, ~:** [teapot *etc.*] warmer

**StPo** *Abk.* **Strafprozessordnung**

**Str.** *Abk.* **Straße** St./Rd.

**StR.** *Abk.* **Studienrat**

**stracks** /ʃtraks/ *Adv.* Ⓐ (*direkt*) straight; Ⓑ (*sofort*) straight away

**Stradivari** /stradiˈva:ri/ *die;* **~, ~[s]** Stradivarius

**straf-, Straf-: ~androhung** *die* threat of punishment; **~anstalt** *die* penal institution; prison; **~antrag** *der* Ⓐ (*des Klägers*) action; legal proceedings *pl.;* **~antrag stellen** bring an action; institute legal proceedings; Ⓑ (*des Staatsanwalts*) petition for a penalty *or* sentence; **~anzeige** *die* reporting of an offence; **[eine] ~anzeige erstatten** report an offence; **~arbeit** *die* imposition (*Brit.*); **~aufschub** *der* (*Rechtsw.*) **[bedingter] ~aufschub** [conditional] deferral of sentence; **~aussetzung** *die* suspension of sentence; **~bank** *die; Pl.* **~bänke** (*Eishockey, Handball*) penalty bench; **~bar** *Adj.* punishable; **das ist ~bar** that is a punishable offence; **sich ~bar machen** make oneself liable to prosecution

**Strafe** /ˈʃtra:fə/ *die;* **~, ~n** punishment; (*Rechtsspr.*) penalty; (*Freiheits~*) sentence; (*Geld~*) fine; **auf dieses Delikt steht eine hohe ~:** this offence carries a heavy penalty; **sie empfand die Arbeit als ~:** she found the work a real drag *or* (*coll.*) bind; **das ist bei ~ verboten/steht unter ~:** it is a punishable offence; **etw. unter ~ stellen** make sth. punishable; **die ~ folgt auf dem Fuße** punishment is swift to follow; **~ muss sein!** discipline is necessary; you'll/he'll *etc.* have to be punished; **das ist die ~ [dafür]** that's what you get; **das ist ja eine ~ Gottes!** it's a real pain [in the neck]; **es ist eine ~, mit ihm arbeiten zu müssen** it's a pain having to work with him; **zur ~:** as a punishment

**strafen** *tr. V.* punish; **ein ~der Blick** a reproachful look; **jmdn. ~d ansehen** give sb. a reproachful look; **jmdn. mit Verachtung ~:** treat sb. with contempt as a punishment; **er ist gestraft genug** (*fig.*) he has been punished enough; **Gott strafe mich, wenn ich lüge!** (*veralt.*) may God strike me down if I am lying; **mit ihm/dieser Arbeit sind wir gestraft** he/this work is a real pain; **das Schicksal hat ihn schwer gestraft** fate has been hard on him; ⇒ *auch* **Lüge**

**Straf-: ~entlassene** *der/die; adj. Dekl.* ex-convict; ex-prisoner; **~erlass, *~erlaß** *der* (*Rechtsw.*) remission [of a/the sentence]; **bedingter ~erlass** conditional remission; **~expedition** *die* punitive expedition

**straff** /ʃtraf/ ❶ *Adj.* Ⓐ (*fest, gespannt*) tight, taut ‹rope, lines, etc.›; firm ‹breasts, skin›; erect ‹posture, figure›; tight ‹rein[s]›; Ⓑ (*energisch*) tight ‹organization, planning, etc.›; strict ‹discipline, leadership, etc.›. ❷ *adv.* Ⓐ (*fest, gespannt*) **die Saiten sind ~ gespannt** the strings are tight; **[zu] ~ sitzen** ‹clothes› be [too] tight; **die Jacke ~ über die Schultern ziehen** pull one's jacket tightly round one's shoulders; **er zog die Zügel ~ an** he pulled the reins tight; **~ zurückgekämmtes Haar** hair combed back tightly; Ⓑ (*energisch*) tightly, strictly ‹organized, planned, etc.›

**straf·fällig** *Adj.* **~ werden** commit a criminal offence; **die Zahl der Straffälligen** the number of offenders; **~e Jugendliche** young offenders

**straffen** ❶ *tr. V.* Ⓐ (*spannen*) tighten; **diese Creme strafft die Haut** this cream firms the skin; **sich** (*Dat.*) **das Gesicht ~ lassen** have a facelift; **den Körper ~:** straighten oneself; draw oneself up; Ⓑ (*raffen*) tighten up ‹text, procedure, organization, etc.›. ❷ *refl. V.* ‹person› straighten oneself, draw oneself up; ‹rope etc.› tighten; ‹body, back› stiffen; ‹posture, bearing› straighten

**straf-, Straf-: ~frei** *Adj.* **jmdn. für ~frei erklären** declare sb. exempt from punishment; **~frei ausgehen** go unpunished; get off [scot-]free (*coll.*); **~freiheit** *die* exemption from punishment; **~gefangene** *der/die* prisoner; **~gericht** *das* (*fig.*) judgement; **ein ~gericht des Himmels** divine judgement; **ein grausames ~gericht abhalten** mete out cruel judgement; **~gesetz** *das* criminal *or* penal law; **~gesetz·buch** *das* criminal *or* penal code; **~justiz** *die* criminal *or* penal justice; **~kammer** *die* (*Rechtsw.*) criminal division (*of a district court*); **~kolonie** *die* penal colony; **~kompanie** *die* punishment battalion; **~lager** *das* penal camp

**sträflich** /ˈʃtrɛ:flɪç/ ❶ *Adj.* criminal. ❷ *adv.* criminally

**Sträfling** /ˈʃtrɛ:flɪŋ/ *der;* **~s, ~e** prisoner

**Sträflings·kleidung** *die* prison clothing; prison clothes *pl.*

**straf-, Straf-: ~los** *Adj.* unpunished; **~mandat** *das* [parking, speeding, *etc.*] ticket; **~maß** *das* sentence; **~minute** *die* Ⓐ (*bes. Eishockey, Handball*) minute of penalty time; **die drei ~minuten** the three-minute penalty *sing.;* Ⓑ (*Rennsport, Springreiten, Biathlon, usw.*) penalty minute; **~mündig** *Adj.* (*Rechtsw.*) of the age of criminal responsibility *postpos.;* **er ist noch nicht ~mündig** he is under the age of criminal responsibility; **~porto** *das* surcharge; **~predigt** *die* (*ugs.*) lecture; **jmdm. eine ~predigt halten** lecture sb.; **~prozess, *~prozeß** *der* criminal proceedings *pl.;* **~prozess·ordnung, *~prozeß·ordnung** *die* (*Rechtsw.*) code of criminal procedure; **~punkt** *der* (*Sport*) penalty point; **~raum** *der* (*bes. Fußball*) penalty area; **~recht** *das* criminal law; **~rechtlich** ❶ *Adj.* criminal *attrib.* ‹case, investigation, responsibility›; **~rechtliche Fragen/Probleme** questions/problems of criminal law; **im ~rechtlichen Sinne** according to criminal law; ❷ *adv.* under criminal law; **etw. ~rechtlich verfolgen** prosecute sth.; **~register** *das* criminal records *pl.;* **~richter** *der,* **~richterin** *die* (*Rechtsw.*) criminal judge; **~sache** *die* criminal case; **~stoß** *der* (*Fußball*) ⇒ **Elfmeter**; **~tat** *die* criminal offence; **~täter** *der,* **~täterin** *die* offender; **~verbüßung** *die* serving [of] one's sentence; **~verfahren** *das* criminal proceedings *pl.;* **~verfolgung** *die* (*Rechtsw.*) [criminal] prosecution; **~|versetzen** *tr. V. nur im Inf. u. Part. gebr.* transfer for disciplinary reasons; **~versetzung** *die* disciplinary transfer; **~verteidiger** *der,* **~verteidigerin** *die* defence lawyer *or* counsel; **~vollzug** *der* penal system; **~würdig** *Adj.* (*Rechtsw.*) punishable; **~zettel** *der* (*ugs.*) [parking, speeding, *etc.*] ticket

**Strahl** /ʃtra:l/ *der;* **~[e]s, ~en** Ⓐ (*Licht, fig.*) ray; (*von Scheinwerfern, Taschenlampen*) beam; **ein ~ fiel durch den Türspalt** a shaft of light came through the crack of the door; Ⓑ (*Flüssigkeit*) jet; **ein dünner ~ Wasser** a thin trickle of water; Ⓒ (*Math., Phys.*) ray

**Strahl·an·trieb** *der* (*Technik*) jet propulsion

**Strahle·mann** *der* (*ugs.*) man/boy with the smiling face

**strahlen** *itr. V.* Ⓐ shine; **ein ~d heller Morgen** a gloriously bright morning; **bei ~dem Wetter** in glorious sunny weather; **eine ~de Schönheit/Stimme** (*fig.*) a radiant beauty/marvellously pure voice; **~d weiß** sparkling white; Ⓑ (*glänzen*) sparkle; Ⓒ (*lächeln*) beam (**vor** + *Dat.* with); **er strahlte über das ganze Gesicht** he was beaming all over his face; Ⓓ (*Physik*) radiate; emit rays

**strahlen-, Strahlen-: ~behandlung** *die* (*Med.*) radiotherapy *no art.;* **~belastung** *die* radioactive contamination; **~biologie** *die* radiobiology *no art.;* **~bündel** *das* (*Optik, Math.*) pencil of rays; **~förmig** ❶ *Adj.* radial; ❷ *adv.* radially; **~pilz** *der* (*Biol.*) ray fungus; **~schutz** *der* radiation protection; **~therapie** *die* (*Med.*) radiotherapy *no art.;* **~tierchen** *das* radiolarian; **~unfall** *der* radiation accident

**Strahler** *der;* **~s, ~** Ⓐ radiator; Ⓑ (*Heiz~*) radiant heater

**strahlig** ❶ *Adj.* radial. ❷ *adv.* radially

**Strahl·triebwerk** *das* jet engine

**Strahlung** *die;* **~, ~en** radiation

**Strahlungs-: ~energie** *die* (*Physik*) radiant energy; **~gürtel** *der* (*Physik*) radiation belt; **~intensität** *die* (*Physik*) intensity of radiation

**Strähne** /ˈʃtrɛ:nə/ *die;* **~, ~n** Ⓐ (*Haare*) strand; **eine graue ~:** a grey streak; Ⓑ (*fig.: Zeitspanne*) streak

**strähnig** ❶ *Adj.* straggly ‹hair›. ❷ *adv.* in strands

**stramm** /ʃtram/ ❶ *Adj.* Ⓐ (*straff*) tight, taut ‹rope, line, etc.›; tight ‹clothes›; Ⓑ (*kräftig*) strapping ‹girl, boy›; sturdy ‹legs, body›; ⇒ *auch* **Max**; Ⓒ (*gerade*) upright, erect ‹posture, etc.›; **eine ~e Haltung einnehmen** stand to attention; Ⓓ (*energisch*) strict ‹discipline›; strict, staunch ‹Marxist, Catholic, etc.›; brisk ‹step›. ❷ *adv.* Ⓐ (*straff*) tightly; **die Hose saß ziemlich ~:** the trousers were rather tight; **der Gurt soll ~ am Körper anliegen** the belt is supposed to be tight; Ⓑ (*kräftig*) sturdily ‹built›; Ⓒ (*energisch*) ‹bring up› strictly; strictly, staunchly ‹Marxist, Catholic, etc.›; ‹hold out› resolutely; Ⓓ (*ugs.: zügig*) ‹work› hard; ‹walk, march› briskly; ‹drive› fast, hard

**stramm|stehen** *unr. itr. V.* stand to *or* at attention

S

**Strampel·höschen** *das*, **Strampel·hose** *die* rompers *pl.*; romper suit; playsuit

**strampeln** /ˈʃtrampl̩n/ *itr. V.* **A** ‹baby› kick [his/her feet] [and wave his/her arms about]; **B** *mit sein* (*ugs.*: *mit dem Rad*) pedal; **C** (*ugs.*: *sich sehr anstrengen*) sweat; struggle

**Strampler** *der*; **~s**, **~** ⇨ **Strampelhöschen**

**Strand** /ʃtrant/ *der*; **~[e]s**, **Strände** /ˈʃtrɛndə/ beach; (*geh. veralt.*: *Flussufer*) bank; strand; (*geh. veralt.*: *Seeufer*) shore; strand; **am ~:** on the beach; **an den ~ gehen** go to the beach; **auf ~ laufen** ‹ship› run aground; **ein Schiff auf ~ setzen** beach a ship

**Strand-:** **~bad** *das* bathing beach (*on river, lake*); **~burg** *die* sand den (*built as a windbreak*); **~café** *das* beach café; **~distel** *die* sea holly

**stranden** *itr. V.*; *mit sein* **A** (*festsitzen*) ‹ship› run aground; (*fig.*) be stranded; **B** (*geh.*: *scheitern*) fail

**Strand-:** **~gut** *das* flotsam and jetsam; **~haubitze** *die*: *in* **voll** *od.* **blau wie eine ~haubitze sein** (*ugs.*) be dead drunk; **~hotel** *das* beach hotel; **~kleid** *das* beach dress; **~korb** *der* basket chair; **~leben** *das* beach life; **~promenade** *die* promenade; **~räuber** *der*, **~räuberin** *die* wrecker; **~segeln** *das* (*Sport*) sand-yachting

**Strang** /ʃtraŋ/ *der*; **~[e]s**, **Stränge** /ˈʃtrɛŋə/ **A** (*Seil*) rope; **jmdn. zum Tod durch den ~ verurteilen** (*geh.*) sentence sb. to be hanged; **B** (*von Wolle, Garn usw.*) hank; skein; **C** (*Nerven~*, *Muskel~*, *Sehnen~*) cord; (*der DNS*) strand; **D** (*Leine*) trace; **über die Stränge schlagen** (*ugs.*) kick over the traces; ⇨ *auch* **reißen** 2 A; **ziehen** 2 A

**strangulieren** /ʃtraŋguˈliːrən/ *tr. V.* strangle

**Strapaze** /ʃtraˈpaːtsə/ *die*; **~**, **~n** strain *no pl.*; **sich von den ~n erholen** recover from the strain *sing.*

**strapaz·fähig** *Adj.* (*österr.*) ⇨ **strapazierfähig**

**strapazieren** **1** *tr. V.* be a strain on ‹person, nerves›; **die tägliche Rasur strapaziert die Haut** shaving daily is hard on the skin; **die Reise würde ihn zu sehr ~:** the journey would be too much [of a strain] for him; **jmds. Geduld ~** (*fig.*) tax sb.'s patience; **wir haben unsere Wanderschuhe/Wintermäntel stark strapaziert** we gave our walking shoes/winter coats a great deal of hard wear; **diese Ausrede ist schon zu oft strapaziert worden** (*fig.*) this excuse has been flogged to death.
**2** *refl. V.* strain *or* tax oneself

**strapazier·fähig** *Adj.* hard-wearing ‹clothes, shoes›; hard-wearing, durable ‹material›; sturdy ‹book›

**Strapazier·fähigkeit** *die* ⇨ **strapazierfähig**: hard-wearingness; durability; sturdiness

**strapaziös** /ʃtrapaˈtsi̯øːs/ *Adj.* wearing

**Straps** /ʃtraps/ *der*; **~es**, **~e** suspender

**Strass**, ***Straß** /ʃtras/ *der*; **~** *od.* **Strasses**, **Strasse** **A** (*Glasfluss*) paste; **B** (*Nachbildung aus ~*) paste gem

**Straßburg** /ˈʃtraːsbʊrk/ (*das*); **~s** ▶ **700** Strasbourg

**Sträßchen** /ˈʃtrɛːsçən/ *das*; **~s**, **~:** little *or* narrow street

**Straße** /ˈʃtraːsə/ *die*; **~**, **~n** ▶ **818** **A** (*in Ortschaften*) street; road; (*außerhalb*) road; (*fig. abwertend*: *Pöbel*) mob; rabble; **auf offener ~:** in [the middle of] the street; **man traut sich abends kaum noch auf die ~:** you hardly dare go out in the evenings any more; **Verkauf über die ~:** take away sales *pl.*; (*von alkoholischen Getränken*) off-licence sales *pl.*; **Jugendliche von der ~ holen** get young people off the streets; **der Mann auf der ~** (*fig.*) the man in the street; **mit jugendlichen Arbeitslosen/Prostituierten kann man hier die ~n pflastern** (*ugs.*) the place is full of young unemployed people/prostitutes (*coll.*); **jmdn. auf die ~ setzen** *od.* **werfen** (*ugs.*) (*aus einer Stellung*) sack sb. (*coll.*); give sb. the sack (*coll.*); (*aus einer Wohnung*) turn sb. out on to the street; **auf der ~ liegen** *od.* **sitzen** *od.* **stehen** (*ugs.*) (*arbeitslos sein*) be out of work; (*ohne Wohnung sein*) be on the streets; **auf die ~ gehen** (*ugs.*) (*demonstrieren*) take to the streets; (*der Prostitution nachgehen*) go on *or* walk the streets; **jmdn. auf die ~ schicken** (*ugs.*) send sb. out on the streets; **sich [nicht] dem Druck der ~ beugen** [not] bow to mob rule; **B** (*Meerenge*) strait[s *pl.*]; **die ~ von Gibraltar/Hormus** the Straits of Gibraltar/Strait of Hormuz

**Straßen-:** **~anzug** *der* lounge suit (*Brit.*); business suit (*Amer.*); **~bahn** *die* tram (*Brit.*); streetcar (*Amer.*); **~bahner** *der*; **~~s**, **~~**, **~bahnerin** *die*; **~~**, **~~nen** (*ugs.*) tramway employee (*Brit.*)

**Straßen·bahn-:** **~fahrer** *der*, **~fahrerin** *die* **A** (*Führer[in]*) tram driver (*Brit.*); **B** (*Benutzer[in]*) tram passenger (*Brit.*); **~halte·stelle** *die* tram stop (*Brit.*); **~linie** *die* tram route (*Brit.*); **die ~linie 24** the number 24 tram (*Brit.*); **~schaffner** *der*, **~schaffnerin** *die* tram conductor (*Brit.*); **~schiene** *die* tramline (*Brit.*); **~wagen** *der* tram[car] (*Brit.*)

**Straßen-:** **~bau** *der* road building *no art.*; road construction *no art.*; **~bekanntschaft** *die*: **sie ist nur eine ~bekanntschaft** she is just someone I talk to when I meet her in the street; **~beleuchtung** *die* street lighting; **~benutzungs·gebühr** *die* ⇨ **Maut**; **~bild** *das* street scene; **mehr und mehr gehörten Uniformen wieder zum ~bild** uniforms were increasingly seen in the streets again; **~café** *das* pavement café; street café; **~decke** *die* road surface; **~dorf** *das* street village; **~ecke** *die* street corner; **~fahrer** *der*, **~fahrerin** *die* (*Rennsport*) road racer; **~feger** *der* **A** ▶ **159** (*bes. nordd.*) road sweeper; **B** (*ugs. scherzh.*: *spannende Fernsehsendung*) programme/series which pulls a huge audience; **~fegerin** *die*; **~~**, **~~nen** ▶ **159** ⇨ **~feger** A; **~fest** *das* street party; **~glätte** *die* slippery road surface; **~graben** *der* ditch [at the side of the road]; **~händler** *der*, **~händlerin** *die* street trader; **~junge** *der* (*abwertend*) street urchin; **~kampf** *der* **A** street fight; street battle; **B** (*Taktik, Strategie*) streetfighting; **~kämpfer** *der*, **~kämpferin** *die* streetfighter; **~karte** *die* road map; **~kehrer** *der*; **~~s**, **~~**, **~kehrerin** *die*; **~~**, **~~nen** ▶ **159** (*bes. südd.*) ⇨ **~feger** A; **~kreuzer** *der* (*ugs. veralt.*) limousine; **~kreuzung** *die* crossroads *sing.*; **~lage** *die* roadholding *no indef. art.*; **eine gute ~lage haben** have good roadholding; hold the road well; **~lärm** *der* street noise; **~laterne** *die* street lamp; **~mädchen** *das* (*abwertend*) streetwalker; **~musikant** *der*, **~musikantin** *die* street musician; busker; **~name** *der* street name; name of a/the street; **~netz** *das* road network; **~rand** *der* roadside; side of the road; **~raub** *der* street robbery; (*gewalttätig*) mugging; **~räuber** *der*, **~räuberin** *die* street robber; (*gewalttätig*) mugger; **~reinigung** *die* street cleaning; **~rennen** *das* (*Rennsport*) road race; **~sammlung** *die* street collection; **~schild** *das* street name sign; **~schlacht** *die* street battle; **~schmutz** *der* (*auf der Straße*) dirt in the street/streets; (*von der Straße*) dirt from the street/streets; **~schuh** *der* walking shoe; **~seite** *die* side of the street/road; (*eines Gebäudes*) street side; **das Fenster ging zur ~seite** the window looked out on [to] the street/road; **~sperre** *die* roadblock; **~sperrung** *die* closing [off] of a/the street/road; **~staub** *der* dust of the street/road; **~theater** *das* **A** street theatre; **B** (*Ensemble*) street theatre group; **~tunnel** *der* road tunnel; **~überführung** *die* (*für Fußgänger*) footbridge; (*für Fahrzeuge*) road bridge; **~unterführung** *die* (*für Fußgänger*) subway; (*für Fahrzeuge*) underpass; **~verhältnisse** *Pl.* road conditions; **~verkauf** *der* **A** (*auf der Straße*) street trading; **B** (*über die Straße*) take away sales *pl.*; (*von alkoholischen Getränken*) off-licence sales *pl.*; **~verkäufer** *der*, **~verkäuferin** *die* street vendor; **~verkehr** *der* traffic; **im ~verkehr** in traffic; **~verkehrs·ordnung** *die* road traffic act; **~zoll** *der* ⇨ **Maut**; **~zug** *der* street; **~zustand** *der* road conditions *pl.*

**Stratege** /ʃtraˈteːgə/ *der*; **~n**, **~n** strategist

**Strategie** /ʃtrateˈgiː/ *die*; **~**, **~n** strategy

**Strategin** *die*; **~**, **~nen**

**strategisch** **1** *Adj.* strategic. **2** *adv.* strategically

**Strato·sphäre** /ʃtrato-/ *die* stratosphere

**Stratus** /ˈʃtraːtʊs/ *der*; **~**, **Strati** (*Met.*) stratus

**Stratus·wolke** *die* stratus cloud

**sträuben** /ˈʃtrɔybn̩/ **1** *tr. V.* ruffle [up] ‹feathers›; bristle ‹fur, hair›. **2** *refl. V.* **A** ‹hair, fur› bristle, stand on end; ‹feathers› become ruffled; **bei dieser Nachricht sträubten sich mir die Haare** the news made my hair stand on end; **B** (*sich widersetzen*) resist; **sich ~, etw. zu tun** resist doing sth.; **sie hat sich mit Händen und Füßen gegen die Versetzung gesträubt** she resisted the transfer with all her might; **die Feder sträubt sich, das zu schildern** (*fig. geh.*) one hesitates *or* is reluctant to put it on paper

**Strauch** /ʃtraux/ *der*; **~[e]s**, **Sträucher** /ˈʃtrɔyçɐ/ shrub

**Strauch·dieb** *der* (*veralt. abwertend*) footpad (*hist.*); **wie ein ~ aussehen** (*ugs.*) look like a tramp

**straucheln** /ˈʃtrauxl̩n/ *itr. V.*; *mit sein* (*geh.*) **A** (*stolpern*) stumble; **sein Fuß strauchelte** (*geh.*) he stumbled; **B** (*scheitern*) fail; **C** (*straffällig werden*) go astray

**Strauch·werk** *das* shrubbery; bushes *pl.*

**Strauß**[1] /ʃtrauːs/ *der*; **~es**, **Sträuße** /ˈʃtrɔysə/ bunch of flowers; (*bes. als Geschenk, zu offiziellem Anlass*) bouquet [of flowers]; (*von kleinen Blumen*) posy

**Strauß**[2] *der*; **~es**, **~e** (*Vogel*) ostrich; **wie der Vogel ~:** like an ostrich

**Strauß**[3] *der*; **~es**, **Sträuße** (*veralt.*) **A** (*Kampf*) battle; **B** (*Streit*) quarrel; **ich habe einen ~ mit dir auszufechten** I have a bone to pick with you

**Sträußchen** /ˈʃtrɔysçən/ *das*; **~s**, **~:** posy

**Straußen-:** **~ei** *das* ostrich egg; **~feder** *die* ostrich feather *or* plume

**Strauß·wirtschaft** *die*: (*bes. südd.*) [*temporarily opened*] *bar selling new wine when a bundle of twigs is displayed*

**Strebe** /ˈʃtreːbə/ *die*; **~**, **~n** brace; strut

**Strebe-:** **~balken** *der* shore; prop; **~bogen** *der* (*Archit.*) flying buttress

**streben** *itr. V.* **A** *mit sein* (*hinwollen*) make one's way briskly; **er strebte zur Tür** he made briskly for the door; **die Pflanzen ~ zum Licht** the plants reach up towards the light; **die Partei strebt an die Macht** the party is reaching out for power; **B** (*trachten*) strive (**nach** for); **danach ~, etw. zu tun** strive to do sth.; **das Streben nach Vollkommenheit** [the] striving for perfection; **C** (*abwertend*) ‹pupil› swot (*Brit. sl.*); cram

**Streben** *das*; **~s** striving (**nach** for); **sein ~ ist darauf gerichtet, die Zustände zu verbessern** his efforts are directed towards improving conditions

**Strebe·pfeiler** *der* (*Archit.*) buttress

**Streber** *der*; **~s**, **~** (*abwertend*) overambitious *or* pushing *or* (*coll.*) pushy person; (*in der Schule*) swot (*Brit. sl.*); cram

**streberhaft**, **streberisch** *Adj.* (*abwertend*) overambitious; pushing; pushy (*coll.*); **ein ~er Schüler** a swot (*Brit. sl.*); grind (*Amer. sl.*)

**Streberin** *die*; **~**, **~nen** ⇨ **Streber**

**Strebe·werk** *das* (*Archit.*) [system *sing.* of] buttresses *pl.*

**strebsam** *Adj.* ambitious and industrious

**Strebsamkeit** *die*; **~:** ambition and industriousness

*old spelling (see note on page 1707)

S

**Streck·bett** *das* (*Med.*) orthopaedic bed

**Strecke** /ˈʃtrɛkə/ *die;* ~, ~**n** [A] (*Weg*~) distance; **über weite** ~**n sah man kein einziges Dorf** for long distances there was not a single village to be seen; **das Land war über weite** ~**n überschwemmt** large parts of the countryside were flooded; **auf der** ~ **bleiben** (*ugs.*) fall by the wayside; [B] (*Abschnitt, Route*) route; (*Eisenbahn*~) line; **er fliegt diese** ~ **oft** he often flies this route; **der Zug hielt auf freier** *od.* **offener** ~: the train stopped between stations; [C] (*Sport*) distance; **viele Zuschauer waren an der** ~: there were a lot of spectators lining the route/track; **die Läufer gehen auf die** ~: the runners are setting off; [D] (*Geom.*) line segment; [E] (*Bergbau*) gallery; [F] (*Jägerspr.*) bag; kill; **ein Tier zur** ~ **bringen** bag *or* kill an animal; **jmdn. zur** ~ **bringen** (*fig.*) hunt sb. down

**strecken** ❶ *tr. V.* [A] (*gerade machen*) stretch ‹arms, legs›; **ein gebrochenes Bein** ~: straighten a broken leg; [B] (*dehnen*) stretch [out] ‹arms, legs, etc.›; **den Hals** ~: crane one's neck; [C] (*lehnen*) stick (*coll.*); **den Kopf aus dem Fenster** ~: stick one's head out of the window (*coll.*); [D] (*größer, länger, breiter machen*) stretch; hammer/roll out ‹metal›; [E] (*verdünnen*) thin down; [F] (*rationieren*) eke out ‹provisions, fuel, etc.›. ❷ *refl. V.* stretch out

**strecken-, Strecken-:** ~**abschnitt** *der* section; ~**arbeiter** *der,* ~**arbeiterin** *die* platelayer; track worker; ~**begehung** *die* track inspection; ~**führung** *die* routing; (*Strecke*) route; ~**netz** *das* route network; (*Eisenbahnw.*) rail network; ~**wärter** *der,* ~**wärterin** *die* track inspector; ~**weise** *Adv.* in places; (*fig.: zeitweise*) at times; **das Buch war** ~**weise langweilig** the book was boring in parts

**Strecker** *der;* ~**s,** ~ ▶ 471 (*Anat.*) extensor

**Streck-:** ~**muskel** *der* ▶ 471 (*Anat.*) extensor [muscle]; ~**verband** *der* (*Med.*) extension *or* traction bandage

**Streetball** /ˈstriːtbɔːl/ *der;* ~**s** streetball

**Streich** /ʃtraiç/ *der;* ~**[e]s,** ~**e** [A] (*geh.: Hieb*) blow; **jmdm. einen** ~ **versetzen** strike sb.; **auf einen** ~ (*veralt.*) at one blow; (*fig.*) at one fell swoop; at one go; [B] (*Schabernack*) trick; prank; **jmdm. einen** ~ **spielen** play a trick on sb.; **mein Gedächtnis hat mir wieder einen** ~ **gespielt** my memory has been playing tricks on me again

**Streichel·einheiten** *Pl.* (*ugs.*) share *sing.* of kindness and affection; (*bei Mitarbeitern*) share *sing.* of encouragement and appreciation

**streicheln** /ˈʃtraiçl̩n/ *tr.* (*auch itr.*) *V.* stroke; (*liebkosen*) stroke; caress; **einem Hund über den Rücken** ~: stroke a dog's back; **er streichelte ihr übers Haar** he stroked her hair

**streichen** ❶ *unr. tr. V.* [A] stroke; **die Geige** ~ (*geh.*) play the violin; ⇒ *auch* **gestrichen** 2, 3; [B] (*an*~) paint; **eine Wand grün/beige** *usw.* ~: paint a wall green/beige *etc.*; **„frisch gestrichen"** 'wet paint'; [C] (*wegstreifen*) sweep ‹crumbs etc.›; **sich** (*Dat.*) **das Haar aus der Stirn** ~: push *or* smooth the hair back from one's forehead; [D] (*drücken*) **Kitt in die Fugen** ~: press putty into the joints; **Tomaten durch ein Sieb** ~: rub *or* press tomatoes through a sieve; [E] (*auftragen*) spread ‹butter, jam, ointment, etc.›; [F] (*be*~) **ein Brötchen [mit Butter]/mit Honig** ~: butter a roll/spread honey on a roll; [G] (*aus*~, *tilgen*) delete; cross out; cancel ‹train, flight›; **jmdn. von der Liste** ~: cross sb. off the list; **Nichtzutreffendes bitte** ~! please delete as appropriate *or* applicable; **etw. aus seinem Gedächtnis** *od.* **seiner Erinnerung** ~: erase sth. from one's memory *or* mind; **einen Auftrag/Zuschuss** ~: cancel an order/a subsidy; [H] (*Rudern*) **die Riemen** ~: back water; [I] (*Seemannsspr. veralt.*) strike ‹sail›; ⇒ *auch* **Flagge**; **Segel**.
❷ *unr. itr. V.* [A] stroke; **jmdm. durch die Haare/über den Kopf** ~: run one's fingers through sb.'s hair/stroke sb.'s head; **er strich sich** (*Dat.*) **nachdenklich über den Bart** he stroked his beard thoughtfully; **mit der Hand über die Tischdecke** ~: smooth the tablecloth with one's hand; [B] (*an*~) paint; [C] *mit sein* (*umhergehen*) wander; [D] (*Geol.*) ‹stratum› strike; (*Geogr.*) ‹mountain range› stretch; [E] *mit sein* (*bes. Jägerspr.*) ‹bird› wing

**Streicher** *der;* ~**s,** ~, **Streicherin** *die;* ~, ~**nen** (*Musik*) string player; **die Streicher:** the strings

**streich·fähig** *Adj.* easy to spread *pred.*

**Streich·holz** *das* match; (*als Spielzeug*) matchstick; **eine Schachtel Streichhölzer** a box of matches

**Streichholz-:** ~**briefchen** *das* book of matches; ~**spiel** *das* game with matchsticks

**Streich-:** ~**instrument** *das* string[ed] instrument; ~**käse** *der* cheese spread; ~**orchester** *das* string orchestra; ~**quartett** *das* string quartet; ~**trio** *das* string trio

**Streichung** *die;* ~, ~**en** [A] (*Tilgung*) deletion; (*Kürzung*) cutting *no indef. art.*; ~**en vornehmen** make deletions/cuts; [B] (*gestrichene Stelle*) deletion; (*Kürzung*) cut

**Streich·wurst** *die* [soft] sausage for spreading; ≈ meat spread

**Streif** /ʃtraif/ *der;* ~**[e]s,** ~**e** (*geh.*) strip; (*Licht*~) shaft

**Streif·band** *das; Pl.* **Streifbänder** wrapper

**Streife** *die;* ~, ~**n** [A] (*Personen*) patrol; [B] (*Streifengang*) patrol; **auf** ~ **gehen/sein** go/be on patrol

**streifen** ❶ *tr. V.* [A] (*leicht berühren*) touch; brush [against]; ‹shot› graze; **jmdn. am Arm/an der Schulter** ~: touch sb. on the arm *or* brush against sb.'s arm/touch sb. on the shoulder; **mit dem Wagen das Garagentor** ~: scrape the garage door with the car; **ein Windhauch streifte ihre Wangen** (*geh.*) she felt a breath of wind on her cheeks; **jmdn. mit einem Blick** ~ (*fig.*) glance fleetingly at sb.; [B] (*kurz behandeln*) touch [up]on ‹problem, subject, etc.›; [C] **den Ring auf den/vom Finger** ~: slip the ring on/off one's finger; **die Ärmel nach oben** ~: pull/push up one's sleeves; **die Butter vom Messer** ~: wipe the butter off the knife; **sich** (*Dat.*) **die Kapuze/den Pullover über den Kopf** ~: pull the hood/slip the pullover over one's head; **sich die Strümpfe von den Beinen** ~: slip one's stockings off; **die Blätter von den Zweigen** ~: strip the leaves from the twigs; strip the twigs of leaves.
❷ *itr. V. mit sein* roam; **durch die Wälder** ~: roam the forests

**Streifen** *der;* ~**s,** ~ [A] (*Linie*) stripe; (*auf der Fahrbahn*) line; **ein heller** ~ **am Horizont** a streak of light on the horizon; **graue** ~ **im Haar haben** have grey streaks in one's hair; [B] (*Stück, Abschnitt*) strip; (*Speck*~) rasher; (*Tresse*) braid; [C] (*ugs.: Film*) film

**Streifen-:** ~**beamte** *der* policeman on patrol duty; ~**beamtin** *die* policewoman on patrol duty; ~**dienst** *der* patrol duty; ~**gang** *der* patrol; ~**muster** *das* striped pattern; **ein Hemd mit** ~**muster** a striped shirt; ~**wagen** *der* patrol car

**streifig** *Adj.* streaky

**Streif-:** ~**licht** *das; Pl.* ~~**er** streak of light; **ein** ~**licht auf etw.** (*Akk.*) **werfen** (*fig.*) highlight sth.; ~**schuss,** *~**schuß** *der* grazing shot; (*Wunde*) graze; ~**zug** *der* expedition; (*fig.*) expedition; journey; (*eines Tieres*) prowl

**Streik** /ʃtraik/ *der;* ~**[e]s,** ~**s** strike; **in den** ~ **treten** come out *or* go on strike; **den** ~ **ausrufen** call a strike; **jmdn. zum** ~ **aufrufen** call sb. out on strike; **mit** ~ **drohen** threaten to strike; threaten strike action; ⇒ *auch* **wild** 1 B

**Streik-:** ~**aufruf** *der* strike call; ~**brecher** *der,* ~**brecherin** *die* strike-breaker; blackleg (*derog.*); scab (*derog.*); ~**drohung** *die* strike threat; threat of strike action

**streiken** *itr. V.* [A] strike; be on strike; (*in den Streik treten*) come out *or* go on strike; strike; [B] (*ugs.: nicht mitmachen*) go on strike; [C] (*ugs.: nicht funktionieren*) pack up (*coll.*); **der Kühlschrank streikt** the fridge has packed up (*coll.*)

**Streikende** *der/die; adj. Dekl.* striker

**Streik-:** ~**front** *die* strike; **an der** ~**front** in the strike/strikes; ~**geld** *das* strike pay; ~**kasse** *die* strike fund; ~**leitung** *die* strike leadership; strike leaders *pl.*; ~**posten** *der* picket; ~**posten beziehen** picket; stand on the picket line; **vor einer Fabrik** ~**posten stehen** picket a factory; ~**recht** *das* right to strike

**Streit** /ʃtrait/ *der;* ~**[e]s** [A] quarrel; argument; (*Zank*) squabble; quarrel; (*Auseinandersetzung*) dispute; argument; ~ **anfangen** start a quarrel *or* an argument; **sie sind im** ~ **auseinander gegangen** they parted in disharmony; **er sucht immer** ~: he is always looking for an argument *or* a quarrel; **die beiden haben oft** ~: those two are always arguing *or* quarrelling *or* fighting; **ein** ~ **der Meinungen** a clash of opinions; **mit jmdm.** ~ **bekommen** get into an argument *or* a quarrel with sb.; **er hat ihn im** ~ **erschlagen** he beat him to death during a quarrel; **miteinander in** ~ **leben** be always at loggerheads with each other; **ein** ~ **um des Kaisers Bart** an argument over nothing; [B] (*veralt.: Kampf*) battle

**Streit·axt** *die* battleaxe

**streit·bar** *Adj.* (*geh.*) [A] pugnacious; [B] (*veralt.: tapfer*) brave; valiant

**streiten** ❶ *unr. itr., refl. V.* quarrel; argue; (*sich zanken*) squabble; quarrel; (*sich auseinander setzen*) argue; have an argument; **die Erben stritten [sich] um den Nachlass** the heirs argued *or* fought over *or* disputed the estate; **darüber lässt sich** ~: one can argue about that; that's a debatable point; **die** ~**den Parteien in einem Prozess** the litigants in a lawsuit; **die Streitenden** the quarrellers. ❷ *unr. itr. V.* (*geh.: kämpfen*) fight

**Streiter** *der;* ~**s,** ~ (*geh.: Kämpfer*) fighter (**für** for, **gegen** against); champion (**für** of)

**Streiterei** *die;* ~, ~**en** arguing *no pl.*, *no indef. art.*; (*Gezänk*) quarrelling *no pl.*; **bei ihnen gibt es immer** ~**en** they are always quarrelling

**Streiterin** *die;* ~, ~**nen** ⇒ **Streiter**

**Streit-:** ~**fall** *der* (*Rechtsw.*) case; (*Kontroverse*) dispute; conflict; **das ist ein** ~**fall** that is a disputed point; **im** ~**fall** in [the] case of dispute *or* conflict; ~**frage** *die* disputed question *or* issue; ~**gespräch** *das* debate; disputation; ~**hahn** *der; Pl.* ~**hähne** (*ugs., oft scherzh.*) quarreller; squabbler; (*fig.: Kampfhahn*) fighter; brawler; ~**hammel** *der* (*fam.*) quarreller

**streitig** *Adj.* [A] disputed ‹question, issue›; **jmdm. jmdn./etw.** ~ **machen** dispute sb.'s right to sb./sth.; [B] (*Rechtsw.*) disputed

**Streitigkeit** *die;* ~, ~**en** [A] quarrel; argument; [B] (*Streitfall*) dispute

**streit-, Streit-:** ~**kräfte** *Pl.* armed forces; ~**macht** *die* (*veralt.*) forces *pl.*; ~**punkt** *der* contentious issue; ~**roß** *das* (*veralt.*) ⇒ **Schlachtross**; ~**sache** *die* [A] dispute; [B] (*Rechtsw.*) ⇒ **Rechtsstreit**; ~**schrift** *die* polemical treatise; ~**sucht** *die* quarrelsomeness; ~**süchtig** *Adj.* quarrelsome; ~**wagen** *der* chariot; ~**wert** *der* amount in dispute

**streng** /ʃtrɛŋ/ ❶ *Adj.* [A] (*hart*) strict ‹teacher, parents, upbringing, principle›; severe ‹punishment›; stringent, strict ‹rule, regulation, etc.›; stringent ‹measure›; rigorous ‹examination, check, test, etc.›; stern ‹reprimand, look›; [B] (*strikt*) strict ‹order, punctuality, diet, instruction, Catholic›; absolute ‹discretion›; complete ‹rest›; ~ **gegen sich selbst sein** be strict with oneself; **im** ~**en Sinne** in the strict sense; [C] (*schnörkellos*) austere, severe ‹cut, collar, style, etc.›; severe ‹hairstyle›; **der** ~**e Aufbau eines Romans** the tight structure of a novel; [D] (*herb*) severe ‹face, features, etc.›; [E] (*durchdringend*) pungent, sharp ‹taste, smell›; **er riecht etwas** ~: he smells a bit strong; [F] (*rau*) severe ‹winter›; sharp, severe ‹frost›.
❷ *adv.* [A] (*hart*) ‹mark, judge, etc.› strictly, severely; ‹punish› severely; ‹look, reprimand›

S

sternly; ~ **durchgreifen** take rigorous action; **B** (*strikt*) strictly; ~ **verboten** strictly prohibited; ~ **genommen** strictly speaking; **C** (*schnörkellos*) **sie trug ein ~ geschnittenes Kostüm** she wore a severe suit; **D** (*durchdringend*) ‹smell› strongly

**Strenge** *die;* ~ **A** ⇒ **streng** A: strictness; severity; stringency; rigour; sternness; **jmdn. mit äußerster ~ bestrafen** punish sb. extremely severely; **B** (*Striktheit*) strictness; **C** (*von [Gesichts]zügen*) severity; **D** (*von Geruch, Geschmack*) pungency; sharpness; **ein Geruch von beißender ~:** a bitingly pungent smell; **E** ⇒ **streng** F.: severity; sharpness; **F** (*Schnörkellosigkeit*) austerity; severity

**streng-, Streng-:** ***~genommen** ⇒ **streng** 2B; **~gläubig** *Adj.* strict; **~gläubigkeit** *die* strict beliefs *pl.*

**strengstens** /ˈʃtrɛŋstn̩s/ *Adv.* [most] strictly

**Streptokokkus** /ʃtrɛptoˈkɔkʊs/ *der;* ~, **Streptokokken** streptococcus

**Strese·mann** *der: formal suit with dark jacket, grey waistcoat, and striped trousers*

**Stress**, ***Streß** /ʃtrɛs/ *der;* **Stresses, Stresse** stress; **im ~ sein** be under stress

**stressen** (*ugs.*) **1** *tr. V.* **jmdn. ~:** put sb. under stress; **vollkommen gestresst sein** be under an enormous amount of stress; **die gestressten Großstädter** the stressed city-dwellers. **2** *itr. V.* be stressful

**stressig** *Adj.* (*ugs.*) stressful

**Stress·situation**, ***Streß·situation** *die* stress situation

**Stretch** /ʃtrɛtʃ/ *der;* ~[e]s, ~es stretch fabric *or* material

**Streu** /ʃtrɔy/ *die;* ~, ~en straw

**Streu·büchse** *die* shaker; (*für Zucker*) shaker; castor; (*für Mehl*) dredger

**streuen** **1** *tr. V.* **A** spread ‹manure, sand, grit›; sprinkle ‹salt, herbs, etc.›; strew, scatter ‹flowers›; (*fig.*) spread ‹rumour›; **den Vögeln Futter ~:** scatter food for the birds; **weit gestreut** (*fig.*) scattered *or* spread over a wide area; **B** (*auch itr.*) (*mit Streugut*) **die Straßen [mit Sand/Salz] ~:** grit/salt the roads; put grit/salt down on the roads; **[den Weg] ~:** put grit/salt *etc.* down [on the path]. **2** *itr. V.* **A** (*beim Schießen*) scatter; **B** (*bes. Physik*) ‹particles, ions, etc.› scatter; **C** (*Med.*) spread

**Streu-:** **~fahrzeug** *das* gritter; gritting lorry; **~gut** *das* grit/salt (*for icy roads etc.*)

**streunen** *itr. V.; meist mit sein* (*oft abwertend*) wander *or* roam about *or* around; **~de Katzen/Hunde** stray cats/dogs; **durch die Straßen/Felder ~:** roam *or* wander the streets/across the fields

**Streuner** *der;* ~s, ~, **Streunerin** *die;* ~, ~nen (*abwertend*) tramp

**Streu-:** **~salz** *das* salt (*for icy roads etc.*); **~sand** *der* **A** grit (*for icy roads etc.*); **B** (*veralt.: zum Trocknen*) sand

**Streusel** *der od. das;* ~s, ~ *crumble [topping] made of butter, sugar, flour;* streusel

**Streusel·kuchen** *der* streusel cake

**Streuung** *die;* ~, ~en **A** (*Verbreitung*) dissemination; **B** (*Ballistik*) scattering; **C** (*Med.*) generalization; metastasis (*Med.*)

**Streu·zucker** *der* granulated sugar

**strich** /ʃtrɪç/ *1. u. 3. Pers. Sg. Prät. v.* **streichen**

**Strich** *der;* ~[e]s, ~e **A** (*Linie*) line; (*in einer Zeichnung*) stroke; line; (*Gedanken~*) dash; (*Schräg~*) diagonal; slash; (*Binde~, Trennungs~*) hyphen; (*Markierung*) mark; **beim Lesen ~e an den Rand machen** sideline passages when reading; **etw. mit groben** *od.* **in großen ~en zeichnen** *od.* (*fig.*) **umreißen** sketch sth. in broad strokes (*lit. or fig.*); **er ist nur noch ein ~ [in der Landschaft]** (*ugs.*) he's as thin as a rake; **keinen ~ tun** *od.* **machen** *od.* **arbeiten** not do a stroke *or* a thing; **jmdm. einen ~ durch die Rechnung/durch etw.** (*Akk.*) **machen** (*ugs.*) mess up *or* wreck sb.'s plans/mess up sb.'s plans for sth.; **dem werden wir einen ~ durch die Rechnung machen!** we'll put a stop to his little game; **einen ~ unter etw.** (*Akk.*) **machen** *od.* **ziehen** put sth. behind one; make a [clean] break with sth.; **unter dem ~:** at the end of the day; all things considered; **unter dem ~ sein** (*ugs.*) not be up to scratch; be below par; **B** (*Winkeleinheit*) point; **C der ~** (*salopp*) (*Prostitution*) [street] prostitution; streetwalking; (*Gegend*) the streetwalkers' patch; the red-light district; **auf den ~ gehen** walk the streets; **D** (*streichende Bewegung*) stroke; **E** (*Pinselführung*) strokes *pl.;* **van Goghs kräftiger ~:** van Gogh's powerful brush strokes *pl. or* brush; **F** (*Streichung*) deletion; **G** (*Bogen~*) bowing *no indef. art.;* **H** (*Haar~, Fell~*) lie; (*eines Teppichs*) pile; (*von Samt o. Ä.*) nap; **gegen den/mit dem ~ bürsten** brush ‹hair, fur› the wrong/right way; brush ‹carpet› against/with the pile; brush ‹velvet› against/with the nap; **jmdm. gegen den ~ gehen** (*ugs.*) go against the grain [with sb.]; **nach ~ und Faden** (*ugs.*) good and proper (*coll.*); well and truly; **jmdn. nach ~ und Faden belügen** (*ugs.*) lie through one's teeth to sb.; **I** (*bes. Jägerspr.*) (*Flug*) flight; (*Schwarm*) flock

**Strich·ätzung** *die* (*Druckw.*) line block *or* plate

**Strichelchen** *das;* ~s, ~: little line; (*dünn*) fine line

**stricheln** /ˈʃtrɪçl̩n/ *tr. V.* **A** (*zeichnen*) sketch in [with short lines]; **eine gestrichelte Linie** a broken line; **B** (*schraffieren*) hatch

**Strich-:** **~junge** *der* (*salopp*) [young] male prostitute; **~kode** *der* bar code

**strichlieren** (*österr.*) ⇒ **stricheln**

**strich-, Strich-:** **~mädchen** *das* (*salopp*) streetwalker; hooker (*Amer. sl.*); **~männchen** *das* matchstick man; **~punkt** *der* semicolon; **~vogel** *der* (*Zool.*) roving bird; **~weise** (*bes. Met.*) **1** *Adv.* ‹rain etc.› in places; **2** *adj.* in places *postpos.;* local; **~zeichnung** *die* line drawing

**Strick**[1] /ʃtrɪk/ *der;* ~[e]s, ~e **A** cord; (*Seil*) rope; **jmdm. aus etw. einen ~ drehen** (*fig.*) use sth. against sb.; **da kann ich mir ja gleich einen ~ nehmen** *od.* **kaufen!** I might as well end it all now; ⇒ *auch* **reißen** 2 A; **ziehen** 2 A; **B** (*fam.: Schlingel*) rascal

**Strick**[2] *das;* ~[e]s (*bes. Mode*) knitted material; **in lässigem ~:** knitted in casual style

**Strick-:** **~arbeit** *die* [piece of] knitting; **~bündchen** *das* knitted welt

**stricken** *tr., itr. V.* knit; **an etw.** (*Dat.*) **~:** be knitting sth.; **eine sauber gestrickte Story** (*fig.*) a neatly constructed story

**Strickerei** *die;* ~, ~en **A** (*Tätigkeit*) knitting; **B** (*Produkt*) piece of knitting

**Strickerin** *die;* ~, ~nen knitter

**Strick-:** **~jacke** *die* cardigan; **~kleid** *das* knitted dress; **~leiter** *die* rope ladder; **~maschine** *die* knitting machine; **~mode** *die* knitwear fashion; **~muster** *das* knitting pattern; (*fig.*) formula; **~nadel** *die* knitting needle; **~waren** *Pl.* knitwear *sing.;* **~zeug** *das* knitting

**Striegel** /ˈʃtriːgl̩/ *der;* ~s, ~: curry-comb

**striegeln** *tr. V.* groom ‹horse›; **gestriegelt und gebügelt** (*fig.*) all spruced up

**Strieme** /ˈʃtriːmə/ *die;* ~, ~n, **Striemen** *der;* ~ns, ~n weal

**Striezel** /ˈʃtriːtsl̩/ *der;* ~s, ~ (*bes. ostd.*) long plaited bun

**strikt** /ʃtrɪkt/ **1** *Adj.* strict; exact ‹opposite›. **2** *adv.* strictly; **ich bin ~ dagegen** I am totally opposed to it

**stringent** /ʃtrɪŋˈgɛnt/ (*geh.*) **1** *Adj.* compelling ‹conclusion, reasoning, proof, argument›. **2** *adv.* ‹prove, deduce› by compelling logic; ‹prove, argue› compellingly

**Stringenz** /ʃtrɪŋˈgɛnts/ *die;* ~ (*geh.*) compelling nature

**Strip** /ʃtrɪp/ *der;* ~s, ~s **A** (*~tease*) strip[-tease]; **B** (*Pflaster*) strip [of sticking plaster]

**Strippe** /ˈʃtrɪpə/ *die;* ~, ~n (*ugs.*) string; **an der ~ hängen** (*fig.*) be on the phone; (*dauernd*) hog the phone (*coll.*); **jmdn. an der ~ haben** (*fig.*) have sb. on the phone *or* line; **jmdn. an die ~ kriegen** (*fig.*) get sb. on the phone; **sich an die ~ hängen** (*fig.*) get on the phone

**strippen** *itr. V.* (*ugs.*) do striptease; strip

**Stripper** *der;* ~s, ~, **Stripperin** *die;* ~, ~nen ▶ 159 (*ugs.*) stripper

**Striptease** /ˈʃtrɪptiːs/ *der od. das;* ~: striptease

**Striptease·tänzerin** *die* ▶ 159 striptease dancer

**stritt** /ʃtrɪt/ *1. u. 3. Pers. Sg. Prät. v.* **streiten**

**strittig** *Adj.* contentious ‹point, problem›; disputed ‹territory›; ‹question› in dispute, at issue; **~ ist nur, ob ...** the only point at issue is whether ...

**Strizzi** /ˈʃtrɪtsi/ *der;* ~s, ~s (*bes. südd., österr.*) **A** (*Zuhälter*) pimp; **B** (*Strolch*) rascal

**Stroh** /ʃtroː/ *das;* ~[e]s straw; **mit ~ gedeckt** ‹roof, cottage› thatched with straw; **es brannte wie ~:** it went up like dry tinder; **~ im Kopf haben** (*ugs.*) have sawdust between one's ears (*coll.*)

**stroh-, Stroh-:** **~ballen** *der* bale of straw; straw bale; **~blond** *Adj.* flaxen-haired ‹person›; straw-coloured, flaxen ‹hair›; **~blume** *die* **A** (*Immortelle*) immortelle; everlasting [flower]; **B** (*Korbblütler*) strawflower; **~dach** *das* roof thatched with straw; **~dumm** *Adj.* (*ugs.*) witless (*coll.*); thick-headed; **~feuer** *das:* **wie ein ~feuer aufflammen** flare up briefly; **das war nur ein ~feuer** (*fig.*) it was just a flash in the pan; **~frau** *die* (*fig.*) front woman; **~gedeckt** *Adj.* ‹roof, house› thatched with straw; **~gelb** *Adj.* straw-coloured; flaxen ‹hair›; **~halm** *der* straw; **sich [wie ein Ertrinkender] an einen ~halm klammern** (*fig.*) grasp at a straw [like a drowning man]; **der letzte ~halm** (*fig.*) the last ray of hope; **nach einem/jedem ~halm greifen** (*fig.*) clutch at a/any straw; **~hut** *der* straw hat

**strohig** *Adj.* strawy; **eine ~e Apfelsine** a dried-up orange; **~ sein/werden/schmecken** be/become/taste like straw

**stroh-, Stroh-:** **~kopf** *der* (*ugs. abwertend*) thickhead; **~mann** *der* (*fig.*) front man; **~puppe** *die* straw doll; **~sack** *der* palliasse; **[ach du] heiliger ~sack!** (*ugs.*) jeepers creepers! (*coll.*); goodness gracious [me]!; **~witwe** *die* (*ugs. scherzh.*) grass widow; **~witwer** *der* (*ugs. scherzh.*) grass widower

**Strolch** /ʃtrɔlç/ *der;* ~[e]s, ~e **A** (*veralt.*) ruffian; **B** (*fam. scherzh.: Junge*) rascal

**strolchen** *itr. V.; mit sein* roam *or* wander [aimlessly] about; **durch die Straßen ~:** roam the streets

**Strom** /ʃtroːm/ *der;* ~[e]s, **Ströme** /ˈʃtrøːmə/ **A** ▶ 306 river; (*von Blut, Schweiß, Wasser, fig.: Erinnerungen, Menschen, Autos usw.*) stream; (*große Menge*) torrent; (*fig.: von Tränen*) flood; **ein reißender ~:** a raging torrent; **in Strömen regnen** *od.* (*ugs.*) **gießen** pour with rain; **in Strömen fließen** (*fig.*) flow freely; **das Blut floss in Strömen** (*fig.*) there was heavy bloodshed; **B** (*Strömung*) current; **mit dem/gegen den ~ schwimmen** (*fig.*) swim with/against the tide (*fig.*); **C** (*Elektrizität*) current; (*~versorgung*) electricity; **das Kabel führt** *od.* **steht unter ~:** the cable is live; **ein ~ führendes Kabel** a live cable; **jmdm. den ~ sperren** *od.* **abstellen** cut off sb.'s electricity supply; **mit ~ betrieben sein** run on electricity; be electric; **der ~ ist ausgefallen** there has been a power failure

**strom-, Strom-:** **~ab** *Adv.* downstream; **~abnehmer** /ˈ----/ *der* (*Technik*) current collector; **~abwärts** *Adv.* downstream; **~auf[wärts]** *Adv.* upstream; **~ausfall** /ˈ---/ *der* power failure

**strömen** /ˈʃtrøːmən/ *itr. V.; mit sein* stream; (*intensiv*) pour; (*fließen*) flow; **~der Regen** pouring rain

**Stromer** *der;* ~s, ~, **Stromerin** *die;* ~, ~nen (*ugs.*) vagabond; roamer

**stromern** *itr. V.; mit Richtungsangabe mit sein* (*ugs.*) roam *or* wander around; **durch die Gegend/Stadt ~:** roam *or* wander around the place/through the town

---

*old spelling (see note on page 1707)

**strom-, Strom-:** *~**führend** ⇒ Strom c; ~**kreis** *der* [electric] circuit; ~**leitung** *die* power line *or* cable; ~**linien·form** *die* streamlined shape; streamlining *no indef. art.;* ~**linien·förmig** *Adj.* streamlined; ~**netz** *das* electricity supply; mains [network]; ~**rechnung** *die* electricity bill; ~**schlag** *der* electric shock; ~**schnelle** *die* rapids *pl.;* ~**stärke** *die* current strength; ~**stoß** *der* electric shock

**Strömung** *die;* ~, ~**en** Ⓐ ▶306 current; (*Met.*) airstream; Ⓑ (*fig.*) (*Bewegung*) movement; (*Tendenz*) trend

**Strom-:** ~**verbrauch** *der* electricity consumption; ~**verbraucher** *der* (*Technik*) current-consuming device; ~**versorgung** *die* electricity *or* power supply; ~**zähler** *der* electricity meter

**Strontium** /ˈʃtrɔntsi̯ʊm/ *das;* ~**s** strontium

**Strophe** /ˈʃtroːfə/ *die;* ~, ~**n** verse; (*einer Ode*) strophe

**Strophen·form** *die* Ⓐ verse form; Ⓑ (*strophische Form*) strophic form

**-strophig** *adj.* **drei~ sein** have three verses; **ein mehr~es/drei~es Lied** a song with several verses/a three-verse song

**strophisch** ❶ *Adj.* strophic. ❷ *adv.* ~ **gestaltet/gebaut** in strophic form

**strotzen** /ˈʃtrɔtsn̩/ *itr. V.* **von** *od.* **vor etw.** (*Dat.*) ~: be full of sth.; **von** *od.* **vor Kraft/Gesundheit** ~: be bursting with strength/health

**strubbelig** /ˈʃtrʊb(ə)lɪç/ *Adj.* tousled; **du bist ja so ~!** your hair is in such a mess

**Strubbel·kopf** *der* (*ugs.*) Ⓐ mop *or* shock of [tousled] hair; Ⓑ (*Mensch*) tousle-head

**strubblig** ⇒ **strubbelig**

**Strudel** /ˈʃtruːdl̩/ *der;* ~**s**, ~ Ⓐ whirlpool; (*kleiner*) eddy; **der ~ der Ereignisse** (*fig.*) the whirl of events; Ⓑ (*bes. südd., österr.: Gebäck*) strudel

**strudeln** *itr. V.* ‹water› eddy, swirl

**Struktur** /ʃtrʊkˈtuːɐ̯/ *die;* ~, ~**en** Ⓐ structure; Ⓑ (*von Stoffen usw.*) texture

**Strukturalismus** /ʃtrʊkturaˈlɪsmʊs/ *der;* ~: structuralism *no art.*

**strukturalistisch** ❶ *Adj.* structuralist. ❷ *adv.* structuralistically

**Struktur·analyse** *die* structural analysis

**strukturell** /ʃtrʊktuˈrɛl/ ❶ *Adj.* structural. ❷ *adv.* structurally

**Struktur·formel** *die* (*Chemie*) structural formula

**strukturieren** *tr. V.* structure; **neu ~:** restructure

**Strukturierung** *die;* ~, ~**en** Ⓐ structuring; organization; Ⓑ (*Struktur*) structure

**struktur-, Struktur-:** ~**politik** *die* economic development policy; structural policy; ~**schwach** *Adj.* (*Wirtsch.*) economically underdeveloped; ~**wandel** *der* structural change

**Strumpf** /ʃtrʊmpf/ *der;* ~[**e**]**s, Strümpfe** /ˈʃtrʏmpfə/ stocking; (*Socke, Knie~*) sock; **lange Strümpfe** stockings; **auf Strümpfen** in stockinged feet/in one's socks

**Strumpf·band** *das; Pl.* **Strumpfbänder** garter; (*Straps*) suspender (*Brit.*); garter (*Amer.*)

**Strümpfchen** /ˈʃtrʏmpfçən/ *das;* ~**s**, ~: little stocking; (*Socke, Kniestrumpf*) little sock

**Strumpf-:** ~**halter** *der* suspender (*Brit.*); garter (*Amer.*); ~**hose** *die* tights *pl.* (*Brit.*); pantyhose (*esp. Amer.*); **eine ~hose** a pair of tights (*Brit.*); ~**maske** *die* stocking mask

**Strunk** /ʃtrʊŋk/ *der;* ~[**e**]**s, Strünke** /ˈʃtrʏŋkə/ stem; stalk; (*Baum~*) stump

**struppig** /ˈʃtrʊpɪç/ *Adj.* shaggy ‹coat, dog, beard›; tangled, tousled ‹hair›

**Struwwel·peter** /ˈʃtrʊvl̩-/ *der* tousle-head

**Strychnin** /ʃtrʏçˈniːn/ *das;* ~**s** strychnine

**Stübchen** /ˈʃtyːpçən/ *das;* ~**s**, ~: [little] room

**Stube** /ˈʃtuːbə/ *die;* ~, ~**n** Ⓐ (*veralt.: Wohnraum*) [living] room; parlour (*dated*); **in der ~ hocken** (*ugs.*) sit around indoors; **die gute ~:** the front room *or* (*dated*) parlour; **immer rein in die gute ~!** (*ugs.*) come on in!; Ⓑ (*Milit.*) [barrack] room

**stuben-, Stuben-:** ~**älteste** *der/die; adj. Dekl.* (*Milit.*) senior man/woman in a/the barrack room; ~**arrest** *der* (*ugs.*) detention (*in one's room*); **[zwei Tage] ~arrest bekommen** be kept in [for two days]; ~**fliege** *die* [common] housefly; ~**hocker** *der* (*ugs. abwertend*) stay-at-home; ~**hockerei** *die;* ~~ (*ugs. abwertend*) sticking (*coll.*) *or* sitting around indoors *no art.;* ~**hockerin** *die;* ~~, ~~**nen** ⇒ ~hocker; ~**kamerad** *der,* ~**kameradin** *die* room-mate; ~**rein** *Adj.* Ⓐ house-trained; Ⓑ (*scherzh.: nicht zotig*) clean ‹joke etc.›; ~**wagen** *der* bassinet; wicker cot

**Stuck** /ʃtʊk/ *der;* ~[**e**]**s** stucco

**Stück** /ʃtʏk/ *das;* ~[**e**]**s**, ~**e** Ⓐ piece; (*kleines*) bit; (*Teil, Abschnitt*) part; **ein ~ Kuchen** a piece *or* slice of cake; **ein ~ Zucker/Seife** a piece *or* lump of sugar/ a piece *or* bar of soap; **ein ~ [Weg** *od.* (*geh.*) **Weges]** a little [way]; a short distance; **ein ~ spazieren gehen** go for a little walk; **ein [gutes] ~ weiterkommen** get a [good] bit further; **ein ~ Autobahn** a section *or* stretch of motorway (*Brit.*) *or* (*Amer.*) freeway; **jmdn. wie ein ~ Dreck/Mist behandeln** (*ugs. abwertend*) treat sb. like dirt; **ein ~ Heimat** a bit of home; **ein gewaltiges/hartes ~ Arbeit** a really big/tough job; **ein ~ Hoffnung/Wahrheit** a ray of hope/a grain of truth; **alles in ~e schlagen** smash everything [to pieces]; **es ist nur ein ~ Papier** it's only a scrap of paper; **sich für jmdn. in ~e reißen lassen** (*ugs.*) do anything for sb.; **im** *od.* **am ~:** unsliced ‹sausage, cheese, etc.›; **aus einem ~ gemeißelt** carved from the solid; **in einem ~** (*ugs.*) ‹talk, rain› non-stop; Ⓑ (*Einzel~*) item; article; (*Exemplar*) specimen; (*Möbel~*) piece [of furniture]; **zwanzig ~ Vieh** twenty head of cattle; **ich nehme 5 ~/5 ~ von den Rosen** I'll take five [of them]/five of the roses; **30 Pfennig das ~, das ~ 30 Pfennig** thirty pfennigs each; **~ für ~:** piece by piece; (*eins nach dem andern*) one by one; **das gute ~** (*oft iron.*) the precious thing; **große ~e auf jmdn. halten** (*ugs.*) think the world of sb.; **Vater, unser bestes ~** (*scherzh.*) father, our pride and joy; ⇒ *auch* **frei** 1 Q; Ⓒ **das ist [ja] ein starkes** *od.* **tolles ~** (*ugs.*) that's a bit much *or* a bit thick (*coll.*); **da hast du dir aber ein [tolles] ~ geleistet** you've [really] gone too far there; **das ist ja ein ~ aus dem Tollhaus!** that's [a piece of] pure lunacy; Ⓓ (*salopp abwertend: Person*) **ein faules/freches ~:** a lazy/cheeky thing *or* devil; **ein dummes** *od.* **blödes ~:** a stupid thing; Ⓔ (*Bühnen~*) play; Ⓕ (*Musik~*) piece

**Stuckateur** /ʃtʊkaˈtøːɐ̯/ *der;* ~**s**, ~**e, Stuckateurin** *die;* ~, ~**nen** [stucco]plasterer

**Stückchen** *das;* ~**s**, ~: [little] piece; bit; **es ist bloß noch ein kleines ~:** it's only another few yards

**Stuck·decke** *die* stucco[ed] ceiling

**stückeln** ❶ *tr. V.* put together ‹sleeve, curtain› with patches. ❷ *itr. V.* sew on patches

**Stücke·schreiber** *der,* **Stücke·schreiberin** *die* playwright

**stück-, Stück-:** ~**gut** *das* [individually] packaged goods *pl.;* ~**lohn** *der* (*Wirtsch.*) piecework pay; (*Akkordsatz*) piece rate; ~**preis** *der* unit price; ~**weise** *Adv.* piece by piece; (*einzeln*) ‹sell› separately; ~**werk** *das:* ~**werk sein/bleiben** be/remain incomplete; ‹book, work of art› remain a torso; **unsere Korrekturen sind nur ~werk, wir müssen das ganze Buch neu bearbeiten** our corrections are only half measures, we must revise the whole book; ~**zahl** *die* (*Wirtsch.*) number of units; **in hohen ~zahlen produzieren** manufacture in large numbers; **eine ~zahl von 300** an output of 300 units

**Student** /ʃtuˈdɛnt/ *der;* ~**en**, ~**en** Ⓐ student; Ⓑ (*österr.: Schüler*) [secondary-school] pupil

**Studenten-:** ~**ausweis** *der* student card; ~**bewegung** *die* student movement; ~**bude** *die* (*ugs.*) student's room; ~**heim** *das* student hostel; students' [hall of] residence; ~**lokal** *das* students' [favourite] haunt; ~**parlament** *das:* students' assembly

**Studentenschaft** *die;* ~, ~**en** student body; **die verfasste ~** (*Hochschulw.*) the students' assembly

**Studenten·verbindung** *die* society; (*für Männer*) fraternity (*Amer.*); (*für Frauen*) sorority (*Amer.*)

**Studentin** *die;* ~, ~**nen** ⇒ Student; ⇒ *auch* -in

**studentisch** *Adj.* student

**Studie** /ˈʃtuːdi̯ə/ *die;* ~, ~**n** study

**studien-, Studien-:** ~**assessor** *der,* ~**assessorin** *die: graduate teacher who has recently passed the second State Examination;* ≈ probationary teacher; ~**aufenthalt** *der* study visit (**in** + *Dat.* to); ~**bewerber** *der,* ~**bewerberin** *die: applicant for a place in higher education;* ~**direktor** *der,* ~**direktorin** *die* Ⓐ deputy headteacher; Ⓑ (*DDR*) *honorary title conferred on a secondary-school teacher;* ~**fach** *das* subject [of study]; ~**freund** *der,* ~**freundin** *die* university/college friend; ~**gang** *der* course of study; ~**gebühr** *die* tuition fee; ~**halber** *Adv.* for study purposes; ~**kolleg** *das* (*Hochschulw.*) preparatory course (*esp. for foreign students*); ~**platz** *der* university/college place; ~**rat** *der,* ~**rätin** *die* ▶91 Ⓐ *established graduate secondary-school teacher* (*Brit.*); *graduate high-school teacher with tenure* (*Amer.*); Ⓑ (*DDR*) *honorary title conferred on a teacher;* ~**referendar** *der,* ~**referendarin** *die* probationary graduate teacher; ~**reise** *die* study trip; ~**zeit** *die* Ⓐ (*Zeit als Student*) time as a student; student days *pl.;* Ⓑ (*Dauer*) period of study

**studieren** /ʃtuˈdiːrən/ ❶ *itr. V.* study; **er studiert in Berlin** he is studying *or* at university in Berlin; **er studiert noch** he is still a student. ❷ *tr. V.* study

**Studierende** *der/die; adj. Dekl.* student

**Studier·stube** *die* (*veralt., scherzh.*) study

**studiert** *Adj.* (*ugs.*) ‹person› who has been to university; ‹painter etc.› with an academic training

**Studierte** *der/die; adj. Dekl.* (*ugs.*) person with a university education

**Studio** /ˈʃtuːdi̯o/ *das;* ~**s**, ~**s** Ⓐ studio; Ⓑ (*Einzimmerwohnung*) [one-room] flatlet (*Brit.*); studio flat (*Brit.*); studio apartment (*Amer.*)

**Studio·bühne** *die* studio theatre

**Studiosus** /ʃtuˈdi̯oːzʊs/ *der;* ~, **Studiosi** (*veralt., scherzh.*) student

**Studium** /ˈʃtuːdi̯ʊm/ *das;* ~**s, Studien** Ⓐ study; (*Studiengang*) course of study; **zum ~ der Medizin zugelassen werden** get a place to study medicine; **das ~ mit dem Staatsexamen abschließen** complete one's studies *or* course [of study] with the State Examination; **neben dem ~ arbeitet sie als Kellnerin** she works as a waitress while she is studying; **während seines ~s** (*als er Student war*) in his student days; Ⓑ (*Erforschung*) study; **Studien über etw.** (*Akk.*) **betreiben** carry out studies into sth.; Ⓒ (*genaues Lesen*) study; **beim ~ der Akten** while studying the files

**Studium generale** *das;* ~: general studies course

**Stufe** /ˈʃtuːfə/ *die;* ~, ~**n** Ⓐ step; (*einer Treppe*) stair; (*Gelände~*) terrace; **„Achtung** *od.* **Vorsicht, ~!"** 'mind the step'; Ⓑ (*Raketen~, Geol., fig.: Stadium*) stage; (*Niveau*) level; (*Steigerungs~, Grad*) degree; (*Rang*) grade; **eine ~ der Entwicklung** a stage of development; **auf einer hohen ~ stehen** be of a high standard; **auf der gleichen ~ stehen [wie …]** be of the same standard [as …]; have the same status [as …]; (*gleichwertig sein*) be equivalent [to …]; **jmdn./etw. mit jmdm./etw. auf eine** *od.* **auf die gleiche ~ stellen** equate sb./sth. with sb./sth.; **zwei Dinge auf die gleiche ~ stellen** equate two things; **sich mit jmdm./etw. auf eine** *od.* **auf die gleiche ~ stellen** put oneself

S

on a level with sb./sth.; [C] (*Technik*) (*Funktions~*) mark; position; (*Geschwindigkeits~*) speed; (*Heiz~*) heat setting; **Gas: ~ III** gas mark III; [D] (*Musik*) degree; **die erste ~ der Tonleiter** the first step on the scale

**stufen** *tr. V.* [A] step; terrace ‹slope›; [B] (*ab~*) grade ‹salaries›; graduate ‹prices›

**stufen-, Stufen-: ~barren** *der* (*Turnen*) asymmetric bars *pl.*; **~heck** *das* (*Kfz-W.*) booted rear; **~leiter** *die* (*fig.*) hierarchy; ladder (*fig.*); **~los** ❶ *Adj.* continuously variable; ❷ *adv.* **~los verstellbar** continuously adjustable; **~plan** *der* phased plan; **~pyramide** *die* (*Kunstwiss.*) step pyramid; **~weise** ❶ *Adv.* in stages *or* phases; ❷ *adj.* phased

**stufig** ❶ *Adj.* layered ‹hair [style]›; terraced ‹terrain›. ❷ *adv.* **~ geschnittenes Haar** layered hair; hair cut in layers; **~ gegliedertes Gelände** terraced terrain

**-stufig** *adj.* -step; (*fig.*) -stage ‹development, rocket, filter, etc›; -phase ‹plan›

**Stuhl** /ʃtu:l/ *der;* **~[e]s, Stühle** /ˈʃty:lə/ [A] chair; [B] (*fig.*) **sein ~ wackelt** his position is threatened *or* no longer secure; **der Minister klebt an seinem ~** (*ugs.*) the minister is not to be shifted [from office]; **jmdm. den ~ vor die Tür setzen** kick sb. out; show sb. the door; **[fast] vom ~ fallen** (*ugs.*) [nearly] have a fit (*coll.*); **jmdn. vom ~ reißen** *od.* **jagen/hauen** (*ugs.*) get sb. excited/take sb.'s breath away; **das hat mich fast** *od.* **bald vom ~ gehauen** (*ugs.*) you could have knocked me down with a feather; **sich zwischen zwei Stühle setzen/zwischen zwei Stühlen sitzen** fall/have fallen between two stools; ⇒ *auch* **elektrisch** 1; [C] (*kath. Kirche*) see; **der ~ Petri** the Holy See *or* See of Rome; ⇒ *auch* **apostolisch** B; **heilig** A; [D] (*Med.*) stool; [E] ⇒ **Stuhlgang** A

**Stuhl·bein** *das* chair leg

**Stühlchen** /ˈʃty:lçən/ *das;* **~s, ~:** little chair

**Stuhl-: ~gang** *der* [A] bowel movement[s]; [B] (*Kot*) stool; **~lehne** *die* [A] (*Rückenlehne*) chair back; [B] (*Armlehne*) chair arm; **~verstopfung** *die* constipation

**Stuka** /ˈʃtu:ka/ *der;* **~s, ~s** (*Milit.*) dive-bomber; (*Ju 87*) stuka

***Stukkateur, *Stukkateurin** ⇒ **Stuckateur, Stuckateurin**

**Stulle** /ˈʃtʊlə/ *die;* **~, ~n** (*nordostd.*) slice of bread; (*Butter~*) piece of bread and butter; (*belegt*) sandwich

**Stulpe** /ˈʃtʊlpə/ *die;* **~, ~n** (*am Ärmel*) turned-up cuff; (*am Stiefel*) bucket-top

**stülpen** /ˈʃtʏlpn̩/ *tr. V.* **etw. auf** *od.* **über etw.** (*Akk.*) **~:** pull/put sth. on to *or* over sth.; **die Taschen nach außen ~:** turn the/one's pockets inside out

**Stulpen·stiefel** *der* bucket-top boot

**stumm** /ʃtʊm/ *Adj.* dumb ‹person›; (*schweigsam*) silent ‹person, reproach, greeting, prayer, etc.›; (*wortlos*) wordless ‹greeting, complaint, prayer, gesture, dialogue›; mute ‹glance, gesture›; (*Theater*) non-speaking ‹part, character›; **~ vor Schreck** speechless with fear; **sie sahen sich ~ an** they looked at one another without speaking *or* in silence; **ein ~er Konsonant/Vokal** (*Sprachw.*) a silent *or* mute consonant/vowel; **das ~e h** the silent h; the h mute; **~er Diener** (*Kleiderständer*) valet; (*Serviertisch*) dumb waiter

**Stumme** *der/die; adj. Dekl.* mute; **die ~n** the dumb

**Stummel** /ˈʃtʊml̩/ *der;* **~s, ~:** stump; (*Bleistift~*) stub; (*Zigaretten~/Zigarren~*) [cigarette/cigar] butt

**Stummel·schwanz** *der* stumpy tail

**Stumm·film** *der* silent film

**Stummheit** *die* dumbness; (*Schweigsamkeit*) silence

**Stumpen** /ˈʃtʊmpn̩/ *der;* **~s, ~:** stumpy cigar

**Stümper** /ˈʃtʏmpɐ/ *der;* **~s, ~** (*abwertend*) botcher; bungler

**Stümperei** *die;* **~, ~en** (*abwertend*) [A] botching; incompetence; [B] (*Ergebnis*) botched job; piece of incompetence

**stümperhaft** (*abwertend*) ❶ *Adj.* incompetent; botched ‹job›; (*laienhaft*) amateurish ‹attempt, drawing›. ❷ *adv.* incompetently; (*laienhaft*) amateurishly

**Stümperin** *die* ⇒ **Stümper**

**stümpern** *itr. V.* (*abwertend*) work incompetently; (*pfuschen*) bungle

**stumpf** /ʃtʊmpf/ ❶ *Adj.* [A] blunt ‹pin, needle, knife, etc.›; snub ‹nose›; flat-topped ‹tower›; (*Math.*) truncated ‹cone, pyramid›; obtuse ‹angle›; [B] (*glanzlos, matt*) dull ‹paint, hair, metal, colour, etc.›; (*rau*) rough ‹stone, wood›; [C] (*Verslehre*) masculine ‹rhyme›; [D] (*abgestumpft, teilnahmslos*) impassive, lifeless ‹person, glance›; impassive, apathetic ‹indifference, resignation›; dulled ‹senses›; blank ‹look, despair›; [E] (*Med.*) contused ‹wound›. ❷ *adv.* (*abgestumpft*) ‹sit, stare› impassively

**Stumpf** *der;* **~[e]s, Stümpfe** /ˈʃtʏmpfə/ stump; **etw. mit ~ und Stiel ausrotten/vernichten** eradicate/destroy sth. root and branch

**Stümpfchen** /ˈʃtʏmpfçən/ *das;* **~s, ~:** [little] stump

**Stumpfheit** *die;* **~** [A] bluntness; [B] (*Abgestumpftheit*) impassiveness; apathy; (*des Blickes*) lifelessness; blankness; (*der Sinne*) dullness

**stumpf-, Stumpf-: ~sinn** *der* [A] apathy; [B] (*Monotonie*) monotony; tedium; **~sinnig** ❶ *Adj.* [A] apathetic; vacant ‹look›; [B] (*monoton*) tedious; dreary; soul-destroying ‹job, work›. ❷ *adv.* [A] apathetically; ‹stare› vacantly; [B] (*monoton*) tediously; monotonously; **~winklig** *Adj.* obtuse-angled ‹triangle, intersection›

**Stund** /ʃtʊnt/ ⇒ **Stunde** B

**Stündchen** /ˈʃtʏntçən/ *das;* **~s, ~** (*fam.*) **[für** *od.* **auf] ein ~:** for an hour or so; **jmds. letztes ~ ist gekommen** *od.* **hat geschlagen** sb.'s last hour has come

**stünde** /ˈʃtʏndə/ *1. u. 3. Pers. Sg. Konjunktiv II v.* **stehen**

**Stunde** /ˈʃtʊndə/ *die;* **~, ~n** [A] ▶ **265**, ▶ **752** hour; **eine ~ Aufenthalt/Pause** an hour's stop/break; a stop/break of an hour; **drei ~n zu Fuß/mit dem Auto** three hours' walk/drive; **120 km in der ~ fahren** do 120 kilometres per hour; **20 Mark [für] die** *od.* **in der** *od.* **pro ~ bekommen** get 20 marks an hour *or* per hour; **jede ~:** once an hour; **nach ~n bezahlt werden** be paid by the hour; **zur vollen ~:** on the hour; **alle halbe ~:** every half hour; **~ um ~, ~n und ~n** [for] hours; [for] hour after hour; **jmds. letzte ~ hat geschlagen** *od.* **ist gekommen** sb.'s last hour has come; **wissen, was die ~ geschlagen hat** (*fig.*) know how things [really] stand; (*wissen, was einem bevorsteht*) know what's in store *or* what one is in for; **die Männer und Frauen der ersten ~** (*einer Partei o. ä.*) the founder members; [B] (*geh.*) (*Zeitpunkt*) hour; (*Zeit*) time; (*Augenblick*) moment; **in ~n der Not/Gefahr** in times of need/danger; **in einer stillen ~:** in a quiet moment; **zu früher/vorgerückter** *od.* **später ~:** at an early/a late hour; **zur ~:** at the present time; **die Gunst der ~ nutzen** make hay while the sun shines (*fig.*); strike while the iron is hot (*fig.*); **seine [große] ~ war gekommen** his big moment had come; **die ~ der Wahrheit** the moment of truth; **die ~ null** [the time of] the new beginning (*esp. in Germany after World War II*); **von Stund an** (*geh. veralt.*) thenceforth (*arch.*); ⇒ *auch* **blau**; **Gebot** E; [C] (*Unterrichtsstunde*) lesson; **in der dritten ~:** in the third period; **eine freie ~:** a free period

**stunden** *tr. V.* **jmdm. einen Betrag/eine Rate** *usw.* **~:** give sb. [extra] time to pay *or* allow sb. to defer payment of a sum/an instalment *etc.*; **können Sie mir den Rest bis morgen ~?** will you give me until tomorrow to pay you the rest?

**stunden-, Stunden-: ~buch** *das* (*Hist., Kunstwiss.*) book of hours; **~gebet** *das* (*kath. Kirche*) *prayer said at the canonical hours*; **~geschwindigkeit** *die:* ▶ **348** **bei/mit einer ~geschwindigkeit von 60 km** at a speed of 60 k.p.h.; **~glas** *das* (*veralt.*) hourglass; **~hotel** *das* sleazy hotel (*which lets rooms by the hour*); **~kilometer** *der* ▶ **348** (*ugs.*) kilometre per hour; k.p.h.; **er fuhr 120 ~kilometer** he was driving at *or* doing 120 k.p.h.; **~lang** ❶ *Adj.* lasting hours *postpos.*; **das ~lange Warten/Stehen** the hours of waiting/standing; ❷ *adv.* for hours; **~lohn** *der* hourly wage; **sie bekommt 12 Mark ~lohn** she gets paid 12 marks an hour *or* per hour; **~plan** *der* timetable; **~schlag** *der* stroke [of the clock]; **mit dem ~schlag** on the stroke of the hour; **~weise** ❶ *Adv.* for an hour or two [at a time]; **er wird ~weise bezahlt** he is paid by the hour; ❷ *adj.* ‹hiring, payment› by the hour; **~zahl** *die* number of hours; (*von Unterrichts~*) number of lessons; **~zeiger** *der* hour hand

**-stündig** *adj.* -hour

**Stündlein** *das;* **~s, ~** ⇒ **Stündchen**

**stündlich** ▶ **752** ❶ *Adj.* hourly. ❷ *adv.* [A] hourly; once an hour; **sich ~ verändern** change from hour to hour *or* from one hour to the next; [B] (*jeden Augenblick*) at any moment; **etw. ~ erwarten** expect sth. hourly

**-stündlich** *adj.* -hourly; **zwei~/halb~:** two-hourly/half-hourly; *adv.* every two hours/half an hour

**Stundung** *die;* **~, ~en** deferment of payment

**Stunk** /ʃtʊnk/ *der;* **~s** (*ugs.*) trouble; **~ machen/anfangen** cause/start trouble

**Stunt** /stant/ *der;* **~s, ~:** stunt

**Stunt·frau** *die* stuntwoman

**Stuntman** /ˈstantmən/ *der;* **~s, Stuntmen** /ˈstantmən/ stuntman

**stupid[e]** /ʃtuˈpi:də/ (*abwertend*) ❶ *Adj.* [A] moronic, empty-headed ‹person›; moronic, vacuous ‹expression›; [B] (*monoton*) soul-destroying. ❷ *adv.* moronically

**Stupidität** /ʃtupidiˈtɛ:t/ *die;* **~** (*abwertend*) [A] moronic stupidity *or* vacuity; [B] (*Monotonie*) deadly monotony *or* tedium

**Stups** /ʃtʊps/ *der;* **~es, ~e** (*ugs.*) push; shove; (*leicht*) nudge

**stupsen** *tr. V.* (*ugs.*) push; shove; (*leicht*) nudge

**Stups·nase** *die* snub nose

**stur** (*ugs.*) ❶ *Adj.* [A] (*abwertend*) (*eigensinnig, unnachgiebig*) obstinate; pigheaded; obstinate, dogged ‹insistence›; (*phlegmatisch*) stolid; dour; **ein ~er Bock** a pigheaded so-and-so (*coll.*); **du ~er Bock!** you're as obstinate as a mule!; **~ wie ein Panzer** stubborn as a mule; **auf ~ schalten** dig one's heels in; **sich ~ stellen, ~ bleiben** not give in; [B] (*unbeirrbar*) dogged; persistent; **~es Geradeausgehen** just keeping straight on; [C] (*abwertend: stumpfsinnig*) tedious; **~es Auswendiglernen** soul-destroying *or* mechanical learning by rote.
❷ *adv.* [A] (*abwertend: eigensinnig, unnachgiebig*) obstinately; [B] (*unbeirrbar*) doggedly; **sie las/redete ~ weiter** she carried on reading/kept on talking regardless; [C] (*abwertend: stumpfsinnig*) tediously; ‹learn, copy› mechanically

**stürbe** /ˈʃtʏrbə/ *1. u. 3. Pers. Sg. Konjunktiv II v.* **sterben**

**Sturheit** *die;* **~** (*ugs. abwertend*) [A] (*Eigensinnigkeit, Unnachgiebigkeit*) obstinacy; pigheadedness; (*phlegmatisches Wesen*) stolidity; dourness; [B] (*Stumpfsinnigkeit*) deadly monotony

**Sturm** /ʃtʊrm/ *der;* **~[e]s, Stürme** /ˈʃtʏrmə/ [A] storm; (*heftiger Wind*) gale; **bei** *od.* **in ~ und Regen** in the wind and rain; **ein ~ im Wasserglas** a storm in a teacup; **das Barometer steht auf ~** (*fig.*) there's a storm brewing; **ein ~ der Begeisterung/des Protests** tumultuous *or* tempestuous applause/a storm of protest; **~ und Drang** (*Literaturw.*) Storm and Stress; ⇒ *auch* **Ruhe** C; [B] (*Milit.: Angriff*) assault (**auf** + *Akk.* on); **der ~ auf die Bastille** (*hist.*) the storming of the Bastille; **etw. im ~ erobern** *od.* **nehmen** (*auch fig.*) take sth. by storm; **gegen etw. ~ laufen** (*fig.*) be up in arms against sth.; **~ klingeln** ring the [door]bell like mad (*coll.*); lean on the [door]bell (*coll.*); [C] (*Sport: die Stürmer*) forward line;

*old spelling (see note on page 1707)

S

**im ~ spielen** play up front; (D) (*österr.: Most*) ⇒ **Federweiße**

**Sturm-: ~abteilung** *die* (*ns.*) *armed and uniformed branch of the NSDAP;* SA; **~angriff** *der* (*Milit.*) assault (**auf** + *Akk.* on); **~bock** *der* (*hist.*) battering ram

**stürmen** /ˈʃtʏrmən/ ❶ *itr. V.* (A) *unpers.* **es stürmt [heftig]** it's blowing a gale; (B) *mit sein* (*rennen*) rush; (*verärgert*) storm; **zum Ausgang ~:** make a rush for the exit; (C) (*Sport: als Stürmer spielen*) play up front *or* as a striker; (D) (*Sport, Milit.: angreifen*) attack. ❷ *tr. V.* (*Milit.*) storm ‹town, position, etc.›; (*fig.*) besiege ‹booking-office, shop, etc.›; **den Saal ~:** force one's way into the hall

**Stürmer** /ˈʃtʏrmɐ/ *der:* **~s, ~** (A) (*Sport*) striker; forward; (B) **~ und Dränger** (*Literaturw.*) Storm and Stress writer; **die ~ und Dränger in der Partei** (*fig.*) the radical faction in the party

**Stürmerin** *die;* **~, ~nen** ⇒ **Stürmer** A

**sturm-, Sturm-: ~flut** *die* storm tide; **~frei** *Adj.* (*scherzh.*) **eine ~freie Bude haben** have a place where one can do as one likes [without interference/objections]; **~gepäck** *das* (*Milit.*) combat pack; **~gepeitscht** *Adj.* (*geh.*) ‹forest, trees› bending before the storm; storm-tossed ‹sea›

**stürmisch** /ˈʃtʏrmɪʃ/ ❶ *Adj.* (A) stormy; (*fig.*) tempestuous, turbulent ‹days, life, times, years›; (B) (*ungestüm*) tempestuous ‹nature, outburst, welcome›; tumultuous ‹applause, welcome, reception›; wild ‹enthusiasm›; passionate ‹lover, embrace, temperament›; vehement ‹protest›; **~es Gelächter** gales of laughter; **er näherte sich mit ~en Schritten** he approached with impetuous steps; **nicht so ~!** calm down!; take it easy!; (C) (*rasant*) meteoric ‹development, growth›; lightning, breakneck ‹speed›. ❷ *adv.* (A) ‹protest› vehemently; ‹embrace› impetuously, passionately; ‹demand› clamorously; ‹applaud› wildly; **jmdn. ~ begrüßen/empfangen** give sb. a tumultuous welcome/reception; (B) (*rasant*) at a tremendous rate *or* speed; at lightning speed

**sturm-, Sturm-: ~laterne** *die* storm lantern (*Brit.*); hurricane lamp; **~lauf** *der:* **im ~lauf** at the double; **~leiter** *die* (*Milit. hist.*) scaling ladder; **~möwe** *die* seamew; common gull; **~reif** *Adj.* (*Milit. hist.*) ready to be stormed *postpos.*; **die Stadt ~reif schießen** soften the town up with a bombardment [preparatory to the assault]; **~schaden** *der* gale *or* storm damage *no pl., no indef. art.;* **~schritt** *der:* **im ~schritt** at the double; **~segel** *das* storm sail; **~tief** *das* (*Met.*) deep low

**Sturm-und-Drang-Zeit** *die* (*Literaturw.*) Storm and Stress period; **in meiner ~** (*fig. scherzh.*) [in the days] when I was sowing my wild oats

**Sturm-: ~vogel** *der* (*Zool.*) petrel; **~warnung** *die* (*Seew.*) gale warning; **~wind** *der* (*dichter., geh.*) tempest (*literary*)

**Sturz** /ʃtʊrts/ *der;* **~es, Stürze** /ˈʃtʏrtsə/ (A) fall (**aus, von** from); (*Unfall*) accident; **ein ~ in die Tiefe** a plunge into the depths; **bei einem ~ vom Pferd** falling off a horse; (B) (*fig.: von Preis, Temperatur usw.*) [sharp] fall, drop (*Gen.* in); (C) (*Verlust des Amtes, der Macht*) fall; (*Absetzung*) overthrow; (*Amtsenthebung*) removal from office; (D) (*Kfz-W.*) camber; (E) *Pl. auch* **~e** (*Fenster~, Tür~*) lintel

**Sturz·bach** *der* [mountain] torrent; (*fig.: von Fragen usw.*) torrent

**stürzen** /ˈʃtʏrtsn̩/ ❶ *itr. V.; mit sein* (A) fall (**aus, von** from); (*in die Tiefe*) plunge; plummet; (*fig.*) ‹temperature, exchange rate, etc.› drop [sharply]; ‹prices› tumble; ‹government› fall, collapse; **beim Rollschuhlaufen/auf dem Eis ~:** have a fall while roller skating/on the ice; **mit dem Pferd/Fahrrad ~:** come off one's horse/bicycle; (B) (*laufen*) rush; dash; **er stürzte ins Zimmer** he burst into the room; **jmdm. in die Arme ~:** hurl *or* fling oneself into sb.'s arms; (C) (*fließen*) stream; pour; (D) (*geh.: steil abfallen*) plunge.
❷ *refl. V.* **sich auf jmdn./etw. ~** (*auch fig.*) pounce on sb./sth.; **sich in etw.** (*Akk.*) **~:** throw oneself *or* plunge into sth.; **sich in die Arbeit ~:** throw oneself into one's work; **sich ins Vergnügen ~:** abandon oneself to pleasure.
❸ *tr. V.* (A) throw; (*mit Wucht*) hurl; **sich aus dem Fenster/von der Brücke ~:** hurl oneself *or* leap out of the window/off the bridge; **sich in die Tiefe ~:** plunge into the depths; **jmdn. ins Verderben/Unglück ~:** plunge sb. into ruin/misfortune; (B) (*umdrehen*) upturn, turn upside-down ‹mould, pot, box, glass, cup›; turn out ‹pudding, cake, etc.›; **„[bitte] nicht ~"** 'this way up'; (C) (*des Amtes entheben*) oust ‹person› [from office]; (*gewaltsam*) overthrow, topple ‹leader, government›

**Sturz-: ~flug** *der* (*Flugw.*) [nose]dive; **im ~flug** in a [nose]dive; **~geburt** *die* (*Med.*) precipitate delivery; **~helm** *der* crash helmet; **~kampf·flugzeug** *das* dive-bomber; **~regen** *der* torrential downpour; **~see** *die,* **~welle** *die* breaking wave; [heavy] sea; (*am Strand usw.*) breaker

**Stuss, *Stuß** /ʃtʊs/ *der;* **Stusses** (*ugs. abwertend*) rubbish; twaddle (*coll.*)

**Stute** /ˈʃtuːtə/ *die;* **~, ~n** mare; (*Esel~*) she-ass

**Stuten** *der;* **~s, ~** (*nordd.*) currant bread; fruit loaf

**Stut[en]-: ~fohlen** *das,* **~füllen** *das* filly

**Stütz** *der;* **~es, ~e** (*Geräteturnen*) support

**Stütze** *die;* **~, ~n** (A) (*auch fig.*) support; (*für die Wäscheleine*) prop; **~n für Kopf, Arme und Füße** head, arm, and footrests; **an jmdm. eine ~ haben** (*fig.*) get support *or* help from sb.; **er ist die ~ der Familie** (*fig.*) he is he mainstay of the family; **die ~n der Gesellschaft** (*fig.*) the pillars of society; (B) (*salopp: Arbeitslosengeld*) dole (*coll.*); **von der ~ leben** live on the dole (*Brit. coll.*)

**stutzen**[1] /ˈʃtʊtsn̩/ *itr. V.* stop short

**stutzen**[2] *tr. V.* trim; dock ‹tail›; clip ‹ear, hedge, wing›; prune ‹tree, bush›

**stützen** /ˈʃtʏtsn̩/ ❶ *tr. V.* (A) support; (*mit Pfosten o. Ä.*) prop up; (*auf~*) rest ‹head, hands, arms, etc.› (**auf** + *Akk.* on); **die Hände in die Seiten/den Kopf in die Hände gestützt** hands on hips/head in hands; **wo sind die Beweise, auf die Sie Ihre Anschuldigungen ~?** where is the evidence to support your accusations *or* on which your accusations are based?; (B) (*Wirtsch.*) support ‹currency, exchange rate, price›; (*niedrig halten*) peg ‹prices›. ❷ *refl. V.* **sich auf jmdn./etw. ~:** lean *or* support oneself on sb./sth.; **sich auf Fakten** (*Akk.*) **~** (*fig.*) ‹theory, statement etc.› be based on facts; **er kann sich auf keinerlei Fakten ~:** he has no facts to support his case

**Stutzen** *der;* **~s, ~** (A) (*Gewehr*) carbine; (B) (*Technik: Rohrstück*) pipe end; spout; (*zum Einfüllen*) filler pipe; (C) (*Kniestrumpf*) [knee] sock (*without a foot*); (*Fußball*) [football] sock

**Stutzer** *der;* **~s, ~** (*veralt. abwertend*) dandy; fop

**stutzerhaft** ❶ *Adj.* dandyish. ❷ *adv.* like a dandy

**Stutz·flügel** *der* (*Musik*) baby grand [piano]

**Stütz·gewebe** *das* ▶471 (*Anat., Biol.*) stroma

**stutzig** *Adj.* **~ werden** begin to wonder; get suspicious; **jmdn. ~ machen** make sb. wonder; make sb. suspicious

**Stütz-: ~korsett** *das* [support] corset; **~mauer** *die* supporting wall; **~pfeiler** *der* [supporting] pillar; **~punkt** *der* (*bes. Milit.*) base; **~rad** *das* stabilizer (*for bicycle*); **~strumpf** *der* support stocking

**Stützung** *die;* **~, ~en** (A) support; **zur ~ seiner Behauptung sagte er ...** in support of his statement, he said ...; (B) (*Wirtsch.*) (*von Währung, Kursen*) support; (*von Preisen*) pegging

**Stützungs·kauf** *der* (*Wirtsch.*) support purchase

**Stütz·verband** *der* (*Med.*) support bandage

**StVO** *Abk.* **Straßenverkehrsordnung**

**stylen** /ˈstaɪlən/ *tr. V.* (*ugs.*) style ‹car etc.›; do up ‹person›; **ein hervorragend gestyltes Modell** a model with outstanding lines

**Styling** /ˈstaɪlɪŋ/ *das;* **~s, ~s** styling

**Styropor** Ⓦⓩ /ʃtyroˈpoːɐ̯/ *das;* **~s** polystyrene [foam]

**Styx** /ʃtʏks/ *der;* **~** (*griech. Myth.*) Styx

**s.u.** *Abk.* **siehe unten** see below

**SU** *Abk.* **Sowjetunion**

**Suada** /ˈzu̯aːda/ *die;* **~, Suaden** (*geh. abwertend*) harangue; diatribe

**Suaheli** /zu̯aˈheːli/ *das;* **~[s]** ▶696 Swahili; ⇒ *auch* **Deutsch**

**subaltern** /zʊp|alˈtɛrn/ (*geh.*) ❶ *Adj.* (A) (*untergeordnet*) subordinate; (B) (*abwertend*) (*unselbstständig*) unoriginal ‹mind, literature›; (*unterwürfig*) servile. ❷ *adv.* (*abwertend: unterwürfig*) in a servile manner

**Subbotnik** /zuˈbɔtnɪk/ *der;* **~[s], ~s** (*DDR*) *voluntary work* (*usually on a Saturday*) *done without payment*

**Sub·dominante** /ˈzʊp-/ *die* (*Musik*) subdominant; (*Dreiklang*) subdominant chord

**Subjekt** /zʊpˈjɛkt/ *das;* **~[e]s, ~e** (A) subject; (B) (*abwertend: Mensch*) creature; type (*coll.*)

**subjektiv** /zʊpjɛkˈtiːf/ ❶ *Adj.* subjective. ❷ *adv.* subjectively

**subjektivieren** *tr. V.* (*geh.*) subjectivize

**Subjektivismus** *der;* **~:** subjectivism

**Subjektivität** /zʊpjɛktiviˈtɛːt/ *die;* **~:** subjectivity

**Subjekt·satz** *der* (*Sprachw.*) subject clause

**Sub-: ~kontinent** *der* (*Geogr.*) subcontinent; **~kultur** *die* (*Soziol.*) subculture

**subkutan** /zʊpkuˈtaːn/ (*Anat., Med.*) ❶ *Adj.* subcutaneous. ❷ *adv.* subcutaneously

**sublim** /zuˈbliːm/ (*geh.*) ❶ *Adj.* subtle; (*erhaben*) sublime. ❷ *adv.* subtly

**Sublimation** /zublimaˈtsi̯oːn/ *die;* **~, ~en** (*Chemie*) sublimation

**sublimieren** *tr., itr. V.* sublimate

**Sublimierung** *die;* **~, ~en** sublimation

**Sublimität** /zublimiˈtɛːt/ *die;* **~** (*geh.*) subtlety

**submarin** *Adj.* submarine

**Subordination** *die* (*bes. Logik*) subordination (**unter** + *Akk.* to)

**subsidiär** /zʊpziˈdi̯ɛːɐ̯/ (*bes. Rechtsw.*) ❶ *Adj.* (A) (*unterstützend*) supplementary ‹measures›; (B) (*als Behelf dienend*) provisional ‹law etc.›. ❷ *adv.* (A) **~ tätig werden** play a supporting role; (B) (*behelfsmäßig*) on a provisional basis

**Subsidiarität** /zʊpzidi̯ariˈtɛːt/ *die;* **~** (*Politik, Soziol.*) subsidiarity *no art.*

**Subskribent** /zʊpskriˈbɛnt/ *der,* **Subskribentin** *die;* **~, ~nen** (*Buchw.*) subscriber

**subskribieren** /zʊpskriˈbiːrən/ (*Buchw.*) ❶ *tr. V.* subscribe to. ❷ *itr. V.* take out a subscription

**Subskription** /zʊpskrɪpˈtsi̯oː/ *die;* **~, ~en** (*Buchw.*) subscription

**Subskriptions·preis** *der* (*Buchw.*) subscription price

**substanziell** ⇒ **substanziell**

**Substantiv** /ˈzʊpstantiːf/ *das;* **~s, ~e** (*Sprachw.*) noun

**substantivieren** *tr. V.* (*Sprachw.*) nominalize

**substantivisch** (*Sprachw.*) ❶ *Adj.* nominal. ❷ *adv.* **~ gebraucht** used as nouns/a noun; nominalized

**Substanz** /zʊpˈstants/ *die;* **~, ~en** (A) (*auch fig.*) substance; (B) (*Grundbestand*) **die ~:** the reserves *pl.*; **etw. geht an die ~** (*fig. ugs.*) (*seelisch, nervlich*) sth. gets you down; (*körperlich*) sth. takes it out of you; **von der ~ zehren** live off' one's reserves *or* capital

**substanziell** /zʊpstanˈtsi̯ɛl/ (*geh.*) ❶ *Adj.* sbustantial. ❷ *adv.* substantially

**substituieren** /zʊpstituˈiːrən/ *tr. V.* (*geh., fachspr.*) replace

**Substitut** /zʊpstiˈtuːt/ *der;* **~en, ~en, Substitutin** *die;* **~, ~nen** assistant manager

**Substitution** /zʊpstituˈtsi̯oːn/ *die;* **~, ~en** (*geh., fachspr.*) replacement

**Substrat** /zʊpˈstraːt/ *das;* **~[e]s, ~e** (*geh., fachspr.*) substratum

S

**subsumieren** /zʊpzu'mi:rən/ *tr. V.* (*geh.*) subsume (**unter** + *Dat. od. Akk.* under)

**subtil** /zʊp'ti:l/ (*geh.*) ❶ *Adj.* subtle. ❷ *adv.* subtly

**Subtilität** /zʊptili'tɛ:t/ *die;* ~, ~**en** (*geh.*) subtlety

**Subtrahend** /zʊptra'hɛnt/ *der;* ~**en**, ~**en** (*Math.*) subtrahend

**subtrahieren** *tr., itr. V.* (*Math.*) subtract

**Subtraktion** /zʊptrak'tsio:n/ *die;* ~, ~**en** (*Math.*) subtraction

**Sub·tropen** *Pl.* (*Geogr.*) subtropics

**sub·tropisch** *Adj.* subtropical

**Subvention** /zʊpvɛn'tsio:n/ *die;* ~, ~**en** (*Wirtsch.*) subsidy

**subventionieren** *tr. V.* (*Wirtsch.*) subsidize

**Sub·version** *die* (*Politik*) subversion

**subversiv** /zʊpvɛr'zi:f/ (*Politik*) ❶ *Adj.* subversive. ❷ *adv.* subversively

**Such-:** ~**aktion** *die* search [operation]; ~**anzeige** *die* Ⓐ missing-person report; Ⓑ (*in der Zeitung*) 'lost' advertisement; ~**bild** *das* ⇨ **Vexierbild**

**Suche** /'zu:xə/ *die;* ~, ~**n** search (**nach** for); **auf der ~ [nach jmdm./etw.] sein** be looking/(*intensiver*) searching [for sb./sth.]; **sich [nach jmdm./etw.] auf die ~ machen, [nach jmdm/etw.] auf die ~ gehen** start searching *or* start a search [for sb./sth.]

**suchen** ❶ *tr. V.* Ⓐ look for; (*intensiver*) search for; **gesucht wird der 54-jährige XY** a search is going on for the 54-year-old XY; **„Kellner/Leerzimmer gesucht"** 'waiter/unfurnished room wanted'; **„Gesucht: Jesse James"** 'Wanted: Jesse James'; **die beiden haben sich gesucht und gefunden** (*ugs.*) those two were made for each other; **solche Menschen/jemanden wie ihn kann man ~** (*ugs.*) you don't come across people like that/someone like him every day; **seinesgleichen ~:** be without equal *or* unequalled; Ⓑ (*bedacht sein auf, sich wünschen*) seek ‹protection, advice, company, warmth, etc.›; look for ‹adventure›; **Kontakt** *od.* **Anschluss ~:** try to get to know people; **Streit ~:** seek a quarrel; **was sucht er denn hier?** what does he want here?; **er hat hier nichts zu ~** (*ugs.*) he has no business [to be] here; **an meinem Schreibtisch hat sie nichts zu ~** (*ugs.*) she's got no right *or* business to be at my desk; Ⓒ (*geh.: trachten*) **~, etw. zu tun** seek *or* endeavour to do sth. ❷ *itr. V.* search; **ich habe überall gesucht** I've looked everywhere; **nach jmdm./etw. ~:** look/search for sb./sth.; **da kannst du lange ~!** (*ugs.*) you're wasting your time looking for that; **sich ~d umsehen** look around; **such, such!** (*an einen Hund*) seek, seek!; **wer sucht, der findet** he who seeks shall find; seek, and ye shall find (*Bibl.*); **S~ spielen** (*landsch.*) play hide-and-seek

**Sucher** *der;* ~**s**, ~ (*Fot.*) viewfinder

**Sucherei** *die;* ~, ~**en** (*ugs., oft abwertend*) [endless] searching *no pl.*

**Such-:** ~**hund** *der* tracker dog; ~**maschine** *die* (*DV*) search engine; ~**meldung** *die* announcement about a missing or wanted person; ~**roboter** *der* (*DV*) ⇨ **Suchmaschine**; ~**schein·werfer** *der* searchlight

**Sucht** /zʊxt/ *die;* ~, **Süchte** /zʏçtə/ *od.* ~**en** Ⓐ addiction (**nach** to); **[bei jmdm.] zur ~ werden** (*auch fig.*) become addictive [in sb.'s case]; Ⓑ *Pl.* **Süchte** (*übermäßiges Verlangen*) craving, obsessive desire (**nach** for); **ihre krankhafte ~, immer alles besser zu wissen** her pathological obsession with knowing better all the time

**süchtig** /'zʏçtɪç/ *Adj.* Ⓐ addicted; **~ machen** (*auch fig.*) be addictive; **~ [nach etw.] sein** (*auch fig.*) be an addict *or* addicted [to sth.]; Ⓑ (*versessen, begierig*) obsessive; **nach etw. ~ sein** be obsessed with sth.

**-süchtig** Ⓐ ‹drug-, heroin-, morphine-, etc.› addicted; **alkohol~ sein** be an alcoholic; Ⓑ (*fig.*) addicted to ‹television›; obsessed with ‹death›; craving for ‹liberation, love, home, sex›

**Süchtige** *der/die; adj. Dekl.,* **Suchtkranke** *der/die* addict

**Sud** /zu:t/ *der;* ~**[e]s**, ~**e** Ⓐ stock; Ⓑ (*Extrakt*) decoction

**Süd**[1] /zy:t/ ▶ 400 Ⓐ (*Seemannsspr., Met.: Richtung*) **nach ~:** southwards; to the south; **aus** *od.* **von ~:** from the south; Ⓑ (*südliches Gebiet, Politik*) South; ⇨ *auch* **Nord**[1] B; Ⓒ *einem Subst. nachgestellt* **Autobahnausfahrt Frankfurt ~:** Frankfurt South motorway (*Brit.*) *or* (*Amer.*) freeway exit; **Europa ~** (*Milit.*) Southern Europe

**Süd**[2] *der;* ~**[e]s**, ~**e** (*Seemannsspr., dichter.*) southerly

**süd-, Süd-:** ~**afrika** (*das*) South Africa; ~**afrikanisch** *Adj.* South African; ~**amerika** (*das*) South America; ~**amerikanisch** *Adj.* South American

**Sudan** /zu'da:n/ (*das*); ~**s** *od. der;* ~**s** Sudan

**Sudanese** *der;* ~**n**, ~**n**, **Sudanesin** *die;* ~, ~**nen** Sudanese

**süd·deutsch** *Adj.* South German; ⇨ *auch* **norddeutsch**

**Süd·deutschland** (*das*) South Germany

**Sudelei** *die;* ~, ~**en** (*ugs. abwertend*) Ⓐ (*das Sudeln*) making *no art.* a [disgusting] mess; Ⓑ (*gesudelte Arbeit*) **[eine] ~ sein** be a [disgusting] mess

**sudeln** /'zu:dl̩n/ *itr. V.* (*ugs. abwertend*) make a [disgusting] mess; (*pfuschen*) make a mess of it; botch it

**Süden** *der;* ~**s** ▶ 400 Ⓐ (*Richtung*) south; ⇨ *auch* **Norden** A; Ⓑ (*Gegend*) southern part; **aus dem ~:** from the south; Ⓒ (*Geogr.*) South; **der tiefe/tiefste ~:** the far South

**Süd·england** (*das*) Southern England; the South of England

**Sudeten** /zu'de:tn̩/ *Pl.* **die ~:** the Sudeten [Mountains]

**Sudeten·deutsche** *der/die* Sudeten German

**Sudetenland** *das;* ~**[e]s** Sudetenland

**süd-, Süd-:** ~**europa** (*das*) Southern Europe; ~**europäisch** *Adj.* Southern European; ~**flanke** *die* (*Met., Milit.*) southern flank; (*Geogr.: eines Gebirges*) southern escarpment; ~**frucht** *die* tropical [or subtropical] fruit; ~**hang** *der* southern slope

**Sud·haus** *das* mashhouse

**Süd-:** ~**insel** *die* South Island; ~**korea** (*das*) South Korea; ~**küste** *die* south coast

**Südländer** /'zy:tlɛndɐ/ *der;* ~**s**, ~, **Südländerin** *die;* ~, ~**nen** Southern European; Mediterranean type

**südländisch** *Adj.* Southern [European]; Mediterranean; Latin ‹temperament›; **~ aussehen** have Latin looks; look like a Southern European

**südlich** ▶ 400 ❶ *Adj.* Ⓐ (*im Süden gelegen*) southern; ⇨ *auch* **Eismeer**; **nördlich** 1 A; **Polarkreis**; **Wendekreis** A; Ⓑ (*nach Süden gerichtet, von Süden kommend*) southerly; Ⓒ (*aus dem Süden kommend, für den Süden typisch*) Southern. ❷ *adv.* southwards; ⇨ *auch* **nördlich** 2. ❸ *Präp. mit Gen.* [to the] south of

**süd-, Süd-:** ~**licht** /'--/ *das; Pl.* ~~**er** Ⓐ (*Polarlicht*) southern lights *pl.*; (*einzelne Erscheinung*) display of the southern lights; Ⓑ (*iron.: Mensch aus Süddeutschland*) South German type; ~**ost**[1] (*Seemannsspr., Met.*) south-east; ⇨ *auch* **Nord**[1] A; **Nordost**[1]; ~**ost**[2] *der* (*Seemannsspr.*) southeaster[ly]; south-easter[ly] [wind]; ~**osten** *der* ▶ 400 south-east; **der ~osten [Englands]** the South-East [of England]; ⇨ *auch* **Norden**; ~**östlich** ▶ 400 ❶ *Adj.* south-eastern; south-easterly ‹direction, wind, course›; ❷ *adv.* **~östlich [von X] liegen** be to the south-east [of X]; ❸ *Präp. mit Gen.* [to the] south-east of; ~**ost·wind** *der* south-east[erly] wind; ~**pol** /'--/ *der* Ⓐ South Pole; Ⓑ (*eines Magneten*) south pole

**Süd·polar-:** ~**gebiet** *das* Antarctic [Region]; ~**meer** *das;* ~**[e]s** Antarctic Ocean

**süd-, Süd-:** ~**pol·expedition** /'------/ *die* expedition to the South Pole; ~**rand** /'--/ *der* southern edge; ~**see** /'--/ *die;* **~: die ~see** the South Seas *pl.*; ~**see·insel** /'----/ *die* South Sea island; ~**seite** /'---/ *die* south side; ~**staaten** /'---/ *Pl.* southern States; ~**süd·ost**[1] (*Seemannsspr., Met.*) south-south-east; ⇨ *auch* **Nord**[1] A; ~**süd·ost**[2] *der* (*Seemannsspr.*) south-south-easterly; ~**süd·osten** *der* south-south-east; ⇨ *auch* **Norden** A; ~**süd·west**[1] (*Seemannsspr., Met.*) south-south-west[erly]; ⇨ *auch* **Nord**[1] A; ~**süd·west**[2] *der* (*Seemannsspr.*) south-south-westerly; ~**südwesten** *der* south-south-west; ⇨ *auch* **Norden** A; ~**tirol** /'---/ (*das*) South Tirol; ~**wand** /'--/ *die* south face; ~**wärts** /'--/ *Adv.* southwards; ~**wein** /'--/ *der* dessert wine; ~**west**[1] (*Seemannsspr., Met.*) south-west; ⇨ *auch* **Nord**[1] A; **Nordwest**[1]; ~**west**[2] *der* (*Seemannsspr.*) southwester[ly]; (*dichter.*) south-west[erly] wind; ~**westafrika** (*das*) South-West Africa; ~**westen** *der* ▶ 400 south-west; **der ~westen [Deutschlands]** the South-West [of Germany]; ⇨ *auch* **Norden** A; ~**wester** *der;* ~~**s**, ~~**:** sou'wester; ~**west·funk** *der* South West German Radio; ~**westlich** ▶ 400 ❶ *Adj.* south-western; south-westerly ‹direction, course, wind›; ❷ *adv.* **~westlich [von X] liegen** be to the south-west [of X]; ❸ *Präp. mit Gen.* [to the] south-west of; ~**west·rundfunk** *der* South West German Radio; ~**west·wind** *der* south-west[erly] wind; ~**wind** /'--/ *der* south *or* southerly wind

**Sues·kanal** /'zu:ɛs-/ *der;* ~**s** Suez Canal

**Suff** /zʊf/ *der;* ~**[e]s** (*salopp*) Ⓐ **im ~:** while under the influence (*coll.*); Ⓑ (*Trunksucht*) boozing (*coll.*); **dem ~ verfallen sein/sich dem ~ ergeben** be/become a victim of the demon drink; be on/take to the bottle (*coll.*)

**süffeln** /'zʏfl̩n/ *tr., itr. V.* (*ugs.*) tipple (*coll.*)

**süffig** *Adj.* (*ugs.*) [very] drinkable; **dieser Wein ist sehr ~:** this wine goes down very well

**Süffisance** /zyfi'zã:s/ *die;* ~ ⇨ **Süffisanz**

**süffisant** /zyfi'zant/ (*geh. abwertend*) ❶ *Adj.* smug. ❷ *adv.* smugly

**Süffisanz** /syfi'zants/ *die;* ~ (*geh. abwertend*) smugness

**Suffix** /zʊ'fɪks/ *das;* ~**es**, ~**e** (*Sprachw.*) suffix

**Suffragette** /zʊfra'gɛtə/ *die;* ~, ~**n** (*hist.*) suffragette; (*veralt. abwertend: Frauenrechtlerin*) campaigner for women's rights

**suggerieren** /zʊge'ri:rən/ *tr. V.* Ⓐ (*geh., Psych.*) suggest; **jmdm. etw. ~:** suggest sth. to sb.; put sth. into sb.'s mind; Ⓑ (*geh.: den Eindruck erwecken*) suggest; give the *or* an impression of; **das musste ~, dass ...** this was bound to give the impression that ...

**Suggestion** /zʊgɛs'tio:n/ *die;* ~, ~**en** Ⓐ (*geh., Psych.*) suggestion; Ⓑ (*geh.: suggestive Wirkung*) suggestive effect *or* power

**suggestiv** /zʊgɛs'ti:f/ (*geh., Psych.*) ❶ *Adj.* suggestive. ❷ *adv.* suggestively

**Suggestiv·frage** *die* leading question

**Suhle** /'zu:lə/ *die;* ~, ~**n** muddy pool

**suhlen** *refl. V.* wallow

**Sühne** /'zy:nə/ *die;* ~, ~**n** (*geh.*) atonement; expiation; **~ [für etw.] leisten** make atonement *or* atone [for sth.]

**sühnen** ❶ *tr., itr. V.* (*abbüßen*) **[für] etw. ~:** atone for *or* pay the penalty for sth. ❷ *tr. V.* (*bestrafen*) punish ‹wrongdoing›

**Sühne-:** ~**opfer** *das* (*Rel.*) expiatory sacrifice; ~**termin** *der* (*Rechtsw.*) conciliation hearing

**Sühn·opfer** *das* ⇨ **Sühneopfer**

**Suite** /'svi:t(ə)/ *die;* ~, ~**n** suite

**Suizid** /zui'tsi:t/ *der od. das;* ~**[e]s**, ~**e** (*bes. Med., Psych.*) suicide

**Sujet** /zy'ʒe/ *das;* ~**s**, ~**s** subject

**Sukkade** /zʊ'ka:də/ *die;* ~, ~**n** candied peel

**Sukkulente** /zʊku'lɛntə/ *die;* ~, ~**n** (*Bot.*) succulent

**sukzessiv** /zʊktsɛ'si:f/ ❶ *Adj.* gradual. ❷ *adv.* gradually

**sukzessive** *Adv.* gradually

**Sulfat** /zʊl'fa:t/ *das;* ~**[e]s**, ~**e** (*Chemie*) sulphate

**Sulfid** /zʊl'fi:t/ *das;* ~**[e]s**, ~**e** (*Chemie*) sulphide

*old spelling (see note on page 1707)

**Sulfit** /zʊlˈfiːt/ *das;* **~s, ~e** (*Chemie*) sulphite
**Sulfonamid** /sʊlfonaˈmiːt/ *das;* **~[e]s, ~e** (*Pharm.*) sulphonamide
**Sulky** /ˈzʊlki/ *das;* **~s, ~s** (*Pferdesport*) sulky
**Sultan** /ˈzʊltaːn/ *der;* **~s, ~e** sultan
**Sultanat** /zʊltaˈnaːt/ *das;* **~[e]s, ~e** sultanate
**Sultanin** *die;* **~, ~nen** sultana
**Sultanine** /sʊltaˈniːnə/ *die;* **~, ~n** sultana
**Sülze** /ˈzʏltsə/ *die;* **~, ~n** Ⓐ diced meat/fish in aspic; (*vom Schweinskopf*) brawn; Ⓑ (*Aspik*) aspic
**sülzen** /ˈzʏltsn̩/ *tr., itr. V.* (*salopp*) ⇒ **quatschen** 1 A, 2
**Sülz·kotelett** *das* boned pork chop in aspic
**Sumerer** /zuˈmeːrɐ/ *der;* **~s, ~, Sumererin** *die;* **~, ~nen** Sumerian
**summ** /zʊm/ *Interj.* buzz
**summa cum laude** /ˈzʊma kʊm ˈlauːdə/ *Adv.* (*Hochschulw.*) with the utmost distinction; *highest of four grades of successful doctoral examination*
**Summand** /zʊˈmant/ *der;* **~en, ~en** (*Math.*) summand
**summarisch** /zʊˈmaːrɪʃ/ (*geh.*) ❶ *Adj.* summary; brief ‹summary›; **ein ~es Verfahren** (*Rechtsw.*) summary proceedings *pl.* ❷ *adv.* summarily; briefly
**summa summarum** /ˈzʊma zʊˈmaːrʊm/ *Adv.* in all; altogether
**Sümmchen** /ˈzʏmçən/ *das;* **~s, ~** (*ugs.*) **ein hübsches** *od.* **nettes ~:** a tidy little sum (*coll.*)
**Summe** /ˈzʊmə/ *die;* **~, ~n** sum
**summen** ❶ *itr. V.* hum; (*lauter, heller*) buzz; **es summt** there's a hum/buzzing. ❷ *tr., auch itr. V.* hum ‹tune, song, etc.›
**Summer** *der;* **~s, ~:** buzzer
**summieren** *refl. V.* add up (**auf** + *Akk.* to); (*anwachsen*) ‹number› grow, increase (**auf** + *Akk.* to)
**Summ·ton** *der; Pl.* **Summtöne** buzzing [tone]; (*leiser*) hum
**Sumpf** /zʊmpf/ *der;* **~[e]s, Sümpfe** /ˈzʏmpfə/ marsh; (*bes. in den Tropen*) swamp; (*fig.*) morass; quagmire; **im ~ stecken bleiben** be stuck in the mire
**Sumpf·dotter·blume** *die* marsh marigold
**sumpfen** *itr. V.* (*salopp*) make whoopee (*coll.*) *or* live it up into the small hours
**Sumpf-: ~fieber** *das* malaria; **~gas** *das* marsh gas; **~gebiet** *das* marsh[land]; (*bes. in den Tropen*) swamp[land]; **~huhn** *das* crake
**sumpfig** *Adj.* marshy
**Sumpf·pflanze** *die* marsh plant
**Sums** /zʊms/ *der;* **~es** (*ugs.*) **viel ~ um etw. machen** make a lot of fuss about sth.
**Sund** /zʊnt/ *der;* **~[e]s, ~e** (*Geogr.*) sound
**Sünde** /ˈzʏndə/ *die;* **~, ~n** sin; (*fig.*) misdeed; transgression; **in ~ leben** (*veralt.*) live in sin; **faul wie die ~:** bone idle; **eine ~ wert sein** (*scherzh.*) be worth a little transgression; ‹food› be naughty but nice; **es ist eine ~ [und Schande]** it's a crying shame
**Sünden-: ~babel** *das* sink of iniquity; **~bekenntnis** *das* confession of one's sins; **~bock** *der* (*ugs.*) scapegoat; **~fall** *der* (*christl. Rel.*) Fall of Man; (*fig.*) fall from grace; **~geld** *das:* **ein ~geld** (*ugs.*) a small fortune; **~pfuhl** *der* (*abwertend*) sink of iniquity; **~register** *das* (*ugs. scherzh.*) catalogue of misdeeds
**Sünder** *der;* **~s, ~, Sünderin** *die;* **~, ~nen** sinner; **armer Sünder** (*veralt.*) condemned man; **sie saß da wie eine arme Sünderin** (*ugs.*) she sat there looking a picture of misery and remorse
**Sünd·flut** *die* ⇒ **Sintflut**
**sündhaft** ❶ *Adj.* Ⓐ sinful; Ⓑ (*ugs.*) **ein ~er Preis/~es Geld** an outrageous price/amount of money. ❷ *adv.* Ⓐ sinfully; Ⓑ (*ugs.: sehr*) outrageously ‹expensive›; stunningly ‹beautiful›; **~ faul** bone idle
**Sündhaftigkeit** *die;* **~:** sinfulness
**sündig** ❶ *Adj.* sinful; (*lasterhaft*) wicked. ❷ *adv.* sinfully
**sündigen** *itr. V.* sin; (*scherzh.: viel essen*) indulge oneself [sinfully]; **gegen die Natur ~** (*fig.*) offend against nature
**Sunnit** /zʊˈniːt/ *der;* **~en, ~en, Sunnitin** *die;* **~, ~nen** Sunnite
**sunnitisch** *Adj.* Sunnite
**super** (*salopp*) ❶ *indekl. Adj.* super (*coll.*); fantastic (*coll.*); **~ aussehen/ sich ~ fühlen** look/feel great (*coll.*). ❷ *adv.* fantastically (*coll.*)
**super-** ultra-‹long, high, fast, modern, masculine, etc.›; **~geheim** top secret; **~günstig** extra cheap
**Super** /ˈzuːpɐ/ *das;* **~s, ~:** four star (*Brit.*); premium (*Amer.*); ⇒ *auch* **Normal**
**Super-** super-‹hero, figure, car, group, etc.›; terrific (*coll.*), tremendous (*coll.*) ‹success, offer, chance, idea, etc.›
**Super-8-Film** *der* super 8 film
**superb** /zuˈpɛrp /,/ **süperb** /zyˈpɛrp/ (*geh.*) ❶ *Adj.* superb. ❷ *adv.* superbly
**Super·benzin** *das* four-star petrol (*Brit.*); premium (*Amer.*)
**Super-: ~ding** *das; Pl.* **~~er** (*salopp*) terrific thing (*coll.*); **~frau** *die* (*ugs.*) superwoman
**Superintendent** /zupɐ|ɪntɛnˈdɛnt/ *der;* **~en, ~en** (*ev. Kirche*) dean
**Superiorität** /zuperi̯oriˈtɛːt/ *die;* **~** (*geh.*) Ⓐ superiority (**über** + *Akk.* in relation to); Ⓑ (*Vormachtstellung*) supremacy (**über** + *Akk.* over)
**super·klug** (*iron.*) ❶ *Adj.* extra clever; smart-aleck (*coll. derog.*). ❷ *adv.* in a smart-aleck way (*coll. derog.*)
**Superlativ** /ˈzuːpɛlatiːf/ *der;* **~s, ~e** (*Sprachw.*) superlative
**superlativisch** *Adj.* (*Sprachw.*) superlative
**super-, Super-: ~mann** *der* (*ugs.*) superman; **~markt** *der* supermarket; **~modern** ❶ *Adj.* ultra-modern; ❷ *adv.* ‹furnished, dressed› in ultra-modern style; **~schlau** *Adj.* (*iron.*) ⇒ **~klug; ~schnell** (*ugs.*) ❶ *Adj.* ultra-fast; ❷ *adv.* at tremendous speed; **~star** *der* superstar
**Süppchen** /ˈzʏpçən/ *das;* **~s, ~:** soup; **sein ~ am Feuer anderer kochen** (*ugs.*) use others for one's own ends
**Suppe** /ˈzʊpə/ *die;* **~, ~n** soup; **jmdm. die ~ versalzen** (*ugs.*) put a spoke in sb.'s wheel; put a spanner in sb.'s works; **jmdm. in die ~ spucken** (*salopp*) mess things up for sb.; ⇒ *auch* **auslöffeln** A; **einbrocken**
**Suppen-: ~einlage** *die: rice, noodles, dumplings, etc. put into a clear soup;* **~fleisch** *das* beef for making soup; **~grün** *das* green vegetables for making soup (*comprising parsley, carrots, celery, and leeks*); **~huhn** *das* boiling fowl; **~kasper** *der* (*ugs.*) poor *or* finicky eater; **~kelle** *die* soup ladle; **~knochen** *der* soup bone; **~löffel** *der* soup spoon; **~nudel** *die* noodle (*for use in soup*); **~schüssel** *die* soup tureen; **~tasse** *die* soup bowl (*with handles*); **~teller** *der* soup plate; **~terrine** *die* soup tureen; **~würfel** *der* stock cube
**suppig** *Adj.* watery; thin
**Supplement** /zʊpleˈmɛnt/ *das;* **~[e]s, ~e** supplement
**Suppositorium** /zʊpoziˈtoːri̯ʊm/ *das;* **~s, Suppositorien** (*Pharm.*) suppository
**supraleitend** *Adj.* (*Physik*) superconducting
**Supra·leiter** *der* (*Physik*) superconductor
**Supra·leitung** *die* (*Physik*) superconductivity
**Supremat** /zupreˈmaːt/ *der od. das;* **~[e]s, ~e** supreme authority
**Sure** /ˈzuːrə/ *die;* **~, ~n** sura
**Surf·brett** /ˈsəːf-/ *das* surfboard
**surfen** /ˈsəːfn̩/ *itr. V.* surf
**Surfer** /ˈsəːfɐ/ *der;* **~s, ~, Surferin** *die;* **~, ~nen** surfer
**Sur·realismus** /zʊreaˈlɪsmʊs/ *der;* **~:** surrealism *no art.*
**Sur·realist** *der,* **Sur·realistin** *die* surrealist
**surrealistisch** ❶ *Adj.* surrealist ‹movement, painting, literature›; surrealistic ‹image, story, scene›. ❷ *adv.* surrealistically; ‹paint› in a surrealistic style; ‹influenced› by surrealism
**surren** /ˈzʊrən/ *itr. V.* Ⓐ (*summen*) hum; ‹camera, fan› whirr; **es surrt** there's a hum/whirr; Ⓑ *mit sein* (*schwirren*) whirr
**Surrogat** /zʊroˈgaːt/ *das;* **~[e]s, ~e** (*geh.*) surrogate
**suspekt** /zʊsˈpɛkt/ ❶ *Adj.* suspicious; **jmdm. ~ sein** seem suspicious to sb.; arouse sb.'s suspicions. ❷ *adv.* suspiciously
**suspendieren** /zʊspɛnˈdiːrən/ *tr. V.* suspend; (*entlassen*) dismiss; **jmdn. vom Dienst/von seinem Amt ~:** suspend/dismiss sb. from his/her post
**Suspendierung, Suspension** /zʊspɛnˈzi̯oːn/ *die;* **~, ~en** suspension; (*Entlassung*) dismissal
**Suspensorium** /zʊspɛnˈzoːri̯ʊm/ *das;* **~s, Suspensorien** (*Med.*) suspensory [bandage]
**süß** /zyːs/ ❶ *Adj.* sweet; (*geh.: lieblich klingend*) melodious; sweet; (*fig.: übertrieben freundlich*) sweet, sugary ‹smile, words›; **er isst gern Süßes** he likes sweet things; he has a sweet tooth; **na, mein Süßer/meine Süße?** well, sweetheart? ❷ *adv.* sweetly; **~ duften** give off a sweet scent; **den Salat ~ anmachen** sweeten the salad dressing; **träum ~!** sweet dreams!; **das hast du ~ gemalt** (*fam.*) you've painted this enchantingly
**Süße** *die;* **~:** sweetness
**süßen** ❶ *tr. V.* sweeten. ❷ *itr. V.* sweeten things; **mit Saccharin ~:** use saccharine as a sweetener
**Süß·holz** *das* liquorice [plant]; **~ raspeln** (*fig. ugs.*) ooze charm
**Süßholz·raspler** *der;* **~s, ~, Süßholz·rasplerin** *die;* **~, ~nen** (*ugs.*) smoothie (*coll.*)
**Süßigkeit** *die;* **~, ~en** Ⓐ (*Bonbon usw.*) sweet (*Brit.*); candy (*Amer.*); **~en** sweets (*Brit.*); candy *sing.* (*Amer.*); (*als Ware*) confectionery *sing.;* Ⓑ (*fig. geh.: Süße*) sweetness
**Süß·kirsche** *die* sweet cherry
**süßlich** ❶ *Adj.* Ⓐ [slightly] sweet; on the sweet side *pred.;* **ein widerlich ~er Geruch/Geschmack** an unpleasantly sickly *or* cloying smell/taste; Ⓑ (*abwertend*) (*sentimental*) sickly mawkish ‹film›; (*heuchlerisch freundlich*) sugary ‹smile etc.›; smarmy (*coll.*) ‹expression, manners›; honeyed ‹words›. ❷ *adv.* (*abwertend*) ‹write, paint› mawkishly *or* in a sickly-sentimental style; ‹smile› smarmily (*coll.*)
**süß-, Süß-: ~most** *der* unfermented fruit juice; **~rahm·butter** *die* sweet cream butter; **~sauer** ❶ *Adj.* sweet-and-sour; (*fig.*) wry ‹smile, face›; **etw. gern ~sauer essen** like eating sth. with a sweet-and-sour sauce; ❷ *adv.* Ⓐ **etw. ~sauer zubereiten** give sth. a sweet-and-sour flavour; Ⓑ (*fig.*) ‹smile› wryly; **~speise** *die* sweet; dessert; **~stoff** *der* sweetener; **~waren** *Pl.* confectionery *sing.;* candy *sing.* (*Amer.*); **~wasser** *das; Pl.* **~:** fresh water; **~wasser·fisch** *der* freshwater fish; **~wein** *der* sweet wine
**Sutane** ⇒ **Soutane**
**Sütterlin·schrift** /ˈzʏtɐliːn-/ *die* Sütterlin script
**SV** *Abk.* **Sportverein** SC
**SVP** *Abk.* **Schweizer Volkspartei**
**svw.** *Abk.* **soviel wie**
**SW** *Abk.* **▶ 400 | Südwest[en]** SW
**Swahili** /svaˈhiːli/ ⇒ **Suaheli**
**Swastika** /ˈsvastika/ *die;* **~, Swastiken** swastika
**Sweatshirt** /ˈswɛt-ʃəːt/ *das;* **~s, ~s** sweatshirt
**SWF** *Abk.* **Südwestfunk**
**Swimmingpool, Swimming-pool** /ˈsvɪmɪŋpuːl/ *der;* **~s, ~s** [swimming] pool
**Swing** /svɪŋ/ *der;* **~[s]** Ⓐ (*Musik*) swing *no art.;* Ⓑ (*Wirtsch.*) swing
**swingen** *itr. V.* Ⓐ (*Musik*) ‹player› swing [it]; ‹music› have a swing [to it]; Ⓑ (*tanzen*) swing
**SWR** *Abk.* **Südwestrundfunk**
**Syllogismus** /zʏloˈgɪsmʊs/ *der;* **~s, Syllogismen** (*Philos.*) syllogism

S

**Sylphe** /ˈzʏlfə/ *der;* **~n, ~n** sylph

**Symbiose** /zʏmˈbi̯oːzə/ *die;* **~, ~n** (*Biol., fig.*) symbiosis (**zwischen** + *Dat.* of); **eine ~ eingehen** (*fig.*) form a symbiotic relationship

**symbiotisch** *Adj.* (*Biol., fig.*) symbiotic

**Symbol** /zʏmˈboːl/ *das;* **~s, ~e** symbol

**symbolhaft** ❶ *Adj.* symbolic (**für** of). ❷ *adv.* symbolically

**Symbolik** /zʏmˈboːlɪk/ *die;* **~:** symbolism

**symbolisch** ❶ *Adj.* symbolic. ❷ *adv.* symbolically

**symbolisieren** ❶ *tr. V.* symbolize. ❷ *refl. V.* be symbolized (**in** + *Dat.* by)

**Symbolismus** *der;* **~:** symbolism; (*Kunstrichtung*) Symbolism *no art.*

**Symbolist** *der;* **~en, ~en, Symbolistin** *die;* **~, ~nen** Symbolist

**symbolistisch** *Adj.* Symbolist

**Symbol·sprache** *die* (*DV*) assembly language

**Symmetrie** /zʏmeˈtriː/ *die;* **~, ~n** symmetry

**Symmetrie·achse** *die* axis of symmetry

**symmetrisch** ❶ *Adj.* symmetrical. ❷ *adv.* symmetrically

**Sympathie** /zʏmpaˈtiː/ *die;* **~, ~n** sympathy; **~ für jmdn. haben** sympathize with *or* have sympathy with sb.; **sich** (*Dat.*) **jmds./alle ~n verscherzen** forfeit sb.'s/everybody's sympathy; **bei aller ~:** with the best will in the world

**Sympathie·streik** *der* sympathy strike; **in ~ [mit jmdm.] treten** strike in sympathy [with sb.]

**Sympathikus** *der;* **~** ▶ 471 (*Anat., Physiol.*) sympathetic nervous system

**Sympathisant** /zʏmpatiˈzant/ *der;* **~en, ~en, Sympathisantin** *die;* **~, ~nen** sympathizer (*Gen.* with)

**sympathisch** ❶ *Adj.* Ⓐ congenial, likeable ‹person, manner›; appealing, agreeable ‹voice, appearance, material›; **jmdm. ~ sein** appeal to sb.; **er war mir gleich ~:** I took to him at once; I took an immediate liking to him; Ⓑ (*Anat., Physiol.*) sympathetic ‹nerve, nervous system, etc.›. ❷ *adv.* in a likeable *or* appealing way; (*angenehm*) agreeably

**sympathisieren** *itr. V.* sympathize (**mit** with); **mit einer Partei ~:** be sympathetic towards a party

**Symphonie** /zʏmfoˈniː/ *usw.* ⇒ **Sinfonie** *usw.*

**Symposion** /zʏmˈpoːzi̯ɔn/ *das;* **~s, Symposien, Symposium** /zʏmˈpoːzi̯ʊm/ *das;* **Symposiums, Symposien** symposium (**über** + Akk., **zu** on)

**Symptom** /zʏmpˈtoːm/ *das;* **~s, ~e** ▶ 474 (*Med., geh.*) symptom (*Gen.*, **für, von** of)

**Symptomatik** /zʏmptoˈmaːtɪk/ *die;* **~** (*Med., geh.*) symptoms *pl.*; symptom complex

**symptomatisch** (*Med., geh.*) ❶ *Adj.* symptomatic (**für** of). ❷ *adv.* symptomatically

**Synagoge** /zynaˈgoːgə/ *die;* **~, ~n** synagogue

**Synästhesie** /zynɛsteˈziː/ *die;* **~, ~n** (*Med., Literaturw.*) synaesthesia

**synchron** /zʏnˈkroːn/ ❶ *Adj.* Ⓐ synchronous; Ⓑ (*Sprachw.*) synchronic. ❷ *adv.* Ⓐ synchronously; Ⓑ (*Sprachw.*) synchronically

**Synchronisation** /zʏnkronizaˈtsi̯oːn/ *die;* **~, ~en** ⇒ **Synchronisierung**

**synchronisch** *Adj.* (*Sprachw.*) synchronic

**synchronisieren** *tr. V.* Ⓐ (*Film*) dub ‹film›; Ⓑ (*Technik, fig.*) synchronize ‹watches, operations, etc.›; fit synchromesh to ‹gearbox›; **alle Gänge sind synchronisiert** (*Kfz-W.*) there is synchromesh on all gears; **synchronisiertes Getriebe** synchromesh gearbox

**Synchronisierung** *die;* **~, ~en** Ⓐ (*Film*) dubbing; Ⓑ (*Technik, fig.*) synchronization; (*Kfz-W.*) fitting of synchromesh (*Gen.* to)

**Synchron-: ~schwimmen** *das* (*Sport*) synchronized swimming; **~sprecher** *der*, **~sprecherin** *die* dubbing actor

**Synchrotron** /ˈzʏnkrotroːn/ *das;* **~s, ~e** *od.* **~s** (*Kernphysik*) synchrotron

**Syndikalismus** /zʏndikaˈlɪsmʊs/ *der;* **~:** syndicalism *no art.*

**syndikalistisch** *Adj.* syndicalist

**Syndikat** /zʏndiˈkaːt/ *das;* **~[e]s, ~e** (*bes. Wirtsch.*) syndicate

**Syndikus** /ˈzʏndikʊs/ *der;* **~, ~se** *od.* **Syndizi** /ˈzʏnditsi/ (*Rechtsspr.*) legal adviser; (*Rechtsanwalt einer Firma*) company lawyer *or* (*Amer.*) attorney

**Syndrom** /zʏnˈdroːm/ *das;* **~s, ~e** ▶ 474 (*Med.*) syndrome

**Synkope** *die;* **~, ~n** Ⓐ /zʏnˈkoːpə/ (*Musik*) syncopation; Ⓑ /ˈzʏnkope/ (*Sprachw.*) syncope

**synkopieren** /zʏnkoˈpiːrən/ *tr. V.* (*Musik, Sprachw.*) syncopate

**synkopisch** *Adj.* (*Musik*) syncopated

**Synodale** /zynoˈdaːlə/ *der/die; adj. Dekl.* synod member

**Synode** /zyˈnoːdə/ *die;* **~, ~n** (*ev., kath. Kirche*) synod

**Synonomie** /zynonyˈmiː/ *die;* **~, ~n** (*Sprachw.*) synonymity

**synonym** /zynoˈnyːm/ (*Sprachw.*) ❶ *Adj.* synonymous. ❷ *adv.* synonymously

**Synonym** /zynoˈnyːm/ *das;* **~s, ~e** (*Sprachw.*) synonym

**Synonym·wörterbuch** *das* dictionary of synonyms

**Synopse** /zyˈnɔpsə/ *die;* **~, ~n, Synopsis** /ˈzyːnɔpsɪs/ *die;* **Synopsis, ~n** Ⓐ textual comparison; Ⓑ (*bibl.*) comparative parallel text of the Synoptic Gospels; Ⓒ (*geh.: Zusammenschau*) overall view; survey

**Synoptiker** *der;* **~s, ~:** synoptist

**syntaktisch** /zʏnˈtaktɪʃ/ (*Sprachw.*) ❶ *Adj.* syntactic. ❷ *adv.* syntactically

**Syntax** /ˈzʏntaks/ *die;* **~, ~en** (*Sprachw.*) syntax

**Synthese** /zʏnˈteːzə/ *die;* **~, ~n** synthesis (*Gen.*, **von, aus** of)

**Synthesizer** /ˈsɪntəsaizɐ/ *der;* **~s, ~** (*Musik*) synthesizer

**Synthetik** /zʏnˈteːtɪk/ *das;* **~s** (*ugs.*) synthetic material

**synthetisch** ❶ *Adj.* synthetic. ❷ *adv.* synthetically

**Syphilis** /ˈzyːfilɪs/ *die;* **~** ▶ 474 (*Med.*) syphilis

**Syrakus** /zyraˈkuːs/ *(das);* **~'** Syracuse

**Syrer** /ˈzyːrɐ/ *der;* **~s, ~, Syrerin** *die;* **~, ~nen** ▶ 553 Syrian

**Syrien** /ˈzyːri̯ən/ *(das);* **~s** Syria

**syrisch** /ˈzyːrɪʃ/ *Adj.* ▶ 553 Syrian

**System** /zʏsˈteːm/ *das;* **~s, ~e** system; **~ in etw.** (*Akk.*) **bringen** introduce some system into sth.; get sth. into some sort of order; **~ haben** be methodical; have system; **hinter etw.** (*Dat.*) **steckt ~:** there's method in sth.

**System-: ~analyse** *die* systems analysis; **~analytiker** *der*, **~analytikerin** *die* ▶ 159 systems analyst

**Systematik** /zʏsteˈmaːtɪk/ *die;* **~, ~en** Ⓐ systematics *sing.*; Ⓑ (*Biol.*) taxonomy

**systematisch** /zʏsteˈmaːtɪʃ/ ❶ *Adj.* systematic. ❷ *adv.* systematically

**systematisieren** *tr. V.* systematize

**system-, System-: ~immanent** ❶ *Adj.* part of the system *pred.*; **~immanente Faktoren** factors inherent in the system; ❷ *adv.* in a manner inherent in the system; **~kritiker** *der*, **~kritikerin** *die* critic of the system; **~los** ❶ *Adj.* unsystematic; ❷ *adv.* unsystematically; **~veränderung** *die* change in the system; **~wette** *die* betting based on an agreed system of permutations; **~zwang** *der* pressure imposed by the system

**Systole** /ˈzʏstole/ *die;* **~, ~n** (*Med.*) systole

**Szenario** /sts̯eˈnaːri̯o/ *das;* **~s, ~s, Szenarium** /sts̯eˈnaːri̯ʊm/ *das;* **~s, Szenarien** (*Theater, Film*) scenario

**Szene** /ˈsts̯eːnə/ *die;* **~, ~n** Ⓐ scene; **hinter der ~:** backstage; behind the scenes; **er erhielt Beifall auf offener ~:** he was applauded during the scene; **die ~ beherrschen** (*fig.*) dominate the scene; **ein Theaterstück in ~ setzen** stage a play; **sich in ~ setzen** (*fig.*) put oneself in the limelight; Ⓑ (*Auseinandersetzung*) scene; **[jmdm.] eine ~ machen** make a scene [in front of sb.]; Ⓒ (*ugs.: bestimmtes Milieu*) scene (*coll.*)

**-szene** *die;* **~, ~n** (*ugs.*) scene (*coll.*); **die Terror[isten]~/Literatur~:** the terrorist/literary scene

**Szenen-: ~applaus** *der* applause during the scene; spontaneous burst of applause; **~folge** *die* sequence of scenes; **~wechsel** *der* (*Theater*) scene change

**Szenerie** /sts̯enəˈriː/ *die;* **~, ~n** Ⓐ (*Bühnendekoration*) set (*Gen.* for); Ⓑ (*Schauplatz*) scene; (*eines Romans*) setting

**szenisch** *Adj.* dramatic; **~e Gestaltung/Effekte** staging/stage effects

**Szepter** /ˈsts̯ɛptɐ/ *das;* **~s, ~** ⇒ **Zepter**

**Szientismus** /sts̯i̯ɛnˈtɪsmʊs/ *der;* **~** (*Fachspr.*) scientism *no art.*

**Szilla** /ˈstsɪla/ *die;* **~, Szillen** (*Bot.*) scilla

**Szylla** /ˈstsʏla/ *in* **zwischen ~ und Charybdis** (*geh.*) between Scylla and Charybdis

S

# T t

**t, T** /te:/ *das;* ~, ~, (*ugs.*) ~**s**, ~**s** t/T; ⇒ *auch* **a, A**

**t** *Abk.* ▶ 353 **Tonne**

**Tab.** *Abk.* **Tabelle**

**Tabak** /'ta(:)bak/ *der;* ~**s**, ~**e** tobacco

**Tabak·monopol** *das* (*Wirtsch.*) tobacco monopoly

**Tabaks-:** ~**beutel** *der* tobacco pouch; ~**dose** *die* tobacco tin; ~**pfeife** *die* [tobacco] pipe

**Tabak-:** ~**steuer** *die* duty *or* tax on tobacco; ~**trafik** /-'---/ *die* (*österr.*) tobacconist['s] [shop]; ~**waren** *Pl.* tobacco *sing.*

**Tabatiere** /taba'tie:rə/ *die;* ~, ~**n** A (*veralt.*) snuff box; B (*österr.*) ⇒ **Tabaksdose**; C (*österr.*) ⇒ **Zigarettenetui**

**tabellarisch** /tabɛ'la:rɪʃ/ ❶ *Adj.* tabular; **ein** ~**er Lebenslauf** a curriculum vitae in tabular form. ❷ *adv.* in tabular form

**Tabelle** /ta'bɛlə/ *die;* ~, ~**n** A (*Übersicht*) table; B (*Sport*) [league/championship] table; **die** ~ **anführen** be at the top of the [league/championship] table

**Tabellen-:** ~**führer** *der* (*Sport*) player in the [league/championship] table; ~**führer sein** be top of the table; ~**führerin** *die* top player in the [league/championship] table; ~**führerin sein** be top of the table; ~**platz** *der* (*Sport*) position *or* place in the [league/championship] table; ~**stand** *der* (*Sport*) state of the [league/championship] table

**tabellieren** *tr. V.* (*Fachspr.*) tabulate

**Tabernakel** /tabɛr'na:kl̩/ *das od. der;* ~**s**, ~ (*kath. Kirche, Archit.*) tabernacle

**Tableau** /ta'blo:/ *das;* ~**s**, ~**s** (*bes. Literaturw.*) tableau

**Tablett** /ta'blɛt/ *das;* ~**[e]s**, ~**s** *od.* ~**e** tray; **jmdm. etw. auf einem silbernen** ~ **servieren** (*fig.*) hand sth. to sb. on a silver platter

**Tablette** *die;* ~, ~**n** tablet

**tabletten-, Tabletten-:** ~**form** *die* tablet form; ~**missbrauch**, *~**mißbrauch** *der* pill abuse; ~**röhrchen** *das* tablet tube; ~**süchtig** *Adj.* addicted to pills *postpos.*

**tabu** /ta'bu:/ *Adj.* taboo

**Tabu** *das;* ~**s**, ~**s** taboo

**tabuieren, tabuisieren** *tr. V.* (*geh.*) **etw.** ~: taboo sth.; make sth. taboo

**Tabula rasa** /'ta:bula 'ra:za/ *in* ~ ~ **machen** make a clean sweep

**Tabulatur** /tabula'tu:ɐ̯/ *die;* ~, ~**en** (*Musik*) tablature

**Taburett** /tabu'rɛt/ *das;* ~**[e]s**, ~**e** (*schweiz.*, *sonst veralt.*) tabouret

**Tabu·wort** *das; Pl.* **Tabuwörter** (*Sprachw.*, *Psych.*) taboo word

**Tacheles** /'taxələs/ *in* **[mit jmdm.]** ~ **reden** (*ugs.*) do some straight talking [to sb.]

**tachinieren** /taxi'ni:rən/ *itr. V.* (*österr. ugs.*) loaf [about]

**Tachinierer** *der;* ~**s**, ~, **Tachiniererin** *die* (*österr. ugs.*) slacker (*coll.*); loafer

**Tachismus** /ta'ʃɪsmʊs/ *der;* ~ (*Kunstwiss.*) tachism *no art.*

**Tacho** /'taxo/ *der;* ~**s**, ~**s** (*ugs.*) speedo (*coll.*)

**Tacho·meter** *der od. das* speedometer

**Tacho·nadel** *die* speedometer needle

**Tacho·stand** *der* (*ugs.: Kilometerstand*) milometer *or* odometer reading

**Tadel** /'ta:dl̩/ *der;* ~**s**, ~ A censure; **jmdm. einen** ~ **erteilen** give sb. a rebuke; rebuke sb.; **ihn trifft kein** ~: he is not to blame; **öffentlicher** ~ (*DDR Rechtsw.*) public censure; B (*im Klassenbuch*) black mark; C (*geh.: Mangel, Makel*) blemish; flaw; **ohne** ~: perfect, flawless ‹figure, copy, etc.›; impeccable ‹dress, appearance, etc.›; irreproachable ‹life, character, person, etc.›

**tadel·los** ❶ *Adj.* A (*makellos*) impeccable; immaculate ‹hair, clothing, suit, etc.›; perfect ‹condition, teeth, pronunciation, German, etc.›; B (*ugs.: sehr gut*) excellent; C /'--'-/ (*ugs.: als Ausruf der Zustimmung*) splendid (*coll.*). ❷ *adv.* A (*makellos*) ‹dress› impeccably, immaculately; ‹fit, speak, etc.› perfectly; ‹live, behave, etc.› irreproachably; B (*ugs.: sehr gut*) **hier wird man** ~ **bedient** the service is excellent here

**tadeln** *tr. V.* **jmdn. [für sein Verhalten** *od.* **wegen seines Verhaltens]** ~: rebuke sb. [for his/her behaviour]; **jmds. Arbeit** ~: criticize sb.'s work; **er hatte an ihr/ihrer Handlungsweise etw. zu** ~: he found some fault with her/the way she behaved; ~**de Worte**/~**der Blick** reproachful words/look

**tadelns·wert** *Adj.* reprehensible

**Tadels·antrag** *der* (*Parl.*) censure motion

**Tafel** /'ta:fl̩/ *die;* ~, ~**n** A (*Schiefer*~) slate; (*Wand*~) blackboard; B (*plattenförmiges Stück*) slab; **eine** ~ **Schokolade** a bar of chocolate; C (*Gedenk*~) plaque; D (*geh.: festlicher Tisch*) table; **die** ~ **aufheben** (*fig.*) rise from the table; E (*Druckw.*) plate

**Tafel-:** ~**apfel** *der* (*Kaufmannsspr.*) dessert apple; ~**auf·satz** *der* centrepiece; ~**berg** *der* (*Geol.*) mesa; ~**besteck** *das* cutlery *or* (*Amer.*) flatware service; ~**bild** *das* (*bild. Kunst*) panel painting

**Täfelchen** /'tɛ:flçən/ *das;* ~**s**, ~ ⇒ **Tafel** B: [small] slab; [small] bar

**tafel-, Tafel-:** ~**fertig** *Adj.* (*Kochk.*) ready to serve *postpos.*; (*noch zu erwärmen*) ready to heat and serve *postpos.*; ~**fertige Gerichte** ready-to-serve/ready-to-heat-and-serve dishes; ~**freuden** *Pl.* (*geh.*) culinary delights; ~**lappen** *der* blackboard cloth; ~**musik** *die* musical entertainment (*provided at a banquet, festive dinner, etc.*)

**tafeln** *itr. V.* (*geh.*) feast

**täfeln** /'tɛ:fl̩n/ *tr. V.* panel

**Tafel-:** ~**obst** *das* [dessert] fruit; ~**runde** *die* (*geh.*) gathering [round a table]; **die** ~**runde des Königs Artus** King Arthur's Round Table; ~**salz** *das* table salt; ~**spitz** *der* (*österr.*) boiled fillet of beef

**Täfelung** *die;* ~, ~**en** A (*das Täfeln*) panelling; B (*Paneel*) [wooden] panelling

**Tafel-:** ~**wasser** *das; Pl.* ~**wässer** [bottled] mineral water; ~**wein** *der* table wine

**Taft** /taft/ *der;* ~**[e]s**, ~**e** taffeta

**Tag** /ta:k/ *der;* ~**[e]s**, ~**e** A ▶ 369 day; **es wird/ist** ~: it's getting/it is light; **solange es noch** ~ **ist** while it's still light; **der** ~ **bricht an** *od.* **graut** *od.* **erwacht/neigt sich** (*geh.*) the day breaks/draws to an end *or* a close; **die** ~**e nehmen ab/zu** the days are getting shorter/longer; **am** ~**[e]** during the day[time]; **am helllichten** ~: in broad daylight; **bei** ~**[e] reisen/ankommen** travel during the day/arrive while it's light; **[drei Stunden] vor** ~ (*geh.*) [three hours] before daylight; **er redet viel, wenn der** ~ **lang ist** (*ugs.*) you can't put any trust in what he says; **sie sind wie** ~ **und Nacht** they are as different as chalk and cheese; **man soll den** ~ **nicht vor dem Abend loben** (*Spr.*) don't count your chickens before they're hatched (*prov.*); **es ist noch nicht aller** ~**e Abend** we haven't yet seen the end of the matter; **guten** ~**!** hello; (*bei Vorstellung*) how do you do?; (*nachmittags auch*) good afternoon; **jmdm. einen guten** ~ **wünschen** wish sb. good day; ~**!** (*ugs.*) hello; hi (*Amer. coll.*); (*nachmittags auch*) afternoon; **bei jmdm. Guten** ~ **sagen** (*ugs.*) pop in to sb. to say 'hello' (*coll.*); **etw. an den** ~ **legen** display sth.; **etw. an den** ~ **bringen** *od.* (*geh.*) **ziehen** bring sth. to light; reveal sth.; **an den** ~ **kommen** come to light; **unter** ~**s** (*landsch.*) during the day [time]; **über/unter** ~**[e]** (*Bergmannsspr.*) above ground/underground; **zu** ~**e** ⇒ **zutage**; B ▶ 833 (*Zeitraum von 24 Stunden*) day; ~ **und Stunde des Treffens stehen fest** the date and time of the meeting are fixed; **welchen** ~ **haben wir heute?** (*Wochentag*) what day is it today? what's today?; (*Datum*) what date is it today?; **heute in/vor drei** ~**en** three days from today/three days ago today; **den** ~ **über** during the day; **einen** ~ **um den anderen** every other day; **jmdm. den** ~ **stehlen** waste sb.'s time; **an diesem** ~: on this day; **dreimal am** ~: three times a day; **früh/spät am** ~**[e]** early/late in the day; **am** ~**e vorher** on the previous day; the day before; **auf den** ~ **[genau]** on the [very] day; ~ **für** ~: every [single] day; **von** ~ **zu** ~: day by day; **in den nächsten** ~**en** in the next few days; **der** ~ **X** the great day; **am folgenden** ~: the next day; **heute ist sein [großer]** ~: it's his big day today; **er hatte heute einen schlechten** ~: today was one of his bad days; **sich** (*Dat.*) **einen schönen/faulen** ~ **machen** (*ugs.*) have a nice/lazy day; **den lieben langen** ~: all day long; **der** ~ **des Herrn** (*christl. Rel.*) the Lord's Day; ~ **der offenen Tür** open day; **der Brief muss/kann jeden** ~ **ankommen** the letter will surely/can arrive any day now; **eines** ~**es** one day; some day; **eines schönen** ~**es** one of these days; **dieser** ~**e werde ich …** in the next few days, I will …; **dieser** ~**e kam ein Mann …** the other day *or* recently, a man came …; **von einem** ~ **auf den anderen** from one day to the next; overnight; **jmdn. von einem** ~ **auf den anderen vertrösten** put sb. off from day to day; **in den** ~ **hinein leben** live from day to day; **den** ~ **über** during the day; C (*Ehren*~, *Gedenk*~) ~ **der deutschen Einheit** (*Bundesrepublik Deutschland*) Day of German Unity; ~ **der Republik** (*DDR*) Republic Day; D *Pl.* ([*Lebens*]*zeit*) days; **sie hat schon bessere** ~**e gesehen** she has seen better days; **seine** ~**e sind gezählt** his days are numbered; **bis in unsere** ~**e** until our day; **auf meine/deine** *usw.* **alten** ~**e** in my/your *etc.* old age; E *Pl.* (*ugs. verhüll.: Menstruation*) period *sing.*; **wenn sie ihre** ~**e hat** when it's her time of the month

**tag-, Tag-:** ~**aktiv** *Adj.* (*Zool.*) diurnal; ~**aus** *Adv.* ~**aus, tagein** day in, day out; day after day; ~**dienst** *der* day duty; ~**dienst haben** be on day duty

**Tage-:** ~**bau** *der; Pl.* ~~**e** (*Bergbau*) A (*Bergbau über Tage*) opencast mining *no art.*; B (*Anlage*) opencast mine; ~**blatt** *das* A (*veralt.: Tageszeitung*) daily [news]paper; B (*in Namen*) **das Offenburger** ~**blatt** the Offenburg Daily News; ~**buch** *das* diary; **[über etw.** (*Akk.*)**]** ~**buch führen** keep a diary [about sth.]; ~**buch·aufzeichnung** *die* diary entry; ~**dieb** *der*, ~**diebin** *die* (*abwertend*) idler; lazybones *sing.*; ~**geld** *das* A (*Verpflegungsbetrag*) daily [expense] allowance; B *Pl.* (*Diäten*) daily [parliamentary] allowance *sing.*; C (*Tagesvergütung*) daily compensation

t

**tag·ein** *Adv.* ⇒ tagaus

**tage-, Tage-: ~lang** ❶ *Adj.*; lasting for days *postpos.*; **das ~lange Warten** the days of waiting; **nach ~langem Regen** after days of rain; ❷ *adv.* for days [on end]; **~lohn** *der* daily *or* day's wage[s]; **im ~lohn arbeiten** be paid by the day; **~löhner** /-lø:nɐ/ *der;* **~~s, ~~, ~löhnerin** *die;* **~~, ~~nen** day labourer

**tagen** *itr. V.* Ⓐ (*konferieren*) meet; **das Gericht/Parlament tagt** the court/parliament is in session; **über etw.** (*Akk.*) **~:** confer about *or* meet to discuss sth.; **bis in den frühen Morgen hinein ~** (*fig.*) celebrate until the early hours; Ⓑ (*geh.: dämmern*) **es tagt** day is breaking *or* dawning

**Tage·reise** *die* day's journey; **nach Passau sind es zehn ~n** it's a ten-day journey to Passau

**Tages-: ~ab·lauf** *der* day; daily routine; **~an·bruch** *der* daybreak; dawn; **~arbeit** *die* day's work; **~aus·flug** *der* day's outing; **~aus·zug** *der* (*Bankw.*) daily statement of account transactions; **~bedarf** *der* daily requirement; **~befehl** *der* (*Milit.*) order of the day; **~creme** *die* (*Kosmetik*) day cream; **~decke** *die* bedspread; **~dessert** *das* dessert *or* (*Brit.*) sweet of the day; **~einnahme** *die* day's takings *pl.*; **~ereignis** *das* event of the day; **~fahrt** *die* day trip; day excursion; **~gespräch** *das* topic of the day; **~karte** *die* Ⓐ (*Gastron.*) menu of the day; Ⓑ (*Fahr-, Eintrittskarte*) day ticket; **~kasse** *die* Ⓐ box office (*open during the day*); Ⓑ (*~einnahme*) day's takings *pl.*; **~kilometer·zähler** *der* trip mileage recorder; **~kurs** *der* (*Börsenw.*) current rate of exchange; **~lauf** *der* daily routine; **~licht** *das* daylight; **bei ~licht** in [the] daylight; **das ~licht scheuen** (*fig.*) shun the light of day; **etw. ans ~licht bringen** *od.* **ziehen** (*fig.*) bring sth. to light; **ans ~licht kommen** (*fig.*) come to light; **~licht·projektor** *der* overhead projector; **~losung** *die* day's password; **~marsch** *der* Ⓐ (*Fußmarsch*) day's hike; Ⓑ (*Strecke eines ~marsches*) day's march; **drei ~märsche entfernt** three days' march away; **~menü** *das* set menu of the day; **~mutter** *die; Pl.* **~mütter** childminder; **~ordnung** *die* agenda; **einen Punkt auf die ~ordnung setzen/von der ~ordnung absetzen** place an item on the agenda/delete an item from the agenda; **an der ~ordnung sein** (*fig.*) be the order of the day; **zur ~ordnung übergehen** (*fig.*) proceed as if nothing had happened; **~ord·nungs·punkt** *der* item on the agenda; **~politik** *die* day-to-day politics *sing.*; **~preis** *der* (*Wirtsch.*) current price; **~presse** *die* daily press; **~ration** *die* daily ration; **~raum** *der* day room; **~satz** *der* Ⓐ (*Rechtsw.: Geldstrafe*) *unit, based on net daily income etc., used to calculate a fine;* Ⓑ (*Unterbringungskosten*) daily rate; **~suppe** *die* soup of the day; **~tour** *die* ⇒ **~fahrt**; **~wanderung** *die* day's hike; **~wanderungen** one-day hikes; **~zeit** *die* time of day; **um diese ~zeit** at this time; **jmdm. die ~zeit [ent]bieten** (*veralt.*) give sb. the time of day; **zu jeder ~- und Nachtzeit** at any time of the day or night; **~zeitung** *die* daily newspaper; daily

**tage·weise** *Adv.* on some days

**Tage·werk** *das* (*veralt. geh.*) day's labour

**Tag·falter** *der* (*Zool.*) butterfly

**tag·hell** ❶ *Adj.* Ⓐ (*durch Tageslicht*) [day]light; Ⓑ (*wie am Tag*) bright as daylight *postpos.* ❷ *adv.* **etw. ist ~ erleuchtet** sth. is very brightly lit [up]

**-tägig** /-tɛːgɪç/ Ⓐ (*... Tage alt*) **ein sechstägiges Küken** a six-day-old chick; Ⓑ (*... Tage dauernd*) **nach dreitägiger Vorbereitung** after three days' preparation; **mit dreitägiger Verspätung** three days late

**täglich** /ˈtɛːklɪç/ ❶ *Adj.* daily. ❷ *adv.* every day; **zweimal ~:** twice a day; **~ zwei Stunden** for two hours a day; **~ drei Tabletten einnehmen** take three tablets daily

*old spelling (see note on page 1707)

**Tag·pfauen·auge** *das* (*Zool.*) peacock butterfly

**tags** *Adv.* Ⓐ by day; in the daytime; Ⓑ **~ zuvor/davor** the day before; **~ darauf** the next *or* following day; the day after

**Tag·schicht** *die* day shift; **~ haben** be on [the] day shift; **in ~ arbeiten** work a day shift

**tags·über** *Adv.* during the day

**tag·täglich** (*intensivierend*) ❶ *Adj.* day-to-day; daily. ❷ *adv.* every single day

**Tag-: ~träumer** *der;* **~träumerin** *die* daydreamer; **~und·nacht·gleiche** *die;* **~~, ~~n** equinox

**Tagung** *die;* **~, ~en** conference

**Tagungs-: ~ort** *der* venue [for a/the conference]; **~teilnehmer** *der,* **~teilnehmerin** *die* participant in a/the conference

**Taifun** /taiˈfuːn/ *der;* **~s, ~e** typhoon

**Taiga** *die;* **~:** taiga

**Taille** /ˈtaljə/ *die;* **~, ~n** waist; **in der ~:** at the waist

**Taillen·weite** *die* waist measurement

**Tailleur** /taˈjøːɐ̯/ *das;* **~s, ~s** (*schweiz.*) tailored suit/coat (*fitted at the waist*)

**taillieren** /taˈjiːrən/ *tr. V.* fit [at the waist]; **ein tailliertes Kostüm** a suit with the jacket fitted at the waist

**Taiwan** /ˈtaivan/ *(das);* **~s** Taiwan

**Taiwaner** *der;* **~s, ~, Taiwanerin** *die;* **~, ~nen** Taiwanese

**Takelage** /takəˈlaːʒə/ *die;* **~, ~n** (*Seew.*) masts and rigging

**takeln** /ˈtaːkl̩n/ *tr. V.* (*Seemannsspr.*) rig

**Takelung** *die;* **~, ~en** (*Seemannsspr.*) rig

**Takt** /takt/ *der;* **~[e]s, ~e** Ⓐ (*Musik*) time; (*Einheit*) bar; measure (*Amer.*); **im ~ bleiben** stay in time; **den ~ [ein]halten** keep in time; **den ~ angeben/schlagen/wechseln** give the beat/beat time/change the time *or* beat; **aus dem ~ kommen** lose the beat; **sich nicht aus dem ~ bringen lassen** not lose the beat; **mit ihm muss ich mal ein paar ~e reden** (*fig. ugs.*) I need to have a serious talk with him; Ⓑ (*rhythmischer Bewegungsablauf*) rhythm; **im/gegen den ~:** in/out of rhythm; **im ~ bleiben** keep the rhythm; **aus dem ~ kommen** lose the rhythm; Ⓒ (*Feingefühl*) tact; **etw. aus ~ tun** do sth. out of tact[fulness]; Ⓓ (*Verslehre*) foot

**takt·fest** (*Musik*) ❶ *Adj.* **ein nicht ganz ~er Pianist** a pianist who has some difficulty keeping time; **~ sein** keep good time. ❷ *adv.* in time

**Takt·gefühl** *das* sense of tact; **etw. mit großem ~ tun** do sth. with great delicacy

**taktieren** *itr. V.* proceed tactically; **vorsichtig/klug ~:** use caution/clever tactics

**Taktik** /ˈtaktɪk/ *die;* **~, ~en [eine] ~:** tactics *pl.*; **die ~ der verbrannten Erde** (*Milit.*) scorched-earth tactics

**Taktiker** *der;* **~s, ~:** tactician

**taktisch** ❶ *Adj.* tactical. ❷ *adv.* tactically; **~ klug vorgehen** use clever *or* good tactics

**takt·los** ❶ *Adj.* tactless. ❷ *adv.* tactlessly

**Taktlosigkeit** *die;* **~, ~en** Ⓐ (*taktlose Art*) tactlessness; Ⓑ (*taktlose Handlung*) piece of tactlessness; **derartige ~en** such tactlessness *sing.*

**Takt-: ~stock** *der* baton; **den ~stock schwingen** (*scherzh.*) wield the baton; **~strich** *der* (*Musik*) bar [line]

**takt·voll** ❶ *Adj.* tactful. ❷ *adv.* tactfully

**Takt·wechsel** *der* (*Musik*) change of time

**Tal** /taːl/ *das;* **~[e]s, Täler** /ˈtɛːlɐ/ valley; **das Vieh zu ~ treiben** drive the cattle down into the valley

**tal·abwärts** *Adv.* down the valley

**Talar** /taˈlaːɐ̯/ *der;* **~s, ~e** robe

**tal·aufwärts** *Adv.* up the valley

**Tal·brücke** *die* bridge across a/the valley

**Tälchen** /ˈtɛːlçən/ *das;* **~s, ~:** [little] valley

**Talent** /taˈlɛnt/ *das;* **~[e]s, ~e** Ⓐ (*Befähigung*) talent (**zu, für** for); **~ für Sprachen haben** have a gift for languages; **sie hat das ~, immer das richtige Wort zu finden** she has a gift for always finding the right word; Ⓑ (*Mensch*) talented person; **junge ~e fördern** promote young talent

**talentiert** /talɛnˈtiːɐ̯t/ *Adj.* talented

**Talent·suche** *die* search for talent; **zur ~ in die Provinz kommen** come in search of talent in the provinces

**Taler** /ˈtaːlɐ/ *der;* **~s, ~** (*hist.*) thaler

**Tal·fahrt** *die* Ⓐ (*Schifffahrt*) passage downstream; Ⓑ (*Fahrt abwärts*) drive down into the valley; (*mit dem Lift*) descent into the valley; (*mit Skiern*) skiing down into the valley; (*fig.*) fall; plunge; **die Wirtschaft befindet sich auf einer ~** (*fig.*) the economy is on the decline

**Talg** /talk/ *der;* **~[e]s, ~e** Ⓐ (*Speisefett*) suet; (*zur Herstellung von Seife, Kerzen usw.*) tallow; Ⓑ (*Haut~*) sebum

**Talg-: ~drüse** *die* sebaceous gland; **~licht** *das; Pl.* **~~er** tallow candle

**Talisman** /ˈtaːlɪsman/ *der;* **~s, ~e** talisman

**Talk** /talk/ *der;* **~[e]s** talc

**talken** /talkn̩/ *itr. V.* appear on a talk show; **über etw. ~:** talk about sth.

**Talk·show** /ˈtɔːkʃoʊ/ *die* (*Ferns.*) talk show; chat show

**Talmi** /ˈtalmi/ *das;* **~s** Ⓐ (*wertloser Schmuck*) imitation *or* cheap jewellery; (*fig.*) tinsel; Ⓑ (*vergoldete Legierung*) pinchbeck

**Talmi·glanz** *der* glitter

**Talmud** /ˈtalmuːt/ *der;* **~[e]s, ~e** Talmud

**Talschaft** *die;* **~, ~en** (*schweiz., westösterr.*) valley people *pl. or* inhabitants *pl.*

**Tal-: ~sohle** *die* valley floor *or* bottom; (*fig.*) depression; **die Wirtschaft befindet sich auf** *od.* **in einer ~sohle** the economy is going through a depression; **~sperre** *die* dam (*with associated reservoir and power station*); **~station** *die* valley station

**Tamarinde** /tamaˈrɪndə/ *die;* **~, ~n** tamarind

**Tamariske** /tamaˈrɪskə/ *die;* **~, ~n** tamarisk

**Tambour** /ˈtambuːɐ̯/ *der;* **~s, ~e** *od.* (*schweiz.*) **~en** (*veralt.*) drummer

**Tambour·major** *der* drum major

**Tamburin** /tambuˈriːn/ *das;* **~s, ~e** tambourine

**Tampon** /ˈtampɔn/ *der;* **~s, ~s** Ⓐ (*Med.: Wattebausch*) tampon; plug; Ⓑ (*Menstruations~*) tampon

**tamponieren** *tr. V.* (*Med.*) plug

**Tamtam** /tamˈtam/ *das;* **~s, ~s** Ⓐ (*Musikinstrument*) tam-tam; Ⓑ (*ugs. abwertend: großer Aufwand*) **[großes] ~:** [a big] fuss; **~ machen** make a fuss

**Tand** /tant/ *der;* **~[e]s** trumpery

**Tändelei** *die;* **~, ~en** Ⓐ (*Spielerei*) dalliance; Ⓑ (*Liebelei*) flirtation

**tändeln** /ˈtɛndl̩n/ *itr. V.* Ⓐ (*spielen*) dally; Ⓑ (*schäkern*) flirt

**Tandem** /ˈtandɛm/ *das;* **~s, ~s** tandem; (*fig.*) pair; **als ~ arbeiten** work in tandem

**Tang** /taŋ/ *der;* **~[e]s, ~e** seaweed

**Tanga** /ˈtaŋga/ *der;* **~s, ~s** tanga

**Tangens** /ˈtaŋgɛns/ *der;* **~, ~** (*Math.*) tangent

**Tangente** /taŋˈgɛntə/ *die;* **~, ~n** Ⓐ (*Math.*) tangent; Ⓑ (*Straße*) ring road; bypass

**tangential** /taŋgɛnˈtsi̯aːl/ (*Math.*) ❶ *Adj.* tangential. ❷ *adv.* tangentially

**Tanger** /ˈtaŋɐ/ *(das);* **~s** ▶ **700** Tangier

**tangieren** /taŋˈgiːrən/ *tr. V.* Ⓐ affect; Ⓑ (*Math.*) be tangent to

**Tango** /ˈtaŋgo/ *der;* **~s, ~s** tango

**Tank** /taŋk/ *der;* **~s, ~s,** (*seltener*) **~e** tank

**Tanke** *die;* **~, ~n** (*salopp*) filling station

**tanken** *tr., itr. V.* fill up; **Benzin/Öl ~:** fill up with petrol (*Brit.*) *or* (*Amer.*) gasoline/oil; **er tankte dreißig Liter [Super]** he put in thirty litres [of four-star]; **hast du schon getankt?** have you already put petrol (*Brit.*) *or* (*Amer.*) gasoline in?; **frische Luft/Sonne ~** (*fig.*) get one's fill of fresh air/sun; **er hat aber reichlich getankt** (*fig. salopp*) he really got tanked up (*sl.*)

t

**Tanker** *der;* **~s, ~:** tanker

**Tanker·flotte** *die* fleet of tankers

**Tank-: ~fahr·zeug** *das* tanker; **~füllung** *die* Ⓐ (*das Füllen*) filling of the tank; Ⓑ **eine ~füllung reicht für ...** one full tank is enough for ...; **~lager** *das* tank farm; **~säule** *die* petrol pump (*Brit.*); gasoline pump (*Amer.*); **~stelle** *die* petrol station (*Brit.*); gas station (*Amer.*); **freie ~stelle** unbranded petrol/gas station; **~wagen** *der* tanker; **~wart** /-vart/ *der;* **~~s, ~~e, ~wartin** *die;* **~~, ~~nen** ▶ 159 petrol pump attendant (*Brit.*)

**Tann** /tan/ *der;* **~[e]s, ~e** (*dichter.*) [pine] forest

**Tanne** /ˈtanə/ *die;* **~, ~n** Ⓐ fir [tree]; **schlank wie eine ~:** slender as a reed; Ⓑ (*Holz*) fir

**Tannen-: ~baum** *der* Ⓐ (*ugs.: Tanne a*) fir tree; Ⓑ (*Weihnachtsbaum*) Christmas tree; **~grün** *das* fir sprigs *pl.*; **~holz** *das* fir; **~nadel** *die* fir needle; **~wald** *der* fir forest; **~zapfen** *der* fir cone; **~zweig** *der* fir branch

**Tansania** /tanˈza:ni̯a/ (*das*); **~s** Tanzania

**Tansanier** /tanˈza:ni̯ɐ/ *der;* **~s, ~, Tansanierin** *die;* **~, ~nen** Tanzanian

**Tantalus·qualen** /ˈtantalʊs-/ *Pl.* **~ leiden** suffer agonizing frustration *sing.*

**Tantchen** *das;* **~s, ~:** auntie (*coll.*)

**Tante** /ˈtantə/ *die;* **~, ~n** Ⓐ aunt; Ⓑ (*Kinderspr.: Frau*) lady; Ⓒ (*ugs.: Frau*) woman

**Tante-Emma-Laden** *der; Pl.* **Tante-Emma-Läden** [small] corner shop

**tantenhaft** ❶ *Adj.* old-maidish; (*belehrend*) nannyish. ❷ *adv.* like an old maid; (*belehrend*) nannyishly

**Tantieme** /tãˈti̯e:mə/ *die;* **~, ~n** Ⓐ (*Gewinnbeteiligung*) percentage of the profits; Ⓑ (*von Künstlern*) royalty

**Tanz** /tants/ *der;* **~es, Tänze** /ˈtɛntsə/ Ⓐ dance; **jmdn. zum ~ auffordern** ask sb. to dance *or* for a dance; **ein ~ auf dem Vulkan** (*fig.*) sitting on a powder keg; **der ~ ums Goldene Kalb** (*fig.*) worship of the golden calf; Ⓑ (*~veranstaltung*) dance; **heute Abend ist ~:** there is dancing this evening; **zum ~ gehen** go dancing; **ein ~ in den Mai/Frühling** a dance to mark the beginning of May/Spring; Ⓒ (*Zank, Auftritt*) song and dance (*fig. coll.*)

**Tanz-: ~abend** *der* evening dance; **~bar** *die* night spot (*coll.*) with dancing; **~bär** *der* dancing bear; **~bein** *das: in* **das ~bein schwingen** (*ugs. scherzh.*) shake a leg (*coll.*); **~boden** *der* dance floor; **~café** *das* coffee house with dancing

**Tänzchen** /ˈtɛntsçən/ *das;* **~s, ~:** [little] dance; **ein ~ wagen** take a turn around the floor

**Tanz·diele** *die* (*veralt.*) dance hall

**tänzeln** /ˈtɛntsl̩n/ *itr. V.* Ⓐ prance; **jmdm. mit ~den Schritten entgegenkommen** skip towards sb.; Ⓑ *mit sein* **sie tänzelte ins Zimmer** she skipped into the room

**tanzen** ❶ *itr. V.* Ⓐ dance; **~ gehen** go dancing; **auf dem Seil ~:** walk the tightrope; **das Schiff tanzt auf den Wellen** the ship is bobbing up and down on the waves; **sich heiß/müde ~:** dance until one is hot/tired; Ⓑ *mit sein* (*sich ~d fortbewegen*) dance; skip. ❷ *tr. V.* **Walzer/Tango ~:** dance a waltz/tango; waltz/tango

**Tänzer** /ˈtɛntsɐ/ *der;* **~s, ~** ▶ 159 Ⓐ dancer; Ⓑ (*Tanzpartner*) dancing partner; Ⓒ (*Balletttänzer*) ballet dancer

**Tanzerei** *die;* **~, ~en** Ⓐ (*ugs.*) [small] dancing party; Ⓑ (*oft abwertend: dauerndes Tanzen*) [continual] dancing *no pl.*

**Tänzerin** *die;* **~, ~nen** ⇒ **Tänzer**

**tänzerisch** ❶ *Adj.* dance-like ‹movement, rhythm, step›; **~e Begabung** talent for dancing. ❷ *adv.* **~ begabt sein** have a talent for dancing; **~ ausgebildet sein** be trained as a dancer; **eine ~ hervorragende Leistung** an outstanding achievement in dance

**Tanz-: ~fläche** *die* dance floor; **~gruppe** *die* dance group; **~kapelle** *die* dance band; **~kurs** *der* dancing class; **~lehrer** *der,* **~lehrerin** *die* dancing teacher; **~lokal** *das* café/restaurant with dancing; **~musik** *die* dance music; **~orchester** *das* dance band; **~partner** *der,* **~partnerin** *die* dancing partner; **~platte** *die* record of dance music; **~platz** *der* [open-air] dance floor; **~saal** *der* dance hall; (*in hotel, castle, etc.*) ballroom; **~schritt** *der* dance step; **~schuh** *der* dance *or* dancing shoe; **~schule** *die* dancing school; school of dancing; **~sport** *der* ballroom *or* competition dancing *no art.*; **~stunde** *die* Ⓐ (*~kurs*) dancing class; **~stunde nehmen, in die ~stunde gehen** take dancing lessons; go to dancing class; Ⓑ (*einzelne Stunde*) dancing lesson; **~tee** *der* tea dance; thé dansant; **~turnier** *das* dancing competition; **~veranstaltung** *die* dance; **~vergnügen** *das* dance

**Taoismus** /taoˈɪsmʊs/ *der;* **~:** Taoism *no art.*

**Tapet** *das: in* **aufs ~ kommen** (*ugs.*) be brought up; come up [for discussion]; **etw. aufs ~ bringen** (*ugs.*) bring sth. up; broach sth.

**Tapete** /taˈpe:tə/ *die;* **~, ~n** wallpaper; **die ~n wechseln** (*ugs.*) have a change of scene

**Tapeten-: ~rolle** *die* roll of wallpaper; **~tür** *die* concealed door; **~wechsel** *der* (*ugs.*) change of scene

**tapezieren** /tapeˈtsi:rən/ *tr. V.* [wall]paper

**Tapezierer** *der;* **~s, ~, Tapeziererin** *die;* **~, ~nen** ▶ 159 paperhanger

**Tapezier-: ~nagel** *der* tack; **~tisch** *der* pasteboard; paperhanger's bench

**tapfer** /ˈtapfɐ/ ❶ *Adj.* brave; courageous; brave ‹child›; **~en Widerstand leisten** resist bravely. ❷ *adv.* Ⓐ bravely; courageously; (*von Kindern*) bravely; **sich ~ halten** be brave; Ⓑ (*kräftig*) ‹eat, drink› heartily; **~ zulangen** have *or* take a big helping

**Tapferkeit** *die;* **~:** courage; bravery

**Tapioka** /taˈpi̯o:ka/ *die;* **~:** tapioca

**Tapir** /ˈta:pi:ɐ̯/ *der;* **~s, ~e** (*Zool.*) tapir

**Tapisserie** /tapɪsəˈri:/ *die;* **~, ~n** tapestry

**tapp** /tap/ *Interj.* patter; **~, ~!** pitter patter!

**tappen** *itr. V.* Ⓐ *mit sein* patter; **in eine Falle ~** (*fig.*) stumble into a trap; Ⓑ (*tastend greifen*) grope (**nach** for)

**täppisch** /ˈtɛpɪʃ/ ❶ *Adj.* awkward; clumsy. ❷ *adv.* awkwardly; clumsily

**Taps** /taps/ *der;* **~es, ~e** (*ugs. abwertend*) clumsy oaf

**tapsig** (*ugs.*) ❶ *Adj.* awkward; clumsy. ❷ *adv.* awkwardly; clumsily

**Tarantel** /taˈrantl̩/ *die;* **~, ~n** (*Zool.*) tarantula; **er sprang wie von der ~ gestochen auf** he jumped up as if something had bitten him

**Tarantella** /taranˈtɛla/ *die;* **~, ~s** *od.* **Tarantellen** (*Musik*) tarantella

**Tarif** /taˈri:f/ *der;* **~s, ~e** Ⓐ (*Preis, Gebühr*) charge; (*Post~, Wasser~*) rate; (*Verkehrs~*) fares *pl.*; (*Zoll~*) tariff; Ⓑ (*~verzeichnis*) list of charges/rates/fares; tariff; **der Fahrpreis beträgt laut ~ 1,20 DM** the fare is fixed at DM 1.20; Ⓒ (*Lohn~*) [wage] rate; (*Gehalts~*) [salary] scale; **weit über/unter ~ verdienen** earn well above/far below the agreed rate

**Tarif-: ~autonomie** *die* [right to] free collective bargaining *no art.* (*without state intervention*); **~gruppe** *die* (*Lohngruppe*) wage group; (*Gehaltsgruppe*) salary group; **~kommission** *die* wages commission

**tariflich** ❶ *Adj.* wage ‹demand, dispute, etc.›. ❷ *adv.* **Löhne und Gehälter sind ~ festgelegt** there are fixed rates for wages and salaries; **die Arbeitszeit ist ~ geregelt** the number of working hours is fixed [by collective agreement]

**tarif-, Tarif-: ~lohn** *der* wage under the collective agreement; **~los** *Adj.* **es herrscht ein ~loser Zustand** no wage agreement is in force; **~partner** *der:* **die ~partner** union and management; employers and employees; **wegen der Unnachgiebigkeit des ~partners** because of the inflexibility of management/the union; **~verhandlung** *die* pay negotiations *pl.*; **~vertrag** *der* pay agreement

**tarnen** /ˈtarnən/ ❶ *tr., itr. V.* camouflage; **seine Aufregung ~** (*fig.*) disguise one's excitement. ❷ *refl. V.* camouflage oneself; (*fig.*) disguise oneself

**Tarn-: ~farbe** *die* camouflage [colour]; **etw. mit ~farbe bemalen** paint sth. with camouflage paint; **~kappe** *die* (*Myth.*) magic hat (*making the wearer invisible*)

**Tarnung** *die;* **~, ~en** (*auch fig.*) camouflage; **zur ~ dienen** serve as camouflage

**Tarock** /taˈrɔk/ *das* (*österr. nur so*) *od. der* taroc

**Tartan·bahn** /ˈtartan-/ *die* Tartan track ®

**Täschchen** /ˈtɛʃçən/ *das;* **~s, ~** ⇒ **Tasche:** [little] bag/pocket

**Tasche** /ˈtaʃə/ *die;* **~, ~n** Ⓐ bag; Ⓑ (*in Kleidung, Koffer, Rucksack usw.*) pocket; Ⓒ (*fig.*) **jmdm. die ~n leeren** (*ugs.*) fleece sb.; **sich** (*Dat.*) **die eigenen ~n füllen** (*ugs.*) line one's own pockets *or* purse; **jmdm. auf der ~ liegen** (*ugs.*) live off sb.; **etw. aus eigener** *od.* **der eigenen ~ bezahlen** pay for sth. out of one's own pocket; **jmdm. etw. aus der ~ ziehen** (*ugs.*) wangle money out of sb. (*coll.*); **[für etw.] tief in die ~ greifen [müssen]** (*ugs.*) [have to] dig deep in *or* into one's pocket [for sth.]; **etw. in die eigene ~ stecken** (*ugs.*) pocket sth.; put sth. in one's own pocket; **in die eigene ~ arbeiten** *od.* **wirtschaften** (*ugs.*) line one's own pocket[s]; **jmdn. in die ~ stecken** (*ugs.*) put sb. in the shade; **sich** (*Dat.*) **in die eigene ~ lügen** (*ugs.*) fool oneself; **etw. in der ~ haben** (*ugs.*) have sth. in one's pocket

**Taschen-: ~buch** *das* paperback; **~buch·ausgabe** *die* paperback edition; **~dieb** *der,* **~diebin** *die* pickpocket; **~fahrplan** *der* pocket timetable; **~format** *das* pocket size; **ein Wörterbuch im ~format** a pocket-size dictionary; **~geld** *das* pocket money; **~kalender** *der* pocket calendar; **~krebs** *der* edible crab; **~lampe** *die* [pocket] torch (*Brit.*) *or* (*Amer.*) flashlight; **~messer** *das* pocket knife; penknife; **~rechner** *der* pocket calculator; **~schirm** *der* telescopic umbrella; **~spiegel** *der* pocket mirror; **~spieler** *der,* **~spielerin** *die* (*veralt.*) conjurer; **~spieler·trick** *der* (*abwertend*) trick; **~tuch** *das; Pl.* **~tücher** handkerchief; **~uhr** *die* pocket watch; **~wörterbuch** *das* pocket dictionary

**Tässchen, *Täßchen** /ˈtɛsçən/ *das;* **~s, ~:** [small] cup

**Tasse** /ˈtasə/ *die;* **~, ~n** Ⓐ cup; **eine ~ Tee** a cup of tea; **trübe ~** (*ugs. abwertend*) drip (*coll.*); **komm, du trübe ~!** come on, don't be such a drip (*coll.*); Ⓑ (*~ mit Untertasse*) cup and saucer; **nicht alle ~n im Schrank haben** (*ugs.*) not be right in the head (*coll.*)

**Tastatur** /tastaˈtu:ɐ̯/ *die;* **~, ~en** keyboard

**Taste** /ˈtastə/ *die;* **~, ~n** Ⓐ (*eines Musikinstruments, einer Schreibmaschine*) key; **[mächtig] in die ~n greifen** start to play with great gusto; Ⓑ (*Fuß~*) pedal [key]; Ⓒ (*am Telefon, Radio, Fernsehgerät, Taschenrechner usw.*) button

**Tast·empfindung** *die* sense of touch

**tasten** ❶ *itr. V.* (*fühlend suchen*) grope, feel (**nach** for); **~de Versuche/Fragen** (*fig.*) tentative attempts/questions. ❷ *refl. V.* (*sich tastend bewegen*) grope *or* feel one's way. ❸ *tr. V.* Ⓐ (*über eine Tastatur eingeben*) key in; Ⓑ (*tastend feststellen*) feel

**Tasten-: ~druck** *der; Pl.* **~drücke** touch of a/the button; **auf ~druck** at the touch of a/the button; **~instrument** *das* keyboard instrument; **~telefon** *das* push-button telephone

**Taster** *der;* **~s, ~** Ⓐ (*Technik: Maschine*) keyboard; Ⓑ ▶ 159 (*Fachspr.: Mensch*) keyboard operator; Ⓒ (*Druck~*) button

**Tasterin** *die;* **~, ~nen** ⇒ **Taster** B

**Tast·sinn** *der* sense of touch

**tat** /ta:t/ *1. u. 3. Pers. Sg. Prät. v.* **tun**

**Tat** *die;* **~, ~en** Ⓐ (*Handlung*) act; (*das Tun*) action; **ein Mann der ~:** a man of action; **jmdm. mit Wort und ~ beistehen** stand by sb. in word and deed; **etw. durch ~en beweisen** prove sth. by one's actions;

t

**zur ~ schreiten** proceed to action; **die gute Absicht/den guten Willen für die ~ nehmen** take the will for the deed; **jmdn. auf frischer ~ ertappen** catch sb. red-handed *or* in the act; **etw. in die ~ umsetzen** put sth. into action *or* effect; **das ist die ~ eines Wahnsinnigen** that is the action of a madman; **eine verbrecherische ~:** a crime; a criminal act; **eine gute ~ vollbringen** do a good deed; **ein Buch über Leben und ~en des ...** a book on the life and exploits of ...; **zu seiner ~ stehen** stand by one's action; **B in der ~** (*verstärkend*) actually; (*zustimmend*) indeed

**Tatar**[1] /ta'taːɐ̯/ *der;* **~en, ~en** Tartar

**Tatar**[2] *das;* **~[s], Tatar·beefsteak** *das* steak tartare

**Tatarin** *die;* **~, ~nen** ⇒ **Tatar**[1]

**tatarisch** *Adj.* Tartar

**tatauieren** /tatau̯'iːrən/ (*Völkerk.*) ⇒ **tätowieren**

**Tat-: ~bestand** *der* **A** facts *pl.* [of the matter *or* case]; **einen ~bestand feststellen** establish the facts [of a matter *or* case]; **B** (*Rechtsw.*) elements *pl.* of an offence; **der ~bestand der vorsätzlichen Tötung** the offence of premeditated murder; **~einheit** *die* (*Rechtsw.*) concomitance of offences; **Mord in ~einheit mit Raub** murder [in concomitance] with robbery

**taten-, Taten-: ~drang** *der* desire *or* thirst for action; **trotz seines hohen Alters war er noch voller ~drang** in spite of his old age he was still full of energy; **~durst** *der* (*geh.*) thirst for action; **er brennt vor ~durst** he is thirsting for action; **~durstig** *Adj.* (*geh.*) thirsty *or* eager for action *postpos.*; **~los** **1** *Adj.* idle; **2** *adv.* idly; **einer Sache** (*Dat.*) **~los zusehen** watch sth. without taking any action

**Täter** /'tɛːtɐ/ *der;* **~s, ~:** culprit; **wer ist der ~?** who did it?; **der ~ hat sich der Polizei gestellt** the person who committed the crime gave himself/herself up to the police; **nach dem ~ fahnden** search *or* look for the person responsible [for the crime]; **die Polizei hat die ~ noch nicht gefunden** the police have not yet found those responsible [for the crime]

**Täterin** *die;* **~, ~nen** ⇒ **Täter**

**Täter·kreis** *der* group of people involved in a/the crime; (*bei mehreren Verbrechen*) group of offenders

**Täterschaft** *die;* **~ A seine ~ ist erwiesen** his responsibility for the crime has been proved; **B** (*schweiz.: Täter*) culprit/culprits

**Tat-: ~form** *die* (*Sprachw.*) ⇒ **Aktiv**[1]; **~her·gang** *der* [course *sing.* of] events *pl.*

**tätig** /'tɛːtɪç/ *Adj.* **A ~ sein** work; **der in unserer Firma ~e Ingenieur** the engineer who works for our firm; **~ werden** (*bes. Amtsspr.*) take action; **~e Reue** (*Rechtsw.*) *remorse for one's crime, accompanied by action to avert its effects;* **B** (*rührig, aktiv*) active; **~e Nächstenliebe** charity [to one's neighbour]; brotherly love; **ein ~er Vulkan** an active vulcano

**tätigen** /'tɛːtɪɡn̩/ *tr. V.* (*Kaufmannsspr., Papierdt.*) transact ‹business, deal, etc.›; **Einkäufe ~:** effect purchases; **Anrufe ~:** put through [telephone] calls

**Tätigkeit** *die;* **~, ~en A** activity; (*Arbeit*) job; **eine fieberhafte ~:** a frenzy of activity; **das gehört zu den ~en einer Hausfrau** that is part of a housewife's work *sing.*; **eine ~ ausüben** do work; do a job; **seine ~ aufnehmen** start work; **nach zweijähriger ~:** after two years' work; **B** (*das In-Betrieb-Sein*) operation; **in ~ treten** come into operation

**Tätigkeits-: ~bereich** *der* sphere *or* field of activity; **~bericht** *der* progress report; **~form** *die* (*Sprachw.*) ⇒ **Aktiv**[1]; **~merkmal** *das* key activity; **~wort** *das; Pl.* **~wörter** (*Sprachw.*) ⇒ **Verb**

*old spelling (see note on page 1707)

**Tat·kraft** *die* energy; drive

**tat·kräftig** **1** *Adj.* energetic, active ‹person›; active ‹help, support›. **2** *adv.* energetically; actively

**tätlich** /'tɛːtlɪç/ **1** *Adj.* physical ‹clash, attack, resistance, etc.›; **gegen jmdn. ~ werden** become violent towards sb. **2** *adv.* physically; **jmdn. ~ angreifen** attack sb. physically; assault sb.

**Tätlichkeit** *die;* **~, ~en** act of violence; **es kam zu ~en** violence occurred

**Tat-: ~mensch** *der* man/woman of action; **~motiv** *das* motive [for a/the crime]; **~ort** *der* scene of a/the crime

**tätowieren** /tɛto'viːrən/ *tr. V.* tattoo; **sich** (*Dat.*) **etw. ~ lassen** have oneself tattooed with sth.

**Tätowierer** *der;* **~s, ~, Tätowiererin** *die;* **~, ~nen ▶ 159** tattooist; tattooer

**Tätowierung** *die;* **~, ~en A** tattoo; **B** (*das Tätowieren*) tattooing

**Tat·sache** *die* fact; **es ist [eine] ~, dass ...** it's a fact that ...; **~!** (*ugs.*) it's true; it's a fact; **~?** (*ugs.*) really?; is that true?; **den ~n entsprechen** be true; **nackte ~n** hard facts; (*scherzh.*) naked bodies; **den ~n ins Auge sehen** face facts; **vollendete ~n schaffen** create a fait accompli; **jmdn. vor die vollendete ~** *od.* **vollendete ~n stellen** present sb. with a fait accompli; ⇒ *auch* **Vorspiegelung**

**Tatsachen-: ~bericht** *der* factual report; **~material** *das* facts *pl.*

**tatsächlich** /'taːtzɛçlɪç/ **1** *Adj.* actual; real; **der ~e Grund** the real reason. **2** *adv.* actually; really; **ist das ~ wahr?** is that really true?; **~?** really?; **ich habe mich ~ geirrt** I was indeed mistaken; **Er hat es geschafft. — Tatsächlich!** He made it. — So he did!

**tätscheln** /'tɛtʃl̩n/ *tr. V.* pat

**tatschen** /'tatʃn̩/ *itr. V.* (*ugs. abwertend*) **an/auf etw.** (*Akk.*) **~:** paw sth.

**Tatter·greis** /'tatɐ-/ *der* (*ugs. abwertend*) doddery old man

**Tatter·greisin** *die* (*ugs. abwertend*) doddery old woman

**Tatterich** /'tatərɪç/ *der;* **~s** (*ugs.*) **einen ~ kriegen** get shaking hands; **er hat einen ~:** his hands are shaking

**tatterig, tattrig** *Adj.* (*ugs.*) shaky ‹hands, movements, etc.›; doddery ‹person›

**tatütata** /ta'tyːta'taː/ *Interj.* pah-paw-pah-paw; **mit „Tatütata" und Blaulicht** with siren wailing and blue light flashing

**tat·verdächtig** *Adj.* suspected; **[dringend] ~ sein** be under [strong] suspicion

**Tat·waffe** *die* weapon [used in the crime]

**Tatze** /'tatsə/ *die;* **~, ~n** (*auch fig. ugs.*) paw

**Tat·zeit** *die:* **[zur] ~:** [at the] time of the crime

**Tau**[1] /tau̯/ *der;* **~[e]s** dew; **vor ~ und Tag** (*dichter.*) before dawn of day

**Tau**[2] *das;* **~[e]s, ~e** (*Seil*) rope

**taub** /taup/ *Adj.* **A** deaf; **~ werden** go deaf; **er war ~ gegen** *od.* **für alle Bitten** (*fig.*) he was deaf to all requests; **auf diesem Ohr ist er ~** (*ugs. scherzh.*) he's deaf to that sort of thing; **B** (*wie abgestorben*) numb; **C** (*leer, unbefruchtet usw.*) empty ‹nut›; unfruitful ‹ear of corn›; unfertilized ‹bird's egg›; dead ‹rock›

**taub·blind** *Adj.* deaf and blind

**Täubchen** /'tɔypçən/ *das;* **~s, ~:** [little] pigeon; (*Turtel~*) [little] dove; **mein ~** (*fig.*) my little dove

**Taube**[1] *die;* **~, ~n** pigeon; (*Turtel~; auch Politik fig.*) dove

**Taube**[2] *der/die; adj. Dekl.* deaf person; deaf man/woman; **die ~n** the deaf

**tauben·blau** *Adj.* greyish-blue

**Tauben·ei** *das* pigeon['s] egg

**taubenei·groß** *Adj.* as big as *or* the size of a golf ball *postpos.*; **~e Stücke** pieces as big as *or* the size of golf balls

**Tauben·schlag** *der* pigeon loft; (*für Turteltauben*) dovecot; **hier geht es zu wie in einem** *od.* **im ~** (*ugs.*) it's like Piccadilly Circus here (*Brit. coll.*); it's like being in the middle of Times Square (*Amer.*)

**Tauber** *der;* **~s, ~, Täuberich** /'tɔybərɪç/ *der;* **~s, ~e** cock pigeon

**Taubheit** *die;* **~:** deafness

**taub-, Taub-: ~nessel** *die* dead nettle; **~stumm** *Adj.* deaf and dumb; **~stumme** *der/die; adj. Dekl.* deaf mute; **~stummen·sprache** *die* deaf-and-dumb language

**tauchen** **1** *itr. V.* **A** *auch mit sein* dive (**nach** for); **früher habe ich viel getaucht** I used to do a lot of skin diving *or* underwater swimming; **er kann zwei Minuten [lang] ~:** he can stay under water for two minutes; **er ist 3 Meter tief getaucht** he dived down three metres; **die Sonne tauchte unter den Horizont** (*fig.*) the sun disappeared *or* sank below the horizon; **B** *mit sein* (*ein~*) dive; (*auf~*) rise; emerge; **er tauchte ins Dunkel des Gartens** (*fig.*) he plunged into the darkness of the garden. **2** *tr. V.* **A** (*ein~*) dip; **der Raum war in Licht getaucht** (*geh.*) the room was bathed in light; **die Landschaft war in Dunkelheit getaucht** (*geh.*) the countryside was shrouded in darkness; **B** (*unter~*) duck

**Tauch·ente** *die* scaup [duck]

**Taucher** *der;* **~s, ~ ▶ 159** diver; (*mit Flossen und Atemgerät*) skin diver

**Taucher-: ~an·zug** *der* diving suit; **~ausrüstung** *die* diving equipment; **~brille** *die* diving goggles *pl.*; **~glocke** *die* diving bell

**Taucherin** *die;* **~, ~nen ▶ 159** ⇒ **Taucher**

**Tauch-: ~gerät** *das* diving equipment *no pl., no indef. art.*; **~maske** *die* diving mask; **~sieder** *der;* **~~s, ~~:** portable immersion heater; **~sport** *der* skin diving *no art.*; **~station** *die:* **auf ~station gehen** (*auf dem U-Boot*) go to one's diving station; (*fig. ugs.*) go to ground; **~tiefe** *die* diving depth

**tauen** **1** *itr. V.* **A** (*unpers.*) **es taut** it's thawing; **B** *mit sein* (*schmelzen*) melt. **2** *tr. V.* melt; thaw

**Tauf·becken** *das* font

**Taufe** *die;* **~, ~n A** (*christl. Rel.: Sakrament*) baptism; **B** (*christl. Rel.: Zeremonie*) christening; baptism; **jmdn. über die ~ halten** *od.* (*veralt.*) **aus der ~ heben** be [a] godparent to sb.; **etw. aus der ~ heben** (*fig. ugs.*) launch sth.

**taufen** *tr. V.* **A** (*die Taufe vollziehen an*) baptize; **katholisch getauft sein** be baptized a Catholic; **B** (*einen Namen geben*) christen ‹child, ship, animal, etc.›; **ein Kind auf den Namen Peter ~:** christen a child Peter; **er wurde nach seinem Großvater [Hermann] getauft** he was named [Hermann] after *or* (*Amer.*) for his grandfather

**Tauf-: ~kapelle** *die* baptistery; **~kleid** *das* christening robe *or* gown

**Täufling** /'tɔyflɪŋ/ *der;* **~s, ~e** child to be baptized; (*Erwachsener*) person to be baptized

**Tauf-: ~name** *der* Christian name; **~pate** *der* godparent; (*männlicher ~pate*) godfather; **~patin** *die* godmother; **~register** *das* register of baptisms; baptismal register

**tau·frisch A** (*feucht vom Tau*) dew-covered; dewy; **B** (*ganz frisch*) fresh; **sie ist auch nicht mehr ganz ~** (*fig.*) she's not exactly a spring chicken any more

**Tauf-: ~schein** *der* certificate of baptism; baptismal certificate; **~stein** *der* font

**taugen** /'tauɡn̩/ *itr. V.* **nichts/wenig** *od.* **nicht viel/etwas ~:** be no/not much/some good *or* use; **zu** *od.* **für etw. ~** ‹person› be suited to sth.; ‹thing› be suitable for sth.; **zu einem** *od.* **zum Lehrer ~** ‹person› make a good teacher; **dazu ~, etw. zu tun** be good at doing sth.; **nicht wissen, was etw. wirklich taugt** not know how useful sth. really is

**Taugenichts** *der;* **~[es], ~e** (*veralt. abwertend*) good-for-nothing

**tauglich** *Adj.* **A** (*geeignet, brauchbar*) **[nicht] ~:** [un]suitable; **der Arzt hat ihn für ~ erklärt, ein Auto zu führen** the doctor has pronounced him fit to drive a car; **B** (*für Militärdienst*) fit [for service]

**Taumel** *der;* **~s A** (*Schwindel, Benommenheit*) [feeling of] dizziness *or* giddiness; **ein**

t

~ **überkam ihn** he was overcome by a feeling of dizziness *or* giddiness; Ⓑ (*Begeisterung, Rausch*) frenzy; fever; **ein ~ der Begeisterung/Leidenschaft** a fever of excitement/passion; **ein ~ des Entzückens/Glücks** a transport of delight/happiness

**taumelig** ❶ *Adj.* dizzy; giddy; **ihm war/wurde ~ vor Glück** he was transported with happiness/went into transports of happiness. ❷ *adv.* ~ **gehen** reel *or* stagger

**taumeln** /'taumḷn/ *itr. V.* Ⓐ *auch mit sein* (*wanken*) reel, sway (**vor** + *Dat.* with); **das Flugzeug begann zu ~:** the aircraft began to roll; Ⓑ *mit sein* (*sich ~d bewegen*) stagger; **in den Abgrund/ins Unglück ~:** tumble into the abyss/plunge into disaster

**tau·nass**, ***tau·naß** *Adj.* wet with dew *postpos.*

**Tau·punkt** *der* (*Physik*) dew point

**Tausch** *der;* ~**[e]s**, ~**e** exchange; **ein guter/schlechter ~:** a good/bad deal; **im ~ gegen** *od.* **für etw.** in exchange for sth.; **etw. durch ~ erwerben** acquire sth. through an exchange; **etw. zum ~ anbieten** offer to exchange sth. for sth.; **etw. im ~ erhalten** receive sth. in exchange

**tauschen** ❶ *tr. V.* exchange (**gegen** for); **Briefmarken/Münzen ~:** exchange *or* swap stamps/coins; **sie tauschten die Partner/Pferde/Plätze** they changed *or* swapped partners/horses/places; **wollen wir ~:** shall we swap (*coll.*); **Küsse ~** (*geh.*) kiss; **einen Händedruck ~:** shake hands. ❷ *itr. V.* **mit den Rollen/Plätzen/Partnern ~:** change *or* swap roles/places/partners; **mit jmdm. ~** (*fig.*) change *or* swap places with sb.

**täuschen** /'tɔyʃn̩/ ❶ *tr. V.* deceive; **ich sah mich in meinen Erwartungen getäuscht** I was disappointed in my expectations; **der Schüler versuchte zu ~:** the pupil tried to cheat; **der Schein täuscht uns oft** appearances are often deceiving; **wenn mich nicht alles täuscht** unless I'm completely mistaken. ❷ *itr. V.* Ⓐ (*irreführen*) be deceptive; Ⓑ (*bes. Sport: ablenken*) make a feint. ❸ *refl. V.* be wrong *or* mistaken (**in** + *Dat.* about); **ich habe mich in ihm getäuscht** I was wrong about him; he disappointed me; **da täuschst du dich aber [gewaltig]** but that's where you're [very much] mistaken

**täuschend** ❶ *Adj.* remarkable, striking ‹similarity, imitation›. ❷ *adv.* remarkably; **jmdm. ~ ähnlich sehen** look remarkably like sb.

**Täuscher** *der;* ~**s**, ~, **Täuscherin** *die;* ~, ~**nen** swindler

**Tausch-:** ~**geschäft** *das* exchange [deal]; **ein gutes ~geschäft machen** make a good deal in an/the exchange; ~**gesellschaft** *die* (*Soziol.*) barter society; ~**handel** *der* Ⓐ bartering; ~**handel treiben** barter; Ⓑ (*Wirtsch.*) trade by barter; ~**objekt** *das* object of barter[ing]

**Täuschung** *die;* ~, ~**en** Ⓐ (*das Täuschen*) deception; **auf eine ~ hereinfallen** be deceived; Ⓑ (*Selbst~*) delusion; illusion; **einer ~ unterliegen** be under an illusion; **er gibt sich der ~ hin, dass ...** he mistakenly believes that ...; **optische ~:** optical illusion

**Täuschungs-:** ~**absicht** *die* intent to deceive; ~**manöver** *das* ploy

**tausend** /'tauznt/ *Kardinalz.* ▶ **841** Ⓐ a *or* one thousand; **einige/mehrere Tausend Zuschauer** a few/several thousand spectators; **Tausend und Abertausend Ameisen** thousands and thousands of ants; ➡ *auch* **acht**; Ⓑ (*ugs.: sehr viele*) thousands of; **noch ~ Sachen zu erledigen haben** still have thousands of *or* a thousand things to do; ~ **Dank/Küsse** a thousand thanks/kisses

**Tausend**[1] *das;* ~**s**, ~**e** *od.* ~ (*nach unbest. Zahlwörtern*) Ⓐ thousand; **ein volles/halbes ~:** a full/half a thousand; a thousand/five hundred; **vom ~:** per thousand; Ⓑ *Pl.* (*große Anzahl*) thousands; ~**e Zuschauer** thousands of spectators; **die Kosten gehen in die ~e** (*ugs.*) the costs run into thousands; **die Tiere starben zu ~en** the animals died in [their] thousands

**Tausend**[2] *die;* ~, ~**en** thousand

**tausend·ein[s]** *Kardinalz.* ▶ **841** a *or* one thousand and one

**Tausender** *der;* ~**s**, ~ Ⓐ (*ugs.*) (*Tausendmarkschein usw.*) thousand-mark/-dollar *etc.* note; (*Betrag*) thousand marks/dollars *etc.*; Ⓑ (*Math.*) thousand

**tausenderlei** *Gattungsz.; indekl.* (*ugs.*) Ⓐ (*von verschiedener Art*) a thousand and one different ‹answers, kinds, etc.›; Ⓑ (*viele*) a thousand and one; ➡ *auch* **hunderterlei**

**tausendfach** *Vervielfältigungsz.* thousandfold; (*ugs.: sehr häufig*) a thousand and one times; **die ~e Menge** a thousand times the amount; ~**en Dank** a thousand thanks; ➡ *auch* **achtfach**

**Tausendfüßer** /'tauzntfy:sɐ/ *der;* ~**s**, ~, **Tausendfüßler** *der;* **Tausendfüßlers, Tausendfüßler** millipede

**Tausend·gülden·kraut** *das* (*Bot.*) centaury

**Tausend·jahr·feier** *die* millenary; millennial; (*Festlichkeit auch*) millenary *or* millennial celebrations *pl.*; ➡ *auch* **Hundertjahrfeier**

**tausend·jährig** *Adj.* Ⓐ (*tausend Jahre alt*) [one-]thousand-year-old; Ⓑ (*tausend Jahre dauernd*) thousand-year[-long]; ~**es Reich** (*ns.*) thousand-year Reich; **Tausendjähriges Reich** (*Theol.*) millennium

**tausendköpfig** *Adj.* thousand-strong; (*fig.*) thousands strong *postpos.*

**Tausend·künstler** *der*, **Tausend·künstlerin** *die* (*ugs. scherzh.*) jack of all trades

**tausend·mal** *Adv.* a thousand times; **ich bitte [dich] ~ um Entschuldigung** (*ugs.*) a thousand pardons *or* apologies; ➡ *auch* **achtmal**

**Tausend·mark·schein** *der* ▶ **337** thousand-mark note

**Tausendsas[s]a** /'tauzntsasa/ *der;* ~**s**, ~**[s]** jack of all trades

**Tausendschönchen** /-ʃø:nçən/ *das;* ~**s**, ~**:** daisy

**tausendst...** *Ordinalz.* ▶ **841** thousandth; ➡ *auch* **acht...**

**tausendstel** /'tauzntstl̩/ *Bruchz.* ▶ **841** thousandth; ➡ *auch* **achtel**

**Tausendstel** *das* (*schweiz. meist* **der**); ~**s**, ~**:** thousandth

**Tausendstel·sekunde** *die;* ~, ~**n** thousandth of a second

**tausend·und·ein[s]** *Kardinalz.* ➡ **tausendein[s]**

**Tautologie** /tautolo'gi:/ *die;* ~, ~**n** (*Rhet., Stilk.*) tautology

**tautologisch** *Adj.* (*Rhet., Stilk.*) tautological; tautologous

**Tau-:** ~**tropfen** *der* dewdrop; ~**wasser** *das; Pl.* ~~**:** meltwater; ~**werk** *das* Ⓐ (*Material*) rope; Ⓑ (*auf einem Schiff*) rigging; ~**wetter** *das* (*auch fig.*) thaw; **gestern war bei uns ~wetter** yesterday we had a thaw; ~**ziehen** *das;* ~~**s** (*auch fig.*) tug-of-war

**Taverne** /ta'vɛrnə/ *die;* ~, ~**n** taverna

**Taxa·meter** /taxa-/ *der* [taxi]meter

**Taxator** /ta'ksa:tɔr/ *der;* ~**s**, ~**en** /taksa'to:rən/, **Taxatorin** *die;* ~, ~**nen** (*Wirtsch.*) valuer

**Taxe** /'taksə/ *die;* ~, ~**n** Ⓐ taxi; Ⓑ (*Gebühr*) charge; Ⓒ (*taxierter Preis*) valuation

**Taxi** /'taksi/ *das;* ~**s**, ~**s** taxi; **mit dem ~:** by taxi *or* in a taxi; ~ **fahren** drive a taxi; (*als Fahrgast*) go by taxi

**taxieren** *tr. V.* Ⓐ (*ugs.: schätzen*) estimate (**auf** + *Akk.* at); **er hat falsch taxiert** his estimate is wrong; **etw. zu hoch/niedrig ~:** overestimate/underestimate sth.; Ⓑ (*den Wert ermitteln von*) value (**auf** + *Akk.* at); **etw. zu hoch/niedrig ~:** overvalue/undervalue sth.; Ⓒ (*ugs.: mustern, prüfen*) size up (*coll.*); Ⓓ (*einschätzen*) assess

**Taxi-:** ~**fahrer** *der;* ~**fahrerin** *die* ▶ **159** taxi driver; ~**fahrt** *die* taxi ride; ~**stand** *der* taxi rank (*Brit.*); taxi stand

**Taxus** /'taksʊs/ *der;* ~, ~**:** yew [tree]

**Tb, Tbc** /te:'be:, te:be:'tse:/ *die;* ~ *Abk.* **Tuberkulose** TB

**Tb-krank** /te:'be:-/ *Adj.* suffering from TB *postpos.;* ~**e Patienten** patients with TB

**Tb-Kranke** /te:'be:-/ *der/die; adj. Dekl.* TB patient; patient with TB

**Teak** /ti:k/ *das;* ~**s**, **Teak·holz** *das* teak

**Team** /ti:m/ *das;* ~**s**, ~**s** team

**Team·arbeit** *die* teamwork

**Team·chef** *der;* **Team·chefin** *die* (*Sport*) team manager

**team·fähig** *Adj.* able to work as part of a team *postpos.;* ~ **sein** be a [good] team player

**Teamwork** /'ti:mwə:k/ *das;* ~**s** teamwork

**Tearoom** /'ti:ru:m/ *der;* ~**s**, ~**s** (*schweiz.*) tearoom (*without alcoholic drinks*)

**Technik** /'tɛçnɪk/ *die;* ~, ~**en** Ⓐ technology; (*Studienfach*) engineering *no art.*; **auf dem neuesten Stand der ~:** incorporating the latest technical advances; **im Zeitalter der ~ leben** live in the technological age *or* age of technology; Ⓑ (*technische Ausrüstung*) equipment; machinery; Ⓒ (*Arbeitsweise, Verfahren*) technique; Ⓓ (*eines Gerätes*) workings *pl.*

**Techniker** *der;* ~**s**, ~, **Technikerin** *die;* ~, ~**nen** ▶ **159** Ⓐ technical expert; Ⓑ (*im Sport, in der Kunst*) technician

**Technikum** /'tɛçnikʊm/ *das;* ~**s**, **Technika** *od.* **Techniken** technical college

**technisch** /'tɛçnɪʃ/ ❶ *Adj.* technical; technological ‹progress, age›; **ein ~er Fehler** a technical fault. ❷ *adv.* technically; ‹interested› in technology; technologically ‹advanced›; ~ **begabt sein** have a technical flair

**technisieren** /tɛçni'zi:rən/ *tr. V.* mechanize

**Technisierung** *die;* ~, ~**en** mechanization

**Techno**[1] /'tɛkno/ *das od. der;* ~**s** techno

**Techno**[2] /'tɛkno/ *der;* ~**s**, ~**s** techno fan

**Technokrat** /tɛçno'kra:t/ *der;* ~**en**, ~**en** technocrat

**Technokratie** /tɛçnokra'ti:/ *die;* ~**:** technocracy

**Technokratin** *die;* ~, ~**nen** technocrat

**technokratisch** *Adj.* technocratic

**Technologie** /tɛçnolo'gi:/ *die;* ~, ~**n** technology

**Technologie·park** *der* science park

**technologisch** ❶ *Adj.* technological. ❷ *adv.* technologically

**Techno·party** *die* techno party

**Techtelmechtel** /tɛçtl̩'mɛçtl̩/ *das;* ~**s**, ~**:** affair

**Teckel** /'tɛkl̩/ *der;* ~**s**, ~**:** dachshund

**Teddy·bär** /'tɛdi-/ *der* teddy bear

**Tedeum** /te'de:ʊm/ *das;* ~**s**, ~**s** Te Deum

**TEE** *Abk.* **Trans-Europ-Express** TEE

**Tee** /te:/ *der;* ~**s**, ~**s** tea; **der ~ muss noch ziehen** the tea must stand *or* brew a while; ~ **machen** make some tea; **einen ~ geben** (*geh.*) give a tea party; **einen im ~ haben** (*fig. ugs.*) be tipsy; have had one over the eight (*coll.*); **abwarten und ~ trinken** (*fig. ugs.*) just wait and see

**Tee-:** ~**beutel** *der* tea bag; ~**butter** *die* (*österr.*) ➡ **Markenbutter**; ~**ei**, *~**-Ei** *das* tea ball; tea egg; ~**gebäck** *das* [tea] biscuits *pl.* (*Brit.*) *or* (*Amer.*) cookies *pl.*; ~**glas** *das; Pl.* ~**gläser** tea glass; ~**kanne** *die* teapot; ~**kessel** *der* tea kettle; ~**licht** *das; Pl.* ~~**er** *od.* ~**e** tea warmer; ~**löffel** *der* teaspoon

**Teen** /ti:n/ *der;* ~**s**, ~**s**, **Teenager** /'ti:neɪdʒə/ *der;* ~**agers**, ~**ager** teenager

**Teenie** /'ti:ni/ *der;* ~**s**, ~**s** (*ugs.*) young teenager

**Tee-:** ~**pause** *die* tea break; ~**pflücker** *der*, ~**pflückerin** *die* tea picker

**Teer** /te:ɐ̯/ *der;* ~**[e]s**, (*Arten:*) ~**e** tar

**Teer·decke** *die* tar surface

**teeren** *tr. V.* tar; **jmdn. ~ und federn** tar and feather sb.

**teer-, Teer-:** ~**farbstoff** *der* aniline dye; ~**fass**, *~**faß** *das* tar barrel; ~**haltig** *Adj.* containing tar *postpos., not pred.*

**Tee·rose** *die* tea rose

**Teer·pappe** *die* bituminous roofing felt

**Tee-:** ~**service** *das* tea service; teaset; ~**sieb** *das* tea strainer; ~**strauch** *der* tea

t

plant; **~stube** *die* tearoom; **~tasse** *die* teacup; **~trinker** *der;* **~trinkerin** *die* tea drinker; **~wagen** *der* tea trolley; **~wasser** *das* water for the tea; ⇒ *auch* **Kaffeewasser**; **~wurst** *die: soft German smoked sausage for spreading;* ≈ meat spread

**Teich** /taiç/ *der;* **~[e]s, ~e** pond; **der große ~** (*ugs. scherzh.: das Meer*) the [herring] pond (*joc.*)

**Teig** /taik/ *der;* **~[e]s, ~e** dough; (*Kuchen~, Biskuit~*) pastry; (*Pfannkuchen~, Waffel~*) batter; (*in Rezepten auch*) mixture; **~ für Fleischklößchen** meatball mixture; **den ~ gehen lassen** let the dough rise

**teigig** *Adj.* Ⓐ (*wie Teig*) doughy; Ⓑ (*blass u. schwammig*) pasty ‹face, skin, complexion›

**Teig-: ~rolle** *die* Ⓐ (*Rolle aus Teig*) roll of dough; Ⓑ (*Nudelholz*) rolling pin; **~waren** *Pl.* pasta *sing.*

**Teil** /tail/ Ⓐ *der;* **~[e]s, ~e** (*etw. von einem Ganzen*) part; **weite ~e des Landes** wide areas of the country; **ein [großer** *od.* **guter] ~ der Presse/Bevölkerung** a [large] section of the press/population; **ich habe das Buch zum größten ~ gelesen** I have read most of the book; **zum ~:** partly; **es waren zum ~ schöne Exemplare** some of them were beautiful specimens; **fünfter ~:** fifth; **den größten ~ des Weges hat er zu Fuß zurückgelegt** he walked most of the way; **ein gut ~ Glück/Mut** a lot of *or* a good bit of luck/courage (*coll.*); Ⓑ *der od. das;* **~[e]s, ~e** (*An~*) share; **sein[en] ~ [schon noch] bekommen** *od.* **kriegen** get one's comeuppance (*coll.*); **sein[en] ~ weghaben** (*ugs.*) have [already] had one's due; (*die verdiente Strafe bekommen haben*) have got what was coming to one; **sich** (*Dat.*) **sein ~ denken** have one's own thoughts on the matter; **ich für mein ~ ...** for my part, I ...; Ⓒ *der od. das;* **~[e]s, ~e** (*Beitrag*) share; **ich will gerne mein[en] ~ dazu beisteuern** I should like to do my share *or* bit; **sein[en] ~ geben** *od.* **[zu etw.] tun** do one's share *or* bit [towards sth.]; Ⓓ *der;* **~[e]s, ~e** (*beteiligte Person[en]; Rechtsw.: Partei*) party; Ⓔ *das;* **~[e]s, ~e** (*Einzel~*) part; **~e des Motors** [component] parts of the engine; **etw. in seine ~e zerlegen** take sth. apart *or* to pieces

**Teil-: ~ansicht** *die* partial view; **~aspekt** *der:* **nur ein ~aspekt des Problems** only one aspect of the problem

**teil·bar** *Adj.* divisible (**durch** by)

**Teilbarkeit** *die;* **~:** divisibility

**Teil-: ~bereich** *der* (*eines Fachs*) branch; (*einer Organisation*) section; **~betrag** *der* instalment; (*einer Rechnung*) item

**Teilchen** *das;* **~s, ~** Ⓐ (*kleines Stück*) [small] part; Ⓑ (*Partikel*) particle; Ⓒ (*bes. nordd.: Gebäckstück*) tart

**Teilchen·beschleuniger** *der;* **~s, ~** (*Kerntechnik*) particle accelerator

**teilen** ❶ *tr. V.* Ⓐ (*zerlegen, trennen*) divide [up]; Ⓑ (*dividieren*) divide (**durch** by); Ⓒ (*auf~*) share (**unter** + *Dat.* among); Ⓓ (*teilweise überlassen, gemeinsam nutzen, teilhaben an*) share; Ⓔ (*in zwei Teile ~*) divide; **das Schiff teilt die Wellen** (*geh.*) the ship cuts through the waves; ⇒ *auch* **Leid** A. ❷ *refl. V.* Ⓐ **sich** (*Dat.*) **etw. [mit jmdm.] ~:** share sth. [with sb.]; **sich** (*Dat.*) **[mit jmdm.] in etw.** (*Akk.*) **~** (*geh.*) share sth. [with sb.]; Ⓑ (*auseinander gehen*) **der Vorhang teilt sich** the curtain opens; **der Weg teilt sich** the road forks; **geteilter Meinung sein** have different views *or* opinions. ❸ *itr. V.* share

**Teiler** *der;* **~s, ~** (*Math.*) factor

**Teil-: ~erfolg** *der* partial success; **~gebiet** *das* branch; **~habe** *die* participation (**an** + *Dat.* in)

**teil|haben** *unr. itr. V.* share (**an** + *Dat.* in)

**Teilhaber** *der;* **~s, ~, Teilhaberin** *die;* **~, ~nen** partner; **stiller Teilhaber** sleeping partner

**Teilhaberschaft** *die;* **~, ~en** participation, (*Anteil*) share (**an** + *Dat.* in)

**teilhaftig** /-ˈhaftɪç/ *Adj.* **in einer Sache** (*Gen.*) **~ werden/sein** (*geh. veralt.*) be blessed with sth.; **eines Anblicks ~ werden** be privy to a sight

**Teil·kasko·versicherung** *die: insurance giving limited cover*

**teil·möbliert** ❶ *Adj.* partially furnished. ❷ *adv.* **~ wohnen** live in partly furnished accommodation

**Teilnahme** /ˈtailna:mə/ *die;* **~, ~n** Ⓐ (*das Mitmachen*) participation (**an** + *Dat.* in); **~ an einem Kurs** attendance at a course; Ⓑ (*Interesse*) interest (**an** + *Dat.* in); Ⓒ (*geh.: Mitgefühl*) sympathy

**teilnahme·berechtigt** *Adj.* eligible (**bei** for)

**Teilnahme·berechtigung** *die* eligibility

**teilnahms·los** *Adj.* (*gleichgültig*) indifferent; (*apathisch*) apathetic

**Teilnahmslosigkeit** *die* (*Gleichgültigkeit*) indifference; (*Apathie*) apathy

**teilnahms·voll** ❶ *Adj.* compassionate. ❷ *adv.* compassionately; **jmdn. ~ ansehen** look at sb. with compassion

**teil|nehmen** /ˈtailne:mən/ *unr. itr. V.* Ⓐ (*dabei sein bei*) **[an etw.** (*Dat.*)**] ~:** attend [sth.]; Ⓑ (*beteiligt sein*) **[an etw.** (*Dat.*)**] ~:** take part [in sth.]; **am Krieg ~:** fight in the war; **an einem Wettkampf ~:** take part in *or* enter a competition; Ⓒ (*als Lernender*) **[an einem Lehrgang] ~:** attend [a course]; **am Unterricht ~:** attend lessons; Ⓓ (*Teilnahme zeigen*) **an jmds. Schmerz/Glück ~:** share sb.'s pain/happiness

**teilnehmend** ⇒ **teilnahmsvoll**

**Teilnehmer** *der;* **~s, ~** Ⓐ participant (*Gen.*, **an** + *Dat.* in); (*bei Wettbewerb auch*) competitor, contestant (**an** + *Dat.* in); Ⓑ (*Fernspr.*) subscriber; **der ~ meldet sich nicht** there is no reply

**Teilnehmerin** *die;* **~, ~nen** ⇒ **Teilnehmer**

**Teilnehmer·zahl** *die* number of participants; (*Sport*) number of competitors

**teils** /tails/ *Adv.* partly; **~ ... ~ ...** partly ... partly ...; **Kostüme, ~ mit Seitenschlitzen** costumes, some with side slits; **Wie hat es dir gestern gefallen? — T~, ~** (*ugs.*) How did you like it yesterday? — So so

**Teil-: ~strecke** *die* (*einer Straße*) stretch; (*einer Buslinie usw.*) stage; (*Rennsport*) stage; **~strich** *der* graduation line; **~stück** *das* piece; part

**Teilung** *die;* **~, ~en** division

**teil·weise** ❶ *Adv.* partly; **~ gut** good in parts. ❷ *adj.* partial

**Teil-: ~zahlung** *die* instalment; **etw. auf ~zahlung kaufen** buy sth. on hire purchase (*Brit.*) *or* (*Amer.*) on installment plan; **~zeit·arbeit** *die* part-time work *no indef. art.;* (*Stelle*) part-time job; **~zeit·beschäftigung** *die* part-time employment *or* work *no indef. art.;* (*Stelle*) part-time job

**Teint** /tɛ̃:/ *der;* **~s, ~s** complexion

**Tektonik** /tɛkˈto:nɪk/ *die;* **~** (*Geol.*) tectonics *sing., no art.*

**tektonisch** *Adj.* tectonic

**tele-, Tele-** /ˈte:le-/ tele-

**Tele-: ~arbeit** *die* teleworking; telecommuting; **~arbeiter** *der* teleworker; telecommuter

**Tele·brief** *der* fax message

**Tele·fax** *das* fax

**Telefon** /ˈte:lefo:n, *auch* teleˈfo:n/ *das;* **~s, ~e** telephone; phone; **ans ~ gehen** answer the [tele]phone; **jmdn. ans ~ rufen** call sb. to the [tele]phone; **am ~ verlangt werden** be wanted on the [tele]phone; **am ~ hängen** (*ugs.*) be on the [tele]phone; **sich ans ~ hängen** (*ugs.*) get on the phone

**Telefon-: ~an·ruf** *der* [tele]phone call; **~anschluss,** ***~an·schluß** *der* telephone; line; **~apparat** *der* telephone

**Telefonat** /telefoˈna:t/ *das;* **~[e]s, ~e** telephone call

**Telefon-: ~buch** *das* [tele]phone book *or* directory; **~gebühr** *die* telephone charge; **~gespräch** *das* telephone conversation; **~häuschen** *das* ⇒ **~zelle**; **~hörer** *der* telephone receiver

**telefonieren** /telefoˈni:rən/ *itr. V.* make a [tele]phone call; **mit jmdm. ~:** talk to sb. [on the telephone]; **nach einem Taxi ~:** [tele]phone a taxi; **du telefonierst zu viel** you're on the phone too much; you're making too many [tele]phone calls; **nach Hause ~:** phone home; **nach England ~:** make a [tele]phone call to England; **lange [mit jmdm.] ~:** be on the telephone [to sb.] for a long time; **er telefoniert gerade** he is on the phone at the moment; **bei jmdm. ~:** use sb.'s [tele]phone

**telefonisch** ❶ *Adj.* telephone; **die ~e Zeitansage** the speaking clock (*Brit. coll.*); the telephone time service; **~e Bestellung** telephone order; order by telephone. ❷ *adv.* by telephone; **jmdm. etw. ~ mitteilen** inform sb. of sth. over the *or* by telephone; **ich bin ~ zu erreichen** *od.* **erreichbar** I can be contacted by telephone; **er hat sich ~ entschuldigt** he telephoned to apologize

**Telefonist** /telefoˈnɪst/ *der;* **~en, ~en, Telefonistin** *die;* **~, ~nen** ▶ **159** telephonist; (*in einer Firma*) switchboard operator

**Telefon-: ~karte** *die* phonecard; **~leitung** *die* telephone line; **~nummer** *die* [telephone number; **~rechnung** *die* [tele]phone bill; **~seelsorge** *die* pastoral advice service; **die ~seelsorge** ≈ the Samaritans (*Brit.*); **~überwachung** *die* telephone surveillance; **~verbindung** *die* telephone line; **~verzeichnis** *das* telephone list; **~zelle** *die* [tele]phone booth *or* (*Brit.*) box; call box (*Brit.*); **~zentrale** *die* telephone exchange

**tele·gen** /teleˈge:n/ *Adj.* telegenic

**Telegraf** /teleˈgra:f/ *der;* **~en, ~en** telegraph

**Telegrafen-: ~amt** *das* telegraph office; **~mast** *der* telegraph pole

**Telegrafie** *die;* **~:** telegraphy *no art.*

**telegrafieren** /telegraˈfi:rən/ *itr., tr. V.* telegraph; **jmdm. ~:** send a telegram to sb.; **nach Berlin ~:** send a telegram to Berlin

**telegrafisch** ❶ *Adj.* telegraphic; **eine ~e Mitteilung** a message by telegraph *or* telegram. ❷ *adv.* by telegraph *or* telegram; **~ überwiesenes Geld** money sent by telegram *or* cable

**Telegramm** *das* telegram

**Telegrammstil** *der* telegram style; telegraphese [style]; **im ~:** in telegraphese

**Telegraph, Telegraphie** *usw.* ⇒ **Telegraf, Telegrafie** *usw.*

**Telekinese** /telekiˈne:zə/ *die;* **~** (*Parapsych.*) telekinesis *no art.*

**Tele·kolleg** *das* ≈ Open University (*Brit.*)

**Tele·objektiv** *das* (*Fot.*) telephoto lens

**Teleologie** /teleoloˈgi:/ *die;* **~** (*Philos.*) teleology *no art.*

**teleo·logisch** /teleoˈlo:gɪʃ/ ❶ *Adj.* teleological. ❷ *adv.* teleologically

**Telepathie** /telepaˈti:/ *die;* **~:** telepathy *no art.*

**telepathisch** ❶ *Adj.* telepathic; **auf ~em Weg** by telepathic means. ❷ *adv.* telepathically

***Telephon, *telephonieren** *usw.:* ⇒ **Telefon, telefonieren** *usw.*

**tele·scheu** *Adj.* camera-shy

**Tele·shopping** *das* teleshopping

**Tele·skop** /teleˈsko:p/ *das;* **~s, ~e** telescope

**Teleskop·antenne** *die* telescopic aerial *or* (*Amer.*) antenna

**Tele·spiel** *das* video game

**Tele·vision** /televiˈzio:n/ *die;* **~:** television *no art.*

**Telex** /ˈte:lɛks/ *das;* **~, ~[e]** telex

**telexen** *itr. V.* telex

**Teller** /ˈtɛlɐ/ *der;* **~s, ~** Ⓐ plate; **ein ~ Suppe** a plate of soup; Ⓑ (*beim Skistock*) basket

**Teller-: ~eisen** *das* (*Jagdw.*) steel jaw trap; **~fleisch** *das* (*bes. österr.*): *pieces of boiled beef or pork served in soup;* **~gericht** *das* (*Gastr.*) one-course meal; **~mine** *die* Teller mine; anti-tank mine; **~rand** *der* rim; edge of a/the plate; **über den eigenen ~rand** (*fig.*) beyond one's own nose; **~wäscher** *der;*

*old spelling (see note on page 1707)

**~~s, ~~, ~wäscherin** *die* dishwasher; **vom ~wäscher zum Millionär werden** go from rags to riches

**Tellur** /tɛˈluːɐ̯/ *das;* **~s** (*Chemie*) tellurium

**Tempel** /ˈtɛmpl̩/ *der;* **~s, ~:** temple

**Tempel-: ~herr** *der* (*hist.*) Templar; **~orden** *der* (*hist.*) Order of the Knights Templars; **~ritter** *der* (*hist.*) Templar; **~schändung** *die* desecration of a/the temple

**Tempera-** /ˈtɛmpəra-/: **~farbe** *die* tempera colour; distemper; **~malerei** *die* **A** (*Maltechnik*) tempera painting *no art.*; painting *no art.* in distemper; **B** (*Bild*) tempera painting

**Temperament** /tɛmpəraˈmɛnt/ *das;* **~[e]s, ~e** **A** (*Wesensart*) temperament; **die vier ~e** the four humours; **eine Sache des ~s** a matter *or* question of temperament; **B** (*Schwung, Lebhaftigkeit*) **eine Frau mit ~:** a lively *or* vivacious woman; a woman with spirit; **[viel] ~ haben** be [very] lively; have [plenty of] spirit; **sie hat kein/wenig ~:** she is not a lively/not a very lively person; **sein ~ reißt alle mit** his vivacity infects everyone; **C** (*Erregbarkeit*) **das ~ geht oft mit mir durch** I often lose my temper; **sein ~ zügeln** control one's temper

**temperament·los** *Adj.* spiritless; lifeless

**Temperaments-: ~aus·bruch** *der* temperamental outburst; **~sache** *die: in* **etw./das ist ~sache** sth./that is a matter *or* question of temperament

**temperament·voll** *Adj.* spirited ‹person, speech, dance, etc.›; lively ‹start etc.›; nippy (*coll.*) ‹car›

**Temperatur** /tɛmpəraˈtuːɐ̯/ *die;* **~, ~en** ▶ 728 **A** (*Wärmezustand*) temperature; **die richtige ~ haben** be [at] the right temperature; **B** (*Körper~*) temperature; **[erhöhte] ~ haben** have *or* be running a temperature; **jmds. ~ messen** take sb.'s temperature

**Temperatur-: ~anstieg** *der* rise in temperature; **~regler** *der* thermostat; **~rück·gang** *der* drop *or* fall in temperature; **~schwankung** *die* fluctuation in temperature; **~sturz** *der* [sudden] fall *or* drop in temperature; **~unterschied** *der* difference in temperature

**temperieren** /tɛmpəˈriːrən/ *tr. V.* bring to the right temperature; **das Zimmer angenehm/richtig ~:** bring the room to a pleasant/the right temperature; **das Wasser ist gut temperiert** the water is [at] the right temperature; **ein schlecht temperierter Wein** a wine at the wrong temperature

**Templer** /ˈtɛmplɐ/ *der;* **~s, ~** (*hist.*) Templar

**Tempo**[1] /ˈtɛmpo/ *das;* **~s, ~s** *od.* **Tempi** **A** *Pl.* **~s** speed; **das ~ erhöhen** speed up; accelerate; **in** *od.* **mit hohem ~:** at high speed; **hier gilt ~ 100** there is a 100 k.p.h. speed limit here; **der hat ein ~ drauf!** (*ugs.*) he's going at quite a *or* (*Brit. coll.*) at a fair old speed!; **~ [~]!** (*ugs.*), **macht mal ein bisschen ~** (*ugs.*) get a move on; **B** (*Musik*) tempo; time; **C** (*Fechten*) period; (*Hieb*) stop cut; (*Stoß*) stop thrust *or* point

**Tempo**[2] Ⓦⓩ *das;* **~s, ~s** (*ugs.*) tissue

**Tempo·limit** *das* ▶ 348 (*Verkehrsw.*) speed limit

**Tempora** ⇒ **Tempus**

**temporal** /tɛmpoˈraːl/ (*Sprachw.*) temporal

**Temporal·satz** *der* (*Sprachw.*) temporal clause

**temporär** /tɛmpoˈrɛːɐ̯/ (*geh.*) **1** *Adj.* temporary. **2** *adv.* temporarily

**Tempo·taschentuch** *das* (*ugs.*) paper tissue *or* handkerchief

**Tempus** /ˈtɛmpʊs/ *das;* **~, Tempora** /ˈtɛmpora/ (*Sprachw.*) ⇒ **Zeitform**

**Tendenz** /tɛnˈdɛnts/ *die;* **~, ~en** **A** trend; **es herrscht die ~/die ~ geht dahin, ... zu ...** there is a tendency to ...; the trend is to ...; **die Preise haben eine steigende/fallende ~:** prices are rising/falling; **B** (*Hang, Neigung*) tendency; **die ~ haben, etw. zu tun** have a tendency to do sth.; **seine Ansichten haben eine ~ zum Dogmatismus** his attitudes tend towards dogmatism; **C** (*oft abwertend: Darstellungsweise*) slant; bias

**tendenziell** /tɛndɛnˈtsi̯ɛl/ **1** *Adj.* **der ~e Fall der Profitrate** the [general] trend towards a drop in profit margins. **2** *adv.* **~ scheint sich eine Verschärfung dieser Krise abzuzeichnen** the trend seems to indicate a deepening of the crisis; **eine ~ faschistische Haltung** an attitude tending towards fascism

**tendenziös** /...ˈtsi̯øːs/ *Adj.* tendentious

**Tendenz·wende** *die* change in a/the trend *or* in direction

**Tender** /ˈtɛndɐ/ *der;* **~s, ~** (*Eisenb., Seew.*) tender

**tendieren** /tɛnˈdiːrən/ *itr. V.* tend **(zu** towards); **er tendiert zu solchen Auffassungen** he tends to [hold] such opinions; **nach links/rechts ~:** tend to[wards] the left/right; **der nach links ~de Flügel dieser Partei** the branch of the party with left-wing leanings

**Teneriffa** /teneˈrɪfa/ *(das);* **~s** Tenerife

**Tenne** /ˈtɛnə/ *die;* **~, ~n** threshing floor (*in barn*)

**Tennis** /ˈtɛnɪs/ *das;* **~:** tennis *no art.*

**Tennis-: ~arm** *der* ▶ 474 (*Med.*) tennis elbow; **~ball** *der* tennis ball; **~platz** *der* tennis court; **~schläger** *der* tennis racket; **~schuh** *der* tennis shoe; **~spiel** *das* **A** (*Tennis*) tennis *no art.*; **B** (*Einzelspiel*) game of tennis; **~spielen** *das;* **~~s** tennis *no art.*; **~spieler** *der*, **~spielerin** *die* tennis player

**Tenor**[1] /teˈnoːɐ̯/ *der;* **~s, Tenöre** /teˈnøːrə/, (*österr. auch:*) **~e** (*Musik*) **A** (*Stimmlage, Sänger*) tenor; **den ~ singen** sing tenor *or* the tenor part; **B** (*im Chor*) tenors *pl.*; tenor voices *pl.*

**Tenor**[2] /ˈteːnɔr/ *der;* **~s** tenor

**Tenor·schlüssel** *der* (*Musik*) tenor clef

**Tentakel** /tɛnˈtaːkl̩/ *der od. das;* **~s, ~** (*Zool., Bot.*) tentacle

**Tenü, Tenue** /təˈnʏ/ *das;* **~s, ~s** (*schweiz.*) style of dress

**Teppich** /ˈtɛpɪç/ *der;* **~s, ~e** carpet; (*kleiner*) rug; **auf dem ~ bleiben** (*fig. ugs.*) keep one's feet on the ground; **etw. unter den ~ kehren** (*fig. ugs.*) sweep sth. under the carpet

**Teppich-: ~boden** *der* fitted carpet; **~fliese** *die* carpet tile; **~kehrer** *der;* **~~s, ~~:** carpet sweeper; **~klopfer** *der* carpet beater; **~stange** *die: frame for beating carpets*

**Term** /tɛrm/ *der;* **~s, ~e** (*Math., Logik, Physik*) term

**Termin** /tɛrˈmiːn/ *der;* **~s, ~e** **A** (*festgelegter Zeitpunkt*) date; (*Anmeldung*) appointment; (*Verabredung*) engagement; **der letzte** *od.* **äußerste ~ für die Zahlung** the deadline *or* final date for payment; **sich** (*Dat.*) **einen ~ geben lassen** make an appointment; **B** (*Rechtsw.*) hearing; **heute ist ~ in Sachen ...** the ... case comes on today

**Terminal** /ˈtøːɐ̯minəl/ *das;* **~s, ~s** terminal

**termin-, Termin-: ~gebunden** *Adj.* scheduled; **~gebunden sein** have a deadline; **~gemäß** **1** *Adj.* on time *postpos.*; **~gemäße Fertigstellung** completion on time *or* schedule; **2** *adv.* on time; on schedule; **~gemäß beginnen** start punctually; **~geschäft** *das* (*Börsenw.*) forward transaction *or* operation

**Termini** ⇒ **Terminus**

**terminieren** /tɛrmiˈniːrən/ *tr. V.* **A** (*befristen*) limit the duration of **(auf** + *Akk.* to); **B** (*zeitlich festlegen*) **eine Veranstaltung** *usw.* **~:** set *or* fix a date for an event *etc.*

**Terminierung** *die;* **~, ~en** scheduling

**Termini technici** ⇒ **Terminus technicus**

**Termin·kalender** *der* appointments book; (*für gesellschaftliche Termine*) engagements diary; **den ~ einhalten** (*fig.*) keep to the schedule

**terminlich** **1** *Adj.* **~e Schwierigkeiten/Grenzen** difficulties/limits with regard to schedule; **~e Gründe** reasons of schedule. **2** *adv.* **es lässt sich ~ vereinbaren** it fits in with the/our/their *etc.* schedule

**Terminologie** /tɛrminoloˈgiː/ *die;* **~, ~n** terminology

**terminologisch** /tɛrminoˈloːgɪʃ/ *Adj.* terminological

**Terminus** /ˈtɛrminʊs/ *der;* **~, Termini** term

**Terminus technicus** /- ˈtɛçnikʊs/ *der;* **~, Termini technici** /...nitsi/ technical term

**Termite** /tɛrˈmiːtə/ *die;* **~, ~n** termite

**Termiten·hügel** *der* termite hill

**Terpentin** /tɛrpɛnˈtiːn/ *das,* (*österr. meist:*) *der;* **~s** **A** (*Harz*) turpentine; **B** (*ugs.: ~öl*) turps *sing.* (*coll.*)

**Terpentin·öl** *das* oil of turpentine

**Terrain** /tɛˈrɛ̃ː/ *das;* **~s, ~s** **A** (*Gelände*) terrain; **~ verlieren** lose ground; **es ist für ihn ein unbekanntes ~** (*fig.*) it is unknown territory to him; **das ~ sondieren** (*fig. geh.*) sound out the situation; **B** (*Baugelände*) building land

**Terrakotta** /tɛraˈkɔta/ *die;* **~, Terrakotten, Terrakotte** *die;* **~, ~n** terracotta

**Terrarium** /tɛˈraːri̯ʊm/ *das;* **~s, Terrarien** terrarium

**Terrasse** /tɛˈrasə/ *die;* **~, ~n** terrace

**terrassen·förmig** **1** *Adj.* terraced. **2** *adv.* in terraces

**Terrassen·haus** *das* block of flats (*Brit.*) *or* (*Amer.*) apartments/house built in terraces on a slope

**Terrazzo** /tɛˈratso/ *der;* **~[s], Terrazzi** terrazzo

**terrestrisch** /tɛˈrɛstrɪʃ/ **1** *Adj.* terrestrial. **2** *adv.* terrestrially

**Terrier** /ˈtɛri̯ɐ/ *der;* **~s, ~:** terrier

**Terrine** /tɛˈriːnə/ *die;* **~, ~n** tureen

**territorial** /tɛritoˈri̯aːl/ *Adj.* territorial

**Territorial-: ~hoheit** *die* territorial sovereignty; **~staat** *der* (*hist.*) territorial state

**Territorium** /tɛriˈtoːri̯ʊm/ *das;* **~s, Territorien** **A** (*Gebiet, Land*) land; territory; **ein unbesiedeltes ~:** uninhabited land *or* territory; **ein riesiges ~:** a huge area *or* region; **B** (*Hoheitsgebiet*) territory

**Terror** /ˈtɛrɔr/ *der;* **~s** **A** terrorism *no art.*; **blutiger ~:** terror and bloodshed; **~ ausüben** use terror tactics; **B** (*ugs.: Zank u. Streit*) trouble; **C** (*ugs.: großes Aufheben*) big row (*coll.*) *or* fuss; **~ machen** raise hell (*coll.*)

**Terror-: ~akt** *der* act of terrorism; **~anschlag** *der* terrorist attack

**terrorisieren** *tr. V.* **A** (*durch Terror unterdrücken*) terrorize; **B** (*ugs.: belästigen*) pester

**Terrorismus** *der;* **~:** terrorism *no art.*

**Terrorist** *der;* **~en, ~en, Terroristin** *die;* **~, ~nen** terrorist

**terroristisch** *Adj.* terrorist

**Terror·welle** *die* wave of terror

**Tertia** /ˈtɛrtsi̯a/ *die;* **~, Tertien** (*Schulw.*) (*veralt.*) fourth and fifth year (*of a Gymnasium*); **B** (*österr.*) third year (*of a Gymnasium*)

**Tertianer** /tɛrˈtsi̯aːnɐ/ *der;* **~s, ~, Tertianerin** *die;* **~, ~nen** (*Schulw.*) **A** (*veralt.*) (*Ober~*) pupil in the fifth year (*of a Gymnasium*); (*Unter~*) pupil in the forth year (*of a Gymnasium*); **B** (*österr.*) pupil in the third year (*of a Gymnasium*)

**tertiär** /tɛrˈtsi̯ɛːɐ̯/ *Adj.* (*Geol.*) Tertiary

**Tertiär** *das;* **~s** (*Geol.*) Tertiary [Period]

**Tertium Comparationis** /ˈtɛrtsi̯ʊm kɔmparaˈtsi̯oːnɪs/ *das;* **~, Tertia Comparationis** (*geh.*) common element (*as a basis for comparison*)

**Terz** /tɛrts/ *die;* **~, ~en** **A** (*Musik*) third; **B** (*Fechten*) tierce

**Terzett** /tɛrˈtsɛt/ *das;* **~[e]s, ~e** **A** (*Musik*) trio; **[im] ~ singen** sing a trio; **B** (*Verslehre*) triplet

**Terzine** /tɛrˈtsiːnə/ *die;* **~, ~n** (*Verslehre*) terza rima

**Tesa·film** Ⓦⓩ /ˈteːza-/ *der;* **~[e]s** Sellotape (*Brit.*) ®; Scotch tape (*Amer.*) ®

**Test** /tɛst/ *der;* **~[e]s, ~s** *od.* **~e** test

**Testament** /tɛstaˈmɛnt/ *das;* **~[e]s, ~e** **A** (*letzte Verfügung eines Erblassers*) will; **das**

t

# Temperaturen

Temperaturen werden in Großbritannien zum Teil noch in Fahrenheit angegeben, obwohl alle Wetterberichte, Schulprüfungen und andere amtliche Quellen die Celsiusskala gebrauchen. In den USA dagegen sind Temperaturen in Fahrenheit noch gang und gäbe.
Um Celsius in Fahrenheit umzurechnen, benutzt man die folgende Formel: Grad in Celsius mal 9 dividiert durch 5 plus 32
(°C x 9 ÷ 5 + 32 = °F).

| | Celsius (°C) | Fahrenheit (°F) | |
|---|---|---|---|
| Siedepunkt | 100 | 212 | Boiling point |
| | 90 | 194 | |
| | 80 | 176 | |
| | 70 | 158 | |
| | 60 | 140 | |
| | 50 | 122 | |
| | 40 | 104 | |
| Körpertemperatur | 37 | 98.4 | Body temperature |
| | 30 | 86 | |
| | 20 | 68 | |
| | 10 | 50 | |
| Gefrierpunkt | 0 | 32 | Freezing point |
| | – 10 | 14 | |
| | – 17,8 | 0 | |
| absoluter Nullpunkt | – 273,15 | – 459.67 | Absolute zero |

## Das Wetter

***Wie viel Grad sind es?***
= What's the temperature?

***Die Außentemperatur beträgt 20 Grad [Celsius]***
= The outside temperature is 20 degrees [centigrade] *od.* (*bes. amerik.*) 68 degrees Fahrenheit

***Höchsttemperaturen um 27 Grad***
= Maximum temperatures around 27 degrees, (*bes. amerik.*) Highs around 80 degrees

***Tiefsttemperaturen um 10 Grad***
= Temperatures falling to 10 degrees, (*bes. amerik.*) Lows around 50 degrees

***Temperaturen um den Gefrierpunkt***
= temperatures around freezing

***zehn Grad unter null***
= ten degrees below freezing

***– 15°C (minus fünfzehn Grad Celsius)***
= – 15°C (minus fifteen degrees centigrade)

***Die Temperatur liegt über/unter dem Gefrierpunkt***
= The temperature is above/below freezing

***In Berlin herrscht die gleiche Temperatur***
= It's the same temperature *od.* The temperature is the same in Berlin

## Bei Personen

***Sie hat erhöhte Temperatur***
= She has a [slight] temperature, Her temperature is above normal

***Er hat [hohes] Fieber/40 Grad Fieber***
= He has a high temperature/a temperature of 40 [centigrade] *od.* 104 [Fahrenheit]

***Wie hoch ist*** od. ***Was ist Ihre Temperatur?***
= What is your temperature?

***Ich habe kein Fieber***
= I haven't got a temperature, My temperature is normal

***Sie hat bei ihm Fieber gemessen***
= She took his temperature

## Bei Dingen

***Bei welcher Temperatur kocht Wasser?***
= What temperature does water boil at?

***Wasser kocht bei 100°C***
= Water boils at 100° *od.* 212°F

***Welche Temperatur hat der Wein?***
= What is the temperature of the wine?

***Der Wein muss die richtige Temperatur haben***
= The wine must be the right temperature

***A hat die gleiche Temperatur wie B***
= A is the same temperature as B

~ **eröffnen** read the will; **ohne Hinterlassung eines ~s sterben** die intestate; **das politische ~** (*fig.*) the political legacy; **er kann sein ~ machen** (*fig. ugs.*) he is [in] for it (*coll.*); **B** (*christl. Rel.*) Testament; **das Alte/Neue ~:** the Old/New Testament

**testamentarisch** /tɛstamɛn'ta:rɪʃ/ **1** *Adj.* testamentary. **2** *adv.* **etw. ~ bestimmen** *od.* **festlegen** *od.* **verfügen** write sth. in one's will

**Testaments-: ~eröffnung** *die* reading of a/the will; **~vollstrecker** *der*, **~vollstreckerin** *die* executor

**Testat** /tɛs'ta:t/ *das;* **~[e]s, ~e A** certification; **B** (*Hochschulw. veralt.: Vorlesungsnachweis*) certificate of attendance

**Test·bild** *das* (*Ferns.*) test card

**testen** *tr. V.* test (**auf** + *Akk.* for)

**Test-: ~fall** *der* test case; **~frage** *die* test question

**testieren** *tr. V.* (*Hochschulw. veralt.*) certify

**Testosteron** /tɛstoste'ro:n/ *das;* **~s** (*Physiol.*) testosterone

**Test-: ~pilot** *der*, **~pilotin** *die* test pilot; **~verfahren** *das* test[ing] procedure

**Tetanus** /'te:tanʊs/ *der;* ~ ▶ 474 (*Med.*) tetanus *no art.*

**Tetanus·schutz·impfung** *die* tetanus vaccination

**Tete-a-Tete**, **Tête-à-tête** /tɛta'tɛ:t/ *das;* **~s, ~s** (*veralt., scherzh.*) tête-à-tête

**Tetraeder** /tetra'|e:dɐ/ *das;* **~s, ~** (*Geom.*) tetrahedron

**Tetralogie** /tetralo'gi:/ *die;* **~, ~n** tetralogy

**teuer** /'tɔyɐ/ **1** *Adj.* **A** expensive; dear *usu. pred.*; **wie ~ war das?** how much did that cost?; **das ist mir zu ~:** that's too expensive *or* too much [for me]; **Kaffee soll wieder teurer werden** coffee is supposed to be going up again; **zu teuren Preisen** at high prices; **teures Geld** (*fig.*) good money; **das ist ihn ~ zu stehen gekommen** (*fig.*) that cost him dear; ⇒ *auch* **Rat** A; **B** (*veralt.: geschätzt*) dear; **teurer Freund!** [my] dear friend!; **[mein] Teuerster!** [my] dearest; (*von Mann zu Mann*) [my] dearest friend; ⇒ *auch* **lieb** 1 D.
**2** *adv.* expensively; dearly; **etw. ~ kaufen/verkaufen** pay a great deal for sth./sell sth. at a high price; **~ essen gehen** eat in an expensive restaurant/expensive restaurants; **sie haben ihren Sieg ~ erkauft** they paid a high price for their victory; **ein ~ erkaufter Sieg** a victory won at a high price; **diese Gemeinheit wird er [mir] ~ bezahlen!** I'll make him pay for that dirty trick!

**Teuerung** *die;* **~, ~en** rise in prices

**Teuerungs-: ~rate** *die* rate of price increases; **~zu·schlag** *der* cost-of-living supplement

**Teufel** /'tɔyfl/ *der;* **~s, ~:** devil; **der ~:** the Devil; **wie der ~ fahren/reiten** drive/ride in daredevil fashion; **armer ~:** poor devil; **der ~ steckt im Detail** it's [always] the little things that cause all the problems; **der ~ ist los** all hell's let loose (*coll.*); **dich reitet wohl der ~!** what's got into you?; **ich weiß auch nicht, was für ein ~ mich da geritten hat** I don't know what got into me; **hol dich/ihn** *usw.* **der ~!** (*salopp*) sod (*Brit. sl.*) *or* (*coll.*) damn you/him *etc.*; **hol's der ~!** (*salopp*) sod (*Brit. sl.*) *or* (*coll.*) damn it!; **der ~ soll dich/ihn/es** *usw.* **holen!** (*salopp*) sod (*Brit. sl.*) *or* (*coll.*) damn you/him/it *etc.*; **in ihn/dich** *usw.* **ist wohl der ~ gefahren** (*salopp*) (*er ist/du bist usw. frech*) what does he think he's/do you think you're *etc.* doing?; (*er ist/du bist usw. leichtsinnig*) he/you *etc.* must be mad; **~ auch!** (*salopp*) damn [it all]! (*coll.*); **das weiß der ~!** (*salopp*) God [only] knows; **weiß der ~, was/wie/wo ...** (*salopp*) God knows what/how/where ...; **hinter etw. her sein wie der ~ hinter der armen Seele** (*ugs.*) be greedy for sth.; **etw. fürchten/scheuen wie der ~ das Weihwasser** (*ugs.*) fear nothing more than sth./avoid sth. like the plague; **den ~ werde ich [tun]!** (*salopp*) like hell [I will]! (*coll.*); **mal bloß nicht den ~ an die Wand!** (*ugs.*) don't invite trouble/(*stärker*) disaster by talking like that!; **des ~s sein** (*ugs.*) be mad; have taken leave of one's senses; **des ~s Gebetbuch** *od.* **Gesangbuch** (*scherzh.*) a pack *or* (*Amer.*) deck of cards; **in ~s Küche kommen** (*ugs.*) get into a hell of a mess (*coll.*); **jmdn. in ~s Küche bringen** (*ugs.*) put sb. in a hell of a mess (*coll.*); **warum musst du den jetzt auf ~ komm raus überholen?** (*ugs.*) why are you so hell-bent on overtaking him now? (*coll.*); **vom ~ besessen sein** (*fig.*) (*verrückt, wahnsinnig*) be mad; (*wild, ungestüm*) be wild; **zum ~ gehen** (*ugs.: kaputtgehen*) be ruined; **scher dich** *od.* **geh zum ~!** (*salopp*) go to hell! (*coll.*); **er soll sich zum ~**

*old spelling (see note on page 1707)

t

**scheren!** (*salopp*) he can go to hell (*coll.*) *or* blazes (*coll.*); **zum** *od.* **beim ~ sein** (*ugs.: kaputt sein*) have had it (*coll.*); be ruined; **jmdn./etw. zum ~ wünschen** (*salopp*) wish sb. in hell/curse sth.; **jmdn. zum ~ jagen** *od.* **schicken** (*salopp*) send sb. packing; **zum ~!** (*salopp*) damn it! (*coll.*); **zum ~ mit dir/damit!** (*salopp*) to hell with you/it! (*coll.*); **wer/wo** *usw.* **zum ~ ...** (*salopp*) who/where *etc.* the hell ... (*coll.*); **wenn man vom ~ spricht[, dann ist er nicht weit]** (*scherzh.*) speak *or* talk of the devil [and he will appear]

**Teufelei** *die;* ~, ~**en** Ⓐ devilry; Ⓑ (*Handlung*) piece of devilry; **diese ~en** this devilry *sing.*

**Teufelin** *die;* ~, ~**nen** (*abwertend*) she-devil

**Teufels-:** ~**austreibung** *die* (*Rel.*) casting-out of devils; exorcism; ~**braten** *der* (*ugs.*) devil; ~**kerl** *der* (*ugs.*) amazing fellow; ~**kreis** *der* vicious circle; ~**messe** *die* Black Mass; ~**rochen** *der* (*Zool.*) devil ray; ~**weib** *das* (*ugs.*) Ⓐ (*bewundernd*) **sie ist ein ~weib** she's some woman (*coll.*); Ⓑ (*abwertend*) she-devil; ~**werk** *das* devil's work *no indef. art.;* ~**zeug** *das* (*ugs.*) terrible stuff (*coll.*)

**teuflisch** ❶ *Adj.* Ⓐ devilish, fiendish ‹plan, trick, etc.›; fiendish, diabolical ‹laughter, pleasure, etc.›; **das Teuflische an dieser Krankheit** the devilish *or* diabolical thing about this illnes; Ⓑ (*ugs.: groß, intensiv*) terrible (*coll.*); dreadful (*coll.*). ❷ *adv.* Ⓐ fiendishly; diabolically; Ⓑ (*ugs.*) terribly (*coll.*); dreadfully (*coll.*)

**Teutone** /tɔy'to:nə/ *der;* ~**n**, ~**n**, **Teutonin** *die;* ~, ~**nen** Teuton

**teutonisch** (*auch fig.*) ❶ *Adj.* Teutonic. ❷ *adv.* Teutonically; in a Teutonic way

**Text** /tɛkst/ *der;* ~**[e]s**, ~**e** Ⓐ text; (*eines Gesetzes, auf einem Plakat*) wording; (*eines Theaterstücks*) script; (*einer Oper*) libretto; **ein Telegramm mit folgendem ~: ...** a telegram which reads/read ...; **weiter im ~!** (*ugs.*) [let's] carry on!; Ⓑ (*eines Liedes, Chansons usw.*) words *pl.;* (*eines Schlagers*) words *pl.;* lyrics *pl.;* Ⓒ (*zu einer Abbildung*) caption

**Text-:** ~**analyse** *die* (*Sprachw.*) text analysis; (*Literaturw.*) textual analysis; ~**aufgabe** *die* (*Schule*) problem; ~**buch** *das* libretto; ~**dichter** *der,* ~**dichterin** *die* librettist

**texten** ❶ *tr. V.* write ‹song, advertisement, etc›. ❷ *itr. V.* ‹composer› write one's own words

**Texter** *der;* ~**s**, ~ ▶ 159 writer; (*in der Werbung*) copywriter

**Text·erfassung** *die* text capture

**Texterin** *die;* ~, ~**nen** ⇒ **Texter**

**textil** *Adj.* textile

**textil-, Textil-:** ~**frei** *Adj.* (*ugs. scherzh.*) nude; ~**gewerbe** *das* textile trade *or* industry; ~**handwerk** *das* textile trade

**Textilien** *Pl.* Ⓐ textiles; Ⓑ (*Fertigwaren*) textile goods

**Textil-:** ~**industrie** *die* textile industry; ~**ingenieur** *der* textile engineer; ~**strand** *der* (*ugs. scherzh.*) beach where there is no nude bathing; ~**waren** *Pl.* textile goods

**text-, Text-:** ~**kritik** *die* textual criticism; ~**kritisch** *Adj.* textual ‹study, commentary›; critical ‹edition›; ~**linguistik** *die* text linguistics *sing., no art.;* ~**sorte** *die* (*Sprachw.*) type of text; ~**stelle** *die* passage [in a/the text]

**Textur** /tɛks'tu:ɐ̯/ *die;* ~, ~**en** (*geh., Geol.*) texture

**Text·verarbeitung** *die* text processing; word processing

**Thai**[1] /tai/ *der;* ~**[s]**, ~**[s]** Thai

**Thai**[2] *das;* ~**s** ▶ 696 (*Sprache*) Thai

**Thailand** (*das*)*;* ~**s** Thailand

**Thailänder** *der;* ~**s**, ~, **Thailänderin** *die;* ~, ~**nen** Thai

**thailändisch** *Adj.* Thai

**Thalamus** /'ta:lamʊs/ *der;* ~, **Thalami** ▶ 471 (*Anat.*) thalamus

**Thälmann·pionier** /'tɛ:l-/ *der* (*DDR*) Thälmann Pioneer

**Theater** /te'a:tɐ/ *das;* ~**s**, ~ Ⓐ theatre; **ins ~ gehen** got to the theatre; **im ~:** at the theatre; **zum ~ gehen** (*ugs.*) go into the theatre; tread the boards; **beim** *od.* **am ~ sein** be *or* work in the theatre; **das englische ~:** English theatre; **~ spielen** act; (*fig.*) play-act; pretend; put on an act; Ⓑ (*fig. ugs.*) fuss; **mach [mir] kein ~!** don't make a fuss; **das ist doch alles nur ~:** that's all just play-acting; **dieses ~ mache ich nicht mehr mit** I'm not having any more to do with this farce; **das war vielleicht ein ~[, bis ich mein Visum hatte]** what a performance *or* (*coll.*) palaver [it was, getting my visa]; **jetzt geht das ~ wieder los!** now we have to go through all 'that performance again

**Theater-:** ~**abonnement** *das* theatre subscription [ticket]; ~**besuch** *der* visit to the theatre; ~**besucher** *der,* ~**besucherin** *die* theatre goer; ~**ferien** *Pl.* theatre holidays; ~**karte** *die* theatre ticket; ~**kasse** *die* theatre box office; ~**kritiker** *der,* ~**kritikerin** *die* theatre *or* drama critic; ~**stück** *das* [stage] play; ~**wissenschaft** *die* theatre studies *pl., no art.;* study of theatre arts

**theatralisch** /tea'tra:lɪʃ/ (*auch fig.*) ❶ *Adj.* theatrical. ❷ *adv.* theatrically

**Theismus** /te'ɪsmʊs/ *der;* ~ (*Philos., Rel.*) theism *no art.*

**Theist** /te'ɪst/ *der;* ~**en**, ~**en**, **Theistin** *die;* ~, ~**nen** (*Philos., Rel.*) theist

**theistisch** (*Philos., Rel.*) ❶ *Adj.* theistic. ❷ *adv.* theistically

**Theke** /'te:kə/ *die;* ~, ~**n** Ⓐ (*Schanktisch*) bar; Ⓑ (*Ladentisch*) counter; **unter der ~** (*fig.*) under the counter

**Thema** /'te:ma/ *das;* ~**s**, **Themen** *od.* ~**ta** Ⓐ subject; topic; (*einer Abhandlung*) subject; theme; (*Leitgedanke*) theme; **das ist für uns kein ~:** that's not a matter for discussion [as far as we are concerned]; **das ~ wechseln** change the subject; **vom ~ abkommen** *od.* **abschweifen** wander off the subject *or* point; **beim ~ bleiben** stick to the subject *or* point; **das ~ verfehlen** go completely off the subject; **damit ist das ~ [für mich] erledigt** [as far as I'm concerned] that's the end of the matter; **lassen wir das ~!** let's drop the subject; ⇒ *auch* **Nummer** A; Ⓑ (*Musik*) theme

**Thematik** /te'ma:tɪk/ *die;* ~, ~**en** theme; (*Themenkreis*) themes *pl.;* (*Themenkomplex*) complex of themes

**thematisch** ❶ *Adj.* (*auch Musik*) thematic; **etw. nach ~en Gesichtspunkten ordnen** arrange sth. according to subject. ❷ *adv.* (*auch Musik*) thematically; (*was das Thema betrifft*) as regards subject matter

**thematisieren** *tr. V.* take as a *or* one's/its theme

**Themen** ⇒ **Thema**

**Themen-:** ~**kreis** *der* group of themes; ~**stellung** *die* presentation of a/the subject; (*Thema*) subject; ~**wahl** *die* choice of subject

**Themse** /'tɛmzə/ *die;* ~ ▶ 306 Thames

**Theologe** /teo'lo:gə/ *der;* ~**n**, ~**n** theologian

**Theologie** /teolo'gi:/ *die;* ~, ~**n** theology *no art.*

**Theologin** *die;* ~, ~**nen** theologian

**theologisch** ❶ *Adj.* theological. ❷ *adv.* theologically

**Theorem** /teo're:m/ *das;* ~**s**, ~**e** theorem

**Theoretiker** /teo're:tikɐ/ *der;* ~**s**, ~, **Theoretikerin** *die;* ~, ~**nen** theoretician; theorist

**theoretisch** /teo're:tɪʃ/ ❶ *Adj.* theoretical. ❷ *adv.* theoretically

**theoretisieren** *itr. V.* (*geh.*) theorize

**Theorie** /teo'ri:/ *die;* ~, ~**n** theory; **das ist graue ~:** that's just pure theory

**Theosophie** /teozo'fi:/ *die;* ~, ~**n** theosophy *no art.*

**theosophisch** ❶ *Adj.* theosophical. ❷ *adv.* theosophically

**Therapeut** /tera'pɔyt/ *der;* ~**en**, ~**en** therapist; therapeutist

**Therapeutik** /tera'pɔytɪk/ *die;* ~ (*Med.*) therapeutics *no art.*

**Therapeutikum** *das;* ~**s**, **Therapeutika** (*Med.*) therapeutic agent

**Therapeutin** *die;* ~, ~**nen** therapist; therapeutist

**therapeutisch** ❶ *Adj.* therapeutic. ❷ *adv.* therapeutically

**Therapie** /tera'pi:/ *die;* ~, ~**n** therapy (**gegen** for); (*fig.*) remedy (**gegen** for); **eine ~ machen** (*ugs.*) undergo *or* have therapy *or* treatment

**therapieren** *tr. V.* treat

**Thermal-:** ~**bad** *das* Ⓐ (*Ort*) thermal spa; Ⓑ (*Bad*) thermal bath; ~**quelle** *die* thermal spring

**Therme** /'tɛrmə/ *die;* ~, ~**n** Ⓐ (*Quelle*) thermal spring; Ⓑ *Pl.* (*Bäder*) baths; thermae

**Thermik** /'tɛrmɪk/ *die;* ~ (*Met.*) thermal

**thermisch** ❶ *Adj.* thermal. ❷ *adv.* thermally

**thermo-, Thermo-** /tɛrmo-/: ~**dynamik** *die* thermodynamics *sing., no art.;* ~**dynamisch** ❶ *Adj.* thermodynamic; ❷ *adv.* thermodynamically; ~**meter** *das* (*österr. u. schweiz.* **der** *od.* **das**) thermometer

**Thermos·flasche** Ⓦⓩ /'tɛrmɔs-/ *die* Thermos flask ®; vacuum flask

**Thermostat** /tɛrmo'sta:t/ *der;* ~**[e]s** *od.* ~**en**, ~**e** *od.* ~**en** thermostat

**Thesaurus** /te'zaurʊs/ *der;* ~, **Thesauren** *od.* **Thesauri** thesaurus

**These** /'te:zə/ *die;* ~, ~**n** thesis

**Thing** /tɪŋ/ *das;* ~**[e]s**, ~**e** (*hist.*) thing

**Thing·platz** *der* (*hist.*) thingstead

**Thomas** /'to:mas/ *der;* ~, ~**se** *in* **ungläubiger ~:** doubting Thomas

**Thora** /to'ra:/ *die;* ~ (*jüd. Rel.*) Torah

**Thora·rolle** *die* (*jüd. Rel.*) Torah [scroll]

**Thriller** /'θrɪlə/ *der;* ~**s**, ~**:** thriller

**Thrombose** /trɔm'bo:zə/ *die;* ~, ~**n** thrombosis

**Thron** /tro:n/ *der;* ~**[e]s**, ~**e** Ⓐ throne; **sein ~ wackelt** (*fig.*) his position is becoming very shaky; Ⓑ (*ugs. scherzh.: Nachttopf*) pot (*coll.*)

**Thron-:** ~**anwärter** *der,* ~**anwärterin** *die* heir apparent; ~**besteigung** *die* accession [to the throne]

**thronen** *itr. V.* sit enthroned; (*fig.: erhöht liegen*) tower

**Thron-:** ~**folge** *die* succession [to the throne]; **die ~folge antreten** succeed [to the throne]; ~**folger** *der;* ~~**s**, ~~, ~**folgerin** *die;* ~~, ~~**nen** heir to the throne; ~**rede** *die* King's/Queen's speech; ~**saal** *der* throne room

**Thuja** /'tu:ja/ *die;* ~, **Thujen**, *österr. auch:* **Thuje** /'tu:jə/ *die;* **Thuje, Thujen** (*Bot.*) thuja

**Thun·fisch** /'tu:n-/ *der* tuna

**Thüringen** /'ty:rɪŋən/ (*das*)*;* ~**s** Thuringia

**Thüringer** ❶ *der;* ~**s**, ~**:** Thuringian ❷ *indekl. Adj.* Thuringian.

**Thüringerin** *die;* ~, ~**nen** ⇒ **Thüringer** 1

**Thüringer Wald** *der* Thuringian Forest

**thüringisch** *Adj.* Thuringian; ⇒ *auch* **badisch**

**Thusnelda** /tʊs'nɛlda/ *die;* ~ (*salopp abwertend*) bird (*sl.*)

**Thymian** /'ty:mi̯a:n/ *der;* ~**s**, ~**e** thyme

**Thymus·drüse** /'ty:mʊs-/ *die* ▶ 471 (*Anat.*) thymus [gland]

**Tiara** /ti'a:ra/ *die;* ~, **Tiaren** tiara

**Tibet** /'ti:bɛt/ (*das*)*;* ~**s** Tibet

**tibetanisch** *Adj.* ⇒ **tibetisch**

**Tibeter** /ti'be:tɐ/ *der;* ~**s**, ~, **Tibeterin** *die;* ~, ~**nen** ▶ 553 Tibetan

**tibetisch** *Adj.* ▶ 553, ▶ 696 Tibetan; ⇒ *auch* **deutsch; Deutsch; Deutsche**[2]

**Tic** /tɪk/ *der;* ~**s** ▶ 474 (*Med.*) tic

**Tick** *der;* ~**[e]s**, ~**s** Ⓐ (*ugs.: Schrulle*) quirk; thing (*coll.*); **du hast wohl einen kleinen ~:** you must be round the bend (*coll.*); Ⓑ ▶ 474 (*Med.*) tic; Ⓒ (*ugs.: Nuance*) tiny bit; shade

**ticken** ❶ *itr. V.* tick; **du tickst wohl nicht richtig** (*salopp*) you must be off your rocker

t

(*coll.*). ❷ *tr. V.* (*salopp: erkennen, merken*) catch on to (*coll.*)

**Ticker** *der;* ~s, ~ (*bes. Pressejargon*) teleprinter; telex

**Ticket** /ˈtɪkət/ *das;* ~s, ~s ticket

**ticktack** /ˈtɪk ˈtak/ *Interj.* tick-tock

**Tide** /ˈtiːdə/ *die;* ~, ~n (*nordd., bes. Seemannsspr.*) tide

**Tiden·hub** *der* tidal range

**tief** /tiːf/ ❶ *Adj.* Ⓐ ▶ 306, ▶ 411 (*auch fig.*) deep; low ‹neckline, bow›; long ‹fall›; **eine fünf Meter ~e Grube** a pit five metres deep; **~es Einatmen** breathing in deeply; Ⓑ (*niedrig*) low ‹table, chair, temperature, tide, level, cloud›; **den Sattel/die Heizung etwas ~er stellen** lower the saddle/turn the heating down a bit; Ⓒ (*intensiv, stark*) deep; intense ‹pain, suffering›; utter ‹misery›; great ‹need, want›; Ⓓ (*weit im Innern gelegen*) **im ~en/~sten Afrika** in the depths of/in darkest Africa; **es freut mich aus ~em Herzen/~ster Seele** I really am delighted; **in ~er/~ster Nacht** in the *or* at dead of night; **im ~en/~sten Winter** in the depths of winter; **im ~sten Mittelalter** in the depths of the middle Ages.
❷ *adv.* Ⓐ (*weit unten*) deep; **100 m ~ in/unter der Erde** 100 metres [down] under the earth; **~ verschneit** covered in deep snow *postpos.*; deep in snow *postpos.*; **er war ~ in Gedanken** he was deep in thought; **die Mütze saß ihm ~ in der Stirn** the cap was low over his forehead; **~ liegend** low-lying ‹area;› deep-set ‹eyes;› **die ~ stehende Sonne** thesun low down on the horizon; **ein moralisch ~ stehender Mensch** a person of little moral principle; Ⓑ (*weit nach unten*) ‹dig, drill› deep; ‹fall, sink› a long way; ‹stoop, bow› low; **~er graben/bohren** dig/drill deeper *or* more deeply; **ein ~ ausgeschnittenes Kleid** a low-cut dress; ⇒ *auch* **Glas**[1] B; Ⓒ (*in nur geringer Höhe*) ‹fly, hover, etc.› low; **~ liegen** be at a lower level; **er wohnt einen Stock ~er** he lives one floor down; Ⓓ (*nach unten*) ‹hang etc.› low; **~er gehen** ‹pilot› go lower ; **einen Stock ~er gehen** go one floor down; **~ herabhängende Äste** low-hanging branches; Ⓔ (*weit innen*) deep; **~ in Afrika/im Dschungel** deep in Africa/in the jungle; Ⓕ (*weit nach innen*) deep; ‹breathe, inhale› deeply; **er sah ihr ~ in die Augen** he looked deep into her eyes; **~er ins All vorstoßen** push deeper into space; **bis ~ in die Nacht/in den Winter** (*fig.*) until deep *or* late into the night/well into winter; **das geht bei ihm nicht sehr ~** (*ugs.*) it doesn't go very deep with him; Ⓖ **er sprach ganz ~:** he spoke in a deep voice; **zu ~ gestimmt** tuned too low; **zu ~ singen** sing flat; **er spielt das Lied ~er/eine Terz ~er** he plays the song in a lower key *or* lower/a third lower; Ⓗ (*intensiv, stark*) ‹feel etc.› deeply; ‹sleep› deeply, soundly; **~ betrübt/bewegt** deeply distressed or saddened/moved; **~ empfunden** deep[ly]-felt; heartfelt ‹thanks, sympathy;› Ⓘ **~ gehend, ~ greifend** ⇒ **tiefgehend, tiefgreifend**; **~ schürfend** ⇒ **tiefschürfend**

**Tief** *das;* ~s, ~s (*Met.*) low; depression; (*fig.*) low

**tief-, Tief-:** **~bau** *der* civil engineering *no art.* (*at or below ground level*); ***~betrübt** ⇒ **tief** 2 H; ***~bewegt** ⇒ **tief** 2h; **~blau** *Adj.* deep blue; **~druck**[1] *der; Pl.* **~drücke** (*Met.*) low pressure; **~druck**[2] *der; Pl.* **~~e** Ⓐ intaglio *or* gravure [printing]; Ⓑ (*Erzeugnis*) intaglio *or* gravure [print]; **~druck·gebiet** *das* (*Met.*) area of low pressure; depression

**Tiefe** *die;* ~, ~n Ⓐ ▶ 411 (*Ausdehnung, Entfernung nach unten*) depth; **eine ~ von 300 m** a depth of 300 metres; **in großen ~n** at great depths; Ⓑ (*weit unten, im Innern gelegener Bereich; auch fig.*) depths *pl.*; **in die ~ stürzen** plunge into the depths; **in der ~ ihres Herzens** (*fig.*) deep down in her heart; ⇒ *auch* **Höhe** H; Ⓒ (*Ausdehnung nach hinten*) depth; **der Schrank hat eine ~ von 60 cm** the cupboard is 60 cm deep; Ⓓ ⇒ **tief** 1 C: depth; intensity; greatness; Ⓔ (*von Tönen, Klängen, Stimmen*) deepness; Ⓕ (*fig.: Tiefgründigkeit*) depth; profundity; Ⓖ *Pl.* (*Akustik*) bass *sing.*; Ⓗ (*Geogr.: Meeres~*) deep

**Tief·ebene** *die* (*Georgr.*) lowland plain

***tief·empfunden** ⇒ **tief** 2 H

**Tiefen-:** **~gestein** *das* (*Geol.*) plutonic rock; **~psychologie** *die* depth psychology *no art.*; **~schärfe** *die* (*Fot.*) ⇒ **Schärfentiefe**; **~wirkung** *die* Ⓐ deep action; Ⓑ (*optisch*) effect of depth

**tief-, Tief-:** **~ernst** ❶ *Adj.* deadly serious; ❷ *adv.* deadly seriously; **~flieger** *der* low-flying aircraft; **~flug** *der* low-altitude flight *no art.*; flying *no art.* at low altitude; **im ~flug** at low altitude; **~gang** *der* (*Schiffbau*) draught; (*fig.*) depth; **~garage** *die* underground car park; **~gefrieren** *unr. tr. V.* [deep-]freeze; **~gehend, ~greifend** ❶ *Adj.* profound; far-reaching; profound, deep ‹crisis›; far-reaching ‹improvement›; ❷ *adv.* profoundly; **~gründig** /-ɡrʏndɪç/ ❶ *Adj.* profound; ❷ *adv.* ‹discuss, examine› in depth; **~gründigkeit** *die;* ~~: profundity; **~kühlen** *tr. V.* [deep-]freeze

**Tief·kühl-:** **~fach** *das* freezer [compartment]; **~kost** *die* frozen food; **~truhe** *die* [chest] freezer *or* deep-freeze

**tief-, Tief-:** **~lader** *der;* ~~s, ~~: low-loader; **~land** *das* lowlands *pl.*; ***~liegend** ⇒ **tief** 2 A; **~punkt** *der* Ⓐ (*fig.*) low [point]; Ⓑ (*Math.: Minimum*) minimum; **~religiös** *Adj.* deeply religious; **~schlaf** *der* deep sleep; **~schlag** *der* (*Boxen*) low punch; punch below the belt (*lit. or fig.*); **~schürfend** ❶ *Adj.* profound; ❷ *adv.* profoundly; **~schwarz** *Adj.* jet-black; **~see** *die* (*Geogr.*) deep sea; **~see·graben** *der* deep-sea trench; **~sinn** *der* profundity; **~sinnig** ❶ *Adj.* profound; ❷ *adv.* profoundly; **~stand** *der* (*auch fig.*) (*tiefer Stand*) low level; (*tiefster Stand*) lowest level; **~stapelei** /-ʃtaːpəˈlai/ *die;* ~~: understatement; (*aus Bescheidenheit*) modesty; **~|stapeln** *itr. V.* understate the case; (*aus Bescheidenheit*) be modest; ***~stehend** ⇒ **tief** 2 A; **~strahler** *der* floodlight

**Tiefst-:** **~temperatur** *die* minimum *or* lowest temperature; **~wert** *der* minimum *or* lowest value

**tief-:** **~traurig** *Adj.* very *or* deeply sad; ***~verschneit** ⇒ **tief** 2 A

**Tiegel** /ˈtiːɡl̩/ *der;* ~s, ~ (*zum Kochen*) pan; (*Schmelz~*) crucible; (*Behälter*) pot

**Tier** /tiːɐ̯/ *das;* ~[e]s, ~e animal; (*in der Wohnung gehaltenes*) pet; **niedere/höhere ~e** lower/higher animals; **er ist ein ~** (*fig.*) he is an animal; **das ist das ~ im Menschen** that's the beast in man; **ein hohes** *od.* **großes ~** (*ugs.*) a big noise (*coll.*) *or* shot (*sl.*)

**tier-, Tier-:** **~art** *die* animal species; species of animal; **~arzt** *der*, **~ärztin** *die* ▶ 159 veterinary surgeon; vet; **~ärztlich** ❶ *Adj.* veterinary; ❷ *adv.* by a veterinary surgeon/veterinary surgeons; **~asyl** *das* animal home

**Tierchen** *das;* ~s, ~: [little] animal; **was für ein possierliches ~!** what a funny little creature!; **jedem ~ sein Pläsierchen** (*ugs.*) each to his own; if that's what he/she wants

**Tier-:** **~fabel** *die* animal fable; **~fänger** *der*, **~fängerin** *die* animal collector; **~freund** *der*, **~freundin** *die* animallover; **~garten** *der* zoo; zoological garden; **~geschichte** *die* animal story

**tierhaft** *Adj.* animal *attrib.* ‹behaviour, warmth, etc.›

**Tier-:** **~halter** *der*, **~halterin** *die* animal owner; **~halter sein** keep an animal/animals; **~haltung** *die* keeping of animals; **~handlung** *die* pet shop; **~heilkunde** *die* ⇒ **~medizin**; **~heim** *das* animal home

**tierisch** ❶ *Adj.* Ⓐ animal *attrib.*; bestial, savage ‹cruelty, crime›; Ⓑ (*ugs.: unerträglich groß*) terrible (*coll.*); **~er Ernst** deadly seriousness; Ⓒ (*Jugendspr.: sehr gut, sehr schön*) great (*coll.*). ❷ *adv.* Ⓐ ‹roar› like an animal; savagely ‹cruel›; Ⓑ (*ugs.: unerträglich*) terribly (*coll.*); deadly ‹monotonous, serious›; baking ‹hot›; perishing (*coll.*) ‹cold›; Ⓒ (*Jugendspr.: sehr*) really; **es hat ~ Spaß gemacht** it was great fun

**tier-, Tier-:** **~kind** *das* baby animal; **~kreis** *der* (*Astron., Astrol.*) zodiac; **~kreis·zeichen** *das* (*Astron., Astrol.*) sign of the zodiac; **er ist im ~kreiszeichen der Jungfrau geboren** he was born under [the sign of] Virgo; **~kunde** *die* zoology *no art.*; **~lieb** *Adj.* animal-loving *attrib.*; fond of animals *postpos.*; **~liebe** *die* love of animals; **~liebend** *Adj.* ⇒ **~lieb**; **~medizin** *die* veterinary medicine; **~mehl** *das* animal meal; **~park** *der* zoo; **~pfleger** *der*, **~pflegerin** *die* ▶ 159 animal keeper; **~quäler** *der;* ~~s, ~~, **~quälerin** *die;* ~~, ~~nen person who is cruel to animals; **ein ~quäler sein** be cruel to animals; **~quälerei** /---ˈ-/ *die* cruelty to animals; **das ist ~quälerei** (*fig. ugs. scherzh.*) that's cruelty to dumb animals (*joc.*); **~reich** *das* animal kingdom; **~schau** *die* menagerie; **~schützer** *der;* ~~s, ~~, **~schützerin** *die;* ~~, ~~nen animal protectionist; **~schutz·verein** *der* society for the prevention of cruelty to animals; animal protection society; **~versuch** *der* animal experiment; **~welt** *die* fauna; **~zucht** *die* [animal] breeding *no art.*

**Tiger** /ˈtiːɡɐ/ *der;* ~s, ~: tiger

**Tiger-:** **~auge** *das* tiger['s] eye; **~hai** *der* tiger shark

**Tigerin** *die;* ~, ~nen tigress

**Tiger·katze** *die* tiger cat; margay

**tigern** *itr. V.; mit sein* (*ugs.*) walk; go

**Tiger·staat** *der* tiger [economy]

**Tilde** /ˈtɪldə/ *die;* ~, ~n tilde

**tilgen** /ˈtɪlɡn̩/ *tr. V.* Ⓐ (*geh.*) delete ‹word, letter, error›; erase ‹record, endorsement›; (*fig.*) wipe out ‹shame, guilt, traces›; Ⓑ (*Wirtsch., Bankw.*) repay; pay off

**Tilgung** *die;* ~, ~en Ⓐ (*geh.*) ⇒ **tilgen** A: deletion; erasure; wiping out; Ⓑ (*Wirtsch., Bankw.*) repayment

**Till** /tɪl/ (*der*) *in* **~ Eulenspiegel** Till Eulenspiegel; (*fig.*) practical joker

**Tilsiter** /ˈtɪlzɪtɐ/ *der;* ~s, ~: Tilsit [cheese]

**Timbre** /ˈtɛ̃ːbr(ə)/ *das;* ~s, ~s timbre

**timen** /ˈtaimən/ *tr. V.* time

**Timing** /ˈtaimɪŋ/ *das;* ~s, ~s timing

**tingeln** /ˈtɪŋl̩n/ *itr. V.* Ⓐ play the [small] clubs/theatres/pubs *etc.*; Ⓑ *mit sein* **er tingelte durch die Hamburger Clubs** he played the Hamburg clubs

**Tingeltangel** /ˈtɪŋl̩taŋl̩/ *das od. der;* ~s, ~ (*veralt. abwertend*) Ⓐ (*Lokal*) cheap nightclub/dance hall; honky-tonk (*coll.*); Ⓑ (*Unterhaltung*) cheap nightclub entertainment

**Tinktur** /tɪŋkˈtuːɐ̯/ *die;* ~, ~en tincture

**Tinnef** /ˈtɪnɛf/ *der;* ~s (*ugs. abwertend*) Ⓐ (*wertloses Zeug*) rubbish; junk; Ⓑ (*Unsinn*) rubbish; nonsense

**Tinte** /ˈtɪntə/ *die;* ~, ~n ink; **das ist klar wie dicke ~** (*ugs.*) that's as clear as daylight; that's crystal clear; **in der ~ sitzen** (*ugs.*) be in the soup (*coll.*)

**tinten-, Tinten-:** **~blau** *Adj.* deep blue; **~fass, *~faß** *das* inkpot; (*eingelassen*) inkwell; **~fisch** *der* cuttlefish; (*Kalmar*) squid; (*Krake*) octopus; **~fleck** *der* ink stain; **~klecks** *der* ink blot; **~kleckser** *der* (*ugs. abwertend*) scribbler; **~stift** *der* ⇒ **Kopierstift**; **~strahl·drucker** *der* (*DV*) ink-jet printer

***Tip, Tipp** /tɪp/ *der;* ~s, ~s Ⓐ (*ugs.: Fingerzeig*) tip; (*an die Polizei*) tip-off; Ⓑ (*bei Toto, Lotto usw.*) [row of] numbers

**tipp, tapp** *Interj.* pitter-patter; pit-a-pat

**Tippel·bruder** /ˈtɪpl̩-/ *der* (*fam.*) tramp

**tippeln** *itr. V.; mit sein* (*ugs.*) walk; **wir mussten nach Hause ~:** we had to foot it home

**tippen** /ˈtɪpn̩/ ❶ *itr. V.* Ⓐ **an/gegen etw.** (*Akk.*) **~:** tap sth.; **an seine Mütze ~:** touch one's cap; **sich** (*Dat.*) **an die Stirn ~:** tap one's forehead; **aufs Gaspedal ~:** touch the accelerator; **daran ist nicht zu ~** (*ugs.*)

*old spelling (see note on page 1707)

t

there's no question about that; Ⓑ (*ugs.: Maschine schreiben*) type; Ⓒ (*ugs.: vermuten*) reckon; **auf jmds. Sieg ~:** tip sb. to win; **darauf hätte ich nicht getippt** I hadn't reckoned with that; **du hast gut/richtig getippt** you were right; Ⓓ (*wetten*) do the pools/lottery *etc.*; **im Lotto ~:** do the lottery. ❷ *tr. V.* Ⓐ tap; **jmdn. auf die Schulter ~:** tap sb. on the shoulder; Ⓑ (*ugs.: mit der Maschine schreiben*) type; Ⓒ (*bei der Registrierkasse*) ring up; Ⓓ (*setzen auf*) choose; **sechs Richtige ~:** make six correct selections

**Tipper** *der;* **~s, ~, Tipperin** *die;* **~, ~nen** person who does the pools/lottery *etc.*

**Tipp-: ~fehler** *der* typing error *or* mistake; **~gemeinschaft** *die* poools/lottery *etc.* syndicate; **~schein** *der* [pools/lottery *etc.*] coupon

**Tippse** /ˈtɪpsə/ *die;* **~, ~n** (*ugs. abwertend*) typist

**tipp·topp** (*ugs.*) ❶ *Adj.* (*tadellos*) immaculate; (*erstklassig*) tip-top. ❷ *adv.* immaculately; **~ in Ordnung** in immaculate *or* tip-top order

**Tipp·zettel** *der* (*ugs.*) ⇒ **Tippschein**

**Tirade** /tiˈraːdə/ *die;* **~, ~n** (*geh. abwertend*) interminable speech; **sich in langen ~n ergehen** talk interminably

**tirilieren** /tiriˈliːrən/ *itr. V.* trill; warble

**Tirol** /tiˈroːl/ (*das*)*;* **~s** [the] Tyrol

**Tiroler** *der;* **~s, ~, Tirolerin** *die;* **~, ~nen** Tyrolese; Tyrolean

**Tisch** /tɪʃ/ *der;* **~[e]s, ~e** Ⓐ table; (*Schreib~*) desk; **er zahlte bar auf den ~:** he paid cash down; **vor/nach ~:** before/after lunch/dinner/the meal *etc.*; **bei ~ sein** *od.* **sitzen** be at table; **zu ~ sein** be having one's lunch/dinner *etc.*; **zu ~ gehen** go to lunch/dinner *etc.*; **vom ~ aufstehen** get up from the table; ‹child› get down [from the table]; **bitte zu ~:** please take your places for lunch/dinner; **es wird gegessen, was auf den ~ kommt!** [you'll] eat what's put on the table!; **ein Gespräch am runden ~:** round-table talks *pl.*; Ⓑ (*fig.*) **am grünen ~, vom grünen ~ aus** merely academically; **reinen ~ machen** (*ugs.*) clear things up; sort things out; **reinen ~ mit etw. machen** (*ugs.*) clear sth. up; sort sth. out; **sich [mit jmdm.] an einen ~ setzen** get round the table [with sb.]; **auf den ~ hauen** (*ugs.*) take a hard line; **etw. auf den ~ legen** (*Angebot machen*) put sth. on the table; (*bezahlen*) lay sth. out; **jmdn. über den ~ ziehen** (*ugs.*) outmanœuvre sb.; **unter den ~ fallen** (*ugs.*) go by the board; **jmdn. unter den ~ trinken** (*ugs.*) drink sb. under the table; **die Füße** *od.* **Beine unter jmds. ~** (*Akk.*) **strecken** (*ugs.*) live under sb.'s roof and eat at sb.'s table; **vom ~ sein** (*ugs.*) be out of the way; ‹subject, topic› be closed; ⇒ *auch* **fegen** 1 B

**Tisch·bein** *das* table leg; leg of the table

**Tischchen** *das;* **~s, ~:** [little] table

**Tisch-: ~dame** *die* dinner partner; **~decke** *die* tablecloth; **~feuerzeug** *das* table lighter; **~fußball** *der* table football; **~gebet** *das* grace; **ein/das ~gebet sprechen** say grace; **~gespräch** *das* breakfast/lunch/dinner conversation; **~herr** *der* dinner partner; **~karte** *die* place card; **~lampe** *die* table lamp

**Tischlein·deck·dich** *das;* **~:** easy life; **was er sucht, ist so eine Art ~:** he's looking to get on the gravy train (*coll.*)

**Tischler** *der;* **~s, ~** ▶ 159 joiner; (*bes. Kunst~*) cabinetmaker

**Tischlerei** *die;* **~, ~en** Ⓐ (*Werkstatt*) joiner's/cabinetmaker's [workshop]; Ⓑ (*Handwerk*) joinery/cabinetmaking

**Tischlerin** *die;* **~, ~nen** ⇒ **Tischler**

**tischlern** ❶ *itr. V.* do woodwork. ❷ *tr. V.* make ‹shelves, cupboard, etc.›

**Tisch-: ~manieren** *Pl.* table manners; **~nachbar** *der*, **~nachbarin** *die* person next to one [at table]; **wer ist dein ~nachbar?** who is sitting next to you?; **~platte** *die* table top; **~rede** *die* after-dinner speech; **~rücken** *das;* **~~s** table-turning *no art. or* -lifting *no art.*; **~tennis** *das* table tennis

**Tisch·tennis-: ~platte** *die* table-tennis table; **~schläger** *der* table-tennis bat

**Tisch-: ~tuch** *das; Pl.* **~tücher** tablecloth; **~vor·lage** *die* handout; **~wäsche** *die* table linen; **~wein** *der* table wine; **~zeit** *die* lunchtime; **wir haben eine halbe Stunde ~zeit** we have half an hour for lunch

**Titan**[1] /tiˈtaːn/ *der;* **~en, ~en** (*Myth., fig.*) Titan

**Titan**[2] *das;* **~s** (*Chemie*) titanium

**titanenhaft** *Adj.* titanic

**titanisch** *Adj.* (*Myth., fig.*) titanic

**Titel** /ˈtiːtl̩/ *der;* **~s, ~** Ⓐ ▶ 91, ▶ 187 title; **unter dem ~ „…"** under the title '…'; Ⓑ (*ugs.: Musikstück, Song usw.*) number

**Titel-: ~anwärter** *der*, **~anwärterin** *die* (*Sport*) title contender; contender for the title; **~bild** *das* Ⓐ cover picture; Ⓑ (*Frontispiz*) frontispiece; **~blatt** *das* title page

**Titelei** *die;* **~, ~en** (*Buchw.*) prelims *pl.*

**Titel-: ~geschichte** *die* cover story *or* article; **~held** *der*, eponymous hero; **~heldin** *die* eponymous heroine; **~kampf** *der* (*Sport*) final; (*Boxen*) title fight; **~rolle** *die* title role; **~schutz** *der* (*Rechtsw.*) copyright (*in a title*); **~seite** *die* Ⓐ (*einer Zeitung, Zeitschrift*) [front] cover; Ⓑ (*eines Buchs*) title page; **~sucht** *die* mania for titles; **~träger** *der*, **~trägerin** *die* Ⓐ titled person; person with a title; Ⓑ (*Sport*) title-holder; **~verteidiger** *der*, **~verteidigerin** *die* (*Sport*) title-holder; (*Mannschaft*) title-holders *pl.*

**Titte** /ˈtɪtə/ *die;* **~, ~n** (*derb*) tit (*coarse*)

**titulieren** /tituˈliːrən/ *tr. V.* Ⓐ (*bezeichnen*) call; **jmdn. als** *od.* **mit „Flasche" ~:** call sb. a dead loss (*coll.*); Ⓑ (*veralt.: mit dem Titel anreden*) address; **jmdn. [als** *od.* **mit] Herr Doktor ~:** address sb. as Doctor

**Titulierung** *die;* **~, ~en** Ⓐ (*Bezeichnung*) name; **gegen seine ~ als … hatte er nichts einzuwenden** he had no objection to being called …; Ⓑ (*veralt.: Anrede mit dem Titel, Nennung des Titels*) title

**Tizian** /ˈtiːtsi̯aːn/ (*der*)*;* **~s** Titian

**tizianrot** *Adj.* Titian [red]

**tja** /tja(ː)/ *Interj.* [yes] well; (*Resignation ausdrückend*) oh, well

**Toast** /toːst/ *der;* **~[e]s, ~e** *od.* **~s** Ⓐ (*getoastetes Brot*) toast; (*Scheibe ~*) piece of toast; Ⓑ (*Trinkspruch*) toast

**Toast·brot** *das* [sliced white] bread for toasting

**toasten** *tr. V.* toast

**Toaster** *der;* **~s, ~:** toaster

**Tobak** /ˈtoːbak/ *der;* **~s** *in* **starker ~ sein** (*ugs.*) be a bit thick (*Brit. coll.*) *or* (*coll.*) much; ⇒ *auch* **Anno**

**Tobel** /ˈtoːbl̩/ *der od. das* (*österr.* **das**)*;* **~s, ~** (*Geogr., österr., schweiz., südd.*) ravine

**toben** /ˈtoːbn̩/ *itr. V.* Ⓐ go wild (**vor** + *Dat.* with); (*fig.*) ‹storm, sea, battle› rage; **wie ein Wilder** *od.* **Berserker ~:** go wild *or* berserk; Ⓑ (*tollen*) romp *or* charge about; Ⓒ *mit sein* (*laufen*) charge

**Toberei** *die;* **~:** romping *or* charging about

**tob-, Tob-: ~sucht** *die* frenzied *or* mad rage; [mad] frenzy; **~süchtig** *Adj.* frenzied; raving mad; **~suchts·anfall** *der* fit of frenzied *or* mad rage; **einen ~suchtsanfall bekommen** *od.* **erleiden** fly into a fit of frenzied rage *or* into a frenzy

**Toccata** /tɔˈkaːta/ ⇒ **Tokkata**

**Tochter** /ˈtɔxtɐ/ *die;* **~, Töchter** /ˈtœçtɐ/ Ⓐ daughter; **die ~ des Hauses** the daughter *or* young lady of the house; **Ihre Frau/Ihr Fräulein ~:** your daughter; **höhere ~:** young lady; Ⓑ (*schweiz.: Mädchen, Bedienstete*) girl; Ⓒ (*Wirtschaftsjargon*) subsidiary

**Töchterchen** /ˈtœçtɐçən/ *das;* **~s, ~:** little daughter; (*Kleinkind*) baby daughter

**Tochter-: ~geschwulst** *die* ▶ 474 (*Med.*) secondary tumour; **~gesellschaft** *die* (*Wirtsch.*) subsidiary [company]

**Tod** /toːt/ *der;* **~[e]s, ~e** (*auch fig.*) death; **es wäre unser aller sicherer ~:** it would mean certain death for us all; **diese Krankheit führt zum ~:** this illness is fatal; **eines natürlichen/gewaltsamen ~es sterben** die a natural/violent death; **jmdn. zum ~e/zum ~ durch den Strang/zum ~ durch Erschießen verurteilen** sentence sb. to death/to death by hanging/to death by firing squad; **~ durch Ersticken/Erfrieren** death by suffocation/freezing to death; **jmdm. den ~ wünschen** wish sb. dead; **bis in den ~:** till death; **das ist kein schöner ~:** that's not a pleasant way to die; **in den ~ gehen** go to one's death; **für jmdn./etw. in den ~ gehen** die for sb./sth.; **jmdn. vom ~[e] erretten** save sb.'s life; **sich zu ~e stürzen/trinken** fall to one's death/drink oneself to death; **zu ~e kommen, den ~ finden** die; lose one's life; **des ~es sein** (*veralt.*) be doomed; **jmdn./etw. auf den ~ nicht leiden/ausstehen können** (*ugs.*) not be able to stand or abide sb./sth.; **er hasste ihn auf den ~:** he utterly detested him; **sich zu ~e schämen/langweilen** be utterly ashamed/bored to death; **zu ~e betrübt** extremely distressed; **etw. zu ~e reiten** (*fig. ugs.*) flog sth. to death (*coll.*); **tausend ~e sterben** (*ugs.*) die a thousand deaths; **sich** (*Dat.*) **den ~ holen** (*ugs.*) catch one's death [of cold]; **der schwarze ~:** the Black Death; **der weiße ~:** death in the snow; **~ und Teufel!** (*veralt.*) by the devil!; **weder ~ noch Teufel fürchten** fear nothing

**tod-: ~bringend** *Adj.* fatal ‹illness, disease, etc.›; deadly, lethal ‹poison etc.›; **~elend** *Adj.* utterly miserable; **~ernst** ❶ *Adj.* deadly serious; ❷ *adv.* deadly seriously; **etw. ~ernst sagen** say sth. in deadly seriousness

**todes-, Todes-: ~ahnung** *die* presentiment *or* premonition of death; **~angst** *die* Ⓐ fear of death; Ⓑ (*große Angst*) extreme fear; **~ängste ausstehen** be scared to death; **~anzeige** *die* Ⓐ (*in einer Zeitung*) death notice; **„~anzeigen"** 'Deaths'; Ⓑ (*Karte*) *card announcing a person's death;* **~art** *die:* **eine schreckliche ~art** a terrible way to die; **~erklärung** *die* (*Rechtsw.*) declaration of death (*of missing person*); **~fall** *der* Ⓐ death; (*in der Familie*) bereavement; Ⓑ (*Versicherungsw.*) **im ~fall** in [the] case *or* in the event of death; **~folge** *die* (*Rechtsw.*) **Körperverletzung mit ~folge** physical injury resulting in death; **~furcht** *die* (*geh.*) fear of death; **~gefahr** *die* mortal danger; **~jahr** *das* year of death; **in seinem ~jahr** in the year of his death; **~kampf** *der* death throes *pl.*; **~kandidat** *der*, **~kandidatin** *die* (*Verurteilte[r]*) condemned man/woman; (*Schwerkranke[r]*) terminal case; **~mutig** ❶ *Adj.* utterly fearless; ❷ *adv.* utterly fearlessly; **~nachricht** *die* news of his/her/their *etc.* death; **~not** *die* (*geh.*) mortal danger; **in ~not** *od.* **~nöten** in mortal danger; **~opfer** *das* death; fatality; **der Unfall forderte drei ~opfer** the accident claimed three lives; **~qual** *die* (*geh.*) [terrible] agony; **~schrei** *der* death cry; **~schuss**, ***~schuß** *der* fatal shot; **war die Abgabe eines ~schusses zulässig?** was it permissible to shoot to kill?; **~schütze** *der*, **~schützin** *die* person who fired the fatal shot; (*Attentäter[in]*) assassin; killer; **~sehnsucht** *die* longing to die; **~spirale** *die* (*Eis-, Rollkunstlauf*) death spiral; **~stoß** *der* death blow; **jmdm./**(*fig.*) **einer Sache den ~stoß geben** deal sb. the death blow/the death blow to sth.; **~strafe** *die* death penalty; **~streifen** *der* death strip; **~stunde** *die* hour of death; **~ursache** *die* cause of death; **~urteil** *das* death sentence; **~verachtung** *die* [utter] fearlessness in the face of death; **etw. mit ~verachtung essen/trinken** (*ugs.*) force sth. down [without showing one's distaste]; **~zelle** *die* death cell

***tod·feind**, **Tod·feind**[1] *in* **jmdm. ~ sein** be sb's deadly enemy

**Tod·feind**[2] *der*, **Tod·feindin** *die* deadly enemy

**tod-: ~geweiht** *Adj.* (*geh.*) doomed [to die]; **~krank** *Adj.* critically ill

**tödlich** /ˈtøːtlɪç/ ❶ *Adj.* Ⓐ fatal ‹accident, illness, outcome, etc.›; lethal, deadly ‹poison, bite, shot, trap, etc.›; lethal ‹dose›; deadly, mortal ‹danger›; [B] (*sehr groß, ausgeprägt*) deadly. ❷ *adv.* [A] fatally; **er ist ~ verunglückt/abgestürzt** he was killed in an accident/he fell to his death; **die Krankheit verläuft in der Regel ~:** the illness is usually fatal; [B] (*sehr*) terribly (*coll.*); **sich ~ langweilen** be bored stiff *or* to death (*coll.*)

**tod-, Tod-: ~müde** *Adj.* dead tired; **~schick** (*ugs.*) ❶ *Adj.* dead smart (*coll.*); ❷ *adv.* dead smartly (*coll.*); **~sicher** (*ugs.*) ❶ *Adj.* sure-fire (*coll.*) ‹system, method, tip, etc.›; **eine ~sichere Sache** a dead certainty *or* (*coll.*) cert; ❷ *adv.* for certain *or* sure; **~sterbens·krank** *Adj.* (*ugs.*) critically ill; **~sünde** *die* (*auch fig.*) deadly *or* mortal sin; **~traurig** ❶ *Adj.* extremely sad; ❷ *adv.* extremely sadly; with extreme sadness; **~unglücklich** *Adj.* (*ugs.*) extremely *or* desperately unhappy

**Toffee** /'tɔfi/ *das;* **~s, ~s** toffee

**Toga** /'to:ga/ *die;* **~, Togen** toga

**Togo** /'to:go/ *(das);* **~s** Togo

**Togoer** *der;* **~s, ~, Togoerin** *die;* **~, ~nen** Togolese

**togoisch** *Adj.* Togolese

**Tohuwabohu** /'to:huva'bo:hu/ *das;* **~s, ~s** chaos; **im ganzen Haus war ein großes ~:** the whole house was in total *or* utter chaos

**toi, toi, toi** /'tɔy 'tɔy 'tɔy/ *Interj.* [A] (*gutes Gelingen!*) good luck!; **~ für deine Prüfung!** good luck in your exam! (*coll.*); [B] (*unberufen!*) touch wood!

**Toilette** /to̯a'lɛtə/ *die;* **~, ~n** [A] toilet; lavatory; **auf die** *od.* **zur ~ gehen** go to the toilet *or* lavatory; **eine öffentliche ~:** a public lavatory *or* convenience; [B] (*geh.: das Sichzurechtmachen*) toilet; **~ machen** make one's toilet; [C] (*geh.: Aufzug*) dress; toilet (*arch.*); **in großer ~:** in full dress

**Toilette-** (*österr.*), **Toiletten-: ~artikel** *der* toiletry; **~becken** *das* lavatory *or* toilet bowl *or* pan; **~frau** *die*, **~mann** *der* lavatory attendant; **~papier** *das* toilet paper; **~seife** *die* toilet soap; **~sitz** *der* lavatory *or* toilet seat

**Tokaier** /to'kai̯ɐ/ *der;* **~s, ~:** Tokay

**Tokio** /'to:ki̯o/ *(das);* **~s** ▶ 700 Tokyo

**Tokioter** /to'ki̯o:tɐ/ ▶ 700 ❶ *der;* **~s, ~:** Tokyoite. ❷ *indekl. Adj.* Tokyo *attrib.*; ⇒ *auch* **Kölner**

**Tokioterin** *die;* **~, ~nen** ⇒ **Tokioter** 1

**Tokkata** /tɔ'ka:ta/ *die;* **~, Tokkaten** (*Musik*) toccata

**tolerant** /tole'rant/ ❶ *Adj.* tolerant **(gegen** of). ❷ *adv.* tolerantly

**Toleranz** *die;* **~, ~en** [A] (*auch Med.*) tolerance; [B] (*Technik*) tolerance

**Toleranz·grenze** *die* [A] limit of tolerance; [B] (*Med.*) tolerance level; [C] (*Technik*) tolerance limit

**tolerierbar** *Adj.* tolerable

**tolerieren** /tole'ri:rən/ *tr. V.* tolerate

**toll** /tɔl/ ❶ *Adj.* [A] (*ugs.*) (*großartig*) great (*coll.*); fantastic (*coll.*); (*erstaunlich*) amazing; (*heftig, groß*) enormous ‹respect›; terrific (*coll.*) ‹noise, storm›; [B] (*wild, ausgelassen, übermütig*) wild; wild, mad ‹tricks, antics›; **die [drei] ~en Tage** the [last three] days of Fasching; [C] (*ugs.: schlimm, übel*) terrible (*coll.*); [D] (*veralt.*) ⇒ **verrückt** 1 A; [E] (*veralt.: ~wütig*) rabid.
❷ *adv.* [A] (*ugs.: großartig*) terrifically well (*coll.*); **~ hast du das gemacht** you've made a great job of that (*coll.*); [B] (*ugs.: heftig, sehr*) ‹rain, snow› like billy-o (*coll.*); **es regnet immer ~er** it's chucking it down harder and harder (*coll.*); [C] (*wild, ausgelassen, übermütig*) **bei dem Fest ging es ~ zu** it was a wild party; [D] (*ugs.: schlimm, übel*) **treibt es nicht zu ~:** don't go too mad; **aber es kommt noch ~er** but that's not all

**Tolle** *die;* **~, ~n** quiff

**tollen** *itr. V.* [A] romp about; [B] *mit sein* romp

**Tollerei** *die;* **~, ~en** (*ugs.*) romping about

**Toll·haus** *das* (*veralt.*) lunatic asylum (*Hist.*); **hier geht es ja zu wie in einem ~:** it's like a madhouse here

**Tollheit** *die;* **~, ~en** (*veralt.*) ⇒ **Verrücktheit**

**toll-, Toll-: ~kirsche** *die* Atropa; **Schwarze ~kirsche** deadly nightshade; belladonna; **~kühn** ❶ *Adj.* daredevil *attrib.*; daring; ❷ *adv.* daringly; **~kühnheit** *die* [A] daring; [B] (*~kühne Handlung*) daredevil *or* daring exploit

**Tollpatsch** /'tɔlpatʃ/ *der;* **~[e]s, ~e** (*ugs.*) clumsy *or* awkward creature

**tollpatschig** (*ugs.*) ❶ *Adj.* clumsy; awkward. ❷ *adv.* clumsily; awkwardly

**toll-, Toll-: ~wut** *die* ▶ 474 rabies *sing.*; **~wütig** *Adj.* rabid

***Tolpatsch** ⇒ **Tollpatsch**

***tolpatschig** ⇒ **tollpatschig**

**Tölpel** /'tœlpl̩/ *der;* **~s, ~** [A] (*abwertend; einfältiger Mensch*) fool; [B] (*Zool.*) (*Gattung Sula*) booby; (*Gattung Morus*) gannet

**tölpelhaft** (*abwertend*) ❶ *Adj.* foolish. ❷ *adv.* foolishly

**Tomahawk** /'tɔmaha:k/ *der;* **~s, ~s** tomahawk

**Tomate** /to'ma:tə/ *die;* **~, ~n** tomato; **du hast wohl ~n auf den Augen!** (*salopp*) you must be blind!; **er wurde rot wie eine ~** (*ugs. scherzh.*) he turned *or* went as red as a beetroot; **du [bist vielleicht eine] treulose ~** (*ugs. scherzh.*) a fine friend you are

**Tomaten-** tomato ‹juice, salad, sauce, soup, etc.›

**Tomaten·mark** *das* tomato purée

**tomaten·rot** *Adj.* brilliant red

**Tombola** /'tɔmbola/ *die;* **~, ~s** *od.* **Tombolen** raffle

**Tommy** /'tɔmi/ *der;* **~s, ~s** (*ugs.: Engländer*) Tommy

**Tomographie** /tomogra'fi:/ *die;* **~** (*Med.*) tomography *no art.*

**Ton**[1] /to:n/ *der;* **~[e]s, ~e** clay

**Ton**[2] *der;* **~[e]s, Töne** /'tø:nə/ [A] (*auch Physik, Musik; beim Telefon*) tone; (*Klang*) note; **der ~ macht die Musik** (*fig. ugs.*) it's not what you say but the way that you say it; **den ~ angeben** (*Musik*) give the note; (*fig.*) (*in der Mode, Kunst usw.*) set the tone; (*in einer Gruppe o. Ä.*) have the most *or* greatest say; **jmdn./etw. in den höchsten Tönen loben** praise sb./sth. to the skies; [B] (*Film, Ferns. usw., ~wiedergabe*) sound; **~ ab!** turn over sound!; **~ läuft** sound running; [C] (*Sprechweise, Umgangs~*) tone; **den richtigen ~ finden** strike the right note; **ich verbitte mir diesen ~!** I will not be spoken to like that!; **sich im ~ vergreifen** adopt the wrong tone; strike the wrong note; **einen unverschämten/frechen** *usw.* **~ anschlagen** adopt an impudent/a cheeky tone; **der gute ~:** good form; **das gehört zum guten ~:** it is considered good form; **hier gehört es zum guten ~, ... zu ...** (*iron.*) here it's the done thing to ... (*coll.*); [D] (*ugs.: Äußerung*) word; **ich möchte keinen ~ mehr hören** I don't want to hear another word; **er konnte keinen ~ herausbringen** he couldn't say a word; **hast du/hat der Mensch [da noch] Töne?** that's just unbelievable; **große Töne reden** *od.* **spucken** (*ugs.*) talk big; [E] (*Farb~*) shade; tone; **~ in ~ gehalten** colour coordinated; [F] (*Akzent*) stress; [G] (*Sprachw.: ~höhe*) tone

**Ton·abnehmer** *der;* **~s, ~:** pick-up

**tonal** /to'na:l/ *Adj.* (*Musik*) tonal

**Tonalität** /tonali'tɛ:t/ *die;* **~** (*Musik*) tonality

**ton-, Ton-: ~angebend** *Adj.* predominant; **~angebend sein** (*in der Mode, Kunst usw.*) set the tone; (*in einer Gruppe o. Ä.*) have the most *or* greatest say; **~arm** *der* pick-up arm; **~art** *die* [A] (*Musik*) key; [B] (*fig.*) tone; **eine andere/schärfere** *usw.* **~art anschlagen** take a stronger *or* tougher line; **~aufnahme** *die* [sound] recording; **~band** *das; Pl.* **~bänder** [A] tape; [B] (*ugs.: ~bandgerät*) tape recorder

**Ton·band-: ~aufnahme** *die* tape recording; **~gerät** *das* tape recorder; **~protokoll** *das* tape transcript

**Ton-: ~blende** *die* (*Rundf., Ferns.*) tone control; **~dichtung** *die* tone poem

**tonen** *tr. V.* (*Fot.*) tone

**tönen** /'tø:nən/ ❶ *itr. V.* [A] (*geh.*) sound; ‹bell› sound, ring; (*schallen, widerhallen*) resound; **mit ~der Stimme** in a resounding voice; **~de Worte/Phrasen** empty words/phrases; [B] (*ugs. abwertend*) boast. ❷ *tr. V.* (*färben*) tint

**Ton·erde** *die* ⇒ **essigsauer**

**tönern** /'tø:nɐn/ *Adj.* clay; ⇒ *auch* **Fuß** C

**Ton-: ~fall** *der* tone; (*Intonation*) intonation; **~film** *der* sound film; talkie (*coll.*); **~folge** *die* sequence of notes; **~frequenz** *die* (*Akustik*) sound frequency; audio frequency; **~gefäß** *das* earthen[ware] vessel; **~geschlecht** *das* (*Musik*) scale; **~höhe** *die* pitch

**Toni** ⇒ **Tonus**

**Tonic** /'tɔnɪk/ *das;* **~[s], ~s** tonic [water]

**Tonika**[1] ⇒ **Tonikum**

**Tonika**[2] /'to:nika/ *die;* **~, Toniken** (*Musik*) tonic

**Tonika-Do** *das;* **~** (*Musik*) Tonika-Doh [method]

**Tonikum** /'to:nikʊm/ *das;* **~s, Tonika** tonic

**Ton·ingenieur** *der*, **Ton·ingenieurin** *die* sound engineer

**tonisch** *Adj.* (*Physiol.*) tonic

**ton-, Ton-: ~kopf** *der* head; **~kunst** *die* (*geh.*) music; **~künstler** *der*, **~künstlerin** *die* (*geh.*) composer; **~lage** *die* (*Musik*) pitch; **~leiter** *die* (*Musik*) scale; **~los** ❶ *Adj.* toneless; ❷ *adv.* tonelessly; **~meister** *der*, **~meisterin** *die* sound engineer, recording engineer

**Tonnage** /tɔ'na:ʒə/ *die;* **~, ~n** (*Seew.*) tonnage

**Tönnchen** /'tœnçən/ *das;* **~s, ~** (*ugs.: dicker Mensch*) dumpling (*coll.*)

**Tonne** /'tɔnə/ *die;* **~, ~n** [A] (*Behälter*) drum; (*Müll~*) bin; (*Regen~*) water butt; [B] ▶ 353 (*Gewicht*) tonne; metric ton; [C] (*ugs.: dicker Mensch*) fatty (*coll.*); [D] (*Seew.*) buoy

**Tonnen·gewölbe** *das* (*Archit.*) barrel *or* tunnel vault

**tonnen·weise** ❶ *Adv.* by the tonne *or* metric ton; (*in großer Menge*) by the ton; **ich habe das Zeug ~:** I've got tons of the stuff (*coll.*). ❷ *adj.* by the ton *postpos.*

**Ton-: ~pfeife** *die* clay pipe; **~setzer** *der*, **~setzerin** *die* (*veralt.*) composer

**Ton-: ~spur** *die* soundtrack; **~störung** *die* (*Rundf., Film, Ferns.*) sound interference; (*durch Geräteschaden usw.*) fault on sound; **~stufe** *die* (*Musik*) note

**Tonsur** /tɔn'zu:ɐ̯/ *die;* **~, ~en** tonsure

**Ton-: ~system** *das* (*Musik*) tone *or* tonic system; **~tafel** *die* clay tablet; **~tauben·schießen** *das;* **~~s** clay-pigeon shooting *no art.*; **~techniker** *der*, **~technikerin** *die* (*Rundf., Ferns., Film*) sound technician; **~träger** *der* sound[-recording and] storage medium; **~umfang** *der* (*Musik*) register; range

**Tönung** *die;* **~, ~en** [A] (*das Tönen*) tinting; [B] (*Farbton*) tint; shade

**Tonus** /'to:nʊs/ *der;* **~, Toni** (*Physiol.*) tone

**Ton·waren** *Pl.* earthenware *sing.*

**top-** ultra ‹modern, topical›

**Top** /tɔp/ *das;* **~s, ~s** (*Mode*) top

**Top-** top; outstanding ‹location, performance, time›

**Topas** /to'pa:s/ *der;* **~es, ~e** topaz

**Topf** /tɔpf/ *der;* **~es, Töpfe** /'tœpfə/ [A] pot; (*Braten~, Schmor~*) casserole; (*Stielkasserolle*) saucepan; **alles in einen ~ werfen** (*fig. ugs.*) lump everything together; [B] (*zur Aufbewahrung*) pot; jar; [C] (*Krug*) jug; [D] (*Nacht~*) chamber pot; po (*coll.*); (*für Kinder*) potty (*Brit. coll.*); [E] (*Blumen~*) [flower]pot; [F] (*salopp: Toilette*) loo (*Brit. coll.*); john (*Amer. coll.*)

*old spelling (see note on page 1707)

**Topf·blume** *die* [flowering] pot plant

**Töpfchen** /'tœpfçən/ *das;* **~s,** ~ ⇒ **Topf** A-D: [small] pot/saucepan/jug *etc.; (Nachttopf)* po *(coll.); (für Kinder)* potty *(Brit. coll.)*

**Topfen** *der;* **~s** *(bayr., österr.)* ⇒ **Quark[1]** A

**Töpfer** /'tœpfɐ/ *der;* **~s,** ~ ▶ 159 potter

**Töpferei** *die;* ~, **~en** (A) *(Handwerk)* pottery *no art.;* (B) *(Werkstatt)* pottery; potter's workshop; (C) *(Erzeugnis)* piece of pottery; **~en** pottery *sing.*

**Töpferin** *die;* ~, **~nen** ▶ 159 potter

**töpfern** ❶ *itr. V.* do pottery. ❷ *tr. V.* make ‹vase, jug, etc.›; **getöpferte Teller** hand-made pottery plates

**Töpfer-:** **~scheibe** *die* potter's wheel; **~ware** *die* pottery *no pl.;* **~waren** pottery *sing.*

**Topf·gucker** *der;* **~s,** ~, **Topf·guckerin** *die;* ~, **~nen** *(scherzh.) Nosy Parker who looks into all the pots and saucepans to see what's cooking*

**top·fit** *Adj.* in *or* on top form *postpos. (gesundheitlich)* in fine fettle; as fit as a fiddle; **jetzt ist der Wagen wieder ~:** the car is in perfect order again now

**Topf-:** **~kuchen** *der* ⇒ **Napfkuchen; ~lappen** *der* oven cloth; **~pflanze** *die* pot plant; **~reiniger** *der* [pot] scourer; scouring pad

**Topinambur** /topinam'bu:ɐ/ *der;* **~s, ~s** *od.* **~e** *od. die;* ~, **~en** Jerusalem artichoke

**Topographie** /topogra'fi:/ *die;* ~, **~n** *(Geogr.)* topography *no art.*

**topographisch** *(Geogr.)* ❶ *Adj.* topographic[al]. ❷ *adv.* topographically

**Topologie** /topolo'gi:/ *die;* ~ *(Math.)* topology *no art.*

**topologisch** *(Math.) Adj.* topological

**Topos** /'tɔpɔs/ *der;* ~, **Topoi** /'tɔpɔy/ (A) *(Literaturw.)* topos; (B) *(geh.: Gemeinplatz)* commonplace

**topp** /tɔp/ *Interj. (veralt.)* done! agreed!

**Topp** *der;* **~s, ~e[n]** *od.* **~s** *(Seemannsspr.)* masthead; **das Schiff war über die ~en geflaggt** the ship was dressed overall

**Topp·segel** *das (Seew.)* topsail

**Topspin** /'tɔpspɪn/ *der;* **~s, ~s** *(bes. Golf, Tennis, Tischtennis)* top spin

**Tor[1]** /to:ɐ/ *das;* **~[e]s, ~e** (A) gate; *(einer Garage, Scheune)* door; *(fig.)* gateway; **vor den ~en der Stadt** just outside the town; ⇒ *auch* **dastehen;** (B) *(Ballspiele)* goal; **mit 3:2 ~en gewinnen** *od.* **siegen** win 3-2 *or* by three goals to two; **im ~ stehen** be in goal; (C) *(Ski)* gate

**Tor[2]** *der;* **~en, ~en** *(geh.: Narr)* fool

**Tor-:** **~aus** *das (Ballspiele)* **der Ball ging ins ~aus** the ball went over the byline *or* went behind; **~bogen** *der* arch[way]

**Torero** /to're:ro/ *der;* **~[s], ~s** torero

**Tores·schluss, *Tores·schluß** *der: in* **kurz vor ~** *(ugs.)* at the last minute *or* the eleventh hour

**Torf** /tɔrf/ *der;* **~[e]s, ~e** peat

**Torf-:** **~ballen** *der* bale of peat; **~moor** *das* peat bog; **~mull** *der* [loose] garden peat

**Tor·frau** *die (Ballspiele)* goalkeeper

**Torheit** *die;* ~, **~en** *(geh.)* (A) foolishness; (B) *(Handlung)* foolish act; **eine [große] ~ begehen** do something [extremely] foolish

**Tor·hüter** *der,* **Tor·hüterin** *die (Ballspiele)* goalkeeper

**töricht** /'tø:rɪçt/ *(geh.)* ❶ *Adj.* foolish ‹behaviour, action, hope›; stupid ‹person, question, smile, face›. ❷ *adv.* ‹behave, act› foolishly; ‹smile, ask› stupidly

**törichterweise** *Adv. (geh.)* foolishly

**Törin** /'tø:rɪn/ *die;* ~, **~nen** fool

**Tor·jäger** *der,* **Tor·jägerin** *die (Ballspiele)* goal scorer

**torkeln** /'tɔrkl̩n/ *itr. V.; mit sein* stagger; reel

**tor-, Tor-:** **~linie** *die (Ballspiele)* [goal-]line; **~los** *Adj. (Ballspiele)* goalless; **~mann** *der; Pl.* **~männer** *od.* **~leute** *(Ballspiele)* goalkeeper

**Törn** /tœrn/ *der;* **~s, ~s** *(Seemannsspr.)* trip

**Tornado** /tɔr'na:do/ *der;* **~s, ~s** tornado

**Tornister** /tɔr'nɪstɐ/ *der;* **~s,** ~ (A) knapsack; (B) *(Schulranzen)* satchel

**torpedieren** /tɔrpe'di:rən/ *tr. V. (Milit., fig.)* torpedo

**Torpedierung** *die;* ~, **~en** *(Milit., fig.)* torpedoing

**Torpedo** /tɔr'pe:do/ *der;* **~s, ~s** torpedo

**Torpedo·boot** *das* torpedo boat

**Tor-:** **~pfosten** *der (Ballspiele)* [goal]post; **~raum** *der (Ballspiele)* goal area; ***~schluß, ~schluss** *der* ⇒ **Toresschluss; ~schluss·panik, *~schluß·panik** *die* last-minute panic; *(Furcht, keinen Partner mehr zu finden)* fear of being left on the shelf; **~schlusspanik haben** *od.* **bekommen** *od.* **kriegen** panic at the last minute/be frightened of being left on the shelf; **~schuss, *~schuß** *der (Ballspiele)* shot [at goal]; **~schütze** *der,* **~schützin** *die (Ballspiele)* [goal] scorer

**Torsi** ⇒ **Torso**

**Torsion** /tɔr'zio:n/ *die;* ~, **~en** *(Physik, Technik, Math.)* torsion

**Torso** /'tɔrzo/ *der;* **~s, ~s** *od.* **Torsi** *(Kunstwiss., auch fig. geh.)* torso

**Tort** /tɔrt/ *der;* **~[e]s** *(ugs. veralt.)* wrong; injury; **jmdm. einen ~ antun** do sb. wrong; **jmdm. etw. zum ~ tun** do sth. to spite sb.

**Törtchen** /'tœrtçən/ *das;* **~s,** ~: tartlet

**Torte** /'tɔrtə/ *die;* ~, **~n** *(Creme~, Sahne~)* gateau; *(Obst~)* [fruit] flan

**Tortelett** /tɔrtə'lɛt/ *das;* **~s, ~s, Tortelette** *die;* **~e, ~en** tartlet

**Torten-:** **~boden** *der* flan case; *(ohne Rand)* flan base; ***~guß, ~guss** *der* glaze; **~heber** *der* cake slice; **~platte** *die* cake plate; **~schaufel** *die* ⇒ **~heber**

**Tortur** /tɔr'tu:ɐ/ *die;* ~, **~en** (A) ordeal; (B) *(veralt.: Folter)* torture

**Tor-:** **~verhältnis** *das (Ballspiele)* goal average; **~wächter** *der,* **~wächterin** *die* (A) gatekeeper; (B) *(Ballspiele)* goalkeeper; **~wart** *der;* **~~s, ~~e, ~wartin** *die;* **~~, ~~nen** *(Ballspiele)* goalkeeper; **~weg** *der* gateway

**tosen** /'to:zn̩/ *itr. V.; mit Richtungsangabe mit sein* ‹sea, surf› roar, rage; ‹storm› rage; ‹torrent, waterfall› roar, thunder; ‹wind› roar; **~der Lärm/Beifall** *(fig.)* thunderous noise/applause

**Toskana** /tɔs'ka:na/ *die;* ~: Tuscany

**tot** /to:t/ *Adj.* (A) dead; **das Kind wurde ~ geboren** the baby was stillborn; **ein ~ geborenes Kind** a stillborn child; **das Projekt war ein ~ geborenes Kind** *(fig.)* the project was stillborn *or* did not get off the ground; **er war auf der Stelle ~:** he died instantly; **~ zusammenbrechen** collapse and die; **~ umfallen** drop dead; **ich will auf der Stelle ~ umfallen, wenn das nicht wahr ist** may I be struck down if it isn't true; **sich ~ stellen** pretend to be dead; play dead; **er ist [politisch] ein ~er Mann** *(fig.)* he is finished [as a politician]; **er ist ein ~er Mann** he is a dead man *or (coll.)* a goner; **halb ~ vor Angst/Schrecken** *usw. (ugs.)* paralysed with fear/shock; **den ~en Mann machen** *(ugs.)* float on one's back; (B) *(abgestorben)* dead ‹tree, branch, leaves, etc.›; (C) *(fig.)* dull ‹colour›; bleak ‹region etc.›; dead ‹town, telephone line, socket, language›; disused ‹railway line›; extinct ‹volcano›; dead, quiet ‹time, period›; useless ‹knowledge›; **ein ~er Flussarm** a backwater; *(Schleife)* an oxbow lake; **das Tote Meer** the Dead Sea; ⇒ *auch* **Briefkasten** B; **Hose** B; **Punkt** D; **Winkel** A

**total** /to'ta:l/ ❶ *Adj.* total. ❷ *adv.* totally

**Total·aus·verkauf** *der* clearance sale

**Totale** *die;* ~, **~n** *od. adj. Dekl.* complete view; *(Film)* long shot

**Totalisator** /totali'za:tɔr/ *der;* **~s, ~en** /-za'to:rən/ totalizator; tote *(coll.)*

**totalitär** /totali'tɛ:ɐ/ *(Politik)* ❶ *Adj.* totalitarian. ❷ *adv.* in a totalitarian way; ‹organized, run› along totalitarian lines

**Totalitarismus** /totalita'rɪsmʊs/ *der;* ~ *(Politik)* totalitarianism *no art.*

**totalitaristisch** ⇒ **totalitär**

**Totalität** /totali'tɛ:t/ *die;* ~, **~en** *(geh.)* totality

**Total-:** **~operation** *die (Med.)* extirpation; *(Gynäkologie)* hysterectomy; **~schaden** *der (Versicherungsw.)* **an beiden Fahrzeugen entstand ~schaden** both vehicles were a write-off

**tot-:** **~|arbeiten** *refl. V. (ugs.)* work oneself to death; **~|ärgern** *refl. V. (ugs.)* get livid *(coll.);* **ich könnte mich ~ärgern** I'm livid *(coll.) or* really furious

**Tote** /'to:tə/ *der/die; adj. Dekl.* dead person; dead man/woman; **die ~n** the dead; **es gab zwei ~:** two people died *or* were killed; there were two fatalities; **wie ein ~r schlafen** sleep like a log; **na, bist du von den ~n auferstanden?** *(ugs. scherzh.)* oh, you're back in the land of the living, are you?; **die ~n soll man ruhen lassen** *(ugs.)* let the dead rest in peace

**Totem** /'to:tɛm/ *das;* **~s, ~s** *(Völkerk.)* totem

**Totem·pfahl** *der* totem pole

**töten** /'tø:tn̩/ *tr., itr. V.* kill; deaden ‹nerve etc.›; **einen kranken Hund ~ lassen** have a sick dog put down; ⇒ *auch* **Blick** A; **Nerv** A

**toten-, Toten-:** **~acker** *der (veralt.)* graveyard; **~ähnlich** *Adj.* deathlike ‹sleep›; **~amt** *das (kath. Kirche)* ⇒ **~messe; ~bahre** *die* bier; **~bett** *das* deathbed; **~blass, *~blaß, ~bleich** *Adj.* deathly pale; pale as death *postpos.;* **~feier** *die* memorial service; **~glocke** *die* death knell; **~gräber** *der;* **~~s, ~~** ▶ 159 (A) gravedigger; (B) *(Zool.)* gravedigger; burying beetle; **~hemd** *das* shroud; **~klage** *die* (A) lamentation *or* bewailing of the dead; (B) *(Literaturw.)* lament; dirge; **~kopf** *der* (A) skull; (B) *(als Symbol)* death's head; *(mit gekreuzten Knochen)* skull and crossbones; **~kult** *der (Völkerk.)* cult of the dead; **~maske** *die* death mask; **~messe** *die (kath. Kirche)* requiem [mass]; **~reich** *das* kingdom of the dead; **~schädel** *der* skull; **~schein** *der* death certificate; **~sonntag** *der: (ev. Kirche) Sunday before Advent on which the dead are commemorated;* **~starre** *die* rigor mortis; **~still** *Adj.* deathly quiet *or* silent; **~stille** *die* deathly quiet *or* silence; **~tanz** *der (bild. Kunst)* Dance of Death; **~wache** *die* vigil by the body; **die ~wache halten** keep vigil by the body

**tot-, Tot-:** **~|fahren** ❶ *unr. tr. V.* [run over and] kill; ❷ *unr. refl. V.* kill oneself; ***~geboren** ⇒ **tot** A; **~geburt** *die* (A) still birth; (B) *(Kind)* still birth; stillborn baby; **ihr erstes Kind war eine ~geburt** her first child was stillborn; **~geglaubte** *der/die; adj. Dekl.* person believed dead; **~gesagte** *der/die; adj. Dekl.* person declared dead; **~|kriegen** *tr. V. (ugs.)* kill; kill, get rid of ‹insect pests, weeds, etc.›; **er/dieser Mantel ist nicht ~zukriegen** *(fig.)* he's irrepressible/this coat just never wears out; **~|lachen** *refl. V. (ugs.)* kill oneself laughing; **zum ~lachen sein** be killing *(coll.);* be killingly funny *(coll.);* **~|laufen** *unr. refl. V. (ugs.)* ‹movement, trend, fashion› peter *or* die out; ‹talks, discussions› peter out; **~|machen** *tr. V. (ugs.)* kill

**Toto** /'to:to:/ *das od. der;* **~s, ~s** (A) *(Pferde~)* tote *(coll.);* **im ~:** on the tote; (B) *(Fußball~)* [football] pools *pl.;* **[im] ~ spielen** do the pools

**Toto-:** **~gewinn** *der* win on the pools/*(coll.)* tote; **~schein** *der* pools coupon/*(coll.)* tote ticket

**tot-, Tot-:** **~|sagen** *tr. V.* declare ‹person› dead; **eine Partei** *usw.* **~sagen** *(fig.)* say a party *etc.* is dead *or* finished; **~|schießen** *unr. tr. V. (ugs.)* **jmdn. ~schießen** shoot sb. dead; **~schlag** *der (Rechtsw.)* manslaughter *no indef. art.;* **~|schlagen** *unr. tr. V.* beat to death; **und wenn du mich ~schlägst** for the life of me; **eher/lieber lasse ich mich ~schlagen** *(ugs.)* I'd rather die *or* be dead; **die Zeit ~schlagen** kill time; **~schläger** *der* (A) *(Mensch)* manslaughterer; (B) *(Waffe)* cosh *(Brit. coll.);* blackjack *(Amer.);* **~schlägerin** *die* ⇒ **schläger** A; **~|schweigen** *unr. tr. V.* hush up; **jmdn. ~schweigen** keep

t

quiet about sb.; *~|**stellen** ⇒ **tot** A; ~|**treten** *unr. tr. V.* trample ‹person› to death; step on and kill ‹insect›

**Tötung** *die;* ~, ~**en** killing; **fahrlässige** ~ (*Rechtsspr.*) manslaughter by culpable negligence

**Tötungs-:** ~**absicht** *die* (*Rechtsw.*) intent *or* intention to kill; ~**versuch** *der* (*Rechtsw.*) attempted murder

**Touch** /tatʃ/ *der;* ~**s**, ~**s** (*ugs.*) touch

**Toupet** /tu'pe:/ *das;* ~**s**, ~**s** toupee

**toupieren** /tu'pi:rən/ *tr. V.* backcomb

**Tour** /tu:ɐ̯/ *die;* ~, ~**en** **A** tour (**durch** of); (*Kletter*~) [climbing] trip; (*kürzere Fahrt, Ausflug*) trip; (*mit dem Auto*) drive; (*mit dem Fahrrad*) ride; (*Zech*~) pub crawl (*Brit. coll.*); **eine ~ machen** go on a tour/trip *or* outing; (*Zech*~) go on a pub crawl (*Brit. coll.*); barhop (*Amer.*); **das ist 'ne ganz schöne ~** (*ugs.*) it's a fair *or* (*Brit. coll.*) fair old way; **B** (*feste Strecke*) route; **die ~ Hamburg-Neapel** the run from Hamburg to Naples; **C** (*Tournee*) tour; **auf ~ gehen** go on tour; **eine ~ durch Europa** a European tour; **D** (*ugs.: Methode*) ploy; **die ~ zieht bei mir nicht** that [one] won't work with me; **etw. auf die sanfte/gemütliche ~ machen** get sth. by soft-soaping/take one's time doing sth.; **seine ~ kriegen/haben** (*ugs.*) get/be in one of one's moods; ⇒ *auch* **krumm** 1 B; **E** (*ugs.: Unternehmen*) plan; **jmdm. die ~ vermasseln** (*ugs.*) put paid to sb.'s [little] plans; **F** (*Technik: Umdrehung*) revolution; rev (*coll.*); **die Maschine kam schnell auf ~en** the machine/engine was soon running at full speed; **jmdn. auf ~en bringen** (*ugs.*) really get sb. going; (*jmdn. böse machen*) get sb. worked up; **auf vollen/höchsten ~en laufen** (*ugs.*) ‹production, preparations, work, etc.› be in full swing; **G** *in* **in einer ~** (*ugs.*) the whole time

**Touren-:** ~**rad** *das* roadster; ~**ski** *der* touring ski; ~**wagen** *der* (*Motorsport*) touring car; ~**zahl** *die* (*Technik*) number of revolutions *or* (*coll.*) revs

**Tourismus** /tu'rɪsmʊs/ *der;* ~: tourism *no art.*

**Tourist** *der;* ~**en**, ~**en** tourist

**Touristen·klasse** *die* tourist class

**Touristik** *die;* ~: tourism *no art.*; tourist industry *or* business

**Touristin** *die;* ~, ~**nen** tourist

**touristisch** ❶ *Adj.* tourist *attrib.* ❷ *adv.* **das Land ist ~ noch kaum erschlossen** the country is still scarcely developed as a tourist area

**Tournedos** /tʊrnə'do:/ *das;* ~ /tʊrnə'do:(s)/, ~**s** tournedos

**Tournee** /tʊr'ne:/ *die;* ~, ~**s** *od.* ~**n** /tʊr'ne:ən/ tour; **auf ~ sein/gehen** be/go on tour

**-tournee** *die* ... tour; **auf Europa~/Deutschland~:** on a European/German tour

**Tower** /'taʊə/ *der;* ~**[s]**, ~**s** (*Flugw.*) [control] tower

**toxisch** /'tɔksɪʃ/ *Adj.* toxic

**Trab** /tra:p/ *der;* ~**[e]s** trot; **im ~:** at a trot; **im ~ reiten** trot; **in [den] ~ fallen** drop into a trot; **sich in ~ setzen** (*ugs.*) get going; get a move on (*coll.*); **jmdn. auf ~ bringen** (*ugs.*) make sb. get a move on; **jmdn. in ~ halten** (*ugs.*) keep sb. on the go (*coll.*)

**Trabant** /tra'bant/ *der;* ~**en**, ~**en** **A** (*Astron.*) satellite; **B** *Pl.* (*fam. scherzh. veralt.: Kinder*) kids (*coll.*)

**Trabanten·stadt** *die* satellite town

**traben** *itr. V.*; *mit sein* (*auch ugs.: laufen*) trot

**Traber** *der;* ~**s**, ~: trotter

**Trab·rennen** *das* trotting; (*einzelne Veranstaltung*) trotting race

**Tracht** /traxt/ *die;* ~, ~**en** **A** (*Volks*~) traditional *or* national costume; (*Berufs*~) uniform; **die ~ der Nonnen** the nuns' dress *or* habit; **B** *in* **eine ~ Prügel** a beating *or* thrashing; (*als Strafe für ein Kind*) a hiding; **C** (*Imkerei*) yield

**trachten** *itr. V.* (*geh.*) strive (**nach** for, after); **all sein** *od.* **sein ganzes Trachten** all his striving *or* endeavours; ⇒ *auch* **Leben** A

**Trachten-:** ~**anzug** *der: suit in the style of a traditional or national costume;* ~**fest** *das: festival at which traditional or national costume is worn;* ~**kapelle** *die: band in traditional or national costume*

**trächtig** /'trɛçtɪç/ pregnant

**Trächtigkeit** *die;* ~, ~**en** pregnancy

**tradieren** /tra'di:rən/ *tr. V.* (*geh.*) hand down, pass on ‹ideas, customs, values, etc.›

**Tradition** /tradi'tsi̯o:n/ *die;* ~, ~**en** tradition; ~ **sein/haben** be a tradition

**Traditionalismus** /traditsi̯ona'lɪsmʊs/ *der;* ~ (*geh.*) traditionalism *no art.*

**Traditionalist** *der;* ~**en**, ~**en**, **Traditionalistin** *die;* ~, ~**nen** (*geh.*) traditionalist

**traditionell** /traditsi̯o'nɛl/ ❶ *Adj.* traditional. ❷ *adv.* traditionally

**traditions-:** ~**bewusst**, *~**bewußt** ❶ *Adj.* tradition-conscious; conscious of tradition *postpos.*; ❷ *adv.* in a tradition-conscious way; ~**reich** *Adj.* rich in tradition *postpos.*

**traf** /tra:f/ *1. u. 3. Pers. Sg. Prät. v.* **treffen**

**träfe** /'trɛ:fə/ *1. u. 3. Pers. Sg. Konjunktiv II v.* **treffen**

**Trafik** /tra'fɪk/ *die;* ~, ~**en** (*österr.*) tobacconist's [shop]

**Trafikant** /trafi'kant/ *der;* ~**en**, ~**en**, **Trafikantin** *die;* ~, ~**nen** (*österr.*) tobacconist

**Trafo** /'tra:fo/ *der;* ~**s**, ~**s** transformer

**träg** /trɛ:k/ ⇒ **träge**

**Trag·bahre** *die* stretcher

**tragbar** *Adj.* **A** portable; **B** wearable ‹clothes›; **C** (*finanziell*) supportable ‹cost, debt, etc.›; **D** (*erträglich, tolerierbar*) bearable; tolerable; **er ist für die Partei nicht mehr ~:** the party can no longer tolerate him

**träge** /'trɛ:gə/ ❶ *Adj.* **A** sluggish; (*geistig*) lethargic; **B** (*Physik*) inert. ❷ *adv.* ⇒ **träge** 1: sluggishly; lethargically

**Trage** *die;* ~, ~**n** **A** (*Bahre*) stretcher; **B** (*Traggestell*) pannier

**Trage·korb** *der* pannier

**tragen** /tra:gn̩/ ❶ *unr. tr. V.* **A** carry; **das Auto wurde aus der Kurve ge~** (*fig.*) the car went off the bend; **B** (*bringen*) take; **vom Wasser/Wind ge~** (*fig.*) carried by water/[the] wind; **C** (*er*~) bear ‹fate, destiny›; bear, endure ‹suffering›; **D** (*halten*) hold; **einen/den linken Arm in der Schlinge ~:** have one's arm/one's left arm in a sling; **E** (*von unten stützen*) support; **die Schwimmweste trägt dich** the life jacket will hold you up; **zum Tragen kommen** ‹advantage, improvement, quality› become noticeable; **ein solcher Boykott kann nur zum Tragen kommen, wenn ...** such a boycott can be effective only if ...; ⇒ *auch* **tragend** 2 A-C; **F** (*belastbar sein durch*) be able to carry *or* take ‹weight›; **der Ast trägt dich nicht** the branch won't take your weight; **G** (*übernehmen, aufkommen für*) bear, carry ‹costs etc.›; take ‹blame, responsibility, consequences›; (*unterhalten, finanzieren*) support; maintain, support ‹school›; **er trägt die Schuld** he is to blame; **die Versicherung trägt den Schaden** the insurance will pay for the damage; **die Organisation trägt sich selbst** the organisation is self-supporting; **H** (*am Körper*) wear ‹clothes, wig, glasses, jewellery, etc.›; have ‹false teeth, beard, etc.›; **man trägt [wieder] Hüte** hats are in fashion [again]; **getragene Kleider** second-hand clothes; **I** (*fig.: haben*) have ‹label etc.›; have, bear ‹title›; bear, carry ‹signature, inscription, seal›; **J** (*hervorbringen*) ‹tree› bear ‹fruit›; ‹field› produce ‹crops›; (*fig.*) yield ‹interest›; **gut/wenig ~** ‹tree› produce a good/poor crop; ‹field› produce a good/poor yield; **K** (*geh.: schwanger sein mit*) be carrying; ⇒ *auch* **Bedenken** B; **getragen** 2, 3; **Sorge** C.
❷ *unr. itr. V.* **A** carry; **wir hatten schwer zu ~:** we were heavily laden; **schwer an etw.** (*Dat.*) **zu ~ haben** have difficulty carrying sth.; find sth. very heavy to carry; (*fig.*) find sth. hard to bear; **das Eis trägt noch nicht** the ice is not yet thick enough to skate/walk *etc.* on; **B** (*am Körper*) **man trägt [wieder] kurz/lang** short/long skirts are in fashion [again]; **C** **der Baum trägt gut** the tree produces a good crop; (*in diesem Sommer*) the tree has a lot of fruit on it ; **D** (*trächtig sein*) be carrying young; **eine ~de Sau/Kuh** a pregnant sow/cow; **E** ([*weit*] *reichen*) ‹voice› carry; ⇒ *auch* **tragend** 2 D.
❸ *unr. refl. V.* **A** **sich gut/schlecht** *usw.* ~ ‹load› be easy/difficult *or* hard *etc.* to carry; **zu zweit trägt sich der Korb besser** two can carry the basket more easily; **B** **der Mantel/Stoff trägt sich angenehm** the coat/material is pleasant to wear; **C** *in* **sich mit etw. ~:** be contemplating sth.; **er trägt sich mit dem Gedanken** *od.* **der Absicht, auszuwandern** he is contemplating [the idea of] emigrating; **D** (*sich kleiden*) dress

**tragend** ❶ *1. Part. von* **tragen.** ❷ *Adj.* **A** (*Stabilität gebend*) load-bearing; supporting ‹wall, column, function, etc.›; **B** (*fig.: grundlegend*) basic, main ‹idea, motif›; **C** (*fig.: wichtig, zentral*) leading, major ‹role, figure›; **D** (*weithin hörbar*) ‹voice› that carries [a long way]

**Träger** /'trɛ:gɐ/ *der;* ~**s**, ~ **A** porter; (*Sänften*~, *Sarg*~) bearer; **B** (*Zeitungs*~) paper boy/girl; delivery boy/girl; **C** (*Bauw.*) girder; [supporting] beam; **D** (*an Kleidung*) strap; (*Hosen*~) braces *pl.*; **E** (*Inhaber*) (*eines Amts*) holder; (*eines Namens, Titels*) bearer; (*eines Preises*) winner; **F** (*fig.: Urheber, treibende Kraft*) moving force; **G** (*fig.: Unterhalter*) **die Schule hat einen privaten ~:** the school is privately maintained; **~ der Arbeitslosenversicherung ist der Staat** unemployment insurance is financed *or* funded by the state; **H** (*fig.: einer Substanz, eines Erregers usw.*) carrier; **I** (*Flugzeug*~) carrier; **J** (*jmd., der etw. als Kleidung, Schmuck usw. trägt*) wearer

**Trägerin** *die;* ~, ~**nen** ⇒ **Träger** A, B, E, F, G, H, J

**träger-, Träger-:** ~**kleid** *das* pinafore dress; ~**los** *Adj.* strapless; ~**rakete** *die* carrier vehicle *or* rocket; ~**rock** *der* skirt with straps

**Trägerschaft** *die;* ~, ~**en** (*einer Schule*) maintenance; **in freier ~ sein** be privately maintained

**Trage-:** ~**tasche** *die* carrier bag; ~**zeit** *die* gestation [period]

**trag-, Trag-:** ~**fähig** *Adj.* able to take a load *or* weight *postpos.*; **eine ~fähige Mehrheit** (*fig.*) a workable majority; ~**fähigkeit** *die* load- *or* weight-bearing capacity; ~**fläche** *die* wing; (*eines Boots*) hydrofoil; ~**flächen·boot** *das* hydrofoil; ~**flügel** *der* ⇒ ~**fläche**; ~**flügel·boot** *das* hydrofoil

**Trägheit** *die;* ~, ~**en** **A** ⇒ **träge** 1 A: sluggishness; lethargy; **B** (*Physik*) inertia

**Trägheits-:** ~**gesetz** *das* (*Physik*) law of inertia; ~**moment** *das* (*Physik*) moment of inertia

**Tragik** /'tra:gɪk/ *die;* ~: tragedy

**Tragiker** *der;* ~**s**, ~: tragedian

**tragi-, Tragi-** /tragi-/: ~**komik** *die* tragicomedy; ~**komisch** ❶ *Adj.* tragicomic; ❷ *adv.* tragicomically; ~**komödie** *die* tragicomedy

**tragisch** /'tra:gɪʃ/ ❶ *Adj.* tragic; **das ist nicht [so] ~** (*ugs.*) it's not the end of the world (*coll.*); **etw. ~ nehmen** take sth. to heart (*coll.*). ❷ *adv.* tragically; **der Film/die Tour endete ~:** the film had a tragic ending/the trip ended in tragedy

**Trag-:** ~**kraft** ⇒ ~**fähigkeit**; ~**last** *die* load; ~**luft·halle** *die* air hall

**Tragöde** /tra'gø:də/ *der;* ~**n**, ~**n** tragedian

**Tragödie** /tra'gø:di̯ə/ *die;* ~, ~**n** tragedy; **er macht immer gleich eine ~ daraus** (*ugs.*) he always acts as if it's the end of the world (*coll.*)

**Tragödien·dichter** *der* tragedian

**Tragödin** *die;* ~, ~**nen** tragedienne

**Trag-:** ~**sessel** *der* sedan [chair]; ~**weite** *die* consequences *pl.*; **von großer ~weite sein** have far-reaching consequences; **ein Ereignis von großer/weltpolitischer**

*old spelling (see note on page 1707)

**~weite** an event of great consequence *or* moment/of moment in world politics; **~zeit** *die* gestation [period]

**Trailer** /'treɪlɐ/ **~s, ~** (*Film*) trailer

**Trainer** /'trɛːnɐ/ *der;* **~s, ~** **A** coach; trainer; (*eines Schwimmers, Tennisspielers*) coach; (*einer Fußballmannschaft*) manager; **B** (*Pferdesport*) trainer

**Trainer·bank** *die; Pl.* **Trainerbänke** (*Sport*) trainer's bench

**Trainerin** *die;* **~, ~nen** ⇒ **Trainer**

**trainieren** ❶ *tr. V.* **A** train; coach; coach ‹swimmer, tennis player›; train ‹horse›; manage ‹football team›; exercise ‹muscles etc.›; **sein Gedächtnis ~** (*fig.*) train one's memory; **darauf trainiert sein, etw. zu tun** be trained to do sth.; **jmdn./ein Tier darauf ~, etw. zu tun** train sb./an animal to do sth.; **ein trainierter Schwimmer/Radfahrer/Bergsteiger** *usw.* a swimmer/cyclist/mountaineer *etc.* [who is] in training; **ein trainierter Körper** a body made fit by training; **B** (*üben, einüben*) practise ‹exercise, jump, etc.›; **C** (*zu Trainingszwecken ausüben*) **Fußball/Tennis ~:** do football/tennis training. ❷ *itr. V.* train; (*Motorsport*) practise; **mit jmdm. ~** ‹trainer› coach sb.; ‹player› train with sb.

**Training** /'trɛːnɪŋ/ *das;* **~s, ~s** (**Fitness~**, *auch fig.: Ausbildung*) training *no indef. art.;* (*Motorsport, fig.*) practice; **Radfahren ist ein gutes ~:** cycling is a good form of training *or* exercise; **sich einem strengen ~ unterziehen** submit oneself to a rigorous training programme; **er hat sich beim ~ verletzt** he injured himself in training/practice; **geistiges ~** (*fig.*) mental exercises *pl.;* **er hat das ~ der Mannschaft übernommen** he has taken over the coaching of the team *or* as coach to the team; **im ~ sein/bleiben** be/keep in training; ⇒ *auch* **autogen**

**Trainings-: ~anzug** *der* track suit; **~hose** *die* track-suit bottoms *pl.;* **~jacke** *die* track-suit top; **~lager** *das; Pl.* **~~:** training camp; **~rückstand** *der* lack of training; **einen ~rückstand haben** be behind with one's training; **~runde** *die* (*Rennsport*) practice lap; **~schuh** *der* training shoe; trainer

**Trakehner** /tra'keːnɐ/ *der;* **~s, ~** (*Pferd*) Trakehner

**Trakt** /trakt/ *der;* **~[e]s, ~e** section; (*Flügel*) wing

**Traktat** /trak'taːt/ *der od. das;* **~[e]s, ~e** **A** (*Abhandlung*) treatise; **B** (*religiöse Flugschrift*) tract

**Traktätchen** /trak'tɛːtçən/ *das;* **~s, ~** (*abwertend*) tract

**traktieren** *tr. V.* **A** set about ‹person, thing›; **jmdn. mit Ohrfeigen/Faustschlägen ~:** slap sb. round the face/punch sb.; **B** (*veralt.: bewirten*) ply (**mit** with)

**Traktor** /'traktɔr/ *der;* **~s, ~en** /-'toːrən/ tractor

**Traktorist** *der;* **~en, ~en, Traktoristin** *die;* **~, ~nen** (*regional*) tractor driver

**trällern** /'trɛlɐn/ *itr., tr. V.* warble

**Tram** /traːm/ *die;* **~, ~s** *od. schweiz. das;* **~s, ~s** (*bes. südd., schweiz.*), **Tram·bahn** *die* (*südd.*) tram (*Brit.*); streetcar (*Amer.*)

**Traminer** /tra'miːnɐ/ *der;* **~s, ~** **A** (*Rebsorte*) Traminer [grape]; **B** (*Weißwein*) Traminer [white wine]

**Tramp** /trɛmp/ *der;* **~s, ~s** tramp; hobo (*Amer.*)

**Trampel** *der od. das;* **~s, ~** (*ugs. abwertend*) clumsy clot (*Brit. sl.*) *or* oaf

**trampeln** ❶ *itr. V.* **A** (*aufstampfen*) **[mit den Füßen] ~:** stamp one's feet; **B** *mit sein* (*abwertend: treten*) trample (**auf** + *Akk.* on). ❷ *tr. V.* trample

**Trampel-: ~pfad** *der* [beaten] path; **~tier** *das* **A** (*Kamel*) Bactrian camel; **B** (*salopp abwertend*) clumsy clot (*Brit. sl.*) *or* oaf

**trampen** /'trɛmpn̩/ *itr. V. mit sein* hitch-hike

**Tramper** *der;* **~s, ~, Tramperin** *die;* **~, ~nen** hitch-hiker

**Trampolin** /'trampoliːn/ *das;* **~s, ~e** trampoline

**Tramway** /'tramve/ *die;* **~, ~s** (*österr.*) tram (*Brit.*); streetcar (*Amer.*)

**Tran** /traːn/ *der;* **~[e]s** **A** (*vom Wal*) train-oil; (*von Fischen*) fish oil; **B** **im ~** (*ugs.*) befuddled; in a daze; (*durch Alkohol, Drogen*) stoned (*sl.*)

**Trance** /'trãːs(ə)/ *die;* **~, ~n** trance; **in ~:** in a trance; **in ~ fallen** go into a trance

**Trance·zustand** *der* trance

**Tranche** /'trãːʃ(ə)/ *die;* **~, ~n** **A** (*Kochk.*) thick slice; **B** (*Wirtsch.*) tranche

**Tränchen** /'trɛːnçən/ *das;* **~s, ~:** [little] tear

**tranchieren** *tr. V.* (*Kochk.*) carve

**Tranchier·messer** *das* carving knife

**Träne** /'trɛːnə/ *die;* **~, ~n** tear; **~ traten ihr in die Augen** tears came into her eyes; **seine ~n trocknen** dry one's eyes; wipe away one's tears; **ihr kommen leicht die ~n** she cries easily; **~n lachen** laugh till one cries *or* till the tears run down one's cheeks; **in ~n aufgelöst sein** be in floods of tears; **in ~n zerfließen** dissolve in tears; **mit einer ~ im Knopfloch** (*scherzh.*) wiping away a tear (*fig.*); **jmdm./einer Sache keine ~ nachweinen** not shed any tears over sb./sth.

**tränen** *itr. V.* ‹eyes› water

**Tränende Herz** *das;* **Tränenden Herzens, Tränenden Herzen** bleeding heart; lyre-flower

**tränen-, Tränen-: ~drüse** *die* ▶ 471 (*Anat.*) tear gland; **auf die ~drüsen drücken** (*fig.*) lay on the agony; **~erstickt** *Adj.* (*geh.*) **mit ~erstickter Stimme** in a voice choked with tears; **~gas** *das* tear gas; **~nass, *~naß** *Adj.* **~nasse Augen/Wangen** tear-stained eyes/cheeks; **~sack** *der* ▶ 471 (*Anat.*) lachrymal sac; **~säcke [unter den Augen]** bags under the eyes; **~überströmt** *Adj.* tear-stained ‹face›

**Tran·funzel** *die* (*ugs. abwertend*) **A** (*trübe Lampe*) miserable lamp; **B** (*langweiliger Mensch*) ponderous dimwit (*coll.*); (*langsamer Mensch*) slowcoach; slowpoke (*Amer.*)

**tranig** *Adj.* **A** (*voller Tran*) ‹meat, fish› full of train-oil; **B** (*wie Tran*) ‹taste› like *or* of train-oil; **C** (*ugs. abwertend: langsam*) sluggish; slow

**trank** /traŋk/ *1. u. 3. Pers. Sg. Prät. v.* **trinken**

**Trank** *der;* **~[e]s, Tränke** (*geh.*) drink; draught (*liter.*)

**Tränke** /'trɛŋkə/ *die;* **~, ~n** watering place; (*Gefäß*) drinking trough

**tränken** *tr. V.* **A** (*auch fig.*) water; **B** (*sich voll saugen lassen*) soak; **ein mit Hohn getränkter Brief** (*fig.*) a letter brimming with scorn

**Tranquilizer** /'træŋkwɪlaɪzə/ *der;* **~s, ~** (*Pharm.*) tranquillizer

**trans-, Trans-** /trans-/: **~aktion** *die* transaction; **~alpin, ~alpinisch** *Adj.* transalpine; **~atlantisch** *Adj.* transatlantic; across the Atlantic *postpos.;* **~-Europ-Express** *der* Trans-Europe Express

**Transfer** /'transfeːɐ̯/ *der;* **~s, ~s** (*bes. Wirtsch., Sport*) transfer

**transferieren** *tr. V.* (*bes. Wirtsch., Sport*) transfer (**auf** + *Akk.*, **in** + *Akk.*, **zu** to)

**Transfer·liste** *die* (*Fußball*) transfer list

**trans-, Trans-: ~formation** *die* transformation; **~formations·grammatik** *die* (*Sprachw.*) transformational grammar; **~formator** /-fɔr'maːtɔr/ *der;* **~~s, ~~en** /-'toːrən/ transformer; **~formator·häuschen** *das* transformer station; **~formieren** *tr. V.* transform (**in** + *Akk.* into, **auf** + *Akk.* to); **~fusion** *die* (*Med.*) transfusion

**transgen** *Adj.* transgenic

**Transistor** /tran'zɪstɔr/ *der;* **~s, ~en** /-'toːrən/ **A** (*Elektronik*) transistor; **B** ⇒ **~radio**

**Transistor·radio** *das* transistor radio

**Transit**[1] /*auch:* '--/ *der;* **~s, ~e** transit

**Transit**[2] /tran'ziːt, *auch:* 'tranzɪt/ *das;* **~s, ~s** transit visa

**Transit·handel** *der* transit trade

**transitiv** /'tranzitiːf/ (*Sprachw.*) ❶ *Adj.* transitive. ❷ *adv.* transitively

**Transit·verkehr** *der* transit traffic

**transkribieren** /transkri'biːrən/ *tr. V.* (*Sprachw.*) transcribe

**Transkription** /transkrɪp'ts̯ioːn/ *die;* **~, ~en** (*Sprachw.*) transcription

**Trans-: ~literation** /-lɪtera'ts̯ioːn/ *die;* **~~, ~~en** (*Sprachw.*) transliteration; **~mission** *die* (*Technik*) transmission; **~missions·riemen** *der* transmission belt

**transparent** /transpa'rɛnt/ *Adj.* **A** transparent; (*Licht durchlassend*) translucent, diaphanous ‹curtain, fabric, etc.›; **B** (*fig.: verständlich*) intelligible

**Transparent** *das;* **~[e]s, ~e** **A** (*Spruchband*) banner; **B** (*Bild*) transparency

**Transparenz** *die;* **~** **A** transparency; (*von Gewebe, Porzellan usw.*) translucence; **B** (*fig.: Verständlichkeit*) intelligibility

**Transpiration** /transpira'ts̯ioːn/ *die;* **~, ~en** **A** (*geh.*) perspiration; **B** (*Bot.*) transpiration

**transpirieren** *itr. V.* (*bes. Med.*) perspire

**trans-, Trans-: ~plantation** /-planta'ts̯ioːn/ *die;* **~~, ~~en** (*Med.*) transplant; (*von Haut*) graft; **~plantieren** /-plan'tiːrən/ *tr. V.* (*Med.*) transplant ‹organ, tissue›; graft ‹skin›; **~ponieren** /-po'niːrən/ *tr. V.* (*Musik*) transpose

**Transport** /trans'pɔrt/ *der;* **~[e]s, ~e** **A** (*Beförderung*) transportation; **beim** *od.* **auf dem ~:** during carriage; **B** (*beförderte Lebewesen od. Sachen*) (*mit dem Zug*) trainload; (*mit mehreren Fahrzeugen*) convoy; (*Fracht*) consignment; shipment; **C** (*Technik*) transport

**transportabel** /transpɔr'taːbl̩/ *Adj.* transportable; mobile ‹field kitchen›; (*tragbar*) portable

**Transport·behälter** *der* container

**Transporter** *der;* **~s, ~** (*Flugzeug*) transport aircraft; (*Auto*) goods vehicle; (*Schiff*) cargo ship

**Transporteur** /-'tøːɐ̯/ *der;* **~s, ~e, Transporteurin** *die;* **~, ~nen** carrier

**transportfähig** *Adj.* moveable

**Transport·flugzeug** *das* transport aircraft

**transportieren** ❶ *tr. V.* **A** transport ‹goods, people›; move ‹patient›; (*fig.*) convey ‹feeling, information, knowledge›; **B** (*Technik: weiterschieben*) transport, wind on ‹film›. ❷ *itr. V.* (*Technik*) ‹camera› wind on

**Transport-: ~kosten** *Pl.* carriage *sing.;* transport costs; **~mittel** *das* means *sing.* of transport; **~unter·nehmen** *das* haulage firm *or* contractor

**Trans·uran** *das* (*Chemie, Physik*) transuranic element

**Tran·suse** *die* (*ugs. abwertend*) ⇒ **Tranfunzel B**

**Transvestit** /transvɛs'tiːt/ *der;* **~en, ~en** transvestite

**transzendent** /transts̯ɛn'dɛnt/ *Adj.* **A** (*Philos.*) transcendent; **B** (*Math.*) transcendental

**transzendental** /transts̯ɛndɛn'taːl/ *Adj.* (*Philos.*) transcendental

**Transzendental·philosophie** *die* transcendental philosophy *no art.*

**Transzendenz** /transts̯ɛn'dɛnts̯/ *die;* **~** **A** transcendency; transcendent nature; **B** (*Philos.*) transcendence

**transzendieren** *tr. V.* (*geh.*) transcend

**Trapez** /tra'peːts̯/ *das;* **~es, ~e** **A** (*Geom.*) trapezium (*Brit.*); trapezoid (*Amer.*); **B** (*im Zirkus o. Ä.*) trapeze

**Trapez-: ~akt** *der* trapeze act; **~künstler** *der,* **~künstlerin** *die* trapeze artist

**Trapezoid** /trapets̯o'iːt/ *das;* **~[e]s, ~e** (*Geom.*) trapezoid (*Brit.*); trapezium (*Amer.*)

**Trappe** /'trapə/ *die;* **~, ~n** bustard

**trappeln** /'trapl̩n/ *itr. V.; mit sein* patter [along]; ‹feet› patter; ‹hoofs› go clip-clop

**Trapper** /'trapɐ/ *der;* **~s, ~, Trapperin** *die;* **~, ~nen** trapper

**Trappist** /tra'pɪst/ *der;* **~en, ~en** Trappist

**Trappisten-: ~käse** *der* Trappist cheese; **~orden** *der* order of Trappists

**Trappistin** *die;* **~, ~nen** Trappistine

**trapsen** /'trapsn/ *itr. V.; mit sein (ugs.)* tramp; clump; ⇒ *auch* **Nachtigall**

**trara** /tra'ra:/ *Interj.* tantara

**Trara** *das;* **~s** *(ugs. abwertend)* razzmatazz *(coll.)*; **viel ~ um etw.** *(Akk.)* **machen** make a great song and dance about sth. *(coll.)*

**Trass, *Traß** /tras/ *der;* **Trasses, Trasse** *(Geol.)* trass

**Trassant** /tra'sant/ *der;* **~en, ~en, Trassantin** *die;* **~, ~nen** *(Finanzw.)* drawer

**Trassat** /tra'sa:t/ *der;* **~en, ~en, Trassatin** *die;* **~, ~nen** *(Finanzw.)* drawee

**Trasse** /'trasə/ *die;* **~, ~n** Ⓐ *(Verkehrsweg)* [marked-out] route *or* line; Ⓑ *(Damm)* [railway/road] embankment

**trat** /tra:t/ *1. u. 3. Pers. Sg. Prät. v.* **treten**

**Tratsch** /tra:tʃ/ *der;* **~[e]s** *(ugs. abwertend)* gossip; tittle-tattle

**tratschen** *itr. V. (ugs. abwertend)* gossip; *(schwatzen)* chatter

**Tratscherei** *die;* **~, ~en** *(ugs. abwertend)* gossiping

**Tratte** /'tratə/ *die;* **~, ~n** *(Finanzw.)* bill [of exchange]

**Trau·altar** *der: in* **[mit jmdn.] vor den ~ treten** *(geh.)* enter into matrimony [with sb.]; **jmdn. zum ~ führen** *(geh. veralt.)* lead sb. to the altar

**Träubchen** /'trɔypçən/ *das;* **~s, ~:** little grape

**Traube** /'traubə/ *die;* **~, ~n** Ⓐ *(Beeren)* bunch; *(von Johannisbeeren o. Ä.)* cluster; Ⓑ *(Wein~)* grape; **jmdm. sind die ~n zu sauer** *(fig.)* it's just sour grapes on sb.'s part; Ⓒ *(Menschenmenge)* bunch; cluster; Ⓓ *(Bot.: Blütenstand)* raceme

**Trauben-: ~hyazinthe** *die* grape hyacinth; **~lese** *die* grape harvest; **~saft** *der* grapejuice; **~zucker** *der* glucose

**trauen** /'trauən/ ❶ *itr. V.* **jmdm./einer Sache ~:** trust sb./sth.; **ich traue dem Braten nicht** *(ugs.)* I think something's up *(coll.)*; it seems fishy to me *(coll.)*; **trau, schau, wem!** make sure you know who you're dealing with; mind you're not taken for a ride *(coll.)*; ⇒ *auch* **Auge** A. ❷ *refl. V.* dare; **sich** *(Akk., selten Dat.)* **~, etw. zu tun** dare [to] do sth.; **du traust dich ja nicht!** you haven't the courage *or* nerve; **sich irgendwohin ~:** dare [to] go somewhere; **ich traue mich nicht in seine Nähe** I daren't go near him. ❸ *tr. V. (verheiraten)* ‹vicar, registrar, etc.› marry; ⇒ *auch* **kirchlich** 1 B, 2; **standesamtlich** 2

**Trauer** /'trauɐ/ *die;* **~** Ⓐ grief **(über** + *Akk.* over); *(um einen Toten)* mourning **(um** + *Akk.* for); **~ haben, in ~ sein** be in mourning; **in stiller/tiefer ~ X** *(in Todesanzeigen)* [much loved and] sadly mourned by X; Ⓑ *(~zeit)* [period of] mourning; Ⓒ *(~kleidung)* mourning

**Trauer-: ~akt** *der* memorial ceremony; *(beim Begräbnis)* funeral ceremony; **~arbeit** *die (Psychol.)* process of grieving; **~fall** *der* bereavement; **~feier** *die* memorial ceremony; *(beim Begräbnis)* funeral ceremony; **~flor** *der* mourning band; black [crape] ribbon; **~gemeinde** *die* [congregation *sing.* of] mourners *pl.*; **~gottes·dienst** *der* funeral service; **~haus** *das* house of mourning; **~jahr** *das* year of mourning; **~karte** *die* [pre-printed] card of condolence; **~kleidung** *die* mourning clothes *pl.*; mourning; **~kloß** *der (ugs. scherzh.)* wet blanket; **~mantel** *der (Zool.)* Camberwell Beauty; mourning cloak [butterfly] *(Amer.)*; **~marsch** *der (Musik)* funeral march; **~miene** *die (ugs.)* long face

**trauern** *itr. V.* Ⓐ mourn; **um jmdn. ~:** mourn for sb.; **die ~den Hinterbliebenen** the bereaved; Ⓑ *(Trauer tragen)* be in mourning

**Trauer-: ~rand** *der* black border *or* edging; **~ränder unter den Nägeln haben** *(fig. scherzh.)* have black *or* grubby fingernails; **~rede** *die* funeral oration; **~schleier** *der* black veil; mourning veil; **~spiel** *das* tragedy; *(fig. ugs.)* deplorable business; **es ist doch ein ~spiel, dass ...** it's quite pathetic that ...; **~weide** *die* weeping willow; **~zeit** *die* period of mourning; **~zug** *der* funeral procession

**Traufe** /'traufə/ *die;* **~, ~n** eaves *pl.*

**träufeln** /'trɔyfln/ *tr. V.* [let] trickle **(in** + *Akk.* into); drip ‹ear drops etc.›

**traulich** /'traulɪç/ ❶ *Adj.* cosy; **in ~er Runde** in a friendly *or* an intimate circle. ❷ *adv.* cosily; *(vertraut)* intimately

**Traulichkeit** *die;* **~:** cosiness; *(Vertrautheit)* intimacy; friendliness

**Traum** /traum/ *der;* **~[e]s, Träume** /'trɔymə/ dream; **sie ist mir im ~ erschienen** she appeared to me in a dream; **wir denken nicht im ~ daran, hier wegzuziehen** we wouldn't dream of moving away from here; **nicht im ~ habe ich mit der Möglichkeit gerechnet, zu gewinnen** I didn't imagine in my wildest dreams that I could win; **Träume sind Schäume** *(Spr.)* dreams are but shadows; **Fliegen war schon immer sein ~:** he had always dreamed of flying; **der ~ ist ausgeträumt,** *(ugs.)* **aus [ist] der ~!** that's the end of 'that dream; 'that dream is over; ⇒ *auch* **kühn** B

**Traum-** dream ‹house, hotel, job, etc.›; ‹house, hotel, woman› of one's dreams; ideal, perfect ‹couple, job›

**Trauma** /'trauma/ *das;* **~s, Traumen** *od.* **~ta** ▸ 474 *(Psych., Med.)* trauma

**traumatisch** *(Psych., Med.)* ❶ *Adj.* traumatic. ❷ *adv.* traumatically

**Traum-: ~bild** *das* vision; *(Wunschbild)* dream; *(idealisiert)* ideal; **~deutung** *die* interpretation of dreams

**träumen** /'trɔymən/ ❶ *itr. V.* dream **(von** of, about); *(unaufmerksam sein)* [day]dream; **[schlaf gut und] träum süß** [sleep well and] sweet dreams; **träum nicht!** pay attention; stop daydreaming. ❷ *tr. V.* dream; **etwas Schreckliches/Schönes ~:** have a terrible/beautiful dream; **er träumte** *od.* *(geh.)* **ihm träumte, er sei ...** he dreamt that he was ...; **das hast du doch nur geträumt!** you must have imagined that; **ich hätte mir nie ~ lassen, dass ...** I should never have imagined it possible that ...; I never imagined that ...

**Traumen** ⇒ **Trauma**

**Träumer** *der;* **~s, ~:** dreamer

**Träumerei** *die;* **~, ~en** daydream; reverie

**Träumerin** *die;* **~, ~nen** dreamer

**träumerisch** ❶ *Adj.* dreamy; *(sehnsüchtig)* wistful. ❷ *adv.* dreamily; *(sehnsüchtig)* wistfully

**Traum·fabrik** *die* dream factory

**traumhaft** ❶ *Adj.* Ⓐ dreamlike; Ⓑ *(ugs.: schön)* marvellous; fabulous *(coll.)*; **~es Glück haben** have a fantastic piece of luck *(coll.)*. ❷ *adv.* Ⓐ as if in a dream; Ⓑ *(ugs.: schön)* fabulously *(coll.)*; **eine ~ eingerichtete Wohnung** a superbly furnished flat

**traum-, Traum-: ~tänzer** *der*, **~tänzerin** *die (abwertend)* wooly-headed idealist; fantasizer; **~verloren** ❶ *Adj.* dreamy; ❷ *adv.* in a dream; dreamily; **~wandlerisch** *Adj.* somnambulistic; **mit ~wandlerischer Sicherheit** with the sureness of a sleepwalker; with instinctive sureness; **~welt** *die* dream world

**traurig** /'traurɪç/ ❶ *Adj.* Ⓐ sad; sad, sorrowful ‹eyes, expression›; unhappy ‹childhood, youth›; unhappy, painful ‹duty›; **ein ~es Kapitel** *(fig.)* a sad story; Ⓑ *(kümmerlich)* sorry, pathetic ‹state etc.›; miserable ‹result›; pitiful, wretched ‹conditions›; down-at-heel ‹area›; **eine ~e Berühmtheit/Rolle** an unfortunate notoriety/role. ❷ *adv.* sadly

**Traurigkeit** *die;* **~:** sadness; sorrow; **eine große/allgemeine ~:** a great/general feeling of sadness

**Trau-: ~ring** *der* wedding ring; **~schein** *der* marriage certificate

**traut** *Adj. (geh.)* Ⓐ *(heimelig)* cosy; secure; **das ~e Familienglück** happiness in the bosom of a/the family; Ⓑ *(vertraut)* familiar; close, intimate ‹friend, family circle›

**Traute** /'trautə/ *die;* **~** *(ugs.)* guts *(coll.)*

**Trauung** *die;* **~, ~en** wedding [ceremony]

**Trau·zeuge** *der*, **Trau·zeugin** *die* witness *(at wedding ceremony)*

**Traveller·scheck** /'trɛvəlɐʃɛk/ *der* traveller's cheque

**Traverse** /tra'vɛrzə/ *die;* **~, ~n** Ⓐ *(Technik)* cross-beam; Ⓑ *(Fechten)* sideways movement to avoid opponent's attack

**Travers·flöte** /tra'vɛrs-/ *die* transverse flute

**Travestie** /travɛs'ti:/ *die;* **~, ~n** travesty

**Trebe** /'tre:bə/ *die: in* **auf ~ sein** *(ugs.)* be a runaway

**Trebegänger** /-gɛŋɐ/ *der;* **~s, ~, Trebegängerin** *die;* **~, ~nen** *(ugs.)* runaway

**Treber** *Pl.* Ⓐ *(Brauereiwesen)* draff *sing.*; Ⓑ *(Weinbau)* marc *sing.*

**Treck** /trɛk/ *der;* **~s, ~s** train, column *(of refugees etc.)*

**Trecker** *der;* **~s, ~:** tractor

**Treff**[1] *das;* **~s, ~s** *(Spielkartenfarbe)* clubs *pl.*; ⇒ *auch* **Pik**[2]

**Treff**[2] /trɛf/ *der;* **~s, ~s** *(ugs.)* Ⓐ *(Treffen)* rendezvous; *(bes. von mehreren Personen)* get-together *(coll.)*; Ⓑ *(Ort)* meeting place

**treffen** ❶ *unr. tr. V.* Ⓐ *(erreichen [und verletzen/schädigen])* hit; ‹punch, blow, object› strike; **jmdn. am Kopf/ins Gesicht ~:** hit *or* strike sb. on the head/in the face; **von einer Kugel tödlich getroffen** fatally wounded by a bullet; **vom Blitz getroffen** struck by lightning; **er fühlte sich von den Vorwürfen nicht getroffen** he did not consider that the reproaches applied to him; **ihn trifft keine Schuld** he is in no way to blame; Ⓑ *(erraten)* hit on; hit ‹right tone›; **du hast genau das Richtige getroffen** you've hit on just the right thing; *(das stimmt haargenau)* you've got it exactly right; **getroffen!** you've got it!; **mit dem Geschenk hast du seinen Geschmack getroffen/nicht getroffen** that present is just the sort of thing he likes/not the sort of thing he likes; **auf dem Foto ist er gut getroffen** the photo is a good likeness of him; that's a good photo of him; Ⓒ *(erschüttern)* affect [deeply]; *(verletzen)* hurt; **jmdn. tief** *od.* **schwer ~:** affect sb. deeply; **es hat ihn in seinem Stolz getroffen** it hurt his pride; Ⓓ *(schaden)* hit; damage; **warum muss es immer mich ~?** why does it always have to be me [who is affected *or* gets it]?; Ⓔ *(begegnen)* meet; **jmdn. zum Mittagessen ~:** meet sb. for lunch; **ich traf ihn zufällig auf der Straße** I happened to run into him in the street; **ihre Blicke trafen sich** *(fig.)* their eyes met; Ⓕ *(vorfinden)* come upon, find ‹anomalies etc.›; **es gut/schlecht ~:** be *or* strike lucky/be unlucky; Ⓖ *(als Funktionsverb)* make ‹arrangements, choice, preparations, decision, etc.›; **eine Vereinbarung** *od.* **Absprache ~:** conclude an agreement. ❷ *unr. itr. V.* Ⓐ ‹person, shot, etc.› hit the target; **nicht ~:** miss [the target]; **ins Schwarze ~:** score a bullseye; Ⓑ *mit sein* **auf etw.** *(Akk.)* **~:** come upon sth.; **auf Widerstand/Ablehnung/Schwierigkeiten ~:** meet with *or* encounter resistance/rejection/difficulties; **auf jmdn./eine Mannschaft ~** *(Sport)* come up against sb./a team. ❸ *unr. refl. V.* Ⓐ **sich mit jmdm. ~:** meet sb.; Ⓑ *(unpers.)* **es trifft sich gut/schlecht** it is convenient/inconvenient

**Treffen** *das;* **~s, ~** Ⓐ meeting; **ein ~ alter Kameraden** a reunion of old comrades; Ⓑ *(Sport)* encounter; **ein faires/spannendes ~:** a fair/exciting contest; Ⓒ *(Milit. veralt.)* encounter; **etw. ins ~ führen** *(fig. geh.)* bring sth. into the attack

**treffend** ❶ *Adj.* apt; apposite ‹remark›; **ein ~es Urteil** an accurate assessment. ❷ *adv.* aptly; **kurz und ~ sagte er ...** he said, short and to the point, ...

**Treffer** *der;* **~s, ~** Ⓐ *(Milit., Boxen, Fechten usw.)* hit; *(Schlag)* blow; *(Ballspiele)* goal; **schwere ~ an Kopf und Körper einstecken** *(Boxen)* take heavy blows *or* punches to the head and body; **er hatte auf zehn Schüsse acht ~:** of his ten shots eight were on target; Ⓑ *(Gewinn)* win; *(Los)* winner

*old spelling (see note on page 1707)

t

**trefflich** (*geh.*) ❶ *Adj.* excellent; splendid ‹person›; first-rate ‹scholar›. ❷ *adv.* excellently; splendidly

**treff-, Treff-: ~punkt** *der* Ⓐ (*Stelle, Ort*) meeting place; rendezvous; Ⓑ (*Geom.*) point of incidence; (*Schnittpunkt*) point of intersection; **~sicher** ❶ *Adj.* with a sure aim *postpos., not pred.*; accurate ‹marksman›; (*fig.*) accurate ‹language, mode of expression›; unerring ‹judgement›; ❷ *adv.* (*auch fig.*) accurately; with unerring accuracy; **~sicherheit** *die* ⇒ **~sicher** 1: accuracy; sureness of aim; (*fig.*) accuracy; unerringness

**Treib-: ~anker** *der* (*Seew.*) sea anchor; **~ball** *der* Ⓐ (*Spiel*) [*informal*] *ball game played by two teams trying to throw the ball over the back line of the opposing team*; Ⓑ (*Badminton*) drive; **~eis** *das* drift-ice

**treiben** /ˈtraibn̩/ ❶ *unr. tr. V.* Ⓐ drive ‹animals, people, leaves, etc.›; (*Fußball*) dribble ‹ball›; **er ließ sich von der Strömung ~:** he let himself be carried along by the current; **die Arbeit trieb ihm den Schweiß auf die Stirn** the effort brought the sweat to his brow; **die Preise in die Höhe ~:** push *or* force up prices; **jmdn. in den Wahnsinn** *od.* **zur Raserei/zur Verzweiflung/in den Tod ~:** drive sb. mad/to despair/to his/her death; Ⓑ (*an~*) drive ‹wheels etc.›; **die ~de Kraft [des Ganzen] ist ...** the moving spirit [behind the whole affair] is ...; **jmdn. zur Eile ~:** make sb. hurry up; Ⓒ (*einschlagen*) drive ‹nail, wedge, stake, etc.› (**in** + *Akk.* into); Ⓓ (*durch Bohrung schaffen*) drive, cut ‹tunnel, gallery› (**in** + *Akk.* into; **durch** through); sink ‹shaft› (**in** + *Akk.* into); Ⓔ (*durchpressen*) force; press; Ⓕ (*sich beschäftigen mit*) go in for ‹farming, cattle breeding, etc.›; study ‹French etc.›; carry on, pursue ‹studies, trade, craft›; **viel Sport ~:** do a lot of sport; go in for sport in a big way; **Handel ~:** trade; **Unfug ~:** get up to mischief; **Unsinn ~:** mess *or* fool about; **was treibt ihr denn hier?** (*ugs.*) what are you up to *or* doing here?; **was habt ihr den ganzen Tag getrieben?** (*ugs.*) what did you do with yourself *or* get up to all day?; ⇒ *auch* **Aufwand** B; **Missbrauch** A; **Scherz**; **Spionage**; **Spott**; Ⓖ (*ugs. abwertend: in Verbindung mit „es"*:) **es wüst/übel/toll ~:** lead a dissolute/bad life/live it up; **es zu toll ~:** overdo it; take things too far; **er hat es zu weit getrieben** he overstepped the mark; he went too far; **es [mit jmdm.] ~** (*ugs. verhüll.: koitieren*) have it off [with sb.] (*sl.*); Ⓗ (*formen*) beat ‹metal, object›; chase ‹silver, gold›; Ⓘ (*Gartenbau*) force ‹plants›; Ⓙ (*aufgehen lassen*) cause ‹dough› to rise.
❷ *unr. itr. V.* Ⓐ *meist, mit Richtungsangabe nur, mit sein* drift; **die Dinge ~ lassen** (*fig.*) let things take their course; **sich ~ lassen** (*fig.*) drift; go with the tide; Ⓑ (*ugs.*) (*harntreibend sein*) get the bladder going; (*schweißtreibend sein*) make you sweat; **ein ~des Mittel** a diuretic/sudorific; Ⓒ (*ausschlagen*) ‹tree, plant› sprout

**Treiben** *das*; **~s**, **~** Ⓐ (*Durcheinander*) bustle; **in der Fußgängerzone herrscht ein lebhaftes ~:** the pedestrian precinct is full of bustling activity; ⇒ *auch* **närrisch** 1 c; Ⓑ (*Tun*) activities *pl.*; doings *pl.*; (*Machenschaften*) wheelings and dealings *pl.*; Ⓒ (*Jägerspr.*) ⇒ **Treibjagd**

**Treiber** *der*; **~s**, **~**, **Treiberin** *die*; **~**, **~nen** (*Jägerspr.*) beater

**Treib-: ~gas** *das* Ⓐ (*für Motoren*) liquefied petroleum gas; LPG; Ⓑ (*in Spraydosen*) propellant; **~gut** *das* flotsam; **~haus** *das* hothouse; **~haus·effekt** *der* greenhouse effect; **~haus·gas** *das* greenhouse gas; **~haus·luft** *die* hothouse atmosphere; (*im Freien*) sultry atmosphere; **~holz** *das* driftwood; **~jagd** *die* (*Jägerspr.*) battue; shoot (*in which game is sent up by beaters*); **eine ~jagd auf kritische Journalisten** (*fig.*) a witch-hunt against critical jounalists; **~mittel** *das* Ⓐ (*Kochk.*) raising agent; Ⓑ (*Chemie: für feste Stoffe*) foaming agent; Ⓒ ⇒ **~gas** B; **~riemen** *der* (*Technik*) drive belt; **~sand** *der* quicksand; **~satz** *der* (*Technik*) [solid] rocket propulsion element; **~schlag** *der* (*Badminton, Golf, Tennis, Tischtennis*) drive; **~stoff** *der* fuel

**treideln** /ˈtraidl̩n/ *tr. V.* (*veralt.*) tow ‹barge› upstream

**treife** /ˈtraifə/ *Adj.* trefa; not kosher *pred.*

**Trema** /ˈtreːma/ *das*; **~s**, **~s** *od.* **~ta** (*Sprachw.*) diaeresis

**tremolieren** *itr. V.* (*Musik*) play/sing with a tremolo

**Tremolo** /ˈtreːmolo/ *das*; **~s**, **~s** *od.* **Tremoli** (*Musik*) tremolo

**Trenchcoat** /ˈtrɛntʃkoʊt/ *der*; **~[s]**, **~s** trench coat

**Trend** /trɛnt/ *der*; **~s**, **~s** trend (**zu** + *Dat.* towards); (*Mode*) vogue; **im ~ liegen** be in vogue

**Trend·setter** *der*; **~s**, **~**, **Trend·setterin** *die*; **~**, **~nen** (*bes. Werbejargon*) trendsetter (*Gen.* in)

**trennbar** *Adj.* Ⓐ (*nicht fest zusammengesetzt*) separable ‹verb, prefix›; Ⓑ (*sich trennen lassend*) **dieses Wort ist [nicht] ~:** this word can[not] be split *or* divided

**trennen** /ˈtrɛnən/ ❶ *tr. V.* Ⓐ separate (**von** from); (*abschneiden*) cut off; sever ‹head, arm›; **der Krieg hatte die Familie getrennt** the war had split up the family; **das Kind von der Mutter ~:** take the child away from the mother; **das Futter aus der Jacke ~:** cut the lining out of the jacket; **nur noch wenige Tage ~ uns von den Ferien** the holidays are only a few days away; Ⓑ (*auf~*) unpick ‹dress, seam›; Ⓒ (*teilen*) divide ‹word, parts of a room etc., fig.: people›; **ein Zaun trennte die Grundstücke** a fence divided the plots from one another; a fence formed the boundary between the plots; **uns ~ Welten** (*fig.*) we are worlds apart; **„st" darf nicht getrennt werden** 'st' cannot be split *or* divided; Ⓓ (*beim Telefon*) **wir wurden getrennt** we were cut off; Ⓔ (*zerlegen*) separate ‹mixture›; Ⓕ (*auseinander halten*) differentiate *or* distinguish between; make a distinction between ‹terms›; **die Arbeit von der Freizeit ~:** keep work separate from leisure.
❷ *itr. V.* (*Rundf., Funkw.*) **gut** *od.* **scharf ~** ‹radio› have good selectivity.
❸ *refl. V.* Ⓐ (*voneinander weggehen*) part [company]; (*fig.*) **die Mannschaften trennten sich 0:0** the game ended in a goalless draw; the two teams drew 0:0; **die Firma hat sich von ihm getrennt** the company has dispensed with his services; Ⓑ (*eine Partnerschaft auflösen*) ‹couple, partners› split up; **sich in Güte ~:** part on good terms; **sie hat sich von ihrem Mann getrennt** she has left her husband; ⇒ *auch* **getrennt**; Ⓒ (*hergeben*) **sich von etw. ~:** part with sth.

**Trenn-: ~schärfe** *die* (*Rundf., Funkw.*) selectivity; **~scheibe** *die* Ⓐ glass partition; Ⓑ (*Schleifscheibe*) cutting disc

**Trennung** *die*; **~**, **~en** Ⓐ (*von Menschen*) separation (**von** from); **in ~ leben** have separated; **die ~ von Tisch und Bett** separation from bed and board; separation without divorce; Ⓑ (*von Gegenständen*) parting; **die ~ von allem irdischen Besitz** parting with all one's worldly goods; Ⓒ (*von Wörtern*) division; Ⓓ (*von Begriffen*) distinction (**von** between)

**Trennungs-: ~linie** *die* (*auch fig.*) dividing line; **~schmerz** *der* pain of separation; **~strich** *der* Ⓐ hyphen; Ⓑ (*fig.*) **einen ~strich ziehen** *od.* **machen** make a [clear] distinction; draw a [clear] line; **er zog einen ~strich zwischen sich und seiner Vergangenheit** he made a clean break with the past

**Trenn·wand** *die* partition

**Trense** /ˈtrɛnzə/ *die*; **~**, **~n** Ⓐ (*Gebiss*) snaffle bit; Ⓑ (*Zaumzeug*) snaffle

**trepp-** /trɛp'-/: **~ab** *Adv.* down the stairs; **~auf** *Adv.* up the stairs

**Treppchen** *das*; **~s**, **~** Ⓐ small staircase; Ⓑ (*Sportjargon*) [winner's] rostrum

**Treppe** /ˈtrɛpə/ *die*; **~**, **~n** Ⓐ staircase; [flight *sing.* of] stairs *pl.*; (*im Freien, auf der Bühne*) [flight *sing.* of] steps *pl.*; **~n steigen** climb stairs; **eine ~ höher/tiefer** one floor *or* flight up/down; **die ~ hinauffallen** (*fig. ugs.*) rise in the world; **die ~ runtergefallen sein** (*fig. ugs. scherzh.*) have been to the sheep shearer's (*joc.*); Ⓑ (*in der Frisur*) step

**Treppen-: ~absatz** *der* half landing; **~geländer** *das* banisters *pl.*; **~giebel** *der* (*Archit.*) stepped gable; **~haus** *das* stairwell; **das Licht im ~haus** the light on the staircase; **~steigen** *das*; **~~s** climbing stairs *no art.*; **~stufe** *die* stair; (*im Freien*) step; **~witz** *der*: **ein ~witz der [Welt]geschichte** one of history's cruel ironies

**Tresen** /ˈtreːzn̩/ *der*; **~s**, **~** (*bes. nordd.*) Ⓐ (*Theke*) bar; Ⓑ (*Ladentisch*) counter

**Tresor** /treˈzoːɐ̯/ *der*; **~s**, **~e** Ⓐ safe; Ⓑ (**~raum**) strongroom

**Tresse** /ˈtrɛsə/ *die*; **~**, **~n** [strip of] braid; (*Rangabzeichen*) stripe

**Trester** /ˈtrɛstɐ/ *Pl.* (*Landw.*) Ⓐ (*von Trauben*) marc; Ⓑ (*von Äpfeln o. Ä.*) pomace

**Trester·brannt·wein** *der* marc

**Tret-: ~boot** *das* pedalo; **~eimer** *der* pedal bin

**treten** /ˈtreːtn̩/ ❶ *unr. itr. V.* Ⓐ *mit sein* (*einen Schritt, Schritte machen*) step (**in** + *Akk.* into, **auf** + *Akk.* on to); **ins Zimmer/in einen Laden ~:** enter the room/a shop; **ans Fenster ~:** go to the window; **zur Seite ~:** step *or* move aside; **von einem Fuß auf den anderen ~:** shift from one foot to the other; **der Schweiß ist ihm auf die Stirn ge~** (*fig.*) the sweat came to his brow; **der Fluss ist über die Ufer ge~** (*fig.*) the river has overflowed its banks; ⇒ *auch* **Stelle** A; Ⓑ (*seinen Fuß setzen*) **auf etw.** (*Akk.*) **~** (*absichtlich*) tread on sth.; (*unabsichtlich; meist mit sein*) step *or* tread on sth.; **jmdm. auf den Fuß ~:** step/tread on sb.'s foot *or* toes; **auf das Gas[pedal]/die Bremse ~:** step on the accelerator/the brake; **kräftig in die Pedale ~:** pedal hard; Ⓒ *mit sein* (*verblasst in Verbindungen mit Substantiven*) **in jmds. Dienste ~:** enter sb.'s service; **in Kontakt** *od.* **Verbindung ~:** get in touch; **in den Ruhestand ~:** go into retirement; ⇒ *auch* **Aktion** C; **Ehestand**; **Hungerstreik**; **Streik**; Ⓓ (*ausschlagen*) kick; **jmdm. an** *od.* **gegen das Schienbein ~:** kick sb. on the shin; **gegen die Tür ~:** kick the door.
❷ *unr. tr. V.* Ⓐ (*Tritt versetzen*) kick ‹person, ball, etc.›; **jmdn. in den Bauch ~:** kick sb. in the stomach; **eine Ecke ~** (*Fußball*) take a corner; **man muss ihn immer ~, damit er etwas tut** (*fig.*) you always have to give him a kick to make him do anything; Ⓑ (*trampeln*) trample, tread ‹path›; **sich** (*Dat.*) **einen Dorn in den Fuß ~:** get a thorn in one's foot; **sich** (*Dat.*) **den Lehm von den Schuhen ~:** stamp the mud off one's shoes; Ⓒ (*mit dem Fuß niederdrücken*) step on ‹brake, pedal›; operate ‹bellows, clutch›; **die Pedale ~:** pedal; Ⓓ (*bei Geflügel: begatten*) tread; mate with

**Treter** *der*; **~s**, **~** (*ugs., oft abwertend*) casual shoe; casual

**Tret-: ~kurbel** *die* crank arm; crank; **~lager** *das* bottom bracket [bearing]; crank bearing; **~mine** *die* anti-personnel mine; **~mühle** *die* (*fig. ugs. abwertend*) treadmill; **in die ~mühle zurückkehren** return to the daily grind (*coll.*); **~roller** *der* pedal-scooter

**treu** /trɔy/ ❶ *Adj.* Ⓐ (*beständig*) faithful, loyal ‹friend, dog, customer, servant, etc.›; faithful ‹husband, wife›; loyal ‹ally, subject›; (*unbeirrt*) staunch, loyal ‹supporter›; **jmdm. ~ sein/bleiben** be/remain true to sb.; **eine ~e Seele** a faithful *or* devoted soul; **jmdm. ~e Dienste leisten** serve sb. faithfully; Ⓑ **sich selbst** (*Dat.*)**/seinem Glauben ~ bleiben** be true to oneself/one's faith; **seinen Grundsätzen ~ bleiben** stick to one's principles; **das Glück/der Erfolg ist ihm ~ geblieben** his luck has held out/success keeps coming his way; ⇒ *auch* **Hand** F; Ⓒ (*ugs.: ~herzig*) ingenuous, trusting ‹eyes, look›.
❷ *adv.* Ⓐ (*beständig*) faithfully; loyally; **~ ergeben/sorgend** devoted; **jmdm. ~ ergeben sein** (*veralt., sonst scherzh.*) be utterly devoted to sb.; Ⓑ (*ugs.: ~herzig*) trustingly; **alles ~ und brav tun** do everything unquestioningly

t

**Treu** ⇒ Treue A

**treu-, Treu-: ~bruch** *der* Ⓐ **landesverräterischer ~bruch** (*DDR Rechtsw.*) state treason; Ⓑ (*hist.: Bruch der Lehnstreue*) felony (*Law Hist.*); **~deutsch** *Adj.* (*ugs., meist abwertend*) typically German; **~doof** (*ugs. abwertend*) ❶ *Adj.* gormlessly naïve (*coll.*); gormless (*coll.*); ❷ *adv.* gormlessly (*coll.*) and naïvely

**Treue** *die;* ~ Ⓐ loyalty; (*von [Ehe]partnern*) fidelity; **jmdm. ~ schwören** swear to be true *or* faithful to sb.; **jmdm. die ~ halten** keep faith with sb.; be loyal to sb.; **meiner Treu!** (*veralt.*) upon my word! (*dated*); **Treu und Glauben** (*Rechtsw.*) equity; **auf Treu und Glauben** (*ugs.*) in good faith; Ⓑ (*Genauigkeit*) accuracy

**Treue·gelöbnis** *das* pledge of loyalty; (*von Ehepartnern*) pledge of fidelity

**Treu·eid** *der* oath of allegiance; (*hist.: im Lehnswesen*) oath of fealty

**Treue-: ~pflicht** *die* (*Rechtsw.*) loyalty to one's employer; (*des Arbeitgebers*) loyalty to one's employee; **~prämie** *die* long-service bonus

***treu·ergeben** ⇒ treu 2 A

**Treue·schwur** *der* oath of loyalty *or* allegiance

**treu-, Treu-: ~hand** *die* Ⓐ (*Wirtschaft*) German privatization agency; Ⓑ (*Rechtsw.*) trusteeship; **~hand·anstalt** *die* (*Wirtschaft*) German privatization agency; **~händer** /-ˈhɛndɐ/ *der;* **~~s**, ~~, **~händerin** *die;* ~~, **~~nen** (*Rechtsw.*) trustee; **~händerisch** ❶ *Adj.* fiduciary; **~händerische Übertragung** assignment on trust. ❷ *adv.* on trust; **etw. ~händerisch verwalten** hold sth. in trust; **~herzig** ❶ *Adj.* ingenuous; (*naiv*) naïve; (*unschuldig*) innocent; ❷ *adv.* ingenuously; (*naiv*) naïvely; (*unschuldig*) innocently; **~herzigkeit** *die;* **~~:** ingenuousness; (*Naivität*) naivety; (*Unschuld*) innocence

**treulich** (*veralt.*) ❶ *Adj.* faithful. ❷ *adv.* faithfully

**treu-, Treu-: ~los** ❶ *Adj.* disloyal, faithless ‹friend, person›; unfaithful ‹husband, wife, lover›; ❷ *adv.* faithlessly; **~losigkeit** *die;* **~~:** disloyalty; faithlessness; (*von [Ehe]partnern*) infidelity; ***~sorgend** ⇒ treu 2 A

**Trevira** Ⓦⓩ /treˈviːra/ *das;* **~:** Trevira ®

**Triangel** /ˈtriːaŋl̩/ *der; österr. das;* **~s**, ~ (*Mus.*) triangle

**Trias** /ˈtriːas/ *die;* ~, ~ Ⓐ (*Geol.*) Triassic; Trias; Ⓑ (*geh.*) trio; trinity

**Trias·formation** *die* (*Geol.*) Triassic system

**Tri·athlet** *der*, **Tri·athletin** *die* triathlete

**Triathlon**[1] /ˈtriːatlɔn/ *das* **~s** triathlon; ~ **trainieren** train for the triathlon

**Triathlon**[2] *der;* **~s**, **~s** triathlon

**Tribun** /triˈbuːn/ *der;* **~s** *od.* **~en**, **~e[n]** (*hist.*) tribune

**Tribunal** /tribuˈnaːl/ *das;* **~s**, **~e** Ⓐ tribunal; Ⓑ (*im antiken Rom*) tribune (*for the municipal authorities in the Forum Romanum*)

**Tribüne** /triˈbyːnə/ *die;* ~, **~n** [grand]stand

**Tribut** /triˈbuːt/ *der;* **~[e]s**, **~e** Ⓐ (*hist.*) tribute *no indef. art.;* Ⓑ (*fig.*) due; **einer Sache** (*Dat.*) **~ zollen** pay the price for sth.; **einen hohen ~ [an Menschenleben] fordern** take a heavy toll [of human lives]

**Trichine** /trɪˈçiːnə/ *die;* ~, **~n** trichina

**trichinös** /trɪçiˈnøːs/ *Adj.* trichinous

**Trichter** /ˈtrɪçtɐ/ *der;* **~s**, ~ Ⓐ funnel; **auf den [richtigen] ~ kommen** (*fig. ugs.*) get the message (*coll.*); ⇒ *auch* **Nürnberger**; Ⓑ (*Granat~, Bomben~, Geogr.*) crater

**Trichter·mündung** *die* estuary

**Trick** /trɪk/ *der;* **~s**, **~s** trick; (*fig.: List*) ploy; **technische ~s** cunning techniques; **den ~ heraushaben** have got the knack

**trick-, Trick-: ~betrüger** *der*, **~betrügerin** *die* confidence trickster; **~film** *der* animated cartoon [film]; **~kiste** *die* (*ugs.*) repertoire of tricks/ploys; bag of tricks; **in die ~kiste greifen** dip into one's bag of tricks; **~reich** ❶ *Adj.* wily; ❷ *adv.* artfully; ‹play› trickily; **~reich geschlagene Bälle** cunningly hit shots

**tricksen** /ˈtrɪksn̩/ (*ugs., bes. Sportjargon*) ❶ *itr. V.* use tricks; work a fiddle (*coll.*); ‹footballer› play trickily. ❷ *tr. V.* fiddle (*coll.*)

**Trick·ski·laufen** *das;* **~s** acrobatic *or* (*Amer. sl.*) hot-dog skiing *no art.*

**Tricktrack** /ˈtrɪktrak/ *das;* **~s**, **~s** tric-trac

**trieb** /triːp/ *1. u. 3. Pers. Sg. Prät. v.* **treiben**

**Trieb** *der;* **~[e]s**, **~e** Ⓐ (*innerer Antrieb*) impulse; (*Drang*) urge; (*Verlangen*) [compulsive] desire; Ⓑ (*Spross*) shoot; Ⓒ (*Technik: Übertragung*) transmission; drive

**trieb-, Trieb-: ~befriedigung** *die* [*esp.* sexual] gratification; **~feder** *die* mainspring; (*fig.*) driving *or* motivating force; (*Beweggrund*) motive (+ *Gen.* behind); **~haft** ❶ *Adj.* compulsive ‹need, behaviour, action, etc.›; carnal ‹sensuality›; **ein ~hafter Mensch** a person ruled by his/her [physical] impulses; ❷ *adv.* compulsively; **~handlung** *die* compulsive act; (*bei Tieren*) instinctive act; **~kraft** *die* (*bes. Soziol.*) driving *or* motivating force; **~stoff** *der* (*schweiz.*) ⇒ **Treibstoff**; **~täter** *der*, **~täterin** *die*, **~verbrecher** *der*, **~verbrecherin** *die: offender committing a crime in gratifying a compulsive desire;* (*Sexualtäter*) sexual offender; **~wagen** *der* (*Eisenb.*) railcar; **~werk** *das* engine

**Trief·auge** *das* watery eye; (*eitrig*) bleary *or* (*Med.*) blear eye

**triefen** /ˈtriːfn̩/ *unr. od. regelm. itr. V.* Ⓐ *mit sein* (*fließen*) (*in Tropfen*) drip; (*in kleinen Rinnsalen*) trickle; Ⓑ (*nass sein*) be dripping wet; ‹nose› run; **~d nass** dripping wet; **von** *od.* **vor Fett/Nässe ~:** be dripping with fat/be dripping wet; **von** *od.* **vor Edelmut ~** (*fig. iron.*) be oozing with nobility

**Trief·nase** *die* runny nose

**trief·nass**, ***trief·naß** *Adj.* dripping wet

**triezen** /ˈtriːtsn̩/ *tr. V.* (*ugs.*) torment; (*plagen*) pester; plague

**triff** /trɪf/ *Imperativ Sg. v.* **treffen**

**trifft** *3. Pers. Sg. Präsens v.* **treffen**

**Trift** /trɪft/ *die;* ~, **~en** Ⓐ (*Strömung*) drift [current]; Ⓑ (*Weide*) common [*esp.* mountain] pasturage; Ⓒ (*Weg*) cattle track

**triften** *tr. V.* raft ‹tree trunks›

**triftig** ❶ *Adj.* good ‹reason, excuse›; valid, convincing ‹motive, argument›. ❷ *adv.* convincingly

**Triftigkeit** *die;* **~:** validity

**Trigonometrie** /trigonomeˈtriː/ *die;* **~:** trigonometry *no art.*

**trigonometrisch** *Adj.* trigonometric; **~er Punkt** triangulation point

**Trikot**[1] /triˈkoː/ *der od. das;* **~s**, **~s** (*Stoff*) cotton jersey

**Trikot**[2] *das;* **~s**, ~ (*ärmellos*) singlet; (*eines Tänzers*) leotard; (*eines Fußballspielers*) shirt; **das gelbe ~** (*Radsport*) the yellow jersey

**Trikotage** /trikoˈtaːʒə/ *die;* ~, **~n** [cotton] jersey garments *pl.;* (*Unterwäsche*) cotton [jersey] underwear

**Triller** /ˈtrɪlɐ/ *der;* **~s**, **~:** trill

**trillern** ❶ *itr. V.* (*Musik*) trill; (*mit vielen T~ singen*) ‹bird, person› warble. ❷ *tr. V.* warble ‹song›

**Triller·pfeife** *die* police/referee's whistle

**Trillion** /trɪˈli̯oːn/ *die;* ~, **~en** quintillion

**Trilogie** /triloˈgiː/ *die;* ~, **~n** trilogy

**Trimester** /triˈmɛstɐ/ *das;* **~s**, ~ (*Hochschulw.*) term

**Trimm-dich-Pfad** *der* keep-fit *or* trim trail

**trimmen** /ˈtrɪmən/ *tr. V.* Ⓐ (*durch Sport*) get ‹person› into shape; **trimm dich durch Sport** keep fit with sport; Ⓑ **etw. auf alt/„Western" usw. ~:** do sth. up to look old/like the wild west *etc.;* Ⓒ (*durch Scheren*) clip ‹dog›; (*durch Bürsten*) groom ‹dog›; Ⓓ (*Seew., Flugw.*) trim ‹ship, aircraft, cargo›; stow ‹barrels, bales, etc.› properly; **Kohlen ~:** take on [a load of] coal

**Trimm-: ~gerät** *das* exerciser; **~trab** *der* jogging *no art.*

**Trinität** /triniˈtɛːt/ *die;* ~ (*christl. Rel.*) Trinity

**Trinitatis** /triniˈtaːtɪs/ (*das*); ~, **Trinitatis·fest** *das* Trinity Sunday *no art.*

**trinkbar** *Adj.* drinkable; **hast du was Trinkbares im Haus?** (*ugs.*) have you anything to drink in the house?

**trinken** /ˈtrɪŋkn̩/ ❶ *unr. itr. V.* drink; **in** *od.* **mit kleinen Schlucken/in großen Zügen ~:** drink in little sips/in big gulps; **lass mich mal [von dem Saft] ~:** let me have a drink [of the juice]; **jmdm. etw. zu ~ geben** give sb. sth. to drink; **was ~ Sie?** what are you drinking?; (*was möchten Sie ~?*) what would you like to drink?; **man merkte, dass er getrunken hatte** one could see that he had been drinking; **auf jmdn./etw. ~:** drink to sb./sth.; **ich trinke auf deine Gesundheit** I'll drink [to] your health; **das Trinken lassen** give up drink. ❷ *unr. tr. V.* drink; **einen Kaffee/ein Bier** *usw.* **~:** have a coffee/beer *etc.;* **ich trinke keinen Tropfen [Alkohol]** I don't drink; I don't touch alcohol; **einen Schluck Wasser ~:** have a drink of water; **einen ~:** have a drink; **einen ~ gehen** (*ugs.*) go for a drink. ❸ *refl. V.* **der Wein trinkt sich gut** the wine is pleasant to drink; **sich satt ~:** drink one's fill; **sich krank/zu Tode ~:** make oneself ill through drink/drink oneself to death

**Trinker** *der;* **~s**, **~:** alcoholic; **ein heimlicher/starker ~:** a secret/heavy drinker

**Trinkerei** *die;* ~, **~en** drinking *no art.*

**Trinker·heil·anstalt** *die* drying-out clinic; detoxification centre

**Trinkerin** *die;* ~, **~nen** ⇒ **Trinker**

**trink-, Trink-: ~fest** *Adj.* **~fest sein** be able to hold one's drink; **ein ~fester Matrose** a sailor used to hard drinking; **~flasche** *die* [drinking] bottle; **~festigkeit** *die* ability to hold one's drink; **~freudig** *Adj.* fond of drinking *pred.;* **~gefäß** *das* drinking vessel (*formal*); **~gelage** *das* (*oft scherzh.*) drinking spree; **~geld** *das* tip; **wie viel ~geld gibst du ihm?** how much do you tip him?; how big a tip do you give him?; **~glas** *das; Pl.* **~gläser** [drinking] glass; **~halle** *die* Ⓐ (*in einem Heilbad*) pump room; Ⓑ (*Kiosk*) refreshment kiosk; (*größer*) refreshment stall; **~halm** *der* [drinking] straw; **~lied** *das* (*veralt.*) drinking song; **~milch** *die* low-fat pasteurized milk; **~spruch** *der* toast (**auf** + *Akk.* to); **einen ~spruch auf jmdn. ausbringen** propose a toast to sb.; **~wasser** *das; Pl.* **~wässer** drinking water; **„kein ~wasser"** 'not for drinking'; **~wasser·aufbereitung** *die* purification of drinking water

**Trio** /ˈtriːo/ *das;* **~s**, **~s** (*Musik, fig.*) trio

**Triole** /triˈoːlə/ *die;* ~, **~n** (*Musik*) triplet

**Trio·sonate** *die* (*Musik*) trio sonata

**Trip** /trɪp/ *der;* **~s**, **~s** Ⓐ (*ugs.: Ausflug*) trip; jaunt; (*untertreibend:*) **ein ~ in die Staaten** a little trip to the States; Ⓑ (*Drogenjargon: Rausch*) trip (*coll.*); **auf dem ~ sein** be tripping (*coll.*); **auf dem religiösen/anarchistischen** *usw.* **~ sein** (*fig. ugs.*) be going through a religious/anarchist *etc.* phase; Ⓒ (*Drogenjargon: Dosis*) fix (*sl.*); **~s werfen** *od.* **schmeißen** pop LSD (*or other hallucinogen*) (*sl.*)

**Tripel-: ~** triple ‹fugue, concerto, etc.›; **~allianz** Triple Alliance

**trippeln** /ˈtrɪpl̩n/ *itr. V.; mit sein* trip; ‹child› patter; (*affektiert*) mince

**Trippel·schritt** *der* short, rapid step; (*affektiert*) mincing step

**Tripper** /ˈtrɪpɐ/ *der;* **~s**, ~ ▶ **474** gonorrhoea; **sich** (*Dat.*) **einen ~ holen** (*ugs.*) get a dose of the clap (*coarse*)

**Triptik** ⇒ **Triptyk**

**Triptychon** /ˈtrɪptyçɔn/ *das;* **~s**, **Triptychen** *od.* **Triptycha** (*Kunstwiss.*) triptych

**Triptyk** /ˈtrɪptʏk/ *das;* **~s**, **~s** triptyque

**trist** /trɪst/ *Adj.* dreary; dismal

**Tristheit** *die;* **~:** dreariness

**Tritons·horn** /ˈtriːtɔns-/ *das* (*Zool.*) triton *or* trumpet shell

**tritt** /trɪt/ *Imperativ Sg. u. 3. Pers. Sg. Präsens v.* **treten**

*old spelling (see note on page 1707)

**Tritt** *der;* **~[e]s, ~e** Ⓐ (*Aufsetzen des Fußes*) step; (*einmalig*) [foot]step; **mit festem ~:** with a firm step *or* tread; ⇒ *auch* **Schritt** A; Ⓑ (*Gleichschritt*) **im ~ marschieren** march in step; **aus dem ~ geraten** *od.* **kommen** get out of step; **ohne ~, marsch!** break step!; **~ fassen** fall in step; (*fig.: sich fangen*) recover oneself; Ⓒ (*Fuß~*) kick; **jmdm. einen ~ versetzen** give sb. a kick; kick sb.; **einen ~ bekommen** *od.* **kriegen** (*fig. ugs.*) be given the push (*Brit. coll.*); get kicked out; Ⓓ (*~brett*) step; Ⓔ (*Bergsteigen*) (*Halt für Füße*) foothold; (*im Eis*) step; Ⓕ (*Gestell*) small stepladder; (*in der Bibliothek*) library steps *pl.*; Ⓖ (*Jägerspr.: Abdruck*) footprint

**Tritt-: ~brett** *das* step; (*an älterem Auto*) running-board; **~brett·fahrer** *der*, **~brett·fahrerin** *die* (*fig. abwertend*) ≈ free rider (*Amer.*); *person who profits from another's work;* **~leiter** *die* stepladder

**Triumph** /tri'ʊmf/ *der;* **~[e]s, ~e** triumph; **~e/einen großen ~ feiern** have a series of triumphs/a great triumph *or* success; be hugely successful/a huge success; **im ~:** in triumph

**triumphal** /triʊm'fa:l/ *Adj.* Ⓐ (*begeisternd*) triumphant ‹success etc.›; **~ sein** be a triumph; Ⓑ (*mit Jubel*) triumphal ‹entry etc.›; **jmdm. einen ~en Empfang bereiten** give sb. a hero's welcome

**Triumphator** /triʊm'fa:tɔr/ *der;* **~s, ~en** /-'to:rən/ Ⓐ (*hist.*) triumphator; Ⓑ (*geh.: Sieger*) conquering hero

**Triumph-: ~bogen** *der* (*Archit.*) triumphal arch; **~geschrei** *das* triumphant cheering *no indef. art.*

**triumphieren** *itr. V.* Ⓐ (*Genugtuung empfinden*) exult; **~d** triumphant; exultant; **~d lachen** laugh triumphantly; Ⓑ (*siegen*) be triumphant *or* victorious; triumph (*lit. or fig.*) (**über** + *Akk.* over)

**Triumph·zug** *der* (*hist.*) triumph; **im ~** (*fig.*) in a triumphal procession

**Triumvirat** /triʊmvi'ra:t/ *das;* **~[e]s, ~e** (*hist.*) triumvirate

**trivial** /tri'vi̯a:l/ ❶ *Adj.* Ⓐ (*platt*) banal; trite; (*unbedeutend*) trivial; Ⓑ (*alltäglich*) humdrum ‹life, career›. ❷ *adv.* (*platt*) banally; ‹say etc.› tritely; ‹written› in a banal style

**Trivialität** *die;* **~, ~en** Ⓐ (*Plattheit, Alltäglichkeit*) banality; triteness; Ⓑ (*platte Äußerung*) banality; (*Gemeinplatz*) commonplace [remark]

**Trivial·roman** *der* light [trashy] novel

**Trochäus** /trɔ'xɛ:ʊs/ *der;* **~, Trochäen** (*Verslehre*) trochee

**trocken** /'trɔkn̩/ ❶ *Adj.* Ⓐ dry; **~en Auges** (*geh.*) dry-eyed; without shedding a tear; **etw. ~ bügeln/reinigen** dry-iron/dry-clean sth.; **sich ~ rasieren** use an electric razor; **noch ~ nach Hause kommen** get home without getting wet; **wieder auf dem Trock[e]nen sein** be on dry land *or* terra firma again; **auf dem Trock[e]nen sitzen** *od.* **sein** (*ugs.*) be completely stuck (*coll.*); (*pleite sein*) be skint (*Brit. sl.*); **~ sitzen** (*ugs.*) have nothing to drink; Ⓑ (*ohne Zutat*) **~es** *od.* (*ugs.*) **~ Brot essen** eat dry bread; Ⓒ (*sachlich-langweilig*) dry, factual ‹account, report, treatise›; bare ‹words, figures›; dull, dry ‹person›; Ⓓ (*unverblümt*) dry ‹humour, remark, etc.›; Ⓔ (*dem Klang nach*) dry ‹laugh, cough, sound›; sharp ‹crack›; clear ‹acoustics›; Ⓕ (*Sportjargon, bes. Boxen, Fußball*) sharp ‹blow›; snappy ‹shot›; **eine ~e Rechte** a straight right. ❷ *adv.* Ⓐ (*sachlich-langweilig*) ‹speak, write› drily, in a matter-of-fact way; Ⓑ (*unverblümt*) drily; Ⓒ (*dem Klang nach*) **das Gewehr knallte kurz und ~:** the rifle went off with a short, sharp report

**Trocken-: ~beeren·aus·lese** *die: wine made from selected grapes left to dry on the vine at the end of the season;* **~blume** *die* dried flower; **~boden** *der* attic drying-room; **~dock** *das* dry dock; **~eis** *das* dry ice; **~futter** *das* (*Landw.*) dry fodder; **~gebiet** *das* (*Geogr.*) arid region; **~gestell** *das* (*für Wäsche*) clothes airer *or* -horse; **~haube** *die* [hood-type] hairdrier

**Trockenheit** *die;* **~, ~en** Ⓐ (*auch fig.*) dryness; Ⓑ (*Dürreperiode*) drought

**trocken-, Trocken-: ~kurs** *der* dry-skiing course; **~|legen** *tr. V.* Ⓐ **ein Baby ~legen** change a baby's nappies (*Brit.*) *or* (*Amer.*) diapers; Ⓑ (*entwässern*) drain ‹marsh, pond, etc.›; **~legung** *die;* **~~, ~~en** draining; **~milch** *die* dried milk; **~rasierer** *der* (*ugs.*) Ⓐ (*Rasierapparat*) electric razor; Ⓑ (*Person*) user of an electric razor; **~|reiben** *unr. tr. V.* rub ‹hair, child, etc.› dry; wipe ‹crockery, window, etc.› dry; **~reinigung** *die* dry-cleaning; **~|schleudern** *tr. V.* spin-dry; **~schwimmen** *das* preparatory swimming exercises *pl.* [on land] (*for learners*); ***~|sitzen** ⇒ **trocken** 1 A; **~spiritus** *der* solid fuel (*for camping-stove*); **~übung** *die* preliminary [swimming/skiing] exercise; (*fig.*) dry run; **~zeit** *die* dry season

**trocknen** ❶ *itr. V.; meist mit sein* dry. ❷ *tr. V.* dry; **die Kleider zum Trocknen aufhängen** hang up the clothes to dry

**Trockner** *der;* **~s, ~:** drier; (*Trockengestell*) airer

**Troddel** /'trɔdl̩/ *die;* **~, ~n** tassel

**Trödel** /'trø:dl̩/ *der;* **~s** (*ugs., oft abwertend*) junk; (*für den Flohmarkt*) jumble

**Trödelei** *die;* **~, ~en** (*ugs. abwertend*) dawdling *no pl.*

**trödeln** *itr. V.* Ⓐ (*ugs., oft abwertend*) dawdle (**mit** over); Ⓑ *mit sein* (*ugs.: schlendern*) saunter

**Trödler** *der;* **~s, ~, Trödlerin** *die;* **~, ~nen** Ⓐ (*ugs. abwertend*) dawdler; slowcoach; slowpoke (*Amer.*); Ⓑ (*ugs.: Händler[in]*) junk dealer; **etw. beim ~ kaufen** buy sth. from *or* at the junk shop

**troff** /trɔf/ *1. u. 3. Pers. Sg. Prät. v.* **triefen**

**trog** /tro:k/ *1. u. 3. Pers. Sg. Prät. v.* **trügen**

**Trog** *der;* **~[e]s, Tröge** /'trø:gə/ (*auch Geol.*) trough

**Troika** /'trɔy̯ka/ *die;* **~, ~s** troika; (*fig.: Führungsgruppe*) triumvirate

**Troja** /'tro:ja/ (*das*); **~s** Troy

**Trojaner** *der;* **~s, ~, Trojanerin** *die;* **~, ~nen** Trojan

**trojanisch** *Adj.* Trojan; **das Trojanische Pferd** (*Myth.; auch fig.*) the Trojan Horse

**Troll** /trɔl/ *der;* **~[e]s, ~e** (*Myth.*) troll

**Troll·blume** *die* globeflower

**trollen** (*ugs.*) *refl. V.* push off (*coll.*); **der Junge trollte sich in sein Zimmer** the boy took himself off to his room

**Trolley·bus** /'trɔli-/ *der* (*bes. schweiz.*) trolleybus

**Trollinger** /'trɔlɪŋɐ/ *der;* **~s, ~:** Trollinger [grape/wine]

**Trommel** /'trɔml̩/ *die;* **~, ~n** Ⓐ (*Schlaginstrument*) drum; **die ~ für jmdn./etw. rühren** (*ugs.*) beat the drum for sb./sth.; Ⓑ (*Behälter; Kabel~, Seil~*) drum

**Trommel-: ~bremse** *die* (*Technik*) drum brake; **~fell** *das* Ⓐ (*bei ~n*) drumhead; Ⓑ (*im Ohr*) eardrum; **~feuer** *das* (*Milit.; auch fig.*) [constant] barrage

**trommeln** ❶ *itr. V.* Ⓐ beat the drum; (*als Beruf, Hobby usw.*) play the drums; Ⓑ (*[auf etw.] schlagen, auftreffen*) drum (**auf** + *Akk.* on, **an** + *Akk.* against); **sie trommelte mit den Fäusten gegen die Tür** she hammered the door with her fists. ❷ *tr. V.* Ⓐ beat [out] ‹march, rhythm, etc.›; Ⓑ **jmdn. aus dem Bett/Schlaf ~:** get sb. out of bed/wake sb. up by hammering on the door

**Trommel-: ~revolver** *der* revolver; **~schlag** *der* drumbeat; **~schlägel, ~schlegel** *der*, **~stock** *der* drumstick; **~wirbel** *der* drum roll

**Trommler** *der;* **~s, ~, Trommlerin** *die;* **~, ~nen** drummer

**Trompete** /trɔm'pe:tə/ *die;* **~, ~n** trumpet; **[eine Melodie] auf der ~ blasen** play [a tune on] the trumpet

**trompeten** ❶ *itr. V.* Ⓐ play the trumpet; (*fig.*) ‹elephant› trumpet; Ⓑ (*ugs. scherzh.: sich laut schnäuzen*) blow one's nose like a foghorn. ❷ *tr. V.* play ‹piece› on the trumpet; (*fig.*) proclaim ‹news etc.› loudly

**Trompeten·stoß** *der* blast on a/the trumpet

**Trompeter** *der;* **~s, ~, Trompeterin** *die;* **~, ~nen** ▶ 159 trumpeter

**Tropen** *Pl.* tropics

**Tropen-** tropical

**Tropen-: ~fieber** *das* ▶ 474 [falciparum] malaria (*Med.*); **~helm** *der* sun helmet; **~koller** *der* tropical madness; **~tauglichkeit** *die* fitness for service/travel in the tropics

**Tropf**[1] /trɔpf/ *der;* **~[e]s, Tröpfe** /'trœpfə/ (*abwertend*) twit (*Brit. coll.*); moron (*coll.*); **armer ~:** poor devil

**Tropf**[2] *der;* **~[e]s, ~e** (*Med.*) drip; **am ~ hängen** be on a drip

**Tröpfchen** /'trœpfçən/ *das;* **~s, ~:** droplet; (*kleine Menge*) drop; (*scherzh.: Wein*) **ein wahrhaft edles ~:** a really fine vintage

**Tröpfchen·infektion** *die* (*Med.*) droplet infection

**tröpfchen·weise** *Adv.* in small drops

**tröpfeln** /'trœpfl̩n/ ❶ *itr. V.* Ⓐ *mit sein* drip (**auf** + *Akk.* on to, **aus, von** from); Ⓑ (*unpers.*) (*ugs.: leicht regnen*) **es tröpfelt** it's spitting [with rain]. ❷ *tr. V.* let ‹sth.› drip (**in** + *Akk.* into, **auf** + *Akk.* on to)

**tropfen** ❶ *itr. V.; mit Richtungsangabe mit sein* drip; ‹tears› fall; **seine Nase tropft** his nose is running; (*unpers.*) **es tropft [vom Dach** *usw.*] water is *or* it's dripping from the roof *etc.*; **es tropft** (*es regnet*) it's spitting [with rain]. ❷ *tr. V.* let ‹sth.› drip (**in** + *Akk.* into, **auf** + *Akk.* on to); **jmdm. eine Tinktur auf die Wunde ~:** pour drops of a tincture into sb.'s wound

**Tropfen** *der;* **~s, ~** Ⓐ drop; **ein paar ~ Parfüm** a few drops of perfume; **es regnet dicke ~:** the rain is falling in large drops *or* spots; **die ersten ~ fallen** the first spots [of rain] are falling; **er hat keinen ~ [Alkohol] getrunken** he hasn't touched a drop; **steter ~ höhlt den Stein** (*Spr.*) constant dropping wears away the stone (*prov.*); persistence gets there in the end; **ein ~ auf den heißen Stein sein** (*fig. ugs.*) be a drop in the ocean; Ⓑ **ein guter/edler ~:** a good/fine vintage

**Tropfen·form** *die* tear shape; **in ~:** tear-shaped *attrib.*

**tropfen·weise** *Adv.* drop by drop; a drop at a time

**tropf-, Tropf-: ~infusion** *die* (*Med.*) intravenous drip; **~nass, *~naß** *Adj.* dripping *or* soaking wet; **~stein·höhle** *die* limestone cave with stalactites and/or stalagmites

**Trophäe** /tro'fɛ:ə/ *die;* **~, ~n** (*hist., Jagd, Sport*) trophy

**tropisch** ❶ *Adj.* tropical. ❷ *adv.* tropically ‹warm›

**Tropo·sphäre** /tropo'sfɛ:rə/ *die;* **~** (*Meteor.*) troposphere

**Tross, *Troß** /trɔs/ *der;* **Trosses, Trosse** Ⓐ (*Milit.*) baggage train; Ⓑ (*Gefolge*) retinue; (*fig.: Zug*) procession [of hangers-on]

**Trosse** /'trɔsə/ *die;* **~, ~n** hawser (*Naut.*)

**Trost** /tro:st/ *der;* **~[e]s** consolation; (*bes. geistlich*) comfort; **jmdm. ~ zusprechen** *od.* **spenden** comfort *or* console sb.; **jmdm. ein/kein ~ sein** be a/no comfort to sb.; **ein schwacher ~!** that's little *or* not much consolation; **in der Arbeit ~ suchen/finden** seek/find solace in work; **als ~:** as a consolation; **nicht [ganz** *od.* **recht] bei ~ sein** (*ugs.*) be out of one's mind; have taken leave of one's senses

**trösten** /'trø:stn̩/ ❶ *tr. V.* comfort, console (**mit** with); **sie wollte sich nicht ~ lassen** she was not to be *or* refused to be comforted; she was inconsolable; **~de Worte** words of comfort; comforting words; **~d den Arm um jmdn. legen** put one's arm around sb. to comfort him/her; **etw. tröstet jmdn.** sth. is a comfort to sb.; **der Gedanke konnte ihn nicht ~:** the thought was no comfort to him. ❷ *refl. V.* console oneself; **sich damit ~, dass ...** console oneself with the thought that ...; **sich mit einer anderen Frau ~:** find consolation with another woman

t

**Tröster** *der;* **~s,** **~, Trösterin** *die;* **~, ~nen** comforter; (*fig.: Sache*) consolation

**tröstlich** *Adj.* comforting

**trost-, Trost-: ~los** *Adj.* Ⓐ (*ohne ~*) hopeless; without hope *postpos.;* (*verzweifelt*) in despair *postpos.;* **mir war ~los zumute, ich fühlte mich ~los** I was in despair; Ⓑ (*deprimierend, öde*) miserable, dreary ‹time, weather, area, food, etc.›; hopeless ‹situation›; **~losigkeit** *die;* **~~** Ⓐ (*einer Person, der Lage usw.*) hopelessness; (*Verzweiflung*) despair; Ⓑ (*Öde*) dreariness; **~pflaster** *das* (*scherzh.*) consolation; **~preis** *der* consolation prize; **~reich** ❶ *Adj.* comforting; ❷ *adv.* comfortingly

**Tröstung** *die;* **~, ~en** comfort *no indef. art.;* **mit den ~en der Kirche versehen sterben** die after having received the last rites

**Trost·wort** *das; Pl.* **Trostworte** word of comfort

**Trott** /trɔt/ *der;* **~[e]s, ~e** Ⓐ (*Gangart*) trot; **im ~ gehen** [go at a] trot; Ⓑ (*leicht abwertend: Ablauf*) routine; **in den alten ~ verfallen** fall back into the same old rut

**Trottel** *der;* **~s, ~** (*ugs. abwertend*) fool; wally (*coll.*)

**trottelhaft** (*ugs. abwertend*) ❶ *Adj.* bumbling ‹idiot, person›; oafish ‹behaviour›. ❷ *adv.* oafishly

**trottelig** (*ugs. abwertend*) ❶ *Adj.* doddery; gaga *pred.* (*sl.*) ❷ *adv.* in a feeble-minded *or* doddery way

**Trotteligkeit** *die;* **~** (*ugs. abwertend*) doddery state; feeble-mindedness

**trotten** *itr. V.; mit sein* trot [along]; (*freudlos*) trudge

**Trottoir** /trɔ'toa:ɐ̯/ *das;* **~s, ~e** *od.* **~s** pavement

**trotz** /trɔts/ *Präp. mit Gen., seltener mit Dat.* in spite of; despite; **~ Frost[s] und Schnee[s]** despite the frost and snow; **~ allem** *od.* **alledem** in spite of everything

**Trotz** *der;* **~es** defiance; (*eines Pferdes*) disobedience; (*Oppositionsgeist*) cussedness (*coll.*); contrariness; **jmdm./einer Sache zum ~:** in defiance of sb./sth.

**Trotz·alter** *das* difficult age

**trotz·dem** /*auch:* '-'-/ ❶ *Adv.* nevertheless; **er tat es ~:** he did it all *or* just the same. ❷ /-'-/ *Konj.* (*ugs.*) although; even though

**trotzen** *itr. V.* Ⓐ (*geh.: widerstehen*) **jmdm./einer Sache ~** (*auch fig.*) defy sb./sth.; **Gefahren/der Kälte ~:** brave dangers/the cold; Ⓑ (*trotzig sein*) be contrary

**trotzig** ❶ *Adj.* defiant; (*widerspenstig*) contrary; bolshie (*coll.*); difficult ‹child›. ❷ *adv.* defiantly

**Trotzkismus** /trɔts'kɪsmʊs/ *der;* **~:** Trotskyism *no art.*

**Trotzkist** *der;* **~en, ~en, Trotzkistin** *die;* **~, ~nen** Trotskyist

**Trotz-: ~kopf** *der* bolshie [little] so-and-so (*coll.*); **~phase** *die* (*Psych.*) ⇒ **~alter**; **~reaktion** *die* act of defiance

**Troubadour** /'tru:badu:ɐ̯/ *der;* **~s, ~e** *od.* **~s** (*hist.*) troubadour; (*fig.: Schlagersänger*) songster

**Trouble** /'trʌbl̩/ *der;* **~s** (*ugs.*) trouble; **~ haben wegen Drogen** be in trouble over drugs

**trüb[e]** /'try:b(ə)/ ❶ *Adj.* Ⓐ (*nicht klar*) murky ‹stream, water›; cloudy ‹liquid, wine, juice›; (*schlammig*) muddy ‹puddle›; (*schmutzig*) dirty ‹glass, window pane›; dull ‹eyes›; **im Trüben fischen** (*ugs.*) fish in troubled waters; Ⓑ (*nicht hell*) dim ‹light›; dull, dismal ‹day, weather›; grey, overcast ‹sky›; dull, dingy ‹red, yellow›; Ⓒ (*gedrückt*) gloomy ‹mood, voice, etc.›; dreary ‹time›; ⇒ *auch* **Tasse** A; Ⓓ (*unerfreulich*) unfortunate, bad ‹experience etc.›; (*zweifelhaft*) dubious ‹sources›. ❷ *adv.* Ⓐ (*nicht hell*) ‹shine, light› dimly; Ⓑ (*gedrückt*) ‹smile, look› gloomily; Ⓒ (*unerfreulich*) **~ laufen** go badly

**Trubel** /'tru:bl̩/ *der;* **~s** [hustle and] bustle; **sie stürzten sich in den dicksten ~:** they plunged into the thick of the hurly-burly; **im ~ der Ereignisse** (*fig.*) in the excitement of the moment; in the rush of events

**trüben** ❶ *tr. V.* Ⓐ make ‹liquid› cloudy; cloud ‹liquid›; ⇒ *auch* **Wässerchen** A; Ⓑ (*beeinträchtigen*) dampen, cast a cloud over ‹mood›; mar ‹relationship›; cloud ‹judgement›; **jmds. Blick [für etw.] ~:** blind sb. [to sth.]. ❷ *refl. V.* Ⓐ ‹liquid› become cloudy; ‹eyes› become dull; ‹sky› darken; Ⓑ (*sich verschlechtern*) ‹relationship› deteriorate; ‹awareness, memory, etc.› become dulled *or* dim

**Trübsal** /'try:pza:l/ *die;* **~, ~e** (*geh.*) Ⓐ (*Leiden*) affliction; Ⓑ (*Kummer*) grief; **~ blasen** (*ugs.*) mope (**wegen** over, about)

**trüb-, Trüb-: ~selig** ❶ *Adj.* Ⓐ (*öde*) dreary, depressing ‹place, area, colour›; dismal ‹house›; Ⓑ (*traurig*) gloomy, melancholy ‹thoughts, mood›; gloomy, miserable ‹face›; ❷ *adv.* (*traurig*) gloomily; **~seligkeit** *die:* Ⓐ (*Ödheit*) dreariness; Ⓑ (*Traurigkeit*) gloom; **~sinn** *der* melancholy; gloom; **~sinnig** ❶ *Adj.* melancholy; gloomy; ❷ *adv.* gloomily

**Trübung** *die;* **~, ~en** Ⓐ clouding; (*des Auges*) dimming; Ⓑ (*Beeinträchtigung*) deterioration; (*der Stimmung*) dampening

**trudeln** /'tru:dl̩n/ *itr. V.* Ⓐ *mit sein* (*rollen*) roll; **auf die Erde ~:** flutter *or* twirl to the ground; **das Flugzeug geriet ins T~:** the plane went into a spin; Ⓑ (*bes. berlin.: würfeln*) play dice

**Trüffel** /'trʏfl̩/ *die;* **~, ~n** *od.* (*ugs.*) *der;* **~s, ~:** truffle

**Trüffel·leber·wurst** *die* liver sausage with truffles

**trug** /tru:k/ *1. u. 3. Pers. Prät. v.* **tragen**

**Trug** *der;* **~[e]s** (*geh.*) deception (**um** over, concerning); ⇒ *auch* **Lug**

**Trug·bild** *das* hallucination; illusion; (*Bild der Fantasie*) figment of the imagination

**trüge** /'try:gə/ *1. u. 3. Pers. Sg. Konjunktiv II v.* **tragen**

**trügen** ❶ *unr. tr. V.* deceive; **dieses Gefühl hatte uns getrogen** this feeling had been a delusion; **wenn mich nicht alles trügt** unless I am very much mistaken. ❷ *unr. itr. V.* be deceptive; ‹feeling, deception› be a delusion; ⇒ *auch* **Schein** B

**trügerisch** ❶ *Adj.* Ⓐ deceptive; false ‹hope, sign, etc.›; treacherous ‹ice›; Ⓑ (*veralt.: auf Betrug zielend*) deceitful; **in ~er Absicht** with intent to deceive. ❷ *adv.* Ⓐ deceptively; Ⓑ (*veralt.: auf Betrug zielend*) deceitfully

**Trug·schluss, *Trug·schluß** *der* Ⓐ wrong conclusion; (*Irrtum*) fallacy; Ⓑ (*Musik*) false *or* deceptive cadence

**Truhe** /'tru:ə/ *die;* **~, ~n** chest

**Trumm** /trʊm/ *das;* **~[e]s, Trümmer** /'trʏmɐ/ (*bes. südd., österr., schweiz.*) large lump; (*großes Exemplar*) whopper (*coll.*); **ein ~ von …** a whopping great … (*coll.*)

**Trümmer** /'trʏmɐ/ *Pl.* (*eines Gebäudes*) rubble *sing.;* (*Ruinen*) ruins; (*eines Flugzeugs usw.*) wreckage *sing.;* (*kleinere Teile*) debris *sing.;* **die Stadt lag in ~n** the town lay in ruins; **eine Stadt in ~ legen** reduce a town to rubble; flatten a town [completely]; **er stand vor den ~n seines Lebens** (*fig.*) he contemplated the ruins of what had once been his life

**Trümmer-: ~feld** *das* expanse of rubble; **~frau** *die* (*hist.*): *woman who cleared away rubble after World War II;* **~grund·stück** *das* bomb site; (*nach einem Erdbeben*) ruined site; **~haufen** *der* pile *or* heap of rubble; **der ~haufen seiner Ehe** (*fig.*) the ruins *pl.* of what had been his marriage

**Trumpf** /trʊmpf/ *der;* **~[e]s, Trümpfe** /'trʏmpfə/ (*auch fig.*) trump [card]; (*Farbe*) trumps *pl.;* **was ist ~?** what are trumps?; **lauter ~** *od.* **Trümpfe haben** have nothing but trumps; **seinen [letzten] ~ ausspielen** (*fig.*) play one's [last] trump card; **alle Trümpfe in der Hand haben** (*fig.*) hold all the [trump] cards; **seine besten Trümpfe aus der Hand geben** (*fig.*) throw away one's greatest advantages; **einen ~ in der Hinterhand haben** (*fig.*) have a card up one's sleeve; **~ sein** (*fig.*) (*das Nötigste sein*) be what matters; be the order of the day; (*Mode sein*) be the in thing

**Trumpf·ass, *Trumpf·as** *das* ace of trumps

**trumpfen** *itr. V.* play a trump

**Trumpf·karte** *die* (*auch fig.*) trump card

**Trunk** /trʊŋk/ *der;* **~[e]s, Trünke** /'trʏŋkə/ (*geh.*) Ⓐ (*Getränk*) drink; beverage (*formal*); Ⓑ (*das Trinken*) **er ist dem ~ verfallen** he is a victim of the demon drink; **sich dem ~ ergeben** take to drink

**trunken** *Adj.* (*geh.; auch fig.*) drunk, intoxicated (**von, vor** + *Dat.* with); **jmdn. ~ machen** make sb. drunk; (*fig.*) intoxicate sb.

**Trunkenbold** /-bɔlt/ *der;* **~[e]s, ~e** (*abwertend*) drunkard

**Trunkenheit** *die;* **~** Ⓐ drunkenness; **im Zustand der ~:** in a state of intoxication; in an intoxicated state; **~ am Steuer** drunken driving; Ⓑ (*geh.: Begeisterung*) [state of] intoxication

**Trunk·sucht** *die* alcoholism *no art.*

**trunk·süchtig** *Adj.* alcoholic; **~ sein** be an alcoholic

**Trupp** /trʊp/ *der;* **~s, ~s** troop; (*von Arbeitern, Gefangenen*) gang; (*von Soldaten, Polizisten*) detachment; squad

**Trüppchen** /'trʏpçən/ *das;* **~s, ~:** [small] group; (*von Soldaten*) small detachment

**Truppe** *die;* **~, ~n** Ⓐ (*Einheit der Streitkräfte*) unit; **nicht von der schnellen ~ sein** (*fig. ugs.*) not be exactly a fast worker; Ⓑ *Pl.* (*Soldaten*) troops; Ⓒ (*Streitkräfte*) [armed] forces *pl.;* (*Heer*) army; **die kämpfende ~:** the front-line *or* combat troops *pl.;* **der Dienst bei der ~:** military service; Ⓓ (*Gruppe von Schauspielern, Artisten*) troupe; company; (*von Sportlern*) squad; (*Mannschaft*) team

**Truppen-: ~ab·zug** *der* withdrawal of troops; troop withdrawal; **~bewegung** *die* troop movement; **~gattung** *die* arm [of the service]; corps; **~konzentration** *die* massing of troops; **~parade** *die* military parade; **~teil** *der* unit; **~übungs·platz** *der* military training area

**Trust** /trast/ *der;* **~[e]s, ~e** *od.* **~s** (*Wirtsch.*) trust

**Trut-** /'tru:t-/: **~hahn** *der; Pl.* **~hähne** turkey [cock]; (*als Braten*) turkey; **~henne** *die* turkey [hen]

**Trutz** /trʊts/ *der;* **~es** (*veralt.*) resistance; **Schutz und ~:** protection and shelter

**Trutz·burg** *die* (*hist.*): *castle built to besiege an enemy castle*

**trutzig** (*veralt.*) ❶ *Adj.* massive, formidable ‹wall, building›. ❷ *adv.* defiantly

**Tschad** /tʃat/ (*der*); **~s** Chad *no art.*

**Tschador** /tʃa'dɔr/ *der;* **~s, ~s** chador

**Tschako** /'tʃako/ *der;* **~s, ~s** (*hist.*) shako

**tschau** /tʃau/ (*ugs.*) ciao (*coll.*); so long (*coll.*)

**Tscheche** /'tʃɛçə/ *der;* **~n, ~n** ▶ 553 Czech

**Tschechei** *die;* **~** (*ugs. veralt.*) Czechoslovakia *no art.*

**Tschechien** (*das;*) **~s** Czech Republic

**Tschechin** *die;* **~, ~nen** ▶ 553 ⇒ **Tscheche**

**tschechisch** ▶ 553, ▶ 696 ❶ *Adj.* Czech. ❷ *adv.* **~ sprechend** Czech-speaking; ⇒ *auch* **deutsch; Deutsch; Deutsche**[2]

**Tschechoslowakei** /tʃɛçoslova'kai/ *die;* **~:** Czechoslovakia *no art.*

**tschechoslowakisch** *Adj.* Czechoslovak[ian]

**Tschetschene** /tʃe'tʃe:nə/ *der;* **~n, ~n** Chechen; **die ~n** the Chechen[s]

**Tschetschenien** /tʃe'tʃe:njən/ *das;* **~s** Chechenia; Chechnya

**tschetschenisch** *Adj.* Chechen

**Tschick** /tʃɪk/ *der;* **~s, ~** (*österr. ugs.*) fag (*Brit. coll.*); (*Zigarettenstummel*) fag end (*Brit. coll.*)

**tschilpen** /'tʃɪlpn̩/ *itr. V.* chirp

**Tschinelle** /tʃi'nɛlə/ *die;* **~, ~n** (*veralt., noch südd., österr.*) cymbal

**tschingderassabum** /tʃɪŋdərasa'bʊm/ *Interj.* crash! crash! boom! boom! (*onomatopoeic for cymbals and drums*)

*old spelling (see note on page 1707)

**tschüs** /tʃy:s/, **tschüss** /tʃʏs/ (*ugs.*) bye (*coll.*); so long (*coll.*)

**Tsd.** *Abk.* **Tausend**

**Tsetse·fliege** /ˈtse:tse-/ *die* tsetse fly

**T-Shirt** /ˈti:ʃə:t/ *das;* **~s, ~s** T-shirt

**T-Träger** *der* (*Bauw.*) T-girder

**TU** *Abk.* **technische Universität**

**Tuba** /ˈtu:ba/ *die;* **~, Tuben** tuba

**Tube** /ˈtu:bə/ *die;* **~, ~n** tube; **eine ~ Zahnpasta** a tube of toothpaste; **auf die ~ drücken** (*fig. ugs.*) step on it (*coll.*); put one's foot down

**Tuberkel·bazillus** /tuˈbɛrkl̩-/ *der* (*Med.*) tubercle bacillus

**tuberkulös** /tubɛrkuˈlø:s/ *Adj.* (*Med.*) tubercular

**Tuberkulose** /tubɛrkuˈlo:zə/ *die;* **~, ~n** ▸ **474** | (*Med.*) tuberculosis *no art.*

**Tuch** /tu:x/ *das;* **~[e]s, Tücher** /ˈty:çɐ/ *od.* **~e** **A** *Pl.* **Tücher** cloth; (*Geschirr~*) dishcloth; (*Bade~*) [bath] towel; (*Kopf~, Hals~*) scarf; **das rote ~ des Matadors** the matador's red cape; **ein rotes ~ für jmdn. sein** (*ugs.*) be like a red rag to a bull for sb.; make sb. see red; **B** *Pl.* **~e** (*Gewebe*) cloth; **C** *Pl.* **~e** (*Seemannsspr.*) ⇒ **Segel~**

**Tuchent** /ˈtʊxn̩t/ *die;* **~, ~en** (*österr.*) feather bed

**Tuch·fühlung** *die* (*scherzh.*) physical contact; (*fig.: Kontakte*) [close] contact; **auf** *od.* **mit ~:** close together

**Tüchlein** *das;* **~s, ~:** [little] handkerchief

**tüchtig** /ˈtʏçtɪç/ **1** *Adj.* **A** efficient ‹secretary, assistant, worker, etc.›; (*fähig*) capable, competent (**in** + *Dat.* at); **freie Bahn dem Tüchtigen!** let ability win through; **B** (*von guter Qualität*) excellent ‹performance, piece of work, etc.›; **~, ~!** (*auch iron.*) well done!; **C** (*ugs.: beträchtlich*) sizeable ‹piece, portion›; big ‹gulp›; hearty ‹eater, appetite›; **eine ~e Tracht Prügel** a good hiding (*coll.*); **ein ~er Schrecken** quite a fright. **2** *adv.* **A** efficiently; (*fähig*) competently; **~ arbeiten** work hard; **B** (*ugs.: sehr*) really ‹cold, warm›; ‹snow, rain› good and proper (*coll.*); ‹eat› heartily; **~ heizen** have the heating up good and high (*coll.*)

**Tüchtigkeit** *die;* **~** **A** efficiency; (*Fähigkeit*) ability; competence; (*Fleiß*) industry; **B** **körperliche ~:** physical fitness

**Tücke** /ˈtʏkə/ *die;* **~, ~n** **A** (*Hinterhältigkeit*) deceit[fulness]; (*List*) guile; scheming *no indef. art.;* (*fig.: des Schicksals*) fickleness; **die ~ des Objekts** the perversity *or* (*coll.*) cussedness of inanimate objects; ⇒ *auch* **List** B; **B** (*hinterhältige Handlung*) wile; ruse; (*Betrug*) deception; **C** ([*verborgene*] *Gefahr/Schwierigkeit*) [hidden] danger/difficulty; (*unberechenbare Eigenschaft*) vagary; **seine ~n haben** ‹engine, machine› be temperamental; have its vagaries; ‹mountain, river, course› be treacherous

**tuckern** /ˈtukɐn/ *itr. V.; mit Richtungsangabe mit sein* chug

**tückisch** **1** *Adj.* **A** (*hinterhältig*) wily; (*betrügerisch*) deceitful; **B** (*gefährlich*) treacherous ‹bend, slope, spot, etc.›; (*Gefahr signalisierend*) menacing ‹look, eyes›. **2** *adv.* **A** (*hinterhältig*) craftily; **B** (*Gefahr signalisierend*) menacingly

**Tuff** /tʊf/ *der;* **~s, ~e** (*Geol.*) **A** tuff; **B** ⇒ **Sinter**

**Tuff·stein** *der* tuff

**Tüftel·arbeit** *die* (*ugs.*) fiddly job

**Tüftelei** *die;* **~, ~en** (*ugs.*) **A** fiddling [about]; (*geistig*) racking one's brains; **B** (*tüftelige Arbeit*) fiddly job

**Tüfteler** *der;* **~s, ~** ⇒ **Tüftler**

**tüfteln** /ˈtʏftl̩n/ *itr. V.* (*ugs.*) fiddle (**an** + *Dat.* with); do finicky work (**an** + *Dat.* on); (*geistig*) rack one's brains, puzzle (**an** + *Dat.* over)

**Tüftler** *der;* **~s, ~, Tüftlerin** *die;* **~, ~nen** (*ugs.*) *person who likes finicky jobs/niggling problems;* (*jmd., der gern Rätselspiele macht*) puzzle freak (*coll.*)

**Tugend** /ˈtu:gn̩t/ *die;* **~, ~en** virtue; **auf dem Pfad der ~ wandeln** keep to the path of virtue *or* the straight and narrow

**tugendhaft** **1** *Adj.* virtuous. **2** *adv.* virtuously; **~ leben** live a life of virtue

**Tukan** /ˈtu:kan/ *der;* **~s, ~e** toucan

**Tüll** /tʏl/ *der;* **~s, ~e** tulle

**Tülle** *die;* **~, ~n** (*bes. nordd.*) spout

**Tüll-:** **~gardine** *die* net curtain; **~spitze** *die* tulle lace

**Tulpe** /ˈtʊlpə/ *die;* **~, ~n** **A** (*Pflanze*) tulip; **B** (*Glas*) tulip glas

**Tulpen-:** **~baum** *der* tulip tree; **~zwiebel** *die* tulip bulb

**tumb** /tʊmp/ *Adj.* (*scherzh.*) guileless; naïve; **~er Tor** simple Simon

**Tumbheit** *die;* **~** (*scherzh.*) guilelessness; ingenuousness

**tummeln** /ˈtʊml̩n/ *refl. V.* **A** (*umhertollen*) romp [about]; (*im Wasser*) splash about; **B** (*bes. westmd., österr., sich beeilen*) stir one's stumps (*coll.*); get a move on (*coll.*)

**Tummel·platz** *der* (*auch fig.*) playground; **ein ~ der Linksradikalen** (*fig.*) a happy hunting ground for left-wing radicals

**Tümmler** /ˈtʏmlɐ/ *der;* **~s, ~** **A** (*Delphin*) bottle-nosed dolphin; **B** (*Taube*) tumbler

**Tumor** /ˈtu:mɔr/ *der;* **~s, ~en** ▸ **474** | /tuˈmo:rən/, *ugs. auch* **~e** /tuˈmo:rə/ (*Med.*) tumour

**Tümpel** /ˈtʏmpl̩/ *der;* **~s, ~:** pond

**Tumult** /tuˈmʊlt/ *der;* **~[e]s, ~e** tumult; commotion; (*Protest*) uproar; **schwere ~e** serious disturbances

**tumultuarisch** /tumʊlˈtu̯a:rɪʃ/ *Adj.* (*geh.*) turbulent; ‹scenes› of uproar

**tun** /tu:n/ **1** *unr. tr. V.* **A** (*machen*) do; **er tat, wie ihm befohlen** he did as he was told; **ich habe anderes zu ~, als hier herumzusitzen** I can't sit around here [all day], I've other things to do; **er tut nichts als meckern** (*ugs.*) he does nothing but moan; **ich weiß nicht, was ich ~ soll** I don't know what to do; **so etwas tut man nicht** that is just not done; **so tu doch etwas!** well, do something [about it], then!; **er hat sein Möglichstes getan** he did his [level] best; **du kannst ~ und lassen, was du willst** you can do just as you please; **was tust du hier/mit dem Messer?** what are you doing here/with that knife?; **dagegen kann man nichts ~:** there is nothing one can do about it; **es hat sich so ergeben, ohne dass ich etwas dazu getan hätte** it turned out that way without my having done anything [towards it]; **was ~?** what is to be done?; **was tut denn die tote Fliege in meiner Suppe?** what's that dead fly doing in my soup?; **man tut, was man kann** one does what one can; one tries one's best; **ich will sehen, was sich ~ lässt** I'll see what can be done; **was tut man nicht alles [...]!** the things I/you *etc.* do [...]!; **B** (*erledigen*) do ‹work, duty, etc.›; **er tut nichts** he doesn't do a thing; **ich muss noch etwas [für die Schule] ~:** I've still got some [school] work to do; **tu's doch!** go on, do it!; **nach getaner Arbeit** when the work is/was done; **mit Geld/einer Entschuldigung** *usw.* **ist es nicht getan** money/an apology *etc.* is not enough; **es ~** (*ugs. verhüll.: koitieren*) do it (*sl.*); ⇒ *auch* **Handschlag** B; **C** [**etwas**] **zu ~ haben** have something to do; **ich hatte dort zu ~/dort geschäftlich zu ~:** I had things/business to do there; **es mit jmdm./etw. zu ~ haben** be dealing with sb./sth.; **wir haben es mit einem gefährlichen Verbrecher zu ~:** we're up against a dangerous criminal; **er hat es mit dem Herzen zu ~** (*ugs.*) he's got heart trouble; **[es] mit jmdm. zu ~ bekommen** *od.* (*ugs.*) **kriegen** get into trouble with sb./sth.; **mit sich [selbst] zu ~ haben** have problems [of one's own]; **[etwas] mit etw./jmdm. zu ~ haben** be concerned with sth./have dealings with sb.; **er hat noch nie [etwas] mit der Polizei zu ~ gehabt** he has never been involved with the police; **mit etw. nichts zu ~ haben** have nothing to do with sth.; not be concerned with sth.; **er hat mit dem Mord nichts zu ~:** he had nothing to do with *or* was not involved in the murder; **mit Kunst hat das kaum etwas zu ~:** that has very little to do with art; **mit jmdm./etw. nichts zu ~ haben wollen** not want [to have] anything to do with sb./sth.; **es ist mir um dich/deine Gesundheit zu ~** (*geh.*) I'm concerned about you/your health; **D** *nimmt die Aussage eines vorher gebrauchten Verbs auf* **ich riet ihm zu verschwinden, was er schleunigst tat** I advised him to disappear, which he did at the double *or* and he did so at the double; **es sollte am nächsten Tag regnen, und das tat es dann auch** it was expected to rain the next day, and it did [so]; **E** *als Funktionsverb* make ‹remark, catch, etc.›; take ‹step, jump›; do ‹deed›; **einen Blick aus dem Fenster ~:** glance out of the window; (*unpers.*) **plötzlich tat es einen furchtbaren Knall** suddenly there was a dreadful bang; **F** (*bewirken*) work, perform ‹miracle›; **seine Wirkung ~:** have its effect; **was tuts?, was tut das schon?** (*ugs.*) so what?; what does it matter?; **das tut nichts** it doesn't matter; ⇒ *auch* **Sache** B; **G** (*an~*) **jmdm. etw. ~:** do sth. to sb.; **jmdm. einen Gefallen ~:** do sb. a favour; **er tut dir nichts** he won't hurt *or* harm you; **der Hund tut nichts** the dog doesn't bite; **H** **es ~** (*ugs.: genügen*) be good enough; **die Schuhe ~ es noch einen Winter** the shoes will do for another winter; **I** (*ugs.: irgendwohin bringen*) put; **Salz an** *od.* **in die Suppe ~:** put salt in *or* add salt to the soup; **den Kleinen zur Oma ~:** take the little boy to granny (*coll.*).

**2** *unr. itr. V.* **A** (*ugs.: funktionieren*) work; **die Kaffeemaschine tut nicht mehr** the coffee machine has had it (*coll.*); **B** **freundlich/geheimnisvoll ~:** pretend to be *or* (*coll.*) act friendly/act mysteriously; **vornehm ~:** act all genteel (*coll.*); **er tut [so], als ob** *od.* **als wenn** *od.* **wie wenn er nichts wüsste** he pretends not to know anything; **er tut nur so [als ob]** he's only pretending; **tu doch nicht so!** stop pretending!.

**3** *unr. refl. V.* (*unpers.*) (*geschehen*) **es hat sich einiges getan** quite a bit has happened; **es tut sich nichts** there's nothing happening.

**4** *Hilfsverb* **A** *betonend* (*ugs.*) **rechnen tut er gut** he's good at arithmetic; **kennen tue ich sie nicht** I don't know her; (*in nicht korrektem Sprachgebrauch*) **ich tu den Fleck einfach nicht wegkriegen** I simply can't get rid of the stain; **B** *zur Umschreibung des Konjunktivs* (*ugs.*) **das täte mich interessieren/freuen** I'd be interested in/pleased about that

**Tun** *das;* **~s** action; activity; **unser nächtliches ~:** our nocturnal activities *pl.;* **jmds. ~ und Treiben** (*geh.*) [all] sb.'s doings

**Tünche** /ˈtʏnçə/ *die;* **~, ~n** **A** (*Farbe*) distemper; wash; **[weiße] ~:** whitewash; **B** (*abwertend: Oberfläche*) veneer (*fig.*)

**tünchen** *tr.* (*auch itr.*) *V.* distemper; **weiß ~:** whitewash

**Tundra** /ˈtʊndra/ *die;* **~, Tundren** tundra

**Tunell** /tuˈnɛl/ *das;* **~s, ~s** (*südd., österr., schweiz.*) ⇒ **Tunnel**

**tunen** /ˈtju:nən/ *tr. V.* (*Kfz-W.*) tune

**Tuner** /ˈtju:nɐ/ *der;* **~s, ~** **A** (*Elektronik*) tuner; **B** (*Kfz-W.*) tuner; tuning expert

**Tunesien** /tuˈne:zi̯ən/ (*das*); **~s** Tunisia

**Tunesier** *der;* **~s, ~, Tunesierin** *die;* **~, ~nen** Tunisian

**tunesisch** *Adj.* Tunisian

**Tun·fisch** ⇒ **Thunfisch**

**Tu·nicht·gut** *der;* **~** *od.* **~[e]s, ~e** good-for-nothing; ne'er-do-well

**Tunika** /ˈtu:nika/ *die;* **~, Tuniken** tunic; (*hist.*) tunica; tunic

**Tunke** /ˈtʊŋkə/ *die;* **~, ~n** (*bes. ostmd.*) sauce; (*Bratensoße*) gravy

**tunken** *tr. V.* (*bes. ostmd.*) dip; dip, dunk ‹biscuit, piece of bread, etc.›

**tunlichst** /ˈtu:nlɪçst/ *Adv.* (*geh.*) **A** (*möglichst*) as far as possible; **B** (*unbedingt*) at all costs; **das hat in Zukunft ~ zu unterbleiben** this must not happen in future at any cost

**Tunnel** /ˈtʊnl̩/ *der;* **~s, ~** *od.* **~s** tunnel

**tunnelieren** *tr. V.* (*österr.*) tunnel through ‹mountain etc.›

**Tunte** /'tʊntə/ *die;* ~, ~**n** **A** *(ugs. abwertend: Frau)* female; **B** *(salopp, auch abwertend: Homosexueller)* queen *(sl.)*

**tuntenhaft, tuntig** ❶ *Adj.* **A** *(ugs. abwertend: tantenhaft)* prissy; **B** *(salopp abwertend: feminin)* poofy *(Brit. coll.)*. ❷ *adv.;* ⇒ **1**: **A** prissily; **B** poofily *(Brit. coll.)*

**Tüpfelchen** /'tʏpflçən/ *das;* ~**s**, ~: dot; **das ~ auf dem i** the final touch

**tüpfeln** *tr. V.* stipple; *(sprenkeln)* speckle

**tupfen** /'tʊpfn̩/ *tr. V.* **A** dab; **sich** *(Dat.)* **den Schweiß von der Stirn ~:** dab the sweat from one's brow; **etw. auf etw.** *(Akk.)* **~:** dab sth. on to sth.; **B** *(mit T~ versehen)* dot; **ein getupftes Kleid** a spotted dress

**Tupfen** *der;* ~**s**, ~: dot; *(größer)* spot

**Tupfer** *der;* ~**s**, ~ **A** *(ugs.)* ⇒ **Tupfen**; **B** *(Med.)* swab

**Tür** /ty:ɐ̯/ *die;* ~, ~**en** door; *(Garten~)* gate; **an die ~ gehen** *(öffnen)* [go and] answer the door; **in der ~ stehen** stand in the doorway; **den Kopf zur ~ hereinstecken** put one's head round the door; **mach die ~ von außen zu!** *(ugs.)* out with you!; out you go!; **jmdm. die ~ einlaufen** *od.* **einrennen** *(fig. ugs.)* keep badgering sb.; **offene ~e einrennen** *(fig.)* be pushing at an open door; **jmdm. die ~ vor der Nase zuschlagen** *(fig.)* slam the door in sb.'s face; **einer Sache** *(Dat.)* **~ und Tor öffnen** *(fig.)* open the door *or* way to sth.; **hinter verschlossenen ~en** behind closed doors; **mit der ~ ins Haus fallen** *(fig. ugs.)* blurt out what one is after; **vor verschlossener ~ stehen** be locked out; **zwischen ~ und Angel** *(fig. ugs.)* in passing; **[ach,] du kriegst die ~ nicht zu!** *(fig. ugs.)* Good Lord!; well I never!; **jmdm. die ~ weisen** *(fig. geh.)* show sb. the door; **vor die ~ gehen** go outside; **jmdn. vor die ~ setzen** *(fig. ugs.)* chuck *(coll.) or* throw sb. out; **vor seiner eigenen ~ kehren** *(fig. ugs.)* set one's own house in order; **Pfingsten steht/die Sommerferien stehen vor der ~** *(fig.)* Whitsun is/the summer holidays are [just] coming up; **der Winter steht vor der ~** *(fig.)* winter is just around the corner

**Tür·angel** *die* door hinge

**Turban** /'tʊrba:n/ *der;* ~**s**, ~**e** turban

**Turbine** /tʊr'bi:nə/ *die;* ~, ~**n** *(Technik)* turbine

**turbinen-, Turbinen-:** ~**antrieb** *der* turbine propulsion; ~**flugzeug** *das* turbojet aircraft; ~**getrieben** *Adj.* turbine-propelled ‹ship, aircraft›; turbine-driven ‹generator›

**Turbo-** /'tʊrbo-/ *(Technik)* turbo-

**Turbo-Prop-Flugzeug** *das* turboprop aircraft

**turbulent** /tʊrbu'lɛnt/ ❶ *Adj.* *(auch Physik, Astron., Met.)* turbulent; *(allzu lebhaft)* chaotic. ❷ *adv.* *(auch Physik, Astron., Met.)* turbulently; *(allzu lebhaft)* chaotically; **bei uns/an den Devisenmärkten geht es ~ zu** things are chaotic [around] here/the exchange markets are in turmoil

**Turbulenz** /tʊrbu'lɛnts/ *die;* ~, ~**en** *(auch Physik, Astron., Met.)* turbulence *no pl.*

**Tür·drücker** *der;* ~**s**, ~ **A** doorknob; **B** *(Türöffner)* [automatic] door-opener

**Turf** /tʊrf/ *(Pferdesport Jargon)* turf

**Tür·griff** *der* door handle

**Türke** /'tʏrkə/ *der;* ~**n**, ~**n** **A** ▶ 553 Turk; **B** *(ugs.)* **einen ~n bauen** tell a cock and bull story/cock and bull stories

**Türkei** *die;* ~**:** Turkey *no art.*

**türken** *tr. V.* *(ugs.)* fake ‹scene, letter, document, etc.›; make up ‹story, report›

**Türken·bund·lilie** *die* turk's-cap lily

**Türkin** *die;* ~, ~**nen** ▶ 553 ⇒ **Türke A**

**türkis** /tʏr'ki:s/ *indekl. Adj.* turquoise

**Türkis**[1] *der;* ~**es**, ~**e** *(Mineral.)* turquoise

**Türkis**[2] *das;* ~ *(Farbe)* turquoise

**türkisch** *Adj.* ▶ 553, ▶ 696 Turkish; ~**er Honig** nougat; ⇒ *auch* **deutsch**; **Deutsch**; **Deutsche**[2]

**türkis·farben** *Adj.* turquoise

**Tür-:** ~**klinke** *die* door handle; ~**klopfer** *der* door knocker

**Turkologie** /tʊrkolo'gi:/ *die;* ~**:** Turkish studies *pl., no art.*

**Turk-:** ~**sprache** *die* Turkic language; ~**volk** *das* Turkic people

**Turm** /tʊrm/ *der;* ~**[e]s**, **Türme** /'tʏrmə/ **A** tower; *(spitzer Kirch~)* spire; steeple; **B** *(Schach)* rook; castle; **C** ⇒ **Sprung~**; **D** *(hist.)* ⇒ **Schuld~**; **Hunger~**; **E** *(Milit.)* turret

**Turmalin** /tʊrma'li:n/ *der;* ~**s**, ~**e** *(Mineral.)* tourmaline

**Turm·bau** *der* building of a/the tower; **der ~ zu Babel** the building of the Tower of Babel

**Türmchen** /'tʏrmçən/ *das;* ~**s**, ~**:** turret

**türmen**[1] ❶ *tr. V.* *(stapeln)* stack up; *(häufen)* pile up. ❷ *refl. V.* be piled up; ‹clouds› gather

**türmen**[2] *itr. V.; mit sein (salopp)* scarper *(Brit. coll.)*; do a bunk *(Brit. coll.)*; beat it *(coll.)*; **aus dem Knast ~:** do a bunk from prison

**turm-, Turm-:** ~**falke** *der* kestrel; ~**haube** *die (Archit.)* cupola; ~**hoch** ❶ *Adj.* towering; ❷ *adv.* **sich ~hoch stapeln** be piled high; ~**hoch mit etw. beladen** piled high with sth.; ~**springen** *das;* ~~**s** high diving *no art.;* ~**uhr** *die* tower clock

**Turn-:** ~**an·zug** *der* leotard; ~**beutel** *der* PE bag

**turnen** /'tʊrnən/ ❶ *itr. V.* **A** *(Sport)* do gymnastics; *(Schulw.)* do gym *or* PE; **sie turnt gut** she's good at gymnastics *or* a good gymnast; *(Schulw.)* she's good at gym *or* PE; **er turnte am Reck/auf der Matte** he was doing *or* performing exercises *or* was working on the horizontal bar/the mat; **B** *mit sein (ugs.: klettern)* clamber; **C** *(ugs.: herumklettern)* clamber about. ❷ *tr. V.* *(Sport)* do, perform ‹exercise, routine›

**Turnen** *das;* ~**s** gymnastics *sing., no art.;* *(Schulw.)* gym *no art.;* PE *no art.*

**Turner** *der;* ~**s**, ~, **Turnerin** *die;* ~, ~**nen** gymnast

**turnerisch** ❶ *Adj.* gymnastic. ❷ *adv.* gymnastically

**Turn-:** ~**fest** *das* gymnastics festival; ~**gerät** *das* gymnastics apparatus; ~**halle** *die* gymnasium; ~**hemd** *das* [gym] singlet; *(für ~unterricht)* gym *or* PE vest; ~**hose** *die (mit langem Bein)* gym trousers *pl.;* *(mit kurzem Bein)* gym shorts *pl.;* *(für ~unterricht)* gym *or* PE shorts *pl.*

**Turnier** /tʊr'ni:ɐ̯/ *das;* ~**s**, ~**e** *(auch hist.)* tournament; *(Reit~)* show; *(Tanz~)* competition; **ein ~ reiten** ride in a tournament

**Turnier-:** ~**pferd** *das* show horse; ~**tanz** *der* **A** *(Tanzsport)* competitive ballroom dancing; **B** *(Tanz)* ballroom dance

**Turn-:** ~**lehrer** *der*, ~**lehrerin** *die* gym *or* PE teacher; ~**schuh** *der* gym shoe; *(Trainingsschuh)* training shoe; trainer *(coll.)*; ~**schuh·generation** *die* youth of the '80s; ~**stunde** *die* gym *or* PE lesson; ~**übung** *die* gymnastics exercise; ~**unterricht** *der* gym *no art.;* PE *no art.*

**Turnüre** /tʊr'ny:rə/ *die;* ~, ~**n** *(Mode, hist.)* bustle

**Turnus** /'tʊrnʊs/ *der;* ~, ~**se** **A** regular cycle; **in einem 4-jährigen ~ stattfinden** take place on a four-year cycle; **er führt das Amt im ~ mit seinen Kollegen** he and his colleagues hold the office in rotation; **B** *(österr.)* ⇒ **Schicht C**

**turnus-:** ~**gemäß** ❶ *Adj.* **die ~gemäße Ablösung des Vorsitzenden erfolgt im April** the chairmanship rotates in April; ❷ *adv.* **er wird den Vorsitz ~gemäß am ersten Januar übernehmen** it will be his turn to take over the chair on 1 January; **~gemäß finden die Verhandlungen in X statt** it is the turn of X to host the negotiations; ~**mäßig** ❶ *Adj.* regular ‹inspection, check, etc.›; ❷ *adv.* on a regular cycle; **~mäßig hat er morgen Nachtdienst** according to the rota he's on duty tomorrow night

**Turn-:** ~**verein** *der* gymnastics club; ~**zeug** *das* gym *or* PE kit

**Tür-:** ~**öffner** *der* door-opener; ~**öffnung** *die* doorway; ~**pfosten** *der* doorpost; door jamb; ~**rahmen** *der* doorframe; ~**schild** *das* sign on a/the door; *(Namensschild)* nameplate; door plate; ~**schloss**, *~**schloß** *das* door lock; ~**schnalle** *die (österr.)* door handle; ~**schwelle** *die* threshold; ~**spalt** *der* crack [of the door]; ~**sturz** *der (Bauw.)* lintel

**turteln** *itr. V.* **A** *(scherzh.: zärtlich sein)* bill and coo; **B** *(veralt.: gurren)* coo

**Turtel·taube** /'tʊrtl̩-/ *die* turtle dove; *(fig.)* lovebird

**Tür·vorleger** *der* doormat

**Tusch** /tʊʃ/ *der;* ~**[e]s**, ~**e** fanfare

**Tusche** *die;* ~, ~**n** **A** Indian *(Brit.) or (Amer.)* India ink; **B** *(nordd., md.: Wasserfarbe)* watercolour; **C** *(ugs.: Wimpern~)* mascara

**Tuschelei** *die;* ~, ~**en** **A** *(das Tuscheln)* whispering; **B** *(Äußerung)* whisper

**tuscheln** /'tʊʃl̩n/ *itr., tr. V.* whisper

**tuschen** ❶ *tr. V.* **A** **etw. ~:** draw sth. in Indian *(Brit.) or (Amer.)* India ink/paint sth. in watercolours; **B** **sich** *(Dat.)* **die Wimpern ~:** put one's mascara on. ❷ *itr. V.* paint in watercolours

**Tusch-:** ~**kasten** *der (nordd., md.)* box of watercolours; **die ist der reinste ~kasten** *(fig.)* she's got all her warpaint on *(coll. joc.)*; ~**zeichnung** *die* pen-and-ink drawing

**Tussi** /'tʊsi/ *die;* ~, ~**s** *(salopp)* female *(derog.)*; *(Mädchen)* bird *(sl.)*; chick *(coll.)*

**tut** /tu:t/ *Interj.* *(Kinderspr.)* beep; toot

**Tütchen** /'ty:tçən/ *das;* ~**s**, ~**:** small bag

**Tüte** /'ty:tə/ *die;* ~, ~**n** **A** bag; **~n kleben** *od.* **drehen** *(fig. ugs.)* be doing time; **das kommt nicht in die ~!** *(fig. ugs.)* not on your life! *(coll.)*; no way!; **B** *(Eis~)* cone; cornet; **C** *(ugs.: beim Alkoholtest)* bag; **in die ~ blasen müssen** be breathalysed; **D** *(salopp: Person)* jerk *(coll.)*

**tuten** /'tu:tn̩/ *itr. V.* hoot; ‹siren, [fog]horn› sound; **das Schiff tutet** the ship sounds its foghorn/hooter; **er wählte die Nummer, und es tutete** he dialled the number, and heard the ringing tone; **er tutete auf seiner Spielzeugtrompete** he tooted on his toy trumpet; ⇒ *auch* **Ahnung C**

**Tutor** /'tu:tɔr/ *der;* ~**s**, ~**en** /tu'to:rən/, **Tutorin** *die;* ~, ~**nen** *(Päd.)* **A** *senior student who helps beginners integrate into student life;* **B** *(Mentor)* tutor

**Tutorium** /tu'to:ri̯ʊm/ *das;* ~, **Tutorien** *(Päd.) seminar conducted by a postgraduate*

**TÜV** /tʏf/ *der;* ~ *Abk.* **Technischer Überwachungsverein** ≈ MOT *(Brit.)*; **ein Auto durch** *od.* **über den ~ bringen** ≈ get a car through its MOT

**Tu·wort** /'tu:-/ *das; Pl.* **Tuwörter** doing word

**Twen** /tvɛn/ *der;* ~**[s]**, ~**s** twenty-to-thirty-year-old; **Mode für ~s** fashions for people in their 20s

**Twist**[1] /tvɪst/ *der;* ~**[e]s**, ~**e** *(Faden)* twist

**Twist**[2] *der;* ~**s**, ~**s** **A** *(Tanz)* twist; **~ tanzen** dance the twist; **B** *(Tennis)* spin

**twisten** *itr. V.* twist; dance the twist

**Tympanon** /'tʏmpanɔn/ *das;* ~**s**, **Tympana** *(Archit.)* tympanum

**Typ** /ty:p/ *der;* ~**s**, ~**en** **A** type; **sie ist genau mein ~** *(ugs.)* she's just my type; **dein ~ wird verlangt** *(salopp)* you're wanted; **dein ~ ist hier nicht gefragt** *(salopp)* we don't want your sort here; **er ist ein dunkler/blonder ~:** he's dark/fair; **die beiden sind ganz verschiedene ~en** they're very different sorts of people; **B** *Gen. auch* ~**en** *(ugs.: Mann)* bloke *(Brit. sl.)*; guy *(coll.)*; **C** *(Technik: Modell) (Auto)* model; *(Flugzeug)* type; **D** *(bes. Philos.)* type

**Type** /'ty:pə/ *die;* ~, ~**n** **A** *(Druck~, Schreibmaschinen~)* type; **B** *(ugs.) (Person)* type; sort; character; *(seltsame Person)* odd type *or* sort *or* character; **eine seltsame/originelle ~:** an odd sort *or* character/an oddball; **C** *(bes. österr.)* ⇒ **Typ D**; **D** *(Fachspr.: Mehl~)* grade

*old spelling (see note on page 1707)

**Typen-:** **~hebel** *der* typebar; **~rad** *das* daisy wheel; **~rad·schreib·maschine** *die* daisy wheel typewriter

**Typhus** /'ty:fʊs/ *der;* ~ ▶474 typhoid [fever]

**Typhus·epidemie** *die* typhoid epidemic

**typisch** ❶ *Adj.* typical (**für** of). ❷ *adv.* typically; **das ist ~ Mann/Frau** that's just typical of a man/woman; **~ Gisela!** typical Gisela!; that's Gisela all over!

**Typo·graph** *der* ▶159 typographer

**Typographie** /typogra'fi:/ *die;* ~, **~n** (*Druckw.*) typography

**Typo·graphin** *die;* ~, **~nen** ▶159 typographer

**typographisch** (*Druckw.*) ❶ *Adj.* typographical. ❷ *adv.* typographically

**Typologie** /typolo'gi:/ *die;* ~, **~n** (*bes. Psych.*) typology

**typologisch** (*bes. Psych.*) ❶ *Adj.* typological. ❷ *adv.* typologically

**Typo·skript** *das; Pl.* **~e** typescript

**Typus** /'ty:pʊs/ *der;* ~, **Typen** (*auch Literaturw., bild. Kunst, Philos.*) type

**Tyrann** /ty'ran/ *der;* **~en, ~en** (*auch fig.*) tyrant

**Tyrannei** *die;* ~, **~en** (*auch fig.*) tyranny

**Tyrannen-:** **~herrschaft** *die* tyranny; tyrannical rule; **~mord** *der* tyrannicide

**Tyrannin** *die;* ~, **~nen** (*auch fig.*) tyrant

**Tyrannis** *die;* ~ (*hist.*) tyranny

**tyrannisch** ❶ *Adj.* tyrannical. ❷ *adv.* tyrannically

**tyrannisieren** *tr. V.* tyrannize

**tyrrhenisch** /tʏ're:nɪʃ/ *Adj.* **Tyrrhenisches Meer** Tyrrhenian Sea

t

# U u

**u, U** /uː/ *das;* ~, ~**:** u, U; ⇒ *auch* **a,** A; **X**
**ü, Ü** /yː/ *das;* ~, ~**:** u umlaut; ⇒ *auch* **a,** A
**U** *Abk.* **Umleitung**
**u.** *Abk.* **und**
**u. a.** *Abk.* **unter anderem**
**u. ä.** *Abk.* **und ähnlich...**
**u. Ä.** *Abk.* **und Ähnliches**
**u. a. m.** *Abk.* **und andere[s] mehr** etc.
**u.** *od.* **U. A. w. g.** *Abk.* **um Antwort wird gebeten** RSVP
**UB** *Abk.* **Universitätsbibliothek**
**U-Bahn** *die* underground (*Brit.*); subway (*Amer.*); (*bes. in London*) tube
**U-Bahnhof** *der,* **U-Bahn-Station** *die* underground station (*Brit.*); subway station (*Amer.*); (*bes. in London*) tube station
**übel** /ˈyːbl̩/ ❶ *Adj.* Ⓐ foul, nasty ‹smell, weather›; bad, nasty ‹headache, cold, taste›; nasty ‹situation, consequences›; sorry ‹state, affair›; foul, (*coll.*) filthy ‹mood›; **nicht** ~ (*ugs.*) not bad at all; **ein übles Ende nehmen** come to a bad end; **eine** ~ **riechende Substanz** an evil-smelling *or* foul-smelling sunstance; Ⓑ ▶ 474 (*unwohl*) **jmdm. ist/wird** ~**:** sb. feels sick; **es kann einem** ~ **werden, wenn man so was hört** hearing that sort of thing is enough to make you sick; Ⓒ (*verwerflich*) bad; wicked; nasty, dirty ‹trick›; **ein übler Bursche** a bad sort (*coll.*) *or* lot; **in üble Gesellschaft geraten** fall in with a bad crowd.
❷ *adv.* Ⓐ **Wie geht's? — Danke, nicht** ~**:** How are things? — Not so bad, thanks; **nicht** ~ **Lust haben, etw. zu tun** have a good mind to do sth.; **etw.** ~ **aufnehmen** take sth. badly; ~ **gelaunt sein** be in a bad mood; **er spielt nicht** ~**:** he plays pretty well; Ⓑ (*nachteilig, schlimm*) badly; **er ist** ~ **dran** he's in a bad way; **jmdm. etw.** ~ **nehmen** hold sth. against sb.; **etw.** ~ **nehmen** *od.* **vermerken** take sth. amiss; take offence at sth.; **nehmen Sie es [mir] bitte nicht** ~**, wenn ich ...** please don't take it amiss *or* be offended if I ...; **jmdm.** ~ **wollen** wish sb. ill; ~ **wollend** malevolent; **jmdn.** ~ **zurichten** give sb. a working over (*coll.*); Ⓒ (*verwerflich*) wickedly
**Übel** *das;* ~**s,** ~ Ⓐ (*Missstand, Ärgernis*) evil; **zu allem** ~**:** on top of everything else; to make matters [even] worse; **ein notwendiges** ~**:** a necessary evil; **das kleinere** ~**:** the lesser evil; **das sind nur kleinere** ~**:** they are just minor annoyances *or* irritations; Ⓑ (*veralt.: Krankheit*) illness; malady; Ⓒ (*veralt.: das Böse*) evil *no art.;* **von** *od.* **vom** ~ **sein** be an evil
**übel-:** *~**gelaunt** ⇒ **gelaunt, übel** 2 A; *~**gesinnt** ⇒ **gesinnt**
**Übelkeit** *die;* ~, ~**en** ▶ 474 nausea; **von einer plötzlichen** ~ **befallen werden** have a sudden feeling of nausea
**übel-, Übel-:** ~**launig** ❶ *Adj.* ill-humoured; ill-tempered; ❷ *adv.* ill-humouredly; ill-temperedly; *~|**nehmen** ⇒ **übel** 2 B; *~**riechend** ⇒ **übel** 1 A; ~**stand** *der* evil; ~**tat** *die* (*geh.*) evil *or* wicked deed; misdeed; ~**täter** *der* wrongdoer; (*Verbrecher*) criminal; (*Verantwortlicher*) culprit; *~|**wollen** ⇒ **übel** 2 B
**üben** /ˈyːbn̩/ ❶ *tr. V.* Ⓐ (*auch itr.*) practise; rehearse ‹scene, play›; practise on ‹musical instrument›; Ⓑ (*trainieren, schulen*) exercise ‹fingers›; train ‹memory›; **mit geübten Händen** with practised hands; Ⓒ (*geh.: bekunden, tun*) exercise ‹patience, restraint, etc.›; commit ‹treason›; take ‹revenge, retaliation›; **Kritik an etw.** (*Dat.*) ~**:** criticize sth. ❷ *refl. V.* **sich in etw.** (*Dat.*) ~**:** practise sth.; **sich in Geduld/Zurückhaltung** ~ (*geh.*) exercise patience/restraint
**über** /ˈyːbɐ/ ❶ *Präp. mit Dat.* Ⓐ (*Lage, Standort*) over; above; (*in einer Rangfolge*) above; **das Bild hängt** ~ **dem Sofa** the picture hangs above the sofa; ~ **jmdm. wohnen** live above sb.; **Nebel lag** ~ **der Wiese** fog hung over the meadow; **zehn Grad** ~ **Null/dem Gefrierpunkt** ten degrees above zero/freezing point; **sie trug eine Jacke** ~ **dem Kleid** she wore a jacket over her dress; ~ **jmdm. stehen** (*fig.*) be above sb.; Ⓑ (*während*) during; ~ **dem Lesen/der Arbeit einschlafen** fall asleep over one's book/magazine *etc.*/over one's work; Ⓒ (*infolge*) because of; as a result of; ~ **der Aufregung vergaß ich, dass ...** in all the excitement I forgot that ...
❷ *Präp. mit Akk.* Ⓐ (*Richtung*) over; (*quer hinüber*) across; ~ **die Straße gehen** go across the road; cross the road; ~ **Karlsruhe nach Stuttgart** via Karlsruhe to Stuttgart; **Tränen liefen ihr** ~ **die Wangen** tears ran down her cheeks; **ihr Rock reicht** ~ **die Knie** her skirt comes down to below the knee; **ein Wettlauf** ~ **eine Distanz von 5 000 Metern** a race over a distance of 5,000 metres; **er zog sich** (*Dat.*) **die Mütze** ~ **die Ohren** he pulled the cap down over his ears; **bis** ~ **die Knöchel im Schlamm versinken** sink up past one's ankles in mud; **es ist zwei Stunden** ~ **die Zeit** it should have happened two hours ago; (*er/sie/es hat schon zwei Stunden Verspätung*) he/she/it is two hours late; **Tennis/seine Tochter geht ihm** ~ **alles** tennis/his daughter means more to him than anything; **italienisches Essen geht ihm** ~ **alles** he loves Italian food more than anything else; Ⓑ (*während*) over; ~ **Mittag** over lunchtime; ~ **das Wochenende nach Hause fahren/zu Hause sein** go/be home for the weekend; ~ **Wochen/Monate** for weeks/months; ~ **Ostern/Weihnachten** over Easter/Christmas; **die ganze Zeit** ~**:** the whole time; **die Woche/den Sommer** ~**:** during the week/summer; **den ganzen Winter/Tag** ~**:** all winter/day long; Ⓒ (*betreffend*) about; ~ **etw. reden/schreiben** talk/write about sth.; **ein Buch** ~ **die byzantinische Kunst** a book about *or* on Byzantine art; **ein Scheck/eine Rechnung** ~ **1 000 Mark** a cheque/bill for 1,000 marks; Ⓓ **Kinder** ~ **10 Jahre** children over ten [years of age]; Ⓔ **Gewalt** ~ **jmdn. haben** have power over sb.; **Wellingtons Sieg** ~ **Napoleon** Wellington's victory over Napoleon; Ⓕ **das geht** ~ **meine Kraft** that's too much for me; **jmdm.** ~ **den Verstand gehen** be beyond sb.; Ⓖ **sie macht Fehler** ~ **Fehler** she makes mistake after mistake; **er hat Schulden** ~ **Schulden** he's up to his ears in debt; Ⓗ (*mittels, durch*) through ‹person›; by ‹post, telex, etc.›; over ‹radio, loudspeaker›; **ich bin** ~ **die Autobahn gekommen** I came along the motorway; **etw.** ~ **alle Sender bringen/ausstrahlen** broadcast sth. on all stations; Ⓘ (*geh. veralt.: bei Verwünschungen*) on; **Schande/Fluch** ~ **ihn!** shame/a curse on him!
❸ *Adv.* Ⓐ (*mehr als*) over; Ⓑ ~ **und** ~**:** all over; **sie war** ~ **und** ~ **mit Schmutz bedeckt** she was covered all over in dirt.
❹ *Adj.* (*ugs.*) Ⓐ (*überlegen*) **jmdm.** ~ **sein** have the edge on sb. (*coll.*); Ⓑ (*übrig*) left [over]; Ⓒ (*zu viel, lästig*) **das ist mir** ~**:** I'm fed up with it (*coll.*)
**über·all** /*od.* --ˈ-/ *Adv.* Ⓐ (*an allen Orten*) everywhere; **sie weiß** ~ **Bescheid** (*auf allen Gebieten*) she knows about everything; Ⓑ (*bei jeder Gelegenheit*) always
**überall-:** ~**her** *Adv.* from all over the place; ~**hin** *Adv.* everywhere
**über·altert** /yːbɐˈ|altɐt/ *Adj.* Ⓐ ‹population› containing a disproportionately high proportion of elderly people; **das Kabinett ist** ~**:** the cabinet has too many elderly members; Ⓑ (*überholt*) outdated; obsolete ‹machine, vehicle, etc.›
**Über·alterung** *die;* ~, ~**en** Ⓐ increase in the proportion of elderly people/workers/members *etc.;* Ⓑ ⇒ **überaltert** B: outdatedness; obsolescence
**Über·angebot** *das* surplus (**an** + *Dat.* of); (*Schwemme*) glut (**an** + *Dat.* of)
**über·ängstlich** ❶ *Adj.* overanxious. ❷ *adv.* overanxiously
**über·anstrengen** *tr. V.* overtax ‹person, energy›; strain ‹eyes, nerves, heart›; **sich** ~**:** overstrain *or* overexert oneself; **überanstreng dich nicht!** (*iron.*) don't strain yourself!
**Über·anstrengung** *die* over exertion; ~ **der Augen/des Herzens** strain on the eyes/heart; **vermeiden Sie jede** ~ **der** *od.* **Ihrer Augen** avoid straining your eyes
**über·antworten** *tr. V.* (*geh.*) Ⓐ (*anvertrauen*) **jmdn./etw. jmdm.** ~**:** entrust sb./sth. to sb.; **die Funde wurden dem Museum überantwortet** the finds were handed over to the museum; Ⓑ (*ausliefern*) **jmdn. dem Gericht** ~**:** hand sb. over to the courts
**über·arbeiten** ❶ *tr. V.* rework; revise ‹text, edition›. ❷ *refl. V.* overwork
**Über·arbeitung** *die;* ~, ~**en** Ⓐ reworking; (*von Text, Manuskript, Ausgabe usw.*) revision; (*überarbeitete Fassung*) revised version; Ⓑ (*Überanstrengung*) overwork
**über·aus** *Adv.* (*geh.*) extremely
**über·backen** *unr. tr. V.* **etw. mit Käse** *usw.* ~**:** top sth. with cheese *etc.* and brown it lightly [under the grill/in a hot oven]; **ein mit Käse** ~**er Auflauf** a soufflé au gratin
**Über·bau** *der; Pl.* ~**e** *od.* ~**ten** (*Philos., Soziol.*) superstructure
**überbeanspruchen** *tr. V.*; **ich überbeanspruche, überbeansprucht, überzubeanspruchen** put too great a strain on ‹heart, circulation, etc.›; strain ‹nerves›; overstrain, overstress ‹material›; overburden, overstretch ‹facilities, services›; overload ‹machine›; make excessive use of ‹right, privilege›; overtax ‹person, body, strenght›; (*mit Arbeit*) overwork ‹person›; (*psychisch*) put too great a strain on ‹person›
**Über·beanspruchung** *die* ⇒ **überbeanspruchen**: straining; overstraining; overstressing; overburdening; overloading; excessive use; overtaxing, overworking; **die** ~ **des Herzens führt zu ...** putting too great a strain on the heart leads to ...
**über|behalten** *unr. tr. V.* (*ugs.*) ⇒ **übrigbehalten**
**Über·bein** *das* ▶ 474 (*Med.*) ganglion
**über|bekommen** *unr. tr. V.* (*ugs.*) Ⓐ (*satt bekommen*) get fed up with (*coll.*); Ⓑ **einen** *od.* **eins** ~**:** get a clout
**überbelasten** *tr. V.*; **ich überbelaste, überbelastet, überzubelasten** Ⓐ overload; Ⓑ (*zu stark in Anspruch nehmen*) overburden ‹person›; place too much strain on ‹bodily organ›

*old spelling (see note on page 1707)

**Über·belastung** *die* Ⓐ overloading; Ⓑ (*zu starke Inanspruchnahme*) overburdening; **die ~ der Leber führt zu ...** placing too much strain on the liver leads to ...

**über·belegt** *Adj.* overcrowded; oversubscribed ‹course›

**Über·belegung** *die* overcrowding; **wegen der ~ des Kurses** because the course is/was oversubscribed

**überbelichten** *tr. V.*; **ich überbelichte, überbelichtet, überzubelichten** (*Fot.*) overexpose

**Über·belichtung** *die* (*Fot.*) overexposure

**Über·beschäftigung** *die* (*Wirtsch.*) overemployment

**überbetonen** *tr. V.*; **ich überbetone, überbetont, überzubetonen** overstress

**Über·bevölkerung** *die* overpopulation

**überbewerten** *tr. V.*; **ich überbewerte, überbewertet, überzubewerten** overvalue; (*überschätzen*) overvalue; overrate; mark ‹pupil, piece of work, gymnast, skater, etc.› too high; **er warnte davor, diesen Faktor überzubewerten** he warned people not to attach too much significance to this factor

**Über·bewertung** *die* overvaluation; (*Überschätzung*) overvaluation; overrating

**überbezahlen** *tr. V.*; **ich überbezahle, überbezahlt, überzubezahlen** overpay

**Über·bezahlung** *die* overpayment

**überbietbar** *Adj.* **kaum noch ~ sein** take some beating; **das ist ein kaum ~es Beispiel für Intoleranz** as an example of intolerance that takes some beating

**über·bieten** *unr. tr. V.* Ⓐ outbid (**um** by); Ⓑ (*übertreffen*) surpass; outdo ‹rival›; break ‹record› (**um** by); exceed ‹target› (**um** by); **das ist kaum noch zu ~:** that takes some beating

**über|bleiben** *unr. itr. V.*; *mit sein* (*ugs.*) ⇒ **übrigbleiben**

**Überbleibsel** /-blaipsl/ *das;* **~s, ~:** remnant; (*einer Kultur*) relic

**über|blenden** *tr. V.* (*Rundf., Ferns., Film*) dissolve

**Über·blick** *der* Ⓐ view; **einen guten ~ über etw.** (*Akk.*) **haben** have a good view over sth.; Ⓑ (*Abriss*) survey; Ⓒ (*Einblick*) overall view *or* perspective; **den ~ über etw.** (*Akk.*) **verlieren** lose track of sth.; **einen ~ über etw.** (*Akk.*) **gewinnen/haben** gain/have an overview of sth.

**über·blicken** *tr. V.* ⇒ **übersehen²** A, B

**über·bordend** *Adj.* exuberant

**über|braten** *unr. tr. V.* **jmdm. eins** *od.* **einen ~** (*ugs.*) belt sb. one

**Über·breite** *die:* **Transport/Ladung mit ~:** wide load; **~ haben** be over normal width

**über·bringen** *unr. tr. V.* deliver; convey ‹greetings, congratulations›

**Über·bringer** *der;* **~s, ~:** bearer

**über·brücken** *tr. V.* Ⓐ (*veralt.*) bridge ‹river, ravine, etc.›; Ⓑ (*fig.*) bridge ‹gap, gulf›; reconcile ‹difference›; **um die finanzielle Notlage zu ~, musste sie ...** to tide herself over the financial crisis, she had to ...

**Überbrückung** *die;* **~, ~en** (*fig.*) bridging; (*von Gegensätzen*) reconciliation; **zur ~ der finanziellen Notlage musste sie ...** to tide herself over the financial crisis, she had to ...

**Überbrückungs-: ~hilfe** *die:* **jmdm. eine ~hilfe gewähren** give sb. interim financial help; **~kredit** *der* (*Finanzw.*) bridging loan

**über·buchen** *tr. V.* overbook

**über·dachen** *tr. V.* roof over; **überdacht** covered ‹terrace, station platform, etc.›

**über·dauern** *tr. V.* survive ‹war, hardship›

**Über·decke** *die* cover; (*auf einem Bett*) bedspread

**über|decken¹** *tr. V.* (*ugs.*) **jmdm. etw. ~:** cover sb. [up] with sth.

**über|decken²** *tr. V.* Ⓐ (*bedecken*) cover; Ⓑ (*verdecken*) cover up

**über·dehnen** *tr. V.* overstretch; strain ‹muscle›

**über·denken** *unr. tr. V.* **etw. ~:** think sth. over

**über·deutlich** ❶ *Adj.* unusually clear. ❷ *adv.* unusually clearly; with unusual clarity; **er hat mir ~ klargemacht, dass ...** he made it only too plain to me that ...

**über·dies** *Adv.* moreover; what is more

**über·dimensional** ❶ *Adj.* inordinately large ‹spectacles, table, statue, etc.›; inordinate ‹love, influence›. ❷ *adv.* enormously ‹enlarged›

**überdosieren** *tr. V.*; **ich überdosiere, überdosiert, überzudosieren: ein Medikament ~:** give/take too large a dose/doses of a medicine

**Über·dosis** *die* overdose

**über·drehen** *tr. V.* Ⓐ overwind ‹watch›; overtighten ‹screw, nut›; Ⓑ (*Technik*) over-rev (*coll.*) ‹engine›; **einen Wagen ~:** over-rev (*coll.*) the engine of a car

**überdreht** *Adj.* (*ugs.*) wound up; (*verrückt*) crazy

**Über·druck¹** *der; Pl.* **Überdrücke** excess pressure; **der Reifen hat ~:** the tyre is over-inflated

**Über·druck²** *der; Pl.* **Über·drucke** (*Philat.*) overprint

**über·drucken** *tr. V.* overprint

**Überdruck·ventil** *das* pressure-relief valve

**Überdruss, *Überdruß** /-drʊs/ *der;* **Überdrusses** surfeit (**an** + *Dat.* of); **etw. bis zum ~ tun** do sth. until one has wearied of it; **das habe ich schon bis zum ~ gehört!** I'm tired of hearing that

**überdrüssig** /-drysɪç/ *Adj.* **jmds./einer Sache ~ sein/werden** be/grow tired of sb./sth.

**über·durchschnittlich** ❶ *Adj.* above average. ❷ *adv.* **sie ist ~ begabt** she is more than averagely gifted *or* talented; **er verdient ~ gut** he earns more than the average

**über·eck** *Adv.* across a/the corner; **die Decke liegt ~ auf dem Tisch** the tablecloth lies diagonally on the table

**Über·eifer** *der* overeagerness; (*zu große Emsigkeit*) overzealousness

**über·eifrig** ❶ *Adj.* overeager; (*zu emsig*) overzealous. ❷ *adv.* overeagerly; (*zu emsig*) overzealously

**über·eignen** *tr. V.* **jmdm. etw. ~:** transfer sth. *or* make sth. over to sb.

**Über·eignung** *die* transfer (**an** + *Akk.* to)

**über·eilen** *tr. V.* rush; **übereilt** overhasty

**über·einander** *Adv.* Ⓐ (*räumlich*) one on top of the other; **sie wohnen ~:** they live one above the other; **ihre Wohnungen liegen ~:** their flats (*Brit.*) *or* (*Amer.*) apartments are situated over each other; **Bretter ~ legen** lay planks one on top of the other; **die Enden des Tuchs ~ schlagen** fold the cloth in the middle so that it is edge to edge; **die Arme/Beine ~ schlagen** fold one's arms/cross one's legs; **mit ~ geschlagenen Armen** with [one's] arms folded; Ⓑ (*fig.: voneinander*) ‹talk etc› about each other; about one another

***übereinander|legen** *usw.* ⇒ **übereinander** A

**überein|kommen** *unr. itr. V.*; *mit sein* agree; come to an agreement

**Überein·kommen** *das;* **~s, ~, Übereinkunft** /-ˈainkʊnft/ *die;* **Übereinkunft, Übereinkünfte** agreement; **ein ~** *od.* **eine Übereinkunft treffen/erzielen** enter into *or* make an agreement/reach [an] agreement

**überein|stimmen** *itr. V.* Ⓐ (*einer Meinung sein*) agree; **mit jmdm. in etw.** (*Dat.*) **~:** agree with sb. on sth.; **wir stimmen darin überein, dass ...** we are in agreement that ...; Ⓑ (*sich gleichen*) ‹colours, styles› match; ‹figures, statements, reports, results› tally, agree; ‹views, opinions› coincide; (*Sprachw.: kongruieren*) agree

**übereinstimmend** ❶ *Adj.* concurrent ‹views, opinions, statements, reports›. ❷ *adv.* **sie stellten ~ fest, dass ...** they agreed in stating that ...; **wir sind ~ der Meinung, dass ...** we share the view that ...

**Überein·stimmung** *die* Ⓐ (*von Meinungen*) agreement (**in** + *Dat.* on); Ⓑ (*Einklang, Gleichheit, Sprachw.: Kongruenz*) agreement (*Gen.* between); **die ~ von** *od.* **zwischen Theorie und Praxis** the correspondence between theory and practice; **in ~ mit einem Vertrag stehen** be in accordance with a contract; **etw. mit etw. in ~ bringen** reconcile sth. with sth.

**über·empfindlich** ❶ *Adj.* oversensitive (**gegen** to); (*Med.*) hypersensitive (**gegen** to). ❷ *adv.* oversensitively; (*Med.*) hypersensitively

**Über·empfindlichkeit** *die* oversensitivity (**gegen** to); (*Med.*) hypersensitivity (**gegen** to)

**übererfüllen** *tr. V.*; **ich übererfülle, übererfüllt, überzuerfüllen** overfulfil

**Über·erfüllung** *die* overfulfilment

**über|essen¹** *unr. tr. V.* **sich** (*Dat.*) **Hamburger/Nugat ~:** eat too many hamburgers/too much nougat

**über·essen²** *unr. refl. V.* **sich** [**an etw.** (*Dat.*)] **~:** gorge oneself [on sth.]

**über|fahren¹** ❶ *unr. tr. V.* **jmdn. ~:** ferry *or* take sb. over. ❷ *unr. itr. V.*; *mit sein* cross over

**über·fahren²** *unr. tr. V.* Ⓐ run over; Ⓑ (*übersehen u. weiterfahren*) go through ‹red light, stop signal, etc.›; Ⓒ (*hinwegfahren über*) cross; go over ‹crossroads›; Ⓓ (*ugs.: überrumpeln*) **jmdn. ~:** catch *or* take sb. unawares

**Über·fahrt** *die* crossing (**über** + *Akk.* of)

**Über·fall** *der* attack (**auf** + *Akk.* on); (*aus dem Hinterhalt*) ambush (**auf** + *Akk.* on); (*mit vorgehaltener Waffe*) hold-up; (*auf eine Bank o. Ä.*) raid (**auf** + *Akk.* on); (*fig. ugs.*) surprise visit

**über·fallen** *unr. tr. V.* Ⓐ attack; raid ‹bank, enemy position, village, etc.›; (*hinterrücks*) ambush; (*mit vorgehaltener Waffe*) hold up; (*fig.: besuchen*) descend on; **jmdn. mit Wünschen/Fragen ~** (*fig.*) bombard sb. with requests/questions; Ⓑ (*überkommen*) ‹tiredness, homesickness, fear› come over; **ein Schauder überfiel mich** a shiver ran through me

**über·fällig** *Adj.* overdue

**Überfall·kommando,** *das* flying squad

**über·fischen** *tr. V.* overfish

**über·fliegen** *unr. tr. V.* Ⓐ (*hinwegfliegen über*) fly over; overfly (*formal*); Ⓑ (*flüchtig lesen*) skim [through]

**über|fließen** *unr. itr. V.*; *mit sein* ⇒ **überlaufen a, b**

**über·flügeln** *tr. V.* outshine; outstrip

**Über·fluss, *Über·fluß** *der* abundance (**an** + *Dat.* of); (*Wohlstand*) affluence; **etw. im ~ haben** have sth. in abundance; **im ~ vorhanden sein** be in abundant *or* plentiful supply; **zu allem ~:** to cap *or* crown it all

**Überfluss·gesellschaft, *Überfluß·gesellschaft** *die* affluent society

**über·flüssig** *Adj.* superfluous; unnecessary ‹purchase, words, work›; (*zwecklos*) pointless; **~e Pfunde** (*ugs. scherzh.*) excess weight *sing.*; **~ zu erwähnen, dass ...** needless to say, ...

**überflüssiger·weise** *Adv.* unnecessarily; (*sinnloserweise*) pointlessly

**über·fluten** *tr. V.* (*auch fig.*) flood

**Über|flutung** *die;* **~, ~en** (*auch fig.*) flooding

**über·fordern** *tr. V.* **jmdn.** [**mit etw.**] **~:** overtax sb. [with sth.]; ask *or* demand too much of sb. [with sth.]; **mit diesem Posten ist er überfordert** this job is too much for him; he is not up to this job

**Über·forderung** *die* Ⓐ **eine** [**körperliche**] **~ für jmdn. sein** be too much for sb. [physically]; **eine intellektuelle ~ für jmdn. sein** ask *or* demand too much of sb. intellectually; Ⓑ (*das Überfordern*) overtaxing

**über·frachten** *tr. V.* overload; (*fig.*) overcharge

**über·fragen** *tr. V.* **da bin ich überfragt** I don't know the answer to that

**über·fremden** *tr. V.* **überfremdet werden/sein** ‹language, culture, etc.› be swamped [by foreign influences]; ‹economy› be dominated [by foreign firms/capital]; ‹country› be dominated [by foreign influences]

U

**Über·fremdung** *die;* ~, ~**en** domination [by foreign influences]; **eine amerikanische** ~ **des Marktes** domination of the market by American capital

**über·fressen** *unr. refl. V.* overeat; **der Hund/**(*salopp*) **sie hat sich an Schokolade** ~: the dog gorged itself/she gorged herself on chocolate

**über·frieren** *unr. itr. V.; mit sein* freeze over; ~**de Nässe** black ice

**Über·fuhr** *die;* ~, ~**en** (*österr.*) ferry

**über|führen¹** *tr. V.* **A** (*an einen anderen Ort bringen*) transfer; **der Tote wurde in seine Heimat übergeführt** the body of the dead man was brought back to his home town/country; **B** (*in einen anderen Zustand bringen*) convert; **etw. in die Praxis** ~: give sth. practical application

**über·führen²** *tr. V.* **A** ⇒ **überführen** A¹; **B** **jmdn. [eines Verbrechens]** ~: find sb. guilty [of a crime]; convict sb. [of a crime]; **C** ⇒ **überführen** B¹

**Über·führung** *die* **A** transfer; **die** ~ **des Toten in seine Heimat** bringing back the body of the dead man to his home town/country; **B** (*eines Verdächtigen*) conviction; **C** (*Brücke*) bridge; (*Hochstraße*) overpass; (*Fußgänger*~) [foot]bridge

**Über·fülle** *die* superabundance; **die** ~ **des Angebots** the excessive amount on offer

**über·füllt** *Adj.* crammed full, chock-full (**von** with); (*mit Menschen*) overcrowded, packed (**von** with); oversubscribed ‹course›

**Über·füllung** *die* overcrowding; „**Wegen** ~ **geschlossen**" 'Full up'

**Über·funktion** *die* ▶ 474 (*Med.*) hyperfunction

**über·füttern** *tr. V.* overfeed

**Über·gabe** *die* **A** handing over (**an** + *Akk.* to); (*einer Straße, eines Gebäudes*) opening; (*von Macht*) handing over; transfer; **B** (*Auslieferung an den Gegner*) surrender (**an** + *Akk.* to)

**Über·gang** *der* **A** crossing; **B** (*Stelle zum Überqueren*) crossing; (*Bahn*~) level crossing (*Brit.*); grade crossing (*Amer.*); (*Fußgängerbrücke*) footbridge; (*an der Grenze, eines Flusses*) crossing point; **C** (*Wechsel, Überleitung*) transition (**zu, auf** + *Akk.* to); **ohne** ~: without any transition

**übergangs-, Übergangs-:** ~**bestimmung** *die* interim regulation; ~**erscheinung** *die* transitional phenomenon; ~**los** **1** *Adj.* without any transition *postpos.;* **2** *adv.* without any transition; ~**lösung** *die* interim *or* temporary solution; ~**mantel** *der* coat for spring and autumn; ~**stadium** *das* transitional stage; ~**zeit** *die* **A** transitional period; **B** (*Frühling*) spring; (*Herbst*) autumn; (*Frühling und Herbst*) spring and autumn

**Über·gardine** *die* curtain

**über·geben** **1** *unr. tr. V.* **A** hand over; pass ‹baton›; **etw. den Flammen** ~ (*fig. geh.*) consign sth. to the flames; **B** (*übereignen*) transfer, make over (*Dat.* to); **C** (*ausliefern*) surrender (*Dat.*, **an** + *Akk.* to); **D** **eine Straße dem Verkehr** ~: open a road to traffic; **das neue Gemeindezentrum wurde seiner Bestimmung** ~: the new community centre was [officially] opened; **E** (*abgeben, überlassen*) **er hat sein Amt** ~: he has handed over his position; **jmdm. etw.** ~: entrust sb. with sth.; **ich übergebe diese Angelegenheit meinem Anwalt** I am placing this matter in the hands of my lawyer.
**2** *unr. refl. V.* (*sich erbrechen*) vomit

**über|gehen¹** *unr. itr. V.; mit sein* **A** pass; **an jmdn./in jmds. Besitz** ~: become sb.'s property; ⇒ *auch* **Fleisch** A; **B** **zu etw.** ~: go over to sth.; **dazu** ~, **etw. zu tun** go over to doing sth.; **zu einem anderen Thema** ~: move on to another subject; **C** **in etw.** (*Akk.*) ~ (*zu etw. werden*) turn into sth.; **in Gärung/Verwesung** ~: begin to ferment/decompose; **ineinander** ~ (*sich vermischen*) merge; **D** **uns gingen die Augen über** we were overwhelmed by the sight; **E** (*Seemannsspr.*) ‹wave› break over the side

**über·gehen²** *unr. tr. V.* **A** (*nicht beachten*) ignore; (*nicht eingehen auf*) **etw. [mit Stillschweigen]** ~: pass sth. over in silence; **B** (*auslassen, überspringen*) skip [over]; **C** (*nicht berücksichtigen*) pass over; **jmdn. bei der Beförderung** ~: pass sb. over for promotion; **jmdn. im Testament** ~: leave sb. out of one's will

**über·genau** **1** *Adj.* over-meticulous. **2** *adv.* over-meticulously

**über·genug** *Adv.* more than enough

**über·geordnet** **1** ⇒ **überordnen**. **2** *Adj.* higher ‹authority, position, court›; greater ‹significance›; superordinate ‹concept›; **einer Sache** (*Dat.*) ~ **sein** ‹authority, position, court› be higher than sth.

**Über·gepäck** *das* (*Flugw.*) excess baggage

**Über·gewicht** *das* **A** ▶ 353 excess weight; (*von Person*) overweight; **[5 kg]** ~ **haben** ‹person› be [5 kilos] overweight; **B** (*fig.*) predominance; **das** ~ **[über jmdn./etw.] haben/gewinnen** be/become predominant [over sb./sth.]; **militärisches** ~ **haben/gewinnen** have/achieve military superiority; **C** **das** ~ **bekommen** *od.* **kriegen** (*ugs.*) ‹person› overbalance

**über·gewichtig** *Adj.* overweight

**über|gießen¹** *unr. tr. V.* **jmdm. etw.** ~: pour sth. over sb.

**über·gießen²** *unr. tr. V.* **etw. mit Wasser/Soße** ~: pour water/sauce over sth.; **sich mit etw.** ~: pour sth. over oneself; **von Licht übergossen sein** (*fig.*) be flooded with light

**über·glücklich** *Adj.* blissfully happy; (*hoch erfreut*) overjoyed

**über·golden** *tr. V.* gild; (*fig. dichter.*) ‹sun› bathe ‹countryside› in gold

**über|greifen** *unr. itr. V.* **A** (*bes. beim Klavierspiel, Turnen*) cross one's hands over; **B** (*sich ausdehnen*) **auf etw.** (*Akk.*) ~: spread to sth.; **auf** *od.* **in jmds. Machtbereich** ~: encroach on sb.'s area of authority

**übergreifend** *Adj.* predominant; (*allumfassend*) all-embracing

**Über·griff** *der* (*unrechtmäßiger Eingriff*) encroachment (**auf** + *Akk.* on); infringement (**auf** + *Akk.* of); (*Angriff*) attack (**auf** + *Akk.* on)

**über·groß** *Adj.* huge; enormous; overwhelming ‹majority›

**Über·größe** *die* outsize; **Kleider/Schuhe** *usw.* **in** ~**n** outsize dresses/shoes *etc.*

**über|haben** *unr. tr. V.* (*ugs.*) **A** (*übergezogen haben*) have ‹coat, jacket, etc.› on; be wearing ‹coat, jacket, etc.›; **B** (*satt haben*) be fed up with (*coll.*); **C** (*übrig haben*) **etw.** ~: have sth. left [over]

**überhand** *in* ~ **nehmen** get out of hand; ‹attacks, muggings, etc.› increase alarmingly; ‹weeds› run riot

***überhand|nehmen** ⇒ **überhand**

**Über·hang** *der* **A** (*Überschuss*) surplus (**an** + *Dat.* of); **B** (*Fels*~, *Archit.*) overhang

**über|hängen¹** *unr. itr. V.; südd., österr., schweiz. mit sein* ‹part of building› overhang; ‹branch› hang over; ‹rock face› form an overhang

**über|hängen²** *tr. V.* **sich** (*Dat.*) **eine Jacke** ~: put a jacket round one's shoulders; **sich** (*Dat.*) **das Gewehr/die Tasche** ~: hang *or* sling the rifle/bag over one's shoulder

**Überhang·mandat** *das* (*Politik*): *seat won in addition to the number a party has gained through proportional representation*

**über·hasten** *tr. V.* rush; **überhastet handeln** act hastily *or* hurriedly

**über·häufen** *tr. V.* **jmdn. mit etw.** ~: heap *or* shower sth. on sb.; **jmdn. mit Ratschlägen/Vorwürfen** ~: bombard sb. with advice/pour reproaches on sb.

**überhaupt** **1** *Adv.* **A** (*insgesamt, im Allgemeinen*) in general; **soweit es** ~ **Zweck hat** as far as there's any point in it at all; ~ **fühlte er sich jetzt wohler** he felt better all round; **er ist** ~ **selten zu Hause** he's not at home much at all; **B** (*meist bei Verneinungen: gar*) ~ **nicht** not at all; **das ist** ~ **nicht wahr** that's not true at all; ~ **keine Zeit haben** have no time at all; not have any time at all; **das kommt** ~ **nicht in Frage** it's quite *or* completely out of the question; ~ **nichts** nothing at all; nothing what[so]ever; **wenn** ~: if at all; **wenn** ~, **dann komme ich morgen** if I come at all, it will be tomorrow; **C** (*überdies, außerdem*) besides; **D** (*besonders*) particularly.
**2** *Partikel* anyway; **wer sind Sie** ~? who are you anyway?; **wer hat dir das** ~ **gesagt?** who told you that anyway?; **was willst du hier** ~? what ar you doing here anyway?; **wie konnte das** ~ **passieren?** how could it happen in the first place?; **das klingt verlockend, aber haben wir** ~ **Geld dafür?** that sounds tempting, but have we got the money for it?; **wissen Sie** ~, **mit wem Sie reden?** do you realize who you're talking to?

**über·heben** *unr. refl. V.* **A** ⇒ **verheben**; **B** (*überheblich sein*) be arrogant

**überheblich** /-'he:plɪç/ **1** *Adj.* arrogant; supercilious ‹grin›. **2** *adv.* arrogantly; ‹grin› superciliously

**Überheblichkeit** *die;* ~: arrogance

**über·heizen** *tr. V.* overheat

**über·hitzen** *tr. V.* (*auch fig.*) overheat

**über·höhen** *tr. V.* raise ‹dike, embankment, etc.›; bank ‹track, curve›

**überhöht** /y:bɐ'hø:t/ *Adj.* (*zu hoch*) excessive

**über|holen¹** **1** *tr., itr. V.* **jmdn.** ~: ferry sb. across. **2** *itr. V.* (*Seemannsspr.*) keel over

**über·holen²** **1** *tr. V.* **A** overtake (*esp. Brit.*); pass (*esp. Amer.*); **B** (*übertreffen*) outstrip; **C** (*wieder instand setzen*) overhaul. **2** *itr. V.* overtake (*esp. Brit.*); pass (*esp. Amer.*)

**Überhol-:** ~**manöver** *das* overtaking (*esp. Brit.*) *or* (*esp. Amer.*) passing manœuvre; ~**spur** *die* overtaking lane (*esp. Brit.*); pass lane (*esp. Amer.*)

**überholt** *Adj.* (*veraltet*) outdated; **durch etw.** ~ **sein** have become outdated as a result of sth.

**Überholung** *die;* ~, ~**en** overhaul; **der Wagen muss zur** ~ **in die Werkstatt** the car has to go into the garage for an overhaul

**Überhol-:** ~**verbot** *das* prohibition of overtaking; „~**verbot**" 'no overtaking' (*esp. Brit.*); 'no passing' (*Amer.*); **hier besteht** ~**verbot** overtaking is prohibited here; ~**vorgang** *der* overtaking *no art.;* **während des** ~**vorgangs** while overtaking

**über·hören** *tr. V.* not hear; **das möchte ich überhört haben** I'll pretend I didn't hear that

**Über·ich, *Über-Ich** *das* (*Psych.*) superego

**über·irdisch** **1** *Adj.* **A** (*himmlisch*) celestial; heavenly; (*übernatürlich*) supernatural; ethereal ‹beauty›; **B** (*veralt.*) ⇒ **oberirdisch** 1. **2** *adv.* **A** (*himmlisch*) celestially; (*übernatürlich*) supernaturally; ethereally ‹beautiful›; **B** (*veralt.*) ⇒ **oberirdisch** 2

**über·kandidelt** /-kandi:dlt/ *Adj.* (*ugs.*) affected

**Über·kapazität** *die* (*Wirtsch.*) overcapacity; ~**en** overcapacity *sing.*

**über|kippen** *itr. V.; mit sein* tip over

**über·kleben** *tr. V.* **die alten Plakate mit neuen** ~: stick new posters over the old ones; **wir überklebten die Anschrift** we stuck something over the address; we covered the address by sticking something over it

**über·klettern** *tr. V.* climb over

**über|kochen** *itr. V.; mit sein* (*auch fig. ugs.*) boil over

**über|kommen¹** *unr. itr. V.; mit sein* (*Seemannsspr.*) ‹water› wash over the deck; ‹wave› break over the side

**über·kommen²** *unr. tr. V.* **Mitleid/Ekel/Furcht überkam mich** I was overcome by pity/revulsion/fear; **ein Gefühl der Verlassenheit überkam sie** a feeling of desolation came over her

**überkommen³** *Adj.* (*geh.*) traditional

**über·kompensieren** *tr. V.;* (*bes. Psych., Wirtsch.*) **ich überkompensiere,**

U

*old spelling (see note on page 1707)

**überkompensiert, überzukompensieren** overcompensate for

**über·kreuzen** ❶ *tr. V.* ⇒ **kreuzen** 1 A. ❷ *refl. V.* cross; **sich ∼de Linien** intersecting lines

**über|kriegen** *tr. V.* (*ugs.*) **jmdn./etw. ∼:** get fed up with sb./sth. (*coll.*)

**über·kronen** *tr. V.* (*Zahnmed.*) crown

**über·krusten** *tr. V.* **das Salz hatte den Boden überkrustet** the ground was encrusted with salt *or* covered with a crust of salt; **von Dreck überkrustete Stiefel** boots caked with dirt

**über·laden¹** *unr. tr. V.* (*auch fig.*) overload

**überladen²** *Adj.* over-ornate ‹façade, style, etc.›; overcrowded ‹shop window›

**über·lagern** *tr. V.* Ⓐ overlie; (*fig.*) combine with; **sich ∼:** combine; **von Sedimentschichten überlagertes Gestein** rock with overlying sedimentary strata; **sich ∼de Gesteinsschichten** superimposed rock strata; Ⓑ (*Physik*) ‹wave› interfere with; ‹force, field› be superimposed on; **sich ∼** ‹waves› interfere; ‹forces, fields› be superimposed

**Über·lagerung** *die* Ⓐ superposition; (*fig.*) combination; Ⓑ (*Physik*) (*von Wellen*) interference; (*von Kräften, Feldern*) superposition

**Überland-** /*od.* --'-/: **∼bus** *der* country bus; **∼leitung** *die* transmission line

**über·lang** *Adj.* unusually long

**Über·länge** *die:* **∼ haben** be unusually long; **eine Ladung mit ∼:** a long load; **„wegen ∼ geänderte Anfangszeiten"** 'starting times changed due to the unusually long running time of the film'

**über·lappen** *tr. V.* (*auch fig.*) overlap

**über|lassen¹** *unr. tr. V.* (*ugs.*) **etw. ∼:** leave sth. over

**über·lassen²** ❶ *unr. tr. V.* Ⓐ (*geben*) **jmdm. etw. ∼:** let sb. have sth.; **er hat mir sein Auto übers Wochenende ∼:** he let me use his car over the weekend; **er hat es mir billig ∼:** he let me have it cheap; Ⓑ **jmdn. jmds. Fürsorge ∼:** leave sb. in sb.'s care; **sich** (*Dat.*) **selbst ∼ sein** be left to one's own devices; Ⓒ **etw. jmdm. ∼** (*etw. jmdn. entscheiden/tun lassen*) leave sth. to sb.; **das bleibt [ganz] dir ∼:** that's [entirely] up to you; **überlass das bitte mir** let that be my concern; let me worry about that; **jmdm. alle Arbeit ∼:** leave sb. to do all the work; **etw. dem Zufall ∼:** leave sth. to chance; Ⓓ **jmdn. seinem Kummer ∼:** leave sb. to cope with his/her grief alone. ❷ *unr. refl. V.* **sich der Leidenschaft/dem Gefühl/den Träumen** *usw.* **∼:** abandon oneself to one's passions/emotions/dreams *etc.*

**über·lasten** *tr. V.* overload; overburden, overstretch ‹facilities, authorities›; put too great a strain on ‹heart, circulation, etc.›; strain ‹nerves›; overstress ‹structure, material›; overtax ‹person›; (*mit Arbeit*) overwork ‹person›; (*psychisch*) put too great a strain on ‹person›

**Überlastung** *die;* **∼, ∼en** ⇒ **überlasten**: overloading; overstretching; straining; overstressing; overtaxing; overworking; **die ständige ∼ führte schließlich zu seinem Zusammenbruch** the continuous strain he was under led eventually to collapse

**Über·lauf** *der* (*auch DV*) overflow

**über|laufen¹** *unr. itr. V.; mit sein* Ⓐ ‹liquid, container› overflow; Ⓑ (*auf die gegnerische Seite überwechseln*) defect; ‹partisan› go over to the other side; **zum Feind/zu den Rebellen ∼:** go over *or* desert to the enemy/the rebels

**über·laufen²** *unr. tr. V.* Ⓐ (*befallen*) seize; **ein Frösteln/Schauer überlief mich, es überlief mich [eis]kalt** a cold shiver ran down my spine; **es überlief sie heiß** a hot flush came over her; Ⓑ (*Sport: hinauslaufen über*) run past; Ⓒ (*Sport: umspielen*) run through, beat ‹defence›

**überlaufen³** *Adj.* overcrowded; oversubscribed ‹course, subject›; **der Arzt ist sehr ∼:** the doctor's list is very full

**Über·läufer** *der* (*auch fig.*) defector

**Überlauf·rohr** *das* overflow pipe

**über·laut** ❶ *Adj.* too loud *pred.;* over-loud ‹voice, laugh›; ‹engine› too noisy *pred.* ❷ *adv.* too loudly

**über·leben** ❶ *tr., auch itr. V.* survive; **das überleb ich nicht!** I'll never get over it!; **du wirst es schon** *od.* **wohl ∼** (*iron.*) you'll survive; **jmdn. ∼:** survive *or* outlive sb. (**um** by). ❷ *refl. V.* become outdated *or* outmoded; **sich überlebt haben** have become outdated; have had its day; **überlebt** outdated; out-of-date

**Über·lebende** *der/die; adj. Dekl.* survivor

**Überlebens·chance** *die* chance of survival

**über·lebens·groß** *Adj.* larger than life-size

**Überlebens·training** *das* survival training; **ein ∼training** a survival-training course

**über|legen¹** ❶ *tr. V.* Ⓐ **jmdm. etw. ∼:** put sth. over sb.; Ⓑ (*ugs.: verhauen*) **jmdn. ∼:** put sb. over one's knee. ❷ *refl. V.* lean over; ‹ship› list

**über·legen²** ❶ *tr. V.* consider; think over *or* about; **etw. noch einmal ∼:** reconsider sth.; **das muss gut überlegt werden** that needs some careful consideration *or* thought; **es wäre zu ∼, ob ...** one might consider whether ...; **es sich anders ∼:** change one's mind; **wenn ich es mir recht überlege, ...** now I come to think of it, ...; **das hättest du dir auch vorher ∼ können** you could have thought about that *or* given that some thought before.
❷ *itr. V.* think; reflect; **überleg doch mal!** think about it!; **ohne zu ∼** (*unbedacht*) without thinking; (*spontan*) without a moment's thought; **ohne lange zu ∼:** without much reflection; **lass mich mal ∼:** let me think; **lange hin und her ∼:** agonize for ages; **ich habe hin und her überlegt** I've turned it over and over in my mind; **am Überlegen sein, ob ...** be thinking over whether ...

**überlegen³** ❶ *Adj.* Ⓐ superior; clear, convincing ‹win, victory›; **jmdm. ∼ sein** be superior to sb. (**an** + *Dat.* in); **zahlenmäßig ∼ sein** be superior in numbers; Ⓑ (*herablassend*) supercilious; superior. ❷ *adv.* Ⓐ in a superior manner; ‹play› much the better: ‹win, argue› convincingly; Ⓑ (*herablassend*) superciliously; superiorly

**Überlegenheit** *die;* **∼:** superiority

**überlegt** /y:bɐ'le:kt/ ❶ *Adj.* carefully considered. ❷ *adv.* in a carefully considered way

**Überlegung** *die;* **∼, ∼en** Ⓐ thought; reflection; **nach reiflicher ∼:** on careful consideration; **mit ∼ handeln** act in a considered way; **einer ∼ wert sein** be worth considering; Ⓑ (*Gedanke*) idea; **∼en** (*Gedankengang*) thoughts; reflections; **∼en zu etw. anstellen** give one's thoughts on sth.

**über|leiten** *itr. V.* **zum nächsten/zu einem neuen Thema ∼** ‹speaker› move on to the next topic; **in etw.** (*Akk.*) **∼:** lead into sth.; **in eine andere Tonart ∼** ‹player› change key

**Über·leitung** *die* transition; **eine ∼ zum nächsten Thema suchen** look for a way of moving on to the next subject

**über·lesen** *unr. tr. V.* overlook; miss

**über·liefern** *tr. V.* hand down; **überlieferte Sitten/Formen** *usw.* traditional customs/forms *etc.;* **in alten Chroniken ist überliefert, dass ...** it is recorded in ancient chronicles that ...

**Über·lieferung** *die* Ⓐ (*etw. Überliefertes*) tradition; **schriftliche ∼en** written records; Ⓑ (*Brauch*) tradition; custom; Ⓒ (*das Überliefern*) handing down

**überlisten** *tr. V.* outwit

**überm** *Präp.* + *Art.* = **über dem**

**Über·macht** *die* superior strength; (*zahlenmäßig*) superior numbers *pl.;* **in der ∼ sein, die ∼ haben** be superior in strength/numbers

**über·mächtig** ❶ *Adj.* Ⓐ superior; Ⓑ (*nicht mehr bezähmbar*) overpowering ‹desire, hatred, urge, etc.›. ❷ *adv.* **∼ loderte das Feuer der Leidenschaft in ihnen** the fire of passion blazed uncontrollably in them; **es zog ihn ∼ in die Ferne** he felt an overpowering desire to travel

**über·malen** *tr. V.* **etw. ∼:** paint sth. over

**über·mannen** *tr. V.* overcome

**Über·maß** *das* excessive amount, excess (**an** + *Dat.* of); **ein ∼ an Arbeit** *od.* **Arbeit im ∼ haben** have an excessive amount of work *or* more than enough work; **etw. im ∼ produzieren** produce sth. in excess; produce an excess of sth.

**über·mäßig** ❶ *Adj.* Ⓐ excessive; Ⓑ (*Musik*) **ein ∼es Intervall** an augmented interval. ❷ *adv.* excessively; **∼ viel essen** eat to excess *or* excessively; **nicht ∼ attraktiv** not especially attractive; **man braucht sich nicht mal ∼ zu beeilen** you don't even need to hurry overmuch

**Über·mensch** *der* superman

**über·menschlich** *Adj.* superhuman; **er hat Übermenschliches geleistet** he has achieved the almost impossible

**über·mitteln** *tr. V.* send; (*als Mittler weitergeben*) pass on, convey ‹greetings, regards, etc.›

**Übermitt[e]lung** *die* sending

**über·morgen** *Adv.* the day after tomorrow

**über·müde** *Adj.* overtired; exhausted

**über·müden** *tr. V.* overtire; **übermüdet** overtired; exhausted

**Übermüdung** *die;* **∼:** overtiredness; exhaustion

**Über·mut** *der* high spirits *pl.;* **etw. aus [lauter]** *od.* **im ∼ tun** do sth. out of [pure] high spirits; **∼ tut selten gut** (*Spr.*) high spirits mustn't get out of hand

**übermütig** /'y:bɐmy:tɪç/ ❶ *Adj.* high-spirited; in high spirits *pred.;* **in ∼er Stimmung** high-spirited; in high spirits. ❷ *adv.* high-spiritedly

**übern** *Präp.* + *Art.* = **über den**

**über·nächst...** *Adj.* ▶ 833 **im ∼en Jahr, ∼es Jahr** the year after next; **∼e Woche** the week after next; **am ∼en Tag** two days later; the next day but one; **∼en Montag** a week on Monday; Monday week; **er wohnt im ∼en Haus** he lives in the next house but one *or* lives two doors away

**über·nachten** *itr. V.* stay overnight; **bei jmdm. ∼:** stay *or* spend the night at sb.'s house/flat (*Brit.*) *or* (*Amer.*) apartment *etc.;* **im Hotel ∼:** stay the night at the hotel; **im Freien ∼:** sleep in the open air

**übernächtigt** /y:bɐ'nɛçtɪçt/ *Adj.* ‹person› tired *or* worn out [through lack of sleep]; tired ‹face, look, etc.›

**Übernachtung** *die;* **∼, ∼en** overnight stay; **∼ und Frühstück** bed and breakfast; **sechs ∼en kosten ...** six nights cost ...

**Übernahme** /'y:bɐna:mə/ *die;* **∼, ∼n** Ⓐ (*von Waren, einer Sendung*) taking delivery *no art.;* (*des Staffelstabs*) receiving *no indef. art.;* (*einer Idee, eines Themas, von Methoden*) adoption, taking over *no indef. art.;* (*einer Praxis, eines Geschäfts, der Macht*) takeover; (*von Wörtern, Ausdrücken*) borrowing (**von** from); **er erklärt sich zur ∼ der Kosten/des Falles bereit** he says he is prepared to meet the cost himself/to take on the case; Ⓑ (*etw. Übernommenes*) borrowing; (*Sendung*) re-broadcast; (*Livesendung*) relay

**über·natürlich** *Adj.* supernatural

**über·nehmen** ❶ *unr. tr. V.* Ⓐ take delivery of ‹goods, consignment›; receive ‹relay baton›; take over ‹power, practice, business, building, school class›; take on ‹job, position, task, role, case, leadership›; undertake to pay ‹costs›; **es ∼, etw. zu tun** take on the job of doing sth.; **das lass mich ∼:** let me do that; ⇒ *auch* **Befehl** B; **Bürgschaft** A; **Garantie** A; **Gewähr**; **Kommando** B; **Steuer¹**; **Verantwortung** A; **Verpflichtung** A; Ⓑ (*bei sich einstellen*) take on ‹staff›; Ⓒ (*Seemannsspr.: an Bord nehmen*) take on board; Ⓓ (*sich zu Eigen machen*) adopt, take over ‹ideas, methods, subject, etc.› (**von** from); borrow ‹word, phrase› (**von** from); **eine Textstelle wörtlich ∼:** use a passage verbatim; **das ZDF hat die Sendung vom britischen Fernsehen übernommen** the programme was re-transmitted/(*als Livesendung*) relayed from British television by ZDF; Ⓔ (*österr. ugs.*) ⇒ **übertölpeln**.
❷ *unr. refl. V.* overdo things *or* it; **er hat sich**

U

beim Training übernommen he overdid things *or* it [while] training; sich mit etw. ∼: take on too much with sth.; übernimm dich nur nicht (*iron.*) don't strain yourself!

**über|ordnen** *tr. V.* Ⓐ etw. einer Sache (*Dat.*) ∼: give sth. precedence over sth.; Ⓑ jmdn. jmdm. ∼: place sb. above sb.; ⇒ *auch* übergeordnet 2

**über·örtlich** (*Amtsspr.*) ❶ *Adj.* regional. ❷ *adv.* regionally

**über·parteilich** ❶ *Adj.* non-party *attrib.*; ein ∼es Komitee an all-party committee; das Amt des Bundespräsidenten ist ∼: the office of Federal President is *or* stands above party politics. ❷ *adv.* in a non-partisan way

**über·pinseln** *tr. V.* (*ugs.*) paint over

**Über·produktion** *die* (*Wirtsch.*, *Med.*) overproduction

**über·prüfbar** *Adj.* checkable; die Angaben waren nicht ∼: the details could not be checked

**über·prüfen** *tr. V.* Ⓐ check (auf + *Akk.* for); check [over], inspect, examine ‹machine, device›; check, inspect, examine ‹papers, luggage›; review ‹issue, situation, results›; (*Finanzw.*) examine, inspect ‹accounts, books›; Ⓑ (*überdenken*) think over; consider; etw. noch mal ∼: think sth. over again; reconsider sth.

**Über·prüfung** *die* Ⓐ ⇒ überprüfen A: checking *no indef. art.* (auf + *Akk.* for); checking [over] *no indef. art.*; inspection; examination; Ⓑ (*Kontrolle*) check; (*des Ausweises, der Geschäftsbücher*) examination; inspection; (*einer Lage, Frage, der Ergebnisse*) review; Ⓒ (*das Überdenken*) consideration; erneute ∼: reconsideration

**über|quellen** *unr. itr. V.*; *mit sein* Ⓐ spill over; Ⓑ (*zu voll sein*) be brimming; die Tribüne quoll von Zuschauern über (*fig.*) the stand was overflowing with spectators

**über·queren** *tr. V.* cross; (*schneiden*) cut across; cross

**über|ragen**[1] *itr. V.* jut out; project

**über·ragen**[2] *tr. V.* Ⓐ (*hinausragen über*) jmdn./etw. ∼: tower above sb./sth.; jmdn. um Kopfeslänge ∼: be a head taller than sb.; der Berg überragt die Ebene the mountain towers over the plain; Ⓑ (*übertreffen*) jmdn. an etw. (*Dat.*) ∼: be head and shoulders above sb. in sth.

**überragend** ❶ *Adj.* outstanding. ❷ *adv.* outstandingly

**überraschen** *tr. V.* surprise; ‹storm, earthquake› take by surprise; (*durch einen Angriff*) take by surprise; catch unawares; jmdn. beim Rauchen/Stehlen ∼: catch sb. smoking/stealing; jmdn. überrascht ansehen look at sb. in surprise; überrascht tun pretend to be surprised; lassen wir uns ∼: let's wait and see; vom Gewitter/vom Regen überrascht werden be caught in the thunderstorm/caught [out] in the rain

**überraschend** ❶ *Adj.* surprising; surprise *attrib.* ‹attack, visit›; (*unerwartet*) unexpected. ❷ *adv.* surprisingly; (*unerwartet*) unexpectedly; die Nachricht kam ∼: the news came as a surprise

**überraschender·weise** *Adv.* surprisingly; (*unerwartet*) unexpectedly

**Überraschung** *die*; ∼, ∼en surprise; zu meiner [großen] ∼: to my [great] surprise; für eine ∼ sorgen cause a surprise; jmdm. eine kleine ∼ mitbringen bring sb. a little something as a surprise

**Überraschungs·moment** *das* element of surprise

**über·reden** *tr. V.* persuade; jmdn. ∼, etw. zu tun persuade sb. to do sth.; talk sb. into doing sth.; jmdn. zum Mitmachen/zu einer Fahrt ∼: persuade sb. to take part/make a journey; talk sb. into taking part/making a journey; ich habe mich zum Kauf eines neuen Autos ∼ lassen I was persuaded to buy *or* was talked into buying a new car

**Überredung** *die*; ∼: persuasion

**Überredungs·kunst** *die* powers *pl.* of persuasion

*old spelling (see note on page 1707)

**über·regional** ❶ *Adj.* national ‹newspaper, radio station›; eine Angelegenheit von ∼er Bedeutung a matter of more than just regional importance; ∼e Veranstaltungen events involving several regions. ❷ *adv.* nationally; ∼ bekannt werden become known outside one's/its own region

**über·reich** ❶ *Adj.* lavish ‹meal, decoration›; abundant, very rich ‹harvest›; ∼ an Bodenschätzen sein be very rich in mineral resources; eine an Ereignissen ∼e Zeit an extremely eventful time; in ∼em Maß vorhanden sein be there in great quantity. ❷ *adv.* jmdn. ∼ beschenken/belohnen lavish gifts on sb./reward sb. lavishly; ∼ verziert sein be lavishly decorated

**über·reichen** *tr. V.* [jmdm.] etw. ∼: present sth. [to sb.]

**über·reichlich** ❶ *Adj.* over-ample; etw. ist in ∼er Fülle vorhanden there is an over abundance of sth. ❷ *adv.* over-amply

**Überreichung** *die*; ∼: presentation

**über·reif** *Adj.* over-ripe

**über·reizen** ❶ *tr. V.* Ⓐ overtax ‹person›; overstrain ‹eyes, nerves, etc.›; [nervlich] überreizt overwrought; Ⓑ (*bes. Skat*) overbid ‹hand›. ❷ *refl. V.* (*bes. Skat*) overbid

**Überreiztheit** *die*; ∼ ⇒ überreizen 1: overtaxed/-strained/-wrought state

**Über·reizung** *die* ⇒ überreizen 1: overtaxing; overstraining; ein Zeichen nervöser ∼: a sign of nervous strain

**über·rennen** *unr. tr. V.* Ⓐ (*Milit.*) overrun; Ⓑ (*umrennen*) run down

**über·repräsentiert** *Adj.* over-represented

**Über·rest** *der* remnant; ∼e (*eines Gebäudes*) remains; ruins; (*einer Mahlzeit*) leftovers; die sterblichen ∼e (*geh. verhüll.*) the mortal remains

**Überroll·bügel** *der* roll bar

**über·rollen** *tr. V.* Ⓐ (*Milit.*) overrun; (*fig.*) overwhelm ‹person›; ‹fashion, craze› sweep through ‹country›; Ⓑ (*hinwegrollen über*) run down

**über·rumpeln** *tr. V.* jmdn. ∼: take sb. by surprise; (*bei einem Angriff*) catch sb. unawares; take sb. by surprise; jmdn. mit etw. ∼: surprise sb. with sth.; take sb. by surprise with sth.

**Überrump[e]lung** *die*; ∼, ∼en surprise attack

**über·runden** *tr. V.* Ⓐ (*Sport*) lap; Ⓑ (*übertreffen*) outstrip

**übers** *Präp.* + *Art.* Ⓐ = über das; Ⓑ ∼ Jahr one year later

**übersät** /y:bɐˈzɛ:t/ *Adj.* mit *od.* von etw. ∼ sein be covered with sth.; (*abwertend*) be strewn with sth.; mit *od.* von Sternen ∼: star-studded; studded with stars *postpos.*

**über·sättigen** *tr. V.* supersaturate ‹solution›; glut ‹market›; satiate ‹public›

**Überschall-:** ∼**flugzeug** *das* supersonic aircraft; ∼**geschwindigkeit** *die* supersonic speed

**über·schatten** *tr. V.* overshadow; cast its/their shadow over; (*fig.*) cast a shadow over

**über·schätzen** *tr. V.* overestimate; overrate ‹writer, performer, book, performance, talent, ability›

**Über·schätzung** *die* ⇒ überschätzen: overestimation; overrating

**überschaubar** *Adj.* eine ∼e Menge/Zahl a manageable quantity/number; das sind ∼e Größen these are quantities one can grasp; das Risiko ist nicht ∼: the risks cannot be calculated; ein ∼er Zeitraum/∼es Gebiet a reasonably short period/small area

**über·schauen** *tr. V.* ⇒ übersehen[2] A, B

**über|schäumen** *itr. V.*; *mit sein* froth over; ∼de Begeisterung bubbling enthusiasm

**über·schlafen** *unr. tr. V.* sleep on ‹matter, problem, etc.›

**Über·schlag** *der* Ⓐ rough calculation *or* estimate; Ⓑ (*Turnen*) handspring; (*am Barren*) forward roll; Ⓒ ⇒ Looping

**über|schlagen**[1] ❶ *unr. tr. V.* die Beine ∼: cross one's legs; mit übergeschlagenen Beinen with [one's] legs crossed. ❷ *unr. itr. V.*; *mit sein* ‹wave› break; ‹spark› jump

**über·schlagen**[2] ❶ *unr. tr. V.* Ⓐ (*auslassen*) skip ‹chapter, page, etc.›; Ⓑ (*ungefähr berechnen*) calculate *or* estimate roughly; make a rough calculation *or* estimate of. ❷ *unr. refl. V.* Ⓐ go head over heels; ‹car› turn over; sich vor Höflichkeit ∼ (*fig.*) fall over oneself to be polite (*coll.*); Ⓑ ‹voice› crack; Ⓒ ‹events, reports, etc.› come thick and fast; die Gedanken überschlugen sich in meinem Kopf the thoughts raced round and round in my head

**überschlagen**[3] *Adj.* (*bes. md.*) lukewarm ‹liquid›; moderately warm ‹room›

**überschlägig** /-ʃlɛ:gɪç/ ❶ *Adj.* [roughly] estimated; rough, approximate ‹estimate›. ❷ *adv.* ‹calculate, estimate› roughly, approximately

**über|schnappen** *itr. V.*; *mit sein* Ⓐ (*ugs.*: *den Verstand verlieren*) go crazy; go round the bend (*coll.*); Ⓑ (*ugs.*: *sich überschlagen*) ‹voice› crack

**über·schneiden** *unr. refl. V.* ‹lines, rays› cross, intersect; (*fig.*) ‹problems, areas of responsibility, events, etc.› overlap

**Überschneidung** *die*; ∼, ∼en ⇒ überschneiden: intersection; (*fig.*) overlapping

**über·schreiben** *unr. tr. V.* Ⓐ entitle; head ‹chapter, section›; Ⓑ (*übertragen*) etw. jmdm. *od.* auf jmdn. ∼: transfer sth. to sb.; make sth. over to sb.

**über·schreien** *unr. tr. V.* shout down

**über·schreiten** *unr. itr. V.* Ⓐ cross; (*fig.*) pass; Überschreiten der Gleise verboten! do not cross the line!; er hat die Siebzig überschritten (*fig.*) he is past seventy; Ⓑ (*hinausgehen über*) exceed ‹authority, powers, budget, speed, limit, deadline, etc.›; das überschreitet jedes Maß that's going too far; die Grenzen des Erlaubten ∼: go beyond what is permissible

**Über·schrift** *die* heading; (*in einer Zeitung*) headline; (*Titel*) title

**Über·schuh** *der* overshoe; galosh *usu. pl.* (*Brit.*)

**über·schuldet** *Adj.* heavily indebted ‹person, firm, country›; heavily mortgaged ‹house, property, etc.›; hoffnungslos ∼ sein ‹person› be hopelessly in debt

**Überschuldung** *die*; ∼, ∼en heavy indebtedness

**Über·schuss**, ***Über·schuß** *der* surplus (an + *Dat.* of)

**überschüssig** /ˈy:bɐʃʏsɪç/ *Adj.* surplus

**über|schütten**[1] *tr. V.* (*ugs.*) spill

**über·schütten**[2] *tr. V.* cover; jmdn./etw. mit Wasser ∼: throw water over sb./sth.; jmdn. mit Vorwürfen/Lob/Ehrungen ∼: heap reproach/praise/honours on sb.; jmdn. mit Fragen ∼: fire questions at sb.; jmdn. mit Geschenken/Geld ∼: shower sb. with presents/lavish money on sb.

**Überschwang** *der*; ∼[e]s exuberance; im ∼ der Begeisterung in one's exuberant enthusiasm; im ∼ der Gefühle out of sheer exuberance

**über·schwänglich** /-ʃvɛŋlɪç/ ❶ *Adj.* effusive ‹words, manner, etc.›; wild ‹joy, enthusiasm›. ❷ *adv.* effusively

**Überschwänglichkeit** *die*; ∼: effusiveness

**über|schwappen** *itr. V.*; *mit sein* ‹liquid, container› slop over

**über·schwemmen** *tr. V.* (*auch fig.*) flood; von Touristen überschwemmt werden (*fig.*) be flooded *or* swamped with tourists; den Markt mit Waren ∼ (*fig.*) flood *or* swamp the market/with goods

**Überschwemmung** *die*; ∼, ∼en flood; (*das Überschwemmen*) flooding *no pl.*; zu ∼en führen lead to flooding *or* floods

**Überschwemmungs-:** ∼**gebiet** *das* flood area; ∼ **gefahr** *die* danger of flooding; ∼**katastrophe** *die* disastrous floods *pl.*

***über·schwenglich** ⇒ überschwänglich

***Überschwenglichkeit** ⇒ Überschwänglichkeit

**Über·see** *in* aus *od.* von ∼: from overseas; in ∼ leben live overseas; nach ∼ auswandern emigrate overseas; Exporte/Post nach ∼: overseas exports/mail; Besitzungen in ∼: overseas possessions

**Übersee-: ~dampfer** *der* ocean-going steamer; **~gebiet** *das* overseas territory; **Britische ~gebiete** British territories overseas; **~hafen** *der* international port; **~handel** *der* overseas trade

**überseeisch** /ˈy:bɐze:ɪʃ/ *Adj.* overseas

**Übersee-: ~kabel** *das* transoceanic cable; **~koffer** *der* cabin trunk

**übersehbar** *Adj.* (*abschätzbar*) assessable; **der Schaden ist noch nicht ~:** the damage cannot yet be assessed

**über|sehen¹** *unr. refl. V.* (*ugs.*) **sich** (*Dat.*) **etw. ~:** get fed up (*coll.*) *or* tired of seeing sth.; **diese Tapete habe ich mir übergesehen** I'm fed up with the sight of this wallpaper

**über·sehen²** *unr. tr. V.* **A** look out over; (*fig.*) survey ‹subject›; **man kann von hier die ganze Bucht ~:** you can look [right] out over the whole bay from here; **etw. gut** *od.* **leicht ~ können** have a good view of sth.; **B** (*abschätzen*) assess ‹damage, situation, consequences, etc.›; **C** (*nicht sehen*) overlook; miss; miss ‹turning, signpost›; **mit seinen roten Haaren ist er nicht zu ~:** you can't miss him with his red hair; **D** (*ignorieren*) ignore

**über·senden** *unr.* (*auch regelm.*) *tr. V.* send; remit, send ‹money›; **die übersandten Waren sind fehlerhaft** the goods sent are faulty; **anbei übersende ich Ihnen …** please find enclosed …

**Über·sendung** *die* sending; (*von Geld*) remittance; sending

**übersetzbar** *Adj.* translatable; **schwer/leicht ~ sein** be difficult/easy to translate

**über|setzen¹** **1** *tr. V.* ferry over. **2** *itr. V.*; *auch mit sein* cross [over]

**über·setzen²** *tr., itr. V.* (*auch fig.*) translate; **etw. ins Deutsche/aus dem Deutschen ~:** translate sth. into/from German

**Über·setzer** *der*, **Übersetzerin** *die*; **~, ~nen** ▶ 159 translator; ⇒ *auch* **-in**

**übersetzt** *Adj.* **A** (*bes. schweiz.: überhöht*) excessive; **B** (*Technik*) **hoch/niedrig ~ sein** have a high/low transmission ratio

**Übersetzung** *die*; **~, ~en** **A** translation; **B** (*Technik*) transmission ratio

**Übersetzungs-: ~büro** *das* translation agency; **~fehler** *der* translation error

**Über·sicht** *die* **A** overall view, overview (**über** + *Akk.* of); **die ~ [über etw.** (*Akk.*)**] verlieren** lose track [of sth.]; **B** (*Darstellung*) survey; (*Tabelle*) summary

**über·sichtlich** **1** *Adj.* clear; ‹crossroads› which allows a clear view. **2** *adv.* clearly

**Übersichtlichkeit** *die*; **~:** clarity; (*einer Kreuzung*) clear layout

**Übersichts·karte** *die* outline map

**über|siedeln¹**, **über·siedeln²** *itr. V.*; *mit sein* move (**nach** to)

**Über·sied[e]lung** /*od.* --'-(-)-/ *die* move (**nach** to)

**Über·siedler** *der*, **Über·siedlerin** *die* migrant

**über·sinnlich** *Adj.* supersensory; (*übernatürlich*) supernatural

**über·spannen** *tr. V.* **A** (*bespannen*) cover; **B** (*zu stark spannen*) over-tension, over-tighten ‹string, cable›; overdraw ‹bow›; over-tension ‹spring›; ⇒ *auch* **Bogen** C; **C** (*sich spannen über*) span ‹river, valley, etc.›

**überspannt** *Adj.* exaggerated ‹ideas, behaviour, gestures›; extreme ‹views›; inflated ‹demands, expectations›

**über·spielen** *tr. V.* **A** (*hinweggehen über*) cover up; cover up, gloss over ‹mistake›; smooth over ‹difficult situation›; **B** (*aufnehmen*) **[auf ein Tonband] ~:** transfer ‹record› to tape; put ‹record› on tape; **[auf ein anderes Tonband] ~:** transfer to another tape; **C** (*Funkw., Ferns.*) transfer; **D** (*Sport*) outplay; **die Abwehr ~:** beat the defence

**über·spitzen** *tr. V.* **etw. ~:** push *or* carry sth. too far; **überspitzt ausgedrückt könnte man sagen, dass …** to exaggerate, one might say that …

**über·sprechen** *unr. tr. V.* **etw. ~:** talk *or* speak over sth.

**über|springen¹** *unr. itr. V.*; *mit sein* **A** ‹spark, fire› jump across; **seine Begeisterung sprang auf uns alle über** (*fig.*) his enthusiasm communicated itself to all of us; **B** (*unvermittelt übergehen zu*) **auf etw.** (*Akk.*) **~:** switch abruptly to sth.

**über·springen²** *unr. tr. V.* **A** jump ‹obstacle›; **B** (*auslassen*) miss out; skip; **eine Klasse ~:** jump a class

**über|sprudeln** *itr. V.*; *mit sein* (*auch fig.*) bubble over (**von** with)

**über·spülen** *tr. V.* ‹water, waves› wash over; **bei Flut überspült** covered at high tide

**über·staatlich** *Adj.* supranational

**über|stehen¹** *unr. itr. V.*; *südd., österr., schweiz. mit sein* jut out; project

**über·stehen²** *unr. tr. V.* come through ‹danger, war, operation›; get over ‹illness›; withstand ‹heat, strain›; ‹boat› weather, ride out ‹storm›; (*überleben*) survive; **das Schlimmste ist jetzt überstanden** we're/they're *etc.* over the worst; the worst is over; **nach überstandener Gefahr** when the danger was over; **das hätten wir** *od.* **das wäre überstanden** that's 'that over with

**über·steigen** *unr. tr. V.* **A** climb over; **B** (*fig.: hinausgehen über*) exceed; **jmds. Fähigkeiten/Kräfte/Mittel ~:** be beyond sb.'s abilities/strength/means; **das übersteigt meinen Horizont** that's above my head

**über·steigern** *tr. V.* push up ‹demands, speed› too far *or* high; **ein übersteigertes Ehrgefühl** an exaggerated sense of honour

**Über·steigerung** *die* excessive increase; (*einer Forderung*) excessive pushing-up

**über·stellen** *tr. V.* transfer ‹convict›; (*an Gericht, Polizei*) hand over (**an** + *Akk.* to)

**über·steuern** **1** *tr. V.* (*Elektrot.*) overdrive. **2** *itr. V.* (*Kfz-W.*) ‹vehicle› oversteer

**über·stimmen** *tr. V.* outvote

**über·strahlen** *tr. V.* **A** (*geh.*) light up; illuminate; **Freude überstrahlte sein Gesicht** (*fig.*) his face lit up with joy; **B** (*fig.: in den Schatten stellen*) outshine

**überstrapazieren** *tr. V.*; **ich überstrapaziere, überstrapaziert, überzustrapazieren** overtax ‹person›; overstrain ‹nerves›; make excessive demands on ‹patience, willingness›; treat ‹car› too roughly; **das Prinzip wird überstrapaziert** the principle is overworked

**über·streichen** *unr. tr. V.* paint over

**über|streifen** *tr. V.* **[sich** (*Dat.*)**] etw. ~:** slip sth. on

**über|strömen¹** *itr. V.*; *mit sein* **A** (*über den Rand strömen*) overflow; **er strömt über vor Glück/Dankbarkeit** (*fig.*) he is brimming *or* bursting with happiness/gratitude; **B** (*geh.: übergehen*) ‹mood, feeling, etc.› communicate itself, spread (**auf** + *Akk.* to)

**über·strömen²** *tr. V.* flood; **von Tränen/Blut überströmt [sein]** [be] streaming with tears/blood; **eine Welle des Glücks überströmte ihn** (*fig.*) a wave of happiness flooded over him

**über|stülpen** *tr. V.* pull on ‹hat etc.›

**Über·stunde** *die*: **er hat eine ~/drei ~n gearbeitet** he did one hour's/three hours' overtime; **~n machen** *od.* **leisten** *od.* (*salopp*) **schieben** do overtime

**Überstunden·zuschlag** *der* overtime supplement; **der ~ beträgt 50%** overtime is paid at time and a half

**über·stürzen** **1** *tr. V.* rush; **nur nichts ~:** don't rush things; take it easy. **2** *refl. V.* rush; (*rasch aufeinander folgen*) ‹events, news, etc.› come thick and fast; **sich bei etw. ~:** rush sth.

**überstürzt** **1** *Adj.* hurried ‹escape, departure›; overhasty ‹decision›. **2** *adv.* ‹decide, act› overhastily; ‹depart› hurriedly

**über·tariflich** **1** *Adj.* **~e Bezahlung/Zulagen** payment/bonuses above agreed rates. **2** *adv.* **jmdn. ~ bezahlen** pay sb. above agreed rates

**über·teuert** *Adj.* over-expensive

**übertölpeln** *tr. V.* dupe; con (*coll.*)

**Übertölpelung** *die*; **~, ~en** duping; conning (*coll.*)

**über·tönen** *tr. V.* drown out

**Über·topf** *der* [decorative] outer pot

**Übertrag** /ˈy:bɐtra:k/ *der*; **~[e]s, Überträge** /-trɛ:gə/ (*bes. Buchf.*) carry-over

**über·tragbar** *Adj.* transferable (**auf** + *Akk.* to); (*auf etw. anderes anwendbar*) applicable (**auf** + *Akk.* to); (*übersetzbar*) translatable; (*ansteckend*) communicable, infectious ‹disease›

**über·tragen** **1** *unr. tr. V.* **A** transfer (**auf** + *Akk.* to); transmit ‹power, torque, etc.› (**auf** + *Akk.* to); communicate ‹disease, illness› (**auf** + *Akk.* to); carry over ‹subtotal›; (*auf etw. anderes anwenden*) apply (**auf** + *Akk.* to); (*übersetzen*) translate; render; **ein Stenogramm in Langschrift ~:** write a piece of shorthand out in longhand; (*mit der Schreibmaschine*) type out a piece of shorthand; **eine Erzählung in Verse ~:** put a story into verse; **etw. ins reine** *od.* **in die Reinschrift ~:** make a fair copy of sth.; **etw. in ein Heft ~:** copy sth. out into a book; **seine Begeisterung** *usw.* **auf jmdn. ~:** communicate one's enthusiasm *etc.* to sb.; **etw. vom** *od.* **aus dem Englischen ins Deutsche ~:** translate sth. from English into German; **in ~er Bedeutung, im ~en Sinne** in a transferred sense; **B** (*senden*) broadcast ‹concert, event, match, etc.›; (*im Fernsehen*) televise; **etw. direkt** *or* **live ~:** broadcast/televise sth. live; **etw. im Fernsehen ~:** televise sth.; **C** (*geben*) **jmdm. Aufgaben/Pflichten** *usw.* **~:** hand over tasks/duties *etc.* to sb.; (*anvertrauen*) entrust sb. with tasks/duties *etc.*; **jmdm. ein Recht ~:** confer a right on sb.; **D** (*Med.: zu lange nicht gebären*) **sie hat ihr Kind ~:** she had a post-term birth; **ein ~es Kind** a post-term infant.
**2** *refl. V.* **sich auf jmdn. ~** ‹disease, illness› be communicated *or* be passed on to sb.; (*fig.*) ‹enthusiasm, nervousness, etc.› communicate itself to sb.

**Über·träger** *der* (*Med.*) carrier

**Übertragung** *die*; **~, ~en** **A** ⇒ **übertragen** 1 A: transference; transmission; communication; carrying over; application; translation; rendering; **die ~ einer Erzählung in Verse** putting a story into verse; **die ~ der Krankheit erfolgt über das Trinkwasser** the disease is spread through drinking water; **B** (*das Senden*) broadcasting; (*Programm, Sendung*) broadcast; (*im Fernsehen*) televising/television broadcast; **C** (*von Aufgaben, Pflichten usw.*) entrusting; (*von Rechten*) conferral; **D** (*Med.: eines Kindes*) post-term birth

**Übertragungs·wagen** *der* outside broadcast vehicle; OB vehicle

**über·trainiert** *Adj.* overtrained

**über·treffen** *unr. tr. V.* **A** surpass, outdo (**an** + *Dat.* in); break ‹record›; **jmdn. an Ausdauer ~:** be superior to sb. in stamina; **jmdn. an Fleiß/Intelligenz ~:** be more diligent/intelligent than sb.; **jmdn. in einem Fach/einem Sport ~:** be better than sb. at a subject/a sport; **in etw.** (*Dat.*) **nicht zu ~ sein** be unbeatable at sth.; **sich selbst ~:** excel oneself; **B** (*übersteigen*) exceed; exceed, surpass ‹expectations›

**über·treiben** *unr. tr. V.* **A** *auch itr.* exaggerate; **B** (*zu weit treiben*) overdo; take *or* carry too far; take *or* push ‹claim, demand› too far; **es mit etw. ~:** take *or* carry sth. too far; **man kann es auch ~:** you can take things *or* go too far

**Übertreibung** *die*; **~, ~en** exaggeration; **er neigt zu ~en** he tends to exaggerate

**über|treten¹** *unr. itr. V.*; *mit sein* **A** *auch mit haben* (*Sport*) step over the line/step out of the circle; **B** (*überwechseln*) change sides; **zu einer anderen Partei ~:** join another party; switch parties; **[von der KPD] zur SPD ~:** switch [from the KPD] to the SPD; **zum Katholizismus/Islam ~:** convert to Catholicism/Islam; **C** (*gelangen*) **in etw.** (*Akk.*) **~:** enter sth.

U

**über·treten²** *unr. tr. V.* break, contravene ‹law›; infringe, violate ‹regulation, prohibition›

**Übertretung** *die;* ~, ~en [A] ⇒ übertreten²: breaking; contravention; infringement; violation; [B] (*Vergehen*) misdemeanour

**Übertretungs·fall** *der:* **im ~[e]** (*Amtsspr.*) if the law is contravened; in the event of an infringement *or* a violation

**übertrieben** /-tri:bn/ ❶ *2. Part. v.* **übertreiben.** ❷ exaggerated; (*übermäßig*) excessive ‹care, thrift, etc.›; **das finde ich reichlich ~:** I really think that's going too far. ❸ *adv.* excessively

**Über·tritt** *der* change of allegiance, switch (**zu** to); (*Rel.*) conversion (**zu** to)

**über·trumpfen** *tr. V.* [A] (*Kartenspiel*) trump; [B] (*übertreffen*) outdo

**über·tünchen** *tr. V.* cover with whitewash; (*fig.*) cover up

**über·übermorgen** *Adv.* in three days' time

**übervölkern** /-'fœlkɐn/ *tr. V.* overpopulate

**Übervölkerung** *die;* ~: overpopulation

**über·voll** *Adj.* overfull; overcrowded, packed ‹room, train, tram, etc.›; packed ‹theatre, cinema›

**über·vorsichtig** ❶ *Adj.* overcautious. ❷ *adv.* overcautiously

**über·vor·teilen** *tr. V.* cheat

**über·wachen** *tr. V.* watch, keep under surveillance ‹suspect, agent, area, etc.›; supervise ‹factory, workers, process›; control ‹traffic›; monitor ‹progress, production process, experiment, patient›; **die Polizei überwacht sein Telefon** the police are monitoring his telephone calls; **er überwacht jeden ihrer Schritte** he watches her every move

**über·wachsen** *unr. tr. V.* overgrow

**Überwachung** *die;* ~, ~en ⇒ überwachen: surveillance; supervision; controlling; monitoring

**Überwachungs·kamera** *die* security camera

**überwältigen** /-'vɛltɪgn̩/ *tr. V.* [A] overpower; [B] (*fig.*) ‹sleep, emotion, fear, etc.› overcome; ‹sight, impressions, beauty, etc.› overwhelm; **von Rührung überwältigt werden** be overcome with emotion

**überwältigend** ❶ *Adj.* overwhelming ‹sight, impression, victory, majority, etc.›; overpowering ‹smell›; stunning ‹beauty›; **das ist nicht [gerade] ~:** that isn't [exactly] anything to write home about (*coll.*). ❷ *adv.* stunningly ‹beautiful›; **das hat er ~ gespielt** he played that quite magnificently

**über·wälzen** *tr. V.* (*bes. Wirtsch.*) pass on ‹costs etc.› (**auf** + *Akk.* to); shift ‹burden, blame, responsibility› (**auf** + *Akk.* on to)

**über|wechseln** *itr. V.; mit sein* [A] cross over (**auf** + *Akk.* to); **auf eine andere Spur ~:** change lanes; move to another lane; [B] (*übertreten*) change sides; **ins feindliche Lager/zur anderen Partei ~:** go over to the enemy/the other party; **von der SPD zur KPD ~:** switch from the SPD to the KPD; [C] (*mit etw. anderem beginnen*) **zu etw. ~:** change over to sth.; **zu einem anderen Thema ~:** turn to another topic; **aufs Gymnasium ~:** go on to grammar school

**über·weisen** *unr. tr. V.* [A] transfer ‹money› (**an, auf** + *Akk.* to); **er bekommt sein Gehalt [auf sein Konto] überwiesen** his salary is paid into his account; [B] (*zu einem anderen Arzt schicken*) refer (**an** + *Akk.* to); **jmdn. in die Klinik ~:** refer sb. to the clinic; [C] (*zuleiten*) refer ‹proposal› (**an** + *Akk.* to); pass on ‹file, application› (**an** + *Akk.* to)

**Über·weisung** *die* [A] transfer (**an, auf** + *Akk.* to); [B] (*Summe*) remittance; [C] (*eines Patienten*) referral (**an** + *Akk.* to); [D] ⇒ **Überweisungsschein**

**Überweisungs-:** **~auftrag** *der* (*Bankw.*) [credit] transfer order; **~formular** *das* (*Bankw.*) [credit] transfer form; **~schein** *der* (*Med.*) certificate of referral

**Über·weite** *die* outsize; **Röcke in ~n** outsize skirts

*old spelling (see note on page 1707)

**über|werfen¹** *unr. tr. V.* throw on ‹clothes›; **er warf dem Pferd eine Decke über** he threw a blanket over the horse

**über·werfen²** *unr. refl. V.* **sich mit jmdm. ~:** fall out with sb.; **sie haben sich überworfen** they have fallen out

**über·wiegen** ❶ *unr. itr. V.* predominate; **es überwog die Einsicht, dass ...** the recognition prevailed that ... ❷ *unr. tr. V.* ‹advantages, disadvantages, etc.› outweigh; ‹emotion, argument› prevail over

**überwiegend** ❶ /*auch* --'--/ *Adj.* overwhelming; **der ~e Teil der Bevölkerung** the majority of the population. ❷ *adv.* mainly

**über·winden** ❶ *unr. tr. V.* [A] overcome ‹resistance›; overcome, surmount ‹difficulty, obstacle, gradient›; conquer ‹capitalism, apartheid, etc.›; overcome, get over ‹fear, inhibitions, disappointment, grief›; get past ‹stage›; [B] (*aufgeben*) overcome ‹doubt, misgivings, reservations, suspicions›; give up ‹way of thinking, point of view›; [C] (*geh.: besiegen*) overcome; vanquish (*literary*). ❷ *unr. refl. V.* overcome one's reluctance; **sich [dazu] ~, etw. zu tun** bring oneself to do sth.; **ich konnte mich nur schwer [dazu] ~, es zu tun** I could hardly bring myself to do it; **dazu konnte ich mich nicht ~:** I could not bring myself to do that

**Über·windung** *die* [A] ⇒ **überwinden** 1 A: overcoming; surmounting; conquest; getting over/past; [B] (*Besiegung*) overcoming; vanquishing (*literary*); [C] (*das Sichüberwinden*) **es war eine große ~ für ihn** it cost him a great effort; **das hat mich viel ~ gekostet** that was a real effort of will for me

**über·wintern** ❶ *itr. V.* [over]winter; spend the winter. ❷ *tr. V.* overwinter ‹plant›

**über·wölben** *tr. V.* arch over

**über·wuchern** *tr. V.* overgrow

**Über·wurf** *der* [A] (*Umhang*) wrap; [B] (*österr.*) ⇒ **Zierdecke**; [C] (*Ringen*) shoulder throw

**Über·zahl** *die* majority; **in der ~ sein** be in the majority; ‹army, enemy› be superior in numbers

**überzählig** /-tsɛlɪç/ *Adj.* surplus; spare; **einige Damen waren ~:** there were a few ladies too many

**über·zeichnen** *tr. V.* [A] (*Börsenw.*) oversubscribe; [B] (*zugespitzt darstellen*) overdraw ‹figure, character, etc.›

**Über·zeit** *die* (*schweiz.*) overtime

**überzeugen** ❶ *tr. V.* convince; (*umstimmen*) persuade; convince; **jmdn. von etw. ~:** convince/persuade sb. of sth. ❷ *itr. V.* be convincing. ❸ *refl. V.* convince *or* satisfy oneself; **sich persönlich** *od.* **mit eigenen Augen [von etw.] ~:** see [sth.] for oneself

**überzeugend** ❶ *Adj.* convincing; convincing, persuasive ‹arguments, proof, words, speech›. ❷ *adv.* convincingly; ‹argue, speak› convincingly, persuasively

**überzeugt** *Adj.* [A] convinced; [B] **von etw. ~ sein** (*etw. hoch einschätzen*) be convinced by sth.; **er ist sehr von sich [selbst] ~:** he's very sure of himself

**Über·zeugung** *die* [A] convincing; (*das Umstimmen*) persuasion; [B] (*feste Meinung*) conviction; **der festen ~ sein, dass ...** be firmly convinced that ...; **zu der ~ kommen** *od.* **gelangen, dass ...** become convinced that ...; **meiner ~ nach ...** I am convinced that ...

**Überzeugungs-:** **~arbeit** *die* propaganda work; **~kraft** *die* power[s] of persuasion; persuasiveness; **mit ~kraft reden** speak persuasively; **~täter** *der,* **~täterin** *die* (*Rechtsspr.*) offender who has acted on grounds of conscience

**über|ziehen¹** *unr. tr. V.* [A] pull on ‹clothes›; [B] **jmdm. eins** *od.* **ein paar ~** (*ugs.*) give sb. a clout

**über·ziehen²** ❶ *unr. tr. V.* [A] **etw. mit etw. ~:** cover sth. with sth.; **die Torte mit Guss ~:** glaze the gateau; **die Betten frisch ~:** put clean sheets on the beds; change the sheets on the beds; **das Land mit Krieg ~** (*fig.*) spread war over the land; [B] overdraw ‹account› (**um** by); **sie hat ihr Konto [um 300 Mark] überzogen** she is [300 marks] overdrawn; **seinen Urlaub ~:** take too much time off; **die Mittagspause um 10 Minuten ~:** take an extra ten minutes over lunch; **die vorgesehene Sendezeit [um drei Minuten] ~:** overrun the programme time [by three minutes]; [C] (*übertreiben*) overdo ‹criticism etc.›; **überzogene Leistungen/Erwartungen/Preiserhöhungen** *usw.* excessive payments/expectations/price increases *etc.* ❷ *unr. itr. V.* [A] overdraw one's account; go overdrawn; [B] (*bei einer Sendung, einem Vortrag*) overrun. ❸ *unr. refl. V.* ‹sky› cloud over, become overcast

**Überzieher** *der;* ~s, ~ [A] (*veralt.: Herrenmantel*) [light] overcoat; [B] (*salopp: Kondom*) johnny (*Brit. sl.*); rubber (*sl.*)

**Überziehungs·kredit** *der* (*Finanzw.*) overdraft facility

**überzüchtet** /y:bɐ'tsʏçtət/ *Adj.* overbred; over-sophisticated ‹engines, systems›

**über·zuckern** *tr. V.* sugar

**Überzug** *der* [A] (*Beschichtung*) coating; [B] (*Bezug*) cover

**üblich** /'y:plɪç/ *Adj.* usual; (*normal*) normal; (*gebräuchlich*) customary; **das ist hier so ~:** that's the accepted *or* (*coll.*) done thing here; **das ist nicht mehr ~:** that's no longer done (*coll.*); **wie ~:** as usual; **sie gebrauchte die ~e Ausrede** she used the same old excuse

**üblicher·weise** *Adv.* usually; generally

**U-Boot** *das* submarine; sub (*coll.*)

**übrig** /'y:brɪç/ *Adj.* remaining *attrib.;* (*ander...*) other; **alle ~en Gäste sind bereits gegangen** all the other guests have already gone; **das/alles ~e erzähle ich dir später** I'll tell you the rest/all the rest later; **die/alle ~en** the/all the rest *or* others; **im ~en** besides; **ein ~es tun** (*geh.*) do one last thing; **es ist etwas ~:** there is some left; **es ist noch Suppe ~:** there is some soup left [over]; **ich habe noch Geld ~:** I [still] have some money left; (*ich habe mehr Geld, als ich brauche*) I [still] have some money to spare; **hast du vielleicht eine Mark [für mich] ~?** can you spare me a mark?; **für jmdn./etw. wenig/nichts ~ haben** have little/no time for sb./sth. (*fig.*); **etw. ~ behalten** have sth. left over; **~ bleiben** be left; remain; ‹food, drink› be left over; **ihm bleibt nichts [anderes** *od.* **weiter] ~, als zu ...** he has no [other] choice but to ...; there is nothing he can do but to ...; **~ lassen** + *Akk.* leave; leave ‹food, drink› over; **lasst mir etwas davon ~:** leave some of it for me; **zu wünschen ~ lassen** leave something to be desired; **sehr** *od.* **viel/nichts zu wünschen ~ lassen** leave much *or* (*coll.*) a lot/nothing to be desired

**übrig-:** ***~|behalten** ⇒ übrig; ***~|bleiben** ⇒ übrig

**übrigens** /'y:brɪgn̩s/ *Adv.* by the way; incidentally

***übrig|lassen** ⇒ übrig

**Übung** /'y:bʊŋ/ *die;* ~, ~en [A] exercise; [B] (*das Üben, Geübtsein*) practice; **das erfordert ~:** that takes practice; **das macht die ~, das ist alles nur ~:** it's [just] a question of practice; **etw. zur ~ tun** do sth. for practice; **außer ~ sein** be out of practice; **~/viel ~/keine ~ haben** have had some/a lot of (*coll.*)/no practice; **aus der ~ kommen** get out of practice; **in der ~ sein/bleiben** be/stay in practice; **~ macht den Meister** (*Spr.*) practice makes perfect (*prov.*); [C] (*Lehrveranstaltung*) class; seminar

**übungs-, Übungs-:** **~buch** *das* book of exercises; (*Lehrbuch*) textbook with exercises; **~halber** *Adv.* for practice; **~munition** *die* (*Milit.*) blank ammunition; **~sache** *die:* **~sache sein** be a matter of practice

**UdSSR** *Abk.* **Union der Sozialistischen Sowjetrepubliken** USSR

**UEFA** /u:'e:fa:/*die;* ~ (*Fußball*) UEFA

**U-Eisen** *das* channel iron

**Ufer** /'u:fɐ/ *das;* ~s, ~ ▶ 306 bank; (*des Meers*) shore; **ans ~ gespült werden** be washed ashore; **der Fluss trat über die ~:** the river burst its banks; **das sichere ~ erreichen** reach dry land; **das Haus liegt direkt am ~:** the house is right by the lake/river/sea

**ufer-, Ufer-: ~befestigung** *die* bank reinforcement; **~böschung** *die* [river/canal] embankment; **~los** *Adj.* limitless; boundless ‹love, indulgence, etc.›; endless ‹discussions, talks, quarrel, subject›; **ins Uferlose gehen** ‹plans, ambitions, etc.› know no bounds; **~promenade** *die* riverside walk; (*am Meer*) promenade; **~straße** *die* riverside/lakeside road; (*am Meer*) coast road

**uff** /ʊf/ *Interj.* oof; phew

**UFO, Ufo** /'u:fo/ *das;* **~[s], ~s** UFO

**u-förmig, U-förmig** *Adj.* U-shaped

**UG** *Abk.* **Untergeschoss**

**Uganda** /u'ganda/ *(das);* **~s** Uganda

**Ugander** /u'gandɐ/ *der;* **~s, ~, Uganderin** *die;* **~, ~nen** ▶553 Ugandan; ⇒ *auch* **-in**

**ugandisch** *Adj.* ▶553 Ugandan

**U-Haft** *die* ⇒ **Untersuchungshaft**

**Uhr** /u:ɐ̯/ *die;* **~, ~en** ▶752 Ⓐ clock; (*Armband~, Taschen~*) watch; (*Wasser~, Gas~*) meter; (*an Messinstrumenten*) dial; gauge; **auf die** *od.* **nach der ~ sehen** look at the time; **ein Arbeiter, der dauernd auf die ~ sieht** a worker who is always clock-watching; **nach meiner ~:** by *or* according to my clock/watch; **jmds. ~ ist abgelaufen** (*fig.*) the sands of time have run out for sb.; **wissen, was die ~ geschlagen hat** (*fig.*) know what's what; know how things stand; **rund um die ~** (*ugs.*) round the clock; Ⓑ (*bei Uhrzeitangaben*) **acht ~:** eight o'clock; **acht ~ dreißig** half past eight; 8.30 /eɪt'θɜ:tɪ/; **wie viel ~ ist es?** what's the time?; what time is it?; **um wie viel ~ treffen wir uns?** [at] what time shall we meet?; when shall we meet?

**Uhr·armband** *das* watch strap

**Uhren·industrie** *die* clock- and watchmaking industry

**Uhr-: ~glas** *das* watch glass; **~kette** *die* watch chain; **~macher,** *der,* **~macherin** *die* ▶159 watchmaker/clockmaker; **~werk** *das* clock/watch mechanism; **~zeiger** *der* clock/watch hand; **~zeiger·sinn** *der:* **im ~zeigersinn** clockwise; **entgegen dem ~zeigersinn** anticlockwise; **~zeit** *die* ▶752 time; **jmdn. nach der ~zeit fragen** ask sb. the time; **hast du [die] genaue ~zeit?** do you have the exact time?

**Uhu** /'u:hu/ *der;* **~s, ~s** eagle owl

**Ukas** /'u:kas/ *der;* **~ses, ~se** (*scherzh.*) edict

**Ukraine** /ukrai̯nə/ *die;* **~:** Ukraine

**Ukrainer** *der;* **~s, ~, Ukrainerin** *die;* **~, ~nen** ▶553 Ukrainian

**ukrainisch** *Adj.* ▶696 Ukrainian; ⇒ *auch* **deutsch**

**UKW** *Abk.* **Ultrakurzwelle** VHF

**UKW-Sender** *der* VHF station; ≈ FM station

**Ulan** /u'la:n/ *der;* **~en, ~en** (*hist.*) uhlan

**Ulk** /ʊlk/ *der;* **~s, ~e** lark (*coll.*); (*Streich*) trick; [practical] joke; **etw. aus ~ sagen/tun** say/do sth. for fun *or* (*coll.*) for a laugh

**ulken** *itr. V.* clown *or* (*coll.*) lark about; **über jmdn./etw. ~:** make fun of sb./sth.

**ulkig** (*ugs.*) ❶ *Adj.* funny. ❷ *adv.* in a funny way

**Ulkus** /'ʊlkʊs/ *das;* **~, Ulzera** ▶474 /'ʊltsera/ (*Med.*) ulcer

**Ulme** /'ʊlmə/ *die;* **~, ~n** Ⓐ elm [tree]; Ⓑ (*Holz*) elm[wood]

**Ultima Ratio** /'ʊltima 'ra:tsi̯o/ *die;* **~ ~** (*geh.*) last resort

**ultimativ** /ʊltima'ti:f/ ❶ *Adj.* Ⓐ ‹demand› made as an ultimatum; **~en Charakter haben** constitute an ultimatum; Ⓑ ultimate; **die ~e Videoanlage** the ultimate video recorder *or* ultimate in video recorders. ❷ *adv.* **etw. ~ fordern** demand sth. in [the form of] an ultimatum; **jmdn. ~ auffordern, etw. zu tun** give sb. an ultimatum to do sth.

**Ultimatum** /ʊlti'ma:tʊm/ *das;* **~s, Ultimaten** ultimatum; **[jmdm.] ein ~ stellen** give *or* set [sb.] an ultimatum

**Ultimo** /'ʊltimo/ *der;* **~s, ~s** last day of the month

**Ultra** /'ʊltra/ *der;* **~s, ~s** extremist

**Ultra·kurz·welle** /ʊltra'kʊrtsvɛlə/ *die* Ⓐ (*Phys., Funkw., Rundf.*) ultra-short wave; Ⓑ (*Rundf.: Wellenbereich*) very high frequency; VHF

**Ultrakurzwellen·sender** *der* very high frequency station; VHF station; ≈ FM station

**ultra-, Ultra-: ~marin** *indekl. Adj.* ultramarine; **~marin** *das;* **~~s** ultramarine; **~montan** *Adj.* (*geh.*) ultramontane; **~schall** /'---/ *der* (*Physik, Med.*) ultrasound

**Ultraschall-: ~behandlung** *die* (*Med.*) ultrasound therapy *or* treatment; (*Technik*) ultrasound treatment; **~untersuchung** *die* (*Med.*) ultrasound examination

**ultra·violett** *Adj.* (*Physik*) ultraviolet

**Ulzera** ⇒ **Ulkus**

**um** /ʊm/ ❶ *Präp. mit Akk.* Ⓐ (*räumlich*) [a]round; **um etw. herum** [a]round sth.; **um das Haus gehen** walk round the house; **das Rad dreht sich um seine Achse** the wheel turns on its axle; **um die Ecke** round the corner; **um sich schlagen** lash *or* hit out; **er warf mit Steinen um sich** he threw stones around *or* about; ⇒ *auch* **greifen** 2 A; **scharen** 2; Ⓑ (*zeitlich*) (*genau*) at; (*etwa*) around [about]; **der Unterricht beginnt um acht [Uhr]** lessons start at eight [o'clock]; **um den 20. August [herum]** around [about] 20 August; **um die Mittagszeit [herum]** around midday; Ⓒ **Tag um Tag/Stunde um Stunde** day after day/hour after hour; **Meter um Meter/Schritt um Schritt** metre by metre/step by step; Ⓓ (*bei Maß- u. Mengenangaben*) by; **die Temperatur stieg um 5 Grad** the temperature rose [by] five degrees; **um 3 cm zu lang sein** be 3 cm too long; **um nichts/einiges/vieles besser sein** be no/somewhat/a lot better; Ⓔ (*südd., österr.: bei Preisangaben*) for.

❷ *Adv.* Ⓐ (*etwa, ungefähr*) around; about; **um [die] 10 Mark/50 Personen [herum]** around *or* about *or* round about ten marks/50 people; Ⓑ (*ugs.: vorüber, vorbei*) over; **um sein** ‹time› be up.

❸ *Konj.* Ⓐ (*final*) **um ... zu** [in order] to; **um es gleich zu sagen, ich kann nicht lange bleiben** I'd better say straight away that I can't stay for long; Ⓑ (*konsekutiv*) **er ist groß genug/ist noch zu klein, um ... zu ...** he is big enough/is still too young to ...; **sie heirateten, um sich schon nach einem Jahr wieder scheiden zu lassen** they got married, only to get divorced again after just one year; ⇒ *auch* **umso**

**um|ackern** *tr. V.* plough over

**um|adressieren** *tr. V.* redirect

**um|ändern** *tr. V.* change; alter; revise ‹text, novel›; alter ‹garment›

**um|arbeiten** *tr. V.* alter ‹garment›; revise, rework ‹text, novel, music›; **einen Roman zu einem Drama/Drehbuch ~:** adapt a novel for the stage/screen

**Umarbeitung** *die;* **~, ~en** (*eines Kleidungsstücks*) alteration; (*eines Romans, Textes, Musikstücks*) revision; reworking; (*zu einem Drehbuch, Drama o. Ä.*) adaptation

**umarmen** *tr. V.* embrace; put one's arms around; (*an sich drücken*) hug; **sie umarmten sich** they embraced/hugged; **sei umarmt [von deiner/deinem ...]** (*als Briefschluss*) lots of love [from ...]

**Umarmung** *die;* **~, ~en** ⇒ **umarmen**: embrace; hug

**Um·bau** *der; Pl.* **~ten** Ⓐ rebuilding; reconstruction; (*kleinere Änderung*) alteration; (*zu etw. anderem*) conversion; (*fig.: eines Systems, einer Verwaltung*) reorganization; **„wegen ~[s] geschlossen"** 'closed for alterations'; **das Gebäude befindet sich im ~:** the building is being rebuilt/altered/converted; Ⓑ (*das Umgebaute*) ⇒ **a**: reconstruction/altered building/conversion

**um|bauen**[1] *tr., auch itr. V.* rebuild; reconstruct; (*leicht ändern*) alter; (*zu etw. anderem*) convert (**zu** into); (*fig.*) reorganize ‹system, administration, etc.›; **das Bühnenbild ~:** change the set; **wir bauen um** we're rebuilding/making alterations

**um·bauen**[2] *tr. V.* surround; **umbauter Raum** interior space

**um|behalten** *unr. tr. V.* keep ‹apron, scarf, etc.› on

**um|benennen** *unr. tr. V.* change the name of, rename ‹street, square, etc.›; **etw. in etw. (Akk.) ~:** change the name of sth. to sth.; rename sth. sth.

**um|beschreiben** *unr. tr. V.* (*Geom.*) circumscribe

**um|besetzen** *tr., auch itr. V.* change ‹team›; recast ‹role, play›; reallocate ‹post, position›

**um|bestellen** *itr. V.* change the order

**um|betten** *tr. V.* Ⓐ **jmdn. ~:** move sb. to another bed; Ⓑ (*in ein anderes Grab legen*) move *or* transfer ‹body› to another grave

**um|biegen** ❶ *unr. tr. V.* bend. ❷ *unr. itr. V.; mit sein* turn; ‹path› bend, turn

**um|bilden** *tr. V.* reorganize, reconstruct ‹department etc.›; reshuffle ‹government, cabinet›; **etw. zu etw. ~** (*Biol.*) develop sth. into sth.

**um|binden** *unr. tr. V.* put on ‹tie, apron, scarf, etc.›

**um|blasen** *unr. tr. V.* blow over

**um|blättern** ❶ *tr. V.* turn [over] ‹page›. ❷ *itr. V.* turn the page/pages

**um|blicken** *refl. V.* Ⓐ look around; **sich nach allen Seiten ~:** look all around; Ⓑ (*zurückblicken*) [turn to] look back (**nach** at)

**Umbra** /'ʊmbra/ *die;* **~** (*Farbe*) umber

**um·branden** *tr. V.* (*geh.*) surge around

**um·brausen** *tr. V.* roar around

**um|brechen**[1] ❶ *unr. tr. V.* Ⓐ bring down ‹telephone pole, tree, etc.›; Ⓑ (*umpflügen*) break up, turn over ‹land›; plough up ‹field›. ❷ *unr. itr. V.; mit sein* collapse; fall down

**um·brechen**[2] *unr. tr. V.* (*Druckw.*) make up

**um|bringen** *unr. tr. V.* kill; **dieses Material ist nicht umzubringen** (*fig. ugs.*) this material is indestructible; **diese Packerei bringt mich fast um** (*fig. ugs.*) all this packing's nearly killing me (*coll.*); **sich vor Höflichkeit ~** (*fig. ugs.*) fall over oneself to be polite (*coll.*); **sich für jmdn. ~** (*fig. ugs.*) do everything for sb.

**Um·bruch** *der* Ⓐ radical change; (*Umwälzung*) upheaval; **im ~ sein** be in a state of flux; Ⓑ (*Druckw.*) make-up; (*Ergebnis*) page proofs *pl.*

**um|buchen** ❶ *tr. V.* Ⓐ change ‹flight, journey route› (**auf** + *Akk.* to); Ⓑ (*Finanzw.*) transfer (**auf** + *Akk.* to). ❷ *itr. V.* change one's booking (**auf** + *Akk.* to)

**Um·buchung** *die* Ⓐ change of booking; **eine ~ Ihres Fluges ist jederzeit möglich** you can change your flight at any time; Ⓑ (*Finanzw.*) transfer (**auf** + *Akk.* to)

**um|datieren** *tr. V.* change the date of; redate ‹contract, letter, etc.›

**um|denken** *unr. itr. V.* revise one's thinking; rethink; **ein Prozess des Umdenkens** a process of rethinking

**um|deuten** *tr. V.* reinterpret; give a new interpretation to

**um|dichten** *tr. V.* adapt, recast ‹poem, song, etc.›

**um|disponieren** *itr. V.* change one's arrangements; make new arrangements

**um·drängen** *tr. V.* crowd round; mob ‹actor, pop star, etc.›

**um|drehen** ❶ *tr. V.* turn round; turn over ‹coin, hand, etc.›; turn ‹key›; turn ‹pockets, bag, garment, sock, etc.› inside out; **jede Mark** *od.* **jeden Pfennig [dreimal] ~** (*ugs.*) watch every penny; **einen Spion ~** (*fig.*) turn a spy. ❷ *refl. V.* turn round; (*den Kopf wenden*) turn one's head; **sich nach jmdm. ~:** turn/turn one's head to look at sb.; **ein Mädchen, nach dem sich die Männer ~:** a girl who turns men's heads. ❸ *itr. V.; auch mit sein* (*ugs.: umkehren*) turn back; (*ugs.: wenden*) turn round

**Um·drehung** *die* turn; (*eines Motors usw.*) revolution; rev (*coll.*); (*eines Planeten*) rotation

**um·einander** *Adv.* **sich ~ kümmern/sorgen** take care of/worry about each other *or*

# Uhrzeit

***Wie viel Uhr ist es?, Wie spät ist es?***
= What time is it?, What's the time?
***Könnten Sie mir sagen, wie spät es ist?***
= Could you tell me the time?
***Wie viel Uhr hast du?***
= What time do you make it?
***Nach meiner Uhr ist es fünf vor/zehn nach neun***
= By my watch it's five to/ten past nine
***Meine Uhr geht vor/nach***
= My watch is fast/slow
***Es war soeben zehn Uhr***
= It's just after *od.* just gone ten [o'clock]
***Es ist elf Uhr vorbei***
= It's gone eleven [o'clock]
***Es ist gleich sieben***
= It's coming up to seven

Im englischsprachigen Raum wird hauptsächlich die 12-Stunden-Uhr verwendet, mit den Zusätzen **a.m.** = ante meridiem = vor Mittag, also morgens, und **p.m.** = post meridiem = nach Mittag, also nachmittags oder abends. Der Ausdruck **o'clock** wird nur bei Uhrzeitangaben verwendet, die sich auf die volle Stunde beziehen. Danach steht statt a.m. bzw. p.m. **in the morning** bzw. **in the afternoon/evening**. Die 24-Stunden-Uhr wird meist nur beim Militär, in der Luftfahrt und für Fahrpläne benutzt. In der folgenden Aufstellung werden Beispiele ihrer hauptsächlich militärischen Form gegeben (jeweils nach dem Schrägstrich).

| GESCHRIEBEN | GESPROCHEN |
|---|---|
| ***1 Uhr***<br>= 1.00 a.m./0100 | ***ein Uhr, eins***<br>one [a.m. *od.* in the morning]/one hundred hours |
| ***13 Uhr***<br>= 1.00 p.m./1300 | ***dreizehn Uhr, ein Uhr mittags***<br>one [p.m. *od.* in the afternoon]/thirteen hundred hours |
| ***2.05 Uhr***<br>= 2.05 a.m./0205 | ***fünf [Minuten] nach zwei, zwei Uhr fünf***<br>five past two [in the morning]/[o] two o five |
| ***14.05 Uhr***<br>= 2.05 p.m./1405 | ***vierzehn Uhr fünf***<br>five past two [in the afternoon]/fourteen o five |
| ***4.15 Uhr***<br>= 4.15 a.m./0415 | ***Viertel od. fünfzehn Minuten nach vier, vier Uhr fünfzehn***<br>four fifteen [a.m.], a quarter past four [in the morning]/[o] four fifteen |
| ***16.15 Uhr***<br>= 4.15 p.m./1615 | ***sechzehn Uhr fünfzehn***<br>four fifteen [p.m.], a quarter past four [in the afternoon] |
| ***5.30 Uhr***<br>= 5.30 a.m./0530 | ***halb sechs, fünf Uhr dreißig***<br>five thirty [a.m.], half past five [in the morning]/[o] five thirty |
| ***17.30 Uhr***<br>= 5.30 p.m./1730 | ***siebzehn Uhr dreißig***<br>five thirty [p.m.], half past five [in the afternoon]/seventeen thirty |
| ***7.45 Uhr***<br>= 7.45 a.m./0745 | ***Viertel od. fünfzehn Minuten vor acht, sieben Uhr fünfundvierzig***<br>seven forty-five [a.m.], a quarter to eight [in the morning]/[o] seven forty-five |
| ***19.45 Uhr***<br>= 7.45 p.m./1945 | ***neunzehn Uhr fünfundvierzig***<br>seven forty-five p.m., a quarter to eight [in the evening]/nineteen forty-five |
| ***0 Uhr, 24 Uhr***<br>= 12.00 [midnight]/0000, 2400* | ***null Uhr, vierundzwanzig Uhr***<br>twelve [o'clock], [twelve] midnight/oo double o, twenty-four hundred hours* |
| ***12 Uhr***<br>= 12 [noon]/1200 | ***zwölf Uhr***<br>twelve [o'clock], [twelve] noon/twelve hundred hours |

*Beim 24-Stunden-System zeigt 0000 = null Uhr den Tagesbeginn an, 2400 = vierundzwanzig Uhr das Tagesende.

## Wann?

***um + Uhrzeit***
= **at** + Uhrzeit
***Er kam um acht Uhr***
= He came at eight o'clock
***Um wie viel Uhr wollen Sie frühstücken?***
= [At] what time do you want breakfast?
***um halb***
= at half past
***um halb neun***
= at half past eight *od.* (*ugs.*) half eight
***Punkt sechs, genau um sechs***
= at six exactly, on the dot of six
***gegen zehn***
= at about ten
***spätestens um zwölf***
= at twelve at the latest
***Es muss bis elf fertig sein***
= It must be ready by eleven
***Ich bin heute bis achtzehn Uhr hier***
= I'll be here until six this evening
***Ich bin erst um sechs dort***
= I won't be there until six
***von 13 bis 14 Uhr geschlossen***
= closed from 1 to 2 p.m.
***stündlich zur vollen Stunde***
= every hour on the hour

U

one another; ~ **besorgt sein** be concerned about each other *or* one another; **sich ~ drehen** revolve around each other
**um|erziehen** *tr. V.* re-educate; **jmdn. zu etw. ~:** re-educate sb. to be *or* as sth.
**um|fahren**[1] *unr. tr. V.* knock over *or* down
**um·fahren**[2] *unr. tr. V.* go round; make a detour round ‹obstruction, busy area›; (*im Auto*) drive *or* go round; (*im Schiff*) sail *or* go round; (*auf einer Umgehungsstraße*) bypass ‹town, village, etc.›
**Umfahrungs·straße** *die* (*österr., schweiz.*) ⇒ **Umgehungsstraße**
**Um·fall** *der* (*ugs. abwertend*) about-face; U-turn
**um|fallen** *unr. itr. V.; mit sein* **A** (*umstürzen*) fall over; **B** (*zusammenbrechen*) collapse; **tot ~:** fall down dead; ~ **wie die Fliegen** go down like flies; **ich falle vor Müdigkeit um** I'm just about ready to drop; **vor Hunger/Durst fast ~:** be faint with hunger/thirst; **vor Schreck fast ~:** nearly die with fright; nearly have a heart attack (*coll.*); **C** (*ugs. abwertend: seine Meinung ändern*) do an about-face; do a U-turn
**Um·fang** *der* **A** circumference; (*eines Quadrats usw.*) perimeter; (*eines Baums, Menschen usw.*) girth; circumference; **er hat**

*old spelling (see note on page 1707)

**einen ganz schönen ~** (*scherzh.*) he has quite a girth; **B** (*Größe*) size; **der Band hat einen ~ von 250 Seiten** the volume contains 250 pages *or* is 250 pages thick; **C** (*Ausmaß*) extent; (*von Wissen*) range; extent; (*einer Stimme*) range; (*einer Arbeit, Untersuchung*) scope; **in vollem ~:** fully; completely; **in großem ~:** on a large scale

**um·fangen** *unr. tr. V.* (*geh.*) embrace; (*fig.*) ‹silence, warmth, etc.› envelop

**umfänglich** /ˈʊmfɛŋlɪç/ *Adj.* extensive; ‹case, parcel, etc.› of considerable size; voluminous, extensive ‹correspondence›

**umfang·reich** *Adj.* extensive; substantial ‹book›

**um·fassen** *tr. V.* **A** grasp; (*umarmen*) embrace; **jmds. Arme/Taille/Knie ~:** grasp *or* clasp sb. round the arms/waist/knees; **jmdn. umfasst halten** hold sb. in one's arms *or* in an embrace; **B** (*enthalten*) contain; (*einschließen*) include; take in; span, cover ‹period›; **C** (*umgeben*) enclose; surround; **D** (*Milit.: umzingeln*) surround; encircle

**umfassend** **1** *Adj.* full ‹reply, information, survey, confession›; extensive, wide, comprehensive ‹knowledge, powers›; broad ‹education›; extensive ‹preparations, measures›. **2** *adv.* ‹inform› fully

**Um·fassung** *die* enclosure

**Um·feld** *das* **A** (*Psych., Soziol.*) milieu; **B** ⇒ **Umgebung A**

**um·flechten** *unr. tr. V.* put wicker round; **eine umflochtene Flasche** a wickered bottle; **eine mit Bast umflochtene Flasche** a raffia-covered bottle

**um|fliegen**[1] *unr. itr. V.; mit sein* (*salopp*) go flying (*coll.*)

**um·fliegen**[2] *unr. tr. V.* fly round

**um·fließen** *unr. tr. V.* flow round

**um|formen** *tr. V.* **A** reshape; remodel; recast, revise ‹poem, novel›; transform ‹person›; **B** (*Elektrot.*) convert

**Um·former** *der* (*Elektrot.*) converter

**Um·formung** *die* **A** ⇒ **umformen A**: reshaping; remodelling; recasting; revision; transformation; **B** (*Elektrot.*) conversion

**Um·frage** *die* survey; (*Politik*) opinion poll; **eine ~ machen** *od.* **veranstalten** carry out a survey/conduct an opinion poll

**um·fried[ig]en** *tr. V.* (*geh.*) ⇒ **einfried[ig]en**

**Umfried[ig]ung** *die;* **~, ~en** (*geh.*) ⇒ **Einfried[ig]ung**

**um|füllen** *tr. V.* **etw. in etw.** (*Akk.*) **~:** transfer sth. into sth.; **der Kaffee muss umgefüllt werden** the coffee has to be put into another container

**um|funktionieren** *tr. V.* change the function of; **etw. zu etw. ~:** turn sth. into sth.

**Um·gang** *der* **A** (*gesellschaftlicher Verkehr*) contact; dealings *pl.;* **jmd. hat guten/schlechten ~:** sb. keeps good/bad company; **mit jmdm. ~ haben/pflegen** associate with sb.; **mit jmdm. keinen ~ haben** have nothing to do with sb.; **er ist kein ~ für dich!** he is not suitable *or* fit company for you; **B** (*das Umgehen*) **den ~ mit Pferden lernen** learn how to handle horses; **im ~ mit Kindern erfahren sein** be experienced in dealing with children; **C** (*bild. Kunst, Archit.*) gallery

**umgänglich** /ˈʊmɡɛŋlɪç/ *Adj.* (*verträglich*) affable; friendly; (*gesellig*) sociable

**umgangs-, Umgangs-: ~formen** *Pl.* manners *pl.;* **~sprache** *die* colloquial language; **die englische ~sprache** colloquial English; **~sprachlich** **1** *Adj.* colloquial; **2** *adv.* colloquially

**um·garnen** *tr. V.* beguile

**um·geben** *unr. tr. V.* **A** surround; ‹hedge, fence, wall, etc.› enclose; ‹darkness, mist, etc.› envelop; **B** **etw. mit etw. ~:** surround sth. with sth.; (*einfrieden*) enclose sth. with sth.; **sich mit jmdm./etw. ~:** surround oneself with sb./sth.

**Umgebung** *die;* **~, ~en** **A** surroundings *pl.;* (*Nachbarschaft*) neighbourhood; (*eines Ortes*) surrounding area; **die nähere/weitere ~ Mannheims** the immediate/broader environs *pl.* of Mannheim; **Wiesbaden und ~:** Wiesbaden and the surrounding area; **B** (*fig.*) milieu; **jmds. nähere ~:** those *pl.* close to sb.; **das Kind braucht seine vertraute ~:** the child needs familiar faces around it

**Um·gegend** *die* (*ugs.*) surrounding area; **die ~ der Stadt** the area surrounding the town

**um|gehen**[1] *unr. itr. V.; mit sein* **A** (*im Umlauf sein*) ‹list, rumour, etc.› go round, circulate; ‹illness, infection› go round; **Angst geht in der Bevölkerung um** fear is spreading in the population; **B** (*spuken*) **hier geht ein Gespenst um** this place is haunted; **im Schloss geht ein Gespenst um** a ghost haunts this castle; the castle is haunted; **C** (*behandeln*) **mit jmdm. freundlich/liebevoll** *usw.* **~:** treat sb. kindly/lovingly *etc.;* **mit etw. sorgfältig/nachlässig** *usw.* **~:** treat sth. carefully/carelessly *etc.;* **er versteht es, mit Kindern umzugehen** he knows how to handle children; **er kann mit Geld nicht ~:** he can't handle money; **mit Pinsel und Farbe ~ können** be able to use a brush and paint; **D** (*verkehren*) **mit jmdm. ~:** associate with sb.; **E** **mit dem Plan/Gedanken ~, etw. zu tun** think of doing sth.; **F** (*bes. nordd.: einen Umweg machen*) make a detour

**um·gehen**[2] *unr. tr. V.* **A** (*herumgehen, -fahren um*) go round; make a detour round ‹obstruction, busy area›; (*auf einer Umgehungsstraße*) bypass ‹town, village, etc.›; **B** (*vermeiden*) avoid; avoid, get round ‹problem, difficulty›; evade ‹question, issue›; **C** (*nicht befolgen*) get round, circumvent ‹law, restriction, etc.›; evade ‹obligation, duty›

**umgehend** **1** *Adj.* immediate. **2** *adv.* immediately

**Umgehung** *die;* **~, ~en** **A** **durch ~ der Innenstadt** by bypassing *or* avoiding the town centre; **B** ⇒ **umgehen**[2] **C**: circumvention; evasion; **das ließe sich nur unter ~ der Bestimmung durchführen** that could only be done by circumventing the regulations; **C** ⇒ **Umgehungsstraße**

**Umgehungs·straße** *die* bypass

**umgekehrt** **1** *Adj.* inverse ‹ratio, proportion›; reverse ‹order›; opposite ‹sign›; **es verhält sich** *od.* **ist genau ~:** the very opposite *or* reverse is true *or* the case. **2** *adv.* inversely ‹proportional›; **vom Englischen ins Deutsche und ~ übersetzen** translate from English into German and vice versa; **~ wirst du kaum erwarten können, dass ...** conversely you can hardly expect that ...

**um|gestalten** *tr. V.* reshape; remodel; redesign ‹square, park, room, etc.›; rework ‹text, music, etc.›; (*reorganisieren*) reorganize; (*verändern*) change; **der Garten wurde zu einem Park umgestaltet** the garden was turned into a park

**um|gießen** *unr. tr. V.* **A** **etw. ~:** pour sth. into another container/into bottles *etc.;* **etw. in etw.** (*Akk.*) **~:** pour sth. into sth.; **B** (*in eine andere Form gießen*) recast

**um·glänzen** *tr. V.* (*dichter.*) **etw. ~:** bathe sth. in light

**um|graben** *unr. tr. V.* dig over

**um·grenzen** *tr. V.* ‹wall, fence, etc.› surround, enclose; (*fig.*) define; delimit

**Umgrenzung** *die;* **~, ~en** **A** ⇒ **umgrenzen**: surrounding; enclosing; (*fig.*) definition; delimitation; **B** (*Grenzlinie*) boundary

**um|gruppieren** *tr. V.* rearrange

**Um·gruppierung** *die* rearrangement

**um|gucken** *refl. V.* (*ugs.*) ⇒ **umsehen**

**um|gürten** *tr. V.* (*veralt.*) put on ‹belt›; **[sich** (*Dat.*)**] das Schwert ~:** gird on one's sword

**um|haben** *unr. tr. V.* **etw. ~:** have sth. on

**um·halsen** *tr. V.* embrace; **sie umhalsten sich** they embraced

**Um·hang** *der* cape

**um|hängen** *tr. V.* **A** **etw. ~:** hang sth. somewhere else; **die Bilder müssen umgehängt werden** the pictures must be changed around; **B** **jmdm./sich einen Mantel/eine Decke ~:** drape a coat/blanket round sb.'s/one's shoulders; **sich** (*Dat.*) **ein Gewehr ~:** sling a rifle from one's shoulder; **sich** (*Dat.*) **einen Fotoapparat ~:** hang *or* sling a camera round one's neck; **jmdm. eine Medaille ~:** hang a medal round sb.'s neck

**Umhänge·tasche** *die* shoulder bag

**um|hauen** *unr. tr. V.* **A** (*fällen*) fell; **B** (*ugs.: niederwerfen*) knock down; floor; **diese Hitze haut einen glatt um** (*salopp*) this heat is enough to knock you over (*coll.*); **schon ein Bier haut mich um** (*salopp*) just one beer's enough to put me under the table (*coll.*); **es hat mich fast umgehauen, als ich davon hörte** (*salopp*) I was flabbergasted when I heard

**um·hegen** *tr. V.* (*geh.*) care lovingly for; **sie umhegt die Kinder mit mütterlicher Liebe** she looks after the children with maternal love

**um·her** *Adv.* around; **weit ~:** all around

**umher-:** ⇒ **herum-**

**umhin|können** *unr. itr. V.* **sie konnte nicht/kaum umhin, das zu tun** she had no/scarcely had any choice but to do it; (*einem inneren Zwang folgend*) she couldn't help/could scarcely help but do it

**um|hören** *refl. V.* keep one's ears open; (*direkt fragen*) ask around; **ich werde mich danach bei** *od.* **unter meinen Kollegen ~:** I'll ask around my workmates (*Brit.*) *or* (*esp. Amer.*) fellow workers

**um·hüllen** *tr. V.* wrap; (*fig.*) ‹mist, fog, etc.› shroud; **jmdn./etw. mit etw. ~:** wrap sb./sth. in sth.

**um·jubeln** *tr. V.* cheer

**um·kämpfen** *tr. V.* fight over ‹position, village, etc.›; contest ‹victory›; **ein heiß umkämpfter Sieg** a hotly contested victory

**Umkehr** /ˈʊmkeːɐ̯/ *die;* **~** (*auch fig.*) turning back; **zur ~ gezwungen werden** be forced to turn back

**umkehr·bar** *Adj.* reversible

**um|kehren** **1** *itr. V.; mit sein* turn back; (*fig. geh.: sich wandeln*) change one's ways; **auf halbem Wege ~** (*fig.*) stop halfway. **2** *tr. V.* **A** turn upside down; turn over ‹sheet of paper›; (*nach links drehen*) turn ‹garment etc.› inside out; (*nach rechts drehen*) turn ‹garment etc.› right side out; **das ganze Haus [nach etw.] ~** (*fig.*) turn the whole house upside down [looking for sth.]; **B** (*ins Gegenteil verkehren*) reverse; invert ‹ratio, proportion›; **C** (*Musik*) invert; **D** (*Logik*) convert ‹proposition›. **3** *refl. V.* be reversed; **der Magen kehrte sich ihm um** (*fig.*) his stomach turned over

**Umkehr·film** *der* (*Fot.*) reversal film

**Umkehrung** *die* **A** reversal; **B** (*Musik*) inversion; **C** (*Logik*) conversion

**um|kippen** **1** *itr. V.; mit sein* **A** fall over; ‹boat› capsize, turn over; ‹vehicle› overturn; **B** (*ugs.: ohnmächtig werden*) keel over; **C** (*ugs. abwertend*) ⇒ **umfallen C**; **D** (*ugs.: umschlagen*) ‹wine› go off; **E** (*Ökologie*) ‹river, lake› reach the stage of biological collapse; **F** (*ugs.: ins Gegenteil umschlagen*) ‹mood› turn; ‹voice› crack. **2** *tr. V.* tip over; knock over ‹lamp, vase, glass, cup›; capsize ‹boat›; turn ‹boat› over; overturn ‹vehicle›

**um·klammern** *tr. V.* clutch; clasp; **seine Hände umklammerten den Griff** his hands gripped *or* clasped the handle; **die Ringer/Boxer ~ sich** the wrestlers are locked together/the boxers are in a clinch; **etw./jmdn. fest umklammert halten** keep a firm grip on sth./clutch sb. tightly

**Umklammerung** *die;* **~, ~en** clutch; clasp; (*mit den Händen*) clutch; grip; clasp; (*Umarmung*) firm embrace; (*Boxen*) clinch

**um·klappbar** *Adj.* fold-down ‹seat›; **~ sein** fold down

**um|klappen** **1** *tr. V.* fold down. **2** *itr. V.; mit sein* (*ugs.: ohnmächtig werden*) keel over

**Umkleide·kabine** *die* changing cubicle

**um|kleiden**[1] (*geh.*) **1** *refl. V.* change; change one's clothes. **2** *tr. V.* **jmdn. ~:** change sb.; change sb.'s clothes

**um·kleiden**[2] *tr. V.* cover

**Umkleide·raum** *der* changing room (*Brit.*); (*im Theater*) green room

U

**um|knicken** ❶ *itr. V.; mit sein* Ⓐ **[mit dem Fuß] ~:** go over on one's ankle; Ⓑ ‹tree, stalk, blade of grass, etc.› bend; ‹branch› bend and snap; **umgeknickte Äste/Halme** snapped branches/bent straws. ❷ *tr. V.* Ⓐ *(falten)* fold ‹page, sheet of paper› over; Ⓑ *(abknicken)* bend over; break ‹flower, stalk›

**um|kommen** *unr. itr. V.; mit sein* Ⓐ die; *(bei einem Unglück, durch Gewalt)* get killed; die; **ich komme um vor Hitze** *(fig. ugs.)* I'm dying in this heat *(coll.)*; **ich komme um vor Hunger/Durst** *(fig. ugs.)* I'm dying of hunger/thirst *(coll.)*; **vor Langeweile ~** *(fig. ugs.)* be bored to death *(coll.)*; die of boredom *(coll.)*; Ⓑ *(ungenießbar werden)* ‹food› go off

**umkränzen** /ʊm'krɛntsn̩/ *tr. V.* garland; *(fig.: umgeben)* encircle

**Um·kreis** *der* Ⓐ surrounding area; **im ~ von 5 km** within a radius of 5 km.; **der ~ der Stadt** the city's environs *pl. or* immediate surroundings *pl.;* **im [näheren] ~ der Stadt** in the [immediate] vicinity of the town; **aus dem ~ des Vorsitzenden hört man, ...** *(fig.)* one learns from those close to the chairman ...; Ⓑ *(Geom.)* circumcircle

**um·kreisen** *tr. V.* circle; ‹spacecraft, satellite› orbit; ‹planet› revolve [a]round; **seine Gedanken umkreisten das Thema** *(fig.)* he kept turning the matter over in his mind

**um|krempeln** *tr. V.* Ⓐ *(aufkrempeln)* turn up ‹cuff›; roll up ‹sleeve, trouser leg›; Ⓑ **das ganze Haus [nach etw.] ~** *(ugs.)* turn the whole house upside down [looking for sth.]; Ⓒ *(ugs.: von Grund auf ändern)* **etw. ~:** give sth. a shake-up; **jmdn. ~:** [completely] change sb.

**um|laden** *unr. tr. V.* transfer ‹goods etc.›

**Um·lage** *die:* **~[n]** share of the cost[s]; *(bei einer Wohnung)* share of the bill[s]; **die ~ beträgt 30 Mark pro Person** the cost is 30 marks per person

**um·lagern** *tr. V.* besiege

**Um·land** *das* surrounding area; **das ~ von Köln** the area around Cologne

**um|lassen** *unr. tr. V. (ugs.)* leave ‹garment, watch, etc.› on

**Um·lauf** *der* Ⓐ rotation; **ein ~ [der Erde um die Sonne] dauert ein Jahr** one revolution [of the earth around the sun] takes a year; Ⓑ *(Zirkulation)* circulation; **in** *od.* **im ~ sein** ‹magazine, report, etc.› be circulating; ‹coin, banknote› be in circulation; **in ~ bringen** *od.* **setzen** circulate ‹report, magazine, etc.›; circulate, put about, start ‹rumour›; bring ‹coin, banknote› into circulation; Ⓒ *(Rundschreiben)* circular

**Umlauf·bahn** *die (Astron., Raumf.)* orbit; **etw. in eine ~ bringen** put sth. into orbit

**um|laufen**[1] ❶ *unr. tr. V.* knock over. ❷ *unr. itr. V.; mit sein* Ⓐ *(rotieren)* rotate; revolve; ‹planet, satellite, etc.› orbit; Ⓑ **~d** *(ringsherum verlaufend)* surrounding; Ⓒ *(kursieren, zirkulieren)* circulate

**um·laufen**[2] *unr. tr. V.* run around; ‹planet, satellite, etc.› orbit

**Um·laut** *der (Sprachw.)* umlaut

**um|lauten** *tr. V. (Sprachw.)* **ein umgelautetes a** an a umlaut; **das „a" wird hier umgelautet** the 'a' takes an umlaut in this case

**um|legen** *tr. V.* Ⓐ *(um einen Körperteil)* put on; **jmdm. etw. ~:** put sth. on sb.; **sich** *(Dat.)* **etw. ~:** put sth. on; **jmdm. eine Stola/Decke ~:** put a stole round sb.'s shoulders/put a blanket round sb.; Ⓑ *(auf den Boden, die Seite legen)* lay down; flatten ‹corn, stalks, etc.›; *(fällen)* fell; Ⓒ *(umklappen)* fold down; turn down ‹collar›; turn up ‹cuff›; throw ‹lever›; turn over ‹calendar-page›; Ⓓ *(ugs.: zu Boden werfen)* floor, knock down ‹person›; Ⓔ *(salopp: ermorden)* **jmdn. ~:** do sb. in *(sl.)*; bump sb. off *(coll.)*; Ⓕ *(verlegen)* transfer ‹patient, telephone call›; **den Termin ~:** change the date **(auf** + *Akk.* to); Ⓖ *(anteilmäßig verteilen)* split, share ‹costs› **(auf** + *Akk.* between); Ⓗ *(derb: koitieren mit)* lay *(sl.)*

*old spelling (see note on page 1707)

**um|leiten** divert; re-route; divert ‹river, stream›

**Um·leitung** *die* diversion; re-routing; **die ~ fahren** take the diversion

**um|lernen** *itr. V.* Ⓐ *(beruflich)* retrain; **auf Feinmechaniker ~:** retrain as a precision engineer; Ⓑ *(seine Anschauungen ändern)* learn to think differently

**umliegend** *Adj.* surrounding ‹area, district›; *(nahe)* nearby ‹building›

**Um·luft** *die (Technik)* recirculated air

**um·mauern** *tr. V.* surround with a wall; **ummauert** walled ‹garden, town›

**um|melden** *tr. V.* **sich ~:** report a change of address; **ein Auto ~:** inform the authorities of a change of ownership of a car/*(am neuen Wohnort)* of the new address of a car's owner

**um|modeln** *tr. V. (ugs.)* change ‹house, flat› round; refashion, alter ‹jacket etc.›

**um|münzen** *tr. V.* **etw. in etw.** *(Akk.)* **~:** convert sth. into sth.; **eine Niederlage in einen Sieg ~** *(fig.: umdeuten)* make a defeat out to be victory

**um·nachtet** *Adj. (geh.)* **[geistig] ~ sein** be [mentally] deranged

**Umnachtung** *die; ~, ~en (geh.)* derangement; **im Zustand der ~, in geistiger ~:** in a state of mental derangement *or* insanity

**um·nebeln** *tr. V. (fig.)* cloud ‹senses, glance›; befog ‹thoughts›; **leicht umnebelt** slightly befuddled

**um|organisieren** *tr. V.* reorganize

**um|packen** ❶ *itr. V.* repack. ❷ *tr. V.* repack; **seine Sachen aus der Reisetasche in einen Koffer ~:** take one's things out of the holdall and pack them into a suitcase

**um|pflanzen** *tr. V.* transplant

**um|pflügen** *tr. V.* plough up

**um|polen** *tr. V. (Elektrot.)* reverse the polarity/connections of; *(fig. ugs.: umwandeln)* convert ‹homosexual›

**um|quartieren** *tr. V.* re-accommodate ‹person› **(in** + *Akk.* in); re-quarter, re-billet ‹troops› **(in** + *Akk.* in); move ‹patient›

**um|rahmen** *tr. V.* frame ‹face etc.›; **eine Feier mit Musik** *od.* **musikalisch ~** *(fig.)* begin and end a ceremony with music; give a ceremony a musical framework

**Um|rahmung** *die; ~, ~en* Ⓐ *(das Umrahmen)* bordering; **musikalische ~** *(fig.)* musical framework; music before and after; Ⓑ *(Umrahmendes)* border; *(fig.)* setting

**um·randen** *tr. V.* ring ‹letter, error, etc.›; border ‹handkerchief, flower bed, etc.›

**umrändert** /ʊm'rɛndɐt/ *Adj.* **schwarz ~:** with a black border; **rot ~e Augen** red-rimmed eyes

**Umrandung** *die; ~, ~en* Ⓐ bordering; Ⓑ *(Umrandendes)* border; surround

**um|räumen** ❶ *tr. V.* rearrange. ❷ *itr. V.* rearrange things

**um|rechnen** *tr. V.* convert **(in** + *Akk.* into); **Waren im Wert von umgerechnet 300 Mark** goods worth the equivalent of 300 marks

**Um·rechnung** *die* conversion **(in** + *Akk.* into)

**Umrechnungs·kurs** *der* exchange rate

**um|reißen**[1] *unr. tr. V.* pull ‹mast, tree› down; knock ‹person› down; ‹wind› tear ‹tent etc.› down

**um·reißen**[2] *unr. tr. V.* outline; summarize ‹subject, problem, situation›; **fest** *od.* **klar** *od.* **scharf umrissen** clearly defined ‹programme›; clear-cut ‹ideas, views›

**um|rennen** *unr. tr. V.* [run into and] knock down

**um·ringen** *tr. V.* surround; *(in großer Zahl)* crowd round

**Um·riss, *Um·riß** *der (auch fig.)* outline; **in Umrissen** in outline

**um|rühren** *tr. (auch itr.) V.* stir; **unter ständigem Umrühren** [while] stirring constantly

**um·runden** *tr. V.* go round ‹lake, town›; *(Raumf.)* orbit; *(Seew.)* round ‹cape›

**um|rüsten** ❶ *tr. V.* Ⓐ *(Technik)* convert **(auf** + *Akk.* to, **zu** into); Ⓑ *(Milit.)* **eine Armee [auf Atomwaffen] ~:** re-equip an army [with nuclear weapons]. ❷ *itr. V.* re-equip; **auf etw.** *(Akk.)* **~:** change over to sth.

**ums** /ʊms/ *Präp.* + *Art.* Ⓐ = **um das;** Ⓑ **~ Leben kommen** lose one's life; **ein Jahr ~ andere** *(geh.)* one year after another; year after year

**um|satteln** *itr. V. (ugs.)* change jobs; ‹student› change courses; **[von etw.] auf etw.** *(Akk.)* **~:** switch [from sth.] to sth.

**Um·satz** *der* turnover; *(Verkauf)* sales *pl.* **(an** + *Dat.* of); **~ machen** *(ugs.)* make money; **1 000 Mark ~ machen** turn over 1,000 marks

**Umsatz-: ~beteiligung** *die* share of the turnover; *(eines Verkäufers)* commission; **~steuer** *die* turnover *or (Amer.)* sales tax

**um|säumen**[1] *tr. V.* hem

**um·säumen**[2] *tr. V. (fig.)* surround

**um|schalten** ❶ *tr. V. (auch fig.)* switch [over] **(auf** + *Akk.* to); move ‹lever›. ❷ *itr. V.* Ⓐ *(auch fig.)* switch *or* change over **(auf** + *Akk.* to); **in den zweiten Gang ~:** change into second gear; **wir schalten jetzt ins Stadion um** now we're going over to the stadium; Ⓑ *(umgeschaltet werden)* **die Ampel schaltet [auf Grün] um** the traffic lights are changing [to green]

**Umschalt·hebel** *der* [changeover] lever

**Um·schau** *die:* **[nach jmdm./etw.] ~ halten** look round *or* out [for sb./sth.]; **„Politische ~"** 'Political Review'

**um|schauen** *refl. V. (bes. südd., österr., schweiz.)* ⇒ **umsehen**

**um|schichten** ❶ *tr. V.* Ⓐ restack; Ⓑ *(Wirtsch.)* restructure ‹investments›; reinvest ‹capital›. ❷ *refl. V. (Soziol.)* be restructured

**um·schichtig** ❶ *Adv.* ‹work› in shifts; **wir müssen ~ essen gehen** we have to eat on a rota basis. ❷ *adj.* shift *attrib.* ‹work›; ‹work› in shifts; ‹lunch break› taken on a rota basis

**Um·schichtung** *die* ⇒ **umschichten** 1, 2: restacking; *(Wirtsch.)* restructuring; reinvestment; *(Soziol.)* restructuring

**um·schiffen** *tr. V.* round ‹headland, cape›; steer clear of ‹rocks, fig.: obstacle›

**Um·schlag** *der* Ⓐ cover; Ⓑ *(Brief~)* envelope; Ⓒ *(Schutz~)* jacket; *(einer Broschüre, eines Heftes)* cover; Ⓓ *(Med.: Wickel)* compress; *(warm)* poultice; Ⓔ *(Hosen~)* turn-up; *(Ärmel~)* cuff; Ⓕ *(Veränderung)* [sudden] change *(Gen.* in); Ⓖ *(Wirtsch.: Güter~)* transfer; trans-shipment

**Umschlag·bahnhof** *der* transfer station

**um|schlagen** ❶ *unr. tr. V.* Ⓐ *(umklappen)* turn up ‹sleeve, collar, trousers›; turn over ‹page›; Ⓑ *(umladen, verladen)* turn round, trans-ship ‹goods›. ❷ *unr. itr. V.; mit sein* ‹weather, mood› change **(in** + *Akk.* into); ‹wind› veer [round]; ‹voice› break; ‹wine› go off; **ins Gegenteil ~:** change completely; become the opposite

**Umschlage·tuch** *das; Pl.* **Umschlage·tücher** shawl

**Umschlag-: ~hafen** *der* port of trans-shipment; **~platz** *der* trans-shipment centre; **~tuch** *das* ⇒ **Umschlagetuch**

**um·schließen** *unr. tr. V.* Ⓐ ‹river, wall› surround; ‹shell, husk, etc.› enclose; ‹hand, fingers, tentacles› clasp, hold; **er umschloss sie mit beiden Armen** he put both arms around her; Ⓑ *(einschließen, umzingeln)* surround, encircle ‹position, enemy›; Ⓒ *(zum Inhalt haben)* embrace

**um·schlingen** *unr. tr. V.* Ⓐ **jmdn./etw. [mit den Armen] ~:** put one's arms around sb./sth.; embrace sb./sth.; **sich umschlungen halten** hold one another in an embrace; **eng umschlungen** in a tight embrace *postpos.;* Ⓑ *(sich schlingen um)* twine [itself] round

**Umschlingung** *die; ~, ~en* embrace; *(einer Boa o. Ä.)* grip

**Um·schluss, *Um·schluß** *der (Rechtsw.)* limited freedom of association *(for prisoners awaiting trial)*

**um·schmeicheln** *tr. V.* heap flattery on; *(fig.)* caress ‹part of body›

**um|schmeißen** *unr. tr. V. (ugs.)* ⇒ **umwerfen** A, B

**um|schnallen** *tr. V.* **[sich** (*Dat.*)**] ~:** buckle on ‹belt, sword›; **jmdm./einem Tier etw. ~:** buckle *or* strap sth. on to sb./an animal

**um|schreiben¹** *unr. tr. V.* A rewrite; B (*übertragen*) transfer ‹money, property› **(auf** + *Akk.* to); C (*transkribieren*) transcribe

**um·schreiben²** *unr. tr. V.* A (*in Worte fassen*) describe; (*definieren*) define ‹meaning, sb.'s task, etc.›; (*paraphrasieren*) paraphrase ‹word, expression›; B (*Sprachw.*) construct **(mit** with); **das Perfekt wird mit „sein" umschrieben** the perfect is conjugated with 'sein'; C (*mit einer Linie umgeben*) outline; (*andeuten*) indicate; **umschrieben** (*Med.*) localized ‹eczema etc.›

**Um·schreibung** *die* A description; (*Definition*) definition; (*Verhüllung*) circumlocution (*Gen.* for); B ⇒ **umschreiben²** B: construction; conjugation

**Um·schrift** *die* A (*Sprachw.*) transcription; B (*bes. Münzk.*) circumscription

**um|schulden** *tr.* (*auch itr.*) *V.* (*Finanzw.*) convert ‹loan›; (*mit längerer Laufzeit*) reschedule ‹loan, debt›

**Umschuldung** *die;* **~, ~en** (*Finanzw.*) loan conversion; (*mit längerer Laufzeit*) extension of credit; rescheduling [of a/the loan/loans]

**um|schulen** ❶ *tr. V.* A **ein Kind [auf eine andere Schule] ~:** transfer a child [to another school]; B (*beruflich*) retrain; **jmdn. auf** *od.* **zum Monteur ~:** retrain sb. as a fitter. ❷ *itr. V.* retrain **(auf** + *Akk.* as)

**Umschulung** *die* A transfer [to another school]; B (*beruflich*) retraining *no pl.* **(auf** + *Akk.* as)

**um|schütten** *tr. V.* A pour [into another container]; decant ‹liquid›; B (*verschütten*) spill

**um·schwärmen** *tr. V.* A swarm around; **von Moskitos umschwärmt werden** be besieged by mosquitoes; B (*fig.*) flock around; **sie war sehr** *od.* **von vielen umschwärmt** she had many admirers

**Um·schweif** *der* circumlocution; **ohne ~e** without beating about the bush; **mach keine [langen] ~e!** get on with it!

**um|schwenken** *itr. V.; mit sein* A ‹person, column› swing round; ‹wind› veer [round]; B (*fig.*) do an about-face

**um·schwirren** *tr. V.* buzz around

**Um·schwung** *der* A complete change; (*in der Politik usw.*) U-turn; volte-face; B (*Turnen*) circle

**um·segeln** *tr. V.* sail round ‹world, island, etc.›; circumnavigate ‹world›; (*fig.*) negotiate ‹obstacle etc.›

**um|sehen** *unr. refl. V.* A look; **sich im Zimmer ~:** look [a]round the room; **sehen Sie sich ruhig um** (*im Geschäft usw.*) by all means have a look round; **du wirst dich noch ~!** (*ugs.*) you're in for a [nasty] shock; **sich nach etw. ~** (*fig.*) be looking *or* on the lookout for sth.; B (*zurücksehen*) look round *or* back; **eine Frau, nach der sich alle Männer ~:** a woman who makes every man turn his head

***um|sein** ⇒ **um** 2 B

**umseitig** ❶ *Adj.* ‹text, illustration, etc.› overleaf. ❷ *adv.* overleaf

**umsetz·bar** *Adj.* (*fig.: umwandelbar*) convertible **(in** + *Akk.* into); **der Vorschlag ist kaum in die Praxis ~:** the suggestion can scarcely be translated into practice

**um|setzen** ❶ *tr. V.* A move; (*auf anderen Sitzplatz*) move to another seat/other seats; (*im Restaurant*) move to another table; (*auf anderen Posten, Arbeitsplatz usw.*) move, transfer **(in** + *Akk.* to); (*in andere Wohnung*) rehouse **(in** + *Akk.* in); (*umpflanzen*) transplant ‹bush etc.›; (*in anderen Topf*) repot ‹plant›; B (*verwirklichen*) implement ‹plan›; translate ‹plan, intention, etc.› into action *or* reality; realize ‹ideas›; **Erlebnisse in Literatur ~:** give experiences literary form; ⇒ *auch* **Praxis** A; **Tat** A; C (*in Waren, Geld usw.*) spend, dispose of ‹money›; **etw. in Geld/Bares ~:** turn sth. into money/cash; **Geld in Schnaps/Geschenke ~:** spend money on schnapps/presents; D (*Wirtsch.*) turn over, have a turnover of ‹x marks etc.›; sell ‹shares, goods›. ❷ *refl. V.* A (*den Sitzplatz wechseln*) move to another seat/other seats; change seats; (*den Tisch wechseln*) move to another table; change tables; B (*sich verwandeln*) transform itself, (*Physik*) be converted **(in** + *Akk.* into)

**Umsetzung** *die;* **~, ~en** A (*auf einen anderen Posten*) transfer **(in** + *Akk.* to); (*in eine andere Wohnung*) rehousing **(in** + *Akk.* in); (*Umpflanzung*) transplant[ing]; (*in einen anderen Topf*) repotting; **durch die ~ des Schülers** by moving the pupil [to another seat/desk]; B (*Verwirklichung*) realization; (*eines Plans*) implementation; (*Umformung*) transformation **(in** + *Akk.* into); (*bes. Technik, Physik*) conversion **(in** + *Akk.* into); **chemische ~en** chemical changes; C (*Wirtsch.: Verkauf*) turnover; sale

**Um·sicht** *die* circumspection; prudence

**um·sichtig** ❶ *Adj.* circumspect; prudent. ❷ *adv.* circumspectly; prudently

**um|siedeln** ❶ *tr. V.* resettle; **nach X umgesiedelt werden** be moved to X. ❷ *itr. V.; mit sein* move **(in** + *Akk.*, **nach** to); **in ein anderes Land ~:** settle in another country; emigrate

**Um·siedler** *der*, **Um·siedlerin** *die* resettled person; (*freiwillig*) resettler

**Um·siedlung** *die* resettlement; **seit meiner ~ aus der DDR in den Westen** since I moved to the West from the GDR

**um|sinken** *unr. itr. V.; mit sein* sink *or* fall to the ground

**umso** *Konj.* **je schneller der Wagen, ~ größer die Gefahr** the faster the car, the greater the danger; **je länger ..., ~ besser ...:** the longer ..., the better ...; **~ besser/schlimmer!** all the better/worse!; **~ mehr, als ...** (*zumal, da ...*) all the more so, as *or* since ...

**um·sonst** *Adv.* A (*unentgeltlich*) free; for nothing; **für ~** (*ugs.*) free, gratis, and for nothing (*joc.*); **~ sein** (*ugs.*) be free [of charge]; not cost anything; **das hast du nicht ~ getan!** (*ugs.*) you'll pay for that!; B (*vergebens*) in vain; C **nicht ~ hat er davor gewarnt** not for nothing did he warn of that

**um·sorgen** *tr. V.* care for; look after

**um·spannen** *tr. V.* A clasp ‹hand, wrist, ankle, etc.›; put one's hands round ‹neck etc.›; B (*fig.: einschieben*) encompass ‹subjects, period›; **alles ~d** all-embracing

**Umspann·werk** *das* (*Elektrot.*) transformer station

**um·spielen** *tr. V.* A ‹smile, light› play about; ‹waves› lap about *or* around; ‹skirt etc.› swirl about *or* around; B (*Ballspiele*) go round ‹defender›

**um|springen** *unr. itr. V.; mit sein* A ‹wind› veer round **(auf** + *Akk.* to); ‹traffic light, fig.: mood› change; B (*ugs. abwertend*) **mit jmdm. grob/übel** *usw.* **~:** treat sb. roughly/badly *etc.*

**um|spulen** *tr. V.* rewind ‹tape, film›

**um·spülen** *tr. V.* wash round; **ein von den Wellen umspültes Riff** a reef washed by the waves

**Um·stand** *der* A (*Gegebenheit*) circumstance; (*Tatsache*) fact; **die näheren Umstände** the particular circumstances; (*Einzelheiten*) the details; **ein glücklicher ~:** a lucky *or* happy chance; **den Umständen entsprechend** as one would expect [in *or* under the circumstances]; **den Umständen entsprechend gut** (*ugs.*) as well as can be expected [given the circumstances]; **das kommt unter gar keinen Umständen in Frage** there is no question of that under any circumstances; **unter allen Umständen** whatever happens; **unter Umständen** possibly; **in anderen Umständen sein** (*ugs.*) be expecting; be in the family way (*coll.*); B (*Aufwand*) business; hassle (*coll.*); **macht keine [großen] Umstände** please don't go to any bother *or* trouble; **das macht gar keine Umstände** it's no bother *or* trouble at all

**umstände·halber** *Adv.* owing to circumstances; **„~ zu verkaufen"** 'forced to sell'; 'genuine reason for sale'

**umständlich** /ˈʊmʃtɛntlɪç/ ❶ *Adj.* involved, elaborate ‹procedure, method, description, explanation, etc.›; elaborate, laborious ‹preparation, check, etc.›; awkward, difficult ‹journey, job›; (*kompliziert*) involved; complicated; (*weitschweifig*) long-winded; (*Umstände machend*) awkward, (*coll.*) pernickety ‹person›; **das ist mir zu ~:** that is too much trouble *or* (*coll.*) hassle [for me]; **es ist etwas ~, mit dem Auto dorthin zu kommen** getting there by car is rather awkward *or* rather a business. ❷ *adv.* in an involved *or* roundabout way; (*weitschweifig*) ‹explain etc.› at great length *or* in a long-winded way; **sie drückt sich manchmal etwas ~ aus** she is sometimes rather long-winded; **er verabschiedete/entschuldigte sich ~:** he made a meal of saying 'goodbye'/'sorry'; **warum einfach, wenns auch ~ geht?** (*iron.*) why do things the easy way if you can make them difficult? (*iron.*)

**Umstands-: ~an·gabe**, **~bestimmung** *die* (*Sprachw.*) adverbial qualification; **~ergänzung** *die* (*Sprachw.*) adverbial complement; **~fürwort** *das* (*Sprachw.*) pronominal adverb; **~kleid** *das* maternity dress; **~kleidung** *die* maternity wear; **~krämer** *der*, **~krämerin** *die* (*ugs. abwertend*) fusspot (*coll.*); **~moden** *Pl.* maternity styles; **~satz** *der* (*Sprachw.*) adverbial clause; **~wort** *das; Pl.* **~wörter** (*Sprachw.*) adverb

**um·stehen** *unr. tr. V.* stand round; surround

**umstehend** ❶ *Adj.* A standing round *postpos.;* **die ~en Personen, die Umstehenden** the bystanders; B (*umseitig*) overleaf *postpos.* ❷ *adv.* overleaf

**um|steigen** *unr. itr. V.* A change **(in** + *Akk.* [on] to); **nach Frankfurt ~:** change for Frankfurt; B (*fig. ugs.*) change over, switch **(auf** + *Akk.* to)

**um|stellen¹** ❶ *tr. V.* A (*anders stellen*) rearrange, change round ‹furniture, books, etc.›; reorder ‹words etc.›; transpose ‹two words›; reshuffle ‹team›; B (*anders einstellen*) reset ‹lever, switch, points, clock›; C (*ändern*) change *or* switch over **(auf** + *Akk.* to). ❷ *refl. V.* adjust **(auf** + *Akk.* to); **er hat sich auf Rohkost umgestellt** he has changed his diet to raw fruit and vegetables. ❸ *itr. V.* switch over **(auf** + *Akk.* to)

**um·stellen²** *tr. V.* surround

**Um·stellung** *die* ⇒ **umstellen¹** 1, 2: A rearrangement; reordering; transposition; redeployment; reshuffle; B resetting; C changeover, switch **(auf** + *Akk.* to); D (*das Sichumstellen*) change; [re]adjustment

**um|stimmen** *tr. V.* (*fig.: zu einer anderen Haltung bewegen*) win ‹person› round; **er ließ sich nicht ~:** he was not to be persuaded; he refused to change his mind

**um|stoßen** *unr. tr. V.* A knock over; B (*rückgängig machen*) reverse ‹judgement, decision›; change ‹plan, decision›; C (*zunichte machen*) upset, wreck ‹plan, theory›

**umstritten** *Adj.* disputed; controversial ‹bill, book, author, proposal, policy, etc.›

**um|strukturieren** *tr. V.* restructure

**um|stülpen** *tr. V.* A turn inside out; (*umkrempeln*) turn *or* roll up ‹trousers, sleeves, etc.›; B (*auskippen*) turn out, empty ‹purse, bag, etc.›; C (*umdrehen*) turn upside down; (*fig.*) turn on its head

**Um·sturz** *der* coup

**um|stürzen** ❶ *tr. V.* overturn; knock over; (*fig.*) topple, overthrow ‹political system, government›. ❷ *itr. V.* overturn; ‹wall, building, chimney› fall down

**Umstürzler** /ˈʊmʃtʏrtslɐ/ *der;* **~s, ~, Umstürzlerin** *die;* **~, ~nen** (*abwertend*) subversive agent

**umstürzlerisch** (*abwertend*) ❶ *Adj.* subversive. ❷ *adv.* **sich ~ betätigen** engage in subversive activities

**Umsturz·versuch** *der* attempted coup

**um|taufen** *tr. V.* **jmdn./**(*ugs.*) **etw. ~:** rename sb./sth.; change sb.'s name/the name of sth. **(auf** + *Akk.* to)

**Um·tausch** *der* exchange; **beim ~:** when exchanging goods/changing money; **reduzierte Ware ist vom ~ ausgeschlossen** sale goods cannot be exchanged

**um|tauschen** *tr. V.* exchange ‹goods, article› (**gegen** for); change ‹dollars, pounds, etc.› (**in** + *Akk.* into)

**um|topfen** *tr. V.* repot ‹plant›

**um·tosen** *tr. V.* (*geh.*) surge around; **von etw. umtost** buffeted by sth.

**Um|triebe** *Pl.* (*abwertend*) [subversive] intrigues; subversion *sing.*

**Um·trunk** *der* communal drink

**um|tun** *unr. refl. V.* (*ugs.*) look [a]round; **sich nach etw. ~:** be on the lookout *or* looking for sth.

**U-Musik** *die* light music

**um|verteilen** *tr. V.* redistribute

**Um·verteilung** *die* redistribution

**um|wälzen** *tr. V.* Ⓐ roll over; **~d** (*fig.*) revolutionary ‹ideas, effect›; epoch-making ‹events›; Ⓑ (*zirkulieren lassen*) circulate ‹water, air›

**Umwälz·pumpe** *die* circulating pump

**Umwälzung** *die; ~, ~en* (*fig.*) revolution

**um|wandeln** ❶ *tr. V.* convert ‹substance, building, etc.› (**in** + *Akk.* into); commute ‹sentence› (**in** + *Akk.* to); (*ändern*) change; alter; **er ist wie umgewandelt** he is a changed man. ❷ *refl. V.* be converted (**in** + *Akk.* into)

**Um·wandlung** *die* conversion (**in** + *Akk.* into); (*einer Strafe*) commutation (**in** + *Akk.* to); (*der Gesellschaft usw.*) transformation

**um|wechseln** *tr. V.* change ‹marks, note, etc.› (**in** + *Akk.* into)

**Um·weg** *der* detour; **auf einem ~ nach Hause fahren** go a long way round *or* make a detour to get home; **auf ~en** by a circuitous *or* roundabout route; (*fig.*) in a roundabout way; **auf dem ~ über** (+ *Akk.*) (*fig.*) [indirectly] via

**Um·welt** *die* Ⓐ environment; Ⓑ (*Menschen*) people *pl.* around sb.; **meine/deine/seine ~:** those *pl.* around me/you/him

**umwelt-, Umwelt-: ~ allergie** *die* environmental allergy; **~bedingt** *Adj.* caused by the *or* one's environment *postpos.*; **~belastung** *die* environmental pollution *no indef. art.*; **~bewusst**, ***~bewußt** *Adj.* environmentally conscious *or* aware; **~feindlich** ❶ *Adj.* inimical to the environment *postpos.*; ecologically undesirable; ❷ *adv.* in an ecologically undesirable way; ‹drive, behave› without regard for the environment; **~forschung** *die* Ⓐ (*Biol.*) ecology; Ⓑ (*Soziol.*) environmental studies *pl.*, *no art. or* science *no art.*; **~freundlich** ❶ *Adj.* environment-friendly; ecologically desirable; ❷ *adv.* in an ecologically desirable way; ‹act› with some regard for the environment; **~ katastrophe** *die* environmental disaster; **~kriminalität** *die* environmental crime; **~politik** *die* ecological policy; **~schäden** *Pl.* environmental damage *sing.*; damage *sing.* to the environment; **~schädlich** ❶ *Adj.* harmful to the environment *postpos.*; ecologically harmful; ❷ *adv.* in an ecologically harmful way; **~schutz** *der* environmental protection *no art.*; conservation of the environment; **~schützer** *der; ~~s, ~~,* **~schützerin** *die; ~~, ~~nen* environmentalist; conservationist; **~sünder** *der*, **~sünderin** *die* (*ugs.*) deliberate polluter of the environment; **~verschmutzung** *die* pollution [of the environment]

**um|wenden** ❶ *regelm.* (*auch unr.*) *tr. V.;* Ⓐ (*auf die andere Seite*) turn over ‹page, joint, etc.›; Ⓑ (*in die andere Richtung*) turn round ‹vehicle, horse›; Ⓒ (*von innen nach außen*) turn ‹garment› inside out. ❷ *unr. od. regelm. refl. V.* turn round

**um·werben** *unr. tr. V.* court; woo

**um|werfen** *unr. tr. V.* Ⓐ knock over; knock ‹person› down *or* over; (*fig. ugs.: aus der Fassung bringen*) bowl ‹person› over; stun ‹person›; (*fig. ugs.: betrunken machen*) knock ‹person› out (*sl.*); **das wirft selbst den stärksten Mann um!** it's more than even the strongest man can take; Ⓑ (*fig. ugs.; umstoßen*) knock ‹plan› on the head (*coll.*); Ⓒ (*umlegen, umhängen*) throw *or* put sth. round sb.'s/one's shoulders

**umwerfend** (*ugs.*) ❶ *Adj.* fantastic (*coll.*); stunning (*coll.*). ❷ *adv.* fantastically [well] (*coll.*); brilliantly; **~ komisch** hilariously funny; **~ schön** stunningly beautiful (*coll.*)

**Um·werfer** *der* derailleur

**um·wickeln** *tr. V.* wrap; bind; (*mit einem Verband*) bandage; **etw. mit Schnur/Draht ~:** wind string/wire round sth.

**um|widmen** *tr. V.* (*Verwaltung*) re-designate (**in** + *Akk.*, **zu** as)

**Um·widmung** *die* (*Verwaltung*) re-designation (**in** + *Akk.* as)

**um·wittern** *tr. V.* (*geh.*) **von Gefahren/einem Geheimnis umwittert sein** be beset *or* fraught with danger/shrouded in mystery

**umwohnend** *Adj.* living in the neighbourhood *postpos.*

**um·wölken** /ʊmˈvœlkn̩/ ❶ *refl. V.* (*geh.*) ‹sky› cloud over; (*fig.*) ‹brow, look› darken. ❷ *tr. V.* shroud; veil

**um|wühlen** *tr. V.* churn *or* plough up

**um·zäunen** *tr. V.* fence round *or* off

**Umzäunung** *die; ~, ~en* Ⓐ (*das Umzäunen*) fencing round *or* off; Ⓑ (*Zaun*) fence, fencing (*Gen.* round)

**um|ziehen** ❶ *unr. itr. V.; mit sein* move (**an** + *Akk.*, **in** + *Akk.*, **nach** to). ❷ *unr. tr. V.* (*umkleiden*) **jmdn./sich ~:** change sb. *or* get sb. changed/change *or* get changed; **sich zum Essen ~:** change for dinner

**um·zingeln** /ʊmˈt͡sɪŋl̩n/ *tr. V.* surround; encircle

**Umzingelung** *die; ~:* encirclement

**Um·zug** *der* Ⓐ move; (*von Möbeln*) removal; **jmdm. beim ~ helfen** help sb. move; help with the removal; Ⓑ (*Festzug*) procession; (*Demonstrationszug*) demonstration

**Umzugs·kosten** *Pl.* removal costs

**UN** /uːˈɛn/ *Pl.* UN *sing.*

**unabänderlich** /ʊn|ap|ˈɛndɐlɪç/ ❶ *Adj.* unalterable; irrevocable ‹decision›; **sich in das Unabänderliche fügen** resign oneself to the inevitable. ❷ *adv.* irrevocably; **das steht ~ fest** that is absolutely certain

**unabdingbar** /ʊn|apˈdɪŋbaːɐ̯/ *Adj.* Ⓐ (*geh.*) indispensable; Ⓑ (*Rechtsspr.*) inalienable

**unabhängig** ❶ *Adj.* independent (**von** of); (*unbeeinflusst*) unaffected (**von** by); **sich ~ machen** go one's own way; ‹colony› become independent. ❷ *adv.* independently (**von** of); **~ voneinander** independently [of one another]; separately; **es kostet 20 Pfennig, ~ von der Gesprächsdauer** it costs 20 pfennigs irrespective *or* regardless of the length of the call; **~ davon, ob .../was .../wo ...** *usw.* irrespective *or* regardless of whether .../what .../where ... *etc.*

**Unabhängigkeit** *die* independence

**Unabhängigkeits·erklärung** *die* declaration of independence

**unabkömmlich** /ʊn|apˈkœmlɪç/ *Adj.* indispensable; **sie ist im Moment ~:** she is otherwise engaged

**unablässig** /ˈʊn|aplɛsɪç/ ❶ *Adj.* incessant; constant ‹repetition›; unremitting ‹effort›. ❷ *adv.* incessantly; constantly

**unabsehbar** ❶ *Adj.* Ⓐ (*fig.*) incalculable, immeasurable ‹extent, damage, etc.›; **in ~er Ferne** (*zeitlich*) in the unforeseeable future; **auf ~e Zeit** far into the future; Ⓑ (*noch nicht vorauszusehen*) unforeseeable ‹consequences›. ❷ *adv.* Ⓐ incalculably; immeasurably; Ⓑ (*in einem noch nicht erkennbaren Ausmaß*) to an unforeseeable extent

**unabsichtlich** ❶ *Adj.* unintentional. ❷ *adv.* unintentionally

**unabweisbar** ❶ *Adj.* irrefutable; absolute ‹necessity›. ❷ *adv.* irrefutably; undeniably

**unabwendbar** *Adj.* inevitable

**unachtsam** ❶ *Adj.* Ⓐ inattentive; **einen Augenblick ~ sein** let one's attention wander for a moment; Ⓑ (*nicht sorgfältig*) careless. ❷ *adv.* (*ohne Sorgfalt*) carelessly

**Unachtsamkeit** *die; ~* Ⓐ inattentiveness; Ⓑ (*mangelnde Sorgfalt*) carelessness

**unähnlich** *Adj.* dissimilar; **jmdm./einer Sache ~ sein** be unlike sb./sth.

**unanfechtbar** *Adj.* incontestable

**unangebracht** *Adj.* inappropriate; misplaced

**unangefochten** *Adj.* unchallenged ‹victor, leadership, etc.›; (*unbestritten*) undisputed, unchallenged ‹assertion, thesis›; (*Rechtsw.*) uncontested ‹verdict, will, etc.›

**unangemeldet** *Adj.* Ⓐ (*unangekündigt*) unexpected ‹visit, guest›; unauthorized ‹demonstration›; **~ kommen** come unannounced; **~ zum Arzt gehen** go to the doctor without an appointment; Ⓑ (*nicht registriert*) unregistered ‹person, participant›; unlicensed ‹television set, radio›

**unangemessen** ❶ *Adj.* unsuitable; inappropriate; unreasonable, disproportionate ‹demand, claim, sentence, etc.›. ❷ *adv.* unsuitably; inappropriately; disproportionately ‹high, low›; **er reagierte völlig ~:** his reaction was out of all proportion; (*unpassend*) his reaction was entirely inappropriate

**unangenehm** ❶ *Adj.* unpleasant (+ *Dat.* for); (*peinlich*) embarrassing, awkward ‹question, situation›; **es ist mir sehr ~, dass ich mich verspätet habe** I am most upset about being late; **die Frage war ihm sichtlich ~:** he clearly found the question embarrassing; **~ werden** ‹person› get *or* turn nasty. ❷ *adv.* unpleasantly; (*peinlich*) **die Frage schien ihn ~ zu berühren** the question appeared to embarrass him; **~ auffallen** make a bad impression

**unangepasst**, ***unangepaßt** ❶ *Adj.* nonconformist. ❷ *adv.* in a nonconformist way

**unangetastet** *Adj.* untouched

**unangreifbar** *Adj.* (*auch fig.*) unassailable; impregnable ‹fortress›; (*unanfechtbar*) irrefutable ‹argument, thesis›; incontestable ‹judgement etc.›

**unannehmbar** *Adj.* unacceptable

**Unannehmlichkeit** *die* trouble; **mit/durch etw. ~en bekommen** get [a lot of (*coll.*)] trouble with sth./as a result of sth.; **~en auf sich** (*Akk.*) **nehmen** take on unpleasant business; **jmdm. ~en bereiten** cause sb. [a lot of (*coll.*)] problems *or* difficulties

**unansehnlich** *Adj.* unprepossessing; plain ‹girl›

**unanständig** ❶ *Adj.* Ⓐ improper; (*anstößig*) indecent ‹behaviour, remark›; dirty ‹joke›; rude ‹word, song›; Ⓑ (*verwerflich*) immoral. ❷ *adv.* Ⓐ improperly; **~ kurze Röcke** indecently short skirts; Ⓑ (*verwerflich*) immorally; Ⓒ (*ugs.; unmäßig, allzu*) disgustingly ‹fat›; indecently ‹often›; **~ viel essen** eat a disgusting amount

**Unanständigkeit** *die* Ⓐ impropriety; indecency; (*Obszönität*) obscenity; Ⓑ (*anstößige Handlung*) impropriety; (*anstößige Äußerung*) obscenity; indecent remark; Ⓒ (*Verwerflichkeit*) immorality; Ⓓ (*verwerfliche Handlung*) immoral action

**unantastbar** *Adj.* inviolable

**unappetitlich** ❶ *Adj.* unappetizing; (*fig.*) unsavoury ‹joke›; unsavoury-looking ‹person›; disgusting ‹washbasin, nails, etc.›. ❷ *adv.* unappetizingly

**Unart** *die* bad habit

**unartig** ❶ *Adj.* naughty. ❷ *adv.* naughtily; ‹behave› badly

**unartikuliert** ❶ *Adj.* inarticulate; (*fig.: nicht ausgedrückt*) unexpressed ‹feeling, thought, desire, etc.›. ❷ *adv.* inarticulately

**unästhetisch** ❶ *Adj.* unpleasant, unsavoury ‹sight etc.›; ugly ‹building etc.›; (*abstoßend*) disgusting. ❷ *adv.* in an unsavoury/a disgusting way

**unaufdringlich** ❶ *Adj.* unassuming ‹person›; (*fig.*) unobtrusive, discreet ‹music, décor, etc.›; discreet ‹perfume, colour, elegance, etc.›. ❷ *adv.* discreetly

**unauffällig** ❶ *Adj.* inconspicuous; unobtrusive ‹scar, defect, skill, behaviour, surveillance, etc.›; discreet ‹signal, elegance›; **sie ist eine eher ~e Erscheinung** she is not at all striking.

*old spelling (see note on page 1707)

❷ *adv.* inconspicuously; unobtrusively; ‹behave, follow, observe, disappear, leave› unobtrusively, discreetly

**unauffindbar** *Adj.* untraceable; **~ sein** *od.* **bleiben** be nowhere to be found

**unaufgefordert** *Adv.* without being asked; **~ eingesandte Manuskripte** unsolicited manuscripts

**unaufgeklärt** *Adj.* Ⓐ unresolved ‹misunderstanding›; unsolved ‹crime, mystery›; Ⓑ (*ignorant*) unenlightened ‹age, person›; (*sexualkundlich*) ignorant of the facts of life *postpos.*

**unaufhaltsam** ❶ *Adj.* inexorable. ❷ *adv.* inexorably

**unaufhörlich** ❶ *Adj.* constant; incessant; continuous ‹rain›. ❷ *adv.* constantly; ‹rain, snow› continuously; **das Telefon klingelte ~:** the telephone was for ever ringing *or* never stopped ringing

**unauflöslich** *Adj.* irreconcilable ‹contradiction etc.›; indissoluble ‹marriage, link›

**unaufmerksam** ❶ *Adj.* inattentive (**gegenüber** to); careless ‹driver›. ❷ *adv.* **sich seinen Gästen gegenüber ~ verhalten** not pay enough attention to one's guests

**Unaufmerksamkeit** *die* inattentiveness; (*Fahrlässigkeit*) carelessness

**unaufrichtig** *Adj.* insincere; **jmdm. gegenüber ~ sein** not be honest with sb.

**Unaufrichtigkeit** *die* Ⓐ insincerity; Ⓑ (*Handlung*) insincere action

**unaufschiebbar** *Adj.* **es war ~:** it could not be put off *or* postponed

**unausbleiblich** *Adj.* inevitable; unavoidable

**unausdenkbar** *Adj.* unimaginable

**unausgefüllt** *Adj.* uncompleted, blank ‹form›; (*fig.*) unfulfilled ‹person›; unfilled ‹time›; empty ‹life›

**unausgeglichen** *Adj.* Ⓐ (*emotional*) [emotionally] unstable ‹person, behaviour›; Ⓑ (*Wirtsch.*) ‹balance of payments› not in balance; unsettled ‹account, debt›; Ⓒ (*unausgewogen*) unbalanced ‹report, relationship, etc.›; unequal ‹distribution›; (*ungleichmäßig*) uneven, changeable ‹climate›

**Unausgeglichenheit** *die* Ⓐ (*eines Menschen*) instability; Ⓑ (*Wirtsch.*) imbalance; Ⓒ (*Unausgewogenheit*) imbalance; (*Ungleichmäßigkeit*) unevenness; inconsistency

**unausgegoren** *Adj.* (*abwertend*) immature

**unausgeschlafen** *Adj.* **[völlig] ~ sein/aussehen** have not had/look as though one has not had [anything like] enough sleep; **~ zur Schule kommen** come to school tired through lack of sleep

**unauslöschlich** ❶ *Adj.* (*geh.*) indelible ‹impression›; unforgettable ‹experience›. ❷ *adv.* indelibly

**unaussprechlich** ❶ *Adj.* Ⓐ inexpressible; Ⓑ (*geh.: unbeschreiblich*) indescribable ‹misery, joy›; unutterable ‹misery, sorrow›. ❷ *adv.* (*geh.*) unutterably; indescribably; ‹suffer, love› beyond expression

**unausstehlich** ❶ *Adj.* unbearable ‹person, noise, smell, etc.›; insufferable ‹person›; intolerable ‹noise, smell›. ❷ *adv.* unbearably; intolerably; insufferably ‹stupid, curious›

**unausweichlich** *Adj.* unavoidable; inevitable

**unbändig** /ˈʊnbɛndɪç/ ❶ *Adj.* Ⓐ boisterous ‹person, horse, temperament›; Ⓑ (*überaus groß/stark*) unbridled, unrestrained ‹desire, longing, joy, merriment›; unbridled, uncontrollable ‹fury, hate, anger›; ravenous ‹hunger›. ❷ *adv.* Ⓐ wildly; Ⓑ (*sehr, äußerst*) unrestrainedly; tremendously (*coll.*); **~ jubeln** *od.* **jauchzen, sich ~ freuen** jump for joy

**unbar** ❶ *Adj.* cashless. ❷ *adv.* ‹pay› without using cash

**unbarmherzig** ❶ *Adj.* (*auch fig.*) merciless; remorseless, unsparing ‹severity›; (*fig.*) very severe ‹winter, cold›; **jmdm. gegenüber** *od.* **gegen jmdn. ~ sein** show sb. no mercy. ❷ *adv.* mercilessly; without mercy

**unbeabsichtigt** ❶ *Adj.* unintentional. ❷ *adv.* unintentionally

**unbeachtet** *Adj.* unnoticed; obscure ‹existence›; **~ leben** live in obscurity; **jmdn./etw. ~ lassen** not take any notice of sb./sth.

**unbeanstandet** ❶ *Adj.* **etw. ~ lassen** let sth. pass; **~ bleiben** be allowed to pass. ❷ *adv.* without objection; **~ durch die Gütekontrolle gehen** be allowed to pass through quality control [without any problems]

**unbeantwortet** *Adj.* unanswered

**unbearbeitet** *Adj.* Ⓐ undealt with *pred.;* which has/have not been dealt with *postpos.;* Ⓑ (*roh*) untreated ‹wood, leather, metal›; (*unbestellt*) uncultivated ‹land, field›; (*nicht redigiert*) unedited ‹manuscript›; (*nicht verändert, adaptiert*) unchanged, unadapted ‹play, version›

**unbebaut** *Adj.* Ⓐ undeveloped ‹site, land›; Ⓑ (*unbestellt*) uncultivated ‹land, area›

**unbedacht** ❶ *Adj.* rash; thoughtless. ❷ *adv.* rashly; thoughtlessly

**unbedarft** ❶ *Adj.* (*ugs.*) Ⓐ inexpert; lay; **er ist literarisch [völlig/ziemlich] ~:** he has no/little idea about literature; Ⓑ (*naiv*) naïve; (*dümmlich*) gormless (*coll.*). ❷ *adv.* naïvely; (*dümmlich*) gormlessly (*coll.*)

**unbedeckt** *Adj.* uncovered; bare; **mit ~em Kopf** bare-headed

**unbedenklich** ❶ *Adj.* Ⓐ harmless, safe ‹substance, drug›; ‹state of health, situation› giving no cause for concern; unobjectionable ‹joke, plan, reading matter›; **es ist nicht ganz ~:** it is to some extent open to objection; Ⓑ (*hemmungslos, skrupellos*) unthinking; unconsidered. ❷ *adv.* without second thoughts

**unbedeutend** ❶ *Adj.* insignificant; minor ‹artist, poet›; slight, minor ‹improvement, change, error›. ❷ *adv.* slightly

**unbedingt** ❶ *Adj.* Ⓐ absolute ‹trust, faith, reliability, secrecy, etc.›; complete ‹rest›; Ⓑ (*Physiol.*) **~e Reflexe** unconditioned reflexes. ❷ *Adv.* absolutely; (*auf jeden Fall*) whatever happens; **etw. ~ tun müssen/wollen** really *or* absolutely have to/be absolutely determined to do sth.; **der Brief muss ~ heute noch weg** the letter really must be posted today; **ich brauche ~ neue Reifen** I need new tyres whatever happens; I really have to have new tyres; **ich brauche jetzt ~ einen Schnaps** I've just got to have a schnapps; **nicht ~:** not necessarily; **nicht ~ nötig** not absolutely necessary; **~!** absolutely!; of course!

**unbeeidigt** *Adj.* (*Rechtsw.*) unsworn; **der Zeuge blieb ~:** the witness was not on *or* under oath

**unbeeindruckt** *Adj.* unimpressed

**unbeeinflusst**, ***unbeeinflußt** *Adj.* uninfluenced; **von jeder Propaganda ~:** not influenced by any propaganda *postpos.*

**unbefahrbar** *Adj.* Ⓐ (*für Landfahrzeuge*) impassable; Ⓑ (*für Wasserfahrzeuge*) unnavigable; not navigable *pred.*

**unbefangen** ❶ *Adj.* Ⓐ (*ungehemmt*) uninhibited; natural, uninhibited ‹behaviour›; **er ist anderen gegenüber ganz ~:** he is perfectly natural with other people; Ⓑ (*unvoreingenommen*) impartial. ❷ *adv.* freely; without inhibition; ‹behave› naturally; **jmdm./einer Sache ~ gegenübertreten** approach sb./sth. with an open mind

**Unbefangenheit** *die* ⇒ **unbefangen** 1 A, B: uninhibitedness; naturalness; impartiality

**unbefleckt** *Adj.* (*geh.*) undefiled; unsullied (*literary*); **die Unbefleckte Empfängnis** (*christl. Rel.*) the Immaculate Conception

**unbefriedigend** *Adj.* unsatisfactory

**unbefriedigt** *Adj.* dissatisfied (**von** with); unsatisfied ‹need, curiosity, desire, etc.›; (*unausgefüllt*) unfulfilled (**von** by); (*sexuell*) [sexually] unsatisfied *or* frustrated

**unbefristet** ❶ *Adj.* for an indefinite *or* unlimited period *postpos.;* indefinite ‹strike›; unlimited ‹visa›. ❷ *adv.* for an indefinite *or* unlimited period

**unbefugt** ❶ *Adj.* unauthorized; **ein Unbefugter** an unauthorized person. ❷ *adv.* without authorization

**unbegabt** *Adj.* ungifted; untalented; **für Sprachen ~ sein** have no talent for languages

**unbegreiflich** *Adj.* incomprehensible (+ *Dat.*, **für** to); incredible ‹love, goodness, stupidity, carelessness, etc.›; **auf ~e Weise** in a baffling *or* mysterious manner

**unbegreiflicherweise** *Adv.* inexplicably

**unbegrenzt** ❶ *Adj.* unlimited; **ein zeitlich ~er Vertrag** a contract with no time limit; **Kosten in ~er Höhe** costs up to an unlimited amount. ❷ *adv.* ‹stay, keep, etc.› indefinitely; ‹trust› absolutely; **ich habe nicht ~ Zeit** I don't have unlimited time

**unbegründet** *Adj.* unfounded, groundless ‹fear, accusation, suspicion›

**unbehaart** *Adj.* hairless; bald ‹head›

**Unbehagen** *das* uneasiness, disquiet; (*Sorge*) concern (**an** + *Dat.* about); **etw. mit ~ feststellen/betrachten** note/watch sth. with concern; **ein leichtes körperliches ~:** a slight physical discomfort; **das bereitet mir ~:** it makes me feel uneasy

**unbehaglich** ❶ *Adj.* uneasy, uncomfortable ‹feeling, atmosphere›; uncomfortable ‹thought, room›; **mir war ~ zumute** I was *or* felt uneasy; **er/es war mir ~:** he/it made me feel uneasy *or* uncomfortable. ❷ *adv.* uneasily; uncomfortably; **~ kühl** uncomfortably *or* unpleasantly cool

**unbehauen** *Adj.* unhewn

**unbehelligt** *Adj.* unmolested; (*ohne Störung*) ‹read, work› undisturbed, in peace; **er gelangte ~ von Journalisten in das Gebäude** he got into the building without being intercepted by journalists; **die Zollbeamten ließen uns ~ passieren** the customs let us through without stopping us

**unbeherrscht** ❶ *Adj.* uncontrolled; intemperate, wild ‹reaction, behaviour, remark›; **er ist ~:** he has no self-control. ❷ *adv.* without any self-control

**Unbeherrschtheit** *die;* **~, ~en** Ⓐ lack of self-control; Ⓑ (*Handlung*) uncontrolled fit; (*Äußerung*) wild outburst

**unbehindert** *Adj.* unhindered; unimpeded

**unbeholfen** ❶ *Adj.* clumsy; awkward. ❷ *adv.* clumsily; awkwardly

**unbeirrbar** ❶ *Adj.* unwavering. ❷ *adv.* unwaveringly; unswervingly

**unbeirrt** ❶ *Adj.* unwavering. ❷ *adv.* without wavering

**unbekannt** ❶ *Adj.* Ⓐ unknown; (*nicht vertraut*) unfamiliar; unidentified ‹caller, donor, flying object›; **das war mir bisher ~:** I didn't know that until now; **es ist mir nicht ~, dass ...** I am not unaware that ...; **sie ist hier ~:** she is not known here; **~e Täter** unknown *or* unidentified culprits; **„Empfänger ~"** 'not known at this address'; **eine ~e Größe** (*Math.; auch scherzh.: Mensch*) an unknown quantity; **ich bin hier ~** (*ugs.*) I'm a stranger here; **[Straf]anzeige gegen ~** (*Rechtsw.*) charge against person or persons unknown; Ⓑ (*nicht vielen bekannt*) little known; obscure ‹poet, painter, etc.›. ❷ *adv.* **„Empfänger ~ verzogen"** 'moved'; 'address unknown'

**Unbekannte**[1] *der/die; adj. Dekl.* unknown *or* unidentified man/woman; (*Fremde[r]*) stranger; **er ist [hier/dem Fernsehpublikum] kein ~er [mehr]** he is no stranger [here/to television viewers]; **der große ~** (*scherzh.*) the mystery man *or* person

**Unbekannte**[2] *die; adj. Dekl.* (*Math.; auch fig.*) unknown

**unbekannterweise** *Adv.* **grüßen Sie ihn/sie ~ [von mir]** give him/her my regards, although we haven't met

**unbekleidet** *Adj.* without any clothes on *postpos.;* bare ‹torso etc.›; naked ‹corpse›

**unbekümmert** ❶ *Adj.* (*unbeschwert*) carefree; (*ohne Bedenken, lässig*) casual; **sie ist [ziemlich] ~:** she doesn't worry [much]; she is [pretty] unconcerned; **um etw. ~ sein** be unconcerned about sth. ❷ *adv.* Ⓐ (*unbeschwert*) in a carefree way; without a care in the world; **~ leben** live a carefree life; Ⓑ (*ohne Bedenken*) without caring *or* worrying;

ganz *od.* **völlig ~:** entirely unconcerned; without a second thought; **er raucht ~ weiter** he happily goes on smoking

**Unbekümmertheit** *die;* ~ **A** carefree manner *or* attitude; carefreeness; **B** (*Bedenkenlosigkeit*) lack of concern

**unbelastet** *Adj.* **A** not under load *postpos.;* **im ~en Zustand** when not under load; **B** (*von Sorgen, Problemen usw.*) free from care *or* worries *postpos.;* **von Sorgen ~:** free from worries; **C** (*ohne Schuld*) **~ sein** have a clean record; **D** (*schuldenfrei*) unmortgaged ‹property, land›

**unbelebt** *Adj.* **A** inanimate ‹nature›; (*anorganisch*) inorganic ‹matter›; **B** (*ohne Lebewesen*) uninhabited; deserted; empty ‹streets›

**unbeleckt** *Adj.* (*salopp*) **von etw. ~ sein** not have a clue about sth. (*coll.*); **sie sind von jeder Kultur ~:** they are complete savages

**unbelehrbar** *Adj.* incorrigible; not accessible to reason *postpos.;* **er ist ~:** he will not learn

**unbeleuchtet** *Adj.* unlit ‹street, corridor, etc.›; ‹vehicle› without [any] lights

**unbelichtet** *Adj.* (*Fot.*) unexposed

**unbeliebt** *Adj.* unpopular (**bei** with)

**Unbeliebtheit** *die* unpopularity

**unbemannt** *Adj.* **A** unmanned; **B** (*scherzh.*) (*ohne Mann*) husbandless (*joc.*); (*ohne Freund*) without a man *postpos.*

**unbemerkt** *Adj., adv.* unnoticed

**unbemittelt** *Adj.* penniless; impecunious; **nicht ganz ~:** not exactly penniless

**unbenommen** *Adj. in* **es ist/bleibt jmdm. ~, zu ...** sb. is/remains free *or* at liberty to ...; **dieses Recht bleibt Ihnen ~:** this remains your right

**unbenutzbar** *Adj.* unusable

**unbenutzt** *Adj.* unused

**unbeobachtet** *Adj.* unobserved; **in einem ~en Augenblick** *od.* **Moment** when no one is/was watching; **wenn er sich ~ fühlt** *od.* **glaubt** when he thinks no one is looking

**unbequem** **1** *Adj.* **A** uncomfortable; **B** (*lästig*) awkward, embarrassing ‹question, opinion›; awkward, troublesome ‹politician etc.›; unpleasant ‹criticism, truth, etc.›; **er wurde ihnen ~:** he became a nuisance *or* an embarrassment to them. **2** *adv.* uncomfortably

**Unbequemlichkeit** *die* **A** lack of comfort; **B** (*Lästigkeit*) awkwardness; **C** (*etw., was unbequem ist*) discomfort

**unberechenbar** **1** *Adj.* unpredictable. **2** *adv.* unpredictably

**unberechtigt** **1** *Adj.* **A** (*ungerechtfertigt*) unjustified; **B** (*unbefugt*) unauthorized. **2** *adv.* **A** (*unbefugt*) without authorization; **B** (*ungerechtfertigt*) without justification; unjustifiably ‹expensive etc.›

**unberücksichtigt** *Adj.* unconsidered; **etw. ~ lassen** leave sth. out of consideration; ignore sth.; **~ bleiben** not be considered; be ignored

**unberufen**[1] *Adj.* **in ~e Hände fallen** fall into the wrong hands

**unberufen**[2] *Interj.* **~ [toi, toi, toi]!** touch wood!; knock on wood! (*Amer.*)

**Unberührbare** *der/die; adj. Dekl.* (*Rel.*) untouchable

**unberührt** *Adj.* **A** untouched; virgin ‹snow, forest, wilderness›; **ein Stück ~er Natur** a stretch of unspoilt countryside; **B** (*geh.: jungfräulich*) in the virgin state; **sie ist noch ~:** she is still a virgin; **C** (*unbeeindruckt*) unmoved (**von** by); **die Nachricht ließ ihn ~:** he was unmoved by the news

**Unberührtheit** *die;* ~ **A** (*natürlicher Zustand*) unspoiled state; **B** (*geh.: Jungfräulichkeit*) virginity; **C** (*das Unbeeindrucktsein*) lack of emotion; impassivity

**unbeschadet** **1** *Präp. mit Gen.* regardless of; notwithstanding. **2** *Adj.* (*veralt.*) ⇒ **unbeschädigt** A, B

**unbeschädigt** *Adj.* **A** undamaged; **B** (*veralt.: unverletzt*) unharmed

**unbescheiden** *Adj.* presumptuous; **wenn ich mir die ~e Frage/Bitte erlauben darf** if you don't mind my asking; **ist es sehr ~, wenn ich Sie bitte ...?** I hope you don't mind my asking you ...

**unbescholten** *Adj.* respectable; (*veralt.: keusch*) chaste ‹girl›; **~ sein** (*Rechtsspr.*) have no [previous] convictions

**Unbescholtenheit** *die;* ~ ⇒ **unbescholten**: respectability; chastity; absence of [previous] convictions

**unbeschrankt** *Adj.* ‹crossing› without gates, with no gates

**unbeschränkt** **1** *Adj.* unlimited; limitless ‹possibilities, power›; (*hist.*) absolute ‹ruler›; **die Teilnehmerzahl ist ~:** there is no limit on the number of participants. **2** *adv.* **für etw. ~ haften** have unlimited liability for sth.

**unbeschreiblich** **1** *Adj.* indescribable; unimaginable ‹fear, beauty›; ‹fear, beauty› beyond description. **2** *adv.* indescribably ‹beautiful›; unbelievably ‹busy›; **~ viele Menschen** an incredible number of people; **sich ~ freuen** be overjoyed

**unbeschrieben** *Adj.* blank, empty ‹piece of paper, page›; ⇒ *auch* **Blatt** B

**unbeschwert** **1** *Adj.* carefree. **2** *adv.* free from care; ‹dance, play› with a light heart

**unbesehen** **1** *Adj.* unquestioning ‹acceptance›. **2** *adv.* without hesitation; **das glaube ich ~:** I don't doubt it for a moment

**unbesiegbar** *Adj.* invincible

**unbesiegt** *Adj.* undefeated ‹army›; unbeaten ‹team, player›

**unbesonnen** **1** *Adj.* impulsive ‹person, nature›; unthinking ‹remark›; (*übereilt*) ill-considered, rash ‹decision, action›. **2** *adv.* ‹act› without thinking; (*übereilt*) rashly

**unbesorgt** *Adj.* unconcerned; **seien** *od.* **bleiben Sie ~!** don't [you] worry; you can set your mind at rest; **du darfst ~ nach Hause gehen** you can go home without worrying/with an easy mind

**unbespielbar** *Adj.* (*Sport*) unplayable ‹pitch›

**unbespielt** *Adj.* blank ‹tape, cassette›

**unbeständig** *Adj.* changeable, unsettled ‹weather›; erratic, inconsistent ‹performance, person, etc.›; inconstant, fickle ‹lover etc.›; (*vergänglich*) transitory ‹love, luck›

**unbestätigt** *Adj.* unconfirmed

**unbestechlich** *Adj.* **A** incorruptible; **B** (*fig.*) uncompromising ‹critic›; incorruptible ‹character›; unerring ‹judgement›; unwavering ‹honesty, love of truth›

**unbestimmbar** *Adj.* unidentifiable ‹plant, sound, colour, etc.›; indeterminable ‹age, distance›; (*Bot., Zool.*) unclassifiable

**unbestimmt** **1** *Adj.* **A** (*nicht festgelegt*) indefinite; indeterminate ‹age, number›; (*ungewiss*) uncertain; **auf ~e Zeit** for an indefinite period; **B** (*ungenau*) vague; **C** (*Sprachw.*) indefinite ‹article, pronoun›; nonfinite ‹verb form›. **2** *adv.* (*ungenau*) vaguely

**Unbestimmtheit** *die* **A** (*Ungenauigkeit*) vagueness; **B** (*Ungewissheit*) uncertainty

**unbestreitbar** **1** *Adj.* indisputable; unquestionable. **2** *adv.* indisputably; unquestionably

**unbestritten** **1** *Adj.* undisputed; **~ ist, dass ...** it is undisputed that ...; there is no disputing that ... **2** *adv.* indisputably

**unbeteiligt** **1** *Adj.* **A** (*passiv, nicht mitwirkend*) uninvolved; **~e Passanten/Zuschauer** passers-by/onlookers who are/were not involved; **ein Unbeteiligter** someone who is/was not involved; an outsider; (*ein Unschuldiger*) an innocent party; **B** (*gleichgültig*) indifferent; detached ‹manner, expression›. **2** *adv.* with a detached *or* indifferent air; **~ dabeistehen** stand by without taking any interest in the proceedings

**unbetont** *Adj.* unstressed

**unbeträchtlich** **1** *Adj.* insignificant; **nicht ~:** not inconsiderable. **2** *adv.* insignificantly; slightly; **nicht ~:** not inconsiderably

**unbeugsam** *Adj.* uncompromising; tenacious; indomitable, unshakeable ‹will, pride›; unwavering, resolute ‹character›

**unbewacht** *Adj.* unsupervised ‹pupils, prisoners, etc.›; unattended ‹car park›; **in einem ~en Moment** when no one is/was watching

**unbewaffnet** *Adj.* unarmed

**unbewältigt** *Adj.* unmastered, uncompleted ‹task›; unresolved ‹conflict, problem›; **unsere ~e Vergangenheit** the past with which we have not come to terms

**unbeweglich** *Adj.* **A** (*bewegungslos*) motionless; still ‹air, water›; fixed ‹gaze, expression›; **~ sitzen/stehen** sit/stand motionless; **B** (*starr*) immovable, fixed ‹part, joint, etc.›; **~es Eigentum** real estate; **ein ~es Fest** an immovable feast; **C** (*nicht mobil*) immobile; **D** (*schwerfällig*) (*geistig*) ponderous; (*körperlich*) slow-moving; slow on one's feet *pred.*

**unbewegt** *Adj.* motionless; fixed ‹expression›

**unbeweibt** *Adj.* (*ugs. scherzh.*) wifeless

**unbewiesen** *Adj.* unproved

**unbewohnbar** *Adj.* uninhabitable; **ein Gebäude für ~ erklären** declare a building unfit for human habitation

**unbewohnt** *Adj.* uninhabited ‹area›; unoccupied ‹house, flat›

**unbewusst**, ***unbewußt** **1** *Adj.* **A** unconscious; **B** (*ungewollt*) unconscious, unintentional ‹distortion, exaggeration, etc.›. **2** *adv.* **A** unconsciously; **B** (*ungewollt*) unconsciously; unintentionally

**Unbewusste**, ***Unbewußte** *das; adj. Dekl.* (*Psych.*) unconscious

**unbezahlbar** *Adj.* **A** (*teuer*) prohibitive; (*zu teuer*) prohibitively expensive ‹article›; **B** (*kostbar*) priceless ‹painting, china›; **meine Sekretärin ist einfach ~** (*ugs.*) my secretary is worth her weight in gold

**unbezahlt** *Adj.* unpaid; ‹goods etc.› not [yet] paid for

**unbezähmbar** *Adj.* uncontrollable; insatiable ‹hunger, thirst, curiosity›

**unbezwinglich** *Adj.* **A** impregnable ‹fortress›; invincible ‹enemy, opponent›; **B** (*fig.: unbezähmbar*) uncontrollable ‹urge›; insatiable ‹hunger, thirst, curiosity, desire›

**Unbilden** /ˈʊnbɪldn̩/ *Pl.* (*geh.*) rigours

**Unbill** /ˈʊnbɪl/ *die;* ~ (*geh.*) (*Unrecht*) wrong; injustice; (*Beschwernis*) rigours *pl.*

**unblutig** **1** *Adj.* **A** bloodless; **B** (*Med.: nichtoperativ*) non-surgical. **2** *adv.* **A** without bloodshed; **B** (*Med.: nichtoperativ*) without [the need for] surgery

**unbot·mäßig** **1** *Adj.* insubordinate; **~e Kritik** disrespectful criticism. **2** *adv.* insubordinately

**Unbot·mäßigkeit** *die* insubordination

**unbrauchbar** *Adj.* unusable; (*untauglich*) useless ‹method, person›; **~ machen** make ‹machine› unserviceable; put ‹machine› out of action; **er ist dafür ~:** he is no use for this

**unbürokratisch** **1** *Adj.* unbureaucratic; **auf möglichst ~e Weise** with as little red tape as possible. **2** *adv.* unbureaucratically; without a great deal of red tape

**unbuß·fertig** *Adj.* impenitent; unrepentant

**unchristlich** **1** *Adj.* **A** unchristian; **B zu ~er Zeit** at an ungodly hour (*coll.*). **2** *adv.* in an unchristian way

**und** /ʊnt/ *Konj.* **A** (*nebenordnend*) and; (*folglich*) [and] so; **das deutsche ~ das französische Volk** the German and French peoples; **zwei ~ drei ist fünf** two and *or* plus three makes five; **es wollte ~ wollte nicht gelingen** it simply *or* just wouldn't work; **es gibt Konservative ~ Konservative** there are conservatives and conservatives; **hoch ~ höher** higher and higher; **~ die anderen/ich?** [and] what about the others/about me?; **~ warum?** why [is that]?; **der ~ der** so-and-so; **zu der ~ der Zeit** at such-and-such a time; **so ~ so ist es gewesen** it was like this; **~?** and?; well?; **ich ~ tanzen?** what, me dance?; **der ~ arbeiten/arm?** what, him work/poor?; ⇒ *auch* **na** A; **ob**[1] C; **wie** 1 C; **B** (*unterordnend*) (*konsekutiv*) **tu mir den Gefallen ~ komm mit** be so kind as to come too; **sei so gut ~ mach das Fenster zu** be so good as to shut the window; **warum bist du auch so leichtsinnig ~**

*old spelling (see note on page 1707)

**schließt dein Fahrrad nicht ab?** why are you so careless as to leave your bicycle unlocked?; **es fehlte nicht viel, ~ der Deich wäre gebrochen** it wouldn't have taken much to breach the dike; (*konzessiv*) **du musst es tun, ~ fällt es dir noch so schwer** you must do it however difficult you may find it; ⇒ *auch* **wenn c**

**Undank** *der* ingratitude; **nur ~ ernten** get no thanks; meet only with ingratitude; **~ ist der Welt Lohn** (*Spr.*) that's all the thanks you get

**undankbar** ❶ *Adj.* [A] ungrateful ‹person, behaviour›; [B] (*wenig lohnend*) thankless ‹task›; unrewarding ‹role, subject, job, etc.›. ❷ *adv.* ungratefully

**undatiert** *Adj.* undated

**undefinierbar** *Adj.* [A] indefinable; [B] (*nicht bestimmbar*) unidentifiable; indeterminable ‹feeling›; indeterminate ‹colour›

**undeklinierbar** *Adj.* (*Sprachw.*) indeclinable

**undenkbar** *Adj.* unthinkable; inconceivable

**undenklich** *Adj.* in **vor ~er Zeit** *od.* **~en Zeiten** an eternity ago; **seit ~er Zeit** *od.* **~en Zeiten** since time immemorial

**undeutlich** ❶ *Adj.* unclear; indistinct; (*ungenau*) vague ‹idea, memory, etc.›. ❷ *adv.* indistinctly; (*ungenau*) vaguely; **du schreibst zu ~:** you don't write clearly enough

**undicht** *Adj.* leaky; leaking; **~ werden** start to leak; develop a leak; **eine ~e Stelle** (*auch fig.*) a leak; **~e Fenster/Türen** windows/doors which do not fit tightly

**undifferenziert** ❶ *Adj.* [A] (*geh.*) indiscriminate ‹criticism›; ‹criticism› which fails to discriminate; overgeneralized, simplistic ‹account›; [B] (*Biol.*) undifferentiated. ❷ *adv.* (*geh.*) in an overgeneralized *or* indiscriminate way

**Unding** *das; in* **ein ~ sein** be preposterous *or* ridiculous

**undiplomatisch** ❶ *Adj.* undiplomatic. ❷ *adv.* undiplomatically

**undiszipliniert** ❶ *Adj.* undisciplined; ‹pupils, class› lacking in discipline. ❷ *adv.* in an undisciplined way

**undogmatisch** ❶ *Adj.* undogmatic. ❷ *adv.* undogmatically

**unduldsam** ❶ *Adj.* intolerant. ❷ *adv.* intolerantly

**undurchdringlich** *Adj.* [A] impenetrable; pitch-dark ‹night›; [B] (*undurchschaubar*) inscrutable ‹person, expression, mask›

**undurchführbar** *Adj.* impracticable

**undurchlässig** *Adj.* impermeable; (*wasserdicht*) watertight; waterproof; (*luftdicht*) airtight

**-undurchlässig** *adj.* **licht~/wasser~/luft~:** lightproof/waterproof/airtight

**undurchschaubar** *Adj.* inscrutable ‹person, plan, etc.›; unfathomable ‹cause, etc.›; **für jmdn. ~ sein** be baffling to sb.

**undurchsichtig** *Adj.* [A] opaque ‹glass›; non-transparent ‹fabric etc.›; dense, impenetrable ‹fog, mist›; [B] (*fig.*) unfathomable, inscrutable ‹plan, intention, role›; shady ‹character, business›

**uneben** *Adj.* uneven; (*holprig*) bumpy ‹road, track›

**Unebenheit** *die; ~, ~en* [A] unevenness; (*Holprigkeit*) bumpiness; [B] (*unebene Stelle*) lumpy *or* uneven patch

**unecht** *Adj.* [A] (*falsch, imitiert*) artificial ‹fur, hair›; false ‹teeth›; imitation ‹jewellery, marble, etc.›; (*gefälscht*) counterfeit ‹notes›; bogus, fake ‹painting›; [B] (*gespielt, vorgetäuscht*) false, insincere ‹friendliness, sympathy, smile, etc.›; simulated ‹enthusiasm, affection, etc.›; [C] (*Math.*) improper ‹fraction›

**unehelich** *Adj.* illegitimate ‹child›; unmarried ‹mother›; **~ geboren sein** be born out of wedlock

**Unehre** *die; ~* (*geh.*) dishonour; **etw. macht jmdm. ~** *od.* **gereicht jmdm. zur ~:** sth. brings dishonour on sb.

**unehrenhaft** ❶ *Adj.* dishonourable. ❷ *adv.* dishonourably; **er wurde ~ aus der Armee entlassen** (*Milit.*) he was given a dishonourable discharge from the army

**unehrlich** ❶ *Adj.* dishonest; **ein ~es Spiel treiben** play a double game. ❷ *adv.* dishonestly; by dishonest means

**Unehrlichkeit** *die* [A] dishonesty; [B] (*Handlung*) dishonest action

**uneigennützig** ❶ *Adj.* unselfish; selfless. ❷ *adv.* unselfishly; selflessly; ‹help› from selfless motives

**Uneigennützigkeit** *die* unselfishness; selflessness

**uneingeschränkt** ❶ *Adj.* unlimited ‹freedom, power, etc.›; absolute ‹trust, authority›; unreserved ‹praise, admiration, recognition›. ❷ *adv.* ‹agree› without reservation

**uneingeweiht** *Adj.* uninitiated

**uneinig** *Adj.* ‹party› divided by disagreement; **[sich** (*Dat.*)**] ~ sein** disagree; be in disagreement; **ich bin [mir] mit ihm darin ~:** I disagree with him on that

**Uneinigkeit** *die* disagreement (**in** + *Dat.* on)

**uneinnehmbar** *Adj.* impregnable

**uneins** *Adj.* **~ sein** be divided (**in** + *Dat.* on); ‹persons, bodies› be at variance *or* at cross purposes (**in** + *Dat.* over); **mit jmdm. ~ sein[, wie ...]** be unable to agree with sb. [how ...]; **er ist mit sich [selbst] ~:** he is undecided *or* cannot decide

**unempfänglich** *Adj.* unreceptive (**für** to)

**unempfindlich** *Adj.* [A] insensitive (**gegen** to); [B] (*nicht anfällig, immun*) immune (**gegen** to, against); [C] (*strapazierfähig*) hard-wearing; (*pflegeleicht*) easy-care *attrib.*

**unendlich** ❶ *Adj.* infinite, boundless ‹space, sea, expanse, fig.: love, care, patience, etc.›; (*zeitlich*) endless; never-ending; (*Math.*) infinite ‹number etc.›; **das Unendliche** the infinite (*Philos.*); infinity (*Math.*); **sich im Unendlichen schneiden** (*Math.*) meet at infinity; **auf ~ stellen** (*Fot.*) focus ‹lens› on infinity; **bis ins Unendliche** (*auch fig.*) endlessly. ❷ *adv.* infinitely ‹lovable, sad›; immeasurably ‹happy›; ‹happy› beyond measure; **~ langsam** with infinite slowness; **~ lang** endless; **~ groß/hoch** of infinite size/height *postpos.*; immensely (*coll.*) large/high; **sich ~ freuen** be tremendously pleased; **~ viele Menschen/Elemente** countless people/an infinite number of elements; **ein ~ ferner Punkt** (*Math.*) a point at an infinite distance; **~ klein** (*Math.*) infinitesimal

**Unendlichkeit** *die; ~* [A] infinity *no def. art.*; (*des Himmels/Ozeans*) infinite expanse; boundlessness; [B] (*geh.: Ewigkeit*) eternity *no def. art.*

**unentbehrlich** *Adj.* indispensable (*Dat.*, **für** to)

**unentgeltlich** /*od.* '----/ ❶ *Adj.* free; **~ sein** be free of charge. ❷ *adv.* free of charge; ‹work› for nothing, without pay

**unentrinnbar** (*geh.*) ❶ *Adj.* inescapable. ❷ *adv.* inescapably

**unentschieden** ❶ *Adj.* [A] unsettled ‹case, matter›; undecided ‹question›; [B] (*Sport, Schach*) drawn ‹game, match›; **bei ~em Spielausgang** if the game ends in a draw; **der Spielstand ist ~:** the scores are level; [C] (*unentschlossen*) indecisive ‹person›. ❷ *adv.* (*Sport, Schach*) **~ spielen** draw; **~ enden** end in a draw; **das Spiel steht 0 : 0 ~:** the game is a goalless draw [so far]

**Unentschieden** *das; ~s, ~* (*Sport, Schach*) draw

**unentschlossen** *Adj.* [A] undecided; [B] (*entschlussunfähig*) indecisive

**Unentschlossenheit** *die* [A] indecision *no def. art.*; [B] (*Entschlussunfähigkeit*) indecisiveness

**unentschuldbar** ❶ *Adj.* inexcusable. ❷ *adv.* inexcusably

**unentschuldigt** ❶ *Adj.* without giving any reason *postpos.*, *not pred.*; **~es Fernbleiben vom Unterricht/Arbeitsplatz** absence from school/work. ❷ *adv.* without giving any reason

**unentwegt** /*od.* --'-/ ❶ *Adj.* [A] (*beharrlich, ausdauernd*) persistent ‹fighter, champion, efforts›; **ein paar Unentwegte** a few stalwarts; [B] (*unaufhörlich*) constant; incessant. ❷ *adv.* [A] (*beharrlich*) persistently; [B] (*unaufhörlich*) constantly; incessantly

**unentwirrbar** ❶ *Adj.* inextricable ‹tangle›; ‹threads, tangle› that cannot be unravelled; (*fig.*) irredeemable ‹muddle, chaos›. ❷ *adv.* inextricably

**unerbittlich** ❶ *Adj.* (*auch fig.*) inexorable; unsparing, unrelenting ‹critic›; relentless ‹battle, struggle›; implacable ‹hate, enemy›; **gegen jmdn. ~ sein** be completely unyielding towards sb. ❷ *adv.* (*auch fig.*) inexorably; relentlessly; **~ durchgreifen** take uncompromising action; **~ gegen jmdn./etw. vorgehen** take ruthless action against sb./sth.

**unerfahren** *Adj.* inexperienced

**unerfindlich** *Adj.* (*geh.*) unfathomable, inexplicable; **es ist mir ~, warum/wie** *usw.* **...** it is a mystery to me why/how *etc.* ...

**unerforschlich** *Adj.* (*geh.*) unfathomable; ⇒ *auch* **Ratschluss**

**unerfreulich** ❶ *Adj.* unpleasant; bad ‹news›; **[etwas] Unerfreuliches** something unpleasant; (*schlechte Nachricht*) bad news. ❷ *adv.* unpleasantly; **~ verlaufen** take a disagreeable course

**unerfüllbar** *Adj.* unrealizable

**unergiebig** *Adj.* (*auch fig.*) unproductive; (*fig.: nicht lohnend*) unrewarding ‹work, subject›

**unergründlich** *Adj.* unfathomable, inscrutable ‹motive, mystery, etc.›; inscrutable ‹expression, smile›

**unerheblich** ❶ *Adj.* insignificant; **nicht ~:** not inconsiderable; **es ist ~, ob ...** it is of no significance *or* importance whether ... ❷ *adv.* insignificantly; [very] slightly

**unerhört** ❶ *Adj.* [A] enormous, tremendous ‹sum, quantity, etc.›; incredible (*coll.*), phenomenal ‹speed, effort, performance, increase›; incredible (*coll.*), fantastic (*coll.*) ‹splendour, luck›; [B] (*abwertend: empörend*) outrageous; scandalous. ❷ *adv.* [A] (*überaus*) incredibly (*coll.*); **~ viel arbeiten** do a fantastic *or* incredible amount of work (*coll.*); [B] (*abwertend: empörend*) outrageously

**unerkannt** ❶ *Adj.* unrecognized; (*nicht identifiziert*) unidentified. ❷ *adv.* without being recognized/identified

**unerklärlich** *Adj.* inexplicable; **es ist mir ~, wie das geschehen konnte** I simply cannot understand how that could happen

**unerlässlich, *unerläßlich** /ʊn|ɛɐ̯ˈlɛslɪç/ *Adj.* indispensable; essential; **es ist ~, ... zu ...** it is essential *or* imperative to ...

**unerlaubt** ❶ *Adj.* ‹entry, parking, absenteeism› without permission; unauthorized ‹parking, entry›; (*illegal*) illegal ‹act›. ❷ *adv.* without authorization *or* permission; (*illegal*) illegally; **der Schule** (*Dat.*) **~ fernbleiben** play truant

**unerledigt** *Adj.* not dealt with *postpos.*; ‹work› not done; unanswered ‹mail, letters›; unprocessed ‹application›

**unermesslich, *unermeßlich** ❶ *Adj.* (*geh.*) [A] (*räumlich*) immeasurable ‹expanse, distance›; boundless ‹spaces›; [B] (*mengen-, zahlenmäßig*) immeasurable, immense ‹wealth, fortune›; **ins Unermessliche** beyond measure; [C] (*überaus groß*) untold ‹suffering, misery, damage›; inestimable ‹value, importance›. ❷ *adv.* immeasurably; ‹rich› beyond measure; **~ viel** an inestimable amount

**unermüdlich** ❶ *Adj.* tireless, untiring (**bei, in** + *Dat.* in). ❷ *adv.* tirelessly

**unernst** *Adj.* frivolous

**unerquicklich** *Adj.* (*geh.*) unpleasant

**unerreichbar** ❶ *Adj.* [A] inaccessible; **in ~er Ferne** *od.* **Entfernung** so distant as to be beyond reach; **sie ist für ihn ~** (*fig.*) she is beyond his reach; [B] (*nicht kontaktierbar*) unobtainable; [C] (*fig.*) unattainable ‹aim, ideal, accuracy, etc.›. ❷ *adv.* [A] (*räumlich*) inaccessibly; [B] (*fig.*) unattainably

**unerreicht** *Adj.* unequalled ‹record, achievement›; **~ bleiben** remain unequalled; ‹goal› not be attained

**unersättlich** *Adj.* insatiable

**unerschlossen** *Adj.* unexploited, undeveloped ‹area›; unexploited, untapped ‹market, resources, deposits›

U

**unerschöpflich** *Adj.* inexhaustible; **ihre Geduld war ~:** there was no end to her patience

**unerschrocken** ❶ *Adj.* intrepid; fearless. ❷ *adv.* intrepidly; fearlessly

**unerschütterlich** ❶ *Adj.* unshakeable; imperturbable ‹calm, equanimity›; tenacious ‹fighter›. ❷ *adv.* unshakeably

**unerschwinglich** ❶ *Adj.* prohibitively expensive; prohibitive ‹price›; **für jmdn. ~ sein** be beyond sb.'s means. ❷ *adv.* prohibitively ‹expensive, high›

**unersetzlich** *Adj.* irreplaceable; irretrievable, irrecoverable ‹loss›; irreparable ‹harm, damage, loss of person›

**unersprießlich** *Adj.* (*geh.*) unprofitable; unproductive

**unerträglich** /od. '----/ ❶ *Adj.* unbearable ‹pain, heat, person, etc.›; intolerable ‹situation, conditions, moods, etc.›; **er/es ist mir ~:** I find him/it unbearable; I cannot stand him/it. ❷ *adv.* unbearably

**unerwähnt** *Adj.* unmentioned; **völlig ~ bleiben** not be mentioned at all

**unerwartet** ❶ *Adj.* unexpected; **es war** *od.* **kam für alle ~:** it came as a surprise to everybody; **etwas Unerwartetes** something unexpected. ❷ *adv.* unexpectedly

**unerwidert** *Adj.* unreturned ‹visit›; unrequited ‹love›; **~ bleiben** ‹greetings› receive no response

**unerwünscht** *Adj.* unwanted; unwelcome ‹interruption, visit, visitor›; undesirable ‹side effects›; **Sie sind hier ~:** you are not wanted *or* welcome here; **ein ~er Ausländer** an undesirable alien

**unerzogen** *Adj.* badly behaved

**UNESCO** /u'nɛsko/ *die;* **~:** UNESCO

**unfähig** *Adj.* Ⓐ **~ sein, etw. zu tun** (*ständig*) be incapable of doing sth.; (*momentan*) be unable to do sth.; **er ist solch eines Verbrechens ~:** he is incapable of such a crime; Ⓑ (*abwertend: inkompetent*) incompetent

**Unfähigkeit** *die* Ⓐ inability; Ⓑ (*Inkompetenz*) incompetence

**unfair** ❶ *Adj.* unfair (**gegen** to). ❷ *adv.* unfairly

**Unfall** *der* accident; **bei einem ~:** in an accident

**unfall-, Unfall-: ~arzt** *der*, **~ärztin** *die* casualty doctor; **zum ~arzt gehen** go to the doctor in the casualty department *or* casualty; **~flucht** *die* (*Rechtsspr.*) **wegen ~flucht** for failing to stop after [being involved in] an accident; **~flucht begehen** fail to stop after [being involved in] an accident; **~folge** *die* consequence *or* effect of an/the accident; **er starb an den ~folgen** he died as a result of the accident; **~frei** ❶ *Adj.* accident-free; free from accidents *postpos.;* ❷ *adv.* without an accident; **~gefahr** *die* risk of accidents/an accident; accident risk; **~kranken·haus** *das* accident *or* casualty hospital; **~opfer** *das* accident victim; **~rente** *die* disability pension (*paid by an accident insurance*); **~station** *die* accident *or* casualty department; **~stelle** *die* scene of an/the accident; **~tod** *der* accidental death; death in an accident; **~ursache** *die* cause of an/the accident; **~versicherung** *die* accident insurance; **~wagen** *der* Ⓐ (*Rettungswagen*) incident vehicle; (*Krankenwagen*) ambulance; Ⓑ (*beschädigter Wagen*) car [that has been] damaged in an/the accident

**unfassbar, *unfaßbar** ❶ *Adj.* incomprehensible; (*unglaublich*) incredible, unimaginable ‹poverty, cruelty, etc.›; **es ist mir ~, wie ...:** it is incomprehensible to me *or* I cannot understand how ... ❷ *adv.* incomprehensibly; incredibly, unimaginably ‹cruel›

**unfehlbar** *Adj.* infallible

**Unfehlbarkeit** *die;* **~:** infallibility

**unfein** ❶ *Adj.* ill-mannered, unrefined ‹behaviour etc.›; unrefined, coarse ‹manner, word›; bad ‹manners›; **das gilt als ~:** it's considered bad manners. ❷ *adv.* ‹behave› badly, in an ill-mannered way

*old spelling (see note on page 1707)

**unfertig** *Adj.* Ⓐ unfinished ‹manuscript, article, etc.›; Ⓑ (*fig.: unreif*) immature

**unfest** (*Sprachw.*) ❶ *Adj.* separable. ❷ *adv.* **~ zusammengesetzte Verben** separable [compound] verbs

**Unflat** /'ʊnfla:t/ *der;* **~[e]s** (*geh. veralt.*) filth

**unflätig** /'ʊnflɛ:tɪç/ (*geh. abwertend*) ❶ *Adj.* coarse ‹behaviour, manners, speech, etc.›; obscene ‹expression, word, curse›; dirty ‹song›. ❷ *adv.* coarsely; obscenely

**unflektiert** *Adj.* (*Sprachw.*) uninflected

**unflott** ❶ *Adj. in* **nicht ~** (*ugs.*) not bad; (*modisch, schick*) quite with it (*coll.*). ❷ *adv.* **nicht ~:** not at all badly; **sie tanzt nicht ~** (*ugs.*) she's a pretty useful dancer (*coll.*)

**unförmig** ❶ *Adj.* shapeless ‹lump, shadow, etc.›; huge ‹legs, hands, body›; bulky, ungainly ‹shape, shoes, etc.›. ❷ *adv.* **~ dick** fat and unshapely *or* bulky; **~ angeschwollen** swollen and unsightly

**unfrankiert** *Adj.* unstamped

**unfrei** ❶ *Adj.* Ⓐ not free *pred.;* subject, dependent ‹people›; ‹life› of bondage *or* without liberty; **die Bauern waren noch ~** (*hist.*) the peasants were still serfs; **sich etwas ~ fühlen** feel a bit tied *or* unable to act freely; Ⓑ (*gehemmt*) inhibited; Ⓒ (*keine Freiheit gewährend*) restrictive ‹education, regime›; Ⓓ (*Postw.*) unstamped. ❷ *adv.* (*gehemmt*) in an inhibited manner

**Unfreie** *der/die; adj. Dekl.* (*hist.*) serf

**Unfreiheit** *die* slavery *no art.;* bondage (*esp. Hist./literary*) *no art.;* **ein Leben in ~:** a life of bondage *or* without freedom

**unfreiwillig** ❶ *Adj.* involuntary; (*erzwungen*) enforced ‹stay›; (*nicht beabsichtigt*) unintended ‹publicity, joke, humour›. ❷ *adv.* involuntarily; without wanting to; (*unbeabsichtigt*) unintentionally

**unfreundlich** ❶ *Adj.* Ⓐ unfriendly (**zu, gegen** to); unkind ‹words, remark›; **ein ~er Akt** (*Politik*) an unfriendly *or* a hostile act; Ⓑ (*fig.*) unpleasant ‹area, climate, environment›; unpleasant, inclement ‹weather, summer›; cheerless ‹room›. ❷ *adv.* in an unfriendly way

**Unfreundlichkeit** *die* Ⓐ unfriendliness; **sie behandelte ihn mit einer solchen ~, dass ...** she treated him in such an unfriendly way that ...; Ⓑ (*Handlung*) unfriendly act; (*Äußerung*) unkind remark

**Unfriede[n]** *der* discord; **in ~ leben/auseinander gehen** live in a state of strife/part in hostility

**unfrisiert** *Adj.* ungroomed ‹hair›; **sie war ~:** she had not done her hair

**unfruchtbar** *Adj.* Ⓐ infertile ‹soil, field, land›; **meine Anregungen fielen auf ~en Boden** (*fig.*) my suggestions fell on stony ground; Ⓑ (*Biol.*) infertile; sterile; **ein Tier ~ machen** sterilize *or* neuter an animal; **die ~en Tage der Frau** the days of infertility; Ⓒ (*fig.*) unfruitful, unproductive ‹discussion, comparison, etc.›; infertile ‹years, period›; ‹idea› which does not lead anywhere

**Unfruchtbarkeit** *die* Ⓐ infertility; Ⓑ (*Biol.*) infertility; sterility; Ⓒ (*fig.*) unproductiveness

**Unfug** /'ʊnfu:k/ *der;* **~[e]s** Ⓐ [piece of] mischief; **allerlei ~ anstellen** get up to all kinds of mischief *or* (*coll.*) monkey business; **grober ~:** public nuisance; **was soll dieser ~?** what's this monkey business? (*coll.*); **lass diesen ~!** stop monkeying about (*coll.*) *or* making a nuisance of yourself; Ⓑ (*Unsinn*) nonsense

**Ungar** /'ʊŋgar/ *der;* **~n, ~n, Ungarin** *die;* **~, ~nen** ▶ 553 Hungarian; ⇨ *auch* **-in**

**ungarisch** ▶ 553, ▶ 696 ❶ *Adj.* Hungarian. ❷ *adv.* in Hungarian; ⇨ *auch* **deutsch; Deutsche**[2]

**Ungarisch** *das;* **~[s]** ▶ 696 Hungarian; ⇨ *auch* **Deutsch**

**Ungarn** (*das*); **~s** Hungary

**ungastlich** ❶ *Adj.* inhospitable. ❷ *adv.* inhospitably

**ungeachtet** *Präp. mit Gen.* (*geh.*) notwithstanding; despite; **~ dessen, dessen ~:** nevertheless; notwithstanding [this]

**ungeahnt** ❶ *Adj.* unsuspected; (*stärker*) undreamt-of *attrib.* ❷ *adv.* unexpectedly

**ungebärdig** ❶ *Adj.* unruly ‹child, horse, etc.›; wild ‹temperament, mountain stream, etc.›. ❷ *adv.* wildly

**ungebeten** ❶ *Adj.* uninvited; (*nicht gern gesehen*) unwelcome. ❷ *adv.* uninvited

**ungebeugt** *Adj.* (*Sprachw.*) uninflected

**ungebildet** *Adj.* uneducated; **ein Ungebildeter** an uneducated person

**ungeboren** *Adj.* unborn

**ungebräuchlich** *Adj.* uncommon; rare; rarely used ‹method, process›

**ungebraucht** *Adj.* unused; mint ‹stamp›

**ungebrochen** *Adj.* Ⓐ (*Physik*) unrefracted ‹rays, waves›; Ⓑ (*fig.*) unbroken ‹will, person›; undiminished ‹strength, courage›

**Ungebühr** *die* (*geh.*) impropriety; **~ vor Gericht** (*Rechtsspr.*) contempt of court

**ungebührlich** (*geh.*) ❶ *Adj.* improper, unseemly ‹behaviour›; unreasonable ‹demand›. ❷ *adv.* ‹behave› improperly; unreasonably ‹high, long, etc.›

**ungebunden** ❶ *Adj.* Ⓐ unbound ‹book etc.›; Ⓑ (*Literaturw.*) **in ~er Rede** in prose; Ⓒ (*frei von Bindungen*) independent; without ties *postpos.;* (*ohne Partner/Partnerin*) unattached. ❷ *adv.* **~ leben** live an independent life *or* a life without ties

**ungedeckt** *Adj.* Ⓐ uncovered ‹cheque, bill of exchange, etc.›; unsecured ‹bond›; Ⓑ unlaid ‹table›; Ⓒ (*ungeschützt*) unprotected; Ⓓ (*Ballspiele*) unmarked ‹player›

**Ungeduld** *die* impatience

**ungeduldig** ❶ *Adj.* impatient. ❷ *adv.* impatiently

**ungeeignet** *Adj.* unsuitable; (*für eine Aufgabe, Stellung*) unsuited (**für, zu** to, for)

**ungefähr** /'ʊŋgəfɛ:ɐ̯/ ❶ *Adj.* approximate; rough ‹idea, outline›. ❷ *Adv.* approximately; roughly; (*mit nachgestellter Zahl*) about; roughly; **~ so** something like this; **so ~** (*ugs.*) more or less; **kannst du mir so ~ sagen, wie/wann** *usw.* **...?** can you give me some idea *or* a rough idea how/when *etc.* ...?; **wann wirst du ~ zurückkommen?** roughly *or* about when will you be back?; **wo ~ ...?** whereabouts ...?; **kannst du es ~ beschreiben?** can you give a rough description?; **ich kann es mir ~ vorstellen** I can imagine; **[wie] von ~:** [as if] by chance; **es kommt nicht von ~[, dass ...]** it's no accident [that ...]

**ungefährdet** *Adj.* safe; (*gesichert*) assured ‹promotion etc.›; ‹play, swim, etc.› in safety

**ungefährlich** ❶ *Adj.* safe; harmless ‹animal, person, illness, etc.›; **nicht ~ sein** be not without danger. ❷ *adv.* safely

**ungefällig** ❶ *Adj.* disobliging, churlish (**gegenüber** to). ❷ *adv.* in a disobliging way; churlishly

**ungefärbt** *Adj.* Ⓐ undyed ‹wool, hair›; ‹food, drink› without colouring matter; Ⓑ (*fig.*) unvarnished ‹truth›; uncoloured, undistorted ‹account›

**ungefragt** *Adj.* unasked

**ungefüge** *Adj.* (*geh.*) Ⓐ cumbersome ‹furniture›; massive, bulky ‹chunk, stature›; massive ‹wall, stone›; ungainly ‹person›; Ⓑ (*schwerfällig*) ponderous ‹style›

**ungehalten** (*geh.*) ❶ *Adj.* annoyed (**über** + *Akk.*, **wegen** about); (*entrüstet*) indignant. ❷ *adv.* indignantly; ‹reply, say› in an aggrieved tone

**ungeheizt** *Adj.* unheated

**ungehemmt** ❶ *Adj.* Ⓐ uninhibited ‹person›; Ⓑ (*uneingeschränkt*) unrestricted, unimpeded ‹movement›; (*fig.*) unrestrained ‹joy, anger, etc.›. ❷ *adv.* Ⓐ without inhibition; Ⓑ (*uneingeschränkt*) ‹develop› unhindered, without hindrance; (*fig.*) ‹cry, laugh, drink, etc.› without restraint

**ungeheuer** ❶ *Adj.* enormous; immense; tremendous ‹strength, energy, effort, enthusiasm, fear, success, pressure, etc.›; vast, immense ‹fortune, knowledge›; (*schrecklich*) terrible (*coll.*), terrific (*coll.*) ‹pain, rage›; **ungeheure Ausgaben** an enormous amount of expense. ❷ *adv.* tremendously; terribly (*coll.*) ‹difficult, clever›

u

**Ungeheuer** *das;* ~**s**, ~ (*auch fig.*) monster
**ungeheuerlich** ❶ *Adj.* monstrous; outrageous. ❷ *adv.* (*ugs.*) terribly (*coll.*)
**Ungeheuerlichkeit** *die;* ~, ~**en** Ⓐ monstrous nature; outrageousness; Ⓑ (*Vorgang*) monstrous *or* outrageous thing
**ungehindert** *Adj.* unimpeded
**ungehobelt** ❶ *Adj.* Ⓐ unplaned ‹wood›; Ⓑ (*grob*) uncouth. ❷ *adv.* uncouthly
**ungehörig** ❶ *Adj.* improper ‹behaviour›; (*frech*) impertinent ‹tone, answer›. ❷ *adv.* improperly; (*frech*) impertinently
**ungehorsam** *Adj.* disobedient (**gegenüber** to)
**Ungehorsam** *der* disobedience (**gegenüber** to)
**ungehört** *Adj.* unheard
**Ungeist** *der* (*geh. abwertend*) pernicious ideology
**ungekämmt** *Adj.* uncombed
**ungeklärt** *Adj.* Ⓐ unsolved ‹question, problem›; unknown ‹cause›; **die Angelegenheit ist noch** ~**:** the matter has yet to be cleared up; Ⓑ (*ungereinigt*) untreated ‹sewage›
**ungekrönt** *Adj.* (*auch fig.*) uncrowned
**ungekündigt** *Adj.* **in** ~**er Stellung** not under notice *postpos.*
**ungekünstelt** ❶ *Adj.* natural; unaffected. ❷ *adv.* naturally; unaffectedly
**ungekürzt** *Adj.* unabridged ‹edition, book›; uncut ‹film, speech›
**ungeladen** *Adj.* Ⓐ unloaded ‹gun, camera›; Ⓑ (*nicht eingeladen*) uninvited ‹guest›
**ungelegen** ❶ *Adj.* inconvenient, awkward ‹time›; ‹visit etc.› at an awkward *or* inconvenient time; **das kommt mir sehr** ~**/nicht** ~**:** that is very inconvenient *or* awkward/quite convenient for me. ❷ *adv.* inconveniently; **komme ich** ~**?** have I come at an inconvenient *or* awkward time?
**Ungelegenheit** *die* inconvenience; **jmdm. große** ~**en machen** *od.* **bereiten** inconvenience sb. greatly
**ungelegt** *Adj. in* **kümmere dich nicht um** ~**e Eier** (*ugs.*) don't cross your bridges before you get to them
**ungelenk** ❶ *Adj.* clumsy; ungainly. ❷ *adv.* clumsily
**ungelenkig** *Adj.* stiff-jointed
**ungelernt** *Adj.* unskilled
**Ungelernte** *der/die; adj. Dekl.* unskilled worker
**ungeliebt** *Adj.* unloved; (*verhüll.: verhasst*) hateful, odious ‹task›; odious ‹school etc.›
**ungelogen** *Adv.* (*ugs.*) honestly
**ungelöscht** *Adj.* (*Chemie*) unslaked ‹lime›
**Ungemach** *das;* ~**[e]s** (*geh. veralt.*) trouble
**ungemacht** *Adj.* unmade
**ungemein** ❶ *Adj.* exceptional ‹progress, popularity›; tremendous ‹advantage, pleasure›. ❷ *adv.* exceptionally; ~ **fleißig** extraordinarily industrious; **das freut mich** ~**:** that pleases me no end (*coll.*)
**ungemütlich** ❶ *Adj.* Ⓐ uninviting, cheerless ‹room, flat›; uncomfortable, unfriendly ‹atmosphere›; Ⓑ (*unangenehm*) unpleasant ‹situation›; **es wird jetzt** ~**:** things are getting nasty; **es wurde ihnen zu** ~**:** things got too unpleasant for them. ❷ *adv.* uncomfortably ‹furnished›; **hier sitzt es sich** ~**:** it's not comfortable sitting here
**ungenannt** *Adj.* anonymous; **ein Ungenannter** an anonymous person
**ungenau** ❶ *Adj.* Ⓐ inaccurate ‹measurement, estimate, thermometer, translation, etc.›; imprecise, inexact ‹definition, formulation, etc.›; (*undeutlich*) vague ‹memory, idea, impression›; Ⓑ (*nicht sorgfältig*) careless ‹work, worker›. ❷ *adv.* Ⓐ inaccurately; ‹define› imprecisely, inexactly; ‹remember› vaguely; **die Uhr geht** ~**:** the clock does not keep good time; Ⓑ (*nicht sorgfältig*) ‹work› carelessly
**Ungenauigkeit** *die* Ⓐ inaccuracy; (*einer Definition*) imprecision; inexactness; Ⓑ (*etwas Ungenaues*) inaccuracy
**ungeniert** /ˈʊnʒeniːɐ̯t/ ❶ *Adj.* free and easy; uninhibited; **er war ganz** ~**:** he was not at all embarrassed *or* concerned. ❷ *adv.* openly; ‹yawn› unconcernedly; (*ohne Scham*) ‹undress etc.› without any embarrassment
**ungenießbar** *Adj.* Ⓐ (*nicht essbar*) inedible; (*nicht trinkbar*) undrinkable; Ⓑ (*fig. ugs.*) unbearable ‹person›; **er ist heute** ~**:** he's in a foul mood today (*sl.*)
**ungenügend** ❶ *Adj.* inadequate; **die Note „ungenügend"/ein U**~ (*Schulw.*) the/an 'unsatisfactory' [mark]. ❷ *adv.* inadequately
**ungenutzt, ungenützt** *Adj.* unused; unexploited ‹resource, energy›; **eine Gelegenheit** ~ **vorübergehen lassen** let an opportunity slip *or* pass by
**ungepflegt** *Adj.* neglected ‹garden, park, car, etc.›; unkempt ‹person, appearance, hair›; uncared-for ‹hands›
**ungerade** *Adj.* odd ‹number›
**ungerecht** ❶ *Adj.* unjust, unfair (**gegen, zu, gegenüber** to). ❷ *adv.* unjustly; unfairly
**ungerechterweise** *Adv.* unjustly; unfairly; **er verdient** ~ **genauso viel wie sie** he earns as much as she does, which is unfair
**ungerechtfertigt** *Adj.* unjustified; unwarranted
**Ungerechtigkeit** *die;* ~, ~**en** injustice; **der Vorwurf der** ~**:** the reproach of being unjust; **so eine** ~**!** how unjust *or* unfair!
**ungeregelt** *Adj.* irregular; disorganized
**ungereimt** *Adj.* Ⓐ (*nicht stimmig*) inconsistent; illogical; (*ugs. abwertend: sinnlos, verworren*) muddled; Ⓑ (*reimlos*) unrhymed
**Ungereimtheit** *die;* ~, ~**en** (*Unstimmigkeit*) inconsistency; (*ugs. abwertend: Unsinnigkeit, Verworrenheit*) muddle
**ungern** *Adv.* reluctantly; **etw.** ~ **tun** not like *or* dislike doing sth.; **Würdest du das bitte tun? — Ungern** Would you do that, please? — I'd rather not
**ungerufen** *Adv.* without being called
**ungerührt** *Adj.* unmoved
**ungesalzen** *Adj.* unsalted
**ungesättigt** *Adj.* (*Chemie*) unsaturated; **mehrfach** ~**:** polyunsaturated
**ungesäuert** *Adj.* unleavened ‹bread›
**ungeschält** *Adj.* unpeeled ‹fruit›; unstripped ‹tree trunk›; ~**er Reis** paddy rice
**ungeschehen** *Adj. in* **etw.** ~ **machen** undo sth.
**Ungeschick** *das* clumsiness; ~ **lässt grüßen!** (*ugs.*) butterfingers!
**Ungeschicklichkeit** *die;* ~, ~**en** Ⓐ clumsiness; ineptitude; Ⓑ (*etwas Ungeschicktes*) piece of clumsiness; (*Fehler*) clumsy mistake
**ungeschickt** ❶ *Adj.* clumsy; awkward ‹movement, formulation, etc.›; **technisch** ~**:** technically inept. ❷ *adv.* clumsily; ‹bow, express oneself, etc.› awkwardly; **sich** ~ **anstellen** show a lack of skill; show oneself to be inept
**ungeschlacht** (*geh.*) ❶ *Adj.* Ⓐ (*unförmig, massig*) huge and ungainly ‹man, animal›; huge, clumsy ‹hands›; clumsy, ungainly ‹limbs, movement›; massive ‹building etc.›; Ⓑ (*grob, unkultiviert*) coarse; uncouth. ❷ *adv.* in an uncouth way
**ungeschlechtlich** (*Biol.*) ❶ *Adj.* asexual. ❷ *adv.* asexually
**ungeschliffen** ❶ *Adj.* Ⓐ uncut ‹diamond etc.›; Ⓑ (*fig. abwertend*) unrefined ‹behaviour, manners›. ❷ *adv.* (*fig. abwertend*) in an unrefined manner
**ungeschmälert** *Adj.* (*geh.*) undiminished; in full measure *postpos.;* (*voll anerkannt*) appreciated to the full *postpos.*
**ungeschminkt** ❶ *Adj.* Ⓐ not made-up *pred.;* without make-up *postpos.;* Ⓑ (*fig.*) unvarnished ‹truth›; uncoloured ‹account›. ❷ *adv.* without holding anything back; **jmdm.** ~ **seine Meinung sagen** give sb. one's honest opinion
**ungeschoren** *Adj.* Ⓐ unshorn; Ⓑ (*fig.*) ~ **bleiben** be left in peace; be spared; ~ **davonkommen** get away with it; (*ohne Schaden*) get away unscathed
**ungeschrieben** *Adj.* unwritten
**ungeschützt** *Adj.* unprotected; (*Wind und Wetter ausgesetzt*) exposed
**ungesehen** *Adj.* unseen
**ungesellig** ❶ *Adj.* Ⓐ unsociable; Ⓑ (*Zool.*) non-gregarious. ❷ *adv.* (*Zool.*) non-gregariously
**ungesetzlich** ❶ *Adj.* unlawful; illegal. ❷ *adv.* unlawfully; illegally
**Ungesetzlichkeit** *die* illegality
**ungesittet** ❶ *Adj.* uncivilized. ❷ *adv.* in an uncivilized manner
**ungestalt** *Adj.* Ⓐ (*geh.*) shapeless; Ⓑ (*veralt.: missgestaltet*) misshapen
**ungestempelt** *Adj.* unstamped ‹licence etc.›; uncancelled ‹stamp›
**ungestillt** *Adj.* (*geh.*) unquenched, unslaked ‹thirst›; unsatisfied, unsated ‹curiosity, desire, greed›
**ungestört** *Adj.* undisturbed; uninterrupted ‹development›; ~ **arbeiten** work in peace *or* without interruption
**ungestraft** ❶ *Adj.* unpunished. ❷ *adv.* with impunity
**ungestüm** /ˈʊnɡəʃtyːm/ (*geh.*) ❶ *Adj.* impetuous, tempestuous ‹person, embrace, nature, etc.›; wild ‹imagination›; violent, fierce ‹wind›; stormy ‹sea›. ❷ *adv.* impetuously
**Ungestüm** *das;* ~**[e]s** impetuosity
**ungesühnt** *Adj.* (*geh.*) unatoned
**ungesund** ❶ *Adj.* (*auch fig.*) unhealthy; (*fig.: übermäßig*) excessive ‹ambition, activity›; **Rauchen ist** ~**:** smoking is bad for you *or* for your health. ❷ *adv.* unhealthily; **er lebt sehr** ~**:** he lives *or* leads a very unhealthy life
**ungesüßt** /ˈʊnɡəzyːst/ *Adj.* unsweetened
**ungetan** *Adj.* still to be done *postpos.;* **etw.** ~ **lassen** leave sth. undone
**ungeteilt** *Adj.* Ⓐ undivided; Ⓑ (*fig.*) unrestricted, absolute ‹power›; undivided ‹attention, interest›; (*einmütig*) unanimous; universal ‹approval, agreement, etc.›
**ungetreu** *Adj.* (*geh.*) disloyal
**ungetrübt** *Adj.* unclouded, perfect ‹happiness›; unalloyed ‹pleasure›; unspoilt, perfect ‹days, relationship›; **seine Freude blieb nicht lange** ~**:** his pleasure did not long remain unsullied
**Ungetüm** /ˈʊnɡətyːm/ *das;* ~**s**, ~**e** monster
**ungeübt** *Adj.* unpractised ‹hand›; **in etw.** ~ **sein** lack practice in sth.
**ungewaschen** *Adj.* unwashed
**ungewiss**, ***ungewiß** *Adj.* uncertain; **eine Fahrt ins Ungewisse** a journey into the unknown; **über etw.** (*Akk.*) **im Ungewissen sein** be uncertain *or* unsure about sth.; **jmdn. [über etw.** (*Akk.*)**] im Ungewissen lassen** leave sb. in the dark *or* keep sb. guessing [about sth.]
**Ungewissheit**, ***Ungewißheit** *die* uncertainty; **in** ~ **sein** be in a state of uncertainty
**ungewöhnlich** ❶ *Adj.* Ⓐ unusual; Ⓑ (*sehr groß*) exceptional ‹strength, beauty, ability, etc.›; outstanding ‹achievement, success›. ❷ *adv.* Ⓐ (*unüblich*) ‹behave› abnormally, strangely; Ⓑ (*enorm*) exceptionally
**ungewohnt** ❶ *Adj.* unaccustomed ‹exertion, heat, cold, load, etc.›; unaccustomed, unusual ‹sight, time›; (*nicht vertraut*) unfamiliar ‹method, work, surroundings, etc.›; **sie sagte es mit** ~**er Schärfe** she said it with a sharpness [that was] unusual for her; **die Arbeit ist ihr** *od.* **für sie noch** ~**:** she is still not used to *or* familiar with the work. ❷ *adv.* unusually
**ungewollt** ❶ *Adj.* unwanted; (*unbeabsichtigt*) unintentional; inadvertent. ❷ *adv.* unintenionally; inadvertently
**ungezählt** *Adj.* Ⓐ (*unzählig*) countless; Ⓑ (*nicht gezählt*) uncounted
**Ungeziefer** /ˈʊnɡət͜siːfɐ/ *das;* ~**s** vermin *pl.*
**ungezogen** ❶ *Adj.* naughty; badly behaved; bad ‹behaviour›; (*frech*) cheeky; **zu jmdm.** ~ **sein** behave badly towards sb.; be cheeky to sb. ❷ *adv.* naughtily; ‹behave› badly
**Ungezogenheit** *die;* ~, ~**en** Ⓐ naughtiness; bad behaviour; Ⓑ (*ungezogene Bemerkung*) ~**en** insolent remarks; **das ist eine** ~**:** that's very naughty/cheeky
**ungezügelt** ❶ *Adj.* unbridled. ❷ *adv.* without restraint

U

**ungezwungen** ❶ *Adj.* natural, unaffected ‹person, behaviour, cheerfulness›; (*nicht förmlich*) informal, free and easy ‹tone, conversation, etc.›. ❷ *adv.* ‹behave› naturally, unaffectedly; ‹talk› freely

**Ungezwungenheit** *die;* ~ ⇒ **ungezwungen** 1: naturalness; unaffectedness; informality

**ungiftig** *Adj.* non-poisonous; non-toxic ‹gas, substance›

**Unglaube[n]** *der* Ⓐ disbelief; incredulity; Ⓑ (*Rel.*) unbelief

**unglaubhaft** *Adj.* implausible

**ungläubig** ❶ *Adj.* Ⓐ disbelieving; incredulous; **~er Thomas** doubting Thomas; Ⓑ (*Rel.*) unbelieving. ❷ *adv.* incredulously; in disbelief

**Ungläubige** *der/die* (*Rel.*) unbeliever

**unglaublich** ❶ *Adj.* Ⓐ incredible; Ⓑ (*ugs.: sehr groß*) incredible (*coll.*), fantastic (*coll.*) ‹speed, amount, luck, etc.›. ❷ *adv.* (*ugs.: äußerst*) incredibly (*coll.*); (*empörend*) ‹behave› in an incredible fashion (*coll.*)

**unglaubwürdig** *Adj.* implausible; untrustworthy, unreliable ‹witness etc.›

**ungleich** ❶ *Adj.* Ⓐ unequal; unequal, different ‹sizes›; odd, unmatching ‹socks, gloves, etc.›; (*unähnlich*) dissimilar ‹characters etc.›; odd ‹couple›; **a [ist] ~ b** (*Math.*) a is not equal to *or* does not equal b; Ⓑ (*ungleichmäßig*) uneven ‹distribution etc.›. ❷ *adv.* Ⓐ unequally; **~ geartet** of different dispositions; Ⓑ (*ungleichmäßig*) unevenly. ❸ *Adv.* (*mit Komparativ*) far ‹larger, more difficult›; (*unvergleichlich*) incomparably ‹better, more beautiful›. ❹ *Präp. mit Dat.* (*geh.*) unlike

**Ungleichgewicht** *das* imbalance

**Ungleichheit** *die* Ⓐ inequality; Ⓑ (*Unterschied*) difference; dissimilarity

**ungleichmäßig** ❶ *Adj.* uneven. ❷ *adv.* Ⓐ unevenly; Ⓑ (*verschieden*) **~ lang** of different lengths

**ungleichnamig** *Adj.* Ⓐ (*Math.*) ‹fractions› with different denominators; Ⓑ (*Physik*) opposite ‹poles›

**Unglück** *das;* **~[e]s, ~e** Ⓐ (*Unfall*) accident; (*Flugzeug~, Zug~*) crash; accident; (*Missgeschick*) mishap; **das ist [doch] kein ~!** that's not a disaster; it doesn't really matter; Ⓑ (*Not*) misfortune; (*Leid*) suffering; distress; **jmdn. ins ~ stürzen** bring ruin *or* disaster on sb.; **sich ins ~ stürzen, in sein ~ rennen** rush headlong into disaster *or* to one's ruin; **es ist ein ~, dass ...** it is a real shame *or* a great pity that ...; Ⓒ (*Pech*) bad luck; misfortune; **~ haben** be unlucky; **das bringt ~:** that's unlucky; **zum ~:** unfortunately; **zu allem ~:** to make matters worse; **das ~ wollte es, dass ...** as luck would have it ...; **~ im Spiel, Glück in der Liebe** unlucky at cards, lucky in love; Ⓓ (*Schicksalsschlag*) misfortune; **ein ~ kommt selten allein** (*ugs.*) it never rains but it pours

**unglücklich** ❶ *Adj.* Ⓐ (*traurig*) unhappy; unhappy, unrequited ‹love›; **er ist ~ darüber, dass ...** he is unhappy that ...; **mach dich nicht ~!** don't do it!; Ⓑ (*nicht vom Glück begünstigt*) unfortunate ‹person›; (*bedauernswert, arm*) hapless ‹person, animal›; **ich Unglücklicher/Unglückliche!** (*geh.*) poor me!; woe is me! (*literary*); **der/die Unglückliche** the unfortunate *or* poor man/woman; Ⓒ (*ungünstig, ungeschickt*) unfortunate ‹moment, combination, meeting, etc.›; unhappy ‹end, choice, solution›; unfortunate, unhappy ‹coincidence, formulation›; clumsy ‹movement›; (*unverdient*) unlucky ‹defeat›; **[bei** *od.* **in etw.** (*Dat.*)**] eine ~e Hand haben** get it wrong [when doing sth.]; **eine ~e Figur abgeben** cut a sorry figure.
❷ *adv.* Ⓐ unhappily; **~ verliebt sein** be unhappy in love; Ⓑ (*ungünstig*) unfortunately; (*ungeschickt*) unhappily, clumsily ‹translated, expressed›; **~ enden** come to an unfortunate end; ‹love affair› end unhappily; **er stürzte so ~, dass ...** he fell so awkwardly that ...; he had such a bad fall that ...

*old spelling (see note on page 1707)

**unglücklicherweise** *Adv.* unfortunately

**Unglücks·botschaft** *die* bad news *sing.*; bad tidings *pl.*

**unglück·selig** *Adj.* Ⓐ (*bedauernswert*) unfortunate, hapless ‹person›; Ⓑ (*verhängnisvoll*) unfortunate, fateful ‹coincidence, combination›; ill-starred, fateful ‹time›; fateful ‹predilection›

**Unglücks-: ~fall** *der* accident; **~rabe** *der* (*ugs.*) unlucky sort (*coll.*); luckless individual (*coll.*); **~stelle** *die* scene of an/the accident; **~zahl** *die* unlucky number

**Ungnade** *die:* *in* **[bei jmdm.] in ~** (*Akk.*) **fallen/in ~** (*Dat.*) **sein** fall/be out of favour [with sb.]

**ungnädig** ❶ *Adj.* bad-tempered; grumpy; (*geh.: schlimm*) unkind ‹fate›. ❷ *adv.* in a bad-tempered way; grumpily

**ungültig** *Adj.* invalid; void (*esp. Law*); spoilt ‹vote, ballot paper›; disallowed ‹goal›; **~e Banknoten** banknotes which are not legal tender; **eine Ehe/ein Tor für ~ erklären** annul a marriage/disallow a goal

**Ungunst** *die* Ⓐ (*geh. veralt.*) disfavour; Ⓑ **zu jmds. ~en** to sb.'s disadvantage; Ⓒ **zu ~en** ⇒ **zuungunsten**

**ungünstig** ❶ *Adj.* Ⓐ unfavourable; unfavourable, poor ‹climate, weather›; (*unglücklich*) unfortunate ‹consequence›; unfortunate, bad ‹shape, layout›; (*unvorteilhaft*) unfavourable, unflattering ‹light, perspective, impression›; unflattering ‹cut of dress›; inconvenient ‹position›; (*schädlich*) harmful ‹effect›; Ⓑ (*unpassend*) inconvenient ‹time›; (*ungeeignet*) inappropriate, inconvenient ‹time, place›; unsuitable ‹colour etc.›. ❷ *adv.* Ⓐ unfavourably; badly ‹designed, laid out›; (*unvorteilhaft*) unflatteringly ‹cut›; **sich ~ auswirken** have a harmful effect; Ⓑ (*unpassend, ungeeignet*) inconveniently

**ungut** *Adj.* Ⓐ uneasy ‹feeling, premonition›; negative ‹impression, expectation›; (*unangenehm*) unpleasant ‹aftertaste, recollection, memories›; Ⓑ *in* **nichts für ~!** no offence [meant]! (*coll.*)

**unhaltbar** *Adj.* Ⓐ untenable ‹thesis, statement, etc.›; Ⓑ (*unerträglich*) unbearable, intolerable ‹conditions, situation›; Ⓒ (*Ballspiele*) unstoppable ‹shot, goal, etc.›

**unhandlich** *Adj.* unwieldy

**Unheil** *das* disaster; **~ anrichten** *od.* **stiften** wreak havoc

**unheilbar** ❶ *Adj.* incurable. ❷ *adv.* incurably; **~ krank** suffering from an incurable disease *postpos.*; incurably ill

**unheil·voll** *Adj.* disastrous; (*verhängnisvoll*) fateful; ominous ‹development›

**unheimlich** ❶ *Adj.* Ⓐ eerie ‹story, figure, place, sound›; eerie, uncanny ‹feeling›; **das/er ist mir ~:** it/he gives me an eerie feeling *or* (*coll.*) the creeps; **mir ist/wird [es] ~:** I have an eerie *or* uncanny feeling; Ⓑ (*ugs.*) (*schrecklich*) terrible (*coll.*) ‹coward, idiot, hunger, headache, etc.›; (*enorm*) terrific (*coll.*) ‹fun, sum, amount, etc.›. ❷ *adv.* Ⓐ eerily; uncannily; Ⓑ (*ugs.; äußerst, sehr*) terribly (*coll.*) ‹fat, nice, etc.›; terrifically (*coll.*) ‹important, large›; incredibly (*coll.*) ‹quick, long›; **~ viel** an incredible *or* a terrific amount (*coll.*); **es macht ~ Spaß** it's terrific fun (*coll.*)

**unhöflich** ❶ *Adj.* impolite. ❷ *adv.* impolitely

**Unhöflichkeit** *die* impoliteness

**Unhold,** *der;* **~[e]s, ~e, Unholdin** *die;* **~, ~nen** Ⓐ fiend; demon; Ⓑ (*abwertend: böser Mensch*) monster

**unhörbar** ❶ *Adj.* inaudible. ❷ *adv.* inaudibly

**unhygienisch** ❶ *Adj.* unhygienic. ❷ *adv.* unhygienically

**uni** /'yni/ *indekl. Adj.* plain, single-colour ‹material etc.›; plain ‹tie›

**Uni** /'ʊni/ *die;* **~, ~s** (*ugs.*) university

**UNICEF** /'u:nitsɛf/ *die;* **~:** UNICEF

**uni·farben** *Adj.* ⇒ **uni**

**Uniform** /'ʊnifɔrm/ *die;* **~, ~en** uniform; **[Staats]bürger in ~:** soldier [in the Bundeswehr]; citizen in uniform; **die ~ ausziehen** (*fig.*) put aside one's uniform; leave the service

**uniformieren** *tr. V.* uniform; **uniformiert** in uniform *postpos.*; uniformed

**Uniformierte** *der/die; adj. Dekl.* man/woman in uniform; (*Polizist*) uniformed [police]man/woman

**Unikat** /uni'ka:t/ *das;* **~[e]s, ~e** ⇒ **Unikum** A

**Unikum** /'u:nikʊm/ *das;* **~s, Unika** *od.* **~s** Ⓐ (*geh.*) **ein ~ sein** be unique; **ein botanisches ~:** a unique botanical specimen; Ⓑ (*ugs.: Original*) [real] character

**uninteressant** *Adj.* Ⓐ uninteresting; (*nicht von Belang*) of no interest *postpos.*; unimportant; **nicht ~:** quite interesting; Ⓑ (*nicht lohnend, nicht attraktiv*) untempting, unattractive ‹offer›; **[für jmdn.] ~ sein** be of no interest [to sb.]

**uninteressiert** *Adj.* uninterested; not interested (**an** + *Dat.* in); **er ist politisch völlig ~:** he is not at all interested in politics

**Union** /u'nio:n/ *die;* **~, ~en** union; **die ~** (*Bundesrepublik Deutschland*) the Union of Christian Democrats and Christian Socialists; the CDU and CSU

**Unions·republik** *die* republic [of the USSR]

**unisono** /uni'zo:no/ *Adv.* (*Musik; auch fig.*) in unison; (*einmütig*) unanimously

**universal** *Adj.* universal; all-embracing ‹education›

**Universal-: ~erbe** *der,* **~erbin** *die* sole heir; **~genie** *das* (*fig.*) universal genius; **~lexikon** *das* general encyclopaedia

**universell** /univɛr'zɛl/ ❶ *Adj.* universal. ❷ *adv.* universally; **~ gebildet sein** have an all-embracing education

**Universität** /univɛrzi'tɛ:t/ *die;* **~, ~en** university; **die ~ Marburg, die Marburger ~:** the University of Marburg; Marburg University; **an der ~** ‹meet, study, etc.› at university; **auf die ~ gehen** (*ugs.*), **die ~ besuchen** go to university

**Universitäts-: ~bibliothek** *die* university library; **~buch·handlung** *die* university bookshop *or* (*Amer.*) bookstore; **„~buchhandlung C. F. Meyer"** 'C. F. Meyer, university booksellers'; **~dozent** *der,* **~dozentin** *die* university lecturer; **~klinik** *die* university hospital; **~stadt** *die* university town; **~studium** *das* study *no art.* at university

**Universum** /uni'vɛrzʊm/ *das;* **~s** universe

**unkameradschaftlich** ❶ *Adj.* uncomradely. ❷ *adv.* in an uncomradely way

**Unke** /'ʊnkə/ *die;* **~, ~n** Ⓐ fire-bellied toad; Ⓑ (*ugs. abwertend: Schwarzseher[in]*) Jeremiah; prophet of doom

**unken** *itr. V.* (*ugs.*) prophesy doom [and destruction] (*joc.*)

**unkenntlich** *Adj.* unrecognizable ‹person, face›; indecipherable ‹writing, stamp›

**Unkenntlichkeit** *die;* **~:** unrecognizable state; (*einer Schrift, eines Stempels*) indecipherable state; **bis zur ~ entstellt** disfigured to the point of being unrecognizable

**Unkenntnis** *die* ignorance; **~ auf einem Gebiet** ignorance of a subject; **etw. aus ~ tun** do sth. from *or* out of ignorance; **jmdn. [über etw.** (*Akk.*)**] in ~ lassen** leave sb. in ignorance [of sth.]; **~ schützt nicht vor Strafe** ignorance [of the law] is no excuse *or* defence

**Unken·ruf** *der* (*fig.*) prophecy of doom

**unkeusch** (*geh.*) ❶ *Adj.* unchaste. ❷ *adv.* unchastely

**Unkeuschheit** *die* unchastity *no art.*

**unklar** *Adj.* Ⓐ (*undeutlich*) unclear; indistinct; (*fig.: unbestimmt*) vague ‹feeling, recollection, idea›; Ⓑ (*nicht klar verständlich*) unclear; Ⓒ (*nicht durchschaubar*) unclear ‹origin, situation, etc.›; (*ungewiss*) uncertain ‹outcome›; **sich** (*Dat.*) **über etw.** (*Akk.*) **im Unklaren sein** be unclear *or* unsure about sth.; **ich bin mir noch im Unklaren, ob ...** I am still not sure *or* certain whether ...; **jmdn. über etw.** (*Akk.*) **im Unklaren lassen** keep sb. guessing about sth.

**Unklarheit** *die* Ⓐ (*Undeutlichkeit*) lack of clarity; indistinctness; Ⓑ (*Unverständlichkeit*) lack of clarity (*Gen.* in); Ⓒ (*Undurchschaubarkeit, Ungewissheit*) uncertainty; **es**

**herrscht noch ~ darüber** it is still uncertain; **D** (*unklarer Punkt*) unclear *or* outstanding point; **falls noch ~en bestehen** if anything is still unclear

**unklug** **1** *Adj.* unwise. **2** *adv.* unwisely

**unkollegial** **1** *Adj.* inconsiderate *or* unhelpful [to one's colleagues]; **er ist [sehr] ~:** he is not [at all] a good colleague. **2** *adv.* not ‹behave› like a good colleague

**unkompliziert** **1** *Adj.* uncomplicated, straightforward ‹person, mechanism, etc.›; straightforward, simple ‹matter, case, problem›; simple ‹fracture› (*Med.*). **2** *adv.* ‹express› straightforwardly, simply

**unkontrollierbar** *Adj.* impossible to check *or* supervise *postpos.*; (*nicht zu beherrschen*) uncontrollable

**unkontrolliert** *Adj.* **A** unsupervised; ‹route› without checkpoints; **B** (*unbeherrscht*) uncontrolled ‹emotions, feelings, outburst›; intemperate ‹words›

**unkonventionell** **1** *Adj.* unconventional. **2** *adv.* unconventionally

**unkonzentriert** **1** *Adj.* lacking in concentration *postpos.*; **du bist heute sehr ~:** you aren't concentrating today. **2** *adv.* without concentrating; **sie arbeitet sehr ~:** she doesn't concentrate at all on her work

**Unkosten** *Pl.* **A** [extra] expense *sing.*; expenses; **mit großen ~ verbunden sein** involve a great deal of expense; **sich in ~ stürzen** dig deep into one's pocket; [really] lash out (*coll.*); **sich in geistige ~ stürzen** (*scherzh.*) strain one's grey matter (*coll.*); **B** (*ugs.: Ausgaben*) costs; expenditure *sing.*

**Unkosten·beitrag** *der* contribution towards expenses

**Unkraut** *das* **A** weeds *pl.*; **~ vergeht nicht** (*ugs. scherzh.*) it would take a great deal to finish off his/her/our sort (*coll.*); **B** (*Art*) weed

**Unkraut·vertilgungsmittel** *das* weedkiller

**unkritisch** **1** *Adj.* uncritical. **2** *adv.* uncritically

**unkultiviert** *Adj.* uncultivated

**unkündbar** *Adj.* permanent ‹position, contract›; irredeemable ‹loan›; **er ist ~:** he cannot be given notice

**unkundig** *Adj.* (*geh.*) ignorant; **einer Sache** (*Gen.*) **~ sein** have no knowledge of sth.; **des Lesens/Schreibens/Deutschen ~:** unable to read/to write/to speak German

**unlängst** *Adv.* (*geh.*) not long ago; recently; **noch ~, ~ noch** only recently

**unlauter** *Adj.* (*geh.*) dishonest; **~er Wettbewerb** (*Rechtsspr.*) unfair competition

**unleidlich** **1** *Adj.* tetchy. **2** *adv.* tetchily

**unlesbar** *Adj.* unreadable

**unleserlich** **1** *Adj.* illegible. **2** *adv.* illegibly

**unleugbar** **1** *Adj.* undeniable; indisputable. **2** *adv.* undeniably; indisputably

**unliebsam** **1** *Adj.* unpleasant; **~es Aufsehen erregen** attract the wrong sort of attention. **2** *adv.* **er ist ~ aufgefallen** he made a bad impression

**unlogisch** **1** *Adj.* illogical. **2** *adv.* illogically

**Unlust** *die* (*Widerwille*) reluctance; (*Lustlosigkeit*) lack of enthusiasm; **mit ~:** with reluctance/without enthusiasm

**unlustig** **1** *Adj.* listless; (*ohne Begeisterung*) unenthusiastic. **2** *adv.* listlessly; (*ohne Begeisterung*) unenthusiastically

**unmännlich** (*abwertend*) **1** *Adj.* unmanly; (*weibisch*) effeminate. **2** *adv.* in an unmanly way

**unmaßgeblich** *Adj.* of no consequence *postpos.*; inconsequential; **nach meiner ~en Meinung** (*scherzh.*) in my humble opinion

**unmäßig** **1** *Adj.* **A** (*übermäßig, maßlos*) immoderate; excessive; **~ im Essen/Trinken sein** eat/drink to excess; **~ in seinen Ansprüchen/Forderungen sein** make excessive claims/demands; **B** (*enorm*) tremendous ‹desire, thirst, fear, etc.›. **2** *adv.* **A** (*übermäßig, allzusehr*) excessively; ‹eat, drink› to excess; **~ viel essen/Geld ausgeben** eat/spend far too much; **B** (*überaus, sehr*) tremendously (*coll.*), terribly ‹surprised, pleased, fond, etc.›

**Unmäßigkeit** *die* immoderation *no art.*

**Unmenge** *die* mass; enormous number/amount; **eine ~ Geld/Bücher, eine ~ von** *od.* **an Geld/Büchern** an enormous amount of money/number of books; **er trinkt ~n [von] Tee** he drinks enormous quantities *or* (*coll.*) gallons of tea

**Unmensch** *der* brute; **ich bin/man ist ja kein ~** (*ugs.*) I'm not inhuman

**unmenschlich** **1** *Adj.* **A** inhuman; brutal; subhuman, appalling ‹conditions›; **B** (*entsetzlich*) terrible (*coll.*), appalling ‹pain, heat, suffering, etc.›. **2** *adv.* **A** in an inhuman way; **B** (*entsetzlich*) appallingly (*coll.*)

**unmerklich** **1** *Adj.* imperceptible. **2** *adv.* imperceptibly

**unmissverständlich, *unmißverständlich** **1** *Adj.* **A** (*eindeutig*) unambiguous; **B** (*offen, direkt*) blunt ‹answer, refusal›; unequivocal ‹language›. **2** *adv.* **A** (*eindeutig*) unambiguously; **B** (*offen, direkt*) bluntly; unequivocally

**unmittelbar** **1** *Adj.* **A** immediate ‹vicinity, past, future›; immediate, next-door ‹neighbour etc.›; **in ~er Strandnähe** right next to the beach; **aus ~er Nähe** ‹shoot› at close quarters, from point-blank range; **B** (*direkt*) direct ‹contact, connection, influence, etc.›; immediate ‹cause, consequence, predecessor, successor›. **2** *adv.* **A** immediately; right ‹behind, next to›; **~ bevorstehen** be imminent; be almost upon us *etc.*; **B** (*direkt*) directly; **ich fahre von dort ~ zum Bahnhof** I'll go straight from there to the station; **etw. ~ erleben** experience sth. at first hand

**unmöbliert** *Adj.* unfurnished

**unmodern** **1** *Adj.* old-fashioned; (*nicht modisch*) unfashionable; **~ werden** go out of fashion. **2** *adv.* in an old-fashioned way; (*nicht modisch*) unfashionably

**unmöglich** **1** *Adj.* **A** impossible; **ich verlange ja nichts Unmögliches [von dir]** I'm not asking [you] for the impossible; **es ist mir ~:** it is impossible for me; **du machst es ihm/mir ~[, zu ...]** you are making it impossible for him/me [to ...]; **B** (*ugs.: nicht akzeptabel, unangebracht*) impossible ‹person, behaviour, colour, ideas, place, etc.›; **~ aussehen** look ridiculous; **jmdn./sich ~ machen** make a fool of sb./oneself; make sb./oneself look ridiculous; **sich bei jmdm. ~ machen** lose sb.'s respect; **C** (*ugs.: erstaunlich, seltsam*) incredible; **an den ~sten Orten** in the most impossible *or* incredible places. **2** *adv.* (*ugs.*) ‹behave› impossibly; ‹dress› ridiculously; **~ angezogen sein** be wearing impossible clothes. **3** *Adv.* (*ugs.: unter keinen Umständen*) **ich/es** *usw.* **kann ~ ...** I/it *etc.* can't possibly ...; **mehr ist ~ zu erreichen** it's impossible to do any more; **das geht ~:** that's out of the question

**Unmoral** *die* immorality *no art.*

**unmoralisch** **1** *Adj.* immoral. **2** *adv.* immorally

**unmotiviert** **1** *Adj.* unmotivated. **2** *adv.* without reason; for no reason

**unmündig** *Adj.* **A** under-age; **~ sein** be under age *or* a minor; **B** (*fig.: geistig unselbstständig*) dependent

**Unmündigkeit** *die*; **~** (*fig.*) dependence

**unmusikalisch** *Adj.* unmusical

**Unmut** *der* (*geh.*) displeasure; annoyance; **seinen ~ an jmdm. auslassen** take it out on sb.

**unnachahmlich** **1** *Adj.* inimitable. **2** *adv.* inimitably

**unnachgiebig** *Adj.* intransigent; **in diesem Punkt ~ sein** be uncompromising in this respect; refuse to yield on this point

**Unnachgiebigkeit** *die* intransigence

**unnachsichtig** **1** *Adj.* merciless; unmerciful; unrelenting ‹severity›. **2** *adv.* mercilessly; ‹punish› unmercifully

**unnahbar** *Adj.* unapproachable

**unnatürlich** **1** *Adj.* unnatural; forced ‹laugh›; artificial ‹material›; ‹death› from unnatural causes; violent ‹death›. **2** *adv.* unnaturally; ‹laugh› in a forced way; ‹speak› affectedly; **er trinkt/schläft ~ viel** he drinks/sleeps an abnormal amount

**Unnatürlichkeit** *die* unnaturalness; (*von Material*) artificiality

**unnormal** **1** *Adj.* abnormal. **2** *adv.* abnormally

**unnötig** **1** *Adj.* unnecessary; needless, pointless ‹heroism›; **~ zu sagen, dass ...** needless to say ... **2** *adv.* unnecessarily

**unnütz** **1** *Adj.* useless ‹stuff, person, etc.›; pointless ‹talk›; wasted ‹words›; pointless, wasted ‹expense, effort›; vain ‹attempt›; **es ist ~, darüber zu streiten** it is no use arguing about it. **2** *adv.* (*unnötig*) needlessly

**UNO** /'u:no/ *die*: **die ~:** the UN

**unökonomisch** **1** *Adj.* uneconomical. **2** *adv.* uneconomically; in an uneconomical way

**unordentlich** **1** *Adj.* **A** untidy; **B** (*ungeregelt*) disorderly ‹life›. **2** *adv.* untidily; ‹tie, treat, etc.› carelessly

**Unordnung** *die* disorder; mess; **so eine ~!** what a mess *or* muddle!; **in dem Zimmer herrschte eine fürchterliche ~:** the room was terribly untidy *or* in a terrible mess (*coll.*); **etw. in ~ bringen** muddle *or* mess sth. up; **in ~ geraten** get into a mess *or* muddle; (*fig.*) ‹equilibrium› become upset

**unorthodox** **1** *Adj.* unorthodox. **2** in an unorthodox way

**Unpaarhufer** *der* (*Zool.*) odd-toed ungulate

**unpaarig** (*Biol.*) **1** *Adj.* unpaired; azygous. **2** *adv.* dissimilarly

**unparteiisch** **1** *Adj.* impartial. **2** *adv.* impartially

**Unparteiische** *der/die; adj. Dekl.* (*Sport*) ⇨ **Schiedsrichter A**

**unpassend** **1** *Adj.* inappropriate; unsuitable ‹dress etc.›. **2** *adv.* inappropriately; unsuitably ‹dressed etc.›

**unpassierbar** *Adj.* impassable

**unpässlich, *unpäßlich** /'ʊnpɛslɪç/ *Adj.* indisposed

**Unpässlichkeit, *Unpäßlichkeit** *die*; **~, ~en** indisposition

**Unperson** *die* unperson

**unpersönlich** **1** *Adj.* impersonal; distant, aloof ‹person›. **2** *adv.* impersonally; ‹answer, write› in impersonal terms

**Unpersönlichkeit** *die* impersonal nature

**unpolitisch** *Adj.* unpolitical; apolitical

**unpopulär** *Adj.* unpopular

**unpraktisch** **1** *Adj.* unpractical. **2** *adv.* in an unpractical way

**unproblematisch** **1** *Adj.* unproblematic; straightforward; **nicht ganz ~:** not without its problems. **2** *adv.* without any problems

**unproduktiv** **1** *Adj.* unproductive. **2** *adv.* unproductively

**unpünktlich** **1** *Adj.* **A** unpunctual ‹person›; **B** (*verspätet*) late, unpunctual ‹payment›. **2** *adv.* late

**Unpünktlichkeit** *die* lateness; lack of punctuality

**unqualifiziert** **1** *Adj.* **A** unqualified, unskilled ‹person›; unskilled ‹work›; **B** (*abwertend: nicht fundiert*) inept ‹remark, criticism›. **2** *adv.* (*abwertend*) ineptly

**unrasiert** *Adj.* unshaven; **~ und fern der Heimat** (*scherzh.*) away from it all and looking pretty disreputable

**Unrast** *die* (*geh.*) restlessness

**Unrat** *der*; **~[e]s** (*geh.*) garbage (*lit. or fig.*); refuse (*Brit.*); **~ wittern** smell a rat (*fig.*)

**unrationell** **1** *Adj.* inefficient. **2** *adv.* inefficiently

**unrealistisch** **1** *Adj.* unrealistic. **2** *adv.* unrealistically

**unrecht** **1** *Adj.* wrong; **auf ~e Gedanken kommen** get wicked ideas. **2** *adv.* wrongly; **jmdm. ~ tun** do sb. an injustice; do wrong by sb.

**Unrecht** *das*; **~[e]s** **A** **~ haben** be wrong; **~ bekommen** be shown to be in the wrong; **jmdm. ~ geben** disagree with sb.; **B** wrong; **im ~ sein** be [in the] wrong; **sich ins ~ setzen** put oneself in the wrong; **ihm**

U

**ist ein ~ geschehen** he has been wronged; **~ tun** do wrong; **zu ~:** wrongly; **nicht zu ~** (*wohlbegründet*) not without [good] reason

**unrechtmäßig** ❶ *Adj.* unlawful; illegal. ❷ *adv.* unlawfully; illegally

**unredlich** (*geh.*) ❶ *Adj.* dishonest. ❷ *adv.* dishonestly

**Unredlichkeit** *die* Ⓐ dishonesty; Ⓑ (*Handlung*) dishonest act

**unreell** *Adj.* unfair ‹deal, price›

**unreflektiert** ❶ *Adj.* (*geh.*) unthinking; (*spontan*) spontaneous ‹tradition›. ❷ *adv.* without thinking; unthinkingly

**unregelmäßig** ❶ *Adj.* irregular. ❷ *adv.* irregularly

**Unregelmäßigkeit** *die* irregularity

**unregierbar** *Adj.* ungovernable

**unreif** *Adj.* Ⓐ unripe; Ⓑ (*nicht erwachsen*) immature

**Unreife** *die* ⇒ **unreif** A, B: unripeness; immaturity

**unrein** *Adj.* Ⓐ (*auch fig.*) impure; bad ‹breath, skin›; (*nicht sauber*) dirty, polluted ‹water, air›; unclear ‹sound›; Ⓑ (*Rel.*) unclean; Ⓒ **etw. ins Unreine schreiben** make a rough copy of sth.; write sth. [out] in rough; **ins Unreine sprechen** *od.* **reden** (*ugs. scherzh.*) talk off the top of one's head

**Unreinheit** *die* Ⓐ ⇒ **unrein** A: impurity; badness; dirtiness; polluted state; lack of clarity; Ⓑ **~en der Haut** skin disorders

**unrentabel** ❶ *Adj.* unprofitable. ❷ *adv.* unprofitably

**unrettbar** ❶ *Adj.* unsavable; beyond hope *pred.* ❷ *adv.* irretrievably ‹lost›

**unrichtig** ❶ *Adj.* incorrect; inaccurate. ❷ *adv.* (*fehlerhaft*) incorrectly

**Unrichtigkeit** *die* Ⓐ (*das Unzutreffendsein*) incorrectness; inaccuracy; Ⓑ (*Fehlerhaftigkeit*) incorrectness; Ⓒ (*etw. Unzutreffendes, Fehler*) inaccuracy

**Unruh** /ˈʊnruː/ *die;* **~, ~en** (*Technik*) balance [wheel] (*of clock*)

**Unruhe** *die* Ⓐ (*auch fig.*) unrest; (*Lärm*) noise; commotion; (*Unrast*) restlessness; agitation; (*Besorgnis*) anxiety; disquiet; **unter den Zuschauern entstand ~:** the audience became restless; Ⓑ (*Unfrieden*) unrest; **~ stiften** stir up trouble; Ⓒ *Pl.* (*Tumulte*) disturbances; unrest *sing.*

**Unruhe-: ~herd** *der* seat of unrest; trouble spot; **~stifter** *der*, **~stifterin** *die* (*abwertend*) troublemaker

**unruhig** ❶ *Adj.* Ⓐ restless; (*besorgt*) anxious; (*nervös*) agitated; jittery; (*fig.*) choppy ‹sea›; busy ‹pattern›; busy, eventful ‹life›; unsettled, troubled ‹time›; **er ist ein ~er Geist** he's a restless creature; **hier ist es mir zum Arbeiten viel zu ~:** there is too much going on [for me] to work here; Ⓑ (*laut*) noisy ‹area etc.›; Ⓒ (*ungleichmäßig*) uneven ‹breathing, pulse, running, etc.›; fitful ‹sleep, motion›; disturbed ‹night›; unsettled ‹life›. ❷ *adv.* Ⓐ restlessly; (*besorgt*) anxiously; **hier geht es sehr ~ zu** there is too much going on here; Ⓑ (*ungleichmäßig*) ‹breathe, run› unevenly; ‹sleep› fitfully

**unrühmlich** ❶ *Adj.* inglorious; ignominious. ❷ *adv.* ignominiously

**unrund** *Adj.* (*Technik*) Ⓐ not perfectly round *pred.*; Ⓑ (*ungleichmäßig*) uneven, rough ‹running of engine›

**uns** /ʊns/ ❶ *Personalpron.* Ⓐ *Akk. des Personalpron.* **wir** us; Ⓑ *Dat. des Personalpron.* **wir; gib es ~:** give it to us; **gib ~ das Geld** give us the money; **wie geht es ~ heute?** (*fam.*) how are we today? (*joc.*); **kommst du zu ~?** are you coming to our place? (*coll.*); **Freunde von ~:** friends of ours; **von ~ aus** as far as we're concerned; **bei ~:** at our home *or* (*coll.*) place; (*in der Heimat*) where I/we live *or* come from; **bei ~ gegenüber, gegenüber von ~:** opposite us *or* our house.
❷ *Reflexivpron. der 1. Pers. Pl.* Ⓐ *refl.* ourselves; **wir schämen ~:** we are ashamed [of ourselves]; **wir waschen ~/~ die Hände** we are washing [ourselves]/our hands; **von ~ aus** (*aus eigenem Antrieb*) on our own initiative; Ⓑ *reziprok* one another; **wir kennen ~ schon** we know one another; we've met; **wir haben ~ gestritten** we had an argument *or* quarrel

**unsachgemäß** ❶ *Adj.* improper. ❷ *adv.* improperly

**unsachlich** ❶ *Adj.* unobjective; **~ werden** lose one's objectivity. ❷ *adv.* without objectivity

**Unsachlichkeit** *die* lack of objectivity

**unsagbar, unsäglich** /ʊnˈzɛːklɪç/ (*geh.*) ❶ *Adj.* indescribable; unutterable. ❷ *adv.* indescribably; unutterably

**unsanft** ❶ *Adj.* rough; hard ‹push, impact›. ❷ *adv.* roughly; **~ geweckt werden** be rudely awoken; **jmdn. ~ zurechtweisen** reprimand sb. curtly *or* rudely

**unsauber** ❶ *Adj.* Ⓐ (*schmutzig*) dirty; Ⓑ (*nachlässig*) untidy, sloppy ‹work, writing, etc.›; Ⓒ (*unklar*) unclear ‹sound›; (*ungenau*) inexact, woolly ‹definition›; Ⓓ (*unlauter*) shady ‹practice, deal, character, etc.›; underhand, dishonest ‹method, means, intention›; (*Sport: unfair*) unsporting, unfair ‹play›. ❷ *adv.* Ⓐ (*nachlässig*) untidily; carelessly; Ⓑ (*unklar*) ‹sing, play› inaccurately; Ⓒ (*Sport: unfair*) unsportingly; unfairly

**Unsauberkeit** *die* Ⓐ dirtiness; lack of cleanliness; Ⓑ (*Nachlässigkeit*) untidiness; sloppiness; Ⓒ (*Unklarheit*) lack of clarity; (*Ungenauigkeit*) woolliness; Ⓓ (*Unehrlichkeit*) shadiness; (*Sport: Unfairness*) unfairness

**unschädlich** *Adj.* harmless; **~ machen** render harmless, neutralize ‹toxic substance, germ. etc.›; put ‹weapon, person› out of action; render ‹bomb etc.› safe; (*verhüll.: durch Tötung*) eliminate ‹person›

**unscharf** ❶ *Adj.* Ⓐ blurred, fuzzy ‹photo, picture›; Ⓑ (*ungenau*) woolly ‹formulation›; **die Grenzen sind ~:** there are no clear-cut borderlines; Ⓒ (*ein ~es Bild ergebend*) ‹lens, optical instrument› with poor definition; (*falsch eingestellt*) out-of-focus. ❷ *adv.* Ⓐ blurred; **durch diese Brille sehe ich alles ganz ~:** everything looks blurred *or* out of focus [to me] through these spectacles; Ⓑ (*ungenau*) unclearly

**unschätzbar** *Adj.* inestimable ‹value etc.›; invaluable ‹service›; priceless ‹riches etc.›

**unscheinbar** *Adj.* inconspicuous; nondescript; unspectacular ‹plumage, blossom›

**unschicklich** (*geh.*) ❶ *Adj.* unseemly; improper. ❷ *adv.* improperly

**unschlagbar** *Adj.* unbeatable ‹opponent, prices, etc.›

**Unschlitt** /ˈʊnʃlɪt/ *das;* **~[e]s, ~e** (*veralt.*) tallow

**unschlüssig** *Adj.* undecided *pred.*; undecisive ‹gesture, attitude›; **ich bin [mir] noch ~, ob ...** I cannot decide whether ...

**unschön** ❶ *Adj.* Ⓐ ugly; unattractive ‹colour, voice›; Ⓑ (*unerfreulich, unfair*) unpleasant, nasty ‹business, incident, weather, conduct, etc.›; ugly ‹scene›. ❷ *adv.* Ⓐ unattractively; Ⓑ (*unfreundlich, unfair*) badly

**Unschuld** *die* Ⓐ innocence; **wegen erwiesener ~:** having been proved innocent; **seine Hände in ~ waschen** (*fig.*) wash one's hands in innocence; Ⓑ (*Naivität*) innocence; (*Jungfräulichkeit*) virginity; **in aller ~:** in all innocence; **eine ~ vom Lande** (*ugs. scherzh.*) a naïve country girl

**unschuldig** ❶ *Adj.* Ⓐ innocent; **an etw.** (*Dat.*) **~ sein** be not guilty of sth.; **er ist an dem Unfall völlig ~:** he was in no way responsible for the accident; Ⓑ (*unverdorben*) innocent; **ein ~es Mädchen** a virgin; **er/sie ist noch ~:** he/she is still a virgin; **den Unschuldigen/die Unschuldige spielen** play the innocent. ❷ *adv.* innocently

**Unschulds-: ~beteuerung** *die* protestation of innocence; **~lamm** *das* (*spött.*) little innocent; **sie sind auch keine ~lämmer** they're no angels; **~miene** *die* innocent expression; **mit ~miene** with an air of innocence

**unschwer** *Adv.* (*geh.*) easily; without difficulty

**unselbständig** ❶ *Adj.* Ⓐ dependent [on other people]; **sei doch nicht immer so ~!** try to be a bit more independent!; Ⓑ (*abhängig*) [financially/economically] dependent; not self-supporting *pred.*; **~e Arbeit** [paid] employment. ❷ *adv.* Ⓐ **[sehr] ~ denken/handeln** not think [at all] for oneself *or* independently/not act [at all] on one's own *or* independently; Ⓑ (*abhängig*) **~ beschäftigte Personen** *od.* **Beschäftigte** persons in employment; employed persons

**Unselbständigkeit** *die* Ⓐ lack of independence; Ⓑ (*Abhängigkeit*) dependence

**unselbstständig** ⇒ **unselbständig**

**Unselbstständigkeit** ⇒ **Unselbständigkeit**

**unselig** *Adj.* (*geh.*) wretched ‹fate, person, etc.›; [extremely] unfortunate ‹situation›; ill-starred ‹inheritance›; (*verhängnisvoll*) disastrous ‹journey, decision, etc.›

**unser**[1] /ˈʊnzɐ/ *Possessivpron. der 1. Pers. Pl.* our; **Vater ~** (*bibl.*) Our Father; **das ist ~s** *od.* (*geh.*) **~es** *od.* (*geh.*) **das ~e** that is ours; **sein Wagen stand neben ~[e]m** *od.* **unsrem** his car was next to ours; **die Unseren** our family; **wir haben das Unsere getan** we have done our share *or* part

**unser**[2] *Gen. des Personalpronomens* **wir** (*geh.*) of us; **wir waren ~ drei** there were three of us; **erbarme dich ~!** have mercy upon us!; **in ~ aller/beider Interesse** in the interest of all/both of us

**unser·einer, unser·eins** *Indefinitpron.* (*ugs.*) the likes of us *pl.*; our sort (*coll.*)

**unserer·seits** *Adv.* for our part

**unseres·gleichen** *indekl. Indefinitpron.* people *pl.* like us; *attr.* **Menschen ~:** people like us

**unseret·halben, unseret·wegen** *Adv.* ⇒ **unsertwegen**

**unseret·willen** *Adv.* ⇒ **unsertwillen**

**unserige** *subst. Possessivpron.* ⇒ **unsrige**

**unseriös** (*abwertend*) ❶ *Adj.* Ⓐ not [quite] the proper thing *pred.*; casual; ‹appearance, manner›; Ⓑ (*niveaulos*) low-quality ‹newspaper›; downmarket ‹publisher›; Ⓒ (*unlauter*) shady, dubious ‹practice, deal›; (*unredlich*) questionable, dishonest ‹method etc.›; (*nicht reell*) dubious ‹firm, pseudo-scientist, faith healer›; dishonest, shady ‹business man›. ❷ *adv.* Ⓐ ‹behave, dress› casually; Ⓑ (*unlauter, unredlich*) dishonestly; unfairly

**unser·seits** ⇒ **unsererseits**

**unsers·gleichen** ⇒ **unseresgleichen**

**unsert·wegen** *Adv.* Ⓐ because of us; on our account; Ⓑ (*was uns angeht*) as far as we are concerned

**unsert·willen** *Adv. in* **um ~:** for our sake[s]

**unsicher** ❶ *Adj.* Ⓐ (*gefährlich*) unsafe; dangerous; (*gefährdet*) at risk *pred.*; insecure ‹job›; **einen Ort ~ machen** (*scherzh.*) honour a place with one's presence (*joc.*); (*sich vergnügen*) have a good time in a place; (*sein Unwesen treiben*) get up to one's tricks in a place; Ⓑ (*unzuverlässig*) uncertain, unreliable ‹method›; unreliable ‹source, person›; Ⓒ (*zögernd*) uncertain, hesitant ‹step›; (*zitternd*) unsteady, shaky ‹hand›; (*nicht selbstsicher*) insecure; diffident; unsure of oneself *pred.*; **ich fühle mich ~:** I don't feel sure of myself; **er ist im Rechnen noch ~:** he still lacks confidence in arithmetic; **jmdn. ~ machen** put sb. off his/her stroke; Ⓓ (*keine Gewissheit habend*) unsure; uncertain; **[sich** (*Dat.*)**] ~ sein[, ob ...]** ‹person› be unsure *or* uncertain [whether ...]; Ⓔ (*ungewiss*) uncertain; **das ist mir zu ~:** that's too uncertain *or* (*coll.*) dodgy for my liking.
❷ *adv.* Ⓐ (*mit Schwierigkeiten*) ‹walk, stand, etc.› unsteadily; **~ fahren** drive without [much] confidence; Ⓑ (*nicht selbstsicher*) ‹smile, look› diffidently

**Unsicherheit** *die* Ⓐ (*Gefährlichkeit*) dangerousness; (*Gefahren*) dangers *pl.*; Ⓑ (*Unzuverlässigkeit*) uncertainty; unreliability; Ⓒ (*Zaghaftigkeit*) unsureness; (*der Schritte o. Ä.*) unsteadiness; Ⓓ (*fehlende Selbstsicherheit*) insecurity; lack of [self-]confidence; Ⓔ

*old spelling (see note on page 1707)

U

(*Ungewissheit*) uncertainty; Ⓕ (*der Arbeitsplätze*) insecurity; (*des Friedens*) instability; Ⓖ (*Unwägbarkeit*) uncertainty

**Unsicherheits·faktor** *der* element of uncertainty

**unsichtbar** *Adj.* invisible (**für** to)

**Unsinn** *der* Ⓐ nonsense; **rede doch keinen ~!** don't talk nonsense *or* rubbish!; **es wäre ~ zu glauben, …** it would be ridiculous to believe …; Ⓑ (*Unfug*) tomfoolery; fooling about *no art.*; **~ machen** *od.* **treiben** mess *or* fool about; **mach [ja] keinen ~:** don't do anything silly; no messing about

**unsinnig** ❶ *Adj.* Ⓐ nonsensical ‹statement, talk, etc.›; absurd, ridiculous ‹demand etc.›; Ⓑ (*ugs.: übermäßig*) terrible (*coll.*) ‹rage, fear, thirst, etc.›. ❷ *adv.* Ⓐ foolishly; stupidly; Ⓑ (*ugs.: übermäßig*) insanely (*coll.*), terribly (*coll.*) ‹expensive›

**Unsitte** *die* bad habit; (*allgemein verbreitet*) bad practice

**unsittlich** ❶ *Adj.* indecent. ❷ *adv.* indecently; **sich jmdm. ~ nähern** make indecent advances to sb.

**unsolid[e]** ❶ *Adj.* Ⓐ flimsy ‹structure›; shoddy ‹work, repair›; (*fig.*) superficial ‹education›; Ⓑ (*ausschweifend*) dissolute ‹person, life›. ❷ *adv.* Ⓐ flimsily ‹made›; shoddily ‹executed›; Ⓑ (*ausschweifend*) **~ leben** live a dissolute life

**unsozial** ❶ *Adj.* unsocial ‹policy, measure, rent, etc.›; antisocial ‹behaviour›. ❷ *adv.* unsocially; ‹behave› antisocially

**unsportlich** ❶ *Adj.* Ⓐ unathletic ‹person›; Ⓑ (*unfair*) unsporting, unsportsmanlike ‹behaviour, play›. ❷ *adv.* (*unfair*) in an unsporting way

**unsr…** ⇒ **unser**[1]

**unsrer·seits** ⇒ **unsererseits**

**unsres·gleichen** ⇒ **unseresgleichen**

**unsrige** /ˈʊnzrɪgə/ *Possessivpron.* (*geh. veralt.*) **der/die/das ~:** ours; our one; **das ~** *od.* **Unsrige** (*unser Anteil*) our share *or* part; (*unser Besitz*) what is/was ours; **die ~n** *od.* **Unsrigen** our family *sing.*

**unstatthaft** *Adj.* inadmissible

**unsterblich** ❶ *Adj.* immortal; (*fig.*) undying ‹love›; **seine Kompositionen sind ~** (*fig.*) his compositions will live for ever. ❷ *adv.* (*ugs.: außerordentlich*) incredibly (*coll.*); **sich ~ in jmdn. verlieben** fall madly in love with sb.; **sich ~ blamieren** make a complete ass of oneself

**Unsterbliche** *der/die; adj. Dekl.* immortal

**Unsterblichkeit** *die* immortality

**Unstern** *der* (*geh.*) unlucky star; **unter einem ~ stehen** be ill-starred

**unstet** (*geh.*) ❶ *Adj.* Ⓐ (*ruhelos*) restless ‹person, glance, thoughts, etc.›; unsettled ‹life›; Ⓑ (*unbeständig*) vacillating ‹person, nature›; (*labil*) unstable ‹person, character›. ❷ *adv.* (*ruhelos*) restlessly

**unstimmig** *Adj.* inconsistent [with the facts]; **[in sich] ~:** inconsistent

**Unstimmigkeit** *die;* **~, ~en** Ⓐ inconsistency; Ⓑ (*etw. Unstimmiges*) discrepancy; Ⓒ (*Meinungsverschiedenheit*) difference [of opinion]

**unstreitig** ❶ *Adj.* indisputable. ❷ *adv.* indisputably

**unstrittig** ❶ *Adj.* Ⓐ uncontentious; Ⓑ ⇒ **unstreitig** 1. ❷ *adv.* ⇒ **unstreitig** 2

**Unsumme** *die* vast *or* huge sum

**unsympathisch** *Adj.* uncongenial, disagreeable ‹person›; unpleasant ‹characteristic, nature, voice›; **er ist mir ~/nicht ~:** I find him disagreeable/quite likeable; I don't like/I quite like him; **der Plan ist mir ~:** the plan is not to my liking

**unsystematisch** ❶ *Adj.* unsystematic. ❷ *adv.* unsystematically

**untad[e]lig** ❶ *Adj.* impeccable ‹behaviour, reputation, etc.›; irreproachable ‹person, life›. ❷ *adv.* impeccably; irreproachably

**Untat** *die* misdeed; evil deed

**untätig** *Adj.* idle; **~ herumsitzen/zusehen** sit around doing nothing/stand idly by

**Untätigkeit** *die* idleness; inactivity

**untauglich** *Adj.* Ⓐ unsuitable ‹applicant›; **~er Versuch** (*Rechtsw.*) attempt doomed to failure; Ⓑ (*für Militärdienst*) unfit [for service] *postpos.*

**unteilbar** *Adj.* Ⓐ indivisible; Ⓑ (*Math.: nicht dividierbar*) prime ‹number›

**unten** /ˈʊntn̩/ *Adv.* Ⓐ down; **hier/da ~:** down here/there; **weiter ~:** further down; **nach ~** (*auch fig.*) downward; **der Weg nach ~:** the way down; **mit dem Gesicht nach ~:** face downwards; **von ~:** from below; **~ liegen** be down below; (*darunter*) lie underneath; **[im Bett] ~ schlafen** sleep in the bottom; Ⓑ (*in Gebäuden*) (*im Erdgeschoss*) downstairs; (*im Hochhaus*) on the bottom floor; **nach ~:** downstairs; **hier ~:** down here; **der Aufzug fährt nach ~/kommt von ~:** the lift (*Brit.*) *or* (*Amer.*) elevator is going down/coming up; Ⓒ (*am unteren Ende, zum unteren Ende hin*) at the bottom; **nach ~ [hin]** towards the bottom; **~ [links] auf der Seite/im Schrank** at the bottom [left] of the page/cupboard; **in der dritten Zeile von ~:** on the third line from the bottom; **die Abbildung ~ links** the illustration bottom left; (*als Bildunterschrift*) **„~ [rechts]"** 'below [right]'; (*auf einem Karton o. Ä.*) **„~"** 'other side up'; **wo** *od.* **was ist [bei dem Karton] ~?** which is the bottom [of the cardboard box]?; **sich ~ herum waschen** wash one's nether regions *or* lower parts (*joc.*); **~ am Tisch** (*fig.*) at the bottom of the table; **100 km weiter ~ am Fluss** 100 km. further downstream; **zwei Häuser weiter ~:** two houses further down [the road]; Ⓓ (*an der Unterseite*) underneath; Ⓔ (*in einer Hierarchie, Rangfolge*) **ziemlich weit/ganz ~ auf der Liste** rather a long way down/right at the bottom of the list; Ⓕ ([*weiter*] *hinten im Text*) below; **weiter ~:** further on; below; **wie ~ angeführt** as stated below; **~ erwähnt** *od.* **genannt** undermentioned (*Brit.*); mentioned below *postpos.;* **von den unten Genannten** of the undermentioned (*Brit.*); of those mentioned below; **~ stehend** following; given below *postpos.;* Ⓖ (*ugs.: im Süden*) **~ in Sizilien/im Süden** down in Sicily/in the south; **hier/dort ~:** down here/there [in the south]; **weiter ~:** further south

**unten·drunter** *Adv.* (*ugs.*) underneath [it/them]

**unten-:** **~durch** *Adv.* through underneath; ⇒ *auch* **durch** 2 K; ***~erwähnt**, ***~genannt** ⇒ **unten** F; **~herum**, **~rum** *Adv.* (*ugs.*) down below; ***~stehend** ⇒ **unten** F

**unter** /ˈʊntɐ/ ❶ *Präp. mit Dat.* Ⓐ (*Lage, Standort, Abhängigkeit, Unterordnung*) under; **~ jmdm. wohnen** live below sb.; **~ der Devise …** according to the motto …; Ⓑ (*weniger, niedriger usw. als*) **Mengen ~ 100 Stück** quantities of less than 100; ⇒ *auch* **Durchschnitt** B; **Gefrierpunkt**; **Preis** A; **Wert** A; Ⓒ (*während*) **~ Mittag/Tags/der Woche** (*bes. südd.*) at *or* around midday/during the day/during the week; Ⓓ (*modal*) **~ Angst/Tränen** in *or* out of fear/in tears; **~ Zittern** trembling; **~ dem Beifall der Menge** applauded by the crowd; ⇒ *auch* **Aufbietung** A; **Einbeziehung**; **Schmerz** A; **Verwendung** A; Ⓔ (*aus einer Gruppe*) among[st]; **~ anderem** among[st] other things; **einer ~ 40 Bewerbern** one of *or* among[st] 40 applicants; Ⓕ (*zwischen*) among[st]; **~ sich** by themselves; **~ uns gesagt** between ourselves *or* you and me; Ⓖ (*Zustand*) **~ Druck/Strom stehen** be under pressure/be live; ⇒ *auch* **Dampf** A; **leiden** A, B; Ⓗ **~ dem Datum des 1. März 1850** (*veralt.*) on 1 March 1850.
❷ *Präp. mit Akk.* Ⓐ (*Richtung, Ziel, Abhängigkeit, Unterordnung*) under; **sich ~ einen Baum setzen** sit under a tree; **die Scheuer war bis ~ die Decke mit Heu gefüllt** the barn was full of hay right up to the roof; Ⓑ (*niedriger als*) **~ null sinken** drop below zero; Ⓒ (*zwischen*) among[st]; **er geht zu wenig ~ Menschen** he has too little to do with people; **~ Strom/Dampf setzen** switch on/put under steam.
❸ *Adv.* less than; **~ 30 [Jahre alt] sein** be under 30 [years of age]; **ein Kind von ~ 4 Jahren** a child of less than *or* under four years

**unter…** *Adj.* Ⓐ lower; bottom; (*ganz unten*) bottom; **das ~e/~ste Stockwerk** the lower/bottom storey; **das Unterste zuoberst kehren** (*ugs.*) turn everything upside down; Ⓑ lower ‹Rhine, Nile, etc.›; Ⓒ (*in der Rangfolge o. Ä.*) lower; lesser ‹authority›; **die ~en Klassen der Schule** the junior classes *or* forms of the school; Ⓓ (*der Oberfläche abgekehrt*) **die ~e Seite [von etw.]** the bottom [of sth.]; **auf der ~en Seite** underneath

**unter-, Unter-:** **~abteilung** *die* Ⓐ department; Ⓑ (*Bot.*) subdivision; **~arm** *der* ▶ 471 forearm; **~art** *die* (*Biol.*) subspecies; **~bau** *der; Pl.* **~~ten** Ⓐ (*Fundament*) foundations *pl.;* Ⓑ (*Grundlage, Basis*) foundation; basis; Ⓒ (*Sockel*) base; Ⓓ (*Straßenbau, Eisenb.*) roadbed; **~bauch** *der* ▶ 471 (*Anat.*) lower abdomen; **~belegt** *Adj.* undersubscribed; half-empty ‹hotel, hospital, etc.›; **~belegung** *die* undersubscription; **~belichten** *tr. V.* (*Fot.*); **ich ~belichte, ~belichtet, ~zubelichten** underexpose; **geistig ~belichtet sein** (*fig. salopp*) be a bit thick *or* (*coll.*) dim; **~belichtung** *die* (*Fot.*) underexposure; **~beschäftigung** *die* (*Wirtsch.*) underemployment; **~besetzt** *Adj.* understaffed; **~bett** *das* underblanket; **~bewerten** *tr. V.;* **ich ~bewerte, ~bewertet, ~zubewerten** undervalue; underrate; mark ‹gymnast, skater› too low; **die Mark wurde ~bewertet** the mark was undervalued; **~bewertung** *die* ⇒ **~bewerten**: undervaluation; underrating *no pl.;* **~bewusstsein**, ***~bewußtsein** *das* subconscious; **~bezahlen** *tr. V.;* **ich ~bezahle, ~bezahlt, ~zubezahlen** underpay; **~bezahlung** *die* underpayment

**unter-, Unter-:** **~bieten** *unr. tr. V.* Ⓐ (*weniger fordern*) undercut (**um** by); **etw. ist [im Niveau] kaum noch zu ~bieten** (*fig.*) sth. is simply rock-bottom [in quality]; Ⓑ (*bes. Sport*) beat ‹record›; **jmds. Rekord ~bieten** be faster than sb.; **~binden** *unr. tr. V.* stop; **~bindung** *die* ending; stopping; **~bleiben** *unr. itr. V.;* *mit sein* **etw. ~bleibt** sth. does not occur *or* happen; **das hat zu ~bleiben!** this must stop

**Unter·boden** *der* (*Kfz-W.*) underside

**Unterboden-:** **~schutz** *der* underseal; **~wäsche** *die* underbody wash; **der Wagen braucht eine ~wäsche** the underside of the car needs washing

**unter·brechen** *unr. tr. V.* interrupt; break ‹journey, silence›; interrupt, break off ‹negotiations, studies›; interrupt, cut off ‹electricity supply›; terminate ‹pregnancy›; **die Telefonverbindung ist unterbrochen worden** the telephone connection has been cut; **wir sind unterbrochen worden** (*im Telefongespräch*) we've been cut off

**Unter·brechung** *die* ⇒ **unterbrechen**: interruption; break (*Gen.* in); termination

**unter·breiten** *tr. V.* (*geh.*) present; **Vorschläge ~:** put suggestions forward

**unter|bringen** *unr. tr. V.* Ⓐ put; **sie konnten die Sachen nicht alle im Kofferraum ~:** they couldn't get *or* fit all the things in the boot (*Brit.*) *or* (*Amer.*) trunk; **er wusste nicht, wo er dieses Gesicht ~ sollte** (*fig.*) he knew the face but couldn't quite place it; Ⓑ (*beherbergen*) put up; **die Kinder sind gut untergebracht** the children are well looked after; Ⓒ (*ugs.*) **jmdn. bei einer Firma/beim Film/als Lehrling ~:** get sb. a job in a company/in films/as an apprentice; Ⓓ (*ugs.: einen Interessenten finden für*) place

**Unterbringung** *die;* **~, ~en** accommodation *no indef. art.*

**unter|buttern** *tr. V.* (*ugs.*) Ⓐ (*unterdrücken*) push aside (*fig.*); Ⓑ (*zusätzlich verbrauchen*) use up

**Unter·deck** *das* lower deck

***unter·der·hand** ⇨ Hand F

**unter·dessen** ⇨ **inzwischen**

**Unter·druck** *der; Pl.* **~drücke** (*Physik, Technik*) low pressure

**unter·drücken** *tr. V.* Ⓐ suppress; hold back ‹comment, question, answer, criticism, etc.›; **ein unterdrücktes Kichern** suppressed giggling; Ⓑ (*niederhalten*) suppress ‹revolution etc.›; oppress ‹minority etc.›

**Unter·drücker** *der*, **Unter·drückerin** *die* (*abwertend*) oppressor

**Unterdrückung** *die;* ~, **~en** Ⓐ (*das Unterdrücken*) suppression; Ⓑ (*das Unterdrücktwerden, -sein*) oppression

**unter·durchschnittlich** ❶ *Adj.* below average. ❷ *adv.* below the average; ~ **verdienen** have below average earnings; ~ **häufig** with below average frequency

**unter·einander** *Adv.* Ⓐ (*räumlich*) one below the other; ~ **liegen** lie *or* be one below *or* underneath the other; Ⓑ (*miteinander*) among[st] ourselves/themselves *etc.*; **sie vertrugen sich gut ~:** they had a good relationship with each other; **die Leitungen ~ verbinden** join the wires together; **sich** (*Dat.*) ~ **helfen** help each other *or* one another

***untereinander|liegen** *usw.* ⇨ **untereinander** A

**unter-, Unter-:** **~entwickelt** *Adj.* underdeveloped; **~ernährt** *Adj.* undernourished; suffering from malnutrition *postpos.;* **~ernährung** *die* malnutrition

**unter-, Unter-:** **~fahren** *unr. tr. V.* drive *or* go under; **~fangen** ❶ *unr. refl. V.* (*geh.*) Ⓐ (*wagen*) dare; venture; Ⓑ (*sich erdreisten*) have the audacity; ❷ *unr. tr. V.* (*Bauw.*) underpin; **~fangen** *das;* **~~s** (*geh.*) venture; undertaking

**unter|fassen** *tr. V.* (*ugs.*) Ⓐ (*einhaken*) **jmdn. ~:** take sb.'s arm; **sie gingen untergefasst** they walked arm in arm; Ⓑ (*stützen*) support

**unter·fertigen** *tr. V.* (*Amtsspr.*) sign

**Unterfertiger** *der;* **~s**, ~, **Unterfertigerin** *die;* ~, **~nen**, **Unterfertigte** *der/die; adj. Dekl.* (*Amtsspr.*) signatory

**unter-, Unter-:** **~fordern** *tr. V.* **jmdn. [mit etw.] ~fordern** ask *or* demand too little of sb. [with sth.]; **~führen** *tr. V.* (*Schrift- u. Druckw.*) put ditto marks for; **~führung** *die* underpass; (*für Fußgänger*) subway (*Brit.*); [pedestrian] underpass (*Amer.*)

**Unter·funktion** *die* ▶ 474 (*Med.*) hypofunction; **[eine] ~ der Schilddrüse** thyroid insufficiency

**unter·füttern** *tr. V.* Ⓐ line ‹garment›; Ⓑ (*unterlegen*) **Fliesen mit einer Dämmschicht ~:** back tiles with a layer of insulating material

**Unter·gang** *der* Ⓐ (*Sonnen~, Mond~ usw.*) setting; Ⓑ (*von Schiffen*) sinking; Ⓒ (*das Zugrundegehen*) decline; (*plötzlich*) destruction; (*von Personen*) downfall; (*der Welt*) end; **der ~ des Römischen Reiches** the fall of the Roman Empire; **er war ihr ~:** he was her ruin; **der Alkohol war ihr ~:** alcohol was the ruin of her *or* was her downfall; **vom ~ bedroht sein** be threatened by destruction; **etw. geht seinem ~ entgegen** sth. is heading for disaster; **etw. ist dem ~ geweiht** sth. is doomed

**Untergangs·stimmung** *die* feelings *pl.* of doom

**unter·gärig** /-gɛːrɪç/ *Adj.* bottom-fermented ‹beer›; bottom-fermenting ‹yeast›

**unter·geben** *Adj.* subordinate

**Untergebene** *der/die; adj. Dekl.* subordinate; **jmds. ~r sein** be subordinate to sb.; **die ~n des Königs** the subjects of the king

**unter-, Unter-:** **~|gehen** *unr. itr. V.; mit sein* Ⓐ ‹sun, star, etc.› set; ‹ship› sink, go down; ‹person› drown, go under; (*fig.*) **sein Stern ist im Untergehen** his star is on the wane; **die Musik ging/seine Worte gingen in dem Lärm ~:** the music was/his words were drowned by *or* lost in the noise; **jmd. geht im Gedränge** *od.* **Gewühl ~:** sb. gets lost in the crowds; Ⓑ (*zugrunde gehen*) come to an end; **davon geht die Welt nicht ~:** it's not the end of the world; **~geordnet** ❶ ⇨ **unterordnen**; ❷ *Adj.* Ⓐ (*weniger wichtig*) secondary ‹role, importance, etc.›; subordinate ‹position, post, etc.›; Ⓑ (*Sprachw.*) subordinate; **~geschoss**, ***~geschoß** *das* basement; **~gestell** *das* Ⓐ (*Fahrgestell*) undercarriage; Ⓑ (*salopp scherzh.: Beine*) legs *pl.;* **~gewicht** *das* ▶ 353 underweight; **[5 kg] ~gewicht haben** be [5 kilos] underweight; **~gewichtig** *Adj.* underweight

**unter-, Unter-:** **~gliedern** *tr. V.* subdivide; **~gliederung** *die* subdivision; **~graben**[1] *unr. tr. V.* undermine (*fig.*); **~graben**[2] *unr. tr. V.* dig in; **~grenze** *die* lower limit; **~grund** *der* Ⓐ (*bes. Landw.*) subsoil; Ⓑ (*Bauw.: Baugrund*) foundation; Ⓒ (*Farbschicht*) background; Ⓓ (*bes. Politik*) underground; **in den ~grund gehen** go underground; **im ~grund** underground

**Untergrund-:** **~bahn** *die* underground [railway] (*Brit.*); subway (*Amer.*); **mit der ~bahn fahren** travel on the *or* by underground (*Brit.*) *or* (*Amer.*) subway; **~bewegung** *die* (*Politik*) underground movement

**unter-, Unter-:** **~gründig** *Adj.* hidden ‹connection, sense›; **~|haken** *tr. V.* (*ugs.*) **jmdn. ~haken** take sb.'s arm; **mit jmdm. ~gehakt gehen** walk arm in arm with sb.; **sich ~haken** link arms; **~halb** ❶ *Adv.* below; **weiter ~halb** further down; **~halb von** below; ❷ *Präp. mit Gen.* below; **~halt** *der* Ⓐ living; Ⓑ (*~haltszahlung*) maintenance; Ⓒ (*Instandhaltung[skosten]*) upkeep; **~|halten**[1] *unr. tr. V.* (*ugs.*) hold underneath

**unter·halten**[2] ❶ *unr. tr. V.* Ⓐ (*versorgen*) support; Ⓑ (*instand halten*) maintain ‹building›; Ⓒ (*betreiben*) run, keep ‹car, hotel›; Ⓓ (*pflegen*) maintain, keep up ‹contact, correspondence›; Ⓔ entertain ‹guest, audience›; **ein ~des Buch** an entertaining book. ❷ *unr. refl. V.* Ⓐ talk; converse; **mit ihm kann man sich gut ~:** he is easy to talk to; one can have a pleasant conversation with him; Ⓑ (*sich vergnügen*) enjoy oneself; **habt ihr euch gut ~?** did you have a good time?

**unterhaltsam** *Adj.* entertaining

**unterhalts-, Unterhalts-:** **~an·spruch** *der* maintenance claim; claim for maintenance; **~berechtigt** *Adj.* entitled to maintenance *postpos.;* **~kosten** *Pl.* maintenance *sing.;* **~pflicht** *die* obligation to pay maintenance; **~pflichtig** *Adj.* obliged to pay maintenance *postpos.;* **~zahlung** *die* maintenance payment

**Unterhaltung** *die* Ⓐ (*Versorgung*) support; Ⓑ (*Instandhaltung*) maintenance; upkeep; **etw. ist in der ~ sehr teuer** the maintenance *or* upkeep of sth. is very expensive; Ⓒ (*Aufrechterhaltung*) maintenance; Ⓓ (*Gespräch*) conversation; Ⓔ (*Zeitvertreib*) entertainment; **ich wünsche gute** *od.* **angenehme ~:** enjoy yourself/yourselves; **ich schreibe zu meiner eigenen ~ Geschichten** I write stories for my own enjoyment

**Unterhaltungs-:** **~elektronik** *die* home electronics *sing., no art.* (*for entertainment purposes*); **~kosten** *Pl.* maintenance costs; (*Kfz-W.*) running costs; **~lektüre** *die* light reading *no art.;* **~literatur** *die* popular fiction; **~musik** *die* light music; **~sendung** *die* entertainment programme

**unter·handeln** *itr. V.* (*bes. Politik*) negotiate (**über** + *Akk.* on)

**Unter·händler** *der*, **Unter·händlerin** *die* (*bes. Politik*) negotiator

**Unter·handlung** *die* (*bes. Politik*) negotiation

**Unter·haus** *das* (*Parl.*) lower house *or* chamber; (*in Großbritannien*) House of Commons; Lower House

**Unter·hemd** *das* vest (*Brit.*); undershirt (*Amer.*)

**unter·höhlen** *tr. V.* Ⓐ hollow out; erode; Ⓑ (*untergraben*) undermine (*fig.*)

**Unter·holz** *das* underwood; undergrowth

**Unter·hose** *die* (*Herren~*) [under]pants *pl.;* (*Damen~*) panties; knickers (*Brit.*); briefs *pl.;* **lange ~n** long underpants; long johns (*coll.*)

**unter·irdisch** ❶ *Adj.* underground; underground, subterranean ‹river, spring, etc.›. ❷ *adv.* underground

**unter·jochen** *tr. V.* subjugate

**Unter·jochung** *die;* **~:** subjugation

**unter|jubeln** *tr. V.* (*ugs.*) **jmdm. etw. ~:** palm sth. off on sb.

**unter·kellern** *tr. V.* **das Haus ist nicht unterkellert** the house doesn't have a cellar

**unter-, Unter-:** **~kiefer** *der* lower jaw; **~kleid** *das* [full-length] slip; **~kleidung** *die* underwear; **~|kommen** *unr. itr. V.; mit sein* Ⓐ (*Unterkunft finden*) find accommodation; Ⓑ (*ugs.: eine Stelle finden*) find *or* get a job; Ⓒ (*ugs.: Interesse finden*) **er versuchte, mit seiner Story woanders ~zukommen** he tried to get his story accepted somewhere else; Ⓓ (*bes. südd., österr.: begegnen*) **so etwas/ein solcher Dummkopf ist mir noch nicht ~gekommen** I've never come across 'anything like it/such a 'fool; **~kommen** *das;* **~~s**, **~~:** accommodation *no indef. art.;* **~körper** *der* lower part of the body; **~|kriechen** *unr. itr. V.; mit sein* (*ugs.*) find shelter; **bei jmdm. ~kriechen** put up at sb.'s (*coll.*); **~|kriegen** *tr. V.* (*ugs.*) Ⓐ (*entmutigen, besiegen*) bring *or* get down; **sich nicht ~kriegen lassen** not let things get one down; Ⓑ ⇨ **unterbringen** A, C

**unter-, Unter-:** **~kühlen** *tr. V.* **jmdn. ~kühlen** reduce sb.'s temperature [below normal]; **er war stark ~kühlt** he was suffering from hypothermia *or* exposure; **~kühlt** *Adj.* dry, factual ‹style›; cool ‹person›; icy ‹tone›; **~kühlung** *die* reduction of body temperature; **er musste mit ~kühlungen in ein Krankenhaus gebracht werden** he was taken to hospital suffering from exposure *or* hypothermia

**Unterkunft** /ˈʊntɐkʊnft/ *die;* ~, **Unterkünfte** /...kynftə/ accommodation *no indef. art.;* lodging *no indef. art.;* **eine gute ~ haben** have good accommodation *or* lodgings; **~ und Frühstück** bed and breakfast; **~ und Verpflegung** board and lodging; **die Unterkünfte der Soldaten** the soldiers' quarters

**Unter·lage** *die* Ⓐ (*Schreib~, Matte o. Ä.*) pad; (*für eine Schreibmaschine usw.*) mat; (*unter einer Matratze, einem Teppich*) underlay; (*zum Schlafen usw.*) base; **ich brauche eine feste ~ zum Schreiben** I need something to rest my paper on so that I can write; **sorgen Sie für eine gute ~** (*ugs. scherzh.*) make sure you've got something in your stomach; Ⓑ *Pl.* (*Akten, Papiere*) documents; papers

**Unter·länge** *die* descender

**Unter·lass**, ***Unter·laß** *der: in* **ohne ~:** incessantly

**unter·lassen** *unr. tr. V.* refrain from [doing]; **Zwischenrufe sind zu ~:** no heckling; **unterlass gefälligst diese Albernheiten** (*ugs.*) kindly stop being so silly; **warum haben Sie es ~, die Angelegenheit zu melden?** why did you omit *or* fail to report the matter?

**Unterlassung** *die;* ~, **~en** omission; failure; **~ der Deklination** (*Sprachw.*) omission of declensional inflexion

**Unterlassungs-:** **~klage** *die* (*Rechtsw.*) application for a restrictive injunction; **~sünde** *die* (*ugs.*) sin of omission

**Unter·lauf** *der* ▶ 306 lower reaches *pl.*

**unter·laufen** ❶ *unr. itr. V.; mit sein* Ⓐ occur; **jmdm. ist ein Fehler/Irrtum ~:** sb. made a mistake; Ⓑ (*ugs.: begegnen*) ⇨ **unterkommen** D. ❷ *unr. tr. V.* Ⓐ evade; get round; Ⓑ (*bes. Fuß-, Handball*) **einen Gegner ~:** charge an opponent who is in the air and knock him to the ground; Ⓒ *mit sein* ‹skin tissue› suffuse with blood; **das Auge war mit Blut** *od.* **blutig ~:** the eye was completely bloodshot

*old spelling (see note on page 1707)

U

**unter|legen**[1] *tr. V.* **A** *(unter etw. legen)* put under[neath]; **jmdm. etw. ~:** put sth. under[neath] sb.; **einer Henne** *(Dat.)* **Eier [zum Brüten] ~:** set a hen [on eggs]; **B** **einem Text einen anderen Sinn ~:** read another meaning into a text

**unter·legen**[2] *tr. V.* **A** *(mit Stoff, Watte o. Ä.)* underlay (**mit** with); **B** **einem Film Musik ~:** put music to a film; **einer Melodie einen Text ~:** put words to a tune

**unter·legen**[3] **1** *2. Part. v.* **unterliegen.** **2** *Adj.* inferior; **jmdm. ~ sein** be inferior to sb. (**an** + *Dat.* in); **jmdm. zahlenmäßig ~ sein** be outnumbered by sb.

**Unterlegene** *der/die; adj. Dekl.* loser

**Unterleg·scheibe** *die* washer

**Unter-:** **~leib** *der* **A** ▶ **471** *(unterer Bauchteil)* lower abdomen; **B** *(verhüll.: weibliche Geschlechtsteile)* pudenda; **~leibs·schmerzen** *Pl.* abdominal pain *sing.*; **~lid** *das* ▶ **471** lower [eye]lid

**unter·liegen** *unr. itr. V.* **A** *mit sein (besiegt werden)* lose; be beaten *or* defeated; **in einem Kampf ~:** lose a fight; **die unterlegene Mannschaft** the losing team; **B** *(unterworfen sein)* be subject to; **es unterliegt keinem Zweifel, dass ...** there is *or* can be no doubt that ...; **einer Täuschung ~:** be mistaken *or* deceived

**Unter·lippe** *die* ▶ **471** lower lip

**unterm** *Präp. + Art.* = **unter dem**

**unter·malen** *tr. V.* accompany; **etw. mit Musik ~:** accompany sth. with music

**Unter·malung** *die; ~, ~en* accompaniment (*Gen.* to)

**unter·mauern** *tr. V.* **A** *(mit Mauern stützen)* underpin; **B** *(mit Argumenten, Fakten absichern)* back up; support

**Untermauerung** *die; ~, ~en* **A** underpinning; *(Mauerwerk)* foundation; **B** *(stützende Argumente)* back-up; support

**unter-, Unter-:** **~|mengen** *tr. V.* mix in; **~mensch** *der (abwertend)* **A** *(brutaler Mensch)* brute; **B** *(ns.: minderwertiger Mensch)* inferior person; subhuman creature; **~miete** *die* subtenancy; sublease; **bei jmdm. in** *od.* **zur ~miete wohnen** be sb.'s subtenant; lodge with sb.; **jmdn. in** *od.* **zur ~miete nehmen** sublet to sb.; **~mieter** *der,* **~mieterin** *die* subtenant; lodger

**unterminieren** /ʊntɐmiˈniːrən/ *tr. V.* undermine

**unter|mischen** *tr. V.* mix in

**untern** *Präp. + Art. (ugs.)* = **unter den**

**unter·nehmen** *unr. tr. V.* **A** *(durchführen)* undertake; make; make ‹attempt›; take ‹steps›; **B** *(Unterhaltsames machen, eingreifen)* do; **viel zusammen ~:** do many things together; **etwas gegen die Missstände ~:** do something about the bad state of affairs

**Unter·nehmen** *das; ~s, ~* **A** *(Vorhaben)* enterprise; venture; undertaking; *(militärische Operation)* operation; **B** *(Firma)* enterprise; concern

**unternehmend** *Adj.* enterprising; active

**Unternehmens-:** **~berater** *der,* **~beraterin** *die* ▶ **159** management consultant; **~form** *die* form *or* type of enterprise; **~führung** *die,* **~leitung** *die* management; **~politik** *die* management policy

**Unternehmer** *der; ~s, ~,* **Unternehmerin** *die; ~, ~nen* employer; *(in der Industrie)* industrialist

**unternehmerisch** **1** *Adj.* entrepreneurial. **2** *adv.* ‹think› in an entrepreneurial *or* businesslike way

**Unternehmerschaft** *die; ~, ~en* employers *pl.*

**Unternehmertum** *das; ~s* **A** employers *pl.*; **B** *(das Unternehmersein)* enterprise *no art.*

**Unternehmung** *die; ~, ~en* ⇒ **Unternehmen**

**Unternehmungs·geist** *der* spirit of enterprise; **er war voller ~:** he was full of initiative

**unternehmungs·lustig** *Adj.* active; **sie ist sehr ~:** she is always out doing things

**unter-, Unter-:** **~offizier** *der* **A** non-commissioned officer; **~offizier vom Dienst** duty NCO; **B** ▶ **91** *(Dienstgrad)* corporal; **~ordnen** **1** *tr. V.* subordinate; **jmdm./einem Ministerium ~geordnet sein** be [made] subordinate to sb./a ministry; **2** *refl. V.* **sich [anderen] nicht ~ordnen können** not be able to accept a subordinate role; **die Politik hat sich der Moral ~zuordnen** politics has to be subordinated to morality; **~ordnend** *Adj. (Sprachw.)* subordinating ‹conjunction›; **~ordnung** *die* **A** subordination; **B** *(Sprachw.)* hypotaxis; **C** *(Biol.: ~gruppe)* suborder; **~pfand** *das (geh.)* pledge (**für** of); **~|pflügen** *tr. V.* plough in *or* under; **~prima** *die (Schulw. veralt.)* eighth year (*of a Gymnasium*); **~primaner** *der,* **~primanerin** *die (Schulw. veralt.)* pupil in the eighth year (*of a Gymnasium*); **~privilegiert** *Adj. (geh.)* underprivileged; **~privilegierte** *der/die; adj. Dekl. (geh.)* underprivileged person; **die ~privilegierten** the underprivileged; **~punkt** *der* **A** subsidiary point; **B** *(unter einem Buchstaben o. Ä.)* dot underneath

**unter·queren** *tr. V.* cross under

**unter·reden** *refl. V. (geh.)* confer (**mit** with)

**Unterredung** *die; ~, ~en* discussion; **er bat ihn um eine ~:** he asked to see him to discuss something [with him]

**unter·repräsentiert** *Adj.* under-represented

**Unterricht** /ˈʊntɐrɪçt/ *der; ~[e]s, ~e* instruction; *(Schul~)* teaching; *(Schulstunden)* classes *pl.*; lessons *pl.*; **der ~ ist beendet** classes *or* lessons are over; **jmdm. ~ [in Musik** *usw.***] geben** give sb. [music *etc.*] lessons; teach sb. [music]; **bei jmdm. ~ [in Russisch] nehmen** have [Russian] lessons from sb.; **zu spät zum ~ kommen** be late for class

**-unterricht** *der:* **Geschichts-/Musik-** *usw.* **~:** history/music *etc.* teaching; *(Unterrichtsstunde)* history/music *etc.* lesson; ⇒ *auch* **Englischunterricht**

**unterrichten** **1** *tr. V.* **A** *(lehren)* teach; **er unterrichtet Englisch** he teaches English; **sie unterrichtet ihre Kinder im Malen** she is teaching her children how to paint; **B** *(informieren)* inform (**über** + *Akk.* of, about); **ich bin bestens/schlecht unterrichtet** I am fully/not well informed. **2** *itr. V. (Unterricht geben)* teach. **3** *refl. V. (sich informieren)* inform oneself (**über** + *Akk.* about)

**unterrichtlich** *Adj.* instructional ‹purpose, problem›; teaching ‹success, work›

**unterrichts-, Unterrichts-:** **~einheit** *die (Päd.)* teaching unit; **~fach** *das* subject; **~frei** *Adj.* free ‹day, hour›; **der Samstag ist ~frei** there are no lessons on Saturday; **nächsten Samstag haben wir ~frei** there is no school this Saturday; **~methode** *die* teaching method; **~stoff** *der* subject matter; **~stunde** *die* lesson; period

**Unterrichtung** *die; ~, ~en* instruction; *(Information)* information

**Unter·rock** *der* **A** [half] slip; **B** ⇒ **Unterkleid**

**unter|rühren** *tr. V.* stir in

**unters** *Präp. + Art.* = **unter das**

**unter·sagen** *tr. V.* forbid; prohibit; **der Arzt untersagte ihm, Alkohol zu trinken** the doctor ordered him not to drink any alcohol; **Rauchen ist strengstens untersagt** smoking is strictly prohibited

**Unter·satz** *der* ⇒ **Untersetzer**

**unter-, Unter-:** **~schätzen** *tr. V.* underestimate ‹amount, effect, meaning, distance, etc.›; underrate ‹writer, performer, book, performance, talent, ability›; **~schätzung** *die* underestimation; **~scheidbar** *Adj.* distinguishable; **~scheiden** **1** *unr. tr. V.* distinguish; **Weizen von Roggen nicht ~scheiden können** not be able to tell the difference between wheat and rye *or* tell wheat from rye; **die Zwillinge sind kaum zu ~scheiden** you can hardly tell the twins apart; **2** *unr. itr. V.* distinguish; differentiate; **zwischen Richtigem und Falschem ~scheiden** tell the difference between right and wrong; **3** *unr. refl. V.* differ (**durch** in, **von** from); **sich durch nichts ~scheiden** be in no way different; **sich dadurch ~scheiden, dass ...** differ in that ...; **in diesem Punkt ~scheiden sich die Parteien überhaupt nicht** on this point there is no difference at all between the parties; **~scheidung** *die (Vorgang)* differentiation; *(Resultat)* distinction

**Unterscheidungs-:** **~merkmal** *das* distinguishing feature; **~vermögen** *das* ability to distinguish; discernment

**unter-, Unter-:** **~schenkel** *der* ▶ **471** shank; lower leg; **~schicht** *die (Soziol.)* lower class; **der ~schicht angehören** be a member of the lower classes *pl.*; **~|schieben**[1] *unr. tr. V.* push under[neath]

**unter·schieben**[2] *unr. tr. V.* **A** *(heimlich zuschieben)* **jmdm. etw. ~:** foist sth. on sb.; **B** *(unterstellen)* **jmdm. etw. ~:** attribute sth. falsely to sb.

**Unter·schied** *der; ~[e]s, ~e* difference; **es lebe der kleine ~!** *(ugs. scherzh.)* vive la petite différence!; **das ist ein ~ wie Tag und Nacht** it's like the difference between black and white; **es ist [schon] ein [großer] ~, ob ...** it makes a [big] difference whether ...; **bei der Beurteilung der Schüler ~e machen** use different methods when assessing the pupils; **ohne ~ der Rasse/des Geschlechts** without regard to *or* discrimination against race/sex; **im ~ zu ihm/zum ~ von ihm** in contrast to him; **zwischen Arbeit und Arbeit ist noch ein ~** *(ugs.)* there is work and there is work *(coll.)*

**unter·schieden** *Adj.* different

**unterschiedlich** **1** *Adj.* different; *(uneinheitlich)* variable; varying. **2** *adv.* **[sehr/ganz] ~:** in [very/quite] different ways; **~ hohe Erträge** yields of varying amount; **etw. sehr ~ einschätzen** give greatly varying estimates of sth.

**Unterschiedlichkeit** *die; ~, ~en* difference (*Gen.* between); *(Uneinheitlichkeit)* variability

**unterschieds·los** **1** *Adj.* uniform; equal ‹treatment›. **2** *adv.* ‹treat› equally; *(ohne Benachteiligung)* without discrimination

**unter|schlagen**[1] *unr. tr. V.* cross ‹legs›; fold ‹arms›

**unter·schlagen**[2] **1** *unr. tr. V.* embezzle, misappropriate ‹money, funds, etc.›; *(unterdrücken)* intercept ‹letter›; withhold, suppress ‹fact, news, information, etc.›. **2** *unr. itr. V.* **er hat ~:** he embezzled money

**Unterschlagung** *die; ~, ~en* ⇒ **unterschlagen**[2]: embezzlement; misappropriation; withholding; suppression; **~en begehen** embezzle sums of money/funds *etc.*

**Unter·schlupf** *der; ~[e]s, ~e* shelter; *(Versteck)* hiding place; hideout

**unter|schlupfen** *(südd.)*, **unter|schlüpfen** *itr. V.; mit sein (ugs.)* hide out; *(Obdach finden)* take shelter (**vor** + *Dat.* from)

**unter·schneiden** *unr. tr. V.* ([*Tisch*]*tennis*) chop

**Unter·schnitt** *der* ([*Tisch*]*tennis*) back spin; underspin

**unter·schreiben** **1** *unr. itr. V.* sign; **mit vollem Namen ~:** sign one's full name. **2** *unr. tr. V.* sign; **diese Behauptung kann ich nicht ~** *(fig. ugs.)* I cannot subscribe to *or* approve this statement

**unter·schreiten** *unr. tr. V.* fall below; **wir haben die veranschlagten Summen/Kosten um 2 Prozent unterschritten** we stayed 2 per cent below the estimated amounts/costs

**Unter·schrift** *die* **A** signature; **seine ~ unter etw.** *(Akk.)* **setzen** put one's signature to sth.; sign sth.; **B** *(Bild~)* caption

**Unterschriften-:** **~aktion** *die* petition; **~liste** *die* list of signatures; **~mappe** *die* signature folder

**unter·schriftlich** *Adv.* by one's signature; **~ bestätigt** signed

**unterschrifts-:** **~berechtigt** *Adj.* **~berechtigt sein** be authorized to sign; have power to sign; **~reif** *Adj.* ready to be signed *pred.*; **ein ~reifer Vertrag** a contract which is ready to be signed

U

**unterschwellig** /-ʃvɛlɪç/ ❶ *Adj.* subliminal. ❷ *adv.* subliminally

**unter-, Unter-:** **~see·boot** *das* submarine; **~seite** *die* underside; (*eines Stoffes*) wrong side; **~sekunda** *die* (*Schulw. veralt.*) sixth year (*of a Gymnasium*); **~sekundaner** *der*, **~sekundanerin** *die* (*Schulw. veralt.*) pupil in the sixth year (*of a Gymnasium*); **~|setzen** *tr. V.* put underneath; **~setzer** *der* mat; (*für Gläser*) coaster; (*für Bügeleisen*) stand

**untersetzt** *Adj.* stocky

**unter|sinken** *unr. itr. V.; mit sein* sink

**unter·spülen** *tr. V.* undermine and wash away

**unterst...** ⇒ unter...

**Unter·stand** *der* Ⓐ (*Schutzbunker*) dugout; Ⓑ (*Unterschlupf*) shelter

**unter|stehen**[1] *unr. itr. V.; südd., österr., schweiz. mit sein* take shelter

**unter|stehen**[2] ❶ *unr. itr. V.* **jmdm. ~:** be subordinate *or* answerable to sb.; **jmdm. untersteht eine Abteilung** sb. is responsible for a department; **diese Ämter ~ dem Ministerium** these offices are under the control of *or* come under the ministry; **ständiger Kontrolle ~:** be under constant supervision. ❷ *unr. refl. V.* dare; **untersteh dich!** [don't] you dare!; **was ~ Sie sich!** how dare you!

**unter|stellen**[1] ❶ *tr. V.* Ⓐ (*zur Aufbewahrung*) keep; store ‹furniture›; Ⓑ (*unter etw.*) put underneath. ❷ *refl. V.* take shelter

**unter·stellen**[2] *tr. V.* Ⓐ (*jmdm. unterordnen, übertragen*) **jmdm. ein Sachgebiet/eine Abteilung ~:** put sb. in charge of a subject/a department; **die Behörde ist dem Ministerium unterstellt** the office is under the ministry; Ⓑ (*annehmen, vermuten*) assume; suppose; **ich unterstelle [einmal], dass ...** I'll [first of all] assume that ...; Ⓒ (*unterschieben*) **jmdm. böse Absichten/schlechte Motive** *usw.* **~:** insinuate *or* imply that sb.'s intentions/motives are bad; **was ~ Sie mir?** what are you trying to accuse me of?

**Unter·stellung** *die* Ⓐ subordination (**unter** + *Akk.* to); Ⓑ (*falsche Behauptung*) insinuation

**unter·steuern** *itr. V.* (*Kfz-W.*) understeer

**unter·streichen** *unr. tr. V.* Ⓐ underline; Ⓑ (*hervorheben*) emphasize; **das kann ich nur ~!** I can only agree with that!

**Unter·streichung** *die;* **~, ~en** Ⓐ underlining; Ⓑ (*das Betonen*) emphasizing

**Unter·stufe** *die* (*Schulw.*) lower school

**unter·stützen** *tr. V.* (*auch DV*) support; **vom Staat unterstützte Einrichtungen** state-funded institutions; **das Mittel unterstützt den Heilungsprozess** the medicine promotes the healing process

**Unter·stützung** *die* Ⓐ support; **der Plan fand bei vielen ~:** the plan was supported by many; Ⓑ (*finanzielle Hilfe*) allowance; (*für Arbeitslose*) [unemployment] benefit *no art.*; **staatliche ~:** state aid

**Unterstützungs·empfänger** *der*, **Unterstützungs·empfängerin** *die* person receiving [unemployment] benefit/an allowance

**unter·suchen** *tr. V.* Ⓐ (*zu erkennen suchen*) examine; Ⓑ (*überprüfen*) test (**auf** + *Akk.* for); Ⓒ (*ärztlich*) examine; **sich ärztlich ~ lassen** have a medical examination *or* check-up; **jmdn. auf seine Arbeitsfähigkeit [hin] ~:** test sb.'s fitness for work; Ⓓ (*aufzuklären suchen*) investigate; **einen Fall gerichtlich ~:** try a case [in court]; Ⓔ (*durchsuchen*) search (**auf** + *Akk.*, **nach** for)

**Untersuchung** *die;* **~, ~en** Ⓐ ⇒ **untersuchen**: examination; test; investigation; search; Ⓑ (*wissenschaftliche Arbeit*) study

**Untersuchungs-:** **~ausschuss**, ***~ausschuß** *der* investigating committee; (*für Unfälle usw.*) committee of inquiry; **~ergebnis** *das* (*der Polizei, des Gerichts*) results *pl.* of an/the investigation; (*Med.*) results *pl.* of a/the test; **~gefängnis** *das* prison (*for people awaiting trial*); **~haft** *die* imprisonment *or* detention while awaiting trial; **jmdn. in ~haft nehmen** commit sb. for trial; **in ~haft sein** *od.* **sitzen** be held on remand; **~häftling** *der* prisoner awaiting trial; remand prisoner; **~kommission** *die* ⇒ **~ausschuss**; **~zimmer** *das* examination room

**unter·tags** *Adv.* (*bes. österr.*) during the day

**untertan** /-taːn/ *Adj.* **in sich** (*Dat.*) **jmdn./etw. ~ machen** (*geh.*) subjugate sb./dominate sth.; **jmdm./einer Sache ~ sein** (*veralt.*) be dominated by sb./be subject to sth.

**Untertan** *der;* **~s** *od.* **~en, ~en** (*hist.*) subject

**Untertanen·geist** *der* (*abwertend*) servile *or* subservient spirit

**untertänig** /-tɛːnɪç/ ❶ *Adj.* subservient; **Ihr ~ster Diener** (*veralt.*) your most obedient *or* humble servant. ❷ *adv.* subserviently

**Untertanin** *die;* **~, ~nen** ⇒ **Untertan**

**Unter·tasse** *die* saucer; **fliegende ~** (*fig.*) flying saucer

**unter|tauchen** ❶ *itr. V.; mit sein* Ⓐ (*im Wasser*) dive [under]; Ⓑ (*verschwinden*) disappear; Ⓒ (*unerkannt leben*) disappear; go underground; **er musste vor der Gestapo [bei Freunden] ~:** he had [to seek shelter with friends] to hide from the Gestapo. ❷ *tr. V.* duck

**Unter·teil** *das od. der* bottom part

**unter·teilen** *tr. V.* Ⓐ (*aufteilen*) divide; Ⓑ (*einteilen, gliedern*) subdivide

**Unter·teilung** *die;* **~, ~en** [sub]division

**Unter·temperatur** *die* subnormal temperature of the body; **der Patient hat ~:** the patient's temperature is below normal

**unter-, Unter-:** **~tertia** *die* (*Schulw. veralt.*) fourth year (*of a Gymnasium*); **~tertianer** *der*, **~tertianerin** *die* (*Schulw. veralt.*) pupil in the fourth year (*of a Gymnasium*); **~titel** *der* Ⓐ subtitle; Ⓑ (*Bildunterschrift*) caption; **~ton** *der; Pl.* **~töne** (*auch Physik, Musik*) undertone; **~tourig** /-tuːrɪç/ (*Technik*) ❶ *Adj.* ‹driving› with *or* at low revs (*coll.*). ❷ *adv.* at low revs (*coll.*)

**unter·treiben** *unr. itr. V.* play things down

**Untertreibung** *die;* **~, ~en** understatement

**unter·tunneln** *tr. V.* tunnel under; tunnel through *or* under ‹mountain›

**unter-, Unter-:** **~vermieten** *tr., itr. V.* sublet; **~vermietung** *die* subletting; **~versichern** *tr. V.* under-insure; **~versicherung** *die* under-insurance; **~versorgen** *tr. V.* under-supply; **ärztlich ~versorgt sein** not be given proper medical treatment; **~versorgung** *die* under-supply (**mit** of); **die ~versorgung der Zellen mit Sauerstoff** the under-supply of the cells with oxygen

**unter·wandern** *tr. V.* infiltrate; **kommunistisch unterwandert** infiltrated by communists

**Unter·wanderung** *die* infiltration *no indef. art.*

**unterwärts** /ˈʊntɐvɛrts/ *Adv.* (*ugs.*) underneath

**Unter·wäsche** *die* underwear

**Unter·wasser-:** **~jagd** *die* (*Tauchsport*) underwater harpooning; **~massage** *die* underwater massage

**unterwegs** *Adv.* Ⓐ (*auf dem Wege irgendwohin*) on the *or* one's/its way; **er ist den ganzen Tag/geschäftlich viel ~:** he is away all day/a great deal on business; **bei ihr ist etwas Kleines ~** (*ugs.*) she is expecting [a happy event]; Ⓑ (*auf, während der Reise*) on the way; **sie waren vier Wochen ~:** they travelled for four weeks; the journey took them four weeks; **sie schickten eine Karte von ~:** they sent a card while they were away; Ⓒ (*nicht zu Hause*) out [and about]

**unter·weisen** *unr. tr. V.* (*geh.*) instruct (**in** + *Dat.* in)

**Unter·weisung** *die* instruction

**Unter·welt** *die;* **~** (*griech. Myth., Verbrechermilieu*) underworld

**unter·weltlich** *Adj.* underworld *attrib.*

**unter·werfen** ❶ *unr. tr. V.* Ⓐ subjugate ‹people, country›; Ⓑ (*unterziehen*) subject (*Dat.* to); **jmds. Post einer genauen Kontrolle ~:** make a close scrutiny of sb.'s correspondence; Ⓒ (*abhängig machen*) **jmdm./einer Sache unterworfen sein** be subject to sb./sth. ❷ *unr. refl. V.* **sich [jmdm./einer Sache] ~:** submit [to sb./sth.]

**Unterwerfung** *die;* **~, ~en** Ⓐ (*das Unterwerfen*) subjugation (**unter** + *Akk.* to); Ⓑ (*das Sichunterwerfen*) submission (**unter** + *Akk.* to)

**unterwürfig** /-vʏrfɪç/ (*abwertend*) ❶ *Adj.* obsequious. ❷ *adv.* obsequiously

**Unterwürfigkeit** *die;* **~** (*abwertend*) obsequiousness

**unter·zeichnen** ❶ *tr. V.* sign. ❷ *refl. V.* (*veralt.*) sign

**Unter·zeichner** *der*, **Unter·zeichnerin** *die*, **Unterzeichnete** *der/die; adj. Dekl.* (*Amtsspr.*) signatory

**Unterzeichnung** *die* signing

**Unter·zeug** *das* (*ugs.*) underwear

**unter|ziehen**[1] *unr. tr. V.* Ⓐ put ‹underwear, jumper, etc.› on underneath; Ⓑ (*Kochk.: vermengen*) fold in

**unter·ziehen**[2] ❶ *unr. refl. V.* **sich einer Sache** (*Dat.*) **~:** undertake sth.; **sich einer Operation** (*Dat.*) **~:** undergo *or* have an operation. ❷ *unr. tr. V.* **etw. einer Untersuchung/Überprüfung/Reinigung** (*Dat.*) **~:** examine/check/clean sth.

**Untiefe** *die* Ⓐ (*seichte Stelle*) shallow; Ⓑ (*große Tiefe*) depth

**Untier** *das* monster; **dieses ~ von einer Katze** (*scherzh.*) this beast of a cat

**untilgbar** *Adj.* (*geh.*) lasting; indelible ‹impression, memory›

**Untote** *der/die* zombie; (*Vampir*) vampire; **die ~n** the undead

**untragbar** *Adj.* unbearable; intolerable; **wirtschaftlich/finanziell ~:** no longer economically/financially viable

**Untragbarkeit** *die;* **~:** intolerableness

**untrainiert** *Adj.* untrained; (*nicht mehr trainiert*) out of training *postpos.*

**untrennbar** *Adj.* inseparable

**untreu** *Adj.* Ⓐ disloyal; **jmdm. ~ werden** be disloyal to sb.; **du bist uns ~ geworden** (*scherzh.*) you've abandoned us (*joc.*); **sich selbst ~ werden** be untrue to oneself; **seinen Grundsätzen ~ werden** abandon one's principles; Ⓑ (*in der Ehe, Liebe*) unfaithful; **jmdm. ~ werden** be unfaithful to sb.

**Untreue** *die* Ⓐ disloyalty; Ⓑ (*in der Ehe, Liebe*) unfaithfulness; Ⓒ (*Rechtsspr.: Veruntreuung*) embezzlement

**untröstlich** *Adj.* inconsolable; **ich bin ~, dass ...** I am extremely sorry that ...

**untrüglich** *Adj.* unmistakable

**untüchtig** *Adj.* incompetent

**Untugend** *die* bad habit

**untunlich** *Adj.* (*veralt.*) impracticable; not sensible; (*unklug*) imprudent

**untypisch** ❶ *Adj.* untypical (**für** of). ❷ *adv.* unusually

**unüberbietbar** *Adj.* unparalleled

**unüberbrückbar** *Adj.* irreconcilable ‹differences, contradictions›

**unüberhörbar** *Adj.* unmistakable

**unüberlegt** ❶ *Adj.* rash. ❷ *adv.* rashly

**Unüberlegtheit** *die;* **~, ~en** Ⓐ rashness; Ⓑ (*unüberlegte Handlung*) rash act

**unüberschaubar** ⇒ **unübersehbar** 1 B, 2

**unübersehbar** ❶ *Adj.* Ⓐ (*offenkundig*) conspicuous; obvious; Ⓑ (*sehr groß*) enormous; immense. ❷ *adv.* (*sehr*) extremely

**unübersetzbar** *Adj.* untranslatable

**unübersichtlich** ❶ *Adj.* unclear; confusing ‹arrangement›; blind ‹bend›; broken ‹country etc.›; (*fig.*) confused ‹affair, matter, conditions, etc.›. ❷ *adv.* unclearly; confusingly ‹arranged›

**Unübersichtlichkeit** *die;* **~: die ~ der Karte/des Geländes** the unclear map/broken country

**unübertragbar** *Adj.* non-transferable; not transferable *pred.*

**unübertrefflich** ❶ *Adj.* superb. ❷ *adv.* superbly

*old spelling (see note on page 1707)

**unübertroffen** *Adj.* unsurpassed

**unüberwindbar, unüberwindlich** *Adj.* insuperable, insurmountable ‹problem, fear, mistrust, etc.›; invincible ‹opponent›

**unüblich** *Adj.* not usual *or* customary *pred.;* unusual

**unumgänglich** *Adj.* [absolutely] necessary

**Unumgänglichkeit** *die;* **~:** absolute necessity

**unumschränkt** /ˈʊn|ʊmʃrɛŋkt/ *Adj.* absolute; **~ herrschen** have absolute rule

**unumstritten** *Adj.* undisputed

**unumwunden** /ˈʊn|ʊmvʊndn̩/ ❶ *Adj.* frank. ❷ *adv.* frankly; openly

**ununterbrochen** ❶ *Adj.* incessant. ❷ *adv.* incessantly

**unveränderbar, unveränderlich** *Adj.* unchangeable, unchanging ‹law, principle›; constant ‹quantity etc.›; permanent ‹mark, scar›; (*nicht zu verändern*) unalterable

**Unveränderlichkeit** *die;* **~** ⇒ **unveränderlich:** unchangeableness; unchangingness; constancy; permanence; unalterableness

**unverändert** *Adj.* unchanged ‹appearance, weather, condition›; unaltered, unrevised ‹edition etc.›; **in seinem Aussehen war er ~:** he had not changed in [his] appearance

**unverantwortlich** ❶ *Adj.* irresponsible. ❷ *adv.* irresponsibly

**Unverantwortlichkeit** *die;* **~:** irresponsibility

**unverarbeitet** *Adj.* [A] raw, unprocessed ‹material›; crude ‹iron, oil, etc.›; [B] (*nicht bewältigt*) raw ‹impression›; raw, undigested ‹thoughts›

**unveräußerlich** *Adj.* [A] (*geh.*) inalienable ‹rights, principles›; [B] (*unverkäuflich*) ‹property› not for sale

**unverbaubar** *Adj.* ‹view› that cannot be spoiled *or* obstructed

**unverbesserlich** *Adj.* incorrigible

**unverbildet** *Adj.* unspoiled

**unverbindlich** ❶ *Adj.* [A] (*nicht bindend*) not binding *pred.;* without obligation *postpos.;* ‹information› without guarantee of correctness; [B] (*zurückhaltend, reserviert*) noncommittal ‹answer, words›; detached, impersonal ‹attitude, person›. ❷ *adv.* ‹send, reserve› without obligation

**Unverbindlichkeit** *die;* **~, ~en** [A] (*eines Angebots usw.*) freedom from obligation; (*einer Person*) detached *or* impersonal manner; **die ~ der Auskunft** the fact that the information is not guaranteed correct; [B] (*unverbindliche Äußerung*) non-committal remark

**unverbleit** *Adj.* unleaded

**unverblümt** /ʊnfɛɐ̯ˈblyːmt/ ❶ *Adj.* blunt; undisguised, open ‹distrust›. ❷ *adv.* bluntly

**unverbraucht** *Adj.* untouched; unspent ‹energy›; fresh ‹air›; **sie ist noch jung und ~:** she is still young and full of energy

**unverbrüchlich** /ʊnfɛɐ̯ˈbryçlɪç/ *Adj.* (*geh.*) inviolable; steadfast

**unverbürgt** *Adj.* unconfirmed ‹report, news, etc.›

**unverdächtig** ❶ *Adj.* free from suspicion *postpos.* ❷ *adv.* in a way that does/did not arouse suspicion

**unverdaulich** *Adj.* indigestible

**unverdaut** *Adj.* undigested

**unverdient** ❶ *Adj.* undeserved ‹luck, praise›; undeserved, unjust ‹accusation, punishment, etc.›. ❷ *adv.* undeservedly

**unverdientermaßen** *Adv.* undeservedly

**unverdorben** *Adj.* unspoilt

**Unverdorbenheit** *die;* **~** (*von Früchten usw.*) freshness; (*sittliche* **~**) innocence

**unverdrossen** ❶ *Adj.* undeterred; (*unverzagt*) undaunted. ❷ *adv.* **~ weitermachen** carry on undaunted

**unverdünnt** *Adj.* undiluted; **er trinkt Whisky ~:** he drinks whisky neat

**unverehelicht** *Adj.* (*bes. Amtsspr.*) unmarried

**unvereinbar** *Adj.* incompatible (**mit** with)

**Unvereinbarkeit** *die;* **~:** incompatibility (**mit** with)

**unverfälscht** ❶ *Adj.* genuine; unadulterated ‹wine etc.›; pure ‹dialect›; unaltered ‹custom, text›. ❷ *adv.* in pure/unaltered form

**unverfänglich** *Adj.* harmless

**unverfroren** ❶ *Adj.* insolent; impudent. ❷ *adv.* insolently; impudently

**Unverfrorenheit** *die;* **~, ~en** [A] insolence; impudence; [B] (*Äußerung, Handlung*) insolent remark; impertinence

**unvergänglich** *Adj.* immortal ‹fame›; unchanging ‹beauty›; abiding ‹recollection›

**Unvergänglichkeit** *die* ⇒ **unvergänglich:** immortality; unchangingness; abidingness

**unvergessen** *Adj.* unforgotten

**unvergesslich, *unvergeßlich** ❶ *Adj.* unforgettable; **dieses Erlebnis wird mir ~ bleiben** *od.* **sein** I shall never forget this experience. ❷ *adv.* unforgettably

**unvergleichbar** *Adj.* incomparable (*Dat.* to, with)

**unvergleichlich** ❶ *Adj.* incomparable (*Dat.* to, with). ❷ *adv.* incomparably

**unverhältnismäßig** *Adv.* unusually

**unverheiratet** *Adj.* unmarried

**unverhofft** /ˈʊnfɛɐ̯hɔft/ ❶ *Adj.* unexpected. ❷ *adv.* unexpectedly; **~ kommt oft** (*Spr.*) always expect the unexpected

**unverhohlen** ❶ *Adj.* unconcealed. ❷ *adv.* openly

**unverhüllt** ❶ *Adj.* [A] (*ohne Umhüllung*) uncovered; [B] (*unverhohlen*) unconcealed. ❷ *adv.* openly

**unverkäuflich** *Adj.* [A] (*nicht zum Verkauf bestimmt*) **~e Ausstellungsstücke** display items that are not for sale; **diese Vase ist ~:** this vase is not for sale; **~es Muster** free sample; [B] (*nicht absetzbar*) unsaleable

**unverkennbar** ❶ *Adj.* unmistakable. ❷ *adv.* unmistakably

**unverlangt** ❶ *Adj.* unsolicited ‹manuscript, photograph›. ❷ *adv.* **~ eingesandt** unsolicited

**unvermählt** *Adj.* (*geh.*) unmarried; unwedded

**unvermeidbar** *Adj.* unavoidable

**unvermeidlich** *Adj.* [A] (*nicht vermeidbar*) unavoidable; (*spött.: obligatorisch*) inevitable; **sich ins Unvermeidliche fügen** submit to *or* accept the inevitable; [B] (*sich als Folge ergebend*) inevitable

**unvermindert** *Adj., adv.* undiminished

**unvermittelt** ❶ *Adj.* sudden; abrupt. ❷ *adv.* suddenly; abruptly

**Unvermögen** *das* lack of ability; **jmds. ~, etw. zu tun** sb.'s inability to do sth.

**unvermögend** *Adj.* without means *postpos.*

**unvermutet** ❶ *Adj.* unexpected. ❷ *adv.* unexpectedly

**Unvernunft** *die* stupidity

**unvernünftig** ❶ *Adj.* stupid; foolish. ❷ *adv.* **er raucht/trinkt ~ viel** he smokes/drinks more than is good for him

**unveröffentlicht** *Adj.* unpublished

**unverpackt** *Adj.* unpacked; unwrapped

**unverputzt** *Adj.* unplastered

**unverrichtet** *Adj.* *in* **~er Dinge** without having achieved anything

**unverrückbar** ❶ *Adj.* unshakeable; immovable; unalterable ‹fact, truth›. ❷ *adv.* unshakeably; immovably; **mein Entschluss steht ~ fest** my decision is absolutely final

**unverschämt** ❶ *Adj.* [A] (*respektlos, impertinent*) impertinent, impudent ‹person, manner, words, etc.›; barefaced, blatant ‹lie›; [B] (*ugs.: sehr groß*) outrageous ‹price, luck, etc.›. ❷ *adv.* [A] impertinently; impudently; ‹lie› barefacedly; blatantly; [B] (*ugs.: sehr*) outrageously ‹expensive›; **du siehst ~ gut aus** you are looking disgustingly well (*joc.*)

**Unverschämtheit** *die;* **~, ~en** [A] impertinence; impudence; (*einer Lüge*) barefacedness; blatancy; [B] (*Äußerung, Handlung*) [piece of] impertinence; **das ist eine ~!** that's outrageous!

**unverschlossen** *Adj.* unlocked; unsealed ‹letter›

**unverschuldet** *Adj.* **ein ~er Verkehrsunfall** an accident which happened through no fault of one's own; **eine ~e Notlage** a plight which is no fault of one's own

**unverschuldetermaßen** *Adv.* through no fault of one's own

**unversehens** *Adv.* suddenly

**unversehrt** *Adj.* unscathed; unhurt; (*unbeschädigt*) undamaged

**Unversehrtheit** *die;* **~:** intactness; **körperliche ~:** freedom from bodily harm

**unversöhnlich** *Adj.* irreconcilable

**Unversöhnlichkeit** *die* irreconcilability

**unversorgt** *Adj.* ‹children, family, etc.› unprovided for

**Unverstand** *der* foolishness; stupidity; **so ein ~!** what foolishness *or* stupidity!

**unverstanden** *Adj.* misunderstood

**unverständig** *Adj.* without understanding *postpos.;* ignorant ‹child›

**Unverständigkeit** *die* lack of understanding

**unverständlich** *Adj.* incomprehensible; (*undeutlich*) unclear ‹pronunciation, presentation, etc.›; **es ist [mir] ~, warum er nicht kommt** I cannot *or* do not understand why he hasn't come

**Unverständlichkeit** *die* incomprehensibility

**Unverständnis** *das* lack of understanding

**unverstellt** *Adj.* normal ‹voice›; unfeigned, genuine ‹joy, passion, etc.›

**unversteuert** *Adj.* untaxed ‹earnings etc.›; duty-free ‹goods, cigarettes›

**unversucht** *in* **nichts ~ lassen** try everything; leave no stone unturned

**unverträglich** *Adj.* [A] (*unbekömmlich*) indigestible; unsuitable ‹medicine›; [B] (*streitsüchtig*) quarrelsome; [C] (*nicht harmonierend*) incompatible ‹blood groups, medicines, transplant tissue›

**Unverträglichkeit** *die* ⇒ **unverträglich:** indigestibility; unsuitability; quarrelsomeness; incompatibility

**unvertraut** *Adj.* unfamiliar

**unvertretbar** *Adj.* unjustifiable

**unverwandt** ❶ *Adj.* fixed; steadfast ‹gaze›. ❷ *adv.* fixedly; steadfastly; **jmdn. ~ anstarren** stare at sb. with a fixed gaze

**unverwechselbar** *Adj.* unmistakable; distinctive

**Unverwechselbarkeit** *die* distinctiveness

**unverwundbar** *Adj.* invulnerable

**Unverwundbarkeit** *die* invulnerability

**unverwüstlich** *Adj.* indestructible; (*fig.*) irrepressible ‹nature, humour›; robust ‹health›

**Unverwüstlichkeit** *die;* **~** ⇒ **unverwüstlich:** indestructibility; irrepressible nature/humour; robustness

**unverzagt** *Adj.* undaunted

**unverzeihlich** *Adj.* unforgivable; inexcusable

**unverzichtbar** *Adj.* indispensable, essential ‹goods, requirements, etc.›; essential ‹measure›; inalienable ‹right›

**unverzinslich** (*Bankw.*) interest-free

**unverzollt** *Adj.* undeclared; **~e Ware** goods on which duty has not been paid

**unverzüglich** ❶ *Adj.* prompt; immediate. ❷ *adv.* promptly; immediately

**unvollendet** *Adj.* unfinished

**unvollkommen** ❶ *Adj.* [A] imperfect; [B] (*unvollständig*) incomplete ‹collection, account, etc.›. ❷ *adv.* [A] imperfectly; **sie beherrscht diese Arbeit nur ~:** she does not have perfect *or* complete command of this work; [B] (*unvollständig*) incompletely

**Unvollkommenheit** *die* [A] (*Fehlerhaftigkeit*) imperfectness; [B] (*Unvollständigkeit*) incompleteness

**unvollständig** ❶ *Adj.* incomplete. ❷ *adv.* **die Tatsachen nur ~ wiedergeben** give an incomplete rendering of the facts; **~ informiert sein** not be fully informed

**Unvollständigkeit** *die* incompleteness

**unvorbereitet** *Adj.* unprepared

**unvoreingenommen** ❶ *Adj.* unbiased; impartial. ❷ *adv.* impartially

**Unvoreingenommenheit** *die* impartiality

**unvorhergesehen** ❶ *Adj.* unforeseen ‹difficulty, event, expenditure›; unexpected ‹visit›. ❷ *adv.* **etw. kommt ganz ~:** sth. happens quite unexpectedly; **~ Besuch bekommen** have an unexpected visitor/unexpected visitors

**unvorhersehbar** *Adj.* unforeseeable

**unvorschriftsmäßig** ❶ *Adj.* contrary to *or* not in accordance with [the] regulations *postpos.*; **die ~e Anwendung eines Geräts** the improper use of a piece of equipment. ❷ *adv.* contrary to [the] regulations; ‹use etc.› improperly; ‹park etc.› illegally

**unvorsichtig** ❶ *Adj.* careless; (*unüberlegt*) rash. ❷ *adv.* carelessly; (*unüberlegt*) rashly

**unvorsichtigerweise** *Adv.* carelessly; (*unüberlegt*) without thinking

**Unvorsichtigkeit** *die* ⇨ **unvorsichtig** 1: [A] carelessness; rashness; [B] (*Handlung usw.*) **eine ~ begehen** do sth. careless/rash; **die ~ begehen, ...** be careless/rash enough ...

**unvorstellbar** ❶ *Adj.* inconceivable; unimaginable. ❷ *adv.* unimaginably; **~ leiden** suffer terribly

**unvorteilhaft** *Adj.* [A] (*nicht attraktiv*) unattractive ‹figure, appearance›; **das Kleid/die Frisur ist sehr ~ für dich** that dress/hairstyle doesn't suit you in the least; [B] (*ohne Vorteil*) unfavourable, poor ‹purchase, exchange›; unprofitable ‹business›

**unwägbar** *Adj.* imponderable; incalculable ‹quantity, behaviour›

**Unwägbarkeit** *die; ~, ~en* [A] imponderability; (*eines Verhaltens*) incalculability; **wegen der ~ der Risiken** because of the incalculable risks; [B] (*etw. Unwägbares*) uncertainty; imponderability

**unwahr** *Adj.* untrue

**unwahrhaftig** *Adj.* (*geh.*) untruthful

**Unwahrheit** *die* [A] untruthfulness; [B] (*Äußerung*) untruth

**unwahrscheinlich** ❶ *Adj.* [A] (*kaum möglich, unglaublich*) improbable; unlikely; **es ist ~, dass er so spät noch kommt** it is unlikely that he'll come so late; **ich halte es für ~[, dass ...]** I think it [is] unlikely that ...; [B] (*ugs.: sehr viel*) incredible (*coll.*). ❷ *adv.* (*ugs.: sehr*) incredibly (*coll.*); **er hat sich ~ gefreut** he was really thrilled (*coll.*)

**Unwahrscheinlichkeit** *die* improbability

**unwandelbar** (*geh.*) ❶ *Adj.* unwavering, steadfast ‹loyalty, love, friendship, attitude, etc.›; immutable ‹laws›. ❷ *adv.* steadfastly

**unwegsam** *Adj.* [almost] impassable

**unweiblich** *Adj.* unfeminine

**unweigerlich** /ʊnˈvaiɡɐlɪç/ ❶ *Adj.* inevitable. ❷ *adv.* inevitably

**unweit** ❶ *Präp. mit Gen.* not far from. ❷ *Adv.* not far (**von** from)

**Unwesen** *das* dreadful state of affairs; **sein ~ treiben** (*abwertend*) be up to one's mischief *or* one's tricks

**unwesentlich** ❶ *Adj.* unimportant; insignificant. ❷ *adv.* slightly; marginally

**Unwetter** *das* [thunder]storm

**unwichtig** *Adj.* unimportant; **Geld ist dabei ~:** the money is irrelevant; **etw. ist jmdm.** *od.* **für jmdn. ~:** sth. is unimportant *or* not important to sb.

**Unwichtigkeit** *die* [A] unimportance; lack of importance; [B] (*etw. Unwichtiges*) unimportant thing; triviality

**unwiderlegbar** ❶ *Adj.* irrefutable. ❷ *adv.* irrefutably

**unwiderruflich** ❶ *Adj.* irrevocable. ❷ *adv.* irrevocably

**unwidersprochen** *Adj.* unchallenged

**unwiderstehlich** *Adj.* irresistible

**Unwiderstehlichkeit** *die; ~:* irresistibility

**unwiederbringlich** (*geh.*) ❶ *Adj.* irretrievable. ❷ *adv.* irretrievably

**Unwiederbringlichkeit** *die; ~:* irretrievability

**Unwille[n]** *der* displeasure; indignation; **jmds. Unwillen erregen** *od.* **hervorrufen** incur sb.'s displeasure

**unwillig** ❶ *Adj.* indignant; angry; (*widerwillig*) unwilling; reluctant. ❷ *adv.* indignantly; angrily; (*widerwillig*) unwillingly; reluctantly

**unwillkommen** *Adj.* unwelcome

**unwillkürlich** ❶ *Adj.* [A] spontaneous ‹cry, sigh›; instinctive ‹reaction, movement, etc.›; [B] (*Physiol.*) involuntary ‹movement etc.›. ❷ *adv.* [A] ‹shout etc.› spontaneously; ‹react, move, etc.› instinctively; [B] (*Physiol.*) ‹move etc.› involuntarily

**unwirklich** (*geh.*) ❶ *Adj.* unreal. ❷ *adv.* **seine Stimme klang ~ fern** his voice sounded distant and unreal

**Unwirklichkeit** *die; ~, ~en* unreality

**unwirksam** *Adj.* ineffective

**Unwirksamkeit** *die* ineffectiveness

**unwirsch** ❶ *Adj.* surly; ill-natured. ❷ *adv.* ill-naturedly

**unwirtlich** *Adj.* inhospitable; rough ‹weather›

**Unwirtlichkeit** *die; ~:* inhospitableness; inhospitality; (*des Wetters*) roughness

**unwirtschaftlich** ❶ *Adj.* uneconomic ‹procedure etc.›; (*nicht sparsam*) uneconomical ‹driving etc.›. ❷ *adv.* ‹work, drive, etc.› uneconomically

**Unwirtschaftlichkeit** *die* economic inefficiency; lack of economy; **der Betrieb musste wegen ~ geschlossen werden** the firm had to be closed down because it was uneconomic

**Unwissen** *das* ignorance

**unwissend** *Adj.* [A] (*unerfahren*) ignorant; innocent ‹child›; [B] (*unbewusst*) unwitting; unknowing

**Unwissenheit** *die; ~* [A] (*Unkenntnis*) ignorance; **~ schützt nicht vor Strafe** ignorance is no defence; [B] (*mangelndes Wissen*) lack of education; (*auf einem bestimmten Gebiet*) lack of knowledge

**unwissenschaftlich** ❶ *Adj.* unscientific. ❷ *adv.* unscientifically

**Unwissenschaftlichkeit** *die; ~:* unscientific nature

**unwissentlich** ❶ *Adj.* unconscious. ❷ *adv.* unknowingly; unwittingly

**unwohl** *Adv.* [A] ▸474 (*nicht wohl*) unwell; **mir ist ~:** I don't feel well; [B] (*unbehaglich*) uneasy; **mir ist ~ bei dem Gedanken** the thought makes me feel uneasy

**Unwohlsein** *das; ~s* ▸474 indisposition; **ein heftiges ~ überkam ihn** he suddenly felt very unwell

**unwohnlich** *Adj.* uncomfortable; unhomely

**Unwucht** *die; ~, ~en* (*Technik*) imbalance

**unwürdig** *Adj.* [A] (*verachtungswürdig*) undignified ‹person, behaviour›; degrading ‹treatment›; [B] (*unangemessen*) unworthy

**Unzahl** *die* huge *or* enormous number

**unzählbar** *Adj.* (*auch Sprachw.*) uncountable

**unzählig** ❶ *Adj.* innumerable; countless. ❷ *adv.* **~ viele Besucher** a huge *or* an enormous number of visitors

***unzähligemal** ⇨ **Mal**[1]

**unzähmbar** *Adj.* untameable ‹animal›; (*fig.*) indomitable ‹person›

**unzart** ❶ *Adj.* indelicate. ❷ *adv.* indelicately

**Unze** /ˈʊntsə/ *die; ~, ~n* ▸353 ounce

**Unzeit** *die: in* **zur ~** (*geh.*) at an inopportune moment

**unzeitgemäß** *Adj.* anachronistic

**unzensiert** *Adj.* uncensored; (*unbenotet*) unmarked; ungraded (*Amer.*)

**unzerbrechlich** *Adj.* unbreakable

**unzerkaut** *Adj.* unchewed

**unzerstörbar** *Adj.* indestructible

**Unzerstörbarkeit** *die; ~:* indestructibility

**unzertrennlich** *Adj.* inseparable

**unziemlich** *Adj.* (*geh.*) unseemly

**unzivilisiert** *Adj.* (*abwertend*) uncivilized

**Unzucht** *die* (*veralt.*) **das ist ~:** this is a sexual offence; **~ [mit jmdm.] treiben** fornicate [with sb.]; **~ mit Abhängigen/Kindern/Tieren** illicit sexual relations *pl.* with dependants/children/animals; **widernatürliche ~:** unnatural sexual act[s]; **gewerbsmäßige ~:** prostitution

**unzüchtig** ❶ *Adj.* obscene ‹letter, gesture›. ❷ *adv.* ‹touch, approach, etc.› indecently; ‹speak› obscenely

**unzufrieden** *Adj.* dissatisfied; (*stärker*) unhappy

**Unzufriedenheit** *die* dissatisfaction; (*stärker*) unhappiness

**unzugänglich** *Adj.* inaccessible ‹area, building, etc.›; unapproachable ‹character, person, etc.›

**Unzugänglichkeit** *die; ~* ⇨ **unzugänglich**: inaccessibility; unapproachability

**unzukömmlich** /ˈʊntsu:kœmlɪç/ *Adj.* (*österr.*) [A] (*nicht zukommend*) undeserved; [B] (*unzulänglich*) inadequate

**unzulänglich** (*geh.*) ❶ *Adj.* insufficient; inadequate. ❷ *adv.* insufficiently; inadequately

**Unzulänglichkeit** *die; ~, ~en* [A] insufficiency; inadequacy; [B] (*etw. Unzulängliches*) inadequacy; shortcoming

**unzulässig** *Adj.* inadmissible; undue ‹influence, interference, delay›; improper ‹method, use, etc.›

**Unzulässigkeit** *die* inadmissibility

**unzumutbar** *Adj.* unreasonable

**Unzumutbarkeit** *die; ~, ~en* [A] (*das Unzumutbarsein*) unreasonableness; [B] (*etw. Unzumutbares*) unreasonable demand

**unzurechnungsfähig** *Adj.* not responsible for one's actions *pred.*; (*geistesgestört*) of unsound mind *postpos.*; **für ~ erklärt werden** be certified insane

**Unzurechnungs·fähigkeit** *die* (*Geistesgestörtheit*) unsoundness of mind

**unzureichend** *Adj.* insufficient; inadequate

**unzusammenhängend** *Adj.* disconnected; incoherent ‹words, ideas›

**unzustellbar** *Adj.* (*Postw.*) undeliverable ‹mail›; **„falls ~, bitte zurück an Absender"** 'if undelivered, please return to sender'; **„~"** 'not known [at this address]'

**unzuträglich** *Adj. in* **jmdm./einer Sache ~ sein** (*geh.*) be detrimental to sb./sth.

**Unzuträglichkeit** *die; ~:* detrimental effect; detrimentalness

**unzutreffend** *Adj.* inappropriate; inapplicable; (*falsch*) incorrect; **„Unzutreffendes bitte streichen"** 'please delete as appropriate'

**unzuverlässig** *Adj.* unreliable

**Unzuverlässigkeit** *die* unreliability

**unzweckmäßig** ❶ *Adj.* unsuitable; (*unpraktisch*) impractical. ❷ *adv.* unsuitably; (*unpraktisch*) impractically

**Unzweckmäßigkeit** *die* ⇨ **unzweckmäßig** 1: unsuitability; impracticality

**unzweideutig** ❶ *Adj.* unambiguous; unequivocal; **etw. mit ~en Worten sagen** say sth. in no uncertain terms. ❷ *adv.* unambiguously; unequivocally; **jmdm. ~ zu verstehen geben, dass ...** tell sb. in no uncertain terms that ...

**Unzweideutigkeit** *die* unambiguousness

**unzweifelhaft** ❶ *Adj.* unquestionable; undoubted. ❷ *adv.* unquestionably; undoubtedly

**Update** /ˈapdeɪt/ *das; ~s, ~s* (*DV*) update

**üppig** ❶ *Adj.* [A] (*voll, dicht*) lush, luxuriant ‹vegetation›; thick ‹hair, beard›; (*fig.*) sumptuous, opulent ‹meal›; rich ‹colour›; [B] (*rundlich, voll*) full ‹bosom, lips›; voluptuous ‹figure, woman›. ❷ *adv.* luxuriantly; (*fig.*) sumptuously

**Üppigkeit** *die; ~* ⇨ **üppig** 1: lushness; luxuriance; thickness; sumptuousness; opulence; richness; fullness; voluptuousness

**up to date** /ˈʌp tə ˈdeɪt/ up to date; **er ist modisch ~:** he wears fashionable clothes; he is fashionably dressed

**Ur·ab·stimmung** *die* [*esp.* strike] ballot

**Ur·adel** *der* ancient nobility

**Ur·ahn[e]** *der* [A] (*Vorfahr*) oldest known ancestor; [B] (*veralt.: Urgroßvater*) great-grandfather

**Ural** *der; ~[s]* Urals *pl.*; Ural Mountains *pl.*

**ur·alt** *Adj.* very old; ancient; **in ~en Zeiten** very long ago; **ein Märchen aus ~en Zeiten** a story of long, long ago

*old spelling (see note on page 1707)

u

**Uran** /u'ra:n/ *das;* **~s** *(Chemie)* uranium

**Uran·erz** *das* uranium ore

**Ur·angst** *die* primeval fear

**Uranus**[1] /'u:ranʊs/ *der;* ~ *(Astron.),* **Uranus**[2] *(der) (Myth.)* Uranus *no def. art.*

**ur·auf·führen** *tr. V.* première, give the first performance of ‹play, concerto, etc.›; première ‹film›; **uraufgeführt werden** ‹film› have its première

**Ur·auf·führung** *die* première; first night *or* performance; *(eines Films)* première; first showing

**urban** /ʊr'ba:n/ *Adj. (geh.)* Ⓐ *(weltmännisch)* urbane; Ⓑ *(städtisch)* urban

**Urbanisation** /ʊrbaniza'tsi̯o:n/ *die;* ~, **~en** urbanization

**urbanisieren** *tr. V.* urbanize

**Urbanistik** /ʊrba'nɪstɪk/ *die;* **~:** town planning and urban development *no art.; (Studienfach)* urban studies *pl., no art.*

**Urbanität** /ʊrbani'tɛ:t/ *die;* **~:** urbanity

**urbar** *in* **ein Stück Land/einen Sumpf/eine Wüste ~ machen** cultivate a piece of land/reclaim a swamp/desert

**Urbarmachung** *die;* ~ *(von Land)* cultivation; *(von Sumpf, Wüste)* reclamation

**Ur·bevölkerung** *die* native population; native inhabitants *pl.*

**Ur·bild** *das* Ⓐ *(Vorbild)* archetype; prototype; Ⓑ *(Inbegriff, Ideal)* perfect example; epitome

**urchig** /'ʊrçɪç/ *Adj. (schweiz.)* ⇒ **urig**

**Ur·christentum** *das* early Christianity *no art.*

**ur·christlich** *Adj.* early Christian

**ur·deutsch** *Adj.* thoroughly *or* totally German

**ur·eigen** *Adj.* very own; **seine ~en Interessen** his own best interests

**Ur·einwohner** *der* native inhabitant; **die australischen ~:** the Australian Aborigines

**Ur·einwohnerin** *die* ⇒ **Ureinwohner**

**Ur·eltern** *Pl.* original ancestors

**Ur·enkel** *der* great-grandson

**Ur·enkelin** *die* great-granddaughter

**Ur·fassung** *die* original version; original

**Ur·fehde** *die (MA.)* oath of truce

**Ur·form** *die* prototype

**Ur·gemeinde** *die* early Christian community

**ur·gemütlich** ❶ *Adj. (ugs.) (behaglich)* extremely cosy; *(bequem)* extremely comfortable. ❷ *adv.* extremely cosily/comfortably

**ur·germanisch** *Adj.* proto-Germanic

**Ur·geschichte** *die* prehistory

**ur·geschichtlich** *Adj.* prehistoric

**Ur·gesellschaft** *die* primitive society

**Ur·gestein** *das* primitive *or* primary rocks *pl.;* **er ist politisches ~** *(fig.)* he is a founding father among politicians

**Ur·gewalt** *die (geh.)* elemental force

**urgieren** /ʊr'gi:rən/ *tr., itr. V. (bes. österr.)* press; urge

**Urgroß-: ~eltern** *Pl.* great-grandparents; **~mutter** *die; Pl.* **~mütter** great-grandmother; **~vater** *der* great-grandfather

**Ur·grund** *der* basis; source; **der ~ alles Seins** the source of all being

**Ur·heber** *der;* **~s,** ~, **Ur·heberin** *die;* ~, **~nen** Ⓐ *(Initiator[in])* originator; initiator; Ⓑ *(bes. Rechtsspr.: Verfasser[in])* author

**Urheber·recht** *das* copyright

**urheber·rechtlich** ❶ *Adj.* copyright *attrib.* ❷ *adv.* ~ **geschützt** copyright[ed]

**Urheberschaft** *die;* **~:** authorship

**Ur·heimat** *die* original home[land]

**urig** /'u:rɪç/ *Adj.* natural ‹person›; real ‹beer›; cosy ‹pub›; **sie ist einfach ~:** she is just different *or* an original

**Urin** /u'ri:n/ *der;* **~s, ~e** *(Med.)* urine; **etw. im ~ haben** *(salopp)* feel sth. in one's bones; have a gut feeling about sth.

**Urinal** /uri'na:l/ *das;* **~s, ~e** urinal

**urinieren** *itr. V.* urinate (**an** + *Akk.* against)

**Ur·instinkt** *der* basic instinct

**Ur·kanton** *der* original canton

**Ur·kirche** *die* early Church

**Ur·knall** *der* big bang

**ur·komisch** *Adj.* extremely funny; hilarious

**Ur·kraft** *die* elemental force

**Ur·kunde** *die;* ~, **~n** document; *(Bescheinigung, Sieger~, Diplom~ usw.)* certificate

**Urkunden·fälschung** *die* forgery *or* falsification of documents/of a/the document

**urkundlich** ❶ *Adj.* documentary. ❷ *adv.* ~ **erwähnt** mentioned in a document/in documents; **~ übereignen** transfer by deed

**Urkunds·beamte** *der,* **Urkunds·beamtin** *die (Rechtsw.)* registrar

**Urlaub** *der;* **~[e]s, ~e** holiday[s] *(Brit.);* vacation; *(bes. Milit.)* leave; **~ haben** have a holiday/have leave; **[sich** *(Dat.)***] ~ nehmen** take a holiday; **auf** *od.* **in** *od.* **im ~ sein** be on holiday/leave; **in ~ gehen/fahren** go on holiday; **unbezahlter ~:** unpaid leave; **~ von der Familie machen** have a holiday away from one's family; **sie machen ~:** they are on holiday; **sie ist noch nicht aus dem ~ zurück** she is still not back from holiday

**-urlaub** *der:* **Schweiz~/Österreich~** *usw.* holiday in Switzerland/Austria *etc.;* **Billig~/Neckermann~:** cheap *or* budget/Neckermann holiday

**urlauben** *itr. V. (ugs.)* holiday; be/go on holiday

**Urlauber** *der;* **~s, ~:** holidaymaker

**-urlauber** *der:* **~s, ~: Sommer~/Winter~/Wochenend~:** summer/winter/weekend holidaymaker; **Billig~/Neckermann~:** person on a cheap *or* budget/Neckermann holiday; **Kreta~/Spanien~:** holidaymaker in *or* on Crete/in Spain

**Urlauberin** *die;* ~, **~nen** ⇒ **Urlauber**

**urlaubs-, Urlaubs-: ~an·schrift** *die* holiday address; **~an·spruch** *der* holiday entitlement; **~geld** *das* holiday pay *or* money; *(gespartes Geld)* holiday money; **~lektüre** *die* holiday reading *no indef. art.;* **~ort** *der* holiday resort; **~pläne** *Pl.* holiday plans; **~reif** *Adj. in* **~reif sein** *(ugs.)* be ready for a holiday; **~reise** *die* holiday [trip]; **eine ~reise ans Meer/ins Gebirge machen** go on holiday to the seaside/go for a holiday in the mountains; **~reisende** *der/die* holidaymaker; **~schein** *der (Milit.)* [leave] pass; **~sperre** *die* Ⓐ *(Milit.)* ban on leave; Ⓑ *(österr.)* holiday closure; **~tag** *der* day of holiday; **zehn ~tage** ten days' holiday; **~vertretung** *die* holiday replacement; **er übernimmt die ~vertretung seines Chefs** he stands in *or* deputizes for his boss when the latter is on holiday; **~zeit** *die* Ⓐ *(Ferienzeit)* holiday period *or* season; Ⓑ *(Zeit des eigenen Urlaubs)* holiday

**Ur·laut** *der* elemental sound; *(schrill)* elemental cry

**Ur·mensch** *der* prehistoric *or* primitive man *no art., no pl.;* early hominid *(as tech. term)*

**Ur·meter** *das (hist.)* standard metre

**Urne** /'ʊrnə/ *die;* ~, **~n** Ⓐ urn; Ⓑ *(Wahl~)* [ballot] box; **zu den ~n gerufen werden** be called to the polls; Ⓒ *(Verlosungs~)* box; *(Lostrommel)* drum

**Urnen-: ~feld** *das* urnfield; **~fried·hof** *der* urn cemetery; cinerarium; **~grab** *das* urn grave

**Urologe** /uro'lo:gə/ *der;* **~n, ~n, Urologin** *die;* ~, **~nen** ▶ 159 urologist

**urologisch** *Adj.* urological

**Ur·oma** *die (fam.)* great-granny *(coll./child lang.)*

**Ur·opa** *der (fam.)* great-grandpa *(coll./child lang.)*

**ur·plötzlich** ❶ *Adj.* extremely sudden. ❷ *adv.* quite suddenly

**Ur·quell** *der (geh.)* [primary] source

**Ur·sache** *die* cause; **aus unbekannter ~:** for no apparent reason; for reasons *pl.* as yet unknown; **die ~ für etw.** the cause of sth.; the reason for sth.; **alle ~ haben, etw. zu tun** have every reason to do sth.; **keine ~!** don't mention it; you're welcome; **kleine ~, große Wirkung** *(Spr.)* great oaks from little acorns grow *(prov.)*

**ur·sächlich** *Adj.* causal; **in ~em Zusammenhang stehen** be causally related (**mit** to); **~ für etw. sein** be the cause of sth.

**Ur·sächlichkeit** *die;* ~, **~en** causality

**Ur·schlamm** *der,* **Ur·schleim** *der* primeval slime; **vom ~ an** *(ugs.)* from the very beginning

**Ur·schrei** *der (Psych.)* primal scream

**Ur·schrift** *die* original

**ur·schriftlich** *Adj.* original ‹version etc.›

**Ur·sendung** *die (Rundf.)* first broadcast performance

**Ur·sprache** *die* Ⓐ *(Sprachw.: Grundsprache)* protolanguage; Ⓑ *(Originalsprache)* original language; **in der ~:** in the original

**Ur·sprung** *der* origin; **vulkanischen ~s sein** be of volcanic origin; **seinen ~ in etw.** *(Dat.)* **haben** originate from sth.

**ur·sprünglich** ❶ *Adj.* Ⓐ *(anfänglich)* original ‹plan, price, form, material, etc.›; initial ‹reaction, trust, mistrust, etc.›; Ⓑ *(unverfälscht, natürlich)* natural. ❷ *adv.* Ⓐ *(anfänglich)* originally; initially; Ⓑ *(unverfälscht, natürlich)* naturally

**Ursprünglichkeit** *die;* **~:** naturalness

**Ursprungs·land** *das (einer Ware)* country of origin *(Commerc.); (einer Person)* native land; *(einer Bewegung, Sitte, Religion usw.)* birthplace

**urst** /u:ɐ̯st/ ❶ *Adj.* great *(coll.);* brilliant *(coll.).* ❷ *adv. (regional Jugendspr.)* really

**Urständ** /'u:ɐ̯ʃtɛnt/ *die: in* **[fröhliche] ~ feiern** be [coming] back with a vengeance

**Ur·strom·tal** *das (Geol.)* glacial valley

**Ur·suppe** *die (Biol.)* primordial soup

**Urteil** *das;* **~s, ~e** judgement; *(Ansicht)* opinion; *(Strafe)* sentence; *(Gerichts~)* verdict; **das ~ lautete auf 10 Jahre Freiheitsstrafe** the sentence was ten years' imprisonment; **über jmdn. das ~ sprechen** pass *or* pronounce judgement on sb.; **sich** *(Dat.)* **selbst das ~ sprechen** sentence oneself; **sich** *(Dat.)* **ein ~ bilden** form an opinion (**über** + *Akk.* about); **ein ~ über etw. fällen** pass *or* pronounce judgement on sth.

**Ur·teilchen** *das* ⇒ **Quark**[2]

**urteilen** *itr. V.* form an opinion; judge; **nach etw. ~:** form an opinion *or* judge according to sth.; **nach seinem Äußeren zu ~:** to judge from his appearance; **über etw./jmdn. ~:** judge sth./sb.; give one's opinion on sth./sb.; **hart ~:** give a harsh opinion; judge harshly; **fachmännisch ~:** give an expert opinion; **~ Sie selbst** judge for yourself/yourselves

**urteils-, Urteils-: ~begründung** *die* opinion; reasons *pl.* for judgement; **~fähig** *Adj.* competent *or* able to judge *postpos.;* **~fähigkeit** *die* competence *or* ability to judge; **~findung** *die;* **~~, ~~en** *(Rechtsspr.)* reaching a/the verdict *no art.;* **~kraft** *die* [power of] judgement; **~spruch** *der* judgement; *(Strafe)* sentence; *(der Geschworenen)* verdict; **~verkündung** *die* pronouncement of judgement; **~vermögen** *das* competence *or* ability to judge

**Ur·text** *der* original

**Ur·tierchen** *das* protozoan

**urtümlich** /'u:ɐ̯ty:mlɪç/ *Adj.* natural ‹landscape etc.›; primitive ‹culture etc.›; *(urweltlich)* primeval ‹plant, animal, landscape›

**Uruguay** /uru'gu̯a:i/ *(das);* **~s** Uruguay

**Uruguayer** /uru'gu̯a:jɐ/ *der;* **~s,** ~, **Uruguayerin** *die;* ~, **~nen** Uruguayan

**Ur·ur-: ~enkel** *der* great-great-grandson; **~enkelin** *die* great-great-granddaughter; **~groß·mutter** *die* great-great-grandmother; **~groß·vater** *der* great-great-grandfather

**Ur·väter·zeit** *die* olden days *or* times *pl.*

**Ur·vertrauen** *das (Päd., Psych.)* sense of basic trust

U

**Ur·viech** *das* (*salopp scherzh.*) real character
**Ur·vogel** *der* (*Paläont.*) archaeopteryx
**Ur·volk** *das* original people
**Ur·wald** *der* primeval forest; **tropischer Urwald** tropical forest; jungle
**ur·weltlich** *Adj.* primeval
**ur·wüchsig** /ˈuːɐ̯vyːksɪç/ *Adj.* natural ‹landscape, power›; earthy ‹language, humour›
**Urwüchsigkeit** *die;* ~ ⇒ **urwüchsig**: naturalness; earthiness
**Ur·zeit** *die* primeval times *pl.;* **vor ~en** in ages past; **seit ~en** since primeval times; (*ugs.: seit längerer Zeit*) since the year dot (*coll.*)
**ur·zeitlich** *Adj.* primeval
**Ur·zelle** *die* primeval cell; (*fig.*) initial germ
**Ur·zeugung** *die* abiogenesis; spontaneous generation
**Ur·zustand** *der* original state
**USA** /uː|ɛs|ˈaː/ *Pl.* USA
**Usambara·veilchen** /uzamˈbaːra-/ *das* African violet
**Usance** /yˈzãːs/ *die;* ~, **~n**, (*schweiz.*), **Usanz** /uˈzants/ *die;* ~, **~en** (*bes. Kaufmannsspr.*) practice
**User** /ˈjuːzɐ/ *der;* **~s**, ~, **Userin** *die;* ~, **~nen** (*bes. DV, Drogenjargon*) user
**usf.** *Abk.* **und so fort** etc.
**Usurpator** /uzʊrˈpaːtɔr/ *der;* **~s**, **~en** /...paˈtoːrən/, **Usurpatorin** *die;* ~, **~nen** usurper
**usurpieren** *tr. V.* usurp
**Usus** /ˈuːzʊs/ *der;* ~ (*ugs.*) custom; **das ist hier so ~:** that's the custom here
**usw.** *Abk.* **und so weiter** etc.
**Utensil** /utɛnˈziːl/ *das;* **~s**, **~ien** /... i̯ən/ piece of equipment; **~ien** equipment *sing.*
**Uterus** /ˈuːterʊs/ *der;* ~, **Uteri** ▶ 471 [... ri] (*Anat.*) uterus
**Utilitarismus** /utilitaˈrɪsmʊs/ *der;* ~ (*Philos.*) utilitarianism *no art.*
**utilitaristisch** *Adj.* utilitarian
**Utopia** /uˈtoːpi̯a/ (*das*)*;* **~s** Utopia
**Utopie** /utoˈpiː/ *die;* ~, **~n** (A) (*Idealvorstellung*) utopian dream; (B) (*ideale Gesellschaftsform*) utopia; (*literarisches Werk*) utopian *or* futuristic work
**utopisch** *Adj.* utopian
**Utopist** *der;* **~en**, **~en**, **Utopistin** *die;* ~, **~nen** utopian dreamer; (*Autor*[*in*]) utopian [author]
**utopistisch** *Adj.* [absurdly] utopian
**u. U.** *Abk.* **unter Umständen**
**UV** *Abk.* **Ultraviolett** UV
**UV-:** **~-Filter** *der* (*Fot.*) UV filter; ultraviolet filter; **~-Strahlen** *Pl.* UV rays; ultraviolet rays
**Ü-Wagen** *der* (*Rundf., Ferns.*) OB van or vehicle
**u. Z.** *Abk.* (*bes. DDR*) **unserer Zeitrechnung** AD
**Uz** /uːts/ *der;* **~es**, **~e** (*ugs.*) joke
**uzen** *tr., itr. V.* (*ugs.*) tease; kid
**Uz·name** *der* (*ugs.*) nickname

u

# V v

**v, V** /vau̯/ *das;* ~, ~: v, V
**v.** *Abk.* **von** (*in Familiennamen*) von
**V** *Abk.* **Volt** V
**Vabanque·spiel** /va'bã:k-/ *das* (*geh.*) dangerous *or* risky game
**Vademekum** /vade'me:kʊm/ *das;* ~s, ~s (*geh. veralt.*) vade mecum
**vag** /va:k/ ⇒ **vage**
**Vagabund** /vaga'bʊnt/ *der;* ~en, ~en (*veralt.*) vagabond
**vagabundieren** *itr. V.* Ⓐ live as a vagabond/ as vagabonds; Ⓑ *mit sein* (*umherziehen*) wander *or* travel around
**Vagabundin** *die;* ~, ~nen ⇒ **Vagabund**
**Vagant** /va'gant/ *der;* ~en, ~en goliard
**Vaganten·dichtung** *die* (*Literaturw.*) goliardic poetry *or* verse
**vage** ❶ *Adj.* vague. ❷ *adv.* vaguely
**Vagheit** *die;* ~: vagueness
**Vagina** /va'gi:na/ *die;* ~, **Vaginen** ▶ 471 (*Anat.*) vagina
**vaginal** *Adj.* (*Anat.*) vaginal
**vakant** /va'kant/ *Adj.* vacant
**Vakanz** /va'kants/ *die;* ~, ~en (*geh.*) vacancy
**Vakuum** /'va:kuʊm/ *das;* ~s, **Vakua** /'va:ku̯a/ *od.* **Vakuen** /... kən/ (*bes. Physik, auch fig.*) vacuum; **im** ~: in a vacuum
**vakuum·verpackt** *Adj.* vacuum-packed
**Valentins·tag** /'va:lɛnti:ns-/ *der* [St] Valentine's Day
**Valenz** /va'lɛnts/ *die;* ~, ~en Ⓐ (*Sprachw.*) valency; Ⓑ (*Chemie*) valence; valency (*Brit.*)
**Valet** /va'lɛt/ *das;* ~s, ~s (*veralt., noch scherzh.*) farewell
**Valuta** /va'lu:ta/ *die;* ~, **Valuten** (*Wirtsch., Bankw.*) foreign currency
**Vamp** /vɛmp/ *der;* ~s, ~s vamp
**Vampir** /'vampi:ɐ̯/ *der;* ~s, ~e Ⓐ vampire; Ⓑ (*Tier*) vampire [bat]
**Vampirin** *die;* ~, ~nen ⇒ **Vampir** A
**Van** /væn/ *der;* ~s, ~s (*Kfz.-W.*) multi-purpose vehicle; MPV
**Vandale** *usw.:* ⇒ **Wandale**
**Vanille** /va'nɪljə/ *die;* ~: vanilla
**Vanille-:** ~**eis** *das* vanilla ice cream; ~**geschmack** *der* vanilla flavour; **Eis mit** ~**geschmack** vanilla-flavoured ice cream; ~**pudding** *der* vanilla pudding; ~**zucker** *der* vanilla sugar
**variabel** /va'ri̯a:bl̩/ ❶ *Adj.* variable. ❷ *adv.* variably
**Variabilität** /vari̯abili'tɛ:t/ *die;* ~ (*geh.*) variability
**Variable** /va'ri̯a:blə/ *die; adj. Dekl.* (*Math., Physik*) variable
**Variante** /va'ri̯antə/ *die;* ~, ~n (*geh.*) variant; variation
**Variation** /varia'tsi̯o:n/ *die;* ~, ~en (*auch Musik*) variation (*Gen.*, **über, zu** on)
**Varietät** /vari̯e'tɛ:t/ *die;* ~, ~en (*bes. Biol.*) variety
**Varieté, Varietee** /vari̯e'te:/ *das;* ~s, ~s variety theatre; (*Aufführung*) variety show; **ins** ~ **gehen** go to a variety show
**variieren** *tr., itr. V.* vary
**Vario·objektiv** /'va:ri̯o-/ *das* (*Fot.*) zoom lens
**Vasall** /va'zal/ *der;* ~en, ~en (*hist., auch fig. abwertend*) vassal
**Vasallen·staat** *der* (*abwertend*) vassal state
**Väschen** /'vɛ:sçən/ *das;* ~s, ~: [little] vase
**Vase** /'va:zə/ *die;* ~, ~n vase
**Vasektomie** /vazɛkto'mi/ *die;* ~, ~n (*Med.*) vasectomy

**Vaseline** /vaze'li:nə/ *die;* ~: Vaseline ®
**Vasen·malerei** *die* vase painting
**vasomotorisch** /vazomo'to:rɪʃ/ *Adj.* (*Physiol.*) vasomotor
**Vater** /'fa:tɐ/ *der;* ~s, **Väter** /'fɛ:tɐ/ Ⓐ father; **er ist** ~ **von drei Kindern** he is the father of three children; **er ist** ~ **geworden** he has become a father; **ein werdender** ~ (*scherzh.*) an expectant father (*joc.*); **grüßen Sie Ihren Herrn** ~! remember me to your father; **er ist ganz der** ~: he is just like his father; **er ist der [geistige]** ~ **dieser Idee** (*fig.*) he thought up this idea; this idea is his; **die Väter der amerikanischen Verfassung** (*fig.*) the [founding] fathers of the American constitution; ~ **Staat** (*scherzh.*) the State; ~ **Rhein** (*dichter.*) the Rhine; Father Rhine (*literary*); **Heiliger** ~ (*kath. Kirche*) Holy Father; **ach, du dicker** ~ (*ugs.*) oh my goodness!; oh heavens!; Ⓑ (*Tier*) sire; Ⓒ (*Rel.*) Father; **Gott** ~: God the Father
**Väterchen** /'fɛ:tɐçən/ *das;* ~s, ~ Ⓐ (*Koseform*) daddy (*coll.*); Ⓑ **[altes]** ~: little old man; Ⓒ ~ **Frost** (*scherzh.*) Jack Frost
**Vater-:** ~**figur** *die* father figure; ~**freuden** *Pl.* ~**freuden entgegensehen** (*meist scherzh.*) be expecting a happy event; be going to be a father; ~**haus** *das* (*geh.*) parental home; **das** ~**haus verlassen** leave one's parents' house; ~**land** *das* fatherland
**vaterländisch** /'--lɛndɪʃ/ *Adj.* (*geh.*) patriotic
**Vaterlands-:** ~**liebe** *die* (*geh.*) love of one's fatherland; patriotism; ~**verräter** *der* (*abwertend*) traitor to one's fatherland
**väterlich** /'fɛ:tɐlɪç/ ❶ *Adj.* Ⓐ (*vom Vater*) his/her *etc.* father's; (*verallgemeinernd*) the father's; (*eines Vaters*) paternal ‹line, love, instincts, etc.›; **das** ~**e Geschäft übernehmen** take over one's father's business; **die** ~**en Pflichten** the duties of a father; Ⓑ (*fürsorglich*) fatherly. ❷ *adv.* in a fatherly way
**väterlicherseits** *Adv.* on the/his/her *etc.* father's side; **meine Großeltern** ~: my paternal grandparents; my grandparents on my father's side
**Väterlichkeit** *die;* ~: fatherliness; (*väterliche Gefühle*) fatherly feeling
**vater-, Vater-:** ~**los** *Adj.* fatherless; ~**los aufwachsen** grow up without a father; ~**mord** *der* patricide; ~**mörder** *der* Ⓐ patricide; Ⓑ (*veralt. scherzh.: Stehkragen*) choker [collar]; ~**mörderin** *die* ⇒ ~**mörder** A; ~**schaft** *die;* ~~, ~~**en** fatherhood; (*bes. Rechtsw.*) paternity; ~**schafts·klage** *die* paternity suit; ~**stadt** *die* (*geh.*) home town; ~**stelle** *die:* **bei** *od.* **an jmdm.** ~**stelle vertreten** take the place of a father to sb.; ~**tag** *der* Father's Day *no def. art.;* ~**tier** *das* (*Landw.*) sire; ~**unser** *das;* ~~**s**, ~~: Lord's Prayer; **das** ~**unser sprechen** say the Lord's Prayer; **drei** ~**unser beten** say three Our Fathers
**Vati** /'fa:ti/ *der;* ~s, ~s (*fam.*) dad[dy] (*coll.*)
**Vatikan** /vati'ka:n/ *der;* ~s Vatican
**vatikanisch** *Adj.* Vatican
**Vatikanstadt** *die;* ~: Vatican City
**V-Ausschnitt** /'fau̯-/ *der* V-neck
**VB** *Abk.* **Verhandlungsbasis: VB 7 800 DM** 7,800 marks o.n.o (*Brit.*)
**v. Chr.** *Abk.* ▶ 207 **vor Christus** BC
**VEB** *Abk.* (*DDR*) **Volkseigener Betrieb**
**Vegetarier** /vege'ta:ri̯ɐ/ *der;* ~s, ~, **Vegetarierin** *die;* ~, ~nen vegetarian

**vegetarisch** ❶ *Adj.* vegetarian. ❷ *adv.* **er isst** *od.* **lebt** *od.* **ernährt sich** ~: he is a vegetarian; he lives on a vegetarian diet
**Vegetarismus** *der;* ~: vegetarianism *no art.*
**Vegetation** /...'tsi̯o:n/ *die;* ~, ~en vegetation *no indef. art.*
**vegetativ** /vegeta'ti:f/ *Adj.* Ⓐ (*Biol.: ungeschlechtlich*) vegetative; Ⓑ (*Physiol., Biol.: unbewusst ablaufend*) autonomic
**vegetieren** *itr. V.* (*oft abwertend*) vegetate; **am Rande der Existenz** ~: eke out a miserable existence
**vehement** /vehe'mɛnt/ (*geh.*) ❶ *Adj.* vehement. ❷ *adv.* vehemently
**Vehemenz** /...'mɛnts/ *die;* ~ (*geh.*) vehemence
**Vehikel** /ve'hi:kl̩/ *das;* ~s, ~ Ⓐ (*oft abwertend: Auto*) vehicle; **ein altes/klappriges** ~: an old crock (*sl.*); Ⓑ (*geh.: Ausdrucksmittel*) vehicle
**Veilchen** /'fai̯lçən/ *das;* ~s, ~ Ⓐ (*Blume*) violet; **wie ein** ~ **im Verborgenen blühen** be modesty itself; go unnoticed; ⇒ *auch* **blau**; Ⓑ (*ugs. scherzh.: blaues Auge*) black eye; shiner (*sl.*)
**veilchen-, Veilchen-:** ~**blau** *Adj.* violet; ~**duft** *der* violet fragrance *or* scent; ~**strauß** *der; Pl.* ~**sträuße** bunch *or* bouquet of violets
**Veits·tanz** /'fai̯ts-/ *der* St Vitus's dance; **einen** ~ **kriegen** (*ugs.*) *od.* **aufführen** (*fig.*) kick up a terrible fuss
**Vektor** /'vɛktɔr/ *der;* ~s, ~en /-'to:rən/ (*Math., Physik*) vector
**Vektor·rechnung** *die* vector algebra; (*im weiteren Sinne*) vector analysis
**velar** /ve'la:ɐ̯/ (*Sprachw.*) ❶ *Adj.* velar. ❷ *adv.* ‹pronounce› as a velar sound
**Velar** *der;* ~s, ~e, **Velar·laut** *der* (*Phon.*) velar sound
**Velo** /'ve:lo/ *das;* ~s, ~s (*schweiz.*) bicycle; bike (*coll.*)
**Velours**[1] /və'lu:ɐ̯/ *der;* ~ /və'lu:ɐ̯s/, ~ /və'lu:ɐ̯s/ (*Stoff*) velour[s]
**Velours**[2] *das;* ~ /və'lu:ɐ̯s/, ~ /və'lu:ɐ̯s/, **Velours·leder** *das* suede
**Vene** /'ve:nə/ *die;* ~, ~n ▶ 471 (*Anat.*) vein
**Venedig** /ve'ne:dɪç/ (*das*); ~s ▶ 700 Venice
**Venen·entzündung** *die* phlebitis *no indef. art.*
**venerisch** /ve'ne:rɪʃ/ *Adj.* (*Med.*) venereal
**Venezianer** /vene'tsi̯a:nɐ/ *der;* ~s, ~, **Venezianerin** *die;* ~, ~nen ▶ 700 Venetian
**venezianisch** *Adj.* ▶ 700 Venetian
**Venezolaner** /venetso'la:nɐ/ *der;* ~s, ~, **Venezolanerin** *die;* ~, ~nen Venezuelan
**venezolanisch** *Adj.* Venezuelan
**Venezuela** /vene'tsu̯e:la/ (*das*); ~s Venezuela
**Venia Legendi** /'ve:ni̯a le'gɛndi/ *die;* ~ (*geh.*) authorization to teach at university after habilitation
**venös** *Adj.* (*Med.*) venous
**Ventil** /vɛn'ti:l/ *das;* ~s, ~e Ⓐ valve; (*fig.*) outlet; Ⓑ (*einer Orgel*) pallet
**Ventilation** /vɛntila'tsi̯o:n/ *die;* ~, ~en ventilation
**Ventilator** /vɛnti'la:tɔr/ *der;* ~s, ~en /...la'to:rən/ ventilator
**ventilieren** *tr. V.* (*geh.*) consider
**Venus**[1] /'ve:nʊs/ *die;* ~ (*Astron.*), **Venus**[2] (*die*) (*Myth.*) Venus *no def. art.*
**Venus·hügel** *der* (*Anat.*) mons Veneris

**verabfolgen** *tr. V.* (*Papierdt. veralt.*) ⇒ **verabreichen**

**verabreden** ❶ *tr. V.* arrange; **ein Erkennungszeichen ~:** agree on a sign to recognize each other by; **am verabredeten Ort** at the agreed place. ❷ *refl. V.* **sich im Park/zum Tennis/für den folgenden Abend ~:** arrange to meet in the park/for tennis/next evening; **sich mit jmdm. ~:** arrange to meet sb.; **mit jmdm. verabredet sein** have arranged to meet sb.; (*formell*) have an appointment with sb.; (*mit dem Freund/der Freundin*) have a date with sb. (*coll.*)

**Verabredung** *die;* **~, ~en** A (*Absprache*) arrangement; **eine ~ treffen** arrange to meet *or* a meeting; **wie auf ~:** as if by arrangement; B (*verabredete Zusammenkunft*) appointment; **eine ~ absagen** call off a meeting *or* an engagement; **ich habe eine ~:** I am meeting sb.; (*formell*) I have an appointment; (*mit meinem Freund/meiner Freundin*) I have a date (*coll.*); **eine ~ für den Abend haben** have an engagement in the evening

**verabreichen** *tr. V.* administer ‹medicine›; give ‹injection, thrashing›

**Verabreichung** *die;* **~, ~en** administration; administering

**verabsäumen** *tr. V.* (*Papierdt.*) neglect; omit

**verabscheuen** *tr. V.* detest; loathe

**verabscheuenswürdig** *Adj.* (*geh.*) detestable; loathsome

**verabschieden** ❶ *tr. V.* A say goodbye to; **sie wurde am Bahnhof verabschiedet** she was seen off at the station; **der Staatsgast wurde auf dem Bonner Flughafen verabschiedet** the official guest was given a farewell at the airport in Bonn; B (*aus dem Dienst*) retire ‹general, civil servant, etc.›; C (*annehmen*) adopt ‹plan, budget›; pass ‹law›. ❷ *refl. V.* **sich [von jmdm.] ~:** say goodbye [to sb.]; (*formell*) take one's leave [of sb.]

**Verabschiedung** *die;* **~, ~en** A leave-taking; B (*aus dem Dienst*) retirement; C (*eines Plans, Etats*) adoption; (*eines Gesetzes*) passing

**verabsolutieren** *tr. V.* make absolute

**verachten** *tr. V.* despise; **ihre Süßspeisen sind nicht zu ~:** her sweets are not to be scoffed at *or* (*coll.*) sneezed at

**Verächter** /fɛɐ̯ˈ|ɛçtɐ/ *der;* **~s, ~, Verächterin** *die;* **~, ~nen** opponent; critic

**verächtlich** /fɛɐ̯ˈ|ɛçtlɪç/ ❶ *Adj.* A (*abschätzig*) contemptuous; B (*verachtenswürdig*) contemptible; despicable; **jmdn./etw. ~ machen** disparage sb./sth.; run sb./sth. down. ❷ *adv.* contemptuously

**Verächtlichkeit** *die;* **~:** contempt; contemptuousness

**Verächtlich·machung** *die;* **~** (*Papierdt.*) disparagement

**Verachtung** *die;* **~:** contempt; **seine ~ aller** *od.* **für alle Konventionen** his contempt for all forms of convention; **jmdn. mit ~ strafen** treat sb. with contempt

**verachtungs·voll** (*geh.*) ⇒ **verächtlich** 1 A, 2

**veralbern** *tr. V.* A (*aufziehen*) **jmdn. ~:** make fun of sb.; **willst du mich ~?** are you trying to make fun of me?; B (*verspotten*) mock

**verallgemeinern** *tr., itr. V.* generalize

**Verallgemeinerung** *die;* **~, ~en** generalization

**veralten** *itr. V.; mit sein* become obsolete; **veraltete Methoden/Wörter** obsolete *or* antiquated methods/obsolete *or* archaic words

**Veranda** /vɛˈranda/ *die;* **~, Veranden** veranda; porch

**veränderbar** *Adj.* changeable; (*Physik*) variable; **nicht mehr ~:** unalterable

**veränderlich** *Adj.* A changeable ‹weather›; variable ‹character, star›; **das Barometer steht auf ~:** the barometer says 'changeable'; B (*veränderbar*) variable

**Veränderliche** *die;* **~n, ~n** (*Math.*) variable

**Veränderlichkeit** *die;* **~, ~en** ⇒ **veränderlich**: changeability; variability

**verändern** ❶ *tr. V.* change; **der Bart verändert ihn stark** the beard makes him look very different. ❷ *refl. V.* A (*anders werden*) change; **sich zu seinem Vorteil/Nachteil ~:** change for the better/worse; (*nur im Aussehen*) look better/worse; B (*die Stellung wechseln*) **sich [beruflich] ~:** change one's job

**Veränderung** *die* change (*Gen.* in); **an etw.** (*Dat.*) **eine ~ vornehmen** change sth.; **berufliche ~:** change of job; **bei uns ist eine ~ eingetreten** our situation has changed

**verängstigen** *tr. V.* frighten; scare; **völlig verängstigt** terrified

**verankern** *tr. V.* fix ‹tent, mast, pole, etc.›; (*mit einem Anker*) anchor; (*fig.*) embody ‹right etc.›

**Verankerung** *die;* **~, ~en** A (*das Befestigen*) fixing; (*mit einem Anker*) anchoring; (*fig.*) embodiment; B (*Halterung*) anchorage; fixture

**veranlagen** *tr. V.* (*Steuerw.*) assess (**mit** at)

**veranlagt** *Adj.* **künstlerisch/praktisch/romantisch ~ sein** have an artistic bent/be practically minded/have a romantic disposition; **ein homosexuell ~er Mann** a man with homosexual tendencies

**Veranlagung** *die;* **~, ~en** A [pre]disposition; **seine homosexuelle/künstlerische/praktische/romantische ~:** his homosexual tendencies *pl.*/artistic bent/practical nature/romantic disposition; **er hat eine ~ zur Fettsucht** he has a tendency towards obesity; B (*Steuerw.*) assessment

**veranlassen** *tr. V.* A cause; induce; **was hat dich zu diesem Schritt/dieser Bemerkung veranlasst?** what caused *or* led you to take this step/make this remark?; **ich fühlte mich veranlasst einzugreifen** I felt obliged to intervene; B (*dafür sorgen, dass etw. getan wird*) **etw. ~:** see to it that sth. is done *or* is carried out; **ich werde alles Weitere/das Nötige ~:** I will take care of *or* see to everything else/I will see [to it] that the necessary steps are taken

**Veranlassung** *die;* **~, ~en** A reason, cause (**zu** for); **äußere ~:** outward reason; B **auf jmds. ~ [hin]** on sb.'s orders

**veranschaulichen** *tr. V.* illustrate

**Veranschaulichung** *die;* **~, ~en** illustration; **zur ~:** as an illustration/as illustrations

**veranschlagen** *tr. V.* estimate (**mit** at); **etw. zu hoch/niedrig ~:** overestimate/underestimate sth.

**Veranschlagung** *die;* **~, ~en** estimate

**veranstalten** *tr. V.* A (*stattfinden lassen*) organize; hold, give ‹party›; hold ‹auction›; do ‹survey›; B (*ugs.: machen, aufführen*) make ‹noise, fuss›

**Veranstalter** *der;* **~s, ~, Veranstalterin** *die;* **~, ~nen** organizer

**Veranstaltung** *die;* **~, ~en** A (*das Veranstalten*) organizing; organization; B (*etw., was veranstaltet wird*) event

**Veranstaltungs·kalender** *der* calendar of events; (*für kürzeren Zeitraum*) diary of events

**verantworten** ❶ *tr. V.* **etw. ~:** take responsibility for sth.; **ich kann das vor Gott/mir selbst/meinem Gewissen nicht ~:** I cannot be responsible for that before God/I cannot justify it to myself/I cannot square that with my conscience. ❷ *refl. V.* **sich für etw. ~:** answer for sth.; **sich vor jmdm. ~:** answer to sb.; **sich vor Gericht für etw. ~:** answer to the courts for sth.; **der Angeklagte hat sich wegen Mordes zu ~:** the accused faces a charge of murder

**verantwortlich** *Adj.* responsible; **der ~e Redakteur** the managing editor; **der für den Einkauf ~e Mitarbeiter** the person responsible for purchasing; **ich fühle mich dafür ~, dass alles klappt** I feel responsible for making sure that everything goes off all right; **für etw. ~ zeichnen** be responsible for *or* in charge of sth.; **jmdm. [gegenüber] ~ sein** be responsible to sb.; **jmdn. für etw. ~ machen** hold sb. responsible for sth.; **die Verantwortlichen** those responsible

**Verantwortlichkeit** *die;* **~, ~en** responsibility

**Verantwortung** *die;* **~, ~en** A responsibility (**für** for); **die Eltern haben** *od.* **tragen die ~ für ihre Kinder** the parents have *or* bear the responsibility for their children; **die ~ für etw. übernehmen** take *or* accept [the] responsibility for sth.; **ich tue es auf deine ~:** you must take responsibility; on your own head be it; **in eigener ~:** on one's own responsibility; off one's own bat (*Brit.*); **jmdn. [für etw.] zur ~ ziehen** call sb. to account [for sth.]; **die Gruppe hat die ~ für den Anschlag übernommen** the group has accepted *or* admitted responsibility for the attack; B (*~sgefühl*) sense of responsibility

**verantwortungs-, Verantwortungs-: ~bewusst, *~bewußt** *Adj.* responsible; **er handelt sehr ~bewusst** he acts in a very responsible manner; **~bewusstsein, *~bewußtsein** *das,* **~gefühl** *das* sense of responsibility; **~los** *Adj.* irresponsible; **~losigkeit** *die;* **~~:** irresponsibility; **~voll** *Adj.* responsible

**veräppeln** /fɛɐ̯ˈ|ɛpl̩n/ *tr. V.* (*ugs.*) **jmdn. ~:** have (*Brit. coll.*) *or* (*Amer. coll.*) put sb. on; **willst du mich ~?** are you having (*Brit. coll.*) *or* (*Amer. coll.*) putting me on?

**verarbeiten** *tr. V.* A use; **~de Industrie** processing industry; **im** *od.* **vom Gehirn verarbeitet** (*fig.*) processed by the brain; **etw. zu etw. ~:** make sth. into sth.; use sth. to make sth.; B (*verdauen*) digest ‹food›; C (*geistig bewältigen*) digest, assimilate ‹film, experience, impressions›; come to terms with ‹disappointment›

**-verarbeitend** *adj.* -processing

**verarbeitet** *Adj.* **gut/schlecht** *usw.* **~:** well/badly *etc.* finished ‹suit, dress, car, etc.›

**Verarbeitung** *die;* **~, ~en** A (*das Verarbeiten*) use; B (*Art der Fertigung*) finish; **Schuhe in erstklassiger ~:** shoes with a first-class finish

**-verarbeitung** *die* -processing

**verargen** *tr. V.* (*geh.*) **jmdm. etw. ~:** hold sth. against sb.

**verärgern** *tr. V.* annoy; **verärgert wandte er sich ab** he turned away in annoyance

**Verärgerung** *die;* **~, ~en** annoyance; **aus ~ über die verspätete Einladung nahm er an dem Empfang nicht teil** he did not attend the reception, because he was annoyed about the late invitation

**verarmen** *itr. V.; mit sein* become poor *or* impoverished; **verarmte Provinzen/verarmter Adel** impoverished provinces/aristocracy

**Verarmung** *die;* **~:** impoverishment

**verarschen** *tr. V.* (*derb*) **jmdn. ~:** take the piss (*coarse*) *or* (*Brit. coll.*) mickey out of sb.; **willst du mich ~?** are you taking the piss (*coarse*) *or* (*Brit. coll.*) mickey?

**verarzten** *tr. V.* (*ugs.*) patch up (*coll.*) ‹person›; fix (*coll.*) ‹wound, injury, etc.›

**verästeln** /fɛɐ̯ˈ|ɛstl̩n/ *refl. V.* (*auch fig.*) branch out

**Veräst[e]lung** *die;* **~, ~en** (*auch fig.*) ramification

**verätzen** *tr. V.* corrode ‹metal etc.›; burn ‹skin, face, etc.›

**Verätzung** *die* corrosion; (*der Haut*) burn

**verausgaben** ❶ *tr. V.* (*Papierdt.*) spend. ❷ *refl. V.* wear oneself out; **sie hat sich total verausgabt** (*finanziell*) she has completely spent out

**veräußerlich** *Adj.* (*bes. Rechtsspr.*) alienable; **nicht ~:** inalienable

**veräußern** *tr. V.* (*bes. Rechtsspr.*) dispose of, sell ‹property›; alienate ‹right›

**Veräußerung** *die* (*bes. Rechtsspr.*) (*von Eigentum*) disposal; sale; (*eines Rechts*) alienation

*old spelling (see note on page 1707)

V

**Verb** /vɛrp/ *das;* **~s, ~en** (*Sprachw.*) verb
**Verba** ⇒ **Verbum**
**verbạcken** *unr. tr. V.* use ‹flour, butter, sugar, etc.› [in baking]
**verbal** /vɛr'ba:l/ *Adj.* ❶ (*auch Sprachw.*) verbal. ❷ *adv.* verbally
**Verbal·injurie** *die;* **~** (*auch Rechtsw.*) verbal injury
**verbalisi̱eren** *tr. V.* (*geh.*) verbalize
**verballhornen** /fɛɐ̯'balhɔrnən/ *tr. V.* corrupt ‹word, phrase›
**Verbạllhornung** *die;* **~, ~en** misuse; corruption
**Verba̱l-: ~phrase** *die* (*Sprachw.*) verbal phrase; **~substantiv** *das* (*Sprachw.*) verbal noun
**Verbạnd** *der* Ⓐ (*Binde*) bandage; dressing; **einen ~ anlegen** apply a dressing; Ⓑ (*von Vereinen, Clubs o. Ä.*) association; Ⓒ (*Milit.: vereinigte Truppenteile*) unit; Ⓓ (*Milit.: Fahrzeug~, Flugzeug~*) formation; Ⓔ (*Gruppe*) group; unit
**Verbạnd-: ~kasten** *der* first-aid box; **~material** *das* dressing materials *pl.*; **~päckchen** *das* packet of dressings
**Verbands·kasten** *usw.* ⇒ **Verbandkasten** *usw.*
**Verbạnd[s]·stoff** *der* dressing [material]
**Verbạnd·zeug** *das* first-aid things *pl.*
**verbạnnen** *tr. V.* (*auch fig.*) banish
**Verbạnnte** *der/die; adj. Dekl.* exile
**Verbạnnung** *die;* **~, ~en** banishment; exile; **in die ~ gehen** go into exile
**Verbạnnungs·ort** *der* place of exile
**verbarrikadi̱eren** ❶ *tr. V.* barricade. ❷ *refl. V.* barricade oneself
**verba̱uen** *tr. V.* Ⓐ (*versperren*) obstruct; block; **jmdm./sich die Zukunft ~** (*fig.*) spoil sb.'s/one's prospects for the future; Ⓑ (*abwertend: unschön bebauen*) spoil; Ⓒ (*zum Bauen verwenden*) use; **sein ganzes Geld ~** (*fig.*) use [up] one's entire money for *or* on building
**verba̱uern** *itr. V.; mit sein* become a country bumpkin
**verbeamten** *tr. V.* make ‹person› a civil servant; (*fig. abwertend*) [over-]bureaucratize
**verbei̱ßen** ❶ *unr. tr. V.* Ⓐ (*unterdrücken*) suppress ‹pain, laughter, anger, feelings›; hold back ‹tears etc.›; Ⓑ (*bes. Jägerspr.: beschädigen*) bite; chew. ❷ *refl. V.* **sich in etw. ~:** bite into sth.; ‹dog› sink its teeth into sth.; (*fig.*) get stuck into sth. (*coll.*)
**verbẹllen** *tr. V.* (*Jägerspr.*) **der Jagdhund verbellte den Bock** the hunting dog barked to show where the buck was
**verbẹrgen** *unr. tr. V.* Ⓐ (*verstecken, auch fig.*) hide; conceal; **jmdn. vor der Polizei verborgen halten** harbour sb.; **sich ~:** hide; **sein Gesicht in den Händen ~:** bury *or* hide one's face in one's hands; Ⓑ (*verheimlichen*) hide; **jmdm. etw. ~, etw. vor jmdm. ~:** keep sth. from sb.; **ich will dir nicht ~, dass ...** I want you to know that ...; I want to make it clear that ...
**verbẹssern** ❶ *tr. V.* Ⓐ improve ‹machine, method, quality›; improve [up]on, better ‹achievement›; beat ‹record›; reform ‹schooling, world›; Ⓑ (*korrigieren*) correct. ❷ *refl. V.* Ⓐ improve; **er hat sich im Skilauf stark verbessert** his skiing has improved a great deal; Ⓑ ([*beruflich*] *aufsteigen*) better oneself
**Verbẹsserung** *die* Ⓐ improvement; **eine ~ der Lage** an improvement in the situation; Ⓑ (*Korrektur*) correction
**verbẹsserungs·fähig** *Adj.* capable of improvement *postpos.*; **es ist noch ~:** it could be improved [on]
**Verbẹsserungs·vorschlag** *der* suggestion for improvement
**verbe̱ugen** *refl. V.* bow (**vor** + *Dat.* to)
**Verbe̱ugung** *die;* **~, ~en** bow; **eine ~ vor jmdm. machen** bow to sb.
**verbe̱ulen** *tr. V.* dent
**verbi̱egen** ❶ *unr. tr. V.* bend. ❷ *unr. refl. V.* bend; buckle; **eine verbogene Wirbelsäule** a curved spine
**Verbi̱egung** *die* bending; buckling; (*der Wirbelsäule*) curvature
**verbiestern** /fɛɐ̯'bi:stɐn/ *tr. V.* (*bes. nordd.: verwirren*) confuse; bewilder
**verbi̱estert** *Adj.* (*ugs.*) grumpy
**verbi̱eten** ❶ *unr. tr. V.* Ⓐ forbid; **jmdm. etw. ~:** forbid sb. sth.; **du hast mir gar nichts zu ~:** you have no right to forbid me [to do] anything; **sie hat ihm das Haus verboten** she forbade him to enter the house; **der Arzt hat mir das Rauchen verboten** the doctor forbade me to smoke; **„Betreten des Rasens/Rauchen verboten!"** 'keep off the grass'/'no smoking'; **das verbietet mir mein Ehrgefühl** (*fig.*) my sense of honour prevents me from doing that; **das verbietet mir mein Geldbeutel** (*fig. scherzh.*) my resources don't run to that; Ⓑ (*für unzulässig erklären*) ban; **so viel Ignoranz müsste verboten werden** (*scherzh.*) such ignorance ought not to be allowed (*joc.*). ❷ *unr. refl. V.* **sich [von selbst] ~:** be out of the question
**verbi̱lden** *tr. V.* bring up wrongly, miseducate ‹person›; **verbildeter Geschmack** (*abwertend*) misguided taste
**verbi̱lligen** ❶ *tr. V.* bring down *or* reduce the cost of; bring down *or* reduce the price of, reduce ‹goods›; **verbilligte Butter/Waren** butter at a reduced price/reduced goods; **verbilligter Eintritt** reduced admission. ❷ *refl. V.* become *or* get cheaper; ‹goods› come down in price, become *or* get cheaper
**Verbi̱lligung** *die* (*von Kosten*) reduction; **eine ~ der Einfuhren** a reduction in the cost of imports; **zur ~ der Einfuhren** to reduce the cost of imports
**verbimsen** /fɛɐ̯'bɪmzn̩/ *tr. V.* (*ugs.*) bash; hit
**verbi̱nden** ❶ *unr. tr. V.* Ⓐ (*bandagieren*) bandage; dress; **jmdm./sich den Fuß ~:** bandage *or* dress sb.'s/one's foot; **jmdn./sich ~:** dress sb.'s/one's wounds; Ⓑ (*zubinden*) bind; **jmdm. die Augen ~:** blindfold sb.; **mit verbundenen Augen** blindfold[ed]; Ⓒ (*zusammenfügen*) join ‹wires, lengths of wood, etc.›; join up ‹dots›; Ⓓ (*zusammenhalten*) hold ‹parts› together; Ⓔ (*in Beziehung bringen*) connect (**durch** by); link ‹towns, lakes, etc.› (**durch** by); **ein paar ~de Worte sprechen** (*fig.*) say a few words as a link; Ⓕ (*verknüpfen*) combine ‹abilities, qualities, etc.›; **die damit verbundenen Anstrengungen/Kosten** *usw.* the effort/cost *etc.* involved; Ⓖ *auch itr.* (*telefonisch*) **jmdn. [mit jmdm.] ~:** put sb. through [to sb.]; **Moment, ich verbinde** one moment, I'll put you through; **falsch verbunden sein** have got the wrong number; Ⓗ *auch itr.* (*in Bezug auf menschliche Beziehungen*) **er war ihr freundschaftlich verbunden** he was bound to her by ties of friendship; **uns verbindet nichts mehr** nothing holds us together any longer; **gemeinsame Erlebnisse ~:** shared experiences draw people together; Ⓘ (*assoziieren*) associate (**mit** with); Ⓙ (*geh. veralt.*) **jmdm. [für etw.] verbunden sein** be obliged to sb. [for sth.]. ❷ *unr. refl. V.* Ⓐ (*zusammenkommen*) (*auch Chemie*) combine (**mit** with); Ⓑ (*in Zusammenhang stehen*) be connected *or* associated (**mit** with); Ⓒ (*sich zusammentun*) join [together]; join forces; **sich zu einer Koalition ~:** join together *or* join forces to form a coalition *or* in a coalition; Ⓓ (*in Gedanken*) be associated (**mit** with); **mit dieser Melodie sind für mich schöne Erinnerungen verbunden** this tune has happy memories for me
**verbi̱ndlich** ❶ *Adj.* Ⓐ (*freundlich*) friendly; (*entgegenkommend*) forthcoming; **eine ~e Verkäuferin** an obliging sales assistant; **~sten Dank!** (*geh.*) a thousand thanks; Ⓑ (*bindend*) obligatory; compulsory; binding ‹agreement, decision, etc.›. ❷ *adv.* Ⓐ (*freundlich*) in a friendly manner; (*entgegenkommend*) in a forthcoming manner; Ⓑ **~ zusagen** definitely agree; **jmdm. etw. ~ zusagen** make sb. a firm offer of sth.
**Verbi̱ndlichkeit** *die;* **~, ~en** Ⓐ (*Freundlichkeit*) friendliness; (*Entgegenkommen*) forthcomingness; Ⓑ (*verpflichtender Charakter*) obligatory *or* compulsory nature; **rechtlich [gesehen] keine ~ haben** have no binding force in law; Ⓒ (*freundliche Äußerung, Handlung*) friendly remark/act; (*entgegenkommende Äußerung, Handlung*) forthcoming comment/gesture; **ein paar ~en sagen** say a few friendly words; Ⓓ (*Pflicht*) obligation; commitment; Ⓔ **~en** (*Kaufmannsspr.: Schulden*) liabilities (**gegen** to)
**Verbi̱ndung** *die* Ⓐ (*das Verknüpfen*) linking; Ⓑ (*Zusammenhalt*) join; connection; Ⓒ (*verknüpfende Strecke*) link; **die kürzeste ~ zwischen zwei Punkten** the shortest line between two points; Ⓓ (*Anschluss durch Telefon, Funk*) connection; **keine ~ mit jmdm./einem Ort bekommen** not be able to get through to sb./a place; **unsere ~ wurde unterbrochen** we were cut off; Ⓔ (*Verkehrs~*) connection (**nach** to); **die ~ zur Außenwelt** connections *pl.* with the outside world; Ⓕ (*Kombination*) combination; **in ~ mit etw.** in conjunction with sth.; Ⓖ (*Bündnis*) association; **eheliche ~** (*geh.*) marriage; **eine ~ mit jmdm. eingehen** enter into association with sb.; (*erotisch*) begin a liaison with sb.; Ⓗ (*Kontakt*) contact; **sich mit jmdm. in ~ setzen, ~ mit jmdm. aufnehmen** get in touch *or* contact with sb.; contact sb.; **in ~ bleiben** keep in touch; **die ~ mit jmdm./etw. nicht abreißen lassen** not lose touch *or* contact with sb./sth.; **seine ~en spielen lassen** pull a few strings (*coll.*); Ⓘ (*Zusammenhang*) connection; **jmdn. mit etw. in ~ bringen** connect sb. with sth.; Ⓙ (*Studenten~*) society; (*für Männer*) fraternity (*Amer.*); (*für Frauen*) sorority (*Amer.*); **eine schlagende ~:** a duelling society *or* (*Amer.*) fraternity; Ⓚ (*das Zusammenfügen*) joining; Ⓛ (*das Zusammengefügtwerden*) bonding; Ⓜ (*bes. Chemie*) (*Stoff*) compound; (*Prozess*) combination
**Verbi̱ndungs-: ~frau** *die* intermediary; (*Agent*) contact [woman] (**zu** with); **~linie** *die* Ⓐ (*verbindende Linie*) connecting line; Ⓑ (*Milit.*) communication line; line of communication; **~mann** *der; Pl.* **~männer** *od.* **~leute** intermediary; (*Agent*) contact [man] (**zu** with); **~offizier** *der* (*Milit.*) liaison officer; **~straße** *die* link road; **~stück** *das* connecting piece; **~student** *der,* **~studentin** *die* member of a students' society; ⇒ *auch* **Verbindung** J; **~tür** *die* connecting door
**Verbi̱ss, *Verbi̱ß** *der* (*Jägerspr.*) damage caused by browsing animals
**verbi̱ssen** ❶ *2. Part. v.* **verbeißen.** ❷ *Adj.* Ⓐ (*hartnäckig*) dogged; doggedly determined; Ⓑ (*verkrampft*) grim. ❸ *adv.* Ⓐ (*hartnäckig*) doggedly; with dogged determination; Ⓑ (*verkrampft*) grimly; Ⓒ (*ugs.: engherzig*) **etw. nicht so ~ sehen** not take sth. so seriously
**Verbi̱ssenheit** *die;* **~:** doggedness; dogged determination
**verbi̱tten** *unr. refl. V.* **sich** (*Dat.*) **etw. ~:** refuse to tolerate sth.; **ich verbitte mir diesen Ton** I will not be spoken to in that tone of voice; **das möchte ich mir verbeten haben** I will not have it
**verbi̱ttern** *tr. V.* embitter; make bitter; **verbittert** embittered; bitter
**Verbi̱tterung** *die;* **~, ~en** bitterness; embitterment
**verblạssen** *itr. V.; mit sein* Ⓐ (*auch fig. geh.*) fade; Ⓑ (*die Leuchtkraft verlieren*) ‹star etc.› fade, pale; ‹sky› grow dim; (*fig.*) pale; ‹memory› fade
**verblä̱uen** *tr. V.* (*ugs.*) bash *or* beat up; do over (*sl.*)
**Verble̱ib** *der;* **~[e]s** (*geh.*) Ⓐ (*Ort*) whereabouts *pl.*; Ⓑ (*das Verbleiben*) staying; **ein weiterer ~:** a longer stay
**verble̱iben** *unr. itr. V.; mit sein* Ⓐ (*sich einigen*) **wie seid ihr denn nun verblieben?** what did you arrange?; **wir sind so verblieben, dass er sich bei mir meldet** we left it that he would contact me; Ⓑ (*geh.: bleiben*) remain; stay; **niemand wusste, wo Sie**

**verblieben waren** nobody knew where you were; **im Amt ~:** remain *or* continue in office; [C] *(im Briefschluss)* remain; **... verbleibe ich Ihr ...** ... I remain, Yours truly, ...; **ich verbleibe mit freundlichen Grüßen Ihr ...** I remain, Yours sincerely, ...; [D] *(übrig bleiben)* remain; **etw. verbleibt jmdm.** sb. has sth. left

**verbleichen** *unr. od. regelm. itr. V.; mit sein* [A] *(auch fig.)* *(blass werden)* fade; [B] *(allmählich erlöschen)* ‹moon› grow pale

**verbleien** /fɛɐ̯ˈblaiən/ *tr. V.* *(Technik)* lead ‹petrol›

**verblenden** *tr. V.* [A] blind; **ein verblendeter Revolutionär** a blind revolutionary; [B] *(Archit.: verkleiden)* face ‹wall, façade, etc.›

**Verblendung** *die; ~, ~en* [A] blindness; [B] *(bes. Archit.: Verkleidung)* facing

***verbleuen** ⇒ **verbläuen**

**Verblichene** /fɛɐ̯ˈblɪçənə/ *der/die; adj. Dekl.* *(geh.)* deceased; **unser teurer ~r** our dear departed brother/leader/friend *etc.*

**verblöden** *itr. V.; mit sein* [A] *(veralt.: schwachsinnig werden)* become feeble-minded; [B] *(ugs.: stumpfsinnig werden)* become a zombie *(coll.)*

**verblüffen** /fɛɐ̯ˈblʏfn̩/ *tr. (auch itr.) V.* astonish; amaze; astound; *(verwirren)* baffle; **seine Offenheit verblüfft** his openness is astonishing; **ich war über seine Antwort verblüfft** I was taken aback by his answer

**verblüffend** **1** *Adj.* astonishing; amazing; astounding. **2** *adv.* astonishingly; amazingly; astoundingly

**Verblüffung** *die; ~, ~en* astonishment; amazement

**verblühen** *itr. V.; mit sein (auch fig.)* fade; **sie war schon verblüht** *(geh.)* her beauty had already faded

**verblümt** /fɛɐ̯ˈbly:mt/ **1** *Adj.* oblique. **2** *adv.* **sich ~ ausdrücken** express oneself in a roundabout *or* an oblique way

**verbluten** *itr. (auch refl.) V.; mit sein* bleed to death

**verbocken** *tr. V.* *(ugs.)* botch; bungle; make a botch-up of

**verbohren** *refl. V.* *(ugs.)* become obsessed **(in** + *Akk.* with)

**verbohrt** *Adj.* *(abwertend)* pigheaded; stubborn; obstinate; *(unbeugsam)* inflexible

**Verbohrtheit** *die; ~* *(abwertend)* pigheadedness; stubbornness; obstinacy; *(Unbeugsamkeit)* inflexibility

**verborgen**[1] *tr. V.* lend out

**verborgen**[2] **1** *2. Part. v.* **verbergen.** **2** *Adj.* [A] *(abgelegen)* secluded; [B] *(nicht sichtbar)* hidden; **es wird ihm nicht ~ bleiben** he shall hear of it; *(nicht entgehen)* it will not escape his notice; **im Verborgenen** out of the public eye; **im Verborgenen blühen** flourish undetected

**Verborgenheit** *die; ~* *(Abgelegenheit)* seclusion

**Verbot** *das; ~[e]s, ~e* ban *(Gen.,* **von** on); **er hat gegen mein ausdrückliches ~ geraucht** he smoked although I had expressly forbidden him to do so; **trotz ärztlichen ~s** against doctor's orders

**Verbots-: ~schild** *das* [A] sign *(prohibiting sth.)*; [B] *(Verkehrsw.)* prohibitive sign; **~tafel** *die* [large] sign *(prohibiting sth.)*

**verbrämen** /fɛɐ̯ˈbrɛ:mən/ *tr. V.* [A] *(einfassen)* trim **(mit** with); [B] *(verschleiern)* dress up *(fig.)*; **wissenschaftlich verbrämter Unsinn** nonsense dressed up as scientific fact

**verbraten** *unr. tr. V.* *(salopp)* blow *(coll.)* ‹money› **(für** on)

**Verbrauch** *der; ~[e]s* [A] consumption; **die Seife ist sparsam im ~:** the soap is economical to use; **zum alsbaldigen ~ bestimmt** for immediate consumption; [B] *(verbrauchte Menge)* consumption **(von, an** + *Dat.* of)

**verbrauchen** **1** *tr. V.* [A] *(verwenden)* use; consume ‹food, drink›; use up ‹provisions›; spend ‹money›; consume, use ‹fuel›; *(fig.)* use up ‹strength, energy›; **das Auto verbraucht 10 Liter [auf 100 Kilometer]** the car does 10 kilometres to the litre; [B] *(verschleißen)* wear out ‹clothing, shoes, etc.›; **die Luft in den Räumen ist verbraucht** the air in the rooms is stale. **2** *refl. V.* *(sich abarbeiten)* wear oneself out; **verbraucht aussehen** look worn out *or* exhausted

**Verbraucher** *der; ~s, ~:* consumer

**verbraucher-: ~feindlich** *Adj.* not in the interests of consumers *postpos.*; **~freundlich** *Adj.* favourable to consumers *postpos.*

**Verbraucherin** *die; ~, ~nen* consumer

**Verbraucher-: ~preis** *der* consumer price; **~schutz** *der* consumer protection

**Verbrauchs·gut** *das* consumer item; **Verbrauchsgüter** consumer goods

**Verbrauch[s]·steuer** *die* *(Steuerw.)* excise [tax]

**verbrechen** *unr. tr. V.* *(scherzh.)* **ich habe nichts verbrochen!** I haven't been up to *or* haven't done anything!; **was hast du verbrochen?** what have you been up to *or* been doing?; **wer hat denn dieses Gedicht verbrochen?** who's responsible for *or* who's the perpetrator of this poem?

**Verbrechen** *das; ~s, ~* *(auch Untat)* crime **(an** + *Dat.*, **gegen** against)

**Verbrechens·bekämpfung** *die* combating of crime; combating crime *no art.*; **für die aktive ~:** for actively combating crime

**Verbrecher** *der; ~s, ~:* criminal; **du kleiner ~!** *(scherzh.)* you little rascal!

**Verbrecher-: ~album** *das* *(veralt.)* ⇒ **~kartei**; **~bande** *die* gang *or* band of criminals

**Verbrecherin** *die; ~, ~nen* criminal

**verbrecherisch** *Adj.* criminal

**Verbrecher-: ~jagd** *die* *(ugs.)* chase after a/the criminal/criminals; **~kartei** *die* criminal records *pl.*; **~syndikat** *das* criminal syndicate

**Verbrechertum** *das; ~s* criminality

**verbreiten** **1** *tr. V.* [A] *(bekannt machen)* spread ‹rumour, lies, etc.›; **er verbreitete, dass ...** he spread it about that ...; **eine Nachricht über den Rundfunk ~:** broadcast an item of news on the radio; [B] *(weitertragen)* spread ‹disease, illness, etc.›; disperse ‹seeds, spores, etc.›; [C] *(erwecken)* radiate ‹optimism, happiness, calm, etc.›; spread ‹fear›; **ihre Gewalttaten verbreiteten überall Entsetzen** their deeds of violence horrified everyone. **2** *refl. V.* [A] *(bekannt werden)* ‹rumour› spread; [B] *(sich ausbreiten)* ‹smell, illness, religion, etc.› spread; [C] *(häufig abwertend: sich äußern)* go on **(über** + *Akk.* about)

**verbreitern** **1** *tr. V.* widen; *(fig.)* broaden ‹basis›. **2** *refl. V.* widen out; get wider

**Verbreiterung** *die; ~, ~en* [A] widening; [B] *(Stelle)* widened section

**Verbreitung** *die; ~, ~en* [A] ⇒ **verbreiten** 1 A, B, C: spreading; broadcasting; dispersal; radiation; **nicht für allgemeine ~ bestimmt** not [intended] for general circulation; [B] *(Ausbreitung)* spread

**Verbreitungs·gebiet** *das* area of distribution; *(einer Tierart)* range

**verbrennen** **1** *unr. itr. V.; mit sein* [A] burn; ‹person› burn to death; **die Dokumente sind verbrannt** the documents were destroyed by fire; **es riecht verbrannt** *(ugs.)* there's a smell of burning; [B] *(verkohlen)* burn; **der Kuchen ist verbrannt** the cake got burnt; [C] *(ausdorren)* scorch; [D] *(Chemie: sich umwandeln)* be converted **(zu** into). **2** *tr. V.* [A] *(ins Feuer geben)* burn; burn, incinerate ‹rubbish›; cremate ‹dead person›; [B] ▶ 474 *(verletzen)* burn; **sich** *(Dat.)* **an der heißen Suppe die Zunge ~:** burn *or* scald one's tongue on the hot soup; **sich** *(Dat.)* **den Mund** *od.* *(derb)* **das Maul** *od.* *(salopp)* **die Schnauze ~** *(fig.)* say too much; ⇒ *auch* **Finger** B; [C] *(ugs.: verbrauchen)* use ‹gas, electricity, etc.›; [D] *(Chemie: umwandeln)* convert

**Verbrennung** *die; ~, ~en* [A] ⇒ **verbrennen** 2 A: burning; incineration; cremation; [B] *(Kfz-W.)* combustion; [C] ▶ 474 *(Wunde)* burn

**Verbrennungs·motor** *der* internal-combustion engine

**verbriefen** *tr. V.* attest

**verbringen** *unr. tr. V.* [A] spend ‹time, holiday, weekend, year, etc.›; [B] *(Papierdt.: bringen)* take

**verbrüdern** *refl. V.* avow friendship and brotherhood; ‹troops› fraternize **(mit** with); *(Politik)* ally oneself/itself

**Verbrüderung** *die; ~, ~en* avowal of friendship and brotherhood; *(von Truppen)* fraternization; *(Politik)* alliance

**verbrühen** *tr. V.* ▶ 474 scald; **sich** *(Dat.)* **den Arm ~:** scald one's arm; **sich ~:** scald oneself

**Verbrühung** *die; ~, ~en* [A] *(das Verbrühen)* scalding; [B] *(Wunde)* scald

**verbuchen** *tr. V.* *(Kaufmannsspr., Finanzw.)* enter; *(fig.)* notch up ‹success, score, etc.›; **etw. auf einem Konto/im Haben ~:** credit sth. to an account/enter sth. on the credit side

**verbuddeln** *tr. V.* *(ugs.)* bury

**Verbum** /ˈvɛrbʊm/ *das; ~s,* **Verben** *od.* *(Sprachw. veralt.)* **Verba** verb

**verbummeln** *tr. V.* *(ugs., oft abwertend)* [A] *(verbringen)* waste, fritter away ‹time, day, afternoon, etc.›; **sie wollten einmal einen ganzen Tag ~:** they wanted to spend a whole day lazing around doing nothing; [B] *(vergessen)* forget [all] about; clean forget; *(verlieren)* lose; *(verlegen)* mislay

**Verbund** *der; ~[e]s, ~e* [A] *(Wirtsch.)* association; **im ~ arbeiten** cooperate; [B] *(Technik)* composite

**Verbund·bau·weise** *die* composite construction

**verbünden** /fɛɐ̯ˈbʏndn̩/ *refl. V.* form an alliance

**Verbundenheit** *die; ~:* closeness **(mit** to); *(mit einem Ort, einer Tradition)* attachment **(mit** to); **aus alter ~:** for the sake of old ties/attachments; **in herzlicher ~:** with deepest sympathy

**verbündet** *Adj.* **[miteinander] ~:** in alliance *postpos.*

**Verbündete** *der/die; adj. Dekl.* ally

**Verbund-: ~glas** *das* *(Technik)* laminated glass; **~netz** *das* grid [system]; **~stein** *der* interlocking paving stone

**verbürgen** **1** *refl. V.* *(bürgen)* vouch **(für** for); **sich für die Kosten ~:** accept liability for the costs. **2** *tr. V.* [A] *(garantieren)* guarantee; **verbürgte Rechte** established rights; [B] *nur im Perf., Plusq. u. im 2. Part. gebr.* *(authentisieren)* verify; authenticate

**verbürgerlichen** **1** *itr. V.; mit sein* become bourgeois. **2** *tr. V.* make bourgeois

**verbüßen** *tr. V.* serve ‹sentence›

**Verbüßung** *die; ~:* serving

**verchromen** *tr. V.* chromium-plate

**Verdacht** /fɛɐ̯ˈdaxt/ *der; ~[e]s, ~e od.* **Verdächte** /fɛɐ̯ˈdɛçtə/ suspicion; **mein ~ hat sich bestätigt/war begründet** my suspicion was confirmed/was well founded; **der ~ der Polizei fiel auf/richtete sich gegen ...** the police suspected ...; **ein ~ stieg in mir auf** I began to suspect something *or* to be suspicious; **er wurde wegen ~s der Steuerhinterziehung verhaftet** he was arrested on suspicion of tax evasion; **~ schöpfen** become suspicious; **jmdn. auf [einen] bloßen ~ hin verhaften lassen** have sb. arrested purely on suspicion; **wen hast du in ~?** who do you suspect?; **ich geriet in [den] ~, das Geld gestohlen zu haben** I was suspected of having stolen the money; **er ist über jeden ~ erhaben** he is above suspicion; **bei dem Patienten besteht ~ auf Meningitis** the patient is suspected of having meningitis; **etw. auf ~ tun** *(ugs.)* do sth. just in case

**verdächtig** /fɛɐ̯ˈdɛçtɪç/ **1** *Adj.* suspicious; **sich ~ machen** arouse suspicion; **er ist dringend der Tat ~:** he is strongly suspected of being the perpetrator. **2** *adv.* suspiciously

**-verdächtig** [A] *(unter Verdacht stehend)* suspected of ...; **mord~:** suspected of murder; [B] *(erwarten lassend)* expected to ...; **ein hit~es Lied** a song expected to be a hit; **der**

*old spelling (see note on page 1707)

**medaillen~e Sportler** the sportsman expected to win a/the medal
**Verdächtige** *der/die; adj. Dekl.* suspect
**verdächtigen** *tr. V.* suspect (*Gen.* of)
**Verdächtigte** *der/die; adj. Dekl.* suspect
**Verdächtigung** *die; ~, ~en* suspicion
**Verdachts·moment** *das* incriminating factor
**verdammen** *tr. V.* **A** (*verwerfen*) condemn; (*Rel.*) damn ‹sinner›; **[Gott] verdamm mich!** damn it (*coll.*); **B** (*zwingen*) condemn (**zu** to); **das ist zum Scheitern verdammt** it is doomed to failure
**verdämmern** (*geh.*) **1** *itr. V.; mit sein* fade. **2** *tr. V.* drowse away
**Verdammnis** *die; ~* (*christl. Theol.*) damnation *no art.*
**verdammt** **1** *Adj.* **A** (*salopp abwertend*) bloody (*Brit. sl.*); damned (*coll.*); **~ [noch mal** *od.* **noch eins]!** damn [it all] (*coll.*); bloody hell (*Brit. sl.*); **~ und zugenäht!** damn and blast [it]! (*coll.*); **so ein ~er Mist!** bloody hell (*Brit. sl.*); **B** (*ugs.: sehr groß*) **einen ~en Hunger haben** be damned hungry (*coll.*); **[ein] ~es Glück haben** be damn[ed] lucky (*coll.*). **2** *adv.* (*ugs.: sehr*) damn[ed] (*coll.*) ‹cold, heavy, beautiful, etc.›; **ich musste mich ~ beherrschen** I had to keep a bloody good grip on myself (*Brit. coll.*)
**Verdammte** *der/die; adj. Dekl.* damned person/man/woman; **die ~n** the damned
**Verdammung** *die; ~, ~en* condemnation; damnation
**verdammungs·würdig** (*geh.*) **1** *Adj.* damnable. **2** *adv.* damnably
**verdampfen** **1** *itr. V.; mit sein* evaporate; vaporize; (*fig.*) ‹anger› abate; ‹person› make oneself scarce (*coll.*). **2** *tr. V.* evaporate; vaporize
**verdanken** *tr. V.* **jmdm./einer Sache etw. ~:** owe sth. to sb./sth.; **ich verdanke meiner Frau wertvolle Anregungen** I have to thank my wife for valuable suggestions; **dass Sie bei uns sind, ~ wir ...** it is thanks *or* due to ... that you are here with us
**verdarb** /fɛɐ̯'darp/ *1. u. 3. Pers. Sg. Prät. v.* **verderben**
**verdaten** *tr. V.* (*DV*) convert into data; (*erfassen*) store away on computer
**verdattert** /fɛɐ̯'datɐt/ *Adj.* (*ugs.*) (*überrascht*) flabbergasted; (*verwirrt*) dazed; stunned; **~ dastehen** stand there flabbergasted/in a daze
**verdauen** /fɛɐ̯'dauən/ **1** *tr. V.* (*auch fig.*) digest; (*fig.*) get over ‹bad experience, shock, blow of fate›; (*Boxerjargon*) take ‹blow›. **2** *itr. V.* digest [one's food]
**verdaulich** /fɛɐ̯'daulɪç/ *Adj.* digestible
**Verdaulichkeit** *die; ~:* digestibility
**Verdauung** *die; ~:* digestion
**Verdauungs-: ~beschwerden** *Pl.* digestive trouble *sing.*; **~spaziergang** *der* (*ugs.*) after-dinner walk; **~störung** *die* poor digestion *no pl.*; **~trakt** *der* ▶ 471 (*Anat.*) digestive *or* alimentary tract
**Verdeck** *das; ~[e]s, ~e* top; hood (*Brit.*); (*bei Kinderwagen*) hood; **mit offenem ~ fahren** drive with the top *or* hood down
**verdecken** *tr. V.* **A** (*nicht sichtbar sein lassen*) hide; cover; **jmdm. die Sicht ~:** block sb.'s view; **B** (*verbergen*) cover; conceal; (*fig.*) conceal ‹intentions etc.›
**verdenken** *unr. tr. V.* **jmdm. etw. nicht ~ [können]** not [be able to] hold sth. against sb.; **kann man ihnen ~, dass sie ... hassen?** can one blame them for hating ...?
**Verderb** *der; ~s* **A** (*von Lebensmitteln*) spoilage; **B** ⇒ **Gedeih**
**verderben** **1** *unr. itr. V.; mit sein* ‹food, harvest› go bad *or* off, spoil; **verdorbene Lebensmittel** food which has gone bad *or* off. **2** *unr. tr. V.* **A** (*unbrauchbar machen*) spoil; (*stärker*) ruin; **daran ist nichts mehr zu ~:** it's in a pretty sorry state anyway; **B** (*zunichte machen*) ruin; spoil ‹appetite, enjoyment, fun, etc.›; **jmdm. die gute Laune ~:** spoil sb.'s good mood; **jmdm. den Abend ~:** ruin sb.'s evening; **C** (*geh.: negativ beeinflussen*) corrupt; deprave; **er will es mit niemandem ~:** he tries to please everybody; he likes to keep in with everybody. **3** *unr. refl. V.* **sich** (*Dat.*) **den Magen/die Augen ~:** give oneself an upset stomach/ruin one's eyesight
**Verderben** *das; ~s* undoing; ruin; (*Theol.*) destruction; **sie sind ins/in ihr ~ gerannt** they rushed headlong towards ruin
**verderben·bringend** *Adj.* disastrous ‹policy›; deadly ‹weapon, disease, etc.›
**Verderber** *der; ~s, ~,* **Verderberin** *die; ~, ~nen* destroyer; **ein ~ der Jugend** a corrupter of youth
**verderblich** *Adj.* **A** perishable ‹food›; **leicht ~:** highly perishable; **B** (*unheilvoll*) pernicious; (*moralisch schädlich*) corrupting; pernicious ‹influence, effect, etc.›
**Verderblichkeit** *die; ~* ⇒ **verderblich**: perishableness; perniciousness; corrupting effect
**verderbt** *Adj.* **A** (*geh. veralt.: verdorben*) corrupt; depraved; **B** (*Literaturw.*) illegible
**Verderbtheit** *die; ~* (*geh. veralt.: Verdorbenheit*) corruptness; depravity
**verdeutlichen** *tr. V.* **etw. ~:** make sth. clear; (*erklären*) explain sth.; **etw. näher ~:** clarify sth. further
**verdeutschen** *tr. V.* **A** (*veralt.: übersetzen*) translate into German; (*eindeutschen*) Germanize ‹name›; **B** (*ugs.: erläutern*) put ‹facts etc.› more plainly; translate ‹instruction, officialese, etc.› into everyday *or* ordinary language
**verdichten** **1** *refl. V.* ‹fog, smoke› thicken, become thicker; (*fig.*) ‹suspicion, rumour› grow; ‹feeling› intensify. **2** *tr. V.* **A** (*Physik, Technik*) compress; (*fig.*) condense ‹events etc.› (**zu** into); **B** (*ausbauen*) increase the density of ‹road network, public transport›
**verdicken** **1** *refl. V.* ‹hard skin› thicken, become thicker; (*anschwellen*) ‹finger, jaw, etc.› swell. **2** *tr. V.* thicken ‹sauce›; (*gelieren lassen*) cause ‹fruit juice etc.› to set
**Verdickung** *die; ~, ~en* **A** thickening; (*Schwellung*) swelling; **B** (*verdickte Stelle*) (*einer Arterie*) thickened section; (*Schwellung*) swelling
**verdienen** **1** *tr. V.* **A** (*in Form von Geld*) earn; **sauer/ehrlich verdientes Geld** hard-/honestly-earned money; **B** (*wert sein*) deserve; **er verdient kein Vertrauen** he doesn't deserve to be trusted; **er hat es nicht besser/nicht anders verdient** he didn't deserve any better/anything else; **womit habe ich das verdient?** what have I done to deserve that?; **er hat die verdiente Strafe bekommen** he got the punishment he deserved. **2** *itr. V.* **beide Eheleute ~:** husband and wife are both wage earners *or* are both earning; **gut ~:** have a good income
**Verdiener** *der; ~s, ~,* **Verdienerin** *die; ~, ~nen* wage earner; **die Mutter ist die Verdienerin:** the mother is the breadwinner
**Verdienst**[1] *der* income; earnings *pl.*
**Verdienst**[2] *das; ~[e]s, ~e* merit; **sich** (*Dat.*) **etw. als** *od.* **zum ~ anrechnen** take the credit for sth.; **er hat sich** (*Dat.*) **große ~e um die Stadt erworben** he made a great contribution to the town
**Verdienst-: ~aus·fall** *der* loss of earnings; **~kreuz** *das: national decoration awarded for service to the community;* **~orden** *der* order of merit
**verdienst·voll** **1** *Adj.* **A** (*lobenswert*) commendable; **B** (*verdient*) ‹person› of outstanding merit. **2** *adv.* (*lobenswert*) commendably
**verdient** **1** *Adj.* **A** ‹person› of outstanding merit; **sich um etw. ~ machen** render outstanding services to sth.; **B** (*gerecht, zustehend*) well-deserved. **2** *adv.* deservedly
**verdientermaßen** *Adv.* deservedly
**Verdikt** /vɛr'dɪkt/ *das; ~[e]s, ~e* (*geh.*) verdict
**verdingen** *unr. od. regelm. refl. V.* (*veralt.*) go into service (**bei** with); go to work (**bei** for)
**verdinglichen** *tr. V.* (*Philos.*) reify
**Verdinglichung** *die; ~, ~en* (*Philos.*) reification
**verdolmetschen** *tr. V.* (*ugs.*) interpret, translate (*Dat.* for)
**verdonnern** *tr. V.* (*salopp*) sentence; **zu einem Bußgeld verdonnert werden** be ordered to pay a fine; **jmdn. dazu ~, etw. zu tun** order *or* make sb. do sth. [as a punishment]; **jmdn. zu einer Strafarbeit ~:** give sb. an imposition
**verdoppeln** **1** *tr. V.* double; (*fig.*) double, redouble ‹efforts etc.›. **2** *refl. V.* double
**Verdopp[e]lung** *die; ~, ~en* doubling
**verdorben** /fɛɐ̯'dɔrbn̩/ *2. Part. v.* **verderben**
**Verdorbenheit** *die; ~:* depravity
**verdorren** /fɛɐ̯'dɔrən/ *itr. V.; mit sein* wither [and die]; ‹meadow› scorch
**verdrängen** *tr. V.* **A** (*wegdrängen*) drive out ‹inhabitants›; (*fig.: ersetzen*) displace; **das Schiff verdrängt 15 000 Tonnen** the ship displaces 15,000 tons; **jmdn. aus seiner Stellung ~:** oust sb. from his/her job; **B** (*Psych.*) repress/(*bewusst*) suppress ‹experience, desire, etc.›
**Verdrängung** *die; ~, ~en* **A** ⇒ **verdrängen A**: driving out; displacement; ousting; **B** (*Psych.*) repression; (*bewusst*) suppression
**Verdrängungs·wettbewerb** *der* (*Kaufmannsspr.*) competition for markets
**verdrecken** (*ugs. abwertend*) **1** *tr. V.* make filthy dirty. **2** *itr. V.; mit sein* get *or* become filthy dirty
**verdrehen** *tr. V.* **A** twist ‹joint›; roll ‹eyes›; **den Hals ~:** twist one's head round; **sich** (*Dat.*) **den Hals ~:** crick one's neck; **jmdm. das Handgelenk ~:** twist sb.'s wrist; ⇒ *auch* **Kopf E**; **B** (*ugs. abwertend: entstellen*) twist ‹words, facts, etc.›; distort ‹sense›
**verdreht** *Adj.* (*ugs. abwertend*) crazy
**Verdrehtheit** *die; ~* (*ugs. abwertend*) (*Verrücktheit*) craziness; (*Verwirrung*) confusion
**verdreifachen** *refl., tr. V.* treble; triple
**verdreschen** *unr. tr. V.* (*ugs.*) thrash
**verdrießen** /fɛɐ̯'dri:sn̩/ *unr. tr. V.* (*geh.*) irritate; annoy; **es sich nicht ~ lassen** (*geh.*) not be put off
**verdrießlich** **1** *Adj.* **A** (*missmutig*) morose; **B** (*geh., veralt.: unangenehm*) irksome ‹task, matter, etc.›. **2** *adv.* (*missmutig*) morosely
**Verdrießlichkeit** *die; ~, ~en* **A** (*Missmut*) moroseness; **B** (*unangehmer Vorgang*) irksome thing/matter *etc.*
**verdross, *verdroß** /fɛɐ̯'drɔs/ *1. u. 3. Pers. Sg. Prät. v.* **verdrießen**
**verdrossen** **1** *2. Part. v.* **verdrießen**. **2** *Adj.* (*missmutig*) morose; (*missmutig und lustlos*) sullen. **3** *adv.* (*missmutig*) morosely; (*missmutig und lustlos*) sullenly
**Verdrossenheit** *die; ~* ⇒ **verdrossen 2**: moroseness; sullenness
**verdrücken** (*ugs.*) **1** *tr. V.* **A** (*essen*) polish off (*coll.*); **B** (*verknautschen*) crumple ‹clothes›. **2** *refl. V.* slip away
**Verdruss, *Verdruß** /fɛɐ̯'drʊs/ *der;* **Verdrusses, Verdrusse** annoyance; (*Unzufriedenheit*) dissatisfaction; discontentment; **jmdm. ~ bereiten** annoy sb.
**verduften** *itr. V.; mit sein* **A** (*Duft verlieren*) ‹coffee› lose its aroma; ‹aroma› go; **B** (*salopp: sich entfernen*) hop it (*Brit. coll.*); clear off (*coll.*)
**verdummen** **1** *tr. V.* **jmdn. ~:** dull sb.'s mind. **2** *itr. V.; mit sein* become stultified
**Verdummung** *die; ~* **A** **die ~ der Massen zum Ziel haben** be aimed at dulling the mind of the masses; **B** (*das Dummwerden*) stultification
**verdunkeln** **1** *tr. V.* **A** darken; (*vollständig*) black out ‹room, house, etc.›; **B** (*verdecken*) darken; (*fig.*) cast a shadow on ‹happiness etc.›; **C** (*bes. Rechtsw.*) obscure ‹facts, situation, etc.›. **2** *refl. V.* darken; grow darker; (*fig.*) ‹expression etc.› darken
**Verdunkelung** *die; ~, ~en* **A** (*das Verdunkeln*) darkening; (*vollständig*) blackout; **B** (*Vorrichtung*) black out blind[s]/curtain[s]; **C** (*bes. Rechtsw.*) obscuring; obscuration
**Verdunkelungs·gefahr** *die* (*Rechtsw.*) danger of suppression of evidence
**Verdunklung** *die; ~, ~en* ⇒ **Verdunkelung**
**verdünnen** *tr. V.* **A** dilute; (*mit Wasser*) water down; dilute; thin [down] ‹paint etc.›; **B**

V

(*dünner machen*) taper [off] ‹stick etc.›; **C** (*Militärjargon*) reduce the number of ‹troops etc.› [in an/the area]

**Verdünner** *der;* **~s, ~, Verdünnungsmittel** *das* thinner; (*in der Industrie*) diluent

**verdünnisieren** *refl. V.* (*salopp*) clear off (*coll.*)

**Verdünnung** *die;* **~, ~en** **A** dilution; (*der Luft*) rarefaction; **B** (*chem. Mittel*) thinner

**verdunsten** **1** *itr. V.; mit sein* evaporate. **2** *tr. V.* evaporate; ‹plant› transpire ‹water›

**Verdunstung** *die;* **~:** evaporation

**verdursten** *itr. V.; mit sein* (*auch fig.*) die of thirst

**verdüstern** **1** *tr. V.* darken; (*fig. geh.*) cast a shadow across. **2** *refl. V.* darken; grow dark; (*fig.*) darken

**verdutzt** /fɛɐ̯ˈdʊtst/ *Adj.* taken aback *pred.;* nonplussed; (*verwirrt*) baffled; **~ hielt er inne** taken aback *or* nonplussed, he paused

**Verdutztheit** *die;* **~:** bafflement

**verebben** *itr. V.; mit sein* (*geh.*) subside

**veredeln** *tr. V.* **A** (*geh.*) ennoble; improve ‹taste›; **B** (*Technik*) refine; beneficiate ‹coal›; **C** (*Gartenbau*) graft

**Vered[e]lung** *die;* **~, ~en** **A** (*geh.*) ennoblement; (*des Geschmacks*) improvement; **B** (*Technik*) refinement; (*von Kohle*) beneficiation; **C** (*Gartenbau*) grafting

**verehelichen** *refl. V.* (*Papierdt., veralt.*) **sich jmdm. ~:** marry sb.; **Else Müller, verehelichte Meyer** Else Meyer, née Müller

**Verehelichung** *die;* **~, ~en** (*Papierdt., veralt.*) marriage (**mit** to)

**verehren** *tr. V.* **A** (*vergöttern*) venerate; revere; **[sehr] verehrte Anwesende!** Ladies and Gentlemen; (*in Briefanreden*) **verehrte gnädige Frau!** [Dear] Madam; **verehrte Frau Müller!** Dear Frau Müller; **B** (*geh.: bewundern*) admire; (*ehrerbietig lieben*) worship; adore; **C** (*scherzh.: schenken*) give; **darf ich Ihnen dieses Buch ~?** may I make you a little gift of this book?

**Verehrer** *der;* **~s, ~, Verehrerin** *die;* **~, ~nen** admirer

**Verehrung** *die* **A** veneration; reverence; **B** (*Bewunderung*) admiration

**verehrungs·würdig** *Adj.* admirable

**vereidigen** /fɛɐ̯ˈ|aidɪɡn̩/ *tr. V.* swear in; **einen Zeugen vor Gericht ~:** swear in a witness; **jmdn. auf etw.** (*Akk.*) **~:** make sb. swear to sth.; **ein vereidigter Sachverständiger** a sworn expert

**Vereidigung** *die;* **~, ~en** swearing in

**Verein** *der;* **~[e]s, ~e** **A** organization; (*zur Förderung der Denkmalspflege usw.*) society; (*der Kunstfreunde usw.*) association; society; (*Sport~*) club; (*fig. ugs.*) crowd (*coll.*); (*kleiner*) bunch (*coll.*); **B** **im ~ [mit]** in conjunction with; together with; **in trautem ~ [mit]** (*scherzh.*) in an unlikely twosome/group [with]

**vereinbar** *Adj.* compatible (**mit** with); **nicht ~:** incompatible; **etw. ist mit etw. nur schwerlich ~:** it is difficult to reconcile sth. with sth.

**vereinbaren** *tr. V.* **A** (*festlegen*) agree; arrange ‹meeting etc.›; **B** (*harmonieren*) **[nicht] zu ~ sein, sich [nicht] ~ lassen** be [in]compatible *or* [ir]reconcilable; **etw. mit etw. [nicht] ~ können** [not] be able to reconcile sth. with sth.

**Vereinbarung** *die;* **~, ~en** **A** (*das Festlegen*) agreeing; (*eines Termins usw.*) arranging; **B** (*Abmachung*) agreement; **eine ~ treffen** come to an agreement

**vereinbarungs·gemäß** **1** *Adj.* as agreed/arranged *postpos.* **2** *adv.* as agreed/arranged

**vereinen** **1** *tr. V.* **A** (*zusammenfassen*) unite; merge ‹businesses› (**zu** into); **B** (*harmonisieren*) reconcile; **C** (*besitzen*) combine; **er vereint alle Kompetenzen in seiner Hand** he combines all responsibilities. **2** *refl. V.* **A** **sich zu gemeinsamem Handeln ~:** join forces; **B** (*vorhanden sein*) combine; **in ihr ~ sich Geist und Anmut** in her, beauty and intellect are united

*old spelling (see note on page 1707)

**vereinfachen** *tr. V.* simplify

**Vereinfachung** *die;* **~, ~en** simplification

**vereinheitlichen** *tr. V.* standardize

**Vereinheitlichung** *die;* **~, ~en** standardization

**vereinigen** **1** *tr. V.* **A** (*zusammenschließen*) unite; merge ‹businesses›; **B** (*zusammenfassen*) bring together; **alle Ämter sind in einer Person vereinigt** all offices are held by the same person; **die Mehrheit der Stimmen auf sich ~:** receive the majority of the votes. **2** *refl. V.* **A** (*sich zusammenschließen*) unite; ‹organizations, firms› merge; (*fig.*) be combined; **B** (*zusammentreffen*) assemble (**zu** for); ‹rivers› meet, merge; **Fulda und Werra ~ sich zur Weser** the Fulda and the Werra meet and form the Weser; **C** (*geh.: sich paaren*) couple

**vereinigt** *Adj.* **Vereinigte Arabische Emirate** United Arab Emirates; **Vereinigtes Königreich [Großbritannien und Nordirland]** United Kingdom [of Great Britain and Northern Ireland]; **Vereinigte Staaten [von Amerika]** United States *sing.* [of America]

**Vereinigung** *die* **A** (*Rechtsw.*) organization; **B** (*Zusammenschluss*) uniting; (*von Unternehmen*) merging; **C** (*geh.: Koitus*) union; **D** (*Zusammentreffen*) assembly; (*von Flüssen*) meeting; merging

**Vereinigungs-:** **~freiheit** *die* ⇒ **Koalitionsfreiheit**; **~menge** *die* (*Math.*) union of sets

**vereinnahmen** *tr. V.* (*Kaufmannsspr.*) take; collect ‹dividend›; (*fig.*) monopolize

**vereinsamen** *itr. V.; mit sein* become [increasingly] lonely *or* isolated

**Vereinsamung** *die;* **~:** loneliness; isolation

**Vereins-:** **~freiheit** *die* freedom of association; **~kamerad** *der,* **~kameradin** *die* fellow club *etc.* member; **~lokal** *das* club's *etc.* local pub (*Brit.*)/meeting room; **~meier** *der;* **~~s, ~~** (*ugs. abwertend*) [real] clubman; enthusiast for club life; **~meierei** *die* (*ugs. abwertend*) enthusiasm for club life

**vereinzeln** *tr. V.* **A** (*geh.*) isolate; **B** (*Forstw., Landw.*) thin out

**vereinzelt** **1** *Adj.* occasional; isolated, occasional ‹shower, outbreak of rain, etc.›; **in ~en Fällen** in isolated cases. **2** *adv.* (*zeitlich*) occasionally; now and then; (*örtlich*) here and there

**Vereinzelung** *die;* **~, ~en** isolation

**vereisen** **1** *itr. V.; mit sein* freeze *or* ice over; ‹wing› ice up; ‹lock› freeze up; **eine vereiste Fahrbahn** an icy carriageway. **2** *tr. V.* (*Med.*) freeze

**Vereisung** *die;* **~, ~en** **A** freezing *or* icing over; (*einer Tragfläche*) icing up; (*eines Schlosses*) freezing up; **B** (*Med.*) freezing

**vereiteln** *tr. V.* thwart; prevent; thwart, foil ‹attempt, plan, etc.›; thwart, frustrate ‹efforts, intentions, etc.›

**Vereitelung** *die;* **~** ⇒ **vereiteln**: thwarting; prevention; foiling; frustrating

**vereitern** *itr. V.; mit sein* go septic; **vereitert sein** be septic; **dieser Zahn ist vereitert** this tooth has an abscess

**Vereiterung** *die* suppuration; (*eines Zahns*) abscess

**verekeln** *tr. V.* **jmdm. etw. ~:** put sb. off sth.

**verelenden** *itr. V.; mit sein* (*geh., Soziol.*) sink into poverty

**Verelendung** *die;* **~, ~en** (*geh., Soziol.*) impoverishment

**Verelendungs·theorie** *die* (*Soziol.*) theory of the pauperization of the proletariat

**verenden** *itr. V.; mit sein* perish; die

**verengen** **1** *refl. V.* narrow; become narrow; ‹pupils› contract; ‹blood vessel› constrict, become constricted. **2** *tr. V.* make narrower; narrow; restrict, narrow ‹field of vision etc.›; make ‹circle, loop› smaller

**Verengung** *die;* **~, ~en** **A** (*das [Sich]verengen*) narrowing; (*eines Blutgefäßes*) constriction; **B** (*verengte Stelle*) narrow part

**vererben** **1** *tr. V.* **A** leave, bequeath ‹property› (*Dat.,* **an** + *Akk.* to); (*fig.: schenken*) bequeath (*joc.*) (*Dat.* to); **B** (*Biol., Med.*) transmit, pass on ‹characteristic, disease›; pass on ‹talent› (*Dat.,* **auf** + *Akk.* to). **2** *refl. V.* (*Biol., Med.*) ‹disease, tendency› be passed on *or* transmitted (**auf** + *Akk.* to)

**vererblich** *Adj.* heritable ‹goods, property›

**Vererbung** *die;* **~, ~en** (*Biol., Med.*) heredity *no art.;* **das ist ~:** it runs in the family

**Vererbungs·lehre** *die* genetics *sing., no art.*

**verewigen** **1** *tr. V.* immortalize; (*andauern lassen*) perpetuate ‹situation etc.›; preserve ‹text› for posterity. **2** *refl. V.* (*ugs.: Spuren hinterlassen*) leave one's mark

**verfahren**[1] **1** *unr. refl. V.* lose one's way. **2** *unr. tr. V.* use up ‹petrol›; **50 DM mit dem Taxi ~:** spend 50 marks on a taxi/taxis. **3** *unr. itr. V.; mit sein* **A** (*handeln*) proceed; **B** (*umgehen*) **mit jmdm./etw. ~:** deal with sb./sth.

**verfahren**[2] *Adj.* dead-end ‹situation›

**Verfahren** *das;* **~s, ~** **A** procedure; (*Technik*) process; (*Methode*) method; **B** (*Rechtsw.*) proceedings *pl.*

**Verfahrens-:** **~frage** *die* question *or* matter of procedure; procedural question *or* matter; **~technik** *die* process engineering *no art.;* **~weise** *die* procedure; method of proceeding; modus operandi

**Verfall** *der* **A** decay; dilapidation; (*fig.: der Preise, einer Währung*) collapse; **mit der Pensionierung begann sein gesundheitlicher ~:** on retirement his health started to deteriorate; **B** (*Auflösung*) decline; **sittlicher ~:** moral degeneracy; **C** (*das Ungültigwerden*) expiry

**-verfall** *der:* **Dollar-/Währungs~:** collapse of the dollar/currency; **Preis~:** collapse of prices

**verfallen** *unr. itr. V.; mit sein* **A** (*baufällig werden*) fall into disrepair; become dilapidated; **B** (*körperlich*) ‹strength› decline; **der Kranke verfiel zusehends** the patient went into a rapid decline; **C** (*untergehen*) ‹empire› decline; ‹morals, morale› deteriorate; **D** (*ungültig werden*) expire; **E** (*hörig werden*) **jmdm. ~:** become a slave; **einem Irrtum ~:** fall a victim to an error; **dem Alkohol ~:** become addicted to alcohol; **jmdm. ~ sein** be completely captivated by sb.; **F** (*geraten*) **in einen Schlummer ~:** sink into a doze; **in den alten Fehler/Ton ~:** make the same old mistake/adopt the same old tone; **G** (*übergehen*) **in seinen Dialekt ~:** lapse into one's dialect; **das Pferd verfiel in [einen] Trab** the horse broke into a trot; **H** **auf jmdn./etw. ~:** think of sb./sth.; **auf einen sonderbaren Gedanken ~:** hit upon a strange idea; **warum seid ihr gerade auf uns ~?** what made you turn to us?; **I** (*zufallen*) **dem Staat ~:** be forfeited to the state

**Verfalls-:** **~datum** *das* use-by date; (*ugs.: Mindesthaltbarkeitsdatum*) best-before date; **~erscheinung** *die* symptom of decline (*Gen.* in); (*in der Sprache*) sign of deterioration

**verfälschen** *tr. V.* distort, misrepresent ‹statement, message›; falsify, misrepresent ‹facts, history, truth›; falsify ‹painting, banknote›; adulterate ‹wine, milk, etc.›

**Verfälschung** *die* ⇒ **verfälschen**: distortion; misrepresentation; falsification; adulteration

**verfangen** **1** *unr. refl. V.* get caught; (*fig.*) become entangled (**in** + *Dat.* in); **sich in Widersprüchen ~** (*fig.*) contradict oneself. **2** *unr. itr. V.* have the desired effect; **wenig/nicht ~:** have little/no effect; **solche Tricks ~ bei mir nicht** such tricks cut no ice with me (*coll.*); such tricks won't get you/him *etc.* anywhere *or* won't work with me

**verfänglich** /fɛɐ̯ˈfɛŋlɪç/ *Adj.* awkward, embarrassing ‹situation, question, etc.›; incriminating ‹evidence, letter, etc.›

**verfärben** **1** *refl. V.* change colour; ‹washing› become discoloured; ‹leaves› turn; **sich rot ~:** change colour to red/be stained red/turn red. **2** *tr. V.* discolour

V

**Verfärbung** *die* [A] *(das [Sich]verfärben)* change of colour; [B] *(verfärbte Stelle)* discoloration; discoloured patch

**verfassen** *tr. V.* write; write, compose ‹poetry›; write, draw up ‹document, law, etc.›; draw up ‹resolution›

**Verfasser** *der;* **~s,** **~, Verfasserin** *die;* **~, ~nen** writer; *(eines Buchs, Artikels usw.)* author; writer

**Verfasserschaft** *die;* **~:** authorship

**Verfassung** *die* [A] *(Politik)* constitution; [B] *(Zustand)* state [of health/mind]; **in guter/schlechter ~ sein** be in good/poor shape; **in bester ~:** on top form; **nicht in der ~ sein, Witze zu machen** not be in a joking mood; be in no mood to joke *or* to make jokes

**verfassung·gebend** *Adj.* constituent ‹assembly, power, etc.›

**verfassungs-, Verfassungs-: ~änderung** *die* constitutional amendment; **~beschwerde** *die (Rechtsw.)* complaint about an infringement/infringements of the constitution *(committed by the State)*; **~bruch** *der* breach of the constitution; **~feindlich** *Adj.* anticonstitutional; **~gericht** *das* constitutional court; **~konform** *Adj.* in conformity with the constitution; **~mäßig** ❶ *Adj.* constitutional; ❷ *adv.* constitutionally; in accordance with a/the constitution; **~schutz** *der* [A] defence *or* protection of the constitution; [B] *(Ämter)* authorities responsible for the defence *or* protection of the constitution

**verfaulen** *itr. V.; mit sein* rot; *(fig.)* ‹system, social order› decay; *(fig.: moralisch)* degenerate

**verfechten** *unr. tr. V. (eintreten für)* advocate, champion ‹theory, hypothesis, etc.›; uphold ‹view›; *(verteidigen)* defend

**Verfechter** *der,* **Verfechterin** *die;* **~, ~nen** advocate; champion

**verfehlen** *tr. V.* [A] *(verpassen)* miss ‹train, person, etc.›; [B] *(vorbeigehen)* miss ‹goal, target, etc.›; **er hat seinen Beruf verfehlt** *(fig.)* he has missed his true vocation *or* is in the wrong job; **eine verfehlte Politik** *(fig.)* an unsuccessful policy; ⇒ *auch* **Thema** A

**Verfehlung** *die;* **~, ~en** misdemeanour; *(Rel.: Sünde)* transgression

**verfeinden** *refl. V.* **sich ~ mit** make an enemy of; **verfeindet sein** be enemies; **sie hatten sich wegen einer Kleinigkeit verfeindet** they had fallen out over a trifling matter

**verfeinern** /fɛɐ̯ˈfainɐn/ ❶ *tr. V.* improve; refine ‹method, procedure, sense›. ❷ *refl. V.* improve; ‹method, procedure, sense› be refined

**Verfeinerung** *die;* **~, ~en** [A] ⇒ **verfeinern** 1, 2: improvement; refinement; **etw. zur ~ tun** do sth. as a refinement; [B] *(etwas Verfeinertes)* refinement

**verfemen** *tr. V. (geh.)* outlaw ‹person, act›; *(verbieten)* ban; *(innerhalb einer Gruppe)* ostracize ‹person›

**Verfemte** *der/die; adj. Dekl. (geh.)* outlaw; *(fig.)* ostracized person

**verfertigen** *tr. V.* produce; make; produce ‹document›

**Verfertigung** *die* production

**verfestigen** ❶ *tr. V.* harden; *(verstärken)* reinforce; strengthen. ❷ *refl. V.* harden; *(verstärkt werden)* be reinforced *or* strengthened; *(sich etablieren)* become firmly established (**zu** + *Dat.* as)

**Verfestigung** *die* hardening; *(Verstärkung)* reinforcement; strengthening

**verfetten** *itr. V.; mit sein* become [too] fat

**verfeuern** *tr. V.* [A] burn; **alles Holz verfeuert haben** have used up all the wood; [B] *(verschießen)* fire; **alle Munition war verfeuert** all the ammunition had been used up

**verfilmen** *tr. V.* [A] film; make a film of; **der Roman wird jetzt verfilmt** the novel is now being made into a film; [B] *(auf Mikrofilm aufnehmen)* microfilm

**Verfilmung** *die;* **~, ~en** [A] *(das Verfilmen)* filming; [B] *(Film)* film [version]

**verfilzen** *itr. V.; mit sein* ‹fabric, garment› felt; become felted; ‹hair› become matted

**verfinstern** ❶ *tr. V.* obscure ‹sun etc.›. ❷ *refl. V. (auch fig.)* darken

**Verfinsterung** *die;* **~, ~en** darkening

**verflachen** ❶ *itr. V.; mit sein* ‹ground› flatten *or* level out, become flatter; ‹water› become shallow; *(fig.)* ‹discussion› become superficial *or* trivial. ❷ *refl. V.* ‹ground› flatten *or* level out. ❸ *tr. V.* flatten; level

**verflechten** *unr. tr. V.* interweave; intertwine; interlace; *(verwickeln)* involve; **[eng/innig] miteinander verflochten sein** *(fig.)* be [closely/intimately] interlinked

**Verflechtung** *die;* **~, ~en** interconnection; *(Verwicklung)* involvement; **eine gegenseitige finanzielle ~:** a financial link-up

**verfliegen** ❶ *unr. refl. V.* ‹pilot› lose one's way; ‹aircraft› get off course. ❷ *unr. itr. V.; mit sein* [A] *(verschwinden)* ‹smoke› disperse, vanish; ‹scent, smell› fade, disappear; ‹mood, tiredness› evaporate; [B] *(sich verflüchtigen)* ‹alcohol etc.› evaporate; [C] *(vorübergehen)* ‹time› fly by; ‹anger› pass

**verfließen** *unr. itr. V.; mit sein* [A] *(verschwimmen)* merge; ‹colours› run; [B] *(geh.: vergehen)* go by; pass

**verflixt** /fɛɐ̯ˈflɪkst/ *(ugs.)* ❶ *Adj.* [A] *(ärgerlich)* akward, unpleasant ‹situation, business, etc.›; [B] *(abwertend: verdammt)* blasted *(Brit.)*; blessed; confounded; **~ [noch mal]!, ~ noch eins!, ~ und zugenäht!** [damn and] blast *(Brit. coll.)*; [C] *(sehr groß)* **er hat ~es Glück gehabt** he was damned lucky *(coll.)*. ❷ *adv. (sehr)* damned *(coll.)*; **das sieht ~ nach Betrug aus** that looks damned close to fraud *(coll.)*

**verflossen** ❶ *2. Part. v.* **verfließen**. ❷ *Adj. (ugs.)* former; **seine ~e Freundin** his ex-girlfriend; **mein Verflossener/meine Verflossene** my ex *(coll.)*

**verfluchen** *tr. V.* curse

**verflucht** ❶ *Adj. (salopp)* [A] *(verdammt)* damned *(coll.)*; bloody *(Brit. sl.)*; **~ [noch mal]!, ~ und zugenäht!** *(derb)* damn [it] *(coll.)*; [B] *(sehr groß)* **wir hatten ~es Glück/Pech** we were damned lucky/unlucky *(coll.)*. ❷ *adv. (sehr)* damned *(coll.)*

**verflüchtigen** ❶ *tr. V. (bes. Chemie)* evaporate. ❷ *refl. V.* [A] *(in Gas übergehen)* ‹alcohol etc.› evaporate; [B] *(sich auflösen)* disperse; ‹smell› disappear; *(fig.)* ‹fear, astonishment› subside; ‹cheerfulness, mockery› vanish; ‹time of youth› be dissipated; [C] *(ugs. scherzh.: sich davonmachen)* make oneself scarce *(coll.)*

**verflüssigen** *(bes. Chemie, Physik)* ❶ *tr. V.* liquefy. ❷ *refl. V.* liquefy; become liquid

**Verflüssigung** *die;* **~, ~en** liquefaction

**verfolgen** *tr. V.* [A] pursue; hunt, track ‹animal›; **jmdn. auf Schritt und Tritt ~:** follow sb. wherever he/she goes; **der Gedanke daran verfolgte ihn** *(fig.)* the thought of it haunted him; **vom Pech verfolgt sein** *(fig.)* be dogged by bad luck; **jmdn. mit Blicken** *od.* **den Augen ~** *(fig.)* follow sb. with one's eyes; [B] *(bedrängen)* plague; **jmdn. mit Bitten ~:** badger sb. with requests; **er verfolgte sie mit seiner Eifersucht** because he was jealous, he would not leave her in peace; [C] *(bedrohen)* persecute; **politisch verfolgt sein** *od.* **werden** be a victim of political persecution; [D] *(folgen)* follow ‹path etc.›; [E] *(zu verwirklichen suchen)* pursue ‹policy, plan, career, idea, purpose, etc.›; [F] *(beobachten)* follow ‹conversation, events, trial, developments, etc.›; [G] **etw. [strafrechtlich] ~:** prosecute sth.

**Verfolger** *der;* **~s, ~, Verfolgerin** *die;* **~, ~nen** pursuer; *(Häscher)* persecutor

**Verfolgte** *der/die; adj. Dekl.* victim of persecution

**Verfolgung** *die;* **~, ~en** [A] *(das Hinterhereilen)* pursuit; **die ~ aufnehmen** take up the chase; [B] *(Bedrohung)* persecution; [C] ⇒ **verfolgen** E: pursuance; [D] **[strafrechtliche] ~:** prosecution

**Verfolgungs-: ~jagd** *die* pursuit; chase; **~rennen** *das (Radsport)* pursuit race; **~wahn** *der (Psych.)* persecution mania

**verformbar** *Adj.* malleable; workable

**verformen** ❶ *tr. V.* [A] make ‹object› go out of shape; distort; [B] *(Technik)* work ‹steel, plastic, etc.›. ❷ *refl. V.* go out of shape; distort; become distorted

**Verformung** *die* distortion

**verfrachten** *tr. V.* transport; *(mit dem Schiff)* ship; **jmdn. ins Bett/in einen Streifenwagen ~** *(fig.)* bundle sb. into bed/into a patrol car

**verfranzen** /fɛɐ̯ˈfrantsn̩/ *refl. V.* [A] *(Fliegerjargon)* stray off course; [B] *(ugs.: sich verirren)* lose one's way

**verfremden** *tr. V.* **[jmdm.] etw. ~:** make sth. [appear] unfamiliar [to sb.]; *(Theaterw., Kunstw.)* distance sth. [from sb.]

**Verfremdung** *die;* **~, ~en** *(Theaterw., Kunstw.)* alienation; distancing

**Verfremdungs·effekt** *der (Theaterw.)* alienation *or* distancing effect

**verfressen**[1] *unr. tr. V. (salopp)* blow *(coll.)* ‹money› on food

**verfressen**[2] *Adj. (salopp abwertend)* piggish *(coll.)*; greedy

**Verfressenheit** *die;* **~** *(salopp abwertend)* piggishness *(coll.)*; greediness

**verfroren** *Adj.* [A] *(durchgefroren)* frozen; freezing cold; [B] *(leicht frierend)* sensitive to the cold; **~ sein** feel the cold

**verfrühen** *refl. V.* arrive *or* come *or* be too early; **diese Maßnahme halte ich für verfrüht** I consider this measure to be premature

**verfügbar** *Adj.* available; **nicht ~:** unavailable

**Verfügbarkeit** *die;* **~:** availability

**verfügen** ❶ *tr. V. (anordnen)* order; *(dekretieren)* decree; **in seinem Testament ~, dass ...** decree in one's will that .... ❷ *itr. V.* [A] *(bestimmen)* **über etw.** *(Akk.)* **[frei] ~ können** be free to decide what to do with sth.; **über jmdn. ~:** tell sb. what to do; **bitte ~ Sie über mich!** *(geh.)* I am at your disposal; [B] *(haben)* **über etw.** *(Akk.)* **~:** have sth. at one's disposal; **über gute Beziehungen/große Erfahrung ~:** have good connections/great experience. ❸ *refl. V. (veralt., scherzh.: sich begeben)* proceed

**Verfügung** *die;* **~, ~en** [A] *(Anordnung)* order; *(Dekret)* decree; **eine ~ erlassen** issue a decree; **seine letztwilligen ~en** his last will and testament; **~en treffen** make provision *sing.*; **„~ von Todes wegen"** *(Amtsspr.)* 'Last Will and Testament'; ⇒ *auch* **einstweilig**; [B] *(Disposition)* **etw. zur ~ haben** have sth. at one's disposal; **jmdm. etw. zur ~ stellen** put sth. at sb.'s disposal; **sein Amt zur ~ stellen** offer to give up one's post *or* office; **jmdm. zur ~ stehen** be at sb.'s disposal; **sich zur ~ halten** hold oneself ready

**Verfügungs·gewalt** *die* power of disposal; **~ über etw.** *(Akk.)* **haben** *(fig.)* have power over sth.

**verführen** ❶ *tr. V.* [A] *(verleiten)* tempt; **jmdn. zum Trinken ~:** encourage sb. to take up drinking; **jmdn. zu einem Bier ~** *(scherzh.)* tempt sb. to a beer; [B] *(sexuell)* seduce. ❷ *itr. V.* **zu etw. ~:** be a temptation to sth.

**Verführer** *der* seducer

**Verführerin** *die* seductress

**verführerisch** ❶ *Adj.* [A] *(verlockend)* tempting; [B] *(aufreizend)* seductive. ❷ *adv.* [A] *(verlockend)* temptingly; [B] *(aufreizend)* seductively

**Verführung** *die* [A] temptation; [B] *(sexuell)* seduction; [C] *(Reiz)* enticement

**verfüttern** *tr. V.* [A] feed (+ *Dat.* to); [B] *(verbrauchen)* use [up] as animal/bird food

**Vergabe** *die* allocation; *(eines Auftrages)* placing; awarding; *(eines Stipendiums, eines Preises)* award

**vergackeiern** /fɛɐ̯ˈgak|ai̯ɐn/ *tr. V. (salopp)* **jmdn. ~:** pull sb.'s leg *(coll.)*

**vergaffen** *refl. V. (ugs.)* **sich in jmdn. ~:** fall for sb.

**vergällen** /fɛɐ̯ˈgɛlən/ *tr. V.* [A] *(verderben)* spoil ‹enjoyment etc.›; sour ‹life›; [B] *(bes. Chemie)* denature; denaturalize

**vergaloppieren** *refl. V. (ugs.)* drop a clanger *(coll.)*; *(zu schnell vorgehen)* fall over oneself

V

**vergammeln** (*ugs.*) ❶ *itr. V.; mit sein* ‹food› go bad. ❷ *tr. V.* waste ‹time›; **den ganzen Sonntag im Bett ~:** idle away the whole of Sunday in bed

**vergammelt** *Adj.* (*ugs. abwertend*) scruffy (*coll.*); tatty (*coll.*); tatty (*coll.*), decrepit ‹vehicle›

**vergangen** /fɛɐ̯ˈgaŋən/ ❶ *2. Part. v.* **vergehen.** ❷ *Adj.* Ⓐ (*vorüber, vorbei*) bygone, former ‹times, years, etc.›; **die ~e Sitzung** the previous *or* last meeting; Ⓑ (*letzt...*) last ‹year, Sunday, week, etc.›; Ⓒ (*ehemalig*) former

**Vergangenheit** *die;* ~, ~**en** Ⓐ (*Zeit*) past; **die jüngste ~:** the recent past; **etw. gehört der ~ an** sth. is a thing of the past; **einen Strich unter die ~ ziehen** let bygones be bygones; Ⓑ (*Leben*) past; (*einer Stadt usw.*) past; history; **eine Frau mit ~:** a woman with a past; Ⓒ (*Grammatik*) past tense

**Vergangenheits·bewältigung** *die* coming to terms with the past

**vergänglich** /fɛɐ̯ˈgɛŋlɪç/ *Adj.* transient; transitory; ephemeral; **alles Irdische ist ~:** all earthly things will pass away

**Vergänglichkeit** *die;* ~**:** transience; transitoriness

**vergären** ❶ *unr. od. regelm. tr. V.* ferment (**zu** into). ❷ *unr. od. regelm. itr. V.; mit sein* (*bes. Chemie*) ferment

**vergasen** *tr. V.* Ⓐ (*bes. Physik*) gasify; Ⓑ (*töten*) gas

**Vergaser** *der;* ~**s**, ~ (*Kfz-W.*) carburettor

**vergaß** /fɛɐ̯ˈga:s/ *1. u. 3. Pers. Sg. Prät. v.* **vergessen**

**Vergasung** *die;* ~, ~**en** Ⓐ (*von Kohle*) gasification; Ⓑ (*Tötung*) gassing; Ⓒ **bis zur ~** (*ugs.*) ad nauseam

**vergattern** *tr. V.* (*bes. Milit.*) remind ‹soldier› of his duties; (*fig.*) reprimand; **jmdn. ~, etw. zu tun** (*fig.*) enjoin sb. to do sth.; **jmdn. zu Stillschweigen ~** (*fig.*) swear sb. to silence

**vergeben** *unr. tr. V.* Ⓐ ▶ 268 *auch itr.* (*geh.: verzeihen*) forgive; **jmdm. etw. ~:** forgive sb. [for] sth.; Ⓑ throw away ‹chance, goal, etc.›; **einen Elfmeter ~:** waste a penalty; Ⓒ (*geben*) place ‹order› (**an** + *Akk.* with); award ‹grant, prize› (**an** + *Akk.* to); **seine Töchter sind alle schon ~:** his daughters are all married [*or* engaged] already; Ⓓ **sich** (*Dat.*) **etwas/nichts ~:** lose/not lose face

**vergebens** ❶ *Adv.* in vain; vainly. ❷ *adj.* **es war ~:** it was of *or* to no avail

**vergeblich** ❶ *Adj.* futile; vain, futile ‹attempt, efforts›; **alles Bitten/Zureden war ~:** all pleading/encouragement was of *or* to no avail; no amount of pleading/encouragement did any good. ❷ *adv.* in vain; vainly

**Vergeblichkeit** *die;* ~**:** futility

**Vergebung** *die;* ~, ~**en** ▶ 268 (*geh.*) forgiveness

**vergegenständlichen** *tr. V.* (*bes. Philos.*) reify; hypostatize

**vergegenwärtigen** /*od.* ---ˈ---/ *refl. V.* **sich** (*Dat.*) **etw. ~:** imagine sth.; (*erinnern*) recall sth.

**Vergegenwärtigung** *die;* ~, ~**en** ⇒ **vergegenwärtigen**: imagining; recalling

**vergehen** ❶ *unr. itr. V.; mit sein* Ⓐ (*verstreichen*) ‹time› pass [by], go by; **es vergeht kein Tag, an dem er nicht anruft** not a day passes by without him ringing up (*Brit.*) *or* (*coll.*) phoning; **wie [doch] die Zeit vergeht!** how time flies!; Ⓑ (*nachlassen*) ‹pain› wear off, pass; ‹pleasure› fade; **ihr verging der Appetit** she lost her appetite; Ⓒ (*sich verflüchtigen*) ‹cloud, scent› disappear; ‹fog› lift; Ⓓ (*geh.: sterben*) pass away; die; Ⓔ (*verschmachten*) die (**vor** + *Dat.* of); **vor Sehnsucht ~:** pine away.
❷ *unr. refl. V.* Ⓐ (*verstoßen*) **sich gegen das Gesetz ~:** violate the law; **sich an fremdem Eigentum ~** (*geh.*) steal another's property; Ⓑ (*sexuell*) **sich an jmdm. ~:** commit indecent assault on sb.; indecently assault sb.

**Vergehen** *das;* ~**s**, ~**:** crime; (*Rechtsspr.*) offence

**vergeigen** *tr. V.* (*ugs.*) botch up ‹test, performance, etc.›; lose ‹game, match›

**vergeistigt** *Adj.* spiritual

**vergelten** *unr. tr. V.* repay (**durch** with); **jmdm. etw. ~:** repay sb. for sth.; **jmds. Freundlichkeit ~:** return sb.'s kindness; **eine Niederlage blutig ~:** take bloody revenge for a defeat; **vergelts Gott!** God bless you!

**Vergeltung** *die* Ⓐ repayment; Ⓑ (*Rache*) revenge; **~ an jmdm./etw. üben** take revenge on sb./sth.; **die ~ eines Unrechts** the avenging of a wrong

**Vergeltungs-:** ~**maßnahme** *die* retaliatory measure; ~**schlag** *der* retaliatory strike

**vergesellschaften** *tr. V.* socialize

**Vergesellschaftung** *die;* ~, ~**en** socialization

**vergessen** /fɛɐ̯ˈgɛsn̩/ ❶ *unr. tr.* (*auch itr.*) *V.* forget; (*liegen lassen*) forget; leave behind; **seine Umgebung/sich völlig ~:** become totally engrossed; **er wird noch einmal seinen Kopf ~** (*ugs.*) he'd forget his head if it wasn't screwed on; **... und nicht zu ~ Tante Erna** ...: and not forgetting Aunt Erna; **das kannst du ~!** (*ugs.*) forget it!; you can forget about that!; **auf etw.** (*Akk.*) **~** (*südd., österr.*) forget sth. ❷ *refl. V.* (*sich nicht beherrschen*) forget oneself

**Vergessenheit** *die;* ~**:** oblivion; **in ~ geraten** fall into oblivion

**vergesslich, *vergeßlich** /fɛɐ̯ˈgɛslɪç/ *Adj.* forgetful

**Vergesslichkeit, *Vergeßlichkeit** *die;* ~**:** forgetfulness

**vergeuden** /fɛɐ̯ˈgɔydn̩/ *tr. V.* waste, squander, waste ‹money›

**Vergeudung** *die;* ~, ~**en** waste; squandering; **so eine ~!** what a waste!

**vergewaltigen** *tr. V.* Ⓐ rape; Ⓑ (*fig.*) oppress ‹nation, people›; violate ‹truth, conscience, law, language, etc.›

**Vergewaltigung** *die;* ~, ~**en** Ⓐ rape; Ⓑ ⇒ **vergewaltigen** B: oppression; violation

**vergewissern** /fɛɐ̯gəˈvɪsɐn/ *refl. V.* make sure (+ *Gen.* of); **der Lehrer vergewisserte sich durch Fragen, ob ...** the teacher ascertained by asking questions whether ...

**Vergewisserung** *die;* ~**:** ascertainment; **nur zur ~:** just as a check

**vergießen** *unr. tr. V.* Ⓐ (*verschütten*) spill; Ⓑ **Tränen ~:** shed tears; **viel Schweiß ~:** sweat blood (*fig.*); ⇒ *auch* **Blut**

**vergiften** *tr. V.* ▶ 474 (*auch fig.*) poison

**Vergiftung** *die;* ~, ~**en** ▶ 474 Ⓐ (*das Vergiften*) poisoning; **~ durch Nahrungsmittel** food poisoning; Ⓑ (*Erkrankung*) poisoning; **~en behandeln** treat cases of poisoning; **an einer ~ sterben** die of poisoning

**Vergil** /vɛrˈgi:l/ (*der*) Virgil

**vergiss, *vergiß** /fɛɐ̯ˈgɪs/ *Imperativ Sg. v.* **vergessen**

**Vergiss·mein·nicht, *Vergiß·mein·nicht** *das;* ~**[e]s**, ~**[e]** forget-me-not

**vergisst, *vergißt** *2. u. 3. Pers. Sg. Präs. v.* **vergessen**

**vergittern** *tr. V.* put a grille on ‹window etc.›; (*mit Stangen*) put bars over ‹window etc.›; **ein vergittertes Fenster** a barred window

**verglasen** *tr. V.* glaze; **das Fenster neu ~:** put new glass in the window

**Verglasung** *die;* ~, ~**en** Ⓐ glazing; Ⓑ (*Glasscheiben*) panes *pl.* of glass

**Vergleich** *der;* ~**[e]s**, ~**e** Ⓐ comparison; **dieser ~ drängt sich einem geradezu auf** one cannot help making this comparison; **dieser ~ hinkt** this is a poor comparison; **das ist doch kein ~!** there is no comparison; **einen ~ anstellen** *od.* **ziehen** draw *or* make a comparison; **er hält dem ~ mit seinem Bruder nicht stand** he doesn't compare *or* stand comparison with his brother; **im ~ zu** *od.* **mit etw.** in comparison with sth.; compared with *or* to sth.; **etw. zum ~ heranziehen** use sth. by way of comparison; Ⓑ (*Sprachw.*) simile; Ⓒ (*Rechtsw.*) settlement; **einen ~ schließen** reach a settlement

**vergleichbar** *Adj.* comparable

**Vergleichbarkeit** *die;* ~**:** comparability

**vergleichen** ❶ *tr. V.* compare (**mit** with, to); **die Uhrzeit ~:** check that one has the correct time; **das ist [doch gar] nicht zu ~:** that [really] doesn't stand comparison *or* compare; **vergleiche Seite** 77 compare page 77; **~de Literaturwissenschaft** comparative literature. ❷ *refl. V.* Ⓐ **sich mit jmdm. ~:** compete with sb.; Ⓑ (*Rechtsw.*) reach a settlement; settle

**vergleichs-, Vergleichs-:** ~**form** *die* (*Sprachw.*) comparative/superlative form; ~**kampf** *der* (*Sport*) friendly match; ~**maß·stab** *der* standard *or* yardstick of comparison; ~**möglichkeit** *die* opportunity for comparison; ~**partikel** *die* (*Sprachw.*) comparative particle; ~**verfahren** *das* (*Rechtsw.*) composition proceedings *pl.*; ~**weise** *Adv.* comparatively

**vergletschern** *itr. V.; mit sein* become glaciated; **vergletschert** glaciated

**verglimmen** *unr. od. regelm. itr. V.; mit sein* ‹fire etc.› [die down and] go out; ‹cigarette, embers› go out

**verglühen** *itr. V.; mit sein* ‹log, wick, fire, etc.› smoulder and go out; ‹glow of sunset› fade; ‹satellite, rocket, wire, etc.› burn out

**vergnügen** /fɛɐ̯ˈgny:gn̩/ ❶ *refl. V.* enjoy oneself; have a good time; **sich beim Tanzen ~:** enjoy oneself dancing. ❷ *tr. V.* amuse

**Vergnügen** *das;* ~**s**, ~**:** pleasure; (*Spaß*) fun; **ein teueres ~** (*ugs.*) an expensive bit of fun (*coll.*); **ein kindliches ~ bei etw. empfinden** take a childlike pleasure *or* delight in sth.; **es ist mir ein ~:** it's a pleasure; **es war mir ein ~, Sie kennen zu lernen** it was a pleasure meeting you; **das ~ ist ganz meinerseits** *od.* **auf meiner Seite** the pleasure is all mine; **mit wem habe ich das ~?** with whom do I have the pleasure of speaking?; **etw. macht jmdm. [großes] ~:** sth. gives sb. [great] pleasure; sb. enjoys sth. [very much]; **sich ein ~ daraus machen, etw. zu tun** derive pleasure from doing sth.; **ich wünsche dir viel ~:** I hope you have a good time *or* enjoy yourself; **viel ~!** (*auch iron.*) have fun!; **mit [dem größten] ~:** with [the greatest of] pleasure; **etw. aus reinem ~** *od.* **nur zum ~ tun** do sth. just for the fun of it *or* for pleasure; **zu meinem ~:** to my great joy

**vergnüglich** ❶ *Adj.* amusing, entertaining ‹play, programme›. ❷ *adv.* amusingly; entertainingly

**vergnügt** ❶ *Adj.* Ⓐ (*in guter Laune*) cheerful; happy ‹smile›; merry ‹group of people›; Ⓑ (*unterhaltsam*) enjoyable. ❷ *adv.* (*in guter Laune*) cheerfully; ‹smile› happily

**Vergnügtheit** *die;* ~**:** cheerfulness

**Vergnügung** *die;* ~, ~**en** Ⓐ (*Zeitvertreib*) pleasure; Ⓑ (*Veranstaltung*) entertainment

**vergnügungs-, Vergnügungs-:** ~**fahrt** *die* pleasure trip; ~**industrie** *die* entertainment industry; ~**lokal** *das* bar providing entertainment; (*Nachtlokal*) nightclub; ~**park** *der* amusement park; ~**reise** *die* pleasure trip; ~**steuer** *die* entertainment tax; ~**sucht** *die* (*oft abwertend*) craving for pleasure; ~**süchtig** *Adj.* pleasure-hungry; ~**viertel** *das* pleasure district

**vergolden** *tr. V.* Ⓐ gold-plate ‹jewellery etc.›; (*mit Blattgold*) gild ‹statue, dome, etc.›; (*mit Gold bemalen*) paint ‹statue, dome, etc.› gold; (*fig.*) ‹evening sun› bathe ‹rooftops etc.› in gold; Ⓑ (*geh.: verklären*) brighten up

**vergönnen** *tr. V.* grant; **es war ihm nicht vergönnt** it was not granted him

**vergotten** *tr. V.* deify

**vergöttern** /fɛɐ̯ˈgœtɐn/ *tr. V.* idolize

**Vergötterung** *die;* ~, ~**en** idolization

**vergöttlichen** *tr. V.* (*göttlich machen*) deify; (*als Gott verehren*) worship [as God]

**vergraben** ❶ *unr. tr. V.* bury; **sein Gesicht in beide Hände** *od.* **in beiden Händen ~:** bury one's face in one's hands. ❷ *unr. refl.*

*old spelling (see note on page 1707)

V

*V.* ‹animal› bury itself (**in** + *Akk. od. Dat.* in); (*fig.*) withdraw from the world; hide oneself away; **sich in die Arbeit/in seine Bücher ~** (*fig.*) bury oneself in one's work/books

**vergrämen** *tr. V.* [A] antagonize; [B] (*Jägerspr.*) scare [off]

**vergrämt** *Adj.* careworn

**vergraulen** *tr. V.* (*ugs.*) put off; **jmdm. etw. ~:** put sb. off sth.

**vergreifen** *unr. refl. V.* [A] **sich im Ton/Ausdruck ~:** adopt the wrong tone/use the wrong expression; **sich in der Wahl seiner Mittel ~:** choose *or* select the wrong means; [B] **sich an etw.** (*Dat.*) **~** (*an fremdem Eigentum*) misappropriate sth.; **sich an der Kasse ~:** put one's hand in the till (*euphem.*); [C] (*tätlich werden*) **sich an jmdm. ~:** assault sb.; (*geschlechtlich missbrauchen*) [indecently] assault sb.; **ich werde mich an der Maschine nicht ~** (*ugs.*) I'm not touching the machine; [D] (*danebengreifen*) ‹musician› play a wrong note

**vergreisen** *itr. V.; mit sein* [A] go senile; **vergreist** senile; [B] (*überaltern*) ‹population› age

**Vergreisung** *die; ~* [A] senescence; [B] (*Überalterung*) ageing

**vergriffen** ❶ *2. Part. v.* **vergreifen**. ❷ *Adj.* out of print *pred.*

**vergröbern** /fɛɐ̯ˈɡrøːbɐn/ ❶ *tr. V.* coarsen. ❷ *refl. V.* become coarser

**Vergröberung** *die; ~, ~en* coarsening; **die Boulevardpresse arbeitet mit ~en** the popular press operates with crude generalizations

**vergrößern** /fɛɐ̯ˈɡrøːsɐn/ ❶ *tr. V.* [A] (*erweitern*) extend ‹room, area, building, etc.›; increase ‹distance›; **sein Repertoire ~:** extend *or* increase *or* enlarge one's repertoire; [B] (*vermehren*) increase; **das Übel ~:** make the trouble worse; [C] (*größer reproduzieren*) enlarge ‹photograph etc.›. ❷ *refl. V.* [A] (*größer werden*) ‹firm, business, etc.› expand; **eine krankhaft vergrößerte Leber** a pathologically enlarged liver; [B] (*zunehmen*) increase; [C] (*ugs.: durch Umzug*) give oneself more space. ❸ *itr. V.* ‹lens etc.› magnify

**Vergrößerung** *die; ~, ~en* [A] ⇒ **vergrößern** 1, 2: extension; increase; enlargement; expansion; [B] (*Foto*) enlargement; **in 100facher ~:** enlarged 100fold

**Vergrößerungs-: ~apparat** *der* (*Fot.*) enlarger; **~glas** *das* magnifying glass; **~spiegel** *der* magnifying mirror

**vergucken** *refl. V.* (*ugs.*) [A] (*sich verlieben*) **sich in jmdn./etw. ~:** fall for sb./sth. (*coll.*); [B] (*falsch sehen*) be mistaken [about what one saw]

**Vergünstigung** *die; ~, ~en* privilege

**vergüten** *tr. V.* [A] (*erstatten*) **jmdm. etw. ~:** reimburse sb. for sth.; **jmdm. seine Unkosten/Auslagen ~:** reimburse sb. for his/her costs/reimburse *or* refund sb.'s expenses; [B] (*bes. Papierdt.: bezahlen*) remunerate, pay for ‹work, services›; **etw. ~:** pay for sth.

**Vergütung** *die; ~, ~en* [A] (*Rückerstattung*) (*von Unkosten*) reimbursement; (*von Auslagen*) reimbursement; refunding; [B] (*Geldsumme*) remuneration

**verh.** *Abk.* **verheiratet** m.

**verhackstücken** *tr. V.* (*ugs.*) [A] (*abwertend: kritisieren*) ‹critic etc.› tear *or* pull to pieces; [B] (*nordd.: besprechen*) discuss

**verhaften** *tr. V.* arrest; **Sie sind verhaftet** you are under arrest

**verhaftet** *Adj.* **einer Sache** (*Dat.*) **~ sein** be trapped in sth.

**Verhaftete** *der/die; adj. Dekl.* person under arrest; man/woman under arrest; arrested man/woman

**Verhaftung** *die; ~, ~en* arrest

**verhageln** *itr. V.; mit sein* be destroyed by hail; ⇒ *auch* **Petersilie**

**verhaken** ❶ *tr. V.* [A] (*zuhaken*) hook up; [B] (*in etw. haken*) hook ‹needle etc.› (**in** + *Dat.* in). ❷ *refl. V.* ‹person› get hooked *or* caught up; ‹zip› get caught

**verhallen** *itr. V.; mit sein* ‹sound› die away; **[ungehört] ~** (*fig.*) ‹call, words, etc.› go unheard *or* unheeded

**verhalten¹** ❶ *unr. refl. V.* [A] (*reagieren*) react; **sich still** *od.* **ruhig ~:** keep quiet; **ich verhielt mich abwartend** I decided to wait and see; [B] (*sich benehmen*) behave; [C] (*beschaffen sein*) be; **die Sache verhält sich nämlich so** this is how things stand *or* the matter stands; [D] (*im Verhältnis stehen*) **a verhält sich zu b wie x zu y** a is to b as x is to y; **die beiden Größen ~ sich zueinander wie 1:10** the two values are in a ratio of 1:10.
❷ *unr. tr. V.* [A] (*geh.: zurückhalten*) restrain, contain ‹anger›; restrain ‹mockery›; contain ‹laughter›; hold back ‹tears, urine›; [B] (*Reiten*) ⇒ **parieren²** c; [C] *auch itr.* (*geh.*) **[den Schritt] ~:** slow down; check one's pace; (*stehen bleiben*) stop

**verhalten²** ❶ *Adj.* [A] (*unterdrückt*) restrained; **mit ~em Tempo** at a measured pace; **mit ~en Schritten** treading quietly; **mit ~em Atem** with bated breath; [B] (*dezent*) restrained, subdued, muted ‹colours›; muted, soft ‹notes, voice, etc.›; [C] (*zurückhaltend*) reserved; **eine ~e Fahrweise** a cautious way of driving. ❷ *adv.* [A] (*unterdrückt*) in a restrained manner; [B] (*zurückhaltend*) in a reserved manner; **~ fahren** drive cautiously; [C] (*dezent*) ‹speak, play, etc.› softly

**Verhalten** *das; ~s* behaviour; (*Vorgehen*) conduct

**verhaltens-, Verhaltens-: ~forschung** *die* behavioural research *no art.*; (*Ethologie*) ethology *no art.*; **~gestört** *Adj.* (*Psych.*) ‹person, child› with a behavioural disorder; **~maßregel** *die* rule of conduct; **~maßregeln für den Notfall** rules governing emergencies; **~muster** *das* behaviour pattern; pattern of behaviour; **~störung** *die* (*Psych.*) behavioural disorder; **~therapie** *die* behavioural therapy; **~weise** *die* behaviour; **~weisen** behaviour patterns; patterns of behaviour

**Verhältnis** /fɛɐ̯ˈhɛltnɪs/ *das; ~ses, ~se* [A] **ein ~ von drei zu eins** a ratio of three to one; **im ~ zu früher** in comparison with *or* compared to earlier times; **der Aufwand stand in keinem ~ zum Erfolg** the expenditure was out of all proportion to the result; [B] (*persönliche Beziehung*) relationship (**zu** with); **zwischen uns** (*Dat.*) **herrscht ein vertrautes ~:** we are on intimate terms; **ein gutes ~ zu jmdm. haben** get on well with sb.; **er hat** *od.* **findet kein [rechtes] ~ zur Musik** he cannot relate to music; [C] (*ugs.: intime Beziehung*) affair; relationship; **mit jmdm. ein ~ haben** have an affair with sb.; **ein ~ mit jmdm. beenden** break up with sb.; break off a relationship with sb.; [D] (*ugs.*) (*Geliebte*) lady friend; (*Geliebter*) man; [E] *Pl.* (*Umstände*) conditions; **in bescheidenen** *od.* **einfachen/gesicherten ~sen leben** live in modest circumstances/be financially secure; **aus bescheidenen** *od.* **einfachen ~sen kommen** come from a humble background; **sie kommt aus kleinen ~sen** she comes from a lower middle-class background; **über seine ~se leben** live beyond one's means

**verhältnis-, Verhältnis-: ~gleichung** *die* (*Math.*) proportion; **~mäßig** *Adv.* relatively; comparatively; **~wahl** *die* proportional representation; **~wahlrecht** *das* [system of] proportional representation; **~wort** *das; Pl.* **~wörter** (*Sprachw.*) preposition

**verhandeln** ❶ *itr. V.* [A] negotiate (**über** + *Akk.* about); [B] (*strafrechtlich*) try a case; (*zivilrechtlich*) hear a case; **das Gericht verhandelt gegen die Terroristen** the court is trying the terrorists. ❷ *tr. V.* [A] **etw. ~:** negotiate over sth.; [B] (*strafrechtlich*) try ‹case›; (*zivilrechtlich*) hear ‹case›

**Verhandlung** *die* [A] (*Besprechung*) **~en** negotiations; **mit jmdm. in ~ stehen** be negotiating with sb.; be [involved *or* engaged] in negotiations *pl.* with sb.; **zu ~en bereit sein** be open to negotiation *sing.*; [B] (*strafrechtlich*) trial; (*zivilrechtlich*) hearing; **die ~ gegen X** the trial of X

**verhandlungs-, Verhandlungs-: ~basis** *die* ⇒ **~grundlage**; **~bereit** *Adj.* ready *or* willing to negotiate *pred.*; **~bereitschaft** *die* readiness *or* willingness to negotiate; **~gegen·stand** *der* subject for/under negotiation; **kein ~gegenstand sein** not be a matter for negotiation; **~grundlage** *die* basis for negotiation[s]; **~partner** *der*, **~partnerin** *die* opposite number [in the negotiations]; **die beiden ~partner** (*die miteinander verhandeln*) the two sides in the negotiations; **~tisch** *der* negotiating table; **~weg** *der*: *in* **auf dem ~weg** by negotiation

**verhangen** *Adj.* overcast

**verhängen** *tr. V.* [A] (*zuhängen*) cover (**mit** with); [B] (*anordnen*) impose ‹fine, punishment› (**über** + *Akk.* on); declare ‹state of emergency, state of siege›; (*Sport*) award, give ‹penalty etc.›

**Verhängnis** /fɛɐ̯ˈhɛŋnɪs/ *das; ~ses, ~se* undoing; **jmdm. zum ~ werden** be sb.'s undoing; **das ~ brach über ihn herein** disaster overtook him

**verhängnis·voll** *Adj.* (*unheilvoll*) disastrous; fatal, disastrous ‹mistake, weakness, hesitation, etc.›; (*schicksalsschwer*) fateful

**Verhängung** *die; ~, ~en* imposition; (*des Ausnahme-, Belagerungszustandes*) declaration

**verharmlosen** *tr. V.* play down

**Verharmlosung** *die; ~, ~en* playing down

**verhärmt** /fɛɐ̯ˈhɛrmt/ *Adj.* careworn

**verharren** *itr. V.* (*geh.*) [A] (*innehalten*) remain; (*plötzlich, kurz*) pause; [B] (*beharren*) **auf seinem Standpunkt ~:** persist in one's view; **in Resignation/Gleichgültigkeit ~:** remain resigned/indifferent

**verharschen** *itr. V.; mit sein* ‹snow› form a crust; ‹wound› form a scab

**verhärten** /fɛɐ̯ˈhɛrtn̩/ ❶ *tr. V.* [A] (*festigen*) harden ‹material etc.›; [B] (*unbarmherzig machen*) harden; make ‹person› hard. ❷ *refl. V.* [A] (*hart werden*) ‹tissue› become hardened; ‹tumour› become scirrhous; [B] (*gefühllos werden*) harden one's heart (**gegen** against); **die Fronten haben sich verhärtet** the positions of the opposing parties have become entrenched

**Verhärtung** *die; ~, ~en* [A] hardening; [B] (*fig.*) becoming hardened; **die ~ der Positionen auf beiden Seiten** the hardening of attitudes on both sides

**verhaspeln** *refl. V.* (*ugs.*) [A] (*sich versprechen*) stumble over one's words; [B] (*sich verwickeln*) become *or* get tangled up

**verhasst, *verhaßt** *Adj.* hated; detested; **es war ihm ~:** he hated *or* detested it; **nichts ist mir so ~ wie ...** there is nothing I detest so much as ...

**verhätscheln** *tr. V.* (*ugs.*) pamper

**Verhätschelung** *die; ~, ~en* (*ugs.*) pampering

**Verhau** /fɛɐ̯ˈhau̯/ *der od. das; ~[e]s, ~e* [A] tangle of branches; (*Dickicht*) thicket; [B] barrier [made of branches]; (*bes. Milit.*) entanglement

**verhauen** (*ugs.*) ❶ *unr. tr. V.* [A] (*verprügeln*) beat up; (*als Strafe*) beat; **jmdm. den Hintern ~:** give sb.'s bottom a good smack[ing]; [B] (*falsch machen*) make a mess of; muck up (*Brit. sl.*). ❷ *unr. refl. V.* (*sich verrechnen*) make a mistake *or* slip; **sich bei etw. mächtig ~:** slip up badly in sth.

**verheben** *unr. refl. V.* do oneself an injury [while lifting sth.]

**verheddern** /fɛɐ̯ˈhɛdɐn/ *refl. V.* [A] (*hängenbleiben*) **sich in etw.** (*Dat.*) **~:** get tangled up in sth.; [B] (*sich verhaspeln*) get muddled up

**verheeren** /fɛɐ̯ˈheːrən/ *tr. V.* devastate; lay waste [to]

**verheerend** *Adj.* [A] (*katastrophal*) devastating; disastrous; [B] (*ugs.: scheußlich*) ghastly (*coll.*); dreadful (*coll.*)

**Verheerung** *die; ~, ~en* devastation *no pl.*; **~[en] anrichten** cause devastation; wreak havoc

**verhehlen** *tr. V.* (*geh.*) conceal; hide; **jmdm. etw. ~:** conceal *or* hide sth. from sb.; **ich kann/will** *od.* **möchte [es] nicht ~, dass**

V

… there is no denying/I have no wish to deny that …

**verheilen** *itr. V.; mit sein* ‹wound› heal [up]

**verheimlichen** *tr. V.* **[jmdm.] etw. ~:** keep sth. secret [from sb.]; conceal *or* hide sth. [from sb.]

**Verheimlichung** *die; ~, ~en* concealment

**verheiraten** ❶ *refl. V.* get married; **sich mit jmdm. ~:** marry sb.; get married to sb.; **er ist mit seiner Firma/Gitarre verheiratet** (*fig.*) he has no time for anything except his company/guitar. ❷ *tr. V.* (*veralt.*) marry (**mit, an** + *Akk.* to); **er hatte zwei Töchter zu ~:** he had two daughters to marry off

**Verheiratete** *der/die; adj. Dekl.* married person; married man/woman; **~** *Pl.* married people; married men/women

**Verheiratung** *die; ~, ~en* marriage

**verheißen** *unr. tr. V.* (*geh.; auch fig.*) promise; **man verhieß ihm eine große Zukunft** a great future was predicted for him; **nichts Gutes ~:** not bode *or* augur well

**Verheißung** *die; ~, ~en* (*geh.*) promise

**verheißungs·voll** ❶ *Adj.* promising; **ein ~er Anfang** a promising *or* an auspicious start. ❷ *adv.* full of promise

**verheizen** *tr. V.* **A** burn; use as fuel; **B** (*abwertend: rücksichtslos einsetzen*) burn out ‹athlete, skier, etc.›; use ‹troops› as cannon fodder; run ‹employee, subordinate, etc.› into the ground

**verhelfen** *unr. itr. V.* **jmdm./einer Sache zu etw. ~:** help sb./sth. to get/achieve sth.; **jmdm. zur Flucht/zum Sieg ~:** help sb. to escape/win

**verherrlichen** *tr. V.* glorify ‹war, violence, deed, etc.›; extol ‹virtues, leader, etc.›; celebrate ‹nature, freedom, peace, etc.›

**Verherrlichung** *die; ~, ~en* ⇒ **verherrlichen**: glorification; extolling; celebration

**verhetzen** *tr. V.* incite; stir up; **die verhetzten Massen** the inflamed masses

**Verhetzung** *die; ~, ~en* incitement; stirring up

**verheult** /fɛɐ̯ˈhɔy̯lt/ *Adj.* (*ugs.*) ‹eyes› red from crying; ‹face› puffy *or* swollen from crying

**verhexen** *tr. V.* (*auch fig.*) bewitch; cast a spell on; **jmdn. in etw.** (*Akk.*) **~:** turn sb. into sth. [by magic]; **es ist wie verhext: kaum setze ich mich hin, klingelt das Telefon** there seems to be a jinx on me today: the moment I sit down, the telephone rings

**verhindern** *tr. V.* prevent; prevent, avert ‹war, disaster, etc.›; **es ließ sich nicht ~, dass er losfuhr** he couldn't be prevented from driving off; no one could stop him [from] driving off; **er ist [dienstlich] verhindert** he is prevented from coming [by business commitments]; he is unable to come [for business reasons]; **ein verhinderter Künstler/Schauspieler** (*ugs.*) a would-be artist/actor

**Verhinderung** *die; ~, ~en* ⇒ **verhindern**: prevention; averting

**verhohlen** /fɛɐ̯ˈhoːlən/ *Adj.* concealed; **kaum ~e Neugier** ill-concealed curiosity

**verhöhnen** /vɛrˈhœnen/ *tr. V.* mock; deride; ridicule

**verhohnepipeln** /fɛɐ̯ˈhoːnəpiːpl̩n/ *tr. V.* (*ugs.*) send up (*coll.*)

**Verhohnepipelung** *die; ~, ~en* send-up (*coll.*)

**Verhöhnung** *die; ~, ~en* **A** mockery; ridiculing; **B** (*Äußerung*) mocking remark

**verhökern** /fɛɐ̯ˈhøːkɐn/ *tr. V.* (*salopp*) flog (*Brit. sl.*)

**Verhör** /fɛɐ̯ˈhøːɐ̯/ *das; ~[e]s, ~e* interrogation; questioning; (*bei Gericht*) examination; **jmdn. ins ~ nehmen** interrogate *or* question sb.; (*fig.*) grill *or* quiz sb.

**verhören** ❶ *tr. V.* (*befragen*) interrogate; question; (*bei Gericht*) examine. ❷ *refl. V.* (*falsch hören*) mishear; hear wrongly; **Hier ist niemand. Du musst dich verhört haben** There's nobody here. You must have been hearing things

**verhornen** *itr. V.; mit sein* keratinize; ‹skin› become horny

**verhüllen** *tr. V.* **A** (*verbergen*) cover; (*fig.*) disguise; mask; **eine verhüllte Drohung** (*fig.*) a veiled threat; **B** (*umgeben*) enshroud; **Wolken verhüllten die Bergspitzen** the mountain tops were veiled *or* shrouded in cloud

**verhüllend** *Adj.* (*Literaturw.*) euphemistic

**Verhüllung** *die; ~, ~en* covering; (*fig.*) disguising

**verhundertfachen** *tr., refl. V.* increase a hundredfold

**verhungern** *itr. V.; mit sein* die of starvation; starve [to death]; **ich bin am V~** (*ugs.*) I'm starving (*fig. coll.*); **Verhungernde** *Pl.* people starving to death; **verhungert aussehen** look half-starved

**verhunzen** /fɛɐ̯ˈhʊntsn̩/ *tr. V.* (*ugs. abwertend*) ruin; mess up; ruin ‹landscape, townscape, etc.›

**verhüten** *tr. V.* prevent; prevent, avert ‹disaster›; **der Himmel verhüte, dass …** heaven forbid that …; **~, dass jmd. etw. tut** prevent sb. [from] doing sth.

**Verhüterli** *das; ~s, ~s* (*ugs. scherzh.*) French letter

**verhütten** *tr. V.* smelt

**Verhüttung** *die; ~, ~en* smelting

**Verhütung** *die; ~, ~en* prevention; (*Empfängnis~*) contraception

**Verhütungs-: ~maßnahmen** *Pl.* contraceptive precautions; **~mittel** *das* contraceptive

**verhutzelt** /fɛɐ̯ˈhʊtsl̩t/ *Adj.* (*ugs.*) wizened ‹person, face›; shrivelled ‹fruit, plant›

**verifizieren** /verifiˈtsiːrən/ *tr. V.* verify

**Verifizierung** *die; ~, ~en* verification

**verinnerlichen** *tr. V.* (*Soziol., Psych.*) internalize

**verinnerlicht** *Adj.* (*vergeistigt*) spiritualized; (*introvertiert*) introverted

**Verinnerlichung** *die; ~, ~en* (*Soziol., Psych.*) internalization

**verirren** *refl. V.* **A** (*abkommen*) get lost; lose one's way; ‹animal› stray; **verirrte Gewehrkugeln** (*fig.*) stray bullets; **B** (*irgendwohin gelangen*) stray (**in, an** + *Akk.* into)

**Verirrung** *die; ~, ~en* aberration

**veritabel** /veriˈtaːbl̩/ *Adj.* (*geh.*) veritable; real

**verjagen** *tr. V.* chase away; (*fig.*) dispel ‹thoughts, cares, etc.›; **jmdn. von Haus und Hof ~:** drive sb. out of house and home

**verjähren** /fɛɐ̯ˈjɛːrən/ *itr. V.; mit sein* come under the statute of limitations; **dieses Verbrechen ist inzwischen verjährt** this crime was committed too long ago to be punishable now

**Verjährung** *die; ~, ~en* limitation; **für Verbrechen wie Völkermord gibt es keine ~:** there is no statute of limitations for crimes like genocide

**Verjährungs·frist** *die* limitation period

**verjazzen** *tr. V.* play in a jazz style; jazz up

**verjubeln** *tr. V.* (*ugs.*) blow (*coll.*) ‹money›

**verjüngen** /fɛɐ̯ˈjʏŋən/ ❶ *tr. V.* rejuvenate ‹person, skin, etc.›; (*jünger aussehen lassen*) make ‹person› look younger; recruit younger blood into ‹team, company, etc.›. ❷ *refl. V.* (*schmaler werden*) taper; become narrower; narrow

**Verjüngung** *die; ~, ~en* **A** (*Jüngerwerden*) rejuvenation; **eine ~ des Politbüros** a recruitment of younger blood into the politburo; **B** (*Schmalerwerden*) tapering; narrowing

**Verjüngungs·kur** *die:* **ich fühle mich reif für eine ~:** I feel in need of being rejuvenated; **die neue Freundin wirkt auf ihn wie eine ~:** his new girlfriend has given him a new lease of life

**verjuxen** *tr. V.* (*ugs.*) **A** (*verjubeln*) blow (*sl.*) ‹money›; **B** (*verulken*) poke fun at

**verkabeln** *tr. V.* connect up [by cable]

**Verkabelung** *die; ~, ~en* installation of cables (*Gen.* in)

**verkalken** *itr. V.; mit sein* **A** ‹tissue› calcify, become calcified; ‹arteries› become hardened; ‹bone› thicken; ‹pipe, kettle, coffee machine, etc.› fur up; **B** (*ugs.: senil werden*) become senile; **er ist schon ziemlich verkalkt** he is already pretty gaga (*coll.*)

**verkalkulieren** *refl. V.* **A** (*falsch berechnen*) miscalculate; **B** (*falsch einschätzen*) miscalculate; make a miscalculation

**Verkalkung** *die; ~, ~en* **A** ⇒ **verkalken A**: calcification; hardening; thickening; furring-up; **B** (*ugs.: Senilität*) senility

**verkannt** /fɛɐ̯ˈkant/ *2. Part. v.* **verkennen**

**verkanten** ❶ *tr. V.* tilt; edge ‹ski›. ❷ *itr., refl. V.* (*sich festklemmen*) get jammed

**verkappt** *Adj.* disguised; **~e Anarchisten** anarchists in disguise

**verkarsten** *itr. V.; mit sein* be karstified

**Verkarstung** *die; ~, ~en* karstification

**verkatert** /fɛɐ̯ˈkaːtɐt/ *Adj.* (*ugs.*) hung-over (*coll.*); **~ aufwachen** wake up with a hangover

**Verkauf** *der* **A** sale; (*das Verkaufen*) sale; selling; **zum ~ stehen** be [up] for sale; **etw. zum ~ anbieten** offer sth. for sale; **B** (*Kaufmannsspr.*) sales *sing. or pl., no art.*

**verkaufen** ❶ *tr. V.* (*auch fig.*) sell (*Dat.*, **an** + *Akk.* to); **sie verkauft ihren Körper** she's a prostitute; **„zu ~"** 'for sale'. ❷ *refl. V.* **A** ‹goods› sell; **sich schlecht/gut ~** ‹goods› sell badly/well; **B** (*ugs.: falsch kaufen*) make a bad buy; **ich habe mich bei den Möbeln verkauft** the furniture was a bad buy

**Verkäufer** *der*, **Verkäuferin** *die* ▶ 159 **A** seller; vendor (*formal*); **B** (*Berufsbez.*) sales *or* shop assistant; salesperson; (*im Außendienst*) salesman/saleswoman; salesperson

**verkäuflich** *Adj.* **A** (*zum Verkauf geeignet*) saleable; marketable; **schwer/leicht ~ sein** be hard/easy to sell; **B** (*zum Verkauf bestimmt*) for sale *postpos.*; **dieses Mittel ist frei ~:** this medicine is available over the counter

**verkaufs-, Verkaufs-: ~aus·stellung** *die* exhibition and sale of works; **~automat** *der* vending machine; **~förderung** *die* sales promotion; **~leiter** *der*, **~leiterin** *die* sales manager; **~offen** *Adj.* **der ~offene Samstag** *od.* **Sonnabend** Saturday on which *or* when the shops are open all day; **~personal** *das* sales staff; **~preis** *der* retail price; **~schlager** *der* big seller; (*Buch*) best seller; **~stand** *der* stall

**Verkehr** *der; ~s* **A** traffic; **den ~ regeln** regulate *or* control the [flow of] traffic; **etw. dem [öffentlichen] ~ übergeben** open sth. to public use; **aus dem ~ ziehen** take ‹coin, banknote› out of circulation; take ‹product› off the market; **jmdn. aus dem ~ ziehen** (*ugs. scherzh.*) put sb. out of circulation (*joc.*); **in [den] ~ bringen** put ‹coin, banknote› into circulation; **B** (*Kontakt*) contact; communication; **diplomatischer ~:** diplomatic relations *pl.*; **keinen ~ mit jmdm. pflegen/den ~ mit jmdm. abbrechen** not/no longer associate with sb.; **C** (*Geschlechts~*) intercourse

**verkehren** ❶ *itr. V.* **A** *auch mit sein* (*fahren*) run; ‹aircraft› fly; **der Dampfer verkehrt zwischen Hamburg und Helgoland** the steamer plies *or* operates *or* goes between Hamburg and Heligoland; **der Bus verkehrt alle 15 Minuten** the bus runs *or* goes every 15 minutes; there's a bus every 15 minutes; **B** (*in Kontakt stehen*) **mit jmdm. ~:** associate with sb.; **wir ~ nur noch über unsere Anwälte/schriftlich miteinander** we only deal with each other through our solicitors/we only have written correspondence with each other; **C** (*zu Gast sein*) **bei jmdm. ~:** visit sb. regularly; **in einem Lokal ~:** frequent a pub (*Brit.*); **in den besten Kreisen ~:** move in the best circles; **D** (*verhüll.: koitieren*) have intercourse; **sexuell ~:** have sexual intercourse. ❷ *tr. V.* (*verdrehen*) turn (**in** + *Akk.* into); **jmds. Absicht ~:** reverse sb.'s intentions; **den Sinn einer Aussage ins Gegenteil ~:** twist the meaning of a statement right round.
❸ *refl. V.* (*sich verwandeln*) turn (**in** + *Akk.* into); **sich ins Gegenteil ~:** change to the opposite

*old spelling (see note on page 1707)

**verkehrs-, Verkehrs-: ~ader** *die* traffic artery; **~ampel** *die* traffic lights *pl.;* **~amt** *das* tourist information office; **~aufkommen** *das* volume of traffic; **~beruhigt** *Adj.* (*Verkehrsw.*) **~beruhigte Zone, ~beruhigter Bereich** traffic-calmed area; **~beruhigung** *die* traffic calming; **~betrieb** *der* transport services *pl.;* **~büro** *das* tourist office; **~chaos** *das* traffic chaos *no indef. art.;* chaos *no indef. art.* on the roads; **~dichte** *die* traffic density; **~erziehung** *die* road safety training; **~flugzeug** *das* commercial aircraft; **~fluss, *~fluß** *der* flow of traffic; **~funk** *der* radio traffic service; **~gefährdung** *die* constituting *no art.* a hazard to other traffic; **eine ~gefährdung darstellen** be *or* constitute a hazard to other traffic; **~hindernis** *das* obstruction to traffic; **~insel** *die* traffic island; refuge; **~knotenpunkt** *der* [traffic] junction; **~kontrolle** *die* traffic check; **~lage** *die* [A] (*Situation*) traffic situation; [B] (*Ortslage*) situation with regard to road and rail links; **eine gute ~lage haben** be well situated with regard to road and rail links; **~lärm** *der* traffic noise; **~meldung** *die* traffic announcement *or* flash; **~minister** *der*, **~ministerin** *die* minister of transport; **~ministerium** *das* ministry of transport; **~mittel** *das* means of transport; **die öffentlichen ~mittel** public transport *sing.;* **~netz** *das* transport system; **~opfer** *das* road accident *or* traffic accident victim; **~polizei** *die* traffic police *pl.;* **~polizist** *der* ▶ 159 traffic policeman; **~polizistin** *die* ▶ 159 traffic policewoman; **~regel** *die* traffic regulation; **~reich** *Adj.* busy ‹crossing, street, etc.›; **~rowdy** *der* road hog; **~schild** *das* traffic sign; road sign; **~sicher** *Adj.* roadworthy ‹vehicle, condition›; **~sicherheit** *die* road safety; (*eines Fahrzeugs*) roadworthiness; **~sprache** *die* lingua franca; **~stockung** *die* traffic hold-up; **~sünder** *der*, **~sünderin** *die* (*ugs.*) traffic offender; **~teilnehmer** *der*, **~teilnehmerin** *die* road user; **~tote** *der/die* person killed on the roads; **weniger ~tote** fewer deaths on the roads; **~unfall** *der* road accident; **~unterricht** *der* road safety instruction; **~verbindung** *die* transport link; **~verhältnisse** *Pl.* [A] (*~verbindungen*) transport links; [B] (*~lage*) traffic conditions; **~weg** *der* traffic route; **~widrig** ❶ *Adj.* contrary to road traffic regulations *postpos.;* ❷ *adv.* contrary to road traffic regulations; **~zeichen** *das* traffic sign; road sign

**verkehrt** ❶ *Adj.* wrong; **das ist gar nicht so ~:** that's not such a bad idea; **es ist sicher nicht ~, das zu tun** there's no harm in doing that; **an den Verkehrten/die Verkehrte kommen** *od.* **geraten** (*ugs.*) come to the wrong person. ❷ *adv.* wrongly; **alles ~ machen** do everything wrong; **sich ~ verhalten** do the wrong thing; ⇒ *auch* **herum** A

**Verkehrung** *die;* ~, **~en** reversal; **eine ~ ins Gegenteil** a change to the opposite

**verkeilen** ❶ *tr. V.* wedge. ❷ *refl. V.* become wedged (**in** + *Akk.* in); **sich ineinander ~:** become wedged together

**verkennen** *unr. tr. V.* fail to recognize; misjudge ‹situation›; fail to appreciate ‹efforts, achievement, etc.›; **es ist nicht zu ~, dass ...** it cannot be denied *or* is undeniable that ...; **ihre Absicht war nicht zu ~:** her intention was unmistakable; **ein verkanntes Genie** an unrecognized genius

**Verkennung** *die;* ~, **~en** ⇒ **verkennen**: failure to recognize/appreciate; misjudgement; **in völliger ~ der Situation** completely misjudging the situation

**verketten** *refl. V.* become interlinked

**Verkettung** *die;* ~, **~en** (*von Zufällen usw.*) chain

**verketzern** *tr. V.* denounce

**Verketzerung** *die;* ~, **~en** denunciation

**verkitschen** *tr. V.* turn ‹novel, film, etc.› into kitsch; sentimentalize ‹song, tune, etc.›

**verkitten** *tr. V.* fill ‹crack, hole, joint, etc.›; put putty round ‹window›

**verklagen** *tr. V.* sue; take proceedings against; take to court; **eine Firma auf Schadenersatz ~:** sue a company for damages

**verklammern** *tr. V.* (*Med.*) close ‹wound› with a clamp/clamps

**verklappen** *tr. V.* dump ‹waste› [at sea]

**Verklappung** *die;* ~, **~en** dumping [at sea]

**verklären** ❶ *tr. V.* (*auch Rel.*) transfigure. ❷ *refl. V.* (*auch fig.*) be transfigured; ‹eyes› shine blissfully

**verklärt** ❶ *Adj.* transfigured, blissful ‹expression, face, etc.›. ❷ *adv.* blissfully

**Verklärung** *die* transfiguration

**verklausulieren** /fɛɐ̯klau̯zu'li:rən/ *tr. V.* [A] (*mit Klauseln versehen*) hedge ‹contract etc.› with qualifying clauses; [B] (*verbergen*) hedge ‹admission of guilt etc.› round with qualifications; **in verklausulierter Form** in a roundabout way

**Verklausulierung** *die;* ~, **~en** [A] (*das Verklausulieren*) involved formulation; [B] (*Formulierung*) qualification

**verkleben** ❶ *itr. V.; mit sein* stick together; **der Pinsel ist verklebt** the bristles of the brush are stuck together. ❷ *tr. V.* [A] (*zusammenkleben*) stick ‹eyelids, eyelashes› together; **verklebte Hände/Haare** sticky hands/matted *or* sticky hair; [B] (*zukleben*) seal up ‹hole›; **eine Wunde mit Heftpflaster ~:** cover a wound with sticking plaster; [C] (*festkleben*) stick [down] ‹floor covering etc.›; **das Schaufenster mit Papier ~:** paper over the shop window; [D] (*verbrauchen*) use up ‹posters, rolls of wallpaper, etc.›

**verkleckern** *tr. V.* (*ugs.*) spill

**verkleiden** *tr. V.* [A] disguise; (*kostümieren*) dress up; **sich ~:** disguise oneself/dress [oneself] up; [B] (*umhüllen, verdecken*) cover; (*verschalen*) line; face ‹façade›

**Verkleidung** *die* [A] disguising; (*das Kostümieren*) dressing up; [B] (*Kostüm*) (*als Tarnung*) disguise; (*bei einer Party usw.*) fancy dress; [C] ⇒ **verkleiden** B: covering; lining; facing; [D] (*Umhüllung*) cover

**verkleinern** /fɛɐ̯'klai̯nɐn/ ❶ *tr. V.* [A] (*kleiner machen*) make smaller; reduce the size of; **den Abstand ~:** reduce *or* decrease the distance; **etw. in verkleinertem Maßstab darstellen** represent sth. on a smaller scale; scale sth. down; [B] (*verringern*) reduce ‹size, number, etc.›; [C] (*schmälern*) belittle ‹person, achievements›; minimize ‹importance, significance›; [D] (*kleiner reproduzieren*) reduce ‹photograph etc.›. ❷ *refl. V.* [A] (*ugs.: sich einschränken*) ‹company etc.› move to smaller premises; ‹family etc.› move to a smaller place; [B] (*kleiner werden*) ‹space, area, etc.› become smaller; [C] (*sich verringern*) ‹number› decrease, grow smaller; ‹circle of friends› grow smaller, shrink. ❸ *itr. V.* ‹lens etc.› make things look *or* appear smaller

**Verkleinerung** *die;* ~, **~en** reduction in size; making smaller; (*des Formats, der Anzahl, des Maßstabs, durch eine Linse*) reduction; (*das Kleinerwerden*) becoming smaller

**Verkleinerungs·form** *die* (*Sprachw.*) diminutive form

**verkleistern** *tr. V.* (*ugs.*) [A] (*zukleben*) fill ‹crack, hole›; (*fig.*) cover up; [B] (*zusammenkleben*) make into a sticky mass

**verklemmen** *refl. V.* get *or* become stuck; ‹door, window› jam, get *or* become jammed

**verklemmt** ❶ *Adj.* inhibited. ❷ *adv.* in an inhibited manner

**Verklemmtheit** *die;* ~: inhibitedness

**verklickern** *tr. V.* (*salopp*) **jmdm. etw. ~:** make sth. clear to sb.; spell sth. out to sb.; (*erklären*) explain sth. to sb. in every detail

**verklingen** *unr. itr. V.; mit sein* ‹sound, voice, song, etc.› fade away; (*fig.*) ‹mood› wear off

**verklumpen** *itr. V.; mit sein* ‹gravy, sauce, etc.› go lumpy

**verknacken** *tr. V.* (*salopp*) **jmdn. zu Gefängnis/einer Geldstrafe ~:** put sb. inside (*sl.*)/slap a fine on sb. (*coll.*); **er wurde zu 18 Monaten verknackt** he got 18 months; **er wurde wegen ein paar Brüchen verknackt** he was done for a couple of break-ins (*sl.*)

**verknacksen** /fɛɐ̯'knaksn̩/ *refl. V.* (*ugs.*) twist, sprain ‹ankle, wrist›; **sich** (*Dat.*) **den Fuß ~:** twist *or* sprain one's ankle

**verknallen** ❶ *tr. V.* (*ugs.: verschießen*) let off ‹firework›; use up ‹ammunition›; **zu Silvester werden unglaubliche Summen verknallt** incredible amounts of money are squandered on fireworks on New Year's Eve. ❷ *refl. V.* (*ugs.: sich verlieben*) fall head over heels in love (**in** + *Akk.* with); **in jmdn. verknallt sein** be crazy about sb. (*coll.*)

**verknappen** ❶ *tr. V.* cut back [on] ‹imports›; **das würde das Wasser noch weiter ~:** that would create even more water shortages. ❷ *refl. V.* run short

**Verknappung** *die;* ~, **~en** cutting back (*Gen.* on); (*der Liquidität*) loss

**verkneifen** *unr. refl. V.* (*ugs.*) [A] **sich** (*Dat.*) **eine Frage/Bemerkung ~:** bite back a question/remark; **ich konnte mir das Lachen/ein Lächeln kaum ~:** I could hardly keep a straight face; I could hardly stop myself laughing/smiling; [B] (*verzichten*) manage *or* do without; **es sich** (*Dat.*) **~, etw. zu tun** stop oneself doing sth.

**verkniffen** ❶ *2. Part. v.* **verkneifen.** ❷ *Adj.* strained ‹expression›; pinched ‹mouth, lips›. ❸ *adv.* in a strained manner; **~ grinsen** force a grin

**verknittern** *tr. V.* crumple; **ein verknittertes Gesicht** (*fig.*) a wrinkled face

**verknöchern** /fɛɐ̯'knœçɐn/ *itr. V.; mit sein* ‹person› become fossilized

**verknorpeln** *itr. V.; mit sein* (*Med.*) become cartilaginous

**Verknorpelung** *die;* ~, **~en** cartilaginification

**verknoten** ❶ *tr. V.* [A] (*verknüpfen*) tie; knot; **zwei Fäden [miteinander] ~:** tie two threads together; [B] (*festbinden*) tie (**an** + *Akk.* to). ❷ *refl. V.* become knotted

**verknüpfen** ❶ *tr. V.* [A] (*knoten*) tie; knot; **die beiden Fäden miteinander ~:** tie *or* knot the two threads together; [B] (*zugleich tun*) combine; [C] (*in Beziehung setzen*) link; (*unwillkürlich*) associate. ❷ *refl. V.* be associated

**Verknüpfung** *die;* ~, **~en** [A] ⇒ **verknüpfen** 1: tying; knotting; combination; linking; association; [B] (*Knoten*) knots *pl.*

**verknusen** /fɛɐ̯'knu:zn̩/ *in* **jmdn./etw. nicht ~ können** (*ugs.*) not be able to stick (*sl.*) *or* stand sb./sth.

**verkochen** ❶ *itr. V.;* mit sein [A] (*verdampfen*) boil away; [B] (*breiig werden, zerfallen*) boil down to a pulp. ❷ *tr. V.* boil (**zu** + *Dat.* to make)

**verkohlen**[1] ❶ *itr. V.* char; become charred. ❷ *tr. V.* burn ‹wood› to charcoal; char

**verkohlen**[2] *tr. V.* (*ugs.*) ⇒ **veräppeln**

**verkommen**[1] *unr. itr. V.; mit sein* [A] (*verwahrlosen*) go to the dogs; (*moralisch, sittlich*) go to the bad; ‹child› go wild; **im tiefsten Elend ~:** sink deeper and deeper into poverty; [B] (*verfallen*) ‹building etc.› go to rack and ruin, fall into disrepair, become dilapidated; ‹garden› run wild; ‹area› become run down; [C] (*herabsinken*) degenerate (**zu** into); [D] (*verderben*) ‹food› go bad; ‹wine, beer› go off

**verkommen**[2] ❶ *2. Part. v.* **~**[1]. ❷ *Adj.* depraved; **ein ~es Subjekt** a dissolute character

**Verkommenheit** *die;* ~: depravity

**verkomplizieren** *tr. V.* complicate

**verkonsumieren** *tr. V.* (*ugs.*) get through; consume

**verkoppeln** *tr. V.* couple; ‹spacecraft› link up

**Verkoppelung** *die;* ~, **~en** coupling; (*von Flugkörpern*) link-up

**verkorken** ❶ *tr. V.* cork [up]. ❷ *itr. V.; mit sein* (*Bot.*) suberize

**verkorksen** /fɛɐ̯'kɔrksn̩/ (*ugs.*) ❶ *tr. V.* make a mess of; mess up; **eine verkorkste Gesellschaft** a screwed-up society (*sl.*). ❷ *refl. V.* **sich** (*Dat.*) **den Magen ~:** upset one's stomach

**verkörpern** ❶ *tr. V.* [A] (*als Schauspieler*) play [the part of]; [B] (*bilden*) embody; ‹person› embody, personify. ❷ *refl. V.* be embodied (**in** + *Dat.* in)

**Verkörperung** *die;* ~, ~**en** embodiment; (*Mensch*) embodiment; personification

**verkosten** *tr. V.* [A] (*bes. österr.: kosten*) try; taste; [B] (*prüfend schmecken*) taste ‹wine›

**verköstigen** /fɛɐ̯ˈkœstɪɡn̩/ *tr. V.* feed; provide with meals

**Verköstigung** *die;* ~, ~**en** [A] feeding; **die** ~ **der Kinder** the provision of the children with meals; [B] (*Kost*) foods; meals *pl.*

**verkrachen** *refl. V.* (*ugs.*) fall out

**verkracht** *Adj.* failed; **er war ein** ~**er Student** he had been a failure at university/college; ⇒ *auch* **Existenz** C

**verkraften** *tr. V.* cope with; **sie hat dieses Erlebnis nie verkraftet** she's never come to terms with this experience

**verkrallen** *refl. V.* dig one's fingers (**in** + *Akk.* into); (*festhalten*) cling (**in** + *Akk./Dat.* to)

**verkramen** *tr. V.* (*ugs.*) mislay

**verkrampfen** *refl. V.* ‹muscle› become cramped; ‹person› go tense, tense up; **verkrampft sitzen/lächeln** sit tensed up/smile tensely

**Verkrampfung** *die;* ~, ~**en** tenseness; tension

**verkratzen** *tr. V.* scratch; **sich** (*Dat.*) **die Beine** ~**:** scratch one's legs

**verkrebst** /fɛɐ̯ˈkreːpst/ *Adj.* (*ugs.*) cancerous

**verkriechen** *unr. refl. V.* ‹animal› creep [away]; ‹person› hide [oneself away]; **sich unter die** *od.* **der Bank** ~**:** crawl *or* creep under the bench; **sich ins Bett** ~ (*ugs.*) crawl into bed (*coll.*); **am liebsten hätte ich mich [in den hintersten Winkel] verkrochen** I'd have liked to crawl away and hide in a corner; I wished the ground would open and swallow me up

**verkrümeln** *refl. V.* (*ugs.: sich entfernen*) slip off *or* away

**verkrümmen** ❶ *refl. V.* double up; ‹spine› become curved. ❷ *tr. V.* bend ‹finger etc.›

**verkrümmt** *Adj.* bent ‹person›; crooked ‹finger›; curved ‹spine›

**Verkrümmung** *die* crookedness; ~ **der Wirbelsäule** curvature of the spine

**verkrüppeln** ❶ *itr. V.; mit sein* ‹tree› become stunted; **verkrüppelt** stunted. ❷ *tr. V.* cripple ‹person›; **verkrüppelte Arme/Füße** deformed arms/crippled feet

**Verkrüppelung** *die;* ~, ~**en** deformity

**verkrusten** *itr. V.; mit sein* form a crust; ‹wound› form a scab; **mit Blut verkrustet** encrusted with blood

**verkühlen** *refl. V.* catch a chill

**Verkühlung** *die* chill

**verkümmern** *itr. V.; mit sein* [A] ‹person, animal› go into a decline; ‹plant etc.› become stunted; ‹muscle, limb› waste away, atrophy; **seelisch** ~ ‹person› become emotionally stunted; [B] ‹talent, emotional life, etc.› wither away; ‹strength› decline, fade; ‹relationship› become less close; ‹trade, initiative› dwindle

**Verkümmerung** *die;* ~, ~**en** ⇒ **verkümmern** B: withering away; declining; fading; becoming less close; dwindling

**verkünden** *tr. V.* announce; pronounce ‹judgement›; promulgate ‹law, decree›; ‹sign, omen› presage; **die Menschenrechte** ~**:** proclaim the rights of man; **seine Miene verkündete nichts Gutes** (*fig.*) his expression did not augur well

**verkündigen** *tr. V.* (*geh.*) [A] (*predigen*) preach; [B] (*bekannt machen*) announce; proclaim; (*mit Nachdruck sagen*) announce; [C] (*ankündigen*) ‹sign, omen› presage

**Verkündigung** *die* [A] (*das Predigen*) preaching; [B] (*Bekanntmachung*) announcement; proclamation; [C] (*das Wort Gottes*) word of God; **die kirchliche** ~**:** the Church's message

**Verkündung** *die;* ~, ~**en** announcement; (*von Urteilen*) pronouncement; (*von Gesetzen, Verordnungen*) promulgation

**verkuppeln** *tr. V.* pair off (**mit** with)

**verkürzen** ❶ *tr. V.* [A] (*verringern*) reduce; (*abkürzen*) shorten; **die Linie erscheint verkürzt** this line appears foreshortened; [B] (*abbrechen*) cut short ‹stay, life›; put an end to, end ‹suffering›; **verkürzte Arbeitszeit** reduced *or* shorter working hours *pl.;* [C] **sich** (*Dat.*) **die Zeit** ~**:** while away the time; make the time pass more quickly; **jmdm. die Winterabende** ~**:** help sb. while away the winter evenings. ❷ *refl. V.* (*kürzer werden*) become shorter; shorten; ‹perspective› become foreshortened. ❸ *itr. V.* (*Ballspiele*) close the gap (**auf** + *Akk.* to)

**Verkürzung** *die* ⇒ **verkürzen** 1 A, B: shortening; reduction; foreshortening; cutting short; ending; **eine** ~ **der Arbeitszeit** a reduction in working hours; **starkes Rauchen hat eine** ~ **der Lebenserwartung um ... zur Folge** heavy smoking reduces life expectancy by ...

**verlachen** *tr. V.* laugh at; **etw. als Unsinn** ~**:** ridicule sth. as nonsense

**verladen** *unr. tr. V.* [A] (*laden*) load; [B] (*ugs.: betrügen*) **jmdn.** ~**:** take sb. for a ride (*coll.*); con sb. (*sl.*); (*Ballspiele*) out-trick sb.

**Verlade·rampe** *die* loading platform

**Verladung** *die* loading

**Verlag** /fɛɐ̯ˈlaːk/ *der;* ~**[e]s**, ~**e** publishing house *or* firm; publisher's; **in welchem** ~ **ist das Buch erschienen?** who published the book?; who is the publisher of the book?

**verlagern** ❶ *tr. V.* shift ‹weight, centre of gravity›; (*an einen anderen Ort*) move; (*fig.*) transfer; shift ‹emphasis›. ❷ *refl. V.* (*auch fig.*) shift; ‹area of high/low pressure etc.› move

**Verlagerung** *die* moving; **eine** ~ **des Schwergewichts** (*fig.*) a shift in emphasis

**Verlags-:** ~**anstalt** *die* publishing house *or* firm; firm of publishers; ~**buch·händler** *der,* ~**buch·händlerin** *die* publisher; ~**haus** *das* publishing house *or* firm; ~**programm** *das* [publisher's] list; ~**wesen** *das* publishing *no art.*

**verlanden** *itr. V.; mit sein* silt up

**Verlandung** *die* silting up

**verlangen** ❶ *tr. V.* [A] (*fordern*) demand; (*wollen*) want; **man kann von ihm nicht** ~**, dass er alles bezahlt** one can't ask *or* expect him to pay everything; **das ist zu viel verlangt** that's asking too much; that's too much to expect; **du verlangst Unmögliches** you're asking the impossible; **die Firma verlangt [von den Bewerbern] EDV-Kenntnisse** the company asks for [applicants with] a knowledge of computers; **die Rechnung** ~**:** ask for the bill; **von jedem wird Pünktlichkeit verlangt** everyone is required *or* expected to be punctual; [B] (*nötig haben*) ‹task etc.› require, call for ‹patience, knowledge, experience, skill, etc.›; **diese Aufgabe verlangt den ganzen Menschen** this task makes demands of the whole person; [C] (*gebieten*) ‹situation, decency› demand; [D] (*berechnen*) charge; **sie verlangte 200 Mark von ihm** she charged him 200 marks; **wie viel verlangst du dafür?** how much are you asking for it?; [E] (*sehen wollen*) ask for, ask to see ‹passport, driving licence, etc.›; [F] (*am Telefon*) ask for; ask to speak to; **du wirst am Telefon verlangt** you're wanted on the phone; [G] *unpers.* (*geh.*) **es verlangt mich, ihn noch einmal zu sehen** I long *or* yearn to see him again.
❷ *itr. V.* (*geh.*) [A] (*bitten*) **nach einem Arzt/Priester** *usw.* ~**:** ask for a doctor/priest *etc.;* **nach einem Glas Wasser** ~**:** ask for a glass of water; [B] (*sich sehnen*) **nach jmdm./etw.** ~**:** long for sb./sth.

**Verlangen** *das;* ~**s**, ~ [A] (*Bedürfnis*) desire (**nach** for); **ein starkes** ~ **nach Schokolade haben** *od.* **verspüren** have a craving for chocolate; [B] (*Forderung*) demand; **auf** ~**:** on request; **auf jmds.** ~**:** at sb.'s request

**verlängern** /fɛɐ̯ˈlɛŋɐn/ ❶ *tr. V.* [A] (*länger machen*) lengthen, make longer ‹skirt, sleeve, etc.›; extend ‹flex, cable, road, etc.›; ⇒ *auch* **Arm** A; **Rücken** A; [B] (*länger gültig sein lassen*) renew ‹passport, driving licence, etc.›; extend, renew ‹contract›; [C] (*länger dauern lassen*) extend, prolong ‹stay, life, suffering, etc.› (**um** by); **ein verlängertes Wochenende** a long weekend; [D] (*verdünnen*) add water *etc.* to ‹sauce, gravy, etc.› (*to make it go further*); [E] (*Ballspiele*) touch ‹cross, corner kick, etc.› on.
❷ *refl. V.* [A] (*länger werden*) become longer; ‹stay, life, suffering, etc.› be prolonged (**um** by); [B] (*länger gültig bleiben*) ‹contract etc.› be extended.
❸ *itr. V.* (*Ballspiele*) touch [the ball] on; **mit dem Kopf** ~**:** head [the ball] on

**Verlängerung** *die;* ~, ~**en** [A] ⇒ **verlängern** 1 A-C: lengthening; renewal; extension; prolongation; [B] (*Ballspiele*) extra time *no indef. art.;* (*nachgespielte Zeit*) injury time *no indef. art.;* **in der/nach** ~**:** in/after extra time; [C] (*Teilstück*) extension

**Verlängerungs·schnur** *die* extension lead *or* (*Amer.*) cord

**verlangsamen** ❶ *tr. V.* **die Fahrt** *od.* **das Tempo/seine Schritte** ~**:** reduce speed/slacken one's pace; slow down. ❷ *refl. V.* slow down; ‹pace› slacken

**Verlangsamung** *die;* ~, ~**en** slowing down; (*des Tempos*) slackening; **zu einer** ~ **des Tempos gezwungen sein** be forced to slow down

**Verlass, *Verlaß** *der: in* **auf jmdn./etw. ist [kein]** ~**:** sb./sth. can[not] be relied *or* depended [up]on; **auf ihn ist kein** ~**:** you can't rely *or* depend on him

**verlassen**[1] ❶ *unr. refl. V.* (*vertrauen*) rely, depend (**auf** + *Akk.* on); **er verlässt sich darauf, dass du kommst** he's relying on you to come; **darauf kannst du dich** ~/**worauf du dich** ~ **kannst** you can depend on *or* be sure of that.
❷ *unr. tr. V.* [A] leave; **die Patientin konnte das Bett** ~**:** the patient was able to get up; [B] (*sich trennen von*) desert; abandon; forsake; leave, desert ‹wife, family, etc.›; **Großvater hat uns für immer** ~ (*verhüll.*) grandfather has been taken from us (*euphem.*); **und da/dann verließen sie ihn** (*ugs.*) and after that I/he *etc.* was at a loss; **der Mut/alle Hoffnung hatte mich** ~ (*fig.*) my courage/all hope had deserted me

**verlassen**[2] ❶ *2. Part. v.* ~[1]. ❷ *Adj.* deserted ‹street, square, village, etc.›; empty ‹house›; (*öd*) desolate ‹region etc.›; **einsam und** ~**:** all alone; ~ **daliegen** be deserted

**Verlassenheit** *die;* ~**:** desertedness; (*Öde*) desolation; **ein Gefühl von** ~**:** a feeling of desolation

**verlässlich, *verläßlich** /fɛɐ̯ˈlɛslɪç/ ❶ *Adj.* reliable; reliable, dependable ‹person›. ❷ *adv.* reliably

**Verlässlichkeit, *Verläßlichkeit** *die;* ~**:** reliability; (*eines Menschen*) reliability; dependability

**verlästern** *tr. V.* malign

**Verlaub** /fɛɐ̯ˈlaup/ *der: in* **mit** ~ (*geh.*) with your permission; **mit** ~ **[gesagt** *od.* **zu sagen]** if you will pardon *or* forgive my saying so

**Verlauf** *der;* ~**[e]s, Verläufe** course; **im** ~**e des Sommers/ihrer Rede** during *or* in the course of the summer/her speech; **der glückliche** ~ **der Revolution** the fortunate outcome of the revolution

**verlaufen** ❶ *unr. itr. V.; mit sein* [A] (*sich erstrecken*) run; [B] (*ablaufen*) ‹test, rehearsal, etc.› go; ‹party etc.› go off; **es ist alles gut** ~**:** everything went [off] well; **die Untersuchung ist ergebnislos** ~**:** the investigation yielded no results; [C] ‹butter, chocolate, etc.› melt; ‹make-up, ink› run. ❷ *unr. itr.* (*auch refl.*) *V.; mit sein* (*sich verlieren*) ‹track, path› disappear (**in** + *Dat.* in). ❸ *unr. refl. V.* [A] (*sich verirren*) get lost; lose one's way; [B] (*auseinander gehen*) ‹crowd etc.› disperse; [C] (*abfließen*) ‹floods› subside

**Verlaufs·form** *die* (*Sprachw.*) progressive *or* continuous form

**verlausen** *itr. V.; mit sein* become infested with lice; **verlaust** louse-ridden; infested with lice *postpos.*

*old spelling (see note on page 1707)

V

**verlautbaren** ❶ *tr. V.* announce [officially]; **offen ~:** state openly; **die Ärzte verlautbarten, dass ...** the doctors issued a bulletin to the effect that .... ❷ *itr. V.; mit sein (geh.)* become known; **es verlautbarte, der Staatschef sei krank** it was reported *or* said that the head of state was ill

**Verlautbarung** *die; ~, ~en* announcement; (*inoffizielle Meldung*) [unofficial] report

**verlauten** ❶ *tr. V.* announce; **er hütete sich davor, ein Wort davon zu ~:** he was careful not to say a word about it. ❷ *itr. V.; mit sein* be reported; **wie verlautet** according to reports; **aus amtlicher Quelle verlautet, dass ...** official reports say that ...; **über ihr Privatleben ließ sie nichts ~:** she let nothing be known about her private life

**verleben** *tr. V.* A (*verbringen*) spend; B (*ugs.: verbrauchen*) spend ‹money› on everyday needs

**verlebendigen** *tr. V.* make ‹text, past, etc.› come alive; imbue ‹portrait, figure› with life

**verlebt** *Adj.* dissipated

**verlegen¹** ❶ *tr. V.* A (*nicht wieder finden*) mislay; B (*verschieben*) postpone (**auf** + *Akk.* until); (*vor~*) bring forward (**auf** + *Akk.* to); **einen Termin ~:** alter an appointment; C (*verlagern*) move; transfer ‹patient›; **die Handlung ins 18. Jahrhundert ~:** transpose *or* shift the action to the 18th century; D (*legen*) lay ‹cable, pipe, carpet, etc.›; E (*versperren*) block, bar ‹way etc.›; block off ‹retreat›; **jmdm. den Weg ~:** block *or* bar sb.'s way; F (*veröffentlichen*) publish.
❷ *refl. V.* (*sich ausrichten*) take up ‹subject, activity, occupation, etc.›; resort to ‹guesswork, flattery, silence, lying, etc.›; **sich auf eine andere Taktik ~:** change [one's] tactics; resort to a different tactic

**verlegen²** ❶ *Adj.* A embarrassed; B **um etw. ~ sein** (*etw. nicht zur Verfügung haben*) be short of sth.; (*etw. benötigen*) be in need of sth.; **nicht/nie um Worte/eine Ausrede ~ sein** not/never be at a loss for words/an excuse. ❷ *adv.* in embarrassment

**Verlegenheit** *die; ~, ~en* A (*Befangenheit*) embarrassment; **in ~ geraten** get *or* become embarrassed; **jmdn. in ~ bringen** embarrass sb.; B (*Unannehmlichkeit*) embarrassing situation; **in finanzieller ~ sein** be in financial difficulties; be financially embarrassed; **ich bin nie in die ~ gekommen** I've never been in that embarrassing situation

**Verlegenheits·lösung** *die* makeshift solution

**Verleger** *der; ~s, ~,* **Verlegerin** *die; ~, ~nen* ▶ 159 publisher; ⇨ *auch* **-in**

**verlegerisch** ❶ *Adj.* publishing; **~e Kenntnisse** knowledge of publishing; **~e Anstrengungen** efforts on the part of the publishers. ❷ *adv.* from the publishing standpoint

**Verlegung** *die; ~, ~en* A (*Verschiebung*) postponement; (*Vor~*) bringing forward *no art.*; **um eine ~ des Termins bitten** ask to change the appointment; B ⇨ **verlegen¹** 1 C: moving; transfer; transposition; shifting; C (*von Kabeln, Rohren, Teppichen usw.*) laying

**verleiden** *tr. V.* **jmdm. etw. ~:** spoil sth. for sb.

**Verleih** *der; ~[e]s, ~e* A (*das Verleihen*) hiring out; (*von Autos*) renting *or* hiring out; B (*Unternehmen*) hire firm *or* company; (*Film~*) distribution company; (*Video~*) video library; (*Auto~*) rental *or* hire firm

**verleihen** *unr. tr. V.* A hire out; rent *or* hire out ‹car›; (*umsonst*) lend [out]; B (*überreichen*) award; bestow, confer ‹award, honour›; **jmdm. einen Orden/Titel ~:** decorate sb./confer a title on sb.; **jmdm. die Ehrenbürgerrechte ~:** give sb. the freedom of the city/town; C (*verschaffen*) give; lend; **er verlieh seinen Worten mit Drohungen Nachdruck** he used threats to lend weight to his words

**Verleiher** *der; ~s, ~,* **Verleiherin** *die; ~, ~nen* hirer; (*Film~*) distributor

**Verleihung** *die; ~, ~en* A ⇨ **verleihen** A: hiring out; renting out; lending [out]; B ⇨ **verleihen** B: awarding; bestowing; conferring; (*Zeremonie*) award; conferment; bestowal

**verleimen** *tr. V.* glue

**verleiten** *tr. V.* **jmdn. dazu ~, etw. zu tun** lead *or* induce sb. to do sth.; (*verlocken*) tempt *or* entice sb. to do sth.; **jmdn. zum Trinken/Stehlen ~:** lead sb. into drinking/stealing; **sich zu voreiligen Schlussfolgerungen ~ lassen** allow oneself to be led into drawing hasty conclusions

**Verleitung** *die:* **sie beschuldigte ihn der ~ zum Meineid** she accused him of inducing *or* encouraging her to commit perjury; **das wäre ~ zum Diebstahl** it would be encouraging theft

**verlernen** *tr. V.* forget; **das Kochen ~:** forget how to cook; **sie hat das Lachen verlernt** (*fig.*) she has forgotten how to laugh

**verlesen¹** ❶ *unr. tr. V.* read out. ❷ *unr. refl. V.* (*falsch lesen*) make a mistake/mistakes in reading; **er hat sich wohl ~:** he must have read it wrongly

**verlesen²** ❶ *2. Part. v.* **~¹**. ❷ *unr. tr. V.* (*auslesen*) sort ‹fruit, vegetables›

**Verlesung** *die; ~, ~en* reading out

**verletzbar** *Adj.* **leicht ~ sein** be easily hurt

**Verletzbarkeit** *die; ~:* **seine ~ war groß** he was very easily hurt; **sie kannte meine ~:** she knew how easily I could be hurt

**verletzen** /fɛɐ̯ˈlɛtsn̩/ *tr. V.* A ▶ 474 (*beschädigen*) injure; (*durch Schuss, Stich*) wound; **ich habe mich am Kopf/mir das Bein verletzt** I injured *or* hurt my head/leg; B (*kränken*) hurt, wound ‹person, feelings›; **verletzte Eitelkeit/verletzter Stolz** injured *or* wounded vanity/pride; **eine ~de Bemerkung** a wounding remark; **sich in seinem Stolz verletzt fühlen** feel that one's pride has been hurt *or* has taken a blow; C (*verstoßen gegen*) violate; infringe; infringe ‹regulation›; break ‹agreement, law›; **das Wahlgeheimnis ~:** breach the secrecy of the vote; **den guten Geschmack ~:** offend against good taste; D (*eindringen in*) violate ‹frontier, airspace, etc.›

**verletzlich** *Adj.* vulnerable; (*empfindlich*) sensitive

**Verletzlichkeit** *die; ~:* vulnerability; (*Empfindlichkeit*) sensitivity

**Verletzte** *der/die; adj. Dekl.* injured person; casualty; (*durch Schuss, Stich*) wounded person; **die ~n** the injured/wounded; the casualties; **bei dem Unfall gab es einen Toten und zwei ~:** one person died and two were injured in the accident; **es gab keine ~n bei der Demonstration** nobody was hurt during the demonstration

**Verletzung** *die; ~, ~en* A ▶ 474 (*Wunde*) injury; **eine ~ am Knie haben** have an injury to one's knee *or* an injured knee; B (*Kränkung*) hurting; wounding; C ⇨ **verletzen** C: violation; infringement; breaking; D (*Grenz~, Luftraum~ usw.*) violation

**verleugnen** *tr. V.* deny; disown ‹friend, relation›; **er kann seine Herkunft nicht ~:** it is obvious where he comes from; **sich selbst ~:** go against *or* betray one's principles

**Verleugnung** *die* denial; (*eines Freundes, Verwandten*) disownment

**verleumden** /fɛɐ̯ˈlɔymdn̩/ *tr. V.* slander; (*schriftlich*) libel

**Verleumder** *der; ~, ~,* **Verleumderin** *die; ~, ~nen* slanderer; (*schriftlich*) libeller

**verleumderisch** *Adj.* slanderous; (*in Schriftform*) libellous

**Verleumdung** *die; ~, ~en* A slander; (*in Schriftform*) libelling; B (*Bemerkung usw.*) slander; (*in Schriftform*) libel

**Verleumdungs·kampagne** *die* smear campaign

**verlieben** *refl. V.* fall in love (**in** + *Akk.* with); **ein verliebtes Pärchen** a pair of lovers; **jmdm. verliebte Blicke zuwerfen** make eyes at sb.; **er ist ganz verliebt in seine Idee** (*fig.*) he is infatuated with his idea; **zum V~ sein/aussehen** (*ugs.*) be/look perfectly sweet

**Verliebte** *der/die; adj. Dekl.* lover; **die beiden ~n** the [two] lovers

**Verliebtheit** *die; ~:* being *no art.* in love; **die ~ dauerte bei ihr nur drei Wochen** she was only in love for three weeks; **in ihrer ~ hatte sie ...** being so much in love, she had ...

**verlieren** /fɛɐ̯ˈliːrən/ ❶ *unr. tr. V.* lose; ‹plant, tree› lose, shed ‹leaves›; **sich (*Dat.*) verloren vorkommen** feel lost; **für jmdn./etw. verloren sein** be lost to sb./sth.; **die Katze verliert Haare** the cat is moulting; **nichts [mehr] zu ~ haben** have nothing [more] to lose; **jmdn./etw. verloren geben** give sb./sth. up for lost; **das hat hier nichts verloren** it has no business to be here.
❷ *unr. itr. V.* lose; **an etw. (*Dat.*) ~:** lose sth.; **sie hat an Reiz verloren** she has lost some of her attraction; **bei jmdm. ~:** become less highly regarded by sb.
❸ *unr. refl. V.* A (*weniger werden*) ‹enthusiasm› subside; ‹reserve etc.› disappear; B (*entschwinden*) vanish; ‹sound› die away; C (*sich verirren*) lose one's way; get lost; D (*sich hingeben*) **er war in Gedanken verloren** he was lost in thought; E (*abschweifen*) digress; **sich in Detailschilderungen ~:** digress into detailed descriptions

**Verlierer** *der; ~s, ~,* **Verliererin** *die; ~, ~nen* loser; **ein schlechter ~:** a bad loser; **der ~ des Autoschlüssels** the person who has lost the car key

**Verlies** /fɛɐ̯ˈliːs/ *das; ~es, ~e* dungeon

**verloben** ❶ *refl. V.* become *or* get engaged, (*arch.*) become betrothed (**mit** to); **verlobt sein** be engaged. ❷ *tr. V.* (*veralt.*) **jmdn. mit jmdm. ~:** betroth sb. to sb. (*arch.*)

**Verlöbnis** /fɛɐ̯ˈløːpnɪs/ *das; ~ses, ~se* (*geh.*) engagement, (*arch.*) betrothal (**mit** to)

**Verlobte** *der/die; adj. Dekl.* **mein ~r** my fiancé *or* (*arch.*) betrothed; **meine ~:** my fiancée *or* (*arch.*) betrothed; **die ~n** the engaged *or* (*arch.*) betrothed couple

**Verlobung** *die; ~, ~en* engagement; betrothal (*arch.*); (*Feier*) engagement party

**Verlobungs·anzeige** *die* engagement announcement

**verlocken** *tr. V.* (*geh.*) tempt; entice; **der See verlockt zum Baden** the lake tempts *or* entices one to bathe in it

**verlockend** *Adj.* tempting; enticing; **das Wetter war nicht gerade ~:** the weather wasn't exactly enticing

**Verlockung** *die* temptation; enticement; **der ~ widerstehen** resist the temptation

**verlogen** /fɛɐ̯ˈloːgn̩/ (*abwertend*) ❶ *Adj.* lying, mendacious ‹person›; false ‹morality, phrases, romanticism, etc.›; insincere ‹compliment›. ❷ *adv.* mendaciously; falsely

**Verlogenheit** *die; ~, ~en* (*eines Menschen*) mendacity; (*einer Moral, Romantik, von Phrasen usw.*) falseness; (*von Komplimenten*) insincerity

**verlohnen** (*geh.*) ❶ *refl.* (*auch itr.*) *V.* be worth while; **es verlohnt sich nicht, das zu tun** it is not worth [while] doing that. ❷ *tr.* (*od. veralt. itr.*) *V.* **das verlohnt die/** (*veralt.*) **der Mühe nicht** it is not worth the trouble

**verlor** /fɛɐ̯ˈloːɐ̯/ *1. u. 3. Pers. Sg. Prät. v.* **verlieren**

**verloren** ❶ *2. Part. v.* **verlieren**.
❷ *Adj.* lost; **[eine] ~e Mühe** a wasted effort; **Lass uns aufhören! Die Sache ist ~:** Let's give up! It's hopeless; **er ist ~:** that's the end of him now; **ohne meine Brille bin ich ~** (*fig.*) I'm lost without my glasses; **~e Eier** poached eggs; **der ~e Sohn** (*bibl.*) the Prodigal Son.
❸ **~ gehen** (*abhanden kommen*) get lost; (*nicht gewonnen werden*) ‹war, battle, etc.› be lost; **deine Postkarte muss wohl verloren gegangen sein** your postcard must have got lost *or* gone astray; **durch diesen Umweg ging uns/ging viel Zeit verloren** we lost a lot of time/a lot of time was lost by this detour; **ein verloren gegangenes**

V

**Buch** a lost book; a book that has gone missing; **an dir ist ein Künstler verloren gegangen** you ought to have been an artist; you would have made a good artist

**Verlorenheit** *die;* **~:** loneliness; isolation

**verlöschen** *unr. itr. V.; mit sein* ‹light, fire, etc.› go out; ‹comet, shooting star› die

**verlosen** *tr. V.* raffle

**Verlosung** *die;* **~, ~en** raffle; draw; (*Ziehung*) draw; (*Vorgang*) raffling

**verlottern** /fɛɐ̯ˈlɔtɐn/ *itr. V.; mit sein (abwertend)* ‹building, town, area, etc.› become run-down; ‹person› go to seed; ‹firm, business› go downhill, go to the dogs

**Verlust** *der;* **~[e]s, ~e** loss (**an** + *Dat.* of); **bei ~:** in the case *or* event of loss; **schwere ~e erleiden** ‹army etc.› suffer heavy losses *or* casualties; **etw. mit ~ verkaufen** sell sth. at a loss

**Verlust·geschäft** *das* loss-making deal *or* transaction; **sonst mache ich ein ~:** otherwise I'll be making a loss

**verlustieren** *refl. V.* (*scherzh.*) amuse oneself; **wir haben uns auf der Party verlustiert** we had fun *or* enjoyed ourselves at the party; **sich mit jmdm. im Bett ~:** have a good time in bed with sb.

**verlustig** *Adj. in* **einer Sache** (*Gen.*) **~ gehen** (*Papierdt.*) lose sth.; (*verwirken*) forfeit *or* lose sth.

**verlust-, Verlust-: ~liste** *die* list of casualties and losses; (*fig.*) casualty list; **~meldung** *die* casualty report; **~reich** *Adj.* Ⓐ (*mit vielen Toten*) ‹battle etc.› involving heavy losses; Ⓑ (*mit finanziellen ~en*) heavily loss-making ‹product, project, etc.›

**vermachen** *tr. V.* **jmdm. etw. ~:** leave *or* bequeath sth. to sb.; (*fig.: schenken, überlassen*) give sth. to sb.; let sb. have sth.

**Vermächtnis** /fɛɐ̯ˈmɛçtnɪs/ *das;* **~ses, ~se** Ⓐ (*Rechtspr.: Legat*) bequest; legacy; (*fig.*) legacy; Ⓑ (*letzter Wille*) last wish

**vermählen** /fɛɐ̯ˈmɛːlən/ (*geh.*) ❶ *refl. V.* **sich [jmdm. od. mit jmdm.] ~:** marry *or* wed [sb.]; (*fig.*) be wedded (**mit** to); **frisch vermählt** newly married. ❷ *tr. V.* (*veralt.*) **seine Tochter mit jmdm. ~:** marry one's daughter to sb.; give one's daughter to sb. in marriage

**Vermählte** *der/die; adj. Dekl.;* (*geh.*) bridegroom/bride; **die ~n** the bride and bridegroom; **die beiden frisch ~n** the newly-married couple; the newly-weds (*coll.*)

**Vermählung** *die;* **~, ~en** (*geh.*) Ⓐ marriage; wedding; Ⓑ (*Fest*) wedding ceremony

**vermaledeit** /fɛɐ̯maleˈdait/ *Adj.* (*ugs. veralt.*) damned; blasted (*Brit.*)

**vermännlichen** *tr. V.* masculinize

**vermarkten** *tr. V.* Ⓐ (*als Ware verkaufen*) exploit commercially; Ⓑ (*Wirtsch.*) market ‹goods etc.›

**Vermarktung** *die;* **~, ~en** Ⓐ commercial exploitation; Ⓑ (*Wirtsch.*) marketing

**vermasseln** /fɛɐ̯ˈmasl̩n/ *tr. V.* (*salopp*) Ⓐ (*verderben*) muck up (*Brit. sl.*); mess up; ruin; Ⓑ (*verhauen*) make a cock-up (*Brit. sl.*) *or* mess of ‹exam etc.›

**Vermassung** *die;* **~, ~en** (*abwertend*) loss of individuality

**vermauern** *tr. V.* Ⓐ (*zumauern*) wall up ‹entrance›; brick up ‹hole, window, etc.›; Ⓑ (*verbrauchen*) use up ‹bricks, sand, etc.› in building a/the wall *etc.*

**vermehren** ❶ *tr. V.* (*größer machen*) increase (**um** by). ❷ *refl. V.* Ⓐ (*größer werden*) increase; Ⓑ (*sich fortpflanzen*) reproduce; ‹bacterium, virus› multiply

**vermehrt** ❶ *Adj.* increased. ❷ *adv.* increasingly; **~ auftreten** occur with increasing frequency

**Vermehrung** *die;* **~, ~en** Ⓐ increase (*Gen.* in); Ⓑ (*Fortpflanzung*) reproduction; (*von Bakterien, Viren*) multiplying

**vermeidbar** *Adj.* avoidable; **die Niederlage wäre ~ gewesen** the defeat could have been avoided

**vermeiden** *unr. tr. V.* avoid; **es lässt sich nicht ~:** it is unavoidable; **es ~, etw. zu tun** avoid doing sth.; **er hatte gehofft, dass der Krieg zu ~ sei** he had hoped that war could be avoided; **ein Gegentor ~:** avoid conceding a goal

**Vermeidung** *die;* **~, ~en** avoidance

**vermeinen** *tr. V.* (*geh.*) think; **er vermeinte, ihre Stimme zu hören** he thought he heard her voice

**vermeintlich** /fɛɐ̯ˈmaintlɪç/ ❶ *Adj.* supposed. ❷ *adv.* supposedly

**vermelden** *tr. V.* report; ‹report› announce

**vermengen** ❶ *tr. V.* Ⓐ (*mischen*) mix (**miteinander** together); Ⓑ (*durcheinander bringen*) mix up; confuse. ❷ *refl. V.* (*sich mischen*) mingle

**vermenschlichen** *tr. V.* anthropomorphize

**Vermenschlichung** *die;* **~, ~en** anthropomorphization

**Vermerk** /fɛɐ̯ˈmɛrk/ *der;* **~[e]s, ~e** note; (*amtlich*) remark; (*Stempel*) stamp; (*im Kalender*) entry

**vermerken** *tr. V.* Ⓐ (*notieren*) make a note of; note [down]; (*in Akten, Wachbuch usw.*) record; **das sei aber nur am Rande vermerkt** but that is only by the way; Ⓑ (*feststellen*) note; ⇒ *auch* **übel** 2 B

**vermessen**[1] ❶ *unr. tr. V.* measure; survey ‹land, site›. ❷ *unr. refl. V.* Ⓐ (*falsch messen*) measure wrongly; Ⓑ (*geh.: sich anmaßen*) **sich ~, etw. zu tun** presume *or* have the presumption to do sth.; **wie konnte er sich ~!** what presumption!

**vermessen**[2] *Adj.* (*geh.*) presumptuous; **darf ich so ~ sein anzunehmen, dass ...** may I be so bold as to assume that ...

**Vermessenheit** *die;* **~, ~en** (*geh.*) presumption; presumptuousness; **das ist eine große ~ von dir** that is very presumptuous of you

**Vermesser** *der;* **~s, ~, Vermesserin** *die;* **~, ~nen** [land] surveyor

**Vermessung** *die* measurement; (*Land~*) surveying

**vermiesen** *tr. V.* (*ugs.*) **jmdm. etw. ~:** spoil sth. for sb.; **jmdm. die Laune/das Vergnügen ~:** spoil sb.'s mood/enjoyment

**vermieten** *tr.* (*auch itr.*) *V.* rent [out], let [out] ‹flat, room, etc.› (**an** + *Akk.* to); hire [out] ‹boat, car, etc.›; **wir ~ auch an Studenten** we also rent *or* let to students; **„Zimmer zu ~"** 'room to let'

**Vermieter** *der* landlord

**Vermieterin** *die* landlady

**Vermietung** *die;* **~, ~en** ⇒ **vermieten**: renting [out]; letting [out]; hiring [out]

**vermindern** ❶ *tr. V.* reduce; decrease; reduce, lessen ‹danger, stress›; lessen ‹admiration, ability›; lower ‹resistance›; reduce ‹debt›. ❷ *refl. V.* decrease; ‹influence, danger› decrease, diminish; ‹resistance› diminish

**vermindert** *Adj.* Ⓐ **~e Zurechnungsfähigkeit** (*Rechtsw.*) diminished responsibility; Ⓑ (*Mus.*) diminished

**Verminderung** *die* ⇒ **vermindern** 1: reduction; decreasing; lessening; lowering; **eine ~ der Einnahmen** a decrease in revenues

**verminen** *tr. V.* mine

**vermischen** ❶ *tr. V.* mix (**miteinander** together); blend ‹teas, tobaccos, etc.›; **Wahres und Erdachtes miteinander ~:** mingle truth and fiction. ❷ *refl. V.* mix; (*fig.*) mingle; ‹races, animals› interbreed; **unter der Rubrik „Vermischtes"** under the heading 'Miscellaneous'

**Vermischung** *die* ⇒ **vermischen**: mixing; blending; (*fig.*) mingling

**vermissen** *tr. V.* Ⓐ (*sich sehnen nach*) miss; Ⓑ (*nicht haben*) **ich vermisse meinen Ausweis** my identity card is missing; **nach dem Brand wurde er vermisst** he was unaccounted for after the fire; **ich vermisse in deiner Küche einen Kühlschrank** I notice that you do not have a fridge in your kitchen; **etw. ~ lassen** lack sth.; be lacking in sth.; **er gilt als** *od.* **ist vermisst** (*fig.*) he is listed as a missing person; **der vermisste Soldat** the missing soldier; **man hat dich in der Vorlesung vermisst** your absence from the lecture was noticed

**Vermisste, *Vermißte** *der/die; adj. Dekl.* missing person

**Vermissten·anzeige, *Vermißten·anzeige** *die:* **~ [von jmdm.] erstatten** report sb. [as] missing

**vermitteln** ❶ *itr. V.* mediate, act as [a] mediator (**in** + *Dat.* in); **~d eingreifen** act as [a] mediator; **~de Worte** conciliating words.
❷ *tr. V.* Ⓐ (*herbeiführen*) arrange; negotiate ‹transaction, ceasefire, compromise›; Ⓑ (*besorgen*) **jmdm. eine Stelle ~:** find sb. a job; find a job for sb.; **jmdm. ein Haus ~:** locate a house for sb.; Ⓒ (*als Mittler tätig sein für*) **das Arbeitsamt vermittelt die Arbeitskräfte an die Firmen** the job centre (*Brit.*) *or* (*Amer.*) employment office places workers with firms; Ⓓ (*weitergeben*) impart ‹knowledge, insight, values, etc.›; communicate, pass on ‹message, information, etc.›; convey, give ‹feeling›; pass on ‹experience›; **jmdm. ein genaues Bild von etw. ~:** convey a precise picture of sth. to sb.; **jmdm. Bildung ~:** educate sb.

**vermittels[t]** *Präp. mit Gen.* (*Papierdt.*) by means of; **~ eines Wörterbuchs** with the help of a dictionary

**Vermittler** *der;* **~s, ~, Vermittlerin** *die;* **~, ~nen** Ⓐ (*Mittler[in]*) mediator; Ⓑ (*Träger[in]*) ⇒ **vermitteln** 2 D: imparter; communicator; conveyer; Ⓒ (*von Berufs wegen*) agent; **der ~ eines Geschäfts** the negotiator of a transaction

**Vermittler·rolle** *die* role of mediator

**Vermittlung** *die;* **~, ~en** Ⓐ (*Schlichtung*) mediation; **seine ~ anbieten** offer to mediate; Ⓑ ⇒ **vermitteln** 2 A: arrangement; negotiation; **durch die ~ eines Beamten** through the good offices of an official; Ⓒ (*das Besorgen*) **die ~ einer Stelle** finding a job for sb.; **die ~ eines Hauses für jmdn.** locating a house for sb.; Ⓓ ⇒ **vermitteln** 2 D: imparting; communicating; passing on; conveying; Ⓔ (*Telefonzentrale*) exchange; (*in einer Firma*) switchboard; (*Telefonist*) operator

**Vermittlungs-: ~ausschuss, *~ausschuß** *der* mediation committee [between the two houses of parliament]; **~gebühr** *die* commission

**vermöbeln** *tr. V.* (*ugs.*) beat up; (*als Strafe*) thrash

**vermodern** *itr. V.; mit sein* decay; rot

**vermöge** *Präp. mit Gen.* (*geh.*) by virtue of

**vermögen** *unr. tr. V.* (*geh.*) **etw. zu tun ~:** be able to do sth.; be capable of doing sth.; **er vermochte [es] nicht, mich zu überzeugen** he was not able to convince me; **wir werden alles tun, was wir [zu tun] ~:** we will do everything we can; **wer vermöchte zu sagen, ob ...** who can say whether ...; **er vermochte nichts dagegen** he could do nothing to prevent it

**Vermögen** *das;* **~s, ~** Ⓐ (*geh.: Fähigkeit*) ability; Ⓑ (*Besitz*) fortune; **er hat ~:** he has money; he is a man of means; **das kostet ja ein ~** (*ugs.*) it costs a fortune; **sein ganzes ~:** all his money

**vermögend** *Adj.* wealthy; well-off; **sie ist eine ~e Frau** she is a woman of means *or* a wealthy woman

**Vermögens-: ~ab·gabe** *die* capital levy; **~bildung** *die:* (*wider*) *creation of wealth by participation of employees in savings and share-ownership schemes;* **~steuer** *die* wealth tax

**Vermögen·steuer** *die* ⇒ **Vermögenssteuer**

**vermögens-, Vermögens-: ~verhältnisse** *Pl.* financial circumstances; **~werte** *Pl.* investments; **~wirksam** ❶ *Adj.* ‹saving› under the employee's savings scheme; **~wirksame Leistungen** employer's contributions to employees' savings schemes; ❷ *adv.* ‹invest› profitably

*old spelling (see note on page 1707)

V

**vermummen** /fɛɐ̯ˈmʊmən/ *tr. V.* Ⓐ *(einhüllen)* wrap up [warmly]; Ⓑ *(verbergen)* disguise; **vermummte Jugendliche** masked youths

**Vermummung** *die;* ~, ~**en** Ⓐ **zur ~ hatten wir ...** in order to disguise ourselves we had ...; **~ soll unter Strafe gestellt werden** wearing a mask is to be made a punishable offence; Ⓑ *(Kleidung)* disguise

**Vermummungs·verbot** *das* ban on wearing masks [during demonstrations]

**vermurksen** *tr. V.* *(ugs.)* mess up; muck up *(Brit. sl.)*

**vermuten** *tr. V.* suspect; **das ist zu ~:** that is what one would suppose *or* expect; we may assume that; **die Untersuchung lässt ~, dass ...** the investigation leads one to suppose that ...; **ich vermute/vermutete ihn in der Bibliothek** I suspect *or* presume he is/supposed *or* presumed he was in the library

**vermutlich** ❶ *Adj.* probable; probable, likely ‹result›; **der ~e Täter** the suspect. ❷ *Adv.* presumably; *(wahrscheinlich)* probably; **[ja,] ~:** [yes,] I suppose so

**Vermutung** *die;* ~, ~**en** supposition; *(Verdacht)* suspicion; **es liegt die ~ nahe, dass ...** it seems a likely supposition that ...; there are grounds for supposing that ...; **die ~ haben, dass ...** presume *or* suppose that ...

**vernachlässigen** *tr. V.* Ⓐ neglect; Ⓑ *(unberücksichtigt lassen)* ignore; disregard

**Vernachlässigung** *die;* ~, ~**en** neglect; *(das Nichtberücksichtigen)* disregard; **unter ~ dieser Erkenntnisse** ignoring these perceptions

**vernageln** *tr. V.* nail up, cover ‹hole etc.›; **mit Brettern vernagelt** boarded up

**vernähen** *tr. V.* Ⓐ stitch [up] ‹tear, wounds›; **den Faden gut ~:** sew the thread in firmly; Ⓑ *(beim Nähen verbrauchen)* use up ‹thread, material›

**vernarben** *itr. V.; mit sein* [form a] scar; heal *(lit. or fig.)*

**Vernarbung** *die;* ~, ~**en** formation of a scar; **die ~ der Wunde dauerte Wochen** the wound took weeks to form a scar

**vernarren** *refl. V.* **sich in jmdn./etw. ~:** become besotted *or* infatuated with sb./sth.; **in jmdn./etw. vernarrt sein** be infatuated with *or (coll.)* crazy about sb./be crazy *(coll.)* abouth sth.

**Vernarrtheit** *die;* ~, ~**en** infatuation **(in** + *Akk.* with)

**vernaschen** *tr. V.* Ⓐ *(für Süßigkeiten ausgeben)* spend on sweets *(Brit.)* or *(Amer.)* candy; Ⓑ *(salopp: geschlechtlich verkehren mit)* lay ‹girl› *(sl.)*; Ⓒ *(salopp: bezwingen, ausschalten)* wipe the floor with *(coll.)* ‹opponent, competitors›

**vernebeln** *tr. V.* shroud ‹area› in fog; *(mit Rauch)* cover ‹area› with a smokescreen; *(fig.)* obscure ‹facts›; **jmdm. das Gehirn ~** *(fig.)* ‹alcohol› befuddle sb.'s brain

**Vernebelung** *die;* ~, ~**en** shrouding in fog/smoke; *(fig.: des Kopfes)* befuddling; clouding; *(der Tatsachen)* obscuration

**vernehmbar** *Adj.* *(geh.)* audible

**vernehmen** *unr. tr. V.* Ⓐ *(geh.: hören, erfahren)* hear; **über seine Absichten nichts ~ lassen** not say anything *or* keep quiet about one's intentions; Ⓑ *(verhören)* question; *(vor Gericht)* examine

**Vernehmen** *das:* *in* **dem/allem ~ nach** from what/all that one hears; **sicherem ~ nach** according to reliable sources

**vernehmlich** ❶ *Adj.* [clearly] audible. ❷ *adv.* audibly; **laut und ~:** loud and clear

**Vernehmung** *die;* ~, ~**en** questioning; *(vor Gericht)* examination

**vernehmungsfähig** *Adj.* in a condition *or* fit to be questioned/examined *postpos.*

**verneigen** *refl. V.* *(geh.)* bow **(vor** + *Dat.* to, *(literary)* before)

**Verneigung** *die;* ~, ~**en** *(geh.)* bow

**verneinen** *tr. (auch itr.) V.* Ⓐ say 'no' to ‹question›; answer ‹question› in the negative; **er verneinte [es]** he said 'no'; **eine ~de Antwort** a negative answer; an answer in the negative; **er schüttelte ~d den Kopf** he shook his head to say 'no'; Ⓑ *(ablehnen)* reject; Ⓒ *(Sprachw.)* negate

**Verneinung** *die;* ~, ~**en** Ⓐ **~ einer Frage** negative answer to a question; Ⓑ *(Ablehnung)* rejection; Ⓒ *(Sprachw.)* negation

**Verneinungs-:** **~fall** *der: in* **im ~falle** *(Papierdt.)* should the answer be in the negative; **~wort** *das; Pl.* **~wörter** *(Sprachw.)* negative [word]

**vernetzen** *tr. V.* *(Chemie, Technik)* interlink

**vernichten** *tr. V.* destroy; exterminate ‹pests, vermin›

**vernichtend** ❶ *Adj.* crushing ‹defeat›; shattering ‹blow›; *(fig.)* devastating ‹criticism›; devastating, withering ‹glance›. ❷ *adv.* **den Feind ~ schlagen** inflict a crushing defeat on the enemy

**Vernichtung** *die;* ~, ~**en** destruction; *(von Schädlingen)* extermination

**Vernichtungs-:** **~lager** *das* extermination camp; **~potenzial** *das* destructive potential; **~waffe** *die* weapon of annihilation

**verniedlichen** *tr. V.* trivialize ‹matter, situation, etc.›; play down ‹guilt, error›

**Verniedlichung** *die;* ~, ~**en** trivialization

**Vernissage** /vɛrnɪˈsa:ʒə/ *die;* ~, ~**n** *(geh.)* private view *(of contemporary artist's exhibition)*

**Vernunft** /fɛɐ̯ˈnʊnft/ *die;* ~**:** reason; **gegen alle [Regeln der] ~:** contrary to all [dictates of] common sense; **ohne ~ handeln** act rashly *or* without thinking; **~ annehmen, zur ~ kommen** see reason; come to one's senses; **jmdn. zur ~ bringen** make sb. see reason

**vernunft-, Vernunft-:** **~begabt** *Adj.* rational; **~ehe** *die,* **~heirat** *die* marriage of convenience

**vernünftig** /fɛɐ̯ˈnʏnftɪç/ ❶ *Adj.* Ⓐ sensible; **es wäre das ~ste gewesen, zu ...** the most sensible thing would have been to ...; **mit ihm kann man kein ~es Wort reden** one can't have a sensible conversation with him; Ⓑ *(ugs.: ordentlich, richtig)* decent; **einen ~en Beruf lernen** learn a proper trade. ❷ *adv.* Ⓐ sensibly; **über etw.** *(Akk.)* **~ diskutieren** have a sensible discussion about sth.; Ⓑ *(ugs.: ordentlich, richtig)* ‹talk, eat› properly; ‹dress› sensibly

**vernünftigerweise** *Adv.* sensibly; **etw. ~ tun** ‹person› have the [good] sense to do sth.

**Vernunft·mensch** *der* [purely] rational person

**vernunft·widrig** ❶ *Adj.* irrational. ❷ *adv.* irrationally

**veröden** ❶ *itr. V.; mit sein* Ⓐ *(menschenleer werden)* become deserted; **verödet** deserted ‹houses, streets, etc›; Ⓑ *(unfruchtbar werden)* ‹land› become barren *or* desolate. ❷ *tr. V.* *(Med.)* treat ‹varicose veins› by injection

**Verödung** *die;* ~, ~**en** ⇒ **veröden**: desertion; desolation; *(Med.)* injection treatment

**veröffentlichen** *tr. V.* publish

**Veröffentlichung** *die;* ~, ~**en** publication

**verordnen** *tr. V.* **[jmdm. etw.] ~:** prescribe [sth. for sb.]; **der Arzt hat mir Bettruhe verordnet** the doctor ordered me to stay in bed

**Verordnung** *die* prescribing; prescription

**verpachten** *tr. V.* lease

**Verpächter** *der;* ~**s**, ~: landlord; lessor *(Law)*

**Verpächterin** *die;* ~, ~**nen** landlady; lessor *(Law)*

**Verpachtung** *die;* ~, ~**en** leasing

**verpacken** *tr. V.* pack; wrap up ‹present, parcel›; **etw. als Geschenk ~:** gift-wrap sth.

**Verpackung** *die* Ⓐ packing; Ⓑ *(Umhüllung)* packaging *no pl.;* wrapping

**Verpackungs·material** *das* packaging [material]

**verpassen** *tr. V.* Ⓐ miss ‹train, person, entry (Mus.), chance, etc.›; Ⓑ *(ugs.: geben)* **jmdm. etw. ~:** give sb. sth.; **jmdm. eins ~:** clout sb. one *(coll.)*

**verpatzen** *tr. V.* *(ugs.)* make a mess of; muck up *(Brit. sl.)*; botch ‹job›; **du hast mir alles verpatzt** you've spoilt it all for me; **eine verpatzte Gelegenheit** a wasted opportunity

**verpennen** *(salopp)* ❶ *itr. V.* oversleep. ❷ *tr. V.* Ⓐ *(vergessen)* forget; Ⓑ *(verschlafen)* sleep through ‹morning etc.›

**verpennt** *Adj.* *(salopp)* half asleep *pred.;* *(fig.)* dozy ‹place›; **total ~:** in a complete sleepy daze

**verpesten** *tr. V.* *(abwertend)* pollute

**Verpestung** *(abwertend) die;* ~, ~**en** pollution

**verpetzen** *tr. V.* *(abwertend)* **jmdn. [beim Lehrer** *usw.***] ~:** tell *or (coll.)* split on sb. [to the teacher *etc.*]

**verpfänden** *tr. V.* pawn ‹article›; mortgage ‹house›; *(fig.)* pledge ‹word, honour›

**Verpfändung** *die* pawning; *(von Hausbesitz)* mortgaging; mortgage

**verpfeifen** *unr. tr. V.* *(ugs. abwertend)* grass *or* split on ‹person› *(coll.)* **(bei** to); sing about ‹plan etc.› *(sl.)*

**verpflanzen** *tr. V.* Ⓐ transplant ‹tree, bush›; *(fig.)* uproot and move ‹person›; Ⓑ *(Med.)* transplant ‹heart etc.›; graft ‹skin›

**Verpflanzung** *die;* ~, ~**en** Ⓐ transplanting; Ⓑ *(Med.)* transplant[ing]; *(von Haut)* graft

**verpflegen** *tr. V.* cater for; feed; **sich selbst ~:** cater for oneself; **nur kalt/im Heim verpflegt werden** only be served cold food/be served one's food in the hostel

**Verpflegung** *die;* ~, ~**en** Ⓐ catering *no indef. art.* *(Gen.* for); Ⓑ *(Nahrung)* food; **Unterkunft und ~:** board and lodging

**Verpflegungs·kosten** *Pl.* cost *sing.* of food *or* meals

**verpflichten** ❶ *tr. V.* Ⓐ oblige; commit; *(festlegen, binden)* bind; *(durch Eid)* swear; **jmdn. auf die Verfassung ~:** make sb. swear *or* promise to uphold the constitution; **zur Verschwiegenheit verpflichtet** sworn to secrecy; **der Kauf des ersten Bandes verpflichtet zur Abnahme des gesamten Werkes** purchase of the first volume is a commitment *or* obliges one to take the complete work; **sich verpflichtet fühlen[, etw. zu tun]** feel obliged [to do sth.]; **das verpflichtet dich zu nichts** that doesn't commit you to anything; **jmdm. verpflichtet sein** be indebted to sb.; **ich bin Ihnen zu Dank verpflichtet** I am indebted *or* obliged to you; Ⓑ *(einstellen, engagieren)* engage ‹actor, manager, etc.›; *(Sport)* sign ‹player›; **jmdn. ans Stadttheater/nach Berlin ~:** take sb. on *or* engage sb. at the Municipal Theatre/for Berlin.
❷ *refl. V.* undertake; promise; **sich zu einer Zahlung ~:** commit oneself to making a payment; **sich vertraglich ~:** sign a contract; bind oneself by contract; **sich bei der Bundeswehr auf 8 Jahre ~:** sign on with the [Federal] Armed Forces for eight years

**Verpflichtung** *die;* ~, ~**en** Ⓐ obligation; commitment; **eine ~ übernehmen** take on an obligation *or* a commitment; **[finanzielle] ~en** [financial] commitments; liabilities; **dienstliche/gesellschaftliche** *usw.* **~en** official/social *etc.* commitments; **ich habe keine anderweitigen ~en** I am not otherwise engaged; I have no other engagements; Ⓑ *(Engagement)* engaging; engagement; *(Sport: eines Spielers)* signing

**verpfuschen** *tr. V.* *(ugs.)* make a mess of; muck up *(Brit. sl.)*; **sich** *(Dat.)* **das Leben/die Karriere ~:** make a mess of one's life/career

**verpissen** *refl. V.* *(salopp)* piss off *(Brit. sl.)*; beat it *(coll.)*

**verplanen** *tr. V.* Ⓐ *(falsch planen)* get the plans wrong for; Ⓑ *(festlegen, einteilen)* book ‹person, time› up; commit ‹money, reprint›; **er hat sein Geld/seine Freizeit schon verplant** his money is already fully committed/his spare time is fully booked

**verplappern** *refl. V.* *(ugs.)* blab *(coll.)*; let the cat out of the bag

V

**verplaudern** ❶ *tr. V.* chat away ‹time›; spend ‹time› chatting. ❷ *refl. V.* go on chatting too long

**verplempern** /fɛɐ̯ˈplɛmpɐn/ (*ugs.*) ❶ *tr. V.* fritter away. ❷ *refl. V.* fritter away one's time/opportunities

**verplomben** *tr. V.* seal

**Verplombung** *die;* ~, ~**en** Ⓐ sealing; Ⓑ (*Plombe*) seal

**verpönt** *Adj.:* scorned; (*tabu*) taboo

**verpoppen** *tr. V.* popularize; (*aufmöbeln*) jazz up

**verprassen** *tr. V.* squander, (*coll.*) blow ‹money, fortune›

**verprellen** *tr. V.* alienate

**verproviantieren** ❶ *tr. V.* supply with food *or* provisions. ❷ *refl. V.* stock up [with food *or* provisions]

**verprügeln** *tr. V.* beat up; (*zur Strafe*) thrash

**verpuffen** *itr. V.; mit sein* go phut; (*fig.*) fizzle out; ‹joke› fall flat

**verpulvern** *tr. V.* (*ugs.*) blow (*coll.*) ‹money›; (*allmählich*) fritter away ‹money›

**verpuppen** *refl. V.* (*Zool.*) pupate

**Verputz** *der* plaster; (*auf Außenwänden*) rendering; (*Rauputz*) roughcast

**verputzen** *tr. V.* Ⓐ (*mit Putz versehen*) plaster; render ‹outside wall›; (*mit Rauputz*) roughcast; Ⓑ (*ugs.: aufessen*) polish off (*coll.*) ‹food›

**Verputzer** *der;* ~**s**, ~, **Verputzerin** *die;* ~, ~**nen** plasterer

**verqualmen** ❶ *itr. V.; mit sein* ‹cigar, cigarette› go out. ❷ *tr. V.* (*ugs. abwertend*) fill ‹room› with smoke; **verqualmt** smoke-filled

**verquält** /fɛɐ̯ˈkvɛːlt/ *Adj.* tormented; in torment *or* agony *pred.*

**verquatschen** (*ugs.*) ❶ *tr. V.* natter away (*coll.*) ‹time›; spend ‹time› nattering (*coll.*). ❷ *refl. V.* blab (*coll.*); let the cat out of the bag

**verquer** ❶ *Adj.* Ⓐ (*schief*) angled, crooked ‹position›; Ⓑ (*absonderlich*) weird, outlandish ‹idea›. ❷ *adv.* Ⓐ (*schief*) at an angle; crookedly; Ⓑ (*absonderlich*) ‹behave› weirdly; Ⓒ **jmdm. geht etw./alles** ~**:** sth./everything is going wrong for sb.

**verquicken** /fɛɐ̯ˈkvɪkn̩/ *tr. V.* combine

**Verquickung** *die;* ~, ~**en** combination

**verquirlen** *tr. V.* mix [with a whisk]; whisk

**verquollen** /fɛɐ̯ˈkvɔlən/ *Adj.* swollen

**verrammeln** *tr. V.* barricade

**verramschen** *tr. V.* (*ugs. abwertend*) ⇒ **verschleudern** A

**verrannt** /fɛɐ̯ˈrant/ *Adj.* obsessed

**Verrat** *der;* ~**[e]s** betrayal (**an** + *Dat.* of); ~ **begehen** (*Politik*) commit [an act of] treason; ~ **an jmdm. begehen** betray sb.

**verraten** ❶ *unr. tr. V.* Ⓐ betray ‹person, cause›; betray, give away ‹secret, plan, etc.› (**an** + *Akk.* to); **wer hat dir das Versteck** ~**?** who told you about the hiding place?; ~ **und verkauft sein** be well and truly in the soup *or* sunk (*coll.*); Ⓑ (*ugs.: mitteilen*) **jmdm. den Grund** *usw.* ~**:** tell sb. the reason *etc.*; Ⓒ (*erkennen lassen*) show, betray ‹feelings, surprise, fear, etc.›; show ‹influence, talent›; Ⓓ (*zu erkennen geben*) give ‹person› away. ❷ *unr. refl. V.* Ⓐ ‹person› give oneself away; Ⓑ (*sich zeigen*) show itself; be revealed

**Verräter** /fɛɐ̯ˈrɛːtɐ/ *der;* ~**s**, ~**:** traitor (*Gen.*, **an** + *Dat.* to)

**Verräterei** *die;* ~, ~**en** treachery

**Verräterin** *die;* ~, ~**nen** traitress

**verräterisch** *Adj.* Ⓐ treacherous ‹plan, purpose, act, etc.›; Ⓑ (*erkennen lassend*) telltale, giveaway ‹look, gesture›; **die Röte in ihrem Gesicht war** ~**:** her red face gave her away

**verrauchen** ❶ *itr. V.; mit sein* ‹smoke, cloud, etc.› clear [away], disappear; (*fig.*) ‹anger etc.› blow over, subside. ❷ *tr. V.* spend ‹money› on smoking

**verräuchern** *tr. V.* fill with smoke; **verräuchert** smoke-filled; smoky

**verraucht** *Adj.* smoke-filled; smoky

**verrauschen** *itr. V.; mit sein* die *or* fade [away]

*old spelling (see note on page 1707)

**verrechnen** ❶ *tr. V.* include, take into account ‹amount etc.›; (*gutschreiben*) credit ‹cheque etc.› to another account. ❷ *refl. V.* (*auch fig.*) miscalculate; make a mistake/mistakes

**Verrechnung** *die* settlement (**mit** by means of); **„nur zur** ~**"** (*Bankw.*) 'not negotiable'; 'a/c payee [only]'

**Verrechnungs-:** ~**einheit** *die* (*Wirtsch.*) clearing unit; ~**scheck** *der* (*Wirtsch.*, *Bankw.*) crossed cheque

**verrecken** *itr. V.; mit sein* (*salopp*) die [a miserable death]; **das tu ich ums Verrecken nicht** there's no way I'll do that

**verregnen** *itr. V.; mit sein* be spoilt *or* ruined by rain; **verregnet** rainy, wet ‹spring, summer, holiday, etc.›; ‹harvest› spoilt by rain

**verreiben** *unr. tr. V.* rub in

**verreisen** *itr. V.; mit sein* go away; **verreist sein** be away

**verreißen** *unr. tr. V.* Ⓐ (*ugs.*) tear ‹book, play, etc.› to pieces; Ⓑ (*ugs.: beim Lenken*) **den Wagen/die Lenkung/das Steuer** ~**:** snatch at the steering; (*als Ausweichmanöver*) swerve

**verrenken** /fɛɐ̯ˈrɛnkn̩/ *tr. V.* Ⓐ (*verletzen*) dislocate; **sich** (*Dat.*) **den Fuß** ~**:** twist one's ankle; Ⓑ (*biegen*) **sich** *od.* **seine Glieder** ~**:** go into *or* perform contortions

**Verrenkung** *die;* ~, ~**en** Ⓐ (*Verletzung*) dislocation; Ⓑ (*Biegung des Körpers*) contortion; ~**en machen** go into *or* perform contortions

**verrennen** *unr. refl. V.* get on the wrong track *or* off course; **sich in etw.** (*Akk.*) ~**:** become obsessed with sth.

**verrenten** *tr. V.* (*Amtsspr.*) retire [on a pension]

**Verrentung** *die;* ~, ~**en** (*Amtsspr.*) retirement [on a pension]

**verrichten** *tr. V.* perform ‹work, duty, etc.›; **seine Notdurft** ~**:** relieve oneself

**Verrichtung** *die* carrying out; performance; **gute** ~**!** (*scherzh. wenn jmd. zur Toilette geht*) have fun!; **die täglichen** ~**en** one's daily tasks

**verriegeln** *tr. V.* bolt

**Verriegelung** *die;* ~, ~**en** Ⓐ (*das Verriegeln*) bolting; Ⓑ (*Vorrichtung*) bolt mechanism; (*Schloss*) lock

**verringern** /fɛɐ̯ˈrɪŋɐn/ ❶ *tr. V.* reduce. ❷ *refl. V.* decrease

**Verringerung** *die;* ~**:** reduction; decrease (*Gen.*, **von** in)

**verrinnen** *unr. itr. V.; mit sein* Ⓐ (*versickern*) seep away; Ⓑ (*geh.: verstreichen*) pass [by]; ‹year, month› elapse, pass

**Verriss**, ***Verriß** *der* (*ugs.*) damning review *or* criticism (**über** + *Akk.* of)

**verrocken** *tr. V.* produce a rock arrangement of ‹piece›

**verrohen** ❶ *tr. V.* brutalize. ❷ *itr. V.; mit sein* become brutal

**Verrohung** *die;* ~, ~**en** brutalization

**verrosten** *itr. V.; mit sein* rust; **verrostet** rusty

**verrotten** *itr. V.; mit sein* rot; ‹building etc.› decay

**verrucht** /fɛɐ̯ˈruːxt/ *Adj.* Ⓐ (*veralt.: ruchlos*) despicable; Ⓑ (*scherzh.: verworfen*) disreputable, seedy ‹quarter etc.›

**Verruchtheit** *die;* ~ Ⓐ despicableness; Ⓑ (*scherzh.: Verworfenheit*) disreputableness; seediness

**verrücken** *tr. V.* move; shift

**verrückt** (*ugs.*) ❶ *Adj.* Ⓐ mad; ~ **werden** go mad *or* insane; **jmdn.** ~ **machen** drive sb. mad; **mach dich doch nicht** ~**!** don't get yourself into a state!; **du bist wohl** ~**!** you must be mad *or* crazy!; **bei diesem Lärm kann man ja** ~ **werden!** this noise is enough to drive you mad *or* (*coll.*) round the bend; **wie** ~**:** like mad *or* crazy (*coll.*); **ich werde** ~**!** I'll be blowed (*sl.*) *or* (*coll.*) damned; ~ **spielen** (*salopp*) ‹person› act crazy (*coll.*); ‹car, machine, etc.› play up; ‹watch, weather› go crazy; Ⓑ (*überspannt, ausgefallen*) crazy ‹idea, fashion, prank, day, etc.›; **so was Verrücktes!** what a crazy idea!; Ⓒ (*begierig, geil*) crazy; **sie macht die Männer** ~**:** she drives men crazy [with desire]; **auf jmdn.** *od.* **nach jmdm/auf etw.** (*Akk.*) ~ **sein** be crazy (*coll.*) *or* mad about sb./sth. ❷ *adv.* crazily; ‹behave› crazily *or* like a madman; ‹paint, dress, etc.› in a mad *or* crazy way

**Verrückte** *der/die; adj. Dekl.* (*ugs.*) madman/madwoman; lunatic

**Verrücktheit** *die;* ~, ~**en** Ⓐ madness; insanity; (*Überspanntheit*) craziness; Ⓑ (*irre Handlung*) act of madness; folly; (*überspannte Idee*) crazy idea

**Verrückt·werden** *das* (*ugs.*) *in* **zum** ~ **sein** be enough to drive you mad *or* (*coll.*) round the bend; **es ist zum** ~ **mit ihm** he's enough to drive anyone scatty (*Brit. coll.*)

**Verruf** *der: in* **in** ~ **kommen** *od.* **geraten** fall into disrepute; **jmdn./etw. in** ~ **bringen** bring sb./sth. into disrepute

**verrufen** *Adj.* disreputable

**verrühren** *tr. V.* stir together; mix

**verrunzelt** *Adj.* wrinkled

**verrußen** ❶ *itr. V.; mit sein* become sooty; ‹sparking plug› soot up; **verrußt** sooty; (*von Ruß bedeckt*) covered in soot *postpos.* ❷ *tr. V.* make sooty

**verrutschen** *itr. V.* slip

**Vers** /fɛrs/ *der;* ~**es**, ~**e** verse; (*Zeile*) line; ~**e schreiben** *od.* (*ugs.*) **schmieden** write verse *or* poetry; **etw. in** ~**e setzen** *od.* **bringen** put sth. into verse; **ein Epos in** ~**en** a verse epic; **sich** (*Dat.*) **einen** ~ **auf etw.** (*Akk.*)**/darauf machen** (*fig.*) make sense of sth./put two and two together

**versachlichen** *tr. V.* make [more] objective

**Versachlichung** *die;* ~**: zur** ~ **der Diskussion beitragen** help to make the discussion more objective

**versacken** *itr. V.; mit sein* (*ugs.*) Ⓐ sink; Ⓑ (*fig.*) ⇒ **versumpfen** B, C

**versagen** ❶ *itr. V.* fail; ‹machine, engine› stop [working], break down; **ihre Stimme versagte** her voice failed. ❷ *tr. V.* (*geh.*) (*nicht gewähren*) **jmdm./sich etw.** ~**:** deny *or* refuse sb. sth./deny oneself sth.; **ein Kind blieb ihr versagt** a child was denied her; **es war ihm versagt, das mitzuerleben** circumstances did not allow him to witness it; **ich konnte es mir nicht** ~**, darauf zu antworten** I could not refrain from answering; ⇒ *auch* **Dienst** D. ❸ *refl. V.* **sich jmdm.** ~**:** refuse to give oneself *or* surrender to sb.

**Versagen** *das;* ~**s** failure; **menschliches** ~**:** human error

**Versager** *der;* ~**s**, ~, **Versagerin** *die;* ~, ~**nen** failure

**Versagung** *die;* ~, ~**en** refusal

**versalzen** ❶ *unr. tr. V.* Ⓐ put too much salt in/on; **die Suppe ist** ~**:** there is too much salt in the soup; the soup is too salty; Ⓑ (*fig. ugs.*) spoil; **jmdm. etw.** ~**:** spoil sth. for sb.; ⇒ *auch* **Suppe**. ❷ *itr. V.; mit sein* (*bes. Ökologie; Bodenk.*) become salty

**versammeln** ❶ *tr. V.* assemble; gather [together]; **seine Leute um sich** ~**:** gather one's people around one. ❷ *refl. V.* assemble; (*weniger formell*) gather; **sich um jmdn./etw.** ~**:** gather round sb./sth.; **vor versammelter Belegschaft sprechen** speak to the assembled staff; ⇒ *auch* **Mannschaft** C

**Versammlung** *die* Ⓐ meeting; (*Partei*~) assembly; (*unter freiem Himmel, bes. politisch*) rally; **auf einer** ~ **sprechen** speak at a meeting/rally; Ⓑ (*Gremium*) assembly; **gesetzgebende/verfassunggebende** ~**:** legislative/constituent assembly; Ⓒ (*das Sichversammeln*) assembly; bringing together *no art.*

**Versammlungs-:** ~**freiheit** *die* freedom of assembly; ~**lokal** *das* meeting place

**Versand** *der;* ~**[e]s** Ⓐ dispatch; **zum** ~ **fertig machen** prepare for dispatch; Ⓑ (*Abteilung*) dispatch department; Ⓒ (*ugs.:* ~*haus*) mail order firm

**Versand·buch·handel** *der* mail order trade

**versanden** *itr. V.; mit sein* Ⓐ fill with sand; ‹harbour etc.› silt up; (*mit Sand bedeckt werden*) be covered with sand; B (*fig. ugs.*) peter *or* fizzle out

**Versand-:** **~geschäft** *das*, **~handel** *der* mail order business; **~haus** *das* mail order firm; **~haus·katalog** *der* mail order catalogue; **~kosten** *Pl.* dispatch costs; carriage *sing.*; (*Post u. Verpackung*) postage and packing

**Versatz-:** **~amt** *das* (*südd.; österr.*) pawnshop; **~stück** *das* A (*Theater*) [movable] piece of scenery; set piece; B (*fig.*) cliché; hackneyed idea; C (*österr.: Pfand*) security

**versaubeuteln** *tr. V.* (*ugs.*) A (*verderben*) mess up; B (*verlieren, verlegen*) lose; mislay

**versauen** *tr. V.* (*salopp*) A (*verschmutzen*) mess up; make mucky (*coll.*); B (*verderben*) foul up (*coll.*)

**versauern** *itr. V.; mit sein* (*ugs.*) waste away; stagnate

**versaufen** ❶ *unr. tr. V.* (*salopp*) drink one's way through. ❷ *unr. itr. V.; mit sein* A (*ugs.: ertrinken*) drown; B (*Bergmannsspr.*) flood

**versäumen** *tr. V.* A (*verpassen*) miss; lose ‹time, sleep›; **da hast du nichts/nicht viel versäumt** you didn't miss anything/miss much; **den versäumten Schlaf nachholen** catch up on lost sleep; B (*vernachlässigen, unterlassen*) neglect ‹duty, task›; **das Versäumte/Versäumtes nachholen** make up for *or* catch up on what one has neglected *or* failed to do; **er versäumte [es] nicht, X zu erwähnen** he did not omit *or* fail to mention X

**Versäumnis** *das;* **~ses, ~se** omission; **die ~se der Eltern gegenüber ihren Kindern** the parents' sins of omission towards their children

**verschachern** *tr. V.* (*abwertend*) sell off

**verschachtelt** *Adj.* higgledy-piggledy ‹streets, town›; **ein ~er Satz** (*fig.*) an encapsulated sentence

**verschaffen** *tr. V.* **jmdm. Arbeit/Geld/Unterkunft** *usw.* **~:** provide sb. with work/money/accommodation *etc.*; get sb. work/money/accommodation *etc.*; **sich** (*Dat.*) **etw. ~:** get hold of sth.; obtain sth.; **sich** (*Dat.*) **Respekt ~:** gain respect; **sich Gewissheit ~:** make sure *or* certain; **es verschaffte mir die Möglichkeit, zu ...** it gave me the opportunity to ...; **was verschafft mir die Ehre?** (*iron.*) to what do I owe this honour?

**verschalen** *tr. V.* line ‹wall, shaft, etc.› [with boards]; (*bedecken*) board up ‹window, hole›

**Verschalung** *die;* **~, ~en** A (*das Verschalen*) lining; boarding; (*eines Fensters*) boarding up; B (*Produkt*) lining; (*aus Brettern*) boarding

**verschämt** /fɛɐ̯ˈʃɛːmt/ ❶ *Adj.* bashful. ❷ *adv.* bashfully

**verschandeln** *tr. V.* (*ugs.*) spoil; ruin; **das Gebäude verschandelt die Landschaft** the building is a blot on the landscape

**Verschandelung** *die;* **~, ~en** (*ugs.*) ruination *no indef. art.*; **eine solche ~ der Gegend** ruining the area like this

**verschanzen** ❶ *refl. V.* (*Milit.*) take up a [fortified] position; (*in einem Graben*) entrench oneself; dig [oneself] in; (*in einem Gebäude*) barricade oneself (**in** + *Dat.* into); **sich in seinem Büro/hinter einer Zeitung ~** (*fig.*) take refuge in one's office/take cover *or* hide behind a newspaper; **sich hinter einer Ausrede/seiner Müdigkeit ~** (*fig.*) hide behind an excuse/use one's tiredness as an excuse ❷ *tr. V.* (*Milit.*) fortify

**Verschanzung** *die;* **~, ~en** (*Milit.*) fortification; (*in Gräben*) entrenchment

**verschärfen** ❶ *tr. V.* A (*steigern*) intensify ‹conflict, difference, desire, etc.›; increase, step up ‹pace, pressure›; B (*strenger machen*) tighten ‹law, control, restriction, etc›; make ‹penalty› more severe; C (*verschlimmern*) make ‹unemployment etc.› worse; aggravate ‹situation, crisis, etc.›. ❷ *refl. V.* A (*sich steigern*) ‹pace, pressure, etc.› increase; ‹pain, tension, conflict, difference› intensify; B (*sich verschlimmern*) get worse

**verschärft** ❶ *Adj.* A (*gesteigert*) increased ‹pressure›; intensified ‹conflict›; more intense ‹training›; B (*strenger*) tighter, stricter ‹control, check, restriction›; more severe ‹reprimand, punishment›; C (*schlimmer geworden*) aggravated. ❷ *adv.* (*strenger*) more strictly

**Verschärfung** *die;* **~, ~en** ⇒ **verschärfen** 1 A-C: intensification; increase; tightening; greater severity; aggravation; worsening

**verscharren** *tr. V.* bury (*just below the surface*); bury ‹person› in a shallow grave

**verschätzen** ❶ *refl. V.* **sich in etw.** (*Dat.*) **~:** misjudge sth.; **wenn du dich da mal nicht verschätzt!** unless you've got it all wrong!. ❷ *tr. V.* misjudge

**verschauen** *refl. V.* (*österr. ugs.*) ⇒ **vergucken** A

**verschaukeln** *tr. V.* (*ugs.*) **jmdn. ~:** take sb. for a ride (*coll.*)

**verscheiden** *unr. itr. V.; mit sein* (*geh.*) pass away

**verscheißen** (*derb*) ❶ *unr. tr. V.* cover with shit (*coarse*); **verschissene Unterhosen** shitty (*coarse*) underpants. ❷ *unr. itr. V.* **in bei jmdm. verschissen haben** (*fig.*) have had it as far as sb. is concerned (*coll.*)

**verscheißern** *tr. V.* (*derb*) **jmdn. ~:** have (*Brit. coll.*) *or* (*Amer. coll.*) put sb. on; **du willst mich wohl ~!** pull the 'other one[, it's got bells on] (*sl.*)

**verschenken** ❶ *tr. V.* A give away; **etw. an jmdn. ~:** give sth. to sb.; B (*ungewollt vergeben*) waste ‹space›; give away ‹points›; **den Sieg ~:** throw away one's chance of winning. ❷ *refl. V.* (*geh.*) **sich [an jmdn.] ~:** throw oneself away [on sb.]

**verscherbeln** /fɛɐ̯ˈʃɛrbl̩n/ *tr. V.* (*ugs.*) flog (*Brit. sl.*) (*Dat.*, **an** + *Akk.* to)

**verscherzen** *refl. V.* **sich** (*Dat.*) **etw. ~:** lose *or* forfeit sth. [through one's own folly]

**verscheuchen** *tr. V.* chase away (*lit. or fig.*); (*durch Erschrecken*) frighten *or* scare away

**verscheuern** *tr. V.* (*ugs.*) flog (*Brit. sl.*) (*Dat.*, **an** + *Akk.* to)

**verschicken** *tr. V.* A ⇒ **versenden**; B **jmdn. zur Kur/an die See** *usw.* **~:** send sb. away to take a cure/to the seaside *etc.*

**Verschickung** *die* A ⇒ **Versendung**; B (*zur Erholung*) sending away [for health reasons] *no indef. art.*

**verschiebbar** *Adj.* A movable; (*verstellbar*) adjustable; B (*aufschiebbar*) which can be put off *postpos.*, *not pred.*

**Verschiebe·bahnhof** *der* marshalling yard

**verschieben** ❶ *unr. tr. V.* A shift; move; **die Grenze wurde um 5 km nach Süden verschoben** the boundary was moved five kilometres to the south *or* further south; **die Perspektive/das ganze Bild ~** (*fig.*) alter *or* change the perspective/the whole picture; B (*aufschieben*) put off, postpone (**auf** + *Akk.* till); **etw. um eine Woche/auf unbestimmte Zeit ~:** postpone sth. for a week/indefinitely; ⇒ *auch* **besorgen** C; C (*ugs.: illegal verkaufen*) traffic in ‹goods›; (*beiseite schaffen*) move illegally; **Waren/Devisen ins Ausland ~:** smuggle goods/currency to a foreign country. ❷ *unr. refl. V.* A get out of place; (*rutschen*) slip; (*Geol.*) ‹continent etc.› shift; **das Kräfteverhältnis hat sich verschoben** (*fig.*) the balance of power has shifted; B (*erst später stattfinden*) be postponed (**um** for); ‹start› be put back *or* delayed (**um** by)

**Verschiebung** *die* A movement; (*fig.: Änderung*) alteration, shift (*Gen.* in); **die ~ der Kontinente** (*Geol.*) the continental shift; B (*zeitlich*) postponement; C (*ugs.: illegaler Handel*) trafficking (**von** in); (*ins Ausland*) smuggling

**verschieden** ❶ *2. Part. v.* **verscheiden**. ❷ *Adj.* A (*nicht gleich*) different (**von** from); **er hat zwei ~e Socken an** he is wearing two odd socks *or* two socks that don't match; **das ist von Fall zu Fall/von Land zu Land ~:** that varies from one case to another/from country to country; B (*vielfältig*) various; **auf ~e Weise** in various ways; **die ~sten ...** all sorts of ...; **die ~sten Theorien** the most diverse theories; **in den ~sten Farben** in the most varied colours; in a whole variety of colours; **die ~en ...** the various ...; C *allein stehend* **Verschiedene** various people; **Verschiedene der Anwesenden** several of those present; **Verschiedenes** various things *pl.*; „**Verschiedenes**" 'miscellaneous'; (*Tagesordnungspunkt*) 'any other business'. ❸ *adv.* differently; **~ groß** of different sizes *postpos.*; different-sized; ‹people› of different heights; **~ schwer/lang** of different weights/lengths *postpos.*

**verschieden·artig** ❶ *Adj.* different in kind *pred.*; (*mehr als zwei*) diverse; **~e Werkzeuge** tools of various [different] kinds; **~e Mittel anwenden** use various different means. ❷ *adv.* diversely; (*auf verschiedene Weise*) in various different ways; **sehr ~ interpretiert werden** be subjected to very diverse interpretations

**Verschiedenartigkeit** *die;* **~:** difference in nature; (*unter mehreren*) diversity; **die ~ der beiden Systeme** the different nature of the two systems

***verschiedene·mal** ⇒ **Mal**[1]

**verschiedenerlei** *unbest. Gattungsz.; indekl.:* A *attr.* various different; B *allein stehend* various different things; **~ Käse** various different kinds of cheese

**verschieden·farbig** ❶ *Adj.* different-coloured; of different colours *postpos.* ❷ *adv.* ‹paint etc› in different colours

**Verschiedenheit** *die;* **~, ~en** difference; dissimilarity; (*unter mehreren*) diversity; (*Unterschied*) difference

**verschiedentlich** *Adv.* on various occasions

**verschießen** ❶ *unr. tr. V.* A (*als Geschoss verwenden*) fire ‹shell, cartridge, etc.›; B (*verbrauchen*) use up ‹ammunition›; **verschossene/nicht verschossene Patronen** spent/unspent *or* live cartridges; ⇒ *auch* **Pulver** B; C **einen Strafstoß ~** (*Fußball*) miss with a penalty. ❷ *unr. refl. V.* (*ugs.*) **[in jmdn.] verschossen sein** be madly in love [with sb.] (*coll.*). ❸ *unr. itr. V.; mit sein* (*verblassen*) fade

**verschiffen** *tr. V.* ship ‹goods, coal›; transport ‹troops, emigrants, etc.› by ship

**Verschiffung** *die;* **~, ~en** shipment; (*von Personen*) transportation [by ship]

**verschimmeln** *itr. V.; mit sein* go mouldy; **verschimmelt** mouldy

**verschlafen**[1] ❶ *unr. itr.* (*auch refl.*) *V.* oversleep. ❷ *unr. tr. V.* A (*schlafend verbringen*) sleep through ‹morning, journey, etc.›; **sein halbes Leben ~:** doze away half one's life; B (*versäumen*) sleep through ‹concert›; not wake up in time for ‹appointment›; not wake up in time to catch ‹train, bus›; (*einschlafen und versäumen*) fall asleep and miss; C (*ugs.: vergessen*) forget about ‹appointment etc.›

**verschlafen**[2] *Adj.* A half asleep; B (*fig.: ruhig, langweilig*) sleepy ‹town, village›

**Verschlag** *der* shed; (*angebaut*) lean-to; (*für Kaninchen*) hutch

**verschlagen**[1] *unr. tr. V.* A **[jmdm.] die Seite ~:** lose sb.'s place *or* page; **die Seite ~** (*im eigenen Buch*) lose one's place *or* page; B **jmdm. den Appetit ~:** rob sb. of his/her appetite; **jmdm. die Sprache** *od.* **Rede/den Atem ~:** leave sb. speechless/take sb.'s breath away; C (*Ballspiele*) mishit ‹ball›; D **das Leben/Schicksal hat ihn nach X ~:** the vagaries of life caused/fate caused him to end up in X; **vom Sturm an eine Küste ~ werden** be driven on to a coast by the gale; **es hat ihn nach Berlin ~:** he landed [up] *or* ended up in Berlin.

**verschlagen**[2] ❶ *Adj.* A (*abwertend: gerissen*) sly; shifty; B (*bes. nordd.: lauwarm*) lukewarm; tepid. ❷ *adv.* (*abwertend: gerissen*) slyly; shiftily

**Verschlagenheit** *die;* **~** (*abwertend*) slyness; shiftiness

**verschlammen** *itr. V.* become *or* get muddy; ‹ditch, river› silt up; **verschlammt** muddy

**verschlampen** (*ugs.*, *bes. südd.*) ❶ *tr. V.* succeed in losing (*iron.*). ❷ *itr. V.; mit sein* (*abwertend*) ‹person› let oneself go; ‹house etc.› get into a bad state; **verschlampt** slovenly; in a slovenly state *postpos.*

V

**verschlanken** *tr. V.* (*Wirtschaftsjargon*) trim [down], reduce ‹production etc.›

**verschlechtern** ❶ *tr. V.* make worse. ❷ *refl. V.* get worse; deteriorate; **sich [finanziell/wirtschaftlich** *usw.*] **~:** be worse off [financially/economically *etc.*]; **er hat sich verschlechtert** he is worse off [now]

**Verschlechterung** *die;* **~, ~en** worsening, deterioration (*Gen.* in); **der Wohnungswechsel bedeutet für ihn keine ~:** his change of flat (*Brit.*) *or* (*Amer.*) apartment leaves him no worse off

**verschleiern** ❶ *tr. V.* Ⓐ veil; (*fig.*) cover, veil ‹sky, moon, etc.›; obscure ‹view›; cloud ‹consciousness›; **Dunst verschleierte die Berge** (*fig.*) a veil of mist hid the mountains; **Tränen verschleierten ihre Augen** *od.* **ihr den Blick** (*fig.*) she could scarcely see through her tears; her vision was blurred by tears; Ⓑ (*fig.: verbergen*) draw a veil over, cover up ‹deception, facts, scandal, etc.›; hide ‹intentions›. ❷ *refl. V.* ‹vision etc.› become blurred; ‹sky› cloud over

**verschleiert** ❶ *Adj.* veiled; misty ‹vision etc.›; fogged ‹photograph›; **mit ~er Stimme** in a husky voice; (*vor Rührung*) in a voice choked with emotion. ❷ *adv.* **ohne Brille sieht er [alles] nur ~:** without [his] glasses he sees everything as in a mist

**Verschleierung** *die;* **~, ~en** Ⓐ veiling; **ohne ~:** without a veil; Ⓑ (*fig.: von Sachverhalten, Motiven*) covering up

**Verschleierungs·taktik** *die* cover-up tactics *pl.*

**verschleifen** *unr. tr. V.* smooth; (*fig.*) slur ‹consonants, vowels›

**verschleimt** *Adj.* congested with phlegm *postpos.*

**Verschleimung** *die;* **~, ~en** mucous congestion

**Verschleiß** /fɛɐ̯ˈʃlai̯s/ *der;* **~es, ~e** Ⓐ (*Abnutzung*) wear *no indef. art.*; wear and tear *sing.*, *no indef. art*; **der Auspuff unterliegt einem sehr hohen/raschen ~:** the exhaust is subject to a great deal of wear and tear/does not last very long; **einen höheren ~ haben** wear more rapidly; have a higher rate of wear; Ⓑ (*Verbrauch*) consumption (**an** + *Dat.* of); **einen hohen ~ an etw.** (*Dat.*) **haben** use up a large amount of sth.; **sie hat einen unheimlichen ~ an Männern** (*ugs. scherzh.*) she gets through men at an incredible rate (*coll.*); Ⓒ (*österr. veralt.: Vertrieb*) sale; retailing

**verschleißen** ❶ *unr. itr. V.*; *mit sein* wear out. ❷ *unr. tr. V.* Ⓐ wear out; (*fig.*) run down, ruin ‹one's nerves, one's health›; use up ‹energy, ability, etc.›; **verschlissen** worn ‹material, suit, etc.›; worn out ‹machine parts etc.›; **sich ~:** wear oneself out; use up all one's energy (**bei** on); Ⓑ (*ugs. scherzh.: verbrauchen*) get through ‹men friends, cleaning-women, etc.›. ❸ *unr.* (*auch regelm.*) *tr. V.* (*österr. veralt.: verkaufen*) sell; retail

**Verschleißer** der; **~s, ~, Verschleißerin** *die;* **~, ~nen** (*österr. veralt.*) retailer

**Verschleiß·erscheinung** *die* sign of wear; (*an einem Menschen*) sign of wear and tear *or* exhaustion

**verschleppen** *tr. V.* Ⓐ carry off ‹valuables, animals›; take away ‹person›; (*bes. nach Übersee*) transport ‹convicts, slaves, etc.›; **in die Sklaverei verschleppt werden** be carried off into slavery; Ⓑ (*weiterverbreiten*) carry, spread ‹disease, bacteria, mud, etc.›; Ⓒ (*verzögern*) delay; (*in die Länge ziehen*) draw out; Ⓓ (*unbehandelt lassen*) let ‹illness› drag on [and get worse]; **verschleppte Krankheit** illness aggravated by neglect

**Verschleppung** *die;* **~, ~en** ⇨ **verschleppen**: Ⓐ carrying off; transportation; Ⓑ carrying; spreading; Ⓒ delaying; drawing out; Ⓓ aggravation by neglect

**verschleudern** *tr. V.* Ⓐ (*billig verkaufen*) sell dirt cheap; (*mit Verlust*) sell at a loss; Ⓑ (*abwertend: verschwenden*) squander

*old spelling (see note on page 1707)

**verschließbar** *Adj.* Ⓐ closable; **[luftdicht] ~:** sealable ‹container etc.›; Ⓑ (*abschließbar*) lockable ‹suitcase, drawer, etc.›

**verschließen** ❶ *unr. tr. V.* Ⓐ close ‹package, tin, pores, mouth, etc›; close up ‹blood vessel, aperture, etc.›; stop ‹bottle›; put a/the bung in ‹barrel›; (*mit einem Korken*) cork *bottle*; **hermetisch verschlossen** hermetically sealed; **etw. luftdicht ~:** make sth. airtight; put an airtight seal on sth.; **die Augen/Ohren [vor etw.** (*Dat.*)] **~** (*fig.*) close one's eyes *or* be blind/turn a deaf ear *or* be deaf [to sth.]; Ⓑ (*abschließen*) lock ‹door, cupboard, drawer, etc.›; lock up ‹house etc.›; ⇨ *auch* **Tür**; Ⓒ (*wegschließen*) lock away (**in** + *Dat. od. Akk.* in); Ⓓ (*versperren*) bar ‹way etc.›; **viele berufliche Möglichkeiten blieben ihm verschlossen** many possible professions remained barred *or* closed to him.
❷ *unr. refl. V.* Ⓐ **sich jmdm. ~:** be closed to sb.; ‹person› shut oneself off from sb.; **er verschloss sich** he shut up like a clam; **der tiefere Sinn verschloss sich ihm** the deeper meaning remained obscure to him; ⇨ *auch* **verschlossen** 2; Ⓑ *in* **sich einer Sache** (*Dat.*) **~:** close one's mind to sth.; (*ignorieren*) ignore sth.

**verschlimmbessern** *tr. V.* (*ugs. scherzh.*) make worse with so-called corrections

**Verschlimmbesserung** *die;* **~, ~en** (*ugs. scherzh.*) so-called correction (*which is wrong*); **das ist eine ~!** that so-called correction has made things worse

**verschlimmern** ❶ *tr. V.* make worse; aggravate ‹state of health›. ❷ *refl. V.* get worse; worsen; ‹position, conditions› deteriorate, worsen

**Verschlimmerung** *die;* **~, ~en** worsening

**verschlingen** ❶ *unr. tr. V.* Ⓐ [inter]twine ‹threads, string, etc.› (**zu** into); **miteinander ~:** intertwine ‹threads, ropes, etc.›; Ⓑ (*essen, fressen*) devour ‹food›; (*fig.*) devour, consume ‹novel, money, etc.›; **jmdn. mit den Augen ~:** devour sb. with one's eyes; **die tobende See verschlang das Schiff** the raging sea engulfed the ship. ❷ *unr. refl. V.* **sich ineinander ~:** become entwined *or* intertwined; ⇨ *auch* **verschlungen**

**verschlissen** *2. Part. v.* **verschleißen** 2

**verschlossen** ❶ *2. Part. v.* **verschließen**. ❷ *Adj.* (*wortkarg*) taciturn, tight-lipped; (*zurückhaltend*) reserved

**Verschlossenheit** *die;* **~:** taciturnity; (*Zurückhaltung*) reserve

**verschlucken** ❶ *tr. V.* Ⓐ swallow ‹food, bone, word, etc.›; (*fig.*) absorb, deaden ‹sound›; absorb, eliminate ‹rays›; Ⓑ (*fig.: unterdrücken*) choke back ‹anger, tears›; hold back ‹remark›. ❷ *refl. V.* choke; **er verschluckte sich beim Essen/Lachen** he choked over his food/with laughing

**verschludern** *tr. V.* (*ugs. abwertend*) ❶ *tr. V.* Ⓐ (*verlieren*) lose; (*verlegen*) mislay; Ⓑ (*vergeuden*) waste ‹material›; throw away ‹money›; Ⓒ (*verderben*) ruin, mess up ‹exercise book› ❷ *itr. V.* go to rack and ruin

**verschlungen** ❶ *2. Part. v.* **verschlingen**. ❷ *Adj.* entwined ‹ornamentation›; winding ‹path etc.›; **er saß mit ~en Armen da** he sat there with arms folded

**Verschluss, *Verschluß** *der* Ⓐ (*am BH, an Schmuck usw.*) fastener; fastening; (*an Taschen, Schmuck*) clasp; (*an Schuhen, Gürteln*) buckle; (*am Schrank, Fenster, Koffer usw.*) catch; (*an Flaschen*) top; (*Stöpsel*) stopper; (*Schraub~*) [screw] top; [screw] cap; (*Tank~*) cap; Ⓑ (*einer Feuerwaffe*) breechblock; Ⓒ (*einer Kamera*) shutter; Ⓓ (*Med.: einer Arterie*) blockage; occlusion; Ⓔ *in* **unter ~ sein/bleiben** be under lock and key; **etw. unter ~ halten** keep sth. under lock and key *or* locked away

**verschlüsseln** *tr. V.* [en]code; (*bes. DV*) encrypt

**Verschlüsselung** *die;* **~, ~en** [en]coding

**Verschluss-, *Verschluß-: ~kappe** *die* top; cap; **~laut** *der* (*Sprachw.*) stop; **~sache** *die* [item of] confidential information; **~sachen** condidential information *sing.*

**verschmachten** *itr. V.*; *mit sein* (*geh.*) fade away (**vor** + *Dat.* from); (*vor Sehnsucht*) pine away

**verschmähen** *tr. V.* (*geh.*) spurn; **verschmähte Liebe** unrequited love

**verschmälern** ❶ *tr. V.* narrow; make narrower (**um** by). ❷ *refl. V.* narrow; become narrower

**verschmausen** *tr. V.* (*ugs. scherzh.*) dig *or* tuck into (*coll.*); (*aufessen*) eat up

**verschmelzen** ❶ *unr. tr. V.* Ⓐ fuse ‹metals›; (*fig.*) fuse, merge (**zu** into, to form); **Kupfer und Zink zu Messing ~:** fuse copper and zinc to make brass; Ⓑ (*verschweißen*) weld together ‹metal parts›. ❷ *unr. itr. V.*; *mit sein* ‹metals, cells› fuse; (*fig.*) ‹firms, images, towns, etc.› merge (**zu** into, to form); **zu einem Ganzen ~:** blend into one

**Verschmelzung** *die;* **~, ~en** Ⓐ fusing, fusion (*lit. or fig.*) (**zu** into); (*von Städten, Firmen usw.*) merging, merger (**zu** into, to form); Ⓑ (*Verschweißung*) weld

**verschmerzen** *tr. V.* get over ‹defeat, disappointment›

**verschmieren** *tr. V.* Ⓐ smear ‹window etc.›; (*beim Schreiben*) mess up ‹paper›; scrawl all over ‹page›; Ⓑ (*verteilen*) spread ‹butter etc.›; smudge ‹ink›; Ⓒ (*verbrauchen*) use up ‹butter, oil, plaster, etc.›; Ⓓ (*zuschmieren*) fill [in] ‹crack, hole, etc.›

**verschmitzt** /fɛɐ̯ˈʃmɪt͜st/ ❶ *Adj.* mischievous; roguish. ❷ *adv.* mischievously; roguishly

**Verschmitztheit** *die;* **~:** mischievousness; roguishness

**verschmoren** *itr. V.*; *mit sein* (*ugs.*) burn; **es riecht verschmort** there's a smell of burning *or* a burnt smell

**verschmust** /fɛɐ̯ˈʃmuːst/ *Adj.* (*ugs.*) ‹child, cat, etc.› that always wants to be cuddled; **er ist [sehr] ~:** he always wants to be cuddled

**verschmutzen** ❶ *itr. V.*; *mit sein* ‹material› get dirty; ‹river etc.› become polluted. ❷ *tr. V.* dirty, soil ‹carpet, clothes›; pollute ‹air, water, etc.›

**Verschmutzung** *die;* **~, ~en** Ⓐ (*der Umwelt*) pollution; Ⓑ (*von Stoffen, Teppichen usw.*) soiling; Ⓒ (*Schmutz*) dirt *no pl.*; **~en** [cases *pl.* of] soiling *sing.*

**verschnaufen** *itr.* (*auch refl.*) *V.* have *or* take a breather

**Verschnauf·pause** *die* breather; rest; **eine ~ einlegen** have *or* take a breather

**verschneiden** *unr. tr. V.* Ⓐ (*durch Schneiden verderben*) cut ‹hair, roses, etc.› all wrong; ruin ‹wood, material, film› by bad/wrong cutting; Ⓑ (*mischen*) blend ‹rum, whisky, etc.›; Ⓒ (*kastrieren*) castrate, geld ‹animal›

**verschneit** *Adj.* snow-covered *attrib.*; covered with snow *postpos.*

**Verschnitt** *der;* **~[e]s, ~e** Ⓐ (*das Mischen*) blending; Ⓑ (*Mischung*) blend (**aus** of); (*fig., meist abwertend*) mixture; combination; Ⓒ (*Abfall*) waste; (*von Holz usw.*) offcuts *pl.*

**-verschnitt** *der:* **ein James-Bond-Verschnitt:** a second-rate James Bond

**verschnörkelt** *Adj.* ornate

**Verschnörkelung** *die;* **~, ~en** ornamentation; (*Schnörkel*) flourish

**verschnupft** /fɛɐ̯ˈʃnʊpft/ ❶ *Adj.* Ⓐ suffering from a cold *postpos.*; **[ganz] ~ sein** have a [bad] cold; Ⓑ (*fig. ugs.: gekränkt*) peeved (*coll.*). ❷ *adv.* in a peeved way (*coll.*); peevishly

**verschnüren** *tr. V.* tie up (**zu** into)

**Verschnürung** *die;* **~, ~en** Ⓐ (*das Verschnüren*) tying up; Ⓑ (*Schnur*) string

**verschollen** /fɛɐ̯ˈʃɔlən/ *Adj.* missing; **er ist ~:** he has disappeared; (*wird vermisst*) he is missing; **sie ließ ihren Mann für ~ erklären** she had her husband declared missing, presumed dead; **er galt seit langem als ~:** for a long time it had been thought he had disappeared

**verschonen** *tr. V.* spare; **von etw. verschont bleiben** be spared by sth.; escape sth.; **jmdn. mit etw. ~:** spare sb. sth.

**verschönen** *tr. V.* brighten up
**verschönern** /fɛɐ̯ˈʃøːnɐn/ *tr. V.* brighten up
**Verschönerung** *die;* ~, ~**en** brightening up; beautification (*joc.*)
**Verschonung** *die* sparing; **er flehte um ~ seines Lebens/der Kinder** he pleaded that his life/the children be spared
**verschorfen** *itr. V.; mit sein* form a scab; **eine verschorfte Wunde** a wound with a scab
**verschrammen** ❶ *tr. V.* scratch. ❷ *itr. V.; mit sein* scratch; get scratched
**verschränken** /fɛɐ̯ˈʃrɛŋkn̩/ *tr. V.* fold ‹arms›; cross ‹legs›; clasp ‹hands›; **mit verschränkten Armen/Händen** with one's arms folded/hands clasped
**Verschränkung** *die;* ~, ~**en** ⇒ **verschränken**: folding; crossing; clasping
**verschrauben** *tr. V.* screw on; **[miteinander]** ~: screw together
**Verschraubung** *die;* ~, ~**en** Ⓐ (*das Verschrauben*) screwing [together]; Ⓑ (*Schraubverbindung*) screw fixing
**verschrecken** *tr. V.* frighten *or* scare [off *or* away]
**verschreiben** ❶ *unr. tr. V.* Ⓐ (*verbrauchen*) use up ‹paper, ink, pencils, etc.›; Ⓑ (*Med.: verordnen*) prescribe ‹medicine, treatment, etc.›; **jmdm. ein Medikament** ~: prescribe a medication for sb.; **sich** (*Dat.*) **etw. für** *od.* **gegen sein Rheuma ~ lassen** get the doctor to prescribe sth. for one's rheumatism; Ⓒ *in* **sich/seine Seele dem Teufel** ~: give oneself/sell one's soul to the devil; Ⓓ (*falsch schreiben*) write incorrectly *or* wrongly. ❷ *unr. refl. V.* Ⓐ (*einen Fehler machen*) make a slip of the pen; **sich beim Datum** ~: make a mistake when writing the date; Ⓑ (*sich widmen*) **sich einer Sache** (*Dat.*) ~: devote oneself to sth.
**Verschreibung** *die;* ~, ~**en** prescription; **mit der ~ von Pillen allein ist es nicht getan** it is not enough simply to prescribe pills
**verschreibungs·pflichtig** *Adj.* available only on prescription *postpos.*
**verschrie[e]n** /fɛɐ̯ˈʃriː[ə]n/ *Adj.* notorious (**wegen** for); **als etw. ~ sein** have the reputation of being sth. (**bei** with)
**verschroben** /fɛɐ̯ˈʃroːbn̩/ ❶ *Adj.* eccentric, cranky ‹person›; cranky, weird ‹ideas›. ❷ *adv.* eccentrically; weirdly
**Verschrobenheit** *die;* ~, ~**en** eccentricity
**verschrotten** *tr. V.* scrap
**Verschrottung** *die;* ~, ~**en** scrapping
**verschrumpeln** *itr. V.; mit sein* (*ugs.*) go shrivelled; **verschrumpelt** shrivelled
**verschüchtern** *tr. V.* intimidate; **verschüchtert** timid; (*adverbial*) timidly
**verschulden** ❶ *tr. V.* be to blame for ‹accident, death, etc.›; (*Fußball usw.*) give away ‹goal, corner›; **sein Unglück selbst** ~: have only oneself to blame for one's misfortune. ❷ *refl. V.* get into debt; **er hat sich dafür hoch ~ müssen** he had to borrow heavily to do that; **sich auf Jahre hinaus** ~: incur debts/a debt that will take years to pay off
**Verschulden** *das;* ~**s** guilt; **durch eigenes/fremdes** ~: through one's own/someone else's fault; **ohne mein** ~: through no fault of my own
**verschuldet** *Adj.* Ⓐ in debt *postpos.* (**bei** to); **hoch** ~: deeply in debt; Ⓑ (*belastet*) mortgaged; **hoch** ~: heavily mortgaged
**Verschuldung** *die;* ~, ~**en** indebtedness *no pl.;* **die hohe ~ des Staates** the state's heavy debts *pl.*
**Verschulung** *die;* ~, ~**en** organization on school lines
**verschusselt** *Adj.* (*ugs.*) ⇒ **schusselig**
**verschütt** *in* ~ **gehen** (*ugs.*) do a vanishing trick *or* disappearing act (*coll.*); (*salopp: umkommen*) go for a burton (*Brit. sl.*)
**verschütten** *tr. V.* Ⓐ spill; Ⓑ (*begraben*) bury ‹person› [alive]; submerge, bury ‹road etc.›; (*fig.*) submerge; **die verschütteten Bergleute** the trapped miners; **ein Verschütteter** one of those buried/trapped; **die Verschütteten** those buried/trapped; **verschüttete Erinnerungen** memories buried in the subconscious
***verschütt|gehen** ⇒ **verschütt**
**verschwägert** /fɛɐ̯ˈʃvɛːɡɐt/ *Adj.* related by marriage *postpos.*
**verschweigen** *unr. tr. V.* conceal ‹truth etc.›; (*verheimlichen*) keep quiet about; **jmdm. etw.** ~: hide *or* conceal sth. from sb.; **du verschweigst mir doch etwas** you're keeping something from me; ⇒ *auch* **verschwiegen** 2
**verschweißen** *tr. V.* weld [together]; **etw. mit etw.** ~: weld sth. to sth.
**verschwenden** *tr. V.* waste (**an** + *Akk.* on); **du verschwendest deine Worte** you are wasting your breath; **sie verschwendete keinen Blick an ihn** she did not give him a single glance
**Verschwender** *der;* ~**s**, ~, **Verschwenderin** *die;* ~, ~**nen** (*von Geld*) spendthrift; (*von Dingen*) wasteful person
**verschwenderisch** ❶ *Adj.* Ⓐ wasteful, extravagant ‹person›; ‹life› of extravagance; Ⓑ (*üppig*) lavish; sumptuous. ❷ *adv.* Ⓐ wastefully, extravagantly; **sie geht ~ mit ihrem Geld um** she is lavish *or* extravagant with her money; Ⓑ (*üppig*) lavishly; sumptuously
**Verschwendung** *die;* ~, ~**en** wastefulness; extravagance; **so eine** ~! what a waste!; ~ **von Steuergeldern** waste *or* squandering of taxpayers' money
**Verschwendungs·sucht** *die* love of extravagance; squandermania (*coll.*)
**verschwiegen** ❶ *2. Part. v.* **verschweigen**. ❷ *Adj.* Ⓐ (*diskret*) discreet; ⇒ *auch* **Grab**; Ⓑ (*still, einsam*) secluded ‹place, bay›; quiet ‹restaurant etc.›; **auf dem ~en Örtchen** (*ugs. scherzh.*) in the smallest room (*joc.*)
**Verschwiegenheit** *die;* ~: secrecy; (*Diskretion*) discretion; ⇒ *auch* **Siegel** B
**verschwimmen** *unr. itr. V.; mit sein* blur; become blurred; **die Zeilen/Buchstaben verschwammen mir vor den Augen** the lines/letters swam in front of my eyes; **ineinander/in eins** ~: merge into one another/into one; ⇒ *auch* **verschwommen** 2
**verschwinden** *unr. itr. V.; mit sein* Ⓐ disappear; vanish; ‹pain, spot, etc.› disappear, go [away]; **seine Zahnschmerzen sind von selbst verschwunden** his toothache went away *or* stopped of its own accord; **die Maus verschwand in ihrem Loch** *od.* **in ihr Loch** the mouse disappeared into its hole; **es ist besser, wir ~/lass uns hier** ~: we'd better/let's make ourselves scarce (*coll.*); **verschwinde [hier]!** off with you!; go away!; hop it! (*coll.*); **ich muss mal ~** (*ugs. verhüll.*) I have to pay a visit (*coll.*) *or* (*Brit. coll.*) spend a penny; **der Müll muss hier** ~: this rubbish must be removed; **jmdn. ~ lassen** take sb. away; (*in einer Anstalt usw.*) put sb. away; (*ermorden*) eliminate sb.; do away with sb.; **etw. ~ lassen** (*wegzaubern*) ‹conjurer› make sth. disappear *or* vanish; (*stehlen*) help oneself to sth. (*coll.*); (*verstecken*) hide sth.; (*unterschlagen, beiseite schaffen*) dispose of sth.; **Zigaretten in seiner Tasche/Karten in seinem Ärmel ~ lassen** slip cigarettes into one's pocket/cards up one's sleeve; Ⓑ (*verborgen sein*) **unter etw.** (*Dat.*) ~: disappear under sth.; be hidden by sth.; Ⓒ **neben jmdm./etw.** ~ (*sehr klein wirken*) be dwarfed by sb./sth.; (*unbedeutend wirken*) pale into insignificance beside sb./sth.
**verschwindend** ❶ *Adj.* tiny. ❷ *adv.* ~ **klein** tiny; minute; ~ **wenig** a tiny amount
**verschwistert** /fɛɐ̯ˈʃvɪstɐt/ *Adj.* **[miteinander] ~ sein** (*Bruder u. Schwester sein*) be brother and sister; (*Brüder u. Schwestern sein*) be brothers and sisters; (*Brüder/Schwestern sein*) be brothers/sisters
**verschwitzen** *tr. V.* Ⓐ make ‹shirt, dress, etc.› sweaty; **verschwitzt** sweaty; **total verschwitzt** soaked in sweat *or* perspiration; Ⓑ (*ugs.: vergessen*) forget; **ich habe es völlig verschwitzt** I clean forgot
**verschwollen** /fɛɐ̯ˈʃvɔlən/ *Adj.* swollen
**verschwommen** ❶ *2. Part. v.* **verschwimmen**. ❷ *Adj.* blurred ‹photograph, vision›; blurred, hazy ‹outline›; vague, woolly ‹idea, concept, formulation, etc.›; vague ‹hope›. ❸ *adv.* ‹express, formulate, refer› vaguely; ‹remember› hazily; **ich sehe alles ganz** ~: everything looks blurred to me
**Verschwommenheit** *die;* ~, ~**en** ⇒ **verschwommen** 2: blurring; haziness; vagueness; woolliness
**verschworen** ❶ *2. Part. v.* **verschwören**. ❷ *Adj.* Ⓐ (*fest zusammenhaltend*) sworn; **ein ~er Haufen** a band of blood brothers; Ⓑ *in* **einer Idee/Sache** (*Dat.*) *usw.* ~ **sein** be dedicated to an idea/a cause *etc.*
**verschwören** *unr. refl. V.* Ⓐ conspire, plot (**gegen** against); **alles scheint sich gegen uns verschworen zu haben** (*fig.*) everything seems to have conspired against us; Ⓑ (*sich verschreiben*) **sich jmdm./einer Sache** ~: dedicate *or* devote oneself to sb./sth.; ⇒ *auch* **verschworen**
**Verschworene** *der/die; adj. Dekl.*, **Verschwörer** *der;* ~**s**, ~, **Verschwörerin** *die;* ~, ~**nen** conspirator
**verschwörerisch** ❶ *Adj.* conspiratorial. ❷ *adv.* conspiratorially
**Verschwörung** *die;* ~, ~**en** conspiracy; plot
**versehen** ❶ *unr. tr. V.* Ⓐ (*ausstatten*) provide; equip ‹car, factory, machine, etc.›; Ⓑ (*ausüben, besorgen*) perform ‹duty etc.›; **bei jmdm. den Haushalt** ~: keep house for sb.; Ⓒ (*innehaben*) hold ‹post, job›; Ⓓ (*kath. Kirche*) administer the last rites *or* sacraments to ‹dying person›. ❷ *unr. refl. V.* Ⓐ (*einen Fehler machen*) make a slip; slip up; Ⓑ *in* **ehe man sich's versieht** before you know where you are; **ehe ich mich's versah** before I knew what was happening
**Versehen** *das;* ~**s**, ~: oversight; slip; **aus** ~: by mistake; inadvertently
**versehentlich** ❶ *Adv.* by mistake; inadvertently. ❷ *adj.* inadvertent
**versehrt** /fɛɐ̯ˈzeːɐ̯t/ *Adj.* disabled
**Versehrte** *der/die; adj. Dekl.* disabled person; **die ~n** the disabled
**Versehrten·sport** *der* sport *no art.* for the disabled
**verselbständigen** *refl. V.* become independent; **sich zu einer eigenen wissenschaftlichen Disziplin** ~: become an independent scientific discipline
**Verselbständigung** *die;* ~, ~**en** gaining *or* achievement of independence
**verselbstständigen** ⇒ **verselbständigen**
**Verselbstständigung** ⇒ **Verselbständigung**
**versenden** *unr.* (*auch regelm.*) *tr. V.* send ‹letter, parcel›; send out ‹invitations›; dispatch ‹goods›
**Versendung** *die* ⇒ **versenden**: sending; sending out; dispatch
**versengen** *tr. V.* scorch; singe ‹hair›
**versenkbar** *Adj.* (*Technik*) foldaway ‹sewing machine›; telescopic ‹aerial›
**versenken** ❶ *tr. V.* Ⓐ sink ‹ship›; sink, dump ‹waste›; lower ‹body, coffin›; **das eigene Schiff** ~: scuttle one's ship; Ⓑ (*verschwinden lassen*) lower, retract ‹aerial, rostrum, etc.›; sink ‹nail, rivet› [flush]; countersink ‹screw›; **die Hände in die Taschen** ~: sink one's hands [deep] into one's pockets. ❷ *refl. V.* (*fig.*) **sich in etw.** (*Akk.*) ~: immerse oneself *or* become engrossed in sth.; **sich in den Anblick von etw.** ~: lose oneself in the contemplation of sth.
**Versenkung** *die* Ⓐ ⇒ **versenken** 1 A, B: sinking; dumping; lowering; scuttling; retraction; countersinking; Ⓑ (*fig.: das Sichversenken*) immersion, absorption (**in** + *Akk.* in); **mystische** ~: mystic contemplation; Ⓒ (*Theater*) trap; **in der ~ verschwinden** (*fig. ugs.*) vanish from the scene; sink into oblivion; **aus der ~ auftauchen** (*fig. ugs.*) re-emerge on the scene
**Vers·epos** *das* epic poem
**Verse·schmied** *der*, **Verse·schmiedin** *die* (*scherzh.*, *abwertend*) rhymester; poetaster

V

**versessen** /fɛɐ̯ˈzɛsn̩/ *Adj.* **auf jmdn./etw. ~ sein** be dead keen on *or* crazy about sb./sth. (*coll.*); **auf peinlichste Genauigkeit ~:** obsessed with scrupulous accuracy; **darauf ~ sein, etw. zu tun** be dying to do sth.

**versetzen** ❶ *tr. V.* Ⓐ move; transfer, move ‹employee›; (*auf einen anderen Platz*) move ‹pupil› [to another seat]; (*in die nächsthöhere Klasse*) move ‹pupil› up, (*Amer.*) promote ‹pupil› (**in** + *Akk.* to); (*umpflanzen*) transplant, move ‹plant›; (*fig.*) transport (**in** + *Akk.* to); **sich ins vorige Jahrhundert versetzt fühlen** (*fig.*) be taken back to the last century; Ⓑ (*nicht geradlinig anordnen*) stagger; **versetzt angeordnet sein** be staggered; Ⓒ (*verpfänden*) pawn; Ⓓ (*verkaufen*) sell; Ⓔ (*ugs.: vergeblich warten lassen*) stand ‹person› up (*coll.*); Ⓕ (*vermischen*) mix; Ⓖ (*erwidern*) retort; Ⓗ **etw. in Bewegung/Tätigkeit ~:** set sth. in motion/operation; **jmdn. in Erstaunen/Unruhe/Angst/Begeisterung ~:** astonish sb./make sb. uneasy/frighten sb./fill sb. with enthusiasm; **jmdn. in die Lage ~, etw. zu tun** put sb. in a position to do sth.; **jmdm. einen Stoß/Fußtritt/Schlag** *usw.* **~:** give sb. a push/kick/deal sb. a blow *etc.*; **jmdm. eine** *od.* **eins ~** (*ugs.*) belt sb. one (*coll.*).
❷ *refl. V.* **sich an jmds. Stelle** (*Akk.*) *od.* **in jmds. Lage** (*Akk.*) **~:** put oneself in sb.'s position *or* place; **sich in jmdn. ~:** put oneself in sb.'s shoes *or* position

**Versetzung** *die;* **~, ~en** Ⓐ moving; (*einer Pflanze*) transplanting; (*eines Schülers*) moving up, (*Amer.*) promotion (**in** + *Akk.* to); (*eines Angestellten*) transfer; move; (*fig.*) transporting; Ⓑ (*Verpfändung*) pawning; Ⓒ (*Verkauf*) selling; sale; Ⓓ (*das Mischen*) mixing; ⇒ *auch* **Ruhestand**

**Versetzungs-: ~konferenz** *die:* (*Schulw.*) *staff meeting to discuss moving pupils to higher classes;* **~zeugnis** *das* (*Schulw.*) end-of-year report (*confirming pupil's move to a higher class*)

**verseuchen** *tr. V.* (*auch fig.*) contaminate; **radioaktiv ~:** contaminate with radioactivity

**Verseuchung** (*auch fig.*) *die;* **~, ~en** contamination

**Vers·fuß** *der* (*Verslehre*) [metrical] foot

**Versicherer** *der;* **~s, ~, Versicherin** *die;* **~, ~nen** insurer

**versichern** ❶ *tr. V.* Ⓐ (*als wahr hinstellen*) assert, affirm ‹sth.›; **etw. hoch und heilig/eidesstattlich ~:** swear blind to sth./attest sth. in a statutory declaration; **jmdm. etw.** *od.* (*geh.*) **jmdn. einer Sache** (*Gen.*) **~:** assure sb. of sth.; **jmdm.** *od.* (*geh.*) **jmdn. ~, dass ...** assure sb. that ...; **seien Sie versichert, dass ...** (*geh.*) you may rest assured that ...; Ⓑ (*vertraglich schützen*) insure (**bei** with); **sein Leben ist hoch/mit 50 000 DM versichert** his life is assured *or* insured for a large sum/50,000 marks.
❷ *refl. V.* (*geh.*) Ⓐ **sich jmds./einer Sache ~:** make sure *or* certain of sb./sth.; Ⓑ (*veralt.: sich bemächtigen*) **sich einer Sache** (*Gen.*) **~:** seize sth.

**Versicherte** *der/die; adj. Dekl.* insured [person]

**Versicherung** *die* Ⓐ (*Beteuerung*) assurance; **eine eidesstattliche ~:** a statutory declaration; Ⓑ (*Schutz durch Vertrag*) insurance; (*Vertrag*) insurance [policy] (**über** + *Akk.* for); (*ugs.: Beitrag, Prämie*) insurance [premium]; **eine ~ abschließen** take out an insurance [policy]; Ⓒ (*Gesellschaft*) insurance [company]

**versicherungs-, Versicherungs-: ~agent** *der,* **~agentin** *die* ▶ 159 insurance broker; **~beitrag** *der* insurance premium; **~betrug** *der* insurance fraud; **~fall** *der* event giving rise to a claim; **~gesellschaft** *die* insurance company; **~karte** *die* Ⓐ (*Sozialversicherung*) insurance *or* contribution card; Ⓑ (*Kfz.-Versicherung*) **die grüne ~karte** the green card; **~kauffrau** *die* insurance saleswoman; **~kaufmann** *der* insurance salesman; **~mathematiker** *der,* **~mathematikerin** *die* actuary; **~nehmer** *der;* **~~s, ~~, ~nehmerin** *die;* **~~, ~~nen** policy holder; **~pflichtig** *Adj.* Ⓐ (*Sozialversicherung*) ‹person› liable for [insurance] contributions; ‹earnings› subject to [insurance] contributions; Ⓑ (*individuell*) subject to compulsory insurance *postpos.*; **~police** *die,* **~schein** *der* insurance policy; **~schutz** *der* insurance cover; **~summe** *die* sum insured; **~vertreter** *der,* **~vertreterin** *die* ▶ 159 insurance agent

**versickern** *itr. V.; mit sein* Ⓐ ‹river etc.› drain *or* seep away; Ⓑ (*fig.: enden*) ‹conversation› fade away; ‹money› drain away

**versieben** *tr. V.* (*ugs.*) Ⓐ (*verlegen*) mislay; Ⓑ (*verderben*) ruin; waste ‹chance›

**versiegeln** *tr. V.* Ⓐ seal; **jmdm. den Mund** *od.* **die Lippen ~** (*fig.*) seal sb.'s lips; silence sb.; Ⓑ (*lackieren, überziehen*) seal ‹floor, paintwork, etc.›

**Versiegelung** *die;* **~, ~en** Ⓐ (*das Versiegeln*) sealing; Ⓑ (*Siegel*) seal; Ⓒ (*Schutzschicht*) protective coating; seal

**versiegen** *itr. V.; mit sein* (*geh.*) dry up; run dry; ‹tears› cease [to flow]; (*fig.*) peter out; ‹energy› run out; **sein nie ~der Humor** his inexhaustible fund of humour

**versiert** /vɛrˈziːɐ̯t/ *Adj.* experienced [and knowledgeable]; **in etw.** (*Dat.*) **~ sein** be well versed in sth.

**Versiertheit** *die;* **~:** experience (**in** + *Dat.* in); (*Wissen*) knowledge (**in** + *Dat.* of)

**versifft** /fɛɐ̯ˈzɪft/ *Adj.* (*ugs.*) filthy

**versilbern** *tr. V.* Ⓐ silver-plate; (*dichter.*) silver; Ⓑ (*ugs.: verkaufen*) turn into cash; flog (*Brit. sl.*)

**versinken** *unr. itr. V.; mit sein* Ⓐ sink; **im Schlamm/Schnee ~:** sink into the mud/snow; **in den Wellen ~:** sink beneath the waves; **im Moor ~:** be sucked into the bog; **ich wäre am liebsten im Erdboden versunken** I wished the ground would [open and] swallow me up; **die Stadt versank im Dunkel** (*fig. geh.*) darkness descended over the town; **eine versunkene Kultur** (*fig.*) a long-vanished civilization; Ⓑ (*fig.*) **~ in** (+ *Akk.*) become immersed in *or* wrapped up in ‹memories, thoughts›; subside, lapse into ‹melancholy, silence, etc.›; **in Gedanken versunken, nickte er** deep *or* lost in thought, he nodded; **er war ganz in ihren Anblick versunken** he was completely absorbed in looking at her

**versinnbildlichen** *tr. V.* symbolize

**Versinnbildlichung** *die;* **~, ~en** symbolic representation

**Version** /vɛrˈzi̯oːn/ *die;* **~, ~en** version

**versippt** *Adj.* related by marriage *postpos.* (**mit** to)

**versklaven** *tr. V.* enslave

**Versklavung** *die;* **~, ~en** enslavement

**Vers·maß** *das* metre

**versnoben** *itr. V.; mit sein* (*abwertend*) become snobbish; turn into a snob; **versnobt** snobbish

**versoffen** /fɛɐ̯ˈzɔfn̩/ ❶ *2. Part. v.* **versaufen.** ❷ *Adj.* (*salopp abwertend*) boozy (*coll.*)

**versohlen** *tr. V.* (*ugs.*) belt ‹person, backside, etc.›; **er muss mal ordentlich versohlt werden** he needs a good hiding (*coll.*)

**versöhnen** /fɛɐ̯ˈzøːnən/ ❶ *refl. V.* **sich [miteinander] ~:** become reconciled; make it up; **sich mit jmdm. ~:** make it up with sb.; **sich mit seinem Schicksal ~:** come to terms with one's fate. ❷ *tr. V.* Ⓐ reconcile; **jmdn. mit jmdm. ~:** reconcile sb. with sb.; **jmdn. mit seinem Schicksal ~:** reconcile sb. to his/her fate; Ⓑ (*besänftigen*) placate; appease

**versöhnlich** ❶ *Adj.* Ⓐ conciliatory; Ⓑ (*erfreulich*) positive; optimistic. ❷ *adv.* Ⓐ in a conciliatory way; ‹say› in a conciliatory tone; Ⓑ (*erfreulich*) ‹end› positively, optimistically

**Versöhnlichkeit** *die;* **~** Ⓐ conciliatory nature; Ⓑ (*Erfreulichkeit*) positive nature; optimism

**Versöhnung** *die;* **~, ~en** Ⓐ reconciliation; Ⓑ (*das Besänftigen*) appeasement; **zu ihrer ~:** in order to placate her

**Versöhnungs·fest** *das* (*jüd. Rel.*) Day of Atonement

**versonnen** ❶ *Adj.* dreamy; (*in Gedanken versunken*) lost in thought *postpos.* ❷ *adv.* dreamily; (*in Gedanken*) lost in thought

**Versonnenheit** *die;* **~;** dreaminess

**versorgen** *tr. V.* Ⓐ supply; **jmdn. mit etw. ~:** supply *or* provide sb. with sth.; **danke, ich bin noch versorgt** I still have plenty, thank you; **seid ihr da drüben noch alle [mit Getränken] versorgt?** have you all got enough to drink over there?; are we looking after you over there?; **hast du den Hund/die Blumen schon versorgt?** have you fed the dog/watered the flowers?; **ich muss mich für die Reise mit Lesestoff ~:** I must get myself something to read on the journey; **das Gehirn ist nicht ausreichend mit Blut versorgt** the blood supply to the brain is not sufficient; Ⓑ (*unterhalten, ernähren*) provide for ‹children, family›; **er hat eine Familie zu ~:** he has a family to support *or* provide for; **versorgt sein** be provided for; Ⓒ (*sorgen für*) look after; attend to, see to ‹heating, garden, etc.›; **er versorgt sich selbst** he looks after himself; he does his own housework; **sie versorgt ihn** *od.* **versorgt ihm den Haushalt** she keeps house for him; **jmdn. ärztlich ~:** give sb. medical care; (*kurzzeitig*) give sb. medical attention

**Versorger** *der;* **~s, ~, Versorgerin** *die;* **~, ~nen** breadwinner; provider

**Versorgung** *die;* **~, ~en** Ⓐ supply[ing]; **die ~ einer Stadt/eines Gebiets/eines Organs mit etw.** the supply of sth. to a town/an area/an organ; **die ~ der Insel erfolgt auf dem Luftwege** the island is supplied by air; supplies reach the island by air; **die ~ des Hundes/der Blumen übernehmen** see to the feeding of the dog/watering of the flowers; Ⓑ (*Unterhaltung, Ernährung*) support[ing]; **zur ~ einer Familie ausreichen** be enough to provide for *or* support a family; **die ~ der Kriegerwitwen/der pensionierten Beamten** making provision for war widows/retired civil servants; Ⓒ (*Bedienung, Pflege*) care; **die ~ des Haushalts** the housekeeping; **die ~ der Heizung/des Gartens** seeing *or* attending to the heating/garden; **die ~ der Heimbewohner ist gut** the people living in the home are well looked after; **ärztliche ~:** medical care *or* treatment; (*kurzzeitig*) medical attention; **die ~ der Wunde** the treatment of the wound; Ⓓ (*Bezüge*) maintenance; (*Sozialhilfe*) benefit

**Versorgungs-: ~anspruch** *der* entitlement to benefit/maintenance; **~ausgleich** *der* (*Rechtsw.*) maintenance settlement; **~lage** *die* supply situation (**bei** with regard to); **~netz** *das* supply network *or* grid

**verspachteln** *tr. V.* Ⓐ fill, put filler in ‹holes, cracks›; Ⓑ (*ugs.: aufessen*) scoff (*coll.*)

**verspannen** ❶ *refl. V.* ‹muscle› tense up; **verspannt** taut ‹muscle›; (*völlig verkrampft*) seized-up ‹back›. ❷ *tr. V.* brace ‹mast etc.›

**Verspannung** *die* Ⓐ ▶ 474 (*Med.: der Muskulatur*) tension; Ⓑ (*eines Mastes o. Ä.*) bracing; (*Seile*) stays *pl.*

**verspäten** *refl. V.* be late; **ich habe mich leider etwas/[um] fünf Minuten verspätet** I am unfortunately a little/five minutes late

**verspätet** *Adj.* late ‹arrival, rose, butterfly›; belated ‹greetings, thanks›; **~ eintreffen** *od.* **ankommen** arrive late

**Verspätung** *die;* **~, ~en** lateness; (*verspätetes Eintreffen*) late arrival; **[fünf Minuten] ~ haben** be [five minutes] late; **eine fünfminütige ~:** a five-minute delay; **mit [fünfminütiger] ~ abfahren/ankommen** leave/arrive [five minutes] late; **seine** *od.* **die ~ aufholen** make up the lost time; **mit dreimonatiger ~:** three months late

**verspeisen** *tr. V.* (*geh.*) consume; partake of

**verspekulieren** ❶ *refl. V.* make a bad speculation; back the wrong horse (*fig.*); **wenn du gedacht hast, ich vergesse das, hast du dich verspekuliert** (*ugs.*) if you thought I would forget about it, you've got another

*old spelling (see note on page 1707)

think coming (*coll.*). ❷ *tr. V.* lose through speculation

**versperren** *tr. V.* Ⓐ block ‹road, entrance›; obstruct ‹view›; **jmdm. den Weg/die Sicht ~:** block sb.'s path/block *or* obstruct sb.'s view; Ⓑ (*bes. österr.: abschließen*) lock

**verspiegeln** *tr. V.* Ⓐ cover ‹wall› with mirrors; Ⓑ (*beschichten*) cover with a reflective surface

**verspielen** ❶ *tr. V.* Ⓐ gamble away; (*fig.: vertun, verwirken*) squander, throw away ‹opportunity, chance›; forfeit ‹right, credibility, sb.'s trust, etc›; Ⓑ (*spielend verbringen*) spend ‹hours, day› playing. ❷ *itr. V.* in **[bei jmdm.] verspielt haben** (*ugs.*) have had it [so far as sb. is concerned] (*coll.*). ❸ *refl. V.* play a wrong note/wrong notes

**verspielt** ❶ *Adj.* (*auch fig.*) playful; fanciful, fantastic ‹form, design, etc.›; **das Kleid ist/wirkt etwas zu ~:** the dress is/seems a little too fanciful. ❷ *adv.* playfully (*lit. or fig.*); ‹dress, designed› fancifully, fantastically

**verspießern** *itr. V.; mit sein* (*abwertend*) become typically bourgeois

**verspinnen** *unr. tr. V.* spin ‹wool› **(zu** into)

**versponnen** ❶ *2. Part. v.* **verspinnen.** ❷ *Adj.* eccentric, odd ‹person›; odd, weird ‹idea›

**Versponnenheit** *die; ~:* eccentricity; oddness; (*einer Idee*) weirdness

**verspotten** *tr. V.* mock; ridicule

**Verspottung** *die; ~, ~en* mocking; ridiculing

**versprechen** ❶ *unr. tr. V.* Ⓐ promise; **jmdm. etw. ~:** promise sb. sth.; **was er verspricht, hält er auch** he keeps his promises; **versprich [mir], pünktlich zu sein** *od.* **dass du pünktlich bist** promise [me] you will be on time; **sich jmdm. ~** (*veralt.*) promise oneself to sb.; **seine Miene/sein Blick versprach nichts Gutes** his expression/glance was ominous; Ⓑ **sich** (*Dat.*) **etw. von etw./jmdm. ~:** hope for sth. *or* to get sth. from sth./sb.; **ich würde mir nicht zu viel davon ~:** I wouldn't set my hopes too high.
❷ *unr. refl. V.* make a slip/slips of the tongue; **ich habe mich nur versprochen** it was just a slip of the tongue [on my part]

**Versprechen** *das; ~s, ~:* promise; **jmdm. das ~ geben, etw. zu tun** promise sb. *or* give sb. a promise to do sth.

**Versprecher** *der; ~s, ~:* slip of the tongue; **ein freudscher ~:** a Freudian slip

**Versprechung** *die; ~, ~en* promise

**versprengen** *tr. V.* Ⓐ (*bes. Milit.*) disperse; scatter; **versprengte Soldaten** soldiers who have/had lost contact with their units; Ⓑ (*verspritzen*) sprinkle ‹water›

**verspritzen** *tr. V.* Ⓐ spray; **darüber ist schon viel Tinte verspritzt worden** (*fig.*) a lot of ink has been spilt over that; Ⓑ (*bespritzen*) spatter ‹windscreen, coat, etc.›

**versprühen** *tr. V.* spray; **Funken ~:** send out a shower of sparks; **Geist** *od.* **Witz ~** (*fig.*) show sparkling wit; scintillate

**verspüren** *tr. V.* feel; **Lust/keine Lust zu etw./Verlangen/kein Verlangen nach etw. ~:** have *or* feel a desire/no desire for sth.

**verstaatlichen** *tr. V.* nationalize

**Verstaatlichung** *die; ~, ~en* nationalization

**verstädtern** /fɛɐ̯ˈʃtɛːtɐn/ *itr. V.; mit sein* become urbanized

**Verstädterung** *die; ~, ~en* urbanization

**Verstand** *der; ~[e]s* (*Fähigkeit zu denken*) reason *no art.;* (*Fähigkeit, Begriffe zu bilden*) mind; (*Vernunft*) [common] sense *no art.;* **Tiere haben keinen ~:** animals do not have the power *or* faculty of reason; **der menschliche ~:** the human mind; **mein** *od.* **der ~ sagt mir, dass ...** reason *or* common sense tells me that ...; **wenn du deinen ~ gebraucht hättest** if you had used your brain *or* had been thinking; **er hat einen klaren ~:** he has a lucid mind; **ich hätte ihm mehr ~ zugetraut** I thought he would have had more sense; **er musste all seinen ~ zusammennehmen** he had to summon up all his mental powers *or* rack his brains; **manchmal zweifle ich an seinem ~:** I sometimes doubt his sanity; **bei klarem ~ bleiben** keep one's mental faculties; **~ und Vernunft** understanding and reason; **~ und Gefühl** head and heart; **das schreckliche Erlebnis hat ihren ~ verwirrt** the terrible experience threw her mind into confusion; **ich verliere noch den ~:** I'll go out of my mind; **hast du denn den ~ verloren** (*ugs.*) have you taken leave of your senses?; are you out of your mind?; **du bist wohl nicht [ganz] bei ~!** (*ugs.*) you must be out of your mind!; **das geht über meinen ~:** that's beyond me; **der Schmerz hat ihn um den ~ gebracht** the pain drove him out of his mind; **seinen ~ versaufen** (*salopp*) drink oneself stupid; **etw. mit ~ trinken/essen/rauchen** really savour sth. [while drinking/eating/smoking it]; ⇒ *auch* **Glück** A; **Sinn** G

**verstandes-, Verstandes-: ~kraft** *die* mental *or* intellectual powers *pl.;* **~mäßig** ❶ *Adj.* rational; intellectual ‹inferiority, superiority›; ❷ *adv.* rationally; intellectually ‹inferior, superior›; **~mensch** *der* rational person

**verständig** /fɛɐ̯ˈʃtɛndɪç/ ❶ *Adj.* sensible; intelligent. ❷ *adv.* sensibly; intelligently

**verständigen** /fɛɐ̯ˈʃtɛndɪgn̩/ ❶ *tr. V.* notify, inform **(von, über** + *Akk.* of). ❷ *refl. V.* Ⓐ make oneself understood; **sich mit jmdm. ~:** communicate with sb.; Ⓑ (*sich einigen*) **sich [mit jmdm.] über/auf etw.** (*Akk.*) **~:** come to an understanding *or* reach agreement [with sb.] about *or.* on sth.

**Verständigkeit** *die; ~:* understanding; intelligence

**Verständigung** *die; ~, ~en* Ⓐ notification; Ⓑ (*das Sichverständlichmachen*) communication *no art.;* **wegen des Lärms war eine ~ praktisch unmöglich** because of the noise, it was almost impossible to make oneself understood; Ⓒ (*Einigung*) understanding; **eine Politik der ~:** a policy of rapprochement; **über diesen Punkt kam es zu keiner ~:** no agreement was reached on this point

**Verständigungs-: ~bereitschaft** *die* readiness to come to an understanding; **~schwierigkeit** *die* difficulty of communication

**verständlich** ❶ *Adj.* Ⓐ comprehensible; (*deutlich*) clear ‹pronunciation, presentation, etc.›; **[leicht] ~:** easily understood; **schwer ~:** difficult to understand; (*bei Lärm*) difficult to make out; **sich ~ machen** make oneself understood; **sich seinen Zuhörern ~ machen** get [one's message] across to one's listeners; **jmdm. etw. ~ machen** make sth. clear to sb.; Ⓑ (*begreiflich, verzeihlich*) understandable; **seine Verärgerung ist mir durchaus ~:** I can fully understand his annoyance.
❷ *adv.* comprehensibly; in a comprehensible way; (*deutlich*) ‹speak, express oneself, present› clearly

**verständlicher·weise** *Adv.* understandably

**Verständlichkeit** *die; ~:* comprehensibility; clarity

**Verständnis** *das; ~ses, ~se* understanding; **dem Leser das ~ erleichtern** make it easier for the reader to understand; **ein ~ für Kunst/Musik** an appreciation of *or* feeling for art/music; **ich habe volles ~ dafür, dass ...** I fully understand that ...; **für so etwas habe ich kein ~:** I have no time for that kind of thing; **für die Unannehmlichkeiten bitten wir um [Ihr] ~:** we ask for your forbearance *or* we apologize for the inconvenience caused

**verständnis-, Verständnis-: ~innig** ❶ *Adj.* knowing, meaningful ‹glance›; ❷ *adv.* knowingly; meaningfully; **~los** ❶ *Adj.* uncomprehending; **der modernen Kunst steht er völlig ~los gegenüber** he has no understanding of *or* feeling for modern art at all; ❷ *adv.* uncomprehendingly; **~losigkeit** *die; ~~:* incomprehension; **voller ~losigkeit** uncomprehendingly; with a complete lack of understanding; **~voll** ❶ *Adj.* understanding; ❷ *adv.* understandingly

**verstärken** ❶ *tr. V.* Ⓐ strengthen; **die Socken sind an den Fersen verstärkt** the socks have reinforced heels; Ⓑ (*zahlenmäßig*) reinforce ‹troops, garrison, etc.› **(um** by); enlarge, augment ‹orchestra, choir› **(um** by); **die Truppen auf 1 500 Mann ~:** bring the troops up to a strength of 1,500 men; Ⓒ (*intensiver machen*) intensify, increase ‹effort, contrast›; strengthen, increase ‹impression, suspicion›; (*größer machen*) increase ‹pressure, voltage, effect, etc.›; (*lauter machen*) amplify ‹signal, sound, guitar, etc.›.
❷ *refl. V.* increase; ⇒ *auch* **verstärkt**

**Verstärker** *der; ~s, ~:* amplifier

**verstärkt** ❶ *Adj.* Ⓐ increased; (*größer*) greater ‹efforts, vigilance, etc.›; **in ~em Maße** to a greater *or* increased extent; Ⓑ (*zahlenmäßig*) enlarged, augmented ‹orchestra, choir, etc.›; reinforced (*Mil.*) ‹unit›. ❷ *adv.* to an increased extent

**Verstärkung** *die; ~, ~en* Ⓐ strengthening; Ⓑ (*zahlenmäßig*) reinforcement (*esp. Mil.*); (*eines Orchesters usw.*) enlargement; Ⓒ (*Intensivierung, Zunahme*) increase (*Gen.* in); (*der Lautstärke*) amplification; **zur ~ einer Sache** (*Gen.*) to increase/amplify sth.; Ⓓ (*zusätzliche Person[en]*) reinforcements *pl.;* Ⓔ (*verstärkendes Element*) reinforcement

**verstauben** *itr. V.; mit sein* get dusty; gather dust (*lit. or fig.*); ⇒ *auch* **verstaubt**

**verstäuben** /fɛɐ̯ˈʃtɔybn̩/ *tr. V.* spray ‹insecticide etc.›

**verstaubt** *Adj.* dusty; covered in dust *postpos.;* (*fig. abwertend*) old-fashioned; outmoded

**verstauchen** *tr. V.* ▶ 474 sprain; **sich** (*Dat.*) **den Fuß/die Hand ~:** sprain one's ankle/wrist

**Verstauchung** *die; ~, ~en* ▶ 474 sprain

**verstauen** *tr. V.* pack **(in** + *Dat. od. Akk.* in[to]); (*bes. im Boot/Auto*) stow **(in** + *Dat. od. Akk.* in); **etw. auf dem Boden/in einem** *od.* **einen Schrank ~:** put *or* (*coll.*) stash sth. away in the loft/a cupboard; **etw. in der Hosentasche ~:** stuff sth. into one's trouser pocket; **er verstaute seine Familie im Auto** (*scherzh.*) he packed his family into the car

**Versteck** *das; ~[e]s, ~e* hiding place; (*eines Flüchtlings, Räubers usw.*) hideout: **~ spielen** play hide-and-seek; **[vor jmdm./voreinander** *od.* **mit jmdm./miteinander] ~ spielen** (*fig.*) hide *or* keep things [from sb./one another]

**verstecken** ❶ *tr. V.* hide **(vor** + *Dat.* from); **jmdn. versteckt halten** keep sb. hidden; **das Haus war in einem Wäldchen versteckt** the house was tucked away in a small wood.
❷ *refl. V.* **sich [vor jmdm./etw.] ~:** hide [from sb./sth.]; **sich versteckt halten** be [in] hiding; (*versteckt bleiben*) remain in hiding; **ich möchte bloß wissen, wo sich meine Brille schon wieder versteckt hat** I should love to know where my glasses have got to; **sich vor** *od.* **neben jmdm. nicht zu ~ brauchen** *od.* **nicht ~ müssen** (*fig.*) not need to fear comparison with sb.; **das ist eine Leistung, mit der er sich nicht ~ muss** it is a performance of which he has no need to be ashamed; **sich vor** *od.* **neben jmdm. ~ müssen** (*fig.*) not be able to compare with sb.; not be a patch on sb. (*coll.*); **sich hinter seinem Chef/seinen Vorschriften** *usw.* **~** (*fig.*) use one's boss (*coll.*)/one's rules and regulations to hide behind; ⇒ *auch* **versteckt**

**Verstecken** *das; ~s* hide-and-seek *no art.*

**Versteck·spiel** *das* game of hide-and-seek; (*fig.*) charade; pretence

**versteckt** *Adj.* hidden; concealed ‹polemics›; veiled ‹threat›; (*heimlich*) secret ‹malice, activity, etc.›; disguised ‹foul›; (*verstohlen*) furtive ‹glance, smile›

**verstehen** ❶ *unr. tr. V.* Ⓐ (*wahrnehmen*) understand; make out; **ich konnte ihn bei dem Lärm nicht ~:** I couldn't make out

V

what he was saying because of the noise; **man versteht [vor Lärm] sein eigenes Wort nicht** one cannot hear oneself speak; **er war am Telefon gut/schlecht/kaum zu ~:** it was easy/difficult/barely possible to understand *or* make out what he was saying on the telephone; (B) *auch itr.* (*begreifen, interpretieren*) understand; **das musst du schon ~:** you must understand *or* see that; **ich verstehe** I understand; I see; **[ich habe] verstanden** understood; I've got it; **wir ~ uns schon** we understand each other; we see eye to eye; **das verstehe [nun] einer!** what is one supposed to make of that?; **du bleibst hier, verstanden** *od.* **verstehst du!** you stay here, understand!; **jmdm. etw. zu ~ geben** give sb. to understand sth.; **das ist in dem Sinne** *od.* **so zu ~, dass ...** it is supposed to mean that ...; **wie soll ich das ~?** how am I to interpret that?; what am I supposed to make of that?; **jmdn./etw. falsch ~:** misunderstand sb./sth.; **versteh mich bitte richtig** *od.* **nicht falsch** please don't misunderstand me *or* get me wrong; **wenn ich [es] recht verstehe** if I understand rightly; **falsch verstandene Loyalität** misunderstood loyalty; **etw. unter etw.** (*Dat.*) **~:** understand sth. by sth.; **was ~ Sie darunter?** what do you think that means?; **jmdn./sich als etw. ~:** see sb./oneself as sth.; consider sb./oneself to be sth.; **er will sich als Christ verstanden wissen** he wants to be seen as *or* to be considered a Christian; ⇒ *auch* **Bahnhof**; **Spaß** B; (C) (*beherrschen, wissen*) **es ~, etw. zu tun** know how to do sth.; **er versteht zu genießen** he knows how to enjoy himself *or* things; **er versteht eine Menge von Autos** he knows a lot about cars; he is quite an expert on cars; **davon verstehe ich nichts/nicht viel** I don't know anything/know much about it. ❷ *unr. refl. V.* (A) **sich mit jmdm. ~:** get on with sb.; **sie ~ sich** they get on well together; (B) (*selbstverständlich sein*) **das versteht sich [von selbst]** that goes without saying; **versteht sich!** (*ugs.*) of course!; (C) (*Kaufmannsspr.: gemeint sein*) **der Preis versteht sich einschließlich Mehrwertsteuer** the price is inclusive of VAT; (D) **sich auf Pferde/Autos** *usw.* (*Akk.*) **~:** know what one is doing with horses/cars; know all about horses/cars; **er versteht sich aufs Dichten** he knows how to write poetry; (E) **sich zu etw. ~** (*veralt.*) agree [reluctantly] to sth.

**versteifen** ❶ *tr. V.* (A) stiffen ‹collar, part of body, etc.›; (B) (*Bauw.: abstützen*) shore up ‹wall, house, excavation, etc.›; brace ‹fence›. ❷ *itr. V.; mit sein* stiffen [up]; become stiff. ❸ *refl. V.* (A) stiffen [up]; become stiff; (B) *in* **sich auf etw.** (*Akk.*) **~:** insist on sth.

**Versteifung** *die;* **~, ~en** (A) stiffening; (B) (*Bauw.*) shoring [up]

**versteigen** *unr. refl. V.* (A) (*sich verirren*) get lost [while climbing]; (*nicht mehr herunterkönnen*) get stuck; get into difficulties; (B) **sich zu einer Behauptung/zu Angriffen gegen jmdn.** *usw.* **~:** have the presumption to make an assertion/attacks on sb. *etc.*; **wie konnte ich mich zu solcher Schwärmerei ~?** how could I get so carried away?; ⇒ *auch* **verstiegen** 2

**versteigern** *tr. V.* auction; **etw. ~ lassen** put sth. up for auction; **auf einer Auktion meistbietend versteigert werden** be sold to the highest bidder at an auction

**Versteigerung** *die* (A) auction *no indef. art.;* **zur ~ kommen** *od.* **gelangen** (*Amtsspr.*) be auctioned; (B) (*Veranstaltung*) auction; **auf einer ~:** at an auction

**versteinern** ❶ *itr. V.; mit sein* ‹plant, animal› fossilize, become fossilized; ‹wood etc.› petrify, become petrified; (*fig. geh.*) ‹person› go rigid; ‹expression, face› harden, become stony; **sie blieb [wie] versteinert stehen** she stopped in her tracks, as rigid as a statue. ❷ *refl. V.* (*geh.*) ‹face, features› harden

*old spelling (see note on page 1707)

**Versteinerung** *die;* **~, ~en** (A) (*das Versteinern*) fossilization; (*von Holz*) petrification; (B) (*Fossil*) fossil

**verstellbar** *Adj.* adjustable

**verstellen** ❶ *tr. V.* (A) (*falsch platzieren*) misplace; put [back] in the wrong place; (B) (*anders einstellen*) adjust ‹seat etc.›; alter [the adjustment of] ‹mirror etc.›; reset ‹alarm clock, points, etc.›; **der Sitz lässt sich in der Höhe ~:** the seat can be adjusted for height; (C) (*versperren*) block, obstruct ‹entrance, exit, view, etc.›; **er verstellte mir den Weg** he blocked my path; he stood in my way; **[jmdm.] den Blick für etw. ~** (*fig.*) obscure sb.'s view of sth.; (D) (*zur Täuschung verändern*) disguise, alter ‹voice, handwriting›.
❷ *refl. V.* (A) (*seine Einstellung, Position verändern*) alter; (*so, dass es falsch eingestellt ist*) get out of adjustment; (B) (*sich anders geben als man ist*) pretend; play-act; **sich vor jmdm. ~:** pretend to sb.

**Verstellung** *die* play-acting; pretence; (*der Stimme, Schrift*) disguising; alteration

**Verstellungs·kunst** *die* [art of] play-acting *no pl.*

**versteppen** *itr. V.; mit sein* become steppe

**versterben** *unr. itr. V.; mit sein* (*geh.*) die; pass away; **mein verstorbener Mann** my late husband; ⇒ *auch* **Verstorbene**

**versteuern** *tr. V.* pay tax on

**verstiegen** ❶ *2. Part. v.* **versteigen.** ❷ *Adj.* whimsical ‹idealist, person›; extravagant, fantastic ‹idea, expectation, etc.›; wild ‹dream, desire›

**Verstiegenheit** *die;* **~, ~en** (A) extravagance; (B) (*etw. Verstiegenes*) extravagant *or* fantastic idea/remark

**verstimmen** ❶ *tr. V.* (A) (*Musik*) put ‹instrument› out of tune; (B) (*schlecht gelaunt machen*) put ‹person› in a bad mood; (*verärgern*) annoy. ❷ *refl. V.* get *or* go out of tune

**verstimmt** *Adj.* (A) (*Musik*) out of tune *pred.;* (B) (*verärgert*) put out, peeved, disgruntled (**über** + *Akk.* by, about); **ein ~er Magen** an upset stomach

**Verstimmung** *die* disgruntled *or* bad mood; **eine leichte ~ hinterlassen** leave a slight sense of annoyance

**verstockt** ❶ *Adj.* obdurate; stubborn. ❷ *adv.* obdurately; stubbornly

**Verstocktheit** *die;* **~:** obduracy; stubbornness

**verstohlen** /fɛɐ̯'ʃtoːlən/ ❶ *Adj.* furtive; surreptitious. ❷ *adv.* furtively; surreptitiously

**verstolpern** *tr. V.* (*Sportjargon*) stumble and miss ‹ball, chance, etc.›

**verstopfen** ❶ *tr. V.* block; **verstopft sein** ‹pipe, drain, jet, nose, etc.› be blocked (**durch, von** with); (*Med.: keinen Stuhlgang haben*) be constipated; **die vielen Autos ~ die Altstadt** the large number of cars causes congestion in the old quarter. ❷ *itr. V.; mit sein* become blocked

**Verstopfung** *die;* **~, ~en** ▸ 474 (*Med.: Stuhl~*) constipation

**verstorben** /fɛɐ̯'ʃtɔrbn̩/ *2. Part. v.* **versterben**

**Verstorbene** *der/die; adj. Dekl.* (*geh.*) deceased

**verstören** *tr. V.* distress

**verstört** *Adj.* distraught; **einen ~en Eindruck machen** appear distraught *or* distressed

**Verstörtheit** *die;* **~:** distressed *or* distraught state; distress

**Verstoß** *der* violation, infringement (**gegen** of); **~ gegen die Etikette/den guten Geschmack** breach of etiquette/offense against good taste

**verstoßen** ❶ *unr. tr. V.* disown; **aus dem Elternhaus ~ werden** be turned out of one's parents' house; **ein Verstoßener** an outcast. ❷ *unr. itr. V.* **gegen etw. ~:** infringe *or* contravene sth.; **gegen die Etikette/den guten Geschmack ~:** commit a breach of etiquette/offend against good taste

**Verstoßung** *die;* **~, ~en** disowning; (*aus dem Elternhaus*) turning out

**verstrahlen** *tr. V.* (A) radiate; (B) (*radioaktiv verseuchen*) contaminate with radiation

**Verstrebung** *die;* **~, ~en** struts *pl.;* (*einzelne Strebe*) strut

**verstreichen** ❶ *unr. tr. V.* (A) (*verteilen*) apply, put on ‹paint›; spread ‹butter etc.›; (B) (*verbrauchen*) use [up] ‹paint›; (C) (*zustreichen*) fill ‹hole, crack›. ❷ *unr. itr. V.; mit sein* (*geh.*) ‹time› pass [by]

**verstreuen** *tr. V.* (A) (*verteilen*) scatter; put down ‹bird food, salt›; (*unordentlich*) strew; **seine Kleider lagen im ganzen Zimmer verstreut** his clothes were scattered *or* strewn all over the room; **verstreute Gehöfte/Aufsätze** isolated *or* scattered farms/isolated essays; (B) (*versehentlich*) spill

**verstricken** ❶ *tr. V.* (A) (*verbrauchen*) use ‹wool› [in knitting]; (B) (*geh.: verwickeln*) **jmdn. in etw.** (*Akk.*) **~:** involve sb. in sth.; draw sb. into sth.; **in etw.** (*Akk.*) **verstrickt [sein]** [be] mixed up *or* involved in sth. ❷ *refl. V.* (A) (*falsch stricken*) make a mistake/mistakes [in knitting]; (B) (*fig.*) **sich in etw.** (*Akk.*) **~:** become entangled *or* caught up in sth.

**Verstrickung** *die;* **~, ~en** involvement (**in** + *Akk.* in)

**verströmen** *tr. V.* exude

**verstrubbeln** *tr. V.* (*ugs.*) tousle

**verstümmeln** *tr. V.* mutilate; (*fig.*) garble ‹report›; chop, mutilate ‹text›; mutilate, do violence to ‹name›; **sich selbst ~:** maim oneself

**Verstümmelung** *die;* **~, ~en** mutilation; (*Selbst~*) self-mutilation; (*fig.: einer Meldung usw.*) garbling

**verstummen** *itr. V.; mit sein* (*geh.*) fall silent; ‹music, noise, conversation› cease; (*allmählich*) die *or* fade away; (*fig.*) ‹rumour, question› go away; **er verstummte vor Schreck** he broke off, terrified; **jmdn. zum Verstummen bringen** silence sb.; **jeder Zweifel verstummte** (*fig.*) every doubt was stilled

**Versuch** *der;* **~[e]s, ~e** (A) attempt; **beim ~, etw. zu tun** in attempting to do sth.; **er hat es gleich beim ersten ~ geschafft** he made it *or* succeeded at the first attempt; **er hat schon mehrmals den ~ gemacht zu ...** he has already made several attempts to ...; **das käme auf einen ~ an** we'll have to try it and see; **einen ~ wäre es wert** it's worth a try; **ich will noch einen letzten ~ mit ihm/damit machen** I'd like to give him/it one more try; (B) (*Experiment*) experiment (**an** + *Dat.* on); (*Probe*) test; (C) (*literarisches Produkt*) attempt; **seine ersten lyrischen/literarischen ~e** his first attempts at poetry/literature; **„~ über das Schöne"** 'Essay on Beauty'; (D) (*Rugby*) try; **einen ~ erzielen** *od.* **legen** score a try

**versuchen** ❶ *tr. V.* (A) try; attempt; **versuchs doch!** (*drohend*) just you try!; (*ermunternd*) just try it!; **es mit jmdm./etw. ~:** give sb./sth. a try; **es bei jmdm. ~:** try sb.; **versuchter Mord** (*Rechtsspr.*) attempted murder; **lass mich mal ~, ob ...** (*ugs.*) let me [try and] see if ...; ⇒ *auch* **Glück** A; (B) (*auch bibl.: in Versuchung führen*) tempt; **versucht sein, etw. zu tun** be tempted to do sth. ❷ *tr., itr. V.* (*probieren*) **den Kuchen/von dem Kuchen ~:** try the cake/some of the cake. ❸ *refl. V.* **sich in/an etw.** (*Dat.*)/**auf einem Instrument/als etw. ~:** try one's hand at sth./at playing an instrument/at being sth.

**Versucher** *der;* **~s, ~, Versucherin** *die;* **~, ~nen** tempter

**versuchs-, Versuchs-: ~anordnung** *die* set-up for an/the experiment/for experiments; **~anstalt** *die* research institute; **~ballon** *der* (A) (*Met.*) sounding balloon; (B) (*fig.*) try-out; (*Gerücht, Vorschlag usw.*) feeler; **einen ~ballon [auf]steigen lassen** fly a kite (*fig.*); put out feelers (*fig.*); **~gelände** *das* testing ground; (*für nukleare Waffen usw.*) test site; **~kaninchen** *das* (*fig.*) guinea pig; **~person** *die* (*bes. Med., Psych.*) test *or* experimental subject; **~stadium** *das* experimental stage; **~tier** *das* experimental animal; **~weise** ❶ *Adv.* on a trial basis; as an experiment; ❷ *adj.* experimental; **~zweck** *der* experimental purpose; **zu ~zwecken**

**gehaltene Tiere** animals kept for experiments

**Versuchung** *die;* ~, ~en temptation; **jmdn. in ~ führen** lead sb. into temptation (*esp. Rel.*); put sb. in the way of temptation; **in ~** (*Akk.*) **kommen** *od.* **geraten[, etw. zu tun]** be *or* feel tempted [to do sth.]

**versumpfen** *itr. V.* Ⓐ become marshy *or* boggy; **versumpft** marshy; boggy; Ⓑ (*ugs. abwertend: verwahrlosen*) go to seed *or* to the dogs; Ⓒ (*ugs.; lange bleiben und trinken*) stay out late boozing (*coll.*)

**versündigen** *refl. V.* **sich an jmdm./etw. ~:** sin against sb./sth.; **sich an seiner Gesundheit ~:** abuse one's health; **versündige dich nicht!** (*als Antwort*) what a [wicked] thing to say/do!

**Versunkenheit** *die;* ~ (*geh.*) [state of] contemplation; deep meditation; **in seiner ~ hatte er ihr Kommen gar nicht bemerkt** he was so deep in thought *or* so engrossed that he had not noticed her coming

**versüßen** *tr. V.* **jmdm./sich etw. ~** (*fig.*) make sth. more pleasant for sb./oneself; (*erträglicher machen*) make sth. more bearable for sb./oneself

**vertäfeln** *tr. V.* panel

**Vertäfelung** *die;* ~, ~en panelling

**vertagen** ❶ *tr. V.* adjourn ‹meeting, debate, etc.› (**auf** + *Akk.* until); postpone ‹decision, verdict› (**auf** + *Akk.* until). ❷ *refl. V.* ‹court› adjourn; ‹meeting› be adjourned

**vertändeln** *tr. V.* (*auch Sport*) fritter away ‹time, chance›

**vertäuen** /fɛɐ̯ˈtɔyən/ *tr. V.* (*Seemannsspr.*) moor

**vertauschen** *tr. V.* Ⓐ exchange; switch; reverse, switch ‹roles›; reverse, transpose ‹poles›; **etw. mit** *od.* **gegen etw. ~:** exchange sth. for sth.; **die Kanzel mit dem Ministersessel ~:** exchange the pulpit for a ministerial post; **die Buchstaben eines Wortes ~:** transpose *or* switch round the letters in a word; Ⓑ (*verwechseln*) mix up

**Vertauschung** *die;* ~, ~en Ⓐ exchange; (*von Buchstaben, Polen usw.*) transposition; (*von Rollen*) reversal; switching; Ⓑ (*Verwechslung*) mixing up; **eine ~:** a mix-up

**Vertäuung** *die;* ~, ~en (*Seemannsspr.*) mooring

**verteidigen** /fɛɐ̯ˈtaidɪgn̩/ ❶ *tr. V.* defend; **der Angeklagte wird sich selbst ~:** the accused will conduct his own defence. ❷ *itr. V.* (*Ballspiele*) defend; (*Verteidiger sein*) be a defender

**Verteidiger** *der;* ~s, ~, **Verteidigerin,** *die;* ~, ~nen Ⓐ (*auch Sport*) defender; **[als] ~ spielen** (*Sport*) play as a defender; Ⓑ (*Rechtsw.*) defence counsel

**Verteidigung** *die;* ~, ~en (*auch Sport, Rechtsw.*) defence; **zur ~ seiner Meinung/der Stadt bereit sein** be ready to defend one's opinion/the town; **jmdn. in die ~ drängen** force sb. on [to] the defensive

**Verteidigungs-: ~bereitschaft** *die* readiness to defend; **~bündnis** *das* defensive alliance; **~drittel** das (*Eishockey*) defence zone; **~haushalt** *der* defence budget; **~minister** *der,* **~ministerin** *die* minister of defence; **~ministerium** *das* ministry of defence; **~rede** *die* (*vor Gericht*) speech for the defence; (*Apologie*) apologia; **~waffe** *die* defensive weapon

**verteilen** ❶ *tr. V.* Ⓐ (*austeilen*) distribute, hand out ‹exercise books, leaflets, prizes, etc.› (**an** + *Akk.* to, **unter** + *Akk.* among); share [out], distribute ‹money, food› (**an** + *Akk.* to, **unter** + *Akk.* among); allocate ‹work›; cast, allocate ‹parts›; **Karten an die Spieler ~:** deal out cards to the players; **ein Drama mit verteilten Rollen lesen** read a play with each part allocated to a different person; Ⓑ (*an verschiedene Plätze bringen*) distribute ‹weight etc.› (**auf** + *Akk.* over); spread ‹cost› (**auf** + *Akk.* among); distribute, spread out ‹cushions etc.›; **Flüchtlinge auf drei Lager ~:** divide up refugees and send them to three camps; Ⓒ (*verstreichen, verstreuen, verrühren usw.*) distribute, spread ‹butter, seed, dirt, etc.›.
❷ *refl. V.* Ⓐ spread out; Ⓑ (*sich ausbreiten, verteilt sein*) be distributed (**auf** + *Akk.* over)

**Verteiler** *der;* ~s, ~ Ⓐ (*Person*) distributor; Ⓑ (*Technik: Zündverteiler*) distributor; Ⓒ (*Bürow.*) distribution list; „~" 'copies to'

**Verteilerin** *die;* ~, ~nen ⇒ **Verteiler** A

**Verteiler·schlüssel** *der* (*Büröw.*) distribution list

**Verteilung** *die* distribution; (*der Rollen, der Arbeit*) allocation; **etw. zur ~ bringen** (*Papierdt.*) distribute sth.; **zur ~ kommen** *od.* **gelangen** (*Papierdt.*) be distributed

**vertelefonieren** *tr. V.* (*ugs.*) spend ‹time› telephoning *or* on the phone; spend ‹money› on telephoning

**verteuern** ❶ *tr. V.* make ‹goods› more expensive. ❷ *refl. V.* become more expensive; **die Lebenshaltung verteuert sich** the cost of living is going up

**Verteuerung** *die* increase *or* rise in price; **die ~ des Kaffees** the increase in the price of coffee

**verteufeln** *tr. V.* condemn; denigrate

**verteufelt** ❶ *Adj.* (*ugs.*) Ⓐ (*verzwickt*) extremely tricky ‹situation, business›; Ⓑ (*äußerst*) fiendish ‹thirst, pain, etc.› ❷ *adv.* (*ugs.*) damned; fiendishly ‹cold›; terribly (*coll.*) ‹similar›; **~!** damn!

**Verteufelung** *die;* ~, ~en condemnation; denigration

**vertiefen** ❶ *tr. V.* Ⓐ deepen (**um** by); make deeper; **eine vertiefte Stelle** a depression; a hollow; Ⓑ (*intensivieren*) deepen ‹knowledge, understanding, love›; deepen, strengthen ‹dislike, friendship, collaboration, etc.›; **ein vertieftes Verständnis** a deeper understanding. ❷ *refl. V.* Ⓐ deepen; become deeper; Ⓑ (*sich konzentrieren*) **sich ~ in** (+ *Akk.*) bury oneself in ‹book, work, etc.›; become deeply involved in ‹conversation›; **in etw.** (*Akk.*) **vertieft sein** be engrossed *or* absorbed in sth.; **in Gedanken vertieft** deep in thought; Ⓒ (*intensiver werden*) ‹friendship› deepen; ‹relations› become closer; ‹hate, conflict› deepen, become more intense

**Vertiefung** *die;* ~, ~en Ⓐ deepening; (*von Freundschaft, Abneigung*) deepening; strengthening; (*von Zusammenarbeit, Beziehungen*) strengthening; (*von Wissen*) consolidation; reinforcement; (*von Hass, Konflikten*) intensification; Ⓑ (*in Gedanken*) absorption (**in** + *Akk.* in); Ⓒ (*Mulde*) depression; hollow

**vertieren** *itr. V.; mit sein* become brutalized; **vertiert** brutalized

**vertikal** /vɛrtiˈka:l/ ❶ *Adj.* vertical; **in ~er Richtung** vertically. ❷ *adv.* vertically

**Vertikale** *die;* ~, ~n Ⓐ (*Linie*) vertical line; Ⓑ (*Lage*) **die ~:** the vertical *or* perpendicular; **etw. in die ~ bringen** *od.* **bewegen** move sth. into a vertical position

**Vertiko** /ˈvɛrtiko/ *das, auch der;* ~s, ~s *small decorated cabinet with a drawer and display shelf on top*

**vertilgen** *tr. V.* Ⓐ (*vernichten*) exterminate ‹vermin›; kill off ‹weeds›; Ⓑ (*ugs.: verzehren*) devour, (*joc.*) demolish ‹food›

**Vertilgung** *die;* ~, ~en Ⓐ (*von Ungeziefer*) extermination; (*von Unkraut*) killing off; Ⓑ (*ugs.: das Verzehren*) demolition (*joc.*)

**Vertilgungs·mittel** *das* (*gegen Unkraut*) weedkiller; (*gegen Insekten*) pesticide

**vertippen** ❶ *refl. V.* Ⓐ make a typing mistake/typing mistakes; (*auf der Rechenmaschine, dem Tastentelefon usw.*) press the wrong number; Ⓑ (*im Lotto, Toto, bei Vorhersagen*) get it wrong. ❷ *tr. V.* mistype ‹word›; type ‹word, letter› wrongly; (*auf der Rechenmaschine, dem Tastentelefon usw.*) get ‹number› wrong

**vertonen** *tr. V.* set ‹text, poem› to music; set, write the music to ‹libretto›; add sound to ‹slides›; add a soundtrack to ‹film›

**Vertonung** *die;* ~, ~en Ⓐ setting [to music]; **die ~ eines Librettos** writing the music to a libretto; **die ~ von Dias/eines Films** adding sound to slides/a soundtrack to a film; Ⓑ (*Werk*) setting

**vertrackt** /fɛɐ̯ˈtrakt/ *Adj.* (*ugs.*) Ⓐ complicated, involved ‹situation, business, etc.›; tricky, intricate ‹job›; Ⓑ (*ärgerlich*) confounded; infuriating; **das ~e Gefühl haben, dass ...** have a nasty feeling that ...

**Vertracktheit** *die;* ~, ~en (*ugs.*) Ⓐ complexity; Ⓑ (*Ärgerlichkeit*) maddening *or* infuriating nature

**Vertrag** *der;* ~[e]s, **Verträge** /...trɛ:gə/ contract; (*zwischen Staaten*) treaty; **mündlicher ~:** verbal agreement; **laut ~:** according to the terms of the contract; **ein ~ auf drei Jahre** a three-year contract; **jmdn. unter ~ nehmen** contract sb.; put sb. under contract; **[bei jmdm.] unter ~ stehen** be under contract [to sb.]

**vertragen** ❶ *unr. tr. V.* Ⓐ endure; tolerate (*esp. Med.*); (*aushalten, leiden können*) stand; bear; take ‹joke, criticism, climate, etc.›; **die Pflanze verträgt keinen Zug/kann Sonne ~:** the plant will not tolerate draughts/can tolerate some sun; **Rauch/Lärm/Belastungen/Aufregung schlecht ~:** not be able to stand too much smoke/noise/strain/excitement; **das Klima [nicht] gut ~:** [not] be able to take the climate; **ich vertrage keinen Kaffee/kein fettes Essen** coffee/fatty food disagrees with me; **den Wein/das Medikament habe ich gut ~:** I was able to drink the wine/take the medicine with no ill effects; **sie verträgt dieses Medikament schlecht/nicht** this medicine doesn't really agree with her/does not agree with her at all; **ich könnte jetzt einen Whisky ~** (*ugs.*) I could do with *or* wouldn't say no to a whisky; **er verträgt eine Menge [Alkohol]/nichts/nicht viel** (*ugs.*) he can hold a lot of drink (*coll.*)/can't hold his drink/can't hold much drink; **er verträgt keine Kritik/keinen Spaß** he cannot take criticism/a joke; **ich kann alles ~, nur nicht das** I can put up with anything but not that; **die Sache verträgt keinen Aufschub** (*geh.*) the matter brooks no delay; Ⓑ (*landsch.: abtragen*) wear out.
❷ *unr. refl. V.* Ⓐ **sich mit jmdm. ~:** get on *or* along with sb.; **sich gut [miteinander] ~:** get on well together; **er verträgt sich mit keinem** he never gets on with anybody; **sie ~ sich wieder** they are friends again; they have made it up; **wir wollen uns wieder ~:** let's make it up *or* let bygones be bygones; **so Kinder, nun vertragt euch wieder** come on children, stop squabbling and call a truce; ⇒ *auch* **Pack**[2]; Ⓑ (*passen*) **sich mit etw. ~:** go with sth.; **die Farben ~ sich nicht [miteinander]** the colours do not go together; **wie verträgt sich das mit seinen christlichen Überzeugungen** how does this square with his Christian convictions?; **so ein Verhalten verträgt sich nicht mit seinem liberalen Anspruch** such behaviour is not consistent with his liberal pretensions

**vertraglich** ❶ *Adj.* contractual. ❷ *adv.* contractually; by contract

**verträglich** /fɛɐ̯ˈtrɛ:klɪç/ *Adj.* Ⓐ digestible ‹food›; **leicht/schwer ~:** easily digestible/indigestible; **ein gut ~es Medikament** a drug which has no side effects; Ⓑ (*umgänglich*) good-natured; easy to get on with *pred.*

**Verträglichkeit** *die;* ~, ~en Ⓐ digestibility; **die ~ eines Medikaments** a drug's lack of side effects; Ⓑ (*Umgänglichkeit*) good nature

**vertrags-, Vertrags-: ~abschluss,** ***~abschluß** *der* completion of [a/the] contract; **~bruch** *der* breach of contract; **~brüchig** *Adj.* in breach of contract *postpos.*; **~brüchig werden/sein** be in breach of contract

**vertrag·schließend** *Adj.* contracting

**vertrags-, Vertrags-: ~entwurf** *der* draft contract/treaty; **~gemäß** *adv.* as per contract; as stipulated in the contract; **~händler** *der,* **~händlerin** *die* authorized *or* appointed dealer; **~partner** *der,* **~partnerin** *die* party to a/the contract; **unser ~partner** our contractual partner; **~schluss,** ***~schluß** *der* ⇒ **~abschluss**; **~spieler**

V

*der*, **~spielerin** *die* (*Fußball*) semi-professional (*under contract to a club*); **~werk** *das* major agreement; (*international*) treaty; **~werkstatt** *die* authorized garage

**vertrauen** *itr. V.* **jmdm./einer Sache ~:** trust sb./sth.; **auf etw.** (*Akk.*) **~:** [put one's] trust in sth.; **auf sein Glück ~:** trust to luck; **ich vertraue darauf, dass ...** I am confident *or* have confidence that ...; **auf Gott ~:** put one's trust in God

**Vertrauen** *das;* **~s** trust; confidence; **~ zu jmdm./etw. haben/fassen** have/come to have confidence in sb./sth.; trust/come to trust sb./sth.; **er hat kein ~ zu sich selbst** he has no confidence in himself *or* self-confidence; **er hat mein volles ~:** I have complete confidence in him; **jmdm. [sein] ~ schenken** put one's trust in sb.; **jmdm. das** *od.* **sein ~ entziehen** withdraw the trust *or* confidence one has/had [placed] in sb.; **jmds. ~ enttäuschen/erschüttern** betray sb.'s trust/destroy sb.'s confidence [in one]; **das Parlament sprach dem Kanzler das ~ aus** parliament passed a vote of confidence in the Chancellor; **sein ~ in jmdn./etw. setzen** put *or* place one's trust in sb./sth.; **sein** *od.* **das ~ zu jmdm. verlieren** lose confidence in sb.; **im ~ [gesagt]** [strictly] in confidence; between you and me; **im ~ auf etw.** (*Akk.*) trusting to *or* in sth.; **im ~ darauf, dass ...** trusting that ...; **ein Mann seines ~s** a man whom he trusts; **jmdn. ins ~ ziehen** take sb. into one's confidence

**vertrauen·erweckend** *Adj.* inspiring *or* that inspires confidence *postpos.*; **einen ~en Eindruck machen** inspire confidence [by one's/it's appearance]; look trustworthy

**vertrauens-, Vertrauens-: ~arzt** *der*, **~ärztin** *die* independent examining doctor (*working for health service, health insurance, etc.*); **~beweis** *der* show of confidence (**für** in); **~bildend** *Adj.* **~bildende Maßnahmen** measures designed to build up trust; **~bruch** *der* breach of trust; (*wenn man Vertrauliches weitersagt*) breach of confidence; **~frage** *die* (*Parl.*) question of confidence; **die ~frage stellen** ask for a vote of confidence; **~frau** *die* A spokeswoman (*Gen.* for); representative; B (*in der Gewerkschaft*) [union] representative; (*in einer Fabrik o. Ä.*) shop steward; **~krise** *die* crisis of confidence; **~lehrer** *der*, **~lehrerin** *die* (*Schulw.*) liaison teacher (*liaising between staff and pupils*); **~mann** *der* A *Pl.* **~männer** *od.* **~leute** spokesman (*Gen.* for); representative; B *Pl.* **~leute** (*in der Gewerkschaft*) [union] representative; (*in einer Fabrik o. Ä.*) shop steward; **~person** *die* person in a position of trust; **~sache** *die* matter *or* question of trust; **~sache sein** be a matter *or* question of trust; **~selig** *Adj.* all too trustful *or* trusting; **~seligkeit** *die* excessive trustfulness; **~stellung** *die* position of trust; **~verhältnis** *das* relationship based on trust; **~voll** ❶ *Adj.* trusting ‹relationship›; ‹collaboration, cooperation› based on trust; (*zuversichtlich*) confident; ❷ *adv.* trustingly; (*zuversichtlich*) confidently; **sich ~voll an jmdn. wenden** turn to sb. with complete confidence; **~würdig** *Adj.* trustworthy; **~würdigkeit** *die* trustworthiness

**vertrauern** *tr. V.* (*geh.*) spend ‹time› in grieving

**vertraulich** ❶ *Adj.* A confidential; B (*freundschaftlich, intim*) familiar ‹manner, tone, etc.›; intimate ‹mood, conversation, whisper›; **er wird gleich ~:** he gets familiar straight away. ❷ *adv.* A confidentially; in confidence; B (*freundschaftlich, intim*) in a familiar way; familiarly

**Vertraulichkeit** *die;* **~, ~en** A confidentiality; B (*vertrauliche Information*) confidence; C (*distanzloses Verhalten*) familiarity; (*Intimität*) intimacy; D (*vertrauliche Handlung*) act of familiarity; (*Äußerung*) familiar remark

**verträumen** *tr. V.* [day]dream away ‹time›

**verträumt** ❶ *Adj.* dreamy; **sie ist zu ~:** she lives too much in a world of dreams. ❷ *adv.* dreamily; idyllically ‹situated›

*old spelling (see note on page 1707)

**Verträumtheit** *die;* **~:** dreaminess; (*idyllischer Charakter*) idyllic nature

**vertraut** /fɛɐ̯ˈtraut/ *Adj.* A close ‹friend etc.›; intimate ‹circle, conversation, etc.›; **sie sind sehr/ein wenig ~ miteinander** they are very close/quite friendly; **mit jmdm. ~ werden** become very friendly *or* close friends with sb.; **auf ~em Fuße** on intimate terms; B (*bekannt*) familiar; **jmdm. ~ sein/werden** be/become familiar to sb.; **er ist mit Pferden ~:** he knows about horses; **mit etw. gut/wenig ~ sein** be well acquainted/have little knowledge of sth.; **jmdn./sich mit etw. ~ machen** familiarize sb./oneself with sth.; **mit diesem Gedanken solltest du dich ~ machen** you should get used to this idea

**Vertraute** *der/die; adj. Dekl.* close friend; **enger ~r** intimate friend

**Vertrautheit** *die;* **~** ⇒ **vertraut**: closeness; intimacy; familiarity

**vertreiben** *unr. tr. V.* A drive out (**aus** of); (*wegjagen*) drive away ‹animal, smoke, clouds, etc.› (**aus** from); **aus der Heimat vertrieben werden** be driven out of *or* expelled from one's homeland; **die vertriebenen Juden** the exiled *or* expelled Jews; **von Haus und Hof vertrieben werden** be turned out of house and home; **jmdn. aus seinem Amt ~:** oust sb. from office; **jmdn. [von seinem Platz] ~:** take sb.'s seat; **bleiben Sie doch ruhig sitzen, ich wollte Sie nicht ~:** please don't get up, I didn't mean to take your place *or* chase you away; **die Müdigkeit/Sorgen ~** (*fig.*) fight off tiredness/drive troubles away; ⇒ *auch* **Zeit** A; B (*verkaufen*) sell

**Vertreibung** *die;* **~, ~en** driving out; (*das Wegjagen*) driving away; (*aus dem Amt*) ousting; (*aus der Heimat*) expulsion

**vertretbar** *Adj.* defensible ‹risk etc.›; tenable, defensible ‹standpoint›; justifiable ‹costs›

**vertreten** ❶ *unr. tr. V.* A stand in *or* deputize for ‹colleague etc.›; ‹teacher› cover for ‹colleague›; **er lässt sich von seinem Staatssekretär ~:** he is sending his permanent secretary as his representative; B (*eintreten für, repräsentieren*) represent ‹person, firm, interests, constituency, country, etc.›; (*Rechtsw.*) act for ‹person, prosecution, etc.›; **er lässt sich durch einen Anwalt ~:** he is getting a lawyer to act for him; **den Fall vertritt Rechtsanwalt Müller** the lawyer defending the case is Müller; **~ sein** be represented (**mit, durch** by); (*anwesend sein*) be present; **schwach/stark ~:** poorly/well represented; C (*einstehen für, verfechten*) support ‹point of view, principle›; hold ‹opinion›; advocate ‹thesis etc.›; pursue ‹policy›; **er vertritt den Standpunkt** *od.* **die Meinung, dass ...** he takes *or* holds the view that ...; **etw. zu ~ haben** be responsible for sth.; D **jmdm. den Weg ~:** bar sb's way. ❷ *unr. refl. V.* **sich** (*Dat.*) **den Fuß ~:** twist one's ankle; **sich** (*Dat.*) **die Füße** *od.* **Beine ~** (*ugs.: sich Bewegung verschaffen*) stretch one's legs

**Vertreter** *der;* **~s, ~** A ▸159 (*Stell~*) deputy; stand-in; (*eines Arztes*) locum (*coll.*); B ▸159 (*Interessen~, Repräsentant*) representative; (*Handels~*) sales representative; commercial traveller; **ein ~ für Staubsauger** a traveller in vacuum cleaners; C (*Verfechter, Anhänger*) supporter; advocate; D (*ugs. abwertend: Kerl, Bursche*) **du bist ein übler/sauberer ~!** you're a nasty piece of work (*coll.*)/a fine one! (*iron.*)

**Vertreterin** *die;* **~, ~nen** ⇒ **Vertreter** A-C

**Vertretung** *die;* **~, ~en** A deputizing; **jmds. ~ übernehmen** stand in *or* deputize for sb.; ‹doctor› act as locum for sb. (*coll.*); **in ~ von Herrn N.** in place of *or* standing in for Mr. N.; **in ~ unterschreiben** sign as a proxy; **in ~ M. Schmidt** (*am Schluss eines Briefes usw.*) p.p. M. Schmidt; B (*Vertreter[in]*) deputy; stand-in; (*eines Arztes*) locum (*coll.*); **ich brauche für morgen eine ~:** I need somebody to take my place *or* stand in for me tomorrow; (*als Lehrer*) I need cover for tomorrow; C (*Delegierte[r]*) representative; (*Delegation*) delegation; **eine diplomatische ~:** a diplomatic mission; **die deutsche ~** (*Sport*) the German team *or* squad; D (*Handels~*) [sales] agency; (*Niederlassung*) agency; branch; E (*Interessen~*) representation; F (*Verfechtung*) advocacy

**Vertretungs·stunde** *die* (*Schulw.*) cover lesson

**vertretungs·weise** *Adv.* as a [temporary] replacement *or* stand-in

**Vertrieb** *der* A sale; marketing; B (*Abteilung*) sales [department]

**Vertriebene** *der/die; adj. Dekl.* expellee [from his/her homeland]

**Vertriebs·gesellschaft** *die* sales *or* marketing company

**vertrimmen** *tr. V.* (*ugs.*) wallop (*coll.*)

**vertrinken** *unr. tr. V.* spend ‹money› on drink

**vertrocknen** *itr. V.; mit sein* dry up; (*fig.*) ‹person› wither, shrivel up

**vertrödeln** *tr. V.* (*ugs. abwertend*) dawdle away, waste ‹time›

**vertrösten** *tr. V.* put ‹person› off (**auf** + *Akk.* until)

**Vertröstung** *die* prevarication

**vertrotteln** *itr. V.; mit sein* go gaga (*coll.*); **vertrottelt** gaga

**vertun** ❶ *unr. tr. V.* waste; **die Mühe war vertan** it was a waste of effort. ❷ *unr. refl. V.* (*ugs.*) make a slip; **wenn du dich da mal nicht vertust!** I think you're a bit wide of the mark there

**vertuschen** *tr. V.* hush up ‹scandal etc.›; keep ‹truth etc.› secret

**Vertuschung** *die;* **~, ~en** hushing up; **eine ~:** a hush-up *or* cover-up

**verübeln** *tr. V.* **jmdm. eine Äußerung** *usw.* **~:** take sb.'s remark *etc.* amiss; **Sie werden es mir nicht ~, wenn ich ...** I hope you won't take it amiss *or* mind if I ...; **das kann man ihm kaum ~:** one can hardly blame him for that

**verüben** *tr. V.* commit ‹crime etc.›; **Streiche ~:** get up to pranks

**verulken** *tr. V.* (*ugs.*) make fun of; take the mickey out of (*Brit. coll*); **du willst mich wohl ~!** you're pulling my leg (*coll.*)

**verunfallen** *itr. V.; mit sein* (*Amtsspr., bes. schweiz.*) have an accident

**Verunfallte** *der/die; adj. Dekl.* (*Amtsspr., bes. schweiz.*) accident victim

**verunglimpfen** /fɛɐ̯ˈ|ʊnglɪmpfn̩/ *tr. V.* (*geh.*) denigrate ‹person, etc.›; sully ‹honour, name, memory›

**Verunglimpfung** *die;* **~, ~en** (*geh.*) ⇒ **verunglimpfen**: denigration; sullying

**verunglücken** *itr. V.; mit sein* A have an accident; ‹car etc.› be involved in an accident; **mit dem Auto/Flugzeug ~:** be in a car/an air accident *or* crash; **beim Segeln ~:** have a sailing accident *or* an accident while sailing; **der verunglückte Fahrer** the driver involved in the accident; B (*scherzh.: misslingen*) go wrong; ‹attempt› fail; ‹cake, sauce, etc.› be a disaster; **verunglückt** unsuccessful

**Verunglückte** *der/die; adj. Dekl.* accident victim; casualty

**verunmöglichen** /*od.* --ˈ---/ *tr. V.* (*bes. schweiz.*) **[jmdm.] etw. ~:** make sth. impossible [for sb.]

**verunreinigen** ❶ *tr. V.* A pollute; contaminate ‹water, milk, flour, oil›; **~de Stoffe** pollutants/contaminants; B (*geh.: beschmutzen*) dirty, soil ‹clothes, floor, etc.›; (*durch Fäkalien*) foul ‹pavement etc.›. ❷ *refl. V.* (*verhüll.*) soil oneself

**Verunreinigung** *die* A pollution; (*von Wasser, Milch, Mehl, Öl*) contamination; B (*Stoff*) pollutant/contaminant; C (*von Kleidern, Fußböden usw.*) soiling; (*von Straßen usw.*) fouling

**verunsichern** *tr. V.* **jmdn. ~:** make sb. feel unsure *or* uncertain; (*sodass er sich gefährdet fühlt*) undermine sb.'s sense of security; **verunsichert** insecure; (*nicht selbstsicher*) unsure of oneself

V

**Verunsicherung** *die* [A] (*das Verunsichern*) **die argumentative ~ der Richter** making the judges uncertain by means of argument; **zur ~ der Bevölkerung dienen** serve to undermine the people's sense of security; [B] (*Unsicherheit*) [feeling of] insecurity

**verunstalten** /fɛɐ̯'|ʊnʃtaltn̩/ *tr. V.* disfigure; **du verunstaltest dich mit dieser Frisur** this hairstyle spoils your looks *or* makes you look terrible

**Verunstaltung** *die; ~, ~en* disfigurement

**veruntreuen** *tr. V.* embezzle

**Veruntreuung** *die; ~, ~en* embezzlement

**verunzieren** *tr. V.* spoil the look of

**verursachen** *tr. V.* cause; **es hat ihm viel Arbeit verursacht** it caused *or* gave him a great deal of work

**Verursacher** *der; ~s, ~,* **Verursacherin** *die; ~, ~nen* cause; person responsible; **der ~ des Unfalls** the person responsible for the accident

**Verursacher·prinzip** *das: principle that the person who causes damage must bear the cost*

**Verursachung** *die; ~:* causing

**verurteilen** *tr. V.* [A] pass sentence on; sentence; **jmdn. zu Gefängnis** *od.* **einer Haftstrafe/drei Monaten Haft ~:** sentence sb. to imprisonment/to three months' imprisonment; **jmdn. zu einer Geldstrafe ~:** impose a fine on sb.; **jmdn. zum Tode ~:** sentence *or* condemn sb. to death; **jmdn. wegen Diebstahl** *usw.* **~:** sentence sb. for theft *etc.*; **der zum Tode Verurteilte** the condemned man; **zum Scheitern verurteilt sein** (*fig.*) be condemned to failure *or* bound to fail; **zum Schweigen verurteilt sein** (*fig.*) be condemned to silence; [B] (*fig.: negativ bewerten*) condemn ‹behaviour, action›

**Verurteilte** *der/die; adj. Dekl.* convicted man/woman

**Verurteilung** *die; ~, ~en* [A] sentencing; **eine ~ zu fünf Jahren Zuchthaus** a sentence of five years' imprisonment; [B] (*fig.*) condemnation

**veruzen** *tr. V.* (*ugs.*) ⇒ **verulken**

**Verve** /'vɛrvə/ *die; ~* (*geh.*) enthusiasm; verve; **mit ~:** enthusiastically

**vervielfachen** ❶ *tr. V.* greatly increase; (*multiplizieren*) multiply ‹number›; **wir müssen unsere Anstrengungen ~:** we must redouble our efforts. ❷ *refl. V.* multiply [several times]; (*fig.*) ‹efforts› be redoubled

**Vervielfachung** *die; ~, ~en* multiplication; (*fig.: der Anstrengungen*) redoubling

**vervielfältigen** *tr. V.* duplicate, make copies of ‹document etc.›

**Vervielfältigung** *die; ~, ~en* [A] duplicating; copying; [B] (*Kopie*) copy

**Vervielfältigungs·zahlwort** *das* (*Sprachw.*) multiplicative

**vervollkommnen** /fɛɐ̯'fɔlkɔmnən/ ❶ *tr. V.* perfect. ❷ *refl. V.* become perfected

**Vervollkommnung** *die; ~, ~en* perfecting; (*Zustand*) perfection

**vervollständigen** ❶ *tr. V.* complete; (*vollständiger machen*) make ‹library etc.› more complete. ❷ *refl. V.* become complete/more complete

**Vervollständigung** *die; ~, ~en* completion/making more complete

**verwachsen**[1] *Adj.* deformed

**verwachsen**[2] *unr. itr. V.; mit sein* [A] ‹wound, scab› heal [up *or* over]; [B] (*zusammenwachsen*) grow together (**mit** with); **zu etw. ~:** grow together to form sth.; grow into sth.; [C] (*fig.*) grow closer (**mit** to); **zu einer Gemeinschaft ~:** grow into a community; **sich mit seiner Umwelt ~ fühlen** feel at one with one's environment

**Verwachsung** *die; ~, ~en* deformity

**verwackeln** (*ugs.*) ❶ *tr. V.* make ‹picture› blurred; **verwackelt** blurred; shaky. ❷ *itr. V.; mit sein* turn out blurred

**verwählen** *refl. V.* misdial; dial the wrong number

**verwahren** ❶ *tr. V.* [A] keep [safe]; (*verstauen*) put away [safely]; [B] (*gefangen halten*) detain, hold ‹person›. ❷ *refl. V.* protest

**verwahrlosen** *itr. V.; mit sein* [A] get in a bad state; ‹house, building› fall into disrepair, become dilapidated; ‹garden, hedge› grow wild, become overgrown; ‹person› let oneself go, (*coll.*) go to pot; **etw. ~ lassen** neglect sth.; allow sth. to get in a bad state; **verwahrlost** neglected; overgrown ‹hedge, garden›; dilapidated ‹house, building›; unkempt ‹person, appearance, etc.›; (*in der Kleidung*) ragged ‹person›; [B] (*sittlich ~*) fall into bad ways; **[sittlich] verwahrlost** depraved

**Verwahrlosung** *die; ~* (*eines Gebäudes*) dilapidation; (*einer Person*) advancing decrepitude; (*sittliche ~*) decline into depravity; **[Zustand der] ~:** state of dilapidation/decrepitude/depravity

**Verwahrung** *die* [A] keeping [in a safe place]; **etw. in ~ geben/nehmen/haben** give/take sth. into safe keeping/hold sth. in safe keeping; **jmdm. etw. in ~ geben** give sth. to sb. for safe keeping; [B] (*Arrest*) detention *no def. art.*; [C] (*Einspruch, Protest*) protest

**verwaisen** *itr. V.* be orphaned; become an orphan; **verwaist** orphaned ‹child›; (*fig.*) lonely, deserted ‹person, place›; unoccupied ‹house›; vacant ‹professorship›

**verwalken** *tr. V.* (*ugs.*) ⇒ **vertrimmen**

**verwalten** *tr. V.* [A] (*betreuen*) administer, manage ‹estate, property, etc.›; run, look after ‹house›; hold ‹money› in trust; [B] (*leiten*) run, manage ‹hostel, kindergarten, etc.›; (*regieren*) administer ‹area, colony, etc.›; govern ‹country›; **die Kanalinseln ~ sich selbst** the Channel Islands are self-governing; [C] (*versehen*) hold ‹office›; carry out, perform ‹task, duty›; [D] (*bürokratisch beherrschen*) **eine verwaltete Gesellschaft** a bureaucratized society

**Verwalter** *der; ~s, ~,* **Verwalterin** *die; ~, ~nen* administrator; (*eines Amts usw.*) manager; (*eines Nachlasses*) trustee

**Verwaltung** *die; ~, ~en* [A] (*Betreuung, Leitung*) administration; management; **etw. unter staatliche ~ stellen** put sth. under State control; **in eigener ~:** under one's own control; [B] (*eines Gebiets*) administration; (*eines Landes*) government; **unter britischer ~:** under British administration *or* rule; [C] (*eines Amtes*) tenure; (*einer Aufgabe*) performance; [D] (*Organ, Behörde, Apparat*) administration; (*eines Betriebes*) management; **die öffentliche/staatliche ~:** the public/state authority

**Verwaltungs-: ~apparat** *der* administrative machine; **~beamte** *der,* **~beamtin** *die* administrative official; administrator; **~bezirk** *der* administrative district; **~gebühr** *die* administrative charge *or* fee; **~gericht** *das* administrative court; **~kosten** *Pl.* administrative costs; **~organ** *das* administrative organ; **~rat** *der* [A] governing body; administrative council; [B] (*schweiz. Wirtsch.*) board of directors

**verwamsen** /fɛɐ̯'vamzn̩/ *tr. V.* (*ugs.*) wallop (*coll.*) ‹child›

**verwandelbar** *Adj.* convertible

**verwandeln** ❶ *tr. V.* [A] convert (**in** + *Akk.*, **zu** into); (*völlig verändern*) transform (**in** + *Akk.*, **zu** into); **er ist/ich fühlte mich wie verwandelt** he's/I felt a different person *or* transformed; **das Sofa lässt sich in ein Bett ~:** the sofa can be converted into a bed; **der Prinz wurde in einen Frosch verwandelt** the prince was turned *or* transformed into a frog; [B] (*Ballspiele*) score from ‹corner, free kick›; convert ‹penalty›. ❷ *refl. V.* **sich in etw.** (*Akk.*) *od.* **zu etw. ~:** turn *or* change into sth.; (*bei chemischen Vorgängen usw.*) be converted into sth.; **die Raupe verwandelt sich in einen Schmetterling** the caterpillar metamorphoses into a butterfly. ❸ *itr. V.* (*Ballspiele*) **er verwandelte [zum 2:0]** he scored [to make it 2-0]

**Verwandlung** *die; ~, ~en* [A] (*das Verwandeln*) conversion (**in** + *Akk.*, **zu** into); (*völlige Veränderung*) transformation (**in** + *Akk.*, **zu** into); [B] (*das Sichverwandeln*) transformation; (*Metamorphose*) metamorphosis

**Verwandlungs·künstler** *der,* **Verwandlungs·künstlerin** *die* quick-change artist

**verwandt**[1] /fɛɐ̯'vant/ *2. Part. v.* **verwenden**

**verwandt**[2] *Adj.* [A] (*auch fachspr.*) related (**mit** to); **mit jmdm.** *od.* (*schweiz.*) **jmdm. ~ sein** be related to sb.; [B] (*fig.: ähnlich*) similar ‹views, ideas, forms›

**Verwandte** *der/die; adj. Dekl.* relative; relation

**Verwandten·besuch** *der* (*Besuch bei Verwandten*) visit to relatives; (*Besuch von Verwandten*) visit from *or* by relatives; **einen ~ machen** visit relatives; **wir erwarten ~:** we are expecting relatives

**Verwandtschaft** *die; ~, ~en* [A] relationship (**mit** to); (*fig.: Ähnlichkeit*) affinity; **zwischen ihnen besteht keine ~:** they are not related [to one another]; [B] (*Verwandte*) relatives *pl.*; relations *pl.*; **die ganze ~:** all one's relatives; **eine große ~ haben** have a large number of relatives; **zur ~ gehören** be one of the family

**verwandtschaftlich** ❶ *Adj.* family ‹ties, relationships, etc.›. ❷ *adv.* **~ miteinander verbunden sein** be related [to each other]

**Verwandtschafts-: ~grad** *der* degree of relationship; **~verhältnis** *das* family relationship; **in einem ~verhältnis zu jmdm. stehen** be related to sb.

**verwanzen** ❶ *itr. V.; mit sein* **verwanzt** bug-ridden. ❷ *tr. V.* (*fig.*) bug

**verwarnen** *tr. V.* warn, caution (**wegen** for)

**Verwarnung** *die; ~, ~en* warning; caution

**verwaschen** *Adj.* [A] washed out, faded ‹jeans, material, inscription, etc.›; [B] (*blass*) washy, watery ‹colour›; blurred ‹lines, contours›; [C] (*fig.*) wishy-washy ‹idea, formulation›

**verwässern** *tr. V.* (*auch fig.*) water down; **verwässert schmecken** taste watery

**Verwässerung** *die* (*auch fig.*) watering down

**verweben** ❶ *tr. V.* [A] weave with; use [for weaving]; [B] *auch unr.* **[miteinander] ~:** interweave ‹threads›; **etw. in etw.** (*Akk.*) **~** (*auch fig.*) weave sth. into sth.; **mit etw. verwoben** (*fig.*) bound *or* caught up with sth. ❷ *unr. refl. V.* (*dichter.*) **sich [zu etw.] ~:** become interwoven [to form *or* into sth.]

**verwechselbar** *Adj.* mistakable (**mit** for); **leicht ~:** easily confused (**mit** with)

**verwechseln** *tr. V.* [A] **[miteinander] ~:** confuse ‹two things/people›; **du musst da irgendetwas ~:** you must be getting mixed up; **er verwechselt immer rechts und links** he always gets mixed up between *or* mixes up right and left; **etw. mit etw./jmdn. mit jmdm. ~:** mistake sth. for sth./sb. for sb.; confuse sth. with sth./sb. with sb.; **Entschuldigung, ich habe Sie [mit jemandem] verwechselt/ich habe die Tür[en] verwechselt** sorry, I thought you were *or* I mistook you for somebody else/I've got the wrong door; **jmdm. zum V~ ähnlich sehen** be the spitting image of sb.; **leicht mit etw. zu ~ sein** be easily confused with sth.; **nicht zu ~ mit …** not to be confused with …; [B] (*vertauschen*) mix up; **jemand hat meinen Regenschirm verwechselt** somebody has taken my umbrella by mistake

**Verwechslung** *die; ~, ~en* [A] [case of] confusion; mistake; **um ~en auszuschließen** to avoid any possibility of confusion; [B] (*Vertauschung*) mixing up; **eine ~:** a mix-up

**verwegen** ❶ *Adj.* daring; (*auch fig.*) audacious. ❷ *adv.* (*auch fig.*) audaciously

**Verwegenheit** *die; ~, ~en* [A] daring; (*auch fig.*) audacity; [B] (*Tat*) act of daring

**verwehen** ❶ *tr. V.* [A] (*zudecken*) cover [over] ‹track, path›; **der Wind verwehte die Spur im Sand** the wind covered up the track in the sand; **vom Schnee verweht** covered in snow; [B] (*wegwehen*) blow away; scatter; **vom Winde verweht** (*fig.*) gone with the wind. ❷ *itr. V.; mit sein* (*geh.*) **im Wind ~:** drift away *or* be lost on the wind

**verwehren** *tr. V.* **jmdm. etw. ~:** refuse *or* deny sb. sth.; **jmdm. ~, etw. zu tun** bar sb. from doing sth.; (*verbieten*) forbid sb. to do sth.; **es verwehrt uns die Sicht** (*fig.*) it obstructs our view

**Verwehung** *die;* ~, ~**en** [snow]drift

**verweichlichen** ❶ *itr. V.; mit sein* grow soft; **ein verweichlichter Mensch** a weakling. ❷ *tr. V.* make soft; **ein verweichlichter Junge** a mollycoddled boy

**Verweichlichung** *die;* ~, ~**en** Ⓐ (*Vorgang*) **die ~ der Jugendlichen verhindern** prevent young people from becoming soft; Ⓑ (*Zustand*) softness; **eine solche Lebensweise führt zur ~:** this way of life makes one soft

**Verweigerer** *der;* ~**s**, ~, **Verweigerin** *die;* ~, ~**nen** Ⓐ rebel; dissident; Ⓑ (*des Kriegsdienstes usw.*) objector (*Gen.* to)

**verweigern** ❶ *tr. V.* refuse; **jmdm. die Erlaubnis/eine Hilfeleistung ~:** refuse sb. permission/assistance; **„Annahme verweigert"** 'delivery refused'; **die Aussage/einen Befehl/die Nahrungsaufnahme ~:** refuse to make a statement/to obey an order/to take food; **den Kriegsdienst ~:** refuse to do military service; be a conscientious objector; **[jmdm.] den Gehorsam ~:** refuse to obey [sb.]; **ein Hindernis ~** (*Pferdesport*) refuse at a jump.
❷ *refl. V.* object; refuse to cooperate; **sich jmdm./einer Sache ~:** refuse to accept sb./sth.; **sich der Gesellschaft ~:** contract out of society; **sich jmdm. [sexuell] ~** (*geh.*) refuse [to have sexual intercourse with] sb.
❸ *itr. V.* Ⓐ (*ugs.: den Kriegsdienst ~*) refuse [to do military service]; be a conscientious objector; Ⓑ (*Pferdesport*) refuse

**Verweigerung** *die;* ~, ~**en** refusal; (*Protest*) protest; **~ des Kriegsdienstes** refusal to do military service; conscientious objection

**Verweil·dauer** *die* length of stay; time spent (*Gen.* by); **die ~ der Speisen im Magen** the period during which food remains in the stomach

**verweilen** *itr. V.* (*geh.*) stay; (*länger als nötig*) linger; **verweile doch** tarry awhile (*literary*); **bei einem Thema/Gedanken ~** (*fig.*) dwell on a theme/thought

**verweint** /fɛɐ̯ˈvaint/ *Adj.* tear-stained ‹face›; ‹eyes› red with tears *or* from crying; ‹person› with a tear-stained face; **sie sah ~ aus/war ~:** she looked as if she had been crying/she had a tear-stained face

**Verweis** *der;* ~**es**, ~**e** Ⓐ reference (**auf** + *Akk.* to); (*Quer~*) cross reference; Ⓑ (*Tadel*) reprimand; rebuke; **jmdm. einen ~ erteilen** *od.* **aussprechen** reprimand *or* rebuke sb.

**verweisen** *unr. tr. V.* Ⓐ **jmdn./einen Fall** *usw.* **an jmdn./etw. ~** (*auch Rechtsspr.*) refer sb./a case *etc.* to sb./sth.; Ⓑ (*wegschicken*) **jmdn. von der Schule/aus dem Saal ~:** expel sb. from the school/send sb. out of the room; **jmdn. des Landes ~:** exile *or* (*Hist.*) banish sb.; **einen Spieler vom Platz ~:** send a player off [the field]; Ⓒ (*Sport*) **jmdn. auf den zweiten Platz ~:** relegate sb. to *or* push sb. into second place; Ⓓ *auch itr.* (*hinweisen*) **[jmdn.] auf etw.** (*Akk.*) **~:** refer [sb.] to sth.; (*durch Querverweis*) cross-refer [sb.] to sth.

**verwelken** *itr. V.; mit sein* ‹flower, leaf› wilt; (*fig.*) ‹fame› fade; **verwelkt** wilted ‹flowers›; withered ‹hands, face›; (*fig.*) faded ‹beauty›

**verweltlichen** ❶ *tr. V.* secularize. ❷ *itr. V.; mit sein* (*geh.*) become worldly *or* secularized

**Verweltlichung** *die;* ~, ~**en** secularization

**verwendbar** *Adj.* usable (**zu, für** for); **es ist mehrfach ~:** it has several uses *or* applications

**Verwendbarkeit** *die;* ~: usability

**verwenden** ❶ *unr. od. regelm. tr. V.* Ⓐ use (**zu, für** for); **ich kann es nicht mehr ~** *od.* **zu nichts mehr ~:** it is no use to me any more; **jmdn./etw. als etw. ~:** use *or* employ sb./sth. as sth.; Ⓑ (*aufwenden*) spend ‹time› (**auf** + *Akk.* on); **viel Energie/Mühe auf etw.** (*Akk.*) **~:** put a lot of energy/effort into sth.; **du solltest mehr Sorgfalt auf deine Schularbeiten ~:** you should take more care with *or* over your school work. ❷ *unr. od. regelm. refl. V.* (*geh.*) **sich [bei jmdm.] für jmdn./etw. ~:** intercede [with sb.] for sb./use one's influence [with sb.] on behalf of sth.

**Verwendung** *die;* ~, ~**en** Ⓐ use; **bei ~ dieses Materials** when using this material; **~ finden** be used; **unter ~ einer Sache** (*Gen.*) *od.* **von etw.** using sth.; **~/keine ~ für etw. haben** have a/no use for sth.; **etw. in ~ nehmen** (*österr.*) put sth. into use *or* service; Ⓑ (*geh.: Fürbitte*) intercession

**verwendungs-, Verwendungs-:** **~fähig** *Adj.* employable; (*als Soldat usw.*) fit for service *postpos.;* **~möglichkeit** *die* [possible] application *or* use; **~weise** *die* application; **es hängt von der ~weise ab** it depends how it is used; **~zweck** *der* application; purpose; **„~zweck"** (*auf Zahlkarten usw.*) 'as payment for'

**verwerfen** ❶ *unr. tr. V.* Ⓐ reject; dismiss ‹thought›; **etw. als unsittlich ~:** condemn sth. as [being] immoral; **einen Antrag/Vorschlag** *usw.* **~:** reject *or* turn down an application/suggestion *etc.;* Ⓑ (*Rechtsw.*) dismiss ‹appeal, action›; overturn, quash ‹judgement›; Ⓒ (*geh., bibl.: verstoßen*) reject ‹person, people›. ❷ *unr. refl. V.* Ⓐ (*sich verziehen*) warp; Ⓑ (*Geol.*) fault; Ⓒ (*Kartenspiel*) put down the wrong cards/cards

**verwerflich** (*geh.*) ❶ *Adj.* reprehensible. ❷ *adv.* reprehensibly

**Verwerflichkeit** *die;* ~ (*geh.*) reprehensibility; reprehensible *or* despicable nature

**Verwerfung** *die;* ~, ~**en** (*Geol.*) fault

**verwertbar** *Adj.* utilizable; usable

**Verwertbarkeit** *die;* ~: usability; **etw. auf seine ~ untersuchen** examine sth. to see if it can/could be utilized

**verwerten** *tr. V.* utilize, use (**zu** for); make use of, exploit ‹suggestion, experience, knowledge, etc.›; put ‹idea› into practice; (*bes. kommerziell*) exploit ‹idea, invention, place, etc.›; **es ist noch zu ~:** it can still be put to good use

**Verwertung** *die* utilization; use; (*bes. kommerziell*) exploitation

**verwesen** *itr. V.; mit sein* decompose

**verweslich** *Adj.* decomposable

**verwestlichen** *itr. V.; mit sein* become westernized

**Verwesung** *die;* ~: decomposition; **in ~ übergehen** start to decompose

**verwetten** *tr. V.* spend ‹money› on betting; **seinen Kopf für etw. ~:** bet anything on sth.

**verwichsen** *tr. V.* (*ugs.*) beat ‹person› up; (*zur Strafe*) give ‹person› a hiding (*coll.*)

**verwickeln** ❶ *refl. V.* Ⓐ get tangled up *or* entangled; Ⓑ (*sich verfangen*) **sich in etw.** (*Akk. od. Dat.*) **~:** get caught [up] in sth.; **sich in Widersprüche ~** (*fig.*) tie oneself up in contradictions. ❷ *tr. V.* involve; **in etw.** (*Akk.*) **verwickelt werden/sein** get/be mixed up *or* involved in sth.

**verwickelt** ❶ *Adj.* involved; complicated. ❷ *adv.* in an involved *or* a complicated way

**Verwicklung** *die;* ~, ~**en** complication

**verwiegen** *unr. refl. V.* get the weight wrong

**verwildern** *itr. V.* Ⓐ ‹garden› become overgrown, go wild; ‹domestic animal› go wild, return to the wild; ‹plant› go *or* grow wild; Ⓑ (*unkultiviert werden*) ‹person› turn wild; (*verwahrlosen*) go to seed; let oneself go

**verwildert** *Adj.* Ⓐ overgrown ‹garden›; ‹animal, plant› which has gone wild; Ⓑ (*unkultiviert*) unkempt, dishevelled ‹person, appearance, etc.›; (*ungehobelt*) uncouth ‹person›; (*ausschweifend*) morally decadent ‹person, society›

**Verwilderung** *die;* ~, ~**en** Ⓐ return to the wild [state]; **die ~ des Gartens schreitet weiter fort** the garden is continuing to get more and more overgrown; Ⓑ (*geh.: von Menschen*) reversion to a primitive state; **die ~ der Sitten** moral decadence

**verwinden** *unr. tr. V.* (*geh.*) get over

**verwinkelt** *Adj.* [narrow and] winding ‹street, corridor›; ‹flat, old quarter› full of nooks and crannies

**verwirken** *tr. V.* (*geh.*) forfeit

**verwirklichen** ❶ *tr. V.* realize ‹dream›; realize, put into practice ‹plan, proposal, idea, etc.›; carry out ‹project, intention›. ❷ *refl. V.* Ⓐ ‹hope, dream› be realized *or* fulfilled; Ⓑ (*sich voll entfalten*) **sich [selbst] ~:** realize one's [full] potential; fulfil oneself

**Verwirklichung** *die;* ~, ~**en** realization; (*eines Wunsches, einer Hoffnung*) fulfilment; **er begann mit der ~ seines Plans** he started to put his plan into practice; **jmdm. bei der ~ eines Projekts helfen** help sb. carry out a project

**verwirren** ❶ *tr. V.* entangle, tangle up ‹thread etc.›; tousle, ruffle ‹hair›. ❷ *tr.* (*auch itr.*) *V.* confuse; bewilder; **jmds. Geist ~** (*geh.*) upset sb.'s mental balance; **das verwirrt [den Zuhörer] nur** it is only confusing [for the listener]; **verwirrt** confused; bewildered; **„Träume ich?", dachte er verwirrt** 'Am I dreaming?' he thought in confusion *or* bewilderment; **~d** bewildering; **~d viele Möglichkeiten** a bewildering number of possibilities. ❸ *refl. V.* ‹thread etc.› become entangled; ‹hair› become tousled *or* ruffled; ‹person, mind› become confused; (*fig.: kompliziert werden*) become confused *or* complicated

**Verwirr·spiel** *das* deliberate confusion *no indef. art.;* **ein ~ mit jmdm. treiben** use intentionally confusing tactics on sb.; **zu einem ~ für jmdn. werden** confuse sb. completely

**Verwirrtheit** *die;* ~: [state of] confusion *or* bewilderment

**Verwirrung** *die;* ~, ~**en** confusion; **jmdn. in ~ bringen** make sb. confused *or* bewildered; **in ~ geraten** become confused *or* bewildered; **im Zustand geistiger ~:** in a disturbed *or* confused mental state

**verwirtschaften** *tr. V.* squander ‹money› by mismanagement

**verwischen** ❶ *tr. V.* smudge ‹signature, writing, etc.›; smear ‹paint›; **alle Spuren ~** (*fig.*) cover up all [one's] tracks. ❷ *refl. V.* become blurred

**verwissenschaftlichen** *tr. V.* make ‹teaching, life› highly scientific; put ‹research, procedure› on a scientific basis

**verwittern** *itr. V.; mit sein* weather

**Verwitterung** *die;* ~, ~**en** weathering

**verwitwet** /fɛɐ̯ˈvɪtvət/ *Adj.* widowed; **Frau Meier, ~e Schmidt** Mrs Meier, the widow of the late Mr Schmidt

**verwohnen** *tr. V.* ruin, make a mess of ‹house, flat›; **das Zimmer sieht verwohnt aus** the room looks badly knocked about

**verwöhnen** /fɛɐ̯ˈvøːnən/ *tr. V.* spoil; **~ Sie sich mit einer Tasse X-Kaffee!** treat yourself to a cup of X coffee; **das Schicksal hat ihn nicht gerade verwöhnt** (*fig.*) fate has not exactly smiled upon him

**verwöhnt** *Adj.* spoilt; (*anspruchsvoll*) discriminating; ‹taste, palate› of a gourmet

**Verwöhnung** *die;* ~: spoiling

**verworfen** /fɛɐ̯ˈvɔrfn̩/ ❶ *2. Part. v.* **verwerfen.** ❷ *Adj.* (*geh.*) depraved ‹person›; dastardly ‹act›

**Verworfenheit** *die;* ~: depravity

**verworren** /fɛɐ̯ˈvɔrən/ *Adj.* confused, muddled ‹ideas, situation, etc.›; confused ‹sound›

**Verworrenheit** *die;* ~: confused nature; confusion

**verwundbar** *Adj.* open to injury *pred.;* (*fig.*) vulnerable; **eine sehr ~e Stelle treffen** (*fig.*) touch a very sensitive spot

**Verwundbarkeit** *die* vulnerability

**verwunden**[1] *2. Part. v.* **verwinden**

**verwunden**[2] *tr. V.* ▶ 474 wound; injure; (*fig. geh.*) wound ‹person, feelings, etc.›

**verwunderlich** *Adj.* surprising

**verwundern** ❶ *tr. V.* Ⓐ surprise; (*erstaunen*) astonish; **verwundert** surprised/astonished (**über** + *Akk.* at); *adv.* in surprise *or* wonderment/astonishment; Ⓑ *in* **zu/nicht zu ~ sein** be surprising/not surprising; be a/no wonder. ❷ *refl. V.* be surprised (**über** + *Akk.* at); (*erstaunt sein*) be astonished (**über** + *Akk.* at)

*old spelling (see note on page 1707)

V

**Verwunderung** *die;* **~:** surprise; (*Staunen*) astonishment; **jmdn. in ~ setzen** surprise/astonish sb.

**Verwundete** *der/die; adj. Dekl.* wounded person; casualty; **die ~n** the wounded

**Verwundung** *die;* ~, **~en** ▶ 474 Ⓐ wounding; Ⓑ (*Wunde, Verletzung*) wound

**verwunschen** *Adj.* enchanted; bewitched

**verwünschen** *tr. V.* Ⓐ curse; Ⓑ (*veralt.*) ⇒ **verzaubern** A

**verwünscht** *Adj.* Ⓐ (*vermaledeit*) accursed; wretched; Ⓑ (*verzaubert*) enchanted; bewitched

**Verwünschung** *die;* ~, **~en** Ⓐ (*das Verfluchen*) cursing; Ⓑ (*Fluch*) curse; oath; Ⓒ (*veralt.*) ⇒ **Verzauberung** A

**verwurschteln** /fɛɐ̯'vʊrʃtl̩n/, **verwursteln** (*ugs.*) ❶ *tr. V.* get ‹thing› in a muddle *or* a tangle. ❷ *refl. V.* get in a muddle *or* a tangle

**verwurzelt** *Adj.* [deeply] rooted; **fest ~** (*auch fig.*) deep-rooted; **in etw.** (*Dat.*) **~ sein** have one's roots in sth.; (*in der Tradition, im Glauben usw.*) be [deeply] rooted in *or* committed to sth.

**Verwurzelung** *die;* **~:** deep rootedness (**mit, in** + *Dat.* in); **trotz seiner ~ in der Tradition** although deeply rooted in tradition

**verwüsten** *tr. V.* devastate

**Verwüstung** *die;* ~, **~en** devastation; **die ~en des Krieges** the ravages of war

**verzagen** *itr. V.; mit sein od. haben* despair; lose heart; **verzagt sein** be despondent

**Verzagtheit** *die;* **~:** despondency; despair

**verzählen** *refl. V.* miscount; **ich verzähle mich dauernd** I keep losing count

**verzahnen** *tr. V.* connect up (**mit** to); (*fig.*) link, dovetail (**mit** with); **miteinander verzahnt** (*fig.*) interconnected

**Verzahnung** *die;* ~, **~en** connection; (*fig.*) link

**verzanken** *refl. V.* (*ugs.*) **sich [mit jmdm. wegen etw.] ~:** fall out [with sb. over sth.]

**verzapfen** *tr. V.* Ⓐ (*landsch.: zapfen*) pull, draw ‹beer etc.›; Ⓑ (*Tischlerei*) tenon; Ⓒ (*ugs. abwertend*) **Blödsinn** *od.* **Mist ~:** come out with *or* produce rubbish

**verzärteln** /fɛɐ̯'tsɛːɐtl̩n/ *tr. V.* mollycoddle

**Verzärtelung** *die;* **~:** mollycoddling

**verzaubern** *tr. V.* Ⓐ cast a spell on; bewitch; **jmdn. in etw.** (*Akk.*) **~:** transform sb. into sth.; **eine verzauberte Prinzessin** a bewitched princess; Ⓑ (*fig.*) enchant

**Verzauberung** *die;* ~, **~en** Ⓐ casting of a/the spell (*Gen.* on); Ⓑ (*fig.*) enchantment

**verzehnfachen** *tr., refl. V.* increase tenfold

**Verzehr** /fɛɐ̯'tseːɐ̯/ *der;* **~[e]s** consumption; **zum alsbaldigen ~ bestimmt** for immediate consumption

**Verzehr·bon** *der* meal voucher; (*für Getränke*) drinks voucher

**verzehren** ❶ *tr. V.* (*auch fig. geh.*) consume; ‹illness etc.› exhaust, debilitate ‹person›; consume, drain [away] ‹strength›; **der Gram verzehrt sie** she is consumed with grief. ❷ *refl. V.* (*geh.*) ‹energy etc.› be consumed; ‹person› eat one's heart out; **sich [in Sehnsucht] nach jmdm. ~:** pine away for sb.; **sich in ohnmächtiger Wut ~:** be consumed with *or* by helpless rage

**Verzehr·zwang** *der* obligation to order (*in a restaurant*)

**verzeichnen** *tr. V.* Ⓐ (*falsch zeichnen*) draw wrongly; Ⓑ (*aufführen*) list; (*eintragen*) enter; (*registrieren*) record; **der Ort ist auf der Karte nicht verzeichnet** the place is not [marked] on the map; **das Wörterbuch verzeichnet das Wort nicht** the dictionary does not list *or* include the word; **große Erfolge/Verluste zu ~ haben** have scored great successes/suffered great losses; **Fortschritte/Erfolge sind nicht zu ~:** no progress was made/there were no successes; Ⓒ (*fig. geh.: zur Kenntnis nehmen*) note; Ⓓ *auch itr.* (*Optik*) ‹lens› distort

**Verzeichnis** /fɛɐ̯'tsaiçnɪs/ *das;* **~ses, ~se** list; (*Register*) index; **ein ~ der lieferbaren Titel** a list *or* catalogue of available titles

**verzeihen** *unr. tr., itr. V.* ▶ 268 forgive; (*entschuldigen*) excuse ‹behaviour, remark, etc.›; **jmdm. [etw.] ~:** forgive sb. [sth. *or* for sth.]; **es sei dir verziehen, ich will es [dir] ~:** you are *or* shall be forgiven; **ich kann es mir nicht ~, dass ich das nicht verhindert habe** I can't *or* I'll never forgive myself for not preventing it; **das ist nicht zu ~:** that's unforgivable/inexcusable; **kannst du mir noch einmal ~?** (*auch iron.*) can you ever forgive me?; **~ Sie [bitte] die Störung** pardon the intrusion; [please] excuse me for disturbing you; **~ Sie [bitte], können Sie mir sagen ...?** excuse me, could you tell me ...?

**verzeihlich** *Adj.* forgivable; excusable; **kaum ~:** almost unforgivable

**Verzeihung** *die;* ~ ▶ 268 forgiveness; **~, können Sie mir sagen, ...?** excuse me, could you tell me ...?; **~!** sorry!; **jmdn. um ~ bitten** apologize to sb.; **ich bitte vielmals um ~:** I do apologize *or* [do] beg your pardon

**verzerren** ❶ *tr. V.* Ⓐ contort ‹face etc.› (**zu** into); Ⓑ (*zerren, überdehnen*) **sich** (*Dat.*) **einen Muskel/eine Sehne ~:** pull *or* strain a muscle/tendon; Ⓒ (*akustisch, optisch*) distort ‹sound, image›; **etw. verzerrt darstellen** (*fig.*) present a distorted account *or* picture of sth.; **seine Stimme klang verzerrt** his voice sounded distorted. ❷ *itr. V.* ‹loudspeaker, mirror, etc.› distort. ❸ *refl. V.* ‹face, features› become contorted (**zu** into)

**Verzerrung** *die;* ~, **~en** Ⓐ (*des Gesichts usw.*) contortion; Ⓑ (*eines Muskels usw.*) strain; pull; Ⓒ (*des Klangs, eines Bildes, der Realität usw.*) distortion

**verzetteln**[1] ❶ *tr. V.* fritter away ‹time, money›; dissipate ‹energy›. ❷ *refl. V.* dissipate one's energies; try to do too many things at once

**verzetteln**[2] *tr. V.* (*auf Zettel schreiben*) put ‹words etc.› on slips

**Verzettelung** *die;* ~, **~en** (*auf Zettel*) transfer to slips

**Verzicht** /fɛɐ̯'tsɪçt/ *der;* **~[e]s, ~e** Ⓐ renunciation (**auf** + *Akk.* of); **ich bin zum ~ auf meinen Anteil bereit** I am prepared to give up my share; **auf etw.** (*Akk.*) **~ leisten** (*geh.*) renounce sth.; Ⓑ (*auf Reichtum, ein Amt usw.*) relinquishment (**auf** + *Akk.* of)

**verzichten** *itr. V.* do without; **~ auf** (+ *Akk.*) (*auskommen ohne*) do without; (*sich enthalten*) refrain *or* abstain from; (*aufgeben*) give up ‹share, smoking, job, etc.›; renounce ‹inheritance›; renounce, relinquish ‹right, privilege›; (*opfern*) sacrifice ‹holiday, salary›; **wenn es nicht mehr für alle reicht, verzichte ich freiwillig** if there isn't enough for everybody I will gladly go without; **auf weitere Ansprüche ~:** waive *or* relinquish further claims; **auf den Thron ~:** renounce one's right to the throne; **auf einen Ministersessel ~:** refuse a ministerial post; **ich verzichte auf deine Hilfe/Ratschläge** I can do without *or* you can keep your help/advice; **[nein danke,] ich verzichte** not for me[, thanks]; **darauf möchte ich nicht [mehr] ~:** I wouldn't be without it now; **darauf kann ich ~** (*iron.*) I can do without that; **auf eine Strafanzeige ~:** not bring a charge; **ich könnte dazu noch einiges sagen, aber ich will darauf ~:** I could add a few things to that, but I will refrain; **auf eine förmliche Vorstellung ~:** dispense with a formal introduction

**Verzicht[s]·erklärung** *die* waiver; disclaimer

**verziehen**[1] *2. Part. v.* **verzeihen**

**verziehen**[2] ❶ *unr. tr. V.* Ⓐ screw up ‹face, mouth, etc.›; **er verzog sein Gesicht zu einer Grimasse/zu einem spöttischen Lächeln** he pulled a face *or* grimaced/put on a derisive smile; ⇒ *also* **Miene**; Ⓑ (*schlecht erziehen*) spoil; **so ein verzogener Bengel!** what a badly brought up *or* spoilt brat!; Ⓒ (*Ballspiele*) mishit ‹ball›; Ⓓ (*Landw.*) thin out ‹seedlings etc.›.
❷ *unr. refl. V.* Ⓐ twist; be contorted; **sein Gesicht verzog sich zu einer Grimasse** his face twisted *or* screwed itself into a grimace; Ⓑ (*aus der Form geraten*) go out of shape; ‹wood› warp; **ein verzogener Rahmen** a distorted frame; **total verzogen sein** be completely out of shape; Ⓒ (*wegziehen*) ‹clouds, storm› move away, pass over: ‹fog, mist› disperse; Ⓓ (*ugs.: weggehen*) take oneself off; **ich verziehe mich jetzt [ins Bett]** I'm off to bed now; **verzieh dich!** (*salopp*) clear (*coll.*) *or* (*coll.*) push off.
❸ *unr. itr. V.; mit sein* move [away]; **„Empfänger [unbekannt] verzogen"** 'no longer at this address'

**verzieren** *tr. V.* decorate

**Verzierung** *die;* ~, **~en** decoration; **überflüssige ~en** superfluous ornamentation *sing.;* **brich dir [bloß/nur] keine ~ ab!** (*fig. ugs.*) don't make [such] a fuss!

**verzinsen** ❶ *tr. V.* pay interest on ‹sum, capital, etc.›; **etw. mit 6% ~:** pay 6% interest on sth. ❷ *refl. V.* **sich [mit 6%] ~:** yield *or* bear [6%] interest

**verzinslich** *Adj.* bearing *or* yielding interest *postpos., not pred.* (**mit, zu** at a rate of)

**Verzinsung** *die;* ~, **~en** [payment of] interest (*Gen.* on)

**verzögern** ❶ *tr. V.* Ⓐ delay (**um** by) ; delay, postpone ‹departure etc.›; **den Baubeginn um zwei Jahre ~:** put back the start of building work [by] two years; Ⓑ (*verlangsamen*) slow down. ❷ *refl. V.* be delayed (**um** by). ❸ *itr. V.* slow down; decelerate

**Verzögerung** *die;* ~, **~en** Ⓐ delaying; delay (*Gen.* in); Ⓑ (*Verlangsamung*) slowing down; (*Technik*) deceleration; Ⓒ (*Verspätung*) delay; hold-up

**Verzögerungs·taktik** *die* delaying tactics *pl.*

**verzollen** *tr. V.* pay duty on

**Verzollung** *die;* ~, **~en** payment of duty (*Gen.* on)

**verzücken** *tr. V.* (*geh.*) enrapture; send into ecstasies; **verzückt** enraptured; in rapture; (*ekstatisch*) ecstatic; **mit verzückter Miene** with a look of ecstasy [on his/her face]

**verzuckern** *tr. V.* Ⓐ sugar ‹almonds›; (*kandieren*) candy ‹fruit›; Ⓑ (*fig.*) ⇒ **versüßen**

**Verzückung** *die;* **~:** ecstasy; rapture; **in ~ geraten** go into ecstasies

**Verzug** *der;* **~[e]s** Ⓐ delay; **~ der Zahlung** delay in payment; late payment; **[mit etw.] im ~ sein/in ~ kommen** *od.* **geraten** be/fall behind [with sth.]; **jmdn./etw. in ~ bringen** delay sb./sth.; hold sb. up/put sth. back; **ohne ~:** without delay; Ⓑ **es ist Gefahr im ~** (*ugs.*) danger is imminent

**Verzugs·zinsen** *Pl.* interest *sing.* on arrears *or* for late payment

**verzweifeln** *itr. V.; meist mit sein* despair; **über etw./jmdn. ~:** despair at sth./of sb.; **am Leben/an den Menschen ~:** despair of life/humanity; **es ist zum V~!** it's enough to drive you to despair; **es ist zum V~ mit dir** you're enough to drive anyone to despair

**verzweifelt** ❶ *Adj.* Ⓐ despairing ‹person, animal›; **~ sein** be in despair *or* full of despair; **ich bin [ganz] ~** (*ratlos*) I'm at my wit's end; Ⓑ desperate ‹situation, attempt, effort, struggle, etc.›. ❷ *adv.* Ⓐ (*entmutigt*) despairingly; Ⓑ (*sehr angestrengt*) desperately

**Verzweiflung** *die;* **~:** despair; **etw. aus ~ tun** do sth. out of despair; **jmdn. zur ~ treiben/bringen** drive sb. to despair

**Verzweiflungs·tat** *die* act of despair

**verzweigen** *refl. V.* branch [out]; **ein weit verzweigtes System/Netz** (*fig.*) a widely branching system/network; **das Unternehmen ist stark verzweigt** (*fig.*) the firm is very diversified

**Verzweigung** *die;* ~, **~en** Ⓐ branching; Ⓑ (*schweiz.*) (*Gabelung*) fork; (*Kreuzung*) crossroads *sing.;* (*Autobahn~*) intersection

**verzwickt** /fɛɐ̯'tsvɪkt/ *Adj.* (*ugs.*) tricky; complicated

**Vesper** /'fɛspɐ/ *die;* ~, **~n** Ⓐ vespers *pl.;* **in die** *od.* **zur ~ gehen** go to vespers; Ⓑ *auch das;* **~s, ~** (*südd.: Zwischenmahlzeit*) snack; **~ machen** have a snack

V

**Vesper·brot** *das (südd.)* sandwiches *pl.*

**vespern** *(bes. südd.)* ❶ *itr. V.* have a snack. ❷ *tr. V.* **etw. ~:** have a snack of sth.

**Vestibül** /vɛsti'by:l/ *das;* **~s, ~e** *(veralt.)* vestibule

**Vesuv** /ve'zu:f/ *der;* **~s** Vesuvius

**Veteran** /vete'ra:n/ *der;* **~en, ~en, Veteranin** *die;* **~, ~nen** *(auch fig.)* veteran

**Veterinär** /veteri'nɛ:ɐ̯/ *der;* **~s, ~e, Veterinärin** *die;* **~, ~nen** veterinary surgeon

**Veterinär·medizin** *die* ⇒ **Tiermedizin**

**Veto** /'ve:to/ *das;* **~s, ~s** veto; **ein ~ gegen etw. einlegen** veto sth.

**Veto·recht** *das* right of veto

**Vetter** /'fɛtɐ/ *der;* **~s, ~n** cousin

**Vettern·wirtschaft** *die (abwertend)* nepotism

**Vexier·bild** /vɛ'ksi:ɐ̯-/ *das* puzzle picture

**v-förmig, V-förmig** /'fau̯-/ *Adj.* V-shaped

**V-Frau** /'fau̯-/ *die* contact [woman]; *(Informantin)* informer

**vgl. vergleiche** cf.

**v.H.** *Abk.* **vom Hundert** per cent

**VHB** *Abk.* **Verhandlungsbasis: ~ 800 DM** 800 marks o.n.o. *(Brit.)*

**VHS** *Abk.* **Volkshochschule**

**via** /'vi:a/ *Präp.* via

**Viadukt** /vi̯a'dʊkt/ *das od. der;* **~[e]s, ~e** viaduct

**Vibraphon** /vibra'fo:n/ *das;* **~s, ~e** *(Musik)* vibraphone

**Vibration** /vibrə'tsi̯o:n/ *die;* **~, ~en** vibration

**Vibrato** /vi'bra:to/ *das;* **~s, ~s** *od.* **Vibrati** *(Musik)* vibrato

**Vibrator** *der;* **~s, Vibratoren** vibrator

**vibrieren** /vi'bri:rən/ *itr. V.* vibrate; ‹voice› quiver, tremble

**video-, Video-** /'vi:deo-/ video

**Video** *das;* **~s, ~s** *(ugs.)* video

**Video-: ~aufzeichnung** *die* video recording; **~band** *das; Pl.* **~bänder** videotape; **~clip** *der* video; **~film** *der* video [film]; **~kamera** *die* video camera; **~kassette** *die* video cassette; **~konferenz** *die* videoconference; **~recorder, ~rekorder** *der* video recorder; **~technik** *die* video technology *no art.* **~text** *der* videotex[t]

**Videothek** /vi:deo'te:k/ *die;* **~, ~en** video library

**Viech** /fi:ç/ *das;* **~[e]s, ~er** Ⓐ *(ugs.: Tier)* creature; Ⓑ *(derb abwertend: Mensch)* bastard *(coll.)*

**Viecherei** *die;* **~, ~en** *(ugs.)* hard grind *or* slog

**Vieh** /fi:/ *das;* **~[e]s** Ⓐ *(Nutztiere)* livestock *sing. or pl.;* **jmdn. wie ein Stück ~ behandeln** treat sb. like an animal; Ⓑ *(Rind~)* cattle *pl.;* Ⓒ ⇒ **Viech**

**Vieh-: ~bestand** *der* stocks *pl.* of animals/cattle; **wie hoch ist der ~bestand dieses Betriebs?** how much livestock does this farm have?; **~futter** *das* animal/cattle feed *or* fodder; **~händler** *der,* **~händlerin** *die* livestock/cattle dealer; **~hirt** *der* herdsman; *(von Rindern)* cowherd **~hirtin** *die* herdswoman; *(von Rindern)* cowherd

**viehisch** ❶ *Adj.* Ⓐ *(abwertend: brutal)* brutish; Ⓑ *(ugs.: immens)* terrible *(coll.)* ‹fear, stupidity, pain›. ❷ *adv.* Ⓐ *(abwertend)* ‹beat, torment› brutally; Ⓑ *(ugs.)* ‹hurt› like hell *(coll.)*; **~ kalt** perishing cold *(coll.)*

**Vieh-: ~markt** *der* livestock/cattle market; **~salz** *das* rock salt; *(als Streusalz)* road salt; **~stall** *der* cowshed; **~tränke** *die* cattle trough; **~treiber** *der,* **~treiberin** *die* [cattle] drover; **~waggon** *der* cattle truck; **~wirtschaft** *die* livestock farming *no art.;* **~zeug** *das (ugs.)* Ⓐ *(Kleinvieh)* animals *pl.;* Ⓑ *(abwertend: lästige Tiere)* creatures *pl.;* **~zucht** *die* [live]stock/cattle breeding *no art.;* **~züchter** *der,* **~züchterin** *die* [live]stock/cattle breeder

**viel** /fi:l/ ❶ *Indefinitpron. u. unbest. Zahlw.* Ⓐ *Sg.* a great deal of; a lot of *(coll.)*; **so/wie/nicht/zu ~:** that/how/not/too much; **wie ~ auch immer** however much; **seine dauernden Besuche werden mir allmählich zu ~:** his constant visits are getting me down *(coll.;)* **was zu ~ ist, ist zu ~:** enough is enough; there must be a limit; **~[es]** *(~e Dinge, vielerlei)* much; **er weiß ~es, aber nicht alles** he knows a great deal, but not everything; **ich kann mich an ~es nicht mehr erinnern** there's much I can't remember; **der ~e Regen** all the rain; **sein ~es Geld** all his money; **gleich ~ Geld/Wasser** the same amount of money/water; **gleich ~ verdienen** earn the same; **in ~er Hinsicht** *od.* **Beziehung** in many respects; **um ~es jünger** a great deal younger; **das ist ein bisschen [sehr] ~!** that's rather too much; **~ Erfreuliches** a great many pleasant things; **er hat in ~em recht** he is right on many points; **er ist nicht ~ über fünfzig** he is not much more than *or* much over fifty; Ⓑ *Pl.* many; **gleich ~[e]** the same number of; **wie ~[e]** how many; **zu ~[e]** too many; **~e hundert** many hundreds of; **die ~en Bäume/Menschen/Probleme** all the trees/people/problems; **seine ~en Kinder** all his children; **~e** *(~e Menschen)* many people; **das wissen nicht ~e** not many people know that; **das wissen ~e nicht** many people don't know that.

❷ *Adv.* Ⓐ *(oft, lange)* a great deal; a lot *(coll.)*; **man redet ~ vom Fortschritt** there is much *or (coll.)* a lot of talk of progress; **er spielt ~ Golf** he plays a lot of golf; **er fährt [nicht] ~ Rad** he does[n't do] a lot of cycling; **~ befahren** busy, much-used ‹road›; **~ beschäftigt** very busy; **~ besucht** much-frequented ‹restaurant, etc.›; much-visited ‹resort, museum, etc.›; **~ gekauft** widely bought; **~ gelesen** widely read; **~ gepriesen** much-praised; **~ geschmäht** much-maligned; much-abused; **ein ~ gefragter Artikel** an article that is in great demand *or* much in demand; **einmal zu ~:** once too often; Ⓑ *(wesentlich)* much; a great deal; a lot *(coll.)*; **~ zu viel** far *or* much too much; **~ zu wenig** far too little; **es geht ihm sehr ~ besser** he is very much better; **~ mehr/weniger** much more/less; **~ zu klein** much too small

**viel-, Viel-: *~befahren** *usw.* ⇒ **viel** 2 A; **~deutig** /-dɔy̆tɪç/ ❶ *Adj.* ambiguous; ❷ *adv.* ambiguously; **~deutigkeit** *die;* **~~:** ambiguity; **~eck** *das* polygon; **~ehe** *die* polygamy *no art.*

**vielerlei** *indekl. unbest. Gattungsz.* Ⓐ *attr.* many different; all kinds *or* sorts of; Ⓑ *subst.* all kinds *or* sorts of things

**vieler·orts** *Adv.* in many places

**viel-, Viel-: ~fach** ❶ *Adj.* Ⓐ multiple; **die ~fache Menge** many times the amount; **ein ~facher Millionär** a multimillionaire; **er ist ~facher Weltmeister** he has been world champion many times over; **auf ~fachen Wunsch unserer Zuschauer** at the request of many of our viewers; Ⓑ *(~fältig)* manifold; many kinds of; ❷ *adv.* many times; *(ugs.: oft)* often; frequently; **ein ~fach geäußerter Wunsch** a wish many times expressed; **~fache** *das; adj. Dekl.* Ⓐ **ein ~faches** many times the amount/number; **die Preise werden ein ~faches von dem betragen, was ...** the prices will be many times greater than ...; **um ein ~faches** many times over; **um ein ~faches schneller/teurer** many times faster/more expensive; Ⓑ *(Math.)* multiple; **~falt** *die;* **~~:** diversity; wide variety; **~fältig** /-fɛltɪç/ ❶ *Adj.* many and diverse; ❷ *adv.* in many different ways; **~farbig,** *(österr.)* **~färbig** *Adj.* multicoloured; **~flach** *das;* **~~[e]s, ~~e** polyhedron; **~fraß** *der;* **~~es, ~~e** Ⓐ *(ugs.: Mensch)* glutton; [greedy-]guts *sing. (sl.)*; Ⓑ *(Tier)* wolverine; ***~gefragt** *usw.* ⇒ **viel** 2 A; **~gestaltig** *Adj.* varied *or* diversified in form *postpos.;* **~gestaltig sein** be varied *or* diversified in form; have many different forms; **~götterei** /-gœtə'rai̯/ *die;* **~~:** polytheism *no art.*

**vielleicht** /fi'lai̯çt/ ❶ *Adv.* Ⓐ perhaps; maybe; **~ kommt er morgen** perhaps *or* maybe he will come tomorrow; he might come tomorrow; **du hast dich ~ geirrt** perhaps you were wrong; you may have been mistaken; **~, dass alles nur ein Missverständnis war** perhaps it was all just a misunderstanding; **hast du den Schirm ~ im Büro liegen lassen?** could it be that you left your umbrella in the office?; Ⓑ *(ungefähr)* perhaps; about; **ein Mann von ~ fünfzig Jahren** a man of perhaps *or* about fifty. ❷ *Partikel* Ⓐ **kannst du mir ~ sagen, ...?** could you possibly tell me ...?; **hast du ~ meinen Bruder gesehen?** have you seen my brother by any chance? Ⓑ *(wirklich)* really; **ich war ~ aufgeregt** I was terribly excited *or* as excited as anything *(coll.)*; **du bist ~ ein Blödmann!** what a stupid idiot you are! *(coll.)*; Ⓒ *(ich bitte dringend, dass ...)* **~ hilfst du mir mal!** would you mind helping me!; Ⓓ *(etwa)* **ist das ~ eine Lösung?** is that supposed to be a solution?; **ist das ~ dein Ernst?** you don't mean that, do you?

**viel-, Viel-: ~mals** *Adv.* **ich bitte ~mals um Entschuldigung** I'm very sorry; I do apologize; **sie lässt ~mals grüßen** she sends her best regards *or* wishes; **danke ~mals** thank you very much; many thanks; **~männerei** /-mɛnə'rai̯/ *die;* **~~:** polyandry *no art.;* **~mehr** /*od.* -'-/ *Konj. u. Adv.* rather; *(im Gegenteil)* on the contrary; **~sagend** ❶ *Adj.* meaningful; ❷ *adv.* meaningfully; **~schichtig** *Adj.* multi-layered; *(fig.: komplex)* complex; **~schreiber** *der,* **~schreiberin** *die (abwertend)* [over-]prolific writer; **~seitig** ❶ *Adj.* versatile ‹person›; varied ‹work, programme, etc.›; **auf ~seitigen Wunsch** by popular request; **diese Küchenmaschine ist sehr ~seitig** this food processor has many uses; ❷ *adv.* **~seitig begabt sein** be versatile; **sich ~seitig verwenden lassen** have many uses; **~seitigkeit** *die;* **~~** ⇒ **~seitig** 1: versatility; variedness; **Kombiwagen sind vor allem wegen ihrer ~seitigkeit so beliebt** estate cars are popular above all because of their many uses; **~sprachig** Adj. multilingual; polyglot; **~staaterei** /-ʃta:tə'rai̯/ *die;* **~~** ⇒ **Partikularismus; ~stimmig** ❶ *Adj.* many-voiced; **ein ~stimmiger Chor** a choir of many voices; ❷ *adv.* in many voices; **~versprechend** ❶ *Adj.* [very] promising; ❷ *adv.* [very] promisingly; **~völker·staat** /'-·--/ *der* multinational state; **~weiberei** /-vai̯bə'rai̯/ *die;* **~~:** polygyny *no art.;* polygamy *no art.;* **~zahl** *die* large number; multitude

**vier** /fi:ɐ̯/ *Kardinalz.* ▶76|, ▶752|, ▶841| four; **alle ~e von sich strecken** *(ugs.)* put one's feet up; **auf allen ~en** *(ugs.)* on all fours; ⇒ *auch* **acht**

**Vier** *die;* **~, ~en** four; **eine ~ schreiben/bekommen** *(Schulw.)* get a D; ⇒ *auch* **Acht**[1]; **Zwei**

**vier-, Vier-** (⇒ *auch* **acht-, Acht-**)**:~achser** *der;* **~~, ~~:** four-axle vehicle; **~achsig** *(Technik)* four-axle *attrib.;* **vierachsig sein** have four axles; **~achtel·takt** /'-'---/ *der (Musik)* four-eight time; **~augen·gespräch** *das (ugs.)* private talk *or* discussion; **~beiner** *der;* **~~s, ~~** *(ugs.)* four-legged friend; **~beinig** *Adj.* four-legged; **~blättrig** *Adj.* four-leaf *attrib.;* four-leaved; **~eck** *das* quadrilateral; *(Rechteck)* rectangle; *(Quadrat)* square; **~eckig** *Adj.* quadrilateral; *(rechteckig)* rectangular; *(quadratisch)* square

**Vierer** *der;* **~s, ~** Ⓐ *(Rudern)* four; Ⓑ *(ugs.: im Lotto)* four winning numbers *pl.;* Ⓒ *(ugs.: Ziffer, beim Würfeln)* four; Ⓓ *(landsch.: Schulnote)* D; Ⓔ *(ugs.: Autobus)* [number] four; Ⓕ *(Golf)* foursome

**Vierer·bob** *der* four-man bob

**viererlei** *Gattungsz.; indekl.* Ⓐ *attr.* four kinds *or* sorts of; four different ‹sorts, kinds, sizes, possibilities›; Ⓑ *subst.* four [different] things

**vier·fach** *Vervielfältigungsz.* fourfold; quadruple; **der ~e Olympiasieger** quadruple Olympic winner; ⇒ *auch* **achtfach**

---

*old spelling (see note on page 1707)

V

**Vier·fache** *das;* **~n;** *adj. Dekl.* **um das ~:** fourfold; by four times the amount; **die Preise sind um das ~ gestiegen** the prices have quadrupled *or* increased four times; **sie verlangen das ~ des normalen Tarifs** they are demanding four times the normal rate; ⇒ *auch* **Achtfache**

**vier-, Vier-: ~farben·druck** /-'---/ *der; Pl.* **~~e** Ⓐ *(Verfahren)* four-colour printing *no art.;* Ⓑ *(einzelnes Stück)* four-colour print; **~farb[en]·stift** *der* four-colour pen; **~flach** *das;* **~~[e]s, ~~, ~flächner** /-flɛçnɐ/ *der;* **~~s, ~~** *(Math.)* tetrahedron; **~füßer** /-fy:sɐ/ *der;* **~~s, ~~** *(Zool.)* quadruped; **~füßig** *Adj.* Ⓐ four-legged; Ⓑ *(Verslehre)* tetrameter; **~füßig sein** be a tetrameter; **~gang·getriebe** *das (Technik)* four-speed gearbox; **~händig** /-hɛndɪç/ ❶ *Adj.* **~händiges Klavierspiel üben** practise piano duets *or* duets on the piano; ❷ *adv.* ‹play› as a duet; **~händig Klavier spielen** play a duet/duets on the piano; **~hundert** *Kardinalz.* ▶ 841 four hundred; **~jährig** *Adj. (4 Jahre alt)* four-year-old *attrib.;* four years old *pred.; (4 Jahre dauernd)* four-year *attrib.;* ⇒ *auch* **achtjährig**; **~jährlich** ❶ *Adj.* four-yearly; ⇒ *auch* **achtjährlich**; ❷ *adv.* every four years

**Vierkant-: ~eisen** *das* square iron; **~holz** *das* squared timber; **~schlüssel** *der* square-section key

**vier·köpfig** *Adj.* four-headed ‹monster›; ‹family, staff› of four

**Vierling** *der;* **~s, ~e** quadruplet

**vier-, Vier-: ~mal** *Adv.* four times; ⇒ *auch* **achtmal**; **~malig** *Adj.* **nach ~maliger Aufforderung** at the fourth request; after being asked four times; ⇒ *auch* **achtmalig**; **~master** *der;* **~~s, ~~:** four-master; **~motorig** *Adj.* four-engined ‹aircraft etc.›; **~rad·an·trieb** *der (Kfz-W.)* four-wheel drive; **~räd[e]rig** /-rɛ:d[ə]rɪç/ *Adj.* four-wheeled; **~schrötig** /-ʃrø:tɪç/ *Adj.* thickset; **~seitig** *Adj.* Ⓐ four-sided ‹figure, object, etc.›; four-page *attrib.* ‹letter, article, etc.›; Ⓑ *(zwischen ~ Beteiligten)* quadripartite ‹agreement, talks, etc.›; **~sitzer** *der;* **~~s, ~~:** four-seater; **~spänner** /-ʃpɛnɐ/ *der;* **~~s, ~~:** four-in-hand; **~spännig** ❶ *Adj.* four-horse ‹coach, carriage, etc.›; ❷ *adv.* with a team of four horses; **~spurig** ❶ *Adj.* four-lane ‹road, motorway›; **~spurig sein** have four lanes; ❷ *adv.* **~spurig befahrbar sein** have all four lanes open; **eine Straße ~spurig ausbauen** widen a road into four lanes; **~stellig** *Adj.* four-figure *attrib.;* ⇒ *auch* **achtstellig**; **~sterne·general** /-'----/ *der (Militärjargon)* four-star general; **~sterne·hotel** /-'----/ *das* four-star hotel; **~stimmig** ❶ *Adj.* four-part ‹harmony, song, etc.›; four-voice ‹choir, group›; ❷ *adv.* **etw. ~stimmig singen** sing sth. in four voices; **~stöckig** *Adj.* four-storey; ⇒ *auch* **achtstöckig**; **~stündig** *Adj.* four-hour *attrib.;* ⇒ *auch* **achtstündig**

**viert** /fi:ɐ̯t/ *in* **wir waren zu ~:** there were four of us; **zu ~ verreisen** go away *or* on holiday in a foursome; ⇒ *auch* **acht²**

**viert...** *Ordinalz.* ▶ 207, ▶ 841 fourth; ⇒ *auch* **acht...**

**vier-, Vier-: ~tägig** *Adj.* four-day *attrib.;* ⇒ *auch* **achttägig**; **~takter** *der;* **~~s, ~~** *(Auto)* car with a four-stroke engine; *(Motor)* four-stroke engine; **~takt·motor** *der (Kfz-W.)* four-stroke engine; **~tausend** *Kardinalz.* ▶ 841 four thousand

**Vierte** *der/die; adj. Dekl.* fourth; ⇒ *auch* **Achte**

**vier-: ~teilen** *tr. V.* quarter; **~teilig** *Adj.* four-part ‹serial, documentary, etc.›; **~teilig sein** be in four parts

**viertel** /'fɪrtl̩/ *Bruchz.* ▶ 752, ▶ 841 quarter; **ein ~ Pfund/eine ~ Million** a quarter of a pound/million; **drei ~ Liter** three quarters of a litre; **um ~/drei ~ acht** *(landsch.)* at [a] quarter past seven; at [a] quarter to eight; **die Flasche ist drei ~ leer** the bottle is three-quarters empty

**Viertel¹** /'fɪrtl̩/ *das (schweiz. meist* **der***);* **~s, ~** ▶ 752, ▶ 841 quarter; **ein ~ Leberwurst** *(ugs.)* a quarter of liver sausage; **ein ~ Wein** *(ugs.)* a quarter-litre of wine; **~ vor/nach eins** [a] quarter to/past one; ⇒ *auch* **akademisch 1**

**Viertel²** *die;* **~, ~** *(Musik)* crotchet *(Brit.;)* quarter *(Amer.)*

**viertel-, Viertel-: ~drehung** *die* quarter turn; **~finale** *das (Sport)* quarter-final; **sich für das ~finale qualifizieren** qualify for the quarter-finals; **~jahr** *das* three months *pl.;* **~jährlich** ❶ *Adj.* quarterly; ❷ *adv.* quarterly; every three months; **~kreis** *der* quadrant; **~liter** *der* quarter of a litre; **~note** *die (Musik)* crotchet *(Brit.);* quarter note *(Amer.);* **~pause** *die* crotchet rest *(Brit.);* quarter rest *(Amer.);* **~pfund** *das* quarter [of a] pound; **~stunde** *die* quarter of an hour; **~stündig** *Adj.* quarter-of-an-hour; fifteen-minute; **~stündlich** ❶ *Adj.* quarter-hourly; every quarter of an hour *postpos.;* ❷ *adv.* every quarter of an hour; **~ton** *der; Pl.* **~töne** *(Musik)* quarter tone

***vierte·mal, *vierten·mal** ⇒ **Mal¹**

**viertens** /'fi:ɐ̯tn̩s/ *Adv.* fourthly; ⇒ *auch* **zweitens**

**Viertonner** *der;* **~s, ~:** four-tonner

**viertürig** /-ty:rɪç/ *Adj.* four-door *attrib.;* **~ sein** have four doors

**Vierung** *die;* **~, ~en** *(Archit.)* crossing

**Vier·viertel·takt** /-'---/ *der (Musik)* four-four time

**Vierwaldstätter See**, *(schweiz.:)* **Vierwaldstättersee** *der* Lake Lucerne

**vier·wöchig** *Adj.* four-week [-long]

**vier-** /'fɪr-/: **~zehn**: *Kardinalz.* ▶ 76, ▶ 752, ▶ 841 fourteen; ⇒ *auch* **achtzehn**; **~zehnjährig** *Adj. (14 Jahre alt)* fourteen-year-old *attrib.;* fourteen years old *pred.; (14 Jahre dauernd)* fourteen-year *attrib.*

**vierzehnt...** /'fɪr-/ *Ordinalz.* ▶ 207 fourteenth; ⇒ *auch* **acht...**

**vier-** /'fɪr-/: **~zehn·tägig** *Adj.* two-week; **unser ~zehntägiger Urlaub** our two-week *or* two weeks' *or* fortnight's holiday; **~zehn·täglich** ❶ *Adj.* fortnightly; ❷ *adv.* fortnightly; every two weeks

**vierzig** /'fɪrtsɪç/ *Kardinalz.* ▶ 76, ▶ 841 forty; ⇒ *auch* **achtzig**

**vierziger** /'fɪrtsɪgɐ/ *indekl. Adj.* **die ~ Jahre** the forties; ⇒ *auch* **achtziger**

**Vierziger¹** *der;* **~s, ~** Ⓐ *(40-jähriger)* forty-year-old; Ⓑ *(ugs.: Autobus)* number forty; Ⓒ *(Wein)* '40's vintage

**Vierziger²** *die;* **~, ~** *(ugs.)* Ⓐ *(Briefmarke)* forty-pfennig/-schilling *etc.* stamp; Ⓑ *(Zigarre)* forty-pfennig cigar; Ⓒ *(Glühbirne)* 40-watt bulb

**Vierziger³** *Pl.* forties; ⇒ *auch* **Achtziger³**

**Vierzigerin** /'----/ *die;* **~, ~nen** forty-year-old

**Vierziger·jahre** /'---'--/ *Pl.* ▶ 76, ▶ 207 forties *pl.*

**vierzig·jährig** /'fɪrtsɪç-/ *Adj. (40 Jahre alt)* forty-year-old *attrib.;* forty years old *pred.; (40 Jahre dauernd)* forty-year *attrib.*

**vierzigst...** /'fɪrtsɪçst .../ *Ordinalz.* ▶ 841 fortieth; ⇒ *auch* **acht...**

**Vierzig·stunden·woche** *die* forty-hour week

**vier-, Vier-: ~zimmer·wohnung** *die* four-room flat *(Brit.) or (Amer.)* apartment; **~zylinder** *der (ugs.)* four-cylinder; **~zylinder·motor** *der* four-cylinder engine

**Vietnam** /vi̯ɛt'nam/ *(das);* **~s** Vietnam

**Vietnamese** /vi̯ɛtna'me:zə/ *der;* **~n, ~n**, **Vietnamesin**, *die;* **~, ~nen** Vietnamese

**vietnamesisch** ▶ 696 ❶ *Adj.* Vietnamese. ❷ *adv.* **wir waren ~ essen** we went to a Vietnamese restaurant *or* for a Vietnamese meal; ⇒ *auch* **deutsch**; **Deutsch**; **Deutsche²**

**Vietnamisierung** *die;* **~:** Vietnamization

**Vietnam·krieg** *der* Vietnam war

**vif** /vi:f/ *(veralt.)* ❶ *Adj.* lively; brisk. ❷ *adv.* briskly

**Vigil** /vi'gi:l/ *die;* **~, ~ien** *(kath. Kirche)* vigil

**Vignette** /vɪn'jɛtə/ *die;* **~, ~n** vignette

**Vikar** /vi'ka:ɐ̯/ *der;* **~s, ~e**, **Vikarin** *die;* **~, ~nen** Ⓐ *(kath. Kirche)* locum tenens; Ⓑ *(ev. Kirche)* ≈ [trainee] curate

**Viktimologie** /vɪktimologi:/ *die;* **~:** victimology *no art.*

**Viktoria** /vɪk'to:ri̯a/ *(die)* Victoria

**viktorianisch** ❶ *Adj.* Victorian. ❷ *adv.* in a Victorian manner

**Villa** /'vɪla/ *die;* **~, Villen** villa

**Villen·viertel** *das* exclusive residential district

**Vinaigrette** /vinɛ'grɛtə/ *die;* **~, ~n** vinaigrette [dressing]

**Viola** /'vi̯o:la/ *die;* **~, Violen** *(Musik)* viola

**violett** /vi̯o'lɛt/ purple; violet

**Violett** *das;* **~s, ~e** *od. ugs.* **~s** purple; violet; *(im Spektrum)* violet

**Violine** /vi̯o'li:nə/ *die;* **~, ~n** *(Musik)* violin

**Violinist** *der;* **~en, ~en, Violinistin**, *die;* **~, ~nen** violinist

**Violin-: ~konzert** *das* violin concerto; **~schlüssel** *der* treble clef

**Violon·cello** /vi̯olɔn'tʃɛlo/ *das* violoncello

**Viper** /'vi:pɐ/ *die;* **~, ~n** viper; adder

**Viren** ⇒ **Virus**

**Virologe** *der;* **~n, ~n** ▶ 159 virologist

**Virologie** /virolo'gi:/ *die;* **~:** virology *no art.*

**Virologin** *die;* **~, ~nen** ▶ 159 virologist

**virtuell** /vɪr'tu̯ɛl/ ❶ *Adj.* Ⓐ potential; Ⓑ *(DV, Optik)* virtual ‹memory, image;› **~e Wirklichkeit** virtual reality. ❷ *adv.* virtually

**virtuos** /vɪr'tu̯o:s/ ❶ *Adj.* virtuoso ‹performance etc.›. ❷ *adv.* in a virtuoso manner

**Virtuose** /vɪr'tu̯o:zə/ *der;* **~n, ~n, Virtuosin** *die;* **~, ~nen** virtuoso

**Virtuosität** *die;* **~:** virtuosity

**virulent** /viru'lɛnt/ *Adj. (Med., geh.)* virulent

**Virus** /'vi:rʊs/ *das;* **~, Viren** /'vi:rən/ virus

**Virus·infektion** *die* ▶ 474 virus infection

**Visa** ⇒ **Visum**

**Visage** /vi'za:ʒə/ *die;* **~, ~n** *(salopp abwertend)* mug *(coll.); (Miene)* expression

**vis-a-vis, vis-à-vis** /viza'vi:/ ❶ *Präp. mit Dat.* opposite. ❷ *Adv.* opposite; **~ von etw./jmdm.** opposite sth./sb.

**Visavis** /viza'vi:/ *das;* **~** /viza'vi:(s)/, **~** /viza'vi:s/ **mein ~:** the person opposite me; **jmdn. zum ~ haben** have sb. opposite one

**Visen** ⇒ **Visum**

**Visier** /vi'zi:ɐ̯/ *das;* **~s, ~e** Ⓐ *(am Helm)* visor; **das ~ herunterlassen** *(fig.)* put up one's guard; **mit offenem ~ kämpfen** *(fig.)* fight out in the open; Ⓑ *(an der Waffe)* backsight; **jmdn. ins ~ nehmen** *(fig. ugs.)* start to keep close tabs on sb.

**visieren** *itr. V.* take aim

**Vision** /vi'zi̯o:n/ *die;* **~, ~en** vision

**visionär** /vizi̯o'nɛ:ɐ̯/ ❶ *Adj.* visionary. ❷ *adv.* in a visionary manner

**Visite** /vi'zi:tə/ *die;* **~, ~n** Ⓐ round; **~ machen** do one's round; **um 10 Uhr war ~:** at 10 o'clock, the doctor did his round; Ⓑ *(veralt.: Besuch)* visit; **zu einer ~:** on a visit

**Visiten·karte** *die* visiting card; **diese gepflegten Grünanlagen sind eine gute ~ für die Stadt** these well-tended parks and gardens are a good advertisement for the town; **seine ~ hinterlassen** *(fig.)* leave one's visiting card *(joc.)*

**Visit·karte** *die (österr.)* ⇒ **Visitenkarte**

**viskos** /vɪs'ko:s/, **viskös** /vɪs'kø:s/ *Adj. (Chemie)* viscous

**Viskose** /vɪs'ko:zə/ *die;* **~** *(Chemie)* viscose

**Viskosität** *die;* **~** *(Chemie)* viscosity

**visuell** /vi'zu̯ɛl/ *(geh.)* ❶ *Adj.* visual. ❷ *adv.* visually

**Visum** /'vi:zʊm/ *das;* **~s, Visa** /'vi:za/ *od.* **Visen** /'vi:zn̩/ visa

**Visum·zwang** *der* visa requirement

**vital** /vi'ta:l/ ❶ *Adj.* Ⓐ *(voller Energie)* vital; energetic; vigorous; **~ sein** be full of life *or* vigour; Ⓑ *(wichtig)* vital. ❷ *adv. (voller Energie)* energetically

**Vitalität** *die;* **~:** vitality

**Vitamin** /vita'mi:n/ *das;* **~s, ~e** Ⓐ vitamin; Ⓑ **~ B** *(ugs. scherzh.)* connections *pl.;* **etw. durch ~ B kriegen** get sth. through knowing the right people

**vitamin-, Vitamin-: ~arm** *Adj.* ‹food, diet, etc.› low in vitamins; **~gehalt** *der* vitamin content; **~mangel** *der* vitamin deficiency;

V

**~reich** *Adj.* rich in vitamins *postpos.;* vitamin-rich; **~stoß** *der* large dose of vitamins; **~tablette** *die* vitamin tablet *or* pill

**Vitrine** /vi'tri:nə/ *die;* ~, **~n** display case; showcase; (*Möbel*) display cabinet

**Vivi·sektion** /vivi-/ *die* (*bes. Med.*) vivisection *no art.*

**vivi·sezieren** *tr. V.* (*bes. Med.*) vivisect

**Vize** /'fi:tsə/ *der;* **~s**, **~s** (*ugs.*) number two (*coll.*)

**Vize-** /'vi:tsə/: **~kanzler** *der*, **~kanzlerin** *die* vice-chancellor; **~könig** *der* viceroy; **~präsident** *der*, **~präsidentin** *die* vice-president

**Vlies** /fli:s/ *das;* **~es**, **~e** fleece

**V-Mann** /'fau-/ *der;* **~[e]s**, **V-Männer** *od.* **V-Leute** contact [man]; (*Informant*) informer

**Vogel** /'fo:gl/ *der;* **~s**, **Vögel** /'fø:gl/ (A) bird; **friss, ~, oder stirb!** (*ugs.*) [you can] like it or lump it! (*coll.*); **der ~ ist ausgeflogen** (*ugs.*) the bird has flown; **[mit etw.] den ~ abschießen** (*ugs.*) take the biscuit [with sth.] (*coll.*); **einen ~ haben** (*salopp*) be off one's rocker *or* head (*coll.*); **jmdm. den ~ zeigen** tap one's forehead at sb. (*as a sign that one thinks he/she is stupid*); (B) (*salopp, oft scherzh.: Mensch*) character; **ein seltsamer** *od.* **komischer ~:** an odd bird *or* character; (C) (*Fliegerspr.: Flugzeug*) machine

**Vogel-: ~bauer** *das od. der* birdcage; **~beer·baum** *der* rowan [tree]; mountain ash; **~beere** *die* rowan berry

**Vögelchen** /'fø:glçən/ *das;* **~s**, **~:** little *or* small bird

**Vogel-: ~dreck** *der* (*ugs.*) bird droppings *pl.;* **~ei** *das* bird's egg

**Vögelei** *die;* ~, **~en** (*derb*) screwing (*coarse*)

**vogel-, Vogel-: ~flug** *der* flight of the birds; **~frei** *Adj.* (*hist.*) outlawed; **jmdn./etw. für ~frei erklären** outlaw sb./sth.; **~futter** *das* bird food; **~häuschen** *das* bird house; **~käfig** *der* birdcage; **~kunde** *die* ornithology *no art.*

**vögeln** /'fø:gln/ *tr., itr. V.* (*derb*) screw (*coarse*); **jmdn./mit jmdm. ~:** screw sb.

**Vogel-: ~nest** *das* bird's nest; **~perspektive** *die* bird's-eye view; **Manhattan aus der ~perspektive** a bird's-eye view of Manhattan; **~scheuche** *die* scarecrow; **~schutz** *der* protection of birds; **~-Strauß-Politik** /--'----/ *die* head-in-the-sand policy; **~-Strauß-Politik treiben** pursue a policy of burying one's head in the sand; **~warte** *die* ornithological institute; **~zug** *der* bird migration

**Vogesen** /vo'ge:zn/ *Pl.* Vosges [Mountains]

**Vöglein** /'fø:glain/ *das;* **~s**, **~:** little bird

**Vogt** /fo:kt/ *der;* **~[e]s**, **Vögte** /'fø:ktə/ (*hist.*) (*eines Gutes, einer Burg usw.*) steward; (*Land~*) governor

**Vogtei** /fo:k'tai/ *die;* ~, **~en** (*hist.*) ⇒ **Vogt**: (*Amt*) stewardship; governorship; (*Sitz*) steward's office; governor's residence

**Vögtin** /'fø:ktın/ *die;* ~, **~nen** ⇒ **Vogt**

**Vokabel** /vo'ka:bl/ *die;* ~, **~n** *od. österr. auch das;* **~s**, **~:** word; vocabulary item; **~n** vocabulary *sing.;* vocab *sing.* (*Sch. coll.*)

**Vokabel·heft** *das* vocabulary *or* (*coll.*) vocab book

**Vokabular** *das;* **~s**, **~e** vocabulary

**vokal** *Adj.* (*Musik*) vocal

**Vokal** /vo'ka:l/ *der;* **~s**, **~e** (*Sprachw.*) vowel

**Vokalisation** *die;* ~, **~en** (*Musik*) vocalization

**vokalisch** (*Sprachw.*) ❶ *Adj.* vocalic; **mit ~em Anlaut** beginning with a vowel. ❷ *adv.* **~ auslauten** end in *or* with a vowel

**Vokalismus** *der;* ~ (*Sprachw.*) vocalism

**Vokalist** *der;* **~en**, **~en**, **Vokalistin** *die;* ~, **~nen** vocalist

**Vokal·musik** *die* vocal music

**Vokativ** /'vo:kati:f/ *der;* **~s**, **~e** (*Sprachw.*) vocative

**Volant** /vo'lã:/ *der, schweiz., österr. meist das;* **~s**, **~s** (A) (*an Kleidungsstücken*) flounce; (B) (*Lenkrad*) steering wheel

**Voliere** /vo'lie:rə/ *die;* ~, **~n** aviary

**Volk** /fɔlk/ *das;* **~[e]s**, **Völker** /'fœlkɐ/ (A) people; **das ~ der Kurden** the Kurdish people; **das irische und das deutsche ~:** the Irish and German peoples; (B) (*Bevölkerung*) people *pl.;* (*Nation*) people *pl.;* nation; **im ~e** among the people; **das ~ befragen** ask the people *or* nation; **das arbeitende/unwissende ~:** the working people/the ignorant masses *pl.;* (C) (*einfache Leute*) people *pl.;* **ein Mann aus dem ~:** a man of the people; **dem ~ aufs Maul schauen** listen to the way the ordinary man speaks; (D) (*ugs.: Leute*) people *pl.;* **viel junges ~:** many young people; **sich unters ~ mischen** go among the people; **etw. unters ~ bringen** make sth. [known to the] public; (E) (*Gruppe*) lot; crowd (*coll.*); **die Spatzen sind ein freches ~** (*fig.*) sparrows are a cheeky lot; (F) (*Bienen~*) colony

**Völkchen** /'fœlkçən/ *das;* **~s**, **~:** lot; crowd (*coll.*)

**völker-, Völker-: ~ball** *der: ball game in which two teams try to get the other side's players out by hitting them with a ball;* **~bund** *der* League of Nations; **~familie** *die* (*geh.*) family of nations; **~freundschaft** *die* international friendship *no art.;* **~kunde** *die* ethnology *no art.;* **~kundler** *der;* **~~s**, **~~**, **~kundlerin** *die;* **~~**, **~~nen** ethnologist; **~mord** *der* genocide; **~recht** *das* international law *no art.;* **~rechtlich** ❶ *Adj.* ‹issue, problem, etc.› of international law; **~rechtliche Verträge** agreements in *or* under international law; **die ~rechtliche Anerkennung eines Staates** the recognition of a state under international law; ❷ *adv.* ‹settle› in accordance with international law; ‹control, regulate› by international law; ‹recognize› under international law

**Völkerschaft** *die;* ~, **~en** people; (*Volksstamm*) tribe

**völker-, Völker-: ~verbindend** ‹idea, event› which brings nations together; **der ~verbindende Charakter des Sports** the ability of sport to bring nations together; **~verständigung** *die* international understanding; understanding between nations; **~wanderung** *die* (A) (*hist.*) migration of peoples; völkerwanderung; (B) (*ugs.*) mass migration; (*Zug*) mass progression

**völkisch** *Adj.* (*veralt., bes. ns.*) national

**volk·reich** *Adj.* heavily populated

**volks-, Volks-: ~abstimmung** *die* plebiscite; **~armee** *die* People's Army; **~armist** /-armıst/ *der;* **~~**, **~~**, **~armistin** *die;* **~~**, **~~nen** member of the People's Army; **~aufstand** *der* national uprising; **~ausgabe** *die* (*veralt.*) popular edition; **~befragung** *die* (*Politik*) referendum; **~begehren** *das* (*Politik*) petition for a referendum; **~belustigung** *die* public entertainment; **~brauch** *der* popular custom; **~bücherei** *die* public library; **~demokratie** people's democracy; **~deutsche** *der/die* ethnic German; **~dichtung** *die* (*Literaturw.*) folk literature *no indef. art.;* **eine ~dichtung** a piece of folk literature; **~eigen** *Adj.* (*DDR*) publicly *or* nationally owned; **~er Betrieb** publicly *or* nationally owned company; **~eigentum** *das* (*DDR*) national[ly owned] property; **~einkommen** *das* (*Wirtsch.*) national income; **~empfinden** *das:* **das [gesunde] ~empfinden** popular sentiment *or* opinion; **~entscheid** *der* (*Politik*) referendum; **~etymologie** *die* (*Sprachw.*) folk *or* popular etymology; **~feind** *der*, **~feindin** *die* enemy of the people; **~fest** *das* public festival; (*Jahrmarkt*) fair; **~front** *die* (*Politik*) popular front; **~gemeinschaft** *die* (*bes. ns.*) national community; **~gemurmel** *das* (*ugs. scherzh.*) mutterings *pl.;* **~genosse** *der*, **~genossin** *die* (*ns.*) national comrade; **~gerichts·hof** *der* (*ns.*) People's Court; **~gesundheit** *die* public health; **~glaube[n]** *der* (*Volksk.*) popular belief; **~held** *der*, **~heldin** *die* folk hero; **~hochschule** *die* adult education centre; **ein Kurs an der ~hochschule** an adult education class; **~initiative** *die* (*schweiz. Politik*) petition for a referendum; **~kammer** *die* (*DDR*) **die ~kammer** the Volkskammer; the People's Chamber; **~kunde** *die* folklore; **~kundler** *der;* **~~s**, **~~**, **~kundlerin** *die;* **~~**, **~~nen** folklorist; **~kundlich** *Adj.* folkloric; **~kundliche Bücher** books on folklore; **~kunst** *die* folk art; **~lied** *das* folk song; **~märchen** *das* folk tale; **~masse** *die* (A) **die ~massen** the people; the masses; (B) (*versammeltes Volk*) crowd [of people]; **~medizin** *die* folk medicine *no art.;* **~mund** *der:* **im ~mund wird das ... genannt** in the vernacular it is called ...; **~musik** *die* folk music; **~nahrungs·mittel** *das* staple food; **~polizei** *die* (*DDR*) People's Police; **~polizist** *der* (*DDR*) People's Policeman; member of the People's Police; **~polizistin** *die* (*DDR*) member of the People's Police; **~rede** *die* (*veralt.*) public address *or* speech; **~reden halten** (*ugs. abwertend*) make a long speech; **halt keine ~reden!** no speechifying! (*coll.*); no long speeches!; **~republik** *die* People's Republic; **die ~republik China** the People's Republic of China; **~schicht** *die* social class; **~schule** *die* (A) (*Bundesrepublik Deutschland und Schweiz veralt.*) *school providing basic primary and secondary education;* (B) (*österr.*) primary school; **~schüler** *der*, **~schülerin** *die* pupil at a 'Volksschule'; **~schul·lehrer** *der*, **~schul·lehrerin** *die* teacher at a 'Volksschule'; **~seele** *die* soul of the people; **die russische ~seele** the soul of the Russian people; **~seuche** *die* national epidemic; **~souveränität** *die* (*Politik*) sovereignty of the people; **~sprache** *die* vernacular [language]; **~stamm** *der* tribe; **~stück** *das* (*Theater*) folk play; **~sturm** *der:* (*ns.*) *German territorial army created towards the end of World War II to help defend the fatherland;* **~tanz** *der* folk dance; **~tracht** *die* traditional costume; (*eines Landes*) national costume; **~trauer·tag** *der* (*Bundesrepublik Deutschland*) national remembrance day; **~tribun** *der* (*hist.*) tribune [of the people]

**Volkstum** *das;* **~:** national character; (*Traditionen*) national customs and traditions

**volkstümlich** /'fɔlksty:mlıç/ ❶ *Adj.* popular; **ein ~er Politiker** a politician of the people *or* with the common touch; **der ~e Name einer Pflanze** the vernacular name of a plant; **~e Preise** popular prices; **eine ~e Einführung** an introduction readily comprehensible to the layman; **sich ~ geben** act the man/woman of the people. ❷ *adv.* **~ schreiben** write in terms readily comprehensible to the layman

**volks-, Volks-: ~verdummung** *die* (*ugs. abwertend*) deliberate deception of the public; **~verhetzung** *die* incitement of the people; **~vermögen** *das* (*Wirtsch.*) national wealth; **~versammlung** *die* (A) public meeting; (B) (*Parlament*) national assembly; **~vertreter** *der*, **~vertreterin** *die* representative of the people; **~vertretung** *die* representative body of the people; **~wahl** *die* (*DDR Politik*) general election; **~weise** *die* folk tune; **~weisheit** *die* old saying; **~wirt** *der*, **~wirtin** *die* economist; **~wirtschaft** *die* national economy; (*Fach*) economics *sing., no art.;* **~wirtschaftler** *der;* **~~s**, **~~**, **~wirtschaftlerin** *die;* **~~**, **~~nen** economist; **~wirtschaftlich** ❶ *Adj.* economic; ❷ *adv.* economically; **~wirtschafts·lehre** *die* economics *sing., no art.;* **~wohl** *das* welfare *or* well-being of the people; **~zählung** *die* [national] census; **~zorn** *der* public anger; **~zugehörigkeit** *die* ethnic origin

**voll** /fɔl/ ❶ *Adj.* (A) full; **der Saal ist ~ Menschen** the room is full of people; **ein Korb ~ [roter] Äpfel** a basket full of [red] apples; **~ von** *od.* **mit etw. sein** be full of sth.; **das Glas ist halb ~** the glass is half full; **beide Hände ~ haben** have both hands full; **~ [von] Dankbarkeit sein** be full of *or* filled with gratitude; **~ Güte/Tatkraft sein** be full of goodness/vigour; **den Kopf ~ haben** (*ugs.*) be preoccupied (**mit**

*old spelling (see note on page 1707)

V

with); **der Saal ist brechend/gestopft ~** (*ugs.*) the room is jam-packed (*coll.*); **die Straßen lagen ~ Schnee** (*ugs.*) the streets were deep in snow; **jeder bekam einen Korb ~:** everybody received a basketful; **mit ~en Backen kauen** eat with bulging cheeks; **aus dem Vollen schöpfen** draw on abundant *or* plentiful resources; **aus dem Vollen leben** *od.* **wirtschaften** live off *or* on the fat of the land; **~e Pulle** *od.* **~[es] Rohr** (*salopp*) ‹drive› flat out; **das Radio auf ~e Pulle drehen** (*salopp*) turn the radio on full blast (*coll.*); **~ laufen** fill up; **etw. ~ laufen lassen** fill sth. [up]; **sich ~ laufen lassen** (*salopp.*) get completely paralytic *or* canned (*Brit. sl.*); **~ schlagen** (*Seemannsspr.*) **become swamped; ~ pumpen** + *Akk.* pump up ‹tyre;› fill up ‹reservoir›; **sich mit Tabletten ~ pumpen** (*fig. ugs.*) pump oneself full of tablets; **~ schmieren** + *Akk.* (*beschmutzen*) smear; (*abwertend: beschreiben, bemalen*) scrawl/draw all over ‹wall etc.›; fill ‹exercise book etc.› with scrawl; **die Mauern mit Parolen ~ schmieren** scrawl *or* daub slogans all over the walls; **etw. ~ laden** load sth. up completely; **~ geladen** fully laden; **etw. ~ füllen** fill sth. up; **etw. ~ gießen** fill sth. [up]; **den Teppich/sich** (*Dat.*) **die Hose mit Wein ~ gießen** (*ugs.*) spill wine all over the carpet/one's trousers; **etw. ~ machen** fill sth. up; (*ugs.: beschmutzen*) get *or* make sth. dirty; **[sich** (*Dat.*)**] die Hosen ~ machen** mess one's pants; **um das Maß ~ zu machen** (*fig.*) to crown *or* cap it all; **etw. ~ packen** pack sth. full; **etw. ~ pfropfen** cram sth. full; **mit etw. ~ gepfropft sein** be crammed full of sth.; **das Zimmer ~ qualmen** (*ugs.*) fill the room with smoke; **sich** (*Dat.*) **den Bauch [mit etw.] ~ schlagen** (*salopp*) stuff oneself *or* one's face [with sth.] (*sl.*); **etw. ~ schreiben** fill sth. [with writing]; **jmdn/etw. ~ spritzen** splash/spray water *etc.* all over sb./sth.; **jmdn./etw. mit etw. ~ spritzen** splash/spray sth. all over sb./sth.; **etw. ~ stopfen** stuff *or* cram sth. full; **jmdn. mit Fakten ~ stopfen** (*ugs.*) pump sb. full of facts; **etw. ~ tanken** fill sth. up; **bitte ~ tanken** fill it up, please; **sich ~ fressen** ‹animal› eat its fill; (*derb*) ‹person› stuff oneself *or* one's face (*sl.*); **~ gefressen sein** (*derb*) ‹person› be stuffed (*sl.*); **sich ~ saufen** (*salopp*) get completely plastered (*sl.*); **sich ~ saugen** ‹leech› suck itself full (*mit* of); ‹sponge› become saturated (*mit* with); **sich ~ stopfen** (*ugs.*) stuff oneself *or* one's face; **er hat sich** (*Dat.*) **die Hosen ~ geschissen** he filled his pants; **er hat den ganzen Teppich ~ gepinkelt** he peed all over the carpet; **soll ich dir dein Glas noch mal ~ schenken?** do you want a refill?; can I give you a refill?; ⇒ *auch* **Lob; Mund;** [B] (*salopp: betrunken*) plastered (*sl.*); canned (*Brit. sl.*); [C] (*üppig*) full ‹figure, face, lip›; thick ‹hair›; ample ‹bosom›; **im Gesicht ~er geworden sein** have filled out *or* be fuller in the face; [D] (*ganz, ~ständig*) full; complete ‹seriousness, success›; **etw. mit ~em Recht tun** be quite right to do sth.; **einen ~en Tag/Monat warten** wait a full *or* whole day/month; **in ~er Fahrt** at full speed; **in ~em Gange sein** be in full swing; **die ~ Wahrheit** the full *or* whole truth; **mit dem ~en Namen unterschreiben** sign one's full name *or* one's name in full; **das Dutzend ist ~:** it's a round dozen; **~es/~stes Verständnis für jmdn. haben** have full/the fullest understanding for sb.; **~e Gewissheit über etw.** (*Akk.*) **haben** be completely certain about sth.; **der Mond ist ~:** the moon is full; **jmdn. nicht für ~ nehmen** not take sb. seriously; **in die Vollen gehen** (*ugs.*) go all out; **etw. ~ machen** (*vervollständigen*) complete sth.; **das Dutzend ~ machen** make up a round dozen; ⇒ *auch* **Brust a; Hals b; Kehle a;** [E] (*kräftig*) full, rich ‹taste, aroma›; rich ‹voice›; [F] **▸ 752** (*ugs.: bei Uhrzeitangaben*) **die Uhr schlug ~:** the clock struck the hour; **fünf nach ~:** five past the hour.
❷ *adv.* [A] (*völlig, ganz*) fully; **~ und ganz** completely; **etw. ~ auslasten** make full use of sth.; **~ verantwortlich für etw. sein** be wholly responsible *or* bear full responsibility for sth.; **~ arbeiten** (*ugs.*) work full-time; **er ist mir ~ in die Seite gefahren** (*salopp*) he drove straight into my side; [B] (*kräftig*) richly; **~ klingen** have a full, rich sound; ⇒ *auch* **voller**

***volladen** ⇒ **voll** 1 A

**Voll·akademiker** *der*, **Voll·akademikerin** *die* university graduate

**voll·auf** /*od.* '--/ *Adv.* completely; fully; **~ genügen/reichen** be quite enough

***vollaufen** ⇒ **voll** 1 A

**voll-, Voll-: ~automatisch** ❶ *Adj.* fully automatic; ❷ *adv.* fully automatically; **~bad** *das* bath; **~bart** *der* full beard; **~bärtig** *Adj.* ‹man› with a full beard; **~beschäftigung** *die* (*Wirtsch.*) full employment *no art.*; **~besitz** *der*: **im ~besitz seiner [geistigen und körperlichen] Kräfte sein** be in full possession of one's [mental and physical] faculties; **~bild** *das* (*Med.*) complete picture; **~blut** *das* [A] thoroughbred; [B] (*Med.*) whole blood; **~blut-** true; **er ist ein ~blutpolitiker/~blutschauspieler** he is a true politician/actor *or* a politician/actor through and through; **~blüter** /-bly:tɐ/ *der;* **~~s, ~~:** thoroughbred; **~blütig** *Adj.* thoroughbred ‹horse›; (*fig.*) full-blooded ‹person›; **~bremsung** *die*: **eine ~bremsung machen** put the brakes full on; **~bringen** /-'--/ *unr. tr. V.* (*geh.*) accomplish; achieve; **es ist ~bracht** (*bibl.*) it is finished; **~busig** /-bu:zɪç/ full-bosomed; buxom; **~dampf** *der* (*Seemannsspr.*) full steam; **mit ~dampf** at full steam *or* speed; (*fig. ugs.*) flat out

**Völle·gefühl** /'fœlə-/ *das* feeling of fullness

**voll·enden** ❶ *tr. V.* complete; finish; **mit vollendetem** *od.* **dem vollendeten 16. Lebensjahr** on reaching the age of 16 *or* completing one's sixteenth year; **vollendeter Mord/Landesverrat** consummated murder/treason; **sein Leben ~** (*fig. geh. verhüll.*) pass away; depart this life; ⇒ *auch* **vollendet**. ❷ *refl. V.* (*geh.*) (*seinen Abschluss finden*) ‹process, transformation, etc.› reach its conclusion; (*vollkommen werden*) reach [its] completion

**vollendet** ❶ *Adj.* accomplished ‹performance›; perfect ‹gentleman, host, manners, reproduction›; **~e Gegenwart/Vergangenheit/Zukunft** (*Sprachw.*) perfect/pluperfect/future perfect; ⇒ *auch* **Tatsache**. ❷ *adv.* ‹play› in an accomplished manner; **~ schön sein** be perfectly beautiful

**vollends** /'fɔlɛnts/ *Adv.* completely; **~ für Behinderte ist das unzumutbar** for disabled people in particular *or* especially it is unreasonable

**Voll·endung** *die* [A] completion; **kurz vor der ~ stehen** be nearing completion; **mit/nach ~ des 65. Lebensjahres** on reaching the age of 65 *or* completing one's sixty-fifth year; [B] (*geh.: Krönung*) culmination; [C] (*Vollkommenheit*) perfection

**voller** *indekl. Adj.* full of; (*erfüllt von*) full of; filled with; **sein Anzug war ~ Flecken** his suit was covered with stains; **ein Leben ~ Arbeit** a life full of *or* filled with work; **~ Widersprüche sein** be full of contradictions

**Völlerei** /fœlə'rai/ *die;* **~, ~en** (*abwertend*) gluttony *no pl.*, *no art.*

**volley** /'vɔli/ *Adv.* (*bes. Fußball, Tennis*) on the volley

**Volley·ball** *der* volleyball

**voll-, Voll-: ~fett** *Adj.* full-fat; ***~|fressen** ⇒ **voll** 1 A; **~führen** /-'--/ *tr. V.* perform, execute ‹somersault, movement›; perform ‹dance, deed›; ***~|füllen** ⇒ **voll** 1 A; **~gas** *das*: **▸ 348** **~gas geben** put one's foot down; **~gas fahren** drive flat out; **mit ~gas** at full throttle; ***~|gießen** ⇒ **voll** 1 A; **~gummi·reifen** *der* solid rubber tyre; **~idiot** *der*, **~idiotin** *die* (*salopp abwertend*) complete idiot (*coll.*)

**völlig** /'fœlɪç/ ❶ *Adj.* complete; total. ❷ *adv.* completely; totally; **du hast ~ recht** you are absolutely right; **das ist ~ unmöglich** that is absolutely impossible; **mit etw. ~ einverstanden sein** be in complete agreement with sth.

**voll-, Voll-: ~inhaltlich** ❶ *Adj.* complete; full; ❷ *adv.* fully; **~jährig** *Adj.* of age *pred.*; **~jährig werden** come of age; attain one's majority; **sie hat zwei ~jährige Kinder** she has two children who are of age; **~jährigkeit** *die;* **~~:** majority *no art.*; **~jurist** *der*, **~juristin** *die* [fully-]qualified lawyer (*who has attained the qualifications necessary to become a judge*); **~kasko·versicherung** *die* fully comprehensive insurance; **~klimatisiert** *Adj.* fully air-conditioned

**voll·kommen** ❶ *Adj.* [A] /-'-- *od.* '---/ (*vollendet*) perfect; [B] /'---/ (*vollständig*) complete; total. ❷ /'---/ *adv.* completely; totally

**Vollkommenheit** *die;* **~:** perfection

**voll-, Voll-: ~korn·brot** *das* wholemeal (*Brit.*) *or* (*Amer.*) wholewheat bread; ***~|machen** ⇒ **voll** 1A, D; **~macht** *die;* **~~, ~~en** [A] authority; **jmdm. [die] ~macht geben/erteilen** give/grant sb. power of attorney; **seine ~macht[en] überschreiten** exceed one's authority; **in ~macht** per procurationem; [B] (*Urkunde*) power of attorney; **~mast** *Adv.* (*Seemannsspr.*) full mast; **auf ~mast** at full mast; **~mast flaggen** hoist a flag/flags to full mast; **~matrose** *der* able-bodied seaman; **~milch** *die* full-cream milk; **~milch·schokolade** *die* full-cream milk chocolate; **~mond** *der* full moon; **es ist/wir haben heute ~mond** there is a full moon tonight; **bei ~mond** at full moon; **~mond·gesicht** *das* (*ugs.*) moon face; **~mundig** ❶ *Adj.* [A] (**~** *im Geschmack*) full-bodied ‹wine, flavour, etc.›; [B] (*abwertend: wichtigtuerisch*) pompous; ❷ *adv.* (*abwertend: wichtigtuerisch*) pompously; **~narkose** *die* (*Med.*) general anaesthetic; **unter ~narkose** under a general anaesthetic; ***~|packen** ⇒ **voll** 1 A; **~pension** *die* full board *no art.*; ***~pfropfen** ⇒ **voll** 1 A; ***~|pumpen** ⇒ **voll** 1 A; ***~|qualmen** ⇒ **voll** 1 A; **~rausch** *der*: **sich** (*Dat.*) **einen ~rausch antrinken** get completely drunk; **etw. im ~rausch tun** do sth. while completely drunk; **~reif** *Adj.* fully ripe; ***~|saufen** ⇒ **voll** 1 A; ***~|saugen** ⇒ **voll** 1 A; ***~|schlagen** ⇒ **voll** 1 A; **~schlank** *Adj.* with a fuller figure *postpos.*, *not pred.*; **ein Modell für ~schlanke Damen** a model for the fuller figure; **~schlank sein** have a fuller figure; ***~|schmieren** ⇒ **voll** 1 A; ***~|schreiben** ⇒ **voll** 1 A; **~sperrung** *die* (*Verkehrsw.*) complete closure; ***~|spritzen** ⇒ **voll** 1 A; **~ständig** ❶ *Adj.* complete; full ‹text, address, etc.›; **nicht ~ständig** incomplete; ❷ *adv.* completely; ‹list› in full; **~ständigkeit** *die;* **~~:** completeness; **der ~ständigkeit halber** for the sake of completeness; ***~|stopfen** ⇒ **voll** 1 A; **~streckbar** /-'--/ *Adj.* (*Rechtsw.*) enforceable; implementable ‹sentence›; **~strecken** /-'--/ *tr. V.* enforce ‹penalty, fine, law›; carry out ‹sentence› (**an** + *Dat.* on); **die ~streckende Gewalt** the executive [power]; **ein Testament ~strecken** execute a will; **~strecker** /-'--/ *der*, **~streckerin** *die;* **~~, ~~nen** (*des Gesetzes*) enforcer; (*eines Testaments*) executor; **~streckung** /-'--/ *die;* **~~, ~~en** ⇒ **vollstrecken**: enforcement; carrying out; execution

**Vollstreckungs·befehl** *der* (*Rechtsw.*) enforcement order; writ of execution

**voll-, Voll-: *~|tanken** ⇒ **voll** 1 A; **~tönend** ❶ *Adj.* sonorous; ❷ *adv.* sonorously; **~treffer** *der* direct hit; **ein ~treffer sein** (*fig.*) hit the bullseye; **~trunken** *Adj.* completely *or* blind drunk; **in ~trunkenem Zustand** in a state of total inebriation; **~trunkenheit** *die* total inebriation *or* intoxication; **~verb** *das* (*Sprachw.*) full verb; **~versammlung** *die* general meeting; **~waise** *die* orphan; **~wertig** *Adj.* full ‹job, member›; [fully] adequate ‹replace ment, substitute, nourishment, diet›; **~zählig** /-tsɛ:lɪç/ *Adj.* complete; **wir bitten um ~zähliges Erscheinen** we request everyone to attend; **sie waren ~zählig erschienen** they had turned out in full strength; **als wir ~zählig [versammelt] waren** when everyone was present

V

**voll·ziehen** ❶ *unr. tr. V.* carry out ‹instruction, action, will›; carry out ‹sentence› (**an** + *Dat.* on); execute, carry out ‹order›; perform ‹sacrifice, ceremony, sexual intercourse›; **die Ehe ~:** consummate the marriage; **die ~de Gewalt** the executive [power]; ❷ *unr. refl. V.* take place; **in ihm hatte sich eine Wandlung ~zogen** a change had come over him *or* taken place in him

**Voll·zug** *der* ⇒ **vollziehen** 1: carrying out; execution; performance; consummation

**Vollzugs-: ~anstalt** *die* penal institution; **~beamte** *der*, **~beamtin** *die* [prison] warder; **~meldung** *die: report that an instruction has been carried out*

**Volontär** /volɔn'tɛ:ɐ̯/ *der;* **~s, ~e** trainee (*receiving a low salary in return for training*)

**Volontariat** /volɔnta'ri̯a:t/ *das;* **~[e]s, ~e** Ⓐ (*Zeit*) period of training; Ⓑ (*Stelle*) traineeship; ⇒ *auch* **Volontär**

**Volontärin** *die;* **~, ~nen** ⇒ **Volontär**

**volontieren** *itr. V.* work as a trainee (**bei** with); ⇒ *auch* **Volontär**

**Volt** /vɔlt/ *das;* **~** *od.* **~[e]s, ~** (*Physik, Elektrot.*) volt

**Volte** /'vɔltə/ *die;* **~, ~n** Ⓐ (*beim Kartenspiel*) sleight of hand; **die** *od.* **eine ~ schlagen** (*fig.*) do a volte-face *or* an about-turn; Ⓑ (*Reiten, Fechten*) volte

**voltigieren** /vɔlti'ʒi:rən/ *itr. V.* perform acrobatics on horseback

**Volt·meter** *das;* **~s, ~** (*Elektrot.*) voltmeter

**Volumen** /vo'lu:mən/ *das;* **~s, ~** ▶ 611 volume

**Volumen-: ~gewicht** *das* ⇒ **Volumgewicht**; **~prozent** *das* ⇒ **Volumprozent**

**Volum·gewicht** *das* weight per [unit] volume

**voluminös** /volumi'nø:s/ *Adj.* voluminous; bulky ‹tome›

**Volum·prozent** *das* per cent by volume

**vom** /fɔm/ *Präp.* + *Art.* Ⓐ = **von dem;** Ⓑ (*räumlich*) from the; **links/rechts ~ Eingang** to the left/right of the entrance; **~ Stuhl aufspringen** jump up out of one's chair; Ⓒ (*zeitlich*) **~ Morgen bis zum Abend** from morning till night; **~ ersten Januar an** [as] from the first of January; Ⓓ (*zur Angabe der Ursache*) **das kommt ~ Rauchen/Alkohol** that comes from smoking/drinking alcohol; **müde ~ Arbeiten/wund ~ Liegen** tired from working/sore from lying; **jmdn. ~ Sehen kennen** know sb. by sight

**Vom·hundert·satz** *der* percentage

**von** /fɔn/ *Präp. mit Dat.* Ⓐ (*räumlich*) from; **nördlich/südlich ~ Mannheim** to the north/south of Mannheim; **rechts/links ~ mir** on my right/left; **~ hier an** *od.* (*ugs.*) **ab** from here on[ward]; **~ Mannheim aus** from Mannheim; **etw. ~ etw. [ab]wischen/[ab]brechen/[ab]reißen** wipe/break/tear sth. off sth.; ⇒ *auch* **aus** 2 C; **her** A; **vorn**[1]; Ⓑ ▶ 207 (*zeitlich*) from; **~ jetzt an** *od.* (*ugs.*) **ab** from now on; **~ heute/morgen an** [as] from today/tomorrow; starting today/tomorrow; **~ Kindheit an** from *or* since childhood; **in der Nacht ~ Freitag auf** *od.* **zu Samstag** during Friday night *or* the night of Friday to Saturday; **das Brot ist ~ gestern** it's yesterday's bread; ⇒ *auch* **her** B; **klein** 1 B; **Mal**[1]; Ⓒ (*anstelle eines Genitivs*) of; **ein Stück ~ dem Kuchen** a slice of the cake; **acht ~ hundert/zehn** eight out of a hundred/ten; **ein Teufel ~ einem Vorgesetzten** a devil of a boss (*coll.*); **die Stimme ~ Caruso** (*ugs.*) Caruso's voice; Ⓓ (*zur Angabe des Urhebers, der Ursache, beim Passiv*) by; **der Roman ist ~ Fontane** the novel is by Fontane; **müde ~ der Arbeit sein** be tired from work[ing]; **etw. ~ seinem Taschengeld kaufen** buy sth. with one's pocket money; **sie hat ein Kind ~ ihm** she has a child by him; ⇒ *auch* **wegen** 2; Ⓔ (*zur Angabe ~ Eigenschaften*) of; **eine Fahrt ~ drei Stunden** a three-hour drive; **Kinder [im Alter] ~ vier Jahren** children aged four; **~ bester Qualität** of the best quality; **ein Mann/eine Frau ~ Charakter** a man/woman of character; **~ größter Bedeutung/Wichtigkeit sein** be of the utmost importance; Ⓕ (*bestehend aus*) of; **ein Ring ~ Gold** a ring of gold; Ⓖ (*als Adelsprädikat*) von; **Alexander ~ Humboldt** Alexander von Humboldt; **mit einer ~ verheiratet sein** (*ugs.*) be married to a woman with a title; Ⓗ (*in Bezug auf*) **er ist ~ Beruf Lehrer** he is a teacher by profession; **klein ~ Statur sein** be small in stature; ⇒ *auch* **her** C; Ⓘ (*über*) about; **~ diesen Dingen spricht man besser nicht** it's better not to speak of such things ⇒ *auch* **Haus** G; **da~; wo~**

**von·einander** *Adv.* from each other *or* one another; **sich ~ trennen** separate *or* part from each other; **sie sind ~ enttäuscht** they are disappointed in each other *or* in one another; **sie halten viel ~:** they think highly of each other

**vonnöten** /fɔn'nø:tn̩/ *Adj. in* **~ sein** be necessary

**vonseiten** *Präp.* + *Gen.* **~ der Direktion** from the management side

**vonstatten** /fɔn'ʃtatn̩/ *Adv. in* **~ gehen** proceed; **der Umzug kann am 15. Juni ~ gehen** the removal can go ahead on 15 June

**Vopo**[1] /'fo:po/ *der;* **~s, ~s** (*ugs.*) ⇒ **Volkspolizist**

**Vopo**[2] *die;* **~** (*ugs.*) ⇒ **Volkspolizei**

**vor** /fo:ɐ̯/ ❶ *Präp. mit Dat.* Ⓐ (*räumlich*) in front of; (*weiter vorn*) ahead of; in front of; (*nicht ganz so weit wie*) before; (*außerhalb*) outside; **~ einem Hintergrund von ...** against a background of ...; **zwei Schritte ~ jmdm. gehen** walk two paces ahead of *or* in front of sb.; **kurz/200 m ~ der Abzweigung** just/200 m. before the turn-off; **~ der Stadt/den Toren der Stadt** outside the town/the gates of the town; **etw. ~ sich haben** (*fig.*) have sth. before one; **das liegt noch ~ mir** (*fig.*) I still have that to come *or* have that ahead of me; Ⓑ ▶ 752 (*zeitlich*) before; **~ Christus** before Christ; B C; **es ist fünf [Minuten] ~ sieben** it is five [minutes] to seven; Ⓒ (*bei Reihenfolge, Rangordnung*) before; **knapp ~ jmdm. siegen** win just ahead *or* in front of sb.; Ⓓ (*in Gegenwart von*) before; in front of; **etw. ~ Zeugen erklären** state sth. before *or* in the presence of witnesses; **sie tanzte ~ ausverkauftem Haus** she danced before *or* to a full house; Ⓔ (*aufgrund von*) with; **~ Freude strahlen** beam with joy; **~ Kälte zittern** shiver with cold; **~ Hunger/Durst umkommen** die of hunger/thirst; **~ Arbeit/Schulden nicht mehr aus und ein wissen** not know which way to turn for work/debts; Ⓕ **~ fünf Minuten/10 Jahren/Wochen** *usw.* five minutes/ten years/weeks ago; **heute/gestern/morgen ~ einer Woche** a week ago today/yesterday/tomorrow.
❷ *Präp. mit Akk.* in front of; **keinen Schritt ~ die Tür tun** *od.* **setzen** not set foot outside the door; **er fuhr bis ~ die Haustür** he drove right up to the front door; **~ sich hin** to oneself; **still ~ sich hin arbeiten** work away quietly; ⇒ *auch* **da~; wo~**.
❸ *Adv.* (*voran*) forward; **Freiwillige ~!** volunteers to the front!; **~ und zurück** backwards and forwards

**vor·ab** *Adv.* beforehand

**Vorab·druck** *der; Pl.* **~e** Ⓐ preprinting; Ⓑ (*gedruckter Text*) preprint

**Vor·abend** *der* evening before; (*fig.*) eve; **das war am ~:** that was the evening before

**Vor·ahnung** *die* premonition; presentiment; **dunkle/schlimme ~en** dark forebodings

**vor·an** /fo'ran/ ❶ *Adv.* (*vorwärts*) forward[s]. ❷ *Präp. mit Dat., nachgestellt* ahead; first; **dem Festzug ~:** at the head of the parade; **allem ~:** first and foremost

**voran-: ~|bringen** *unr. tr. V.* make progress with ‹work, project, etc.›; **die Sache des Friedens ~bringen** advance *or* further the cause of peace; **jmdn./etw. ein gutes Stück ~bringen** bring sb./sth. a good step further; **~|gehen** *unr. itr. V.; mit sein* Ⓐ go first *or* ahead; **jmdm. ~gehen** go ahead of sb.; **[jmdm.] mit gutem Beispiel ~gehen** (*fig.*) set [sb.] a good example; Ⓑ (*Fortschritte machen*) make progress; **rasch/nur schleppend ~gehen** make rapid/only slow progress; **es geht mit der Arbeit/dem Schreiben nicht [so recht] ~:** the work/writing is not making [much] progress; Ⓒ ⇒ **vorausgehen** B; **~|kommen** *unr. itr. V.; mit sein* Ⓐ make headway; **gut ~kommen** make good headway *or* progress; Ⓑ (*Fortschritte machen*) make progress; **die Arbeit kommt gut/nicht ~:** the work is making good progress *or* coming along well/not making any progress; **beruflich ~kommen** get on in one's job

**Vor·ankündigung** *die* advance announcement; **ohne ~:** without any advance *or* prior notice

**Vor·anmeldung** *die* booking; (*für einen Kursus*) registration

**voran-: ~|schreiten** *unr. itr. V.; mit sein* (*geh.*) Ⓐ lead the way; Ⓑ (*fortschreiten*) progress; advance; **~|stellen** *tr. V.* place *or* put first; **dem Buch ist eine Einleitung ~gestellt** the book starts *or* begins with an introduction; **~|treiben** *unr. tr. V.* push ahead

**Vor·anzeige** *die* advance announcement

**Vor·arbeit** *die* preliminary work *no pl.*

**vor|arbeiten** ❶ *itr. V.* put in some hours in advance; **einen Tag/zwei Tage ~:** work a day/two days in advance. ❷ *refl. V.* work one's way forward; **sich auf den zweiten Platz ~:** work one's way up to second place

**Vor·arbeiter** *der* foreman

**Vor·arbeiterin** *die* forewoman

**vor·aus** ❶ /-'-/ *Präp. mit Dat., nachgestellt* in front; **jmdm. weit ~ sein** be a long way in front *or* far ahead of sb.; **jmdm./seiner Zeit ~ sein** (*fig.*) be ahead of sb./one's time. ❷ *Adv.* Ⓐ **im Voraus** /'--/ in advance; Ⓑ (*Seemannsspr.*) ahead; **Volldampf ~!** full steam ahead!

**voraus-, Voraus-: ~|ahnen** *tr. V.* have a presentiment of; **~ahnen, dass ...** have a presentiment that ...; **~|berechnen** *tr. V.* (*auch fig.*) calculate in advance; **~|bestimmen** *tr. V.* determine in advance; **~|eilen** *itr. V.; mit sein* hurry on ahead; **jmdm. ~eilen** hurry on ahead of sb.; **~|fahren** *unr. itr. V.; mit sein:* ⇒ **vorfahren** C; **~|gehen** *unr. itr. V.; mit sein* Ⓐ go [on] ahead; **ihm geht der Ruf ~, sehr streng zu sein** (*fig.*) he has the reputation of being very strict; Ⓑ (*zeitlich*) **einem Ereignis ~gehen** precede an event; **dem Entschluss gingen lange Überlegungen ~:** the decision was preceded by *or* followed lengthy deliberations; **~gegangene Misserfolge** previous failures; **wie im Vorausgehenden bereits dargestellt worden ist** as has already been shown above; **~|haben** *unr. tr. V.* **jmdm./einer Sache etw. ~haben** have the advantage of sth. over sb./sth.; **er hat ihm [an diplomatischem Geschick] viel/nichts ~:** he has a great/no advantage over him [with regard to diplomatic skill]; **~|laufen** *unr. itr. V.; mit sein* run on ahead *or* in front; **~|planen** ❶ *itr. V.* plan ahead; ❷ *tr. V.* **etw. ~planen** plan sth. in advance; **~sage** *die* ⇒ **Vorhersage**; **~|sagen** *tr. V.* predict; **jmdm. die Zukunft ~sagen** foretell *or* predict sb.'s future; **~|schauen** *itr. V.* look ahead; **~schauende Planung/Politik** foresighted planning/policy; **~|schicken** *tr. V.* Ⓐ send [on] ahead; Ⓑ (*einleitend sagen*) say first; **ich muss folgendes ~schicken** I must start *or* begin by saying the following; **~sehbar** *Adj.* foreseeable; **~|sehen** *unr. tr. V.* foresee; **das war [doch] ~zusehen/ließ sich nicht ~sehen** that was foreseeable/unforeseeable; **~|setzen** *tr. V.* Ⓐ (*als gegeben ansehen*) assume; **etw. als bekannt ~setzen** assume sth. is known; **er setzte stillschweigend/als selbstverständlich ~, dass ...** he took it for granted that ...; **Ihr Einverständnis ~setzend** assuming *or* provided that you agree; **~gesetzt, [dass] ...** provided [that] ...; Ⓑ (*erfordern*) require ‹skill, experience, etc.›; presuppose ‹good organization, planning, etc.›; **~setzung** *die;* **~, ~,**

*old spelling (see note on page 1707)

**~~en** Ⓐ (*Annahme*) assumption; (*Prämisse*) premiss; Ⓑ (*Vorbedingung*) prerequisite; **unter der ~setzung, dass ...** on condition *or* on the pre-condition that ...; **etw. zur ~setzung haben/machen** have sth. as/make sth. a pre-condition *or* prerequisite; **er hat die besten ~setzungen für den Job** he has the best qualifications for the job; **~sicht** *die* foresight; **aller ~sicht nach** in all probability; **in weiser ~sicht** (*scherzh.*) with great foresight; **~sichtlich** ❶ *Adj.* anticipated; expected; ❷ *adv.* probably; **der Abflug wird sich ~sichtlich verzögern** the departure is expected to be delayed; **~zahlung** *die* advance payment

**Vor·bau** *der; Pl.* **~ten** Ⓐ porch; Ⓑ (*salopp scherzh.: Busen*) [well-developed] bust; Ⓒ *s.* **Lenkervorbau**

**vor|bauen** *itr. V.* make provision; **der kluge Mann baut vor** (*Spr.*) a wise man makes provision for the future; **um vorzubauen, habe ich gleich gesagt, dass ...** to avoid any problems, I said straight away that ...

**Vor·bedacht** *der: in* **mit** *od.* (*seltener*) **aus ~:** intentionally; deliberately

**Vor·bedingung** *die* [pre]condition; **~en stellen** set preconditions

**Vorbehalt** /ˈfo:ɐ̯bəhalt/ *der;* **~[e]s, ~e** reservation; **etw. nur unter ~ tun** do sth. only with reservations; **unter dem ~, dass ...** with the reservation that ...; **ohne ~:** unreservedly; without reservation

**vor|behalten** *unr. tr. V.* reserve; **sich** (*Dat.*) **etw. ~:** reserve oneself sth.; reserve sth. [for oneself]; **sich** (*Dat.*) **das Recht ~, etw. zu tun** reserve the right to do sth.; **„Änderungen ~"** 'subject to alterations'; **alle Rechte ~** (*Druckw.*) all rights reserved; **jmdm. ~ sein/bleiben** ‹decision› be left [up] to sb.; ‹discovery, revision work, etc.› be left to sb.; **die ersten Sitzreihen waren den Ehrengästen ~:** the first rows of seats were reserved for the guests of honour

**vorbehaltlich** *Präp. mit Gen.* (*Papierdt.*) subject to

**vorbehalt·los** ❶ *Adj.* unreserved; unconditional. ❷ *adv.* unreservedly; without reservation[s]

**vor·bei** *Adv.* Ⓐ (*räumlich*) past; by; **der Wagen war schon [an uns] ~:** the car was already past [us] *or* had already gone past *or* by [us]; **an etw.** (*Dat.*) **~:** past sth.; **[wieder] ~!** missed [again]!; Ⓑ ▶ 752 (*zeitlich*) past; over; (*beendet*) finished; over; **es ist acht Uhr ~** (*ugs.*) it is past *or* gone eight o'clock; **~ ist ~:** what's past is past; ⇒ *auch* **aus** 2 A

**vorbei-: ~|bringen** *unr. tr. V.* (*ugs.*) drop off; drop round with; **kannst du mir das Buch heute Abend ~bringen?** can you drop the book off at my place this evening?; **~|dürfen** *unr. itr. V.* (*ugs.*) be allowed past *or* by; **an jmdm./etw. ~dürfen** be allowed past *or* by sb./sth.; **darf/dürfte ich mal bitte ~?** can/could I come *or* get past *or* by, please?; **~|fahren** ❶ *unr. itr. V.; mit sein* Ⓐ drive/ride past; pass; **an jmdm. ~fahren** drive/ride past *or* pass sb.; Ⓑ (*ugs.: einen kurzen Besuch machen*) **[bei jmdm./der Post] ~fahren** drop in (*coll.*) [at sb.'s/at the post office]; ❷ *tr. V.* (*ugs.*) **kannst du mich schnell beim Bahnhof ~fahren?** can you just run me to the station?; (*absetzen*) can you just drop me off at the station?; **~|führen** *itr. V.* ‹path, road, etc.› go *or* run past; **an etw.** (*Dat.*) **~führen** go *or* run past sth.; **daran führt kein Weg ~** (*fig.*) there's no getting around it; **~|gehen** *unr. itr. V.; mit sein* Ⓐ pass; go past; **an jmdm./etw. ~gehen** pass *or* go past sb./sth.; **der Schuss/Schlag ist [am Ziel] ~gegangen** the shot/blow missed [its mark *or* target]; **an der Wirklichkeit ~gehen** (*fig.*) miss the truth; **im Vorbeigehen** (*auch fig.*) in passing; Ⓑ (*ugs.: einen kurzen Besuch machen*) **[bei jmdm./der Post] ~gehen** drop in (*coll.*) [at sb.'s/at the post office]; Ⓒ (*vergehen*) pass; **keine Gelegenheit ~gehen lassen** not let an *or* let no opportunity slip *or* pass; Ⓓ (*Sport*) **an jmdm. ~gehen** pass *or* go past *or* overtake sb.; **~|kommen** *unr. itr. V.; mit sein* Ⓐ pass; **an etw.** (*Dat.*) **~kommen** pass sth.; Ⓑ (*ugs.: einen kurzen Besuch machen*); **[bei jmdm.] ~kommen** drop in (*coll.*) [at sb.'s]; Ⓒ (*~gehen, -fahren können*) get past *or* by; **daran kommt man nicht ~** (*fig.*) there's no getting around *or* away from that; **~|können** *unr. itr. V.* (*ugs.*) be able to get past *or* by; **~|lassen** *unr. tr. V.* (*ugs.*) let past *or* by; **jmdn. an etw.** (*Dat.*) **~lassen** let sb. past *or* by sth.; **~|marschieren** *itr. V.; mit sein* march past; **an jmdm./etw. ~marschieren** march past sb./sth.; **~|müssen** *unr. itr. V.* (*ugs.*) have to pass *or* go past; **an jmdm./etw. ~müssen** have to pass *or* go past sb./sth.; **~|planen** *itr. V.* **an etw.** (*Dat.*) **~planen** plan without regard to sth.; **~|reden** *itr. V.* **an etw.** (*Dat.*) **~reden** talk round sth. without getting to the point; **am Wesentlichen ~reden** miss the essential point; **aneinander ~reden** talk at cross purposes; **~|schießen** ❶ *unr. itr. V.* Ⓐ (*danebenschießen*) miss; **[am Ziel] ~schießen** miss [the target]; Ⓑ *mit sein* (*~fahren, -fliegen*) ‹car etc.› shoot past; **an jmdm./etw. ~schießen** shoot past sb./sth.; ❷ *unr. tr. V.* **den Ball am Tor ~schießen** shoot wide of the goal; **~|ziehen** *unr. itr. V.; mit sein* pass by; (*überholen*) pass; go past; overtake; **an jmdm./etw. ~ziehen** pass by sb./sth.; (*jmdn./etw. überholen*) pass *or* go past *or* overtake sb.

**vor·belastet** *Adj.* handicapped (**durch** by); **erblich ~ sein** have an inherited defect

**Vor·bemerkung** *die* preliminary remark

**vor|bereiten** *tr. V.* Ⓐ prepare; **jmdn./sich auf** *od.* **für etw. ~:** prepare sb./oneself for sth.; **sich [in Latein] nicht vorbereitet haben** not be prepared [in Latin]; **auf diese Reaktion war ich nicht vorbereitet!** I was unprepared for that reaction!; Ⓑ (*die Vorarbeiten machen für*) prepare for; **ein Fest/eine Reise ~:** prepare for *or* make preparations for a party/trip

**Vor·bereitung** *die;* **~, ~en** preparation; **~en [für** *od.* **zu etw.] treffen** make preparations for sth.; **in ~ sein** be in preparation

**Vor·besitzer** *der,* **Vor·besitzerin** *die* previous owner

**Vor·besprechung** *die* Ⓐ preliminary discussion[s *pl.*]; Ⓑ (*Rezension*) advance review

**vor|bestellen** *tr. V.* order in advance

**Vor·bestellung** *die* advance order

**vor·bestimmt** *Adj.* predestined

**vor·bestraft** *Adj.* (*Amtsspr.*) with a previous conviction/previous convictions *postpos., not pred.;* **[zweimal/mehrfach] ~ sein** have [two/several] previous convictions

**Vor·bestrafte** *der/die; adj. Dekl.* person with a previous conviction/previous convictions

**vor|beten** ❶ *itr. V.* lead the prayer/prayers. ❷ *tr. V.* Ⓐ **jmdm. das Vaterunser** *usw.* **~:** say the Lord's Prayer *etc.* [aloud] to sb.; Ⓑ (*ugs.*) reel off ‹list, text, explanation, etc.›

**Vorbeuge·haft** *die* preventive custody

**vor|beugen** ❶ *tr. V.* bend ‹head, upper body› forward; **sich ~:** lean *or* bend forward. ❷ *itr. V.* **einer Sache** (*Dat.*) *od.* **gegen etw. ~:** prevent sth.; **einer Gefahr ~:** avert a danger; **~de Maßnahmen** preventive measures; **Vorbeugen ist besser als Heilen** (*Spr.*) prevention is better than cure (*prov.*)

**Vor·beugung** *die* prevention (**gegen** of); **zur ~:** as a preventive

**Vorbeugungs·maßnahme** *die* preventive measure

**Vor·bild** *das* model; **jmdm. als ~ dienen** serve sb. as a model; **jmdm. ein gutes ~ sein** be a good example to sb.; set sb. a good example; **sich** (*Dat.*) **jmdn./etw. zum ~ nehmen** take sb. as a model *or* model oneself on sb./take sth. as a model

**vor·bildlich** ❶ *Adj.* exemplary. ❷ *adv.* in an exemplary way *or* manner

**Vor·bildung** *die:* **die nötige/theoretische ~ besitzen** have the necessary knowledge and training/the theoretical background; **über eine mangelhafte ~ verfügen** have inadequate knowledge and training; have an inadequate background

**vor|bohren** *tr. V.* pre-drill

**Vor·bote** *der,* **Vor·botin** *die* harbinger

**vor|bringen** *unr. tr. V.* say; **eine Frage/Forderung/ein Anliegen ~:** ask a question/make a demand/express a desire; **Argumente ~:** present *or* state arguments; **Beweise ~:** produce evidence; **dagegen lässt sich viel ~:** there's much to be said against it

**vor·christlich** *Adj.* pre-Christian; **das dritte ~e Jahrhundert** the third century before Christ

**Vor·dach** *das* canopy

**vor|datieren** *tr. V.* Ⓐ postdate ‹cheque, letter, etc.›; Ⓑ (*zurückdatieren*) antedate

**vor|dem** /*od.* '-–/ *Adv.* Ⓐ (*geh.: zuvor*) before; Ⓑ (*veralt.: früher*) in [the] olden days

**Vor·denker** *der,* **Vor·denkerin** *die* (*Politikjargon*) guiding intellectual force

**vorder...** /ˈfɔrdɐ.../ *Adj.* front; **die ~en Reihen** the front rows; **die ~sten Reihen** the rows at the very front; **der V~e Orient** the Middle East

**vorder-, Vorder-: ~achse** *die* front axle; **~ansicht** *die* front view; **~asien** (*das*) the Middle East; the Near East; **~bein** *das* foreleg; **~gebäude** *das* front building; **~grund** *der* foreground; **im ~grund stehen** (*fig.*) be prominent *or* to the fore; **bei seiner Entscheidung standen diese Überlegungen im ~grund** (*fig.*) these considerations were uppermost in his mind when taking his decision; **etw. in den ~grund stellen** *od.* **rücken** (*fig.*) give priority to sth.; place special emphasis on sth.; **in den ~grund treten** *od.* **rücken** (*fig.*) come to the fore; **sich in den ~grund spielen** *od.* **schieben** *od.* **drängen** (*fig.*) push oneself forward; **~gründig** /-gryndɪç/ ❶ *Adj.* superficial; ❷ *adv.* superficially; **~hand** *Adv.* for the time being; for the present; **~haus** *das* house facing the street/square *etc.*

**Vorder·indien** (*das*) the Indian Peninsula

**vorder-, Vorder-: ~lader** *der;* **~~s, ~~** (*Waffenkunde*) muzzle-loader; **~lastig** *Adj.* bow-heavy ‹ship›; nose-heavy ‹aircraft›; **~lauf** *der* (*Jägerspr.*) foreleg; **~mann** *der* person in front; **ihr/sein ~mann** the person in front of her/him; **jmdn. auf ~mann bringen** (*ugs.*) lick sb. into shape; **den Garten/Haushalt auf ~mann bringen** (*ugs.*) get the garden/house shipshape; **~pfote** *die* front paw; **~rad** *das* front wheel; **~rad·antrieb** *der* front-wheel drive; **~reifen** *der* front tyre; **~seite** *die* front; (*einer Münze, Medaille*) obverse; **~sitz** *der* front seat

**vorderst...** ⇒ **vorder...**

**Vorder-: ~steven** *der* (*Seemannsspr.*) stem; **~teil** *das od. der* front [part]; **~zahn** *der* front tooth

**vor|drängen** *refl. V.* push [one's way] forward *or* to the front; (*fig.*) push oneself forward; **sich bis an etw.** (*Akk.*) **~:** push [one's way] forward to sth.; **sich an der Kasse/in der Schlange ~:** push to the front at the check-out/push to the front of the queue *or* (*Amer.*) line

**vor|dringen** *unr. itr. V.; mit sein* push forward; advance; **in den Weltraum ~:** push forward into space; **bis zu jmdm. ~** (*fig.*) reach sb.; get as far as sb.

**vor·dringlich** ❶ *Adj.* Ⓐ priority *attrib.* ‹treatment›; **eine ~e Angelegenheit** a matter of priority; Ⓑ (*dringlich*) urgent; **unser ~stes Anliegen ist es, ...** our main *or* overriding concern is ... ❷ *adv.* Ⓐ as a matter of priority; Ⓑ as a matter of urgency

**Vor·druck** *der; Pl.* **~e** form

**vor·ehelich** *Adj.* premarital

**vor·eilig** ❶ *Adj.* rash. ❷ *adv.* rashly; **~ den Schluss ziehen, dass ...** jump to the conclusion that ...

**vor·einander** *Adv.* Ⓐ one in front of the other; Ⓑ (*einer dem anderen gegenüber*) opposite each other; face to face; **Geheimnisse ~ haben/Gefühle ~ verbergen** have secrets/hide feelings from each other; **Hochachtung/Furcht ~ haben** have great respect for each other/be afraid of each other

V

**vor·eingenommen** *Adj.* prejudiced; biased; **für/gegen jmdn. ~ sein** be prejudiced in sb.'s favour/against sb.; **jmdm. gegenüber ~ sein** be prejudiced towards sb.

**Vor·eingenommenheit** *die;* ~, ~**en** prejudice; bias; **politische ~:** political bias

**Vor·einstellung** *die* (*DV*) default

**vorenthalten** *unr. tr. V.*; **ich enthalte vor** (*od. seltener:* **vorenthalte**), **vorenthalten, vorzuenthalten: jmdm. etw. ~:** withhold sth. from sb.; **jmdm. eine Nachricht ~:** keep *or* withhold news from sb.

**Vor·entscheidung** *die* preliminary decision; **mit diesem Tor war eine ~ gefallen** this goal decided the course of the match

**vor·erst** /*od.* -'-/ *Adv.* for the present; for the time being

**Vor·essen** *das* (*schweiz.*) stew

**vor|exerzieren** *tr. V.* (*ugs.*) demonstrate

**vorfabriziert** *adj.* pre-fabricated; (*fig.*) ready-made ‹opinion, solution›

**Vorfahr** /-fa:ɐ̯/ *der;* ~**en** *od. selten* ~**s**, ~**en**, **Vorfahre** *der;* ~**n**, ~**n** forefather; ancestor

**vor|fahren** *unr. itr. V.*; *mit sein* **A** (*ankommen*) drive/ride up; **vor dem Hotel/Haus ~:** drive/ride up outside the hotel/house; **B** (*weiter nach vorn fahren*) ‹person› drive *or* move forward; ‹car› move forward; **C** (*vorausfahren*) drive *or* go on ahead

**Vorfahrin** *die;* ~, ~**nen** [female] ancestor

**Vor·fahrt** *die* (*Verkehrsw.*) right of way; „~ **beachten/gewähren!**" 'give way'; **weil er die ~ nicht beachtete** because he failed to give way; **jmdm. die ~ nehmen** fail to give way to sb.

**Vorfahrt[s]-:** ~**schild** *das* (*Verkehrsw.*) right of way sign; ~**straße** *die* main road; ~**zeichen** *das* (*Verkehrsw.*) ⇒ ~**schild**

**Vor·fall** *der* **A** incident; occurrence; **B** ▶ 474 (*Med.*) prolapse

**vor|fallen** *unr. itr. V.*; *mit sein* **A** (*sich ereignen*) happen; occur; **ist etwas [Besonderes] vorgefallen?** has anything [special] happened?; **B** (*nach vorn fallen*) fall forward

**vor|feiern** *tr., itr. V.* celebrate early *or* ahead of time

**Vor·feld** *das* **A** (*eines Flughafens*) apron; **B** (*Basketball*) front court; **C** (*fig.*) **im ~:** in advance; **im ~ des Parteitages** in the run-up to the party conference

**Vor·film** *der* supporting film

**vor|finden** ❶ *unr. tr. V.* find. ❷ *unr. refl. V.* be to be found

**vor|flunkern** *tr. V.* (*ugs.*) **jmdm. ~, dass ...** spin sb. a yarn that ...; **sie flunkerte ihm irgendetwas vor** she told him some fib or other

**Vor·form** *die* early form

**Vor·freude** *die* anticipation; **voller ~ auf etw.** (*Akk.*) **sein** be full of [happy] anticipation of sth.

**Vor·frühling** *der* early spring

**vor|fühlen** *itr. V.* **bei jmdm. ~:** sound sb. out; **ich habe bei ihnen vorgefühlt, was ...** I sounded them out about *or* as to what ...

**vor|führen** *tr. V.* **A** bring forward; **jmdn. dem Richter ~:** bring sb. before the judge; **er wurde zur Vernehmung vorgeführt** he was brought for questioning; **B** (*zeigen*) show; **wann führst du uns deinen Freund vor?** when are you going to introduce your boyfriend to us?; **C** (*demonstrieren*) demonstrate; **jmdm. etw. ~:** demonstrate sth. to sb.; **D** (*darbieten*) show ‹film, slides, etc.›; present ‹circus act, programme›; perform ‹play, trick, routine›

**Vorführ·gerät** *das* (*Projektor*) projector

**Vor·führung** *die* **A** bringing forward; **der Richter ordnete die ~ des Gefangenen an** the judge ordered the prisoner to be brought forward; **B** (*das Zeigen*) showing; exhibiting; **C** (*das Demonstrieren*) demonstration; **D** (*das Darbieten*) ⇒ **vorführen** D: showing; presentation; performance; **E** (*Veranstaltung*) ⇒ **vorführen** D: show; presentation; performance

**Vorführ·wagen** *der* demonstration car *or* model

**Vor·gabe** *die* **A** (*Sport*) handicap; **B** (*Richtlinie*) guideline

**Vorgabe·zeit** *die* (*Wirtsch.*) [target] time for the job/project *etc.*

**Vor·gang** *der* **A** occurrence; event; **chemische/physikalische** *usw.* **Vorgänge** chemical/physical *etc.* processes; **B** (*Amtsspr.*) file; **der ~ XY** the file on XY

**Vorgänger** /-gɛŋɐ/ *der;* ~**s**, ~, **Vorgängerin** *die;* ~, ~**nen** (*auch fig.*) predecessor

**Vor·garten** *der* front garden

**vor|gaukeln** *tr. V.* **jmdm. ~, dass ...** lead sb. to believe that ...; **jmdm. eine heile Welt ~:** lead sb. to believe in a perfect *or* an ideal world

**vor|geben** *unr. tr. V.* **A** (*vortäuschen*) pretend; **B** (*Sport*) **jmdm. eine Runde/50 m/15 Punkte ~:** give sb. a lap [start]/[a start of] 50 m/[a lead of] 15 points; **C** (*im Voraus festlegen*) set in advance; **vorgegebene Normen/Werte** pre-determined standards/preset values; **ein vorgegebenes Programm** a preset programme

**Vor·gebirge** *das* promontory

**vor·geblich** *Adj.*; *adv.* ⇒ **angeblich**

**vor·gedruckt** *Adj.* pre-printed

**vor·gefasst**, ***vor·gefaßt** *Adj.* preconceived

**vorgefertigt** *Adj.* ⇒ **vorfabriziert**

**Vor·gefühl** *das* presentiment; **im ~ solchen Glücks** in anticipation of such happiness

**vor|gehen** *unr. itr. V.*; *mit sein* **A** (*ugs.: nach vorn gehen*) go forward; **an die Tafel/zum Altar ~:** go up to the blackboard/the altar; **B** (*vorausgehen*) go on ahead; **jmdn. ~ lassen** let sb. go first; **C** ‹clock› be fast; ⇒ *auch* **nachgehen** D; **D** (*einschreiten*) **gegen jmdn./etw. ~:** take action against sb./sth.; **gesetzlich gegen jmdn./etw. ~:** take legal action *or* proceedings against sb./sth.; **mit etw./mit Strenge gegen jmdn./etw. ~:** use sth. on/take strict measures against sb./sth.; **E** (*verfahren*) proceed; **F** (*sich abspielen*) happen; go on; **was geht hier vor?** what is happening *or* going on here?; **in jmdm. ~:** go on inside sb.; **mit ihm war eine Veränderung vorgegangen** there had been a change in him; a change had taken place in him; **G** (*Vorrang haben*) have priority; come first; **allem anderen ~:** have priority *or* take precedence over everything else

**Vor·gehen** *das;* ~**s** action

**vor·gelagert** *Adj.* **die [der Küste] ~en Inseln** the offshore islands; the islands situated off the coast

**vor·genannt** *Adj.* (*Amtsspr.*) aforementioned; aforesaid

**Vor·geplänkel** *das* preliminary skirmishing *no indef. art.*

**Vor·gericht** *das* ⇒ **Vorspeise**

**Vor·geschichte** *die* **A** prehistory *no art.*; **B** (*Begebenheiten*) history

**vor·geschichtlich** *Adj.* prehistoric

**Vor·geschmack** *der* foretaste

**vor·geschritten** *Adj.* (*geh.*) late ‹hour›; advanced ‹age›

**Vor·gesetzte** *der/die; adj. Dekl.* superior

**Vor·gespräch** *das* preliminary discussion

**vor·gestern** *Adv.* the day before yesterday; ~ **Mittag/Abend/früh** the day before yesterday at midday/the evening before last/the morning of the day before yesterday; **er ist von ~** (*ugs.*) he is old-fashioned *or* behind the times; **Ansichten/Konventionen von ~** (*ugs.*) old-fashioned *or* outdated views/conventions

**vor·gestrig** *Adj.* of the day before yesterday *postpos.*

**vor|glühen** *tr., itr. V.* (*Kfz-W.*) preheat

**vor|greifen** *unr. itr. V.* **A** **jmdm. [bei** *od.* **in/mit etw.] ~:** anticipate sb. *or* jump in ahead of sb. [in/with sth.]; **einer Sache** (*Dat.*) **~:** anticipate sth.; **B** (*in einer Erzählung*) jump ahead

**Vor·griff** *der* anticipation (**auf** + *Akk.* of); (*bei einer Erzählung*) jump *or* leap ahead (**auf** + *Akk.* to); **im ~ auf etw.** (*Akk.*) in anticipation of sth.

**vor|haben** *unr. tr. V.* intend; (*geplant haben*) plan; **er hat eine Reise vor** *od.* **er hat vor, eine Reise zu machen** he intends going on a journey/plans to go on a journey; **hast du heute Abend etwas vor?** have you anything planned *or* any plans for this evening?; are you doing anything this evening?; **wenn du nichts Besseres vorhast** if you have nothing better to do; **er hat Großes mit seinem Sohn vor** he has great plans for his son

**Vor·haben** *das;* ~**s**, ~ (*Plan*) plan; (*Projekt*) project

**Vor·halle** *die* (*eines Tempels*) portico; (*Eingangshalle*) entrance hall; (*eines Theaters, Hotels*) foyer

**vor|halten** ❶ *unr. tr. V.* **A** hold up; **sich** (*Dat.*) **etw. ~:** hold sth. [up] in front of oneself; **jmdn. mit vorgehaltener Schusswaffe bedrohen** threaten sb. at gunpoint; ⇒ *auch* **Hand** F; **B** (*zum Vorwurf machen*) **jmdm. etw. ~:** reproach sb. for sth. ❷ *unr. itr. V.* (*ugs., auch fig.*) last

**Vor·haltungen** *Pl.* **jmdm. [wegen etw.] ~ machen** reproach sb. [for sth.]

**Vor·hand** *die* **A** (*Sport, bes. Tennis*) forehand; ⇒ *auch* **Rückhand**; **B** (*beim Pferd*) forehand; **C** (*Kartenspiel*) lead; **in der ~ sein** have the lead

**vorhanden** /-'handn̩/ *Adj.* existing; (*verfügbar*) available; **~ sein** exist *or* be in existence/be available; **ein Vorratsraum ist hier leider nicht ~:** unfortunately there is no storeroom here; **von dieser Sorte ist noch genügend ~:** there's still plenty of this sort left

**Vorhanden·sein** *das;* ~**s** existence

**Vor·hang** *der* (*auch Theater*) curtain; **viele Vorhänge bekommen** (*Theater*) get a large number of curtain calls; ⇒ *auch* **eisern** 1A

**Vorhänge·schloss**, ***Vorhänge·schloß** *das* padlock

**Vorhang-:** ~**stange** *die* curtain rod; ~**stoff** *der* curtain material; curtaining

**Vor·haut** *die* ▶ 471 foreskin; prepuce

**vor|heizen** *tr. V.* put the heating on in ‹room etc.› [to warm it up in advance]; **im vorgeheizten Ofen** in a preheated oven

**vor·her** /*od.* -'-/ beforehand; (*davor*) before; **am Abend ~:** [on] the evening before; [on] the previous evening; **das ist drei Wochen ~ passiert** it happened three weeks earlier *or* before

**vorher-, Vorher-:** ~**|bestimmen** *tr. V.* determine in advance; predetermine; **alles ist vom Schicksal/von Gott ~bestimmt** everything is foreordained by fate/preordained by God; ~**bestimmung** *die* predetermination; (*Prädestination*) predestination; ~**|gehen** *unr. itr. V.*; *mit sein* **in den ~gehenden Wochen** in the preceding weeks; in the weeks before; **wie im Vorhergehenden erläutert** as explained above

**vorherig** /*od.* '---/ *Adj.* prior ‹notice, announcement, warning›; previous ‹discussion, agreement›; **um ~e Bezahlung bitten** request payment in advance

**Vor·herrschaft** *die* supremacy; dominance

**vor|herrschen** *itr. V.* predominate; **die ~de Meinung/der ~de Geschmack** the predominant *or* prevailing opinion/taste

**vorher-, Vorher-:** ~**sage** *die* prediction; (*des Wetters*) forecast; ~**|sagen** *tr. V.* predict; forecast ‹weather›; ~**sehbar** *Adj.* ⇒ **voraussehbar**; ~**|sehen** *unr. tr. V.* ⇒ **voraussehen**

**vor|heucheln** *tr. V.* **[jmdm.] etw. ~:** feign sth. [to sb.]; **er heuchelte ihr Liebe vor** he pretended to love her

**vor·hin** /*od.* -'-/ *Adv.* a short time *or* while ago; **sie ist ~ erst angekommen** she has only just arrived; **das ist der Junge von ~** (*ugs.*) that's the boy who we saw a short time ago *or* just now

***vor·hinein, Vor·hinein** *in* **im ~** (*bes. österr.*) in advance

**Vor·hof** *der* **A** ▶ 471 (*Anat.*) atrium; **B** (*vorderer Hof*) forecourt; **für uns war es**

---

*old spelling (see note on page 1707)

V

**schon der ~ zur Seligkeit** (*fig.*) to us it was almost perfect bliss

**Vor·hölle** *die* (*kath. Rel.*) limbo *no art.*

**Vor·hut** *die;* ~, **~en** advance guard; (*fig.*) vanguard

**vorig** *Adj.* Ⓐ ▶ 207 last; Ⓑ (*schweiz.*) (*übrig*) left over *postpos.*; (*verfügbar*) spare; **etw. ~ lassen** leave sth. over; **~e Zeit haben** have some spare time

**vor·industriell** *Adj.* pre-industrial

**Vor·jahr** *das* previous year

**vor·jährig** *Adj.* of the previous year

**vor|jammern** *tr. V.* (*ugs.*) **jmdm. etw. ~:** moan *or* whine to sb. about sth.

**Vor·kämpfer** *der,* **Vor·kämpferin** *die* pioneer; **ein ~ der Freiheit** a pioneering champion of freedom

**vor|kauen** *tr. V.* (*fig. ugs.*) spell out; **jmdm. etw. ~:** spell sth. out for sb.; spoon-feed sth. to sb.

**Vorkaufs·recht** *das* (*Rechtsw.*) right of first refusal

**Vorkehr** /-ke:ɐ̯/ *die;* ~, **~en** (*schweiz.*) precaution

**Vorkehrungen** *Pl.* precautions; **~ [gegen etw.] treffen** take precautions [against sth.]

**Vor·kenntnis** *die* background knowledge

**vor|knöpfen** *tr. V.* (*ugs.*) **sich** (*Dat.*) **jmdn. [ordentlich/kräftig] ~:** give sb. a [proper/good] talking-to (*coll.*)

**vor|kochen** *tr., itr. V.* cook in advance

**vor|kommen** *unr. itr. V.; mit sein* Ⓐ (*sich ereignen*) happen; **dass mir so etwas nicht wieder vorkommt!** I hope I never experience anything like that again; **so etwas ist mir noch nie vorgekommen** nothing like that has ever happened to me before; Ⓑ (*vorhanden sein*) occur; **das Tier/die Pflanze kommt nur im Gebirge vor** the animal/plant is found only in the mountains; **in einer Erzählung ~** ‹character, figure› appear in a story; Ⓒ (*erscheinen*) seem; **das Lied kommt mir bekannt vor** I seem to know the song; **es kam mir [so] vor, als ob …** I felt *or* it seemed as if …; **du kommst dir wohl schlau vor** I suppose you think you're clever; **das kommt dir nur so vor** it just seems like that to you; **ich komme mir überflüssig vor** I feel [as if I am] superfluous; **wie kommst du mir eigentlich vor?** (*ugs.*) who do you think you are?; Ⓓ (*ugs.: nach vorne kommen*) come forward; **an die Tafel ~:** come up to the blackboard; Ⓔ (*her~*) come out; **hinter/unter etw.** (*Dat.*) **~:** come out from behind/under sth.; **unter dem Schnee ~** ‹flower› come up out of the snow

**Vorkommen** *das;* **~s,** ~ Ⓐ (*das Auftreten*) occurrence; (*einer Krankheit*) incidence; Ⓑ (*Geol.: Lagerstätte*) deposit

**Vorkommnis** /-kɔmnɪs/ *das;* **~ses, ~se** incident; occurence

**vor|kosten** *tr. V.* sample in advance

**Vor·kriegszeit** *die* pre-war period

**vor|laden** *unr. tr. V.* summon; summon, subpoena ‹witness›

**Vor·ladung** *die* summons; **eine ~ vor Gericht** a summons to appear in court; **eine gerichtliche/polizeiliche ~:** a court/police summons; **die ~ eines Zeugen beantragen** apply for a witness to be summoned *or* subpoenaed

**Vor·lage** *die* Ⓐ ⇒ **vorlegen** 1A: presentation; showing; production; submission; tabling; introduction; **gegen ~ einer Sache** (*Gen.*) on production *or* presentation of sth.; Ⓑ (*Entwurf*) draft; (*Gesetzentwurf*) bill; Ⓒ (*Muster*) pattern; (*Modell*) model; **~n zum Stricken** knitting patterns; **etw. von einer ~ abschreiben** copy sth.; **etw. als ~ benutzen** use sth. as a model; **nach einer/ohne ~ zeichnen** draw from/without a model; Ⓓ (*Ballspiele, bes. Fußball*) forward pass; **eine ~ geben/schlagen** make a forward pass; lay the ball forward; Ⓔ (*Skisport*) vorlage; forward lean; Ⓕ (*Kaufmannsspr.*) advance; **[für etw.] in ~ treten** advance the money [for sth.]

**Vor·land** *das* Ⓐ (*vor einem Gebirge*) foothills *pl.*; Ⓑ (*Deich~*) foreshore

**vor|lassen** *unr. tr. V.* Ⓐ (*ugs.: den Vortritt lassen*) **jmdn. ~:** let sb. go first *or* in front; Ⓑ (*empfangen*) admit; let in

**vor|laufen** *unr. itr. V.; mit sein* (*ugs.*) Ⓐ (*ugs.: nach vorn laufen*) run forward; Ⓑ ⇒ **vorauslaufen**

**Vor·läufer** *der,* **Vor·läuferin** *die* precursor; forerunner

**vor·läufig** ❶ *Adj.* temporary; provisional ‹diagnosis, settlement, result, successor›; interim ‹order, agreement›. ❷ *adv.* for the time being; for the present; **jmdn. ~ festnehmen** detain sb. temporarily; take sb. into temporary custody

**vor·laut** ❶ *Adj.* forward. ❷ *adv.* forwardly

**vor|leben** *tr. V.* **jmdm. etw. ~:** set sb. an example of sth. [in the way one lives]

**Vor·leben** *das* past life; past

**Vorlege-: ~besteck** *das* [set of] serving cutlery; **~gabel** *die* serving fork; **~löffel** *der* serving spoon

**vor|legen** ❶ *tr. V.* Ⓐ present; show, produce ‹certificate, identity card, etc.›; show ‹sample›; submit ‹evidence›; table, introduce ‹parliamentary bill›; (*veröffentlichen*) publish; Ⓑ **jmdm./sich eine Frage ~:** pose sb./oneself a question; Ⓒ (*anbringen vor*) **eine Kette/einen Riegel ~:** put a chain on *or* across/a bolt across; Ⓓ (*geh.: aufgeben*) serve ‹food›; **jmdm. etw. ~:** serve sb. with sth.; serve sth. to sb.; Ⓔ (*bes. Fußball*) **jmdm./sich den Ball ~:** lay the ball on for sb./tap the ball on; Ⓕ **ein scharfes Tempo ~:** set a fast pace.
❷ *refl. V.* lean forward

**Vorleger** *der;* **~s,** ~ (*vor der Badewanne, dem Waschbecken*) mat; (*vor dem Bett*) rug

**Vor·leistung** *die* advance concession

**vor|lesen** *unr. tr., itr. V.* read aloud *or* out; read ‹story, poem, etc.› aloud; **jmdm. [etw.] ~:** read [sth.] to sb.; **lies schon vor!** read it out!; read out what it says!; **aus seinen Werken ~:** read from one's works

**Vor·lesung** *die* lecture; (*~sreihe*) series *or* course of lectures

**Vorlesungs·verzeichnis** *das* lecture timetable

**vor·letzt...** *Adj.* ▶ 833 last but one; next to last; penultimate ‹page, episode, etc.›; **mein ~es Exemplar** my last copy but one; my next to last copy; **~es Mal** the time before last; **im ~en Jahr/Sommer** the year/summer before last; **seit ~er Woche** since the week before last

**vorlieb** *in* **mit jmdm./etw. ~ nehmen** put up with sb./sth.; (*sich begnügen*) make do with sb./sth.

**Vor·liebe** *die* preference; [special] fondness *or* liking; **eine ~ für jmdn./etw. haben** be fond of sb./be fond of *or* partial to sth.; **etw. mit ~ tun** particularly like doing sth.

***vorlieb|nehmen** ⇒ **vorlieb**

**vor|liegen** *unr. itr. V.* Ⓐ **jmdm. ~** ‹application, complaint, plans, etc.› be with sb.; **das Beweismaterial liegt dem Gericht vor** the evidence is before *or* has been submitted to the court; **die Ergebnisse liegen uns noch nicht vor** we do not have the results yet; **die mir ~de Ausgabe/~den Ergebnisse** the edition/results in front of me; **im ~den Fall, in ~dem Fall** in the present case; Ⓑ (*bestehen*) be [present]; exist; ‹symptom› be present; ‹book› be available; **gegen ihn liegt nichts vor** there is nothing against him; **hier liegt ein Irrtum/Missverständnis vor** there is a mistake/misunderstanding here; **ein Verschulden des Fahrers liegt nicht vor** the driver is/was not to blame; Ⓒ *südd., österr., schweiz. mit sein* (*ugs.: vorgelegt sein*) ‹chain, bolt, etc.› be on *or* across

**vor|lügen** *unr. tr. V.* (*ugs.*) **jmdm. etwas ~:** lie to sb.; **er hat uns vorgelogen, dass er die Prüfung bestanden habe** he lied to us, pretending he had passed the examination

**vorm** /fo:ɐ̯m/ *Präp.* + *Art.* Ⓐ = **vor dem;** Ⓑ (*räumlich*) in front of the; Ⓒ (*zeitlich, bei Reihenfolge, Rangordnung*) before the; **~ Frühstück** before breakfast

**vor|machen** *tr. V.* (*ugs.*) Ⓐ (*vorführen*) **jmdm. etw. ~:** show sb. sth.; **ihm macht niemand was vor** there is no one better than him; no one can teach him anything; Ⓑ (*vortäuschen*) **jmdm. etwas ~:** kid (*coll.*) *or* fool sb.; **mir kannst du nichts ~:** you can't kid (*coll.*) *or* fool me; **wir wollen uns nichts ~:** let's not kid (*coll.*) *or* fool ourselves; **mach mir doch nichts vor** don't try and kid me (*coll.*); **der lässt sich von keinem was ~:** he's nobody's fool; ⇒ *auch* **Dunst** B; **X**

**Vor·macht** *die* supremacy *no art.*

**Vormacht·stellung** *die* [position of] supremacy *no art.*; **sich** (*Dat.*) **eine ~ sichern** secure [a position of] supremacy

**vormalig** /-ma:lɪç/ *Adj.* former

**vormals** /-ma:ls/ *Adv.* formerly

**Vor·mann** *der* foreman

**Vor·marsch** *der* (*auch fig.*) advance; **auf dem** *od.* **im ~ sein** ‹army› be advancing *or* on the advance; (*fig.*) ‹ideas, new development, etc.› be gaining ground

**Vor·märz** *der* (*hist.*): *period in German history from 1815 until the March 1848 revolution*

**vor|merken** *tr. V.* make a note of; **ein Zimmer ~ lassen** reserve a room; **ich habe Sie für den Kurs/für Montag vorgemerkt** I've put you down for the course/for Monday

**Vor·mieter** *der,* **Vor·mieterin** *die* previous tenant

***vor·mittag** ⇒ **Vormittag**

**Vor·mittag** *der* morning; **am [späten] ~:** [late] in the morning; **am frühen ~:** during the first part of the morning; **heute/morgen/Freitag ~:** this/tomorrow/Friday morning

**vor·mittäglich** *Adj.* morning

**vor·mittags** *Adv.* ▶ 752 in the morning

**Vormittags·stunde** *die* morning hour

**Vor·monat** *der* previous *or* preceding month

**Vor·mund** *der;* **~[e]s, ~e** *od.* **Vormünder, Vormundin** *die;* **~, ~nen** guardian; **einen Vormund bestellen** appoint a guardian; **ich brauche keinen Vormund** (*fig.*) I don't need anyone telling me what to do

**Vormundschaft** *die;* **~, ~en** guardianship; **die ~ über** *od.* **für jmdn. übernehmen** become sb.'s guardian; **jmdn. unter jmds. ~ stellen** place sb. under sb.'s guardianship

**Vormundschafts·gericht** *das: court dealing with matters of guardianship*

**vorn**[1] /fɔrn/ *Adv.* at the front; **das Zimmer liegt nach ~ [raus]** (*ugs.*) the room faces the front; **~ am Haus/in der Schlange** at the front of the house/queue *or* (*Amer.*) line; **ganz ~ sitzen** sit right at the front; **das Kleid wird ~ zugeknöpft** the dress buttons up at the front *or* in front; **~ im Bild** in the foreground of the picture; **nach ~ schauen** look in front *or* to the front; **nach ~ gehen/kommen** go/come to the front; **~ im Buch** at the front of the book; **[gleich] da ~:** [just] over there; **weiter ~:** up ahead; a bit further on; **der Wind/Schlag kam von ~:** the wind/blow came from the front; **noch einmal von ~ anfangen** start afresh; start from the beginning again; **es geht wieder von ~ los** it is starting all over again; **von ~ bis hinten** (*ugs.*) from beginning to end; **das ist von ~ bis hinten gelogen** it's all lies from beginning to end

**vorn**[2] /fo:ɐ̯n/ *Präp.* + *Art.* (*ugs.*) = **vor den**

**Vor·name** *der* first *or* Christian name

**vorne** *Adv.* ⇒ **vorn**[1]

**vornehm** /'fo:ɐ̯ne:m/ ❶ *Adj.* Ⓐ (*nobel*) noble ‹character, behaviour, gesture, etc.›; **~e Gesinnung** noble-mindedness; Ⓑ (*der Oberschicht angehörend, kultiviert*) distinguished; **zur ~en Welt/Gesellschaft/zu den ~en Kreisen gehören** be part of high society; **~e Blässe/~es Getue** genteel pallor/behaviour; Ⓒ (*von adliger Herkunft*) noble; Ⓓ (*elegant*) exclusive ‹district, hotel, restaurant, resort›; elegant ‹villa, clothes›; elegant, distinguished ‹appearance›; Ⓔ **~st...** (*geh.: vorrangig*) primary ‹duty, task, function, source of income, etc.›.

V

❷ *adv.* Ⓐ (*nobel*) nobly; Ⓑ (*elegant*) elegantly

**vor|nehmen** *unr. tr. V.* Ⓐ **sich** (*Dat.*) **etw.** ~: plan sth.; **sich** (*Dat.*) ~, **etw. zu tun** plan to do sth.; **sich** (*Dat.*) ~, **mit dem Rauchen aufzuhören** resolve to give up smoking; Ⓑ (*ugs.: sich beschäftigen mit*) get busy with; **nimm dir ein Buch vor und lies!** pick up a book and read!; Ⓒ (*ugs.: zur Rede stellen*) **sich jmdn.** ~: give sb. a talking-to (*coll.*); Ⓓ (*durchführen*) carry out, make ‹examination, search, test›; perform ‹action, ceremony›; make ‹correction, change, division, choice, selection›; take ‹measurements›

**Vornehmheit** *die;* ~ ⇒ **vornehm** 1 A-D: nobility; exclusivity; elegance; **seine** ~ **beeindruckte sie** she was impressed by his distinguished manner; **die** ~ **seiner Erscheinung** his distinguished appearance

**vornehmlich** *Adv.* (*geh.*) above all; primarily

**Vornehm·tuerei** /*od.* ----'-/ *die;* ~ (*abwertend*) affectation

**vor|neigen** *tr., refl. V.* lean forward; **in vorgeneigter Haltung** bent forward

**vorne·weg** *Adv.* ⇒ **vorweg**

**vorn-:** ~**herein** *in* **von** *od.* (*schweiz.*) **zum** *od.* **im** ~**herein** from the start *or* outset *or* beginning; ~**über** *Adv.* forwards

**vornüber|fallen** *unr. itr. V.; mit sein* fall forwards

**Vor·ort** *der* suburb

**Vorort·zug** *der* suburban train

**Vor·platz** *der* forecourt

**Vor·posten** *der* (*Milit., auch fig.*) outpost

**vor|preschen** *itr. V.; mit sein* (*fig.*) rush ahead

**Vor·programm** *das* supporting programme

**vor|programmieren** *tr. V.* (*auch fig.*) preprogramme

**vor|ragen** *itr. V.* project; jut out

**Vor·rang** *der* Ⓐ **[den]** ~ **[vor jmdm./etw.] haben** have priority *or* take precedence [over sb./sth.]; **jmdn. mit** ~ **bedienen** give sb. priority service; **jmdm./einer Sache den** ~ **geben** give sb./sth. priority; Ⓑ (*bes. österr.: Vorfahrt*) right of way

**vorrangig** /-raŋıç/ ❶ *Adj.* priority *attrib.* ‹treatment, task, objective›; ~ **sein** be a matter of priority *or* of prime importance; **von** ~**er Bedeutung** of prime *or* utmost importance; **jmds.** ~**es Anliegen/Ziel sein** be sb.'s primary concern/goal; **zu den** ~**sten Aufgaben gehören** be one of the prime *or* most important tasks. ❷ *adv.* **jmdn.** ~ **behandeln** give sb. priority treatment; **etw.** ~ **erledigen** deal with sth. as a matter of priority

**Vorrang·stellung** *die* position of prime importance; (*eines Landes*) supremacy

**Vor·rat** *der* supply, stock (**an** + *Dat.* of); **etw. auf** ~ **kaufen/herstellen** stock up with *or* on sth./produce stocks of sth.; **ein** ~ **an Witzen** (*fig.*) a stock of jokes; **solange der** ~ **reicht** while stocks last

**vorrätig** /-rɛːtıç/ *Adj.* in stock *postpos.;* **etw.** ~ **haben** have sth. in stock; **etw. nicht** ~ **haben** be out of [stock of] sth.

**Vorrats-:** ~**kammer** *die* pantry; larder; ~**keller** *der* cellar storeroom; ~**raum** *der* storeroom

**Vor·raum** *der* anteroom

**vor|rechnen** *tr. V.* **jmdm. etw.** ~: work sth. out *or* calculate sth. for sb.; **jmdm. seine Fehler** ~ (*fig.*) enumerate sb.'s mistakes

**Vor·recht** *das* privilege

**Vor·rede** *die* Ⓐ (*Vorwort*) preface; foreword; Ⓑ (*einleitende Worte*) introductory remarks *pl.;* **sich nicht lange bei** *od.* **mit der** ~ **aufhalten** not take long over the introductions

**Vor·redner** *der*, **Vor·rednerin** *die* previous speaker; **mein Vorredner:** the previous speaker

**vor|reiten** *unr. itr. V.; mit sein* ride on ahead

**Vor·reiter** *der*, **Vor·reiterin** *die:* **den Vorreiter/die Vorreiterin machen,** ~ **sein** lead the way

*old spelling (see note on page 1707)

**Vor·richtung** *die* device

**vor|rücken** ❶ *tr. V.* move forward; advance ‹chess piece›. ❷ *itr. V.; mit sein* move forward; (*Milit.*) advance; **mit dem Turm** ~ (*Schach*) advance the rook; **auf den 5. Platz** ~: move up to fifth place; **zu vorgerückter Stunde** (*geh.*) at a late hour

**Vor·ruhestand** *der* early retirement

**Vor·ruhestands·regelung** *die* regulation enabling employees to take early retirement

**Vor·runde** *die* (*Sport*) preliminary *or* qualifying round

**vors** *Präp.* + *Art.* Ⓐ = **vor das;** Ⓑ in front of the; **jmdm.** ~ **Auto laufen** run in front of sb.'s car

**vor|sagen** *tr. V.* Ⓐ *auch itr.* **jmdm. [die Antwort]** ~: tell sb. the answer; (*flüsternd*) whisper the answer to sb.; Ⓑ (*aufsagen*) recite; **sich** (*Dat.*) **etw.** ~: recite sth. to oneself

**Vor·saison** *die* start of the season; early [part of the] season

**Vor·satz** *der* intention; **den** ~ **fassen, etw. zu tun** resolve to do sth.; make a resolution to do sth.; **den** ~ **haben, etw. zu tun** intend to do sth.; have the intention of doing sth.; **mit** ~: with intent; **der Weg zur Hölle ist mit guten Vorsätzen gepflastert** (*Spr.*) the road to hell is paved with good intentions (*prov.*)

**Vorsatz·blatt** *das* (*Buchw.*) endpaper

**vorsätzlich** /-zɛtslıç/ ❶ *Adj.* intentional; deliberate; wilful ‹murder, arson, etc.›. ❷ *adv.* intentionally; deliberately

**Vor·schau** *die* preview

**Vor·schein** *der: in* **etw. zum** ~ **bringen** reveal sth.; bring sth. to light; **zum** ~ **kommen** appear; (*entdeckt werden*) come to light; **sie griff in ihre Tasche und brachte eine Tüte zum** ~: she delved into her pocket and produced a bag; **wieder zum** ~ **kommen** reappear

**vor|schieben** ❶ *unr. tr. V.* Ⓐ push ‹bolt› across; ⇒ *auch* **Riegel** A; Ⓑ (*nach vorn schieben*) push forward; **den Kopf/die Schultern** ~: stick one's head forward/put one's shoulders forward; **die Unterlippe** ~: stick out one's bottom lip; Ⓒ (*für sich handeln lassen*) **jmdn.** ~: use sb. as a front man; Ⓓ (*als Vorwand nehmen*) use as a pretext *or* excuse; **die Verabredung war nur vorgeschoben** the appointment was only an excuse.
❷ *unr. refl. V.* push forward; ‹air mass, glacier› advance

**vor|schießen** *unr. tr. V.* **jmdm. Geld** ~: advance sb. money

**vor|schlafen** *unr. itr. V.* (*ugs.*) stock up on sleep

**Vorschlag** *der* suggestion; proposal; **das ist ein** *od.* **das nenn ich einen** ~**!** what a good *or* (*coll.*) great suggestion *or* idea!; **auf** ~ **von ...** at the suggestion of ...; **ein** ~ **zur Güte** (*scherzh.*) a conciliatory proposal

**vor|schlagen** *unr. tr. V.* **[jmdm.] etw.** ~: suggest *or* propose sth. [to sb.]; **jmdn. für/als etw.** ~: propose sb. for/as sth.

**Vorschlag·hammer** *der* sledgehammer

**vor|schmecken** *itr. V.* **der Knoblauch schmeckt vor** there is too strong a taste of garlic; it tastes too strongly of garlic; **das Gewürz soll nicht** ~: [the flavour of] the spice should not stand out

**vor·schnell** *Adj., adv.* ⇒ **voreilig**

**vor·schreiben** *unr. tr. V.* stipulate, lay down, set ‹conditions›; lay down ‹rules›; prescribe ‹dose›; **er wollte uns** ~, **was wir zu tun hätten** he wanted to tell us *or* dictate to us what to do; **ich lasse mir [von dir] nichts** ~: I won't be told what to do [by you]; I won't be dictated to [by you]; **das Gesetz schreibt vor, dass ...** the law lays down *or* provides that ...; **wie es der Brauch vorschreibt** as custom dictates *or* demands; **die vorgeschriebene Geschwindigkeit/Zahl/Dosis** the prescribed speed/number/dose

**Vor·schrift** *die* instruction; order; (*gesetzliche od. amtliche Bestimmung*) regulation; **ich lasse mir von dir keine** ~**en machen** I won't be told what to do by you; I won't be dictated to by you; **das ist** ~: that's/those are the regulations; **das verstößt** *od.* **ist gegen die** ~: it's against the rules *or* regulations; **die Medizin nach** ~ **einnehmen** take the medicine as directed; **Dienst nach** ~ **machen** work to rule

**vorschrifts·mäßig** ❶ *Adj.* correct; proper. ❷ *adv.* correctly; properly

**Vor·schub** *der: in* **jmdm./einer Sache** ~ **leisten** encourage sb./encourage *or* promote *or* foster sth.

**Vorschul·alter** *das* preschool age

**Vor·schule** *die* nursery school

**Vorschul·erziehung** *die* preschool education

**vor·schulisch** *Adj.* preschool

**Vor·schuss, *Vor·schuß** *der* advance; **er bekam 500 Mark** ~: he received an advance of 500 marks

**Vorschuss·lorbeeren, *Vorschuß·lorbeeren** *Pl.* premature praise *sing.*

**vor|schützen** *tr. V.* plead as an excuse; **wichtige Geschäfte/Krankheit** ~: pretend one has important business/feign illness; **Unwissenheit** ~: plead ignorance; ⇒ *auch* **Müdigkeit**

**vor|schwärmen** *tr. V.* **jmdm. von jmdm./etw.** ~: rave about sb./sth. to sb. (*coll.*)

**vor|schweben** *itr. V.* **jmdm. schwebt etw./jmd. vor** sb. has sth./sb. in mind

**vor|schwindeln** *tr. V.* (*ugs.*) **jmdm.** ~, **dass ...** kid sb. that ... (*coll.*); **sie wollte den anderen nichts** ~: she didn't want to kid the others (*coll.*)

**vor|sehen** ❶ *unr. tr. V.* Ⓐ (*planen*) plan; **wie vorgesehen** as planned; **die Eröffnung ist für den 21. März vorgesehen** the opening is scheduled *or* planned for 21 March; Ⓑ (*einsetzen, verwenden wollen*) **etw. für/als etw.** ~: intend sth. for/as sth.; **die Gelder sind für den Neubau einer Schule vorgesehen** the money is earmarked for the building of a school; **jmdn. für/als etw.** ~: designate sb. for/as sth.; Ⓒ (*festlegen*) ‹law, plan, contract, etc.› provide for.
❷ *unr. refl. V.* (*sich in Acht nehmen*) **sich [vor jmdm./etw.]** ~: be careful [of sb./sth.]; **sieh dich vor dem Hund vor** be careful of *or* mind the dog; **sieh dich vor, dass du nicht krank wirst** be careful *or* take care you don't become ill

**Vorsehung** *die;* ~: Providence *no art.*

**vor|setzen** *tr. V.* Ⓐ (*nach vorn setzen*) move forward; **den rechten/linken Fuß** ~: put one's right/left foot forward; **sich** ~ (*ugs.*) come/go and sit at the front; Ⓑ (*zu essen, trinken geben*) **jmdm. etw.** ~: serve sb. sth.; (*fig.*) serve *or* dish sb. up sth.

**Vor·sicht** *die* care; (*bei Risiko, Gefahr*) caution; care; (*Umsicht*) circumspection; caution; **hier ist** ~ **geboten/nötig** caution/care is advisable/needed here; **alle** ~ **außer Acht lassen** throw [all] caution to the winds; **zur** ~: as a precaution; to be on the safe side; **er ist mit** ~ **zu genießen** (*ugs.*) you should be wary of *or* careful with him; **was er sagt, ist mit** ~ **zu genießen** (*ugs.*) what he says should be taken with caution; ~**!** be careful!; watch *or* look out!; „~, **Glas**" 'glass — handle with care'; „~, **bissiger Hund**" 'beware of the dog'; ~ **an der Bahnsteigkante** stand back from the edge of the platform; „~, **Stufe!**" 'mind the step!'; „~, **Steinschlag**" 'danger, falling rocks'; „~, **frisch gestrichen**" 'wet paint'; ~ **ist die Mutter der Porzellankiste** (*ugs.*), ~ **ist besser als Nachsicht** (*ugs. scherzh.*) better safe than sorry

**vorsichtig** /-zıçtıç/ ❶ *Adj.* careful; (*bei Risiko, Gefahr*) cautious; careful; (*umsichtig*) circumspect; cautious; guarded ‹remark, hint, question, optimism›; cautious, conservative ‹estimate›; **sei** ~**!** be careful!, take care! ❷ *adv.* carefully; with care; ~ **optimistisch** guardedly *or* cautiously optimistic; **etw.** ~ **andeuten** hint at sth. cautiously; ~ **geschätzt** at a conservative estimate

**vorsichts·halber** *Adv.* as a precaution; to be on the safe side

V

**Vorsichts·maßnahme** *die* precautionary measure; precaution

**Vor·silbe** *die* [monosyllabic] prefix

**vor|singen** ❶ *unr. tr. V.* **[jmdm.] etw. ~:** sing sth. [to sb.]; **ich singe euch die erste Strophe vor** I'll sing you the first verse. ❷ *unr. itr. V.* Ⓐ **[jmdm.] ~:** sing [to sb.]; **wenn er ~ soll** when he has to sing in public *or* in front of people; Ⓑ *(zur Prüfung)* have *or* take a singing test; **bei der Oper ~:** audition for *or* have an audition with the opera company

**vor·sintflutlich** *Adj. (ugs.)* antiquated

**Vor·sitz** *der* chairmanship; **den ~ haben** *od.* **führen** be the chairman; be in the chair; *(im Gericht)* preside over the trial; **er hat** *od.* **führt bei der Tagung den ~:** he is chairing the conference; **den ~ übernehmen** *(eines Vereins)* take over the chairmanship *or* presidency; *(bei einer Tagung, Sitzung)* take the chair; **unter dem ~ von ...** under the chairmanship of ...

**vor|sitzen** *unr. itr. V.* **einer Versammlung/Kommission** *(Dat.)* **~:** chair a *or* preside over a meeting/commission

**Vorsitzende** *der/die; adj. Dekl.* chair[person]; *(bes. Mann)* chairman; *(Frau auch)* chairwoman

**Vor·sorge** *die* precautions *pl.*; *(für den Todesfall, Krankheit, Alter)* provisions *pl.*; *(Vorbeugung)* prevention; **~ treffen** take precautions (**gegen** against)/make provisions (**für** for); **für den Fall einer Krankheit ~ treffen** make provisions in case of illness; **~ treffen, dass ...** take precautions/make provisions so that ...

**vor|sorgen** *itr. V.* **für etw. ~:** make provisions for sth.; provide for sth.

**Vorsorge·untersuchung** *die (Med.)* medical check-up

**vorsorglich** ❶ *Adj.* precautionary ‹measure, check-up, etc.›. ❷ *adv.* as a precaution; to be on the safe side

**Vor·spann** *der (Film, Ferns.)* opening credits *pl.*

**Vor·speise** *die* starter; hors d'œuvre

**vor|spiegeln** *tr. V.* **jmdm. ~, dass ...** delude sb. into believing that ...; **er spiegelte ihnen eine Notlage vor** he deluded them into believing *or* led them to believe that he was in a plight; **Unwissenheit/Krankheit ~:** feign ignorance/illness

**Vor·spiegelung** *die:* **das ist [eine] ~ falscher Tatsachen** these are falsehoods presented as if they were facts; **unter ~ falscher Tatsachen** under false pretences

**Vor·spiel** *das* Ⓐ *(Theater)* prologue; *(Musik)* prelude; Ⓑ *(vorm Geschlechtsakt)* foreplay; Ⓒ *(als Prüfung)* practical examination; *(bei Bewerbungen)* audition

**vor|spielen** ❶ *tr. V.* Ⓐ **jmdm. ein Musikstück/eine Szene ~:** play a piece of music to *or* for sb./act out *or* perform a scene for *or* in front of sb.; Ⓑ *(vorspiegeln)* **jmdm. etw. ~:** feign sth. to sb.; **spiel uns doch nichts vor!** don't try and fool us!; **jmdm. Theater/eine Komödie ~:** put on an act for sb. ❷ *itr. V.* Ⓐ **jmdm. ~:** play to *or* for sb.; **einer Jury ~:** perform in front of a jury; Ⓑ *(bei einer Bewerbung)* audition, have an audition (**bei** for); **jmdn. ~ lassen** audition sb.

**Vor·sprache** *die (österr.)* visit (**bei** to)

**vor|sprechen** ❶ *unr. tr. V.* Ⓐ *(zum Nachsprechen)* **jmdm. etw. ~:** pronounce *or* say sth. first for sb.; **einem Zeugen den Eid ~:** say the oath for the witness to repeat; Ⓑ *(zur Prüfung)* recite. ❷ *unr. itr. V.* Ⓐ *(zur Prüfung)* recite one's examination piece; *(bei Bewerbungen)* audition; **am Staatstheater ~:** audition for the State Theatre; **jmdn. ~ lassen** audition sb.; Ⓑ *(einen Besuch machen)* **bei jmdm. [in einer Angelegenheit] ~:** call on sb. about a matter; **bei** *od.* **auf einer Behörde ~:** call at an office

**vor|springen** *unr. itr. V.; mit sein* Ⓐ *(ugs.)* **hinter einem Auto ~:** jump out from behind a car; Ⓑ *(weit hervorstehen)* jut out; project; **ein ~des Kinn** a prominent chin

**Vor·sprung** *der* Ⓐ *(vorspringender Teil)* projection; *(Fels~)* ledge; Ⓑ *(räumlicher, zeitlicher Vorteil)* lead; **einen [knappen] ~ [vor jmdm.] haben** have a [slight] lead [over sb.]; be [slightly] ahead [of sb.]; **jmdm. einen ~ geben** give sb. a start; **jmdm. zehn Schritte/einen zehnminütigen ~ geben** give sb. ten paces'/ten minutes' start

**Vor·stadt** *die* suburb; **in der ~ wohnen** live in the suburbs

**vor·städtisch** *Adj.* suburban

**Vor·stand** *der* Ⓐ *(leitendes Gremium) (einer Firma)* board [of directors]; *(eines Vereins, einer Gesellschaft)* executive committee; *(einer Partei)* executive; **im ~ sein** be on the board/executive committee/executive; Ⓑ *(Leiter)* chairman

**Vorstands·mitglied** *das* ⇒ **Vorstand** A: member of the board; board member; member of the executive committee; member of the executive

**vor|stehen** *unr. itr. V.* Ⓐ *(her~)* ‹house, roof, etc.› project, jut out; ‹teeth, chin› stick out; ‹cheek-bones› be prominent; **~de Zähne/Augen** buck teeth *or* projecting teeth/bulging eyes; Ⓑ *(geh.: leiten)* **einer Institution/dem Haushalt ~:** be the head of an institution/the household; **einem Geschäft/einer Abteilung ~:** be in charge of *or* run a business/department

**vorstehend** *Adj.* above *attrib.* ‹explanation, remarks, etc.›; **im Vorstehenden** above; **das Vorstehende** the above

**Vorsteher** *der;* **~s, ~:** head; *(einer Schule)* headmaster; *(einer Gemeinde)* chairman; *(eines Klosters)* abbot

**Vorsteher·drüse** *die* ▶ 471 prostate [gland]

**Vorsteherin** *die;* **~, ~nen** head; *(einer Schule)* headmistress; *(eines Klosters)* abbess

**Vorsteh·hund** *der* pointer; *(langhaarig)* setter

**vorstell·bar** *Adj.* conceivable; imaginable; **es ist durchaus/[nur] schwer ~, dass ...** it is quite/scarcely conceivable that ...

**vor|stellen** ❶ *tr. V.* Ⓐ *(nach vorn stellen)* put ‹leg, foot, etc.› out *or* forward; **die Uhr [um eine Stunde] ~:** put the clock forward [one hour]; Ⓑ *(bekannt machen mit; auch fig.)* introduce; **jmdn./sich jmdm. ~:** introduce sb./oneself to sb.; Ⓒ *(bei Bewerbung)* **sich ~:** come/go for [an] interview; **sich beim Personalleiter ~:** go for an interview with the personnel director; Ⓓ *(darstellen)* represent; **er stellt etwas vor** *(ugs.) (sieht gut aus)* he looks good; *(gilt als Persönlichkeit)* he is somebody; Ⓔ *(zur Untersuchung)* **sich dem Arzt ~:** go to see the doctor.
❷ *refl. V.* Ⓐ **sich** *(Dat.)* **etw. ~:** imagine sth.; **stell dir vor, wir würden gewinnen** imagine we won; **ja, stell dir vor!** just imagine!; **ich habe mir das Wochenende ganz anders vorgestellt** the weekend was not at all what I had imagined; **ich kann ihn mir gut als Lehrer ~:** I can easily imagine *or* see him as a teacher; **was haben Sie sich** *(Dat.)* **als Preis vorgestellt?** what price did you have in mind?; **man stelle sich** *(Dat.)* **bitte einmal vor, dass ...** just imagine that ...; **das muss man sich** *(Dat.)* **[ein]mal ~!** just imagine *or* picture it!; Ⓑ **sich** *(Dat.)* **unter etw.** *(Dat.)* **etw. ~:** understand sth. by sth.; **darunter kann ich mir nichts ~:** it doesn't mean anything to me

**vorstellig** /ˈfoːɐ̯ʃtɛlɪç/ *Adj.* in **bei jmdm./etw. ~ werden** *(Papierdt.)* approach sb./sth.

**Vor·stellung** *die* Ⓐ *(Begriff)* idea; **jmdm. eine ~ von etw. geben** give sb. an idea of sth.; **sich** *(Dat.)* **von jmdm./etw. eine ~ machen** picture sb./sth.; **er macht sich** *(Dat.)* **keine ~ [davon], welche Mühe das kostet** he has no idea how much effort that costs; **das entspricht ganz/nicht meinen ~en** that is exactly/not what I had in mind; Ⓑ *(Fantasie)* imagination; **das geht über alle ~ hinaus** it is unimaginable; Ⓒ *(Aufführung)* performance; *(im Kino)* showing; **eine starke/schwache ~ geben** *(fig.)* perform well/badly; Ⓓ *(das Bekanntmachen)* introduction; Ⓔ *(Präsentation)* presentation; Ⓕ *(bei einer Bewerbung)* interview; **zur ~ kommen** come for [an] interview

**Vorstellungs-: ~gespräch** *das* interview; **~kraft** *die* [powers *pl.* of] imagination; **~vermögen** *das* ⇒ **~kraft**

**Vor·stopper** *der,* **Vor·stopperin** *die (Fußball)* central defender

**Vor·stoß** *der* advance; **einen ~ in ein Gebiet/in den Weltraum unternehmen** push forward *or* advance into an area/venture into space; **einen ~ bei der Geschäftsleitung unternehmen** *(fig.)* make an approach to management

**vor|stoßen** *unr. itr. V.; mit sein* advance; push forward; **in den Weltraum ~:** venture into space

**Vor·strafe** *die (Rechtsw.)* previous conviction

**Vorstrafen·register** *das* ⇒ **Strafregister**

**vor|strecken** *tr. V.* Ⓐ stretch ‹arm, hand› out; stick out ‹stomach›; **den Kopf/Hals ~:** crane one's neck forward; Ⓑ *(auslegen)* advance ‹money, sum›

**vor|streichen** *unr. tr. V.* **etw. ~:** give sth. an undercoat; undercoat sth.

**Vor·stufe** *die* preliminary stage

**vor|stürmen** *itr. V.; mit sein* rush *or* charge forward

**Vor·tag** *der* day before; previous day; **am ~ der Prüfung** the day before *or* on the eve of the examination

**vor|tanzen** ❶ *tr. V.* **der Tanzlehrer tanzte ihnen den Foxtrott vor** the dancing teacher showed them *or* demonstrated how to dance the foxtrot. ❷ *itr. V.* demonstrate one's dancing ability; **jmdm. ~:** dance in front of sb.

**vor|tasten** *refl. V. (auch fig.)* feel one's way forward

**vor|täuschen** *tr. V.* feign ‹interest, illness, etc.›; simulate ‹reality etc.›; fake ‹crime›

**Vor·täuschung** *die* ⇒ **vortäuschen**: feigning; simulation; faking; **unter ~ falscher Tatsachen** under false pretences

**Vor·teil** /*od.* ˈfɔrtail/ *der* Ⓐ advantage; **~e und Nachteile einer Sache gegeneinander abwägen** weigh up the pros and cons *or* the advantages and disadvantages of sth.; **einen ~ aus etw. ziehen** derive an *or* some advantage from sth.; benefit from sth.; **auf seinen [eigenen] ~ bedacht sein** have an eye to the main chance *or* to one's own interests; **jmdm. gegenüber im/sehr im ~ sein** have an/a great advantage over sb.; **[für jmdn.] von ~ sein** be advantageous [to sb.]; **sich zu seinem ~ verändern** change for the better; Ⓑ *(Fußball, Hockey, Rugby usw.)* advantage; **~ gelten lassen, auf ~ erkennen** ‹referee› play advantage; Ⓒ *(Tennis)* advantage; **~ Aufschläger** ad in

**vorteilhaft** ❶ *Adj.* advantageous. ❷ *adv.* advantageously; **sich auf etw.** *(Akk.)* **~ auswirken** have a favourable *or* beneficial effect on sth.; **sich ~ kleiden** wear clothes that suit one

**Vortrag** /-traːk/ *der;* **~[e]s, Vorträge** /-trɛːɡə/ Ⓐ *(Rede)* talk; *(wissenschaftlich)* lecture; **einen ~ halten** give a talk/lecture; Ⓑ *(Darbietung)* presentation; performance; *(eines Gedichts)* recitation; rendering

**vor|tragen** *unr. tr. V.* Ⓐ *(darbieten)* perform ‹gymnastic routine etc.›; sing ‹song›; perform, play ‹piece of music›; recite ‹poem›; Ⓑ *(darlegen)* present ‹case, matter, request, demands›; lodge, make ‹complaint›; express ‹wish, desire›; **ich habe ihm die Gründe für meinen Entschluss vorgetragen** I told him the reasons for my decision

**Vortragende** *der/die; adj. Dekl.* speaker; *(bei wissenschaftlichem Vortrag)* lecturer

**Vortrags-: ~reihe** *die* series of lectures/talks; **~reise** *die* lecture tour

**vor·trefflich** ❶ *Adj.* excellent; splendid; superb ‹singer, player, swimmer, etc.›; **~ schmecken** taste excellent *or* superb. ❷ *adv.* excellently; splendidly; ‹sing, play, swim, etc.› superbly; **sich ~ für etw. eignen** be perfectly *or* excellently suited for sth.

V

**Vortrefflichkeit** *die;* **~:** excellence

**vor|treiben** *unr. tr. V.* drive ‹tunnel, shaft›

**vor|treten** *unr. itr. V.; mit sein* step forward

**Vor·tritt** *der* **A** **jmdm. den ~ lassen** (*auch fig.*) let sb. go first; **Damen haben den ~:** ladies first; **B** (*schweiz.*) ⇒ **Vorfahrt**

**Vortrupp** *der* advance guard; (*fig.*) vanguard

**vor|turnen** *tr. V.* **[jmdm.] eine Übung ~:** perform a gymnastic exercise [in front of sb.]; (*zur Nachahmung*) demonstrate a gymnastic exercise [to sb.]

**Vor·turner** *der*, **Vor·turnerin** *die* demonstrator [gymnast]

**vorüber** *Adv.* **A** (*zeitlich*) over; **~ sein** be over; ‹pain› be gone; ‹danger› be past; **die Gelegenheit ist noch nicht ~:** the opportunity has not yet passed *or* is still there; **das ist aus und ~** (*ugs.*) that is [all] over and done with; **B** (*räumlich*) past; **an etw.** (*Dat.*) **~:** past sth.

**vorüber|gehen** *unr. itr. V.; mit sein* **A** go *or* walk past; pass by; **an jmdm./etw. ~:** go past sb./sth.; pass sb./sth.; (*achtlos*) pass sb./sth. by; **im V~:** in passing; (*fig.: nebenbei*) in a trice; **B** (*fig.*) **an jmdm./etw. ~:** ignore sb./sth.; **die Krise ist an uns** (*Dat.*) **vorübergegangen** the crisis passed us by *or* left us untouched; ⇒ *auch* **Kelch A**; **spurlos 2**; **C** (*vergehen*) pass; ‹pain› go; ‹storm› pass, blow over; **das geht vorüber** (*ugs.*) (*tröstend*) it'll pass; (*scherzh. iron.*) that won't last long; **eine Gelegenheit ~ lassen** let an opportunity slip; miss an opportunity

**vorübergehend** ❶ *Adj.* temporary; passing ‹interest, infatuation›; brief ‹illness, stay›. ❷ *adv.* temporarily; (*auf kurze Zeit*) for a short time; briefly

**Vor·urteil** *das* bias; (*voreilige Schlussfolgerung*) prejudice (**gegen** against, towards); **gegen etw. ~e haben** *od.* (*geh.*) **hegen** be biased/prejudiced against *or* towards sth.

**vorurteils-, Vorurteils-:** **~frei**, **~los** ❶ *Adj.* open-minded; ❷ *adv.* open-mindedly; **~losigkeit** *die;* **~~:** open-mindedness

**Vor·väter** *Pl.* forefathers

**Vor·vergangenheit** *die* (*Sprachw.*) pluperfect

**Vor·verkauf** *der* advance sale of tickets; advance booking; **Karten im ~ besorgen** buy tickets in advance; **im ~ kosten die Karten 20 Mark** the tickets cost 20 marks if bought in advance

**Vorverkaufs·kasse** *die* advance ticket office; (*im Theater*) box office

**vor|verlegen** *tr. V.* **A** (*zeitlich*) bring forward (**auf** + *Akk.* to; **um** by); **B** (*räumlich*) move forward; (*Milit.*) push forward ‹front, position›

**vor·veröffentlichen** *tr. V.* arrange advance publication of; **vorveröffentlicht werden** appear in advance publication

**Vor·verurteilung** *die* condemnation in advance of trial

**vor·vor·gestern** *Adv.* (*ugs.*) three days ago; the day before the day before yesterday

**vor|wagen** *refl. V.* dare to go forward *or* (*Mil.*) advance; **sich zu weit ~:** venture too far forward; (*fig.*) stick one's neck out too far (*coll.*)

**Vorwahl** *die* **A** (*Politik*) preliminary election; (*in den USA*) primary; **B** (*Fernspr.*) dialling code

**Vor·wahlkampf** *der* (*Politik*) advance election campaign

**Vorwähl·nummer** *die* (*Fernspr.*) dialling code

**Vorwand** *der;* **~[e]s, Vorwände** pretext; (*Ausrede*) excuse; **etw. zum ~ nehmen** use sth. as a pretext/an excuse; **unter dem ~, dass ...** giving as one's pretext that ...

**vor|wärmen** *tr. V.* warm ‹bed, room, teapot, etc.› beforehand; (*bes. Technik*) preheat ‹air, oven, etc.›

**vor|warnen** *tr. V.* **jmdn. ~:** give sb. advance warning; warn sb. [in advance]; **vorgewarnt sein** be forewarned

**Vor·warnung** *die* [advance] warning; **~ geben** give an early *or* advance warning

*old spelling (see note on page 1707)

**vor·wärts** *Adv.* forwards; (*weiter*) onwards; (*mit der Vorderseite voran*) facing forwards; **~ marsch!** (*Milit.*) forward, march!; **~!** (*weiter!*) come on!; **den Wagen ~ einparken** park the car nose first; **ein Schritt ~** (*auch fig.*) a step forwards; **mach mal [etwas] ~!** (*ugs.*) get a move on! (*coll.*); **eine Rolle/ein Salto ~:** a forward roll/somersault; **das Buch kenne ich ~ und rückwärts** I know the book inside out; **~ gehen** (*fig.*) make progress; **mit der Arbeit will es nicht ~ gehen** the work just isn't getting anywhere; **~ kommen** (*fig.*) make progress; (*im Beruf, Leben*) get on *or* ahead; **~ bringen** + *Akk.* advance ‹plan, process, cause›; allow ‹person› to make progress

**vorwärts-, Vorwärts-:** ***~|bringen** ⇒ **vorwärts**; **~gang** *der* forward gear; ***~|gehen** ⇒ **vorwärts**; ***~|kommen** ⇒ **vorwärts**; **~strategie** *die* strategy of attack; **~verteidigung** *die* (*Milit.*) forward defence

**Vor·wäsche** *die* prewash

**Vorwasch·gang** *der* prewash programme

**vor·weg** *Adv.* **A** (*vorher*) beforehand; **um es ~ zu sagen, ...** let me say right away ...; **B** (*voraus*) in front; ahead; **~ marschieren** march at the head of the column; **C** (*vor allem*) above all

**Vor·weg** *der: in* **im ~[e]** in anticipation

**Vorwegnahme** *die;* **~:** anticipation

**vorweg|nehmen** *unr. tr. V.* anticipate; **um das Ergebnis vorwegzunehmen, ...** to come straight to the result ...

**Vor·wehe** *die* (*Med.*) early contraction

**vor·weihnachtlich** ❶ *Adj.* pre-Christmas. ❷ *adv.* **~ gestimmt** in a pre-Christmas mood; **~ dekoriert** adorned with Christmas decorations

**Vor·weihnachtszeit** *die* pre-Christmas period

**vor|weisen** *unr. tr. V.* produce; **~ können, vorzuweisen haben** (*fig.*) possess ‹knowledge, experience, etc.›

**vor|werfen** *unr. tr. V.* **A** (*zum Vorwurf machen*) **jmdm. etw. ~:** reproach sb. with sth.; (*beschuldigen*) accuse sb. of sth.; **jmdm. ~, etw. getan zu haben** reproach sb. with *or* accuse sb. of doing *or* having done sth.; **jmdm. Parteilichkeit/Rücksichtslosigkeit ~:** accuse sb. of being biased/careless; **ich habe mir nichts vorzuwerfen** I've nothing to reproach myself for; **sie haben sich** (*Dat.*) **[gegenseitig] nichts vorzuwerfen** one is as bad as the other; **B** (*hinwerfen*) **etw. den Tieren [zum Fraß] ~:** throw sth. to the animals [as food]; **C** (*nach vorn werfen*) throw ‹head, ball, etc.› forward

**Vor·werk** *das* **A** (*veralt.: eines Guts*) outlying farm; **B** (*hist.: einer Festung*) outworks *pl.*

**vor|wiegen** *unr. itr. V.* predominate

**vor·wiegend** *Adv.* mainly

**Vor·wissen** *das* previous *or* existing knowledge; (*über einen bestimmten Sachverhalt*) foreknowledge; prior knowledge

**Vor·witz** *der* bumptiousness; (*eines Kindes*) pertness; (*Anmaßung*) presumption; (*Neugier*) excessive curiosity

**vor·witzig** ❶ *Adj.* bumptious; pert ‹child›; (*anmaßend*) presumptuous ‹speech etc.›; (*neugierig*) curious. ❷ *adv.* (*anmaßend*) presumptuously

**vor|wölben** ❶ *tr. V.* push out ‹stomach etc.›. ❷ *refl. V.* bulge; ‹curtain, sail› billow [out]; **vorgewölbt** puffed-out ‹chest›; pouting ‹lips›

**Vor·wort** *das; Pl.* **~e** foreword; preface

**Vor·wurf** *der* reproach; (*Beschuldigung*) accusation; **jmdm. etw. zum ~ machen** reproach sb. with sth.; **jmdm. [wegen etw.] einen ~/Vorwürfe machen** reproach sb. [for sth.]; **sich** (*Dat.*) **[wegen etw.] [bittere] Vorwürfe machen** reproach *or* blame oneself [bitterly] [for sth.]; **..., sagte er mit leisem ~ [in der Stimme]** ..., he said in a tone of gentle reproach

**vorwurfs·voll** ❶ *Adj.* reproachful. ❷ *adv.* reproachfully

**vor|zählen** *tr. V.* **[jmdm.] Geld** *usw.* **~:** count out money *etc.* for sb.

**Vor·zeichen** *das* **A** (*Omen*) omen; **B** (*Math.*) [algebraic] sign; **unter anderen/mit veränderten ~** (*fig.*) under different/changed conditions; **C** (*Musik*) sharp/flat [sign]; (*für Tonart*) key signature

**vor|zeichnen** *tr. V.* **A** make a preparatory sketch for ‹picture etc.›; **B** (*zur Nachahmung*) **jmdm. etw ~:** draw sth. for sb. to copy; **C** (*im Voraus festlegen*) lay down, set out ‹policy etc.›; (*vorschreiben*) prescribe ‹path›

**vorzeigbar** *Adj.* presentable

**vor|zeigen** *tr. V.* produce, show ‹passport, ticket, etc.›; show ‹hands, fingernails›

**Vor·zeit** *die* prehistory; **in grauer ~:** in the dim and distant past

**vorzeitig** ❶ *Adj.* premature ‹birth, death, ageing›; early ‹retirement›. ❷ *adv.* prematurely; **~ pensioniert werden** be retired early

**Vorzeitigkeit** *die;* **~** (*Sprachw.*) anteriority

**vor·zeitlich** *Adj.* prehistoric

**Vor·zensur** *die* **A** preliminary censorship; **B** (*Schulw.*) classwork mark (*to be combined with examination marks in deciding the final grading*)

**vor|ziehen** *unr. tr. V.* **A** (*lieber mögen*) prefer; (*bevorzugen, besser behandeln*) favour, give preference to ‹person›; **etw. einer Sache** (*Dat.*) **~:** prefer sth. to sth.; **ich ziehe ihn seinem Bruder vor** I prefer him to *or* like him better than his brother; **das jüngste Kind wird oft [den anderen] vorgezogen** the youngest child is often given preference [over the others]; **B** (*zuziehen*) draw ‹curtain›; **C** (*vorverlegen*) bring forward ‹date› (**um** by); **der Arzt hat mich vorgezogen** (*ugs.*) the doctor gave me priority; **vorgezogene Wahlen** early elections; **D** (*nach vorn ziehen*) pull forward; (*Milit.*) move ‹troops› forward

**Vor·zimmer** *das* **A** outer office; anteroom; **B** (*österr.: Diele*) hall

**Vorzimmer·dame** *die* receptionist

**Vor·zug** *der* **A** preference (**gegenüber** over); **jmdm./einer Sache den ~ geben** prefer sb./sth.; (*Vorrang*) give precedence to sb./sth.; **den ~ haben** be preferred/take precedence; **B** (*gute Eigenschaft*) good quality; merit; (*Vorteil*) advantage; **C** (*österr. Schulw.: Auszeichnung*) distinction; **D** (*Vorrecht, Vergünstigung*) privilege

**vorzüglich** /fo:ɐ̯ˈtsy:klɪç/ ❶ *Adj.* excellent; first-rate; (*in Briefen*) **mit ~er Hochachtung** (*veralt.*) yours faithfully; your obedient servant (*dated*); **~ schmecken** taste excellent. ❷ *adv.* excellently; **~ speisen** have an excellent meal

**Vorzüglichkeit** *die;* **~, ~en** excellence

**vorzugs-, Vorzugs-:** **~aktie** *die* (*Wirtsch.*) preference share; **~milch** *die* best quality milk; **~weise** *Adv.* (*hauptsächlich*) primarily; (*besonders*) especially; particularly; (*am liebsten*) preferably

**Vota, Voten** ⇒ **Votum**

**votieren** /voˈti:rən/ *itr. V.* (*geh.*) vote

**Votiv·bild** *das* votive picture

**Votum** /ˈvo:tʊm/ *das;* **~s, Vota** *od.* **Voten** **A** vote; **B** (*geh.: Urteil*) judgment

**Voyeur** /vo̯aˈjø:ɐ̯/ *der;* **~s, ~e** voyeur

**Voyeurin** *die;* **~, ~nen** voyeuse; voyeur

**VP** *Abk.* (*DDR*) **Volkspolizei**

**VR** *Abk.* **Volksrepublik**

**vulgär** /vʊlˈgɛ:ɐ̯/ ❶ *Adj.* vulgar. ❷ *adv.* in a vulgar way; **er drückt sich sehr ~ aus** he uses very vulgar language

**Vulgarität** /vʊlgariˈtɛ:t/ *die;* **~, ~en** vulgarity

**Vulgär·latein** *das* vulgar Latin

**Vulkan** /vʊlˈka:n/ *der;* **~s, ~e** volcano; **wie auf einem ~ leben** be sitting on a powder keg; ⇒ *auch* **Tanz A**

**Vulkan·ausbruch** *der* volcanic eruption

**vulkanisch** *Adj.* volcanic

**Vulkanisier·anstalt** *die* (*veralt.*) vulcanizing plant

**vulkanisieren** *tr. V.* vulcanize

**Vulkanismus** *der;* **~:** vulcanism *no art.*

**Vulva** /ˈvʊlva/ *die;* **~, Vulven** vulva

**v. u. Z.** *Abk.* **vor unserer Zeit[rechnung]** BC

V

# W w

**w, W** /ve:/ *das;* **~s, ~:** w, W

**W** *Abk.* A **West, Westen** W.; B **Watt** W.

**WAA** *Abk.* **Wiederaufbereitungsanlage**

**Waadt** /va[:]t/ *die;* ~, **Waadt·land** *das* Vaud *no art.*

**Waage** /'va:gə/ *die;* ~, **~n** A [pair *sing.* of] scales *pl.; (Gold~, Apotheker~ usw.)* balance; *(Brücken~)* weighbridge; **etw. mit der ~ wiegen** weigh sth. on the scales; **er bringt 80 kg auf die ~** *(ugs.)* he tips the scales at 80 kilos; **sich** *(Dat.) od.* **einander die ~ halten** balance out; balance one another; ⇒ *auch* **Zünglein** B; B *(Astrol., Astron.)* **[die] ~:** Libra; **er ist [eine] ~:** he is a Libra *or* Libran

**waage-, Waage-: ~balken** *der* balance *or* scale beam; **~recht** ❶ *Adj.* horizontal; ❷ *adv.* horizontally; **~rechte** *die; adj. Dekl.* A *(Linie)* horizontal line; horizontal; B *(Lage)* horizontal position; **in der ~n** horizontal; level; *(flach liegend)* flat

**waag·recht** ⇒ **waagerecht**

**Waag·schale** *die* scale pan; **etw. in die ~schale werfen** *(fig.)* bring sth. to bear

**wabb[e]lig** /'vab(ə)lɪç/ *Adj. (ugs.)* wobbly; flabby ‹muscles, flesh›

**Wabe** /'va:bə/ *die;* ~, **~n** honeycomb

**Waben·honig** *der* comb honey

**wabern** *itr. V. (geh.)* A ‹smoke, mist, cloud› swirl, drift; ‹steam› billow; *(fig.)* fluctuate; B *(flackern, lodern)* ‹flames etc.› flicker

**wach** /vax/ ❶ *Adj.* A awake; **in ~em** *od.* **im ~en Zustand** in a state of wakefulness; **jmdn. ~ machen** wake sb. up; **jmdn. ~ küssen** wake sb. with a kiss; **sich ~ halten** stay awake; **er wurde früh ~:** he woke up early; **~ halten** + *Akk.* keep ‹interest, memory, etc.› alive; B *(aufmerksam, rege)* alert ‹mind, eyes, etc.›; attentive ‹audience›; lively, keen ‹interest›; **mit ~em Verstand** with an alert *or* lively mind. ❷ *adv.* alertly; attentively

**Wach-: ~ablösung** *die* changing of the guard/watch; **eine politische ~ablösung** *(fig.)* a change of political leadership; **~boot** *das* patrol boat; **~dienst** *der (Milit.)* guard *or* sentry duty; *(Seew.)* watch [duty]; **~dienst haben** *(Milit.)* be on guard *or* sentry duty; *(Seew.)* be on watch; have the watch

**Wache** /'vaxə/ *die;* ~, **~n** A *(Wachdienst) (Milit.)* guard *or* sentry duty; *(Seew.)* watch [duty]; *(Seew.: Zeitabschnitt)* watch; **~ haben** *od.* **halten** *(Milit.)* be on guard *or* sentry duty; *(Seew.)* be on watch; have the watch; **~ schieben** *(ugs.)* do sentry duty; **~ gehen** *(Seemannsspr.)* do watch duty; **~ stehen** *(Milit.)* stand on guard; *(Ausschau halten)* keep lookout; B *(Wächter)* guard; *(Milit.: Posten)* sentry; **eine ~ aufstellen** post a guard/sentry; C *(Mannschaft) (Milit.)* guard; *(Seew.)* watch; D *(Wachlokal)* guardroom; *(Gebäude)* guardhouse; *(Polizei~)* police station

**wachen** *itr. V.* A *(geh.: wach sein)* be awake; B *(um jmdn. zu betreuen)* **bei jmdm. ~:** stay up at sb.'s bedside; sit up with sb.; C **über etw.** *(Akk.)* **~:** watch over *or* keep an eye on sth.; *(über~)* supervise sth.; **er wachte darüber, dass ...** he watched carefully to ensure that ...

**wach-, Wach-: ~habend** *Adj.* **~habender Offizier** *(Milit.)* duty officer; *(Seew.)* officer of the watch; **~habende** *der; adj. Dekl. (Milit.)* person on guard; guard; *(Seew.)* watch; ***~|halten** ⇒ **wach** 1 A

**Wachheit** *die;* **~:** alertness; *(Scharfsinn)* acuity

**Wach-: ~hund** *der* guard dog; watchdog; **~lokal** *das (Milit.)* guardroom; **~mann** *der; Pl.* **~männer** *od.* **~leute** ▶ 159 A watchman; B *(österr.: Polizist)* policeman; **~mannschaft** *die (Milit.)* guard detachment

**Wacholder** /va'xɔldɐ/ *der;* **~s, ~** A juniper; B *(Schnaps) spirit from juniper berries;* ≈ gin

**Wacholder-: ~beere** *die* juniper berry; **~schnaps** *der* ⇒ **Wacholder** B

**wach-, Wach-: ~posten** *der (Milit.)* guard; sentry; **~|rufen** *unr. tr. V.* awaken, rouse ‹enthusiasm, ambition, etc.›; evoke, bring back ‹memory, past›; **~|rütteln** *tr. V.* rouse *or* shake ‹person› out of his/her apathy; stir ‹conscience›

**Wachs** /vaks/ *das;* **~es, ~e** wax; **er wurde weich wie ~:** he became really amenable; **~ in jmds. Hand** *od.* **Händen sein** *(fig.)* be like wax in sb.'s hands

**Wachs·abdruck** *der; Pl.* **Wachsabdrücke** wax impression

**wachsam** /'vaxza:m/ ❶ *Adj.* watchful; vigilant; **sei ~!** be on your guard!. ❷ *adv.* vigilantly

**Wachsamkeit** *die;* **~:** vigilance

**Wachs-: ~bild** *das* wax relief; **~bohne** *die* wax bean

**wachsen**[1] *unr. itr. V.; mit sein* A grow; ‹shadow› lengthen; ‹building› rise; **sich** *(Dat.)* **einen Bart ~ lassen** grow a beard; **sich** *(Dat.)* **die Haare/die Fingernägel ~ lassen** let one's hair/fingernails grow long; **hoch gewachsen** tall; **ein schlank gewachsener Mann** a slimly-built man; **er ist mit seiner Verantwortung gewachsen** *(fig.)* he has grown with his responsibilities; B *(fig.: allmählich entstehen)* evolve [naturally]; **eine gewachsene Stadt** a city which has evolved naturally; **eine gewachsene Ordnung** an organic order; C *(fig.: größer werden)* grow; ‹wealth, danger, etc.› grow, increase; ‹flood, tide› rise; ‹tension, excitement, anger, astonishment› grow, mount

**wachsen**[2] *tr. V.* wax; *(polieren)* wax-polish

**wächsern** /'vɛksɐn/ *Adj. (geh.: bleich)* waxen

**Wachs-: ~figur** *die* waxwork; wax figure; **~figuren·kabinett** *das* waxworks *sing. or pl.;* waxworks museum; **wir waren im ~figurenkabinett** we went to see the waxworks; **~kerze** *die* wax candle; **~malerei** *die* encaustic; **~mal·kreide** *die* wax crayon

**Wach·soldat** *der,* **Wach·soldatin** *die* A sentry; B *(eines Garderegiments)* Guard

**Wachspapier** *das* waxed paper

**wächst** /vɛkst/ *2. u. 3. Pers. Sg. Präsens v.* **wachsen**

**Wachs·tafel** *die* wax tablet

**Wach·stube** *die* A *(Milit.)* guardroom; B *(Polizeiwache)* duty room

**Wachs·tuch** *das* A *Pl.* **~e** *(Material)* oilcloth; B *Pl.* **Wachs·tücher** *(Tischtuch)* oilcloth tablecloth

**Wachstum** /'vakstu:m/ *das;* **~s** growth; **im ~ zurückgeblieben** stunted ‹tree etc.›; underdeveloped ‹person›

**wachstums-, Wachstums-: ~fördernd** *Adj.* promoting growth *postpos.;* **~fördernd wirken** promote growth; **~hemmend** *Adj.* inhibiting growth *postpos.;* **~hemmend wirken** inhibit growth; **~hormon** *das* growth hormone; **~rate** *die (bes. Wirtsch.)* growth rate; **~störung** *die* growth disorder

**wachs·weich** *Adj.* A as soft as butter *postpos.;* B *(fig.: ängstlich, gefügig)* [weak and] submissive

**Wacht** /vaxt/ *die;* ~, **~en** *(geh.)* guard *or* sentry duty; **~ haben** *od.* **halten** be on guard *or* sentry duty

***Wächte** ⇒ **Wechte**

**Wachtel** /'vaxtl̩/ *die;* ~, **~n** quail

**Wächter** /'vɛçtɐ/ *der;* **~s, ~:** guard; *(Leib~)* bodyguard; *(Nacht~, Turm~)* watchman; *(Park~)* [park]-keeper; *(fig.)* guardian

**Wächterin** *die;* ~, **~nen** ⇒ **Wächter**

**Wacht-: ~meister** *der* ▶ 91 A *(Dienstgrad der Polizei)* constable *(Brit.)*; patrolman *(Amer.)*; B *(ugs.: Polizist)* policeman; *(als Anrede)* **Herr ~meister** officer; C *(Milit. hist.)* sergeant; **~meisterin** *die* ▶ 91 A *(Dienstgrad der Polizei)* constable *(Brit.)*; patrolwoman *(Amer.)*; B *(ugs.: Polizistin)* policewoman; **~posten** *der* ⇒ **Wachposten**

**Wach·traum** *der* daydream; waking dream

**Wach[t]·turm** *der* watchtower

**Wach- und Schließ·gesellschaft** *die* property security company

**Wach-: ~zimmer** *das (österr.)* [police] duty room; **~zustand** *der* waking state

**wackelig** ❶ *Adj.* A *(nicht stabil)* wobbly ‹chair, table, etc.›; loose ‹tooth›; shaky, rickety ‹structure›; rickety ‹car, furniture›; B *(ugs.: kraftlos, schwach)* frail ‹person›; frail, doddery ‹old person›; **~ auf den Beinen sein** be a bit shaky on one's feet; C *(fig. ugs.: gefährdet, bedroht)* dodgy *(Brit. coll.)* ‹business›; insecure, shaky ‹job›; **er steht in der Schule/in Latein ziemlich ~:** things are dodgy for him at school *(Brit. coll.)*/his Latin is somewhat shaky. ❷ *adv.* **~ stehen** be wobbly; *(nicht fest gefügt sein)* be shaky/rickety

**Wackel·kontakt** *der (Elektrot.)* loose connection

**wackeln** /'vakl̩n/ *itr. V.* A wobble; ‹post etc.› move about; ‹tooth etc.› be loose; ‹house, window, etc.› shake; **mit dem Kopf/den Ohren/den Hüften ~:** waggle *or* wag one's head/ears/wiggle one's hips; **der Hund wackelte mit dem Schwanz** the dog wagged its tail; B *mit sein (ugs.: gehen)* ‹person› totter; C *(ugs.: gefährdet, bedroht sein)* ‹job, government› be insecure; ‹firm› be in a dodgy *(Brit. coll.) or* shaky state

**Wackel·peter** *der;* **~s, ~** *(ugs.)* wobbly jelly

**wacker** /'vakɐ/ *(veralt.)* ❶ *Adj.* A *(rechtschaffen)* upright; decent; *(iron.)* trusty; worthy; B *(tüchtig)* good; **ein ~er Zecher/Esser** a hearty drinker/eater; C *(tapfer, mutig)* valiant. ❷ *adv.* A *(tapfer)* valiantly; **sich ~ halten/schlagen** put up a good show; B *(tüchtig)* ‹eat, drink, etc.› heartily

**Wacker·stein** *der (veralt.)* lump of rock

**wacklig** /'vaklɪç/ ⇒ **wackelig**

**Wade** /'va:də/ *die;* ~, **~n** ▶ 471 *(Anat.)* calf

**Waden-: ~bein** *das* ▶ 471 *(Anat.)* fibula; **~krampf** *der* ▶ 474 cramp in one's calf; **einen ~krampf bekommen** get cramp in one's calf; **~wickel** *der* leg compress

**Waffe** /'vafə/ *die;* ~, **~n** A *(auch fig.)* weapon; *(Feuerwaffe)* firearm; **~n tragen** bear arms; **der Kriegsdienst mit der ~:** service under arms; **unter ~n stehen** *od.* **sein** be under arms; **jmdn. zu den ~n rufen** call sb. to arms; **zu den ~n rufen** issue a call to arms; **die ~n strecken** lay down one's arms; *(fig.)* give up the struggle; **jmdn. mit seinen eigenen ~n schlagen** *(fig.)* defeat sb. with his own arguments; B *(veralt.: Waffengattung)* arm [of the service]

**Waffel** /'vafl̩/ *die;* ~, **~n** A waffle; *(dünne ~, Eis~)* wafer; B *(Eistüte)* cone

**Waffel·eisen** *das* waffle iron

**waffen-, Waffen-: ~arsenal** *das* arsenal [of weapons]; (*Versteck*) cache of arms; **~besitz** *der* possession of a firearm/firearms; **~bruder** *der* (*geh.*) brother- *or* comrade-in-arms; **~gang** *der* (*geh.*) engagement; (*fig.*) clash; **~gattung** *die* Ⓐ (*Truppengattung*) arm [of the service]; Ⓑ (*Teilstreitkraft*) armed service; **~gewalt** *die* armed force; **mit ~gewalt** by force of arms; **~handel** *der* arms trade; arms trading; **~händler** *der*, **~händlerin** *die* arms dealer; **~kammer** *die* (*Milit.*) armoury; **~lager** *das* arsenal; **~rock** *der* (*veralt.*) tunic; **~ruhe** *die* ceasefire; **~schein** *der* firearms licence; **~schmied** *der* armourer; **~schmiede** *die* (*geh.*) armoury; **~schmuggel** *der* gun-running; **~-SS** *die* (*ns.*): *armed divisions of the SS;* Waffen-SS; **~starrend** *Adj.* (*geh.*) armed to the teeth *postpos.;* **~still·stand** *der* armistice; [permanent] ceasefire; **~stillstands·abkommen** *das* armistice agreement; **~stillstands·linie** *die* ceasefire line; **~technik** *die* arms technology *no art.*

**wägbar** /ˈvɛːkbaːɐ̯/ *Adj.* **nicht ~:** imponderable; **ein kaum ~es Risiko** a risk which it is barely possible to gauge

**Wage·mut** *der* daring; audacity

**wage·mutig** *Adj.* daring; audacious

**wagen** /ˈvaːgn̩/ ❶ *tr. V.* risk; **[es] ~, etw. zu tun** dare to do sth.; **einen Versuch/eine Wette ~:** dare to make an attempt/a bet; risk an attempt/a bet; **eine Bitte/Behauptung ~:** venture a request/statement; **wer nicht wagt, der nicht gewinnt** (*Spr.*), **frisch gewagt ist halb gewonnen** (*Spr.*) nothing ventured, nothing gained; ⇒ *auch* **gewagt** 2. ❷ *refl. V.* **sich irgendwohin/nicht irgendwohin ~:** venture somewhere/not dare to go somewhere; **sich an etw.** (*Akk.*) **~:** dare to tackle sth.; venture to tackle sth.

**wägen** /ˈvɛːgn̩/ *unr. od. regelm. tr. V.* Ⓐ ⇒ **wiegen**[1] 2; Ⓑ (*geh.: ab~*) weigh up ‹pros and cons etc.›

**Wagen** *der;* **~s, ~** Ⓐ (*PKW*) car; (*Omnibus*) bus; (*LKW*) truck; lorry (*Brit.*); (*Liefer~*) van; Ⓑ (*Pferde~*) cart; (*Kutsche*) coach; carriage; (*Plan~*) wagon; (*Zirkus~, Wohn~*) caravan (*Brit.*); trailer (*esp. Amer.*); **der Große ~** (*Astron.*) the Plough; the Big Dipper (*Amer.*); (*Ursa Major*) the Great Bear; **der Kleine ~** (*Astron.*) the Little Dipper (*Amer.*); (*Ursa Minor*) the Little Bear; **jmdm. an den ~ fahren** (*fig. ugs.*) give sb. what for (*coll.*); pitch into sb. (*coll.*); **sich [nicht] vor jmds. ~** (*Akk.*) **spannen lassen** (*fig. ugs.*) not let sb. lead one by the nose; Ⓒ (*Eisenbahn~*) (*Personen~*) coach; carriage; (*Güter~*) truck; wagon; car (*Amer.*); (*Straßenbahn~*) car; Ⓓ (*Kinder~, Puppen~*) pram (*Brit.*); baby carriage (*Amer.*); (*Sport~*) pushchair (*Brit.*); stroller (*Amer.*); Ⓔ (*Hand~*) handcart; Ⓕ (*Einkaufs~*) [shopping] trolley; Ⓖ (*Schreibmaschinen~*) carriage; Ⓗ (*Servier~, Tee~*) trolley

**Wagen-: ~burg** *die* Ⓐ (*hist.*) [defensive] circle of wagons; Ⓑ *urban, gypsy-style encampment;* **~heber** *der* jack; **~ladung** *die* truckload; lorryload (*Brit.*); **~park** *der* vehicle pool; **~pflege** *die* car care; **~plane** *die* tarpaulin; **~rad** *das* cartwheel; **~rennen** *das* (*hist.*) chariot race; **~schlag** *der* (*geh.*) ⇒ **~tür**; **~schmiere** *die* cart grease; **~tür** *die* Ⓐ (*einer Kutsche*) carriage door; Ⓑ (*eines Autos*) car door; **~wäsche** *die* car wash

**Waggon** /vaˈgɔŋ, *südd., österr.:* vaˈgoːn/ *der;* **~s, ~s,** *südd., österr.:* **~s, ~e** Ⓐ (*Güterwagen*) wagon; truck (*Brit.*); car (*Amer.*); Ⓑ (*veralt.: Personenwagen*) carriage; coach

**waggon·weise** *Adv.* by the wagonload

**waghalsig** ❶ *Adj.* daring; risky ‹speculation›; (*leichtsinnig*) reckless ‹driver, rider›. ❷ *adv.* daringly; ‹speculate› riskily; (*leichtsinnig*) recklessly

**Wagnerianer** /vaːgnəˈri̯aːnɐ/ *der;* **~s, ~, Wagnerianerin** *die;* **~, ~nen** Wagnerian

**wagnerianisch** *Adj.* Wagnerian

**Wagnis** /ˈvaːknɪs/ *das;* **~ses, ~se** daring exploit *or* feat; (*Risiko*) risk

**Wahl** /vaːl/ *die;* **~, ~en** Ⓐ choice; **eine/seine ~ treffen** make a/one's choice; **jmdm. die ~ lassen** let sb. choose; **es gibt/mir bleibt** *od.* **ich habe keine [andere] ~:** there is/I have no choice *or* alternative; **vor die ~ gestellt, nach A oder B zu fahren** faced with the choice between going to A or B; **es stehen drei Menüs zur ~:** there are three set meals to choose from; **die ~ fiel auf ihn** the choice fell on him; **in die engere ~ kommen** be short-listed *or* put on the shortlist (*Brit.*); **das Mädchen seiner ~** (*geh.*) his intended; **wer die ~ hat, hat die Qual** (*Spr.*) it's agonizing to have to choose; Ⓑ (*in ein Gremium, Amt usw.*) election; **die ~[en] zum Bundestag vom 6. März** the election[s] [to the Bundestag] of 6 March; **in Hessen ist ~** *od.* **sind ~en** there are elections in Hessen; **ich werde nicht zur ~ gehen** I am not going to vote; **sich zur ~ stellen** stand *or* (*Amer.*) run for election; **jmdn. zur ~ vorschlagen** suggest sb. as a candidate; nominate sb.; **seine ~ zum Präsidenten** his election as President *or* to the Presidency; **geheime ~:** secret ballot; Ⓒ (*Güteklasse*) **erste/zweite/dritte ~:** best/second/third quality; **die Socken sind zweite ~:** the socks are seconds

**Wahl-** *in* **~berliner/~bayer** *usw.* (*scherzh.*) Berliner/Bavarian *etc.* by adoption

**Wahl-: ~alter** *das* voting age; **~aus·gang** *der* election result

**wählbar** *Adj.* Ⓐ eligible for election *postpos.;* **diese Partei ist für mich einfach nicht ~:** I just couldn't vote for this party; Ⓑ (*passiv wahlberechtigt*) eligible to stand for election *postpos.*

**wahl-, Wahl-: ~benachrichtigung** *die* polling card; **~berechtigt** *Adj.* eligible *or* entitled to vote *postpos.;* **~berechtigte** *der/die; adj. Dekl.* person entitled to vote; **~beteiligung** *die* turnout; **die ~beteiligung lag bei 81%** there was an 81% turnout; **~bezirk** *der* ward

**wählen** /ˈvɛːlən/ ❶ *tr. V.* Ⓐ choose; (*aus~*) select ‹station, programme, etc.›; **seine Worte [sorgfältig/genau] ~:** choose one's words [carefully]; **sich** (*Dat.*) **jmdn. zum Vorbild ~:** take sb. as one's model; model oneself on sb.; ⇒ *auch* **gewählt** 2, 3; Ⓑ (*Fernspr.*) dial ‹number›; Ⓒ (*durch Stimmabgabe*) elect; **jmdn. ins Parlament/in den Vorstand ~:** elect sb. to Parliament/to the board; **jmdn. zum Vorsitzenden ~:** elect sb. as chairman; Ⓓ (*stimmen für*) vote for ‹party, candidate›.
❷ *itr. V.* Ⓐ choose; **zwischen zwei Möglichkeiten** (*Dat.*) **~:** choose between two possibilities; **haben Sie schon gewählt?** (*im Lokal*) are you ready to order?; Ⓑ (*Fernspr.*) dial; Ⓒ (*stimmen*) vote; **konservativ/grün ~:** vote Conservative/for the Greens; **wann wird in Hessen gewählt?** when are the elections in Hessen?

**Wähler** *der;* **~s, ~:** voter

**Wähler·auftrag** *der* mandate [given by the electorate]

**Wahl·ergebnis** *das* election result

**Wählerin** *die;* **~, ~nen** voter

**Wähler·initiative** *die* Ⓐ voters' campaign; Ⓑ (*Gruppe*) voters' action group

**wählerisch** *Adj.* choosy; particular **(in** + *Dat.* about); **er war in seiner Ausdrucksweise nicht sehr ~:** his choice of vocabulary was not exactly refined

**Wählerschaft** *die;* **~, ~en** electorate; **die ~ der SPD** the SPD's voters *pl.;* those who vote for the SPD

**Wähler-: ~stimme** *die* vote; **~verzeichnis** *das* electoral register *or* roll

**wahl-, Wahl-: ~fach** *das* (*Schulw.*) optional subject; **~frei** *Adj.* optional; **~gang** *der* ballot; **~geheimnis** *das* secrecy *or* confidentiality of the ballot; **~geschenk** *das* pre-election bonus; **~gesetz** *das* electoral law; **~heimat** *die* adopted country/place of residence; **~helfer** *der*, **~helferin** *die* Ⓐ election worker; Ⓑ (*Helfer[in] im Wahlkampf*) supporter (*at election time*); **~kabine** *die* polling booth; **~kampf** *der* election campaign; **~kreis** *der* constituency; **~leiter** *der*, **~leiterin** *die* returning officer (*Brit.*); election official (*Amer.*); **~liste** *die* list of candidates; **~lokal** *das* polling station; **~los** ❶ *Adj.* indiscriminate; random; ❷ *adv.* indiscriminately; at random; **~los durcheinander** ‹eat, drink, read› in any *or* (*coll.*) any old order; **~mann** *der; Pl.* **~männer** elector (*elected by and representing other voters*); **~möglichkeit** *die* choice; (*Alternative*) alternative; **~nacht** *die* election night; **~niederlage** *die* election defeat; **~periode** *die* legislative period; (*eines Amtsträgers*) term in office; **~pflicht** *die* compulsory voting; **~plakat** *das* election poster; **~programm** *das* election manifesto; **~propaganda** *die* election propaganda; **~recht** *das* Ⓐ **[aktives] ~recht** right to vote; (*einer Gruppe*) franchise; **[passives] ~recht** right to stand [as a candidate] for election; Ⓑ (*Rechtsvorschriften*) electoral law; **~rede** *die* election speech

**Wähl·scheibe** *die* (*Fernspr.*) dial

**wahl-, Wahl-: ~schein** *der* voting permit (*esp. for postal voter*); **~sieg** *der* election victory; **~spruch** *der* motto; **~system** *das* electoral system; **~tag** *der* election day; polling day; **~urne** *die* ballot box; **~verfahren** *das* electoral procedure; **~verhalten** *das* voting habits *pl.;* **~versammlung** *die* election meeting; **~versprechen** *das* election promise; **~verteidiger** *der*, **~verteidigerin** *die* (*Rechtsw.*) *defence lawyer chosen by the defendant;* **~verwandtschaft** *die* (*geh.*) feeling of affinity; **~vorschlag** *der* nomination; **~weise** *Adv.* as desired; to choice; **~weise ... oder ...** either ... or ... [as desired]; **~wiederholung** *die* (*Fernspr.*) redial

**Wahn** /vaːn/ *der;* **~[e]s** Ⓐ mania; Ⓑ (*Täuschung*) delusion; **sie ließ ihn in diesem ~:** she let him go on believing this; **er ist in dem ~ befangen** *od.* **lebt in dem ~, dass ...** he is labouring under the delusion that ...

**wähnen** /ˈvɛːnən/ *tr. V.* (*geh.*) think [mistakenly]; imagine; **jmdn. in Sicherheit** *od.* **sicher ~:** imagine *or* think sb. is safe

**wahn-, Wahn-: ~idee** *die* ⇒ **~vorstellung**; **~sinn** *der* Ⓐ insanity; madness; **jmdn. in den ~sinn treiben** drive sb. insane; **in ~sinn** *od.* **dem ~sinn verfallen** go insane; Ⓑ (*ugs.: Unvernunft*) madness; lunacy; **das ist ja ~sinn!** that's just crazy!; Ⓒ (*salopp*) **~sinn!** incredible! (*coll.*); amazing!; **dieser Film ist einfach ~sinn** this film is just fantastic (*coll.*); **~sinnig** ❶ *Adj.* Ⓐ (*geistesgestört*) insane; mad; **~sinnig werden** go insane; **du machst mich noch ~sinnig!** (*ugs.*) you're driving me round the bend (*coll.*); **wie ~sinnig** (*ugs.*) like mad *or* crazy (*coll.*); **ich werde ~sinnig!** (*ugs.*) fantastic! (*coll.*); Ⓑ (*ugs.: ganz unvernünftig*) mad; crazy; **so etwas ~sinniges!** what a crazy idea!; Ⓒ (*ugs.: groß, heftig, intensiv*) terrific (*coll.*) ‹effort, speed, etc.›; terrible (*coll.*) ‹fright, job, pain›. ❷ *adv.* (*ugs.*) incredibly (*coll.*); terribly (*coll.*); **ich habe ~sinnig viel zu tun** I'm terribly *or* terrifically busy (*coll.*)

**Wahnsinnige** *der/die; adj. Dekl.* maniac; madman/madwoman

**Wahnsinnig·werden** *in* **es ist zum ~/zum ~ mit ihm** it's/he's enough to drive you round the bend *or* up the wall (*coll.*)

**Wahn·sinns-: ~idee** *die* Ⓐ crazy idea (*coll.*); Ⓑ (*salopp: großartige Idee*) great *or* fantastic idea (*coll.*); **~tat** *die* insane act; act of madness

**wahn-, Wahn-: ~vorstellung** *die* delusion; **~witz** *der* lunacy; insanity; **~witzig** ❶ *Adj.* Ⓐ insane; Ⓑ (*ugs.: allzu groß, stark usw.*) insane, lunatic ‹speed›; terrible (*coll.*), awful ‹pain›. ❷ *adv.* (*ugs.*) insanely (*coll.*) ‹fast, expensive›; incredibly (*coll.*) ‹high›; ‹hurt› like hell (*coll.*)

**wahr** /vaːɐ̯/ ❶ *Adj.* Ⓐ true; **[das] ist ja gar nicht ~!** that's just not true!; **davon ist kein Wort ~:** there isn't a word of truth in

*old spelling (see note on page 1707)

W

it; **nicht ~?** *translation depends on preceding verb form;* **du hast Hunger, nicht ~?** you're hungry, aren't you?; **nicht ~, er weiß es doch?** he does know, doesn't he?; **du hast es vergessen, nicht ~?** you've forgotten it, haven't you?; **das darf [doch] nicht ~ sein!** I don't believe it!; **etw. ~ machen** carry sth. out; **so ~ ich hier stehe** as surely as I stand here; **so ~ mir Gott helfe** so help me God; **was ~ ist, muss ~ bleiben** facts are facts; **das ist schon gar nicht mehr ~** (*ugs.*) that was donkey's years ago (*coll.*); **daran ist etwas Wahres** there's a grain of *or* some truth in that; **B** (*wirklich*) real ‹reason, motive, feelings, joy, etc.›; actual ‹culprit›; (*echt*) true, real ‹friend, friendship, love, art›; (*regelrecht*) veritable ‹miracle›; **es war eine ~e Pracht** it was really *or* truly magnificent; **im ~sten Sinne des Wortes** in the truest sense of the word; **das ist nicht das Wahre** (*ugs.*) it's not exactly ideal; it's not quite the thing; **das ist doch das einzig Wahre** (*ugs.*) that's just what the doctor ordered (*coll.*); ⇒ *auch* **Jakob.** **2** *adv.* **~ sprechen** (*geh.*) speak true (*literary*)

**wahren** *tr. V.* (*geh.*) preserve, maintain ‹balance, equality, neutrality, etc.›; maintain, assert ‹authority, right›; keep ‹promise, secret›; (*verteidigen*) defend, safeguard ‹interests, rights, reputation›; **Anstand ~:** observe the proprieties; ⇒ *auch* **Distanz B; Form E; Gesicht[1] A; Schein B**

**währen** /ˈvɛːrən/ *itr. V.* (*geh.*) last; **ein lange ~der Prozess** a process of long duration; **immer ~:** perpetual; eternal, everlasting ‹bliss, friendship, memory›; **der immer ~de Kalender** the perpetual calendar; **was lange währt, wird endlich gut** (*Spr.*) it will be/was worth it in the end

**während** /ˈvɛːrənt/ **1** *Konj.* **A** (*zeitlich*) while; **B** (*adversativ*) whereas. **2** *Präp. mit Gen.* during; (*über einen Zeitraum von*) for; **~ des ganzen Tages** all day [long]

**während·dem** (*ugs.*), **während·des** (*geh.*), **während·dessen** *Adv.* in the meantime; meanwhile

**wahr|haben** *unr. tr. V.* *in* **etw. nicht ~ wollen** not want to admit sth.

**wahrhaft** (*geh.*) **1** *Adj.* true; genuine. **2** *adv.* truly

**wahrhaftig** **1** *Adj.* (*geh.*) truthful ‹person›; (*wahr*) true, truthful ‹statement›; **der ~e Gott** the true God; **~er Gott!** good God!. **2** *adv.* really; genuinely; **das habe ich nicht gewollt, ~ nicht!** I didn't want that, really I didn't!; **wirklich und ~:** really and truly

**Wahrhaftigkeit** *die;* **~** (*geh.*) truthfulness

**Wahrheit** *die;* **~, ~en** truth; **die ~ eines Berichts** the accuracy *or* faithfulness of an account; **in ~:** in truth; in reality; **die ~ sagen** *od.* (*geh.*) **sprechen** tell *or* speak the truth; **um der ~ willen ...** to be truthful ...

**wahrheits-, Wahrheits-:** **~beweis** *der* proof of truth; **~findung** *die;* **~~, ~~en** (*Rechtsw.*) ascertainment of the truth; **~gehalt** *der* truth; **~gemäß** **1** *Adj.* truthful; accurate ‹information›; **2** *adv.* truthfully; **~getreu** **1** *Adj.* truthful; faithful, accurate ‹account›; **2** *adv.* truthfully; ‹portray› faithfully, accurately; **~liebe** *die* love of truth; **~liebend** *Adj.* honest

**wahrlich** *Adv.* (*geh.*) really; truly; **~, ich sage euch: ...** (*bibl.*) verily I say unto you, ...

**wahrnehmbar** *Adj.* perceptible; (*hörbar*) audible

**wahr|nehmen** *unr. tr. V.* **A** (*mit den Sinnen erfassen*) perceive; discern; (*spüren*) feel; detect ‹sound, smell›; (*bemerken*) notice; be aware of; (*erkennen, ausmachen*) make out; discern; detect, discern ‹atmosphere, undertone›; **er nimmt alles, was um ihn herum vorgeht, genau wahr** he takes in everything going on around him; **B** (*nutzen*) take advantage of ‹opportunity›; exploit ‹advantage›; exercise ‹right›; **die Vorfahrt ~:** exercise one's right of way; **C** (*vertreten*) look after ‹sb.'s interests, affairs›; **D** (*erfüllen, ausführen*) carry out, perform ‹function, task, duty›; fulfil ‹responsibility›

**Wahrnehmung** *die;* **~, ~en** **A** perception; (*eines Sachverhalts*) awareness; (*eines Geruchs, eines Tons*) detection; **B** (*Nutzung*) (*eines Rechts*) exercise; (*einer Gelegenheit, eines Vorteils*) exploitation; **C** (*Vertretung*) representation; **in ~ von jmds. Interessen** in sb's interest; **D** (*einer Funktion, Aufgabe, Pflicht*) performance; execution; (*einer Verantwortung*) fulfilment

**Wahrnehmungs·vermögen** *das* faculty of perception

**wahr·sagen, wahr|sagen** **1** *itr. V.* tell fortunes; **sich** (*Dat.*) **[von jmdm.] ~ lassen** have one's fortune told [by sb.]; **aus den Karten/den Handlinien ~:** read the cards/palms. **2** *tr. V.* predict, foretell ‹future›; **sie hat ihm gewahrsagt, dass er ...** she predicted that he ...

**Wahrsager** *der;* **~s, ~:** fortune teller

**Wahrsagerei** *die;* **~:** fortune telling *no def. art.*

**Wahrsagerin** *die;* **~, ~nen** fortune teller

**Wahrsagung** *die;* **~, ~en** prediction

**währschaft** /ˈvɛːɐ̯ʃaft/ *Adj.* (*schweiz.*) durable ‹material›; solid ‹roof›; wholesome ‹food›; strong ‹coffee›; reliable ‹workman›

**wahrscheinlich** **1** *Adj.* probable; likely; **~ klingen** sound plausible; **wenig ~:** not very likely; **das halte ich für das Wahrscheinlichste** I think that's the most likely answer; **nicht im Bereich des Wahrscheinlichen liegen** be beyond the bounds of probability. **2** *adv.* probably

**Wahrscheinlichkeit** *die;* **~, ~en** probability (*also Math.*); likelihood; **mit einiger/hoher** *od.* **großer ~:** quite/very probably; **aller ~ nach** in all probability

**Wahrscheinlichkeits-:** **~grad** *der* degree of probability; **~rechnung** *die* (*Math.*) probability calculus

**Wahrung** *die;* **~:** preservation; maintenance; (*eines Versprechens, Geheimnisses*) keeping; (*von Interessen, Rechten, Ruf*) defence; safeguarding; **die ~ des Anstandes** the observation of the proprieties

**Währung** *die;* **~, ~en** ▶ **337** currency

**Währungs-:** **~block** *der; Pl.* **~blöcke** currency bloc; **~einheit** *die* currency unit; monetary unit; **~reform** *die* currency reform; **~reserve** *die* currency reserve; **~schlange** *die* (*Wirtsch.*) [EC] currency snake; **~system** *das* currency system; **~union** *die* currency union; **~-, Wirtschafts- und Sozialunion** social, economic, and currency union

**Wahr·zeichen** *das* symbol; (*einer Stadt, einer Landschaft*) [most famous] landmark

**Waise** /ˈvaizə/ *die;* **~, ~n** orphan; **er/sie ist ~:** he/she is an orphan

**Waisen-:** **~haus** *das* orphanage; **~kind** *das* orphan; **~knabe** *der* (*veralt.*) orphaned boy; **gegen jmdn. der reinste ~knabe sein** (*ugs.*) be a mere novice compared to sb.; **~rente** *die* orphan's [social] benefit

**Wal** /vaːl/ *der;* **~[e]s, ~e** whale

**Wald** /valt/ *der;* **~[e]s, Wälder** /ˈvɛldɐ/ wood; (*größer*) forest; **die Tiere des ~es** the animals of the forest; **im ~ spazieren gehen** go walking in the woods; **viel ~:** a great deal of woodland; **in/durch ~ und Feld** *od.* **Flur** in/through woods and fields; **ein ~ von Masten/Antennen** (*fig.*) a forest of masts/aerials; **ich glaub, ich steh im ~** (*salopp*) I don't believe this!; you can't be serious!; **den ~ vor [lauter] Bäumen nicht sehen** (*fig.*) not see the wood for the trees; **wie man in den ~ hineinruft, so schallt es heraus** (*Spr.*) you are treated as you treat others

**Wald-:** **~ameise** *die* wood ant; **~arbeiter** *der,* **~arbeiterin** *die* ▶ **159** forestry worker; **~bestand** *der* forests *pl.;* (*Fläche*) area of forest; **~brand** *der* forest fire

**Wäldchen** /ˈvɛltçən/ *das* copse; spinney

**Wald·einsamkeit** *die* (*dichter.*) woodland solitude

**Wald·erdbeere** *die* wild strawberry

**Waldes-:** **~rauschen** *das;* **~~s** (*dichter.*) forest murmurs *pl.;* **~saum** *der* (*dichter.*) edge of the woods/forest

**Wald-:** **~frevel** *der* ⇒ **Forstfrevel**; **~gebiet** *das* forest area; **~geist** *der* woodland sprite; **~gott** *der* (*Myth.*) forest god; **~göttin** *die* (*Myth.*) forest goddess; **~horn** *das* French horn; (*Jagdhorn*) [large] hunting horn

**waldig** *Adj.* wooded

**Wald-:** **~land** *das* woodland; **~lauf** *der:* **[einen] ~lauf machen** go jogging through the woods; **~lehr·pfad** *der* woodland nature trail; **~meister** *der* (*Bot.*) woodruff

**Waldorf-** /ˈvaldɔrf/: **~salat** *der* (*Kochk.*) Waldorf salad; **~schule** *die* Rudolf Steiner school

**wald-, Wald-:** **~rand** *der* edge of the woods *or* the forest; **~reich** *Adj.* densely wooded; **~schrat** *der* hobgoblin; woodland gnome; **~spaziergang** *der* walk in the woods; **~sterben** *das;* **~~s** death of the forest [as a result of pollution]; **~stück** *das* piece of woodland; **~tier** *das* forest *or* woodland animal

**Waldung** *die;* **~, ~en** forest

**Wald·weg** *der* forest path; (*für Fahrzeuge*) forest track

**Wales** /weɪlz/ (*das*); **~'** Wales

**Wal-:** **~fang** *der* whaling *no def. art.;* **auf ~fang gehen/sein** go/be whaling; **~fänger** *der* ▶ **159** whaler; **~fisch** *der* (*ugs.*) whale

**Walhall, Walhalla** /valˈhal(a)/ (*das*); **~s** Valhalla

**Waliser** /vaˈliːzɐ/ *der;* **~s, ~** ▶ **553** Welshman

**Waliserin** *die;* **~, ~nen** ▶ **553** Welshwoman

**walisisch** /vaˈliːzɪʃ/ ▶ **553**, ▶ **696** **1** *Adj.* Welsh; **das Walisische** Welsh. **2** *adv.* **etw. ~ aussprechen** pronounce sth. the Welsh way

**walken** /ˈvalkn̩/ *tr. V.* full ‹cloth›; roll ‹sheet metal›; tumble ‹leather›

***Walkie-talkie, Walkie-Talkie** /ˈwɔːkiˈtɔːki/ *das;* **~s, ~s** walkie-talkie

**Walkman** (Wz) /ˈwɔkmən/ *der;* **~s, Walkmen** /ˈwɔkmən/ Walkman ®; personal stereo

**Walküre** /valˈkyːrə/ *die;* **~, ~n** (*nord. Myth., fig.*) Valkyrie

**Wall** /val/ *der;* **~[e]s, Wälle** /ˈvɛlə/ earthwork; embankment; rampart (*esp. Mil.*); (*fig.*) wall

**Wallach** /ˈvalax/ *der;* **~[e]s, ~e** gelding

**wallen** *itr. V.* **A** (*brodeln*) boil; **der Zorn brachte sein Blut zum W~** (*fig. geh.*) anger made his blood boil; **B** (*geh.: aufgewühlt sein*) ‹sea, waves› seethe, churn; **C** *mit Richtungsangabe mit sein* (*geh.*) ‹mist, steam› swirl; **D** **~des Haar/~de Gewänder** (*geh.*) flowing hair/robes

**wall-, Wall-:** **~fahren** *itr. V.; mit sein* make a pilgrimage; **~fahrer** *der,* **~fahrerin** *die* pilgrim; **~fahrt** *die* pilgrimage; **eine ~fahrt machen** go on a pilgrimage

**Wall·fahrts-:** **~kirche** *die* pilgrimage church; **~ort** *der* place of pilgrimage

**Wall·graben** *der* moat

**Wallis** /ˈvalɪs/ *das;* **~:** Valais; **im/aus dem ~:** in/from Valais

**Wallone** /vaˈloːnə/ *der;* **~n, ~n** Walloon

**Wallonien** /vaˈloːniən/ (*das*); **~s** Wallonia

**Wallonin** *die;* **~, ~nen** Walloon

**wallonisch** *Adj.* ▶ **696** Walloon

**Wallung** *die:* **~, ~en** ▶ **474** **A** (*geh.*) **in ~ sein** be seething *or* churning; **in ~ geraten** start to seethe *or* churn; **in ~ bringen** make ‹sea, water, etc.› churn; **B** (*fig. geh.*) **er** *od.* **sein Blut war/geriet in ~:** he *or* his blood was seething/began to seethe; (*vor Leidenschaft*) his feelings were in turmoil *or* inflamed/became inflamed; **jmdn.** *od.* **jmds. Blut in ~ bringen** (*vor Wut, Ärger*) make sb.'s blood boil; (*vor Leidenschaft*) inflame sb. *or* sb.'s feelings; **C** (*Med.*) ⇒ **Hitzewallung**

**Walm·dach** /ˈvalm-/ *das* hipped roof

**Wal·nuss, *Wal·nuß** /ˈvalnʊs/ *die* walnut

**Walnuss·baum, *Walnuß·baum** *der* walnut tree

**Walpurgis·nacht** /valˈpʊrgɪs-/ *die* Walpurgis Night *no art.*

W

**Wal·ross**, ***Wal·roß** /ˈvalrɔs/ *das; Pl.* **~rosse** walrus

**Wal·statt** *die (dichter. veralt.)* field of battle; **auf der ~ bleiben** *(veralt.)* fall in battle

**walten** /ˈvaltn̩/ ❶ *itr. V. (geh.)* Ⓐ ‹good sense, good spirit› prevail; ‹peace, silence, harmony, etc.› reign; **rohe Kräfte haben hier gewaltet** brutal forces have been at work here; **Vorsicht/Gnade/Milde/Strenge** *usw.* **~ lassen** exercise caution/mercy/leniency/rigour *etc.*; **Vernunft ~ lassen** be reasonable; Ⓑ *(veralt.: das Regiment führen)* rule (**über** + *Akk.* over); ⇒ *auch* **Amt** B, **schalten** 2 D. ❷ *tr. V. in* **das walte Gott** *(geh.)*/*(salopp scherzh.)* **Hugo** may God grant that this be so/I hope to God it is

**Walz** *die; ~* ⇒ **Walze** E

**Walze** /ˈvaltsə/ *die; ~, ~n* Ⓐ roller; *(Straßen~)* [road] roller; *(Schreib~)* platen; *(Tiefdruck~)* gravure cylinder; Ⓑ *(eines mechanischen Musikinstruments)* barrel; *(hist.: eines Phonographen)* cylinder; **er spielt immer wieder die alte ~** *(ugs.)* he always comes out with the same old story; Ⓒ *(Geom.)* cylinder; Ⓓ *(Walzwerk)* rolling mill; Ⓔ *(veralt.)* **auf der ~ sein/auf die ~ gehen** be on/take to the road; **ein Handwerksbursche auf der ~:** an itinerant journeyman

**walzen** ❶ *tr. V.* roll ‹field, road, steel, etc.›. ❷ *itr. V. (veralt., scherzh.)* Ⓐ *mit Richtungsangabe mit sein (Walzer tanzen)* waltz; Ⓑ *mit sein (reisen)* rove; *(zu Fuß)* hike

**wälzen** /ˈvɛltsn̩/ ❶ *tr. V.* Ⓐ roll ‹round object›; heave ‹heavy object›; *(drehen)* roll ‹person etc.› over; *(fig.)* shove ‹blame, responsibility› (**auf** + *Akk.* on); **die Arbeit auf jmdn. ~:** lumber sb. with the work; Ⓑ *(ugs.: studieren)* pore over ‹books etc.›; Ⓒ *(Kochk.: wenden)* **etw. in Mehl** *usw.* **~:** toss sth. in flour *etc.*; Ⓓ *(ugs.: diskutieren, nachdenken über)* mull over ‹plans, problem, etc.›.
❷ *refl. V.* roll; *(auf der Stelle)* roll about *or* around; *(im Krampf, vor Schmerzen)* writhe around; **sich schlaflos im Bett ~:** toss and turn in bed, unable to sleep; **sich vor Lachen ~** *(ugs.)* fall about laughing; **Menschenmengen wälzten sich durch die Straßen** crowds of people thronged through the streets

**Walzen·dynamo** *der* tread-driven dynamo

**walzen·förmig** *Adj.* cylindrical

**Walzer** *der; ~s, ~:* waltz; **kannst du ~ tanzen?** can you waltz?

**Wälzer** *der; ~s, ~ (ugs.)* hefty tome

**Walzer-: ~musik** *die* waltz music; **~takt** *der* waltz time

**Walz-: ~stahl** *der* rolled steel; **~straße** *die (Technik)* roll train; **~werk** *das* rolling mill

**Wampe** /ˈvampə/ *die; ~, ~n (ugs. abwertend)* pot belly

**Wams** /vams/ *das; ~es,* **Wämser** /ˈvɛmzɐ/ Ⓐ *(hist.: Untergewand zur Rüstung)* gambeson; Ⓑ *(veralt.: Jacke)* doublet

**wand** *1. u. 3. Pers. Sg. Prät. v.* **winden**

**Wand** /vant/ *die; ~,* **Wände** /ˈvɛndə/ Ⓐ wall; *(Trenn~)* partition; **die eigenen vier Wände** one's own four walls; **..., dass die Wände wackeln** *(ugs.)* ... almost fit to raise the roof *(coll.)*; **jmdn. an die ~ stellen** *(verhüll. ugs.)* put sb. up against a wall *(euphem.)*; **da kann man die Wände hochgehen** *(fig.)* it's enough to drive you up the wall *(coll.)*; **jmdn. an die ~ drücken** *(fig.)* push sb. into the background; **jmdn. an die ~ spielen** *(fig.)* outclass sb.; *(durch Manöver ausschalten)* outmanœuvre sb.; **bei ihm redet man gegen eine ~** *(fig.)* talking to him is like talking to a brick wall; **sie wohnen ~ an ~:** they live next door to one another; they are neighbours; **die Wände haben Ohren** *(ugs.)* walls have ears; Ⓑ *(bewegliche Trenn~)* screen; **spanische ~:** folding screen; Ⓒ *(eines Behälters, Schiffs)* side; *(eines Zeltes)* wall; side; *(Biol.)* septum; *(Anat.)* wall; Ⓓ *(Fels~)* face; wall; Ⓔ *(Wolken~)* bank of cloud

*old spelling (see note on page 1707)

**Wandale** /vanˈdaːlə/ *der; ~n, ~n,* **Wandalin** *die; ~, ~nen* Ⓐ *(hist.)* Vandal; Ⓑ *(fig.)* vandal

**Wandalismus** /vandaˈlɪsmʊs/ *der; ~:* vandalism

**Wand·behang** *der* wall hanging

**Wandel** /ˈvandl̩/ *der; ~s* change; **im ~ der Zeiten/der Jahrhunderte** through the ages/over the centuries

**Wandel·anleihe** *die (Bankw.)* convertible loan

**wandelbar** *Adj.* changeable; variable ‹size, number›

**Wandel-: ~gang** *der* promenade; *(im Theater)* foyer; **~halle** *die* lobby; *(im Theater)* foyer

**wandeln** ❶ *refl. V.* change (**in** + *Akk.* into). ❷ *tr. V. (verändern)* change; **etw. in etw.** *(Akk.)* **~** *(geh.)* change *or* turn sth. into sth. ❸ *itr. V.; mit sein (geh.)* stroll; ⇒ *auch* **Leiche**; **Lexikon** A

**Wander-: ~ameise** *die* army ant; **~ausstellung** *die* touring exhibition; **~bühne** *die* touring company; **~bursche** *der* journeyman *(travelling from place to place)*; **~düne** *die* wandering dune

**Wanderer** *der; ~s, ~* Ⓐ walker; *(der weite Wege zurücklegt)* rambler; hiker; Ⓑ *(dichter.: Reisender)* traveller

**Wander-: ~falke** *der* peregrine falcon; **~gewerbe** *das* itinerant trade; **~heuschrecke** *die* migratory locust

**Wanderin** *die; ~, ~nen* ⇒ **Wanderer**

**Wander-: ~jahr** *das* year of travel; *(eines Handwerkers)* journeyman year; **~karte** *die* rambler's [path] map; **~kleidung** *die* rambling *or* hiking clothes *pl.*; **~leben** *das* unsettled life; *(von Nomaden)* nomadic life; **~lied** ramblers' *or* hikers' song

**wandern** /ˈvandɐn/ *itr. V.; mit sein* Ⓐ hike; ramble; *(ohne Angabe des Ziels)* go hiking *or* rambling; Ⓑ *(ugs.: gehen)* wander *(lit. or fig.)*; *(fig.)* ‹glance, eyes, thoughts› roam, wander; Ⓒ *(ziehen, reisen)* travel; *(ziellos)* roam; ‹exhibition, circus, theatre› tour, travel; ‹animal, people, tribe› migrate; *(fig.)* ‹cloud, star› drift; **~de Stämme** nomadic tribes; Ⓓ *(sich verlagern)* ‹glacier, dune, island› move, shift; *(innerhalb des Körpers)* ‹kidney etc.› be displaced; ‹foreign body› migrate; Ⓔ *(ugs.: befördert werden)* land; **in den Papierkorb/Müll** *usw.* **~:** land *or* be thrown in the waste-paper basket/rubbish bin *etc.*; Ⓕ *(fig.: weitergegeben werden)* be handed *or* passed on

**Wander-: ~niere** *die* ▶474 *(Med.)* floating kidney; **~pokal** *der* challenge cup; **~prediger** *der* itinerant preacher; **~ratte** *die* brown rat

**Wanderschaft** *die; ~:* travels *pl.*; **die Zeit der ~:** the years *pl.* of travel; **auf [der] ~ sein/auf [die] ~ gehen** be on/set off on one's travels; **ein Handwerksbursche auf [der] ~:** a travelling *or* an itinerant journeyman

**Wander·schuh** *der* hiking shoe

**Wanders·mann** *der; Pl.* **Wanders·leute** *(veralt.)* wayfarer

**Wander-: ~stock** *der* staff; **~tag** *der* day's hike *(for a class or school)*

**Wanderung** *die; ~, ~en* Ⓐ hike; walking tour; *(sehr lang)* trek; **eine ~ machen** go on a hike/tour/trek; Ⓑ *(Zool., Soziol.)* migration

**Wanderungs·bewegung** *die (Soziol.)* migration; migratory movement

**Wander-: ~verein** *der* ramblers' association; **~vogel** *der* Ⓐ *(ugs.: begeisterter Wanderer)* keen hiker; Ⓑ *in* **der ~vogel** *(hist.) ramblers' association, founded 1895, precursor of the German youth movement;* Ⓒ *(Mitglied)* member of the *Wandervogel*; **~weg** *der* footpath *(constructed for ramblers)*; **~zirkus** *der* travelling circus

**Wand-: ~gemälde** *das* mural; **~haken** *der* [wall] hook; **~kalender** *der* calendar; **~lampe** *die*, **~leuchte** *die* wall light

**Wandlung** *die; ~, ~en* Ⓐ change; *(grundlegend)* transformation; Ⓑ *(kath. Rel.)* transubstantiation; *(in der Messe)* consecration of the bread and wine

**wandlungs·fähig** *Adj.* adaptable

**Wand·malerei** *die* mural painting; wall painting; *(Bild)* mural; wall painting

**Wandrer** *der; ~s, ~* ⇒ **Wanderer**

**Wandrerin** *die; ~, ~nen* ⇒ **Wanderin**

**Wand-: ~schirm** *der* folding screen; **~schrank** *der* wall cupboard *or (Amer.)* closet; *(Einbauschrank)* built-in cupboard *or (Amer.)* closet; *(für Kleidung)* built-in wardrobe *or (Amer.)* closet; **~spiegel** *der* wall mirror; **~tafel** *die* [wall] blackboard

**wandte** /ˈvantə/ *1. u. 3. Pers. Prät. v.* **wenden**

**Wand-: ~teller** *der* wall [display] plate; **~teppich** *der* wall hanging; tapestry; **~uhr** *die* wall clock

**Wandung** *die; ~, ~en (von Gefäßen usw.)* side; *(von Organen)* wall

**Wand-: ~verkleidung** *die (außen)* facing; *(innen)* wall covering; *(Täfelung)* wall panelling; **~zeitung** *die* wall newspaper

**Wange** /ˈvaŋə/ *die; ~, ~n* Ⓐ ▶471 *(geh.)* cheek; **~ an ~:** cheek to cheek; **ihm stieg das Blut in die ~n** the blood rose to his cheeks; Ⓑ *(Technik)* cheek; *(einer Treppe)* stringer; *(einer Leiter)* stile

**Wangen·kuss**, ***Wangen·kuß** *der:* **jmdm. einen ~ geben** kiss sb's cheek

**Wankel·motor** *der* Wankel engine

**Wankel·mut** *der (geh.)* vacillation

**wankelmütig** /-myːtɪç/ *Adj. (geh.)* vacillating

**wanken** /ˈvaŋkn̩/ *itr. V.* Ⓐ *(schwanken)* sway; ‹person› totter; *(unter einer Last)* stagger; **ins W~ geraten** *od.* **kommen** begin to sway/totter; **nicht ~ und nicht weichen** *(geh.)* not budge an inch; Ⓑ *mit sein (unsicher gehen)* stagger; totter; **~den Schrittes** *(geh.)* with unsteady gait; Ⓒ *(geh.: bedroht sein)* ‹government, empire, etc.› totter; **ins W~ geraten** begin to totter; ‹theory, faith, etc.› become shaky; **ins W~ bringen** make ‹monarchy, government, etc.› totter; shake ‹resolve, faith›; Ⓓ *(geh.: unsicher sein/werden)* ‹person› waver, vacillate; **[in etw.** *(Dat.)***] ~d werden** begin to waver *or* vacillate [in sth.]; **jmdn. ~d machen** make sb. waver

**wann** /van/ *Adv.* ▶752 when; **~ kommst du morgen?** when *or* [at] what time are you coming tomorrow?; **~ ist dieses Jahr Ostern?** when *or* on what date does Easter fall this year?; **seit ~ wohnst du dort?** how long have you been living there?; **seit ~ sind Delphine Fische/bin ich dein Laufbursche?** *(iron.)* since when have dolphins been fish/have I been your errand boy?; **bis ~ kann ich noch anrufen?** until when *or* how late can I still phone?; **von ~ an ...?** from when ...?; **von ~ bis ~ gilt es?** for what period is it valid?; **bis ~ ist das Essen fertig?** [by] when will the food be ready?; **ich weiß nicht, ~:** I don't know when; **du kannst kommen, ~ du willst** you can come when[ever] you like; **~ [auch] immer** *(geh.)* whenever

**Wanne** *die; ~, ~n* bath[tub]; *(Öl~)* sump; *(Fot.)* [wash] tank; **in die ~ steigen** get into the bath

**Wannen·bad** *das* bath

**Wanst** /vanst/ *der; ~[e]s,* **Wänste** /ˈvɛnstə/ *(ugs. abwertend)* belly; *(dicker Bauch)* potbelly; **sich den ~ voll schlagen** stuff oneself *(coll.)*

**Want** /vant/ *die; ~, ~en (Schiffbau)* shroud

**Wanze** /ˈvantsə/ *die; ~, ~n (Bett~, Abhör~)* bug *(coll.)*

**Wappen** /ˈvapn̩/ *das; ~s, ~:* coat of arms; **~ oder Zahl?** heads or tails?

**Wappen-: ~feld** *das (Her.)* quarter; **~kunde** *die* heraldry *no art.*; **~schild** *der od. das (Her.)* shield; **~spruch** *der* motto; **~tier** *das* heraldic beast

**wappnen** *refl. V. (geh.)* Ⓐ forearm oneself; **sich gegen etw. ~:** prepare [oneself] for sth.; **[gegen etw.] gewappnet sein** be forearmed [against sth.]

**war** /vaːɐ̯/ *1. u. 3. Pers. Sg. Prät. v.* **sein**

**Waran** /vaˈraːn/ *der; ~s, ~e (Zool.)* monitor lizard

**warb** /varp/ *1. u. 3. Pers. Sg. Prät. v.* **werben**

**ward** /vart/ *(geh.) 1. u. 3. Pers. Sg. Prät. v.* **werden**

**Ware** /'va:rə/ *die;* ~, ~**n** Ⓐ ~**[n]** goods *pl.;* Ⓑ *(einzelne* ~*)* article; commodity *(Econ., fig.)*; *(Erzeugnis)* product; **neue** ~ **bekommen** receive new stock; **die Händler preisen ihre** ~**n an** the traders are vaunting the excellence of their wares; **heiße** ~ *(ugs.)* hot goods; Ⓒ *(Kaufmannsspr.: Stoff)* material

**Waren-:** ~**an·gebot** *das* supply [of goods]; *(Sortiment)* range of goods; ~**annahme** *die* Ⓐ acceptance of goods; **„keine** ~**annahme"** no deliveries; Ⓑ *(Annahmestelle)* goods reception; **„**~**annahme"** 'goods in'; ~**auf·zug** *der* goods lift *(Brit.) or (Amer.)* elevator; ~**ausfuhr** *die* export of goods; ~**aus·gabe** *die* Ⓐ issue of goods; Ⓑ *(Ausgabestelle)* goods collection point; ~**begleit·schein** *der (Zollw.)* [customs] bond note; ~**bestand** *der* stock; ~**börse** *die (Wirtsch.)* commodity exchange; ~**einfuhr** *die* import of goods; ~**haus** *das* department store; ~**korb** *der (Statistik)* basket of goods; ~**lager** *das (einer Fabrik o. Ä.)* stores *pl.; (eines Geschäftes)* stockroom; *(größer)* warehouse; *(Bestand)* stocks *pl.;* ~**muster** *das,* ~**probe** *die* sample; ~**sendung** *die (Postw.)* parcel containing samples *(sent at a special rate)*; ~**test** *der* product test; ~**umsatz** *der* turnover of goods; ~**umschlag** *der* volume of goods handled; ~**zeichen** *das* trade mark

**warf** /varf/ *1. u. 3. Pers. Sg. Prät. v.* **werfen**

**warm** /varm/; **wärmer** /'vɛrmɐ/, **wärmst...** /'vɛrmst.../ ❶ *Adj.* Ⓐ warm; hot ‹meal, food, bath, spring›; hot, warm ‹climate, country, season, etc.›; ~**e Küche** hot food; **das Essen** ~ **machen/stellen** heat up the food/keep the food warm *or* hot; **im Warmen sitzen/ins Warme kommen** sit in/come into the warm; ~ **halten** ‹coat, blanket, etc.› keep one warm; **etw.** ~ **halten** keep sth. warm; **sich** *(Dat.)* **jmdn.** ~ **halten** *(fig. ugs.)* keep on the right side of sb.; **mir ist/wird** ~**:** I feel warm/I'm getting warm; *(zu* ~*)* I feel hot/I'm getting hot; **den Motor** ~ **laufen lassen** warm up the engine; ~ **laufen/sich** ~ **laufen** warm up; **„**~**"** *(auf Wasserhahn)* 'hot'; ~**e Miete** ⇒ **Warmmiete**; Ⓑ *(herzlich)* warm ‹sympathy, appreciation, words, etc.›; *(lebhaft)* enthusiastic ‹agreement›; keen, lively ‹interest›; **[mit jmdm./etw.]** ~ **werden** *(ugs.)* warm [to sb./sth.]; **mir wurde ganz** ~ **ums Herz** *(geh.)* I felt a warm glow [of emotion]; Ⓒ *(salopp abwertend: homosexuell)* gay *(coll.)*; queer *(sl.)*; **ein** ~**er Bruder** *(salopp abwertend)* a queer *(sl.)*; a fag *(Amer. sl. derog.)*.

❷ *adv.* warmly; ~ **essen/duschen** have a hot meal/shower; ~ **sitzen/schlafen** sit/sleep in the warm; **sich** ~ **anziehen/zudecken** dress up/cover oneself up warmly

**warm-, Warm-:** ~**blut** *das: cross between heavy and light breeds;* ≈ cross-bred horse; ~**blüter** /-bly:tɐ/ *der;* ~~**s**, ~~ *(Zool.)* warm-blooded creature; ~**blütig** /-bly:tɪç/ *Adj. (Zool.)* warm-blooded

**Warme** *der; adj. Dekl. (salopp abwertend)* queer *(sl.)*; fag *(Amer. sl. derog.)*

**Wärme** /'vɛrmə/ *die;* ~**:** warmth; *(Hitze; auch Physik)* heat; **wir haben drei Grad** ~**:** it is three degrees above zero; **spezifische** ~ *(Physik)* specific heat

**wärme-, Wärme-:** ~**austauscher** *der;* ~~**s**, ~~ *(Technik)* heat-exchanger; ~**belastung** *die* Ⓐ *(Ökologie)* thermal pollution; Ⓑ *(Technik)* thermal stress; ~**beständig** *Adj.* heat-resistant; ~**dämmend** *Adj.* insulating [against heat loss]; ~**einheit** *die* thermal unit; ~**energie** *die* thermal energy; ~**gewitter** *das (Met.)* heat thunderstorm; ~**grad** *der* Ⓐ *Pl.* degrees above zero; **wir hatten** ~**grade** the temperature was above zero; Ⓑ *(Temperatur)* temperature; ~**haushalt** *der* Ⓐ *(der Erde)* heat balance; Ⓑ *(des Körpers)* heat regulation; ~**isolation** *die* thermal insulation; ~**kraftwerk** *das* thermal power station; ~**lehre** *die (Physik)* theory of heat; *(Thermodynamik)* thermodynamics *sing., no art.*

**wärmen** ❶ *tr. V.* warm; *(auf*~*)* warm up ‹food, drink›; **jmdn./sich/sich [gegenseitig]** ~**:** warm sb./oneself/each other up. ❷ *itr. V.* be warm; *(warm halten)* keep one warm; **die Sonne wärmt kaum noch** the sun has hardly any warmth now

**Wärme-:** ~**pumpe** *die (Technik)* heat pump; ~**speicher** *der* thermal store; ~**strahlung** *die* thermal radiation; ~**technik** *die* heat technology *no art.;* ~**verlust** *der* heat loss

**Wärm·flasche** *die* hot-water bottle

**warm-, Warm-:** ~**front** *die (Met.)* warm front; *~**|halten** ⇒ **warm** 1 A; ~**halte·platte** *die* hotplate; ~**herzig** ❶ *Adj.* warm-hearted; ❷ *adv.* warm-heartedly; ~**herzigkeit** *die;* ~~: warm-heartedness; warmth; *~**|laufen** ⇒ **warm** 1 A; ~**luft** *die* warm air; ~**miete** *die (ugs.)* rent inclusive of heating; **es kostet 500 Mark** ~**miete** the rent, inclusive of heating, is 500 marks

**wärmstens** /'vɛrmstn̩s/ *Adv.* ~ **empfehlen** warmly recommend

**Warm·wasser** *das* hot water

**Warm·wasser-:** ~**bereiter** *der;* ~~**s**, ~~**:** water heater; boiler; ~**heizung** *die* hot-water heating; ~**versorgung** *die* hot-water supply

**Warn-:** ~**blink·anlage** *die (am Bahnübergang)* flashing warning lights *pl.; (am Kfz)* hazard warning lights *pl.;* ~**blinker** *der (ugs.)* hazard warning lights *pl.;* ~**blink·leuchte** *die* flashing warning light; ~**dreieck** *das (Kfz-W.)* hazard warning triangle

**warnen** /'varnən/ *tr. (auch itr.) V.* warn **(vor** + *Dat.* of, about); **jmdn. [davor]** ~, **etw. zu tun** warn sb. against doing sth.; **vor dem Betreten des Eises wird gewarnt** you are warned to beware of thin ice; **die Polizei warnt vor Nebel/vor Taschendieben** the police have issued a fog warning/a warning against pickpockets; **ich bin jetzt gewarnt** I have been warned; I know now to be careful; **ein** ~**des Beispiel** a cautionary example; **er hob** ~**d den Zeigefinger** he raised an admonitory finger

**Warn-:** ~**kreuz** *das (Verkehrsw.)* warning cross; ~**lampe** *die* warning light; ~**ruf** *der* Ⓐ warning shout; Ⓑ *(eines Tiers)* warning cry; ~**schild** *das* warning sign; ~**schuss**, *~**schuß** *der* warning shot; ~**signal** *das* warning signal; ~**streik** *der* token strike; ~**system** *das* warning system

**Warnung** *die;* ~, ~**en** warning **(vor** + *Dat.* of, about); **lass dir das eine** ~ **sein!** let that be a warning to you!; **das ist meine letzte** ~**:** that's the last warning I shall give you; I shan't warn you again

**Warn·zeichen** *das* warning sign; *(Schall*~*, Leuchtzeichen)* warning signal

**Warschau** /'varʃau/ *(das);* ~**s** ▶ **700** War-saw

**Warschauer** ▶ **700** ❶ *der;* ~**s**, ~**:** citizen of Warsaw; *(geborener* ~*)* native of Warsaw. ❷ *indekl. Adj.* Warsaw

**Warschauerin** *die;* ~, ~**nen** ⇒ **Warschauer** 1

**Warte** /'vartə/ *die;* ~, ~**n** *(geh.)* **[hohe]** ~**:** vantage point; *(fig.: Standpunkt)* **von jmds.** ~ **aus [gesehen]** [seen] from sb.'s standpoint

**Warte-:** ~**frau** *die (veralt.)* [*esp.* toilet] attendant; ~**frist** *die* ⇒ ~**zeit** B; ~**halle** *die* waiting room; *(Flugw.)* departure lounge; ~**liste** *die* waiting list; **auf** ~**liste** *(Flugw.)* on standby

**warten** /'vartn̩/ ❶ *itr. V.* wait **(auf** + *Akk.* for); **warte mal!** wait a moment!; just a moment!; **na warte!** *(ugs.)* just you wait!; **„bitte** ~**!"** 'wait'; *(am Telefon)* 'hold the line please'; **da kannst du lange** ~**!** *(iron.)* you'll have a long wait; you'll be lucky *(iron.)*; **auf sich** ~ **lassen** take one's/its time; **nicht lange auf sich** ~ **lassen** not be long in coming; **das lange W**~ **war völlig umsonst gewesen** the long wait had been all for nothing; **wir wollen mit dem Essen** ~, **bis alle da sind** we'll hold the meal until everybody's here; **sie wollen mit dem Heiraten noch [etwas]** ~**:** they want to wait a little before getting married; **darauf habe ich schon lange gewartet** *(iron.)* I've seen that coming [for a long time]; **auf dich/den haben wir gerade noch gewartet** *(iron.)* you were/he was all we needed; **Sie können [gleich] drauf** ~**:** you might as well wait for it; **so lange** ~**/mit etw.** ~, **bis es zu spät ist** leave it/leave sth. until it's too late.

❷ *tr. V.* service ‹car, machine, etc.›

**Wärter** /'vɛrtɐ/ *der;* ~**s**, ~ ▶ **159** attendant; *(Tier*~*, Zoo*~*, Leuchtturm*~*)* keeper; *(Kranken*~*)* orderly; *(Gefängnis*~*)* warder; *(Schranken*~*)* crossing keeper

**Warte·raum** *der* waiting room

**Wärter·häuschen** *das* attendant's hut; *(Schranken*~*)* crossing-keeper's hut

**Wärterin** *die;* ~, ~**nen** ▶ **159** ⇒ **Wärter**

**Warte-:** ~**saal** *der* waiting room; ~**schleife** *die (Flugw.)* turning loop; ~**zeit** *die* Ⓐ wait; **nach einer** ~**zeit von einer Stunde** after waiting for an hour; Ⓑ *(festgesetzte Frist)* waiting period; ~**zimmer** *das* waiting room

**-wärts** /-vɛrts/ *adv.* ‹north-, south-, up-, down-, etc.›wards; **seit**~**:** sideways

**Wartung** *die;* ~, ~**en** service; *(das Warten)* servicing; *(Instandhaltung)* maintenance; **der Wagen muss zur** ~**:** the car has to go to be serviced *or* go for servicing

**wartungs·frei** *Adj.* maintenance-free

**warum** /va'rʊm/ *Adv.* why; ~ **nicht?** why not?; ~ **nicht gleich so?** why not do that in the first place?; **nach dem Warum fragen** ask the reason why

**Warze** /'vartsə/ *die;* ~, ~**n** Ⓐ wart; Ⓑ *(Brust*~*)* nipple

**Warzen-:** ~**hof** *der* ▶ **471** *(Anat.)* nipple areola; ~**schwein** *das* warthog

**warzig** *Adj.* warty

**was** /vas/ ❶ *Interrogativpron. Nom. u. Akk. u. (nach Präp.) Dat. Neutr.;* ⇒ *auch (Gen.)* **wessen** 1 B what; ~ **kostet das?** what *or* how much does that cost?; ~ **ist er [von Beruf]?** what's his job?; **[das ist] gut,** ~**?** *(ugs.: nicht?)* not bad, eh?; ~ **ist?,** ~ **denn?** *(*~ *ist denn los?)* what is it?; what's up?; ~ **denn, willst du etwa schon gehen?** you're not going already, are you?; **ach** ~**!** *(ugs.)* oh, come on!; of course not!; **für** ~ **brauchst du es?** *(ugs.)* what do you need it for?; **mit** ~ **beschäftigt er sich?** *(ugs.)* how does he occupy his time?; ~ **der alles weiß!** what a lot he knows!; ~ **es [nicht] alles gibt!** *(Ding)* what will they think of next?; *(Ereignis)* the things people will do!; **und** ~ **nicht alles** *(ugs.)* and so on ad infinitum; ~ **[auch] immer** whatever; ~ **für ein .../**~ **für ...** what sort *or* kind of ...; ~ **für ein Auto hat er?,** *(ugs.)* ~ **hat er für ein Auto?** what kind of car has he got?; ~ **für Möglichkeiten haben wir?** *(ugs.)* what possibilities do we have?; **Hast du den Apfel gegessen? — Was fürn Apfel?** *(ugs.)* Did you eat the apple? — What apple?; ~ **für ein Unsinn/Glück/gemeiner Kerl!** *(ugs.)* what nonsense/luck/*(coll.)* what a mean so-and-so!; **Wars ein Sturm? — Und** ~ **für einer!** Was it a storm? — Not half! *(coll.) or* And then some! *(coll.)*.

❷ *Relativpron. Nom. u. Akk. u. (nach Präp.) Dat. Neutr.;* ⇒ *auch (Gen.)* **wessen** 2 B Ⓐ **[das,]** ~**:** what; **alles,** ~ **...** everything *or* all that ...; **alles,** ~ **ich weiß** all [that] I know; **das Beste,** ~ **du tun kannst** the best thing that you can do; **das,** ~ **du nicht mehr brauchst** the things *pl. or* what you no longer need; ~ **er nicht kennt, [das] isst er nicht** he won't eat anything he doesn't know; **vieles/manches/nichts/dasselbe/etwas,** ~ **...** much/many things/nothing/the same one/something that ...; ~ **mich betrifft/das anbelangt, [so] ...** as far as I'm/that's concerned, ...; Ⓑ *weiterführend* which; **er hat zugesagt,** ~ **mich gefreut hat** he agreed, which pleased me; **es hat geregnet,** ~ **uns aber nicht gestört hat** it rained, but that didn't bother us; Ⓒ *(ugs.: wer)* ~ **ein ganzer Kerl ist, [der] wehrt sich** anyone worth his salt will put up a fight; Ⓓ *(landsch.: derjenige, der/diejenige, die)* ~ **unser Vater ist, der sagt immer**

... our father always says ...; Ⓔ (*landsch.: der, die, das*) **die Frieda, ~ unsere Jüngste ist** Frieda, who is our youngest. ❸ *Indefinitpron. Nom. u. Akk. u.* (*nach Präp.*) *Dat. Neutr.* (*ugs.*) Ⓐ (*etwas*) something; (*in Fragen, Verneinungen*) anything; **er hat kaum ~ gesagt** he hardly said anything *or* a thing; **ist ~?** is anything wrong?; **wenn er ~ gesehen hätte ...** if he had seen anything; **haben die ~ miteinander?** is there something between them?; **so ~:** such a thing; something like that; **nein, so ~!** you don't say!; **so ~ könnte mir nicht passieren** nothing like that could happen to me; **gibt es hier so ~ wie'n Klo?** there isn't a loo (*Brit.*) *or* (*Amer.*) john here, is there? (*coll.*); **er ist so ~ wie'n Professor** he's a professor *or* something of the sort; **so ~ Dummes/Ärgerliches!** how stupid/annoying!; **gibt es ~ Neues?** Is there any news?; **aus ihm wird mal/wird nie ~:** he'll make something of himself/he'll never come to anything; **das will ~ heißen** that really means something; Ⓑ (*ein Teil*) some; **ich bekomme auch ~:** I get some too; Ⓒ (*landsch.: ein wenig*) a little; a bit; **noch ~ Geld/Milch** some more money/milk; **~ lauter** a bit louder. ❹ *Adv.* (*ugs.*) Ⓐ (*warum, wozu*) why; what ... for; **~ stehst du hier herum?** what are you standing around here for?; Ⓑ (*wie*) how; **~ hast du dich verändert!** how you've changed; **lauf, ~ du kannst!** run as fast as you can!; Ⓒ (*inwiefern*) **~ kümmerts dich?** what does it matter to you?

**wasch-, Wasch-: ~aktiv** *Adj.* detergent; **~an·lage** *die* washing plant; (*Autowaschanlage*) car wash; (*Scheibenwaschanlage*) windscreen washer; **~an·leitung** *die* washing instructions *pl.*; **~automat** *der* washing machine

**wasch·bar** *Adj.* washable

**Wasch-: ~bär** *der* racoon; **~becken** *das* washbasin; **~benzin** *das* cleaning fluid (*with petrol base*); **~beton** *der* exposed aggregate concrete; **~brett** *das* washboard

**Wäsche** /ˈvɛʃə/ *die;* **~, ~n** Ⓐ (*zu waschende Textilien*) washing; (*für die Wäscherei*) laundry; **jmdm. die ~ machen** do sb.'s washing; **schmutzige ~ waschen** (*fig.*) wash [one's] dirty linen in public; Ⓑ (*Unterwäsche*) underwear; **dumm/verdutzt aus der ~ gucken** (*ugs.*) look stupid/flabbergasted; **jmdm. an die ~ gehen/wollen** (*salopp*) go for sb./try to get at sb.; Ⓒ (*das Waschen*) washing *no pl.*; (*einmalig*) wash; **bei/nach der ersten ~:** when washed for the first time/after the first wash; **in der ~ sein** be in the wash; **etw. in die** *od.* **zur ~ tun** put sth. in the wash; **bei uns ist heute große ~:** we're doing a big wash today; Ⓓ (*Waschanlage*) washing plant

**Wäsche·beutel** *der* laundry bag

**wasch·echt** *Adj.* Ⓐ colour-fast ‹textile, clothes›; fast ‹colour›; Ⓑ (*fig.: echt*) genuine; pukka (*coll.*)

**Wäsche-: ~garnitur** *die* set of underwear; **~klammer** *die* clothes peg (*Brit.*); clothespin (*Amer.*); **~korb** *der* laundry basket; (*für nasse ~*) clothes basket; **~leine** *die* clothes line

**waschen** ❶ *unr. tr. V.* Ⓐ wash; **sich ~:** wash [oneself]; have a wash; **jmdm./sich die Hände/das Gesicht** *usw.* **~:** wash sb.'s/one's hands/face *etc.*; **Wäsche ~:** do the/some washing; **sich ge~ haben** (*fig. ugs.*) be quite something; Ⓑ (*fig. ugs.*) launder ‹money›. ❷ *unr. itr. V.* do the washing

**Wäsche·puff** *der* linen basket (*Brit.*), clothes hamper (*Amer.*) (*with upholstered lid*)

**Wäscherei** *die;* **~, ~en** laundry

**Wäscherin** *die;* **~, ~nen** laundrywoman

**Wäsche-: ~schleuder** *die* spin drier; **~spinne** *die* rotary clothes drier; **~ständer** *der* clothes airer; **~tinte** *die* marking ink; **~trockner** *der* Ⓐ (*Maschine*) tumble-drier; Ⓑ (*Gestell*) clothes airer; **~zeichen** *das* linen mark

*old spelling (see note on page 1707)

**wasch-, Wasch-: ~frau** *die* washerwoman; **~gang** *der* washing cycle; **~gelegenheit** *die* washing facilities *pl.*; **~hand·schuh** *der* flannel mitt (*Brit.*); shower/bath mitt (*Amer.*); **~küche** *die* Ⓐ laundry room; Ⓑ (*ugs.: dichter Nebel*) pea-souper; **~lappen** *der* Ⓐ [face] flannel; washcloth (*Amer.*); Ⓑ (*ugs. abwertend*) (*Weichling*) softie (*coll.*); (*Feigling*) sissy; **~lauge** *die* soapy water; soapsuds *pl.*; **~maschine** *die* washing machine; **~maschinen·fest** *Adj.* machine washable; **~mittel** *das* detergent; **~muschel** *die* (*österr.*) washbasin; **~programm** *das* washing programme; **~pulver** *das* washing powder; **~raum** *der* washing room; **~salon** *der* launderette; laundromat (*Amer.*); **~schüssel** *die* washing bowl; **~straße** *die* [automatic] car wash

**wäscht** /vɛʃt/ *3. Pers. Sg. Präsens v.* **waschen**

**Wasch-: ~tag** *der* washday; **~tisch** *der* washstand

**Waschung** *die;* **~, ~en** (*Rel., Med.*) ablution

**Wasch-: ~wasser** *das* washing water; **~weib** *das* (*salopp abwertend: Klatschbase*) gossip; **~zettel** *der* (*Buchw.*) blurb; **~zeug** *das* washing things *pl.*; **~zwang** *der* (*Psych.*) obsession with washing oneself

**Wasser** /ˈvasɐ/ *das;* **~s, ~/Wässer** /ˈvɛsɐ/ Ⓐ water; **ins ~ gehen** enter the water; (*zum Schwimmen*) go for a swim; (*verhüll.: sich ertränken*) drown oneself; **warst du schon im ~?** have you been in the water?; (*zum Schwimmen*) have you been for a swim?; **sich über ~ halten** (*auch fig.*) keep one's head above water (*lit. or fig.*); **direkt am ~:** right by the water; (*am Meer*) right by the sea; **ein Boot zu ~ lassen** put out *or* launch a boat; **auflaufendes/ablaufendes ~:** incoming/outgoing tide; **unter ~ stehen** be under water; be flooded; **etw. unter ~ setzen** flood sth.; **zu ~:** by sea; **ihre Überlegenheit zu ~:** their naval superiority; **der Transport zu ~:** transport by water; **~ treten** paddle (*for therapeutic purposes*); (*strampeln*) tread water; Ⓑ (*fig.*) **ins ~ fallen** fall through; **das ~ steht ihm bis zum Hals** he's up to his neck in trouble; (*verschuldet sein*) he's up to his eyes in debt; **reinsten ~s** par excellence; **bis dahin fließt noch viel ~ den Bach** *od.* **Fluss** *od.* **Rhein** *usw.* **hinunter** a lot of water will have flowed under the bridge by then; **nahe am ~ gebaut haben** (*ugs.*) be rather weepy *or* tearful; **mit allen ~n gewaschen sein** know all the tricks; **jmdm. das ~ abgraben** pull the carpet from under sb.'s feet; leave sb. high and dry; **~ ziehen** (*ugs.*) ‹stockings, socks› be at half mast; **~ hat keine Balken** (*Spr.*) you must either sink or swim; **stille ~ sind tief** (*Spr.*) still waters run deep (*prov.*); **die kochen auch nur mit ~** (*ugs.*) they're no different from the rest of us; **bei ~ und Brot sitzen** be doing time [in prison]; **jmdm. nicht das ~ reichen können** not be able to hold a candle to sb.; not be a patch on sb. (*coll.*); ⇒ *auch* **Mühle** A; Ⓒ *Pl.* **Wässer** (*Mineral~, Tafel~*) mineral water; (*Heil~*) water; Ⓓ *Pl.* **die ~ des Ganges** (*geh.*) the waters of the Ganges; Ⓔ *Pl.* **~** (*Gewässer*) **ein fließendes/stehendes ~:** a moving/stagnant stretch of water; Ⓕ (*Schweiß*) sweat; (*Urin*) water; urine; (*Speichel*) saliva; (*Gewebsflüssigkeit*) fluid; **~ lassen** pass water; **sein ~ abschlagen** (*salopp*) have a slash (*sl.*); **ihm lief das ~ im Mund[e] zusammen** his mouth watered; **~ in den Beinen haben** have fluid in one's legs; ⇒ *auch* **Blut**; **Rotz** A; Ⓖ *Pl.* **Wässer** (*Lösung, Lotion usw.*) lotion; (*Mund~*) mouthwash; (*Duft~*) scent; (*Kölnisch ~*) cologne

**wasser-, Wasser-: ~abweisend** *Adj.* water-repellent; **~ader** *die* [underground] watercourse; **~arm** *Adj.* ‹area› suffering from a water shortage; **~aufbereitung** *die* water treatment; **~bad** *das* (*Kochk.*) bain-marie; **~ball** *der* Ⓐ beachball; Ⓑ (*Spiel*) water polo; **~baller** *der;* **~~s, ~~, ~ballerin** *die;* **~~, ~~nen** water polo player; **~bau** *der* hydraulic engineering *no art.*; **~becken** *das* pool; (*~tank*) water tank; **~bett** *das* waterbed; **~büffel** *der* water buffalo; **~burg** *die* moated castle

**Wässerchen** /ˈvɛsɐçən/ *das;* **~s, ~** Ⓐ **er sieht aus, als könnte er kein ~ trüben** (*fig.*) he looks as though butter wouldn't melt in his mouth; Ⓑ ⇒ **Wasser** G; Ⓒ (*scherzh.: Wodka*) vodka

**wasser-, Wasser-: ~dampf** *der* steam; **~dicht** *Adj.* Ⓐ waterproof ‹clothing, watch, etc.›; watertight ‹container, seal, etc.›; Ⓑ (*fig. ugs.*) watertight ‹alibi, contract›; **~druck** *der; Pl.* **~drücke** water pressure; **~eimer** *der* bucket; **~fahrzeug** *das* vessel; watercraft; **~fall** *der* waterfall; **reden wie ein ~fall** (*ugs.*) talk non-stop; **~farbe** *die* watercolour; **~fläche** *die* expanse of water; **~flasche** *die* water bottle; **~floh** *der* water flea; **~flugzeug** *das* seaplane; **~führend** *Adj.* water-bearing; **~gehalt** *der* water content; **~gekühlt** *Adj.* water-cooled; **~glas** *das* Ⓐ (*Gefäß*) glass; tumbler; ⇒ *auch* **Sturm** A; Ⓑ (*Chemie*) water glass; **~glätte** *die:* **bei ~glätte** in wet and slippery conditions; **~graben** *der* Ⓐ ditch; (*um eine Burg*) moat; Ⓑ (*Reiten, Leichtathletik*) water jump; **~hahn** *der; Pl.* **~hähne**, *fachspr.* **~en** water tap; faucet (*Amer.*); **~haushalt** *der* Ⓐ (*Physiol.*) water balance; Ⓑ (*Ökologie, Bodenk.*) hydrologic balance; **~hose** *die* (*Met.*) waterspout; **~huhn** *das* coot

**wässerig** /ˈvɛsərɪç/ ⇒ **wässrig**

**wasser-, Wasser-: ~kasten** *der* water tank; (*im WC*) cistern; **~kessel** *der* kettle; **~kopf** *der* ▶ 474 hydrocephalus (*Med.*); **der ~kopf der Bürokratie** (*fig.*) excessive bureaucracy; **~kraft** *die* water power; **~kraftwerk** *das* hydroelectric power station; **~kreislauf** *der* water cycle; **~krug** *der* water jug; **~kühlung** *die* water-cooling system; **mit ~kühlung** water-cooled; **~lache** *die* puddle [of water]; **~lauf** *der* watercourse; (*Bach*) stream; **~leiche** *die* (*ugs.*) body of a drowned person; **~leitung** *die* Ⓐ water pipe; (*Hauptleitung*) water main; **unter der/die ~leitung** (*ugs.*) under the tap; **die ~leitung aufdrehen/zudrehen** (*ugs.*) turn the tap on/off; Ⓑ (*Aquädukt*) aqueduct; **~linie** *die* (*Schifffahrt*) waterline; **~loch** *das* waterhole; **~mann** *der* Ⓐ (*Myth.*) merman; Ⓑ (*Astron., Astrol.*) **[der] ~mann** Aquarius; Ⓒ (*Astrol.: Mensch*) Aquarian; **~masse** *die* mass *or* torrent of water; **~melone** *die* watermelon; **~messer** *der;* **~~s, ~~:** water meter; **~mühle** *die* watermill

**wassern** *itr. V.; mit sein* (*Flugw., Zool.*) land [on the water]; (*Raumf.*) splash down

**wässern** /ˈvɛsɐn/ ❶ *tr. V.* Ⓐ (*einweichen*) soak; (*Phot.*) wash ‹negative, print›; Ⓑ (*bewässern*) water. ❷ *itr. V.* (*geh.*) water; **eine ~de Wunde** a suppurating wound

**wasser-, Wasser-: ~nixe** *die* (*Myth.*) water nymph; **~ober·fläche** *die* surface of the water; **~pfeife** *die* hookah; water pipe; **~pflanze** *die* aquatic plant; **~pistole** *die* water pistol; **~pumpe** *die* water pump; **~rad** *das* waterwheel; **~ratte** *die* Ⓐ water rat; Ⓑ (*ugs. scherzh.*) keen swimmer; (*Kind*) water baby; **~rohr** *das* water pipe; **~rohrbruch** *der* burst pipe; **~säule** *die* head of water; **~schaden** *der* water damage *no pl., no indef. art.*; (*durch Überschwemmung*) flood damage *no pl., no indef. art.*; **~scheide** *die* (*Geogr.*) watershed; **~scheu** *Adj.* scared of water; **~schlange** *die* water snake; **~schlauch** *der* [water] hose; **~schloss**, ***~schloß** *das* (*mit ~graben*) moated [residential] castle; (*an einem kleinen See o. Ä.*) [residential] castle set on a lake; **~schutz·gebiet** *das* water conservation area; **~schutz·polizei** *die* river/lake police; **~ski**[1] *der* waterski; **~ski fahren** waterski; **~ski**[2] *das;* **~skis** waterskiing *no art.*; **~speier** *der;* **~~s, ~~:** (*Archit.*) gargoyle; **~spiegel** *der* Ⓐ (*Oberfläche*) surface [of the water]; Ⓑ (*Niveau*) water level; **~spiele** *Pl.* waterworks *pl.*; **~sport** *der* water sport *no art.*; **~sportler** *der*, **~sportlerin** *die* water sports enthusiast; **~spülung** *die* flush; flushing system; **~stand** *der* water level; **~stands·anzeiger** *der* water gauge;

**~stands·meldung** *die* water level report (*on the radio*); **~stelle** *die* watering place

**Wasser·stoff** *der* hydrogen

**Wasser·stoff-: ~bombe** *die* hydrogen bomb; **~per·oxid, ~per·oxyd, ~super·oxid, ~super·oxyd** *das* (*Chemie*) hydrogen peroxide

**Wasser-: ~strahl** *der* jet of water; **~straße** *die* waterway; **~sucht** *die* ▶ 474 (*Med.*) dropsy; **~tank** *der* water tank; **~temperatur** *die* water temperature; **~tiefe** *die* depth of the water; **bei einer ~tiefe von nur 0,50 m** when the water is/was only 0.5 m. deep; **~träger** *der*, **~trägerin** *die* water carrier; (*fig.*) dogsbody (*coll.*); **~treten** *das;* **~~s** treading water *no art.;* **~tropfen** *der* drop of water; **~turm** *der* water tower; **~uhr** *die* Ⓐ water clock; Ⓑ (*volkst.: ~messer*) water meter; **~verbrauch** *der* water consumption; **~verdunster** *der;* **~~s, ~~:** humidifier; **~verschmutzung** *die* water pollution; **~versorgung** *die* water supply; **~vogel** *der* waterbird; aquatic bird; **~vorrat** *der* water reserves *pl.;* water supply; **~waage** *die* spirit level; **~weg** *der* water route; **auf dem ~weg** by water; **~welle** *die* shampoo and set; **~werfer** *der* water cannon; **~werk** *das* waterworks *sing.;* **~wirtschaft** *die* water management; **~zähler** *der* water meter; **~zeichen** *das* watermark

**wässrig, *wäßrig** /ˈvɛs(ə)rɪç/ *Adj.* Ⓐ watery; ⇒ *auch* **Mund**; Ⓑ (*Chemie*) aqueous ‹solution›

**waten** /ˈva:tn̩/ *itr. V.; mit sein* wade

**Waterkant** /ˈva:tɐkant/ *die;* ~ (*nordd.*) [North German] coast

**watscheln** /ˈvatʃl̩n/ *itr. V.; mit sein* waddle

**Watschen** /ˈva:tʃn̩/ *die;* ~, ~ (*bayr., österr. ugs.*) ⇒ **Ohrfeige**

**Watt**[1] /vat/ *das;* **~[e]s, ~en** mudflats *pl.*

**Watt**[2] *das;* **~s,** ~ (*Technik, Physik*) watt; **die Glühlampe hat 100 ~:** it is a 100-watt lightbulb

**Watte** /ˈvatə/ *die;* **~, ~n** cotton wool; (*als Polsterung*) wadding

**Watte·bausch** *der* wad of cotton wool

**Watten·meer** *das* tidal shallows *pl.* (*covering mudflats*)

**wattieren** *tr. V.* wad; (*gesteppt*) quilt ‹garment›; pad ‹shoulder etc.›

**wattiert** *Adj.* quilted; padded ‹shoulder etc., envelope›

**Watt·sekunde** *die* (*Physik, Technik*) joule; watt-second

**Wat·vogel** *der* (*Zool.*) wading bird; wader

**wau, wau** /vau̯, vau̯/ *Interj.* (*Kindersp*r.) bow-wow; woof-woof

**Wauwau** *der;* **~s, ~s** (*Kinderspr.*) bow-wow (*child lang.*)

**WC** *Abk. engl.* **watercloset** toilet; WC

**WDR** *Abk.* **Westdeutscher Rundfunk** West German Radio

**weben** /ˈve:bn̩/ ❶ *regelm.* (*geh., fig. auch unr.*) *tr., itr. V.* weave. ❷ *unr. refl. V.* (*geh.*) ‹legend› be woven (**um** around)

**Weber** *der;* **~s, ~** ▶ 159 weaver

**Weberei** *die;* **~, ~en** Ⓐ weaving *no art.;* Ⓑ (*Betrieb*) weaving mill

**Weberin** *die;* **~, ~nen** ▶ 159 weaver

**Weber·knecht** *der* (*Zool.*) daddy-long-legs

**Web-: ~fehler** *der* flaw [in the weave]; **~kante** *die* selvage

**Website** /ˈwebˈsaɪt/ *die;* **~, ~s** (*DV*) Web site

**Web·stuhl** *der* loom

**Wechsel** /ˈvɛksl̩/ *der;* **~s,** ~ Ⓐ (*das Auswechseln*) change; (*Geld~*) exchange; (*Ballspiele*) (*Seiten~*) changeover; (*Spieler~*) substitution; **fliegender** ~ (*Handball, Eishockey*) substitution without stopping play; Ⓑ (*Aufeinanderfolge*) alternation; **der ~ der Jahreszeiten** the rotation *or* succession of the seasons; **im ~:** alternately; (*bei mehr als zwei*) in rotation; **im ~ mit ...** alternating with ...; **in täglichem/regelmäßigem ~:** in daily/regular rotation; **im ~ der Zeiten/Jahre/Jahreszeiten** over the ages/years/through the changing seasons; Ⓒ (*das Überwechseln*) move; (*Sport*) transfer; Ⓓ (*Bankw.*) bill of exchange (**über** + *Akk.* for); Ⓔ (*ugs. veralt.: monatliches Unterhaltsgeld*) monthly allowance; Ⓕ (*Jägerspr.*) game path

**Wechsel-: ~bad** *das:* **ein ~bad nehmen, ~bäder machen** dip one's feet/arms *etc.* in alternate hot and cold water; **~balg** *der Pl.* **~bälge** *od.* **~bälger** changeling; **~beziehung** *die* interrelation; **in [einer] ~beziehung zueinander** *od.* **miteinander stehen** be interrelated; **~dienst** *der* shift work; **im ~dienst arbeiten** work shifts; **~fälle** *Pl.* vicissitudes; ups and downs (*coll.*); **~geld** *das* ▶ 337 change; **~gesang** *der* antiphonal chant; (*Art des Gesangs*) antiphony *no art.*

**wechsel·haft** *Adj.* changeable

**Wechsel-: ~jahre** *Pl.* change of life *sing.;* menopause *sing.;* **in die ~jahre kommen** reach the menopause; **die ~jahre des Mannes** the male menopause; **~kasse** *die* office issuing change; **~kurs** *der* exchange rate

**wechseln** ❶ *tr. V.* Ⓐ change ‹subject, socks, job, doctor, etc.›; **das Hemd ~:** change one's shirt; **die Wohnung ~:** move home; **ein Hemd/ein Paar Socken zum Wechseln** a spare shirt/pair of socks; ⇒ *auch* **Besitzer** A; Ⓑ ([*aus*]*tauschen*) exchange ‹letters, words, glances, etc.›; **mit jmdm. den Platz ~:** change places with sb.; **sie wechselten die Plätze** they changed places; ⇒ *auch* **Ring** A; Ⓒ ▶ 337 (*um~*) change ‹money, note, etc.› (**in** + *Akk.* into); **kannst du mir 100 Mark ~?** can you change 100 marks for me?; **einen Hunderter in fünf Zwanziger/einen Schein in Münzen/Mark in Lire ~:** change a hundred for five twenties/a note into coins/marks into lire.

❷ *itr. V.* Ⓐ (*sich ändern*) change; **auf Rot ~** ‹traffic light› change to red; **mit ~dem Erfolg** with varying success; **~de Bewölkung, ~d wolkig** *od.* **bewölkt** (*bei Wettervorhersagen*) variable cloud; **Wind aus ~den Richtungen** wind variable; Ⓑ *mit sein* (*über~*) move; (*Jägerspr.*) ‹game› change its habitat; **über die Grenze ~:** get across the frontier; Ⓒ ([*sich*] *ab~*) alternate; (*aufeinander folgen*) succeed one another; **Geschlechtsverkehr mit [häufig] ~den Partnern** sexual intercourse with frequent changes of partner; Ⓓ (*herausgeben*) **ich kann nicht ~:** I haven't any change

**wechsel-, Wechsel-: ~objektiv** *das* (*Fot.*) interchangeable lens; **~rahmen** *der* picture frame (*with a removable back*); **~schicht** *die* alternating shift; **in ~schicht arbeiten** work alternate shifts; **~schritt** *der* changeover step; **~seitig** ❶ *Adj.* mutual; **~seitiger Zusammenhang** interconnection; **~seitige Abhängigkeit** interdependence; ❷ *adv.* mutually; **sich ~seitig beeinflussen** influence each other; **~seitigkeit** *die;* **~, ~en** reciprocity; **~spiel** *das* interplay; **das ~spiel des Zufalls** (*geh.*) the vagaries *pl.* of chance; **~ständig** *Adj.* (*Bot.*) alternate ‹leaves›; **~strom** *der* (*Elektrot.*) alternating current; **~stube** *die* bureau de change; **~voll** *Adj.* chequered ‹history›; **ein ~volles Leben/Schicksal** a life full of vicissitudes; **~wähler** *der,* **~wählerin** *die* (*Politik*) floating voter; **~warm** *Adj.* (*Zool.*) cold-blooded; **~weise** *Adv.* alternately; **~wirkung** *die* interaction

**Wechsler** /ˈvɛkslɐ/ *der;* **~s, ~** (*bibl.*) money changer

**Wechte** /ˈvɛçtə/ *die;* **~, ~n** [snow] cornice

**Weck·dienst** *der* [telephone] alarm call service

**wecken** /ˈvɛkn̩/ *tr. V.* Ⓐ **jmdn. [aus dem Schlaf] ~:** wake sb. [up]; **der Kaffee weckte seine Lebensgeister** (*fig.*) the coffee revived his spirits; Ⓑ (*fig.: hervorrufen*) arouse, awaken ‹interest, curiosity›; arouse ‹anger›; awaken ‹desire, misgiving›

**Wecken**[1] *das;* **~s** morning call; (*Mil.*) reveille

**Wecken**[2] *der;* **~s,** ~ (*südd., österr.*) Ⓐ (*Brötchen*) oblong roll; Ⓑ (*Brot*) oblong loaf

**Wecker** *der;* **~s,** ~ Ⓐ alarm clock; **jmdm. auf den ~ gehen** *od.* **fallen** (*ugs.*) get on sb.'s nerves; Ⓑ (*ugs.: Uhr*) big fat watch

**Weck·glas** Ⓦⓩ *das; Pl.* **Weckgläser** preserving jar

**Weck·ruf** *der* morning call

**Wedel** *der;* **~s,** ~ Ⓐ (*Staub~*) feather duster; Ⓑ (*Palm~, Farn~*) [palm/fern] frond

**wedeln** ❶ *itr. V.* Ⓐ ‹tail› wag; **[mit dem Schwanz] ~** ‹dog› wag its tail; (*winken*) **mit der Hand/einem Tuch ~:** wave one's hand/a handkerchief; Ⓑ *mit Richtungsangabe mit sein* (*Ski*) wedel. ❷ *tr. V.* **Krümel vom Tisch ~:** flap crumbs off the table

**weder** /ˈve:dɐ/ *Konj.* **~ A noch B** neither A nor B

**weg** /vɛk/ *Adv.* Ⓐ ▶ 265 away; (*verschwunden, ~gegangen*) gone; **~ sein** be away; (*~gegangen*) be gone; **er ist schon seit einer Stunde ~:** he left an hour ago; **~ sein** (*fig. ugs.*) (*eingeschlafen sein*) have dropped off; (*bewusstlos sein*) be out [cold]; **er war sofort ~:** he was out like a light; **[von jmdm./etw.] ~ sein** (*fig. ugs.*) be knocked sideways [by sb./sth.] (*coll.*); **[immer] ~ damit!** [let's] chuck it away (*coll.*); **~ mit dir!** away *or* off with you!; **~ da!** get away from there!; **Hände ~ [von meiner Kamera]!** hands off [my camera]!; **Kopf ~!** move your head!; **[nur] ~ von hier!, nichts wie ~!** let's hop it (*sl.*); let's make ourselves scarce (*coll.*); **und ~ ist/war er, und schon ist/war er ~:** and he is/was gone; **weit ~:** far away; a long way away; **weit ~ von der Schule** a long way from the school; **100 Meter von der Straße ~:** 100 metres from the road; ⇒ *auch* **Fenster**; Ⓑ **von ... ~** (*ugs.: unmittelbar von*) straight off *or* from; **von der Schule ~ eingezogen werden** be conscripted straight from school; Ⓒ **über einen Schock/Schrecken** *usw.* **~ sein** (*ugs.*) have got over a shock/fright *etc.*

**Weg** /ve:k/ *der;* **~[e]s, ~e** Ⓐ (*Fuß~*) path; (*Feld~*) track; **„kein öffentlicher ~"** 'no public right of way'; **am ~[e]** by the wayside; **er kennt hier ~ und Steg** (*geh.*) he knows every inch of this area; Ⓑ (*Zugang*) way; (*Passage, Durchgang*) passage; **sich** (*Dat.*) **einen ~ durch etw. bahnen** clear a path *or* way through sth.; **jmdm. im ~[e] stehen** *od.* (*auch fig.*) **sein** be in sb.'s way; **einer Sache** (*Dat.*) **im ~[e] stehen** (*fig.*) stand in the way of sth.; **sich** (*Dat.*) **selbst im ~[e] stehen** (*fig.*) be one's own worst enemy; **geh [mir] aus dem ~[e]** get out of the *or* my way; **jmdm. aus dem ~[e] gehen** (*fig.*) keep out of sb's way; avoid sb.; **einer Gefahr/Situation/Diskussion** *usw.* **aus dem ~[e] gehen** (*fig.*) keep clear of a danger/avoid a situation/discussion *etc.;* **jmdn./etw. aus dem ~[e] räumen** (*fig.*) get rid of sb./sth.; **jmdm. den ~ abschneiden** head sb. off; **jmdm. den ~ versperren, sich jmdm. in den ~ stellen, jmdm. in den ~ treten** block sb.'s path; Ⓒ ▶ 818 (*Route, Verbindung*) way; route; **[jmdn.] nach dem ~ fragen** ask [sb.] the way; **wir haben denselben ~:** we're going the same way; **wohin/woher des ~[e]s?** (*veralt., scherzh.*) wither goest/whence comest thou? (*arch./joc.*); **des ~es kommen** (*geh.*) draw near; approach; **seines ~es** *od.* **seiner ~e gehen** (*geh.*) go on one's way; **eigene** *od.* **seine eigenen ~e gehen** (*fig.*) go one's own way; **das liegt auf dem/meinem ~:** that's on the/my way; **er ist mir über den ~ gelaufen** (*fig. ugs.*) I ran *or* bumped into him; **jmdm. nicht über den ~ trauen** (*fig.*) not trust sb. an inch; **neue ~e beschreiten** *od.* **gehen** (*fig.*) break new ground; **den ~ der Tugend verlassen** leave the path of virtue; **den ~ des geringsten Widerstands gehen** take the line of least resistance; **hier trennen sich unsere ~e** (*auch fig.*) this is where we part company; **seinen ~ machen** (*fig.*) make one's way [in the world]; Ⓓ ▶ 265 (*Strecke, Entfernung*) distance; (*Gang*) walk; (*Reise*) journey; **es sind 2 km/10 Minuten ~:** it is a distance of two kilometres/it is ten minutes' walk; **zwei Stunden ~:** two hours' journey; **er hat noch einen weiten ~ vor sich** (*Dat.*) he still has a long way to go; **den ~**

W

# Wegbeschreibung

## Die Fragen

1. ***Wie komme ich zum Bahnhof?***
= How do I get to the station?
2. ***Wie kommt man am besten zum Museum?***
= Which is the best way to the museum?
3. ***Geht es hier zum White Hart Hotel?***
= Am I right for the White Hart Hotel ?
4. ***Wo ist hier die nächste Bank?***
= Where is the nearest bank?
5. ***Gibt es hier in der Nähe eine Apotheke?***
= Is there a chemist's near here?
6. ***Wie weit ist es zum Krankenhaus?***
= How far is it to the hospital?
7. ***Können Sie mir sagen, wo es hier ein gutes Restaurant gibt?***
= Can you direct me to a good restaurant?

## Die Antworten

1. ***Gehen Sie die erste Straße rechts, dann die zweite links, dann immer nur geradeaus bis zur Kreuzung. Biegen Sie rechts ein und dann sehen Sie den Bahnhof vor sich***
= Take the first turning on the right, then the second on the left, then go straight on as far as the junction. Turn right and you will see the station in front of you
2. ***Am besten, Sie gehen hier an der Ampel über die Straße, dann die Gasse entlang, die links am Theater vorbeiführt. Sie kommen dann gegenüber vom Museum heraus***
The best way is to cross over here at the lights and go down the alleyway along the left side of the theatre. You will come out opposite the museum
3. ***Nein, Sie sind zu weit gegangen/gefahren. Gehen/Fahren Sie zurück zur Kreuzung und biegen Sie links ab. Das Hotel liegt etwa hundert Meter weiter auf der rechten Seite***
No, you've come too far. Go back to the crossroads and turn left, you'll find the hotel about a hundred yards further on on the right
4. ***Am Marktplatz ist eine Filiale von Barclays. Biegen Sie dort drüben rechts ein, Sie kommen dann nach ein paar hundert Metern zum Marktplatz***
= There is a branch of Barclays on the market place, which is a couple of hundred yards along that turning over there on the right
5. ***In der nächsten Straße links ist eine, allerdings nur eine kleine. Falls Sie eine größere brauchen, müssen Sie mit der Linie 11 ins Zentrum fahren***
= There's one in the next street on the left, but it's only small. If you want a bigger one you'll have to take the number 11 bus into the centre
6. ***Es liegt etwa zwei Kilometer von hier an der Hauptstraße nach Cardiff. Am besten nehmen Sie ein Taxi, die Busse fahren nämlich nicht sehr oft***
= It's about a mile and a half from here on the main Cardiff road. You'd best take a taxi as the buses aren't very frequent
7. ***Tut mir Leid, ich bin auch fremd hier***
= Sorry, I'm a stranger here myself

**abkürzen** take a short cut; **auf dem kürzesten ~:** by the shortest route; **auf halbem ~[e]** (*auch fig.*) halfway; **sich auf den ~ machen** set off; **jmdm. einen guten Ratschlag mit auf den ~ geben** (*fig.*) give sb. some good advice for his/her future life; **etw. in die ~e leiten** get sth. under way; **jmdn. auf seinem letzten ~ begleiten** (*geh.*) accompany sb. on his/her last journey; **auf dem besten ~ sein, etw. zu tun** (*meist iron.*) be well on the way towards doing sth.; **er ist** *od.* **befindet sich auf dem ~[e] der Besserung** he's on the road to recovery; **viele ~e führen nach Rom** (*Spr.*) all roads lead to Rome; **E** (*ugs.: Besorgung*) errand; **einen ~ machen** do *or* run an errand; **jmdm. einen ~ abnehmen** run an errand for sb.; **F** (*Methode*) way; (*Mittel*) means; **ich sehe keinen anderen ~:** I can't see any alternative; **auf diesem ~[e]** by this means; in this way; **auf schnellstem ~[e]** as speedily as possible; **auf legalem/diplomatischem ~[e]** through legal/diplomatic channels; **auf friedlichem/gütlichem ~[e]** by peaceful/amicable means; **auf schriftlichem ~[e]** by letter; **auf kaltem ~[e]** (*ugs.*) without bothering about the niceties; **G zu ~e** ⇒ **zuwege**

**Weg·bereiter** *der;* **~s, ~, Wegbereiterin** *die;* **~, ~nen** forerunner; **er war ein Wegbereiter des Sozialismus** he helped pave the way for socialism

**weg-: ~|blasen** *unr. tr. V.* blow away; **wie ~geblasen sein** have vanished; **~|bleiben** *unr. itr. V.; mit sein* **A** (*nicht kommen*) stay away; (*nicht nach Hause kommen*) stay out; **B** (*ugs.: aussetzen*) ‹engine› stop; ‹electricity› go off; **mir blieb die Luft ~:** I was left gasping; **C** (*ugs.: ~gelassen werden*) be left out; **~brechen** *unr. itr. V.; mit sein* disappear; **es ist uns ein wichtiger Markt weggebrochen** we have lost an important market; **~|bringen** *unr. tr. V.* **A** take away; (*zur Reparatur, Wartung usw.*) take in; **B** (*ugs., bes. südd.*) ⇒ **~kriegen**; **~|denken** *unr. tr. V.* **sich** (*Dat.*) **etw. ~denken** imagine sth. is not there; **er ist aus unserem Team nicht [mehr] ~zudenken** I/we can't imagine our team without him; **~|diskutieren** *tr. V.* **es lässt sich nicht ~diskutieren** its existence cannot be argued away; **~|dürfen** *unr. itr. V.* be allowed to go away; (*ausgehen dürfen*) be allowed to go out; **ich darf hier nicht ~:** I can't leave here

**Wege·geld** *das* **A** mileage charge; **B** (*veralt.: Straßenzoll*) road toll

**Wegelagerei** *die;* **~:** highway robbery

**Wegelagerer** *der;* **~s, ~:** highwayman

**Wegelagerin** *die;* **~, ~nen** highwaywoman

**wegen** **1** *Präp. mit Gen., in bestimmten Fällen auch mit Dat./mit endungslosem Nomen* **A** (*zur Angabe einer Ursache, eines Grundes*) because of; owing to; **~ des schlechten Wetters,** (*geh.*) **des schlechten Wetters ~:** because of the bad weather; **[nur] ~ Peter/**(*ugs.*) **euch** all because of Peter/you; **~ Hochwasser[s]** owing to flooding; **von Berufs ~:** for professional reasons; **~ mir** (*ugs., bes. südd.*) because of me; (*was mich betrifft*) as far as I'm concerned; **~ Umbau[s] geschlossen** closed for alterations; **~ Mangel[s] an Beweisen** owing to lack of evidence; **B** (*zur Angabe eines Zwecks, Ziels*) for [the sake of]; **~ einer Tagung nach X fahren** go to X for a conference; **er ist ~ dringender Geschäfte verreist** he's away on urgent business; **C** (*um ... willen*) for the sake of; **~ der Kinder/**(*ugs.*) **dir** for the children's/your sake; **D** (*bezüglich*) about; regarding; **ich habe ~ morgen noch eine Frage** I've another question about tomorrow. **2** *in* **von ~!** (*ugs.*) you must be joking!; **von ~ lauwarm/billig!** lukewarm/cheap? not on your life!

**Wegerich** /ˈveːgərɪç/ *der;* **~s, ~e** (*Bot.*) plantain

**Weges·rand** *der* (*geh.*) **am ~:** by the wayside

**weg-, Weg-: ~|essen** *unr. tr. V.* eat up; **jmdm. alles ~essen** eat up all sb.'s food; **~|fahren** **1** *unr. itr. V.; mit sein* **A** leave; (*im Auto*) drive off; (*losfahren*) set off; **wann seid ihr in Kiel ~gefahren?** when did you leave Kiel?; **B** (*irgendwohin fahren*) go away. **2** *unr. tr. V.* drive away; (*mit dem Handwagen/Boot/Schubkarren*) take away; **~fahr·sperre** *die* (*Kfz.-W.*) immobilizer; **~fall** *der* ending; (*Einstellung*) discontinuation; **in ~fall kommen** (*Papierdt.*) be discontinued; **~|fallen** *unr. itr. V.; mit sein* be discontinued; (*nicht mehr zutreffen*) ‹reason› no longer apply; (*~gelassen werden*) be omitted; **~|fegen** *tr. V.* (*auch fig.*) sweep away; **~|fliegen** *unr. itr. V.; mit sein* fly away; (*~geschleudert/~geblasen werden*) fly off; **~|führen** *tr.,* *itr. V.* lead away; **das führt vom Thema ~:** this takes us away from the subject

**Weg·gab[e]lung** *die* fork [in the path/road]

**Weg·gang** *der* departure

**weg|geben** *unr. tr. V.* **A** **etw. zur Reparatur ~:** take sth. to be repaired; **ich gebe meine Wäsche weg** I send my washing to the laundry; **B** (*verschenken*) give away

**Weg·gefährte** *der,* **Weg·gefährtin** *die* (*auch fig.*) fellow-traveller

**weg-: ~|gehen** *unr. itr. V.* **A** leave; (*ugs.: ausgehen*) go out; (*ugs.: ~ziehen*) move away; **von jmdm. ~gehen** leave sb.; **geh ~!** go away!; **geh mir [bloß] ~ damit!** (*ugs.*) you can keep that!; **B** (*verschwinden*) ‹spot, fog, etc.› go away; **C** (*sich entfernen lassen*) ‹stain› come out; **D** (*ugs.: verkauft werden*) sell; **~|gießen** *unr. tr. V.* pour away; **~|gucken** *itr. V.* ⇒ **~sehen**; **~|haben** *unr. tr. V.* (*ugs.*) **A** have got rid of ‹dirt, stain, etc.›; **etw. ~haben wollen** want to get rid of sth.; **B** (*bekommen haben*) have got ‹punishment, cold, etc.›; **einen ~haben** (*betrunken sein*) have had one too many (*coll.*); (*nicht bei Verstand sein*) be off one's rocker (*coll.*); ⇒ *auch* **Fett** A; **Teil** B; **C** (*können, wissen*) **in Literatur/auf einem Gebiet [et]was ~haben** know a thing or two about literature/on a subject; **D** (*begriffen haben*) **er hatte es sofort ~:** he immediately got the hang of it (*coll.*); ⇒ *auch* **Ruhe** F; **~|holen** (*ugs.*) **1** *tr. V.* take away; **2** *refl. V.* **sich** (*Dat.*) **was ~holen** catch something; **~hören** *itr. V.* not listen; **er konnte nicht ~hören** he couldn't help listening; **~|jagen** *tr. V.* chase away; **~|kommen** *unr. itr. V.; mit sein* **A** get away; (*~gehen können*) manage to go out; **mach, dass du [hier] ~kommst!** (*ugs.*) come on, hop it! (*coll.*); make yourself scarce!

*old spelling (see note on page 1707)

W

(*coll.*); [B] (*abhanden kommen*) go missing; [C] **gut/schlecht** *usw.* **[bei etw.] ~kommen** (*ugs.*) come off well/badly *etc.* [in sth.]; [D] (*ugs.: davon ~kommen*) get off; [E] (*ugs.*) ⇒ **hinwegkommen**; [F] (*ugs.: loskommen*) **von jmdm. ~kommen** get away from sb.; **vom Rauchen ~kommen** give up smoking; **~|können** *unr. itr. V.* [A] be able to leave *or* get away; (*ausgehen können*) be able to go out; [B] (*~geworfen werden können*) **die Zeitung kann ~:** the paper can be thrown away

**Weg·kreuz** *das* wayside cross

**weg-: ~|kriegen** *tr. V.* get rid of ‹cold, pain, etc.›; get out, get rid of ‹stain›; shift, move ‹stone, tree trunk›; **er ist von seinem Spielzeug kaum ~zukriegen** you can hardly tear him away from his toys; **~|lassen** *unr. tr. V.* [A] **jmdn. ~lassen** let sb. go; (*ausgehen lassen*) let sb. go out; [B] (*auslassen*) leave out; omit; **die Soße ~lassen** do without the sauce; give the sauce a miss; **~|laufen** *unr. itr. V.; mit sein* run away (**von, vor** + *Dat.* from); **von zu Hause ~laufen** run away from home; **seine Frau ist ihm ~gelaufen** (*ugs.*) his wife has gone *or* run off and left him (*coll.*); **die Arbeit läuft [dir] nicht ~** (*ugs.*) the work will keep; **~|legen** *tr. V.* (*beiseite legen*) put aside; (*an seinen Platz legen*) put away; (*aus der Hand legen*) put down; **~|leugnen** *tr. V.* (*ugs.*) deny ‹sth.› out of existence; **~|loben** *tr. V.* **jmdn. ~loben** get rid of sb. by singing his/her praises; **~|machen** (*ugs.*) ❶ *tr. V.* get rid of; remove ‹wart›; delete ‹comma etc.›; **[sich (*Dat.*)] ein Kind ~machen lassen** (*salopp*) get rid of a baby (*before birth*); ❷ *itr. V.; mit sein* (*landsch.: ~ziehen*) go off; **~|müssen** *unr. itr. V.* [A] have to leave; (*loskommen müssen*) have to get away; **ich muss kurz ~:** I've got to go out for a short while; [B] (*entfernt werden müssen*) have to be removed; ‹furniture etc.› have to be moved; (*~gebracht werden müssen*) ‹letter etc.› have to go; (*~geworfen werden müssen*) have to be thrown away; **du musst da ~:** you'll have to move; **der Diktator muss ~:** the dictator must go; **~|nehmen** *unr. tr. V.* [A] (*entfernen*) take away; remove; move ‹head, arm›; **nimm die Finger da ~!** [keep your] fingers off!; **[das/etwas] Gas ~nehmen** take one's foot off/ease up on the accelerator; [B] (*entziehen, entwenden*) **jmdm. etw. ~nehmen** take sth. away from sb.; (*einem Besitzer*) **er hat mir das Buch ~genommen** he's taken my book; **dem Freund die Freundin ~nehmen** pinch one's friend's girlfriend (*coll.*); **jmdm. den Turm** *usw.* **~nehmen** (*Schachspiel*) take sb.'s rook *etc.*; **du nimmst mir das [ganze] Licht ~:** you're in my light; [C] (*beanspruchen, einnehmen*) take up ‹space, time›; **~|packen** *tr. V.* put away; **~|putzen** *tr. V.* [A] clean off ‹marks etc.›; [B] (*ugs.: aufessen, trinken*) polish off (*coll.*)

**Weg·rand** *der* wayside; **Blumen/Gasthöfe am ~:** wayside flowers/inns

**weg-: ~|rationalisieren** *tr. V.* cut ‹staff, jobs› as part of a rationalization programme; **~|räumen** *tr. V.* clear away ‹dishes, rubbish, snow, etc.›; remove ‹obstacles, difficulties›; (*an seinen Platz tun*) tidy *or* put away; **~|rennen** *unr. itr. V.; mit sein* (*ugs.*) run away (**vor** + *Dat.* from); **~|schaffen** *tr. V.* get rid of; (*~räumen*) clear away; (*~bringen*) take away; **~|schauen** *itr. V.* (*bes. südd., österr., schweiz.*) look away; **~|scheren** *refl. V.* clear off (*coll.*); **~|schicken** *tr. V.* [A] send off ‹letter, parcel›; [B] send ‹person› away; **~|schieben** *unr. tr. V.* push away; **~|schleichen** *unr. itr., refl. V.; itr. mit sein* creep away; **~|schleppen** ❶ *tr. V.* [A] (*~tragen*) carry *or* lug off *or* away; [B] (*abschleppen*) tow ‹car, rig, etc.› away; ❷ *refl. V.* drag oneself away; **~|schließen** *unr. tr. V.* lock away; **~|schmeißen** *unr. tr. V.* (*ugs.*) chuck away (*coll.*); **~|schnappen** *tr. V.* (*ugs.*) **jmdm. etw. ~schnappen/vor der Nase ~schnappen** snatch sth. away from sb./from under sb.'s nose; **jmdm. die Freundin ~schnappen** pinch sb.'s girlfriend (*coll.*); **~|schütten** *tr. V.* pour away; **~|sehen** *unr. itr. V.* [A] look away; [B] (*ugs.*) ⇒ **hinwegsehen**; **~|sollen** *unr. itr. V.* **er soll jetzt ~:** he is to *or* should leave now; **diese Sachen sollen ~:** these things are to go; **das Plakat soll ~:** the poster is to be removed; **~|spülen** *tr. V.* [A] wash away; [B] (*ugs.: spülen*) wash up; **~|stecken** *tr. V.* [A] put away; [B] (*fig. ugs.: hinnehmen*) take, accept ‹blow›; swallow ‹insult›; **einen ~stecken** (*derb*) have a poke (*coarse*); **~|stellen** *tr. V.* put away; move ‹car› out of the way; (*beiseite stellen*) put aside; **~|stoßen** *unr. tr. V.* push *or* shove away

**Weg·strecke** *die* stretch [of road]; (*Entfernung*) distance

**weg-: ~|tragen** *unr. tr. V.* carry away; **~|treten** ❶ *unr. tr. V.* kick away; ❷ *unr. itr. V.; mit sein* step away; (*zurücktreten*) step back; (*Milit.*) dismiss; **~getreten!** (*Milit.*) dismiss!; **[etwas] ~getreten sein** (*fig. ugs.*) be [somewhat] distracted; **~|tun** *unr. tr. V.* (*ugs.*) [A] put away; [B] (*~werfen*) throw away

**wegweisend** *Adj.* pioneering; **~ sein/werden** show the way forward (**für** to)

**Wegweiser** *der;* **~s, ~** [A] signpost; [B] (*fig.: Buch*) guide

**weg-: ~|werfen** *unr. tr. V.* (*auch fig.*) throw away; **das ist doch ~geworfenes Geld** (*ugs.*) that's money down the drain (*coll.*); **~werfend** *Adj.* dismissive ‹gesture, remark›

**Weg·werf-: ~flasche** *die* disposable *or* non-returnable bottle; **~gesellschaft** *die* (*abwertend*) throwaway society; **~mentalität** *die* (*abwertend*) use-and-throw-away attitude

**weg-: ~|wischen** *tr. V.* wipe away; (*fig.*) erase ‹memory›; dispel ‹fear, doubt›; dismiss ‹objection›; **~|wollen** *unr. itr. V.* want to go *or* leave; (*loskommen wollen*) want to get away; (*ausgehen wollen*) want to go out; (*verreisen wollen*) want to go away; **~|zaubern** *tr. V.* spirit away; **wie ~gezaubert sein** have vanished into thin air

**Weg·zehrung** *die* (*geh.*) provisions *pl.* for the journey

**weg-: ~|zerren** *tr. V.* drag away; **~|ziehen** ❶ *unr. tr. V.* pull away; pull *or* draw back ‹curtain›; pull off ‹blanket›; **jmdm. den Stuhl ~ziehen** pull away sb.'s chair [from under him/her]; ❷ *unr. itr. V.; mit sein* [A] (*umziehen*) move away; **aus X ~ziehen** leave X; move from X; [B] (*wandern*) ‹animals, nomads, etc.› leave [on their migration]

**Weg·zug** *der* move; **nach ihrem ~ aus Berlin** after moving [away] from Berlin

**weh**[1] *Interj.* (*veralt.*) **o ~:** alas; **~ mir!** woe is me! (*arch.*)

**weh**[2] /veː/ *Adj.* [A] (*ugs.: schmerzend*) sore; **einen ~en Finger haben** have a sore *or* bad finger; [B] (*geh.: schmerzlich*) painful; **ein ~es Lächeln** a sad smile; [C] (*geh.: schmerzlich*) **ihr ist ~ ums Herz** her heart aches; she is sore at heart; **ein ~es Gefühl** an aching feeling; ⇒ *auch* **wehtun**

**Weh** *das;* **~[e]s** (*geh.*) sorrow; grief

**wehe** *Interj.* woe betide you/him *etc.;* **~ [dir], wenn du ...** woe betide you if you ...

**Wehe**[1] /ˈveːə/ *die;* **~, ~n die ~n setzten ein** the contractions started; she went into labour; **~n haben** have contractions; **in den ~n liegen** be in labour

**Wehe**[2] *die;* **~, ~n** drift

**wehen** ❶ *itr. V.* [A] (*blasen*) blow; [B] (*flattern*) flutter; **ihre Haare wehten im Wind** her hair was blowing about in the wind; **mit ~den Rockschößen** with coat-tails flapping; [C] *mit sein* ‹leaves, snowflakes, scent› waft. ❷ *tr. V.* blow

**weh-, Weh-: ~klage** *die* (*geh.*) lamentation; **~klagen** *itr. V.* (*geh.*) lament; **über etw.** (*Akk.*) **~klagen** lament *or* bewail sth.; **~leidig** (*abwertend*) ❶ *Adj.* [A] (*überempfindlich*) soft; **sei nicht so ~leidig!** don't be so soft *or* such a sissy; [B] (*weinerlich*) whining *attrib.;* **ein ~leidiges Gesicht machen** look sorry for oneself; ❷ *adv.* self-pityingly; (*weinerlich*) whiningly; **~mut** *die;* **~~** (*geh.*) melancholy *or* wistful nostalgia; **~mütig** ❶ *Adj.* melancholically *or* wistfully nostalgic; ❷ *adv.* with melancholy *or* wistful nostalgia

**wehmuts·voll** (*geh.*) ⇒ **wehmütig**

**Wehr**[1] *die;* **~, ~en** [A] *in* **sich [gegen jmdn./etw.] zur ~ setzen** make a stand [against sb./sth.]; resist [sb./sth.]; [B] ⇒ **Feuer~**; [C] ⇒ **~macht**

**Wehr**[2] *das;* **~[e]s, ~e** weir

**Wehr-: ~beauftragte** *der/die: parliamentary commissioner for the armed forces;* **~bereichs·kommando** *das* military district command

**Wehr·dienst** *der* military service *no art.;* **zum ~ einberufen werden** be called up; **seinen ~ ableisten** do one's military service

**wehr·dienst-, Wehr·dienst-: ~pflichtig** *Adj.* ⇒ **wehrpflichtig**; **~verweigerer** *der* conscientious objector; **~verweigerung** *die* conscientious objection

**wehren** ❶ *refl. V.* [A] (*körperlich Widerstand leisten*) defend oneself; put up a fight; **sich tapfer/mit aller Kraft ~:** defend oneself *or* resist bravely/with all one's might; ⇒ *auch* **Haut** A; [B] (*sich verwahren*) **sich gegen etw. ~:** fight against sth.; **gegen so etwas weiß ich mich zu ~:** I know how to deal with that sort of thing; [C] (*sich sträuben*) **sich [dagegen] ~, etw. zu tun** resist having to do sth. ❷ *itr. V.* (*geh.: einschreiten gegen*) **jmdm./einer Sache ~:** fight sb./fight [against] sth. ❸ *tr. V.* (*geh. veralt.*) ⇒ **verwehren**

**wehr-, Wehr-: ~ersatzdienst** *der* ⇒ **Ersatzdienst**; **~erziehung** *die* (*bes. DDR*) defence education; **~experte** *der,* **~expertin** *die* defence expert; **~fähig** *Adj.* fit for military service *postpos.;* **~gang** *der* (*hist.*) battlemented parapet; **~haft** *Adj.* [A] (*fähig, sich zu verteidigen*) able to defend oneself *postpos.;* [B] (*befestigt*) fortified; **~kirche** *die* fortified church; **~kraft** *die* military strength; **~kraft·zersetzung** *die* (*Milit., bes. ns.*) undermining of military strength; **~los** *Adj.* defenceless; **jmdm./einer Sache ~los ausgeliefert sein** be defenceless against sb./sth.; **~losigkeit** *die;* **~~:** defencelessness; **~macht** *die* armed forces *pl.;* **~mann** *der* [A] *Pl.* **~männer** *od.* **~leute** ⇒ **Feuerwehrmann**; [B] (*schweiz.: Soldat*) soldier; **~pass,** ***~paß** *der* service record [book]; **~pflicht** *die* military service; conscription; **die allgemeine ~pflicht** compulsory military service; **~pflichtig** *Adj.* liable for military service *postpos;* **~pflichtige** *der/die; adj. Dekl.* person liable for military service; **~sold** *der* military pay; **~übung** *die* reserve duty [re]training exercise

**weh|tun** *unr. itr. V.* ▶474 (*ugs.*) hurt; **mir tut der Magen/Kopf/Rücken weh** my stomach/head/back is aching *or* hurts; **mir tut der Hals weh** my throat is sore; **jmdm./sich ~:** hurt sb./oneself

**Weh·weh** *das;* **~s, ~s** (*Kinderspr.*) hurt; **hast du ein ~?** have you hurt yourself?

**Wehwehchen** *das;* **~s, ~:** little complaint

**Weib** /vaip/ *das;* **~[e]s, ~er** [A] (*veralt.: weibliches Wesen, ugs.: Frau*) woman; female (*derog.*); **sie ist ein tolles ~:** she's a bit of all right (*coll.*); [B] (*veralt., noch scherzh.: Ehefrau*) wife; **~ und Kind [haben]** [have a] wife and family; **er nahm sie zum ~[e]** he took her for his wife

**Weibchen** *das;* **~s, ~** [A] (*weibliches Tier*) female; [B] (*abwertend: Frau*) female; **er degradiert sie zum ~:** he reduces her to the role of dumb female; [C] (*veralt., noch fam. scherzh.: Ehefrau*) little woman (*joc.*)

**Weiber-: ~feind** *der* woman-hater; misogynist; **~geschichten** *Pl.* (*salopp*) affairs; **~held** *der* (*ugs.*) ladykiller; **~wirtschaft** *die* (*abwertend*) **das ist ja hier die reinste ~wirtschaft** the whole place seems to be run by women *or* females

**weibisch** (*abwertend*) ❶ *Adj.* womanish; effeminate. ❷ *adv.* womanishly; effeminately

W

**weiblich** ❶ *Adj.* [A] female; [B] (*für die Frau typisch*) feminine; [C] (*Sprachw.*) feminine ‹noun, declension, gender›; (*Verslehre*) female ‹rhyme›. ❷ *adv.* femininely

**Weiblichkeit** *die;* ~ [A] (*weibliche Art*) femininity; [B] (*Gesamtheit der Frauen*) women *pl.*; **die holde** ~ (*veralt.*) the fair sex

**Weibs-:** **~bild** *das* [A] (*ugs.*) woman; [B] (*salopp abwertend*) female; **~stück** *das* (*salopp abwertend*) bitch (*sl.*)

**weich** /vaiç/ ❶ *Adj.* [A] (*auch fig.*) soft; soft, mellow ‹sound, voice›; **ein ~es** *od.* **~ gekochtes Ei** a soft-boiled egg; **ein Ei ~ kochen** soft-boil an egg; **ein ~es Herz** *od.* **Gemüt haben** be soft-hearted; **~ werden** (*ugs.*) soften; weaken; **jmdn. ~ machen** (*ugs.*) soften sb. up; [B] (*nicht scharf u. streng*) soft, gentle ‹features›; gentle ‹mouth, face›. ❷ *adv.* softly; ‹brake› gently; **~ landen** *od.* **aufsetzen** make a soft landing; ⇒ *auch* **betten** 1 A

**Weich·bild** *das:* **wir nähern uns dem ~ der Stadt** we're approaching the outskirts of the town; **noch im ~ der Stadt liegen** be still just in[side] the town

**Weiche**[1] *die;* ~, **~n** [A] (*Flanke*) flank; [B] (*Weichheit*) softness

**Weiche**[2] *die;* ~, **~n** points *pl.* (*Brit.*); switch (*Amer.*); **die ~ stellen** set the points; **die ~n [für etw.] stellen** (*fig.*) set the course [for sth.]

**weichen**[1] ❶ *itr. V.; mit sein* (*weich werden*) soak. ❷ *tr. V.* (*ein~*) soak

**weichen**[2] *unr. itr. V.; mit sein* [A] (*sich entfernen*) move; **nicht von jmds. Seite ~:** not move from *or* leave sb.'s side; **das Blut wich aus ihrem Gesicht** (*geh.*) the blood drained from her face; [B] (*Platz machen*) **vor jmdm./einer Sache ~:** give way to sb./sth.; **dem Feind ~:** retreat from the enemy; **vor jmdm./etw. zur Seite ~:** step *or* move out of the way of sb./sth.; **die Bäume sind dem Neubau gewichen** the trees have gone to make room for the new building; **die Spannung wich großer Erleichterung** (*fig.*) [the] tension gave way to great relief; ⇒ *auch* **wanken** A; [C] (*nachlassen*) subside; **die Angst/Spannung wich von ihm** the fear/tension left him

**Weichen·steller** *der;* **~s**, **~:** pointsman (*Brit.*); switchman (*Amer.*)

**Weichen·stellerin** *die;* ~, **~nen** pointswoman (*Brit.*); switchwoman (*Amer.*)

***weich·gekocht** ⇒ **weich** 1 A

**Weichheit** *die;* ~ [A] (*auch fig.*) softness; (*eines Tons, der Stimme*) mellowness; **die ~ seines Gemüts** (*fig.*) his soft-heartedness; [B] ⇒ **weich** 1 B: softness; gentleness

**weich-, Weich-:** **~herzig** ❶ *Adj.* soft-hearted; ❷ *adv.* soft-heartedly; **~herzigkeit** *die;* **~~:** soft-heartedness; **~holz** *das* softwood; **~käse** *der* soft cheese

**weichlich** ❶ *Adj.* soft; (*ohne innere Festigkeit*) weak. ❷ *adv.* softly

**Weichling** *der;* **~s**, **~e** (*abwertend*) weakling

**weich-, Weich-:** ***~|machen** ⇒ **weich** 1 A; **~macher** *der* (*Chemie, Technik*) plasticizer; **~schalig** *Adj.* soft-shelled ‹crustacean›; soft-skinned ‹fruit›

**Weichsel** /ˈvaiksl/ *die;* **~:** Vistula

**Weichsel·kirsche** *die* (*landsch.*) ⇒ **Sauerkirsche**

**Weich-:** **~spüler** *der;* **~~s**, **~~** (*Werbespr.*), **~spülmittel** *das* [fabric] softener; **~teile** *Pl.* ▶ 471 [A] (*Anat.*) soft parts; [B] (*ugs.: Genitalien*) privates; **~tier** *das* mollusc; **~zeichner** *der* (*Fot.*) soft-focus lens

**Weide**[1] /ˈvaidə/ *die;* ~, **~n** willow

**Weide**[2] *die;* ~, **~n** pasture; **auf der ~ sein** be at pasture; **die Kühe auf die** *od.* **zur ~ treiben** drive the cows to pasture

**Weide-:** **~fläche** *die* pasture; **~land** *das* pasture[land]; grazing land

**weiden** ❶ *itr., tr. V.* graze. ❷ *refl. V.* [A] (*geh.: sich erfreuen*) **er** *od.* **sein Auge weidete sich an dem herrlichen Anblick** he feasted his eyes on the glorious sight; [B] (*abwertend: schadenfroh beobachten*) gloat over; revel in; **sich an jmds. Schmerz** (*Dat.*) **~:** gloat over sb.'s pain

**Weiden-:** **~baum** *der* willow tree; **~gerte** *die* willow rod; (*zum Korbflechten*) osier; (*kleiner*) wicker; **~kätzchen** *das* willow catkin

**Weide-:** **~platz** *der* pasture; **~wirtschaft** *die* pastoral farming *no art.*

**weidlich** *Adv.* **etw. ~ ausnutzen** make full use of sth.; **sich ~ über etw. lustig machen** have a good laugh at sth.; **sie mussten sich ~ plagen** they really had to slave away

**Weid·mann** *der* (*geh.*) huntsman; hunter

**weid·männisch** ❶ *Adj.* hunting, huntsman's *attrib.* ‹expression, terminology, customs›. ❷ *adv.* in the manner of a huntsman; like a huntsman

**Weidmanns·heil** *Interj.* good hunting

**Weid·werk** *das* [art of] hunting

**weid·wund** *Adj.* **ein ~ geschossenes Tier** an animal shot in the belly [and fatally wounded]

**weigern** /ˈvaigɐn/ ❶ *refl. V.* refuse; **sich ~, etw. zu tun** refuse to do sth. ❷ *tr. V.* (*veralt.: ver~*) **jmdm. etw. ~:** refuse *or* deny sb. sth.

**Weigerung** *die;* ~, **~en** refusal

**Weih·bischof** *der* (*kath. Kirche*) suffragan bishop

**Weihe**[1] *die;* ~, **~n** [A] (*Rel.: Einweihung*) consecration; dedication; [B] (*kath. Kirche: Priester~, Bischofs~*) ordination; **die niederen/höheren ~n** (*hist.*) the minor/major orders; [C] (*geh.: Erhabenheit*) solemnity

**Weihe**[2] *die;* ~, **~n** (*Zool.*) harrier

**weihen** *tr. V.* [A] (*Rel.: durch Weihe heiligen*) consecrate; [B] (*kath. Kirche: ordinieren*) ordain; **jmdn. zum Priester/Bischof ~:** ordain sb. priest/consecrate sb. bishop; [C] (*Rel.: durch Weihe zueignen*) dedicate (*Dat.* to); [D] (*geh.: preisgeben*) **dem Tod[e]/dem Untergang geweiht sein** be doomed to die/to fall; [E] (*geh.: widmen*) dedicate

**Weiher** *der;* **~s**, ~ (*bes. südd.*) [small] pond

**Weihe·stätte** *die* (*geh.*) holy place

**weihe·voll** *Adj.* (*geh.*) solemn

**Weih-:** **~gabe** *die* (*bes. kath. Kirche*) votive offering; **~nacht** *die* (*geh.*) ⇒ **Weihnachten**

**weihnachten** *itr. V.* (*unpers.*) **es weihnachtet bereits/es fängt an zu ~:** Christmas has already started/Christmas is starting

**Weihnachten** *das;* ~, ~ ▶ 369 Christmas; **frohe** *od.* **fröhliche** *od.* **gesegnete ~!** Merry *or* Happy Christmas!; **grüne ~:** Christmas without snow; **zu** *od.* (*bes. südd.*) **an/über ~:** at *or* for/over Christmas

**weihnachtlich** ❶ *Adj.* Christmassy. ❷ *adv.* **~ geschmückt/gedeckt sein** be decorated/set for Christmas; **ihr war ~ zumute** she was in a Christmassy mood

**Weihnachts-:** **~abend** *der* Christmas Eve; **~baum** *der* Christmas tree; **~einkauf** *der* Christmas purchase; **~einkäufe** Christmas shopping *sing.*; **~feier** *die* Christmas party; **~feiertag** *der:* **der erste/zweite ~feiertag** Christmas Day/Boxing Day; **~ferien** *Pl.* Christmas holidays; **~fest** *das* ▶ 369 Christmas; **~gans** *die* Christmas goose; **~gebäck** *das* Christmas biscuits *pl.* (*Brit.*) *or* (*Amer.*) cookies *pl.*; **~geld** *das* Christmas bonus; **~geschäft** *das* Christmas trade; **~geschenk** *das* Christmas present *or* gift; **~geschichte** *die* Christmas story; **~gratifikation** *die* Christmas bonus; **~karte** *die* Christmas card; **~lied** *das* Christmas carol; **~mann** *der* [A] Father Christmas; Santa Claus; [B] (*ugs.: Dummkopf*) silly idiot (*coll.*); **~markt** *der* Christmas fair; **~spiel** *das* (*Literaturw.*) nativity play; **~stern** *der* [A] Christmas star; [B] (*Pflanze*) poinsettia; **~stollen** *der* Christmas Stollen; **~tag** *der* ⇒ **~feiertag**; **~zeit** *die* Christmas time; **in der ~zeit** at Christmas time

**Weih-:** **~rauch** *der* incense; **jmdm. ~rauch streuen** (*geh.*) eulogize sb.; **~wasser** *das* (*kath. Kirche*) holy water; **~wasser·becken** *das* (*kath. Kirche*) stoup

**weil** /vail/ *Konj.* because

**weiland** *Adv.* (*veralt.*) (*vormals*) formerly; (*einst*) once

**Weilchen** *das;* **~s** little while

**Weile** *die;* **~:** while; **eine ganze** *od.* (*geh.*) **geraume ~:** a good while; **eine ~ dauern** take a while; **vor einer ~:** a while ago; **damit hat es noch [gute] ~** (*geh.*) there is still [plenty of] time; ⇒ *auch* **Ding**[1] C; **eilen** 1 A

**weilen** *itr. V.* (*geh.*) (*ver~*) stay; (*sein*) be; **zu Besuch bei jmdm. ~:** be on a visit to sb.; be visiting sb.; **er weilt nicht mehr unter uns** (*Dat.*) *od.* **unter den Lebenden** (*verhüll.*) he is no longer among *or* with us

**Weiler** *der;* **~s**, **~:** hamlet

**Weimarer Republik** *die* Weimar Republic

**Wein** /vain/ *der;* **~[e]s**, **~e** [A] wine; **im ~ ist** *od.* **liegt Wahrheit** (*Spr.*) in vino veritas; **jmdm. reinen ~ einschenken** (*fig.*) tell sb. the truth; **neuen ~ in alte Schläuche füllen** (*fig.*) pour new wine into old bottles (*prov.*); [B] (*Reben*) vines *pl.*; **wilder ~:** Virginia creeper; [C] (*~trauben*) grapes *pl.*

**Wein-:** **~[an]bau** *der* wine-growing *no art.*; **~bauer** *der;* **~~n**, **~~n**, **~bäuerin** *die* winegrower; **~beere** *die* [A] grape; [B] (*südd., österr., schweiz.: Rosine*) raisin; **~beißer** *der;* **~~s**, **~~** (*österr.*) [A] (*Gebäck*) iced ginger biscuit; [B] (*~kenner*) wine connoisseur; **~beißerin** *die;* **~~**, **~~nen** ⇒ **Weinbeißer** B; **~berg** *der* vineyard; **~berg·schnecke** *die* [edible] snail; **~brand** *der* brandy

**weinen** ❶ *itr. V.* cry; (*aus Trauer, Kummer*) cry; weep; **um jmdn. ~:** cry *or* weep for sb.; **über jmdn./etw. ~:** cry over *or* about sb./sth.; **vor Glück/Wut ~:** cry with happiness/anger; **vor Freude ~:** cry *or* weep for *or* with joy; **es ist zum Weinen** it's enough to make you weep; **es ist zum Weinen mit dir** (*ugs.*) you're enough to make anyone weep; **leise ~d abziehen** (*fig. ugs.*) leave with one's tail between one's legs. ❷ *tr. V.* shed ‹tears›; **sich** (*Dat.*) **die Augen rot ~:** make one's eyes red with crying; **sich in den Schlaf ~:** cry oneself to sleep

**weinerlich** ❶ *Adj.* tearful; weepy; **ein ~es Gesicht machen** look on the verge of tears *or* as if one is about to cry. ❷ *adv.* tearfully

**wein-, Wein-:** **~essig** *der* wine vinegar; **~fass**, ***~faß** *das* wine barrel *or* cask; **~flasche** *die* wine bottle; **~garten** *der* vineyard; **~gegend** *die* winegrowing region; **~geist** *der* ethyl alcohol; ethanol; **~glas** *das* wineglass; **~gut** *das* vineyard; **~händler** *der*, **~händlerin** *die* ▶ 159 wine merchant; **~handlung** *die* wine merchant's; **~hauer** *der*, **~hauerin** *die;* **~~**, **~~nen** (*österr.*) winegrower; **~jahr** *das* vintage; **~karte** *die* wine list; **~keller** *der* window cellar; **~kenner** *der*, **~kennerin** *die* wine connoisseur; **~königin** *die* wine queen (*representing a particular wine region for the year*); **~krampf** *der* crying fit; fit of crying; **~küfer** *der* cellarman; **~küferin** *die* cellarwoman; **~lese** *die* grape harvest; **~lokal** *das* wine bar; **~probe** *die* window tasting [session]; **~rebe** *die* [A] grapevine; [B] (*Ranke*) [grapevine] shoot; **~rot** *Adj.* wine-red; wine-coloured; **~schaum·creme** *die* (*Kochk.*) zabaglione; **~selig** *Adj.* merry on *or* with wine *pred.*; **in ~seliger Stimmung sein** be merry on *or* with wine; **~stein** *der* cream of tartar; **~stock** *der; Pl.* **~stöcke** [grape]vine; **~straße** *die* wine route; **~stube** *die* wine bar; **~traube** *die* grape; **~trinker** *der*, **~trinkerin** *die* wine drinker; **~verkoster** *der*, **~~s**, **~~**, **~verkosterin** *die;* **~~**, **~~nen** wine taster

**weise** /ˈvaizə/ ❶ *Adj.* wise; **ein Weiser** a wise man; **die drei Weisen aus dem Morgenland** the three Wise Men from the East. ❷ *adv.* wisely

**-weise** (*bei Mengen- und Maßangaben*) by the ...; **kilo~/meter~/liter~/eimer~** *usw.* by the kilo/metre/litre/bucketful *etc.*; in kilos/metres/litres/bucketfuls *etc.*; **monats~/wochen~/stunden~:** by the month/week/hour; **paar~:** in pairs

*old spelling (see note on page 1707)

**Weise** *die;* ~, ~**n** Ⓐ *(Art, Verfahren)* way; **auf diese/andere** ~: this way/ [in] another way; **auf die eine oder andere** ~: in one way or another; **auf meine** ~: in my own way; **auf geheimnisvolle** ~: in a mysterious manner; mysteriously; **in gewisser** ~: in certain respects; **in keiner** ~: in no way; Ⓑ *(Melodie)* tune; melody

**weisen** ❶ *unr. tr. V.* Ⓐ *(geh.: zeigen)* show; **jmdm. etw.** ~: show sb. sth.; ⇒ *auch* **Tür**; Ⓑ *(ver~)* **jmdn. aus dem Zimmer** ~: send sb. out of the room; **jmdn. aus dem Land/von der Schule** ~: expel sb. from the country/from the school; **etw. von sich** ~ *(fig.)* reject sth.; ⇒ *auch* **Hand** F; **Schranke** B. ❷ *unr. itr. V. (irgendwohin zeigen)* point; **mit der Hand auf etw.** *(Akk.)* ~: point to sth.; **nach Norden** ~: point North; **eine Idee, die in die Zukunft weist** a forward-looking idea

**Weisheit** *die;* ~, ~**en** Ⓐ wisdom; **die** ~ **mit Löffeln gefressen haben** *(ugs.)* know it all; know all the answers; **er hat die** ~ **[auch] nicht mit Löffeln gefressen** *(ugs.)* he is not all that bright; **der** ~ **letzter Schluss** the answer to everything; **mit seiner** ~ **am Ende sein** be at one's wit's end; Ⓑ *(Erkenntnis)* wise insight; *(Spruch)* wise saying; **deine** ~**en kannst du für dich behalten** *(spött.)* you can keep your pearls of wisdom to yourself

**Weisheits·zahn** *der* ▶ 471 wisdom tooth

**weis|machen** *tr. V. (ugs.)* **das kannst du mir nicht** ~! you can't expect me to swallow that!; **du willst mir doch nicht** ~, **dass ...?** you're not trying to make me believe *or (coll.)* to kid me that ...; **er lässt sich** *(Dat.)* **nichts** ~: you can't fool him; he's not to be fooled; **das kannst du anderen** ~! tell that to the marines *(coll.)*

**weiß**[1] /vais/ *1. u. 3. Pers. Sg. Präsens v.* **wissen**

**weiß**[2] ❶ *Adj.* Ⓐ white; ~**e Ostern/Weihnachten** Easter with snow/white Christmas; **das Weiße Meer** the White Sea; **Weißer Sonntag** *(christl. Kirche)* Low Sunday; **der** ~**e Sport** tennis; **er/sie ist** ~ **geworden** his/her hair has turned white; ⇒ *auch* **Fleck** B; **Haus** A; **Tod**; **Weste**; Ⓑ *(Kaufmannsspr.)* unbranded ‹product›. ❷ *adv.* white; ~ **gepunktet** with white dots *postpos., not pred.;* ~ **glühend** white-hot

**Weiß** *das;* ~**[es]**, ~: white

**weis-, Weis-:** ~**sagen** *tr. V.* Ⓐ *auch itr. (prophezeien)* prophesy; foretell; Ⓑ *(ahnen lassen)* forebode; ~**sager** *der;* ~~**s**, ~~: prophet; ~**sagerin** *die;* ~~, ~~**nen** prophetess; ~**sagung** *die;* ~~, ~~**en** prophecy

**weiß-, Weiß-:** ~**bier** *das: light, highly effervescent, top-fermented beer made from wheat and barley;* weiss beer; ~**blech** *das* tin plate; ~**blond** *Adj.* ash-blond/-blonde; ~**brot** *das* white bread; **ein** ~**brot** a white loaf; ~**buch** *das (Politik)* White Paper; ~**burgunder** *der* white burgundy; ~**dorn** *der; Pl.* ~~**e** hawthorn

**Weiße**[1] *die;* ~, ~**n** Ⓐ whiteness; Ⓑ ⇒ **Berliner**[1] 1

**Weiße**[2] *der/die; adj. Dekl.* white; white man/woman

**Weiße-Kragen-Kriminalität** *die* white-collar crime *no art.*

**weißeln** *(südd., österr., schweiz.)*, **weißen** *tr. V.* paint white; *(tünchen)* whitewash

**weiß-, Weiß-:** ~**gardist** *der (hist.)* member of the White Guard; *~**glühend** ⇒ **weiß**[2] 2; ~**glut** *die* white heat; **jmdn. [bis] zur** ~**glut bringen** *od.* **reizen** *od.* **treiben** *(ugs.)* make sb. livid *(Brit. coll.)*; ~**gold** *das* white gold; ~**haarig** *Adj.* white-haired; ~**haarig sein** have white hair; ~**herbst** *der* ≈ rosé wine; ~**käse** *der (bes. nordd.)* ⇒ **Quark**; ~**kohl** *der, (bes. südd., österr.)* ~**kraut** *das* white cabbage

**weißlich** *Adj.* whitish

**Weiß-:** ~**macher** *der* whitener; ~**russland**, *~**rußland** *(das)* White Russia

**weißt** *2. Pers. Sg. Präsens v.* **wissen**

**weiß-, Weiß-:** ~**tanne** *die* silver fir; ~**wal** *der* white whale; ~**wand·reifen** *der* white-wall tyre; ~**|waschen** *unr. tr. V. (ugs.)* **jmdn./sich** ~**waschen** clear sb.'s/one's name; ~**wein** *der* white wine; ~**wurst** *die* veal sausage

**Weisung** *die;* ~, ~**en** Ⓐ *(geh., sonst Amtsspr.)* instruction; *(Direktive)* directive; **auf** *od.* **nach** ~ **[von jmdm.]** on *or* in accordance with [sb.'s] instructions; ~ **geben/erhalten/haben, etw. zu tun** give/receive/have instructions to do sth.; Ⓑ *(Rechtsw.)* [court] order; **jmdm. die** ~ **erteilen, etw. zu tun** order sb. to do sth.

**weisungs-, Weisungs-:** ~**befugnis** *die* authority to issue instructions/directives; ~**gebunden** *Adj.* subject to instructions/directives *postpos.;* ~**gemäß** *Adv.* in accordance with instructions; as instructed

**weit** /vait/ ❶ *Adj.* Ⓐ ▶ 818 *(räumlich ausgedehnt)* wide; *(fig.)* broad ‹concept›; **in die** ~**e Welt ziehen** go out into the big wide world; ~**e Kreise** *od.* **Teile der Bevölkerung** *(fig.)* large *or* broad sections of the population; **im** ~**eren Sinn** *(fig.)* in the broader sense; **das Weite suchen** *(fig.)* take to one's heels; ⇒ *auch* **Feld** E; Ⓑ *(locker sitzend)* wide; **jmdm. zu** ~ **sein** ‹clothes› be too loose on sb.; **einen Rock [in der Taille]** ~**er machen** let out a skirt [at the waist]; Ⓒ *(streckenmäßig ausgedehnt, lang)* long ‹way›; **einen** ~**en Blick [über die Gegend] haben** have a wide view [over the area].
❷ *adv.* Ⓐ *(räumlich ausgedehnt)* ~ **geöffnet** wide open; ~ **verbreitet** ⇒ **weitverbreitet**; ~ **bekannt** widely known; ~ **gereist** widely travelled; ~ **verzweigt** ⇒ **weitverzweigt**; ~ **herumgekommen sein** have got around a good deal; have travelled widely; ~ **und breit war niemand zu sehen** there was no one to be seen anywhere; **den besten Fisch** ~ **und breit kriegst du in diesem Restaurant** this restaurant has the best fish for miles around; Ⓑ ▶ 265, ▶ 818 *(streckenmäßig ausgedehnt, lang)* far; ~**er** further; farther; **am** ~**esten** [the] furthest *or* farthest; **es ist noch** ~: it is still a long way; **sehr** ~ **gehen** walk a very long way; **hast du es** ~? do you have far to go?; ~ **[entfernt** *od.* **weg] wohnen** live a long way away *or* off; live far away; **zwei Häuser** ~**er wohnen** live two houses further *or* farther on; **15 km** ~ **[von hier]** 15 km. away [from here]; **5,80 Meter** ~ **springen** jump [a distance of] 5.80 metres; **von** ~**em** from a distance; **von** ~ **her** from far away; **es würde zu** ~ **führen, das alles jetzt zu analysieren** it would be too much to analyse it all now; **das geht zu** ~ *(fig.)* that is going too far; **etw. zu** ~ **treiben, es mit etw. zu** ~ **treiben** *(fig.)* overdo sth.; carry sth. too far; **mit etw. [nicht]** ~ **kommen** *(fig.)* [not] get far with sth.; **so** ~, **so gut** so far, so good; ~ **blickend** ⇒ **weitblickend**; ~ **gehend** ⇒ **weitgehend**; ~ **reichend** ⇒ **weitreichend**; ⇒ *auch* **entfernt** A; **hersein** C; Ⓒ *(zeitlich entfernt)* ~ **nach Mitternacht** well past midnight; ~ **zurückliegen** be a long way back *or* a long time ago; Ⓓ *(in der Entwicklung)* far; **sehr** ~ **mit etw. sein** have got a long way with sth.; **wie** ~ **seid ihr?** how far have you got?; **wir wollen es gar nicht erst so** ~ **kommen lassen** we do not want to let it come to that; **so** ~ **ist es schon mit dir gekommen?** have things come to that with you?; **er wird es einmal** ~ **bringen** he will go far one of these days; ~ **fortgeschritten** *od.* **gediehen sein** be far advanced; Ⓔ *(~aus)* far; **jmdn.** ~ **übertreffen** surpass sb. by far *or* by a long way; **bei** ~**em** by far; by a long way; **bei** ~**em nicht!** not by a long way!; **bei** ~**em nicht so gut wie ...** nowhere near as good as ...; **das ist bei** ~**em nicht alles** that's not all by a long way; **bei** ~**em hübscher als ...** far prettier than ...; **etw. bei** ~**em übertreffen** far exceed sth.; ⇒ *auch* **gefehlt** 2; **weiter**

**-weit** *Adj., adv.* **europa**~**/hessen**~: throughout Europe/Hessen *postpos.*

**weit-, Weit-:** ~**ab** *Adv.* far away; ~**aus** *Adv.* far ‹better, worse, etc.›; **der** ~**aus beste** *od.* ~**aus der beste Reiter** by far *or* far and away the best rider; *~**bekannt** ⇒ **weit** 2A; ~**blick** *der* far-sightedness; **politischen** ~**blick haben** be politically far-sighted; **ihm fehlt der** ~**blick** he lacks vision; ~**blickend** *Adj.* far-sighted

**Weite** *die;* ~, ~**n** Ⓐ *(räumliche Ausdehnung)* expanse; Ⓑ *(bes. Sport: Entfernung)* distance; Ⓒ *(eines Kleidungsstückes)* width; Ⓓ *(Größe, Durchmesser)* width

**weiten** ❶ *tr. V.* widen. ❷ *refl. V.* widen; ‹pupil› dilate; *(fig.)* ‹chest› swell

**weiter** *Adv.* Ⓐ ⇒ **weit** 2; Ⓑ further; farther; **halt, nicht** ~! stop, don't go any further; ~! go on!; **er hat immer** ~ **gelacht/geschwatzt** he carried on laughing/chattering; **nur immer** ~ **so!** keep it up!; **und so** ~: and so on; **und so** ~ **und so fort** and so on and so forth; Ⓒ *(~hin, anschließend)* then; **was geschah** ~? what happened then *or* next?; Ⓓ *(außerdem, sonst)* ~ **nichts, nichts** ~: nothing more *or* else; ~ **weiß ich nichts von der Sache** that's all I know about it; **ich brauche** ~ **nichts** I don't need anything else; there's nothing else I need; **er wollte** ~ **nichts als ...** all he wanted was ...; **Was ist los? — Ach, nichts** ~: What's the matter — Oh, nothing in particular; **das macht** ~ **nichts** *od.* **ist nicht** ~ **schlimm** it isn't that important; it doesn't really matter; **wenn es** ~ **nichts ist** if 'that's all

**weiter...** *Adj. (zusätzlich)* further; ~**e zwei Jahre warten** wait a further two years *or* two more years; **ohne** ~**e Umstände** without any fuss; **die** ~**e Entwicklung abwarten** await further developments; **im** ~**en Verlauf zeigte sich, dass ...** it later became clear that ...; **bis auf** ~**es** for the time being; **„bis auf** ~**es geschlossen"** 'closed until further notice'; **des Weiteren** *(geh.)* furthermore; ⇒ *auch* **ohne** 1 C

**weiter-, Weiter-:** ~**|arbeiten** *itr. V.* continue *or* carry on working; ~**|bestehen** *unr. itr. V.* continue to exist; ~**|bilden** *tr. V.* ⇒ **fortbilden**; ~**bildung** *die* ⇒ **Fortbildung**; ~**|bringen** *unr. tr. V.* **die Diskussion/Auskunft/sein Ratschlag brachte uns nicht** ~: the discussion/information/his advice did not get us any further [forward]; ~**|entwickeln** *tr., refl. V.* develop [further]; **er hat sich im letzten Jahr auffallend** ~**entwickelt** he has matured noticeably in the last year; ~**entwicklung** *die* [further] development; ~**|erzählen** *tr. V.* Ⓐ continue telling; Ⓑ *(~sagen)* pass on; **erzähl das nicht** ~: don't tell anyone; ~**|fahren** *unr. itr. V.; mit sein* continue [on one's way]; *(~reisen)* travel on; ~**fahrt** *die* continuation of one's journey; **angenehme** ~**fahrt!** enjoy the rest of your journey; **auf der** ~**fahrt nach X trafen wir ...** continuing our journey to X we met ...; ~**flug** *der* connecting flight; onward flight; **auf unserem** ~**flug** as we continued our flight; **Passagiere zum** ~**flug nach New York** passengers continuing on to New York; ~**|führen** ❶ *tr. V.* Ⓐ *(fortführen)* continue; Ⓑ *(voranbringen)* **das führt uns nicht** ~: that does not get us any further *or* anywhere; ❷ *itr. V.* continue; ~**führende Schulen** secondary schools; ~**gabe** *die* Ⓐ passing on; Ⓑ *(Sport)* pass; ~**|geben** *unr. tr. V.* Ⓐ pass on; Ⓑ *(Sport)* pass; ~**|gehen** *unr. itr. V.; mit sein* Ⓐ go on; **bitte** ~**gehen, nicht stehen bleiben!** please move along *or* keep moving, don't stop!; Ⓑ *(sich fortsetzen, noch nicht aufhören)* continue; go on; **der Weg geht nicht** ~: the path does not go any further; **die Geschichte/Sache geht** ~: there's more to come; **das Leben geht** ~: life goes on; **so kann es nicht** ~**gehen** it cannot go on like this; **so kann es mit uns nicht** ~**gehen** we cannot go on like this; **wie soll es denn nun** ~**gehen?** what is going to happen now?; ~**|helfen** *unr. itr. V.* **jmdm. [mit etw.]** ~**helfen** help sb. [with sth.]; ~**hin** *Adv.* Ⓐ *(immer noch)* still; Ⓑ *(künftig)* in future; **etw.** ~**hin tun** continue to do sth. [in future]; Ⓒ *(außerdem)* in addition; ~**|kommen** *unr. itr. V.; mit sein* Ⓐ get

W

further; **mach, dass du ~kommst** (*ugs.*) clear off (*coll.*); **B** (*Fortschritte machen*) make progress *or* headway; **im Leben/Beruf ~kommen** get on in life/one's career; **~|können** *unr. itr. V.* (*ugs.*) **A** be able to go on; **geradeaus können wir nicht ~:** we can't go *or* get any further straight on; **B** (*bei einer Aufgabe*) **nicht ~können** get stuck; be unable to go on; **~|laufen** *unr. itr. V.; mit sein* **A** (*~gehen*) walk on; carry on walking; **B** (*in Betrieb bleiben, auch fig.*) keep going; **C** (*fortgeführt werden*) continue; ‹agreement, insurance› run; **~|leben** *itr. V.* **A** (*am Leben bleiben*) go on living; **B** (*seine Existenz fortsetzen*) continue *or* carry on one's life; **C** (*nach dem Tod fortleben*) live on; **~|leiten** *tr. V.* pass on ‹news, information, etc.›; forward ‹letter, parcel, etc.›; **~|machen** (*ugs.*) **1** *itr. V.* carry on; go on; **~machen!** (*Milit.*) carry on; as you were; **2** *tr. V.* **etw. ~machen** carry on with sth.; **~|müssen** *unr. itr. V.* (*ugs.*) have to be on one's way; **ich muss ~:** I must be on my way; **~|reden** *itr. V.* go on *or* carry on talking; **sie ließ mich nicht ~reden** she would not let me carry on [with what I was saying]; **~|reichen** *tr. V.* pass on; **~reise** *die* ⇨ **~fahrt**

**weiters** *Adv.* (*österr.*) ⇨ **ferner**

**weiter-: ~|sagen** *tr. V.* pass on; **sag es nicht ~:** don't tell anyone; **~|schicken** *tr. V.* forward; send on; send ‹person› on; **~|sehen** *unr. itr. V.* see; **morgen werden wir ~sehen** we'll see what we can do tomorrow; **~|spielen** *tr., itr. V.* **A** go on *or* carry on playing; **der Schiedsrichter ließ ~spielen** the referee allowed play to continue; **B** (*Sport: abspielen*) pass; **~|sprechen** *unr. itr. V.* go on *or* carry on speaking *or* talking

**Weiterungen** *Pl.* complications; difficulties

**weiter-, Weiter-: ~|verarbeiten** *tr. V.* process; **~verarbeitung** *die* processing; **~|verfolgen** *tr. V.* follow up ‹clue, case, etc.›; continue to follow ‹developments, events, etc.›; pursue further ‹idea, line of thought, etc.›; **~verkauf** *der* resale; **nicht zum ~verkauf bestimmt** not for resale; **~|verkaufen** *tr. V.* resell; **~|wissen** *unr. itr. V.* **A** **nicht [mehr] ~wissen** be at one's wit's end; **B** (*bei einem Rätsel, einer Aufgabe usw.*) be stuck; **~|wollen** *unr. itr. V.* (*ugs.*) want to go on; **das Pferd wollte nicht ~:** the horse would not go any further; **~|zahlen** *tr., auch itr. V.* continue *or* go on paying; continue to pay; **das Gehalt wird ~gezahlt** the salary continues to be paid; **~|ziehen** *unr. itr. V.; mit sein* move on

**weit-, Weit-: ~gehend** **1** *Adj.* extensive, wide, sweeping ‹powers›; far-reaching ‹support, concessions, etc.›; wide ‹support, agreement, etc.›; general ‹renunciation›. **2** *adv.* to a large *or* great extent; **~gereist** ⇨ **weit** 2A; **~her** *Adv.* (*geh.*) from afar; **~herzig** **1** *Adj.* generous; liberal ‹interpretation›; **2** *adv.* generously; ‹interpret› liberally; **~hin** *Adv.* **A** (*~ umher*) for miles around; **B** (*~gehend*) to a large *or* great extent; **~läufig** **1** *Adj.* **A** (*ausgedehnt*) extensive; (*geräumig*) spacious; **B** (*entfernt*) distant; **C** (*ausführlich*) lengthy; long-winded; **2** *adv.* **A** (*ausgedehnt*) spaciously; **B** (*entfernt*) distantly; **C** (*ausführlich*) at length; long-windedly; **~maschig** *Adj.* wide-meshed; **~räumig** **1** *Adj.* spacious ‹room, area, etc.›; wide ‹gap, space›; **2** *adv.* spaciously; **etw. ~räumig umfahren** give sth. a wide berth; **~reichend** **1** *Adj.* **A** long-range; **B** (*umfangreich und gewichtig*) far-reaching ‹importance, consequences›; sweeping ‹changes, powers›; extensive ‹relations, influence›; **~reichende Freiheiten** a large *or* great degree of freedom; **2** *adv.* extensively; to a large extent; **~schuss**, ***~schuß** *der* (*Sport*) long-range shot; **~schweifig** **1** *Adj.* long-winded; **2** *adv.* long-windedly; **~sicht** *die* far-sightedness; **~sichtig** **1** *Adj.* long-sighted; (*fig.*) far sighted; **2** *adv.* (*fig.*) far-sightedly; **~sichtigkeit** *die;* **~~:** long-sightedness; (*fig.*) far-sightedness; **~|springen** *unr. itr. V.; mit sein; nur im Inf. u. Part. gebr.* (*Sport*) do the long jump (*Brit.*) *or* broad jump (*Amer.*); **~sprung** *der* (*Sport*) long jump (*Brit.*); broad jump (*Amer.*); **~verbreitet** *Adj.* widespread; common; common ‹plant, animal›; **~verzweigt** *Adj.* extensive ‹network›; ‹firm› with many [different] branches; **eine ~verzweigte Verwandtschaft haben** have numerous branches in one's family; **~winkel·objektiv** *das* wide-angle lens

***old spelling (see note on page 1707)**

**Weizen** /'vaitsn̩/ *der;* **~s** wheat

**Weizen-: ~bier** *das* ⇨ **Weißbier**; **~brot** *das* wheat bread; **ein ~brot** a wheat loaf; a loaf of wheat bread; **~keim** *der* wheat germ *no pl.;* **~keim·öl** *das* wheat-germ oil; **~mehl** *das* wheat flour

**welch** /vɛlç/ **1** *Interrogativpron.* **A** (*bei Wahl aus einer unbegrenzten Menge*) what; **aus ~em Grund?** for what reason?; **~e Folgen wird das haben?** what will be the consequences of that?; **um ~e Zeit?** [at] what time?; **B** (*bei Wahl aus einer begrenzten Menge*) (*adj.*) which; (*subst.*) which one; **an ~em Tag/in ~em Jahr?** on which day/in which year?; **~e Folgen auch immer** whatever the consequences; **~er/~e/~es auch immer** whichever one; **~er/~e/~es von [den] beiden** which of the two; **C** (*geh.: was für ein*) what a; (*oft unflektiert*) **~ reizendes Geschöpf!** what a charming creature!; **~ ein Zufall/Glück!** what a coincidence/how fortunate!.
**2** *Relativpron.* (*bei Menschen*) who; (*bei Sachen*) which; (*unflektiert, Papierdt.*) **X, Y und Z, ~ Letztere/Letzterer/Letzteres …** X, Y, and Z, the latter of whom/which …
**3** *Indefinitpron.* some; **ich habe keine Seife — hast du ~e?** I have no soap — have you any?; **es gibt ~e, die behaupten, dass …** (*ugs.*) there are some [people] *or* those who claim that …

**welcher·art** *Adv.* what kind of; **es ist gleichgültig, ~ seine Überlegungen waren** it's irrelevant what his considerations were

**welcher·lei** *indekl. Interrogativadj.* whatever

**Welfe** /'vɛlfə/ *der;* **~n, ~n** (*hist.*) Guelph

**welk** /vɛlk/ *Adj.* withered ‹skin, hands, etc.›; wilted ‹leaves, flower›; limp ‹lettuce›; shrivelled ‹breasts›; **sein Gesicht sah ~ aus** his face looked old and tired

**welken** *itr. V.; mit sein* ‹plant, flower› wilt; (*fig.*) ‹beauty› fade; ‹woman› age

**Well·blech** *das* corrugated iron

**Wellblech·dach** *das* corrugated-iron roof

**Welle** /'vɛlə/ *die;* **~, ~n** **A** ▶ **411** (*auch fig.*) wave; **sein Grab in den ~n finden** (*geh.*) go to *or* find a watery grave; **grüne ~** (*Verkehrsw.*) linked *or* synchronised traffic lights; **grüne ~ bei 70 km/h** traffic lights phased *or* synchronized for 70 km per hour; **[hohe] ~n schlagen** (*fig.*) cause a [major] stir; **die weiche ~** (*fig. ugs.*) the soft approach *or* line; **B** (*im Haar*) wave; **sich** (*Dat.*) **~n legen lassen** have one's hair waved; **C** (*Physik*) wave; (*Rundf.: Frequenz*) wavelength; **D** (*Technik*) shaft; **E** (*wellenförmige Erhebung*) undulation; **F** (*Gymnastik*) circle

**wellen** **1** *tr. V.* (*wellig formen*) wave ‹hair›; corrugate ‹iron, metal›. **2** *refl. V.* **A** (*wellig sein*) ‹hair› be wavy; ‹ground, carpet› undulate; ‹stairs› be uneven; **B** (*wellig werden*) ‹carpet, stairs› become uneven

**wellen-, Wellen-: ~bad** *das* artificial wave pool; **~bereich** *der* (*Rundf.*) waveband; **~berg** *der* crest [of a/the wave]; **~brecher** *der* breakwater; **~förmig** **1** *Adj.* wavy ‹line, outline, seam, etc.›; wavelike ‹motion, movement, etc.›; **2** *adv.* ‹be propagated› in the form of waves *or* as waves; **~gang** *der* swell; **ein starker/leichter ~gang** a strong/light swell; **bei starkem ~gang** in heavy seas; **~länge** *die* (*Physik*) wavelength; **[mit jmdm.] auf der gleichen ~länge liegen** (*fig. ugs.*) be on the same wavelength [as sb.]; **~linie** *die* wavy line; **~reiten** *das* surfing *no art.;* **~sittich** *der* budgerigar; **~tal** *das* trough [of a/the wave]

**Well·fleisch** *das* boiled belly pork

**Well·horn·schnecke** *die* whelk

**wellig** *Adj.* wavy ‹hair›; undulating ‹scenery, hills, etc.›; uneven ‹surface, track, etc.›

**Well·pappe** *die* corrugated cardboard

**Welpe** /'vɛlpə/ *der;* **~n, ~n** (*Hund*) whelp; pup; (*Wolf, Fuchs*) whelp; cub

**Wels** /vɛls/ *der;* **~es, ~e** catfish

**welsch** /vɛlʃ/ *Adj.* **A** (*schweiz.*) **die ~e Schweiz** French[-speaking] Switzerland; **B** (*veralt.: romanisch*) Latin; **C** (*veralt. abwertend: fremdländisch*) foreign

**Welschland** *das;* **~[e]s** (*schweiz.*) French [-speaking] Switzerland;

**welsch-, Welsch-: ~schweizer** *der* (*schweiz.*) French[-speaking] Swiss [man]; **~schweizerin** *die* (*schweiz.*) French [-speaking] Swiss [woman/girl]; **~schweizerisch** *Adj.* (*schweiz.*) French Swiss

**Welt** /vɛlt/ *die;* **~, ~en** **A** world; **auf der ~:** in the world; **in der ganzen ~ bekannt sein** be known worldwide *or* all over the world; **eine Reise um die ~:** a round-the-world tour; **die schönste Frau der ~:** the most beautiful woman in the world; **in seiner eigenen ~ leben** live in a world of one's own; **die Alte/Neue ~:** the Old/New World; **die Dritte/Vierte ~:** the Third/Fourth World; **zwölf Mark, das ist doch nicht die ~!** (*ugs.*) twelve marks, that's not the earth! (*coll.*); **nicht die ~ kosten** (*ugs.*) not cost the earth (*coll.*); **die ~ ist klein** *od.* **ein Dorf** (*scherzh.*) it's a small world; **davon geht die ~ nicht unter** (*ugs.*) it's not the end of the world; **auf die** *od.* **zur ~ kommen** be born; **auf der ~ sein** have been born; **aus aller ~:** from all over the world; **nicht aus der ~ sein** (*ugs.*) not be at the other end of the earth; **in aller ~:** throughout the world; all over the world; **in alle ~:** all over the world; **um nichts in der ~, nicht um alles in der ~:** not for anything in the world *or* on earth; **um alles in der ~** (*ugs.*) for heaven's sake; **die ganze ~** (*fig.*) the whole world; **so etwas hat die ~ noch nicht gesehen** (*fig. ugs.*) it is/was incredible *or* fantastic (*coll.*); **alle ~** (*fig. ugs.*) the whole world; everybody; **vor aller ~** (*fig. ugs.*) in front of everybody; **eine verkehrte ~:** a topsy-turvy world; **mit sich und der ~ zufrieden sein** be content with life; **aus der ~ schaffen** resolve ‹problem, dispute, etc.›; **Kinder in die ~ setzen** (*ugs.*) have children; **Gerüchte in die ~ setzen** start rumours; **wer/was/wo/warum in aller ~ …?** (*ugs.*) who/what/where/why on earth …?; **er/sie ist nicht von dieser ~** (*geh.*) he/she is not of this world; **zur ~ bringen** bring into the world; give birth to; **eine Dame/ein Mann von ~:** a woman/man of the world; **die gelehrte ~:** the world of scholars; **die vornehme ~:** high society; ⇨ *auch* **Brett** D; **nobel** 1 B; **B** (*~all*) universe; (*Planetensystem*) planetary system; (*Sternensystem*) galaxy; **uns trennen ~en** (*fig.*) we are worlds apart

**welt-, Welt-: ~abgeschieden** *Adj.* remote; **~all** *das* universe; cosmos; **~anschaulich** **1** *Adj.* ideological; **2** *adv.* ideologically; **~anschauung** *die* world view; Weltanschauung; **~atlas** *der* atlas of the world; **~aus·stellung** *die* world fair; **~bank** *die* World Bank; **~bekannt** *Adj.* known all over the world *pred.;* world-famous ‹artist, author, etc.›; **~berühmt** *Adj.* world-famous; **~best…** *Adj.* world's best *attrib.;* best … in the world; **der/die ~beste** the world champion; **~bestleistung** *die* (*Sport*) world record; **~bestzeit** *die* (*Sport*) world record time; **~bewegend** **1** *Adj.* world-shaking; **nicht ~bewegend sein** (*ugs. spött.*) be nothing to write home about (*coll.*); **2** *adv.* **er spielt nicht [gerade] ~bewegend** (*ugs. spött.*) his playing isn't [exactly] anything to write home about (*coll.*); **~bild** *das* world view; conception of the world; **~bürger** *der*, **~bürgerin** *die* citizen of the world; cosmopolite

**Welten·bummler** *der*, **Welten·bummlerin** *die* globetrotter

**Welt·erfolg** *der* worldwide success

**Welter·gewicht** *das* welterweight

**welt-, Welt-: ~erschütternd** ⇨ **~bewegend**; **~flucht** *die* withdrawal from the world; **~fremd** **1** *Adj.* unworldly; **2** *adv.*

W

unrealistically; **~frieden** *der* world peace; **~geist** *der* (*Philos.*) world spirit; **~geistliche** *der* (*kath. Kirche*) secular priest; **~geltung** *die* international standing; **~gericht** *das* (*Rel.*) Last Judgement; **~geschichte** *die* Ⓐworld history *no art.*; **in der ~geschichte umherreisen** (*ugs. scherzh.*) travel around all over the place; Ⓑ(*Werk*) history of the world; **~geschichtlich** ❶*Adj.* **ein ~geschichtliches Ereignis, ein Ereignis von ~geschichtlicher Bedeutung** an important event in world history; ❷*adv.* **~geschichtlich gesehen** *od.* **betrachtet** [viewed] from the point of view of world history; **~gesundheits·organisation** *die* World Health Organization; **~gewandt** *Adj.* sophisticated; **~handel** *der* world trade; **~herrschaft** *die* world domination; **~hilfs·sprache** *die* international auxiliary language; **~karte** *die* map of the world; **~kind** *das* (*dichter.*) worldling; **~klasse** *die* world class; **~klasse sein, zur ~klasse gehören** be world-class; **~klug** ❶*Adj.* worldly-wise; ❷*adv.* in a worldly-wise manner; **~krieg** *der* world war; **der erste** *od.* **Erste/zweite** *od.* **Zweite ~krieg** the First/Second World War; World War I/II; **~kugel** *die* globe

**wẹltlich** *Adj.* Ⓐ(*irdisch, sinnlich*) worldly; Ⓑ(*nicht geistlich*) secular

**wẹlt-, Wẹlt-: ~literatur** *die* world literature *no art.*; **~macht** *die* world power; **~mann** *der* man of the world; **~männisch** /-mɛnɪʃ/ ❶*Adj.* sophisticated; ❷*adv.* in a sophisticated manner; **~marke** *die* international make; **~markt** *der* (*Wirtsch.*) world market; **~meer** *das* ocean; **die sieben ~meere** the seven seas; **~meister** *der*, **~meisterin** *die* world champion; **die Mannschaft ist ~meister** the team are world champions; **~meisterschaft** *die* world championship; **die ~meisterschaft im Fußball** the [football] World Cup; **~musik** *die* world music; **~offen** ❶*Adj.* Ⓐ(*aufgeschlossen*) open-minded; Ⓑ(*für alle ~ offen*) open to the world *postpos.*; ❷*adv.* open-mindedly; **~öffentlichkeit** *die:* **die Meinung der ~öffentlichkeit** world opinion; **an die ~öffentlichkeit appellieren** make an appeal to the people of the world; **~ordnung** *die* world order; **~politik** *die* world politics *pl.*; **~politisch** ❶*Adj.* **~politische Auswirkungen/Bedeutung haben** have an effect on world politics/be important in world politics; **das ~politische Klima** the climate in world politics; ❷*adv.* in terms of *or* from the point of view of world politics; **~raum** *der* space *no art.*

**Wẹltraum-: ~fahrer** *der*, **~fahrerin** *die* space traveller; **~fahrt** *die* space travel *no art.*; **~station** *die* space station

**wẹlt-, Wẹlt-: ~reich** *das* empire; **~reise** *die* world tour; **eine ~reise machen** go round the world; **~reisende** *der/die* globetrotter; **~rekord** *der* world record; **~rekordler** *der*, **~rekordlerin** *die* world record holder; **~religion** *die* world religion; **~revolution** *die* world revolution; **~ruf** *der* worldwide reputation; **~ruf haben** have a worldwide reputation; **von ~ruf** with a worldwide reputation *postpos.*, *not pred.*; **~schmerz** *der* world-weariness; Weltschmerz; **~sicherheits·rat** *der* (*Pol.*) [United Nations] Security Council; **~sprache** *die* world language; **~stadt** *die* cosmopolitan city; **~star** *der* international star; **~um·segler** *der*, **~um·seglerin** *die* circumnavigator of the globe; **~umspannend** *Adj.* global; **~untergang** *der* end of the world; **~untergangs·stimmung** *die* mood of black despair; (*in der Natur*) **es herrschte ~untergangsstimmung** it was as if the end of the world were approaching; **~uraufführung** *die* world première; **~verbesserer** *der;* **~~s, ~~, ~verbesserin** *die;* **~~, ~~nen** (*iron.*) **ein ~verbesserer/eine ~verbesserin** someone who thinks he/she can set the world to rights; **~weit** ❶*Adj.* worldwide; ❷*adv.* throughout *or* all over the world; **~wirtschaft** *die* world economy; **~wirtschafts·krise** *die* world economic crisis; **~wunder** *das:* **die sieben ~wunder** the Seven Wonders of the World; **etw. wie ein ~wunder anstaunen** stare at sth. as if it were from another planet; **~zeit·uhr** *die* clock showing times around the world

**wem** /veːm/ *Dat. von* **wer** ❶*Interrogativpron.* to whom; who ... to; **~ hast du das Buch geliehen?** to whom did you lend the book?; who did you lend the book to?; **mit/von/zu ~:** with/from/to whom; who ... with/from/to. ❷*Relativpron.* the person to whom ...; the person who ... to; **~ der Schal gehört** the person to whom the scarf belongs; the person the scarf belongs to; **~ so etwas nicht selbst passiert ist** anyone to whom this has never happened; **~ es auch [immer]** *od.* **~ immer es passiert ist** (*geh.*) whoever it was it happened to. ❸*Indefinitpron.* (*ugs.: jemandem*) to somebody *or* someone; **gehört das ~?** does this belong to anybody?; **telefoniert sie mit ~?** is she on the phone to somebody?

**Wẹm·fall** *der* dative [case]

**wen** /veːn/ *Akk. von* **wer** ❶*Interrogativpron.* whom; who (*coll.*); **an/für ~:** to/for whom ...; who ... to/for; **an ~ schreibst du?** to whom are you writing? who are you writing to?; **~ von ihnen kennst du?** which [one] of these do you know? ❷*Relativpron.* the person whom; **~ das nicht überzeugt** anyone who is not convinced by that; **~ [auch] immer** (*geh.*) whoever; no matter whom. ❸*Indefinitpron.* (*ugs.: jemanden*) somebody; someone; **suchst du ~?** are you looking for somebody?

**Wẹnde¹** *die;* **~, ~n** Ⓐ(*Veränderung*) change; **eine ~ zum Besseren/Schlechteren** a change for the better/worse; Ⓑ*in* **um die ~ des Jahrhunderts** at the turn of the century; Ⓒ(*Turnen*) front vault; Ⓓ(*Seemannsspr.*) turn

**Wẹnde²** *der;* **~n, ~n** Wend

**Wẹnde·hals** *der* (*ugs. abwertend*) turncoat; renegade

**Wẹnde·kreis** *der* Ⓐ(*Geogr.*) tropic; **der nördliche ~, der ~ des Krebses** the Tropic of Cancer; **der südliche ~, der ~ des Steinbocks** the Tropic of Capricorn; Ⓑ(*Kfz-W.*) turning circle

**Wẹndel** *die;* **~, ~n** (*Technik*) coil

**Wẹndel·treppe** *die* spiral staircase

**Wẹnde-: ~manöver** *das* turning manœuvre; **~marke** *die* (*Sport*) turning mark

**wẹnden¹** ❶*tr., auch itr. V.* (*auf die andere Seite*) turn [over]; toss ‹pancake, cutlet, etc.›; (*in die entgegengesetzte Richtung*) turn [round]; **einen Mantel ~:** turn a coat inside out; **bitte ~!** please turn over; ⇒ *auch* **drehen** 1 A. ❷*itr. V.* Ⓐturn [round]; Ⓑ(*Seemannsspr.*) tack. ❸*refl. V.* **sich zum Besseren/Schlechteren ~:** take a turn for the better/worse; **das Glück hat sich gewendet** (*geh.*) his/her *etc.* luck has turned; ⇒ *auch* **Blatt** E

**wẹnden²** ❶*unr.* (*auch regelm.*) *tr. V.* Ⓐ(*in eine andere Richtung drehen*) turn; **den Kopf ~:** turn one's head; **keinen Blick von jmdm. ~:** not take one's eyes off sb.; **er wandte seine Schritte nach links** (*geh.*) he turned his steps to the left; Ⓑ(*geh.: auf~*) spend; **viel Zeit/Geld an** *od.* **auf etw.** (*Akk.*) **~:** spend a great deal of time/money on sth.; **viel Mühe an** *od.* **auf etw.** (*Akk.*) **~:** take a great deal of trouble over sth.
❷*unr.* (*auch regelm.*) *refl. V.* Ⓐ‹person› turn; **das Glück hat sich von ihm gewandt** *od.* **gewendet** (*fig. geh.*) his good fortune deserted him; Ⓑ(*sich richten*) **sich an jmdn. [um Rat/Hilfe] ~:** turn to sb. [for advice/help]; **sich mit einer Bitte an jmdn. ~:** ask a favour of sb.; **ich habe mich schriftlich dorthin gewandt** I've written there; **an wen soll ich mich ~?** whom should I approach?; **sich an eine höhere Instanz/die richtige Adresse ~:** go to a higher authority/the right address; **das Buch wendet sich an junge Leser** (*fig.*) the book is addressed to *or* intended for young readers; **sich gegen jmdn./etw. ~:** oppose sb./sth.; Ⓒ(*geh.: sich anschicken*) **sich zum Gehen/zur Flucht ~:** get ready *or* prepare to go/flee

**Wẹnde-: ~platz** *der* turning area; **~punkt** *der* turning point; (*Geom.: einer Kurve*) point of inflexion

**wẹndig** ❶*Adj.* Ⓐagile; nimble; manœuvrable ‹vehicle, boat, etc.›; Ⓑ(*gewandt*) astute. ❷*adv.* Ⓐ(*beweglich*) agilely; nimbly; Ⓑ(*gewandt*) astutely

**Wẹndigkeit** *die;* **~** Ⓐagility; nimbleness; (*eines Flugzeugs*) manœuvrability; Ⓑ(*Gewandtheit*) astuteness

**Wẹndin** *die;* **~, ~nen** ⇒ **Wende²**

**Wẹndung** *die;* **~, ~en** Ⓐ(*Änderung der Richtung*) turn; **eine ~ um 180°** a 180° turn; Ⓑ(*Veränderung*) change; **eine unerwartete/entscheidende ~:** an unexpected/decisive turn of events; **eine ~ zum Besseren/Schlechteren** a turn for the better/worse; Ⓒ(*Biegung*) bend; Ⓓ(*Rede~*) expression

**Wẹn·fall** *der* accusative [case]

**wẹnig** /ˈveːnɪç/ ❶*Indefinitpron. u. unbest. Zahlw.* Ⓐ*Sg.* little; **sie besitzt nur ~ Schmuck** she owns only a little *or* doesn't own much jewellery; **das ~e Geld reicht nicht aus** this small amount of money is not enough; **~ Zeit/Geld haben** not have much *or* have little time/money; **das ist ~:** that isn't much; **dazu kann ich ~ sagen** I can't say much about that; **nicht ~ Mühe/Arbeit/Zeit kosten** take quite a lot of effort/work/time; **zu ~:** too little; **zu ~ Zeit/Geld haben** not have enough time/money; **ein Exemplar/50 Mark zu ~:** one copy too few/50 marks too little; **nur ~es** only a little; **um [ein] ~es älter** (*veralt.*) a little older; Ⓑ*Pl.* a few; **es sind nur noch ~e Wochen bis ...** there are only a few weeks to go until ...; **bis auf ~e/mit ~en Ausnahmen** apart from/with a few exceptions; **nur ~ Leute waren unterwegs** only a few people were about; **~ Chancen haben, etw. zu tun** have little chance of doing sth.; **sie hatte ~ Bücher/Freunde** she had few books/friends; **mit ~en Worten** in a few words; **die ~en, die davon wussten** the few who knew about it; **nur ~e haben teilgenommen** only a few took part; **einer von** *od.* **unter ~en** one of only a few; **nicht ~e** quite a few.
❷*Adv.* little; **nur ~ besser** only a little better; **er war ~ erbaut** he was not particularly pleased; **wir waren nicht ~ erstaunt/erfreut** we were more than a little astonished/pleased; **~ mehr** not much more; **das ist ~ nett von ihr** that is not very nice of her; **ein ~:** a little; **ein ~ zusammensitzen/ausruhen** sit together for a little while/rest a little; **das nützt [mir] ~:** it won't do [me] much good; **ich komme nur ~ in die Stadt** I don't often get into town; **wir gehen ~ ins Theater** we don't go much to the theatre; **zu ~ schlafen/sich zu ~ bewegen** get too little or not get enough sleep/exercise

**wẹniger** ❶*Komp. von* **wenig;** *Indefinitpron. u. unbest. Zahlw.* (+ *Sg.*) less; (+ *Pl.*) fewer; **immer ~:** less and less; **du wirst [ja] immer ~** (*ugs.*) you're wasting away. ❷*Komp. von* **wenig;** *Adv.* less; **es kommt ~ auf Quantität als auf Qualität an** quantity is less important than quality; **~ schön als praktisch** more practical than attractive; **das ist ~ angenehm/erfreulich/schön** that is not very pleasant/pleasing/nice; **nichts ~ als ...** nothing less than ...; **je mehr ich darüber nachdenke, umso ~ überzeugt es mich** the more I think about it, the less it convinces me; ⇒ *auch* **mehr** 1. ❸*Konj.* less; **fünf ~ drei** five, take away three

**Wẹnigkeit** *die;* **~:** small amount; **meine ~** (*scherzh.*) yours truly

**wẹnigst...** ❶*Sup. von* **wenig;** *Indefinitpron. u. unbest. Zahlw.* least; **damit habe ich die ~e Arbeit** *od.* **am ~sten Arbeit** that gives me the least work; **am ~en** least; **sie hat am ~en [geschenkt] bekommen** she received the fewest presents; **in den ~en Fällen/für die ~en Menschen** in very few cases/for very few people; **nur die ~en** only

W

very few; **das ~e, was wir tun können** the least we can do; **das ist noch das ~e, ...** worse still, ... ❷ *Sup. von* **wenig; *Adv.*** **am ~en** the least; **das hätte ich am ~en erwartet** that's the last thing I should have expected; **das konnte sie am ~en leiden** it was what she hated most

**wenigstens** *Adv.* at least

**wenn** /vɛn/ *Konj.* Ⓐ (*konditional*) if; **außer ~:** unless; **und [selbst] ~:** even if; **~ es sein muss, komme ich mit** If I have to, I'll come along; **~ es nicht anders geht** if there's no other way; **~ du schon rauchen musst** if you 'must smoke; **~ nicht, dann nicht** if not, it doesn't matter; **~ das Wörtchen ~ nicht wär[, wär mein Vater Millionär]** (*scherzh.*) if only, if only; Ⓑ (*temporal*) when; **jedes Mal,** *od.* **immer, ~:** whenever; **~ du dich erst einmal eingearbeitet hast ...** once you've got used to the work ...; Ⓒ (*konzessiv*) **~ ... auch** even though; **~ es auch schwer ist** even though it is hard; **und ~ es [auch] noch so spät ist ...** no matter how late it is ...; however late it is ...; **[und] ~ auch!** (*ugs.*) even so; all the same; Ⓓ (*in Wunschsätzen*) if only; **~ ich doch** *od.* **nur** *od.* **bloß wüsste, ob ...** if only I knew whether ...; **~ er doch käme!** if only he would come

**Wenn** *das;* **~s, ~** *od.* (*ugs.*) **~s: das ~ und Aber, die ~[s] und Aber[s]** the ifs and buts

**wenn·gleich** *Konj.* (*geh.*) even though; although

**wenn·schon** *Adv.* **~ [nicht] ..., dann ...** even if [not] ..., then ...; **[na** *od.* **und] ~!** (*ugs.*) so what?; **~, dann ...** if that's how it is, then ...; **~, dennschon** (*ugs.*) if you're going to do something, you may as well do it properly; no half measures!

**Wenzel**[1] /ˈvɛntsl̩/ (*der*) Wenceslas

**Wenzel**[2] *der;* **~s, ~** (*Kartenspiele*) jack; knave

**wer** /veːɐ̯/ *Nom. Mask. u. Fem.; s. auch* (*Gen.*) **wessen;** (*Dat.*) **wem;** (*Akk.*) **wen** ❶ *Interrogativpron.* who; **~ alles ist dabei gewesen?** which people were there?; who was there?; **~ von ...** which of; **~ weiß wie viel/wie oft/wie lange** *usw.* who knows how much/how often/how long *etc.*; **~ da?** (*Milit.*) who goes there?; **was glaubt er eigentlich, ~ er ist?** who does he think he is? ❷ *Relativpron.* the person who; (*jeder, der*) anyone *or* anybody who; **~ es auch [immer]** *od.* **~ immer es getan hat** (*geh.*) whoever did it. ❸ *Indefinitpron.* (*ugs.: jemand*) someone; somebody; (*in Fragen, Konditionalsätzen*) anyone; anybody; **ist da ~?** is anyone there?; **~ sein** be somebody

**Werbe-: ~abteilung** *die* advertising *or* publicity department; **~agentur** *die* advertising agency; **~aktion** *die* advertising campaign; **~block** *der; pl.* **~blöcke** commercial break; **~feldzug** *der* advertising campaign; **~fernsehen** *das* television commercials *pl.*; **~film** *der* advertising *or* promotional *or* publicity film; **~funk** *der* radio commercials *pl.*; **~gag** *der* publicity gimmick (*coll.*); **~geschenk** *das* [promotional] free gift; **~kampagne** *die* ⇒ **~feldzug; ~leiter** *der,* **~leiterin** *die* advertising manager

**werben** /ˈvɛrbn̩/ ❶ *unr. itr. V.* Ⓐ advertise; **für etw. ~:** advertise sth.; **für eine Partei ~:** canvass for a party; Ⓑ (*geh.: sich bemühen*) **~ um** try to enlist ‹subscribers, helpers, etc.›; recruit ‹soldier, mercenary, etc.›; **um Wählerstimmen ~:** seek to attract votes; **um jmds. Gunst/Freundschaft ~:** court sb.'s favour/friendship; **um eine Frau ~:** court a woman. ❷ *unr. tr. V.* attract ‹readers, customers, etc.›; recruit ‹soldiers, members, staff, etc.›

**werbe-, Werbe-: ~schrift** *die* prospectus; advertising brochure; **~sendung** *die* mailshot; **ich will keine ~sendungen bekommen** I don't want any junk mail; **~slogan** *der* advertising slogan; **~spot** *der* commercial; advertisement; ad (*coll.*); **~sprache** *die* advertising jargon; **~spruch** *der* advertising slogan **~text** *der* advertising copy *no pl.*; **~texter** *der,* **~texterin** *die* advertising copywriter; **~träger** *der* advertising medium; **~trommel** *die: in* **[für jmdn./etw.] die ~trommel rühren** *od.* **schlagen** beat *or* thump the drum [for sb./sth.]; **~wirksam** ❶ *Adj.* effective ‹advertisement etc.›; **~wirksam sein** be good publicity *or* a good advertisement; **dieser Slogan ist wenig ~wirksam** this slogan is not very effective publicity *or* not a very effective advertisement; ❷ *adv.* effectively ‹worded etc.›

**Werbung** *die;* **~, ~en** Ⓐ (*Reklame, Propaganda*) advertising; **für etw. ~ machen** advertise sth.; **für ein neues Buch/einen Kandidaten viel ~ machen** give a lot of publicity to a new book/a candidate; Ⓑ ⇒ **Werbeabteilung;** Ⓒ (*geh.: Bemühen um jmds. Gunst*) courtship *no pl.*

**Werbungs·kosten** *Pl.* (*Steuerw.*) advertising costs

**Werde·gang** *der* Ⓐ (*Laufbahn*) career; Ⓑ (*Entwicklungsgang*) development

**werden** /ˈveːɐ̯dn̩/ ❶ *unr. itr. V.; mit sein; 2. Part.* **geworden** Ⓐ become; get; **älter ~:** get *or* grow old[er]; **du bist aber groß/schlank geworden!** you've grown so tall/slim; **wahnsinnig** *od.* **verrückt ~:** go mad; **gut ~:** turn out well; **das muss anders ~:** things have to change; **wach ~:** wake up; **rot ~:** go *or* turn red; **das Wetter wurde schlechter** the weather got worse; **er ist 70 [Jahre alt] geworden** he has had his 70th birthday *or* has turned 70; **heute soll es/wird es heiß ~:** it's supposed to get/it's going to be hot today; **mir wird übel/heiß/schwindelig** I feel sick/I'm getting hot/dizzy; **Arzt/Professor ~:** become a doctor/professor; **was willst du einmal ~?** what do you want to be when you grow up?; **Vater ~:** become a father; **Erster/Letzter ~:** be *or* come first/last; **das Kind wird ein Junge** the baby is going to be a boy; **was soll das ~?** what is that going to be?; **eine ~de Mutter** a mother-to-be; an expectant mother; Ⓑ (*sich entwickeln*) **zu etw. ~:** become sth.; **das Wasser wurde zu Eis** the water turned into ice; **was soll aus dir ~?** what is to become of you?; **aus Liebe wurde Hass** love turned into hate; **aus ihm ist nichts/etwas geworden** he hasn't got anywhere/has got somewhere in life; **daraus wird nichts ~:** nothing will come of it/that!; **Von wegen! Daraus wird nichts!** You must be joking! No chance!; Ⓒ (*unpers.*) (*sich einem bestimmten Zeitpunkt nähern*) **es wird [höchste] Zeit** it is [high] time; **es wird ein Jahr, seit ...** it will be a year since ...; **es wird 10 Uhr** it is nearly 10 o'clock; **es wird Tag/Nacht** day is dawning/night is falling; **es wird Herbst** autumn is coming; Ⓓ (*entstehen*) come into existence; **es werde Licht!** (*bibl.*) let there be light!; **jeder Tag, den Gott ~ lässt** every day that God gives *or* grants us; **was nicht ist, [das] kann noch ~:** things can change; **im Werden sein** be coming into being; Ⓔ (*ugs.*) **sind die Fotos [etwas] geworden?** have the photos turned out [well]?; **wirds bald?** (*ugs.*) hurry up!; **was soll nur ~?** what's going to happen now? **nicht mehr** *od.* **wieder ~** (*salopp*) flip one's lid (*coll.*); **ich werd nicht mehr** *od.* **wieder!** (*salopp*) well, I'm blowed! (*sl.*); Ⓕ (*geh. veralt.: widerfahren*) **ihm soll [sein] Recht ~:** he shall have justice.
❷ *Hilfsverb; 2. Part.* **worden** Ⓐ (*zur Bildung des Futurs*) **wir ~ uns um ihn kümmern** we will take care of him; **dem werd ichs zeigen!** (*ugs.*) I'll show him (*coll.*); **dir werd ich helfen!** (*ugs.*) I'll give you what for (*coll.*); **wer wird denn gleich weinen!** you're not going to cry, are you?; **Sie ~ entschuldigen** (*ugs.*) excuse me[, please]; **es wird gleich regnen** it is going to rain any minute; **wir ~ nächste Woche in Urlaub fahren** we are going on holiday next week; Ⓑ (*als Ausdruck der Vermutung*) **es wird um die 80 Mark kosten** it will cost around 80 marks; **sie ~ [wohl] im Garten sein** they are probably in the garden; **er wird doch nicht [etwa] krank sein?** he wouldn't be ill, would he?; **sie wird schon wissen, was sie tut** she must know what she's doing; Ⓒ (*zur Bildung des Passivs*) **du wirst gerufen** you are being called; **er wurde gebeten** he was asked; **ihm wurde gesagt** he was told; **es wurde gelacht/gesungen/getanzt** there was laughter/singing/dancing; **jetzt wird aber geschlafen!** right, it's time to go to sleep now!; **unser Haus wird renoviert** our house is being renovated; Ⓓ (*zur Umschreibung des Konjunktivs*) **was würdest du tun?** what would you do?; **würdest du bitte etwas für mich besorgen?** would you mind getting something for me?; **ich würde kommen** I would come

**Wer·fall** *der* nominative [case]

**werfen** /ˈvɛrfn̩/ ❶ *unr. tr. V.* Ⓐ throw; drop ‹bombs›; **die Tür ins Schloss ~:** slam the door shut; **jmdn. aus dem Saal ~** (*fig. ugs.*) throw sb. out of the hall; **eine Frage in die Debatte ~** (*fig.*) throw *or* inject a question into the debate; **neue Waren auf den Markt ~** (*fig.*) bring new products on to the market; **Bilder an die Wand ~** (*fig.*) project pictures on the wall; **einen kurzen Blick in den Spiegel/in die Zeitung ~** (*fig.*) cast a glance in the mirror/at the paper; Ⓑ (*ruckartig bewegen*) throw; **den Kopf in den Nacken ~:** throw *or* toss one's head back; **die Arme in die Höhe ~:** throw one's arms up; Ⓒ (*erzielen*) throw; **eine Sechs ~:** throw a six; **ein Tor ~** (*Handball, Wasserball*) shoot *or* throw a goal; Ⓓ (*Ringen, Judo: nieder~*) throw, floor ‹opponent›; Ⓔ (*bilden*) **Falten ~:** wrinkle; crease; **Blasen ~:** bubble; **[einen] Schatten ~:** cast [a] shadow; Ⓕ (*gebären*) give birth to.
❷ *unr. itr. V.* Ⓐ throw; **mit etw. [nach jmdm.] ~:** throw sth. [at sb.]; **mit Geld/Fremdwörtern/Schimpfwörtern** *usw.* **um sich ~** (*fig.*) throw [one's] money around/bandy foreign words about/bandy curses *etc.* about; Ⓑ (*Junge kriegen*) give birth; ‹dog, cat› litter.
❸ *unr. refl. V.* Ⓐ throw oneself; **sich vor einen Zug ~:** throw oneself under a train; **sich jmdm. in die Arme/zu Füßen ~:** throw oneself into sb.'s arms/at sb.'s feet; **sich auf eine neue Aufgabe ~** (*fig.*) throw oneself into a new task; **sich in die** *od.* **seine Kleider ~** (*fig.*) throw on one's clothes; Ⓑ (*sich verziehen*) buckle; ‹wood› warp

**Werfer** *der;* **~s, ~, Werferin** *die;* **~, ~nen** thrower; (*Baseball*) pitcher; (*Cricket*) bowler

**Werft** /vɛrft/ *die;* **~, ~en** shipyard; dockyard; (*Flugw.*) hangar

**Werft·arbeiter** *der,* **Werft·arbeiterin** *die* shipyard worker

**Werg** /vɛrk/ *das;* **~[e]s** tow

**werk-, Werk-** (*Betrieb*) ⇒ **werk[s]-, Werk[s]-:**

**Werk** /vɛrk/ *das;* **~[e]s, ~e** Ⓐ (*Arbeit*) work; **am ~[e] sein** be at work; **sich ans ~ machen, ans ~ gehen** set to *or* go to work; **ins ~ setzen** carry out ‹attack, strategy, etc.›; put ‹agreement, plan, etc.› into effect; set ‹arrangements, events› in motion; **zu ~e gehen** (*geh.*) proceed; Ⓑ (*Tat*) work; **~e der Nächstenliebe** works of charity; **das ist dein ~!** that is your doing *or* handiwork; **du tätest ein gutes ~, wenn ...** (*scherzh.*) you would be doing me/him/us *etc.* a favour if ...; Ⓒ (*geistiges, künstlerisches Erzeugnis*) work; **ein neues ~ beginnen** begin a new piece of work; Ⓓ (*Betrieb, Fabrik*) factory; plant; works *sing. or pl.*; (*Belegschaft*) works *sing. or pl.*; **ab ~:** ex works; Ⓔ (*Trieb~*) mechanism; **das ~ einer Uhr/Orgel** the works *pl.* of a clock/organ

**Werk·bank** *die; Pl.* **Werkbänke** workbench

**werkeln** *itr. V.* Ⓐ (*bes. südd., österr.*) work; Ⓑ (*herumbasteln*) potter around *or* about

**werken** *itr. V.* work

**Werken** *das;* **~s** (*Schulw.*) handicraft

**werk-, Werk-: ~getreu** ❶ *Adj.* faithful to the spirit of the original *postpos.*; **eine ~getreue Inszenierung** a production which is/

*old spelling (see note on page 1707)

was faithful to the original; ❷ *adv.* ‹stage, present, produce› in a manner faithful to the original; **~lehrer** *der*, **~lehrerin** *die* [handi]craft teacher; **~meister** *der* foreman; **~meisterin** *die* forewoman

**Werk[s]-: ~angehörige** *der/die* factory *or* works employee; **~arzt** *der*, **~ärztin** *die* factory *or* works doctor; **~bücherei** *die* factory *or* works library

**Werk·schutz** *der* Ⓐ factory *or* works security; Ⓑ (*Personen*) factory *or* works security service

**werk[s]-, Werk[s]-: ~eigen** *Adj.* factory- *or* company-owned; **~fahrer** *der*, **~fahrerin** *die* (*Motorsport*) works driver; **~gelände** *das* factory *or* works premises *pl.*; **~halle** *die* workshop; **~kantine** *die* works canteen; **~leitung** *die* factory *or* works management; **~spionage** *die* industrial espionage

**Werk-: ~statt** *die*, **~stätte** *die* workshop; (*Kfz-W.*) garage; **~stoff** *der* material; **~stoff·prüfung** *die* testing of materials; material testing; **~stück** *das* workpiece; **~verkehr** *der* works transport

**Werk[s]·wohnung** *die* company-owned flat (*Brit.*) *or* (*Amer.*) apartment

**werk-, Werk-: ~tag** *der* working day; workday; **~tags** *Adv.* on weekdays; **~tätig** *Adj.* working; **~tätige** *der/die; adj. Dekl.* worker; **die Zahl der ~tätigen** the number of people in work; **~treue** *die* faithfulness to the original; **~unterricht** *der* [handi]craft instruction *no art.*; (*Unterrichtsstunde*) [handi]craft lesson; ⇒ *auch* **Englischunterricht**; **~verzeichnis** *das* (*Musik*) catalogue of works; **~zeug** *das* Ⓐ (*auch fig.*) tool; Ⓑ (*Gesamtheit*) tools *pl.*

**Werkzeug-: ~kasten** *der* toolbox; **~macher** *der*, **~macherin** *die* tool maker; **~maschine** *die* machine tool

**Wermut** /'ve:ɐ̯mu:t/ *der;* **~[e]s, ~s** Ⓐ (*Pflanze*) wormwood; Ⓑ (*Wein*) vermouth

**Wermut·bruder** *der* (*ugs. abwertend*) wino (*coll.*)

**Wermuts·tropfen** *der* (*geh.*) drop of bitterness

**Wermut·wein** *der* vermouth

**wert** /ve:ɐ̯t/ *Adj.* Ⓐ (*geh.*) esteemed; (*als Anrede*) **~e Genossen!** my dear comrades; **Ihr ~es Schreiben** (*Kaufmannsspr. veralt.*) your esteemed letter; **wie ist Ihr ~er Name, bitte?** (*geh.*) may I have your name, please?; Ⓑ ▶337 *in* **etw. ~ sein** be worth sth.; **das ist nichts ~:** this is worth nothing *or* worthless; **der Teppich ist sein Geld nicht ~:** the carpet is not worth the money; **jmds./einer Sache ~ sein** deserve sb./sth.; **das ist nicht der Erwähnung ~:** this is not worth mentioning; **Berlin ist immer eine Reise ~:** Berlin is always worth a visit; **jmdn./etw. einer Sache** (*Gen.*) **[für] ~ erachten** (*geh.*) consider sb./sth. worthy of sth.; ⇒ *auch* **Rede** C

**Wert** *der;* **~[e]s, ~e** Ⓐ (*Preis*) value; **im ~ steigen/fallen** increase/decrease in value; **an ~ gewinnen/verlieren** gain/lose in value; **im ~[e] von ...** worth ...; **etw. unter [seinem] ~ verkaufen** sell sth. for less than its value; Ⓑ (*positive Bedeutung*) value; **einer Sache** (*Dat.*) **großen ~ beimessen** attach great value to sth.; **sich** (*Dat.*) **seines [eigenen] ~es bewusst sein** be conscious of one's own importance; **das hat [doch] keinen ~!** (*ugs.: ist sinnlos*) there's no point; **~ auf etw.** (*Akk.*) **legen** set great store by *or* on sth.; Ⓒ (*Zahlen~*) value; (*als Ergebnis*) result; Ⓓ *Pl.* (*~sachen*) valuable objects; objects of value; Ⓔ (*Briefmarke*) denomination; Ⓕ *Pl.* (*~papiere*) securities

**wert-, Wert-: ~arbeit** *die* high-quality workmanship; **~beständig** *Adj.* of lasting value *postpos.*; stable ‹currency, investment, etc.›; **~beständig bleiben/sein** retain its value; **~brief** *der* (*Postw.*) registered letter

**werten** *tr., itr. V.* Ⓐ judge; assess; **etw. als besondere Leistung ~:** rate sth. as a special achievement; **etw. als Erfolg/Misserfolg ~:** regard sth. as *or* consider sth. a success/failure; **etw. hoch/gering ~:** rate sth. highly/not rate sth. very highly; **diese Leistung kann nicht hoch genug gewertet werden** this achievement cannot be regarded highly enough; **etw. kritisch/moralisch ~:** judge sth. critically/from a moral point of view; Ⓑ (*Sport*) **etw. hoch/niedrig ~:** award high/low points to sth.; **der schlechteste Sprung wird nicht gewertet** the worst jump is not counted

**wert·frei** ❶ *Adj.* detached; impartial; neutral ‹term›. ❷ *adv.* with detachment; impartially

**Wert·gegenstand** *der* valuable object; object of value; **Wertgegenstände** valuables

**-wertig** (*Chemie, Sprachw.*) -valent; **zwei~/drei~:** bivalent/trivalent

**Wertigkeit** *die;* **~, ~en** (*Chemie, Sprachw.*) valency (*Brit.*); valence (*Amer.*)

**wert-, Wert-: ~los** *Adj.* worthless; valueless; **~marke** *die* stamp; (*Essenmarke usw.*) ticket; **~maßstab** *der* standard [of value]; **~minderung** *die* depreciation; reduction in value; **~paket** *das* (*Postw.*) registered parcel; **~papier** *das* (*Wirtsch.*) security; **~papier·börse** *die* stock exchange; **~sache** *die* valuable item *or* object; **~sachen** valuables; **~schätzung** *die* (*geh.*) esteem; high regard; **~schöpfung** *die* (*Wirtsch.*) added value; **~sendung** *die* (*Postw.*) registered item; **~steigerung** *die* appreciation; increase in value; **~stoff** *der* recyclable material; **~system** *das* system of values; value system

**Wertung** *die;* **~, ~en** judgement; (*Sport*) **er erreichte ~en über 16** he was given scores [of] over 16; **noch in der ~ sein** be still in the competition/race *etc.*

**wert-, Wert-: ~urteil** *das* value judgement; **~voll** *Adj.* valuable; (*moralisch*) estimable ‹person, quality›; **~vorstellung** *die* [concept *sing.* of] values *pl.*; **~zeichen** *das* stamp; **~zuwachs** *der* appreciation [in value]

**Wer·wolf** *der* (*Myth.*) werewolf

**wes** /vɛs/ *Gen. v.* **wer** (*veralt.*) ⇒ **wessen**; ⇒ *auch* **Brot** A; **Geist** C

**Wesen** /'ve:zn̩/ *das;* **~s, ~** Ⓐ (*Natur*) nature; (*Art, Charakter*) character; nature; **ein freundliches/kindliches ~ haben** have a friendly/childlike nature *or* manner; **von liebenswürdigem ~ sein** have a pleasant nature; Ⓑ (*Mensch*) creature; soul; **ein weibliches/männliches ~:** a woman *or* female/a man *or* male; Ⓒ (*Lebe~*) being; creature; **es war kein menschliches ~ zu sehen** there was not a [living] soul in sight; **ein höheres ~:** a higher being; **das höchste ~:** the Supreme Being; Ⓓ (*Philos.*) essence; Ⓔ (*veralt.: Tun u. Treiben*) hustle and bustle; **sein ~ treiben** ‹child› romp *or* play around; ‹ghost› be abroad, go around; ‹thief› be at work; **viel ~s/kein ~ [aus *od.* um *od.* von etw.] machen** (*ugs.*) make a lot of fuss/not make a fuss [about sth.]

**wesenhaft** (*geh.*) ❶ *Adj.* intrinsic. ❷ *adv.* intrinsically

**wesens-, Wesens-: ~art** *die* nature; character; **~eigen** *Adj.* characteristic; **jmdm./einer Sache ~eigen sein** be characteristic of sb./sth.; **~fremd** *Adj.* foreign to sb.'s/sth.'s nature *postpos.*; **~gemäß** *Adj.* **etw. ist jmdm. [nicht] ~gemäß** sth. is [not] in keeping with sb.'s nature; **~verwandt** *Adj.* who are similar in character *or* nature *postpos., not pred.*; **~verwandt sein** be similar in character *or* nature; **~zug** *der* trait; characteristic

**wesentlich** ❶ *Adj.* fundamental (**für** to); **sich auf das Wesentliche beschränken** limit oneself to [the] essentials; **von ~er Bedeutung** of considerable importance; **im Wesentlichen** essentially. ❷ *adv.* (*weit, um vieles*) considerably; much; **es wäre mir ~ lieber, wenn wir ...** I would much rather we ...; **sich von etw. ~ unterscheiden** be very *or* considerably different from sth.; **nichts ~ Neues enthalten** contain nothing substantially new

**Wes·fall** *der* genitive [case]

**wes·halb** *Adv.* ⇒ **warum**

**Wesir** /ve'zi:ɐ̯/ *der;* **~s, ~e** vizier

**Wespe** /'vɛspə/ *die;* **~, ~n** wasp

**Wespen-: ~nest** *das* wasp's nest; **in ein ~nest stechen** (*fig. ugs.*) stir up a hornets' nest; **sich in ein ~nest setzen** (*fig.*) bring a hornets' nest [down] about one's ears; **~stich** *der* wasp sting; **~taille** *die* wasp waist

**wessen** *Gen. von* **wer** *u.* **was** ❶ *Interrogativpron.* Ⓐ (*von* **wer**) whose; Ⓑ (*von* **was**) **~ wird er beschuldigt?** what is he accused of?; **~ hat er sich schuldig gemacht** what is he guilty of?. ❷ *Relativpron.* Ⓐ (*von* **wer**) **~ er gedachte, war seine Mutter** the person [whom] he was thinking about was his mother; Ⓑ (*von* **was**) **[das,] ~ er sich rühmt, ist ...** what he prides himself on his ...

**wessent·wegen** *Interrogativadv.* (*geh.*) on whose account; because of whom

**wessent·willen** *Interrogativadv. in* **um ~** (*geh.*) for whose sake

**Wessi** /'vɛsi/ *der;* **~s, ~s** (*ugs.*) Westerner; West German

**Wessiland** (*das*)*;* **~s** (*salopp, bes. berlin.*) West Germany

**West**[1] /vɛst/ ▶400 Ⓐ (*bes. Seemannsspr., Met.: Richtung*) west; Ⓑ (*westliches Gebiet, Politik*) West; ⇒ *auch* **Ost**[1] B; Ⓒ *einem Subst. nachgestellt* (*westlicher Teil, westliche Lage*) West; ⇒ *auch* **Süd**[1] C

**West**[2] *der;* **~[e]s, ~e** (*Seemannsspr.*) westerly; (*dichter.*) west wind

**West·afrika** (*das*) West Africa

**West-Berlin, Westberlin** (*das*) West Berlin

**West·berliner** ❶ *der* West Berliner. ❷ *indekl. Adj.* West Berlin

**West·berlinerin** *die* ⇒ **Westberliner** 1

**west-, West-: ~besuch** *der* (*ugs.*) visitor/visitors *pl.* from West Germany; **~besuch haben** have a visitor/visitors from West Germany; **~deutsch** ❶ *Adj.* Ⓐ (*Politik*) West German; Ⓑ (*Geogr.*) Western German; ❷ *adv.* in a Western German manner; **~deutsche** *der/die* Ⓐ (*Politik*) West German; Ⓑ (*Geogr.*) Western German; **~deutschland** (*das*) Ⓐ (*Politik*) West Germany; Ⓑ (*Geogr.*) Western Germany

**Weste** /'vɛstə/ *die;* **~, ~n** waistcoat (*Brit.*); vest (*Amer.*); **eine schuss- *od.* kugelsichere ~:** a bulletproof vest; **eine weiße *od.* reine *od.* saubere ~ haben** (*ugs.*) have a clean record; **jmdm. etw. unter die ~ jubeln** (*fig. ugs.*) shift *or* push sth. on to sb.

**Westen** *der;* **~s** ▶400 Ⓐ (*Richtung*) west; **nach ~:** westwards; to the west; **im/aus *od.* von *od.* vom ~:** in/from the west; ⇒ *auch* **Norden** A; Ⓑ (*Gegend*) West; **im ~:** in the West; **der Wilde ~:** the Wild West; ⇒ *auch* **Norden** B; Ⓒ (*Geogr.*) **der ~:** the West; Ⓓ (*Politik*) **der ~** (*Westeuropa u. die USA*) the West; (*die [alte] BRD*) the West; West Germany

**Westen·tasche** *die* waistcoat (*Brit.*) *or* (*Amer.*) vest pocket; **etw. wie seine ~ kennen** (*ugs.*) know sth. like the back of one's hand *or* inside out

**Westentaschen·format** *das: in* **in *od.* im ~:** pocket-size[d] ‹calculator etc.›; (*ugs. spött. fig.*) small-time ‹politician etc.›; tinpot ‹dictator›

**Western** *der;* **~[s], ~:** western

**West·europa** (*das*) Western Europe

**west·europäisch** *Adj.* West[ern] European; **~e Zeit** Greenwich Mean Time

**Westfale** /-'fa:lə/ *der;* **~n, ~n** Westphalian

**Westfalen** (*das*)*;* **~s** Westphalia

**Westfälin** /-'fɛ:lɪn/ *die;* **~, ~nen** Westphalian

**westfälisch** *Adj.* Westphalian; **der Westfälische Friede** (*hist.*) the Treaty of Westphalia; ⇒ *auch* **deutsch**; **Deutsch** A; **badisch**

**west-, West-: ~fernsehen** *das* (*ugs.*) West German television; **~flanke** *die* (*Milit., Geogr.*) western flank; (*Met.*) western edge; **~geld** *das* (*ugs.*) West German money; **~germanisch** *Adj.* West Germanic; **~gote** *der*, **~gotin** *die* West Goth; Visigoth; **~hang** *der* western slope

**West·indien** (*das*) the West Indies *pl.*

**west·indisch** *Adj.* West Indian

**West·küste** *die* west[ern] coast

**Westler** *der;* **~s, ~, Westlerin** *die;* **~, ~nen** (*ugs.*) West German

**westlich** ❶ *Adj.* ▶ 400 Ⓐ (*im Westen*) western; **15 Grad ~er Länge** 15 degrees west [longitude]; **das ~e Frankreich** western France; **~st** westernmost; **der ~ste Punkt** the most westerly point; Ⓑ (*nach, aus dem Westen*) westerly; Ⓒ (*aus dem Westen kommend, für den Westen typisch*) Western, Ⓓ (*Politik*) Western; ⇒ auch **östlich** 1 D. ❷ *adv.* westwards; **~ von ...** [to the] west of ... ❸ (*Präp. mit Gen.*) [to the] west of

**west-, West-: ~mächte** *Pl.* (*Politik*) Western powers; **~mark** *die; Pl.* **~~** (*ugs.*) West German mark; **~nordwest**[1] /--'-/ (*Seemannsspr., Met.*) west-north-west; ⇒ auch **Nord**[1] A; **~nordwest**[2] /--'-/ *der* (*Seemannsspr.*) west-north-wester[ly]; **~nordwesten** /--'--/ *der* west-north-west; ⇒ auch **Norden** A; **~östlich** ❶ *Adj.* west-to-east; from west to east *postpos.* ❷ *adv.* [from] west to east

**West·preußen** (*das*) West Prussia

**west-, West-: ~reise** *die* (*ugs.*) trip to the West; **~seite** *die* western side; **~sender** *der* (*ugs.*) radio station in the West; **~südwest**[1] /--'-/ (*Seemannsspr., Met.*) west-south-west; ⇒ auch **Nord**[1] A; **~südwest**[2] /--'-/ *der* (*Seemannsspr.*) west-south-wester[ly]; **~südwesten** /--'--/ *der* west-south-west; ⇒ auch **Norden** A; **~teil** *der* western part; **~wall** *der* (*hist.*) Siegfried Line; **~wärts** *Adv.* ▶ 400 Ⓐ (*nach Westen*) [to the] west; Ⓑ (*im Westen*) in the west; **~wind** *der* west[erly] wind; **~zone** *die* (*hist.*) Western zone

**wes·wegen** *Adv.* ⇒ **warum**

**Wett-: ~annahme** *die* betting office; bookmaker's; **~bewerb** *der;* **~~[e]s, ~~e** Ⓐ competition; **in einem ~bewerb siegen** win a competition; **sehr gut im ~bewerb liegen** have a good chance of winning the competition; **außer ~bewerb laufen** run as an unofficial competitor; Ⓑ (*Wirtsch.: Konkurrenz*) competition *no indef. art.*; **unlauterer ~bewerb** (*Rechtsw.*) unfair competition; **~bewerber** *der,* **~bewerberin** *die* competitor

**wettbewerbs-, Wettbewerbs-: ~bedingung** *die* competition condition; **~bedingungen** conditions *or* terms of a/the competition; **~beschränkung** *die* (*Wirtsch.*) restraint of trade; **~fähig** *Adj.* competitive; **~verzerrung** *die* (*Wirtsch.*) distortion of normal trading conditions

**Wett·büro** *das* betting-office; bookmaker's

**Wette** /'vɛtə/ *die;* **~, ~n** bet; **die ~ ging um 100 Mark** the bet was 100 marks; **was gilt die ~?** how much do you want to bet?; what do you bet?; **eine ~ [mit jmdm.] abschließen** make a bet [with sb.]; **[ich gehe] jede ~ [ein], dass ...** I bet you anything [you like] that ...; **mit jmdm. um die ~ laufen** *od.* **rennen** race sb.; **die Jungen schwammen um die ~:** the boys raced each other at swimming; **um die ~ arbeiten/singen** (*fig.*) try to outdo each other at hard work/singing

**Wett·eifer** *der* competitiveness

**wett·eifern** *itr. V.* **mit jmdm. [um etw.] ~:** compete with sb. [for sth.]; **miteinander ~:** compete with each other

**wetten** ❶ *itr. V.* bet; **mit jmdm. ~:** have a bet with sb.; **mit jmdm. um etw. ~:** bet sb. sth.; **auf etw.** (*Akk.*) **~:** bet on sth.; put one's money on sth.; **[wollen wir] ~?** [do you] want to bet?; **~ [dass]?** (*ugs.*) you can bet on it; it's a dead cert (*Brit. sl.*) *or* (*Amer. coll.*) sure-fire thing; **ich wette hundert zu eins, dass ...** (*ugs.*) I'll bet [you] a hundred to one that ...; **so haben wir nicht gewettet** (*ugs.*) that was not the deal *or* not what we agreed; **auf Platz/Sieg ~:** make a place bet/bet on a win.
❷ *tr. V.* **10 Mark ~:** bet 10 marks

**Wetter**[1] *das;* **~, ~** Ⓐ weather; **bei jedem ~:** in all weathers; **es ist schönes ~:** the weather is good *or* fine; **was haben wir heute für ~?** what's the weather like today?; **falls das ~ es zulässt** weather permitting; **nach dem ~ sehen** see what the weather is like; **bei solchem ~ jagt man keinen Hund vor die Tür** the weather is/was not fit for a dog to be out in; **ein ~ zum Eierlegen** (*salopp*) fantastic *or* marvellous weather (*coll.*); **bei jmdm. gut ~ machen** (*fig. ugs.*) get on the right side of sb.; butter sb. up; **um gut[es] ~ bitten** (*fig. ugs.*) try to make it up; Ⓑ (*Un~*) storm; **alle ~!** (*veralt.*) by Jove!; Ⓒ *Pl.* (*Bergbau*) **schlagende ~:** firedamp

**Wetter**[2] *der;* **~s, ~:** better

**wetter-, Wetter-: ~amt** *das* meteorological office; **~aussichten** *Pl.* weather outlook *sing.*; **~bericht** *der* weather report; (*Voraussage*) weather forecast; **~besserung** *die* improvement in the weather; **~beständig** *Adj.* weatherproof

**Wetterchen** *das;* **~s** (*ugs.*) fantastic (*coll.*) *or* lovely weather

**wetter-, Wetter-: ~dienst** *der* weather *or* meteorological service; **~fahne** *die* weathervane; **~fest** *Adj.* weather-resistant; **~fleck** *der* (*österr.*) weatherproof cape; **~frosch** *der* Ⓐ (*ugs.*) *tree frog kept as a means of predicting the weather;* Ⓑ (*scherzh.*) weatherman; **~fühlig** *Adj.* sensitive to [changes in] the weather *postpos.*; **~fühligkeit** *die;* **~~:** sensitivity to [changes in] the weather; **~gott** *der* weather god; **~hahn** *der; Pl.* **~hähne** weathercock

**Wetterin** *die;* **~, ~nen** better

**wetter-, Wetter-: ~karte** *die* weather chart; weather map; **~kunde** *die* meteorology *no art.*; **~lage** *die* weather situation; (*fig.*) situation; climate; **~lampe** *die* (*Bergbau*) safety lamp; **~leuchten** *itr. V.* (*unpers.*) **es ~leuchtet** there is summer lightning; **es begann zu ~leuchten** flashes of [summer] lightning began to appear; **~leuchten** *das;* **~~s** sheet (*esp. summer*) lightning *no indef. art.*; (*fig.*) first ominous signs *pl.*; **~mantel** *der* ⇒ **Regenmantel**

**wettern** *itr. V.* (*ugs.: schimpfen*) curse; **gegen** *od.* **über etw./jmdn. ~:** loudly denounce sth./sb.

**wetter-, Wetter-: ~prognose** *die* weather forecast; **~regel** *die* saying about the weather; **~satellit** *der* weather satellite; **~schacht** *der* (*Bergbau*) ventilation shaft; **~scheide** *die* weather *or* meteorological divide; **~seite** *die* windward side; side exposed to the weather; **~station** *die* weather station; **~sturz** *der* sudden fall in temperature; **~um·schlag** *der* change in the weather; **~vorhersage** *die* weather forecast; **~warte** *die* weather station; **~wendisch** *Adj.* (*abwertend*) capricious; unpredictable

**wett-, Wett-: ~fahrt** *die* race; **eine ~fahrt machen** have a race; **~kampf** *der* competition; **jmdn. zum ~kampf auffordern** challenge sb. to a contest; **~kämpfer** *der,* **~kämpferin** *die* competitor; **~lauf** *der* race; **einen ~lauf machen** run a race; **ein ~lauf mit der Zeit/dem Tod** (*fig.*) a race against time/with death; **~läufer** *der,* **~läuferin** *die* runner; **~|machen** *tr. V.* (*ugs.*) Ⓐ (*ausgleichen*) make up for; **etw. durch etw. ~machen** make up for sth. with sth.; (*wieder gutmachen*) make good (loss, mistake, etc.); Ⓑ (*sich erkenntlich zeigen für*) do something in return for; **~rennen** *das* (*auch fig.*) race; **ein ~rennen machen** have *or* run a race; **~rüsten** *das;* **~~s** arms race; **~schwimmen** *das* swimming contest; **~streit** *der* contest; (*fig.*) conflict; **mit jmdm./etw. in ~streit liegen/treten** be competing/compete with sb./sth.; **~streiten** *unr. itr. V.; nur im Inf. gebr.* compete

**wetzen** /'vɛtsn̩/ ❶ *tr. V.* sharpen; whet; **der Vogel wetzt seinen Schnabel an einem Stein** the bird rubs its beak on a stone. ❷ *itr. V.; mit sein* (*ugs.*) dash

**Wetz-: ~stahl** *der* steel; **~stein** *der* whetstone

**WEZ** *Abk.* **Westeuropäische Zeit** GMT

**WG** *Abk.* **Wohngemeinschaft**

**WGB** *Abk.* **Weltgewerkschaftsbund** WFTU

**Whiskey** /'vɪski/ *der;* **~s, ~s** whiskey; [American/Irish] whisky

**Whisky** /'vɪski/ *der;* **~s, ~s** whisky; **ein ~ mit Eis/[mit] Soda** whisky on the rocks/and soda

**Whist** /vɪst/ *das;* **~[e]s** whist

**wich** /vɪç/ *1. u. 3. Pers. Sg. Prät. v.* **weichen**

**Wichs** /vɪks/ *der;* **~es, ~e,** (*österr.:*) *die;* **~, ~en** (*Studentenspr.*) **in [vollem/voller] ~ erscheinen** appear in full regalia *or* full [gala] dress

**Wichse** *die;* **~, ~n** (*ugs.*) Ⓐ (*Schuhcreme*) [shoe] polish; Ⓑ (*Schläge*) a hiding (*coll.*); **dann kriegst du** *od.* **dann gibts ~:** you'll get a good hiding (*coll.*)

**wichsen** ❶ *tr. V.* (*ugs.*) Ⓐ polish; Ⓑ (*landsch.: schlagen*) **jmdn. ~:** give sb. a good hiding (*coll.*); **jmdm. eine ~:** box sb.'s ears. ❷ *itr., tr. V.* (*derb: masturbieren*) wank (*Brit. coarse*); jerk off (*coarse*)

**Wichser** *der;* **~s, ~** (*derb*) wanker (*Brit. coarse*)

**Wicht** /vɪçt/ *der;* **~[e]s, ~e** Ⓐ (*fam.: kleines Kind*) little rascal *or* imp (*joc.*); Ⓑ (*abwertend: männliche Person*) [insignificant] creature; **armer ~:** poor devil

**Wichtel** *der;* **~s, ~** Ⓐ ⇒ **Wichtelmännchen**; Ⓑ (*bei den Pfadfinderinnen*) brownie

**Wichtel·männchen** *das* gnome; (*Kobold*) goblin

**wichtig** /'vɪçtɪç/ *Adj.* important; **nimm die Sache nicht so ~:** don't take the matter so seriously; **es ist mir ~ zu wissen, ob ...** it is important to me to know if ...; **nichts Wichtigeres zu tun haben[, als ...]** (*auch iron.*) have nothing better to do [than ...]; **das Wichtigste ist, dass du schweigst** the most important thing is that you remain silent; **Wichtiges zu tun haben** have important things to do; **sich ~ machen** *od.* **tun** (*ugs. abwertend*) be full of one's own importance; **sich mit etw. ~ machen** be pompous about sth.; **sich** (*Dat.*) **~ vorkommen** (*ugs. abwertend*) be full of oneself; **sich sehr ~ nehmen** (*ugs.*) be full of self-importance

**Wichtigkeit** *die;* **~:** importance; **einer Sache** (*Dat.*) **[große/besondere] ~ beimessen** *od.* **beilegen** attach [great/particular] importance to sth.

**Wichtigtuer** /-tu:ɐ/ *der;* **~s, ~** (*ugs. abwertend*) pompous ass

**Wichtigtuerei** *die;* **~, ~en** (*ugs. abwertend*) pomposity; pompousness *no pl.*

**Wichtigtuerin** *die;* **~, ~nen** ⇒ **Wichtigtuer**

**wichtigtuerisch** ❶ *Adj.* self-important; pompous. ❷ *adv.* in a self-important manner; (behave, act) pompously

**Wicke** /'vɪkə/ *die;* **~, ~n** vetch; (*im Garten*) sweet pea

**Wickel** *der;* **~s, ~:** compress; **jmdm. einen ~ machen** put a compress on sb.; **jmdn. am** *od.* **beim ~ haben/nehmen** (*fig. ugs.*) have/grab sb. by the scruff of his/her neck

**Wickel-: ~gamasche** *die* puttee; **~kind** *das* baby; infant; **~kommode** *die* baby's changing table

**wickeln** *tr. V.* Ⓐ (*schlingen*) wind; **Wolle zu einem Knäuel ~:** wind wool into a ball; **etw. auf/um etw.** (*Akk.*) **~:** wind sth. on to sth./round sth.; Ⓑ (*eindrehen*) **sich/jmdm. die Haare ~:** put one's/sb.'s hair in curlers *or* rollers; Ⓒ (*ein~*) wrap; **etw./jmdn./sich in etw.** (*Akk.*) **~:** wrap sth./sb./oneself in sth.; **er hat sich [fest] in seinen Mantel gewickelt** he wrapped his coat tightly [a]round himself; Ⓓ (*windeln*) **ein Kind ~:** change a baby's nappy; **der Kleine ist frisch gewickelt** the baby has had his nappy changed; Ⓔ (*bandagieren*) bandage; Ⓕ (*aus~*) unwrap; **etw./jmdn./sich aus etw. ~:** unwrap sth./sb./oneself from sth.; **das Buch aus dem Papier ~:** take the book out of the wrapping paper; Ⓖ (*ab~*) unwind (thread, wool, etc.) (**von** from); Ⓗ *in* **schief** *od.* **falsch gewickelt sein** (*ugs.*) be very much mistaken

**Wickel-: ~rock** *der* wrapover skirt; **~tisch** *der* baby's changing table

**Wicklung** *die;* **~, ~en** (*Elektrot.*) winding

**Widder** /'vɪdɐ/ *der;* **~s, ~** Ⓐ (*Tier*) ram; Ⓑ (*Astron., Astrol.*) Aries; **sie/er ist [ein] ~:** she/he is [an] Aries

*old spelling (see note on page 1707)

W

**wider** /'vi:dɐ/ *Präp. mit Akk.* Ⓐ (*geh., veralt.*) against; Ⓑ (*geh.: entgegen*) contrary to; ~ **[alles] Erwarten** contrary to [all] expectations; ~ **besseres Wissen/alle Vernunft** against one's better knowledge/all reason; ~ **Willen** against one's will

**wider-, Wider-:** **~borstig** ❶ *Adj.* unruly, unmanageable ‹hair›; (*fig.*) rebellious ‹person›; unruly, rebellious ‹child›; **sich ~borstig zeigen** be rebellious; ❷ *adv.* rebelliously; **~fahren** /--'--/ *unr. itr. V.; mit sein* (*geh.*) **etw. ~fährt jmdm.** sth. happens to sb.; **jmdm. ~fährt eine große Freude/ein schweres Leid** sb. experiences great joy/great sorrow; **ihm ist [ein] Unrecht ~fahren** he has been done an injustice; **jmdm. Gerechtigkeit ~fahren lassen** see that justice is done to sb.; **~haken** *der* barb; **~hall** *der* echo; (*fig.*) **[bei jmdm.] ~hall finden** meet with a [positive] response [from sb.]; **großen ~hall finden** meet with a wide response; **~|hallen** *itr. V.* echo; resound (**von** with); **der Schuss hallte von den Bergwänden ~:** the shot echoed from the mountainsides; **~legen** /--'--/ *tr. V.* **etw. ~legen** refute *or* disprove sth.; **jmdn. ~legen** prove sb. wrong; **~legung** /--'--/ *die; ~~, ~~en* refutation

**widerlich** (*abwertend*) ❶ *Adj.* Ⓐ (*Ekel erregend*) revolting; repulsive; ~ **schmecken/riechen** taste/smell revolting; Ⓑ (*höchst unsympathisch, kaum erträglich*) repugnant, repulsive ‹person, behaviour, etc.›; awful ‹headache etc.›. ❷ *adv.* Ⓐ (*Ekel erregend*) revoltingly; Ⓑ (*verabscheuungswürdig*) ‹behave, act› in a repugnant *or* repulsive manner; Ⓒ (*unangenehm*) awfully ‹cold, hot, sweet, etc.›

**Widerlichkeit** *die; ~, ~en* (*abwertend*) Ⓐ repulsiveness; Ⓑ (*Äußerung/Handlung*) revolting remark/action

**Widerling** *der; ~[e]s, ~e* (*abwertend*) repulsive creature

**widern** /'vi:dɐn/ *tr., itr. V.* (*veralt.*) ⇒ **ekeln** 2

**wider-, Wider-:** **~natürlich** *Adj.* unnatural; **~part** *der; ~~[e]s, ~~e* (*geh.*) adversary; **jmdm. ~part bieten** resist sb.; **~raten** /--'--/ *unr. itr. V.* (*geh. veralt.*) **jmdm. ~raten, etw. zu tun** advise sb. against doing sth.; **~rechtlich** ❶ *Adj.* illegal; unlawful; **~rechtliches Betreten eines Geländes/Gebäudes** trespass[ing] on a property/unlawful *or* illegal entry to a building; ❷ *adv.* illegally; unlawfully; **~rechtlichkeit** *die* illegality; unlawfulness; **~rede** *die* Ⓐ argument; contradiction; **keine ~rede!** don't argue!; no arguing!; **ohne ~rede** without [any] argument *or* protest; Ⓑ ⇒ **Gegenrede** A; **~rist** *der* (*Zool.*) withers *pl.*; **~ruf** *der* (*einer Aussage*) retraction; (*eines Befehls, einer Anordnung, Erlaubnis usw.*) revocation; withdrawal; **[bis] auf ~ruf** until revoked *or* cancelled; **~rufen** /--'--/ *unr. tr., auch itr. V.* retract, withdraw ‹statement, claim, confession, etc.›; revoke, cancel ‹order, permission, etc.›; repeal ‹law›; **~ruflich** ❶ *Adj.* revocable ‹permission, power of attorney›; ❷ *adv.* until further notice; **~sacher** *der; ~~s, ~~,* **~sacherin** *die; ~~, ~~nen* (*geh.*) adversary; opponent; **~schein** *der* (*geh.*) reflection; **~setzen** /--'--/ *refl. V.* **sich jmdm./einer Sache ~setzen** oppose sb./sth.; **sich einer Aufforderung ~setzen** refuse to comply with a demand; **~setzlich** /*od.* --'--/ ❶ *Adj.* rebellious; **sich ~setzlich zeigen** be rebellious; ❷ *adv.* rebelliously; **~setzlichkeit** /*od.* --'---/ *die; ~~, ~~en* Ⓐ (*Haltung*) rebelliousness; Ⓑ (*Handlung*) rebellious action; **~sinn** *der* absurdity; **~sinnig** *Adj.* absurd; **~spenstig** /-ʃpɛnstɪç/ ❶ *Adj.* unruly; rebellious; wilful; unruly, unmanageable ‹hair›; stubborn ‹horse, mule, etc.›; ❷ *adv.* wilfully; rebelliously; **~spenstigkeit** *die; ~~, ~~en* Ⓐ (*Haltung*) unruliness; rebelliousness; wilfulness; (*von Haaren*) unruliness; unmanageableness; (*von Pferden usw.*) stubbornness; Ⓑ (*Handlung*) unruly *or* rebellious *or* wilful behaviour *no pl.*; **~|spiegeln** /--'--/ ❶ *tr. V.* reflect; (*als Spiegelbild*) mirror; (*fig.*) reflect; ❷ *refl. V.* be reflected; (*als Spiegelbild*) be mirrored; (*fig.*) be reflected; **~sprechen** *unr. itr. V.* Ⓐ (*Einwände erheben*) contradict; **jmdm./einer Sache/sich [selbst] ~sprechen** contradict sb./sth./oneself; **der Betriebsrat hat der Entlassung ~sprochen** the works committee has opposed the dismissal; Ⓑ (*im Gegensatz stehen zu*) contradict, be inconsistent with ‹facts, truth, etc.›; **sich** (*Dat.*) **~sprechende Aussagen/Nachrichten** conflicting statements/news reports; **~spruch** *der* Ⓐ (*Widerrede, Protest*) opposition; protest; **es erhob sich allgemeiner ~spruch** there was a general protest; **nicht den geringsten ~spruch dulden** not tolerate the slightest argument; **auf ~spruch stoßen** meet with opposition *or* protests; **etw. ohne ~spruch hinnehmen** accept sth. without argument; Ⓑ (*etw. Unvereinbares*) contradiction; **ein ~spruch in sich** (*Dat.*) **[selbst] sein** be a contradiction in terms; **sich** (*Akk.*) **in ~sprüche verwickeln** get entangled *or* caught up in contradictions; **in ~spruch zu** *od.* **mit etw. stehen** contradict sth.; be contradictory to sth.; **in ~spruch zu etw. geraten** come into conflict with sth.; Ⓒ (*Philos.*) contradiction; **~sprüchlich** ❶ *Adj.* contradictory ‹news, statements, etc.›; inconsistent ‹behaviour, attitude, etc.›; ❷ *adv.* **er verhielt sich sehr ~sprüchlich** his behaviour was very inconsistent; **~sprüchlichkeit** *die; ~~, ~~en* Ⓐ (*Eigenschaft*) contradictoriness; inconsistency; Ⓑ (*Äußerung, Handlung*) contradiction; **~spruchs·los** ❶ *Adj.* unprotesting; uncontradicting; ❷ *adv.* without opposition *or* protest

**Wider·stand** *der* Ⓐ resistance (**gegen** to); **jmdm./einer Sache ~ leisten** resist sb./sth.; put up resistance to sb./sth.; **an jmds. ~** (*Dat.*) **scheitern** collapse in the face of sb.'s resistance; **bei jmdm. auf ~ stoßen** meet with *or* encounter resistance from sb.; **zum bewaffneten ~ aufrufen** call [people] to arms; Ⓑ (*Hindernis*) opposition; **allen Widerständen zum Trotz** despite all opposition; ⇒ *auch* **Weg** C; Ⓒ (*Widerstandbewegung*) **der ~:** the Resistance; Ⓓ (*Mech., Elektrot.*) resistance; (*Elektrot.: Schaltungselement*) resistor

**widerstands-, Widerstands-:** **~bewegung** *die* resistance movement; **~fähig** *Adj.* robust; resistant ‹material etc.›; hardy ‹animal, plant›; **~fähig gegen** *od.* **gegenüber etw. sein** be resistant to sth.; **~fähigkeit** *die* robustness; (*von Material usw.*) resistance; (*von Tier, Pflanze*) hardiness; **~fähigkeit gegen etw.** resistance to sth.; **~kämpfer** *der,* **~kämpferin** *die* resistance fighter; **~kraft** *die* resistance; **~los** ❶ *Adj.* without resistance *postpos.*; ❷ *adv.* without resistance

**wider-, Wider-:** **~stehen** *unr. itr. V.* Ⓐ (*nicht nachgeben*) **[jmdm./einer Sache] ~stehen** resist [sb./sth.]; Ⓑ (*standhalten*) **jmdm./einer Sache ~stehen** withstand sb./sth.; **~streben** *itr. V.* Ⓐ (*zu~ sein*) **etw. ~strebt jmdm.** sb. dislikes *or* detests sth.; **das ~strebt meinem Taktgefühl** that goes against my sense of tact; **es ~strebt jmdm., etw. zu tun** sb. dislikes doing sth. *or* is reluctant to do sth.; Ⓑ (*geh.: sich ~setzen*) **einer Sache** (*Dat.*) **~streben** oppose sth.; **~d nachgeben/einwilligen** give in/agree reluctantly; **~streben** *das; ~~s* reluctance; **trotz anfänglichem ~streben** after some initial reluctance; **~streit** *der* conflict; **in** *od.* **im ~streit mit etw. leben/stehen** be/live in conflict with sth.; **~streitend** *Adj.* conflicting; **~wärtig** /-vɛrtɪç/ (*abwertend*) ❶ *Adj.* Ⓐ (*unangenehm*) disagreeable, unpleasant ‹conditions, situation, etc.›; Ⓑ (*ekelhaft, abscheulich*) revolting, repugnant ‹smell, taste, etc.›; objectionable, offensive ‹person, behaviour, attitude, etc.›; **das ist mir ~wärtig** I find that offensive *or* objectionable; **~wärtig riechen/schmecken** smell/taste revolting; ❷ *adv.* ‹behave, act, etc.› in an objectionable *or* offensive manner; **~wärtigkeit** *die; ~~, ~~en* Ⓐ offensiveness; objectionableness; repulsiveness; Ⓑ (*Umstand*) disagreeable *or* unpleasant circumstance; **~wille** *der* aversion (**gegen** to); **einen ~willen gegen jmdn./etw. haben** *od.* **empfinden** have/experience an aversion to sb./sth.; **etw. mit ~willen essen/tun** eat sth. with distaste/do sth. with reluctance *or* reluctantly; **~willig** ❶ *Adj.* (*unwillig*) reluctant; unwilling; ❷ *adv.* reluctantly; unwillingly; **etw. nur ~willig tun** do sth. only with reluctance; **~wort** *das; Pl.* **~~e: ~worte geben** answer back; **etw. ohne [ein] ~wort tun** do sth. without argument *or* protest; **keine ~worte dulden** not tolerate any argument; **keine ~worte!** no arguments!

**widmen** /'vɪtmən/ ❶ *tr. V.* Ⓐ (*zueignen*) **jmdm. ein Buch/Gedicht/eine Sinfonie** *usw.* **~:** dedicate a book/poem/symphony *etc.* to sb.; Ⓑ (*verwenden für/auf*) **etw. jmdm./einer Sache ~:** devote sth. to sb./sth.; **jmdm./einer Sache seine Liebe/Aufmerksamkeit ~:** give sb./sth. one's love/attention. ❷ *refl. V.* (*sich beschäftigen mit*) **sich jmdm./einer Sache ~:** attend to sb./sth.; (*ausschließlich*) devote oneself to sb./sth.; **heute kann ich mich dir ganz ~:** I can devote myself to you entirely today

**Widmung** *die; ~, ~en* dedication (**an** + *Akk.* to)

**widrig** /'vi:drɪç/ *Adj.* unfavourable, adverse ‹wind, circumstances, fate, etc.›

**widrigen·falls** *Adv.* (*bes. Amtsspr.*) otherwise

**Widrigkeit** *die; ~, ~en* adversity

**wie** ❶ *Interrogativadv.* Ⓐ (*auf welche Art u. Weise*) how; **~ heißt er/das?** what is his/its name?; what is he/that called?; **~ [bitte]?** [I beg your] pardon?; (*entrüstet*) I beg your pardon!; **~ war das?** (*ugs.*) what was that?; what did you say?; **~ meinen?** (*scherzh.*) [I beg your] pardon?; **~ kommt es, dass ...?** how is it that ...?; **~ das?** (*ugs.*) how did that come about?; **~ käme ich denn dazu?** why should I?; Ⓑ (*durch welche Merkmale gekennzeichnet*) **~ war das Wetter?** what was the weather like?; how was the weather?; **~ ist dein neuer Chef?** what is your new boss like? (*coll.*); how is your new boss? (*coll.*); **~ geht es ihm?** how is he?; **~ war es in Spanien?** what was Spain like?; what was it like in Spain?; **~ findest du das Bild?** what do you think of the picture?; **~ gefällt er dir?** how do you like him?; **~ wärs mit ...** how about ...; **~ wäre es, wenn du dir die Schuhe putztest?** how about [you] cleaning your shoes?; **Gott, ~ du aussiehst!** God, just look at yourself!; Ⓒ (*in welchem Grade*) how; **~ lange/groß/hoch/oft?** how long/big/high/often?; **~ sehr haben wir uns das gewünscht!** how badly we wanted that!; **~ spät ist es?** what time is it?; **~ alt bist du?** how old are you?; **~ er läuft!** how fast he runs!; **und ~!** and how! (*coll.*); Ⓓ (*ugs.: nicht wahr*) **das hat dir Spaß gemacht, ~?** you enjoyed that, didn't you?; **das ärgert dich wohl, ~?** that does annoy you, doesn't it?

❷ *Relativadv.* **[die Art,] ~ er es tut** the way *or* manner in which he does it; **die Preise steigen in dem Maße, ~ die Löhne erhöht werden** prices are rising at the same rate as wages; **~ man es auch [immer] macht, es ist ihr nie recht** whatever you do *or* whichever way you do it she's never happy with it; **~ er das wieder geschafft hat!** he's done it again — how does he manage it?

❸ *Konj.* Ⓐ *Vergleichspartikel* as; **[so] ... ~ ...** as ... as ...; **das Buch ist so unterhaltend ~ lehrreich** the book is as entertaining as it is instructive; **er kam so schnell ~ möglich** he came as quickly as possible; **~ gewöhnlich** *od.* **üblich/immer** as usual/always; **ein Mann ~ er** a man like him; **es geht dir [so] ~ mir** you're like me; **er macht es [genauso] ~ du** he does it [just] like you [do]; **~ durch ein Wunder** as if by a miracle; **er kann spielen ~ kein Zweiter** no one can touch him when it comes to playing; **ich fühlte mich ~ ...** I felt as if I were ...; **„N" ~ „Nordpol"** N for November; Ⓑ (*zum Beispiel*) like; such as; **Entwicklungsländer ~ [zum Beispiel] Somalia oder Tansania** developing countries such as Somalia or Tanzania [for example]; ~

**folgt** as follows; **~ schon der Name sagt** as the name already implies; **~ wenn** as if *or* though; C (*und, so~*) as well as; both; **Männer ~ Frauen** men as well as women; both men and women; D (*temporal: als*) **~ ich an seinem Fenster vorbeigehe, höre ich ihn singen** as I pass by his window I hear him singing; **~ ich die Tür öffne, steht doch tatsächlich Christine vor mir** when I open the door, who is standing there but Christine; E (*ugs.: außer*) **wir hatten nichts ~ Ärger [damit]** we had nothing but trouble [with it]; **nichts ~ hin!** come on, let's go!; ⇒ *auch* **nichts**; F (*nicht standardsprachlich: als*) than

**Wiedehopf** /ˈviːdəhɔpf/ *der;* **~[e]s, ~e** hoopoe

**wieder** /ˈviːdɐ/ *Adv.* A again; **etw. ~ aufbauen** reconstruct *or* rebuild sth.; **etw. ~ aufbereiten** (*Kerntechnik*) reprocess sth.; **~ aufführen** + *Akk.* revive ‹play›; rerun, reshow ‹film›; **~ aufnehmen** + *Akk.* resume; take up ‹subject, idea› again; re-establish ‹relations, contact›; **ein Verfahren ~ aufnehmen** (*Rechtsspr.*) reopen a case; **jmdn. ~ aufrichten** give fresh heart to sb.; **~ auftauchen** turn up again; **~ beleben** + *Akk.* revive, resuscitate ‹person›; revive, resurrect ‹friendship, custom, etc.›; **etw. ~ entdecken** rediscover sth.; **jmdn./etw. ~ erkennen** recognize sb./sth.; **er war kaum ~ zu erkennen** he was almost inrecognizable; **etw. ~ eröffnen** reopen sth.; **jmdn. ~ erwecken** revive sb.; bring back *or* restore sb. to life; **etw. ~ erwecken** (*fig.*) revive *or* reawaken sth.; **~ finden** + *Akk.* find again; regain ‹composure, dignity, courage, etc.›; **die Handschuhe haben sich ~ gefunden** the gloves have been found; **jmdn./etw. ~ sehen** see sb./sth. again; **etw. ~ tun** do sth. again; **ein Land ~ vereinigen** reunify a country; **etw. ~ verwenden** reuse sth.; **jmdn. ~ wählen** re-elect sb.; **je/nie ~:** ever/never again; **~ mal** *od* **mal ~ ins Kino gehen** go to the cinema again some time; **immer ~,** (*geh.*) **~ und ~:** again and again; time and [time] again; **es regnet schon ~:** it's raining again; **das Buch ist ~ ein Bestseller** the book is another best seller; **nie ~ Krieg!** no more war!; **wie du ~ aussiehst!** just look at yourself again!; **was ist denn jetzt schon ~ los?** what's happened 'now?; **alles ist ~ beim Alten** everything is back as it was before; **etw. ~ an seinen Platz zurückstellen** put sth. back in its place; **ich bin gleich ~ da** I'll be right back (*coll.*); I'll be back in a minute; **willst du schon ~ gehen?** are you going already?; **gib es ihm ~ zurück** (*ugs.*) give it back to him!; B **einige ..., andere ... und ~ andere ...** some ..., others ..., and yet others ...; **das ist ~ etwas anderes** that is something else again; C (*andererseits, anders betrachtet*) **das ist auch ~ wahr** that's true enough; **da hast du auch ~ Recht** you're right there; **so schlimm ist es auch ~ nicht** it's not as bad as all that; D (*meinerseits, deinerseits usw.*) in turn; E (*auch*) likewise; also; F (*ugs.: noch*) **wie heißt er ~?** what's his name again?; **wo/wann war das [gleich] ~?** where/when was that again?

**wieder-, Wieder-: ~aufbau** *der* reconstruction; rebuilding; **der wirtschaftliche ~aufbau** economic recovery; ***~auf|bauen** ⇒ **wieder** A; ***~auf|bereiten** ⇒ **wieder** A; **~aufbereitung** *die* recycling; (*bes. Kerntechnik*) reprocessing; **~aufbereitungs·anlage** *die* recycling plant; (*Kerntechnik*) reprocessing plant; ***~auf|führen** ⇒ **wieder** A; **~aufführung** *die* (*eines Theaterstücks*) revival; (*eines Films*) rerun; **~aufnahme** *die* A resumption; (*von Beziehungen*) re-establishment; **die ~aufnahme eines Verfahrens** (*Rechtsspr.*) the resumption *or* reopening of proceedings; B (*als Mitglied*) readmittance; C (*eines Theaterstücks*) revival; **~aufnahme·verfahren** *das* (*Rechtsspr.*) retrial; ***~auf|nehmen, *~auf|richten** ⇒ **wieder** A; **~aufrüstung** *die* rearmament; ***~auf|tauchen** ⇒ **wieder** A

**wieder-, Wieder-: ~beginn** *der* recommencement; resumption; **~|bekommen** *unr. tr. V.* get back; **du bekommst es ~:** you'll get it back; ***~|beleben** ⇒ **wieder** A; **~belebungs·versuch** *der* attempt at resuscitation; **bei jmdm. ~belebungsversuche machen** attempt to revive *or* resuscitate sb.; **~bewaffnung** *die* rearmament; **~|bringen** *unr. tr. V.* bring back

**Wieder·einsetzung** *die* reinstatement

**wieder-, Wieder-: *~|entdecken** ⇒ **wieder** A; **~entdeckung** *die* rediscovery; ***~|erkennen** ⇒ **wieder** A; **~|erobern** *tr. V.* recapture ‹territory›; regain ‹position, title, etc.›; **~eroberung** *die* ⇒ **~erobern**: recapture; regaining; ***~|eröffnen** ⇒ **wieder** A; **~eröffnung** *die* reopening; ***~|erwecken, *~|finden** ⇒ **wieder** A; **~gabe** *die* A (*Darstellung, Schilderung*) report; account; B (*Übersetzung*) rendering; C (*Reproduktion; in Ton u. Bild*) reproduction; D (*Aufführung*) rendition; **~|geben** *unr. tr. V.* A (*zurückgeben*) give back; return; B (*berichten*) report; give an account of; (*~holen*) repeat; (*ausdrücken*) express; (*zitieren*) quote; **etw. gekürzt ~geben** give a shortened version of sth.; C (*übersetzen*) render; D (*darstellen*) portray; depict; **die Gebirge sind auf der Landkarte in Braun ~gegeben** the mountains are shown in brown on the map; E (*hörbar, sichtbar machen*) reproduce; **~geburt** *die* A (*Rel.*) reincarnation; B (*christl. Rel., fig. geh.*) rebirth; **~|gewinnen** *unr. tr. V.* recover ‹lost item, money, etc.›; regain ‹composure, equilibrium, etc.›

***wieder·gut|machen** ⇒ **gutmachen** A

**Wiedergutmachung** *die;* **~, ~en** A reparation; **die ~ des Unrechts fordern** demand that the injustice be made good; B (*Leistung*) compensation

**wieder|haben** *unr. tr. V.* (*auch fig.*) have back

**wieder-, Wieder-: ~her|stellen** *tr. V.*; **ich stelle wieder her** A re-establish ‹contact, peace›; B (*reparieren*) restore ‹building›; C (*~ gesund machen*) **jmdn. ~herstellen** restore sb. to health; get sb. on his/her feet again; **~herstellung** *die* A re-establishment; B (*~instandsetzung*) restoration; C (*Genesung*) recovery; **bis zu seiner völligen ~herstellung** until he has completely recovered *or* is fully restored to health; **~holbar** *Adj.* repeatable; **das ist nicht ~holbar** it cannot be repeated; **~holen** ❶ *tr. V.* A repeat; replay ‹football match›; retake ‹penalty kick›; resit, retake ‹exam›; **eine Wahl ~holen** hold an election again; rehold an election; B (*nochmals sagen*) repeat, reiterate ‹question, demand, offer, etc.›; C (*repetieren*) revise ‹lesson, vocabulary, etc.›; ❷ *refl. V.* A (*~ dasselbe sagen*) repeat oneself; B (*erneut geschehen*) happen again; C (*~kehren*) be repeated; recur

**wieder|holen** *tr. V.* fetch *or* get back

**wiederholt** ❶ *Adj.* repeated; **zum ~en Male** yet again. ❷ *adv.* repeatedly

**Wiederholung** *die;* **~, ~en** A repetition; (*eines Fußballspiels usw.*) replay; (*eines Freistoßes, Elfmeters usw.*) retaking; (*einer Sendung*) repeat; (*einer Aufführung*) repeat performance; **eine ~ der Wahl ist notwendig** the election must be held again *or* reheld; B (*des Schuljahrs, einer Prüfung usw.*) repeating; **eine ~ der Prüfung ist nicht möglich** it is not possible to resit *or* retake the exam; C (*von Fragen, Forderungen, Angeboten usw.*) repetition; reiteration; D (*von Lernstoff*) revision

**Wiederholungs-: ~fall** *der:* **in im ~fall** (*bes. Amtsspr.*) in the event of [any] recurrence; **~täter** *der,* **~täterin** *die* (*Kriminologie*) habitual offender; **~zahlwort** *das* (*Sprachw.*) multiplicative; **~zeichen** *das* (*Musik*) repeat sign

**Wieder·hören** *das:* **in [auf] ~!** goodbye! (*at end of telephone call*)

**Wieder·instandsetzung** *die* reconstruction

**wieder-, Wieder-: ~|käuen** /-kɔyən/ ❶ *itr. V.* ruminate; chew the cud; ❷ *tr. V.* A chew again; B (*fig. abwertend*) rehash; **~käuer** *der;* **~~s, ~~:** ruminant; **~kehr** *die;* **~~** (*geh.*) A (*Rückkehr*) return; B (*~holung*) recurrence; (*Jahrestag*) anniversary; **~|kehren** *itr. V.; mit sein* (*geh.*) A (*zurückkehren*) return; B (*sich noch einmal ereignen*) come again; **eine nie ~kehrende Gelegenheit** a chance that will never come again; the chance of a lifetime; C (*sich wiederholen*) be repeated; recur; **~|kommen** *unr. itr. V.; mit sein* A (*zurückkommen*) return; come back; B (*noch einmal kommen*) come back *or* again; C (*sich noch einmal ereignen*) ‹opportunity, past› come again; **~|kriegen** *tr. V.* (*ugs.*) ⇒ **~bekommen**; **~kunft** /-kʊnft/ *die;* **~~** (*geh.*) return; **die ~kunft Christi** the Second Coming of Christ; **~schauen** *das:* **in [auf] ~schauen!** (*südd., österr.*) goodbye!; **~|sehen** *unr. tr. V.* see again; **sich ~sehen** see each other *or* meet again; **~sehen** *das;* **~~s, ~~:** reunion; **~sehen mit Berlin/der Heimat** return to Berlin/one's homeland; **sie stießen auf ein baldiges ~sehen an** they drank to seeing each other again soon; **~sehen macht Freude** (*scherzh.*) I'd like to have it back some time; **[auf] ~sehen!** goodbye!; **jmdm. Auf ~sehen sagen** say goodbye to sb.; **[auf] ~sehen nächsten Monat/in London** goodbye until we meet again next month/in London

**Wiedersehens·freude** *die* pleasure of seeing sb./each other again

**wieder-, Wieder-: ~täufer** *der* (*Rel.*) anabaptist; ***~|tun** ⇒ **wieder** A; **~um** *Adv.* A (*erneut*) again; B (*andererseits*) on the other hand; **so weit würde ich ~um nicht gehen** I wouldn't, however, go that far; C (*meiner-, deinerseits usw.*) in turn; ***~|vereinigen** ⇒ **wieder** A; **~vereinigung** *die* reunification; **~verheiratung** *die* remarriage; ***~|verwenden** ⇒ **wieder** A; **~verwendung** *die* reuse; **~vorlage** *die* (*bes. Amtsspr.*) **zur ~vorlage** for resubmission; to be resubmitted; **~wahl** *die* re-election; **sich zur ~wahl stellen** stand *or* run for re-election; ***~|wählen** ⇒ **wieder** A

**Wiege** /ˈviːɡə/ *die;* **~, ~n** (*auch fig.*) cradle; **seine ~ stand in Sachsen** (*geh.*) he was born in Saxony; his birthplace was in Saxony; **es ist ihm nicht an der ~ gesungen worden, dass ...** he would never have dreamt *or* could never have foreseen that ...; **eine solche Karriere ist ihm nicht an der ~ gesungen worden** he would never have dreamt of such a career; **von der ~ an** (*geh.*) from the day he/she was born; **von der ~ bis zur Bahre** (*scherzh.*) from the cradle to the grave

**Wiege·messer** *das* chopping knife (*with curved blade used by rocking to and fro*)

**wiegen**[1] ▶ 353 ❶ *unr. itr. V.* weigh; **was** *od.* **wie viel wiegst du?** how much do you weigh?; what weight *or* how heavy are you?; **schwer ~** (*fig.*) carry weight. ❷ *unr. tr. V.* weigh; **etw. gut/knapp ~:** weigh sth. generously/short; **gewogen und zu leicht befunden** (*fig.*) weighed [in the balance] and found wanting

**wiegen**[2] ❶ *tr. V.* A (*schaukeln, hin u. her bewegen*) rock; shake ‹head› (*in doubt*); **die Hüften ~:** sway one's hips; **einen ~den Gang haben** have a rolling gait; B (*zerkleinern*) chop [up] (*with a Wiegemesser*). ❷ *refl. V.* ‹boat, cradle, etc.› rock; ‹person, branch, etc.› sway; **sich in den Hüften ~:** sway one's hips; **sich in der Hoffnung ~, dass ...** cherish *or* nurture the hope that ...

**Wiegen-: ~fest** *das* (*geh.*) birthday; **~lied** *das* lullaby; cradle song

**wiehern** /ˈviːɐn/ *itr. V.* A whinny; (*lauter*) neigh; B (*fig. ugs.*) **vor Lachen ~:** roar with laughter; **[das ist ja] zum ~!** that's a scream! (*coll.*); **sich ~d auf die Schenkel schlagen** slap one's thigh with a bellow of laughter; **~des Gelächter** uproarious laughter

**Wien** /viːn/ (*das*); **~s** ▶ 700 Vienna

**Wiener**[1] *der;* **~s, ~** ▶ 700 Viennese

**Wiener**[2] *Adj.* Viennese; **~ Würstchen** wiener; frankfurter; **~ Schnitzel** Wiener schnitzel; **der ~ Kongress** the Congress of

*old spelling (see note on page 1707)

W

Vienna; **die ~ Sängerknaben/Philharmoniker** the Vienna Boys' Choir/Vienna Philharmonic

**Wiener**[3] *die;* ~, ~: wiener [sausage]

**Wienerin** *die;* ~, **~nen** Viennese

**wienerisch** *Adj.* ▶ 700 Viennese; **das Wienerische** the Viennese dialect

**wienern** *tr. V. (ugs.)* polish; shine

**wies** /'vi:s/ *1. u. 3. Pers. Sg. Prät. v.* **weisen**

**Wiese** /'vi:zə/ *die;* ~, **~n** meadow; *(Rasen)* lawn; **auf der grünen ~** *(fig.)* out in the [open] country

**Wiesel** /'vi:zl̩/ *das;* **~s**, ~: weasel; **wie ein ~ laufen** run like a hare; ⇒ *auch* **flink** 1

**wiesel·flink** ❶ *Adj.* nimble. ❷ *adv.* quick as a flash

**wieseln** *itr. V.; mit sein* scurry

**Wiesen-:** **~blume** *die* meadow flower; **~grund** *der (geh.)* meadowland; **~schaum·kraut** *das* lady's smock

**wie·so** *Interrogativadv.* why

***wie·viel** ⇒ **viel** 1A, B, **Uhr** B, **Seite** C

**wie·viel·mal** /od. -'--/ *Interrogativadv.* how many times

**wievielt** /od. '--/ *in* **zu ~ [wart ihr]?** how many [of you were there]?

**wievielt...** /od. '--/ *Interrogativadj.* ▶ 207, ▶ 841 **zum ~en Mal bitte ich dich das nun?** how many times *or* how often have I asked you?; **als ~er Läufer ist er durchs Ziel gekommen?** in what position did he finish?; **die ~e Querstraße ist das von hier aus?** how many turnings is that from here?; **der ~e Band?** which number volume?; **beim ~en Versuch hat es geklappt?** how many attempts did it take?; **der ~e ist heute?** what is the date today?; **am ~en?** [on] what date?

**wie·weit** *Interrogativadv.* to what extent; how far

**wie·wohl** *Konj. (geh. veralt.)* although

**Wigwam** /'vɪkvam/ *der;* **~s**, **~s** wigwam

**Wikinger** /'vi:kɪŋɐ/ *der;* **~s**, ~, **Wikingerin** *die;* ~, **~nen** Viking

**wild** /vɪlt/ ❶ *Adj.* Ⓐ wild; rugged, wild ‹countryside, area, etc.›; untouched, uncultivated ‹land, soil›; wild, unruly ‹hair, beard, etc.›; **Geranien kommen ~ vor** geraniums grow wild; **~e Triebe** rank shoots; **~es Fleisch** *(Med.)* proud flesh; **~ lebende Tiere** wild animals; animals living in the wild; **~ wachsende Pflanzen** wild plants; Ⓑ *(nicht [behördlich] genehmigt, nicht angemeldet)* unauthorized; illegal; **~e Taxis** unlicensed taxis; **~es Parken** illegal parking; **in ~er Ehe leben** *(veralt.)* live in sin; **~er Streik** wildcat strike; Ⓒ *(heftig, gewaltig)* wild ‹panic, flight, passion, desire, etc.›; fierce ‹battle, anger, determination, look›; **~ auf etw.** *(Akk.)* **sein** *(ugs.)* be mad *or* crazy about sth. *(coll.)*; **~ auf jmdn.** *od.* **nach jmdm. sein** *(ugs.)* be mad *or* crazy *or* wild about sb. *(coll.)*; ⇒ *auch* **Jagd** E; Ⓓ *(wütend)* furious ‹cursing, shouting, etc.›; **~ werden** get furious; **jmdn. ~ machen** make sb. furious; infuriate sb.; **den ~en Mann spielen** *(ugs.)* get heavy *(coll.)*; Ⓔ *(unbändig, ungestüm)* wild, unruly ‹child›; Ⓕ *(maßlos, wüst)* wild ‹speculation, claim, rumour, accusation›; vile ‹oaths, curses›; **halb so** *od.* **nicht so ~ sein** *(ugs.)* not be as bad as all that *(coll.)*; Ⓖ *(primitiv)* savage; wild; *(abwertend: unzivilisiert)* uncivilized; **ein ~er Haufen** a pack of savages; **der wilde Mann** *(Myth.)* the wild man of the woods.
❷ *adv.* Ⓐ wildly; **die Haare hingen ihr ~ ins Gesicht** her hair hung wildly about her face; **alles ging ~ durcheinander** everything was in chaos; **~ bewegtes Wasser** turbulent water; **~ entschlossen sein** *(ugs.)* be absolutely determined; **wie ~ um sich schlagen** hit out *or* lash out wildly; **wie ~** *(ugs.)* like mad *(coll.)*; Ⓑ *(ordnungswidrig)* illegally; **~ zelten/bauen** camp/build in an unauthorized place

**Wild** *das;* **~[e]s** Ⓐ *(Tiere, Fleisch)* game; Ⓑ *(einzelnes Tier)* [wild] animal

**Wild-:** **~bach** *der* mountain torrent; **~bahn** *die: in* **in freier ~bahn** in the wild; **~bret** /-brɛt/ *das;* **~s** *(geh.)* game; **~dieb** *der,* **~diebin** *die* poacher

**Wilde** *der/die; adj. Dekl.* savage; **wie ein ~r/eine ~/die ~n** *(ugs.)* like a mad thing/like mad things *(coll.)*

**Wild·ente** *die* wild duck

**Wilderei** *die;* ~, **~en** poaching *no pl., no art.*

**Wilderer** *der;* **~s**, ~, **Wilderin** *die;* ~, **~nen** poacher

**wildern** ❶ *itr. V.* Ⓐ poach; go poaching; Ⓑ ‹cat, dog› kill game. ❷ *tr. V.* poach

**wild-, Wild-:** **~fang** *der* wild creature; **er ist ein kleiner ~fang** he is a wild little thing; **sie war ein richtiger ~fang** she was a real tomboy; **~fremd** *Adj.* completely strange; **~fremder Mensch/~fremde Leute** complete stranger/strangers; **~gans** *die* wild goose; **~gehege** *das* game enclosure

**Wildheit** *die;* ~: wildness; *(eines Volkes usw.)* savageness

**wild-, Wild-:** **~hüter** *der,* **~hüterin** *die* ▶ 159 gamekeeper; **~katze** *die* wild cat; ***~lebend** ⇒ **wild** 1A; **~leder** *das* suede; **~ledern** *Adj.* suede

**Wildnis** *die;* ~, **~se** wilderness

**wild-, Wild-:** **~park** *der* game park; **~pferd** *das* wild horse; **~pflanze** *die* wild plant; **~romantisch** *Adj.* wild and romantic; romantically wild; **~sau** *die* wild sow; **~schaden** *der* damage *no pl., no indef. art.* caused by game

**wild-, Wild-:** **~schwein** *das* wild boar; ***~wachsend** ⇒ **wild** 1A; **~wasser** *das; Pl.* **~~:** mountain torrent; **~wasser·rennen** *das* wild-water racing; *(einzelne Veranstaltung)* wild water race; **~wechsel** *der* Ⓐ *(Weg, Pfad)* game path; Ⓑ *(Vorgang)* game crossing; **~west** /-'vɛst/ *in* **in/aus** *usw.* **~west** in/from *etc.* the Wild West; **~west·film** *der* western; Wild West film; **~wuchs** *der* rank growth

**Wilhelm** /'vɪlhɛlm/ *(der)* William; **~ der Eroberer** William the Conqueror; ⇒ *auch* **Friedrich ~**

**wilhelminisch** /vɪlhɛl'mi:nɪʃ/ *Adj.* Wilhelminian

**will** /vɪl/ *1. u. 3. Pers. Sg. Präsens v.* **wollen**

**Wille** *der;* **~ns** will; *(Wunsch)* wish; *(Absicht)* intention; **der ~ zur Macht** the will to power; **guter/böser ~:** goodwill/ill will; **es war kein böser ~ von mir** there was no ill will intended; **etw. aus freiem ~n tun** do sth. of one's own free will; **seinen ~n durchsetzen** get one's own way; **sie hat den festen ~n, es zu tun** she firmly intends to do it; **er hat seinen eigenen ~n** he has a mind of his own; **sie ist voll guten ~ns** she is very well-intentioned; **lass ihm seinen ~n** let him have his way; **beim besten ~n nicht** not with the best will in the world; **wo ein ~ ist, ist auch ein Weg** *(Spr.)* where there's a will, there's a way *(prov.)*; **letzter ~:** will; last will and testament *(formal)*; **mit ~n** intentionally; **ich musste wider ~n lachen** I couldn't help laughing; **jmdm. zu ~n sein** *(geh.)* do sb.'s bidding; **sie war ihm zu ~n** *(veralt.)* she let him have his way with her

**willen** *Präp. mit Gen. in* **um jmds./einer Sache ~:** for sb.'s/sth.'s sake

**Willen** *der;* **~s** ⇒ **Wille**

**willen·los** ❶ *Adj.* will-less; **völlig ~ sein** have no will of one's own. ❷ *adv.* will-lessly

**Willenlosigkeit** *die;* ~: lack of will

**willens** *Adj. in* **~ sein, etw. zu tun** *(geh.)* be willing to do sth.; **ich bin nicht ~, es zu tun** I have no intention of doing it

**willens-, Willens-:** **~akt** *der* act of will; **~anstrengung** *die* effort of will; **unter größter ~anstrengung** by a huge effort of will; **~bildung** *die:* **die politische ~bildung** the formulation of political demands and objectives; **~erklärung** *die (bes. Rechtsw.)* declaration of intent; **~freiheit** *die* freedom of will; **~kraft** *die* will power; strength of will; **~schwach** *Adj.* weak-willed; **~schwäche** *die* weakness of will; **~stark** *Adj.* strong-willed; **~stärke** *die* strength of will

**willentlich** /'vɪləntlɪç/ ❶ *Adj.* deliberate. ❷ *adv.* deliberately; on purpose

**willfahren** /od. '---/ *itr. V. (geh.)* **ich willfahre, willfahrt** *od.* **gewillfahrt, zu willfahren: [jmdm.] ~:** obey [sb.]; do sb.'s bidding; **jmds. Bitte** *(Dat.)* **~:** comply with sb.'s request

**willfährig** /'vɪlfɛ:rɪç *od.* -'--/ *Adj.* compliant; **jmdm. ~ sein** submit to sb.'s will; **sich** *(Dat.)* **jmdn. ~ machen** make sb. submit to one's will

**Willfährigkeit** /od. -'---/ *die;* ~ *(geh.)* compliance

**Williams Christ·birne** /'vɪljamz 'krɪst-/ *die* Bartlett pear

**willig** ❶ *Adj.* willing; obedient ‹horse›; ⇒ *auch* **Geist**[1] A. ❷ *adv.* willingly

**will·kommen** *Adj.* welcome; **jmdm. ~ sein** be welcome to sb.; **~ zu Hause/in Mannheim!** welcome home/in Mannheim!; **jmdn. ~ heißen** welcome sb.; **ich möchte Sie herzlich ~ heißen** a very warm welcome to you

**Will·kommen** *das od. (selten) der;* **~s**, ~: welcome; **jmdm. ein herzliches ~ bereiten** *od.* **bieten** give sb. a warm welcome

**Willkommens-:** **~gruß** *der* welcome; **~trunk** *der* welcoming drink

**Will·kür** *die;* ~: arbitrary use of power; *(einer Entscheidung, Handlung o. Ä.)* arbitrariness; **jmds. ~** *(Dat.)* **preisgegeben** *od.* **ausgeliefert sein** be at sb.'s mercy; **das ist die reine ~:** that is purely arbitrary

**Willkür-:** **~akt** *der* arbitrary act; **~herrschaft** *die* tyranny

**willkürlich** ❶ *Adj.* arbitrary; *(vom Willen gesteuert)* voluntary ‹muscle, movement, etc.›. ❷ *adv.* arbitrarily; *(vom Willen gesteuert)* voluntarily

**Willkür·maßnahme** *die* arbitrary measure

**wimmeln** /'vɪmln̩/ *itr. V.* Ⓐ *(sich bewegen)* **Insekten/Ratten ~ dort** the place is swarming with insects/rats; Ⓑ *(voll sein)* **von Menschen ~:** be teeming *or* swarming with people; **von Fischen/Läusen/Ungeziefer ~:** be teeming with fish/swarming with lice/vermin; **in dem Artikel wimmelt es von Fehlern** the article is teeming with mistakes

**wimmern** /'vɪmɐn/ *itr. V.* whimper; **zum Wimmern [sein]** *(ugs.)* [be] simply pathetic

**Wimpel** /'vɪmpl̩/ *der;* **~s**, ~: pennant

**Wimper** /'vɪmpɐ/ *die;* ~, **~n** Ⓐ [eye]lash; **ohne mit der ~ zu zucken** without batting an eyelid; Ⓑ *(Biol.)* cilium

**Wimpern·tusche** *die* mascara

**Wimper·tierchen** *das* ciliate; infusorian

**Wind** /vɪnt/ *der;* **~[e]s**, **~e** Ⓐ wind; **bei ~ und Wetter** in all weathers; **[schnell] wie der ~:** like the wind; Ⓑ *(fig.)* **hier weht [jetzt] ein schärferer/anderer/frischer ~** *(ugs.)* things have tightened up a lot here [now]/things are different here [now]/there's a much fresher feel to the place [now]; **wissen/merken, woher der ~ weht** *(ugs.)* know/notice which way the wind's blowing; **~ machen** *(ugs.)* brag; **viel ~ um etw. machen** *(ugs.)* make a great fuss about sth.; **~ von etw. bekommen** *od.* **kriegen** *(ugs.)* get wind of sth.; **jmdm. den ~ aus den Segeln nehmen** *(ugs.)* take the wind out of sb.'s sails; **sich** *(Dat.)* **den ~ um die Nase** *od.* **Ohren wehen lassen** *(ugs.)* see a bit of life *or* the world; **gegen den/mit dem ~ segeln** swim against/with the tide; **etw. in den ~ schlagen** turn a deaf ear *or* pay no heed to sth.; **in den ~ reden** waste one's breath; **alle Appelle waren in den ~ gesprochen** all appeals were in vain; **in alle [vier] ~e** in all directions; **ihre Kinder sind in alle ~e zerstreut** her children are scattered to the four corners of the earth; **sein Mäntelchen nach dem ~e hängen** be a trimmer; **wer ~ sät, wird Sturm ernten** *(Spr.)* sow the wind and reap the whirlwind *(prov.)*; Ⓒ *(Blähung)* wind; **einen ~ fahren lassen** break wind

**Wind-:** **~beutel** *der* Ⓐ *(Gebäck)* cream puff; Ⓑ *(abwertend: Person)* frivolous and irresponsible person; **~bö[e]** *die* gust of wind

W

**Winde** *die;* ~, ~**n** Ⓐ *(Technik)* winch; Ⓑ *(Bot.)* bindweed; convolvulus

**Wind·ei** *das* wind egg; *(fig. abwertend)* dud

**Windel** /ˈvɪndl̩/ *die;* ~, ~**n** nappy *(Brit.)*; diaper *(Amer.)*; **damals lagst du noch in [den] ~n** you were still in nappies then; **noch in den ~n liegen** *od.* **stecken** *(fig.)* ‹project etc.› still be in its infancy

**Windel·höschen** *das* nappy pants *pl.*

**windeln** *tr. V.* **ein Baby ~:** put a baby's nappy *(Brit.) or (Amer.)* diaper on

**windel·weich** *Adj. (ugs.)* soft; **jmdn. ~ schlagen** *od.* **hauen** beat the living daylights out of sb. *(coll.)*

**winden**[1] ❶ *unr. tr. V.* Ⓐ *(geh.)* make ‹wreath, garland›; **Blumen zu einem/in einen Kranz ~:** bind flowers into a wreath; make a wreath out of flowers; **etw. um etw. ~:** wind sth. around sth.; **jmdm. etw. aus der Hand ~:** wrest sth. from sb.'s hand; Ⓑ *(mit einer Winde bewegen)* winch.
❷ *unr. refl. V.* Ⓐ ‹plant, tendrils› wind **(um** around); ‹snake› coil [itself], wind itself **(um** around); Ⓑ *(sich krümmen)* writhe; **sich vor Schmerzen/in Krämpfen ~:** writhe in pain/convulsions; **sich vor Verlegenheit ~:** squirm with embarrassment; **sich vor Lachen ~:** fall about laughing; **sich ~ wie ein Aal** *(fig.)* try to wriggle out of it; Ⓒ *(sich schlängeln)* ‹path, river› wind [its way]; **sich durch etw. ~:** wind one's/its way through sth.

**winden**[2] *itr. V.; unpers.* **es windet** it's windy

**Windes·eile** *die* in **in** *od.* **mit ~:** in next to no time; **sich in ~ verbreiten** spread like wildfire

**wind-, Wind-:** ~**fang** *der* porch; ~**geschützt** *Adj.* sheltered from the wind *postpos.;* sheltered; **diese Pflanzen müssen ~geschützt stehen** these plants must be kept sheltered from the wind; ~**geschwindigkeit** *die* wind speed; ~**harfe** *die* wind harp; aeolian harp; ~**hauch** *der* breath of wind; ~**hose** *die (Met.)* whirlwind; ~**hund** *der* Ⓐ greyhound; **Afghanischer ~hund** Afghan hound; Ⓑ *(ugs. abwertend)* careless and unreliable sort *(coll.)*

**windig** *Adj.* Ⓐ windy; Ⓑ *(ugs. abwertend)* shady; dubious ‹excuse, morality›; empty ‹words, talk, hope›

**Wind-:** ~**jacke** *die* windcheater *(Brit.)*; windbreaker *(Amer.)*; ~**jammer** *der; Pl.* ~~**s**, ~~**:** *(Seemannsspr.)* windjammer; ~**kanal** *der* Ⓐ *(Technik)* wind tunnel; Ⓑ *(an der Orgel)* wind trunk; ~**licht** *das; Pl.* ~~**er** table lantern *(with candle in glass container)*; ~**mühle** *die* windmill; **gegen** *od.* **mit ~mühlen kämpfen** *(fig.)* tilt at windmills; ~**mühlen·flügel** *der* windmill sail; ~**pocken** *Pl.* ▶ 474 chickenpox *sing.;* ~**rad** *das* Ⓐ wind wheel; Ⓑ ⇒ ~**rädchen**; ~**rädchen** *das* windmill; ~**richtung** *die* wind direction; ~**rose** *die* compass card

**Winds·braut** *die (dichter.)* gale; *(Wirbelwind)* whirlwind

**wind-, Wind-:** ~**schatten** *der* lee; ~**schief** *Adj. (oft abwertend)* crooked; ~**schlüpfig**, ~**schnittig** *Adj.* streamlined; ~**schutz·scheibe** *die* windscreen *(Brit.)*; windshield *(Amer.)*; ~**spiel** *das* [small] greyhound; ~**stärke** *die* force of the wind; ~**stärke 7/9** *usw.* wind force 7/9 *etc.;* ~**still** *Adj.* windless; still; **es war völlig ~still** there was no wind at all; **ein ~stilles Plätzchen** a sheltered spot; a spot out of the wind; ~**stille** *die* calm; **es herrschte völlige ~stille** there was no wind at all; ~**stoß** *der* gust of wind; ~**surfer** *der,* ~**surferin** *die* windsurfer; ~**surfing** *das* windsurfing *no art.*

**Windung** *die;* ~, ~**en** Ⓐ *(Krümmung)* bend; *(eines Flusses)* meander; *(des Darms, Gehirns)* convolution; Ⓑ *(spiralförmiger Verlauf)* spiral; *(einer Spule o. Ä.)* winding; Ⓒ *(schlangenartige Bewegung)* wriggling

**Wind·zug** *der* breeze

**Wingert** /ˈvɪŋɐt/ *der;* ~**s**, ~**e** *(westmd., schweiz.)* ⇒ **Weinberg**

*old spelling (see note on page 1707)

**Wink** /vɪŋk/ *der;* ~**[e]s**, ~**e** Ⓐ *(Zeichen)* sign; *(mit dem Kopf)* nod; Ⓑ *(Hinweis)* hint; *(Ratschlag)* tip; hint; *(an die Polizei)* tip-off; **ein ~ mit dem Zaunpfahl** *(scherzh.)* a strong hint

**winke** *in:* ~, ~ **machen** *(Kinderspr.)* wave

**Winkel** /ˈvɪŋkl̩/ *der;* ~**s**, ~ Ⓐ *(Math.)* angle; **toter ~:** blind spot; Ⓑ *(Ecke; auch fig.)* corner; **in allen Ecken und ~n suchen** search every nook and cranny; Ⓒ *(Ort)* corner; spot; Ⓓ *(Werkzeug)* [carpenter's] square; *(T-förmig)* T-square; Ⓔ *(milit. Rangabzeichen)* chevron; Ⓕ (~*eisen*) angle iron

**winkel-, Winkel-:** ~**advokat** *der,* ~**advokatin** *die (abwertend)* shady lawyer; ~**eisen** *das (Technik)* angle iron; ~**förmig** *Adj.* angled; ~**funktion** *die (Math.)* trigonometrical function; ~**halbierende** *die; adj. Dekl. (Math.)* bisector of a/the angle

**winkelig** *Adj.* twisty ‹streets›; **ein ~es Haus** a house full of odd corners

**Winkel-:** ~**maß** *das* measure of angle; ~**messer** *der;* ~~**s**, ~~**:** protractor; ~**schleifer** *der* angle grinder; ~**zug** *der* shady trick *or* move

**winken** ❶ *itr. V.* Ⓐ wave; **jmdm. ~:** wave to sb.; **mit etw. ~:** wave sth.; **mit dem Kopf ~:** nod [one's head]; Ⓑ *(auffordern heranzukommen)* **jmdm. ~:** beckon sb. over; **einem Taxi ~:** hail a taxi; Ⓒ *(in Aussicht stehen)* **etw. winkt jmdm.** sth. is in prospect for sb.; **dem Sieger winkt eine Flasche Sekt** the winner will receive a bottle of champagne. ❷ *tr. V.* Ⓐ *(heran~)* beckon; **jmdn. zu sich ~:** beckon sb. over [to one]; **der Polizist winkte den Wagen zur Seite** the policeman waved the car over [to the side]; Ⓑ *(signalisieren)* signal

**Winker** *der;* ~**s**, ~**:** trafficator; indicator

**winklig** *Adj.* ⇒ **winkelig**

**winseln** /ˈvɪnzl̩n/ *itr. V.* Ⓐ ‹dog› whimper; Ⓑ *(abwertend)* whine; **um Gnade/sein Leben ~:** whine and beg for mercy/one's life

**Winter** /ˈvɪntɐ/ *der;* ~**s**, ~ ▶ 431 winter; **über den ~:** over [the] winter; ⇒ *auch* **Frühling**

**winter-, Winter-:** ~**abend** *der* winter['s] evening; ~**anfang** *der* beginning of winter; **am 22. Dezember ist ~anfang** 22 December is the first day of winter; ~**einbruch** *der* onset of winter; ~**fahr·plan** *der* winter timetable; ~**fell** *das* winter coat; ~**fest** *Adj.* Ⓐ winter *attrib.* ‹clothing›; **ein ~festes Haus** a house that can withstand the rigours of winter; Ⓑ ⇒ ~**hart**; ~**frucht** *die* ⇒ ~**getreide**; ~**garten** *der* conservatory; ~**getreide** *das (Landw.)* winter grain; ~**halb·jahr** *das:* **während des ~halbjahrs/im ~halbjahr** from October to March; ~**hart** *Adj. (Bot.)* hardy; ~**hilfswerk** *das: (ns.) relief organization in Nazi Germany providing clothes, fuel, food, etc. for the needy;* ~**jasmin** *der* winter jasmine; ~**kleid** *das* Ⓐ *(auch fig.)* winter dress; Ⓑ *(Zool.)* winter coat; *(von Vögeln)* winter plumage; ~**kleidung** *die* winter clothes *pl. or* clothing; ~**landschaft** *die* winter landscape

**winterlich** ▶ 431 ❶ *Adj.* wintry; winter *attrib.* ‹clothing, break›. ❷ *adv.* ~ **kalt/öde** cold/bare and wintry; ~ **warm angezogen** dressed in warm winter clothes

**Winter-:** ~**luft** *die* winter air; ~**mantel** *der* winter coat; ~**mode** *die* winter fashions *pl.; (eines Modehauses)* winter collection; ~**monat** *der* winter month; ~**nacht** *die* winter['s] night; ~**olympiade** *die* Winter Olympics *pl.;* ~**quartier** *das* Ⓐ *(Milit.)* winter quarters *pl.;* Ⓑ *(Zool.)* wintering grounds *pl.;* ~**reifen** *der* winter tyre; ~**ruhe** *die (Zool.)* winter dormancy; ~**ruhe halten** have a period/periods of winter inactivity

**winters** *Adv.* in winter

**Winter-:** ~**saat** *die (Landw.) (Saatgut)* winter seed; *(Pflanzen)* young winter corn; ~**sachen** *Pl.* winter things; ~**saison** *die* winter season

**Winters·anfang** *der* ⇒ **Winteranfang**

**Winter-:** ~**schlaf** *der (Zool.)* hibernation; ~**schlaf halten** hibernate; ~**schlussverkauf**, *~**schlußverkauf** *der* winter sale[s *pl.*]; ~**schuh** *der* winter shoe; ~**semester** *das* winter semester; ~**sonnenwende** *die* winter solstice; ~**spiele** *Pl.* Winter Games; **die Olympischen ~spiele** the Winter Olympics; ~**sport** *der* winter sports *pl.;* **in den ~sport fahren** go on a winter sports holiday; ~**sportler** *der* winter sportsman; ~**sportlerin** *die* winter sportswoman

**Winters·zeit** *die* ⇒ **Winterzeit**

**Winter-:** ~**tag** *der* winter['s] day; ~**urlaub** *der* winter holiday; ~**wetter** *das* winter weather; ~**zeit** *die* wintertime; **zur ~zeit** in [the] wintertime

**Winzer** /ˈvɪntsɐ/ *der;* ~**s**, ~, **Winzerin** *die;* ~, ~**nen** ▶ 159 winegrower

**winzig** /ˈvɪntsɪç/ ❶ *Adj.* tiny; tiny, minute ‹portion, writing›. ❷ *adv.* **er schreibt ~:** he has tiny *or* minute writing; ~ **klein** tiny; minute

**Winzigkeit** *die;* ~, ~ Ⓐ tininess; minuteness; Ⓑ *(Kleinigkeit)* tiny thing; triviality

**Winzling** /ˈvɪntslɪŋ/ *der;* ~**s**, ~**e** tiny person/animal/thing; **er/sie/es ist ein ~:** he/she/it is a tiny little thing

**Wipfel** /ˈvɪpfl̩/ *der;* ~**s**, ~**:** treetop

**Wippe** /ˈvɪpə/ *die;* ~, ~**n** see-saw

**wippen** *itr. V.* bob up and down; *(hin und her)* bob about; *(auf einer Wippe)* see-saw; **er ließ das Kind auf den Knien ~:** he bounced the child [up and down] on his knees; **er wippte in den Knien** he bobbed up and down, bending at the knees; **mit dem Fuß ~:** jiggle one's foot up and down; **mit dem Schwanz ~:** jerk its tail up and down

**wir** /viːɐ̯/ *Personalpron.; 1. Pers. Pl. Nom.* we; ~ **beide** *od.* **beiden** we two; the two of us; **sie weiß mehr als ~:** she knows more than we do; she knows more than us *(coll.)*; **nicht nur ~ würden profitieren** we shouldn't be the only ones to profit; **Wer hat das getan? — Wir nicht!** Who did it? — It wasn't us! *or* We didn't!; **Wer kommt mit? — Wir!** Who's coming? — We are!; **Wer ist es? — Wir sinds!** Who is it? — It's us!; **wie fühlen ~ uns heute?** *(zu einem Patienten)* how are we feeling today?; ⇒ *auch (Gen.)* **unser**; *(Dat.)* **uns**; *(Akk.)* **uns**

**wirb** /vɪrp/ *Imperativ Sg. v.* **werben**

**Wirbel** /ˈvɪrbl̩/ *der;* ~**s**, ~ Ⓐ *(kreisende Bewegung) (im Wasser)* whirlpool; vortex; *(in der Luft)* whirlwind; *(kleiner)* eddy; *(von Rauch, beim Tanz)* whirl; **alles drehte sich in einem ~ um ihn** everything was whirling round him; **ein ~ der Leidenschaft** *(fig.)* a whirlpool of passions; Ⓑ *(Trubel)* hurly-burly; **der ~ der Ereignisse** the whirl of events; Ⓒ *(Aufsehen)* fuss; **um jmdn./etw. ~ machen** make a fuss about sb./sth.; Ⓓ ▶ 471 *(Anat.)* vertebra; Ⓔ *(Haar~)* crown; *(vorne)* cowlick; Ⓕ *(Trommel~)* [drum] roll; Ⓖ *(Musik, bei Streichinstrumenten)* tuning peg

**Wirbellose** *Pl.; adj. Dekl. (Zool.)* invertebrates

**wirbeln** ❶ *itr. V.* Ⓐ *mit sein* whirl; ‹water, snowflakes› swirl; **jmdm. durch den Kopf ~** *(fig.)* ‹thoughts› race through sb.'s head; Ⓑ *auch mit sein (in kreisender Bewegung sein)* ‹propeller, wheel, etc.› whirl; Ⓒ *(einen Wirbel schlagen)* ‹drum› roll; ‹drummer› beat a roll. ❷ *tr. V.* swirl ‹leaves, dust›; whirl ‹dancer›

**Wirbel-:** ~**säule** *die* ▶ 471 *(Anat.)* vertebral column; spinal column; ~**sturm** *der* cyclone; ~**tier** *das (Zool.)* vertebrate; ~**wind** *der* whirlwind; *(fig., meist scherzh.)* bundle of energy

**wirbt** /vɪrpt/ *3. Pers. Sg. Präsens v.* **werben**

**wird** /vɪrt/ *3. Pers. Sg. Präsens v.* **werden**

**wirf** /vɪrf/ *Imperativ Sg. v.* **werfen**

**wirft** *3. Pers. Sg. Präsens v.* **werfen**

**wirken** /ˈvɪrkn̩/ ❶ *itr. V.* Ⓐ *(eine Wirkung haben)* have an effect; **wirkt die Tablette schon?** is the tablet beginning to take effect yet?; **es wirkte erst nach einer Stunde** it only took effect after an hour; **schmerzstillend/einschläfernd ~:** have a pain-killing/

soporific effect; **gegen etw. ~:** be effective against sth.; **bei jmdm. ~:** have an effect on sb.; **seine Worte wirkten ermutigend** his words were encouraging; **ihre Heiterkeit wirkte ansteckend** her cheerfulness was infectious; **lassen Sie die Farben und Klänge auf sich ~:** let the colours and sounds sink in; **Sauerstoff wirkt dabei als Katalysator** oxygen acts as a catalyst; **B** (*erscheinen*) seem; appear; **neben ihm wirkt sie ausgesprochen klein** she seems decidedly small beside him; **sie wirkt sehr nett** she seems very nice; **er wirkt auf mich sehr sympathisch** I find him very congenial; **C** (*beeindrucken*) ‹person› make an impression (**auf** + *Akk.* on); ‹picture, design, etc.› be effective; **D** (*tätig sein*) work; **da wirkt ein verborgener Mechanismus** a hidden mechanism is operating there. **2** *tr. V.* **A** (*geh.: be~, vollbringen*) bring about; do ‹good, harm›; ⇒ *auch* **Wunder** A; **B** (*Textilw.*) knit

**Wirker** *der;* **~s, ~:** knitter

**Wirkerei** *die;* **~, ~en** **A** (*Herstellung*) knitting; **B** (*Betrieb*) knitwear factory

**Wirkerin** *die;* **~, ~nen** knitter

**wirklich** **1** *Adj.* real; actual, real ‹event, incident, state of affairs›; real, true ‹friend›. **2** *Adv.* really; (*in der Tat*) actually; really; **nein, ~?** no, really?; **er ist es ~:** it really is him; **~ und wahrhaftig** really and truly

**Wirklichkeit** *die;* **~, ~en** reality; **~ werden** become a reality; ‹dream› come true; **in ~:** in reality; **auf den Boden der ~ zurückkehren** come back down to earth (*fig.*)

**wirklichkeits-, Wirklichkeits-:** **~fern** **1** *Adj.* unrealistic; **2** *adv.* unrealistically; **~form** *die* (*Sprachw.*) indicative; **~fremd** **1** *Adj.* unrealistic; **er ist ~fremd** he is out of touch with reality; **2** *adv.* unrealistically; **~getreu** **1** *Adj.* faithful; **2** *adv.* faithfully; **~nah** **1** *Adj.* realistic; **2** *adv.* realistically; **~sinn** *der* sense of realism

**wirksam** /ˈvɪrkza:m/ **1** *Adj.* effective; **mit dem 1. Juli ~ werden** (*Amtsspr.*) take effect from 1 July. **2** *adv.* effectively

**Wirksamkeit** *die;* **~:** effectiveness

**Wirk·stoff** *der* active agent

**Wirkung** *die;* **~, ~en** **A** effect (**auf** + *Akk.* on); **ohne ~ bleiben** have no effect; **seine ~ verfehlen** fail to have the desired effect; **seine ~ tun** ‹drug, medicine, etc.› take effect; ‹treatment, therapy› be effective; **mit ~ vom 1. Juli** (*Amtsspr.*) with effect from 1 July; **B** (*Physik*) action

**wirkungs-, Wirkungs-:** **~bereich** *der* **A** area of activity; **sie fühlte sich in ihrem häuslichen ~bereich wohl** she felt quite happy in her domestic domain; **B** (*Milit.*) range; **~dauer** *die:* **eine kurze/lange ~dauer haben** be effective for a short/long period; **~feld** *das* sphere of activity; **~grad** *der* effectiveness; (*Technik*) efficiency; **~los** **1** *Adj.* ineffective; **2** *adv.* ineffectively; **~losigkeit** *die;* **~~:** ineffectiveness; **~mechanismus** *der* mode of action; **~stätte** *die* (*geh.*) workplace; **~voll** **1** *Adj.* effective; **2** *adv.* effectively; **~weise** *die* (*eines Wirkstoffs*) mode of action; **die ~weise eines Mechanismus/ökonomischer Gesetze** the way a mechanism works/economic laws operate

**Wirk·waren** *Pl.* knitwear *sing.;* (*Strümpfe, Socken*) hosiery *sing.*

**wirr** /vɪr/ **1** *Adj.* **A** (*unordentlich*) tousled ‹hair, beard›; tangled ‹ropes, roots›; **ein ~es Durcheinander** a chaotic muddle; **B** (*unklar, verwirrt*) confused; muddled, confused ‹thoughts›; **mir war ~ im Kopf** my head was reeling. **2** *adv.* **A** (*unordentlich*) **das Haar hing ihr ~ ins Gesicht** her tousled hair hung over her face; **alles lag ~ durcheinander** everything lay in a chaotic muddle; **B** (*verworren*) **sie träumte ~:** she had confused dreams; **~ reden** talk in a confused way; **C** (*verwirrt*) in confusion

**Wirren** *Pl.* turmoil *sing.*

**Wirr·kopf** *der* (*abwertend*) muddle-headed person; **ein ~ sein** be muddle-headed

**wirr·köpfig** **1** *Adj.* muddle-headed. **2** *adv.* muddle-headedly

**Wirrnis** /ˈvɪrnɪs/ *die;* **~, ~se** (*geh.*) confusion; **die ~se der Revolution** the chaos *sing.* of the revolution

**Wirrsal** /ˈvɪrza:l/ *das;* **~[e]s, ~e** *od.* **die; ~, ~e** (*geh.*) ⇒ **Wirrnis**

**Wirrwarr** /-var/ *der;* **~s** chaos; (*von Stimmen*) clamour; (*von Meinungen*) welter; (*von Haaren, Wurzeln, Vorschriften*) tangle

**Wirsing** /ˈvɪrzɪŋ/ *der;* **~s, Wirsing·kohl** *der* savoy [cabbage]

**Wirt** /vɪrt/ *der;* **~[e]s, ~e** **A** landlord; ⇒ *auch* **Rechnung**; **B** (*Biol.*) host

**Wirtel** /ˈvɪrtl/ *der;* **~s, ~** ⇒ **Spinnwirtel**

**Wirtin** *die;* **~, ~nen** landlady

**Wirtschaft** *die;* **~, ~en** **A** economy; (*Geschäftsleben*) commerce and industry; **in die ~ gehen** become a business man/woman; **die freie ~:** the free market economy; **B** (*Gast~*) public house (*Brit.*); pub (*Brit.*); bar (*Amer.*); **C** (*Haushalt*) household; **jmdm. die ~ führen** keep house for sb.; **D** (*ugs. abwertend: Unordnung*) mess; shambles *sing.;* **E** (*landwirtschaftlicher Betrieb*) [small] farm; **F** (*das Haushalten*) housekeeping

**wirtschaften** **1** *itr. V.* **A** **mit dem Geld gut ~:** manage one's money well; **mit Verlust/Gewinn ~:** run at a loss/profit; **wenn weiter so gewirtschaftet wird wie bisher** if things continue to be run as they have been up to now; **B** (*sich zu schaffen machen*) busy oneself. **2** *tr. V.* **eine Firma konkursreif/in den Ruin ~:** bring a company to the brink of bankruptcy/ruin a company; **er hat den Hof zugrunde gewirtschaftet** he brought the farm to rack and ruin

**Wirtschafter** *der;* **~s, ~** **A** (*Wirtsch.: Unternehmer*) entrepreneur; (*Industrieller*) industrialist; **B** (*in landwirtschaftlichem Betrieb*) farm manager

**Wirtschafterin** *die;* **~, ~nen** **A** ⇒ **Wirtschafter**; **B** (*Haushälterin*) housekeeper

**Wirtschaftler** *der;* **~s, ~, Wirtschaftlerin** *die;* **~, ~nen** **A** ⇒ **Wirtschaftswissenschaftler**; **B** ⇒ **Wirtschafter** A

**wirtschaftlich** **1** *Adj.* **A** (*die Wirtschaft betreffend*) economic; **B** (*finanziell*) financial; **C** (*sparsam, rentabel*) economical. **2** *adv.;* *s. Adj.* **a, b, c** economically; financially

**Wirtschaftlichkeit** *die;* **~:** economic viability

**wirtschafts-, Wirtschafts-:** **~abkommen** *das* economic agreement; **~aufschwung** *der* economic upturn; **~berater** *der,* **~beraterin** *die* economic adviser; **~beziehungen** *Pl.* economic relations; **~block** *der; Pl.* **~blöcke** economic bloc; **~buch** *das* ⇒ **Haushaltsbuch**; **~flüchtling** *der* economic refugee; **~form** *die* economic system; **~führer** *der,* **~führerin** *die* leading figure in commerce and industry; **~führung** *die* (*eines Landes*) management of the economy; (*eines Betriebs*) financial management; **~gebäude** *Pl.* domestic offices; **~geld** *das* ⇒ **Haushaltsgeld**; **~gemeinschaft** *die* economic community; **~geographie** *die* economic geography *no art.;* **~gymnasium** *das: grammar school placing emphasis on economics, law, and business studies;* **~hilfe** *die* economic aid *no indef. art.;* **~hochschule** *die* business school *or* college; **~ingenieur** *der,* **~ingenieurin** *die* industrial engineer; **~jahr** *das* ⇒ **Geschäftsjahr**; **~kapitän** *der,* **~kapitänin** *die* captain of industry; **~krieg** *der* economic war; (*Kriegsführung*) economic warfare; **~kriminalität** *die* economic crime *no art.;* **~krise** *die* economic crisis; **~lage** *die* economic situation; **~leben** *das* economic life; (*Geschäftsleben*) business life; **ein Mann aus dem ~leben** a man from the business world; **~lenkung** *die* economic control; **~minister** *der,* **~ministerin** *die* minister for economic affairs; **~ministerium** *das* ministry of economic affairs; **~ordnung** *die* economic system; **~politik** *die* economic policy; **~politisch** **1** *Adj.* relating to economic policy *postpos.;* economic policy *attrib.* ‹measures, decisions›; **2** *adv.* from the point of view of economic policy; **~prüfer** *der,* **~prüferin** *die* ▶ 159 auditor; **~recht** *das* commercial law; **~spionage** *die* industrial espionage; **~standort** *der* ⇒ **Standort** C; **~system** *das* economic system; **~teil** *der* business section; **~union** *die* economic union; ⇒ *auch* **Währungsunion**; **~verband** *der* employers' association; **~wachstum** *das* economic growth; **~wissenschaft** *die* economics *no art.;* economic science *no art.;* **~wissenschaftler** *der,* **~wissenschaftlerin** *die* ▶ 159 economist; **~wunder** *das* (*ugs.*) economic miracle; **~zeitung** *die* financial newspaper; **~zweig** *der* economic sector

**Wirts-:** **~haus** *das* pub (*Brit.*); (*mit Unterkunft*) inn; pub (*Brit.*); **~leute** *Pl.* landlord and landlady; **~pflanze** *die* (*Biol.*) host plant; **~stube** *die* bar

**Wisch** /vɪʃ/ *der;* **~[e]s, ~e** (*salopp abwertend*) piece *or* bit of paper

**wischen** **1** *itr., tr. V.* wipe; **etw. von etw. ~:** wipe sth. off *or* from sth.; **er wischte sich** (*Dat.*) **die Stirn** he wiped his brow; **sich** (*Dat.*) **den Schlaf aus den Augen ~:** wipe the sleep from one's eyes; **mit der Hand/einem Lappen über den Tisch ~:** wipe the table with one's hand/a cloth; **versehentlich mit dem Ärmel über die Zeichnung ~:** accidentally brush one's sleeve across the drawing; **Staub ~:** do the dusting; dust; **jmdm. eine ~** (*ugs.*) give sb. a clout round the face. **2** *itr. V.;* *mit sein* (*huschen*) ‹person› slip; ‹mouse, lizard› scurry; ‹cat› dart

**Wischer** *der;* **~s, ~** ⇒ **Scheibenwischer**

**Wischiwaschi** /vɪʃiˈvaʃi/ *das;* **~s** (*salopp abwertend*) wish-wash

**Wisch-:** **~lappen** *der,* **~tuch** *das; Pl.* **~tücher** cloth

**Wisent** /ˈvi:zɛnt/ *der;* **~s, ~e** wisent; aurochs

**Wismut** /ˈvɪsmu:t/ *das;* **~[e]s** bismuth

**wispern** /ˈvɪspɐn/ *itr., tr. V.* whisper

**wiss-,** ***wiß-, Wiss-,** ***Wiß-:** **~begier, ~begierde** *die* thirst for knowledge; **~begierig** *Adj.* eager for knowledge; ‹child› eager to learn

**wissen** /ˈvɪsn/ **1** *unr. tr. V.* know; **ich weiß [es]** I know; **ich weiß [es] nicht** I don't know; **etw. genau ~:** know sth. for certain; **ich weiß [mir] keinen anderen Rat/kein größeres Vergnügen, als ...** I can't think of anything other/I know of no greater pleasure than ...; **soviel ich weiß** as far as I know; **ich weiß ein gutes Lokal** I know [of] a good pub (*Brit.*); **er weiß es nicht anders** he knows no better; **er weiß immer alles besser** he always knows better; **ich wüsste nicht, dass ich dich um deinen Rat gebeten hätte** I am not aware of having asked your advice; **nicht, dass ich wüsste** not so far as I know; not that I know of; **ich möchte nicht ~, wieviel das gekostet hat** I hardly dare think how much it cost; **woher soll ich das ~?** how should I know?; **weißt du [was], wir fahren einfach dorthin** I'll tell you what, let's just go there; **jmdn. etw. ~ lassen** let sb. know sth.; **ein ~der Blick/ein ~des Lächeln** a knowing look/smile; **nicht mehr weiter ~:** not know what to do next; **was weiß ich** (*ugs.*) I don't know; **man kann nie ~** (*ugs.*) you never know; **gewusst, wie!** (*ugs.*) it's easy when you know how; **was ich nicht weiß, macht mich nicht heiß** (*Spr.*) what I don't know doesn't hurt me; **von jmdm./etw. nichts [mehr] ~ wollen** want to have nothing [more] to do with sb./sth.; **jmd. will es ~** (*ugs.*) sb. wants to put himself/herself to the test; **er tut, als sei es wer weiß wie wichtig** (*ugs.*) he behaves as if it were incredibly important (*coll.*); **dies und noch wer weiß was alles** (*ugs.*) this and heaven knows what else [too]; **ich hätte wer weiß was darum gegeben** (*ugs.*) I'd have given almost anything for it; **ich weiß sie in Sicherheit/glücklich** (*geh.*) I know she's safe/happy; **ich wusste**

**ihn in Gefahr** (*geh.*) I knew him to be in danger; **ich wollte diese Äußerung nicht als Vorwurf verstanden ~** (*geh.*) I didn't mean what I said to be taken as a reproach; **sich zu benehmen ~:** know how to behave oneself; **er wusste zu berichten, dass ...** he was able to report that ...; **ich weiß nichts mit ihm anzufangen** he isn't my type of person; **Sie müssen ~, dass ...** (*erklärend*) I should tell you that ...; **ich weiß ihren Namen nicht mehr** I can't remember her name; **weißt du noch, wie arm wir damals waren?** do you remember how poor we were then?; ⇨ *auch* **Glocke** A; **Gott** A, B; **Stunde** A.

❷ *unr. itr. V.* **von etw./um etw. ~:** know about sth.; **ich weiß von nichts** I don't know anything about it

**Wịssen** *das;* **~s** knowledge; **ein großes ~ haben** be very knowledgeable; **meines/unseres ~s** to my/our knowledge; **ohne jmds. ~:** without sb.'s knowledge; **mit jmds. ~:** with sb.'s knowledge; **wider** *od.* **gegen besseres ~:** against one's better judgement; **nach bestem ~ und Gewissen** to the best of one's knowledge and belief; **~ ist Macht** (*Spr.*) knowledge is power (*prov.*)

**Wịssenschaft** *die;* **~, ~en** science; **die ~ hat ...** science has ...; **in der ~ tätig sein** be a scientist; **etw. ist eine ~ für sich** (*ugs.*) there's a real art to sth.

**Wịssenschafter** *der;* **~s, ~, Wịssenschafterin** *die;* **~, ~nen** (*österr. u. schweiz.*), **Wịssenschaftler** *der;* **~s, ~, Wịssenschaftlerin** *die;* **~, ~nen** ▶ **159** academic; (*Natur~*) scientist

**wịssenschaftlich** ❶ *Adj.* scholarly; (*natur~*) scientific; **~er Assistent** ≈ assistant lecturer; **~er Rat** ≈ lecturer; assistant professor (*Amer.*). ❷ *adv.* in a scholarly manner; (*natur~*) scientifically; **das ist ~ nicht haltbar** that is not scientifically tenable; **~ arbeiten** (*als Wissenschaftler tätig sein*) work as a scholar/scientist

**Wịssenschaftlichkeit** *die;* **~** ⇨ **wissenschaftlich**: scholarliness; scientific rigour; **die ~ einer Untersuchung infrage stellen** question whether a piece of research has been conducted in a proper scholarly/scientific manner

**Wịssenschafts-: ~betrieb** *der* (*ugs.*) academic activity; (*in den Naturwissenschaften*) scientific activity; **~theorie** *die* philosophy of science

**wịssens-, Wịssens-: ~drang** *der,* **~durst** *der* thirst for knowledge; **~gebiet** *das* area *or* field of knowledge; **~lücke** *die* gap in sb's knowledge; **~stand** *der* state of knowledge; **~wert** *Adj.* **~wert sein** be worth knowing; **eine ~werte Tatsache** a fact worth knowing; **das Buch enthält viel ~wertes** the book contains a great deal of valuable and interesting information

**wissentlich** /ˈvɪsn̩tlɪç/ ❶ *Adj.* deliberate. ❷ *adv.* knowingly; deliberately

**witschen** /ˈvɪtʃn̩/ *itr. V.; mit sein* (*ugs.*) slip

**wittern** /ˈvɪtɐn/ ❶ *itr. V.* sniff the air. ❷ *tr. V.* get wind of; scent; (*fig.: ahnen*) sense

**Wịtterung** *die;* **~, ~en** Ⓐ (*Wetter*) weather *no indef. art;* Ⓑ (*Jägerspr.*) (*Geruchssinn*) sense of smell; (*Geruch*) scent; **~ nehmen, die ~ aufnehmen** pick up the scent; **~ von etw. bekommen** (*auch fig.*) get wind of sth.; Ⓒ (*Spürsinn*) **eine/keine ~ für etw. haben** have a/no instinct for sth.

**wịtterungs-, Wịtterungs-: ~bedingt** *Adj.* caused by the weather *postpos.;* **~einfluss, *~einfluß** *der* effect of the weather; **~umschlag** *der* change in the weather; **~verhältnisse** *Pl.* weather conditions

**Witwe** /ˈvɪtvə/ *die;* **~, ~n** widow; **~ werden** be widowed; **grüne ~** (*ugs. scherzh.*) *suburban housewife left alone at home during the day while her husband is at work*

**Wịtwen-: ~rente** *die* widow's pension; **~schaft** *die;* **~~:** widowhood; **~schleier** *der* widow's veil; **~tröster** *der* (*ugs. scherzh.*) skirt-chaser (*coll.*) with a preference for widows; **~verbrennung** *die* suttee

**Wịtwer** *der;* **~s, ~:** widower; **~ werden** be widowed

**Wịtwerschaft** *die;* **~:** widowhood

**Witz** /vɪts/ *der;* **~es, ~e** Ⓐ joke; **~e reißen** (*ugs.*) crack jokes; **das ist der [ganze] ~:** that's the whole point; **der ~ ist nämlich der, dass ...** the thing about it is that ...; **ich mache keine ~e** I'm not joking; **das soll wohl ein ~ sein** you/he *etc.* must be joking; **mach keine ~e!** come off it! (*coll.*); Ⓑ (*Geist, Esprit, veralt.: Klugheit*) wit; **mit ~:** wittily

**Wịtz-: ~blatt** *das* humorous magazine; **~blatt·figur** *die* joke figure; **~bold** /-bɔlt/ *der;* **~~[e]s, ~~e** joker; (*der jmdm. einen Streich spielt*) practical joker; prankster

**Witzelei** *die;* **~, ~en** Ⓐ teasing; Ⓑ (*witzelnde Bemerkung*) joke

**witzeln** /ˈvɪtsl̩n/ *itr. V.* joke (**über** + *Akk.* about)

**Wịtz·figur** *die* Ⓐ (*in Witzen*) joke character; Ⓑ (*ugs. abwertend*) figure of fun; **du ~!** you clown!

**wịtzig** ❶ *Adj.* Ⓐ (*spaßig*) funny; amusing; Ⓑ (*ugs.: seltsam*) funny; odd; Ⓒ (*einfallsreich*) imaginative. ❷ *adv.; s. Adj.* **a, b, c** amusingly; oddly; imaginatively

**Wịtzigkeit** *die;* **~** Ⓐ wit; **von umwerfender ~ sein** be hilariously funny; Ⓑ ⇨ **Witz** B

**wịtz·los** ❶ *Adj.* Ⓐ (*ohne Witz*) dull; Ⓑ (*ugs.: sinnlos*) pointless. ❷ *adv.* (*ohne Witz*) unimaginatively

**WM** *Abk.* **Weltmeisterschaft**

**WNW** *Abk.* ▶ **400** **Westnordwest[en]** WNW

**wo** /vo:/ ❶ *Adv.* Ⓐ (*interrogativ*) where; **~ gibts denn so was!** (*ugs.*) who ever heard of such a thing!; ⇨ *auch* **ach** 1 E; **hindenken**; Ⓑ (*relativisch*) where; (*temporal*) when; **überall, ~:** wherever; **~ immer er auch sein mag** wherever he may be; Ⓒ (*indefinit*) (*ugs.*) somewhere; **wenn du ihn ~ sehen solltest** if you should see him anywhere. ❷ *Konj.* Ⓐ (*da, weil*) seeing that; Ⓑ (*obwohl*) although; when; Ⓒ (*falls*) **~ möglich** if possible; **~ nicht ..., so doch ...** if not ..., then ...

**wo·anders** *Adv.* somewhere else; elsewhere; **sie ist mit ihren Gedanken ganz ~:** she's miles away (*coll.*)

**wob** /vo:p/ *1. u. 3. Pers. Sg. Prät. v.* **weben**

**wo·bei** *Adv.* Ⓐ (*interrogativ*) **~ hast du sie ertappt?** what did you catch her doing?; **~ ist es kaputtgegangen?** how did it get broken?; Ⓑ (*relativisch*) **er gab sechs Schüsse ab, ~ einer der Täter getötet wurde** he fired six shots — one of the criminals was killed; **so viel zu den Statistiken, ~ [aber] zu beachten ist, dass ...** that concludes our remarks on the statistics, though it should be noted that ...; **sie sagte nein, ~** (*indem*) **sie vermied, mich anzusehen** she said 'no', avoiding looking at me as she did so; *NB The word occurs in North German coll. usage in two parts, e.g.* **wo hast du sie bei ertappt?**

**Woche** /ˈvɔxə/ *die;* **~, ~n** ▶ **833** week; **in dieser/der nächsten/der letzten ~:** this/next/last week; **heute in/vor einer ~:** a week today/a week ago today; **zweimal die** *od.* **in der ~:** twice a week

**Wọchen-: ~bett** *das:* **im ~bett liegen** be lying in; **im ~bett sterben** die soon after childbirth; **~blatt** *das* weekly

**Wọchenend-: ~aus·gabe** *die* weekend edition; **~bei·lage** *die* weekend supplement

**wọchen-, Wọchen-: ~ende** *das* weekend; **schönes ~ende!** have a nice weekend!; **~end·haus** *das* weekend house; **~fluss, *~fluß** *der* (*Med.*) lochia; **~karte** *die* weekly season ticket; **~lang** ❶ *Adj.* lasting weeks *postpos;* ❷ *adv.* for weeks [on end]; **~lohn** *der* weekly wages *pl.;* **~markt** *der* weekly market; **~schau** *die* (*bes. früher*) weekly newsreel; **~schrift** *die* weekly; **~stunde** *die* (*Schulw.*) period per week; **~tag** *der* ▶ **833** weekday (*including Saturday*); **welcher ~tag ist heute?** what day of the week is it?; **~tags** *Adv.* on weekdays [and Saturdays]

**wöchentlich** /ˈvœçn̩tlɪç/ ❶ *Adj.* weekly. ❷ *adv.* weekly; **es werden ~ ca. 50 Briefe beantwortet** some fifty letters are answered every week; **~ einmal** once a week; **wir treffen uns ~:** we meet once a week

**-wöchentlich** ❶ *Adj.* -weekly. ❷ *adv.* every ... weeks; ⇨ *auch* **achtwöchentlich**

**wọchen·weise** *Adv.* for a week at a time

**Wọchen·zeitung** *die* weekly newspaper

**-wöchig** /-vœçɪç/ Ⓐ (... *Wochen alt*) ... -week-old; **ein achtwöchiges Kind** an eight-week-old baby; Ⓑ (... *Wochen dauernd*) ... week's/weeks'; ... -week; **eine vierwöchige Kur** a four-week course of treatment; **mit dreiwöchiger Verspätung** three weeks late

**Wöchnerin** /ˈvœçnərɪn/ *die;* **~, ~nen** woman who has just given birth; puerpera (*Med.*)

**Wọ̈chnerinnen·station** *die* maternity ward

**Wodka** /ˈvɔtka/ *der;* **~s, ~s** vodka

**wo·durch** *Adv.* Ⓐ (*interrogativ*) how; **~ unterscheidet sie sich von den anderen?** in what way is she different from the others?; Ⓑ (*relativisch*) as a result of which; **alles, ~ er sich verletzt fühlen könnte** anything that might offend him; ⇨ *auch* **wobei** *NB*

**wo·fern** *Konj.* (*veralt.*) provided that

**wo·für** *Adv.* Ⓐ (*interrogativ*) for what; **~ brauchst du es?** what do you need it for?; **~ hältst du mich?** what do you take me for?; **~ interessierst du dich?** what are you interested in?; Ⓑ (*relativisch*) for which; **er ist nicht das, ~ er sich ausgibt** he's not what he claims to be; ⇨ *auch* **wobei** *NB*

**wog** /vo:k/ *1. u. 3. Pers. Sg. Prät. v.* **wiegen**

**Woge** /ˈvo:gə/ *die;* **~, ~n** (*auch fig.*) wave; **die ~n glätten** (*fig.*) pour oil on troubled waters

**wo·gegen** ❶ *Adv.* Ⓐ (*interrogativ*) against what; what ... against; **~ ist sie allergisch?** what is she allergic to?; Ⓑ (*relativisch*) against which; which ... against; **..., ~ nichts einzuwenden ist** to which there is no objection; ⇨ *auch* **wobei** *NB* ❷ *Konj.* whereas

**wogen** /ˈvo:gn̩/ *itr. V.* (*geh.*) ‹sea› surge; (*fig.*) ‹corn› wave; ‹crowd› surge; ‹battle› rage; **mit ~dem Busen** (*fig.*) with heaving bosom

**wo·her** *Adv.* Ⓐ (*interrogativ*) where ... from; **~ weißt du das?** how do you know that?; **~ kennst du ihn?** where do you know him from?; **[ach] ~ denn!, ach ~!** (*ugs.*) good heavens, no!; not at all!; **~ bist du so braun?** how did you get so brown?; Ⓑ (*relativisch*) where ... from; ⇨ *auch* **wobei** *NB*

**wohin** *Adv.* Ⓐ (*interrogativ*) where [... to]; **~ damit?** (*ugs.*) where shall I put it/them?; **~ so spät/eilig?** where are you/is he *etc.* going so late/in such a hurry?; Ⓑ (*relativisch*) where; **er ging ins Zimmer, ~ ihm die anderen folgten** he went into the room, and the others followed him in; Ⓒ (*indefinit*) **ich muss mal ~** (*ugs. verhüll.*) I've got to pay a visit *or* a call (*euphem.*); ⇨ *auch* **wobei** *NB*

**wo·hinein** *Adv.* ⇨ **worein**

**wo·hingegen** *Konj.* whereas

**wo·hinter** *Adv.* Ⓐ (*interrogativ*) behind what; what ... behind; **~ habt ihr euch versteckt?** what did you hide behind?; Ⓑ (*relativisch*) behind which; ⇨ *auch* **wobei** *NB*

**wohl** /vo:l/ ❶ *Adv.* Ⓐ (*gesund*) well; **jmdm. ist nicht ~, jmd. fühlt sich nicht ~:** sb. does not feel well; Ⓑ (*behaglich*) at ease; happy; **es sich ~ sein lassen** spoil oneself; **mir ist nicht recht ~ bei der Sache** the whole thing makes me a bit uneasy; **lass es dir ~ ergehen!** enjoy yourself!; **leb ~!/leben Sie ~!** farewell!; **~ oder übel** whether I/you *etc.* want to or not; Ⓒ (*durchaus*) well; **ich bin mir dessen ~ bewusst** I'm quite *or* perfectly conscious of that; Ⓓ (*ungefähr*) about; **~ 100 Gäste** 100 or so guests; about 100 guests; Ⓔ (*veralt.: gewiss*) **sehr ~[, der** *od.* **mein Herr]** certainly

*old spelling (see note on page 1707)

W

# Wochentage

| DEUTSCH | ENGLISCH | ABKÜRZUNG |
|---|---|---|
| *Sonntag* | Sunday | Sun |
| *Montag* | Monday | Mon |
| *Dienstag* | Tuesday | Tues |
| *Mittwoch* | Wednesday | Wed |
| *Donnerstag* | Thursday | Thurs |
| *Freitag* | Friday | Fri |
| *Samstag* | Saturday | Sat |

Es ist zu beachten, dass im englischsprachigen Raum die Woche am Sonntag beginnt und am Samstag endet.

## Wann?

Wie beim Datum wird *am* + Wochentag mit **on** übersetzt (ohne **the**). Dieses **on** kann nicht ausgelassen werden.

***Ich fahre [am] Mittwoch nach Kairo***
= I am going to Cairo on Wednesday

Selbstverständlich wird aber, wenn es sich um einen bestimmten, näher beschriebenen Tag handelt, ein Artikel eingesetzt.

***am letzten Sonntag vor Pfingsten***
= on the last Sunday before Whitsun

***Es geschah an einem verregneten Montag***
= It happened on a wet Monday

Aber:

***Eines [schönen] Samstags trafen wir uns im Zoo***
= One [fine] Saturday we met at the zoo

## Wiederholtes

Hier fällt das **on** vor **every, most** und **some** weg. Vor der Pluralform (**Mondays, Fridays** usw.) fehlt das **on** im amerikanischen Englisch, wird aber im britischen Englisch meist nicht weggelassen.

***Ich fahre freitags/jeden Freitag nach Hause***
= I go home [on] Fridays/every Friday

***jeden zweiten Donnerstag***
= every other Thursday

***jeden dritten Montag***
= every third Monday

***fast jeden Samstag***
= almost every Saturday, most Saturdays

***manchmal am Mittwoch***
= sometimes on a Wednesday, some Wednesdays

***ab und zu am Freitag***
= occasionally on a Friday, on the occasional *od.* odd Friday

## Vergangenes und Künftiges

***letzten Donnerstag***
= last Thursday

***am vorangehenden Donnerstag***
= [on] the preceding Thursday

***vorletzten Donnerstag***
= [on] the Thursday before last

***Donnerstag vor einer Woche***
= a week ago on Thursday

***Ich werde sie [am] nächsten*** od. ***kommenden Montag sehen***
= I will see her next Monday *od.* this [coming] Monday

***Ich habe sie am [darauf] folgenden Montag gesehen***
= I saw her the following *od.* the next Monday

***übernächsten Montag***
= the Monday after next

***Montag in einer Woche***
= a week on Monday

***ab Samstag***
= from Saturday [on]

***Es muss bis Freitag fertig sein***
= It must be ready by Friday

## Tageszeiten

***[am] Montagmorgen, Montag früh***
= on Monday morning

***[am] Dienstagmittag***
= midday on Tuesday

***[am] Mittwochnachmittag***
= on Wednesday afternoon

***[am] Donnerstagabend***
= on Thursday evening; (*am späten Abend*) on Thursday night

***Freitagnacht***
= on Friday night

Und wenn es regelmäßig geschieht:

***montagmorgens***
= on Monday mornings

***dienstagmittags***
= midday on Tuesdays

***mittwochnachmittags***
= on Wednesday afternoons

***donnerstagabends***
= on Thursday evenings; (*am späten Abend*) on Thursday nights

***freitagnachts***
= on Friday nights

## Heute

***Welchen Tag haben wir heute?***
What day is it today?

***Heute ist Dienstag***
= It's Tuesday [today]

## Adjektive und Zusammensetzungen

Im Englischen gibt es keine Adjektive, die dem deutschen *sonntäglich*, *sonntägig* usw. entsprächen. Man verwendet das Substantiv, mit oder ohne **'s**:

***sein sonntäglicher Spaziergang***
= his [regular] Sunday walk

***ein sonntägiger Spaziergang***
= a Sunday walk, a walk on a Sunday

***ein Sonntagsfahrer***
= a Sunday driver

***die Sonntagszeitungen***
= the Sunday papers

Vergleiche aber:

***die Zeitung von Dienstag***
= Tuesday's paper

Ferner:

***die Züge am Montag***
= Monday's trains

***die Schulstunden am Mittwoch***
= Wednesday's lessons

W

[, sir]; very good [, sir]; (F) (*geh.: gut*) well; **er tat es, ~ wissend, dass ...** he did it knowing full well that ...; **~ ausgewogen** well-balanced; **~ bedacht** well-considered; [carefully] considered ‹reply, judgement›; well *or* carefully thought-out ‹plan›; **~ bedacht vorgehen** proceed in a carefully considered way *or* with careful consideration; **~ begründet** well-founded; (*berechtigt*) well-justified; **~ bekannt** well-known; **~ beraten** well-advised; **~ beleibt** corpulent; **~ dosiert** carefully measured; **~ durchdacht** carefully thought-out; **~ geordnet** well-ordered; **~ überlegt** well-considered; carefully considered ‹decision›; **~ versehen** well-provided (**mit** with); **~ verwahrt** safely stored; (*unter Verschluss*) safely locked away; **~ temperiert** ‹room› at a pleasant temperature;

‹wine› at the correct temperature; **das ~ temperierte Klavier** the Well-Tempered Clavier; **G** (*jedoch*) **...**, **~ aber ...** but ...; however ...; **hier gibt es keine Ratten, ~ aber Mäuse** there are no rats here, but there are mice; **H** (*geh.*) **~ dem, der ...!** happy the man who ...; **~ dir, dass du das nicht machen musst** count yourself lucky not to have to do that; **jmdm. ~ tun** show sb. kindness; **es tut ihm ~:** it does him good; **jmdm. ~ wollen** wish sb. well; **I** (*zwar*) **~ versprach ich hinzugehen, aber ...** I may have promised to go, but ... **2** *Partikel* **A** (*vermutlich*) probably; **er wird ~ bald kommen** I imagine he'll come soon; **~ kaum** hardly; **du bist ~ nicht recht bei Verstand?** have you taken leave of your senses?; **dir ist ~ schlecht?** aren't you feeling well?; **was/warum/wie ~?** but what/why/how?; **na** *od.* **ja, was/warum/wie ~?** need you ask what/why/how?; **das mag ~ sein** that may well be; **es wird ~ gleich Schluss sein** I imagine it's nearly over; **das wird ~ so sein** that's probably the case; **ich habe ~ nicht recht gehört** I don't think I could have heard right; **B** (*verstärkend*) **wirst du ~ herkommen!** will you come here!; **siehst du ~!** there, you see!; **man wird doch ~ fragen dürfen** there's nothing wrong in asking, is there?

**Wohl** *das;* **~[e]s** welfare; well-being; **das allgemeine/öffentliche ~:** the public good; **zu jmds. ~:** for sb.'s benefit *or* good; **auf jmds. ~ trinken** drink sb.'s health; **[auf] dein ~!** your health!; **zum ~!** cheers!; **das ~ und Weh[e]** (*geh.*) the weal and woe

**wohl-, Wohl-: ~an** /-'-/ *Interj.* (*veralt.*) [well,] come now; **~anständig** (*veralt.*) **1** *Adj.* respectable; proper ‹behaviour›; **2** *adv.* respectably; ‹behave› properly; **~auf** /-'-/ *Adj.* (*geh.*) **~auf sein** be well *or* in good health; ***~ausgewogen**, ***~bedacht** ⇨ **wohl** 1 F; **~befinden** *das* well-being; ***~begründet** ⇨ **wohl** 1 F; **~behagen** *das* sense of well-being; **mit ~behagen** with a sense of well-being; **etw. mit ~behagen essen** eat sth. with relish; **~behalten** *Adj.* safe and well ‹person›; undamaged ‹thing›; ***~bekannt**, ***~beleibt**, ***~beraten** ⇨ **wohl** 1 F; **~bestallt** *Adj.* (*geh.*) wellestablished; ***~dosiert** ⇨ **wohl** 1 F; ***~durchdacht** ⇨ **wohl** 1 F; **~ergehen** *das* ⇨ **~befinden**; **~erzogen** *Adj.* well brought-up; **~erzogenheit** *die;* **~~** (*geh.*) good upbringing; (*gute Manieren*) good manners *pl.*; **~fahrt** *die* **A** (*geh.:* **~***ergehen*) welfare; **B** (*öffentliche Fürsorge*) **von der ~fahrt betreut werden** be looked after by the welfare services; **von der ~fahrt leben** (*ugs.*) live on welfare

**Wohlfahrts-: ~marke** *die* (*Postw.*) charity stamp; **~pflege** *die* social welfare *no art.*; **~staat** *der* welfare state

**wohl-, Wohl-: ~feil 1** *Adj.* **A** (*preiswert*) inexpensive; **B** (*geistlos, platt*) trite; **2** *adv.* cheaply; **etw. ~feil verkaufen/erstehen** sell/buy sth. cheap; **~geboren** *Adj.* (*veralt.*) **Euer ~geboren** Your Honour; **Seiner ~geboren** to His Honour; **~gefallen** *das* pleasure; **sein ~gefallen an jmdm. haben** have a great liking for sb.; **an etw.** (*Dat.*) **~gefallen finden** take pleasure in sth.; **sich in ~gefallen auflösen** (*scherzh.*) (*ein gutes Ende finden*) end well; ‹difficulties, misunderstandings› be cleared up; (*entzweigehen, auseinander fallen*) ‹clothes, book, etc.› fall apart; (*verschwinden*) vanish into thin air; **~gefällig 1** *Adj.* **A** (**~***gefallen ausdrückend*) ‹smile, look› of pleasure; **B** (*veralt.: angenehm*) pleasing; agreeable; **2** *adv.* **A** (*mit* **~***gefallen*) with pleasure; **B** (*veralt.: angenehm*) **die Speisen ~gefällig darreichen** serve the food in a way that is pleasing *or* agreeable to the eye; **~geformt** *Adj.* well-formed; **~gefühl** *das* sense of well-being; **~gelitten** *Adj.* (*geh.*) well-liked; **~gemerkt** *Adv.* please note; mark you; **~gemut** /-gəmu:t/ (*geh.*) **1** *Adj.* cheerful; **2** *adv.* cheerfully; **~genährt** *Adj.* (*meist spött.*) well-fed; ***~geordnet** ⇨ **wohl** 1 F; **~geraten** *Adj.* (*geh.*) fine *attrib.* ‹child›; successful ‹piece of work, translation, etc.›; **ihre Kinder sind ~geraten** their children have turned out well; **~geruch** *der* (*geh.*) pleasant *or* agreeable aroma; (*von Blumen*) agreeable fragrance; **alle ~gerüche Arabiens** (*scherzh. od. iron.*) all the perfumes of Arabia; **~gesetzt** *Adj.* (*geh.*) well-turned ‹compliment›; well-chosen ‹words›; well-worded ‹speech›; **~gesinnt** *Adj.* well-disposed; **jmdm./einer Sache ~gesinnt sein** be well-disposed towards sb./sth.; **der Wettergott war uns nicht ~gesinnt** the weather was unkind to us; **~gestalt** (*veralt.*), **~gestaltet** *Adj.* (*geh.*) well-shaped; well-proportioned ‹body›; **~getan 1** *2. Part. v.* **~tun; 2** *Adj.* *in* **~getan sein** (*veralt.*) be well done; **~habend** *Adj.* prosperous; **~habenheit** *die;* **~~:** prosperity

**wohlig 1** *Adj.* pleasant; agreeable; (*gemütlich*) cosy. **2** *adv.* ‹sigh, purr, etc.› with pleasure; ‹stretch oneself› luxuriously

**wohl-, Wohl-: ~klang** *der* (*geh.*) melodious *or* pleasing sound; **~klingend** *Adj.* (*geh.*) melodious; **~laut** *der* (*geh.*) ⇨ **~klang**; **~leben** *das* (*geh.*) good living; **~meinend** *Adj.* (*geh.*) well-meaning; **~proportioniert** *Adj.* (*geh.*) well-proportioned; **~riechend** *Adj.* (*geh.*) fragrant; **~schmeckend** *Adj.* (*geh.*) delicious; **~sein** *das:* **[zum] ~sein!** your health!; **~stand** *der* prosperity; **zu ~stand gelangen** achieve a degree of prosperity; **bei dir ist wohl der ~stand ausgebrochen!** (*scherzh.*) have you won the pools *or* something?

**Wohlstands-: ~gesellschaft** *die* (*abwertend*) affluent society; **~kriminalität** *die* (*Rechtsspr.*) crime characteristic of the affluent society; **~müll** *der* (*abwertend*) refuse produced by the affluent society

**wohl-, Wohl-: ~tat** *die* **A** (*gute Tat*) good deed; (*Gefallen*) favour; **jmdm. eine ~tat erweisen** do sb. a good turn; **auf die ~taten anderer angewiesen sein** be dependent on the kindness of others; **B** (*Genuss*) blissful relief; **~täter** *der* benefactor; **~täterin** *die* benefactress; **~tätig** *Adj.* charitable; **~tätigkeit** *die* charity; charitableness

**Wohltätigkeits-: ~basar** *der* charity bazaar; **~konzert** *das* charity concert; **~veranstaltung** *die* charity event

**wohl-, Wohl-: *~temperiert** ⇨ **wohl** 1 F; **~tuend 1** *Adj.* agreeable; **eine ~tuende Wirkung haben** have a beneficial effect; **2** *adv.* agreeably; ***~|tun**, ***~überlegt** ⇨ **wohl** 1 F; **~verdient** *Adj.* well-earned, well-deserved ‹reward, honour, success, etc.›; well-deserved ‹punishment, fate›; **~verhalten** *das* good behaviour *no indef. art.*; ***~versehen** ⇨ **wohl** 1F; **~verstanden** *Adv.* (*geh.*) ⇨ **~gemerkt**; ***~verwahrt** ⇨ **wohl** 1 F; **~weislich** /-vaislıç/ *Adv.* deliberately; ***~|wollen** ⇨ **wohl** 1 F; **~wollen** *das;* **~~s** goodwill; **jmdn. mit ~wollen betrachten** regard sb. benevolently; **~wollend 1** *Adj.* benevolent; favourable ‹judgement, opinion›; **2** *adv.* benevolently; ‹judge, consider› favourably

**Wohn-: ~anhänger** *der* caravan; trailer (*Amer.*); **~anlage** *die* residential estate; **~bau** *der; Pl.* **~~ten** residential building; **~bereich** *der* living rooms *pl.*; (*eines Zimmers*) living area; **~bezirk** *der* **A** residential district; **B** (*DDR*) district; **~block** *der; Pl.* **~~s**, *od.* **~blöcke** residential block

**wohnen** *itr. V.* live; (*kurzfristig*) stay; (*fig. dichter.*) dwell; **sie ~ sehr hübsch** they have a lovely home; (*der Lage nach*) they live in a lovely spot; **ich wohne in der Leibnizstraße** 7 I live/am staying at [number] 7 Leibnizstrasse; **wo ~ Sie?** where do you live/where are you staying?

**wohn-, Wohn-: ~fläche** *die* living space; **eine Wohnung mit 50 m² ~fläche** a flat (*Brit.*) *or* (*Amer.*) apartment with 50 sq.m. floor area; **~gebäude** *das* residential building; **~gebiet** *das*, **~gegend** *die* residential area; **~geld** *das* housing benefit; **~gemeinschaft** *die* group sharing a flat (*Brit.*) *or* (*Amer.*) apartment/house; **unsere ~gemeinschaft** the group who share our flat (*Brit.*) *or* (*Amer.*) apartment/house; **in einer ~gemeinschaft leben** live in a shared flat (*Brit.*) *or* (*Amer.*) apartment/house; share a flat (*Brit.*) *or* (*Amer.*) apartment/house; **in diesem Haus wohnt eine studentische ~gemeinschaft/wohnen nur ~gemeinschaften** a group of students is sharing this house/the flats (*Brit.*) *or* (*Amer.*) apartments in this house are all shared; **~haft** *Adj.* resident (**in** + *Dat.* in); **~haus** *das* [dwelling] house; **~heim** *das* (*für Alte, Behinderte*) home; (*für Obdachlose, Lehrlinge*) hostel; (*für Studenten*) hall of residence; **~komplex** *der* residential complex; **~küche** *die* combined kitchen and living room; **~kultur** *die* style of home furnishing; **~lage** *die:* **unsere ~lage ist optimal** our house/flat (*Brit.*) *or* (*Amer.*) apartment is ideally situated; **in ruhiger/guter ~lage** in a quiet/good area; **~landschaft** *die* (*bes. Werbesprache*): *arrangement of furniture etc. to give an impressive 'landscape' effect*

**wohnlich 1** *Adj.* homely. **2** *adv.* **~ eingerichtet** furnished in a homely way

**Wohnlichkeit** *die;* **~:** homeliness

**Wohn-: ~mobil** *das;* **~~s, ~~e** motor home; motor caravan; **~ort** *der* place of residence; **~raum** *der* **A** living room; **B** (**~***fläche*) living space; **~siedlung** *die* residential estate; (*mit gleichartigen Häusern*) housing estate; **~silo** *der od. das* (*abwertend*) [anonymous] tower block *or* high-rise block; **~sitz** *der* place of residence; domicile (*formal*); **seinen ~sitz in Hamburg haben** live *or* (*formal*) be domiciled in Hamburg; **ohne festen ~sitz** of no fixed abode; **ohne festen ~sitz sein** have no fixed abode; **~stube** *die* (*landsch.*) living room

**Wohnung** *die;* **~, ~en A** flat (*Brit.*); apartment (*Amer.*); (*Wohneinheit*); home; dwelling (*formal*); **B** (*Unterkunft*) lodging; **freie ~ haben** have free lodging; **~ nehmen** (*veralt.*) take up residence

**Wohnungs-: ~amt** *das* housing department; **~bau** *der* housing construction; **der soziale ~bau** (*Amtsspr.*) public-sector housebuilding; **~inhaber** *der*, **~inhaberin** *die* occupant (*of a dwelling*); **~markt** *der* housing market; **~miete** *die* rent; **~not** *die* housing crisis; serious housing shortage; **~schlüssel** *der* key to the flat (*Brit.*) *or* (*Amer.*) apartment; **~suche** *die* search for a flat (*Brit.*) *or* (*Amer.*) apartment; **auf ~suche sein** be flat-hunting; **~suchende** *der/die; adj. Dekl.* person looking for a flat (*Brit.*) *or* (*Amer.*) apartment; **~tausch** *der* flat-swap (*coll.*); exchange of flats (*Brit.*) *or* (*Amer.*) apartments; **~tür** *die* door of the flat (*Brit.*) *or* (*Amer.*) apartment

**Wohnung-: ~suche** ⇨ **Wohnungssuche**; **~suchende** ⇨ **Wohnungssuchende**

**Wohnungs·wechsel** *der* move to a new flat (*Brit.*) *or* (*Amer.*) apartment

**Wohn-: ~verhältnisse** *Pl.* living conditions; **~viertel** *das* residential district; **~wagen** *der* caravan; trailer (*Amer.*); **~zimmer** *das* **A** living room; **B** (*Einrichtung*) set of living room furniture

**wölben** /'vœlbn̩/ **1** *tr. V.* curve; arch ‹brows, shoulders›; cup ‹hand›; bend ‹metal›; vault, arch ‹roof, ceiling›; **eine gewölbte Decke** a vaulted ceiling; **die Brust ~:** swell out one's chest. **2** *refl. V.* curve; ‹sky, bridge, ceiling› arch; ‹chest› swell; ‹stomach, muscles› bulge; ‹metal› bend; **eine gewölbte Stirn** a domed forehead

**Wölbung** *die;* **~, ~en** curve; (*einer Decke, des Himmels*) arch; vault; (*von Augenbrauen*) arch; (*eines Bauches, Muskels*) bulge

**Wolf** /vɔlf/ *der;* **~[e]s, Wölfe** /'vœlfə/ **A** wolf; **ein ~ im Schafspelz sein** (*fig.*) be a wolf in sheep's clothing; **mit den Wölfen heulen** (*fig. ugs.*) run with the pack; **unter die Wölfe geraten** (*fig.*) be ruthlessly exploited; **B** (*ugs.: Fleisch~*) mincer; **jmdn. durch den ~ drehen** (*fig. salopp*) put sb. through the mill; **C** (*volkst.: Wundsein*) intertrigo *no art.* (*Med.*); *soreness caused by the rubbing of areas of the skin against each*

*old spelling (see note on page 1707)

*other;* **sich** (*Dat.*) **einen ~ laufen** make oneself sore between the legs through walking too much

**Wölfin** /ˈvœlfɪn/ *die;* ~, **~nen** [wolf] bitch

**wölfisch** *Adj.* wolfish; ravenous ‹hunger›

**Wölfling** /ˈvœlflɪŋ/ *der;* **~s, ~e** Cub

**Wolfram** /ˈvɔlfram/ *das;* **~s** (*Chemie*) tungsten

**Wolfs-: ~hund** *der* (*volkst.*) Alsatian [dog]; **Irischer ~hund** Irish wolfhound; **~hunger** *der* (*ugs.*) ravenous hunger; **ich habe einen ~hunger!** I'm ravenous!; **~kind** *das* (*Myth.*) wolf child; **~milch** *die* (*Bot.*) spurge; **~rachen** *der* (*volkst.*) cleft palate; **~spinne** *die* wolf spider

**Wolga** /ˈvɔlga/ *die;* ~ ▶306 Volga

**Wölkchen** /ˈvœlkçən/ *das;* **~s, ~:** small cloud

**Wolke** /ˈvɔlkə/ *die;* ~, **~n** (*auch Mineral.*) cloud; **'ne ~ sein** (*berlin. salopp*) be fantastic (*coll.*); **auf ~n** *od.* **in den ~n schweben** (*fig.*) have one's head in the clouds; **aus allen ~n fallen** (*fig. ugs.*) be completely stunned; **eine ~ von Tüll** billows of tulle

**wolken-, Wolken-: ~bank** *die; Pl.* **~bänke** bank of cloud; **~bildung** *die* formation of cloud; **es wird zu stärkerer ~bildung kommen** it will become very cloudy *or* overcast; **~bruch** *der* cloudburst; **~bruch·artig** *Adj.* torrential; **~decke** *die* [unbroken] cloud *no indef. art.;* **die ~decke riss auf** the clouds broke; **~feld** *das* (*Met.*) cloud field; **~fetzen** *der* wisp of cloud; **~kratzer** *der* skyscraper; **~kuckucks·heim** *das* cloud cuckoo land; **im ~kuckucksheim** in cloud cuckoo land; **~los** *Adj.* cloudless; **~schleier** *der* veil of cloud; **~verhangen** *Adj.* overcast; **~wand** *die* wall of cloud

**wolkig** *Adj.* **A** (*auch Fot., Chemie, Mineral.*) cloudy; **B** (*unklar, verschwommen*) vague; vague, hazy ‹idea, concept›

**Woll·decke** *die* [woollen] blanket

**Wolle** /ˈvɔlə/ *die;* ~, **~n** **A** wool; (*fig.: Haar*) hair; **in der ~ gefärbt** dyed-in-the-wool; **sich in die ~ kriegen** (*fig. ugs.*) quarrel (**wegen** over); **sich in der ~ haben** *od.* **liegen** (*fig. ugs.*) be at loggerheads; **B** (*Jägerspr.*) hair; (*von Hasen, Kaninchen*) fur

**wollen**[1] *Adj.* woollen

**wollen**[2] **1** *unr. Modalverb; 2. Part.* ~ **A** **etw. tun ~** (*den Wunsch haben, etw. zu tun*) want to do sth.; (*die Absicht haben, etw. zu tun*) be going to do sth.; **wir wollten gerade gehen** we were just about to go; **das Buch habe ich immer lesen ~:** I've always wanted to read that book; **ich will lieber zu Hause bleiben** I'd rather stay at home; **was will man da machen?** (*ugs.*) what can you do?; **ohne es zu ~:** without intending to; **ich wollte Sie fragen, ob ...** I wanted to ask you if ...; **wenn Sie bitte Platz nehmen ~:** would you like to take a seat/take your seats?; **~ Sie mich entschuldigen?** would you excuse me?; **wenn ich mich darum auch noch kümmern wollte, ...** if I were to see to that as well, then ...; **na gut, ich will [mal] nicht so sein** (*ugs.*) all right, I don't want to be awkward; **dann will ich nichts gesagt haben** (*ugs.*) I take it all back; **das will ich meinen!** (*ugs.*) I absolutely agree; **wir ~ sehen** we'll see; **B** (*in Aufforderungen*) **man wolle bitte darauf achten, dass ...** please note that ...; **wollt ihr Ruhe geben/damit aufhören!** (*ugs.*) will you be quiet/stop that!; **~ Sie bitte so freundlich sein und das heute noch erledigen** would you be so kind as to do it today; **C** (*in Bezug auf bezweifelte Behauptungen*) **er will ein Dichter sein** he claims to be a poet; **sie will es [nicht] gesehen haben** she claims [not] to have seen it; **D** (*sich in der gewünschten Weise verhalten*) **die Wunde will nicht heilen** the wound [just] won't heal; **der Motor wollte nicht anspringen** the engine wouldn't start; **es will nicht gelingen** it just won't work; **es will mir nicht einleuchten, dass ...** I can't really see that ...; **E** (*müssen*) **etw. will getan sein** sth. needs *or* (*coll.*) has got to be done; **das will gelernt sein** it has to be learned; **F** (*einen bestimmten Zweck, eine bestimmte Funktion haben*) be intended to; **die Aktion will die Leute über ... aufklären** the purpose of the campaign is to inform people about ...; **G das will nichts heißen/nicht viel sagen** that doesn't mean anything/much.

**2** *unr. itr. V.* **A du musst nur ~, dann geht es auch** you only have to want to enough *or* have the will, then it's possible; **ob du willst oder nicht** whether you want to or not; **ganz wie du willst** just as you like; **wenn du willst, könnten wir ...** if you want [to], we could ...; **du kannst es halten, wie du willst** you can do just as you like; **das ist, wenn man so will, ...** that is, if you like, ...; **[na] dann ~ wir mal!** (*ugs.*) [right,] let's get started!; **B** (*ugs.: irgendwohin zu gehen wünschen*) **ich will nach Hause/ans Meer** I want to go home/to go to the seaside; **ich will hier raus** I want to get out of here; **zu wem ~ Sie?** whom do you want to see?; **er wollte zum Theater** he wanted to become an actor; **C** *verneint* (*ugs.: funktionieren*) **der Motor will nicht** the engine won't go; **seine Beine/Gelenke/Augen ~ nicht mehr** his legs/joints/eyes just aren't up to it any more.

**3** *unr. tr. V.* **A** want; **das wollte ich nicht** I didn't mean to do that; **das habe ich nicht gewollt** I never meant that to happen; **~, dass jmd. etw. tut** want sb. to do sth.; **er will nicht, dass du ihm hilfst** he doesn't want you to help him; **er wollte nur euer Bestes** he only wanted what's best for you; **er will es nicht anders** he wouldn't have it any other way; **da ist nichts [mehr] zu ~** (*ugs.*) there's nothing we/you *etc.* can do about it; **was du nicht willst, dass man dir tu, das füg auch keinem anderen zu** (*Spr.*) do as you would be done by (*prov.*); **ich wollte, er wäre hier/es wäre vorbei** I wish he were here/it were over; **B** (*ugs.: zum Gedeihen brauchen*) need; **C** (*ugs.: schaden*) **jmdm. nichts ~ können** be unable to harm sb.; **was kann sie mir schon ~?** what can she do to me?

**Woll·gras** *das* cotton grass

**wollig** *Adj.* woolly

**Woll-: ~jacke** *die* woollen cardigan; **~kleid** *das* woollen dress; **~knäuel** *das* ball of wool; **~sachen** *Pl.* woollen things; woollies (*coll.*); **~socke** *die* woollen sock; **~stoff** *der* woollen cloth; **~strumpf** *der* woollen stocking; (*Kniestrumpf*) woollen sock

**Wollust** /ˈvɔlʊst/ *die;* ~, **Wollüste** /ˈvɔlʏstə/ (*geh.*) lust; (*Sinnlichkeit*) sensuality; (*großes Vergnügen*) delight; **etw. mit wahrer ~ tun** take great delight in doing sth.

**wollüstig** /ˈvɔlʏstɪç/ (*geh.*) **1** *Adj.* lustful; (*sinnlich*) sensual. **2** *Adj.* lustfully; (*sinnlich*) sensually

**wo·mit** *Adv.* **A** (*interrogativ*) **~ schreibst du?** what do you write with?; (*more formal*) with what do you write?; **~ habe ich das verdient?** what have I done to deserve that?; **B** (*relativisch*) **~ du schreibst** which *or* that you write with; (*more formal*) with which you write; **~ ich nicht sagen will, dass ...** by which I don't mean to say that ...; **~ er nicht gerechnet hatte, war ...** what he had not reckoned with was ...; **~ du es auch machst, ...** whatever you do it with ...; ⇒ *auch* **wobei** *NB*

**wo·möglich** *Adv.* possibly

**wo·nach** *Adv.* **A** (*interrogativ*) after what; what ... after; **~ suchst du?** what are you looking for?; **~ riecht es?** what does it smell of?; **~ richtet ihr euch?** what do you go by?; **~ verlangte er?** what did he ask for?; **B** (*relativisch*) after which; which ... after; **alles, ~ er verlangte** all he asked for; **etwas, ~ sie sich sehnte** something she longed for; **eine Vorschrift, ~ ...** a regulation according to which ...; ⇒ *auch* **wobei** *NB*

**Wonne** /ˈvɔnə/ *die;* ~, **~n** (*geh.*) bliss *no pl.;* ecstasy; (*etw., was Freude macht*) joy; delight; **es war eine ~, ihr zuzuhören** she was a joy *or* delight to listen to; **das Kind ist ihre ganze ~:** the child is her great joy; **es ist eine wahre ~:** it's sheer delight; **Würdest du helfen? — Aber mit ~!** (*scherzh.*) Would you help? — Of course, I'd be delighted!

**Wonne-: ~monat** (*geh.*), **~mond** (*veralt.*) *der* May *no art.;* **im ~monat [Mai]** in the merry month of May; **~proppen** *der* (*ugs. scherzh.*) chubby cherub

**wonnig** *Adj.* sweet

**woran** /voˈran/ *Adv.* **A** (*interrogativ*) **~ hast du dich verletzt?** what did you hurt yourself on?; **~ hat sie sich gelehnt?** what did she lean against?; **man weiß nicht, ~ man ist** you don't know where you are; **~ ist sie gestorben?** what did she die of?; **~ denkst du?** what are you thinking of?; **B** (*relativisch*) **nichts, ~ man sich verletzen/lehnen könnte** nothing one could hurst oneself on/one could lean against; **alles, ~ er sich erinnern konnte** everything he could remember

**worauf** /voˈrauf/ **A** (*interrogativ*) **~ sitzt er?** what is he sitting on?; **~ wartest du?** what are you waiting for?; **~ will er hinaus?** what is he getting at?; **B** (*relativisch*) **es gab nichts, ~ er sich hätte setzen können** there was nothing for him to sit on; **etwas, ~ ich schreiben kann** something to write on; **etwas, ~ man sich verlassen kann** something one can rely on; **etwas, ~ ich Sie hinweisen sollte, ist ...** something I ought to point out to you is ...; **das Einzige, ~ es jetzt ankommt** the only thing that matters now; **es gab nichts, ~ er sich hätte freuen können** there was nothing for him to look forward to; **C** (*relativisch: ~hin*) whereupon

**worauf·hin** *Adv.* **A** (*interrogativ*) **~ hat er das getan?** what made him do it?; what was the cause of his doing it?; **B** (*relativisch*) whereupon

**woraus** /voˈraus/ *Adv.* **A** (*interrogativ*) **~ ist das Zitat?** where is the quotation from?; **~ trinken wir den Wein?** what shall we drink the wine from?; **~ ist das Gewebe?** what is the fabric made of?; **~ schließt du das?** what do you infer that from?; **B** (*relativisch*) **es gab nichts, ~ wir den Wein hätten trinken können** there was nothing for us to drink the wine out of; **es gab nichts, ~ sie Werkzeuge machen konnten** there was nothing for them to make tools from; **..., ~ ich schließe, dass ...** ... from which I conclude that ...

**worden** /ˈvɔrdn̩/ *2. Part. v.* **werden** 2

**worein** /voˈrain/ *Adv.* **A** (*interrogativ*) in what; what ... in; **B** (*relativisch*) in which; which ... in; **..., ~ sie sich schickte** ..., to which she resigned herself; ..., which she resigned herself to

**worin** /voˈrɪn/ *Adv.* **A** (*interrogativ*) in what; what ... in; **~ willst du es verschicken?** what do you want to send it in?; **ich weiß nicht, ~ der Unterschied liegt** I don't know what the difference is; **B** (*relativisch*) in which; which ... in; **..., ~ ich mit dir übereinstimme** ..., which I agree with you on

**Work·shop** /ˈwəːkʃɔp/ *der;* **~s, ~s** workshop

**World·cup** /ˈwəːldkʌp/ *der* (*Sport*) World Cup

**Wort** /vɔrt/ *das;* **~[e]s, Wörter** /ˈvœrtɐ/ *od.* **~e** **A** *Pl.* **Wörter**, *auch:* **~e** word; **~ für ~:** word for word; **DM 1 000 (in ~en: tausend)** DM 1,000 (in words: one thousand); **in des ~es wahrster Bedeutung, im wahrsten Sinne des ~es** in the truest sense of the word; **Liebe ist ein großes ~:** love is a big word; **das treffende** *od.* **passende ~:** the right word; **B** *Pl.* **~e** (*Äußerung*) word; **zwischen uns ist kein böses ~ gefallen** not a harsh word has passed between us; **das ist das erste ~, das ich [davon] höre** that's the first I've heard of it; **mir fehlen die ~e** I'm lost for words; **davon ist kein ~ wahr** not a word of it is true; **darüber ist kein ~ gefallen** not a word was said about it; **spar dir deine ~e!** don't waste your breath!; **in ~ und Tat** in word and deed; **eine Sprache in ~ und Schrift beherrschen** have a written and

W

spoken command of a language; **das ~ an jmdn. richten** address sb.; **ein paar ~e sprechen** say a few words; **ein ~ mit jmdm. sprechen** have a word with sb.; **bei ihm ist jedes zweite ~ Geld** he's always talking about money; **nicht viele ~e machen** not beat about the bush; **ich verstehe kein ~:** I don't understand a word [of it]; **auf ein ~!** (*veralt.*) can I have a word with you?; **auf jmds. ~e hören** listen to what sb. says; **etw. in ~e fassen** put sth. into words; **mit einem ~:** in a word; **mit anderen ~en** in other words; **ich glaube dir aufs ~:** I can well believe it; **jmdn. [nicht] zu ~ kommen lassen** [not] let sb. get a word in; **kein ~ mehr!** not another word!; **etw. mit keinem ~ erwähnen** not say a word about sth.; not mention sth. at all; **man verstand sein eigenes ~ nicht** you could not hear yourself speak; **die ~e gut zu setzen wissen** (*geh.*) have a way with words; **jmdm. aufs ~ folgen** *od.* **gehorchen** obey sb.'s every word; **dein ~ in Gottes Ohr!** let's hope you're right!; **ein ~ gab das andere** one thing led to another; **hast du [da noch] ~e?** what do you say to that?; **das ist das letzte/mein letztes ~:** that's the/my last word on the matter; **[immer] das letzte ~ haben wollen/müssen** want to have/have to have the last word; **Dr. Meyer hat das ~:** it's Dr Meyer's turn to speak; **das ~ ergreifen** *od.* **nehmen** start to speak; **das ~ führen** be the main speaker; **das große ~ haben** *od.* **führen** talk big; **jmdm. das ~ geben** *od.* **erteilen/entziehen** call upon sb. to speak/to finish speaking; **jmdm. das ~ verbieten** forbid sb. to speak; **einer Sache das ~ reden** (*geh.*) speak out in favour of sth.; **für jmdn. ein [gutes] ~ einlegen** put in a [good] word for sb.; **jmdm. das ~ aus dem Munde nehmen** take the words out of sb.'s mouth; **jmdm. das ~ im Munde herumdrehen** twist sb.'s words; **kein ~/kein weiteres ~ über etw.** (*Akk.*) **verlieren** not spend time discussing sth./not say another word about sth.; **jmdm. ins ~ fallen** interrupt sb.; **ums ~ bitten** ask to speak; **sich zu ~ melden** indicate one's wish to speak; Ⓒ *Pl.* **~e** (*Spruch*) saying; (*Zitat*) quotation; **geflügelte ~e** well-known sayings and quotations; **das bekannte ~ Schillers** the well-known quotation from Schiller; Ⓓ *Pl.* **~e** (*geh.: Text*) words *pl.*; **in ~ und Bild** in words and pictures; **das geschriebene/gedruckte ~:** the written/printed word; Ⓔ *Pl.* **~e** (*Versprechen*) word; **[sein] ~ halten** keep one's word; **sein ~ brechen** break one's word; **jmdm. sein ~ [auf etw.** (*Akk.*)**] geben** give sb. one's word [on sth.]; **auf mein ~!** I give you my word; **jmdn. beim ~ nehmen** take sb. at his/her word; **[bei jmdm.] im ~ sein** have made a promise [to sb.]; Ⓕ (*christl. Rel., Theol.*) Word

**wort-, Wort-: ~art** *die* (*Sprachw.*) part of speech; **~bedeutung** *die* word meaning; meaning of a/the word; **~bildung** *die* (*Sprachw.*) word formation; **~bruch** *der* breaking one's word *no art.*; **~brüchig** *Adj.* **~brüchig werden** break one's word

**Wörtchen** /'vœrtçən/ *das;* **~s, ~:** little word; **noch ein ~ mit jmdm. zu reden haben** (*ugs.*) have a bone to pick with sb.; **[bei** *od.* **in etw.** (*Dat.*)**] ein ~ mitzureden haben** (*ugs.*) have some say [in sth.]

**Wörter-: ~buch** *das* dictionary; **~verzeichnis** *das* word index

**wort-, Wort-: ~familie** *die* (*Sprachw.*) word family; **~feld** *das* (*Sprachw.*) word field; **~fetzen** *Pl.* scraps of conversation; **~forschung** *die* lexicology *no art.*; **~führer** *der*, **~führerin** *die* spokesman/spokeswoman; spokesperson; **sich zum ~führer einer Gruppe/Sache machen** make oneself the spokesman of a group/cause; **~gefecht** *das* battle of words; **~geklingel** *das* (*abwertend*) fine-sounding verbiage; **~geplänkel** *das* banter *no indef. art;* **~geschichte** *die* etymology *no art.;* **~getreu** ❶ *Adj.* word-for-word; ❷ *adv.* word for word; **~gewaltig** ❶ *Adj.* powerfully eloquent; ❷ *adv.* with powerful eloquence; **~gewandt** ❶ *Adj.* eloquent; ❷ *adv.* eloquently; **~gottes·dienst** *der* (*christl. Kirche*): *service centred on the sermon and readings from the Scriptures;* **~gut** *das* vocabulary; **~hülse** *die* (*abwertend*) [empty] cliché; **~inhalt** *der* (*Sprachw.*) word meaning; meaning of a/the word; **~karg** ❶ *Adj.* taciturn ‹person›; laconic ‹reply, greeting, etc.›; **ein ~karger Mann** a man of few words; ❷ *adv.* taciturnly; ‹reply, greet, etc.› laconically; **~kargheit** *die* ⇨ **~karg:** taciturnity; laconicism; **~klauberei** /-klau bə'rai/ *die;* **~~, ~~en** quibbling; **solche ~klaubereien ändern nichts an der Tatsache, dass ...** such quibbles do not alter the fact that ...; **~laut** *der* wording; **im [vollen] ~laut** verbatim

**Wörtlein** *das;* **~s, ~** ⇨ **Wörtchen**

**wörtlich** /'vœrtlɪç/ ❶ *Adj.* Ⓐ (*wortgetreu*) word-for-word; ⇨ *auch* **Rede** E; Ⓑ (*der eigentlichen Bedeutung entsprechend*) literal. ❷ *adv.* Ⓐ (*wortgetreu*) word-for-word; ‹copy, repeat› verbatim, word-for-word; **das hat sie ~ gesagt** those were her very words; Ⓑ (*der eigentlichen Bedeutung entsprechend*) literally

**wort-, Wort-: ~los** ❶ *Adj.* silent; wordless; unspoken ‹agreement, understanding›; ❷ *adv.* without saying a word; **~meldung** *die:* **gibt es noch ~meldungen?** does anyone else wish to speak?; **es liegen keine weiteren ~meldungen vor** no one else wishes to speak; **~reich** ❶ *Adj.* Ⓐ (*mit vielen ~en*) verbose; Ⓑ (*reich im ~schatz*) **eine ~reiche Sprache** a language with a rich vocabulary; ❷ *adv.* (*mit vielen ~en*) verbosely; ‹apologize, thank› profusely; **~schatz** *der* vocabulary; **~schöpfung** *die* Ⓐ word-coining *no art.;* Ⓑ (**~**) neologism; new coinage; **~schwall** *der* torrent of words; **~sinn** *der* sense of a word/the word[s]; **~spiel** *das* play on words; (*mit ähnlich klingenden Wörtern*) pun; play on words; **~stamm** *der* (*Sprachw.*) stem of a/the word; **~stellung** *die* (*Sprachw.*) word order; **~streit** *der* ⇨ **~gefecht**; **~ungetüm** *das* overlong monstrosity of a word; **~wahl** *die* choice of word; **~wechsel** *der* exchange of words; **mit jmdm. einen ~wechsel haben** exchange words with sb.; **~witz** *der* pun; **~wörtlich** ❶ *Adj.* word-for-word; ❷ *adv.* word for word; **etw. ~wörtlich nehmen** take sth. literally

**wor·über** *Adv.* Ⓐ (*interrogativ*) over what ...; what ... over; **~ bist du gestolpert?** what did you trip over?; **~ lachst du?** what are you laughing about?; Ⓑ (*relativisch*) over which; which ... over; **es gibt nichts, ~ wir sprechen könnten** we have nothing to talk about

**worum** *Adv.* Ⓐ (*interrogativ*) around what; what ... around; **~ bat er?** what did he ask for?; **~ geht es denn?** what is it about then?; Ⓑ (*relativisch*) around which; which ... around; **alles, ~ er bat** everything he asked for

**worunter** *Adv.* Ⓐ (*interrogativ*) under what; what ... under; **~ leidet er?** what is he suffering from?; Ⓑ (*relativisch*) under which; which ... under; **etwas, ~ er besonders leidet, ist ...** something he particularly suffers from is ...

**wo·selbst** *Adv.* (*veralt.*) where

**Wotan** /'vo:tan/ (*der*) Wotan

**wo·von** *Adv.* Ⓐ (*interrogativ*) from where; where ... from; **~ soll er leben?** what is he supposed to live on?; **~ redest du?** what are you talking about?; **~ ist er müde/krank?** what has made him tired/ill?; Ⓑ (*relativisch*) from which; which ... from; **das, ~ er sprach** what he was talking about; ⇨ *auch* **wobei** *NB*

**wo·vor** *Adv.* Ⓐ (*interrogativ*) in front of what; what ... in front of; **~ stand er?** what was he standing in front of?; **~ hast du Angst?** what are you afraid of?; Ⓑ (*relativisch*) in front of which; which ... in front of; **das, ~ er sie gewarnt hatte** what he had warned her about; **das einzige, ~ ich Angst habe** the only thing I am afraid of; ⇨ *auch* **wobei** *NB*

**wo·zu** *Adv.* Ⓐ (*interrogativ*) to what; what ... to; (*wofür*) what ... for; **~ brauchst du das Geld?** what do you need the money for?; **~ hast du dich entschlossen?** what have you decided [on]?; **~ hat sie ihn gezwungen?** what did she force him to do?; **~ diese Umstände?** why all this fuss?; **~ denn?** (*zu welchem Zweck*) what for?; (*als Ausdruck der Ablehnung*) why should I/you *etc.?;* **weißt du, ~ das gut sein soll?** do you know what the point of it is supposed to be?; Ⓑ (*relativisch*) **dann habe ich gebügelt, ~ ich keine Lust hatte** then I did some ironing, which I had no inclination to do; **~ du dich auch entschließt** whatever you decide on; **er will studieren, ~ er allerdings das Abitur braucht** he wants to go to university but for that he needs the Abitur; ⇨ *auch* **wobei** *NB*

**Wrack** /vrak/ *das;* **~[e]s, ~s** *od.* **~e** wreck; (*fig.: Mensch*) [physical] wreck; **ein seelisches/nervöses ~** (*fig.*) a mental/nervous wreck

**wrang** /vraŋ/ *1. und 3. Pers. Sg. Prät. v.* **wringen**

**Wrasen** /'vra:zn̩/ *der;* **~s, ~** (*nordd.*) steam

**wringen** /'vrɪŋən/ *unr. tr. V.* (*bes. nordd.*) wring

**WS** *Abk.* **Wintersemester**

**WSV** *Abk.* **Winterschlussverkauf**

**WSW** *Abk.* **▶ 400 | Westsüdwest[en]** WSW

**Wucher** /'vu:xɐ/ *der;* **~s** profiteering; (*beim Verleihen von Geld*) usury; **18 Prozent Zinsen: das ist ja ~!** 18 per cent interest: that's extortionate!; **[mit etw.] ~ treiben** profiteer [on sth.]; (*beim Verleihen von Geld*) charge an extortionate rate/extortionate rates of interest [on sth.]

**Wucher·blume** *die* chrysanthemum

**Wucherer** *der;* **~s, ~, Wucherin** *die;* **~, ~nen** profiteer; (*beim Verleihen von Geld*) usurer

**wuchern** *itr. V.* Ⓐ *auch mit sein* (*stark wachsen*) ‹plants, weeds, etc.› proliferate, run wild; (*fig.*) be rampant; **eine ~de Geschwulst** a cancerous tumour; **krebsartig ~** (*fig.*) grow like a cancer; **eine ~de Fantasie** (*fig.*) an imagination that runs wild; Ⓑ (*Wucher treiben*) **[mit etw.] ~:** profiteer [on sth.]; (*beim Verleihen von Geld*) lend [sth.] at extortionate interest rates

**Wucher·preis** *der* extortionate price

**Wucherung** *die;* **~, ~en** growth

**Wucher·zins** *der; Pl.* **~en** extortionate rate of interest

**wuchs** /vu:ks/ *1. u. 3. Pers. Sg. Prät. v.* **wachsen**

**Wuchs** *der;* **~es** Ⓐ (*Wachstum*) growth; Ⓑ (*Gestalt*) stature; **klein/groß von ~ sein** ‹person› be small/tall in stature

**Wucht** /vʊxt/ *die;* **~** Ⓐ force; (*von Schlägen*) power; weight; **mit voller ~:** with full force; **mit voller ~ zuschlagen** hit with all one's might; Ⓑ *in* **eine ~ sein** (*salopp*) be absolutely fantastic (*coll.*); Ⓒ (*bes. ostmd.: Schläge*) beating; (*als Strafe für Kind*) hiding (*coll.*); beating

**wuchten** *tr. V.* heave

**wuchtig** ❶ *Adj.* Ⓐ (*voller Wucht*) powerful; mighty; Ⓑ (*schwer, massig*) massive. ❷ *adv.* powerfully

**Wühl·arbeit** *die* (*fig.*) subversive activities *pl.;* subversion

**wühlen** /'vy:lən/ ❶ *itr. V.* Ⓐ (*graben*) dig; (*mit der Schnauze, dem Schnabel*) root (**nach** for); ‹mole› tunnel, burrow; **er wühlte in ihren Locken** he tousled her hair; Ⓑ (*ugs.: suchen*) rummage [around] (**nach** for); Ⓒ (*fig.: Wühlarbeit leisten*) engage in subversive activities *or* subversion (**gegen** against); Ⓓ (*ugs.: schwer arbeiten*) graft (*Brit. coll.*); slave away. ❷ *tr. V.* burrow; tunnel out ‹burrow›. ❸ *refl. V.* **sich in etw.** (*Akk.*)**/durch etw. ~:** burrow into/through sth.; **die Autos wühlten sich durch den Schlamm** the cars churned their way through the mud

**Wühler** *der;* **~s, ~** Ⓐ (*Zool.*) cricetine; Ⓑ (*fig.: Subversiver*) subversive; Ⓒ (*ugs.: fleißig Arbeitender*) grafter (*Brit. coll.*)

*old spelling (see note on page 1707)

W

**Wühlerin** *die;* ~, **~nen** ⇒ **Wühler** B, C

**Wühl-: ~maus** *die* one of the Microtinae (*the voles and lemmings*); (*Kleine ~maus*) European pine vole; (*Schermaus*) European water vole; **~tisch** *der* (*ugs.*) bargain counter

**Wulst** /vʊlst/ *der;* **~[e]s, Wülste** /ˈvʏlstə/ *od.* **~e** Ⓐ bulge; (*Fett~*) roll of fat; (*an einer Flasche, einem Reifen*) bead; Ⓑ (*Heraldik*) wreath; Ⓒ (*Archit.*) torus

**wulstig** *Adj.* bulging; thick ‹lips›

**wumm** /vʊm/ *Interj.* boom

**wummern** /ˈvʊmɐn/ *itr. V.* ‹machine, engine› hum; **mit den Fäusten gegen etw. ~:** drum one's fists against sth.

**wund** /vʊnt/ *Adj.* ▶ 474 sore; **sich ~ laufen** walk until one's feet are sore; **sich ~ liegen** get bedsores (**an** + *Dat.* on); **sich** (*Dat.*) **den Rücken ~ liegen** get bedsores on one's back; **ich habe mir die Finger ~ geschrieben** (*ugs.*) I've worn my fingers to the bone with all that writing; ⇒ *auch* **Fuß** B; **Punkt** D; **reiben** 1 A

**Wund-: ~arzt** *der* (*hist.*) surgeon; **~brand** *der* ▶ 474 (*Med.*) gangrene

**Wunde** *die;* ~, **~n** wound; **alte ~n wieder aufreißen** (*fig.*) open up old wounds; **der Krieg hat dem Land tiefe ~n geschlagen** (*fig.*) the war has left deep scars on the country; ⇒ *auch* **Salz**

***wunder, Wunder**[1] (*ugs.*) *in* (*ugs.*) **er denkt, er sei ~ wer** he thinks he's really something; **sie glaubt, sie sei ~ wie klug** she thinks she's ever so *or* oh so clever (*coll.*); **er glaubt, ~ was geleistet zu haben** he thinks he's achieved something fantastic (*coll.*); **ich dachte, ~ was es da alles zu sehen gibt** I thought there would be all sorts of fantastic things to see; **er bildet sich ~ was darauf ein** he's terribly pleased with himself about it (*coll.*)

**Wunder**[2] *das;* **~s,** ~ Ⓐ miracle; **~ tun** work *or* perform miracles; **~ wirken** (*fig. ugs.*) work wonders; **o ~!** wonders will never cease!; **ein/kein ~ sein** (*ugs.*) be a/no wonder; **was ~, wenn ...?** small *or* no wonder that ...; **er wird sein blaues ~ erleben** (*ugs.*) he's in for a nasty shock; Ⓑ (*etw. Außergewöhnliches, Erstaunliches*) wonder; **ein ~ an ...** (*Dat.*) a miracle of ...; **ein technisches ~:** a technological marvel

**wunderbar** ❶ *Adj.* Ⓐ (*übernatürlich erscheinend*) miraculous; **das grenzt ans Wunderbare** it's bordering on the miraculous; **auf ~e Weise** miraculously; Ⓑ (*sehr schön, herrlich*) wonderful; marvellous. ❷ *adv.* Ⓐ (*sehr schön, herrlich*) wonderfully; marvellously; Ⓑ (*ugs.: sehr*) wonderfully

**wunder-, Wunder-: ~ding** *das; Pl.* **~~e** amazing thing; (*ugs.: Gegenstand*) wonder; **~doktor** *der* (*spött.*) miracle-working doctor; **~glaube** *der* belief in miracles; **~gläubig** *Adj.* ‹person› who believes in miracles; **~gläubig sein** believe in miracles; **~heiler** *der;* **~~s,** ~~, **~heilerin** *die;* ~~, **~~nen** faith healer; **~heilung** *die* miraculous cure; **~hübsch** ❶ *Adj.* wonderfully pretty; ❷ *adv.* quite beautifully; **~kerze** *die* sparkler; **~kind** *das* child prodigy; **~knabe** *der* boy prodigy; **~lampe** *die* magic lamp; **~land** *das* wonderland

**wunderlich** ❶ *Adj.* strange; odd. ❷ *adv.* strangely; oddly

**Wunderlichkeit** *die;* ~, **~en** Ⓐ strangeness; oddness; Ⓑ (*etwas Wunderliches*) oddity

**Wunder·mittel** *das* miracle cure (**gegen** for)

**wundern** ❶ *tr. V.* surprise; **mich wundert** *od.* **es wundert mich, dass ...** I'm surprised that ...; **es würde** *od.* **sollte mich [nicht] ~, wenn ...** I should [not] be surprised *or* it would [not] surprise me if ... ❷ *refl. V.* **sich über jmdn./etw. ~:** be surprised at sb./sth.; **du wirst dich [noch mal] ~** (*ugs.*) you're in for a shock; you've got a surprise in store; **ich muss mich doch sehr über dich ~:** I really am surprised at you

**wunder|nehmen** *unr. tr. V.* (*geh.*) **etw. nimmt jmdn. wunder** sth. surprises sb.

**wunders** ⇒ **Wunder**[1]

**wundersam** (*geh.*) ❶ *Adj.* strange. ❷ *adv.* **ihr wurde ~ zumute** she had a strange feeling

**wunder-, Wunder-: ~schön** ❶ *Adj.* simply beautiful; (*herrlich*) simply wonderful; ❷ *adv.* quite beautifully; (*einwandfrei*) perfectly; **~tat** *die* miracle; **~täter** *der,* **~täterin** *die* miracle worker; **~tätig** *Adj.* miraculous; **~tier** *das* strange and wonderful animal; **~tüte** *die* surprise packet; **~voll** ❶ *Adj.* wonderful; marvellous; ❷ *adv.* wonderfully; marvellously; **~waffe** *die* superweapon; **~welt** *die* wonderworld; **~werk** *das* marvel

**wund-, Wund-: ~fieber** *das* ▶ 474 (*Med.*) traumatic fever; wound fever; **~infektion** *die* ▶ 474 (*Med.*) wound infection; ***~|liegen** ⇒ **wund**; **~mal** *das; Pl.* **~~e** (*bes. Rel.*) scar; **die ~male Christi** Christ's stigmata; **~pflaster** *das* sticking plaster; **~rand** *der* (*Med.*) edge of a/the wound; **~rose** *die* ▶ 474 (*Med.*) St Anthony's fire; erysipelas (*Med.*); **~sein** *das* ▶ 474 soreness; **~starrkrampf** *der* ▶ 474 (*Med.*) tetanus

**Wunsch** /vʊnʃ/ *der;* **~[e]s, Wünsche** /ˈvʏnʃə/ Ⓐ wish (**nach** to have); (*Hoffen, Sehnen*) desire (**nach** for); **sich** (*Dat.*) **einen ~ erfüllen/versagen** grant/deny oneself something one wants; **haben Sie [sonst] noch einen ~?** will there be anything else?; **jmds. ~ und Wille sein** be something sb. most earnestly desires; **auf jmds. ~:** at sb.'s wish; **auf allgemeinen ~ [hin]** in response to popular demand; **alles geht** *od.* **läuft nach ~:** everything's going as we want/he wants *etc.*; **dein ~ ist mir Befehl** (*scherzh.*) your wish is my command; **der ~ ist der Vater des Gedankens** (*scherzh.*) the wish is father to the thought; ⇒ *auch* **fromm** C; Ⓑ *Pl.* ▶ 369 (*zu bestimmten Anlässen*) wishes; **mit den besten/herzlichsten Wünschen** with best/warmest wishes; **beste Wünsche zum Geburtstag** many happy returns of the day

**wünschbar** *Adj.* (*bes. schweiz.*) desirable

**Wunsch-: ~bild** *das* desired ideal; **~denken** *das* wishful thinking

**Wünschel-** /ˈvʏnʃl̩-/: **~rute** *die* divining rod; **~rutengänger** *der,* **~rutengängerin** *die* diviner

**wünschen** /ˈvʏnʃn̩/ *tr. V.* Ⓐ **sich** (*Dat.*) **etw. ~:** want sth.; (*im Stillen*) wish for sth.; **jmdm. Erfolg/nichts Gutes/den Tod ~:** wish sb. success/no good/wish sb. dead; **er wünschte sich** (*Dat.*) **ein Rad zum Geburtstag** he asked for a cycle for his birthday; **du darfst dir [von mir] etwas ~:** you can have a present [from me] — what would you like?; **sich** (*Dat.*) **jmdn. als** *od.* **zum Freund ~:** want to have sb. as a friend; **alles, was du dir nur ~ kannst** everything you could wish for; **er war so, wie man sich** (*Dat.*) **einen Lehrer wünscht** he was just as one would want a teacher to be; **was wünschst du dir?** what would you like?; **ich wünschte, du wärest hier** I wish you were here; **jmdn. weit fort ~:** wish sb. far away; **ich wünschte mich auf eine einsame Insel** I wished I were on a desert island; Ⓑ ▶ 369 (*in formelhaften W~*) wish; **jmdm. alles Gute/frohe Ostern ~:** wish sb. all the best/a happy Easter; **jmdm. gute Nacht ~:** wish *or* bid sb. good night; **sie wünschte ihm gute Besserung** she said she hoped he would soon get better; Ⓒ *auch itr. V.* (*begehren*) want; **was ~ Sie?, Sie ~?** (*von einem Bediensteten gesagt*) yes, madam/sir?; (*von einem Kellner gesagt*) what would you like?; (*von einem Verkäufer gesagt*) can I help you?; **er wünscht, dass du gehst** he wants you to go; **ganz, wie Sie ~:** just as you like; **solange Sie es ~:** as long as you wish *or* like; **die gewünschte Auskunft** the information asked for; **ich wünsche das nicht** I do not wish it; **dein Chef wünscht dich zu sprechen** your boss would like to speak to you; **etw. lässt [viel]/lässt nichts zu ~ übrig** sth. leaves a great deal/nothing to be desired; **es verlief alles wie gewünscht** everything went as we/he *etc.* had wanted

**wünschens·wert** *Adj.* desirable

**wunsch-, Wunsch-: ~form** *die* (*Sprachw.*) ⇒ **Optativ**; **~gegner** *der,* **~gegnerin** *die* (*bes. Sport*) ideal opponent; **~gemäß** ❶ *Adv.* as desired; (*einer Bitte gemäß*) as requested; ❷ *adj.* **die ~gemäße Ausführung eines Auftrags** the performance of a task as desired/requested; **~kind** *das* wanted child; **~konzert** *das* request concert; (*im Rundfunk*) request programme; **~los** ❶ *Adj.* [perfectly] contented; perfect ‹happiness›; ❷ *adv.* **~los glücklich sein** be perfectly contented; **~satz** *der* (*Sprachw.*) optative sentence; **~traum** *der* wishful dream; (*unrealistisch*) pipe dream; **~vorstellung** *die* wishful notion; **~zettel** *der* list of things one would like; (*zum Geburtstag o. Ä.*) list of presents one would like

**wupp** /vʊp,/ **wupp·dich, wupps** *Interj.* (*ugs.*) woomph (*coll.*)

**wurde** /ˈvʊrdə/ *1. u. 3. Pers. Sg. Prät. v.* **werden**

**würde** /ˈvʏrdə/ *1. u. 3. Pers. Sg. Konjunktiv II v.* **werden**

**Würde** *die;* ~, **~n** Ⓐ dignity; **seine ~ bewahren** preserve one's dignity; **sich in seiner ~ verletzt fühlen** feel that one's dignity has been affronted; **etw. mit ~ tragen** bear sth. with dignity; (*scherzh.*) bear up well in spite of sth.; **unter jmds. ~ sein** be beneath sb.'s dignity; **unter aller ~ sein** be beneath contempt; Ⓑ (*Rang*) rank; (*Amt*) office; (*Titel*) title; (*Auszeichnung*) honour; **die ~ eines Professors** the title of professor; **zu höchsten ~n gelangen** attain high office

**würde·los** ❶ *Adj.* undignified; (*schimpflich*) disgraceful. ❷ *adv.* in an undignified way; (*schimpflich*) disgracefully

**Würdelosigkeit** *die;* ~ ⇒ **würdelos**: lack of dignity; disgracefulness

**Würden·träger** *der,* **Würden·trägerin** *die* dignitary

**würde·voll** ❶ *Adj.* dignified. ❷ *adv.* with dignity

**würdig** ❶ *Adj.* Ⓐ (*würdevoll*) dignified; Ⓑ (*wert*) worthy; suitable ‹occasion›; **jmds./einer Sache [nicht] ~ sein** [not] be worthy of sb./sth.; **sich jmds./einer Sache [nicht] ~ erweisen** *od.* **zeigen** prove oneself [not] worthy of sb./sth. ❷ *adv.* Ⓐ (*würdevoll*) with dignity; ‹dressed› in a dignified manner; Ⓑ (*angemessen*) worthily; ‹celebrate› in a/the appropriate manner; **jmdn. ~ zu vertreten wissen** make a worthy deputy for sb.

**würdigen** *tr. V.* Ⓐ (*anerkennen, beachten*) recognize; (*schätzen*) appreciate; (*lobend hervorheben*) acknowledge; **etw. zu ~ wissen** appreciate sth.; Ⓑ (*für wert halten*) **jmdn. einer Sache** (*Gen.*) **~:** deem sb. worthy of sth.; **jmdn. keines Blickes/keiner Antwort ~:** not deign to look at/answer sb.

**Würdigkeit** *die;* ~ Ⓐ (*Würde*) dignity; Ⓑ (*Wert*) worth

**Würdigung** *die;* ~, **~en** ⇒ **würdigen** A: recognition; appreciation; acknowledgement; **in ~ einer Sache** (*Gen.*) in recognition of sth.

**Wurf** /vʊrf/ *der;* **~[e]s, Würfe** /ˈvʏrfə/ Ⓐ throw; (*beim Baseball*) pitch; (*beim Kegeln*) bowl; (*gezielt aufs Tor*) shot; Ⓑ (*das Werfen*) throwing/pitching/bowling; **zum ~ ausholen** draw back one's arm ready to throw; **beim ~:** when throwing/pitching/bowling; Ⓒ (*Zool.*) litter; Ⓓ (*gelungenes Werk*) successful work; success; **mit dieser Erfindung ist ihm ein großer ~ gelungen** this invention has been a great success for him

**Wurf·bahn** *die* trajectory

**Würfel** /ˈvʏrfl̩/ *der;* **~s,** ~ Ⓐ (*auch Math.*) cube; **Gemüse/Fleisch in ~ schneiden** dice vegetables/meat; Ⓑ (*Spiel~*) dice; die (*formal*); **die ~ sind gefallen** (*fig.*) the die is cast

**Würfel·becher** *der* dice cup
**Würfel·muster** *das* check pattern
**würfeln** ❶ *itr. V.* throw the dice; (*mit Würfeln spielen*) play dice; **du bist mit Würfeln dran** it's your turn to throw; **hast du schon gewürfelt?** have you already thrown *or* had your throw?; **um etw. ~:** play dice for sth.; **darum ~, wer anfangen soll** throw a/the dice to see who should start. ❷ *tr. V.* Ⓐ throw; Ⓑ (*in Würfel schneiden*) dice ‹vegetables, meat›
**Würfel-: ~spiel** *das* Ⓐ (*Glücksspiel*) dice; (*einzelne Partie*) game of dice; Ⓑ (*Brettspiel*) dice game; **~zucker** *der* cube sugar; lump sugar
**Wurf-: ~geschoss, *~geschoß** *das* missile; **~kreis** *der* (*Sport*) throwing circle; **~scheibe** *die* discus; **~sendung** *die* ⇒ **Postwurfsendung**; **~speer** *der,* **~spieß** *der* (*hist.*) spear; **~taube** *die* (*Schießsport*) clay pigeon; **~tauben·schießen** *das;* **~~s** (*Schießsport*) clay-pigeon shooting *no art.*
**Würge-: ~engel** *der* (*bes. christl. Rel.*) Angel of Death; **~griff** *der* (*auch fig.*) stranglehold; **~mal** *das; Pl.* **~~e** *od.* **~mäler** strangle *or* strangulation mark
**würgen** /ˈvʏrgn̩/ ❶ *tr. V.* Ⓐ strangle; throttle; (*fig.*) ‹tie, collar› strangle; **~de Angst** (*fig.*) choking fear; Ⓑ (*ugs.: zwängen*) **etw. in etw.** (*Akk.*) **~:** stuff sth. into sth. ❷ *itr. V.* Ⓐ (*Brechreiz haben*) retch; Ⓑ (*mühsam schlucken*) **an etw.** (*Dat.*) **~:** have to force sth. down; ⇒ *auch* **hängen²** 1 D
**Würger** *der;* **~s, ~** Ⓐ strangler; Ⓑ (*Zool.*) shrike
**Würgerin** *die* ⇒ **Würger** A
**Wurm¹** /vʊrm/ *der;* **~[e]s, Würmer** /ˈvʏrmɐ/ worm; (*Made*) maggot; **von Würmern befallen sein** have worms/be maggoty; **da ist** *od.* **sitzt der ~ drin** (*fig. ugs.*) there's something wrong there; **jmdm. die Würmer aus der Nase ziehen** (*fig. ugs.*) get sb. to spill the beans (*fig. sl.*); **den ~** *od.* **Würmer baden** (*ugs. scherzh.*) be fishing
**Wurm²** *das;* **~[e]s, Würmer** (*fam.*) little mite
**wurmen** *tr., auch itr. V.* (*ugs.*) **jmdn. ~:** rankle with sb.; **so was wurmt [einen] schon** that sort of thing rankles
**Wurm·fort·satz** *der* ▶ 471 | (*Anat.*) appendix
**wurmig** *Adj.,* **wurm·stichig** *Adj.* worm-eaten; (*madig*) maggoty
**Wurscht** /vʊrʃt/ (*ugs.*) *in* **jmdm. ist jmd./etw. ~:** sb. doesn't care about sb./sth.; **das ist mir vollkommen** *od.* **völlig ~:** I couldn't care less about that; **ach, mir ist alles ~!** oh, what do I care!
**wurscht·egal** *Adj.* (*ugs.*) ⇒ **wurstegal**
**Wurst** /vʊrst/ *die;* **~, Würste** /ˈvʏrstə/ Ⓐ sausage; **es geht um die ~** (*fig. ugs.*) the crunch has come; **mit der ~ nach der Speckseite** *od.* **dem Schinken werfen** (*fig. ugs.*) use a sprat to catch a mackerel (*fig. coll.*); Ⓑ (*wurstähnliches Gebilde*) roll; **den Teig zu einer ~ formen** roll the dough into a sausage shape; **eine ~ machen** (*fam.*) do a big one (*child lang.*); Ⓒ (*ugs.*) ⇒ **Wurscht**
**Wurst·brot** *das* open sausage sandwich; (*mit Streichwurst*) open meat-spread sandwich; (*zusammengeklappt*) sausage/meat-spread sandwich
**Würstchen** /ˈvʏrstçən/ *das;* **~s, ~** Ⓐ [small] sausage; **Frankfurter/Wiener ~:** frankfurter/wienerwurst; **heiße ~:** hot sausages; Ⓑ (*ugs., oft abwertend*) nobody; (*hilfloser Mensch*) poor soul; **ein armes ~:** a poor soul; Ⓒ **[ein] ~ machen** (*Kinderspr.*) do [poo]poos (*child lang.*)
**Würstchen·bude** *die* sausage stand
**wurst·egal** *Adj.* (*ugs.*) *in* **~ sein** not matter in the slightest; **das ist mir ~:** I couldn't care less [about that]
**Wurstel** /ˈvʊrstl̩/ *der;* **~s, ~** (*bayr., österr.*) clown
**Würstel** /ˈvʏrstl̩/ *das;* **~s, ~** (*bes. österr.*) sausage
**Wurstelei** *die;* **~, ~en** (*ugs. abwertend*) pottering about *no pl.*
**wursteln** *itr. V.* (*ugs.*) ❶ potter; **an etw.** (*Dat.*) **~:** potter about with sth. ❷ *refl. V.* **sich durchs Leben ~:** muddle [along] through life
**Wurst-: ~finger** *der* podgy finger; **~haut** *die* sausage skin
**wurstig** (*ugs.*) ❶ *Adj.* couldn't-care-less *attrib.* ‹attitude, behaviour, reply›; **er ist ein ~er Typ** *od.* **ist ~:** he couldn't care less about anything. ❷ *adv.* in a couldn't-care-less way
**Wurstigkeit** *die;* **~** (*ugs.*) couldn't-care-less attitude
**Wurst-: ~salat** *der: piquant salad with pieces of sausage, onion rings, boiled eggs and/or cheese;* **~suppe** *die* sausage soup; **~waren** *Pl.* sausages; **~zipfel** *der* end of a/the sausage
**württembergisch** /ˈvʏrtəmbɛrgɪʃ/ *Adj.* of/from Württemberg; ⇒ *auch* **badisch**
**Würze** /ˈvʏrtsə/ *die;* **~, ~n** Ⓐ (*Gewürz*) spice; seasoning; Ⓑ (*Aroma*) aroma; (*fig.*) spice; ⇒ *auch* **Kürze** C
**Wurzel** /ˈvʊrtsl̩/ *die;* **~, ~n** Ⓐ (*auch fig.*) root; **~[n] fassen** take root; **~n schlagen** take root; (*fig.: heimisch werden*) put down roots; **ich stehe hier schon so lange, dass ich bald ~n schlage** (*scherzh.*) I've been standing here so long I'll soon grow roots; **seine ~n in etw.** (*Dat.*) **haben** (*fig.*) have its roots in sth.; **die ~ allen Übels** (*fig.*) the root of all evil; **das Übel an der ~ fassen** *od.* **packen** (*fig.*) strike at the root of the problem; **etw. mit der ~ ausrotten** (*fig.*) eradicate sth. completely; Ⓑ ▶ 841 | (*Math.*) root; **~n ziehen** calculate roots; **aus einer Zahl die ~ ziehen** extract the [square] root of a number; **die dritte ~ aus** *od.* **von 8** the cube root of 8; Ⓒ (*bes. nordd.*) carrot; Ⓓ (*der Hand*) wrist; (*des Fußes*) ankle; (*eines Nagels, der Nase*) root; Ⓔ (*Sprachw.*) root
**Wurzel-: ~ballen** *der* root ball; **~behandlung** *die* (*Zahnmed.*) root treatment; **~bürste** *die* stiff brush; (*zum Scheuern*) [stiff] scrubbing brush *or* (*Amer.*) scrub brush
**Würzelchen** /ˈvʏrtsl̩çən/ *das;* **~s, ~:** rootlet
**Wurzel·haut·entzündung** *die* ▶ 474 | (*Med.*) periodontitis *no indef. art.*
**wurzelig** *Adj.* full of roots *postpos.*
**Wurzel·knolle** *die* tuber
**wurzel·los** *Adj.* without roots *postpos.;* (*auch fig.*) rootless
**Wurzel·losig·keit** *die;* **~:** lack of roots; (*fig.*) rootlessness
**wurzeln** *itr. V.* Ⓐ (*Wurzeln schlagen*) take root; **flach ~:** have shallow roots; **das Misstrauen wurzelt tief in ihm** (*fig.*) his mistrust is deep-rooted; Ⓑ **in etw.** (*Dat.*) **~** (*seinen Ursprung haben in*) be rooted in sth.; (*verursacht sein durch*) have its roots in sth.
**Wurzel-: ~spross, *~sproß** *der* (*Bot.*) root sucker; **~stock** *der; Pl.* **~stöcke** Ⓐ (*Bot.*) rootstock; rhizome; Ⓑ (*eines Baumes*) stump and roots *pl.;* **~werk** *das* roots *pl.*
**würzen** /ˈvʏrtsn̩/ *tr. V.* season; (*fig.*) spice; **Humor würzt das Leben** (*fig.*) humour is the spice of life
**würzig** ❶ *Adj.* tasty; full-flavoured ‹beer, wine›; aromatic ‹fragrance, smell, tobacco›; tangy ‹air›; (*scharf*) spicy. ❷ *adv.* **sie kocht nicht ~ genug** she doesn't use enough seasoning
**Würzigkeit** *die;* **~** ⇒ **würzig** 1: tastiness; full flavour; aromatic fragrance; tanginess; spiciness
**wusch** /vuːʃ/ *1. u. 3. Pers. Sg. Prät. v.* **waschen**
**Wuschel·haar** *das* (*ugs.*) frizzy *or* fuzzy hair
**wuschelig** *Adj.* (*ugs.*) frizzy; fuzzy
**Wuschel·kopf** *der* (*ugs.*) Ⓐ (*Haar*) shock *or* mop of frizzy *or* fuzzy hair; Ⓑ (*Mensch*) frizzy-haired *or* fuzzy-haired man/girl *etc.;* man/girl *etc.* with frizzy *or* fuzzy hair
**wuscheln** /ˈvʊʃl̩n/ *tr., itr. V.* tousle; **in jmds. Haar ~:** tousle sb.'s hair
**wuselig** *Adj.* (*bes. südd., md.*) busy; bustling
**wuseln** /ˈvuːzl̩n/ *itr. V.* (*bes. südd., md.*) Ⓐ *mit sein* (*sich flink bewegen*) scurry; Ⓑ (*sich beschäftigen*) bustle around
**wusste, *wußte** /ˈvʊstə/ *1. und 3. Pers. Sg. Prät. v.* **wissen**
**wüsste, *wüßte** /ˈvʏstə/ *1. und 3. Pers. Sg. Konjunktiv II v.* **wissen**
**wüst** /vyːst/ ❶ *Adj.* Ⓐ (*öde*) desolate; Ⓑ (*unordentlich*) chaotic; tangled, tousled ‹hair, beard, etc.›; wild ‹appearance›; **ein ~es Durcheinander herrschte dort** it was utter chaos *or* an utter shambles there; Ⓒ (*abwertend: wild, ungezügelt*) wild; furious ‹fight, shoot-out›; Ⓓ (*abwertend: unanständig*) rude; coarse ‹oath, abuse›; Ⓔ (*abwertend: furchtbar, abscheulich*) terrible; foul (*sl.*), terrible (*coll.*) ‹weather›. ❷ *adv.* Ⓐ (*unordentlich*) chaotically; **das Haar hing ihr ~ ins Gesicht** her hair straggled down over her face; Ⓑ (*abwertend: wild, ungezügelt*) wildly; **sie habens ~ getrieben** they had a wild time; Ⓒ (*abwertend: unanständig*) ‹swear, abuse sb.› coarsely; Ⓓ (*abwertend: furchtbar, abscheulich*) terribly; **sie haben ihn ~ zugerichtet** they really knocked him about
**Wust** /vuːst/ *der;* **~[e]s** (*abwertend*) jumble; (*fig.*) welter; **ein ~ von Daten/Vorschriften** a mass of data/regulations
**Wüste** *die;* **~, ~n** desert; (*Eis~*) waste; (*fig.*) wasteland; **jmdn. in die ~ schicken** (*ugs.*) give sb. the push (*coll.*)
**wüsten** *itr. V.* **mit etw. ~:** squander sth.
**Wüstenei** *die;* **~, ~en** Ⓐ (*Einöde*) waste land; Ⓑ (*scherzh.: Unordnung*) shambles *sing.;* chaos *no indef. art.*
**Wüsten-: ~fuchs** *der* fennec; **~klima** *das* desert climate; **~sand** *der* desert sand[s *pl.*]; **~schiff** *das* (*dichter.*) ship of the desert
**Wüstling** *der;* **~s, ~e** (*abwertend*) lecher; debauchee
**Wut** /vuːt/ *die;* **~:** rage; fury; **auf jmdn. eine ~ haben** be furious with sb.; **seine ~ an jmdm. auslassen** vent one's rage *or* fury on sb.; **in ~ geraten** *od.* **kommen** get furious; **jmdn. in ~ bringen** infuriate sb.; **eine ~ im Bauch haben** (*ugs.*) be livid (*Brit. coll.*)
**Wut-: ~an·fall** *der* fit of rage; **~ausbruch** *der* outburst of rage *or* fury
**wüten** /ˈvyːtn̩/ *itr. V.* (*auch fig.*) rage; (*zerstören*) wreak havoc
**wütend** ❶ *Adj.* Ⓐ furious; angry ‹voice, mob›; **auf** *od.* **über jmdn. ~ sein** be furious with sb.; **er war ~ auf sie, weil sie ihn warten ließ** he was furious with her for keeping him waiting; **über etw.** (*Akk.*) **~ sein** be furious about sth.; Ⓑ (*sehr groß, heftig*) raging ‹pain, hatred, etc.›; fierce ‹proponent, defender›. ❷ *adv.* Ⓐ furiously; in a fury; Ⓑ (*heftig*) furiously
**wut·entbrannt** ❶ *Adj.* infuriated; furious. ❷ *adv.* in a fury
**Wüterich** /ˈvyːtərɪç/ *der;* **~s, ~e** (*abwertend*) hot-tempered person; (*Gewaltmensch*) brute
**wut·schnaubend** ❶ *Adj.* snorting with rage *pred.* ❷ *adv.* snorting with rage
**Wutz** /vʊts/ *die;* **~, ~en** *od.* **der; ~en, ~en** (*bes. westmd.*) pig
**Wz** *Abk.* **Warenzeichen** TM; ®

W

**x, X¹** /ɪks/ *das;* ~, ~**:** x, X; **Herr/die Stadt X** Mr X/the town of X; **jmdm. ein X für ein U vormachen** (*fig.*) dupe sb.; **er lässt sich** (*Dat.*) **kein X für ein U vormachen** you can't fool him; he's not easily fooled; ⇨ *auch* **a, A**

**x²** *unbest. Zahlwort* (*ugs.*) umpteen (*coll.*)

**x-Achse** *die* (*Math.*) x-axis

**Xanthippe** /ksan'tɪpə/ *die;* ~, ~**n** (*abwertend*) harridan

**X-Beine** *Pl.* knock knees; ~ **haben** have knock knees; be knock-kneed

**x-beinig** *Adj.* knock-kneed

**x-beliebig** *Adj.* (*ugs.*) **irgendein** ~**er/irgendeine** ~**e/irgendein** ~**es** any old (*coll. attrib.*); **jeder** ~**e Ort** any old place (*coll.*); **der Ort ist** ~**:** any old place will do (*coll.*); **denk dir eine** ~**e Zahl** think of a number, any old number (*coll.*); **irgendwelche** ~**en Leute** just anybody; **ich tue das nicht für jeden x-Beliebigen** I don't do it for just anybody

**X-Chromosom** *das* (*Biol.*) X-chromosome

**x-fach** ❶ *Vervielfältigungsz.* **die** ~**e Menge** (*Math.*) x times the amount; (*ugs.*) umpteen times the amount (*coll.*). ❷ *adv.* (*ugs.*) ~ **erprobt sein** have been tested umpteen times (*coll.*) *or* any number of times

**x-fache, *X-fache** *das;* ~**n: das** ~ **einer Zahl** (*Math.*) X times a number; **das** ~ **seines normalen Einkommens** (*ugs.*) umpteen times his normal income (*coll.*)

**X-Haken** *der* picture hook

**x-mal** *Adv.* (*ugs.*) umpteen times (*coll.*); any number of times

**X-Strahlen** *Pl.* (*Physik*) X-rays

**x-t...** *Ordinalz.* ▶841 Ⓐ (*Math.*) xth; Ⓑ (*ugs.*) umpteenth (*coll.*)

***x-te·mal, *x-ten·mal** ⇨ **Mal¹**

**Xylophon** /ksylo'fo:n/ *das;* ~**s,** ~**e** xylophone

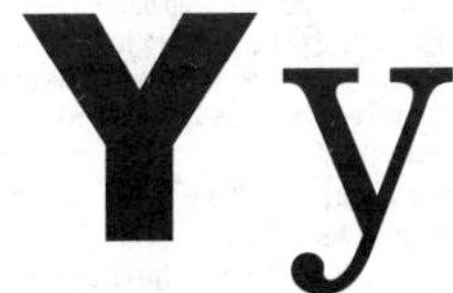

**y, Y** /'ʏpsilɔn/ *das;* ~, ~**:** y, Y; ⇨ *auch* **a, A**

**y-Achse** *die* (*Math.*) y-axis

**Yacht** ⇨ **Jacht**

**Yankee** /'jɛnki/ *der;* ~**s,** ~**s** (*oft abwertend*) Yankee (*Brit. coll.*); Yank (*Brit. coll.*)

**Y-Chromosom** *das* (*Biol.*) Y-chromosome

**Yen** /jɛn/ *der;* ~**[s],** ~**[s]** ▶337 yen

**Yeti** /'je:ti/ *der;* ~**s,** ~**s** yeti

**Yoga** ⇨ **Joga**

**Yogi[n]** ⇨ **Jogi[n]**

**Youngster** /'jʌŋstə/ *der;* ~**s,** ~**[s]** (*Sport*) youngster

**Yo-Yo** /jo'jo: *od.* 'jo:'jo:/ *das;* ~**s,** ~**s** yo-yo

**Ypsilon** /'ʏpsilɔn/ *das;* ~**[s],** ~**s** y, Y; (*im griechischen Alphabet*) upsilon

**Ysop** /'i:zɔp/ *der;* ~**s,** ~**e** hyssop

**Yucca** /'jʊka/ *die;* ~, ~**s** yucca

# Zz

**z, Z** /tsɛt/ *das;* ~, ~: z, Z; ⇒ *auch* **a, A**

**zach** /tsax/ *Adj.* (*bes. ostmd.*) timid

**zack** /tsak/ *Interj.* (*salopp*) **~! ~!** (*beeil dich*) get a move on! (*coll.*); make it snappy! (*coll.*); **bei ihm muss alles ~, ~ gehen** he likes things done at the double; **und ~, ~ wars fertig** and in a flash it was done

**Zack** *in* **auf ~ sein** (*ugs.*) (*tüchtig sein*) be on the ball (*coll.*) *or* one's toes; (*funktionieren*) be in good shape; **jmdn./etw. auf ~ bringen** (*ugs.*) knock sb./sth. into shape (*coll.*)

**Zacke** *die;* ~, **~n** point; (*eines Bergkamms, eines Diagramms*) peak; (*einer Säge, eines Kamms*) tooth; (*einer Gabel, Harke*) prong

**zacken** *tr. V.* serrate; pink ‹cloth, seam, hem›; **mit gezacktem Rand** with a serrated edge

**Zacken** *der;* **~s,** ~ **A** ⇒ **Zacke**; **B** (*fig.*) **sich** (*Dat.*) **keinen ~ aus der Krone brechen** (*ugs.*) not lose face; **dir bricht kein ~ aus der Krone, wenn du mithilfst!** (*ugs.*) it wouldn't hurt you to help out; **einen [kleinen] ~ [in der Krone] haben** (*ugs.*) be [a bit] tipsy

**zackig** **1** *Adj.* **A** (*gezackt*) jagged; (*mit kleinen, regelmäßigen Zacken*) serrated; **B** (*schneidig*) dashing; smart; rousing ‹music›; brisk ‹orders, tempo›; lively ‹organization›. **2** *adv.* **A** (*gezackt*) jaggedly; **B** (*schneidig*) smartly; ‹play music› rousingly; **..., aber mach ein bisschen ~!** ..., and make it snappy! (*coll.*)

**zag** /tsa:k/ (*geh.*) **1** *Adj.* timid; (*fig.*) tentative ‹hope›. **2** *adv.* timidly; (*fig.*) tentatively

**zagen** *itr. V.* (*geh.*) hesitate (**vor** + *Dat.* in the face of); **zögern und ~:** keep hesitating; **~d** hesitant[ly]

**zaghaft** **1** *Adj.* timid; (*zögernd*) hesitant; tentative. **2** *adv.* timidly; (*zögernd*) hesitantly; tentatively

**Zaghaftigkeit** *die;* **~:** timidity; (*Zögern*) hesitancy

**Zagheit** *die;* ~ (*geh.*) timidity

**zäh** /tsɛ:/ **1** *Adj.* **A** (*fest*) tough; heavy ‹dough, soil›; (*dickflüssig*) glutinous; viscous ‹oil›; **B** (*schleppend*) sluggish, dragging ‹conversation›; **C** (*widerstandsfähig*) tough ‹person›; **D** (*beharrlich*) tenacious; tough ‹negotiations›; dogged ‹resistance›; **mit ~em Fleiß** by dint of sheer hard work. **2** *adv.* **A** (*schleppend*) sluggishly; **B** (*beharrlich*) tenaciously; ‹resist› doggedly

***Zäheit** ⇒ **Zähheit**

**zäh·flüssig** *Adj.* glutinous; viscous ‹oil›; thick ‹soup›; heavy ‹dough›; (*fig.: langsam*) slow-moving ‹traffic›; **die Verhandlungen waren ~** (*fig.*) the negotiations were hard going

**Zäh·flüssigkeit** *die* glutinousness; (*von Öl*) viscosity; (*von Soße, Suppe*) thickness

**Zähheit** *die;* **~:** **A** (*Festigkeit*) toughness; (*des Teigs, Bodens*) heaviness; (*Dickflüssigkeit*) glutinousness; (*von Öl*) viscosity; **B** (*schleppendes Tempo*) sluggishness; **C** (*Widerstandsfähigkeit*) toughness; (*der Konstitution*) robustness; **D** (*Beharrlichkeit*) tenacity; (*des Widerstands*) doggedness

**Zähigkeit** *die;* ~ **A** (*Widerstandsfähigkeit*) toughness; **B** (*Beharrlichkeit*) tenacity; **mit ~:** tenaciously

**Zahl** /'tsa:l/ *die;* ~, **~en ▶ 841** number; (*Ziffer*) numeral; (*Zahlenangabe, Geldmenge*) figure; **er nannte keine ~en** he did not give any figures; **in die/aus den roten ~en kommen** go into/get out of the red; **in den roten/schwarzen ~en** in the red/black; **mit ~en umgehen können** be good with figures; **[fünf/sieben] an der ~:** [five/seven] in number; **in großer ~:** in great numbers; **Leiden ohne** *od.* (*veralt.*) **sonder ~:** suffering beyond measure

**Zahl·adjektiv** *das* numeral adjective

**zahlbar** *Adj.* (*Kaufmannsspr.*) payable

**zählbar** *Adj.* countable

**zählebig** *Adj.* hardy ‹plant, animal›; **ein ~es Vorurteil** a prejudice which dies hard

**zahlen** **1** *tr. V.* **▶ 337** **A** pay ‹price, amount, rent, tax, fine, etc.› (**an** + *Akk.* to); **jmdm. 200 Mark ~, 200 Mark an jmdn. ~:** pay sb. 200 marks; **einen hohen Preis ~** (*auch fig.*) pay a high price; **B** (*ugs.: für eine Dienstleistung*) pay for ‹taxi, repair, etc.›; **jmdm. etw. ~:** pay for sth. for sb.; **zahlst du mir ein Bier?** will you buy me a beer?. **2** *itr. V.* pay; **er will nicht ~:** he won't pay [up]; **er zahlt noch an seinem Auto** he is still paying off his car; **in Dollar** *od.* **mit Dollars ~:** pay in dollars; **~ bitte!** (*im Lokal*) [can I/we have] the bill, please!; **die Firma zahlt gut/schlecht** the firm pays well/badly

**zählen** /'tsɛ:lən/ **1** *itr. V.* **A** count; **ich zähle bis drei** I'll count up to three; **B** (*geh.: vorhanden sein*) **nach Tausenden/Millionen ~:** number thousands/millions; **C** (*gehören*) **zu einer Gruppe** *usw.* **~:** be one of *or* belong to a group *etc.*; **diese Tage zählten zu den schönsten seines Lebens** these days were among *or* were some of the most wonderful in his life; **D** (*gültig/wichtig sein*) count; **die Pause zählt nicht als Arbeitszeit** the break does not count as working time; **bei ihm** *od.* **für ihn zählt nur Erfolg** for him the only thing that counts is success; **E** (*vertrauen*) **auf jmdn./etw. ~:** count on sb./sth.

**2** *tr. V.* **A** count; **Geld auf den Tisch ~:** count money out on to the table; **B** (*geh.: eine bestimmte Anzahl haben*) number; **die Stadt zählt 500 000 Einwohner** the town has 500,000 inhabitants; **er zählt 90 Jahre** he is 90 years of age; **seine Tage sind gezählt** (*fig.*) his/its days are numbered; **C** (*als zugehörig betrachten*) **jmdn. zu seinen Freunden ~:** count sb. among one's friends; **D** (*wert sein*) be worth; **E** (*werten*) **das Tor wurde nicht gezählt** the goal was not counted *or* didn't count

**zahlen-, Zahlen-:** **~folge** *die* sequence *or* series of numbers; **~gedächtnis** *das* memory for figures; **~kombination** *die* combination (*for a lock*); **~lotterie** *die*, **~lotto** *das: lottery in which entrants guess which set of figures will be drawn at random from a fixed sequence of numbers;* **~mäßig** **1** *Adj.* numerical; **2** *adv.* numerically; **~mystik** *die* numerology *no art.*; **~schloss**, ***~schloß** *das* combination lock

**Zähler** *der;* **~s,** ~ **A** (*Messgerät*) meter; **B** (*Math.*) numerator

**Zähler·stand** *der* meter reading; **den ~ ablesen** read the meter

**zahl-, Zahl-:** **~grenze** *die* fare stage; **~karte** *die* (*Postw.*) paying-in slip; **~kellner** *der*, **~kellnerin** *die: waiter/waitress to whom payment is made;* **~los** *Adj.* countless; innumerable

**Zahl·meister** *der*, **Zahl·meisterin** *die* **▶ 159** (*auch fig.*) paymaster; (*auf Schiffen*) purser

**zahl·reich** **1** *Adj.* numerous; large ‹family, group, audience›; **seine ~e Nachkommenschaft** his numerous descendants. **2** *adv.* in large numbers

**Zahl·tag** *der* pay day

**Zahlung** *die;* ~, **~en ▶ 337** payment; **etw. in ~ nehmen/geben** (*Kaufmannsspr.*) take/give sth. in part exchange; take sth. as a trade-in/trade sth. in

**Zählung** *die;* ~, **~en** counting; **eine ~:** a count

**zahlungs-, Zahlungs-:** **~anweisung** *die: postal order paid by the postman to the payee in person;* **~aufforderung** *die* notice to pay; demand for payment; **~aufschub** *der* deferment of payment; **~bedingungen** *Pl.* (*Wirtsch.*) terms of payment; **~befehl** *der* (*Rechtsspr. veralt.*) order to pay; **~bilanz** *die* (*Wirtsch.*) balance of payments; **~empfänger** *der*, **~empfängerin** *die* payee; **~erleichterung** *die* easy terms *pl.*; **~fähig** *Adj.* solvent; **~fähigkeit** *die* solvency; **~frist** *die* period for payment; credit period; **~kräftig** *Adj.* (*ugs.*) affluent; **~mittel** *das* means of payment; **~termin** *der* date for payment (**für** of); **~unfähig** *Adj.* insolvent; **~unfähigkeit** *die* insolvency; **~verkehr** *der* payments *pl.*; transactions *pl.*; **~weise** *die* method of payment (*Gen.* for); **~ziel** *das* (*Kaufmannsspr.*) ⇒ **~frist**

**Zähl·werk** *das* counter

**Zahl-:** **~wort** *das; Pl.* **~wörter** (*Sprachw.*) numeral; **~zeichen** *das* numeral

**zahm** /tsa:m/ **1** *Adj.* (*auch fig.*) tame. **2** *adv.* (*auch fig.*) tamely

**zähmen** /'tsɛ:mən/ *tr. V.* **A** (*auch fig.*) tame; subdue ‹forces of nature›; **B** (*geh.*) restrain ‹curiosity, impatience, etc.›

**Zähmung** *die;* ~, **~en** taming

**Zahn** /tsa:n/ *der;* **~[e]s, Zähne** /'tsɛ:nə/ **A ▶ 471** tooth; (*Raubtier~*) fang; (*an einer Briefmarke usw.*) serration; **Zähne** (*an einer Briefmarke usw.*) perforations; **sich** (*Dat.*) **einen ~ ziehen lassen** have a tooth out; **die dritten Zähne** (*scherzh.*) dentures; **B** (*fig.*) **der ~ der Zeit** (*ugs.*) the ravages *pl.* of time; **der ~ der Zeit hat an diesem Haus genagt** (*ugs.*) time has left its mark on this house; **jmdm. diesen** *od.* **den ~ ziehen** (*ugs.*) put paid to this idea [of sb.'s] (*coll.*); **[jmdm.] die Zähne zeigen** (*ugs.*) show [sb.] one's teeth; **die Zähne zusammenbeißen** (*ugs.*) grit one's teeth; **sich** (*Dat.*) **an jmdm./etw. die Zähne ausbeißen** (*ugs.*) get nowhere with sb./sth.; **lange Zähne machen, mit langen Zähnen essen** (*ugs.*) make a face over one's food; **jmdn. auf den ~ fühlen[, ob ...]** (*ugs.*) sound sb. out [to see whether ...]; **bis an die Zähne bewaffnet** armed to the teeth; **etw. mit Zähnen und Klauen verteidigen** (*ugs.*) defend sth. tooth and nail; **C** (*ugs.: Geschwindigkeit*) **einen ganz schönen ~ draufhaben** be going like the clappers (*Brit. coll.*); **mit einem höllischen ~:** at a hell of a lick (*coll.*); **einen ~ zulegen** (*ugs.*) get a move on (*coll.*); **D** (*Jugendspr. veralt.*) piece *or* bit of skirt (*sl.*); **ein steiler ~:** a piece of hot stuff (*coll.*)

**zahn-, Zahn-:** **~arzt** *der*, **~ärztin** *die* **▶ 159** dentist; (*mit chirurgischer Ausbildung*) dental surgeon; **~ärztlich** **1** *Adj.* dental ‹treatment etc.›; **~ärztlicher Befund** dentist's findings *pl.*; **2** *adv.* **jmdn. ~ärztlich behandeln** give sb. dental treatment; **~ärztlich empfohlen** recommended by dentists; **~behandlung** *die* dental treatment; **~bein** *das* (*Biol.*) dentine; **~belag** *der* [dental] plaque; **~bürste** *die* toothbrush

**Zahn·creme** *die* ⇒ **Zahnpasta**

**zähne-, Zähne-:** **~fletschend** *Adj.* baring its/their teeth *postpos.*; (*knurrend*) snarling;

*old spelling (see note on page 1707)

# Zahlen

## Kardinalzahlen = Cardinal numbers

0 **(*null*)** = nought (*bes. brit.*), zero[1]
1 **(*eins, ein...*)** = one
2 **(*zwei*)** = two
3 **(*drei*)** = three
4 **(*vier*)** = four
5 **(*fünf*)** = five
6 **(*sechs*)** = six
7 **(*sieben*)** = seven
8 **(*acht*)** = eight
9 **(*neun*)** = nine
10 **(*zehn*)** = ten
11 **(*elf*)** = eleven
12 **(*zwölf*)** = twelve
13 **(*dreizehn*)** = thirteen
14 **(*vierzehn*)** = fourteen
15 **(*fünfzehn*)** = fifteen
16 **(*sechzehn*)** = sixteen
17 **(*siebzehn*)** = seventeen
18 **(*achtzehn*)** = eighteen
19 **(*neunzehn*)** = nineteen
20 **(*zwanzig*)** = twenty
21 **(*einundzwanzig*)** = twenty-one
22 **(*zweiundzwanzig*)** = twenty-two
30 **(*dreißig*)** = thirty
40 **(*vierzig*)** = forty
50 **(*fünfzig*)** = fifty
60 **(*sechzig*)** = sixty
70 **(*siebzig*)** = seventy
80 **(*achtzig*)** = eighty
90 **(*neunzig*)** = ninety
100 **([*ein*]*hundert*)** = a *od.* one hundred[2]
101 **([*ein*]*hundert*[*und*]*eins*, [*ein*]*hundert*[*und*]*ein...*)** = a *od.* one hundred and one (*brit.*), a *od.* one hundred one (*amerik.*)
555 **(*fünfhundert*[*und*]*fünfundfünfzig*)** = five hundred and fifty-five (*brit.*), five hundred fifty-five (*amerik.*)
1,000 **([*ein*]*tausend*)** = a *od.* one thousand[2]
1,001 **([*ein*]*tausend*[*und*]*eins*, [*ein*]*tausend*[*und*]*ein...*)** = a *od.* one thousand and one (*brit.*), a *od.* one thousand one (*amerik.*)
1,200 **([*ein*]*tausendzweihundert od. zwölfhundert*)** = one thousand two hundred, twelve hundred
100,000 **([*ein*]*hunderttausend*)** = a *od.* one hundred thousand
1,000,000 **(*eine Million*)** = a *od.* one million
3,536,000 **(*drei Millionen fünfhundertsechsunddreißigtausend*)** = three million[3] five hundred and thirty-six (*brit.*) *od.* (*amerik.*) five hundred thirty-six thousand
1,000,000,000 **(*eine Milliarde*)** = a *od.* one billion, a *od.* one thousand million
1,000,000,000,000 **(*eine Billion*)** = a *od.* one trillion, a *od.* one million million

### ANMERKUNGEN

[1] 'Nought' wird hauptsächlich im britischen Englisch, 'zero' dagegen im amerikanischen Englisch für die Ziffer 0 verwendet. Wenn man eine Zahl ausspricht, die eine Null enthält, sagt man entweder 'oh' oder (besonders im amerikanischen Sprachraum) 'zero':

***Die Vorwahl für London (Mitte) ist 0171***
= The code for central London is 0171 (oh-one-seven-one *od.* (*bes. amerik.*) zero-one-seven-one)

***der Peugeot 46***
= the Peugeot 406 (four-oh-six)

***Sie haben 4:0 gewonnen***
= They won 4-0 (four-nil *od.* (*amerik.*) four-zero)

***Den ersten Satz gewann sie 6:0***
= She won the first set 6-0 (six-love)

***Tiefsttemperaturen um 4 Grad unter Null***
Temperatures falling to *od.* (*bes. amerik.*) Lows around 4 degrees below zero

[2] **one** sagt man statt **a**, wenn man die Genauigkeit der Ziffer betonen will; **a hundred** (und **a thousand, a million** usw.) ist aber viel häufiger, vor allem bei zusammengesetzten Zahlen (z.B. **a hundred and twenty**).

[3] Wie bei **hundred** und **thousand** verwendet man die Pluralform **millions** nicht in Zahlen, da **million** hier kein Substantiv ist; das gilt auch für unbestimmte Zahlwörter:

***einige/ein paar Millionen [Pfund]***
= several/a couple of million [pounds]

**millions** kommt nur in ungenauen Ausdrücken vor, wie etwa:

***Man kann Millionen von Pfund/Dollar verdienen***
= One can earn millions [of pounds/dollars]

***Hunderte von Millionen***
= hundreds of millions

## Brüche = Fractions

| | | | |
|---|---|---|---|
| 1/2 | a half | 1 1/2 | one and a half |
| 1/3 | a third | 5 2/3 | five and two thirds |
| 1/4 | a quarter | 2 3/4 | two and three quarters |
| 1/5 | a fifth | 4 4/5 | four and four fifths |
| 1/8 | an eighth | 8 7/8 | eight and seven eighths |
| 1/32 | one thirty-second | 10/71 | ten seventy-firsts |

Zur Bildung der Brüche dienen also die (substantivisch gebrauchten) Formen der Ordinalzahlen.

***zwei Drittel des Weges***
= two thirds of the distance

***drei Viertel aller Offiziere***
= three quarters of all officers

Nach dem Bruch folgt bei Maßeinheiten **of a**, und die Einheit steht dementsprechend im Singular.

***ein Viertelliter***
= a quarter of a litre

***fünf achtel Meilen***
= five eighths of a mile

***sechs hundertstel Sekunden***
= six hundredths of a second

**ZAHLEN** (FORTSETZUNG)

## Ordinalzahlen = Ordinal numbers

***1.* (*erst...*)** = 1st (first)
***2.* (*zweit...*)** = 2nd (second)
***3.* (*dritt...*)** = 3rd (third)
***4.* (*viert...*)** = 4th (fourth)
***5.* (*fünft...*)** = 5th (fifth)
***6.* (*sechst...*)** = 6th (sixth)
***7.* (*sieb[en]t...*)** = 7th (seventh)
***8.* (*acht...*)** = 8th (eighth)
***9.* (*neunt...*)** = 9th (ninth)
***10.* (*zehnt...*)** = 10th (tenth)
***11.* (*elft...*)** = 11th (eleventh)
***12.* (*zwölft...*)** = 12th (twelfth)
***13.* (*dreizehnt...*)** = 13th (thirteenth)
***14.* (*vierzehnt...*)** = 14th (fourteenth)
***15.* (*fünfzehnt...*)** = 15th (fifteenth)
***16.* (*sechzehnt...*)** = 16th (sixteenth)
***17.* (*siebzehnt...*)** = 17th (seventeenth)
***18.* (*achtzehnt...*)** = 18th (eighteenth)
***19.* (*neunzehnt...*)** = 19th (nineteenth)
***20.* (*zwanzigst...*)** = 20th (twentieth)
***21.* (*einundzwanzigst...*)** = 21st (twenty-first)
***22.* (*zweiundzwanzigst...*)** = 22nd (twenty-second)
***30.* (*dreißigst...*)** = 30th (thirtieth)
***40.* (*vierzigst...*)** = 40th (fortieth)
***50.* (*fünfzigst...*)** = 50th (fiftieth)
***60.* (*sechzigst...*)** = 60th (sixtieth)
***70.* (*siebzigst...*)** = 70th (seventieth)
***80.* (*achtzigst...*)** = 80th (eightieth)
***90.* (*neunzigst...*)** = 90th (ninetieth)
***100.* ([*ein*]*hundertst...*)** = 100th ([one] hundredth)
***101.* ([*ein*]*hundert*[*und*]*erst...*)** = 101st ([one] hundred and first (*brit.*), [one] hundred first (*amerik.*))
***555.* (*fünfhundert*[*und*]*fünfundfünfzigst...*)** = 555th (five hundred and fifty-fifth (*brit.*), five hundred fifty-fifth (*amerik.*))
***1 000.* ([*ein*]*tausendst...*)** = 1,000th ([one] thousandth)
***1 001.* ([*ein*]*tausend*[*und*]*erst...*)** = 1,001st (one thousand and first (*brit.*), one thousand first (*amerik.*))
***1 200.* ([*ein*]*tausendzweihundertst... od. zwölfhundertst...*)** = 1,200th (one thousand two hundredth, twelve hundredth)
***100 000.* ([*ein*]*hunderttausendst...*)** = 100,000th ([one] hundred thousandth)
***1 000 000.* (*millionst...*)** = 1,000,000th ([one] millionth)
***3 536 000.* (*drei Millionen fünfhundertsechsunddreißigtausendst...*)** = 3,536,000th (three million five hundred and thirty-six (*brit.*) *od.* (*amerik.*) five hundred thirty-six thousandth)
***1 000 000 000.* (*milliardst...*)** = 1,000,000,000th ([one] billionth, [one] thousand millionth)
***1 000 000 000 000.* (*billionst...*)** = 1,000,000,000,000th ([one] trillionth, one million millionth)

## Dezimalzahlen = Decimal numbers

0,1 = 0.1 (point one, oh *od.* (*brit.*) nought *od.* (*amerik.*) zero point one)
0,015 = 0.015 ([oh] point oh *od.* (*brit.*) [nought] point nought *od.* (*amerik.*) [zero] point zero one five)
1,43 = 1.43 (one point four three)
11,70 = 11.70 (eleven point seven oh)
12,$\bar{3}$ = 12.$\bar{3}$ (twelve point three recurring)

## Rechnen

7 + 3 = 10 (seven plus three is *od.* equals ten)
10 – 3 = 7 (ten minus three is *od.* equals seven)
10 x 3 = 30 (ten times three is *od.* equals thirty)
30 ÷ 3 = 10 (thirty divided by three is *od.* equals ten)

## Potenzen = Powers

$3^2$ = ***drei hoch zwei*** = three squared
$3^3$ = ***drei hoch drei*** = three cubed
$3^{10}$ = ***drei hoch zehn*** = three to the power of ten
$\sqrt{25}$ = **[*Quadrat*]*wurzel aus fünfundzwanzig*** = the square root of twenty-five

···➤ Altersangaben | Datum | Entfernung | Fläche
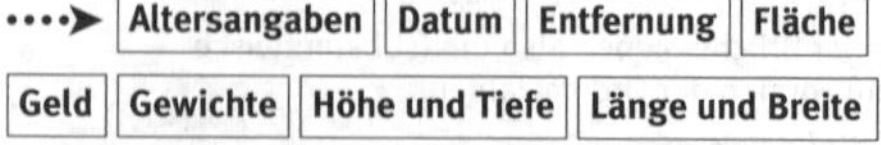
Geld | Gewichte | Höhe und Tiefe | Länge und Breite
Rauminhalt | Temperaturen | Uhrzeit

**~klappern** *das;* **~~s** chattering teeth *pl.;* ⇨ *auch* **heulen** B; **~klappernd** *Adj.* with chattering teeth *postpos.;* **~knirschend** *adv.* gnashing one's teeth; cursing silently; **~knirschend nachgeben** give in with bad grace *or* under protest

**zahnen** *itr. V.* ‹baby› be teething

**zahn-, Zahn-: ~ersatz** *der* denture; **~fäule** *die* tooth decay; dental caries *(Med.)*; **~fleisch** *das* ▶ 471 gum; *(als Ganzes)* gums *pl.;* **auf dem ~fleisch gehen** *(fig. ugs.)* be absolutely knackered *(Brit. coll.)*; be tuckered [out] *(Amer. coll.)*; **~fleisch·bluten** *das;* **~~s** bleeding gums *pl.;* **~füllung** *die* filling; **~hals** *der* neck of a/the tooth; **~heilkunde** *die* dentistry *no art.;* **~klinik** *die* dental clinic; **~kranz** *der* **A** sprocket [wheel]; **B** *(~kranzpaket)* rear sprocket [cluster]; **~krone** *die* crown [of a/the tooth]; **~laut** *der (Sprachw.)* dental; **~los** *Adj.* toothless; **~lücke** *die* gap in one's teeth; **~medizin** *die* dentistry *no art.;* **~pasta** /-pasta/ *die;* **~~**, **~pasten** toothpaste; **~pflege** *die* dental care; **~prothese** *die* dentures *pl.;* [set *sing.* of] false teeth *pl.;* **~pulver** *das* tooth powder; **~putz·becher** *der* tooth mug; **~rad** *das* gearwheel; *(für Ketten)* sprocket; **~rad·bahn** *die* rack railway; **~schmelz** *der* enamel; **~schmerzen** *Pl.* ▶ 474 toothache *sing.;* **~seide** *die* dental floss; **~spange** *die* [tooth] brace; **~stein** *der* tartar; **~stocher** *der;* **~~s**, **~~:** toothpick; **~stumpf** *der* [tooth] stump; **~techniker** *der*, **~technikerin** *die* dental technician; **~wal** *der* toothed whale; **~weh** *das (ugs.)* toothache; **~wurzel** *die* root of a/the tooth

**Zähre** /ˈtsɛːrə/ *die;* **~**, **~n** *(dichter. veralt.)* tear[drop]

**Zaire** /zaˈiːr/ *(das);* **~s** Zaire

**Zairer** /zaˈiːrɐ/ *der;* **~s**, **~**, **Zairerin** *die;* **~**, **~nen** Zairese

**Zampano** /ˈtsampano/ *der;* **~s**, **~s** golden boy; **er ist ein richtiger ~:** everything just falls into his lap

**Zander** /ˈtsandɐ/ *der;* **~s**, **~:** zander

**Zange** /ˈtsaŋə/ *die;* **~**, **~n** **A** *(Werkzeug)* pliers *pl.;* *(Eiswürfel~, Wäsche~, Zucker~)* tongs *pl.;* *(Geburts~)* forceps *pl.;* *(Kneif~)* pincers *pl.;* *(Loch~)* punch; **eine ~:** a pair of pliers/tongs/forceps/pincers/a punch; **jmdn. in die ~ nehmen** *(fig. ugs.)* put the screws on sb.; *(Fußballjargon)* crowd sb. out; **jmdn. in der ~ haben** *(fig. ugs.)* have sb. where one wants him/her; **B** *(bei Tieren)* pincer

**Zangen·geburt** *die* forceps delivery

**Zank** /tsaŋk/ *der;* **~[e]s** squabble; row; **[um** *od.* **über etw.** *(Akk.)***] in ~ geraten** start squabbling [over sth.]

**Zank·apfel** *der* bone of contention

**zanken** ❶ *refl. (auch itr.) V.* squabble, bicker (**um** *od.* **über** + *Akk.* over). ❷ *itr. V. (bes. ostmd.: schimpfen)* **[mit jmdm.] ~:** scold [sb.]

**Zänkerei** *die;* **~**, **~en** [minor] squabbling *no pl. or* squabbles *pl.*

**zänkisch** *Adj.* quarrelsome

**Zäpfchen** /ˈtsɛpfçən/ *das;* **~s**, **~** **A** suppository; **B** ▶ 471 *(Anat.)* uvula

**Zäpfchen-r, Zäpfchen-R** *das (Sprachw.)* uvular r

**zapfen** /ˈtsapfn̩/ *tr. V.* tap, draw ‹beer, wine›; **kannst du mir zwei Pils ~?** can you draw me two Pils?

**Zapfen** *der;* **~s**, **~** **A** *(Bot.)* [pine/fir] cone; **B** *(Stöpsel)* bung; **C** *(Eis~)* icicle; **D** *(Holzverarb.)* tenon

**Zapfen·streich** *der (Milit.)* **A** *(Signal)* last post *(Brit.)*; taps *pl. (Amer.)*; **der Große ~:** the tattoo; **B** *(Ende der Ausgehzeit)* time for return to barracks

**Zapfer** *der;* **~s**, **~:** barman

**Zapferin** *die;* **~**, **~nen** barmaid

**Zapf-: ~hahn** *der; Pl.* **~hähne**, *fachspr.* **~~en** tap; **~säule** *die* petrol pump *(Brit.)*; gasoline pump *(Amer.)*

**zappelig** *Adj. (ugs.)* **A** wriggly; fidgety ‹child›; **B** *(nervös)* jittery *(coll.)*

**zappeln** /ˈtsapl̩n/ *itr. V.* wriggle; ‹child› fidget; **mit den Beinen/Armen ~:** wave one's legs/arms about; **jmdn. ~ lassen** *(fig. ugs.)* keep sb. on tenterhooks; *(im Unklaren lassen)* keep sb. guessing

**Zappelphilipp** *der;* **~s**, **~e** *od.* **~s** *(ugs.)* fidgety child; fidget

**zappen** /ˈzɛpn̩/ *(ugs.)* ❶ *itr. V.* zap *(coll.)*. ❷ *refl. V.* zap *(coll.)*; **sich durch die Frühstückssendungen/zwanzig Kanäle ~:** zap through the breakfast programmes/twenty channels

**zappenduster** /ˈtsapn̩ˈduːstɐ/ *Adj. (ugs.)* pitch-dark; **es ist ~** *(fig.)* things look black *or* hopeless

**Zar** /tsaːɐ̯/ *der;* **~en**, **~en** *(hist.)* Tsar

**Zaren·reich** *das (hist.)* tsardom

**Zarewitsch** /tsaˈreːvɪtʃ/ *der;* **~[e]s**, **~e** *(hist.)* Tsarevitch

**Zarge** /ˈtsargə/ *die;* **~**, **~n** **A** *(Rahmen)* frame; **B** *(eines Saiteninstruments)* side wall; rib

**Zarin** *die;* **~**, **~nen** *(hist.)* Tsarina

**Zarismus** *der;* **~** *(hist.)* tsarism *no art.*

**zaristisch** *Adj. (hist.)* tsarist

**zart** /tsaːɐ̯t/ ❶ *Adj.* **A** delicate; soft ‹skin›; tender ‹bud, shoot›; fragile, delicate ‹china›; fine ‹silk, lace›; delicate, frail ‹health, constitution, child›; **im ~en Alter von sechs Jahren** *(geh.)* at the tender age of six; **das ist nichts für ~e Seelen** *od.* **Gemüter** it is not at all suitable for sensitive souls; **B** *(weich)* tender ‹meat, vegetables›; soft ‹filling›; fine ‹biscuits›; **C** *(leicht)* gentle ‹kiss, touch›; delicate ‹colour, complexion, fragrance, etc.›; soft ‹pastel colours›; soft, gentle ‹voice, sound, tune›; **D** *(einfühlsam, zärtlich)* tender ‹care, feelings›; **E** *(zurückhaltend)* delicate ‹reference›; gentle ‹hint›; faint ‹smile›.
❷ *adv.* **A** *(empfindlich)* delicately; **B** *(leicht)* delicately ‹coloured, fragrant›; ‹kiss, touch› gently; **C** *(zärtlich, einfühlsam)* tenderly; **D** *(zurückhaltend)* ‹hint› gently; ‹smile› faintly

**zart-, Zart-: ~besaitet** *Adj.* highly sensitive; **~bitter** *Adj.* plain ‹chocolate›; **~blau** *Adj.* pale blue; **~fühlend** ❶ *Adj.* tactful; ❷ *adv.* tactfully; **~gefühl** *das* tact; delicacy of feeling

**Zartheit** *die;* **~** **A** delicacy; *(der Haut)* softness; *(von Porzellan)* fragility; *(von Spitzen, Seide)* fineness; *(der Gesundheit, Konstitution, eines Kindes)* delicateness; *(Sensibilität)* sensitivity; **B** *(von Fleisch, Gemüse)* tenderness; **C** *(Leichtheit) (eines Kusses, einer Berührung)* gentleness; *(einer Farbe, des Teints, eines Dufts)* delicacy; *(der Stimme, des Tons, einer Melodie)* softness; gentleness; **D** *(Zärtlichkeit)* tenderness; **E** *(Zurückhaltung)* delicacy

**zärtlich** /ˈtsɛːɐ̯tlɪç/ ❶ *Adj.* **A** tender; loving; **~ werden** *(verhüll.)* start petting; **B** *(geh.: fürsorglich)* loving; caring. ❷ *adv.* **A** *(liebevoll)* tenderly; lovingly; **B** *(geh.: fürsorglich)* lovingly; caringly

**Zärtlichkeit** *die;* **~**, **~en** **A** *(Zuneigung)* tenderness; affection; **B** *(Liebkosung)* caress; **es kam zu ~en zwischen ihnen** they became intimate; **~en austauschen** become intimate; **C** *(Fürsorglichkeit)* loving care

**zart·rosa** *Adj.* pale pink

**Zaster** /ˈtsastɐ/ *der;* **~s** *(salopp)* dough *(coll.)*

**Zäsur** /tsɛˈzuːɐ̯/ *die;* **~**, **~en** **A** *(Verslehre, Musik)* caesura; **B** *(geh.) (Einschnitt)* break; *(Wendepunkt)* turning point

**Zauber** /ˈtsaubɐ/ *der;* **~s**, **~** **A** *(auch fig.)* magic; *(magische Handlung)* magic trick; *(Bann)* [magic] spell; **einen großen ~ auf jmdn. ausüben** have a great fascination for sb.; **er ist ihrem ~ erlegen** he has fallen under her spell; **der ~ des Verbotenen** the fascination of what is forbidden; ⇨ *auch* **faul** 1 C; **B** *(ugs. abwertend: Aufheben)* fuss; **ich halte nichts von dem ganzen ~:** the whole palaver means nothing to me *(coll.)*; **C** *(ugs.: Zeug)* stuff

**Zauberei** *die;* **~**, **~en** **A** *(das Zaubern)* magic; **B** *(Zaubertrick)* magic trick

**Zauberer** *der;* **~s**, **~:** magician

**zauber-, Zauber-: ~flöte** *die:* **„Die ~flöte"** 'The Magic Flute'; **~formel** *die* magic spell; *(fig.: Patentlösung)* magic formula; panacea; **~haft** ❶ *Adj.* enchanting; delightful; ❷ *adv.* enchantingly; delightfully

**Zauberin** *die;* **~**, **~nen** **A** sorceress; **B** *(Zauberkünstlerin)* conjurer

**zauberisch** *(geh.)* ❶ *Adj.* **A** *(traumhaft)* magical; **B** *(bezaubernd)* enchanting. ❷ *adv.* **A** *(traumhaft)* magically; **B** *(bezaubernd)* enchantingly

**zauber-, Zauber-: ~kraft** *die* magic[al] *or* supernatural powers *pl.;* **~kräftig** *Adj.* with magic properties *postpos., not pred.;* **ein ~kräftiger Trank** a magic potion; **~kunst** *die* **A** magic *no art.;* *(eines Bühnenkünstlers)* magic *no art.;* conjuring *no art.;* **B** *(magische Fähigkeit)* magic; **~künstler** *der*, **~künstlerin** *die* conjurer; magician

**zaubern** ❶ *itr. V.* **A** *(Zauberkraft ausüben)* do magic; **ich kann doch nicht ~!** *(ugs.)* I can't work miracles; **B** *(Zaubertricks ausführen)* do conjuring tricks. ❷ *tr. V. (auch fig.)* conjure; conjure up ‹palace, horse, etc.›; **eine Taube aus dem Hut ~:** produce a dove out of a hat; **ein vorzügliches Essen auf den Tisch ~** *(fig.)* conjure up an excellent meal

**Zauber-: ~stab** *der* magic wand; **~trank** *der* magic potion; **~trick** *der* conjuring trick

**Zauderer** *der;* **~s**, **~**, **Zauderin** *die;* **~**, **~nen** waverer; ditherer

**zaudern** /ˈtsaudɐn/ *itr. V. (geh.)* delay; **mit etw. ~:** delay in doing sth.; **zu lange ~:** procrastinate for too long

**Zaum** /tsaum/ *der;* **~[e]s**, **Zäume** /ˈtsɔymə/ **A** bridle; **B** *(geh.)* **jmdn./etw. im ~ halten** keep sb./sth. in check *or* under control; **sich/seine Zunge im ~ halten** restrain *or* control oneself/control one's tongue; **seine Gefühle/Leidenschaften im ~ halten** control one's feelings/passions

**zäumen** /ˈtsɔymən/ *tr. V.* bridle ‹horse›

**Zaum·zeug** *das* bridle

**Zaun** /tsaun/ *der;* **~[e]s**, **Zäune** /ˈtsɔynə/ fence; **einen Streit/Krieg vom ~ brechen** *(fig.)* suddenly start a quarrel/war

**Zaun-: ~gast** *der* onlooker; **~könig** *der (Zool.)* wren; **~pfahl** *der* fence post; ⇨ *auch* **Wink** B; **~winde** *die (Bot.)* hedge bindweed

**Zausel** *der;* **~s**, **~** *(landsch. abwertend)* fellow; **ein alter ~:** an old buffer *(coll.)*

**zausen** /ˈtsauzn̩/ *tr. V. (auch fig.)* ruffle; ruffle, tousle ‹hair›

**z. B.** *Abk.* **zum Beispiel** e.g.

**z. b. V.** *Abk.* **zur besonderen Verwendung**

**ZDF** *Abk.* **Zweites Deutsches Fernsehen** Second German Television Channel

**Zebra** /ˈtseːbra/ *das;* **~s**, **~s** *(Zool.)* zebra

**Zebra·streifen** *der* zebra crossing *(Brit.)*; pedestrian crossing

**Zebu** /ˈtseːbu/ *der od. das;* **~s**, **~s** *(Zool.)* zebu

**Zech·bruder** *der (ugs. abwertend)* **A** drinking pal *(coll.)*; **B** *(Trinker)* boozer *(coll.)*; tippler

**Zeche** *die;* **~**, **~n** **A** *(Rechnung)* bill *(Brit.)*; check *(Amer.)*; **eine hohe ~ machen** run up a large bill; **die ~ prellen** *(ugs.)* leave without paying [the bill]; **die ~ bezahlen müssen** *(fig.)* have to foot the bill *or* pay the price; **B** *(Grube)* pit; mine

**zechen** /ˈtsɛçn̩/ *itr. V. (veralt., scherzh.)* tipple

**Zecher** *der;* **~s**, **~**, **Zecherin** *die;* **~**, **~nen** *(veralt., scherzh.)* tippler

**Zech-: ~gelage** *das (veralt., scherzh.)* drinking bout; **~genosse** *der*, **~genossin** *die (veralt., scherzh.)* drinking companion; **~kumpan** *der*, **~kumpanin** *die (ugs. abwertend)* drinking pal *(coll.)*; **~preller** *der;* **~~s**, **~~:** *person who leaves without paying the bill;* bill-dodger; **~prellerei** *die;* **~~**, **~~en** *leaving without paying the bill;* bill-dodging; **~prellerin** *die;* **~~**, **~~nen** ⇨ **~preller**; **~tour** *die (ugs.)* pub crawl *(Brit. coll.)*; **eine ~tour unternehmen** go on a pub crawl *(Brit. coll.)*; barhop *(Amer. coll.)*

**Zecke** /ˈtsɛkə/ *die;* ~, ~**n** (*Zool.*) tick
**Zeder** /ˈtseːdɐ/ *die;* ~, ~**n** cedar
**Zedern·holz** *das* cedarwood
**Zeh** /tseː/ *der;* ~**s**, ~**en**, **Zehe** *die;* ~, ~**n** [A] ▶ 471 toe; **jmdm. auf die ~en treten** (*auch fig.*) tread on sb.'s toes; [B] (*Knoblauchzehe*) clove
**Zehen-:** ~**nagel** *der* ▶ 471 toenail; ~**spitze** *die:* ▶ 471 **auf ~spitzen** on tiptoe; **sich auf die ~spitzen stellen** stand on tiptoe
**zehn** /tseːn/ *Kardinalz.* ▶ 76, ▶ 752, ▶ 841 ten; ⇒ *auch* **acht**[1]
**Zehn** *die;* ~, ~**en** ten; ⇒ *auch* **Acht**[1] A, D, E, G
**zehn-, Zehn-** ⇒ *auch* **acht-, Acht-:** ~**eck** *das* decagon; ~**eckig** *Adj.* decagonal; ~**ender** *der;* ~~**s**, ~~ (*Jägerspr.*) ten-pointer
**Zehner** *der;* ~**s**, ~ [A] (*ugs.: Geldschein, Münze*) ten; [B] (*ugs.: Autobus*) number ten; [C] (*Math.*) ten; **die ~ addieren** add up the tens; [D] (*Sprungturm*) ten-metre platform; ⇒ *auch* **Achter** D
**Zehner·karte** *die* ticket for ten trips/visits *etc.*
**zehnerlei** *Gattungsz.; indekl.* [A] *attr.* ten kinds *or* sorts of; ten different ‹sorts, sizes, etc.›; [B] *subst.* ten [different] things
**Zehner-:** ~**packung** *die* packet of ten; ~**stelle** *die* (*Math.*) **in der ~stelle** in the tens; ~**system** *das* (*Math.*) ⇒ **Dezimalsystem**; ~**ziffer** *die* (*Math.*) figure in the tens
**zehn·fach** *Vervielfältigungsz.* tenfold; **die ~e Menge** ten times the quantity; ⇒ *auch* **achtfach**
**Zehnfache** *das; adj. Dekl.* **das ~:** ten times as much; **um ein ~s/um das ~:** ten times; ⇒ *auch* **Achtfache**
**zehn-, Zehn-:** ~**finger·system** *das* touch [-typing] system; **im ~fingersystem schreiben** touch-type; ~**flach** *das;* ~~**[e]s**, ~~**e**, ~**flächner** *der;* ~~**s**, ~~ (*Math.*) decahedron; ~**jahres·feier**, ~**jahr·feier** *die* tenth anniversary celebration; ~**jährig** *Adj.* (*10 Jahre alt*) ten-year-old *attrib.;* ten years old *postpos.;* (*10 Jahre dauernd*) ten-year *attrib.;* ⇒ *auch* **achtjährig**; ~**jährlich** ❶ *Adj.* ten-yearly; ❷ *adv.* every ten years; ⇒ *auch* **achtjährlich**; ~**kampf** *der* (*Sport*) decathlon; ~**kämpfer** *der* decathlete; ~**mal** *Adv.* ten times; **und wenn du dich ~mal langweilst** it doesn't matter 'how bored you are; ⇒ *auch* **achtmal**; ~**malig** *Adj.* **nach ~maligem Läuten** after ringing ten times; ⇒ *auch* **achtmalig**; ~**mark·schein** *der* ▶ 337 ten-mark note; ~**pfennig·[brief]marke** *die* ten-pfennig stamp; ~**pfennig·stück** *das* ▶ 337 ten-pfennig piece; ~**seitig** *Adj.* ten-sided; ten-page *attrib.* ‹letter, article, etc.›; ~**stöckig** *Adj.* ten-storey ‹building›; ⇒ *auch* **achtstöckig**
**zehnt** /tseːnt/ *in* **wir waren zu ~:** there were ten of us; ⇒ *auch* **acht**[2]
**zehnt...** *Ordinalz.* ▶ 207, ▶ 841 tenth; ⇒ *auch* **acht...**
**zehn-:** ~**tägig** *Adj.* (*10 Tage alt*) ten-day-old *attrib.;* (*10 Tage dauernd*) ten-day *attrib.;* ⇒ *auch* **achttägig**; ~**tausend** *Kardinalz.* ▶ 841 ten thousand; **die oberen ~tausend** (*fig.: die vornehmen Leute*) the élite of society
**Zehnte**[1] *der;* ~**n**, ~**n** (*hist.*) tithe
**Zehnte**[2] *der/die; adj. Dekl.* tenth; ⇒ *auch* **Achte**
**zehn·teilig** *Adj.* ten-piece ‹tool set etc.›; ten-part ‹serial›; ⇒ *auch* **achtteilig**
**zehntel** /ˈtseːntl/ *Bruchz.* ▶ 841 tenth; ⇒ *auch* **achtel**
**Zehntel** *das* (*schweiz. meist* **der**); ~**s**, ~: ▶ 841 tenth
**Zehntel-:** ~**liter** *der* tenth of a litre; ~**sekunde** *die* tenth of a second
***zehnte·mal**, ***zehnten·mal** ⇒ **Mal**[1]
**zehntens** *Adv.* tenthly
**Zehn·tonner** *der;* ~**s**, ~: ten-tonner
**zehren** /ˈtseːrən/ *itr. V.* [A] (*leben*) **von etw. ~:** live on *or* off sth.; **von Erinnerungen** *usw.* ~ (*fig.*) sustain oneself on memories *etc.;* [B] (*geh.: schwächen*) drain sb.'s strength; take it out of sb.; [C] (*zusetzen*) **an jmdm./jmds. Kräften ~:** wear sb. down/sap sb.'s strength
**Zehr·geld** *das* (*veralt.*) money for the journey
**Zeichen** /ˈtsaiçn̩/ *das;* ~**s**, ~ [A] (*Gebärde*) sign; (*Laut, Wink*) signal; **das ~ zum Angriff** the signal to attack; **jmdm. ein ~ geben** signal to sb.; **zum ~, dass ...** to show that ...; as a sign that ...; **zum** *od.* **als ~ ihrer Versöhnung** as a sign *or* token of their reconciliation; [B] (*Markierung*) mark; (*Waren~*) [trade] mark; (*am Briefkopf*) reference; **sein ~ unter ein Schriftstück setzen** initial a document; **seines/ihres ~s** (*veralt., scherzh.*) by trade/profession; **[ein] ~ setzen** set an example; point the way; [C] (*Symbol*) sign; (*Chemie, Math., auf Landkarten usw.*) symbol; (*Satz~*) punctuation mark; (*Musik*) accidental; **das ~ des Kreuzes** the sign of the cross; [D] (*An~*) sign; indication; (*einer Krankheit*) sign; symptom; **ein ~ dafür, dass ...** a [sure] sign that ...; **wenn nicht alle ~ trügen** unless I am very much mistaken; **es geschehen noch ~ und Wunder** wonders will never cease (*iron.*); **die ~ der Zeit erkennen** see which way the wind's blowing (*fig.*); [E] (*Tierkreis~*) sign [of the zodiac]; **ich bin im ~ des Krebses** *usw.* **geboren** I was born under the sign of Cancer *etc.;* **im** *od.* **unter dem ~ von etw. stehen** (*geh.*) be much influenced by sth.
**zeichen-, Zeichen-:** ~**block** *der; Pl.* ~**blöcke** *od.* ~~**s** sketch pad; ~**brett** *das* drawing board; ~**dreieck** *das* set square; ~**erklärung** *die* legend; ~**feder** *die* drawing pen; ~**haft** (*geh.*) ❶ *Adj.* symbolic; ❷ *adv.* symbolically; ~**heft** *das* drawing book; ~**kohle** *die* charcoal (*in stick form*); ~**lehrer** *der,* ~**lehrerin** *die* drawing teacher; ~**papier** *das* drawing paper; ~**setzung** *die;* ~~, ~~**en** punctuation; ~**sprache** *die* sign language; ~**stift** *der* drawing pencil; ~**trick·film** *der* animated cartoon; ~**unterricht** *der* drawing lessons *pl.;* (*Schulfach*) art *no art.;* ⇒ *auch* **Englischunterricht**; ~**winkel** *der* set square
**zeichnen** ❶ *tr. V.* [A] (*malen, darstellen*) draw; (*fig.*) portray ‹character›; **ein Bild von dem Geschehen ~** (*fig.*) describe what happened; [B] (*markieren*) **das Fell ist schön/auffallend gezeichnet** the fur has beautiful/striking markings; **er war vom Alter/von der Krankheit gezeichnet** (*fig.*) age/sickness had left its mark on him; **ein vom Tode Gezeichneter** (*fig. geh.*) a man already bearing the mark of death; [C] (*bes. Kaufmannsspr.*) sign ‹cheque›; subscribe for ‹share, loan›.
❷ *itr. V.* [A] draw; **ich zeichne schon länger daran** I have been working on this drawing for quite a while; [B] (*bes. Kaufmannsspr.: unterschreiben*) sign; **für etw. [verantwortlich] ~** (*fig.*) be responsible for sth.
**Zeichnen** *das;* ~**s** drawing; **technisches ~:** technical drawing
**Zeichner** *der;* ~**s**, ~, **Zeichnerin** *die;* ~, ~**nen** ▶ 159 [A] graphic artist; (*Technik*) draughtsman/-woman; [B] (*Kaufmannsspr.*) subscriber
**zeichnerisch** ❶ *Adj.* ‹fault› of draughtsmanship; ‹talent› as a draughtsman/-woman *or* for drawing; **exakte ~e Wiedergabe** exact portrayal in a drawing. ❷ *adv.* **~ begabt sein** have a talent for drawing; **etw. ~ darstellen** make a drawing of sth.
**Zeichnung** *die;* ~, ~**en** [A] drawing; (*fig.: von Figuren*) portrayal; [B] (*bei Tieren und Pflanzen*) markings *pl.;* [C] (*Kaufmannsspr.*) subscription
**zeichnungs·berechtigt** *Adj.* (*Kaufmannsspr.*) with signatory powers *postpos.;* **~ sein** have signatory powers
**Zeige·finger** *der* index finger; forefinger; **der erhobene ~** (*fig.*) the wagging *or* monitory finger
**zeigen** /ˈtsaiɡn̩/ ❶ *tr. V.* point; **[mit dem Finger/einem Stock] auf jmdn./etw. ~:** point [one's finger/a stick] at sb./sth.; **nach Norden/zwölf ~:** point [to the] north/to twelve o'clock.
❷ *tr. V.* show; **jmdm. etw. ~:** show sb. sth.; show sth. to sb.; **jmdm. sein Zimmer ~:** show sb. to his/her room; **dem werd ichs ~!** (*ugs.*) I'll show him!; **er hat es allen seinen Konkurrenten gezeigt** (*ugs.*) he showed all his competitors just how it was done; **zeig mal, was du kannst** show [us] what you can do.
❸ *refl. V.* [A] (*sich sehen lassen*) appear; **er zeigt sich selten in der Öffentlichkeit** he is rarely seen in public; **mit ihr kann man sich überall ~:** you can take her anywhere; **er wollte sich von seiner besten Seite ~:** he wanted to show himself to advantage; [B] (*sich erweisen*) prove to be; **es wird sich ~, wer daran schuld war** time will tell who was responsible; **es hat sich gezeigt, dass ...** it turned out that ...; **sich als etw. ~:** prove *or* turn out to be sth.
**Zeiger** *der;* ~**s**, ~: pointer; (*Uhr~*) hand
**Zeige·stock** *der; Pl.* ~**stöcke** pointer
**Zeig·finger** *der* (*schweiz.*) ⇒ **Zeigefinger**
**zeihen** /ˈtsaiən/ *unr. tr. V.* (*geh.*) **jmdn. einer Sache** (*Gen.*) **~:** indict sb. of sth.
**Zeile** /ˈtsailə/ *die;* ~, ~**n** [A] line; **jmdm. ein paar ~n schreiben** drop sb. a line; **vielen Dank für Ihre ~:** many thanks for your letter; **mit zwei ~n Abstand** with double spacing; **zwischen den ~n lesen** (*fig.*) read between the lines; [B] (*Reihe*) row; (*des Fernsehbildes*) line
**Zeilen-:** ~**ab·stand** *der* [line] spacing; (*in gedrucktem Text*) leading; ~**bau·weise** *die* ribbon development; ~**gieß·maschine** *die* Linotype (P) machine; ~**honorar** *das* payment by the line; ~**sprung** *der* (*Verslehre*) enjambment
**-zeilig** /-tsailɪç/ -line; **zwei~ sein** have two lines
**Zeisig** /ˈtsaizɪç/ *der;* ~**s**, ~**e** (*Zool.*) siskin
**zeit** /tsait/ *Präp. mit Gen. in* **~ meines** *usw.*/**unseres** *usw.* **Lebens** all my *etc.* life/our *etc.* lives
**Zeit** *die;* ~, ~**en** [A] time *no art.;* **im Laufe der ~:** in the course of time; **mit der ~:** with time; in time; (*allmählich*) gradually; **die ~ arbeitet für/gegen jmdn.** time is on sb.'s side/is against sb.; **die ~ heilt alle Wunden** (*Spr.*) time is a great healer; **kommt ~, kommt Rat** (*Spr.*) take your time and you'll find an answer; **keine ~ verlieren dürfen** have no time to lose; **die ~ drängt** time is pressing; there is [precious] little time; **~ ist Geld** (*Spr.*) time is money (*prov.*); **sich** (*Dat.*) **die ~ [mit etw.] vertreiben** pass the time [with/doing sth.]; **jmdm. ~/drei Tage** *usw.* **~ lassen** give sb. time/three days *etc.;* **sich** (*Dat.*) **~ lassen** *od.* **nehmen** take one's time; **sich** (*Dat.*) **~ für jmdn./etw. ~ nehmen** make time for sb./sth.; **etw. hat ~, mit etw. hat es ~:** there's no hurry about sth.; **auf ~ spielen** (*Sportjargon*) play for time; **eine ~ lang** for a while *or* a time; ⇒ *auch* **nachtschlafend**; **sparen**; **stehlen**; **totschlagen**; [B] (*~punkt*) time; **ihre/seine ~ ist gekommen** (*geh. verhüll.*) her/his time has come; **außer der ~, außerhalb der üblichen ~:** at an unusual time; **seit der** *od.* **dieser ~:** since that time; **um diese ~:** at this time; **vor der ~:** prematurely; early; **zu jeder ~:** at any time; **zur rechten ~:** at the right time; **wer nicht kommt zur rechten ~, der muss essen, was übrig bleibt** (*Spr.*) the early bird catches the worm (*prov.*); **zu welcher ~?** at what time?; when?; **zu bestimmten ~en** at certain times; **alles zu seiner ~:** all in good time; **es ist/wird [langsam] ~** *od.* **ist an der ~:** it's time/[just] about time; **es ist [aller]höchste ~[, dass wir uns wehren]** it's high time [we fought back]; **von ~ zu ~:** from time to time; **zur ~** ⇒ **zurzeit**; [C] (*~abschnitt, Lebensabschnitt*) time; period; (*Geschichtsabschnitt*) age; period; **die schönste ~ des Lebens** *od.* **im Leben** the best time of one's life; **er hat ~en, in denen ...** he has times *or* periods when ...; **die erste ~:** at first; **auf ~:** temporarily; **ein Vertrag auf ~:** a fixed-term contract; **ein Zug der**

*old spelling (see note on page 1707)

Z

**~:** a feature of the times; **mit der ~ gehen** move with the times; **der Geist der ~:** the spirit of the age; **die ~, als es noch kein Telefon gab** the days *pl.* before there were telephones; **andere ~en, andere Sitten** things are different now; **in früheren ~en** in former times; in the old days; **zu meiner ~:** in my day; **in der nächsten ~, in nächster ~:** in the near future; **für alle ~:** for ever; for all time; **in der letzten** *od.* **in letzter** *od.* **in jüngster ~:** recently; **zu allen ~en** always; at all times; **zu keiner ~:** at no time; never; **hier bin ich die längste ~ gewesen** (*ugs.*) I've been here for long enough; **seit ewigen ~en** (*ugs.*) for ages (*coll.*); **seit undenklichen ~en** from time immemorial; **vor ~en** (*dichter.*) long ago; in days gone by; **zu ~en von jmdm./etw.** in sb.'s day/at the time of sth.; ⇒ *auch* **lieb** 1 D; **D** (*Sport: ~raum*) time; **gute ~en laufen** do good times; **die ~ bei etw. stoppen** time sth.; **E** (*Sport: Wettbewerbsdauer*) **einen Vorsprung über die ~ bringen** retain one's lead until the end of the game; **über die ~ kommen** (*Boxen*) go the distance; **F** (*Sprachw.*) tense

**zeit-, Zeit-: ~abschnitt** *der* period; **~alter** *das* age; era; **~angabe** *die* **A** statement regarding time; **er konnte keine genaue ~angabe machen** he could not be precise about the time; **B** (*Sprachw.*) expression of time; **~ansage** *die* (*im Radio*) time check; (*am Telefon*) speaking clock; **~arbeit** *die* (*Wirtsch.*) temporary work; work as a temp (*coll.*); **~aufwand** *der:* **viel ~aufwand erfordern** take up a great deal of time; **den ~aufwand verringern** reduce the time needed; **~bedingt** *Adj.* arising from prevailing circumstances *postpos.;* (*vorübergehend*) temporary; **~begriff** *der* concept of time; **~bestimmung** *die* (*Sprachw.*) expression of time; **~bombe** *die* (*auch fig.*) time bomb; **~dauer** *die* duration; **~dokument** *das* contemporary document; **~druck** *der* pressure of time; **unter ~druck** under pressure; **unter ~druck stehen/in ~druck kommen** be/become pressed for time; be/come under pressure [of time]; **~ein·teilung** *die* timing; **mit seiner ~einteilung nie zurechtkommen** never succeed in organizing one's time properly

**Zeiten-: ~folge** *die* (*Sprachw.*) sequence of tenses; **~wende** *die* turning point in history

**zeit-, Zeit-: ~erscheinung** *die* transient phenomenon; **~ersparnis** *die* time-saving; **das bedeutete keine ~ersparnis** it did not save any time; **~faktor** *der* time factor; **~form** *die* (*Sprachw.*) tense; **in der ~form der Gegenwart** in the present tense; **~gebunden** *Adj.* characteristic of its/their time *postpos.;* **~gebunden sein** be an expression *or* a reflection of its/their time; **~gefühl** *das* sense of time; **~geist** *der* spirit of the age; **~gemäß** *Adj.* (*modern*) up-to-date; (*aktuell*) topical ‹theme›; contemporary ‹views›; (*in der Vergangenheit*) in keeping with the period *postpos.;* **~genosse** *der,* **~genossin** *die* **A** contemporary; **B** (*Mitmensch*) fellow man/woman; **ein seltsamer ~genosse** a strange individual (*coll.*); **prominente ~genossen waren anwesend** leading figures [of the day] were present; **~genössisch** /-gənœsɪʃ/ *Adj.* contemporary; **~geschehen** *das:* **das [aktuelle] ~geschehen** current events *pl.;* **~geschichte** *die* **A** **die ~geschichte** the modern age; our age; **B** (*Disziplin*) contemporary history *no art.;* **~geschichtlich** ❶ *Adj.* **A** (*zeitlich*) contemporary ‹source etc.›; **B** (*fachlich*) **~geschichtlicher Unterricht** contemporary-history teaching; ❷ *adv.* **A** historically; **B** (*fachlich*) from the point of view of contemporary history; **~geschmack** *der* contemporary taste; **~gewinn** *der* ⇒ **~ersparnis**; **~gleich** ❶ *Adj.* **A** (*Sport*) ‹runners etc.› with the same time; **B** ⇒ **gleichzeitig** 1; ❷ *adv.* ⇒ **gleichzeitig** 2

**zeitig** *Adj., adv.* early

**zeitigen** *tr. V.* (*geh.*) produce, yield ‹result, success, etc.›; provoke, precipitate ‹uproar›

**zeit-, Zeit-: ~karte** *die* (*Verkehrsw.*) season ticket; **~kritik** *die* appraisal *or* analysis of contemporary issues; **~kritisch** ❶ *Adj.* ‹essay, article, film› analysing contemporary issues; **~kritische Themen** contemporary issues; ❷ *adv.* ‹examine› in the light of contemporary issues; ***~lang** ⇒ **Zeit** A; **~läuf[t]e** /-lɔyf(t)ə/ *Pl.* (*geh.*) times; **über alle ~läuf[t]e hinweg** for all time; **~lebens** *Adv.* all one's life

**zeitlich** ❶ *Adj.* **A** ‹length, interval› in time; chronological ‹order, sequence›; **in großem/kurzem ~en Abstand** at long/short intervals; **B** (*Rel.*) temporal; **das Zeitliche segnen** (*verhüll.*) pass on (*euphem.*); (*scherzh.*) come to grief. ❷ *adv.* **A** with regard to time; **ich kann es ~ nicht einrichten** I can't fit it in time-wise (*coll.*); **wenn es der Beruf ~ erlaubt** if one's job leaves enough time

**zeit-, Zeit-: ~lohn** *der* (*Wirtsch.*) time-work rate; (*Stundenlohn*) hourly rate; **~los** ❶ *Adj.* timeless; classic ‹fashion, shape›; ❷ *adv.* timelessly; **~los eingerichtet** furnished in a classic *or* timeless style; **~lupe** *die* (*Film*) slow motion; **~lupen·tempo** *das:* **in im ~lupentempo** at a crawl; at a snail's pace; **~mangel** *der* lack of time; **aus ~mangel, wegen ~mangel[s]** owing to lack of time; **~maß** *das* speed; (*von Musik usw.*) tempo; **~messer** *der;* **~~s, ~~:** timepiece; **~nah[e]** ❶ *Adj.* topical ‹play etc.›; ‹teaching, syllabus› relevant to the present day; ❷ *adv.* topically; **~nehmer** *der;* **~~s, ~~, ~nehmerin** *die;* **~~, ~~nen** timekeeper; **~not** *die* **in ~not geraten** *od.* **kommen** become pressed for time; **in ~not machte er einen falschen Zug** (*Schach*) in time pressure he made a wrong move; **~plan** *der* schedule; **~punkt** *der* moment; **zum jetzigen ~punkt** at the present moment; at this point in time; **~raffer** *der;* **~~s, ~~:** (*Film*) timelapse; **etw. im ~raffer zeigen** show sth. speeded up; **~raubend** *Adj.* time-consuming; **~raum** *der* period; **über einen ~raum von fünf Tagen** for a period of five days; **~rechnung** *die* calendar; **vor unserer ~rechnung** BC; before Christ; **unserer/christlicher ~rechnung** AD; Anno Domini; **~schrift** *die* magazine; (*bes. wissenschaftlich*) journal; periodical; **~soldat** *der,* **~soldatin** *die: soldier serving for a fixed period;* **~spanne** *die* period; **~springen** *das;* **~~s, ~~** (*Pferdesport*) jumping against the clock; **~strafe** *die* (*Sport*) sending off for a specified time; (*im Eishockey*) penalty; **~strömung** *die* prevailing trend; **~umstände** *Pl.* prevailing circumstances; **die damaligen ~umstände** the circumstances prevailing at the time

**Zeitung** *die;* **~, ~en** [news]paper; **[die] ~ lesen** read the paper; **bei einer ~ arbeiten** work for a newspaper; **er ist von der ~** (*ugs.*) he's from the press; **eine Anzeige in die ~ setzen** put an advertisement in the paper

**Zeitungs-: ~abonnement** *das* newspaper subscription; **~annonce** *die,* **~anzeige** *die* newspaper advertisement; **~artikel** *der* newspaper article; **~ausschnitt** *der* newspaper cutting; **~austräger** *der,* **~austrägerin** *die* newspaper deliverer; **~ente** *die* (*ugs.*) false [newspaper] report; canard; **~frau** *die* newspaper seller; (*Austrägerin*) newspaper deliverer; **~inserat** *das* newspaper advertisement; **~leser** *der,* **~leserin** *die* newspaper reader; **~meldung** *die* newspaper report; **~notiz** *die* newspaper item; **~papier** *das* **A** (*alte Zeitung[en]*) newspaper; **B** (*unbedruckt*) newsprint; **~ständer** *der* newspaper rack; **~träger** *der,* **~trägerin** *die* ⇒ **~austräger**; **~verkäufer** *der,* **~verkäuferin** *die* newspaper seller; news vendor; **~wissenschaft** *die* (*Hochschulw.*) journalistic studies *pl., no art.*

**zeit-, Zeit-: ~unterschied** *der* time difference; **~verschwendung** *die* waste of time; **[reine** *od.* **pure] ~verschwendung sein** be a [pure *or* complete] waste of time; **~vertreib** *der;* **~~[e]s, ~~e** pastime; **zum ~vertreib** to pass the time; **~weilig** ❶ *Adj.* temporary; ❷ *adv.* **A** (*vorübergehend*) temporarily; for a time; **B** (*gelegentlich*) occasionally; at times; **~weise** *Adv.* **A** (*gelegentlich*) occasionally; at times; (*von ~ zu ~*) from time to time; **~weise Regen** occasional rain; **B** (*vorübergehend*) for a time; for a while; **~wende** *die* **A** **vor/nach der ~wende** BC/AD; before Christ/Anno Domini; **um die ~wende** about the time of the birth of Christ; **B** ⇒ **Zeitenwende**; **~wort** *das; Pl.* **~wörter** (*Sprachw.*) verb; **~zeichen** *das* (*Rundf., Funkw.*) time signal; **~zone** *die* time zone; **~zünder** *der* time fuse

**zelebrieren** /tsele'bri:rən/ *tr. V.* **A** (*kath. Kirche*) celebrate ‹mass›; conduct ‹service, wedding›; **B** (*feierlich ausführen*) make ‹meal, event, etc.› into a ritual; **C** (*ehren*) honour

**Zelebrität** /tselebri'tɛ:t/ *die;* **~, ~en** (*geh.*) celebrity

**Zelle** /'tsɛlə/ *die;* **~, ~n** cell; (*Telefon~*) [telephone] booth *or* (*Brit.*) box; **die [kleinen] grauen ~n** (*scherzh.*) one's grey matter *sing.*

**Zeller** *der;* **~s** (*österr. ugs.*) celeriac

**Zell-: ~gewebe** *das* (*Biol.*) cell tissue; **~gift** *das* (*Biol., Med.*) cytotoxin; **~kern** *der* (*Biol.*) cell nucleus; **~stoff** *der* **A** cellulose; **B** (*Material*) cellulose wadding; **~teilung** *die* (*Biol.*) cell division

**Zellulitis** /tsɛlu'li:tɪs/ *die;* **~, Zellulitiden** /tsɛluli'ti:dn̩/ **▶ 474** (*Med.*) cellulitis

**Zelluloid** /tsɛlu'lɔyt/ *das;* **~[e]s** celluloid

**Zellulose** /tsɛlu'lo:zə/ *die;* **~, ~n** cellulose

**Zell·wolle** *die* rayon

**Zelt** /tsɛlt/ *das;* **~[e]s, ~e** tent; (*Fest~*) marquee; (*Zirkus~*) big top; **das himmlische ~** (*fig. dichter.*) the canopy of heaven (*literary*); **seine ~e irgendwo aufschlagen** (*fig.*) settle down somewhere; **seine ~e abbrechen** (*fig.*) up sticks (*coll.*); decamp

**zelten** *itr. V.* camp; **wir waren ~:** we went camping; **„Z~ verboten"** 'no camping'

**Zelt-: ~lager** *das* camp; **~pflock** *der* tent peg; **~plane** *die* tarpaulin; **~platz** *der* camping site; campsite

**Zement** /tse'mɛnt/ *der;* **~[e]s, ~e** cement

**Zement·boden** *der* concrete floor

**zementieren** *tr. V.* **A** cement; **zementierte Wege** concrete paths; **B** (*fig.: festlegen*) make ‹division, situation, etc.› permanent; **weiter zementiert werden** ‹prejudice, opinion› become further entrenched

**Zen** /zɛn/ *das;* **~[s], Zen-Buddhismus** *der* (*Rel.*) Zen [Buddhism] *no art.*

**Zenit** /tse'ni:t/ *der;* **~[e]s** zenith; **im ~ stehen** be at its zenith; **er stand im ~ seines Ruhms** (*fig. geh.*) he was at the peak of his fame

**zensieren** /tsɛn'zi:rən/ ❶ *tr. V.* **A** (*Schulw.*) mark, (*Amer.*) grade ‹essay etc.›; **B** (*der Zensur unterziehen*) censor ‹article, film, etc.›. ❷ *itr. V.* (*Schulw.*) **streng/milde ~:** mark *or* (*Amer.*) grade severely/leniently

**Zensierung** *die;* **~, ~en** (*Schulw.*) marking; grading (*Amer.*)

**Zensor** /'tsɛnzɔr/ *der;* **~s, ~en** /tsɛn'zo:rən/ censor

**Zensur** /tsɛn'zu:ɐ̯/ *die;* **~, ~en** **A** (*Schulw.: Note*) mark; grade (*Amer.*); **~en austeilen** (*fig.*) mete out praise and blame (*literary*); **B** (*Kontrolle*) censorship; **C** (*Behörde*) censors *pl.*

**zensurieren** *tr. V.* (*österr.*) ⇒ **zensieren** 1 B

**Zentaur** /tsɛn'tauɐ̯/ *der;* **~en, ~en** (*Myth.*) centaur

**Zenti-** /tsɛnti-/: **~gramm** /--'gram/ *das* centigram; **~liter** /--'li:tɐ/ *der, auch: das* **▶ 611** centilitre; **~meter** /--'me:tɐ/ *der, auch: das* **▶ 489** centimetre; **~meter·maß** *das* [centimetre] measuring tape

**Zentner** /'tsɛntnɐ/ *der;* **~s, ~** **▶ 353** **A** centner; metric hundredweight; **B** (*österr., schweiz.*) centner; 100 kilograms

**zentner-, Zentner-: ~gewicht** *das* centner *or* fifty-kilogram weight; (*fig.: große Last*) massive weight; **~last** *die* hundredweight load; **ihr fiel eine ~last vom Herzen**

Z

(*fig.*) that was a load off her mind; **~schwer** ❶ *Adj.* weighing over a hundredweight *postpos., not pred.*; (*äußerst schwer*) massively heavy; ❷ *adv.* **~schwer auf jmdm. lasten** (*fig.*) weigh heavily on sb.; **~weise** *Adv.* by the hundredweight

**zentral** /tsɛn'tra:l/ ❶ *Adj.* central. ❷ *adv.* centrally

**Zentral·afrikanische Republik** *die* Central African Republic

**Zentral·bank** *die; Pl.* **~en** (*Finanzw.*) central bank

**zentral·beheizt** *Adj.* centrally heated; (*durch Fernwärme*) heated by a district heating system

**Zentrale** *die;* **~, ~n** Ⓐ (*zentrale Stelle*) head *or* central office; (*der Polizei, einer Partei*) headquarters *sing. or pl.*; (*Funk~*) control centre; (*fig.: Mittelpunkt*) centre; **das Gehirn ist die ~ für das Nervensystem** the brain is the control centre of the nervous system; Ⓑ (*Telefon~*) [telephone] exchange; (*eines Hotels, einer Firma o. Ä.*) switchboard; Ⓒ (*Geom.*) line passing through the centres of two circles

**Zentral·heizung** *die* central heating

**Zentralisation** /tsɛntraliza'tsi̯o:n/ *die;* **~, ~en** centralization

**zentralisieren** *tr. V.* centralize

**Zentralisierung** *die;* **~, ~en** centralization

**Zentralismus** *der;* **~:** centralism *usu. no art.*

**zentralistisch** ❶ *Adj.* centralist. ❷ *adv.* centralistically

**Zentral-: ~komitee** *das* Central Committee; **~nerven·system** *das* ▶471 (*Anat.*) central nervous system; **~organ** *das* official organ; **~speicher** *der* (*DV*) main memory

**Zentren** ⇨ Zentrum

**zentrieren** ❶ *tr. V.* centre (**um** on). ❷ *refl. V.* **sich um etw. ~:** be centred around sth.

**Zentrierung** *die;* **~, ~en** centring

**zentrifugal** /tsɛntrifu'ga:l/ (*Physik*) ❶ *Adj.* centrifugal. ❷ *adv.* centrifugally

**Zentrifugal·kraft** *die* (*Physik*) centrifugal force

**Zentrifuge** *die;* **~, ~n** centrifuge

**zentripetal** /tsɛntripe'ta:l/ (*Physik*) ❶ *Adj.* centripetal. ❷ *adv.* centripetally

**Zentripetal·kraft** *die* (*Physik*) centripetal force

**Zentri·winkel** /'tsɛntrivɪŋkl/ *der* (*Geom.*) central angle

**Zentrum** /'tsɛntrʊm/ *das;* **~s, Zentren** centre; **im ~:** at the centre; (*im Stadt~*) in the town/city centre; **im ~ des öffentlichen Interesses stehen** (*fig.*) be the focus of public interest

**Zephir** /'tse:fɪr/ *der;* **~s, ~e** (*dichter. veralt.*) zephyr

**Zeppelin** /'tsɛpəli:n/ *der;* **~s, ~e** Zeppelin

**Zepter** /'tsɛptɐ/ *das, auch: der;* **~s, ~:** sceptre; **das ~ übernehmen** (*fig.*) take the helm; **das ~ führen** *od.* (*scherzh.*) **schwingen** (*fig.*) wield the sceptre

**zerbeißen** *unr. tr. V.* bite in two; ‹flea, mosquito, etc.› bite ‹person etc.› all over

**zerbersten** *unr. itr. V.; mit sein* burst apart; **zerborstene Mauern** smashed walls

**zerbomben** *tr. V.* bomb to pieces; destroy by bombing; **zerbombt** bombed ‹streets, houses›

**zerbrechen** ❶ *unr. itr. V.; mit sein* break [into pieces]; smash [to pieces]; ‹glass› shatter; (*fig.*) ‹marriage, relationship› break up; **an seinem Kummer ~** (*fig. geh.*) be broken down by grief. ❷ *unr. tr. V.* break; smash, shatter ‹dishes, glass›

**zerbrechlich** *Adj.* Ⓐ fragile; **„Vorsicht, ~!“** 'fragile; handle with care'; Ⓑ (*zart, schwach*) frail

**Zerbrechlichkeit** *die;* **~** Ⓐ fragility; Ⓑ (*Zartheit, Schwachheit*) frailty

**zerbröckeln** ❶ *itr. V.; mit sein* (*auch fig.*) crumble away. ❷ *tr. V.* break into small pieces

**zerbröseln** ❶ *itr. V.; mit sein* crumble. ❷ *tr. V.* crumble up

*old spelling (see note on page 1707)

**zerdehnen** *tr. V.* Ⓐ (*dehnen*) stretch [out of shape]; Ⓑ (*verlängern*) draw out ‹plot, scenes›; drawl ‹word, vowel›

**zerdeppern** /tsɛɐ̯'dɛpɐn/ *tr. V.* (*ugs.*) smash ‹window, china, glass›

**zerdrücken** *tr. V.* Ⓐ (*zerquetschen*) mash ‹potatoes, banana›; Ⓑ (*zusammendrücken*) squash ‹fly etc.›; stub out ‹cigarette›; **eine Träne ~** (*fig. spöttisch*) shed a tear; Ⓒ (*ugs.: zerknittern*) crease ‹clothes›

**Zeremonie** /tseremo'ni:/ *die;* **~, ~n** ceremony; (*fig.*) ritual

**Zeremoniell** /tseremo'ni̯ɛl/ *das;* **~s, ~e** ceremonial

**Zeremonien·meister** *der* master of ceremonies

**Zeremonien·meisterin** *die* master of ceremonies; mistress of ceremonies (*rare*)

**zerfahren** ❶ *Adj.* distracted; scrappy ‹play›. ❷ *adv.* distractedly; ‹play› scrappily, without concentration

**Zerfall** *der;* **~[e]s, Zerfälle** Ⓐ disintegration; (*eines Organismus, fig.: der Moral*) breakdown; (*einer Leiche*) decomposition; (*eines Gebäudes*) decay; Ⓑ (*Kernphysik*) decay

**zerfallen**[1] *unr. itr. V.; mit sein* Ⓐ (*auch fig.*) disintegrate (**in** + *Akk.*, **zu** into); ‹building› fall into ruin, decay; ‹corpse› decompose, decay; **~de Mauern/Ruinen** crumbling walls/ruins; **zu Staub ~:** crumble into dust; **Moral und Kultur waren ~** (*fig.*) morals and culture had broken down *or* fallen into decay; Ⓑ (*unterteilt sein*) **in Phasen/Teile** *usw.* **~:** be divided into phases/parts *etc.*; Ⓒ (*Kernphysik*) decay

**zerfallen**[2] *Adj.* **mit jmdm. ~ sein** have fallen out with sb.; **mit sich und der Welt ~ sein** be at odds with oneself and the world

**Zerfalls·produkt** *das* (*bes. Kernphysik*) decay product

**zerfasern** *itr. V.; mit sein* fray

**zerfetzen** *tr. V.* Ⓐ (*zerstören*) rip *or* tear to pieces; rip *or* tear up ‹letter etc.› (**in** + *Akk.* into); (*fig.*) tear apart ‹body, limb›; Ⓑ (*kritisieren*) tear ‹book, play, etc.› to pieces *or* shreds

**zerfleddern** *tr. V.* wear out ‹book etc.›; **das Buch ist zerfleddert** the book is falling apart

**zerfleischen** *tr. V.* tear ‹person, animal› limb from limb; **sich ~** (*auch fig.*) tear each other apart; ‹country› tear itself apart

**Zerfleischung** *die;* **~, ~en** tearing apart *no art.*

**zerfließen** *unr. itr. V.; mit sein* Ⓐ (*schmelzen*) melt [away]; **in** *od.* **vor Mitleid ~** (*fig.*) dissolve with pity; **das Geld ist ihr unter den Händen zerflossen** the money ran through her fingers (*fig.*); Ⓑ (*auseinander fließen*) ‹paint, ink› run; ‹shapes› dissolve; **~de Konturen/Grenzen** blurred outlines/limits

**zerfransen** ❶ *itr. V.; mit sein* fray. ❷ *tr. V.* fray; (*zerreißen*) tear

**zerfressen** *unr. tr. V.* Ⓐ (*fressen*) eat away; ‹moth etc.› eat holes in; **von Motten ~:** motheaten; Ⓑ (*zersetzen*) corrode ‹metal›; eat away ‹bone›; **Kummer/Eifersucht zerfrisst ihm das Herz** (*fig.*) he is consumed with grief/jealousy

**zerfurchen** *tr. V.* Ⓐ rut ‹track etc.›; Ⓑ furrow ‹brow, face›

**zergehen** *unr. itr. V.; mit sein* melt; (*in Wasser, im Mund*) ‹tablet etc.› dissolve; **auf der Zunge ~:** melt in the mouth

**zergliedern** *tr. V.* Ⓐ dissect ‹plant, animal, corpse›; Ⓑ analyse ‹behaviour, process, etc.›; **Sätze ~:** parse sentences

**Zergliederung** *die* Ⓐ dissection; Ⓑ (*Analyse*) analysis; (*von Sätzen*) parsing

**zergrübeln** *refl. V.* **sich** (*Dat.*) **den Kopf** *od.* **das Hirn ~:** rack one's brains

**zerhacken** *tr. V.* chop up (**zu** into); (*in Wut*) hack to pieces

**zerhauen** *unr. tr. V.* chop up

**zerkauen** *tr. V.* chew [up]

**zerkleinern** /tsɛɐ̯'klainɐn/ *tr. V.* chop up ‹vegetables, meat, wood›; (*zerkauen*) chew up ‹food›; (*zermahlen*) crush ‹rock etc.›

**Zerkleinerung** *die;* **~, ~en** chopping up; (*Zerkauung*) chewing; (*Zermahlung*) crushing

**zerklüftet** *Adj.* fissured ‹landscape›; craggy ‹mountains›; deeply indented ‹coastline›

**zerknallen** ❶ *itr. V.; mit sein* burst [with a bang]. ❷ *tr. V.* burst ‹bag etc.› [with a bang]

**zerknautschen** *tr. V.* (*ugs.*) crumple

**zerknicken** ❶ *tr. V.* snap. ❷ *itr. V.; mit sein* snap

**zerknirscht** ❶ *Adj.* remorseful. ❷ *adv.* remorsefully

**Zerknirschung** *die;* **~:** remorse

**zerknittern** *tr. V.* crease; crumple; **ein zerknittertes Gesicht** a wrinkled face

**zerknüllen** *tr. V.* crumple up [into a ball]

**zerkochen** ❶ *itr. V.; mit sein* get overcooked; **zu Brei ~:** cook to a pulp; **zerkocht** overcooked. ❷ *tr. V.* overcook

**zerkratzen** *tr. V.* scratch

**zerkrümeln** ❶ *tr. V.* crumble up. ❷ *itr. V.; mit sein* break into crumbs; crumble

**zerlassen** *unr. tr. V.* (*Kochk.*) melt

**zerlegen** *tr. V.* Ⓐ (*auseinander nehmen*) dismantle; take to pieces; strip, dismantle ‹engine›; **etw. in seine Bestandteile ~:** reduce sth. to its component parts; **einen Lichtstrahl in die Farben des Spektrums ~:** split up a ray of light into the colours of the spectrum; Ⓑ (*zerschneiden*) cut up ‹animal, meat›; carve ‹joint›; dissect ‹corpse›

**zerlesen** *unr. tr. V.* read ‹book etc.› again and again until it looks worn out; **ein [völlig] ~es Exemplar** a well-thumbed copy

**zerlumpt** *Adj.* ragged ‹clothes, person›; **~ sein** ‹clothes› be in tatters, be torn; **~ herumlaufen** go about in rags

**zermahlen** *unr. tr. V.* grind

**zermalmen** /tsɛɐ̯'malmən/ *tr. V.* crush

**zermartern** *refl. V.* **in sich** (*Dat.*) **den Kopf** *od.* **das Hirn ~:** rack one's brains

**zermürben** *tr. V.* wear ‹person› down; **~d** wearing; trying

**Zermürbung** *die* wearing down *no art.*; (*Milit.*) attrition

**Zermürbungs·krieg** *der* war of attrition

**zernagen** *tr. V.* gnaw away

**zerpflücken** *tr. V.* Ⓐ pick ‹flower, lettuce, etc.› apart; Ⓑ (*fig.: kritisch analysieren*) pull ‹play, book, etc.› to pieces; destroy ‹alibi, reputation›

**zerplatzen** *itr. V.; mit sein* burst; **vor Wut ~** (*fig.*) explode [with anger]

**zerquetschen** *tr. V.* crush; mash ‹potatoes›; **es kostet 20 Mark und ein paar Zerquetschte** (*ugs.*) it costs 20 marks and a bit

**zerraufen** *tr. V.* tousle ‹hair›

**Zerr·bild** *das* distorted image

**zerreden** *tr. V.* talk over and over; do *or* flog ‹subject› to death (*coll.*)

**zerreiben** *unr. tr. V.* crush ‹spices, paint colours, etc.›; grind ‹corn›; (*fig.*) crush, wipe out ‹enemy›

**zerreißen** ❶ *unr. tr. V.* Ⓐ (*auseinander reißen*) tear up; (*in kleine Stücke*) tear to pieces; ‹animal› tear ‹prey› limb from limb; dismember ‹prey›; break ‹thread›; **ich könnte ihn ~!** I could tear him limb from limb!; **sich [fast] ~ [um jmdn.]** [nearly] kill oneself [for sb. *or* to help sb.]; **ich kann mich nicht ~:** I can't be in two places at once; **Schüsse zerrissen die Stille** shots rent the silence; Ⓑ (*beschädigen*) tear ‹stocking, trousers, etc.› (**an** + *Dat.* on).
❷ *unr. itr. V.; mit sein* Ⓐ (*auseinander gehen*) ‹thread, string, rope› break; **die Bande zwischen ihnen waren zerrissen** (*fig.*) the bonds between them had parted; **ihre Nerven war zum Zerreißen gespannt** her nerves were stretched to breaking point; Ⓑ (*kaputtgehen*) ‹paper, cloth, etc.› tear; **zerrissene Kleider/Schuhe** ragged clothes/worn-out shoes

**Zerreiß·probe** *die* acid test

**zerren** /'tsɛrən/ ❶ *tr. V.* Ⓐ drag; **etw. an die Öffentlichkeit ~** (*fig.*) drag sth. into the limelight; Ⓑ **sich** (*Dat.*) **einen Muskel/eine Sehne ~:** pull a muscle/tendon. ❷ *itr. V.* **an etw.** (*Dat.*) **~:** tug *or* pull at sth.

Z

**zerrinnen** *unr. itr. V.* melt; (*fig.*) ‹time, years› pass; **seine Hoffnungen/Träume/Pläne zerrannen [in nichts]** (*geh.*) his hopes/dreams vanished/plans came to nothing; **jmdm. unter den Händen/Fingern ~:** slip through sb.'s fingers

**zerrissen** /tsɛɐ̯ˈrɪsn̩/ ❶ *2. Part. v.* **zerreißen.** ❷ *Adj.* **[innerlich] ~:** at odds with oneself

**Zerrissenheit** *die; ~:* inner turmoil

**Zerr·spiegel** *der* distorting mirror

**Zerrung** *die; ~, ~en* pulled muscle; (*Sehnen~*) pulled tendon

**zerrupfen** *tr. V.* tear to bits

**zerrütten** /tsɛɐ̯ˈrʏtn̩/ *tr. V.* ruin ‹health›; shatter ‹nerves›; ruin, wreck ‹marriage›; **aus zerrütteten Familienverhältnissen stammen** come from a broken home; **die Finanzen sind zerrüttet** the finances are in a disastrous state

**Zerrüttung** *die; ~, ~en* (*der Gesundheit*) ruining; (*der Nerven*) shattering; (*einer Ehe*) [irretrievable] breakdown; (*einer Familie*) break-up

**Zerrüttungs·prinzip** *das* (*Rechtsw.*) principle of irretrievable breakdown (*of a marriage*)

**zersägen** *tr. V.* saw up

**zerschellen** *itr. V.; mit sein* be dashed *or* smashed to pieces

**zerschlagen**[1] ❶ *unr. tr. V.* smash ‹plate, windscreen, etc.›; smash up ‹furniture›; (*fig.*) smash ‹spy ring etc.›; crush ‹enemy, attack›; break up ‹cartel›. ❷ *unr. refl. V.* ‹plan, deal› fall through

**zerschlagen**[2] *Adj.* worn out; whacked (*Brit. coll.*); tuckered [out] (*Amer. coll.*); shattered (*Brit. coll.*)

**Zerschlagung** *die; ~, ~en* smashing; destruction; (*eines Gegners, Widerstands*) crushing; **die ~ der Kartelle** the breaking up of cartels

**zerschmelzen** *unr. itr. V.; mit sein* (*auch fig.*) melt

**zerschmettern** *tr. V.* smash; shatter ‹glass, leg, bone›; (*fig.*) crush ‹army, enemy›

**zerschneiden** *unr. tr. V.* Ⓐ (*schneiden*) cut; (*in Stücke*) cut up; (*in zwei Teile*) cut in two; carve ‹joint›; **von tiefen Furchen zerschnitten** deeply rutted; Ⓑ (*verletzen*) cut [into] ‹skin etc.›

**zerschnippeln** *tr. V.* (*ugs.*) cut up *or* snip into small pieces

**zerschunden** /tsɛɐ̯ˈʃʊndn̩/ *Adj.* covered in scratches *postpos.*

**zersetzen** ❶ *tr. V.* Ⓐ (*auflösen*) corrode ‹metal›; decompose ‹organism›; Ⓑ (*untergraben*) subvert ‹ideals›; undermine ‹morale›; **~de Schriften** subversive writings. ❷ *refl. V.* decompose; ‹wood, compost› rot

**Zersetzung** *die; ~, ~en* Ⓐ ⇒ **zersetzen** 2: decomposition; rotting; Ⓑ ⇒ **zersetzen** 1 B: subversion; undermining

**Zersetzungs·prozess, *Zersetzungs·prozeß** *der* process of decomposition

**zersiedeln** *tr. V.* (*Amtsspr.*) overdevelop ‹area›; spoil ‹area› by overdevelopment

**Zersied[e]lung** *die* overdevelopment

**zerspalten** *unr.* (*auch regelm.*) *tr. V.* (*auch fig.*) split [up]; (*Chemie*) break down ‹compounds› (**in** + *Akk.* into)

**zersplittern** ❶ *itr. V.; mit sein* ‹wood, bone› splinter; ‹glass› shatter; **das Land war in viele Kleinstaaten zersplittert** the country was fragmented into many small states. ❷ *tr. V.* splinter; shatter ‹glass›

**zersprengen** *tr. V.* Ⓐ (*sprengen*) blow up; (*in Stücke*) blow to pieces; Ⓑ (*auseinander treiben*) scatter ‹army›

**zerspringen** *unr. itr. V.; mit sein* Ⓐ shatter; (*Sprünge bekommen*) crack; (*fig.*) ‹heart› burst (**vor** + *Dat.* with); **der Kopf wollte mir ~ vor Schmerzen** my head was splitting; I had a splitting headache; Ⓑ (*geh.: zerreißen*) ‹string etc.› break

**zerstampfen** *tr. V.* Ⓐ (*zerkleinern*) pound, crush ‹spices etc.›; mash ‹potatoes›; Ⓑ (*beschädigen*) trample down ‹field etc.›

**zerstäuben** *tr. V.* spray

**Zerstäuber** *der; ~s, ~:* atomizer

**zerstechen** *unr. tr. V.* Ⓐ (*stechen*) sting all over; ‹mosquitoes› bite all over; Ⓑ (*beschädigen*) jab holes in ‹cushion etc.›; puncture, slit ‹tyre›; **ihre Venen sind ganz zerstochen** her veins are covered in needle marks

**zerstieben** *unr.* (*auch regelm.*) *itr. V.; mit sein* (*geh.*) scatter; ‹crowd› disperse; (*fig.*) ‹sadness, nightmare› vanish; **in alle Winde ~:** disappear without trace

**zerstörbar** *Adj.* destructible; **leicht ~ sein** be easily destroyed *or* broken

**zerstören** *tr. V.* destroy; ‹hooligan› smash up, vandalize ‹telephone box etc.›; (*fig.*) ruin ‹landscape, health, life›; dash, destroy ‹hopes, dreams›; wreck, destroy ‹marriage›; **durch ein Feuer/Erdbeben zerstört** destroyed in *or* by a fire/an earthquake; **~de Gewalt** destructive power; **zerstörte Städte** ruined cities

**Zerstörer** *der; ~s, ~* Ⓐ (*Schiff*) destroyer; Ⓑ (*Person*) destroyer; wrecker; (*Rowdy*) vandal

**Zerstörerin** *die; ~, ~nen* ⇒ **Zerstörer** B

**zerstörerisch** ❶ *Adj.* destructive. ❷ *adv.* **~ wirken** have a destructive effect

**Zerstörung** *die* destruction; (*durch Rowdys*) smashing up; vandalization; (*der Gesundheit, Existenz*) ruin[ation]; (*einer Ehe*) wrecking; destruction; (*von Hoffnungen*) dashing; destruction

**Zerstörungs·wut** *die* destructive frenzy

**zerstoßen** *unr. tr. V.* crush ‹berries etc.›; (*im Mörser*) pound, crush ‹peppercorns etc.›

**zerstreiten** *unr. refl. V.* **sich mit jmdm. ~:** fall out with sb.; **untereinander zerstritten sein** be at loggerheads

**zerstreuen** ❶ *tr. V.* Ⓐ scatter; (*auseinander treiben*) disperse ‹crowd›; (*fig.*) **zerstreut liegende Gehöfte** scattered farms; **in alle Welt zerstreut** scattered to the four winds; Ⓑ (*unterhalten*) **jmdn./sich ~:** entertain sb./oneself; (*ablenken*) take sb.'s/one's mind off things; **sich ein wenig ~:** enjoy oneself a little; **sich mit** *od.* **durch etw. ~:** pass the time with sth.; Ⓒ (*beseitigen*) allay ‹fear, doubt, suspicion›; dispel ‹worry, concern›. ❷ *refl. V.* disperse; (*schneller*) scatter

**zerstreut** ❶ *Adj.* distracted; (*vergesslich*) absent-minded; **ein ~er Professor** (*ugs. scherzh.*) an absent-minded professor. ❷ *adv.* absent-mindedly

**Zerstreutheit** *die; ~:* absent-mindedness

**Zerstreuung** *die; ~, ~en* diversion; (*Unterhaltung*) entertainment; **~ suchen** look for a distraction [to take one's mind off things]

**zerstückeln** *tr. V.* break ‹sth.› up into small pieces; (*zerschneiden*) cut *or* chop sth. up into small pieces; dismember ‹corpse›

**Zerstückelung** *die; ~, ~en* breaking up; (*Zerschneidung*) cutting *or* chopping up; (*einer Leiche*) dismembering

**zerteilen** ❶ *tr. V.* divide into pieces; (*zerschneiden*) cut into pieces; cut up; **das Schiff zerteilte die Wellen** (*fig.*) the ship sliced through the waves. ❷ *refl. V.* part

**zerteppern** /tsɛɐ̯ˈtɛpɐn/ ⇒ **zerdeppern**

**Zertifikat** /tsɛrtifiˈkaːt/ *das; ~[e]s, ~e* certificate; **~ Deutsch als Fremdsprache** diploma in German as a foreign language

**zertrampeln** *tr. V.* trample all over ‹flower bed etc.›; trample ‹child etc.› underfoot

**zertrennen** *tr. V.* take apart; unpick ‹dress›

**zertreten** *unr. tr. V.* stamp on; stamp out ‹cigarette, match›; stamp on, crush ‹insect› underfoot

**zertrümmern** *tr. V.* smash; smash, shatter ‹glass›; smash up ‹furniture›; wreck ‹car, boat›; reduce ‹building, city› to ruins

**Zervelat·wurst** /tsɛrvəˈlaːt-/ *die* cervelat [sausage]

**zerwühlen** *tr. V.* churn up ‹bedclothes, soil›; make a mess of, tousle ‹hair›

**Zerwürfnis** /tsɛɐ̯ˈvʏrfnɪs/ *das; ~ses, ~se* (*geh.*) quarrel; dispute; (*Bruch*) rift

**zerzausen** *tr. V.* ruffle; ruffle, tousle ‹hair›; **zerzaust aussehen** look dishevelled; **vom Wind zerzauste Bäume** windswept trees

**Zeter** *das:* in **~ und Mord[io] schreien** (*ugs.*) scream blue murder (*coll.*); raise hell (*coll.*)

**zetern** /ˈtseːtɐn/ *itr. V.* (*abwertend*) (*schimpfen*) scold [shrilly]; (*sich beklagen*) moan (**über** + *Akk.* about); **gegen den Sittenverfall ~:** declaim against the decay of morals

**Zettel** /ˈtsɛtl̩/ *der; ~s, ~:* slip *or* piece of paper; (*mit einigen Zeilen*) note; (*Bekanntmachung*) notice; (*Formular*) form; (*Kassen~*) receipt; (*Hand~*) leaflet; (*Stimm~*) [ballot] paper

**Zettel-: ~kasten** *der* index on slips of paper; **~wirtschaft** *die* (*ugs. abwertend*) jumble of bits of paper

**Zeug** /tsɔyk/ *das; ~[e]s, ~e* Ⓐ (*ugs., oft abwertend: Sachen*) stuff; **fürchterliches ~ träumen** dream awful things; **sie hat** *od.* **in ihr steckt das ~ zu etw.** (*fig.*) she has what it takes to be sth. *or* has the makings of sth.; **was das ~ hält** (*fig. ugs.*) for all one's worth; ‹drive› hell for leather; **sich [für jmdn./etw. mächtig** *od.* **tüchtig] ins ~ legen** (*fig.*) do one's utmost [for sb./sth.]; Ⓑ (*ugs.: Unsinn*) **dummes/albernes ~** (*Gerede*) nonsense; rubbish; **dummes ~ machen** mess about; Ⓒ (*Kleidung*) things *pl.*; **jmdm. etwas am ~ flicken** (*ugs.*) pin something on sb.; Ⓓ (*veralt.: Tuch*) cloth

**Zeuge** /ˈtsɔygə/ *der; ~n, ~n* witness; **~ von etw. sein/werden** be a witness to sth.; witness sth.; **~ der Anklage/Verteidigung** (*Rechtsw.*) witness for the prosecution/defence; **die ~n Jehovas** the Jehovah's Witnesses; **die Ruinen sind ~n der Vergangenheit** (*fig.*) the ruins bear witness to the past

**zeugen**[1] *itr. V.* give evidence; testify; **von etw. ~** (*fig.*) testify to sth.; (*zeigen*) display sth.; **das zeugt nicht gerade für seine Uneigennützigkeit** (*fig.*) that doesn't say much for his unselfishness

**zeugen**[2] *tr. V.* procreate; ‹man› father ‹child›; (*fig.*) engender; bring about; **Kinder ~:** reproduce; have children

**Zeugen·aussage** *die* testimony; witness's statement

**Zeugenschaft** *die; ~:* testimony

**Zeugen-: ~stand** *der* witness box (*Brit.*); witness stand (*Amer.*); **~vernehmung** *die* examination of the witness/witnesses

**Zeug·haus** *das* (*bes. Milit. hist.*) armoury

**Zeugin** *die; ~, ~nen* witness

**Zeugnis** *das; ~ses, ~se* Ⓐ (*Schulw.*) report; **~ der Reife** ⇒ **Abitur~**; Ⓑ (*Arbeits~*) reference; testimonial; **ich kann ihm nur das beste ~ ausstellen** (*fig.*) I can't speak too highly of him; Ⓒ (*Gutachten*) certificate; Ⓓ (*geh.: Beweis*) evidence; **~se einer früheren Kulturstufe** evidence *or* testimony of an earlier stage of civilization; Ⓔ (*veralt.: Aussage*) testimony; **falsches ~ ablegen** bear false witness

**Zeugs** *das; ~* (*ugs. abwertend*) stuff; (*einzelne Dinge*) things *pl.*

**Zeugung** *die; ~, ~en* procreation; (*eines Kindes*) fathering

**zeugungs-, Zeugungs-: ~akt** *der* act of procreation *or* reproduction; **~fähig** *Adj.* fertile; **~fähigkeit** *die* fertility

**Zeus** (*der*) Zeus

**ZGB** *Abk.* (*DDR, Schweiz*) **Zivilgesetzbuch**

**z. Hd.** *Abk.* **zu Händen; zu Handen** (*österr.*) attn.

**Zibebe** /tsiˈbeːbə/ *die; ~, ~n* (*österr., südd.*) sultana

**Zichorie** /tsɪˈçoːri̯ə/ *die; ~:* chicory

**Zicke** /ˈtsɪkə/ *die; ~, ~n* Ⓐ (*Ziege*) she goat; nanny goat; Ⓑ (*Schimpfwort*) ⇒ **Ziege** B; Ⓒ *Pl.* (*ugs.: Dummheiten*) stupid tricks; monkey business (*coll.*); **~n machen** mess about; (*Schwierigkeiten machen*) make trouble; **mach bloß keine ~n!** none of your monkey business! (*coll.*)

**zickig** (*ugs. abwertend*) ❶ *Adj.* prim; (*prüde*) prudish. ❷ *adv.* primly; (*prüde*) prudishly

**Zicklein** *das; ~s, ~:* kid

**Zickzack** *der; ~[e]s, ~e* zigzag; **im ~:** in a zigzag; **sie fuhren im ~ durch den Verkehr** they zigzagged through the traffic

Z

**Zick·zack·kurs** *der* zigzag line; **im ~:** in a zigzag [line]

**Ziege** /ˈt̮siːgə/ *die;* ~, ~**n** Ⓐ goat; Ⓑ (*Schimpfwort: Frau*) **dumme** *od.* **blöde ~:** stupid cow (*sl. derog.*); **eingebildete ~:** stuck-up female (*derog.*)

**Ziegel** /ˈt̮siːgl̩/ *der;* ~**s**, ~ Ⓐ brick; Ⓑ (*Dach~*) tile

**Ziegel·dach** *das* tiled roof

**Ziegelei** *die;* ~, ~**en** brickworks *sing.*

**ziegel·rot** *Adj.* brick-red

**Ziegel·stein** *der* brick

**Ziegen-:** ~**bart** *der* goat's beard; (*ugs.: Spitzbart*) goatee beard; ~**bock** *der* he- *or* billy goat; ~**käse** *der* goat's cheese; ~**leder** *das* goatskin; ~**milch** *die* goat's milk; ~**peter** *der;* ~**s**, ~ (*ugs.*) mumps *sing.*

**zieh** /t̮siː/ *1. u. 3. Pers. Sg. Prät. v.* **zeihen**

**Zieh-:** ~**brunnen** *der* draw-well; ~**eltern** *Pl.* (*veralt.*) foster-parents

**ziehen** /ˈt̮siːən/ ❶ *unr. tr. V.* Ⓐ pull; (*sanfter*) draw; (*zerren*) tug; (*schleppen*) drag; **jmdn. an sich ~:** draw sb. to one; **jmdn. am Ärmel ~:** pull sb. by the sleeve; **sie zogen ihn mit Gewalt ins Auto** they dragged him into the car by force; **er zog die Knie bis unters Kinn** he drew his knees up under his chin; **das Auto nach rechts/links ~:** pull the car over to the left/right; **das Flugzeug nach oben/unten ~:** put the plane into a climb/descent; **die Rollläden nach oben ~:** roll up the shutters; **ein Hemd** *usw.* **durchs Wasser ~:** give a shirt *etc.* a quick rinse; **die Gardinen vor das Fenster ~:** draw the curtains [across the window]; **Perlen auf eine Schnur ~:** thread pearls/beads on to a string; **den Hut ins Gesicht ~:** pull one's hat down over one's face; **einen Pullover über das Hemd ~:** put a pullover on over one's shirt; **~ und ablegen** (*DV*) drag and drop; Ⓑ (*fig.*) **es zog ihn zu ihr/zu dem Ort** he felt drawn to her/to the place; **es zog ihn in die Ferne** he felt an urge to travel; **alle Blicke auf sich ~:** attract *or* capture all the attention; **jmds. Zorn/Unwillen** *usw.* **auf sich ~:** incur sb.'s anger/displeasure *etc.;* **etw. nach sich ~:** result in sth.; entail sth.; **gewisse Folgen nach sich ~:** have certain consequences; Ⓒ (*heraus~*) pull out ‹nail, cork, organ-stop, etc.›; extract ‹tooth›; take out, remove ‹stitches, splinter›; draw ‹cord, sword, pistol›; **den Ring vom Finger ~:** pull *or* take one's ring off one's finger; **den Hut ~:** raise *or* (*dated*) doff one's hat; **etw. aus der Tasche ~:** take sth. out of one's pocket; (*aus Automaten*) **Zigaretten/Süßigkeiten** *usw.* **~:** get cigarettes/sweets *etc.* from a slot machine; **die [Quadrat]wurzel ~** (*Math.*) extract the square root; Ⓓ (*dehnen*) stretch ‹elastic etc.›; stretch out ‹sheets etc.›; ⇒ *auch* **Blase** A; **Faden**[1]; Ⓔ (*Gesichtspartien bewegen*) make ‹face, grimace›; **die Augenbrauen nach oben ~:** raise one's eyebrows; **die Stirn in Falten ~:** wrinkle *or* knit one's brow; (*missmutig*) frown; **die Mundwinkel nach unten ~:** pull down the corners of one's mouth; Ⓕ (*bei Brettspielen*) move ‹chessman etc.›; Ⓖ (*einatmen*) **Luft durch die Nase ~:** breathe *or* draw in air; **er zog den Rauch in die Lungen** he inhaled the smoke [into his lungs]; Ⓗ (*zeichnen*) draw ‹line, circle, arc, etc.›; Ⓘ (*anlegen*) dig ‹trench›; build ‹wall›; erect ‹fence›; put up ‹washing line›; run, lay ‹cable, wires›; draw ‹frontier›; trace ‹loop›; follow ‹course›; **sich** (*Dat.*) **einen Scheitel ~:** make a parting [in one's hair]; Ⓙ (*auf~*) grow ‹plants, flowers›; breed ‹animals›; **den Burschen werde ich mir noch ~** (*ugs.*) I'll knock the lad into shape yet (*coll.*); Ⓚ (*verblasst; auch als Funktionsverb*) draw ‹lesson, conclusion, comparison›; ⇒ *auch* **Konsequenz** A; **Rechenschaft**; **Verantwortung** A; Ⓛ (*herstellen*) make ‹candles›; draw ‹wire, pipes›; Ⓜ (*spannen*) mount ‹picture› (**auf** + *Akk.* to); fit ‹string› (**auf** + *Akk.* to); Ⓝ (*beim Sprechen*) draw out ‹vowel›; Ⓞ (*in sich aufnehmen*) ‹plant› draw [up] ‹water, nourishment› (**aus** from); (*gewinnen*) extract ‹oil, ore› (**aus** from); **Profit/Nutzen aus etw. ~** (*fig.*) derive profit/benefit from sth.; Ⓟ (*Finanzw.*) **einen Wechsel auf jmdn. ~:** draw a bill on sb.; Ⓠ (*schlagen*) **jmdm. etw. über den Kopf ~:** hit sb. over the head with sth.; Ⓡ (*Waffenkunde*) rifle ‹barrel›.

❷ *unr. itr. V.* Ⓐ (*reißen*) pull; **an etw.** (*Dat.*) **~:** pull on sth.; **der Hund zieht an der Leine** the dog is straining at the leash; **an einem** *od.* **am gleichen** *od.* **an demselben Strang** *od.* **Strick ~** (*fig.*) be pulling in the same direction; Ⓑ (*funktionieren*) ‹stove, pipe, chimney› draw; **ausgezeichnet/nicht richtig ~** (*Kfz-W.*) ‹car, engine› pull really well/not pull properly; Ⓒ *mit sein* (*um~*) move (**nach, in** + *Akk.* to); **aufs Land ~:** move [out] into the country; **zu jmdm. ~:** move in with sb.; Ⓓ *mit sein* (*gehen*) go; (*marschieren*) march; (*umherstreifen*) roam; rove; (*fortgehen*) go away; leave; ‹fog, clouds› drift; **durch etw. ~:** pass through sth.; **in den Krieg ~:** go *or* march off to war; **an die Front ~:** move up to the front; **jmdn. ungern ~ lassen** be sorry to see sb. go; **die Schwalben ~ nach Süden** the swallows are flying southwards; Ⓔ (*saugen*) draw; **an einer Zigarette/Pfeife ~:** draw on a cigarette/pipe; **an einem Strohhalm ~:** suck at a straw; **lass mich mal an deiner Zigarette ~:** let me have a puff of your cigarette; Ⓕ ‹tea, coffee› draw; Ⓖ (*Kochk.*) simmer; Ⓗ (*unpers.*) **es zieht [vom Fenster her]** there's a draught [from the window]; **es zieht mir an den Beinen** there's a draught round my legs; Ⓘ (*ugs.: ankommen*) sell; ‹trick› work; **das zieht bei mir nicht** that won't wash *or* won't cut any ice with me (*coll.*); Ⓙ (*schmerzen*) **es zieht [mir] im Rücken** I've got backache; **~de Schmerzen** aches; **ein leichtes/starkes Ziehen im Bauch** a slight/intense stomach ache.

❸ *unr. refl. V.* Ⓐ (*sich erstrecken*) ‹road› run, stretch; ‹frontier› run; **eine Narbe zog sich über sein ganzes Gesicht** there was a scar right across his face; **der Weg** *o. Ä.* **zieht sich** the journey *etc.* goes on and on; Ⓑ (*sich ver~*) warp; get out of shape

**Zieher** *der;* ~**s**, ~, **Zieherin** *die;* ~, ~**nen** (*salopp*) pickpocket

**Zieh-:** ~**harmonika** *die* piano accordion; ~**kind** *das* (*veralt.*) foster-child; ~**mutter** *die; Pl.* ~**mütter** (*veralt.*) foster-mother

**Ziehung** *die;* ~, ~**en** draw; **die ~ des Hauptgewinns** the draw for the main prize

**Zieh·vater** *der* Ⓐ (*veralt.*) foster-father; Ⓑ (*fig.*) sponsor; patron

**Ziel** /t̮siːl/ *das;* ~**[e]s**, ~**e** Ⓐ (*Punkt, Ort*) destination; **am ~ der Reise angelangen** reach the end of one's journey; reach one's destination; **mit unbekanntem ~ abreisen** leave for an unknown destination; Ⓑ (*Sport*) finish; (*~linie*) finishing line; (*Pferderennen*) finishing post; **im ~:** at the finish; **das ~ erreichen** finish; **als Erster das ~ erreichen** *od.* **durchs ~ gehen** finish first; cross the finishing line first; ‹horse› be first past the [finishing] post; Ⓒ (*~scheibe; auch Milit.*) target; **[weit] über das ~ [hinaus]schießen** (*fig. ugs.*) go over the top; overstep the mark; Ⓓ (*Zweck*) aim; goal; **sein ~ erreichen** achieve one's objective *or* aim; **[das] ~ unserer Bemühungen ist es, ... zu ...** the object of our efforts is to ...; **mit dem ~, etw. zu tun** with the aim of doing sth.; **sich** (*Dat.*) **ein ~ setzen** *od.* **stecken** set oneself a goal; **sich** (*Dat.*) **etw. zum ~ setzen** set oneself *or* take sth. as one's aim; **etw. zum ~ haben** have sth. as one's/its goal; **Beharrlichkeit führt zum ~:** if at first you don't succeed, try, try, and try again; Ⓔ (*Ende*) **einer Sache** (*Dat.*) **ein ~ setzen** put an end to sth.

**ziel-, Ziel-:** ~**bahn·hof** *der* destination; ~**band** *das; Pl.* ~**bänder** (*Sport*) finishing tape; ~**bewusst**, *~**bewußt** ❶ *Adj.* purposeful; determined; **sehr ~bewusst sein** know exactly where one is going; ❷ *adv.* purposefully; determinedly

**zielen** *itr. V.* Ⓐ (*mit einer Waffe*) aim (**auf** + *Akk.*, **nach** at); **genau ~:** take careful aim; **ein gut gezielter Schuss/Wurf** an accurate *or* well-aimed shot/throw; Ⓑ (*sich richten*) **auf jmdn./etw. ~** ‹reproach, plan, efforts, etc.› be aimed at sb./sth.

**zielend** *Adj.* (*Sprachw.*) transitive

**ziel-, Ziel-:** ~**fern·rohr** *das* telescopic sight; ~**foto** *das* (*Sport*) photograph of a/the finish; photo-finish photograph; ~**gerade** *die* (*Sport*) finishing straight; ~**gerichtet** ❶ *Adj.* purposeful; Ⓑ *adv.* purposefully; ~**gruppe** *die* target group; ~**kamera** *die* (*Sport*) photo-finish camera; ~**linie** *die* (*Sport*) finishing line; ~**los** ❶ *Adj.* aimless; ❷ *adv.* aimlessly; ~**losigkeit** *die;* ~~: aimlessness; ~**orientiert** ❶ *Adj.* goal-oriented; purposeful; ❷ *adv.* with a clear goal/clear goals in view; purposefully; ~**richter** *der*, ~**richterin** *die* finish judge; ~**scheibe** *die* (*auch fig.*) target (*Gen.* for); ~**setzung** *die;* ~~, ~~**en** aims *pl.;* objectives *pl.;* ~**sicher** ❶ *Adj.* Ⓐ (*treffsicher*) accurate; Ⓑ (*~gerichtet*) decisive, purposeful ‹steps›; confident ‹grip›; ❷ *adv.* Ⓐ (*treffsicher*) accurately; Ⓑ (*~gerichtet*) decisively; (*zuversichtlich*) confidently; ~**sicherheit** *die* accuracy; ~**sprache** *die* (*Sprachw.*) target language; ~**strebig** ❶ *Adj.* Ⓐ purposeful; Ⓑ (*energisch*) single-minded ‹person›; ❷ *adv.* Ⓐ purposefully; Ⓑ (*energisch*) single-mindedly; ~**strebigkeit** *die;* ~~ ⇒ ~**strebig**: Ⓐ purposefulness; Ⓑ single-mindedness; ~**wahl** *die* (*Fernspr.*) one-touch dialling

**ziemen** /ˈt̮siːmən/ (*veralt.*) ❶ *refl. V.* be seemly; **das ziemt sich einfach nicht** that just is not done (*coll.*). ❷ *itr. V.* **jmdm./einer Sache ~:** befit sb./sth.; be fitting for sb./sth.

**Ziemer** *der;* ~**s**, ~ ⇒ **Ochsenziemer**

**ziemlich** ❶ *Adj.* (*ugs.*) fair, sizeable ‹quantity, number›; **eine ~e Frechheit/Weile** quite a cheek/while; **mit ~er Lautstärke** quite loudly; **er kommt mit ~er Sicherheit** he is more or less certain to come; **ich weiß mit ~er Sicherheit, dass ...** I am fairly *or* reasonably certain that ... ❷ *adv.* Ⓐ quite; fairly; (*etwas intensiver*) pretty; **du kommst ~ spät** you're rather late; **~ viele Leute** quite a few people; Ⓑ (*ugs.: fast*) pretty well; more or less; **er ist so ~ in meinem Alter** he's more or less my age

**ziepen** /ˈt̮siːpn̩/ (*bes. nordd.*) ❶ *itr. V.* **es ziepte ihr im Kreuz** she had a twinge in her back. ❷ *tr. V.* tweak (**an** + *Dat.* by); **jmdn. an den Haaren ~:** give sb.'s hair a tug

**Zier** /t̮siːɐ̯/ *die;* ~ (*veralt.*) ⇒ **Zierde**

***Zierat** ⇒ **Zierrat**

**Zierde** *die;* ~, ~**n** (*auch fig.*) ornament; embellishment; **zur ~:** as decoration; **jmdm. zur ~ gereichen** (*fig.*) be a credit to sb.; **[die] ~ des Landes** (*fig.*) the pride of the nation; **eine ~ des Landes** (*fig.*) one of the country's jewels

**Zier·decke** *die* ornamental bedspread

**zieren** ❶ *tr. V.* (*geh.*) adorn; decorate ‹room›. ❷ *refl. V.* be coy; (*sich bitten lassen*) need some coaxing *or* pressing; **zier dich nicht so!** don't make such a fuss!; don't be so coy!

**Ziererei** *die;* ~, ~**en** (*abwertend*) coyness *no indef. art., no pl.;* (*Zögern*) hedging *no indef. art., no pl.;* (*Pose*) posturing *no indef. art.*

**Zier-:** ~**garten** *der* ornamental garden; (*Blumengarten*) flower garden; ~**leiste** *die* [decorative] moulding; (*an der Decke*) cornice; (*am Auto*) trim

**zierlich** ❶ *Adj.* dainty; delicate; petite, dainty ‹woman, figure›. ❷ *adv.* daintily; delicately

**Zierlichkeit** *die;* ~: daintiness; delicateness; (*einer Frau, Gestalt*) petiteness; daintiness

**Zier·pflanze** *die* ornamental plant

**Zierrat** /ˈt̮siːraːt/ *der;* ~**[e]s**, ~**e** (*geh.*) ornament[ation]; **bloßer ~ sein** be purely ornamental; **reich an ~en** richly decorated *or* ornamented

**Zier-:** ~**stich** *der* (*Handarb.*) ornamental stitch; ~**strauch** *der* ornamental shrub

**Ziffer** /ˈt̮sɪfɐ/ *die;* ~, ~**n** Ⓐ (*Zahlzeichen*) numeral; (*in einer mehrstelligen Zahl*) digit; figure; **arabische/römische ~n** arabic/

*old spelling (see note on page 1707)

roman numerals; Ⓑ (*Unterabschnitt*) subsection; clause

**Ziffer·blatt** *das* dial; face

**-zig, zig** /tsɪç/ *unbest. Zahlwort* (*ugs.*) umpteen (*coll.*)

**Zigarettchen** *das;* **~s, ~** (*ugs.*) ciggy (*coll.*)

**Zigarette** /tsiga'rɛtə/ *die;* **~, ~n** cigarette

**Zigaretten-: ~asche** *die* cigarette ash; **~automat** *der* cigarette machine; **~etui** *das* cigarette case; **~kippe** *die* cigarette end; **~länge** *die* (*ugs.*) *in* **auf** *od.* **für eine ~länge** just for a smoke; **~papier** *das* cigarette paper; **~pause** *die* (*ugs.*) break for a smoke; **~raucher** *der*, **~raucherin** *die* cigarette smoker; **~schachtel** *die* cigarette packet; **~spitze** *die* cigarette holder

**Zigarillo** /tsiga'rɪlo/ *der od. das;* **~s, ~s** cigarillo; small cigar

**Zigarre** /tsi'garə/ *die;* **~, ~n** Ⓐ cigar; Ⓑ (*ugs.: Rüffel*) telling-off; rocket (*Brit. coll.*); **jmdm. eine ~ verpassen** give sb. a dressing down *or* (*Brit. coll.*) rocket

**Zigarren-: ~abschneider** *der* cigar cutter; **~asche** *die* cigar ash; **~raucher** *der*, **~raucherin** *die* cigar smoker; **~stummel** *der* cigar stub

**Zigeuner** /tsi'gɔynɐ/ *der;* **~s, ~, Zigeunerin,** *die;* **~, ~nen** Ⓐ gypsy; Ⓑ (*ugs.: Tramp*) vagabond

**Zigeuner-: ~kapelle** *die* gypsy band; **~musik** *die* gypsy music; **~primas** *der* leading fiddle player [of a gypsy band]; **~schnitzel** *das* (*Kochk.*): *veal or pork escalope in a spicy sauce with green peppers, tomato, etc.*; **~sprache** *die* Romany [language]

**zig·mal** *Adv.* (*ugs.*) umpteen times (*coll.*)

**zigst ...** ▶ 841 (*ugs.*) umpteenth (*coll.*)

**zig·tausend** *unbest. Zahlwort* (*ugs.*) umpteen thousand (*coll.*)

**Zikade** /tsi'ka:də/ *die;* **~, ~n** (*Zool.*) cicada

**Zimbal** /'tsɪmbal/ *das;* **~s, ~e** *od.* **~s** (*Musik*) cimbalom

**Zimbel** /'tsɪmbl̩/ *die;* **~, ~n** (*Musik*) cymbal

**Zimmer** /'tsɪmɐ/ *das;* **~s, ~** room; **auf/in sein ~ gehen** go to one's room

**Zimmer-: ~antenne** *die* indoor aerial *or* (*Amer.*) antenna; **~arbeit** *die* carpentry *no indef. art.*; **~arbeiten** carpentry work *sing.*; **~brand** *der* room fire; **~decke** *die* ceiling

**Zimmerer** *der;* **~s, ~, Zimmerin** *die;* **~, ~nen** carpenter

**Zimmer-: ~flucht** *die* suite [of rooms]; **~hand·werk** *das* carpentry *no art.*; **~kellner** *der* room waiter; **~kellnerin** *die* room waitress; **~lautstärke** *die* domestic listening level; **das Radio auf ~lautstärke stellen** turn the radio down to a reasonable volume [so as not to disturb the neighbours]; **~linde** *die* African hemp; **~mädchen** *das* chambermaid; **~mann** *der; Pl.* **~leute** carpenter; **~meister** *der*, **~meisterin** *die* master carpenter;

**zimmern** ❶ *tr. V.* make ‹shelves, coffin, etc.›. ❷ *itr. V.* do carpentry; **an einem Regal ~:** be making a bookshelf

**Zimmer-: ~nummer** *die* room number; **~pflanze** *die* house plant; indoor plant; **~suche** *die* room-hunt; **bei der ~suche** when room-hunting; **auf ~suche sein** be looking for a room; **~temperatur** *die* room temperature; **~theater** *das* studio theatre; **~vermittlung** *die* accommodation office

**zimperlich** /'tsɪmpɐlɪç/ (*abwertend*) ❶ *Adj.* timid; (*leicht angeekelt*) squeamish; (*prüde*) prissy; (*übertrieben rücksichtsvoll*) overscrupulous; **sei nicht ~ mit ihnen** don't go easy on them. ❷ *s. Adj.:* timidly; squeamishly; prissily; overscrupulously; **die Polizei ging nicht gerade ~ mit ihr um** the police didn't exactly treat her with kid gloves

**Zimperlichkeit** *die;* **~, ~en** (*abwertend*) timidity; (*Neigung zum Ekel*) squeamishness; (*Prüderie*) prissiness; (*übertriebene Rücksicht*) overscrupulousness; excessive scruples *pl.*

**Zimt** /tsɪmt/ *der;* **~[e]s, ~e** Ⓐ cinnamon; Ⓑ (*ugs. abwertend: Zeug*) rubbish; **so ein ~!** what a load of rubbish! (*coll.*)

**Zimt-: ~stange** *die* cinnamon stick; **~ziege** *die* (*Schimpfwort: Frau*) cow (*sl. derog.*)

**Zink¹** /tsɪŋk/ *das;* **~[e]s** zinc

**Zink²** *der;* **~[e]s, ~en** (*Musik*) cornetto

**Zink-: ~blech** *das* zinc [sheet]; **~blende** *die* zinc blende

**Zinke** *die;* **~, ~n** prong; (*eines Kammes*) tooth; (*Holzverarb.*) dovetail

**zinken** *tr. V.* (*ugs.*) mark ‹cards›

**Zinken** *der;* **~s, ~** Ⓐ (*Gaunerspr.*) [crook's/beggar's] secret sign *or* mark; Ⓑ (*ugs. scherzh.: Nase*) conk (*coll.*)

**Zink-: ~leim·verband** *der* (*Med.*) Unna's paste dressing; **~salbe** *die* (*Med.*) zinc oxide ointment

**Zinn** /tsɪn/ *das;* **~[e]s** Ⓐ (*Metall*) tin; Ⓑ (*Gegenstände*) pewter[ware]

**Zinne** *die;* **~, ~n** Ⓐ merlon; **~n** battlements; Ⓑ (*schweiz.: Dachterrasse*) roof terrace

**Zinn·figur** *die* pewter figure; (*Zinnsoldat o. Ä.*) tin figure;

**Zinnie** /'tsɪni̯ə/ *die;* **~, ~n** (*Bot.*) zinnia

**Zinn·kraut** *das* common horsetail

**Zinnober** /tsɪ'no:bɐ/ *der;* **~s, ~:** Ⓐ cinnabar; Ⓑ *österr.: das;* **~s** (**~rot**) vermilion; Ⓒ (*salopp abwertend*) (*wertloses Zeug*) junk; rubbish; (*Unsinn*) twaddle; **~ machen** make a big fuss

**zinnober·rot** *Adj.* vermilion

**Zinn-: ~soldat** *der* tin soldier; **~teller** *der* pewter plate

**Zins** /tsɪns/ *der;* **~es, ~en** *od.* **~e** Ⓐ *Pl.* **~en** (*Geld*) interest; **~en tragen** *od.* **bringen** earn interest; **zu 8% ~en** at 8% interest; **bei einem ~ von 8%** at 8% interest; **die ~en sind gestiegen** interest rates have gone up; **jmdm. etw. mit ~en** *od.* **mit ~ und ~eszins zurückzahlen** (*fig.*) make sb. pay dearly for sth.; Ⓑ *Pl.* **~e** (*südd., österr., schweiz.: Mietzins*) rent

**Zins·erhöhung** *die* increase in the rate of interest

**Zinses·zins** *der; Pl.* **~en** compound interest

**zins-, Zins-: ~fuß** *der* interest rate; **~günstig** (*Finanzw.*) ❶ *Adj.* at a favourable rate of interest *postpos.*; low-interest ‹credit, loan›; high-interest, high-yield ‹savings scheme, investment, etc.›; ❷ *adv.* at a favourable rate of interest; **~los** ❶ *Adj.* interest-free; ❷ *adv.* free of interest; **~pflichtig** *Adj.* liable to interest *postpos.*; **... ist ~pflichtig** interest is payable on ...; **~politik** *die* policy on interest rates; **~rechnung** *die* calculation of interest; **~satz** *der* interest rate; **~senkung** *die* reduction of interest rates

**Zionismus** /tsio'nɪsmʊs/ *der;* **~:** Zionism *no art.*

**Zionist** *der;* **~en, ~en, Zionistin,** *die;* **~, ~nen** Zionist

**zionistisch** *Adj.* Zionist

**Zipfel** /'tsɪpfl̩/ *der;* **~s, ~** (*einer Decke, eines Tisch-, Handtuchs usw.*) corner; (*Wurst~, eines Halstuchs*) [tail] end; (*einer ~mütze*) point; (*Spitze eines Sees usw.*) tip

**zipfelig** *Adj.* uneven ‹hem›; ‹coat, skirt› with an uneven hem

**Zipfel·mütze** *die* [long-]pointed cap

**Zipp** Ⓦⓩ /tsɪp/ *der;* **~s, ~s** (*österr.*) zip

**Zipperlein** /'tsɪpɐlai̯n/ *das;* **~** (*ugs. veralt.*) gout

**Zipp·verschluss, *Zipp·verschluß** *der* (*österr.*) zip fastener

**Zirbel-** /'tsɪrbl̩/: **~drüse** *die* (*Biol.*) pineal gland; **~kiefer** *die* Swiss [stone] pine; arolla pine

**Zirconium** (*fachspr.*) ⇒ **Zirkonium**

**zirka** /'tsɪrka/ *Adv.* about; approximately

**Zirkel** /'tsɪrkl̩/ *der;* **~s, ~** Ⓐ (*Gerät*) [pair *sing.* of] compasses *pl.*; Ⓑ (*Kreis, Gruppe; beim Pferdesport*) circle; Ⓒ ⇒ **Zirkeldefinition; Zirkelschluss**

**Zirkel-: ~definition** *die* circular definition; **~kasten** *der* compasses case

**zirkeln** ❶ *tr. V.* (*genau abmessen*) measure out precisely; **gezirkelt** precisely laid out; **er zirkelte den Ball genau in die linke obere Ecke** (*Fußballjargon*) he placed the ball with precision in the top left-hand corner. ❷ *itr. V.* (*ugs.: sehr genau arbeiten*) try to get things just right

**Zirkel·schluss, *Zirkel·schluß** *der* circular argument

**Zirkonium** /tsɪr'ko:ni̯ʊm/ *das;* **~s** zirconium

**zirkular** /tsɪrku'la:ɐ̯/ (*Physik, Fot.*) ❶ *Adj.* circular ❷ *adv.* circularly

**Zirkulation** /tsɪrkula'tsi̯o:n/ *die;* **~, ~en** Ⓐ circulation; Ⓑ (*Fechten*) circular parry

**zirkulieren** *itr. V.; auch mit sein* circulate

**Zirkumflex** /tsɪrkʊm'flɛks/ *der;* **~es, ~e** (*Sprachw.*) circumflex

**Zirkus** /'tsɪrkʊs/ *der;* **~, ~se** Ⓐ circus; Ⓑ (*ugs.*) (*Trubel*) hustle and bustle; (*Krach*) to-do; rumpus (*coll.*); (*Umstände*) **mach nicht so einen ~!** don't make such a fuss!

**Zirkus-: ~pferd** *das* circus horse; **~vorstellung** *die* circus performance; **~zelt** *das* big top

**zirpen** /'tsɪrpn̩/ *itr. V.* chirp

**Zirren** ⇒ **Zirrus**

**Zirrhose** /tsɪ'ro:zə/ *die;* **~, ~n** ▶ 474 (*Med.*) cirrhosis

**Zirrus** /'tsɪrʊs/ *der;* **~, ~** *od.* **Zirren, Zirrus·wolke** *die* (*Met.*) cirrus [cloud]

**zirzensisch** /tsɪr'tsɛnzɪʃ/ *Adj.* circus *attrib.*

**zisalpin** /tsɪs|al'pi:n/ *Adj.* cisalpine

**Zischelei** *die;* **~, ~en** whispering

**zischeln** /'tsɪʃl̩n/ *tr. V.* whisper angrily

**zischen** /'tsɪʃn̩/ ❶ *itr. V.* Ⓐ hiss; ‹hot fat› sizzle; Ⓑ *mit sein* hiss; (*ugs.: flitzen*) whizz. ❷ *tr. V.* Ⓐ (*zischend sprechen*) hiss; Ⓑ **ein Bier/einen ~** (*ugs.*) knock back a beer (*coll.*)/knock one back (*coll.*)

**Zisch·laut** *der* (*Sprachw.*) sibilant

**Ziseleur** /tsize'lø:ɐ̯/ *der;* **~s, ~e, Ziseleurin** *die* engraver

**Ziselier·arbeit** *die* engraving; (*von Gold, Silber*) chasing *no indef. art.*; (*Produkt*) piece of engraved/chased work

**ziselieren** /tsize'li:rən/ *tr., itr. V.* engrave; chase ‹gold, silver›

**Ziselierung** *die;* **~, ~en** engraving; (*von Gold, Silber*) chasing

**Zisterne** /tsɪs'tɛrnə/ *die;* **~, ~n** [underground] tank *or* cistern

**Zisterzienser** /tsɪstɛr'tsi̯ɛnzɐ/ *der;* **~s, ~, Zisterziensserin** *die;* **~, ~nen** Cistercian [monk/nun]

**Zisterzienser·orden** *der* Cistercian order

**Zitadelle** /tsita'dɛlə/ *die;* **~, ~n** citadel

**Zitat** /tsi'ta:t/ *das;* **~[e]s, ~e** quotation (**aus** from); **falsches ~:** misquotation

**Zitaten-: ~sammlung** *die* collection of quotations; **~schatz** *der* store of quotations

**Zither** /'tsɪtɐ/ *die;* **~, ~n** zither

**Zither·spieler** *der*, **Zither·spielerin** *die* zither player

**zitieren** /tsi'ti:rən/ *tr., itr. V.* Ⓐ quote (**aus, nach** from); (*Rechtspr.: anführen*) cite; **..., ich zitiere: „...“** ... and I quote: '...'; (*wie er usw. sich ausdrückt*) '...', as he *etc.* puts it; **falsch ~:** misquote; Ⓑ (*vorladen, rufen*) summon (**vor** before, **zu** to)

**Zitronat** /tsitro'na:t/ *das;* **~[e]s** candied lemon peel

**Zitrone** /tsi'tro:nə/ *die;* **~, ~n** lemon; **jmdn. ausquetschen wie eine ~** (*ugs.*) (*ausfragen*) pump sb.; (*ausbeuten*) bleed sb. dry

**zitronen-, Zitronen-: ~falter** *der* brimstone butterfly; **~gelb** *Adj.* lemon yellow; **~limonade** *die* lemonade; **~melisse** *die* lemon balm; **~presse** *die* lemon squeezer; **~saft** *der* lemon juice; **~säure** *die* (*Chemie*) citric acid; **~schale** *die* lemon peel

**Zitrus·frucht** /'tsitrʊs-/ *die* citrus fruit

**Zitter-: ~aal** *der* electric eel; **~gras** *das* quaking grass

**zittern** /'tsɪtɐn/ *itr. V.* Ⓐ tremble (**vor** + *Dat.* with); (*vor Kälte*) shiver; ‹needle, arrow, leaf, etc.› quiver; (*flimmern*) ‹air› shimmer; (*beben*) ‹walls, windows› shake; **mit ~der Stimme** in a trembling *or* quavering voice; Ⓑ (*Angst haben*) tremble; quake; **vor jmdm./etw. ~:**

be terrified of sb./sth.; **er zittert vor der Prüfung** he's scared stiff (*coll.*) about the exam; **mit Zittern und Zagen** in fear and trembling; **um jmdn./etw. ~:** be very worried about sb./sth.; **für jmdn. ~:** be anxious for sb.; [C] *mit sein* (*salopp: gehen*) **nach Hause ~:** slope off home (*coll.*)

**Zitter-: ~pappel** *die* aspen; **~partie** *die* (*Sportjargon, auch fig.*) nail-biting affair; **~rochen** *der* torpedo ray

**zittrig** ❶ *Adj.* shaky; doddery ‹old man›. ❷ *adv.* shakily

**Zitze** /'tsɪtsə/ *die;* ~, ~n teat

**Zivi** /'tsi:vi/ *der;* ~s, ~s (*ugs.*) ⇒ **Zivildienstleistende**

**zivil** /tsi'vi:l/ ❶ *Adj.* [A] civilian ‹life, population›; non-military ‹purposes›; civil ‹aviation, marriage, law, defence›; ⇒ *auch* **Ersatzdienst;** [B] (*annehmbar*) decent; reasonable. ❷ *adv.* decently; reasonably

**Zivil** *das;* ~s [A] civilian clothes *pl.;* **Polizist in ~:** plain-clothes policeman; [B] (*schweiz.: Familienstand*) marital status

**Zivil-: ~beruf** *der* civilian profession *or* job; **~bevölkerung** *die* civilian population; **~courage** *die* courage of one's convictions; **~diener** *der* (*österr.*) ⇒ **Ersatzdienstleistende;** **~dienst** *der* ⇒ **Ersatzdienst;** **~dienst·leistende** *der; adj. Dekl.,* **~dienstler** /-di:nstlɐ/ *der;* ~~s, ~~ (*ugs.*) ⇒ **Ersatzdienstleistende;** **~ehe** *die* civil marriage; **~flughafen** *der* civil airport; **~gericht** *das* civil court; **~gesetz·buch** (*schweiz., DDR*) civil code

**Zivilisation** /tsiviliza'tsio:n/ *die;* ~, ~en civilization; **eine hohe/niedrige ~:** a high/low level of civilization; **fortschreitende ~:** progressively increasing degree of civilization

**Zivilisations·krankheit** *die* disease of modern civilization *or* society

**zivilisations·müde** *Adj.* weary of modern civilization *postpos.*

**zivilisatorisch** /tsiviliza'to:rɪʃ/ ❶ *Adj.* ‹development, level, standard› of civilization. ❷ *adv.* with regard to civilization

**zivilisieren** *tr. V.* civilize

**zivilisiert** ❶ *Adj.* civilized. ❷ *adv.* in a civilized way

**Zivilist** *der;* ~en, ~en civilian

**Zivil-: ~kammer** *die* (*Rechtsw.*) *chamber for civil matters;* **~klage** *die* (*Rechtsw.*) private action *or* prosecution; **~kleidung** *die* civilian clothes *pl;* **~leben** *das* civilian life; **~luftfahrt** *die* civil aviation; **~person** *die* civilian; **~prozess,** ***~prozeß** *der* (*Rechtsw.*) civil action; **~prozess·ordnung,** ***~prozeß·ordnung** *die* (*Rechtsw.*) civil procedure; **~recht** *das* civil law; **~richter** *der,* **~richterin** *die* civil judge; **~sache** *die* (*Rechtsw.*) civil case; **~schutz** *der* civil defence; **~trauung** *die* civil wedding; **~verfahren** *das* (*Rechtsw.*) civil proceedings *pl.*

**ZK** *Abk.* **Zentralkomitee**

**Zloty** /'zlɔti/ *der;* ~s, ~s zloty

**Znüni** /'tsny:ni/ *der od. das;* ~s, ~ (*schweiz.*) mid-morning snack

**Zobel** /'tso:bl/ *der;* ~s, ~: sable

**Zobel·pelz** *der* sable [fur]

**zockeln** /'tsɔkl̩n/ ⇒ **zuckeln**

**Zofe** /'tso:fə/ *die;* ~, ~n (*hist.*) lady's maid

**Zoff** /tsɔf/ *der;* ~s (*ugs.*) rowing (*coll.*); squabbling; **~ machen** cause trouble; **mit jmdm. ~ haben** have a set-to with sb.

**zog** *1. u. 3. Pers. Sg. Prät. v.* **ziehen**

**zögerlich** /'tsø:gəlɪç/ ❶ *Adj.* hesitant; tentative. ❷ *adv.* hesitantly; tentatively

**zögern** *itr. V.* hesitate; **ich zögere nicht zu behaupten, dass ...** I have no hesitation in saying that ...; **mit der Antwort ~:** hesitate before answering; **mit der Abreise ~:** delay one's departure; **ohne zu ~:** without hesitation; **nach einigem Zögern** after a moment's hesitation; **~d vorangehen** proceed hesitantly

*old spelling (see note on page 1707)

**Zögling** /'tsø:klɪŋ/ *der;* ~s, ~e (*veralt.*) boarding pupil; boarder

**Zölibat** /tsøli'ba:t/ *das od. der;* ~[e]s, ~e celibacy *no art.*

**Zoll**[1] /tsɔl/ *der;* ~[e]s, **Zölle** /'tsœlə/ [A] (*Abgabe*) [customs] duty; **auf dieser Ware liegt kein/ein hoher ~:** there is no duty/a high rate of duty on this article; **die Zölle senken** reduce rates of duty *or* [customs] tariffs; [B] (*hist.: Benutzungsgebühr*) toll; **~ erheben** charge a toll; [C] (*Behörde*) customs *pl.*

**Zoll**[2] *der;* ~[e]s, ~ ▶ 489 inch; **ein Nagel von 2 ~:** a two-inch nail; **von 4 ~ Durchmesser** 4 inches in diameter; **keinen ~ nachgeben** *od.* **weichen** (*fig.*) not give *or* budge an inch; **jeder ~** *od.* **~ für ~ ein Gentleman** (*fig.*) every inch a gentleman

**zoll-, Zoll-: ~abfertigung** *die* customs clearance; **die ~abfertigung passieren** go through custom; **bei der ~abfertigung** at the customs; **~amt** *das* customs house *or* office; **~ausland** *das: region outside one's own customs area;* **~beamte** *der,* **~beamtin** *die* ▶ 159 customs officer; **~breit** *Adj.* inch-wide; **~breit** *der;* ~~, ~~: **keinen ~breit zurückweichen** (*fig.*) not budge an inch

**zollen** *tr. V.* (*geh.*) **jmdm. etw. ~:** accord sb. sth.; **jmdm. Respekt/Bewunderung ~:** show sb. respect/admiration; **jmdm. Lob ~:** bestow praise upon sb.; **jmdm. Anerkennung ~:** give sb. recognition; **jmdm. Beifall ~:** applaud sb.; **jmdm./einer Sache Tribut ~:** pay tribute to sb./sth.

**zoll-, Zoll-: ~erklärung** *die* customs declaration; **~fahndung** *die* customs investigation; **~formalität** *die* customs formality; **~frei** ❶ *Adj.* duty-free; free of duty *pred.;* ❷ *adv.* free of duty; **~gebiet** *das* customs area; **sich auf britischem ~gebiet befinden** be in the British customs area; **~grenz·bezirk** *der* frontier area under customs surveillance; **~grenze** *die* limit of a/the customs area; **~inland** *das* domestic customs area; **~kontrolle** *die* customs examination *or* check; **zur ~kontrolle gehen** go to customs for clearance

**Zöllner** /'tsœlnɐ/ *der;* ~s, ~, **Zöllnerin** *die;* ~, ~nen [A] (*ugs. veralt.*) customs officer; [B] (*hist.: Steuereintreiber*) tax collector; (*bibl.*) publican

**zoll-, Zoll-: ~pflichtig** *Adj.* dutiable; **~schranke** *die* customs barrier; **~station** *die,* **~stelle,** *die* customs post; **~stock** *der* folding rule; **~union** *die* customs union; **~verein** *der* (*hist.*) **der Deutsche ~verein** the German customs union; the Zollverein

**Zombie** /'tsɔmbi/ *der;* ~[s], ~s zombie

**Zone** /'tso:nə/ *die;* ~, ~n [A] zone; (*für Telefongespräche*) charge zone; (*für öffentlichen Nahverkehr*) fare zone; [B] **die ~** (*ugs. veralt.*) East Germany

**Zonen-: ~grenze** *die* [A] **die ~grenze** (*ugs. veralt.*) the East German border; [B] (*hist.: zwischen Besatzungszonen*) zonal frontier; **~rand·gebiet** *das* area along the East German border; **~zeit** *die* zone time

**Zoo** /tso:/ *der;* ~s, ~s zoo; **im/in den ~:** at/to the zoo

**Zoo·handlung** *die* pet shop

**Zoologe** /tsoo'lo:gə/ *der;* ~n, ~n ▶ 159 zoologist

**Zoologie** *die;* ~: zoology *no art.*

**Zoologin** *die;* ~, ~nen ▶ 159 zoologist

**zoologisch** ❶ *Adj.* zoological; **~er Garten** zoological gardens *pl.;* **~er Bedarf** *pet foods and accessories pl.* ❷ *adv.* zoologically; **~ interessiert/beschlagen** interested in/knowledgeable about zoology

**Zoom**[1] /zu:m/ *das;* ~s, ~s (*Film, Fot.: Objektiv*) zoom

**Zoom**[2] *der;* ~s, ~s (*Film: Aufnahme*) zoom shot

**zoomen** /'zu:mən/ *itr., tr. V.* (*Film*) zoom

**Zoom·objektiv** *das* (*Film, Fot.*) zoom lens

**Zoo-: ~tier** *das* zoo animal; **~wärter** *der,* **~wärterin** *die* ▶ 159 zookeeper

**Zopf** /tsɔpf/ *der;* ~[e]s, **Zöpfe** /'tsœpfə/ [A] plait; (*am Hinterkopf*) pigtail; **sich** (*Dat.*) **Zöpfe flechten** plait one's hair [into pigtails]; **falscher ~:** false braid; **einen alten ~ abschneiden** (*fig.*) put an end to an antiquated custom *or* practice; [B] (*Backwerk*) plait

**Zopf·band** *das; Pl.* **Zopfbänder** pigtail ribbon

**Zöpfchen** /'tsœpfçən/ *das;* ~s, ~: small plait/pigtail

**Zopf-: ~muster** *das* cable pattern; **~spange** *die* hairslide (*Brit.*), barnette (*Amer.*) (*for a pigtail*); **~stil** *der* (*Kunstwiss.*): *plain style of the late 18th century;* **~zeit** *die* (*Kunstwiss.*) age of the Zopfstil

**Zorn** /tsɔrn/ *der;* ~[e]s anger; (*stärker*) wrath; fury; **ihn packte der ~:** he flew into a rage; **einen ~ auf jmdn. haben** (*ugs.*) be furious with sb.; **jmds. ~ erregen** anger sb.; **der ~ der Götter** the wrath of the Gods; **vor ~ kochen** be boiling with rage; **gerechter ~:** righteous anger; **im ~:** in a rage; in anger

**Zorn-: ~ader** *die: in* **jmdm. schwillt die ~ader** (*geh.*) sb. flies into a rage; **~ausbruch** *der* angry outburst; fit of rage

**Zornes-: ~ader** ⇒ **Zornader;** **~falte** *die* (*geh.*) vertical line [on the brow]; angry furrow; **~röte** *die* (*geh.*) *in* **jmdm. die ~röte ins Gesicht treiben** make sb. flush with anger; **jmdm. steigt die ~röte ins Gesicht** sb. flushes with anger

**zornig** ❶ *Adj.* furious; **~ über etw.** furious about sth.; **~ auf** *od.* **über jmdn.** furious with sb. ❷ *adv.* furiously

**Zorn·röte** *die* ⇒ **Zornesröte**

**Zote** /'tso:tə/ *die;* ~, ~n dirty joke

**Zoten·reißer** *der;* ~s, ~, **Zoten·reißerin** *die;* ~, ~nen (*abwertend*) teller of dirty jokes

**zotig** ❶ *Adj.* smutty; dirty ‹joke›. ❷ *adv.* smuttily

**Zotte** /'tsɔtə/ *die;* ~, ~n [A] (*Haarbüschel*) shaggy tuft [of hair]; [B] ▶ 471 (*Anat.*) villus

**Zottel** /'tsɔtl/ *die;* ~, ~n (*ugs.*) [A] ⇒ **Zotte** A; [B] *Pl.* (*abwertend: Haare*) shaggy locks

**Zottel·haar** *das* (*ugs.*) shaggy *or* unkempt hair

**zottelig** ❶ *Adj.* shaggy. ❷ *adv.* **die Haare hingen ihr ~ ins Gesicht** her hair hung shaggily over her face

**Zottel·kopf** *der* (*ugs.*) [A] (*Frisur*) shaggy hair; [B] (*Person*) shaggy-haired type

**zotteln** *itr. V.; mit sein* (*ugs.*) saunter; amble

**Zottel·trab** *der* jogtrot

**zottig** *Adj.* shaggy

**ZPO** *Abk.* **Zivilprozessordnung**

**Z-Soldat** *der* (*Militärjargon*) ⇒ **Zeitsoldat**

**Ztr.** *Abk.* **Zentner** cwt.

**zu** /tsu:/ ❶ *Präp. mit Dat.* [A] (*Richtung*) to; **zu ... hin** towards ...; **er kommt zu mir** (*besucht mich*) he is coming to my place; [B] (*zusammen mit*) with; **zu dem Käse gab es Wein** there was wine with the cheese; **das passt nicht zu Bier/zu dem Kleid** that doesn't go with beer/with that dress; [C] (*Lage*) at; **zu beiden Seiten** on both sides; **zu seiner Linken** (*geh.*) on his left; **es ist zu Wasser und zu Lande zu erreichen** it can be reached by water and overland; **er kam zu dieser Tür herein** he came in by this door; **der Dom zu Speyer** (*veralt.*) Speyer Cathedral; **er wurde zu Köln geboren** (*veralt.*) he was born in Cologne; **das Gasthaus zu den drei Eichen** the Three Oaks Inn; **der Graf zu Mansfeld** the Count of Mansfeld; [D] (*zeitlich*) at; **zu Weihnachten** at Christmas; **was schenkst du ihnen zu Weihnachten?** what will you give them for Christmas?; **er will zu Ostern verreisen** he wants to go away for Easter; **zu Anfang des Jahres** at the beginning of the year; **zu dieser Stunde** at this time; **zu meiner Zeit** in my day; ⇒ *auch* **Lebzeiten;** [E] (*Art u. Weise*) **zu meiner Zufriedenheit/Überraschung** to my satisfaction/surprise; **zu seinem Vorteil/Nachteil** to his advantage/disadvantage; **zu niedrigen**

Z

# zu, zum, zur

## Wohin? = to

***Sie gehen zur Schule/zur Arbeit***
= They are going to school/to work

Es ist zu beachten, dass bei diesen Ausdrücken im Englischen kein Artikel verwendet wird.

Beim Modalverb mit *zu* darf **go** im Englischen nicht fehlen:

***Er will morgen zu ihr***
= He wants to go and see her tomorrow

***Ich muss zum Arzt***
= I must go to the doctor's *od.* to see the doctor

Aber:

***Er geht zum Militär/Theater***
= He is going into the army/the theatre

Adverbiale Zusätze wie *hin*, *hinaus*, *herüber* usw. verlangen andere Übersetzungen:

***zur Küste hin***
= towards the coast

***zur Tür herein/hinaus***
= in through/out of the door

***Sie sah zu mir herüber/zum Himmel hinauf***
= She looked across at me/up at the sky

Beim übertragenen Gebrauch, der eine ***Verwandlung*** kennzeichnet, verwendet man oft auch **into**:

***Das Wasser wurde zu Eis***
= The water turned [in]to ice

***Der Junge war zu einem Mann geworden***
= The boy had grown into a man

***Die Zutaten zu einem Brei verrühren***
= Mix the ingredients [in]to a paste

***Das machte ihn zum Märtyrer***
= This made him into a martyr

Aber:

***Ich machte/ernannte ihn zu meinem Vertreter***
= I made/appointed him my representative

Wenn man ein ***Verhältnis*** beschreiben will, sagt man auch **to**:

***in einem Verhältnis von drei zu eins***
= in a ratio of three to one

Beim Spielstand aber wird das **to** meist ausgelassen, außer wenn die Worte ‘goals’, ‘points’, ‘games’, ‘sets’ usw. verwendet werden:

***Das Ergebnis war zwei zu null***
= The final score was two-nil *od.* two goals/points *etc.* to nil

## Wo? Wann? Wie viel? = at

**1. ORT**

***Ich bleibe zu Hause***
= I am staying at home

***Er lag zu ihren Füßen***
= He lay at her feet

***Zu ebener Erde haben wir fünf Zimmer***
= We have five rooms at ground level *od.* on the ground floor

Aber:

***zu beiden Seiten***
= on both sides

***zu meiner Linken***
= on my left

**2. ZEIT**

***zu Anfang/Ende des Jahres***
= at the beginning/end of the year

***Zu Ostern/Zu Weihnachten/Zum Wochenende wollen wir verreisen***
= We want to go away at *od.* for Easter/Christmas/the weekend

***Sie bekommen es zu gegebener Zeit***
= You will get it at the appropriate time

***Er kam zu später Stunde*** (geh.)
= He came at a late hour

Aber:

***Es tritt zum 1. Januar in Kraft***
= It comes into force on January 1st

***Es muss [bis] zum 31. August fertig werden***
= It must be finished by August 31st

***zu diesem Anlass***
= on this occasion

***zum ersten/letzten Mal***
= for the first/last time

**3. PREIS**

***Sie verkaufen alles zu niedrigsten Preisen***
= They sell everything at rock-bottom prices

***Kartoffeln zu 70 Pfennig das Pfund***
= Potatoes at *od.* for 70 pfennigs a pound

Aber:

***sechs Briefmarken zu sieben Schilling***
= six seven schilling stamps

## Was ist der Zweck? = for

***Zu diesem Zweck gibt es einen Notruf***
= There is an emergency line for this purpose

***Sie fährt zu einer Besprechung nach Berlin***
= She is going to Berlin for a meeting

***Das haben wir nur zum Spaß gemacht***
= We only did it for fun

***das Öl zur Schmierung*** od. ***zum Schmieren der Nockenwelle***
= the oil for the lubrication of *od.* for lubricating the camshaft

Hier verwendet man auch **to** + Infinitiv:

***Zum Lesen braucht er eine Brille***
= He needs spectacles for reading *od.* to read with

***etwas zum Schreiben***
= something to write with

***ein paar Worte zur Beruhigung***
= a few words to set your mind at rest

Aber:

***ein paar Worte zur Einführung/Erklärung/Entschuldigung***
= a few words by way of introduction/explanation/apology

Wenn es sich um den Anlass für ein Geschenk oder dergleichen handelt, sagt man auch **for**:

***Er hat es mir zu Weihnachten/zum Geburtstag geschenkt***
= He gave it me for Christmas/my birthday

***Zum 30. Jubiläum überreichte ihm die Firma eine Uhr***
= For *od.* On the occasion of his 30th anniversary the firm presented him with a clock

## Womit zusammen? = with

***Diese Bluse kannst du zu dem Rock tragen***
= You can wear this blouse with that skirt

***Zum Essen gab es Rotwein***
= There was red wine with the meal

## Worüber? = on

***Es gibt mehrere Bücher zu diesem Thema***
= There are several books on this subject

***Was meinen Sie zu dieser Entwicklung?***
= What is your opinion on this development?

***Er wurde zur Sache vernommen***
= He was questioned on the matter

**Preisen** at low prices; **zu Deutsch** (*fig.*) in plain German; in words of one syllable; (*bei Mengenangaben o. Ä*) **zu Dutzenden/zweien** by the dozen/in twos; **sie sind zu einem Drittel/zu 50% arbeitslos** a third/50% of them are jobless; **zu einem großen Teil** largely; to a large extent; **F** (*ein Zahlenverhältnis ausdrückend*) **ein Verhältnis von 3 zu 1** a ratio of 3 to 1; **das Ergebnis war 2 zu 1** the result was 2-1 *or* 2 to 1; **G** (*einen Preis zuordnend*) at; for; **Stoff zu zwanzig Mark der Meter** cloth at *or* for twenty marks a metre; **fünf Briefmarken zu fünfzig [Pfennig]** five 50-pfennig stamps; **H** (*eine Zahlenangabe zuordnend*) **ein Fass zu zehn Litern** a ten-litre barrel; **Portionen zu je einem Pfund** portions weighing a pound each; **I** (*Zweck*) for; **zu einer weiteren Behandlung nach X fahren** go to X for further treatment; **sie sagte das zu seiner Beruhigung** she said it to allay his fears; **Stoff zu einem Kleid** material for a dress; **J** (*Ziel, Ergebnis*) into; **zu etw. werden** turn into sth.; **die Kartoffeln zu einem Brei zerstampfen** mash the potatoes into a puree; **das hat ihn zu meinem Freund gemacht** that made him my friend; **zu Staub zerfallen** crumble into dust; **K** (*über*) about; on; **sich zu etw. äußern** comment on sth.; **zu welchem Thema spricht er?** what is he going to speak about?; **was sagst du zu meinem Vorschlag?** what do you say to my proposal?; **L** (*gegenüber*) **freundlich/hässlich zu jmdm. sein** be friendly/nasty to sb.; **Liebe zu jmdm. empfinden** have feelings of love towards sb.; ⇒ *auch* **zum**; **zur**.

**❷** *Adv.* **A** (*allzu*) too; **zu sehr** too much; **er ist zu alt, um diese Reise zu unternehmen** he is too old to undertake this journey; **das ist ja zu schön/komisch!** that's really wonderful/hilarious!; that's too wonderful/hilarious for words!; **B** *nachgestellt* (*Richtung*) towards; **der Grenze zu** towards the border; **dem Fenster zu stand ein Polizist** a policeman stood over towards the window; **C** (*ugs.*) **~ sein** ‹door, window› be shut; ‹shop› have shut; (*fig.: betrunken sein*) be tight (*coll.*); **Augen/Tür zu!** shut your eyes/the door!; **D** (*ugs.: Aufforderung*) **nur zu!** (*fang/fangt an!*) get going!; get down to it!; (*mach/macht weiter!*) get on with it!; **dort gehst du richtig, nur zu!** you're going the right way, just keep going!; **Wir sind fertig. — Na, dann zu!** We're ready. — Right, let's go!.

**❸** *Konj.* **A** (*mit Infinitiv*) to; **ich bat ihn zu helfen** I asked him to help; **du hast zu gehorchen** you must obey; **was gibts da zu lachen?** what is there to laugh about?; **er ist heute nicht zu sprechen** he is not available today; **die Wände sind noch zu streichen** the walls still have to be painted; **das ist nicht zu glauben** it is unbelievable; **Haus zu verkaufen/vermieten** house for sale/to let; **B** (*mit 1. Part.*) **die zu gewinnenden Preise** the prizes to be won; **die zu erledigende Post** the letters *pl.* to be dealt with

**zu·aller·erst** *Adv.* first of all; (*hauptsächlich*) above all else

**zu·aller·letzt** *Adv.* last of all

**zu|arbeiten** *itr. V.* **jmdm. ~:** assist sb. [with preparatory work]

**zu|bauen** *tr. V.* **A** develop, build on ‹land›; **B** (*ugs.: versperren*) block ‹entrance, door›; obstruct ‹view›

**Zubehör** /ˈtsu:bəhø:ɐ̯/ *das;* **~[e]s, ~e** *od. schweiz.* **~den** accessories *pl.;* (*eines Staubsaugers, Mixers o. Ä.*) attachments *pl.;* (*Ausstattung*) equipment; **mit allem ~:** with all accessories *pl.;* fully equipped ‹workshop, kitchen, etc.›

**zu|beißen** *unr. itr. V.* bite; **einen Hund ärgern, bis er zubeißt** tease a dog until he bites one

**zu|bekommen** *unr. tr. V.* get ‹suitcase, door, etc.› shut; get the top on ‹bottle›; get ‹clothes, buttons› done up; manage to repair ‹leak›; manage to mend ‹hole›

**Zuber** /ˈtsu:bɐ/ *der;* **~s, ~** (*bes. südd.*) tub

**zu|bereiten** *tr. V.* prepare ‹meal, food, cocktail, etc.›; make up ‹medicine, ointment›; (*kochen*) cook ‹fish, meat, etc.›

**Zu·bereitung** *die;* **~, ~en** preparation; (*von Arznei*) making up; (*Kochen*) cooking

**zu|betonieren** *tr. V.* concrete over; cover in concrete

**Zu·bett·gehen** *das;* **~s vorm/beim ~:** before/on going to bed

**zu|bewegen** **❶** *tr. V.* **etw. auf jmdn./etw. ~:** move sth. towards sb./sth. **❷** *refl. V.* **sich auf etw. ~:** move towards sth.

**zu|billigen** *tr. V.* **jmdm. etw. ~:** grant *or* allow sb. sth.; **jmdm. ~, dass er in gutem Glauben gehandelt hat** accept that sb. acted in good faith; **dem Angeklagten mildernde Umstände ~:** allow the accused's plea of extenuating circumstances

**Zu·billigung** *die;* **~, ~en** granting; allowing; **er wurde unter ~ mildernder Umstände für schuldig befunden** he was found guilty but with extenuating circumstances

**zu|binden** *unr. tr. V.* tie [up]

**zu|blinzeln** *itr. V.* **jmdm. ~:** wink at sb.

**zu|bringen** *unr. tr. V.* **A** (*verbringen*) spend; **B** (*landsch.*) ⇒ **zubekommen**

**Zu·bringer** *der;* **~s, ~** (*Verkehrsw.*) **A** (*Straße*) access *or* feeder road; **B** (*Verkehrsmittel*) shuttle; (*Flughafenbus o. Ä.*) courtesy bus

**Zu·brot** *das* bit extra *or* on the side; **er ist auf ein ~ angewiesen** he is forced to earn a bit on the side

**zu|buttern** *tr., itr. V.* (*ugs.*) chip in (*coll.*)

**Zucchetto** /tsuˈkɛto/ *der;* **~s, Zucchetti** (*schweiz.*), **Zucchino** /tsuˈki:no/ *der;* **~s, Zucchini** courgette (*Brit.*); zucchini (*Amer.*)

**Zucht** /tsʊxt/ *die;* **~, ~en** **A** (*Züchtung*) (*von Tieren*) breeding; (*von Pflanzen*) cultivation; breeding; (*von Bakterien, Perlen*) culture; **B** (*~ergebnis*) (*von Tieren*) breed; (*von Pflanzen*) variety; strain; (*von Bakterien*) culture; strain; **ein Pferd aus deutscher ~:** a German-bred horse; **Pflanzen/Tiere aus meiner ~:** plants which I have grown/animals which I have bred; **C** (*Einrichtung*) breeding establishment; (*für Pferde*) stud; (*für Pflanzen*) plant breeding establishment; **D** (*geh.: Disziplin*) discipline; **für ~ und Ordnung sorgen** keep order; **jmdn. in strenge ~ nehmen** take sb. firmly in hand

**Zucht-: ~bulle** *der* breeding bull; **~eber** *der* breeding boar

**züchten** /ˈtsʏçtn̩/ *tr. V.* (*auch fig.*) breed; cultivate ‹plants›; culture ‹bacteria, pearls›

**Züchter** *der;* **~s, ~, Züchterin,** *die;* **~, ~nen** breeder; (*von Pflanzen*) grower [of new varieties]; plant breeder

**Zucht·haus** *das* **A** (*Gefängnis*) [long-stay] prison; penitentiary (*Amer.*); **B** (*Strafe*) [severest form of] imprisonment; imprisonment in a penitentiary (*Amer.*); (*mit Zwangsarbeit*) penal servitude (*hist.*)

**Zuchthäusler** /-hɔysləɐ/ *der;* **~s, ~, Zuchthäuslerin** *die;* **~, ~nen** (*veralt.*) convict

**Zuchthaus·strafe** *die* [severe] prison sentence; sentence to a penitentiary (*Amer.*); **eine lebenslange ~:** life imprisonment; a life sentence

**Zucht·hengst** *der* stud horse; breeding stallion

**züchtig** (*veralt.*) **❶** *Adj.* demure. **❷** *adv.* demurely

**züchtigen** /ˈtsʏçtɪgn̩/ *tr. V.* (*geh.*) beat; thrash; (*fig.: bestrafen*) castigate

**Züchtigung** *die;* **~, ~en** (*geh.*) beating; thrashing; (*fig.: Bestrafung*) castigation; **körperliche ~:** corporal punishment

**zucht·los** (*veralt.*) **❶** *Adj.* undisciplined; (*unzüchtig*) licentious. **❷** *adv.* without discipline; in an undisciplined way; (*unzüchtig*) licentiously

**Zuchtlosigkeit** *die;* **~, ~en** (*veralt.*) **A** lack of discipline; (*Unzüchtigkeit*) licentiousness; **B** (*Verhalten*) impropriety

**Zucht-: ~perle** *die* cultured pearl; **~tier** *das* breeding animal

**Züchtung** *die;* **~, ~en** **A** (*das Züchten*) breeding; (*von Pflanzen*) cultivation; **B** (*Zuchtergebnis*) strain

**zuck** /tsʊk/ ⇒ **ruck, zuck**

**zuckeln** /ˈtsʊkl̩n/ *itr. V.; mit sein* saunter; amble; (*schleppend*) trail; ‹cart etc.› trundle

**Zuckel·trab** *der* (*ugs.*) jogtrot

**zucken** *itr. V.; mit Richtungsangabe mit sein* twitch; ‹body, arm, leg, etc.› jerk; (*vor Schreck*) start; ‹flames› flicker, flare up; ‹light, lightning› flicker, flash; ‹whip› flick (**nach** at); ‹dragonfly› flick; ‹clock-hand› jerk; **er zuckte zur Seite** he jumped to one side; **mit der Hand ~:** jerk one's hand; **mit den Achseln/Schultern ~:** shrug one's shoulders; **er ertrug den Schmerz, ohne auch nur zu ~:** he bore the pain without even flinching; **es zuckte in seinem Gesicht/um ihren Mund** his face twitched/there was a twitch around her mouth

**zücken** /ˈtsʏkn̩/ *tr. V.* draw ‹sword, dagger, knife›; (*scherzh.*) take out, produce ‹wallet, notebook, camera, etc.›

**Zucker** *der;* **~s, ~** **A** sugar; **~ sein** (*fig. salopp*) be fabulous (*coll.*); **B** (*Medizinjargon*) ⇒ **Blutzuckerspiegel**; **C** (*ugs.: ~krankheit*) diabetes; **~ haben** be a diabetic

**Zucker·bäcker** *der,* **Zucker·bäckerin** *die* (*veralt., bes. südd., österr.*) confectioner

**Zuckerbäcker·stil** *der* (*Archit.*) wedding cake style

**Zucker·brot** *das: in* **mit ~ und Peitsche** with a carrot and a stick

**zucker-, Zucker-: ~dose** *die* sugar bowl; **~erbse** *die* edible-podded *or* mangetout pea; **~guss, *~guß** *der* icing; **~hut** *der* sugar loaf; **~krank** *Adj.* diabetic; **~krankheit** *die* diabetes

**Zuckerl** *das;* **~s, ~[n]** (*südd., österr.*) sweet (*Brit.*); candy (*Amer.*); (*fig.*) sweetener; enticement

**Zucker-: ~lecken** *das* ⇒ **Honiglecken**; **~lösung** *die* sugar solution; (*sirupartig*) syrup

**zuckern** *tr. V.* sugar

**zucker-, Zucker-: ~puppe** *die* (*ugs.*) sweet little thing; sweetie (*coll.*); **~rohr** *das* sugar cane; **~rübe** *die* sugar beet; **~schlecken** *das* ⇒ **Honiglecken**; **~stange** *die* stick of rock; **~streuer** *der* sugar caster; **~süß** **❶** *Adj.* as sweet as sugar *postpos.;* beautifully sweet; (*fig. abwertend*) saccharine, sugary ‹picture, smile, etc.›; **❷** *adv.* **~süß lächeln** (*fig. abwertend*) give a saccharine *or* sugary smile; **~wasser** *das* sugar water; **~watte** *die* candyfloss; **~zange** *die* sugar tongs *pl.;* **~zeug** *das* (*veralt.*) sweet things *pl.;* confectionery

**zuckrig** *Adj.* sugary

**Zuckung** *die;* **~, ~en** twitch; **letzte ~en** death throes

**Zu·decke** *die* (*ugs.*) cover

**zu|decken** *tr. V.* cover up; cover [over] ‹well, ditch›; **sich ~:** tuck oneself up; **gut/warm zugedeckt** well/warmly tucked up

**zu·dem** *Adv.* (*geh.*) moreover; furthermore

**zu|denken** *unr. tr. V.* (*geh.*) **jmdm. etw. ~:** intend sth. for sb.

**zu|diktieren** *tr. V.* **jmdm. etw. ~:** impose sth. on sb.

**zu|drehen** **❶** *tr. V.* **A** (*abdrehen*) turn off ‹tap, heating, water, gas›; (*schließen*) screw ‹valve, container› shut; **B** (*zuwenden*) **jmdm. den Kopf/Rücken ~:** turn one's head towards/one's back on sb. **❷** *refl. V.* **sich jmdm./etw. ~:** turn to *or* towards sb./sth.

**zu·dringlich** **❶** *Adj.* pushy (*coll.*), pushing ‹person, manner›; (*sexuell*) importunate ‹person, manner›; prying ‹glance›; **er wurde ~:** he began to force his attentions on her/me/*etc.* **❷** *adv.* importunately

**Zu·dringlichkeit** *die;* **~, ~en** **A** pushiness (*coll.*); (*in sexueller Hinsicht*) importunate

*old spelling (see note on page 1707)

Z

manner; **B** (*Handlung*) **~en** insistent advances *or* attentions

**zu|drücken** ❶ *tr. V.* press shut; push ‹door› shut; **er drückte ihr die Gurgel** *od.* **Kehle zu** he choked *or* throttled her; **sie drückte ihm** (*dem Toten*) **die Augen zu** she closed his eyes. ❷ *itr. V.* press

**zu|eignen** *tr. V.* (*geh.*) **jmdm. etw. ~:** dedicate sth. to sb.

**Zu·eignung** *die; ~, ~en* dedication

**zu|eilen** *itr. V.; mit sein* **auf jmdn./etw. ~:** hurry *or* rush towards sb./sth.

**zu·einander** *Adv.* to one another; (*zusammen*) together; **~ finden** come together; (*fig.: sich einigen*) find common ground; **~ halten** stick together; **~ kommen** meet up; get together; **~ stehen** stand by one another; stick together; **Liebe ~ empfinden** have feelings of love towards one another; **gut/schlecht ~ passen** ‹things› go well together/not match; ‹people› be well-/ill-suited

***zueinander|finden** *usw.:* ⇨ **zueinander**

**zu|erkennen** *unr. tr. V.* **jmdm. ein Recht ~:** grant sb. a right; **jmdm. eine Entschädigung/einen Preis ~:** award sb. compensation/a prize; **jmdm. einen Titel ~:** confer a title on sb.

**Zuerkennung** *die; ~, ~en* (*eines Rechts*) granting; (*einer Entschädigung, eines Preises*) award; (*eines Titels*) conferring

**zu·erst** *Adv.* **A** first; **ich muss ~ einmal etwas essen** I must have something to eat first; **er war ~ da** he was here first; he was the first to come; **wer ~ kommt, wird ~ bedient** first come, first served; **mit dem Kopf ~ ins Wasser springen** jump into the water head first; **B** (*anfangs*) at first; to start with; **C** (*erstmals*) first; for the first time

**Zu·erwerb** *der* ⇨ **Nebenerwerb**

**Zuerwerbs·betrieb** *der* (*Landw.*): *holding which does not provide an adequate income without supplementation from non-agricultural work*

**zu|fächeln** *tr. V.* **jmdm. etw. ~:** waft sth. towards sb.; **jmdm./sich Kühlung ~:** fan sb./oneself

**zu|fahren** *unr. itr. V.; mit sein* **A** (*sich zubewegen*) **auf jmdn./etw. ~:** head towards sb./sth.; (*zusteuern*) drive at *or* aim for sb./sth.; **auf jmdn./etw. zugefahren kommen** come towards sb./sth.; **B** (*ugs.: los-, weiterfahren*) get a move on (*coll.*); **fahr zu!** step on it! (*coll.*)

**Zu·fahrt** *die* **A** access [for vehicles]; **die ~ zum Stadion erfolgt über die B 27** the stadium is approached along the B 27; **B** (*Straße, Weg*) access road; (*zum Haus*) driveway

**Zufahrts·straße** *die* access road; **~ zur Innenstadt** road leading to the town centre

**Zu·fall** *der* chance; (*zufälliges Zusammentreffen von Ereignissen*) coincidence; **es war [ein] reiner ~:** it was pure chance *or* coincidence; **der ~:** chance; **es ist kein ~, dass ...** it is no accident that ...; **durch ~:** by chance *or* accident; **ich habe durch ~ gesehen, wo sie es versteckt hat** I happened to see where she hid it; **dass wir uns dort begegneten, war ~:** our meeting there was a coincidence; **das ist aber ein ~/was für ein ~!** what a coincidence!; **der ~ wollte es, dass das Seil riss** by a stroke of fate *or* as chance would have it, the rope broke; **der ~ hat uns dorthin geführt** fate led us there; **etw. dem ~ überlassen** leave sth. to chance; **das verdankt er nur einem ~:** he owes it to chance

**zu|fallen** *unr. itr. V.; mit sein* **A** (*sich schließen*) ‹door etc.› slam shut; ‹eyes› close; **ihm fielen [vor Müdigkeit] die Augen zu** his eyelids were drooping [with tiredness]; **B** (*zuteil werden, zukommen*) **jmdm. ~** ‹task› fall to sb.; ‹prize, inheritance› go to sb.; **ihm fällt alles nur so zu** everything just drops into his lap; **die Verantwortung fällt ihm zu** the responsibility is his

**zu·fällig** ❶ *Adj.* accidental; chance *attrib.* ‹meeting, acquaintance›; random ‹selection›; **~e Ereignisse/Prozesse** (*Math.*) random events/processes. ❷ *adv.* by chance; **ich bin ~ hier vorbeigekommen** I just happened to be passing; **wissen Sie ~, wie spät es ist?** (*ugs.*) do you by any chance know the time?; **~ habe ich den Brief bei mir** as it happens, I have the letter on me; **es ist nicht ~ so, dass ...** it is no accident *or* coincidence that ...

**zufälliger·weise** *Adv.* ⇨ **zufällig 2**

**Zu·fälligkeit** *die* **A** accidental nature; fortuitousness; (*des Zusammentreffens von Ereignissen*) coincidental nature; **B** (*zufälliges Ereignis*) coincidence; chance occurrence

**Zufalls-:** **~auswahl** *die* random selection; **~bekanntschaft** *die* chance acquaintance; **~ergebnis** *das* chance result; **~fund** *der* chance find; **~generator** *der* (*Musik*) random generator; **~größe** *die* (*Math.*) ⇨ **~variable**; **~treffer** *der* fluke; **~variable** *die* (*Math.*) random variable; **~zahl** *die* (*Math.*) random number; **~ziffer** *die* (*Math.*) random digit

**zu|fassen** *itr. V.* **A** (*zugreifen*) make a snatch *or* grab; **B** (*ugs.*) ⇨ **zupacken B**

**zu|faxen** *tr. V.* **jmdm. etw. ~:** fax sth. to sb.; fax sb. sth.; **etw. zugefaxt erhalten** receive sth. by fax

**zu|fliegen** *unr. itr. V.; mit sein* **A** **auf jmdn./etw. ~:** fly towards sb./sth.; **es kam auf mich zugeflogen** it came flying towards me; **B** (*geflogen kommen*) **jmdm. ~** ‹bird› fly into sb.'s house; **ihm fliegen die Herzen zu** (*fig.*) all hearts surrender to his charms; **ihr fliegt in der Schule alles nur so zu** (*fig.*) school work comes easily to her; **die Einfälle fliegen ihm nur so zu** (*fig.*) he is never short of inspiration; **C** (*ugs.: zufallen*) ‹door, window, etc.› slam shut

**zu|fließen** *unr. itr. V.; mit sein* **A** **einer Sache** (*Dat.*) **~:** flow towards sth.; (*in etw. hineinfließen*) flow into sth.; **B** (*zukommen*) **jmdm./einer Sache ~** ‹money etc.› go to sb./sth.

**Zu·flucht** *die* refuge (**vor** + *Dat.* from); (*vor Unwetter o. Ä.*) shelter (**vor** + *Dat.* from); **[seine] ~ zu etw. nehmen** (*fig.*) resort to sth.

**Zufluchts-:** **~ort** *der*, **~stätte** *die* place of refuge; sanctuary

**Zu·fluss**, ***Zu·fluß** *der* **A** (*das Zufließen*) inflow; supply; (*fig.*) influx; **B** (*Gewässer*) feeder stream/river

**zu|flüstern** *tr. V.* **jmdm. etw. ~:** whisper sth. to sb.

**zu·folge** *Präp. mit Dat.; nachgestellt* according to; **sein Vorschlag, dem ~ das Haus versteigert werden soll** his proposal that the house should be put up for auction

**zu·frieden** ❶ *Adj.* contented; (*befriedigt*) satisfied; **mit etw. ~ sein** be satisfied with sth.; **bist du jetzt ~?** are you satisfied [now]?; **ein ~es Gesicht machen** look contented *or* satisfied; **wir können ~ sein** we can't complain; **sich ~ geben** be satisfied; **sich mit etw. nicht ~ geben wollen** refuse to accept sth.; **damit gebe ich mich nicht ~:** I cannot accept that; **jmdn. ~ stellen** satisfy sb.; **jmdn./etw. ~ lassen** leave sb./sth. alone; **lass mich damit ~!** stop going on at me about it! (*coll.*); **ich bin es ~** (*veralt.*) it's all right with me. ❷ *adv.* contentedly

***zufrieden|geben** ⇨ **zufrieden 1**

**Zufriedenheit** *die; ~:* contentment; (*Befriedigung*) satisfaction; **zu meiner vollen ~:** to my complete satisfaction

***zufrieden|lassen**, ***zufrieden|stellen** ⇨ **zufrieden 1**

**zufriedenstellend** ❶ *Adj.* satisfactory. ❷ *adv.* satisfactorily

**zu|frieren** *unr. itr. V.; mit sein* freeze over

**zu|fügen** *tr. V.* **A** **jmdm. etw. ~:** inflict sth. on sb.; **jmdm. Schaden/[ein] Unrecht ~:** do sb. harm/an injustice; **jmdm. eine Beleidigung/Kränkung ~:** insult/hurt sb.; ⇨ *auch* **wollen**; **B** (*hin~*) **etw. einer Sache** (*Dat.*) **~:** add sth. to sth.

**Zufuhr** /ˈtsuːfuːɐ̯/ *die; ~, ~en:* supply; (*Material*) supplies *pl.*; **die ~ milder Meeresluft** the stream of mild sea air

**zu|führen** ❶ *itr. V.* **auf etw.** (*Akk.*) **~:** lead towards sth. ❷ *tr. V.* **A** (*zuleiten*) **einer Sache** (*Dat.*) **etw. ~:** supply sth. to sth.; supply sth. with sth.; **dem Motor Kraftstoff ~:** supply fuel to the engine; supply the engine with fuel; **B** (*bringen*) **einer Firma Kunden/einer Partei Mitglieder ~:** bring new customers to a firm/new members to a party; **die Stute dem Hengst ~:** bring the mare to the stallion; **etw. seiner eigentlichen Bestimmung ~:** devote sth. to its proper purpose; **jmdn. der gerechten Strafe ~:** ensure that sb. gets condign punishment

**Zu·fuß·gehen** *das; ~s* walking

**Zug** /tsuːk/ *der; ~[e]s, Züge* /ˈtsyːɡə/ **A** (*Bahn*) train; (*Straßenbahn*) tram (*Brit.*); streetcar (*Amer.*) (*consisting of two or more cars*); (*Last~*) truck *or* (*Brit.*) lorry and trailer; **ich nehme lieber den ~** *od.* **fahre lieber mit dem ~:** I prefer to go by train *or* rail; **jmdn. vom ~ abholen/zum ~ bringen** meet sb. off/take sb. to the train; **jmdn. in den ~ setzen** (*ugs.*) put sb. on the train; **B** (*Gespann von ~tieren*) team; **ein ~ Ochsen** a team *or* yoke of oxen; **C** (*Kolonne*) column; (*Um~*) procession; (*Demonstrations~*) march; (*Vogelschar*) flock; **D** (*das Ziehen*) pull; traction (*Phys.*); (*fig.*) **das ist der ~ der Zeit** this is the modern trend *or* the way things are going; **die Sache hat einen ~ ins Lächerliche** there's something ridiculous about it; **dem ~ des Herzens folgen** follow the promptings of one's heart; **E** (*Vorrichtung*) pull; (*einer Posaune*) slide; **F** (*Wanderung*) migration; (*Streif~, Beute~, Diebes~*) expedition; **G** (*beim Brettspiel*) move; **du bist am ~:** it's your move; **etw. ~ um ~ erledigen** (*fig.*) deal with sth. step by step; **Leistung/Erfüllung ~ um ~** (*Rechtsw.*) simultaneous performance; **zum ~e kommen** (*fig.*) get a chance; **H** (*Schluck*) swig (*coll.*); mouthful; (*großer Schluck*) gulp; **einen tiefen ~ [von etw.] nehmen** take a big gulp *or* (*literary*) deep draught [of sth.]; **das Glas auf einen** *od.* **in einem ~ leeren** empty the glass at one go; **einen Roman in einem ~ durchlesen** (*fig.*) read a novel at one sitting; **er hat einen guten ~** (*ugs.*) he can really knock it back (*coll.*); **etw. in vollen Zügen genießen** (*fig.*) enjoy sth. to the full; **I** (*beim Rauchen*) pull; puff; drag (*coll.*); **J** (*Atem~*) breath; **in tiefen** *od.* **vollen Zügen** in deep breaths; **in den letzten Zügen liegen** (*ugs.*) be at death's door; (*fig. scherzh.*) ‹car, engine, machine› be at its last gasp; ‹project etc.› be on the last lap; **K** (*~luft; beim Ofen*) draught; **im ~ sitzen** sit in a draught; **der Kamin hat einen schlechten/guten ~:** the fire draws badly/well; **L** (*Gesichts~*) feature; trait; (*Wesens~*) characteristic; trait; **seine Züge** his features; **in ihrem Gesicht lag ein ~ von Strenge** there was a hint of severity in her face; **die Stadt trägt noch dörfliche Züge** the town still has something of the village about it; **das ist ein charakteristischer ~ an ihm** it is a characteristic of his; **das war kein schöner ~ von ihr** that did her no credit; **M** (*landsch.: Schublade*) drawer; **N** (*Bewegung eines Schwimmers/Ruderers*) stroke; **O** (*ugs.: Disziplin*) discipline; **jmdn. gut im ~ haben** have sb. well trained *or* under control; **in etw.** (*Dat.*) **ist ~** (*ugs.*) sth. has punch; **~ in etw.** (*Akk.*) **bringen** get sth. organized; **P** (*Milit.: Einheit*) platoon; **Q** (*Schulw.: Zweig*) side; **R** (*Höhen~*) range; chain; **die Züge des Odenwalds** the hills of the Odenwald; **S** (*Abluftrohr*) flue; **T** (*Schrift~; Strich*) stroke; **mit klaren Zügen geschrieben** written in a clear hand; **in großen/groben Zügen** (*fig.*) in broad outline

**Zu·gabe** *die* **A** (*Geschenk*) [free] gift; **B** (*im Konzert, Theater*) encore; **C** (*das Zugeben*) addition; **unter sparsamer ~ von Wasser** adding water sparingly

**Zug·ab·teil** *das* [train] compartment (*Brit.*)

**Zu·gang** *der* **A** (*Weg*) access; (*Eingang*) entrance; **B** (*das Betreten, Hineingehen*) access; **~ verboten!** no admittance!; **er hat jederzeit ~ zum Chef** he can see the boss (*coll.*) at any time; **C** (*fig.*) access; **~ zu jmdm./etw. finden** be able to relate to sb./sth.; **D** (*das Hinzukommen*) (*von Personen*) intake; (*von Patienten*) admission; (*Zuwachs*) increase (**von** in); **E** (*Person, Sache*) (*Patient*) new admission; (*Soldat*) new recruit; (*Buch*) [new] accession; (*Ware*) new stock item

**zu·gange** *in* **irgendwo/mit jmdm./einer Sache ~ sein** (*ugs.*) be busy *or* occupied somewhere/with sb./sth.

**zugänglich** /ˈt̮suːgɛŋlɪç/ *Adj.* **A** (*Zugang bietend*) accessible; (*geöffnet*) open; **schwer ~:** difficult to reach *pred.*; **die Zimmer sind von der Terrasse her ~:** the rooms can be reached from the terrace; **B** (*zur Verfügung stehend*) available (*Dat.*, **für** to); (*verständlich*) accessible (*Dat.*, **für** to); **schwer ~es Material** material that is difficult to obtain; **C** (*aufgeschlossen*) approachable ‹person›; **für neue Ideen** *usw.* **~ sein** be amenable *or* receptive to new ideas *etc;* **allem Schönen** *od.* **für alles Schöne ~ sein** respond to all that is beautiful

**Zugänglichkeit** *die;* **~ A** accessibility; **schlechte ~:** difficulty of access; **B** (*Aufgeschlossenheit*) receptiveness (**gegenüber** to)

**Zug-: ~anschluss, *~anschluß** *der* [train] connection; **~begleiter** *der* **A** (*Schaffner*) guard; **B** (*Faltblatt*) train schedule leaflet; **~begleiterin** *die* ⇒ **~begleiter** A; **~brücke** *die* drawbridge

**zu·geben** *unr. tr. V.* **A** (*hinzufügen*) add (*Dat.* to); **[jmdm.] etw. ~:** give [sb.] sth. as an extra; **der Sänger gab noch ein Lied zu** the singer sang another song as an encore; **B** (*gestehen, zugestehen*) admit; admit, confess ‹guilt, complicity›; admit to, confess to ‹deed, crime›; **sie gab zu, es gestohlen zu haben** she admitted stealing it *or* having stolen it; **ich gebe zu, dass ich mich geirrt habe** I admit [that] I was wrong; **gibs doch endlich zu!** come on, admit it!; **du wirst mir ~** *od.* **du wirst doch ~ müssen, dass ...** you have to admit that ...; **es war, zugegeben, viel Glück dabei** true, there was a lot of luck involved; **C** (*erlauben*) allow; permit; **er wollte nicht ~, dass ich allein reise** he would not allow me to *or* let me travel alone

**zu·gegebener·maßen** *Adv.* admittedly

**zu·gegen** *Adj. in* **~ sein** (*geh.*) be present

**zu|gehen** *unr. itr. V.; mit sein* **A** (*sich nähern*) **auf jmdn./etw. ~:** approach sb./sth.; **sie sollten endlich aufeinander ~** (*fig.*) they should try to come together at last; **dem Ende ~:** be coming to an end; **es geht auf Weihnachten zu** it is coming up to for Christmas; **er geht schon auf die Achtzig zu** he is coming up to eighty; **B** (*ugs.: vorangehen*) get a move on (*coll.*); step on it (*coll.*); **C** (*Amtsspr.*) **jmdm. ~:** be sent to sb.; **jmdm. etw. ~ lassen** send sth. to sb.; **D** *unpers.* (*geschehen, verlaufen*) **hier/dort geht es ... zu** things are ... here/there; **ich weiß, wie es zugegangen ist** I know what went on; **auf dem Fest ging es fröhlich zu** it was very jolly at the party; **es müsste seltsam ~, wenn das nicht gelänge** something remarkable would have to happen for that not to succeed; **es geht nicht mit rechten Dingen zu** there is something fishy going on (*coll.*); **E** (*ugs.: sich schließen*) close; shut; **F** (*ugs.: sich schließen lassen*) **die Tür/der Knopf geht nicht zu** the door will not shut/the button will not fasten; **der Reißverschluss geht schwer zu** the zip is difficult to do up; **G** ⇒ **zulaufen** E

**Zu·geherin** *die;* **~, ~nen, Zu·geh·frau** *die* (*bes. südd., österr.*) cleaning lady; (*Haushaltshilfe*) home help

**zu|gehören** *itr. V.* (*geh.*) **jmdm./einer Sache ~:** belong to sb./sth.

**zu·gehörig** *Adj.* belonging to it/them *postpos., not pred.;* (*begleitend*) accompanying; **der Kreis und die ~en Gemeinden** the district and the communities belonging to it; **einer Sache** (*Dat.*) **~:** belonging to sth.; **sich jmdm./einer Sache** (*Dat.*) **~ fühlen** have a feeling of belonging [to sb./sth.]

**Zugehörigkeit** *die;* **~:** belonging (**zu** to); (*Mitgliedschaft*) membership (**zu** of)

**Zugehörigkeits·gefühl** *das* sense of belonging

**zu·geknöpft** *Adj.* (*fig. ugs.*) tight-lipped; (*nicht zugänglich*) unapproachable

**Zügel** /ˈt̮syːgl̩/ *der;* **~s, ~ A** rein; **ein Pferd am ~ führen** lead a horse by the reins; **einem Pferd in die ~ fallen** stop a horse by seizing the reins; **B** (*fig.*) **die ~ [fest] in der Hand haben** be [firmly] in control; have things [firmly] under control; **die ~ straffer anziehen** tighten up on things; **jmdm./seiner Fantasie** *usw.* **~ anlegen** clamp down on sb./curb one's imagination *etc.;* **die ~ schießen lassen** let things take their course; **die ~ schleifen lassen** *od.* **lockern** slacken the reins

**zügel·los** (*fig.*) ❶ *Adj.* unrestrained; unbridled ‹rage, passion›; limitless ‹ambition›; frantic ‹rush, retreat›; **ein ~es Leben führen** live a life of licentious indulgence. ❷ *adv.* without restraint; **~ leben** live a life of licentious indulgence

**Zügellosigkeit** *die;* **~, ~en** lack of restraint; (*Unzüchtigkeit*) licentiousness

**zügeln** *tr. V.* **A** rein [in] ‹horse›; **B** (*fig.*) curb, restrain ‹feeling, desire, curiosity, etc.›; **sich ~:** restrain oneself

**Zügelung** *die;* **~, ~en** curbing; restraining

**Zu·gereiste** *der/die; adj. Dekl.* newcomer

**zu|gesellen** *refl. V.* **sich jmdm./einer Sache ~:** join sb./sth.

**Zu·geständnis** *das* concession (**an** + *Akk.* to)

**zu|gestehen** *unr. tr. V.* **A** (*anerkennen*) grant ‹right, claim, share, etc.›; allow ‹discount, commission, time›; **jmdm. ~, etw. zu tun** give sb. permission to do sth.; **B** (*zugeben*) admit; concede; **du wirst mir ~ müssen, dass ...** you have to admit that ...

**zu·getan** ❶ *2. Part. v.* **zutun**. ❷ *Adj. in* **jmdm. [herzlich] ~ sein** (*geh.*) be [very] attached to sb.; **den schönen Künsten ~ sein** have a penchant for the fine arts

**Zu·gewinn** *der* gain (**an** + *Dat.* in)

**Zugewinn·gemeinschaft** *die* (*Rechtsw.*): *separate property with equal division of property acquired after marriage*

**Zu·gezogene** *der/die; adj. Dekl.* newcomer

**zug·fest** *Adj.* tensile ‹steel etc.›; **sehr ~ sein** have great tensile strength

**Zug·führer** *der,* **Zug·führerin** *die* **A** (*Eisenb.*) guard; **B** (*Milit.*) platoon sergeant

**zu|gießen** *unr. tr., itr. V.* add (*Dat.* to); **darf ich [dir] ~?** may I top you up (*Brit. coll.*) *or* (*Amer. coll.*) put a top on it?

**zugig** *Adj.* draughty, (*im Freien*) windy ‹corner etc.›

**zügig** /ˈt̮syːgɪç/ ❶ speedy; rapid; **mit ~er Geschwindigkeit, in ~er Fahrt** at a good *or* brisk speed. ❷ *adv.* speedily; rapidly

**Zügigkeit** *die;* **~:** speediness; rapidity

**Zug·kraft** *die* **A** (*Physik*) (*verformend*) tensile force; (*beschleunigend*) traction force; **B** (*fig.*) attraction

**zug·kräftig** *Adj.* effective ‹publicity›; powerful ‹argument›; convincing ‹evidence›; influential ‹name›; catchy ‹title, slogan›; **ein ~er Schauspieler/Film** an actor who/film which is a big draw; **~ sein** ‹film, actor, etc.› be a big draw

**zu·gleich** *Adv.* at the same time; **er ist Maler und Dichter ~:** he is both a painter and a poet

**Zug-: ~luft** *die* draught; **~luft [ab]bekommen** be in a draught; **~maschine** *die* tractor; (*von Sattelzug*) tractor [unit]; **~nummer** *die* **A** ⇒ **Zugpferd** B; **B** (*Eisenb.*) train number; **~personal** *das* train crew; **~pferd** *das* **A** (*Pferd*) draughthorse; **B** (*fig.: Attraktion*) big draw; crowd-puller; **C** (*treibende Kraft*) dynamo; **~pflaster** *das* (*Med.*) cantharidal plaster

**zu|greifen** *unr. itr. V.* **A** take hold; **er kann nicht richtig ~:** he cannot grasp things properly; **rasch ~:** make a quick grab; **B** (*sich bedienen*) help oneself; (*fig.: handeln*) take action; **er sah seine Chance und griff zu** (*fig.*) he saw his chance and acted at once; **C** (*fleißig arbeiten*) **[hart** *od.* **kräftig] ~:** [really] knuckle down to it; **wenn viele Hände mit ~:** when plenty of people lend a hand

**Zu·griff** *der* **A** grasp; **sich dem ~ der Polizei entziehen** escape the clutches of the police; **B** (*Zugang*) access (**auf** + *Akk.* to)

**zu·grunde** *Adv. in* **A ~ gehen** (*sterben*) die (**an** + *Dat.* of); (*zerstört werden*) be destroyed (**an** + *Dat.* by); ‹marriage› founder (**an** + *Dat.* owing to); ‹person› go under; (*finanziell*) be ruined; ‹company› go to the wall; **an sich selbst ~ gehen** destroy oneself; **~ richten** destroy; (*finanziell*) ruin ‹company, person›; **B etw. ~ legen** use sth. as a basis; **etw. einer Sache** (*Dat.*) **~ legen** base sth. on sth.; **etw. liegt einer Sache ~:** sth. is based on sth.; **das diesem Urteil ~ liegende Gesetz** the law which gives rise to this verdict

**Zugrunde·legung** *die;* **~: unter** *od.* **bei ~ dieser Umstände** on the basis of these facts

**Zugs-** (*österr.*) ⇒ **Zug-**

**Zug-: ~schaffner** *der,* **~schaffnerin** *die* ticket inspector; **~telefon** *das* train telephone; **~tier** *das* draught animal

**zu|gucken** *itr. V.* (*ugs.*) ⇒ **zusehen**

**Zug·unglück** *das* train crash

**zu·gunsten** ❶ *Präp. mit Gen.* in favour of; **eine Sammlung ~ der Flutopfer** a collection for the flood victims. ❷ *Adv.* **~ von** in favour of

**zu·gut** *in* **etw. ~ haben** (*schweiz., südd.*) be owed sth.; **du hast [bei mir] 10 Mark ~:** you've got ten marks to come [from me]

**zu·gute** *Adv. in* **jmdm. seine Jugend/Unerfahrenheit** *usw.* **~ halten** (*geh.*) take sb.'s youth/inexperience *etc.* into consideration; make allowances for sb.'s youth/inexperience *etc.;* **sich** (*Dat.*) **etwas/viel auf etw.** (*Akk.*) **~ tun** *od.* **halten** (*geh.*) be proud/very proud of sth.; **jmdm./einer Sache ~ kommen** stand sb./sth. in good stead; **jmdm. etw. ~ kommen lassen** let sb. have the benefit of *or* let sb. benefit from sth.

**Zug-: ~verbindung** *die* **A** (*Eisenbahnverbindung*) rail *or* (*Amer.*) railroad service; **B** (*~anschluss*) [train] connection; **~verkehr** *der* rail *or* (*Amer.*) railroad traffic; **~vogel** *der* migratory bird; **~zeit** (*Zool.*) *die* period of migration; **~zwang** *der* **A** (*fig.*) pressure to take action; **unter ~zwang stehen, in ~zwang sein** be under pressure to take action; **jmdn. in ~zwang bringen** put sb. under pressure; **B** (*Schach*) zugzwang

**zu|haben** *unr. itr. V.* (*ugs.*) **A** ‹shop, office› be shut *or* closed; **wir haben montags zu** we are closed on Mondays; **B** (*zubekommen haben*) **endlich hat sie den Koffer/Reißverschluss zu** at last she's managed to shut the suitcase/do up the zip

**zu|haken** *tr. V.* hook up; do up the hooks on

**zu|halten** ❶ *unr. tr. V.* hold closed; (*nicht öffnen*) keep closed; **jmdm./sich die Augen/den Mund** *usw.* **~:** put one's hand[s] over sb.'s/one's eyes/mouth *etc.;* **sich** (*Dat.*) **die Nase ~:** hold one's nose. ❷ *itr. V.* **auf etw.** (*Akk.*) **~:** head for sth.

**Zuhälter** /ˈt̮suːhɛltɐ/ *der;* **~s, ~:** pimp

**Zuhälterei** *die;* **~:** pimping; (*Rechtsw.*) living off the earnings of prostitution

**zu·handen** ❶ *Adj.* **jmdm. ~ sein** be available to sb.; be at sb.'s disposal. ❷ *Präp. mit Gen.* (*österr., schweiz.*) **~ Herrn B** for the attention of Herr B. ❸ *Adv.* (*österr., schweiz.*) **~ von Herrn B** for the attention of Herr B

**zu|hängen** *tr. V.* cover ‹window, cage›

**zu|hauen** ❶ *unr. itr. V.* **A** (*ugs.*) bang *or* slam ‹door, window› shut; **B** (*behauen*) hew into shape. ❷ *unr. itr. V.* (*ugs.*) hit *or* strike out

*old spelling (see note on page 1707)

Z

**zu·hauf** *Adv.* (*geh.*) in great numbers

**zu·hause** *Adv.* (*österr., schweiz.*) ⇒ **daheim**

**Zu·hause** *das;* **~s** home

**zu|heilen** *itr. V.; mit sein* heal [over]

**Zuhilfenahme** /tsu'hɪlfəna:mə/ *die;* **~:** utilization; **ohne/unter ~ einer Sache** (*Gen.*)/**von etw.** without/with the aid of sth.

**zu·hinterst** *Adv.* right at the back; **~ in der Schublade/auf dem Regal** right at the back of the drawer/of the shelf

**zu|hören** *itr. V.* **jmdm./einer Sache ~:** listen to sb./sth.; **nun hör mal zu** now listen; (*leicht drohend*) now [you] listen here; **er kann gut ~:** he's a good listener

**Zu·hörer** *der,* **Zu·hörerin** *die* listener; **sie merkte, dass sie einen ~ hatte** she noticed that somebody was listening

**Zuhörerschaft** *die;* **~:** audience

**zu·innerst** *Adv.* (*geh.*) deep down; in one's heart of hearts; **~ aufgewühlt** moved to the depths of one's soul

**zu|jubeln** *itr. V.* **jmdm. ~:** cheer sb. [on]

**Zu·kauf** *der* additional purchase/purchases; **~ an Grund und Boden** purchase of more land

**zu|kehren** *tr. V.* turn (*Dat.* to); **jmdm. den Rücken/das Gesicht ~:** turn one's back on sb./one's face towards sb.

**zu|klappen** **1** *tr. V.* close; fold ‹penknife› shut; (*mit Wucht*) slam ‹lid› shut. **2** *itr. V.; mit sein* ‹window, lid, etc.› click to *or* shut; (*mit Wucht*) slam shut

**zu|kleben** *tr. V.* **A** (*verschließen*) seal ‹letter, envelope›; **B** (*bekleben*) cover

**zu|klinken** *tr. V.* [click] shut

**zu|knallen** (*ugs.*) **1** *tr. V.* slam. **2** *itr. V.; mit sein* slam

**zu|kneifen** *unr. tr. V.* squeeze ‹eye[s]› shut; shut ‹eye[s]› tight; shut ‹mouth› tightly

**zu|knöpfen** *tr. V.* button up

**zu|knoten** *tr. V.* knot; tie up

**zu|kommen** *itr. V.; mit sein* **A** (*sich nähern*) **auf jmdn. ~:** approach sb.; (*zu jmdm. kommen*) come up to sb.; **er/der Stier/das Auto kam direkt auf mich zu** he/the bull/the car came straight towards me; **er ahnte nicht, was noch auf ihn ~ sollte** (*fig.*) he had no idea what he was in for; **die Dinge auf sich ~ lassen** (*fig.*) take things as they come; **wir werden in der Angelegenheit noch auf Sie ~:** we shall be coming back to you on this matter; **B** (*geh.*) (*zuteil/übermittelt werden*) **jmdm. ~:** reach sb.; ‹inheritance› come to sb.; **jmdm. etw. ~ lassen** (*schicken*) send sb. sth.; (*schenken*) give sb. sth.; **jmdm./einer Sache Pflege/Aufmerksamkeit ~ lassen** devote care/attention to sth.; **C** (*gebühren*) **jmdm. kommt etw. zu/nicht zu** sb. is entitled/not entitled to sth.; sb. has a right/no right to sth.; (*etw. ist jmdm. angemessen/nicht angemessen*) sth. befits/does not befit sb.; **dir kommt diese Entscheidung nicht zu** this decision is not up to you; this is not your decison; **D** (*beizumessen sein*) **dieser Entdeckung kommt große Bedeutung zu** great significance must be attached to this discovery

**zu|korken** *tr. V.* cork

**zu|kriegen** *tr. V.* (*ugs.*) ⇒ **zubekommen**

**Zukunft** /'tsu:kʊnft/ *die;* **~, Zukünfte** /'tsu:kynftə/ **A** future; **das wird die ~ lehren** time will tell; **für alle ~:** for all time; **~/keine ~ haben** have a/no future; **in naher/ferner ~:** in the near *or* immediate/distant future; **in ~:** in future; **einer Sache** (*Dat.*) **gehört die ~:** the future belongs to sth.; **seine [politische] ~ schon hinter sich** (*Dat.*) **haben** (*scherzh.*) be over the hill [politically]; **mit/ohne ~:** with/without a future; **ich wünsche Ihnen alles Gute für Ihre weitere ~:** I wish you all the best for the future; **B** (*Grammatik*) future [tense]; **erste** *od.* **unvollendete/zweite** *od.* **vollendete ~:** future/future perfect [tense]

**zu·künftig** **1** *Adj.* future. **2** *Adv.* in future

**Zukünftige** *der/die; adj. Dekl.* (*ugs.*) **mein ~r/meine ~:** my husband/wife-to-be; my intended (*joc.*)

**zukunfts-, Zukunfts-:** **~aussichten** *Pl.* prospects for the future; **~forschung** *die* futurology *no art.;* **~musik** *die* (*fig.*) *in* **~musik sein** be very much in the future; (*als utopisch anzusehen sein*) be pie in the sky; **~perspektive** *die* prospects *pl.* for the future; future prospects *pl.;* **~roman** *der* novel set in the future; **~sicherung** *die* safeguarding *no art.* the future; **etwas für die ~sicherung tun** do something to secure *or* safeguard the future

**zukunft[s]·weisend** *Adj.* forward-looking; pointing the way forward *postpos.*

**zu|lächeln** *itr. V.* **jmdm./sich ~:** smile at sb./each other

**zu|lachen** *itr. V.* **jmdm. ~:** give sb. a friendly laugh

**Zulage** *die* (*vom Arbeitgeber*) extra pay *no indef. art.;* additional allowance *no indef. art.;* (*vom Staat*) benefit

***zu·lande** ⇒ **Land** E

**zu|langen** *itr. V.* **A** (*ugs.: sich bedienen*) tuck in (*coll.*); **B** (*ugs.: zupacken*) [really] knuckle down to it

**zu|länglich** (*geh.*) **1** *Adj.* adequate. **2** *adv.* adequately

**zu|lassen** *unr. tr. V.* **A** (*erlauben, dulden*) allow; permit; **solches Unrecht darf man nicht ~:** such injustice must not be permitted; **ich lasse keine Ausnahme zu** I do not allow *or* permit any exceptions; **das lässt nur einen/keinen anderen Schluss zu** that permits of *or* allows only one/no other conclusion; **B** (*teilnehmen lassen*) admit; **jmdn. bei etw. ~:** admit sb. to sth.; **C** (*mit einer Erlaubnis, Lizenz usw. versehen*) **jmdn. als Arzt ~:** register sb. as a doctor; **eine Partei ~** (*Politik*) permit a party to exist; **der Anwalt ist beim Amtsgericht Mannheim zugelassen** the lawyer is registered to practise at Mannheim district court; **jmdn. zum Studium/zum Studium der Medizin ~:** accept sb. at university/to study medicine; **jmdn. zu einer Prüfung ~:** allow *or* permit sb. to take an examination; **der Bulle ist zur Zucht zugelassen** the bull is registered for breeding; **D** (*zur Benutzung, zur Anwendung, zum Verkauf usw. freigeben*) allow; permit; **ein Medikament ~:** approve a medicine [for sale]; **für den öffentlichen Verkehr/für Autobahnen [nicht] zugelassen sein** [not] be authorized for use on public highways/motorways (*Brit.*) *or* (*Amer.*) freeways; **E** (*Kfz-W.*) register ‹vehicle›; **auf jmdn./jmds. Namen zugelassen sein** be registered in sb.'s name; **F** (*geschlossen lassen*) leave closed *or* shut; leave ‹letter› unopened; leave ‹collar, coat› fastened [up]

**zu·lässig** *Adj.* permissible; admissible ‹appeal›; **~e [Höchst]geschwindigkeit** [maximum] permissible speed; [upper] speed limit

**Zulässigkeit** *die;* **~:** permissibility; (*einer Berufung*) admissibility

**Zulassung** *die;* **~, ~en** **A** (*Erlaubnis, Lizenz*) **~ als Arzt** registration as a doctor; **~ zur Teilnahme/zur Prüfung beantragen** apply for permission to attend/to take *or* (*Brit.*) sit an examination; **ihm ist die ~ zum Studium/zum Medizinstudium erteilt worden** he has been accepted at university/to study medicine; **B** (*Freigabe*) approval; authorization; **C** (*Kfz-W.*) registration; **D** (*Kfz-W. ugs.*) ⇒ **Kraftfahrzeugschein**

**zulassungs·pflichtig** *Adj.* liable *or* subject to registration *postpos.*

**Zulassungs·stelle** *die* vehicle registration office

**zu·lasten** **1** *Präp. mit Gen.* **die Kosten gehen ~ des Käufers/der Staatskasse** the costs are borne by the purchaser/the public purse. **2** *Adv. in* **~ von: dies muss ~ von Millionen Arbeitnehmern gehen** the cost of this must be borne by millions of workers; **hässliche Verallgemeinerungen ~ von Minderheiten** nasty generalizations at the expense of minorities

**Zu·lauf** *der* **A** **[großen** *od.* **starken** *od.* **viel] ~ haben** ‹shop, restaurant, etc.› enjoy a large clientele, be very popular; ‹doctor, lawyer› have a large practice, be very much in demand; **mehr** *od.* **größeren ~ haben** ‹shop, restaurant, etc.› enjoy an increased clientele, be more popular; ‹doctor, lawyer› have a larger practice, be more in demand; **der ~ war so groß, dass das Gastspiel verlängert werden musste** the guest performance was so popular that its run had to be extended; **B** (*zulaufende Menge*) inflow; **C** (*Rohr, Leitung*) intake

**zu|laufen** *unr. itr. V.; mit sein* **A** **auf jmdn./etw. ~** (*auch fig.*) run towards sb./sth.; **auf jmdn./etw. zugelaufen kommen** come running towards sb./sth.; **einer Sache** (*Dat.*) **~** (*geh.*) run towards sth.; **B** **jmdm. ~** ‹cat, dog, etc.› adopt sb. as a new owner; **ein zugelaufener Hund** a stray dog that has adopted us/them *etc.;* **C** (*hin~*) ‹water etc.› run in; **warmes Wasser ~ lassen** run [some] warm water in; **D** (*sich verjüngen*) taper; **spitz/konisch/keilförmig ~:** taper to a point; **E** (*ugs.: schnell laufen*) get one's skates on (*Brit. sl.*); get a move on (*coll.*)

**zu|legen** **1** *refl. V.* **sich** (*Dat.*) **etw. ~:** get oneself sth.; **er hat sich einen Bart zugelegt** (*ugs.*) he has grown a beard; **sich einen Künstlernamen ~:** adopt a pseudonym. **2** *itr. V.* (*ugs.*) **A** (*sein Tempo steigern*) step on it (*coll.*); **B** (*wachsen, stärker werden*) ‹sales, output, turnover, etc.› increase; **der Dollar hat [um vier Pfennige] zugelegt** the dollar has risen [four pfennigs]; **sie könnten bei Neuwahlen ~:** the could improve their position if there were fresh elections. **3** *tr. V.* (*ugs.*) add; **wenn meine Eltern noch 100 Mark ~, kann ich mir das Fahrrad kaufen** if my parents put in a hundred marks, I can afford the bicycle; **einen Schritt/**(*ugs.:*) **Zahn ~:** get a move on (*coll.*)

**zu·leid[e]** *in* **jmdm. etwas/nichts ~ tun** hurt *or* harm sb./not [do anything to] hurt *or* harm sb.; ⇒ *auch* **Fliege** A

**zu|leiten** *tr. V.* **A** feed; supply; supply ‹nourishment›; feed ‹signal›; channel ‹sewage›; **B** (*zukommen lassen*) send; forward

**Zu·leitung** *die* **A** supply; **B** (*Übersendung, Zustellung*) sending; forwarding; **C** (*Rohr, Kabel usw.*) feed line

**zu·letzt** *Adv.* **A** (*zum Schluss, nach allem anderen*) last [of all]; **~ liest du es noch einmal durch** finally, read it through again; **an sich selbst denkt sie immer ~:** she always thinks of herself last; **sich** (*Dat.*) **etw. für ~ aufheben** save sth. till last; **B** (*als Letzter/Letzte/Letztes*) last; **er kommt immer ~:** he always comes last; he is always [the] last; **das ~ geborene Kind** the child born last; **C** (*fig.: am wenigsten*) least of all; **darauf wäre ich ~ gekommen** that's the last thing I should have thought of; **nicht ~:** not least; **D** (*das letzte Mal*) last; **ich habe ihn ~ gestern Abend gesehen** I last saw him yesterday evening; **E** (*schließlich, am Ende*) in the end; **bis ~:** [right up] to *or* until the end

**zu·liebe** *Adv.* **jmdm./einer Sache ~:** for sb.'s sake/for the sake of sth.

**Zu·liefer·betrieb** *der* supplier (*Gen.* to)

**zu|löten** *tr. V.* solder; solder up ‹hole›

**Zu·luft** *die* (*Technik*) incoming air

**zum** /tsʊm/ *Präp. + Art.* **A** = **zu dem; B** (*räumlich: Richtung*) to the; **ein Fenster ~ Hof** a window on to *or* facing the yard; **~ Hof liegen** face the yard; **wo geht es ~ Stadion?** which is the way to the stadium?; **C** (*räumlich: Lage*) **etw. ~ Fenster hinauswerfen** throw sth. out of the window; **die Gaststätte „Zum Lamm"** the 'Lamb Inn'; **D** (*Zusammengehörigkeit, Hinzufügung*) **Milch ~ Tee/Sahne ~ Kuchen nehmen** take milk with [one's] tea/have cream with one's cake; **E** (*zeitlich*) at the; **spätestens ~ 15. April** by 15 April at the latest; **~ Schluss/richtigen Zeitpunkt** at the end/the right moment; **F** (*Zweck*) **ein Gerät ~ Schneiden** an instrument for cutting [with]; **hol dir was ~ Schreiben** get something to write with; **~ Spaß/Vergnügen** for fun/pleasure; **~ Lesen braucht er eine Brille** he needs glasses for reading; **~**

Z

**Schutz** as *or* for protection; **etw. ~ Essen/Lesen** (*österr.*) sth. to eat/read; **~ Schwimmen gehen** go swimming; **G** (*Folge*) **~ Nachteil des Kunden** to the disadvantage of the customer; **~ Ärger/Leidwesen seines Vaters** to the annoyance/sorrow of his father; **~ Nutzen der Allgemeinheit** for the benefit of the general public; **es ist ~ Verrücktwerden** it is enough to drive you mad; **das ist gar nicht ~ Lachen** it's no laughing matter; (*in Bezug auf etwas Sichtbares*) it's nothing to laugh at; **H** (*sonstige Verwendungen*) **jmdn. ~ Direktor ernennen/~ Kanzler wählen** appoint sb. director/elect sb. chancellor; **~ Dieb werden** become a thief; **sich** (*Dat.*) **etw. ~ Ziel setzen** set oneself sth. as a goal; **~ Ersten, ~ Zweiten, ~ Dritten!** (*bei Versteigerung*) going, going, gone!; **~ Funk/Fernsehen/Film wollen** want to go *or* get into radio/television/films

**zu|machen** **1** *tr. V.* close; shut; fasten, do up ‹dress›; seal ‹envelope, letter›; turn off ‹tap›; put the top on ‹bottle›; (*stilllegen*) close *or* shut down ‹factory, mine, etc.›; **den Laden ~** (*ugs.: auflösen*) shut up shop; **ich habe kein Auge zugemacht** I didn't sleep a wink. **2** *itr. V.* **A** close; shut; **der Laden hat zugemacht** (*ugs.*) the place has closed down; **B** (*ugs., bes. nordd.: sich beeilen*) get a move on (*coll.*)

**zu·mal** **1** *Adv.* especially; particularly; **~ da ...** especially *or* particularly since ... **2** *Konj.* especially *or* particularly since

**zu|marschieren** *itr. V.; mit sein* **auf jmdn./etw. ~:** march towards sb./sth.

**zu|mauern** *tr. V.* wall *or* brick up

**zu·meist** *Adj.* in the main; for the most part

**zu|messen** *unr. tr. V.* (*geh.*) **A** (*zuteilen*) **jmdm. seine Essensration ~:** issue sb. with his food ration; **ihm war nur eine kurze Zeit für seine Lebensarbeit zugemessen** (*fig.*) he was only allotted a few short years for his life's work; **B** ⇒ **beimessen**

**zumindest** *Adv.* at least; **so schien es ~:** at least, that is how it seemed; **~ hätte er sich entschuldigen müssen** he should at least have apologized

**zumutbar** *Adj.* reasonable; **das ist ihm kaum/durchaus/nicht ~:** one can scarcely/quite well/not expect that of him; **das ist ihr körperlich nicht ~:** that is asking too much of her physically; **im Rahmen des Zumutbaren** within the bounds of what is reasonable

**Zumutbarkeit** *die; ~:* reasonableness

**zu·mute** *Adj.* in **jmdm. ist unbehaglich/elend** *usw.* **~:** sb. feels uncomfortable/wretched *etc.*; **mir war merkwürdig ~:** I had a peculiar *or* strange feeling; **mir wurde ganz komisch ~:** I felt quite funny; a funny feeling came over me; **ich kann mir gut vorstellen, wie dir ~ ist** I can well imagine how you feel; **mir war nicht danach ~:** I didn't feel like it *or* in the mood; **mir war nicht nach Lachen/Ironie ~:** I did not feel in the mood for laughing/irony; **mir war zum Weinen ~:** I felt like crying

**zu|muten** *tr. V.* **A** (*abverlangen*) **jmdm. etw. ~:** expect *or* ask sth. of sb.; **willst du mir etwa ~, dass ich die ganze Zeit herumsitze und warte?** do you expect me to *or* are you asking me to sit around here the whole time and wait?; **diesen kleinen Umweg können wir ihm schon ~:** I do not think this small detour would be asking too much of him; **diese Arbeit möchte ich ihm nicht ~:** I would not like to ask him to do this work *or* impose this work on him; **das ist ihm durchaus/nicht zu~:** it is perfectly reasonable to/one cannot expect *or* ask that of him; **seinem Körper/seinem Wagen zu viel ~:** overtax oneself physically/ask too much of one's car; **sich** (*Dat.*) **etw. ~:** undertake sth.; **sich zu viel ~:** take on too much; overdo it; **B** (*antun*) **jmdm. etw. ~:** expect sb. to put up with sth.; **diesen Lärm können wir den Nachbarn nicht ~:** we cannot expect the neighbours to put up with this noise; **so eine winzige Schrift kann man keinem ~:** nobody can be expected to read such tiny writing; **diesen Anblick wollte ich ihm nicht ~:** I wanted to spare him this sight

**Zumutung** *die; ~, ~en* **A** (*Ansinnen*) unreasonable demand; imposition; **eine ~ sein** be unreasonable; **etw. als [eine] ~ empfinden** consider sth. unreasonable; **B** (*Belästigung*) imposition; **etw. ist [einfach] eine ~:** sth. is [simply *or* just] too much; **eine ~ für jmdn. sein** be an imposition on sb.; **der Film/die Schauspielerin war eine ~:** the film/actress was appalling; **das Essen war eine ~:** the meal was an affront

**zu·nächst** **1** *Adv.* **A** (*als Erstes*) first; (*anfangs*) at first; **~ einmal** first; **~ ..., zum Zweiten ..., zum Dritten ..., schließlich ...** firstly *or* in the first place *or* for one thing ..., secondly ..., thirdly ..., lastly ...; **B** (*im Moment, vorläufig*) for the moment; for the time being. **2** *Präp. + Dat.* (*geh.*) next to; **jmdm./einer Sache ~:** next to sb./sth.

**zu|nageln** *tr. V.* nail up; **etw. mit Brettern ~:** board sth. up

**zu|nähen** *tr. V.* sew up; ⇒ *auch* **verdammt** 1 A; **verflixt** 1 B

**Zunahme** /ˈt͡suːnaːmə/ *die; ~, ~n* increase (*Gen.*, **an** + *Dat.* in)

**Zu·name** *der* surname; last name

**Zünd·blättchen** *das* percussion cap

**zündeln** /ˈt͡sʏndl̩n/ *itr. V.* (*bes. südd., österr.; auch fig.*) play with fire

**zünden** /ˈt͡sʏndn̩/ **1** *tr. V.* ignite ‹gas, fuel, etc.›; detonate ‹bomb, explosive device, etc.›; let off ‹fireworks›; fire ‹rocket›. **2** *itr. V.* ‹rocket, engine› fire; ‹candle, lighter, match› light; ‹gas, fuel, explosive› ignite; (*fig.*) arouse enthusiasm; **bei ihm hat es gezündet** (*ugs.*) he's cottoned *or* caught on (*coll.*); the penny's dropped (*coll.*); **der ~de Funke** (*auch fig.*) the igniting spark

**zündend** *Adj.* (*fig.*) stirring, rousing ‹speech, song, effect, tune, etc.›; exciting ‹rhythm›

**Zunder** /ˈt͡sʊndɐ/ *der; ~s* **A** tinder; **trocken wie ~:** dry as tinder; tinder-dry; **B** (*fig. ugs.*) *in* **jmdm. ~ geben** lay into sb. (*coll.*); **~ kriegen** get it in the neck (*coll.*)

**Zünder** *der; ~s, ~* **A** (*Waffent.*) igniter; (*für Bombe, Mine*) detonator; **B** *Pl.* (*österr.*) matches

**Zünd-:** **~holz** *das* (*bes. südd., österr.*) match; **~holz·schachtel** *die* (*bes. südd., österr.*) matchbox; **~hütchen** *das; ~~s, ~~:* percussion cap; **~kabel** *das* (*Kfz-W.*) ignition lead; (*from coil to distributor*) coil lead; (*from distributor to plugs*) plug lead; **~kapsel** *die* ⇒ **Sprengkapsel**; **~kerze** *die* spark[ing] plug; **~plättchen** *das* percussion cap; **~schloss, *~schloß** *das* (*Kfz-W.*) ignition [lock]; **der Schlüssel steckt im ~schloss** the key is in the ignition; **~schlüssel** *der* (*Kfz-W.*) ignition key; **~schnur** *die* fuse; **~spule** *die* spark coil; **~stoff** *der* (*fig.*) fuel for conflict; **zum ~stoff eines Konflikts werden** become the trigger for a conflict; **die Rede enthält einigen ~stoff** the speech contains some explosive material

**Zündung** *die; ~, ~en* **A** ⇒ **zünden** 1: ignition; detonation; letting off; firing; **B** (*Kfz-W.: Anlage*) ignition; **die ~ einstellen** adjust the timing

**Zünd·verteiler** *der* (*Kfz-W.*) distributor

**Zünd·zeitpunkt** *der* (*Kfz-W.*) ignition time; **den ~ einstellen/verstellen** set/alter the ignition timing

**zu|nehmen** **1** *unr. itr. V.* **A** increase (**an** + *Dat.* in); ‹moon› wax; **an Größe/Länge** *usw.* **~:** increase in size/length *etc.*; **an Erfahrung/Macht ~:** gain [in] experience/power; **in ~dem Maße** to an increasing extent *or* degree; increasingly; **mit ~dem Alter** with advancing age; **die Tage nehmen zu** the days are drawing out *or* getting longer; **B** ▶ **353** (*schwerer werden*) put on *or* gain weight; **er hat [um] ein Kilo zugenommen** he has put on *or* gained a kilo. **2** *unr. tr.* (*auch itr.*) *V.* (*Handarb.*) increase

**zunehmend** *Adv.* increasingly; **sich ~ vergrößern/verschlechtern** get increasingly bigger/worse

**zu|neigen** **1** *itr. V.* incline *or* be inclined towards; **ich neige mehr dieser Ansicht/Auffassung zu** I tend *or* incline more towards this view. **2** *refl. V.* **A** (*geh.: sich angezogen fühlen von*) be *or* feel drawn to; **er ist ihr sehr/in Liebe zugeneigt** he is attracted to *or* fond of her/is drawn to her by feelings of love and affection; **der den Künsten zugeneigte Fürst** the prince, who is/was fond of the arts; **B** (*sich neigen nach*) **jmdm./einer Sache ~:** lean towards sb./sth.; **sich dem/seinem Ende ~** (*fig.*) draw to a close

**Zu·neigung** *die; ~, ~en* affection; **[eine] starke ~ zu jmdm. haben/empfinden** have/feel [a] strong *or* deep affection for *or* towards sb.; **~ zu jmdm. fassen** become fond of sb.

**Zunft** /t͡sʊnft/ *die; ~, Zünfte* /ˈt͡sʏnftə/ (*hist.*) guild; **die ~ der Bäcker** the bakers' guild; **die ~ der Journalisten** (*scherzh.*) the journalistic fraternity; **zu welcher ~ gehört er?** (*scherzh.*) what does he do for a living?

**zünftig** /ˈt͡sʏnftɪç/ **1** *Adj.* **A** (*ugs.*) proper; **eine ~e Tracht Prügel/Ohrfeige** a good thrashing/box on the ears; **er sieht richtig ~ aus in seiner Tracht** he really looks the genuine article in his costume; **ein ~es Bier trinken** drink a decent beer; **B** (*hist.*) guild *attrib.* ‹craftsman, traditions, etc.›. **2** *adv.* (*ugs.*) properly; **~ Skat spielen** have a decent game of skat

**Zunge** /ˈt͡sʊŋə/ *die; ~, ~n* **A** ▶ **471** tongue; **einen bitteren Geschmack auf der ~ haben** have a bitter taste in one's mouth; **dem Hund hing die ~ heraus** the dog's tongue was hanging out; **[jmdm.] die ~ herausstrecken** put one's tongue out [at sb.]; **auf der ~ zergehen** melt in one's mouth; **mit der ~ anstoßen** (*ugs.*) lisp; **B** (*fig.*) **mit schwerer ~:** with a thick tongue; in a slurred voice; **eine spitze** *od.* **scharfe/lose ~ haben** have a sharp/loose tongue; **mit doppelter** *od.* **gespaltener ~ sprechen** (*geh.*) be two-faced; **böse ~n behaupten, dass ...** malicious gossip has it that ...; malicious tongues are saying that ...; **seine ~ hüten** *od.* **zügeln** *od.* **im Zaum halten** guard *or* mind one's tongue; **der Wein hatte ihm die ~ gelöst** the wine had loosened his tongue; **ich musste mir auf die ~ beißen** I had to bite my tongue; **lieber beiße ich mir die ~ ab** (*ugs.*) I would bite my tongue off first; **der Name liegt mir auf der ~:** the name is on the tip of my tongue; **etw. auf der ~ haben** have sth. on the tip of one's tongue; **sich** (*Dat.*) **die ~ abbrechen** tie one's tongue in knots; **bei dem Namen bricht man sich** (*Dat.*) **die ~ ab** that name is a real tongue-twister; **jmdm. leicht** *od.* **glatt von der ~ gehen** trip easily off sb.'s tongue; **Liebe ist ein Wort, das mir nur schwer von der ~ geht** I find it difficult to say the word 'love'; **er ließ den Namen/das Wort auf der ~ zergehen** he rolled the name/word around his tongue; **mit [heraus]hängender ~:** with [one's/its] tongue hanging out; **er hat eine feine** *od.* **verwöhnte ~** (*fig.*) he has a delicate palate; **C** (*eines Blasinstruments*) reed; (*einer Orgel*) tongue; (*einer Waage*) needle; pointer; (*eines Schuhs*) tongue; **D** (*geh.: Sprache*) tongue

**züngeln** /ˈt͡sʏŋl̩n/ *itr. V.* **A** ‹snake etc.› dart its tongue in and out; **B** *mit Richtungsangabe mit sein* ‹flame› flicker; dart; ‹water› lick; **die Flammen züngelten aus dem Dach** tongues of flame leapt up out of the roof

**zungen-, Zungen-:** **~brecher** *der* (*ugs.*) tongue-twister; **~fertig** **1** *Adj.* eloquent; **2** *adv.* eloquently; **~fertigkeit** *die* eloquence; **~kuss, *~kuß** *der* French kiss; **~schlag** *der* way *or* manner of speaking; **ein falscher ~schlag** a slip of the tongue; **~spitze** *die* tip of the tongue; **~spitzen-r, ~spitzen-R** *das* (*Sprachw.*) apical R; **~wurst** *die* tongue sausage

**Zünglein** /ˈt͡sʏŋlain/ *das; ~s, ~* **A** [little] tongue; **B** (*einer Waage*) [small] needle *or*

*old spelling (see note on page 1707)

pointer; **das ~ an der Waage sein** (*fig.*) tip the scales

**zu·nichte** *Adj. in* **etw. ~ machen** ruin sth.; **jmds. Hoffnungen ~ machen** shatter *or* dash sb.'s hopes; **jmds. Anstrengungen/Pläne ~ machen** ruin *or* wreck sb.'s efforts/plans; **~ werden/sein** be ruined/shattered *or* dashed/ruined *or* wrecked

**zu|nicken** *itr. V.* **jmdm./sich ~:** nod to sb./one another

**zu·nutze** *Adj. in* **sich** (*Dat.*) **etw. ~ machen** (*nutzen*) make use of sth.; (*ausnutzen*) take advantage of sth.

**zu·oberst** *Adv.* [right] on [the] top; **ganz ~:** right on [the] top; on the very top; ⇒ *auch* **unter...** A

**zuordenbar** *Adj.* **A** relatable; **einander ~e Elemente** elements that can be related to each other; **B** (*sich zurechnen lassend*) assignable; **einer Sache** (*Dat.*) **~ sein** be classifiable as sth.

**zu|ordnen** *tr. V.* **A** relate (*Dat.* to); **einem Bild ein Wort ~:** relate a word to a picture; **einer Sache** (*Dat.*) **eine Zahl/einen Wert ~:** assign a number/value to sth.; **B** (*zurechnen*) **jmdn./etw. einer Sache** (*Dat.*) **~:** classify sb./sth. as belonging to sth.; **Organismen, die sich den Tieren ~ lassen** organisms which can be classified as animals; **C** (*zuweisen*) assign (*Dat.* to); **D** (*beimessen*) attribute, attach (*Dat.* to)

**Zu·ordnung** *die* **A** relating; **die ~ x→y** (*Math.*) the relation x→y; **B** (*Zurechnung*) classification; **C** (*Zuweisung*) assigning, assignment (*Dat.* to)

**zu|packen** *itr. V.* **A** grab it/them; **fest ~ können** be able to grab things and grip them tightly; **der Hund stellte den Dieb und packte zu** the dog caught the thief and sank its teeth into him; **bei dem günstigen Angebot habe ich zugepackt** (*fig.*) the offer was a good one and I jumped at it; **B** (*fig.: energisch ans Werk gehen*) knuckle down to it; **er hat eine sehr ~de Art** he has a very vigorous, purposeful manner

**zu·pass, *zu·paß** *in* **jmdm. ~ kommen** come [to sb.] at just the right time *or* moment

**zu|passen** *tr. V.* **jmdm. den Ball ~:** pass the ball to sb.

**zupfen** /ˈtsʊpfn̩/ ❶ *itr. V.* **an etw.** (*Dat.*) **~:** pluck *or* pull at sth.; **sich** (*Dat.*) **am Ohrläppchen ~:** pull [at] one's ear lobe; **an einer Gitarre/an den Saiten ~:** pluck a guitar/the strings. ❷ *tr. V.* **A etw. aus/von** *usw.* **etw. ~:** pull sth. out of/from *etc.* sth.; **sie zupfte ihm ein paar Fusseln vom Pullover** she pulled *or* picked a few pieces of fluff off his pullover; **B** (*aus~*) pull out; pluck ‹eyebrows›; pull up ‹weeds›; **C** pluck ‹string, guitar, tune›; **D jmdn. am Ärmel/Bart ~:** pull *or* tug [at] sb.'s sleeve/beard

**Zupf-: ~geige** *die* (*veralt.*) guitar; **~instrument** *das* plucked [string] instrument

**zu|pflastern** *tr. V.* pave over

**zu|pressen** *tr. V.* press shut

**zu|prosten** *itr. V.* **jmdm. ~:** drink sb.'s health; raise one's glass to sb.

**zur** /tsuːɐ̯/ *Präp. + Art.* **A** = **zu der; B** (*räumlich, fig.: Richtung*) to the; **~ Schule/Arbeit gehen** go to school/work; **ein Fenster ~ Straße** a window on to the street; **~ Straße liegen** face the street; **wo geht es ~ Post?** which is the way to the post office?; **C** (*räumlich: Lage*) **~ Tür hereinkommen** come [in] through the door; **~ Rechten** to *or* on the right; **die Gaststätte „Z~ Rose"** the 'Rose Inn'; **D** (*Zusammengehörigkeit, Hinzufügung*) **~ Hasenkeule empfehle ich einen Rotwein** I recommend a red wine with the haunch of hare; **E** (*zeitlich*) at the; **~ Stunde/Zeit** at the moment; at present; **~ Adventszeit** at Advent time; **~ Jahreswende** at New Year; **rechtzeitig ~ Buchmesse** in [good] time for the book fair; **F** (*Zweck*) **ein Gerät ~ Zerkleinerung von Gemüse** a device for chopping up vegetables; **~ Entschuldigung** by way of [an] excuse; **~ Inspektion in die Werkstatt müssen** have to go in for a check-up; **G** (*Folge*) **~ vollen Zufriedenheit ihres Chefs** to the complete satisfaction of her boss; **~ allgemeinen Erheiterung** to everybody's amusement; **H** (*sonstige Verwendungen*) **sie wurde ~ Direktorin ernannt/~ Präsidentin gewählt** she was appointed director/elected president; **~ Diebin werden** become a thief; **die Wahlen ~ Knesseth** elections to the Knesset

**zu·rande** *in* **mit etw. ~ kommen** (*ugs.*) [not] able to cope with sth.; **mit jmdm. [nicht] ~ kommen** (*ugs.*) [not] get on with sb.

**zu·rate** *in* **mit sich ~ gehen** give the matter a lot of thought; **jmdn./etw. ~ ziehen** consult sb./sth.

**zu|raten** *unr. itr. V.;* **ich würde/kann dir nur ~:** I would advise you to do so/I can only recommend it; **auf jmds. Z~ [hin]** on sb.'s advice *or* recommendation; **ich möchte [dir] weder zu- noch abraten** I should not like to advise you one way or the other

**zu|raunen** *tr. V.* **jmdm. etw. ~:** whisper sth. to sb.

**Zürcher** /ˈtsʏrçɐ/ ❶ *indekl. Adj.* Zurich *attrib.* ❷ *der;* **~s, ~:** inhabitant/native of Zurich; **er ist ~:** he is from Zurich; ⇒ *auch* **Kölner**

**zürcherisch** *Adj.* Zurich *attrib.;* **~ sein** ‹area:› belong to *or* be part of Zurich

**zu|rechnen** *tr. V.* **A** (*zuordnen*) **jmdn./etw. einer Sache** (*Dat.*) **~:** class sb./sth. as belonging to sth.; **solche Wörter rechnen wir den Adverbien zu** such words are classed as adverbs; **B** (*anlasten, zuschreiben*) **jmdm. etw. ~:** attribute *or* ascribe sth. to sb.; **die Folgen hast du dir selbst zuzurechnen:** you've only got yourself to blame for the consequences; **C** (*hinzufügen*) **etw. einer Sache** (*Dat.*) **~:** add sth. to sth.

**zurechnungs·fähig** *Adj.* **A** sound of mind *pred.;* **B** (*Rechtsw.: schuldfähig*) responsible [for one's actions]

**Zurechnungs·fähigkeit** *die* **A** soundness of mind; **B** (*Rechtsw.: Schuldfähigkeit*) responsibility [for one's actions]

**zurecht-, Zurecht-: ~|biegen** *unr. tr. V.* bend into shape; **er wird die Sache schon wieder ~biegen** (*fig.*) he will get things straightened out *or* sorted out again; **im Internat werden sie den Jungen schon ~biegen** (*fig.*) they will soon lick the boy into shape at boarding school; **~|finden** *unr. refl. V.* find one's way [around]; **sich in einem Fahrplan/Kursbuch ~finden** find one's way around a timetable; **er findet sich im Leben/in der Welt nicht [mehr] ~:** he is not able to cope with life/the world [any longer]; **~|kommen** *unr. itr. V.; mit sein* **A** get on (**mit** with); **wir kommen gut miteinander ~:** we get on well [with each other]; **mit etw. ~kommen** cope with sth.; **ich komme auch ohne Geschirrspülmaschine/mit meinem Gehalt [ganz gut] ~:** I manage *or* cope *or* get on [very well] without a dishwasher/on my salary; **mit einem Problem/den Kindern ~kommen** cope with *or* handle a problem/the children; **B** (*ugs.: rechtzeitig kommen*) come in time; **~|legen** *tr. V.* **A** lay out [ready]; **jmdm. etw. ~legen** lay sth. out ready for sb.; **sich** (*Dat.*) **den Ball ~legen und schießen** spot the ball and shoot; **B** (*fig.*) get ready; prepare; **sich** (*Dat.*) **ein Gegenargument/eine Erwiderung ~gelegt haben** have a counter-argument/reply ready; **~|machen** *tr. V.* (*ugs.*) **A** (*vorbereiten*) get ready; **B** (*herrichten*) do up; **C jmdn./sich ~machen** get sb. ready/get [oneself] ready; (*schminken*) make sb. up/put on one's make-up; **sich** (*Dat.*) **die Haare ~machen** do one's hair; **~|rücken** *tr. V.* put *or* set ‹chair, crockery, etc.› in place; straighten ‹tie›; adjust ‹spectacles, hat, etc.›; (*fig.: richtig stellen, korrigieren*) put straight; **jmdm. einen Stuhl ~rücken** put *or* set a chair in place for sb.; ⇒ *auch* **Kopf** A; **~|schneiden** *unr. tr. V.* cut to size/shape; trim ‹fringe, beard, hedge›; (*herstellen*) cut out (**aus** of); **~|setzen** ❶ *tr. V.* adjust ‹spectacles, hat, etc.›; ❷ *refl. V.* settle oneself; **~|stellen** *tr. V.* put *or* set ‹chair, crockery, etc.› in place; **~|stutzen** *tr. V.* trim ‹hedge, beard, hair etc.›; **jmdn./etw. ~stutzen** (*fig.*) sort *or* straighten sb. out/get *or* knock sth. into shape; **~|weisen** *unr. tr. V.* rebuke; reprimand ‹pupil, subordinate, etc.›; **~weisung** *die* ⇒ **~weisen**: rebuke; reprimand

**zu|reden** *itr. V.* **jmdm. ~:** persuade sb.; (*ermutigen*) encourage sb.; **jmdm. gut ~:** encourage sb.; **gutes Z~:** persuasion; **erst nach langem Z~:** only after a great deal of persuasion

**zu·reichend** (*geh.*) ⇒ **zulänglich**

**zu|reiten** ❶ *unr. tr. V.* break [in] ‹horse›. ❷ *unr. itr. V.; mit sein* **auf jmdn./etw. ~:** ride towards sb./sth.; **auf jmdn./etw. zugeritten kommen** come riding towards sb./sth.

**Zürich** /ˈtsyːrɪç/ (*das*); **~s** ▶ **700** Zurich

**zürich·deutsch** ❶ *Adj.* Zurich-German. ❷ *adv.* in Zurich German; ⇒ *auch* **deutsch; Deutsch**

**Zürich·see** *der;* **~s** Lake [of] Zurich

**zu|richten** *tr. V.* **A** (*verletzen*) injure; **sie haben ihn übel zugerichtet** they [really] knocked him about; **übel zugerichtet** badly injured; **B** (*beschädigen*) make a mess of; **C** (*landsch.: zubereiten, vorbereiten*) prepare; (*Technik: zuschneiden*) cut to size/shape; **D** (*Lederherstellung, Kürschnerei, Textilind.*) dress, finish ‹leather, fur, etc.›; **E** (*Druckw.*) make ready

**zu|riegeln** *tr. V.* bolt

**zürnen** /ˈtsʏrnən/ *itr. V.* (*geh.*) **jmdm. ~:** be angry with sb.

**zurren** /ˈtsʊrən/ *tr. V.* (*Seemannsspr.*) lash down

**Zur·schau·stellung** *die* exhibition; display

**zu·rück** *Adv.* **A** back; **ich bin gleich [wieder] ~:** I'll be right back (*coll.*); **sei bitte zum Essen ~:** please be back in time for lunch/dinner *etc;* **einen Schritt ~ machen** take a step backwards; **~!** get *or* go back!; **„~ an Absender"** 'return to sender'; **... und 10 Pfennig ~:** ... and 10 pfennigs change; ⇒ *auch* **Dank** A; **hin** D; **Natur** A; **B** (*weiter hinten; auch fig.*) behind; **[mit etw.] ~ sein** (*fig.: im Rückstand*) be behind [with sth.]

**Zurück** *das:* in **es gibt [für jmdn.] kein ~ [mehr]** there is no going back [for sb.]

**zurück-, Zurück-: ~|begleiten** *tr. V.* **jmdn. ~begleiten** accompany sb. back; **~|behalten** *unr. tr. V.* **A** keep [back]; retain; **B** (*nicht mehr loswerden*) be left with ‹scar, heart defect, etc.›; **~|bekommen** *unr. tr. V.* get back; **Sie bekommen noch 10 Mark ~:** you get 10 marks change; **er bekommt es von mir [doppelt] ~** (*fig.*) I'll pay him back [twice over]; **~|beordern** *tr. V.* order back; **~|besinnen** *unr. refl. V.* **sich auf etw.** (*Akk.*) **~besinnen** remember sth.; think back to sth.; **~|beugen** ❶ *tr. V.* bend back; ❷ *refl. V.* lean *or* bend back; **~|bilden** *refl. V.* (*Biol.*) **A** ‹swelling› go down; ‹uterus› contract; ‹symptoms› disappear; (*atrophieren*) ‹limb, organ, etc.› atrophy; **B** (*im Laufe der Stammesentwicklung*) ‹limb, organ› be lost; **~|bleiben** *unr. itr. V.; mit sein* **A** remain *or* stay behind; **B** (*nicht mithalten*) lag behind; (*fig.*) fall behind; **hinter den Erwartungen ~bleiben** fall short of expectations; **in seiner Entwicklung ~bleiben** ‹child› be retarded *or* backward in its development; **C** (*bleiben*) remain; **von der Krankheit ist [bei ihm] nichts ~geblieben** the illness has left no lasting effects [on him]; **D** (*wegbleiben*) stay *or* keep back; ⇒ *auch* **zurückgeblieben; ~|blenden** *itr. V.* (*Film; auch fig.*) flash back; **in/auf etw.** (*Akk.*) **~blenden** flash back to sth.; **~|blicken** *itr. V.* **A** look back (**auf** + *Akk.* at); (*sich umblicken*) look back *or* round; **B** (*fig.*) **auf etw.** (*Akk.*) **~blicken** look back on sth.; **~|bringen** *unr. tr. V.* **A** (*wieder herbringen*) bring back; return; (*wieder hinbringen*) take back; return; **jmdn. ins Leben/in die Wirklichkeit ~bringen** (*fig.*) bring sb. back to life/reality; **B** (*ugs.: ~werfen*) set back; **~|datieren** *tr. V.* antedate, backdate ‹letter, cheque, etc.›; antedate ‹event, artefact, etc.›; **~|denken** *unr. itr. V.* think back (**an** + *Akk.* to); **so weit ich ~denken kann** as far as I can remember *or* recall;

Z

**~|drängen** *tr. V.* force back; drive back ‹enemy›; **den Drogenmissbrauch ~drängen** (*fig.*) fight drug abuse; **~|drehen** *tr. V.* Ⓐ turn back; turn down ‹heating, volume, etc.›; **das Rad der Geschichte ~drehen** (*fig.*) turn back the wheel of history; Ⓑ (*rückwärts drehen*) turn backwards; **~|dürfen** *unr. itr. V.* be allowed [to go] back *or* to return; **das Fleisch darf nicht in die Kühltruhe ~:** the meat must not go back in the freezer; **~|eilen** *itr. V.*; *mit sein* hurry back; **~|erbitten** *unr. tr. V.* (*geh.*) **etw. ~erbitten** ask for sth. to be returned; **etw. von jmdm. ~erbitten** ask sb. to return sth.; **~|erhalten** *unr. tr. V.* (*geh.*) be given back; get back; **anliegend erhalten Sie Ihre Bewerbungsunterlagen ~:** please find enclosed your application, which we are returning to you; **~|erinnern** *refl. V.* **sich an etw.** (*Akk.*) **~erinnern** remember *or* recall sth.; **~|erlangen** *tr. V.* (*geh.*) regain; **~|erobern** *tr. V.* win back ‹votes, majority, etc.›; regain ‹power, position, etc.›; recapture ‹territory, town, etc.›; **~|erstatten** *tr. V.* refund; **jmdm. etw. ~erstatten** refund sth. to sb.; **~|erwarten** *tr. V.* **jmdn. ~erwarten** expect sb. back; **~|fahren** ❶ *unr. itr. V.*; *mit sein* Ⓐ go back; return; (*als Autofahrer*) drive back; (*mit dem Fahrrad, Motorrad usw.*) ride back; Ⓑ (*nach hinten fahren*) go back[wards]; Ⓒ (*~weichen*) start back; (*entsetzt*) recoil; ❷ *unr. tr. V.* Ⓐ **jmdn./etw. ~fahren** drive sb./sth. back; Ⓑ (*Technikjargon*) reduce the output of ‹power plant, refinery, etc.›; cut back ‹delivery, production, budget, etc.›; **~|fallen** *unr. itr. V.*; *mit sein* Ⓐ fall back; Ⓑ (*nach hinten fallen*) fall back[wards]; Ⓒ (*fig.: in Rückstand geraten*) fall behind; Ⓓ (*fig.: auf einen niedrigeren Rang*) drop (**auf** + *Akk.* to); Ⓔ (*fig.: in einen früheren Zustand*) **in etw.** (*Akk.*) **~fallen** fall back into sth.; **in den alten Trott ~fallen** slip back into the old routine; Ⓕ (*fig.*) **an jmdn. ~fallen** ‹property› revert to sb.; Ⓖ (*fig.*) **auf jmdn. ~fallen** ‹actions, behaviour, etc.› reflect [up]on sb.; **deine Gemeinheiten werden eines Tages auf dich [selbst] ~fallen** your meanness will recoil [up]on you one day; **~|faxen** *tr., itr. V.* fax back; **jmdm. etw. ~faxen** fax sth. back to sb.; **~|finden** *unr. itr. V.* find one's way back; **~|fliegen** ❶ *unr. itr. V.*; *mit sein* fly back; ❷ *unr. tr. V.* **jmdn./etw. ~fliegen** fly sb./sth. back; **~|fließen** *unr. itr. V.*; *mit sein* flow back; **~|fordern** *tr. V.* **etw. ~fordern** ask for sth. back; (*nachdrücklicher*) demand sth. back; **~|fragen** *itr. V.* answer with a question; **„...?", fragte er ~:** '...?', he asked in return; **~|führen** ❶ *tr. V.* Ⓐ **jmdn. ~führen** take sb. back; Ⓑ (*~bewegen*) **etw. ~führen** move sth. back; return sth.; Ⓒ **etw. auf etw.** (*Akk.*) **~führen** (*auf Ursprung*) trace sth. back to sth.; (*auf Ursache*) attribute sth. to sth.; put sth. down to sth.; (*auf einfachere Form*) reduce sth. to sth.; ❷ *itr. V.* lead back; **es führt kein anderer Weg ~:** there is no other way back; **~|geben** ❶ *unr. tr. V.* Ⓐ give back; return; hand in ‹driver's licence, membership card›; return ‹goods, unused ticket, etc.›; relinquish ‹mandate, office, etc.›; take back ‹defective goods›; give back ‹freedom›; **jmdm. etw. ~geben** give sth. back to sb.; return sth. to sb.; Ⓑ (*erwidern*) reply; ❷ *unr. tr.* (*auch itr.*) *V.* (*Ballspiele*) Ⓐ return ‹ball, puck, service, pass, throw›; **[den Ball] an jmdn. ~geben** return the ball to sb.; Ⓑ (*nach hinten geben*) **[den Ball] ~geben** pass the ball back; **~geblieben** ❶ *2. Part. v.* **~bleiben;** ❷ *Adj.* retarded; **~|gehen** *unr. itr. V.*; *mit sein* Ⓐ go back; return; (*sich ~bewegen*) ‹pick-up arm, indicator, needle, etc.› return; Ⓑ (*nach hinten gehen*) go back; ‹enemy› retreat; **in die Geschichte/bis in die Jahre meiner Kindheit ~gehen** (*fig.*) go back into history/to the years of my childhood; Ⓒ (*verschwinden*) ‹bruise, ulcer› disappear; ‹swelling, inflammation› go down; ‹pain› subside; Ⓓ (*sich verringern*) decrease; go down; ‹fever› abate; ‹flood› subside; ‹business› fall off; Ⓔ (*~geschickt werden*) be returned *or* sent back; **ein Essen ~gehen lassen** send a meal back; Ⓕ **auf jmdn. ~gehen** (*jmds. Werk sein*) go back to sb.; (*von jmdm. abstammen*) originate from *or* be descended from sb.; **der Name geht auf ein lateinisches Wort ~:** the name comes from a Latin word; Ⓖ (*sich ~bewegen lassen*) ‹lever etc.› go back; **~|gewinnen** *unr. tr. V.* Ⓐ win back; regain ‹confidence, title, strength, freedom, etc.›; Ⓑ (*Wirtsch.*) reclaim, recover ‹raw materials etc.›; **~gezogen** ❶ *2. Part. v.* **~ziehen;** ❷ *Adj.* secluded; ❸ *adv.* **~gezogen leben** lead a withdrawn life; (*an abgelegenem Ort*) live a secluded life; **~gezogenheit** *die;* **~~:** seclusion; **~|greifen** *unr. itr. V.* **auf jmdn./etw. ~greifen** fall back on sb./sth.; **~|haben** *unr. tr. V.* have back; **hast du es inzwischen ~?** have you got it back yet?; **ich will es ~haben** I want it back; **~|halten** ❶ *unr. tr. V.* Ⓐ **jmdn. ~halten** hold sb. back; **eine dringende Angelegenheit hielt mich in Köln ~:** an urgent matter kept *or* detained me in Cologne; **er war durch nichts ~zuhalten** there was no stopping him; nothing would stop him; Ⓑ (*am Vordringen hindern*) keep back ‹crowd, mob, etc.›; Ⓒ (*behalten*) withhold ‹news, letter, parcel, etc.›; Ⓓ (*nicht austreten lassen*) hold back ‹tears etc.›; **sein Wasser ~halten** hold one's water; Ⓔ (*von etw. abhalten*) **jmdn. ~halten** stop sb.; **jmdn. von etw. ~halten** keep sb. from sth.; **jmdn. davon ~halten, etw. zu tun** stop sb. doing sth.; keep sb. from doing sth.; ❷ *unr. refl. V.* Ⓐ (*sich zügeln, sich beherrschen*) restrain *or* control oneself; Ⓑ (*nicht aktiv werden*) **sich in einer Diskussion ~halten** keep in the background in a discussion; ❸ *unr. itr. V.* **mit etw. ~halten** (*etw. nicht äußern*) keep sth. to oneself; **~haltend** ❶ *Adj.* Ⓐ reserved; subdued, muted ‹colour›; Ⓑ (*kühl, reserviert*) cool, restrained ‹reception, response›; Ⓒ (*Wirtsch.: schwach*) slack ‹demand›; Ⓓ (*sparsam*) **mit etw. ~haltend** ‹person› who is/was sparing with sth.; sparing with sth. *pred.;* ❷ *adv.* Ⓐ ‹behave› with reserve *or* restraint; **eine ~haltend gemusterte Tapete** a wallpaper with a subdued pattern; Ⓑ (*kühl, reserviert*) coolly; **das Publikum/Bonn reagierte ~haltend** the public's response was cool/Bonn's response was cautious; **sich ~haltend zu etw. äußern** be cautious in one's comments on sth.; **~haltung** *die* Ⓐ reserve; **~haltung üben** (*geh.*) exercise restraint; **sich** (*Dat.*) **~haltung auferlegen** (*geh.*) adopt an attitude of reserve; Ⓑ (*Kühle, Reserviertheit*) coolness; reserve; **ein Buch mit ~haltung aufnehmen** give a book a cool reception; Ⓒ (*Wirtsch.: geringe Kaufbereitschaft*) caution; **~|holen** *tr. V.* Ⓐ fetch back; get back ‹money›; bring back ‹satellite, missile›; **jmdn. ~holen** bring sb. back; Ⓑ (*~rufen*) call back; **~|kämmen** *tr. V.* comb back; backcomb; **seine ~gekämmten Haare** his backcombed hair; **~|kaufen** *tr. V.* buy back; repurchase; **~|kehren** *itr. V.*; *mit sein* return; come back (**von, aus** from); **zu jmdm. ~kehren** return *or* go back to sb.; **~|klappen** *tr. V.* tip back ‹seat›; lift back ‹lid›; fold back ‹flap›; **~|kommen** *unr. itr. V.*; *mit sein* Ⓐ come back; return; ‹letter› come back, be returned; Ⓑ (*~gelangen*) get back; Ⓒ **~kommen auf** (+ *Akk.*) come back to ‹subject, question, point, etc.›; **auf ein Angebot ~kommen** come back on an offer; Ⓓ (*ugs.: ~befördert werden*) go back; **~|können** *unr. itr. V.* be able to go back *or* return; **nicht ans Ufer ~können** not be able to get back to the bank; **jetzt können wir nicht mehr ~** (*fig.*) there's no going *or* turning back now; **~|kriegen** *tr. V.* ⇒ **~bekommen; ~|lassen** *unr. tr. V.* Ⓐ leave; Ⓑ (*~kehren lassen*) **jmdn. ~lassen** allow sb. to return; let sb. return; **~|lassung** *die;* **~~: unter ~lassung einer Sache/jmds.** leaving sth./sb. behind; **~|laufen** *unr. itr. V.*; *mit sein* Ⓐ run back; Ⓑ (*ugs.: ~gehen*) come/go back; Ⓒ (*sich ~bewegen*) run back; **das Tonband ~laufen lassen** run the tape back; **~|legen** ❶ *tr. V.* Ⓐ put back; Ⓑ (*nach hinten beugen*) lean *or* lay ‹head› back; Ⓒ (*reservieren*) put aside, keep (*Dat.,* **für** for); Ⓓ (*sparen*) put away; put by; Ⓔ (*hinter sich bringen*) cover ‹distance›; ❷ *refl. V.* lie back; (*sich ~lehnen, ~neigen*) lean back; **~|lehnen** *refl. V.* lean back; **~|liegen** *unr. itr. V.* Ⓐ **das Ereignis/das liegt einige Jahre ~:** the event took place/that was several years ago; **in den ~liegenden Jahren** in the past [few] years; Ⓑ (*bes. Sport*) be behind; **mit 2:3 Toren ~liegen** be 3-2 behind; **~|melden** *refl. V.* report back (**bei** to); **~|müssen** *unr. itr. V.* Ⓐ have to go back *or* return; Ⓑ (*~befördert werden müssen*) have to go back; **~|nehmen** *unr. tr. V.* Ⓐ take back; Ⓑ (*widerrufen*) take back; **ich nehme alles ~ [und behaupte das Gegenteil** (*scherzh.*)**]** I take it all back; Ⓒ (*rückgängig machen*) revoke, rescind ‹decision, ban, etc.›; withdraw ‹complaint, legal action›; **einen Zug ~nehmen** (*Brettspiele*) take a move back; **~|pfeifen** *unr. tr. V.* Ⓐ whistle ‹dog› back; Ⓑ (*fig. salopp*) **jmdn. ~pfeifen** call sb. off; **~|prallen** *itr. V.*; *mit sein* Ⓐ bounce back (**von** off); ‹bullet› ricochet (**von** from); Ⓑ (*fig.*) start back; (*entsetzt*) recoil; **~|rechnen** *itr. V.* reckon back; **~|reichen** ❶ *tr. V.* hand back; ❷ *itr. V.* go back (**in** + *Akk.* to); **~|rollen** ❶ *tr. V.* Ⓐ roll back; Ⓑ (*nach hinten rollen*) roll back[wards]; ❷ *itr. V.*; *mit sein* Ⓐ roll back; Ⓑ (*nach hinten rollen*) roll back [wards]; **~|rufen** ❶ *unr. tr. V.* Ⓐ call back; recall ‹ambassador›; **jmdn. ins Leben ~rufen** (*fig.*) bring sb. back to life; Ⓑ (*anrufen*) call *or* (*Brit.*) ring back; Ⓒ **jmdm./sich etw. ins Gedächtnis** *od.* **in die Erinnerung ~rufen** remind sb. of sth./call sth. to mind; Ⓓ (*als Antwort, nach hinten rufen*) call *or* shout back; Ⓔ (*Wirtsch.*) recall ‹defective goods, car, etc.›; ❷ *unr. itr. V.* (*anrufen*) call *or* (*Brit.*) ring back; **~|schalten** *itr. V.* Ⓐ switch *or* turn back; Ⓑ (*beim Autofahren*) change down; **~|schaudern** *itr. V.*; *mit sein* shrink back (**vor** + *Dat.* from); **~|schauen** *itr. V.* (*bes. südd., österr., schweiz.*) ⇒ **~blicken; ~|scheuen** *itr. V.*; *mit sein* ⇒ **~schrecken²; ~|schicken** *tr. V.* send back; **~|schieben** *unr. tr. V.* Ⓐ push back; draw back ‹bolt, curtains›; Ⓑ (*nach hinten schieben*) push back[wards]; **~|schlagen** ❶ *unr. tr. V.* Ⓐ (*nach hinten schlagen*) fold back ‹cover, hood, etc.›; turn down ‹collar›; (*zur Seite schlagen*) pull *or* draw back ‹curtains›; Ⓑ (*durch einen Schlag ~befördern*) hit back; (*mit dem Fuß*) kick back; Ⓒ (*zum Rückzug zwingen, abwehren*) beat off, repulse ‹enemy, attack›; ❷ *unr. itr. V.* Ⓐ hit back; ‹enemy› strike back, retaliate; Ⓑ *mit sein* ‹pendulum› swing back; ‹starting handle› kick back; ‹wave› crash back; Ⓒ **auf etw.** (*Akk.*) **~schlagen** (*fig.*) have repercussions on sth.; **~|schneiden** *unr. tr. V.* cut back ‹plant, shoot, etc.›; **~|schrauben** *tr. V.* reduce ‹demand, wage, consumption, etc.›; lower ‹expectations›; **~|schrecken¹** *tr. V.* **jmdn. ~schrecken** deter sb.; **~|schrecken²** *regelm., veralt. unr. itr. V.*; *mit sein* Ⓐ shrink back; recoil; Ⓑ **vor etw.** (*Dat.*) **~schrecken** (*fig.*) shrink from sth.; **er schreckt vor nichts ~:** he will stop at nothing; **~|sehnen** *refl. V.* **sich nach der Geborgenheit seines Elternhauses ~sehnen** long to return to the security of one's parents' home; **sich zu jmdm./nach Italien ~sehnen** long to be back with sb./in Italy; **~|senden** *unr. od. regelm. tr. V.* (*geh.*) ⇒ **~schicken; ~|setzen** ❶ *tr. V.* Ⓐ put back; Ⓑ (*nach hinten setzen*) move back; Ⓒ (*~fahren*) move back; reverse; back; Ⓓ (*benachteiligen*) **jmdn. ~setzen** neglect sb.; **sich ~gesetzt fühlen** feel neglected; ❷ *refl. V.* Ⓐ sit down again (**an** + *Akk.* at); Ⓑ (*sich weiter nach hinten setzen*) move back; ❸ *itr. V.* (*~fahren*) move back[wards]; reverse; back; **~setzung** *die;* **~~, ~~en** neglect; (*Kränkung*) insult; slight; **~|spielen** *tr. V.* (*Ballspiele*) **den Ball ~spielen** pass *or* play the ball back; **~|springen** *unr. itr. V.*; *mit sein* Ⓐ jump back; ‹indicator needle etc.› spring back; ‹ball› bounce back; Ⓑ (*nach hinten springen*) jump back[wards]; Ⓒ (*weiter hinten liegen*) be set back; **~|stecken** ❶ *tr. V.* Ⓐ put back; Ⓑ (*nach hinten stecken*) move back; ❷ *itr. V.* (*ugs.*) lower one's sights; **~|stehen** *unr. itr. V.* Ⓐ stand back; be set

*old spelling (see note on page 1707)

Z

back; Ⓑ (*fig.: übertroffen werden*) be left behind; **hinter jmdm. ~stehen** take second place to sb.; Ⓒ (*fig.: verzichten*) miss out; **~|stellen** ❶ *tr. V.* Ⓐ put back; Ⓑ (*nach hinten stellen*) move back; Ⓒ (*niedriger einstellen*) turn down ‹heating›; put back ‹clock›; Ⓓ (*reservieren*) put aside, keep (*Dat.*, **für** for); Ⓔ (*vorläufig befreien*) **jmdn. vom Wehrdienst ~stellen** defer sb.'s military service; defer sb. (*Amer.*); **sollen wir ihn schon einschulen oder noch ~stellen lassen?** shall we start him at school now or delay it a while?; Ⓕ (*aufschieben*) postpone; defer; Ⓖ (*hintanstellen*) put aside ‹reservations, doubts, etc.›; Ⓗ (*österr.: ~geben*) return; ❷ *refl. V.* go *or* get back; **stell dich an deinen Platz ~!** get back in *or* go back to your place!; **~|stoßen** ❶ *unr. tr. V.* Ⓐ push back; Ⓑ (*von sich stoßen*) push away; ❷ *unr. itr. V.*; *mit sein* ⇒ **~setzen** 3; **~|streifen** *tr. V.* pull back; pull up ‹sleeve›; **~|stufen** *tr. V.* downgrade (**in** + *Akk.* to); **~|treten** *unr. itr. V.* Ⓐ *mit sein* step back; **bitte von der Bahnsteigkante ~treten** please stand back from the edge of the platform; Ⓑ *mit sein* (*von einem Amt*) resign; step down; ‹government› resign; **als Vorsitzender/von einem Amt ~treten** step down as chairman/resign from an office; Ⓒ *mit sein* (*von einem Vertrag, einer Vereinbarung usw.*) withdraw (**von** from); back out (**von** of); Ⓓ *mit sein* (*fig.: in den Hintergrund treten*) become less important; fade in importance; **hinter/gegenüber etw.** (*Dat.*) **~treten** take second place to sth.; **~|tun** *unr. tr. V.* put back; **~|übersetzen** *tr. V.* translate back; **~|verfolgen** *tr. V.* trace back; **~|verlangen** *tr. V.* demand back; **~|versetzen** ❶ *tr. V.* Ⓐ move *or* transfer back; Ⓑ (*fig.*) take *or* transport back; ❷ *refl. V.* think oneself back (**in** + *Akk.* to); **~|weichen** *unr. itr. V.*; *mit sein* draw back (**vor** + *Dat.* from); back away; (*~schrecken*) shrink back, recoil (**vor** + *Dat.* from); **er wich keinen Schritt/Zentimeter ~:** he stood his ground; **~|weisen** *unr. tr. V.* Ⓐ send back; **jmdn. an der Grenze ~weisen** turn sb. back at the frontier; Ⓑ (*abweisen, nicht akzeptieren*) reject ‹proposal, question, demand, application, etc.›; turn down, refuse ‹offer, request, invitation, help, etc.›; turn away ‹petitioner, unwelcome guest›; Ⓒ (*sich verwahren gegen*) repudiate ‹accusation, claim, etc.›; **~weisung** *die* ⇒ **~weisen** A–C: sending back; turning back; rejection; turning down; refusal; turning away; repudiation; **~|wenden** *unr. od. regelm. tr. u. refl. V.* turn back; **~|werfen** ❶ *unr. tr. V.* Ⓐ throw back; **den Kopf/sein Haar ~werfen** throw *or* toss one's head back/toss one's hair back; Ⓑ (*reflektieren*) reflect ‹light, sound›; Ⓒ (*Milit.*) repulse ‹enemy›; Ⓓ (*fig.: in einer Entwicklung*) set back; ❷ *unr. refl. V.* throw oneself back; **~|wirken** *itr. V.* react (**auf** + *Akk.* [up]on); **~|wollen** ❶ *unr. itr. V.* want to go back; ❷ *unr. tr. V.* (*ugs.*) **etw. ~wollen** want sth. back; **~|zahlen** *tr. V.* pay back; **~|ziehen** ❶ *unr. tr. V.* Ⓐ pull back; draw back ‹bolt, curtains, one's hand, etc.›; **es zieht ihn in die Heimat/zu ihr ~** (*fig.*) he is drawn back to his homeland/to her; Ⓑ (*abziehen, ~beordern*) withdraw, pull back ‹troops›; withdraw, recall ‹ambassador›; Ⓒ (*rückgängig machen*) withdraw; cancel ‹order, instruction›; Ⓓ (*wieder aus dem Verkehr ziehen*) withdraw ‹coin, stamp, etc.›; ❷ *unr. refl. V.* withdraw (**aus, von** from); ‹troops› withdraw, pull back; **sich von** *od.* **aus der Politik/aus dem Showgeschäft/aus dem Berufsleben ~ziehen** retire from politics/show business/professional life; **sich aufs Land/in sein Zimmer ~ziehen** retreat to the country/retire to one's room; ⇒ *auch* **zurückgezogen**; ❸ *unr. itr. V.*; *mit sein* go back; return; **~|zucken** *itr. V.*; *mit sein* flinch; (*erschrocken*) start back; **mit der Hand ~zucken** jerk one's hand away

**Zu·ruf** *der* shout; **durch ~ wählen/abstimmen** vote by acclamation

**zu|rufen** *unr. tr. V.* **jmdm. etw. ~:** shout sth. to sb.

**zur·zeit** *Adv.* at the moment; at present

**Zu·sage** *die* Ⓐ (*auf eine Einladung hin*) acceptance; (*auf eine Stellenbewerbung hin*) offer; Ⓑ (*Versprechen*) promise; undertaking; **jmdm. die** *od.* **seine ~ geben, etw. zu tun** promise sb. that one will do sth.; **ich kann Ihnen keine ~n machen** I cannot make you any promises

**zu|sagen** ❶ *itr. V.* Ⓐ (*auf eine Einladung hin*) **[jmdm.] ~/fest ~:** accept/give sb. a firm acceptance; Ⓑ (*auf ein Angebot hin*) accept; **sie haben fest zugesagt** (*auf eine Stellenbewerbung hin*) they made me/him *etc.* a firm offer [of a job]; Ⓒ (*gefallen*) **jmdm. ~:** appeal to sb. ❷ *tr. V.* Ⓐ promise; **jmdm. etw. ~:** promise sb. sth.; **sein Kommen ~:** promise to come; **jmdm. sein Kommen ~:** promise sb. that one will come; Ⓑ ⇒ **Kopf** A

**zusammen** /tsu'tsamən/ *Adv.* together; **mit jmdm. ~ sein** (*zusammenleben*) be *or* live with sb.; **wir bestellten uns ~ eine Flasche Wein** we ordered a bottle of wine between us; **wir haben ~ ein Auto** we own a car between us; **alle/alles ~:** all together; **ihr seid alle ~ Feiglinge!** (*ugs.*) you're cowards, the whole lot of you (*coll.*); **guten Abend/schöne Ferien** *usw.* **~!** (*ugs.*) good evening/have a good holiday, everyone *or* all of you!; **er verdient mehr als alle anderen ~:** he earns more than the rest of us/them put together

**zusammen-, Zusammen-: ~arbeit** *die* cooperation *no indef. art.*; **~|arbeiten** *itr. V.* cooperate; work together; (*kollaborieren*) collaborate; **mit ihm könnte ich nicht ~arbeiten** I could not work with him; **~|ballen** ❶ *tr. V.* **[zu einem Klumpen] ~ballen** make into a ball; ❷ *refl. V.* mass together; **dunkle Wolken ballten sich ~:** dark clouds loomed; **~ballung** *die*; **~, ~en** concentration; **eine ~ballung von Städten** a conglomeration of towns; **~|bauen** *tr. V.* assemble; put together; **~|beißen** *unr. tr. V.* **die Zähne ~beißen** clench one's teeth together; ⇒ *auch* **Zahn** B; **~|bekommen** *unr. tr. V.* Ⓐ get together, raise ‹money, rent, etc.›; manage to collect ‹signatures›; Ⓑ (*~gesetzt/~gebaut usw. bekommen*) get together; Ⓒ (*fig. ugs.*) remember; **~|betteln** *tr. V.* **sich** (*Dat.*) **etw. ~betteln** manage to collect sth. by begging; **~|binden** *unr. tr. V.* tie together; **jmdm. die Hände auf dem Rücken ~binden** tie sb.'s hands behind his/her back; **sich** (*Dat.*) **das Haar ~binden** tie one's hair; **~|bleiben** *unr. itr. V.*; *mit sein* stay together; **~|brauen** ❶ *tr. V.* (*ugs.*) concoct ‹drink›; ❷ *refl. V.* (*fig.*) ‹storm, bad weather, trouble, etc.› be brewing; ‹disaster› loom; **da braut sich was ~:** there's something brewing there; **~|brechen** *unr. itr. V.*; *mit sein* Ⓐ (*einstürzen*) collapse; Ⓑ (*zu Boden sinken*) ‹person, animal› collapse; (*fig.*) ‹person› break down; **nervlich ~brechen** have a nervous breakdown; Ⓒ (*fig.*) collapse; ‹order, communications, system, telephone network› break down; ‹theory› collapse, break down; ‹traffic› come to a standstill, be paralysed; ‹attack, front, resistance› crumble; **für ihn brach eine Welt ~:** his whole world collapsed; **~|bringen** *unr. tr. V.* Ⓐ bring together; bring ‹chemicals› into contact with each other; **die Ziege mit einem Bock ~bringen** put the nanny goat together with a billy goat; **jmdn. mit jmdm. ~bringen** bring sb. together with sb.; Ⓑ (*ugs., bes. südd.*) ⇒ **~bekommen**; **~bruch** *der* Ⓐ (*eines Menschen*) collapse; (*psychisch, nervlich*) breakdown; **dem ~bruch nahe sein** be near to collapse/breakdown; Ⓑ (*fig.*) ⇒ **~brechen** C: collapse; breakdown; crumbling; **es kam zu einem ~bruch des Verkehrs** traffic came to a standstill *or* was paralysed; **~|drängen** ❶ *tr. V.* push together; herd ‹crowd› together; (*fig.*) condense ‹story, report, facts, etc.›; ❷ *refl. V.* crowd together; (*fig.*) be concentrated (**auf** + *Akk.* into); **~|drücken** *tr. V.* Ⓐ press together; (*komprimieren*) compress ‹gas›; Ⓑ (*zerdrücken*) crush; **~|fahren** ❶ *unr. itr. V.*; *mit sein* Ⓐ collide (**mit** with); **zwei Autos sind ~gefahren** two cars have collided [with each other]; Ⓑ (*~zucken*) start; jump; ❷ *unr. tr. V.* (*ugs.*) smash up ‹vehicle›; run over ‹person, animal›; **~fall** *der* coincidence; **~|fallen** *unr. itr. V.*; *mit sein* Ⓐ collapse; **in sich ~fallen** (*auch fig.*) collapse; ‹fire› die down; **das ganze Lügengebäude fiel in sich ~** (*fig.*) the whole tissue of lies fell apart; Ⓑ (*~sinken, schrumpfen*) **[in sich] ~fallen** ‹cake› sink [in the middle]; ‹froth, foam, balloon, etc.› collapse; Ⓒ ‹person› become emaciated; Ⓓ (*zeitlich*) **[zeitlich] ~fallen** coincide; fall at the same time; Ⓔ (*räumlich*) coincide; **~|falten** *tr. V.* fold up; **~|fassen** *tr. V.* Ⓐ put together; **einzelne Verbände in einer Dachorganisation ~fassen** bring individual associations together in one umbrella organization; Ⓑ (*in eine kurze Form bringen*) summarize; **etw. in einem Satz ~fassen** sum sth. up *or* summarize sth. in one sentence; **~fassend kann man sagen ...** to sum up *or* in summary, one can say ...; **~fassung** *die* ⇒ **~fassen** A, B: putting together; bringing together; summary; **~|fegen** *tr. V.* (*bes. nordd.*) sweep together; **~|finden** *unr. refl. V.* Ⓐ get together; Ⓑ (*~treffen*) meet up; **~|flicken** *tr. V.* Ⓐ (*auch fig.*) patch up; Ⓑ ⇒ **~stoppeln**; **~|fließen** *unr. itr. V.*; *mit sein* ‹rivers, streams› flow into each other, join up; (*fig.*) ‹colours› run together; ‹sounds› blend together; **~fluss**, ***~fluß** *der* ▶ **306** confluence; **~|fügen** ❶ *tr. V.* fit together; **was Gott ~gefügt hat, das soll der Mensch nicht scheiden** what therefore God hath joined together, let not man put asunder; ❷ *refl. V.* fit together; **sich zu einem Ganzen ~fügen** fit together to form a whole; **~|führen** *tr. V.* bring together; **getrennte Familien wieder ~führen** reunite divided families; **~|gehen** *unr. itr. V.*; *mit sein* Ⓐ (*sich verbünden, sich ~tun*) join forces (**mit** with); (*fusionieren*) ‹firms› merge; Ⓑ (*~passen*) go together; Ⓒ (*ugs.: ~laufen, ~fließen usw.*) join up; meet; Ⓓ (*ugs.: sich ~fügen, verbinden usw. lassen*) fit together; meet; **~|gehören** *itr. V.* belong together; **~gehörig** *Adj.* [closely] related *or* connected ‹subjects, problems, etc.›; matching *attrib.* ‹pieces of tea service, cutlery, etc.›; **die ~gehörigen Teile/Fotos** the parts/photographs which belong together; **~gehörigkeit** *die*; **~: tiefe ~gehörigkeit mit jmdm. fühlen** have a deep sense *or* feeling of unity with sb.; **die beiden verbindet ein starkes Gefühl der ~gehörigkeit** the two of them are joined by a strong sense *or* feeling of belonging together; **~gehörigkeits·gefühl** *das* sense *or* feeling of belonging together; **~genommen** *Adj.* **alle diese Dinge ~genommen** all these things together; **~gewürfelt** *Adj.* oddly assorted; **ein bunt ~gewürfelter Haufen** a motley collection of people; **~|haben** *unr. tr. V.* (*ugs.*) have got together; **~halt** *der* cohesion; **keinen/einen guten ~halt haben** have no/good cohesion; **~|halten** ❶ *unr. tr. V.* Ⓐ hold together; Ⓑ (*beisammenhalten*) keep together; **sein Geld ~halten** be careful with one's money; ❷ *unr. itr. V.* Ⓐ hold together; Ⓑ (*fig.*) ‹friends, family, etc.› stick together; **~hang** *der* connection; (*einer Geschichte, Rede*) coherence; (*Kontext*) context; **was er sagte, hatte keinen ~hang** what he said was incoherent; **in [keinem] ~hang mit etw. stehen** be [in no way] connected with sth.; **die historischen/gesellschaftlichen ~hänge kennen** know the historical/social context; **etw. mit etw. in ~hang bringen** connect sth. with sth.; make a connection between sth. and sth.; **im ~hang mit ...** in connection with ...; **etw. aus dem ~hang lösen/reißen** take sth. out of [its] context; **~|hängen** *unr. itr. V.* Ⓐ be joined [together]; **in ~hängenden Sätzen** in coherent sentences; **~hängender Text** continuous text; **~hängend erzählen** relate in a coherent manner; Ⓑ (*fig.*) **mit etw. ~hängen** (*zu etw. eine Beziehung haben*) be related to sth.; (*durch etw.* [*mit*] *verursacht sein*) be the result of sth.; **das hängt damit ~, dass ...** that is connected with *or* has to do with the fact that ...; **die damit ~hängenden Fragen**

the related issues; **~hang·los** ❶ *Adj.* incoherent, disjointed ‹speech, story, etc.›; **~hanglos nebeneinander stehen** stand disconnectedly side by side; ❷ *adv.* ‹speak› incoherently; **~|hauen** *unr. tr. V.* (*ugs.*) [A] (*zerschlagen*) smash up; [B] (*verprügeln*) **jmdn. ~hauen** beat sb. up; [C] (*abwertend: nachlässig anfertigen*) knock together ‹furniture›; knock off (*coll.*) ‹homework, task, etc.›; **~|heften** *tr. V.* [A] staple together; (*Buchbinderei*) stitch together; [B] (*Schneiderei*) tack *or* baste together; **~|kauern** *refl. V.* huddle [up]; **sich ängstlich ~kauern** cower; **~|kaufen** *tr. V.* buy; **~|kehren** *tr. V.* (*bes. südd.*) ⇒ **~fegen**; **~klappbar** *Adj.* folding; **~klappbar sein** fold up; **~|klappen** ❶ *tr. V.* [A] fold up; [B] (*~schlagen*) **die Hacken/Absätze ~klappen** click one's heels; ❷ *itr. V.*; *mit sein* (*ugs.*) collapse; **~|klauben** *tr. V.* (*südd.*, *österr.*) gather together; **~|kleben** *tr.*, *itr. V.* stick together; **~|kneifen** *unr. tr. V.* press ‹lips› together; screw ‹eyes› up; **~|knüllen** *tr. V.* crumple up; (*fest*) screw up; **~|kommen** *unr. itr. V.*; *mit sein* [A] meet; **mit jmdm. ~kommen** meet sb.; [B] (*zueinander kommen; auch fig.*) get together; [C] (*~treffen, gleichzeitig auftreten*) occur *or* happen together; **heute kommt bei mir aber auch alles ~!** (*ugs.*) everything's going wrong at once today!; [D] (*sich summieren, sich sammeln*) accumulate; **da werden schon so an die 50 Leute ~kommen** there are sure to be getting on for 50 people there altogether; **~|koppeln** *tr. V.* couple together; dock ‹spacecraft›; **~|krachen** *itr. V.*; *mit sein* (*ugs.*) [A] collapse with a crash; **er ist mit dem Stuhl ~gekracht** he crashed to the floor with the chair; [B] (*~stoßen*) ‹vehicles› crash [into each other], collide [with each other]; **mit einem Auto ~krachen** crash *or* collide with a car; **~|krampfen** *refl. V.* ‹hands› clench; ‹stomach, chest› tighten; **es krampfte sich in mir alles ~:** I tensed up inside; **~|kratzen** *tr. V.* (*ugs.*) scrape together ‹money, savings, etc.›; **~|kriegen** *tr. V.* (*ugs.*) ⇒ **~bekommen**; **~|krümmen** *refl. V.* double up; writhe

**Zusammenkunft** /tsu'zamənkʊnft/ *die;* ~, **Zusammenkünfte** /... kʏnftə/ meeting

**zusammen-:** **~|läppern** *refl. V.* (*ugs.*) mount up; **~|laufen** *unr. itr. V.*; *mit sein* [A] ‹people, crowd› gather, congregate; [B] (*~fließen*) ‹rivers, streams› flow into each other, join up; [C] (*sich sammeln*) ‹water, oil, etc.› collect; [D] (*sich vereinigen*) converge; (*Geom.*) intersect; [E] (*ineinander laufen*) ‹colours› run together; **~|leben** *itr. V.* live together; **~leben** *das* living together *no art.*; **das eheliche/menschliche ~leben** married life/man's social existence; **~|legen** ❶ *tr. V.* [A] put *or* gather together; [B] (*~falten*) fold [up]; [C] (*miteinander verbinden*) amalgamate, merge ‹classes, departments, etc.›; combine ‹events›; [D] put ‹patients, guests, etc.› together [in the same room]; [E] (*aneinander legen*) fold ‹hands, arms›; ❷ *itr. V.* club together; pool our/your/their money; **~|leimen** glue *or* stick together; **~|lesen** *unr. tr. V.* gather; **~|nähen** *tr. V.* [A] sew together; **etw. mit etw. ~nähen** sew sth. to sth.; [B] (*durch Nähen reparieren*) sew up; **~|nehmen** ❶ *unr. tr. V.* [A] summon *or* muster up ‹courage, strength, understanding›; [B] collect ‹thoughts, wits›; ⇒ *auch* **~genommen**; ❷ *unr. refl. V.* get *or* take a grip on oneself; **nimm dich ~!** pull yourself together!; **~|packen** ❶ *tr. V.* pack up; (*~verpacken*) pack up together; ❷ *itr. V.* pack up; **~|passen** *itr. V.* ‹colours, clothes, furniture› go together; ‹persons› be suited to each other; **mit etw. ~passen** go with sth.; **~|fantasieren** *refl. V.* (*ugs.*) **sich** (*Dat.*) **etw. ~fantasieren** dream up sth.; invent sth.; (*im Fieber*) imagine

**Zusammenprall** *der;* ~[e]s, ~e collision; (*fig.*) clash

**zusammen-, Zusammen-:** **~|prallen** *itr. V.*; *mit sein* collide (**mit** with); (*fig.*) clash; **~|pressen** *tr. V.* [A] squeeze; (*komprimieren*) compress ‹gas›; [B] (*aneinander pressen*) press ‹lips, hands› together; **~|raffen** *tr. V.* gather up ‹possessions, papers, etc.›; bundle up ‹clothes›; **~|rasseln** *itr. V.*; *mit sein* (*ugs.*) ⇒ **~krachen** B; **~|rechnen** *tr. V.* add up; **einen Betrag mit einem anderen ~rechnen** add one amount to another; **~|reimen** *refl. V.* (*ugs.*) [A] **sich** (*Dat.*) **etw. ~reimen** work sth. out [for oneself]; **ich kann mir das nur so ~reimen** that's the only way I can make sense of it; [B] (*~passen, ~gehören*) **wie reimt sich das ~?** how does that tally?; **~|reißen** *unr. refl. V.* (*ugs.*) ⇒ **~nehmen** 2; **~|ringeln** *refl. V.* ‹snake› coil itself up; **~|rollen** ❶ *tr. V.* roll up; ❷ *refl. V.* ‹cat, dog, etc.› curl up; ‹hedgehog› roll [itself] up [into a ball]; **~|rotten** *refl. V.* (*abwertend*) ‹crowds, groups, etc.› band together; ‹youths› gang together *or* up; (*in Aufruhr*) form a mob; **~rottung** *die;* ~~, ~~**en** (*abwertend*) gathering; **auf der Straße kam es zu ~rottungen** mobs [of hooligans] gathered in the street; **~|rücken** ❶ *tr. V.* move ‹chairs, tables, etc.› together; ❷ *itr. V.*; *mit sein* (*auch fig.*) move closer together; **~|rufen** *unr. tr. V.* call together; **~|sacken** *itr. V.*; *mit sein* (*ugs.*) [A] (*einstürzen*) **[in sich] ~sacken** collapse; [B] (*zu Boden sinken*) ‹person› collapse; [C] (*eine schlaffe Haltung annehmen*) **[in sich] ~sacken** slump; **~|scharen** *refl. V.* gather; **~schau** *die* survey; **aus der ~schau beider ergibt sich ...** looking at *or* viewing the two together shows ...; **~|scheißen** *unr. tr. V.* (*salopp*) **jmdn. ~scheißen** tear sb. off a strip (*coll.*); **~|schlagen** ❶ *unr. tr. V.* [A] strike *or* bang together; clap ‹hands› [together]; **die Hacken ~schlagen** click one's heels; [B] (*verprügeln*) beat up; [C] (*zertrümmern*) smash up *or* to pieces; [D] (*~falten*) fold up; ❷ *unr. itr. V.*; *mit sein* **über jmdm./etw. ~schlagen** engulf sb./sth.; (*fig.*) ‹disaster, misfortune› overtake sb./sth.; **~|schließen** ❶ *unr. refl. V.* join together; ‹firms› merge, amalgamate; **sich im Kampf für/gegen etw. ~schließen** unite in the struggle for/against sth.; ❷ *unr. tr. V.* lock together; **~schluss**, ***~schluß** *der* joining together; union; (*von Firmen*) merger; amalgamation; **~|schmelzen** *unr. itr. V.*; *mit sein* melt [away]; (*fig.*) ‹supplies, savings, etc.› dwindle (**auf** + *Akk.* to); **~|schneiden** *unr. tr. V.* (*Film, Ferns., Rundf.: kürzen*) cut; **~|schnüren** *tr. V.* [A] tie up (**zu** in); [B] (*einschnüren*) lace in ‹waist›; **der Anblick schnürte mir das Herz ~** (*geh.*) the sight tore at my heart[strings]; **~|schrecken** *unr. od. regelm. itr. V.*; *mit sein* start; jump; **~|schreiben** *unr. tr. V.* [A] write together; [B] (*abwertend: verfassen*) dash off ‹report, letter, etc.›; **was für einen Unsinn hast du denn da ~geschrieben!** what a lot of rubbish you've written there; **~schreibung** *die* writing together *or* as one word; **beachten Sie bitte die ~schreibung solcher Bezeichnungen** please remember that such terms are written together *or* as one word; **~|schrumpfen** *itr. V.*; *mit sein* shrivel [up]; (*fig.*) dwindle; **~|schustern** *tr. V.* (*ugs. abwertend*) cobble together; **~|schweißen** *tr. V.* weld together; **etw. mit etw. ~schweißen** weld sth. to sth.; **die Gefahr hat sie noch enger ~geschweißt** (*fig.*) the danger forged even stronger bonds between them; ***~|sein** ⇒ **zusammen**; **~sein** *das* [A] being together *no art.*; [B] (*Treffen*) get-together; **~|setzen** ❶ *tr. V.* [A] put together; **Steine zu einem Mosaik ~:** put stones together to make a mosaic; [B] (*herstellen*) make; **ein ~gesetztes Wort/Verb** a compound word/verb; [C] (*~bauen, ~montieren*) assemble; put together; [D] (*beieinander sitzen lassen*) seat *or* put together; **jmdn. mit jmdm. ~:** seat *or* put sb. next to sb.; ❷ *refl. V.* [A] **sich aus etw. ~:** be made up *or* composed of sth.; **wie setzt sich das Gremium ~?** how is the committee made up?; [B] (*sich zueinander setzen*) sit together; **sich mit jmdm. ~:** sit next to sb.; [C] (*zu einem Gespräch*) get together; **~setzung** *die;* ~~, ~~**en** [A] putting together; [B] (*Aufbau*) composition; „**~setzung: ...**" (*als Aufschrift auf Medikamentenpackung*) 'ingredients: ...'; [C] (*Sprachw.*) compound; **~|sinken** *unr. itr. V.*; *mit sein* [A] **[in sich] ~sinken** collapse; ‹fire› die down; ‹dough› sink; [B] (*zu Boden sinken*) **[in sich] ~sinken** slump to the ground; (*eine schlaffe Haltung einnehmen*) slump; **ohnmächtig/tot ~sinken** collapse in a faint/fall down dead; **~|sitzen** *unr. itr. V.* [A] sit together; **mit jmdm. ~sitzen** sit next to sb.; [B] (*miteinander verbunden sein*) be joined together; **~|sparen** *tr. V.* save up; **sich** (*Dat.*) **ein Auto/Fahrrad ~sparen** save up and buy a car/bicycle; **~spiel** *das* [A] (*von Musikern*) ensemble playing; (*von Darstellern*) ensemble acting; (*einer Mannschaft*) teamwork; [B] (*fig.*) interplay; **~|spielen** *itr. V.* [A] play together; ‹actors› act together; **mit jmdm. ~spielen** play/act with sb.; [B] (*fig.*) ‹forces, influences, etc.› work together, combine; **~|stauchen** *tr. V.* [A] compress; [B] (*fig. ugs.*) **jmdn. ~stauchen** tear sb. off a strip (*coll.*); **~|stecken** ❶ *tr. V.* [A] fit together; join up ‹extension cables›; [B] (*mit einer Nadel, Spange usw.*) pin together; ⇒ *auch* **Kopf** A; ❷ *itr. V.* (*ugs.*) be together; **~|stehen** *unr. itr. V.* [A] stand together; **mit jmdm. ~stehen** stand with sb.; [B] (*fig.: ~halten*) stand by one another; **~|stellen** ❶ *tr. V.* [A] put together; [B] (*aus einzelnen Teilen gestalten*) put together ‹programme, film, book, menu, exhibition, team, delegation›; draw up ‹list, timetable›; compile ‹report, broadcast›; work out ‹route, tour›; make up ‹bouquet, flower arrangement›; [C] (*in einer Übersicht, Liste usw.*) draw together; compile ‹facts, data›; [D] (*kombinieren*) combine; ❷ *refl. V.* stand together; **~stellung** *die* [A] ⇒ **~stellen** 1 B: putting together; drawing up; compilation; working out; making up; [B] (*Übersicht*) survey; (*von Tatsachen, Daten*) compilation; [C] (*Kombination*) combination; **~|stimmen** *itr. V.* [A] ‹instruments› harmonize; ‹colours, furniture› match, go together; **mit etw. ~stimmen** go with sth.; [B] (*stimmig sein*) agree (**mit** with); **~|stoppeln** *tr. V.* (*abwertend*) cobble together; **~stoß** *der* collision; (*fig.*) clash (**mit** with); **bei dem ~stoß [der beiden Züge]** in the collision [between the two trains]; **~|stoßen** *unr. itr. V.*; *mit sein* collide (**mit** with); **wir stießen mit den Köpfen ~:** we banged *or* bumped our heads; **~|strömen** *itr. V.*; *mit sein* [A] ‹rivers, streams› flow into one another, join up; [B] (*~laufen, ~kommen*) congregate; **~|stückeln** *tr. V.* (*ugs.*) patch together; **~|stürzen** *itr. V.*; *mit sein* collapse; ‹mine shaft, roof› cave in, collapse; **~|suchen** *tr. V.* collect bit by bit; hunt out ‹information› bit by bit; **~|tragen** *unr. tr. V.* collect; **~|treffen** *unr. itr. V.*; *mit sein* [A] meet; **mit jmdm. ~treffen** meet sb.; [B] (*zeitlich*) coincide; **~treffen** *das* [A] meeting; [B] **ein merkwürdiges ~treffen von Zufällen** a peculiar set of coincidences; **~|treiben** *unr. tr. V.* herd together; **~|treten** *unr. itr. V.*; *mit sein* meet (**zu** for); ‹parliament› assemble; **~|trommeln** *tr. V.* (*ugs.*) round up; **~|tun** (*ugs.*) ❶ *unr. tr. V.* put together; ❷ *unr. refl. V.* get together (**mit** with); **~|wachsen** *unr. itr. V.*; *mit sein* grow together; join [up]; ‹bones› knit together; (*fig.*) ‹towns› merge into one; **~gewachsen sein** be joined; ‹bones› have knitted together; **~|werfen** *unr. tr. V.* (*ugs.*) lump together; **~|wirken** *itr. V.* combine; **~|zählen** *tr. V.* add up; **~|ziehen** ❶ *unr. tr. V.* [A] draw *or* pull together; draw *or* pull ‹noose, net› tight; **die Brauen ~ziehen** knit one's brows; **die Säure zieht einem den Mund ~:** the sourness makes you pucker up your mouth; [B] (*konzentrieren*) mass ‹troops, police›; [C] (*addieren*) add up *or* together; (*~fassen*) simplify ‹mathematical expression›; ❷ *unr. refl. V.* [A] ‹skin, muscle, heart› contract; ‹face› tighten up; ‹wound› close up; [B] ⇒ **~brauen** 2; ❸ *unr. itr. V.*; *mit sein* move in together; **mit jmdm. ~ziehen** move in with sb.; **~|zimmern** *tr. V.* (*ugs.*) knock together; (*fig. abwertend*) cobble together; **~|zucken** *itr. V.*; *mit sein* start; jump

**Zu·satz** *der* [A] addition; **unter ~ von etw.** while adding sth.; **ohne ~ von ...** without

*old spelling (see note on page 1707)

the addition of ...; without adding ...; **B** (*Zugesetztes, Additiv*) additive; **C** (*zusätzlicher Teil*) addition; (*zu einem Vertrag*) rider; additional clause; (*Nachtrag*) addendum; (*zu einem Brief*) postscript; (*zu einem Testament*) codicil

**Zusatz·bremsleuchte** *die* (*Kfz-W.*) high-level brake light

**zusätzlich** /ˈt̮suːzɛt̮slɪç/ **1** *Adj.* additional; **2** *adv.* in addition

**zu·schanden** *Adv.* *in* **etw. ~ machen** wreck *or* ruin sth.; **ein Auto ~ fahren/ein Pferd ~ reiten** wreck a car/ruin a horse by bad riding; **~ werden** be wrecked *or* ruined

**zu|schanzen** *tr. V.* (*ugs.*) **jmdm./sich etw. ~:** wangle sth. for sb./oneself (*coll.*)

**zu|schauen** *itr. V.* (*südd., österr., schweiz.*) ⇒ **zusehen**

**Zu·schauer** *der*, **Zu·schauerin** *die*; **~, ~nen** spectator; (*im Theater, Kino*) member of the audience; (*an einer Unfallstelle*) onlooker; (*Fernseh~*) viewer; **die ~:** the spectators; the crowd *sing.*; (*im Theater, Kino*) the audience *sing.*; (*an einer Unfallstelle*) the onlookers; (*Fernseh~*) the audience *sing.*; the viewers

**Zuschauer·raum** *der* auditorium

**zu|schaufeln** *tr. V.* fill in [with a shovel/shovels]

**zu|schicken** *tr. V.* send; **jmdm. etw. ~:** send sth. to sb.; send sb. sth.; **sich** (*Dat.*) **etw. ~ lassen** send for sth.

**zu|schieben** *unr. tr. V.* **A** push ‹drawer, door› shut; **den Riegel ~:** put the bolt across; **B** (*fig.: zuweisen*) **jmdm. die Schuld/Verantwortung ~:** lay the blame/responsibility on sb.

**zu|schießen** **1** *unr. tr. V.* **A** **jmdm. den Ball ~:** kick *or* pass the ball to sb.; **B** (*als Zuschuss geben*) contribute (**zu** towards); **Geld zu etw. ~:** contribute [money] *or* put money towards sth.; **jmdm. 200 Mark ~:** give sb. 200 marks towards it. **2** *unr. itr. V.*; *mit sein* **auf jmdn./etw. zugeschossen kommen** come shooting towards sb.

**Zu·schlag** *der* **A** additional *or* extra charge; (*für Nacht-, Feiertagsarbeit, Arbeitserschwernisse*) additional *or* extra payment; **der Intercity-Zug kostet [5 Mark] ~:** you have to pay a supplement [of 5 marks] on an intercity train; **B** (*Eisenb.*) supplement ticket; **C** (*bei einer Versteigerung*) acceptance of a/the bid; **der ~ erfolgt an Herrn X** *od.* **wird Herrn X erteilt** the lot is knocked down to Mr X *or* goes to Mr X; **D** (*bei Ausschreibung eines Auftrags*) acceptance of a/the tender; **jmdm. den ~ für etw. geben** give sb. the contract for sth.; **den ~ bekommen** *od.* **erhalten** get the contract

**zu|schlagen** **1** *unr. tr. V.* **A** bang or slam ‹door, window, etc.› shut; close ‹book›; (*heftig*) slam ‹book› shut; **B** **jmdm. etw. ~** (*bei einer Versteigerung*) knock sth. down to sb.; (*bei Ausschreibung eines Auftrags, durch Gerichtsbeschluss*) award sth. to sb.; **C** (*angliedern*) annex (*Dat.* to); **D** (*als Zuschlag erheben*) add on; **das Porto wird dem Preis zugeschlagen** the price does not include postage.
**2** *unr. itr. V.* **A** *mit sein* ‹door, trap› slam *or* bang shut; **B** (*einen Schlag führen*) throw a blow/blows; (*losschlagen*) hit *or* strike out; (*fig.*) ‹army, police, murderer› strike; **er schlug kräftig zu** he threw a powerful blow; **schlag doch zu!** [go on,] hit it/me/him *etc.*; **C** (*salopp: zugreifen*) jump at it; (*beim Essen*) have a good nosh-up (*coll.*); (*beim Trinken*) knock it back (*coll.*)

**zuschlag·pflichtig** /-ˈpflɪçtɪç/ *Adj.* (*Eisenb.*) ‹train› on which on supplement is payable

**Zuschlag·stoff** *der* (*Hüttenw.*) flux; (*Bauw.*) aggregate

**zu|schließen** **1** *unr. tr. V.* lock. **2** *unr. itr. V.* lock up

**zu|schnappen** *itr. V.* **A** *mit sein* snap shut; **B** (*zubeißen*) snap; **der Hund schnappt zu, wenn man ihn neckt** if you tease him the dog will snap at you

**zu|schneiden** *unr. itr. V.* cut out ‹material etc.› (**zu, für** for); saw ‹plank, slat› to size; cut out ‹dress, jacket›; **auf jmdn./etw. zugeschnitten sein** (*fig.*) be tailor-made for sb./sth.; **auf jmds. Geschmack zugeschnitten** geared to sb.'s taste

**zu|schneien** *itr. V.*; *mit sein* snow in *or* up

**Zu·schnitt** *der* **A** (*von Kleidung*) cut; (*fig.*) character; (*Format*) calibre; **B** (*das Zuschneiden*) (*von Kleidung*) cutting [out]; (*von Platten usw.*) sawing to size

**zu|schnüren** *tr. V.* tie up; **sich** (*Dat.*) **die Schuhe ~:** tie *or* do up one's shoes; ⇒ *auch* **Kehle**

**zu|schrauben** *tr. V.* screw the lid *or* top on ‹jar, flask›; screw ‹lid, top› on

**zu|schreiben** *unr. tr. V.* **A** **jmdm./einem Umstand etw. ~:** attribute sth. to sb./a circumstance; **jmdm. das Verdienst/die Schuld an etw.** (*Dat.*) **~:** credit sb. with/blame sb. for sth.; **das hast du dir selbst zu~:** you only have yourself to blame [for this]; **jmdm./einer Sache eine Eigenschaft ~:** ascribe a characteristic *or* quality to sb./sth.; credit sb./sth. with a quality; **B** (*überschreiben*) **einem Konto eine Summe ~:** transfer a sum to an account

**Zu·schrift** *die* letter; (*auf eine Anzeige*) reply

**zu·schulden** *Adv.* **sich** (*Dat.*) **[irgend]etw. ~ kommen lassen** do [any] wrong

**Zu·schuss, *Zu·schuß** *der* contribution (**zu** towards); (*regelmäßiger ~*) allowance; **[staatlicher] ~:** state subsidy (**für, zu** towards); **ich gebe dir einen kleinen ~:** I'll give you something towards it

**Zuschuss·betrieb, *Zuschuß·betrieb** *der* subsidized concern

**zu|schustern** *tr. V.* (*ugs.*) **A** **jmdm. einen Posten** *usw.* **~:** organize a job *etc.* for sb.; **B** (*zuschießen*) contribute (**zu** towards)

**zu|schütten** *tr. V.* **A** fill in ‹ditch etc.›; **B** (*ugs. hinzufügen*) pour on, add ‹water etc.›

**zu|sehen** *unr. itr. V.* **A** watch; **jmdm. [bei einem Spiel/beim Arbeiten** *usw.*] **~:** watch sb. [playing a game/working *etc.*]; **bei näherem Z~:** on closer examination; if you look more closely; **vom [bloßen] Z~:** [simply] by watching; **er musste ~, wie sein Haus niederbrannte** he had to stand by and watch his house burn down; **wir dürfen diesem Unrecht nicht tatenlos ~:** we cannot stand idly by and allow this injustice; **B** (*dafür sorgen, sich darum bemühen*) make sure; see to it; **sieh zu, dass ...** see that ...; make sure that ...; **er soll ~, wie er das hinkriegt** he'll just have to manage somehow; **sieh zu, wo du bleibst!** you're on your own

**zusehends** /ˈt̮suːzeːənt̮s/ *Adv.* visibly

**Zu·seher** *der*, **Zu·seherin** *die* (*österr.*) ⇒ **Zuschauer**

***zu·sein** ⇒ **zu** 2 C

**zu|senden** *unr. od. regelm. tr. V.* ⇒ **zuschicken**

**Zu·sendung** *die* **A** (*das Zusenden*) sending; **ich bitte um ~ des Vertrages** I would ask that the contract be sent to me; **B** (*Zugesandtes*) (*Brief*) letter; (*Paket*) parcel; (*Warensendung*) consignment

**zu|setzen** **1** *tr. V.* **A** **[zu] einem Stoff etw. ~:** add sth. to a substance; **B** (*zuzahlen*) pay out; **er hat nichts [mehr] zu~** (*fig.*) he has no strength left in him. **2** *itr. V.* (*ugs.*) **jmdm. ~** (*jmdn. angreifen*) go for sb.; (*beim Verhör*) grill sb.; (*jmdn. bedrängen*) pester *or* badger sb.; ‹mosquitoes etc.› plague sb.; ‹illness, heat› take a lot out of sb.; ‹death, divorce› be a heavy blow for sb.; **einer Sache** (*Dat.*) **~** (*beschädigen*) damage sth.

**zu|sichern** *tr. V.* **jmdm. etw. ~:** promise sb. sth.; assure sb. of sth.

**Zu·sicherung** *die* promise; assurance

**zu|sperren** (*südd., österr.*) **1** *tr. V.* lock. **2** *itr. V.* lock up

**Zu·spiel** *das* (*Ballspiele*) passing; (*einzelner Spielzug*) pass

**zu|spielen** **1** *itr. V.* (*Ballspiele*) pass. **2** *tr. V.* **A** (*Ballspiele*) **jmdm. den Ball ~:** pass the ball to sb.; **B** (*fig.: zukommen lassen*) **der Presse Informationen ~:** leak information to the press

**zu|spitzen** **1** *tr. V.* **A** sharpen to a point; **B** (*fig.: verschärfen*) aggravate ‹position, crisis›; intensify ‹competition, conflict, etc.›; **C** (*fig.: pointieren*) make ‹question, answer› pointed. **2** *refl. V.* become aggravated

**Zu·spitzung** *die*; **~, ~en** **A** (*fig.: Verschärfung*) aggravation; (*der Konkurrenz, eines Konflikts*) intensification; **B** (*fig.: Pointierung*) pointed emphasis

**zu|sprechen** **1** *unr. tr. V.* **A** **er sprach ihr Trost/Mut zu** his words gave her comfort/courage; **sich** (*Dat.*) **selbst Mut ~:** give oneself courage; **B** (*zuerkennen*) **jmdm. ein Erbe** *usw.* **~:** award sb. an inheritance *etc.*; **die Kinder der Mutter/dem Vater ~:** award custody of the children to the mother/father; **C** (*zuschreiben*) **jmdm./einer Sache etw. ~:** ascribe sth. to sb./sth. **2** *unr. itr. V.* **A** (*zureden*) **jmdm. ermutigend/tröstend** *usw.* **~:** speak encouragingly/comfortingly to sb.; **B** (*geh.*) **dem Essen/den Getränken ~:** partake of the food/drinks

**Zu·spruch** *der* (*geh.*) **A** (*Zureden*) words *pl.*; **Worte des ~s** (*tröstend*) words of comfort; (*ermutigend*) words of encouragement; **B** (*Anklang*) **[bei jmdm.] ~ finden** be popular [with sb.]

**Zu·stand** *der* **A** condition; (*bes. abwertend*) state; **in rohem/gefrorenem ~:** in the raw/frozen state; raw/frozen; **in flüssigem ~:** in liquid form; **in betrunkenem ~:** while under the influence of alcohol; **in bewusstlosem ~:** in a state of unconsciousness; unconscious; **geistiger/gesundheitlicher ~:** state of mind/health; **der ~ des Patienten** the patient's condition; **er war in einem schlimmen ~:** he was in a bad way; **Zustände kriegen** *od.* **bekommen** (*ugs.*) have a fit (*coll.*); **B** (*Stand der Dinge*) state of affairs; situation; **Zustände** conditions; **das sind ja [schöne] Zustände!** that's a fine state of affairs!; these are fine goings-on!; **das ist doch kein ~!** that just won't do (*coll.*); ⇒ *auch* **Rom**

**zu·stande** *in* **~ bringen** + *Akk.* manage to do; [manage to] bring about ‹agreement, coalition, etc.›; **~ kommen** come into being; (*geschehen*) take place; **es wollte kein Gespräch ~ kommen** it was impossible to get a conversation going

**zu·ständig** *Adj.* **A** appropriate, proper, relevant ‹authority, office, etc.›; **das ~e Gericht** the court of jurisdiction; **von ~er Seite** by the proper authority; **[für etw.] ~ sein** (*verantwortlich*) be responsible [for sth.]; (*kompetent*) be competent [to deal with sth.]; ‹court› have jurisdiction [in sth.]; **dafür sind wir nicht ~:** it's not our responsibility/we are not competent to decide that; **B** (*österr. Amtsspr.*) **nach Wien ~ sein** be domiciled in Vienna

**Zuständigkeit** *die*; **~, ~en** (*Verantwortlichkeit*) responsibility; (*Kompetenz*) competence; (*eines Gerichts*) jurisdiction

**Zuständigkeits·bereich** *der* (*Verantwortlichkeit*) area of responsibility; (*Kompetenz*) range of competence; **das fällt in den ~ des Innenministeriums** it is within the responsibility/competence of the Ministry of the Interior

**Zustands-:** **~passiv** *das* (*Sprachw.*) passive of condition; **~verb** *das* (*Sprachw.*): *verb describing a state*

**zu·statten** *Adv.* *in* **jmdm./einer Sache ~ kommen** be a help *or* be useful to sb./for sth.; (*von Vorteil sein*) be of advantage to sb./sth.

**zu|stecken** *tr. V.* **A** pin up ‹tear›; pin together ‹curtains etc.›; **B** (*heimlich geben*) **jmdm. etw. ~:** slip sb. sth.

**zu|stehen** *unr. itr. V.* **etw. steht jmdm. zu** sb. is entitled to sth.; **ein Urteil über ihn steht mir nicht zu** it is not for me to judge him

**zu|steigen** *unr. itr. V.*; *mit sein* get on; **ist noch jemand zugestiegen?** (*im Bus*) any more fares, please?; (*im Zug*) ≈ tickets, please!

**zu|stellen** *tr. V.* [A] block ‹entrance, passage, etc.›; [B] (*bringen*) deliver ‹letter, parcel, etc.›; **jmdm. etw. ~:** deliver sth. to sb.; (*zuschicken*) send sb. sth.; **jmdm. ein Schriftstück ~:** serve a writ on sb.

**Zu·steller** *der;* **~s, ~, Zu·stellerin** *die;* **~, ~nen** [A] deliverer; [B] (*Postbote/-botin*) postman/postwoman

**Zu·stellung** *die* delivery; (*Zusendung*) submission

**zu|steuern** ❶ *itr. V.; mit sein* **auf jmdn./etw. ~:** head for sb./sth.; **einer Sache** (*Dat.*) **~:** head for sth. ❷ *tr. V.* [A] **etw. auf jmdn./etw. ~:** steer *or* drive sth. towards sb./sth.; [B] (*ugs.*) ⇒ **beisteuern**

**zu|stimmen** *itr. V.* agree; **jmdm. [in einem Punkt] ~:** agree with sb. [on a point]; **~d nicken** nod in agreement; **einer Sache** (*Dat.*) **~:** agree to sth.; **einem Gesetzentwurf ~** ‹parliament› pass *or* approve a bill; **dem kann ich nur ~:** I quite agree

**Zu·stimmung** *die* (*Billigung*) approval (**zu** of); (*Einverständnis*) agreement (**zu** to, with); (*Plazet*) consent (**zu** to); **[allgemeine] ~ finden** meet with [general] approval; **die ~ der Eltern** the parents' consent; **jmdm. seine ~ zu etw. geben** give sb. one's consent to *or* for sth.; **nicht ohne/nur mit jmds. ~:** not without/only with the agreement *or* consent of sb.

**zu|stopfen** *tr. V.* [A] plug, stop up ‹hole, crack›; plug ‹ears›; [B] (*mit Nadel und Faden*) darn, mend ‹hole›

**zu|stöpseln** *tr. V.* [A] put a stopper in ‹bottle›; (*mit Korken*); put a cork in, cork ‹bottle›; [B] put a plug in ‹basin›; plug ‹drain etc.›

**zu|stoßen** ❶ *unr. tr. V.* push ‹door etc.› shut; (*mit dem Fuß, heftig*) kick ‹door etc.› shut. ❷ *unr. itr. V.* [A] strike out; (*mit einem Messer usw.*) make a stab; stab; ‹snake etc.› strike; [B] *mit sein* **jmdm. ~:** happen to sb.; **wenn mir etwas zustößt** if anything should happen to me

**zu|streben** *itr. V.; mit sein* **einer Sache** (*Dat.*) *od.* **auf etw.** (*Akk.*) **~:** make for sth.; (*fig.*) strive for *or* aim at sth.

**Zu·strom** *der* [A] (*von Luft, fig.: Geld usw.*) flow; [B] (*von Menschen*) influx; stream; **starken** *od.* **großen ~ haben** have a great influx of people

**zu|stürmen** *itr. V.; mit sein* **auf jmdn./etw. ~:** charge towards sb./sth.

**zu|stürzen** *itr. V.; mit sein* **auf jmdn./etw. ~/zugestürzt kommen** rush/come rushing towards sb./sth.; (*direkt heran*) rush/come rushing up to sb./sth.

**zu|tage** *Adv. in:* **~ kommen** *od.* **treten** become visible (*lit. or fig.*); ‹stream› come to the surface; (*ans Licht kommen*) ‹documents etc.› come to light, be revealed; ‹story› come out, be made public; (*fig.: erkennbar werden*) become evident; ‹differences etc.› come into the open; **etw. ~ bringen** *od.* **fördern** (*aus der Tasche usw.*) produce sth.; (*fig.: erkennbar machen*) bring sth. to light; reveal sth.; **offen** *od.* **klar ~ liegen** be perfectly clear *or* evident

**Zu·tat** *die* ingredient

**zu·teil** *Adv.* (*geh.*) *in* **jmdm./einer Sache ~ werden** be granted *or* accorded to sb./sth.; **ihm wurde die Ehre ~, die Ansprache halten zu dürfen** he was accorded the honour of giving the address; **jmdm. etw. ~ werden lassen** accord sb. sth.; bestow sth. on sb.; **einer Sache** (*Dat.*) **mehr Aufmerksamkeit ~ werden lassen** devote more attention to sth.

**zu|teilen** *tr. V.* [A] **jmdm. jmdn./etw. ~:** allot *or* assign sb./sth. to sb.; [B] (*als Ration*) **jmdm. seine Portion ~:** mete out his/her share to sb.; **den Kindern das Essen ~:** ration *or* share out the food to the children; **die zugeteilte Menge** the allocated amount

**Zu·teilung** *die* [A] allotting, assigning (**an** + *Akk.* to); [B] (*als Ration*) sharing out, allocation (**an** + *Akk.* to); (*eines Mandats, Quartiers*) allocation, assignment (**an** + *Akk.* to); **es gab Fleisch nur auf ~:** meat was only to be had on rations; [C] (*Ration*) allocation, ration (**an** + *Dat.* of)

**zuteilungs·reif** *Adj.* (*Wirtsch.*) mature

**zu·tiefst** *Adv.* profoundly; **~ verletzt** deeply hurt *or* offended

**zu|tragen** ❶ *unr. refl. V.* (*geh.*) take place; occur. ❷ *unr. tr. V.* **jmdm. etw. ~:** carry sth. to sb. (*fig.: mitteilen*) report sth. to sb.; **jmdm. Nachrichten/Gerüchte** *usw.* **~:** pass on news/rumours *etc.* to sb.

**Zu·träger** *der,* **Zu·trägerin** *die* informer

**zuträglich** /ˈt͜suːtrɛːklɪç/ *Adj.* healthy ‹climate›; **jmdm./einer Sache ~ sein** be good for sb./sth.; be beneficial to sb./sth.

**Zuträglichkeit** *die;* **~:** beneficial effect; (*des Klimas*) healthiness

**zu|trauen** *tr. V.* **jmdm. etw. ~:** believe sb. [is] capable of [doing] sth.; **den Mut hätte ich ihm gar nicht zugetraut** I should never have thought he had the courage; **ich hätte ihm mehr Taktgefühl zugetraut** I should have thought he had more tact; **ihm ist alles zu~:** I wouldn't put anything past him; **das hätte ich ihm nicht zugetraut** I should never have thought it of him; **das ist ihm [durchaus] zu~:** I could [well] believe it of him; **sich** (*Dat.*) **etw. ~:** think one can do *or* is capable of doing sth.; **trau dir nicht zu viel zu** don't take on too much; don't overdo it; **er traut sich** (*Dat.*) **zu wenig zu** he has too little self-confidence

**Zutrauen** *das;* **~s** confidence, trust (**zu** in); **~ zu sich selbst** self-confidence

**zutraulich** ❶ *Adj.* trusting; trustful. ❷ *adv.* trustingly; trustfully

**Zutraulichkeit** *die;* **~:** trust[fulness]

**zu|treffen** *unr. itr. V.* [A] be correct; **der Vorwurf trifft zu** the reproach is justified; [B] **auf** *od.* **für jmdn./etw. ~:** apply to sb./sth.

**zutreffend** ❶ *Adj.* [A] correct; (*treffend*) accurate; **es ist ~, dass ...** it is correct *or* the case that ...; [B] (*geltend*) applicable; relevant; **Zutreffendes bitte ankreuzen** please mark with a cross where applicable. ❷ *adv.* correctly; (*treffend*) accurately

**zu|treiben** *unr. itr. V.; mit sein* **jmdm./einer Sache ~, auf jmdn./etw. ~** (*auch fig.*) be carried along *or* drift towards sb./sth.

**zu|trinken** *unr. itr. V.* **jmdm. ~:** raise one's glass and drink to sb.

**Zu·tritt** *der* entry; admittance; **„kein ~", „~ verboten"** 'no entry'; 'no admittance'; **jmdm. den ~ verweigern** refuse sb. admission; **~ [zu etw.] haben** have access [to sth.]

**zu|tun** *unr. tr. V.* **kein Auge ~:** not sleep a wink

**Zu·tun** *das;* **~s** *in* **ohne jmds. ~:** without sb.'s being involved; **es geschah ohne mein ~:** I had nothing to do with it

**zu·ungunsten** ❶ *Präp. mit Gen.* to the disadvantage of ❷ *Adv.* **~ von** to the disadvantage of

**zu·unterst** *Adv.* right at the bottom; ⇒ *auch* **ober...** A

**zuverlässig** /ˈt͜suːfɛɐ̯lɛsɪç/ ❶ *Adj.* reliable; (*verlässlich*) dependable ‹person›. ❷ *adv.* [A] reliably; **er arbeitet sehr ~:** he is a very reliable worker; [B] (*mit Gewissheit*) ‹confirm› with certainty; ‹know› for sure, for certain

**Zuverlässigkeit** *die;* **~:** reliability; (*Verlässlichkeit*) dependability

**Zuversicht** /t͜suːˈfɛɐ̯zɪçt/ *die;* **~:** confidence

**zuversichtlich** ❶ *Adj.* confident; **sich ~ geben** express one's confidence. ❷ *adv.* confidently

**Zuversichtlichkeit** *die;* **~:** confidence

***zuviel** ⇒ **viel; gut** 1 A; **kriegen** 1 A; **sagen** 1 C

**Zu·viel** *das;* **~s** excess (**an** + *Dat.* of)

**zu·vor** *Adv.* before; **tags/im Jahr ~:** the day/year before

**zu·vorderst** *Adv.* right at the front

**zuvörderst** /t͜suˈfœrdɐst/ *Adv.* (*veralt.*) first and foremost

**zuvor|kommen** *unr. itr. V.; mit sein* [A] **jmdm. ~:** beat sb. to it; get there first; [B] **einer Sache** (*Dat.*) **~:** anticipate *or* forestall sth.

**zuvorkommend** ❶ *Adj.* obliging; (*höflich*) courteous. ❷ *adv.* obligingly; (*höflich*) courteously

**Zuvorkommenheit** *die;* **~:** courteousness; courtesy

**Zu·wachs** *der;* **~es, Zuwächse** /ˈt͜suːvɛksə/ increase (*Gen.,* **an** + *Dat.* in); **~ an Besuchern/Mitgliedern** increase in the number of visitors/members; **wirtschaftlicher ~:** economic growth; **die Familie hat ~ bekommen** there has been an addition to the family; **der Mantel ist auf ~ genäht** the coat has been made [on the large side] to allow room to grow into

**-zuwachs** *der* increase in ‹income, capital, exports, votes, expenditure, productivity, population, etc.›; **Lohn-/Gehalts~:** wage/salary increase

**zu|wachsen** *unr. itr. V.; mit sein* [A] ‹wound› heal [over]; [B] (*bewachsen/überwachsen werden*) become overgrown; **mit etw. zugewachsen sein** be overgrown with sth.; [C] (*zuteil werden*) **jmdm./einer Sache ~:** fall *or* be granted to sb./sth.

**Zuwachs·rate** *die* (*bes. Wirtsch.*) growth rate

**Zu·wanderer** *der,* **Zu·wanderin** *die* immigrant

**zu|wandern** *itr. V.; mit sein* immigrate

**Zu·wanderung** *die* immigration

**zu|warten** *itr. V.* wait

**zu·wege** *Adv. in* **etw. ~ bringen** [manage to] achieve sth.; **gut/schlecht ~ sein** (*ugs.*) be in good shape/a bad way

**zu·weilen** *Adv.* (*geh.*) now and again; at times

**zu|weisen** *unr. tr. V.* **jmdm. etw. ~:** allocate *or* allot sb. sth.

**zu|wenden** ❶ *unr. od. regelm. refl. V.* [A] **sich jmdm./einer Sache ~** (*auch fig.*) turn to sb./sth.; (*sich widmen*) devote oneself to sb./sth.: [B] (*geh.: gehen*) **er wandte sich dem Ausgang zu** he moved towards the exit. ❷ *unr. od. regelm. tr. V.* [A] **jmdm./einer Sache etw. ~:** turn sth. to[wards] sb./sth.; **jmdm. den Rücken ~:** turn one's back on sb.; [B] (*geben, zuteil werden lassen*) **jmdm. Geld ~:** give *or* donate money to sb.

**Zu·wendung** *die* [A] (*Aufmerksamkeit*) [loving] attention *or* care; [B] (*Geldgeschenk*) gift of money; (*Unterstützung*) [financial] contribution; (*Geldspende*) donation; **auf ~en angewiesen sein** be dependent on financial support *sing. or* contributions

***zu·wenig** ⇒ **wenig; viel** 2 B

**zu|werfen** *unr. tr. V.* [A] slam ‹door, lid›; [B] **jmdm. etw. ~:** throw sth. to sb.; throw sb. sth.; **jmdm. einen bösen/giftigen Blick ~:** look daggers at sb.; ⇒ *auch* **Ball** A; **Blick** A; **Kusshand**

**zuwider** ❶ *Adj.* [A] **jmdm. ~ sein** be repugnant to sb.; **Spinat ist mir äußerst ~:** I absolutely detest spinach; [B] (*geh.: nicht förderlich*) **jmdm./einer Sache** (*Dat.*) **~ sein** ‹circumstances, weather, etc.› be against sb./sth. ❷ *Präp. mit Dat.; nachgestellt* contrary to *attrib.*

**zuwider-, Zuwider-: ~|handeln** *itr. V.* **dem Gesetz/einer Vorschrift** *usw.* **~handeln** contravene *or* infringe the law/a regulation *etc.*; **einer Anordnung/einem Verbot ~handeln** defy an instruction/a ban; **~handelnde** *der/die; adj. Dekl.* offender; **~|laufen** *unr. itr. V.; mit sein* **einer Sache** (*Dat.*) **~laufen** go against *or* run counter to sth.

**zu|winken** *itr. V.* **jmdm./einander ~:** wave to sb./one another

**zu|zahlen** *tr. V.* pay ‹five marks etc.› extra; **einen Betrag ~:** pay an additional sum

**zu|zählen** *tr. V.* [A] (*dazurechnen*) add on; [B] (*zurechnen*) **etw. einem Gebiet/Zeitalter ~:** assign sth. to an area/era

**zu·zeiten** *Adv.* (*geh.*) ⇒ **zuweilen**

**zu|ziehen** ❶ *unr. tr. V.* [A] pull ‹door› shut; draw ‹curtain›; pull *or* draw ‹knot, net› tight; do up ‹zip›; [B] call in ‹expert, specialist›. ❷ *unr. refl. V.* [A] **sich** (*Dat.*) **eine Krankheit/Infektion ~:** catch an illness/contract an infection; **sich** (*Dat.*) **einen Schädelbruch**

*old spelling (see note on page 1707)

Z

~: sustain a fracture of the skull; **sich** (*Dat.*) **jmds. Zorn/Vorwürfe ~:** incur sb.'s anger/reproaches; Ⓑ(*sich schließen*) ‹knot, noose› tighten, get tight. ❸ *unr. itr. V.; mit sein* move here *or* into the area

**Zu·zug** *der* Ⓐ influx; Ⓑ(*Genehmigung*) settlement permit

**zuzüglich** /'tsu:tsy:klıç/ *Präp. mit Gen.* plus; **400 Mark ~ [der] Heizungskosten** 400 marks plus *or* not including heating

**Zuzugs·genehmigung** *die* settlement permit

**zu|zwinkern** *itr. V.* **jmdm. ~:** wink at sb.

**zwacken** /'tsvakn̩/ *tr., auch itr. V.* (*ugs.*) ⇨ **zwicken**

**zwang** /tsvaŋ/ *1. u. 3. Pers. Sg. Prät. v.* **zwingen**

**Zwang** *der;* **~[e]s, Zwänge** /'tsvɛŋə/ Ⓐ compulsion; **unter ~ handeln** act under duress; **Kinder ohne ~ erziehen** bring children up without constraint; **auf jmdn. ~ ausüben** exert pressure on sb.; force sb.'s hand; **der ~ der Verhältnisse** the force of circumstance[s]; **soziale Zwänge** social constraints; the constraints of society; **unmittelbarer ~** (*Rechtsspr.*) direct coercion; **das ist freiwilliger ~** (*iron.*) it's voluntary but compulsory; Ⓑ(*unwiderstehlicher Drang*) irresistible urge; **aus einem ~ [heraus] handeln** act under a compulsion *or* on an irresistible impulse; Ⓒ(*Beschränkung*) constraint; compulsion; **sich** (*Dat.*) **~ antun** *od.* **auferlegen** restrain oneself; exercise self-restraint; **tu dir keinen ~ an!** feel free!; don't force yourself! (*iron.*); **ohne [jeden] ~:** without any constraint; ‹speak› [quite] freely *or* openly; Ⓓ (*Pflicht, Verpflichtung*) obligation; **es besteht kein ~ zur Teilnahme/zum Kauf** there is no obligation to take part/to buy anything

**zwängen** /'tsvɛŋən/ ❶ *tr. V.* squeeze; **Bücher in seine Aktentasche ~:** cram books into one's briefcase. ❷ *refl. V.* squeeze [oneself]

**zwanghaft** ❶ *Adj.* Ⓐ compulsive; (*als Ausdruck einer Zwangsneurose*) obsessive; **~e Vorstellung** obsession; Ⓑ ⇨ **gezwungen** 2. ❷ *adv.* Ⓐ compulsively; Ⓑ ⇨ **gezwungen** 3

**zwanglos** ❶ *Adj.* Ⓐ informal; casual, free and easy ‹behaviour›; Ⓑ(*unregelmäßig*) haphazard ‹arrangement›; **in ~er Folge** at irregular intervals. ❷ *adv.* Ⓐ informally; freely; **es ging dort ziemlich ~ zu** things were pretty free and easy there; Ⓑ (*unregelmäßig*) haphazardly ‹arranged›

**Zwanglosigkeit** *die;* ~ Ⓐ informality; Ⓑ (*Unregelmäßigkeit*) haphazard *or* casual manner

**zwangs-, Zwangs-: ~anleihe** *die* (*Wirtsch.*) compulsory loan; **~arbeit** *die* forced labour; **~ernährung** *die* force-feeding *no indef. art.;* **~handlung** *die* (*Psych.*) compulsive act; **~herrschaft** *die* tyranny; despotism; **~jacke** *die* straitjacket; **~lage** *die* predicament; **jmdn. in eine ~lage bringen** put sb. in a predicament; **~läufig** /-lɔyfıç/ ❶ *Adj.* inevitable; ❷ *adv.* inevitably; **~maßnahme** *die* coercive measure; sanction; **~neurose** *die* (*Psych.*) compulsion *or* obsessive-compulsive neurosis; **~räumung** *die* [enforced] eviction; **~versteigern** *tr. V., nur im Inf. u. Part.* (*Rechtsw.*) put up for compulsory auction; **~versteigerung** *die* (*Rechtsw.*) [compulsory] auction; **~vollstreckung** *die* (*Rechtsw.*) [compulsory] execution; **~vorstellung** *die* (*Psych.*) obsession; **~weise** ❶ *Adv.* compulsorily; (*mit Gewalt*) by force; ❷ *adj.* compulsory; enforced ‹evacuation etc.›; **~weise Ernährung** force-feeding

**zwanzig** /'tsvantsıç/ *Kardinalz.* ▶ 76, ▶ 752, ▶ 841 twenty; ⇨ *auch* **achtzig**

**Zwanzig** *die;* **~, ~en** twenty

**zwanziger** *indekl. Adj.* **die ~ Jahre** the twenties; ⇨ *auch* **achtziger**

**Zwanziger**[1] *der;* **~s, ~** Ⓐ(*20-Jähriger*) twenty-year-old; (*Mann von 20 bis 29*) man in his twenties; Ⓑ twenty-mark/franc/schilling *etc.* note; ⇨ *auch* **Achtziger**[1] B, C

**Zwanziger**[2] *die;* **~, ~** (*ugs.*) twenty-pfennig/centimes/schilling *etc.* stamp

**Zwanziger**[3] *Pl.* twenties; **die goldenen** *od.* **wilden ~:** the roaring twenties; **in den ~n sein** be in one's twenties

**Zwanziger·jahre** *Pl.* ▶ 76, ▶ 207 twenties *pl.*

**zwanzig·jährig** *Adj.* (*20 Jahre alt*) twenty-year-old *attrib.;* (*20 Jahre dauernd*) twenty-year *attrib.;* ⇨ *auch* **achtjährig**

**Zwanzig·mark·schein** *der* ▶ 337 twenty-mark note

**Zwanzig·pfennig·marke** *die* twenty-pfennig stamp

**zwanzigst...** *Ordinalz.* ▶ 207, ▶ 841 twentieth; ⇨ *auch* **acht...**; **achtzigst...**

**zwar** /tsva:ɐ̯/ *Adv.* Ⓐ admittedly; **ich war ~ dabei, habe aber trotzdem nichts gesehen** I was indeed *or* I 'was there, but I didn't see anything; **ich weiß es ~ nicht genau, aber ...** I'm not absolutely sure [I admit,] but ...; Ⓑ *in* **und ~:** to be precise; **er ist Zahnarzt, und ~ ein guter** he is a dentist, and a good one at that; **ich komme heute, und ~ um fünf Uhr** I'm coming today, at five o'clock [to be precise]; **verschwinde hier, und ~ sofort!** clear off (*coll.*), and I mean now!

**Zweck** /tsvɛk/ *der;* **~[e]s, ~e** Ⓐ purpose; **zu diesem ~:** for this purpose; **zum ~ der Fortbildung** for the purposes of further education; **was ist der ~ Ihrer Reise?** what is the purpose of your journey?; **seinen ~ erfüllen** serve its purpose; **Geld für einen guten/wohltätigen ~:** money for a good cause/for a charity; **das ist [nicht] der ~ der Übung** (*ugs.*) that is [not] the object *or* point of the exercise; ⇨ *auch* **heiligen** A; **Mittel** A; Ⓑ(*Sinn*) point; **es hat keinen/wenig ~ [, das zu tun]** it's pointless *or* there is no point/there is little *or* not much point [in doing that]; **ohne [jeden] Sinn und ~:** completely pointless

**zweck-, Zweck-: ~bau** *der; Pl.* **~~ten** functional building; **~dienlich** ❶ *Adj.* appropriate; helpful, relevant ‹information etc.›; **wäre es nicht ~dienlicher, wenn ...?** wouldn't it be more to the point if ...?; ❷ *adv.* **~dienlich verwendet werden** be used for an appropriate purpose; **~entfremden** *tr. V.* use for another purpose; (*durch Umbau*) convert sth. to another use; (*für den falschen ~*) misuse; **etw. als etw. ~entfremden** use sth. as sth.; **die Gelder sind ~entfremdet [verwendet] worden** the money has been diverted from its proper use; **~entfremdung** *die* use/conversion for another purpose; (*von Geldern*) diversion [from its proper use]; **~entsprechend** ❶ *Adj.* appropriate; suitable; ❷ *adv.* appropriately; **~frei** ❶ *Adj.* ‹research› without any specific purpose; pure ‹science›; ❷ *adv.* without any specific purpose; **~gebunden** *Adj.* (*Finanzw.*) [to be used] for a specified purpose

**zweckhaft** ❶ *Adj.* purposeful; **nicht ~ sein** have no purpose. ❷ *adv.* purposefully; with purpose

**zweck-, Zweck-: ~los** *Adj.* pointless; **~losigkeit** *die;* **~~:** pointlessness; **~mäßig** ❶ *Adj.* appropriate; expedient ‹behaviour, action›; functional ‹building, fittings, furniture›; ❷ *adv.* appropriately ‹arranged, clothed›; ‹act› expediently; ‹equip, furnish› functionally; **~mäßigkeit** *die* appropriateness; (*einer Handlung*) expediency; (*eines Gebäudes*) functionalism; **~optimismus** *der* expedient optimism; **~propaganda** *die* [calculated *or* targeted] propaganda

**zwecks** *Präp. mit Gen.* (*Papierdt.*) for the purpose of; **~ Heirat** with a view to marriage

**zweck·voll** *Adj.; adv.* ⇨ **zweckmäßig**

**zwei** /tsvai/ *Kardinalz.* ▶ 76, ▶ 752, ▶ 841 two; **wir ~:** we two; the two of us; **sie gehen ~ und ~** *od.* **zu ~en nebeneinander** they are walking in pairs; **sie waren/kamen zu ~en** there were two of them/two of them came; **für ~ essen/arbeiten** eat enough for two/do the work of two people; **dazu gehören immer noch ~!** (*ugs.*) it takes two [to do that]!; **das ist so sicher, wie ~ mal ~ vier ist** (*ugs.*) it's as sure as eggs is eggs (*coll.*); ⇨ *auch* **acht**[1]

**Zwei** *die;* **~, ~en** Ⓐ(*Zahl*) two; Ⓑ(*Schulnote*) B; **eine ~ schreiben/bekommen** get a B; **er hat die Prüfung mit ~ bestanden** he got a B in the examination; ⇨ *auch* **Acht**[1] A, D, E, G

**zwei-, Zwei-** ⇨ *auch* acht-, Acht-: **~ad[e]rig** *Adj.* (*Elektrot.*) two-core; **~bändig** *Adj.* two-volume; **~beiner** *der;* **~~s, ~~, ~beinerin** *die;* **~~, ~~nen** (*scherzh.*) human [being]; **~bett·zimmer** *das* twin-bedded room; **~deutig** /-dɔytıç/ ❶ *Adj.* Ⓐ ambiguous; equivocal ‹smile›; Ⓑ(*fig.: schlüpfrig*) suggestive ‹remark, joke›; ‹novel, film, etc.› full of double entendre; ❷ *adv.* Ⓐ ambiguously; ‹smile› equivocally; Ⓑ(*fig.: schlüpfrig*) suggestively; **~deutigkeit** *die;* **~~, ~~en** Ⓐ ambiguity; (*fig.: Schlüpfrigkeit*) suggestiveness; Ⓑ(*zweideutige Äußerung*) ambiguity; (*schlüpfrige Äußerung*) double entendre; **~dimensional** /-dimɛnzi̯ona:l/ ❶ *Adj.* two-dimensional; ❷ *adv.* two-dimensionally; in two dimensions; **~drittel·mehrheit** *die* two-thirds majority; **~ein·halb** *Bruchz.* ▶ 841 two and a half

**Zweier** *der;* **~s, ~** Ⓐ(*ugs. Schulnote*) **einen ~ haben/schreiben** get a B; Ⓑ (*ugs.: Münze*) two-pfennig piece; Ⓒ(*Ruderboot*) pair; **im ~ ohne Steuermann** in the coxless pairs; Ⓓ(*Golf*) twosome; (*Wettkampf*) single; twosome

**zweierlei** *Gattungsz.; indekl.* Ⓐ *attr.* two sorts *or* kinds of; two different ‹sizes, kinds, etc.›; odd ‹socks, gloves›; **mit ~ Maß messen** use double standards; **auf ~ Art** in two different ways; Ⓑ *subst.* two [different] things; **es ist ~, ob man es sagt oder [ob man es] auch tut** it is one thing to say it and another [thing] to do it; **Ordnung und Ordnung sind ~:** there is order and order

**zwei-, Zwei-: ~fach** *Vervielfältigungsz.* double; (*~mal, um den Faktor 2*) twice; **die ~fache Menge/Länge** double *or* twice the amount/length; **in ~facher Vergrößerung/Verkleinerung** enlarged to twice its size/reduced to half-size; **der ~fache Vater** the father of two; **in ~facher Hinsicht** in two respects; **~fach gesichert** double-locked; **~fach gegen die Vorschriften verstoßen** infringe the regulations in two ways; **etw. ~fach vergrößern/verkleinern** enlarge sth. to twice its size/reduce sth. to half-size; ⇨ *auch* **achtfach**; **~fache** *das; adj. Dekl.* **das ~fache kosten** cost twice as much; cost double [the amount]; **ein Foto um das ~fache vergrößern** enlarge a photo to twice its size; ⇨ *auch* **Achtfache**; **~familien·haus** *das* two-family house; duplex (*esp. Amer.*); **~farbig** ❶ *Adj.* two-coloured; two-tone ‹scarf, paintwork, etc.›; ❷ *adv.* in two colours

**Zweifel** /'tsvaifl̩/ *der;* **~s, ~:** doubt (**an** + *Dat.* about); **in ~ geraten, ~ bekommen** become doubtful; **ich habe keinen ~ daran/[gewisse] ~ daran, dass ...** I am in no doubt that/in some doubt whether ...; **ich habe da so meine ~** *od.* **bin [mir] darüber im ~:** I have my doubts about that; **ich bin mir noch im ~, ob ...** I am still uncertain whether ...; **etw. in ~ ziehen** question sth.; **[für jmdn.] außer ~ stehen** be beyond doubt [as far as sb. is concerned]; **über jeden** *od.* **allen ~ erhaben sein** be beyond any shadow of a doubt; **er ließ keinen ~ daran, dass ...** he left no doubt [in anyone's mind] that ...; **jmdn. [über etw.** (*Akk.*)**] [nicht] im ~ lassen** leave sb. in [no] doubt [about sth.]; **daran** *od.* **darüber besteht kein ~, daran gibt es keinen ~:** there is no doubt about it; **mir kommen ~:** I am beginning to have my doubts; **kein ~, ...** there is/was no doubt about it, ...; **ohne ~:** without [any] doubt; **im ~:** in case of doubt; if in doubt

**zweifelhaft** *Adj.* Ⓐ doubtful; Ⓑ(*fragwürdig*) dubious; (*suspekt*) suspicious

**zweifel·los** *Adv.* undoubtedly; without [any] doubt

Z

**zweifeln** *itr. V.* doubt; **wenn man zweifelt** if one is in doubt *or* has any doubts; **an jmdm./etw. ~:** doubt sb./sth.; have doubts about sb./sth.; **man hat lange daran gezweifelt** it has long been in doubt *or* uncertain; **~ daran, dass ..., ~, ob ...** doubt whether ...; **er hat nie daran gezweifelt, dass ...** he never doubted that ...; **daran ist nicht zu ~:** there can be no doubt about it

**zweifels-, Zweifels-: ~fall** *der* case of doubt; doubtful *or* problematic case; **im ~fall[e]** in case of doubt; if in doubt; **~frei** ❶ *Adj.* definite; **~frei sein** be beyond doubt; ❷ *adv.* beyond [any] doubt; **~ohne** *Adv.* undoubtedly; without doubt

**zwei·flammig** *Adj.* two-burner ‹cooker›

**Zweifler** *der;* **~s, ~, Zweiflerin** *die;* **~, ~nen** doubter

**zweiflerisch** ❶ *Adj.* doubtful; (*skeptisch*) sceptical. ❷ *adv.* doubtfully; (*skeptisch*) sceptically

**zweiflüg[e]lig** *Adj.* two-winged

**Zwei·fronten·krieg** *der* war on two fronts; **einen ~ führen** (*fig.*) fight on two fronts

**Zweig** /tsvaik/ *der;* **~[e]s, ~e** Ⓐ [small] branch; (*meist ohne Blätter*) twig; **auf keinen grünen ~ kommen** (*ugs.*) not get anywhere; (*finanziell*) not become well off; Ⓑ (*einer Familie*) branch; Ⓒ (*Unterabteilung, Branche*) (*einer Wissenschaft usw.*) branch; (*eines Gymnasiums usw.*) side

**Zweig·betrieb** *der* subsidiary; (*Filiale*) branch

**zwei-, Zwei-: ~geschlechtig** *Adj.* (*Biol.*) hermaphroditic; bisexual; **~geschossig** *Adj., adv.* ⇒ **~stöckig**; **~gespann** *das* Ⓐ pair of horses/oxen; Ⓑ (*Wagen*) carriage and pair; Ⓒ (*fig.*) duo; two-man band; **~gestrichen** *Adj.* (*Musik*) two-line ‹octave›; **das ~gestrichene A** the A two above middle C; **das ~gestrichene C** the C above middle C; **~geteilt** *Adj.* divided; divided in two *postpos.*

**Zweig·geschäft** *das* branch

**zwei·gleisig** ❶ *Adj.* two-track; double-track; (*fig.*) two-way ‹therapy, treatment›. ❷ *adv.* Ⓐ ‹run› on two tracks; **eine Strecke ~ ausbauen** add a second track [to a section]; Ⓑ (*fig.*) **~ fahren** follow a dual-track policy

**Zweig-: ~stelle** *die* branch [office]; **~werk** *das* subsidiary plant

**zwei·händig** /-hɛndɪç/ ❶ *Adj.* two-handed. ❷ *adv.* ‹hold on, catch ball, etc.› with both hands; ‹type, play› with two hands

**Zweiheit** *die;* **~** (*geh.*) duality

**zwei-, Zwei-: ~höck[e]rig** *Adj.* two-humped; **~hundert** *Kardinalz.* ▶841 two hundred; **~jährig** *Adj.* Ⓐ (**~** *Jahre alt*) two-year-old *attrib.;* (**~** *Jahre dauernd*) two-year *attrib.;* Ⓑ (*Bot.*) biennial ‹plant›; ⇒ *auch* **achtjährig**; **~jährlich** ❶ *Adj.* two-yearly *attrib.;* biennial; ⇒ *auch* **achtjährlich**; ❷ *adv.* every two years; biennially; **~kammer·system** *das* (*Politik*) bicameral system; **~kampf** *der* Ⓐ single combat; (*Duell*) duel; **jmdn. im ~kampf töten** kill sb. in single combat/a duel; Ⓑ (*Sport*) man-to-man tussle; duel; **~keim·blättrig** *Adj.* (*Bot.*) dicotyledonous; **~köpfig** *Adj.* Ⓐ two-headed; Ⓑ (*aus* **~** *Personen bestehend*) two-person *attrib.;* of two [people] *postpos.;* **~kreis·bremse** *die* (*Kfz-W.*) dual-circuit braking system; **~mal** *Adv.* twice; **das wird er sich** (*Dat.*) **~mal überlegen** he'll think twice about that; ⇒ *auch* **achtmal**; **~malig** *Adj.* **nach ~maligem Versuch** after trying twice; after two tries; ⇒ *auch* **achtmalig**; **~mark·stück** *das* two-mark piece; **~monats·schrift** *die* bimonthly [periodical]; **~motorig** *Adj.* twin-engined; **~parteien·system** *das* two-party system; **~pfennig·stück** *das* two-pfennig piece; **~phasen·strom** *der* (*Physik, Elektrot.*) two-phase current; **~phasig** *Adj.* (*Physik, Elektrot.*) two-phase; **~-plus-vier-Gespräche** *Pl.* (*Politik*) two plus four talks; **~polig** *Adj.* (*Physik, Elektrot.*) double-pole; two-core ‹cable›; two-pin ‹plug, socket›; **~rad** *das* two-wheeler; **~räd[e]rig** *Adj.* two-wheeled; **~reiher** *der* double-breasted suit/coat/jacket; **~reihig** ❶ *Adj.* Ⓐ in two rows *postpos.;* double ‹chain›; Ⓑ (*mit* **~** *Knopfreihen*) double-breasted ‹suit, coat›; ❷ *adv.* in two rows

**Zweisamkeit** *die;* **~, ~en** togetherness; partnership

**zwei-, Zwei-: ~schläfrig** *Adj.* double ‹bed›; **~schneidig** *Adj.* double-edged; **ein ~schneidiges Schwert** (*fig.*) a double-edged sword; **~seitig** ❶ *Adj.* Ⓐ double-sided; two-sided; Ⓑ (**~** *Seiten lang*) two page ‹letter, article, etc.›; Ⓒ (*bilateral*) bilateral ‹treaty, agreement, etc.›; ❷ *adv.* Ⓐ on two *or* both sides; **~seitig tragbar** reversible ‹anorak, coat›; Ⓑ (*bilateral*) bilaterally; **~silbig** ❶ *Adj.* two-syllable *attrib.;* ❷ *adv.* ‹pronounced› as two syllables; **~sitzer** *der;* **~~s, ~~:** two-seater; **~sitzig** *Adj.* two-seater *attrib.;* **~spaltig** ❶ *Adj.* two-column; ⇒ *auch* **achtspaltig**; ❷ *adv.* ‹printed, set› in two columns; **~spänner** *der;* **~~s, ~~:** carriage and pair; **~spännig** ❶ *Adj.* drawn by two horses *postpos.;* ❷ *adv.* **~spännig fahren** drive [in] a carriage and pair; **~sprachig** ❶ *Adj.* bilingual; ‹sign› in two languages; ❷ *adv.* bilingually; ‹written› in two languages; ‹published› in a bilingual edition; **~sprachigkeit** *die;* **~~:** bilingualism; **~spurig** ❶ *Adj.* Ⓐ two-lane ‹road, motorway›; (*Eisenb.*) double-track ‹railway›; Ⓑ two-track ‹vehicle›; Ⓒ two- *or* twin-track ‹recording›; ❷ *adv.* Ⓐ in two lanes; **~spurig ausbauen** make ‹road› dual carriageway; dual ‹road›; widen ‹railway› to two tracks; Ⓑ ‹record› on two tracks; **~stellig** *Adj.* two-figure *attrib.* ‹number, sum›; **~stellige Stimmenverluste** loss of more than 10% of votes; **~stimmig** ❶ *Adj.* two-part *attrib.;* ❷ *adv.* in two parts; **~stöckig** ❶ *Adj.* two-storey *attrib.;* **~stöckig sein** have two storeys *or* floors; **ein ~stöckiges Bett** a bunk bed; ❷ *adv.* ‹build› two storeys high; **~strahlig** *Adj.* twin-engined ‹jet aircraft›; **~stündig** *Adj.* two-hour *attrib.;* (*Schulw.*) double period *attrib.* ‹test, examination›; **nach ~stündiger Wartezeit** after waiting for two hours; **~stündlich** ❶ *Adj.* two-hourly *attrib.;* ❷ *adv.* every two hours

**zweit** /'tsvait/ *in* **wir waren zu ~:** there were two of us; **sie sind zu ~ verreist** the two of them went away together; **sie schlafen je zu ~ in den Zimmern** they sleep two to a room; **zu ~ lebt man billiger als allein** two can live cheaper than one; ⇒ *auch* **acht²**

**zweit...** *Ordinalz.* ▶207, ▶841 Ⓐ second; **jeder ~e Einwohner** every other *or* second inhabitant; **jeder Zweite** every other one; Ⓑ (*zweitbest...*) second; **~er Klasse fahren/liegen** travel second-class/be in a second-class hospital bed; Ⓒ (*ander..., weiter...*) second; other; **ich habe noch einen ~en** I have a second one; (*als Ersatz*) I have a spare; **wie kein Zweiter** as no one else can; like nobody else; **ein ~er Al Capone** (*fig.*) a second Al Capone; ⇒ *auch* **erst...**

**zwei-, Zwei-: ~tägig** *Adj.* (*2 Tage alt*) two-day-old *attrib.;* (*2 Tage dauernd*) two-day *attrib.;* ⇒ *auch* **achttägig**; **~täglich** ❶ *Adj.* **in ~täglichem Wechsel** on a two-day rota; ❷ *adv.* every two days; **~takter** *der;* **~~s, ~~** (*Kfz-W.*) Ⓐ (*Motor*) two-stroke engine; Ⓑ (*ugs.: Fahrzeug*) two-stroke; **~takt·motor** *der* (*Kfz-W.*) two-stroke engine

**zweit·ältest ...** *Adj.* second oldest; **der/die Zweitälteste** the second oldest

**zwei·tausend** *Kardinalz.* ▶207, ▶841 two thousand

**Zwei·tausender** *der: mountain more than two thousand metres high*

**Zweit·ausfertigung** *die* [second] copy; duplicate

**zweit·best...** *Adj.* second best; **der/die Zweitbeste** the second best

**Zwei·teiler** *der* Ⓐ (*Badeanzug, Kleid*) two-piece; (*Kostüm, Anzug*) two-piece suit; Ⓑ (*Ferns.*) two-part film/programme

**zwei·teilig** *Adj.* two-piece ‹suit, bathing suit, suite, etc.›; two-part ‹film, programme›; two-volume ‹dictionary, novel›; ⇒ *auch* **achtteilig**

***zweite·mal, *zweiten·mal** ⇒ **Mal¹**

**zweitens** *Adv.* secondly; in the second place

**Zweite[r]-Klasse-Abteil** *das* second-class compartment

**zweit-, Zweit-: ~frisur** *die* wig; **~größt...** *Adj.* second biggest *or* largest; **~klassig** ❶ *Adj.* second-rate; **als ~klassig behandelt werden** be treated as a second-class citizen/as second-class citizens; ❷ *adv.* **die Mannschaft hat nur ~klassig gespielt** the team's performance was second-rate; **~klässler, *~kläßler** *der;* **~~s, ~~, ~klässlerin** *die;* **~~, ~~nen** (*südd., schweiz.*) pupil in second class of primary school; second-year pupil; **~platzierte** *der/die; adj. Dekl.* (*Sport*) runner-up; **~rangig** /-raŋɪç/ *Adj.* Ⓐ (*nicht vordringlich*) of secondary importance *postpos.;* **von ~rangiger Bedeutung sein** be of secondary importance; Ⓑ (**~klassig**) second-rate; **~schlüssel** *der* second *or* spare key; **~stimme** *die* second vote

**zwei·türig** *Adj.* two-door ‹car›; ‹room› with two doors

**Zweit-: ~wagen** *der* second car; **~wohnung** *die* second home

**zwei-, Zwei-: ~viertel·takt** /-'fɪrtl̩-/ *der* (*Musik*) two-four time; **im ~vierteltakt** in two-four time; **~wertig** *Adj.* Ⓐ (*Chemie*) bivalent; Ⓑ (*Sprachw.*) two-place *attrib.;* **~wöchentlich** ❶ *Adj.* fortnightly; ❷ *adv.* every fortnight *or* two weeks; ⇒ *auch* **achtwöchentlich**; **~wöchig** *Adj.* (*zwei Wochen alt*) two-week-old *attrib.;* (*2 Wochen dauernd*) two-week *attrib.;* fortnight's *attrib.;* **~zeiler** *der;* **~~s, ~~:** couplet; **~zeilig** *Adj.* two-line *attrib.;* (*Maschinenschreiben*) **in ~zeiligem Abstand** double-spaced; **~zeiliger Leerraum** double-spacing; **~zimmer·wohnung** /-'----/ *die* two-room flat (*Brit.*) *or* (*Amer.*) apartment; **~zügig** *Adj.* ‹school› with two main subject areas

**Zwerch·fell** /'tsvɛrç-/ *das* ▶471 (*Anat.*) diaphragm

**zwerchfell·erschütternd** ❶ *Adj.* side-splitting; screamingly funny. ❷ *adv.* side-splittingly, screamingly ‹funny›

**Zwerg** /tsvɛrk/ *der;* **~[e]s, ~e** Ⓐ dwarf; Ⓑ (*Garten~*) gnome; Ⓒ (*abwertend: unbedeutender Mensch*) [little] squirt (*coll.*); wretch

**zwergenhaft** *Adj.* dwarfish

**Zwerg·huhn** *das* bantam

**Zwergin** *die;* **~, ~nen** dwarf

**zwerg-, Zwerg-: ~pudel** *der* miniature *or* toy poodle; **~schule** *die* single-class school; **~staat** *der* miniature state; **~wuchs** *der* (*Biol.*) dwarfism *no art.;* stunted growth *no art.;* **~wüchsig** /-vy:ksɪç/ *Adj.* (*Biol.*) dwarf-like ‹race, people›; dwarf, miniature ‹tree, plant›

**Zwetsche** /'tsvɛtʃə/ *die;* **~, ~n** Ⓐ damson plum; Ⓑ (*Baum*) damson plum [tree]

**Zwetschen-: ~baum** *der* damson plum tree; **~kern** *der* plum stone; **~kuchen** *der* plum flan; **~mus** *das* plum purée; **~schnaps** *der,* **~wasser** *das; Pl.* **~wässer** plum brandy

**Zwetschge** /'tsvɛtʃgə/ *die;* **~, ~n** (*bes. südd., schweiz.*) ⇒ **Zwetsche**

**Zwetschken·knödel** /'tsvɛtʃkn̩-/ *der* (*Kochk.*) plum dumpling

**Zwickel** /'tsvɪkl̩/ *der;* **~s, ~** Ⓐ (*Schneiderei*) gusset; Ⓑ (*Archit.*) spandrel; (*einer Kuppel*) pendentive; Ⓒ (*salopp*) ⇒ **Zweimarkstück**

**zwicken** /'tsvɪkn̩/ ❶ *tr., auch itr. V.* (*bes. südd., österr.*) Ⓐ pinch; **jmdm.** *od.* **jmdn. in den Arm ~:** pinch sb.'s arm; Ⓑ (*plagen*) **jmdn. ~:** give sb. twinges; **es zwickte und zwackte ihn überall** he had twinges *or* little aches and pains all over. ❷ *itr. V.* ‹trousers, skirt› pinch

**Zwicker** *der;* **~s, ~:** pince-nez

**Zwick·mühle** *die* Ⓐ double mill; Ⓑ (*fig.: Dilemma*) dilemma; **in der ~ sitzen** *od.* **sein** *od.* **stecken** be in a dilemma

**Zwie·back** /'tsvi:bak/ *der;* **~[e]s, ~e** *od.* **Zwiebäcke** /'tsvi:bɛkə/ rusk; (*unzählbar*) rusks *pl.*

*old spelling (see note on page 1707)

Z

**Zwiebel** /ˈt͡sviːbl̩/ *die;* ~, ~**n** Ⓐ onion; (*Blumen*~) bulb; Ⓑ (*ugs. scherzh.: Taschenuhr*) pocket watch; turnip (*sl.*); Ⓒ (*ugs. scherzh.: Haarknoten*) bun

**Zwiebel-:** ~**kuchen** *der* (*Kochk.*) onion pie; ~**muster** *das* onion pattern

**zwiebeln** *tr. V.* (*ugs.*) keep on at ‹person›; give ‹person› a hard time

**Zwiebel-:** ~**ring** *der* onion ring; ~**schale** *die* onion skin; ~**suppe** *die* onion soup; ~**turm** *der* onion tower

**zwie-**, **Zwie-:** ~**fach** *Adj.*; *adv.* (*veralt.*) ⇒ **zweifach**; ~**fältig** *Adj.*; *adv.* (*veralt.*) ⇒ **zweifach**; ~**gespräch** *das* (*geh.*) dialogue; ~**laut** *der* (*Sprachw.*) diphthong; ~**licht** *das* Ⓐ (*Dämmerlicht*) twilight; Ⓑ (*Mischung von Dämmer- und Kunstlicht*) half-light (*that is unpleasant for the eye*); Ⓒ **ins** ~**licht geraten** (*fig.*) become suspect; ‹person› come under suspicion; ~**lichtig** *Adj.* shady; dubious; ~**spalt** *der;* ~~**[e]s**, ~~**e** *od.* ~**spälte** /-ʃpɛltə/ Ⓐ ([*innerer*] *Widerspruch*) [inner] conflict; **in einen** ~**spalt geraten** get into a state of conflict; Ⓑ (*Kluft*) rift; split; ~**spältig** /-ʃpɛltɪç/ *Adj.* conflicting ‹mood, feelings›; discordant ‹impression›; (*widersprüchlich*) contradictory ‹nature, attitude, person, etc.›; ~**spältigkeit** *die;* ~~: conflicting *or* contradictory nature; ~**sprache** *die* (*geh.*) dialogue; **mit jmdm./etw.** ~**sprache halten** commune with sb./sth.; ~**tracht** *die* (*geh.*) discord; ~**tracht säen** sow the seeds of discord

**Zwille** /ˈt͡svɪlə/ *die;* ~, ~**n** (*nordd.*) Ⓐ ⇒ **Astgabel**; Ⓑ (*Schleuder*) catapult

**Zwilling** /ˈt͡svɪlɪŋ/ *der;* ~**s**, ~**e** Ⓐ twin; Ⓑ *Pl.* (*Astrol.*) Gemini; the Twins; **er/sie ist [ein]** ~: he/she is a Gemini

**Zwillings-:** ~**bruder** *der* twin brother; ~**geburt** *die* twin birth; ~**paar** *das* pair of twins; ~**schwester** *die* twin sister

**Zwing·burg** *die* fortress, stronghold (*for the subjugation of the population*)

**zwingen** /ˈt͡svɪŋən/ ❶ *unr. tr. V.* Ⓐ force; **jmdn. zu etw.** ~, **jmdn. [dazu]** ~, **etw. zu tun** force *or* compel sb. to do sth.; make sb. do sth.; **jmdn. zu einem Geständnis** ~: force sb. into a confession *or* to make a confession; **sich zu etw. gezwungen sehen** find oneself forced *or* compelled to do sth.; **man kann ihn nicht dazu** ~: he can't be forced *or* made to do it; Ⓑ (*geh.*) **jmdn. in/auf** *usw.* **etw.** (*Akk.*) ~: force sb. into/on to *etc.* sth.
❷ *unr. refl. V.* force oneself; **sich [dazu]** ~, **etw. zu tun** force oneself to do sth.; **sich zum Schreiben/Essen** ~: force oneself to write/make oneself eat; ⇒ *auch* **gezwungen** 2, 3

**zwingend** *Adj.* compelling ‹reason, logic›; conclusive ‹proof, argument›; imperative, absolute ‹necessity›

**Zwinger** *der;* ~**s**, ~ Ⓐ (*Hunde*~) kennel; (*ganze Anlage, auch Zucht*) kennels *pl.*; Ⓑ (*Gehege*) compound; enclosure; (*für Bären*) bear pit

**zwinkern** /ˈt͡svɪŋkɐn/ *itr. V.* **[mit den Augen]** ~: blink; (*als Zeichen*) wink; **jmdn.** ~**d ansehen** wink at sb.; look at sb. with a wink

**zwirbeln** /ˈt͡svɪrbl̩n/ *tr. V.* twirl; twist

**Zwirn** /t͡svɪrn/ *der;* ~**[e]s**, ~**e** [strong] thread *or* yarn

**Zwirns·faden** *der* [strong] thread

**zwischen** /ˈt͡svɪʃn̩/ *Präp. mit Dat./Akk.* Ⓐ (*räumlich, zeitlich, fig.*) between; Ⓑ (*räumlich: unter, inmitten*) among[st]

**zwischen-**, **Zwischen-:** ~**akt** *der* interlude; ~**akt·musik** *die* incidental music; (*einzelnes Stück*) entr'acte; ~**applaus** *der* spontaneous applause (*during a performance*); ~**aufenthalt** *der* stopover; ~**bemerkung** *die* interjection; ~**bescheid** *der* provisional notification; (*Entscheidung*) interim decision; ~**bilanz** *die* (*Wirtsch.*) interim balance; (*fig.*) provisional appraisal; ~**blutung** *die* (*Med.*) intermenstrual *or* mid-cyclical bleeding; ~**buch·handel** *der* wholesale book trade; ~**deck** *das* (*Schiffbau*) Ⓐ 'tween-deck; Ⓑ (*Raum*) 'tween-decks *sing.*; **im** ~**deck** 'tween-decks; ~**ding** *das* ⇒ **Mittelding**; ~**drin** /-ˈ-/ *Adv.* (*ugs.*) ⇒ ~**durch** A; ~**durch** /-ˈ-/ *Adv.* Ⓐ (*zeitlich*) between times; (~ *zwei Zeitpunkten*) in between; (*von Zeit zu Zeit*) from time to time; (*in der* ~*zeit*) in the mean time; **das mache ich mal irgendwann** ~**durch** I'll fit that in whenever I have time; **iss nicht so viel** ~**durch** don't eat so much between meals; Ⓑ (*räumlich*) here and there; ~**eis·zeit** *die* interglacial period; ~**ergebnis** *das* interim result; (*einer Untersuchung*) interim findings *pl.*; (*Sport*) latest score; ~**examen** *das* ⇒ ~**prüfung**; ~**fall** *der* incident; **es kam zu schweren/blutigen** ~**fällen** there were serious/violent incidents; ~**frage** *die* question; **jmdm. eine** ~**frage stellen** interrupt sb. to ask a question; ~**gas** *das* (*Kfz-W.*) ~**gas geben** *od.* **mit** ~**gas schalten** double-declutch; ~**gericht** *das* (*Kochk.*) entrée (*Brit.*); ~**geschoss**, *~**geschoß** *das* mezzanine; ~**größe** *die* intermediate size; (*bei Schuhen*) half-size; ~**handel** *der* (*Wirtsch.*) intermediate trade; (*Großhandel*) wholesale trade; (~*händler*) middleman; ~**händler** *der* (*Wirtsch.*) middleman; (*fig.*) go-between; ~**hirn** *das* ▶ 471 (*Anat.*) diencephalon; ~**hoch** *das* (*Met.*) ridge of high pressure; ~**kiefer[knochen]** *der* ▶ 471 (*Anat.*) intermaxillary; premaxilla; ~**lager** *das* temporary *or* interim storage facility; ~**lagern** *tr. V.* store temporarily; ~|**landen** *itr. V.*; *mit sein* **in X** ~**landen** land in X on the way; ~**landung** *die* stopover; ~**lauf** *der* (*Sport*) [intermediate] heat; ~**lösung** *die* interim solution; ~**mahlzeit** *die* snack [between meals]; ~**menschlich** ❶ *Adj.* interpersonal ‹relations›; ‹contacts› between people; ❷ *adv.* on a personal level; ~**musik** *die* musical interlude; ~**prüfung** *die* intermediate examination; ~**raum** *der* space; gap; (*Lücke*) gap; **eine Zeile** ~**raum lassen** leave a space of one line; (*Maschinenschreiben*) double-space; ~**reich** *das* (*geh.*) twilight world; ~**ruf** *der* interruption; **viele** ~**rufe** a great deal of heckling *sing.*; ~**rufer** *der*, ~**ruferin** *die* heckler; ~**runde** *die* (*Sport*) intermediate round; ~**satz** *der* (*Sprachw.*) parenthetic clause; parenthesis; ~|**schalten** *tr. V.* (*Elektrot.*) insert ‹resistance, amplifier, etc.› in a circuit; ~**spiel** *das* (*Musik-, Theaterstück*) intermezzo; (*in einem Solokonzert/Gesangsstück*) linking passage; (*fig.*) interlude; ~**spurt** *der* (*Sport*) spurt; burst [of speed]; ~**staatlich** *Adj.* international; ~**stadium** *das* intermediate stage; ~**station** *die* Ⓐ stop; stopping place; Ⓑ (~*aufenthalt*) stop; **dort machten wir einen Tag** ~**station** we stopped there for a day; ~**stecker** *der* (*Elektrot.*) adaptor; ~**stück** *das* connecting *or* middle piece; (*Verbindungsstück*) connector; (*Adapter*) adaptor; ~**stufe** *die* intermediate stage; ~**summe** *die* subtotal; ~**text** *der* linking text; ~**ton** *der; Pl.* ~**töne** shade; nuance; (*fig.*) nuance; ~**tür** *die* connecting door; ~**wand** *die* dividing wall; partition; ~**wirt** *der* (*Biol., Med.*) intermediate host; ~**zeit** *die* Ⓐ interim; (*länger*) intervening period; **in der** ~**zeit** in the mean time; Ⓑ (*Sport*) split time; ~**zeitlich** *Adv.* (*bes. Amtsspr.*) in the mean time; ~**zeugnis** *das* (*Schulw.*) intermediate report; (*Arbeitswelt*) [intermediate] performance appraisal

**Zwist** /t͡svɪst/ *der;* ~**[e]s**, ~**e** (*geh.*) strife *no indef. art.*; (*Fehde*) feud; dispute; **in** *od.* **im** ~ **leben** live in a state of strife; **den alten** ~ **begraben** bury the hatchet

**Zwistigkeit** *die;* ~, ~**en** (*geh.*) dispute

**zwitschern** /ˈt͡svɪt͡ʃɐn/ ❶ *itr.* (*auch tr.*) *V.* chirp. ❷ *tr. V.* *in* **einen** ~ (*salopp*) have a drink

**Zwitter** /ˈt͡svɪtɐ/ *der;* ~**s**, ~ (*Biol., Med.*) hermaphrodite; **ein** ~ **aus A und B** (*fig.*) a cross between A and B

**Zwitter·stellung** *die* ambiguous position

**zwittrig** *Adj.* (*Biol., Med.*) hermaphroditic

**zwo** /t͡svoː/ *Kardinalz.* ▶ 841 (*ugs.; bes. zur Verdeutlichung*) ⇒ **zwei**

**zwölf** /t͡svœlf/ *Kardinalz.* ▶ 76, ▶ 752, ▶ 841 twelve; ~ **Uhr mittags/nachts** [twelve o'clock] midday/midnight; **es ist fünf [Minuten] vor** ~ (*fig.*) we are on the brink; ⇒ *auch* **acht**[1]

**zwölf-**, **Zwölf-** twelve-; ⇒ *auch* **acht-**, **Acht-**

**Zwölf** *die;* ~, ~**en** twelve; ⇒ *auch* **Acht**[1] A, E, G

**Zwölf-:** ~**eck** *das* (*Geom.*) dodecagon; ~**ender** *der;* ~~**s**, ~~: Ⓐ (*Jägerspr.*) royal [stag]; Ⓑ (*scherzh. veralt.*) *soldier with twelve years service*

**Zwölfer** *der;* ~**s**, ~: twelve; ⇒ *auch* **Achter** C, D

**zwölferlei** *Gattungsz.; indekl.* Ⓐ *attr.* twelve sorts *or* kinds of; twelve different ‹sorts, sizes, etc.›; Ⓑ *subst.* twelve [different] things

**zwölf-**, **Zwölf-:** ~**fach** *Vervielfältigungsz.* twelvefold; **die** ~**fache Menge** twelve times the quantity; ⇒ *auch* **achtfach**; ~**fache** *das; adj. Dekl.*; **das** ~**fache** twelve times as much; **um ein** ~**faches** *od.* **um das** ~**fache** twelve times; ⇒ *auch* **Achtfache**; ~**finger·darm** *der* ▶ 471 (*Anat.*) duodenum; ~**fingerdarm·geschwür** *das* ▶ 474 (*Med.*) duodenal ulcer; ~**hundert** *Kardinalz.* ▶ 841 one thousand two hundred; twelve hundred; ~**jährig** *Adj.* (*12 Jahre alt*) twelve-year-old *attrib.*; twelve years old *pred.*; (*12 Jahre dauernd*) twelve-year *attrib.*; ⇒ *auch* **achtjährig**; ~**kampf** *der* (*Turnen*) twelve-exercise event; ~**mal** *Adv.* twelve times; ⇒ *auch* **achtmal**; ~**meilen·zone** /-ˈ----/ *die* twelve-mile zone

**zwölft** /t͡svœlft/ *in* **wir waren zu** ~: there were twelve of us; ⇒ *auch* **acht**[2]

**zwölft...** *Ordinalz.* ▶ 207, ▶ 841 twelfth; ⇒ *auch* **acht...**

**zwölf·tausend** *Kardinalz.* twelve thousand

**zwölf·teilig** *Adj.* twelve-piece ‹set›; twelve-part ‹serial etc.›; ⇒ *auch* **achtteilig**

**zwölftel** *Bruchz.* ▶ 841 twelfth; ⇒ *auch* **achtel**

**Zwölftel** *das* (*schweiz. meist der*) ~**s**, ~ ▶ 841 twelfth

*__zwölfte·mal__, *__zwölften·mal__ ⇒ **Mal**[1]

**zwölftens** *Adv.* twelfthly

**Zwölf·ton·musik** *die* twelve-tone music

**zwot...** /t͡svoːt.../ *Ordinalz.* (*ugs.; bes. bei Datumsangaben*) ⇒ **zweit...**

**zwotens** *Adv.* (*ugs.*) secondly

**Zyan** /t͡sy̆aːn/ *das;* ~**s** (*Chemie*) cyanogen

**Zyanid** /t͡sy̆aˈniːt/ *das;* ~**s**, ~**e** (*Chemie*) cyanide

**Zyan·kali** *das;* ~**s** (*Chemie*) potassium cyanide

**Zyklen** ⇒ **Zyklus**

**zyklisch** /ˈt͡syːklɪʃ/ ❶ *Adj.* cyclic[al]. ❷ *adv.* cyclically; as a cycle

**Zykloide** /t͡sykloˈiːdə/ *die;* ~, ~**n** (*Math.*) cycloid

**Zyklon** /t͡syˈkloːn/ *der;* ~**s**, ~**e** (*Met.*) cyclone

**Zyklop** /t͡syˈkloːp/ *der;* ~**en**, ~**en** (*griech. Myth.*) Cyclops

**Zyklopen·mauer** *die* (*Archäol., Bauw.*) Cyclopean wall

**zyklothym** /t͡sykloˈtyːm/ *Adj.* (*Psych., Med.*) cyclothymic

**Zyklotron** /ˈt͡syːklotroːn/ *das;* ~**s**, ~**s** *od.* ~**e** (*Kernphysik*) cyclotron

**Zyklus** /ˈt͡syːklʊs/ *der;* ~, **Zyklen** (*auch Math.*) cycle

**Zylinder** /t͡siˈlɪndɐ/ *der;* ~**s**, ~ Ⓐ (*Geom., Technik*) cylinder; (*einer Lampe*) chimney; Ⓑ (*Hut*) top hat

**Zylinder-:** ~**hut** *der* top hat; ~**kopf** *der* cylinder head

**zylindrisch** ❶ *Adj.* cylindrical. ❷ *adv.* cylindrically

**Zyniker** *der;* ~**s**, ~, **Zynikerin** *die;* ~, ~**nen** cynic

**zynisch** /ˈt͡syːnɪʃ/ ❶ *Adj.* cynical. ❷ *adv.* cynically

**Zynismus** *der;* ~, **Zynismen** Ⓐ cynicism; Ⓑ (*Äußerung*) cynical remark

**Zypern** /ˈtsy:pɐn/ *(das);* **~s** Cyprus
**Zyprer** /ˈtsy:prɐ/ *der;* **~s,** **~,** **Zyprerin** *die;* **~,** **~nen** Cypriot
**Zypresse** /tsyˈprɛsə/ *die;* **~,** **~n** cypress
**Zypriot** /tsypriˈo:t/ *der;* **~en,** **~en,** **Zypriotin** *die;* **~,** **~nen** ▶ 553 Cypriot
**zypriotisch, zyprisch** *Adj.* ▶ 553 Cypriot
**Zyste** /ˈtsystə/ *die;* **~,** **~n** ▶ 474 *(Med.)* cyst
**Zytologie** /tsytoloˈgi:/ *die;* **~** *(Biol.)* cytology *no art.*
**z. Z., z. Zt.** *Abk.* **zur Zeit**

Z

# German correspondence



····➤ You will also find useful information in the lexical boxes **Letter writing** and **Greetings**.

### Invitation to a wedding

Sehr geehrte Frau Gustav,
sehr geehrter Herr Gustav,

am Donnerstag, den 2. Mai 1998 heiratet unsere Tochter Christa. Sie haben ihre Vermählungsanzeige sicher bereits erhalten. Wir als Brauteltern möchten Sie nun ganz persönlich zur Feier einladen, denn Sie haben viele Jahre als Freunde des Hauses den Lebensweg unserer Tochter begleitet. Bitte machen Sie uns die Freude und nehmen Sie an ihrer Hochzeit teil.

Ursula und Dieter Zimmermann

### Accepting a wedding invitation

Sehr geehrte Frau Heiner,
sehr geehrter Herr Heiner,

vielen Dank für die Einladung zur Hochzeit Ihrer Tochter.

Es freut uns sehr, dass Sie uns zu den Freunden Ihrer Familie zählen, und wir werden selbstverständlich gerne kommen.

Mit den besten Grüßen

Lotte und Franz Dernbach

### Good wishes for the New Year

Harfenstr. 17 30.12.98
90081 Würzburg

Liebe Karin, lieber Ferdinand,

euch und euren Kindern wünsche ich von Herzen ein glückliches neues Jahr. Ich hoffe, ihr hattet ein schönes Weihnachtsfest und es geht euch allen gut. Es kommt mir vor, als hätten wir uns eine Ewigkeit nicht gesehen.

Für mich wird das neue Jahr wohl ziemlich unruhig werden, denn ich will meine Wohnung verkaufen. Ich möchte mir ein kleines Haus etwas näher an meinem Arbeitsort kaufen.

Ich würde euch sehr gerne mal wieder sehen. Ich schlage vor, dass wir uns am Abend in der Stadt treffen, wenn ihr das nächste Mal in Würzburg seid. Ruft doch einfach ein paar Tage vorher an, damit wir etwas ausmachen können.

Mit herzlichen Grüßen

Euer Thomas

### Thanks for New Year wishes

Dürerstraße 8 08.01.98
59272 Ahlen

Liebe Helen,

ganz vielen Dank für deine guten Wünsche zum neuen Jahr. Ich habe mich sehr gefreut, nach so langer Zeit mal wieder ein Lebenszeichen von dir zu bekommen und zu erfahren, wie es dir in der letzten Zeit ergangen ist. Ich werde dir einen "richtigen" Brief schreiben, sobald ich etwas mehr Zeit habe. Heute wollte ich dir nur schnell sagen, wie sehr ich mich darüber freue, dass wir wieder Kontakt miteinander haben. Außerdem möchte ich vorschlagen, dass ihr mich besucht, wenn du im Februar mit John in Deutschland bist. Ihr könntet dann gerne bei mir wohnen. Das Haus bietet reichlich Platz.

Herzliche Grüße

Deine Karin

### Condolences: formal

Calvinstr. 89 30.10.98
63540 Hanau

Sehr geehrte Frau Aichstädter,

gestern haben wir vom Tod Ihres Gatten erfahren. Wir waren davon sehr betroffen und fühlen uns in Ihrer Trauer mit Ihnen verbunden.

Wir hoffen, dass Sie in Ihrer großen Familie die teilnehmende Unterstützung erfahren, die Ihnen helfen wird, über den schmerzlichen Verlust hinwegzukommen.

Mit stillem Gruß

Ihre Hanna und Karl Moser

### Thanks for condolences: formal

Martinstraße 9 20.9.98
45130 Essen

Sehr geehrter Herr Knopf,

für Ihre Anteilnahme und Ihre freundlichen Worte des Trostes danke ich Ihnen von Herzen. Auch dafür, dass Sie mir Ihre tatkräftige Unterstützung angeboten haben, möchte ich mich herzlich bedanken. Es ist gut zu wissen, dass ich jederzeit darauf zurückkommen kann - auch wenn ich im Moment glücklicherweise mit allem einigermaßen zurechtkomme.

Herzliche Grüße von Ihrer

Adelheid Bauer

### Condolences: informal

Burgweg 45
73033 Göppingen

4. Juni 1998

Liebe Frau Haberer,

über den Tod Ihres Mannes sind wir sehr traurig. Wir haben mit ihm einen wirklichen Freund verloren, der - wenn auch nur über den nachbarlichen Gartenzaun hinweg - an unserem Leben immer freundlichen Anteil nahm und uns nicht selten Trost und Rat spendete. Wir werden ihn vermissen.

Bitte lassen Sie es uns doch wissen, wenn wir Ihnen auf irgendeine Weise helfen können.

In herzlichem Gedenken

Ihre Marion und Walter König

### Thanks for condolences: informal

An der Tonkuhle 26. 3. 97
26131 Oldenburg

Liebe Frau Seitz,

mit dem lieben Brief, den Sie mir aus Anlass des plötzlichen Todes meines geliebten Mannes geschrieben haben, haben Sie mir sehr geholfen. Ich danke Ihnen von ganzem Herzen.

Dafür, dass Sie an der Beerdigung nicht teilnehmen konnten, habe ich selbstverständlich das größte Verständnis. Aber wenn Sie es einrichten können, besuchen Sie mich doch in der nächsten Zeit einmal. Sie würden mir damit wirklich eine große Freude machen.

Herzlichst

Ihre Marianne Becker

### Thanking for a wedding gift

Häherweg 9
81827 München

23. Juli 98

Liebe Kathleen, lieber Douglas,

wir möchten euch ganz herzlich für den wunderschönen Fotoband über Schottland danken, den ihr uns zu unserer Hochzeit geschenkt habt. Er erinnert uns so an unsere Zeit in Glasgow und an die Freunde, die wir dort seitdem haben.

Auch war es schön, mal wieder zu hören, wie es euch geht. Kommt doch bei Gelegenheit mal bei uns vorbei. Wir haben jetzt viel Platz und würden uns freuen, wenn ihr uns für ein paar Tage besuchen würdet.

Herzliche Grüße

Eure Lisa und Dirk

### Enquiry to the tourist office

Silvia Sommer
Tannenweg 23
48149 Münster

24. April 1998

Verkehrsverein Heidelberg e. V.
Friedrich-Ebert-Anlage 2
69117 Heidelberg

Hotels und Pensionen in Heidelberg

Sehr geehrte Damen und Herren,

würden Sie mir bitte freundlicherweise eine Liste der Hotels und Pensionen (der mittleren Kategorie) am Ort zusenden?

Daneben bin ich an Informationen über Busfahrten zu den Sehenswürdigkeiten der Umgebung in der zweiten Augusthälfte interessiert.

Mit vielem Dank im Voraus und freundlichen Grüßen

Silvia Sommer

Silvia Sommer

### Booking a hotel room

Theodor Schnebel
Weerthplatz 6
32756 Detmold

24.02.98

Hotel "Goldener Pflug"
Ortsstraße 7
69235 Steinbach

Zimmerreservierung 2. - 11. 8. 98

Sehr geehrte Damen und Herren,

ich wurde durch die Broschüre "Hotels und Pensionen im Naturpark Odenwald" (Ausgabe 1997) auf ihr Haus aufmerksam.

Ich würde gerne für die Zeit vom 2. bis 11. August (neun Nächte) ein ruhiges, möglichst nicht zur Straße gelegenes Doppelzimmer reservieren.

Falls Sie in der fraglichen Zeit etwas Passendes frei haben, informieren Sie mich doch bitte über den Preis und darüber, ob sie eine Anzahlung wünschen.

Mit freundlichen Grüßen

Theodor Schnebel

### Cancelling a hotel booking

Tobias Schwarz
Gartenstr. 19
76530 Baden-Baden

16. Juli 1997

Hotel Deutscher Hof
Hauptstr. 102
68293 Mannheim

Stornierung meiner Zimmerreservierung
(bestätigt mit Schreiben vom 7.7.98)

Sehr geehrte Damen und Herren,

zu meinem Bedauern sehe ich mich genötigt, meine Reservierung für die Zeit vom 2. bis 18. August rückgängig zu machen.

Würden Sie so freundlich sein, den von mir angezahlten Betrag (DM 200,00) auf mein Ihnen bekanntes Konto zurückzuüberweisen?

Mit bestem Dank im Voraus und freundlichen Grüßen

Ihr

Tobias Schwarz

## Letting your house

Marlies Günther
Borkenweg 34
53127 Bonn

12. Mai 1998

Ihr Schreiben vom 8. Mai

Sehr geehrte Frau Schmitt, sehr geehrter Herr Schmitt,

vielen Dank für Ihre Anfrage wegen unseres Ferienhauses, das in der von Ihnen genannten Zeit noch frei ist.

Das Haus hat drei Schlafzimmer, zwei Bäder, ein großes Wohnzimmer, ein Esszimmer, eine Küche und einen etwa sechshundert Quadratmeter großen Garten. Alle wichtigen Läden sind in etwa fünf Minuten zu Fuß zu erreichen. Großenkneten ist ein kleines Dorf im Naturpark Wildeshauser Geest, nur etwa vierzig Autominuten von Bremen entfernt.

Die Miete beträgt 900,00 DM pro Woche. Eine Anzahlung von zehn Prozent, zahlbar sofort nach Vertragsabschluss, dient uns als Sicherheit. Sie wird im Falle Ihres Rücktritts nicht erstattet. Der Restbetrag ist spätestens eine Woche nach Ende des Aufenthalts fällig.

Zu Ihrer Information legen wir diesem Schreiben ein Foto unseres Hauses bei.

Wir würden uns freuen, bald von Ihnen zu hören.

Mit freundlichen Grüßen

Marlies Günter

Marlies Günther

## Renting a holiday house

FELIX SONDERMANN
XANTENER STRAßE 89
46286 DORSTEN

4. April 98

Ihre Anzeige in der "Zeit"

Sehr geehrte Frau Kaiser, sehr geehrter Herr Kaiser,

ich habe ihre Annonce in der "Zeit" gelesen und bin eventuell daran interessiert, Ihr Ferienhaus in Dänemark für zwei Wochen im Juli zu mieten. Wären Sie so freundlich, mir mitzuteilen, ob und gegebenenfalls wann das Haus im Juli noch zu haben ist?

Falls es bereits vergeben ist, wüsste ich gern, ob die Möglichkeit besteht, es im nächsten Jahr für zwei Wochen im August zu mieten. (Ich kenne die Gegend, in der es liegt, bereits von einem früheren Aufenthalt und möchte sehr gerne wieder einmal ein paar Wochen dort verbringen.)

Ich freue mich darauf, von Ihnen zu hören.

Mit freundlichen Grüßen

Felix Sondermann

## Booking a caravan site

Willi Schenk 16.06.97
Austraße 8
90763 Fürth

Herrn Arthur Müller
56789 Waldfeld
Dorfstr. 31

Stellplatzreservierung

Sehr geehrter Herr Müller,

ich habe Ihre Anschrift dem ACDA-Campingführer 1996 entnommen und möchte für die Woche von Sonntag, 17.8. bis Samstag, 24.8. einen Stellplatz für einen Wohnanhänger reservieren. Ich würde mit meiner Frau und unseren drei Kindern kommen.

Würden Sie mir freundlicherweise mitteilen, ob Sie meine Reservierung annehmen können und ob Sie gegebenenfalls eine Anzahlung wünschen?

Außerdem wäre ich Ihnen dankbar für eine kurze Wegbeschreibung von der Autobahn A 3 aus, auf der wir aus südlicher Richtung anreisen würden.

Ich freue mich darauf, bald von Ihnen zu hören und verbleibe mit freundlichen Grüßen

Ihr

W. Schenk

W. Schenk

## Enquiry to a caravan site

**Camilla Stumpf**
**Saalgasse 10**
**60311 Frankfurt**

02.05.97

Camping am See
Frau Bettina Sattler
Auweg 6-10
87654 Waldenkirchen

Reservierung eines Mietwohnwagens

Sehr geehrte Frau Sattler,

Ihre Anlage wurde mir von meinem Bekannten Herrn Stephan Seidel empfohlen, der, wie Sie wissen, schon mehrmals bei Ihnen Urlaub gemacht hat. Ich würde nun gerne mit meinen beiden Söhnen (neun und vierzehn Jahre alt) drei Wochen im Juli bei Ihnen verbringen.

Würden Sie mir freundlicherweise nähere Informationen über die in dieser Zeit noch zur Verfügung stehenden Wohnwagen und deren Mietpreise geben? Außerdem wäre ich Ihnen dankbar, wenn Sie mir Informationsmaterial über die Gegend zukommen lassen könnten.

Mit vielem Dank im Voraus und freundlichen Grüßen

Camilla Stumpf

Camilla Stumpf

### Asking for a theatre programme listing

Georg Dorn
Peiner Landstraße 78
31135 Hildesheim

12. Mai 1998

Hotel Stetter
Gartenstr. 32
26122 Oldenburg

Sehr geehrte Damen und Herren,

meine Frau und ich werden in der Woche vom 19. bis 25. Juli in Ihrem Hause zu Gast sein (Reservierung vom 27. 6.) und möchten Sie um eine kleine Gefälligkeit bitten: Würden Sie so freundlich sein und uns einen Spielplan des Staatstheaters sowie Informationen über Reservierungsmöglichkeiten besorgen? Sollten Sie dazu nicht in der Lage sein, so teilen Sie uns doch bitte mit, an welche Stelle wir uns wenden können.

Wir freuen uns sehr auf unseren Aufenthalt bei Ihnen.

Mit freundlichen Grüßen

Georg Dorn

### To a teacher: apologizing for sick child's absence

Johannes Timm
Ahornstraße 40
40667 Meerbusch

09.11.98

Städtisches Gymnasium
Frau Oberstudienrätin
Dr. Mara Kunze
Lessingstraße 67
40666 Meerbusch

Sehr geehrte Frau Dr. Kunze,

unsere Tochter Elke liegt mit einer fiebrigen Erkältung im Bett. Der Arzt sagte, wir sollten sie frühestens in der nächsten Woche wieder zur Schule schicken.

Bitte entschuldigen Sie ihr Fehlen. Vielen Dank.

Mit freundlichen Grüßen

Ihr

Johannes Timm

### To a school about admission

Sheila Evans-Wüst
35 Prince Edward Road
Oxford OX7 3AA

23. Februar 1998

Herrn Oberstudiendirektor
Dr. Erwin Kachelmann
Lessinggymnasium
Kantstraße 9
79797 Freiburg

Sehr geehrter Herr Dr. Kachelmann,

wir werden im Sommer dieses Jahres von England nach Freiburg ziehen und sind auf der Suche nach einem passenden Gymnasium für unseren zehnjährigen Sohn Jakob. Jakob ist, da mein Mann Deutscher ist, zweisprachig und hat die Grundschule in Oxford absolviert.

Das Lessinggymnasium wurde uns von Herrn und Frau Sautter empfohlen, deren Tochter Clara Ihre Schule seit zwei Jahren besucht.

Wenn Sie bereit wären, unseren Sohn zum Beginn des neuen Schuljahrs aufzunehmen, würden wir uns freuen, Näheres über die Schule und die Modalitäten der Anmeldung zu erfahren.

Wir werden vom 21. Mai an in Freiburg sein und könnten dann jederzeit zur Besichtigung der Schule und zu einem Gespräch zu Ihnen kommen.

Mit freundlichen Grüßen

Sheila Evans-Wüst

Sheila Evans-Wüst

### To a university about admission as a research student

Thomas Emmler
Donaustr. 56
91052 Erlangen

11.11.98

Herrn
Prof. Dr. Helmut Schulte
Institut für Komparatistik
Peterssstraße 54
28282 Bremen

Sehr geehrter Herr Professor Schulte,

ich wende mich auf Anraten von Herrn Dr. Michael Wagner in Erlangen, der dort meine Magisterarbeit betreut hat, an Sie.

Ich würde gerne an Ihr Institut kommen, um bei Ihnen zu promovieren. Eine Übersicht über meine bisherige Forschungstätigkeit, eine Skizze der mir vorschwebenden Dissertation sowie ein Lebenslauf liegen diesem Schreiben bei.

Ich würde mich sehr freuen, wenn Sie bereit wären, mich als Doktoranden anzunehmen. Um mein Vorhaben finanzieren zu können, werde ich gegebenenfalls ein Stipendium der Deutschen Forschungsgemeinschaft beantragen.

Ich freue mich darauf, von Ihnen zu hören und verbleibe mit freundlichen Grüßen

Ihr

Thomas Emmler

Anlagen

### Asking for an estimate

Karl Esser
Karlstraße 23
23554 Lübeck

30.07.98

Firma
Anton Schmidt
Am Graben 8
23456 Lübeck

Sehr geehrter Herr Schmidt,

in dem in meiner oben stehenden Adresse genannten Haus, das ich kürzlich erworben und bezogen habe, sind die Fensterrahmen erneuerungsbedürftig. Ich möchte Sie bitten, mir ein entsprechendes Angebot zu unterbreiten.

Wenn Sie so freundlich sein wollen, mich kurz anzurufen, können wir einen Termin vereinbaren, sodass Sie sich die Fenster zunächst ansehen können.

Mit freundlichen Grüßen

Karl Esser

Karl Esser

### Asking for work to be undertaken

Manfred Scherer
Brahmsbogen 33
06124 Halle

12.09.98

Firma
Sanitär Grimmig
Kanalstraße 25
06060 Halle

Ihr Schreiben vom 09.09.98

Sehr geehrte Damen und Herren,

ich bin mit Ihrem Kostenvoranschlag einverstanden und möchte Ihnen nun den Auftrag erteilen, den verrosteten Heizkörper zu ersetzen.

Bitte teilen Sie mir mit, wann Sie die Arbeiten ausführen können, damit ich es einrichten kann, dass ich zu der Zeit im Hause bin.

Mir würde es am besten an einem Mittwoch- oder Donnerstagnachmittag passen.

Mit freundlichen Grüßen

Manfred Scherer

### Complaining about a delay

Dieter Winterbauer
Bülowstraße 20
10783 Berlin

*9. Mai 1998*

*Bilderrahmungsservice*
*Johannes Schmich*
*Sandweg 8*
*10784 Berlin*

*Sehr geehrter Herr Schmich,*

*ich habe vor sechs Wochen ein großes Ölgemälde zur Rahmung bei Ihnen abgegeben. Seinerzeit haben Sie mir versichert, es würde mir innerhalb von drei Wochen in meine Wohnung geliefert werden. Da es bis heute noch nicht bei mir angekommen ist, frage ich mich, ob es etwa irgendwelche unvorhergesehenen Probleme gibt.*

*Seien Sie bitte so freundlich und rufen Sie mich umgehend an, damit ich erfahre, wann Sie mir das gerahmte Bild zu bringen gedenken. Ich hoffe recht bald, denn ich bin sehr gespannt auf das Ergebnis Ihrer Arbeit.*

*Mit freundlichen Grüßen*

*Dieter Winterbauer*

### Complaining about quality of work

Helmut Sommer
Dolberger Str. 21
59077 Hamm

28. April 1998

Fa.
Klaus & Söhne
Bahnhofstraße 7
59078 Hamm

Reklamation

Sehr geehrte Damen und Herren,

wie ich Ihnen bereits telefonisch mitgeteilt habe, bin ich mit der Ausführung Ihrer Arbeiten am Freisitz meines Hauses keineswegs zufrieden. In dem betonierten Bereich zeigen sich bereits jetzt große Risse und in dem gepflasterten Teil haben sich etliche Steine gelockert oder gesenkt. Abgesehen von der ästhetischen Seite ist es momentan geradezu gefährlich, den Bereich zu betreten.

Ich bitte Sie daher mit Nachdruck, umgehend für Abhilfe zu sorgen.

Ihre Rechnung werde ich selbstverständlich erst begleichen, wenn dies zu meiner vollen Zufriedenheit erfolgt ist.

Mit freundlichen Grüßen

Helmut Sommer

## Looking for a placement in a company

James Carter 30.03.98
67 Liverpool Rd.
Birmingham
BH3 5FF

Fa.
WareSoft GmbH
Frankfurter Str. 78
63067 Offenbach

Bewerbung um eine Praktikantenstelle

Sehr geehrte Damen und Herren,

im Rahmen eines Fortbildungsprogramms im Zusammenhang mit meiner derzeitigen Stelle als Informatiker in Birmingham muss ich im Sommer dieses Jahres für wenigstens zwei Monate in einem deutschsprachigen Land bei einer Firma der Computerbranche arbeiten.

Da ich Ihre Firma durch Frau Jean Evans, die im vorigen Jahr für zwei Monate bei Ihnen war, kenne, erlaube ich mir, bei Ihnen anzufragen, ob Sie mir eine geeignete Praktikantenstelle anbieten könnten.

In der Anlage finden Sie meinen Lebenslauf und ein Empfehlungsschreiben.

In der Hoffnung auf eine positive Antwort verbleibe ich mit freundlichen Grüßen

James Carter

Anlagen

## Enquiring about work[1]

Joseph Bauer 30.04.98
Gotenstraße
81925 München

Frau
Marianne Lösch
Fremdspracheninstitut
Langenbrücker Straße 65
91919 Erlangen

Bewerbung

Sehr geehrte Frau Lösch,

von meinem Kollegen Fritz Langenberg, der bis vor kurzem bei Ihnen beschäftigt war, weiß ich, dass Sie im kommenden September neue Mitarbeiter einstellen wollen.

Ich bin derzeit als Lehrer für Deutsch als Fremdsprache beim Goethe-Institut beschäftigt. Da mein Vertrag jedoch auf Ende Juni dieses Jahres befristet ist, suche ich nach einem neuen Betätigungsfeld.

Wie Sie meinem Lebenslauf entnehmen können, bringe ich die notwendigen Qualifikationen sowie einschlägige Berufserfahrung mit.

Zu einem Vorstellungsgespräch stehe ich ab dem 22. Juni jederzeit zur Verfügung. Sie können mich ab diesem Datum unter der folgenden Adresse erreichen:

c/o Gerber
Voltastraße 67
91056 Erlangen
Tel.: (09131) 786546

Mit freundlichen Grüßen

Joseph Bauer

Anlage

## Enquiring about work[2]

Friederike Sauer
Mühlstr. 65
71640 Ludwigsburg

20. September 1998

Innenarchitekturbüro
Winter & Co.
Kegelstraße 9
70707 Stuttgart

Bewerbung

Sehr geehrte Damen und Herren,

ich wende mich an Sie in der Hoffnung, dass Sie mir eventuell eine Stelle anbieten können. Wie Sie meinem Lebenslauf entnehmen können, bin ich diplomierte Innenarchitektin und verfüge über beträchtliche Berufserfahrung. Ich bin erst kürzlich aus Paris zurückgekehrt, wo ich die letzten fünf Jahre tätig war, und habe nun den Wunsch, in einem kleinen Team hier im Stuttgarter Raum zu arbeiten.

Ich hoffe, von Ihnen zu hören, und würde Ihnen gerne auch Arbeitsproben vorlegen.

Mit freundlichen Grüßen

Friederike Sauer

Anlage

## Replying to a job advertisement

Ernst Wagner 30.02.98
Jörgstr. 65
74076 Heilbronn

Softwarehaus
WSO GmbH
Kanalstr. 75
75757 Pforzheim

Ihre Stellenanzeige im Tagblatt vom 12.02.98

Sehr geehrte Damen und Herren,

ich interessiere mich für die von Ihnen im "Tagblatt" vom 12. Februar ausgeschriebene Stelle eines Programmierers und würde mich freuen, wenn Sie mir nähere Informationen über die Stelle sowie ein Bewerbungsformular zuschicken könnten.

Ich bin derzeit auf der Basis eines demnächst auslaufenden Zeitvertrags bei der Firma WareSoft GmbH in Heilbronn tätig und verfüge über die geforderten Qualifikationen sowie über enschlägige Berufserfahrung

Ich freue mich darauf, von Ihnen zu hören.

Mit freudlichen Grußen

Ernst Wagner

Curriculum Vitae[1]

## Lebenslauf

Gerd Seibelt
Schillerweg 16
51143 Köln

Tel. (02 21) 53 19 67

geboren am 30. 06. 1960 in Köln, ledig

**Ausbildung**

| | |
|---|---|
| 1976 | mittlere Reife, Theodor-Heuss-Realschule Köln |
| 1976 - 1979 | Lehre zum Industriekaufmann bei der Schmidt OHG, Düsseldorf |
| | Abschlussprüfung: gut |
| 1981 - 1984 | Abendgymnasium in Düsseldorf, Abschluss Abitur |

**Berufstätigkeit**

| | |
|---|---|
| 08/79 - 12/85 | Sachbearbeiter Rechnungslegung, Schmidt OHG, Düsseldorf |
| | Hausinterne Fortbildung zum Fachwirt Personalwesen |
| 01/86 - 09/90 | Gruppenleiter in der Personalabteilung, Schnodt & Mai, Köln |
| | Verantwortlich für Auszubildende, Praktikanten, Aushilfskräfte |
| seit 10/90 | Leiter der Personalabteilung, Schnodt & Mai, Köln |
| | Übernahme aller personalwirtschaflichen Aufgaben, insbesondere |
| | Entwicklung eines hausinternen Fortbildungswesens |
| | Begleitend verschiedene Führungskräfteseminare (z. B. Motivation von Mitarbeitern) |

Curriculum Vitae[2]

**Andrea Krauße - Wendlandstr. 13 - 81249 München - (0 89) 13 07 25**

| | |
|---|---|
| **Geburtdatum, -ort** | 22.02.1960, Heidelberg |
| **Familienstand** | ledig |
| **Schulbildung, -abschluss** | mittlere Reife<br>Realschule II, Heidelberg |
| **Berufsausbildung** | kaufmännische Lehre<br>Abschlussprüfung 1982: sehr gut |
| **Besondere Kenntnisse** | gute Englischkenntnisse (Wirtschaftsenglisch)<br>Steno: 180 Silben<br>400 Schreibmaschinenanschläge<br>Textverarbeitung (Word 6)<br>Computer-"Führerschein" |
| **Jetzige Position** | Direktionssekretärin |

| **Datum**<br>VON BIS | **Praktische Tätigkeiten** | **Fortbildung** |
|---|---|---|
| **09/77 - 12/82** | kaufmännische Lehre<br>Walter Hoffmann, Heidelberg<br>Verpackungsmaschinen | Abendlehrgang<br>Abschluss: gepr. Sekretärin |
| **01/83 - 08/88** | Abteilungssekretärin<br>Feldmeier AG, Stuttgart<br>Papierwarenfabrik | 2-jähr. Abendlehrgang<br>Berlitz-School<br>Abschluss: IHK-gepr. |
| **09/88 - 10/90** | Direktionssekretärin<br>Siemens AG, München<br>Vertrieb | |
| **seit 11/90** | Direktionssekretärin<br>6-monatiger Computerabendkurs<br>Eberhard Zimmer GmbH<br>Textildruckmaschinen, München | ConTrol data:<br>BASIC-Programmierkurs |

Tätigkeitsmerkmale: Selbstständige Korrespondenz in Englisch; Assistenz bei Marketingaufgaben; selbstständige Lohn- und Gehaltsabrechnung aller Mitarbeiter

## Applying for a job as an au pair

Susan Atkins
5 Avon Crescent
Kenilworth
Warwickshire CV8 2PQ

3. März 1998

Frau
Franziska Rosner
Internationale Ferienjob-Agentur
Schillerstaße 32
56566 Koblenz

Aupairstelle in Deutschland

Sehr geehrte Frau Rosner,

ich suche eine Ferienbeschäftigung als Aupairmädchen. Ich habe mit dieser Art Arbeit schon bei mehreren Aufenthalten in der Schweiz Erfahrungen gesammelt. Aber dieses Mal möchte ich gerne nach Deutschland gehen.

In der Anlage finden Sie meinen Lebenslauf sowie die Zeugnisse der drei schweizerischen Familien, bei denen ich war.

Ich könnte von Ende Juni bis Anfang September bleiben. Würden Sie mir bitte mitteilen, ob ich eine Arbeitserlaubnis benötige und ob Sie mir gegebenenfalls eine beschaffen könnten?

Mit vielem Dank im Voraus und freundlichen Grüßen

Susan Atkins

Anlagen

## Offering a job as an au pair

Helga Neubert
Unterseestraße 50
78467 Konstanz

3. April 98

Liebe Julia,

vielen Dank für deine Bewerbung. Von etlichen Bewerberinnen bist du diejenige, der ich die Aupairstelle am liebsten geben möchte.

Könntest du am 5. Juni anfangen und bis zum 5. September bleiben? Dann sind die Ferien zu Ende und unsere Söhne fahren wieder ins Internat.

Wir würden wöchentlich zweihundert Mark bezahlen und du hättest ein eigenes Zimmer und jedes zweite Wochenende frei. Lass es mich bitte wissen, wenn du noch irgendwelche Fragen hast.

Ich würde mich sehr freuen, wenn du unser Angebot annehmen würdest. Bitte gib uns möglichst bald Bescheid.

Beste Grüße

Helga Neubert

## Asking for a reference

Torsten Kruse
Franzstr. 53
47441 Moers

28.11.98

Herrn
Dr. Karsten Matern
Lessingstraße 20
47474 Moers

Sehr geehrter Herr Dr. Matern,

wie Sie ja wissen, ist meine derzeitige Anstellung befristet und wird in etwa drei Monaten auslaufen.

Ich habe mich daher beim Verlag Köpke in Herten um eine Stelle als Korrektor beworben und mir erlaubt, Sie als Referenz anzugeben.

Ich hoffe, dass Sie die Freundlichkeit haben, ein paar Zeilen zu schreiben, falls man Sie darum bitten sollte. Mit ein wenig Glück könnte ich beim Verlag Köpke endlich eine Dauerstellung finden und ich danke Ihnen schon heute für Ihre Hilfe.

Mit freundlichem Gruß

Ihr

Torsten Kruse

## Thanking for a reference

Jens Kettler
Kieselstr.
41472 Neuss

30. April 97

Herrn
Volker Grimm
Turnerstraße 54
51515 Köln

Lieber Herr Grimm,

ich möchte mich ganz herzlich bei Ihnen bedanken. Sie haben mir bei meiner Bewerbung um eine Redakteursstelle beim "Kunstmagazin" durch Ihr Empfehlungsschreiben sehr geholfen.

Ich nehme an, dass es auch Sie freuen wird zu hören, dass man mir den Posten angeboten hat und dass ich bereits in drei Wochen beginnen werde. Ich bin so froh, dass es nun endlich einmal geklappt hat und würde mich am liebsten gleich morgen in die Arbeit stürzen.

Noch einmal ganz herzlichen Dank!

Mit herzlichem Gruß

Ihr

Jens Kettler

## Accepting a job

Oliver Zahn
Hansastr. 43
26723 Emden

31. März 1998

Werbeagentur
Fissler & Partner
Großkopfstr. 44
30303 Hannover

Sehr geehrter Herr Fissler,

ich freue mich sehr, dass Sie sich dafür entschieden haben, die freie Stelle in Ihrem Team durch mich neu zu besetzen. Ich nehme Ihr Angebot hiermit gerne an.

Ich kann, wie ich Ihnen bereits bei unserem Gespräch sagte, am ersten August beginnen, früher allerdings leider wirklich nicht.

Würden Sie mir bitte noch mitteilen, wann genau ich mich am ersten August bei Ihnen einfinden soll?

Ich freue mich sehr auf die Arbeit bei Ihnen.

Mit freundlichen Grüßen

Ihr

Oliver Zahn

## Refusing a job

Christoph Höfer
Weidengrund 7
58515 Lüdenscheid

5. November 1998

Frau Ursula Jaspers
Zahntechnik GmbH
Am Hang 21
33333 Bielefeld

Sehr geehrte Frau Jaspers,

ich möchte mich ganz herzlich dafür bedanken, dass Sie mir die Stelle, um die ich mich bei Ihnen beworben habe, anbieten.

Zu meinem Bedauern muss ich Ihr freundliches Angebot nun aber doch ablehnen, da mein derzeitiger Arbeitgeber mir völlig überraschend ein Angebot gemacht hat, das so attraktiv war, dass ich es trotz allem nicht ausschlagen mochte.

Ich hoffe, Sie haben ein wenig Verständnis für meine Entscheidung.

Mit freundlichen Grüßen

Christoph Höfer

## Giving a reference

Dr. Adalbert Fiedler
Zeppelinstr. 43
70193 Stuttgart

14. August 1998

Produktdesign GmbH
Neckarstr. 70
71717 Ludwigsburg

Ihr Schreiben vom 6. August

Sehr geehrte Damen und Herren,

ich freue mich über die Gelegenheit, Frau Luise Gebhard bei ihrer Bewerbung um die Stelle einer Designerin in Ihrem Hause zu unterstützen.

Während ihres Studiums habe ich Frau Gebhard als eine herausragende Studentin kennnen gelernt. Sie hat originelle und spannende Ideen - die sie auch umzusetzen weiß. Ihre Magisterarbeit, die ich betreut habe, ist exzellent.

Frau Gebhard ist eine angenehme, fleißige und verlässliche Frau, und ich kann sie ohne jede Einschränkung empfehlen.

Mit freundlichem Gruß

Dr. A. Fiedler

## Resigning from a post

Walter Schreiber
Fördestraße 25
24944 Flensburg

3. Oktober 1998

Frau Dr. Elfriede Singer
im Hause
Kündigung

Liebe Frau Singer,

mit diesem Brief möchte ich Ihnen mitteilen, dass ich mein Arbeitsverhältnis mit Wirkung zum 31. August kündige.

Der Entschluss ist mir nicht leicht gefallen, da ich mich bei der Arbeit in Ihrer Redaktion immer sehr wohl gefühlt habe - bis es am Anfang dieses Jahres zu den bekannten Veränderungen an der Spitze des Verlages kam.

Seither ist es mir aber beim besten Willen nicht mehr möglich, mich in der Redaktion so einzubringen, wie Sie es von Ihren Mitarbeitern erwarten können und wie ich es unter anderen Umständen auch liebend gern täte.

Ich hoffe, dass Sie Verständnis für meinen Schritt haben und wünsche Ihnen alles Gute für die Zukunft.

Mit besten Grüßen

Ihr Walter Schreiber

# Englische Musterbriefe



····➤ Weitere nützliche Hinweise finden sich in den Informationsboxen **Briefeschreiben** und **Grüße**.

### Einladung zu einer Hochzeit

23 Chapel Lane
Little Bourton
Northampton
NN19 1AZ

*Mr and Mrs Peter Thompson*
*request the pleasure of your company*
*at the marriage of their daughter*

*Hannah*
*to*
*Mr Steve Warner*

*at one o'clock*
*on Saturday 25th July*
*St. Mary's Church, Northampton*

R.S.V.P

### Dank für eine Einladung zur Hochzeit

Schillerstraße
35041 Marburg
Germany.

22/8/98

Dear Joe,

Thanks for your letter. I was delighted to hear that you two are getting married, and I'm sure you'll be very happy together. I will do my best to come to the wedding, it'd be such a shame to miss it.

I think your plans for a small wedding sound just the thing, and I feel honoured to be invited. I wonder if you have decided where you are going for your honeymoon yet? I look forward to seeing you both soon. Beate sends her congratulations.

Best wishes,

Erik

### Zum neuen Jahr

Flat 3, Alice House
44 Louis Gardens
London W5.

January 2nd 1998

Dear Arthur and Gwen,

Happy New Year! This is just a quick note to wish you all the best for 1998. I hope you had a good Christmas, and that you're both well. It seems like a long time since we last got together.

My New Year should be busy as I am trying to sell the flat. I want to buy a small house nearer my office and I'd like a change from the flat since I've been here nearly six years now. I'd very much like to see you, so why don't we get together for an evening next time you're in town? Do give me a ring so we can arrange a date.

With all good wishes from

Lance

### Antwort auf einen Neujahrsgruß

19 Wrekin Lane
Brighton
BN7 8ZT

6th January 1998

My dear Katrin,

Thank you so much for your letter and New Year's wishes. It was great to hear from you after all this time, and to get all your news from the past year. I'll write a "proper" reply later this month, when I've more time. I just wanted to tell you now how glad I am that we are in touch again, and to say that if you do come over in February I would love you to come and stay — I have plenty of room for you and Stephan.

All my love,

Helen

**Kondolenzbrief (förmlich)**

Larch House
Hughes Lane
Sylvan Hill
Sussex

22 June 1998

Dear Mrs Robinson,

I would like to send you my deepest sympathies on your sad loss. It came as a great shock to hear of Dr Robinson's terrible illness, and he will be greatly missed by everybody who knew him, particularly those who, like me, had the good fortune to have him as a tutor. He was an inspiring teacher and a friend I am proud to have had. I can only guess at your feelings. If there is anything I can do please do not hesitate to let me know.

With kindest regards,
Yours sincerely,

Malcolm Smith

**Dank für Beileid (förmlich)**

55A Morford Lane
Bath
BA1 2RA

4 September 1998.

Dear Mr Schenk,

I am most grateful for your kind letter of sympathy. Although I am saddened by Rolf's death, I am relieved that he did not suffer at all.

The funeral was beautiful. Many of Rolf's oldest friends came and their support meant a lot to me. I quite understand that you could not come over for it, but hope you will call in and see me when you are next in the country.

Yours sincerely,

Maud Allen

**Kondolenzbrief (informell)**

18 Giles Road
Chester CH1 1ZZ
Tel: 01224 123341

May 21st 1998

My dearest Victoria,

I was so shocked to hear of Raza's death. He seemed so well and cheerful when I saw him at Christmas time. It is a terrible loss for all of us, and he will be missed very deeply. You and the children are constantly in my thoughts.

My recent operation prevented me from coming to the funeral and I am very sorry about this. I will try to come up to see you at the beginning of July, if you feel up to it. Is there anything I can do to help?

With much love to all of you
from

Penny

**Dank für Beileid (informell)**

122 Chester Street
Mold
Clwyd
CH7 1VU

15 November 1998

Dearest Rob,

Thank you very much for your kind letter of sympathy. Your support means so much to me at this time.

The whole thing has been a terrible shock, but we are now trying to pick ourselves up a little. The house does seem very empty.

With thanks and very best wishes from us all,

Love,

Elizabeth

## Dank für ein Hochzeitsgeschenk

Mill House
Mill Lane
Sandwich
Kent
CT13 OLZ

June 1st 1998

Dear Len and Sally,

We would like to thank you most warmly for the lovely book of photos of Scotland that you sent us as a wedding present. It reminds us so vividly of the time we spent there and of the friends we made.

It was also good to get all your news. Do come and see us next time you are back on leave - we have plenty of room for guests.

Once again many thanks, and best wishes for your trip to New Zealand.

Kindest regards from

Peter and Claire

## An das Fremdenverkehrsbüro

Am Grün 280
9026 Klagenfurt
Austria

4th May 1998

The Regional Tourist Office
3 Virgin Road
Canterbury
CT1A 3AA

Dear Sir/Madam,

Please send me a list of local hotels and guest houses in the medium price range. Please also send me details of local coach tours available during the last two weeks in August.

Thanking you in advance,

Yours faithfully,

Dirk Müller

Dirk Müller

## Hotelzimmerreservierung

35 Prince Edward Road
Oxford OX7 3AA
Tel: 01865 322435

The Manager
Brown Fox Inn
Dawlish
Devon

23rd April 1998

Dear Sir or Madam,

I noticed your hotel listed in the "Inns of Devon" guide for last year and wish to reserve a double (or twin) room from August 2nd to 11th (nine nights). I would like a quiet room at the back of the Hotel, if one is available.

If you have a room free for this period please let me know the price, what this covers, and whether you require a deposit.

Yours faithfully,

Charles Fairhurst

## Stornierung einer Hotelzimmerreservierung

**Message for:** The Manager, The Black Bear Hotel
**Address:** 14 Valley Road, Dorchester
**Fax Number:** (01305) 367492

**From:** Ulrike Fischer
**Date:** 16 March 1998
Number of pages including this page: 1

---

Sonnenblickallee 61
80339 München
Germany

Dear Sir or Madam,

I am afraid that I must cancel my booking for August 2nd-18th. I would be very grateful if you could return my £50.00 deposit at your early convenience.

Yours faithfully,

Ulrike Fischer

### Vermietung eines Ferienhauses

Mrs M Henderson
333a Sisters Avenue
Battersea
London SW3 0TR
Tel: 0171-344 5657

23/4/98

Dear Mr and Mrs Neubauer,

Thank you for your letter of enquiry about our holiday home. The house is available for the dates you mention. It has three bedrooms, two bathrooms, a big lounge, a dining room, a large modern kitchen and a two-acre garden. It is five minutes' walk from the shops. Newick is a small village near the Sussex coast, and only one hour's drive from London.

The rent is £250 per week; 10% (non-refundable) of the total amount on booking, and the balance 4 weeks before arrival. Should you cancel the booking after that, the balance is returnable only if the house is re-let. Enclosed is a photo of the house. We look forward to hearing from you soon.

Yours sincerely,

Margaret Henderson

Margaret Henderson

### Anmietung eines Ferienhauses

*23c Tollway Drive*
*Lydden*
*Kent*
*CT33 9ER*
*(01304 399485)*

*4th June 1998*

*Dear Mr and Mrs Murchfield,*

*I am writing in response to the advertisement you placed in "Home Today" (May issue). I am very interested in renting your Cornish cottage for any two weeks between July 24th and August 28th. Please would you ring me to let me know which dates are available?*

*If all the dates are taken, perhaps you could let me know whether you are likely to be letting out the cottage next year, as this is an area I know well and want to return to.*

*I look forward to hearing from you.*

*Yours sincerely,*

*Michael Settle.*

### Reservierung eines Stellplatzes auf einem Campingplatz

Biegenstraße 54
53639 Königswinter 1
Germany

25th April 1998

Mr and Mrs F. Wilde
Peniston House
Kendal
Cumbria
England

Dear Mr and Mrs Wilde,

I found your caravan site in the Tourist Board's brochure and would like to book in for three nights, from July 25th to 28th. I have a caravan with a tent extension and will be coming with my wife and two children. Please let me know if this is possible, and if you require a deposit. Would you also be good enough to send me instructions on how to reach you from the M6?

I look forward to hearing from you.

Yours sincerely,

Jürgen Lang

Jürgen Lang

### Anmietung eines Wohnwagens auf einem Campingplatz

**22 Daniel Avenue**
**Caldwood**
**Leeds LS8 7RR**
**Tel: 01532 9987676**

3 March 1998

Dear Mr Vale,

Your campsite was recommended to me by a friend, James Dallas, who has spent several holidays there. I am hoping to come with my two boys aged 9 and 14 for three weeks this July.

Would you please send me details of the caravans for hire, including mobile homes, with prices and dates of availability for this summer. I would also appreciate some information on the area, and if you have any brochures you could send me this would be very helpful indeed.

Many thanks in advance.

Yours sincerely,

Frances Goodheart

Frances Goodheart.

### Bitte um Zusendung eines Theaterspielplans

3 Cork Road
Dublin 55
Ireland
Tel: (1) 3432255

23/5/98

The Manager
Plaza Hotel
Old Bromwood Lane
Victoria
London

Dear Sir or Madam,

My wife and I have booked a room in your hotel for the week beginning 10th July 1998. We would be very grateful if you could send us the theatre listings for that week, along with some information on how to book tickets in advance. If you are unable to provide this information, could you please advise us on where we could get it from? We are looking forward to our visit very much.

Yours faithfully,

Ryan Friel

Mr RYAN FRIEL

### Entschuldigungsschreiben für ein Schulkind

23 Tollbooth Lane
Willowhurst
Sussex BN27 9UK

Tuesday 19 March

Dear Mr Jessel,

I am writing to let you know that my son Roger is unwell and will probably not be in school for the rest of the week. He has flu, and the doctor said that he should be able to go back to school sometime next week, but I will let you know if this is not the case.

Yours sincerely,

Louisa Finch

### Anmeldung eines Kindes an einer Schule

Schloßtreppe 187
2456 Hamburg 65
Germany
2nd April 1998

Mr T Allen, BSc, DipEd.
Headmaster
Twining School
Walton
Oxon
OX44 23W

Dear Mr Allen,

I shall be moving to Walton from Germany this summer and am looking for a suitable school for my 11-year-old son, Markus. Markus is bilingual (his father is English) and has just completed his primary schooling in Hamburg. Your school was recommended to me by the Simpsons, whose son Bartholomew is one of your pupils.

If you have a vacancy for next term, please send me details. I shall be in Walton from 21 May, and could visit the school any time after that to discuss this with you.

Yours sincerely,

Katharina Smith

Katharina Smith (Mrs)

### Bewerbung um einem Studienplatz

43 Wellington Villas
York
YO6 93E

2.2.98

Dr T Benjamin,
Department of Fine Art
University of Brighton
Falmer Campus
Brighton
BN3 2AA

Dear Dr Benjamin,

I have been advised by Dr Kate Rellen, my MA supervisor in York, to apply to do doctoral studies in your department.

I enclose details of my current research and also my tentative Ph.D proposal, along with my up-to-date curriculum vitae, and look forward to hearing from you. I very much hope that you will agree to supervise my Ph.D. If you do, I intend to apply to the Royal Academy for funding.

Yours sincerely,

Alice Nettle

### Anfrage an einen Handwerksbetrieb

*"Pond Cottage"*
*Marsh Road*
*Cambridge*
*CB2 9EE*

*01223 456454*

---

**Message for:** Shore Builders Ltd
**Address:** 667, Industrial Drive, Cambridge CB12 9RR
**Fax Number:** (01223) 488322

**From:** T H Meadows
**Date:** June 21st 1998
Number of pages including this page: 1

---

Dear Sirs.

I have just purchased the above cottage in which several window frames are rotten. I would be glad if you could call and give me a written estimate of the cost of replacement (materials and labour). Please telephone before calling.

Yours faithfully,

T H Meadows

### Auftrag an einen Handwerksbetrieb

The Garden House
Willow Road
Hereford

Tel: 01432 566885

9th September 1998.

Rouche Building Co
33 Hangar Lane
Hereford

Dear Sirs,

I accept your estimate of £195 for replacing the rusty window frame.

Please would you phone to let me know when you will be able to do the work, as I will need to take time off to be there. A Wednesday or Thursday afternoon would suit me best.

Yours faithfully,

Steven Hartwell

### Mahnung wegen Lieferverzugs

19 Colley Terrace
Bingley
Bradford

Tel: 01274 223447

*4.5.98*

*Mr J Routledge*
*'Picture This'*
*13 High End Street*
*Bradford*

*Dear Mr Routledge,*

*I left a large oil portrait with you six weeks ago for framing. At the time you told me that it would be delivered to me within three weeks at the latest. Since the portrait has not yet arrived I wondered if there was some problem?*

*Would you please telephone to let me know what is happening, and when I can expect the delivery? I hope it will not be too long, as I am keen to see the results.*

*Yours faithfully,*

*Mrs. J J Escobado*

### Reklamation an einen Handwerksbetrieb

112 Victoria Road
Chelmsford
Essex CM1 3JJ

Tel: 01621 33433

Allan Deal Builders
35 Green St
Chelmsford
Essex CM3 4RJ

ref. WL/45/LPO

Dear Sirs,

I confirm my phone call, complaining that the work carried out by your firm on our patio last week is not up to standard. Large cracks have already appeared in the concrete area and several of the slabs in the paved part are unstable. Apart from anything else, the area is now dangerous to walk on.

Please send someone round this week to re-do the work. In the meantime I am of course withholding payment.

Yours faithfully,

W. Nicholas Cotton

### Bewerbung um eine Praktikantenstelle

Nanssensweg 39
50733 Köln
Germany

5th February 1998

Synapse & Bite Plc
3F Well Drive
Dolby Industrial Estate
Birmingham BH3 5FF

Dear Sirs,

As part of my advanced training relating to my current position as a junior systems trainee in Köln, I have to work for a period of not less than two months over the summer in a computing firm in Britain or Ireland. Having heard of your firm from Frau Schultz who worked there in 1992, I am writing to you in the hope that you will be able to offer me a placement for about eight weeks this summer.

I enclose my C.V. and a letter of recommendation.

Hoping you can help me, I remain,

Yours faithfully,

Heike Schmidt

Encls.

### Blindbewerbung[1]

23 Ave Rostand
7500 Paris
France

6th May 1998

Mrs J Allsop
Lingua School
23 Handle St
London SE3 4ZK

Dear Mrs Allsop,

My colleague Robert Martin, who used to work for you, tells me that you are planning to appoint extra staff this September. I am currently teaching German as a Foreign Language at the Goethe Institüt in Paris.

You will see from my CV (enclosed) that I have appropriate qualifications and experience. I will be available for interview after the 22nd June, and may be contacted after that date at the following address:

c/o Lewis
Dexter Road
London NE2 6KQ
Tel: 0171 335 6978

Yours sincerely,

Steffi Newman

Encl.

### Blindbewerbung[2]

23 Bedford Mews
Dock Green
Cardiff
CF 23 7UU

(01222) 3445656

2nd August 1998

Marilyn Morse Ltd
Interior Design
19 Churchill Place
Cardiff CF4 8MP

Dear Sir or Madam,

I am writing in the hope that you might be able to offer me a position in your firm as an interior designer. As you will see from my enclosed CV, I have a BA in interior design and plenty of experience. I have just returned from Bonn where I have lived for 5 years, and I am keen to join a small team here in Cardiff.

I would be happy to take on a part-time position until something more permanent became available. I hope you will be able to make use of my services, and should be glad to bring round a folio of my work.

Yours faithfully,

K J Dixon (Mrs)

Encls.

### Bewerbung auf eine Stellenanzeige hin

16 Andrew Road
Inverness IV90 OLL
Phone: 01463 34454

13th February 1998

The Personnel Manager
Pandy Industries PLC
Florence Building
Trump Estate
Bath BA55 3TT

Dear Sir or Madam,

I am interested in the post of Deputy Designer, advertised in the "Pioneer" of 12th February, and would be glad if you could send me further particulars and an application form.

I am currently nearing the end of a one-year contract with Bolney & Co, and have relevant experience and qualifications, including a BSc in Design Engineering and an MSc in Industrial Design.

Thanking you in anticipation, I remain,

Yours faithfully,

A Aziz

**Lebenslauf**[1]

| | |
|---|---|
| **Name:** | Mary Phyllis Hunt (née Redshuttle) |
| **Address:** | 16 Victoria Road<br>Brixton<br>LONDON SW12 5HU |
| **Telephone:** | 0181-677968 |
| **Nationality:** | British |
| **Date of Birth:** | 11/3/63 |
| **Marital Status:** | Divorced, one child (4 years old) |
| **Education/Qualifications:** | |
| 1985-6 | University of Essex Business School<br>Postgraduate Diploma in Business Management with German |
| 1981-3 & 1984-5 | London School of Economics,<br>Department of Business Studies<br>BSc First Class Honours in Business Studies with Economics |
| 1983-4 | Year spent in Bonn, studying business German at evening classes and working in various temporary office jobs |
| 1974-1981 | Colchester Grammar School for Girls<br>7 'O' Levels<br>4 'A' Levels: Mathematics (A), History (A), Economics (A), German (B) |
| **Past Employment:** | |
| 1987-89 | Trainee manager, Sainsway Foodstores PLC,<br>69-75 Aylestone Street<br>London EC5A 9HB |
| 1989-91 | Assistant Manager, Sainsway Foodstores PLC, Lincoln Arcade, Faversham, Kent |
| 1991-2 | Assistant Purchasing Officer,<br>Delicatessen International<br>77 rue Baudelaire<br>75012 Paris, France |
| 1992-present | Deputy Manager, Retail Outlets Division,<br>Delicatessen International, Riverside House,<br>22 Charles St, London EC7X 4JJ |
| **Other Interests:** | Tennis and Swimming<br>Judo - brown belt<br>Wine tasting and vineyards |
| **References:** | Mr J Byers-Ellis<br>Manager, Retail Outlets Division<br>Delicatessen International<br>Riverside House<br>22 Charles St, London EC7X 4JJ |

[As present employer is not yet aware of this application, please inform me before contacting him]

| | |
|---|---|
| | Dr Margaret McIntosh<br>Director of Studies<br>University of Essex Business School<br>Colchester CR3 5SA |

**Lebenslauf**[2]

**Name:** HEIDER Sarah Delores

**Address:** 1123 Cedar Ave
Evanston
Illinois 60989
USA

**Date of Birth:** 9.27.56

**Marital Status:** Married, 4 children (aged 8-14)

**Education:**

PhD degree in Shakespearean Poetics and Gender, Northwestern University, Evanston, Illinois, defended 1987

A.M. degree in English and American Literature, University of Pennsylvania, Philadelphia, completed 1981

B.A. degree (English Major), University of Berkeley, California

**Professional Experience:**

| | |
|---|---|
| 1996-present | Associate Professor, Department of English, Northwestern University |
| 1992-96 | Assistant Professor (Renaissance Studies), Department of English, Northwestern University |
| 1987-91 | Assistant Professor, Department of English, University of Pennsylvania |
| 1984-87 | Research Assistant to Prof D O'Leary (Feminism & Shakespearean Poetics) Northwestern University |
| 1983-84 | Research Assistant, Dept of Women's Studies Prof K. Anders (Representations of Renaissance Women), Northwestern University |
| 1981-83 | Teaching Assistant, Renaissance Drama, Northwestern University |

**Academic Awards and Honours:**

Wallenheimer Research Fellow, 1996-97

Milton Wade Predoctoral Fellow, 1983-84

Pankhurst/Amersham Foundation Graduate Fellow, 1981-83

Isobella Sinclair Graduate Fellow, 1981-82

**Research Support:** See list attached

**Publications:** See list attached

**Other Professional Activities & Membership of Professional Organizations:**

President, Renaissance Minds Committee, 1996-present

Member, UPCEO (University Professors Committee for Equal Opportunities), 1988-present

Advisor, Virago Press Renaissance series, Virago, London, 1992-94

Advisor, Pandora Press, NY office, NY, 1991

## Suche nach einer Aupairstelle

St. Johnann Straße 84A
8008 Zürich
Switzerland

+41 (1) 221-2623

15 April 1998

Miss D Lynch
Home from Home Agency
3435 Pine Street
Cleveland, Ohio 442233

Dear Miss Lynch,

I am seeking summer employment as an au pair. I have experience of this type of work in Britain but would now like to work in the USA.
I enclose my C.V, and copies of testimonials from three British families.

I would be able to stay from the end of June to the beginning of September. Please let me know if I need a work permit, and if so, whether you can get one for me.

Yours sincerely,

Elke Petersen

Encls.

## Anbieten einer Aupairstelle

89 Broom St
Linslade
Leighton Buzzard
Beds
LU7 7TJ

4th March 1998

Dear Julie,

Thank you for your reply to our advertisement for an au pair. Out of several applicants, I decided that I would like to offer you the job.

Could you start on the 5th June and stay until the 5th September when the boys go back to boarding school? The pay is £50 a week and you will have your own room and every second weekend free. Please let me know if you have any questions.

I look forward to receiving from you your confirmation that you accept the post.

With best wishes,

Yours sincerely,

John L. King

## Bitte um ein Empfehlungsschreiben

8 Spright Close
Kelvindale
Glasgow GL2 0DS

Tel: 0141-357 6857

23rd February 1998

Dr M Mansion
Department of Civil Engineering
University of East Anglia

Dear Dr Mansion,

As you may remember, my job here at Longiron & Co is only temporary. I have just applied for a post as Senior Engineer with Bingley & Smith in Glasgow and have taken the liberty of giving your name as a referee.

I hope you will not mind sending a reference to this company should they contact you. With luck, I should find a permanent position in the near future, and I am very grateful for your help.

With best regards,

Yours sincerely,

Helen Lee

## Dank für ein Empfehlungsschreiben

The Stone House
Wallop
Cambs
CB13 9RQ

8/9/98

Dear Capt. Dominics,

I would like to thank you for writing a reference to support my recent application for the job as an assistant editor on the Art Foundation Magazine.

I expect you'll be pleased to know that I was offered the job and should be starting in three weeks' time. I am very excited about it and can't wait to start.

Many thanks once again,

Yours sincerely,

Molly (Valentine)

### Annahme eines Stellenangebots

16 Muddy Way
Wills
Oxon
OX23 9WD
Tel: 01865 76754

Your ref: TT/99/HH 4 July 1998

Mr M Flynn
Mark Building
Plews Drive
London
NW4 9PP

Dear Mr Flynn,

I was delighted to receive your letter offering me the post of Senior Designer, which I hereby accept.

I confirm that I will be able to start on 31 July but not, unfortunately, before that date. Can you please inform me where and when exactly I should report on that day? I very much look forward to becoming a part of your design team.

Yours sincerely,

Nicholas Plews

### Ablehnung eines Stellenangebots

4 Menchester St
London
NW6 6RR
Tel: 0181-334 5343

Your ref: 099/PLK/001 9 July 1998

Ms J Jamieson
Vice-President
The Nona Company
98 Percy St
YORK
YO9 6PQ

Dear Ms Jamieson,

I am very grateful to you for offering me the post of Instructor. I shall have to decline this position, however, with much regret, as I have accepted a permanent post with my current firm.

I had believed that there was no possibility of my current position continuing after June, and the offer of a job, which happened only yesterday, came as a complete surprise to me. I apologize for the inconvenience to you.

Yours sincerely,

J D Salam

### Empfehlungsschreiben

DEPT OF DESIGN

University of Hull
South Park Drive
Hull HL5 9UU
Tel: 01646 934 5768
Fax: 01646 934 5766

Your ref. DD/44/34/AW 5/3/98

Dear Sirs,

Mary O'Donnel. Date of birth 21-3-57

I am glad to be able to write most warmly in support of Ms O'Donnel's application for the post of Designer with your company.

During her studies, Ms O'Donnel proved herself to be an outstanding student. Her ideas are original and exciting, and she carries them through - her MSc thesis was an excellent piece of work. She is a pleasant, hard-working and reliable person and I can recommend her without any reservations.

Yours faithfully,

Dr A A Jamal

### Kündigung des Arbeitsverhältnisses

Editorial Office

Modern Living Magazine
22 Salisbury Road, London W3 9TT
Tel: 0171-332 4343 Fax: 0171-332 4354

To: Ms Ella Fellows 6 June 1998

General Editor.

Dear Ella,

I am writing to you, with great regret, to resign my post as Commissioning Editor with effect from the end of August.

As you know, I have found the recent management changes increasingly difficult to cope with. It is with great reluctance that I have come to the conclusion that I can no longer offer my best work under this management.

I wish you all the best for the future,

Yours sincerely,

Elliot Ashford-Leigh

# Useful phrases according to function / Formulierungshilfen für verschiedene Situationen

## 1. Saying thank you

### For a letter

*personal letter*: Vielen *od.* Herzlichen Dank für deinen Brief / für deine freundlichen Zeilen.

*fairly formal letter*: Ich bedanke mich für Ihren Brief.

*formal business letter*: Wir bestätigen dankend den Eingang *od.* Empfang Ihres Schreibens [vom 5. 9. 99].

### For an invitation

Herzlichen Dank für die Einladung [zum Abendessen/ zu Deiner Party]. Ich werde bestimmt kommen und freue mich schon sehr darauf. / Leider kann ich nicht kommen, weil …

Ich bedanke mich für Ihre freundliche Einladung [zum Abendessen / zum Empfang / zur Hochzeit Ihrer Tochter], die ich gerne annehme / die ich leider nicht annehmen kann[, da ich schon anderweitig verpflichtet bin] (*formell*).

### For a gift

Vielen / Herzlichen / Tausend Dank für das reizende Geschenk / für die schönen Blumen. Das war doch wirklich nicht nötig. / Es war sehr lieb / sehr nett von dir. Du hast meinen Geschmack genau getroffen. / Es ist genau das, was ich wollte.

### For help / donations

Ich bin Ihnen sehr dankbar für die viele Mühe, die Sie sich [meinetwegen] gemacht haben / dass Sie sich [meinetwegen] soviel Mühe gemacht haben.

Ich kann dir gar nicht sagen, wie dankbar Erich und ich dir sind, dass du uns so hilfreich zur Seite gestanden hast.

Haben Sie herzlichsten Dank für Ihre wertvolle Hilfe. / Ich möchte Ihnen unseren herzlichsten Dank für Ihre wertvolle Hilfe aussprechen.

Ich möchte Ihnen im Namen der Abteilung / meiner Kollegen unseren aufrichtigen Dank für Ihre großzügige Spende ausdrücken (*formell*).

## 1. Dank

### Für einen Brief

*persönlicher Brief*: Many thanks / Thanks for your letter.
Thank you for your letter.

*Geschäftsbrief*: We thank you for your letter of 6 September 1989.

*formeller Geschäftsbrief*: We acknowledge with thanks your letter of the 6. 9. 1999.

### Für eine Einladung

Many thanks for the invitation [to dinner / to your party]. I'd love to come and I'm really looking forward to it. / Unfortunately I can't come because … (*coll.*)

Richard Edwards has [great] pleasure in accepting / [greatly] regrets he is unable to accept Susan Stewart's kind invitation to dinner / the kind invitation of the Cultural Attaché to a reception / Mr and Mrs David Banks' kind invitation to the wedding of their daughter (*formal*).

*oder*:
Richard Edwards thanks … for his/her/their kind invitation to …, which he has pleasure in accepting / which he regrets he is unable to accept [due to a previous engagement] (*formal*).

### Für ein Geschenk

Thank you very much / (*coll.*) Many thanks / Thank you [ever (*coll.*)] so much for the delightful present / for the lovely flowers.

You really shouldn't have [bothered] (*coll.*). / It was really sweet / kind of you. It's just what I wanted.

### Für Hilfeleistungen / Spenden

I am most grateful for / I greatly appreciate all the trouble you have taken [on my behalf].

Jim and I cannot thank you enough for helping us out.

Please accept / May I offer you our warmest thanks for your valuable assistance (*formal*).

I would like to offer you on behalf of the department / my colleagues our most sincere *or* grateful thanks for your generous donation (*formal*).

## 2. Greetings

### On a postcard

Schöne / Viele / Herzliche Grüße aus Freiburg / Spanien
Es grüßen recht herzlich Stephan und Inge

## 2. Grüße

### Auf einer Postkarte

Greetings / Best wishes from the Outer Hebrides
Wish you were here!
All best wishes [from] Helen and Norman

**For a birthday**

Herzliche Grüße / Herzlichen Glückwunsch / Alles Gute zum Geburtstag

**Zum Geburtstag**

Many happy returns [of the day]
Happy Birthday
All good *or* best wishes for your birthday

**For Christmas [and the New Year]**

Frohe *od.* Fröhliche Weihnachten / Ein gesegnetes *od.* frohes Weihnachtsfest [und viel Glück im neuen Jahr / und die besten Wünsche zum neuen Jahr / und einen guten Rutsch ins neue Jahr]

**Zu Weihnachten [und zum neuen Jahr]**

[Best wishes for] a Merry *or* Happy Christmas and a Prosperous New Year
Christmas Greetings

**For Easter**

Frohe *od.* Fröhliche Ostern / Ein frohes Osterfest

**Zu Ostern**

[Best wishes for a] Happy Easter

**For a wedding**

Dem glücklichen Paar viel Freude am Hochzeitstag [und viel Glück im künftigen gemeinsamen Leben]

**Zu einer Hochzeit**

Every good wish to the happy couple / to the bride and bridegroom on their wedding day [and in the years to come]

**For an exam**

Viel Erfolg bei der bevorstehenden Prüfung
Alles Gute zum Abitur

**Zu einer Prüfung**

Every success in your [forthcoming] exams
All good wishes for your A-levels / GCSEs

**For a house move**

Viel Glück im neuen Heim

**Zum Umzug**

Every happiness in your new home

**For an illness**

Gute Besserung!

**Bei einem Krankheitsfall**

Get well soon!
All best wishes for a speedy recovery

## 3. Congratulations

Herzlichen Glückwunsch / Herzliche Glückwünsche / Ich gratuliere / Wir gratulieren [herzlichst] zum neuen Baby / zur bestandenen Prüfung / zum neuen Job / zur Beförderung / zur Verlobung.

Ich habe mich sehr über deinen Erfolg bei der Prüfung gefreut. Das hast du gut gemacht!

Ich habe / Wir haben mit großer Freude von deiner / eurer bevorstehenden Vermählung gehört. Herzlichen Glückwunsch und alles Gute für die Zukunft!

## 3. Gratulation

Congratulations / Many congratulations / I/We congratulate you [most sincerely] on the [arrival of the] new baby / on passing the exam / on the new job / on your promotion / on your engagement.

I was delighted to hear of your success in the exam. Well done!

I/We have just heard the wonderful news of your forthcoming marriage and offer you my/our sincerest *or* heartiest congratulations and best wishes for your future happiness.

## 4. Apologizing, expressing regret

Es tut mir aufrichtig Leid / Ich bedaure sehr, dass ich Ihnen so viel Kummer bereitet habe.

Ich muss mich bei Ihnen entschuldigen, dass ich Sie fälschlicherweise beschuldigt habe.

Ich nehme alles zurück und bitte vielmals / tausendmal um Entschuldigung.

Nimm es mir nicht übel, dass ich nicht früher geschrieben habe. / Es tut mir Leid, dass du so lange auf ein Lebenszeichen von mir warten musstest.

Ich muss mich für die so späte Beantwortung Ihres Briefes entschuldigen / muss mich entschuldigen, dass diese Geburtstagswünsche so verspätet eintreffen.

## 4. Entschuldigung, Bedauern

I am really *or* genuinely sorry / I greatly *or* very much regret that I have caused you so much trouble.

I owe you an apology / Please accept my humble apology for the wrongful accusation.

I take back all that I said and apologize unreservedly.

Sorry not to have written earlier. / (*joc.*) I'm sorry you've had to wait such a long time for any sign of life.

I must apologize for the delay in replying to your letter / for being so late with these birthday wishes.

Ich bitte [vielmals] um Entschuldigung / muss Sie für meinen Fehler um Verzeihung bitten.

I beg you to / I must ask you to forgive / excuse my mistake (*formal*).

Bitte entschuldigen Sie mein Versehen.

Please excuse my oversight.

Verzeih! Es war alles nur ein dummes Missverständnis.

Sorry! It was all a stupid misunderstanding.

Zu unserem Bedauern müssen wir Ihnen mitteilen, dass wir diesen Artikel nicht mehr führen (*formell*).

We regret to have to inform you / To our regret we must inform you that we no longer stock this item (*formal*).

Leider können wir dieses Teil nicht einzeln liefern.

Unfortunately we cannot supply this part separately.

## 5. Cancelling a visit

Leider wird aus meinem geplanten Besuch zu Weihnachten nichts werden. / Leider kann ich deine / eure Einladung nicht annehmen, da etwas dazwischengekommen ist. Meine Mutter ist schwer krank. / Ich habe mir das Bein gebrochen. / Ich muss wegen dringender Geschäfte verreisen. Kannst du mich auch bei deiner Schwester entschuldigen? Es tut mir sehr Leid / Ich finde es wirklich schade, dass wir uns nicht sehen werden.

## 5. Absagen

Unfortunately / (*coll.*) I'm afraid I can't come to see you as arranged at Christmas / we can't accept your invitation for the 9th owing to unforeseen circumstances. My mother is seriously ill. / I have broken my leg. / I have to go away on urgent business. Please tell your sister from me how sorry I am / (*formal*) convey my apologies to your sister. It is a great disappointment to me. / I shall really miss seeing you.

## 6. Expressing sympathy

Du Arme / Armer! Es tut mir wirklich Leid, dass du diese Operation vor dir hast.

Inge erzählte mir von deinem Unfall. Du tust mir wirklich Leid. / Du hast mein volles Mitgefühl, dass du so etwas durchmachen musstest. / Ich kann es dir nachfühlen, was du durchgemacht hast, und hoffe, dass es dir bald wieder besser geht.

## 6. Teilnahme

You poor thing! I am sorry to hear that you have to have this operation (*coll.*).

Francis told me of your accident. I feel really sorry for you / I feel for you / I sympathize with you having to go through such an experience, and I hope you will soon be on the mend.

## 7. Condolences

Zutiefst erschüttert lasen / hörten wir vom Tode Ihres / deines Mannes.

Ich möchte Ihnen unser aufrichtiges Beileid zu Ihrem schweren Verlust ausdrücken. / Bitte nehmen Sie mein tief empfundenes Mitgefühl zu diesem schweren Verlust entgegen. / Ich möchte Ihnen meine herzliche Anteilnahme zu diesem schweren Verlust aussprechen. / Wir möchten dir unsere tiefe Anteilnahme *od.* unser aufrichtiges Beileid ausdrücken.

Wir sind alle in Gedanken bei dir. Lass es uns bitte wissen, wenn wir dir irgendwie behilflich sein können.

## 7. Kondolenz

I was/We were deeply saddened / It was a great shock to read / hear of the death of your husband.

I would like to assure you of our deepest sympathy in your tragic loss (*formal*). / You have all my/our sympathy in this great loss. / I/We would like to say how sorry I am/we are. / I/We would like to express my/our sincere condolences (*formal*).

I am/We are all thinking of you at this time / You are very much in my/our thoughts. Please let me know if there is anything I/we can do.

## 8. Invitations

Möchtest du und Georg / Möchtet ihr beide am 14. zu uns zum Abendessen kommen? Wir haben unsere neuen Nachbarn eingeladen, und ich dachte, ihr würdet sie auch gerne kennen lernen.

Es würde uns sehr freuen, wenn Sie und Ihre Frau am 14. um 20 Uhr zu uns zum Abendessen kommen könnten. Außer Ihnen haben wir unsere neuen Nachbarn, Herrn und Frau Meyer, eingeladen.

## 8. Einladungen

I wonder if you and Betty could make it / Would you and Betty be free for dinner on the 14th? We are having our new neighbours, the Wilsons, round, and I'm sure you'd like to meet them (*coll.*).

We would be very pleased if you and your wife could come to dinner / join us for dinner on the evening of the 14th. We have also invited our new neighbours, Bill and Angela Wilson.

*Invitations to a party are usually by word of mouth; there is no set form for written invitations.*

Please come to Jennifer's 40th birthday party from 8 o'clock on 23rd September at 12 Parkhurst Gardens, SW4.

Buffet and disco RSVP 0181-323 1279

*formell, auf einer Karte:*

David Bruce
at Home
Sunday December 5th at 12.00 noon

RSVP Wine and cheese

*Invitations to a wedding are usually only to the reception, and are preceded or accompanied by a wedding announcement, which occasionally is an invitation as well:*

Irene Brinkmann Stefan Hopf

Wir heiraten am Samstag, dem 24. April 1999, um 14 Uhr in der Pfarrkirche Landsberg.

[Zu dieser Feier laden wir euch herzlich ein.]

Goethestraße 12 Ulrichsweg 4
Landsberg Altötting

*Bei einer Hochzeit wird gewöhnlich zur Trauungszeremonie und zu einem anschließenden Empfang eingeladen. Freunde können auch eine „Evening Invitation" erhalten, die sich nur auf eine Party nach dem Empfang bezieht.*

*more formal style:*
Dr. Heinrich und Frau Gertrud Brinkmann geben die bevorstehende Vermählung ihrer Tochter Irene mit Stefan Hopf bekannt.

Die Trauung findet am Samstag, dem 24. April 1999, um 14 Uhr in der Pfarrkirche Landsberg statt.

*formell, in gedruckter Form:*
Mr and Mrs James Merriweather request the pleasure of your company at the wedding of their daughter Jane to Timothy Wade at St. Swithin's Church, Compton Abbas, on Saturday June 26th 1999 at 3 p.m. [and afterwards at the Golden Cross Hotel]
RSVP

Es wäre wirklich sehr schön, wenn du im September mit uns nach Italien kommen könntest. / Wir planen für den September eine Italienreise und dachten uns, du möchtest vielleicht mit uns kommen.

It would be wonderful if you could come with us / join us on our trip to Scotland in September. / We are going to Scotland in September and wonder if you would be interested in coming along.

Wäre es vielleicht möglich, dass du zu Ostern zu uns kommst? Hans besucht zu der Zeit einen Kurs, du könntest also in seinem Zimmer schlafen.

Is there any chance that you could come and stay with us at Easter? Edward will be away on a course so you could have his room.

## 9. Requests

Könntest du mich bitte am Donnerstag anrufen? / (*formeller*:) Wäre es Ihnen möglich, mich Donnerstag anzurufen?

Ich wäre Ihnen für die Zusendung eines Musters dankbar.

Ich wäre Ihnen dankbar, wenn Sie mir in dieser Situation behilflich sein könnten.

Ich möchte Sie bitten, das schriftlich zu bestätigen.

Wäre es Ihnen vielleicht möglich, den Empfang für uns zu organisieren?

Wir bitten um postwendende Bezahlung *od.* Begleichung der Rechnung.

### Requesting information

Könnten Sie mir bitte die Preise Ihrer Elektroherde mitteilen / Auskunft über Ihre Elektroherde geben?

Ich möchte nicht neugierig sein, aber ich wüsste gern, wo Sie dieses Kleid gekauft haben.

Ich wäre Ihnen dankbar, wenn Sie mir mitteilen könnten, wo ich Ersatzteile bekommen kann.

Bitte teilen Sie uns unbedingt Ihre neue Anschrift mit (*formell*). / Vergiss nicht, uns deine neue Adresse zu schreiben.

## 9. Bitten

Please could you give me a ring on Thursday / Would you be so good *or* kind as to telephone me on Thursday?

I would be grateful if you could send me a sample.

I would be grateful for *or* would appreciate your help in this matter.

Would you please confirm this in writing? / Would you mind confirming this in writing?

Could you possibly / Would it be possible for you to organize the reception for us?

I must ask you to let us have / (*höfliche Forderung*:) Kindly let us have your payment by return of post.

### Um Auskunft

Please could you tell me / let me know the prices / send me details of your range of electric cookers.

I don't wish to seem inquisitive, but I'd love to know where you bought that dress.

I would be very grateful for any information you can give me on the availability of spare parts.

Do not forget to inform us of (*formal*) / let us know your new address.

**Requesting clarification**

Wir bitten um eine Erklärung für Ihre Abreise. / Könnten Sie uns bitte den Grund Ihrer Abreise angeben? / Bitte erklären Sie uns, warum Sie [überraschend] abgereist sind.

Ich wäre Ihnen dankbar, wenn Sie mir den zweiten Absatz Ihres Briefes genauer erklärten.

Bitte teilen Sie uns mit, warum Sie die Waren nicht mehr annehmen wollen.

**Um Klarstellung / Erklärung**

Please could you give the reason for your departure / explain the reason for your departure *or* why you have left.

I would be grateful if you could clarify the second paragraph in your letter.

May I ask you why you no longer want the goods?

## 10. Explaining

Bitte berücksichtigen Sie, dass ich keine Gelegenheit hatte, die Rede vorzubereiten.

Er hat wegen fehlender Aufstiegsmöglichkeiten gekündigt. / Er hat gekündigt, weil es für ihn keine Aufstiegsmöglichkeiten gab.

Aufgrund seiner Einstellung mir gegenüber werde ich ihn in Zukunft nicht mehr beschäftigen.

Die verspätete Lieferung ergab sich aus Gründen, auf die wir keinen Einfluss hatten.

## 10. Erklärung, Begründung

You must understand / You will appreciate that I have had no time to prepare a speech.

The reason why he left (*coll.*) / The reason for his departure was the lack of prospects. / He left because of *or* on account of the lack of prospects / because there were no prospects of promotion.

In view of *or* In the light of *or* Given his uncooperative attitude I am not giving him any more work.

The delay in delivery is due to circumstances beyond our control.

## 11. Advice, suggestions

Ich finde, du solltest es [lieber] deinem Vater überlassen.

[Wenn ich dir einen Rat geben darf –] frag doch Herrn Klee.

Ich schlage vor, wir fahren mit dem Zug. / Darf ich vorschlagen, mit dem Zug zu fahren?

Ich würde dir raten, nicht hinzugehen.

Ich würde vorschlagen, sie alle auf einmal einzuladen. / Wenn du mich fragst – ich würde sie alle auf einmal einladen.

An deiner Stelle würde ich das Geld annehmen.

Wenn ich die Möglichkeit hätte, würde ich nicht zögern.

Vor allen Dingen nimm dir warme Kleidung mit. / Nimm dir auf alle Fälle warme Kleidung mit.

Geben Sie ihm das Geld unter keinen Umständen.

Sieh zu *od.* Achte darauf, dass du genug Essen im Haus hast.

Ich würde Ihnen raten / Es wäre [vielleicht] ratsam *od.* gut, es Ihrer Frau zu sagen.

Es ist immer gut, ein paar Sicherungen in Reserve zu haben.

Es ist oft von Vorteil / Es hat seine Vorteile / Vieles spricht dafür, die Sache selbst zu erledigen.

Du solltest dir mal überlegen, ob du Dein Kind nicht zu Hause bekommen möchtest.

Und wenn ich dir das Geld leihen würde?

## 11. Ratschläge, Vorschläge

I think you should *or* ought to let your father do it.

[If I may make a suggestion –] why don't you ask Mrs Potterton?

I suggest we take the train. / Might I suggest we take the train?

My advice would be / I would advise you not to go.

My idea would be to invite them all at once. / If you ask me *or* ask my opinion *or* want my advice, I would invite them all at once.

If I were you I would just take the money.

[If I were] given the chance, I wouldn't hesitate.

Be sure to take / Whatever you do, take warm clothes with you.

Under no circumstances let him have the money.

Make sure you have enough food in the house.

It might be / would be a good idea / wise / advisable / as well to tell your wife about it.

It is always a good idea / wise / advisable / as well to have spare fuses handy.

There is something / a lot to be said for doing the job oneself.

You should consider [the possibility of] having the baby at home.

What if *or* Suppose I were to lend you the money?

Vielleicht hättest du Lust, deinen Onkel zu besuchen / (*ugs.*) Wie wär's mit einem Besuch bei deinem Onkel, während du hier bist?

You might like / care to visit your uncle. / (*coll.*) How about going to see your uncle while you are here?

## 12. Instructions, need, compulsion

## 12. Anweisung, Bedürfnis, Zwang

Die Stange mit beiden Händen anfassen und fest drücken.

[You should] place both hands on the bar and push hard.

Das Papier wird wie folgt in die Maschine eingeführt / ist wie folgt in die Maschine einzuführen.

The paper is inserted in the machine as follows: ...

Sehen Sie bitte zu, dass Sie bis 7 Uhr hier sind.

Please *or* Kindly ensure that / see to it that you are here by 7 a.m.

Sie müssen / sollen sich bei Ankunft beim Dienst habenden Feldwebel melden. / Sie melden sich bei Ankunft beim Dienst habenden Feldwebel.

You must / You are to / You will report to the duty sergeant on arrival.

Du hast zu tun, was ich sage, da gibts nichts!

You have [got] to do as I say, there are no two ways about it.

Für den Posten müssen Sie eine Lehrerausbildung haben / ist eine Lehrerausbildung Voraussetzung.

You have to have *or* You need a teaching qualification in order to be considered / A teaching qualification is a requirement for this post.

Es ist [absolut] notwendig / unbedingt angeraten / Pflicht *od.* Vorschrift, Schutzkleidung zu tragen.

It is essential / necessary / indispensable / obligatory *or* compulsory to wear protective clothing.

Alle sind verpflichtet, die Erklärung zu unterschreiben.

Everyone is obliged / required to sign this declaration.

Er wurde von den Einbrechern gezwungen, den Safe zu öffnen.

He was forced by the thieves to open the safe.

Muss ich wirklich jetzt kommen? / Ich muss doch nicht etwa jetzt kommen?

Do I really / Surely I don't have to come now?

Sie dürfen keinesfalls Alkohol zu sich nehmen, nachdem Sie diese Pillen genommen haben.

Under no circumstances *or* On no account must you drink alcohol after taking these pills.

## 13. Approval / disapproval

## 13. Billigung / Missbilligung

Ich mag es / mag es nicht *od.* Es gefällt mir / gefällt mir nicht, wie er mich ansieht.

I like / don't like *or* object to the way he looks at me.

Ich liebe / hasse diese Musik *od.* kann diese Musik nicht ausstehen.

I love / hate *or* (*coll.*) can't stand this music.

Das ist genau das, was ich will. / Genau das will ich nicht.

This is just what I want / what I don't want.

Ich bin von Jazz begeistert *od.* bin ein [begeisterter] Jazzfan. / Ich habe für Jazz nichts übrig.

I am keen on jazz *or* a jazz enthusiast *or* a jazz fan. / I dislike jazz.

Ich stimme diesem Programm völlig / keineswegs zu *od.* bin mit diesem Programm völlig / gar nicht einverstanden.

I approve of *or* endorse *or* am in favour of this policy. / I disapprove of *or* am against *or* opposed to this policy.

Sie unterstützt *od.* befürwortet diesen Plan / ist gegen diesen Plan.

She supports *or* backs this plan. / She opposes this plan.

Er ist ein Befürworter / Gegner von Tierversuchen *od.* ist für / gegen Tierversuche.

He is a supporter / opponent of animal experiments.

Ich bewundere ihn *od.* schätze ihn sehr *od.* habe eine hohe Meinung von ihm / schätze ihn wenig *od.* habe eine schlechte Meinung von ihm.

I admire *or* have a high regard for *or* a high opinion of him. / I have little regard for *or* a low opinion of him.

| | |
|---|---|
| Sie stehen Ihrer Bewerbung wohlwollend / ablehnend gegenüber. | They view your application favourably / unfavourably *or* take a favourable / unfavourable view of your application. |

## 14. Permitting / forbidding | 14. Erlaubnis / Verbot

| | |
|---|---|
| Du darfst es ihm sagen / darfst es ihm nicht sagen. | You may tell him [if you wish] / may not *or* must not tell him. |
| Es ist uns erlaubt / nicht erlaubt, die Gefangenen zu besuchen. | We are allowed *or* permitted / not allowed *or* permitted to visit the prisoners. |
| Rauchen ist hier gestattet / verboten *od.* nicht gestattet. | Smoking is allowed *or* permitted / forbidden *or* prohibited in here. |
| Ich habe nichts dagegen, wenn Sie sich den Tag freinehmen wollen. / Ich muß Ihnen verbieten, weiteren Urlaub zu nehmen. / Ich bin nicht damit einverstanden, dass Sie weiteren Urlaub nehmen. | I have no objection to *or* nothing against your taking the day off. / I [expressly] forbid you to take / I cannot agree to your taking any more time off work. |

## 15. Desires, intentions | 15. Wünsche, Absichten

| | |
|---|---|
| Was willst du werden, wenn du groß bist? | What do you want to be when you grow up? |
| Ich möchte gern Pilot werden, aber das geht aus gesundheitlichen Gründen nicht. | I would like to be a pilot, but my health is not good enough. |
| Ich will / möchte gern nach Italien fahren. | I want to go / I would like to go to Italy. |
| Mich zieht es an den Nil. / Mein großer Wunsch ist es, eine Reise auf dem Nil zu machen. | I have a great desire / longing to take a trip on the Nile. |
| Du kannst gehen, wenn du willst. | You can go if you wish *or* want. |
| Sie hat es sich in den Kopf gesetzt / Ihr größter Wunsch ist, Archäologie zu studieren. | She has set her heart on studying *or* wants above all else to study archaeology. |
| Ich habe es mir zum Ziel gesetzt, ihn unter allen Umständen zu einem Geständnis zu bewegen. | I mean *or* intend *or* propose to make him confess, come what may. |
| Bitte teilen Sie mir mit, was Sie vorhaben / teilen Sie mir Ihre Pläne mit. | Please let me know your intentions / what your plans are *or* what you have in mind. |
| Glaubst du, sie hat ihn wirklich bewusst ermuntert? – Ja, sie wollte ihn eindeutig [dazu] anstiften. | Do you think she really intended *or* meant to encourage him? – Yes, she had every intention of leading him on. |
| Mein Ziel ist es / Es ist meine Absicht / Ich habe vor, die beiden Firmen zu fusionieren. | My intention *or* What I have in mind is to / I am planning to merge the two companies. |
| Sein Ziel ist es / Er plant, hier eine Fabrik zu bauen. | His aim *or* object is to build a factory here. |
| Mir kommt es allein darauf an, dass es die Arbeiter besser haben. | My sole aim *or* purpose is to better the workers' lot. |
| Ich habe keineswegs vor / die Absicht, Sie zu entlassen. | I have no intention of dismissing you. |

## 16. Opinions | 16. Meinungen

| | |
|---|---|
| Ich halte sie für / Meiner Meinung nach ist sie / Ich finde, sie ist die größte Blues-Sängerin. | I think she is / In my opinion she is / I believe her to be the greatest living blues singer. |
| Meiner Ansicht *od.* Meinung nach / So wie ich es sehe, sind neue Gesetze keine Lösung. | To my mind / In my opinion / As I see it, further legislation is not the answer. |
| Ich finde / Ich habe den Eindruck, dass junge Leute heute allgemein höflicher sind. | [Personally] I find *or* reckon / have the impression that young people are generally politer nowadays. |
| Ich habe das Gefühl, man will uns den Vertrag aufzwingen. | I feel we are being pushed into accepting the deal. |

Meine Meinung ist / Ich bin der Meinung, dass Frauen noch immer benachteiligt sind.

My view [of the matter] / My opinion is that women are still underprivileged.

Wie ich über die Sache denke, ist dir offensichtlich nicht wichtig.

My feelings / thoughts on the matter are evidently of no importance to you.

Mit seiner Reaktion auf den Vorschlag hatte niemand gerechnet.

His reaction to the proposal was quite unexpected.

Wie er es sieht, liegt die Zukunft der Firma in der Lebensmittelherstellung.

He sees the future of the company as lying in food manufacturing.

Was ist Ihre Meinung dazu? / Wie sehen Sie die Sache?

What is your opinion on this / your view of the matter?

Ich teile Ihre Meinung *od.* Ansicht. / Ich bin ganz Ihrer Meinung.

I share your opinion *or* point of view. / I agree entirely with what you say.

Wir sind uns völlig / teilweise / im Großen und Ganzen einig. / Wir sind einer Meinung.

We are in complete / partial / broad agreement / thinking on the same lines.

Das Ergebnis seiner Ermittlungen stimmt nicht mit Ihren Aussagen überein / untermauert Ihre Aussagen nicht.

The results of the investigation do not agree with *or* are not consistent with / do not bear out *or* corroborate your claims.

Ich bin völlig anderer Meinung / kann Ihrer Meinung nicht zustimmen *od.* beipflichten / kann Ihre Ansicht nicht teilen.

I completely disagree *or* cannot agree at all with your view / with what you say. / I cannot accept your view / what you say.

Einigen wir uns [doch] darauf, dass wir in diesem Punkt verschiedener Meinung sind!

We must agree to differ on this.

## 17. Right / wrong

## 17. Richtig / falsch

Ich sehe es jetzt ein, du hattest Recht und ich Unrecht.

I see now you were right and I was wrong.

Sie haben diese Behauptung mit Recht angezweifelt – sie stimmt tatsächlich nicht.

You were quite right to query this assertion – it is indeed incorrect.

Es war nicht richtig, dass sie ihn entlassen haben. / Sie hätten ihn nicht entlassen sollen.

They were wrong *or* It was wrong of them to dismiss him. / They should not have dismissed him.

Seine Position anzufechten war falsch, obgleich es zu der Zeit richtig erschien.

Challenging his position was the wrong thing to do, even though it seemed the right thing at the time.

Du hast Recht / Unrecht, dass ... *od.* Deine Annahme, dass ..., ist richtig / falsch.

You are correct / wrong in your assumption that ... *or* Your assumption that ... is correct / wrong.

Diese Behauptung steht im krassen Widerspruch zu den Tatsachen, soweit sie uns bekannt sind.

To say this is flying in the face of the facts *or* contrary to the facts as we know them.

## 18. Doubt / certainty

## 18. Zweifel / Sicherheit

Ich bin nicht sicher / Ich weiß es nicht [genau] / Ich kann es nicht mit Sicherheit sagen, ob er kommen wird.

I'm not sure *or* certain / I don't know [for sure] / I cannot say with any certainty whether he will come.

Er weiß noch immer nicht / ist noch immer unentschieden, welche Schritte er unternehmen soll. / Er fragt sich noch immer, was er machen soll.

He is still uncertain *or* undecided as to what action to take. / He is still wondering what to do.

Es bestehen immer noch Zweifel, ob der Plan auch ausgeführt werden kann / ob das Projekt eine Zukunft hat.

There is still considerable doubt about *or* as to the feasibility of the plan / surrounding the future of the project.

Es ist zweifelhaft / fraglich / [sehr] die Frage, ob wir dadurch etwas gewinnen können.

It is a matter for debate *or* debatable / doubtful whether we will gain anything by this.

Ich habe meine Zweifel [an seinen Fähigkeiten].

I have my doubts [about his competence].

Man kann kaum erwarten, dass er solchen Bedingungen zustimmt, aber man weiß ja nie.

One can hardly expect him to agree to such terms, but you never know.

Ich bin [ganz *od.* absolut] sicher *od.* [fest] davon überzeugt, dass sie es getan hat.

I'm [quite *or* absolutely] certain *or* sure / positive *or* convinced that she did it.

Wir sind ganz zuversichtlich *od.* voller Zuversicht, dass wir gewinnen werden.

We are [quietly] confident that we will win.

Es besteht kein Zweifel / Es steht außer Zweifel / Es ist unbestreitbar *od.* nicht zu leugnen, dass sie die beste Chefin ist, die wir je hatten.

There can be no doubt *or* question / It is beyond doubt *or* question *or* dispute / It is indisputable *or* undeniable that she is the best boss we have had.

Niemand kann abstreiten *od.* leugnen, dass er viel Erfahrung auf diesem Gebiet hat.

Nobody can deny that he has great experience in this field.

Es wird bestimmt einige Zeit Unruhe geben.

There is bound to be a period of unrest.

## 19. Expressions of feeling

## 19. Gefühlsäußerungen

### Amazement

### Erstaunen

Ich war erstaunt darüber / Mit Erstaunen hörte ich, dass du Innsbruck verlassen hast.

I was surprised / (*stronger*) amazed *or* astonished to hear that you had left Glasgow.

Zu meinem Erstaunen *od.* Zu meiner großen Überraschung stimmte sie ohne Widerrede zu.

To my surprise / (*stronger*) amazement *or* astonishment she agreed without a murmur.

Er war wie vom Blitz getroffen / wie vom Donner gerührt, als er merkte, dass sein Freund ihn betrogen hatte.

He was thunderstruck *or* flabbergasted *or* dumbfounded when he discovered his best friend had tricked him.

Ich war fassungslos / erschüttert, als ich es erfuhr.

I was stunned / (*stronger*) shattered by the news.

Die Nachricht war ein Schock für uns / war ein Blitz aus heiterem Himmel / kam völlig unerwartet.

The news was quite a shock / a bombshell / a bolt from the blue / took us all by surprise.

Der Bau dieses Schiffes war eine enorme / erstaunliche Leistung für die damalige Zeit.

The building of this ship was a staggering *or* an astounding achievement for its time.

Die Kombination von gelbem Hemd und rosaroten Hosen war schon etwas schockierend.

The combination of a yellow shirt and pink trousers was rather startling.

### Disappointment

### Enttäuschung

Das Scheitern des Projekts war eine bittere Enttäuschung / ein harter Schlag für ihn / bedeutete einen schweren Rückschlag für ihn.

The failure of the project was a bitter disappointment / a heavy blow / a serious setback for him.

Seine Hoffnungen wurden zunichte [gemacht], als man seine Bitte ablehnte.

His hopes were dashed when his request was refused.

Wir waren bitter enttäuscht *od.* bestürzt / [sehr] ernüchtert.

We were bitterly disappointed *or* sick with disappointment / dismayed / [completely] disenchanted.

Ich fühlte mich im Stich gelassen / betrogen, als er sein Versprechen nicht hielt.

I felt [badly] let down / betrayed when he went back on his promise.

Unser Jahresgewinn entsprach nicht den Erwartungen *od.* war nicht so hoch wie erwartet.

Our annual profits have not come up to *or* have fallen short of expectations.

Sie sahen alle niedergeschlagen / deprimiert / niedergeschmettert aus.

They all looked dejected / crestfallen / (*coll.*) down in the dumps after their defeat.

Alle unsere Bemühungen, die Umweltverschmutzung zu bekämpfen, wurden zunichte gemacht.

All our attempts to combat environmental pollution have been frustrated.

# A a

**A**[1], **a**[1] /eɪ/ *n., pl.* **As** *or* **A's** Ⓐ (*letter*) A, a, *das;* **from A to Z** von A bis Z; **A road** Straße 1. Ordnung; ≈ Bundesstraße, *die;* Ⓑ **A** (*Mus.*) A, a, *das;* **A sharp** ais, Ais, *das;* **A flat** as, As, *das;* Ⓒ (*example*) A, a; **if A says to B: …:** wenn A zu B sagt: …; Ⓓ (*Naut.*) **A 1** in erstklassigem Zustand; Ⓔ **A 1** (*coll.*) eins a (*ugs.*); **I'm feeling absolutely A 1** ich fühle mich eins a (*ugs.*) *od.* erstklassig; Ⓕ (*paper size*) **A 1, A 2, A 3,** *etc.* [DIN] A 1, A 2, A 3 *usw.;* **a pad of A 4 [paper]** ein [DIN-]A4-Block; Ⓖ (*Sch., Univ.: mark*) Eins, *die;* **he got an A [in French]** er bekam [in Französisch] „sehr gut" *od.* eine Eins

**A**[2] *abbr.* **answer**

**a**[2] /ə, *stressed* eɪ/ *indef. art.* Ⓐ ein/eine/ein; **he is a gardener/a Frenchman** er ist Gärtner/Franzose; **she did not say a word** sie sagte kein Wort; ⇒ *also* **many** 1 B; **quite**; **such** 1 A; Ⓑ (*per*) pro; **£40 a year** 40 Pfund pro Jahr; **it's 20p a pound** es kostet 20 Pence das Pfund; **two a penny** zwei Stück [für] einen Penny; **six a side** sechs auf jeder Seite

**AA** *abbr.* Ⓐ (*Brit.*) **Automobile Association** *britischer Automobilklub;* Ⓑ **anti-aircraft** Flugabwehr-; Fla-; **AA gun** Flak, *die;* Ⓒ **Alcoholics Anonymous**

**AB** *abbr.* Ⓐ **able rating** *or* **seaman;** Ⓑ (*Amer. Univ.*) **Bachelor of Arts**

**aback** /əˈbæk/ *adv.* **be taken ~:** erstaunt sein (**by** über + *Akk.*); **I've never seen her so taken ~:** ich habe sie noch nie so betroffen gesehen

**abacus** /ˈæbəkəs/ *n., pl.* **~es** *or* **abaci** /ˈæbəsaɪ/ Abakus, *der*

**abandon** /əˈbændən/ ❶ *v.t.* Ⓐ (*forsake*) verlassen ‹Ort›; verlassen, im Stich lassen ‹Person›; aussetzen ‹Kind, Tier›; aufgeben ‹Prinzip›; stehen lassen ‹Auto›; aufgeben, fallen lassen ‹Gedanken, Plan›; **~ hope** die Hoffnung aufgeben; **~ ship** das Schiff verlassen; **~ ship!** alle Mann von Bord!; Ⓑ (*surrender*) **~ sth. to the enemy** etw. dem Feind übergeben *od.* überlassen; Ⓒ (*yield*) **~ oneself to sth.** sich einer Sache (*Dat.*) hingeben; Ⓓ (*give up*) ablegen ‹Gewohnheit›; abbrechen ‹Spiel›; sich trennen von ‹Reichtümern, Besitz›; hingeben (*geh.*) ‹Reichtum, Geld und Gut›.
❷ *n., no pl.* Unbekümmertheit, *die;* Ungezwungenheit, *die;* **with ~:** unbekümmert; ungezwungen

**abandoned** /əˈbændənd/ *adj.* Ⓐ (*deserted*) verlassen, ausgesetzt ‹Kind, Tier›; **~ property** herrenloses Gut; Ⓑ (*profligate*) verworfen, verkommen ‹Person›; lasterhaft ‹Benehmen›

**abandonment** /əˈbændənmənt/ *n., no pl.* Ⓐ (*giving up*) (*of right, claim*) Preisgabe, *die;* Abtretung, *die;* (*of plan, property*) Aufgabe, *die;* Ⓑ (*carefreeness*) Zwanglosigkeit, *die;* Unbekümmertheit, *die;* Ⓒ (*self-surrender*) Sichgehenlassen, *das;* Hingabe, *die* (**to** an + *Akk.*)

**abase** /əˈbeɪs/ *v.t.* demütigen, erniedrigen ‹Person›; **~ oneself** sich erniedrigen

**abashed** /əˈbæʃt/ *adj.* beschämt; verlegen; **feel ~:** beschämt sein; **be ~ [by sth.]** sich [durch etw.] aus der Fassung bringen lassen

**abate** /əˈbeɪt/ *v.i.* [an Stärke *od.* Intensität] abnehmen; nachlassen; ‹Zorn, Eifer, Sturm:› abflauen, nachlassen

**abatement** /əˈbeɪtmənt/ *n., no pl.* Abnahme, *die;* Nachlassen, *das;* (*of a nuisance*) Beseitigung, *die;* ⇒ *also* **noise abatement**; **smoke abatement**

**abattoir** /ˈæbətwɑː(r)/ *n.* Schlachthof, *der;* ([*part of*] *building*) Schlachthaus, *das*

**abbess** /ˈæbɪs/ *n.* Äbtissin, *die*

**abbey** /ˈæbɪ/ *n.* Ⓐ Abtei, *die;* Ⓑ (*church*) Abteikirche, *die;* **the A~** (*Brit.*) die Abteikirche von Westminster

**abbot** /ˈæbət/ *n.* Abt, *der*

**abbreviate** /əˈbriːvɪeɪt/ *v.t.* abkürzen ‹Wort usw.›; **~ 'Saint' to 'St'** Saint mit St. abkürzen

**abˈbreviated dialling** *n., no pl.* (*Teleph.*) Kurzwahl, *die*

**abbreviation** /əbriːvɪˈeɪʃn/ *n.* (*of word etc.*) Abkürzung, *die*

**ABC** /eɪbiːˈsiː/ *n.* Ⓐ (*alphabet*) Abc, *das;* **as easy as ~:** kinderleicht; Ⓑ (*fig.: rudiments*) Abc, *das;* Einmaleins, *das*

**abdicate** /ˈæbdɪkeɪt/ *v.t.* abdanken; **~ [the throne]** auf den Thron verzichten; dem Thron entsagen (*geh.*); **~ one's rights** auf seine Rechte verzichten

**abdication** /æbdɪˈkeɪʃn/ *n.* (*by monarch*) Abdankung, *die;* Thronverzicht, *der;* **the ~ of his rights** der Verzicht auf seine Rechte

**abdomen** /ˈæbdəmɪn, æbˈdəʊmɪn/ *n.* (*Anat.*) Bauch, *der;* Unterleib, *der;* Abdomen, *das* (*fachspr.*)

**abdominal** /æbˈdɒmɪnl/ *adj.* (*Anat.*) Bauch-; Abdominal- (*fachspr.*)

**abduct** /əbˈdʌkt/ *v.t.* entführen

**abduction** /əbˈdʌkʃn/ *n.* Entführung, *die*

**abeam** /əˈbiːm/ *adv.* (*Naut.*) querab; dwars; **~ of the ship** dwarsschiffs

**abed** /əˈbed/ *adv.* (*arch.*) im Bett; zu Bett (*veralt.*)

**Aberdeen** /ˈæbədiːn/ *n.* **~ [Angus]** Angusrind, *das;* **~ [terrier]** Scotchterrier *od.* Schottische Terrier, *der*

**Aberdonian** /æbəˈdəʊnɪən/ ❶ *adj.* aus Aberdeen; Aberdeener. ❷ *n.* Aberdeener, *der*/ Aberdeenerin, *die*

**aberrant** /əˈberənt/ *adj.* abweichend, (*bes. fachspr.*) anomal ‹Verhalten, Exemplar›

**aberration** /æbəˈreɪʃn/ *n.* Ⓐ (*straying, lit. or fig.*) Abweichung, *die;* (*deviation*) Abweichung, *die;* Anomalie, *die* (*bes. fachspr.*); (*lapse, moral slip*) Verirrung, *die;* **mental ~[s** *pl.***]** geistige Verirrung; Ⓑ (*Optics, Astron.*) Aberration, *die*

**abet** /əˈbet/ *v.t.,* **-tt-** (*support*) helfen (+ *Dat.*); unterstützen; **aid and ~:** Beihilfe leisten (+ *Dat.*); **aiding and ~ting [a criminal]** (*Law*) Beihilfe [bei einem Verbrechen]

**abeyance** /əˈbeɪəns/ *n.* Ⓐ (*suspension*) **be in/fall into ~:** zeitweilig außer Kraft sein/ treten; Ⓑ (*Law*) **be in ~** ‹[Adels]titel:› [vorübergehend] abgeschafft sein

**abhor** /əbˈhɔː(r)/ *v.t.,* **-rr-** hassen; (*loathe*) verabscheuen

**abhorrence** /əbˈhɒrəns/ *n.* Ⓐ *no pl.* (*loathing*) Abneigung, *die* (**of** gegen); Abscheu, *der* (**of** vor + *Dat.*); **hold sth. in ~:** einen Abscheu vor etw. (*Dat.*) haben; Ⓑ (*detested thing*) Gräuel, *der*

**abhorrent** /əbˈhɒrənt/ *adj.* (*disgusting*) abscheulich ‹Benehmen, Gedanke, Person›; **be ~ to sb.** jmdm. zuwider sein

**abide** /əˈbaɪd/ ❶ *v.i.,* **abode** /əˈbəʊd/ *or* **~d** Ⓐ *usu.* **~d: ~ by** befolgen ‹Gesetz, Regel, Vorschrift›; [ein]halten ‹Versprechen›; Ⓑ (*continue*) fortdauern; fortbestehen; (*remain*) bleiben; verweilen (*geh.*). ❷ *v.t.* Ⓐ (*tolerate*) ertragen; **I can't ~ dogs** ich kann Hunde nicht ausstehen; Ⓑ (*submit to*) hinnehmen ‹Urteil, Entscheidung, Kritik›

**abiding** /əˈbaɪdɪŋ/ *attrib. adj.* bleibend, beständig ‹Liebe›; dauerhaft ‹Verbindung, Freundschaft›

**ability** /əˈbɪlɪtɪ/ *n.* Ⓐ (*capacity*) Können, *das;* Fähigkeit, *die;* **have the ~ to do sth.** etw. können *od.* (*geh.*) vermögen; **make use of one's ~** *or* **abilities** seine Fähigkeiten einsetzen; **have the ~ to type/do shorthand** Maschine schreiben können/Kurzschrift beherrschen *od.* können; **to the best of my ~:** soweit es in meinen Kräften steht; Ⓑ *no pl.* (*cleverness*) Intelligenz, *die;* **she is a girl of great ~:** sie ist ein sehr intelligentes Mädchen; **it depends on his ~ at school** es hängt von seinen Leistungen in der Schule ab; Ⓒ (*talent*) Begabung, *die;* Talent, *das;* Anlagen *Pl.;* **he shows** *or* **has great musical ~:** er ist musikalisch sehr begabt; **she has a natural ~ for teaching** sie hat eine natürliche Begabung zur Lehrerin

**abject** /ˈæbdʒekt/ *adj.* Ⓐ (*miserable*) elend; erbärmlich; **in the most ~ poverty** in bitterster Armut; Ⓑ (*self-abasing, submissive*) unterwürfig

**abjectly** /ˈæbdʒektlɪ/ *adv.* Ⓐ (*miserably*) erbärmlich; Ⓑ (*submissively*) unterwürfig

**abjectness** /ˈæbdʒektnɪs/ *n., no pl.* Ⓐ (*misery*) Erbärmlichkeit, *die;* Ⓑ (*submissiveness*) Unterwürfigkeit, *die*

**abjuration** /æbdʒʊəˈreɪʃn/ *n.* (*of belief, religion*) Abschwören, *das*

**abjure** /əbˈdʒʊə(r)/ *v.t.* abschwören (+ *Dat.*) ‹Glauben, Religion›; sich lossagen von ‹Theorie, Weltanschauung›

**ablative** /ˈæblətɪv/ (*Ling.*) ❶ *adj.* Ablativ-; **~ case** Ablativ, *der.* ❷ *n.* Ablativ, *der;* ⇒ *also* **absolute** C

**ablaut** /ˈæblaʊt/ *n.* (*Ling.*) Ablaut, *der*

**ablaze** /əˈbleɪz/ *pred. adj.* in Flammen; **be ~:** in Flammen stehen; (*fig.*) glühen (**with** vor + *Dat.*); **be ~ with light** hell erleuchtet sein

**able** /ˈeɪbl/ *adj.* Ⓐ **be ~ to do sth.** etw. können; **I'd love to come but I don't know if I'll be ~ [to]** ich würde sehr gern kommen, aber ich weiß nicht, ob es mir möglich sein wird; **I think you'd be better/more ~ to do it than I would** ich glaube, Sie sind eher dazu in der Lage als ich; Ⓑ (*competent*) fähig; tüchtig; (*talented*) begabt; fähig

**able: ~-bodied** /ˈeɪblbɒdɪd/ *adj.* kräftig; stark; tauglich ‹Soldat, Matrose›; **~ ˈrating, ~ ˈseaman** *n.* Vollmatrose, *der*

**ablution** /əˈbluːʃn/ *n., usu. in pl.* Ⓐ (*ceremony*) Waschung, *die;* Ablution, *die* (*Rel.*); (*joc.: washing*) Wäsche, *die;* **perform one's ~s** sich waschen; Ⓑ *in pl.* sanitäre Anlagen

**ably** /ˈeɪblɪ/ *adv.* geschickt; gekonnt

**abnormal** /æbˈnɔːml/ *adj.* Ⓐ (*deviant*) abnorm ‹Gestalt, Größe›; a[b]normal ‹Interesse, Verhalten›; **mentally/physically ~:** geistig/physisch anomal *od.* krank; Ⓑ (*irregular*) ungewöhnlich; a[b]normal

**abnormality** /æbnɔːˈmælɪtɪ/ *n.* Ⓐ (*deviation*) Abnormität, *die;* Anomalie, *die;* Ⓑ (*irregularity*) Ungewöhnlichkeit, *die;* Regelwidrigkeit, *die;* Abnormität, *die*

**abnormally** /æbˈnɔːməlɪ/ *adv.* (*untypically*) ungewöhnlich; abnorm; (*unusually*) ungewöhnlich

**Abo** /ˈæbəʊ/ *n., pl.* **~s** (*Austral. sl. derog.*) Eingeborene, *der/die*

**aboard** /əˈbɔːd/ ❶ *adv.* (*on or in ship etc.*) an Bord; **a bus with 30 passengers ~:** ein Bus mit 30 Fahrgästen; **all ~!** alle Mann an Bord!; (*bus, train*) alle[s] einsteigen! ❷ *prep.* an Bord; **~ an ocean liner** an Bord eines Überseedampfers; **~ the bus/train** im Bus/ Zug; **~ ship** an Bord

**abode**[1] /əˈbəʊd/ *n.* (*formal/joc.: dwelling place*) Wohnstätte, *die;* Bleibe, *die;* **of no fixed ~:** ohne festen Wohnsitz

a

**abode**[2] ⇒ **abide**

**abolish** /əˈbɒlɪʃ/ *v.t.* abschaffen; abschaffen, aufheben ‹Gesetz›

**abolishment** /əˈbɒlɪʃmənt/, **abolition** /æbəˈlɪʃn/ *ns.* Abschaffung, *die;* (*of law*) Abschaffung, *die;* Aufhebung, *die;* (*of slavery*) Abschaffung, *die;* Abolition, *die*

**abolitionist** /æbəˈlɪʃənɪst/ *n.* Abolitionist, *der; attrib.* abolitionistisch

**ˈA-bomb** *n.* Atombombe, *die*

**abominable** /əˈbɒmɪnəbl/ *adj.* abscheulich; scheußlich; widerwärtig; **the A~ Snowman** der Schneemensch; der Yeti

**abominably** /əˈbɒmɪnəblɪ/ *adv.* abscheulich; scheußlich; widerwärtig

**abominate** /əˈbɒmɪneɪt/ *v.t.* verabscheuen

**abomination** /əbɒmɪˈneɪʃn/ *n.* Ⓐ *no pl.* (*abhorrence*) Abscheu, *der* (**of** vor + *Dat.*); Ⓑ (*object of disgust*) Abscheulichkeit, *die*

**aboriginal** /æbəˈrɪdʒɪnl/ ❶ *adj.* Ⓐ einheimisch ‹Pflanze, Tier, Bevölkerung›; **the ~ inhabitants of this region** die Ureinwohner *od.* die Urbevölkerung dieser Region; Ⓑ (*in Australia*) **A~ tribes** Aboriginesstämme; **A~ customs** Brauchtum der Aborigines. ❷ *n.* Ureinwohner, *der;* (*in Australia*) **A~:** [australischer] Ureinwohner

**aborigine** /æbəˈrɪdʒɪnɪ/ *n.* Ureinwohner, *der;* Urbewohner, *der;* (*in Australia*) **A~:** [australischer] Ureinwohner

**abort** /əˈbɔːt/ ❶ *v.i.* Ⓐ (*Med.*) eine Fehlgeburt haben; abortieren (*Med.*); Ⓑ (*fail*) misslingen; scheitern. ❷ *v.t.* Ⓐ (*Med.*) **~ a baby** eine Schwangerschaftsunterbrechung durchführen; [ein Baby] abtreiben; **~ a woman** bei einer Frau eine Schwangerschaftsunterbrechung durchführen; Ⓑ (*fig.: end*) vorzeitig beenden; abbrechen ‹Projekt, Unternehmen›; Ⓒ (*Aeronaut., Astronaut.*) abbrechen; aufgeben ‹Rakete›

**abortion** /əˈbɔːʃn/ *n.* Ⓐ (*deliberate*) Schwangerschaftsunterbrechung, *die;* Abtreibung, *die;* **have/get an ~:** die Schwangerschaft unterbrechen lassen; **back-street ~:** illegale Abtreibung (*durch Engelmacherin*); Ⓑ (*involuntary*) Früh- *od.* Fehlgeburt, *die;* Abort, *der* (*Med.*); Ⓒ (*monstrosity*) Missgeburt, *die*

**abortionist** /əˈbɔːʃənɪst/ *n.* abtreibender Arzt/abtreibende Ärztin; **back-street ~:** Engelmacherin, *die*/Engelmacher, *der* (*ugs.*)

**aˈbortion pill** *n.* Abtreibungspille, *die*

**abortive** /əˈbɔːtɪv/ *adj.* misslungen ‹Plan›; fehlgeschlagen ‹Versuch›; **be ~:** ein Fehlschlag sein

**abound** /əˈbaʊnd/ *v.i.* Ⓐ (*be plentiful*) reichlich *od.* in Hülle und Fülle vorhanden sein *od.* da sein; Ⓑ **~ in sth.** an etw. (*Dat.*) reich sein; **the English language ~s in idioms** die englische Sprache ist reich an Redensarten; **~ with** voll sein von; wimmeln von ‹Lebewesen›

**about** /əˈbaʊt/ ❶ *adv.* Ⓐ (*all around*) rings[her]um; (*here and there*) überall; **all ~:** ringsumher; **strewn/littered ~ all over the room** überall im Zimmer verstreut; **there must be some kitchen utensils ~:** irgendwo müssen hier ein paar Küchengeräte herumliegen; Ⓑ (*near*) **be ~:** da sein; hier sein; **is John ~?** ist John da?; **there was nobody ~:** es war niemand da; Ⓒ **be ~ to do sth.** gerade etw. tun wollen; im Begriff sein, etw. zu tun; (*Amer.: intend*) beabsichtigen, etw. zu tun; **I was just ~ to go shopping when ...:** ich wollte gerade einkaufen gehen, als ...; Ⓓ (*active*) **be out and ~:** aktiv sein; etwas unternehmen; **be up and ~:** auf sein (*ugs.*); Ⓔ ▶ 912, ▶ 1012 (*approximately*) ungefähr; **[at] ~ 5 p.m.** ungefähr um *od.* gegen 17 Uhr; **Here I am! — And ~ time too!** (*coll.*) Hier bin ich. — Langsam wird es auch Zeit!; **it's ~ time somebody told him a thing or two** (*coll.*) langsam wird es Zeit, dass ihm mal jemand die Meinung sagt; **I've had [just] ~ enough of this** (*coll.*) ich habe [endgültig] genug *od.* (*salopp*) die Nase voll davon; Ⓕ (*round*) herum; rum (*ugs.*); **the battery is the wrong way ~:** die Batterie ist falsch [herum] eingebaut; **~ turn!**, (*Amer.*) **~ face!** (*Mil.*) kehrt!; ⇒ *also* **about-turn**; Ⓖ (*in rotation*) **[week and] week ~:** in wöchentlichem Wechsel; **[turn and] turn ~:** abwechselnd; **we take turn ~ at [the] cooking** wir wechseln uns mit dem Kochen ab

❷ *prep.* Ⓐ (*all around*) um [... herum]; **there was litter lying ~ the park/streets** überall im Park/auf den Straßen lag der Abfall herum; **walk ~ the garden** im Garten herumgehen; **man ~ town** ⇒ **town** A; Ⓑ (*with*) **have sth. ~ one** etw. [bei sich] haben; **have you got a match ~ you?** haben Sie vielleicht ein Streichholz?; ⇒ *also* **wit**[1] B; Ⓒ (*concerning*) **a talk/an argument/a question ~ sth.** ein Gespräch über etw. (*Akk.*)/Streit wegen etw./eine Frage zu etw.; **talk/laugh ~ sth.** über etw. (*Akk.*) sprechen/lachen; **cry ~ sth.** wegen etw. weinen; **know ~ sth.** von etw. wissen; **what was it ~?** worum ging es?; **what is/was all that ~?** worum geht/ging es denn?; ⇒ *also* **do**[1] 1 B; **what** 5 A; Ⓓ (*occupied with*) **be ~ sb.'s business** für jmdn. arbeiten *od.* tätig sein; **what are you/is he ~?** was hast du/hat er vor?; was führst du/führt er im Schilde?; **mind what you're ~:** pass auf!; sieh dich vor!; sei vorsichtig!; **be quick/brief ~ it** beeil dich!; (*in speaking*) fasse dich kurz!; **while you're ~ it** da Sie gerade dabei sind. ⇒ *also* **go about** 2

**about-ˈface, about-ˈturn** ❶ *ns.* (*lit. or fig.*) Kehrtwendung, *die.* ❷ *vs. i.* kehrtmachen; **~!** kehrt!

**above** /əˈbʌv/ ❶ *adv.* Ⓐ (*position*) oben; oberhalb; (*higher up*) darüber; (*on top*) oben; (*upstream*) weiter oben; **up ~:** oben; droben (*bes. südd.*); **from ~:** von oben [herab]; **~ right** rechts oben; oben rechts; Ⓑ (*direction*) nach oben; hinauf; (*upstream*) stromauf[wärts]; Ⓒ (*earlier in text*) weiter oben; **see ~, p. 123** siehe oben, S. 123; Ⓓ (*upstairs*) (*position*) oben; (*direction*) nach oben; **the flat/floor ~:** die Wohnung/das Stockwerk *od.* die Etage darüber *od.* über uns/ihnen *usw.*; **on the floor ~:** eine Etage höher; Ⓔ (*in heaven*) [droben] im Himmel; **from ~:** vom Himmel [herab *od.* hoch].

❷ *prep.* Ⓐ (*position*) über (+ *Dat.*); (*upstream from*) oberhalb (+ *Gen.*); **my brother is head and shoulders ~ me** mein Bruder ist zwei Köpfe größer als ich; (*fig.*) mein Bruder ist mir haushoch überlegen; **~ the general noise was heard ...:** durch den allgemeinen Lärm hindurch konnte man ... hören; **~ oneself** (*in high spirits*) übermütig; aufgekratzt (*ugs.*); (*conceited*) größenwahnsinnig (*ugs.*); **~ board** einwandfrei; korrekt; ⇒ *also* **average** 1 A; **ground**[1] 1 A, B; **head** 1 B; **par** A, D; Ⓑ (*direction*) über (+ *Akk.*); **the sun rose ~ the horizon** am Horizont ging die Sonne auf; Ⓒ (*more than*) über (+ *Akk.*); **will anyone go ~ £2,000?** bietet jemand mehr als 2 000 Pfund?; **he valued honour ~ life** er stellte die Ehre über das Leben; **be ~ criticism/suspicion/reproach** über jede Kritik/jeden Verdacht/allen Vorwurf erhaben sein; **that's ~ me** das ist mir zu hoch (*ugs.*); **you ought to be ~ all that at your age** du solltest in deinem Alter über so etwas stehen (*ugs.*); **~ all [else]** vor allem; insbesondere; ⇒ *also* **over** 1 G; **station** 1 D; Ⓓ (*ranking higher than*) über (+ *Dat.*); **she's in the class ~ me** sie ist eine Klasse über mir *od.* höher als ich.

❸ *adj.* (*earlier*) obig ‹Erklärung, Aufzählung, Ziffern›; (**~*mentioned***) oben genannt.

❹ *n.* **the ~:** das Obige; (*person[s]*) der/die Obengenannte/die Obengenannten

**above: ~ board** *pred. adj.* einwandfrei; korrekt; **~-mentioned** /əˈbʌvmenʃnd/, **above-named** /əˈbʌvneɪmd/ *adjs.* oben genannt; oben erwähnt

**abracadabra** /æbrəkəˈdæbrə/ *n.* Abrakadabra, *das;* Hokuspokus, *der*

**abrade** /əˈbreɪd/ *v.t.* (*scrape off*) abschaben; abschürfen ‹Haut›

**abrasion** /əˈbreɪʒn/ *n.* Ⓐ (*Med.*) Abschürfung, *die;* Ⓑ (*graze*) Hautabschürfung, *die*

**abrasive** /əˈbreɪsɪv/ ❶ *adj.* Ⓐ scheuernd; Scheuer-; (*scratchy*) kratzig; Ⓑ (*fig.: harsh*) aggressiv; herausfordernd ‹Ton›; **an ~ remark** eine barsche Bemerkung. ❷ *n.* Scheuermittel, *das;* Schleifmittel, *das* (*Technik*)

**abreast** /əˈbrest/ *adv.* Ⓐ nebeneinander; Seite an Seite; **walk/ride three ~:** zu dritt nebeneinander gehen/fahren; Ⓑ (*fig.*) **keep ~ of** *or* **with sth.** sich über etw. (*Akk.*) auf dem Laufenden halten

**abridge** /əˈbrɪdʒ/ *v.t.* Ⓐ (*condense*) kürzen; Ⓑ (*curtail*) einschränken; beschneiden ‹Rechte, Freiheiten, Privilegien›

**abridg[e]ment** /əˈbrɪdʒmənt/ *n.* Ⓐ (*shortening*) Kürzung, *die;* Ⓑ (*summary*) (*of text*) Kurzfassung, *die;* (*of book*) Epitome, *die* (*Literaturw.*); Abriss, *der*

**abroad** /əˈbrɔːd/ *adv.* Ⓐ (*overseas*) im Ausland; (*direction*) ins Ausland; **have you ever been ~?** waren Sie schon mal im Ausland?; **are you going ~?** fahren Sie ins Ausland?; **from ~:** aus dem Ausland; Ⓑ (*widely*) in alle Richtungen; **the news was spread ~ that ...:** überall verbreitete sich die Nachricht, dass ...; (*at large*) **there is a rumour ~ that ...:** es geht ein Gerücht um, dass ...

**abrogate** /ˈæbrəgeɪt/ *v.t.* annullieren ‹Vertrag›; aufheben, außer Kraft setzen ‹Gesetz, Vorschrift›

**abrogation** /æbrəˈgeɪʃn/ *n., no pl.* ⇒ **abrogate**: Annullierung, *die;* Aufhebung, *die;* Außerkraftsetzung, *die*

**abrupt** /əˈbrʌpt/ *adj.* Ⓐ (*sudden*) abrupt, plötzlich ‹Ende, Abreise, Wechsel›; **come to an ~ halt** ‹Fahrzeug:› plötzlich *od.* abrupt anhalten; Ⓑ (*disconnected*) zusammenhanglos ‹Schreibstil›; Ⓒ (*brusque*) schroff, barsch ‹Art, Ton›; Ⓓ (*steep*) jäh, steil ‹Abhang›; stark ‹Gefälle›; (*fig.*) plötzlich ‹Zunahme, Abnahme, Anstieg›

**abruptly** /əˈbrʌptlɪ/ *adv.* Ⓐ (*suddenly*) abrupt; plötzlich; Ⓑ (*disconnectedly*) zusammenhanglos; unzusammenhängend; Ⓒ (*brusquely*) schroff; barsch; Ⓓ (*steeply*) jäh; steil; (*fig.*) plötzlich ‹zunehmen, abnehmen›

**abruptness** /əˈbrʌptnɪs/ *n., no pl.* ⇒ **abrupt**: Ⓐ Plötzlichkeit, *die;* Ⓑ Zusammenhanglosigkeit, *die;* Ⓒ Schroffheit, *die;* Barschheit, *die;* Ⓓ Steilheit, *die;* Jähe, *die* (*veralt.*); (*fig.*) Plötzlichkeit, *die*

**ABS** *abbr.* **anti-lock brake** *or* **braking system** ABS

**abscess** /ˈæbsɪs/ *n.* (*Med.*) Abszess, *der*

**abscond** /əbˈskɒnd/ *v.i.* Ⓐ (*depart*) sich entfernen; [heimlich] verschwinden (*ugs.*); Ⓑ (*flee*) flüchten; fliehen

**abseil** /ˈæbseɪl, ˈæbzaɪl/ (*Mount.*) ❶ *v.i.* abseilen. ❷ *n.* Abseilen, *das*

**absence** /ˈæbsəns/ *n.* Ⓐ Abwesenheit, *die;* (*from work*) Fernbleiben, *das;* **his ~s from school** sein Fehlen in der Schule; **how long was your ~ from home?** wie lange waren Sie von zu Hause fort?; **~ makes the heart grow fonder** Abwesenheit verstärkt die Zuneigung; ⇒ *also* **leave**[1] B; Ⓑ (*lack*) **the ~ of sth.** der Mangel an etw. (*Dat.*); das Fehlen von etw.; **in the ~ of concrete evidence** mangels konkreter Beweise; Ⓒ **~ [of mind]** Geistesabwesenheit, *die;* Zerstreutheit, *die*

**absent** ❶ /ˈæbsənt/ *adj.* Ⓐ abwesend; **be ~:** nicht da sein; **be ~ from school/work** in der Schule/am Arbeitsplatz fehlen; **for all those ~ from the last meeting** für alle, die beim letzten Treffen nicht anwesend waren; **I'm afraid he's ~ in America at the moment** er ist zur Zeit leider in Amerika; **he's ~ on leave** er ist auf Urlaub; **be ~ without leave** sich unerlaubt entfernt haben; **~ voter** Briefwähler, *der*/-wählerin, *die;* Ⓑ (*lacking*) **be ~:** fehlen; Ⓒ (*abstracted*) geistesabwesend; zerstreut.
❷ /əbˈsent/ *v. refl.* **~ oneself [from sth.]** [einer Sache (*Dat.*)] fernbleiben

**absentee** /æbsənˈtiː/ *n.* Fehlende, *der/die;* Abwesende, *der/die;* **there were a few ~s** ein paar fehlten; **~ landlord** nicht auf seinem Gut lebender Gutsherr

**absenteeism** /æbsənˈtiːɪzm/ *n., no pl.* [häufiges] Fernbleiben; (*without good reason*) Krankfeiern, *das* (*ugs.*)

**absently** /'æbsəntlɪ/ *adv.* [geistes]abwesend

**absent-minded** /æbsənt'maɪndɪd/ *adj.* geistesabwesend; (*habitually*) zerstreut

**absent-mindedly** /æbsənt'maɪndɪdlɪ/ *adv.* geistesabwesend

**absent-mindedness** /æbsənt'maɪndɪdnɪs/, **absentness** /'æbsəntnɪs/ *ns., no pl.* Geistesabwesenheit, *die;* (*habitual*) Zerstreutheit, *die*

**absinth** /'æbsɪnθ/ *n.* A (*liqueur*) **~[e]** Absinth, *der;* B (*essence*) Wermutextrakt, *der;* C (*Bot.: wormwood*) Wermut, *der*

**absolute** /'æbsəlu:t, 'æbsəlju:t/ *adj.* A (*complete, not relative*) absolut; unumstößlich ‹Beweis, Tatsache›; unbestreitbar ‹Tatsache›; ausgemacht ‹Lüge, Schurkerei, Skandal›; (*unconditional*) fest ‹Versprechen›; streng ‹Verpflichtung›; **~ alcohol** reiner Alkohol; ⇒ *also* **zero** 1 C; B (*unrestricted*) absolut ‹Monarchie, Herrscher›; uneingeschränkt ‹Macht›; unumschränkt ‹Herrscher›; **~ majority** absolute Mehrheit; C (*Ling.*) absolut ‹Verb›; (*uninflected*) ungebeugt; unflektiert; **ablative ~:** Ablativus absolutus, *der;* **accusative/genitive/nominative ~:** absoluter Akkusativ/Genitiv/Nominativ; **~ construction** absolute Konstruktion; D (*Philos.*) absolut; **the ~:** das Absolute

**absolutely** /'æbsəlu:tlɪ, 'æbsəlju:tlɪ/ *adv.* A absolut; strikt ‹ablehnen›; völlig ‹verrückt›; entschieden ‹bestreiten›; ausgesprochen ‹kriminell, schlimm, ekelhaft›; **you're ~ right!** du hast völlig Recht; B (*positively*) regelrecht; **~ fabulous/gorgeous** echt toll (*ugs.*); **I say ~ no** ich sage entschieden nein; **~ not!** auf keinen Fall!; C (*unconditionally*) mit absoluter Sicherheit ‹behaupten, glauben, beweisen›; strikt ‹sich weigern›; D (*without qualification, independently*) absolut; E (*Ling.*) absolut; F /æbsə'lu:tlɪ/ (*coll.: yes indeed*) hundertprozentig (*ugs.*)

**absolute: ~ 'pitch** *n.* (*Mus.*) (*ability*) absolutes Gehör; (*standard*) absolute Tonhöhe; **~ temperature** *n.* (*Phys.*) absolute Temperatur

**absolution** /æbsə'lu:ʃn, æbsə'lju:ʃn/ *n.* A (*release*) Lossprechung, *die* (**from** von); (*forgiveness of wrongdoing*) Vergebung, *die;* B (*Relig.*) (*forgiveness*) Vergebung, *die;* (*release*) Erlass, *der* (**from** *Gen.*); **the priest pronounced ~:** der Priester erteilte [die] Absolution

**absolutism** /'æbsəlu:tɪzm, 'æbsəlju:tɪzm/ *n., no pl.* (*Polit.*) Absolutismus, *der*

**absolve** /əb'zɒlv/ *v.t.* A (*release*) **~ from** entbinden von ‹Pflichten›; vergeben ‹Sünde, Verbrechen›; lossprechen von ‹Schuld›; (*Relig.*) Absolution erteilen (+ *Dat.*); B (*acquit*) freisprechen (*Rechtsw.*)

**absorb** /əb'sɔ:b, əb'zɔ:b/ *v.t.* A aufsaugen ‹Flüssigkeit›; aufnehmen ‹Flüssigkeit, Nährstoff, Wärme›; resorbieren (*Med.*); absorbieren (*fachspr.*); (*fig.*) in sich aufnehmen ‹Wissen›; **~ a price increase** Mehrkosten auffangen; B (*reduce in strength*) absorbieren; abfangen ‹Schlag, Stoß›; C (*incorporate*) absorbieren ‹Chemikalie›; eingliedern, integrieren ‹Abteilung, Gemeinde›; inkorporieren (*Rechtsw.*) ‹Gemeinde›; **be ~ed by** *or* **into the crowd** von der Menge verschluckt werden; D (*consume*) aufzehren ‹Kraft, Zeit, Vermögen›; aufnehmen ‹Importe, Arbeitskräfte›; E (*engross*) ausfüllen ‹Person, Interesse, Gedanken›

**absorbed** /əb'sɔ:bd, əb'zɔ:bd/ *adj.* versunken; **be/get ~ in sth.** in etw. (*Akk.*) vertieft sein/sich in etw. (*Akk.*) vertiefen; **be/get ~ in sb.** von jmdm. gefangen genommen sein/werden; **he's totally ~ in his passion/work** er geht völlig in seiner Leidenschaft/Arbeit auf; **be/get ~ by sth./sb.** von etw./jmdm. [völlig] in Anspruch genommen sein/werden

**absorbency** /əb'sɔ:bənsɪ, əb'zɔ:bənsɪ/ *n.* Saugfähigkeit, *die*

**absorbent** /əb'sɔ:bənt, əb'zɔ:bənt/ ❶ *adj.* saugfähig; absorbierend (*fachspr.*); **~ cotton** (*Amer.*) Watte, *die.* ❷ *n.* (*substance*) Absorbens (*Chemie, Med.*); (*material*) absorbierendes Material

**absorbing** /əb'sɔ:bɪŋ, əb'zɔ:bɪŋ/ *adj.* faszinierend

**absorption** /əb'sɔ:pʃn, əb'zɔ:pʃn/ *n.* A (*incorporation, physical process*) Absorption, *die* (*fachspr.*); Resorption, *die* (*Med.*); B (*of department, community*) Integration, *die;* (*of effort*) Aufnahme, *die;* (*of goods*) Abnahme, *die;* C (*engrossment*) (*in reading, watching*) Versunkenheit, *die;* **their ~ in each other** ihr vollkommenes Aufgehen ineinander

**abstain** /əb'steɪn/ *v.i.* A enthaltsam sein; **~ from sth.** sich einer Sache (*Gen.*) enthalten; B **~ [from voting]** sich der Stimme enthalten

**abstainer** /əb'steɪnə(r)/ *n.* A Antialkoholiker, *der;* Abstinenzler, *der;* B (*in vote*) **an ~** *jmd., der sich der Stimme enthält*

**abstemious** /əb'sti:mɪəs/ *adj.*, **abstemiously** /əb'sti:mɪəslɪ/ *adv.* enthaltsam

**abstemiousness** /əb'sti:mɪəsnɪs/ *n., no pl.* Enthaltsamkeit, *die*

**abstention** /əb'stenʃn/ *n.* A Enthaltung, *die;* **~ from sex** sexuelle Enthaltsamkeit; B **~ from the vote/from voting** Stimmenthaltung, *die;* **how many ~s were there?** wie viele Personen enthielten sich der Stimme?

**abstinence** /'æbstɪnəns/ *n.* A (*abstaining*) Abstinenz, *die;* **total ~:** völlige Abstinenz; B (*moderation*) Entsagung, *die*

**abstinent** /'æbstɪnənt/ *adj.* abstinent

**abstract** ❶ /'æbstrækt/ *adj.* abstrakt; **~ noun** (*Ling.*) Abstraktum, *das;* **the ~:** das Abstrakte; **in the ~:** abstrakt; **~ expressionism** ⇒ **action painting.** ❷ *n.* A (*summary*) Zusammenfassung, *die;* Abstract, *das* (*fachspr.*); (*of book*) Inhaltsangabe, *die;* B (*idea*) Abstraktum, *das;* C (*Art*) abstraktes [Kunst]werk. ❸ /æb'strækt/ *v.t.* A (*remove*) wegnehmen; (*euphem.: steal*) entwenden, (*ugs.*) stibitzen (**from** aus); B (*summarize*) zusammenfassen ‹Bericht, Referat›

**abstracted** /æb'stræktɪd/ *adj.*, **abstractedly** /æb'stræktɪdlɪ/ *adv.* [geistes]abwesend

**abstraction** /æb'strækʃn/ *n.* A (*removal*) Entnahme, *die;* (*euphem.: stealing*) Entwendung, *die;* B *no pl.* (*absence of mind*) Geistesabwesenheit, *die;* Zerstreutheit, *die;* C (*idea*) Abstraktion, *die;* **he talks in ~s** er spricht in abstrakten Begriffen

**abstractly** /'æbstræktlɪ/ *adv.* abstrakt

**abstractness** /'æbstræktnɪs/ *n., no pl.* Abstraktheit, *die*

**abstractor** /æb'stræktə(r)/ *n.: Verfasser[in] von Abstracts*

**abstruse** /æb'stru:s/ *adj.*, **abstrusely** /æb'stru:slɪ/ *adv.* abstrus

**abstruseness** /æb'stru:snɪs/ *n., no pl.* Abstrusität, *die*

**absurd** /əb'sɜ:d/ *adj.* absurd; (*ridiculous*) lächerlich; **the theatre of the ~:** das absurde Theater

**absurdity** /əb'sɜ:dɪtɪ/ *n.* Absurdität, *die*

**absurdly** /əb'sɜ:dlɪ/ *adv.* lächerlich; **he is ~ afraid of ...:** er hat eine krankhafte Angst vor (+ *Dat.*) ...

**ABTA** *abbr.* (*Brit.*) **Association of British Travel Agents** *Vereinigung der britischen Reiseveranstalter*

**abundance** /ə'bʌndəns/ *n.* A **[an] ~ of sth.** eine Fülle von etw.; **an ~ of love/energy** ein Übermaß an Liebe/Energie (*Dat.*); **in ~:** in Hülle und Fülle; B (*profusion*) Überfluss, *der;* C (*wealth*) Reichtum, *der*

**abundant** /ə'bʌndənt/ *adj.* reich ‹Auswahl›; übergroß ‹Interesse, Begeisterung›; **an ~ supply of fish/fruit** Fisch/Obst im Überfluss; **~ proof/reason** mehr als genug Beweise/Gründe; **be ~:** reichlich vorhanden sein; **~ in** reich an (+ *Dat.*)

**abundantly** /ə'bʌndəntlɪ/ *adv.* reichlich; **I made it ~ clear that ...:** ich habe es mehr als deutlich zum Ausdruck gebracht, dass ...

**abuse** ❶ /ə'bju:z/ *v.t.* A (*misuse*) missbrauchen ‹Macht, Recht, Autorität, Vertrauen›; (*maltreat*) peinigen, quälen ‹Tier›; schaden (+ *Dat.*) ‹Motor›; **sexually ~:** sexuell missbrauchen; B (*insult*) beschimpfen. ❷ /ə'bju:s/ *n.* A (*misuse*) Missbrauch, *der;* B (*unjust or corrupt practice*) Missstand, *der;* C (*insults*) Beschimpfungen *Pl.;* **a term of ~:** ein Schimpfwort

**abusive** /ə'bju:sɪv/ *adj.* beleidigend; **~ language** Beleidigungen; Beschimpfungen; **become** *or* **get ~:** ausfallend werden

**abut** /ə'bʌt/ ❶ *v.i.*, **-tt-:** A (*border*) **~ on** grenzen an (+ *Akk.*); B (*end*) **~ on/against** stoßen *od.* angrenzen an (+ *Akk.*); (*rest*) **~ on** ruhen auf (+ *Dat.*). ❷ *v.t.* A (*border on*) angrenzen an (+ *Akk.*); B (*end on*) anstoßen an (+ *Akk.*)

**abutment** /ə'bʌtmənt/ *n.* Widerlager, *das*

**abysmal** /ə'bɪzml/ *adj.* A (*bottomless*) unergründlich ‹Tiefe›; (*fig.*) grenzenlos ‹Unwissenheit›; B (*coll.: bad*) katastrophal (*ugs.*)

**abyss** /ə'bɪs/ *n.* (*lit. or fig.*) Abgrund, *der;* **the ~ of space/the sea** die unendliche Tiefe des Weltraums/der See

**Abyssinia** /æbɪ'sɪnɪə/ *pr. n.* (*Hist.*) Abessinien (*das*)

**AC** *abbr.* (*Electr.*) **alternating current** Ws

**a/c** *abbr.* **account**

**acacia** /ə'keɪʃə/ *n.* (*Bot.*) Akazie, *die;* **[false] ~:** Robinie, *die*

**academe** /'ækədi:m/ *n.* (*literary*) Akademie, *die;* (*university*) Alma Mater, *die;* **the grove[s] of A~:** die akademischen Gefilde

**academic** /ækə'demɪk/ ❶ *adj.* A (*scholarly*) akademisch; wissenschaftlich ‹Fach, Studium›; **an ~ person/thinker** ein Theoretiker; **he's better on the ~ side** das Theoretische liegt ihm mehr; B (*of university etc.*) akademisch; **~ year** Universitätsjahr, *das;* C (*abstract, formal*) akademisch. ❷ *n.* Wissenschaftler, *der*/Wissenschaftlerin, *die;* (*scholar*) Gelehrte, *der*/*die*

**academical** /ækə'demɪkl/ ❶ *adj.* akademisch. ❷ *n. in pl.* akademische Tracht

**academically** /ækə'demɪkəlɪ/ *adv.* A (*intellectually*) wissenschaftlich; **be ~ very able** große intellektuelle Fähigkeiten haben; B (*educationally*) **~ [speaking]** was die akademische Ausbildung betrifft

**academician** /əkædə'mɪʃn/ *n.* Akademiemitglied, *das*

**academy** /ə'kædəmɪ/ *n.* A (*society*) Akademie, *die;* **Royal A~ [of Arts]** *Akademie der Künste in Großbritannien;* B (*school*) höhere Bildungsanstalt; (*college*) Akademie, *die*

**acanthus** /ə'kænθəs/ *n.* (*Bot.*) Akanthus, *der;* Bärenklau, *die od. der*

**ACAS** /'eɪkæs/ *abbr.* (*Brit.*) **Advisory Conciliation and Arbitration Service** *staatliche Schlichtungsstelle*

**accede** /æk'si:d/ *v.i.* A (*assent*) zustimmen (**to** *Dat.*); B beitreten (**to** *Dat.*) ‹Abkommen, Bündnis›; antreten ‹Amt›; **~ [to the throne]** den Thron besteigen

**accelerate** /ək'seləreɪt/ ❶ *v.t.* beschleunigen; erhöhen ‹Geschwindigkeit, Notwendigkeit›. ❷ *v.i.* sich beschleunigen; ‹Auto[fahrer], Läufer:› beschleunigen; ‹Autofahrer:› Gas geben (*ugs.*)

**acceleration** /əkselə'reɪʃn/ *n.* Beschleunigung, *die;* **the ~ of economic growth** das verstärkte wirtschaftliche Wachstum

**accelerator** /ək'seləreɪtə(r)/ *n.* A (*Motor Veh.*) **~ [pedal]** Gas[pedal], *das;* B (*Phys.*) Beschleuniger, *der*

**accent** ❶ /'æksənt/ *n.* A (*prominence by stress*) Akzent, *der;* (*mark*) Akzent, *der;* Akzentzeichen, *das;* B ▶ 1275 (*pronunciation*) Akzent, *der;* (*note in sb.'s voice*) Unterton, *der;* C *in pl.* (*speech*) Ton[fall], *der;* D (*Mus.*) Akzent, *der;* E (*rhythmical stress*) Betonung, *die;* F (*emphasis*) Akzent, *der;* **the ~ is on ...:** der Akzent liegt auf (+ *Dat.*) ...; G (*distinctive character*) Gepräge, *das;* H (*contrasting detail*) [Farb]akzent, *der.* ❷ /ək'sent/ *v.t.* (*stress, lit. or fig.*) betonen; (*mark*) mit Akzent[en] versehen

**accentual** /ək'sentjʊəl/ *adj.* akzentuierend

**accentuate** /ək'sentjʊeɪt/ *v.t.* betonen; vertiefen ‹Eindruck, Erinnerung, Feindschaft›; verstärken ‹Schmerz, Kummer›

**accentuation** /əksentjʊ'eɪʃn/ *n.* Betonung, *die*

**accept** /ək'sept/ *v.t.* A ▶ 924 (*be willing to receive*) annehmen; aufnehmen ‹Mitglied›; (*take*

a

*formally*) entgegennehmen ‹Dank, Spende, Auszeichnung›; übernehmen ‹Verantwortung, Aufgabe›; (*agree to*) annehmen ‹Vorschlag, Plan, Heiratsantrag, Einladung›; ~ **sb. for a job/school** jmdm. eine Einstellungszusage geben/jmdn. in eine Schule aufnehmen; ~ **sb. for a course** jmdn. in einen Lehrgang aufnehmen; ~ **sb. on to the staff** jmdn. in die Belegschaft aufnehmen; ~ **sb. into the Church/the family** jmdn. in die Kirche/in die Familie aufnehmen; **get sth. ~ed** dafür sorgen, dass etw. angenommen wird; ~ **sth. for publication** etw. zur Veröffentlichung annehmen; **B** (*approve*) akzeptieren; **he is ~ed in the best circles** er ist in den besten Kreisen eingeführt; ~ **sb. as a member of the group** jmdn. als Mitglied der Gruppe anerkennen; **C** (*acknowledge*) akzeptieren; **it is ~ed that ...:** es ist unbestritten, dass ...; **an ~ed fact** eine anerkannte Tatsache; **an ~ed opinion** eine verbreitete Ansicht; ~ **sb. for what he is** jmdn. so nehmen, wie er ist; **D** (*believe*) ~ **sth. [from sb.]** [jmdm.] etw. glauben; **E** (*heed*) beherzigen ‹Rat, Warnung›; **F** (*tolerate*) hinnehmen; ~ **losing a job** sich mit einer Kündigung abfinden; **he won't ~ that** er wird das nicht ohne weiteres hinnehmen; **G** (*Commerc.*) annehmen ‹Scheck›

**acceptability** /əksepta'bɪlɪtɪ/ *n., no pl.* Annehmbarkeit, *die;* (*of salary, price, risk*) Angemessenheit, *die;* (*agreeableness*) Annehmlichkeit, *die*

**acceptable** /ək'septəbl/ *adj.* **A** (*suitable, reasonable*) akzeptabel; **damaged banknotes are not ~:** beschädigte Banknoten können nicht angenommen werden; **B** (*agreeable*) annehmbar ‹Preis, Gehalt›; angenehm ‹Person›; **would the salary be ~ to you?** wäre das Gehalt annehmbar für Sie?

**acceptably** /ək'septəblɪ/ *adv.* **A** (*suitably, agreeably*) angenehm ‹nahe, wenig›; **be ~ priced** nicht zu teuer sein; **B** (*reasonably*) vernünftig; **she sings ~ well** sie singt ganz akzeptabel; **C** (*adequately*) hinreichend

**acceptance** /ək'septəns/ *n.* **A** (*willing receipt*) Annahme, *die;* (*of gift, offer*) Annahme, *die;* Entgegennahme, *die;* (*of duty, responsibility*) Übernahme, *die;* (*in answer*) Zusage, *die;* (*welcome*) Aufnahme, *die;* (*agreement*) Annahme, *die;* Zustimmung, *die* (**of** zu); **[letter of] ~:** schriftliche Zusage, *die;* **she gave her ~ to his proposal of marriage** sie gab ihm ihr Jawort; **B** *no pl.* (*approval*) Billigung, *die;* **C** *no pl.* (*acknowledgement*) Anerkennung, *die;* (*of excuse, explanation*) Annahme, *die;* **that fact has gained general ~:** diese Tatsache wird allgemein anerkannt; **D** *no pl.* (*heeding*) Beachtung, *die;* **E** *no pl.* (*toleration*) (*of a fact*) Hinnahme, *die;* (*of behaviour*) Duldung, *die;* **F** (*Commerc.:* [*engagement to honour*] *bill etc.*) Akzept, *das*

**access** /'ækses/ **1** *n.* **A** *no pl., no art.* (*entering*) Zutritt, *der* (**to** zu); (*by vehicles*) Einfahren, *das* (**into** in + *Akk.*); **this doorway is the only means of ~:** diese Tür ist der einzige Zugang; **'no entry except for ~'** „Anlieger[verkehr] frei"; **B** (*admission*) **gain** *or* **obtain** *or* **get ~:** Einlass finden; **C** *no pl.* (*opportunity to use or approach*) Zugang, *der* (**to** zu); **the father has ~ to the children** der Vater hat ein Recht zum Umgang mit den Kindern; **she was not allowed ~ to her personal file** man verweigerte ihr die Einsichtnahme in ihre Personalakte; **D** (*accessibility*) **easy/difficult of ~:** leicht/schwer zugänglich; **E** (*way* [*in*]) Zugang, *der;* (*road*) Zufahrt, *die;* (*door*) Eingang, *der.*
**2** *v.t.* (*Computing*) ~ **the file/drive** *etc.* auf die Datei/das Laufwerk *usw.* zugreifen

**accessary** /ək'sesərɪ/ **1** *n.* ⇒ **accessory** 2 D. **2** *adj.* beteiligt (**to** an + *Dat.*)

**accessibility** /əksesɪ'bɪlɪtɪ/ *n., no pl.* **A** (*reachability*) **the easy ~ of the beach** der leichte Zugang zum Strand; **B** (*approachability, availability, understandability*) Zugänglichkeit, *die*

**accessible** /ək'sesɪbl/ *adj.* **A** (*reachable*) **[more] ~ [to sb.]** [besser] erreichbar [für jmdn.]; **B** (*available, open, understandable*) zugänglich (**to** für)

**accession** /ək'seʃn/ *n.* **A** Amtsantritt, *der;* (*to position, estate*) Übernahme, *die* (**to** *Gen.*); ~ **to the throne** Thronbesteigung, *die;* **B** (*being added*) Zugang, *der;* **C** (*thing added*) **new ~s to the library** Neuerwerbungen der Bibliothek; **D** (*joining*) Beitritt, *der* (**to** zu)

**accessory** /ək'sesərɪ/ **1** *adj.* ~ **[to sth.]** zusätzlich [zu etw.]. **2** *n.* **A** (*accompaniment*) Extra, *das;* **B** *in pl.* (*attachments*) Zubehör, *das;* **one of the accessories** eines der Zubehörteile; **C** (*dress article*) Accessoire, *das;* **D** ~ **[to a crime]** Mittäter [bei einem Verbrechen]; ~ **before the fact** Anstifter, *der;* ~ **after the fact** Begünstiger, *der*

**'access road** *n.* Zufahrtsstraße, *die*

**accidence** /'æksɪdəns/ *n.* (*Ling.*) Formenlehre, *die*

**accident** /'æksɪdənt/ *n.* **A** (*unlucky event*) Unfall, *der;* **road ~:** Verkehrsunfall, *der;* **meet with/have an ~:** einen Unfall erleiden/haben; ~ **rate** Unfallziffer, *die;* **B** (*chance*) Zufall, *der;* (*unfortunate chance*) Unglücksfall, *der;* **by ~:** zufällig; **by an** *or* **some ~ of fate** durch eine Laune des Schicksals; **C** (*mistake*) Versehen, *das;* **by ~:** versehentlich; **D** (*mishap*) Missgeschick, *das;* **chapter of ~s** (*coll.*) Pechsträhne, *die;* **have a chapter of ~s** vom Pech verfolgt sein; **~s will happen** das kommt schon mal vor

**accidental** /æksɪ'dentl/ **1** *adj.* (*fortuitous*) zufällig; (*unintended*) unbeabsichtigt; ~ **death** Tod durch Unfall. **2** *n.* (*Mus.*) Akzidens, *das* (*fachspr.*); Vorzeichen, *das*

**accidentally** /æksɪ'dentəlɪ/ *adv.* (*by chance*) zufällig; (*by mistake*) versehentlich

**'accident-prone** *adj.* ~ **person** Unfäller, *der* (*Psych.*); **he was the most ~ of the children** er hatte von den Kindern immer die meisten Unfälle; **he's such an ~ boy** mit dem Jungen ist aber auch immer irgendwas (*ugs.*)

**acclaim** /ə'kleɪm/ **1** *v.t.* (*welcome*) feiern; (*hail as*) ~ **sb. king** jmdn. zum König ausrufen. **2** *n., no pl.* **A** (*welcome*) Beifall, *der;* **B** (*approval*) Anerkennung, *die*

**acclamation** /æklə'meɪʃn/ *n.* **A** *no pl.* (*approval of plan or proposal*) Beifall, *der;* **B** *usu. in pl.* (*shouting*) Beifallsbekundung, *die*

**acclimatisation, acclimatise** ⇒ **acclimatiz-**

**acclimatization** /əklaɪmətaɪ'zeɪʃn/ *n.* (*lit. or fig.*) Akklimatisation, *die*

**acclimatize** /ə'klaɪmətaɪz/ *v.t.* (*lit. or fig.*) akklimatisieren; ~ **sth./sb. to sth.** etw./jmdn. an etw. (*Akk.*) gewöhnen; ~ **oneself, get** *or* **become ~d** sich akklimatisieren; ~ **oneself** *or* **get** *or* **become ~d to sth.** sich an etw. (*Akk.*) gewöhnen

**accolade** /'ækəleɪd, ækə'leɪd/ *n.* (*gesture*) Akkolade, *die;* (*fig.*) (*praise*) **~[s]** Lob, *das;* (*approval, acknowledgement*) Anerkennung, *die*

**accommodate** /ə'kɒmədeɪt/ *v.t.* **A** (*lodge*) unterbringen; (*hold, have room for*) Platz bieten (+ *Dat.*); **B** (*oblige*) gefällig sein (+ *Dat.*)

**accommodating** /ə'kɒmədeɪtɪŋ/ *adj.* (*obliging*) zuvorkommend; (*compliant*) entgegenkommend

**accommodatingly** /ə'kɒmədeɪtɪŋlɪ/ *adv.* (*obligingly*) zuvorkommend

**accommodation** /əkɒmə'deɪʃn/ *n.* **A** *no pl.* (*lodgings*) Unterkunft, *die;* **can you provide us with [some] ~ for the night?** können Sie uns ein Nachtquartier besorgen?; ~ **is very expensive in Oxford** Wohnungen/Zimmer sind in Oxford sehr teuer; **there is a lack of good hotel ~ in this town** in dieser Stadt fehlt es an guten Hotels; **student ~ is getting more expensive** Studentenunterkünfte *od.* -wohnungen werden [immer] teurer; **B** (*space*) **there is ~ for 500 people in this auditorium** in diesem Auditorium haben 500 Personen Platz; **C** *in pl.* (*Amer.: lodgings*) Unterkunft, *die*

**accommo'dation address** *n.* Gefälligkeitsadresse, *die*

**accompaniment** /ə'kʌmpənɪmənt/ *n.* **A** (*lit. or fig.; also Mus.*) Begleitung, *die;* **B** (*thing*) Begleiterscheinung, *die*

**accompanist** /ə'kʌmpənɪst/ *n.* (*Mus.*) Begleiter, *der*/Begleiterin, *die*

**accompany** /ə'kʌmpənɪ/ *v.t.* (*go along with; also Mus.*) begleiten; **the ~ing booklet** die beiliegende Broschüre

**accomplice** /ə'kʌmplɪs, ə'kɒmplɪs/ *n.* Komplize, *der*/Komplizin, *die*

**accomplish** /ə'kʌmplɪʃ, ə'kɒmplɪʃ/ *v.t.* (*perform*) vollbringen ‹Tat›; erfüllen ‹Aufgabe›; (*complete*) vollenden ‹Kunstwerk, Bauwerk›; (*achieve*) erreichen; verwirklichen ‹Ziel, Wunsch›

**accomplished** /ə'kʌmplɪʃt, ə'kɒmplɪʃt/ *adj.* fähig; **he is an ~ speaker/dancer** er ist ein erfahrener Redner/vollendeter Tänzer

**accomplishment** /ə'kʌmplɪʃmənt, ə'kɒmplɪʃmənt/ *n.* **A** *no pl.* (*completion*) Vollendung, *die;* (*of deed*) Ausführung, *die;* (*of task*) Erfüllung, *die;* (*of aim*) Verwirklichung, *die;* **B** (*achievement*) Leistung, *die;* (*skill*) Fähigkeit, *die*

**accord** /ə'kɔːd/ **1** *v.i.* ~ **[with sth.]** [mit etw.] übereinstimmen. **2** *v.t.* (*formal: grant*) ~ **sb. sth.** jmdm. etw. gewähren. **3** *n.* **A** (*volition*) **of one's own ~:** aus eigenem Antrieb; von selbst; **of its own ~:** von selbst; **B** (*harmonious agreement*) Übereinstimmung, *die;* **with one ~:** geschlossen; **C** (*harmony*) Harmonie, *die;* **be in ~ with** harmonieren mit; **D** (*treaty*) Übereinkunft, *die*

**accordance** /ə'kɔːdəns/ *n.* **in ~ with** in Übereinstimmung mit; gemäß (+ *Dat.*)

**according** /ə'kɔːdɪŋ/ *adv.* **A** ~ **as** (*depending on how*) je nachdem wie; (*depending on whether*) je nachdem ob; **B** ~ **to** nach; **act ~ to the rules** sich an die Regeln halten; ~ **to how** je nachdem wie; ~ **to him** (*opinion*) seiner Meinung nach; (*account*) nach seiner Aussage; ~ **to circumstances/the season** den Umständen/der Jahreszeit entsprechend

**accordingly** /ə'kɔːdɪŋlɪ/ *adv.* (*as appropriate*) entsprechend; (*therefore*) folglich

**accordion** /ə'kɔːdɪən/ *n.* Akkordeon, *das;* ~ **pleats** Plisseefalten

**accost** /ə'kɒst/ *v.t.* ansprechen

**account** /ə'kaʊnt/ **1** *v.t.* (*consider*) halten für; ansehen als.
**2** *n.* **A** (*Finance*) (*reckoning*) Rechnung, *die;* (*statement*) Auflistung, *die;* Aufstellung, *die;* (*invoice*) Rechnung, *die;* **money of ~** (*Finance*) Rechnungseinheit, *die;* ~ **rendered** ⇒ **render** E; **keep ~s/the ~s** Buch/die Bücher führen; **settle** *or* **square ~s with sb.** (*lit. or fig.*) mit jmdm. abrechnen; **on ~:** auf Rechnung; a conto; **on one's [own] ~:** auf eigene Rechnung; auf eigenes Risiko; (*fig.*) von sich aus; **B** (*at bank, shop*) Konto, *das;* **an ~ with** *or* **at a bank** ein Konto bei einer Bank; **pay sth. into one's ~:** etw. auf sein Konto einzahlen; **draw sth. out of one's ~:** etw. von seinem Konto abheben; **on ~:** auf Rechnung; **joint ~:** gemeinsames Konto; Gemeinschaftskonto, *das;* **C** (*statement of facts*) Rechenschaft, *die;* **give** *or* **render an ~ for sth.** über etw. (*Akk.*) Rechenschaft ablegen; **call sb. to ~:** jmdn. zur Rechenschaft ziehen; **give a good ~ of oneself** seinen Mann stehen; **D** (*consideration*) **take ~ of sth., take sth. into ~:** etw. berücksichtigen; **take no ~ of sth./sb., leave sth./sb. out of ~:** etw./jmdn. unberücksichtigt lassen *od.* nicht berücksichtigen; **don't change your plans on my ~:** ändert nicht meinetwegen eure Pläne; **on ~ of** wegen; **on no ~, not on any ~:** auf [gar] keinen Fall; **E** (*importance*) **of some/little/no ~:** von/von geringer/ohne Bedeutung; **F** (*performance*) Interpretation, *die;* **G** (*report*) **an ~ [of sth.]** ein Bericht [über etw. (*Akk.*)]; **give a full ~ of sth.** ausführlich über etw. (*Akk.*) berichten *od.* Bericht erstatten; **by** *or* **from all ~s** nach allem, was man hört; **H** (*advantage*) **turn sth. to [good] ~:** aus etw. Nutzen *od.* Vorteil ziehen

~ **for** *v.t.* **A** (*give reckoning*) Rechenschaft *od.* Rechnung ablegen über (+ *Akk.*); **B** (*explain*) erklären; **I can't ~ for that** ich kann mir das nicht erklären; **C** (*represent in amount*) ausmachen; ergeben; **D** (*kill, destroy, capture*) zur Strecke bringen

**accountability** /əkaʊntəˈbɪlɪtɪ/ *n., no pl.* Verantwortlichkeit, *die* (**to** gegenüber)

**accountable** /əˈkaʊntəbl/ *adj.* verantwortlich; (*explicable*) erklärlich; **be ~ to sb.** jmdm. Rechenschaft schuldig sein; **be ~ for sth.** für etw. verantwortlich sein

**accountancy** /əˈkaʊntənsɪ/ *n., no pl.* Buchhaltung, *die*

**accountant** /əˈkaʊntənt/ *n.* ▶ 1261 [Bilanz-]buchhalter, *der*/[Bilanz]buchhalterin, *die*; ⇒ *also* **chartered accountant**

**acˈcount holder** *n.* Kontoinhaber, *der*/-inhaberin, *die*

**accounting** /əˈkaʊntɪŋ/ *n.* **A** *no pl.* (*Finance*) Buchführung, *die*; **B** (*explanation*) **there's no ~ for it** das ist nicht zu erklären; **there's no ~ for taste[s]** über Geschmack lässt sich [nicht] streiten

**acˈcount number** *n.* Kontonummer, *die*

**accredit** /əˈkredɪt/ *v.t.* **A** (*vouch for*) bestätigen; **B** (*send as representative*) **be ~ed to sb.** bei jmdm. akkreditiert sein

**accredited** /əˈkredɪtɪd/ *adj.* anerkannt ‹Schule, Anstalt, Buch, Regierung›; akkreditiert ‹Botschafter, Diplomat›; zugelassen ‹Journalist›

**accretion** /əˈkri:ʃn/ *n.* **A** (*combination*) Verschmelzung, *die*; **B** (*growth*) Wachstum, *das*; (*of power*) Anwachsen, *das*

**accrue** /əˈkru:/ *v.i.* ‹Zinsen:› auflaufen; **~ to sb.** ‹Macht, Ansehen:› jmdm. zuwachsen; ‹Reichtümer, Einnahmen:› jmdm. zufließen

**accrued** /əˈkru:d/ *adj.* anfallend ‹Ausgaben, Gewinne›; aufgelaufen ‹Schulden, Zinsen›; entstanden ‹Vorteile, Kontakte›

**accumulate** /əˈkju:mjʊleɪt/ **1** *v.t.* (*gather*) sammeln; machen, (*fachspr.*) akkumulieren ‹Vermögen›; (*in a pile*) zusammentragen; (*along the way*) einsammeln; (*produce*) einbringen ‹Zinsen, Gewinne, Undank, Kritik› (**for sb.** jmdm.); **it's amazing how much stuff you ~ in the space of a year** es ist erstaunlich, wie viel Zeug sich bei einem in einem Jahr so ansammelt. **2** *v.i.* ‹Menge, Staub:› sich ansammeln; ‹Schnee, Geld:› sich anhäufen; ‹Schlamm:› sich absetzen

**accumulation** /əkju:mjʊˈleɪʃn/ *n.* [An]sammeln, *das*; (*being accumulated*) Anhäufung, *die*; (*growth*) Zuwachs, *der* (**of** an + *Dat.*); (*mass*) Menge, *die*

**accumulator** /əˈkju:mjʊleɪtə(r)/ *n.* **A** (*Electr.*) Akkumulator, *der*; Akku, *der* (*ugs.*); Sammler, *der*; **B** (*bet*) Kumulativwette, *die*

**accuracy** /ˈækjʊrəsɪ/ *n.* Genauigkeit, *die*

**accurate** /ˈækjʊrət/ *adj.* genau; akkurat (*geh.*); (*correct*) richtig; getreu ‹Wiedergabe›; **the description of the man turned out to be completely ~:** die Beschreibung des Mannes erwies sich als völlig korrekt; **is the clock ~?** geht die Uhr richtig *od.* genau?

**accurately** /ˈækjʊrətlɪ/ *adv.* (*precisely*) genau; exakt; (*correctly*) richtig; korrekt; (*faithfully*) getreu; genau; **the landscape is represented ~:** die Landschaft ist naturgetreu dargestellt

**accursed**, (*arch.*) **accurst** /əˈkɜ:st/ *adj.* **A** (*ill-fated*) verflucht; verwünscht; **B** (*involving misery*) unselig; **C** (*coll.: detestable*) verflixt (*ugs.*); verdammt (*ugs.*)

**accusation** /ækju:ˈzeɪʃn/ *n.* **A** (*accusing*) Anschuldigung, *die* (**of** gegen); Anklage, *die* (*Rechtsw.*); (*being accused*) Beschuldigung, *die*; **B** (*charge*) Vorwurf, *der*; **make an ~/make ~s about sb./sth.** eine Anschuldigung/Anschuldigungen gegen jmdn./wegen etw. vorbringen

**accusative** /əˈkju:zətɪv/ (*Ling.*) **1** *adj.* Akkusativ-; akkusativisch; **~ case** Akkusativ, *der*. **2** *n.* Akkusativ, *der*

**accusatory** /əˈkju:zətərɪ/ *adj.* anklagend ‹Blick, Stimme, Schweigen›

**accuse** /əˈkju:z/ *v.t.* (*charge*) beschuldigen; bezichtigen (*geh.*); (*Law*) (*indict*) anklagen; **~ sb. of cowardice** jmdm. Feigheit vorwerfen; **what are you accusing me of?** wessen beschuldigt *od.* bezichtigt ihr mich?; was werft ihr mir vor?; **the children were ~d of stealing apples** die Kinder wurden beschuldigt, Äpfel gestohlen zu haben; **~ sb. of theft/murder** jmdn. wegen Diebstahl[s]/Mord[es] anklagen; jmdn. des Diebstahls/Mordes anklagen (*geh.*); **the ~d** der/die Angeklagte/die Angeklagten

**accuser** /əˈkju:zə(r)/ *n.* Ankläger, *der*/Anklägerin, *die*

**accusing** /əˈkju:zɪŋ/ *adj.* anklagend; **point an ~ finger at sb.** (*lit. or fig.*) anklagend mit dem Finger auf jmdn. zeigen

**accusingly** /əˈkju:zɪŋlɪ/ *adv.* anklagend; (*reproachfully*) vorwurfsvoll

**accustom** /əˈkʌstəm/ *v.t.* **~ sb./sth. to sth.** jmdn./etw. an etw. (*Akk.*) gewöhnen; **~ sb. to doing sth.** jmdn. daran gewöhnen, etw. zu tun; **grow/be ~ed to sth.** sich an etw. (*Akk.*) gewöhnen/an etw. (*Akk.*) gewöhnt sein; **I'm not ~ed to being called rude names** ich bin nicht gewohnt, dass man mich beschimpft

**accustomed** /əˈkʌstəmd/ *attrib. adj.* gewohnt; üblich

**ace** /eɪs/ **1** *n.* **A** (*Cards, Tennis*) Ass, *das*; **~ of trumps/diamonds** Trumpf-/Karoass, *das*; **B** (*fig.*) **an ~ up one's sleeve** ein Trumpf in der Hand; **play one's ~:** seinen Trumpf ausspielen; **hold all the ~s** alle Trümpfe auf *od.* in der Hand haben; **C** (*champion, outstanding person*) Ass, *das*; (*pilot*) erfolgreicher Kampfflieger; **D** (*hair's breadth*) **he was within an ~ of doing it/of winning** er hätte es um ein Haar getan/hätte um ein Haar gewonnen. **2** *adj.* (*coll.*) klasse (*ugs.*); spitze (*ugs.*)

**acerbic** /əˈsɜ:bɪk/ *adj.* scharf ‹Worte, Kritik, Zunge›; rau ‹Umgangston, Temperament›

**acerbity** /əˈsɜ:bɪtɪ/ *n., no pl.* ⇒ **acerbic**: Schärfe, *die*; Rauheit, *die*

**acetate** /ˈæsɪteɪt/ *n.* (*Chem.*) Acetat, *das*; **~ fibre/silk** Acetatfaser/-seide, *die*

**acetic** /əˈsi:tɪk/ *adj.* (*Chem.*) essigsauer; **~ acid** Essigsäure, *die*

**acetone** /ˈæsɪtəʊn/ *n.* Aceton, *das*

**acetylene** /əˈsetɪli:n/ *n.* Acetylen, *das*

**ache** /eɪk/ **1** *v.i.* **A** ▶ 1232 schmerzen; wehtun; **whereabouts does your leg ~?** wo tut [dir] das Bein weh?; **I'm aching all over** mir tut alles weh; **her heart ~s with love** (*fig.*) das Herz tut ihr weh vor Liebe; **B** (*fig.: long*) **~ for sb./sth.** sich nach jmdm./etw. verzehren; **~ to do sth.** darauf brennen, etw. zu tun. **2** *n.* ▶ 1232 Schmerz, *der*; **~s and pains** Wehwehchen, *die*

**achievable** /əˈtʃi:vəbl/ *adj.* (*accomplishable*) durchführbar; (*attainable*) erreichbar ‹Ziel, Standard›

**achieve** /əˈtʃi:v/ *v.t.* zustande bringen; ausführen ‹Aufgabe, Plan›; erreichen ‹Ziel, Standard, Absicht›; herstellen, herbeiführen ‹Frieden, Harmonie›; erzielen ‹Rekord, Leistung, Erfolg›; erfüllen ‹Zweck›; finden ‹Seelenfrieden›; es bringen zu, erlangen ‹Berühmtheit, Anerkennung›; erlangen ‹gutes Aussehen›; **he ~d great things** er hat Großes geleistet; **he's ~d what he set out to do** er hat erreicht, was er sich (*Dat.*) vorgenommen hat; **he'll never ~ anything [in life]** er wird es [im Leben] nie zu etwas bringen

**achievement** /əˈtʃi:vmənt/ *n.* **A** *no pl.* ⇒ **achieve**: Zustandebringen, *das*; Ausführung, *die*; Erreichen, *das*; Herstellung, *die*; Herbeiführung, *die*; Erzielen, *das*; Erfüllung, *die*; Finden, *das*; Erlangen, *das*; **the task is impossible of ~:** die Aufgabe ist undurchführbar; **for these people ~ is measured in terms of money** für diese Leute wird Erfolg am Geld gemessen; **B** (*thing accomplished*) Leistung, *die*; Errungenschaft, *die*

**Achilles** /əˈkɪli:z/ *pr. n.* Achilles (*der*); ⇒ *also* **heel**[1] 1 A; **tendon**

**achy** /ˈeɪkɪ/ *adj.* **feel ~:** Schmerzen haben; **I feel ~ all over** mir tut alles weh

**acid** /ˈæsɪd/ **1** *adj.* **A** (*sour*) sauer; (*fig.: biting*) bissig; **B** (*Chem., Agric., Geol.*) sauer ‹Reaktion, Lösung, Boden, Gesteine›. **2** *n.* **A** Säure, *die*; **B** (*sl.: LSD*) Acid, *das*

**acid: ~ drop** *n.* (*Brit.*) saurer *od.* saures Drops; **~ head** *n.* (*sl.*) Säurekopf, *der* (*salopp*); LSD-Schlucker, *der* (*salopp*); **~ house** *n* Acidhouse, *das*; *attrib.* **~ house music/party** Acidhousemusik, *die*/Acidhouseparty, *die*

**acidic** /əˈsɪdɪk/ *adj.* **A** (*sour*) säuerlich; (*fig.*) bissig; **B** (*Chem., Agric., Geol.*) sauer

**acidity** /əˈsɪdɪtɪ/ *n.* Säure, *die*; Acidität, *die* (*fachspr.*); Säuregrad, *der*; (*excessive*) Übersäuerung, *die*; (*fig.*) Bissigkeit, *die*

**acidly** /ˈæsɪdlɪ/ *adv.* (*fig.*) bissig

**acidosis** /æsɪˈdəʊsɪs/ *n., pl.* **acidoses** /æsɪˈdəʊsi:z/ (*Med.*) Acidose, *die*

**acid: ~ rain** *n.* saurer Regen; **~ test** *n.* Goldprobe, *die*; (*fig.*) Feuerprobe, *die*

**acknowledge** /əkˈnɒlɪdʒ/ *v.t.* **A** (*admit*) zugeben, eingestehen ‹Tatsache, Notwendigkeit, Fehler, Schuld›; (*accept*) sich bekennen zu ‹einer Verantwortung, Pflicht, Schuld›; anerkennen ‹Schulden›; (*take notice of*) grüßen ‹Person›; (*recognize*) anerkennen ‹Autorität, Recht, Forderung, Notwendigkeit›; **an ~d expert** ein anerkannter Fachmann; **he won't ~ himself beaten** er gibt sich nicht geschlagen; **~ sb./sth. [as *or* to be] sth.** jmdn./etw. als etw. anerkennen; **he was ~d [as] the world's greatest living poet** er galt als der Welt größter lebender Dichter; **~ sb. [as] capable of doing sth.** jmdn. für fähig halten, etw. zu tun; **B** (*express thanks for*) sich erkenntlich zeigen für ‹Dienste, Bemühungen, Gastfreundschaft›; erwidern ‹Gruß›; **C** (*confirm receipt of*) bestätigen ‹Empfang, Bewerbung›; **~ a letter** den Empfang eines Briefes bestätigen

**acknowledg[e]ment** /əkˈnɒlɪdʒmənt/ *n.* **A** (*admission of a fact, necessity, error, guilt*) Eingeständnis, *das*; (*acceptance of a responsibility, duty, debt*) Bekenntnis, *das* (**of** zu); (*recognition of authority, right, claim*) Anerkennung, *die*; **B** (*thanks, appreciation*) (*of services, friendship*) Dank, *der* (**of** für); (*of greetings*) Erwiderung, *die*; **a grateful ~ of the services you have rendered to the community** eine dankbare Anerkennung Ihrer Verdienste um die Gemeinschaft; **C** (*confirmation of receipt*) Bestätigung [des Empfangs/einer Bewerbung]; **letter of ~:** Bestätigungsschreiben, *das*; **D** (*author's*) Danksagung, *die*; **'~s'** „Dank"

**acme** /ˈækmɪ/ *n.* Gipfel, *der*; Höhepunkt, *der*

**acne** /ˈæknɪ/ *n.* ▶ 1232 (*Med.*) Akne, *die*

**acolyte** /ˈækəlaɪt/ *n.* **A** (*Eccl.*) Ministrant, *der*; Messdiener, *der*; **B** (*fig.: follower*) Gefolgsmann, *der*

**aconite** /ˈækənaɪt/ *n.* (*Bot.*) Eisenhut, *der*; Sturmhut, *der*; Akonit, *das* (*fachspr.*)

**acorn** /ˈeɪkɔ:n/ *n.* Eichel, *die*

**acoustic** /əˈku:stɪk/ *adj.* **A** akustisch; **B** (*Mus.*) **~ guitar** Konzertgitarre, *die*; (*in pop, folk, etc.*) akustische Gitarre

**acoustically** /əˈku:stɪkəlɪ/ *adv.* akustisch

**acoustics** /əˈku:stɪks/ *n. pl.* **A** (*properties*) Akustik, *die*; akustische Verhältnisse *Pl.*; **B** *constr. as sing.* (*science*) Akustik, *die*

**acquaint** /əˈkweɪnt/ *v.t.* **~ sb./oneself with sth.** jmdn./sich mit etw. vertraut machen; **be ~ed with sb.** mit jmdm. bekannt sein

**acquaintance** /əˈkweɪntəns/ *n.* **A** *no pl.* Vertrautheit, *die*; **~ with sb.** Bekanntschaft mit jmdm.; **a passing ~:** eine flüchtige Bekanntschaft; **make the ~ of sb.** jmds. Bekanntschaft machen; jmdn. kennen lernen; **B** (*person*) Bekannte, *der*/*die*

**acquiesce** /ækwɪˈes/ *v.i.* einwilligen (**in** in + *Akk.*); (*under pressure*) sich fügen; **you must not ~ in everything [they say]** du darfst nicht allem zustimmen [,was sie sagen]

**acquiescence** /ækwɪˈesəns/ *n.* **A** *no pl.* (*acquiescing*) Einwilligung, *die* (**in** in + *Akk.*); (*state*) Ergebenheit, *die*; **B** (*assent*) Zustimmung, *die*

**acquiescent** /ækwɪˈesənt/ *adj.* fügsam; ergeben

**acquire** /əˈkwaɪə(r)/ *v.t.* **A** sich (*Dat.*) anschaffen ‹Gegenstände›; (*gain*) erwerben ‹Land, Besitz, Wohlstand, Kenntnisse›; sammeln ‹Erfahrungen›; ernten ‹Lob›; **B** (*take on*) annehmen ‹Tonfall, Farbe, Aussehen, Gewohnheit›; **last year the orchestra ~d a new leader** letztes Jahr erhielt das Orchester einen neuen Konzertmeister; **I have ~d a few unwanted**

a

**pounds** ich habe leider ein paar Pfund[e] zugenommen; **~d characteristics** (*Biol.*) erworbene Eigenschaften; **~ the habit of smoking** sich (*Dat.*) das Rauchen angewöhnen; **~ a taste for sth.** Geschmack an etw. (*Dat.*) gewinnen; **this wine is an ~d taste** an diesen Wein muss man sich erst gewöhnen

**acquirement** /əˈkwaɪəmənt/ *n.* ⇒ **acquisition A**

**acquisition** /ækwɪˈzɪʃn/ *n.* **A** (*of goods, wealth, land*) Erwerb, *der;* (*of knowledge*) Aneignung, *die;* Erwerb, *der;* (*of attitude, habit*) Annahme, *die;* **B** (*thing*) Anschaffung, *die*

**acquisitive** /əˈkwɪzɪtɪv/ *adj.* raffsüchtig; **~ instinct** Sammeltrieb, *der;* **the ~ society** die nach Besitz strebende Gesellschaft

**acquisitiveness** /əˈkwɪzɪtɪvnɪs/ *n., no pl.* Raffgier, *die*

**acquit** /əˈkwɪt/ *v.t.*, **-tt-:** **A** (*Law*) freisprechen; **~ sb. of sth.** jmdn. von etw. freisprechen; **he was ~ted on all three charges** er wurde in allen drei Anklagepunkten freigesprochen; **B** (*discharge*) **~ oneself of** erfüllen ‹Pflichten›; **~ oneself well** seine Sache gut machen; **if you ~ yourself well in the test** wenn du in der Prüfung gut abschneidest

**acquittal** /əˈkwɪtl/ *n.* **A** (*Law*) Freispruch, *der;* **B** (*performance*) Erfüllung, *die;* Erledigung, *die*

**acre** /ˈeɪkə(r)/ *n.* **A** ▶ **928** (*measure*) Acre, *der;* ≈ Morgen, *der;* **B** *in pl.* (*land*) Grund und Boden, *der;* **broad ~s** weites Land

**acreage** /ˈeɪkərɪdʒ/ *n.* **what is the ~ of your estate?** wie viel Land *od.* wie viele Morgen hat Ihr Gut?; **a farm of small ~:** ein Hof mit kleiner Anbaufläche

**acrid** /ˈækrɪd/ *adj.* beißend ‹Geruch, Dämpfe, Rauch›; bitter ‹Geschmack›

**acrimonious** /ækrɪˈməʊnɪəs/ *adj.* bitter; aggressiv ‹Haltung›; bissig ‹Bemerkung›; erbittert ‹Streit, Diskussion›

**acrimoniously** /ækrɪˈməʊnɪəslɪ/ *adv.* bitter; erbittert ‹angreifen›

**acrimony** /ˈækrɪmənɪ/ *n., no pl.* Bitterkeit, *die;* (*of attitude*) Aggressivität, *die;* (*of comment, criticism, etc.*) Bissigkeit, *die;* (*of argument, discussion*) Erbitterung, *die*

**acrobat** /ˈækrəbæt/ *n.* ▶ **1261** (*lit. or fig.*) Akrobat, *der*/Akrobatin, *die;* **a mental/intellectual ~:** ein Geistesakrobat

**acrobatic** /ækrəˈbætɪk/ *adj.* (*lit. or fig.*) akrobatisch

**acrobatics** /ækrəˈbætɪks/ *n., no pl.* Akrobatik, *die;* **mental ~:** Gehirnakrobatik, *die*

**acronym** /ˈækrənɪm/ *n.* Akronym, *das;* Initialwort, *das*

**across** /əˈkrɒs/ **1** *adv.* **A** (*to intersect*) [quer] darüber; **B** (*from one side to the other*) darüber; (*in crossword puzzle*) waagerecht; (*from here to there*) hinüber; **go ~ to the enemy** (*fig.*) zum Feind übergehen; **measure** *or* **be 9 miles ~:** 9 Meilen breit sein; **C** (*on the other side*) drüben; **~ there/here** [da] drüben/hier drüben; **~ from** gegenüber von; **just ~ from us there is a little shop** bei uns ist gleich gegenüber ein kleiner Laden; **D** *with verbs* (*towards speaker*) herüber-; (*away from speaker*) hinüber-; **swim ~:** herüber-/hinüberschwimmen.
**2** *prep.* **A** (*crossing*) über (+ *Akk.*); **right ~ the field** quer über das Feld; **a double yellow line ~ an entrance** eine gelbe Doppellinie vor einer Einfahrt; **B** (*from one side to the other of*) über (+ *Akk.*); **we went ~ the Atlantic** wir überquerten den Atlantik; **protest meetings ~ Canada** Protestversammlungen in ganz Kanada; **~ the board** pauschal; **a pay rise ~ the board** eine pauschale *od.* generelle Lohnerhöhung; **C** (*on the other side of*) auf der anderen Seite (+ *Gen.*); **~ the ocean/river** jenseits des Meeres/Flusses

**aˈcross-the-board** *adj.* pauschal; **an ~ pay rise** eine pauschale *od.* generelle Lohnerhöhung

**acrostic** /əˈkrɒstɪk/ *n.* Akrostichon, *das*

**acrylic** /əˈkrɪlɪk/ **1** *adj.* aus Acryl *nachgestellt;* Acryl-; **~ paint/fibre** Acrylfarbe, *die*/Acrylfaser, *die.* **2** *n.* Acryl, *das*

**act** /ækt/ **1** *n.* **A** (*deed*) Tat, *die;* (*official action*) Akt, *der;* **an ~ of God** höhere Gewalt; **an ~ of mercy** ein Gnadenakt; **an ~ of kindness** ein Akt *od.* Zeichen der Güte; **an ~ of folly** eine Dummheit; **Acts [of the Apostles]** (*Bibl.*) *constr. as sing.* Apostelgeschichte, *die;* **B** (*process*) **be in the ~ of doing sth.** gerade dabei sein, etw. zu tun; **he was caught in the ~ [of stealing]** er wurde [beim Stehlen] auf frischer Tat ertappt; **they were caught in the [very] ~:** sie wurden in flagranti ertappt; **C** (*in a play*) Akt, *der;* Aufzug, *der* (*geh.*); **a five-~ play** ein Drama in fünf Akten; **a one-~ play** ein Einakter; **D** (*theatre performance*) Akt, *der;* Nummer, *die;* (*performer*) Darsteller, *der*/Darstellerin, *die;* **the ~ consisted of four jugglers** die Truppe bestand aus vier Jongleuren; **get in on the ~** (*fig. coll.*) ins Geschäft einsteigen; mitmischen (*ugs.*); **he/she will be a hard ~ to follow** (*fig.*) das macht ihm/ihr so leicht keiner nach; **get one's ~ together** (*coll.*) sich am Riemen reißen (*ugs.*); **E** (*pretence*) Theater, *das;* Schau, *die* (*ugs.*); **it's all an ~ with her** sie tut nur so; **put on an ~** (*coll.*) eine Schau abziehen (*ugs.*); Theater spielen; **get into the** *or* **in on the ~** (*sl.*) in das Geschäft einsteigen; mitmischen (*ugs.*); **F** (*decree*) Gesetz, *das;* **Act of Parliament** Parlamentsakte, *die.*
**2** *v.t.* **A** (*perform*) spielen ‹Stück›; **B** (*play role of*) spielen ‹Rolle›; **he's a famous film producer and really ~s the part** (*fig.*) er ist ein berühmter Filmproduzent und benimmt sich auch so; ⇒ *also* **fool**[1] 1 B.
**3** *v.i.* **A** (*perform actions*) handeln; reagieren; **~ upon the instructions you were given** folgen Sie den Anweisungen wie gegeben; **~ [up]on sb.'s advice** jmds. Rat [-schlag] (*Dat.*) folgen; **~ quickly** schnell reagieren *od.* handeln; **B** (*behave*) sich verhalten; (*function*) **~ as sb.** als jmd. fungieren *od.* tätig sein; **~ as sth.** als etw. dienen; **C** (*perform special function*) ‹Person:› handeln; ‹Gerät, Ding:› funktionieren; ‹Substanz, Mittel:› wirken; **~ for** *or* **~ on behalf of sb.** für jmdn. *od.* in jmds. Auftrag tätig werden; jmdn. vertreten; **~ to prevent sth.** ‹Vorrichtung, Gerät:› zur Verhütung von etw. dienen; **D** (*perform play etc.; lit. or fig.*) spielen; schauspielern (*ugs.*); **she wants to ~ on stage/in films** sie will zum Theater/Film; **E** (*have effect*) **~ on sth.** auf etw. (*Akk.*) wirken *od.* einwirken

**~ ˈout** *v.t.* **A** vorspielen, nachmachen ‹Bewegungen, Handlung›; **B** (*Psych.*) abreagieren ‹Spannung, Ärger›

**~ ˈup** *v.i.* (*coll.*) Theater machen (*ugs.*); ‹Auto, Magen:› Zicken machen (*ugs.*), verrückt spielen (*salopp*); **the kids have been ~ing up like mad today** die Kinder haben heute total verrückt gespielt (*salopp*)

**acting** /ˈæktɪŋ/ **1** *adj.* (*temporary*) stellvertretend; (*in charge*) geschäftsführend; amtierend. **2** *n., no pl.* (*Theatre etc.*) die Schauspielerei; **she's studying ~:** sie ist auf der Schauspielschule; **an ~ career** eine Karriere als Schauspieler; **she does a lot of ~ in her spare time** sie spielt in ihrer Freizeit viel Theater

**action** /ˈækʃn/ *n.* **A** (*doing sth.*) Handeln, *das;* **what kind of ~ do you think is necessary?** welche Schritte *od.* Maßnahmen halten Sie für notwendig?; **his quick ~ saved the boy's life** sein schnelles Eingreifen rettete dem Jungen das Leben; **a man of ~:** ein Mann der Tat; **take ~:** Schritte *od.* etwas unternehmen; Maßnahmen ergreifen; **see sth. in ~:** etw. in Betrieb sehen; **put a plan into ~:** einen Plan in die Tat umsetzen; **come into ~:** in die Tat umgesetzt werden; **put sth. out of ~:** etw. außer Betrieb setzen; **be/be put out of ~:** außer Betrieb sein/gesetzt werden; **a film full of ~:** ein Film mit viel Handlung; **B** (*effect*) **the ~ of salt on ice** die Wirkung von Salz auf Eis; **C** (*act*) Tat, *die;* **she is impulsive in her ~s** sie handelt sehr impulsiv; **D** (*Theatre*) Handlung, *die;* Geschehen, *das;* **where the ~ is** (*coll.*) wo was los ist (*ugs.*); **hey, man, where's the ~?** (*coll.*) du, sag mal, wo ist hier was los? (*ugs.*); **get a piece of the ~** (*coll.*) mitmachen; **E** (*legal process*) [Gerichts]verfahren, *das;* **bring an ~ against sb.** eine Klage *od.* ein Verfahren gegen jmdn. anstrengen; **F** (*fighting*) Gefecht, *das;* Kampf, *der;* **he died in ~:** er ist [im Kampf] gefallen; **go into ~:** Kampfhandlungen aufnehmen; **we all went into ~** (*fig.*) wir machten uns alle an die Arbeit; **G** (*movement*) Bewegung, *die;* (*mechanism*) Mechanismus, *der;* (*of piano, organ*) Mechanik, *die*

**actionable** /ˈækʃənəbl/ *adj.* [gerichtlich] verfolgbar *od.* strafbar

**action: ~ committee, ~ group** *ns.* [Eltern-/Bürger- *usw.*]initiative, *die;* **~-packed** *adj.* spannend ‹Buch, Roman›; **an ~-packed film** ein Film mit viel Aktion; **an ~-packed holiday** ein Aktivurlaub; **~ painting** *n.* Action-Painting, *das;* abstrakter Expressionismus; **~ ˈreplay** *n.* Wiederholung [in Zeitlupe]; **~ stations** *n. pl.* (*Mil.; also fig.*) Stellung, *die;* **go to ~ stations** Stellung beziehen; **~ stations!** in die Stellungen!

**activate** /ˈæktɪveɪt/ *v.t.* **A** in Gang setzen ‹Vorrichtung, Mechanismus›; auslösen ‹Mechanismus›; **~d by concern for public morality** getrieben von der Sorge um die öffentliche Moral; **B** (*Chem., Phys.*) aktivieren; **~d carbon** *or* **charcoal** Aktivkohle, *die*

**activation** /æktɪˈveɪʃn/ *n.* Aktivierung, *die*

**active** /ˈæktɪv/ *adj.* **A** aktiv; wirksam ‹Kraft, Mittel›; praktisch ‹Gebrauch, Versuch, Kenntnisse›; tätig ‹Vulkan›; rege ‹Verstand, Gesellschaft›; **a very ~ child** ein sehr lebhaftes Kind; **take an ~ interest in sth.** reges Interesse an etw. (*Dat.*) zeigen; regen Anteil an etw. (*Dat.*) nehmen; **take an ~ part in sth.** sich aktiv an etw. (*Dat.*) beteiligen; **he's still ~ as an author** er arbeitet noch als Schriftsteller; **maintain an ~ knowledge of current affairs** im politischen Tagesgeschehen auf dem Laufenden bleiben; **~ carbon** Aktivkohle, *die;* **on ~ service** *or* (*Amer.*) **duty** (*Mil.*) im aktiven Dienst; ⇒ *also* **list**[1] 1 A; **B** (*Ling.*) aktiv[isch]; **~ voice** Aktiv, *das*

**actively** /ˈæktɪvlɪ/ *adv.* aktiv; **be ~ engaged in sth.** intensiv mit etw. beschäftigt sein; **be ~ interested in sth.** ein reges Interesse an etw. (*Dat.*) zeigen

**activeness** /ˈæktɪvnɪs/ *n., no pl.* Aktivität, *die;* (*of mind*) Regsamkeit, *die;* (*of person*) Regheit, *die*

**activist** /ˈæktɪvɪst/ *n.* Aktivist, *der*/Aktivistin, *die*

**activity** /ækˈtɪvɪtɪ/ *n.* **A** *no pl.* Aktivität, *die;* **military ~:** militärischer Einsatz; **~ in the field of reform** reformerische Aktivitäten; **B** (*exertion*) aktive Tätigkeit; rege [Mit]arbeit; **C** *usu. in pl.* (*action*) Aktivität, *die;* (*occupation*) Betätigung, *die;* **she has so many social activities** sie ist gesellschaftlich so aktiv; **classroom activities** schulische Tätigkeiten; **outdoor activities** Betätigung an der frischen Luft; **a new sporting ~:** eine neue Sportart; **~ holiday** Aktivurlaub, *der;* **some activities offered by the youth centre** einige Veranstaltungen des Jugendzentrums

**actor** /ˈæktə(r)/ *n.* **A** Schauspieler, *der;* **B** ⇒ **actress**

**actress** /ˈæktrɪs/ *n.* Schauspielerin, *die*

**actual** /ˈæktʃʊəl/ *adj.* **A** (*real*) eigentlich, tatsächlich ‹Lage, Gegebenheiten›; wirklich ‹Name, Gegenstand›; konkret ‹Beispiel›; **what was the ~ time of his arrival?** wann genau ist er angekommen?; **what is the ~ position now?** wie ist eigentlich der Stand der Dinge?; **it's an ~ fact** das ist eine Tatsache *od.* ein Faktum; **in ~ fact** tatsächlich; **no ~ crime was committed** es wurde kein eigentliches Verbrechen begangen; **B** (*current*) derzeitig; **the ~ situation** der gegenwärtige Stand der Dinge

**actuality** /æktʃʊˈælɪtɪ/ *n.* Wirklichkeit, *die;* Realität, *die;* **the ~ of the situation** die reale *od.* wirkliche Lage; **in ~:** in Wirklichkeit; **when her dream became an ~:** als ihr Traum Wirklichkeit wurde

**actually** /ˈæktʃʊəlɪ/ *adv.* (*in fact*) eigentlich; (*by the way*) übrigens; (*believe it or not*) sogar; **~, to tell you the truth ...:** also, um die Wahrheit zu sagen, ...; **~, I must be going** ich muss jetzt wirklich gehen; **I'm ~ quite capable of looking after myself** im Übrigen bin ich gut in der Lage, für mich selbst zu sorgen; **he ~ had the cheek to suggest ...:** er hatte tatsächlich die Unverfrorenheit, vorzuschlagen ...

**actuarial** /æktʃʊ'eərɪəl/ *adj.* versicherungsmathematisch

**actuary** /'æktʃʊərɪ/ *n.* ▶**1261** Versicherungsmathematiker, *der;* Aktuar, *der*

**actuate** /'æktʃʊeɪt/ *v.t.* (*activate*) antreiben ‹Maschine›; in Bewegung setzen ‹Vorgang›; auslösen ‹Mechanismus, Reaktion›

**actuation** /æktʃʊ'eɪʃn/ *n.* (*of machine*) Antrieb, *der;* (*of mechanism*) Auslösen, *das*

**acumen** /'ækjʊmen/ *n.* Scharfsinn, *der;* **business ~:** Geschäftssinn, *der;* **political ~:** politische Klugheit

**acupressure** /'ækjʊpreʃə(r)/ *n.* (*Med.*) Akupressur, *die*

**acupuncture** /'ækjupʌnktʃə(r)/ *n.* (*Med.*) Akupunktur, *die*

**acute** /ə'kju:t/ *adj.*, **~r** /ə'kju:tə(r)/, **~st** /ə'kju:tɪst/ **A** (*penetrating*) scharf ‹Kritik›; genau ‹Beobachtung›; wach ‹Bewusstsein›; **B** (*Geom.*) **~ angle** spitzer Winkel; **C** (*Med.*) akut ‹Krankheit, Stadium›; **D** (*critical*) akut ‹Gefahr, Knappheit, Situation, Mangel›; **E** (*keen*) fein ‹Geruchssinn›; heftig ‹Schmerz›; **F** (*Ling.*) **~ accent** Akut, *der;* **G** (*sharp*) scharf ‹Schneide›; fein ‹Spitze›

**acutely** /ə'kju:tlɪ/ *adv.* **A** (*penetratingly*) genau[estens] ‹sich bewusst sein, durchdenken, beobachten›; **B** (*Med.*) akut; **he is ~ ill with pneumonia** er hat eine akute Lungenentzündung; **C** (*critically*) äußerst; (*keenly*) äußerst; überaus; intensiv ‹fühlen›

**acuteness** /ə'kju:tnɪs/ *n.*, *no pl.* **A** (*of criticism*) Schärfe, *die;* (*of observation*) Genauigkeit, *die;* (*of understanding*) Scharfsinn, *der;* **B** (*Med.*) Akutheit, *die;* **C** (*of pain, sensation*) Heftigkeit, *die;* **D** (*of sense, hearing, etc.*) Feinheit, *die;* **E** (*of cutting edge*) Schärfe, *die;* (*of point*) Feinheit, *die*

**AD** *abbr.* ▶**1055** **Anno Domini** n. Chr.; (*bes. DDR*) u. Z.

**ad** /æd/ *n.* (*coll.*) Annonce, *die;* Inserat, *das;* **small ad** Kleinanzeige, *die;* **TV ads** Werbespots im Fernsehen

**adage** /'ædɪdʒ/ *n.* Sprichwort, *das*

**adagio** /ə'dɑ:dʒjəʊ/ (*Mus.*) **1** *adv.* adagio. **2** *adj.* Adagio-; langsam; ruhig. **3** *n.*, *pl.* **~s** Adagio, *das*

**Adam** /'ædəm/ *pr. n.* (*first man*) Adam (*der*); **he doesn't know me from ~:** er hat keine Ahnung, wer ich bin

**adamant** /'ædəmənt/ *adj.* unnachgiebig; **be ~ that ...:** darauf bestehen, dass ...

**Adam's 'apple** *n.* Adamsapfel, *der*

**adapt** /ə'dæpt/ **1** *v.t.* **A** (*adjust*) anpassen (**to** *Dat.*); umbauen ‹Auto›; variieren ‹Frisur, Kleidung›; umstellen ‹Maschine› (**to** auf + *Akk.*); **this room can easily be ~ed to individual tastes** dieses Zimmer lässt sich leicht auf den persönlichen Geschmack abstimmen; **your eyes will quickly ~ themselves to the dark** deine Augen werden sich schnell an die Dunkelheit gewöhnen; **~ oneself to sth.** sich an etw. (*Akk.*) gewöhnen; **this furnace can be ~ed to take coal or oil** dieser Ofen lässt sich auf Kohle oder Öl einstellen; **be ~ed for doing sth.** darauf eingestellt sein, etw. zu tun; **B** (*modify*) adaptieren, bearbeiten ‹Text, Theaterstück›; **~ed for TV by ...:** für das Fernsehen bearbeitet von ...; **~ sth. from sth.** etw. nach etw. bearbeiten.
**2** *v.i.* **A** ‹Tier, Auge:› sich anpassen (**to** an + *Akk.*); **B** (*to surroundings, circumstances*) sich gewöhnen (**to** an + *Akk.*)

**adaptability** /ədæptə'bɪlɪtɪ/ *n.*, *no pl.* (*to way of life or environment*) Anpassungsfähigkeit, *die* (**to** *or* **for** an + *Akk.*)

**adaptable** /ə'dæptəbl/ *adj.* anpassungsfähig; vielseitig ‹Maschine›; flexibel ‹Planung›; **be ~ to** *or* **for sth.** an etw. (*Akk.*) angepasst werden können

**adaptation** /ædəp'teɪʃn/ *n.* **A** *no pl.* Anpassung, *die* (**to** an + *Akk.*); (*of garment*) Veränderung, *die;* (*of system, machine*) Umstellung, *die* (**to** auf + *Akk.*); **B** (*version*) Adap[ta]tion, *die;* (*of story, text*) Bearbeitung, *die;* **C** (*Biol.*) Adaptation, *die;* Anpassung, *die*

**adaptor** (**adapter**) /ə'dæptə(r)/ *n.* (*device*) Adapter, *der;* **a four-socket ~:** eine Vierfachsteckdose

**ADC** *abbr.* (*Mil.*) **aide-de-camp**

**add** /æd/ **1** *v.t.* hinzufügen (**to** *Dat.*); hinzufügen, anfügen ‹weitere Worte›; beisteuern ‹Ideen, Vorschläge› (**to** zu); dazusetzen ‹Namen, Zahlen›; **~ two and two** zwei und zwei zusammenzählen; **~ two numbers together** zwei Zahlen addieren; **~ the flour to the liquid** geben Sie das Mehl in die Flüssigkeit; **we have ~ed a number of new books to our collection** wir haben unsere Sammlung um ein paar neue Bücher erweitert.
**2** *v.i.* **~ to** vergrößern ‹Schwierigkeiten, Einkommen›; verbessern ‹Ruf›; **~ [together] to give** *or* **make the desired amount** zusammen den gewünschten Betrag ergeben

**~ 'up** **1** *v.i.* **A these figures ~ up to 30** diese Zahlen ergeben zusammen[gezählt] 30; **these things ~/it ~s up** (*fig. coll.*) all diese Dinge summieren sich/das summiert sich alles; **~ up to sth.** (*fig.*) auf etw. hinauslaufen; **B** (*make sense*) einen Sinn ergeben. **2** *v.t.* zusammenzählen

**added** /'ædɪd/ *attrib. adj.* zusätzlich; **~ to this** außerdem; obendrein

**addendum** /ə'dendəm/ *n.*, *pl.* **addenda** /ə'dendə/ (*thing to be added*) Nachtrag, *der;* Addendum, *das* (*veralt.*); (*addition*) Zusatz, *der;* *in pl.* (*in book etc.*) Addenda *Pl.*

**adder** /'ædə(r)/ *n.* (*Zool.*) Viper, *die*

**addict** **1** /ə'dɪkt/ *v.t.* **be ~ed** süchtig sein; **become ~ed [to sth.]** [nach etw.] süchtig werden; **be ~ed to alcohol/smoking/drugs** alkohol-/nikotin-/drogensüchtig sein. **2** /'ædɪkt/ *n.* Süchtige, *der/die;* (*fig. coll.*) [begeisterte] Anhänger, *der*/Anhängerin, *die;* **become an ~:** süchtig werden; **drug/heroin ~s** Drogen-/Heroinsüchtige *Pl.*; **a TV ~** (*fig. coll.*) ein Fernsehnarr

**addiction** /ə'dɪkʃn/ *n.* Sucht, *die;* (*fig. coll.*) Fimmel, *der* (*ugs.*); **an ~ to sth.** die Sucht nach etw.; **~ to heroin** Heroinsucht, *die*

**addictive** /ə'dɪktɪv/ *adj.* **be ~:** süchtig machen; (*fig. coll.*) zu einer Sucht werden

**'adding machine** *n.* Rechenmaschine, *die*

**addition** /ə'dɪʃn/ *n.* **A** *no pl.* Hinzufügen, *das;* (*of ingredient*) Dazugeben, *das;* (*adding up*) Addieren, *das;* (*process*) Addition, *die;* **in ~:** außerdem; **in ~ to** zusätzlich zu; **B** (*thing added*) Ergänzung, *die* (**to** zu); **we are expecting a new ~ to our family** wir erwarten Familienzuwachs

**additional** /ə'dɪʃənl/ *adj.* zusätzlich; **~ details** weitere Einzelheiten

**additionally** /ə'dɪʃənəlɪ/ *adv.* außerdem

**additive** /'ædɪtɪv/ **1** *n.* Zusatz, *der.* **2** *adj.* zusätzlich; (*to be added*) weiter

**addled** /'ædld/ *adj.* **A** (*rotten*) verdorben; faul; **B** (*muddled*) verwirrt ‹Gedanken›; benebelt ‹Kopf›

**'add-on** **1** *n.* (*accessory*) Zubehörteil, *das;* (*for electrical appliance*) Zusatzgerät, *das;* (*addition*) Zusatz, *der.* **2** *adj.* **~ accessory** Zubehörteil, *das;* (*for electrical appliance*) Zusatzgerät, *das;* **sth. can be bought as an ~ feature/accessory for sth.** etw. ist als Zubehör zu einer Sache erhältlich

**address** /ə'dres/ **1** *v.t.* **A** **~ sth. to sb./sth.** etw. an jmdn./etw. richten; **you must ~ your complaint to ...:** richten Sie Ihre Beschwerde an (+ *Akk.*) ...; **~ oneself to sb./sth.** sich an jmdn./etw. wenden; **B** ▶**1286** (*mark with ~*) adressieren (**to** an + *Akk.*); mit Anschrift versehen; **C** (*speak to*) anreden ‹Person›; sprechen zu ‹Zuhörern›; **~ sb. as sth.** jmdn. mit etw. *od.* als etw. anreden; **D** (*give attention to*) angehen ‹Problem›; **E** (*apply*) **~ oneself to sth.** sich zu etw. anschicken.
**2** *n.* **A** ▶**1286** (*on letter or envelope*) Adresse, *die;* Anschrift, *die;* (*place of residence*) Wohnsitz, *der;* **of no fixed ~:** ohne festen Wohnsitz; **B** (*discourse*) Ansprache, *die;* Rede, *die;* **C** (*skill*) Gewandtheit, *die;* **D** *in pl.* (*courteous approach*) Werben, *das;* **pay one's ~es to sb.** (*arch.*) jmdm. den Hof machen; **E** (*Computing*) Adresse, *die*

**ad'dress book** *n.* Adressenbüchlein, *das*

**addressee** /ædre'si:/ *n.* Adressat, *der*/Adressatin, *die;* Empfänger, *der*/Empfängerin, *die*

**ad'dress label** *n.* Adressenaufkleber, *der*

**adduce** /ə'dju:s/ *v.t.* anführen

**adenoids** /'ædɪnɔɪdz/ *n. pl.* (*Med.*) Rachenmandel- *od.* Nasenpolypen *Pl.;* Rachenmandelwucherungen *Pl.*

**adept** /'ædept, ə'dept/ **1** *adj.* geschickt (**in, at** in + *Dat.*). **2** *n.* Kenner, *der*/Kennerin, *die;* Meister, *der*/Meisterin, *die*

**adequacy** /'ædɪkwəsɪ/ *n.*, *no pl.* **A** (*sufficiency*) Adäquatheit, *die;* Angemessenheit, *die;* **B** (*suitability*) Eignung, *die;* **C** (*bare sufficiency*) Zulänglichkeit, *die;* **D** (*proportionateness*) **the ~ of sth. to sth.** die Angemessenheit einer Sache für etw.

**adequate** /'ædɪkwət/ *adj.* **A** (*sufficient*) ausreichend; angemessen ‹Bezahlung, Wohnraum›; **B** (*barely sufficient*) hinreichend; zulänglich; **my grant is ~ and no more** mein Stipendium reicht gerade so aus; **C** (*suitable*) angemessen; **he couldn't find ~ words** ihm fehlten die richtigen *od.* passenden Worte; **D** (*proportionate*) **~ [to sth.]** einer Sache (*Dat.*) angemessen

**adequately** /'ædɪkwətlɪ/ *adv.* **A** (*sufficiently*) ausreichend; **are you ~ prepared for your exam?** haben Sie sich auf die Prüfung in ausreichender Weise vorbereitet?; **these children are not ~ nourished** diese Kinder sind unterernährt; **B** (*barely sufficiently*) hinreichend; zulänglich; **C** (*suitably*) angemessen ‹gekleidet, qualifiziert usw.›

**adhere** /əd'hɪə(r)/ *v.i.* **A** (*stick*) haften, (*by glue*) kleben (**to** an + *Dat.*); **~ [to each other]** ‹zwei Dinge:› zusammenkleben; **B** (*give support*) **~ to sth./sb.** an jmdm./einer Sache festhalten; **~ to a party/policy** eine Partei/Politik unterstützen; **C** (*keep*) **~ to** festhalten an (+ *Dat.*) ‹Programm, Brauch, Gewohnheit›; sich halten an (+ *Akk.*) ‹Abmachung, Versprechen, Regel›; **we must ~ strictly to the schedule** wir müssen uns genau an den Zeitplan halten

**adherence** /əd'hɪərəns/ *n.*, *no pl.* **A** (*to party, leader, policy*) Unterstützung, *die* (**to** *Gen.*); **B** (*to programme, agreement, promise, schedule*) Einhalten, *das* (**to** *Gen.*); (*to decision, tradition, principle*) Festhalten, *das* (**to** an + *Dat.*); (*to rule*) Befolgen, *das* (**to** *Gen.*)

**adherent** /əd'hɪərənt/ *n.* Anhänger, *der*/Anhängerin, *die*

**adhesion** /əd'hi:ʒn/ *n.* **A** *no pl.* (*sticking*) Haften, *das* (**to** an + *Dat.*); (*by glue*) Kleben, *das* (**to** an + *Dat.*); **B** *no pl.* (*support*) Unterstützung, *die* (**to** *Gen.*); (*to agreement*) Einhalten, *das* (**to** *Gen.*)

**adhesive** /əd'hi:sɪv/ **1** *adj.* (*adherent*) klebrig; gummiert ‹Briefmarke, Umschlag›; Klebe‹band, -schicht›; **be ~:** kleben/gummiert sein; **~ plaster** Heftpflaster, *das;* ⇒ *also* **tape** 1 A. **2** *n.* Klebstoff, *der;* Klebemittel, *das*

**ad hoc** /æd 'hɒk/ **1** *adv.* ad hoc. **2** *adj.* Adhoc-

**adieu** /ə'dju:/ **1** *int.* adieu; leb/lebt wohl; **we bid** *or* **wish you ~:** leb/lebt wohl. **2** *n.*, *pl.* **~s** *or* **~x** /ə'dju:z/ Adieu *od.* Lebewohl, *das*

**ad infinitum** /æd ɪnfɪ'naɪtəm/ *adv.* ad infinitum (*geh.*); ohne Ende

**adipose** /'ædɪpəʊs/ *adj.* adipös (*fachspr.*); verfettet; **~ tissue** Fettgewebe, *das*

**adjacent** /ə'dʒeɪsənt/ *adj.* angrenzend; Neben-; **~ to** (*position*) neben (+ *Dat.*); (*direction*) neben (+ *Akk.*); **he sat in the ~ room** er saß im Zimmer nebenan

**adjectival** /ædʒɪk'taɪvəl/ *adj.* (*Ling.*) adjektivisch; **~ endings** Adjektivendungen

**adjective** /'ædʒɪktɪv/ *n.* (*Ling.*) Adjektiv, *das;* Eigenschaftswort, *das*

a

**adjoin** /əˈdʒɔɪn/ ❶ *v.t.* grenzen an (+ *Akk.*); **the room ~ing ours** das Zimmer neben unserem. ❷ *v.i.* aneinander grenzen; nebeneinander liegen; **an ~ing field** ein angrenzendes *od.* benachbartes Feld; **in the ~ing room** im Zimmer daneben *od.* nebenan

**adjourn** /əˈdʒɜːn/ ❶ *v.t.* (*break off*) unterbrechen; (*put off*) aufschieben. ❷ *v.i.* (*suspend proceedings*) sich vertagen; **let's ~ to the sitting room/pub** begeben wir uns ins Wohnzimmer/(*ugs.*) in die Kneipe

**adjournment** /əˈdʒɜːnmənt/ *n.* (*suspending*) (*of court*) Vertagung, *die;* (*of meeting*) Unterbrechung, *die*

**adjudge** /əˈdʒʌdʒ/ *v.t.* (*pronounce*) **~ sb./sth. [to be] sth.** jmdn./etw. für etw. erklären *od.* befinden

**adjudicate** /əˈdʒuːdɪkeɪt/ *v.i.* (*in court, tribunal*) als Richter tätig sein; (*in contest*) Preisrichter sein (**at** bei, in + *Dat.*)

**adjudication** /ədʒuːdɪˈkeɪʃn/ *n.* Ⓐ (*judging*) Beurteilung, *die;* **expert ~:** Expertenmeinung, *die;* Ⓑ (*decision*) Entscheidung, *die*

**adjudicator** /əˈdʒuːdɪkeɪtə(r)/ *n.* Schiedsrichter, *der*/Schiedsrichterin, *die;* (*in contest*) Preisrichter, *der*/Preisrichterin, *die*

**adjunct** /ˈædʒʌŋkt/ *n.* Ⓐ Anhängsel, *das;* (*effect*) Neben- *od.* Begleiterscheinung, *die;* Ⓑ (*Ling.*) Adjunkt, *das*

**adjuration** /ædʒʊəˈreɪʃn/ *n.* [inständige] Bitte; Beschwörung, *die*

**adjure** /əˈdʒʊə(r)/ *v.t.* inständig bitten; beschwören

**adjust** /əˈdʒʌst/ ❶ *v.t.* Ⓐ richtig [an]ordnen ‹Gegenstände, Gliederung›; ändern ‹Gegebenheiten›; zurechtmachen ‹Frisur›; zurechtrücken ‹Hut, Krawatte›; (*regulate*) regulieren, regeln ‹Geschwindigkeit, Höhe usw.›; [richtig] einstellen ‹Gerät, Mechanismus, Bremsen, Vergaser, Motor, Zündung›; (*adapt*) entsprechend ändern ‹Plan, Bedingungen›; angleichen ‹Gehalt, Lohn, Zinsen›; **~ sth. [to sth.]** etw. [an etw. (*Akk.*)] anpassen *od.* [auf etw. (*Akk.*)] einstellen; **please ~ your watches** bitte stellen Sie Ihre Uhren richtig; **'do not ~ your set'** „Störung"; Ⓑ (*assess*) berechnen ‹Schaden›; regulieren ‹Versicherungsansprüche›; eichen ‹Maß, Gewicht›; **such discrepancies can be ~ed** solche Unstimmigkeiten können ausgeglichen *od.* beigelegt werden.
❷ *v.i.* **~ [to sth.]** sich [an etw. (*Akk.*)] gewöhnen *od.* anpassen; ‹Gerät, Maschine usw.:› sich [auf etw. (*Akk.*)] einstellen lassen; **the eye soon ~s to the dark** das Auge gewöhnt sich schnell an die Dunkelheit; **~ to new conditions/a requirement** sich auf neue Verhältnisse/eine Forderung einstellen

**adjustable** /əˈdʒʌstəbl/ *adj.* einstellbar (**to** auf + *Akk.*); verstellbar, justierbar ‹Gerät›; regulierbar ‹Temperatur›

**adjustment** /əˈdʒʌstmənt/ *n.* Ⓐ (*of layout, plan*) Ordnung, *die;* (*of things*) Anordnung, *die;* (*of device, engine, machine*) Einstellung, *die;* (*of hair, clothing*) Zurechtmachen, *das;* (*to situation, lifestyle*) Anpassung, *die* (**to** an + *Akk.*); (*of eye*) Adaption, *die;* Gewöhnung, *die;* **some ~s are necessary on your car engine** an Ihrem Motor muss einiges neu *od.* richtig eingestellt werden; **she made a few minor ~s to her manuscript** sie brachte an ihrem Manuskript ein paar kleinere Korrekturen an; Ⓑ (*of insurance claim, damage*) Schadensfestsetzung, *die;* Ⓒ (*settlement*) (*of claims or damages*) Regulierung, *die;* Ⓓ (*device*) Einstellvorrichtung, *die*

**adjutant** /ˈædʒʊtənt/ *n.* Ⓐ (*Mil.*) Adjutant, *der;* Ⓑ (*Ornith.*) **~ [bird]** Indischer Marabu

**ad lib** /æd ˈlɪb/ *adv.* zwanglos, nach Belieben

**ad-lib** ❶ *adj.* (*unprepared, improvised*) Stegreif-, improvisiert ‹Rede, Vortrag›; **give an ~ rendering** improvisieren. ❷ *v.i.*, **-bb-** (*coll.*) improvisieren

**Adm.** *abbr.* **admiral** Adm.

**'adman** *n.* Werbe-, Reklamefachmann, *der*

**admin** /ˈædmɪn/ *n.* (*coll.*) Verwaltung, *die;* **an ~ problem** ein Verwaltungsproblem

**administer** /ædˈmɪnɪstə(r)/ *v.t.* Ⓐ (*manage*) verwalten; führen ‹Geschäfte, Regierung›; regieren ‹Land›; Ⓑ (*give, apply*) spenden ‹Trost›; leisten, gewähren ‹Hilfe, Unterstützung›; austeilen, verabreichen ‹Schläge, Prügel›; verabreichen, geben ‹Medikamente›; spenden, geben ‹Sakramente›; anwenden ‹Disziplinierungsmaßnahmen›; **~ justice [to sb.]** [über jmdn.] Recht sprechen; **~ punishment to sb.** jmdn. bestrafen; **~ an oath to sb.** jmdn. vereidigen; jmdm. einen Eid abnehmen; **~ treatment to sb.** jmdn. behandeln

**administration** /ədmɪnɪˈstreɪʃn/ *n.* Ⓐ (*management, managing*) Verwaltung, *die;* Ⓑ (*giving, applying*) (*of sacraments*) Spenden, *das;* Geben, *das;* (*of discipline*) Anwendung, *die;* (*of medicine*) Verabreichung, *die;* (*of aid, relief*) Gewährung, *die;* **~ of justice** Rechtspflege, *die;* **~ of an oath** Eidesabnahme, *die;* Ⓒ (*ministry, government*) Regierung, *die;* (*Amer.: President's period of office*) Amtszeit, *die;* Ⓓ (*Law*) **~ of the estate** Nachlassverwaltung, *die*

**administrative** /ədˈmɪnɪstrətɪv/ *adj.* Verwaltungs-; administrativ ‹Angelegenheit, Geschick, Fähigkeit›; **~ work** Verwaltungsarbeit, *die;* **an ~ job** ein Verwaltungsposten

**administrator** /ədˈmɪnɪstreɪtə(r)/ *n.* ▶ **1261** Ⓐ (*manager*) Administrator, *der;* Verwalter, *der;* (*sb. capable of organizing*) Organisator, *der;* Ⓑ (*performing official duties*) Verwaltungsbeamte/-angestellte, *der;* Ⓒ (*of deceased person's estate*) Verwalter, *der;* Testamentsvollstrecker, *der*

**admirable** /ˈædmərəbl/ *adj.* bewundernswert; erstaunlich; (*excellent*) vortrefflich; ausgezeichnet

**admirably** /ˈædmərəblɪ/ *adv.* bewundernswert; erstaunlich; (*excellently*) vortrefflich

**admiral** /ˈædmərəl/ *n.* Ⓐ ▶ **1617** Admiral, *der;* **A~ of the Fleet** (*Brit.*) Großadmiral, *der;* Ⓑ (*butterfly*) **red ~:** Admiral, *der*

**Admiralty** /ˈædmərəltɪ/ *n.* **~ [Board]** (*Hist.*) *britisches Marineministerium*

**admiration** /ædməˈreɪʃn/ *n.*, *no pl.* Ⓐ Bewunderung, *die* (**of, for** für); Ⓑ (*object of ~*) **be the ~ of sb.** von jmdm. bewundert werden

**admire** /ədˈmaɪə(r)/ *v.t.* bewundern (**for** wegen)

**admirer** /ədˈmaɪərə(r)/ *n.* Bewunderer, *der*/Bewunderin, *die;* (*suitor*) Verehrer, *der*/Verehrerin, *die*

**admiring** /ədˈmaɪərɪŋ/ *adj.*, **admiringly** /ədˈmaɪərɪŋlɪ/ *adv.* bewundernd

**admissibility** /ədmɪsɪˈbɪlɪtɪ/ *n.*, *no pl.* Zulässigkeit, *die*

**admissible** /ədˈmɪsɪbl/ *adj.* Ⓐ akzeptabel ‹Plan, Vorschlag›; erlaubt, zulässig ‹Abweichung, Schreibung›; Ⓑ (*Law*) zulässig; **that is not ~ evidence** das ist kein vor Gericht zugelassener Beweis *od.* zugelassenes Beweisstück

**admission** /ədˈmɪʃn/ *n.* Ⓐ (*entry*) Zutritt, *der;* **~ to university** Zulassung [zum Studium] an einer Universität; **~ costs** *or* **is 50p** der Eintritt kostet 50 Pence; **charge for ~:** Eintrittspreis, *der;* Ⓑ (*charge*) Eintritt, *der;* Ⓒ (*confession*) Eingeständnis, *das* (**of,** to *Gen.*); **by** *or* **on one's own ~:** nach eigenem Eingeständnis

**admission: ~ charge, ~ fee, ~ price** *ns.* Eintrittspreis, *der;* **~ money** *n.* Eintrittsgeld, *das;* **~ ticket** *n.* Eintrittskarte, *die*

**admit** /ədˈmɪt/ ❶ *v.t.*, **-tt-:** Ⓐ (*let in*) hinein-/hereinlassen; **persons under the age of 16 not ~ted** kein Zutritt für Jugendliche unter 16 Jahren; **~ sb. to a school/club** jmdn. in eine Schule/einen Klub aufnehmen; **'this ticket ~s two'** „Eintrittskarte für zwei Personen"; **be ~ted to hospital** ins Krankenhaus eingeliefert werden; Ⓑ (*accept as valid*) **if we ~ that argument/evidence** wenn wir davon ausgehen, dass dieses Argument zutrifft/dass diese Beweise erlaubt sind; Ⓒ (*acknowledge*) zugeben; eingestehen; **~ sth. to be true** zugeben *od.* eingestehen, dass etw. wahr ist; **~ to being guilty/drunk** zugeben, schuldig/betrunken zu sein; Ⓓ (*have room for*) Platz bieten (+ *Dat.*).
❷ *v.i.*, **-tt-: ~ of sth.** etw. zulassen *od.* erlauben

**admittance** /ədˈmɪtəns/ *n.* Zutritt, *der;* **no ~ [except on business]** Zutritt [für Unbefugte] verboten

**admittedly** /ədˈmɪtɪdlɪ/ *adv.* zugegeben[ermaßen]; **~ he is very young** zugegeben, er ist sehr jung

**admixture** /ədˈmɪkstʃə(r)/ *n.* Ⓐ *no pl.* (*mixing*) [Ver]mischen, *das;* Vermengen, *das;* Ⓑ (*ingredient*) Zusatz, *der;* Beimischung, *die*

**admonish** /ədˈmɒnɪʃ/ *v.t.* ermahnen; (*reproach*) ermahnen; tadeln

**admonishment** /ədˈmɒnɪʃmənt/, **admonition** /ædməˈnɪʃn/ *ns.* Ermahnung, *die;* (*reproach*) Ermahnung, *die;* Tadel, *der*

**ad nauseam** /æd ˈnɔːzɪæm, æd ˈnɔːsɪæm/ *adv.* bis zum Überdruss

**ado** /əˈduː/ *n.*, *no pl.*, *no art.* **without more** *or* **with no further ~:** ohne weiteres Aufhebens

**adobe** /əˈdəʊbɪ, əˈdəʊb/ *n.* (*brick*) Adobe, *der;* ungebrannter Lehmziegel

**adolescence** /ædəˈlesns/ *n.*, *no art.* die Zeit des Erwachsenwerdens; die Adoleszenz (*Med.*)

**adolescent** /ædəˈlesnt/ ❶ *n.* Heranwachsende, *der/die.* ❷ *adj.* heranwachsend ‹Person›; pubertär ‹Benehmen›

**adopt** /əˈdɒpt/ *v.t.* Ⓐ adoptieren; aufnehmen ‹Tier›; **we ~ed a refugee family** wir übernahmen die Patenschaft für eine Flüchtlingsfamilie; Ⓑ (*take over*) annehmen, übernehmen ‹Kultur, Sitte›; annehmen ‹Glaube, Religion›; Ⓒ (*take up*) übernehmen, sich aneignen ‹Methode›; einnehmen ‹Standpunkt, Haltung›; **that's not the right attitude to ~:** das ist nicht die richtige Einstellung; Ⓓ (*approve*) annehmen; billigen; **the meeting ~ed the motion** die Versammlung stimmte dem Antrag zu

**adoption** /əˈdɒpʃn/ *n.* Ⓐ Adoption, *die;* Ⓑ (*taking over*) (*of culture, custom*) Annahme, *die;* Übernahme, *die;* (*of belief*) Annahme, *die;* Ⓒ (*taking up*) (*of method*) Aneignung, *die;* Übernahme, *die;* (*of point of view*) Einnahme, *die;* Ⓓ (*approval*) Annahme, *die*

**adoptive** /əˈdɒptɪv/ *adj.* adoptiert; **~ son/mother** Adoptivsohn, *der*/-mutter, *die*

**adorable** /əˈdɔːrəbl/ *adj.*, **adorably** /əˈdɔːrəblɪ/ *adv.* bezaubernd; hinreißend

**adoration** /ædəˈreɪʃn/ *n.* Ⓐ Verehrung, *die;* Ⓑ (*worship of gods etc.*) Anbetung, *die*

**adore** /əˈdɔː(r)/ *v.t.* Ⓐ innig *od.* über alles lieben; **his adoring girlfriend/fans** seine schmachtende Freundin/schmachtenden Fans; Ⓑ (*coll.: like greatly*) **~ sth.** für etwas schwärmen; **~ doing sth.** etw. sehr, sehr gern *od.* (*ugs.*) für sein Leben gern tun; Ⓒ (*worship*) anbeten ‹Götter usw.›

**adorn** /əˈdɔːn/ *v.t.* schmücken; **~ oneself** sich schön machen

**adornment** /əˈdɔːnmənt/ *n.* Ⓐ *no pl.* Verschönerung, *die;* Ⓑ (*ornament*) Verzierung, *die;* **~s** Schmuck, *der*

**adrenal** /əˈdriːnl/ (*Anat.*) ❶ *adj.* **~ glands** Nebennieren *Pl.* ❷ *n.* Nebenniere, *die*

**adrenalin,** (*Amer.* ®) /əˈdrenəlɪn/ *n.* (*Physiol., Med.*) Adrenalin, *das*

**Adriatic** /eɪdrɪˈætɪk/ *pr. n.* **~ [Sea]** Adriatisches Meer; Adria, *die*

**adrift** /əˈdrɪft/ *pred. adj.* Ⓐ **be ~:** treiben; **cut a boat ~:** die Halteleine eines Bootes durchschneiden; Ⓑ (*fig.: exposed*) verloren; preisgegeben; **turn sb. ~:** jmdn. sich (*Dat.*) selbst überlassen

**adroit** /əˈdrɔɪt/ *adj.* geschickt; gewandt; **be ~ at sth./doing sth.** gewandt *od.* geschickt in etw. (*Dat.*) sein

**adroitly** /əˈdrɔɪtlɪ/ *adv.* geschickt; gewandt

**adroitness** /əˈdrɔɪtnɪs/ *n.*, *no pl.* Geschicklichkeit, *die;* Gewandtheit, *die*

**adulation** /ædjʊˈleɪʃn/ *n.*, *no pl.* (*praise*) Beweihräucherung, *die;* (*admiration of person*) Vergötterung, *die*

**adult** /ˈædʌlt, əˈdʌlt/ ❶ *adj.* erwachsen ‹Person›; reif ‹Verhalten›; ausgewachsen ‹Tier, Pflanze›; **this play is suitable only for ~ audiences** dieses Stück ist nur für Erwachsene geeignet; **an ~ film/book** *etc.* ein Film/Buch *usw.* [nur] für Erwachsene; **behave in an ~ manner** sich wie ein Erwachsener benehmen. ❷ *n.* Erwachsene, *der/die;* '**~s only**' „Nur für Erwachsene"; **~ education** Erwachsenenbildung, *die*

**adulterate** /əˈdʌltəreɪt/ *v.t.* verunreinigen; panschen ‹Wein, Milch›

**adulteration** /ədʌltəˈreɪʃn/ *n.* Verunreinigung, *die;* (*of wine, milk*) Panschen, *das*

**adulterer** /əˈdʌltərə(r)/ *n.* Ehebrecher, *der*

**adulteress** /əˈdʌltərɪs/ *n.* Ehebrecherin, *die*

**adulterous** /əˈdʌltərəs/ *adj.* ehebrecherisch

**adultery** /əˈdʌltərɪ/ *n., no pl.* Ehebruch, *der*

**adulthood** /ˈædʌlthʊd, əˈdʌlthʊd/ *n., no pl.* Erwachsenenalter, *das;* **reach ~:** erwachsen werden

**adumbrate** /ˈædəmbreɪt/ *v.t.* Ⓐ (*outline*) umreißen; skizzieren; Ⓑ (*suggest faintly*) andeuten; Ⓒ (*foreshadow*) ankündigen

**advance** /ədˈvɑːns/ ❶ *v.t.* Ⓐ (*move forward*) vorrücken lassen; Ⓑ (*put forward*) vorbringen ‹Plan, Meinung, These›; Ⓒ (*bring forward*) vorverlegen ‹Termin›; Ⓓ (*promote*) befördern; Ⓔ (*further*) fördern; **~ one's own interests** [nur] die eigenen Interessen verfolgen; Ⓕ (*pay before due date*) vorschießen; **~ sb. a week's pay** jmdm. einen Wochenlohn [als] Vorschuss geben; (*loan*) **the bank ~d me two thousand pounds** die Bank lieh mir zweitausend Pfund; Ⓖ (*increase*) erhöhen.
❷ *v.i.* Ⓐ (*move forward; also Mil.*) vorrücken; ‹Prozession:› sich vorwärts bewegen; **~ towards sb./sth.** ‹Person:› auf jmdn./etw. zugehen; **he ~d towards me** er kam auf mich zu; Ⓑ (*fig.: make progress*) Fortschritte machen; vorankommen; Ⓒ (*increase*) steigen.
❸ *n.* Ⓐ (*forward movement*) Vorrücken, *das;* (*fig.: progress*) Fortschritt, *der;* **any ~ on £30?** [bietet] jemand mehr als 30 Pfund?; Ⓑ *usu. in pl.* (*personal overture*) Annäherungsversuch, *der;* Ⓒ (*payment beforehand*) Vorauszahlung, *die;* (*on salary*) Vorschuss, *der* (**on** auf + *Akk.*); (*loan*) Darlehen, *das;* Ⓓ **in ~:** im Voraus; **be in ~ of one's age** seiner Zeit voraus sein; **send sb./sth. in ~:** jmdn./etw. vorausschicken

**adˈvance booking** *n.* (*for a film, play*) [vorherige] Kartenreservierung; (*of a table in a restaurant*) [vorherige] Tischreservierung

**advanced** /ədˈvɑːnst/ *adj.* fortgeschritten; **he has ~ ideas** er hat Ideen, die seiner Zeit voraus sind; **be ~ in years** in fortgeschrittenem Alter sein; **~ level** ⇒ **A level**; **~ studies** weiterführende Studien

**advance ˈguard** *n.* (*lit. or fig.*) Vorhut, *die*

**advancement** /ədˈvɑːnsmənt/ *n., no pl.* Ⓐ (*promotion*) Aufstieg, *der;* Ⓑ (*furtherance*) Förderung, *die*

**advance: ~ ˈnotice** *n.* **a week's ~ notice** Benachrichtigung eine Woche [im] Voraus; **give sb. ~ notice of sth.** jmdn. im Voraus von etw. in Kenntnis setzen; **~ ˈpayment** *n.* Vorauszahlung, *die*

**advantage** /ədˈvɑːntɪdʒ/ *n.* Ⓐ (*better position*) Vorteil, *der;* **give sb. an ~ over sb.** für jmdn. einen Vorteil gegenüber jmdm. bedeuten *od.* ein Vorteil gegenüber jmdm. sein; **gain an ~ over sb.** sich (*Dat.*) einen Vorteil gegenüber jmdm. verschaffen; **have an ~ over sb.** jmdm. gegenüber im Vorteil sein; **take [full/unfair] ~ of sth.** etw. [voll/unfairerweise] ausnutzen; **take ~ of sb.** jmdn. ausnutzen; (*euphem.: seduce*) jmdn. missbrauchen; **don't let them take ~ of you** lass dich nicht von ihnen ausnutzen; **have the ~ of sb.** [jmdm. gegenüber] in der besseren Position sein; **we shall show our range of products to ~:** wir werden unser Sortiment vorteilhaft ausstellen; **be seen to better ~:** vorteilhafter aussehen; Ⓑ (*benefit*) Vorteil, *der;* '**ability to type [would be] an ~**' „Schreibmaschinenkenntnisse von Vorteil"; **it could be done/we could do it with ~:** es wäre von Vorteil, wenn es getan würde/wenn wir es täten; **be to one's ~:** für jmdn. von Vorteil sein; **something to your ~:** etwas, was für dich von Vorteil ist; **turn sth. to [one's] ~:** etw. ausnutzen; Ⓒ (*Tennis*) Vorteil, *der;* **~ in/out** Vorteil Aufschläger/Rückschläger

**advantageous** /ædvənˈteɪdʒəs/ *adj.* vorteilhaft ‹Verfahren, Übereinkunft›; günstig ‹Lage›; **be [mutually] ~:** [für beide Seiten] von Vorteil sein; **be ~ to sb.** für jmdn. von Vorteil sein

**advantageously** /ædvənˈteɪdʒəslɪ/ *adv.* **we could ~ discuss this** es wäre von Vorteil, wenn wir das besprächen; **be ~ placed** günstig gelegen sein; **compare ~ with sth.** gegenüber etw. günstig abschneiden

**advent** /ˈædvənt/ *n., no pl.* Ⓐ (*of thing*) Beginn, *der;* Anfang, *der;* **before the ~ of the railways** vor dem Aufkommen der Eisenbahn; Ⓑ *no art.* **A~** (*season*) Advent, *der*

**adventitious** /ædvənˈtɪʃəs/ *adj.* zufällig

**adventure** /ədˈventʃə(r)/ *n.* Abenteuer, *das;* **in a spirit of ~:** voller Abenteuerdrang

**adˈventure: ~ holiday** *n* Abenteuerurlaub, *der;* **they organize ~s** sie bieten Abenteuerurlaub an; **~ playground** *n.* (*Brit.*) Abenteuerspielplatz, *der*

**adventurer** /ədˈventʃərə(r)/ *n.* Abenteurer, *der;* (*derog.: speculator*) Glücksritter, *der*

**adventuress** /ədˈventʃərɪs/ *n.* Abenteu[r]erin, *die*

**adventurism** /ədˈventʃərɪzm/ *n., no pl.* Abenteuerlust, *die;* Wagemut, *der;* (*Polit.*) Abenteuerpolitik, *die*

**adventurous** /ədˈventʃərəs/ *adj.* Ⓐ (*venturesome*) abenteuerlustig; **~ spirit** Abenteuergeist, *der;* Ⓑ (*filled with adventures*) abenteuerlich; Ⓒ (*enterprising*) kühn

**adverb** /ˈædvɜːb/ *n.* (*Ling.*) Adverb, *das;* Umstandswort, *das;* **~ of time/place** Zeit-/Ortsadverb, *das*

**adverbial** /ədˈvɜːbɪəl/ *adj.* (*Ling.*) adverbial

**adverbially** /ədˈvɜːbɪəlɪ/ *adv.* (*Ling.*) adverbial

**adversary** /ˈædvəsərɪ/ *n.* (*enemy*) Widersacher, *der*/Widersacherin, *die;* (*opponent*) Kontrahent, *der*/Kontrahentin, *die*

**adverse** /ˈædvɜːs/ *adj.* Ⓐ (*hostile*) ablehnend (**to** gegenüber); **an ~ response** eine abschlägige Antwort; Ⓑ (*unfavourable*) ungünstig ‹Bedingung, Entwicklung›; negativ ‹Bilanz, Urteil›; nachteilig ‹Auswirkung›; **developments ~ to our interests** für unsere Interessen nachteilige Entwicklungen; Ⓒ (*contrary*) widrig ‹Wind, Umstände›

**adversely** /ˈædvɜːslɪ/ *adv.* Ⓐ (*hostilely*) ablehnend; Ⓑ (*unfavourably*) nachteilig

**adversity** /ədˈvɜːsɪtɪ/ *n.* Ⓐ *no pl.* Not, *die;* **in ~:** in der Not; in Notzeiten; Ⓑ *usu. in pl.* (*misfortune*) Widrigkeit, *die*

**advert** /ˈædvɜːt/ (*Brit. coll.*) ⇒ **advertisement**

**advertise** /ˈædvətaɪz/ ❶ *v.t.* werben für ‹Güter, Waren›; (*by small ad*) inserieren ‹Auto, Haus›; ausschreiben ‹Stelle›; **~ one's intentions** seine Absichten bekannt geben; **~ one's presence** seine Anwesenheit bekannt machen. ❷ *v.i.* werben; (*in newspaper*) inserieren; annoncieren; **~ on television** Werbung im Fernsehen machen; **~ for sb./sth.** jmdn./etw. [per Inserat] suchen

**advertisement** /ədˈvɜːtɪsmənt/ *n.* Anzeige, *die;* **TV ~:** Fernsehspot, *der;* **classified ~:** Kleinanzeige, *die* ; **his behaviour is not a good ~ for the firm** (*fig.*) sein Verhalten ist für das Unternehmen keine gute Reklame

**advertiser** /ˈædvətaɪzə(r)/ *n.* (*in newspaper*) Inserent, *der*/Inserentin, *die;* (*on radio, TV*) Auftraggeber/Auftraggeberin [der Werbesendung]

**advertising** /ˈædvətaɪzɪŋ/ *n., no pl., no indef. art.* Werbung, *die;* **~ agency/campaign/industry** Werbeagentur, *die*/-kampagne, *die*/-branche, *die*

**Advertising ˈStandards Authority** *n.* (*Brit.*) Werbeaufsichtsbehörde

**advice** /ədˈvaɪs/ *n.* Ⓐ *no pl., no indef. art.* (*counsel*) Rat, *der;* **seek ~ from sb.** bei jmdm. Rat suchen; **my ~ to you would be ...:** ich würde dir raten ...; **he doesn't listen to ~:** er hört nicht auf Ratschläge; **on sb.'s ~:** auf jmds. Rat (*Akk.*) hin; **a piece of ~:** ein Rat[schlag]; **give sb. a piece** *or* **bit of ~:** jmdm. einen guten Rat geben; **if you ask** *or* **want my ~:** wenn du meinen Rat hören willst; **take ~ [from sb.]** [jmdn.] um Rat fragen; **take sb.'s ~:** jmds. Rat (*Dat.*) folgen; **take legal ~:** sich juristisch beraten lassen; Ⓑ (*formal notice*) Bescheid, *der;* Avis, *der od. das* (*Kaufmannsspr.*)

**advisability** /ədvaɪzəˈbɪlɪtɪ/ *n., no pl.* Ratsamkeit, *die;* **consider the ~ of doing sth.** erwägen, ob es ratsam ist, etw. zu tun

**advisable** /ədˈvaɪzəbl/ *adj.* ratsam

**advise** /ədˈvaɪz/ ❶ *v.t.* Ⓐ (*offer advice to*) beraten; **please ~ me** bitte geben Sie mir einen Rat; **~ sb. to do sth.** jmdm. raten, etw. zu tun; **~ sb. not to do** *or* **against doing sth.** jmdm. abraten, etw. zu tun; **what would you ~ me to do?** wozu würdest du mir raten?; Ⓑ (*recommend*) **~ sth.** zu etw. raten; Ⓒ (*inform*) unterrichten, informieren (**of** über + *Akk.*); **keep me ~d** halten Sie mich auf dem Laufenden.
❷ *v.i.* Ⓐ raten; **~ on sth.** bei etw. beraten; **please ~:** erbitte Rat; Ⓑ (*Amer.: consult*) **~ with sb.** sich mit jmdm. beraten

**advised** /ədˈvaɪzd/ *adj.* **[well-]~:** wohl überlegt; **be well/better ~** ‹Person:› wohl beraten/besser beraten sein

**advisedly** /ədˈvaɪzɪdlɪ/ *adv.* bewusst

**adviser, advisor** /ədˈvaɪzə(r)/ *n.* Berater, *der*/Beraterin, *die*

**advisory** /ədˈvaɪzərɪ/ *adj.* beratend; **~ committee** Beratungsausschuss, *der;* **in an ~ capacity** in beratender Funktion

**advocaat** /ædvəˈkɑːt/ *n.* Eierlikör, *der*

**advocacy** /ˈædvəkəsɪ/ *n., no pl.* **sb.'s ~ of sth.** jmds. Engagement *od.* Eintreten für etw.

**advocate** ❶ /ˈædvəkət/ *n.* ▶ **1261** (*of a cause*) Befürworter, *der*/Befürworterin, *die;* Fürsprecher, *der*/Fürsprecherin, *die;* (*for a person*) Fürsprecher, *der*/Fürsprecherin, *die;* (*Law: professional pleader*) [Rechts]anwalt, *der*/[Rechts]anwältin, *die;* **Faculty of A~s** [schottische] Anwaltskammer, *die;* **Lord A~:** [schottische] Generalstaatsanwalt, *der.*
❷ /ˈædvəkeɪt/ *v.t.* Ⓐ (*recommend*) befürworten; empfehlen; **~ a policy** für eine Politik eintreten; **~ that ...:** dafür plädieren, dass ...; Ⓑ (*defend*) verteidigen; eintreten für

**advt.** *abbr.* **advertisement**

**adze** (*Amer.:* **adz**) /ædz/ *n.* Dechsel, *die*

**Aegean** /iːˈdʒiːən/ *pr. n.* **~ [Sea]** Ägäisches Meer; Ägäis, *die*

**aegis** /ˈiːdʒɪs/ *n.* Ⓐ (*auspices*) **under the ~ of sb./sth.** unter der Ägide (*geh.*) *od.* Schirmherrschaft von jmdm./etw.; Ⓑ (*protection*) Schutz, *der*

**Aeneid** /ˈiːnɪɪd/ *n.* Äneis, *die*

**aeon** /ˈiːən/ *n.* (*age*) Äon, *der* (*geh.*)

**aerate** /ˈeəreɪt/ *v.t.* Ⓐ (*charge with gas*) [mit Kohlendioxid] anreichern; **~d water** kohlensaures Wasser; Ⓑ (*Agric., Hort.*) durchlüften

**aerial** /ˈeərɪəl/ ❶ *adj.* Ⓐ (*in the air*) Luft-; **~ root** Luftwurzel, *die;* **~ cableway** *or* **ropeway** *or* **railway** Seilbahn, *die;* Ⓑ (*atmospheric*) atmosphärisch; Ⓒ (*Aeronaut.*) Luft-; **~ bombardment** Bombardierung [aus der Luft]; **~ photograph/photography** Luftaufnahme, *die*/Luftaufnahmen; **~ spraying** Besprühung aus der Luft.
❷ *n.* Antenne, *die*

**aero-** /eərə/ *in comb.* Aero-

**aerobatics** /eərəˈbætɪks/ *n.* Ⓐ *no pl.* Kunstflug, *der;* Aerobatik, *die;* Ⓑ *pl.* (*feats of flying skill*) fliegerische Kunststücke

**aerobic** /eəˈrəʊbɪk/ *adj.* aerob (*Biol.*)

**aerobics** /eəˈrəʊbɪks/ *n., no pl.* Aerobic, *das*

**aerodrome** /ˈeərədrəʊm/ *n.* (*Brit. dated*) Aerodrom, *das* (*veralt.*); Flugplatz, *der*

**aerodyˈnamic** *adj.* aerodynamisch

**aerodyˈnamics** *n., no pl.* Aerodynamik, *die*

**aero-engine** /ˈeərəʊendʒɪn/ *n.* (*Aeronaut.*) Flug[zeug]motor, *der*

**ˈaerofoil** *n.* Tragfläche, *die;* Tragflügel, *der* (*fachspr.*); (*on car*) Heckspoiler, *der*

**ˈaerogram[me]** ⇒ **air letter**

**aeronautic** /eərəˈnɔːtɪk/, **aeronautical** /eərəˈnɔːtɪkl/ *adj.* aeronautisch

**aeronautics** /eərə'nɔ:tɪks/ *n., no pl.* Aeronautik, *die*

**aeroplane** /'eərəpleɪn/ *n. (Brit.)* Flugzeug, *das*

**aerosol** /'eərəsɒl/ *n.* Ⓐ *(spray)* Spray, *der od. das;* *(container)* ~ **[spray]** Spraydose, *die;* Ⓑ *(system of particles)* Aerosol, *das*

**'aerospace** *n., no pl., no art.* Erdatmosphäre und Weltraum; *(technology)* Luft- und Raumfahrt, *die*

**aesthete** /'i:sθi:t/ *n.* Ästhet, *der*/Ästhetin, *die*

**aesthetic** /i:s'θetɪk/ ❶ *adj.* ästhetisch; schöngeistig ‹Person, Epoche›. ❷ *n.* **the Hegelian ~:** die hegelsche Ästhetik

**aesthetically** /i:s'θetɪkəlɪ/ *adv.* ästhetisch

**aestheticism** /i:s'θetɪsɪzm/ *n., no pl.* Ästhetizismus, *der*

**aesthetics** /i:s'θetɪks/ *n., no pl.* Ästhetik, *die*

**aether** ⇒ **ether** B

**aetiology** /i:tɪ'ɒlədʒɪ/ *n. (Med., Philos.)* Ätiologie, *die*

**AF** *abbr.* **audio frequency**

**afar** /ə'fɑ:/ *adv.* ~ **[off]** weit fort; in weiter Ferne; **from ~:** aus der Ferne

**AFC** *abbr. (Brit.)* **Association Football Club** *Fußballverein*

**affability** /æfə'bɪlɪtɪ/ *n., no pl.* Freundlichkeit, *die;* **the boss's back-slapping ~:** die joviale Leutseligkeit des Chefs

**affable** /'æfəbl/ *adj.* freundlich; **he is on ~ terms with everyone** er versteht sich mit allen gut

**affably** /'æfəblɪ/ *adv.* freundlich

**affair** /ə'feə(r)/ *n.* Ⓐ *(concern, matter)* Angelegenheit, *die;* **it's not my ~:** es geht mich nichts an; **that's 'his ~:** das ist seine Sache; **the Dreyfus ~:** die Dreyfus-Affäre; Ⓑ *in pl. (everyday business)* Geschäfte *Pl.;* [tägliche] Arbeit; *(business dealings)* Geschäfte *Pl.;* **state of ~s** Lage, *die;* ⇒ *also* **current** 1 C; **foreign** C; **state** 1 D; Ⓒ *(love ~)* Affäre, *die;* **have an ~ with sb.** eine Affäre *od.* ein Verhältnis mit jmdm. haben; Ⓓ *(occurrence)* Geschichte, *die (ugs.);* Angelegenheit, *die;* Ⓔ *(coll.: thing)* Ding, *das;* **our house is a tumbledown ~:** unser Haus ist eine Bruchbude *(ugs.);* Ⓕ ~ **of honour** Ehrenhandel, *der*

**affect**[1] /ə'fekt/ *v.t. (pretend to have)* nachahmen; imitieren; *(pretend to feel or do)* vortäuschen; spielen; **the boy ~ed indifference** der Junge tat so, als sei es ihm gleichgültig; **~ to do sth.** vorgeben, etw. zu tun

**affect**[2] *v.t.* Ⓐ *(produce effect on)* sich auswirken auf (+ *Akk.*); **damp had ~ed the spark plugs** Feuchtigkeit hatte die Zündkerzen in Mitleidenschaft gezogen; **plant growth is ~ed by the amount of rainfall** das Wachstum der Pflanzen wird von der Niederschlagsmenge beeinflusst; Ⓑ *(emotionally)* betroffen machen; **be ~ed by sth.** von etw. betroffen sein; Ⓒ ‹Vorschrift:› betreffen; ‹Krankheit:› infizieren ‹Person›; befallen ‹Pflanze›

**affectation** /æfek'teɪʃn/ *n.* Ⓐ *(studied display)* Verstellung, *die;* *(artificiality)* Affektiertheit, *die;* Ⓑ *no pl. (pretence)* ~ **of sth.** Vortäuschung von etw.

**affected** /ə'fektɪd/ *adj.* affektiert; gekünstelt ‹Sprache, Stil›

**affectedly** /ə'fektɪdlɪ/ *adv.* affektiert

**affectedness** /ə'fektɪdnɪs/ *n., no pl.* Affektiertheit, *die*

**affecting** /ə'fektɪŋ/ *adj.* rührend; ergreifend

**affectingly** /ə'fektɪŋlɪ/ *adv.* in ergreifender Weise; rührend

**affection** /ə'fekʃn/ *n.* Ⓐ *(kindly feeling)* Zuneigung, *die;* **have** *or* **feel ~ for sb./sth.** für jmdn. Zuneigung empfinden/an etw. *(Dat.)* hängen; **gain** *or* **win sb.'s ~s** jmds. Zuneigung gewinnen; **she was held in great ~ by many people** viele hatten sie in ihr Herz geschlossen; **have a place in sb.'s ~s** einen festen Platz in jmds. Herzen einnehmen; **lots of love and ~** *(close of letter)* alles Liebe und Gute; Ⓑ *(Med.: illness)* Affektion, *die*

**affectionate** /ə'fekʃənət/ *adj.* anhänglich ‹Person, Kind, [Haus]tier›; liebevoll ‹Umarmung›; zärtlich ‹Lächeln, Erinnerung›; **your ~ son** *(in letter)* Dein dich liebender Sohn

**affectionately** /ə'fekʃənətlɪ/ *adv.* liebevoll; **yours ~:** viele Grüße und Küsse

**affidavit** /æfɪ'deɪvɪt/ *n. (Law)* **[sworn] ~:** eidesstattliche Versicherung; **swear an ~:** eine eidesstattliche Versicherung abgeben

**affiliate** /ə'fɪlɪeɪt/ ❶ *v.t.* Ⓐ *(attach)* **be ~d to** *or* **with sth.** an etw. *(Akk.)* angegliedert *od.* angeschlossen sein; **the organization is not politically ~d** die Organisation ist politisch nicht gebunden; Ⓑ *(adopt)* aufnehmen ‹Mitglied›; angliedern ‹Vereinigung›; **be an ~d member of an organization** einer Organisation angeschlossen sein. ❷ *n. (person)* assoziiertes Mitglied; *(organization)* Zweigorganisation, *die;* Affiliation, *die (Wirtsch.)*

**affiliation** /əfɪlɪ'eɪʃn/ *n.* Angliederung, *die* **(to, with** an + *Akk.*); ~ **order** *gerichtliche Feststellung der Vaterschaft und Festsetzung der Unterhaltsverpflichtung für ein nichteheliches Kind*

**affinity** /ə'fɪnɪtɪ/ *n.* Ⓐ *(relationship)* Verwandtschaft, *die* **(to** mit); Ⓑ *(liking)* Neigung, *die* **(for** zu); **feel an ~ to** *or* **for sb./sth.** sich zu jmdm./etw. hingezogen fühlen; Ⓒ *(structural resemblance)* Affinität, *die;* Verwandtschaft, *die;* *(fig.)* Verwandtschaft, *die* **(with, to** mit); **the ~ of sth. to** *or* **with sth.** die Affinität von etw. zu etw.

**affirm** /ə'fɜ:m/ ❶ *v.t. (assert)* bekräftigen ‹Absicht›; beteuern ‹Unschuld›; *(state as a fact)* bestätigen; ~ **sth. to sb.** jmdm. etw. versichern. ❷ *v.i. (Law) ohne religiöse Beteuerung schwören*

**affirmation** /æfə'meɪʃn/ *n.* Ⓐ *(of intention)* Bekräftigung, *die;* *(of fact)* Bestätigung, *die;* *(of quality)* Versicherung, *die;* Ⓑ *(Law)* eidesstattliche Erklärung

**affirmative** /ə'fɜ:mətɪv/ ❶ *adj.* affirmativ; bestätigend ‹Erklärung›; bejahend, zustimmend ‹Antwort›; ~ **vote** Jastimme, *die.* ❷ *n.* Bejahung, *die;* **answer in the ~:** bejahend antworten; **the answer is in the ~:** die Antwort ist „ja“ *od.* positiv

**affirmative 'action** *n. (Amer.)* positive Diskriminierung *(fachspr.);* Bevorzugung, *die*

**affirmatively** /ə'fɜ:mətɪvlɪ/ *adv.* **answer ~:** bejahend antworten

**affix** ❶ /ə'fɪks/ *v.t.* Ⓐ *(fix)* ~ **sth. to sth.** etw. an etw. *(Dat.)* befestigen; **the stamp had not been properly ~ed to the letter** die Marke war nicht richtig auf den Brief geklebt worden; Ⓑ *(impress)* aufdrücken; ~ **one's stamp/seal upon sth.** seinen Stempel/sein Siegel auf etw. *(Akk.)* drücken; Ⓒ *(add)* beifügen; ~ **one's signature [to sth.]** seine Unterschrift [unter etw. *(Akk.)*] setzen. ❷ /'æfɪks/ *n. (Ling.)* Affix, *das*

**afflict** /ə'flɪkt/ *v.t. (physically)* plagen; *(mentally)* quälen; peinigen; **be ~ed with sth.** von etw. befallen sein

**affliction** /ə'flɪkʃn/ *n.* Ⓐ *no pl. (distress)* Bedrängnis, *die;* **endure sorrow and ~:** Kummer und Leid ertragen; Ⓑ *(cause of distress)* Leiden, *das;* **bodily ~s** körperliche Gebrechen

**affluence** /'æfluəns/ *n., no pl.* Ⓐ *(wealth)* Reichtum, *der;* Ⓑ *(plenty)* Überfluss, *der*

**affluent** /'æfluənt/ ❶ *adj.* Ⓐ *(wealthy)* reich; **the ~ society** die Überflussgesellschaft; Ⓑ *(abounding)* reichhaltig; ~ **in** reich an (+ *Dat.*). ❷ *n. (of river)* Nebenfluss, *der;* *(of lake)* Zufluss, *der*

**afford** /ə'fɔ:d/ *v.t.* Ⓐ sich *(Dat.)* leisten; **be able to ~ sth.** sich *(Dat.)* etw. leisten können; **be able to ~:** aufbringen können ‹Geld›; erübrigen können ‹Zeit›; **be able to ~ to do sth.** es sich *(Dat.)* leisten können, etw. zu tun; **sb. can ill ~ sth.** jmd. kann sich *(Dat.)* etw. kaum leisten; **we can well ~ to look critically at our dietary habits** uns täte es sehr gut, sich *(Dat.)* die eigenen Essgewohnheiten einmal kritisch zu betrachten; Ⓑ *(provide)* bieten; gewähren ‹Schutz›; bereiten ‹Vergnügen›; ~ **sb. sth.** jmdm. etw. bieten/gewähren/bereiten

**affordable** /ə'fɔ:dəbl/ *adj.* erschwinglich

**afforest** /ə'fɒrɪst/ *v.t.* aufforsten

**afforestation** /əfɒrɪ'steɪʃn/ *n.* Aufforstung, *die*

**affray** /ə'freɪ/ *n.* Schlägerei, *die*

**affront** /ə'frʌnt/ ❶ *v.t. (insult)* beleidigen; *(offend)* kränken; vor den Kopf stoßen *(ugs.).* ❷ *n. (insult)* Affront, *der (geh.)* **(to** gegen); Beleidigung, *die* **(to** *Gen.*); *(offence)* Kränkung, *die* **(to** *Gen.*)

**Afghan** /'æfgæn/ ▶ **1275**, ▶ **1340** ❶ *adj.* afghanisch; ⇒ *also* **English** 1. ❷ *n.* Ⓐ *(person)* Afghane, *der*/Afghanin, *die;* Ⓑ *(language)* Afghanisch, *das;* ⇒ *also* **English** 2 A

**Afghan 'hound** *n.* Afghane, *der*

**Afghanistan** /æf'gænɪstɑ:n/ *pr. n.* Afghanistan *(das)*

**aficionado** /əfɪsjə'nɑ:dəʊ/ *n., pl.* **~s** Liebhaber, *der*/Liebhaberin, *die*

**afield** /ə'fi:ld/ *adv.* **far ~** *(direction)* weit hinaus; *(place)* weit draußen; **we didn't go farther ~ than ...:** wir gingen nicht weiter hinaus als bis zu ...; **from as far ~ as ...:** von so weit her wie ...; **go too far ~** *(fig.)* sich zu weit entfernen

**afire** /ə'faɪə(r)/ *pred. adj.* **[set] ~:** in Brand [setzen *od.* stecken]; **be ~:** in Flammen stehen

**aflame** /ə'fleɪm/ *pred. adj.* **be ~:** in Flammen stehen

**afloat** /ə'fləʊt/ *pred. adj.* Ⓐ *(floating)* über Wasser; flott ‹Schiff›; **get a boat ~:** ein Boot flottmachen; Ⓑ *(at sea)* auf See; **be ~:** auf dem Meer treiben; Ⓒ *(awash)* **be ~:** unter Wasser stehen

**afoot** /ə'fʊt/ *pred. adj.* Ⓐ *(astir)* auf den Beinen; Ⓑ *(under way)* im Gange; **set ~:** in Gang setzen; aufstellen ‹Plan›; **plans were ~ to ...:** es gab Pläne, zu ...; **there's trouble ~:** es gibt Ärger

**aforementioned** /ə'fɔ:menʃnd/, **aforesaid** /ə'fɔ:sed/ *adjs.* oben erwähnt *od.* genannt

**aforethought** /ə'fɔ:θɔ:t/ *adj.* **with malice ~:** mit Vorbedacht

**a fortiori** /eɪ fɔ:tɪ'ɔ:raɪ/ *adv.* erst recht

**afoul** /ə'faʊl/ *adv. (Amer.)* verwickelt **(of** in + *Akk.*); **fall** *or* **run ~ of sth.** sich in etw. *(Akk.)* verwickeln; *(fig.)* mit etw. in Konflikt geraten

**afraid** /ə'freɪd/ *pred. adj.* **[not] be ~ [of sb./sth.]** [vor jmdm./etw.] [keine] Angst haben; **be ~ lest ...:** befürchten, dass ...; **be ~ to do sth.** Angst davor haben, etw. zu tun; **be ~ of doing sth.** Angst haben, etw. zu tun; **I'm ~ [that] we must assume that ...:** leider müssen wir annehmen, dass ...; **I'm ~ so/not** ich fürchte ja/nein

**afresh** /ə'freʃ/ *adv.* von neuem; **every word has been translated ~:** jedes Wort ist neu übersetzt worden

**Africa** /'æfrɪkə/ *pr. n.* Afrika *(das);* ⇒ *also* **black** 1 C

**African** /'æfrɪkən/ ❶ *adj.* ▶ **1340** afrikanisch; **sb. is ~:** jmd. ist Afrikaner/Afrikanerin. ❷ *n.* Ⓐ ▶ **1340** Afrikaner, *der*/Afrikanerin, *die;* Ⓑ *(Amer.: Black African)* Neger, *der*/Negerin, *die*

**African 'violet** *n. (Bot.)* Usambaraveilchen, *das*

**Afrikaans** /æfrɪ'kɑ:ns/ *n.* ▶ **1275** Afrikaans, *das;* ⇒ *also* **English** 2 A

**Afrikaner** /æfrɪ'kɑ:nə(r)/ *n.* ▶ **1340** Afrika[a]nder, *der*/Afrika[a]nderin, *die*

**Afro** /'æfrəʊ/ ❶ *adj.* Afro-; ~ **look** Afrolook, *der.* ❷ *n., pl.* **~s** Afrolook, *der*

**Afro-** /æfrəʊ/ *in comb.* afro-/Afro-

**Afro-A'merican** ❶ *adj.* afroamerikanisch. ❷ *n.* Afroamerikaner, *der*/-amerikanerin, *die*

**Afro-Carib'bean** ❶ *adj.* afrokaribisch. ❷ *n.* Mensch afrokaribischer Herkunft *od.* Abstammung

**aft** /ɑ:ft/ *adv. (Naut., Aeronaut.)* achtern; **go ~:** nach achtern gehen

**after** /'ɑ:ftə(r)/ ❶ *adv.* Ⓐ *(later)* danach; **two days ~:** zwei Tage danach *od.* später; **soon/shortly ~:** bald/kurz danach *od.* darauf; **long ~:** lange danach; Ⓑ *(behind)* hinterher.

❷ *prep.* Ⓐ ▶ **1012** *(following in time)* nach; **~ six months** nach sechs Monaten; **~ you** nach Ihnen; **~ you with the salt** *(coll.)* kann ich das Salz nach dir haben?; **time ~**

time wieder und wieder; **day ~ day** Tag für Tag; **it is a quarter ~ ten o'clock** (*Amer.*) es ist Viertel nach zehn; **B** (*behind*) hinter (+ *Dat.*); (*in pursuit of*) **be/shout ~ sb.** hinter jmdm. her sein/herrufen; **what are you ~?** was suchst du denn?; (*to questioner*) was willst du wirklich wissen?; **she's only ~ his money** sie ist nur hinter seinem Geld her; **C** (*about*) **ask ~ sb./sth.** nach jmdm./etw. fragen; **D** (*next in importance to*) nach; **E** (*in spite of*) nach; **~ all** schließlich; **so you've come ~ all!** du bist also doch gekommen!; **I think I'll have a beer ~ all** ich glaube, ich trinke doch ein Bier; **so we took the train ~ all** wir haben den Zug schließlich doch genommen; **F** (*as a result of*) **~ what has happened** nach dem, was geschehen ist; **~ seeing that film/reading that book** nach diesem Film/diesem Buch; **G** (*in allusion to, in imitation of*) nach; **named ~:** benannt nach; **a picture ~ Rubens** ein Bild nach Rubens.
**3** *conj.* nachdem.
**4** *adj.* **A** (*later*) später; **in ~ years** in späteren Jahren; **B** (*Naut.*) Achter-

**after: ~birth** *n.* Nachgeburt, *die;* **~care** *n., no pl.* (*after hospital stay*) Nachsorge, *die;* (*after prison sentence*) Resozialisierung, *die;* **~-dinner speaker** *n.* Tischredner, *der;* **~-'dinner speech** *n.* Tischrede, *die;* **~-effect** *n., usu. in pl.* Nachwirkung, *die;* **~life** *n.* Leben nach dem Tod

**aftermath** /ˈɑ:ftəmæθ, ˈɑ:ftəmɑ:θ/ *n., no pl.* Nachwirkungen *Pl.;* **the ~ of the war** die Folgen *od.* Auswirkungen des Krieges; **in the ~ of sth.** nach etw.

**afternoon** /ɑ:ftəˈnu:n/ *n.* ▶**1012**, ▶**1056**, ▶**1191** Nachmittag, *der; attrib.* Nachmittags-; **this/tomorrow ~:** heute/morgen Nachmittag; **during the ~:** im Laufe des Nachmittags; **[early/late] in the ~:** am [frühen/späten] Nachmittag; (*regularly*) [früh/spät] nachmittags; **at three in the ~:** um drei Uhr nachmittags; **on Monday ~s/~:** Montag nachmittags/[am] Montagnachmittag; **one ~:** eines Nachmittags; **~s, of an ~:** nachmittags; **the other ~:** neulich nachmittags; **~, all!** (*coll. greeting*) Tag, zusammen!; ⇒ *also* **good 1 M**

**afters** /ˈɑ:ftəz/ *n. pl.* (*Brit. coll.*) Nachtisch, *der*

**after: ~-sales service** *n.* Kundendienst, *der;* **~shave** *n.* Aftershave, *das;* **~shock** *n.* Nachbeben, *das;* **~taste** *n.* Nachgeschmack, *der;* **~thought** *n.* nachträglicher Einfall; nachträgliche Idee; **be added as an ~thought** erst später hinzukommen

**afterwards** /ˈɑ:ftəwədz/ (*Amer.:* **afterward** /ˈɑ:ftəwəd/) *adv.* danach

**again** /əˈgen, əˈgeɪn/ *adv.* **A** (*another time*) wieder; **see a film ~:** einen Film noch einmal sehen; **play/sing a tune ~:** eine Melodie noch einmal spielen/singen; **not ~!** nicht schon wieder!; **~ and ~, time and [time] ~:** immer wieder; **back ~:** wieder zurück; **go back there ~:** wieder dorthin gehen; **as much ~:** noch einmal so viel; **half as much/many ~:** noch einmal halb so viel/so viele; **come ~** (*coll.: would you say that ~?*) wie bitte?; **B** (*besides*) **[there] ~:** außerdem; **C** (*on the other hand*) **[then/there] ~:** andrerseits

**against** /əˈgenst, əˈgeɪnst/ *prep.* **A** (*in opposition to, to the disadvantage of, in contrast to*) gegen; **those ~ the motion** diejenigen, die gegen den Antrag sind; **as ~:** gegenüber; **be ~ sb.'s doing sth.** dagegen sein, dass jmd. etw. tut; **B** (*into collision with, in contact with*) gegen; **lean sth. ~ sth.** etw. gegen etw. lehnen; **C** (*in preparation for*) gegen; **protect sth. ~ frost** etw. vor Frost schützen; **save money ~ a rainy day** Geld für schlechte Zeiten sparen; **be warned ~ sth./doing sth.** vor etw. (*Dat.*) gewarnt werden/davor gewarnt werden, etw. zu tun; **D** (*in return for*) gegen; **rate of exchange ~ the dollar** Wechselkurs des Dollar

**agape** /əˈgeɪp/ *adj.* **with mouth ~:** mit offenem Mund; **be ~** ‹Person:› den Mund aufsperren (**with** vor)

**agaric** /ˈægərɪk/ *n.* (*Bot.*) Blätterpilz, *der*

**agate** /ˈægət/ *n.* (*Min.*) Achat, *der*

**agave** /əˈgeɪvɪ/ *n.* (*Bot.*) Agave, *die*

**age** /eɪdʒ/ **1** *n.* **A** ▶**912** Alter, *das;* **the boys' ~s are 7, 6, and 3** die Jungen sind 7, 6 und 3 Jahre alt; **what ~ are you?, what is your ~?** wie alt bist du?; **at the ~ of** im Alter von; **at what ~:** in welchem Alter; **be six years of ~:** sechs Jahre alt sein; **children of six years of ~ and under** Kinder [im Alter] von sechs Jahren und darunter; **when I was your ~:** als ich so alt war wie du; **he looks his ~:** man sieht ihm sein Alter an; **come of ~:** mündig *od.* volljährig werden; (*fig.*) den Kinderschuhen entwachsen; **be over ~:** die vorgeschriebene Altersgrenze überschritten haben; **be/look under ~:** zu jung sein/aussehen; **she's now of an ~ when she ...:** sie ist jetzt in dem Alter, in dem sie ...; **be** *or* **act your ~** (*coll.*) sei nicht so kindisch; **B** (*advanced ~*) Alter, *das;* **her ~ is catching up with her** sie merkt jetzt doch, dass sie alt wird; **her face was wrinkled with ~:** ihr Gesicht war vom Alter zerfurcht; **~ before beauty** (*joc.*) Alter vor Schönheit; **C** (*generation*) Generation, *die;* **D** (*great period*) Zeitalter, *das;* **wait [for] ~s** *or* **an ~ for sb./sth.** (*coll.*) eine Ewigkeit auf jmdn./etw. warten; **take/be ~s** *or* **an ~** (*coll.*) eine Ewigkeit dauern; **she took ~s looking for the book** (*coll.*) sie suchte eine Ewigkeit nach dem Buch; **I'll be ~s yet** (*coll.*) ich brauche noch eine Ewigkeit.
**2** *v.t.* **A** altern lassen; altern (*selten*); **sth. ~s sb./sth. prematurely** etw. lässt jmdn./etw. frühzeitig alt werden; **B** (*mature*) reifen lassen; altern (*fachspr.*)
**3** *v.i.* altern

**'age bracket** *n.* Altersstufe, *die*; **children in the 9–13 ~:** Kinder im Alter von 9–13 Jahren

**aged** **1** *adj.* **A** /eɪdʒd/ ▶**912** **be ~ five** fünf Jahre alt sein; **a boy ~ five** ein fünfjähriger Junge; **B** /eɪdʒd/ (*matured*) gealtert ‹Wein, Käse, Brandy›; **C** /ˈeɪdʒɪd/ (*elderly*) bejahrt. **2** /ˈeɪdʒɪd/ *n. pl.* **the ~:** die alten Menschen

**'age group** *n.* Altersgruppe, *die*

**ageism** /ˈeɪdʒɪzm/ *n.* Diskriminierung aufgrund des Alters

**ageist** /ˈeɪdʒɪst/ *adj.* das Alter diskriminierend

**ageless** /ˈeɪdʒlɪs/ *adj.* nicht alternd ‹Person›; (*eternal*) zeitlos

**age: ~ limit** *n.* Altersgrenze, *die;* **~-long** *adj.* jahrhundertelang

**agency** /ˈeɪdʒənsɪ/ *n.* **A** (*action*) Handeln, *das;* **through/by the ~ of sth.** durch [die Einwirkung von] etw.; **through/by the ~ of sb.** durch jmds. Vermittlung; **B** (*business establishment*) Geschäftsstelle, *die;* (*news/advertising ~*) Agentur, *die;* (*United Nations department*) (*major*) Sonderorganisation, *die;* (*minor*) Unterorganisation, *die*

**agenda** /əˈdʒendə/ *n.* (*lit. or fig.*) Tagesordnung, *die*; Agenda, *die;* **[be] on the ~:** auf der Tagesordnung *od.* Agenda [stehen]; **six items on the ~:** sechs Tagesordnungspunkte; **be high on the ~:** obenan *od.* ganz oben auf der Tagesordnung *od.* Agenda stehen; **have a hidden ~:** heimliche Absichten hegen *od.* verfolgen

**agent** /ˈeɪdʒənt/ *n.* **A** [treibende] Kraft; (*Ling.*) Agens, *das;* **be a free ~:** sein eigener Herr sein; **B** (*substance*) Mittel, *das;* **an oxidizing ~:** ein Oxidationsmittel; **C** (*one who acts for another*) Vertreter, *der*/Vertreterin, *die;* **D** (*spy*) Agent, *der*/Agentin, *die*

**agent provocateur** /ɑ:ʒɑ̃ prɒvɒkəˈtɜ:(r)/ *n., pl.* **agents provocateurs** /ɑ:ʒɑ̃ prɒvɒkəˈtɜ:(r)/ Agent provocateur, *der*

**age: ~-old** *adj.* uralt; **~ range** *n.* Altersstufe, *die*; **teach English across a very large ~ range** Schüler der verschiedensten Altersstufen in Englisch unterrichten; ⇒ *also* **age bracket**

**agglomerate** /əˈglɒməreɪt/ *v.t.* agglomerieren

**agglomeration** /əglɒməˈreɪʃn/ *n.* (*mass*) Agglomeration, *die* (*bes. fachspr.*); Anhäufung, *die*

**aggrandizement** /əˈgrændɪzmənt/ *n., no pl.* Vergrößerung, *die;* (*of power, influence*) Ausdehnung, *die;* **his personal ~:** die Glorifizierung seiner Person

**aggravate** /ˈægrəveɪt/ *v.t.* **A** verschlimmern ‹Krankheit, Zustand, Situation›; verschärfen ‹Streit›; **B** (*coll.: annoy*) aufregen; ärgern; **be ~d by sth.** sich über etw. (*Akk.*) ärgern *od.* aufregen

**aggravating** /ˈægrəveɪtɪŋ/ *adj.* (*coll.*) ärgerlich; lästig ‹Kind, Lärm›

**aggravation** /ægrəˈveɪʃn/ *n., no pl.* **A** Verschlimmerung, *die;* (*of dispute*) Verschärfung, *die;* **B** (*coll.: annoyance*) Ärger, *der*

**aggregate** **1** /ˈægrɪgət/ *n.* **A** (*sum total*) Gesamtmenge, *die;* (*assemblage*) Ansammlung, *die;* **in the ~:** in seiner/ihrer Gesamtheit; **B** (*Building*) [Beton]zuschlag, *der;* **C** (*Geol.*) Aggregat, *das.* **2** *adj.* (*collected into one*) zusammengefügt; (*collective*) gesamt; **the ~ amount** der Gesamtbetrag. **3** /ˈægrɪgeɪt/ *v.t.* **A** verbinden ‹Material, Stoff› (**into** zu); ansammeln ‹Reichtum›; **B** (*unite*) vereinigen; (*coll.: amount to*) sich [insgesamt] belaufen auf (+ *Akk.*); **audiences aggregating 7 million** insgesamt 7 Millionen Zuhörer/Zuschauer

**aggregation** /ægrɪˈgeɪʃn/ *n.* Ansammlung, *die;* Aggregation, *die* (*bes. fachspr.*)

**aggression** /əˈgreʃn/ *n.* **A** *no pl.* Aggression, *die;* **B** (*unprovoked attack*) Angriff, *der;* **C** *no pl.* (*Psych.*) Aggression, *die*

**aggressive** /əˈgresɪv/ *adj.* aggressiv; angriffslustig ‹Kämpfer›; heftig ‹Angriff›

**aggressively** /əˈgresɪvlɪ/ *adv.* aggressiv, herausfordernd ‹handeln, reagieren›; (*forcefully*) aggressiv, wirkungsvoll, dynamisch ‹verkaufen, anbieten›; **the product was marketed ~:** die Werbung für das Produkt hatte Biss

**aggressiveness** /əˈgresɪvnɪs/ *n., no pl.* Aggressivität, *die*

**aggressor** /əˈgresə(r)/ *n.* Aggressor, *der*

**aggrieve** /əˈgri:v/ *v.t.* **A** (*treat unfairly*) ungerecht behandeln; **feel [oneself] much ~d at** *or* **over sth.** sich durch etw. ungerecht behandelt fühlen; **B** **~d** (*resentful*) verärgert; (*offended*) gekränkt

**aggro** /ˈægrəʊ/ *n., no pl.* (*Brit. sl.*) Zoff, *der* (*ugs.*); Krawall, *der;* **they are looking for ~:** sie suchen Streit

**aghast** /əˈgɑ:st/ *pred. adj.* (*horrified*) bestürzt, erschüttert (**at** über + *Akk.*); (*terrified*) erschrocken (**at** über + *Akk.*); **we stood ~ as ...:** wir standen wie versteinert, als ...

**agile** /ˈædʒaɪl/ *adj.* beweglich; agil (*geh.*); flink, behänd[e] ‹Bewegung›

**agility** /əˈdʒɪlɪtɪ/ *n., no pl.:* ⇒ **agile**: Beweglichkeit, *die;* Flinkheit, *die;* Behändigkeit, *die;* **mental ~:** geistige Behändigkeit *od.* Beweglichkeit

**agitate** /ˈædʒɪteɪt/ **1** *v.t.* **A** (*shake*) schütteln; (*stir up*) aufrühren; **B** (*disturb*) beunruhigen; erregen. **2** *v.i.* **~ for/against sth.** für/gegen etw. agitieren

**agitation** /ædʒɪˈteɪʃn/ *n.* **A** (*shaking*) Schütteln, *das;* (*stirring up*) Aufrühren, *das;* **B** (*emotional disturbance*) Erregung, *die;* **C** (*campaign*) Agitation, *die*

**agitator** /ˈædʒɪteɪtə(r)/ *n.* **A** Agitator, *der;* **B** (*device*) Rührwerk, *das*

**AGM** *abbr.* **Annual General Meeting** JHV

**agnostic** /ægˈnɒstɪk/ **1** *adj.* agnostizistisch. **2** *n.* Agnostiker, *der*/Agnostikerin, *die*

**agnosticism** /ægˈnɒstɪsɪzm/ *n., no pl.* Agnostizismus, *der*

**ago** /əˈgəʊ/ *adv.* **ten years ~:** vor zehn Jahren; **[not] long ~:** vor [nicht] langer Zeit; **that was a long while ~:** das war vor langer Zeit; **how long ~ is it that ...?** wie lange ist es her, dass ...?; **no longer ~ than last Sunday** nicht vor letztem Sonntag; (*only last Sunday*) erst letzten Sonntag

**agog** /əˈgɒg/ *pred. adj.* gespannt (**for** auf + *Akk.*); **be ~ to hear the news** gespannt darauf sein, die Neuigkeiten zu hören

a

# Age

## How old?

***How old is she?, What age is she?***
= Wie alt ist sie?

***She is forty [years old]*** or (more formal) ***forty years of age***
= Sie ist vierzig [Jahre alt]

***He has just turned sixty***
= Er ist gerade sechzig geworden

***at the age of twenty***
= im Alter von zwanzig Jahren, mit zwanzig

***Life begins at forty***
= Mit vierzig fängt das Leben an

***a man of fifty*** or ***aged fifty***
= ein fünfzigjähriger Mann, ein Fünfzigjähriger

***a girl of ten***
= ein zehnjähriges Mädchen

***a thirty-year-old [man]***
= ein Dreißigjähriger

***a thirty-year-old [woman]***
= eine Dreißigjährige

***an eighty-year-old pensioner***
= ein achtzigjähriger Rentner

***They have an eight-year-old and a five-year-old***
= Sie haben ein achtjähriges und ein fünfjähriges Kind

## Older and younger

***I'm older than you [are]***
= Ich bin älter als du

***She's younger than him*** or ***than he is***
= Sie ist jünger als er

***He's four years older than me*** or (more formal) ***four years my senior***
= Er ist vier Jahre älter als ich

***You are twenty years younger than her*** or (more formal) ***twenty years her junior***
= Du bist zwanzig Jahre jünger als sie

***They are the same age***
= Sie sind gleich alt *or* gleichaltrig

***She is [exactly] the same age as John***
= Sie ist [genau]so alt wie John

## Approximate ages

***He's about fifty***
= Er ist ungefähr fünfzig *or* um die fünfzig

***She's just over sixty***
= Sie ist etwas über sechzig

***He's nearly seventy*** or ***just under seventy***
= Er ist fast *or* bald siebzig

***He's getting on for seventy***
= Er geht auf die siebzig zu *or* wird bald siebzig

***She's in her sixties***
= Sie ist in den Sechzigern

***He's in his late/early sixties***
= Er ist Ende/Anfang sechzig

***Jane's in her mid-forties***
= Jane ist Mitte vierzig

***He's still a teenager*** or ***in his teens***
= Er ist noch ein Teenager *or* in den Teenagerjahren

***Her son's just ten***
= Ihr Sohn ist gerade zehn geworden

***She's barely twelve***
= Sie ist noch keine zwölf Jahre alt

***games for the under-twelves***
= Spiele für Kinder unter 12 Jahren

***only for the over-eighties***
= nur für Leute über achtzig

**agonize** /ˈægənaɪz/ ❶ *v.i.* Ⓐ (*suffer agony*) Todesqualen erleiden; Ⓑ (*fig.: struggle*) ringen; **~ over sth.** sich (*Dat.*) den Kopf über etw. (*Akk.*) zermartern. ❷ *v.t.* quälen; **an ~d scream** ein qualerfüllter Schrei; **an agonizing wait** (*fig.*) eine qualvolle Wartezeit

**agony** /ˈægənɪ/ *n.* Todesqualen *Pl.*; **suffer ~/agonies** Todesqualen erleiden; **die in ~:** qualvoll sterben; **in an ~ of indecision/anticipation** (*fig.*) in qualvoller Unentschlossenheit/Erwartung; **death ~, last ~:** Agonie, *die;* Todeskampf, *der*

**agony: ~ aunt** *n.* (*coll.*) Briefkastentante, *die* (*ugs. scherzh.*); **~ column** *n.* (*Brit. coll.*) Ⓐ *Zeitungsspalte für private Mitteilungen („Persönliches“)*; Ⓑ (*advice column*) *Spalte für die „Briefkastentante“*

**agoraphobia** /ægərəˈfəʊbɪə/ *n.* (*Psych.*) Agoraphobie, *die;* Platzangst, *die*

**agoraphobic** /ægərəˈfəʊbɪk/ *adj.* (*Psych.*) an Agoraphobie *od.* Platzangst leidend; **be ~:** an Agoraphobie *od.* Platzangst leiden

**agrarian** /əˈgreərɪən/ *adj.* Agrar-; (*relating to agricultural matters*) agrarisch

**agree** /əˈgriː/ ❶ *v.i.* Ⓐ (*consent*) einverstanden sein; **~ to** *or* **with sth./to do sth.** mit etw. einverstanden sein/damit einverstanden sein, etw. zu tun; **we can only ~ to differ** *or* **disagree** wir können nur darin übereinstimmen, dass wir nicht übereinstimmen; Ⓑ (*hold similar opinion*) einer Meinung sein; **they ~d [with me]** sie waren derselben Meinung [wie ich]; **~ with sb. about** *or* **on sth./that …:** jmdm. in etw. (*Dat.*) zustimmen/jmdm. darin zustimmen, dass …; **I ~:** stimmt; **I couldn't ~ more** ich bin völlig deiner Meinung; **do you ~ with what I say?** stimmst du darin mit mir überein?; Ⓒ (*reach similar opinion*) **~ on sth.** sich über etw. (*Akk.*) einigen; **we could not ~ on how …:** wir konnten uns nicht darüber einigen, wie …; Ⓓ (*harmonize*) übereinstimmen; **sth. ~s with sth.** etw. stimmt mit etw. überein; **make ~:** zur Übereinstimmung bringen; **~ closely** weitgehend übereinstimmen; Ⓔ (*suit*) **~ with sb.** ‹Essen:› jmdm. bekommen; Ⓕ (*Ling.*) übereinstimmen.
❷ *v.t.* Ⓐ (*reach agreement about*) vereinbaren; Ⓑ (*consent to*) **~ sth.** einer Sache (*Dat.*) zustimmen

**agreeable** /əˈgriːəbl/ *adj.* Ⓐ (*pleasing*) angenehm ‹Überraschung, Person, Abend, Stimme›; erfreulich ‹Anblick›; Ⓑ (*willing to agree*) **be ~ [to sth.]** [mit etw.] einverstanden sein

**agreeableness** /əˈgriːəbəlnɪs/ *n., no pl.* **the ~ of his company** seine angenehme Gesellschaft; **the ~ of the taste/climate** der angenehme Geschmack/das angenehme Klima

**agreeably** /əˈgriːəblɪ/ *adv.* angenehm; **~ surprised** angenehm überrascht; **we were ~ entertained** wir wurden auf angenehme Weise *od.* nett unterhalten

**agreed** /əˈgriːd/ *adj.* einig; vereinbart ‹Summe, Zeit›; **be ~ that …/about sth.** sich (*Dat.*) darüber einig sein, dass …/sich (*Dat.*) über etw. (*Akk.*) einig sein; **it was ~ that …:** man war sich (*Dat.*) darüber einig, dass …; **~!** einverstanden!

**agreement** /əˈgriːmənt/ *n.* Ⓐ Übereinstimmung, *die;* (*mutual understanding*) Übereinkunft, *die;* **be in ~ [about sth.]** sich (*Dat.*) [über etw. (*Akk.*)] einig sein; **I'm in ~ with what you say** ich stimme darin mit dir überein; **enter into an ~:** eine Übereinkunft treffen; **come to** *or* **reach an ~ with sb. [about sth.]** mit jmdm. eine Einigung [über etw. (*Akk.*)] erzielen; Ⓑ (*treaty*) Abkommen, *das;* Ⓒ *no pl., no indef. art.* (*state of harmony*) Übereinstimmung, *die;* Ⓓ (*Law*) Abkommen, *das;* Vertrag, *der;* **legal ~:** rechtliche Vereinbarung; Ⓔ (*Ling.*) Übereinstimmung, *die*

**agribusiness** /ˈægrɪbɪznɪs/ *n.* ≈ Agrarindustrie, *die*

**agrichemical** /ˈægrɪkemɪkl/ *n.* Agrochemikalie, *die*

**agricultural** /ægrɪˈkʌltʃərl/ *adj.* landwirtschaftlich; **~ worker** Landarbeiter, *der*

**agriculturalist** /ægrɪˈkʌltʃərəlɪst/ ⇒ **agriculturist**

**agriculture** /ˈægrɪkʌltʃə(r)/ *n.* Landwirtschaft, *die*

**agriculturist** /ægrɪˈkʌltʃərɪst/ *n.* ▶ 1261 Landwirtschaftsexperte, *der;* (*farmer*) Landwirt, *der*

**agrimony** /ˈægrɪmənɪ/ *n.* (*Bot.*) Odermennig, *der*

**aground** /əˈgraʊnd/ *pred. adj.* auf Grund gelaufen; **go** *or* **run ~:** auf Grund laufen

**ague** /ˈeɪgjuː/ *n.* ▶ 1232 (*fever*) Wechselfieber, *das* (*veralt.*); (*shivering fit*) Schüttelfrost, *der*

**ah** /ɑː/ *int.* ach; (*of pleasure*) ah

**aha** /ɑːˈhɑː/ *int.* aha

**ahead** /əˈhed/ *adv.* Ⓐ (*further forward in space*) voraus; **the way ~ was blocked** der Weg vor uns/ihnen *usw.* war versperrt; **~ of sb./sth.** vor jmdm./etw.; **right** *or* **straight ~ of us** (*directly in line*) genau vor uns (*Dat.*); **keep going straight ~** (*straight forwards*) gehen Sie immer geradeaus; Ⓑ (*fig.*) **be ~ of the others** den anderen voraus sein; **be ~ on points** nach Punkten führen; **get ~:** vorwärts kommen; Ⓒ (*further forward in time*) **~ of us lay three days of intensive training** vor uns lagen drei Tage intensives Training; **Britain is eight hours**

~ **of Los Angeles** in Großbritannien ist es acht Stunden später als in Los Angeles; **finish ~ of schedule** *or* **time** früher als geplant fertig werden; **get home ~ of sb.** eher *od.* früher nach Hause kommen als jmd.; **we've got ~ of ourselves** (*fig.*) wir sind zu schnell vorgegangen; **there is no point in looking too far ~:** es hat keinen Sinn, zu weit in die Zukunft zu planen

**ahoy** /əˈhɔɪ/ *int.* (*Naut.*) ahoi

**AI** *abbr.* Ⓐ **artificial intelligence** KI; Ⓑ **artificial insemination** KB

**aid** /eɪd/ ❶ *v.t.* Ⓐ ~ **sb. [to do sth.]** jmdm. helfen[, etw. zu tun]; ~**ed by** unterstützt von; **the finances have been ~ed by donations** die Finanzen sind durch Spenden aufgebessert worden; ⇒ *also* **abet**; Ⓑ (*promote*) fördern. ❷ *n.* Ⓐ *no pl.* (*help*) Hilfe, *die;* **come to sb.'s ~, go to the ~ of sb.** jmdm. zu Hilfe kommen; **with the ~ of sth./sb.** mithilfe einer Sache (*Gen.*)/mit jmds. Hilfe; mithilfe von etw./jmdm.; **in ~ of sb./sth.** zugunsten von jmdm./etw.; **what's [all] this in ~ of?** (*coll.*) wozu soll das [Ganze *od.* alles] gut sein?; ⇒ *also* **foreign aid**; Ⓑ (*source of help*) Hilfsmittel, *das* (**to** für)

**aide** /eɪd/ *n.* Ⓐ ⇒ **aide-de-camp**; Ⓑ (*assistant*) Berater, *der*/Beraterin, *die*

**aide-de-camp** /eɪddəˈkɑ̃ː/ *n., pl.* **aides-de-camp** /eɪddəˈkɑ̃ː/ (*Mil.*) Adjutant, *der*

**aide-mémoire** /ˈeɪdmemwɑː(r)/ *n.* (*aid to memory*) Gedächtnisstütze, *die*

**Aids** /eɪdz/ *n., no pl., no art.* ▶ 1232 Aids (*das*); ~ **victim** Aidsopfer, *das;* ~ **virus** Aids-Virus, *der,* (*fachspr.*) *das*

ˈ**Aids-related** *adj.* ~ **disease/illness** durch Aids hervorgerufene Krankheit

**aikido** /ˈaɪkɪdəʊ/ *n.* (*Sport*) Aikido, *das*

**ail** /eɪl/ *v.t.* (*arch.: trouble*) plagen; **what ~s him?** was ist mit ihm?

**ailing** /ˈeɪlɪŋ/ *adj.* (*sickly*) kränklich

**ailment** /ˈeɪlmənt/ *n.* Gebrechen, *das;* **minor ~:** leichte Erkrankung

**aim** /eɪm/ ❶ *v.t.* ausrichten ‹Schusswaffe, Rakete›; ~ **sth. at sb./sth.** etw. auf jmdn./etw. richten; **that remark was not ~ed at you** (*fig.*) diese Bemerkung war nicht gegen Sie gerichtet; ~ **a blow/shot/book at sb.** nach jmdm. schlagen/auf jmdn. schießen/ein Buch nach jmdm. werfen.
❷ *v.i.* Ⓐ zielen; ~ **at sth./sb.** auf etw./jmdn. zielen; ~ **high/wide** [zu] hoch/[zu] weit zielen; ~ **high** (*fig.*) sich (*Dat.*) ein hohes Ziel stecken *od.* setzen; Ⓑ (*intend*) ~ **to do sth.** *or* **at doing sth.** beabsichtigen, etw. zu tun; **please ~ to be back by 4 p.m.** versuche bitte, bis 16 Uhr zurück zu sein; ~ **at** *or* **for sth.** (*fig.*) etw. anstreben; **I'm not quite sure what you're ~ing at** (*fig.*) ich weiß nicht recht, worauf Sie hinauswollen.
❸ *n.* Ⓐ Ziel, *das;* **his ~ was true** er hatte genau gezielt; **take ~ [at sth./sb.]** [auf etw./jmdn.] zielen; **take ~ at the target** das Ziel anvisieren; Ⓑ (*purpose*) Ziel, *das*

**aimless** /ˈeɪmlɪs/ *adj.* ziellos ‹Leben, Aktivität›; sinnlos ‹Vorhaben, Beschäftigung›

**aimlessly** /ˈeɪmlɪslɪ/ *adv.* ziellos

**aimlessness** /ˈeɪmlɪsnɪs/ *n.* Ziellosigkeit, *die*

**ain't** /eɪnt/ (*coll.*) Ⓐ = **am not, is not, are not;** ⇒ **be**; Ⓑ = **has not, have not;** ⇒ **have** 2

**air** /eə(r)/ ❶ *n.* Ⓐ Luft, *die;* **take the ~:** [frische] Luft schöpfen (*geh.*); **be in the ~** (*fig.*) (*be spreading*) ‹Gerücht, Idee:› in der Luft liegen; (*be uncertain*) ‹Plan, Projekt:› in der Luft hängen; **be up in the ~** ‹Plan, Projekt:› in der Luft hängen; **be walking on ~** (*fig.*) wie auf Wolken schweben (*ugs.*); **by ~:** mit dem Flugzeug; **travel by ~:** fliegen; **send a letter by ~:** einen Brief mit *od.* per Luftpost schicken; **from the ~:** aus der Vogelperspektive; Ⓑ (*breeze*) Lüftchen, *das;* Ⓒ (*Radio, Telev.*) **be/go on the ~:** senden; ‹Programm, Sendung:› gesendet werden; **be/go off the ~:** nicht/nicht mehr senden; ‹Programm:› beendet sein/werden; Ⓓ (*appearance*) **there was an ~ of absurdity about the whole exercise** die ganze Übung hatte etwas Absurdes; **his newspaper stories have the ~ of fiction** seine Zeitungsgeschichten haben etwas Fiktives; Ⓔ (*bearing*) Auftreten, *das;* (*facial expression*) Miene, *die;* ~**s and graces** Allüren *Pl.* (*abwertend*); **give oneself** *or* **put on ~s** sich aufspielen; Ⓕ (*Mus.*) Melodie, *die.*
❷ *v.t.* Ⓐ (*ventilate*) lüften ‹Zimmer, Matratze, Kleidung›; Ⓑ (*finish drying*) nachtrocknen ‹Wäsche›; Ⓒ (*parade*) zur Schau tragen; Ⓓ (*make public*) [öffentlich] darlegen.
❸ *v.i.* (*be ventilated*) lüften

**air:** ~ **bag** *n.* (*Motor Veh.*) Airbag, *der;* **side ~ bag** Seitenairbag, *der;* ~**bed** *n.* Luftmatratze, *die;* ~**borne** *adj.* ~**borne bacteria** in der Luft befindliche Bakterien; ~**borne freight** Luftfracht, *die;* ~**borne troops** Luftlandetruppen *Pl.;* **be ~borne** sich in der Luft befinden; **become ~borne** sich in die Luft erheben; ~ **brake** *n.* Druckluftbremse, *die;* (*flap*) Luftbremse, *die;* ~ **brick** *n.* Lüftungsstein, *der* (*Bauw.*); ~**brush** *n.* Spritzpistole, *die;* ~ **bubble** *n.* Luftblase, *die;* ~ **bus** *n.* Airbus, *der;* ~**-conditioned** *adj.* klimatisiert; ~ **conditioner** *n.* Klimaanlage, *die;* ~ **conditioning** *n., no pl.* Klimatisierung, *die;* (*system*) Klimaanlage, *die;* ~**-cooled** *adj.* luftgekühlt; ~ **corridor** *n.* (*Aeronaut.*) Luftkorridor, *der;* ~ **cover** *n.* Deckung aus der Luft

**aircraft** /ˈeəkrɑːft/ *n., pl. same* Luftfahrzeug, *das;* (*aeroplane*) Flugzeug, *das*

**aircraft:** ~ **carrier** *n.* (*Navy*) Flugzeugträger, *der;* ~ **noise** *n.* Fluglärm, *der*

**air:** ~ **crew** *n.* Besatzung, *die;* Flugpersonal, *das;* ~ **cushion** *n.* Ⓐ Luftkissen, *das;* Ⓑ ~**-cushion vehicle** Luftkissenfahrzeug, *das*

**Airedale** /ˈeədeɪl/ *n.* Airedaleterrier, *der*

**airer** /ˈeərə(r)/ *n.* Wäscheständer, *der*

**air:** ~ **fare** *n.* Flugpreis, *der;* ~ **ferry** *n.* (~*craft*) [im Pendelluftverkehr eingesetztes] Flugzeug; (*service*) Pendelluftverkehr, *der;* ~**field** *n.* Flugplatz, *der;* ~ **filter** *n.* Luftfilter, *der od. das;* ~**foil** (*Amer.*) ⇒ **aerofoil**; ~ **force** *n.* Luftstreitkräfte *Pl.;* Luftwaffe, *die;* ~**frame** *n.* (*Aeronaut.*) Flugwerk, *das;* ~ **freshener** *n.* Lufterfrischer, *der;* Luftverbesserer, *der;* ~**gun** *n.* Luftgewehr, *das;* ~ **hostess** *n.* ▶ 1261 Stewardess, *die*

**airily** /ˈeərɪlɪ/ *adv.* (*flippantly*) leichthin

**airiness** /ˈeərɪnɪs/ *n., no pl.* (*flippancy*) Unbekümmertheit, *die*

**airing** /ˈeərɪŋ/ *n.* Auslüften, *das;* **these clothes need a good ~:** diese Kleider müssen gründlich gelüftet werden; **give a problem an ~** (*fig.*) ein Problem an die Öffentlichkeit bringen; ~ **cupboard** Trockenschrank, *der*

**airless** /ˈeəlɪs/ *adj.* stickig ‹Zimmer, Büro›; windstill ‹Nacht›

**air:** ~ **letter** *n.* Luftpostleichtbrief, *der;* Aerogramm, *das;* ~**lift** ❶ *n.* Luftbrücke, *die* (**of** für); ❷ *v.t.* auf dem Luftweg *od.* über eine Luftbrücke transportieren; ~**line** *n.* Fluggesellschaft, *die;* Fluglinie, *die; attrib.* ~**line pilot** ▶ 1261 [für eine Fluggesellschaft fliegender] Pilot; ~ **liner** *n.* Verkehrsflugzeug, *das;* ~**lock** *n.* Ⓐ (*stoppage*) Luftblase, *die;* Ⓑ (*of spacecraft etc.*) Luftschleuse, *die;* ~ **mail** *n.* Luftpost, *die;* **by ~ mail** mit *od.* per Luftpost; ~**mail** *v.t.* mit *od.* per Luftpost befördern; ~**man** /ˈeəmən/ *n., pl.* ~**men** /ˈeəmən/ Flieger, *der;* ~ **mile** *n.* Flugmeile, *die;* ~**-minded** *adj.* am Fliegen interessiert; ~**miss** *n.* (*Aeronaut.*) Beinahezusammenstoß, *der;* ~**plane** (*Amer.*) ⇒ **aeroplane**; ~ **play** *n., no pl.* (*Radio*) *das Spielen einer Platte im Radio;* **the record receives** *or* **gets no/a great deal of ~play** die Platte wird [überhaupt] nicht/wird sehr häufig im Radio gespielt; ~ **pocket** *n.* (*Aeronaut.*) Luftloch, *das;* ~ **pollution** *n.* Luftverschmutzung, *die;* ~**port** *n.* Flughafen, *der;* ~ **port tax** Flughafengebühr, *die;* ~ **power** *n.* Schlagkraft der Luftwaffe; ~ **pressure** *n.* Luftdruck, *der;* ~ **pump** *n.* Luftpumpe, *die;* ~ **raid** *n.* Luftangriff, *der;* ~**-raid precautions** Luftschutz, *der;* ~**-raid shelter** Luftschutzraum, *der;* ~**-raid warden** Luftschutzwart, *der;* ~ **rifle** *n.* Luftgewehr, *das;* ~**screw** *n.* (*Aeronaut.*) Luftschraube, *die* (*Technik*); ~**-sea** ˈ**rescue** *n.* Seenotrettungseinsatz aus der Luft; ~**ship** *n.* Luftschiff, *das;* ~ **show** *n.* Flugschau, *die;* ~**sick** *adj.* luftkrank; ~**sickness** *n.* Luftkrankheit, *die;* ~**space** *n.* Luftraum, *der;* ~ **speed** *n.* (*Aeronaut.*) Eigengeschwindigkeit, *die;* ~**stream** *n.* (*Meteorol.*) Luftströmung, *die;* ~ **strike** *n.* Luftschlag, *der;* ~**strip** *n.* Start-und-Lande-Bahn, *die;* ~ **terminal** *n.* [Air]terminal, *der od. das;* ~**tight** *adj.* luftdicht; ~**time** *n.* Sendezeit, *die;* ~**-to-~** *adj.* Luft-Luft-; ~**-to-~ refuelling** Betanken in der Luft; ~ **traffic** *n.* (*Aeronaut.*) Flugverkehr, *der; attrib.* ~**-traffic control** (*Aeronaut.*) Flugsicherung, *die;* ~**-traffic controller** ▶ 1261 (*Aeronaut.*) Fluglotse, *der;* ~**waves** *n. pl.* Äther, *der;* ~**way** *n.* Ⓐ (*Aeronaut.*) Luftstraße, *die;* Ⓑ (*Anat.*) Luftröhre, *die;* Ⓒ (*ventilation shaft*) Lüftungsschacht, *der;* ~**woman** *n.* Fliegerin, *die;* ~**worthy** *adj.* (*Aeronaut.*) lufttüchtig

**airy** /ˈeərɪ/ *adj.* Ⓐ luftig ‹Büro, Zimmer›; windig ‹Küste›; Ⓑ (*poet.: lofty*) **the ~ mountain** der in luftige Höhen hinaufragende Berg; Ⓒ (*superficial*) vage; (*flippant*) leichtfertig

**airy-fairy** /eərɪˈfeərɪ/ *adj.* (*coll. derog.*) aus der Luft gegriffen ‹Plan›; versponnen ‹Idee, Vorstellung›

**aisle** /aɪl/ *n.* Gang, *der;* (*lateral section of church*) Seitenschiff, *das;* **have the audience rolling in the ~s** (*coll.*) das Publikum dazu bringen, dass es sich vor Lachen kugelt; **walk down the ~ with sb.** (*fig.*) mit jmdm. vor den Traualtar treten

**aitch** /eɪtʃ/ *n.* H, h, *das;* **drop one's ~es** das h [im Anlaut] nicht aussprechen

**Aix-la-Chapelle** /eɪkslɑːʃæˈpel/ *pr. n.* ▶ 1626 Aachen (*das*)

**ajar** /əˈdʒɑː(r)/ *pred. adj.* **be** *or* **stand [slightly] ~:** einen [winzigen] Spaltbreit offen stehen; **leave ~:** offen lassen

**a.k.a.** *abbr.* **also known as** al.

**akimbo** /əˈkɪmbəʊ/ *adv.* **with arms ~:** die Arme in die Seite gestemmt

**akin** /əˈkɪn/ *pred. adj.* Ⓐ verwandt; **look ~:** sich (*Dat.*) ähnlich sehen; Ⓑ (*fig.*) ähnlich; **be ~ to sth.** einer Sache (*Dat.*) ähnlich sein

**alabaster** /ˈæləbɑːstə/ ❶ *n.* Alabaster, *der.* ❷ *adj.* alabastern; **an ~ sculpture** eine Alabasterskulptur

**à la carte** /ɑː lɑː ˈkɑːt/ ❶ *adv.* à la carte. ❷ *adj.* **the ~ menu** das Menü à la carte

**alack** /əˈlæk/ *int.* (*arch.*) o weh; ~**-a-day** ach und weh

**alacrity** /əˈlækrɪtɪ/ *n., no pl.* Eilfertigkeit, *die;* **accept with ~:** mit [großer] Bereitwilligkeit annehmen

**Aladdin's** /əˈlædɪnz/**:** ~ **cave** *n.: Ort, an dem man Kostbarkeiten in großer Fülle findet;* ~ **lamp** *n.* Aladins Wunderlampe

**à la mode** /ɑː lɑː ˈməʊd/ *adj.* Ⓐ in Mode; à la mode (*veralt.*); **be ~:** Mode sein; Ⓑ (*Cookery*) in Wein geschmort; Ⓒ (*Amer. Gastr.*) **pie ~:** Kuchen mit Eis

**alarm** /əˈlɑːm/ ❶ *n.* Ⓐ Alarm, *der;* **give** *or* **raise the ~:** Alarm schlagen; Ⓑ (*fear*) Angst, *die;* (*uneasiness*) Besorgnis, *die;* **jump up in ~:** erschreckt aufspringen; **spread ~ and despondency** allgemeine Angst und Mutlosigkeit erzeugen; Ⓒ (*mechanism*) Alarmanlage, *die;* (*of ~ clock*) Weckmechanismus, *der;* (*signal*) Warnsignal, *das;* **sound the ~:** die Alarmanlage betätigen; Ⓓ ⇒ **alarm clock**.
❷ *v.t.* Ⓐ (*make aware of danger*) aufschrecken; (*call into action*) alarmieren; Ⓑ (*cause anxiety to*) beunruhigen

**aˈlarm:** ~ **bell** *n.* Alarmglocke, *die;* Warnsignal, *das;* **the ~ bells started ringing [in my head]** (*fig.*) in meinem Kopf fing ein rotes Lämpchen an zu leuchten; ~ **call** *n.* Weck[an]ruf, *der;* ~ **clock** *n.* Wecker, *der*

**alarming** /əˈlɑːmɪŋ/ *adj.* alarmierend

**alarmingly** /əˈlɑːmɪŋlɪ/ *adv.* in alarmierendem Maße

**alarmist** /əˈlɑːmɪst/ ❶ *n.* Panikmacher, *der.* ❷ *adj.* ‹Reden, Behauptungen› von Panikmachern

**alarum** /əˈlɑːrəm/ *n.* ~**s and excursions** (*joc.*) Lärm und Getümmel

a

a

**alas** /ə'læs, ə'lɑːs/ ❶ *int.* ach. ❷ *adv.* (*unfortunately*) leider Gottes

**Alaska** /ə'læskə/ Ⓐ *pr. n.* Alaska (*das*); Ⓑ *n.* (*Cookery*) **baked ∼:** ≈ Überraschungsomelett, *das;* Omelette surprise, *die*

**Albania** /æl'beɪnɪə/ *pr. n.* Albanien (*das*)

**Albanian** /æl'beɪnɪən/ ▶ **1275**, ▶ **1340** ❶ *adj.* albanisch; **sb. is ∼:** jmd. ist Albaner/Albanerin; ⇒ *also* **English** 1. ❷ *n.* Ⓐ (*person*) Albaner, *der*/Albanerin, *die;* Ⓑ (*language*) Albanisch, *das;* ⇒ *also* **English** 2 A

**albatross** /'ælbətrɒs/ *n.* (*Ornith., Golf*) Albatros, *der*

**albeit** /ɔːl'biːɪt/ *conj.* (*literary*) wenn auch; obgleich (*geh.*)

**albino** /æl'biːnəʊ/ *n., pl.* **∼s** Albino, *der*

**Albion** /'ælbɪən/ *n.* (*literary/poet.*) Albion, *das;* **perfidious ∼:** das perfide Albion

**album** /'ælbəm/ *n.* Ⓐ Album, *das;* Ⓑ (*record, set of records*) Album, *das;* **four-record ∼:** Kassette mit vier Langspielplatten; Ⓒ (*record holder*) Kassette, *die*

**albumen** /'ælbjʊmɪn/ *n.* Ⓐ Albumen, *das;* Eiweiß, *das;* Ⓑ (*Bot.*) Nährgewebe, *das*

**alchemist** /'ælkəmɪst/ *n.* Alchimist, *der;* Alchemist, *der*

**alchemy** /'ælkəmɪ/ *n., no pl.* (*lit. or fig.*) Alchimie, *die;* Alchemie, *die*

**alcohol** /'ælkəhɒl/ *n.* Alkohol, *der*

**'alcohol-free** *adj.* alkoholfrei

**alcoholic** /ælkə'hɒlɪk/ ❶ *adj.* alkoholisch; **∼ smell/taste** Alkoholgeruch, *der*/-geschmack, *der;* **∼ stupor** Vollrausch, *der.* ❷ *n.* Alkoholiker, *der*/Alkoholikerin, *die*

**Alcoholics A'nonymous** *n.* die Anonymen Alkoholiker

**alcoholism** /'ælkəhɒlɪzm/ *n., no pl.* Alkoholismus, *der;* Trunksucht, *die*

**alcopop** /'ælkəʊpɒp/ *n.: alkoholhaltiges Erfrischungsgetränk*

**alcove** /'ælkəʊv/ *n.* Alkoven, *der;* (*in garden wall, hedge*) Nische, *die*

**aldehyde** /'ældɪhaɪd/ *n.* (*Chem.*) Aldehyd, *der;* (*acetaldehyde*) Acetaldehyd, *der*

**alder** /'ɔːldə(r)/ *n.* (*Bot.*) Erle, *die;* **∼ buckthorn** Faulbaum, *der*

**alderman** /'ɔːldəmən/ *n., pl.* **aldermen** /'ɔːldəmən/ Ⓐ Stadtrat, *der;* Alderman, *der;* Ratsherr, *der* (*veralt.*); Ⓑ (*Amer., Austral.*) *gewähltes Mitglied einer Stadtverwaltung*

**ale** /eɪl/ *n.* Ⓐ Ale, *das;* Ⓑ (*Hist.*) Bier, *das*

**aleatoric** /eɪlɪə'tɔːrɪk/, **aleatory** /'eɪlɪətərɪ/ *adjs.* aleatorisch

**'alehouse** *n.* (*Hist.*) [Bier]schenke, *die*

**alert** /ə'lɜːt/ ❶ *adj.* Ⓐ (*watchful*) wachsam; **be ∼ for trouble** auf der Hut sein; **be ∼ to sth.** mit etw. rechnen; Ⓑ (*physically lively*) lebhaft; (*mentally lively*) aufgeweckt; (*attentive*) **the ∼ listener** der aufmerksame Zuhörer. ❷ *n.* Ⓐ (*warning*) Alarmsignal, *das;* Ⓑ (*state of preparedness*) Alarmbereitschaft, *die;* **air-raid ∼:** Fliegeralarm, *der;* **be on the ∼ [for/against sth.]** [vor etw. (*Dat.*)] auf der Hut sein. ❸ *v.t.* alarmieren; **∼ sb. [to sth.]** jmdn. [vor etw. (*Dat.*)] warnen

**alertly** /ə'lɜːtlɪ/ *adv.* aufmerksam

**alertness** /ə'lɜːtnɪs/ *n., no pl.* Wachsamkeit, *die;* **∼ of mind** geistige Beweglichkeit

**A level** /'eɪ levl/ *n.* (*Brit. Sch.*) Ⓐ ≈ Abitur, *das;* Abschluss der Sekundarstufe II; **take one's ∼s** ≈ das Abitur machen; Ⓑ *attrib.* ≈ Abitur-; **∼ French** ≈ Französisch als Abiturfach; **∼ papers** ≈ Abiturarbeiten

**alexandrine** /ælɪg'zændrɪn/ *n.* (*Pros.*) Alexandriner, *der*

**alfalfa** /æl'fælfə/ *n.* (*Bot.*) Luzerne, *die;* Alfalfa, *die*

**alfresco** /æl'freskəʊ/ ❶ *adv.* im Freien. ❷ *adj.* ‹Unterhaltung, Essen› im Freien

**alga** /'ælgə/ *n., pl.* **∼e** /'ældʒiː, 'ælgiː/ (*Bot.*) Alge, *die*

**algebra** /'ældʒɪbrə/ *n.* (*Math.*) Algebra, *die*

**algebraic** /ældʒɪ'breɪɪk/ *adj.* (*Math.*) algebraisch

**Algeria** /æl'dʒɪərɪə/ *pr. n.* Algerien (*das*)

**Algerian** /æl'dʒɪərɪən/ ▶ **1340** ❶ *adj.* algerisch; **sb. is ∼:** jmd. ist Algerier/Algerierin. ❷ *n.* Algerier, *der*/Algerierin, *die*

**Algiers** /æl'dʒɪəz/ *pr. n.* ▶ **1626** Algier (*das*)

**algorithm** /'ælgərɪðm/ *n.* (*Math., Computing*) Algorithmus, *der*

**alias** /'eɪlɪəs/ ❶ *adv.* alias. ❷ *n.* angenommener Name; (*of criminal*) falscher Name

**alibi** /'ælɪbaɪ/ *n.* Alibi, *das;* (*coll.: excuse*) Ausrede, *die*

**Alice** /'ælɪs/ *n.* **an ∼-in-Wonderland situation** eine völlig groteske Situation

**alien** /'eɪlɪən/ ❶ *adj.* Ⓐ (*strange*) fremd; **be ∼ to sb.** jmdm. fremd sein; Ⓑ (*foreign*) ausländisch; (*from another world*) außerirdisch; Ⓒ (*different*) **be ∼ from sth.** einer Sache (*Dat.*) fremd sein; Ⓓ (*repugnant*) **be ∼ to sb.** jmdm. zuwider sein; Ⓔ (*contrary*) **cruelty was ∼ to her nature** Grausamkeit lag ihr völlig fern; **fascism is ∼ to our democratic beliefs** der Faschismus steht in krassem Gegensatz zu unserer demokratischen Überzeugung.
❷ *n.* Ⓐ (*Admin.: foreigner*) Ausländer, *der*/Ausländerin, *die;* Ⓑ (*a being from another world*) Außerirdische, *der/die*

**alienate** /'eɪlɪəneɪt/ *v.t.* Ⓐ (*estrange*) befremden ‹Person›; zerstören ‹Zuneigung›; verlieren ‹Unterstützung›; **his gaffes have ∼d many of his supporters** durch seine Ausrutscher hat er sich (*Dat.*) viele seiner Anhänger entfremdet; **feel ∼d from society** sich der Gesellschaft entfremdet fühlen; Ⓑ (*divert*) entziehen (**from** *Dat.*)

**alienation** /eɪlɪə'neɪʃn/ *n., no pl.* Ⓐ Entfremdung, *die;* Ⓑ (*Theatre*) Verfremdung, *die*

**alight**[1] /ə'laɪt/ *v.i.* Ⓐ aussteigen; **∼ from a vehicle** aus einem Fahrzeug aussteigen; **∼ from a horse** von einem Pferd absitzen; Ⓑ ‹Vogel:› sich niedersetzen; ‹Flugzeug, Schneeflocken:› landen

**alight**[2] *pred. adj.* (*on fire*) **be/catch ∼:** brennen; **set sth. ∼:** etw. in Brand setzen; **the upper storey was well ∼:** das obere Stockwerk brannte lichterloh

**align** /ə'laɪn/ *v.t.* Ⓐ (*place in a line*) ausrichten; **the posts must be ∼ed** die Pfosten müssen in einer Linie ausgerichtet werden; Ⓑ (*bring into line*) in eine Linie bringen; **∼ the wheels** (*Motor Veh.*) die Spur einstellen

**alignment** /ə'laɪnmənt/ *n.* Ⓐ Ausrichtung, *die;* **in/out of ∼:** [genau] ausgerichtet/nicht richtig ausgerichtet; **the wheels are in/out of ∼** (*Motor Veh.*) die Spur ist richtig/falsch eingestellt; Ⓑ (*Polit.*) Gruppierung, *die;* Ausrichtung, *die*

**alike** /ə'laɪk/ ❶ *pred. adj.* ähnlich; (*indistinguishable*) [völlig] gleich. ❷ *adv.* gleich; in gleicher Weise; **winter and summer ∼:** Sommer wie Winter; **all of us ∼ are concerned, this concerns us all ∼:** es geht uns alle gleichermaßen an

**alimentary** /ælɪ'mentərɪ/ *adj.* Nahrungs-; alimentär (*Med.*); **∼ organ/system** Verdauungsorgan/-system, *das*

**alimentary ca'nal** *n.* (*Anat.*) Verdauungskanal, *der*

**alimentation** /ælɪmən'teɪʃn/ *n., no pl.* (*formal*) Ernährung, *die*

**alimony** /'ælɪmənɪ/ *n.* Unterhaltszahlung, *die*

**alive** /ə'laɪv/ *pred. adj.* Ⓐ lebendig; lebend; **stay ∼:** am Leben bleiben; **if I'm still ∼ in thirty years' time** wenn ich in dreißig Jahren noch am Leben bin; **any man ∼:** jeder x-Beliebige; **no man ∼:** kein Mensch auf der ganzen Welt; **man ∼!** (*coll.*) Menschenskind!; **keep one's hopes ∼:** nicht die Hoffnung verlieren; **keep sb.'s hopes ∼:** jmdn. noch hoffen lassen; **keep a matter ∼:** eine Sache offen halten; **the issue is still ∼:** die Angelegenheit ist immer noch offen; **come ∼:** wieder aufleben; ‹Ereignis:› wieder lebendig werden; Ⓑ (*Electr.*) eingeschaltet ‹Mikrofon›; **be/become ∼** ‹Draht:› unter Strom stehen/gesetzt werden; Ⓒ (*aware*) **be ∼ to sth.** sich (*Dat.*) einer Sache (*Gen.*) bewusst sein; **he's always ∼ to new ideas** er ist neuen Ideen gegenüber immer aufgeschlossen; Ⓓ (*brisk*) rege; munter; **be ∼ and kicking** gesund und munter sein; **look ∼!** ein bisschen munter!; Ⓔ (*swarming*) **be ∼ with sth.** von etw. wimmeln

**alkali** /'ælkəlaɪ/ *n., pl.* **∼s** *or* **∼es** (*Chem.*) Alkali, *das;* **∼ metal** Alkalimetall, *das*

**alkaline** /'ælkəlaɪn/ *adj.* (*Chem.*) alkalisch; **∼ earth** Erdalkali, *das;* alkalische Erde

**all** /ɔːl/ ❶ *attrib. adj.* Ⓐ (*entire extent or quantity of*) ganz; **∼ England** ganz England; **∼ day** den ganzen Tag; **∼ the snow/milk/food** der ganze *od.* aller Schnee/die ganze *od.* alle Milch/das ganze *od.* alles Essen; **∼ the family** die ganze Familie; **for ∼ that** trotz allem; **∼ his life** sein ganzes Leben; **∼ my money** all mein Geld; mein ganzes Geld; **stop ∼ this noise/shouting!** hör mit dem Krach/Geschrei auf!; **what's ∼ this noise/shouting about?** was soll der [ganze] Krach/das [ganze] Geschrei?; **thank you for ∼ your hard work** danke für all deine Anstrengungen; **get away from it ∼:** einmal von allem abschalten; **that says it ∼:** das sagt alles; **∼ hail!** Heil!; Ⓑ (*entire number of*) alle; **∼ the books** alle Bücher; **∼ my books** all[e] meine Bücher; **in ∼ our houses** in allen unseren Häusern; **where are ∼ the glasses?** wo sind all die Gläser *od.* (*ugs.*) die ganzen Gläser?; **∼ ten men** alle zehn Männer; **we ∼ went to bed** wir gingen alle schlafen; **aren't we ∼?** trifft das nicht für uns alle zu?; **∼ you children can stay here** ihr Kinder könnt alle hier bleiben; **∼ the others** alle anderen; **∼ those present** alle Anwesenden; **be ∼ things to ∼ men** es allen recht machen [wollen]; **∼ Goethe's works** sämtliche Werke Goethes; **why he of ∼ people?** warum ausgerechnet er?; **of ∼ the nitwits!** so ein Schwachkopf!; **∼ manner of things** alles Mögliche; **∼ manner of sausages** die verschiedensten Wurstsorten; **people of ∼ ages** Menschen jeden Alters; **with ∼ her faults** trotz all ihrer Fehler; **A∼ Fools' Day** der 1. April; **A∼ Saints' Day** Allerheiligen; **A∼ Souls' Day** Allerseelen; Ⓒ (*any whatever*) jeglicher/jegliche/jegliches; Ⓓ (*greatest possible*) **in ∼ innocence** in aller Unschuld; **with ∼ speed** so schnell wie möglich. ⇒ *also* **four** 2 C; **kind** 1 A; **that** 2 A; **time** 1 A, B, F; **way** 1 A.
❷ *n.* Ⓐ (**∼** *persons*) alle; **∼ present** alle Anwesenden; **one and ∼:** [alle] ohne Ausnahme; **goodbye, one and ∼!** Wiedersehen, alle zusammen!; **∼ and sundry** Krethi und Plethi; **∼ of us** wir alle; **the happiest/most beautiful of ∼:** der/die Glücklichste/die Schönste unter allen; **the best pupils of ∼:** die besten Schüler [von allen]; **most of ∼:** am meisten; **he ran fastest of ∼:** er lief am schnellsten; Ⓑ (*every bit*) **∼ of it/the money** alles/das ganze *od.* alles Geld; Ⓒ **∼ of** (*coll.: as much as*) **be ∼ of seven feet tall** gut sieben Fuß groß sein; Ⓓ (**∼** *things*) alles; **∼ that I possess** alles, was ich besitze; **∼ I need is the money** ich brauche nur das Geld; **not ∼ of the missing antiques have been recovered** nicht alle [der] fehlenden Antiquitäten sind wieder gefunden worden; **when ∼ is said and done** alles in allem; **∼ is lost** alles ist verloren; **∼ is not lost** es ist nicht alles verloren; **he wants ∼ or nothing** er will alles oder nichts; **it's ∼ or nothing** es geht ums Ganze; **that is ∼:** das ist alles; **it is not ∼ it might be** es lässt zu wünschen übrig; **the most beautiful of ∼:** der/die/das Schönste von allen; **most of ∼:** am meisten; **for ∼ you say, I still like her** trotz allem, was du sagst, mag ich sie immer noch; **give one's ∼:** sein Letztes geben; **lose one's ∼:** sein ganzes Hab und Gut verlieren; **it was ∼ but impossible** es war fast unmöglich; **it was ∼ I could do not to laugh** ich konnte mir das Lachen kaum verbeißen; **∼ in ∼:** alles in allem; **sb's ∼ in ∼:** jmds. Ein und Alles; **it's ∼ the same** *or* **∼ one to me** es ist mir ganz egal *od.* völlig gleichgültig; **that's ∼ very well** *or* **fine** das ist alles schön und gut; **sth. and ∼:** mitsamt etw.; **can I help you at ∼?** kann ich Ihnen irgendwie behilflich sein?; **I do not know at ∼:** ich weiß wirklich nicht; **I do not care at ∼:** es ist mir völlig gleich; **you are not disturbing me at ∼:** du störst mich nicht im Geringsten; **were you surprised at ∼?** warst du denn überrascht?; **if you go to Venice at ∼:**

wenn du überhaupt nach Venedig fährst; **is he there at ~?** ist er überhaupt da?; **he is not stupid at ~:** er ist keineswegs dumm; **he is not at ~ stupid** er ist gar nicht *od.* überhaupt nicht dumm; **she has no talent at ~:** sie hat gar *od.* überhaupt kein Talent; **nothing at ~:** gar nichts; **not at ~ happy/well** überhaupt nicht glücklich/gesund; **not at ~!** überhaupt nicht!; (*acknowledging thanks*) gern geschehen!; nichts zu danken!; **if at ~:** wenn überhaupt; **in ~:** insgesamt; ⇒ *also* **time** 1 C; **E** (*Sport*) **two [goals] ~:** zwei zu zwei; (*Tennis*) **thirty ~:** dreißig beide.

**3** *adv.* ganz; **~ but** fast; **he ~ but fell down** er wäre fast heruntergefallen; **dressed ~ in white** ganz in Weiß [gekleidet]; **~ the better/worse [for that]** um so besser/schlimmer; **I feel ~ the better for it** das hat mir wirklich gut getan; **~ the more reason to do sth.** um so mehr sollte man etw. tun; **~ at once** (*suddenly*) plötzlich; (*simultaneously*) alle[s] zugleich; **~ too soon** allzu schnell; **go ~ serious** (*coll.*) ganz ernst werden; **be ~ 'for sth.** (*coll.*) sehr für etw. sein; **her latest play is ~ about ...:** in ihrem jüngsten Stück geht es um ...; **be ~ 'in** (*exhausted*) total *od.* völlig erledigt sein (*ugs.*); **go ~ out [to do sth.]** alles daransetzen[, etw. zu tun]; **be ~ ready [to go]** (*coll.*) fertig [zum Weggehen] sein (*ugs.*); **sth. is ~ right** etw. ist in Ordnung; (*tolerable*) etw. ist ganz gut; **did you get home ~ right?** sind Sie gut nach Hause gekommen?; **I'm ~ right** mir geht es ganz gut; **work out ~ right** gut gehen; klappen (*ugs.*); **that's her, ~ right** das ist sie, ganz recht; **yes, ~ right** ja, gut; **is it ~ right if I go in?** kann ich reingehen?; **it's ~ right for you/him** *etc.*, **but ...** (*coll.*) es passt dir/ihm *usw.*, aber ...; **it's ~ right by** *or* **with me** das ist mir recht; **lie ~ round the room** überall im Zimmer herumliegen; **it was agreed ~ round that ...:** alle waren [damit] einverstanden, dass ...; **order drinks ~ round** Getränke für alle bestellen; **better ~ round** in jeder Hinsicht besser; **be ~ there** (*coll.*) voll da sein (*ugs.*); **I don't think he's ~ there** (*coll.*) ich glaube, er ist nicht ganz da (*ugs.*); **~ the same** trotzdem; **it's ~ the same to me** es ist mir einerlei; **if it's ~ the same to you** wenn du nichts dagegen hast; **the A~ Blacks** (*coll.*) *die neuseeländische Rugbynationalmannschaft*

**Allah** /ˈælə/ *pr. n.* Allah (*der*)

**all: ~-A'merican** *adj.* **the ~-American football team** die beste Footballmannschaft der ganzen USA; **the ~-American boy** der typisch amerikanische Junge; **~-around** (*Amer.*) ⇒ **~-round**

**allay** /əˈleɪ/ *v.t.* **A** vermindern; trüben, dämpfen ‹Freude, Glück›; zerstreuen ‹Besorgnis, Befürchtungen›; **B** (*alleviate*) stillen ‹Hunger, Durst›; lindern ‹Schmerz›

**all: ~-'clear** *n.* Entwarnung, *die;* **sound the ~-clear** entwarnen; **~-day** *adj.* ganztägig ‹Ausflug, Versammlung›

**allegation** /ælɪˈgeɪʃn/ *n.* Behauptung, *die;* **make ~s against sb.** Beschuldigungen gegen jmdn. erheben; **reject all ~s of corruption** jeglichen Vorwurf der Korruption zurückweisen

**allege** /əˈledʒ/ *v.t.* **~ that ...:** behaupten, dass ...; **~ criminal negligence** den Vorwurf grober Fahrlässigkeit erheben

**alleged** /əˈledʒd/ *adj.*, **allegedly** /əˈledʒɪdlɪ/ *adv.* angeblich

**allegiance** /əˈli:dʒəns/ *n.* Loyalität, *die* (**to** gegenüber); **swear ~ to king and country** dem König und dem Vaterland Treue schwören; **oath of ~:** Treueeid, *der;* **some supporters changed their ~ from Liverpool to Everton** einige Fans sind von Liverpool zu Everton umgeschwenkt

**allegorical** /ælɪˈgɒrɪkl/ *adj.* allegorisch

**allegory** /ˈælɪgərɪ/ *n.* Allegorie, *die;* (*emblem*) Sinnbild, *das*

**allegro** /æˈleɪgrəʊ, æˈlegrəʊ/ (*Mus.*) **1** *adv.* allegro. **2** *n.*, *pl.* **~s** Allegro, *das*

**all-e'lectric** *adj.* vollelektrisch; **our house is ~:** in unserem Haus ist alles elektrisch

**'all-embracing** *adj.* alles umfassend

**Allen key** ® /ˈælən ki:/ *n.* Inbusschlüssel, *der* (Wz)

**allergic** /əˈlɜ:dʒɪk/ *adj.* allergisch (**to** gegen)

**allergy** /ˈælədʒɪ/ *n.* **A** (*Med.*) Allergie, *die* (**to** gegen); **B** (*fig. coll.*) **have an ~ to sth.** auf etw. (*Akk.*) allergisch reagieren

**alleviate** /əˈli:vɪeɪt/ *v.t.* abschwächen

**alleviation** /əli:vɪˈeɪʃn/ *n.*, *no pl.* Abschwächung, *die*

**alley**[1] /ˈælɪ/ *n.* **A** [schmale] Gasse; (*between flower beds or gardens*) Pfad, *der;* (*avenue*) Allee, *die;* **be up sb.'s ~** (*coll.*) jmds. Fall sein (*ugs.*); **this problem is just** *or* **right up his ~** (*coll.*) für dieses Problem ist er genau der Richtige; **B** (*skittle ~*) Bahn, *die*

**alley**[2] ⇒ **ally**[2]

**'all-fired** (*Amer. coll.*) *adj.*, *adv.* verdammt

**alliance** /əˈlaɪəns/ *n.* Bündnis, *das;* (*league*) Allianz, *die;* **~ with other groups would increase our influence** ein Bündnis mit anderen Gruppen würde unseren Einfluss vergrößern; **in ~ with sb./sth.** im Verein mit jmdm./etw.

**allied** /ˈælaɪd/ *adj.* **be ~ to** *or* **with sb./sth.** mit jmdm./etw. verbündet sein; **German is more closely ~ to English than to French** das Deutsche ist mit dem Englischen enger verwandt als mit dem Französischen; **the A~ Powers** die Alliierten

**alligator** /ˈælɪgeɪtə(r)/ *n.* (*Zool.*) Alligator, *der;* (*skin*) Krokodilleder, *das*

**'alligator clip** *n.* Krokodilklemme, *die*

**all: ~-important** *adj.* entscheidend; **~-in** *adj.* Pauschal-; **it costs £350 ~-in** es kostet 350 Pfund alles inklusive; **~-in wrestling** Freistilringen, *das*

**alliteration** /əlɪtəˈreɪʃn/ *n.* Stabreim, *der;* Alliteration, *die*

**alliterative** /əˈlɪtərətɪv/ *adj.* stabreimend; alliterierend

**'all-night** *adj.* die ganze Nacht dauernd ‹Sitzung›; nachts durchgehend geöffnet ‹Gaststätte›

**allocate** /ˈæləkeɪt/ *v.t.* zur Verfügung stellen ‹Geld, Mittel›; **~ sth. to sb./sth.** jmdm./einer Sache etw. zuweisen *od.* zuteilen

**allocation** /æləˈkeɪʃn/ *n.* Verteilung, *die;* (*ration*) Zuteilung, *die*

**allot** /əˈlɒt/ *v.t.*, **-tt-: ~ sth. to sb.** jmdm. etw. zuteilen; **you will be ~ted fifty pounds** es werden Ihnen fünfzig Pfund bewilligt; **we ~ted two hours to the task** wir haben zwei Stunden für diese Arbeit vorgesehen; **~ shares** Aktien ausgeben

**allotment** /əˈlɒtmənt/ *n.* **A** Zuteilung, *die;* **B** (*Brit.: plot of land*) Gartenparzelle, *die;* ≈ Schrebergarten, *der;* **C** (*share*) Anteil, *der*

**all: ~-out** *attrib. adj.* mit allen [verfügbaren] Mitteln *nachgestellt;* **~-over** *attrib. adj.* **~-over tan** nahtlose Bräune

**allow** /əˈlaʊ/ **1** *v.t.* **A** (*permit*) **~ sth.** etw. erlauben *od.* zulassen *od.* (*förmlicher*) gestatten; **~ sb. to do sth.** jmdm. erlauben, etw. zu tun; **be ~ed to do sth.** etw. tun dürfen; **will you be ~ed to?** darfst du?; **~ sb./oneself sth.** jmdm./sich etw. erlauben; **sb. is ~ed sth.** jmdm. ist etw. erlaubt; **~ sth. to happen** zulassen, dass etw. geschieht; **~ yourself to be convinced** lassen Sie sich überzeugen; **~ sb. in/out/past/through** jmdn. hinein-/hinaus-/vorbei-/durchlassen; **you are not ~ed in/out/past/through** Sie dürfen nicht hinein/hinaus/vorbei/durch; **~ sb. a discount/5% interest** jmdm. Rabatt/5% Zinsen geben; **B** (*agree*) zugeben; **C** (*Law*) bestätigen ‹Anspruch›; **~ the appeal** der Berufung (*Dat.*) stattgeben; **D** (*Sport*) **the referee ~ed the goal** der Schiedsrichter gab das Tor.

**2** *v.i.* **~ of sth.** etw. zulassen *od.* erlauben; **~ for sth.** etw. berücksichtigen; **we started very early, to ~ for delays** wir begannen sehr früh, um etwaige Verzögerungen auffangen zu können

**allowable** /əˈlaʊəbl/ *adj.* zulässig

**allowance** /əˈlaʊəns/ *n.* **A** Zuteilung, *die;* (*money for special expenses*) Zuschuss, *der;* **your luggage ~ is 44 kg.** Sie haben 44 kg Freigepäck; **tax ~:** Steuerfreibetrag, *der;* **clothing ~:** Kleidergeld, *das;* **B make ~s for sth./sb.** etw./jmdn. berücksichtigen; **make ~ for errors** eventuelle Fehler einkalkulieren; **C** (*Commerc.*) Ermäßigung, *die*

**alloy** **1** /ˈælɔɪ/ *n.* Legierung, *die;* (*inferior metal added*) unedles Metall; **~ steel** Sonderstahl, *der.* **2** /əˈlɔɪ/ *v.t.* legieren; (*debase*) geringhaltiger machen

**all: ~-points bulletin** *n.* (*Amer.*) Fahndungsaufruf, *der;* **~-'powerful** *adj.* allmächtig; **~-purpose** *adj.* Universal-; Allzweck-; **~-risks** *attrib. adj.* **an ~-risks insurance** eine alle gängigen Risiken abdeckende Versicherung; **~-round** *adj.* Allround-; **~-'rounder** *n.* Allroundtalent, *das;* (*Sport*) Allroundspieler, *der*/-spielerin, *die*

**'allspice** *n.* Pimentbaum, *der;* (*berry*) Piment, *der*

**'all-time** *adj.* **~ record** absoluter Rekord; **~ favourites** *or* **greats** unvergessene Publikumslieblinge; **~ high/low** höchster/niedrigster Stand aller Zeiten

**allude** /əˈlju:d, əˈlu:d/ *v.i.* **~ to sth./sb.** sich auf etw./jmdn. beziehen; (*covertly*) auf etw./jmdn. anspielen

**allure** /əˈljʊə(r)/ **1** *v.t.* locken; (*fascinate*) faszinieren; **~ sb. to do sth.** jmdn. dazu verlocken, etw. zu tun; **~d by thoughts of stardom** durch die Aussicht auf eine glänzende Karriere verlockt. **2** *n.*, *no pl.* Verlockung, *die;* (*personal charm*) Charme, *der*

**allurement** /əˈljʊəmənt/ *n.* Verlockung, *die;* (*charm*) **she displayed all her ~s** sie ließ all ihre Reize spielen

**alluring** /əˈljʊərɪŋ/ *adj.* verlockend; **an ~ appeal** eine Verlockung

**allusion** /əˈlju:ʒn, əˈlu:ʒn/ *n.* **A** Hinweis, *der;* **in an ~ to** unter Bezugnahme auf (+ *Akk.*); **B** (*covert reference*) Anspielung, *die* (**to** auf + *Akk.*)

**allusive** /əˈlju:sɪv, əˈlu:sɪv/ *adj.* **be ~ to sth.** auf etw. (*Akk.*) anspielen

**alluvial** /əˈlu:vɪəl/ *adj.* (*Geol.*) angeschwemmt; **~ soil** Alluvialboden, *der*

**'all-weather** *attrib. adj.* Allwetter-

**ally**[1] **1** /əˈlaɪ, ˈælaɪ/ *v.t.* **~ oneself with sb./sth.** sich mit jmdm./etw. verbünden; ⇒ *also* **allied**. **2** /ˈælaɪ/ *n.* Verbündete, *der/die;* **my old friend and ~:** mein alter Freund und Kampfgefährte; **the Allies** die Alliierten

**ally**[2] /ˈælɪ/ *n.* (*besonders schöne*) Murmel (*aus Alabaster od. Glas*)

**Alma Mater** /ælmə ˈmeɪtə(r), ælmə ˈmɑ:tə(r)/ *n.* Alma Mater, *die*

**almanac** /ˈɔ:lmənæk, ˈɒlmənæk/ *n.* Almanach, *der*

**almighty** /ɔ:lˈmaɪtɪ/ **1** *adj.* **A** allmächtig; **the A~:** der Allmächtige; **God A~!** (*coll.*) großer Gott!; **he acts as if he were God A~:** er tut, als ob er der liebe Gott selber wäre; **B** (*coll.: very great, hard, etc.*) mächtig. **2** *adv.* (*coll.*) mächtig

**almond** /ˈɑ:mənd/ *n.* **A** Mandel, *die;* **sweet/bitter ~:** Süß-/Bittermandel, *die;* **~ eyes** Mandelaugen; **B** (*tree*) Mandelbaum, *der*

**almoner** /ˈɑ:mənə(r)/ *n.* (*Brit.*) Sozialbetreuer, *der*/-betreuerin, *die* (*eines Krankenhauses*)

**almost** /ˈɔ:lməʊst/ *adv.* fast; beinahe; **she ~ fell** sie wäre fast gefallen

**alms** /ɑ:mz/ *n.*, *no pl.* Almosen, *das*

**'almshouse** *n.* Armenhaus, *das*

**aloe** /ˈæləʊ/ *n.* **A** Aloe, *die;* **B** *in pl.* (*Pharm.*) Aloe, *die;* Aloesaft, *der*

**aloft** /əˈlɒft/ *adv.* **A** (*position*) (*literary*) hoch droben (*dichter.*); (*Naut.*) [oben] in der Takelage *od.* im Rigg; **B** (*direction*) (*literary*) empor (*dichter.*); (*Naut.*) in die Takelage; in das Rigg; **go ~:** in die Takelage *od.* in das Rigg klettern; aufentern (*Seemannsspr.*)

**alone** /əˈləʊn/ **1** *pred. adj.* allein; alleine (*ugs.*); **be [all] ~:** [ganz] allein sein; **she likes to be ~ sometimes** manchmal ist sie gern [für sich] allein; **when his parents died he was left ~ [in the world]** als seine Eltern starben, stand er ganz allein da; **he was not ~ in the belief that ...:** er stand nicht allein mit der Überzeugung, dass ...

❷ *adv.* allein; **you ~ can help me** nur du *od.* du allein kannst mir helfen; **the problem/money was his ~:** es war einzig und allein sein Problem/Geld; **this fact ~:** schon allein dies; **go it ~:** es im Alleingang tun

**along** /ə'lɒŋ/ ❶ *prep.* **A** *(position)* entlang (+ *Dat.*); **~ one side of the street** auf der einen Straßenseite; **all ~ the wall** die ganze *od.* an der ganzen Mauer entlang; **B** *(direction)* entlang (+ *Akk.*); **walk ~ the riverbank/street** am Ufer *od.* das Ufer/die Straße entlanglaufen; **creep ~ a wall** eine Mauer *od.* an einer Mauer entlangschleichen. ❷ *adv.* **A** *(onward)* weiter; **he came running ~:** er kam herbei- *od.* angelaufen; **leaves carried ~ by the wind** vom Wind fortgetragenes Laub; **he saw the train steaming ~ in the distance** er sah den Zug in der Ferne vorbei- *od.* vorüberdampfen; **the snake was slithering ~ in the tall grass** die Schlange glitt durch das hohe Gras; **B** *(with one)* **bring/take sb./sth. ~:** jmdn./etw. mitbringen/mitnehmen; **C** *(there)* **I'll be ~ shortly/as soon as I can** ich komme gleich/sobald ich kann; **D** **all ~:** die ganze Zeit [über]

**alongside** /əlɒŋ'saɪd/ ❶ *adv.* daneben; längsseits (*Seemannsspr.*); **~ the quay** am Kai; **~ of** ⇒ **2.** ❷ *prep.* *(position)* neben (+ *Dat.*); längsseits (*Seemannsspr.*) (+ *Gen.*); *(direction)* neben (+ *Akk.*); längsseits heran an (*Seemannsspr.*) (+ *Akk.*); (*fig.*) neben (+ *Dat.*); **work ~ sb.** mit jmdm. zusammen arbeiten/(*fig.*) zusammenarbeiten

**aloof** /ə'lu:f/ ❶ *adv.* abseits; **stand ~ from the others** abseits der anderen stehen; **hold ~ from sb.** sich von jmdm. fernhalten; sich abseits von jmdm. halten; **keep ~:** Distanz wahren; **keep ~ from sb.** sich von jmdm. absondern *od.* fernhalten. ❷ *adj.* distanziert; reserviert

**aloofness** /ə'lu:fnɪs/ *n., no pl.* Reserviertheit, *die;* Distanz[iertheit], *die*

**aloud** /ə'laʊd/ *adv.* laut; **read [sth.] ~:** [etw.] vorlesen; **think ~:** laut denken

**alp** /ælp/ *n.* *(pasture)* Alp, *die;* ⇒ *also* **Alps**

**alpaca** /æl'pækə/ *n.* **A** *(Zool.)* Alpaka, *das;* **B** *(wool)* Alpaka, *das;* Alpakawolle, *die;* *(fabric)* Alpaka, *der*

**alpenhorn** /'ælpənhɔ:n/ *n.* Alphorn, *das*

**alpenstock** /'ælpənstɒk/ *n.* Bergstock, *der*

**alpha** /'ælfə/ *n.* **A** *(letter)* Alpha, *das;* **the A~ and Omega** das A und O; **B** *(Sch., Univ.: mark)* Eins, *die*

**alphabet** /'ælfəbet/ *n.* Alphabet, *das;* Abc, *das;* **the phonetic/Cyrillic ~:** das phonetische/kyrillische Alphabet

**alphabetical** /ælfə'betɪkl/ *adj.* alphabetisch; **in ~ order** in alphabetischer Reihenfolge; alphabetisch geordnet

**alphabetically** /ælfə'betɪkəlɪ/ *adv.* alphabetisch; nach dem Alphabet

**alphabetize** /'ælfəbetaɪz/ *v.t.* alphabetisieren; nach dem Alphabet ordnen

**alpha: ~ particles** *n. pl.* (*Phys.*) Alphateilchen *Pl.;* **~ rays** *n. pl.* (*Phys.*) Alphastrahlen *Pl.*

**alpine** /'ælpaɪn/ ❶ *adj.* **A** alpin; Hochgebirgs-; **~ region/climate/vegetation** Hochgebirgsregion, *die*/-klima, *das*/alpine Vegetation; **~ flowers** Alpen-, Gebirgsblumen; **~ garden** Alpengarten, *der;* Alpinum, *das;* **~ skiing/event** alpiner Skisport/Wettbewerb; **B** **A~:** Alpen-. ❷ *n.* (*Bot.*) Alpenblume, *die;* [Hoch]gebirgspflanze, *die*

**Alpinist, alpinist** /'ælpɪnɪst/ *n.* Alpinist, *der*/ Alpinistin, *die*

**Alps** /ælps/ *pr. n. pl.* **the ~:** die Alpen

**already** /ɔ:l'redɪ/ *adv.* schon; **it's ~ 8 o'clock** *or* **8 o'clock ~:** es ist schon 8 Uhr; **He's here. — A~?** Er ist hier. — Schon [so früh]?; **she's ~ got ten children** sie hat schon *od.* bereits zehn Kinder

**Alsace** /æl'sæs/ *pr. n.* Elsass, *das;* **~-Lorraine** Elsass-Lothringen (*das*)

**Alsatian** /æl'seɪʃn/ ❶ *adj.* elsässisch. ❷ *n.* **A** *(person)* Elsässer, *der*/Elsässerin, *die;* **B** *(dog)* [deutscher] Schäferhund

**also** /'ɔ:lsəʊ/ *adv.* auch; *(moreover)* außerdem; **I'm going, and John is ~ going** *or* **John is going ~:** ich gehe, und John geht auch *od.* ebenfalls; **he's writing a book and ~ translating one** er schreibt ein Buch und übersetzt auch *od.* außerdem eines; **he's writing and ~ translating a book** er schreibt ein Buch und übersetzt es auch

**'also-ran** *n.* **be an ~** ‹Hund, Pferd:› [immer nur] hintere Plätze/einen hinteren Platz belegen; **he remained an ~ all his life** (*fig.*) er kam sein ganzes Leben lang auf keinen grünen Zweig (*ugs.*)

**altar** /'ɔ:ltə(r), 'ɒltə(r)/ *n.* **A** *(Communion table)* Altar, *der;* **lead sb. to the ~** (*fig.*) jmdn. zum Traualtar führen; **B** *(for sacrifice)* Opferstätte, *die;* Opfertisch, *der*

**'altarpiece** *n.* Altarbild, -gemälde, *das*

**alter** /'ɔ:ltə(r), 'ɒltə(r)/ ❶ *v.t.* **A** *(change)* ändern; verändern ‹Stadt, Wohnung›; **That's wrong. It will have to be ~ed** Das ist falsch. Es muss geändert werden; **have a dress ~ed** ein Kleid ändern lassen; **B** (*Amer.: castrate, spay*) sterilisieren. ❷ *v.i.* sich verändern; **he has ~ed a lot since then** *(in appearance)* er hat sich seitdem stark verändert; *(in character)* er hat sich seitdem sehr geändert

**alteration** /ɔ:ltə'reɪʃn, ɒltə'reɪʃn/ *n.* Änderung, *die;* *(of text)* Abänderung, *die;* *(of house)* Umbau, *der;* **without any ~s** ohne jede Änderung; **we're having some ~s done to the house** wir bauen um

**altercation** /ɔ:ltə'keɪʃn, ɒltə'keɪʃn/ *n.* Auseinandersetzung, *die;* Streiterei, *die*

**alter ego** /æltər 'egəʊ, æltər 'i:gəʊ/ *n., pl.* **~s** Alter Ego, *das* (*geh.*)

**alternate** ❶ /ɔ:l'tɜ:nət, ɒl'tɜ:nət/ *adj.* **A** *(in turn)* sich abwechselnd; **John and Mary come on ~ days** John und Mary kommen abwechselnd einen um den anderen Tag; *(together)* John und Mary kommen jeden zweiten Tag; **she goes shopping and goes to work on ~ Saturdays** sie geht abwechselnd jeden zweiten Samstag arbeiten und einkaufen; **~ leaves** (*Bot.*) wechselständige Blätter; **~ angles** (*Math.*) Wechselwinkel *Pl.;* **B** ⇒ **alternative** 1.
❷ *n.* **A** *(deputy)* Vertreter, *der*/Vertreterin, *die;* **B** *(substitute)* Alternative, *die.*
❸ /'ɔ:ltəneɪt, 'ɒltəneɪt/ *v.t.* abwechseln lassen; **she has only two summer dresses, so she ~s them** sie hat nur zwei Sommerkleider, deshalb trägt sie sie abwechselnd; **he ~s his days off and** *or* **with his working days** er hat abwechselnd einen Tag frei und geht einen Tag zur Arbeit.
❹ *v.i.* sich abwechseln; alternieren (*fachspr.*)

**alternately** /ɔ:l'tɜ:nətlɪ, ɒl'tɜ:nətlɪ/ *adv.* abwechselnd

**'alternating current** *n.* (*Electr.*) Wechselstrom, *der*

**alternation** /ɔ:ltə'neɪʃn, ɒltə'neɪʃn/ *n.* Wechsel, *der;* **~ of generations** (*Biol.*) Generationswechsel, *der*

**alternative** /ɔ:l'tɜ:nətɪv, ɒl'tɜ:nətɪv/ ❶ *adj.* alternativ; Alternativ-; **~ possibility** Ausweich- *od.* Alternativmöglichkeit, *die;* **~ suggestion** Alternativ- *od.* Gegenvorschlag, *der;* **~ route** Alternativstrecke, *die;* *(to avoid obstruction etc.)* Ausweichstrecke, *die;* **we'll try to get you on an ~ flight** wir werden versuchen, Ihren Flug umzubuchen; **the ~ society** die alternative Gesellschaft; **~ fuel** Alternativkraftstoff, *der* (*für Verbrennungsmotoren*); **~ medicine** Alternativmedizin, *die.*
❷ *n.* **A** *(choice)* Alternative, *die;* Wahl, *die;* **if I had the ~:** wenn ich vor die Wahl *od.* Alternative gestellt würde; wenn ich vor der Wahl *od.* Alternative stünde; **we have no ~ [but to ...]** wir haben keine andere Wahl[, als zu ...]; **that left me** *or* **I was left with no ~:** mir blieb keine andere Wahl; **B** *(possibility)* Möglichkeit, *die;* **we have two ~s: either we press forward or we turn back** wir haben zwei Möglichkeiten: weiterzufahren oder umzukehren; **there is no [other] ~:** es gibt keine Alternative *od.* andere Möglichkeit; **what are the ~s?** welche Alternativen gibt es?

**alternatively** /ɔ:l'tɜ:nətɪvlɪ, ɒl'tɜ:nətɪvlɪ/ *adv.* oder aber; **or ~:** oder aber auch

**alternator** /'ɔ:ltəneɪtə(r), 'ɒltəneɪtə(r)/ *n.* (*Electr.*) Wechselstromgenerator, *der*

**although** /ɔ:l'ðəʊ/ *conj.* obwohl; **~ quite clever, he still makes mistakes** obwohl er ziemlich klug ist, macht er trotzdem *od.* doch Fehler

**altimeter** /'æltɪmi:tə(r)/ *n.* Höhenmesser, *der*

**altitude** /'æltɪtju:d/ *n.* ▶ **1210** *(height)* Höhe, *die;* **what is our ~?** wie hoch sind wir?; **at what ~ are we flying?** wie hoch *od.* in welcher Höhe fliegen wir?; **from this ~:** aus dieser Höhe; **what is the ~ of ...?** wie hoch liegt ...?; **at an ~ of 2,000 ft.** ≈ in einer Höhe von 600 Metern; **at high ~:** in großer Höhe; **gain/lose ~:** [an] Höhe gewinnen/verlieren

**alto** /'æltəʊ/ *n., pl.* **~s** (*Mus.*) *(voice, part)* Alt, *der;* *(male singer)* Alt, *der;* Altist, *der;* Altsänger, *der;* *(female singer)* Alt, *der;* Altistin, *die;* Altsängerin, *die;* **~ saxophone/clarinet** Altsaxophon, *das*/Altklarinette, *die;* **~ clef** Altschlüssel, *der*

**altogether** /ɔ:ltə'geðə(r)/ ❶ *adv.* völlig; *(on the whole)* im Großen und Ganzen; *(in total)* insgesamt; **not ~ [true/convincing]** nicht ganz [wahr/überzeugend]. ❷ *n.* **in the ~** (*coll.*) im Evas-/Adamskostüm

**altruism** /'æltrʊɪzm/ *n., no pl.* Altruismus, *der;* Uneigennützigkeit, *die*

**altruist** /'æltrʊɪst/ *n.* Altruist, *der* (*geh.*)

**altruistic** /æltrʊ'ɪstɪk/ *adj.,* **altruistically** /æltrʊ'ɪstɪkəlɪ/ *adv.* altruistisch; uneigennützig

**alum** /'æləm/ *n.* (*Chem.*) Alaun, *der*

**alumina** /ə'lu:mɪnə/ *n.* Aluminiumoxyd, (*fachspr.*) -oxid, *das;* Tonerde, *die*

**aluminium** /æljʊ'mɪnɪəm/ *n.* (*Brit.*) Aluminium, *das; attrib.* **~ foil** Alufolie, *die*

**aluminize** /ə'lu:mɪnaɪz/ *v.t.* aluminieren

**aluminum** /ə'lu:mɪnəm/ (*Amer.*) ⇒ **aluminium**

**alumna** /ə'lʌmnə/ *n., pl.* **~e** /ə'lʌmni:/ (*Amer.*) Absolventin, *die*

**alumnus** /ə'lʌmnəs/ *n., pl.* **alumni** /ə'lʌmnaɪ/ (*Amer.*) Absolvent, *der;* **we are both alumni of Harvard** wir sind beide ehemalige Harvard-Studenten

**alveolar** /æl'vɪələ(r), ælvɪ'əʊlə(r)/ *adj.* **A** (*Anat.*) **~ ridge** Alveolarfortsatz, *der;* **B** (*Phonet.*) alveolar; Alveolar-

**always** /'ɔ:lweɪz, 'ɔ:lwɪz/ *adv.* *(at all times)* immer; *(repeatedly)* ständig; [an]dauernd (*ugs.*); *(whatever the circumstances)* jederzeit; **he ~ comes on Monday** er kommt immer am Montag; **he is ~ making fun of other people** er macht sich dauernd *od.* ständig über andere lustig; **don't worry, I can ~ sleep on the floor** keine Sorge, ich kann jederzeit *od.* ohne weiteres auf dem Fußboden schlafen; **you can ~ come by train if you prefer** ihr könnt ja auch mit der Bahn kommen, wenn euch das lieber ist

**alyssum** /'ælɪsəm/ *n.* (*Bot.*) Steinkraut, *das*

**Alzheimer's disease** /'æltshaɪmez dɪzi:z/ *n.* ▶ **1232** Alzheimerkrankheit, *die*

**AM** *abbr.* **amplitude modulation** AM

**am** ⇒ **be**

**a.m.** /eɪ'em/ ▶ **1012** ❶ *adv.* vormittags; **[at] one/four ~:** [um] ein/vier Uhr nachts *od.* morgens *od.* früh; **[at] five/eight ~:** [um] fünf/acht Uhr morgens *od.* früh; **[at] nine ~:** [um] neun Uhr morgens *od.* früh *od.* vormittags; **[at] ten/eleven ~:** [um] zehn/elf Uhr vormittags. ❷ *n.* Vormittag, *der;* **Monday/this ~:** Montagvormittag/heute Vormittag

**amalgam** /ə'mælgəm/ *n.* **A** *(lit. or fig.: mixture)* Mischung, *die;* **B** *(alloy)* Amalgam, *das*

**amalgamate** /ə'mælgəmeɪt/ ❶ *v.t.* vereinigen; verschmelzen (*geh.*); amalgamieren (*geh.*) ‹Rassen›; zusammenlegen ‹Abteilungen›; fusionieren ‹Firmen›. ❷ *v.i.* sich vereinigen; ‹Firmen:› fusionieren; ‹Abteilungen:› zusammengelegt werden

**amalgamation** /əmælgə'meɪʃn/ *n.* **A** *(action)* Vereinigung, *die;* *(of races)* Verschmelzung, *die* (*geh.*); Amalgamierung, *die* (*geh.*); (*of firms*) Fusion, *die;* (*of departments*) Zusammenlegung, *die;* Ⓑ (*result*) Vereinigung, *die;* **his 'theory' is an ~ of various ideas** seine „Theorie" besteht aus einer Mischung *od.* (*geh.*) ist ein Amalgam der verschiedensten Ideen

**amanuensis** /əmænjʊ'ensɪs/ *n., pl.* **amanuenses** /əmænjʊ'ensi:z/ Sekretär, *der*

**amaryllis** /æmə'rɪlɪs/ *n.* (*Bot.*) Ⓐ (*plant of genus A~*) Amaryllis, *die;* Ⓑ (*plant of related genus*) Amaryllisgewächs, *das*

**amass** /ə'mæs/ *v.t.* [ein]sammeln; **what a lot of books you have ~ed over the years!** was für eine Menge Bücher sich bei dir während der Jahre angesammelt *od.* angehäuft hat!; **~ a [large] fortune** ein [großes] Vermögen anhäufen

**amateur** /'æmətə(r)/ *n.* Ⓐ (*non-professional*) Amateur, *der;* Ⓑ (*derog.: trifler*) Amateur, *der;* Dilettant, *der;* Ⓒ *attrib.* Amateur-; Laien-; **~ actor/theatre** Amateur- *od.* Laienschauspieler/Amateur- *od.* Laientheater; **when he retired he took up ~ photography/writing** als Rentner fing er an zu fotografieren/schriftstellern

**amateurish** /'æmətərɪʃ/ *adj.* (*derog.*) laienhaft; amateurhaft

**amateurishness** /'æmətərɪʃnɪs/ *n.* Dilettantismus, *der*

**amateurism** /'æmətərɪzm/ *n., no pl.* Amateursport, *der;* (*as qualifying principle*) Amateurstatus, *der*

**amatory** /'æmətərɪ/ *adj.* erotisch; Liebes-; **~ poems/letters/affairs** Liebesgedichte/-briefe/-affären; **~ advances** amouröse Avancen (*geh.*)

**amaze** /ə'meɪz/ *v.t.* verblüffen; verwundern; **be ~d [by sth.]** [über etw. (*Akk.*)] verblüfft *od.* verwundert sein

**amazement** /ə'meɪzmənt/ *n., no pl.* Verblüffung, *die;* Verwunderung, *die*

**amazing** /ə'meɪzɪŋ/ *adj.* (*remarkable*) erstaunlich; (*astonishing*) verblüffend; **'~ value'** „sensationell günstig"

**amazingly** /ə'meɪzɪŋlɪ/ *adv.* Ⓐ *as sentence-modifier* (*remarkably*) erstaunlicherweise; (*astonishingly*) verblüffenderweise; Ⓑ erstaunlich; **~ stupid** außerordentlich *od.* (*ugs.*) selten dumm

**Amazon**[1] /'æməzən/ *pr. n.* ▸1480 **the ~:** der Amazonas *od.* (*veralt.*) Amazonenstrom

**Amazon**[2] *n.* Ⓐ (*Mythol.: female warrior*) Amazone, *die;* Ⓑ (*fig.*) Mannweib, *das* (*abwertend*); Amazone, *die* (*veralt.*)

**ambassador** /æm'bæsədə(r)/ *n.* Ⓐ ▸1261, ▸1617 Botschafter, *der*/Botschafterin, *die;* (*on particular mission*) Sonderbotschafter, *der;* Gesandte, *der* (*hist.*); **~ to a country/court** Botschafter in einem Land/an einem Hof; Ⓑ (*messenger*) Abgesandte, *der/die;* Beauftragte, *der/die*

**ambassadorial** /æmbæsə'dɔ:rɪəl/ *adj.* Botschafter-; eines/des Botschafters *nachgestellt;* (*of envoy*) Gesandten-; eines/des Gesandten *nachgestellt*

**amber** /'æmbə(r)/ ❶ *n.* Ⓐ Bernstein, *der;* Ⓑ (*traffic light*) Gelb, *das;* **when the ~ is flashing** bei gelbem Blinklicht. ❷ *adj.* Bernstein-; aus Bernstein *nachgestellt;* (*colour*) bernsteinfarben; gelb ‹Verkehrslicht›

**ambergris** /'æmbəgrɪs, 'æmbəgri:s/ *n.* Amber, *der;* Ambra, *die*

**ambiance** /ɑ̃bɪ'ɑ̃s/ ⇒ **ambience**

**ambidexterity** /æmbɪdeks'terɪtɪ/ ⇒ **ambidextrousness**

**ambidextrous** /æmbɪ'dekstrəs/ *adj.* beidhändig; ambidexter (*fachspr.*)

**ambidextrously** /æmbɪ'dekstrəslɪ/ *adv.* beidhändig

**ambidextrousness** /æmbɪ'dekstrəsnɪs/ *n., no pl.* Beidhändigkeit, *die*

**ambience** /'æmbɪəns/ *n.* Ambiente, *das* (*geh.*); Milieu, *das;* Atmosphäre, *die;* **the ~ of the theatre** das Ambiente des Theaters; das Theatermilieu; die Theateratmosphäre

**ambient** /'æmbɪənt/ *adj.* Umgebungs-; **~ pressure/air** Umgebungsdruck, *der*/-luft, *die*

**ambiguity** /æmbɪ'gju:ɪtɪ/ *n.* Zweideutigkeit, *die;* Doppelsinnigkeit, *die* (*geh.*); (*having several meanings*) Mehrdeutigkeit, *die;* Ambiguität, *die* (*Sprachw.*)

**ambiguous** /æm'bɪgjʊəs/ *adj.* zweideutig; doppelsinnig (*geh.*); (*with several meanings*) mehrdeutig; ambig (*Sprachw.*); nicht eindeutig klassifizierbar ‹Pflanze, Tier›; **her smile was ~:** ihr Lächeln war zweideutig

**ambiguously** /æm'bɪgjʊəslɪ/ *adv.* zweideutig; doppelsinnig (*geh.*); (*with several meanings*) mehrdeutig; ambig (*Sprachw.*); **smile ~:** zweideutig lächeln

**ambiguousness** /æm'bɪgjʊəsnɪs/ *n., no pl.* Zweideutigkeit, *die;* Doppelsinnigkeit, *die* (*geh.*); (*having several meanings*) Mehrdeutigkeit, *die*

**ambit** /'æmbɪt/ *n.* Gebiet, *das;* Bereich, *der;* **the ~ of sb.'s experience/competence** jmds. Erfahrungs-/Kompetenz- *od.* Zuständigkeitsbereich

**ambition** /æm'bɪʃn/ *n.* Ehrgeiz, *der;* (*aspiration*) Ambition, *die;* Wunsch, *der;* **you can never fulfil every ~:** man kann nie all seine Ambitionen verwirklichen

**ambitious** /æm'bɪʃəs/ *adj.* ehrgeizig; ambitioniert (*geh.*) ‹Person›; **she was very ~ for him to succeed** ihr ganzer Ehrgeiz war es, dass er Erfolg hatte; **be ~ to do sth.** von dem Ehrgeiz erfüllt sein, etw. zu tun

**ambitiously** /æm'bɪʃəslɪ/ *adv.* voller Ehrgeiz; von Ehrgeiz erfüllt

**ambitiousness** /æm'bɪʃəsnɪs/ *n., no pl.* Ehrgeiz, *der;* ehrgeiziges Streben; **the ~ of his proposal/the new project** das Ehrgeizige an seinem Plan/an dem neuen Projekt

**ambivalence** /æm'bɪvələns/ *n., no pl.* Ambivalenz, *die*

**ambivalent** /æm'bɪvələnt/ *adj.* ambivalent

**amble** /'æmbl/ ❶ *v.i.* Ⓐ ‹Reiter:› im Passgang reiten; ‹Pferd:› im Passgang gehen; (*ride at easy pace*) im Schritt reiten; Ⓑ (*fig.: walk slowly*) schlendern; gemütlich gehen. ❷ *n.* Ⓐ Passgang, *der;* Ⓑ (*fig.*) Schlendern, *das*

**ambrosia** /æm'brəʊzɪə/ *n., no pl.* Ambrosia, *die*

**ambulance** /'æmbjʊləns/ *n.* Ⓐ (*vehicle*) Krankenwagen, *der;* Ambulanz, *die;* (*Mil.*) Sanitätswagen, *der;* Sanka, *der* (*bes. Soldatenspr.*); Ⓑ (*Mil.: mobile hospital*) Feldlazarett, *das;* Ambulanz, *die*

**ambulance: ~ chaser** *n.* (*Amer.*) *Anwalt oder sein Agent, der Unfallopfer dazu überredet, auf Schadenersatz zu klagen;* **~ driver** *n.* ▸1261 Fahrer eines/des Krankenwagens; **~ man** *n.* ▸1261 Sanitäter, *der;* **~ service** *n.* Rettungsdienst, *der;* **~ worker** *n.* ▸1261 Sanitäter, *der*/Sanitäterin, *die*

**ambulant** /'æmbjʊlənt/ *adj.* gehfähig ‹Patient›; ambulant ‹Behandlung›

**ambush** /'æmbʊʃ/ ❶ *n.* (*concealment*) Hinterhalt, *der;* (*troops concealed*) im Hinterhalt liegende Truppe; **lie in ~** (*lit. or fig.*) im Hinterhalt liegen; **arrange an ~:** einen Überfall aus dem Hinterhalt führen. ❷ *v.t.* [aus dem Hinterhalt] überfallen

**ameba** /ə'mi:bə/ (*Amer.*) ⇒ **amoeba**

**ameliorate** /ə'mi:lɪəreɪt/ ❶ *v.t.* verbessern. ❷ *v.i.* sich verbessern; besser werden

**amelioration** /əmi:lɪə'reɪʃn/ *n.* [Ver]besserung, *die*

**ameliorative** /ə'mi:lɪərətɪv/ *adj.* verbessernd; bessernd ‹Einfluss›; **~ measures/effect** Verbesserungsmaßnahmen *Pl.*/-effekt, *der*

**amen** /ɑ:'men, eɪ'men/ ❶ *int.* amen; **say '~' to sth.** Ja und Amen zu etw. sagen. ❷ *n.* Amen, *das*

**amenability** /əmi:nə'bɪlɪtɪ/ *n., no pl.* Ⓐ (*responsiveness*) Zugänglichkeit, *die* (**to** für); Ⓑ (*of phenomenon etc.*) Unterworfenheit, *die* (**to** unter + *Akk.*)

**amenable** /ə'mi:nəbl/ *adj.* Ⓐ (*responsive*) zugänglich, aufgeschlossen ‹Person› (**to** *Dat.*); **he simply isn't ~ to reason/advice** er ist Vernunftgründen/Ratschlägen einfach nicht zugänglich; **~ to kindness** für Freundlichkeit empfänglich; Ⓑ (*subject*) unterworfen ‹Sache› (**to** *Dat.*); **be ~ to the laws of nature/rules of grammar** den Naturgesetzen/Regeln der Grammatik unterworfen sein *od.* gehorchen

**amend** /ə'mend/ *v.t.* (*correct*) berichtigen; (*improve*) abändern, ergänzen ‹Gesetzentwurf, Antrag›; ändern ‹Verfassung›; [ver]bessern ‹Situation›

**amendment** /ə'mendmənt/ *n.* (*to motion*) Abänderungsantrag, *der;* (*to bill*) Änderungsantrag, *der;* (*to Constitution*) Änderung, *die* (**to** *Gen.*); Amendement, *das* (*Dipl.*); (*of situation*) [Ver]besserung, *die*

**amends** /ə'mendz/ *n. pl.* **make ~ [to sb.]** es [bei jmdm.] wieder gutmachen; **make ~ for sth.** etw. wieder gutmachen

**amenity** /ə'mi:nɪtɪ/ *n.* Ⓐ *no pl.* (*pleasantness*) Annehmlichkeiten *Pl.;* Ⓑ (*pleasant feature*) (*of residence*) Attraktivität, *die;* Wohnqualität, *die;* (*of locality*) Attraktivität, *die;* Reiz, *der;* **the amenities of a town** die kulturellen und Freizeiteinrichtungen einer Stadt; **social amenities** öffentliche Freizeiteinrichtungen; **with every ~, including showers, central heating, etc.** mit allem Komfort inklusive Duschen, Zentralheizung usw.

**amenity: ~ bed** *n.* (*Brit.*) ≈ Privatbett [in einem öffentlichen Krankenhaus]; **~ centre** *n.* Freizeitzentrum, *das*

**America** /ə'merɪkə/ *pr. n.* Ⓐ Amerika (*das*); Ⓑ **the ~s** Nord-, Süd- und Mittelamerika

**American** /ə'merɪkən/ ▸1275, ▸1340 ❶ *adj.* amerikanisch; **sb. is ~:** jmd. ist Amerikaner/Amerikanerin; **~ English** amerikanisches Englisch; **~ studies** Amerikanistik, *die;* ⇒ *also* **English** 1; **legion** B. ❷ *n.* Ⓐ (*person*) Amerikaner, *der*/Amerikanerin, *die;* Ⓑ (*language*) Amerikanisch, *das;* ⇒ *also* **English** 2 A

**American: ~ 'football** *n.* Football, *der;* **~ 'Indian** ▸1340 ❶ *n.* Indianer, *der*/Indianerin, *die;* ❷ *adj.* indianisch

**Americanisation, Americanise** ⇒ **Americaniz-**

**Americanism** /ə'merɪkənɪzm/ *n.* Ⓐ (*Ling.*) Amerikanismus, *der;* Ⓑ (*attachment*) Amerikanertum, *das*

**Americanization** /əmerɪkənaɪ'zeɪʃn/ *n.* Ⓐ Amerikanisierung, *die;* Ⓑ (*naturalization*) Einbürgerung [in Amerika]

**Americanize** /ə'merɪkənaɪz/ *v.t.* Ⓐ amerikanisieren; Ⓑ (*naturalize*) [in Amerika] einbürgern

**American: ~ 'organ** *n.* (*Mus.*) amerikanische Orgel; **~ plan** *n.* (*Amer. Hotel Managem.*) Vollpension, *die*

**Amerindian** /æmə'rɪndɪən/ ▸1340 ❶ *adj.* indianisch; **~ languages** Indianersprachen; **~ peoples** Indianer *Pl.* ❷ *n.* Indianer, *der*/Indianerin, *die*

**amethyst** /'æmɪθɪst/ *n.* Amethyst, *der*

**AMEX** /'æmeks/ *abbr.* **American Stock Exchange** A.S.E.

**amiability** /'eɪmɪəbɪlɪtɪ/ *n., no pl.* ⇒ **amiable**: Umgänglichkeit, *die;* Freundlichkeit, *die;* Entgegenkommen, *das*

**amiable** /'eɪmɪəbl/ *adj.* umgänglich; freundlich ‹Person›; entgegenkommend ‹Haltung›; **be in an ~ mood** gut gelaunt sein

**amiably** /'eɪmɪəblɪ/ *adv.* freundlich; **be ~ disposed towards sb./sth.** jmdm./einer Sache wohlgesinnt sein

**amicability** /æmɪkə'bɪlɪtɪ/ *n., no pl.* Freundschaftlichkeit, *die*

**amicable** /'æmɪkəbl/ *adj.* freundschaftlich ‹Gespräch, Beziehungen›; gütlich ‹Einigung›; friedlich ‹Lösung›; **~ relations with one's neighbours** ein freundnachbarliches Verhältnis

**amicably** /'æmɪkəblɪ/ *adv.* in [aller] Freundschaft; **get on ~ with one's neighbours** mit seinen Nachbarn gut auskommen

**amid** /ə'mɪd/ *prep.* inmitten; (*fig.: during*) bei; **~ the fighting** mitten im Gefecht

**amidships** /ə'mɪdʃɪps/ (*Amer.:* **amidship** /ə'mɪdʃɪp/) *adv.* (*position*) mittschiffs; Mitte Schiff (*Seemannsspr.*); (*direction*) [nach] mittschiffs; **hit sb. ~** (*fig. coll.*) jmdn. in den Bauch schlagen/treffen

a

**amidst** /ə'mɪdst/ ⇒ **amid**

**amino acid** /əmi:nəʊ 'æsɪd/ *n.* (*Chem.*) Aminosäure, *die*

**Amish** /'ɑ:mɪʃ, 'eɪmɪʃ, 'æmɪʃ/ *adj.* Amisch; **the ~ Mennonites** die Amischen

**amiss** /ə'mɪs/ ❶ *pred. adj.* Ⓐ (*wrong*) verkehrt; falsch; **is anything ~?** stimmt irgendetwas nicht?; ist irgendetwas nicht in Ordnung?; Ⓑ (*out of place*) fehl am Platz[e]; unangebracht. ❷ *adv.* **take sth. ~:** etw. übel nehmen; **come** *or* **go ~:** ungelegen kommen; **a glass of wine would not come** *or* **go ~:** ein Glas Wein wäre nicht verkehrt

**amity** /'æmɪtɪ/ *n.* Freundschaft, *die;* gutes Einvernehmen

**ammeter** /'æmɪtə(r)/ *n.* (*Electr.*) Amperemeter, *das;* Strommesser, *der*

**ammo** /'æməʊ/ *n., no pl.* (*Mil. coll.*) Muni, *die* (*Milit. ugs.*)

**ammonia** /ə'məʊnɪə/ *n.* Ammoniak, *das;* **~ water** Salmiakgeist, *der;* Ammoniaklösung, *die*

**ammunition** /æmjʊ'nɪʃn/ *n., no pl., no indef. art.* (*lit. or fig.*) Munition, *die*

**amnesia** /æm'ni:zɪə/ *n.* (*Med.*) Amnesie, *die;* Gedächtnisschwund, *der*

**amnesty** /'æmnɪstɪ/ *n.* Amnestie, *die;* **grant an ~ to sb.** jmdn. amnestieren; **they were released under an ~:** sie wurden im Rahmen einer Amnestie freigelassen

**amniocentesis** /æmnɪəʊsen'ti:sɪs/ *n.* (*Med.*) Fruchtwasserentnahme, *die*

**amoeba** /ə'mi:bə/ *n., pl.* **~s** *or* **~e** /ə'mi:bi:/ (*Zool.*) Amöbe, *die*

**amok** /ə'mɒk/ *adv.* **run ~:** Amok laufen

**among[st]** /ə'mʌŋ(st)/ *prep.* Ⓐ unter (+ *Dat.; seltener:* + *Akk.*); **~ us/you/friends** unter uns/euch/Freunden; **~ other things** unter anderem; **~ others** unter anderen; Ⓑ (*in/into the middle of, surrounded by*) zwischen (+ *Dat./Akk.*); **hide ~ the bushes** sich im Gebüsch verstecken; **~ tall trees** inmitten hoher Bäume; **she was sitting ~ her children** sie saß im Kreise ihrer Kinder; **there are some weeds ~ the flowers** zwischen den Blumen wächst Unkraut; **a village ~ the hills** ein Dorf in den Bergen; **I saw him ~ the crowd** ich habe ihn in der Menge gesehen; Ⓒ (*in the practice or opinion of, in the number of*) unter (+ *Dat.*); **~ men/scientists** unter Männern/Wissenschaftlern; **who is the tallest ~ you?** wer ist der größte von *od.* (*geh.*) unter euch?; **I count him ~ my friends** ich zähle ihn zu meinen Freunden; **that painting is reckoned ~ his best works** das Bild zählt zu seinen besten Werken; Ⓓ (*between*) unter (+ *Dat.; seltener:* + *Akk.*); **share the sweets ~ yourselves** teilt euch die Bonbons; **we only have five pounds ~ us** wir haben zusammen nur fünf Pfund; **he distributed his wealth ~ the poor** er verteilte sein Vermögen an die *od.* unter die *od.* unter den Armen; Ⓔ (*reciprocally*) **they often quarrel ~ themselves** sie streiten oft miteinander; sie streiten sich oft; **we often disagree ~ ourselves** wir sind [untereinander] oft verschiedener Meinung; Ⓕ (*jointly*) **~ you/them** *etc.* gemeinsam; zusammen

**amoral** /eɪ'mɒrəl/ *adj.* amoralisch

**amorous** /'æmərəs/ *adj.* verliebt; amourös ‹Abenteuer, Beziehung›; **~ glances** verliebte Blicke; **~ advances** Annäherungsversuche *Pl.;* amouröse Avancen *Pl.* (*veralt., scherzh.*); **an ~ novel/poem** ein Liebesroman/-gedicht; **be ~ of sb.** (*literary*) in jmdn. verliebt sein

**amorously** /'æmərəslɪ/ *adv.* verliebt

**amorousness** /'æmərəsnɪs/ *n., no pl.* Verliebtheit, *die*

**amorphous** /ə'mɔ:fəs/ *adj.* Ⓐ (*shapeless, unorganized*) formlos; amorph ‹Masse›; (*fig.*) chaotisch ‹Stil›; Ⓑ (*Min., Chem.*) amorph

**amortization** /əmɔ:taɪ'zeɪʃn/ *n.* (*Finance*) Ⓐ (*of assets*) Abschreibung, *die;* Ⓑ (*of debt, mortgage*) Tilgung, *die;* Amortisation, *die*

**amortize** /ə'mɔ:taɪz/ *v.t.* (*Finance*) abschreiben ‹Vermögenswerte›; tilgen, amortisieren ‹Schuld, Hypothek›

**amount** /ə'maʊnt/ ❶ *v.i.* **~ to sth.** sich auf etw. (*Akk.*) belaufen; (*fig.*) auf etw. (*Akk.*) hinauslaufen; einer Sache (*Dat.*) gleichkommen; **the cost/debts/fees/profits ~ed to ...:** die Kosten/Schulden/Gebühren/Gewinne beliefen sich auf ... (*Akk.*); **all these arguments/proposals don't ~ to much** diese Argumente/Vorschläge bringen alle nicht viel; **my savings don't ~ to very much** meine Ersparnisse sind nicht gerade groß; **what this all ~s to is that ...:** zusammenfassend kann man sagen, dass ...
❷ *n.* Ⓐ (*total*) Betrag, *der;* Summe, *die;* (*full significance*) volle Bedeutung *od.* Tragweite; Ⓑ **the ~ of a bill** die Höhe einer Rechnung; Ⓒ (*quantity*) Menge, *die;* **an ~ of rain/patience** eine Menge Regen/Geduld; **large ~s of money** beträchtliche Geldsummen; **a tremendous ~ of** (*coll.*) wahnsinnig viel (*ugs.*); **no ~ of money will make me change my mind** und wenn man mir noch so viel Geld gibt: Meine Meinung werde ich nicht ändern; **no ~ of talking will settle the matter** so viel wir auch darüber reden, wir werden zu keinem Ergebnis kommen; ⇒ *also* **any** 1 E

**amour** /ə'mʊə(r)/ *n.* Affäre, *die;* Liebschaft, *die*

**amour propre** /æmʊə 'prɒpr/ *n., no pl.* Ⓐ (*self-esteem*) Ehrgefühl, *das;* Selbstachtung, *die;* Ⓑ (*vanity*) Eitelkeit, *die*

**amp** /æmp/ *n.* Ⓐ (*Electr.*) Ampere, *das;* Ⓑ (*coll.: amplifier*) Verstärker, *der*

**ampere** /'æmpeə(r)/ *n.* (*Electr.*) Ampere, *das*

**ampersand** /'æmpəsænd/ *n.* Et-Zeichen, *das*

**amphetamine** /æm'fetəmɪn, æm'fetəmi:n/ *n.* Amphetamin, *das*

**amphibian** /æm'fɪbɪən/ ❶ *adj.* Ⓐ (*Zool.*) amphibisch; **~ animal** amphibisches Lebewesen; Amphibie, *die;* Lurch, *der;* Ⓑ (*Mil.*) ⇒ **amphibious** B. ❷ *n.* Ⓐ (*Zool.*) Amphibie, *die;* Lurch, *der;* Ⓑ (*vehicle*) Amphibienfahrzeug, *das*

**amphibious** /æm'fɪbɪəs/ *adj.* Ⓐ (*Biol.*) amphibisch; **toads are ~:** Kröten sind Amphibien; Ⓑ (*operating on land or water*) amphibisch; zu Lande und zu Wasser einsetzbar; **~ vehicle/tank/aircraft** Amphibienfahrzeug, *das*/-panzer, *der*/-flugzeug, *das;* **~ warfare/operations/forces** amphibische Kriegsführung/Operationen/Streitkräfte

**amphitheatre** (*Amer.:* **amphitheater**) /'æmfɪθɪətə(r)/ *n.* Ⓐ Amphitheater, *das;* Ⓑ (*Geog.: hollow*) Kessel, *der;* Ⓒ (*fig.: arena*) Schauplatz, *der*

**amphora** /'æmfərə/ *n., pl.* **~e** /'æmfəri:/ *or* **~s** Amphora, Amphore, *die*

**ample** /'æmpl/ *adj.,* **~r** /'æmplə(r)/, **~st** /'æmplɪst/ Ⓐ (*spacious*) weitläufig ‹Garten, Räume›; groß ‹Ausdehnung›; (*extensive, abundant*) reichhaltig ‹Mahl, Bibliographie›; ausführlich, umfassend ‹Behandlung eines Themas›; weit reichend, umfassend ‹Vollmachten, Machtbefugnisse›; Ⓑ (*enough*) **~ room/food** reichlich Platz/zu essen; **this hall is ~ in size for the party** dieser Saal bietet reichlich Platz für die Feier; Ⓒ (*stout*) üppig ‹Busen›; stattlich ‹Erscheinung›

**amplification** /æmplɪfɪ'keɪʃn/ *n.* Ⓐ (*Phys.*) Verstärkung, *die;* Ⓑ (*enlargement*) weitere *od.* zusätzliche Erläuterungen; Ⓒ (*of knowledge, wisdom, etc.*) Erweiterung, *die;* Vertiefung, *die*

**amplifier** /'æmplɪfaɪə(r)/ *n.* Verstärker, *der*

**amplify** /'æmplɪfaɪ/ ❶ *v.t.* Ⓐ verstärken ‹Ton›; Ⓑ (*enlarge on*) weiter ausführen, näher *od.* ausführlicher erläutern ‹Erklärung, Bericht›; Ⓒ (*enhance*) erweitern, vertiefen ‹Wissen, Kenntnisse›. ❷ *v.i.* auf Einzelheiten (*Akk.*) eingehen; **~ on sth.** etw. näher erläutern

**amplitude** /'æmplɪtju:d/ *n.* Ⓐ (*Electr.*) Amplitude, *die;* Schwingungsweite, *die;* **~ modulation** Amplitudenmodulation, *die;* Ⓑ (*Phys.*) Amplitude, *die;* größte Ausschlagweite; Ⓒ *no pl.* (*breadth*) Breite, *die;* Weite, *die;* (*abundance*) Fülle, *die;* (*wide range*) Breite, *die*

**amply** /'æmplɪ/ *adv.* (*spaciously, abundantly*) reichlich ‹breit, belohnen›; zur Genüge ‹zeigen, demonstrieren›

**ampoule** /'æmpu:l/ *n.* Ampulle, *die*

**amputate** /'æmpjʊteɪt/ *v.t.* amputieren

**amputation** /æmpjʊ'teɪʃn/ *n.* Amputation, *die*

**amputee** /æmpjʊ'ti:/ *n.* Amputierte, *der/die*

**Amtrack** ® /'æmtræk/*n.: amerikanische Eisenbahngesellschaft*

**amuck** /ə'mʌk/ ⇒ **amok**

**amulet** /'æmjʊlɪt/ *n.* (*lit. or fig.*) Amulett, *das*

**amuse** /ə'mju:z/ *v.t.* Ⓐ (*interest*) unterhalten; **keep a child ~d** ein Kind richtig beschäftigen; **~ oneself with sth.** sich mit etw. beschäftigen; **~ oneself by doing sth.** sich (*Dat.*) die Zeit damit vertreiben, etw. zu tun; Ⓑ (*make laugh or smile*) belustigen; amüsieren; **be ~d by** *or* **at sth.** sich über etw. (*Akk.*) amüsieren

**amusement** /ə'mju:zmənt/ *n.* Belustigung, *die;* (*pastime*) Freizeitbeschäftigung, *die;* **all the ~s on offer at the seaside** das gesamte Freizeitangebot am Meer; **in the ~s** in der Spielhalle

**a'musement arcade** *n.* Spielhalle, *die*

**amusing** /ə'mju:zɪŋ/ *adj.,* **amusingly** /ə'mju:zɪŋlɪ/ *adv.* amüsant

**an**[1] /ən, *stressed* æn/ *indef. art.* ⇒ *also* **a**[2]: ein/eine/ein; **an elephant/Englishman** ein Elefant/Engländer; **an hour/historical play** eine Stunde/ein historisches Stück; **an LP** eine LP

**an**[2] /æn/ *conj.* (*arch./dial.*) so (*veralt.*); **an I meet him** so ich ihn treffe

**anabolic steroid** /ænəbɒlɪk 'stɪərɔɪd, ænəbɒlɪk 'sterɔɪd/ *n.* (*Physiol.*) anaboles Steroid; Anabolikum, *das*

**anachronism** /ə'nækrənɪzm/ *n.* Anachronismus, *der*

**anachronistic** /ənækrə'nɪstɪk/ *adj.* anachronistisch; zeitwidrig

**anaconda** /ænə'kɒndə/ *n.* (*Zool.*) Anakonda, *die*

**anaemia** /ə'ni:mɪə/ *n., no pl.* ▶ **1232** (*Med.*) Blutarmut, *die;* Anämie, *die;* ⇒ *also* **pernicious**

**anaemic** /ə'ni:mɪk/ *adj.* (*Med.*) blutarm; anämisch; (*fig.*) blutleer; saft- und kraftlos

**anaerobic** /æneə'rəʊbɪk/ *adj.* (*Biol.*) anaerob

**anaesthesia** /ænɪs'θi:zɪə/ *n.* (*Med.*) (*absence of sensation*) Empfindungslosigkeit, *die;* Anästhesie, (*fachspr.*) Anaesthesia, *die;* (*artificially induced*) Narkose, *die;* **general ~:** [Voll]narkose, *die;* Allgemeinanästhesie, *die* (*fachspr.*); **local ~:** örtliche Betäubung; Lokalanästhesie, *die* (*fachspr.*)

**anaesthetic** /ænɪs'θetɪk/ ❶ *adj.* (*Med.*) anästhetisch; betäubend. ❷ *n.* Anästhetikum, *das;* **give sb. an ~:** jmdm. eine Narkose geben; (*local*) jmdn. betäuben; **be under an ~:** in Narkose liegen; **general ~:** Narkotikum, *das;* Narkosemittel, *das;* **local ~:** Lokalanästhetikum, *das*

**anaesthetist** /ə'ni:sθətɪst/ *n.* ▶ **1261** (*Med.*) Anästhesist, *der*/Anästhesistin, *die;* Narkose[fach]arzt, *der*/-ärztin, *die*

**anaesthetization** /əni:sθətaɪ'zeɪʃn/ *n.* Betäubung, *die;* (*fig.*) Abstumpfung, *die* (**to** gegenüber)

**anaesthetize** /ə'ni:sθətaɪz/ *v.t.* narkotisieren; betäuben; anästhesieren (*fachspr.*); (*fig.*) abstumpfen (**to** gegenüber); **become ~d to sth.** (*fig.*) gegenüber etw. abstumpfen

**anagram** /'ænəgræm/ *n.* Anagramm, *das*

**anagrammatic** /ænəgrə'mætɪk/, **anagrammatical** /ænəgrə'mætɪkl/ *adj.* anagrammatisch

**anal** /'eɪnl/ *adj.* Ⓐ (*Anat.*) anal; Anal-; After-; **~ region** Analbereich, *der;* **~ canal** Afterkanal, *der;* Ⓑ (*Psych.*) **~ stage** anale Phase; **~ eroticism** Analerotik, *die*

**analgesia** /ænæl'dʒi:zɪə/ *n.* (*Med.*) Analgesie, *die*

**analgesic** /ænæl'dʒi:sɪk/ (*Med.*) ❶ *adj.* analgetisch. ❷ *n.* Analgetikum, *das*

**analog** (*Amer.*) ⇒ **analogue**

**analogical** /ænəˈlɒdʒɪkl/ *adj.* Ⓐ analog; Analogie-; **~ reasoning** Analogiedenken, *das;* Ⓑ (*expressing analogy*) metonymisch ‹Wort, Ausdruck›

**analogous** /əˈnæləgəs/ *adj.* vergleichbar; analog; **be ~ to sth.** einer Sache (*Dat.*) entsprechen

**analogously** /əˈnæləgəslɪ/ *adv.* analog

**analogue** /ˈænəlɒg/ *n.* Entsprechung, *die;* Analogon, *das* (*geh.*); **~ computer** Analogrechner, *der;* **~ watch** Analoguhr, *die*

**analogy** /əˈnælədʒɪ/ *n.* Ⓐ (*agreement; also Ling.*) Analogie, *die;* Ⓑ (*similarity*) Parallele, *die;* Analogie, *die;* **draw an ~ between/with** eine Parallele ziehen zwischen (+ *Dat.*)/zu; Ⓒ (*Logic*) Analogie, *die;* **use an argument by ~/argue by ~:** einen Analogieschluss/Analogieschlüsse ziehen

**analysable** /ˈænəlaɪzəbl/ *adj.* analysierbar; zerlegbar ‹Satz›

**analyse** /ˈænəlaɪz/ *v.t.* Ⓐ analysieren; kritisch untersuchen ‹Literatur›; Ⓑ (*Chem.*) untersuchen (**for** auf + *Akk.*); Ⓒ (*Ling.*) [zer]gliedern; Ⓓ (*Psych.*) analysieren (*fachspr.*); psychoanalytisch behandeln; **get ~d** sich einer [Psycho]analyse unterziehen

**analysis** /əˈnælɪsɪs/ *n., pl.* **analyses** /əˈnælɪsiːz/ Ⓐ Analyse, *die;* (*Chem., Med.: of sample*) Untersuchung, *die;* (*statement*) Analyse, *die;* [Lage]beurteilung, *die;* **in the final** *or* **last** *or* **ultimate ~:** letzten Endes; Ⓑ (*Math.*) Analysis, *die;* Ⓒ (*Psych.*) Analyse, *die*

**analyst** /ˈænəlɪst/ *n.* ▶ **1261** Ⓐ Laboratoriumsingenieur, *der;* Laborfachmann, *der* (*ugs.*); Ⓑ (*Econ., Polit., etc.*) Experte, *der;* Fachmann, *der;* Ⓒ (*Psych.*) Analytiker, *der*/Analytikerin, *die*

**analytic** /ænəˈlɪtɪk/ *adj.* analytisch

**analytical** /ænəˈlɪtɪkl/ *adj.* Ⓐ analytisch ‹Methode, Sprache, Begabung›; Ⓑ **~ geometry** analytische Geometrie

**analytically** /ænəˈlɪtɪkəlɪ/ *adv.* analytisch

**analyze** (*Amer.*) ⇒ **analyse**

**anapaest** (*Amer.:* **anapest**) /ˈænəpiːst/ *n.* (*Pros.*) Anapäst, *der*

**anaphora** /əˈnæfərə/ *n.* (*Lit.*) Anapher, *die*

**anarchic** /əˈnɑːkɪk/, **anarchical** /əˈnɑːkɪkl/ *adj.* anarchisch; (*anarchistic*) anarchistisch

**anarchism** /ˈænəkɪzm/ *n., no pl.* Anarchismus, *der*

**anarchist** /ˈænəkɪst/ *n.* Anarchist, *der*/Anarchistin, *die*

**anarchistic** /ænəˈkɪstɪk/ *adj.* anarchistisch

**anarchy** /ˈænəkɪ/ *n., no pl.* Anarchie, *die;* (*fig.: disorder*) Chaos, *das*

**anathema** /əˈnæθəmə/ *n.* Ⓐ *no pl., no art.* (*detested thing*) ein Gräuel; **be ~ to sb.** jmdm. verhasst *od.* ein Gräuel sein; Ⓑ *no pl., no art.* (*accursed thing*) **be ~:** verflucht sein; Ⓒ (*curse of God*) Fluch, *der;* (*curse of Church*) Anathema, *das;* Kirchenbann, *der*

**anathematize** /əˈnæθəmətaɪz/ ❶ *v.t.* verdammen; verfluchen; ‹Kirche, Papst:› in den Bann tun. ❷ *v.i.* fluchen

**anatomical** /ænəˈtɒmɪkl/ *adj.,* **anatomically** /ænəˈtɒmɪkəlɪ/ *adv.* anatomisch

**anatomist** /əˈnætəmɪst/ *n.* Anatom, *der;* (*dissector*) Anatomiegehilfe, *der;* (*fig.*) Sezierer, *der;* Analytiker, *der*

**anatomize** /əˈnætəmaɪz/ *v.t.* sezieren; (*fig.*) analysieren; sezieren

**anatomy** /əˈnætəmɪ/ *n., no pl.* Ⓐ Anatomie, *die;* (*dissection*) Sektion, *die;* Ⓑ (*joc.: body*) Anatomie, *die* (*scherzh.*); **a certain part of his ~:** ein bestimmter Körperteil; Ⓒ (*fig.: analysis*) Anatomie, *die;* Analyse, *die*

**ANC** *abbr.* **African National Congress** ANK

**ancestor** /ˈænsestə(r)/ *n.* Vorfahr, *der;* Ahn[e], *der;* (*fig.*) Ahn[e], *der*

**ancestral** /ænˈsestrəl/ *adj.* angestammt ‹Grundbesitz, Land›; **~ portraits** Ahnenbilder

**ancestry** /ˈænsestrɪ/ *n.* Ⓐ (*lineage*) Abstammung, *die;* Herkunft, *die;* Ⓑ (*ancestors*) Vorfahren *Pl.;* Ⓒ *no pl.* (*ancient descent*) Familientradition, *die*

**anchor** /ˈæŋkə(r)/ ❶ *n.* Anker, *der;* **lie at ~:** vor Anker liegen; **come to** *or* **cast** *or* **drop ~:** vor Anker gehen; **weigh ~:** den Anker lichten; ⇒ *also* **drag** 2 E. ❷ *v.t.* Ⓐ verankern; vor Anker legen; (*secure*) befestigen (**to** an + *Dat.*); Ⓑ (*fig.*) **be ~ed to sth.** an etw. (*Akk.*) gefesselt sein. ❸ *v.i.* ankern

**anchorage** /ˈæŋkərɪdʒ/ *n.* Ⓐ (*place for anchoring*) Ankerplatz, *der;* Ankergrund, *der* (*geh.*); Ⓑ (*anchoring, lying at anchor*) Ankern, *das;* Ⓒ (*fig.*) [Rück]halt, *der*

**anchorite** /ˈæŋkəraɪt/ *n.* (*lit. or fig.*) Einsiedler, *der*

**anchor:** **~man** *n.* Ⓐ (*Sport*) (*in tug-of-war*) hinterster *od.* letzter Mann; (*in relay race*) Schlussläufer, *der;* (*Mountaineering*) Seilletzte, *der;* **he is the ~man of the company** (*fig.*) er ist die Stütze der Firma; Ⓑ ▶ **1261** (*Telev., Radio*) Moderator, *der;* Redakteur im Studio, *der;* **~ ring** *n.* Ankerring, *der*

**anchovy** /ˈæntʃəvɪ, ænˈtʃəʊvɪ/ *n.* An[s]chovis, *die;* Sardelle, *die*

**anchovy:** **~ ˈpear** *n.* An[s]chovisbirne, *die;* **~ ˈtoast** *n.* Toast mit An[s]chovispaste

**ancien régime** /ɑ̃sjɛ̃ reɪˈʒiːm/ *n., pl.* **anciens régimes** /ɑ̃sjɛ̃ reɪˈʒiːm/ Ancien Régime, *das;* (*fig.*) alte Regierungsform

**ancient** /ˈeɪnʃənt/ ❶ *adj.* Ⓐ (*belonging to past*) alt; (*pertaining to antiquity*) antik; **~ Rome/Greece** das alte *od.* antike Rom/Griechenland; **in ~ times** im Altertum; **~ history** Alte Geschichte, *die;* **that's ~ history; everybody knows it** (*fig.*) das ist längst ein alter Hut (*ugs.*), jeder weiß das; **the ~ Greeks** die alten Griechen; **A~ Greek** Altgriechisch, *das;* **~ Egypt** Altägypten (*das*); Ⓑ (*old*) alt; historisch ‹Gebäude usw.›; **~ monument** (*Brit. Admin.*) [offiziell anerkanntes] historisches Denkmal; [offiziell anerkannte] historische Stätte; **~ lights** (*Law*) *Fenster, die mindestens 20 Jahre lang Lichtzutritt hatten, der nicht durch bauliche Maßnahmen behindert werden darf.*

❷ *n.* Ⓐ **the ~s** Menschen der Antike; (*authors*) die Schriftsteller der Antike; Ⓑ **the A~ of Days** (*literary*) der Allvater; Ⓒ (*arch.: old man*) Alte, *der*

**anciently** /ˈeɪnʃəntlɪ/ *adv.* in alten Zeiten; (*in antiquity*) in der Antike; im Altertum

**ancillary** /ænˈsɪlərɪ/ ❶ *adj.* Ⓐ (*auxiliary*) **be ~ to sth.** für etw. Hilfsdienste leisten; **be ~ to medicine** eine Hilfswissenschaft der Medizin sein; Ⓑ (*subordinate*) zweitrangig; **~ industries** Zulieferindustrien; **~ services** Hilfeleistungen; **~ worker** Hilfskraft, *die;* **~ subject** Nebenfach, *das;* **a network of ~ roads** ein Netz von Verbindungsstraßen. ❷ *n.* (*Brit.*) Hilfskraft, *die*

**and** /ənd, *stressed* ænd/ *conj.* Ⓐ und; **two hundred ~ forty** zweihundert[und]vierzig; **a knife, fork, ~ spoon** Messer, Gabel und Löffel; **there are books ~ books** es gibt Bücher und Bücher; es gibt sone Bücher und solche (*salopp*); **two ~ two are four** zwei und zwei ist *od.* sind vier; **[by] two ~ two** in Zweierreihen; **~/or** und/oder; Ⓑ *expr. condition* und; **take one more step ~ I'll shoot** noch einen Schritt, und ich schieße; **do that ~ you'll regret it** wenn du das tust, wirst du es noch bedauern; Ⓒ *expr. continuation* und; **she cried ~ cried** sie weinte und weinte; **he tried ~ tried to open it** er versuchte immer wieder, es zu öffnen; **for weeks ~ weeks/years ~ years** wochen-/jahrelang; **for miles ~ miles** meilenweit; **better ~ better** immer besser

**andante** /ænˈdæntɪ/ (*Mus.*) ❶ *adv.* andante; gemessen. ❷ *adj.* ruhig. ❸ *n.* Andante, *das*

**Andean** /ænˈdiːən/ *adj.* (*Geog.*) Anden-

**Andes** /ˈændiːz/ *pr. n. pl.* Anden *Pl.*

**andiron** /ˈændaɪən/ *n.* Feuerbock, *der*

**Andorra** /ænˈdɔːrə/ *pr. n.* Andorra (*das*)

**Andrew** /ˈændruː/ *pr. n.* (*as name of saint*) Andreas (*der*)

**androgynous** /ænˈdrɒdʒɪnəs/ *adj.* (*Biol.*) zwittrig

**anecdotal** /ˈænɪkdəʊtl/ *adj.* anekdotisch; anekdotenhaft

**anecdote** /ˈænɪkdəʊt/ *n.* Anekdote, *die;* **he is never without a witty ~:** er ist nie um eine witzige Geschichte verlegen

**anemia, anemic** (*Amer.*) ⇒ **anaem-**

**anemometer** /ænɪˈmɒmɪtə(r)/ *n.* (*Meteorol.*) Anemometer, *das;* Windmesser, *der*

**anemone** /əˈnemənɪ/ *n.* Anemone, *die;* (*pasque flower*) Kuhschelle, *die;* ⇒ *also* **sea anemone; wood anemone**

**aneroid** /ˈænərɔɪd/ *adj.* **~ barometer** Aneroidbarometer, *das*

**anesthesia** *etc.* (*Amer.*) ⇒ **anaesthesia** *etc.*

**anew** /əˈnjuː/ *adv.* Ⓐ aufs Neue; erneut; **let's start ~:** fangen wir noch einmal von vorne an; Ⓑ (*in a new form*) neu; **he decided to start life ~ in Australia** er beschloss, in Australien ein neues Leben zu beginnen

**angel** /ˈeɪndʒl/ *n.* Ⓐ (*lit. or fig.*) Engel, *der;* **evil ~:** böser Geist; **good ~:** guter Engel; **be on the side of the ~s** (*fig.*) auf der Seite der Guten stehen; **be an ~ and ...** (*coll.*) sei so lieb und ...; ⇒ *also* **guardian angel;** Ⓑ (*Commerc. coll.*) Finanzier, *der*

**angel:** **~ cake** *n., no pl.* Biskuitkuchen, *der;* **~ fish** *n.* Kaiserfisch, *der;* Engelfisch, *der*

**angelic** /ænˈdʒelɪk/ *adj.* Ⓐ (*of angel[s]*) Engels-; Ⓑ (*like angel[s]*) engelhaft; engelgleich (*geh.*); **an ~ child** ein Kind wie ein Engel; **she looked ~:** sie sah wie ein Engel aus

**angelica** /ænˈdʒelɪkə/ *n.* Ⓐ (*Bot., Cookery, Med.*) Angelika, *die;* Engelwurz, *die;* Ⓑ (*candied*) kandierte Angelika

**angelus** /ˈændʒɪləs/ *n.* (*RC Ch.*) Angelus, *der od. das;* **~ bell** Angelusläuten, *das*

**anger** /ˈæŋgə(r)/ ❶ *n., no pl.* (*wrath*) Zorn, *der* (**at** über + *Akk.*); (*fury*) Wut, *die* (**at** über + *Akk.*); **be filled with ~:** erzürnt/wütend sein; **in [a moment of] ~:** im Zorn/in der Wut. ❷ *v.t.* verärgern; (*infuriate*) erzürnen (*geh.*)/wütend machen; **be ~ed by sth.** über etw. (*Akk.*) verärgert/erzürnt/wütend sein

**angina [pectoris]** /ænˈdʒaɪnə (ˈpektərɪs)/ *n., no pl.* ▶ **1232** (*Med.*) Angina Pectoris, *die*

**angle**[1] ❶ *n.* Ⓐ (*Geom.*) Winkel, *der;* **acute/obtuse/right ~:** spitzer/stumpfer/rechter Winkel; **at an ~ of 60°** im Winkel von 60°; **at an ~:** schief; **at an ~ to the wall** schräg zur Wand; Ⓑ (*corner*) Ecke, *die;* (*recess*) Winkel, *der;* Ⓒ (*direction*) Perspektive, *die;* Blickwinkel, *der;* (*fig.*) Gesichtspunkt, *der;* Aspekt, *der;* **the photo isn't taken from a flattering ~:** die Aufnahme ist aus einem unvorteilhaften [Blick]winkel gemacht; **the committee examined the matter from various ~s** der Ausschuss prüfte die Angelegenheit von verschiedenen Seiten; **looking at it from a commercial ~:** aus kaufmännischer Sicht betrachtet

❷ *v.t.* Ⓐ [aus]richten; Ⓑ (*coll.: bias*) färben ‹Nachrichten, Formulierung›.

❸ *v.i.* [im Winkel] abbiegen; **the road ~s sharply to the left** die Straße biegt scharf nach links ab

**angle**[2] *v.i.* angeln; (*fig.*) **~ for sth.** sich um etw. bemühen; **~ for compliments** nach Komplimenten fischen; **~ for an opportunity** eine Gelegenheit suchen

**Angle** /ˈæŋgl/ *n.* Angehöriger/Angehörige des Volksstammes der Angeln; **the ~s** die Angeln

**ˈangle brackets** *n. pl.* spitze Klammern

**angled** /ˈæŋgəld/ *adj.* (*angular*) eckig ‹Form, Figur›; (*placed obliquely*) schief; (*fig.*) tendenziös, gefärbt ‹Bericht, Kommentar›; **acute-/obtuse-/right-~:** spitz-/stumpf-/rechtwinklig

**angle:** **~dozer** /ˈæŋgldəʊzə(r)/ *n.* Seitenräumer, *der;* **~ grinder** *n.* Winkelschleifer, *der;* (*with cutting disc*) Flex, *die;* **~ iron** *n.* Winkeleisen, *das;* **~-parking** *n.* Schrägparken, *das*

**angler** /ˈæŋglə(r)/ *n.* Ⓐ Angler, *der*/Anglerin, *die;* Ⓑ **~[fish]** Angler, *der;* Seeteufel, *der*

**Anglican** /ˈæŋglɪkən/ ❶ *adj.* anglikanisch. ❷ *n.* Anglikaner, *der*/Anglikanerin, *die*

**Anglicanism** /ˈæŋglɪkənɪzm/ *n., no pl.* Anglikanismus, *der*

a

**Anglicism** /'æŋglɪsɪzm/ *n.* Ⓐ (*word or idiom*) Anglizismus, *der;* Ⓑ (*Englishness*) englische Eigenart
**Anglicize** /'æŋglɪsaɪz/ *v.t.* anglisieren
**angling** /'æŋglɪŋ/ *n.* Angeln, *das*
**Anglist** /'æŋglɪst/ *n.* Anglist, *der*/Anglistin, *die*
**Anglistics** /æŋ'glɪstɪks/ *n., no pl.* Anglistik, *die*
**Anglo-** /æŋgləʊ/ *in comb.* anglo-/Anglo-; **he's an ~Cypriot** er ist Zyprer britischer Herkunft
**Anglo-A'merican** ▶ 1340 ❶ *adj.* angloamerikanisch; **an ~ agreement** ein englisch-/britisch-amerikanischer Vertrag. ❷ *n.* Angloamerikaner, *der*/Angloamerikanerin, *die*
**Anglo-'Catholic** ❶ *n.* Anglokatholik, *der*/Anglokatholikin, *die.* ❷ *adj.* anglokatholisch
**Anglo-'French** ❶ *adj.* englisch-/britisch-französisch; (*Ling.*) anglofranzösisch; anglonormannisch. ❷ *n.* (*Ling.*) Anglonormannisch, *das;* Anglofranzösisch, *das*
**Anglo-'German** *adj.* englisch-/britisch-deutsch
**Anglo-'Indian** ▶ 1340 ❶ *adj.* angloindisch. ❷ *n.* Anglo-Inder, *der*/Anglo-Inderin, *die*
**Anglomania** /æŋgləʊ'meɪnɪə/ *n.* Anglomanie, *die*
**Anglo-'Norman** ❶ *adj.* anglonormannisch. ❷ *n.* (*dialect*) Anglonormannisch, *das*
**Anglophile** /'æŋgləʊfaɪl/ ❶ *n.* Anglophile, *der/die.* ❷ *adj.* anglophil
**Anglophobia** /æŋgləʊ'fəʊbɪə/ *n.* Anglophobie, *die*
**anglophone** /'æŋgləʊfəʊn/ ❶ *adj.* anglophon. ❷ *n.* Anglophone, *der/die*
**Anglo-'Saxon** ▶ 1340 ❶ *n.* Angelsachse, *der*/Angelsächsin, *die;* (*language*) Angelsächsisch, *das;* (*Amer. coll.: English*) Englisch, *das.*
❷ *adj.* angelsächsisch; (*Amer. coll.: English*) englisch
**Angola** /æŋ'gəʊlə/ *pr. n.* Angola (*das*)
**Angolan** /æn'gəʊlən/ ▶ 1340 ❶ *adj.* angolanisch; **sb. is ~:** jmd. ist Angolaner/Angolanerin. ❷ *n.* Angolaner, *der*/Angolanerin, *die*
**angora** /æŋ'gɔ:rə/ *n.* Angora‹katze, -ziege, -kaninchen›; **~ [wool]** Angorawolle, *die;* Mohair, *der*
**angrily** /'æŋgrɪlɪ/ *adv.* verärgert; (*stronger*) zornig
**angry** /'æŋgrɪ/ *adj.* Ⓐ böse; verärgert ‹Person, Stimme, Geste›; (*stronger*) zornig; wütend; **be ~ at** *or* **about sth.** wegen etw. böse sein; **he was ~ at being asked** er war verärgert darüber, dass man ihn fragte; **be ~ with** *or* **at sb.** mit jmdm. *od.* auf jmdn. böse sein; sich über jmdn. ärgern; **be in an ~ mood** schlechter Laune *od.* böse sein; **get ~:** böse werden; **get** *or* **make sb. ~:** jmdn. verärgern; (*stronger*) jmdn. wütend machen; Ⓑ (*fig.*) drohend, bedrohlich ‹Wolke, Himmel›; Ⓒ (*inflamed and painful*) böse, schlimm ‹Riss, Wunde›; **an ~ red** eine entzündliche Röte
**angst** /æŋst/ *n.* neurotische Angst; (*remorse*) Schuldgefühl, *das*
**anguish** /'æŋgwɪʃ/ *n., no pl.* Qualen *Pl.;* **he shuddered with ~:** er erschauerte vor Schmerz
**anguished** /'æŋgwɪʃt/ *adj.* qualvoll; gequält ‹Herz, Gewissen›
**angular** /'æŋgjʊlə(r)/ *adj.* Ⓐ (*having angles*) eckig ‹Gebäude, Struktur, Gestalt›; Ⓑ (*lacking plumpness, stiff*) knochig ‹Körperbau›; kantig ‹Gesicht›; Ⓒ (*measured by angle*) angular; winklig; **~ momentum** (*Phys.*) Drehimpuls, *der;* Drall, *der;* **~ motion** (*Phys.*) Kreisbewegung, *die;* **~ velocity** (*Phys.*) Winkelgeschwindigkeit, *die;* (*Electr.*) Kreisfrequenz, *die;* (*Mech.*) Umlauf- *od.* Drehgeschwindigkeit, *die*
**angularity** /æŋgjʊ'lærɪtɪ/ *n., no pl.* Eckigkeit, *die;* **the ~ of his handwriting** seine eckige Handschrift
**anhydride** /æn'haɪdraɪd/ *n.* (*Chem.*) Anhydrid, *das*
**anhydrous** /æn'haɪdrəs/ *adj.* (*Chem.*) [kristall]wasserfrei; nichtwässrig

**aniline** /'ænɪli:n, 'ænɪlaɪn, 'ænɪlɪn/ *n.* Anilin, *das;* **~ dye** künstlicher Farbstoff, *der;* (*made from ~*) Anilinfarbstoff, *der*
**animal** /'ænɪməl/ ❶ *n.* Ⓐ Tier, *das;* (*quadruped*) Vierbeiner, *der;* (*any living being*) Lebewesen, *das;* **~ rights** *das Recht der Tiere auf Leben und Unversehrtheit;* **~ rights activists** aktive Tierschützer; **domestic ~:** Haustier, *das;* ⇒ *also* **kingdom** D; Ⓑ (*fig. coll.*) **there is no such ~ as a 'typical' criminal** so etwas wie den „typischen" Verbrecher gibt es gar nicht; **that's a queer sort of ~:** das ist 'ne Sorte für sich (*ugs.*); Ⓒ (*fig.: ~ instinct; brute*) Tier, *das;* **don't be such an ~!** benimm dich doch mal wie ein Mensch!
❷ *adj.* Ⓐ tierisch; **~ behaviour/breeding** Tierverhalten, *das*/Tierzucht, *die;* **~ spirits** Lebensfreude, *die;* Ⓑ (*from ~s*) tierisch ‹Produkt, Klebstoff, Öl›; Ⓒ (*carnal, sexual*) körperlich ‹Bedürfnisse, Triebe, Wünsche›; tierisch, animalisch ‹Veranlagung, Natur›
**animalcule** /ænɪ'mælkju:l/ *n.* Mikroorganismus, *der*
**animal: A~ Libe'ration Front** *n.* Tierbefreiungsfront, *die;* **~ lover** *n.* Tierfreund, *der*/-freundin, *die;* **~ pro'tectionist** *n.* Tierschützer, *der*/-schützerin, *die;* **~ 'rights** *n. pl.* Tierrechte *Pl.; attrib.* **~ rights supporter** Tierrechtler, *der*/Tierrechtlerin, *die*
**animate** ❶ /'ænɪmeɪt/ *v.t.* Ⓐ (*enliven*) beleben; Ⓑ (*inspire*) anregen; (*to do sth. mischievous*) animieren; **~ sb. with enthusiasm** jmdn. mit Begeisterung erfüllen; **he was ~d by a passion for truth** er war von einer leidenschaftlichen Wahrheitsliebe beseelt; Ⓒ (*breathe life into*) mit Leben erfüllen. ❷ /'ænɪmət/ *adj.* beseelt ‹Leben, Körper›; belebt ‹Objekt, Welt›; lebendig ‹Seele›
**animated** /'ænɪmeɪtɪd/ *adj.* lebhaft ‹Diskussion, Unterhaltung, Ausdruck, Gebärde›; lebendig ‹Darstellung›; **~ cartoon** Zeichentrickfilm, *der*
**animatedly** /'ænɪmeɪtɪdlɪ/ *adv.* lebhaft
**animation** /ænɪ'meɪʃn/ *n.* Ⓐ *no pl.* Lebhaftigkeit, *die;* Ⓑ (*Cinemat.*) Animation, *die*
**animator** /'ænɪmeɪtə(r)/ *n.* ▶ 1261 (*Cinemat.*) Animator, *der*/Animatorin, *die*
**animism** /'ænɪmɪzm/ *n., no pl.* (*Relig.*) Animismus, *der*
**animosity** /ænɪ'mɒsɪtɪ/ *n.* Animosität, *die* (*geh.*), Feindseligkeit, *die* (**against, towards** gegen)
**anion** /'ænaɪən/ *n.* (*Phys.*) Anion, *das*
**anise** /'ænɪs/ *n.* (*Bot.*) Anis, *der*
**aniseed** /'ænɪsi:d/ *n.* Anis[samen], *der*
**anisette** /ænɪ'zet/ *n.* Anislikör, *der;* Anisette, *der*
**ankle** /'æŋkl/ *n.* ▶ 966 (*joint*) Fußgelenk, *das;* (*part of leg*) Knöchelgegend, *die;* Fessel, *die*
**ankle: ~-deep** *adj.* knöcheltief; **~ sock** *n.* Socke, *die;* (*esp. for children*) Söckchen, *das*
**anklet** /'æŋklɪt/ *n.* Ⓐ Fußkettchen, *das;* Ⓑ (*Amer.*) ⇒ **ankle sock**
**annalist** /'ænəlɪst/ *n.* Annalist, *der*
**annals** /'ænəlz/ *n. pl.* (*lit. or fig.*) Annalen *Pl.;* **in the ~ of human history** in der Geschichte *od.* in den Annalen der Menschheit
**Anne** /æn/ *pr. n.* (*Hist., as name of ruler, saint, etc.*) Anna (*die*)
**anneal** /ə'ni:l/ *v.t.* ausglühen ‹Stahl›; kühlen ‹Glas›
**annelid** /'ænəlɪd/ *n.* (*Zool.*) Ringelwurm, *der*
**annex** ❶ /ə'neks/ *v.t.* Ⓐ (*add*) angliedern (**to** *Dat.*); anbauen ‹Gebäude›; (*append*) anfügen ‹Bemerkungen› (**to** *Dat.*); Ⓑ (*incorporate*) annektieren ‹Land, Territorium›; (*coll.: take without right*) sich (*Dat.*) unter den Nagel reißen (*ugs.*) ‹Gegenstände›; Ⓒ (*attach*) (*as an attribute*) zuschreiben (**to** *Dat.*); verbinden (**to** mit); (*as a condition*) verbinden (**to** mit); (*as a consequence*) binden, knüpfen (**to** an + *Akk.*).
❷ /'æneks/ *n.* (*supplementary building*) Anbau, *der;* Annexbau, *der* (*selten*); (*built-on extension*) Erweiterungsbau, *der;* (*appendix*) (*to document*) Zusatz, *der;* Annex, *der* (*geh.*); (*to treaty*) Anhang, *der;* Annex, *der* (*geh.*)
**annexation** /ænɪk'seɪʃn/ *n.* Ⓐ (*of land*) Annexion, *die;* Annektierung, *die;* Ⓑ (*as an attribute*) Verknüpfung, *die* (**to** mit)

**annexe** ⇒ **annex** 2
**annihilate** /ə'naɪəleɪt/ *v.t.* Ⓐ vernichten ‹Armee, Flotte, Bevölkerung, Menschheit›; zerstören ‹Stadt, Land›; Ⓑ (*fig.*) zunichte machen; am Boden zerstören ‹Person›
**annihilation** /ənaɪə'leɪʃn/ *n.* Ⓐ ⇒ **annihilate**: Vernichtung, *die;* Zerstörung, *die;* (*fig.*) Verderben, *das;* Untergang, *der;* **the party's ~:** der Untergang der Partei; Ⓑ (*Phys.*) Paarvernichtung, *die*
**anniversary** /ænɪ'vɜ:sərɪ/ *n.* Jahrestag, *der;* **wedding ~:** Hochzeitstag, *der;* **the university celebrated its 500th ~:** die Universität feierte ihr 500jähriges Jubiläum *od.* Bestehen; **the ~ of Shakespeare's birth** [die Wiederkehr von] Shakespeares Geburtstag; **the ~ of his death** sein Todestag
**Anno Domini** /ænəʊ 'dɒmɪnaɪ/ ❶ *adv.* ▶ 1055 nach Christi Geburt; **~ 62** [im Jahre] 62 nach Christi Geburt. ❷ *n.* (*coll.*) das Alter
**annotate** /'ænəteɪt/ *v.t.* kommentieren; mit Anmerkungen versehen
**annotation** /ænə'teɪʃn/ *n.* (*act*) Kommentierung, *die;* (*comment*) Anmerkung, *die*
**announce** /ə'naʊns/ *v.t.* bekannt geben; ansagen ‹Programm›; (*over Tannoy etc.*) durchsagen; (*in newspaper*) anzeigen ‹Heirat usw.›; (*make known the approach of; fig.: signify*) ankündigen
**announcement** /ə'naʊnsmənt/ *n.* Bekanntgabe, *die;* (*over Tannoy etc.*) Durchsage, *die;* **they made an ~ over the radio that ...:** sie gaben im Radio bekannt, dass ...; **did you read the ~ of his death in the paper?** haben Sie seine Todesanzeige in der Zeitung gelesen?
**announcer** /ə'naʊnsə(r)/ *n.* ▶ 1261 Ansager, *der*/Ansagerin, *die;* Sprecher, *der*/Sprecherin, *die*
**annoy** /ə'nɔɪ/ *v.t.* Ⓐ ärgern; **his late arrival ~ed me** ich habe mich über sein spätes Kommen geärgert; **her remarks ~ everybody** ihre Bemerkungen sind allen lästig; Ⓑ (*harass*) schikanieren
**annoyance** /ə'nɔɪəns/ *n.* Verärgerung, *die;* (*nuisance*) Plage, *die;* **[much] to my/his ~:** [sehr] zu meiner/seiner Verärgerung; **a look of ~:** ein Blick der Verärgerung; **having a pub next door to one's house is a constant ~:** wenn man eine Kneipe nebenan hat, ist das ein ständiges Ärgernis
**annoyed** /ə'nɔɪd/ *adj.* **be ~ [at** *or* **with sb./sth.]** ärgerlich [auf *od.* über jmdn./über etw.] sein; **be ~ to find that ...:** sich darüber ärgern, dass ...; **he got very ~:** er hat sich darüber sehr geärgert
**annoying** /ə'nɔɪɪŋ/ *adj.* ärgerlich; lästig ‹Gewohnheit, Person›; **the ~ part of it is that ...:** das Ärgerliche daran *od.* was einen daran ärgert ist, dass ...
**annual** /'ænjʊəl/ ❶ *adj.* Ⓐ (*reckoned by the year*) Jahres-; **~ income/subscription/rent/turnover/production/leave/salary** Jahreseinkommen, *das*/-abonnement, *das*/-miete, *die*/-umsatz, *der*/-produktion, *die*/-urlaub, *der*/-gehalt, *das;* **~ rainfall** jährliche Regenmenge; Ⓑ (*recurring yearly*) [all]jährlich ‹Ereignis, Feier›; Jahres‹bericht, -hauptversammlung›; Ⓒ (*Bot.*) einjährig, (*fachspr.*) annuell ‹Pflanze›; **~ ring** (*Bot.*) Jahresring, *der.*
❷ *n.* Ⓐ (*Bot.*) einjährige Pflanze; Ⓑ (*Bibliog.*) Jahrbuch, *das;* Jahresschrift, *die;* (*of comic etc.*) Jahresalbum, *das*
**annually** /'ænjʊəlɪ/ *adv.* (*per year*) jährlich; (*once a year*) [all]jährlich
**annuity** /ə'nju:ɪtɪ/ *n.* (*grant, sum payable*) Jahresrente, *die;* (*investment*) Rentenversicherung, *die*
**annul** /ə'nʌl/ *v.t.*, **-ll-** (*abolish*) annullieren, für ungültig erklären ‹Gesetz, Vertrag, Ehe, Testament›; auflösen ‹Vertrag›
**annular** /'ænjʊlə(r)/ *adj.* ringartig; ringförmig
**annulment** /ə'nʌlmənt/ *n.* (*of law, treaty, marriage, will*) Annullierung, *die;* (*of treaty also*) Auflösung, *die*
**Annunciation** /ənʌnsɪ'eɪʃn/ *n.* Ⓐ (*Eccl.*) **the ~:** Mariä Verkündigung; **Feast of the ~:**

Fest der Verkündigung Mariä; (B) **a~** Ankündigung, *die*

**annunciator** /əˈnʌnsɪeɪtə(r)/ *n.* (*indicator*) [elektrische] Anzeige

**annus mirabilis** /ænəs mɪˈrɑːbɪlɪs/ *n., no pl.* Wunderjahr, *das;* wundersames Jahr

**anode** /ˈænəʊd/ *n.* (*Electr.*) Anode, *die*

**anodize** /ˈænədaɪz/ *v.t.* anodisieren; **anodizing** anodische Behandlung

**anodyne** /ˈænədaɪn/ ❶ *adj.* (*Med.*) schmerzstillend; analgetisch (*fachspr.*); (*fig.*) wohltuend; (*soothing*) einlullend; **the ~ aspects of modern life** die Segnungen des modernen Lebens (*iron.*). ❷ *n.* (*Med.*) Schmerzmittel, *das;* Analgetikum, *das;* (*fig.*) Wohltat, *die*

**anoint** /əˈnɔɪnt/ *v.t.* (*esp. Relig.*) salben; **~ sb. king** jmdn. zum König salben

**anomalous** /əˈnɒmələs/ *adj.* (A) (*abnormal*) anomal, anormal ‹Lage, Verhältnisse, Zustand›; ungewöhnlich ‹Situation, Anblick›; (B) (*Ling.: irregular*) unregelmäßig

**anomalously** /əˈnɒmələslɪ/ *adv.* (A) außergewöhnlich; (B) (*Ling.*) unregelmäßig ‹deklinieren, konjugieren›

**anomaly** /əˈnɒməlɪ/ *n.* Anomalie, *die;* Absonderlichkeit, *die;* (*exception*) Ausnahme, *die*

**anon** /əˈnɒn/ *adv.* (A) (*arch./literary: soon*) bald; (B) (*coll.: later*) später; **more of that ~!** mehr davon später!; **see you ~:** bis später [dann]

**anon.** /əˈnɒn/ *abbr.* **anonymous [author]** anon.

**anonymity** /ænəˈnɪmɪtɪ/ *n.* Anonymität, *die*

**anonymous** /əˈnɒnɪməs/ *adj.* anonym

**anonymously** /əˈnɒnɪməslɪ/ *adv.* anonym; **he phoned ~:** er machte einen anonymen Anruf; **he dresses rather ~:** er kleidet sich sehr unauffällig

**anorak** /ˈænəræk/ *n.* Anorak, *der*

**anorexia** /ænəˈreksɪə/ *n.* Anorexie, *die* (*Med.*); Appetitlosigkeit, *die;* Magersucht, *die* (*volkst.*); **~ nervosa** /ænəreksɪə nɜːˈvəʊsə/ nervöse Anorexie (*Med.*); Anorexia nervosa, *die* (*Med.*)

**anorexic** /ænəˈreksɪk/ *adj.* anorektisch (*fachspr.*); magersüchtig; **be ~:** an Anorexie (*Med.*) *od.* Magersucht leiden

**another** /əˈnʌðə(r)/ ❶ *pron.* (A) (*additional*) noch einer/eine/eins; ein weiterer/eine weitere/ein weiteres; **yet ~:** noch einer/eine/eins; **one thing leads to ~:** eines ergibt sich aus dem anderen; **We have lots of apples. Please have ~:** Wir haben eine ganze Menge Äpfel. Nimm dir doch noch einen; **send a copy to the customer and keep ~ for reference** schicken Sie eine Kopie an den Kunden, und eine weitere nehmen Sie für unsere Unterlagen; **there's one school in the neighbourhood already and ~ [which is] being built** es gibt schon eine Schule in der Gegend, und eine zweite ist gerade im Bau; (B) (*counterpart*) wieder einer/eine/eins; **such ~:** noch so einer/so eine/so eins; (C) (*Brit. Law*) **X versus Y and ~:** X gegen Y und andere; (D) (*different*) ein anderer/eine andere/ein anderes; **she ran off with/married ~:** sie brannte mit einem anderen durch (*ugs.*)/heiratete einen anderen; **making a mistake is one thing, but lying deliberately is quite ~:** einen Fehler zu machen ist eine Sache, aber absichtlich zu lügen ist ganz etwas anderes; **they said one to ~:** sie sagten zueinander; **in one way or ~:** so oder so; irgendwie; **for one reason or ~:** aus irgendeinem Grund; **A. N. Other** (*Brit.*) N. N.; ⇒ *also* **one** 1 F, 3 B.
❷ *adj.* (A) (*additional*) noch einer/eine/eins; ein weiterer/eine weitere/ein weiteres; **give me ~ chance** gib mir noch [einmal] eine Chance; **after ~ six weeks** nach weiteren sechs Wochen; **~ 100 pounds** weitere 100 Pfund; **he didn't say ~ word** er sagte nichts mehr; **he hasn't ~ day to live** er hat keinen Tag länger zu leben; **he hasn't ~ penny left** er hat keinen Pfennig mehr; **it'll take ~ few years** es wird noch ein paar Jahre [länger] dauern; (B) (*a person like*) ein neuer/eine neue/ein neues; ein zweiter/eine zweite/ein zweites; **~ Chaplin** ein neuer *od.* zweiter Chaplin; (C) (*different*) ein anderer/eine andere/ein anderes; **ask ~ person** fragen Sie jemand anderen *od.* anders; **~ time, don't be so greedy** sei beim nächsten Mal nicht so gierig; **I'll do it ~ time** ich tu's ein andermal; **[and] [there's] ~ thing** [und] noch etwas; **it's one thing to make a request, ~ thing to order** zu bitten ist eine Sache, zu befehlen eine andere; **that's quite ~ problem** das ist wieder ein anderes Problem; **~ place** (*Brit. Parl.*) die andere Kammer [dieses Parlaments]; ⇒ *also* **tomorrow** A

**anschluss** /ˈænʃlʊs/ *n.* (*Hist.*) Anschluss, *der;* **the ~ of Austria by Germany** der Anschluss Österreichs [an Deutschland]

**answer** /ˈɑːnsə(r)/ ❶ *n.* (A) (*reply*) Antwort, *die* (**to** auf + *Akk.*); (*reaction*) Reaktion, *die;* **I tried to phone him, but there was no ~:** ich habe versucht, ihn anzurufen, aber es hat sich niemand gemeldet; **do you have any ~ to the accusations made against you?** haben Sie irgendetwas auf die Anschuldigungen gegen Sie zu erwidern?; **there is no ~ to that** dem ist nichts mehr hinzuzufügen; **by way of [an] ~:** als Antwort; **in ~ to sth.** als Antwort *od.* Reaktion auf etw. (*Akk.*); **he always has an ~ [ready]** er hat immer eine Antwort parat; **make ~** (*formal*) [eine] Antwort geben; (B) (*to problem*) Lösung, *die* (**to** *Gen.*); (*to calculation*) Ergebnis, *das;* **have** *or* **know all the ~s** (*coll.*) alles wissen.
❷ *v.t.* (A) beantworten ‹Brief, Frage›; antworten auf (+ *Akk.*) ‹Frage, Hilferuf, Einladung, Inserat›; (*react to*) erwidern ‹Geste, Schlag›; (*respond to*) eingehen auf (+ *Akk.*) ‹Angebot, Vorschlag›; eingehen auf (+ *Akk.*), erfüllen ‹Bitte›; sich stellen zu ‹Beschuldigung›; erhören ‹Gebet›; erfüllen ‹Wunsch›; **~ sb.** jmdm. antworten; **~ me!** antworte [mir]!; **~ a question** eine Frage beantworten; auf eine Frage antworten; (B) **~ the door/bell** an die Tür gehen; (C) (*be satisfactory for*) genügen (+ *Dat.*); entsprechen (+ *Dat.*); **the flat ~ed his purpose very well** die Wohnung entsprach *od.* genügte seinen Anforderungen vollauf; **her desires were fully ~ed** ihren Wünschen wurde vollauf entsprochen; ⇒ *also* **telephone** 1.
❸ *v.i.* (A) (*reply*) antworten; **~ to sth.** sich zu etw. äußern; (B) (*be responsible*) **~ for sth.** für etw. die Verantwortung übernehmen; **~ to sb.** jmdm. [gegenüber] Rechenschaft ablegen; **one day you will have to ~ for your crimes** eines Tages wirst du dich für deine Verbrechen verantworten müssen; **he has a lot to ~ for** er hat vieles zu verantworten; (C) (*correspond*) **~ to a description** einer Beschreibung (*Dat.*) entsprechen; (D) (*be satisfactory*) **~ for a purpose/intention** sich für einen Zweck/ein Vorhaben eignen; (E) **~ to the name of ...:** auf den Namen ... hören

**~ ˈback** *v.i.* widersprechen; Widerworte haben (*ugs.*); **he's always ready to ~ back** er gibt einem gern Kontra (*ugs.*); **don't ~ back!** keine Widerworte!

**answerable** /ˈɑːnsərəbl/ *adj.* (*responsible*) **be ~ to sb.** jmdm. [gegenüber] verantwortlich sein; **be ~ for sb./sth.** für jmdn./etw. verantwortlich sein

**answering: ~ machine** *n.* (*Teleph.*) Anrufbeantworter, *der;* **~ service** *n.* (*Teleph.*) Fernsprechauftragsdienst, *der*

**ˈanswerphone** (*Brit.*) ⇒ **answering machine**

**ant** /ænt/ *n.* Ameise, *die;* **white ~:** Termite, *die;* weiße Ameise (*volkst.*); **have ~s in one's pants** (*coll.*) nicht stillsitzen können

**antacid** /ænˈtæsɪd/ ❶ *n.* Antazidum, *das.* ❷ *adj.* Magensäure bindend

**antagonism** /ænˈtægənɪzm/ *n.* Feindseligkeit, *die* (**towards, against** gegenüber); (*between two*) Antagonismus, *der* (*geh.*); **the ~ between the two families** die Feindschaft zwischen den beiden Familien

**antagonist** /ænˈtægənɪst/ *n.* Gegner, *der*/Gegnerin, *die;* (*in debate etc.*) Kontrahent, *der*/Kontrahentin, *die*

**antagonistic** /æntægəˈnɪstɪk/ *adj.* feindlich ‹Mächte, Prinzipien›; feindselig ‹Kritik›; antagonistisch, gegensätzlich ‹Interessen›; **be ~ towards sth.** gegen etw. eingestellt sein; **be ~ towards sb.** jmdn. anfeinden

**antagonize** /ænˈtægənaɪz/ *v.t.* (A) (*evoke hostility or enmity of*) sich (*Dat.*) zum Feind machen; vor den Kopf stoßen (*ugs.*); (B) (*counteract*) entgegenwirken (+ *Dat.*); **~ one another** sich gegenseitig bekämpfen

**antarctic** /æntˈɑːktɪk/ ❶ *adj.* antarktisch; **A~ explorer** Antarktisforscher, *der;* **A~ Circle/Ocean** südlicher Polarkreis/Südpolarmeer, *das.* ❷ *pr. n.* **the A~:** die Antarktis

**Antarctica** /æntˈɑːktɪkə/ *pr. n.* die Antarktis

**ante** /ˈæntɪ/ ❶ *n.* (*in poker etc.*) Einsatz, *der;* **up the ~** (*fig. coll.*) den Einsatz erhöhen. ❷ *v.t.* setzen; **~ [up] £10** 10 Pfund setzen; **can you ~ up £1,000 to buy this plot of land?** können Sie 1000 Pfund zum Kauf dieses Grundstücks aufbringen?

**ˈanteater** *n.* (*Zool.*) Ameisenfresser, *der*

**antecedent** /æntɪˈsiːdənt/ ❶ *adj.* vorher-, vorausgehend ‹Faktoren, Elemente, Prinzipien›; **be ~ to sth.** einer Sache (*Dat.*) vorausgehen. ❷ *n.* (A) (*preceding event*) früherer Umstand; vorangegangenes Ereignis; (*preceding thing*) Vorläufer, *der;* (B) *in pl.* (*past history*) **sb.'s ~s** jmds. Vorleben

**antechamber** /ˈæntɪtʃeɪmbə(r)/ *n.* Vorzimmer, *das*

**antedate** /æntɪˈdeɪt/ *v.t.* (A) (*precede*) voraus-, vorangehen (+ *Dat.*); (B) (*give earlier date to*) zurückdatieren

**antediluvian** /æntɪdɪˈljuːvɪən, æntɪdɪˈluːvɪən/ *adj.* (*lit. or fig.*) vorsintflutlich

**antelope** /ˈæntɪləʊp/ *n.* (A) (*Zool.*) Antilope, *die;* (B) (*leather*) Antilopenleder, *das*

**antenatal** /æntɪˈneɪtl/ *adj.* (A) (*concerning pregnancy*) Schwangerschafts-; Schwangeren-; **~ care** Schwangerenfürsorge, *die;* **~ clinic** Klinik für werdende Mütter; (B) (*before birth*) vorgeburtlich; prä- *od.* antenatal (*fachspr.*)

**antenna** /ænˈtenə/ *n.* (A) *pl.* **~e** /ænˈteniː/ (*Zool.*) Fühler, *der;* Antenne, *die* (*fachspr.*); (B) *pl.* **~s** (*tech, Amer.: aerial*) Antenne, *die*

**antepenultimate** /æntɪpɪˈnʌltɪmət/ *adj.* drittletzt...

**ante-post** /æntɪˈpəʊst/ *adj.* (*Horseracing*) **~ betting** Wetten vor dem Renntag

**anterior** /ænˈtɪərɪə(r)/ *adj.* (A) (*to the front*) vorder...; **be in an ~ position** vorn sein; (B) (*prior*) früher...; **be ~ to sth.** einer Sache (*Dat.*) vorausgehen

**ante-room** /ˈæntɪruːm, ˈæntɪrʊm/ *n.* Vorraum, *der;* (*waiting room*) Warteraum, *der*

**antheap** /ˈænthiːp/ *n.* Ameisenhaufen, *der;* Ameisenhügel, *der;* **this human ~** (*fig.*) dieses Menschengewimmel

**anthem** /ˈænθəm/ *n.* (A) (*Eccl. Mus.*) Chorgesang, *der;* (B) (*song of praise*) Jubel-, Preisgesang, *der* (*geh.*); Hymne, *die;* ⇒ *also* **national anthem**

**anther** /ˈænθə(r)/ *n.* (*Bot.*) Staubbeutel, *der*

**anthill** /ˈænthɪl/ ⇒ **antheap**

**anthologist** /ænˈθɒlədʒɪst/ *n.* Herausgeber, *der*/Herausgeberin, *die* [einer Anthologie/von Anthologien]

**anthology** /ænˈθɒlədʒɪ/ *n.* (*of poetry, prose, songs*) (*by different writers*) Anthologie, *die;* (*by one writer*) Auswahl, *die*

**anthracite** /ˈænθrəsaɪt/ *n.* Anthrazit, *der*

**anthrax** /ˈænθræks/ *n., no pl., no indef. art.* ▶ 1232 (*Med., Vet. Med.*) Milzbrand, *der;* Anthrax, *der* (*fachspr.*)

**anthropocentric** /ænθrəpəʊˈsentrɪk/ *adj.* anthropozentrisch

**anthropoid** /ˈænθrəpɔɪd/ ❶ *adj.* (A) (*manlike*) menschenähnlich; anthropoid; **~ ape** Menschenaffe, *der;* (B) (*coll. derog.: apelike*) affenartig (*abwertend*). ❷ *n.* Anthropoid[e], *der;* Menschenaffe, *der*

**anthropological** /ænθrəpəˈlɒdʒɪkl/ *adj.* anthropologisch

**anthropologist** /ænθrəˈpɒlədʒɪst/ *n.* ▶ 1261 Anthropologe, *der*/Anthropologin, *die*

**anthropology** /ænθrəˈpɒlədʒɪ/ *n., no pl.* Anthropologie, *die*

**anthropomorphic** /ænθrəpəʊˈmɔːfɪk/ *adj.* anthropomorphisch

a

**anti** /'æntɪ/ ❶ *prep.* gegen; **be ~ sth.** gegen etw. sein; Gegner von etw. sein. ❷ *adj.* ablehnend; **young people are all so ~ these days** die jungen Leute heutzutage sind gegen alles *od.* lehnen einfach alles ab. ❸ *n.* Gegner, *der;* Widersacher, *der*

**anti-** /æntɪ/ *pref.* anti-/Anti-

**anti: ~-a'bortion** *attrib. adj.* **~-abortion protester** Abtreibungsgegner, *der*/Abtreibungsgegnerin, *die;* **~-abortion protest/law** Protest/Gesetz gegen Abtreibung; **~-abortion demonstration/movement** Antiabtreibungsdemonstration, *die*/-bewegung, *die;* **~-abortionist** /æntɪə'bɔːʃənɪst/ *n.* Abtreibungsgegner, *der*/-gegnerin, *die;* **~-'aircraft** *adj.* (*Mil.*) Flugabwehr-; **~-aircraft gun** Flak, *die;* **~-aircraft battery** Flakbatterie, *die*

**antibiotic** /æntɪbaɪ'ɒtɪk/ ❶ *adj.* antibiotisch. ❷ *n.* Antibiotikum, *das*

**'antibody** *n.* (*Physiol.*) Antikörper, *der*

**antic** /'æntɪk/ *n.* (*trick*) Mätzchen, *das* (*ugs.*); (*of clown*) Possen, *der*

**Antichrist** /'æntɪkraɪst/ *n.* Antichrist, *der*

**anticipate** /æn'tɪsɪpeɪt/ *v.t.* Ⓐ (*expect*) erwarten; (*foresee*) voraussehen; **~ rain/trouble** mit Regen/Ärger rechnen; Ⓑ (*discuss or consider before due time*) vorwegnehmen; antizipieren; **don't ~ your income** gib dein Einkommen nicht im Voraus aus; Ⓒ (*forestall*) **~ sb./sth.** jmdm./einer Sache zuvorkommen

**anticipation** /æntɪsɪ'peɪʃn/ *n., no pl.* Erwartung, *die;* **in ~ of sth.** in Erwartung einer Sache (*Gen.*); **she was looking forward to the event with ~:** sie sah dem Ereignis erwartungsvoll entgegen; **thanking you in ~:** Ihnen im Voraus dankend

**anticipatory** /æn'tɪsɪpətərɪ/ *adj.* vorwegnehmend

**anti'clerical** *adj.* antiklerikal; kirchenfeindlich

**anticli'mactic** *adj.* [auf enttäuschende Weise] abfallend; **the film has an ~ ending** der Film hat ein enttäuschendes Ende

**anti'climax** *n.* Ⓐ (*ineffective end*) Abstieg, *der;* Abfall, *der;* Ⓑ (*Lit.*) Antiklimax, *die*

**anti'clockwise** ❶ *adv.* gegen den Uhrzeigersinn. ❷ *adj.* gegen den *od.* entgegen dem Uhrzeigersinn *nachgestellt;* linksläufig (*Technik*); **in an ~ direction** gegen den *od.* entgegen dem Uhrzeigersinn

**anticor'rosive** *adj.* Rostschutz-

**anti'cyclone** *n.* (*Meteorol.*) Hochdruckgebiet, *das;* Antizyklone, *die* (*Met.*)

**antidepressant** /æntɪdɪ'presənt/ *n.* (*Med.*) Antidepressivum, *das*

**antidote** /'æntɪdəʊt/ *n.* Gegengift, -mittel, *das* (**for, against** gegen); (*fig.*) Gegenmittel, *das* (**to** gegen)

**'antifreeze** *n.* Gefrierschutzmittel, *das;* Frostschutzmittel, *das*

**antigen** /'æntɪdʒən/ *n.* (*Physiol.*) Antigen, *das*

**'anti-hero** *n.* Antiheld, *der*

**anti'histamine** *n.* (*Med.*) Antihistamin[ikum], *das*

**'antiknock** *n.* (*Motor Veh.*) Antiklopfmittel, *das*

**Antilles** /æn'tɪliːz/ *pr. n. pl.* Antillen *Pl.*

**'anti-lock** *adj.* Antiblockier-; **~ brake** *or* **braking system** Antiblockiersystem, *das*

**antimacassar** /æntɪmə'kæsə(r)/ *n.* Schonbezug, *der*

**'antimatter** *n.* (*Phys.*) Antimaterie, *die*

**antimony** /'æntɪmənɪ/ *n.* Antimon, *das*

**antinomy** /æn'tɪnəmɪ/ *n.* Antinomie, *die*

**'anti-novel** *n.* Antiroman, *der*

**anti'nuclear** *adj.* Anti-Atom[kraft]-

**'antiparticle** *n.* (*Phys.*) Antiteilchen, *das*

**antipathetic** /æntɪpə'θetɪk/, **antipathetical** /æntɪpə'θetɪkl/ *adj.* Ⓐ (*averse, opposed*) **be ~ to sb./sth.** jmdm./einer Sache abgeneigt sein; eine Antipathie gegen jmdn./etw. haben; Ⓑ (*arousing antipathy*) **be ~ to sb.** jmdm. zuwider sein

**antipathy** /æn'tɪpəθɪ/ *n.* Antipathie, *die;* Abneigung, *die;* **~ to** *or* **for sb./sth.** Abneigung gegen jmdn./etw.

**anti-person'nel** *adj.* gegen Menschen gerichtet; **~ bomb** Splitterbombe, *die;* **~ mine** Schützenmine, *die*

**antiperspirant** /æntɪ'pɜːspɪrənt/ ❶ *adj.* schweißhemmend; **~ spray** Deodorantspray, *der od. das.* ❷ *n.* Antitranspirant, *das*

**antiphonal** /æn'tɪfənəl/ *adj.* (*Eccl. Mus.*) **~ singing** Wechselgesang, *der*

**antipodal** /æn'tɪpədl/ *adj.* (*Australasian*) australisch und ozeanisch

**antipodean** /æntɪpə'diːən/ *adj.* ⇒ **antipodal**

**antipodes** /æn'tɪpədiːz/ *n. pl.* entgegengesetzte *od.* antipodische Teile der Erde; (*Australasia*) Australien und Ozeanien

**'antipope** *n.* (*Hist.*) Gegenpapst, *der*

**antiquarian** /æntɪ'kweərɪən/ ❶ *adj.* Ⓐ (*of antiquity*) antik; Altertums-; **~ research** Altertumsforschung, *die;* **~ writings** antike Schriften; **~ society** Gesellschaft für Altertumsforschung; Ⓑ **~ bookshop** *or* **bookseller's** Antiquariat, *das;* Antiquariatsbuchhandlung, *die;* **~ bookseller** ▶ **1261** Antiquar, *der;* Antiquariatsbuchhändler, *der.* ❷ *n.* (*collector*) Antiquitätensammler, *der*

**antiquarianism** /æntɪ'kweərɪənɪzm/ *n., no pl.* Liebhaberei für Altertümer; Altertümelei, *die* (*auch abwertend*)

**antiquary** /'æntɪkwərɪ/ ⇒ **antiquarian 2**

**antiquated** /'æntɪkweɪtɪd/ *adj.* (*old-fashioned*) antiquiert; veraltet; (*out of date*) überholt

**antique** /æn'tiːk/ ❶ *adj.* Ⓐ antik ‹Möbel, Schmuck usw.›; (*as an ~*) antiquarisch ‹Wert, Bedeutung›; **furniture of ~ design** Möbel im antiken Stil; Ⓑ (*existing since old times*) antik ‹Philosophie, Literatur, Kultur, Volk, Kunst, Ideen›; (*antiquated*) altertümlich ‹Sprache, Ansicht, Verhalten›. ❷ *n.* ▶ **1261** Antiquität, *die;* **~ dealer** Antiquitätenhändler, *der*/-händlerin, *die;* **~ shop** Antiquitätenladen, *der*

**antiquity** /æn'tɪkwɪtɪ/ *n.* Ⓐ *no pl.* (*ancientness*) Alter, *das;* **a city/law/fossil of great ~:** eine uralte Stadt/ein uraltes Gesetz/Fossil; Ⓑ *no pl., no art.* (*old times*) Altertum, *das;* Antike, *die;* (*the ancients*) Antike, *die;* **in ~:** im Altertum; in der Antike; Ⓒ *in pl.* (*ancient relics*) Altertümer *Pl.;* (*ancient customs*) altertümliche Bräuche

**anti-'roll bar** ⇒ **roll bar**

**antirrhinum** /æntɪ'raɪnəm/ *n.* (*Bot.*) Löwenmaul, *das*

**anti-'Semite** *n.* Antisemit, *der*/-semitin, *die;* Judenfeind, *der*/-feindin, *die*

**anti-Se'mitic** *adj.* antisemitisch; judenfeindlich

**anti-Semitism** /æntɪ'semɪtɪzm/ *n., no pl.* Antisemitismus, *der;* Judenhass, *der*

**anti'sepsis** *n., no pl.* (*Med.*) Antisepsis, *die*

**anti'septic** ❶ *adj.* Ⓐ antiseptisch; keimtötend; Ⓑ (*scrupulously clean*) aseptisch; keimfrei; (*sterile*) keimfrei; steril; (*fig.: unfeeling*) gefühllos. ❷ *n.* Antiseptikum, *das*

**anti'social** *adj.* Ⓐ asozial; Ⓑ (*unsociable*) ungesellig ‹Person›; unwirtlich ‹Ort›

**anti'static** *adj.* antistatisch

**anti-'tank gun** *n.* (*Mil.*) Panzerabwehrkanone, *die*

**anti: ~-'terrorist** *attrib. adj.* antiterroristisch; **~-'theft** *attrib. adj.* Antidiebstahl-

**antithesis** /æn'tɪθəsɪs/ *n., pl.* **antitheses** /æn'tɪθəsiːz/ Ⓐ (*thing*) Gegenstück, *das* (**of,** to zu); **these two concepts are the ~ of each other** diese beiden Begriffe sind Gegensätze; Ⓑ (*state*) Gegensatz, *der;* (*Rhet.: contrast of ideas*) Antithese, *die;* **stand in ~ to sth.** einer Sache (*Dat.*) antithetisch gegenüberstehen; **the ~ of** *or* **between two things** der Gegensatz zwischen zwei Dingen

**antithetic** /æntɪ'θetɪk/, **antithetical** /æntɪ'θetɪkl/ *adj.* Ⓐ (*opposite*) gegensätzlich; (*consisting of opposites*) antithetisch; **be ~ to sth.** zu etw. einer Sache im Gegensatz stehen; Ⓑ (*Rhet.*) antithetisch

**anti: ~'toxin** *n.* (*Med.*) Antitoxin, *das;* **~'trust** *adj.* (*Amer.*) Kartell-; Antitrust-; **~trust law** Kartellgesetz, *das;* **~'virus** *attrib. adj.* (*Computing*) Antivirus-; **~virus software** Antivirensoftware, *die*

**antivivisectionism** /æntɪvɪvɪ'sekʃənɪzm/ *n., no pl.* Ablehnung der Vivisektion

**antivivisectionist** /æntɪvɪvɪ'sekʃənɪst/ *n.* Vivisektionsgegner, *der*/-gegnerin, *die*

**antler** /'æntlə(r)/ *n.* (*branch of horn*) Geweihsprosse, *die;* (*horn*) Stange, *die* (*Jägerspr.*); **a pair of ~s** ein Geweih *od.* (*Jägerspr.*) Gehörn

**antonym** /'æntənɪm/ *n.* Antonym, *das;* Gegen[satz]wort, *das*

**antonymous** /æn'tɒnɪməs/ *adj.* antonym

**Antwerp** /'æntwɜːp/ *pr. n.* ▶ **1626** Antwerpen (*das*)

**anus** /'eɪnəs/ *n.* (*Anat.*) After, *der;* Anus, *der*

**anvil** /'ænvɪl/ *n.* (*also Anat.*) Amboss, *der*

**anxiety** /æŋ'zaɪətɪ/ *n.* Ⓐ (*state*) Angst, *die;* (*concern about future*) Sorge, *die* (**about** wegen); **anxieties** Sorgen *Pl.;* **cause sb. ~:** jmdm. Angst/Sorgen machen; Ⓑ (*desire*) Verlangen, *das* (**for** nach); **his ~ to do sth.** sein Verlangen danach, etw. zu tun

**anxious** /'æŋkʃəs/ *adj.* Ⓐ (*troubled*) besorgt; **days of ~ waiting** Tage bangen Wartens; **be ~ about sth./sb.** um etw./jmdn. besorgt sein; **we were all so ~ about you** wir haben uns (*Dat.*) alle solche Sorgen um Sie gemacht; Ⓑ (*eager*) sehnlich; **be ~ for sth.** ungeduldig auf etw. (*Akk.*) warten; **have an ~ desire to do sth.** ängstlich darauf bedacht sein, etw. zu tun; **he is ~ to please** er ist bemüht zu gefallen; **he is ~ to learn another language** er will unbedingt noch eine Sprache lernen; Ⓒ (*worrying*) **an ~ time** eine Zeit banger Sorge; **two ~ days of waiting** zwei Tage bangen Wartens

**anxiously** /'æŋkʃəslɪ/ *adv.* Ⓐ besorgt; Ⓑ (*eagerly*) sehnsüchtig; **always ~ eager to help** immer eifrig darauf bedacht, zu helfen

**any** /'enɪ/ ❶ *adj.* Ⓐ (*some*) [irgend]ein/eine; **have you ~ wool/~ statement to make?** haben Sie Wolle/[irgend]eine Erklärung abzugeben?; **if you have ~ difficulties** wenn du irgendwelche Schwierigkeiten hast; **not ~:** kein/keine; **that isn't ~ way to behave** das ist keine Art, sich zu benehmen; **without ~:** ohne jeden/jede/jedes; **if you've ~ spare time** *or* **time to spare** wenn du Zeit hast *od.* hättest; **we haven't ~ time to lose** wir haben keine Zeit zu verlieren; **have you ~ idea of the time?** hast du eine Ahnung, wie spät es ist?; **~ news of Peter yet?** schon was von Peter gehört?; Ⓑ (*one*) ein/eine; **there isn't ~ hood on this coat** dieser Mantel hat keine Kapuze; **a book without ~ cover** ein Buch ohne Deckel; Ⓒ (*all*) jeder/jede/jedes; **to avoid ~ delay** um jede Verzögerung zu vermeiden; Ⓓ (*every*) jeder/jede/jedes; **~ and every** jeder/jede/jedes beliebige; **~ fool knows that!** das weiß doch jedes Kind!; **~ time** *or* **on ~ occasion [when] I went there** jedes Mal *od.* immer, wenn ich dorthin ging; **[at] ~ time** jederzeit; **[at] ~ time of day** zu jeder Tageszeit; Ⓔ (*whichever*) jeder/jede/jedes [beliebige]; **choose ~ [one] book/~ books you like** suchen Sie sich (*Dat.*) irgendein Buch/irgendwelche Bücher aus; **choose ~ two numbers** nimm zwei beliebige Zahlen; **do it ~ way you like** machen Sie es, wie immer Sie wollen; **cook the meat [in] ~ way/[for] ~ length of time you wish** kochen Sie das Fleisch, wie/so lange Sie wollen; **visit us [at] ~ time** besuchen Sie uns, wann [immer] Sie wollen; **~ day/minute [now]** jeden Tag/jede Minute; **[at] any time [now]** jederzeit; **~ moment now the bomb will explode** die Bombe wird jeden Moment explodieren; **you can count on him ~ time** (*coll.*) du kannst dich jederzeit auf ihn verlassen; **I'd prefer Mozart ~ day** (*coll.*) ich würde Mozart allemal (*ugs.*) *od.* jederzeit vorziehen; **not [just] ~ house** nicht irgendein beliebiges Haus; **take ~ amount you wish** nehmen Sie, so viel Sie wollen; **~ amount of** jede Menge (*ugs.*); **the room was filled with ~ amount of decorations/~ number of film stars** das Zimmer war reich geschmückt/in dem Zimmer war ein Heer von Filmstars; ⇒ *also* **case¹** A; **old** 1 D; **rate** 1 F; Ⓕ (*an appreciable*) ein nennenswerter/eine nennenswerte/ein nennenswertes; **she**

**didn't stay ~ length of time** sie ist nicht sehr lange geblieben; **he couldn't walk ~ distance without feeling exhausted** er konnte keine längere Strecke gehen, ohne sich erschöpft zu fühlen; **if he drinks ~ amount he gets roaring drunk** wenn er einmal etwas mehr trinkt, ist er gleich sternhagelvoll (*salopp*).
**2** *pron.* **A** (*some*) *in condit., interrog., or neg. sentence* (*replacing sing. n.*) einer/eine/ein[e]s; (*replacing collect. n.*) welcher/welche/welches; (*replacing pl. n.*) welche; **not ~:** keiner/keine/kein[e]s/*Pl.* keine; **without ~:** ohne; **I need to buy some sugar, we haven't got ~ at the moment** ich muss Zucker kaufen, wir haben im Augenblick keinen; **Here are some sweets. Would you like ~?** Hier sind ein paar Bonbons. Möchtest du welche?; **they ate all the cake and didn't leave ~ for us** *or* **without leaving ~ for us** sie haben den ganzen Kuchen gegessen und uns nichts übrig gelassen; **hardly ~:** kaum welche/welches; **Tea? No, I don't want ~ at the moment, thanks** Tee? Nein danke, im Moment nicht; **not known to ~ except ...:** keinem *od.* niemandem bekannt außer ...; **Here is a list of the books I need. Do you have ~ of them in stock?** Hier ist eine Liste mit den Büchern, die ich brauche. Haben Sie [irgend]welche davon vorrätig?; **I haven't seen ~ of my friends for years** ich habe seit Jahren keinen von meinen Freunden gesehen; **is there ~ of that cake left?** ist noch etwas [von dem] Kuchen übrig?; **is there ~ of you who would be willing to help?** wäre irgendjemand von Ihnen bereit zu helfen?; **he is not having ~ of it** (*fig. coll.*) er will nichts davon wissen; **B** (*no matter which*) irgendeiner/irgendeine/irgendein[e]s/irgendwelche *Pl.*; **you have to pick a number between 1 and 10, ~ you like** du musst eine Zahl zwischen 1 und 10 ziehen, irgendeine; **you can choose three books, ~ [of them] you like** Sie können sich (*Dat.*) drei Bücher aussuchen, egal welche; **Which numbers? — A~ between 1 and 10** Welche Zahlen? — Irgendwelche zwischen 1 und 10.
**3** *adv.* **do you feel ~ better today?** fühlen Sie sich heute [etwas] besser?; **if it gets ~ colder** wenn es noch kälter wird; **he didn't seem ~ [the] wiser after that** danach schien er auch nicht klüger zu sein; **I can't wait ~ longer** ich kann nicht [mehr] länger warten; **the occasional jokes do not make the book ~ [the] less boring** durch die gelegentlichen Witze wird das Buch keineswegs interessanter; **I don't feel ~ [the] better** mir ist kein bisschen wohler; **not ~ too happy about it** nicht gerade glücklich darüber; ⇒ *also* **more** 1 A, 3 D, I

**'anybody** *n. & pron.* **A** (*whoever*) jeder; **~ and everybody** jeder Beliebige; **B** (*somebody*) [irgend]jemand; **how could ~ be so cruel?** wie kann man nur so grausam sein?; **there wasn't ~ willing to help** es war niemand bereit zu helfen; **there's never ~ at home when I phone** es ist nie jemand zu Hause, wenn ich anrufe; **I've never seen ~ who ...:** ich habe noch keinen gesehen, der ...; **he is a match for ~ with his strength** bei seiner Kraft kann er sich mit jedem *od.* jedermann messen; **~ but** jeder[mann] außer; **The score is 1 : 1. It's ~'s match now** Es steht 1 : 1. Das Spiel ist jetzt offen; **what will happen is ~'s guess** was geschehen wird, [das] weiß keiner; **he's not [just] ~:** er ist nicht [einfach] irgendwer; **C** (*important person*) jemand; wer (*ugs.*); **everybody who was ~ was there** alles, was Rang und Namen hatte, war da

**'anyhow** *adv.* **A** ⇒ **anyway**; **B** (*haphazardly*) irgendwie; **he dresses ~:** er kleidet sich ohne Überlegung; **the furniture was arranged ~:** die Möbel waren wahllos irgendwo hingestellt; **all ~:** ganz unordentlich

**'anyone** ⇒ **anybody**

**'anyplace** (*Amer. coll.*) ⇒ **anywhere**

**'anything** **1** *n. & pron.* **A** (*whatever thing*) was [immer]; alles, was; **you may do ~ you wish** Sie können [alles] tun, was Sie möchten; **~ and everything** alles Mögliche; **B** (*something*) irgendetwas; **is there ~ wrong with you?** fehlt Ihnen [irgend] etwas?; **have you done ~ silly?** hast du [irgend]etwas Dummes gemacht?; **can we do ~ to help you?** können wir Ihnen irgendwie helfen?; **I don't want ~ [further] to do with him** ich möchte nichts [mehr] mit ihm zu tun haben; **I've never seen ~ like it in my life** ich habe noch nie in meinem Leben so etwas gesehen; **he can hardly see ~ without his glasses** ohne seine Brille kann er kaum etwas sehen; **C** (*a thing of any kind*) alles; **~ like that** so etwas; **as ... as ~** (*coll.*) wahnsinnig ... (*ugs.*); **not for ~ [in the world]** um nichts in der Welt; **I will do ~ in my power to help you** ich werde alles tun, was in meiner Macht steht, um Ihnen zu helfen; **the temperature is ~ from 30 to 40 degrees** die Temperatur liegt irgendwo zwischen 30 und 40 Grad; **~ but** (**~ except**) alles außer; (*far from*) alles andere als; **Cheap? The house was ~ but!** Billig war das Haus? Von wegen!; **prices are rising like ~** (*coll.*) die Preise steigen wie nur was *od.* wie verrückt (*ugs.*); **we don't want [just] ~:** wir wollen nicht einfach irgendetwas [Beliebiges].
**2** *adv.* **not ~ like as ... as** keineswegs so ... wie

**'anyway** *adv.* **A** (*in any case, besides*) sowieso; **we wouldn't accept your help ~:** wir würden von Ihnen sowieso keine Hilfe annehmen; **B** (*at any rate*) jedenfalls; **~, I must go now** wie dem auch sei, ich muss jetzt gehen

**'anywhere** **1** *adv.* **A** (*in any place*) (*wherever*) überall, wo; wo [immer]; (*somewhere*) irgendwo; **can you see my bag ~?** siehst du meine Tasche irgendwo?; **the price could be ~ between £30 and £40** der Preis könnte irgendwo zwischen 30 Pfund und 40 Pfund liegen; **not ~ near as ... as** (*coll.*) nicht annähernd so ... wie; **~ but ...:** überall, außer ...; überall, nur nicht ...; **[just] ~:** überall; **not just ~:** nicht überall; **B** (*to any place*) (*wherever*) wohin [auch immer]; (*somewhere*) irgendwohin; **have you ever been ~ by plane?** sind Sie je mit dem Flugzeug [irgendwohin] geflogen?; **I wouldn't go ~ near that island again** ich würde nicht wieder auch nur in die Nähe der Insel fahren; **~ but ...:** überallhin, außer ...; überallhin, nur nicht ...; **[just] ~:** [einfach] irgendwohin.
**2** *pron.* **if there's ~ you'd like to see** wenn es irgendetwas gibt, was du sehen möchtest; **have you found ~ to live yet?** haben Sie schon eine Wohnung gefunden?; **is there ~ we can stay for the night?** können wir hier irgendwo übernachten?; **there's never ~ open for milk after 6 p.m.** nach 18 Uhr kann man nirgends mehr Milch bekommen; **~ but ...:** überall, außer ...; **[just] ~:** irgendein x-beliebiger Ort; **from ~ hot** von irgendwo, wo es warm ist; **from ~ in the world** aus aller Welt

**aorta** /eɪ'ɔːtə/ *n.* (*Anat.*) Aorta, *die*

**apace** /ə'peɪs/ *adv.* (*arch./literary*) rasch; geschwind (*veralt.*)

**apart** /ə'pɑːt/ *adv.* **A** (*separately*) getrennt; **with one's legs ~:** mit gespreizten Beinen; **a few problems ~:** einige Probleme ausgenommen; **~ from ...** (*except for*) außer ...; bis auf ... (+ *Akk.*); (*in addition to*) außer ...; **everybody ~ from one person** alle außer einem; **he took me ~ in order to speak to me alone** er nahm mich zur Seite, um allein mit mir zu sprechen; **a race ~:** ein Volk für sich; **B** (*into pieces*) auseinander; **he took the engine ~:** er nahm den Motor auseinander; **the toy came ~ in his hands** das Spielzeug zerbrach in seinen Händen; **take ~** (*fig.*) (*criticize*) auseinander nehmen (*ugs.*) ‹Theaterstück, Theoretiker, Politiker›; (*analyse*) zergliedern; (*coll.: defeat*) vernichtend schlagen; **take a poem/play/book ~:** ein Gedicht/Stück/Buch zergliedern *od.* [im Einzelnen] analysieren; **C** **~ [from]** (*to a distance*) weg [von]; (*at a distance*) **ten kilometres ~:** zehn Kilometer voneinander entfernt; **they have moved far ~ from each other** sie sind weit voneinander weggezogen; **they are miles** *or* **worlds ~ [from each other] in their tastes** zwischen ihren Geschmäckern liegen Welten

**apartheid** /ə'pɑːtheɪt/ *n., no pl., no art.* Apartheid, *die;* (*fig.*) Diskriminierung, *die*

**apartment** /ə'pɑːtmənt/ *n.* **A** (*room*) Apartment, *das;* Appartement, *das;* **~s** (*in a mansion etc.*) Räume *Pl.;* Räumlichkeiten *Pl.;* **B** (*esp. Amer.*) Wohnung, *die;* **~ house** Appartementhaus, *das*

**apathetic** /æpə'θetɪk/ *adj.* apathisch (**about** gegenüber); (*not feeling emotion*) gleichgültig

**apathetically** /æpə'θetɪkəlɪ/ *adv.* apathisch; (*without emotion*) gleichgültig

**apathy** /'æpəθɪ/ *n., no pl.* Apathie, *die* (**about** gegenüber); (*lack of emotion*) Gleichmut, *der*

**APB** *abbr.* (*Amer.*) **all-points bulletin**

**ape** /eɪp/ **1** *n.* **A** (*tailless monkey*) [Menschen]affe, *der;* (*monkey*) Affe, *der;* **man is descended from the ~s** der Mensch stammt vom Affen ab; **B** (*imitator*) Nachahmer, *der;* Nachäffer, *der* (*abwertend*); **C** (*apelike person*) Affe, *der;* **go ~** (*coll.*) verrückt werden (*ugs.*); durchdrehen (*ugs.*).
**2** *v.t.* nachahmen; nachäffen (*abwertend*)

**apelike** /'eɪplaɪk/ *adj.* wie ein Affe *nachgestellt*

**Apennines** /'æpɪnaɪnz/ *pr. n. pl.* Apenninen *Pl.*

**aperçu** /æpɜː'sjuː/ *n.* **A** (*summary*) kurzer Überblick (**of** über + *Akk.*); **B** (*insight*) Aperçu, *das*

**aperient** /ə'pɪərɪənt/ **1** *adj.* abführend; **this preparation is mildly/strongly ~:** dieses Präparat ist ein schwaches/starkes Abführmittel. **2** *n.* Abführmittel, *das*

**aperitif** /ə'perɪtiːf, əperɪ'tiːf/ *n.* Aperitif, *der*

**aperture** /'æpətʃə(r)/ *n.* **A** (*opening*) Öffnung, *die;* **B** (*Optics, Photog., etc.*) Blende, *die*

**APEX** /'eɪpeks/ *abbr.* **Advance Purchase Excursion** *reduzierter Flugtarif bei Vorauszahlung*

**apex** /'eɪpeks/ *n., pl.* **~es** *or* **apices** /'eɪpɪsiːz/ (*tip*) Spitze, *die;* (*of heart, lung, etc.*) Spitze, *die;* Apex, *der* (*fachspr.*); (*fig.*) Gipfel, *der;* Höhepunkt, *der*

**apfelstrudel** /'æpfəlstruːdl/ *n.* Apfelstrudel, *der*

**aphasia** /ə'feɪzɪə/ *n.* (*Med.*) Aphasie, *die*

**aphid** /'eɪfɪd/ *n.* (*Zool.*) Blattlaus, *die*

**aphorism** /'æfərɪzm/ *n.* (*pithy statement*) Aphorismus, *der;* (*maxim*) Maxime, *die*

**aphoristic** /æfə'rɪstɪk/ *adj.* aphoristisch

**aphrodisiac** /æfrə'dɪzɪæk/ (*Med.*) **1** *adj.* aphrodisisch. **2** *n.* Aphrodisiakum, *das*

**apiarist** /'eɪpɪərɪst/ *n.* ▶ **1261** Bienenzüchter, *der;* Imker, *der*

**apiary** /'eɪpɪərɪ/ *n.* Bienenhaus, *das*

**apices** *pl. of* **apex**

**apiece** /ə'piːs/ *adv.* je; **we took two bags ~:** wir nahmen je zwei Beutel; **they cost a penny ~:** die kosten einen Penny das Stück; **books/five books at £1 ~:** jedes Buch ein Pfund/fünf Bücher zu je einem Pfund

**apish** /'eɪpɪʃ/ *adj.* **A** (*apelike*) affenartig; **B** (*imitative*) sklavisch [nachahmend]; **C** (*silly*) affig (*ugs.*)

**aplenty** /ə'plentɪ/ *adv.* in [Hülle und] Fülle

**aplomb** /ə'plɒm/ *n.* Sicherheit [im Auftreten]; Aplomb, *der* (*geh.*)

**apocalypse** /ə'pɒkəlɪps/ *n.* **A** (*event*) Apokalypse, *die;* **B** (*Relig.*) (*revelation*) Offenbarung, *die;* (*book*) Apokalypse, *die;* Offenbarung, *die*

**apocalyptic** /əpɒkə'lɪptɪk/, **apocalyptical** /əpɒkə'lɪptɪkl/ *adj.* **A** (*dramatic*) apokalyptisch; **B** (*Relig.*) (*of revelation*) apokalyptisch; (*of book*) Offenbarungs-; der Offenbarung *nachgestellt*

**Apocrypha** /ə'pɒkrɪfə/ *n.* (*Bibl.*) Apokryphen *Pl.*

a

# Apologizing

## Fairly formal

***I owe you an apology*** or ***I must apologize for accusing you wrongly***
= Ich muss mich bei Ihnen entschuldigen, dass ich Sie fälschlich beschuldigt habe

***Please accept my humble apology***
= Ich bitte vielmals um Entschuldigung

***I take back all that I said and apologize unreservedly***
= Ich nehme alles zurück und bitte tausendmal um Entschuldigung

***I greatly*** or ***very much regret that I have had to disappoint you***
= Ich bedaure sehr, dass ich Sie enttäuschen musste

***I must ask you to forgive*** or ***excuse my mistake***
= Ich muss Sie für meinen Fehler um Verzeihung bitten

***Please excuse my oversight***
= Bitte entschuldigen Sie mein Versehen

***Please forgive me for being so late with these birthday wishes***
= Bitte entschuldigen Sie, dass diese Geburtstagswünsche so verspätet eintreffen

***I must apologize for the delay in replying to your letter***
= Ich muss mich entschuldigen, dass ich Ihren Brief erst so spät beantworte

***I am sorry*** or ***I regret to have to inform you that ...***
= Ich muss Ihnen leider mitteilen, dass ...
Ich bedaure, Ihnen mitteilen zu müssen, dass ...

## Less formal

***I really am sorry that I've let you down***
= Es tut mir aufrichtig Leid, dass ich dich im Stich gelassen habe

***I'm sorry to be such a nuisance***
= Tut mir Leid, dass ich dir so viel Mühe mache

***Sorry!*** (*e.g. when you bump into someone*)
= Entschuldigung!

***Sorry to bother you, but can you tell me ...***
= Entschuldigung, wenn ich störe, aber können Sie mir sagen ...

***I'm sorry, but*** or ***Unfortunately I'll have to go now***
= Leider muss ich jetzt gehen

***Sorry, but I can't help***
= Tut mir Leid, da kann ich nicht helfen

***Don't be cross that I haven't written before***
= Sei mir nicht böse *or* Nimm es mir nicht übel, dass ich nicht früher geschrieben habe

***Forgive me! It was all a stupid misunderstanding***
= Verzeih! Es war alles nur ein dummes Missverständnis

**apocryphal** /ə'pɒkrɪfl/ *adj.* Ⓐ (*of doubtful origin*) apokryph; zweifelhaft; (*invented*) apokryph; unecht; Ⓑ (*of the Apocrypha*) apokryph

**apogee** /'æpədʒi:/ *n.* Ⓐ (*highest point*) Höhepunkt, *der;* Gipfel[punkt], *der;* Ⓑ (*Astron.*) Apogäum, *das;* Erdferne, *die*

**apolitical** /eɪpə'lɪtɪkl/ *adj.* apolitisch; unpolitisch

**Apollo** /ə'pɒləʊ/ *pr. n.* Apoll[o], *der*

**apologetic** /əpɒlə'dʒetɪk/ *adj.* Ⓐ entschuldigend; **~ words** Worte der Entschuldigung; **an ~ person** jmd., der sich dauernd entschuldigt; **he wrote a very ~ letter** er schrieb einen Brief, in dem er sich vielmals entschuldigte; **he was most ~ about ...:** er entschuldigte sich vielmals für ...; Ⓑ (*diffident*) zaghaft ‹Lächeln, Ton›; zurückhaltend, bescheiden ‹Wesen, Art›

**apologetically** /əpɒlə'dʒetɪkəlɪ/ *adv.* Ⓐ entschuldigend; **he wrote very ~ to say that he ...:** er schrieb mit großem Bedauern, dass er ...; Ⓑ (*diffidently*) zaghaft; bescheiden

**apologetics** /əpɒlə'dʒetɪks/ *n., no pl.* Apologetik, *die*

**apologia** /æpə'ləʊdʒɪə/ *n.* Apologie, *die*

**apologist** /ə'pɒlədʒɪst/ *n.* Apologet, *der*/Apologetin, *die*

**apologize** /ə'pɒlədʒaɪz/ *v.i.* Ⓐ ▶ 924 sich entschuldigen; **~ to sb. for sth./sb.** sich bei jmdm. für etw./jmdn. entschuldigen; Ⓑ (*defend one's actions*) sich rechtfertigen

**apology** /ə'pɒlədʒɪ/ *n.* Ⓐ ▶ 924 Entschuldigung, *die;* **make an ~ [to sb.] for sth.** sich für etw. [bei jmdm.] entschuldigen; **an ~ to sb. for sth.** eine Entschuldigung bei jmdm. für etw.; **you owe him an ~/he deserves an ~ from you** Sie müssen sich bei ihm entschuldigen; **please accept our apologies** wir bitten vielmals um Entschuldigung; **she was full of apologies for her mistake** sie entschuldigte sich vielmals für ihren Fehler; Ⓑ (*defence*) Rechtfertigung, *die;* Ⓒ (*poor substitute*) **an ~ for a ...:** ein erbärmliches Exemplar von ...; **what's this ~ for a meal?** was ist denn das für eine kärgliche *od.* armselige Mahlzeit?

**apoplectic** /æpə'plektɪk/ *adj.* apoplektisch; **~ stroke** *or* **fit** Schlaganfall, *der*

**apoplexy** /'æpəpleksɪ/ *n.* Apoplexie, *die* (*fachspr.*); Schlaganfall, *der;* **a fit of ~:** ein Schlaganfall

**apostasy** /ə'pɒstəsɪ/ *n.* Apostasie, *die*

**apostate** /ə'pɒstət/ ❶ *n.* Abtrünnige, *der/die;* Renegat, *der;* Apostat, *der* (*Rel.*). ❷ *adj.* abtrünnig; [von einer Partei/Glaubensrichtung] abgefallen

**a posteriori** /eɪ pɒsterɪ'ɔ:raɪ/ ❶ *adv.* a posteriori. ❷ *adj.* aposteriorisch

**apostle** /ə'pɒsl/ *n.* (*lit. or fig.*) Apostel, *der;* **the A~s** die [zwölf] Apostel; **A~s' Creed** Apostolisches Glaubensbekenntnis; Apostolikum, *das* (*fachspr.*)

**apostolic** /æpə'stɒlɪk/ *adj.* apostolisch

**apostrophe** /ə'pɒstrəfɪ/ *n.* Ⓐ (*sign*) Apostroph, *der;* Auslassungszeichen, *das;* Ⓑ (*Rhet.: exclamatory passage*) Apostrophe, *die*

**apostrophize** /ə'pɒstrəfaɪz/ *v.t.* apostrophieren

**apothecary** /ə'pɒθɪkərɪ/ *n.* Ⓐ (*arch.*) Apotheker, *der*/Apothekerin, *die;* Ⓑ **apothecaries' measure/weight** Apothekermaß/-gewicht, *das*

**apotheosis** /əpɒθɪ'əʊsɪs/ *n., pl.* **apotheoses** /əpɒθɪ'əʊsi:z/ Ⓐ (*deification*) Apotheose, *die* (*auch fig.*); Vergöttlichung, *die;* Ⓑ (*deified ideal*) Gott, *der*/Göttin, *die;* Ⓒ (*ultimate point*) Gipfelpunkt, *der;* Apotheose, *die* (*geh.*)

**appal** (*Amer.:* **appall**) /ə'pɔ:l/ *v.t.*, **-ll-** (*dismay*) entsetzen; (*terrify*) erschrecken; **your behaviour ~s me!** ich bin entsetzt über dein Benehmen!; **obscenity ~s her** sie empört sich über Obszönitäten

**appalling** /ə'pɔ:lɪŋ/ *adj.* (*dismaying*) entsetzlich; (*terrifying*) schrecklich; (*coll.: very bad*) fürchterlich; scheußlich

**apparatchik** /æpə'rɑ:tʃɪk/ *n., pl.* **~s** *or* **~i** /æpə'rɑ:tʃɪki:/ Apparatschik, *der*

**apparatus** /æpə'reɪtəs/ *n.* (*equipment*) Gerät, *das;* (*gymnastic ~*) Geräte *Pl.;* (*machinery, lit. or fig.*) Apparat, *der;* **a piece of ~:** ein Apparat

**apparel** /ə'pærəl/ ❶ *n.* Kleidung, *die;* Gewänder *Pl.* (*geh.*). ❷ *v.t.*, (*Brit.*) **-ll-** (*arch.*) gewanden (*veralt.*); kleiden (*auch fig.*)

**apparent** /ə'pærənt/ *adj.* Ⓐ (*clear*) offensichtlich ‹Ziel, Zweck, Wirkung, Begeisterung, Interesse›; offenbar ‹Bedeutung, Wahrheit›; **it soon became ~ that ...:** es zeigte sich bald, dass ...; **the meaning was/became clearly ~ to all of us** die Bedeutung war/wurde uns allen deutlich klar; **heir ~:** recht- *od.* gesetzmäßiger Erbe; **he is the heir ~ to the throne** er ist der rechtmäßige Thronfolger; Ⓑ (*seeming*) scheinbar; **be only ~:** nur scheinbar sein; **this was only the ~ truth** das schien nur die Wahrheit zu sein

**apparently** /ə'pærəntlɪ/ *adv.* Ⓐ (*clearly*) offensichtlich; offenbar; Ⓑ (*seemingly*) scheinbar; **he was not asleep, but only ~ so** er schien nur zu schlafen

**apparition** /æpə'rɪʃn/ *n.* Ⓐ (*appearance*) [Geister]erscheinung, *die;* Ⓑ (*ghost*) Gespenst, *das*

**appeal** /ə'pi:l/ ❶ *v.i.* Ⓐ (*Law etc.*) Einspruch erheben *od.* einlegen (**to** bei); **~ to a court** bei einem Gericht Berufung einlegen; **~ against sth.** gegen etw. Einspruch/Berufung einlegen; **~ from a judgement** gegen ein Urteil Berufung einlegen; Ⓑ (*refer*) **~ to** verweisen auf ‹Erkenntnisse, Tatsachen›; Ⓒ (*make earnest request*) **~ to sb. for sth./to do sth.** jmdn. um etw. ersuchen/jmdn. ersuchen, etw. zu tun; **I ~ to you to give generously** ich appelliere an Sie *od.* ich ersuche Sie, großzügig zu spenden; Ⓓ (*address oneself*) **~ to sb./sth.** an jmdn./etw. appellieren; **this type of music ~s to the senses rather than the intellect** solche Musik spricht eher das Gefühl an als den Verstand; Ⓔ (*be attractive*) **~ to sb.** jmdm. zusagen; **how does that ~?** könnte dir das gefallen? **this music does not ~ to their tastes** diese Musik ist nicht ihr Geschmack; Ⓕ (*Cricket*) Einspruch erheben.
❷ *v.t.* überweisen ‹Sache, Fall usw.›.
❸ *n.* Ⓐ (*Law etc.*) Einspruch, *der* (**to** bei); (*to higher court*) Berufung, *die* (**to** bei); **an ~ against** *or* **from a judgement** Berufung gegen eine Entscheidung; **lodge an ~ with sb.** bei jmdm. Einspruch/Berufung einlegen; **acquittal on ~:** Freispruch in der Berufung; **right of ~:** Einspruchs-/Berufungsrecht, *das;* **there is no ~ against this decision** gegen diese Entscheidung gibt es keine Einspruchs-/Berufungsmöglichkeit; **Court of A~:** Berufungsgericht, *das;* Appellationsgericht, *das* (*veralt.*); Ⓑ (*reference*) Berufung, *die;* Verweisung, *die;* **make an ~ to sth.** sich auf etw. (*Akk.*) berufen; auf etw. (*Akk.*) verweisen; Ⓒ (*imploring request*) Appell, *der;* Aufruf, *der;* **an ~ to sb. for sth.** eine Bitte an jmdn. um etw.; **make an ~ to sb.** eine dringende Bitte an jmdn. richten; an

jmdn. appellieren; **D** (*addressing oneself*) Appell, *der;* Aufruf, *der;* **make an ~ to sb.** einen Appell an jmdn. richten; **the ~ of the music is to the senses rather than the intellect** die Musik spricht eher das Gefühl an als den Verstand; **E** (*attraction*) Reiz, *der;* Anziehungskraft, *die;* **a Rolls Royce has a certain class ~:** ein Rolls Royce ist etwas für Standesbewusste; **F** (*Cricket*) Einspruch, *der*

**appealable** /əˈpiːləbl/ *adj.* gerichtlich anfechtbar; appellabel (*veralt.*)

**appealing** /əˈpiːlɪŋ/ *adj.* **A** (*imploring*) flehend; **B** (*attractive*) ansprechend ‹Farbe, Geschichte, Stil›; verlockend ‹Essen, Idee›; reizvoll ‹Haus, Beruf, Baustil›; angenehm ‹Stimme, Charakter›

**appealingly** /əˈpiːlɪŋlɪ/ *adv.* ansprechend

**appear** /əˈpɪə(r)/ *v.i.* **A** (*become visible, be seen, arrive*) erscheinen; ‹Licht, Mond:› auftauchen; ‹Symptom, Darsteller:› auftreten; (*present oneself*) auftreten; (*Sport*) spielen; **he was ordered to ~ at the police station/before the court** er wurde zum Polizeirevier geladen/vom Gericht vorgeladen; **he ~ed in court charged with murder** er stand wegen Mordes vor Gericht; **B** (*occur*) vorkommen; ‹Irrtum:› vorkommen, auftreten; ‹Ereignis:› vorkommen, eintreten; (*be manifest*) ‹Einstellung, Meinung:› sich zeigen; **C** (*seem*) ~ **[to be] ...:** scheinen ... [zu sein]; **try to ~ relaxed** versuch, entspannt zu erscheinen; **you could at least ~ to be interested** du könntest zumindest so tun, als ob du interessiert wärest; **~ to do sth.** scheinen, etw. zu tun; **she only ~s to be asleep** es hat nur den Anschein, als schlafe sie; **D** (*be published*) erscheinen; herauskommen

**appearance** /əˈpɪərəns/ *n.* **A** (*becoming visible*) Auftauchen, *das;* (*of symptoms*) Auftreten, *das;* (*arrival*) Erscheinen, *das;* (*of performer, speaker, etc.*) Auftritt, *der;* **make an** *or* **one's ~:** erscheinen; **make a public ~:** in der Öffentlichkeit auftreten; **put in an ~:** sich sehen lassen; **B** (*look*) Äußere, *das;* **outward ~:** äußere Erscheinung; **~s** Äußerlichkeiten *Pl.;* **the house had a shabby ~:** das Haus hatte ein schäbiges Aussehen; **his ~ of being nervous** sein nervöses Auftreten; **to judge by ~s, to all ~s** allem Anschein nach; **for the sake of ~s, to keep up ~s** um den Schein zu wahren; **C** (*semblance*) Anschein, *der;* **~s to the contrary, ...:** entgegen allem Anschein ...; **~s can be deceptive** der Schein trügt; **D** (*occurrence*) Auftreten, *das;* Vorkommen, *das;* **E** (*publication*) Veröffentlichung, *die;* Erscheinen, *das*

**appease** /əˈpiːz/ *v.t.* **A** (*make calm*) besänftigen; (*Polit.*) beschwichtigen; **B** (*soothe*) lindern ‹Leid, Schmerz, Not›; mildern ‹Beunruhigung, Erregung›; (*satisfy*) befriedigen ‹Verlangen, Lust›; stillen ‹Hunger, Durst›

**appeasement** /əˈpiːzmənt/ *n.* ⇨ **appease**: Besänftigung, *die;* Beschwichtigung, *die;* Linderung, *die;* Milderung, *die;* Befriedigung, *die;* Stillen, *das*

**appellant** /əˈpelənt/ (*Law*) **1** *n.* Berufungskläger, *der*/-klägerin, *die;* Appellant, *der* (*veralt.*). **2** *adj.* Berufungs-; Appellations- (*veralt.*)

**appellate** /əˈpelət/ *adj.* (*Law*) Berufungs-; Appellations- (*veralt.*); **~ judge/hearing** Berufungsrichter, *der*/-verfahren, *das*

**appellation** /æpəˈleɪʃn/ *n.* (*name, nomenclature*) Bezeichnung, *die;* (*way of addressing*) Anrede, *die*

**append** /əˈpend/ *v.t.* **~ sth. to sth.** etw. an etw. (*Akk.*) anhängen; (*add*) etw. einer Sache (*Dat.*) anfügen; **~ one's signature to a document** seine Unterschrift unter ein Dokument setzen

**appendage** /əˈpendɪdʒ/ *n.* **A** Anhängsel, *das;* (*addition*) Anhang, *der;* **he feels as if he has become a mere ~ to the household** er fühlt sich im Haus nur noch als fünftes Rad am Wagen; **B** (*accompaniment*) Zu-, Beigabe, *die* (**to** zu)

**appendectomy** /æpenˈdektəmɪ/, **appendicectomy** /əpendɪˈsektəmɪ/ *ns.* (*Med.*) Blinddarmoperation, *die* (*volkst.*); Appendektomie, *die* (*fachspr.*)

**appendices** *pl. of* appendix

**appendicitis** /əpendɪˈsaɪtɪs/ *n.* ▶ **1232** Blinddarmentzündung, *die* (*volkst.*); Appendizitis, *die* (*fachspr.*)

**appendix** /əˈpendɪks/ *n., pl.* **appendices** /əˈpendɪsiːz/ *or* **~es** **A** Anhang, *der* (**to** zu); **B** ▶ **966** (*Anat.*) **[vermiform]** /ˈvɜːmɪfɔːm/ **~:** Blinddarm, *der* (*volkst.*); Wurmfortsatz [des Blinddarms]

**appertain** /æpəˈteɪn/ *v.i.* **~ to sth.** (*relate*) sich auf etw. (*Akk.*) beziehen; (*belong*) zu etw. gehören; (*be appropriate*) zu etw. dazugehören

**appetite** /ˈæpɪtaɪt/ *n.* **A** (*for food*) Appetit, *der* (**for** auf + *Akk.*); **~ for sex** Lust auf Sex; **B** (*fig.: desire*) Verlangen, *das* (**for** nach); **~ for knowledge** Wissensdrang, *der;* Wissensdurst, *der;* **~ for life** Lebenshunger, *der;* Lebensgier, *die*

**appetizer** /ˈæpɪtaɪzə(r)/ *n.* Appetitanreger, *der;* (*on menu*) Vorspeise, *die;* **act as an/be an ~:** appetitanregend wirken

**appetizing** /ˈæpɪtaɪzɪŋ/ *adj.* appetitlich ‹Anblick, Speise, Geruch›; appetitanregend ‹Getränk, Geschmack›

**appetizingly** /ˈæpɪtaɪzɪŋlɪ/ *adv.* appetitanregend

**applaud** /əˈplɔːd/ **1** *v.i.* applaudieren; [Beifall] klatschen. **2** *v.t.* applaudieren (+ *Dat.*); Beifall spenden (+ *Dat.*); (*approve of, welcome*) billigen ‹Entschluss›; (*praise*) loben, anerkennen ‹Versuch, Bemühungen›

**applause** /əˈplɔːz/ *n.* Applaus, *der;* (*praise*) Lob, *das;* Anerkennung, *die;* **give ~:** Applaus *od.* Beifall spenden; **get ~:** Applaus *od.* Beifall ernten

**apple** /ˈæpl/ *n.* Apfel, *der;* **the ~ of sb.'s eye** (*fig.*) jmds. Liebling

**apple: ~ 'brandy** *n.* Apfelschnaps, *der;* **~ cart** *n.* **upset the ~ cart** (*fig.*) die Pferde *od.* Gäule scheu machen (*ugs.*); **~-'green** **1** *adj.* apfelgrün; **2** *n.* Apfelgrün, *das;* **~jack** (*Amer.*) ⇨ **~ brandy;** **~ 'pie** *n.* gedeckte Apfeltorte; **~ pie bed** *Bett, in dem das Betttuch aus Scherz so gefaltet ist, dass man die Beine nicht ausstrecken kann;* **in ~ pie order** picobello (*ugs.*); tadellos in Ordnung; **~ 'sauce** *n.* Apfelmus, *das;* **~ tree** *n.* Apfelbaum, *der*

**appliance** /əˈplaɪəns/ *n.* (*utensil*) Gerät, *das;* (*aid*) Hilfsmittel, *das;* (*fire engine*) Feuerlöschfahrzeug, *das*

**applicability** /æplɪkəˈbɪlɪtɪ/ *n.* **A** Anwendbarkeit, *die* (**to** auf + *Akk.*); **B** (*appropriateness*) Eignung, *die* (**to** für)

**applicable** /ˈæplɪkəbl, əˈplɪkəbl/ *adj.* **A** anwendbar (**to** auf + *Akk.*); **B** (*appropriate*) geeignet; angebracht; zutreffend ‹Fragebogenteil usw.›; **the ~ documents** die entsprechenden Unterlagen

**applicant** /ˈæplɪkənt/ *n.* Bewerber, *der*/Bewerberin, *die* (**for** um); (*claimant*) Antragsteller, *der*/Antragstellerin, *die*

**application** /æplɪˈkeɪʃn/ *n.* **A** (*putting*) Auftragen, *das* (**to** auf + *Akk.*); (*administering*) Anwendung, *die;* (*of heat, liquids*) Zufuhr, *die;* (*employment; of rule etc.*) Anwendung, *die;* **the ~ of new technology** der Einsatz neuer Technologien; **this rule is of** *or* **has universal ~:** diese Regel beansprucht allgemeine Gültigkeit; **B** (*request*) Bewerbung, *die* (**for** um); (*for passport, licence, etc.*) Antrag, *der* (**for** auf + *Akk.*); **~ form** Antragsformular, *das;* **available on ~:** auf Anfrage erhältlich; **~ for a passport** Antrag auf Erteilung eines Passes; **C** (*diligence*) Fleiß, *der* (**to** bei); (*with enthusiasm*) Eifer, *der* (**to** für); **D** (*Med.: lotion, poultice, etc.*) Mittel, *das;* **E** (*Computing*) Applikation, *die*

**applicator** /ˈæplɪkeɪtə(r)/ *n.* Applikator, *der*

**appliqué** /æˈpliːkeɪ/ **1** *n.* Applikationsstickerei, *die.* **2** *adj.* appliziert

**apply** /əˈplaɪ/ **1** *v.t.* **A** anlegen ‹Verband›; auftragen ‹Creme, Paste, Farbe› (**to** auf + *Akk.*); zuführen ‹Wärme, Flüssigkeit› (**to** *Dat.*); **~ the brakes** bremsen; die Bremse betätigen; **~ gentle pressure to the tube** drücken Sie leicht auf die Tube; **~ pressure to sb.** (*fig.*) jmdn. unter Druck setzen; **B** (*make use of*) anwenden; **applied linguistics/mathematics** angewandte Sprachwissenschaft/Mathematik; **C** (*devote*) richten, lenken ‹Gedanken, Überlegungen, Geist› (**to** auf + *Akk.*); verwenden ‹Zeit, Energie› (**to** auf + *Akk.*); **~ oneself [to sth.]** sich (*Dat.*) Mühe geben [mit etw.]; sich [um etw.] bemühen; **~ oneself to a task** sich an eine Aufgabe machen. **2** *v.i.* **A** (*have relevance*) zutreffen (**to** auf + *Akk.*); (*be valid*) gelten; **things which don't ~ to us** Dinge, die uns nicht betreffen; **B** (*address oneself*) **~ [to sb.] for sth.** [jmdn.] um etw. bitten *od.* (*geh.*) ersuchen; (*for passport, licence, etc.*) [bei jmdm.] etw. beantragen; (*for job*) sich [bei jmdm.] um etw. bewerben

**appoint** /əˈpɔɪnt/ *v.t.* **A** (*fix*) bestimmen; festlegen ‹Zeitpunkt, Ort›; **~ that ...:** anordnen, dass ...; **B** (*choose for a job*) einstellen; (*assign to office*) ernennen; **~ sb. [to be** *or* **as] sth./to do sth.** jmdn. zu etw. ernennen/jmdn. dazu berufen, etw. zu tun; **~ sb. to sth.** jmdn. in etw. (*Akk.*) einsetzen; **he was ~ed governor** er wurde zum Gouverneur bestellt *od.* ernannt; **~ sb. one's heir** jmdn. als seinen Erben einsetzen

**appointed** /əˈpɔɪntɪd/ *adj.* **A** (*fixed*) vereinbart; verabredet; **B** **well/badly ~:** gut/schlecht ausgestattet *od.* eingerichtet ‹Zimmer usw.›

**appointee** /əpɔɪnˈtiː/ *n.* Ernannte, *der/die;* Berufene, *der/die*

**appointment** /əˈpɔɪntmənt/ *n.* **A** (*fixing*) Festlegung, *die;* Festsetzung, *die;* **B** (*assigning to office*) Ernennung, *die;* Berufung, *die;* (*Law*) Verfügung, *die* (**of** über + *Akk.*); (*being assigned to office*) Ernennung, *die* (**as** zum/zur); (*to job*) Einstellung, *die;* **~ to a position** Berufung auf einen Posten; **by ~ to Her Majesty the Queen, makers of fine confectionery** königlicher Hoflieferant für feines Konfekt; **C** (*office*) Stelle, *die;* Posten, *der;* **a teaching ~:** eine Stelle als Lehrer/Lehrerin; **D** (*arrangement*) Termin, *der;* **dental ~:** Termin beim Zahnarzt; **make an ~ with sb.** sich (*Dat.*) von jmdm. einen Termin geben lassen; **by ~:** nach Anmeldung; mit Voranmeldung; **E** *usu. in pl.* (*equipment etc.*) Ausstattung, *die*

**apportion** /əˈpɔːʃn/ *v.t.* **A** (*allot*) **~ sth. to sb.** jmdm. etw. zuteilen; **B** (*portion out*) [gleichmäßig] verteilen (**among** an + *Akk.*); aufteilen (**among** unter + *Akk.*)

**apportionment** /əˈpɔːʃnmənt/ *n.* **A** (*allotting*) Zuteilung, *die* (**to** an + *Akk.*); **B** (*portioning out*) Verteilung, *die* (**among** an + *Akk.*); Aufteilung, *die* (**among** unter + *Akk.*)

**apposite** /ˈæpəzɪt/ *adj.* (*appropriate*) passend; geeignet; (*well chosen*) treffend; **~ to sth.** zutreffend auf etw. (*Akk.*); **these remarks are very ~ to the matter** diese Bemerkungen treffen die Sache genau

**appositely** /ˈæpəzɪtlɪ/ *adv.* (*appropriately*) in passender *od.* geeigneter Weise

**appositeness** /ˈæpəzɪtnɪs/ *n., no pl.* (*appropriateness*) Angemessenheit, *die*

**apposition** /æpəˈzɪʃn/ *n.* (*Ling.*) Apposition, *die;* **in ~ [to sth.]** in Apposition [zu etw.]

**appraisal** /əˈpreɪzl/ *n.* (*evaluation*) Bewertung, *die;* (*of property*) Taxierung, *die;* Schätzung, *die;* **what ~ do you give/what is your ~ of the situation?** wie beurteilen Sie die Situation?

**appraise** /əˈpreɪz/ *v.t.* (*evaluate*) bewerten; (*value*) schätzen; taxieren; **can you ~ the extent of the damage?** können Sie das Ausmaß des Schadens abschätzen?

**appreciable** /əˈpriːʃəbl/ *adj.* (*perceptible*) nennenswert ‹Unterschied, Einfluss›; spürbar ‹Veränderung, Wirkung, Erfolg›; merklich ‹Verringerung, Anstieg›; (*considerable*) beträchtlich; erheblich

**appreciably** /əˈpriːʃəblɪ/ *adv.* (*perceptibly*) spürbar ‹verändern›; merklich ‹sich unterscheiden›; (*considerably*) beträchtlich; erheblich

**appreciate** /əˈpriːʃɪeɪt, əˈpriːsɪeɪt/ **1** *v.t.* **A** (*[correctly] estimate value or worth of*) [richtig] einschätzen; (*understand*) verstehen; (*be aware of*) sich (*Dat.*) bewusst sein (+ *Gen.*); (*be receptive to*) Gefallen finden an (+ *Dat.*); **~ that/what ...:** verstehen, dass/was ...; **B** (*be grateful for*) anerkennen; schätzen; (*enjoy*) genießen; **I'd really ~ that** das wäre sehr nett von dir; **a stamped addressed envelope would be ~d** bitte einen frankierten Rückumschlag beilegen. ❷ *v.i.* im Wert steigen

**appreciation** /əpri:ʃɪ'eɪʃn, əpri:sɪ'eɪʃn/ *n.* **A** *([right] estimation)* [richtige] Einschätzung; *(understanding)* Verständnis, *das* (**of** für); *(awareness)* Bewusstsein, *das; (sensitivity)* Sinn, *der* (**of** für); **B** *(gratefulness)* Dankbarkeit, *die; (enjoyment)* Gefallen, *das* (**of** an + *Dat.*); **in grateful ~ of** *or* **for your help** in dankbarer Anerkennung Ihrer Hilfe; **C** *(rise in value)* Wertsteigerung, *die;* **D** *(review)* [positive] Kritik; Würdigung, *die*

**appreciative** /ə'pri:ʃətɪv/ *adj.* **A be ~ of sth./sb.** *(aware of)* fähig sein, etw./jmdn. [richtig] einzuschätzen; **she is very ~ of music** sie hat viel Sinn für Musik; **be ~ of sb.'s plight** für jmds. Not Verständnis aufbringen; **B** *(grateful)* dankbar (**of** für); *(approving)* anerkennend

**apprehend** /æprɪ'hend/ *v.t.* **A** *(arrest)* festnehmen; fassen; **B** *(perceive)* wahrnehmen; vernehmen ‹Stimme, Geräusch›; einsehen ‹Wahrheit›; *(understand)* erfassen; begreifen; **C** *(anticipate)* vorausahnen; befürchten ‹Unglück›

**apprehension** /æprɪ'henʃn/ *n.* **A** *(arrest)* Festnahme, *die;* Verhaftung, *die;* **B** *(uneasiness)* Besorgnis, *die;* **C** *(conception)* Auffassung, *die;* Ansicht, *die* (**of** über + *Akk.*); *(understanding)* Verständnis, *das*

**apprehensive** /æprɪ'hensɪv/ *adj.* *(uneasy)* besorgt; **~ of sth.** besorgt wegen etw.; **be ~ of doing sth.** ein ungutes Gefühl haben, etw. zu tun; **be ~ that ...:** befürchten, dass ...; **~ for sb./sb.'s safety** besorgt um jmdn./jmds. Sicherheit

**apprehensively** /æprɪ'hensɪvlɪ/ *adv.* *(uneasily)* besorgt

**apprehensiveness** /æprɪ'hensɪvnɪs/ *n.* Besorgnis, *die* (**of** wegen); **~ that ...:** Sorge, dass ...; **~ for sb./sb.'s safety** Besorgtheit um jmdn./jmds. Sicherheit

**apprentice** /ə'prentɪs/ ❶ *n.* *(learner)* Lehrling, *der* (**to** bei); *(to a painter)* Schüler, *der* (**to** *Gen.*); *(beginner)* Neuling, *der;* Anfänger, *der; (jockey)* angehender Jockey. ❷ *v.t.* in die Lehre geben (**to** bei); **be ~d [to sb.]** [bei jmdm.] in der Lehre sein *od.* in die Lehre gehen; **become ~d** eine Lehre beginnen

**apprenticeship** /ə'prentɪsʃɪp/ *n.* *(training)* Lehre, *die* (**to** bei); *(learning period)* Lehrzeit, *die;* Lehrjahre *Pl.;* **serve an/one's ~:** eine/seine Lehre machen; *(fig.)* ein/sein Volontariat machen

**apprise** /ə'praɪz/ *v.t.* unterrichten; in Kenntnis setzen; **~ sb. that ...:** jmdn. darüber unterrichten *od.* davon in Kenntnis setzen, dass ...; **~ sb. of sth.** jmdn. über etw. *(Akk.) od.* von etw. unterrichten; **be ~d of sth.** über etw. *(Akk.)* unterrichtet sein

**appro** /'æprəʊ/ *n.* *(Brit.)* **on ~** *(Commerc. coll.)* = **on approval;** ⇒ **approval B**

**approach** /ə'prəʊtʃ/ ❶ *v.i.* *(in space)* sich nähern; näher kommen; ‹Soldaten:› [heran]anrücken; ‹Sturm usw.:› aufziehen; *(in time)* nahen; **the train now ~ing platform 1** der auf Gleis 1 einfahrende Zug; **the time is fast ~ing when you will have to ...:** es wird nicht mehr lange dauern und du musst ...
❷ *v.t.* **A** *(come near to)* sich nähern (+ *Dat.*); *(set about)* herangehen an (+ *Akk.*); angehen ‹Problem, Aufgabe, Thema›; **B** *(be similar to)* verwandt sein (+ *Dat.*); **C** *(approximate to)* nahe kommen (+ *Dat.*); **the temperature/weight ~es 100 °C/50 kg** die Temperatur/das Gewicht beträgt nahezu 100 °C/50 kg; **a performance ~ing perfection** eine an Perfektion grenzende Aufführung; **few writers can ~ Shakespeare** wenige Dichter reichen an Shakespeare heran; **D** *(appeal to)* sich wenden an (+ *Akk.*); **E** *(attempt to influence)* herantreten an (+ *Akk.*); **F** *(make advances to)* sich heranmachen an (+ *Akk.*).
❸ *n.* **A** [Heran]nahen, *das; (treatment)* Ansatz, *der* (**to** zu); *(attitude)* Einstellung, *die* (**to** gegenüber); **a new ~:** eine neue Sicht; **B** *(similarity)* Ähnlichkeit, *die* (**to** mit); **C** *(approximation)* Annäherung, *die;* **some sort of ~ to a timetable** ein ungefährer Zeitplan; **D** *(appeal)* Herantreten, *das* (**to** an + *Akk.*); **make an ~ to sb. concerning sth.** wegen etw. an jmdn. herantreten; sich wegen etw. an jmdn. wenden; **E** *(attempt to influence)* Vorstoß, *der* (**to** bei); **F** *(advance)* Annäherungsversuche; **make ~es to sb.** Annäherungsversuche bei jmdm. machen; **G** *(access)* Zugang, *der; (road)* Zufahrtsstraße, *die; (fig.)* Zugang, *der;* **H** *(Aeronaut.)* Landeanflug, *der;* Approach, *der*

**approachability** /əprəʊtʃə'bɪlɪtɪ/ *n.* **A** *(friendliness)* Umgänglichkeit, *die; (receptiveness)* Empfänglichkeit, *die;* **B** *(accessibility)* Zugänglichkeit, *die*

**approachable** /ə'prəʊtʃəbl/ *adj.* **A** *(friendly)* umgänglich; *(receptive)* empfänglich; **B** *(accessible)* zugänglich; erreichbar

**ap'proach road** *n.* Zufahrtsstraße, *die*

**approbate** /'æprəbeɪt/ *v.t.* *(Amer.)* genehmigen; approbieren *(veralt.)*

**approbation** /æprə'beɪʃn/ *n.* *(sanction)* Genehmigung, *die; (Relig.)* Approbation, *die; (approval)* Zustimmung, *die;* Einverständnis, *das;* **parental ~:** elterliches Einverständnis; Einwilligung der Eltern; **meet with/get sb.'s ~:** jmds. Zustimmung finden

**appropriate** ❶ /ə'prəʊprɪət/ *adj.* *(suitable)* geeignet (**to, for** für); *(peculiar)* eigen (**to** *Dat.*); **I feel it is ~ on such an occasion to say a few words** ich halte es für angebracht, bei einem solchen Anlass ein paar Worte zu sagen; **a style ~ to a man of his age and importance** ein Stil, der einem Mann in seinem Alter und seiner Stellung entspricht; **the ~ authority** die zuständige Behörde.
❷ /ə'prəʊprɪeɪt/ *v.t.* **A** *(take possession of)* sich *(Dat.)* aneignen; sich bemächtigen (+ *Gen.*); *(take to oneself)* **~ sth. [to oneself]** etw. in [seinen] Besitz nehmen; etw. mit Beschlag belegen; **B** *(reserve)* **~ sth. [to/for sth.]** etw. [zu/für etw.] bestimmen

**appropriately** /ə'prəʊprɪətlɪ/ *adv.* gebührend; passend ‹dekoriert, gekleidet, genannt›

**appropriateness** /ə'prəʊprɪətnɪs/ *n., no pl.* Angemessenheit, *die; (of remarks, words)* Angebrachtheit, *die*

**appropriation** /əprəʊprɪ'eɪʃn/ *n.* Besitzergreifung, *die; (taking to oneself)* Aneignung, *die;* In-Beschlag-Nehman, *das; (reservation)* Bestimmung, *die*

**approval** /ə'pru:vl/ *n.* **A** *(sanctioning) (of plan, project, expenditure)* Genehmigung, *die; (of proposal, reform, marriage)* Billigung, *die; (agreement)* Zustimmung, *die;* Einwilligung, *die* (**for** in + *Akk.*); **letter of ~:** Genehmigungsschreiben, *das;* **B** *(esteem)* Lob, *das;* Anerkennung, *die;* **does the plan meet with your ~?** findet der Plan Ihre Zustimmung?; **murmurs of ~:** zustimmendes Gemurmel; **on ~** *(Commerc.)* zur Probe; *(to view)* zur Ansicht

**approve** /ə'pru:v/ ❶ *v.t.* **A** *(sanction)* genehmigen ‹Plan, Projekt, Ausgaben›; billigen ‹Vorschlag, Reform, Heirat›; *(commend)* loben; anerkennen; **~d hotel** empfohlenes Hotel; **~d school** *(Brit. Hist.)* Erziehungsheim, *das;* Besserungsanstalt, *die (veralt.)*; **B** *(find good)* gutheißen; für gut halten. ❷ *v.i.* **~ of** billigen; zustimmen (+ *Dat.*) ‹Plan›; einverstanden sein mit ‹Tätigkeiten, Gewohnheiten, Verhalten›; **they don't ~ of her going out with boys** sie sind nicht damit einverstanden, dass sie mit Jungen ausgeht

**approving** /ə'pru:vɪŋ/ *adj.* zustimmend, beipflichtend ‹Worte›; anerkennend, bewundernd ‹Blicke›

**approvingly** /ə'pru:vɪŋlɪ/ *adv.* ⇒ **approving:** zustimmend; anerkennend

**approx.** /ə'prɒks/ *abbr.* **approximately** ca.

**approximate** ❶ /ə'prɒksɪmət/ *adj.* *(fairly correct)* ungefähr *attr.;* **the figures given here are only ~:** dies hier sind nur ungefähre Zahlen. ❷ /ə'prɒksɪmeɪt/ *v.t.* **A** *(make similar)* **~ sth. to sth.** etw. einer Sache *(Dat.)* anpassen; **B** *(come near to)* nahe kommen (+ *Dat.*); annähernd erreichen (+ *Akk.*). ❸ *v.i.* **sth. ~s to sth.** etw. gleicht einer Sache *(Dat.)* annähernd

**approximately** /ə'prɒksɪmətlɪ/ *adv.* *(roughly)* ungefähr; *(almost)* fast; **the answer is ~ correct** die Antwort stimmt ungefähr; **very ~:** ganz grob

**approximation** /əprɒksɪ'meɪʃn/ *n.* **A** Annäherung, *die* (**to** an + *Dat.*); Angleichung, *die* (**to** an + *Dat.*); **B** *(estimate)* Annäherungswert, *der;* **at** *or* **as a rough ~ I'd say ...:** grob geschätzt würde ich sagen ...

**appurtenances** /ə'pɜ:tɪnənsɪz/ *n. pl.* **A** *(belongings, appendages)* Zubehör, *das;* **he had all the ~ of 'the good life'** er hatte alles, was zum „guten Leben" gehört; **... and all the ~:** ... mit allem Zubehör; **B** *(accessories)* Attribute

**APR** *abbr.* **annualized percentage rate** Jahreszinssatz, *der*

**Apr.** *abbr.* **April** Apr.

**après-ski** /æpreɪ'ski:/ *n., no pl.* Après-Ski, *der; attrib.* Après-Ski-

**apricot** /'eɪprɪkɒt/ ❶ *n.* **A** *(fruit, tree)* Aprikose, *die;* **~ jam** Aprikosenmarmelade, *die;* **~ brandy** Apricot-Brandy, *der;* Aprikosenlikör, *der;* **B** *(colour)* Aprikosenfarbe, *die;* Apricot, *das.* ❷ *adj.* aprikosenfarben

**April** /'eɪprəl/ *n.* ▶ **1055** April, *der;* **~ fool** April[s]narr, *der;* **make an ~ fool of sb.** jmdn. in den April schicken; **'~ fool!'** „April, April!"; **~ Fool's Day** der 1. April; **~ showers** typisches Aprilwetter; ⇒ *also* **August**

**a priori** /eɪ praɪ'ɔ:raɪ/ ❶ *adv.* von vornherein; a priori *(Philos.).* ❷ *adj.* apriorisch

**apron** /'eɪprən/ *n.* **A** *(garment)* Schürze, *die;* **be tied to sb.'s ~ strings** jmdm. an der Schürze *od.* am Schürzenzipfel hängen; **B** *(on airfield)* Vorfeld, *das;* **C** *(Theatre)* **~ [stage]** Vorbühne, *die*

**apropos** /æprə'pəʊ, 'æprəpəʊ/ ❶ *adv.* **A** *(to the purpose)* passend; *(just when wanted)* zur Hand; **B ~ of** *(in respect of)* in Bezug auf (+ *Akk.*); hinsichtlich (+ *Gen.*); **C** *(incidentally)* apropos; übrigens; da wir gerade davon sprechen. ❷ *adj.* passend; treffend ‹Bemerkung›. ❸ *prep.* *(coll.)* apropos

**apse** /æps/ *n.* *(Archit.)* Apsis, *die*

**apt** /æpt/ *adj.* **A** *(suitable)* passend ‹Ausdruck, Geschenk›; angemessen ‹Reaktion›; treffend ‹Zitat, Bemerkung›; **B** *(tending)* **be ~ to do sth.** dazu neigen, etw. zu tun; **C** *(quick-witted)* begabt (**at** für); **be ~ at doing sth.** eine Gabe dafür haben, etw. zu tun

**aptitude** /'æptɪtju:d/ *n.* **A** *(propensity)* Neigung, *die; (ability)* Begabung, *die;* **linguistic ~:** Sprachbegabung, *die;* **learning ~:** Lernfähigkeit, *die;* **~ test** Eignungstest, *der;* **B** *(suitability)* Eignung, *die*

**aptly** /'æptlɪ/ *adv.* passend; **~ chosen words** treffend gewählte Worte

**aptness** /'æptnɪs/ *n., no pl.* **A** *(suitability)* Angemessenheit, *die;* **the ~ of his replies** die Treffsicherheit seiner Antworten; **B** *(tendency)* Neigung, *die;* **C** *(quick-wittedness)* Begabung, *die* (**at** für)

**aqualung** /'ækwəlʌŋ/ *n.* Tauchgerät, *das*

**aquamarine** /ækwəmə'ri:n/ ❶ *n.* **A** *(colour)* Aquamarin, *das;* **B** *(stone)* Aquamarin, *der.* ❷ *adj.* aquamarin[farben]

**aquaplane** /'ækwəpleɪn/ ❶ *v.i.* **A** ‹Reifen:› aufschwimmen; ‹Fahrzeug:› [durch Aquaplaning] ins Rutschen geraten; **B** *(use ~)* Wasserski laufen. ❷ *n.* Monoski, *der;* Wasserski, *der*

**aquaplaning** /'ækwəpleɪnɪŋ/ **A** Aquaplaning, *das;* **B** *(Sport)* Wasserski, *das*

**aqua regia** /ækwə 'ri:dʒɪə/ *n.* *(Chem.)* Königswasser, *das;* Goldscheidewasser, *das*

**aquarelle** /ækwə'rel/ *n.* *(technique)* Aquarellmalerei, *die; (product)* Aquarell, *das*

**Aquarian** /ə'kweərɪən/ *n.* *(Astrol.)* Wassermann, *der*

**aquarium** /ə'kweərɪəm/ *n., pl.* **~s** *or* **aquaria** /ə'kweərɪə/ Aquarium, *das*

**Aquarius** /ə'kweərɪəs/ *n.* *(Astrol., Astron.)* der Wassermann; der Aquarius; ⇒ *also* **Aries**

**aquatic** /ə'kwætɪk/ ❶ *adj.* **A** aquatisch; Wasser-; **~ plant/bird** Wasserpflanze, *die*/-vogel, *der;* **B** *(Sport)* Wassersport-; **~ sports** Wassersportarten. ❷ *n.* **A** *(plant)*

Wasserpflanze, *die;* (*animal*) Wassertier, *das;* **B** *in pl.* (*Sport*) Wassersport, *der*

**aquatint** /'ækwətɪnt/ *n.* (*technique*) Aquatinta, *die;* (*product*) Aquatintaarbeit, *die*

**aqueduct** /'ækwɪdʌkt/ *n.* Aquädukt, *der od. das*

**aqueous** /'eɪkwɪəs, 'ækwɪəs/ *adj.* (*containing water, watery*) wässerig; wässrig; aquatisch (*fachspr.*); ~ **vapour/content** Wasserdampf/-gehalt, *der*

**aqueous 'humour** *n.* (*Anat.*) Kammerwasser, *das;* Humor aquosus (*fachspr.*)

**aquifer** /'ækwɪfə(r)/ *n.* (*Geol.*) Wasser führende Schicht

**aquilegia** /ækwɪ'li:dʒɪə/ *n.* (*Bot.*) [Gemeine] Akelei

**aquiline** /'ækwɪlaɪn/ *adj.* adlerartig; Adler-; ~ **eye/nose** Adlerauge, *das*/-nase, *die*

**Arab** /'ærəb/ **1** *adj.* ▶ 1340 arabisch; ~ **horse** Araber, *der.* **2** *n.* **A** ▶ 1340 Araber, *der*/Araberin, *die;* **desert** ~: Beduine, *der;* **B** (*Arabian horse*) Araber, *der;* **C** **street arab** Betteljunge, *der*

**arabesque** /ærə'besk/ *n.* **A** Arabeske, *die;* **B** (*Ballet*) Arabesque, *die*

**Arabia** /ə'reɪbɪə/ *pr. n.* Arabien (*das*)

**Arabian** /ə'reɪbɪən/ **1** *adj.* arabisch; **the** ~ **Nights** Tausendundeine Nacht. **2** *n.* Araber, *der*/Araberin, *die*

**Arabic** /'ærəbɪk/ **1** *adj.* arabisch; **gum a**~ Gummiarabikum, *das;* **a**~ **numerals** arabische Ziffern; ⇨ *also* **English** 1. **2** *n.* ▶ 1275 Arabisch, *das;* ⇨ *also* **English** 2 A

**arabis** /'ærəbɪs/ *n.* (*Bot.*) Gänsekresse, *die*

**Arab-Is'raeli** *attrib. adj.* ▶ 1340 arabisch-israelisch

**Arabist** /'ærəbɪst/ *n.* Arabist, *der*/Arabistin, *die*

**arable** /'ærəbl/ **1** *adj.* bebaubar, landwirtschaftlich nutzbar ‹Land›; ~ **land** (*cultivated*) Ackerland, *das;* ~ **crops** landwirtschaftliche Nutzpflanzen. **2** *n.* Ackerland, *das*

**Araby** /'ærəbɪ/ *pr. n.* (*poet.*) Arabien (*das*)

**arachnid** /ə'ræknɪd/ *n.* (*Zool.*) Spinnentier, *das;* **the** ~**s** die Spinnentiere *od.* (*fachspr.*) Arachn[o]iden

**Araldite** ® /'ærəldaɪt/ *n.* Araldit, *das* Ⓦᶻ

**Aramaic** /ærə'meɪɪk/ ▶ 1275 **1** *adj.* aramäisch. **2** *n.* Aramäisch, *das*

**araucaria** /ærɔ:'keərɪə/ *n.* (*Bot.*) Araukarie, *die*

**arbiter** /'ɑ:bɪtə(r)/ *n.* (*judge*) Richter, *der;* (*arbitrator*) Vermittler, *der;* (*controller*) Herr, *der,* (*geh.*) Gebieter, *der* (**of** über + *Akk.*)

**arbitrage** /'ɑ:bɪtrɑ:ʒ/ *n.* (*St. Exch.*) Arbitrage, *die*

**arbitrarily** /'ɑ:bɪtrərɪlɪ/ *adv.* **A** (*at random*) willkürlich; arbiträr (*geh.*); (*capriciously*) aus einer Laune heraus; **B** (*unrestrainedly*) rücksichtslos; **C** (*despotically*) willkürlich

**arbitrariness** /'ɑ:bɪtrərɪnɪs/ *n., no pl.* **A** (*randomness*) Willkür, *die;* Willkürlichkeit, *die;* Arbitrarität, *die* (*geh.*); (*capriciousness*) Launenhaftigkeit, *die;* **B** (*unrestrainedness*) Rücksichtslosigkeit, *die;* **C** (*despotism*) Willkür, *die*

**arbitrary** /'ɑ:bɪtrərɪ/ *adj.* **A** (*random*) willkürlich; arbiträr; (*capricious*) launenhaft; launisch ‹Idee›; **B** (*unrestrained*) rücksichtslos ‹Vorgehen, Bestrafung, Wesen, Haltung›; **C** (*despotic*) willkürlich; ~ **rule** Willkürherrschaft, *die*

**arbitrate** /'ɑ:bɪtreɪt/ **1** *v.t.* schlichten, beilegen ‹Streit›; ~ **a difference of opinion** eine Meinungsverschiedenheit beseitigen. **2** *v.i.* ~ **[upon sth.]** [in einer Sache] vermitteln *od.* als Schiedsrichter fungieren; ~ **between parties** zwischen Parteien vermitteln

**arbitration** /ɑ:bɪ'treɪʃn/ *n.* Vermittlung, *die;* (*in industry*) Schlichtung, *die;* **go to** ~: einen Schlichter anrufen *od.* einschalten; ‹Konflikt:› einem Schlichter vorgelegt werden; **take sth. to** ~: etw. einem Schlichter vorlegen

**arbitrator** /'ɑ:bɪtreɪtə(r)/ *n.* (*mediator*) Vermittler, *der;* (*in industry*) Schlichter, *der;* (*arbiter*) Schiedsrichter, *der;* (*judge*) Richter, *der*

**arbor**[1] /'ɑ:bə(r)/ *n.* (*axle*) Welle, *die;* Spindel, *die;* (*Amer.: tool holder*) Dorn, *der;* Aufsteckhalter, *der;* Träger, *der*

**arbor**[2] (*Amer.*) ⇨ **arbour**

**Arbor Day** /'ɑ:bə deɪ/ *n.* (*Amer., Austral.*) Tag des Baumes

**arboreal** /ɑ:'bɔ:rɪəl/ *adj.* (*of trees*) Baum-; (*inhabiting trees*) Baum-; auf Bäumen lebend; **be** ~: auf Bäumen leben

**arboretum** /ɑ:bə'ri:təm/ *n., pl.* **arboreta** /ɑ:bə'ri:tə/ *or* ~**s** Arboretum, *das;* Baumgarten, *der*

**arboriculture** /'ɑ:bərɪkʌltʃə(r)/ *n.* Baumzucht, *die*

**arbor vitae** /ɑ:bə 'vaɪti:, ɑ:bə 'vi:taɪ/ *n.* (*Bot.*) Lebensbaum, *der*

**arbour** /'ɑ:bə(r)/ *n.* (*Brit.*) Laube, *die*

**arbutus** /ɑ:'bju:təs/ *n.* Arbutus, *der;* Erdbeerbaum, *der;* **trailing** ~ (*Amer.*) kriechende Heide

**arc** /ɑ:k/ *n.* **A** [Kreis]bogen, *der;* **B** (*Electr.*) Lichtbogen, *der;* ~ **lamp,** ~ **light** Lichtbogenlampe, *die;* ~ **welding** Lichtbogen-, Elektroschweißung, *die*

**arcade** /ɑ:'keɪd/ *n.* Arkade, *die;* **shopping** ~: Einkaufspassage, *die*

**Arcadian** /ɑ:'keɪdɪən/ *adj.* arkadisch

**arcane** /ɑ:'keɪn/ *adj.* geheimnisvoll; undurchschaubar; **an** ~ **secret** ein verborgenes Geheimnis

**arch**[1] /ɑ:tʃ/ **1** *n.* Bogen, *der;* (*curvature; of foot*) Wölbung, *die;* (*of bridge*) Bogen, *der;* Joch, *das;* (*vault*) Gewölbe, *das.* **2** *v.i.* sich wölben; ‹Ast, Glied:› sich biegen. **3** *v.t.* **A** (*furnish with* ~) mit Bogen versehen; ~**ed gateway** Torbogen, *der;* ~**ed in the Gothic manner** mit gotischem/gotischen Bogen; **B** (*form into* ~) beugen ‹Rücken, Arm›; **the cat** ~**ed its back** die Katze machte einen Buckel

**arch**[2] *adj.* schelmisch; kokett

**arch-** *pref.* Erz-; ~**villain** Erzschurke, *der;* Erzgauner, *der*

**archaeological** /ɑ:kɪə'lɒdʒɪkl/ *adj.* archäologisch; ~ **dig** [Aus]grabung, *die*

**archaeologist** /ɑ:kɪ'ɒlədʒɪst/ *n.* ▶ 1261 Archäologe, *der*/Archäologin, *die;* Altertumsforscher, *der*/-forscherin, *die*

**archaeology** /ɑ:kɪ'ɒlədʒɪ/ *n.* Archäologie, *die;* Altertumskunde, *die;* **marine/industrial** ~: Unterwasser-/Industriearchäologie, *die*

**archaic** /ɑ:'keɪɪk/ *adj.* (*out of use*) veraltet; archaisch; (*antiquated*) altertümlich; überholt ‹Methode, Gesetz›; **an** ~ **typewriter** (*coll.*) eine museumsreife *od.* vorsintflutliche Schreibmaschine

**archaically** /ɑ:'keɪɪkəlɪ/ *adv.* (*in out-of-use style*) altertümlich, (*deliberately*) altertümelnd ‹sich ausdrücken, schreiben›

**archaism** /'ɑ:keɪɪzm/ *n.* Archaismus, *der*

**archangel** /'ɑ:keɪndʒl/ *n.* Erzengel, *der*

**arch'bishop** *n.* ▶ 1617 Erzbischof, *der*

**arch'bishopric** *n.* **A** (*office*) Amt des Erzbischofs; **B** (*diocese*) Erzbistum, *das*

**arch'deacon** *n.* Archi-, Erzdiakon, *der*

**arch'deaconry, arch'deaconship** *ns.* Archidiakonat, *das od. der*

**arch'diocese** ⇨ **archbishopric** B

**arch'duchess** *n.* (*Hist.*) Erzherzogin, *die*

**arch'duke** *n.* (*Hist.*) Erzherzog, *der*

**arch-'enemy** *n.* (*chief enemy*) Erzfeind, *der;* (*the Devil*) ⇨ **arch-fiend**

**archeology** *etc.* (*Amer.*) ⇨ **archaeology** *etc.*

**archer** /'ɑ:tʃə(r)/ *n.* **A** Bogenschütze, *der;* **B** (*Astrol.*) **the A**~: der Schütze; **under the sign of the A**~: im Zeichen des Schützen

**'archerfish** *n.* Schützenfisch, *der*

**archery** /'ɑ:tʃərɪ/ *n., no pl.* Bogenschießen, *das*

**archetypal** /'ɑ:kɪtaɪpl/ *adj.* (*original*) archetypisch (*geh.*); (*typical*) typisch; prototypisch; **he was the** ~ **film director** er war der Prototyp des Regisseurs

**archetype** /'ɑ:kɪtaɪp/ *n.* (*original*) Urfassung, *die;* Archetyp, *der;* (*typical specimen*) Prototyp, *der;* Archetyp, *der*

**arch-'fiend** *n.* Erzfeind, *der;* Satan, *der*

**archiepiscopal** /ɑ:kɪɪ'pɪskəpl/ *adj.* erzbischöflich

**archiepiscopate** /ɑ:kɪɪ'pɪskəpət/ ⇨ **archbishopric** A

**Archimedes** /ɑ:kɪ'mi:di:z/ *n.* ~**' principle** (*Phys.*) das Archimedische Prinzip

**archipelago** /ɑ:kɪ'peləgəʊ/ *n., pl.* ~**s** *or* ~**es** Archipel, *der;* (*islands*) Inselgruppe, *die;* (*sea*) Inselmeer, *das*

**architect** /'ɑ:kɪtekt/ *n.* **A** ▶ 1261 (*designer*) Architekt, *der*/Architektin, *die;* Baumeister, *der* (*geh.*); **naval** ~: Schiffskonstrukteur, *der;* Schiffbauer, *der;* ⇨ *also* **landscape architect**; **B** (*maker, creator*) Schöpfer, *der;* (*fig.*) Urheber, *der;* **the** ~ **of one's own fate/fortune** seines [eigenen] Glückes Schmied

**architectonic** /ɑ:kɪtek'tɒnɪk/ *adj.* **A** architektonisch; **B** (*constructive*) schöpferisch ‹Fähigkeiten, Kraft›

**architectural** /ɑ:kɪ'tektʃərl/ *adj.* architektonisch; ~ **style** Baustil, *der*

**architecture** /'ɑ:kɪtektʃə(r)/ *n.* **A** Architektur, *die;* Baukunst, *die* (*geh.*); (*style*) Bauweise, *die;* Architektur, *die;* **naval/railway/bridge** ~: Schiff[s]-/Eisenbahn-/Brückenbau, *der;* **B** (*structure, lit. or fig.*) Konstruktion, *die;* **C** (*Computing*) [System]architektur, *die*

**architrave** /'ɑ:kɪtreɪv/ *n.* (*beam*) Architrav, *der;* Epistylion, *das;* (*moulding*) Archivolte, *die*

**archival** /ɑ:'kaɪvəl/ *adj.* archivalisch

**archive** /'ɑ:kaɪv/ **1** *n., usu. in pl.* Archiv, *das.* **2** *v.t.* archivieren

**archivist** /'ɑ:kɪvɪst/ *n.* ▶ 1261 Archivar, *der*/Archivarin, *die*

**archly** /'ɑ:tʃlɪ/ *adv.* schelmisch; kokett

**archness** /'ɑ:tʃnɪs/ *n., no pl.* Schalkhaftigkeit, *die;* (*of woman*) Koketterie, *die*

**arch-'traitor** *n.* Erzverräter, *der*

**'archway** *n.* (*vaulted passage*) Gewölbegang, *der;* Tunnel, *der;* (*arched entrance*) Durchgang, *der;* Torbogen, *der*

**arctic** /'ɑ:ktɪk/ **1** *adj.* (*lit. or fig.*) arktisch; **A**~ **Circle/Ocean** nördlicher Polarkreis/Nordpolarmeer, *das.* **2** *pr. n.* **the A**~: die Arktis. **3** *n.* (*Amer.: overshoe*) hoher Überschuh

**arctic:** ~ **'fox** *n.* Polarfuchs, *der;* ~ **'tern** *n.* Küstenseeschwalbe, *die*

**ardency** /'ɑ:dənsɪ/ *n., no pl.* Eifer, *der* (**in** bei); (*of feeling, desire, etc.*) Leidenschaftlichkeit, *die;* Heftigkeit, *die;* (*of admiration, prayer, belief, poem*) Inbrunst, *die*

**Ardennes** /ɑ:'den/ *pr. n. pl.* Ardennen *Pl.*

**ardent** /'ɑ:dənt/ *adj.* **A** (*eager*) begeistert ‹Anhänger, Theaterbesucher, Interesse, Gefolgsmann›; (*fervent*) glühend ‹Bewunderer, Leidenschaft›; hitzig ‹Temperament, Wesen›; brennend ‹Wunsch›; feurig ‹Rede, Liebhaber›; leidenschaftlich ‹Gedicht, Liebesbrief, Anbetung›; innigst, (*geh.*) inbrünstig ‹Hoffnung, Liebe›

**ardently** /'ɑ:dəntlɪ/ *adv.* (*eagerly*) begeistert; (*fervently*) glühend; **hope** ~: inbrünstig (*geh.*) *od.* inständig hoffen

**ardour** (*Brit.; Amer.:* **ardor**) /'ɑ:də(r)/ *n.* (*warm emotion*) Leidenschaft, *die;* (*passionate emotion*) Inbrunst, *die* (*geh.*); (*fervour*) Eifer, *der;* ~ **for reform/learning** Reformeifer, *der*/Wissensdurst, *der*

**arduous** /'ɑ:djʊəs/ *adj.* schwer, anstrengend ‹Aufgabe, Arbeit, Unterfangen›; hart ‹Arbeit, Tag, Zeit›; beschwerlich ‹Reise, Aufstieg, Fahrt›

**arduously** /'ɑ:djʊəslɪ/ *adv.* (*laboriously*) beschwerlich

**arduousness** /'ɑ:djʊəsnɪs/ *n., no pl.* (*difficulty*) Mühe, *die;* Beschwerlichkeit, *die*

**are**[1] /ɑ:(r)/ *n.* Ar, *das*

**are**[2] ⇨ **be**

**area** /'eərɪə/ *n.* **A** ▶ 928 (*surface measure*) Flächenausdehnung, *die;* **the floor** ~ **is 15 square metres** der Fußboden hat eine Fläche von 15 Quadratmetern; **what is the** ~ **of your farm?** wie groß ist Ihr Hof?; **B** (*region*) Gelände, *das;* (*of wood, marsh, desert*) Gebiet, *das;* (*of city, country*) Gegend, *die;* (*of*

a

## Area (square measure)

| | | | |
|---|---|---|---|
| 1 square inch (sq. in.) | = 6,45 cm² (sechs Komma vier fünf Quadratzentimeter) | | |
| 144 square inches | = 1 square foot (sq. ft) | = 929 cm² (neunhundertneunundzwanzig Quadratzentimeter) | |
| 9 square feet | = 1 square yard (sq. yd) | = 0,836 m² (null Komma acht drei sechs Quadratmeter) | |
| 4,840 square yards | = 1 acre | = 0,4 ha (null Komma vier Hektar) | |
| 640 acres | = 1 square mile | = 2,59 km² (zwei Komma fünf neun Quadratkilometer) | |

***What is the area of the room?***
= Wie viel Quadratmeter hat das Zimmer?
***The area of the room is 180 square feet***
= Das Zimmer hat 16,72 Quadratmeter [Fläche]
***2,000 square feet of office space***
≈ 186 Quadratmeter Bürofläche
***He farms 1,000 acres [of land]***
≈ Er bewirtschaftet 400 Hektar [Land]
***a farm of 1,000 acres***
≈ ein 400 Hektar großer Bauernhof, ein Bauernhof von 400 Hektar
***an area of about 40 square miles***
≈ eine Fläche von etwa 100 Quadratkilometern

*skin, wall, etc.*) Stelle, *die;* **a poor ~ of the town** eine arme Gegend der Stadt; **it happened in this ~:** es ereignete sich hier in der Nähe; **in the Hamburg ~:** im Hamburger Raum; **in the ~ of ...** (*fig.*) um ... herum; **an ~ of ground** ein Grundstück *od.* Gelände *od.* Areal; **C** (*defined space*) Bereich, *der;* **parking/picnic/sports ~:** Park-/Picknick-/Sportplatz, *der;* **no-smoking ~:** Nichtraucherzone, *die;* **D** (*subject field*) Gebiet, *das;* **in the ~ of electronics/medicine** auf dem Gebiet *od.* im Bereich der Elektronik/Medizin; **E** (*scope*) Raum, *der;* **~ of choice** Wahlmöglichkeiten *Pl.;* **~ of responsibility** Verantwortungsbereich, *der;* **F** (*sunken court*) Vorhof, *der*

**'area code** *n.* (*Amer. Teleph.*) Gebietsvorwahl[nummer], *die*

**areaway** /'eərɪəweɪ/ (*Amer.*) ⇒ **area F**

**areca** /'ærɪkə, ə'ri:kə/ *n.* Arekapalme, *die;* **~ nut** Arekanuss, *die*

**arena** /ə'ri:nə/ *n.* (*at circus, bullfight*) Arena, *die;* (*in equestrianism*) Dressurviereck, *das;* (*fig.: scene of conflict*) Bühne, *die;* Schauplatz, *der;* (*fig.: sphere of action*) Bereich, *der;* **the political ~:** die politische Arena; **enter the ~** (*fig.*) die Arena betreten; auf den Plan treten; **~ stage** Arenabühne, *die;* **~ theatre** Arenatheater, *das*

**aren't** /ɑ:nt/ (*coll.*) = **are not;** ⇒ **be**

**areola** /ə'ri:ələ/ *n., pl.* **~e** /ə'ri:əli:/ (*Anat.*) (*of nipple*) Warzenhof, *der;* (*of eye*) *an die Pupille grenzender Teil der Iris*

**argent** /'ɑ:dʒənt/ (*esp. Her.*) **1** *n.* Silber, *das.* **2** *adj.* silbern

**Argentina** /ɑdʒən'ti:nə/ *pr. n.* Argentinien (*das*)

**Argentine** /'ɑ:dʒəntaɪn/ **1** *pr. n.* **the ~:** Argentinien (*das*). **2** *adj.* argentinisch

**Argentinian** /ɑ:dʒən'tɪnɪən/ ▶ **1340** **1** *adj.* argentinisch; **sb. is ~:** jmd. ist Argentinier/Argentinierin. **2** *n.* Argentinier, *der*/Argentinierin, *die*

**argillaceous** /ɑ:dʒɪ'leɪʃəs/ *adj.* (*of clay*) tonig; tonhaltig; (*like clay*) tonartig

**argle-bargle** /ɑ:gl'bɑ:gl/ ⇒ **argy-bargy**

**argon** /'ɑ:gɒn/ *n.* (*Chem.*) Argon, *das*

**argonaut** /'ɑ:gənɔ:t/ *n.* **A** (*Zool.*) Papierboot, *das;* **B A~** (*Mythol.*) Argonaut, *der*

**argosy** /'ɑ:gəsɪ/ *n.* (*Hist./poet.: merchant vessel*) Handelsschiff, *das*

**argot** /'ɑ:gəʊ/ *n.* Argot, *das od. der;* **thieves' ~:** Rotwelsch, *das;* **that class/group has its own ~:** diese Klasse/Gruppe hat ihren eigenen Jargon *od.* Slang

**arguable** /'ɑ:gjʊəbl/ *adj.* **A** fragwürdig ‹Angelegenheit, Punkt›; **it's not an ~ point at all** das ist überhaupt keine Frage; **it's ~ whether ...:** es ist noch die Frage, ob ...; **B it is ~ that ...** (*can reasonably be argued that*) man kann sich auf den Standpunkt stellen, dass ...

**arguably** /'ɑ:gjʊəblɪ/ *adv.* möglicherweise

**argue** /'ɑ:gju:/ **1** *v.t.* **A** (*maintain*) **~ that ...:** die Ansicht vertreten, dass ...; **B** (*treat by reasoning*) darlegen ‹Grund, Standpunkt, Fakten›; **I don't want to ~ the point now** lassen wir für den Moment diesen Punkt noch ungeklärt; **~ sth. away** etw. wegdiskutieren; **C** (*persuade*) **~ sb. into doing sth.** jmdn. dazu überreden, etw. zu tun; **~ sb. out of doing sth.** [es] jmdm. ausreden, etw. zu tun; **D** (*prove*) **~ sb. [to be] sb./sth.** der Beweis dafür sein, dass jmd. jmd./etw. ist; **E** (*indicate*) **~ sth.** von etw. zeugen
**2** *v.i.* **~ with sb.** sich mit jmdm. streiten; **~ against sb.** jmdm. widersprechen; **~ for/against sth.** für/gegen etw. eintreten; sich für/gegen etw. aussprechen; **~ about sth.** sich über/um etw. (*Akk.*) streiten; **none of your arguing!** keine Widerrede!

**argument** /'ɑ:gjʊmənt/ *n.* **A** (*reason*) Begründung, *die;* **~s for/against sth.** Argumente für/gegen etw.; **B** *no pl.* (*reasoning process*) Argumentieren, *das;* **the powers of logical ~:** das Vermögen, logisch zu argumentieren; **assume sth. for ~'s sake** etw. rein theoretisch annehmen; **C** (*debate*) Auseinandersetzung, *die;* **get into an ~/get into ~s with sb.** mit jmdm. in Streit geraten; **D** (*summary*) Kurzfassung, *die;* Zusammenfassung, *die;* **E** (*Math.*) Argument, *das*

**argumentation** /ɑ:gjʊmen'teɪʃn/ *n.* **A** *no pl.* (*reasoning*) Argumentieren, *das;* **his powers of ~:** seine Fähigkeit, zu argumentieren; **B** (*debate*) Gezänk, *das*

**argumentative** /ɑ:gjʊ'mentətɪv/ *adj.* **A** (*fond of arguing*) widerspruchsfreudig; (*quarrelsome*) streitlustig; streitsüchtig; **B** (*logical*) argumentativ

**Argus** /'ɑ:gəs/ *n.* **A** (*butterfly*) Augenfalter, *der;* **B** (*Ornith.*) Arguspfau, *der*

**argy-bargy** /ɑ:dʒɪ'bɑ:dʒɪ/ (*joc.*) **1** *n.* Hickhack, *der od. das* (*ugs.*); Streiterei, *die.* **2** *v.i.* sich herumstreiten (*ugs.*) (**about** über + *Akk.*)

**aria** /'ɑ:rɪə/ *n.* (*Mus.*) Arie, *die*

**Arian¹** /'eərɪən/ *n.* (*Astrol.*) Widder, *der*

**Arian²** ⇒ **Aryan**

**arid** /'ærɪd/ *adj.* **A** (*dry; also fig.*) trocken ‹Klima, Land›; **B** (*barren*) dürr; karg; **C** (*Geog.*) arid; **~ zone** Trockengürtel, *der*

**aridity** /ə'rɪdɪtɪ/ *n., no pl.* **A** (*dryness of land, heat; also fig.*) Trockenheit, *die;* (*Geog.*) Aridität, *die;* **B** (*barrenness*) Kargheit, *die*

**aridness** /'ærɪdnɪs/ ⇒ **aridity**

**Aries** /'eəri:z/ *n.* (*Astrol., Astron.*) der Widder; der Aries; **under [the sign of] ~, the Ram** im Zeichen des Aries *od.* des Widders; **he/she is an ~:** er/sie ist [ein] Widder; **first point of ~:** Frühlingspunkt, *der;* Widderpunkt, *der*

**aright** /ə'raɪt/ *adv.* recht ‹hören, sich erinnern›

**arise** /ə'raɪz/ *v.i.,* **arose** /ə'rəʊz/, **arisen** /ə'rɪzn/ **A** (*originate*) entstehen; (*literary: be born*) geboren werden; **hatred has ~n in their hearts** Hass ist in ihren Herzen aufgekeimt (*geh.*); **B** (*present itself*) auftreten; ‹Gelegenheit:› sich bieten; **a crisis has ~n in Turkey** in der Türkei ist es zu einer Krise gekommen; **new hopes have** *or* **hope has ~n that ...:** man hat wieder Hoffnung geschöpft, dass ...; **C** (*result*) **~ from** *or* **out of sth.** von etw. herrühren; **D** (*Hist.: stand up*) **~, Sir Robert!** erhebt euch, Sir Robert!; **E** ‹Sonne, Nebel:› aufsteigen; **F** ‹See, Sturm:› anschwellen; **G** (*rise from the dead*) auferstehen

**aristocracy** /ærɪ'stɒkrəsɪ/ *n.* Aristokratie, *die;* (*fig.*) **an ~ of ...:** eine Elite von ...

**aristocrat** /'ærɪstəkræt/ *n.* Aristokrat, *der*/Aristokratin, *die;* **an ~ among wines** (*fig.*) ein besonders edler Wein

**aristocratic** /ærɪstə'krætɪk/ *adj.* **A** aristokratisch; Aristokraten-; adelig; Adels-; **B** (*grand*) exklusiv ‹Luxus, Pracht etc.›; (*distinguished*) vornehm ‹Aussehen, Auftreten›; (*refined*) kultiviert; fein ‹Manieren, Sitten›; (*stylish, fine*) edel ‹Qualität, Geschmack, Gesichtszüge, Wein, Möbel›

**aristocratically** /ærɪstə'krætɪkəlɪ/ *adv.* aristokratisch

**Aristotelian** /ærɪstə'ti:lɪən/ *adj.* aristotelisch

**Aristotle** /'ærɪstɒtl/ *pr. n.* Aristoteles (*der*)

**arithmetic¹** /ə'rɪθmətɪk/ *n.* **A** (*science*) Arithmetik, *die;* **B** (*computation*) Rechnen, *das;* **mental ~:** Kopfrechnen, *das;* **there are several mistakes in your ~:** du hast dich mehrmals verrechnet

**arithmetic²** /ærɪθ'metɪk/, **arithmetical** /ærɪθ'metɪkl/ *adj.* arithmetisch; **arithmetical progression** arithmetische Progression; (*sequence/series*) arithmetische Folge/Reihe

**ark** /ɑ:k/ *n.* **sth. looks as if it came [straight] out of the ~:** etw. sieht vorsintflutlich aus; ⇒ *also* **Noah's ark**

**arm¹** /ɑ:m/ *n.* **A** ▶ **966** (*limb*) Arm, *der;* **~ in ~ [with each other]** Arm in Arm; **[be] at ~'s length [from]** auf Armeslänge [entfernt sein von]; **keep sb. at ~'s length** (*fig.*) eine gewisse Distanz zu jmdm. wahren; **as long as sb.'s ~** (*fig.*) ellenlang; **cost sb. an ~ and a leg** (*fig.*) jmdn. eine Stange Geld kosten (*ugs.*); **on sb.'s ~:** an jmds. Arm (*Dat.*); **under one's ~:** unter dem Arm; **a babe** *or* **a child in ~s** ein kleines Kind; **in sb.'s ~s** in jmds. Armen; **fall into each other's ~s** sich (*Dat.*) in die Arme fallen; **take sb. in one's ~s** jmdn. in die Arme nehmen *od.* (*geh.*) schließen; **the lovers were found dead in each other's ~s** die beiden Liebenden wurden eng umschlungen tot aufgefunden; **with open ~s** (*lit. or fig.*) mit offenen Armen; **within ~'s reach** (*lit. or fig.*) in Reichweite; **be within ~'s reach of safety** fast in Sicherheit sein; **B** (*sleeve*) Ärmel, *der;* (*support*) Armlehne, *die;* **C** (*branch*) Ast, *der;* **D** (*~-like thing*) Arm, *der*

**arm²** **1** *n.* **A** *usu. in pl.* (*weapon*) Waffe, *die;* **possession/export of ~s** Waffenbesitz/-export, *der;* **small ~s** Handfeuerwaffen; **bear ~s** (*be armed*) bewaffnet sein; (*serve as soldier*) Waffen tragen; **in ~s** bewaffnet; **lay down one's ~s** die Waffen niederlegen; **take up ~s** zu den Waffen greifen; **under ~s** bewaffnet; unter Waffen; **up in ~s** (*lit.*) kampfbereit; **be up in ~s about sth.** (*fig.*)

wegen etw. in Harnisch *od.* aufgebracht sein; **~s dealer** Waffenhändler, *der;* **B** *in pl.* (*heraldic device*) Wappen, *das;* (*inn sign*) **'The King's/Waterman's Arms'** ≈ „Zum König/Fährmann"; ⇒ *also* **coat of arms**; **C** *in pl.* (*military profession*) Kriegs- *od.* Militärdienst, *der;* **D** (*military grouping*) Waffengattung, *die.*
**2** *v.t.* **A** (*furnish with weapons*) bewaffnen; mit Waffen ausrüsten ‹Schiff›; **B** (*furnish with tools etc.*) ausrüsten; bewaffnen (*fig.*); **~ oneself with sth.** sich mit etw. wappnen; **~ed with all advantages/virtues** mit allen Vorteilen/Tugenden ausgestattet; **C** scharf machen ‹Bombe usw.›

**armada** /ɑːˈmɑːdə/ *n.* Armada, *die*

**armadillo** /ɑːməˈdɪləʊ/ *n., pl.* **~s** (*Zool.*) Gürteltier, *das*

**Armageddon** /ɑːməˈgedən/ *n.* Armageddon, *das* (*geh.*)

**armament** /ˈɑːməmənt/ *n.* **A** (*weapons etc.*) **~[s]** Kriegsgerät, *das;* **B** (*force*) Streitmacht, *die;* **C** *no pl.* (*process*) (*of persons*) Bewaffnung, *die;* (*of boat*) Ausrüstung, *die*

**armature** /ˈɑːmətʃə(r)/ *n.* **A** (*Biol.: defensive covering*) Schutzkleid, *das;* **B** (*sculptor's framework*) Knebel, *der;* Reiter, *der;* **C** (*Magn., Electr.*) Anker, *der*

**arm: ~band** *n.* Armbinde, *die;* **~chair 1** *n.* Sessel, *der;* **2** *adj.* **~chair politician/strategist** politischer Amateur/Amateurstratege, *der;* **~chair critic** Hobby- *od.* Amateurkritiker, *der;* **~chair travel** Reisen in der Fantasie

**armed** /ɑːmd/ *adj.* bewaffnet; mit Geschützen bestückt ‹Schiff›; **~ forces** Streitkräfte *Pl.;* **~ neutrality** bewaffnete Neutralität

**-armed** *adj. in comb.* (*with arms*) mit ... Armen; (*with sleeves*) -ärm[e]lig; **long-/brown-~:** mit langen/braunen Armen; **two-~:** zweiarmig

**Armenia** /ɑːˈmiːnɪə/ *pr. n.* Armenien (*das*)

**Armenian** /ɑːˈmiːnɪən/ ▶ 1275, ▶ 1340 **1** *adj.* armenisch; **sb. is ~:** jmd. ist Armenier/Armenierin; ⇒ *also* **English** 1. **2** *n.* **A** (*person*) Armenier, *der*/Armenierin, *die;* **B** (*language*) Armenisch, *das;* ⇒ *also* **English** 2 A

**armful** /ˈɑːmfʊl/ *n.* **an ~ of fruit** ein Arm voll Obst; **with an ~ of gifts** mit einem Arm voll Geschenken; **flowers by the ~:** ganze Arme voll Blumen

**'armhole** *n.* Armloch, *das*

**armistice** /ˈɑːmɪstɪs/ *n.* (*cessation from hostilities; also fig.*) Waffenstillstand, *der;* (*short truce*) Waffenruhe, *die;* **A~ Day** *Gedenktag des Endes des 1. Weltkriegs*

**armless** /ˈɑːmlɪs/ *adj.* (*without arms*) ohne Arme; armlos; (*without sleeves*) ohne Ärmel; ärmellos

**armlet** /ˈɑːmlɪt/ *n.* (*band*) Armbinde, *die;* (*bracelet*) Armring, *der;* Armreif, *der*

**'armlock** *n.* (*Wrestling*) Armschlüssel, *der*

**armor** (*Amer.*) ⇒ **armour**

**armorer** (*Amer.*) ⇒ **armourer**

**armorial** /ɑːˈmɔːrɪəl/ *adj.* Wappen-; heraldisch; **~ bearings** Wappen, *das;* Wappenschild, *der*

**armory** (*Amer.*) ⇒ **armoury**

**armour** /ˈɑːmə(r)/ (*Brit.*) **1** *n.* **A** *no pl.* (*Hist.*) Rüstung, *die;* **suit of ~:** Harnisch, *der;* **B** *no pl.* (*steel plates*) Panzerung, *die;* Panzer, *der;* **C** *no pl.* (*~ed vehicles*) Panzerfahrzeuge; **D** (*steel plate*) **~ [plate]** Panzerplatte, *die;* Panzerblech, *das;* **~-clad** gepanzert; Panzer-; **E** *no pl.* (*protective covering*) Panzer, *der.* **2** *v.t.* (*furnish with protective cover*) ausrüsten; armieren ‹Kabel›; (*toughen*) panzern ‹Glas›; (*with steel plates*) verkleiden; **~ed car/train** gepanzerter Wagen/Zug; Panzerwagen/-zug, *der;* **~ed cable** bewehrtes *od.* armiertes Kabel; **~ed division** Panzerdivision, *die;* **~ed glass** Panzerglas, *das*

**armourer** /ˈɑːmərə(r)/ *n.* (*Brit.*) (*maker of arms etc.*) Waffenschmied, *der* (*hist.*); Waffentechniker, *der*

**armoury** /ˈɑːmərɪ/ *n.* (*Brit.*) **A** (*array of weapons*) Waffenarsenal, *das;* (*fig.*) Arsenal, *das;* **one of the strongest weapons in the British ~:** eine der stärksten britischen Waffen; **B** (*arsenal*) [Waffen]arsenal, *das;* Waffenkammer, *die;* **C** (*Amer.: drill hall*) Exerzierhalle, *die*

**arm: ~pit** *n.* Achselhöhle, *die;* **~rest** *n.* Armlehne, *die*

**arms: ~ control** *n.* Rüstungskontrolle, *die; attrib.* Rüstungskontroll-; **~ race** *n.* Rüstungswettlauf, *der*

**army** /ˈɑːmɪ/ *n.* **A** (*fighting force*) Heer, *das;* **standing ~:** stehendes Heer; **mercenary ~:** Söldnerheer, *das;* **Napoleon's ~:** die Armee Napoleons; **B** *no pl., no indef. art.* (*military profession*) Militär, *das;* **be in the ~:** beim Militär sein; **go into** *or* **join the ~:** zum Militär gehen; (*as a career*) die Militärlaufbahn einschlagen; **leave the ~:** aus dem Militärdienst ausscheiden; **C** (*large number*) Heer, *das;* **an ~ of workmen/officials/ants** ein Heer von Arbeitern/Beamten/Ameisen

**army: ~ corps** *n.* Armeekorps, *das;* **A~ List** *n.* (*Brit.*) Rangliste des Heeres

**arnica** /ˈɑːnɪkə/ *n.* Arnika, *die*

**aroma** /əˈrəʊmə/ *n.* (*fragrance*) Duft, *der*

**aromatherapy** /ərəʊməˈθerəpɪ/ *n., no pl.* Aromatherapie, *die*

**aromatic** /ærəˈmætɪk/ **1** *adj.* (*fragrant*) aromatisch (*auch Chem.*); duftend ‹Blütenblätter, Nelken usw.›; (*pleasant*) angenehm würzig. **2** *n.* Duftstoff, *der*

**arose** ⇒ **arise**

**around** /əˈraʊnd/ **1** *adv.* **A** (*on every side*) **[all] ~:** überall; **he waved his arms ~:** er ruderte mit den Armen; **all ~ there was nothing but trees** ringsumher *od.* ringsherum gab es nichts als Bäume; **B** (*round*) herum; **come ~ to sb.'s house** bei jmdm. vorbeikommen; **show sb. ~:** jmdn. herumführen; **pass the hat ~:** den Hut herumgehen lassen; **have to get ~ to doing sth.** [endlich] einmal daran denken müssen, etw. zu tun; **look ~, have a look ~:** sich [ein bisschen] umsehen *od.* umschauen; **C** (*coll.: near*) in der Nähe; **have you seen my hat ~?** hast du irgendwo meinen Hut gesehen?; **we'll always be ~ when you need us** wir werden immer da sein, wenn du uns brauchst; **D** (*coll.: in existence*) vorhanden; **there's not/you don't see much leather ~ these days** zur Zeit gibt es/sieht man nur wenig Leder; **E** (*in various places*) **ask/look ~:** herumfragen/-schauen; **travel ~ within England** in England herumreisen; **he's been ~** (*fig.*) er ist viel herumgekommen. ⇒ *also* **go around**; **hang around**.
**2** *prep.* **A** um [... herum]; rund um; **they had their arms ~ each other** sie hielten sich umschlungen; **darkness closed in ~ us** die Dunkelheit umfing uns (*geh.*) *od.* schloss uns ein; **he wore a coat ~ his shoulders** er hatte einen Mantel um die Schultern gelegt; **B** (*here and there in*) **we went ~ the town** wir gingen durch die Stadt; **~ the garden you'll find ...:** im Garten findet man ...; **C** (*here and there near*) **~ London** um London herum; **D** (*round*) um [... herum]; **~ the back of the house** (*position*) hinter dem Haus; (*direction*) hinter das Haus; **E** (*approximately at*) **~ 3 o'clock** ungefähr um 3 Uhr; gegen 3 Uhr; **I saw him somewhere ~ the station** ich habe ihn irgendwo am Bahnhof gesehen; **F** (*approximately equal to*) etwa; ungefähr; **sth. [costing] ~ £2** etw. für um die *od.* ungefähr 2 Pfund

**arousal** /əˈraʊzl/ *n.* **A** (*awakening*) Aufwachen, *das;* **B** (*excitement, also sexual*) Erregung, *die;* (*calling into existence*) (*of interest, enthusiasm*) Erweckung, *die;* (*of hatred, passion*) Erregung, *die*

**arouse** /əˈraʊz/ *v.t.* **A** (*awake*) [auf]wecken; **~ sb. from his sleep** jmdn. aus dem Schlaf reißen; **B** (*excite*) erregen; (*call into existence*) erwecken ‹Interesse, Begeisterung›; erregen ‹Hass, Leidenschaften usw.›; **be sexually ~d by sth./sb.** durch etw./jmdn. sexuell erregt werden; **~ suspicion** Verdacht erregen

**arpeggio** /ɑːˈpedʒɪəʊ/ *n., pl.* **~s** (*Mus.*) Arpeggio, *das*

**arr.** *abbr.* **A** (*Mus.*) **arranged by** Arr.; **B** **arrives** Ank.

**arrack** /ˈærək/ *n.* Arrak, *der*

**arraign** /əˈreɪn/ *v.t.* (*indict*) vor Gericht bringen, anklagen (**for** wegen); (*accuse*) beschuldigen; **~ sb. for sth.** jmdm. die Schuld an etw. (*Dat.*) geben

**arraignment** /əˈreɪnmənt/ *n.* (*indictment*) Anklageerhebung, *die;* (*accusation*) Beschuldigung, *die;* **the ~ of them, their ~:** die Anklageerhebung gegen sie

**arrange** /əˈreɪndʒ/ **1** *v.t.* **A** (*order*) anordnen; (*adjust*) in Ordnung bringen; **the seating was ~d so that ...:** die Sitzreihen waren so angeordnet, dass ...; **B** (*Mus., Radio, etc.: adapt*) bearbeiten; **C** (*settle beforehand*) ausmachen, vereinbaren ‹Termin›; **~ the catering for a party** sich um Essen und Trinken für eine Feier kümmern; **D** (*plan*) planen ‹Urlaub›; aufstellen ‹Stundenplan›; **don't ~ anything for next Saturday** nimm dir für nächsten Sonnabend nichts vor; **E** (*resolve*) beilegen; ins Reine bringen ‹Beziehungen›.
**2** *v.i.* **A** (*plan*) sorgen (**for** für); **~ for sb./sth. to do sth.** veranlassen *od.* dafür sorgen, dass jmd./etw. etw. tut; **can you ~ to be at home when ...?** kannst du es so einrichten, dass du zu Hause bist, wenn ...?; **~ about sth.** etw. in die Wege leiten; **she ~d about getting him a work permit** sie leitete alles in die Wege, damit er eine Arbeitserlaubnis bekam; **B** (*agree*) **they ~d to meet the following day** sie verabredeten sich für den nächsten Tag; **~ with sb. about sth.** sich mit jmdm. über etw. (*Akk.*) einigen; **~ with sb. about doing sth.** sich mit jmdm. darüber einigen, etw. zu tun

**arrangement** /əˈreɪndʒmənt/ *n.* **A** (*ordering, order*) Anordnung, *die;* (*thing ordered*) Arrangement, *das;* **seating ~:** Anordnung der Sitze; **B** (*Mus., Radio, etc.: adapting, adaptation*) Bearbeitung, *die;* Arrangement, *das;* **a guitar ~:** eine Bearbeitung *od.* ein Arrangement für Gitarre; **C** (*settling beforehand*) Vereinbarung, *die;* Übereinkunft, *die;* (*of plans*) Aufstellung, *die;* **by ~:** nach Vereinbarung *od.* Absprache; **D** *in pl.* (*plans*) Vorkehrungen; **make ~s** Vorkehrungen treffen; **we have made ~s for you to be picked up from the airport** wir haben veranlasst, dass Sie vom Flughafen abgeholt werden; **holiday ~s** Urlaubsvorbereitungen; **~s about security** Sicherheitsvorkehrungen; **E** (*agreement*) Vereinbarung, *die;* **make an ~ to do sth.** vereinbaren *od.* die Vereinbarung treffen, etw. zu tun; **the ~ is that ...:** die Vereinbarung lautet, dass ...; **F** (*resolution*) Einigung, *die;* **make an ~:** eine Einigung erzielen; **I'm sure we can come to some ~ about ...:** wir können uns sicher irgendwie einigen über (+ *Akk.*) ...

**arrant** /ˈærənt/ *adj.* Erz‹lump, -schurke, -lügner, -feigling›; dreist ‹Lüge, Missbrauch, Anmaßung›; unverhüllt ‹Grobheit, Heuchelei, Begierde›; **~ nonsense** barer Unsinn

**arras** /ˈærəs/ *n.* A[r]razzo, *der*

**array** /əˈreɪ/ **1** *v.t.* (*formal: dress*) kleiden; schmücken; **~ sb. in sth.** jmdn. in etw. (*Akk.*) kleiden *od.* (*geh.*) hüllen; **~ sth. with sth.** etw. mit etw. schmücken. **2** *n.* (*ordered display*) Reihe, *die*

**arrears** /əˈrɪəz/ *n. pl.* (*debts*) Schulden *Pl.;* Rückstände *Pl.;* (*remainder*) **there were huge ~ of work to be done/letters to be answered** es war noch eine Menge Arbeit aufzuholen/es mussten noch zahlreiche Briefe beantwortet werden; **the work on the building is badly in ~:** man ist mit den Arbeiten an dem Gebäude beträchtlich in Verzug [geraten]; **be in ~ with sth.** mit etw. im Rückstand sein; **be paid in ~:** rückwirkend bezahlt werden

**arrest** /əˈrest/ **1** *v.t.* **A** (*stop*) aufhalten; zum Stillstand bringen ‹Fluss›; **~ judgement** (*Law*) ein/das Urteil aufheben; **B** (*seize*) verhaften, (*temporarily*) festnehmen ‹Person›; beschlagnahmen ‹Sache›; **C** (*catch*) erregen

‹Aufmerksamkeit, Interesse›; (*catch attention of*) fesseln; faszinieren. **2** *n.* **A** (*stoppage*) Stillstand, *der;* **~ of judgement** (*Law*) Aussetzung des/eines Verfahrens; **cardiac ~:** Herzstillstand, *der;* **B** (*legal apprehension*) (*of person*) Verhaftung, *die;* (*temporary*) Festnahme, *die;* (*of thing*) Beschlagnahme, *die;* **under ~:** festgenommen; **he was put under police/military ~:** er wurde in Polizeigewahrsam genommen/unter Arrest gestellt

**arrestable** /əˈrestəbl/ *adj.* **be an ~ act/offence** ein Grund zur Festnahme sein

**arris** /ˈærɪs/ *n.* (*Archit.*) [Dach]grat, *der*

**arrival** /əˈraɪvl/ *n.* **A** Ankunft, *die;* (*fig.: at decision etc.*) Gelangen, *das* (**at** zu); (*of mail etc.*) Eintreffen, *das;* (*coming*) Kommen, *das;* Nahen, *das;* **it marked his ~ in the literary world** damit hat er sich in der literarischen Welt etabliert; **'~'** „Ankunft"; **~s hall** Ankunftshalle, *die;* **B** (*appearance*) Auftauchen, *das;* **the ~ of buds in springtime** das Sprießen der Knospen im Frühling; **C** (*person*) Ankömmling, *der;* (*thing*) Lieferung, *die;* **new ~** (*coll.: newborn baby*) Neugeborene, *das;* **how's the new ~?** (*coll.*) wie gehts dem neuen Erdenbürger?; **new ~s** Neuankömmlinge; **late ~s at the theatre** verspätet eintreffende Theaterbesucher

**arrive** /əˈraɪv/ *v.i.* **A** ankommen; **when do we ~ at Frankfurt?** wann kommen wir in Frankfurt an? **~ at a conclusion/an agreement** zu einem Schluss/einer Einigung kommen; **we've ~d at stalemate** wir sind in eine Sackgasse geraten; **the train is just arriving** der Zug läuft gerade ein; **B** (*establish oneself*) es schaffen; arrivieren (*geh.*); **with this book he ~d** mit diesem Buch hat er es geschafft; **C** (*be brought*) eintreffen; (*coll.: be born*) ankommen; **what time does the mail usually ~?** wann kommt die Post normalerweise?; **D** (*come*) ‹Stunde, Tag, Augenblick:› kommen; **the time has ~d when ...:** jetzt ist der Zeitpunkt gekommen, wo ...

**arrogance** /ˈærəgəns/ *n., no pl.* Arroganz, *die;* (*presumptuousness*) Anmaßung, *die;* Überheblichkeit, *die*

**arrogant** /ˈærəgənt/ *adj.* arrogant; (*presumptuous*) überheblich; anmaßend

**arrogantly** /ˈærəgəntlɪ/ *adv.* arrogant; penetrant ‹überlegen, stolz›; (*presumptuously*) anmaßend; überheblich; anmaßenderweise ‹behaupten, verlangen›

**arrogate** /ˈærəgeɪt/ *v.t.* (*claim*) **~ sth. to oneself** etw. für sich in Anspruch nehmen; sich (*Dat.*) etw. anmaßen

**arrow** /ˈærəʊ/ **1** *n.* (*missile*) Pfeil, *der;* (*pointer*) [Hinweis-, Richtungs]pfeil, *der;* **as straight as an ~:** schnurgerade. **2** *v.t.* mit einem Pfeil/mit Pfeilen markieren

**arrow: ~head** *n.* **A** Pfeilspitze, *die;* **B** (*Bot.*) Pfeilkraut, *das;* **~ key** *n.* (*Computing*) Cursortaste, *die;* Pfeiltaste, *die;* **~root** *n.* **A** (*plant*) Pfeilwurz, *die;* **B** (*starch*) Arrowroot, *das* (*Stärkemehl*)

**arse**[1] /ɑːs/ *n.* (*coarse*) Arsch, *der* (*derb*); **move your ~!** sei nicht so lahmarschig! (*derb*)

**~ a'bout, ~ around** *v. i.* (*Brit. coarse*) herumalbern (*ugs.*); herumblödeln (*ugs.*)

**arse**[2] ⇨ **ass**[1] 2

**arse: ~hole** *n.* (*coarse*) Arschloch, *das* (*derb*); **~-licking** *n., no pl.* (*coarse*) Arschkriecherei, *die* (*derb*); Schleimscheißerei, *die* (*derb*)

**arsenal** /ˈɑːsənl/ *n.* (*store*) [Waffen]arsenal, *das;* Waffenlager, *das;* (*fig.*) Arsenal, *das*

**arsenic** /ˈɑːsənɪk/ *n.* (*Chem.*) **A** Arsenik, *das;* **B** (*element*) Arsen, *das*

**arson** /ˈɑːsn/ *n.* Brandstiftung, *die*

**arsonist** /ˈɑːsənɪst/ *n.* Brandstifter, *der*/Brandstifterin, *die*

**art** /ɑːt/ *n.* **A** Kunst, *die;* **the ~s** ⇨ **fine art c**; **B** (*skill, skilled activity*) Kunst, *die;* **works of ~:** Kunstwerke *Pl.;* **~ needlework/music/film** künstlerische Handarbeit/Kunstmusik/Kunstfilm; **~s and crafts** Kunsthandwerk, *das;* Kunstgewerbe, *das;* **he is a master of his ~:** er ist ein Meister [in] seiner Kunst; **translation is an ~:** Übersetzen ist eine Kunst; **C** *in pl.* (*branch of study*) Geisteswissenschaften; **he's an ~s student** er studiert Geisteswissenschaften; **faculty of ~s** philosophische Fakultät; **he has an ~s degree** er hat das Abschlussexamen der philosophischen Fakultät [gemacht]; **Bachelor/Master of Arts** Bakkalaureus/Magister der philosophischen Fakultät; **D** (*knack*) Kunst, *die;* (*stratagem*) Kunstgriff, *der;* Kniff, *der* (*ugs.*); **an ~ in itself** eine Kunst für sich; **E** (*cunning*) List, *die*

**art: ~ collection** *n.* Kunstsammlung, *die;* **~ collector** *n.* Kunstsammler, *der;* **~ college** ⇨ **~ school**

**art deco** /ɑːt ˈdekəʊ/ *n., no pl.* Art déco, *der*

**artefact** /ˈɑːtɪfækt/ *n.* Artefakt, *das*

**arterial** /ɑːˈtɪərɪəl/ *adj.* **A** (*of artery*) arteriell; **B** (*principal*) Haupt-; **~ road** Hauptverkehrsstraße, *die*

**arteriosclerosis** /ɑːtɪərɪəʊskləˈrəʊsɪs/ *n., pl.* **arterioscleroses** /ɑːtɪərɪəʊskləˈrəʊsiːz/ ▶ 1232 (*Med.*) Arteriosklerose, *die* (*fachspr.*); Arterienverkalkung, *die*

**artery** /ˈɑːtərɪ/ *n.* **A** ▶ 966 (*Anat.*) Schlagader, *die;* Arterie, *die* (*bes. fachspr.*); **B** (*fig.: road etc.*) [Haupt]verkehrsader, *die*

**artesian** /ɑːˈtiːzɪən, ɑːˈtiːʒən/ *adj.* **~ well** artesischer Brunnen

**'art form** *n.* (*form of composition*) Kunstform, *die;* [Kunst]gattung, *die;* (*medium of expression*) Kunst[form], *die*

**artful** /ˈɑːtfl/ *adj.* schlau; raffiniert; **~ dodger** Schlawiner, *der*

**artfully** /ˈɑːtfəlɪ/ *adv.* schlau; raffiniert

**artfulness** /ˈɑːtflnɪs/ *n., no pl.* Schlauheit, *die;* Raffiniertheit, *die*

**'art gallery** *n.* Kunstgalerie, *die*

**arthritic** /ɑːˈθrɪtɪk/ (*Med.*) **1** *adj.* arthritisch; **she's got ~ joints in her fingers** sie hat Arthritis in den Fingergelenken. **2** *n.* Arthritiker, *der*/Arthritikerin, *die*

**arthritis** /ɑːˈθraɪtɪs/ *n.* ▶ 1232 (*Med.*) Arthritis, *die* (*fachspr.*); Gelenkentzündung, *die*

**arthropod** /ˈɑːθrəpɒd/ *n.* (*Zool.*) Gliederfüßler, *der;* **the ~s** die Arthropoden

**Arthur** /ˈɑːθə(r)/ *pr. n.* **King ~:** König Artus

**artic** /ɑːˈtɪk/ *n.* (*coll.*) Zug, *der* (*ugs.*); Sattelschlepper, *der* (*ugs.*)

**artichoke** /ˈɑːtɪtʃəʊk/ *n.* **[globe] ~:** Artischocke, *die;* **Jerusalem ~:** Topinambur, *der;* (*edible part*) Topinamburwurzel, *die*

**article** /ˈɑːtɪkl/ **1** *n.* **A** (*of constitution, treaty*) Artikel, *der;* (*of creed*) Glaubensartikel, *der;* (*of indictment*) [Anklage]punkt, *der;* (*of agreement*) [Vertrags]punkt, *der;* (*of the law*) Paragraph, *der;* (*in dictionary etc.*) Eintrag, *der;* **~s [of association]** Satzung, *die;* **~s of apprenticeship/employment** Lehr-/Arbeitsvertrag, *der;* **~ of faith** (*fig.*) Glaubensbekenntnis, *das* (*fig.*); **B** (*in magazine, newspaper*) Artikel, *der;* (*in technical journal*) Beitrag, *der;* Aufsatz, *der;* **C** (*Ling.*) Artikel, *der;* Geschlechtswort, *das;* **definite/indefinite ~:** bestimmter/unbestimmter Artikel; **D** (*particular part, thing*) Artikel, *der;* **woollen ~s [of clothing]** Wollsachen; **an ~ of furniture/clothing** ein Möbel-/Kleidungsstück; **an ~ of value** ein Wertgegenstand; **toilet ~s** Toilettenartikel.

**2** *v.t.* in die Lehre geben (**to** bei); **be ~d to sb.** bei jmdm. in der Lehre sein

**articled** /ˈɑːtɪkld/ *adj.* **~ clerk** (*Law*) Rechtspraktikant, *der*/-praktikantin, *die;* ≈ Rechtsreferendar, *der*/-referendarin, *die*

**articulate 1** /ɑːˈtɪkjʊlət/ *adj.* **A** (*clear*) verständlich; **B** (*eloquent*) redegewandt; **be ~/not very ~:** sich gut/nicht sehr gut ausdrücken [können]; **C** (*jointed*) gegliedert; Glieder-; (*distinctly joined*) aus Einzelgliedern; mit Gelenken. **2** /ɑːˈtɪkjʊleɪt/ *v.t.* **A** *usu. in pass.* durch Gelenke/ein Gelenk verbinden; **~d lorry** Sattelzug, *der;* Sattelschlepper, *der* (*ugs.*); **B** (*pronounce*) [deutlich] aussprechen; (*utter, express*) artikulieren; in Worte fassen. **3** *v.i.* **A** (*speak distinctly*) artikuliert sprechen; deutlich sprechen; **~ clearly** klar und deutlich sprechen; **B** (*speak*) sprechen; **C** (*form a joint*) **~ with sth.** mit etw. ein Gelenk bilden

**articulately** /ɑːˈtɪkjʊlətlɪ/ *adv.* **A** (*clearly*) klar; deutlich; **B** (*coherently*) klar; **he expresses himself very ~:** er drückt sich sehr klar aus

**articulateness** /ɑːˈtɪkjʊlətnɪs/ *n., no pl.* (*clarity*) Deutlichkeit, *die;* (*coherence*) Klarheit, *die*

**articulation** /ɑːtɪkjʊˈleɪʃn/ *n.* **A** (*clear speech*) deutliche Aussprache; **his ~ is good** er hat eine deutliche Aussprache; **B** (*coherent speech*) flüssige Ausdrucksweise; (*act of speaking*) Artikulation, *die;* [Laut]bildung, *die*

**artifact** (*Amer.*) ⇨ **artefact**

**artifice** /ˈɑːtɪfɪs/ *n.* **A** (*cunning*) List, *die;* Raffinement, *das* (*geh.*); **B** (*device*) Trick, *der;* List, *die;* **C** (*skill*) Geschick, *das;* Geschicklichkeit, *die*

**artificial** /ɑːtɪˈfɪʃl/ *adj.* **A** (*not natural*) künstlich; Kunst-; (*not real*) unecht; imitiert; (*~ly produced*) künstlich; Kunst-; synthetisch [hergestellt]; **~ sweetener** Süßstoff, *der;* **~ limb** Prothese, *die;* **~ eye** Glasauge, *das;* **B** (*affected, insincere*) gekünstelt; unecht; **she's ~ and two-faced** sie verstellt sich; **~ politeness** gekünstelte *od.* gespielte Höflichkeit; **she wore an ~ smile for the cameras** für die Fotografen setzte sie ein einstudiertes Lächeln auf; **her ~ enthusiasm** ihre gespielte Begeisterung

**artificial: ~ ho'rizon** *n.* Kreiselhorizont, *der;* **~ insemi'nation** *n.* künstliche Besamung; **~ in'telligence** *n.* künstliche Intelligenz

**artificiality** /ɑːtɪfɪʃɪˈælɪtɪ/ *n., no pl.* **A** (*unnaturalness*) Künstlichkeit, *die;* **B** (*unreality*) Unechtheit, *die;* **C** (*affectedness*) Affektiertheit, *die;* Geziertheit, *die;* (*formality*) Förmlichkeit, *die;* (*insincerity*) Gekünsteltheit, *die*

**artificial: ~ 'kidney** ⇨ **kidney machine**; **~ 'language** *n.* Kunstsprache, *die*

**artificially** /ɑːtɪˈfɪʃəlɪ/ *adv.* **A** (*unnaturally*) künstlich; unnatürlich; **the food has been ~ flavoured** die Lebensmittel sind mit künstlichem Geschmacksstoff versetzt; **~ produced diamonds/pearls** synthetische Diamanten/künstliche Perlen; **B** (*affectedly, insincerely*) affektiert; geziert

**artificialness** /ɑːtɪˈfɪʃəlnɪs/ ⇨ **artificiality**

**artificial respi'ration** *n.* künstliche Beatmung

**artillery** /ɑːˈtɪlərɪ/ *n.* Artillerie, *die*

**artilleryman** /ɑːˈtɪlərɪmən/ *n., pl.* **artillerymen** /ɑːˈtɪlərɪmən/ Artillerist, *der*

**artisan** /ˈɑːtɪzn, ɑːtɪˈzæn/ *n.* [Kunst]handwerker, *der*

**artist** /ˈɑːtɪst/ *n.* ▶ 1261 **A** (*exponent of a fine art*) Künstler, *der*/Künstlerin, *die;* (*fig.*) Künstler, *der*/Künstlerin, *die;* Könner, *der*/Könnerin, *die;* **he's an ~ in words/rhetoric** er ist ein Wort-/Redekünstler; **she's an ~ in cookery** sie ist eine Kochkünstlerin; **he's a real ~ at his job** er ist ein echter Könner seines Fachs; **B** ⇨ **artiste**

**artiste** /ɑːˈtiːst/ *n.* Artist, *der*/Artistin, *die;* Künstler, *der*/Künstlerin, *die;* **circus ~s** Zirkusartisten *Pl.*

**artistic** /ɑːˈtɪstɪk/ *adj.* **A** (*of art*) Kunst-; künstlerisch; **~ movements such as Expressionism** Kunstrichtungen, zum Beispiel der Expressionismus; **the ~ world** die Welt der Kunst; **B** (*of artists*) Künstler-; künstlerisch; **~ circles** Künstlerkreise; **C** (*made with art*) kunstvoll; Kunst-; **~ designs** kunstvolle Muster; **a truly ~ piece of poetry/writing** ein dichterisches/schriftstellerisches Kunstwerk; **D** (*naturally skilled in art*) künstlerisch veranlagt *od.* begabt; **she's quite ~:** sie ist künstlerisch ziemlich begabt; **have ~ leanings** künstlerische Neigungen haben; **E** (*appreciative of art*) kunstverständig; **~ sense** Kunstverständnis, *das*

**artistically** /ɑːˈtɪstɪkəlɪ/ *adv.* **A** (*in art*) künstlerisch; in der Kunst; (*from an artist's viewpoint*) künstlerisch [gesehen]; **B** (*with

a

## As

When used as a preposition or conjunction to mean *like*, the usual translation is **wie**:

***as usual***
= wie gewöhnlich

***as explained below***
= wie unten erklärt

***as so often***
= wie so oft

***as you may have heard***
= wie Sie vielleicht gehört haben

***as was the custom there***
= wie es dort Sitte war

Note also:

***a coat the same colour as mine***
= ein Mantel in derselben Farbe wie meiner

***a writer such as Dickens***
= ein Schriftsteller wie Dickens

However if the sense is *in the manner of* or *in the function of*, the translation is **als** (note that *a/an* is not translated):

***dressed as a sailor***
= als Matrose gekleidet

***He works as an engineer***
= Er arbeitet als Ingenieur

***my duty as a father***
= meine Pflicht als Vater

In comparisons (*as ... as ...*) the first *as* is translated by **so**, but this is often omitted in set similes:

***She is as old as my mother***
= Sie ist so alt wie meine Mutter

***This car is not as fast as yours***
= Dieses Auto ist nicht so schnell wie deins

***He is not as good a cook as you***
= Er ist kein so guter Koch wie du

***He is as wily as a fox***
= Er ist schlau wie ein Fuchs

Where a verb such as *can/could* or *want/like* comes after the *as*, **wie** is usually omitted:

***Come as quickly as you can***
= Komm, so schnell du kannst

***Take as much as you like***
= Nimm, so viel du willst

And where the sense of *as ... as* is the same as *however*, the translation is *wie ... auch*:

***As fast as we rowed*** (= *However fast we rowed*), ***the others rowed faster***
= Wie schnell wir auch ruderten, die anderen ruderten schneller

For the conjunction in time expressions, the translations are **als** (with the sense of *when*) or **während** (with the sense of *while*):

***As I stepped into the house, I heard her voice***
= Als ich in das Haus hineintrat, hörte ich ihre Stimme

***As we were talking, the doorbell rang***
= Während wir uns unterhielten, klingelte es

And expressing a reason with the sense of *since*, the translation is **da**:

***As I am going to London I can take it with me***
= Da ich nach London fahre, kann ich es mitnehmen

---

*art)* kunstvoll ‹geschmückt, gestaltet›; **C** künstlerisch ‹begabt, veranlagt›; **be ~ interested/appreciative** an Kunst interessiert sein/einen Sinn für Kunst haben

**artistry** /'ɑːtɪstrɪ/ *n., no pl.* **A** *(artistic pursuit)* künstlerisches Schaffen; **B** *(artistic ability)* künstlerische Fähigkeit[en]; künstlerisches Geschick; *(artistic quality)* Kunst, *die;* künstlerischer Wert

**artless** /'ɑːtlɪs/ *adj.* **A** *(guileless)* arglos; **~ piety** schlichte Frömmigkeit; **B** *(simple)* schmucklos; schlicht; **~ beauty/grace** natürliche Schönheit/Anmut

**artlessly** /'ɑːtlɪslɪ/ *adv.* **A** *(guilelessly)* arglos; **B** *(simply)* schmucklos; schlicht

**artlessness** /'ɑːtlɪsnɪs/ *n., no pl.* **A** *(guilelessness)* Arglosigkeit, *die;* **B** *(simplicity)* Schmucklosigkeit, *die;* Schlichtheit, *die*

**art: ~ nouveau** /ɑː nuː'vəʊ/ *n.* Jugendstil, *der;* **~ paper** *n.* Kunstdruckpapier, *das*

**'arts centre** *n.* Kunstzentrum, *das*

**art: ~ school** *n.* Kunsthochschule, *die;* **~work** *n.* Bildmaterial, *das*

**arty** /'ɑːtɪ/ *adj.* *(coll.)* auf Künstler machend; **he's an ~ type** er ist so ein Künstlertyp; **~ furniture** auf Kunst gemachte Möbel; **an ~ design** ein pseudokünstlerisches Muster; **~-[and-]crafty** *(joc.)* auf Kunstgewerbe gemacht

**arum** /'eərəm/ *n.* *(Bot.)* Aronstab, *der;* **~ lily** Zimmercalla, *die*

**Aryan** /'eərɪən/ ▶ 1275 **1** *adj.* indogermanisch; arisch *(veralt.)*. **2** *n.* **A** *(language)* Indogermanisch, *das;* Arisch, *das (veralt.)*; **B** *(person)* Arier, *der*/Arierin, *die (bes. ns.)*; Indogermane, *der*/Indogermanin, *die*

**as** /əz, *stressed* æz/ **1** *adv. in main sentence (in same degree)* **as ... [as ...]** so ... [wie ...]; **as soon as possible** so bald wie möglich; **almost as tall as ...:** fast so groß wie ...; **half as much** halb soviel; **you know as well as I do that ...:** Sie wissen genauso gut wie ich, dass ...; **they did as much as they could** sie taten, was sie konnten; **as good a ... [as ...]** ein so guter ... [wie ...]/eine so gute ... [wie ...]/ein so gutes ... [wie ...].

**2** *rel. adv. or conj. in subord. clause* **A** *expr. degree* **[as *or* so] ... as ...:** [so ...] wie ...; **as ... as possible** so ... wie möglich; **as ... as you can** so ...[, wie] Sie können; **come as quickly as you can** kommen Sie, so schnell Sie können; **quick as a flash** blitzschnell; **as recently as [this morning]** erst [heute Morgen]; **as early as [tomorrow]** schon *od.* bereits *od.* gleich [morgen]; **B** *(though)* **... as he** *etc.* **is/was** obwohl er *usw.* ... ist/war; **intelligent as she is/was, ...:** obwohl sie ziemlich intelligent ist/war, ...; **safe as it might be, ...:** obwohl es vielleicht ungefährlich ist, ...; **C** *(however much)* **try as he might/would, he could not concentrate** sosehr er sich auch bemühte, er konnte sich nicht konzentrieren; **push/strain/pull as he might/would, ...:** wie sehr er auch drückte/sich anstrengte/zog, ...; **D** *expr. manner* wie; **as you may already have heard, ...:** wie Sie vielleicht schon gehört haben, ...; **as we are all well aware, ...:** wie wir alle sehr wohl wissen, ...; **as we had hoped/expected ...:** wie erhofft/erwartet, ...; **as it were** sozusagen; gewissermaßen; **as you were!** Kommando zurück!; **E** *expr. time* als; während; **as and when** wann immer; **as we climbed the stairs** als wir die Treppe hinaufgingen; **as we were talking** während wir uns unterhielten; **he knew her as a teenager** er kannte sie schon, als sie noch ein Teenager war; **F** *expr. reason* da; **as we're now all assembled** da wir jetzt vollzählig sind; **G** *expr. result* **so ... as to ...** so ... zu; **would you be so kind as to help us?** würden Sie so freundlich sein und uns helfen?; **H** *expr. purpose* **so as to ...** um ... zu ...; **I** *expr. illustration* wie [z. B.]; **industrial areas, as the north-east of England for example** Industriegebiete wie z. B. der Nordosten Englands.

**3** *prep.* **A** *(in the function of)* als; **as an artist** als Künstler; **speaking as a parent, ...:** als Mutter/Vater ...; **B** *(like)* wie; **he's treated as an outcast** er wird wie ein Ausgestoßener behandelt; **they regard him as a fool** sie halten ihn für einen Dummkopf.

**4** *rel. pron.* *(which)* **fool as he was he did not notice the obvious dangers** dumm, wie er war, sah er die Gefahren nicht; **as is our custom** wie immer; **they danced, as was the custom there** sie tanzten, wie es dort Sitte war; **he was shocked, as were we all** er war wie wir alle schockiert; **it was him/the earthquake as did it** *(uneducated)* er ists gewesen/das Erdbeben wars; **the same as ...:** der-/die-/dasselbe wie ...; **such as** wie zum Beispiel; **they enjoy such foreign foods as ...:** sie essen gern ausländische Lebensmittel wie ...

**5** **as far** ⇒ far 1 D; **as for ...:** was ... angeht *od.* betrifft *od.* anbelangt; **as from ...:** von ... an; **you will receive a pension as from your 60th birthday** vom 61. Lebensjahr an bekommen Sie Rente; **you are dismissed as from today** Sie sind mit sofortiger Wirkung entlassen; **as [it] is** wie die Dinge liegen; wie es aussieht; **I'll take the dress as it is** ich nehme das Kleid, wie es ist; **the place is untidy enough as it is** es ist schon liederlich genug[, wie es jetzt ist]; **as of ...:** von ... an; **as of 31 December annually** am 31. 12. jeden Jahres; **as to** hinsichtlich (+ *Gen.*); **nothing further was mentioned as to holiday plans** von Urlaubsplänen wurde nichts weiter gesagt; **as was** wie es einmal war; **Miss Tay as was** das frühere Fräulein Tay; **as yet** bis jetzt; noch; **as yet the plan is only under discussion** der Plan wird noch diskutiert

**a.s.a.p.** *abbr.* **as soon as possible**

**asbestos** /æz'bestɒs, æs'bestɒs/ *n.* **A** *(fabric)* Asbest, *der;* **B** *(mineral)* Amiant, *der*

**asbestosis** /æzbes'təʊsɪs, æsbes'təʊsɪs/ *n., no pl.* ▶ 1232 *(Med.)* Asbestose, *die*

a

(*fachspr.*); Staublungenerkrankung, *die;* **suffer from ~:** eine Staublunge haben

**ascend** /əˈsend/ ❶ *v.i.* [A] (*go up*) hinaufgehen *od.* -steigen; (*climb up*) hinaufklettern; (*by vehicle*) hinauffahren; (*come up*) heraufkommen; **the lift ~ed** der Aufzug fuhr nach oben; **Christ ~ed into heaven** Christus fuhr auf gen Himmel (*geh.*); **~ in the lift** mit dem Aufzug hinauffahren; [B] (*rise*) [höher]steigen; aufsteigen; **the helicopter ~ed slowly** der Hubschrauber stieg langsam höher; **the water ~s to above the level of this line** das Wasser steigt über die Marke; [C] (*slope upwards*) ‹Hügel, Straße:› ansteigen; **the stairs ~ very steeply** die Treppe ist sehr steil; [D] (*in quality, rank, etc.*) aufsteigen; [E] (*in pitch*) höher werden. ❷ *v.t.* [A] (*go up*) hinaufsteigen, hinaufgehen ‹Treppe, Leiter, Berg›; **~ a rope** an einem Seil hochklettern; [B] (*come up*) **we saw a fireman ~ing the ladder towards us** wir sahen einen Feuerwehrmann die Leiter heraufsteigen; [C] (*go along*) hinauffahren ‹Straße›; [D] **~ the throne** den Thron besteigen

**ascendancy** /əˈsendənsɪ/ *n., no pl.* beherrschender Einfluss; Vorherrschaft, *die;* **gain/have the ~ over sb.** die Vorherrschaft über jmdn. gewinnen/haben

**ascendant** /əˈsendənt/ *n.* [A] (*Astrol.*) Aszendent, *der;* [B] **in the ~:** im Aufsteigen begriffen; **his popularity was now firmly in the ~:** seine Beliebtheit nahm beständig zu

**ascension** /əˈsenʃn/ *n.* [A] (*going up*) Auffahrt, *die;* **right ~** (*Astron.*) Rektaszension, *die;* [B] **[the] A~** (*Relig.*) [Christi] Himmelfahrt

**Aˈscension Day** *n.* Himmelfahrtstag, *der*

**ascent** /əˈsent/ *n.* [A] (*going up, rise; also fig.*) Aufstieg, *der;* **our ~ in the lift/up the hill** unsere Auffahrt mit dem Lift/unser Aufstieg den Berg hinauf; [B] (*way; also fig.*) Aufstieg, *der;* [C] (*slope*) Steigung, *die;* [D] (*steps*) Aufgang, *der*

**ascertain** /æsəˈteɪn/ *v.t.* feststellen; ermitteln ‹Fakten, Daten›

**ascertainable** /æsəˈteɪnəbl/ *adj.* feststellbar; zu ermittelnd ‹Fakten, Daten›

**ascertainment** /æsəˈteɪnmənt/ *n.* Feststellung, *die;* (*of facts, data*) Ermittlung, *die;* (*of information*) Beschaffung, *die*

**ascetic** /əˈsetɪk/ ❶ *adj.* asketisch. ❷ *n.* [A] Asket, *der*/Asketin, *die;* [B] (*Relig. Hist.*) Eremit, *der;* Klausner, *der*

**ascetically** /əˈsetɪkəlɪ/ *adv.* asketisch

**asceticism** /əˈsetɪsɪzm/ *n., no pl.* Askese, *die*

**ascribe** /əˈskraɪb/ *v.t.* zuschreiben (**to** *Dat.*); **~ sth. to sth./sb.** (*regard as belonging*) etw. einer Sache/jmdm. zuschreiben; (*attribute, impute*) etw. auf etw./jmdn. zurückführen

**ascription** /əˈskrɪpʃn/ *n.* ⇒ **ascribe**: Zuschreiben, *das;* Zurückführen, *das*

**asepsis** /eɪˈsepsɪs/ *n., no pl.* [A] (*absence of sepsis*) Asepsis, *die;* Keimfreiheit, *die* (*fachspr.*); [B] (*aseptic method*) Aseptik, *die* (*fachspr.*); keimfreie Wundbehandlung

**aseptic** /eɪˈseptɪk/ *adj.* aseptisch

**asexual** /eɪˈsekʃʊəl/ *adj.* [A] (*without sexuality*) asexuell; [B] (*Biol.: without sex*) asexual; ungeschlechtig; **~ reproduction** ungeschlechtliche Vermehrung

**ash[1]** /æʃ/ *n.* [A] (*tree*) Esche, *die;* [B] (*wood*) Eschenholz, *das.* ⇒ *also* **mountain ash**

**ash[2]** *n.* [A] (*powdery residue*) Asche, *die;* **layer of ~:** Ascheschicht, *die;* **cigarette ~:** Zigarettenasche, *die;* **sweep up the ~[es]** die Asche auffegen; [B] *in pl.* (*remains*) Asche, *die;* **in ~es** in Schutt und Asche; ⇒ *also* **sackcloth;** [C] (*Cricket*) **the Ashes** *imaginäre Trophäe für den Gewinner einer Serie von Vergleichswettkämpfen zwischen den Mannschaften Englands und Australiens*

**ashamed** /əˈʃeɪmd/ *adj., usu. pred.* beschämt; **we were ~:** wir schämten uns *od.* waren beschämt; **be ~ [of sb./sth.]** sich [jmds./einer Sache wegen] schämen; **you ought to be ~ of yourselves for telling lies** ihr solltet euch schämen zu lügen; **be/feel ~ for sb./sth.** sich für jmdn./etw. schämen; **be ~ to do sth.** sich schämen, etw. zu tun; **I'm ~ to have to say/admit that I told a white lie** ich muss leider *od.* zu meiner Schande zugeben, dass ich eine Notlüge erzählt habe; **he was not ~ to stand up and say that ...:** er schämte sich nicht, aufzustehen und zuzugeben, dass ...

**ash: ~ bin** *n.* Mülleimer, *der;* **~ blonde** ❶ *adj.* aschblond; ❷ *n.* Aschblonde, *der/die;* **~can** (*Amer.*) ⇒ **~ bin**

**ashen** /ˈæʃn/ *adj.* [A] (*ash-coloured*) aschfarben; aschfahl ‹Gesicht›; **~ grey** aschgrau; [B] (*of ashes*) aus Asche; Asche-

**ashore** /əˈʃɔː(r)/ *adv.* (*position*) an Land; am Ufer; (*direction*) an Land; ans Ufer; **go/be ~:** an Land gehen/sein

**ˈashpan** *n.* Aschkasten, *der*

**ashram** /ˈæʃrəm/ *n.* Ashram, *das od. der*

**ash: ~tray** *n.* Aschenbecher, *der;* **~ tree** ⇒ **ash[1]** A; **Ash ˈWednesday** *n.* Aschermittwoch, *der;* **~wood** ⇒ **ash[1]** B

**Asia** /ˈeɪʃə/ *pr. n.* Asien (*das*); **~ ˈMinor** Kleinasien (*das*)

**Asian** /ˈeɪʃən, ˈeɪʒən/, **Asiatic** /eɪʃɪˈætɪk/ ❶ *adj.* asiatisch. ❷ *n.* Asiat, *der*/Asiatin, *die*

**aside** /əˈsaɪd/ ❶ *adv.* beiseite; zur Seite; **stand ~!** treten Sie zur Seite!; **I pulled the curtain ~:** ich zog den Vorhang zur Seite; **~ from sb./sth.** außer jmdm./etw.; **take sb. ~:** jmdn. beiseite nehmen. ❷ *n.* [A] (*in a play*) Apart, *das;* Beiseitesprechen, *das;* [B] (*incidental remark*) [beiläufige] Bemerkung

**asinine** /ˈæsɪnaɪn/ *adj.* (*stupid*) dämlich; **don't be so ~:** sei kein Esel

**asininity** /æsɪˈnɪnɪtɪ/ *n.* Dämlichkeit, *die*

**ask** /ɑːsk/ ❶ *v.t.* [A] fragen; **~ [sb.] a question** [jmdm.] eine Frage stellen; **~ sb.'s name** nach jmds. Namen fragen; **~ sb. [sth.]** jmdn. [nach etw.] fragen; **I was ~ed some awkward questions by the boss** der Chef stellte mir einige unangenehme Fragen; **~ sb. about sth.** jmdn. nach etw. fragen; **I ~ you!** (*coll.*) ich muss schon sagen!; **if you ~ ˈme** (*coll.*) [also,] wenn du mich fragst; **~ me another** (*coll.*) frag mich was Leichteres (*ugs.*); [B] (*seek to obtain*) **~ sth.** um etw. bitten; **~ sb.'s advice on sth.** jmdn. wegen etw. um Rat fragen; **how much are you ~ing for that car?** wie viel verlangen Sie für das Auto?; **~ a favour of sb., ~ sb. a favour** jmdn. um einen Gefallen bitten; **~ sb. to do sth.** jmdn. [darum] bitten, etw. zu tun; **you have only to ~:** du brauchst es nur zu sagen; **~ a lot of sb.** viel von jmdm. verlangen; **it's ~ing a lot** es ist viel verlangt; **~ing price** geforderter Preis; **it's yours for the ~ing** du kannst es gern haben; [C] (*invite*) einladen; **~ sb. to dinner** jmdn. zum Essen einladen; **~ sb. out** jmdn. einladen; **the boss ~ed me up to his office** der Chef hat mich gebeten, in sein Büro hinaufzukommen. ❷ *v.i.* **you may well ~:** du hast allen Grund zu fragen; **~ after sb./sth.** nach jmdm./etw. fragen; **~ after sb.'s health** fragen, wie es jmdm. [gesundheitlich] geht; **~ for sth./sb.** etw./jmdn. verlangen; **~ for it** (*coll.: invite trouble*) es herausfordern; es so *od.* nicht anders haben wollen; ⇒ *also* **trouble** 1 A

**askance** /əˈskæns, əˈskɑːns/ *adv.* [A] (*sideways*) von der Seite; [B] (*suspiciously*) **look ~ [at sb./sth.]** [über jmdn./etw.] befremdet sein

**askew** /əˈskjuː/ ❶ *adv.* schief; (*awry*) **the wind had blown all her clothes ~:** der Wind hatte ihre ganze Kleidung in Unordnung gebracht. ❷ *pred. adj.* schief; (*awry*) in Unordnung

**asleep** /əˈsliːp/ *pred. adj.* [A] (*lit. or fig.*) schlafend; (*euphem.: dead*) entschlafen (*geh.*); **be/lie ~:** schlafen; **he seems to be ~:** er scheint zu schlafen; **fall ~:** einschlafen; **has the government fallen ~?** (*fig.*) schläft die Regierung?; **the old man fell ~** (*euphem.*) der alte Mann schlief [für immer] ein; [B] (*numb*) eingeschlafen ‹Arm, Bein›

**asocial** /eɪˈsəʊʃl/ *adj.* (*antisocial*) asozial; (*not social*) ungesellig; asozial; (*inconsiderate*) rücksichtslos

**asp** /æsp/ *n.* (*Zool.*) (*Vipera aspis*) Aspisviper, *die;* (*Naja haje*) Uräusschlange, *die*

**asparagus** /əˈspærəgəs/ *n.* Spargel, *der;* **~ fern** (*Bot.*) Asparagus, *der*

**aspect** /ˈæspekt/ *n.* [A] Aspekt, *der;* [B] (*expression*) Gesichtsausdruck, *der;* (*appearance*) **[physical] ~:** Erscheinungsbild, *das;* [C] (*position looking in a given direction*) Lage, *die;* (*front*) Seite, *die;* **have a southern ~:** nach Süden liegen; [D] (*Ling., Astrol.*) Aspekt, *der*

**aspectual** /æˈspektjʊəl/ *adj.* (*Ling.*) aspektisch

**aspen** /ˈæspən/ *n.* (*Bot.*) Espe, *die*

**asperity** /æˈsperɪtɪ/ *n., no pl.* [A] (*harshness*) Schroffheit, *die;* [B] (*roughness*) Rauheit, *die*

**aspersion** /əˈspɜːʃn/ *n.* Verunglimpfung, *die;* **cast ~s on sb./sth.** jmdn./etw. in den Schmutz ziehen

**asphalt** /ˈæsfælt/ ❶ *n.* Asphalt, *der.* ❷ *v.t.* asphaltieren

**asphyxia** /æˈsfɪksɪə/ *n., no pl.* (*Med.*) Asphyxie, *die* (*fachspr.*); schwere Atemstörung; Erstickung, *die*

**asphyxiate** /æˈsfɪksɪeɪt/ (*Med.*) ❶ *v.t.* ersticken; **be ~d by sth.** an etw. (*Dat.*) ersticken. ❷ *v.i.* ersticken

**asphyxiation** /æsfɪksɪˈeɪʃn/ *n.* (*Med.*) Erstickung, *die;* **death by ~:** Erstickungstod, *der*

**aspic** /ˈæspɪk/ *n.* (*jelly*) Aspik, *der*

**aspidistra** /æspɪˈdɪstrə/ *n.* (*Bot.*) Schusterpalme, *die;* Aspidistra, *die* (*fachspr.*)

**aspirant** /əˈspaɪərənt, ˈæspərənt/ ❶ *adj.* aufstrebend. ❷ *n.* Aspirant, *der*/Aspirantin, *die;* Bewerber, *der*/Bewerberin, *die;* **an ~ to high office** ein Bewerber für ein hohes Amt

**aspirate** ❶ /ˈæspərət/ *adj.* (*Phonet.*) aspiriert; behaucht. ❷ *n.* (*Phonet.*) Aspirata, *die;* behauchter [Verschluss]laut. ❸ /ˈæspəreɪt/ *v.t.* [A] (*Phonet.*) aspirieren; [B] (*draw by suction*) absaugen

**aspiration** /æspəˈreɪʃn/ *n.* [A] Streben, *das;* Aspiration, *die* (*geh.*); **your ~[s] for** *or* **after success** dein Streben nach Erfolg; **have ~s to sth.** nach etw. streben; [B] (*Phonet.*) Aspiration, *die;* Behauchung, *die*

**aspire** /əˈspaɪə(r)/ *v.i.* **~ to** *or* **after sth.** nach etw. streben; **~ to be sth.** danach streben, etw. zu sein; **I once ~d to be an actor** ich wollte einmal [unbedingt] Schauspieler werden

**aspirin** /ˈæspərɪn/ *n.* (*Med.*) Aspirin ⓦⓩ, *das;* Kopfschmerztablette, *die*

**aspiring** /əˈspaɪərɪŋ/ *adj.* aufstrebend

**ass[1]** /æs/ ❶ *n.* (*Zool.; also fig.*) Esel, *der;* **make an ~ of oneself** sich blamieren. ❷ *v.i.* (*coll.*) **~ about** *or* **around** herumalbern (*ugs.*)

**ass[2]** (*Amer.*) ⇒ **arse[1]**

**assail** /əˈseɪl/ *v.t.* [A] angreifen; [B] (*fig.*) in Angriff nehmen ‹Hindernis, Aufgabe›; **~ sb. with questions/insults** jmdn. mit Fragen/Beleidigungen überschütten; **I was ~ed with doubts** mich überkamen Zweifel; **the noise ~ed our ears** der Lärm dröhnte in unseren Ohren

**assailant** /əˈseɪlənt/ *n.* Angreifer, *der*/Angreiferin, *die*

**assassin** /əˈsæsɪn/ *n.* [A] Mörder, *der*/Mörderin, *die;* [B] (*Hist.*) Assassine, *der*

**assassinate** /əˈsæsɪneɪt/ *v.t.* ermorden; **be ~d** einem Attentat zum Opfer fallen

**assassination** /əsæsɪˈneɪʃn/ *n.* Mord, *der* (**of** an + *Dat.*); **~ attempt** Attentat, *das* (**on** auf + *Akk.*); ⇒ *also* **character assassination**

**assault** /əˈsɔːlt/ ❶ *n.* [A] Angriff, *der;* (*fig.*) Anschlag, *der;* (*euphem.: rape*) Vergewaltigung, *die;* **verbal ~s** verbale Angriffe; [B] (*Mil.*) Sturmangriff, *der;* **~ craft** Sturmboot, *das;* **~ course** Hindernisstrecke, *die;* Hindernisparcours, *der;* [C] (*Law*) [Androhung einer] Tätlichkeit; ⇒ *also* **battery** B. ❷ *v.t.* [A] (*lit. or fig.*) angreifen; (*euphem.: rape*) vergewaltigen; missbrauchen (*geh.*); [B] (*Mil.*) stürmen; angreifen

**assay** /əˈseɪ/ ❶ *n.* [A] Probe, *die;* **A~ Office** [*amtliches*] *Labor für die Analyse von Edelmetallen o. Ä.;* [B] (*Chem.*) Analyse, *die.*

**2** *v.t.* **A** prüfen ‹Metall, Erz›; **B** (*Chem.*) analysieren; **C** (*show on* ~) enthalten

**assemblage** /ə'semblɪdʒ/ *n.* **A** (*of things, persons*) Ansammlung, *die;* **B** (*process*) (*bringing together*) Zusammentragen, *das;* (*fitting together*) Zusammensetzen, *das;* (*coming together*) Zusammenkunft, *die*

**assemble** /ə'sembl/ **1** *v.t.* **A** zusammentragen ‹Beweise, Material, Sammlung›; zusammenrufen ‹Menschen›; **a team was ~d, and work began** ein Team wurde zusammengestellt, und die Arbeit begann; **B** (*fit together*) zusammenbauen. **2** *v.i.* sich versammeln

**assembly** /ə'semblɪ/ *n.* **A** (*coming together, meeting, deliberative body*) Versammlung, *die;* (*in school*) (*tägliche Versammlung aller Schüler und Lehrer zur*) Morgenandacht; **B** (*fitting together*) Zusammenbau, *der;* Montage, *die;* **C** (*assembled unit*) Einheit, *die*

**as'sembly line** *n.* Fließband, *das;* **work/be produced on an ~:** am Fließband arbeiten/produziert werden

**assent** /ə'sent/ **1** *v.i.* zustimmen; **~ to sth.** einer Sache (*Dat.*) zustimmen. **2** *n.* Zustimmung, *die;* **royal ~:** Zustimmung des Königs/der Königin; **by common ~:** nach allgemeiner Auffassung

**assert** /ə'sɜ:t/ *v.t.* **A** geltend machen; **~ oneself** sich durchsetzen; **B** (*declare*) behaupten; beteuern ‹Unschuld›

**assertion** /ə'sɜ:ʃn/ *n.* **A** Geltendmachen, *das;* **B** (*declaration*) Behauptung, *die;* **~ of innocence** Unschuldsbeteuerung, *die;* **make an ~:** eine Behauptung aufstellen

**assertive** /ə'sɜ:tɪv/ *adj.* energisch ‹Person›; bestimmt ‹Ton, Verhalten›; fest ‹Stimme›; (*dogmatic*) rechthaberisch

**assertiveness** /ə'sɜ:tɪvnɪs/ *n., no pl.* Bestimmtheit, *die;* (*dogmatism*) Rechthaberei, *die*

**assess** /ə'ses/ *v.t.* **A** (*evaluate*) einschätzen; beurteilen; **B** (*value*) schätzen; taxieren; **C** (*fix amount of*) festsetzen ‹Steuer, Bußgeld usw.› (**at** auf + *Akk.*); **D** (*tax*) veranlagen

**assessment** /ə'sesmənt/ *n.* **A** (*evaluation*) Einschätzung, *die;* Beurteilung, *die;* **B** (*valuation*) Schätzung, *die;* Taxierung, *die;* **C** (*fixing amount of damages or fine*) Festsetzung, *die;* (*of tax*) Veranlagung, *die;* **D** (*tax to be paid*) Steuerbescheid, *der*

**assessor** /ə'sesə(r)/ *n.* ▶ **1261** **A** (*tax inspector*) ≈ Finanzbeamte, *der*/Finanzbeamtin, *die;* **B** (*adviser to judge*) (*als Beisitzer fungierender*) Sachverständiger

**asset** /'æset/ *n.* **A** Vermögenswert, *der;* **my [personal] ~s** mein [persönlicher] Besitz; **B** (*fig.*) (*useful quality*) Vorzug, *der* (**to** für); (*person*) Stütze, *die;* (*thing*) Hilfe, *die*

**'asset-stripping** *n.* (*Commerc.*) *Ankauf unrentabler Unternehmen, von denen einzelne Teile gewinnbringend weiterverkauft werden*

**asseverate** /ə'sevəreɪt/ *v.t.* beteuern

**asseveration** /əsevə'reɪʃn/ *n.* Beteuerung, *die*

**assiduity** /æsɪ'dju:ɪtɪ/ *n.* **A** *no pl.* (*diligence*) Eifer, *der;* (*conscientiousness*) Gewissenhaftigkeit, *die;* **B** (*obsequious attention*) Beflissenheit, *die*

**assiduous** /ə'sɪdjʊəs/ *adj.* **A** (*diligent*) eifrig; (*conscientious*) gewissenhaft; **we made ~ efforts** wir unternahmen alle Anstrengungen; **B** (*obsequiously attentive*) beflissen

**assiduously** /ə'sɪdjʊəslɪ/ *adv.* **A** (*diligently*) gewissenhaft; **B** (*with obsequious attentiveness*) beflissen

**assiduousness** /ə'sɪdjʊəsnɪs/ ⇒ **assiduity A**

**assign** /ə'saɪn/ **1** *v.t.* **A** (*allot*) **~ sth. to sb.** jmdm. etw. zuweisen; **B** (*appoint*) zuteilen; **~ sb. to a job/task** jmdn. mit einer Arbeit/Aufgabe betrauen; **~ sb. to do sth.** jmdn. damit betrauen, etw. zu tun; **~ sb. to a post** jmdn. auf einen Posten berufen; **C** (*specify*) festsetzen ‹Zeit, Datum, Grenzwert›; **D** (*ascribe*) angeben; **~ a cause to sth.** einen Grund für etw. angeben; **~ an event to a date** ein Ereignis einer Zeit zuschreiben. **2** *n.* (*Law*) Rechtsnachfolger, *der*

**assignable** /ə'saɪnəbl/ *adj.* **A** (*allottable*) zuteilbar; **be ~ to sb.** jmdm. zugeteilt werden können; **B** (*specifiable*) bestimmbar; **C** (*ascribable*) angebbar

**assignation** /æsɪg'neɪʃn/ *n.* **A** (*appointment*) **sb.'s ~ to a job/task** jmds. Betrauung mit einer Arbeit/Aufgabe; **sb.'s ~ to a post** jmds. Berufung auf einen Posten; **B** (*allotment*) Zuteilung, *die;* (*of property*) Übereignung, *die;* **C** (*attribution*) Zuordnung, *die;* **D** (*Amer.: illicit lovers' meeting*) Stelldichein, *das;* **~ house** Bordell, *das*

**assignee** /əsaɪ'ni:/ *n.* **A** (*agent*) Bevollmächtigte, *der/die;* **B** ⇒ **assign 2**

**assignment** /ə'saɪnmənt/ *n.* **A** (*allotment*) Zuteilung, *die;* (*of property*) Übereignung, *die;* (*document*) Übereignungsurkunde, *die;* **B** (*task*) Aufgabe, *die;* (*Amer. Sch. and Univ.*) Arbeit, *die;* Aufgabe, *die;* **C** (*attribution*) (*of date*) Bestimmung, *die;* (*of reason, cause*) Aufgabe, *die*

**assimilate** /ə'sɪmɪleɪt/ *v.t.* **A** (*make like*) angleichen; **~ sth. with** *or* **to sth.** etw. an etw. (*Akk.*) angleichen; **B** (*absorb*) (*Biol.*) assimilieren; **C** (*fig.*) aufnehmen ‹Informationen, Einflüsse usw.›; **D** (*Ling.*) angleichen

**assimilation** /əsɪmɪ'leɪʃn/ *n.* **A** (*making or becoming like*) Angleichung, *die* (**to, with** an + *Akk.*); **B** (*Biol.: absorbing*) Assimilation, *die;* **C** (*fig.*) (*of information, influences, etc.*) Aufnahme, *die;* (*of people*) Integration, *die;* **D** (*Ling.*) Assimilation, *die*

**assist** /ə'sɪst/ **1** *v.t.* (*help*) helfen (+ *Dat.*); voranbringen ‹Vorgang, Prozess›; **~ sb. to do** *or* **in doing sth.** jmdm. helfen, etw. zu tun; **~ sb. with sth.** jmdm. bei etw. helfen. **2** *v.i.* **A** (*help*) helfen; **~ with sth./in doing sth.** bei etw. helfen/helfen, etw. zu tun; **B** (*take part*) mitarbeiten; **~ in sth.** an etw. (*Dat.*) mitarbeiten; **~ in an operation** bei einer Operation assistieren

**assistance** /ə'sɪstəns/ *n., no pl.* Hilfe, *die;* **give ~ to sb.** jmdm. behilflich sein; jmdm. helfen; **be of ~ [to sb.]** [jmdm.] behilflich sein; [jmdm.] helfen

**assistant** /ə'sɪstənt/ ▶ **1261** **1** *n.* (*helper*) Helfer, *der*/Helferin, *die;* (*subordinate*) Mitarbeiter, *der*/Mitarbeiterin, *die;* (*of professor, artist*) Assistent, *der*/Assistentin, *die;* (*in shop*) Verkäufer, *der*/Verkäuferin, *die.* **2** *attrib. adj.* **~ manager** stellvertretender Geschäftsführer; **~ editor** Redaktionsassistent, *der;* **~ professor** (*Amer.*) ≈ Assistenzprofessor, *der*

**assizes** /ə'saɪzɪz/ *n. pl.* (*Brit. Law Hist.*) *regelmäßige Gerichtstage in den verschiedenen Grafschaften*

**associate** **1** /ə'səʊʃɪət, ə'səʊsɪət/ *n.* **A** (*partner*) Partner, *der*/Partnerin, *die;* Kompagnon, *der;* (*colleague*) Kollege, *der*/Kollegin, *die;* (*companion*) Gefährte, *der*/Gefährtin, *die* (*geh.*); Kamerad, *der*/Kameradin, *die;* (*of gangster*) Komplize, *der*/Komplizin, *die;* **B** (*subordinate member*) außerordentliches Mitglied.

**2** *adj.* ▶ **1261** beigeordnet; (*allied*) verwandt; außerordentlich ‹Mitglied usw.›; **~ judge** Beisitzer, *der;* **~ professor** (*Amer.*) ≈ außerordentlicher Professor.

**3** /ə'səʊʃɪeɪt, ə'səʊsɪeɪt/ *v.t.* **A** (*join*) in Verbindung bringen; **be ~d** in Verbindung stehen; **B** (*connect in the mind*) in Verbindung bringen; assoziieren (*Psych.*); **~ sth. with sth.** etw. mit etw. assoziieren (*Psych.*) *od.* verbinden; **C** **~ oneself with sth.** sich einer Sache (*Dat.*) anschließen.

**4** *v.i.* **~ with sb.** mit jmdm. verkehren *od.* Umgang haben; (*for common purpose*) sich zusammenschließen

**associateship** /ə'səʊʃɪətʃɪp, ə'səʊsɪətʃɪp/ *n.* außerordentliche Mitgliedschaft

**association** /əsəʊsɪ'eɪʃn/ *n.* **A** (*organization*) Verband, *der;* Vereinigung, *die;* **an ~ of residents** eine Vereinigung von Anwohnern; **articles** *or* **deeds of ~:** Satzung, *die;* **B** (*mental connection*) Assoziation, *die;* **~ of ideas** Gedankenassoziation, *die;* **have ~s for sb.** bei jmdm. Assoziationen hervorrufen; **C** **A~ football** (*Brit.*) Fußball, *der;* **D** (*connection*) Verbindung, *die;* **E** (*contact with people*) Kontakt, *der;* (*cooperation*) Zusammenarbeit, *die;* **business ~:** geschäftliche Zusammenarbeit

**associative** /ə'səʊʃɪətɪv, ə'səʊsɪətɪv/ *adj.* assoziativ

**assonance** /'æsənəns/ *n.* (*Pros.*) Assonanz, *die*

**assorted** /ə'sɔ:tɪd/ *adj.* gemischt ‹Bonbons, Sortiment›; **cardigans of ~ kinds** verschiedenerlei Strickjacken; **an ~ bunch of people** ein zusammengewürfelter Haufen Leute; ⇒ *also* **ill-assorted**

**assortment** /ə'sɔ:tmənt/ *n.* Sortiment, *das;* **a good ~ of hats [to choose from]** eine gute Auswahl an Hüten; **an ~ of ideas** eine Reihe von Ideen; **an odd ~ of players** eine seltsame Mischung von Spielern

**Asst.** *abbr.* **Assistant** Ass.

**assuage** /ə'sweɪdʒ/ *v.t.* stillen; (*soothe*) besänftigen ‹Person, Ärger›; lindern ‹Schmerz, Sorge›

**assume** /ə'sju:m/ *v.t.* **A** voraussetzen; ausgehen von; **~ sb.'s innocence** von jmds. Unschuld ausgehen; jmds. Unschuld voraussetzen; **he's not so stupid as we ~d him to be** er ist nicht so dumm, wie wir angenommen haben; **B** (*undertake*) übernehmen ‹Amt, Pflichten›; **C** (*take on*) annehmen ‹Namen, Rolle›; gewinnen ‹Aspekt, Bedeutung›; **under an ~d name** unter einem Decknamen; **D** (*formal: put on oneself*) anlegen (*geh.*) ‹Gewand›; **E** (*simulate*) vortäuschen ‹Freude, Trauer, Unwissenheit›

**assuming** /ə'sju:mɪŋ/ *adj.* **A** **~ that ...:** vorausgesetzt, dass ...; **B** (*presumptuous*) anmaßend

**assumption** /ə'sʌmpʃn/ *n.* **A** Annahme, *die;* **going on the ~ that ...:** vorausgesetzt, dass ...; **B** (*undertaking*) Übernahme, *die;* **~ of power/office** Macht-/Amtsübernahme, *die;* **C** (*simulation*) Vortäuschung, *die;* (*of look, air*) Aufsetzen, *das;* **with an ~ of indifference** mit scheinbarer Gleichgültigkeit; **D** **the A~** (*Relig.*) Mariä Himmelfahrt

**assurance** /ə'ʃʊərəns/ *n.* **A** Zusicherung, *die;* **I give you my ~ that ...:** ich versichere Ihnen, dass ...; **I can give you no ~ that ...:** ich kann Ihnen nicht versprechen, dass ...; **B** *no pl.* (*self-confidence*) Selbstsicherheit, *die;* **C** *no pl.* (*certainty*) Sicherheit, *die;* **D** *no pl.* (*impudence*) Dreistigkeit, *die;* **E** *no pl.* (*Brit.: insurance*) Versicherung, *die*

**assure** /ə'ʃʊə(r)/ *v.t.* **A** versichern (+ *Dat.*); **you're safe now, I ~ you** ich versichere dir, du bist jetzt in Sicherheit; **~ sb. of sth.** jmdn. einer Sache (*Gen.*) versichern (*geh.*); **B** (*convince*) **~ sb./oneself** jmdn./sich überzeugen; **C** (*make certain or safe*) gewährleisten; **D** (*Brit.: insure*) versichern

**assured** /ə'ʃʊəd/ *adj.* gesichert ‹Tatsache›; gewährleistet ‹Erfolg›; **be ~ of sth.** sich (*Dat.*) einer Sache (*Gen.*) sicher sein

**assuredly** /ə'ʃʊərɪdlɪ/ *adv.* gewiss; gewisslich (*geh., veralt.*)

**Assyrian** /ə'sɪrɪən/ ▶ **1275**, ▶ **1340** **1** *adj.* assyrisch. **2** *n.* Assyrer, *der*/Assyrerin, *die*

**aster** /'æstə(r)/ *n.* Aster, *die;* **China ~:** Sommeraster, *die*

**asterisk** /'æstərɪsk/ **1** *n.* Sternchen, *das;* Asteriskus, *der* (*Druckw.*). **2** *v.t.* mit einem Sternchen versehen

**astern** /ə'stɜ:n/ *adv.* (*Naut., Aeronaut.*) achtern; (*towards the rear*) achteraus; **~ of sth.** hinter etw. (*Dat.*); **full speed ~!** volle Kraft zurück!; **go ~:** achteraus fahren; **fall ~:** achteraus sacken

**asteroid** /'æstərɔɪd/ *n.* (*Astron.*) Asteroid, *der*

**asthma** /'æsmə/ *n.* ▶ **1232** (*Med.*) Asthma, *das*

**asthmatic** /æs'mætɪk/ (*Med.*) **1** *adj.* asthmatisch. **2** *n.* Asthmatiker, *der*/Asthmatikerin, *die*

**astigmatism** /ə'stɪgmətɪzm/ *n.* (*Med., Optics*) Astigmatismus, *der*

**astir** /ə'stɜ:(r)/ *pred. adj.* in Bewegung; (*out of bed*) auf den Beinen; (*excited*) in Aufruhr

**astonish** /ə'stɒnɪʃ/ *v.t.* erstaunen; **you ~ me** (*iron.*) wer hätte das gedacht; **he was ~ed**

a

**to hear that ...:** er war erstaunt zu hören, dass ...

**astonishing** /əˈstɒnɪʃɪŋ/ *adj.* erstaunlich

**astonishingly** /əˈstɒnɪʃɪŋlɪ/ *adv.* erstaunlich; *as sentence-modifier* **~ [enough], no one has yet ...** erstaunlicherweise hat noch niemand ...

**astonishment** /əˈstɒnɪʃmənt/ *n., no pl.* Erstaunen, *das;* **in utter ~:** äußerst erstaunt

**astound** /əˈstaʊnd/ *v.t.* verblüffen; [sehr] überraschen; **you ~ me** (*iron.*) das überrascht mich aber sehr

**astounding** /əˈstaʊndɪŋ/ *adj.* erstaunlich

**astrakhan** /æstrəˈkæn/ *n.* (*fleece, cloth*) Astrachan, *der*

**astral** /ˈæstrl/ *adj.* astral; **~ body** Astralleib, *der;* **~ spirits** Sterngeister

**astray** /əˈstreɪ/ **1** *adv.* in die Irre; **sb. goes ~:** jmd. verirrt sich; **sth. goes ~** (*is mislaid*) etw. wird verlegt; (*is lost*) etw. geht verloren; **lead ~:** irreführen; **go/lead ~** (*fig.*) in die Irre gehen/führen; (*into sin*) vom rechten Weg abkommen/abbringen. **2** *pred. adj.* **be ~:** sich verirrt haben; (*fig.: be in error*) sich irren; ‹Rechnung:› abwegig sein

**astride** /əˈstraɪd/ **1** *adv.* rittlings ‹sitzen›; breitbeinig ‹stehen›; **with one's legs ~:** mit gespreizten Beinen; **~ of sth.** rittlings auf etw. (*Dat./Akk.*). **2** (*Air Force*) *prep.* **A** rittlings auf (+ *Dat.*); **B** (*extending across*) zu beiden Seiten (+ *Gen.*)

**astringency** /əˈstrɪndʒənsɪ/ *n., no pl.* Schärfe, *die;* (*of wine, fruit*) Säure, *die;* (*severity*) Schärfe, *die;* (*of judgement*) Strenge, *die*

**astringent** /əˈstrɪndʒənt/ **1** *adj.* **A** herb, streng ‹Geruch, Geschmack›; stechend, beißend ‹Geruch›; sauer ‹Obst, Wein›; **B** (*styptic*) adstringierend (*Med.*); blutstillend; **C** (*severe*) scharf; beißend; streng ‹Urteil›. **2** *n.* Adstringens, *das*

**astro-** /æstrəʊ/ *in comb.* astro-/Astro-

**astrologer** /əˈstrɒlədʒə(r)/ *n.* ▶ **1261** Astrologe, *der*/Astrologin, *die*

**astrological** /æstrəˈlɒdʒɪkl/ *adj.* astrologisch

**astrology** /əˈstrɒlədʒɪ/ *n., no pl.* Astrologie, *die*

**astronaut** /ˈæstrənɔːt/ *n.* ▶ **1261** Astronaut, *der*/Astronautin, *die*

**astronautical** /æstrəˈnɔːtɪkl/ *adj.* astronautisch; **~ research** Weltraumforschung, *die;* **~ engineering** Raumfahrttechnik, *die*

**astronautics** /æstrəˈnɔːtɪks/ *n., no pl.* Astronautik, *die;* Raumfahrt, *die*

**astronomer** /əˈstrɒnəmə(r)/ *n.* ▶ **1261** Astronom, *der*/Astronomin, *die*

**astronomical** /æstrəˈnɒmɪkl/ *adj.*, **astronomically** /æstrəˈnɒmɪkəlɪ/ *adv.* (*lit. or fig.*) astronomisch

**astronomy** /əˈstrɒnəmɪ/ *n., no pl.* Astronomie, *die*

**astrophysical** /æstrəʊˈfɪzɪkl/ *adj.* astrophysikalisch

**astrophysicist** /æstrəʊˈfɪzɪsɪst/ *n.* ▶ **1261** Astrophysiker, *der*/Astrophysikerin, *die*

**astrophysics** /æstrəʊˈfɪzɪks/ *n., no pl.* Astrophysik, *die*

**astute** /əˈstjuːt/ *adj.* scharfsinnig ‹Beobachter, Bemerkung›; (*skilful*) geschickt

**astutely** /əˈstjuːtlɪ/ *adv.* scharfsinnig ‹bemerken, entscheiden›; (*skilfully*) geschickt

**astuteness** /əˈstjuːtnɪs/ *n., no pl.* Scharfsinnigkeit, *die;* (*skill*) Geschick, *das*

**asunder** /əˈsʌndə(r)/ *adv.* (*literary*) auseinander; **tear sth. ~:** etw. zerreißen

**asylum** /əˈsaɪləm/ *n.* Asyl, *das;* **grant sb. ~:** jmdm. Asyl gewähren; **seek ~:** um Asyl bitten *od.* nachsuchen; **political ~:** politisches Asyl; *attrib.* **~ seeker** Asylsuchende, *der/die*

**asymmetric** /æsɪˈmetrɪk, eɪsɪˈmetrɪk/, **asymmetrical** /æsɪˈmetrɪkl, eɪsɪˈmetrɪkl/ *adj.* asymmetrisch; unsymmetrisch; **~ bars** (*Sport*) Stufenbarren, *der*

**asymmetry** /æˈsɪmɪtrɪ, eɪˈsɪmɪtrɪ/ *n.* Asymmetrie, *die*

**asynchronous** /eɪˈsɪŋkrənəs/ *adj.* asynchron; **~ motor** Asynchronmotor, *der*

**at** /ət, *stressed* æt/ *prep.* **A** *expr. place* an (+ *Dat.*); **at the station** am Bahnhof; **at the baker's/butcher's/grocer's** beim Bäcker/Fleischer/Kaufmann; **at the chemist's** in der Apotheke/Drogerie; **at the supermarket** im Supermarkt; **at my mother's** bei meiner Mutter; **at home** zu Hause; **at the party** auf der Party; **at the office/hotel** im Büro/Hotel; **at school** in der Schule; **at Dover** in Dover; **B** ▶ **1012** *expr. time* **at Christmas/Easter/Whitsun** [zu *od.* an] Weihnachten/Ostern/Pfingsten; **at six o'clock** um sechs Uhr; **at midnight** um Mitternacht; **at midday** am Mittag; mittags; **at dawn** im Morgengrauen; **at [the age of] 40** mit 40; im Alter von 40; **at this/the moment** in diesem/im Augenblick *od.* Moment; **at any time** jederzeit; **at irregular intervals** in unregelmäßigen Abständen; **at the first attempt** beim ersten Versuch; **C** *expr. price* **at £2.50 [each]** zu *od.* für [je] 2,50 Pfund; **petrol is charged at 5p per mile** die Benzinkosten werden mit 5 Pence pro Meile berechnet; **D she's still 'at it** sie ist immer noch dabei; **while we're/you're** *etc.* **'at it** wenn wir/du *usw.* schon dabei sind/bist *usw.*; **so while I was 'at it,...:** und wo *od.* da ich schon dabei war...; **at that** (*at that point*) dabei; (*at that provocation*) daraufhin; (*moreover*) noch dazu; (*nevertheless*) trotzdem; **this is where it's at** (*coll.*) da ist was los (*ugs.*)

**atavism** /ˈætəvɪzm/ *n.* Atavismus, *der*

**atavistic** /ætəˈvɪstɪk/ *adj.* atavistisch

**ataxia** /əˈtæksɪə/ *n., no pl.* (*Med.*) Ataxie, *die;* **locomotor ~:** lokomotorische Ataxie

**ate** ⇨ **eat**

**atheism** /ˈeɪθɪɪzm/ *n., no pl.* Atheismus, *der*

**atheist** /ˈeɪθɪɪst/ *n.* Atheist, *der*/Atheistin, *die*

**Athenian** /əˈθiːnɪən/ **1** *adj.* athenisch; **the ~ people** die Athener; **~ history** die Geschichte Athens. **2** *n.* Athener, *der*/Athenerin, *die*

**Athens** /ˈæθɪnz/ *pr. n.* ▶ **1626** Athen (*das*)

**atherosclerosis** /æθərəʊskləˈrəʊsɪs/ *n., pl.* **atheroscleroses** /æθərəʊskləˈrəʊsiːz/ (*Med.*) Atherosklerose, *die*

**athlete** /ˈæθliːt/ *n.* Athlet, *der*/Athletin, *die;* Sportler, *der*/Sportlerin, *die;* (*runner, jumper*) Leichtathlet, *der*/Leichtathletin, *die;* **~'s foot** ▶ **1232** (*Med.*) Athletenfuß, *der* (*fachspr.*); Fußpilz, *der*

**athletic** /æθˈletɪk/ *adj.* sportlich; (*robust*) athletisch; **~ sports** Leichtathletik, *die;* **any reasonably ~ person** jeder einigermaßen sportliche Mensch; **the goalkeeper made an ~ save** der Torwart zeigte eine Glanzparade

**athletically** /æθˈletɪkəlɪ/ *adv.* sportlich; athletisch ‹gebaut›

**athleticism** /æθˈletɪsɪzm/ *n., no pl.* Sportlichkeit, *die*

**athletics** /æθˈletɪks/ *n., no pl.* **A** Leichtathletik, *die;* **B** (*Amer.: physical sports*) Sport, *der*

**at-'home** *n.: festgesetzter Tag, an dem man zu festgesetzter Zeit zwanglos Gäste empfängt;* Jour fixe, *der* (*veralt.*)

**athwart** /əˈθwɔːt/ **1** *adv.* **A** (*literary: from side to side*) quer (to zu); **B** (*Naut.*) dwars. **2** *prep.* **A** (*literary: from side to side of*) quer über (+ *Dat./Akk.*); **B** (*Naut.*) dwars zu

**Atlantic** /ətˈlæntɪk/ **1** *adj.* atlantisch; **~ Ocean** Atlantischer Ozean; **~ coast** Atlantikküste, *die.* **2** *pr. n.* Atlantik, *der*

**atlas** /ˈætləs/ (*also Anat.*) Atlas, *der;* **~ of the world** Weltatlas, *der*

**ATM** *abbr.* **automated teller machine**

**atmosphere** /ˈætməsfɪə(r)/ *n.* **A** (*lit. or fig.*) Atmosphäre, *die;* **the ~ of the Earth** die Erdatmosphäre; **B** (*air in a place*) Luft, *die*

**atmospheric** /ætməˈsferɪk/ *adj.* **A** atmosphärisch; **~ moisture** Luftfeuchtigkeit, *die;* **B** (*fig.: evocative*) stimmungsvoll

**atmospherics** /ætməˈsferɪks/ *n. pl.* (*Radio*) atmosphärische Störungen

**atoll** /ˈætɒl, əˈtɒl/ *n.* Atoll, *das*

**atom** /ˈætəm/ *n.* **A** Atom, *das;* **B** (*fig.*) **not an ~ of truth** kein Körnchen Wahrheit; **not a single ~ of evidence** nicht der Schatten eines Beweises

**'atom bomb** ⇨ **atomic bomb**

**atomic** /əˈtɒmɪk/ *adj.* (*Phys.*) Atom-

**atomic: ~ 'bomb** *n.* Atombombe, *die;* **~ 'energy** *n., no pl.* Atomenergie, *die;* **~ 'mass** ⇨ **~ weight; ~ 'number** *n.* (*Phys., Chem.*) Kernladungszahl, *die;* Ordnungszahl, *die;* **~ 'power** *n., no pl.* Atomkraft, *die;* **~ 'warfare** *n., no pl.* Atomkrieg, *der;* **~ 'weight** *n.* (*Phys., Chem.*) Atomgewicht, *das*

**atomization** /ætəmaɪˈzeɪʃn/ *n.* Atomisierung, *die;* (*of liquid*) Zerstäubung, *die*

**atomize** /ˈætəmaɪz/ *v.t.* atomisieren; zerstäuben ‹Flüssigkeit›

**atomizer** /ˈætəmaɪzə(r)/ *n.* Zerstäuber, *der*

**atonal** /eɪˈtəʊnl, əˈtəʊnl/ *adj.* (*Mus.*) atonal

**atone** /əˈtəʊn/ *v.i.* es wieder gutmachen; **~ for sth.** etw. wieder gutmachen

**atonement** /əˈtəʊnmənt/ *n.* **A** (*atoning*) Buße, *die;* (*reparation*) Wiedergutmachung, *die;* **make ~ for sth.** für etw. Buße tun; **B** (*Relig.*) Versöhnung, *die;* **Day of A~:** Versöhnungsfest, *das;* Jom Kippur, *der;* **the A~:** das Sühneopfer [Christi]

**atonic** /əˈtɒnɪk/ *adj.* (*Phonet., Pros.*) unbetont; atonisch (*veralt.*)

**atop** /əˈtɒp/ **1** *adv.* obendrauf; **~ of sth.** [oben] auf etw. (*Dat./Akk.*). **2** *prep.* [oben] auf (+ *Dat./Akk.*)

**atrium** /ˈeɪtrɪəm/ *n., pl.* **atria** /ˈeɪtrɪə/ *or* **~s** **A** (*Anat.*) Vorhof, *der;* Atrium, *das* (*fachspr.*); **B** (*Archit., Roman Ant.*) Atrium, *das*

**atrocious** /əˈtrəʊʃəs/ *adj.* grauenhaft; scheußlich ‹Wetter, Benehmen›

**atrociously** /əˈtrəʊʃəslɪ/ *adv.* grauenhaft; scheußlich ‹sich benehmen›

**atrocity** /əˈtrɒsɪtɪ/ *n.* **A** *no pl.* (*extreme wickedness*) Grauenhaftigkeit, *die;* **B** (*atrocious deed*) Gräueltat, *die* (*geh.*); Grausamkeit, *die;* **C** (*coll.: repellent thing*) Widerwärtigkeit, *die*

**atrophy** /ˈætrəfɪ/ **1** *n.* **A** (*Med.*) Atrophie, *die*; Verkümmerung, *die;* **muscular ~:** Muskelatrophie, *die* (*Med.*); Muskelschwund, *der;* **B** (*emaciation*) Abmagerung, *die;* (*fig.*) Verfall, *der.* **2** *v.i.* atrophieren (*Med.*); verkümmern

**atropine** /ˈætrəpɪn, ˈætrəpiːn/ *n.* (*Med.*) Atropin, *das*

**attach** /əˈtætʃ/ **1** *v.t.* **A** (*fasten*) befestigen (**to** an + *Dat.*); anhängen ‹Wagen› (**to** an + *Dat.*); **please find ~ed a copy of the letter** beigeheftet ist eine Kopie des Briefes; **B** (*join*) **~ oneself to sth./sb.** sich einer Sache/jmdm. anschließen; **C** (*assign*) **be ~ed to sth.** einer Sache (*Dat.*) zugeteilt sein; **is there a car ~ed to the job?** ist die Stelle mit einem Dienstwagen verbunden?; **the research unit is ~ed to the university** die Forschungsabteilung ist der Universität (*Dat.*) angegliedert; **D** (*fig.: ascribe*) zuschreiben; **~ no blame to sb.** jmdm. keine Schuld geben; **I can't ~ a name to that face** ich kann diesem Gesicht keinen Namen zuordnen; **E** (*attribute*) beimessen; **~ importance/meaning to sth.** einer Sache (*Dat.*) Gewicht/Bedeutung beimessen; **F** (*Law*) pfänden ‹Eigentum›; festnehmen ‹Person›. **2** *v.i.* **no blame ~es to sb.** jmdn. trifft keine Schuld; **suspicion ~es to sb.** der Verdacht fällt auf jmdn.

**attachable** /əˈtætʃəbl/ *adj.* **A** **be ~ to sth.** an etw. (*Dat.*) befestigt werden können; **B** (*Law*) pfändbar ‹Gut, Ware›

**attaché** /əˈtæʃeɪ/ *n.* Attaché, *der;* **cultural/military/press/naval ~:** Kultur-/Militär-/Presse-/Marineattaché, *der*

**at'taché case** *n.* Diplomatenkoffer, *der*

**attached** /əˈtætʃt/ *adj.* (*emotionally*) **be ~ to sb./sth.** an jmdm./etw. hängen; **become ~ to sb./sth.** jmdn./etw. lieb gewinnen

**attachment** /əˈtætʃmənt/ *n.* **A** (*act or means of fastening*) Befestigung, *die;* **the ~ of a recording device to a telephone** der Anschluss eines Aufnahmegerätes an ein Telefon; **B** (*accessory*) Zusatzgerät, *das;* **blender ~:** Mixaufsatz, *der;* **C** (*ascribing*) Zuordnung, *die;* **the ~ of blame would be premature at this stage** es wäre in diesem

# At

## Where?

**an** + dative describes position:

***at the corner of the street*** = an der Straßenecke

***at the side*** = an der Seite

***at the royal court*** = am königlichen Hof

But note

***at the top/bottom*** = oben/unten

***at the top of the pile*** = oben auf dem Stapel

***at the front/back*** = vorne/hinten

***at the bottom of page 4*** = auf Seite 4 unten

***at the back of the house*** = (*inside*) hinten im Haus; (*outside*) hinterm Haus

When referring to someone's house or shop, **bei** + dative is used:

***at my uncle's*** = bei meinem Onkel

***at the baker's*** = beim Bäcker

***at the Robinsons*** = bei Robinsons

***at Woolworth's*** = bei Woolworth

Note that there is usually no article with a name.

In the case of buildings, **an** indicates the general area (including outside), while **in** is used for the inside:

***They are at the theatre*** (*i.e. inside*) = Sie sind im Theater

***We met at the theatre*** (*i.e. inside/just outside*) = Wir trafen uns im/am Theater

**bei** is also often used for a place of work:

***He works at the bank*** = Er arbeitet bei der Bank

but in the case of most offices and shops it is **in**:

***at the bookshop*** = in der Buchhandlung

***at the office*** = im Büro

***at the supermarket*** = im Supermarkt

***at the travel agent's*** = im Reisebüro

Cf. also:

***at school*** = in der Schule

***at a party*** = auf einer Party

***at university*** = auf der Universität

With place names, use **in**:

***You have to change at Cologne*** = Sie müssen in Köln umsteigen

## When?

With an actual time, at is translated by **um**:

***at 9 a.m.*** = um 9 Uhr (morgens)

***at 9 p.m.*** = um 9 Uhr abends *or* 21 Uhr

***at midday/midnight*** = um zwölf Uhr mittags/um Mitternacht

But note

***at a late hour*** = zu später Stunde

***at night*** = bei Nacht

***at sunrise/sunset*** = bei Sonnenaufgang/Sonnenuntergang

With the main church festivals, *at* is either not translated or **zu** (or in South Germany **an**) is used:

***She's coming at Christmas/Easter*** = Sie kommt [zu *or* an] Weihnachten/Ostern

Cf. also:

***at [5 minute] intervals*** = in Abständen [von 5 Minuten]

***at this moment*** = in diesem Augenblick

***at any moment*** or ***at any time*** = jederzeit

## How old?

***at [the age of] sixty*** = im Alter von sechzig

***at her age*** = in ihrem Alter

***too old at forty*** = mit vierzig schon zu alt

## How much?

Expressing price, the translation is **zu**:

***two pounds at fifty pence a pound*** = zwei Pfund zu fünfzig Pence das Pfund

***six oranges at 30p each*** = sechs Orangen zu 30 Pence das Stück

***at the same price*** = zum gleichen Preis

## With superlatives

***She was at her most charming*** = Sie zeigte sich von ihrer charmantesten Seite

***I am not at my best in the morning*** = Morgens bin ich nicht gerade in Höchstform

***This is an example of Czech music at its most captivating*** = Das ist eines der reizvollsten Beispiele tschechischer Musik

---

Stadium verfrüht, jemandem die Schuld zu geben; Ⓓ (*attribution*) Beimessung, *die;* Ⓔ (*affection*) Anhänglichkeit, *die* (**to** an + *Akk.*); **his ~ to that party** seine Sympathie für diese Partei; **have an ~ for sb.** an jmdm. hängen; Ⓕ (*Law*) Pfändung, *die*

**attack** /əˈtæk/ ❶ *v.t.* Ⓐ angreifen; (*ambush, raid*) überfallen; (*fig.: criticize*) attackieren; **a woman was ~ed and raped** eine Frau wurde überfallen und vergewaltigt; Ⓑ (*affect*) ‹Krankheit:› befallen; Ⓒ (*start work on*) in Angriff nehmen; **she ~ed the washing-up** sie machte sich an den Abwasch; Ⓓ (*take action against*) vorgehen gegen; Ⓔ (*act harmfully on*) angreifen ‹Metall, Oberfläche›.
❷ *v.i.* angreifen; **~ in strength** in großer Zahl angreifen.
❸ *n.* Ⓐ (*on enemy*) Angriff, *der;* (*on person*) Überfall, *der;* (*fig.: criticism*) Attacke, *die;* Angriff, *der;* **air ~:** Luftangriff, *der;* **be under ~:** angegriffen werden; **come under ~ from all directions** (*fig.*) von allen Seiten attackiert *od.* angegriffen werden; Ⓑ (*start*) Inangriffnahme, *die* (**on** *Gen.*); **make a spirited ~ on sth.** etw. beherzt in Angriff nehmen; Ⓒ (*of illness, lit. or fig.*) Anfall, *der;* **the girls got an ~ of the giggles** die Mädchen mussten furchtbar kichern; Ⓓ (*Sport*) Angriff, *der;* Ⓔ (*Mus.*) [präziser] Einsatz; (*on piano*) Anschlag, *der;* Attacke, *die* (*Jazz*)

**attacker** /əˈtækə(r)/ *n.* (*also Sport*) Angreifer, *der*/Angreiferin, *die*

**attacking** /əˈtækɪŋ/ *adj.* offensiv ‹Spielweise, Spieler›; angreifend ‹Truppen›

**attain** /əˈteɪn/ ❶ *v.t.* erreichen ‹Ziel, Wirkung›; **~ power** an die Macht gelangen; **the author ~ed his ambition** der Autor erreichte sein Ziel; **she ~ed her hope** ihre Hoffnung erfüllte sich. ❷ *v.i.* **~ to sth.** zu etw. gelangen; **~ to success** Erfolg haben; **~ to power** an die Macht gelangen

**attainability** /əteɪnəˈbɪlɪtɪ/ *n., no pl.* Erreichbarkeit, *die*

**attainable** /əˈteɪnəbl/ *adj.* erreichbar ‹Ziel›; realisierbar ‹Hoffnung, Ziel›

**attainder** /əˈteɪndə(r)/ *n.* (*Hist.*) Verlust von Recht und Besitz (*als Folge eines Todesurteils oder der Ächtung*)

**attainment** /əˈteɪnmənt/ *n.* Ⓐ *no pl.* Verwirklichung, *die;* **be impossible of ~:** unmöglich zu erreichen sein; Ⓑ (*thing attained*) Leistung, *die*

**attar** /ˈætə(r)/ *n.* Rosenöl, *das;* Attar, *der* (*veralt.*)

**attempt** /əˈtempt/ ❶ *v.t.* Ⓐ versuchen; **~ to do sth.** versuchen, etw. zu tun; Ⓑ (*try to accomplish*) sich versuchen an (+ *Dat.*); (*try to conquer*) angreifen; **candidates should ~ 5 out of 10 questions** die Kandidaten sollten 5 von 10 Fragen zu beantworten versuchen.
❷ *n.* Versuch, *der;* **make an ~ at sth.** sich an etw. (*Dat.*) versuchen; **make an ~ to do sth.** den Versuch unternehmen, etw. zu tun; **he will make an ~ on the 800 m record**

**tonight** er wird heute Abend einen Rekordversuch über 800 m unternehmen; **make an ~ on sb.'s life** ein Attentat *od.* einen Mordanschlag auf jmdn. verüben

**attend** /ə'tend/ ❶ *v.i.* Ⓐ (*give care and thought*) aufpassen; (*apply oneself*) **~ to sth.** auf etw. (*Akk.*) achten; (*deal with sth.*) sich um etw. kümmern; **everyone had their own tasks to ~ to** jeder musste sich um seine eigenen Aufgaben kümmern *od.* sich seinen eigenen Aufgaben widmen; Ⓑ (*be present*) anwesend sein; **~ at sth.** bei etw. anwesend sein; **the chiropodist ~s on Wednesdays** der Fußpfleger ist [immer] mittwochs da; Ⓒ (*wait*) bedienen; aufwarten (*veralt.*); **~ on sb.** jmdn. bedienen; jmdm. aufwarten (*veralt.*).
❷ *v.t.* Ⓐ (*be present at*) teilnehmen an (+ *Dat.*); (*go regularly to*) besuchen; **his lectures are well ~ed** seine Vorlesungen werden gut besucht; Ⓑ (*follow as a result from*) sich ergeben aus; **be ~ed by sth.** etw. zur Folge haben; Ⓒ (*accompany*) verbunden sein mit; **may good luck ~ you** (*formal*) möge das Glück dir hold sein (*geh.*); Ⓓ (*wait on*) bedienen; aufwarten (*veralt.*) (+ *Dat.*); Ⓔ ‹Arzt:› behandeln

**attendance** /ə'tendəns/ *n.* Ⓐ (*being present*) Anwesenheit, *die;* (*going regularly*) Besuch, *der* (**at** *Gen.*); **regular ~ at school** regelmäßiger Schulbesuch; **your ~ record is very poor** Sie haben reichlich oft gefehlt; Ⓑ (*number of people present*) Teilnehmerzahl, *die;* **there was only a small ~ for sth.** etw. wurde nur schwach besucht; **~s at churches are declining** die Zahl der Kirchenbesucher geht zurück; Ⓒ **be in ~:** anwesend sein; **the ladies in ~:** die anwesenden Damen; **in close ~:** in unmittelbarer Nähe. ⇒ *also* **dance** 2 A

**attendance: ~ allowance** *n.* (*Brit.*) *Sozialversicherungsleistung für Personen, die die Pflege einer pflegebedürftigen Person besorgen;* **~ centre** *n.* (*Brit.*) Jugendarrestanstalt (*in der Freizeitarrest verbüßt wird*)

**attendant** /ə'tendənt/ ❶ *n.* Ⓐ ▶1261 (*person providing service*) **[lavatory] ~:** Toilettenmann, *der*/Toilettenfrau, *die;* **[cloakroom] ~:** Garderobenmann, *der*/Garderobenfrau, *die;* **museum ~:** Museumswärter, *der;* Ⓑ (*member of entourage*) Begleiter, *der*/Begleiterin, *die.* ❷ *adj.* begleitend; **~ circumstances** Begleitumstände; **its ~ problems/risks** die damit verbundenen Probleme/Risiken; **be ~ upon sth.** mit etw. verbunden sein

**attender** /ə'tendə(r)/ *n.* (*person present*) Anwesende, *der/die;* **regular ~s will know ...:** wer regelmäßig teilnimmt, wird wissen, ...

**attention** /ə'tenʃn/ ❶ *n.* Ⓐ *no pl.* Aufmerksamkeit, *die;* **your careful ~ would be much appreciated** ich wäre Ihnen dankbar, wenn Sie gut aufpassen würden; **pay ~ to sb./sth.** jmdn./etw. beachten; **pay ~!** gib Acht!; pass auf!; **hold sb.'s ~:** jmds. Interesse wach halten; **attract [sb.'s] ~:** [jmdn.] auf sich (*Akk.*) aufmerksam machen; **catch sb.'s ~:** jmds. Aufmerksamkeit erregen; **bring sth. to sb.'s ~:** jmds. Aufmerksamkeit auf etw. (*Akk.*) lenken; jmdn. auf etw. (*Akk.*) aufmerksam machen; **call** *or* **draw sb.'s ~ to sb./sth.** jmds. Aufmerksamkeit auf jmdn./etw. lenken; jmdn. auf jmdn./etw. aufmerksam machen; **~ Miss Jones** (*on letter*) zu Händen [von] Miss Jones; Ⓑ *no pl.* (*consideration*) **give sth. one's personal ~:** sich einer Sache (*Gen.*) persönlich annehmen; **we are giving your enquiry our fullest ~:** wir bearbeiten Ihre Anfrage mit der größten Sorgfalt; Ⓒ *in pl.* (*ceremonious politeness*) Aufmerksamkeit, *die;* **show sb. little ~s** jmdm. kleine Aufmerksamkeiten erweisen; **pay [one's] ~s to sb.** jmdm. den Hof machen (*veralt.*); Ⓓ (*Mil.*) Grundstellung, *die;* Habachtstellung, *die;* **stand to ~:** stillstehen; strammstehen.
❷ *int.* Ⓐ Achtung!; **~ all shipping** Achtung! An alle Schiffe!; Ⓑ (*Mil.*) stillgestanden!

**attentive** /ə'tentɪv/ *adj.* Ⓐ (*paying attention*) aufmerksam; **be ~ to sth.** auf etw. (*Akk.*) achten; Ⓑ (*heedful*) **be more ~ to one's studies** sich gewissenhafter seinen Studien widmen; **be [more] ~ to sb.'s warnings** auf jmds. Warnungen hören; Ⓒ (*assiduous*) aufmerksam; **he was very ~ to the ladies** er war den Damen gegenüber sehr aufmerksam *od.* zuvorkommend

**attentively** /ə'tentɪvlɪ/ *adv.* aufmerksam

**attentiveness** /ə'tentɪvnɪs/ *n., no pl.* Aufmerksamkeit, *die*

**attenuate** /ə'tenjʊeɪt/ *v.t.* Ⓐ (*make thin*) dünn machen; dünnflüssig machen ‹Öl›; Ⓑ (*reduce, lit. or fig.*) abschwächen; dämpfen ‹Schall, Ton›; Ⓒ (*Electr.*) [ab]schwächen; dämpfen ‹Welle, Schwingung›

**attenuation** /ətenjʊ'eɪʃn/ *n.* ⇒ **attenuate** A, B, C: Verdünnung, *die;* Abschwächung, *die;* Dämpfung, *die*

**attest** /ə'test/ ❶ *v.t.* (*certify validity of*) bestätigen; beglaubigen ‹Unterschrift, Urkunde›. ❷ *v.i.* (*bear witness*) **~ to sth.** etw. bezeugen; (*fig.*) von etw. zeugen

**attestation** /ætɪ'steɪʃn/ *n.* Bestätigung, *die*

**attic** *n.* Ⓐ (*storey*) Dachgeschoss, *das;* oberstes Stockwerk; Ⓑ (*room*) Dachboden, *der;* (*habitable*) Dachkammer, *die;* Mansarde, *die*

**Attic** /'ætɪk/ ❶ *adj.* attisch; **~ dialect** attischer Dialekt; **~ salt** *or* **wit** attisches Salz; attischer Witz. ❷ *n.* attischer Dialekt

**attire** /ə'taɪə(r)/ ❶ *n., no pl.* Kleidung, *die.* ❷ *v.t.* kleiden; **be ~d in sth.** in etw. (*Akk.*) gekleidet sein; **~ oneself** sich kleiden

**attitude** /'ætɪtju:d/ *n.* Ⓐ (*posture, way of behaving*) Haltung, *die;* **in a defensive/threatening ~:** in abwehrender/drohender Haltung; **strike an ~:** eine Haltung einnehmen; Ⓑ (*mode of thinking*) **~ [of mind]** Einstellung, *die* (**to[wards]** zu); Ⓒ (*Aeron.*) Fluglage, *die*

**attitudinize** /ætɪ'tju:dɪnaɪz/ *v.i.* sich in Szene setzen

**attn.** *abbr.* **for the attention of** z. H[d].

**attorney** /ə'tɜ:nɪ/ *n.* ▶1261 Ⓐ (*legal agent*) Bevollmächtigte, *der/die;* **power of ~:** Vollmacht, *die;* Ⓑ (*Amer.: lawyer*) [Rechts]anwalt, *der*/[Rechts]anwältin, *die*

**Attorney-'General** *n., pl.* **Attorneys-General** *oberster Justizbeamter bestimmter Staaten;* ≈ Generalbundesanwalt, *der;* (*in USA*) ≈ Justizminister, *der*

**attract** /ə'trækt/ *v.t.* Ⓐ (*draw*) anziehen; auf sich (*Akk.*) ziehen ‹Interesse, Blick, Kritik›; ‹Köder, Attraktion:› anlocken; **the party launched a publicity campaign to ~ new members** die Partei startete eine Werbekampagne, um neue Mitglieder zu gewinnen; Ⓑ (*arouse pleasure in*) anziehend wirken auf (+ *Akk.*); **what ~s me about the girl** was ich an dem Mädchen anziehend finde; Ⓒ (*arouse interest in*) reizen (**about** an + *Dat.*); **I am ~ed by that idea** der Gedanke reizt mich

**attractant** /ə'træktənt/ *n.* Lockmittel, *das*

**attraction** /ə'trækʃn/ *n.* Ⓐ Anziehung, *die;* (*force, lit. or fig.*) Anziehung[skraft], *die;* **I cannot see the ~ of going to horror films** ich kann nichts Besonderes daran finden, in Gruselfilme zu gehen; **the possibility of promotion has little ~ for me** die Möglichkeit, befördert zu werden, reizt mich nur wenig; Ⓑ (*fig.: thing that attracts*) Attraktion, *die;* (*charm*) Verlockung, *die;* Reiz, *der;* Ⓒ (*Ling.*) Attraktion, *die*

**attractive** /ə'træktɪv/ *adj.* Ⓐ anziehend; **~ power/force** Anziehungskraft, *die;* Ⓑ (*fig.*) attraktiv; reizvoll ‹Vorschlag, Möglichkeit, Idee›

**attractively** /ə'træktɪvlɪ/ *adv.* reizvoll

**attractiveness** /ə'træktɪvnɪs/ *n., no pl.* Attraktivität, *die*

**attributable** /ə'trɪbjʊtəbl/ *adj.* **be ~ to sb./sth.** jmdm./einer Sache zuzuschreiben sein; **this comment is not ~:** dieser Kommentar muss anonym bleiben

**attribute** ❶ /'ætrɪbju:t/ *n.* Ⓐ (*quality*) Attribut, *das;* Eigenschaft, *die;* **punctuality is not one of her ~s** Pünktlichkeit ist nicht gerade eine ihrer Stärken; Ⓑ (*symbolic object*) Attribut, *das;* Ⓒ (*Ling.*) Attribut, *das.*
❷ /ə'trɪbju:t/ *v.t.* (*ascribe, assign*) zuschreiben (**to** *Dat.*); (*refer*) zurückführen (**to** auf + *Akk.*)

**attribution** /ætrɪ'bju:ʃn/ *n.* (*ascribing, assigning*) Zuordnung, *die* (**to** *Dat.*); (*referring*) Zurückführung, *die* (**to** auf + *Akk.*)

**attributive** /ə'trɪbjʊtɪv/ *adj.*, **attributively** /ə'trɪbjʊtɪvlɪ/ *adv.* (*Ling.*) attributiv

**attrition** /ə'trɪʃn/ *n., no pl.* Ⓐ (*wearing down*) Zermürbung, *die;* **war of ~** (*lit. or fig.*) Zermürbungskrieg, *der;* Ⓑ (*friction, abrasion*) Abrieb, *der*

**attune** /ə'tju:n/ *v.t.* Ⓐ (*bring into accord*) aufeinander abstimmen; Ⓑ (*fig.: make accustomed*) gewöhnen (**to** an + *Akk.*); **be ~d to sth.** auf etw. (*Akk.*) eingestellt sein

**atypical** /eɪ'tɪpɪkl, ə'tɪpɪkl/ *adj.* atypisch; untypisch

**aubergine** /'əʊbəʒi:n/ *n.* Aubergine, *die*

**aubrietia** /ɔ:'bri:ʃə/ *n.* (*Bot.*) Blaukissen, *das;* Aubrietie, *die* (*fachspr.*)

**auburn** /'ɔ:bən/ *adj.* rötlich braun

**auction** /'ɔ:kʃn/ ❶ *n.* Ⓐ Auktion, *die;* Versteigerung, *die;* **sell sth. by ~:** etw. durch Versteigerung verkaufen; **be put up for ~:** zur Versteigerung kommen; versteigert werden; **Dutch ~:** Abschlag, *der;* Ⓑ (*Cards*) Bieten, *das.* ❷ *v.t.* versteigern

**auctioneer** /ɔ:kʃə'nɪə(r)/ *n.* ▶1261 Auktionator, *der*/Auktionatorin, *die*

**audacious** /ɔ:'deɪʃəs/ *adj.* (*daring*) kühn; verwegen; (*impudent*) dreist

**audaciously** /ɔ:'deɪʃəslɪ/ *adv.* (*daringly*) kühn; (*impudently*) dreist

**audacity** /ɔ:'dæsɪtɪ/ *n., no pl.* Ⓐ (*daringness*) Kühnheit, *die;* Verwegenheit, *die;* Ⓑ (*impudence*) Dreistigkeit, *die*

**audibility** /ɔ:dɪ'bɪlɪtɪ/ *n.* Hörbarkeit, *die*

**audible** /'ɔ:dɪbl/ *adj.* hörbar; **every word was ~ through the wall** man konnte jedes Wort durch die Wand hören; **the child's voice was scarcely ~:** die Stimme des Kindes war kaum zu hören

**audibly** /'ɔ:dɪblɪ/ *adv.* hörbar; **whisper sth. quite ~:** etw. recht vernehmlich flüstern

**audience** /'ɔ:dɪəns/ *n.* Ⓐ (*listeners, spectators*) Publikum, *das;* **cinema/concert ~s have increased** die Zahl der Kino-/Konzertbesucher hat zugenommen; Ⓑ (*formal interview*) Audienz, *die* (**with** bei); **private ~:** Privataudienz, *die;* Ⓒ (*readers*) Publikum, *das;* Leserkreis, *der*

**audio** /'ɔ:dɪəʊ/ *adj.* Ton-; **~ frequency** Tonfrequenz, *die;* **~ range** Hörbereich, *der;* **~ equipment** Audioanlage, *die*

**audio: ~book** *n.* Hörbuch, *das;* **~ cassette** *n.* Audiokassette, *die;* Tonkassette, *die;* **~ engineer** *n.* Toningenieur, *der*/-ingenieurin, *die;* **~ typist** *n.* ▶1261 Phonotypist, *der*/-typistin, *die;* **~-'visual** *adj.* audiovisuell (*fachspr.*)

**audit** /'ɔ:dɪt/ ❶ *n.* **~ [of the accounts]** Rechnungsprüfung, *die* (*Wirtsch.*); **the ~ of the firm's books** die Revision der Firmengeschäftsbücher. ❷ *v.t.* Ⓐ prüfen; Ⓑ (*Amer.: attend*) als Gasthörer belegen

**audition** /ɔ:'dɪʃn/ ❶ *n.* (*singing*) Probesingen, *das;* (*dancing*) Vortanzen, *das;* (*acting*) Vorsprechen, *das;* **~s are being held today** heute ist Probesingen/Vortanzen/Vorsprechen. ❷ *v.i.* (*sing*) vorsingen; probesingen; (*dance*) vortanzen; (*act*) vorsprechen; **~ for a part** für eine Rolle vorsprechen. ❸ *v.t.* vorsingen/vortanzen/vorsprechen lassen

**auditor** /'ɔ:dɪtə(r)/ *n.* ▶1261 Buchprüfer, *der*/-prüferin, *die;* Rechnungsprüfer, *der*/-prüferin, *die*

**auditorium** /ɔ:dɪ'tɔ:rɪəm/ *n., pl.* **~s** *or* **auditoria** /ɔ:dɪ'tɔ:rɪə/ Zuschauerraum, *der*

**auditory** /'ɔ:dɪtərɪ/ *adj.* Ⓐ (*concerned with hearing*) Gehör-; auditiv (*Med.*); Ⓑ (*received by the ear*) akustisch; auditiv (*Med.*)

**au fait** /əʊ 'feɪ/ *pred. adj.* vertraut (**with** mit); au fait (*geh.*); (*up to date*) auf dem Laufenden

**Aug.** *abbr.* **August** Aug.

**Augean** /ɔ:'dʒi:ən/ *adj.* überaus schmutzig; **~ stables** (*lit. or fig.*) Augiasstall, *der*

**auger** /'ɔ:gə(r)/ *n.* (*for wood*) Handbohrer, *der;* Stangenbohrer, *der* (*Technik*); (*for soil*) Erdbohrer, *der* (*Technik*)

**aught¹** /ɔ:t/ *n., no pl., no art.* (*arch./poet.*) [irgend]etwas

**aught²** ⇒ **ought²**

**augment** ❶ /ɔ:g'ment/ *v.t.* verstärken ‹Armee›; verbessern ‹Einkommen›; aufstocken ‹Fonds, finanzielle Mittel›; **∼ed interval** (*Mus.*) übermäßiges Intervall. ❷ *v.i.* zunehmen; ‹Reserven:› zunehmen, anwachsen; ‹Lärm:› zunehmen, anschwellen

**augmentation** /ɔ:gmən'teɪʃn/ *n., no pl.* Ⓐ (*enlargement*) Erweiterung, *die;* (*of funds, finances*) Aufstockung, *die;* (*growth*) Anstieg, *der;* Zunahme, *die;* Ⓑ (*Mus.*) Augmentation, *die*

**au gratin** ⇒ **gratin**

**augur** /'ɔ:gə(r)/ ❶ *n.* Ⓐ (*Roman Ant.*) Augur, *der;* Ⓑ (*soothsayer*) Augur, *der* (*geh.*). ❷ *v.t.* Ⓐ (*portend*) bedeuten; versprechen ‹Erfolg›; Ⓑ (*foretell*) prophezeien (**of, for** *Dat.*). ❸ *v.i.* **∼ well/ill for sth./sb.** ein gutes/schlechtes Zeichen für etw./jmdn. sein

**augury** /'ɔ:gjʊrɪ/ *n.* Vorzeichen, *das*

**august** /ɔ:'gʌst/ *adj.* Ⓐ (*venerable*) ehrwürdig; (*noble*) erlaucht; Ⓑ (*majestic*) großartig; eindrucksvoll

**August** /'ɔ:gəst/ *n.* ▶ **1055** August, *der;* **in ∼:** im August; **last/next ∼:** letzten/nächsten August; **the first of/on the first of ∼** *or* **on ∼ [the] first** der erste/am ersten August; **1[st] ∼** (*as date on document*) 1. August; **every ∼:** jeden August; jedes Jahr im August; **an ∼ day** ein Augusttag; **from ∼ to October** von August bis Oktober

**Augustine¹** /ɔ:'gʌstɪn/ *pr. n.* Augustinus (*der*)

**Augustine²** *n.* Augustiner, *der*

**Augustinian** /ɔ:gʌ'stɪnɪən/ ❶ *adj.* Augustinisch ‹Lehre›; **∼ monk** Augustinermönch, *der.* ❷ *n.* (*monk*) Augustiner, *der*

**auk** /ɔ:k/ *n.* (*Ornith.*) Alk, *der*

**auld** /ɔ:ld/ *adj.* (*Scot.*) ⇒ **old; for ∼ lang syne** um der guten, alten Zeiten willen

**au naturel** /əʊ nætjə'rel/ *adv., pred. adj.* (*Gastr.*) nature; au naturel

**aunt** /ɑ:nt/ *n.* Tante, *die;* **A∼ Sally** *Wurfspiel [auf dem Jahrmarkt], bei dem mit Stöcken oder Bällen auf eine Holzfigur geworfen wird;* (*target doll*) ≈ Schießbudenfigur, *die;* (*fig.*) Zielscheibe, *die* (*fig.*); **my sainted ∼!** du liebe Güte!

**auntie, aunty** /'ɑ:ntɪ/ *n.* (*coll.*) Tantchen, *das;* (*with name*) Tante, *die;* **do you love A∼ Betty?** magst du die liebe Tante Betty?

**au pair** /əʊ 'peə(r)/ ❶ *n.* Aupairmädchen, *das.* ❷ *adj.* **∼ girl** Aupairmädchen, *das*

**aura** /'ɔ:rə/ *n., pl.* **∼e** /'ɔ:ri:/ *or* **∼s** Ⓐ (*atmosphere, Med.*) Aura, *die;* **have an ∼ about one** von einer Aura umgeben sein; **an ∼ of mystery** eine Aura des Geheimnisvollen; Ⓑ (*subtle emanation*) Aura, *die;* Fluidum, *das*

**aural** /'ɔ:rl/ *adj.* akustisch; aural (*Med.*); **∼ specialist** Ohrenarzt, *der*

**aureola** /ɔ:'ri:ələ/, **aureole** /'ɔ:rɪəʊl/ *n.* (*Art*) Aureole, *die;* (*around head*) Nimbus, *der*

**au revoir** /əʊ rə'vwɑ:(r)/ ❶ *int.* auf Wiedersehen. ❷ *n.* **say one's ∼s** Auf Wiedersehen sagen

**auricle** /'ɔ:rɪkl/ *n.* Ⓐ (*external ear*) Ohrmuschel, *die;* Auricula, *die* (*Med.*); Ⓑ (*Anat.: of heart*) Atrium, *das* (*fachspr.*); Vorhof, *der;* Herzohr, *das;* Ⓒ (*Bot.*) Blattöhrchen, *das;* Aurikel, *die*

**auricular** /ɔ:'rɪkjʊlə(r)/ *adj.* Ⓐ (*of the ear*) Ohr-; aurikular (*Med.*); (*by the ear*) akustisch; **∼ witness** Ohrenzeuge, *der;* **∼ confession** (*Relig.*) Ohrenbeichte, *die;* Ⓑ (*Anat.: of auricle of heart*) Vorhof-

**auriferous** /ɔ:'rɪfərəs/ *adj.* (*Geol.*) goldhaltig

**aurora** /ɔ:'rɔ:rə/ *n., pl.* **∼s** *or* **∼e** /ɔ:'rɔ:ri:/ Polarlicht, *das;* **∼ borealis** /bɔ:rɪ'eɪlɪs/ Nordlicht, *das;* **∼ australis** /ɔ:'streɪlɪs/ Südlicht, *das*

**auscultation** /ɔ:skəl'teɪʃn/ *n., no pl.* (*Med.*) Auskultation, *die* (*fachspr.*); Abhorchen, *das*

**auspice** /'ɔ:spɪs/ *n.* Ⓐ *in pl.* **under the ∼s of sb./sth.** unter jmds./einer Sache Auspizien (*geh.*) *od.* Schirmherrschaft; Ⓑ (*sign*) Auspizium, *das* (*geh.*); Vorzeichen, *das;* **under favourable ∼s** unter günstigen Auspizien (*geh.*) *od.* Vorzeichen

**auspicious** /ɔ:'spɪʃəs/ *adj.* Ⓐ (*favourable*) günstig; viel versprechend ‹Anfang›; Ⓑ (*fortunate*) glückhaft (*geh.*); glücklich

**auspiciously** /ɔ:'spɪʃəslɪ/ *adv.* Ⓐ (*favourably*) viel versprechend; Ⓑ (*fortunately*) glücklich

**Aussie** /'ɒzɪ, 'ɒsɪ/ (*coll.*) ❶ *adj.* australisch. ❷ *n.* Ⓐ Australier, *der*/Australierin, *die;* Ⓑ (*Australia*) Australien (*das*)

**austere** /ɒ'stɪə(r), ɔ:'stɪə(r)/ *adj.* Ⓐ (*morally strict, stern*) streng; unbeugsam ‹Haltung›; Ⓑ (*severely simple*) karg; Ⓒ (*ascetic*) asketisch ‹Leben›

**austerely** /ɒ'stɪəlɪ, ɔ:'stɪəlɪ/ *adv.* Ⓐ (*morally, strictly, sternly*) streng; Ⓑ (*severely simply*) karg; **∼ simple** karg und schlicht; Ⓒ (*ascetically*) asketisch ‹leben›

**austereness** /ɒ'stɪənɪs, ɔ:'stɪənɪs/ ⇒ **austerity A, B**

**austerity** /ɒ'sterɪtɪ, ɔ:'sterɪtɪ/ *n.* Ⓐ *no pl.* (*moral strictness*) Strenge, *die;* Ⓑ *no pl.* (*severe simplicity*) Kargheit, *die;* Ⓒ *no pl.* (*lack of luxuries*) wirtschaftliche Einschränkung; Austerity, *die* (*Wirtsch.*); Ⓓ *in pl.* (*deprivations*) Entbehrungen; (*for religious reasons*) Entsagungen

**Australasia** /ɒstrə'leɪʃə, ɔ:strə'leɪʃə/ *pr. n.* Australien und der südwestliche Pazifik

**Australasian** /ɒstrə'leɪʃn, ɔ:strə'leɪʃn/ *adj.* **∼ peoples/cultures** Völker/Kulturen Australiens und des südwestlichen Pazifiks; **∼ region** australische Region (*Zool.*)

**Australia** /ɒ'streɪlɪə, ɔ:'streɪlɪə/ *pr. n.* Australien (*das*)

**Australian** /ɒ'streɪlɪən, ɔ:'streɪlɪən/ ▶ **1340** ❶ *adj.* australisch; **∼ bear** Beutelbär, *der;* Koala, *der;* **sb. is ∼:** jmd. ist Australier/Australierin; **∼ [National] Rules football** *australische Art des Football.* ❷ *n.* Australier, *der*/Australierin, *die*

**Austria** /'ɒstrɪə, 'ɔ:strɪə/ *pr. n.* Österreich (*das*); **∼-Hungary** (*Hist.*) Österreich-Ungarn (*das*)

**Austrian** /'ɒstrɪən, 'ɔ:strɪən/ ▶ **1340** ❶ *adj.* österreichisch; **sb. is ∼:** jmd. ist Österreicher/Österreicherin. ❷ *n.* Österreicher, *der*/Österreicherin, *die*

**Austro-Hungarian** /ɒstrəʊhʌŋ'geərɪən, ɔ:strəʊhʌŋ'geərɪən/ *adj.* (*Hist.*) österreichisch-ungarisch

**autarchic** /ɔ:'tɑ:kɪk/, **autarchical** /ɔ:'tɑ:kɪkl/ *adj.* Ⓐ (*sovereign*) unabhängig; selbstständig; Ⓑ (*despotic*) despotisch

**autarchy** /'ɔ:tɑ:kɪ/ *n., no pl.* Autarchie, *die* (*veralt.*); (*of state, region*) Unabhängigkeit, *die;* Selbstständigkeit, *die;* (*of ruler, government, regime*) unumschränkte Herrschaft

**autarky** /'ɔ:tɑ:kɪ/ *n., no pl.* Autarkie, *die*

**authentic** /ɔ:'θentɪk/ *adj.* (*reliable; also Mus.*) authentisch; (*genuine*) authentisch; echt; berechtigt ‹Anspruch›; unverfälscht ‹Akzent›

**authentically** /ɔ:'θentɪkəlɪ/ *adv.* (*genuinely*) **his accent was ∼ upper-class** er sprach im unverfälschten Tonfall der Oberschicht

**authenticate** /ɔ:'θentɪkeɪt/ *v.t.* authentifizieren; **∼ sth.** die Echtheit einer Sache (*Gen.*) bestätigen; **∼ information/a report** eine Information/einen Bericht bestätigen; **I succeeded in authenticating my claim** es gelang mir, meinen Anspruch zu beweisen

**authentication** /ɔ:θentɪ'keɪʃn/ *n., no pl.* Bestätigung der Echtheit; (*of information, report*) Bestätigung, *die*

**authenticity** /ɔ:θen'tɪsɪtɪ/ *n., no pl.* Echtheit, *die;* Authentizität, *die;* (*of claim*) Berechtigung, *die;* (*of information, report*) Zuverlässigkeit, *die*

**author** /'ɔ:θə(r)/ ❶ *n.* Ⓐ ▶ **1261** (*writer*) Autor, *der*/Autorin, *die;* (*profession*) Schriftsteller, *der*/Schriftstellerin, *die;* **the ∼ of the book/article** der Autor *od.* Verfasser des Buches/Artikels; **the ∼s of the 19th century** die Autoren *od.* Schriftsteller des 19. Jahrhunderts; Ⓑ (*originator*) Vater, *der.* ❷ *v.t.* (*write*) verfassen

**authoress** /'ɔ:θərɪs/ *n.* ▶ **1261** Autorin, *die*

**authorisation, authorise** ⇒ **authoriz-**

**authoritarian** /ɔ:θɒrɪ'teərɪən/ ❶ *adj.* autoritär. ❷ *n.* autoritäre Person; **be an ∼:** autoritär sein

**authoritarianism** /ɔ:θɒrɪ'teərɪənɪzm/ *n., no pl.* Autoritarismus, *der* (*Psych.*); autoritäre Einstellung

**authoritative** /ɔ:'θɒrɪtətɪv/ *adj.* Ⓐ (*recognized as reliable*) autoritativ; maßgebend; zuverlässig ‹Bericht, Information›; (*official*) amtlich; Ⓑ (*commanding*) Respekt einflößend

**authoritatively** /ɔ:'θɒrɪtətɪvlɪ/ *adv.* Ⓐ (*reliably*) zuverlässig ‹berichten›; (*officially*) offiziell; **he talked ∼ about his specialist field** er sprach als Fachmann über sein Spezialgebiet; Ⓑ (*commandingly*) mit Bestimmtheit

**authoritativeness** /ɔ:'θɒrɪtətɪvnɪs/ *n., no pl.* Ⓐ (*reliability*) Zuverlässigkeit, *die;* (*official nature*) amtlicher Charakter; Ⓑ (*commanding quality*) Bestimmtheit, *die;* (*of person*) entschiedenes Auftreten; **the ∼ of his manner** seine Respekt einflößende Art

**authority** /ɔ:'θɒrɪtɪ/ *n.* Ⓐ *no pl.* (*power*) Autorität, *die;* (*delegated power*) Befugnis, *die;* **have the/no ∼ to do sth.** berechtigt *od.* befugt/nicht befugt sein, etw. zu tun; **you have my ∼:** Sie haben meine Zustimmung; **have/exercise ∼ over sb.** Weisungsbefugnis gegenüber jmdm. haben; **on one's own ∼:** in eigener Verantwortung; **[be] in ∼:** verantwortlich [sein]; **be under sb.'s ∼:** jmdm. unterstehen; **those in ∼:** die Verantwortlichen; Ⓑ (*person having power*) Autorität, *die;* (*body having power*) **the authorities** die Behörde[n]; **the highest legal ∼:** die höchste rechtliche Instanz; Ⓒ (*expert, book, quotation*) Autorität, *die;* (*evidence*) Quelle, *die;* **what is your ∼ for your assertion?** worauf stützt du deine Behauptung?; **on the ∼ of Darwin** nach Darwin; **have it on the ∼ of sb./sth. that …:** durch jmdn./etw. wissen, dass …; **have it on good ∼ that …:** aus zuverlässiger Quelle wissen, dass …; Ⓓ *no pl.* (*weight of testimony*) Autorität, *die;* **give** *or* **add ∼ to sth.** einer Sache (*Dat.*) Gewicht ver[leihen; Ⓔ *no pl.* (*power to influence*) Autorität, *die;* Ⓕ *no pl.* (*masterfulness*) Souveränität, *die*

**authorization** /ɔ:θəraɪ'zeɪʃn/ *n.* Genehmigung, *die;* Autorisation, *die;* **obtain/give ∼:** die Genehmigung einholen/erteilen

**authorize** /'ɔ:θəraɪz/ *v.t.* Ⓐ (*give authority to*) ermächtigen; bevollmächtigen; autorisieren; **∼ sb. to do sth.** jmdn. ermächtigen, etw. zu tun; **entry is permitted only to ∼d personnel** Unbefugten ist der Zutritt verboten; Ⓑ (*sanction*) genehmigen; **∼ sth.** etw. genehmigen; einer Sache (*Dat.*) zustimmen; **the A∼d Version** *engl. Fassung der Bibel von 1611*

**authorship** /'ɔ:θəʃɪp/ *n., no pl.* Ⓐ *no art.* (*occupation*) Schriftstellerei, *die;* Ⓑ (*origin*) Autorschaft, *die;* **of unknown ∼:** von einem unbekannten Autor *od.* Verfasser

**autistic** /ɔ:'tɪstɪk/ *adj.* (*Psych., Med.*) autistisch

**auto** /'ɔ:təʊ/ *n., pl.* **∼s** (*Amer. coll.*) Auto, *das*

**auto-** /ɔ:təʊ/ *in comb.* auto-/Auto-

**autobahn** /'ɔ:təbɑ:n/ *n., pl.* **∼s** *or* **∼en** /'ɔ:təbɑ:nən/ [deutsche] Autobahn

**autobi'ographer** *n.* Autobiograph, *der*/Autobiographin, *die*

**autobio'graphic, autobio'graphical** *adj.* autobiographisch

**autobi'ography** *n.* Autobiographie, *die*

**autocade** /'ɔ:təʊkeɪd/ (*Amer.*) ⇒ **motorcade**

**autoclave** /'ɔ:təkleɪv/ *n.* Autoklav, *der*

**autocracy** /ɔ:'tɒkrəsɪ/ *n.* Autokratie, *die*

**autocrat** /'ɔ:təkræt/ *n.* Autokrat, *der*

**autocratic** /ɔ:tə'krætɪk/ *adj.* autokratisch

**'autocross** *n., no pl.* Autocross, *das*

**Autocue** ® /'ɔ:təʊkju:/ *n.* Teleprompter Ⓦⓩ, *der*

**'autofocus** *n., no pl.* (*Photog.*) Autofokus, *der*

**autogenic** /ɔ:təʊ'dʒenɪk/ *adj.* autogen; **∼ training** autogenes Training

a

**autogenous** /ɔ:ˈtɒdʒɪnəs/ *adj.* (*Med.*, *Industry*) autogen; ~ **welding** autogene Schweißung; Autogenschweißen, *das*

**ˈautogiro** *n.*, *pl.* ~**s** Autogiro, *das*

**autograph** /ˈɔ:təgrɑ:f/ ❶ *n.* Ⓐ (*signature*) Autogramm, *das;* Ⓑ (*manuscript*) Autograph, *das;* (*signed document*) **the original** ~: das Original. ❷ *v.t.* Ⓐ (*sign*) signieren; Ⓑ (*write with one's own hand*) mit eigener Hand schreiben

**autogyro** ⇒ **autogiro**

**auto-imˈmune** *adj.* (*Med.*) autoimmun; ~ **response** Autoimmunantwort, *die*

**automat** /ˈɔ:təmæt/ *n.* (*Amer.*) Ⓐ (*slot machine*) [Münz]automat, *der;* Ⓑ (*cafeteria*) Automatenrestaurant, *das*

**automate** /ˈɔ:təmeɪt/ *v.t.* automatisieren

**automated ˈteller machine** *n.* Geldautomat, *der*

**automatic** /ɔ:təˈmætɪk/ ❶ *adj.* automatisch; ~ **weapons** automatische Waffen; Schnellfeuerwaffen; ~ **writing** automatisches Schreiben; ~ **gear system**, ~ **transmission** Automatikgetriebe, *das;* **his reaction was completely** ~: er reagierte ganz automatisch; **disqualification is** ~ **after two false starts** die Disqualifikation erfolgt automatisch nach zwei Fehlstarts; ~ **pilot** ⇒ **autopilot**.
❷ *n.* (*weapon*) automatische Waffe; (*vehicle*) Fahrzeug mit Automatikgetriebe; (*tool, apparatus*) Automat, *der*

**automatically** /ɔ:təˈmætɪkəlɪ/ *adv.* automatisch

**automation** /ɔ:təˈmeɪʃn/ *n.*, *no pl.* Automation, *die;* (*automatic control*) Automatisierung, *die;* automatische Steuerung

**automatism** /ɔ:ˈtɒmətɪzm/ *n.*, *no pl.* (*Biol.*, *Med.*, *Psych.*) Automatismus, *der*

**automaton** /ɔ:ˈtɒmətən/ *n.*, *pl.* ~**s** *or* **automata** /ɔ:ˈtɒmətə/ Automat, *der*

**automobile** /ˈɔ:təməbi:l/ *n.* (*Amer.*) Auto, *das*

**automotive** /ɔ:təˈməʊtɪv/ *adj.* Kraftfahrzeug-; ~ **industry** Auto[mobil]industrie, *die;* ~ **workers** Arbeiter in der Auto[mobil]industrie; ~ **products** Erzeugnisse der Auto[mobil]industrie

**autonomic** /ɔ:təˈnɒmɪk/ *adj.* Ⓐ (*Physiol.*) autonom; unbedingt ‹Reflex›; Ⓑ ⇒ **autonomous**

**autonomous** /ɔ:ˈtɒnəməs/ *adj.* (*also Philos.*) autonom

**autonomy** /ɔ:ˈtɒnəmɪ/ *n.*, *no pl.* (*also Philos.*) Autonomie, *die;* ~ **of action** autonomes Handeln

**ˈautopilot** *n.* Autopilot, *der;* **[fly] on** ~: mit Autopilot [fliegen]

**autopsy** /ˈɔ:tɒpsɪ, ɔ:ˈtɒpsɪ/ *n.* Ⓐ (*postmortem*) Autopsie, *die;* Obduktion, *die;* (*fig.*) Manöverkritik, *die;* Ⓑ (*personal inspection*) Prüfung durch persönliche Inaugenscheinnahme; Autopsie, *die* (*fachspr.*)

**auto:** ~**save** (*Computing*) ❶ *n.* automatisches Speichern; ❷ *v.t.* automatisch speichern; ~**-suggestion** *n.* Autosuggestion, *die;* ~**timer** *n.* [automatische] Schaltuhr

**autumn** /ˈɔ:təm/ *n.* ▶ **1504** (*lit. or fig.*) Herbst, *der;* **in** ~ **1969, in the** ~ **of 1969** im Herbst 1969; **in early/late** ~: im Frühherbst/Spätherbst; **last/next** ~: letzten/nächsten Herbst; ~ **is a beautiful time of the year** der Herbst ist eine schöne Jahreszeit; ~ **weather/fashions** Herbstwetter, *das*/Herbstmoden

**autumnal** /ɔ:ˈtʌmnl/ *adj.* (*lit. or fig.*) herbstlich; (*blooming or maturing in autumn*) Herbst-; ~ **flower** Herbstblume, *die*

**autumn ˈcrocus** *n.* Herbstzeitlose, *die*

**auxiliary** /ɔ:gˈzɪljərɪ/ ❶ *adj.* Ⓐ (*helping*) Hilfs-; auxiliar (*fachspr.*); **be** ~ **to sth.** etw. unterstützen *od.* fördern; ~ **troops** Hilfstruppen; Ⓑ (*subsidiary*) zusätzlich; Zusatz-; Ⓒ (*Ling.*) ~ **verb** Hilfsverb, *das.* ❷ *n.* Ⓐ ▶ **1261** Hilfskraft, *die;* **medical** ~: ärztliches Hilfspersonal; Ⓑ *in pl.* (*Mil.*) Hilfstruppen; Ⓒ (*Ling.*) Hilfsverb, *das*

**AV** *abbr.* **Authorized Version;** ⇒ **authorized** B

**avail** /əˈveɪl/ ❶ *n.*, *no pl.*, *no art.* Nutzen, *der;* **be of no** ~: nichts nützen; nutzlos *od.* vergeblich sein; **to no** ~: vergebens; **of what** ~ **is it ...?** was nützt es ...? ❷ *v.i.* Ⓐ (*be of profit*) etwas nützen *od.* fruchten; **it will not** ~: es wird nichts nützen *od.* fruchten; Ⓑ (*afford help*) helfen. ❸ *v.t.* nützen; **it will** ~ **you nothing** es wird dir nichts nützen. ❹ *v. refl.* ~ **oneself of sth.** von etw. Gebrauch machen; ~ **oneself of an opportunity** eine Gelegenheit nutzen

**availability** /əveɪləˈbɪlɪtɪ/ *n.*, *no pl.* Vorhandensein, *das;* **the** ~ **of sth.** die Möglichkeit, etw. zu bekommen; **I'll find out about the** ~ **of tickets** ich werde mich erkundigen, ob Karten zu bekommen sind; **the likely** ~ **of spare parts** die voraussichtliche Lieferbarkeit von Ersatzteilen; **the** ~ **of accommodation** das Zimmer-/Wohnungsangebot

**available** /əˈveɪləbl/ *adj.* Ⓐ (*at one's disposal*) verfügbar; **make sth.** ~ **to sb.** jmdm. etw. zur Verfügung stellen; **be** ~: zur Verfügung stehen; Ⓑ (*capable of use*) gültig ‹Fahrkarte, Angebot›; Ⓒ (*obtainable*) erhältlich; lieferbar ‹Waren›; verfügbar ‹Unterkunft, Daten›; **have sth.** ~: etw. zur Verfügung haben; **nobody was** ~ **for comment** niemand stellte sich für einen Kommentar zur Verfügung

**avalanche** /ˈævəlɑ:nʃ/ ❶ *n.* (*lit. or fig.*) Lawine, *die.* ❷ *v.i.* **mud** ~**d down** eine Lawine von Schlamm stürzte herab

**avant-garde** /ævɑ̃ˈgɑ:d/ ❶ *adj.* avantgardistisch. ❷ *n.* Avantgarde, *die*

**avarice** /ˈævərɪs/ *n.*, *no pl.* Geldgier, *die;* Habsucht, *die;* ~ **for sth.** (*fig.*) Gier nach etw.

**avaricious** /ævəˈrɪʃəs/ *adj.* geldgierig; habsüchtig; (*fig.*) gierig (**for** nach); ~ **for power** machtgierig

**Ave.** *abbr.* **Avenue**

**Ave [Maria]** /ˈɑ:veɪ (məˈrɪə)/ *n.* Ave[-Maria], *das*

**avenge** /əˈvendʒ/ *v.t.* rächen; **be** ~**d**/~ **oneself on sb.** sich an jmdm. rächen; **be** ~**d for sth.** sich für etw. rächen

**avenger** /əˈvendʒə(r)/ *n.* Rächer, *der*/Rächerin, *die* (*geh.*)

**avenue** /ˈævənju:/ *n.* (*broad street*) Avenue, *die;* Boulevard, *der;* (*tree-lined road; Brit.: approach to country house*) Allee, *die;* (*fig.*) Weg, *der* (**to** zu); ~ **of approach** Zugang, *der;* **all** ~**s of escape were closed** jeder Ausweg war versperrt; ⇒ *also* **explore** B

**aver** /əˈvɜ:(r)/ *v.t.*, **-rr-** beteuern; **what one expert** ~**s, another denies** was der eine Fachmann mit Nachdruck bestätigt, das bestreitet der andere

**average** /ˈævərɪdʒ/ ❶ *n.* Ⓐ Durchschnitt, *der;* **the** ~ **is about ...:** der Durchschnitt liegt bei [ungefähr] ...; **on [the** *or* **an]** ~: im Durchschnitt; durchschnittlich; im Schnitt (*ugs.*); **above/below** ~: über/unter dem Durchschnitt; **law of** ~**s** Wahrscheinlichkeitsgesetz, *das;* Ⓑ (*arithmetic mean*) Mittelwert, *der;* **batting** ~ (*Baseball, Cricket*) Durchschnittsleistung als Schlagmann; **bowling** ~ (*Cricket*) Durchschnittsleistung als Werfer; Ⓒ (*Insurance*) Havarie, *die;* ~ **adjustment** Dispache, *die.*
❷ *adj.* Ⓐ durchschnittlich; ~ **speed** durchschnittliche Geschwindigkeit; Durchschnittsgeschwindigkeit, *die;* **he is of** ~ **height** er ist mittelgroß; Ⓑ (*mediocre*) durchschnittlich; mittelmäßig.
❸ *v.t.* Ⓐ (*find the* ~ *of*) den Durchschnitt ermitteln von; Ⓑ (*amount on* ~ *to*) durchschnittlich betragen; **the planks** ~**d three metres in length** die Bretter waren durchschnittlich drei Meter lang; **these things** ~ **themselves out** so etwas gleicht sich aus; Ⓒ (*do on* ~) einen Durchschnitt von ... erreichen; **she** ~**s four novels a year** sie schreibt durchschnittlich vier Romane im Jahr; **the train** ~**d 90 m.p.h.** der Zug fuhr im Durchschnitt mit 144 Kilometern pro Stunde.
❹ *v.i.* ~ **out at** im Durchschnitt betragen

**averagely** /ˈævərɪdʒlɪ/ *adv.* durchschnittlich

**averse** /əˈvɜ:s/ *pred. adj.* **be** ~ **to** *or* **from sth.** einer Sache (*Dat.*) abgeneigt sein; **be** ~ **to** *or* **from doing sth.** abgeneigt sein, etw. zu tun

**aversion** /əˈvɜ:ʃn/ *n.* Ⓐ *no pl.* (*dislike*) Abneigung, *die;* Aversion, *die;* **have/take an** ~ **to** *or* **from sth.** eine Abneigung *od.* Aversion gegen etw. haben/bekommen; ~ **therapy** (*Psych.*) Aversionstherapie, *die;* Ⓑ (*object*) **be sb.'s** ~: jmdm. ein Gräuel sein; **my pet** ~ **is ...:** ein besonderer Gräuel ist mir ...

**avert** /əˈvɜ:t/ *v.t.* Ⓐ (*turn away*) abwenden ‹Blick, Gesicht, Aufmerksamkeit›; Ⓑ (*prevent*) abwenden ‹Katastrophe, Schaden, Niederlage›; verhüten ‹Unfall›; verhindern ‹Fehlschlag›

**aviary** /ˈeɪvɪərɪ/ *n.* Vogelhaus, *das;* Aviarium, *das*

**aviation** /eɪvɪˈeɪʃn/ *n.*, *no pl.*, *no art.* Ⓐ (*operating of aircraft*) Luftfahrt, *die;* ~ **fuel** Flugbenzin, *das;* Ⓑ (*aircraft manufacture*) Flugzeugbau, *der;* ~ **industry** Flugzeugindustrie, *die;* Luftfahrtindustrie, *die*

**aviator** /ˈeɪvɪeɪtə(r)/ *n.* ▶ **1261** Flieger, *der*/Fliegerin, *die*

**avid** /ˈævɪd/ *adj.* (*enthusiastic*) begeistert; passioniert; **be** ~ **for sth.** (*eager, greedy*) begierig auf etw. (*Akk.*) sein

**avidity** /əˈvɪdɪtɪ/ *n.*, *no pl.* (*enthusiasm*) Begeisterung, *die;* (*greed*) Begierde, *die*

**avidly** /ˈævɪdlɪ/ *adv.* (*enthusiastically*) eifrig; begeistert ‹annehmen›; (*greedily*) begierig

**avionics** /eɪvɪˈɒnɪks/ *n.* Ⓐ *no pl.* Bordelektronik, *die;* Avionik, *die;* Ⓑ *constr. as pl.* (*systems*) Bordelektr[on]ik, *die;* Avionik, *die*

**avocado** /ævəˈkɑ:dəʊ/ *n.*, *pl.* ~**s:** ~ **[pear]** Avocado[birne], *die;* (*tree*) Avocado, *die*

**avocation** /ævəˈkeɪʃn/ *n.* (*minor occupation*) Nebenbeschäftigung, *die;* (*coll.: vocation*) Beruf, *der*

**avocet** /ˈævəset/ *n.* (*Ornith.*) Säbelschnäbler, *der*

**avoid** /əˈvɔɪd/ *v.t.* Ⓐ (*keep away from*) meiden ‹Ort›; ~ **an obstacle/a cyclist** einem Hindernis/Radfahrer ausweichen; ~ **the boss when he's in a temper** geh dem Chef aus dem Weg, wenn er schlechte Laune hat; Ⓑ (*refrain from*) vermeiden; ~ **doing sth.** vermeiden, etw. zu tun; **you can hardly** ~ **seeing her** du wirst kaum umhinkönnen, sie zu sehen; Ⓒ (*escape*) vermeiden; **they wore masks to** ~ **recognition** sie trugen Masken, um nicht erkannt zu werden

**avoidable** /əˈvɔɪdəbl/ *adj.* vermeidbar; **if it is [at all]** ~: wenn es sich [irgend] vermeiden lässt

**avoidance** /əˈvɔɪdəns/ *n.*, *no pl.* Vermeidung, *die;* **the** ~ **of accidents** das Vermeiden von Unfällen; die Unfallverhütung; ~ **of death duties** Umgehung der Erbschaftssteuer

**avoirdupois** /ævədjʊˈpɔɪz/ ❶ *adj.* Avoirdupois-. ❷ *n.* Ⓐ Avoirdupois, *das;* Ⓑ (*joc.: bodily weight*) Gewicht, *das*

**avow** /əˈvaʊ/ *v.t.* bekennen; ~ **oneself [to be] sth.** sich als etw. bekennen; **an** ~**ed opponent/supporter** ein erklärter Gegner/Befürworter

**avowal** /əˈvaʊəl/ *n.* Bekenntnis, *das;* **on your own** ~: wie Sie selbst erklärt haben

**avowedly** /əˈvaʊɪdlɪ/ *adv.* erklärtermaßen

**avuncular** /əˈvʌŋkjʊlə(r)/ *adj.* onkelhaft

**aw** /ɔ:/ *int. expr. remonstrance, commiseration* oh; *expr. disgust* bah; **aw, bad luck!** so ein Pech!

**AWACS** /ˈeɪwæks/ *abbr.* **Airborne Warning and Control Systems** AWACS

**await** /əˈweɪt/ *v.t.* erwarten; **disaster** ~**s us if ...:** uns erwartet eine Katastrophe, wenn ...; **the long** ~**ed visit** der lang ersehnte Besuch

**awake** /əˈweɪk/ ❶ *v.i.*, **awoke** /əˈwəʊk/, **awoken** /əˈwəʊkn/ (*lit. or fig.*) erwachen; **we awoke to the sound of rain on the windows** als wir erwachten, hörten wir den Regen gegen die Fenster prasseln; **one day I shall** ~ **to find myself a rich man** eines Tages werde ich aufwachen und ein reicher Mann sein; ~ **to sth.** einer Sache (*Gen.*) gewahr werden; **when she awoke to her surroundings** als sie gewahr wurde, wo sie sich befand.

a

**❷** *v.t.*, **awoke, awoken** (*lit. or fig.*) wecken; **~ sb. to sth.** (*fig.*) jmdm. etw. bewusst machen; **be awoken to sth.** (*fig.*) einer Sache (*Gen.*) gewahr werden.
**❸** *pred. adj.* (*lit. or fig.*) wach; **wide ~:** hellwach; **lie ~:** wach liegen; **be ~ to sth.** (*fig.*) sich (*Dat.*) einer Sache (*Gen.*) bewusst sein

**awaken** /ə'weɪkn/ **❶** *v.t.* (*esp. fig.*) ⇒ **awake** 2. **❷** *v.i.* (*esp. fig.*) ⇒ **awake** 1

**awakening** /ə'weɪknɪŋ/ *n.* Erwachen, *das;* **a rude ~** (*fig.*) ein böses Erwachen

**award** /ə'wɔ:d/ **❶** *v.t.* (*grant*) verleihen, zuerkennen ‹Preis, Auszeichnung›; zusprechen ‹Sorgerecht, Entschädigung›; gewähren ‹Zahlung, Gehaltserhöhung›; **~ sb. sth.** jmdm. etw. verleihen/zusprechen/gewähren; **sb. is ~ed sth.** jmdm. wird etw. verliehen/zugesprochen/gewährt; **he was ~ed the prize** der Preis wurde ihm zuerkannt; **the referee ~ed a penalty [to Arsenal]** der Schiedsrichter erkannte auf Strafstoß [für Arsenal].
**❷** *n.* **A** (*judicial decision*) Schiedsspruch, *der;* **B** (*payment*) Entschädigung[ssumme], *die;* (*grant*) Stipendium, *das;* **make an ~ to sb.** jmdm. finanzielle Unterstützung gewähren; **C** (*prize*) Auszeichnung, *die;* Preis, *der*

**a'ward-winning** *adj.* preisgekrönt

**aware** /ə'weə(r)/ *adj.* **A** *pred.* (*conscious*) **be ~ of sth.** sich (*Dat.*) einer Sache (*Gen.*) bewusst sein; **be ~ that ...:** sich (*Dat.*) [dessen] bewusst sein, dass ...; **what made you ~ that ...?** woran bemerkten Sie, dass ...?; **the patient was ~ of everything going on around him** der Patient bekam alles mit, was um ihn herum vorging; **as far as I am ~:** soweit ich weiß; **not that I am ~ of** nicht, dass ich wüsste; **B** (*well-informed*) informiert

**awareness** /ə'weənɪs/ *n., no pl.* (*consciousness*) Bewusstsein, *das;* **raise public ~ of sth.** etw. der Öffentlichkeit zu Bewusstsein bringen; etw. ins allgemeine Bewusstsein bringen

**awash** /ə'wɒʃ/ *pred. adj.* auf gleicher Höhe mit dem Wasserspiegel; **be ~** (*flooded*) unter Wasser stehen; (*fig.*) **be ~ with money** im Geld schwimmen

**away** /ə'weɪ/ **❶** *adv.* **A** (*at a distance*) entfernt; **~ in the distance** weit in der Ferne; **two feet ~ [from sth.]** zwei Fuß entfernt [von etw.]; **play ~** (*Sport*) auswärts spielen; **Christmas is still months ~:** bis Weihnachten dauert es noch Monate; **B** (*to a distance*) weg; fort; **get ~ from it all** ⇒ **all** 1 A; **~ with you/him!** weg *od.* fort mit dir/ihm!; **throw sth. ~:** etw. wegwerfen *od.* fortwerfen; **~ we go!** los gehts!; **C** (*absent*) nicht da; **be ~ on business** geschäftlich außer Haus sein; **be ~ [from school] with a cold** wegen einer Erkältung [in der Schule] fehlen; **he's ~ in France/on holiday** er ist zur Zeit in Frankreich/im Urlaub; **D** (*towards or into non-existence*) **die/fade ~:** verhallen; **gamble one's money ~:** sein Geld verspielen; **drink the evening ~:** den Abend mit Trinken verbringen; **the water has all boiled ~:** das ganze Wasser ist verkocht; **idle one's time ~:** seine Zeit vertrödeln; **E** (*constantly*) unablässig; **work ~ on sth.** ohne Unterbrechung an etw. (*Dat.*) arbeiten; **laugh ~ at sth.** unablässig über etw. (*Akk.*) lachen; **they were singing ~:** sie sangen aus voller Kehle; **F** (*without delay*) gleich ‹fragen usw.›; **fire ~** (*lit. or fig.*) losschießen (*ugs.*).
**❷** *adj.* (*Sport*) auswärts *präd.;* Auswärts-; **the next match is ~:** das nächste Spiel ist auswärts; **~ match** Auswärtsspiel, *das;* **~ team** Gastmannschaft, *die*

**awe** /ɔ:/ **❶** *n.* Ehrfurcht, *die* (**of** vor + *Dat.*); **be** *or* **stand in ~ of sb.** jmdn. fürchten; (*feel respect*) Ehrfurcht vor jmdm. haben; **hold sb. in ~:** jmdn. ehrfürchtig respektieren. **❷** *v.t.* Ehrfurcht einflößen (+ *Dat.*); **be ~d by sth.** sich von etw. beeindrucken *od.* einschüchtern lassen; **be ~d into silence** beeindruckt *od.* eingeschüchtert schweigen; **in an ~d voice** mit ehrfurchtsvoller Stimme

**aweigh** /ə'weɪ/ *pred. adj.* (*Naut.*) aus dem Grund

**'awe-inspiring** *adj.* Ehrfurcht gebietend

**awesome** /'ɔ:səm/ *adj.* überwältigend; eindrucksvoll ‹Schweigen›; übergroß ‹Verantwortung›

**awe: ~stricken, ~struck** *adj.* [von Ehrfurcht] ergriffen; ehrfurchtsvoll ‹Ausdruck, Staunen›

**awful** /'ɔ:fl/ *adj.* **A** furchtbar; fürchterlich; **too ~ for words** (*coll.*) unbeschreiblich schlecht; **be an ~ lot better/worse** (*coll.*) ein ganzes Stück besser/schlechter sein; **not an ~ lot better/worse** (*coll.*) nicht gerade viel besser/schlechter; **an ~ lot of money/people** (*coll.*) ein Haufen Geld/Leute (*ugs.*); **an ~ long time/way** (*coll.*) eine furchtbar lange Zeit/ein furchtbar weiter Weg; **B** (*commanding reverence*) Ehrfurcht gebietend; (*solemnly impressive*) eindrucksvoll; **~ silence** feierliche Stille

**awfully** /'ɔ:fəlɪ, 'ɔ:flɪ/ *adv.* furchtbar; **not ~** (*coll.*) nicht besonders; **thanks ~** (*coll.*) tausend Dank

**awfulness** /'ɔ:flnɪs/ *n., no pl.* **A** (*terribleness*) Furchtbarkeit, *die;* **B** (*impressive solemnity*) [eindrucksvolle *od.* Ehrfurcht gebietende] Feierlichkeit

**awhile** /ə'waɪl/ *adv.* eine Weile; **not yet ~:** so bald nicht

**awkward** /'ɔ:kwəd/ *adj.* **A** (*ill-adapted for use*) ungünstig; **be ~ to use** unhandlich sein; **the parcel is ~ to carry** das Paket ist schlecht zu tragen; **B** (*clumsy*) unbeholfen; **be at an ~ age** in einem schwierigen Alter sein; **C** (*embarrassing, embarrassed*) peinlich; **feel ~:** sich unbehaglich fühlen; **D** (*difficult*) schwierig, unangenehm ‹Person›; ungünstig ‹Zeitpunkt›; schwierig, peinlich ‹Lage, Dilemma›; ⇒ *also* **customer** B

**awkwardly** /'ɔ:kwədlɪ/ *adv.* **A** (*badly*) ungünstig ‹geformt, angebracht›; **B** (*clumsily*) ungeschickt, unbeholfen ‹gehen, sich ausdrücken›; ungeschickt, unglücklich ‹fallen, sich ausdrücken›; **C** (*embarrassingly*) peinlicherweise; (*embarrassedly*) peinlich berührt; betreten; **D** (*unfavourably*) ungünstig ‹gelegen›

**awkwardness** /'ɔ:kwədnɪs/ *n., no pl.* ⇒ **awkward**: **A** Unhandlichkeit, *die;* **the ~ of the design puts me off** das ungünstige Design stößt mich ab; **B** Unbeholfenheit, *die;* **C** Peinlichkeit, *die;* **a moment of ~:** ein peinlicher Augenblick; **D** (*of person*) unangenehmes Wesen; (*of situation, position*) Schwierigkeit, *die*

**awl** /ɔ:l/ *n.* Ahle, *die;* Pfriem, *der*

**awn** /ɔ:n/ *n.* Granne, *die*

**awning** /'ɔ:nɪŋ/ *n.* (*on wagon*) Plane, *die;* (*on house*) Markise, *die;* (*of tent*) Vordach, *das;* (*on ship*) Sonnensegel, *das*

**awoke, awoken** ⇒ **awake**

**AWOL** /'eɪwɒl/ *adj.* (*Mil.*) unerlaubt von der Truppe entfernt; **go ~:** sich unerlaubt von der Truppe entfernen

**awry** /ə'raɪ/ **❶** *adv.* schief; **your coat has pulled your scarf [all] ~:** deine Jacke hat deinen Schal ganz verzogen; **go ~** (*fig.*) schiefgehen (*ugs.*); ‹Plan:› fehlschlagen.
**❷** *pred. adj.* schief; unordentlich; **your tie is all ~:** deine Krawatte sitzt ganz schief; **our clothes were all ~:** unsere Kleidung war völlig in Unordnung; **now our plans are utterly ~** (*fig.*) nun sind unsere Pläne völlig fehlgeschlagen

**axe** (*Amer.:* **ax**) /æks/ **❶** *n.* **A** Axt, *die;* Beil, *das;* **have an ~ to grind** (*fig.*) sein eigenes Süppchen kochen (*ugs.*); **B** (*fig.: reduction*) **the ~:** radikale Kürzung; Rotstift, *der;* **on which sector will the ~ fall next?** welcher Sektor wird als nächster dem Rotstift zum Opfer fallen? ⇒ *also* **take** 1 F. **❷** *v.t.* (*reduce*) [radikal] kürzen; (*eliminate*) [radikal] einsparen ‹Stellen›; (*dismiss*) entlassen; (*abandon*) aufgeben ‹Projekt›

**axes** *pl. of* **axe, axis**

**axial** /'æksɪəl/ *adj.* axial; Achsen-; Axial-

**axil** /'æksɪl/ *n.* (*Bot.*) Blattachsel, *die;* (*of tree*) Winkel zwischen Ast und Stamm

**axiom** /'æksɪəm/ *n.* Axiom, *das*

**axiomatic** /æksɪə'mætɪk/ *adj.* axiomatisch; **I have taken it as ~ that ...:** ich gehe von dem Grundsatz aus, dass ...

**axis** /'æksɪs/ *n., pl.* **axes** /'æksi:z/ **A** Achse, *die;* **~ of rotation** Rotationsachse, *die;* **B** (*Polit.*) Achse, *die;* **the A~** (*Hist.*) die Achse; **the A~ powers** (*Hist.*) die Achsenmächte; **C** (*Bot.*) Sprossachse, *die;* **D** (*Anat., Physiol.*) Axis, *der*

**axle** /'æksl/ *n.* Achse, *die*

**'axle grease** *n.* Wagenschmiere, *die*

**ay**[1] /aɪ/ **❶** *adv.* **A** (*in voting; arch./dial.*) ja; **answer ay** mit Ja antworten; **B** (*Naut.*) **ay, ay, sir!** jawohl, Herr Kapitän!/Admiral! *etc.*
**❷** *n., pl.* **ayes** /aɪz/ (*answer*) Ja, *das;* (*vote*) Jastimme, *die;* **the ayes have it** die Mehrheit ist dafür

**ay**[2] *int.* **ay me!** (*arch./poet.*) oje!

**ayatollah** /aɪə'tɒlə/ *n.* Ajatollah, *der*

**aye**[1] ⇒ **ay**[1]

**aye**[2] /eɪ/ *adv.* (*arch.: ever*) all[e]zeit (*veralt.*); **for ~:** auf ewig

**azalea** /ə'zeɪlɪə/ *n.* (*Bot.*) Azalee, *die*

**Azerbaijan** /æzəbaɪ'dʒɑ:n/ *pr. n.* Aserbaidschan (*das*); Aserbeidschan (*das*)

**azimuth** /'æzɪməθ/ *n.* (*Astron.*) Azimut, *der*

**Azores** /ə'zɔ:z/ *pr. n. pl.* Azoren *Pl.*

**Aztec** /'æztek/ ▶ **1275**, ▶ **1340** **❶** *adj.* aztekisch. **❷** *n.* **A** (*person*) Azteke, *der*/Aztekin, *die;* **B** (*language*) Aztekisch, *das*

**azure** /'æʒjə(r), 'eɪʒjə(r)/ **❶** *n.* **A** (*sky blue*) Azur[blau], *das;* **B** (*Her.*) Blau, *das;* **C** (*literary: unclouded sky*) Azur, *der.* **❷** *adj.* **A** (*sky-blue*) azurblau; azurn; **B** (*Her.*) blau

b

# B b

**B, b** /biː/ *n., pl.* **Bs** *or* **B's** **A** (*letter*) B, b, *das;* **B road** Straße 2. Ordnung; ≈ Landstraße, *die;* **B film** *or* (*Amer.*) **movie** Vorfilm, *der;* **B B** (*Mus.*) H, h, *das;* **B flat** B, b, *das;* **C** (*example*) B, b (*ohne Artikel*); **D B** (*Sch., Univ.: mark*) Zwei, *die;* **he got a B** er bekam „gut" *od.* eine Zwei

**B.** *abbr.* **A** (*Univ.*) **Bachelor; B bishop** Bisch.; (*Chess*) L; **C** (*on pencil*) **black** B

**BA** *abbr.* **A** (*Univ.*) **Bachelor of Arts;** ⇒ *also* **B.Sc.**; **B British Academy** *geisteswissenschaftliche akademische Institution in Großbritannien;* **C British Association** *naturwissenschaftliche akademische Institution in Großbritannien*

**b.** *abbr.* **A born** geb.; **B** (*Cricket*) **bowled by** ausgeschlagen durch Tortreffer von

**baa** /bɑː/ ❶ *n.* Blöken, *das.* ❷ *v.i.,* **~ed** *or* **~'d** /bɑːd/ mähen; blöken

**BAA** *abbr.* **British Airports Authority** *britische Flughafenbehörde*

**'baa-lamb** *n.* (*child lang.*) Bählämmchen, *das;* Bählamm, *das*

**baba** /'bɑːbɑː/ *n.* **[rum] ~:** [Rum]baba, *das; mit Rumsirup getränktes Gebäck*

**babble** /'bæbl/ ❶ *v.i.* **A** (*talk incoherently*) stammeln; **~ [away** *or* **on]** ‹Baby:› [vor sich (*Akk.*) hin] lallen *od.* plappern; **B** (*talk foolishly*) [dumm] schwatzen; **a babbling idiot** ein dummer Schwätzer; **C** (*talk excessively*) **~ away** *or* **on** quasseln (*ugs.*); **D** (*murmur*) ‹Bach:› plätschern. ❷ *v.t.* **A** (*divulge foolishly*) ausplaudern; **~ sth. to sb.** etw. bei jmdm. ausplaudern; **B** (*utter incoherently*) stammeln. ❸ *n.* **A** (*incoherent speech*) Gestammel, *das;* (*childish or foolish speech*) Gelalle, *das;* **B** (*idle talk*) Geschwätz, *das;* **C** (*murmur of water*) Geplätscher, *das;* **D** (*Teleph.*) unverständliches Gemurmel

**babbler** /'bæblə(r)/ *n.* **A** (*chatterer, teller of secrets*) Plaudertasche, *die;* **B** (*Ornith.*) Timalie, *die;* Lärmdrossel, *die* (*veralt.*)

**babe** /beɪb/ *n.* **A** (*inexperienced person*) Anfänger, *der*/Anfängerin, *die;* **be a ~:** noch nicht trocken hinter den Ohren sein (*ugs.*); **B** (*guileless person*) Lamm, *das;* **~s in the wood** hilflose Lämmchen; **C** (*Amer. sl.: young woman*) Kleine, *die* (*ugs.*); **I love you, ~:** ich liebe dich, Kleines; **D** (*young child*) kleines Kind; **as innocent as a new-born ~:** unschuldig wie ein neugeborenes Kind; ⇒ *also* **mouth** 1 A

**babel** /'beɪbl/ *n.* **A** (*scene of confusion*) Durcheinander, *das;* **B** (*noisy medley*) **~ of voices** [lautes] Stimmengewirr; **tower of B~** (*fig.*) gigantisches Projekt; **C** (*confusion of tongues*) babylonisches Sprachengewirr

**baboon** /bə'buːn/ *n.* (*Zool.*) Pavian, *der;* (*fig. derog.: person*) Neandertaler, *der;* Halbaffe, *der*

**babushka** /bə'bʊʃkə/ *n.* Kopftuch, *das*

**baby** /'beɪbɪ/ ❶ *n.* **A** Baby, *das;* **have a ~/ be going to have a ~:** ein Kind bekommen; **she is having a ~ in May** sie bekommt im Mai ein Kind; **she has a young ~:** sie hat ein kleines Baby; **mother and ~ are doing fine** Mutter und Kind sind wohlauf; **a ~ boy/girl** ein kleiner Junge/ein kleines Mädchen; **throw out** *or* **away the ~ with the bathwater** (*fig.*) das Kind mit dem Bade ausschütten; **be left holding** *or* **carrying the ~** (*fig.*) die Sache ausbaden müssen (*ugs.*); der Dumme sein (*ugs.*); **leave sb. carrying the ~** (*fig.*) jmdn. die Sache ausbaden lassen (*ugs.*); **it's your/his** *etc.* **~** (*fig.*) das ist dein/sein *usw.* Bier (*ugs.*); **reference books are Jones's ~:** um Nachschlagewerke muss sich Jones kümmern; **B** (*youngest member*) Jüngste, *der/die;* (*male also*) Benjamin, *der;* **the ~ of the family** das Küken der Familie; **C** (*childish person*) **be a ~:** sich wie ein kleines Kind benehmen; **D** (*young animal*) Junge, *das;* **~ bird/giraffe** junger Vogel/junge Giraffe; Vogeljunge, *das*/Giraffenjunge, *das;* **E** (*small thing*) **be a ~:** winzig sein; **~ [car]** Miniauto, *das;* Kleinwagen, *der;* **~ [bottle]** Miniflasche, *die;* **F** (*coll.: sweetheart*) Schatz, *der;* (*in pop song also*) Baby, *das;* **G** (*sl.: young woman*) Kleine, *die* (*ugs.*); **H** (*coll.: person*) Typ, *der;* (*thing*) Ding, *das* (*ugs.*); **this ~** (*the speaker himself*) unsereiner (*ugs.*).

❷ *v.t.* wie ein kleines Kind behandeln; (*be easy on*) mit Samthandschuhen anfassen

**baby: ~ boom** *n.* Babyboom, *der;* **~-bouncer** *n. federnd aufgehängter Sitz für Kleinkinder, in dem sie durch Wippen ihre Beine kräftigen sollen;* **~ buggy** *n.* (*Amer.*) Kinderwagen, *der;* **~ car** ⇒ **baby** 1 E; **~ carriage** *n.* (*Amer.*) Kinderwagen, *der;* **~ clothes** *n. pl.* Babykleidung, *die;* **~-doll** *adj.* **~-doll pyjamas/nightdress** Babydoll, *das;* **~ face** *n.* **A** (*face*) Kindergesicht, *das;* **B** (*person*) Milchgesicht, *das* (*leicht abwertend*); **~ food** *n.* Babynahrung, *die;* **~ 'grand** *n.* (*Mus.*) Stutzflügel, *der*

**babyhood** /'beɪbɪhʊd/ *n., no pl.* frühe Kindheit

**babyish** /'beɪbɪɪʃ/ *adj.* kindlich ‹Aussehen›; kindisch ‹Benehmen, Person›; **don't be so ~:** benimm dich nicht wie ein kleines Kind

**baby: ~-minder** *n.* Tagesmutter, *die;* **~ powder** *n.* Babypuder, *der;* **~sit** *v.i., forms as* **sit** 1 babysitten (*ugs.*); auf das Kind/die Kinder aufpassen; **she ~sits for us** sie kommt zu uns zum Babysitten; **~sitter** *n.* Babysitter, *der;* **~sitting** *n.* Babysitting, *das;* **~-snatch** *v.i.* ⇒ **cradle-snatch**; **~-snatcher** *n.* **A** Kindesentführer, *der;* **B** (*fig. coll.*) *jmd., der mit einer sehr viel jüngeren Person eine Liebesbeziehung eingeht;* **~-snatching** *n.* **A** Kindesentführung, *die;* **B You can't ask her out. That would be ~-snatching** (*fig. coll.*) Du kannst sie nicht einladen. Das wäre Verführung einer Minderjährigen (*scherzh.*); **~-talk** *n.* Babysprache, *die;* **~ walker** *n.* Laufstuhl, *der;* **~ wipe** *n.* feuchtes Baby[pflege]tuch

**baccarat** /'bækərɑː/ *n.* Bakkarat, *das*

**Bacchanalia** /bækə'neɪlɪə/ *n. pl.* **A** (*drunken revelry*) Bacchanal, *das* (*geh.*); **B** (*Greek and Roman Ant.*) Bacchanalien *Pl.*

**Bacchanalian** /bækə'neɪlɪən/ ❶ *adj.* bacchantisch. ❷ *n.* Bacchant, *der* (*geh.*)

**baccy** /'bækɪ/ *n.* (*coll.*) Tabak, *der*

**bachelor** /'bætʃələ(r)/ *n.* **A** (*unmarried man*) Junggeselle, *der;* **B** (*Univ.*) Bakkalaureus, *der;* Bachelor, *der;* **B~ of Arts/Science** Bakkalaureus der philosophischen Fakultät/der Naturwissenschaften

**bachelor: ~ flat** *n.* Junggesellenwohnung, *die;* **~ girl** *n.* Junggesellin, *die*

**bachelorhood** /'bætʃələhʊd/ *n., no pl.* Junggesellendasein, *das*

**bacillary** /bə'sɪlərɪ/ *adj.* (*Biol., Med.*) bazillär

**bacillus** /bə'sɪləs/ *n., pl.* **bacilli** /bə'sɪlaɪ/ (*Biol., Med.*) **A** (*rod-shaped bacterium*) Bazillus, *der;* **B** (*pathogenic bacterium*) Bakterie, *die;* Bazillus, *der* (*veralt.*)

**back** /bæk/ ❶ *n.* **A ▶ 966** (*of person, animal*) Rücken, *der;* **stand ~ to ~:** Rücken an Rücken stehen; **give** *or* **make a ~:** sich bücken; **as soon as my ~ was turned** (*fig.*) sowie ich den Rücken gedreht hatte; **behind sb.'s ~** (*fig.*) ⇒ **behind** 2 B; **be on one's ~:** [auf dem Rücken] liegen; (*fig.: be ill*) im Bett liegen; flachliegen (*salopp*); auf der Nase liegen (*ugs.*); **turn one's ~ on sb.** jmdm. den Rücken zuwenden; (*fig.: abandon sb.*) jmdn. im Stich lassen; **turn one's ~ on sth.** (*fig.*) etw. vernachlässigen; sich um etw. nicht kümmern; **don't turn your ~ on this chance** lass dir diese Chance nicht entgehen; **get** *or* **put sb.'s ~ up** (*fig.*) jmdn. wütend machen; **be glad to see the ~ of sb./sth.** (*fig.*) froh sein, jmdn./etw. nicht mehr sehen zu müssen; **have one's ~ to the wall** (*fig.*) mit dem Rücken zur Wand stehen; **be at sb.'s ~** (*fig.*) (*in support*) hinter jmdm. stehen; (*in pursuit*) jmdm. auf den Fersen sein; **with sb. at one's ~** (*fig.*) gefolgt von jmdm.; **get off my ~** (*fig. coll.*) lass mich zufrieden; **have sb./sth. on one's ~** (*fig.*) jmdn./etw. am Hals haben (*ugs.*); **you look as if you had the cares of the world on your ~:** du siehst aus, als ob die Sorgen der ganzen Welt auf dir lasten; **put one's ~ into sth.** (*fig.*) sich für etw. mit allen Kräften einsetzen; **you're not exactly putting your ~ into this work** (*fig.*) du strengst dich bei dieser Arbeit nicht genug an; ⇒ *also* **break** 1 C, 2 B; **B** (*outer or rear surface*) Rücken, *der;* (*of vehicle*) Heck, *das;* **the car went into the ~ of me** (*coll.*) das Auto ist mir hinten reingefahren (*ugs.*); **with the ~ of one's hand** mit dem Handrücken; **know sth. like the ~ of one's hand** (*fig.*) etw. wie seine Westentasche kennen; **the ~ of one's/the head** der Hinterkopf; **the ~ of the leg** (*below knee*) die Wade; **C** (*of book*) (*spine*) [Buch]rücken, *der;* (*final pages*) Ende, *das;* **at the ~ [of the book]** hinten [im Buch]; **D** (*of dress*) Rücken, *der;* (*of knife*) [Messer]rücken, *der;* **E** (*more remote part*) hinterer Teil; **at the ~ [of sth.]** hinten [in etw. (*Dat.*)]; im hinteren Teil [von etw.]; **F** (*inside car*) Rücksitz, *der;* Fond, *der* (*seltener*); (*of chair*) [Rücken]lehne, *die;* (*of material*) linke Seite; (*of house, cheque*) Rückseite, *die;* (*~ wall*) Rückseite, *die;* Rückwand, *die;* **~-to-~ houses** (*Brit.*) *Häuser, deren Rückseiten eng aneinander gebaut sind;* **~ to front** verkehrt rum; **please get to the ~ of the queue** bitte, stellen Sie sich hinten an; **we squeezed five people into the ~ [of the car]** wir zwängten fünf Personen auf die Rücksitze [des Wagens]; **the coat hook was on the ~ of the door** der Kleiderhaken befand sich hinten an der Tür; **there's something at the ~ of my mind** ich habe da noch etwas im Hinterkopf; **in ~ of sth.** (*Amer.*) hinter etw. (*Dat.*); ⇒ *also* **beyond** 3; **G** (*Sport*) (*player*) Verteidiger, *der;* (*position*) **he played at ~ this week** diese Woche hat er als Verteidiger gespielt; **H** (*of ship*) Kiel, *der;* **I the Backs** *die Uferanlagen hinter einigen Colleges in Cambridge (England).*

❷ *adj., no comp.; superl.* **~most** /'bækməʊst/ **A** (*situated behind*) hinter...; **from the ~most of the three lines** von der hintersten der drei Linien; **B** (*of the past*) früher; **~ issue** alte Ausgabe; **C** (*overdue*) rückständig ‹Lohn, Steuern›; **D** (*remote*) abgelegen ‹Ort, Straße›; **E** (*reversed*) **~ motion** Rückwärtsbewegung, *die;* **~ flow** Rückfluss, *der;* **F** (*Cricket*) **~ play** *das Schlagen des Balles hinter der Schlagmallinie;* **G** (*Phonet.*) **~ vowel** Hinterzungenvokal, *der.*

❸ *adv.* **A** (*to the rear*) zurück; **step ~:** zurücktreten; **play ~** (*Cricket*) zurücktreten, um zu schlagen; **B** (*behind*) zurück; weiter hinten; **we passed a pub two miles ~:** wir sind vor zwei Meilen an einem Pub vorbeigefahren; **~ and forth** hin und her; **~ of sth.** (*Amer.*) hinter etw. (*Dat.*); Ⓒ (*at a distance*) **the house stands a long way ~ from the road** das Haus steht weit von der Straße zurück; Ⓓ (*to original position, home*) [wieder] zurück; **I got my letter ~:** ich habe meinen Brief zurückbekommen; **the journey ~:** die Rückfahrt/der Rückflug; **there and ~:** hin und zurück; Ⓔ (*to original condition*) wieder; Ⓕ (*in the past*) zurück; **go a long way ~:** weit zurückgehen; **a week/month ~:** vor einer Woche/vor einem Monat; Ⓖ (*in return*) zurück; **I got a letter ~:** er/sie hat mir wiedergeschrieben.

❹ *v.t.* Ⓐ (*assist*) helfen (+ *Dat.*); unterstützen ‹Person, Sache›; Ⓑ (*bet on*) wetten *od.* setzen auf (+ *Akk.*) ‹Pferd, Gewinner, Favorit›; **~ the wrong/right horse** (*lit. or fig.*) aufs falsche/richtige Pferd setzen (*ugs.*); **~ X to beat Y** darauf wetten, dass X gegen Y gewinnt; **the horse which is most heavily ~ed** das Pferd, auf das am meisten gesetzt wurde; Ⓒ (*cause to move ~*) zurücksetzen [mit] ‹Fahrzeug›; rückwärts gehen lassen ‹Pferd›; **how did you manage to ~ the car into that lamp post?** wie hast du es nur fertig gebracht, rückwärts gegen den Laternenpfahl zu fahren?; **~ water** rückwärts rudern; Ⓓ (*put or act as a ~ to*) [an der Rückseite] verstärken; Ⓔ (*endorse*) indossieren ‹Wechsel, Scheck›; Ⓕ (*lie at the ~ of*) **~ sth.** hinten an etw. (*Akk.*) grenzen; Ⓖ (*Mus.*) begleiten.

❺ *v.i.* zurücksetzen; ‹Wind:› [sich] gegen den Uhrzeigersinn drehen; **~ into/out of sth.** rückwärts in etw. (*Akk.*)/aus etw. fahren; **~ on to sth.** hinten an etw. (*Akk.*) grenzen; **~ and fill** (*Amer.*) sich hin und her bewegen; (*fig.*) schwanken

**~ a'way** *v.i.* zurückweichen; (*fig.*) zurückschrecken

**~ 'down** *v.i.* (*fig.*) nachgeben; einen Rückzieher machen (*ugs.*); ⇒ *also* **back-down**

**~ 'off** ⇒ **~ away**

**~ 'out** *v.i.* rückwärts herausfahren; (*fig.*) einen Rückzieher machen (*ugs.*); **~ out of sth.** (*fig.*) von etw. zurücktreten

**~ 'up** ❶ Ⓐ *v.t.* unterstützen; untermauern ‹Anspruch, Geschichte, These›; Ⓑ (*Computing*) sichern ‹Daten, Dokumente›; **~ up a file on to a floppy disk** von einer Datei eine Sicherungskopie auf Diskette machen. ❷ *v.i.* Ⓐ ‹Wasser:› sich [auf]stauen; Ⓑ (*reverse*) zurücksetzen; Ⓒ (*Amer.: form queue of vehicles*) sich stauen. ⇒ *also* **~-up**

**back: ~ache** *n., no pl.* ▶ 1232 Rückenschmerzen *Pl.*; **~ 'bench** *n.* (*Brit. Parl.*) hintere Sitzreihe; **a ~-bench MP** ein Parlamentsabgeordneter [aus den hinteren Reihen]; **~-bencher** /bæk'bentʃə(r)/ *n.* (*Brit. Parl.*) [einfacher] Abgeordneter/[einfache] Abgeordnete; (*derog.*) Hinterbänkler, *der* (*abwertend*); **~biter** *n.* Verleumder, *der*/Verleumderin, *die*; **~biting** *n.* Verleumdung, *die*; Hetzerei, *die* (*ugs.*); **~blocks** *n. pl.* (*Austral., NZ*) ≈ Hinterland, *das; dünn besiedeltes, abgelegenes Land im Landesinneren;* **~ boiler** *n.* (*Brit.*) (*hinter dem Ofen o. Ä. angebrachter*) Boiler; **~bone** *n.* Wirbelsäule, *die;* Rückgrat, *das* (*auch fig.*); (*Amer.: of book*) [Buch]rücken, *der*; **to the ~bone** (*fig.*) durch und durch; **~-breaking** *adj.* äußerst mühsam; gewaltig ‹Anstrengung›; **~-breaking work** Knochenarbeit, *die*; **~ 'burner** *n.* **put sth. on the ~ burner** (*fig. coll.*) etw. zurückstellen; **~chat** *n., no pl.* (*coll.*) [freche] Widerrede; **none of your ~chat!** keine Widerrede!; **~cloth** *n.* (*Brit. Theatre*) Prospekt, *der*; **~comb** *v.t.* zurückkämmen; **~ copy** ⇒ **~ number**; **~date** *v.t.* zurückdatieren (**to** auf + *Akk.*); **~ 'door** *n.* Hintertür, *die* (*auch fig.*); **~-door** *adj.* (*fig.*) Hintertreppen- (*abwertend*); **~-down** *n.* (*coll.*) Rückzieher, *der* (*ugs.*); **~drop** ⇒ **~cloth**

**backer** /'bækə(r)/ *n.* Geldgeber, *der*; (*of horse*) Wetter, *der*

**back: ~fill** *v.t.* [wieder] auffüllen; **~fire** ❶ /'--/ *n.* Fehlzündung, *die*; ❷ /-'-/ *v.i.* knallen; (*fig.*) fehlschlagen; **it ~fired on me/him** *etc.* der Schuss ging nach hinten los (*ugs.*); **~-formation** *n.* (*Ling.*) (*word*) rückgebildetes Wort; (*action*) Rückbildung, *die*

**backgammon** /'bækgæmən/ *n.* (*game*) Backgammon, *das*; ≈ Tricktrack, *das*; ≈ Puff, *das*

**back: ~ground** *n.* Ⓐ (*lit. or fig.*) Hintergrund, *der*; (*social status*) Herkunft, *die*; (*education*) Ausbildung, *die*; (*experience*) Erfahrung, *die*; **be in the ~ground** im Hintergrund stehen; **he comes from a poor ~ground** er stammt aus ärmlichen Verhältnissen; **against this ~ground** vor diesem Hintergrund; **~ground heating** *Heizung, die automatisch für eine erträgliche Zimmertemperatur sorgt;* **~ground music** Hintergrundmusik, *die*; Ⓑ **~ground [information]** Hintergrundinformation, *die*; Ⓒ (*Radio*) Störgeräusch, *das*; **~hand** (*Tennis etc.*) ❶ *adj.* Rückhand-; ❷ *n.* Rückhand, *die*; **~handed** /bæk'hændɪd/ *adj.* Ⓐ **~-handed slap** Schlag mit dem Handrücken; **~-handed stroke** (*Tennis*) Rückhandschlag, *der*; Ⓑ (*fig.*) indirekt; zweifelhaft ‹Kompliment›; **~hander** /bæk'hændə(r)/ *n.* Ⓐ (*stroke*) Rückhandschlag, *der* (*Tennis usw.*); (*blow*) Schlag [mit dem Handrücken]; Ⓑ (*coll.: bribe*) Schmiergeld, *das*

**backing** /'bækɪŋ/ *n.* Ⓐ (*material*) Rückenverstärkung, *die*; **leather ~:** Rückseite aus Leder; **the silver ~ of a mirror** die silberne Beschichtung eines Spiegels; Ⓑ (*support*) Unterstützung, *die*; **the President has a large ~:** der Präsident kann sich auf eine große Anhängerschaft stützen; Ⓒ (*betting*) **there was much ~ of the favourite** es wurden viele Wetten auf den Favoriten abgeschlossen; Ⓓ (*Mus.: accompaniment*) Begleitung, *die*

**back: ~ issue** ⇒ **~ number**; **~lash** *n.* Rückstoß, *der*; (*excessive play in machine*) Spiel, *das*; (*fig.*) Gegenreaktion, *die*; **a right-wing ~lash** eine Gegenbewegung nach rechts

**backless** /'bæklɪs/ *adj.* rückenfrei ‹Kleid›

**back: ~list** *n.* Verzeichnis der lieferbaren Titel; Backlist, *die* (*Verlagsw.*); **~log** *n.* Rückstand, *der*; **~log of work** Arbeitsrückstand, *der*; **a large ~log of unfulfilled orders** ein großer Überhang an unerledigten Aufträgen; **~marker** *n.* Ⓐ (*lagging behind other competitors*) Schlusslicht, *das* (*ugs. fig.*); Ⓑ *jmd., der ohne Vorgabe od. mit dem größten Handicap startet;* **~ 'number** *n.* Ⓐ (*of periodical, magazine*) alte Nummer; Ⓑ (*fig. coll.*) **these methods are a [real] ~ number** diese Methoden sind [reichlich] rückständig; **not every star is a ~ number when he is 60** nicht jeder Star ist mit 60 abgeschrieben; **~pack** ❶ *n.* Rucksack, *der*; ❷ *v.i.* mit dem Rucksack [ver]reisen; **~packer** *n.* Rucksackreisende, *der/die*; Rucksacktourist, *der*/-touristin, *die*; (*hiker*) Wanderer, *der*/Wanderin, *die* mit Rucksack; **~packing** *n., no pl.* das [Ver]reisen mit dem Rucksack; (*hiking*) das Wandern mit dem Rucksack; *attrib.* ‹Reise usw.› mit dem Rucksack; **~ passage** *n.* (*Anat. coll.*) After, *der*; **~ pay** *n.* ausstehender Lohn/ausstehendes Gehalt; **he was reinstated with ~ pay** er wurde wieder eingestellt und erhielt eine Lohn-/Gehaltsnachzahlung; **she was awarded £7,850 in ~ pay** sie erhielt eine Nachzahlung von £7,850; **~-'pedal** *v.i.* Ⓐ die Pedale rückwärts treten; (*brake*) mit dem Rücktritt bremsen; Ⓑ (*fig.*) einen Rückzieher machen (*ugs.*); **~rest** *n.* Rückenlehne, *die*; **~ 'room** *n.* Hinterzimmer, *das*; **in the ~ room** (*fig.*) hinter verschlossenen Türen; **~room boys** (*coll.*) Experten im Hintergrund (*bes. Wissenschaftler, die an Geheimprojekten arbeiten*); **~scratcher** *n.* Rückenkratzer, *der*; **~scratching** *n.* (*fig. coll.*) **[mutual] ~scratching** Klüngelei, *die* (*abwertend*); **~ 'seat** *n.* Rücksitz, *der*; (*in bus, coach*) hinterer Sitzplatz; **take a ~ seat** (*fig.*) in den Hintergrund treten; **be in the ~ seat** (*fig.*) im Hintergrund stehen; **~-seat driver** *besserwisserischer Beifahrer, der immer dazwischenredet;* (*fig.*) Neunmalkluge, *der/die*; **~side** *n.* Hinterteil, *das* (*ugs.*); Hintern, *der* (*ugs.*); **get [up] off one's ~side** seinen Hintern heben (*ugs.*); **~sight** *n.* Visier, *das*; **~slapping** *adj.* (*fig.*) plump-vertraulich; **~slider** *n.* Abtrünnige, *der/die*; **~space** *v.i.* die Rücktaste betätigen; **~'stage** ❶ *adj.* hinter der Bühne; **~stage activities** (*fig.*) Aktivitäten hinter den Kulissen; ❷ *adv.* Ⓐ **go ~stage** hinter die Bühne gehen; **wait ~stage for the artist** hinter der Bühne auf den Künstler warten; Ⓑ (*fig.*) hinter den Kulissen; **~'stair[s]** ⇒ **~-door**; **~'stairs** *n. pl.* Hintertreppe, *die*; **~stitch** ❶ *v.t. & i.* steppen; ❷ *n.* Steppstich, *der*; **~stitch seam** Steppnaht, *die*; **~ street** kleine Seitenstraße; **from the ~ streets of Naples** ≈ aus den Hinterhöfen Neapels; ⇒ *also* **abortion** A; **abortionist**; **~stroke** *n.* (*Swimming*) Rückenschwimmen, *das*; **do** *or* **swim the ~stroke** rückenschwimmen; **~ talk** (*Amer.*) ⇒ **~chat**; **~track** *v.i.* wieder zurückgehen; (*fig.*) eine Kehrtwendung machen; **~-up** *n.* Ⓐ (*support*) Unterstützung, *die*; **a racing driver needs a large ~-up crew** ein Rennfahrer muss eine große Crew hinter sich haben; Ⓑ (*reserve*) Reserve, *die*; **~-up supplies** Vorräte für den Bedarfs- *od.* Notfall; **~-up [copy]** (*Computing*) Sicherungskopie, *die*; Ⓒ (*Amer.: queue of vehicles*) Stau, *der*; **a ~-up of cars** eine Autoschlange; Ⓓ **~-up light** (*Amer.*) Rückfahrscheinwerfer, *der*

**backward** /'bækwəd/ ❶ *adj.* Ⓐ (*directed to rear*) rückwärts gerichtet; Rückwärts-; **~ movement** Rückwärtsbewegung, *die*; **the ~ slant to his handwriting** seine nach links geneigte Handschrift; Ⓑ (*reluctant, shy*) zurückhaltend; **be ~ in coming forward** (*joc.*) sich zurückhalten; Ⓒ (*slow, retarded*) zurückgeblieben ‹Kind›; (*underdeveloped*) rückständig, unterentwickelt ‹Land, Region›; **~ in sth.** in etw. (*Dat.*) zurückgeblieben; **~ in his studies** mit seinem Studium im Rückstand. ❷ *adv.* ⇒ **backwards**

**'backward-looking** *adj.* rückwärts gewandt

**backwardness** /'bækwədnɪs/ *n., no pl.* Ⓐ (*reluctance, shyness*) Zurückhaltung, *die*; Ⓑ (*of child*) Zurückgebliebenheit, *die*; (*of country, region*) Rückständigkeit, *die*; **the child's ~ in school** dass das Kind in der Schule zurückgeblieben ist/war

**backwards** /'bækwədz/ *adv.* Ⓐ nach hinten; **the child fell [over] ~ into the water** das Kind fiel rückwärts ins Wasser; **bend** *or* **fall** *or* **lean over ~ to do sth.** (*fig. coll.*) sich zerreißen, um etw. zu tun (*ugs.*); Ⓑ (*oppositely to normal direction*) rückwärts; **~ and forwards** (*to and fro, lit. or fig.*) hin und her; Ⓒ (*into a worse state*) **go ~:** sich verschlechtern; **under his leadership the country is going ~:** unter seiner Führung verschlechtert sich die Lage des Landes; Ⓓ (*into past*) **look ~:** an frühere Zeiten denken; Ⓔ (*reverse way*) rückwärts; von hinten nach vorn; **you're doing everything ~:** du machst ja alles verkehrt herum; **know sth. ~:** etw. in- und auswendig kennen

**back: ~wash** *n.* Rückstrom, *der* (**from** *Gen.*); (*fig.*) Auswirkungen *Pl.*; **in the ~wash of** (*fig.*) als Folge von; **~water** *n.* totes Wasser; (*fig.*) Kaff, *das* (*ugs. abwertend*); **this town is too much of a ~water** diese Stadt ist zu provinziell; **~woods** *n. pl.* abgelegene Wälder; unerschlossene Waldgebiete; (*fig.*) hinterste Provinz; **~woodsman** *n.* ≈ Waldbewohner, *der*; (*uncouth person*) Hinterwäldler, *der* (*spött.*); **~ 'yard** *n.* Hinterhof, *der*; (*Amer.: garden*) Garten, *der* [hinter dem Haus]; **in one's own ~ yard** (*fig.*) vor der eigenen Haustür

**bacon** /'beɪkn/ *n.* [Frühstücks]speck, *der*; **~ and eggs** Eier mit Speck; **bring home the ~** (*fig. coll.*) es schaffen; (*der Ernährer sein*) die Brötchen verdienen (*ugs.*); **save one's ~** (*fig.*) die eigene *od.* seine Haut retten

**bacteria** *pl. of* **bacterium**

**bacterial** /bæk'tɪərɪəl/ *adj.* bakteriell

**bactericide** /bæk'tɪərɪsaɪd/ *n.* Bakterizid, *das*

**bacteriological** /bæktɪərɪə'lɒdʒɪkl/ *adj.* bakteriologisch; **~ warfare** Bakterienkrieg, *der*

**bacteriologist** /bæktɪərɪˈɒlədʒɪst/ *n.* Bakteriologe, *der*/Bakteriologin, *die*

**bacteriology** /bæktɪərɪˈɒlədʒɪ/ *n.* Bakteriologie, *die*

**bacterium** /bækˈtɪərɪəm/ *n., pl.* **bacteria** /bækˈtɪərɪə/ Bakterie, *die*

**bad** /bæd/ ❶ *adj.*, **worse** /wɜːs/, **worst** /wɜːst/ Ⓐ schlecht; (*worthless*) wertlos, ungedeckt ‹Scheck›; (*counterfeit*) falsch ‹Münze, Banknote›; (*rotten*) schlecht, verdorben ‹Fleisch, Fisch, Essen›; faul ‹Ei, Apfel›; (*unpleasant*) schlecht, unangenehm ‹Geruch›; **do a ~ job on sth.** bei etw. schlecht arbeiten; **sth. gives sb. a ~ name** etw. trägt jmdm. einen schlechten Ruf ein; **sb. gets a ~ name** jmd. kommt in Verruf; **she is in ~ health** sie hat eine angegriffene Gesundheit; **she has a ~ complexion** sie hat einen unreinen Teint; **be ~ at doing sth.** etw. nicht gut können; **be a ~ liar** ein schlechter Lügner sein; **[some] ~ news** schlechte *od.* schlimme Nachrichten; **~ breath** Mundgeruch, *der;* **he is having a ~ day** er hat einen schwarzen Tag; **~ hair day** (*coll.*) schlechter Tag; **I'm having a ~ hair day** (*coll.*) heute geht bei mir alles schief; **~ business** ein schlechtes Geschäft; **it is a ~ business** (*fig.*) das ist eine schlimme Sache; **in the ~ old days** in den schlimmen Jahren; **not ~** (*coll.*) nicht schlecht; nicht übel; **not so ~** (*coll.*) gar nicht so schlecht *od.* übel; **things weren't so ~** (*coll.*) es war alles nicht so schlimm; **sth. is not a ~ idea** etw. ist keine schlechte Idee; **not half ~** (*coll.*) [gar] nicht schlecht; **sth. is too ~** (*coll.*) etw. ist ein Jammer; **that was too ~ of him** (*coll.*) das war rücksichtslos von ihm; **too ~!** (*coll.*) so ein Pech! (*auch iron.*); **go ~:** schlecht werden; **in a ~ sense** im schlechten Sinne; Ⓑ (*noxious*) schlecht; schädlich; **it is ~ for you** es ist schlecht für dich; es schadet dir; Ⓒ (*wicked*) schlecht; (*immoral*) schlecht; verdorben; unmoralisch ‹Buch, Heft›; (*naughty*) ungezogen, böse ‹Kind, Hund›; Ⓓ (*offensive*) **[use] ~ language** Kraftausdrücke [benutzen]; Ⓔ (*in ill health*) **she's ~ today** es geht ihr heute schlecht; **have a ~ arm/finger** einen schlimmen Arm/Finger haben (*ugs.*); **I have a ~ pain** ich habe schlimme Schmerzen; **be in a ~ way** in schlechtem Zustand sein; Ⓕ (*serious*) schlimm, böse ‹Sturz, Krise›; schwer ‹Fehler, Krankheit, Unfall, Erschütterung›; hoch ‹Fieber›; schrecklich ‹Feuer›; Ⓖ (*coll.: regretful*) **a ~ conscience** ein schlechtes Gewissen; **feel ~ about sth./not having done sth.** etw. bedauern/bedauern, dass man etw. nicht getan hat; **I feel ~ about him/her** ich habe seinetwegen/ihretwegen ein schlechtes Gewissen; Ⓗ (*Commerc.*) **a ~ debt** eine uneinbringliche Schuld (*Wirtsch.*); Ⓘ (*Law: invalid*) ungültig. ⇒ *also* **book** 1 A; **egg**[1]; **form** 1 H; **hat** B; **lot** C; **luck** A; **patch** 1 A; **penny** C; **temper** 1 A; **worse** 1; **worst** 1. ❷ *n.* Ⓐ (*ill fortune*) Schlechte, *das;* Ⓑ (*debit*) **be £100 to the ~:** mit 100 Pfund in der Kreide stehen (*ugs.*); Ⓒ (*ruin*) **go to the ~:** auf die schiefe Bahn geraten. ⇒ *also* **worse** 3. ❸ *adv.* (*Amer. coll.*) ⇒ **badly**

**baddish** /ˈbædɪʃ/ *adj.* ziemlich schlecht

**baddy** /ˈbædɪ/ *n.* (*coll.*) Schurke, *der;* **the goodies and the baddies** die Guten und die Bösen (*oft iron.*)

**bade** ⇒ **bid** 1 C, D, E

**badge** /bædʒ/ *n.* Ⓐ (*as sign of office, membership, support*) Abzeichen, *das;* (*larger*) Plakette, *die;* Ⓑ (*symbol*) Symbol, *das;* Ⓒ (*thing revealing quality or condition*) Kennzeichen, *das*

**badger** /ˈbædʒə(r)/ ❶ *n.* Dachs, *der.* ❷ *v.t.* **~ sb. [into doing/to do sth.]** jmdm. keine Ruhe lassen[, bis er/sie etw. tut]; **~ sb. with questions** jmdn. mit Fragen löchern (*ugs.*); **don't ~ her out of her wits!** mach sie nicht verrückt! (*ugs.*)

ˈ**badger baiting** *n.* Dachshetze, *die*

**badinage** /ˈbædɪnɑːʒ/ *n.* Spöttelei, *die*

ˈ**bad lands** *n. pl.* (*Amer.*) Badlands *Pl.*

**badly** /ˈbædlɪ/ *adv.*, **worse** /wɜːs/, **worst** /wɜːst/ Ⓐ schlecht; Ⓑ (*seriously*) schwer ‹verletzt, beschädigt›; sehr ‹schief sein, knarren›; **he hurt himself ~:** er hat sich (*Dat.*) schwer verletzt; **he has got it ~:** es hat ihn schlimm erwischt (*ugs.*); **be ~ beaten** schwer verprügelt werden (*ugs.*); (*in game, battle*) vernichtend geschlagen werden; Ⓒ (*urgently*) dringend; **want sth. [so] ~:** sich (*Dat.*) etw. [so] sehr wünschen; Ⓓ (*coll.: regretfully*) **feel ~ about sth.** etw. [sehr] bedauern; **I don't feel too ~ about it** es macht mir nicht so viel aus. ⇒ *also* **worse** 2; **worst** 2

ˈ**bad man** *n.* (*Amer.*) Bösewicht, *der*

**badminton** /ˈbædmɪntən/ *n.* Federball, *der;* (*als Sport*) Badminton, *das*

ˈ**bad mouth** *n.* (*Amer. coll.*) Klatsch, *der* (*ugs.*)

ˈ**bad-mouth** *v.t.* (*Amer. coll.*) klatschen über (+ *Akk.*) (*ugs.*)

**badness** /ˈbædnɪs/ *n., no pl.* ⇒ **bad**: Schlechtigkeit, *die;* Verdorbenheit, *die;* Ungezogenheit, *die;* Ungültigkeit, *die;* **the ~ in him** seine innere Schlechtigkeit

**bad-tempered** /bædˈtempəd/ *adj.* griesgrämig

**BAe** *abbr.* **British Aerospace** *britisches Unternehmen, das Flugzeuge und Raumschiffe herstellt*

**baffle** /ˈbæfl/ ❶ *v.t.* Ⓐ (*perplex*) **~ sb.** jmdm. unverständlich sein; jmdn. vor ein Rätsel stellen; Ⓑ (*stop progress of*) aufhalten. ❷ *n.* **~[ plate]** Prallfläche, *die* (*Technik*); **~[ board]** (*of loudspeaker*) Schallwand, *die*

**baffled** /ˈbæfld/ *adj.* verwirrt; **be ~:** vor einem Rätsel stehen

**bafflement** /ˈbæflmənt/ *n.* Verwirrung, *die*

**baffling** /ˈbæflɪŋ/ *adj.* rätselhaft

**bag** /bæg/ ❶ *n.* Ⓐ Tasche, *die;* (*sack*) Sack, *der;* (*hand~*) [Hand]tasche, *die;* (*of plastic*) Beutel, *der;* (*small paper ~*) Tüte, *die;* **a ~ of cement** ein Sack Zement; **~ and baggage** (*fig.*) mit Sack und Pack; **be a ~ of bones** (*fig.*) nur Haut und Knochen sein; **[whole] ~ of tricks** (*fig.*) Trickkiste, *die* (*ugs.*); **have exhausted one's [whole] ~ of tricks** sein Pulver verschossen haben (*ugs.*); **leave sb. holding the ~** (*Amer. fig.*) jmdm. den schwarzen Peter zuschieben; **his nomination is in the ~** (*fig. coll.*) er hat die Nominierung in der Tasche (*ugs.*); **freedom was as good as in the ~** (*coll.*) die Freiheit war so gut wie gewonnen; ⇒ *also* **cat** A; **mixed ~;** Ⓑ (*Hunting: amount of game*) Jagdbeute, *die;* Strecke, *die* (*Jägerspr.*); **make** *or* **secure a good ~** (*lit. or fig.*) reiche Jagdbeute/(*fig.*) Beute machen; Ⓒ *in pl.* (*coll.: large amount*) **~s of** jede Menge (*ugs.*); Ⓓ *in pl.* (*Brit. dated: trousers*) Hose, *die;* Ⓔ (*puffiness*) **have ~s under** *or* **below one's eyes** Tränensäcke haben; Ⓕ (*sl. derog.: woman*) **[old] ~:** alte Schlampe (*ugs. abwertend*); Ⓖ (*coll.: current interest, activity*) **what's your ~?** auf was stehst du [zur Zeit]? (*ugs.*).

❷ *v.t.*, **-gg-** Ⓐ (*put in sacks*) in Säcke füllen; einsacken (*fachspr.*); (*put in plastic ~s*) in Beutel füllen; (*put in small paper ~s*) in Tüten füllen; eintüten (*fachspr.*); Ⓑ (*Hunting*) erlegen, erbeuten ‹Tier›; Ⓒ (*claim possession of*) sich (*Dat.*) schnappen (*ugs.*); (*euphem.: steal*) klauen (*ugs.*); (*Brit. Sch. coll.: claim*) **~s I go first!** erster!

**bagatelle** /bægəˈtel/ *n.* Ⓐ (*trifle*) Nebensächlichkeit, *die;* Ⓑ (*Mus.*) Bagatelle, *die* (*fachspr.*); kurzes Musikstück

**bagel** /ˈbeɪgl/ *n. hartes, ringförmiges Hefegebäck*

**bagful** /ˈbægfʊl/ *n.* ⇒ **bag** 1 A: **a ~ of** ein Sack [voll]/eine Tasche/ein Beutel/eine Tüte [voll]

**baggage** /ˈbægɪdʒ/ *n.* Ⓐ Gepäck, *das;* **mental/cultural ~** (*fig.*) geistiges/kulturelles Rüstzeug; ⇒ *also* **bag** 1 A; Ⓑ (*Mil.*) Gepäck, *das;* Ⓒ (*joc.: woman*) Flittchen, *das* (*abwertend*); (*saucy girl*) Fratz, *der* (*ugs.*)

**baggage: ~ allowance** *n.* Freigepäck, *das;* **be over/within one's ~ allowance** Übergepäck/kein Übergepäck haben; **~ car** *n.* (*Amer.*) Gepäckwagen, *der;* **~ check** *n.* Gepäckkontrolle, *die;* (*Amer.: ticket*) Gepäckschein, *der;* **~ handler** *n.* Gepäckverlader, *der*/Gepäckverladerin, *die;* **~ handling** *n.* Gepäckverladung, *die; attrib.* Gepäckverladungs-; **~ reclaim** *n.* Gepäckausgabe, *die;* **~ room** *n.* (*Amer.*) Gepäckaufbewahrung, *die;* **~ tag** *n.* (*Amer.*) Kofferanhänger, *der*

**bagginess** /ˈbægɪnɪs/ *n., no pl.* Schlaffheit, *die;* **the ~ of these old trousers** die Ausgebeultheit dieser alten Hose

**baggy** /ˈbægɪ/ *adj.* weit [geschnitten] ‹Kleid›; schlaff [herabhängend] ‹Haut›; (*through long use*) ausgebeult ‹Hose›

**Baghdad** /bægˈdæd/ *pr. n.* ▶ **1626** Bagdad (*das*)

**bag: ~pipe** *adj.* Dudelsack-; **~pipe[s]** *n.* Dudelsack, *der;* **~piper** *n.* Dudelsackpfeifer, *der*

**baguette** /bæˈget/ *n.* Baguette, *die;* [französisches] Stangenweißbrot

**bah** /bɑː/ *int.* bah

**Bahamas** /bəˈhɑːməz/ *pr. n. pl.* **the ~:** die Bahamainseln

**Bahamian** /bəˈheɪːmɪən/ ❶ *adj.* bahamisch. ❷ *n.* Bahamer, *der*/Bahamerin, *die*

**bail**[1] /beɪl/ ❶ *n.* Ⓐ Sicherheitsleistung, *die* (*Rechtsw.*); (*financial*) Kaution, *die;* (*personal*) Bürgschaft, *die;* **grant sb. ~:** jmdm. die Freilassung gegen Kaution bewilligen; **give sb. ~ on payment of the sum of ...:** jmdn. gegen eine Kaution in Höhe von ... freilassen; **be [out] on ~:** gegen Kaution auf freiem Fuß sein; **the judge refused ~ to the accused** der Richter lehnte es ab, den Angeklagten gegen Kaution freizulassen; **put** *or* **release sb. on ~:** jmdn. gegen Kaution freilassen; **forfeit one's** *or* (*coll.*) **jump** *or* (*coll.*) **skip [one's] ~:** die Kaution verfallen lassen [und nicht vor Gericht erscheinen]; Ⓑ (*person[s] acting as surety*) Bürge, *der;* **go ~ for sb.** für jmdn. Bürge sein; **go ~ for sb./sth.** (*fig.*) für jmdn./etw. bürgen *od.* geradestehen.

❷ *v.t.* Ⓐ (*entrust*) anvertrauen; Ⓑ (*release*) gegen Kaution freilassen; Ⓒ (*go ~ for*) bürgen für; **~ sb. out** jmdn. gegen Bürgschaft freibekommen; (*fig.*) jmdn. aus der Klemme helfen (*ugs.*)

**bail**[2] *n.* (*Cricket*) Querstab, *der*

**bail**[3] *v.t.* (*scoop*) **~ [out]** ausschöpfen

**~ out** *v.i.* (*Aeronaut.*) ‹Pilot:› abspringen *od.* (*Fliegerspr.*) aussteigen

**bailey** /ˈbeɪlɪ/ *n.* (*wall*) Burgmauer, *die;* (*outer court*) Zwinger, *der;* (*inner court*) Burghof, *der;* **the Old B~:** das Old Bailey (*oberster Strafgerichtshof für London*)

ˈ**Bailey bridge** *n.* Bailey-Brücke, *die* (*Brücke aus vorgefertigten Teilen, die in kurzer Zeit errichtet werden kann*)

**bailiff** /ˈbeɪlɪf/ *n.* ▶ **1261** Ⓐ ≈ Justizbeamte, *der;* Büttel, *der* (*veralt.*); (*performing distraints*) Gerichtsvollzieher, *der;* (*serving writs*) Gerichtsbote, *der* (*veralt.*); Ⓑ (*agent of landlord*) Verwalter, *der;* Vogt, *der* (*hist.*); Ⓒ (*Amer. Admin.: court official*) ≈ Gerichtsbeamte, *der*

**bailiwick** /ˈbeɪlɪwɪk/ *n.* Ⓐ (*Hist.*) Amtsbezirk eines Bailiffs; Vogtei, *die;* Ⓑ (*joc.*) Reich, *das* (*fig.*)

**bairn** /beən/ *n.* (*Scot./N. Engl./literary*) Kind, *das*

**bait**[1] /beɪt/ ❶ *v.t.* Ⓐ mit einem Köder versehen ‹Falle›; beködern ‹Angelhaken›; Ⓑ (*torment with dogs*) **~ sth. [with dogs]** die Hunde auf etw. (*Akk.*) hetzen; **the badger was ~ed to death** der Dachs wurde von den Hunden totgebissen; Ⓒ (*fig.: torment*) herumhacken auf (+ *Dat.*) (*ugs.*); (*in playful manner*) necken; **~ sb. with questions** jmdn. mit Fragen zusetzen (*ugs.*). ❷ *n.* (*lit. or fig.*) Köder, *der;* **live ~:** lebender Köder; **rise to** *or* **take the ~** (*fig.*) anbeißen

**bait**[2] ⇒ **bate**[2]

**baize** /beɪz/ *n.* (*Textiles*) Fries, *der*

**bake** /beɪk/ ❶ *v.t.* Ⓐ (*cook*) backen; **~d apple** Bratapfel, *der;* **~d beans** gebackene Bohnen [in Tomatensoße]; **~d potato** [in der Schale] gebackene Kartoffel; Ⓑ (*harden*) brennen ‹Ziegel, Keramik›; ausdörren ‹Erde, Boden, Land›. ❷ *v.i.* Ⓐ backen; gebacken werden; (*fig.: be hot*) **I'm baking!** mir ist wahnsinnig heiß! (*ugs.*); Ⓑ (*be hardened*) ‹Ziegel, Keramik:›

gebrannt werden; ‹Boden, Erde:› ausdorren. ❸ *n.* (*Amer.: party*) Party [, bei der Gebackenes gegessen wird]

**bake: ~apple** *n.* (*Can.*) [getrocknete] Moltebeere; **~house** *n.* Backstube, *die*

**bakelite** /ˈbeɪkəlaɪt/ *n.* Bakelit, *das*

**baker** /ˈbeɪkə(r)/ *n.* ▶ 1261 Bäcker, *der;* **at the ~'s** beim Bäcker; in der Bäckerei; **go to the ~'s** zum Bäcker *od.* zur Bäckerei gehen; **a ~'s dozen** 13 Stück

**bakery** /ˈbeɪkərɪ/ *n.* Bäckerei, *die*

**baking** /ˈbeɪkɪŋ/ *adv.* **it's ~ hot today, isn't it?** eine Hitze wie im Backofen ist das heute, nicht wahr?

**baking: ~ dish** *n.* Auflaufform, *die;* **~ powder** *n.* Backpulver, *das;* **~ sheet** *n.* Backblech, *das;* **~ soda** *n.* Natron, *das;* **~ tin** *n.* Backform, *die;* **~ tray** *n.* Kuchenblech, *das*

**Balaclava** /bæləˈklɑːvə/ *n.* **~ [helmet]** Balaklavamütze, *die* (*Wollmütze, die Kopf und Hals bedeckt und nur das Gesicht frei lässt*)

**balalaika** /bæləˈlaɪkə/ *n.* Balalaika, *die*

**balance** /ˈbæləns/ ❶ *n.* A (*instrument*) Waage, *die;* **~ [wheel]** Unruh, *die;* B **the B~** (*Astrol.*) die Waage; ⇨ *also* **archer** B; C (*fig.*) **be** *or* **hang in the ~:** in der Schwebe sein; **the prisoners' lives are in the ~:** das Leben der Gefangenen ist bedroht; D (*even distribution*) Gleichgewicht, *das;* (*correspondence*) Übereinstimmung, *die;* (*due proportion*) ausgewogenes Verhältnis; (*Art: harmony*) Ausgewogenheit, *die;* **strike a ~ between** den Mittelweg finden zwischen (+ *Dat.*); **the ~ of sb.'s mind** jmds. seelisches Gleichgewicht; **~ of power** ⇨ **power** 1 F; E (*counterpoise*) Gegengewicht, *das;* Ausgleich, *der;* F (*steady position*) Gleichgewicht, *das;* **keep/lose one's ~:** das Gleichgewicht halten/verlieren; (*fig.*) sein Gleichgewicht bewahren/verlieren; **off [one's] ~** (*lit. or fig.*) aus dem Gleichgewicht; **throw sb. off [his] ~** (*lit. or fig.*) jmdn. aus dem Gleichgewicht werfen; G (*preponderating weight or amount*) Bilanz, *die;* **the ~ of evidence appears to be in his favour** die Beweise scheinen zu seinen Gunsten zu überwiegen; H (*Bookk.: difference*) Bilanz, *die;* (*state of bank account*) Kontostand, *der;* (*statement*) Auszug, *der;* **on ~** (*fig.*) alles in allem; **~ sheet** Bilanz, *die;* I (*Econ.*) **~ of payments** Zahlungsbilanz, *die;* **~ of trade** Handelsbilanz, *die;* J (*surplus amount*) **~ [in hand]** Überschuss, *der;* **you may keep the ~:** der Rest ist für Sie; K (*remainder*) Rest, *der.*
❷ *v.t.* A (*weigh up*) abwägen; **~ sth. with** *or* **by** *or* **against sth. else** etw. gegen etw. anderes abwägen; B (*bring into or keep in ~*) balancieren; auswuchten ‹Rad›; **~ oneself** balancieren; C (*equal, neutralize*) ausgleichen; **~ each other, be ~d** sich (*Dat.*) die Waage halten; D (*make up for, exclude dominance of*) ausgleichen; E (*Bookk.*) bilanzieren.
❸ *v.i.* A (*be in equilibrium*) balancieren; **do these scales ~?** ist diese Waage im Gleichgewicht?; **balancing act** (*lit. or fig.*) Balanceakt, *der;* B (*Bookk.*) ausgeglichen sein; bilanzieren (*Kaufmannsspr.*)

**balanced** /ˈbælənst/ *adj.* ausgewogen; ausgeglichen ‹Person, Team, Gemüt›

**Balaton** /ˈbælətɒn/ *pr. n.* **Lake ~:** der Plattensee; der Balaton (*DDR*)

**balcony** /ˈbælkənɪ/ *n.* Balkon, *der;* (*Amer. Theatre: dress circle*) erster Rang

**bald** /bɔːld/ *adj.* A kahl ‹Person, Kopf›; kahlköpfig, glatzköpfig ‹Person›; **he is ~:** er ist kahl[köpfig] *od.* hat eine Glatze; **go ~:** eine Glatze bekommen; B (*plain*) einfach, schmucklos ‹Stil, Rede, Prosa›; schlicht ‹Appell›; knapp, nackt ‹Behauptung›; C (*coll.: worn smooth*) abgefahren ‹Reifen›

**'bald eagle** *n.* Weißkopf-Seeadler, *der*

**balderdash** /ˈbɔːldədæʃ/ *n.*, *no pl.*, *no indef. art.* A Unsinn, *der;* dummes Zeug (*ugs.*); B (*jumble of words*) Wortsalat, *der*

**bald: ~head** *n.* A kahlköpfiger *od.* glatzköpfiger Mensch; Kahlkopf, *der* (*ugs.*); Glatzkopf, *der* (*ugs.*); B (*Ornith.*) Amerikanische Pfeifente; **~-headed** *adj.* glatzköpfig; kahlköpfig

**balding** /ˈbɔːldɪŋ/ *adj.* mit beginnender Glatze *nachgestellt;* **be ~:** kahl werden

**baldly** /ˈbɔːldlɪ/ *adv.* unverhüllt; offen; knapp und klar ‹zusammenfassen, umreißen›; **simply and ~:** schlicht und einfach; **to put it ~:** um es geradeheraus zu sagen

**baldness** /ˈbɔːldnɪs/ *n.*, *no pl.* ⇨ **bald** A, B: Kahlheit, *die;* Einfachheit, *die;* Schlichtheit, *die;* Knappheit, *die*

**'baldpate** ⇨ **baldhead**

**baldric** /ˈbɔːldrɪk/ *n.* (*Hist.*) Bandelier, *das*

**bale**[1] /beɪl/ ❶ *n.* Ballen, *der.* ❷ *v.t.* (*pack*) in Ballen verpacken; zu Ballen binden ‹Heu›

**bale**[2] *n.* (*arch./poet.*) A (*evil*) Unheil, *das* (*geh.*); B (*woe*) Elend, *das*

**bale**[3] ⇨ **bail**[3]

**Balearic Islands** /bælɪˈærɪk aɪləndz/ *pr. n. pl.* Balearen *Pl.*

**baleful** /ˈbeɪlfl/ *adj.* unheilvoll; (*malignant*) böse

**balefully** /ˈbeɪlfəlɪ/ *adv.* unheilvoll; (*malignantly*) böse

**balk** /bɔːk, bɔːlk/ ❶ *n.* A (*ridge*) Rain, *der;* B (*timber beam*) Balken, *der;* C (*tie beam*) Binderbalken, *der* (*Bauw.*); ≈ Dachbalken, *der;* D (*hindrance*) Hindernis, *das* (**to** für); E *no indef. art.* (*Billiards*) *markierte Fläche auf dem Billardtisch, wo die Kugel nicht direkt gespielt werden darf;* F (*Baseball*) *Art Foul des Werfers.*
❷ *v.t.* A [be]hindern; **they were ~ed in their plan/undertaking** *etc.* ihr Plan/Unternehmen *usw.* wurde blockiert; **they were ~ed of their prey** sie wurden um ihre Beute gebracht; B (*avoid*) ausweichen (+ *Dat.*) ‹Person, Gespräch›; sich entziehen (+ *Dat.*) ‹Verantwortung, Aufgabe, Gespräch›.
❸ *v.i.* sich sträuben (**at** gegen); ‹Pferd:› scheuen (**at** vor + *Dat.*)

**Balkan** /ˈbɔːlkn/ ❶ *adj.* Balkan-. ❷ *n. pl.* **the ~s** der Balkan; die Balkanländer

**Balkanize** /ˈbɔːlkənaɪz/ *v.t.* balkanisieren

**ball**[1] /bɔːl/ ❶ *n.* A Kugel, *die;* **the animal rolled itself into a ~:** das Tier rollte sich [zu einer Kugel] zusammen; B (*Sport, incl. Golf, Polo*) Ball, *der;* (*Billiards etc., Croquet*) Kugel, *die;* **the ~ is in your court** (*fig.*) jetzt bist du am Zug (*fig.*); **have the ~ at one's feet** (*fig.*) alle Möglichkeiten *od.* Chancen haben; **keep one's eye on the ~** (*fig.*) die Sache im Auge behalten; **keep the ~ rolling** (*fig.*) die Sache in Schwung halten; **start the ~ rolling** (*fig.*) den Anfang machen; **be on the ~** (*fig. coll.*) voll da sein (*salopp*); (*be alert*) auf Zack sein (*ugs.*); **play ~:** Ball spielen; (*fig. coll.: cooperate*) mitmachen; **play ~ with sb.** mit jmdm. Ball spielen; (*fig. coll.: cooperate*) mit jmdm. zusammenarbeiten; C (*missile*) Kugel, *die;* D (*round mass*) Kugel, *die;* (*of wool, string, fluff, etc.*) Knäuel, *das;* **two ~s of wool** zwei Wollknäuel *od.* Knäuel Wolle; **~ of clay** Lehmklumpen, *der;* E (*Anat.: rounded part*) Ballen, *der;* **~ of the hand/foot** Hand-/Fußballen, *der;* F *in pl.* (*coarse: testicles*) Eier *Pl.* (*derb*); **~s!** (*fig.*) Scheiß! (*salopp abwertend*); *constr. as sing.* **make a ~s of sth.** (*fig.*) bei etw. Scheiße bauen (*derb*).
❷ *v.t.* zusammenballen; zerknüllen ‹Papier›; ballen ‹Faust›

**~ 'up** (*Brit.*) *see* **balls up**

**ball**[2] *n.* (*dance*) Ball, *der;* **give a ~:** einen Ball geben *od.* veranstalten; **have [oneself] a ~** (*fig. coll.*) sich riesig amüsieren (*ugs.*); **open the ~:** den Ball eröffnen; (*fig.*) den Tanz beginnen

**ballad** /ˈbæləd/ *n.* A Lied, *das;* (*narrative*) Ballade, *die;* Lied, *das;* B (*poem*) Ballade, *die*

**balladry** /ˈbælədrɪ/ *n.* Balladendichtung, *die*

**ball and 'socket joint** *n.* Kugelgelenk, *das*

**ballast** /ˈbæləst/ *n.* A Ballast, *der;* **be in ~:** auf Ballastfahrt sein (*Seemannsspr.*); B (*fig.: sth. that gives stability*) stabilisierender Faktor; C (*coarse stone etc.*) Schotter, *der*

**ball: ~ 'bearing** *n.* (*Mech.*) Kugellager, *das;* **~boy** *n.* Balljunge, *der;* **~ clay** *n.* (*Amer. Min.*) Pfeifenton, *der;* **~cock** *n.* Schwimmer[regel]ventil, *das* (*Technik*); **~ control** *n.* Ballführung, *die*

**ballerina** /bæləˈriːnə/ *n.* ▶ 1261 Ballerina, *die;* **prima ~:** Primaballerina, *die*

**ballet** /ˈbæleɪ/ *n.* Ballett, *das;* **~ dancer** Balletttänzer, *der*/-tänzerin, *die*

**ball: ~ game** *n.* A Ballspiel, *das;* B (*Amer.*) Baseballspiel, *das;* **a whole new ~ game** (*fig. coll.*) eine ganz neue Geschichte (*ugs.*); **a different ~ game** (*fig. coll.*) eine andere Sache; **~girl** *n.* Ballmädchen, *das*

**ballistic** /bəˈlɪstɪk/ *adj.* ballistisch; **~ missile** ballistische Rakete; **go ~** (*fig. coll.*) ausrasten (*salopp*)

**ballistics** /bəˈlɪstɪks/ *n.*, *no pl.* Ballistik, *die*

**ball: ~ joint** ⇨ **ball and socket joint**; **~ lightning** *n.* Kugelblitz, *der*

**balloon** /bəˈluːn/ ❶ *n.* A Ballon, *der;* **hot-air ~:** Heißluftballon, *der;* **when the ~ goes up** (*fig.*) wenn es losgeht (*ugs.*); B (*toy*) Luftballon, *der;* C (*coll.: in strip cartoon etc.*) Sprechblase, *die;* D (*drinking glass*) Schwenker, *der;* Schwenkglas, *das.* ❷ *v.i.* A sich blähen; B (*travel in ~*) im Ballon fahren. ❸ *v.t.* (*hit, kick*) hoch in die Luft schlagen

**balloon 'tyre** *n.* Ballonreifen, *der*

**ballot** /ˈbælət/ ❶ *n.* A (*voting*) Abstimmung, *die;* **[secret] ~:** geheime Wahl; **hold** *or* **take a ~:** abstimmen; B (*vote*) Stimme, *die;* **cast one's ~:** seine Stimme abgeben; C (*ticket, paper*) Stimmzettel, *der.* ❷ *v.i.* abstimmen; **~ for sb./sth.** für jmdn./etw. stimmen. ❸ *v.t.* abstimmen lassen; eine Abstimmung vornehmen bei

**ballot: ~ box** *n.* Wahlurne, *die;* **~ paper** *n.* Stimmzettel, *der*

**ball: ~park** *n.* (*Amer.*) Baseballfeld, *das;* **your estimate is not in the right ~park** (*fig.*) mit deiner Schätzung liegst du völlig falsch (*ugs.*); **~ pen, ~point, ~point 'pen** *ns.* Kugelschreiber, *der;* **~room** *n.* Tanzsaal, *der;* **~room dancing** *n.* Gesellschaftstanz, *der*

**balls 'up** *v.t.* (*coarse*) Scheiße bauen bei (*derb*)

**balls-up** /ˈbɔːlzʌp/ (*coarse*) *n.* Scheiß, *der* (*salopp abwertend*); **make a ~ of sth.** bei etw. Scheiße bauen (*derb*)

**'ball-tampering** *n.*, *no pl.*: *die Manipulierung der Balloberfläche beim Kricketspiel*

**bally** /ˈbælɪ/ (*Brit. dated euphem.*) *adj.*, *adv.* verdammt (*salopp*)

**ballyhoo** /bælɪˈhuː/ *n.* A (*publicity*) [Reklame]rummel, *der* (*ugs.*); **create a great deal of ~ over sth.** einen großen Rummel um etw. veranstalten (*ugs.*); B (*nonsense*) Geschrei, *das* (*abwertend*)

**balm** /bɑːm/ *n.* A (*lit. or fig.*) Balsam, *der;* B (*fragrance*) [aromatischer] Duft; C (*tree*) Balsambaum, *der;* D (*herb*) Melisse, *die;* **~ of Gilead** Gileadbalsam, *der*

**balmy** /ˈbɑːmɪ/ *adj.* A (*yielding balm*) Balsam liefernd; B (*fragrant*) wohlriechend; balsamisch (*geh.*); C (*soft, mild*) mild; D (*coll.: crazy*) bescheuert (*salopp*); E (*soothing, healing*) lindernd

**baloney** ⇨ **boloney** A

**balsa** /ˈbɔːlsə, ˈbɒlsə/ *n.* A (*tree*) Balsabaum, *der;* B (*wood*) **~[ wood]** Balsaholz, *das*

**balsam** /ˈbɔːlsəm, ˈbɒlsəm/ *n.* A (*lit. or fig.; also Med., Chem.*) Balsam, *der;* **Canada ~:** Kanadabalsam, *der;* B (*tree*) Balsambaum, *der;* C (*plant of genus Impatiens*) Springkraut, *das;* (*garden flower*) Gartenbalsamine, *die;* (*touch-me-not*) Rührmichnichtan, *das*

**balsam 'fir** *n.* Balsamtanne, *die*

**balsamic vinegar** /bælsæmɪk ˈvɪnɪgə(r)/ *n.* Balsamessig, *der*

**Balt** /bɔːlt, bɒlt/ *n.* Balte, *der*/Baltin, *die*

**Baltic** /ˈbɔːltɪk, ˈbɒltɪk/ ❶ *pr. n.* Ostsee, *die.* ❷ *adj.* baltisch; **~ coast** Ostseeküste, *die;* **the ~ Sea** die Ostsee; **the ~ States** das Baltikum

**baluster** /ˈbæləstə(r)/ *n.* A (*pillar*) Baluster, *der;* Docke, *die;* B (*post*) Geländerpfosten, *der;* (*balustrade*) Balustrade, *die*

**balustrade** /bæləˈstreɪd/ *n.* Balustrade, *die*

**bamboo** /bæmˈbuː/ *n.* A (*stem*) Bambus, *der;* Bambusrohr, *das;* B (*grass*) Bambus, *der;* **~ curtain** (*Polit.*) Bambusvorhang, *der;* **~ shoots** Bambussprossen

**bamboozle** /bæm'bu:zl/ *v.t.* (*coll.*) **A** (*mystify*) verblüffen; **B** (*cheat*) reinlegen (*ugs.*); **～ sb. into doing sth.** jmdn. [durch Tricks] dazu bringen, etw. zu tun; jmdn. so reinlegen, dass er etw. tut; **～ sb. out of sth.** jmdm. etw. abluchsen (*salopp*)

**ban** /bæn/ **1** *v.t.*, **-nn-** verbieten; **～ sb. from doing sth.** jmdm. verbieten, etw. zu tun; **he was ～ned from driving/playing** er erhielt Fahr-/Spielverbot; **～ sb. from a place** jmdm. die Einreise/den Zutritt *usw.* verbieten; **～ sb. from a pub/the teaching profession** jmdm. Lokalverbot erteilen/jmdn. vom Lehrberuf ausschließen. **2** *n.* Verbot, *das;* **place a ～ on sth.** etw. mit einem Verbot belegen; **the ～ placed on these drugs** das Verbot dieser Drogen; **lift the ～ on sth.** das Verbot einer Sache (*Gen.*) aufheben

**banal** /bə'nɑ:l, bə'næl/ *adj.* banal

**banality** /bə'nælɪtɪ/ *n.* Banalität, *die*

**banana** /bə'nɑ:nə/ *n.* **A** (*fruit*) Banane, *die;* **a hand of ～s** eine Hand Bananen (*fachspr.*); **go ～s** (*Brit. coll.*) verrückt werden (*salopp*); überschnappen (*ugs.*); **B** (*plant*) Bananenstaude, *die*

**banana: ～ republic** *n.* (*derog.*) Bananenrepublik, *die* (*abwertend*); **～ skin** *n.* Bananenschale, *die;* **～ 'split** *n.* Bananensplit, *das*

**band** /bænd/ **1** *n.* **A** Band, *das;* **a ～ of light/colour** ein Streifen Licht/Farbe; **B** (*range of values*) Bandbreite, *die* (*fig.*); **income ～:** ≈ Gehaltsstufe, *die;* **C** (*of frequency or wavelength*) **long/medium ～:** Langwellen-/Mittelwellenband, *das;* **high-frequency ～:** Hochfrequenzbereich, *der;* **D** (*organized group*) Gruppe, *die;* (*of robbers, outlaws, etc.*) Bande, *die;* **B～ of Hope** *Organisation jugendlicher Abstinenzler;* **E** (*of musicians*) [Musik]kapelle, *die;* (*pop group, jazz ～*) Band, *die;* Gruppe, *die;* (*dance ～*) [Tanz]kapelle, *die;* (*military ～*) Militärkapelle, *die;* (*brass ～*) Blaskapelle, *die;* **if or when the ～ begins to play** (*fig. coll.*) wenn es ernst wird; **F** *in pl.* (*part of legal, clerical, or academic dress*) Beffchen, *das;* **G** (*ring round bird's leg*) Beringung, *die;* **H** (*Amer.*) (*herd*) Herde, *die;* (*of birds, insects*) Schwarm, *der;* **I** *in pl.* (*arch.: sth. that restrains*) Bande *Pl.* ⇒ *also* **beat** 1 D.
**2** *v.t.* **A ～ sth.** ein Band um etw. machen; **B** (*form into a league*) vereinigen; **C** (*mark with stripes*) bändern; **～ed** (*Biol.*) Streifen-; gestreift.
**3** *v.i.* **～ together [with sb.]** sich [mit jmdm.] zusammenschließen

**bandage** /'bændɪdʒ/ **1** *n.* (*for wound, fracture*) Verband, *der;* (*for fracture, as support*) Bandage, *die;* (*for blindfolding*) Binde, *die.* **2** *v.t.* verbinden ‹[offene] Wunde usw.›; bandagieren ‹[verstauchtes] Gelenk usw.›

**'Band Aid** ® *n.* ≈ Hansaplast ⓌⓏ, *das*

**b. & b.** /bi: ən 'bi:/ *abbr.* **bed & breakfast**

**'bandbox** *n.* Bandschachtel, *die* (*veralt.*); ≈ Hutschachtel, *die*

**bandicoot** /'bændɪku:t/ *n.* **A** (*Ind.: rat*) Bandikutratte, *die;* **B** (*Austral.: marsupial*) Bandikut, *der;* Beuteldachs, *der*

**bandit** /'bændɪt/ *n.* Bandit, *der*

**banditry** /'bændɪtrɪ/ *n.* Banditen[un]wesen, *das*

**'bandmaster** *n.* Kapellmeister, *der*

**bandoleer, bandolier** /bændə'lɪə(r)/ *n.* Schultergürtel, *der;* Bandelier, *das* (*veralt.*)

**'bandsaw** *n.* Bandsäge, *die*

**bandsman** /'bændzmən/ *n., pl.* **bandsmen** /'bændzmən/ Mitglied der/einer Kapelle/Band

**band: ～stand** *n.* Musikertribüne, *die;* (*circular*) Konzertpavillon, *der;* **～wagon** *n.* Wagen der Musikkapelle; **climb or jump on [to] the ～wagon** (*fig.*) auf den fahrenden Zug aufspringen (*fig.*); **～width** *n.* (*Communications*) Bandbreite, *die*

**bandy**[1] /'bændɪ/ *v.t.* **A** (*toss to and fro*) hin- und herspielen; **B** (*fig.*) herumerzählen (*ugs.*) ‹Geschichte›; **be bandied from mouth to mouth** von Mund zu Mund gehen; **insults were being bandied about** Beschimpfungen flogen hin und her; **C** (*discuss*) **～ about** hin und her diskutieren; **D** (*exchange*) wechseln; **they were ～ing blows** sie tauschten Schläge aus; **don't ～ words with me** ich wünsche keine Diskussion

**bandy**[2] *adj.* krumm; **he has ～ legs or is ～-legged** er hat O-Beine (*ugs.*); **～-legged person** o-beinige Person (*ugs.*)

**bane** /beɪn/ *n.* Ruin, *der;* **he is the ～ of my life** er ist der Nagel zu meinem Sarg (*ugs.*)

**bang**[1] /bæŋ/ **1** *v.t.* **A** knallen (*ugs.*); schlagen; zuknallen (*ugs.*), zuschlagen ‹Tür, Fenster, Deckel›; **～ one's head on or against the ceiling** mit dem Kopf an die Decke knallen (*ugs.*) *od.* schlagen; **I could ～ their heads together** (*fig.*) ich könnte ihre Köpfe gegeneinander schlagen; **she ～ed down the receiver** sie knallte den Hörer auf die Gabel (*ugs.*); **he ～ed the nail in** er haute den Nagel rein (*ugs.*); ⇒ *also* **brick wall**; **B** (*sl.: copulate with*) bumsen (*salopp*).
**2** *v.i.* **A** (*strike*) **～ [against sth.]** [gegen etw.] schlagen *od.* (*ugs.*) knallen; **～ at the door** gegen die Tür hämmern; **B** (*make sound of blow or explosion*) knallen; ‹Kanonen:› donnern; ‹Trommeln:› dröhnen; **～ away at sth.** auf etw. (*Akk.*) ballern (*ugs.*); **～ shut** zuknallen (*ugs.*); zuschlagen; **a door is ～ing somewhere** irgendwo schlägt eine Tür.
**3** *n.* **A** (*blow*) Schlag, *der;* **give your radio a good ～:** hau mal kräftig gegen dein Radio (*ugs.*); **B** (*noise*) Knall, *der;* **the party went off with a ～** (*fig.*) die Party war eine Wucht (*ugs.*). ⇒ *also* **big bang**; **whimper** 1.
**4** *adv.* **A** (*with impact*) mit voller Wucht; **B** (*explosively*) **go ～** ‹Gewehr, Feuerwerkskörper:› krachen; **the balloon went ～ and exploded** der Ballon explodierte mit einem lauten Knall; **C ～ goes sth.** (*fig.: sth. ends suddenly*) aus ist es mit etw.; **～ went £50** 50 Pfund waren weg; **D ～ off** (*coll.: immediately*) sofort; **answer ～ off** wie aus der Pistole geschossen antworten (*ugs.*); **E** (*coll.: exactly*) genau; **you are ～ on time** du bist pünktlich auf die Minute (*ugs.*); **～ on [the] target** genau richtig; **～ on** genau *od.* gerade; **F ～-up** (*Amer. coll.: first-class*) Klasse (*ugs.*).
**5** *int.* peng

**bang**[2] **1** *v.t.* (*esp. Amer.*) gerade abschneiden ‹Haare›. **2** *n. inpl.* (*esp. Amer.: fringe*) Pony, *der*

**banger** /'bæŋə(r)/ *n.* (*coll.*) **A** (*sausage*) Würstchen, *das;* **B** (*firework*) Kracher, *der* (*ugs.*); **C** (*car*) Klapperkiste, *die* (*ugs.*)

**Bangladesh** /bæŋglə'deʃ/ *pr. n.* Bangladesch (*das*)

**Bangladeshi** /bæŋglə'deʃɪ/ ▶ **1340** **1** *adj.* bangalisch. **2** *n.* Bangali, *der/die*

**bangle** /'bæŋgl/ *n.* Armreif, *der*

**banian** /'bænɪən/ *n.* (*Bot.*) **～[ tree]** Banyanbaum, *der*

**banish** /'bænɪʃ/ *v.t.* verbannen (**from** aus); bannen ‹Furcht›

**banishment** /'bænɪʃmənt/ *n.* Verbannung, *die* (**from** aus)

**banister** /'bænɪstə(r)/ *n.* **A** (*uprights and rail*) [Treppen]geländer, *das;* **B** *usu. in pl.* (*upright*) Geländerpfosten, *der*

**banjo** /'bændʒəʊ/ *n., pl.* **～s** *or* **～es** Banjo, *das*

**bank**[1] /bæŋk/ **1** *n.* **A** (*slope*) Böschung, *die;* **B** ▶ **1480** (*at side of river*) Ufer, *das;* **C** (*elevation in bed of sea or river*) Bank, *die;* **D** (*mass*) **a ～ of clouds/fog** eine Wolken-/Nebelbank; **a ～ of snow** eine Schneewehe; **E** (*artificial slope*) Überhöhung, *die* (*Verkehrsw.*). **2** *v.t.* **A** (*build higher*) überhöhen (*Verkehrsw.*); **B** (*heap*) **～ [up]** aufschichten; **～ [up] the fire with coal** Kohlen auf das Feuer schichten; **C** in die Kurve legen ‹Flugzeug›. **3** *v.i.* **A** (*rise*) **～ [up]** ‹Rauch, Wolken:› sich aufschichten; **B** ‹Flugzeug:› sich in die Kurve legen

**bank**[2] **1** *n.* **A** (*Commerc., Finance*) Bank, *die;* **central ～:** Zentralbank, *die;* **the B～** (*Brit.*) die Bank von England; **cry/laugh all the way to the ～** (*fig. coll.*) sich für seinen Erfolg entschuldigen (*iron.*)/aus seiner Freude über seinen Erfolg keinen Hehl machen; **B** (*Gaming*) Bank, *die;* ⇒ *also* **blood bank**; **bottle bank**. **2** *v.i.* **A** (*keep ～*) Bankier sein; **B** (*keep money*) **～ at/with ...:** ein Konto haben bei ...; **C ～ on sth.** (*fig.*) auf etw. (*Akk.*) zählen. **3** *v.t.* zur Bank bringen

**bank**[3] *n.* **A** (*row*) Reihe, *die;* **B** (*tier*) **～ [of oars]** Ruderreihe, *die*

**bankable** /'bæŋkəbl/ *adj.* bankfähig; (*fig.*) erfolgversprechend

**bank: ～ account** *n.* Bankkonto, *das;* **～ balance** *n.* Kontostand, *der;* **～ bill** *n.* (*Brit.*) Bankakzept, *der;* (*Amer.:* **～note**) Banknote, *die;* **～ book** *n.* Sparbuch, *das;* **～ card** *n.* Scheckkarte, *die;* **～ charges** *n. pl.* Kontoführungskosten *Pl.;* **～ clerk** *n.* ▶ **1261** Bankangestellte, *der/die;* **～ draft** *n.* Bankakzept, *das*

**banker** /'bæŋkə(r)/ *n.* ▶ **1261** (*Commerc., Finance*) Bankier, *der;* Banker, *der* (*ugs.*); **let me be your ～:** lassen Sie mich Ihnen Geld leihen

**banker's: ～ card** ⇒ **bank card**; **～ draft** ⇒ **～ draft**; **～ 'order** ⇒ **order** 1 O

**bank 'holiday** *n.* **A** Bankfeiertag, *der;* **B** (*Brit.: public holiday*) Feiertag, *der*

**banking** /'bæŋkɪŋ/ *n.* Bankwesen, *das;* **a career in ～:** die Banklaufbahn; *attrib.* **～ hours** Schalterstunden *Pl.;* Öffnungszeiten *Pl.* (*der Bank*); **it is ～ practice** es ist banküblich; **new ～ arrangements** neue Bankverhältnisse

**bank: ～ loan** *n.* Bankdarlehen, *das;* **take out a ～ loan** bei einer Bank einen Kredit *od.* ein Darlehen aufnehmen; **～ manager** *n.* ▶ **1261** Zweigstellenleiter [einer/der Bank]; **～note** *n.* Banknote, *die;* Geldschein, *der;* **～ raid** *n.* Banküberfall, *der;* **～ rate** *n.* Diskontsatz, *der;* **～ robber** *n.* Bankräuber, *der;* **～roll 1** *n.* finanzielle Mittel *Pl.;* **2** *v.t.* finanziell unterstützen

**bankrupt** /'bæŋkrʌpt/ **1** *n.* **A** (*Law*) Gemeinschuldner, *der;* **become a ～:** Gemeinschuldner werden; **be declared a ～:** zum Gemeinschuldner erklärt werden; **B** (*insolvent debtor*) Bankrotteur, *der.* **2** *adj.* **A** bankrott; **go ～:** in Konkurs gehen; Bankrott machen; bankrottieren (*veralt.*); **B** (*fig.*) **morally ～:** moralisch bankrott (*fig.*). **3** *v.t.* bankrott machen

**bankruptcy** /'bæŋkrʌptsɪ/ *n.* Konkurs, *der;* Bankrott, *der;* **go into ～:** in Konkurs gehen; Bankrott machen; **～ proceedings** Konkursverfahren, *das*

**bank: ～ statement** *n.* Kontoauszug, *der;* **～ transfer** *n.* Banküberweisung, *die*

**banner** /'bænə(r)/ **1** *n.* **A** (*flag, ensign; also fig.*) Banner, *das;* **join or follow the ～ of** dem Banner (+ *Gen.*) folgen; **B** (*on two poles*) Spruchband, *das;* Transparent, *das;* **C** (*sth. used as symbol*) Symbol, *das.* **2** *adj.* **A** (*conspicuous*) **～ headline** Balkenüberschrift, *die;* **B** (*Amer.: pre-eminent*) herausragend

**bannister** ⇒ **banister**

**bannock** /'bænək/ *n.* (*Scot., N. Engl.*) *rundes, flaches Brot*

**banns** /bænz/ *n. pl.* Aufgebot, *das;* **publish/put up the ～:** das Aufgebot verkünden/aushängen; **forbid the ～:** Einspruch [gegen die Eheschließung] erheben

**banquet** /'bæŋkwɪt/ **1** *n.* Bankett, *das* (*geh.*). **2** *v.i.* **A** [festlich] tafeln (*geh.*); bankettieren (*veralt.*); **～ing hall** Bankettsaal, *der;* **B** (*carouse*) zechen (*geh.*)

**banshee** /'bænʃi:/ *n.* (*Ir., Scot.*) Banshee, *die* (*Myth.*); ≈ Weiße Frau

**bantam** /'bæntəm/ *n.* Zwerg-, Bantamhuhn, *das*

**'bantamweight** *n.* (*Boxing etc.*) Bantamgewicht, *das;* (*person also*) Bantamgewichtler, *der*

**banter** /'bæntə(r)/ **1** *n.* **A** heiterer Spott; **B** (*remarks*) Spöttelei, *die* (**on** über + *Akk.*); (*joking back and forth*) spöttisches Geplänkel. **2** *v.t.* aufziehen (**about** mit). **3** *v.i.* spötteln

**Bantu** /bæn'tu:/ ❶ *n.* Ⓐ *pl. same or* **~s** Bantu, *der/die;* Ⓑ *(language group)* Bantu, *das;* Bantusprachen. ❷ *adj.* Bantu-

**Bantustan** /bæntʊ'stɑ:n/ *n.* (*S. Afr.*) Bantuheimatland, *das*

**banyan** ⇒ **banian**

**baobab** /'beɪəbæb/ *n.* (*Bot.*) Baobab, *der;* Affenbrotbaum, *der*

**BAOR** *abbr.* **British Army of the Rhine** Britische Rheinarmee

**bap** /bæp/ *n.* ≈ Brötchen, *das*

**baptise** ⇒ **baptize**

**baptism** /'bæptɪzm/ *n.* Taufe, *die;* **~ is the first sacrament** die Taufe ist das erste Sakrament; **~ of fire** (*fig.*) Feuertaufe, *die;* **~ of blood** (*fig.*) Bluttaufe, *die* (*Rel.*)

**baptismal** /bæp'tɪzml/ *adj.* Tauf-; ‹Wiedergeburt, Reinigung› durch die Taufe; **~ certificate** Taufschein, *der;* **~ name** Taufname, *der*

**Baptist** /'bæptɪst/ ❶ *n.* Ⓐ Baptist, *der*/Baptistin, *die;* Ⓑ **John the ~:** Johannes der Täufer. ❷ *adj.* **the ~ Church/a ~ chapel** die Kirche/eine Kapelle der Baptisten

**baptize** /bæp'taɪz/ *v.t.* taufen; **be ~d a Catholic/Protestant** katholisch/protestantisch getauft werden; **what name were you ~d by?** auf welchen Namen wurden Sie getauft?

**bar¹** /bɑ:(r)/ ❶ *n.* Ⓐ *(long piece of rigid material)* Stange, *die;* (*shorter, thinner also*) Stab, *der;* (*of gold, silver*) Barren, *der;* **a ~ of soap** ein Stück Seife; **a ~ of chocolate** ein Riegel Schokolade; (*slab*) eine Tafel Schokolade; Ⓑ *(Sport)* Stab, *der;* (*of high ~*) [Reck]stange, *die;* (*of parallel ~s*) [Barren]holm, *der;* (*cross~*) [Sprung]latte, *die;* **high** *or* **horizontal ~:** Reck, *das;* **parallel ~s** Barren, *der;* Ⓒ *(heating element)* Heizelement, *das* (*Elektrot.*); Ⓓ *(band)* Streifen, *der;* (*on medal*) silberner Querstreifen; (*Her.*) Balken, *der;* Ⓔ *(rod, pole)* Stange, *die;* (*of cage, prison*) Gitterstab, *der;* **behind ~s** (*in prison*) hinter Gittern; (*into prison*) hinter Gitter; Ⓕ *(barrier, lit. or fig.)* Barriere, *die* **(to** für); **a ~ on recruitment/promotion** ein Einstellungs-/Beförderungsstopp; Ⓖ *(for refreshment)* Bar, *die;* (*counter*) Theke, *die;* Ⓗ *(Law: place at which prisoner stands)* ≈ Anklagebank, *die;* **the prisoner at the ~:** der/die Angeklagte; **be judged at the ~ of conscience/of public opinion** (*fig.*) sich vor dem Gewissen/der öffentlichen Meinung verantworten müssen; Ⓘ *(Law: particular court)* Gerichtshof, *der;* **be called to the ~:** als Anwalt vor höheren Gerichten zugelassen werden; **be called within the ~:** zum Anwalt der Krone ernannt werden; **the B~:** die höhere Anwaltschaft; **the inner ~:** die Anwaltschaft der Krone; **the outer ~** *die Anwälte, die nicht Anwälte der Krone sind;* **he was reading for the ~:** er bereitete sich auf die Zulassung als Anwalt vor höheren Gerichten vor; Ⓙ *(Mus.)* Takt, *der;* **~[-line]** Taktstrich, *der;* Ⓚ *(sandbank, shoal)* Barre, *die;* Sandbank, *die.*

❷ *v.t.*, **-rr-:** Ⓐ *(fasten)* verriegeln; **~red window** vergittertes Fenster; Ⓑ *(keep)* **~ sb. in/out** jmdn. ein-/aussperren; Ⓒ *(obstruct)* sperren ‹Straße, Weg› **(to** für); **~ sb.'s way** jmdm. den Weg versperren; Ⓓ *(prohibit, hinder)* verbieten; **~ sb. from doing sth.** jmdn. daran hindern, etw. zu tun; Ⓔ *(not consider)* unberücksichtigt lassen; Ⓕ *(mark)* mit Streifen versehen; **~red [with colourful stripes]** [bunt]gestreift; **~red with brown** braun gestreift; Ⓖ *(Law)* ausschließen.

❸ *prep.* abgesehen von; **~ any accidents** falls nichts passiert; **~ none** ohne Einschränkung; **bet two to one ~ one** (*Racing*) zwei zu eins auf alle außer einem wetten

**bar²** *n.* (*Meteorol., Phys.*) Bar, *das*

**barb** /bɑ:b/ ❶ *n.* Ⓐ Widerhaken, *der;* (*fig.*) Gehässigkeit, *die;* **~s of ridicule** gehässige Spötteleien; Ⓑ *(of fish)* Bartfaden, *der;* Bartel, *die;* Ⓒ *(of feather)* Fahne, *die.* ❷ *v.t.* mit Widerhaken versehen

**Barbadian** /bɑ:'beɪdɪən/ ▶1340 ❶ *adj.* barbadisch; **sb. is ~:** jmd. ist Barbadier/Barbadierin. ❷ *n.* Barbadier, *der*/Barbadierin, *die*

**Barbados** /bɑ:'beɪdəʊz, bɑ:'beɪdɒs/ *pr. n.* Barbados (*das*)

**barbarian** /bɑ:'beərɪən/ ❶ *n.* (*lit. or fig.*) Barbar, *der.* ❷ *adj.* (*lit. or fig.*) barbarisch; **a ~ king** ein Barbarenkönig

**barbaric** /bɑ:'bærɪk/ *adj.* barbarisch; primitiv ‹Kleidung, Schmuck›

**barbarically** /bɑ:'bærɪkəlɪ/ *adv.* barbarisch

**barbarism** /'bɑ:bərɪzm/ *n.* Ⓐ *no pl.* Barbarei, *die;* (*rudeness also*) Unkultiviertheit, *die;* Ⓑ *no pl.* *(departing from normal standards)* Barbarismus, *der* (*Sprachw., Kunstwiss.*); Ⓒ *(instance)* [barbarische] Grausamkeit

**barbarity** /bɑ:'bærɪtɪ/ *n.* Ⓐ *no pl.* Grausamkeit, *die;* **he treats criminals with ~:** er behandelt Verbrecher äußerst barbarisch; Ⓑ *(instance)* Barbarei, *die*

**barbarous** /'bɑ:bərəs/ *adj.* barbarisch

**barbarously** /'bɑ:bərəslɪ/ *adv.* auf barbarische Art und Weise; barbarisch

**barbarousness** /'bɑ:bərəsnɪs/ *n., no pl.* Rohheit, *die*

**Barbary 'ape** *n.* (*Zool.*) Magot, *der;* Berberaffe, *der*

**barbecue** /'bɑ:bɪkju:/ ❶ *n.* Ⓐ *(party)* Grillparty, *die;* Barbecue, *das;* Ⓑ *(food)* Grillgericht, *das;* Barbecue, *das; attrib.* **~ sauce** Grillsoße, *die;* Barbecuesoße, *die;* Ⓒ *(fireplace with frame)* Grill, *der;* Ⓓ *(frame)* Grill, *der;* Bratrost, *der;* Barbecue, *das.* ❷ *v.t.* grillen

**barbed wire** /bɑ:bd 'waɪər/ *n.* Stacheldraht, *der;* **~ fence** Stacheldrahtzaun, *der*

**barbel** /'bɑ:bl/ *n.* Ⓐ *(Zool.)* Barbe, *die;* Ⓑ *(filament)* Bartfaden, *der;* Bartel, *der*

**'barbell** *n.* Hantel, *die*

**barber** /'bɑ:bə(r)/ *n.* ▶1261 Friseur, *der;* Barbier, *der* (*veralt.*); **go to the ~'s** zum Friseur gehen; **~'s pole** *spiralig rot und weiß gestreifter Stab als Ladenschild des Friseurs*

**barberry** /'bɑ:bərɪ/ *n.* Ⓐ *(shrub)* Berberitze, *die;* Sauerdorn, *der;* Ⓑ *(berry)* Berberitzenbeere, *die;* Sauerdornbeere, *die*

**barber: ~shop** *n.* (*Amer.*) **~shop harmony** Barbershopharmonie, *die; vokale Harmonik mit paralleler Stimmführung;* **~shop singing/quartet** Barbershopgesang, *der*/-quartett, *das;* **~'s shop** *n.* (*Brit.*) Friseursalon, *der*

**barbican** /'bɑ:bɪkən/ *n.* (*Hist.*) Barbakane, *die;* Torvorwerk, *das*

**barbiturate** /bɑ:'bɪtjʊrət/ *n.* (*Chem.*) Barbiturat, *das*

**barcarole** /bɑ:kə'rəʊl/, **barcarolle** /bɑ:kə'rɒl/ *n.* (*Mus.*) Barkarole, *die*

**Barcelona** /bɑ:sɪ'ləʊnə/ *pr. n.* ▶1626 Barcelona (*das*); **~ nut** Barcelonanuss, *die* (*eine Haselnusssorte*)

**bar: ~ chart** *n.* Stabdiagramm, *das;* **~ code** *n.* Strichcode, *der*

**bard** /bɑ:d/ *n.* Barde, *der;* **the B~ [of Avon]** Shakespeare

**bardic** /'bɑ:dɪk/ *adj.* bardisch (*veralt.*)

**bare** /beə(r)/ ❶ *adj.* Ⓐ nackt; **expose a ~ back to the sun** den nackten Rücken der Sonne aussetzen; **walk with** *or* **in ~ feet** barfuß gehen; **in one's ~ skin** nackt [und bloß]; Ⓑ *(hatless)* **with one's head ~:** ohne Hut; Ⓒ *(leafless)* kahl; Ⓓ *(unfurnished)* kahl; nackt ‹Boden›; Ⓔ *(unconcealed)* **lay ~ sth.** etw. aufdecken; Ⓕ *(unadorned)* nackt, ungeschminkt ‹Wahrheit, Tatsache›; grob ‹Skizze›; nackt, kahl ‹Wand›; ⇒ *also* **bone** 1 A; Ⓖ *(empty)* leer; Ⓗ *(scanty)* knapp ‹Mehrheit›; [sehr] gering ‹Menge, Teil›; Ⓘ *(mere)* äußerst ‹Notwendige›; karg ‹Essen, Leben›; nur geringe ‹Möglichkeit›; bloß ‹Gedanke›; **the ~ necessities of life** das zum Leben Notwendigste; Ⓙ *(without tools)* **do sth. with one's ~ hands** etw. mit den *od.* seinen bloßen Händen tun; Ⓚ *(unprovided with)* **~ of sth.** ohne etw.; **the land was ~ of any vegetation** das Land war völlig vegetationslos.
❷ *v.t.* Ⓐ *(uncover)* entblößen ‹Kopf, Arm, Bein›; ziehen ‹Schwert›; bloßlegen ‹Draht eines Kabels›; **~ one's back to the sun** seinen Rücken der Sonne aussetzen; Ⓑ *(reveal)* blecken ‹Zähne›; **she ~d her heart to him** (*fig.*) sie schüttete ihm ihr Herz aus

**bare: ~back** ❶ *adj.* ‹Reiter, Reiten› auf ungesatteltem Pferd; ❷ *adv.* ohne Sattel; **~faced** *adj.*, **~faced[ly]** /beə'feɪsɪd(lɪ)/ *adv.* (*fig.*) unverhüllt; **~foot** ❶ *adj.* barfüßig; **he is ~foot** er ist barfuß *od.* barfüßig; **~foot doctor** Barfußarzt, *der;* ❷ *adv.* barfuß; **~handed** /beə'hændɪd/ ❶ *adj.* **he was ~handed** (*without gloves*) er trug keine Handschuhe; (*without weapon*) er war unbewaffnet; ❷ *adv.* mit bloßen Händen; **~headed** /beə'hedɪd/ ❶ *adj.* **he was ~headed** er trug keine Kopfbedeckung; ❷ *adv.* ohne Kopfbedeckung; **~-legged** *adj.* mit bloßen Beinen

**barely** /'beəlɪ/ *adv.* Ⓐ *(only just)* kaum; knapp ‹vermeiden, entkommen›; Ⓑ *(scantily)* karg

**bare-'midriff** *adj.* taillenfrei ‹Kleid›

**'bar end** *n.* Lenkerhörnchen, *das*

**bareness** /'beənɪs/ *n., no pl.* ⇒ **bare** 1 C, D, F: Kahlheit, *die;* Nacktheit, *die;* Kargheit, *die*

**'barfly** *n.* (*coll.*) Kneipenhocker, *der*/-hockerin, *die* (*ugs.*)

**bargain** /'bɑ:gɪn/ ❶ *n.* Ⓐ *(agreement)* Abmachung, *die;* **an unequal ~:** ein ungleicher Handel; **into the ~,** (*Amer.*) **in the ~:** darüber hinaus; **make** *or* **strike a ~ to do sth.** sich darauf einigen, etw. zu tun; **I'll make a ~ with you** ich mache dir ein Angebot; **they got the best of the ~:** sie haben den besseren Teil bekommen; **a ~'s a ~:** was einmal abgemacht ist, gilt; Ⓑ *(thing acquired)* Kauf, *der;* **a good/bad ~:** ein guter/schlechter Kauf; Ⓒ *(thing offered cheap)* günstiges Angebot; (*thing acquired cheaply*) guter Kauf; **a definite ~:** ein absolutes Sonderangebot. ⇒ *also* **best** 3 E; **hard** 1 A.
❷ *v.i.* Ⓐ *(discuss)* handeln; **~ for** *or* **on sth.** um etw. handeln; Ⓑ **~ for** (*expect*): **more than one had ~ed for** mehr, als man erwartet hatte; **~ for sth.** mit etw. rechnen.
❸ *v.t.* **~ away** sich (*Dat.*) abhandeln lassen

**bargain: ~ 'basement** *n.* Tiefgeschoss mit Sonderangeboten; **~ counter** *n.* Tisch mit Sonderangeboten; **~ hunter** *n.* Schnäppchenjäger, *der*/-jägerin, *die*

**bargaining** /'bɑ:gɪnɪŋ/ *n.* Handel, *der;* (*negotiating*) Verhandlungen; **~ position** Verhandlungsposition, *die;* **~ counter** (*fig.*) Trumpf [für Verhandlungen]; ⇒ *also* **collective bargaining**

**bargain: ~ offer** *n.* Sonderangebot, *das;* **~ price** *n.* Sonderpreis, *der*

**barge** /bɑ:dʒ/ ❶ *n.* Ⓐ Kahn, *der;* **freight/cargo ~:** Fracht-/Lastkahn, *der;* Ⓑ *(for State occasions)* Prunkschiff, *das* (*veralt.*).
❷ *v.i.* Ⓐ *(lurch)* **~ into sb.** jmdn. anrempeln; **~ against sth.** gegen etw. taumeln; Ⓑ **~ about the house** im Haus herumtoben; Ⓑ **~ in** (*intrude*) hineinplatzen/hereinplatzen (*ugs.*); **he ~d in on us** er platzte bei uns herein (*ugs.*)

**bargee** /bɑ:'dʒi:/(*Brit.*), **barge-man** (*Amer.*) *ns.* ▶1261 Flussschiffer, *der*

**'bargepole** *n.* Stake, *die* (*nordd.*); **I wouldn't touch him/that** *etc.* **with [the end of] a ~!** (*fig.*) ich würde ihn/das *usw.* nicht mit der Beißzange anfassen! (*ugs.*)

**baritone** /'bærɪtəʊn/ (*Mus.*) ❶ *n.* Bariton, *der;* (*voice, part also*) Baritonstimme, *die.* ❷ *adj.* **~ voice** Baritonstimme, *die*

**barium** /'beərɪəm/ *n.* (*Chem.*) Barium, *das;* **~ meal** Kontrastbrei, *der* (*mit Bariumsulfat*)

**bark¹** /bɑ:k/ ❶ *n.* Ⓐ *(of tree)* Borke, *die;* Rinde, *die;* Ⓑ *(for tanning, dyeing)* [Gerber]lohe, *die.* ❷ *v.t.* Ⓐ *(abrade)* aufschürfen; Ⓑ *(strip ~ from)* entrinden

**bark²** ❶ *n.* (*lit. or fig.*) Bellen, *das;* **his ~ is worse than his bite** (*fig.*) er ist nicht so bissig, wie er tut; ≈ Hunde, die bellen, beißen nicht. ❷ *v.i.* Ⓐ *(lit. or fig.)* bellen; **~ at sb.** jmdn. anbellen; **be ~ing up the wrong tree** auf dem Holzweg sein; Ⓑ **~ at** (*abuse*) anblaffen (*salopp*); Ⓒ *(speak loudly and curtly)* brüllen; Ⓓ *(Amer.: act as tout)* den Ausrufer machen. ❸ Ⓐ *v.t.* bellen; Ⓑ (*bellow*) **~ [out] orders to sb.** jmdm. Befehle zubrüllen

**bark**[3] *n.* (*poet.: ship*) Schiff, *das*

**'barkeep** (*Amer.*), **'barkeeper** *n.* Barkeeper, *der;* (*owner*) Wirt, *der*

**barker** /'bɑːkə(r)/ *n.* Ausrufer, *der*

**barley** /'bɑːlɪ/ *n.* Gerste, *die;* ⇒ *also* **pearl barley**

**barley: ~corn** *n.* (*grain*) Gerstenkorn, *das;* **~-mow** *n.* Gerstenschober, *der* (*bes. südd.*); **~ sugar** *n.* Gerstenzucker, *der;* **~ water** *n.* Gerstenwasser, *das* (*veralt.*)

**barm** /bɑːm/ *n.* Hefe, *die;* Bärme, *die* (*nordd.*)

**bar: ~maid** *n.* ▶ 1261 (*Brit.*) Bardame, *die;* **~man** /'bɑːmən/ *n., pl.* **~men** /'bɑːmən/ ▶ 1261 Barmann, *der;* Schankkellner, *der*

**bar mitzvah** /bɑː'mɪtzvə/ *n.* **A** (*boy*) Bar-Mizwa, *der;* **B** (*ceremony*) Bar-Mizwa, *die*

**barmy** /'bɑːmɪ/ *adj.* (*coll.: crazy*) bescheuert (*salopp*)

**barn** /bɑːn/ *n.* **A** (*Brit.: for grain etc.*) Scheune, *die;* (*Amer.: for implements etc.*) Schuppen, *der;* (*Amer.: for animals*) Stall, *der;* **B** (*derog.*) [großer, hässlicher] Schuppen

**barnacle** /'bɑːnəkl/ *n.* **A** (*Zool.*) Rankenfüßer, *der;* **B** ~ **[goose]** Weißwangengans, *die*

**barn: ~ dance** *n.* ≈ Schottische, *der;* **~ door** *n.* Scheunentor, *das;* **be as big as a ~ door** (*fig.*) nicht zu verfehlen sein

**barney** /'bɑːnɪ/ *n.* (*coll.*) Krach, *der* (*ugs.*); **have a ~:** Krach haben (*ugs.*)

**barn: ~ owl** *n.* Schleiereule, *die;* **~storm** *v.i.* durch die Provinz ziehen *od.* tingeln; **~stormer** *n.* tingelnder Schauspieler; (*Amer.: politician*) Politiker [im Wahlkampf in der Provinz]; (*Amer.: aviator*) [Kunstflug]pilot [auf Tournee durch die Provinz]; **~storming** /'bɑːnstɔːmɪŋ/ *adj.* mitreißend; **~yard** *n.* Wirtschaftshof, *der*

**barograph** /'bærəgrɑːf/ *n.* Barograph, *der*

**barometer** /bə'rɒmɪtə(r)/ *n.* (*lit. or fig.*) Barometer, *das*

**barometric** /bærə'metrɪk/ *adj.* barometrisch; **~ pressure** Luftdruck, *der*

**baron** /'bærn/ *n.* ▶ 1617 **A** (*holder of title*) Baron, *der;* Freiherr, *der;* **B** (*merchant*) **coal/oil ~:** Kohlen-/Ölmagnat, *der;* **C** (*powerful person*) Papst, *der* (*fig.*); **press ~:** Pressezar, *der;* **D** (*Hist.: holder of land*) Baron, *der;* **E** (*sirloin*) **~ of beef** [ungeteiltes] Lendenstück; Baron, *der* (*Kochk.*)

**baroness** /'bærənɪs/ *n.* ▶ 1617 Baronin, *die;* Freifrau, *die*

**baronet** /'bærənɪt/ *n.* Baronet, *der*

**baronetcy** /'bærənɪtsɪ/ *n.* Stand/Titel eines Baronets

**baronial** /bə'rəʊnɪəl/ *adj.* freiherrlich

**barony** /'bærənɪ/ *n.* **A** Baronie, *die;* Baronat, *das;* **B** (*Scot.: manor*) Landgut, *das*

**baroque** /bə'rɒk/ **1** *n.* Barock, *das.* **2** *adj.* **A** barock; **~ painting/literature** Barockmalerei/-literatur, *die;* **~ painter/writer** Maler/Schriftsteller des Barock; **B** (*grotesque*) barock

**barouche** /bə'ruːʃ/ *n.* (*Hist.*) Kalesche, *die*

**barque** /bɑːk/ *n.* Bark, *die*

**barrack**[1] /'bærək/ *n. usu. in pl., often constr. as sing.* **A** (*for soldiers*) Kaserne, *die;* **B** (*for temporary housing*) Baracke, *die;* **C** (*plain, dull building*) Kaserne, *die*

**barrack**[2] **1** *v.i.* buhen (*ugs.*). **2** *v.t.* ausbuhen (*ugs.*)

**barrack: ~-room 'lawyer** *n.* Feldwebeltyp, *der* (*abwertend*); **~ 'square** *n.* Kasernenhof, *der*

**barracouta** /bærə'kuːtə/, **barracuda** /bærə'kuːdə/ *n., pl. same or* **~s; A** *usu.* **-uda** (*sea fish*) Barrakuda, *der;* Pfeilhecht, *der;* **B** *usu.* **-outa** (*food fish*) Atun, *der*

**barrage** /'bærɑːʒ/ *n.* **A** (*Mil.*) Sperrfeuer, *das;* (*fig.*) **a ~ of questions/insults** ein Bombardement von Fragen/Beleidigungen; **a ~ of cheers** stürmischer Jubel; **B** (*dam*) Talsperre, *die;* Staustufe, *die;* **C** (*Fencing, Showjumping, etc.*) Stechen, *das*

**'barrage balloon** *n.* Sperrballon, *der*

**barramundi** /bærə'mʌndɪ/ *n.* (*Zool.*) Barramundi, *der*

**barre** /bɑː(r)/ *n.* (*Ballet*) Stange, *die*

**barrel** /'bærl/ *n.* **A** (*vessel*) Fass, *das;* (*of metal, for oil, fuel, tar, etc.*) Tonne, *die;* Fass, *das;* (*measure*) Barrel, *das;* **be over a ~** (*fig.*) in der Klemme sitzen (*ugs.*); **have sb. over a ~** (*fig.*) jmdn. in der Zange haben (*ugs.*); **scrape the ~** (*fig.*) das Letzte zusammenkratzen (*ugs.*); **B** (*revolving cylinder*) Walze, *die;* **C** (*of pump*) Stiefel, *der;* (*of engine-boiler*) Trommel, *die;* (*of pen or pencil*) Schaft, *der;* **D** (*of gun*) Lauf, *der;* (*of cannon etc.*) Rohr, *das*

**barrel: ~-chested** /'bærltʃestɪd/ *adj.* **a ~-chested man** ein Mann mit einem breiten, gewölbten Brustkorb; **~house** *n.* (*Amer.*) Kneipe, *die; attrib.* **~house music** [einfache, laute] Jazzmusik; **~-organ** *n.* (*Mus.*) Leierkasten, *der;* Drehorgel, *die;* **~ vault** *n.* (*Archit.*) Tonnengewölbe, *das*

**barren** /'bærn/ **1** *adj.* **A** unfruchtbar ‹Person, Tier, Pflanze, Land›; kinderlos ‹Ehe›; gelt (*Jägerspr., Landw.*) ‹Wild, Ziege, Rind›; **B** (*meagre, dull*) nutzlos ‹Handlung, Arbeit›; mager ‹Ergebnis›; unfruchtbar ‹Periode, Beziehung›; fruchtlos ‹Diskussion›; **be ~ of results** wenig Erfolg haben. **2** *n.* **~[s]** Ödland, *das*

**barrenness** /'bærnnɪs/ *n., no pl.* **A** Unfruchtbarkeit, *die;* (*of marriage*) Kinderlosigkeit, *die;* **B** ⇒ **barren** B: Nutzlosigkeit, *die;* Magerkeit, *die;* Unfruchtbarkeit, *die;* Fruchtlosigkeit, *die*

**barrette** /bə'ret/ *n.* (*Amer.*) Haarspange, *die*

**barricade** /bærɪ'keɪd/ **1** *n.* Barrikade, *die;* **a ~ of silence** (*fig.*) eine Mauer des Schweigens. **2** *v.t.* verbarrikadieren

**barrier** /'bærɪə(r)/ *n.* **A** (*fence*) Absperrung, *die;* Barriere, *die;* (*at railway, frontier*) Schranke, *die;* **B** (*gate of railway station*) Sperre, *die;* **C** (*obstacle, lit. or fig.*) Barriere, *die;* **a ~ to progress** ein Hindernis für den Fortschritt; **break the class ~:** die Klassenschranken durchbrechen; ⇒ *also* **sound barrier**

**barrier: ~ cream** *n.* Schutzcreme, *die;* **~ reef** *n.* Barrier- *od.* Wallriff, *das*

**barring** /'bɑːrɪŋ/ *prep.* außer im Falle (+ *Gen.*); **~ accidents** falls nichts passiert; **~ the possibility of rain** falls es nicht vielleicht regnet

**barrister** /'bærɪstə(r)/ *n.* ▶ 1261 **A** (*Brit.*) **~[-at-law]** Barrister, *der;* ≈ [Rechts]anwalt/-anwältin vor höheren Gerichten; **B** (*Amer.: lawyer*) [Rechts]anwalt, *der*/-anwältin, *die*

**barroom** /'bɑːruːm/ *n.* (*Amer.*) Bar, *die*

**barrow**[1] /'bærəʊ/ *n.* **A** Karre, *die;* Karren, *der;* **B** ⇒ **wheelbarrow**

**barrow**[2] *n.* (*Archaeol.*) Hügelgrab, *das*

**'barrow boy** *n.* ▶ 1261 (*Brit.*) Straßenhändler, *der*

**bar 'sinister** *n.* (*Her.*) Bastardfaden, *der*

**Bart.** *abbr.* **baronet**

**'bartender** *n.* ▶ 1261 Barkeeper, *der;* Schankkellner, *der*

**barter** /'bɑːtə(r)/ **1** *v.t.* [ein]tauschen; **~ sth. for sth. [else]** etw. für *od.* gegen etw. [anderes] [ein]tauschen; **~ away sth.** etw. verspielen (*fig.*). **2** *v.i.* Tauschhandel treiben; **they ~ed for cigarettes with books and clothes** sie tauschten Bücher und Kleidung gegen Zigaretten. **3** *n.* Tauschhandel, *der;* **~ of opinions/ideas** (*fig.*) Gedankenaustausch, *der*

**barytes** /bə'raɪtiːz/ *n.* (*Min.*) Baryt, *der*

**basal** /'beɪsl/ *adj.* **A** (*Med., Biol.*) basal; **~ cell** Basalzelle, *die;* **B** (*fundamental*) grundlegend; fundamental. ⇒ *also* **metabolism**

**basalt** /'bæsɔːlt, bə'sɔːlt/ *n.* Basalt, *der*

**bascule** /'bæskjuːl/ *n.* Baskule, *die* (*veralt.*); **~ bridge** Klappbrücke, *die*

**base**[1] /beɪs/ **1** *n.* **A** (*of lamp, pyramid, wall, mountain, microscope*) Fuß, *der;* (*of cupboard, statue*) Sockel, *der;* (*fig.*) (*support*) Basis, *die;* Fundament, *das;* (*principle*) Ausgangsbasis, *die;* (*main ingredient*) Grundbestandteil, *der;* (*of make-up*) Grundlage, *die;* (*Photog.: support for film etc.*) Unterlage, *die;* (*Ling.: root*) Wurzel, *die;* (*Ling.: primary morpheme*) Stamm, *der;* **shake the very ~ of sth.** (*fig.*) etw. in seinen Grundfesten erschüttern; **glue has a flour ~:** die Grundsubstanz von Leim ist Mehl; **a sauce which has a tomato ~:** eine Soße auf Tomatenbasis (*Kochk.*); **B** (*Mil.*) Basis, *die;* Stützpunkt, *der;* **C** (*Baseball*) Mal, *das;* **get to first ~** (*fig. coll.*) [wenigstens] etwas erreichen; **he didn't get to first ~ with her** er konnte bei ihr überhaupt nicht landen (*ugs.*); **be off ~** (*fig. coll.*) falsch liegen (*ugs.*); **D** (*Archit.*) Basis, *die;* **E** (*Geom.*) Basis, *die;* (*of triangle also*) Grundlinie, *die;* (*of solid also*) Grundfläche, *die;* **F** (*Chem.*) Base, *die;* **G** (*Surv.*) Basis, *die;* **H** (*Math.: number*) Basis, *die;* Grundzahl, *die;* **I** (*Bot., Zool.*) Basis, *die;* (*of leaf*) Blattgrund, *der;* **J** (*Her.*) Schildfuß, *der.* **2** *v.t.* **A** **be ~d on sth.** sich auf etw. (*Akk.*) gründen; **~ sth. on sth.** etw. auf etw. (*Dat.*) aufbauen; **~ one's hopes on sth.** seine Hoffnung auf etw. (*Akk.*) gründen; **a book ~d on newly discovered papers** ein Buch, das auf neu entdeckten Dokumenten basiert; **B** *in pass.* (*have chief station or means*) **be ~d in Paris** (*permanently*) in Paris sitzen; (*temporarily*) in Paris sein; **a submarine ~d on Malta** ein U-Boot, das seinen Stützpunkt auf Malta hat; **computer-~d accountancy** Buchführung über Computer; **land-~d forces** landgestützte Streitkräfte; **C** **~ oneself on** sich stützen auf (+ *Akk.*)

**base**[2] *adj.* **A** (*morally low*) niederträchtig; niedrig ‹Beweggrund›; **B** (*cowardly*) feige; (*selfish*) selbstsüchtig; (*mean*) niederträchtig; **C** (*degrading*) entwürdigend

**baseball** /'beɪsbɔːl/ *n.* Baseball, *der*

**base: ~ board** *n.* (*Amer.*) Fußleiste, *die;* **~born** *adj.* (*arch.*) von niederer Herkunft; (*illegitimate*) unehelich; **~ camp** *n.* Basislager, *das;* **~ 'coin** *n.* entwertete Münze; **~ hit** *n.* (*Baseball*) *Schlag, der dem Schlagmann ermöglicht, das erste Mal zu erreichen*

**baseless** /'beɪslɪs/ *adj.* unbegründet

**baselessly** /'beɪslɪslɪ/ *adv.* grundlos

**baselessness** /'beɪslɪsnɪs/ *n., no pl.* Haltlosigkeit, *die*

**base: ~line** *n.* Grundlinie, *die;* **~load** *n.* (*Electr.*) Grundlast, *die*

**basely** /'beɪslɪ/ *adv.* niederträchtig

**baseman** /'beɪsmən/ *n., pl.* **basemen** /'beɪsmən/ (*Baseball*) Malspieler, *der*

**basement** /'beɪsmənt/ *n.* Souterrain, *das;* Kellergeschoss, *das;* (*esp. in department store*) Untergeschoss, *das;* Tiefgeschoss, *das;* **a ~ flat** eine Souterrain- *od.* Kellerwohnung

**base 'metal** *n.* unedles Metall

**baseness** /'beɪsnɪs/ *n., no pl.* Niedrigkeit, *die;* Niederträchtigkeit, *die*

**'base rate** *n.* **A** (*Finance*) Eckzins, *der;* **B** (*wage*) Grundlohn, *der*

**bases** *pl. of* **base** *or* **basis**[1]

**bash** /bæʃ/ **1** *v.t.* [heftig] schlagen; **~ one's head against sth.** sich (*Dat.*) den Kopf [heftig] an etw. (*Dat.*) anschlagen; **~ sth. in** etw. einschlagen; **the car was badly ~ed in** *or* **up** das Auto war völlig verbeult; **~ sb. up** jmdn. zusammenschlagen; **he was badly ~ed up** er wurde schlimm zusammengeschlagen; **queer ~ing** (*sl.*) Zusammenschlagen von Schwulen (*ugs.*); **union ~ing** Einprügeln auf die Gewerkschaften. **2** *n.* **A** [heftiger] Schlag; **B** (*coll.: attempt*) Versuch, *der;* **have a ~ at sth.** etw. [mal] probieren *od.* versuchen; **C** (*coll.: party*) Fete, *die* (*ugs.*)

**bashful** /'bæʃfl/ *adj.* **A** (*shy*) schüchtern; **B** (*shamefaced*) verschämt

**bashfully** /'bæʃfəlɪ/ *adv.* ⇒ **bashful**: schüchtern; verschämt

**bashfulness** /'bæʃflnɪs/ *n., no pl.* ⇒ **bashful**: Schüchternheit, *die;* Verschämtheit, *die*

**basic** /'beɪsɪk/ *adj.* **A** (*fundamental*) grundlegend; **~ structure/principle/element/vocabulary** Grundstruktur, *die*/-prinzip, *das*/-bestandteil, *der*/-wortschatz, *der;* **be ~ to sth.** wesentlich für etw. sein; **have a ~ knowledge of sth.** Grundkenntnisse einer Sache (*Gen.*) haben; **~ problem/reason/issue** Hauptproblem, *das*/-grund, *der*/-sache, *die;* Ⓑ *(standard minimum)* **~ wages/salary** Grundlohn, *der*/Grundgehalt, *das;* **the length of a ~ working day is 8 hours** ein normaler Arbeitstag dauert 8 Stunden; Ⓒ *(Chem., Geol.)* basisch. ⇒ *also* **basics**

**basically** /ˈbeɪsɪkəlɪ/ *adv.* im Grunde; grundsätzlich ‹übereinstimmen›; *(mainly)* hauptsächlich

**basic: ~ ˈdye** *n. (Chem.)* basischer Farbstoff; **B~ ˈEnglish** *n.* Basic English, *das; auf einem sehr einfachen Grundwortschatz beruhendes Englisch;* **~ ˈindustry** *n.* wichtiger Industriezweig

**basics** /ˈbeɪsɪks/ *n. pl.* **stick to the ~:** beim Wesentlichen bleiben; **the ~ of maths/cooking** die Grundlagen der Mathematik/das Abc der Kochkunst; **go** *or* **get back to ~** *(when learning)* sich [zuerst] Grundkenntnisse aneignen; *(return to moral values)* wieder auf die [moralischen] Grundwerte zurückkommen; **he doesn't understand the ~ of honesty** er weiß überhaupt nicht, was Ehrlichkeit ist

**basic ˈslag** *n.* Thomasschlacke, *die (Hüttenw.); (finely ground)* Thomasmehl, *das (Landw.)*

**basidium** /bəˈsɪdɪəm/ *n., pl.* **basidia** /bəˈsɪdɪə/ *(Bot.)* Basidie, *die;* Sporenständer, *der*

**basil** /ˈbæzɪl/ *n. (Bot.)* **[sweet] ~:** Basilikum, *das;* **bush ~:** Buschbasilikum, *das*

**basilica** /bəˈzɪlɪkə/ *n. (Archit., Eccl.)* Basilika, *die*

**basilisk** /ˈbæzɪlɪsk/ *n. (Mythol., Zool.)* Basilisk, *der;* **~ stare** *(fig.)* Basiliskenblick, *der*

**basin** /ˈbeɪsn/ *n.* Ⓐ Becken, *das; (wash~)* Waschbecken, *das; (bowl)* Schüssel, *die;* Ⓑ *(depression)* Becken, *das; (artificial)* Bassin, *das;* Becken, *das;* Ⓒ *(of river etc.)* Becken, *das;* **the ~ of the Amazon, the Amazon ~:** das Amazonasbecken; Ⓓ *(harbour)* [Hafen]becken, *das;* Ⓔ *(valley)* [Tal]kessel, *der;* Ⓕ *(Geol.)* Becken, *das*

**basinful** /ˈbeɪsnfʊl/ *n.* **ten ~s of water** zehn Schüsseln [voll] Wasser; **have had a ~ of sth.** *(fig. coll.: more than enough)* von etw. die Nase voll haben *(ugs.)*

**basis** /ˈbeɪsɪs/ *n., pl.* **bases** /ˈbeɪsiːz/ Ⓐ *(ingredient)* Grundbestandteil, *der;* Ⓑ *(foundation, principle, common ground)* Basis, *die;* Grundlage, *die;* **rest on a ~ of conjecture** sich auf Vermutungen gründen; **meet on a purely friendly ~:** einander auf rein freundschaftlicher Basis begegnen; **on a first come first served ~:** nach dem Prinzip „Wer zuerst kommt, mahlt zuerst"; Ⓒ *(beginning)* Ausgangspunkt, *der*

**bask** /bɑːsk/ *v.i.* Ⓐ sich [wohlig] wärmen; sich aalen *(ugs.);* **~ in the sun** sich sonnen; sich in der Sonne aalen *(ugs.);* Ⓑ *(fig.)* sich sonnen (**in** in + *Dat.*)

**basket** /ˈbɑːskɪt/ *n.* Ⓐ Korb, *der; (smaller, for bread etc.)* Körbchen, *das; (of chip pan)* Drahteinsatz, *der;* **wire ~:** Drahtkorb, *der;* Ⓑ *(quantity)* **a ~ [full] of plums/apples** ein Korb [voll] Pflaumen/Äpfel; **sell ~s of sth.** [ganze] Körbe voll etw. verkaufen; etw. körbeweise verkaufen; Ⓒ *(protection for hand)* Korb, *der; (Fencing)* Glocke, *die;* Ⓓ *(of typewriter)* **[type] ~:** Typenkorb, *der;* Ⓔ *(Basketball)* Korb, *der;* **make** *or* **score a ~:** einen Korb werfen; Ⓕ *(Econ.)* **~ of currencies** Währungskorb, *der*

**basket: ~ball** *n.* Basketball, *der;* **~ case** *n. (coll.)* Schwerbeschädigte ohne Arme und Beine; *(fig.)* hoffnungsloser Fall; **~ chair** *n.* Korbsessel, *der;* **~ clause** *n.* Generalklausel, *die*

**basketful** /ˈbɑːskɪtfʊl/ ⇒ **basket** B

**basketry** /ˈbɑːskɪtrɪ/ ⇒ **basketwork**

**basket: ~ weave** *n.* Panamabindung, *die (Weberei);* **~work** *n. (art)* Korbflechterei, *die; (collectively)* Korbwaren; **a piece of ~work** ein Korbgeflecht; **~work is his hobby** Korbflechten ist sein Hobby

**basking ˈshark** *n.* Riesenhai, *der*

**Basle** /bɑːl/ ▶ **1626** ❶ *pr. n.* Basel *(das).* ❷ *attrib. adj.* Baseler

**Basque** /bæsk, bɑːsk/ ❶ *adj.* ▶ **1275**, ▶ **1340** baskisch; **the ~ Country** das Baskenland. ❷ *n.* Ⓐ ▶ **1275**, ▶ **1340** Baske, *der*/Baskin, *die; (language)* Baskisch, *das;* Ⓑ **b~** *(of bodice)* Schößchen, *das;* Ⓒ **b~** *(bodice)* Schößchenjacke, *die*

**bas-relief** /ˈbæsrɪliːf/ *n. (Art)* Basrelief, *das*

**bass¹** /bæs/ *n., pl. same or* **~es** *(Zool.)* Barsch, *der; (Perca fluviatilis)* [Fluss]barsch, *der*

**bass²** /bæs/ *n. (fibre)* Bast, *der*

**bass³** /beɪs/ *(Mus.)* ❶ *adj.* Bass-; **~ voice** Bassstimme, *die.* ❷ *n.* Ⓐ Bass, *der; (voice, part)* Bass, *der;* Bassstimme, *die; (singer)* Bassist, *der;* Bass, *der;* Ⓑ *(coll.) (double ~)* [Kontra]bass, *der; (~ guitar)* Bass, *der;* Ⓒ **figured** *or* **thorough ~:** Generalbass, *der; (theory)* Generalbasslehre, *die;* ⇒ *also* **ground¹**

**bass**/beɪs/**: ~ clef** *n. (Mus.)* Bassschlüssel, *der;* **~ drum** *n.* große Trommel

**basset** /ˈbæsɪt/ *n.* **~[-hound]** Basset, *der*

**bass guiˈtar** /beɪs/ *n.* Bassgitarre, *die*

**bassinet** /bæsɪˈnet/ *n.* Stubenwagen, *der;* Korb[kinder]wagen, *der; (cradle)* Korbwiege, *die*

**bassist** /ˈbeɪsɪst/ *n.* Bassist, *der*/Bassistin, *die*

**basso** /ˈbæsəʊ/ *n., pl.* **~s** *or* **bassi** /ˈbæsiː/ *(Mus.)* Basso, *der*

**bassoon** /bəˈsuːn/ *n. (Mus.)* Fagott, *das*

**bassoonist** /bəˈsuːnɪst/ *n. (Mus.)* Fagottist, *der*/Fagottistin, *die*

**bass: ~ player** *n.* Bassist, *der*/Bassistin, *die;* **~ viol** /beɪs ˈvaɪəl/ *n.* Gambe, *die;* Kniegeige, *die (veralt.); (Amer.: double ~)* Bassgeige, *die;* Kontrabass, *der*

**bast** /bæst/ *n.* Bast, *der*

**bastard** /ˈbɑːstəd/ ❶ *adj.* Ⓐ unehelich; Ⓑ *(hybrid)* verfälscht ‹Sprache, Stil›; Ⓒ *(Bot., Zool.)* Bastard-. ❷ *n.* Ⓐ uneheliches Kind; unehelicher Sohn/uneheliche Tochter; Bastard, *der (hist.);* Ⓑ *(sl.) (disliked person)* Schweinehund, *der (derb);* Mistkerl, *der (derb); (disliked thing)* Scheißding, *das (derb);* **you old ~!** *(in friendly exclamation)* alter Schwede! *(salopp);* **the poor ~!** *(unfortunate person)* das arme Schwein! *(ugs.)*

**bastard: ~ title** *n. (Printing)* Schmutztitel, *der;* **~ wing** *n. (Zool.)* Afterflügel, *der*

**bastardy** /ˈbɑːstədɪ/ *n., no pl.* uneheliche Herkunft; Unehelichkeit, *die*

**baste¹** /beɪst/ *v.t. (stitch)* heften; reihen

**baste²** *v.t.* Ⓐ [mit Fett/Bratensaft] begießen ‹Fleisch›; Ⓑ *(thrash, cudgel)* prügeln

**bastion** /ˈbæstɪən/ *n.* Bastei, *die; (fig.)* Bastei, *die;* Bastion, *die;* Bollwerk, *das*

**bat¹** /bæt/ *n. (Zool.)* Fledermaus, *die;* **blind as a ~** *(fig.)* blind wie ein Maulwurf; **have ~s in the belfry** *(fig. coll.)* einen Dachschaden haben *(ugs.);* **sb. drives like a ~ out of hell** *(sl.)* jmd. fährt, als ob der Teufel hinter ihm her wäre *(ugs.)*

**bat²** ❶ *n.* Ⓐ *(Sport)* Schlagholz, *das; (for table tennis)* Schläger, *der;* **do sth. off one's own ~** *(fig.)* etw. auf eigene Faust tun; **his earnings off his own ~:** das, was er selbst verdient[e]; **carry one's ~** *(Cricket) als Schlagmann während eines Durchgangs nicht ausscheiden;* **right off the ~** *(Amer. fig.)* sofort; Ⓑ *(act of using ~)* Schlag, *der;* Ⓒ *usu. in pl. (implement to guide aircraft)* Kelle, *die;* Ⓓ *(batsman)* Schlagmann, *der.* ❷ *v.i.,* **-tt-** Ⓐ *(Sport)* schlagen; Ⓑ *(coll.: move)* **~ around the town** in der Stadt rummachen *(ugs.);* **~ away** sich wegmachen *(ugs.).* ❸ *v.t.,* **-tt-** Ⓐ schlagen; Ⓑ *(Baseball)* **~ in two runs** zwei Läufe holen *(ugs.)*

**bat³** *n. (Brit. coll.: pace)* Tempo, *das;* **at an awful ~:** mit einem Affenzahn *(salopp)*

**bat⁴** *v.t.,* **-tt-: ~ one's eyes/eyelids** [mit den Augen/Augenlidern] blinzeln *od.* zwinkern; **he never ~ted an eyelid** *(fig.: betrayed no emotion)* er hat nicht mit der Wimper gezuckt; **without ~ting an eyelid** *(fig.)* ohne mit der Wimper zu zucken

**batch** /bætʃ/ *n.* Ⓐ *(of loaves)* Schub, *der;* Ⓑ *(of people)* Gruppe, *die;* Schwung, *der (ugs.); (of letters, books, files, papers)* Stapel, *der;* Schwung, *der (ugs.); (of rules, regulations)* Bündel, *das*

**batch: ~ file** *n. (Computing)* Stapeldatei, *die;* **~ ˈprocessing** *n. (Computing)* Schub-, Stapelverarbeitung, *die;* **~ production** *n.* Stapelfertigung, *die*

**bate¹** /beɪt/ *v.t.* **with ~d breath** mit angehaltenem *od. (geh.)* verhaltenem Atem; **~ one's breath** den Atem verhalten *(geh.)*

**bate²** *n. (Brit. coll.)* Rage, *die (ugs.);* **be in a [terrible] ~:** [schrecklich] in Rage sein; **get/fly into a ~:** in Rage geraten

**bath** /bɑːθ/ ❶ *n., pl.* **~s** /bɑːðz/ Ⓐ Bad, *das;* **have** *or* **take a ~:** ein Bad nehmen; Ⓑ *(vessel)* **~[tub]** Badewanne, *die;* **room with ~:** Zimmer mit Bad; Ⓒ *usu. in pl. (building)* Bad, *das;* **[swimming] ~s** Schwimmbad, *das;* Ⓓ **Order of the B~** *(Brit.)* Orden vom Bade. ❷ *v.t. & i.* baden

**bath: B~ ˈbrick** *n.* Putzstein, *der;* **B~ ˈbun** *n.* ≈ Rosinenbrötchen mit Zuckerguss; **~ cap** *n.* Badekappe, *die;* Bademütze, *die;* **~ chair** *n.* Rollstuhl, *der;* **~ cube** *n. pl.* Badesalzwürfel, *der*

**bathe** /beɪð/ ❶ *v.t.* Ⓐ baden; Ⓑ *(moisten)* baden ‹Wunde, Körperteil›; **~d with** *or* **in sweat** schweißüberströmt ‹Gesicht, Person›; in Schweiß gebadet ‹Person›; **~d with** *or* **in tears** tränenüberströmt; Ⓒ *(envelop)* **sunlight ~d the gardens** Sonne lag über den Gärten *(geh.);* **~d in sunlight** von der Sonne beschienen. ❷ *v.i.* baden; **go bathing** baden gehen. ❸ *n.* Bad, *das (im Meer usw.);* **take** *or* **have a ~:** baden; ein Bad nehmen

**bather** /ˈbeɪðə(r)/ *n.* Ⓐ Badende, *der/die;* Ⓑ *in pl. (Austral.: garment)* Badeanzug, *der*

**bathetic** /bəˈθetɪk/ *adj.* bathisch *(geh.)*

**bathing** /ˈbeɪðɪŋ/ *n.* Baden, *das;* '**~ prohibited'** „Baden verboten!"

**bathing: ~ beach** *n.* Badestrand, *der;* **~ beauty, ~ belle** *ns.* Badenixe, *die;* **~ cap** *n.* Badekappe, *die;* Bademütze, *die;* **~ costume** *n.* Badeanzug, *der;* **~-machine** *n. (Hist.)* Badekarren, *der;* **~ suit** *n.* Badeanzug, *der;* **~ trunks** *n. pl.* Badehose, *die*

**ˈbath mat** *n.* Badematte, *die*

**bathos** /ˈbeɪθɒs/ *n., no pl. (Lit., Rhet.)* Bathos, *das (geh.);* Umschlag ins Triviale; *(anticlimax)* Antiklimax, *die (Stilk.)*

**bath: ~robe** *n.* Bademantel, *der;* **~room** *n.* Badezimmer, *das;* **~ salts** *n. pl.* Badesalz, *das;* **~time** *n.* Badezeit, *die;* **~ towel** *n.* Badetuch, *das;* **~tub** ⇒ **bath** 1 B; **~water** *n.* Badewasser, *das;* ⇒ *also* **baby** 1 A

**batik** /ˈbætɪk, bəˈtiːk/ *n.* Batik, *der od. die*

**batiste** /bəˈtiːst/ ❶ *n.* Batist, *der.* ❷ *adj.* batisten; **~ dress/blouse** Batistkleid, *das*/Batistbluse, *die*

**batman** /ˈbætmən/ *n., pl.* **batmen** /ˈbætmən/ *(Mil.)* [Offiziers]bursche, *der*

**baton** /ˈbætn/ *n.* Ⓐ *(staff of office)* Stab, *der;* Baton, *der (veralt.);* **Field Marshal's ~:** Marschallstab, *der;* Ⓑ *(truncheon)* Schlagstock, *der;* Ⓒ *(Mus.)* Taktstock, *der;* **conductor's ~:** Dirigentenstab, *der;* Ⓓ *(for relay race)* [Staffel]stab, *der;* Staffelholz, *das;* Ⓔ *(Her.)* ≈ Schrägbalken, *der;* **~ sinister** Bastardfaden, *der*

**bats** /bæts/ *pred. adj. (coll.)* bekloppt *(salopp);* **go ~:** überschnappen *(ugs.)*

**batsman** /ˈbætsmən/ *n., pl.* **batsmen** /ˈbætsmən/ *(Sport)* Schlagmann, *der;* **~'s wicket** *für den Schlagmann günstige Spielbahn*

**battalion** /bəˈtæljən/ *n. (lit. or fig.)* Bataillon, *das;* **~s of** *(fig.)* ganze Bataillone von; **God is for the big ~s** Gott ist mit dem Stärkeren

**batten¹** /ˈbætn/ ❶ *n.* Ⓐ *(piece of timber)* Latte, *die;* Ⓑ *(Naut.)* Latte, *die;* Ⓒ *(bar, strip of wood)* Leiste, *die.* ❷ *v.t. (Naut.)* **~ down** [ver]schalken ‹Luke›

**batten²** *v.i.* Ⓐ **~ on sth.** sich an etw. *(Dat.)* gütlich tun; *(grow fat)* sich mästen mit etw.; Ⓑ *(thrive)* **~ on** sich mästen auf Kosten (+ *Gen.*)

**batter¹** /ˈbætə(r)/ ❶ *v.t.* Ⓐ *(strike)* einschlagen auf (+ *Akk.*); **~ down/in** einschlagen; **~ sth. to pieces** etw. zerschmettern *od.* in Stücke schlagen; **he ~ed his head against**

**the wall** er schlug seinen Kopf gegen die Wand; Ⓑ (*attack with artillery*) beschießen; bombardieren (*Milit. veralt.*); ~ **down** zusammenschießen; Ⓒ (*fig.: handle severely*) bombardieren; ~ **sb. into exhaustion** jmdn. völlig zermürben; Ⓓ (*bruise, damage*) übel zurichten; ramponieren (*ugs.*); **~ed baby** misshandeltes Baby; **~ed wife** misshandelte Ehefrau; geschlagene Frau; **~ed wives' home** Frauenhaus, *das;* **~ed by the gales** vom Sturm stark beschädigt; **a ~ed car** ein verbeultes Auto.
❷ *v.i.* heftig klopfen; **they ~ed at** *or* **against the door** sie hämmerten gegen die Tür

**batter²** *n.* (*Cookery*) [Back]teig, *der;* (*for pancake*) [Eierkuchen]teig, *der;* (*for waffle*) [Waffel]teig, *der*

**batter³** *n.* (*Baseball*) Schlagmann, *der*

**battering ram** /'bætərɪŋ ræm/ *n.* Rammbock, *der*

**battery** /'bætərɪ/ *n.* Ⓐ (*series; also Mil., Electr.*) Batterie, *die;* **a ~ of specialists** (*fig.*) eine ganze Reihe von Spezialisten; ⇒ *also* **recharge** 1; Ⓑ (*Law*) **[assault and] ~:** tätlicher Angriff; Ⓒ (*Psych.*) Testreihe, *die;* Ⓓ (*Baseball*) *Werfer und Fänger;* Ⓔ (*Agric.*) Legebatterie, *die*

**battery: ~ charger** *n.* Batterieladegerät, *das;* ~ **'chicken** *n.* Batteriehuhn, *das;* ~ **'farming** *n.* Batteriehaltung, *die;* ~ **'hen** *n.* Batteriehuhn, *das;* **~-operated** *adj.* batteriebetrieben

**batting** /'bætɪŋ/ *n.* (*Sport*) Schlagen, *das;* ⇒ *also* **average** 1 B

**battle** /'bætl/ ❶ *n.* Ⓐ (*fight*) Schlacht, *die;* **the ~ at Amman** die Schlacht bei Amman; **they went out to ~:** sie zogen in die Schlacht; **do** *or* **give ~:** kämpfen; **join ~ with sb.** jmdm. eine Schlacht liefern; **die in ~:** [in der Schlacht] fallen; Ⓑ (*fig.: contest*) Kampf, *der;* ~ **for life** Kampf ums Überleben; ~ **of words** Wortgefecht, *das;* ~ **of ideas/wits** Wettstreit der Ideen/geistiger Wettstreit; ⇒ *also* **fight** 2 C; Ⓒ (*victory*) Sieg, *der;* **the ~ is to the strong** der Sieg gehört den Starken; **sth./that is half the ~:** mit etw./damit ist schon viel gewonnen. ⇒ *also* **pitch¹** 2 F.
❷ *v.i.* ~ **with** *or* **against sth.** mit *od.* gegen etw. kämpfen; ~ **for sth.** für etw. kämpfen.
❸ *v.t.* Ⓐ kämpfen gegen; Ⓑ ~ **one's way through the crowd** sich durch die Menge kämpfen

**battle: ~axe** *n.* Streitaxt, *die;* (*coll.: woman*) Schreckschraube, *die* (*ugs. abwertend*); **~cruiser** *n.* (*Navy*) Schlachtkreuzer, *der;* ~ **cry** *n.* Schlachtruf, *der*

**battle: ~dress** *n.* (*Mil.*) (*for general service*) Arbeitsanzug, *der;* (*for field service*) Kampfanzug, *der;* ~ **fatigue** *n.* Frontkoller, *der* (*ugs.*); Frontneurose, *die;* **~field, ~ground** *ns.* Schlachtfeld, *das;* **~-lines** *n. pl.* Kampflinien

**battlement** /'bætlmənt/ *n., usu. in pl.* Ⓐ Zinne, *die;* Ⓑ (*roof*) mit Zinnen bewehrtes Dach

**battlemented** /'bætlməntɪd/ *adj.* mit Zinnen bewehrt

**battle: ~ 'royal** *n.* [heftiger] Kampf (*auch fig.*); (*everyone for himself*) Kampf jeder gegen jeden; **~ship** *n.* Schlachtschiff, *das;* **~-weary** *adj.* kampfesmüde

**batty** /'bætɪ/ *adj.* (*coll.*) bekloppt (*salopp*); **go** *or* **become ~:** überschnappen (*ugs.*)

**'batwing sleeve** *n.* Fledermausärmel, *der*

**bauble** /'bɔ:bl/ *n.* Ⓐ (*trinket*) Flitter, *der;* **little ~s** kleine, wertlose Schmuckstücke; Ⓑ (*toy*) Spielzeug, *das;* **dolls and other ~s** Puppen und anderes Spielzeug; Ⓒ (*Hist.: jester's emblem*) Narrenzepter, *das;* Ⓓ (*worthless thing*) Talmi, *der;* **be a ~/be ~s** Talmi sein

**baulk** ⇒ **balk**

**bauxite** /'bɔ:ksaɪt/ *n.* (*Min.*) Bauxit, *der*

**Bavaria** /bə'veərɪə/ *pr. n.* Bayern (*das*)

**Bavarian** /bə'veərɪən/ ▶ 1275, ▶ 1340 ❶ *adj.* bay[e]risch; **sb. is ~:** jmd. ist Bayer/Bayerin. ❷ *n.* Ⓐ (*person*) Bayer, *der*/Bayerin, *die;* Ⓑ (*dialect*) Bay[e]risch[e], *das;* Bairisch[e], *das*

**bawdily** /'bɔ:dɪlɪ/ *adv.* zweideutig, (*stronger*) obszön ‹lachen, schreiben›

**bawdiness** /'bɔ:dɪnɪs/ *n., no pl.* ⇒ **bawdy** 1: Zweideutigkeit, *die;* Obszönität, *die*

**bawdy** /'bɔ:dɪ/ ❶ *adj.* zweideutig, (*stronger*) obszön ‹Witz, Geschichte, Sprache›; obszön ‹Person›. ❷ *n.* Zweideutigkeit, *die;* (*stronger*) Obszönität, *die*

**'bawdy house** *n.* (*arch.*) Bordell, *das*

**bawl** /bɔ:l/ ❶ *v.t.* brüllen; ~ **sth. at sb.** jmdm. etw. zubrüllen; ~ **[out] one's wares** seine Waren ausschreien; ~ **sb. out** (*coll.*) jmdn. zusammenstauchen (*ugs.*). ❷ *v.i.* brüllen; ~ **out to sb.** nach jmdm. brüllen; ~ **at sb.** jmdn. anbrüllen

**bay¹** *n.* (*of sea*) Bucht, *die;* (*larger also*) Golf, *der;* **the B~ of Bengal** der Golf von Bengalen; **Hudson's B~:** die Hudsonbai; **the B~ of Pigs** die Schweinebucht

**bay²** *n.* Ⓐ (*division of wall*) Joch, *das* (*Archit.*); Ⓑ (*space in room*) Erker, *der;* Ⓒ (*recess, compartment*) Lagerraum, *der;* (*in barn*) Banse, *die;* **sick~** (*Navy*) Schiffshospital, *das;* (*Mil.*) Sanitätsbereich, *der;* (*in school, college, office*) Krankenzimmer, *das;* Ⓓ (*of railway line*) ≈ Nebengleis, *das;* Ⓔ (*platform*) *Bahnsteig an einem Nebengleis;* (*in bus station*) Haltestelle, *die*

**bay³** ❶ *n.* (*bark*) Gebell, *das;* Gelaut, *das* (*Jägerspr.*); **at ~:** gestellt; **be at ~** (*fig.*) mit dem Rücken zur Wand stehen (*fig.*); **hold** *or* **keep sb./sth. at ~** (*fig.*) jmdn./etw. vom Leib halten; **stand at ~** (*fig.*) sich [den Verfolgern] stellen. ❷ *v.i.* bellen; ~ **at sb./sth.** jmdn./etw. anbellen. ❸ *v.t.* anbellen

**bay⁴** /beɪ/ *n.* Ⓐ (*Bot.*) Lorbeer[baum], *der;* Ⓑ *in pl.* (*wreath*) **[garland of] ~s** Lorbeer[kranz], *der*

**bay⁵** ❶ *adj.* braun ‹Pferd›. ❷ *n.* Braune, *der*

**bay: ~berry** *n.* Pimentbaum, *der;* **~leaf** *n.* (*Cookery*) Lorbeerblatt, *das*

**bayonet** /'beɪənɪt/ ❶ *n.* Bajonett, *das;* Seitengewehr, *das;* **with fixed ~s** mit aufgepflanzten Bajonetten. ❷ *v.t.* mit dem Bajonett *od.* Seitengewehr aufspießen; ~ **sb. to death** jmdn. mit dem Bajonett erstechen

**bayonet: ~ fitting** *n.* Bajonettfassung, *die;* ~ **plug** *n.* Stecker mit Bajonettverschluss *od.* -fassung; ~ **socket** *n.* Steckdose mit Bajonettfassung

**bay: ~ 'rum** *n.* Pimentöl, *das;* ~ **'window** *n.* Erkerfenster, *das*

**bazaar** /bə'zɑ:(r)/ *n.* (*oriental market*) Basar, *der;* (*large shop*) Kaufhaus, *das;* Basar, *der* (*DDR*); (*sale*) [Wohltätigkeits]basar, *der*

**bazooka** /bə'zu:kə/ *n.* (*Mil.*) Bazooka, *die;* (*smaller*) Panzerfaust, *die*

**BBC** *abbr.* **British Broadcasting Corporation** BBC, *die*

**bbl.** *abbr.* **barrels** (*esp. of oil*)

**BC** *abbr.* ▶ 1055 **before Christ** v. Chr.; (*bes. DDR*) v. u. Z.

**BD** *abbr.* **Bachelor of Divinity** Bakkalaureus der Theologie; ⇒ *also* **B. Sc.**

**BDS** *abbr.* **Bachelor of Dental Surgery** Bakkalaureus der Zahnheilkunde; ⇒ *also* **B. Sc.**

**be** /bi:/ *v., pres. t.* **I am** /əm, *stressed* æm/, *neg.* (*coll.*) **ain't** /eɪnt/, **he is** /ɪz/, *neg.* (*coll.*) **isn't** /'ɪznt/; **we are** /ə(r), *stressed* ɑ:(r)/, *neg.* (*coll.*) **aren't** /ɑ:nt/; *p. t.* **I was** /wəz, *stressed* wɒz/, *neg.* (*coll.*) **wasn't** /'wɒznt/, **we were** /wə(r), *stressed* wɜ:(r), weə(r)/, *neg.* (*coll.*) **weren't** /wɜ:nt, weənt/; *pres. p.* **being** /'bi:ɪŋ/; *p. p.* **been** /bɪn, *stressed* bi:n/ ❶ *copula* Ⓐ *indicating quality or attribute* sein; **she'll be ten next week** sie wird nächste Woche zehn; **she is a mother/an Italian** sie ist Mutter/Italienerin; **being a Frenchman, he naturally took an interest in politics** als Franzose interessierte er sich natürlich für Politik; **not being a cat lover, I kept well away** da ich nicht gerade ein Katzenfreund bin, hielt ich mich fern; **he is being nice to them/sarcastic** er ist nett zu ihnen/jetzt ist er sarkastisch; **he has always been lazy** er ist schon immer faul gewesen; **be sensible!** sei vernünftig!; Ⓑ *in exclamations* **was she pleased!** war sie [vielleicht] froh!; **isn't he stupid!** ist er nicht [wirklich] dumm!; **aren't you a big boy!** was bist du schon für ein großer Junge!; Ⓒ **will be** *indicating supposition* **[I dare say] you'll be a big boy by now** du bist jetzt sicher schon ein großer Junge; **you'll be relieved to hear that** du wirst erleichtert sein, das zu hören; Ⓓ *indicating physical or mental welfare or state* sein; sich fühlen; **be ill/unwell** krank sein/sich nicht wohl fühlen; **I am well** es geht mir gut; **I am hot** mir ist heiß; **I am freezing** mich friert; es friert mich; **how are you/is she?** wie gehts (*ugs.*)/geht es ihr?; Ⓔ *identifying the subject* **he is the person I was speaking of** er ist es, von dem ich sprach; **it is the 5th today** heute haben wir den Fünften; **who's that?** wer ist das?; **it is she, it's her** sie ists; **it is Joe who came** Joe ist gekommen; **if I were you** wenn ich du *od.* an deiner Stelle wäre; Ⓕ *indicating profession, pastime, etc.* **be a teacher/a footballer** Lehrer/Fußballer sein; **she wants to be a surgeon** sie möchte Chirurgin werden; Ⓖ *with possessive* **it is/was hers** es ist/war ihrs; es gehört/gehörte ihr; **this book is your uncle's** dieses Buch gehört deinem Onkel; Ⓗ *indicating intended recipient* **it's for you** es ist für dich; Ⓘ (*cost*) kosten; **how much are those eggs?** was kosten die Eier da?; **that will be 76p** das macht 76 Pence; Ⓙ (*equal*) sein; **two times three is six, two threes are six** zweimal drei ist *od.* sind *od.* gibt sechs; **sixteen ounces is a pound** sechzehn Unzen sind *od.* ergeben ein Pfund; Ⓚ (*constitute*) ausmachen; bilden; **London is not England** London ist nicht [gleich] England; Ⓛ (*mean*) bedeuten; **he was everything to her** er bedeutete ihr alles; **seeing is believing** was man [selbst] sieht, glaubt man; Ⓜ (*represent*) darstellen; stehen für; bedeuten; **let x be 3** [angenommen] x sei 3.
❷ *v.i.* Ⓐ (*exist*) [vorhanden] sein; existieren; **can such things be?** kann es so etwas geben?; kann so etwas vorkommen?; **I think, therefore I am** ich denke, also bin ich; **there is/are ...:** es gibt ...; **there are no such things** es gibt nichts dergleichen; so etwas gibt es nicht; **once upon a time there was a princess** es war einmal eine Prinzessin; **to be or not to be** Sein oder Nichtsein; **the powers that be** die maßgeblichen Stellen; die da oben (*ugs.*); **for the time being** vorläufig; **Miss Jones that was** das frühere Fräulein Jones; **be that as it may** wie dem auch sei; Ⓑ (*remain*) bleiben; **I shan't be a moment** *or* **second** ich komme gleich; noch eine Minute; **she has been in her room for hours** sie ist schon seit Stunden in ihrem Zimmer; **let it be** lass es sein; **let him/her be** lass ihn/sie in Ruhe; Ⓒ (*attend*) sein; **is he here?** ist er hier?; Ⓓ *indicating position in space or time* **he's upstairs** er ist oben; **how long has he been here?** wie lange ist er schon hier?; Ⓔ (*be situated*) sein; **Hungary is in the heart of Europe** Ungarn liegt im Herzen Europas; **the chair is in the corner** der Stuhl steht *od.* ist in der Ecke; **here you are** (*on arrival*) da bist du/da seid ihr [ja]; (*on giving sb. sth.*) so, bitte!; Ⓕ (*happen, occur, take place*) stattfinden; sein; **where will the party be?** wo ist die Party?; wo findet die Party statt?; Ⓖ (*go, come*) **be off with you!** geh/geht!; **I'm off** *or* **for home** ich gehe jetzt nach Hause; **she's from Australia** sie stammt *od.* ist aus Australien; **are you for London?** wollen Sie nach London?; sind Sie auf dem Weg nach London?; **be on one's way** unterwegs *od.* auf dem Wege sein; Ⓗ (*on visit etc.*) sein; **have you [ever] been to London?** bist du schon einmal in London gewesen?; **has anyone been?** ist jemand da gewesen?; **has the postman been?** war der Briefträger *od.* die Post schon da?; Ⓘ **be for/against sth./sb.** für/gegen etw./jmdn. sein; **How kind she is. She's been and tidied the room** (*coll.*) Wie nett sie ist. Sie hat doch wirklich das Zimmer aufgeräumt; **the children have**

**been at the biscuits** die Kinder waren an den Keksen (*ugs.*); **I've been into this matter** ich habe mich mit der Sache befasst. **3** *v. aux.* **A** *forming passive* werden; **the child was found** das Kind wurde gefunden; **German is spoken in this shop** in diesem Geschäft wird Deutsch gesprochen; **B** (*arch.*) *forming past tenses of verbs of motion* sein; **the sun is set** die Sonne ist untergegangen; **when I got there she was gone** als ich hinkam, war sie schon [weg]gegangen; **Christ is risen** (*Relig.*) Christ[us] ist auferstanden *od.* (*dichter. veralt.*) erstanden; **the prisoner is fled** der Gefangene ist geflohen; **C** *forming continuous tenses, active* **he is reading** er liest [gerade]; er ist beim Lesen; **I am leaving tomorrow** ich reise morgen [ab]; **the train was departing when I got there** der Zug fuhr gerade ab, als ich ankam; **D** *forming continuous tenses, passive* **the house is/was being built** das Haus wird/wurde [gerade] gebaut *od.* ist/war im Bau; **E** *expr. obligation* **be to** sollen; **I am to inform you** ich soll Sie unterrichten; **you are to report to the police** Sie sollen sich bei der Polizei melden; **he is to clean the house thoroughly** er soll das ganze Haus gründlich putzen; **he is to be admired** er ist zu bewundern; **F** *expr. arrangement* **the Queen is to arrive at 3 p.m.** die Königin soll um 15 Uhr eintreffen; **he is to be there** er soll dort sein; **I am to go** ich soll gehen; **G** *expr. possibility* **the car is for sale** das Auto ist zu verkaufen; **it was not to be seen** es war nicht zu sehen; **there was nothing to be seen** es war nichts zu sehen; **I was not to be sidetracked** ich ließ mich nicht ablenken; **H** *expr. destiny* **they were never to meet again** sie sollten sich nie wieder treffen; **I** *expr. condition* **if I were to tell you that …, were I to tell you that …** wenn ich dir sagen würde, dass … **4** **bride-/husband-to-be** zukünftige Braut/zukünftiger Ehemann; **mother-/father-to-be** werdende Mutter/werdender Vater; **the be-all and end-all** das A und O

**beach** /'bi:tʃ/ **1** *n.* Strand, *der;* **~ area** Strandzone, *die;* **on the ~:** am Strand; *attrib.* **~ hat/suit/shoe** Strandhut/-anzug/-schuh, *der.* **2** *v.t.* auf [den] Strand setzen ‹Schiff usw.›; ans Ufer ziehen ‹Boot, Wal›

**beach: ~ball** *n.* Wasserball, *der;* **~comber** /'bi:tʃkəʊmə(r)/ *n.* **A** Strandgutsammler, *der;* **B** (*wave*) große Brandungswelle; **~head** *n.* (*Mil.*) Brückenkopf, *der;* **~ volleyball** *n.* Beachvolleyball, *das;* **~wear** *n.* Strandkleidung, *die*

**beacon** /'bi:kn/ *n.* **A** Leucht-, Signalfeuer, *das;* (*Naut.*) Leuchtbake, *die;* **B** (*Brit.*) (*hill*) leicht sichtbarer Hügel (*für ein Signalfeuer*); **C** (*lighthouse, tower, etc.*) Leuchtfeuer, *das;* **D** (*radio station*) Funkfeuer, *das;* **E** (*signal light*) Signalleuchte, *die;* (*for aircraft*) Landelicht, *das;* **F** (*fig.*) Leitstern, *der*

**bead** /bi:d/ **1** *n.* **A** Perle, *die;* **~s** Perlen *Pl.;* Perlenkette, *die;* **tell one's ~s** den Rosenkranz beten; **~s of dew** Tautropfen *od.* (*geh.*) -perlen; **~s of perspiration** *or* **sweat** Schweißtropfen *od.* -perlen; **B** (*gunsight*) Kornspitze, *die;* Korn, *das;* **draw a ~ on sb./sth.** auf jmdn./etw. zielen; **C** (*tyre edge*) ⇒ **beading** C; **D** (*Archit.*) ⇒ **beading** B. **2** *v.t.* mit Perlen/perlenartiger Verzierung versehen

**beading** /'bi:dɪŋ/ *n.* **A** Perlenstickerei, *die;* **B** (*Archit.*) Perl- *od.* Rundstab, *der;* Abdeckstab, *der;* **C** (*tyre edge*) Wulst, *der od. die*

**beadle** /'bi:dl/ *n.* ▶ **1261** (*Brit.*) (*Hist.: of church*) Kirchendiener, *der;* (*with more responsibility, esp. Scot.*) Küster, *der;* (*of university*) Pedell, *der*

**beady** /'bi:dɪ/ *adj.* **~ eyes** Knopfaugen; **those ~ eyes of hers don't miss anything** ihrem wachsamen Blick entgeht nichts; **I've got my ~ eye on you** ich lasse dich nicht aus den Augen

**'beady-eyed** *adj.* mit Knopfaugen *nachgestellt;* (*watchful*) mit wachen Augen *nachgestellt*

**beagle** /'bi:gl/ *n.* Beagle, *der*

**beak**[1] /bi:k/ *n.* Schnabel, *der;* (*of turtle, octopus*) Mundwerkzeug, *das;* (*fig.: large, hooked nose*) Hakennase, *die;* Zinken, *der* (*salopp*)

**beak**[2] *n.* (*Brit. coll.*) **A** (*magistrate, judge*) Kadi, *der* (*ugs.*); **B** (*schoolmaster*) Pauker, *der*

**beaked** /bi:kt/ *adj.* geschnäbelt

**beaker** /'bi:kə(r)/ *n.* **A** (*cup*) Becher, *der;* **B** (*Chem.*) Becherglas, *das*

**'be-all** ⇒ **be** 4

**beam** /bi:m/ **1** *n.* **A** (*timber etc.*) Balken, *der;* **behold the ~ in thine own eye** (*Bibl.*) sieh den Balken in deinem eigenen Auge; **B** (*in loom*) Baum, *der;* **C** (*Agric.: in plough*) Grindel, *der;* Pflugbaum, *der;* **D** (*in balance*) Waagebalken, *der;* **E** (*Naut.*) (*ship's breadth*) [größte] Schiffsbreite; (*side of ship*) [Schiffs]seite, *die;* **~s** Decksbalken; **on the ~:** querschiffs; **on the port ~:** backbords; **broad in the ~** (*fig. coll.*) breithüftig; **F** (*ray etc.*) [Licht]strahl, *der;* **~ of light** Lichtstrahl, *der;* **the car's headlamps were on full ~:** die Scheinwerfer des Wagens waren aufgeblendet; **G** (*Aeronaut., Mil., etc.: guide*) Peil- *od.* Leitstrahl, *der;* (*course*) **come in on the ~:** auf dem Peil- *od.* Leitstrahl ein- *od.* anfliegen; **be off ~** (*fig. coll.*) danebenliegen (*ugs.*); **be on the ~** (*fig. coll.*) richtig liegen (*ugs.*); **H** (*smile*) Strahlen, *das.* **2** *v.t.* **A** **~ [forth]** ausstrahlen; **B** (*broadcast*) aussenden; ausstrahlen ‹Wellen, Licht, Rundfunkprogramm›; (*fig.: aim*) **~ at** [hin]zielen auf (+ *Akk.*); **~ towards** richten *od.* lenken auf (+ *Akk.*); **this magazine is ~ed at housewives** die Zielleser[schaft] dieser Illustrierten sind Hausfrauen. **3** *v.i.* **A** (*shine*) strahlen; glänzen; **the sun ~ed down** die Sonne strahlte vom Himmel; **B** (*smile*) strahlen; **~ at sb.** jmdn. anstrahlen

**'beam-ends** *n. pl.* **the ship is on her ~:** das Schiff liegt auf der Seite; **be on one's ~** (*fig.*) pleite (*ugs.*) *od.* in großer Geldnot sein

**beaming** /'bi:mɪŋ/ *adj.* strahlend

**bean** /bi:n/ **1** *n.* **A** Bohne, *die;* **full of ~s** (*fig. coll.*) putzmunter (*ugs.*); quietschlebendig (*ugs.*); **he hasn't [got] a ~** (*fig. coll.*) er hat keinen roten Heller (*ugs.*); **not worth a ~** (*coll.*) nicht die Bohne *od.* keinen Pfifferling wert (*ugs.*); ⇒ *also* **old** 1 D; **spill**[1] 1 B; **B** (*Amer. coll.: head*) Birne, *die* (*fig. salopp*). **2** *v.t.* (*Amer. coll.: hit*) **~ sb.** jmdm. eins auf die Birne geben (*salopp*)

**bean: ~bag** *n.* **A** *mit Bohnen gefülltes Säckchen zum Spielen;* **B** (*cushion*) Knautschsessel, *der;* **~ curd** *n.* Soja[bohnen]quark, *der;* **~ feast** *n.* (*Brit. coll.*) Gelage, *das;* (*employees' annual dinner*) Betriebsfeier, *die*

**beano** /'bi:nəʊ/ *n., pl.* **~s** (*Brit. coll.*) Gelage, *das*

**bean: ~pole** *n.* (*lit. or fig.*) Bohnenstange, *die;* **~sprout** *n.* Sojabohnenkeim, *der;* **~stalk** *n.* Bohnenstängel, *der;* **~stick** *n.* Bohnenstange, *die*

**bear**[1] /beə(r)/ *n.* **A** Bär, *der;* **be like a ~ with a sore head** (*coll.*) ein richtiger Brummbär sein (*ugs.*); **B** (*fig.*) Tollpatsch, *der* (*ugs.*); **C** (*Astron.*) **Great/Little B~:** Großer/Kleiner Bär; **D** (*St. Exch.*) Baissier, *der*

**bear**[2] **1** *v.t.,* **bore** /bɔ:(r)/, **borne** /bɔ:n/ **A** (*show*) tragen ‹Wappen, Inschrift, Unterschrift›; aufweisen, zeigen ‹Merkmal, Spuren, Ähnlichkeit, Verwandtschaft›; **~ a resemblance** *or* **likeness to sb.** Ähnlichkeit mit jmdm. haben; **B** (*be known by*) tragen, führen ‹Namen, Titel›; **C** **~ some/little relation to sth.** einen gewissen/wenig Bezug zu etw. haben; **D** (*poet./formal: carry*) tragen ‹Waffe, Last›; mitgebracht haben, mit sich führen ‹Geschenk, Botschaft›; **I was borne along by the fierce current** die starke Strömung trug mich mit [sich]; **be borne in upon sb.** jmdm. klar werden; jmdm. zu[m] Bewusstsein kommen; **E** (*endure, tolerate*) ertragen, erdulden ‹Schmerz, Kummer›; *with neg.* ertragen, aushalten ‹Schmerz›; ausstehen, leiden ‹Geruch, Lärm›; **he couldn't ~ the misery** er konnte das Elend nicht ertragen; **I can't ~ watching her eat** ich kann ihr beim Essen einfach nicht zusehen; **I can't ~ salami** ich kann Salami einfach nicht ausstehen; **F** (*sustain*) tragen, übernehmen ‹Verantwortlichkeit, Kosten›; auf sich (*Akk.*) nehmen ‹Schuld›; tragen, aushalten ‹Gewicht›; **G** (*be fit for*) vertragen; **it does not ~ repeating** *or* **repetition** das lässt sich unmöglich wiederholen; (*is not important*) es lohnt sich nicht, das zu wiederholen; **his language won't ~ repeating** man kann seine [gemeinen] Ausdrücke gar nicht wiederholen; **it will not ~ scrutiny** es hält einer Überprüfung nicht stand; **it does not ~ thinking about** daran darf man gar nicht denken; **~ comparison with sth.** den *od.* einen Vergleich mit etw. aushalten; einem *od.* dem Vergleich mit etw. standhalten; **H** (*carry in the mind*) hegen ‹Hass, Liebe›; **~ sb. a grudge** *or* **a grudge against sb.** jmdm. gegenüber nachtragend sein; **~ sb. malice** *or* **malice towards sb.** jmdm. grollen; einen Groll auf jmdn. hegen; **~ sth. in mind** an etw. (*Akk.*) denken; etw. nicht vergessen; **~ in mind that …:** vergiss nicht, dass …; merk dir, dass …; **I** (*give birth to*) gebären ‹Kind, Junges›; ⇒ *also* **born**; **J** (*yield*) tragen ‹Blumen, Früchte usw.›; bringen, tragen ‹Zinsen›; **his efforts bore no result** (*fig.*) seine Bemühungen hatten *od.* brachten keinen Erfolg; **~ fruit** (*fig.*) Früchte tragen (*geh.*); **K** (*bring sth. needed*) leisten ‹Hilfe›; **~ witness** *or* **testimony to sth.** von etw. zeugen *od.* Zeugnis ablegen; **~ sb. company** jmdm. Gesellschaft leisten; **~ a hand** helfen; **~ a hand in an undertaking** bei einem Vorhaben helfen; **L** (*behave*) **~ oneself well/with dignity** sich gut betragen *od.* benehmen/Würde zeigen. **2** *v.i.,* **bore, borne** **A** **the path ~s [to the] left** der Weg führt [nach] links; **he bore right** er hielt sich [nach] rechts; **B** **bring to ~:** aufbieten ‹Kraft, Energie›; ausüben ‹Druck›; **bring one's influence to ~:** seinen Einfluss geltend machen

**~ a'way** *v.t.* wegtragen; davontragen ‹Preis usw.›; **be borne away** fort- *od.* davongetragen werden

**~ 'down** **1** *v.t.* niederdrücken; überwältigen ‹Feind›; **be borne down by the weight of …:** von der Last (+ *Gen.*) gebeugt sein. **2** *v.i.* **~ down on sb./sth.** auf jmdn./etw. zusteuern; sich jmdm./einer Sache schnell nähern; ‹Schiff:› auf jmdn./etw. zu- *od.* lossegeln; ‹Wagen:› auf jmdn./etw. zufahren *od.* -steuern

**~ 'off** ⇒ **~ away**

**~ on** ⇒ **~ upon**

**~ 'out** *v.t.* **A** hinaustragen; **B** (*fig.*) bestätigen ‹Bericht, Erklärung›; **~ sb. out** jmdm. Recht geben; **~ sb. out in sth.** jmdn. in etw. (*Dat.*) bestätigen

**~ 'up** **1** *v.t.* halten; [unter]stützen. **2** *v.i.* **A** durchhalten; ausharren (*geh.*); **~ up well under sth.** etw. gut ertragen; **B** (*Naut.*) abfallen

**~ upon** *v.t.* (*relate to*) sich beziehen auf (+ *Akk.*); Bezug haben auf (+ *Akk.*); im Zusammenhang stehen mit

**~ with** *v.t.* **~ with sb./sth.** mit jmdm./etw. Nachsicht haben; **~ with sth. for the time being** etw. vorübergehend auf sich (*Akk.*) nehmen; **if you'll ~ with me a little longer** wenn Sie sich vielleicht noch einen Moment gedulden wollen

**bearable** /'beərəbl/ *adj.* zum Aushalten *nachgestellt;* erträglich ‹Situation, Beruf›

**bear: ~-baiting** *n.* (*Hist.*) Bärenhatz, *die;* **~ cub** *n.* Bärenjunge, *das*

**beard** /bɪəd/ **1** *n.* **A** Bart, *der;* **full ~:** Vollbart, *der;* **small pointed ~:** Spitzbart, *der;* **B** (*Bot.*) Grannen. **2** *v.t.* trotzen (+ *Dat.*); Trotz bieten (+ *Dat.*); **~ the lion in his den** (*fig.*) sich in die Höhle des Löwen wagen

**bearded** /'bɪədɪd/ *adj.* bärtig; **be ~:** einen Bart haben; **a ~ gentleman** ein Herr mit Bart

**bearer** /'beərə(r)/ *n.* **A** (*carrier*) Träger, *der*/Trägerin, *die;* (*of letter, message, cheque, banknote*) Überbringer, *der*/Überbringerin, *die;* **cheque to ~:** Inhaberscheck, *der;* **payable to ~:** zahlbar an Überbringer *od.* Inhaber ‹Scheck›; **I am the ~ of glad tidings** ich bringe euch eine frohe Botschaft; **B the ~ of shares/bonds** der Aktionär/Obligationär; **~ share/bond** Inhaberaktie/Inhaberschuldverschreibung, *die*

**bear: ~ garden** *n.* (*fig.*) Tollhaus, *das* (*fig.*); **~ hug** *n.* kräftige Umarmung

**bearing** /'beərɪŋ/ *n.* **A** (*behaviour*) Verhalten, *das;* Gebaren, *das* (*geh.*); (*deportment*) [Körper]haltung, *die;* **B** (*endurance*) Ertragen, *das;* Erdulden, *das;* **beyond** *or* **past [all] ~:** unerträglich; nicht zum Aushalten; **C** (*relation*) Zusammenhang, *der;* Bezug, *der;* **consider sth. in all its ~s** etw. in seiner ganzen Tragweite betrachten; **have some/no ~ on sth.** relevant/irrelevant *od.* von Belang/belanglos für etw. sein; **D** (*significance*) Bedeutung, *die;* [tieferer] Sinn; **the ~ of a remark** die Bedeutung *od.* der Sinn einer Bemerkung; **E** (*Mech. Engin.*) Lager, *das;* **F** (*compass ~*) Lage, *die;* Position, *die;* **take a compass ~:** den Kompasskurs feststellen; **get one's ~s** sich orientieren; (*fig.*) sich zurechtfinden; **I have lost my ~s** (*lit. or fig.*) ich habe die Orientierung verloren; **G** (*Her.*) Wappenbild, *das*

**bearish** /'beərɪʃ/ *adj.* **A** brummig; unfreundlich; **B** (*St. Exch.*) baissierend; auf Baisse spekulierend ‹Kapitalanleger›

**'bear market** *n.* (*St. Exch.*) Markt mit fallenden Preisen; Baissemarkt, *der*

**'bearskin** *n.* **A** Bärenfell, *das;* Bärenhaut, *die;* **B** (*Mil.*) Bärenfellmütze, *die*

**beast** /bi:st/ *n.* Tier, *das;* (*quadruped*) Vierbeiner, *der;* (*ferocious, wild*) Bestie, *die;* (*fig.: brutal person*) roher, brutaler Mensch; Bestie, *die* (*abwertend*); (*disliked person*) Scheusal, *das* (*abwertend*); **it was a ~ of a winter** das war ein scheußlicher Winter; **the B~** (*Bibl.*) das Tier; **man and ~:** Mensch und Tier

**beastliness** /'bi:stlmɪs/ *n., no pl.* (*coll.*) Scheußlichkeit, *die*

**beastly** /'bi:stlɪ/ *adj., adv.* (*coll.*) scheußlich

**beat** /bi:t/ **1** *v.t.*, **~, beaten** /'bi:tn/ **A** (*strike repeatedly*) schlagen ‹Trommel, Rhythmus, Eier, Teig›; klopfen ‹Teppich›; hämmern ‹Gold, Silber usw.›; **~ the dust out of a carpet/cushion** einen Teppich/ein Polster ausklopfen; **~ a path through sth.** sich (*Dat.*) einen Weg durch etw. bahnen; **~ one's breast** (*lit. or fig.*) sich (*Dat.*) an die Brust schlagen; **~ its chest** ‹Affe:› sich (*Dat.*) gegen die Brust trommeln; **~ some sense into sb.** jmdm. Vernunft einprügeln; **~ the bounds** (*Brit.*) die Grenzen der Gemarkung abgehen; **~ one's brains** sich (*Dat.*) den Kopf zerbrechen; **~ it** (*coll.*) sich verdrücken (*ugs.*); **~ it!** (*coll.*) hau ab! (*ugs.*); verschwinde!; **B** (*hit*) schlagen; [ver]prügeln; **be ~en to death** totgeschlagen *od.* -geprügelt werden; **C** (*defeat*) schlagen ‹Mannschaft, Gegner›; (*surmount*) in den Griff bekommen ‹Inflation, Arbeitslosigkeit, Krise›; **~ the deadline** den Termin noch einhalten; **D** (*surpass*) brechen ‹Rekord›; übertreffen ‹Leistung›; **hard to ~:** schwer zu schlagen; **you can't ~** *or* **nothing ~s French cuisine** es geht [doch] nichts über die französische Küche; **~ that!** das soll mal einer nachmachen!; **~ everything** (*coll.*), **~ the band** (*coll.*) alles in den Schatten stellen; **~ sb. to it** jmdm. zuvorkommen; **can you ~ it?** ist denn das zu fassen?; **E** (*circumvent*) umgehen; **~ the system** sich gegen das bestehende System durchsetzen; **F** (*perplex*) **it ~s me how/why ...:** es ist mir ein Rätsel, wie/warum ...; **G ~ time** den Takt schlagen; **H** (*Hunting*) **~ the bushes/water** den Treiber machen; **I** *p.p.* **~: I'm ~** (*coll.: exhausted*) ich bin geschafft (*ugs.*) *od.* erledigt (*ugs.*). ⇒ *also* **beaten** 2.

**2** *v.i.*, **~, beaten** **A** (*throb*) ‹Herz:› schlagen, klopfen; ‹Puls:› schlagen; **my heart seemed to stop ~ing** ich dachte, mir bleibt das Herz stehen; **B** ‹Sonne:› brennen (**on** auf + *Akk.*); ‹Wind, Wellen:› schlagen (**on** auf + *Akk.*, **against** gegen); ‹Regen, Hagel:› prasseln, trommeln (**against** gegen); **C ~ about the bush** um den [heißen] Brei herumreden (*ugs.*); **D** (*knock*) klopfen, pochen (**at** an + *Dat.*); **E** (*Naut.*) kreuzen.

**3** *n.* **A** (*stroke, throbbing*) Schlag, *der;* Schlagen, *das;* (*rhythm*) Takt, *der;* **his heart missed a ~:** ihm stockte das Herz; **~ [music]** Beat, *der;* Beatmusik, *die;* **B** (*Mus.*) Schlag, *der;* (*of metronome, baton*) Taktschlag, *der;* **C** (*Phys.*) Schwebung, *die;* **D** (*of policeman, watchman*) Runde, *die;* (*habitual round*) übliche Runde; (*area*) Revier, *das;* **be off sb.'s [usual] ~** (*fig.*) nicht in jmds. Fach schlagen; **E** (*Hunting*) Treibjagd, *die;* **F did you ever see the ~ of that?** (*Amer. coll.*) hast du so etwas schon mal gesehen?; **G** (*Amer. Journ.: scoop*) Knüller, *der* (*ugs.*)

**~ a'bout** *v.i.* [herum]suchen

**~ 'back** *v.t.* zurückschlagen ‹Feind›

**~ 'down** **1** *v.i.* ‹Sonne:› herniederbrennen; ‹Regen:› niederprasseln. **2** *v.t.* **A** einschlagen ‹Tür›; **B** (*in bargaining*) herunterhandeln

**~ 'in** *v.t.* einschlagen; demolieren (*ugs.*)

**~ 'off** *v.t.* abwehren, zurückschlagen ‹Angriff›

**~ 'out** *v.t.* **A** heraushämmern ‹Rhythmus, Melodie›; aushämmern ‹Metall›; ausschlagen ‹Feuer›; **B** (*Amer.: defeat*) aus dem Feld schlagen ‹Konkurrenten›

**~ 'up** *v.t.* **A** zusammenschlagen ‹Person›; schlagen ‹Sahne usw.›; **B** (*attract*) anwerben ‹Rekruten›

**beaten** /'bi:tn/ **1** ⇒ **beat** 1, 2. **2** *adj.* **A a ~ track** *or* **path** ein Trampelpfad; **off the ~ track** (*remote*) weit abgelegen; weitab vom Schuss (*ugs.*); **he has always kept to the ~ track** (*fig.*) er ist immer in den gewohnten Bahnen geblieben; **go off the ~ track** (*fig.*) vom üblichen Weg abweichen; **B** (*hammered*) gehämmert ‹Silber, Gold›; **C** (*exhausted, dejected*) erschöpft, (*ugs.*) erledigt ‹Person›

**beater** /'bi:tə(r)/ *n.* **A** (*Cookery*) Rührbesen, *der;* **B** (*Hunting*) Treiber, *der;* **C** (*carpet ~*) [Teppich]klopfer, *der*

**beatific** /bi:ə'tɪfɪk/ *adj.* beglückend; (*blissful*) beglückt, selig ‹Lächeln›

**beatification** /bɪætɪfɪ'keɪʃn/ *n.* (*Relig.*) Seligsprechung, *die;* Beatifikation, *die*

**beatify** /bɪ'ætɪfaɪ/ *v.t.* (*Relig.*) selig sprechen; beatifizieren

**beating** /'bi:tɪŋ/ *n.* **A** (*punishment*) **a ~:** Schläge *Pl.;* Prügel *Pl.;* **a good ~:** eine gehörige Tracht Prügel (*ugs.*); **B** (*defeat*) Niederlage, *die;* **give sb. a good ~:** jmdm. eine schwere Niederlage zufügen; **take** *or* **get a [sound] ~:** eine [schwere] Niederlage hinnehmen [müssen]; **C** (*surpassing*) **take some/a lot of ~:** nicht leicht zu übertreffen sein/seinesgleichen suchen

**beatitude** /bɪ'ætɪtju:d/ *n.* **A** (*blessedness*) [Glück]seligkeit, *die;* **B** *in pl.* Seligpreisungen

**'beat-up** *adj.* (*coll.*) ramponiert (*ugs.*)

**beau** /bəʊ/ *n., pl.* **~x** /bəʊz/ *or* **~s** **A** (*ladies' man*) Frauenheld, *der;* (*fop*) Beau, *der* (*geh.*); Dandy, *der* (*geh.*); **B** (*Amer.: boyfriend*) Galan, *der* (*veralt.*); Verehrer, *der*

**Beaufort scale** /'bəʊfət skeɪl/ *n.* (*Meteorol.*) Beaufortskala, *die*

**Beaujolais** /'bəʊʒəleɪ/ *n.* Beaujolais, *der*

**beaut** /bju:t/ (*Austral., NZ, & Amer. sl.*) **1** *n.* Prachtexemplar, *das;* (*woman*) Schönheit, *die.* **2** *adj.* klasse (*ugs.*)

**beauteous** /'bju:tɪəs/ *adj.* (*poet.*) wunderschön; herrlich

**beautician** /bju:'tɪʃn/ *n.* **▶1261** Kosmetiker, *der*/Kosmetikerin, *die*

**beautification** /bju:tɪfɪ'keɪʃn/ *n.* Verschönerung, *die;* (*of the body*) Schönheitspflege, *die*

**beautiful** /'bju:tɪfl/ *adj.* [ausgesprochen] schön; wunderschön ‹Augen, Aussicht, Blume, Kleid, Morgen, Musik, Schmuck›; (*enjoyable, impressive*) großartig; **the B~ People** die Hippies; **~ letters** (*Amer.*) Belletristik, *die;* schöne Literatur; **small is ~:** klein ist schön

**beautifully** /'bju:tɪfəlɪ/ *adv.* wunderbar; (*coll.: very well*) prima (*ugs.*); (*coll.: very*) wunderbar, schön ‹weich, warm›; **you did [that] ~:** du hast es prima gemacht

**beautify** /'bju:tɪfaɪ/ *v.t.* verschönern; schöner machen; (*adorn*) [aus]schmücken; **~ oneself** sich schönmachen (*ugs.*)

**beauty** /'bju:tɪ/ *n.* **A** *no pl.* Schönheit, *die;* (*of action, response*) Eleganz, *die;* (*of idea, simplicity, sacrifice*) Größe, *die;* **~ is only skin deep** man kann nicht nach dem Äußeren urteilen; **be a thing of ~:** wunderschön sein; **B** (*person or thing*) Schönheit, *die;* (*animal*) wunderschönes Tier; **she is a real ~:** sie ist wirklich eine Schönheit; **B~ and the Beast** die Schöne und das Tier; **They've just bought a new car. It's a ~:** Sie haben sich (*Dat.*) gerade einen neuen Wagen gekauft. Er ist wunderbar; **C** (*exceptionally good specimen*) Prachtexemplar, *das;* **that last goal was a ~:** dieses letzte Tor war ein richtiges Bilderbuchtor; **D** (*beautiful feature*) Schöne, *das;* **her eyes are her great ~:** das Schöne an ihr sind ihre Augen; **the ~ of it/of living in California** das Schöne *od.* Gute daran/am Leben in Kalifornien

**beauty: ~ competition, ~ contest** *ns.* Schönheitswettbewerb, *der;* **~ parlour** ⇒ **~ salon;** **~ queen** *n.* Schönheitskönigin, *die;* **~ salon** *n.* Schönheitssalon, *der;* Kosmetiksalon, *der;* **~ spot** *n.* Schönheitsfleck, *der;* (*patch*) Schönheitspflästerchen, *das;* (*place*) schönes Fleckchen [Erde]; **a local ~ spot** ein Ausflugsziel am Ort; **~ treatment** *n.* Schönheitsbehandlung, *die*

**beaux** *pl. of* **beau**

**beaver** /'bi:və(r)/ **1** *n.* **A** *pl. same or* **~s** Biber, *der;* Biberratte, *die;* **eager ~** (*fig. coll.*) Übereifrige, *der/die;* (*esp. at school*) Streber, *der*/Streberin, *die;* **B** (*fur*) Biber[pelz], *der.* **2** *v.i.* (*Brit.*) **~ away** schuften (*ugs.*); eifrig arbeiten (**at** an + *Dat.*)

**beaver: B~board** ® *n.* (*Amer.*) Hartfaserplatte, *die;* **~ lamb** *n.* Biberlamm, *das*

**becalmed** /bɪ'kɑ:md/ *adj.* **be ~:** in einer Flaute *od.* Windstille treiben

**became** ⇒ **become**

**because** /bɪ'kɒz/ **1** *conj.* weil; **one of the reasons why she stopped is ~ she was tired** einer der Gründe, warum sie aufhörte, ist, dass sie müde war; **he is popular ~ handsome** er ist beliebt, weil er gut aussieht; **that is ~ you don't know German** das liegt daran, dass du kein Deutsch kannst. **2** *adv.* **~ of** wegen (+ *Gen.*); **don't come just ~ of me** nur meinetwegen brauchen Sie nicht zu kommen; **~ of which he ...:** weswegen er ...

**beck¹** /bek/ *n.* (*dial.: brook*) [Wild]bach, *der*

**beck²** *n.* **be at sb.'s ~ and call** jmdm. zur Verfügung stehen; **have sb. at one's ~ and call** jmdn. zur Verfügung haben; ganz über jmdn. verfügen können

**beckon** /'bekn/ **1** *v.t.* **A** winken; **~ sb. in/over** jmdn. herein-/herbei- *od.* herüberwinken; **B** (*fig.: invite*) locken; rufen. **2** *v.i.* **A ~ to sb.** jmdm. winken *od.* ein Zeichen geben; jmdn. zu sich winken; **B** (*fig.: be inviting*) locken

**become** /bɪ'kʌm/ **1** *copula, forms as* **come** werden; **~ a politician/dentist** Politiker/Zahnarzt werden; **~ a hazard/nuisance/rule** zu einem Risiko/zu einer Plage/zur Regel werden; **~ popular/angry** beliebt/böse werden; **~ accustomed** *or* **used to sb./sth.** sich an jmdn./etw. gewöhnen. **2** *v.i., forms as* **come** werden; **what has ~ of him?** was ist aus ihm geworden?; **what has ~ of that guidebook/courier?** wo ist der Reiseführer geblieben?; **what is to ~ of you?** was soll bloß aus dir werden?. **3** *v.t., forms as* **come** **A** ⇒ **befit;** **B** (*suit*) **~ sb.** jmdm. stehen; zu jmdm. passen

**becoming** /bɪ'kʌmɪŋ/ *adj.* **A** (*fitting*) schicklich (*geh.*); geziemend (*geh.*); **it is not ~ for a young lady to ...:** es ziemt sich für eine junge Dame nicht, zu ...; **B** (*flattering*) vorteilhaft, kleidsam ‹Hut, Kleid, Frisur›

**becquerel** /'bekərel/ *n.* (*Phys.*) Becquerel, *das*

**bed** /bed/ **1** *n.* **A** Bett, *das;* (*without bedstead*) Lager, *das;* **they talked together till ~** (*coll.*) sie unterhielten sich, bis sie ins Bett gingen; **he's very fond of his ~:** er liegt gerne im Bett; **be/lie in ~:** im Bett sein/liegen; **~ and board** (*lodging*) Unterkunft und

Verpflegung; (*marital relations*) Tisch und Bett; **~ and breakfast** Zimmer mit Frühstück; **a ~ and breakfast place** eine Frühstückspension; **get into/out of ~:** ins *od.* zu Bett gehen/aufstehen; **go to ~:** zu *od.* ins Bett gehen; **go to ~ with sb.** (*fig.*) mit jmdm. ins Bett gehen (*ugs.*); **the newspaper has gone to ~** (*fig.*) die Zeitung ist im Druck; **make the ~:** das Bett machen; **put sb. to ~:** jmdn. zu *od.* ins Bett bringen; **put a paper to ~** (*fig.*) eine Zeitung in Druck geben; **life isn't a** *or* **is no ~ of roses** (*fig.*) das Leben ist kein reines Vergnügen; **his life isn't exactly a ~ of roses** (*fig.*) er ist nicht gerade auf Rosen gebettet; **~ of sickness** (*literary*) Krankenlager, *das* (*geh.*); **have got out of ~ on the wrong side** (*fig.*) mit dem linken Fuß zuerst aufgestanden sein; **as you make your ~ so you must lie on it** (*prov.*) wie man sich bettet, so liegt man; **take to one's ~:** sich krank ins Bett legen; **be confined to ~:** ans Bett gefesselt sein (*fig.*); **be brought to ~** (*literary*) niederkommen (**of** mit); entbunden werden (**of** von); **B** (*flat base*) Unterlage, *die;* (*of machine*) Bett, *das;* (*of road, railway, etc.*) Unterbau, *der;* Kies-/Schotterbett, *das;* (*of billiard table*) Schieferplatte (*die mit grünem Kammgarntuch bespannt ist*); **C** (*in garden*) Beet, *das;* (*for osiers etc.*) Pflanzung, *die;* **D** (*of sea, lake*) Grund, *der;* Boden, *der;* (*of river*) Bett, *das;* **E** (*layer*) Schicht, *die;* **F** (*of oysters etc.*) Bank, *die.*
**2** *v.t.*, **-dd- A** ins Bett legen; **B** (*fig. coll.*) beschlafen ‹Frau›; **C** (*plant*) setzen ‹Pflanze, Sämling›.
**3** *v.i.*, **-dd-** zu *od.* ins Bett gehen; schlafen gehen; **he ~s with his mistress** (*fig.*) er schläft mit seiner Geliebten

**~ 'down 1** *v.t.* mit Streu versorgen ‹Pferd usw.›; **the troops were ~ded down in a barn** die Soldaten wurden über Nacht in einer Scheune einquartiert; **the farmer ~ded down the tramp** der Bauer beherbergte den Landstreicher. **2** *v.i.* kampieren; **she ~s down with her boyfriend** (*fig.*) sie schläft mit ihrem Freund

**~ 'in** *v.t.* einlassen

**~ 'out** *v.t.* auspflanzen ‹Pflanzen›

**B. Ed.** /bi: 'ed/ *abbr.* **Bachelor of Education** Bakkalaureus der Erziehungswissenschaften; ⇒ *also* **B. Sc.**

**bedazzle** /bɪ'dæzl/ *v.t.* **A** blenden; **B** (*confuse*) verwirren

**bed: ~bug** *n.* [Bett]wanze, *die;* **~chamber** *n.* **A** (*arch.*) Schlafgemach, *das* (*veralt.*); Schlafzimmer, *das;* **B the Royal Bedchamber** das königliche Schlafgemach; **Lady/Gentleman of the Bedchamber** königliche Hofdame/königlicher Kammerjunker; **~clothes** *n. pl.* Bettzeug, *das;* **turn down** *or* **back the ~clothes** das Bett aufdecken

**beddable** /'bedəbl/ *adj.* (*coll.*) **be ~:** was fürs Bett sein (*ugs.*)

**bedding** /'bedɪŋ/ *n., no pl., no indef. art.* **A** Matratze und Bettzeug; (*for animal*) Streu, *das;* **B** (*Geol.*) Lagerung, *die;* Schichtung, *die*

**'bedding plant** *n.* Freilandpflanze, *die*

**beddy-byes** /'bedɪbaɪz/ *n.* (*child lang.*) Heiabett, *das* (*Kinderspr.*); Heia, *die* (*Kinderspr.*); **off to ~:** ab in die Heia *od.* ins Heiabett

**bedeck** /bɪ'dek/ *v.t.* schmücken; **~ oneself** sich aufputzen (*abwertend*); **~ed with flags** mit Fahnen geschmückt; fahnengeschmückt

**bedevil** /bɪ'devl/ *v.t.*, (*Brit.*) **-ll- A** (*spoil*) verderben; durcheinander bringen ‹System›; **B** (*plague, afflict*) heimsuchen; **that family is ~led by bad luck** diese Familie ist vom Pech verfolgt; **C** (*torment*) quälen; peinigen (*geh.*); **~ sb.'s life** jmdm. das Leben zur Hölle machen

**bed: ~fast** *adj.* (*arch.*) bettlägerig; **~fellow** *n.* Bettgenosse, *der*/-genossin, *die;* **make** *or* **be strange ~fellows** (*fig.*) ‹Personen:› ein merkwürdiges Gespann sein; ‹Staaten, Organisationen:› eine eigenartige Kombination sein; **~head** *n.* Kopfende des Bettes; **~jacket** *n.* Bettjacke, *die*

**bedlam** /'bedləm/ *n.* Chaos, *das;* Durcheinander, *das;* **absolute ~:** ein totales Chaos *od.* Durcheinander; **it is [like] ~ in here** hier geht es zu wie im Irrenhaus

**'bedlinen** *n.* Bettwäsche, *die*

**bedouin** /'bedu:ɪn/ *n., pl. same* Beduine, *der*/Beduinin, *die*

**bed: ~pan** *n.* Bettschüssel, *die;* Bettpfanne, *die;* **~plate** *n.* Grundplatte, *die;* Bodenplatte, *die;* **~post** *n.* Bettpfosten, *der*

**bedraggle** /bɪ'drægl/ *v.t.* [nass und] schmutzig machen; **~d** [nass und] verschmutzt *od.* schmutzig

**bed: ~ rest** *n.* Bettruhe, *die;* **~ridden** *adj.* bettlägerig; **~rock** *n.* Felssohle, *die;* (*fig.*) Basis, *die;* Fundament, *das;* **get** *or* **reach down to ~rock** (*fig.*) zum Kern der Sache kommen; einer Sache (*Dat.*) auf den Grund gehen; **~ roll** *n.* zusammengerolltes Bettzeug; **~room** *n.* Schlafzimmer, *das;* **~room comedy/farce** Schlafzimmerkomödie, *die;* **~room scene** Bettszene, *die;* **she has ~room eyes** sie hat einen Schlafzimmerblick (*ugs.*); **a two-~room[ed] house** ein Haus mit zwei Schlafzimmern; **~ set'tee** *n.* Bettcouch, *die;* **~side** *n.* Seite des Bettes, *die;* **be at the ~side** am Bett sein; **~side table/lamp** Nachttisch, *der*/Nachttischlampe, *die;* **~side reading** Bettlektüre, *die;* **a ~side book** ein Buch als Bettlektüre; **have a good ~side manner** ‹Arzt:› gut mit Kranken umgehen können; **~sit, ~'sitter** *ns.* (*coll.*), **~'sitting room** *n.* (*Brit.*) Wohnschlafzimmer, *das;* **~socks** *n. pl.* Bettsocken; **~sore** *n.* wundgelegene Stelle; **get ~sores** sich wundliegen; **~spread** *n.* Tagesdecke, *die;* **~stead** /'bedsted/ *n.* Bettgestell, *das;* **~straw** *n.* (*Bot.*) **[Our] Lady's ~straw** Echtes Labkraut; **~table** *n.* Krankentisch, *der;* **~time** *n.* Schlafenszeit, *die;* **it's past the children's ~time** die Kinder müssten schon im Bett sein; **will you have it finished by ~time?** bist du vor dem Schlafengehen damit fertig?; **a ~time story** eine Gutenachtgeschichte; **a novel that makes good ~time reading** ein Roman, den man gut vor dem Einschlafen lesen kann

**beduin** ⇒ **bedouin**

**'bed-wetting** *n.* Bettnässen, *das*

**bee** /bi:/ *n.* **A** Biene, *die;* **she's such a busy ~** (*fig.*) sie ist so ein fleißiges Mädchen; **as busy as a ~** (*fig.*) bienenfleißig; **have a ~ in one's bonnet** (*fig.*) einen Fimmel *od.* Tick haben (*ugs.*); **she thinks she's the ~'s knees** (*fig. coll.*) sie hält sich für die Größte (*ugs.*); **B** (*Amer.*) (*meeting*) *nachbarliche Versammlung zu gemeinsamer Arbeit;* (*party*) Fest, *das;* ⇒ *also* **spelling bee**

**Beeb** /bi:b/ *n.* (*Brit. coll.*) **the ~:** die BBC

**beech** /bi:tʃ/ *n.* **A** (*tree*) Buche, *die;* (*Austral.*) Scheinbuche, *die;* **B** (*wood*) Buche, *die;* Buchenholz, *das; attrib.* buchen

**beech: ~-marten** *n.* Steinmarder, *der;* **~-mast** *n.* Bucheckern *Pl.;* **~-nut** *n.* [Buch]ecker, *die;* **~wood** ⇒ **beech B**

**'bee-eater** *n.* (*Ornith.*) Bienenfresser, *der*

**beef** /bi:f/ **1** *n.* **A** *no pl.* Rindfleisch, *das;* Rind, *das;* **B** *no pl.* (*coll.: muscles*) Muskeln; **have plenty of ~:** sehr muskulös sein; **there's a great deal of ~ on him** er ist ganz schön mit Muskeln bepackt (*ugs.*); **C** *usu. in pl.* **beeves** /bi:vz/ *or* (*Amer.*) **~s** (*ox*) Mastrind, *das;* **D** *pl.* **~s** (*coll.: complaint*) Meckerei, *die* (*ugs.*). **2** *v.t.* **~ up** stärken. **3** *v.i.* (*coll.*) meckern (*ugs.*) (**about** über + *Akk.*)

**beef: ~burger** *n.* Beefburger, *der;* **~cake** *n.* (*Amer. coll.*) Muskeln *Pl.;* Bizeps, *der* (*ugs.*); **~ cattle** *n. pl.* Mastrinder; **~eater** *n.* (*Brit.*) Beefeater, *der;* **~steak** *n.* Beefsteak, *das;* **~steak fungus** Leberpilz, *der;* **~ 'tea** *n.* Kraftbrühe, *die;* Fleischbrühe, *die*

**beefy** /'bi:fɪ/ *adj.* **A** (*like beef*) wie Rindfleisch *nachgestellt;* Rindfleisch-; **B** (*coll.: muscular*) muskulös; (*fleshy*) massig

**bee: ~hive** *n.* Bienenstock, *der;* (*rounded*) Bienenkorb, *der;* (*fig.: scene of activity*) Taubenschlag, *der;* (*hairstyle*) toupierte Hochfrisur; **~-keeper** *n.* ▶ **1261** Imker, *der*/Imkerin, *die;* Bienenzüchter, *der*/-züchterin, *die;* **~-keeping** *n.* ▶ **1261** Imkerei, *die;* Bienenhaltung, *die;* Bienenzucht, *die;* **~line** *n.* **make a ~line for sth./sb.** schnurstracks auf etw./jmdn. zustürzen

**been** ⇒ **be**

**beep** /bi:p/ **1** *n.* Piepton, *der;* (*of car horn*) Tuten, *das.* **2** *v.i.* piepen; ‹Signalhorn:› hupen; **~ at sb.** jmdn. anhupen; **a ~ing sound** ein Piepton. **3** *v.t.* (*esp. Amer.*) ⇒ **bleep 3**

**beeper** /'bi:pə(r)/ *n.* Piepser, *der*

**beer** /bɪə(r)/ *n.* Bier, *das;* **order two ~s** zwei Bier bestellen; **brew various ~s** verschiedene Biere *od.* Biersorten brauen; **life is not all ~ and skittles** (*fig.*) das Leben ist kein reines Vergnügen; **small ~:** Dünnbier, *das* (*ugs.*); (*fig.: trifles*) Nebensächlichkeiten *Pl.;* Kleinigkeiten *Pl.;* **that firm's turnover is only small ~:** der Umsatz dieser Firma ist kaum der Rede wert; **he is only small ~:** er hat nichts zu sagen

**beer: ~ barrel** *n.* Bierfass, *das;* **~ belly** *n.* (*coll.*) Bierbauch, *der* (*ugs.*); **~ bottle** *n.* Bierflasche, *die;* **~ can** *n.* Bierdose, *die;* **~ cellar** *n.* Bierkeller, *der;* **~ crate** *n.* Bierkasten, *der;* **~ drinker** *n.* Biertrinker, *der;* **~ engine** *n.* Bierpumpe, *die;* **~ garden** *n.* Biergarten, *der;* **~ glass** *n.* Bierglas, *das;* **~ hall** *n.* Bierhalle, *die;* **~house** *n.* (*Brit.*) Bierschenke, *die;* Bierstube, *die;* **~ making** *n.* Brauerei, *die;* **~ mat** *n.* Bierdeckel, *der;* Bieruntersetzer, *der;* **~ money** *n.* Geld für Getränke; **~ mug** *n.* Bierkrug, *der;* **~ pump** ⇒ **~ engine;** **~-swilling** *adj.* (*coll.*) biersaufend (*salopp*)

**beery** /'bɪərɪ/ *adj.* **A** ‹Person› mit Bierfahne; **~ taste/smell** Biergeschmack, *der*/Biergeruch, *der;* **B** (*tipsy*) bierselig

**beestings** /'bi:stɪŋz/ *n. pl.* (*Agric.*) Biestmilch, *die*

**beeswax** /'bi:zwæks/ *n.* Bienenwachs, *das*

**beet** /bi:t/ *n.* Rübe, *die;* **red ~:** rote Bete *od.* Rübe; **white ~:** weiße Rübe; Wasserrübe, *die;* **~ sugar** Rübenzucker, *der*

**beetle[1]** /'bi:tl/ *n.* Käfer, *der;* **as blind as a ~** (*fig.*) blind wie ein Maulwurf

**beetle[2]** *n.* (*tool*) Holzhammer, *der;* (*machine*) Kalander, *der*

**beetle[3]** *v.i.* **A** ‹Brauen:› vorstehen; ‹Felsen:› überhängen, vorstehen; **B ~ along/off/past** (*coll.*) ‹Mensch:› entlangpesen/abhauen/vorbeirennen (*ugs.*); ‹Auto:› entlang-/weg-/vorbeibrummen (*ugs.*)

**beetle: ~-browed** /bi:tl'braʊd/ *adj.* finster aussehend; **~ 'brows** *n. pl.* buschige [vorstehende] Augenbrauen; **~-crusher** *n.* Quadratlatschen, *der*

**'beetroot** *n.* rote Beete *od.* Rübe

**beeves** ⇒ **beef 1 C**

**befall** /bɪ'fɔ:l/ **1** *v.i., forms as* **fall 2** sich begeben (*geh.*); geschehen. **2** *v.t., forms as* **fall 2** widerfahren (+ *Dat.*)

**befit** /bɪ'fɪt/ *v.t.*, **-tt-** (*be seemly for*) sich ziemen *od.* gebühren für (*geh.*); **it ill ~s you to do that** es steht Ihnen schlecht an, das zu tun; **she behaved as ~ted a lady** sie benahm sich, wie es sich für eine Dame gebührte

**befitting** /bɪ'fɪtɪŋ/ *adj.* gebührend (*geh.*); schicklich ‹Benehmen› (*geh.*)

**befog** /bɪ'fɒg/ *v.t.*, **-gg-: A** (*confuse*) verwirren; ‹Drogen, Alkohol:› benebeln, umnebeln; **B** (*obscure*) verunklaren ‹Sachverhalt, Thema›

**befool** /bɪ'fu:l/ *v.t.* täuschen; **be ~ed** sich täuschen lassen

**before** /bɪ'fɔ:(r)/ **1** *adv.* **A** (*of time*) vorher; zuvor; **the day ~:** am Tag zuvor; **long ~:** lange vorher *od.* zuvor; **not long ~:** kurz vorher; **our friendship is less close than ~:** unsere Freundschaft ist nicht mehr so eng wie früher *od.* vorher; **the noise continued as ~:** der Lärm ging nach wie vor weiter; **you should have told me so ~:** das hättest du mir vorher *od.* früher *od.* eher sagen sollen; **I've seen that film ~:** ich habe den Film schon [einmal] gesehen; **I've heard that ~:** das habe ich schon einmal gehört; **I wish I had known that ~:** hätte ich das nur früher gewusst; **I'll give it to you on your birthday and not ~:** ich gebe es dir an deinem Geburtstag und nicht eher; **B** (*ahead in position*) vor[aus]; **C** (*in* *front*) voran; **go/ride ~:** voran- *od.* vorausgehen/-reiten.

❷ *prep.* A ▸1055 (*of time*) vor; **the day ~ yesterday** vorgestern; **the year ~ last** vorletztes Jahr; **the year ~ that** das Jahr davor; **the time ~ that** das vorige Mal; **old/die ~ one's time** frühzeitig gealtert/sterben; **it was [well] ~ my time** das war [lange] vor meiner Zeit; **since ~ the operation/war** schon vor der Operation/dem Krieg; **~ now** vorher; früher; **~ Christ** vor Christus; vor Christi Geburt; **he got there ~ me** er war vor mir da; **~ then** vorher; **~ long** bald; **~ leaving, he phoned/I will phone** bevor er wegging, rief er an/bevor ich weggehe, rufe ich an; **~ tax** brutto; vor [Abzug (*Dat.*) der] Steuern; B (*position*) vor (+ *Dat.*); (*direction*) vor (+ *Akk.*); **~ my very eyes** vor meinen Augen; **go ~ a committee/court of law** vor einen Ausschuss/ein Gericht kommen; **be brought/appear ~ the judge** vor den Richter gebracht werden/vor dem Richter erscheinen; C (*under the action of*) vor (+ *Dat.*); **sail ~ the wind** vor dem Wind segeln; ⇒ *also* **carry** 1 A; D (*awaiting*) **have one's future/life ~ one** seine Zukunft/sein Leben noch vor sich (*Dat.*) haben; (*confronting*) **the matter ~ us** das uns (*Dat.*) vorliegende Thema; die Sache, die uns (*Akk.*) betrifft; **the task ~ us** die Aufgabe, die vor uns (*Dat.*) liegt; **the problem ~ them** das Problem, vor dem sie stehen/standen; E (*ahead of in sequence*) vor (+ *Dat.*); **he's ~ her in class** in der Klasse ist er besser als sie; **he puts work ~ everything** die Arbeit ist ihm wichtiger als alles andere; **~ all else she is a teacher** in erster Linie ist sie Lehrerin; **~ everything else** (*as most important*) vor allem; vor allen Dingen; **ladies ~ gentlemen** Damen haben [den] Vortritt; F (*rather than*) vor; **death ~ dishonour** lieber tot als ehrlos; **right ~ might** Macht darf nicht vor Recht gehen.

❸ *conj.* A bevor; **it'll be ages ~ I finish this** es wird eine Ewigkeit dauern, bis ich damit fertig bin; **shortly/long ~ I met you** kurz/lange bevor ich dich kennen lernte; B (*rather than*) bevor; ehe

**beforehand** /bɪˈfɔːhænd/ ❶ *adv.* vorher; (*in anticipation*) im Voraus; **I found out about it ~:** ich habe es schon vorher herausgefunden; **whereas five minutes ~ it had been sunny, ...:** während die Sonne vor fünf Minuten noch geschienen hatte, ... ❷ *pred. adj.* **be ~ with** (*early*) vorzeitig tun; (*premature, overhasty*) voreilig sein mit

**befoul** /bɪˈfaʊl/ *v.t.* A verschmutzen ‹Gebäude›; verpesten ‹Luft›; B (*fig.*) beschmutzen ‹Namen›; vergiften ‹Atmosphäre›

**befriend** /bɪˈfrend/ *v.t.* A (*act as a friend to*) sich anfreunden mit; B (*help*) sich annehmen (+ *Gen.*)

**befuddle** /bɪˈfʌdl/ *v.t.* A (*make drunk*) benebeln; B (*confuse*) verwirren; konfus machen

**beg** /beg/ ❶ *v.t.*, **-gg-** A betteln um; erbetteln ‹Lebensunterhalt›; **~ one's bread** sich (*Dat.*) sein Brot erbetteln; B (*ask earnestly*) bitten; **he ~ged her not to go** er bat sie, doch nicht zu gehen; **she ~ged to come with us** sie bat darum, mit uns kommen zu dürfen; **~ that sth. be done** darum bitten, dass etw. getan wird; **I ~ to inform you that ...** (*formal*) ich erlaube mir, Sie davon in Kenntnis zu setzen, dass ... (*geh.*); **I ~ to differ** da bin ich [aber] anderer Meinung; **~ sb. for sth.** jmdn. um etw. bitten; C (*ask earnestly for*) **~ sth.** um etw. bitten; **~ sth. of sb.** etw. von jmdm. erbitten; **~ a favour [of sb.]** [jmdn.] um einen Gefallen bitten; **~ forgiveness** um Verzeihung bitten; **~ leave** *or* **permission to do sth.** um Erlaubnis bitten, etw. tun zu dürfen; ⇒ *also* **pardon** 1 B; D **~ the question** (*evade difficulty*) der Frage (*Dat.*) ausweichen.

❷ *v.i.*, **-gg-** A ‹Bettler:› betteln (**for** um); ‹Hund:› Männchen machen; betteln; **a ~ging letter** ein Bettelbrief; **go [a-]~ging** keinen Abnehmer finden; B (*ask earnestly*) bitten (**for** um); **~ of sb. to do sth.** jmdn. [darum] bitten, etw. zu tun; **~ off** sich entschuldigen [lassen]

**began** ⇒ **begin**

**begat** ⇒ **beget**

**beget** /bɪˈget/ *v.t.*, **begot** /bɪˈgɒt/ *or* (*arch.*) **begat** /bɪˈgæt/, **begotten** /bɪˈgɒtn/ A (*arch.: procreate*) zeugen; **God's only begotten son** Gottes eingeborener Sohn; B (*literary: cause*) zeugen; gebären (*geh.*)

**beggar** /ˈbegə(r)/ ❶ *n.* A Bettler, *der*/Bettlerin, *die*; **~s can't be choosers** (*prov.*) man kann es sich (*Dat.*) eben nicht immer aussuchen; B (*coll.: person*) Arme, *der/die*; **poor ~:** armer Teufel; **a poor old ~:** ein armer alter Mann; **be a lucky/lazy/cheeky ~:** ein Glückspilz/Faulpelz/frecher Kerl sein (*ugs.*); **be a funny little ~:** ein drolliger Fratz sein (*ugs.*). ❷ *v.t.* A an den Bettelstab bringen; arm machen; B (*outshine*) in den Schatten stellen; **~ description** unbeschreiblich sein

**beggarly** /ˈbegəlɪ/ *adj.* erbärmlich; erbarmungswürdig ‹Person›; (*fig.*) erbärmlich; (*ungenerous*) engherzig ‹Einstellung›; armselig ‹Bezahlung›

**beggary** /ˈbegərɪ/ *n.* [Bettel]armut, *die*; **be reduced to ~:** bettelarm werden

**begin** /bɪˈgɪn/ ❶ *v.t.*, **-nn-**, **began** /bɪˈgæn/, **begun** /bɪˈgʌn/ A **~ sth.** [mit] etw. beginnen; **~ a new bottle** eine neue Flasche anbrechen; **she began life in a small village** sie verbrachte ihre ersten Lebensjahre in einem kleinen Dorf; **~ school** in die Schule kommen; eingeschult werden; **when do you ~ your retirement?** wann gehen Sie in Pension?; **~ doing** *or* **to do sth.** anfangen *od.* beginnen, etw. zu tun; **I began to slip** ich kam ins Rutschen; **I am ~ning to get annoyed** so langsam werde ich ärgerlich; B **not ~ to do sth.** (*coll.: make no progress towards doing sth.*): **the film does not ~ to compare with the book** der Film lässt sich nicht annähernd mit dem Buch vergleichen; **she didn't even ~ to grasp it** sie hat es nicht einmal ansatzweise verstanden; **the authorities couldn't even ~ to assess the damage** die Behörden konnten den Schaden nicht einmal grob abschätzen.

❷ *v.i.* **-nn-**, **began**, **begun** anfangen; beginnen (*oft geh.*); **when the world began** als die Erde entstand; **where does the river ~?** wo entspringt der Fluss?; **~ning student** (*Amer.*) Anfänger, *der*/-Anfängerin, *die*; **~ning next month** vom nächsten Monat an; **~ at the beginning** von vorne anfangen; **~ [up]on sth.** etw. anfangen; **~ with sth./sb.** bei *od.* mit etw./jmdm. anfangen *od.* beginnen; **to ~ with** zunächst *od.* zuerst einmal; **it is the wrong book, to ~ with** das ist schon einmal das falsche Buch

**beginner** /bɪˈgɪnə(r)/ *n.* Anfänger, *der*/Anfängerin, *die*; **~'s luck** Anfängerglück, *das*

**beginning** /bɪˈgɪnɪŋ/ *n.* ▸1055 Anfang, *der*; Beginn, *der*; **at** *or* **in the ~:** am Anfang; **at the ~ of February/the month** Anfang Februar/des Monats; **myths about the ~ of the world** Mythen über die Entstehung der Welt; **at the ~ of the day** zu Beginn des Tages; **from ~ to end** von Anfang bis Ende; von vorn bis hinten; **from the [very] ~:** [ganz] von Anfang an; **have its ~s in sth.** seine Anfänge *od.* seinen Ursprung in etw. (*Dat.*) haben; **small ~s** kleine Anfänge; **[this is] the ~ of the end** [das ist] der Anfang vom Ende; **go back to the ~:** wieder von vorne anfangen; **make a ~ with sth.** mit etw. anfangen

**begone** /bɪˈgɒn, bɪˈgɔːn/ *v.i. in imper. and inf. only* (*arch.*) **~!** fort!; hinweg! (*veralt.*); **tell sb. to ~:** jmdn. sagen, dass er sich fortmachen solle

**begonia** /bɪˈgəʊnɪə/ *n.* (*Bot.*) Begonie, *die*; Schiefblatt, *das*

**begorra** /bɪˈgɒrə/ *int.* (*Ir.*) Jesses

**begot, begotten** ⇒ **beget**

**begrudge** /bɪˈgrʌdʒ/ *v.t.* A (*envy*) **~ sb. sth.** jmdm. etw. missgönnen; **I don't ~ their buying a car** ich gönne ihnen, dass sie sich (*Dat.*) ein Auto kaufen; B (*give reluctantly*) **I ~ the time/money I have to spend** es ist mir leid um die Zeit/das Geld; C (*be dissatisfied with*) **~ doing sth.** etw. ungern tun; **he did not ~ the fact that ...:** er war nicht darüber verärgert, dass ...

**beguile** /bɪˈgaɪl/ *v.t.* A (*delude*) betören; verführen; **~ sb. into doing sth.** jmdn. dazu verführen, etw. zu tun; **be ~d by sb./sth.** sich von jmdm./etw. täuschen lassen; B (*cheat*) betrügen; **~ sb. [out] of sth.** jmdn. um etw. betrügen; **~ sb. into doing sth.** jmdn. verleiten, etw. zu tun; C (*divert attention from*) vertreiben; (*charm*) bezaubern; (*amuse*) unterhalten

**beguiling** /bɪˈgaɪlɪŋ/ *adj.* verführerisch; betörend ‹Einfluss›; verlockend ‹Zeitvertreib›

**begun** ⇒ **begin**

**behalf** /bɪˈhɑːf/ *n.*, *pl.* **behalves** /bɪˈhɑːvz/: **on** *or* (*Amer.*) **in ~ of sb./sth.** (*as representing sb./sth.*) für jmdn./etw.; (*more formally*) im Namen von jmdm./etw.; **on** *or* (*Amer.*) **in sb.'s/my ~** (*for sb.'s/my benefit*) zugunsten von jmdm./zu meinen Gunsten; **don't fret on my ~:** mach dir meinetwegen keine Sorgen

**behave** /bɪˈheɪv/ ❶ *v.i.* A sich verhalten; sich benehmen; ‹Chemikalien:› reagieren; **how do you ~ under stress?** wie verhältst du dich bei Stress?; **he ~s more like a friend to them** er behandelt sie mehr wie Freunde; **~ well/badly** sich gut/schlecht benehmen *od.* betragen; **~ well/badly towards sb.** jmdn. gut/schlecht behandeln; **my car hasn't been behaving too well of late** mein Auto hat mir in letzter Zeit ziemlich viel Ärger gemacht; **well-/ill-** *or* **badly/nicely ~d** brav/ungezogen/lieb (*ugs.*); B (*do what is correct*) brav sein; sich benehmen; sich betragen. ❷ *v. refl.* **~ oneself** sich benehmen; **~ yourself!** benimm dich!

**behavior** *etc.* (*Amer.*) ⇒ **behaviour** *etc.*

**behaviour** /bɪˈheɪvjə(r)/ *n.* A (*conduct*) Verhalten, *das* (**towards** gegenüber); Benehmen, *das* (**towards** gegenüber); (*of child*) Betragen, *das*; **be on one's good/best ~:** sein bestes Benehmen an den Tag legen; **put sb. on his/her best ~:** jmdm. raten, sich gut zu benehmen; B (*moral conduct*) Verhalten, *das*; **his ~ towards her** sein Verhalten ihr gegenüber; C (*of ship*) Seeverhalten, *das*; (*of machine*) Eigenschaften *Pl.*; (*of substance*) Verhalten, *das*; D (*Psych.*) Verhalten, *das*; **~ therapy** Verhaltenstherapie, *die*

**behavioural** /bɪˈheɪvjərl/ *adj.* Verhaltens-; **~ similarities** Ähnlichkeiten im Verhalten

**behavioural 'science** *n.* Verhaltensforschung, *die*

**behaviourism** /bɪˈheɪvjərɪzm/ *n.*, *no pl.* (*Psych.*) Behaviorismus, *der*

**behaviourist** /bɪˈheɪvjərɪst/ *n.* (*Psych.*) Behaviorist, *der*/Behavioristin, *die*

**behead** /bɪˈhed/ *v.t.* enthaupten, köpfen ‹Person›

**beheld** ⇒ **behold**

**behest** /bɪˈhest/ *n.*, *no pl.* (*literary*) **at sb.'s ~:** auf jmds. Geheiß (*Akk.*)

**behind** /bɪˈhaɪnd/ ❶ *adv.* A (*at rear of sb./sth.*) hinten; **from ~:** von hinten; **be ~:** dahinter sein; **the person ~:** der Hintermann; **come from ~:** von hinten kommen; (*fig.*) aufholen; **he glanced ~ before moving off** er schaute nach hinten, bevor er losfuhr; **you go ahead and we'll follow on ~:** geh du vor, und wir kommen hinterher; **the church tower and the mountain ~:** der Kirchturm und der Berg dahinter; B (*further back*) **[be] miles ~:** kilometerweit [zurückliegen]; **[be] years/weeks ~:** Jahre/Wochen im Rückstand *od.* Verzug [sein]; **leave sb. ~:** jmdn. zurücklassen; (*move faster*) jmdn. hinter sich (*Dat.*) lassen; **fall ~:** zurückbleiben; (*fig.*) in Rückstand geraten; **lag ~:** zurückbleiben; (*fig.*) im Rückstand sein; **be ~:** hinten sein; (*be late*) im Verzug sein; C (*in arrears*) **be/get ~ with one's payments/rent** mit seinen Zahlungen/der Miete *usw.* im Rückstand *od.* Verzug sein/in Rückstand *od.* Verzug geraten; D (*remaining after one's departure*) **leave sth. ~:** etw. zurücklassen; **he left his gloves ~ by mistake** er ließ seine Handschuhe versehentlich liegen; er vergaß seine Handschuhe; **stay ~:** dableiben; (*as punishment*) nachsitzen.

❷ *prep.* Ⓐ (*at rear of, on other side of; fig.: hidden by*) hinter (+ *Dat.*); **he stepped out from ~ the wall** er trat hinter der Mauer hervor; **he came from ~ her/a bush** er kam von hinten/er kam hinter einem Busch hervor; **one ~ the other** hintereinander; **the person ~ him** sein Hintermann; **~ sb.'s back** (*fig.*) hinter jmds. Rücken (*Dat.*); **what was ~ his words?** was verbirgt sich hinter seinen Worten?; Ⓑ (*towards rear of*) hinter (+ *Akk.*); **I don't want to go ~ his back** ich will nicht hinter seinem Rücken handeln; **put ~ one** vergessen; **put the past ~ one** einen Strich unter die Vergangenheit ziehen; **look ~ the façade** (*fig.*) hinter die Fassade blicken; Ⓒ (*further back than*) hinter (+ *Dat.*); **they were miles ~ us** sie lagen meilenweit hinter uns (*Dat.*) zurück; **be ~ the times** nicht auf dem Laufenden sein; **fall ~ sb./sth.** hinter jmdn./etw. zurückfallen; **lag ~ sb./sth.** hinter jmdm./etw. bleiben; Ⓓ (*past*) hinter (+ *Dat.*); **my youth is now ~ me** meine Jugend liegt jetzt hinter mir; **all that trouble is ~ me** ich habe den ganzen Ärger hinter mir; Ⓔ (*later than*) **be/run ~ schedule** im Rückstand *od.* Verzug sein; **~ time** im Rückstand *od.* Verzug; Ⓕ (*in support of*) hinter (+ *Dat.*); **I'm right ~ you in all you do** ich stehe hinter dir in allem, was du tust; **the man ~ the project** der Mann, der hinter dem Projekt steht; **he has a lot of money ~ him** er verfügt über viel Geld; Ⓖ (*in the tracks of*) hinter (+ *Dat.*); **he followed ~ her on his bike** er fuhr ihr mit dem Fahrrad hinterher; Ⓗ (*remaining after departure of*) **she left nothing ~ her but an old photograph** sie hinterließ nichts als eine alte Fotografie.

❸ *n.* (*buttocks*) Hintern, *der* (*ugs.*); Hinterteil, *das* (*ugs.*)

**behindhand** /bɪ'haɪndhænd/ *pred. adj.* Ⓐ **be/get ~ with one's payments/rent** mit seinen Zahlungen/der Miete im Rückstand *od.* Verzug sein/in Rückstand *od.* Verzug geraten; **I am getting ~ in my work** ich komme mit meiner Arbeit in Verzug; **the farmers are ~ with their harvesting** die Bauern sind mit der Ernte zurück *od.* im Rückstand; Ⓑ (*out of date, behind time*) zurück; **she is about twenty years ~ in her style of dress/taste in music** sie hinkt der Mode/dem Musikgeschmack etwa zwanzig Jahre hinterher; Ⓒ (*backward*) **be ~ in sth./doing sth.** mit etw. zurückhaltend *od.* zögerlich sein/etw. zurückhaltend *od.* zögerlich tun

**behold** /bɪ'həʊld/ *v.t.*, **beheld** /bɪ'held/ (*arch./literary*) Ⓐ erblicken (*geh.*); Ⓑ *in imper.* siehe/sehet!

**beholden** /bɪ'həʊldn/ *pred. adj.* **be ~ to sb. [for sth.]** jmdm. [für etw.] verpflichtet *od.* verbunden sein

**beholder** /bɪ'həʊldə(r)/ *n.* (*arch./literary*) Betrachter, *der;* Beschauer, *der;* **beauty is in the eye of the ~:** schön ist, was gefällt

**behove** /bɪ'həʊv/ *v.t. impers.* (*arch./literary*) **it ~s sb. to do sth.** es [ge]ziemt *od.* schickt sich für jmdn., etw. zu tun (*geh.*); **it ill ~s sb. to do sth.** es steht jmdm. schlecht an, etw. zu tun (*geh.*)

**beige** /beɪʒ/ ❶ *n.* Beige, *das.* ❷ *adj.* beige

**being** /'bi:ɪŋ/ ❶ *pres. part. of* **be.** ❷ *n.* Ⓐ *no pl., no art.* (*existence*) Dasein, *das;* Leben, *das;* Existenz, *die;* **in ~:** bestehend; **bring sth. into ~:** etw. einführen; **call into ~:** ins Leben rufen; **come into ~:** entstehen; **when the new system comes into ~:** wenn das neue System eingeführt wird; Ⓑ (*anything, esp. person, that exists*) Wesen, *das;* Geschöpf, *das;* **the Supreme B~:** das höchste Wesen; Ⓒ (*constitution, nature, essence*) Sein, *das;* **my very ~ cried out in protest** mein Innerstes schrie aus Protest auf

**bejewelled** (*Amer.:* **bejeweled**) /bɪ'dʒu:əld/ *adj.* mit Edelsteinen geschmückt; juwelengeschmückt

**belabour** (*Brit.; Amer.:* **belabor**) /bɪ'leɪbə(r)/ *v.t.* Ⓐ (*beat*) einschlagen auf (+ *Akk.*); (*fig.*) überhäufen; Ⓑ ⇒ **labour 3 B**

**belated** /bɪ'leɪtɪd/ *adj.* verspätet

**belatedly** /bɪ'leɪtɪdlɪ/ *adv.* verspätet; nachträglich

**belay** /bɪ'leɪ, *Mount. also* 'bi:leɪ/ ❶ *v.t.* belegen ‹Tau, Seil›; (*Mount.*) anseilen; **~ [there]!** (*Naut.*) belegen!; **~ing pin** (*Naut.*) Belegklampe, *die.* ❷ *n.* (*Mount.*) Selbstsicherung, *die;* (*rock*) Felskopf, *der*

**bel canto** /bel 'kæntəʊ/ *n.* (*Mus.*) Belcanto, Belkanto, *der*

**belch** /beltʃ/ ❶ *v.i.* heftig aufstoßen; rülpsen (*ugs.*); **flames ~ed forth from the furnace** Flammen schlugen aus dem Ofen. ❷ *v.t.* ausstoßen ‹Rauch, Flüche usw.›; [aus]speien ‹Asche›; **the car exhaust was ~ing clouds of smoke** aus dem Auspuff quollen Rauchschwaden. ❸ *n.* Rülpser, *der* (*ugs.*)

**beleaguer** /bɪ'li:gə(r)/ *v.t.* (*lit. or fig.*) belagern

**belfry** /'belfrɪ/ *n.* Glockenturm, *der;* (*bell space*) Glockenstube, *die*

**Belgian** /'beldʒən/ ▶ **1340** ❶ *n.* Belgier, *der*/Belgierin, *die.* ❷ *adj.* belgisch; **sb. is ~:** jmd. ist Belgier/Belgierin

**Belgium** /'beldʒəm/ *pr. n.* Belgien (*das*)

**Belgrade** /bel'greɪd/ *pr. n.* ▶ **1626** Belgrad (*das*)

**belie** /bɪ'laɪ/ *v.t.*, **belying** /bɪ'laɪɪŋ/ (*fail to fulfil*) enttäuschen ‹Versprechen, Vorstellung›; (*give false notion of*) hinwegtäuschen über (+ *Akk.*) ‹Tatsachen, wahren Zustand›; (*fail to justify*) nicht gerecht werden (+ *Dat.*) ‹einer Erwartung, Theorie›; (*fail to corroborate*) im Widerspruch stehen zu

**belief** /bɪ'li:f/ *n.* Ⓐ Vertrauen, *das;* Glaube[n], *der;* **have great ~ in sth.** großes Vertrauen zu etw. haben; **~ in sth.** Glaube an etw. (*Akk.*); **beyond** *or* **past ~:** unglaublich; **it is my ~ that ...:** ich bin der Überzeugung, dass ...; **in the ~ that ...:** in der Überzeugung, dass ...; **to the best of my ~:** meines Wissens; Ⓑ (*Relig.*) Glaube[n], *der*

**believable** /bɪ'li:vəbl/ *adj.* glaubhaft; glaubwürdig

**believe** /bɪ'li:v/ ❶ *v.i.* Ⓐ **~ in sth.** (*put trust in truth of*) an etw. (*Dat.*) glauben; **I ~ in him** ich vertraue ihm; **I ~ in free medical treatment for all** ich bin für die kostenlose ärztliche Behandlung aller; **I don't ~ in going to the dentist** ich halte nicht viel von Zahnärzten; Ⓑ (*have faith*) glauben (**in** an + *Akk.*) ‹Gott, Himmel usw.›; Ⓒ (*suppose, think*) glauben; denken; **I ~ so/not** ich glaube schon/nicht; **Mr Smith, I ~:** Herr Smith, nehme ich an.

❷ *v.t.* Ⓐ **~ sth.** etw. glauben; **I ~d his words** ich glaubte seinen Worten; **I can well ~ it** das glaub ich gerne; **if you ~ that, you'll ~ anything** wers glaubt, wird selig (*ugs. scherzh.*); **[I] don't ~ a word of it** [ich] glaube kein Wort [davon]; **don't you ~ it** glaub das [ja] nicht; **~ it or not** ob du es glaubst oder nicht; **would you ~ [it]** (*coll.*) stell dir mal vor (*ugs.*); **I'd never have ~d it of her** das hätte ich ihr nie zugetraut; **~ sb.** jmdm. glauben; **I don't ~ you** das glaube ich dir nicht; **they would have us ~ that ...:** sie wollen uns glauben machen, dass ...; **~ [you] me** glaub/glaubt mir!; **I [can] ~ you** ich kann es dir nachfühlen; **I couldn't ~ my eyes/ears** ich traute meinen Augen/Ohren nicht; Ⓑ (*be of opinion that*) glauben; der Überzeugung sein; **she ~d it to be wrong** sie hielt es für falsch; **he is ~d to be in the London area** man vermutet ihn im Raum London; **people ~d her to be a witch** die Leute hielten sie für eine Hexe; **make ~ [that ...]** so tun, als ob ...

**believer** /bɪ'li:və(r)/ *n.* Ⓐ Gläubige, *der/die;* Ⓑ **be a great** *or* **firm ~ in sth.** viel von etw. halten; **I'm a firm ~ in being strict with children** ich bin sehr für eine strenge Kindererziehung; **I'm no great ~ in taking exercise** ich halte nicht viel von körperlicher Bewegung

**Belisha beacon** /bəli:ʃə 'bi:kn/ *n.* (*Brit.*) *gelbes Blinklicht an Zebrastreifen*

**belittle** /bɪ'lɪtl/ *v.t.* herabsetzen; schlecht machen; schmälern ‹Erfolg, Verdienste, Rechte›; **don't ~ yourself** mach dich nicht schlechter, als du bist

**belittlement** /bɪ'lɪtlmənt/ *n.* Herabsetzung, *die;* Schlechtmachen, *das*

**bell** /bel/ ❶ *n.* Ⓐ Glocke, *die;* (*smaller*) Glöckchen, *das;* **clear as a ~:** glockenklar; (*understandable*) [ganz] klar und deutlich; **sound as a ~:** kerngesund ‹Person›; völlig intakt ‹Gerät, Gegenstand›; Ⓑ (*device to give ~-like sound*) Klingel, *die;* **electric ~:** elektrisches Läutewerk; Ⓒ (*ringing*) Läuten, *das;* **the ~ has gone** es hat geläutet *od.* geklingelt; **there's the ~:** es läutet *od.* klingelt; **was that the ~?** hat es geläutet *od.* geklingelt?; Ⓓ (*Boxing*) Gong, *der;* Ⓔ (*Naut.*) **one ~/eight ~s** ein Glas/acht Glasen; Ⓕ (*Bot.*) Glöckchen, *das;* Kelch, *der.* ❷ *v.t.* **~ the cat** (*fig.*) der Katze (*Dat.*) die Schelle umhängen (*ugs.*)

**belladonna** /belə'dɒnə/ *n.* Ⓐ (*Bot.*) Belladonna, *die;* (*drug*) Atropin, *das;* Ⓑ **~ lily** Belladonnalilie, *die* (*südafrik. Amaryllis*)

**bell: ~-bottomed** *adj.* ausgestellt; **~boy** *n.* (*Amer.*) [Hotel]boy, *der;* [Hotel]page, *der;* **~-buoy** *n.* (*Naut.*) Glockenboje, *die*

**belle** /bel/ *n.* Schönheit, *die;* Schöne, *die;* **~ of the ball** Ballkönigin, *die*

**belles-lettres** /bel'letr/ *n. pl.* schöngeistige Literatur; Belletristik, *die*

**bell: ~flower** *n.* Glockenblume, *die;* **~hop** (*Amer.*) ⇒ **bellboy**

**bellicose** /'belɪkəʊs/ *adj.* kriegerisch, kriegslustig ‹Stimmung, Nation›; streitsüchtig ‹Person›

**belligerence** /bɪ'lɪdʒərəns/, **belligerency** /bɪ'lɪdʒərənsɪ/ *n.*, *no pl.* Kriegslust, *die;* (*of person*) Kampfeslust, *die;* Streitlust, *die*

**belligerent** /bɪ'lɪdʒərənt/ ❶ *adj.* kriegslustig, kriegerisch, kampflustig ‹Nation›; streitlustig ‹Person, Benehmen›; aggressiv ‹Rede›; **~ powers** Krieg führende Mächte. ❷ *n.* Krieg führendes Land; Krieg führende Partei; (*opponent*) Gegner, *der*

**bellow** /'beləʊ/ ❶ *v.i.* ‹Tier, Person:› brüllen; **~ at sb.** jmdn. anbrüllen; **~ for sth./sb.** lauthals nach etw./jmdm. schreien. ❷ *v.t.* **~ out** brüllen ‹Befehl›; grölen ‹Lied›. ❸ *n.* Brüllen, *das*

**bellowing** /'beləʊɪŋ/ *n.* Gebrüll, *das*

**bellows** /'beləʊz/ *n. pl.* Ⓐ Blasebalg, *der;* (*Mus.*) Bälge *Pl.;* **a pair of ~:** ein Blasebalg; Ⓑ (*Phot.*) Balgen, *der*

**bell: ~ pull** *n.* Glockenzug, *der;* Klingelzug, *der;* **~ push** *n.* Klingeltaster, *der* (*fachspr.*); Klingel, *die;* **~-ringer** *n.* Glöckner, *der;* **~-ringing** *n.* Glockenläuten, *das;* **~ rope** *n.* Glockenseil, *das;* **~-shaped** *adj.* glockenförmig; **~ tent** *n.* Rundzelt, *das;* **~ tower** *n.* Glockenturm, *der;* **~wether** *n.* Leithammel, *der*

**belly** /'belɪ/ ❶ *n.* Bauch, *der;* (*womb*) Leib, *der;* (*stomach*) Magen, *der;* **go ~ up** (*coll.: go bankrupt*) Pleite gehen (*ugs.*). ❷ *v.t.* blähen; **the wind bellied [out] the sails** der Wind blähte die Segel. ❸ *v.i.* **~ [out]** ‹Segel:› sich blähen, schwellen

**belly: ~ache** ❶ *n.* Bauchschmerzen *Pl.;* Bauchweh, *das* (*ugs.*); ❷ *v.i.* (*sl.*) jammern (**about** über + *Akk.*); **~aching** *n.* (*sl.*) Gejammer, *das* (*ugs. abwertend*); **~ button** *n.* (*coll.*) Bauchnabel, *der;* **~ dance** *n.* Bauchtanz, *der;* **~ dancer** *n.* Bauchtänzerin, *die*

**bellyful** /'belɪfʊl/ *n.* **a ~ of food** eine ordentliche Portion Essen (*ugs.*); **have had a ~ of sth.** (*fig.*) von etw. die Nase voll haben (*ugs.*)

**belly: ~ landing** *n.* (*Aeronaut.*) Bauchlandung, *die;* **~ laugh** *n.* dröhnendes Lachen; **he gave a great ~ laugh** er lachte lauthals los

**belong** /bɪ'lɒŋ/ *v.i.* Ⓐ (*be rightly assigned*) **~ to sb.** jmdm. gehören; **~ to sth.** zu etw. gehören; **power ~s to the workers** (*as slogan*) alle Macht den Arbeitern; Ⓑ **~ to** (*be member of*) **~ to a club** einem Verein angehören; **she ~s to a trade union/the club** sie ist Mitglied einer Gewerkschaft/des Vereins; **~ to a church/the working class/another generation** einer Kirche/der Arbeiterklasse/einer anderen Generation (*Dat.*) angehören; Ⓒ (*be rightly placed*) **feel that one doesn't ~:** das Gefühl haben, fehl am

Platze zu sein *od.* dass man nicht dazugehört; **he doesn't really ~ anywhere** er ist nirgendwo wirklich zu Hause; **a sense of ~ing** ein Zugehörigkeitsgefühl; **where does this ~?** wo gehört das hin?; **the cutlery ~s in this drawer** das Besteck gehört in diese Schublade; **~ outside** nach draußen gehören; **~ together** zusammengehören; **this item doesn't ~ under this heading** dieser Punkt fällt nicht unter diese Rubrik

**belongings** /bɪˈlɒŋɪŋz/ *n. pl.* Habe, *die;* Sachen *Pl.;* **personal ~:** persönlicher Besitz; persönliches Eigentum; **all our ~:** unsere gesamte Habe; unser ganzes Hab und Gut

**beloved** /bɪˈlʌvɪd/ ❶ *adj.* geliebt; lieb; teuer; **be ~** /bɪˈlʌvd/ **by** *or* **of sb.** von jmdm. geliebt werden; jmdm. lieb und teuer sein; **in ~ memory of my husband, in memory of my ~ husband** in treuem Angedenken an meinen geliebten *od.* teuren Mann. ❷ *n.* Geliebte, *der/die;* **my ~** (*iron.*) mein Lieber/meine Liebe; **dearly ~** (*Relig.*) liebe Brüder und Schwestern im Herrn; liebe Gemeinde

**below** /bɪˈləʊ/ ❶ *adv.* A (*position*) unten; unterhalb; (*lower down*) darunter; (*downstream*) weiter unten; **it is on the shelf ~:** es ist auf dem [Regal]brett darunter; **down ~:** unten; drunten (*bes. südd.*); **from ~:** von unten [herauf]; **~ left** links unten; unten links; B (*direction*) nach unten; hinunter; hinab (*geh.*); (*downstream*) stromab[wärts]; **if you glance ~:** wenn Sie nach unten blicken *od.* (*geh.*) hinabblicken; C (*later in text*) unten; **see [p. 123] ~:** siehe unten[, S. 123]; **as described in detail ~:** wie [weiter] unten ausführlich beschrieben; **please sign ~:** bitte hier unterschreiben; **a photo with a caption ~:** ein Foto mit einer Bildunterschrift; D (*downstairs*) (*position*) unten; (*direction*) nach unten; (*Naut.*) unter Deck; **go ~:** unter Deck gehen; **the flat/floor ~:** die Wohnung/das Stockwerk *od.* die Etage darunter *od.* unter uns/ihnen *usw.;* **on the floor ~:** eine Etage tiefer; E (**~** *zero*) **frosts of ten and twenty ~:** Fröste von zehn und zwanzig Grad unter Null; F (*Relig.*) **on earth ~:** [hier] auf Erden; **here ~:** hienieden (*geh.*); G (*in hell*) drunten. ❷ *prep.* A (*position*) unter (+ *Dat.*); unterhalb (+ *Gen.*); (*downstream from*) unterhalb (+ *Gen.*); **down ~ us was a huge abyss** tief unter uns war ein riesiger Abgrund; **his hair is well ~ shoulder level** sein Haar reicht bis weit über die Schultern; ⇒ *also* **average** 1 A; **par** A, D; B (*direction*) unter (+ *Akk.*); **the sun sank ~ the horizon** die Sonne ging am Horizont unter; **he went ~ deck** (*Naut.*) er ging unter Deck; C (*ranking lower than*) unter (+ *Dat.*); **she's in the class ~ me** sie ist eine Klasse unter mir *od.* tiefer als ich; **~-zero temperatures** Temperaturen unter Null; **the temperature is well ~ zero** die Temperatur liegt weit unter Null; **~ the breadline** unter dem Existenzminimum; D (*unworthy of*) **it is ~ him** es ist unter seiner Würde

**belt** /belt/ ❶ *n.* A Gürtel, *der;* (*for carrying tools, weapons, ammunition, etc.*) Gurt, *der;* (*on uniform*) Koppel, *das;* **he wears both ~ and braces** (*fig.*) er sichert etw. doppelt und dreifach; er glaubt, doppelt genäht hält besser; **hit below the ~** (*lit. or fig.*) unter die Gürtellinie schlagen; **under one's ~** ‹Essen usw.› im Bauch; **with a couple of drinks under his ~:** mit ein paar Drinks intus (*ugs.*); **with all those qualifications under his ~:** mit all den Zeugnissen in der Tasche; ⇒ *also* **tighten** 1 A; B (*strip*) Gurt, *der;* (*of colour, trees*) Streifen, *der;* (*region*) Gürtel, *der;* **industrial ~:** Industrierevier, *das;* **~ of warm air/low pressure** Warmluft-/Tiefdruckgürtel, *der;* **coal/oil ~:** Kohlerevier, *das*/Ölgebiet, *das;* C (*of machine gun cartridges*) Gurt, *der;* D (*Mech. Engin.: drive ~*) Riemen, *der;* E (*coll.: heavy blow*) Schlag, *der;* **give sb. a ~:** jmdm. eine runterhauen (*ugs.*).
❷ *v.t.* (*hit*) schlagen; **I'll ~ you [one]** (*coll.*) ich hau dir eine runter (*ugs.*).
❸ *v.i.* (*coll.*) **~ up/down the motorway** über die Autobahn rasen; **he ~ed off as fast as his legs would carry him** er rannte davon, so schnell er konnte

**~ along** *v.i.* (*coll.*) rasen (*ugs.*)

**~ out** *v.t.* (*coll.*) schmettern; voll herausbringen ‹Rhythmus›; (*on piano*) hämmern

**~ 'up** *v.i.* A (*Amer. coll., Brit. coll. joc.: put seat~ on*) sich anschnallen; sich angurten; B (*Brit. coll.: be quiet*) die Klappe halten (*salopp*)

**belting** /ˈbeltɪŋ/ *n.* A **give sb. a [good] ~** (*coll.*) jmdm. eine [ordentliche] Tracht Prügel verabreichen (*ugs.*); B (*material*) Gürtelstoff, *der;* (*of leather*) Riemenleder, *das*

**belying** ⇒ **belie**

**bemoan** /bɪˈməʊn/ *v.t.* beklagen

**bemuse** /bɪˈmjuːz/ *v.t.* verwirren; (*stupefy*) verblüffen

**bemused** /bɪˈmjuːzd/ *adj.* verwirrt

**bench** /bentʃ/ *n.* A Bank, *die;* (*seat across boat*) Ducht, *die;* (*Sport: for reserves*) Reservebank, *die;* Ersatzbank, *die;* B (*Law*) **on the ~:** auf dem Richterstuhl; **he was given a seat on the ~:** er wurde zum Richter ernannt; C (*office of judge*) Richteramt, *das;* **be raised to the B~:** zum Richter ernannt werden; D (*lawcourt*) **Queen's/King's B~** (*Brit.*) *Abteilung des obersten Gerichts, die sich mit Kriminalfällen befasst;* E (*Brit. Parl.*) Bank, *die;* Reihe, *die;* ⇒ *also* **backbench; cross-bench; front bench;** F (*work table*) Werkbank, *die;* (*gold or silversmith's*) Werkbrett, *das;* (*carpenter's*) Hobelbank, *die;* (*in laboratory*) [Labor]tisch, *der*

**bench: ~mark** *n.* Höhenmarke, *die;* (*fig.*) Maßstab, *der;* Fixpunkt, *der;* **~marking** *n., no pl.* Benchmarking, *das* (*fachspr.*); Leistungsvergleich, *der;* **~ 'seat** *n.* Sitzbank, *die;* **~ test** *n.* Test auf dem Prüfstand

**bend¹** /bend/ ❶ *n.* A (*bending*) Beuge, *die;* Beugung, *die;* **a ~ of the body/the knee** eine Rumpf-/Kniebeuge; B (*curve*) (*in road*) Kurve, *die;* **there is a ~ in the road** die Straße macht eine Kurve; **a ~ in the river** eine Flussbiegung; **be round the ~** (*fig. coll.*) spinnen (*ugs.*); verrückt sein (*ugs.*); **go round the ~** (*fig. coll.*) überschnappen (*ugs.*); durchdrehen (*ugs.*); **drive sb. round the ~** (*fig. coll.*) jmdn. wahnsinnig *od.* verrückt machen (*ugs.*); C ▶ **1232** | **the ~s** (*Med. coll.*) Taucherkrankheit, *die.*
❷ *v.t.,* **bent** /bent/ A (*force out of straightness*) biegen; verbiegen ‹Nadel, Messer, Eisenstange, Ast›; spannen ‹Bogen›; beugen ‹Arm, Knie›; anwinkeln ‹Arm, Bein›; krumm machen ‹Finger›; **~ sth. at an angle** etw. umbiegen; **~ sth. back/forward/up/down** etw. nach hinten/vorne/oben/unten biegen; **'please do not ~'** (*on envelope*) „bitte nicht knicken!"; **~ sth. back into shape** etw. zurückbiegen; etw. wieder in Form biegen; **~ the law** (*fig.*) das Gesetz beugen; ⇒ *also* **rule** 1 A; B (*fix*) **be bent on sth.** zu etw. entschlossen sein; auf etw. (*Akk.*) versessen *od.* erpicht sein; **on pleasure bent** (*dated*) vergnügungssüchtig; **~ one's energies on sth.** (*dated*) seine ganze Kraft auf etw. (*Akk.*) verwenden; **~ oneself to sth.** sich auf etw. (*Akk.*) konzentrieren; C (*coll.: pervert*) missbrauchen; pervertieren; manipulieren ‹Ergebnis›; D (*direct*) **we must ~ our steps home** wir müssen unsere Schritte heimwärts lenken (*geh.*); **he bent his mind on** *or* **to the problem** er dachte ernst über das Problem nach; **~ an ear** sich umhören; E (*force to submit*) unterwerfen; gefügig machen; F (*Naut.*) festmachen; befestigen ‹Tau›.
❸ *v.i.,* **bent** A sich biegen; sich krümmen; ‹Äste:› sich neigen; **the road ~s** die Straße macht eine Kurve; **the road ~s for two miles** die Straße ist auf zwei Meilen kurvenreich; **the river ~s/~s in and out** der Fluss macht eine Biegung/schlängelt sich; B (*bow*) sich bücken; (*fig.*) sich beugen; **~ to** *or* **before sb.** (*fig.*) sich jmdm. beugen; **catch sb. ~ing** (*fig. coll.*) jmdn. [in einer peinlichen Lage] erwischen

**~ 'down** *v.i.* sich bücken; sich hinunterbeugen

**~ 'over** *v.i.* sich nach vorn beugen; sich bücken; ⇒ *also* **backwards** A

**bend²** *n.* A (*Naut.*) Knoten, *der;* Schlinge, *die;* B (*Her.*) Schrägbalken, *der;* **~ sinister** schräglinker Balken; Schräglinksbalken, *der*

**bendable** /ˈbendəbl/ *adj.* biegbar

**bended** /ˈbendɪd/ *adj.* **on ~ knee[s]** auf [den] Knien

**bender** /ˈbendə(r)/ *n.* (*coll.*) Besäufnis, *das* (*salopp*)

**bendy** /ˈbendɪ/ *adj.* (*coll.*) A biegsam; B (*winding*) gewunden ‹Pfad, Straße›

**beneath** /bɪˈniːθ/ ❶ *prep.* A (*unworthy of*) **~ sb.** jmds. unwürdig; unter jmds. Würde (*Dat.*); **~ sb.'s dignity** unter jmds. Würde (*Dat.*); **marry ~ one** nicht standesgemäß heiraten; unter seinem Stand heiraten; **~ contempt** verachtenswert; unter aller Kritik; B (*under*) unter (+ *Dat.*). ❷ *adv.* darunter

**Benedictine** ❶ *n.* A /benɪˈdɪktɪn/ (*monk/nun*) Benediktiner, *der*/Benediktinerin, *die;* B ® /benɪˈdɪktiːn/ (*liqueur*) Benediktiner, *der.* ❷ *adj.* Benediktiner-

**benediction** /benɪˈdɪkʃn/ *n.* (*Relig.*) Benediktion, *die;* Segnung, *die;* **pronounce/say the ~** (*before meal*) um den Segen Gottes bitten; (*after meal*) das Dankgebet sprechen *od.* sagen

**benefaction** /benɪˈfækʃn/ *n.* A (*gift*) Spende, *die;* (*endowment*) Schenkung, *die;* Stiftung, *die;* B (*doing good*) Wohltat, *die*

**benefactor** /ˈbenɪfæktə(r)/ *n.* Wohltäter, *der;* (*patron*) Stifter, *der;* Gönner, *der*

**benefactress** /ˈbenɪfæktrɪs/ *n.* Wohltäterin, *die;* (*patroness*) Stifterin, *die;* Gönnerin, *die*

**benefice** /ˈbenɪfɪs/ *n.* (*Eccl.*) Benefizium, *das*

**beneficence** /bɪˈnefɪsəns/ *n.* Mildtätigkeit, *die;* (*active kindness*) Güte, *die*

**beneficent** /bɪˈnefɪsənt/ *adj.* (*showing active kindness*) gütig; (*doing good*) wohltätig; mildtätig

**beneficial** /benɪˈfɪʃl/ *adj.* A nutzbringend; nützlich; vorteilhaft ‹Einfluss›; günstig ‹Klima›; **be ~ to sth./sb.** zum Nutzen von etw./jmdm. sein; **a good night's sleep is very ~:** ein guter Schlaf ist sehr erholsam; B (*Law*) nutznießerisch; **~ owner** Nießbraucher, *der*

**beneficially** /benɪˈfɪʃəlɪ/ *adv.* ⇒ **beneficial** A: nutzbringend; nützlich; vorteilhaft; günstig

**beneficiary** /benɪˈfɪʃərɪ/ *n.* Nutznießer, *der*/Nutznießerin, *die*

**benefit** /ˈbenɪfɪt/ ❶ *n.* A Vorteil, *der;* Vorzug, *der* (*geh.*); **be of ~ to sb./sth.** jmdm./einer Sache von Nutzen sein; **have the ~ of** den Vorteil *od.* (*geh.*) Vorzug (+ *Gen.*) haben; **derive ~ from sth., get some ~ from sth.** aus etw. Nutzen ziehen; von etw. profitieren; **not get much ~ from sth.** wenig Nutzen aus etw. ziehen; nicht viel von etw. profitieren; **did you get much ~ from your holiday?** hat dir der Urlaub viel genützt?; **without the ~ of** ohne das Zutun (+ *Gen.*); **with the ~ of** mithilfe (+ *Gen.*); **to sb.'s ~:** zu jmds. Nutzen; **for sb.'s ~:** in jmds. Interesse (*Dat.*); im Interesse von jmdm.; **for the ~ of sth.** im Interesse einer Sache (*Gen.*); **for the ~ of future generations** im Interesse künftiger Generationen; **for the ~ of anyone who/all those who ...** (*iron.*) allen/all denen zuliebe, die ... (*iron.*); **give sb. the ~ of the doubt** im Zweifelsfall zu jmds. Gunsten entscheiden; **give sb. the ~ of sth.** jmdm. etw. zugute kommen lassen (*iron.*); B (*allowance*) Beihilfe, *die;* **social security ~:** Sozialhilfe, *die;* Hilfe zum Lebensunterhalt (*Amtsspr.*); **supplementary ~** (*Brit.*) zusätzliche Hilfe zum Lebensunterhalt; **unemployment ~:** Arbeitslosenunterstützung, *die;* **sickness ~:** Krankengeld, *das;* **disablement ~:** Invalidenrente, *die;* **child ~** (*Brit.*) Kindergeld, *das;* **maternity ~:** Mutterschaftsgeld, *das;* **~ club** *or* **society** Versicherungsverein auf Gegenseitigkeit; C **~ [performance/match/concert]** Benefizveranstaltung, *die* /-spiel, *das* /-konzert, *das;* D **without ~ of clergy** (*joc.*) ohne kirchlichen Segen.
❷ *v.t.* **~ sb./sth.** jmdm./einer Sache nützen *od.* gut tun; **these facilities/discoveries**

**have ~ed the area/humanity** diese Einrichtungen/Entdeckungen sind dem Gebiet/der Menschheit zugute gekommen *od.* haben dem Gebiet/der Menschheit Nutzen gebracht. ❸ *v.i.* **~ by/from sth.** von etw. profitieren; aus etw. Nutzen ziehen; **~ from experience** aus Erfahrung lernen; **how do I/will my son ~?** was habe ich/hat mein Sohn davon?

**'benefit tourism** *n.* Sozialhilfetourismus, *der*

**Benelux** /'benɪlʌks/ *pr. n.* **the ~ countries** die Beneluxländer

**benevolence** /bɪ'nevələns/ *n., no pl.* (*desire to do good*) Güte, *die;* (*of ruler*) Milde, *die;* (*of despot, the authorities*) Wohlwollen, *das*

**benevolent** /bɪ'nevələnt/ *adj.* Ⓐ (*desiring to do good*) gütig; mild ‹Herrscher›; wohlwollend ‹Behörde, Despot›; **~ despotism** aufgeklärter Absolutismus; Ⓑ *attrib.* (*charitable*) wohltätig, mildtätig ‹Institution, Verein›; Ⓒ (*kind and helpful*) hilfsbereit; **a ~ smile/air** ein gütiges Lächeln/gütiger Gesichtsausdruck

**benevolently** /bɪ'nevələntlɪ/ *adv.* gütig ‹lächeln›

**Bengali** /beŋ'gɔ:lɪ/ ▶ 1275, ▶ 1340 ❶ *n.* Ⓐ (*person*) Bengale, *der*/Bengalin, *die;* Ⓑ (*language*) Bengali, *das.* ❷ *adj.* bengalisch

**benighted** /bɪ'naɪtɪd/ *adj.* (*fig.*) unwissend, (*ugs.*) unbedarft ‹Person›; finster ‹Gegend, Zeitalter›; obskur ‹Philosophie, Politik, Sitten›

**benign** /bɪ'naɪn/ *adj.* Ⓐ (*gracious, gentle*) gütig ‹Person, Aussehen, Verständnis›; mildtätig ‹Gabe, Geschenk›; wohlwollend ‹Person, Verhalten›; (*mild*) mild, heilsam ‹Klima, Sonne›; (*fortunate*) günstig ‹Stern, Einfluss, Ergebnis, Aspekt›; Ⓑ (*Med.*) gutartig, (*fachspr.*) benigne ‹Tumor›

**benignity** /bɪ'nɪgnɪtɪ/ *n., no pl.* Ⓐ Wohlwollen, *das;* Ⓑ (*Med.*) Gutartigkeit, *die*

**benignly** /bɪ'naɪnlɪ/ *adv.* gütig; wohlwollend

**benison** /'benɪzən/ *n.* (*arch.*) Segen, *der*

**bent**[1] /bent/ ❶ ⇒ **bend**[1] 2, 3. ❷ *n.* Neigung, *die;* Hang, *der;* Schlag, *der;* **have a ~ for sth.** einen Hang zu etw. *od.* eine Vorliebe für etw. haben; **those with *or* of an artistic ~:** Menschen mit einer künstlerischen Ader *od.* Veranlagung; **follow one's ~:** seiner Neigung *od.* seinen Neigungen folgen; **to the top of one's ~:** nach Herzenslust. ❸ *adj.* Ⓐ krumm; gebogen; Ⓑ (*Brit. sl.: corrupt*) link (*salopp*); nicht ganz sauber (*salopp*) ‹Händler usw.›; Ⓒ (*Brit. coll. derog.: homosexual*); schwul (*ugs.*); andersrum *präd.* (*ugs.*)

**bent**[2] *n.* (*Bot.*) Straußgras, *das;* (*stiff flower stalk*) Halm, *der;* (*heath*) Heide, *die*

**benumb** /bɪ'nʌm/ *v.t.* Ⓐ gefühllos machen ‹Glieder›; **~ed** gefühllos; **~ed with cold** starr vor Kälte; Ⓑ (*fig.: stupefy*) lähmen; betäuben ‹Sinne, Gefühle›; **he was ~ed with panic/grief** er war vor Entsetzen/Kummer gelähmt

**Benzedrine**, ® /'benzɪdri:n/ *n.* (*Med.*) Benzedrin, *das*

**benzene** /'benzi:n/ *n.* (*Chem.*) Benzol, *das;* **~ ring** Benzolring, *der*

**benzine** /'benzi:n/ *n.* Leichtbenzin, *das*

**bequeath** /bɪ'kwi:ð/ *v.t.* Ⓐ **~ sth. to sb.** jmdm. etw. vermachen *od.* hinterlassen; Ⓑ (*fig.*) überliefern ‹Märchen, Legende, Zeugnisse›; vererben ‹Tradition›

**bequest** /bɪ'kwest/ *n.* Legat, *das* (**to** an + *Akk.*); **make a ~ to sb. of sth.** jmdm. etw. vermachen

**berate** /bɪ'reɪt/ *v.t.* schelten

**bereave** /bɪ'ri:v/ *v.t.* **~ A of B** B (*Dat.*) A nehmen; **be ~d [of sb.]** jmdn. verlieren; **a disaster ~d him of his father** er hat seinen Vater durch ein Unglück verloren; **the ~d** der/die Hinterbliebene/die Hinterbliebenen;

**bereavement** /bɪ'ri:vmənt/ *n.* Trauerfall, *der;* **he sympathized with her in her ~:** er sprach ihr sein Beileid aus; **on account of their recent ~:** aufgrund ihres Trauerfalles

**bereft** /bɪ'reft/ *pred. adj.* **be ~ of sth.** etw. verloren haben

**beret** /'bereɪ, 'berɪ/ *n.* Baskenmütze, *die;* (*as military headdress*) Barett, *das*

**bergamot** /'bɜ:gəmɒt/ *n.* Ⓐ (*tree*) Bergamotte, *die;* Bergamottenbaum, *der;* Ⓑ (*perfume*) Bergamottparfüm, *das;* Ⓒ (*herb*) Zitronenminze, *die;* Pfefferminze, *die;* **~ oil** Bergamottöl, *das*

**beriberi** /berɪ'berɪ/ *n.* ▶ 1232 (*Med.*) Beriberi, *die*

**berk** /bɜ:k/ *n.* (*Brit. sl.*) Dussel, *der* (*ugs.*); Spinner, *der* (*ugs.*); Blödmann, *der* (*salopp*)

**Berlin** /bɜ:'lɪn/ ▶ 1626 ❶ *pr. n.* Berlin (*das*). ❷ *attrib. adj.* Berliner; (*Ling.*) berlinisch

**Berliner** /bɜ:'lɪnə(r)/ *n.* Berliner, *der*/Berlinerin, *die*

**Bermuda** /bə'mju:də/ *pr. n.* die Bermudainseln; **the ~s** die Bermudas; **~s, ~ shorts** Bermudashorts

**Berne** /bɜ:n/ ▶ 1626 ❶ *pr. n.* Bern (*das*). ❷ *attrib. adj.* Berner

**berry** /'berɪ/ *n.* Beere, *die;* ⇒ *also* **brown** 1

**berserk** /bə'sɜ:k, bə'zɜ:k/ *adj.* rasend; **go ~:** durchdrehen (*ugs.*); **he went ~ with an axe** er wütete mit einem Beil

**berth** /bɜ:θ/ ❶ *n.* Ⓐ (*adequate space*) Seeraum, *der* (*der für ein Schiff erforderlich ist*); **give the rocks a wide ~:** Abstand zu den Felsen halten; gut frei von den Felsen halten (*fachspr.*); **give sb./sth. a wide ~** (*fig.*) jmdm./einer Sache aus dem Weg gehen; einen großen Bogen um jmdn./etw. machen; Ⓑ (*ship's place at wharf*) Liegeplatz, *der;* Ⓒ (*sleeping place*) (*in ship*) Koje, *die;* Kajütenbett, *das;* (*in train*) Schlafwagenbett, *das;* (*in aircraft*) Sleeper, *der;* **a 4-~ caravan** ein Vierpersonenanhänger; Ⓓ (*job*) Stelle, *die;* **find a cushy ~:** eine bequeme Stelle *od.* einen bequemen Job finden. ❷ *v.t.* festmachen ‹Schiff›. ❸ *v.i.* ‹Schiff:› festmachen, anlegen

**beryl** /'berɪl/ *n.* Beryll, *der*

**beryllium** /bɪ'rɪlɪəm/ *n.* (*Chem.*) Beryllium, *das*

**beseech** /bɪ'si:tʃ/ *v.t.*, **besought** /bɪ'sɔ:t/ *or* **~ed** (*literary*) flehen um, (*geh.*) erflehen ‹Gnade, Vergebung›; anflehen ‹Person›; **~ sb. to do sth.** jmdn. anflehen *od.* inständig bitten, etw. zu tun; **~ sb. for sth.** jmdn. um etw. anflehen; **I ~ you** ich flehe dich an

**beseeching** /bɪ'si:tʃɪŋ/ *adj.*, **beseechingly** /bɪ'si:tʃɪŋlɪ/ *adv.* flehend; flehentlich (*geh.*)

**beset** /bɪ'set/ *v.t.*, *forms as* **set** 1 Ⓐ heimsuchen; plagen; ‹Probleme, Zweifel, Versuchungen:› bedrängen; **sth. is ~ with troubles** etw. steckt voller Schwierigkeiten/Probleme; **~ by doubts** von Zweifeln geplagt; Ⓑ (*hem in*) umgeben; einschließen; (*occupy and make impassable*) belagern; blockieren; versperren; **~ting sin** Untugend, *die*

**beside** /bɪ'saɪd/ *prep.* Ⓐ (*close to*) neben (+ *Dat.*); an (+ *Dat.*); **~ the sea/lake** am Meer/See; **walk ~ the river** am Fluss entlanggehen; **sit/stand ~ sb.** neben jmdm. sitzen/stehen; **sit down/go and stand ~ sb.** sich neben jmdn. setzen/stellen; Ⓑ (*compared with*) neben (+ *Dat.*); Ⓒ (*wide of*) weit entfernt von ‹Problem, Frage›; **be ~ the point** nichts damit zu tun haben; Ⓓ **~ oneself with joy/grief** außer sich vor Freude/Kummer

**besides** /bɪ'saɪdz/ ❶ *adv.* außerdem; **he was a historian ~:** er war außerdem noch Historiker; **do/say sth. [else] ~:** sonst noch etw. tun/sagen; **~, we don't need it** außerdem brauchen wir es nicht; **whatever she may have done ~:** was sie sonst noch getan haben mag. ❷ *prep.* außer; **~ us [there were others]** außer uns [waren noch andere da]; **~ my husband and me** außer meinem Mann und mir; **~ which, he was late** und obendrein *od.* außerdem kam er zu spät; **he said nothing ~ that** er sagte weiter *od.* sonst nichts

**besiege** /bɪ'si:dʒ/ *v.t.* (*lit. or fig.*) belagern; **be ~d with letters/offers/requests/enquiries** mit Briefen/Angeboten/Bitten/Anfragen überschüttet *od.* überhäuft werden

**besieger** /bɪ'si:dʒə(r)/ *n.* Belagerer, *der*

**besmear** /bɪ'smɪə(r)/ *v.t.* verschmieren; **~ed with blood** blutverschmiert

**besmirch** /bɪ'smɜ:tʃ/ *v.t.* (*lit. or fig.*) beschmutzen (*geh.*); besudeln (*geh.*) **~ sb.'s name** jmds. Namen besudeln *od.* beflecken

**besom** /'bi:zəm/ *n.* [Reisig]besen, *der*

**besot** /bɪ'sɒt/ *v.t.*, **-tt-** betören; **be ~ted by *or* with the idea that ...:** von der Idee besessen sein, dass ...; **~ted with alcohol** berauscht *od.* benommen vom Alkohol; **be ~ted by *or* with sb.** in jmdn. vernarrt sein

**besought** ⇒ **beseech**

**bespatter** /bɪ'spætə(r)/ *v.t.* bespritzen; vollspritzen

**bespeak** /bɪ'spi:k/ *v.t.*, *forms as* **speak** 2 Ⓐ (*suggest*) zeugen von; verraten; Ⓑ (*reserve*) reservieren; vorbestellen

**bespectacled** /bɪ'spektəkld/ *adj.* bebrillt

**bespoke** /bɪ'spəʊk/ ❶ ⇒ **bespeak.** ❷ *attrib. adj.* **~ overcoat** maßgeschneiderter Mantel; **~ boots** Stiefel nach Maß; **~ tailor** Maßschneider, *der*

**bespoken** ⇒ **bespeak**

**best** /best/ ❶ *adj. superl. of* **good** Ⓐ best...; **be ~ [of all]** am [aller]besten sein; **the ~ thing about it was ...:** das Beste daran war ...; **the ~ thing to do is to apologize** das Beste ist, sich zu entschuldigen; **the very ~ people** die feinen Leute; **may the ~ man win!** auf dass der Beste gewinnt!; Ⓑ (*most advantageous*) best...; günstigst...; **which *or* what is the ~ way?** wie ist es am besten *od.* günstigsten?; **it's ~ to travel via Paris** am besten fährt man über Paris; **think it ~ to do sth.** es für das Beste halten, etw. zu tun; **do as you think ~ *or* what you think is ~:** mach, was du für richtig hältst; Ⓒ (*greatest*) größt...; **the ~ part of the day/money** der größte Teil des Tages/Geldes; **[for] the ~ part of an hour** fast eine ganze Stunde.

❷ *adv. superl. of* **well**[2] 2 am besten; **like sth. ~ of all** etw. am liebsten mögen; **as ~ we could** so gut wir konnten; **as ~ you can** so gut es geht; **you know ~:** Sie müssen es [am besten] wissen; **you'd ~ be going now** am besten gehen Sie jetzt; **he is ~ known for his etchings** er ist vor allem für seine Kupferstiche bekannt; **he is the person ~ able to do it/to cope** er ist der Fähigste, um das zu tun/damit fertig zu werden; **I was not ~ pleased to discover that ...** (*iron.*) ich war gar nicht begeistert, als ich entdeckte, dass ... (*iron.*).

❸ *n.* Ⓐ **the ~:** der/die/das Beste; **the wine was not of the ~:** der Wein war nicht von der besten Qualität; **their latest record is their ~:** ihre letzte Platte ist die beste; Ⓑ (*clothes*) beste Sachen; Sonntagskleider *Pl.;* **wear one's [Sunday] ~:** seine Sonntagskleider tragen; sich in Schale werfen (*ugs.*); Ⓒ **play the ~ of three [games]** um zwei Gewinnsätze spielen; **the ~ of it is ...** (*also iron.*) das Beste daran ist ...; der Witz dabei ist ... (*iron.*); **get *or* have the ~ of it** gut damit fahren; gut dabei wegkommen; **get the ~ out of sth./sb.** das Beste aus etw./jmdm. herausholen; **that's the ~ of having a car** das ist das Beste an einem Auto; **he is not in the ~ of health** es geht ihm nicht sehr gut; **bring out the ~ in sb.** jmds. beste Seiten zum Vorschein bringen; **all the ~!** alles Gute!; Ⓓ **the ~** *pl.* die Besten; **they are the ~ of friends** sie sind die besten Freunde; **with the ~ of intentions** in bester Absicht; **from the ~ of motives** aus den edelsten Motiven [heraus]; **get six of the ~** (*coll.*) Prügel beziehen; verdroschen werden (*ugs.*); **[sb. is] one of the ~** (*coll.*) [jmd. ist] ein feiner Kerl; **she can down a pint of beer/play tennis with the ~ of them** (*coll.*) beim Biertrinken/Tennisspielen macht ihr keiner was vor (*ugs.*); Ⓔ **at ~:** bestenfalls; **be at one's ~:** in Hochform sein; **an example of modern architecture at its ~:** eines der gelungensten Beispiele moderner Architektur; **[even] at the ~ of times** schon normalerweise; **it is [all] for the ~:** es ist [doch] nur zum Guten; **he did it [all] for the ~:** er hat es [doch] nur gut gemeint; **hope for the ~:** das Beste hoffen; **do one's ~:** sein Bestes *od.* Möglichstes tun; **he is doing his ~ to ruin me** (*iron.*) er tut sein

b

Möglichstes, mich zu ruinieren; **do the ~ you can** machen Sie es so gut Sie können; **it's not good, but it's the ~ I can do** es ist nicht gut, aber mehr kann ich nicht tun; **look one's ~:** möglichst gut aussehen; **make the ~ of oneself** das Beste aus sich machen; **make the ~ of it/things** das Beste daraus machen; **make the ~ of a bad job** *or* **bargain** (*coll.*) das Beste daraus machen; **to the ~ of one's ability** nach besten Kräften; so gut man kann; **to the ~ of my belief/knowledge** meines Wissens; **she wants/has the ~ of everything** sie will immer nur/hat von allem das Beste. ❹ *v.t.* (*Sport*) schlagen; (*outwit*) übervorteilen

**best: ~-before date** *n.* Mindesthaltbarkeitsdatum, *das;* **~-dressed** *attrib. adj.* bestgekleidet; **~ 'end** *n.* (*Gastr.*) Filet, *das;* **~ 'friend** *n.* bester Freund/beste Freundin; **be ~ friends with sb.** sehr gut mit jmdm. befreundet sein; **~-hated** *attrib. adj.* (*iron.*) bestgehasst (*iron.*)

**bestial** /ˈbestɪəl/ *adj.* (*of or like a beast*) tierisch; (*brutish, barbarous*) barbarisch; (*savage*) brutal; (*depraved*) bestialisch; tierisch

**bestiality** /bestɪˈælɪtɪ/ *n.* Ⓐ Bestialität, *die;* (*savagery*) Brutalität, *die;* Ⓑ (*sodomy*) Sodomie, *die*

**bestir** /bɪˈstɜː(r)/ *v. refl.*, **-rr-** sich aufraffen

**best: ~-kept** *attrib. adj.* bestgepflegt; bestgehütet ‹Geheimnis›; **the ~-kept village in England** das schönste Dorf Englands; **~-known** *attrib. adj.* bekanntest...; **~-laid** *attrib. adj.* bestüberlegt ‹Pläne›; **~-loved** *attrib. adj.* meistgeliebt; **~ 'man** *n.* Trauzeuge, *der* (*des Bräutigams*)

**bestow** /bɪˈstəʊ/ *v.t.* verleihen ‹Titel›; schenken ‹Gunst, Wohlwollen›; zuteil werden lassen ‹Ehre, Segnungen›; **~ sth. [up]on sb.** jmdm. etw. verleihen/schenken/zuteil werden lassen

**bestowal** /bɪˈstəʊəl/ *n.* Verleihung, *die* (**[up]on** an + *Akk.*); (*of land*) Schenkung, *die*

**'best-quality** *attrib. adj.* der Spitzenklasse *nachgestellt;* erstklassig

**bestride** /bɪˈstraɪd/ *v.t.*, *forms as* **stride** 3 sich rittlings setzen auf (+ *Akk.*); (*position*) rittlings sitzen auf (+ *Dat.*) ‹Mauer, Bank›

**best: ~ 'seller** *n.* Bestseller, *der;* (*author*) Bestsellerautor, *der;* **~-selling** *attrib. adj.* meistverkauft ‹Schallplatte›; **~-selling book/novel** Bestseller, *der;* **a ~-selling author/novelist** ein Bestsellerautor

**bet** /bet/ ❶ *v.t.*, **-tt-**, **~** *or* **~ted** Ⓐ wetten; **I ~ him £10** ich habe mit ihm um 10 Pfund gewettet; **he ~ £10 on that horse** er hat 10 Pfund auf das Pferd gesetzt; Ⓑ (*coll.: be confident*) wetten; **I ~ he's late** wetten, dass er zu spät kommt?; **[I] ~ you I know where he got it from** wetten, dass ich weiß, woher er es hat?; **[you can] ~ your life** darauf kannst du Gift nehmen (*ugs.*); **[I] ~ you [anything]** ich gehe jede Wette darauf ein; **I'll ~ he tells them he's swum the Channel** ich wette, er erzählt ihnen, dass er den Kanal durchschwommen hat; **~ [you] I 'can** und ob ich kann; **you '~ [I am/he will etc.]** und ob; allerdings.
❷ *v.i.*, **-tt-**, **~** *or* **~ted** Ⓐ wetten (**for** um); **~ on sth.** auf etw. (*Akk.*) setzen; Ⓑ (*coll.: be confident*) **the shops will be closed, I'll ~:** ich wette, die Geschäfte sind geschlossen; **[do you] want to ~?** [wollen wir] wetten? ⇒ *also* **boot**[1] 1 A; **bottom** 2 B.
❸ *n.* Ⓐ Wette, *die;* (*sum*) Wetteinsatz, *der;* **make** *or* **have a ~ with sb. on sth.** mit jmdm. über etw. (*Akk.*) wetten; **accept** *or* **take a ~ on sth.** eine Wette auf etw. (*Akk.*) eingehen; **lay a ~ on sth.** auf etw. (*Akk.*) wetten; Ⓑ (*fig. coll.: choice*) Tipp, *der;* **be a bad/good/safe ~:** ein schlechter/guter/sicherer Tipp sein; **it's a fair ~ that ...:** du kannst ziemlich sicher sein, dass ...; **be sb.'s best ~:** das Beste sein; **my ~ is that ...:** ich wette, dass ...

**beta** /ˈbiːtə/ *n.* Ⓐ (*letter*) Beta, *das;* Ⓑ (*Sch., Univ.: mark*) Zwei, *die*

**beta-blocker** /ˈbiːtəblɒkə(r)/ *n.* (*Med.*) Beta[rezeptoren]blocker, *der*

**betake** /bɪˈteɪk/ *v. refl.*, *forms as* **take** 1 (*literary*) sich begeben; **~ oneself somewhere** sich irgendwohin begeben

**beta: ~ particles** *n. pl.* (*Phys.*) Betateilchen *Pl.;* **~ rays** *n. pl.* (*Phys.*) Betastrahlen *Pl.*

**betel** /ˈbiːtl/ *n.* (*Bot.*) Betel, *der;* **~ nut** Betelnuss, *die*

**bête noire** /beɪt ˈnwɑː(r)/ *n.*, *pl.* **bêtes noires** /beɪt ˈnwɑː(r)/ Gräuel, *der*

**bethink** /bɪˈθɪŋk/ *v. refl.*, **bethought** /bɪˈθɔːt/ (*literary*) sich besinnen

**betide** /bɪˈtaɪd/ (*literary*) ❶ *v.t.* geschehen (+ *Dat.*) (*veralt., geh.*); **woe ~ you if ...:** wehe dir, wenn ...; **whatever ~s you** was Ihnen auch immer geschieht. ❷ *v.i.* geschehen

**betimes** /bɪˈtaɪmz/ *adv.* (*literary*) beizeiten

**betoken** /bɪˈtəʊkn/ *v.t.* Ⓐ (*indicate*) ankündigen ‹Frühjahr, Krieg›; Ⓑ (*suggest*) hindeuten auf (+ *Akk.*)

**betony** /ˈbetənɪ/ *n.* (*Bot.*) Ziest, *der*

**betook** ⇒ **betake**

**betray** /bɪˈtreɪ/ *v.t.* Ⓐ verraten (**to** an + *Akk.*); missbrauchen ‹jmds. Vertrauen›; **~ oneself** sich verraten; **~ the fact that ...:** verraten, dass ...; Ⓑ (*lead astray*) fehlleiten

**betrayal** /bɪˈtreɪəl/ *n.* Verrat, *der;* **~ of one's friends/country** Verrat an seinen Freunden/seinem Vaterland; **an act of ~:** ein Verrat; **a ~ of trust** ein Vertrauensbruch

**betroth** /bɪˈtrəʊð/ *v.t.* (*arch.*) versprechen (*veralt.*); **be ~ed to sb.** jmdm. versprochen sein (*veralt.*)

**betrothal** /bɪˈtrəʊðl/ *n.* (*dated*) Verlöbnis, *das*

**betrothed** /bɪˈtrəʊðd/ (*dated*) ❶ *adj.* versprochen (*veralt.*). ❷ *n.* Anverlobter, *der*/Anverlobte, *die* (*veralt.*)

**better** /ˈbetə(r)/ ❶ *adj.* ▶ **1232** *compar. of* **good** 1 besser; **I have something ~ to do** ich habe etwas Besseres zu tun; **do you know of anything ~?** kennst du etwas Besseres?; **that's ~:** so ists schon besser; **~ and ~:** immer besser; **~ still, let's phone** oder noch besser: Rufen wir doch an; **be much ~** (*recovered*) sich viel besser fühlen; **he is much ~ today** es geht ihm heute schon viel besser; **get ~** (*recover*) besser werden; **I am/my ankle is getting ~:** mir/meinem Knöchel geht es besser; **so much the ~:** umso besser; **she is none the ~ for it** das hat ihr nichts genützt; **she is much the ~ for having been to university** es hat ihr sehr genützt, dass sie studiert hat; **my ~ feelings/nature** mein besseres Ich; **be ~ than one's word** mehr tun, als man versprochen hat; **my/his ~ half** (*joc.*) meine/seine bessere Hälfte (*scherzh.*); **the ~ part of sth.** (*greater part*) der größte Teil einer Sache (*Gen.*); **[for] the ~ part of an hour** fast eine ganze Stunde; **he is no ~ than a criminal** er kommt einem Kriminellen gleich; **she's no ~ than she should be** (*euphem.*) sie ist auch nicht gerade eine Heilige; **on ~ acquaintance** bei näherer Bekanntschaft; ⇒ *also* **all** 3.
❷ *adv. compar. of* **well**[2] 2 Ⓐ (*in a ~ way*) besser; **I hope you do ~ in future** hoffentlich haben Sie in Zukunft mehr Glück; (*by your own efforts*) ich hoffe, dass Sie es in Zukunft besser machen werden; Ⓑ (*to a greater degree*) mehr; **the ~ to do sth.** um etw. besser tun zu können; **you cannot do ~ than ...:** das Beste, was du tun kannst, ist ...; **I like Goethe ~ than Schiller** ich mag Goethe lieber als Schiller; **he is ~ liked than Carter** er ist beliebter als Carter; Ⓒ **he would do ~ to ask first** er sollte lieber *od.* besser zuerst fragen; Ⓓ **know ~ than ...:** es besser wissen als ...; **you ought to know ~ than to ...:** du solltest es besser wissen und nicht ...; Ⓔ **go one ~ [than sb.]**, (*Amer.*) **go sb. one ~:** jmdn. überbieten; Ⓕ **you'd ~ not tell her** Sie erzählen es ihr besser nicht; **I'd ~ begin by introducing myself** ich stelle mich besser zuerst einmal vor; **I'd ~ be off now** ich gehe jetzt besser; **hadn't you ~ ask first?** sollten Sie nicht besser zuerst fragen?; **I promise I'll clear up after the party — You'd ~!** Ich verspreche, dass ich nach der Party aufräume — Das will ich aber auch hoffen. ⇒ *also* **better off**.
❸ *n.* Ⓐ Bessere, *das;* **we hope for ~:** wir erhoffen uns (*Dat.*) mehr; **get the ~ of sb./sth.** jmdn./etw. unterkriegen (*ugs.*); **exhaustion got the ~ of him** seine Erschöpfung machte ihm schwer zu schaffen; **be a change for the ~:** eine vorteilhafte Veränderung sein; **for ~, for worse** in Freud und Leid; **for ~ or for worse** was immer daraus werden wird; **I thought ~ of it** ich habe es mir anders überlegt; Ⓑ *in pl.* Leute, die höher stehen; **one's ~s** Leute, die über einem stehen *od.* die einem überlegen sind.
❹ *v.t.* Ⓐ (*surpass*) übertreffen; Ⓑ (*improve*) verbessern; **~ oneself** (*rise socially*) sich verbessern

**'better-class** *attrib. adj.* besser, feiner ‹Leute›; vornehm ‹Vorort, Familie›

**betterment** /ˈbetəmənt/ *n.*, *no pl.* Verbesserung, *die*

**better: ~ 'off** *adj.* Ⓐ (*financially*) [finanziell] besser gestellt; Ⓑ **he is ~ off than I am** ihm geht es besser als mir; **be ~ off than sb.** besser als jmd. dran sein (*ugs.*); **be ~ off without sth./sb.** ohne etw./jdmn. besser dran sein; **~-quality** *attrib. adj.* qualitativ besser; **~-than-average** *attrib. adj.* überdurchschnittlich [gut/viel]; **earn a ~-than-average income** überdurchschnittlich viel verdienen

**betting** /ˈbetɪŋ/ ❶ *n.* Wetten, *das;* **there was heavy ~ on that horse** auf das Pferd wurde sehr viel gesetzt; **what's the ~ it rains?** (*fig.*) ob es wohl regnen wird? ❷ *attrib. adj.* Wett-; **I'm not a ~ man** ich wette nicht

**'betting office**, **'betting shop** *ns.* Wettbüro, *das*

**between** /bɪˈtwiːn/ ❶ *prep.* Ⓐ (*position*) zwischen (+ *Dat.*); (*direction*) zwischen (+ *Akk.*); **it is not far ~ the two places** die beiden Orte liegen nicht weit auseinander; **~ then and now** zwischen damals und jetzt; **~ now and the end of term** bis zum Ende des Trimesters; **there's nothing to choose ~ them** sie unterscheiden sich durch nichts; **[in] ~:** zwischen; Ⓑ (*amongst*) unter (+ *Dat.*); **the work was divided ~ the volunteers** die Arbeit wurde zwischen den Freiwilligen aufgeteilt; **~ ourselves, ~ you and me** unter uns (*Dat.*) gesagt; **that's [just] ~ ourselves** das bleibt aber unter uns (*Dat.*); Ⓒ (*by joint action of*) **~ them/the four of them they succeeded in dislodging the stone** gemeinsam/zu viert gelang es ihnen, den Stein zu lösen; **we ate it up ~ us** wir haben es zusammen *od.* gemeinsam aufgegessen; Ⓓ (*shared by*) **~ us we had 40p** wir hatten zusammen 40 Pence; **we had three tents ~ the five of us** wir hatten drei Zelte für uns fünf; **there is nothing ~ us** wir haben nichts miteinander; **it's all over ~ us** es ist aus zwischen uns (*Dat.*) (*ugs.*).
❷ *adv.* **[in] ~:** dazwischen; (*in time*) zwischendurch; **the space ~:** der Zwischenraum

**between: ~times**, **~whiles** *advs.* in der Zwischenzeit

**betwixt** /bɪˈtwɪkst/ ❶ *prep.* (*arch./poet.*) zwischen. ❷ *adv.* Ⓐ (*arch./poet.*) dazwischen; Ⓑ **~ and between** (*coll.*) zwischen beiden

**bevel** /ˈbevl/ ❶ *n.* (*slope*) Schräge, *die;* **~ edge** Schrägkante, *die;* **~ gear** Kegelradgetriebe, *das.* ❷ *v.t.*, (*Brit.*) **-ll-** abschrägen

**beverage** /ˈbevərɪdʒ/ *n.* (*formal*) Getränk, *das*

**bewail** /bɪˈweɪl/ *v.t.* beklagen; (*lament*) bejammern

**beware** /bɪˈweə(r)/ *v.t. & i.*; *only in imper. and inf.* **~ [of] sth./sb.** sich vor jmdm./etw. hüten *od.* in Acht nehmen; **~ of doing sth.** sich davor hüten, etw. zu tun; '**~ of black ice/falling masonry**' „Vorsicht, Glatteis/herabfallendes Mauerwerk!"; '**~ of pickpockets**' „vor Taschendieben wird gewarnt"; '**~ of the dog**' „Vorsicht, bissiger Hund!"; **~ [of] how ...** darauf Acht geben, wie ...; ~

**that you do not succumb to the temptation** hüte dich davor, der Versuchung zu erliegen

**bewilder** /bɪˈwɪldə(r)/ *v.t.* verwirren; **be ~ed by sth.** durch *od.* von etw. verwirrt werden/sein

**bewildering** /bɪˈwɪldərɪŋ/ *adj.* verwirrend

**bewilderment** /bɪˈwɪldəmənt/ *n., no pl.* Verwirrung, *die;* **in total ~:** völlig verwirrt

**bewitch** /bɪˈwɪtʃ/ *v.t.* verzaubern; verhexen; (*fig.*) bezaubern

**bewitching** /bɪˈwɪtʃɪŋ/ *adj.* bezaubernd

**bewitchingly** /bɪˈwɪtʃɪŋlɪ/ *adv.* bezaubernd; **smile ~ at sb.** jmdn. mit einem bezaubernden Lächeln ansehen

**beyond** /bɪˈjɒnd/ ❶ *adv.* Ⓐ (*in space*) jenseits; (*on other side of wall, mountain range, etc.*) dahinter; **the world ~:** das Jenseits; Ⓑ (*in time*) darüber hinaus; Ⓒ (*in addition*) daneben; außerdem; **and nothing ~:** und weiter nichts *od.* nichts weiter. ❷ *prep.* Ⓐ (*at far side of*) jenseits (+ *Gen.*); **when we get ~ the river, we'll stop** wenn wir den Fluss überquert haben, machen wir Halt; Ⓑ (*in space: after*) nach; **all we saw was ruin ~ ruin** wir sahen eine Ruine nach der anderen; Ⓒ (*later than*) nach; **she never looks** *or* **sees ~ the present** sie sieht *od.* blickt nie über die Gegenwart hinaus; **I shan't wait ~ an hour/~ 6 o'clock** ich warte nicht länger als eine Stunde/nicht länger als bis 6 Uhr; Ⓓ (*out of reach, comprehension, range*) über ... (+ *Akk.*) hinaus; **it's [far** *or* (*coll.*) **way] ~ me/him** *etc.* (*too difficult*) das ist mir/ihm *usw.* [bei weitem] zu schwer; (*incomprehensible*) das ist mir/ihm *usw.* [völlig] unverständlich; **be ~ the power of anyone's imagination** jedermanns Vorstellungsvermögen (*Akk.*) übersteigen; **your work is ~ all praise** Ihre Arbeit kann man nicht genug loben; **~ reproach** tadellos; **that is ~ my powers/competence** das liegt nicht in meiner Macht/überschreitet meine Befugnisse; **be ~ sb.'s capabilities/understanding** jmds. Fähigkeiten/Begriffsvermögen (*Akk.*) übersteigen; Ⓔ (*surpassing, exceeding*) mehr als; **I succeeded ~ my wildest hopes** mein Erfolg übertraf meine kühnsten Hoffnungen; **they're living ~ their means** sie leben über ihre Verhältnisse; Ⓕ (*more than*) weiter als; **he can't yet walk ~ a few steps** er kann noch nicht weiter als ein paar Schritte gehen; ⇒ *also* **joke** 1 A; Ⓖ (*besides*) außer; **there's nothing you can do ~ writing to him regularly** Sie können nichts weiter tun, als ihm regelmäßig [zu] schreiben; **~ this/that** weiter.
❸ *n.* **the B~:** das Jenseits; **at the back of ~:** am Ende der Welt

**b.f.**[1] /biː ˈef/ *n.* (*Brit. euphem.*) Blödmann, *der* (*salopp*)

**b.f.**[2] *abbr.* (*Bookk.*) **brought forward** Übertrag

**BFPO** *abbr.* **British Forces Post Office** *Postdienst der britischen Streitkräfte*

**b.h.p.** *abbr.* (*Mech. Engin.*) **brake horsepower**

**biannual** /baɪˈænjʊəl/ *adj.* halbjährlich

**biannually** /baɪˈænjʊəlɪ/ *adv.* zweimal jährlich

**bias** /ˈbaɪəs/ ❶ *n.* Ⓐ (*tendency*) Neigung, *die;* **have a ~ towards** *or* **in favour of sth./sb.** etw./jmdn. bevorzugen; **have a ~ against sth./sb.** gegen etw./jmdn. eingenommen sein; **be of** *or* **have a conservative ~:** konservativ eingestellt sein; Ⓑ (*prejudice*) Voreingenommenheit, *die;* **be without ~:** unvoreingenommen sein; Ⓒ (*Statistics*) systematischer Fehler; Bias, *das* (*fachspr.*); Ⓓ (*Dressmaking*) schräger Schnitt; **cut on the ~:** schräg zum Fadenlauf schneiden; **~ binding** Schrägband, *das.* ❷ *v.t.*, **-s-** *or* **-ss-** beeinflussen; **be ~ed towards** *or* **in favour of sth./sb.** für etw./jmdn. eingestellt sein; **they are ~ed in favour of women** sie bevorzugen Frauen; **be ~ed against sth./sb.** gegen etw./jmdn. voreingenommen sein; **a ~ed account** eine gefärbte *od.* tendenziöse Darstellung; **a ~ed jury/judge** befangene Geschworene/ein befangener Richter/eine befangene Richterin

**bib** /bɪb/ ❶ *n.* Ⓐ (*for baby*) Lätzchen, *das;* Ⓑ (*of apron etc.*) Latz, *der;* **put on one's best ~ and tucker** (*joc.*) sich in Schale werfen (*ugs.*). ❷ *v.i.*, **-bb-** (*arch.*) trinken

**Bible** /ˈbaɪbl/ *n.* Ⓐ (*Christian*) Bibel, *die;* Ⓑ (*of other religion*) heiliges Buch; (*fig.: authoritative book*) Bibel, *die*

**Bible: ~ class** *n.* Bibelstunde, *die;* **~ ˈoath** *n.* Eid auf die Bibel

**biblical** /ˈbɪblɪkl/ *adj.* biblisch; Bibel-

**bibliographer** /bɪblɪˈɒgrəfə(r)/ *n.* ▶ **1261** Bibliograph, *der*/Bibliographin, *die*

**bibliographic** /bɪblɪəˈgræfɪk/, **bibliographical** /bɪblɪəˈgræfɪkl/ *adj.* bibliographisch

**bibliography** /bɪblɪˈɒgrəfɪ/ *n.* Ⓐ (*list*) Bibliographie, *die;* Schriftenverzeichnis, *das;* Ⓑ (*study*) Bibliographie, *die*

**bibliophile** /ˈbɪblɪəfaɪl/ *n.* Bibliophile, *der/die*

**bibulous** /ˈbɪbjʊləs/ *adj.* trunksüchtig

**bicarb** /ˈbaɪkɑːb/ *n.* (*coll.*) Natron, *das*

**bicarbonate** /baɪˈkɑːbəneɪt/ *n.* Ⓐ (*Cookery*) **~ [of soda]** Natron, *das;* Ⓑ (*Chem.*) doppeltkohlensaures Natrium

**bicentenary** /baɪsenˈtiːnərɪ, baɪsenˈtenərɪ/, **bicentennial** /baɪsenˈtenɪəl/ ❶ *adjs.* Zweihundertjahr-; **~ celebrations** Zweihundertjahrfeier, *die.* ❷ *ns.* Zweihundertjahrfeier, *die*

**biceps** /ˈbaɪseps/ *n.* Ⓐ (*Anat.*) Bizeps, *der;* Ⓑ (*muscularity*) Muskeln *Pl.;* Bizeps, *der* (*ugs.*)

**bicker** /ˈbɪkə(r)/ *v.i.* zanken; streiten; **~ with sb. about** *or* **over sth.** sich mit jmdm. um etw. zanken *od.* streiten

**bickering** /ˈbɪkərɪŋ/ *n.* Gezänk, *das;* Zankerei, *die* (*ugs.*)

**bicycle** /ˈbaɪsɪkl/ ❶ *n.* Fahrrad, *das; attrib.* Fahrrad-; **ride a ~:** [mit dem] Fahrrad fahren; Rad fahren; **by ~:** mit dem [Fahr]rad. ❷ *v.i.* Rad fahren; **he ~s to work** er fährt mit dem Fahrrad zur Arbeit

**bicycle: ~ clip** *n.* Hosenklammer, *die;* **~ courier** *n.* Fahrradkurier, *der*/Fahrradkurierin, *die;* **~ kick** *n.* (*Football*) Fallrückzieher, *der;* **~ lane** *n.* (*reserved for cyclists*) Radfahrstreifen, *der;* (*with priority for cyclists*) Schutzstreifen, *der* [für Radfahrer]; **~ messenger** *n.* Fahrradkurier. *der*/Fahrradkurierin, *die;* **~ path** *n.* [Fahr]radweg, *der;* **~ rack** *n.* Fahrradständer, *der*

**bid** /bɪd/ ❶ *v.t.* Ⓐ **-dd-**, **~** (*at auction*) bieten; **what am I ~?** was höre ich?; was wird geboten?; **~ up the price** den Preis in die Höhe treiben; Ⓑ **-dd-**, **~** (*Cards*) reizen; Ⓒ **-dd-**, **bade** /bæd/ *or* **~**, **bidden** /ˈbɪdn/ *or* **~** (*arch./poet.: command*) heißen (*geh.*); **~ sb. do sth.** jmdn. etw. tun heißen; **do as you are ~[den]** tu, was man dich geheißen hat; Ⓓ **-dd-**, **bade** *or* **~**, **bidden** *or* **~** (*invite*) einladen; **he bade her be seated** er bat sie, Platz zu nehmen; Ⓔ **-dd-**, **bade** *or* **~**, **bidden** *or* **~: ~ sb. welcome** jmdn. willkommen heißen; **~ sb. goodbye** sich von jmdm. verabschieden; **~ sb./** (*coll.*) **sth. farewell**, **~ farewell to sb./** (*coll.*) **sth.** jmdm./einer Sache Lebewohl sagen; **~ sb. good day** jmdm. einen guten Tag wünschen. ❷ *v.i.*, **-dd-**, **~** Ⓐ werben (**for** um); **the President is ~ding for re-election** der Präsident bewirbt sich um die Wiederwahl; **~ fair to be sth.** etw. zu werden versprechen; Ⓑ (*at auction*) bieten; Ⓒ (*Cards*) bieten; reizen.
❸ *n.* Ⓐ (*at auction*) Gebot, *das;* **make a ~ of £9 for sth.** 9 Pfund für etw. bieten; Ⓑ (*fig.: attempt*) Bemühung, *die;* **make a ~ for sth.** sich um etw. bemühen; **he made a strong ~ for the Presidency** er griff nach dem Präsidentenamt; **in his absence they made a ~ for power** in seiner Abwesenheit versuchten sie, die Macht an sich (*Akk.*) zu reißen; **a ~ for fame and fortune** ein Versuch, berühmt und reich zu werden; **the prisoner made a ~ for freedom** der Gefangene versuchte, die Freiheit zu erlangen; **his ~ to save the crew failed** sein Versuch, die Besatzung zu retten, scheiterte; Ⓒ (*Cards*) Ansage, *die;* **make no ~:** passen; **it's your ~:** Sie bieten!

**biddable** /ˈbɪdəbl/ *adj.* (*obedient*) fügsam

**bidden** ⇒ **bid** 1 C, D, E

**bidder** /ˈbɪdə(r)/ *n.* Bieter, *der*/Bieterin, *die;* **the highest ~:** der/die Höchstbietende

**bidding** /ˈbɪdɪŋ/ *n.* Ⓐ (*at auction*) Steigern, *das;* Bieten, *das;* **open the ~:** das erste Gebot machen; **~ was brisk** es wurde lebhaft *od.* rege geboten; ⇒ *also* **force** 2 I; Ⓑ (*command*) Geheiß, *das* (*geh.*); **at sb.'s ~:** auf jmds. Geheiß (*Akk.*); **do sb.'s ~:** tun, was einem von jmdm. befohlen wird; Ⓒ (*Cards*) Bieten, *das;* Reizen, *das*

**ˈbidding prayer** *n.* Bittgebet, *das*

**bide** /baɪd/ ❶ *v.t.* **~ one's time** den rechten Augenblick abwarten. ❷ *v.i.* (*arch./dial.: remain*) ausharren; **~ awhile** *or* (*Scot.*) **a wee** ein Weilchen warten

**bidet** /ˈbiːdeɪ/ *n.* Bidet, *das*

**biennial** /baɪˈenɪəl/ ❶ *adj.* Ⓐ (*lasting two years*) zweijährig; bienn (*fachspr.*), zweijährig ‹Pflanze›; Ⓑ (*once every two years*) zweijährlich. ❷ *n.* (*Bot.*) zweijährige Pflanze; Bienne, *die* (*fachspr.*)

**biennially** /baɪˈenɪəlɪ/ *adv.* alle zwei Jahre

**bier** /bɪə(r)/ *n.* Totenbahre, *die*

**biff** /bɪf/ (*coll.*) ❶ *n.* Klaps, *der* (*ugs.*); **he gave her a ~ on the head** er haute ihr auf den Kopf. ❷ *v.t.* hauen; **he ~ed me on the head with a book** er hat mir ein Buch auf den Kopf geknallt (*ugs.*)

**bifocal** /baɪˈfəʊkl/ (*Optics*) ❶ *adj.* Bifokal-. ❷ *n. in pl.* Bifokalgläser *Pl.*

**bifurcate** /ˈbaɪfəkeɪt/ ❶ *v.i.* sich gabeln. ❷ *v.t.* gabelförmig teilen

**bifurcation** /baɪfəˈkeɪʃn/ *n.* (*division*) Aufspaltung, *die;* (*point*) Gabelung, *die;* (*branch*) Zweig, *der*

**big** /bɪg/ ❶ *adj.* Ⓐ (*in size*) groß; schwer, heftig ‹Explosion, Zusammenstoß›; schwer ‹Unfall, Niederlage›; hart ‹Konkurrenz›; teuer ‹Preis›; reichlich ‹Mahlzeit›; **earn ~ money** das große Geld verdienen; **he is a ~ man/she is a ~ woman** (*tall*) er/sie ist eine lange Latte (*ugs.*); (*fat*) er/sie ist wohlbeleibt; **she is a ~ girl** (*joc.: busty*) sie hat einen ganz schönen Balkon (*ugs.*); **the ~ expense of moving house** die hohen Umzugskosten; **~ words** geschraubte Ausdrücke (⇒ *also* G); **in a ~ way** (*coll.*) im großen Stil; **he fell in love with her in a ~ way** er verliebte sich heftig in sie; **carry/wield a ~ stick** (*fig.*) den großen Knüppel schwingen (*ugs.*); Ⓑ (*of largest size, larger than usual*) groß ‹Appetit, Zehe, Buchstabe›; **~ game** Großwild, *das;* **Conservatism with a ~ C** (*fig.*) Konservati[vi]smus par excellence *od.* in Reinkultur; Ⓒ **~ger** (*worse*) schwerer; **the ~ger the crime the more severe the penalty** je schwerer das Verbrechen, desto härter die Strafe; **~gest** (*worst*) größt...; **he is the ~gest liar/idiot** er ist der größte Lügner/Idiot; Ⓓ (*grown up, elder*) groß; **you're ~ enough to know better** du bist groß *od.* alt genug, um es besser zu wissen; Ⓔ (*important*) groß; wichtig ‹Nachricht, Entscheidung›; **the ~ story in the papers today is ...:** das Hauptthema in den Zeitungen von heute ist ...; **a ~ man** ein wichtiger Mann (⇒ *also* A); **the B~ Three/Four** *etc.* die Großen Drei/Vier *usw.;* Ⓕ (*coll.: outstanding*) groß ‹Augenblick, Chance›; **what's the ~ hurry?** warum die große Eile?; Ⓖ (*boastful*) angeberisch (*ugs.*); großspurig (*ugs.*); **get** *or* **grow/be too ~ for one's boots** *or* **breeches** (*coll.*) größenwahnsinnig werden/sein (*ugs.*); **~ talk** Großsprecherei, *die;* **~ talker** Großsprecher, *der*/Großsprecherin, *die;* **~ words** große Worte (⇒ *also* A); Ⓗ (*coll.: generous*) großzügig; nobel (*oft iron.*); **that's ~ of you** (*iron.*) wie nobel!; Ⓘ (*coll.: keen*) **be ~ on sth.** großen Wert auf etw. (*Akk.*) legen; Ⓙ (*coll.: popular*) **be ~** ‹Schauspieler, Popstar:› gut ankommen. ⇒ *also* **idea** E.
❷ *adv.* groß; **come/go over ~:** groß ankommen (*ugs.*) (**with** bei); **talk ~:** groß daherreden (*ugs.*); **think ~:** im großen Stil planen

**bigamist** /ˈbɪgəmɪst/ *n.* Bigamist, *der*/Bigamistin, *die*

**bigamous** /ˈbɪgəməs/ *adj.* bigamistisch

**bigamy** /ˈbɪgəmɪ/ *n.* Bigamie, *die*

**big:** ~ **band** *n.* (*Mus.*) Bigband, *die;* ~ **ˈbang** *n.* Urknall, *der;* **Big Ben** *n.* Big Ben (*der*); *Glocke/Uhr im Turm des Parlamentsgebäudes in London;* **Big ˈBrother** *n.* der Große Bruder; ~ **ˈbusiness** *n.* das Großkapital; ~ **ˈcheese** *n.* (*coll.: person*) hohes Tier (*ugs.*); ~ **ˈdeal** ⇒ **deal¹** 3 A; ~ **ˈdipper** *n.* **A** (*Brit.: at fair*) Achterbahn, *die;* **B** (*Astron.*) ⇒ **dipper** D; ~ **end** *n.* (*Motor Veh.*) Pleuelfuß, *der;* ~ **game** *n.* Großwild, *das;* ~**-game hunting** Großwildjagd, *die;* ~**head** *n.* (*coll.*) Fatzke, *der* (*ugs. abwertend*); ~**-ˈheaded** *adj.* (*coll.*) eingebildet; ~**-ˈhearted** *adj.* großherzig

**bight** /baɪt/ *n.* **A** (*loop*) Schlaufe, *die;* **B** (*curve*) (*in coast*) Bucht, *die;* (*in river*) Krümmung, *die;* Schleife, *die*

**big:** ~ ~**mouth** *n.* (*fig. coll.*) **have a ~ mouth** ein Schwätzer/eine Schwätzerin sein (*ugs.*); ~**mouth** *n.* (*coll.*) **be a ~ mouth** ein Angeber/eine Angeberin sein (*ugs.*); ~ **ˈname** *n.* (*person*) Größe, *die;* ~ **ˈnoise** *n.* (*coll.*) hohes Tier (*ugs.*)

**bigot** /ˈbɪgət/ *n.* bornierter Mensch; (*Relig.*) bigotter Mensch

**bigoted** /ˈbɪgətɪd/ *adj.* borniert; (*Relig.*) bigott

**bigotry** /ˈbɪgətrɪ/ *n.* Borniertheit; (*Relig.*) Bigotterie, *die*

**big:** ~ **shot** ⇒ ~ **noise**; ~ **time** *n.* **be in the ~ time** (*coll.*) eine große Nummer sein (*ugs.*); **make it [in]to** *or* **hit the ~ time** (*sl.*) groß herauskommen (*ugs.*); ~ **ˈtop** *n.* Zirkuszelt, *das;* ~ **ˈwheel** *n.* **A** (*at fair*) Riesenrad, *das;* **B** (*coll.: person*) hohes Tier (*ugs.*); ~**wig** *n.* (*coll.*) hohes Tier (*ugs.*)

**bijou** /ˈbiːʒuː/ **1** *n., pl.* ~**x** /ˈbiːʒuː/ Schmuckstück, *das;* (*fig.*) Juwel, *das.* **2** *adj.* exquisit

**bike** /baɪk/ (*coll.*) **1** *n.* (*bicycle*) Rad, *das;* (*motorcycle*) Maschine, *die.* **2** *v.i.* (*by bicycle*) Rad fahren; radeln (*ugs., bes. südd.*); mit dem Fahrrad fahren; (*by motorcycle*) [mit dem] Motorrad fahren

**bike:** ~ **courier** ⇒ ~ **messenger**; ~ **lane** (*esp. Amer.*) ⇒ **bicycle lane**; ~ **messenger** *n.* ▶ 1261 (*on motorbike*) Motorradkurier, *der*/Motorradkurierin, *die;* (*on bicycle*) Fahrradkurier, *der*/Fahrradkurierin, *die;* ~ **path** (*esp. Amer.*) ⇒ **bicycle path**

**biker** /ˈbaɪkə(r)/ *n.* (*cyclist*) Radfahrer, *der*/Radfahrerin, *die;* Biker, *der* (*Jargon*); (*motorcyclist*) Motorradfahrer, *der*/Motorradfahrerin, *die;* Biker, *der* (*Jargon*)

**bikini** /bɪˈkiːnɪ/ *n.* Bikini, *der;* ~ **briefs** Slip, *der*

**bilateral** /baɪˈlætərl/ *adj.* bilateral

**bilaterally** /baɪˈlætərəlɪ/ *adv.* bilateral; **the two countries agreed ~ on disarmament** beide Länder einigten sich darauf abzurüsten

**bilberry** /ˈbɪlbərɪ/ *n.* Blau-, Heidelbeere, *die*

**bile** /baɪl/ *n.* **A** (*Physiol.*) Gallenflüssigkeit, *die;* **B** (*Med.*) Gallenleiden, *das;* **C** (*fig.: peevishness*) Verdrießlichkeit, *die;* Übellaunigkeit, *die*

**bilge** /bɪldʒ/ *n.* **A** Bilge, *die;* **B** (*filth*) angesammelter Schmutz im Kielraum; (*fig. coll.: nonsense*) Quatsch, *der;* Unsinn, *der*

**bilge:** ~**-keel** *n.* Kimm- *od.* Bilge[n]kiel, *der;* ~**-water** *n.* Bilge[n]wasser, *das*

**bilingual** /baɪˈlɪŋgwəl/ *adj.* zweisprachig; bilingual (*fachspr.*) ‹Person›; bilinguisch (*fachspr.*) ‹Buch, Ausgabe›

**bilingualism** /baɪˈlɪŋgwəlɪzm/ *n., no pl.* Bilingualismus, *der;* Zweisprachigkeit, *die*

**bilious** /ˈbɪljəs/ *adj.* (*Med.*) Gallen-; biliös (*fachspr.*); (*fig.: peevish*) verdrießlich; ~ **attack** Gallenanfall, *der;* Gallenkolik, *die;* **a ~ green** ein unappetitliches Grün

**biliousness** /ˈbɪljəsnɪs/ *n., no pl.* Gallenbeschwerden *Pl.;* Gallenleiden, *das;* (*fig.*) Reizbarkeit, *die;* Verdrießlichkeit, *die*

**bilk** /bɪlk/ *v.t.* **A** (*evade payment to*) prellen ‹Gläubiger, Kellner usw.›; **B** (*evade payment of*) nicht bezahlen ‹Schuld, Rechnung usw.›; ~ **payment** nicht bezahlen *od.* Zahlung unterlassen; **C** (*cheat*) betrügen; ~ **sb. of sth.** jmdn. um etw. betrügen

**bill¹** /bɪl/ **1** *n.* **A** (*of bird*) Schnabel, *der;* **B** (*promontory*) Landzunge, *die;* **C** (*Naut.: point of anchor fluke*) Spitze, *die.* **2** *v.i.* ‹Vögel:› schnäbeln; ‹Personen:› sich liebkosen; ~ **and coo** ‹Vögel:› schnäbeln und gurren; ‹Personen:› [miteinander] turteln

**bill²** *n.* **A** (*Hist.: weapon*) Hellebarde, *die;* **B** (*for lopping*) Hippe, *die*

**bill³** **1** *n.* **A** (*Parl.*) Gesetzentwurf, *der;* Gesetzesvorlage, *die;* **B** (*note of charges*) Rechnung, *die;* **could we have the ~, please?** wir möchten zahlen; **a ~ for £10** eine Rechnung über 10 Pfund (*Akk.*); (*amount*) **a large ~:** eine hohe Rechnung; **a ~ of £10** eine Rechnung von 10 Pfund; **C** (*poster*) Plakat, *das;* **ˈ[stick] no ~sˈ** „Plakate ankleben verboten"; **D** (*programme*) Programm, *das;* **what's on the ~?** was steht auf dem Programm?; **top the ~, be top of the ~:** der Star [des Abends *usw.*] sein; ~ **of fare** Speisekarte, *die;* (*fig.*) [bunter] Programmreigen; **E** (*Law*) Klageschrift, *die;* **F** ▶ 1328 (*Amer.: banknote*) Banknote, *die;* [Geld]schein, *der;* **a 50-dollar ~:** ein Fünfzigdollarschein; **G** ~ **[of exchange]** (*Commerc.*) Wechsel, *der;* Tratte, *die* (*fachspr.*); **H** ~ **of health** Gesundheitsattest *od.* -zeugnis, *das;* **give sb./sth. a clean ~ of health** (*fig.*) jmdm./einer Sache ein gutes/einwandfreies Zeugnis ausstellen; ~ **of lading** Konnossement, *das;* Seefrachtbrief, *der;* ~ **of quantities** (*Brit.*) Kostenvoranschlag, *der* (*Aufstellung der Kosten/Dimensionen eines Bauwerks*); ~ **of sale** Kaufvertrag, *der;* Verkaufsurkunde, *die.*

**2** *v.t.* **A** (*announce*) ankündigen; **he is ~ed to appear next week at the Palace Theatre** er soll nächste Woche im Palace Theatre auftreten; **B** (*advertise*) durch Anschlag bekannt machen *od.* bekannt geben; **C** (*charge*) eine Rechnung ausstellen (+ *Dat.*); ~ **sb. for sth.** jmdm. etw. in Rechnung stellen *od.* berechnen

**ˈbillboard** *n.* Anschlagbrett, *das od.* -tafel, *die;* Plakattafel, *die;* Reklametafel, *die*

**billet¹** /ˈbɪlɪt/ **1** *n.* **A** (*quarters*) Quartier, *das;* Unterkunft, *die;* (*for soldiers*) Truppenunterkunft, *die;* Ortsunterkunft, *die;* **B** (*job*) Stellung, *die;* Posten, *der.* **2** *v.t.* **A** (*quarter*) unterbringen, einquartieren (**with, on** bei; **in** in + *Dat.*); **B** (*provide quarters for*) ‹Einwohner:› ein Quartier stellen (+ *Dat.*)

**billet²** *n.* **A** (*of wood*) Holzscheit, -klotz, *der;* **B** (*bar*) kleine Metallstange; **C** (*Archit.*) Spannkeil, *der*

**billet-doux** /bɪlɪˈduː/ *n., pl.* **billets-doux** /bɪlɪˈduːz/ Liebesbrief, *der;* Billetdoux, *das* (*veralt.*)

**bill:** ~**fold** *n.* (*Amer.*) Brieftasche, *die;* ~**head** *n.* gedrucktes Rechnungsformular; ~**hook** ⇒ **bill²** B

**billiard**/ˈbɪljəd/**:** ~ **ball** *n.* Billardkugel, *die;* ~ **cue** *n.* Queue, *das;* Billardstock, *der;* ~ **player** *n.* Billardspieler, *der;* ~ **room** *n.* Billardzimmer, *das*

**billiards** /ˈbɪljədz/ *n.* Billard[spiel], *das;* **a game of ~:** eine Partie Billard; **bar ~** (*Brit.*) *Billardspiel, bei dem die Löcher, in die die Kugeln gespielt werden müssen, nicht an den Seiten, sondern über die Tischplatte verteilt sind*

**ˈbilliard table** *n.* Billardtisch, *der*

**billion** /ˈbɪljən/ *n.* ▶ 1352 **A** (*thousand million*) Milliarde, *die;* **B** (*esp. Brit. dated: million million*) Billion, *die*

**billionaire** /bɪljəˈneə(r)/ *n.* (*Amer.*) Milliardär, *der*

**billow** /ˈbɪləʊ/ **1** *n.* **A** (*surging mass*) Masse, *die;* ~ **of smoke** Rauchwolke, *die;* ~ **of fog** Nebelschwaden, *der;* **a ~ of flame** eine Feuerwalze; **B** (*arch.: wave*) Woge, *die;* ~**s** (*poet.: sea*) Wogen *Pl.* (*dichter.*). **2** *v.i.* ‹Ballon, Segel:› sich [auf]blähen; ‹See, Meer:› wogen, sich [auf]türmen; ‹Rauch:› in Schwaden aufsteigen; ‹Kleid, Vorhang:› sich bauschen

**billowy** /ˈbɪləʊɪ/ *adj.* wogend ‹See, Kornfeld›; gebläht ‹Segel›; in Schwaden ziehend ‹Rauch›; bauschig ‹Rock›

**bill:** ~**poster,** ~**sticker** *ns.* ▶ 1261 Plakat[an]kleber, *der*

**billy¹** /ˈbɪlɪ/ *n.* (*pot*) Kochgeschirr, *das*

**billy²** *n.* **A** ⇒ **billy goat**; **B** ~ **[club]** (*Amer.*) [Gummi]knüppel, *der*

**ˈbillycan** ⇒ **billy¹**

**ˈbilly goat** *n.* Ziegenbock, *der*

**billy-o** /ˈbɪlɪəʊ/ *n.* (*coll.*) **like ~:** wie verrückt (*ugs.*); **they are fighting like ~:** sie prügeln sich wie die Wilden (*ugs.*)

**bimbo** /ˈbɪmbəʊ/ *n.* (*coll. derog.*) Puppe, *die* (*salopp*)

**bimetallic** /baɪmɪˈtælɪk/ *adj.* bimetallisch; ~ **strip** Bimetall, *das;* Bimetallstreifen, *der*

**bimonthly** /baɪˈmʌnθlɪ/ **1** *adj.* **A** (*two-monthly*) zweimonatlich; alle zwei Monate erscheinend ‹Zeitschrift›/stattfindend ‹Treffen, Ereignis›; **B** (*twice-monthly*) zweimal im Monat erscheinend ‹Zeitschrift›/stattfindend ‹Treffen, Ereignis›. **2** *adv.* **A** (*two-monthly*) alle zwei Monate; **B** (*twice monthly*) zweimal im Monat

**bin** /bɪn/ *n.* **A** (*for storage*) Behälter, *der;* (*for coal*) Kohlenkasten, *der;* (*for fruit*) [Obst]kiste, *die;* (*for bread*) Brotkasten, *der;* (*for wine*) Weinregal, *das;* **B** (*for rubbish*) (*inside house*) Abfalleimer, *der;* Mülleimer, *der;* (*outside house*) Mülltonne, *die;* (*in public place*) Abfallkorb, *der*

**binary** /ˈbaɪnərɪ/ **1** *adj.* **A** binär; zweizählig; ~ **system** binäres System; **B** (*Math.*) ~ **digit** binäre Ziffer; Dualzahl, *die;* ~ **number** binäre Zahl; **C** (*Biol.*) ~ **fission** äquale Zellteilung; **D** (*Mus.*) ~ **form** zweiteilige Form; ~ **measure** gerader Takt; **E** (*Astron.*) ~ **star** Doppelstern, *der;* **F** (*Chem.*) ~ **compound** binäre Verbindung; Zweifachverbindung, *die.* **2** *n.* (*Astron.*) Doppelstern, *der*

**ˈbin bag** *n.* Müllbeutel, *der*

**bind** /baɪnd/ **1** *v.t.,* **bound** /baʊnd/ **A** (*tie*) fesseln ‹Person, Tier›; (*bandage*) wickeln, binden ‹Glied, Baum›; verbinden ‹Wunde› (**with** mit); **he was bound hand and foot** er war/wurde an Händen und Füßen gefesselt; **they bound the animal's legs together** sie fesselten das Tier an den Beinen; ~ **sb. to sth.** jmdn. an etw. (*Akk.*) fesseln *od.* binden; ~ **sth. to sth.** etw. an etw. (*Akk.*) binden; **B** (*fasten together*) zusammenbinden; (*fig.: unite*) verbinden; **C** ~ **books** Bücher binden; **D be bound up with sth.** (*fig.*) eng mit etw. verbunden *od.* verknüpft sein; eng mit etw. zusammenhängen; **E** (*oblige*) ~ **sb./oneself to sth.** jmdn./sich an etw. (*Akk.*) binden; **this agreement ~s us** wir sind an diese Abmachung gebunden; **be bound to do sth.** (*required*) verpflichtet sein, etw. zu tun; **be bound by law** von Gesetzes wegen verpflichtet sein; **be bound to secrecy** zur Verschwiegenheit verpflichtet sein; ⇒ *also* **honour** 1 D; **F be bound to do sth.** (*certain*) etw. ganz bestimmt tun; **it is bound to rain** es wird bestimmt *od.* sicherlich regnen; **G I'm bound to say that ...** (*feel obliged*) ich muss schon sagen, dass ...; ich fühle mich verpflichtet zu sagen, dass ...; **I'm bound to agree** ich glaube, ich stimme überein; **H** (*constipate*) verstopfen; **I** (*Cookery*) binden; **J** (*indenture*) durch Lehrvertrag binden ‹Lehrling›; **he was bound [apprentice] for 3 years** er ging drei Jahre in die Lehre; **K** (*Law*) ~ **sb. over [to keep the peace]** jmdn. verwarnen *od.* rechtlich verpflichten[, die öffentliche Ordnung zu wahren]; **I'll be bound** (*fig.*) ganz gewiss; auf mein Wort; **L** (*coll.: bore*) langweilen; ~ **sb. stiff** jmdn. zu Tode langweilen; **M** (*encircle*) ~ **one's hair with flowers** sich (*Dat.*) Blumen ins Haar binden; **N** (*edge*) einfassen ‹Stoffkante usw.› (**with** mit).

**2** *v.i.,* **bound** **A** (*cohere*) binden; ‹Lehm, Ton:› fest *od.* hart werden; ‹Zement:› abbinden; **B** (*be restricted*) blockieren; ‹Kolben:› sich festfressen; **the window frame ~s easily** der Fensterrahmen verklemmt sich leicht; **C** (*coll.: complain*) meckern (*ugs.*) (**about** über + *Akk.*).

**3** *n.* **A** (*Bot.*) Ranke, *die;* **B** (*Mus.*) Bindebogen, *der;* Bindungszeichen, *das;* Bindung, *die;* **C** (*coll.: nuisance*) **be a ~:** recht lästig sein; **what a ~!** wie unangenehm *od.* lästig!; **D be in a ~** (*Amer. coll.*) in einer Klemme sitzen (*ugs.*)

**binder** /'baɪndə(r)/ *n.* **A** (*substance*) Bindemittel, *das;* Binder, *der;* **B** (*book~*) Buchbinder, *der*/-binderin, *die;* **C** (*Agric.*) [Mäh]binder, *der;* Bindemäher, *der;* **D** (*tie beam*) Bundbalken, *der;* Binderbalken, *der;* **E** (*cover*) (*for papers*) Hefter, *der;* (*for magazines*) Mappe, *die;* **F** (*bondstone*) Binder, *der;* Bindestein, *der*

**bindery** /'baɪndərɪ/ *n.* Buchbinderei, *die*

**binding** /'baɪndɪŋ/ **1** *adj.* bindend, verbindlich ‹Vertrag, Abkommen› **(on** für). **2** *n.* **A** (*cover of book*) [Buch]einband, *der;* **B** (*edge*) (*of carpet, material, etc.*) [Einfass]band, *das;* Besatz, *der;* **C** (*on ski*) Bindung, *die*

**bindweed** /'baɪndwi:d/ *n.* (*Bot.*) Winde, *die*

**binge** /bɪndʒ/ *n.* (*coll.: drinking bout*) Sauferei, *die* (*salopp*); **go/be out on a ~:** auf Sauftour gehen/sein (*salopp*)

**bingo** /'bɪŋgəʊ/ **1** *n., no pl.* Bingo, *das;* **~ hall** Bingohalle, *die.* **2** *int.* peng; zack

**'bin liner** *n.* Müllbeutel, *der*

**binnacle** /'bɪnəkl/ *n.* (*Naut.*) Kompasshaus, *das*

**binocular** /bɪ'nɒkjʊlə(r)/ **1** *adj.* binokular. **2** *n. in pl.* **[pair of] ~s** Fernglas, *das;* Binokular, *das*

**bint** /bɪnt/ *n.* (*coll. derog.*) Weib[stück], *das*

**bio-** /baɪəʊ/ *in comb.* Bio-; Lebens-

**bio'active** *adj.* bioaktiv; biologisch aktiv

**bio'chemical** *adj.* biochemisch

**bio'chemist** *n.* ▶ **1261** Biochemiker, *der*/Biochemikerin, *die*

**bio'chemistry** *n.* Biochemie, *die*

**biode'gradable** *adj.* biologisch abbaubar

**biode'grade** *v.i.* sich biologisch abbauen

**biodi'versity** *n., no pl.* biologische Vielfalt

**bioengi'neering** *n.* **A** Biotechnik, *die;* **a ~ process** ein biotechnisches Verfahren; **B** (*genetic engineering*) Gentechnologie, *die*

**bio'ethics** *n.* Bioethik, *die*

**'biogas** *n.* Biogas, *das*

**bio'genesis** *n., no pl.* Biogenese, *die*

**biogenic** /baɪə'dʒenɪk/ *adj.* biogenetisch

**biographer** /baɪ'ɒgrəfə(r)/ *n.* ▶ **1261** Biograph, *der*/Biographin, *die*

**biographic** /baɪə'græfɪk/, **biographical** /baɪə'græfɪkl/ *adj.* biographisch

**biography** /baɪ'ɒgrəfɪ/ *n.* Biographie, *die;* (*branch of literature*) biographische Literatur

**biological** /baɪə'lɒdʒɪkl/ *adj.* biologisch

**biological: ~ 'clock** *n.* biologische Uhr; **~ con'trol** *n.* biologische Schädlingsbekämpfung; **~ 'warfare** *n.* biologische Kriegführung; Bakterienkrieg, *der*

**biologically** /baɪə'lɒdʒɪkəlɪ/ *adv.* biologisch

**biologist** /baɪ'ɒlədʒɪst/ *n.* ▶ **1261** Biologe, *der*/Biologin, *die*

**biology** /baɪ'ɒlədʒɪ/ *n.* Biologie, *die*

**'biomass** *n.* Biomasse, *die*

**biometric** /baɪə'metrɪk/, **biometrical** /baɪə'metrɪkl/ *adj.* biometrisch

**bionic** /baɪ'ɒnɪk/ *adj.* bionisch

**bionics** /baɪ'ɒnɪks/ *n.* Bionik, *die*

**biopic** /'baɪəʊpɪk/ *n.* (*coll.*) Filmbiographie, *die*

**biopsy** /'baɪɒpsɪ/ *n.* Biopsie, *die*

**'biorhythm** *n.* Biorhythmus, *der*

**bioscope** /'baɪəskəʊp/ *n.* (*S. Afr.*) Filmtheater, *das;* Kino, *das*

**'biosphere** *n.* Biosphäre, *die*

**bio'synthesis** *n.* Biosynthese, *die*

**biotech'nology** *n.* Biotechnik, *die*

**biotope** /'baɪətəʊp/ *n.* Biotop, *der od. das*

**bipartisan** /baɪpɑ:tɪ'zæn, baɪ'pɑ:tɪzæn/ *adj.* Zweiparteien-

**bipartite** /baɪ'pɑ:taɪt/ *adj.* (*having two parts*) zweiteilig; (*involving two parties*) zweiseitig ‹Dokument, Abkommen›

**biped** /'baɪped/ *n.* Bipede, *der;* Zweifüßer, *der*

**biplane** /'baɪpleɪn/ *n.* Doppeldecker, *der*

**birch** /bɜ:tʃ/ **1** *n.* **A** (*tree*) Birke, *die;* **B** ⇒ **birch-rod. 2** *v.t.* mit der Rute züchtigen

**'birch bark** *n.* Birkenrinde, *die*

**birching** /'bɜ:tʃɪŋ/ *n.* [Tracht] Prügel, *die;* **~ should be made illegal** die Prügelstrafe sollte verboten werden

**'birch rod** *n.* [Birken]rute, *die*

**bird** /bɜ:d/ *n.* **A** Vogel, *der;* **the ~ is** *or* **has flown** (*fig.*) der Vogel ist ausgeflogen (*fig.*); **~s of a feather flock together** (*prov.*) Gleich und Gleich gesellt sich gern (*Spr.*); **it's [strictly] for the ~s** (*coll.*) das kannste vergessen (*salopp*); **get the ~** (*be hissed etc.*) ausgepfiffen werden; (*be dismissed*) entlassen werden; **give sb. the ~** (*hiss sb.*) jmdn. auspfeifen; (*dismiss sb.*) jmdn. entlassen; **kill two ~s with one stone** (*fig.*) zwei Fliegen mit einer Klappe schlagen; **a ~ in the hand is worth two in the bush** (*prov.*) ein Spatz in der Hand ist besser als eine Taube auf dem Dach (*Spr.*); **like a ~** (*without difficulty or hesitation*) einfach so; **a little ~ told me** mein kleiner Finger sagt mir das; **tell sb. about the ~s and the bees** (*euphem.*) jmdm. erzählen, wo die kleinen Kinder herkommen; **B** (*sl.: girl*) Mieze, *die* (*salopp*); **C** (*coll.: person*) Vogel, *der* (*ugs.*); **a queer ~:** ein komischer Kauz *od.* Vogel; **a gay old ~:** ein lustiger alter Knabe; **D** *no art.* (*sl.: imprisonment*) Knast, *der* (*ugs.*); **do ~:** Knast schieben (*salopp*). ⇒ *also* **early bird**

**bird: ~ bath** *n.* Vogelbad, *das;* **~brained** *adj.* (*coll.*) **A** (*stupid*) gehirnamputiert (*salopp*); **~brained person** Mensch mit einem Spatzenhirn (*salopp*); **B** (*flighty*) flatterhaft; **~cage** *n.* Vogelkäfig, *der;* Vogelbauer, *das od. der;* **~ call** *n.* Vogelruf, *der;* (*instrument*) Lockpfeife, *die;* **~ fancier** *n.* Vogelfreund, *der*/-freundin, *die;* (*breeder*) Vogelzüchter, *der*/-züchterin, *die*

**birdie** /'bɜ:dɪ/ **1** *n.* **A** Vögelchen, *das;* **B** (*Golf*) Birdie, *das;* ein Schlag unter Par. **2** *v.t.* einen Schlag unter Par spielen

**bird: ~lime** *n.* Vogelleim, *der;* **~ of 'paradise** *n.* Paradiesvogel, *der;* **~ of 'passage** *n.* (*lit. or fig.*) Zugvogel, *der;* **~ sanctuary** *n.* Vogelschutzgebiet, *das;* **~seed** *n.* Vogelfutter, *das;* **~'s-eye** *n.* (*Bot.*) Gamander-Ehrenpreis, *der;* **~'s-eye 'view** *n.* Vogelperspektive, *die;* **have/get a ~'s-eye view of sth.** (*lit. or fig.*) etw. aus der Vogelperspektive sehen; **~'s nest** *n.* Vogelnest, *das;* **~'s nest soup** Schwalbennestersuppe, *die;* **~ strike** *n.* Kollision von Flugzeug und Vogel; **~ table** *n.* Futterstelle für Vögel; **~watcher** *n.* Vogelbeobachter, *der*/-beobachterin, *die;* **~-watching** *n., no pl., no indef. art.* das Beobachten von Vögeln

**biretta** /bɪ'retə/ *n.* (*Eccl.*) Birett, *das*

**Biro** ® /'baɪrəʊ/ *n., pl.* **~s** Kugelschreiber, *der;* Kuli, *der* (*ugs.*)

**birth** /bɜ:θ/ *n.* **A** Geburt, *die;* **at the/at ~:** bei der Geburt; **[deaf] from** *or* **since ~:** von Geburt an [taub]; **date and place of ~:** Geburtsdatum und -ort; **land of my ~:** Land meiner Väter (*geh.*); **give ~** ‹Frau:› entbinden; gebären (*geh.*); ‹Tier:› jungen; werfen; **she gave ~ prematurely** sie hatte eine Frühgeburt; **give ~ to a child** von einem Kind entbunden werden; ein Kind gebären (*geh.*) *od.* zur Welt bringen; **B** (*coming into existence*) (*of movement, fashion, etc.*) Aufkommen, *das;* (*of party, company*) Gründung, *die;* (*of nation*) Geburt, *die;* (*of new era*) Anbruch, *der;* Geburt, *die;* **the ~ of an idea** die Geburt einer Idee; **come to ~:** geboren werden; ‹Ära:› anbrechen; **give ~ to sth.** etw. entstehen lassen; **C** (*parentage*) Geburt, *die;* Abkunft, *die* (*geh.*); **of good/low** *or* **humble ~:** aus gutem Hause *od.* guter Familie/von niedriger Abstammung; **of high ~:** von hoher Geburt; [von] edler Abkunft (*geh.*); **be a German by ~:** Deutsche[r] von Geburt sein; [ein] gebürtiger Deutscher/[eine] gebürtige Deutsche sein; **sb.'s right by ~:** jmds. angeborenes Recht

**birth: ~ certificate** *n.* Geburtsurkunde, *die;* **~ control** *n.* Geburtenkontrolle *od.* -regelung, *die;* **~day** *n.* ▶ **1191** Geburtstag, *der;* **when is your ~day?** wann haben Sie Geburtstag?; *attrib.* **~day card** Geburtstagskarte, *die;* **~day party** Geburtstagsfeier, *die;* (*with music and dancing*) Geburtstagsparty, *die;* (*children's*) Kindergeburtstag, *der;* **~day present** Geburtstagsgeschenk, *das;* **~day honours** (*Brit.*) Titel- und Ordensverleihungen *Pl.* (*am offiziellen Geburtstag des britischen Monarchen*); **[be] in his/her ~day suit** (*coll. joc.: naked*) im Adams-/Evaskostüm [sein]

**'birthing pool** /'bɜ:θɪŋ/ *n.* Gebärwanne, *die*

**birth: ~mark** *n.* Muttermal, *das;* **~place** *n.* Geburtsort, *der;* (*house*) Geburtshaus, *das;* **~ rate** *n.* Geburtenrate *od.* -ziffer, *die;* **~right** *n.* Geburtsrecht, *das;* (*right of first-born*) Erstgeburtsrecht, *das;* **~stone** *n.* Monatsstein, *der*

**biscuit** /'bɪskɪt/ **1** *n.* **A** (*Brit.*) Keks, *der;* **coffee and ~s** Kaffee und Gebäck; **~ tin** Keksdose, *die;* **B** (*Amer.: roll*) [weiches] Brötchen; **C** (*colour*) Beige, *das;* **D** (*pottery*) Biskuit, *das.* ⇒ *also* **take** 1 C. **2** *adj.* beige

**bisect** /baɪ'sekt/ *v.t.* (*into halves*) in zwei Hälften teilen; halbieren; (*into two*) in zwei Teile teilen

**bisection** /baɪ'sekʃn/ *n.* (*into halves*) Halbierung, *die;* (*into two*) Zweiteilung, *die*

**bisector** /baɪ'sektə(r)/ *n.* Halbierende, *die*

**bisexual** /baɪ'seksjʊəl/ **1** *adj.* **A** (*Biol.*) zwittrig; doppelgeschlechtig; **B** (*attracted by both sexes*) bisexuell. **2** *n.* Bisexuelle, *der/die*

**bisexuality** /baɪseksjʊ'ælɪtɪ/ *n., no pl.* ⇒ **bisexual** 1: Zwittrigkeit, *die;* Doppelgeschlechtigkeit, *die;* Bisexualität, *die*

**bish** /bɪʃ/ *n.* (*Brit. dated coll.*) Fehler, *der*

**bishop** /'bɪʃəp/ *n.* **A** ▶ **1617** (*Eccl.*) Bischof, *der; as voc.* Herr Bischof; **B** (*Chess*) Läufer, *der*

**bishopric** /'bɪʃəprɪk/ *n.* **A** (*office*) Bischofsamt, *das;* Bischofswürde, *die;* **B** (*diocese*) Bistum, *das;* Diözese, *die*

**'bishop sleeve** *n.* Puffärmel, *der*

**bismuth** /'bɪzməθ/ *n.* (*Chem., Med.*) Wismut, *das*

**bison** /'baɪsn/ *n.* (*Zool.*) **A** (*Amer.: buffalo*) Bison, *der;* **B** (*European*) Wisent, *der*

**bisque** /bɪsk/ **A** (*porcelain*) Biskuit, *das;* **B** (*Gastr.*) Fischcremesuppe, *die*

**bistort** /'bɪstɔ:t/ *n.* (*Bot.*) Wiesenknöterich, *der*

**bistro** /'bi:strəʊ/ *n., pl.* **~s** Bistro, *das*

**bit[1]** /bɪt/ *n.* **A** (*for horse*) Gebiss, *das;* Gebissstange, *die;* **take the ~ between one's teeth** (*fig.*) aufmüpfig werden (*ugs.*); **B** (*of drill*) [Bohr]einsatz, *der;* Bohrer, *der;* (*of key*) [Schlüssel]bart, *der;* (*of soldering iron*) Lötkolben[kopf], *der*

**bit[2]** *n.* **A** (*piece*) Stück, *das;* (*smaller*) Stückchen, *das;* **a little ~:** ein kleines Stückchen; **a ~ of cheese/wood/cough/sugar** ein bisschen *od.* etwas Käse/ein Stück Holz/etwas Kohle/ein bisschen *od.* etwas Zucker; **a ~ of trouble/luck** ein wenig Ärger/Glück; **the best ~s** die besten Teile; **it cost quite a ~:** es kostete ziemlich viel; **have a ~ of cheek** ein bisschen frech sein; **a ~ of all right** (*coll.*) gar nicht übel (*ugs.*); **a ~ [of stuff]** (*coll.: woman*) ein netter *od.* toller Käfer (*ugs.*); **~ by ~:** Stück für Stück; (*gradually*) nach und nach; **smashed to ~s** in tausend Stücke zersprungen; **sb./sth. is blown to ~s** jmd. wird zerrissen/etw. wird in die Luft gesprengt; **he was thrilled to ~s** (*coll.*) er hat sich wahnsinnig gefreut (*ugs.*); **~s and bobs** Krimskrams, *der* (*ugs.*); Kram, *der* (*ugs.*); **~s and pieces** Verschiedenes; **do one's ~:** seinen Teil tun *od.* dazu beitragen; (*fair share also*) das Seine tun; **not a** *or* **one ~** (*not at all*) überhaupt nicht; **sb./sth. is not a ~ of use** jmd. ist zu nichts zu gebrauchen/mit etw. kann man überhaupt nichts anfangen; **it is not a ~ of use complaining** es hat überhaupt keinen Sinn, sich zu beklagen; **not a ~ of it** ganz im Gegenteil; **he is every ~ as clever as you are** er ist genauso schlau wie du; **B a ~** (*somewhat*): **a ~ tired/late/too early** ein bisschen müde/spät/zu früh; **a little ~, just a ~:** ein klein bisschen; **quite a ~:** um einiges ‹besser, stärker, hoffnungsvoller›; **with a ~ more practice** mit etwas mehr Übung; **C a ~ of** (*rather*):

b

**be a ~ of a coward/bully** ganz schön feige *od.* ein ziemlicher Feigling sein/den starken Mann markieren (*ugs.*); **every politician has to be a ~ of a showman** jeder Politiker muss auch etwas von einem Schauspieler an sich (*Dat.*) haben; **a ~ of a disappointment** eine ganz schöne Enttäuschung; **D** (*Brit.*) **~s of furniture** [armselige] Möbel; **~s of children** kleine Kinder; **E** (*short time*) **[for] a ~:** eine Weile; **a little ~, just a ~:** ein klein bisschen; **wait a ~ longer** noch ein Weilchen warten; **F** (*short distance*) **a ~:** ein Stückchen; **a ~ closer** ein bisschen näher; **a little ~, just a ~:** ein kleines Stückchen; **G** (*coin*) Münze, *die;* **sixpenny/threepenny ~** (*Brit. Hist.*) Sixpence-/Dreipencestück, *das;* **H** (*Amer.: $12\frac{1}{2}$ cents*) **two ~s** 25 Cent; **four/six ~s** 50/75 Cent; **I** (*role*) **a ~ [part]** eine kleine Rolle

**bit³** *n.* (*Computing*) Bit, *das*

**bit⁴** ⇒ **bite** 1, 2

**bitch** /bɪtʃ/ **1** *n.* **A** (*dog*) Hündin, *die;* (*vixen*) Füchsin, *die;* **B** (*sl. derog.: woman*) Miststück, *das;* Schlampe, *die* (*salopp*); ⇒ *also* **son**; **C** (*coll.: grumble*) **have a ~ about sth.** über etw. (*Akk.*) meckern (*ugs.*). **2** *v.i.* (*coll.*) meckern (*ugs.*) (**about** über + *Akk.*). **3** *v.t.* **~ sth. [up]** (*coll.*) etw. verpfuschen (*ugs.*) *od.* (*salopp*) versauen

**bitchy** /ˈbɪtʃɪ/ *adj.* (*coll.*) gemein; gehässig; **be/get ~ about sb.** gehässige Bemerkungen über jmdn. machen/anfangen, gehässige Bemerkungen über jmdn. zu machen

**bite** /baɪt/ **1** *v.t.*, **bit** /bɪt/, **bitten** /ˈbɪtn/ beißen; (*sting*) ‹Moskito usw.:› stechen; **~ one's nails** an den Nägeln kauen; (*fig.*) wie auf Kohlen sitzen; **~ one's lip** (*lit. or fig.*) sich (*Dat.*) auf die Lippen beißen; **he won't ~ you** (*fig. coll.*) er wird dich schon nicht beißen; **I've been bitten** (*fig.: swindled*) ich bin reingelegt worden (*ugs.*) *od.* hereingefallen; **once bitten twice shy** (*prov.*) einmal und nie wieder!; **~ the hand that feeds one** (*fig.*) sich [seinem Gönner gegenüber] undankbar zeigen; **~ the dust** (*fig.*) daran glauben müssen (*ugs.*); **be bitten with an idea** von einer Idee besessen sein; **what's biting** *or* **bitten you/him?** (*fig. coll.*) was ist mit dir/ihm los?; was hast du/hat er denn? **2** *v.i.*, **bit, bitten A** beißen; (*sting*) stechen; ‹Rad:› fassen, greifen; ‹Schraube:› fassen; (*take bait, lit. or fig.*) anbeißen; **B ~ at sth.** nach etw. schnappen; **C** (*have an effect*) sich auswirken; greifen; **D have sth. to ~ on** (*fig.*) etw. haben, worauf man sich stützen kann; **~ on the bullet** (*fig.*) die Zähne zusammenbeißen.
**3** *n.* **A** (*act*) Biss, *der;* (*piece*) Bissen, *der;* (*wound*) Bisswunde, *die;* (*by mosquito etc.*) Stich, *der;* **he took a ~ of the apple** er biss in den Apfel; **can I have a ~?** darf ich mal [ab]beißen?; **take one ~ at a time** immer nur einen Bissen auf einmal nehmen; **put the ~ on [sb.]** (*Amer. coll.*) jmdn. unter Druck setzen; **B** (*taking of bait*) [An]beißen, *das;* **I haven't had a ~ all day** es hat den ganzen Tag noch keiner angebissen; **wait for a ~:** darauf warten, dass einer *od.* ein Fisch anbeißt; **C** (*food*) Happen, *der;* Bissen, *der;* **I haven't had a ~ [to eat] since breakfast** ich habe seit dem Frühstück nichts mehr gegessen; **have a ~ to eat** eine Kleinigkeit essen; **come and have a ~ to eat** komm und iss eine Kleinigkeit (*ugs.*); **D** (*grip*) **these old tyres have no ~:** diese alten Reifen fassen *od.* greifen nicht [mehr]; **E** (*incisiveness*) Bissigkeit, *die;* Schärfe, *die;* **we need new laws that will have more ~:** wir brauchen neue Gesetze, die besser greifen; **F** (*Dent.*) Biss, *der;* normale Bissstellung

**~ 'back** *v.t.* **~ sth. back** etw. unterdrücken; **~ back one's words/a remark** sich (*Dat.*) seine Worte/eine Bemerkung verkneifen

**~ 'off** *v.t.* abbeißen; **the dog bit off the man's ear** der Hund hat dem Mann ein Ohr abgebissen; **~ sb.'s head off** (*fig.*) jmdm. den Kopf abreißen; **~ off more than one can chew** (*fig.*) sich (*Dat.*) zu viel zumuten; sich übernehmen

**biter** /ˈbaɪtə(r)/ *n.* **the ~ bit** mit den eigenen Waffen geschlagen; (*in deception also*) der betrogene Betrüger; **it's a case of the ~ bit** wer andern eine Grube gräbt, fällt selbst hinein (*Spr.*)

**'bite-size** *adj.* mundgerecht

**biting** /ˈbaɪtɪŋ/ *adj.* (*stinging*) beißend; schneidend ‹Kälte, Wind›; (*sarcastic*) scharf ‹Angriff, Worte›; beißend ‹Kritik›; bissig, sarkastisch ‹Bemerkung, Kommentar›

**bitten** ⇒ **bite** 1, 2

**bitter** /ˈbɪtə(r)/ **1** *adj.* **A** bitter; **~ orange** (*Bot.*) Pomeranze, *die;* **~ lemon** (*drink*) Bitter lemon, *das;* **B** (*fig.*) scharf, heftig ‹Antwort, Bemerkung, Angriff›; bitter ‹Kampf, Kälte, Enttäuschung, Tränen›; verbittert ‹Person›; erbittert ‹Feind›; scharf, bitterkalt ‹Wind, Wetter›; streng ‹Winter›; **~ experience** bittere Erfahrung; **to the ~ end** bis zum bitteren Ende; **be/feel ~ [about sth.]** [über etw. (*Akk.*)] bitter *od.* verbittert sein. ⇒ *also* **pill** B. **2** *n.* **A** (*bitterness*) Bitterkeit, *die;* **B** *in pl.* (*liquors*) Magenbitter, *der;* **C** (*Brit.: beer*) bitteres Bier (*halbdunkles, obergäriges Bier*)

**bitterly** /ˈbɪtəlɪ/ *adv.* bitterlich ‹weinen, sich beschweren›; bitter ‹erwidern›; erbittert ‹kämpfen, sich widersetzen›; scharf ‹kritisieren›; **~ cold** bitterkalt; **he ~ resented the unfounded accusations** er war äußerst erbittert über die unbegründeten Beschuldigungen; **be ~ opposed to sth.** ein erbitterter Gegner einer Sache (*Gen.*) sein

**bittern** /ˈbɪtən/ *n.* (*Ornith.*) Rohrdommel, *die*

**bitterness** /ˈbɪtənɪs/ *n.*, *no pl.* Bitterkeit, *die;* (*of reply, remark, attack*) Schärfe, *die;* Heftigkeit, *die;* (*of person*) Verbitterung, *die;* (*of wind*) bittere Kälte

**bitter-'sweet** *adj.* (*lit. or fig.*) bittersüß

**bitty** /ˈbɪtɪ/ *adj.* zusammengestoppelt (*abwertend*); zusammengestückelt

**bitumen** /ˈbɪtjʊmən/ *n.* Bitumen, *das*

**bituminous** /bɪˈtju:mɪnəs/ *adj.* bituminös; **~ coal** Stein- *od.* Fettkohle, *die;* Bituminit, *das*

**bivalve** /ˈbaɪvælv/ **1** *adj.* **A** (*Zool.*) zweischalig ‹Muschel›; zweiklappig ‹Schale›; **B** (*Biol.*) zweiklappig ‹Frucht›. **2** *n.* (*Zool.*) Muschel, *die*

**bivouac** /ˈbɪvʊæk/ **1** *n.* Biwak, *das;* Lager, *das.* **2** *v.i.*, **-ck-** biwakieren; im Freien übernachten

**bi-weekly** /baɪˈwi:klɪ/ **1** *adj.* **A** (*two-weekly*) zweiwöchentlich; alle zwei Wochen erscheinend ‹Zeitschrift›/stattfindend ‹Treffen, Ereignis›; **B** (*twice-weekly*) zweimal in der Woche erscheinend ‹Zeitschrift›/stattfindend ‹Treffen, Ereignis›. **2** *adv.* **A** (*two-weekly*) alle zwei Wochen; **B** (*twice weekly*) zweimal in der Woche

**biz** /bɪz/ *n.* (*coll.*) Geschäft, *das*

**bizarre** /bɪˈzɑ:(r)/ *adj.* bizarr; (*eccentric*) exzentrisch; (*grotesque, irregular*) grotesk

**bk.** *abbr.* **book** Bch.

**blab** /blæb/ (*coll.*) **1** *v.i.*, **-bb-** quatschen (*abwertend*). **2** *v.t.*, **-bb-** ausplaudern

**black** /blæk/ **1** *adj.* **A** schwarz; (*very dark*) dunkel; (*dirty*) **as ~ as coal** *or* **ink** kohlrabenschwarz; ⇒ *also* **face** 1 A; **B** (*dark-clothed*) schwarz [gekleidet]; **C B~** (*dark-skinned*) schwarz; **B~ man/woman/child** Schwarze, *der*/Schwarze, *die*/schwarzes Kind; **B~ people** Schwarze *Pl.;* **B~ ghettos** von Schwarzen bewohnte Gettos; **B~ Africa** Schwarzafrika (*das*); **D** (*looking gloomy*) düster; **things look ~:** es sieht böse *od.* düster aus; **~ clouds** dunkle Wolken; **E** (*fig.: wicked*) schwarz ‹Gedanken›; **~ ingratitude** grober Undank; **F** (*evil*) schändlich; **he is not as ~ as he is painted** er ist nicht so schlecht, wie er dargestellt wird; **get some ~ looks** finster angesehen werden; **give sb. a ~ look** jmdn. finster ansehen; **G** (*dismal*) **a ~ day** ein schwarzer Tag; **be in a ~ mood** deprimiert sein; **~ despair** tiefe Verzweiflung; **H** (*macabre*) schwarz ‹Witz, Humor›; **I** (*not to be handled*) bestreikt ‹Lastwagen, Schiff›.
**2** *n.* **A** (*colour*) Schwarz, *das;* (*in roulette*) Noir, *das;* **B B~** (*person*) Schwarze, *der*/*die;* **C** (*credit*) **[be] in the ~:** in den schwarzen Zahlen [sein]; **D** (*Bot.: fungus*) Brand, *der;* **E** (*Snooker*) schwarze Kugel; **F** (**~ clothes**) **dressed in ~:** schwarz gekleidet.
**3** *v.t.* **A** (*blacken*) schwärzen; **~ sb.'s eye** jmdm. ein blaues Auge machen; **~ one's face** sich schwarz anmalen; **~ one's shoes** seine Schuhe wichsen; **B** (*declare ~*) bestreiken ‹Betrieb›; boykottieren ‹Arbeit›

**~ 'out** **1** *v.t.* verdunkeln. **2** *v.i.* das Bewusstsein verlieren. ⇒ *also* **~out**

**black: ~ and 'blue** *pred. adj.* grün und blau; **~ and 'white** **1** *pred. adj.* (*in writing*) schwarz auf weiß; (*Cinemat., Photog., etc.*) schwarzweiß; (*fig.: comprising only opposite extremes*) Schwarzweiß-; **2** *n.* **[sth. is there/down] in ~ and white** (*in writing*) [etw. steht] schwarz auf weiß [geschrieben]; **this film is in ~ and white** dieser Film ist in schwarzweiß; **see/portray** *etc.* **things in ~ and white** (*fig.*) schwarzweiß malen; **~-and-white** *attrib. adj.* Schwarzweiß-; **~ 'art** *n.* schwarze Kunst, *die;* Magie, *die;* **~ball** *v.t.* stimmen gegen; **~ 'beetle** *n.* (*Zool.*) Küchenschabe, *die;* **~berry** /ˈblækbərɪ/ *n.* Brombeere, *die;* **go ~berrying** Brombeeren pflücken gehen; **~bird** *n.* Amsel, *die;* **~board** *n.* [Wand]tafel, *die;* **~ 'books** *n. pl.* **be in sb.'s ~ books** bei jmdm. schlecht angeschrieben sein; **~ 'box** *n.* (*flight recorder*) Flugschreiber, *der;* (*apparatus with concealed mechanism*) Black box, *die;* **~ 'bread** *n.* Schwarzbrot, *das;* **~buck** *n.* (*Zool.*) Hirschziegenantilope, *die;* **~ 'cap** *n.* (*Brit. Law Hist.*) *gefaltetes Tuch aus schwarzer Seide, das der Richter früher auf dem Kopf trug, wenn er ein Todesurteil verkündete;* **~cap** *n.* (*Ornith.*) Mönchsgrasmücke, *die;* **~cock** *n.* (*Ornith.*) Birkhahn, *der;* **B~ Country** *n.* (*Brit.*) *Industriegebiet von Staffordshire und Warwickshire;* **~'currant** *n.* schwarze Johannisbeere; **B~ 'Death** *n.* schwarzer Tod; **~ 'earth** *n.* (*Geol.*) Schwarzerde, *die;* Tschernosjom, *der od. das* (*fachspr.*); **~ e'conomy** *n.* Schattenwirtschaft, *die*

**blacken** /ˈblækn/ *v.t.* **A** (*make dark[er]*) verfinstern ‹Himmel›; (*make black[er]*) schwärzen; **the ancient buildings were ~ed by centuries of smoke and grime** die alten Bauwerke waren durch die Jahrhunderte rauch- und rußgeschwärzt; **B** (*fig.: defame*) verunglimpfen; **~ sb.'s [good] name** jmds. [guten] Namen beschmutzen; **~ the picture** schwarz malen

**black: ~ 'eye** *n.* **A** (*bruised*) blaues Auge (*fig.*); Veilchen, *das* (*ugs.*); **B** (*dark*) **~ eyes** schwarze Augen; **~-eyed** *adj.* schwarzäugig; **be ~-eyed** schwarze Augen haben; **~-face** *n.* **A** (*sheep*) Schaf mit schwarzem Gesicht; **B** (*make-up*) Schminke für eine Negerrolle; **~fly** *n.* (*Zool.*) **A** (*aphid*) Blattlaus, *die;* **B** (*thrips*) Schwarze Fliege; **B~ 'Forest** *pr. n.* Schwarzwald, *der;* **B~ Forest 'gateau** *n.* Schwarzwälder [Kirschtorte], *die;* **B~ Friar** *n.* Dominikaner, *der;* **~ 'frost** ⇒ **frost** 1 A; **~ grouse** *n.* (*Ornith.*) Birkhuhn, *das*

**blackguard** /ˈblægɑ:d/ **1** *n.* (*scoundrel*) Schurke, *der;* Lump, *der;* (*foul-mouthed person*) Schandmaul, *das* (*geh. abwertend*). **2** *adj.* (*scoundrelly*) schurkisch (*veralt.*); gemein; (*foul-mouthed*) unflätig. **3** *v.t.* (*call a ~*) **~ sb.** jmdn. einen Lumpen *od.* Schurken schimpfen; (*abuse*) in unflätiger Weise schimpfen über (+ *Akk.*)

**blackguardly** /ˈblægɑ:dlɪ/ *adj.* gemein

**black: ~head** *n.* **A** (*Ornith.*) Bergente, *die;* **B** (*pimple*) Mitesser, *der;* **~ 'hole** *n.* **A** (*Astron.*) schwarzes Loch; **B** (*esp. Mil.: gaol*) Bunker, *der;* **~ 'ice** *n.* Glatteis, *das*

**blacking** /ˈblækɪŋ/ *n.* schwarze Schuhcreme

**blackish** /ˈblækɪʃ/ *adj.* schwärzlich

**black: ~jack** *n.* **A** (*flag*) schwarze Piratenflagge; **B** (*Amer.: bludgeon*) Totschläger, *der;* **C** (*Cards*) Vingt-[et-]un, *das;* **D** (*vessel*) lederner (*außen mit Teer überzogener*) Trinkbecher; **~lead** /ˈblækled/ **1** *n.* Graphit, *der;* **2** *v.t.* schwärzen; **~leg** **1** *n.* **A** (*Brit.: strike-breaker*) Streikbrecher, *der*/-brecherin, *die;* **B** (*swindler*) *jmd., der bei Pferderennen od. anderen Glücksspielen falsch spielt;* **2** *v.i.*

Streikbrecher/-brecherin sein; ~ **'letter** *n.* (*Gothic type*) gotische Schrift; (*Schwabacher type*) Schwabacher [Schrift], *die;* (*Fraktur*) Fraktur, *die;* ~ **list** *n.* schwarze Liste; **~list** *v.t.* auf die schwarze Liste setzen

**blackly** /'blæklɪ/ *adv.* Ⓐ (*darkly, gloomily*) düster; Ⓑ (*angrily*) finster

**black: ~mail** ❶ *v.t.* erpressen; **~mail sb. into doing sth.** jmdn. durch Erpressung dazu zwingen, etwas zu tun; ❷ *n.* Erpressung, *die;* **sheer/emotional ~mail** glatte/psychologische Erpressung; **B~ Maria** /blæk mə'raɪə/ *n.* grüne Minna (*ugs.*); ~ **'mark** *n.* (*fig.*) Makel, *der;* **a ~ mark against sb.** ein Makel, der an jmdm. haftet; ~ **'market** *n.* schwarzer Markt; ~ **marketeer** /blæk mɑːkɪ'tɪə(r)/ *n.* Schwarzhändler, *der/-händlerin, die;* ~ **'mass** *n.* Ⓐ (*Satanist mass*) schwarze Messe; Ⓑ (*requiem mass*) Totenmesse, *die*

**blackness** /'blæknɪs/ *n., no pl.* Ⓐ (*black colour*) Schwärze, *die;* **the ~ of the sky** das Schwarz des Himmels; Ⓑ (*darkness*) Finsternis, *die;* (*fig.: wickedness*) Abscheulichkeit, *die*

**'blackout** *n.* Ⓐ Verdunkelung, *die;* (*Theatre, Radio*) Blackout, *der;* **news ~:** Nachrichtensperre, *die;* Ⓑ (*Med.*) **I had a ~:** ich verlor das Bewusstsein

**black: ~ 'pudding** *n.* Blutwurst, *die;* **B~ 'Rod** *n.* (*Brit. Parl.*) *Zeremonienmeister des britischen Oberhauses;* **B~ 'Sea** *pr. n.* Schwarze Meer, *das;* ~ **'sheep** *n.* (*lit. or fig.*) schwarzes Schaf; **~shirt** *n.* (*Polit.*) Schwarzhemd, *das;* **~smith** *n.* ▶ 1261 Schmied, *der;* ~ **spot** *n.* (*fig.*) schwarzer Fleck; (*dangerous*) Gefahrenstelle, *die;* ~ **'tea** *n.* schwarzer Tee; **~thorn** *n.* (*Bot.*) Schwarzdorn, *der;* ~ **'tie** *n.* schwarze Fliege (*zur Smokingjacke getragen*); **~top** *n.* (*Amer. Road Constr.*) Schwarzdecke, *die;* ~ **'velvet** *n.* (*drink*) *Mixgetränk mit Champagner und Starkbier;* ~ **'widow** *n.* (*Zool.*) Schwarze Witwe

**bladder** /'blædə(r)/ *n.* ▶ 966 (*Anat., Zool., Bot.*) Blase, *die*

**'bladderwrack** *n.* (*Bot.*) Blasentang, *der*

**blade** /bleɪd/ *n.* Ⓐ (*of sword, knife, dagger, razor, plane*) Klinge, *die;* (*of chisel, scissors, shears*) Schneide, *die;* (*of saw, oar, paddle, spade, propeller*) Blatt, *das;* (*of paddle wheel, turbine*) Schaufel, *die;* Ⓑ (*of grass etc.*) Spreite, *die;* Ⓒ (*sword*) Schwert, *das;* Klinge, *die* (*geh. veralt.*); Ⓓ (*person*) zackiger, schneidiger Bursche (*veralt.*)

**blah** /blɑː/, **blah-blah** /'blɑːblɑː/ *n.* (*coll.*) Blabla, *das*

**blahs** /blɑːz/ *n. pl.* (*Amer. coll.*) Frust, *der* (*ugs.*)

**blame** /bleɪm/ ❶ *v.t.* Ⓐ (*hold responsible*) ~ **sb. [for sth.]** jmdm. die Schuld [an etw. (*Dat.*)] geben; **always get ~d for sth.** immer an etw. (*Dat.*) schuld sein sollen; **don't ~ me [if ...]** geben Sie nicht mir die Schuld[, wenn ...]; ~ **sth. [for sth.]** etw. [für etw.] verantwortlich machen; **be to ~ [for sth.]** an etw. (*Dat.*) schuld sein; ~ **sth. on sb./sth.** jmdn./etw. für etw. verantwortlich machen; Ⓑ (*reproach*) ~ **sb./oneself** jmdn./sich Vorwürfe machen; **I don't ~ you/him** (*coll.*) ich kann es Ihnen/ihm nicht verdenken; **who can ~ her?** wer kann es ihr verdenken?; **don't ~ yourself** machen Sie sich (*Dat.*) keine Vorwürfe; **have only oneself to ~:** die Schuld bei sich selbst suchen müssen; **blaming oneself never helps** Selbstvorwürfe helfen nichts.
❷ *n.* Ⓐ (*responsibility*) Schuld, *die;* **lay** *or* **put the ~ on sb. [for sth.]** jmdm. [an etw. (*Dat.*)] die Schuld geben; **bear the ~ [for sth.]** die Schuld [an etw. (*Dat.*)] tragen; **get the ~:** die Schuld bekommen; **take the ~ [for sth.]** die Schuld [für etw.] auf sich (*Akk.*) nehmen; Ⓑ (*censure*) Tadel, *der*

**blameable** /'bleɪməbl/ *adj.* tadelnswert

**blameless** /'bleɪmlɪs/ *adj.*, **blamelessly** /'bleɪmlɪslɪ/ *adv.* untadelig

**blameworthy** /'bleɪmwɜːðɪ/ *adj.* tadelnswert

**blanch** /blɑːnʃ/ ❶ *v.t.* Ⓐ (*whiten*) bleichen; abziehen ‹Mandeln›; (*make pale*) erbleichen lassen; Ⓑ (*Cookery: scald*) blanchieren; überbrühen. ❷ *v.i.* (*grow pale*) bleich werden

**blancmange** /blə'mɒnʒ/ *n.* Flammeri, *der*

**blanco** /'blæŋkəʊ/ (*Mil.*) ❶ *n., no pl.* weißes Mittel zum Wachsen. ❷ *v.t.* [weiß] wachsen

**bland** /blænd/ *adj.* (*gentle, suave*) verbindlich; freundlich ‹Art, Stimmung›; (*mild*) mild ‹Luft›; (*not irritating, not stimulating*) mild ‹Medizin, Nahrung›; (*unexciting*) farblos

**blandish** /'blændɪʃ/ *v.t.* (*flatter*) schmeicheln (+ *Dat.*); (*cajole*) beschwatzen

**blandishment** /'blændɪʃmənt/ *n.* (*flattery*) Schmeichelei, *die;* (*cajolery*) Beschwatzen, *das;* (*allurement*) Verlockung, *die*

**blandly** /'blændlɪ/ *adv.* (*gently*) verbindlich; (*mildly*) mild

**blandness** /'blændnɪs/ *n., no pl.;* ⇒ **bland**: Verbindlichkeit, *die;* Freundlichkeit, *die;* Milde, *die;* Farblosigkeit, *die*

**blank** /blæŋk/ ❶ *adj.* Ⓐ leer; kahl ‹Wand, Fläche›; Ⓑ (*empty*) frei; **leave a ~ space** Platz frei lassen; Ⓒ (*fig.*) leer, ausdruckslos ‹Gesicht, Blick›; **look ~:** ein verdutztes Gesicht machen; **give sb. a ~ look** jmdn. verdutzt ansehen.
❷ *n.* Ⓐ (*space*) Lücke, *die;* **my mind was a ~:** ich hatte ein Brett vor dem Kopf; **his memory was a ~:** er hatte keinerlei Erinnerung; Ⓑ (*document with ~s*) Vordruck, *der;* Ⓒ (*lottery ticket*) Niete, *die;* **draw a ~:** eine Niete ziehen; (*fig.*) kein Glück haben; Ⓓ (*domino*) *Dominostein mit ein od. zwei Leerfeldern;* Ⓔ (*cartridge*) Platzpatrone, *die;* Ⓕ (*Num.*) Schrötling, *der;* Ⓖ (*dash*) Lücke, *die;* (*euphemism*) Gedankenstrich, *der;* Punkt, Punkt, Punkt

**blank: ~ 'cartridge** *n.* Platzpatrone, *die;* ~ **'cheque** *n.* Blankoscheck, *der;* (*fig.*) Blankovollmacht, *die;* **give sb. a ~ cheque** (*fig.*) jmdm. freie Hand *od.* eine Blankovollmacht geben

**blanket** /'blæŋkɪt/ ❶ *n.* Ⓐ Decke, *die;* **wet '~** (*fig.*) Trauerkloß, *der* (*ugs.*); **be born on the wrong side of the ~** (*fig.*) unehelich geboren sein; Ⓑ (*thick layer*) Decke, *die;* **a ~ of snow** eine Schneedecke; **a ~ of fog/cloud** eine Nebel-/Wolkendecke; Ⓒ (*Printing*) Gummituch, *das.* ❷ *v.t.* Ⓐ (*cover*) zudecken; Ⓑ (*stifle*) ersticken. ❸ *adj.* umfassend; **~ agreement** Pauschalabkommen, *das;* **~ term** Allerweltswort, *das*

**'blanket stitch** *n.* Festonstich, *der*

**blankety** /'blæŋkɪtɪ/ *adj.* (*euphem.*) ~ **[blank]** verflixt (*ugs.*); **what the ~ blank ...?** was zum Kuckuck ...? (*ugs.*); **call sb./sth. a ~ blank** jmdn./etw. zum Kuckuck wünschen (*ugs.*)

**blankly** /'blæŋklɪ/ *adv.* verdutzt

**blankness** /'blæŋknɪs/ *n., no pl.* Ⓐ (*of surface etc.*) Leere, *die;* **the ~ of the wall** die kahle Wand; Ⓑ (*expressionlessness*) Ausdruckslosigkeit, *die;* **the ~ of his expression** sein nichts sagender Gesichtsausdruck

**blank: ~ test** *n.* Blindversuch, *der;* ~ **'verse** *n.* (*Pros.*) Blankvers, *der*

**blanquette** /blɑ̃'ket/ *n.* (*Cookery*) [Kalbs]frikassee, *das*

**blare** /bleə(r)/ ❶ *v.i.* ‹Lautsprecher:› plärren; ‹Trompete:› schmettern. ❷ *v.t.* ~ **[out]** [hinaus]plärren ‹Worte›; [hinaus]schmettern ‹Melodie›. ❸ *n.* (*of loudspeaker, radio, voice*) Plärren, *das;* (*of trumpet, trombone*) Schmettern, *das*

**blarney** /'blɑːnɪ/ ❶ *n.* (*cajoling*) Schmeichelei, *die;* (*nonsense*) Geschwätz, *das.* ❷ *v.i.* schmeicheln. ❸ *v.t.* ~ **sb.** jmdm. schmeicheln; **don't be ~ed into doing it** lass dich nicht beschwatzen, das zu tun

**blasé** /'blɑːzeɪ/ *adj.* blasiert

**blaspheme** /blæs'fiːm/ *v.i.* lästern

**blasphemous** /'blæsfəməs/ *adj.* lästerlich, blasphemisch ‹Bemerkung, Eid, Fluch›

**blasphemy** /'blæsfəmɪ/ *n.* Blasphemie, *die;* **~ is a sin** Gotteslästerung ist eine Sünde

**blast** /blɑːst/ ❶ *n.* Ⓐ (*gust*) **a ~ [of wind]** ein Windstoß; Ⓑ (*sound*) Tuten, *das;* **he gave a ~ on his trumpet** er ließ seine Trompete erschallen; **give one ~ of the horn** einmal ins Horn stoßen; Ⓒ (*Metallurgy etc.: air current*) Gebläseluft, *die;* **at full ~** (*fig.*) auf Hochtouren *Pl.;* Ⓓ (*of explosion*) Druckwelle, *die;* (*coll.: explosion*) Explosion, *die;* Ⓔ (*coll.: reprimand*) Standpauke, *die* (*ugs.*). ❷ *v.t.* Ⓐ (*blow up*) sprengen ‹Felsen›; (*coll.: kick*) donnern ‹Fußball›; Ⓑ (*wither*) verdorren lassen; Ⓒ (*curse*) ~ **you/him!** zum Teufel mit dir/ihm! ❸ *v.i.* (*coll.: shoot*) **start ~ing away** drauflosschießen (**at** auf + *Akk.*); ❹ *int.* **[oh] ~!** [oh] verdammt!

~ **'off** *v.i.* abheben; ⇒ *also* **blast-off**

**blasted** /'blɑːstɪd/ *adj.* (*damned*) verdammt (*salopp*); verflucht (*salopp*)

**blast: ~ furnace** *n.* Hochofen, *der;* **~-hole** *n.* Sprengloch, *das;* **~-off** *n.* Abheben, *das*

**blatancy** /'bleɪtənsɪ/ *n., no pl.* ⇒ **blatant**: Eklatanz, *die;* Unverhohlenheit, *die;* Unverfrorenheit, *die;* Krassheit, *die;* Lärmen, *das;* Plärren, *das;* Aufdringlichkeit, *die*

**blatant** /'bleɪtənt/ *adj.* Ⓐ (*flagrant*) eklatant; offensichtlich; Ⓑ (*unashamed*) unverhohlen; unverfroren ‹Lüge›; Ⓒ (*noisy*) lärmend; plärrend ‹Geräusch, Musikbox›; Ⓓ (*visually obtrusive*) aufdringlich

**blatantly** /'bleɪtəntlɪ/ *adv.* ⇒ **blatant**: eklatant; unverhohlen; unverfroren; lärmend; plärrend; aufdringlich

**blaze**[1] /bleɪz/ ❶ *n.* Ⓐ (*conflagration*) Feuer, *das;* **it took hours to put out the ~:** es dauerte Stunden, bis das Feuer *od.* der Brand gelöscht war; Ⓑ (*display*) **a ~ of lights** ein Lichtermeer; **a ~ of colour** eine Farbenpracht; ein Farbenmeer; Ⓒ (*fig.: full light*) Glanz, *der;* **in a ~ of glory** mit Glanz und Gloria; Ⓓ (*fig.: outburst*) Ausbruch, *der;* **[in] a ~ of temper** in einem Wutausbruch; Ⓔ (*coll.*) **go to ~s!** scher dich zum Teufel! (*salopp*); **like ~s** wie verrückt (*ugs.*) ‹arbeiten, rennen usw.›; **what the ~s [are you doing]?** was zum Teufel [machst du da]? (*salopp*); **how the ~s am I supposed to ...?** wie zum Teufel soll ich ...?
❷ *v.i.* Ⓐ (*burn*) brennen; **the house was already blazing when the firemen arrived** das Haus stand schon in Flammen als die Feuerwehr ankam; **a blazing fire** ein hell loderndes Feuer; **the blazing sun** die glühende Sonne; **a blazing hot day** ein glühend heißer Tag; Ⓑ (*be brilliantly lighted*) [er]strahlen; ‹Schnee:› glänzen; Ⓒ (*emit light*) strahlen; **the spotlight ~d down on them** der Scheinwerfer strahlte sie an; Ⓓ (*fig.: with anger etc.*) ‹Augen:› glühen; **a blazing row** ein heftiger Streit; Ⓔ (*show bright colours*) leuchten

~ **a'way** *v.i.* Ⓐ (*shoot*) [drauf]losschießen (**at** auf + *Akk.*); Ⓑ (*work*) loslegen (**at** mit)

~ **'up** *v.i.* Ⓐ (*burst into ~*) aufflammen; Ⓑ (*in anger*) aufbrausen

**blaze**[2] ❶ *n.* (*on animal's head*) Blesse, *die;* (*on tree*) Markierung, *die.* ❷ *v.t.* markieren, kennzeichnen ‹Baum, Weg, Pfad›; ~ **a trail** einen Weg markieren; ~ **a** *or* **the trail** (*fig.*) den Weg bahnen

**blaze**[3] *v.t.* (*proclaim*) verkünden; ~ **sth. abroad** etw. ausposaunen (*ugs.*)

**blazer** /'bleɪzə(r)/ *n.* Blazer, *der*

**blazing 'star** *n.* (*Amer. Bot.*) Prachtscharte, *die*

**blazon** /'bleɪzn/ *v.t.* Ⓐ (*Her.*) blasonieren; ‹Wappen›; Ⓑ (*fig.*) (*paint*) ausmalen; (*proclaim*) verkünden

**bleach** /bliːtʃ/ ❶ *v.t.* bleichen ‹Wäsche, Haar, Knochen›. ❷ *v.i.* bleichen. ❸ *n.* (*substance*) Bleichmittel, *das;* (*process*) Bleiche, *die*

**bleaching** /'bliːtʃɪŋ/: ~ **agent** *n.* Bleichmittel, *das;* ~ **powder** *n.* Bleichpulver, *das*

**bleak**[1] /bliːk/ *adj.* Ⓐ (*bare*) öde ‹Landschaft, Berg, Insel, Ebene, Hügel›; karg ‹Zimmer›; Ⓑ (*chilly*) rau; kalt ‹Wetter, Tag›; Ⓒ (*unpromising*) düster; ~ **prospect[s]** trübe Aussichten

**bleak**[2] *n.* (*Zool.*) Ukelei, *der*

**bleakly** /'bliːklɪ/ *adv.* Ⓐ düster ‹anschauen›; Ⓑ kalt ‹wehen›

**bleakness** /'bliːknɪs/ *n., no pl.* Ⓐ (*of prospect*) Düsterkeit, *die;* Ⓑ (*of weather*) Kälte, *die*

**bleary** /'blɪərɪ/ *adj.* trübe ‹Augen›; **look ~-eyed** verschlafen aussehen; einen verschleierten Blick haben

**bleat** /bli:t/ ❶ *v.i.* ‹Schaf, Kalb:› blöken; ‹Ziege:› meckern; (*fig.*) jammern; (*plaintively*) meckern. ❷ *v.t.* ~ **[out]** herunterplärren ‹Entschuldigungen, Klagen›. ❸ *n.* ⇒ 1: Blöken, *das;* Geblök, *das;* Meckern, *das;* (*fig.*) Gejammer, *das* (*ugs.*); (*plaintive*) Gemecker, *das* (*ugs.*)

**bled** ⇒ **bleed**

**bleed** /bli:d/ ❶ *v.i.*, **bled** /bled/ bluten; ~ **for the cause/one's country** für die Sache/die Heimat sein Blut geben (*dichter.*). ❷ *v.t.*, **bled** Ⓐ (*draw blood from, lit. or fig.*) zur Ader lassen; ~ **sb. white** (*fig.*) jmdn. den letzten Pfennig kosten (*ugs.*); ‹Erpresser:› jmdn. bis aufs Hemd ausziehen (*ugs.*); Ⓑ (*extract fluid, air, etc. from*) entlüften ‹Bremsen, Heizkörper›

**bleeder** /'bli:də(r)/ *n.* Ⓐ (*haemophiliac*) Bluter, *der;* Ⓑ (*Brit. coarse: unpleasant person*) Scheißer, *der* (*derb*)

**bleeding** /'bli:dɪŋ/ ❶ *n.* (*loss of blood*) Blutung, *die.* ❷ *adj.* (*Brit. coarse: damned*) Scheiß-; **don't stand there the whole ~ time doing nothing!** steh da nicht die ganze Zeit so blöd rum, ohne was zu tun! (*salopp*). ❸ *adv.* (*Brit. coarse*) ~ **awful** total beschissen (*derb*); **I don't ~ care!** das ist mir scheißegal! (*salopp*); **don't be ~ stupid!** sei doch nicht so saublöd! (*salopp*)

**bleeding 'heart** *n.* Ⓐ (*Bot.*) Tränendes Herz; Flammendes Herz; Ⓑ (*coll.: person*) mitfühlende Seele

**bleep** /bli:p/ ❶ *n.* Piepen, *das;* **two faint ~s** zwei schwache Piepser. ❷ *v.i.* ‹Geigerzähler, Funksignal:› piepen. ❸ *v.t.* ~ **sb.** jmdn. über seinen Kleinempfänger *od.* (*ugs.*) Piepser rufen

**bleeper** /'bli:pə(r)/ *n.* Kleinempfänger, *der;* Piepser, *der* (*ugs.*)

**blemish** /'blemɪʃ/ ❶ *n.* Ⓐ (*stain*) Fleck, *der;* (*on fruit*) Stelle, *die;* Ⓑ (*defect, lit. or fig.*) Makel, *der;* **be without a ~:** makellos sein; **her only ~ was her quick temper** ihr einziger Fehler war ihr aufbrausendes Wesen. ❷ *v.t.* Ⓐ (*spoil*) verunstalten; Ⓑ (*fig.*) ~ **sth.** einer Sache (*Dat.*) schaden

**blench** /blenʃ/ *v.i.* zurückschrecken

**blend** /blend/ ❶ *v.t.* Ⓐ (*mix*) mischen ‹Whisky-, Tee-, Tabaksorten›; Ⓑ (*make indistinguishable*) vermischen. ❷ *v.i.* Ⓐ sich mischen lassen; **pink does not ~ with orange** Rosa verträgt sich nicht mit Orange; ~ **in with/into sth.** [gut] zu etw. passen/mit etw. verschmelzen; Ⓑ ‹Whisky-, Tee-, Tabaksorten:› sich [harmonisch] verbinden. ❸ *n.* (*mixture*) Mischung, *die*

**blender** /'blendə(r)/ *n.* Ⓐ (*person*) [Ver]mischer, *der;* Ⓑ (*apparatus*) Mixer, *der;* Mixgerät, *das*

**Blenheim** /'blenɪm/ *pr. n.* **the Battle of ~:** die Schlacht von Höchstädt

**bless** /bles/ *v.t.*, **blessed** /blest/ *or* **blest** /blest/ Ⓐ (*consecrate, pronounce blessing on*) segnen; **she did not have a penny to ~ herself with** (*fig.*) sie besaß keinen Pfennig *od.* (*ugs.*) keinen roten Heller; **they have been ~ed with a son** sie wurden mit einem Sohn gesegnet; **[God] ~ you** Gottes Segen; (*as thanks*) das ist sehr lieb von dir/Ihnen; (*to person sneezing*) Gesundheit!; **goodbye and God ~:** Wiedersehen, [und] mach's/macht's gut!; ~ **you, I wouldn't dream of it** mein Gott, ich denke gar nicht daran; ~ **me!, I'm blest!,** ~ **my soul!** du meine Güte! (*ugs.*); ~ **me if it isn't Sid** ja das ist doch Sid!; Ⓑ (*call holy*) preisen; (*attribute one's good fortune to*) **they ~ed their stars/guardian angel that ...:** sie priesen dankbar das Glück/ihren Schutzengel dafür, dass ...

**blessed** ❶ [blest] *p. t. and p. p. of* **bless.** ❷ /'blesɪd, *pred.* blest/ *adj.* Ⓐ **be ~ with sth.** (*also iron.*) mit etw. gesegnet sein; Ⓑ (*revered*) heilig ‹Gott, Mutter Maria›; (*in Paradise*) selig; (*RC Ch.: beatified*) selig; (*blissful*) beglückend; Ⓒ *attrib.* (*euphem.: cursed*) verdammt (*salopp*)

**blessedness** /'blesɪdnɪs/ *n., no pl.* (*happiness*) Glückseligkeit, *die;* (*enjoyment of divine favour*) Seligkeit, *die*

**blessing** /'blesɪŋ/ *n.* Ⓐ (*declaration or bestowal of divine favour, grace at table*) Segen, *der;* **do sth. with sb.'s ~** (*fig.*) etw. mit jmds. Segen tun (*ugs.*); **give sb./sth. one's ~** (*fig.*) jmdm./etw. seinen Segen geben (*ugs.*); Ⓑ (*divine gift*) Segnung, *die;* **count one's ~s** (*fig.*) dankbar sein; Ⓒ (*fig.: welcome thing*) Segen, *der;* **what a ~!** welch ein Segen!; **be a ~ in disguise** sich schließlich doch noch als Segen erweisen; ⇒ *also* **mixed blessing**

**blest** ⇒ **bless;** (*poet.*) ⇒ **blessed** 2

**blether** /'bleðə(r)/ ❶ *v.i.* schwafeln (*ugs.*); sülzen (*ugs.*); **go on ~ing** weiterschwafeln *od.* -sülzen. ❷ *n.* Geschwafel, *das;* Gesülze, *das* (*ugs.*)

**blew** ⇒ **blow**[1] 1, 2

**blight** /blaɪt/ ❶ *n.* Ⓐ (*plant disease*) Brand, *der;* (*fig.: malignant influence*) Fluch, *der;* Geißel, *die;* **fascism — a ~ on the twentieth century** Faschismus — ein Fluch des zwanzigsten Jahrhunderts; Ⓑ (*fig.: unsightly urban area*) Schandfleck, *der;* Ⓒ (*Brit.: aphid*) Blattlaus, *die.* ❷ *v.t.* Ⓐ (*affect with ~*) **be ~ed** von Brand befallen werden/sein; Ⓑ (*spoil*) beeinträchtigen ‹Schönheit›; überschatten ‹Freude, Leben›; (*frustrate*) zunichte machen ‹Hoffnung›; **a ~ed area** eine heruntergekommene Gegend

**blighter** /'blaɪtə(r)/ *n.* (*Brit. coll.*) Ⓐ **the poor ~:** der arme Kerl; Ⓑ (*derog.*) Lümmel, *der* (*abwertend*); (*thing*) Mistding, *das* (*salopp*)

**blimey** /'blaɪmɪ/ *int.* (*Brit. sl.*) Mensch (*salopp*)

**blimp** /blɪmp/ *n.* Ⓐ (*Brit.*) **[Colonel] B~** *Personifikation des stockkonservativen Engländers;* Ⓑ (*airship*) unstarres Kleinluftschiff

**blimpish** /'blɪmpɪʃ/ *adj.* reaktionär

**blind** /blaɪnd/ ❶ *adj.* Ⓐ blind ‹Person, Tier›; **a ~ man/woman** ein Blinder/eine Blinde; **[be] as ~ as a bat** stockblind [sein] (*ugs.*); ~ **in one eye** auf einem Auge blind; **go** *or* **become ~:** blind werden; erblinden; **turn a ~ eye [to sth.]** (*fig.*) [bei etw.] ein Auge zudrücken; Ⓑ (*Aeronaut.*) ~ **landing/flying** Blindlandung, *die*/Blindflug, *der;* Ⓒ (*without foresight*) blind; **a ~ policy** eine kurzsichtige *od.* unbesonnene Politik; Ⓓ (*unreasoning*) blind ‹Vorurteil, Weigerung, Gehorsam, Vertrauen›; Ⓔ (*oblivious*) **be ~ to sth.** blind gegenüber etw. sein; Ⓕ (*reckless*) blind ‹Hast›; rasend ‹Geschwindigkeit›; Ⓖ (*not ruled by purpose*) blind ‹Wut, Zorn›; dunkel ‹Instinkt›; kopflos ‹Panik›; Ⓗ (*concealed*) verdeckt ‹Graben›; unsichtbar ‹Hindernis›; Ⓘ (*walled up*) blind ‹Tür, Fenster›; Ⓙ (*coll.: drunk*) blau (*ugs.*); **get ~:** sich voll laufen lassen (*ugs.*); Ⓚ **a ~** (*coll.: any whatever*): **he doesn't do a ~ thing [to help her]** er rührt keinen Finger[, um ihr zu helfen]; **not a ~ bit of** überhaupt kein/keine; **it didn't do a ~ bit of good** es hat überhaupt nichts genützt; **you didn't take a ~ bit of notice** du hast dich überhaupt nicht darum gekümmert.
❷ *adv.* Ⓐ blindlings; **the pilot had to fly/land ~:** der Pilot musste blind fliegen/landen; Ⓑ (*completely*) ~ **drunk** stockbetrunken (*ugs.*); **swear ~:** hoch und heilig versichern; Ⓒ (*Cookery*) **bake sth. ~:** etw. blind backen.
❸ *n.* Ⓐ (*screen*) Jalousie, *die;* (*of cloth*) Rollo *das;* (*of shop*) Markise, *die;* Ⓑ (*Amer. Hunting: hide*) Jagdschirm, *der;* Ⓒ (*pretext*) Vorwand, *der;* (*cover*) Tarnung, *die;* **be a ~ for sth.** als Tarnung für etw. dienen; Ⓓ (*Brit. dated coll.: drinking bout*) **go on a ~:** eine Sauftour machen (*salopp*); Ⓔ *pl.* **the ~:** die Blinden *Pl.;* **it's [a case of] the ~ leading the ~** (*fig.*) das ist, wie wenn ein Blinder einen Lahmen [spazieren] führt.
❹ *v.t.* (*lit. or fig.*) blenden; **be ~ed** (*accidentally*) das Augenlicht verlieren; ~ **sb. to the fact that ...:** jmdn. gegenüber der Tatsache blind machen, dass ...; **he was ~ed by his infatuation** er war von seiner eigenen Verliebtheit geblendet *od.* verblendet; ~ **sb. with science** jmdn. mit großen Worten beeindrucken.
❺ *v.i.* (*Brit. coll.: go heedlessly*) rasen; ~ **along** rumrasen (*ugs.*)

**blind:** ~ **'alley** *n.* (*lit. or fig.*) Sackgasse, *die;* ~ **'corner** *n.* unübersichtliche Kurve; ~ **'date** *n.* Verabredung mit einem/einer Unbekannten

**blinder** /'blaɪndə(r)/ *n.* Ⓐ **play a ~** (*Sport*) sich selbst übertreffen; Ⓑ *usu. in pl.* (*Amer.: blinker*) Scheuklappe, *die*

**'blindfold** ❶ *v.t.* die Augen verbinden (+ *Dat.*); **the conjurer asked to be ~ed** der Zauberer bat darum, ihm die Augen zu verbinden. ❷ *adj.* mit verbundenen Augen *nachgestellt;* **he was ~ all the time** er hatte die ganze Zeit die Augen verbunden; **I could do that ~** (*fig.*) das könnte ich mit verbundenen Augen [tun]. ❸ *n.* Augenbinde, *die*

**blind 'gut** *n.* (*Anat.*) Blinddarm, *der*

**blinding** /'blaɪndɪŋ/ *adj.* blendend ‹Licht, Sonnenlicht, Blitz›; grell ‹Strahl›; **a ~ headache** rasende Kopfschmerzen *Pl.*

**blindly** /'blaɪndlɪ/ *adv.* [wie] blind; wie ein Blinder; (*fig.*) blindlings

**blind man's 'buff** *n.* Blindekuh *o. Art.*

**blindness** /'blaɪndnɪs/ *n., no pl.* Ⓐ Blindheit, *die;* Ⓑ (*lack of foresight*) Blindheit, *die* (**to** gegenüber); (*unreasonableness*) Verblendung, *die*

**blind:** ~ **side** *n.* (*Rugby*) ungeschützte Seite; (*fig.*) schwache Seite (*fig.*); ~ **spot** *n.* (*Anat.*) blinder Fleck; (*Motor Veh.*) toter Winkel; (*fig.: weak spot*) schwacher Punkt; **~worm** *n.* (*Zool.*) Blindschleiche, *die*

**blink** /blɪŋk/ ❶ *v.i.* Ⓐ blinzeln; Ⓑ (*shine intermittently*) blinken; (*shine momentarily*) aufblinken. ❷ *v.t.* Ⓐ ~ **back/away one's tears** seine Tränen blinzelnd zurückhalten; ~ **one's eyes** mit den Augen zwinkern; Ⓑ (*fig.: ignore*) die Augen verschließen vor (+ *Dat.*); ignorieren ‹Tatsache›. ❸ *n.* Ⓐ (*blinking*) Blinzeln, *das;* **he gave one or two ~s** er blinzelte ein paarmal; Ⓑ (*intermittent light*) Blinken, *das;* (*momentary gleam*) Aufblinken, *das;* Ⓒ (*coll.*) **be on the ~:** kaputt sein (*ugs.*)

**blinker** /'blɪŋkə(r)/ ❶ *n. in pl.* Scheuklappen; **have/put ~s on** (*lit. or fig.*) Scheuklappen tragen/anlegen. ❷ *v.t.* Scheuklappen anlegen (+ *Dat.*); **this horse has to be ~ed** dieses Pferd muss Scheuklappen tragen; **be ~ed** (*fig.*) borniert sein

**blinking** /'blɪŋkɪŋ/ (*Brit. coll. euphem.*) ❶ *adj.* verflixt (*ugs.*); **it's a ~ nuisance** das ist echt verdammt ärgerlich (*ugs.*). ❷ *adv.* verflixt (*ugs.*); **I don't ~ [well] care** das kümmert mich verflixt wenig; **it's ~ raining** verflixt [und zugenäht], es regnet

**blip** /blɪp/ ❶ *v.t.*, **-pp-** hauen. ❷ *n.* Ⓐ (*sound*) (*of bursting bubble*) leiser Knall; (*on magnetic tape*) leises Knacken; (*act*) Schlag, *der;* Ⓑ (*Radar: image*) Echozeichen, *das*

**bliss** /blɪs/ *n.* (*joy*) [Glück]seligkeit, *die;* Glück, *das;* (*gladness*) Freude, *die;* **his idea of ~:** seine Vorstellung vom Glücklichsein

**blissful** /'blɪsfl/ *adj.* [glück]selig; ~ **ignorance** (*iron.*) selige Unwissenheit

**blissfully** /'blɪsfəlɪ/ *adv.* ~ **happy** glückselig; **be ~ unaware** *or* **ignorant [of sth.]** (*iron.*) in seliger Unwissenheit [von etw.] sein

**blister** /'blɪstə(r)/ ❶ *n.* (*on skin, plant, metal, paintwork*) Blase, *die.* ❷ *v.t.* Blasen hervorrufen auf (+ *Dat.*) ‹Metall, Anstrich, Haut›. ❸ *v.i.* ‹Haut, Pflanze:› Blasen bekommen; ‹Metall, Anstrich:› Blasen werfen

**blistering** /'blɪstərɪŋ/ *adj.* **a ~ attack** ein erbitterter Angriff; **a ~ criticism** eine ätzende Kritik; **a ~ pace** ein mörderisches Tempo

**'blister pack** *n.* Sichtpackung, *die*

**blithe** /blaɪð/ *adj.* Ⓐ (*poet.: joyous*) fröhlich; heiter; Ⓑ (*casual*) unbekümmert

**blithely** /'blaɪðlɪ/ *adv.* ~ **ignore sth.** sich unbekümmert über etw. (*Akk.*) hinwegsetzen

**blithering** /'blɪðərɪŋ/ *adj.* (*coll.*) Ⓐ (*utter*) total; völlig; **a ~ idiot** ein alter Idiot (*salopp*); Ⓑ (*senselessly talkative*) quatschig (*salopp*) ‹Kommentator, Journalist›

**B. Litt.** /bi: 'lɪt/ *abbr.* **Bachelor of Letters** Bakkalaureus der Literaturwissenschaften; ⇒ *also* **B. Sc.**

**blitz** /blɪts/ (*coll.*) ❶ *n.* Ⓐ (*Hist.*) Luftangriff, *der* (**on** auf + *Akk.*); **during the [London]**

**~:** während der Luft- *od.* Bombenangriffe [auf London]; Ⓑ (*fig.: attack*) Großaktion, *die (fig.)*; **have a ~ on one's room** in seinem Zimmer gründlich sauber machen. ❷ *v.t.* [schwer] bombardieren

**blizzard** /ˈblɪzəd/ *n.* Schneesturm, *der*

**bloat** /bləʊt/ ❶ *v.t.* aufblähen; **dead bodies ~ed by the water** vom Wasser aufgedunsene Leichen. ❷ *v.i.* aufschwellen; aufschwemmen

**bloated** /ˈbləʊtɪd/ *adj.* Ⓐ (*having overeaten*) aufgedunsen; **I feel ~:** ich bin voll (*ugs.*); Ⓑ **be ~ with pride/wealth** aufgeblasen sein/im Geld schwimmen

**bloater** /ˈbləʊtə(r)/ *n.* Bückling, *der*

**blob** /blɒb/ *n.* Ⓐ (*drop*) Tropfen, *der;* (*small mass*) Klacks, *der* (*ugs.*); (*of butter etc.*) Klecks, *der;* Ⓑ (*spot of colour*) Fleck, *der*

**bloc** /blɒk/ *n.* (*Polit.*) Block, *der;* **the Eastern ~/Eastern ~ countries** (*Hist.*) der Ostblock/die Ostblockstaaten; **the Western ~ [countries]** die westlichen Staaten; **the anti-EU ~:** der Anti-EU-Block; **~ vote** ⇒ **block vote**

**block** /blɒk/ ❶ *n.* Ⓐ (*large piece*) Klotz, *der;* **~ of wood** Holzklotz, *der;* Ⓑ (*for chopping on*) Hackklotz, *der;* Ⓒ (*for beheading on*) Richtblock, *der;* (*for hammering on, for mounting horse from*) Klotz, *der;* (*toy building brick*) Bauklotz, *der;* **be a chip off the old ~:** ganz der Vater sein; **be on the ~** (*Amer.*) zur Versteigerung angeboten werden; Ⓓ (*large mass of concrete or stone, building stone*) Block, *der;* Ⓔ (*coll.: head*) **knock sb.'s ~ off** jmdm. eins überziehen (*salopp*); Ⓕ (*building*) [Häuser]block, *der;* **~ of flats/offices** Wohnblock, *der*/Bürohaus, *das;* Ⓖ (*Amer.: area between streets*) Block, *der;* **on this/our ~:** in diesem/unserem Block; **six ~s away** sechs Blocks weiter; Ⓗ (*large quantity*) Masse, *die;* **a ~ of shares** ein Aktienpaket; **a ~ of seats** mehrere nebeneinander liegende Sitze; **in the cheapest ~ of seats** im billigsten Block; Ⓘ (*pad of paper*) Block, *der;* Ⓙ (*obstruction*) Verstopfung, *die;* Ⓚ (*traffic jam*) [Verkehrs]stau, *der;* Ⓛ (*mental barrier*) **a mental ~:** eine geistige Sperre; Mattscheibe *o. Art.* (*salopp*); **a psychological ~:** ein psychologischer Block; Ⓜ (*Printing*) Klischee, *das;* Ⓝ (*pulley*) Block, *der;* **~ and tackle** Flaschenzug, *der;* Ⓞ (*Athletics*) Startblock, *der.*

❷ *v.t.* Ⓐ (*obstruct*) blockieren, versperren ‹Tür, Straße, Durchgang, Sicht›; verstopfen ‹Rohr, Nase, Abfluss›; blockieren, verhindern ‹Fortschritt›; abblocken ‹Ball, Torschuss›; Ⓑ (*Commerc.*) einfrieren ‹Investitionen, Guthaben›; **~ed currency** nicht frei konvertierbare Währung; Ⓒ (*emboss*) prägen

**~ 'in** *v.t.* ausfüllen ‹Umrisse, Zeichnung›; abdecken ‹Kamin, Fenster usw.›

**~ 'off** *v.t.* [ab]sperren ‹Straße›; blockieren ‹Rohr, Verkehr›

**~ 'out** *v.t.* ausschließen ‹Licht, Lärm›; retuschieren ‹Foto›; abdecken ‹Matrize, Schablone›

**~ 'up** *v.t.* verstopfen; versperren, blockieren ‹Eingang›

**blockade** /blɒˈkeɪd/ ❶ *n.* Blockade, *die.* ❷ *v.t.* blockieren

**blockage** /ˈblɒkɪdʒ/ *n.* Block, *der;* (*of pipe, gutter*) Verstopfung, *die*

**block: ~board** *n.* Tischlerplatte, *die;* **~ 'booking** *n.* Gruppenbuchung, *die;* **~buster** *n.* Ⓐ (*bomb*) [große] Fliegerbombe; Ⓑ (*fig.*) Knüller, *der* (*ugs.*); **~ 'capital** *n.* Blockbuchstabe, *der;* **~ diagram** *n.* Blockdiagramm, *das;* **~ 'grant** *n.* Pauschalsubvention, *die;* **~head** *n.* Dummkopf, *der* (*abwertend*); **~ heater** *n.* Nachtspeicherheizung, *die;* **~house** *n.* Blockhaus, *das;* **~ 'letters** *n. pl.* Blockschrift, *die;* **~ 'vote** *n.* Stimmenblock, *der*

**bloke** /bləʊk/ *n.* (*Brit. coll.*) Typ, *der* (*ugs.*)

**blond** /blɒnd/ ⇒ **blonde** 1

**blonde** /blɒnd/ ❶ *adj.* blond ‹Haar, Person›; hell ‹Teint›. ❷ *n.* Blondine, *die*

**blood** /blʌd/ ❶ *n.* Ⓐ ▶966 Blut, *das;* **sb.'s ~ boils** (*fig.*) jmd. ist in Rage; **it makes my ~ boil** es bringt mich in Rage; **sb.'s ~ turns** *or* **runs cold** (*fig.*) jmdm. erstarrt das Blut in den Adern; **draw first ~** (*lit. or fig.*) den ersten Treffer erzielen; **be after** *or* **out for sb.'s ~** (*fig.*) es auf jmdn. abgesehen haben; **taste ~** (*fig.*) Blut lecken; **it's like getting ~ out of** *or* **from a stone** das ist fast ein Ding der Unmöglichkeit; **[a policy of] ~ and iron** Blut und Eisen; Ⓑ (*relationship*) Blutsverwandtschaft, *die;* **~ is thicker than water** (*prov.*) Blut ist dicker als Wasser; Ⓒ (*race*) Blut, *das;* Geblüt, *das* (*geh.*); **of noble ~:** von edlem Geblüt; **fresh** *or* **new ~:** frisches Blut; **young ~:** Nachwuchs, *der;* **sth. is in sb.'s ~:** etw. liegt jmdm. im Blut; Ⓓ (*passion*) **his ~ is up** er ist in Rage; **do sth. in cold ~:** etw. kaltblütig tun; **[there is] bad ~ [between them]** [es gibt] böses Blut [zwischen ihnen].

❷ *v.t.* Ⓐ **has this hound been ~ed yet?** ist dieser Spürhund schon an Blut gewöhnt?; Ⓑ (*fig.*) **he was ~ed in the Battle of Leipzig** er bestand seine Feuertaufe in der Völkerschlacht bei Leipzig

**blood: ~ and 'thunder** *n.* Mord und Totschlag; **~-and-thunder stories** Schauer- und-Schund-Geschichten; **~ bank** *n.* Blutbank, *die;* **~bath** *n.* Blutbad, *das;* **~ brother** *n.* (*by birth*) leiblicher Bruder; (*by ceremony*) Blutsbruder, *der;* **~ cell** *n.* Blutkörperchen, *das;* **~ clot** *n.* Blutgerinnsel, *das;* **~ count** *n.* Blutbild, *das;* **carry out a ~ count** das Blutbild bestimmen; **~-curdling** *adj.* Grauen erregend; **~ donor** ⇒ **donor** B; **~ feud** *n.* Blutrache, *die;* **~ group** *n.* Blutgruppe, *die;* **~ heat** *n.* Körpertemperatur, *die;* **~hound** *n.* Bluthund, *der;* (*fig.*) Spürhund, *der*

**bloodless** /ˈblʌdlɪs/ *adj.* Ⓐ (*without bloodshed*) unblutig; **a ~ coup** ein unblutiger Staatsstreich; Ⓑ (*without blood, pale*) blutleer; Ⓒ (*unemotional*) gefühllos

**blood: ~-letting** *n.* (*Med. Hist.; also fig.*) Aderlass, *der;* **~lust** *n.* Blutgier, *die;* **~ money** *n.* Blutgeld, *das;* **~ orange** *n.* Blutorange, *die;* **~ poisoning** *n.* Blutvergiftung, *die;* **~ pressure** *n.* Blutdruck, *der;* **~ 'pudding** *n.* ≈ Blutwurst, *die;* **~-red** *adj.* blutrot; **~ relation** *n.* Blutsverwandte, *der/die;* **~ sample** *n.* Blutprobe, *die;* **~shed** *n.* Blutvergießen, *das;* **~shot** *adj.* blutunterlaufen; **~ sports** *n. pl.* Hetzjagd, *die;* **~stain** *n.* Blutfleck, *der;* **~stained** *adj.* (*lit. or fig.*) blutbefleckt; **~stock** *n.* Vollblutpferde *Pl.;* **~stone** *n.* Blutstein, *der;* **~stream** *n.* Blutstrom, *der;* **~sucker** *n.* (*leech*) Blutegel, *der;* (*fig.: extortioner*) Blutsauger, *der;* **~ sugar** *n.* Blutzucker, *der* (*Med.*); **~ test** *n.* Blutprobe, *die;* **~thirsty** *adj.* blutdürstig (*geh.*); blutrünstig; **~ transfusion** *n.* Bluttransfusion, *die;* **~ vessel** *n.* Blutgefäß, *das*

**bloody** /ˈblʌdɪ/ ❶ *adj.* Ⓐ blutig; (*running with blood*) blutend; (*like blood*) blutrot; (*loving bloodshed*) blutrünstig; **give sb. a ~ nose** (*lit., or fig. coll.*) jmdm. eins auf die Nase geben; Ⓑ (*sl.: damned*) verdammt (*salopp*); **you ~ fool!** du Vollidiot! (*salopp*); **~ hell!** verdammt noch mal! (*salopp*); Ⓒ (*Brit.*) *as intensifier* einzig; **he didn't leave me a ~ penny** er ließ mir keinen roten Heller; **that/he is a ~ nuisance** das ist vielleicht ein Mist (*salopp*)/der geht einem vielleicht *od.* ganz schön auf den Wecker (*ugs.*).

❷ *adv.* Ⓐ (*sl.: damned*) verdammt (*salopp*); **don't be so ~ stupid!** sei doch nicht so verdammt blöde! Ⓑ (*Brit.*) *as intensifier* verdammt (*salopp*); **not ~ likely!** denkste! (*salopp*); **I don't ~ [well] like it!** ich kann das, verdammt noch mal, nicht leiden!

❸ *v.t.* (*make ~*) blutig machen; (*stain with blood*) mit Blut beflecken

**bloody: B~ 'Mary** *n.* Bloody Mary, *der od. die* (*ein Cocktail*); **~-'minded** *adj.* stur (*ugs.*)

**bloom** /bluːm/ ❶ *n.* Ⓐ Blüte, *die;* **be in ~:** in Blüte stehen; **have come into ~:** blühen; Ⓑ (*on fruit*) Flaum, *der;* (*flush*) rosige Gesichtsfarbe; Ⓒ (*prime*) Blüte, *die;* **in the ~ of youth** in der Blüte der Jugend; **come into ~:** erblühen. ❷ *v.i.* blühen; (*fig.: flourish*) in Blüte stehen

**bloomer** /ˈbluːmə(r)/ *n.* (*Brit.*) Ⓐ (*coll.: error*) Schnitzer, *der;* Ⓑ (*loaf*) Langbrot, *das*

**bloomers** /ˈbluːməz/ *n. pl.* Ⓐ [Damen]pumphose, *die;* (*coll.: knickers*) Schlüpfer, *der;* Ⓑ (*Hist.: costume*) weite Damenhose (*zum Radfahren*)

**blooming** /ˈbluːmɪŋ/ (*Brit. coll. euphem.*) ❶ *adj.* verflixt (*ugs.*); **oh, you ~ idiot!** du Trottel! (*ugs.*). ❷ *adv.* verflixt (*ugs.*)

**blooper** /ˈbluːpə(r)/ *n.* (*Amer. coll.*) [peinlicher] Fehler, *der;* Patzer, *der* (*ugs.*); **make** *or* **pull a ~:** einen Bock schießen (*ugs.*)

**blossom** /ˈblɒsəm/ ❶ *n.* Ⓐ (*flower*) Blüte, *die;* Ⓑ *no pl., no indef. art.* (*mass of flowers*) Blüte, *die;* Blütenmeer, *das* (*geh.*); **be in ~:** in [voller] Blüte stehen *od.* sein; **have come into ~:** blühen. ❷ *v.i.* Ⓐ blühen; **the trees ~ed early this year** die Baumblüte begann dieses Jahr schon früh; Ⓑ (*fig.*) blühen; ‹Mensch:› aufblühen; erblühen (*geh.*); **~ [out] into a statesman/poet** sich zu einem Staatsmann/Dichter entwickeln

**blot** /blɒt/ ❶ *n.* Ⓐ (*spot of ink*) Tintenklecks, *der;* (*stain*) Fleck, *der;* (*blemish*) Makel, *der;* Schandfleck, *der;* **a ~ on the landscape** (*lit. or fig.*) ein Schandfleck in der Landschaft; Ⓑ (*fig.*) Makel, *der;* **a ~ on sb.'s character** ein Fleck auf jmds. weißer Weste (*fig.*); ⇒ *also* **escutcheon**.

❷ *v.t.*, **-tt-:** Ⓐ (*dry*) ablöschen ‹Tinte, Schrift, Papier›; Ⓑ (*spot with ink*) beklecksen; verklecksen; (*fig.: disgrace*) beflecken ‹Namen, guten Ruf›; **~ one's copybook** (*fig. coll.*) sich unmöglich machen

**~ 'out** *v.t.* Ⓐ (*obliterate*) einen Klecks machen auf (+ *Akk.*); unleserlich machen ‹Schrift›; Ⓑ (*obscure*) verdecken ‹Sicht›; **thick smoke/fog ~ted out the enemy ship/the mountains** dichter Rauch/Nebel verdeckte [die Sicht auf] das feindliche Schiff/die Berge; Ⓒ auslöschen ‹Leben, Menschheit, Erinnerung›; dem Erdboden gleichmachen, ausradieren ‹Stadt, Land›

**blotch** /blɒtʃ/ *n.* (*on skin*) Fleck, *der;* (*patch of ink etc.*) Klecks, *der*

**blotchy** /ˈblɒtʃɪ/ *adj.* (*skin*) fleckig; (*with wet blotches*) verkleckst

**blotter** /ˈblɒtə(r)/ *n.* Ⓐ Schreibunterlage, *die;* Ⓑ (*Amer.*) (*record book*) Kladde, *die;* (*Police: record of arrests*) [Polizei]register, *das*

**'blotting paper** *n.* Löschpapier, *das*

**blotto** /ˈblɒtəʊ/ *pred. adj.* (*coll.*) [sternhagel]voll (*salopp*)

**blouse** /blaʊz/ *n.* Bluse, *die*

**blow**[1] /bləʊ/ ❶ *v.i.*, **blew** /bluː/, **blown** /bləʊn/ Ⓐ ‹Wind:› wehen; ‹Sturm:› blasen; ‹Luft:› ziehen; **there is a gale ~ing out there** es stürmt draußen; **the wind blew in gusts** es wehte ein böiger Wind; der Wind war böig; **there's a draught ~ing** es zieht; **cold air blew down every corridor** auf allen Gängen war es kalt und zugig; Ⓑ (*exhale*) blasen; **~ on one's tea to cool it** in den Tee pusten, um ihn abzukühlen; **~ on one's hands to warm them** in die Hände hauchen, um sie zu wärmen; **~ hot and cold** (*fig.*) einmal hü und einmal hott sagen; Ⓒ (*puff, pant*) ‹Person:› schwer atmen, schnaufen; ‹Tier:› schnaufen; Ⓓ (*eject air and water*) ‹Wal:› spritzen; Ⓔ (*be sounded by ~ing*) geblasen werden; ‹Trompete, Flöte, Horn, Pfeife usw.:› ertönen; Ⓕ (*be driven by ~ing*) geblasen *od.* geweht werden; ‹Blätter, Schneeflocken, Seifenblasen:› [durch die Luft] fliegen; **a few leaves blew along the road** einige Blätter wirbelten *od.* (*dichter.*) tanzten die Straße entlang; Ⓖ (*melt*) ‹Sicherung, Glühfaden:› durchbrennen; Ⓗ (*coll.: depart*) abhauen (*salopp*).

❷ *v.t.*, **blew, blown** (⇒ *also* **m**): Ⓐ (*breathe out*) [aus]blasen, ausstoßen ‹Luft, Rauch›; Ⓑ (*send by ~ing*) **~ sb. a kiss** jmdm. eine Kusshand zuwerfen; Ⓒ (*drive by ~ing*) treiben ‹Blätter, Schnee, Staub usw.›; Ⓓ (*make by ~ing*) blasen ‹Glas›; machen ‹Seifenblasen›; Ⓔ (*sound*) blasen ‹Trompete, Flöte, Horn, Pfeife usw.›; **~ one's own trumpet** (*fig.*) sein Eigenlob singen; Ⓕ (*send jet of air at*) anblasen ‹Feuer›; (*gently*) anhauchen; Ⓖ (*clear*) ausblasen ‹Ei›; **~ one's nose** sich (*Dat.*) die Nase putzen; [sich] schnäuzen (*geh.*); Ⓗ (*send flying*) schleudern; **~ sth. to pieces** etw. in die Luft sprengen; **it ~s your mind** (*coll.*) da flippst du aus (*ugs.*); **this dope will ~ your mind**

(*coll.*) der Stoff hier haut voll rein (*salopp*); **~ one's top** *or* (*Amer.*) **stack** (*coll.*) in die Luft gehen (*ugs.*); **I** (*cause to melt*) durchbrennen lassen ‹Sicherung, Glühlampe›; durchhauen (*ugs.*) ‹Sicherung›; **J** (*break into*) sprengen, aufbrechen ‹Tresor, Safe›; aufbrechen ‹Schloss›; **K** (*coll.: reveal*) verraten ‹Plan, Komplizen›; ⇒ *also* **cover** 1 I; **gaff²**; **L** **be ~n** (*out of breath*) erschöpft sein; **M** *p. t., p. p.* **~ed** (*coll.: curse*) **[well,] I'm** *or* **I'll be ~ed** ich werde verrückt! (*salopp*); **I'll be ~ed if I'll do it!** ich denk' nicht [im Traum] dran, das zu tun (*ugs.*); **well, I'll be ~ed if it isn't old Sid!** Mensch[enskind], wenn das nicht der alte Sid ist! (*ugs.*); **~ you, Jack!** du kannst mich mal gern haben! (*salopp*); **~ you, Jack, I'm all right** [das ist] dein Pech *od.* Problem *od.* Bier (*ugs.*); **~!** [so ein] Mist! (*ugs.*); **~ the expense** es ist doch Wurscht, was es kostet (*ugs.*); **N** (*coll.: squander*) verpulvern, verplempern (*ugs.*) ‹Geld, Mittel, Erbschaft›; **he blew all his winnings on gambling** er hat seinen ganzen Gewinn verspielt; **he blew all his money on women** er hat sein ganzes Geld für Frauen ausgegeben; **~ it** (*lose opportunity*) es vermasseln (*salopp*).
❸ *n.* **A** (*wind*) Sturm, *der;* **B** (*inhaling of fresh air*) **we went outside for a ~:** wir gingen raus, um etwas frische Luft zu schnappen (*ugs.*); **C** (*~ing of instrument*) **he gave a loud/long ~ on his trumpet** er ließ einen lauten/langen Trompetenstoß erschallen; **D** (*~ing of nose*) **he gave his nose a [good] ~:** er schnäuzte sich [gründlich] (*geh.*); **have a good ~:** putz dir mal ordentlich die Nase

**~ a'way** ❶ *v.i.* wegfliegen. ❷ *v.t.* **A** wegblasen; **B** (*Amer. coll.: shoot dead*) umblasen (*ugs.*); **C** (*coll.: defeat utterly*) vernichtend schlagen; (*Football, Tennis, etc.*) vom Platz fegen (*ugs.*); **D** (*coll.: disprove*) wegfegen ‹Meinung, Vorschlag›; über den Haufen werfen (*ugs.*) ‹Theorie›; **E** (*coll.: impress*) anmachen (*ugs.*); **be ~n away by sb./sth.** von jmdm./etw. [hin und] weg sein (*ugs.*); **we were ~n away by the news** die Neuigkeiten haben uns umgehauen (*ugs.*); **F** **be ~n away** (*coll.: become intoxicated*) high werden (*coll.*)

**~ 'down** ❶ *v.i.* umgeblasen werden. ❷ *v.t.* umblasen

**~ 'in** ❶ *v.t.* zum Einsturz bringen ‹Haus, Mauer›; **the gale blew the windows in** der Sturm drückte die Fenster ein. ❷ *v.i.* **A** ‹Luft:› hereinkommen; ‹Staub:› hereingeweht werden; **B** (*coll.: enter*) hereinschneien; hereinplatzen

**~ 'off** ❶ *v.i.* **A** weggeblasen werden; **B** (*Brit. sl.: break wind*) pup[s]en (*fam.*). ❷ *v.t.* wegblasen; ‹Explosion:› wegreißen

**~ 'out** ❶ *v.t.* **A** (*extinguish*) ausblasen ‹Kerze, Lampe›; **B** (*by explosion*) **the explosion blew all the windows out** durch die Explosion flogen alle Fensterscheiben raus; **~ sb.'s/one's brains out** jmdm./sich eine Kugel durch den Kopf jagen (*ugs.*). ❷ *v.i.* ‹Reifen:› platzen; ‹Kerze, Lampe:› ausgeblasen werden. ❸ *v. refl.* ‹Sturm:› sich legen. ⇒ *also* **~-out**

**~ 'over** ❶ *v.i.* umgeblasen werden; ‹Streit, Sturm:› sich legen; **wait till the whole thing ~s over** (*fig.*) warte, bis sich die Sache gelegt hat. ❷ *v.t.* umblasen

**~ 'up** ❶ *v.t.* **A** (*shatter*) [in die Luft] sprengen; **B** (*inflate*) aufblasen ‹Ballon›; aufpumpen ‹Reifen›; **C** (*coll.: reprove*) in der Luft zerreißen (*ugs.*); **D** (*coll.: enlarge*) vergrößern ‹Foto, Seite›; **E** (*coll.: exaggerate*) hochspielen, aufbauschen ‹Ereignis, Bericht›. ❷ *v.i.* **A** (*explode*) explodieren; **B** (*arise suddenly*) ‹Krieg, Konflikt, Sturm:› ausbrechen; **C** (*lose one's temper*) [vor Wut] explodieren (*ugs.*); in die Luft gehen (*ugs.*). ⇒ *also* **~-up**

**blow²** *n.* **A** (*stroke*) Schlag, *der;* (*with axe*) Hieb, *der;* (*jolt, push*) Stoß, *der;* **in** *or* **at one ~** (*lit. or fig.*) mit einem Schlag; **come to ~s** handgreiflich werden; **a ~-by-~ description/account** eine Beschreibung/ein Bericht in allen Einzelheiten; **strike a ~ for sb./sth.** (*fig.*) jmdm./einer Sache einen großen Dienst erweisen; **strike a ~ against sb./sth.** (*fig.*) jmdm./einer Sache einen [schweren] Schlag versetzen; **B** (*disaster*) [schwerer] Schlag, *der* (*fig.*) (**to** für); Schicksalsschlag, *der;* Tiefschlag, *der;* **come as** *or* **be a ~ to sb.** ein schwerer Schlag für jmdn. sein; **suffer a ~:** einen Schock erleiden

**'blow-dry** *v.t.* fönen

**blower** /'bləʊə(r)/ *n.* **A** (*apparatus*) Gebläse, *das;* **B** (*Brit. coll.: telephone*) **on the ~:** an der Strippe; **get on the ~:** sich an die Strippe hängen; **I spoke to him on the ~ yesterday** ich habe gestern mit ihm telefoniert

**blow: ~fish** *n.* Kugelfisch, *der;* **~fly** *n.* Schmeißfliege, *die;* **~hole** *n.* **A** (*Zool.*) Atemloch, *das;* Spritzloch, *das;* **B** (*Metallurgy*) Abzugsloch, *das;* **~ job** *n.* (*coarse*) Blasmusik, *die* (*fig. vulg.*); **give sb. a ~-job** jmdm. einen blasen (*vulg.*); **~lamp** *n.* Lötlampe, *die*

**blown** ⇒ **blow¹** 1, 2

**blow: ~-out** *n.* **A** (*burst tyre*) Reifenpanne, *die;* **B** (*coll.: meal*) feudales Essen (*ugs.*); **we had a good ~-out at the Savoy** wir sind im Savoy richtig feudal essen gewesen (*ugs.*); **~pipe** *n.* (*weapon*) Blasrohr, *das;* (*tool*) Lötrohr, *das* (*Chemie*); (*Glass-blowing*) Glasmacherpfeife, *die;* **~torch** (*Amer.*) ⇒ **~lamp**; **~-up** *n.* (*coll.: enlargement*) Vergrößerung, *die*

**blowy** /'bləʊɪ/ *adj.* windig; (*windswept*) stürmisch

**blowzy** /'blaʊzɪ/ *adj.* **A** (*red-faced*) rotbäckig; **she had a ~, well-fed appearance** sie war pausbäckig und wohlgenährt; **B** (*coarse-looking*) schlampig; verwildert; **C** (*slatternly*) schlampig ‹Frau›

**blub** /blʌb/ *v.i.*, **-bb-** (*coll.*) heulen (*ugs.*); plärren (*ugs.*)

**blubber** /'blʌbə(r)/ ❶ *n.* **A** (*whale-fat*) Walspeck, *der;* **B** (*coll.: weeping*) Geplärr[e], *das* (*ugs.*); Heulen, *das* (*ugs.*). ❷ *v.i.* (*coll.: weep*) heulen (*ugs.*); plärren (*ugs.*); jammern

**bludgeon** /'blʌdʒn/ ❶ *n.* Knüppel, *der.* ❷ *v.t.* niederknüppeln; **~ sb. to death** jmdm. [mit einem Knüppel] totschlagen

**blue¹** /bluː/ ❶ *adj.* **A** blau; **be ~ with cold/rage** blau gefroren/rot vor Zorn sein; ⇒ *also* **face** 1 A; **B** (*depressed*) **be/feel ~:** niedergeschlagen sein/sich bedrückt *od.* deprimiert fühlen; **C** (*Brit. Polit.: conservative*) konservativ; ≈ schwarz (*ugs.*); **D** (*pornographic*) pornographisch; Porno-; **~ film** *or* **movie** Porno[film], *der;* **~ jokes** unanständige Witze.
❷ *n.* **A** (*colour*) Blau, *das;* **B** (*blueness*) Bläue, *die;* **C** (*Snooker*) blaue Kugel; **D** (*~ clothes*) **dressed in ~:** blau gekleidet; **the boys in ~** (*Brit. coll.: police*) die Blauen (*ugs.*); **E** (*Brit. Univ.*) **be a/get a** *or* **one's ~:** die Universität bei Sportwettkämpfen vertreten haben/vertreten; **F** (*whitener*) Waschblau, *das;* Wäscheblau, *das;* **G** (*sky*) Himmelsblau, *das;* **out of the ~** (*fig.*) aus heiterem Himmel (*ugs.*); völlig unerwartet (*ugs.*); **disappear into the ~** (*fig.*) sich in nichts auflösen; **H** (*Polit.: Conservative*) Konservative, *der/die;* ≈ Schwarze, *der/die* (*ugs.*); **I** (*butterfly*) Bläuling, *der;* **J** **the ~s** (*melancholy*) Niedergeschlagenheit; **have the ~s** niedergeschlagen *od.* deprimiert sein; **get the ~s** schwermütig *od.* melancholisch werden; **K** **the ~s** (*Mus.*) der Blues; **play/sing the ~s** Blues spielen/singen; **play a ~s** einen Blues spielen.
❸ *v.t.* (*make ~*) blau machen; bläuen ‹Stahl, Wäsche›

**blue²** *v.t.* (*Brit. coll.: squander*) verpulvern, verplempern ‹Geld, Erbe›

**blue: ~ baby** *n.* (*Med.*) blausüchtiger Säugling; **~bell** *n.* (*campanula*) [blaue Wiesen]glockenblume, *die;* (*wild hyacinth*) Sternhyazinthe, *die;* **~berry** /bluːbərɪ/ *n.* Heidelbeere, *die;* Blaubeere, *die;* **~bird** *n.* (*of N. Amer.*) Elfenblauvogel, *der;* (*of S. and S.E. Asia*) Rotkehlhüttensänger, *der;* **~ 'blood** *n.* blaues Blut; **~-'blooded** *adj.* blaublütig; **~ book** *n.* **A** (*Brit. Parl.*) Blaubuch, *das;* **B** (*Amer. Polit.*) *eine Art Who's Who;* **~bottle** *n.* **A** (*Zool.*) Schmeißfliege, *die;* **B** (*Bot.*) Kornblume, *die;* **~ 'cheese** *n.* Blauschimmelkäse, *der;* Edelpilzkäse, *der;* **~ 'chip** *n.* (*Poker*) blaue Spielmarke, *die;* **~-chip share** *n.* (*St. Exch.*) erstklassiges Wertpapier; Blue chip, *der* (*fachspr.*); **~-'collar** *adj.* **~-collar worker** Arbeiter, *der*/Arbeiterin, *die;* **~-collar union** Arbeitergewerkschaft, *die;* **~-eyed** *adj.* blauäugig; **be ~-eyed** blaue Augen haben; **~-eyed 'boy** *n.* (*fig. coll.*) Goldjunge, *der;* **~fish** *n.* Blaubarsch, *der;* **~ 'fit** *n.* (*coll.*) **have a ~ fit** Zustände kriegen (*ugs.*); **~ grass** *n.* (*Amer.: Poa pratensis*) Wiesenrispengras, *das;* **~ gum** *n.* (*Bot.*) Blaugummibaum, *der;* Fieberbaum, *der;* **~jacket** *n.* (*fig.*) Blaujacke, *die* (*ugs.*); **~ 'jeans** *n. pl.* Blue jeans *Pl.;* **~ 'moon** *n.* **once in a ~ moon** alle Jubeljahre (*ugs.*); **~ 'mould** *n.* essbare Schimmelpilze *Pl.;* **~ 'murder** *n.* **cry** *or* **scream ~ murder** (*coll.*) Zeter und Mordio schreien (*ugs.*)

**blueness** /'bluːnɪs/ *n.*, *no pl.* Bläue, *die*

**blue: ~ 'pencil** *n.* (*fig.*) blauer Farbstift; ≈ Rotstift, *der;* **~-'pencil** *v.t.* mit dem Rotstift gehen an ‹Text›; zensieren ‹Nachricht›; **B~ 'Peter** *n.* (*Naut.*) Blauer Peter; **~print** *n.* **A** Blaupause, *die;* **B** (*fig.*) Plan, *der;* Entwurf, *der;* **~ 'ribbon** *n.* **A** (*ribbon of the Garter*) das blaue Band des Hosenbandordens; **B** (*distinction*) höchste Auszeichnung; erster Preis; **C** (*sign of teetotalism*) *Abzeichen eines Temperenzlervereins;* **~stocking** *n.* Blaustrumpf, *der;* **she was too much of a ~stocking** sie war zu blaustrümpfig; **~ 'streak** *n.* (*coll.*) **he ran like a ~ streak** er rannte wie ein geölter Blitz (*ugs.*); **~throat** *n.* (*Ornith.*) Blaukehlchen, *das;* **~ tit** *n.* (*Ornith.*) Blaumeise, *die;* **~ 'water** *n.* hohe See; **~ 'whale** *n.* Blauwal, *der*

**bluff¹** /blʌf/ ❶ *n.* (*act*) Täuschungsmanöver, *das;* Bluff, *der* (*ugs.*); **it's nothing but a ~:** das ist bloß [ein] Bluff; ⇒ *also* **call** 2 C. ❷ *v.i. & t.* bluffen (*ugs.*)

**bluff²** ❶ *n.* (*headland*) Kliff, *das;* Steilküste, *die;* (*inland*) Steilhang, *der.* ❷ *adj.* **A** (*abrupt, blunt, frank, hearty*) raubeinig (*ugs.*); **B** (*perpendicular*) steil; schroff ‹Felswand, Abhang, Küste›; breit ‹Schiffsbug›

**bluffness** /'blʌfnɪs/ *n.*, *no pl.* Raubeinigkeit, *die* (*ugs.*)

**bluish** /'bluːɪʃ/ *adj.* bläulich

**blunder** /'blʌndə(r)/ ❶ *n.* [schwerer] Fehler; **make a ~:** einen [schweren] Fehler machen; einen Bock schießen (*ugs.*). ❷ *v.i.* **A** (*make mistake*) einen [schweren] Fehler machen; **B** (*move blindly*) tappen; **he ~ed about the darkened room/down the corridor** er tappte in dem dunklen Zimmer umher/den Flur entlang. ❸ *v.t.* (*mismanage*) falsch machen

**blunderbuss** /'blʌndəbʌs/ *n.* (*Arms Hist.*) Donnerbüchse, *die* (*veralt.*)

**blunt** /blʌnt/ ❶ *adj.* **A** stumpf; **a ~ instrument** ein stumpfer Gegenstand; **B** (*outspoken*) direkt; unverblümt; **he was quite ~ about his opinion/dislike** er machte aus seiner Meinung/Abneigung überhaupt keinen Hehl; **C** (*uncompromising*) glatt (*ugs.*) ‹Ablehnung›. ❷ *v.t.* **~ [the edge of]** stumpf machen ‹Messer, Schwert, Säge›; dämpfen ‹Begeisterung, Mut›; mildern ‹Trauer, Enttäuschung›; **~ the edge of one's appetite** sich (*Dat.*) den Appetit verderben

**bluntly** /'blʌntlɪ/ *adv.* **A** (*outspokenly*) direkt, unverblümt ‹sprechen, antworten›; **B** (*uncompromisingly*) glatt ‹ablehnen›

**bluntness** /'blʌntnɪs/ *n.*, *no pl.* ⇒ **blunt** 1: Stumpfheit, *die;* Direktheit, *die;* Unverblümtheit, *die;* **he was shocked by the ~ of her refusal** ihre glatte Absage hat ihn regelrecht schockiert (*ugs.*)

**blur** /blɜː(r)/ ❶ *v.t.*, **-rr-** **A** (*smear*) verwischen, verschmieren ‹Schrift, Seite›; **B** (*make indistinct*) verwischen ‹Schrift, Farben, Konturen›; **become ~red** ‹Farben, Schrift:› verwischt werden; **C** (*dim*) trüben ‹Sicht, Wahrnehmung›; **my vision is ~red** ich sehe alles verschwommen; mir [ver]schwimmt alles vor [den] Augen; **her eyes were ~red by tears** ihre Augen schwammen in Tränen. ❷ *n.* **A** (*smear*) [verschmierter] Fleck, *der;* **B** (*dim image*) verschwommener Fleck

**blurb** /blɜ:b/ *n.* Klappentext, *der;* Waschzettel, *der*

**blurt** /blɜ:t/ *v.t.* hervorstoßen ‹Worte, Beschimpfung›; ~ **sth. out** mit etw. herausplatzen (*ugs.*)

**blush** /blʌʃ/ ❶ *v.i.* Ⓐ erröten (*geh.*); rot werden; **make sb.** ~: jmdn. erröten (*geh.*) *od.* rot werden lassen; Ⓑ (*be ashamed*) sich schämen (**at** bei). ❷ *n.* Ⓐ (*reddening*) Erröten, *das* (*geh.*); **spare sb.'s ~es** jmdn. nicht in Verlegenheit bringen; Ⓑ (*rosy glow*) Röte, *die;* **the ~ of dawn** (*literary*) der rosige Schimmer der Morgenröte; Ⓒ (*glance*) **at [the] first ~:** auf den ersten Blick

**blusher** /ˈblʌʃə(r)/ *n.* Rouge, *das*

**bluster** /ˈblʌstə(r)/ ❶ *v.i.* Ⓐ ‹Wind:› tosen, brausen; Ⓑ ‹Person:› sich aufplustern (*ugs.*). ❷ *v.t.* ~ **one's way out of sth.** etw. lautstark abstreiten; **you can't ~ your way out of this one** diesmal kannst du dich nicht großartig aus der Affäre ziehen. ❸ *n.* Ⓐ (*blowing of wind*) Tosen, *das;* Brausen, *das;* Ⓑ (*talk, threats*) Schreierei, *die* (*ugs.*); Geschrei, *das* (*abwertend*)

**blustery** /ˈblʌstərɪ/ *adj.* stürmisch ‹Wetter, Wind›

**BM** *abbr.* Ⓐ ⇒ **MB**; Ⓑ **British Museum** Britisches Museum

**B. Mus.** /bi:ˈmʌz/ *abbr.* **Bachelor of Music** Bakkalaureus der Musik; ⇒ *also* **B. Sc.**

**BMX** *abbr.* **bicycle moto-cross** BMX; ~ **[bike]** BMX-Rad, *das*

**BO** *abbr.* (*coll.*) **body odour** Körpergeruch, *der*

**boa** /ˈbəʊə/ *n.* Ⓐ (*Zool.*) Boa, *die;* (*python*) Riesenschlange, *die;* Ⓑ (*garment*) Boa, *die*

**boa constrictor** /ˈbəʊə kənstrɪktə(r)/ *n.* Boa constrictor, *die;* (*python*) Riesenschlange, *die*

**boar** /bɔ:(r)/ *n.* Ⓐ (*male pig*) Eber, *der;* Ⓑ (*wild*) Keiler, *der;* Ⓒ (*guinea pig*) Bock, *der*

**board** /bɔ:d/ ❶ *n.* Ⓐ Brett, *das;* **as flat as a ~:** flach; ‹Frau› flach wie ein Bügelbrett; **bare ~s** bloße Dielen; Ⓑ (*black~*) Tafel, *die;* Ⓒ (*notice~*) Schwarzes Brett; Ⓓ (*in game*) Brett, *das;* Ⓔ (*spring~*) [Sprung]brett, *das;* Ⓕ (*material*) Spanplatte, *die;* Ⓖ (*meals*) Verpflegung, *die;* **~ and lodging** Unterkunft und Verpflegung; **full ~:** Vollpension, *die;* Ⓗ (*table*) **a festive ~:** ein festlich gedeckter Tisch; Ⓘ (*Admin. etc.*) Amt, *das;* Behörde, *die;* **gas/water/electricity ~:** Gas-/Wasser-/Elektrizitätsversorgungsgesellschaft, *die;* ~ **[of examiners]** [Prüfungs]kommission, *die;* ~ **of inquiry** Untersuchungsausschuss, *der;* ~ **of trustees** Kuratorium, *das;* ~ **[of interviewers]** Gremium, *das* (*zur Auswahl von Bewerbern*); (*Univ.*) Berufungskommission, *die;* ~ **of trade** (*Amer.*) Handelskammer, *die;* **B~ of Trade** (*Brit. Hist.*) Handelsministerium, *das;* Ⓙ (*Commerc., Industry*) ~ **[of directors]** Vorstand, *der;* (*supervisory ~*) Aufsichtsrat, *der;* (*in public body*) Verwaltungsrat, *der;* **chairman of the ~:** Vorstands-/Aufsichtsrats-/Verwaltungsratsvorsitzende, *der/die;* Ⓚ (*Naut., Aeronaut., Transport*) **on ~:** an Bord; **on ~ the ship/plane** an Bord des Schiffes/Flugzeugs; **on ~ the train/bus** im Zug/Bus; **go on ~ the train/bus** in den Zug/Bus einsteigen; **take sb. on ~** (*fig. coll.*) jmdn. aufnehmen; **take sth. on ~** (*fig. coll.*) (*consume*) etw. zu sich nehmen; (*accept*) etw. annehmen; Ⓛ **the ~s** (*Theatre*) die Bühne; Ⓜ **go by the ~:** ins Wasser fallen; **your high principles will have to go by the ~:** du musst deine hohen Grundsätze über Bord werfen. ⇒ *also* **above** 2 A; **across** 2 B. ❷ *v.t.* Ⓐ ⇒ ~ **up**; Ⓑ (*provide with lodging*) in Pension nehmen; Ⓒ (*go on ~*) ~ **the ship/plane** an Bord des Schiffes/Flugzeugs gehen; ~ **the train/bus** in den Zug/Bus einsteigen; Ⓓ (*come alongside*) längsseits herankommen an (+ *Akk.*); (*force one's way on ~*) entern; Ⓔ (*interview*) ~ **sb.** mit jmdm. ein Vorstellungsgespräch führen. ❸ *v.i.* Ⓐ (*lodge*) [in Pension] wohnen (**with** bei); Ⓑ (*~ an aircraft*) an Bord gehen; **'flight L 5701 now ~ing [at] gate 15'** „Passagiere des Fluges L 5701 bitte zum Flugsteig 15"

~ **'out** ❶ *v.i.* in Pension wohnen. ❷ *v.t.* in Pension geben

~ **'up** *v.t.* mit Brettern vernageln

**boarder** /ˈbɔ:də(r)/ *n.* Ⓐ (*lodger*) Pensionsgast, *der;* Ⓑ (*Sch.*) Internatsschüler, *der*/-schülerin, *die;* Interne, *der/die* (*veralt.*); Ⓒ (*Naut.*) Enterer, *der*

**'board game** *n.* Brettspiel, *das*

**boarding**/ˈbɔ:dɪŋ/:~ **house** *n.* Pension, *die;* **~-party** *n.* Enterkommando, *das;* **~-pass** *n.* Bordkarte, *die;* ~ **school** *n.* Internat, *das*

**board:** ~ **meeting** *n.* Vorstands-/Aufsichtsrats-/Verwaltungsratssitzung, *die;* **~room** *n.* Sitzungssaal, *der;* (*fig.: top management*) Vorstandsetage, *die;* **~-sailing** ⇒ **windsurfing**; **~walk** *n.* (*Amer.*) Bohlenweg, *der;* (*in yard, trench, etc.*) Holzrost, *der*

**boast** /bəʊst/ ❶ *v.i.* prahlen (**of, about** mit); **that's nothing to ~ about** das ist kein Grund zum Prahlen. ❷ *v.t.* prahlen mit; (*possess*) sich rühmen (+ *Gen.*); **our school ~s a fine playing field** unsere Schule nennt einen sehr schönen Sportplatz ihr Eigen. ❸ *n.* Ⓐ Prahlerei, *die;* **his favourite ~ is that ...:** am liebsten prahlt er damit, dass ...; Ⓑ (*cause of pride*) Stolz, *der*

**boaster** /ˈbəʊstə(r)/ *n.* Aufschneider, *der*/Aufschneiderin, *die* (*ugs.*)

**boastful** /ˈbəʊstfl/ *adj.* prahlerisch; großspurig ‹Erklärung, Behauptung›; ~ **stories** Angebergeschichten (*ugs.*)

**boastfully** /ˈbəʊstfəlɪ/ *adv.* großspurig; **talk ~ of sth.** mit etw. prahlen

**boastfulness** /ˈbəʊstfəlnɪs/ *n., no pl.* Großspurigkeit, *die*

**boat** /bəʊt/ ❶ *n.* Ⓐ Boot, *das;* **ship's ~:** Beiboot, *das;* **go by ~:** mit dem Schiff fahren; **push the ~ out** (*fig. coll.*) ein Fass aufmachen (*ugs.*); **be in the same ~** (*fig.*) im gleichen Boot sitzen; ⇒ *also* **burn**[1] 2 A; **miss** 2 D; **rock**[2] 1 B; Ⓑ (*ship*) Schiff, *das;* Ⓒ (*for sauce etc.*) Sauciere, *die.* ❷ *v.i.* **go ~ing** eine Bootsfahrt machen

**boat:** ~ **deck** *n.* Bootsdeck, *das;* ~ **drill** *n.* Bootsmanöver, *das*

**boater** /ˈbəʊtə(r)/ *n.* Ⓐ (*person*) Bootsfahrer, *der*/-fahrerin, *die;* Ⓑ (*hat*) steifer Strohhut; Kreissäge, *die* (*ugs.*)

**boatful** /ˈbəʊtfʊl/ *n.* Bootsladung, *die*

**boat:** **~hook** *n.* Bootshaken, *der;* **~house** *n.* Bootshaus, *das;* **~load** *n.* Bootsladung, *die;* **~man** /ˈbəʊtmən/ *n., pl.* **~men** /ˈbəʊtmən/ Ⓐ (*hiring*) Bootsverleiher, *der;* Ⓑ (*providing transport*) Bootsführer, *der;* ~ **people** *n. pl.* Boatpeople *Pl.;* Bootsflüchtlinge; ~ **race** *n.* Regatta, *die;* **the B~ Race** die Oxford-Cambridge-Regatta; **~swain** /ˈbəʊsn/ *n.* Bootsmann, *der;* **~swain's chair** Bootsmannsstuhl, *der;* ~ **train** *n.* Zug mit Schiffsanschluss

**bob**[1] /bɒb/ ❶ *v.i.*, **-bb-** Ⓐ ~ **[up and down]** sich auf und nieder bewegen; (*jerkily*) auf und nieder schnellen; ‹[Pferde]schwanz:› [auf und nieder] wippen; **the poppies ~bed in the breeze** der Mohn wiegte sich im Wind [hin und her]; **a cork was ~bing on the waves** ein Korken tanzte auf den Wellen [auf und nieder]; ~ **up** hochschnellen; Ⓑ (*curtsy*) knicksen. ❷ *n.* (*curtsy*) Knicks, *der*

**bob**[2] ❶ *n.* Ⓐ (*weight*) Gewicht, *das;* Ⓑ (*hairstyle*) Bubikopf, *der.* ❷ *v.t.*, **-bb-** kurz schneiden ‹Haar›; **wear one's hair ~bed** einen Bubikopf tragen

**bob**[3] *n., pl. same* (*Brit. coll.*) Ⓐ (*Hist.: shilling*) Schilling, *der;* (*fig.*) **she's got** *or* **she's worth a few ~, she's not short of a ~ or two** sie hat schon ein paar Mark; Ⓑ (*5p*) Fünfer, *der* (*ugs.*); **two/ten ~:** 10/50 Pence

**bob**[4] *n.* (*coll.*) **~'s your uncle** die Sache ist geritzt (*ugs.*); fertig ist der Lack (*ugs.*)

**bob**[5] *n.* (*~sled*) Bob, *der*

**bobbin** /ˈbɒbɪn/ *n.* Spule, *die*

**'bobbin lace** *n.* Klöppelspitze, *die*

**bobble** /ˈbɒbl/ *n.* Pompon, *der;* Bommel, *die* (*bes. nordd.*)

**bobby** /ˈbɒbɪ/ *n.* (*Brit. coll.*) Bobby, *der* (*ugs.*); Schupo, *der* (*ugs. veralt.*)

**bobby:** ~ **pin** *n.* (*Amer.*) Haarklemme, *die;* ~ **socks** *n. pl.* Söckchen; **~-soxer** /ˈbɒbɪsɒksə(r)/ *n.* Backfisch, *der*

**'bobcat** *n.* (*Amer.*) [Rot]luchs, *der*

**bob:** **~sled**, **~sleigh** *ns.* Bob[schlitten], *der;* **~stay** *n.* (*Naut.*) Wasserstag, *das;* **~tail** *n.* (*horse*) *Pferd mit gestutztem Schwanz;* (*dog*) *Hund mit kupiertem Schwanz*

**bock** /bɒk/ *n.* Bock[bier], *das*

**bod** /bɒd/ *n.* (*Brit. coll.*) Mensch, *der;* **~s** Leute; **odd ~:** seltsamer Typ (ugs.)

**bode** /bəʊd/ ❶ *v.i.* ~ **ill/well** nichts Gutes/einiges erhoffen lassen. ❷ *v.t.* Ⓐ (*foretell*) prophezeien; Ⓑ (*portend*) bedeuten; ~ **no good** nichts Gutes ahnen lassen

**bodega** /bəˈdi:gə/ *n.* Bodega, *die*

**bodice** /ˈbɒdɪs/ *n.* (*part of dress*) Oberteil, *das;* (*undergarment, part of dirndl*) Mieder, *das*

**'bodice-ripper** /ˈbɒdɪsrɪpə(r)/ *n.* (*coll.*) Verführungsschnulze, *die*

**-bodied** /bɒdɪd/ *in comb.* von ... Körperbau; **big-~:** von großem, schwerem Körperbau; **a wide-~ aircraft** ein Flugzeug mit breitem Rumpf

**bodiless** /ˈbɒdɪlɪs/ *adj.* körperlos ‹Gespenst›; **a ~ head** ein Kopf ohne Rumpf

**bodily** /ˈbɒdɪlɪ/ ❶ *adj.* körperlich; organisch ‹Krankheit›; ~ **harm** Körperverletzung, *die;* ~ **needs** leibliche Bedürfnisse; ~ **organs** Körperorgane. ❷ *adv.* **he lifted her ~:** er hob sie einfach hoch; **the audience rose ~:** das Publikum stand geschlossen auf

**bodkin** /ˈbɒdkɪn/ *n.* Ⓐ (*needle*) Durchziehnadel, *die;* Ⓑ (*hairpin*) lange Haarnadel; Ⓒ (*tool*) Ahle, *die*

**body** /ˈbɒdɪ/ ❶ *n.* Ⓐ ▶ 966 (*of person*) Körper, *der;* Leib, *der* (*geh.*); (*of animal*) Körper, *der;* **bend one's ~ forward** den Oberkörper nach vorne beugen; **the ~ of Christ** der Leib Christi; **enough to keep ~ and soul together** genug, um am Leben zu bleiben; **do sth. ~ and soul** etw. mit aller Kraft tun; Ⓑ (*corpse*) Leiche, *die;* Leichnam, *der* (*geh.*); **over my dead ~!** nur über meine Leiche; Ⓒ (*coll.: person*) Mensch, *der;* (*woman also*) Person, *die;* **she/he is a very kind ~:** sie ist ein sehr netter Mensch/er ist ein sehr netter Kerl; Ⓓ (*group of persons*) Gruppe, *die;* (*having a particular function*) Organ, *das;* (*military force*) [Truppen]verband, *der;* **government ~:** staatliche Einrichtung; **charitable ~:** Wohltätigkeitsorganisation, *die;* **student ~:** Studentenschaft, *die;* **in a ~:** geschlossen; Ⓔ (*mass*) **a huge ~ of water** große Wassermassen; Ⓕ (*main portion*) Hauptteil, *der;* Ⓖ (*Motor Veh.*) Karosserie, *die;* (*Railw.*) Aufbau, *der;* (*aircraft fuselage*) Rumpf, *der;* Ⓗ (*majority*) Gros, *das;* Ⓘ (*collection*) Sammlung, *die;* **a ~ of knowledge** ein Wissensschatz; **a ~ of facts** Tatsachenmaterial, *das;* Ⓙ (*of soup or gravy*) Substanz, *die;* (*of wine*) Körper, *der;* **have no great ~:** nicht sehr gehaltvoll sein/nicht sehr viel Körper haben. ⇒ *also* **corporate** A; **foreign** D; **heavenly** B; **politic** 1 C. ❷ *v.t.* ~ **sth. forth** etw. verkörpern *od.* versinnbildlichen

**body:** ~ **bag** *n.* Leichensack, *der;* ~ **blow** *n.* Körperstoß, *der* (*Boxen*); (*fig.*) schwerer Schlag; **~building** ❶ *n.* Bodybuilding, *das;* ❷ *adj.* **~building food** Aufbaukost, *die;* ~ **clock** ⇒ **biological clock**; ~ **colour** *n.* Deckfarbe, *die;* ~ **fascism** *n.* Körperfaschismus, *der;* ~ **fluids** *n. pl.* Körperflüssigkeiten; **~guard** *n.* ▶ 1261 (*single*) Leibwächter, *der;* (*group*) Leibwache, *die;* ~ **hair** *n.* Körperhaar, *das;* ~ **language** *n.* Körpersprache, *die;* ~ **odour** *n.* Körpergeruch, *der;* ~ **piercing** *n., no pl.* Piercing, *das;* ~ **search** *n.* Leibesvisitation, *die;* **~snatcher** *n.* Leichenräuber, *der;* ~ **stocking** *n.* Bodystocking, *der;* ~ **weight** *n.* Körpergewicht, *das;* **~work** *n., no pl.* (*Motor Veh.*) Karosserie, *die*

**Boer** /ˈbəʊə(r), bʊə(r)/ ❶ *n.* Bure, *der*/Burin, *die.* ❷ *adj.* **the ~ War** der Burenkrieg

**boffin** /ˈbɒfɪn/ *n.* (*Brit. coll.*) Eierkopf, *der* (*salopp*)

**bog** /bɒg/ ❶ *n.* Ⓐ Moor, *das;* (*marsh, swamp*) Sumpf, *der;* Ⓑ (*Brit. sl.: lavatory*) Lokus, *der* (*salopp*). ❷ *v.t.*, **-gg-:** **be ~ged**

b

## The body

German uses the definite article for parts of the body where English uses the possessive adjective, as long as it is clear whose body part it is (which usually means that it belongs to the person who is the subject of the sentence):

***He raised his hand***
= Er hob die Hand

***She closed her eyes***
= Sie schloss die Augen

But

***She closed his eyes***
= Sie schloss ihm die Augen

***She passed her hand over my forehead***
= Sie fuhr mir mit der Hand über die Stirn

From the last two examples it can be seen that where the owner of the part of the body is not the subject, i.e. not doing the action, German uses the dative of the personal pronoun plus the definite article. This also applies when the owner of the body part is responsible for the action (often an injury), but in this case the pronoun is reflexive (which only makes a difference in the third person):

***I've broken my leg***
= Ich habe mir das Bein gebrochen

***He dislocated his arm***
= Er hat sich (*Dat.*) den Arm ausgerenkt

***You nearly dislocated his arm***
= Du hast ihm fast den Arm ausgerenkt

***She hit her head on the beam***
= Sie hat sich den Kopf am Balken angestoßen *or* ist mit dem Kopf gegen den Balken gestoßen

***Can you put some cream on my back [for me]?***
= Kannst du mir den Rücken mit Creme einreiben?

Note the same construction with a noun:

***She massaged her son's back***
= Sie massierte ihrem Sohn den Rücken

Note also the following impersonal construction:

***My head is spinning***
= Mir dreht sich *or* schwirrt der Kopf

***My feet were tingling***
= Es kribbelte mir *or* mich in den Füßen

····➤ Illnesses

### Body features

There are many adjectives in German ending in **-ig** describing features corresponding to English adjectives ending in *-ed:*

***blue-eyed***
= blauäugig

***long-legged***
= langbeinig

***dark-haired***
= dunkelhaarig

These are usually used attributively, i.e. before the noun, not separately:

***a long-legged blonde***
= eine langbeinige Blondine

but

***He is blue-eyed***
= Er hat blaue Augen

***She is dark-haired***
= Sie hat dunkle Haare

····➤ Colours, Height, Weight

**down** festsitzen (*fig.*); nicht weiterkommen; **get ~ged down in details** (*fig.*) sich in Details verzetteln

**bogey** /'bəʊgɪ/ *n.* **A** (*Golf: one stroke over par*) Bogey, *das;* **B** ⇒ **bogy**

**boggle** /'bɒgl/ *v.i.* **A** (*be startled*) sprachlos sein; **the imagination ~s at the thought** der Gedanke übersteigt die Vorstellungskraft; **the mind ~s [at the thought]** bei dem Gedanken wird einem schwindlig; **B** (*hesitate, demur*) **~ at** *or* **about sth.** etw. höchst ungern tun

**boggy** /'bɒgɪ/ *adj.* sumpfig; morastig

**bog 'oak** *n.* Mooreiche, *die*

**'bog-standard** *adj.* (*coll.*) stinknormal (*salopp*)

**bogus** /'bəʊgəs/ *adj.* falsch; gefälscht ‹Geld, Schmuck, Dokument›; **~ firm** Schwindelfirma, *die;* **the claim/deal was ~:** die Behauptung/das Geschäft war reiner Schwindel

**bogy** /'bəʊgɪ/ *n.* **A B~** (*the Devil*) der Gottseibeiuns; **B** (*evil spirit*) Gespenst, *das;* **~ man** Schreckgestalt, *die;* **C** (*bugbear*) Schreckgespenst, *das;* **D** (*Brit. coll.: piece of dried mucus*) Popel, *der* (*ugs.*)

**Bohemia** /bəʊ'hi:mɪə/ *pr. n.* Böhmen (*das*)

**Bohemian** /bəʊ'hi:mɪən/ **1** *adj.* **A** (*socially unconventional*) unkonventionell; unbürgerlich; **a ~ person** ein Bohemien; **B** (*Geog.*) böhmisch; **he/she is ~:** er ist Böhme/sie ist Böhmin. **2** *n.* **A** (*socially unconventional person*) Bohemien, *der;* **B** (*native of Bohemia*) Böhme, *der*/Böhmin, *die*

**bohemianism** /bəʊ'hi:mɪənɪzm/ *n., no pl.* unkonventioneller Lebensstil

**boil[1]** /bɔɪl/ **1** *v.i.* **A** kochen; (*Phys.*) sieden; **the kettle's ~ing** das Wasser im Kessel kocht; **keep the pot ~ing** (*fig.*) (*get a living*) sich über Wasser halten; (*keep sth. going*) dafür sorgen, dass es weitergeht; **B** (*fig.*) ‹Wasser, Wellen:› schäumen, brodeln; **C** (*fig.: be angry*) kochen; schäumen (**with** vor + *Dat.*); **D** (*fig. coll.: be hot*) sehr heiß sein; **I'm ~ing** mir ist heiß; **be ~ing [hot]** sehr heiß sein; ‹Wasser:› kochend heiß sein; **a ~ing hot August day** ein glühend heißer Augusttag.
**2** *v.t.* **A** kochen; **~ sth. dry** etw. verkochen; **it is necessary to ~ the water** man muss das Wasser abkochen; **~ed potatoes** Salzkartoffeln; **~ the kettle** das Wasser heiß machen; **~ed shirt** gestärktes Frackhemd; **go and ~ your head** (*fig. coll.*) du kannst mir den Buckel herunterrutschen (*salopp*); **B** (*make by ~ing*) kochen ‹Seife›; **~ed sweet** (*Brit.*) hartes [Frucht]bonbon; Hartkaramelle, *die* (*fachspr.*).
**3** *n.* Kochen, *das;* **come to/go off the ~:** zu kochen anfangen/aufhören; (*fig.*) sich zuspitzen/sich wieder beruhigen; **bring to the ~:** zum Kochen bringen; (*fig.*) auf die Spitze treiben

**~ a'way** *v.i.* **A** (*continue boiling*) weiterkochen; **B** (*evaporate completely*) verkochen

**~ 'down 1** *v.i.* einkochen; **~ down to sth.** (*fig.*) auf etw. (*Akk.*) hinauslaufen. **2** *v.t.* einkochen; (*fig.*) kurz zusammenfassen

**~ 'over** *v.i.* überkochen

**~ 'up 1** *v.t.* kochen. **2** *v.i.* kochen; (*fig.*) sich zuspitzen

**boil[2]** *n.* (*Med.*) Furunkel, *der*

**boiler** /'bɔɪlə(r)/ *n.* **A** Kessel, *der;* **B** (*hot-water tank*) Boiler, *der;* **C** (*for laundry*) [Wasch]kessel, *der*

**boiler: ~house** *n.* Kesselhaus, *das;* **~maker** *n.* ▶ **1261** Kesselschmied, *der;* **~ room** *n.* Kesselraum, *der;* **~ suit** *n.* Overall, *der*

**boiling** /'bɔɪlɪŋ/ **1** ⇒ **boil[1]** 1, 2. **2** *n.* **the whole ~** (*coll.*) der ganze Krempel (*ugs.*)

**boiling: ~ point** *n.* ▶ **1603** Siedepunkt, *der;* **be at/reach ~ point** (*fig.*) auf dem Siedepunkt sein/den Siedepunkt erreichen; **~-ring** *n.* Kochspirale, *die*

**boisterous** /'bɔɪstərəs/ *adj.* **A** (*noisily cheerful*) ausgelassen; **B** (*rough*) wild; rau ‹Wind, See, Witterung›

**boisterously** /'bɔɪstərəslɪ/ *adv.* ⇒ **boisterous**: ausgelassen; wild

**bold** /bəʊld/ *adj.* **A** (*courageous*) mutig; (*daring*) kühn; **B** (*forward*) keck; kühn ‹Worte›; **make so ~ [as to ...]** so kühn sein[, zu ...]; ⇒ *also* **brass** 1 A; **C** (*striking*) auffallend, kühn ‹Farbe, Muster›; kräftig ‹Konturen›; fett ‹Schlagzeile›; **bring out in ~ relief** deutlich hervortreten lassen; **D** (*vigorous*) kühn; ausdrucksvoll ‹Stil, Beschreibung›; **E** (*Printing*) fett; (*secondary ~*) halbfett; **in ~ [type]** im Fettdruck

**bold: ~-face, ~-faced** ⇒ **bold** E

**boldly** /'bəʊldlɪ/ *adv.* **A** (*courageously*) mutig; (*daringly*) kühn; **B** (*forwardly*) dreist; **C** (*strikingly*) kräftig ‹hervortreten›; mit kühnem Schwung ‹signieren, malen›; auffällig ‹mustern›

**boldness** /'bəʊldnɪs/ *n., no pl.* **A** (*courage, daring*) Kühnheit, *die;* **B** (*forwardness*) Dreistigkeit, *die;* **C** (*strikingness*) Kühnheit, *die;* (*of description, style*) Ausdruckskraft, *die;* (*of an outline, of lettering*) Deutlichkeit, *die;* (*of pattern*) Auffälligkeit, *die*

**bole** /bəʊl/ *n.* (*trunk*) [Baum]stamm, *der*

**bolero** /bə'leərəʊ/ *n., pl.* **~s** Bolero, *der*

**Bolivia** /bə'lɪvɪə/ *pr. n.* Bolivien (*das*)

**Bolivian** /bə'lɪvɪən/ ▶ **1340** **1** *adj.* bolivianisch; **sb. is ~:** jmd. ist Bolivianer/Bolivianerin. **2** *n.* Bolivianer, *der*/Bolivianerin, *die*

**boll** /bəʊl/ *n.* Samenkapsel, *die*

**bollard** /'bɒləd/ *n.* (*Brit.*) Poller, *der*

**bollocks** /'bɒləks/ (*coarse*) **1** *n. pl.* Eier (*derb*). **2** *int.* Scheiße

**'boll weevil** *n.* Baumwollkapselkäfer, *der*

**bologna** /bə'ləʊnjə/ *n.* (*Amer.*) **~ [sausage]** ≈ Mortadella, *die*

**boloney** /bə'ləʊnɪ/ *n.* **A** (*coll.*) Quatsch, *der* (*ugs.*); **B** (*Amer.: sausage*) ⇒ **bologna**

**Bolshevik** /'bɒlʃɪvɪk/ *n.* **A** (*Hist.*) Bolschewik, *der;* **B** (*coll.: revolutionary*) Bolschewist, *der*/Bolschewistin, *die* (*ugs.*)

**bolshie, bolshy** /'bɒlʃɪ/ *adj.* (*coll.: uncooperative*) aufsässig; rotzig (*salopp*)

**bolster** /'bəʊlstə(r)/ ❶ *n.* (*pillow*) Nackenrolle, *die;* (*wedge-shaped*) Keilkissen, *das.* ❷ *v.t.* (*fig.*) stärken; **~ sb. up** jmdm. Mut machen; **~ sth. up** etw. stärken; **~ up a regime/one's status** ein Regime stützen/seinen Status aufpolieren (*ugs.*)

**bolt¹** /bəʊlt/ ❶ *n.* **A** (*on door or window*) Riegel, *der;* (*on gun*) Kammerverschluss, *der;* **B** (*metal pin*) Schraube, *die;* (*without thread*) Bolzen, *der;* **C** (*of crossbow*) Bolzen, *der;* **shoot one's ~** (*fig.*) sein Pulver verschießen; **D** **~ [of lightning]** Blitz[strahl], *der;* **[like] a ~ from the blue** (*fig.*) wie ein Blitz aus heiterem Himmel; **E** (*sudden dash*) **make a ~ for freedom** einen Fluchtversuch machen; **make a ~ for it** das Weite suchen.
❷ *v.i.* **A** davonlaufen; ‹Pferd:› durchgehen; ‹Fuchs, Kaninchen:› [mit einem Satz] flüchten; **~ out of the shop** aus dem Laden rennen; **B** (*Hort., Agric.*) vorzeitig Samen bilden; ‹Salat, Kohl:› schießen; **C** (*Amer. Polit.*) abspringen (*ugs.*).
❸ *v.t.* **A** (*fasten with ~*) verriegeln; **~ sb. in/out** jmdn. einsperren/aussperren; **B** (*fasten with ~s with/without thread*) verschrauben/mit Bolzen verbinden; **~ sth. to sth.** etw. an etw. (*Akk.*) schrauben/mit Bolzen befestigen; **C** (*gulp down*) **~ [down]** hinunterschlingen ‹Essen›; hinunterstürzen ‹Getränk›; **D** aufjagen ‹Fuchs, Kaninchen usw.›.
❹ *adv.* **~ upright** kerzengerade

**bolt²** *v.t.* (*sift*) sieben

**bolt: ~-hole** *n.* (*lit. or fig.*) Schlupfloch, *das;* **~-on** *adj.* aufschraubbar

**Bolzano** /bɒl'zɑ:nəʊ/ *pr. n.* Bozen (*das*)

**bomb** /bɒm/ ❶ *n.* **A** Bombe, *die;* **go like a ~** (*fig. coll.*) ein Bombenerfolg sein; **my new car goes like a ~:** mein neues Auto ist die reinste Rakete; **go down a ~ with** (*fig. coll.*) ein Bombenerfolg sein bei; **B** (*coll.: large sum of money*) **a ~:** 'ne Masse Geld (*ugs.*); **C** (*Amer. coll.: failure*) Reinfall, *der* (*ugs.*). ❷ *v.t.* bombardieren; **~ a pub** einen Bombenanschlag auf eine Kneipe verüben. ❸ *v.i.* **A** Bomben werfen; **~ing raid** Bombenangriff, *der;* **B** (*coll.: fail*) durchfallen; **C** (*coll.: travel fast*) rasen

**~ 'out** *v.t.* ausbomben

**bombard** /bɒm'bɑ:d/ *v.t.* (*Mil.*) beschießen; bombardieren (*veralt.*); (*fig.*) bombardieren

**bombardier** /bɒmbə'dɪə(r)/ *n.* (*Brit. Mil.*) Unteroffizier [bei der Artillerie]

**bombardment** /bɒm'bɑ:dmənt/ *n.* Beschuss, *der;* Bombardierung, *die* (*veralt.*); (*fig.*) Bombardierung, *die*

**bombast** /'bɒmbæst/ *n.*, *no pl.* Schwulst, *der;* Bombast, *der*

**bombastic** /bɒm'bæstɪk/ *adj.* bombastisch; schwülstig

**bomb: ~ bay** *n.* Bombenschacht, *der;* **~ blast** *n.* (*blast wave*) Druckwelle, *die;* (*explosion*) Bombenexplosion, *die;* **~ disposal** *n.* Räumung von Bomben; *attrib.* **~ disposal expert** Experte für die Räumung von Bomben; **~ disposal squad** Bombenräumkommando, *das*

**bombe** /bɔ̃b/ *n.* (*Gastr.*) Eisbombe, *die*

**bomber** /'bɒmə(r)/ *n.* **A** (*Air Force*) Bomber, *der* (*ugs.*); **B** (*terrorist*) Bombenattentäter, *der*/-attentäterin, *die;* Bombenleger, *der*/-legerin, *die* (*ugs.*)

**'bomber jacket** *n.* Bomberjacke, *die*

**bombing** /'bɒmɪŋ/ *n.* Bombardierung, *die*

**bomb: ~proof** *adj.* bombenfest; **~ scare** *n.* Bombendrohung, *die;* **~shell** *n.* Bombe, *die;* (*fig.*) Sensation, *die;* **come as a** *or* **be something of a ~shell** wie eine Bombe einschlagen; **a blonde ~shell** eine Superblondine; **~-site** *n.* Trümmergrundstück, *das;* (*larger area*) Trümmerfeld, *das*

**bona fide** /bəʊnə 'faɪdɪ/ ❶ *adj.* (*genuine*) echt; (*sincere*) ehrlich; redlich; **~ contract** in gutem Glauben abgeschlossener Vertrag; **~ purchaser** gutgläubiger Erwerber. ❷ *adv.* (*genuinely*) wahrhaftig; (*sincerely*) ehrlich; redlich; (*in good faith*) in gutem Glauben; bona fide (*geh.*)

**bonanza** /bə'nænzə/ ❶ *n.* **A** (*unexpected success*) Goldgrube, *die* (*fig.*); **B** (*large output*) reiche Ausbeute. ❷ *adj.* äußerst ertragreich ‹Farm, Geschäftsjahr›

**bon-bon** /'bɒnbɒn/ *n.* Praline, *das*

**bonce** /bɒns/ *n.* (*Brit. coll.: head*) Birne, *die* (*salopp*)

**bond** /bɒnd/ ❶ *n.* **A** Band, *das;* **B** *in pl.* (*shackles, lit. or fig.*) Fesseln; Bande (*dichter. veralt.*); **C** (*uniting force*) Band, *das;* **D** (*adhesion*) **the ~ will be instantaneous/unbreakable** die Haftwirkung wird sofort eintreten/die Teile werden absolut fest aneinander kleben; **E** (*Commerc.*) (*debenture*) Anleihe, *die;* Schuldverschreibung, *die;* (*deed*) Schuldschein, *der;* **goods in ~:** Waren unter Zollverschluss; **F** (*agreement*) Übereinkommen, *das;* (*covenant*) Bund, *der;* **my word is [as good as] my ~:** was ich verspreche, das halte ich auch; **G** (*Insurance*) ≈ Vertrauensschadenversicherung, *die;* **H** (*Building*) [Mauer]verband, *der;* **English ~:** Blockverband, *der;* **I** ⇒ **bond paper;** **J** (*Chem.*) Bindung, *die.*
❷ *v.t.* **A** (*join securely*) zusammenfügen (**to** mit); **B** (*Building*) im Verband legen; **C** (*Commerc.*) unter Zollverschluss nehmen; ⇒ *also* **bonded A**

**bondage** /'bɒndɪdʒ/ *n.*, *no pl.* Sklaverei, *die* (*auch fig.*); (*sexual perversion*) Bondage, *das;* Fesseln, *das;* **in ~ to sb.** als jmds. Sklave/Sklavin (*auch fig.*)

**bonded** /'bɒndɪd/ *adj.* **A** (*Commerc.*) unter Zollverschluss; **~ goods** Zolllagergut, *das;* **~ warehouse** Zolllager, *das;* **~ debt** fundierte Schuld (*Finanzw.*); **B** (*cemented, reinforced*) verstärkt

**'bond: ~paper** *n.* Dokumentenpapier, *das;* (*for general use*) feines Schreibpapier; **~stone** *n.* (*Building*) Binder, *der;* **~-washing** *n.* (*Finance*) *Umwandlung von zu versteuernden Dividendengewinnen in steuerfreie Kapitalerträge*

**bone** /bəʊn/ ❶ *n.* **A** ▶ 966 Knochen, *der;* (*of fish*) Gräte, *die;* **~s** (*fig.: remains*) Gebeine *Pl.* (*geh.*); **be chilled to the ~** (*fig.*) völlig durchgefroren sein; **cut prices to the ~:** die Preise äußerst scharf kalkulieren; **pare expenditure to the ~:** sich radikal einschränken; **work one's fingers to the ~** (*fig.*) bis zum Umfallen arbeiten; **I feel it in my ~s** (*fig.*) ich habe es im Gefühl; **make old ~s** (*fig.*) alt werden; **the bare ~s** (*fig.*) die wesentlichen Punkte; (*of a story*) die Grundzüge; **close to the** *or* **near the ~** (*fig.*) (*indecent*) gewagt; (*destitute*) am Rande des Existenzminimums; **come** *or* **get close to** *or* **near the ~** (*fig.*) [ziemlich] gewagt sein; ⇒ *also* **dry 1 A;** **B** (*material*) Knochen, *der;* (*ivory*) Elfenbein, *das;* **C** (*stiffener*) (*in collar*) Kragenstäbchen, *das;* (*in corset*) Korsettstange, *die;* **D** (*subject of dispute*) **have/find a ~ to pick with sb.** mit jmdm. ein Hühnchen zu rupfen haben (*ugs.*)/einen Grund finden, mit jmdm. Streit anzufangen; **~ of contention** Zankapfel, *der;* **make no ~s about sth./doing sth.** keinen Hehl aus etw. machen/sich nicht scheuen, etw. zu tun. ❷ *v.t.* den/die Knochen herauslösen aus, ausbeinen ‹Fleisch, Geflügel›; entgräten ‹Fisch›. ❸ *v.i.* **~ up on sth.** (*coll.*) etw. büffeln (*ugs.*)

**bone: ~ 'china** *n.* Knochenporzellan, *das;* **~ 'dry** *adj.* knochentrocken (*ugs.*); **~fish** *n.* (*Amer.*) Grätenfisch, *der;* **~head** *n.* (*coll.*) Holzkopf, *der* (*salopp abwertend*); **~-headed** *adj.* (*coll.*) blöd (*ugs. abwertend*); **~-'idle, ~ 'lazy** *adjs.* stinkfaul (*salopp*); **~ marrow** *n.* (*Anat.*) Knochenmark, *das;* **~meal** *n.* Knochenmehl, *das*

**boner** /'bəʊnə(r)/ *n.* (*coll.*) grober Schnitzer; **pull a ~:** sich (*Dat.*) einen groben Schnitzer leisten

**bone: ~-shaker** *n.* Klapperkiste, *die* (*salopp*); **~ 'weary** *adj.* völlig erschöpft

**bonfire** /'bɒnfaɪə(r)/ *n.* **A** (*at celebration*) Freudenfeuer, *das;* **B~ Night** (*Brit.*) [Abend des] Guy Fawkes Day (*mit Feuerwerk*); **B** (*for burning rubbish*) Feuer, *das;* **make a ~ of sth.** (*lit. or fig.*) etw. verbrennen

**bongo** /'bɒŋgəʊ/ *n.*, *pl.* **~s** *or* **~es** (*drum*) Bongo, *das od. die*

**bonhomie** /'bɒnəmi:/ *n.*, *no pl.* Bonhomie, *die* (*geh.*); Jovialität, *die*

**bonk** /bɒŋk/ (*Brit.*) ❶ *v.t.* **A** (*coll.: hit*) hauen; **B** (*sl.: copulate with*) bumsen (*salopp*). ❷ *v.i.* (*sl.: copulate*) bumsen (*salopp*)

**bonkers** /'bɒŋkəz/ *adj.* (*coll.*) verrückt (*salopp*); wahnsinnig (*ugs.*); **go ~:** überschnappen (*ugs.*); **be ~:** spinnen (*ugs. abwertend*)

**bon mot** /bɔ̃ 'məʊ, bɒn 'məʊ/ *n.*, *pl.* **bons mots** /bɔ̃ 'məʊ, bɒn 'məʊ/ Bonmot, *das*

**bonnet** /'bɒnɪt/ *n.* **A** (*woman's*) Haube, *die;* Bonnet, *das* (*hist.*); (*child's*) Häubchen, *das;* (*Scotch cap*) [Schotten]mütze, *die;* ⇒ *also* **bee A;** **B** (*Brit. Motor Veh.*) Motor- *od.* Kühlerhaube, *die*

**bonny** /'bɒnɪ/ *adj.* **A** (*fine*) prächtig ‹Bursche, Schiff›; herrlich ‹Land, Stadt, Anblick›; **B** (*healthy-looking*) prächtig ‹Baby›; gesund ‹Gesicht›; **C** (*Scot. and N. Engl.: comely*) hübsch

**bonsai** /'bɒnsaɪ/ *n.* **A** (*tree*) Bonsai[baum], *der;* **B** *no pl.*, *no art.* (*method*) Bonsai, *das*

**bonus** /'bəʊnəs/ *n.* **A** zusätzliche Leistung; **B** (*to shareholders, insurance-policy holder*) Bonus, *der;* (*to employee*) **Christmas ~:** Weihnachtsgratifikation, *die;* **cost-of-living ~:** Teuerungszulage, *die;* **production ~:** Leistungsprämie, *die;* **C** (*advantage*) Pluspunkt, *der*

**bon vivant** /bɔ̃ vi:'vɑ̃/ *n.*, *pl.* **~s** *or* **bons vivants** /bɔ̃ vi:'vɑ̃/ Gourmet, *der;* Feinschmecker, *der*

**bon voyage** /bɔ̃ vwɑ:'jɑ:ʒ/ *int.* glückliche Reise

**bony** /'bəʊnɪ/ *adj.* **A** (*of bone*) beinern; knöchern; Knochen-; (*like bone*) knochenartig; **B** (*big-boned*) grobknochig; **C** (*skinny*) knochendürr (*ugs.*); spindeldürr; **D** (*full of bones*) grätig ‹Fisch›; ‹Fleisch› mit viel Knochen; **be ~:** viele Gräten/Knochen haben

**boo** /bu:/ ❶ *int.* (*to surprise sb.*) huh; (*expr. disapproval, contempt*) buh; **he wouldn't say '~' to a goose** er ist sehr schüchtern; **cries of '~'** Buhrufe. ❷ *n.* Buh, *das* (*ugs.*). ❸ *v.t.* ausbuhen (*ugs.*); **he was ~ed off the stage** er wurde so ausgebuht, dass er die Bühne verließ (*ugs.*). ❹ *v.i.* buhen (*ugs.*)

**boob** /bu:b/ (*Brit. coll.*) ❶ *n.* **A** (*mistake*) Fehler, *der;* Schnitzer, *der* (*ugs.*); **B** (*simpleton*) Dussel, *der* (*salopp*); Blödian, *der* (*ugs. abwertend*); **C** (*breast*) Titte, *die* (*derb*). ❷ *v.i.* einen Schnitzer machen (*ugs.*)

**booboo** /'bu:bu:/ (*coll.*) ⇒ **boob 1 A**

**booby** /'bu:bɪ/ *n.* **A** Trottel, *der* (*ugs. abwertend*); **B** (*Ornith.*) Tölpel, *der*

**booby: ~hatch** *n.* (*Amer. sl.*) Klapsmühle, *die* (*salopp*); **~ prize** *n.* *Preis für den schlechtesten Teilnehmer an einem Wettbewerb;* **~ trap** *n.* **A** *Falle, mit der man jmdm. einen Streich spielen will;* **B** (*Mil.*) versteckte Sprengladung; **~-trap** *v.t.* **A** [für einen Streich] präparieren; **B** (*Mil.*) **the bomb/the door had been ~-trapped** die Bombe war präpariert worden/an der Tür war eine versteckte Sprengladung angebracht worden

**boodle** /'bu:dl/ *n.* (*coll.*) Zaster, *der* (*salopp*); (*for bribery*) Schmiergeld, *das* (*ugs.*)

**book** /bʊk/ ❶ *n.* **A** Buch, *das;* **in ~ form** in Buchform; als Buch; **be a closed ~ [to sb.]** (*fig.*) [jmdm. *od.* für jmdn.] ein Buch mit sieben Siegeln sein; **the ~ of Job** das Buch Hiob; **the ~ of fate** (*fig.*) das Schicksal; **the ~ of life** (*fig.*) das Buch des Lebens (*Rel.*); das Lebensbuch (*Rel.*); **the [Good] B~:** das Buch der Bücher; die Bibel; **throw the ~ at sb.** (*fig.*) jmdn. kräftig zusammenstauchen (*ugs.*); **bring to ~** (*fig.*) zur Rechenschaft ziehen; **in my ~** (*fig.*) meiner Ansicht *od.* Meinung nach; **it won't suit my ~** (*fig.*) es passt mir nicht; **be in sb.'s good/bad ~s** (*fig.*) bei jmdm. gut/schlecht angeschrieben sein; **that's not in the ~** (*fig. coll.*) das geht nicht; **I can read you like a ~** (*fig.*) ich kann in dir lesen wie in einem Buch; **do sth.** *or* **play it/speak by the ~** (*fig.*) sich an die Regeln halten/ganz korrekte Angaben machen; **speak** *or* **talk like a ~** (*fig.*) sich geschraubt ausdrücken (*ugs. abwertend*); **take a leaf out of sb.'s ~** (*fig.*) sich (*Dat.*) jmdn. zum Vorbild nehmen; **you could take a leaf out of his ~:** du könntest dir von ihm eine

Scheibe abschneiden (*ugs.*); ⇒ *also* **black books**; **open** 1 K; **B** (*for accounts*) Kontood. Rechnungsbuch, *das;* (*for notes*) [Notiz]buch, *das;* (*for exercises*) [Schreib]heft, *das;* **C** (*telephone directory*) Telefonbuch, *das;* **be in the ~:** im Telefonbuch stehen; **D** (*coll.: magazine*) Magazin, *das;* Illustrierte, *die;* **E** *in pl.* (*records, accounts*) Bücher; **do the ~s** die Abrechnung machen; **balance the ~s** die Bilanz machen *od.* ziehen; ⇒ *also* **keep** 1 H; **F** *in pl.* (*list of members*) **be on the ~s** auf der [Mitglieds]liste *od.* im Mitgliederverzeichnis stehen; **G** (*record of bets*) Wettbuch, *das;* **make** *or* **keep a ~ on sth.** Wetten auf etw. (*Akk.*) annehmen; **H** **~ of tickets** Fahrscheinheft, *das;* **~ of stamps/matches** Briefmarkenheft/Streichholzbriefchen, *das;* **~ of samples** Musterbuch, *das;* **I** (*in poem*) Gesang, *der;* **J** (*libretto*) Textbuch, *das;* (*playscript*) Textvorlage, *die;* **~ of words** Textbuch, *das;* (*fig.*) Arbeitsanweisungen *Pl.*

**2** *v.t.* **A** (*engage in advance*) buchen ‹Reise, Flug, Platz [im Flugzeug]›; [vor]bestellen ‹Eintrittskarte, Tisch, Zimmer, Platz [im Theater]›; anmelden ‹Telefongespräch›; engagieren, verpflichten ‹Künstler, Orchester›; **be fully ~ed** ‹Vorstellung:› ausverkauft sein; ‹Flug[zeug]:› ausgebucht sein; ‹Hotel:› voll belegt *od.* ausgebucht sein; **B** (*enter in ~*) eintragen; (*for offence*) aufschreiben (*ugs.*) (**for** wegen); **C** (*issue ticket to*) **we are ~ed on a flight to Athens** man hat für uns einen Flug nach Athen gebucht.

**3** *v.i.* buchen; (*for travel, performance*) vorbestellen

**~ 'in 1** *v.i.* sich eintragen; **we ~ed in at the Ritz** wir sind im Ritz abgestiegen. **2** *v.t.* **A** (*make reservation for*) Zimmer/ein Zimmer vorbestellen *od.* reservieren für; **we're ~ed in at the Dorchester** unsere Zimmer sind im Dorchester reserviert; **B** (*register*) eintragen

**~ 'up 1** *v.i.* buchen. **2** *v.t.* buchen; **the guest house is ~ed up** die Pension ist ausgebucht *od.* voll belegt

**bookable** /'bʊkəbl/ *adj.* **be ~:** vorbestellt werden können; ‹Flug, Urlaub:› gebucht werden können

**book: ~binder** *n.* ▶ 1261 Buchbinder, *der*/-binderin, *die;* **~binding** *n.*, *no pl.* Buchbinderei, *die;* **~case** *n.* Bücherschrank, *der;* **~ club** *n.* Buchklub, *der;* Buchgemeinschaft, *die;* **~ends** *n. pl.* Buchstützen

**bookie** /'bʊkɪ/ *n.* ▶ 1261 (*coll.*) Buchmacher, *der*

**booking** /'bʊkɪŋ/ *n.* **A** Buchung, *die;* (*of ticket*) Bestellung, *die;* (*of table, room, seat*) Vorbestellung, *die;* **~ for the concert opens today** der Vorverkauf für das Konzert beginnt heute; **make/cancel a ~:** buchen/eine Buchung rückgängig machen; (*for tickets*) bestellen/abbestellen; **change one's ~:** umbuchen; (*for tickets*) umbestellen; **B** (*of performer*) Engagement, *das*

**booking: ~ clerk** *n.* ▶ 1261 Schalterbeamte, *der*/-beamtin, *die;* Fahrkartenverkäufer, *der*/-verkäuferin, *die;* **~ hall** *n.* Schalterhalle, *die;* **~ office** *n.* (*in station*) [Fahrkarten]schalter, *der;* (*in theatre*) [Theater]kasse, *die;* (*selling tickets in advance*) Vorverkaufsstelle, *die*

**bookish** /'bʊkɪʃ/ *adj.* **A** (*studious*) gelehrt; (*addicted to reading*) **be ~:** ein Bücherwurm sein; **B** (*as in books*) schriftsprachlich; papieren (*abwertend*)

**book: ~ jacket** *n.* Schutzumschlag, *der;* **~keeper** *n.* ▶ 1261 Buchhalter, *der*/Buchhalterin, *die;* **~keeping** *n.* Buchführung, *die;* Buchhaltung, *die*

**booklet** /'bʊklɪt/ *n.* Broschüre, *die*

**book: ~-lover** *n.* Bücherfreund, *der;* **~maker** *n.* ▶ 1261 (*in betting*) Buchmacher, *der;* **~making** *n.*, *no pl.* **A** (*in betting*) Buchmacherei, *die;* **B** (*compiling books*) Kompilation, *die;* **~man** *n.* Literat, *der;* **~mark 1** *n.* **A** Lesezeichen, *das;* Buchzeichen, *das;* **B** (*Computing*) Lesezeichen, *das;* **2** *v.t.* (*Computing*) mit einem Lesezeichen versehen; **~marker** *n.* Lesezeichen, *das;* Buchzeichen, *das;* **~mobile** /'bʊkməbi:l/ *n.* (*Amer.*) Fahrbücherei, *die;* **~ page** *n.* **A** (*in newspaper*) *Seite mit Buchrezensionen;* ≈ Literaturseite, *die;* **B** (*page of ~*) Buchseite, *die;* **~plate** *n.* Exlibris, *das;* **~ post** *n.*, *no pl.* Büchersendung, *die;* **~rest** *n. Halter für das aufgeschlagene Buch;* **~ review** *n.* Buchbesprechung, *die;* **~seller** *n.* ▶ 1261 Buchhändler, *der*/-händlerin, *die;* **~shelf** *n.* Bücherbord, *das;* **on my ~shelves** in meinen Bücherregalen; **~shop** *n.* Buchhandlung, *die;* Buchladen, *der;* **~stall** *n.* Bücherstand, *der;* **~store** (*Amer.*) ⇒ **~shop**

**booksy** /'bʊksɪ/ *adj.* (*coll.*) hochgestochen (*ugs. abwertend*) ‹Stil, Ausdruck, Konversation›; hochgelahrt (*scherzh.*) ‹Person›

**book: ~ token** *n.* Büchergutschein, *der;* **~ trough** *n.* Bücherständer, *der;* **~ value** *n.* (*Bookk.*) Buchwert, *der;* **~work** *n.* Bücherstudium, *das;* **~worm** *n.* (*lit. or fig.*) Bücherwurm, *der*

**boom¹** /bu:m/ *n.* **A** (*for camera or microphone*) Ausleger, *der;* **B** (*Naut.*) Baum, *der;* **C** (*floating barrier*) [schwimmende] Absperrung

**boom² 1** *v.i.* **A** dröhnen; ‹Kanone, Wellen, Brandung:› dröhnen, donnern; ‹Vogel:› [dumpf] rufen; **B** ‹Geschäft, Verkauf, Stadt, Gebiet:› sich sprunghaft entwickeln; ‹Preise, Aktien:› rapide steigen; **business is ~ing** das Geschäft boomt *od.* erlebt einen Boom; die Geschäfte florieren. **2** *n.* **A** (*of person*) Gebrüll, *das;* (*of gun, waves*) Dröhnen, *das;* Donnern, *das;* (*of bird*) [dumpfes] Rufen; [dumpfer] Ruf; **B** (*in business*) [sprunghafter] Aufschwung; Boom, *der;* (*in prices*) [rapider] Anstieg; *attrib.* **a ~ area** ein Gebiet, das sich sprunghaft entwickelt; **a ~ year** ein Boomjahr; **C** (*period of economic expansion*) Hochkonjunktur, *die;* Boom, *der; attrib.* **the ~ years** die Jahre der Hochkonjunktur

**~ 'out 1** *v.i.* ‹Stimme:› dröhnen; ‹Kanone:› donnern, dröhnen. **2** *v.t.* brüllen ‹Kommando, Befehl›

**boomerang** /'bu:məræŋ/ **1** *n.* (*lit. or fig.*) Bumerang, *der.* **2** *v.i.* (*fig.*) sich als Bumerang erweisen

**booming** /'bu:mɪŋ/ *adj.* **A** (*deep, resonant*) donnend ‹Stimme›; schallend ‹Lachen›; dröhnend ‹Klang› **B** (*Econ.*) boomend (*ugs.*) ‹Wirtschaft, Konjunktur, Tourismus›

**'boom town** *n. Stadt in sprunghaftem Aufschwung*

**boon** /bu:n/ *n.* **A** (*blessing*) Segen, *der;* Wohltat, *die;* **be a tremendous ~** *or* **a ~ and a blessing to sb.** ein wahrer Segen für jmdn. sein; **B** (*request, favour*) Gunst, *die* (*geh.*)

**'boon companion** *n.* Kumpan, *der*

**boondoggle** /'bu:ndɒgl/ (*Amer.*) **1** *n.* sinnlose Arbeit. **2** *v.i.* sinnlos arbeiten

**boor** /bʊə(r)/ *n.* Rüpel, *der* (*abwertend*)

**boorish** /'bʊərɪʃ/ *adj.*, **boorishly** /'bʊərɪʃlɪ/ *adv.* flegelhaft (*abwertend*); rüpelhaft (*abwertend*)

**boorishness** /'bʊərɪʃnɪs/ *n.*, *no pl.* Flegelei, *die* (*abwertend*); Rüpelei, *die* (*abwertend*)

**boost** /bu:st/ **1** *v.t.* **A** steigern; ankurbeln ‹Wirtschaft›; in die Höhe treiben ‹Preis, Wert, Aktienkurs›; stärken, heben ‹Selbstvertrauen, Moral›; (*increase reputation of*) aufbauen; (*recommend vigorously*) anpreisen; **B** (*coll.: push from below*) hochschieben; hochheben; **C** (*Electr.*) erhöhen ‹Spannung›; **D** (*Radio*) verstärken ‹Signal›. **2** *n.* **A** Auftrieb, *der;* (*increase*) Zunahme, *die;* **give sb./sth. a ~:** jmdn./einer Sache Auftrieb geben; **be given a ~:** Auftrieb erhalten; **give sales/production a ~:** den Verkauf/die Produktion ankurbeln

**booster** /'bu:stə(r)/ *n.* **A** (*Med.*) **~ [shot** *or* **injection]** Auffrischimpfung, *die;* **B** (*Astronaut.*) **~ [rocket/motor]** Starthilfsrakete, *die*/Starthilfstriebwerk, *das*

**'booster cushion, 'booster seat** *ns.* Sitzerhöhung, *die*

**boot¹** /bu:t/ **1** *n.* **A** Stiefel, *der;* **get the ~** (*fig. coll.*) rausgeschmissen werden (*ugs.*); **give sb. the ~** (*fig. coll.*) jmdn. rausschmeißen (*ugs.*); **give sb. a ~ up the backside** (*fig. coll.*) jmdm. den Marsch blasen (*salopp*); **as tough as old ~s** (*fig. coll.*) zäh wie Leder; **put the ~ in** (*coll.*) ihn/sie *usw.* [brutal] treten; **put the ~ in!** (*coll.*) tritt ihn/sie *usw.* zusammen! (*ugs.*); **the ~ is on the other foot** (*fig.*) es ist genau umgekehrt; **you can bet your ~s that ...** (*fig. coll.*) ..., darauf kannst du Gift nehmen (*ugs.*); ⇒ *also* **big** 1 G; **die¹** 1 A; **heart** 1 C; **B** (*Brit.: of car*) Kofferraum, *der;* **C** (*Hist.: torture*) spanischer Stiefel.

**2** *v.t.* **A** (*coll.*) treten; kicken (*ugs.*) ‹Ball›; **~ sb. out** (*fig. coll.*) jmdn. rausschmeißen (*ugs.*); **B** (*Computing*) **~ [up]** booten

**boot²** *n.* **to ~:** noch dazu; obendrein

**bootable** /'bu:təbl/ *adj.* (*Computing*) bootbar ‹System›; **~ disk** Bootdiskette, *die*

**boot: ~black** (*Amer.*) ⇒ **shoeblack**; **~ disk** *n.* (*Computing*) Bootdiskette, *die*

**booted** /'bu:tɪd/ *adj.* gestiefelt

**bootee** /bu:'ti:/ *n.* (*infant's*) Babyschuh, *der;* (*woman's*) Stiefelette, *die*

**booth** /bu:ð/ *n.* **A** Bude, *die;* **B** (*telephone ~*) Telefonzelle, *die;* **C** (*polling ~*) Wahlkabine, *die*

**'bootleg 1** *v.t.* schmuggeln; (*sell/make*) schwarz (*ugs.*) *od.* illegal verkaufen/brennen. **2** *adj.* geschmuggelt; (*sold/made*) schwarz (*ugs.*) *od.* illegal verkauft/gebrannt

**bootlegger** /'bu:tlegə(r)/ *n.* ⇒ **bootleg** 1: Schmuggler, *der;* Schwarzhändler *der;* Schwarzbrenner, *der*

**'bootlicker** *n.* (*derog.*) Speichellecker, *der* (*abwertend*)

**boots** /bu:ts/ *n. sing.* (*Brit. dated*) Hausbursche, *der*

**boot: ~ sale** *n.* (*Brit.*) *eine Art Flohmarkt, bei dem die Verkaufsgegenstände im Kofferraum des Autos ausgelegt werden;* **~strap** *n.* (*Computing*) Bootstrapping, *das;* **~straps** *n. pl.* **pull oneself up** *or* **raise oneself by one's own ~straps** (*fig.*) sich aus eigener Kraft hocharbeiten

**booty** /'bu:tɪ/ *n.*, *no pl.* Beute, *die*

**booze** /bu:z/ (*coll.*) **1** *v.i.* saufen (*salopp*). **2** *n.*, *no pl.* **A** (*drink*) Alkohol, *der;* **B** (*drinking bout*) Besäufnis, *das* (*salopp*); **go/be on the ~:** [einen] saufen gehen/saufen (*salopp*)

**'booze cruise** *n.* **A** (*coll.: drunken cruise*) Sauftour, *die* (*auf Fähren*); **B** (*Brit. coll.: to buy cheap alcohol*) *Fahrt mit der Fähre, um billig Alkohol zu kaufen*

**boozer** /'bu:zə(r)/ *n.* (*coll.*) **A** (*one who boozes*) Säufer, *der*/Säuferin, *die* (*derb*); **B** (*Brit. public house*) Kneipe, *die* (*ugs.*)

**'booze-up** *n.* (*coll.*) Besäufnis, *das* (*salopp*); **have a ~:** saufen gehen (*salopp*)

**boozy** /'bu:zɪ/ *adj.* (*coll.*) betrunken; blau *nicht attr.* (*ugs.*); (*addicted to drink*) versoffen (*salopp*)

**bop** /bɒp/ (*coll.*) **1** *v.i.* (*zur Popmusik*) tanzen. **2** *n.* Tanz, *der* (*zur Popmusik*); **have a ~:** tanzen; **put on a ~:** eine Tanzfete (*ugs.*) veranstalten

**bopper** /'bɒpə(r)/ *n.* (*coll.*) *jmd., der zur Popmusik tanzt*

**borage** /'bɒrɪdʒ/ *n.* (*Bot.*) Borretsch, *der*

**borax** /'bɔ:ræks/ *n.* (*Chem.*) Borax, *der*

**Bordeaux** /bɔ:'dəʊ/ *n.*, *pl. same* /bɔ:'dəʊz/ Bordeaux[wein], *der*

**bordel** /bɔ:'del/, *n. pl.* **~s, bordello** /bɔ:'deləʊ/ *n.*, *pl.* **~los** (*Amer.*) Bordell, *das*

**border** /'bɔ:də(r)/ **1** *n.* **A** Rand, *der;* (*of tablecloth, handkerchief, dress*) Bordüre, *die;* **B** (*of country*) Grenze, *die;* **the B~[s]** die Grenze; **north of the B~** (*in Scotland*) in Schottland; **C** (*flower bed*) Rabatte, *die;* ⇒ *also* **herbaceous**. **2** *attrib. adj.* Grenz ‹stadt, -gebiet, -streit›. **3** *v.t.* **A** (*adjoin*) [an]grenzen an (+ *Akk.*); **be ~ed by** [an]grenzen an (+ *Akk.*); **B** (*put a ~ to, act as ~ to*) umranden; einfassen; **C** (*resemble closely*) grenzen an (+ *Akk.*). **4** *v.i.* **~ on** ⇒ **3** A, C

**borderer** /'bɔ:dərə(r)/ *n.* Grenzbewohner, *der*/-bewohnerin, *die*

**border: ~land** Grenzgebiet, *das;* (*fig.*) Grenzbereich, *der;* **~line 1** *n.* Grenzlinie, *die;* (*fig.*) Grenze, *die;* **2** *adj.* **sb./sth. is ~line** (*fig.*) jmd. ist/etw. liegt auf der Grenze; **a ~line case/candidate/type**

(*fig.*) ein Grenzfall; **B~ terrier** *n.* Borderterrier, *der*

**bore¹** /bɔ:(r)/ ❶ *v.t.* (*make hole in*) bohren; **~ the rock/the wood** ein Loch in das Gestein/das Holz bohren; **~ rock/wood** Gestein/Holz bohren; **~ one's way through sth.** sich durch etw. hindurchbohren. ❷ *v.i.* (*drill*) bohren (**for** nach). ❸ *n.* [A] (*of firearm, engine cylinder*) Bohrung, *die* (*Technik*); (*of tube, pipe*) Innendurchmesser, *der;* [B] (*calibre*) Kaliber, *das;* [C] ⇒ **borehole**

**bore²** ❶ *n.* [A] (*nuisance*) **it's a real ~:** es ist wirklich ärgerlich; **what a ~!** wie ärgerlich!; **she is a real ~:** sie kann einem wirklich auf die Nerven gehen; [B] (*dull person*) Langweiler, *der* (*ugs. abwertend*). ❷ *v.t.* (*weary*) langweilen; **sb. is ~d with sth.** etw. langweilt jmdn.; **sb. is ~d with life** jmdn. ödet alles an (*ugs.*); **I'm ~d** ich langweile mich; ich habe Langeweile; **~ sb. to death** *or* **to tears** (*coll.*) jmdn. zu Tode langweilen

**bore³** *n.* (*tidewave*) Flutbrandung, *die;* Bore, *die*

**bore⁴** ⇒ **bear²**

**boredom** /ˈbɔ:dəm/ *n., no pl.* Langeweile, *die;* **with a look of utter ~ on one's face** mit einem völlig gelangweilten Gesichtsausdruck

**ˈborehole** *n.* Bohrloch, *das*

**borer** /ˈbɔ:rə(r)/ *n.* (*tool*) Bohrer, *der*

**boring** /ˈbɔ:rɪŋ/ *adj.* langweilig

**born** /bɔ:n/ ❶ **be ~:** geboren werden; **I was ~ in England** ich bin *od.* wurde in England geboren; **he was ~ of rich parents** *or* **~ rich** er war das Kind reicher Eltern; **he was ~ into a rich family** er wurde in eine reiche Familie hineingeboren; **a new era was ~:** eine neue Ära brach an; **be ~ again** (*fig.*) wieder geboren werden; **I wasn't ~ yesterday** (*fig.*) ich bin nicht von gestern (*ugs.*); **there's one ~ every minute** (*coll.*) die Dummen werden nicht alle; **be ~ of sth.** (*fig.*) aus etw. entstehen; **be ~ blind/lucky** blind von Geburt sein/ein Glückskind sein; **be ~ a poet** zum Dichter geboren sein; **be ~ to sth.** (*fig.*) zu etw. geboren *od.* bestimmt sein; **be ~ to command** zum Befehlen geboren sein; **sb. is ~ to be hanged** jmdm. ist ein schlimmes Ende vorbestimmt.
❷ *adj.* [A] geboren; **you don't know you are ~** (*coll.*) du kannst dich nicht beklagen; **~ again** (*fig.*) wieder geboren; **in all my ~ days** (*fig. coll.*) in meinem ganzen Leben; mein Lebtag (*ugs. veralt.*); ⇒ *also* **breed** 1 C; [B] (*destined to be*) **be a ~ orator** *or* **an orator ~:** der geborene Redner *od.* zum Redner geboren sein; [C] (*complete*) **a ~ fool** ein völliger Narr

**borne** ⇒ **bear²**

**boron** /ˈbɔ:rɒn/ *n.* (*Chem.*) Bor, *das*

**borough** /ˈbʌrə/ *n.* [A] (*Brit. Hist.: town with corporation*) Borough, *das; Stadt mit Selbstverwaltung;* **the ~ of Brighton** ≈ die Stadt Brighton; [B] (*Brit.: town sending members to Parliament*) Borough, *das; Stadt[bezirk] mit Vertretung im Parlament;* [C] (*Amer.*) **the ~ of ...** (*town*) die Stadt ...; (*village*) die Gemeinde ...

**borrow** /ˈbɒrəʊ/ ❶ *v.t.* [A] [sich (*Dat.*)] ausleihen; [sich (*Dat.*)] borgen; entleihen, ausleihen ‹Buch, Schallplatte usw. aus der Leihbücherei›; [sich (*Dat.*)] leihen ‹Geld von der Bank›; [sich (*Dat.*)] leihen, [sich (*Dat.*)] borgen ‹Geld›; **~ sth. from sb.** [sich (*Dat.*)] etw. von *od.* bei jmdm. borgen *od.* [aus]leihen; [B] (*fig.*) übernehmen ‹Idee, Methode, Meinung›; entlehnen ‹Wort, Ausdruck aus einer anderen Sprache›; **sb. is living on ~ed time** jmds. Uhr ist abgelaufen. ❷ *v.i.* borgen; (*from bank*) Kredit aufnehmen (**from** bei)

**borrowed ˈlight** *n.* [A] (*reflected light*) indirektes Licht; [B] (*internal window*) Innenfenster, *das*

**borrower** /ˈbɒrəʊə(r)/ *n.* (*from bank*) Kreditnehmer, *der;* (*from library*) Entleiher, *der*

**borrowing** /ˈbɒrəʊɪŋ/ *n.* (*from bank*) Kreditaufnahme, *die* (**from** bei); (*from library*) Entleihen, *das;* Ausleihen, *das;* (*fig.*) Übernahme, *die;* **'haute couture' is a ~ from French** „Haute couture“ ist eine Entlehnung aus dem Französischen

**borsch** /bɔ:ʃ/ *n.* Borschtsch, *der*

**Borstal** /ˈbɔ:stl/ *n.* (*Brit.*) Erziehungsheim, *das;* Besserungsanstalt für jugendliche Straftäter

**bortsch** /bɔ:tʃ/ ⇒ **borsch**

**borzoi** /ˈbɔ:zɔɪ/ *n.* Barsoi, *der*

**bosh** /bɒʃ/ *n., no pl., no indef. art.* (*coll.*) Quatsch, *der* (*ugs. abwertend*)

**bos'n** /ˈbəʊsn/ ⇒ **boatswain**

**Bosnia** /ˈbɒznɪə/ *n.* Bosnien (*das*)

**Bosnia-Herzegovina** /bɒznɪəhɜ:tsəgəˈvi:nə/ *pr. n.* Bosnia und Herzegovina (*das*)

**Bosnian** /ˈbɒznɪən/ ▶ **1340** ❶ *adj.* bosnisch; **sb. is ~:** jmd. ist Bosnier/Bosnierin. ❷ *n.* Bosnier, *der*/Bosnierin, *die*

**bosom** /ˈbʊzəm/ *n.* [A] (*person's breast*) Brust, *die;* Busen, *der* (*dichter. veralt.*); [B] (*of dress*) ≈ Vorderseite des Oberteils; (*of blouse*) ≈ Vorderteil, *das;* (*space between breast and garment*) Busen, *der* (*dichter. veralt.*); [C] (*fig.: enfolding relationship*) Schoß, *der* (*geh.*); **in the ~ of one's family** im Schoße der Familie; *attrib.* **a ~ friend** ein guter Freund; ein Busenfreund; [D] (*fig.: seat of thoughts or emotions*) Brust, *die;* **lay bare one's ~ to sb.** jmdm. sein Herz ausschütten; [E] (*fig.: surface*) Oberfläche, *die;* [F] *in pl.* (*Amer.: breasts*) Busen, *der;* Brüste; [G] (*Amer.: shirt front*) Hemdbrust, *die;* (*as separate garment*) Vorhemd, *das*

**bosomy** /ˈbʊzəmɪ/ *adj.* vollbusig

**Bosphorus** /ˈbɒsfərəs/ *pr. n.* Bosporus, *der*

**boss¹** /bɒs/ *n.* [A] (*metal knob, stud*) Bosse, *die* (*Kunstwiss.*); (*on shield*) Schildbuckel, *der od. die;* [B] (*protuberance*) Verdickung, *die;* [C] (*Archit.*) Schlussstein, *der*

**boss²** (*coll.*) ❶ *n.* [A] (*master*) Boss, *der* (*ugs.*); Chef, *der;* **OK, you're the ~:** du bist der Boss; **who's the ~ in your household?** wer bestimmt bei euch zu Hause?; [B] (*Amer. Polit.*) [Partei]boss, *der* (*ugs.*). ❷ *v.t.* **~ sth.** bei etw. das Sagen haben; **~ sb. [about** *or* **around]** jmdn. herumkommandieren (*ugs.*)

**ˈboss-eyed** *adj.* (*coll.*) schielend; **be ~:** schielen

**bossiness** /ˈbɒsɪnɪs/ *n., no pl.* herrische Art

**bossy** /ˈbɒsɪ/ *adj.* (*coll.*) herrisch; **don't be so ~:** hör auf herumzukommandieren (*ugs.*)

**bosun, bo'sun** /ˈbəʊsn/ ⇒ **boatswain**

**botanical** /bəˈtænɪkl/ *adj.* botanisch; **~ garden[s]** botanischer Garten

**botanist** /ˈbɒtənɪst/ *n.* ▶ **1261** Botaniker, *der*/Botanikerin, *die*

**botany** /ˈbɒtənɪ/ *n., no pl.* Botanik, *die;* Pflanzenkunde, *die*

**botch** /bɒtʃ/ ❶ *n.* (*bungled work*) ⇒ **2** A: Pfuscherei, *die* (*ugs. abwertend*); Patzer, *der* (*ugs.*); **make a ~ of sth.** bei etw. pfuschen (*ugs. abwertend*). ❷ *v.t.* [A] (*bungle*) pfuschen bei (*ugs. abwertend*) ‹Reparatur, Arbeit›; patzen bei (*ugs.*) ‹Vortrag, Stabwechsel›; **a ~ed job** eine gepfuschte Arbeit (*ugs. abwertend*); [B] (*repair badly*) [notdürftig] flicken. ❸ *v.i.* ⇒ **2** A: pfuschen (*ugs. abwertend*); patzen (*ugs.*)

**~ ˈup** *v.t.* [A] (*bungle*) verpfuschen (*ugs. abwertend*); [B] (*repair badly*) [notdürftig] flicken

**both** /bəʊθ/ ❶ *adj.* beide; **we ~ like cooking** wir kochen beide gern; **~ these books are expensive** die[se] Bücher sind beide teuer; **~ [the] brothers** beide Brüder; **~ our brothers** unsere beiden Brüder; **~ ways** (*Brit. Racing*) = **each way** ⇒ **each** 1; **you can't have it ~ ways** beides [zugleich] geht nicht; ⇒ *also* **cut** 2 A.
❷ *pron.* beide; **~ [of them] are dead** beide sind tot; **they are ~ dead** sie sind beide tot; **~ of you/them are ...:** ihr seid/sie sind beide ...; **for them ~:** für sie beide; **Love or hate? — B~:** Liebe oder Hass? — Beides; **go along to bed, ~ of you** ihr geht jetzt ins Bett, alle beide.
❸ *adv.* **~ A and B, A and B ~:** sowohl A als [auch] B; **~ brother and sister are dead** sowohl der Bruder als auch die Schwester sind tot; **~ you and I** wir beide; **he and I were ~ there** er und ich waren beide da; **she was ~ singing and playing** sie hat gesungen und zugleich gespielt

**bother** /ˈbɒðə(r)/ ❶ *v.t.* [A] *in pass.* (*take trouble*) **I can't be ~ed [to do it]** ich habe keine Lust[, es zu machen]; **I can't be ~ed with details like that** ich kann mich nicht mit solchen Kleinigkeiten abgeben *od.* befassen; **can't you even be ~ed to dress properly?** kannst du dich nicht einmal richtig anziehen?; **I can't be ~ed with people who ...:** ich habe nichts übrig für Leute, die ...; [B] (*annoy*) lästig sein *od.* fallen (+ *Dat.*); ‹Lärm, Licht:› stören; ‹Schmerz, Wunde, Zahn, Rücken:› zu schaffen machen (+ *Dat.*); **I'm sorry to ~ you, but ...:** es tut mir leid, dass ich Sie damit belästigen muss, aber ...; **don't ~ me now** lass mich jetzt in Ruhe!; [C] (*worry*) Sorgen machen (+ *Dat.*); ‹Problem, Frage:› beschäftigen; **I'm not ~ed about him/the money** seinetwegen/wegen des Geldes mache ich mir keine Gedanken; **what's ~ing you/is something ~ing you?** was hast du denn/hast du etwas?; **~ oneself** *or* **one's head about sth.** sich (*Dat.*) über etw. (*Akk.*) den Kopf zerbrechen (*ugs.*); ⇒ *also* **hot** 1 F; [D] (*coll.: confound*) **~ it!** wie ärgerlich!; **~ him/her/you/this car!** zum Kuckuck mit ihm/ihr/dir/diesem Auto!
❷ *v.i.* (*trouble oneself*) **~ to do that** sich damit aufhalten, das zu tun; **don't ~ to do sth.** Sie brauchen etw. nicht zu tun; **she didn't even ~ to ask** sie hielt es nicht mal für nötig, zu fragen; **you needn't have ~ed to come** Sie hätten wirklich nicht zu kommen brauchen; **you needn't/shouldn't have ~ed** das wäre nicht nötig gewesen; **don't ~!** nicht nötig!; **~ with sth./sb.** sich mit etw./jmdm. aufhalten; **~ about sth./sb.** sich (*Dat.*) über etw./jmdn. Gedanken machen.
❸ *n.* [A] (*nuisance*) **what a ~!** wie ärgerlich!; **it's a real/such a ~:** es ist wirklich lästig; [B] (*trouble*) Ärger, *der;* **it's no ~ [for me]** es macht mir gar nichts aus; **the children were no ~ at all** wir hatten mit den Kindern überhaupt keine Schwierigkeiten; **have a spot of ~ with sth.** Schwierigkeiten mit etw. haben; **without any ~ at all** ohne irgendwelche Schwierigkeiten; **it's not worth the ~:** es lohnt nicht; **I'm sorry to have put you to all this ~:** es tut mir leid, Ihnen soviel Umstände gemacht zu haben; **if it isn't too much ~:** wenn es nicht zu viel Mühe macht; **go to the ~ of doing sth.** sich (*Dat.*) die Mühe machen, etw. zu tun.
❹ *int.* (*coll.*) wie ärgerlich!

**botheration** /bɒðəˈreɪʃn/ *int.* ⇒ **bother** 4

**bothersome** /ˈbɒðəsəm/ *adj.* lästig; unleidlich ‹Kind›

**bottle** /ˈbɒtl/ ❶ *n.* [A] Flasche, *die;* **a beer ~:** eine Bierflasche; **a ~ of beer** eine Flasche Bier; [B] (*fig. coll.: alcoholic drink*) **be too fond of the ~:** dem Alkohol zu sehr zugetan sein; **be on the ~:** trinken; ⇒ *also* **hit** 1 K; [C] (*gas cylinder*) **a ~ of gas** eine Gasflasche; [D] (*Brit. coll.: courage, confidence*) Mumm, *der* (*ugs.*); **lose one's ~:** sich (*Dat.*) den Schneid abkaufen lassen (*ugs.*).
❷ *v.t.* [A] (*put into ~s*) in Flaschen [ab]füllen; [B] (*store in ~s*) in Flaschen lagern *od.* aufheben; **~d beer** Flaschenbier, *das;* **~d gas** Flaschengas, *das;* [C] (*preserve in jars*) einmachen

**~ ˈup** *v.t.* [A] (*conceal*) in sich (*Dat.*) aufstauen; [B] (*entrap*) einschließen

**bottle: ~ bank** *n.* Altglasbehälter, *der;* **~-fed** *adj.* mit der Flasche gefüttert; **~-fed babies** Flaschenkinder

**bottleful** /ˈbɒtlfʊl/ *n.* **a ~ of shampoo** eine Flasche Schampon

**bottle: ~ glass** *n.* Flaschenglas, *das;* **~-green** ❶ *n.* Flaschengrün, *das;* ❷ *adj.* flaschengrün; **~neck** *n.* (*fig.*) Flaschenhals, *der* (*ugs.*); (*in production process also*) Engpass, *der;* **~ opener** *n.* Flaschenöffner, *der;* **~ party** *n.* Bottleparty, *die;* **~ top** *n.* Flaschenverschluss, *der*

**bottom** /ˈbɒtəm/ ❶ *n.* [A] (*lowest part*) unteres Ende; (*of cup, glass, box, chest*) Boden, *der;* (*of valley, canyon, crevasse, well, shaft*) Sohle, *die;* (*of canyon, crevasse, well also*)

b

Grund, *der;* (*of hill, slope, cliff, stairs*) Fuß, *der;* **the ~ of the valley** die Talsohle; **[be] at the ~ of the page/list** unten auf der Seite/Liste [sein]; **[be] in the ~ of the box/glass** am Boden des Kastens/Glases [sein]; unten im Kasten/Glas [sein]; **the ~ of my coat/dress is all muddy** mein Mantel/Kleid ist unten ganz schmutzig; **the book right at the ~ of the pile** das Buch ganz unten im Stapel; **~ up** auf dem Kopf; verkehrt herum; **~s up!** (*coll.*) hoch die Tassen!; **the ~ fell** *or* **dropped out of her world/the market** (*fig.*) für sie brach eine Welt zusammen/der Markt brach zusammen; **knock the ~ out of sth.** (*fig.*) etw. zusammenbrechen lassen; ⇨ *also* **false bottom**; **B** ▶966 (*buttocks*) Hinterteil, *das* (*ugs.*); Po[dex], *der* (*fam.*); **C** (*of chair*) Sitz, *der;* Sitzfläche, *die;* **D** (*of sea, lake*) Grund, *der;* **on the ~:** auf dem Grund; **go to the ~:** [ver]sinken; **send a ship to the ~:** ein Schiff in den Grund bohren *od.* versenken; **touch ~:** Grund haben; (*fig.*) den Tiefpunkt erreichen; **E** (*farthest point*) **at the ~ of the garden/street** hinten im Garten/am Ende der Straße; ⇨ *also* **heart** 1 B; **F** (*underside*) Unterseite, *die;* **G** (*fig.*) **start at the ~:** ganz unten anfangen; **be ~ of the class/league** der/die Letzte in der Klasse sein/Tabellenletzte[r] sein; **H** *usu. in pl.* **~[s]** (*of track suit, pyjamas*) Hose, *die;* **I** (*fig.: basis, origin*) **be at the ~ of sth.** hinter etw. (*Dat.*) stecken (*ugs.*); einer Sache (*Dat.*) zugrunde liegen; **get to the ~ of sth.** einer Sache (*Dat.*) auf den Grund kommen; **at ~:** im Grunde genommen; **J** (*Naut.*) Schiffsboden, *der;* **~ up** kieloben; **K** (*Brit. Motor Veh.*) **in ~:** im ersten Gang.

❷ *adj.* **A** (*lowest*) unterst...; (*lower*) unter...; **B** (*fig.: last*) letzt...; **be ~:** der/die/das Letzte sein; **you can bet your/I'd [be willing to] bet my ~ dollar** (*fig. coll.*) jede Wette (*ugs.*).

❸ *v.i.* **~ [out]** ‹Preise:› den tiefsten Stand erreichen; ‹Rezession, Rückgang:› den tiefsten Punkt erreichen

**bottom:** ~ **'dog** ⇨ **underdog**; ~ **'drawer** *n.* (*fig.*) Aussteuer, *die;* **put sth. [away] in one's ~ drawer** etw. für die Aussteuer beiseite legen

**bottomless** /'bɒtəmlɪs/ *adj.* bodenlos; unendlich tief ‹Meer, Ozean›; (*fig.: inexhaustible*) unerschöpflich; **the ~ pit** der Abgrund der Hölle

**bottom 'line** *n.* (*fig. coll.*) **the ~:** das Fazit

**'botulism** /'bɒtju:lɪzm/ *n., no pl., no art.* ▶1232 (*Med.*) Botulismus, *der*

**boudoir** /'bu:dwɑ:(r)/ *n.* Boudoir, *das* (*veralt.*); Damenzimmer, *das* (*veralt.*)

**bouffant** /'bu:fã/ *adj.* voll und duftig, füllig ‹Haar, Frisur›; bauschig ‹Kleidung›

**bough** /baʊ/ *n.* Ast, *der*

**bought** ⇨ **buy** 1

**bouillabaisse** /bu:jə'beɪs/ *n.* (*Gastr.*) Bouillabaisse, *die*

**bouillon** /'bu:jɔ̃/ *n.* (*Cookery*) Bouillon, *die;* **~ cube** Brühwürfel, *der*

**boulder** /'bəʊldə(r)/ *n.* Felsbrocken, *der*

**'boulder clay** *n.* (*Geol.*) Geschiebelehm, *der;* (*with many boulders*) Blocklehm, *der*

**boulevard** /'bu:ləvɑ:d/ *n.* Boulevard, *der*

**boult** ⇨ **bolt²**

**bounce** /baʊns/ ❶ *v.i.* **A** springen; (*on bumpy road*) ‹Auto:› holpern; **the ball ~d twice** der Ball sprang zweimal auf; **~ up and down on sth.** auf etw. (*Dat.*) herumspringen; **B** (*coll.: be rejected by bank*) ‹Scheck:› platzen(*ugs.*); **it won't ~:** er ist gedeckt; **C** (*rush*) **~ about** herumspringen *od.* -hüpfen; **~ into/out of the room** ins/aus dem Zimmer stürmen; **~ in/out** hereinplatzen/hinausstürzen.

❷ *v.t.* **A** aufspringen lassen ‹Ball›; **he ~d the baby on his knee** er ließ das Kind auf den Knien reiten; **B** (*Amer. coll.: dismiss*) rausschmeißen (*ugs.*); an die Luft setzen (*ugs.*).

❸ *n.* **A** (*rebound*) Aufprall, *der;* **on the ~:** beim Aufprall; **B** (*rebounding power*) ≈ Elastizität, *die;* (*fig.: energy*) Schwung, *der;* **there's plenty of/not much ~ in the ball** der Ball springt sehr gut/nicht besonders gut

~ **'back** *v.i.* zurückprallen; (*fig.*) ‹Person:› [plötzlich] wieder da sein

~ **'off** ❶ *v.i.* abprallen. ❷ *v.t.* **~ sth. off sth.** etw. von etw. abprallen lassen; **~ off sth.** von etw. abprallen; ‹Signal:› von etw. reflektiert werden

**bouncer** /'baʊnsə(r)/ *n.* (*coll.*) **A** Rausschmeißer, *der* (*ugs.*); **B** (*Cricket*) hoch aufspringender Ball

**bouncing** /'baʊnsɪŋ/ *adj.* kräftig; stramm

**bouncy** /'baʊnsɪ/ *adj.* **A** gut springend ‹Ball›; federnd ‹Matratze, Bett›; **B** (*fig.: lively*) munter

**bound¹** /baʊnd/ ❶ *n.* **A** *usu. in pl.* (*limit*) Grenze, *die;* **within the ~s of possibility** *or* **the possible** im Bereich des Möglichen; **keep sth. within ~s** etw. in Grenzen halten; **increase beyond all ~s** über alle Maßen ansteigen; **the ball is out of ~s** der Ball hat die Spielbahn verlassen; **go beyond the ~s of decency** die Grenzen des Anstands verletzen; **sth. is out of ~s [to sb.]** der Zutritt zu etw. ist [für jmdn.] verboten; **the pub is out of ~s** das Betreten des Lokals ist verboten; **beyond the ~s of human knowledge** jenseits der menschlichen Erkenntnisfähigkeit; **there are no ~s to his ambition** sein Ehrgeiz kennt keine Grenzen; **know no ~s** (*fig.*) keine Grenzen kennen; **keep within the ~s of reason/propriety** vernünftig/im Rahmen bleiben; **B** (*of territory*) Grenze, *die;* ⇨ *also* **beat** 1 A.

❷ *v.t., usu. in pass.* begrenzen; **be ~ed by sth.** durch etw. begrenzt werden; **sth. is ~ed by sth.** (*fig.*) einer Sache (*Dat.*) sind durch etw. Grenzen gesetzt

**bound²** ❶ *v.i.* (*spring*) hüpfen; springen; **~ with joy** vor Freude hüpfen; **~ into the room** ins Zimmer stürzen; **the dog came ~ing up** der Hund kam angesprungen. ❷ *n.* (*spring*) Satz, *der;* **at** *or* **with one ~:** mit einem Satz; ⇨ *also* **leap** 3

**bound³** *pred. adj.* ▶1024 **be ~ for home/Frankfurt** auf dem Heimweg/nach Frankfurt unterwegs sein; **homeward ~:** auf dem Weg nach Hause; **where are you ~ for?** wohin geht die Reise?; **all passengers ~ for Zürich** alle Passagiere nach Zürich

**bound⁴** ⇨ **bind** 1, 2

**boundary** /'baʊndərɪ/ *n.* Grenze, *die*

**bounden** /'baʊndn/ *attrib. adj.* **~ duty** Pflicht und Schuldigkeit

**bounder** /'baʊndə(r)/ *n.* (*dated coll.*) Lump, *der* (*abwertend*)

**boundless** /'baʊndlɪs/ *adj.* grenzenlos

**bounteous** /'baʊntɪəs/ *adj.* (*rhet.*) ⇨ **bountiful**

**bountiful** /'baʊntɪfl/ *adj.* (*generous*) großzügig; gütig ‹Gott›; (*plentiful*) reichlich ‹Ernte, Gaben, Ertrag›; **Lady B~:** gute Fee

**bountifully** /'baʊntɪfəlɪ/ *adv.* (*generously*) großzügig; (*plentifully*) reichlich

**bounty** /'baʊntɪ/ *n.* **A** (*reward*) Kopfgeld, *das;* (*for capturing animal*) Fangprämie, *die;* (*for shooting animal*) Abschussprämie, *die;* **B** (*Commerc.*) Subvention, *die;* **C** (*gift*) Gabe, *die*

**bouquet** /bʊ'keɪ, bəʊ'keɪ, 'bu:keɪ/ *n.* **A** (*bunch of flowers*) Bukett, *das;* [Blumen]strauß, *der;* **bride's ~:** Brautstrauß, *der;* Brautbukett, *das;* **B** (*fig.: praise*) **get a ~:** gelobt werden; **he gets all the ~s** ihm gilt alles Lob; **be meant as a ~:** als Kompliment gemeint sein; **C** (*perfume of wine*) Bukett, *das;* Blume, *die*

**bouquet garni** /bʊkeɪ gɑ:'ni:/ *n., pl.* **bouquets garnis** /bʊkeɪ gɑ:'ni:/ (*Cookery*) Kräutersträußchen, *das;* Bouquet garni, *das* (*fachspr.*)

**bourbon** /'bɜ:bən, 'bʊəbən/ *n.* (*Amer.*) **~ [whiskey]** Bourbon, *der*

**bourgeois** /'bʊəʒwɑ:/ ❶ *n., pl. same* **A** (*middle-class person*) Bürger, *der*/Bürgerin, *die;* **the ~** *pl.* die bürgerliche Mittelklasse; **B** (*person with conventional ideas, selfish materialist*) Spießbürger, *der* (*abwertend*); Spießer, *der*/Spießerin, *die* (*abwertend*); **C** (*capitalist*) Bourgeois, *der* (*marx.*).

❷ *adj.* **A** (*middle-class*) bürgerlich; **B** (*conventional, selfishly materialist*) spießbürgerlich (*abwertend*); **C** (*capitalistic*) bourgeois (*marx.*)

**bourgeoisie** /bʊəʒwɑ:'zi:/ *n.* **A** Bürgertum, *das;* **B** (*capitalist class*) Bourgeoisie, *die* (*marx.*)

**bout** /baʊt/ *n.* **A** (*spell*) Periode, *die;* **B** (*contest*) Wettkampf, *der;* **C** (*fit*) Anfall, *der;* **~ of temper** Wutanfall, *der;* **he's out on one of his drinking ~s again** er ist mal wieder auf einer seiner Zechtouren (*ugs.*)

**boutique** /bu:'ti:k/ *n.* Boutique, *die*

**bovine** /'bəʊvaɪn/ *adj.* **A** (*of ox*) Rinder-; **B** (*of genus Bos*) **be a ~ animal** zu den Stirnrindern gehören; **C** (*fig.*) (*heavy*) grob; (*stupid*) erzdumm; (*sluggish*) träge

**bovver** /'bɒvə(r)/ *n.* (*coll.*) Zoff, *der* (*ugs.*)

**bow¹** /bəʊ/ ❶ *n.* **A** (*curve*) Bogen, *der;* **B** (*weapon*) Bogen, *der;* **have two strings to one's ~:** eine Alternative haben; ⇨ *also* **longbow**; **C** ⇨ **saddle-bow**; **D** (*Mus.*) Bogen, *der;* (*stroke*) [Bogen]strich, *der;* **up/down ~:** Auf-/Abstrich, *der;* **E** (*tied knot or ribbon*) Schleife, *die;* **tie the shoelace in a ~:** den Schnürsenkel zu einer Schleife binden; **F** (*Amer.: of spectacle frame*) Bügel, *der.* ❷ *v.t.* streichen ‹Violine, Viola usw.›. ❸ *v.i.* den Bogen führen

**bow²** /baʊ/ ❶ *v.i.* **A** (*submit*) sich beugen (**to** *Dat.*); **B** **~ [down to** *or* **before sb./sth.]** (*bend*) sich [vor jmdm./etw.] verbeugen *od.* verneigen; **C** (*incline head*) **~ [to sb.]** sich [vor jmdm.] verbeugen; **a ~ing acquaintance with sth.** eine flüchtige Bekanntschaft mit etw.; **~ out** sich formell verabschieden; **~ out of sth.** sich von etw. zurückziehen; ⇨ *also* **scrape** 2 E.

❷ *v.t.* **A** (*cause to bend*) beugen; **~ed down by** *or* **with care/responsibilities/age** (*fig.*) von Sorgen/Verpflichtungen niedergedrückt/vom Alter gebeugt; ⇨ *also* **knee** A; **B** (*show by ~ing*) **he ~ed his acknowledgement of the applause** er verbeugte sich zum Dank für den Applaus; **~ sb. in/out** jmdn. unter Verbeugungen hinein-/hinausgeleiten.

❸ *n.* Verbeugung, *die;* **make one's ~** (*make entrance*) sich vorstellen; (*make exit*) sich [formell] verabschieden; **take a ~:** sich [unter Applaus] verbeugen; **they ought to** *or* **can take a ~** (*fig.*) sie verdienen Hochachtung

**bow³** /baʊ/ *n.* (*Naut.*) **A** *usu. in pl.* Bug, *der;* **in the ~s** im Bug; **on the ~:** am Bug; **shot across the ~s** (*fig.*) Schuss vor den Bug (*ugs.*); **B** (*rower*) Bugmann, *der*

**bowdlerize** /'baʊdləraɪz/ *v.t.* zensieren; **a ~d version** eine „gereinigte" Fassung

**bowel** /'baʊəl/ *n.* **A** ▶966 (*Anat.*) **~s** *pl.*, (*Med.*) **~:** Darm, *der;* **B** *in pl.* (*interior*) Innere, *das;* **in the ~s of the library/the earth** in den Katakomben der Bibliothek/im Inneren der Erde

**bower** /baʊə(r)/ *n.* **A** (*enclosed by foliage*) Laube, *die;* (*summer house*) Sommerhaus, *das;* **B** (*poet.*) (*inner room*) Gemach, *das* (*geh.*); (*boudoir*) Boudoir, *das*

**'bowerbird** *n.* Laubenvogel, *der*

**bowl¹** /bəʊl/ *n.* **A** (*basin*) Schüssel, *die;* (*shallower*) Schale, *die;* **mixing/washing-up ~:** Rühr-/Abwaschschüssel, *die;* **soup ~:** Suppentasse, *die;* **sugar ~:** Zuckerdose, *die;* **a ~ of water** eine Schüssel/Schale Wasser; **a ~ of soup** eine Tasse Suppe; **B** (*~-shaped part*) schalenförmiger Teil; (*of WC*) Schüssel, *die;* (*of spoon*) Schöpfteil, *der;* (*of pipe*) [Pfeifen]kopf, *der;* **C** (*amphitheatre*) Freilufttheater, *das;* (*Sport*) Stadion, *das;* **D** (*Amer.: region*) Senke, *die*

**bowl²** ❶ *n.* **A** (*ball*) Kugel, *die;* (*in skittles*) [Kegel]kugel, *die;* (*in tenpin bowling*) [Bowling]kugel, *die;* **B** *in pl.* (*game*) Bowlsspiel, *das;* Bowls, *das.* ❷ *v.i.* **A** (*play ~s*) Bowls spielen; (*play skittles*) kegeln; (*play tenpin bowling*) bowlen; **B** (*go along*) rollen; **~ along** dahinrollen; **C** (*Cricket*) werfen. ❸ *v.t.* **A** (*roll*) rollen lassen; **~ sb./sth. over** jmdn./etw. umwerfen; **~ sb. over** (*fig.*) jmdn. überwältigen *od.* (*ugs.*) umhauen; **B** (*Cricket etc.*) werfen; **~ [down] the wicket**

das Tor einwerfen; **~ the batsman [out]/side out** den Schlagmann/die Mannschaft ausschlagen

**bow** /bəʊ/: **~-'legged** *adj.* krummbeinig; o-beinig (*ugs.*); **be ~-legged** krumme Beine *od.* (*ugs.*) O-Beine haben; **~ 'legs** *n. pl.* krumme Beine; O-Beine *Pl.* (*ugs.*)

**bowler**[1] /'bəʊlə(r)/ *n.* Ⓐ (*Cricket etc.*) Werfer, *der;* Ⓑ (*at bowls*) Bowlsspieler, *der*/Bowlsspielerin, *die;* (*at bowling*) Bowlingspieler, *der*/Bowlingspielerin, *die*

**bowler**[2] *n.* **~ [hat]** Bowler, *der*

**'bowl fire** *n.* Heizsonne, *die*

**bowline** /'bəʊlɪn/ *n.* Ⓐ **~ [knot]** Palstek, *der;* Ⓑ (*Naut.: rope*) Buline, *die* (*Seemannsspr.*)

**bowling** /'bəʊlɪŋ/ *n.* **[tenpin] ~:** Bowling, *das;* **go ~:** bowlen gehen

**bowling: ~ alley** *n.* (*for tenpin ~*) Bowlingbahn, *die;* (*for skittles*) Kegelbahn, *die;* **~ average** ⇒ **average** 1 B; **~ crease** *n.* (*Cricket*) Wurflinie, *die;* **~ green** *n. Rasenfläche für Bowls*

**bowman**[1] /'bəʊmən/ *n., pl.* **bowmen** /'bəʊmən/ (*archer*) Bogenschütze, *der*

**bowman**[2] /'baʊmən/ *n., pl.* **bowmen** /'baʊmən/ (*Naut.*) Bugmann, *der*

**bowser** /'baʊzə(r)/ *n.* (*tanker*) Tankwagen, *der*

**bow: ~sprit** /'bəʊsprɪt/ *n.* (*Naut.*) Bugspriet, *der od. das;* **~string** /'bəʊstrɪŋ/ *n.* Bogensehne, *die;* **~ tie** /bəʊ'taɪ/ *n.* Fliege, *die;* [Smoking-/Frack]schleife, *die;* **~ window** /bəʊ'wɪndəʊ/ *n.* Erkerfenster, *das*

**bow-wow** /'baʊwaʊ/ ❶ *n.* Ⓐ (*dog's bark*) Gebell, *das;* Ⓑ (*child lang.: dog*) Wauwau, *der* (*Kindersprr.*). ❷ *int.* wauwau

**box**[1] /bɒks/ *n.* (*Bot.*) Ⓐ (*tree*) Buchsbaum, *der;* Ⓑ (*wood*) Buchsbaumholz, *das*

**box**[2] ❶ *n.* Ⓐ (*container*) Kasten, *der;* (*bigger*) Kiste, *die;* (*made of cardboard, thin wood, etc.*) Schachtel, *die;* **a ~ of cigars** eine Schachtel Zigarren; **pencil ~:** Federkasten, *der;* **jewellery ~:** Schmuckkasten, *der;* **cigar ~:** Zigarrenkiste, *die;* **cardboard ~:** [Papp]karton, *der;* (*smaller*) [Papp]schachtel, *die;* **shoe~:** Schuhkarton, *der;* **~ of matches** Streichholzschachtel, *die;* Ⓑ (**~ful**) **she emptied the whole ~ of beads on to the floor** sie hat die ganze Schachtel [mit] Perlen auf die Erde geschüttet; Ⓒ **the ~** (*coll.: television*) der Kasten (*ugs. abwertend*); die Flimmerkiste (*scherzh.*); Ⓓ (*coachman's seat*) [Kutsch]bock, *der;* Ⓔ (*at newspaper office*) ≈ Chiffre, *die;* Ⓕ (*in theatre etc.*) Loge, *die;* (*in restaurant etc.*) ≈ Nische, *die;* Ⓖ (*compartment*) **[loose] ~:** Box, *die;* ⇒ *also* **horsebox;** Ⓗ (*country house*) Hütte, *die;* Ⓘ (*casing*) Kasten, *der;* (*cricketer's etc. shield*) ≈ Suspensorium, *das;* Ⓙ (*confined area*) Viereck, *das;* (*enclosed by printed lines*) Kasten, *der;* Ⓚ (*Footb. coll.: penalty area*) Strafraum, *der;* Ⓛ (*Baseball*) Box, *die.*

❷ *v.t.* ⇒ **1** A: [in eine Schachtel/in Schachteln *usw.*] verpacken; **~ the compass** (*Naut.*) alle Kompasspunkte der Reihe nach aufzählen; (*fig.*) einmal die Runde machen

**~ 'in** *v.t.* Ⓐ (*enclose in ~*) in einem Gehäuse unterbringen; Ⓑ (*enclose tightly*) einklemmen; **feel ~ed in** sich eingeengt fühlen

**~ 'up** *v.t.* Ⓐ (*enclose in ~*) ⇒ **~** 1 A: [in eine Schachtel/in Schachteln *usw.*] verpacken; Ⓑ (*confine*) einzwängen; **I'd hate to be ~ed up anywhere with him** ich wäre nur äußerst ungern irgendwo mit ihm eingesperrt

**box**[3] ❶ *n.* (*slap, punch*) Schlag, *der;* **he gave him a ~ on the ear[s]** er gab ihm eine Ohrfeige. ❷ *v.t.* Ⓐ (*slap, punch*) schlagen; **he ~ed his ears** *or* **him round the ears** er ohrfeigte ihn; **get one's ears ~ed** eine Ohrfeige bekommen; Ⓑ (*fight with fists*) **~ sb.** gegen jmdn. boxen. ❸ *v.i.* boxen (**with, against** gegen); **~ clever** (*coll.*) auf Draht sein (*ugs.*)

**Box and Cox** /bɒks ənd 'kɒks/ *n.* (*two persons who take turns*) **like ~:** im ständigen Wechsel; **be like ~:** sich ständig abwechseln

**box: ~ barrage** *n.* Sperrfeuer, *das;* **~ camera** *n.* Box, *die;* **~car** *n.* (*Amer. Railw.*) gedeckter [Güter]wagen

**boxer** /'bɒksə(r)/ *n.* Ⓐ ▶1261 Boxer, *der;* Ⓑ (*dog*) Boxer, *der*

**'boxer shorts** *n. pl.* Boxershorts *Pl.*

**boxful** /'bɒksfʊl/ *n.* **a ~ of chocolates** *etc.* eine [ganze] Schachtel Pralinen *usw.*

**'box girder** *n.* Kastenträger, *der* (*Technik*)

**boxing** /'bɒksɪŋ/ *n.* Boxen, *das;* **professional/amateur ~:** Berufs-/Amateurboxen, *das*

**boxing: B~ Day** *n.* (*Brit.*) zweiter Weihnachtsfeiertag; **~ glove** *n.* Boxhandschuh, *der;* **~ match** *n.* Boxkampf, *der;* **~ ring** *n.* Boxring, *der*

**box: ~ junction** *n.* (*Brit.*) *gelb markierter Kreuzungsbereich, in den man bei Stau nicht einfahren darf;* **~-kite** *n.* Kastendrachen, *der;* **~ number** *n.* (*at newspaper office*) Chiffre, *die;* (*at post office*) Postfach, *das;* **my post office ~ number is ...:** meine Postfachnummer ist ...; **~ office** *n.* Kasse, *die;* (*fig.*) **be ~ office, be a ~ office success** ein Kassenerfolg sein; **be good/bad ~ office** gut/schlecht ankommen (**among** bei); **~ pew** *n.* geschlossener Chorstuhl; **~-pleat** *n.* Quetschfalte, *die;* **~room** *n.* (*Brit.*) Abstellraum, *der;* **~ score** *n.* [tabellarischer] Spielbericht; ≈ Spielbogen, *der;* **~-spanner** *n.* (*Brit.*) Steckschlüssel, *der;* **~-spring** *n.* Sprungfeder, *die;* **~wood** ⇒ **box**[1] B

**boy** /bɔɪ/ ❶ *n.* Ⓐ Junge, *der;* **baby ~:** kleiner Junge; **~s' school** Jungenschule, *die;* **a ~'s name** ein Jungenname; **a little Italian ~:** ein kleiner Italiener; **[my] ~** (*as address*) [mein] Junge; **here/sit/come on ~!** (*to dog*) hier!/sitz!/komm!; **good ~!** (*to dog*) guter Hund!; **the ~s** (*male friends*) die Kumpels (*salopp*); **come on, ~s!** los, Jungs!; **~s will be ~s** so sind Jungs/Männer nun mal; **jobs for the ~s** Vetternwirtschaft, *die* (*abwertend*); **the Smith ~s** die Jungen von Smiths; ⇒ *also* **old boy;** Ⓑ (*servant*) Boy, *der.* ❷ *int.* **[oh] ~:** Junge, Junge! (*ugs.*)

**boy-and-'girl** *adj.* teenagerhaft; Teenager‹romanze, -liebe›

**'boy band** *n.* Boyband, *die*

**boycott** /'bɔɪkɒt/ ❶ *v.t.* boykottieren. ❷ *n.* Boykott, *der*

**'boyfriend** *n.* Freund, *der*

**boyhood** /'bɔɪhʊd/ *n.* Kindheit, *die*

**boyish** /'bɔɪɪʃ/ *adj.* jungenhaft; **she had a ~ haircut/figure** sie hatte einen Knabenhaarschnitt/eine knabenhafte Figur

**Boyle's Law** /'bɔɪlz lɔː/ *n.* (*Phys.*) Boyle-Mariotte-Gesetz, *das*

**boy: ~meets-'girl** *attrib. adj.* Liebes‹geschichte, -film›; **~ 'scout** ⇒ **scout**[1] 1 A

**bozo** /'bəʊzəʊ/ *n.* (*esp. Amer. coll.*) Trottel, *der* (*ugs. abwertend*)

**BP** *abbr.* Ⓐ **boiling point** SP; Ⓑ **British Petroleum** BP; Ⓒ (*Med.*) **British Pharmacopoeia** *amtliches britisches Arzneimittelverzeichnis*

**Bp.** *abbr.* **bishop** Bf.

**BR** *abbr.* (*Hist.*) **British Rail[ways]** *britische Eisenbahngesellschaft*

**bra** /brɑː/ *n.* BH, *der* (*ugs.*)

**Br.** *abbr.* Ⓐ **British** brit.; Ⓑ **Brother** Br.

**brace** /breɪs/ ❶ *n.* Ⓐ (*buckle*) Schnalle, *die;* (*connecting piece*) Klammer, *die;* (*Dent.*) [Zahn]spange, *die;* [Zahn]klammer, *die;* Ⓑ *in pl.* (*trouser straps*) Hosenträger; Ⓒ *pl. same* (*pair*) **a/two ~ of** zwei/vier; (*derog.*) **a ~ of twins/servants** ein Zwillings-/Dienerpaar; Ⓓ (*Printing, Mus.*) geschweifte Klammer; Akkolade, *die;* Ⓔ (*strut*) Strebe, *die;* Ⓕ (*Naut.*) Brasse, *die.* ⇒ *also* **brace and bit.**

❷ *v.t.* Ⓐ (*fasten*) befestigen; (*stretch*) spannen; (*string up*) anspannen; (*with struts*) stützen; **~ up one's courage** seinen ganzen Mut zusammennehmen; Ⓑ (*support*) stützen; Ⓒ (*Naut.*) brassen.

❸ *v. refl.* **~ oneself** (*lit. & fig.*) sich zusammennehmen; **~ oneself [up] for sth.** (*fig.*) sich auf etw. (*Akk.*) [innerlich] vorbereiten

**brace and 'bit** *n.* Bohrwinde, *die*

**bracelet** /'breɪslɪt/ *n.* Ⓐ (*band*) Armband, *das;* (*chain*) Kettchen, *das;* (*bangle*) Armreif, *der;* Ⓑ *in pl.* (*coll.: handcuffs*) Brasselett, *das* (*Gaunerspr.*)

**bracer** /'breɪsə(r)/ (*coll.: tonic*) Muntermacher, *der* (*ugs. scherzh.*)

**brachial** /'breɪkɪəl/ *adj.* (*Anat.*) brachial

**bracing** /'breɪsɪŋ/ *adj.* belebend

**bracken** /'brækn/ *n.* [Adler]farn, *der*

**bracket** /'brækɪt/ ❶ *n.* Ⓐ (*support, projection*) Konsole, *die;* (*of iron*) Krageisen, *das;* (*of stone*) Kragstein, *der;* (*lamp support*) Lampenhalter, *der;* Ⓑ (*mark*) Klammer, *die;* **open/close ~s** Klammer auf/zu; Ⓒ (*group*) Gruppe, *die;* **social ~:** Gesellschaftsschicht, *die.* ❷ *v.t.* Ⓐ (*enclose in ~s*) einklammern; Ⓑ (*couple with brace*) mit einer Klammer verbinden; (*fig.*) in Verbindung bringen

**brackish** /'brækɪʃ/ *adj.* brackig

**bract** /brækt/ *n.* (*Bot.*) Braktee, *die*

**brad** /bræd/ *n.* [flacher] Drahtstift

**bradawl** /'brædɔːl/ *n.* [flache] Ahle

**brae** /breɪ/ *n.* (*Scot.*) (*bank*) [Ufer]böschung, *die;* (*hillside*) Hang, *der*

**brag** /bræg/ ❶ *n.* (*boast, boasting*) Prahlerei, *die;* **his ~ is that ...:** er prahlt damit, dass ... ❷ *v.i.*, **-gg-** prahlen (**about** mit). ❸ *v.t.*, **-gg-** prahlen; **he ~s that he has a Rolls Royce** er prahlt damit, dass er einen Rolls-Royce hat

**braggart** /'brægət/ ❶ *n.* Prahler, *der*/Prahlerin, *die.* ❷ *adj.* prahlerisch

**brahmin** /'brɑːmɪn/ *n.* Brahmane, *der*

**brahminism** /'brɑːmɪnɪzm/ *n.* Brahmanismus, *der*

**braid** /breɪd/ ❶ *n.* Ⓐ (*plait*) Flechte, *die* (*geh.*); Zopf, *der;* (*band entwined with hair*) Haarband, *das;* Flechtband, *das* (*veralt.*); Ⓑ (*decorative woven band*) Borte, *die;* Ⓒ (*on uniform*) Litze, *die;* (*with metal threads*) Tresse, die. ❷ *v.t.* Ⓐ (*plait; arrange in ~s*) flechten; Ⓑ zusammenbinden ‹Haare›; Ⓒ (*trim with ~*) mit Borten/Litzen/Tressen besetzen

**braiding** /'breɪdɪŋ/ *n.* (*bands*) Bänder; (*decorative woven bands*) Borten

**Braille** /breɪl/ *n.* Blindenschrift, *die*

**brain** /breɪn/ ❶ *n.* Ⓐ ▶966 Gehirn, *das;* **have [got] sex/food/money on the ~:** nur Sex/Essen/Geld im Kopf haben; **he's got her on the ~:** sie geht ihm nicht aus dem Kopf; **use your ~[s]** gebrauch deinen Verstand; **he's got a good ~:** er ist ein kluger Kopf; **you need ~s for that** dafür braucht man Verstand; **he didn't have the ~s to do it** er war zu dumm, es zu tun; **~ versus brawn** Köpfchen gegen Muskelkraft; **get your ~ in gear before opening your mouth!** (*coll.*) schalt erst mal dein Gehirn ein, bevor du den Mund aufmachst!; **I need a cup of strong coffee in the morning to help me get my ~ in gear** (*coll.*) ich brauche morgens eine Tasse starken Kaffee, um wach zu werden; ⇒ *also* **rack**[1] 2 C; Ⓑ *in pl.* (*Gastr.*) Hirn, *das;* Ⓒ (*coll.: clever person*) **she's the ~[s] of the class** sie ist die Intelligenteste in der Klasse; **he's a terrific ~:** er ist wahnsinnig intelligent (*ugs.*); **the ~ behind the business** der Kopf des Unternehmens.

❷ *v.t.* den Schädel einschlagen (+ *Dat.*); **I'll ~ you!** (*coll.*) du kriegst gleich eins auf die Rübe! (*ugs.*)

**brain: ~child** *n.* (*coll.*) Geistesprodukt, *das;* **that system was my own ~child** ich war der geistige Vater dieses Systems; **~-dead** *adj.* Ⓐ (*Med.*) hirntot; Ⓑ (*coll. derog.*) hirnlos (*abwertend*) ‹Person›; hirnverbrannt (*abwertend*), hirnrissig (*abwertend*) ‹Ansicht, Idee›; **~ drain** *n.* (*coll.*) Abwanderung [von Wissenschaftlern]; Braindrain, *der*

**brainless** /'breɪnlɪs/ *adj.* (*stupid*) hirnlos

**brain: ~ power** *n.* geistige Leistung; **his ~ power will get him far** mit seiner Intelligenz wird er es weit bringen; **~stem** *n.* ▶1261 (*Anat.*) Hirnstamm, *der;* **~storm** *n.* Ⓐ Anfall geistiger Umnachtung; Ⓑ (*Amer. coll.*) ⇒ **~wave** B; **~storming** *n.*

b

Brainstorming, *das;* ~**s trust** *n.* Expertengremium, *das;* ~ **surgeon** *n.* Gehirnchirurg, *der;* ~**-teaser** *n.* Denk[sport]aufgabe, *die;* ~ **trust** *n.* (*Amer.*) [beratendes] Expertengremium; Braintrust, *der;* ~ **tumour** *n.* Gehirntumor, *der;* ~**-twister** ⇒ ~**-teaser**; ~**wash** *v.t.* einer Gehirnwäsche unterziehen; ~**wash sb. into doing sth.** jmdm. [ständig] einreden, etw. zu tun; ~**washing** *n.* Gehirnwäsche, *die;* ~**wave** *n.* Ⓐ (*Physiol.*) Hirnstromwelle, *die;* Ⓑ (*coll.: inspiration*) genialer Einfall; ~**work** *n.* Kopfarbeit, *die*

**brainy** /'breɪnɪ/ *adj.* intelligent

**braise** /breɪz/ *v.t.* (*Cookery*) schmoren

**brake**[1] /breɪk/ ❶ *n.* (*apparatus; coll.: pedal etc.*) Bremse, *die;* **sth. acts as a ~ on sth.** etw. bremst etw.; **apply** *or* **put on the ~s** die Bremse betätigen; (*fig.*) zurückstecken; **put the ~[s] on sth.** (*fig.*) etw. bremsen; **put the ~[s] on spending** die Ausgaben einschränken. ❷ *v.t. & i.* bremsen; ~ **hard** scharf bremsen

**brake**[2] *n.* (*Bot.*) Adlerfarn, *der*

**brake**[3] *n.* (*thicket*) Dickicht, *das*

**brake**[4] *n.* Ⓐ (*wagonette*) Break, *der od. das;* Ⓑ (*estate car*) Kombi[wagen], *der*

**brake:** ~ **block** *n.* Bremsklotz, *der;* ~ **cable** *n.* Bremszug, *der;* Bremsseil, *das;* ~ **drum** *n.* Bremstrommel, *die;* ~ **fluid** *n.* Bremsflüssigkeit, *die;* ~ **horsepower** *n.* Bremsleistung, *die;* Nutzleistung, *die;* ~ **light** *n.* Bremslicht, *das;* ~ **lining** *n.* Bremsbelag, *der;* ~ **pad** *n.* Bremsbelag, *der;* ~ **shoe** *n.* Bremsbacke, *die;* ~**-van** *n.* (*Railw.*) Bremswagen, *der*

**braking** /'breɪkɪŋ/ *n.* Bremsen, *das*

'**braking distance** *n.* Bremsweg, *der*

**bramble** /'bræmbl/ *n.* Ⓐ (*shrub*) Dornenstrauch, *der;* (*blackberry bush*) Brombeerstrauch, *der;* Ⓑ (*fruit*) Brombeere, *die*

**Bramley** /'bræmlɪ/ *n. englischer Kochapfel*

**bran** /bræn/ *n.* Kleie, *die*

**branch** /brɑːnʃ/ ❶ *n.* Ⓐ (*bough*) Ast, *der;* (*twig*) Zweig, *der;* Ⓑ (*of nerve, artery, antlers*) Ast, *der;* (*of river*) [Neben]arm, *der;* (*of road, pipe, circuit*) Abzweigung, *die;* (*of railway*) Nebenstrecke, *die;* (*of family* [*of languages*], *subject*) Zweig, *der;* (*local establishment*) Zweigstelle, *die;* (*shop*) Filiale, *die.* ❷ *v.i.* Ⓐ sich verzweigen; Ⓑ (*tend*) ~ **away from sth.** sich von etw. wegentwickeln; Ⓒ (*diverge*) ~ **into sth.** sich in etw. (*Akk.*) aufspalten

~ '**forth** ⇒ ~ 2 A

~ '**off** *v.i.* abzweigen; (*fig.*) sich abspalten

~ '**out** *v.i.* Ⓐ ⇒ ~ 2 A; Ⓑ (~ *off*) abzweigen (**from** von); Ⓒ (*fig.*) ~ **out into sth.** sich auch mit etw. befassen; ~ **out on one's own** sich selbstständig machen

**branch:** ~ **line** *n.* (*Railw.*) Nebenstrecke, *die;* ~ **manager** *n.* ▶ 1261 Filialleiter, *der*/-leiterin, *die;* ~ **office** *n.* Zweigstelle, *die*

**brand** /brænd/ ❶ *n.* Ⓐ (*trade mark*) Markenzeichen, *das;* (*goods of particular make*) Marke, *die;* (*fig.: type*) Art, *die;* ~ **of washing powder/soap** Waschpulvermarke, *die*/Seifenmarke, *die;* Ⓑ (*permanent mark, stigma*) Brandmal, *das;* (*on sheep, cattle*) Brandzeichen, *das;* (*on cigar box, crate*) eingebranntes Zeichen; ~ **of Cain** Kainsmal, *das;* Ⓒ (*burning log etc.*) [Feuer]brand, *der* (*veralt.*); (*charred log etc.*) verkohltes Holzscheit; (*poet.: torch*) Brand, *der* (*geh.*); Ⓓ (*Bot.: blight*) Brand, *der;* Ⓔ (*poet.: sword*) Schwert, *das.*

❷ *v.t.* Ⓐ (*burn*) mit einem Brandzeichen markieren ‹Tier›; Ⓑ (*stigmatize* [*as*]) ~ [**as**] brandmarken als ‹Verräter, Verbrecher usw.›; Ⓒ (*Brit.: label with trade mark*) mit einem Markenzeichen versehen; ~**ed goods** Markenware, *die;* Ⓓ (*impress*) einbrennen (**upon** *Dat. od.* in + *Akk.*)

**brand:** ~ **awareness** *n.* Markenbewusstsein, *das;* ~ **image** *n.* Markenimage, *das*

'**branding iron** *n.* Brandeisen, *das*

**brandish** /'brændɪʃ/ *v.t.* schwenken; schwingen ‹Waffe›

**brand:** ~ **leader** *n.* (*product*) marktführendes Produkt; (*company*) Marktführer, *der;* (*brand*) führende Marke; ~ **name** *n.* Markenname, *der;* ~**-'new** *adj.* nagelneu (*ugs.*); brandneu (*ugs.*); **is the car ~-new?** ist der Wagen [fabrik]neu?

**brandy** /'brændɪ/ *n.* Weinbrand, *der*

**brandy:** ~ **ball** *n.* (*Brit.*) Weinbrandtrüffel, *die;* ~ **butter** *n.* ≈ Kognakbutter, *die; Creme aus Butter, Zucker und Brandy;* ~ **snap** *n. mit Schlagsahne gefülltes knuspriges Röllchen mit Ingwergeschmack*

**brant** /brænt/ (*Amer.*) ⇒ **brent**

'**bran tub** *n. mit Kleie o. ä. gefüllte Kiste, aus der man Geschenke herausfischen kann*

**brash**[1] /bræʃ/ *adj.* Ⓐ (*self-assertive*) dreist; (*garish*) auffällig ‹Kleidung›; knallig ‹Farbe›; Ⓑ (*rash*) unüberlegt

**brash**[2] *n.* Ⓐ (*loose rock*) [**stone**] ~: Trümmergestein, *das;* Ⓑ (*loose ice*) Eistrümmer *Pl.*

**brash**[3] *n.* (*Med.*) saures Aufstoßen

**brashly** /'bræʃlɪ/ *adv.* ⇒ **brash**[1]: dreist; auffällig; unüberlegt

**brashness** /'bræʃnɪs/ *n., no pl.* ⇒ **brash**[1]: Dreistigkeit, *die;* Unüberlegtheit, *die*

**brass** /brɑːs/ ❶ *n.* Ⓐ Messing, *das;* **do sth. as bold as ~:** die Unverfrorenheit haben, etw. zu tun; Ⓑ (*inscribed tablet*) Grabplatte aus Messing; Ⓒ [**horse**] ~**es** Messinggeschirr, *das;* Ⓓ **the** ~ (*Mus.*) das Blech (*fachspr.*); die Blechbläser; Ⓔ ⇒ **brassware**; Ⓕ *no pl., no indef. art.* (*Brit. coll.: money*) Kies, *der* (*salopp*); Ⓖ [**top**] ~ (*coll.: officers, leaders of industry etc.*) hohe Tiere (*ugs.*). ❷ *attrib. adj.* Messing-; ~ **player** (*Mus.*) Blechbläser, *der.* ❸ *v.t.* **be ~ed off** [**doing sth.**] (*coll.*) es satt haben[, etw. zu tun] (*ugs.*); **be ~ed off with** *or* **about sb./sth.** (*coll.*) jmdn./etw. satt haben (*ugs.*)

**brass** '**band** *n.* Blaskapelle, *die*

**brasserie** /'bræsərɪ/ *n.* Bierlokal, *das;* (*more fashionable*) Brasserie, *die*

**brass:** ~ '**farthing** *n.* **not a ~ farthing** kein Pfennig (*ugs.*); **he doesn't care a ~ farthing about it** es interessiert ihn nicht für fünf Pfennige (*ugs.*); ~ **hat** *n.* (*coll.*) hohes Tier (*ugs.*)

**brassica** /'bræsɪkə/ *n.* (*Bot.*) Kohlpflanze, *die;* Brassica, *die* (*Bot.*)

**brassière** /'bræsːeə(r), 'bræzjə(r)/ *n.* (*formal*) Büstenhalter, *der*

**brass:** ~ '**plate** *n.* Messingschild, *das;* ~ **rubbing** *n.* Ⓐ *no pl., no indef. art.* Frottage, *die* (*von Messingtafeln*); (*impression*) Frottage, *die* (*einer Messingtafel*); ~ '**tacks** *n. pl.* **get** *or* **come down to ~ tacks** (*coll.*) zur Sache kommen; ~**ware** *n., no pl.* Messingteile; (*utensils, candlesticks, etc.*) Messinggerät, *das*

**brassy** /'brɑːsɪ/ *adj.* Ⓐ (*in colour*) messing-; (*in sound*) blechern; Ⓑ (*impudent*) dreist; (*pretentious*) auffällig

**brat** /bræt/ *n.* (*derog.: child*) Balg, *das od. der* (*ugs., meist abwertend*); (*young rascal*) Flegel, *der*

**bravado** /brə'vɑːdəʊ/ *n., pl.* ~**es** *or* ~**s** Mut, *der;* **be full of ~:** sehr mutig tun; **do sth. out of ~:** so waghalsig sein, etw. zu tun; (*as pretence*) den starken Mann markieren wollen und etw. tun (*ugs.*)

**brave** /breɪv/ ❶ *adj.* Ⓐ mutig; (*able to endure sth.*) tapfer; **be ~!** nur Mut!/sei tapfer!; Ⓑ (*literary: splendid*) stattlich; prachtvoll; **make a ~ show** einen prächtigen Anblick bieten; **a ~ new world** eine schöne neue Welt. ❷ *n.* [indianischer] Krieger. ❸ *v.t.* trotzen (+ *Dat.*); mutig gegenübertreten (+ *Dat.*) ‹Kritiker, Interviewer›; ~ **it out** sich durch nichts einschüchtern lassen

**bravely** /'breɪvlɪ/ *adv.* Ⓐ mutig; (*showing endurance*) tapfer; Ⓑ (*literary: splendidly*) stattlich; prachtvoll

**bravery** /'breɪvərɪ/ *n., no pl.* Mut, *der;* (*endurance*) Tapferkeit, *die*

**bravo** /brɑː'vəʊ/ *int.* bravo; **shouts of '~'** Bravorufe

**bravura** /brə'vʊərə/ *n.* Bravour, *die;* ~ **piece/passage** (*Mus.*) Bravourstück, *das*

**braw** /brɔː/ *adj.* (*Scot.*) schön

**brawl** /brɔːl/ ❶ *v.i.* Ⓐ sich schlagen; Ⓑ ‹Bach:› rauschen. ❷ *n.* Schlägerei, *die*

**brawn** /brɔːn/ *n.* Ⓐ (*muscle*) Muskel, *der;* (*muscularity*) Muskeln; **he's got some ~:** er hat ganz schön starke Muskeln; **you need a bit of ~ for that** dafür brauchst du schon ein paar Muskeln; ⇒ *also* **brain** 1 A; Ⓑ (*chopped pig's head*) ≈ Presskopf, *der;* (*in aspic jelly*) Schweinskopfsülze, *die*

**brawny** /'brɔːnɪ/ *adj.* muskulös

**bray** /breɪ/ ❶ *n.* (*of ass*) Iah, *das.* ❷ *v.i.* ‹Esel:› iahen, schreien; ‹Person:› wiehern

**braze** /breɪz/ ❶ *v.t.* [hart]löten. ❷ *n.* [Hart]lötung, *die*

**brazen** /'breɪzn/ ❶ *adj.* Ⓐ dreist; (*shameless*) schamlos; Ⓑ (*of brass*) Messing-; aus Messing *nachgestellt;* messingen (*selten*); Ⓒ (*harsh-sounding*) metallisch; Ⓓ (*brass-coloured*) ~ [**yellow**] messinggelb; **a ~ yellow** ein Messinggelb. ❷ *v.t.* ~ [**out**] trotzen (+ *Dat.*); ~ **it out** (*deny guilt*) es abstreiten; (*not admit guilt*) es nicht zugeben

'**brazen-faced** ⇒ **brazen** 1 A

**brazenly** /'breɪznlɪ/ *adv.* dreist; (*shamelessly*) schamlos

**brazenness** /'breɪznnɪs/ *n., no pl.* Dreistigkeit, *die;* (*shamelessness*) Schamlosigkeit, *die*

**brazier** /'breɪzɪə(r), 'breɪʒə(r)/ *n.* Kohlenbecken, *das*

**Brazil** /brə'zɪl/ *n.* Ⓐ *pr. n.* Brasilien (*das*); Ⓑ ⇒ **Brazil nut**

**Brazilian** /brə'zɪlɪən/ ▶ 1340 ❶ *adj.* brasilianisch; **sb. is ~:** jmd. ist Brasilianer/Brasilianerin. ❷ *n.* Brasilianer, *der*/Brasilianerin, *die*

**Bra'zil nut** *n.* Paranuss, *die*

**breach** /briːtʃ/ ❶ *n.* Ⓐ (*violation*) Verstoß, *der* (**of** gegen); ~ **of faith/duty** Vertrauensbruch, *der*/Pflichtverletzung, *die;* ~ **of the peace** Störung von Ruhe und Ordnung; (*by noise only*) ruhestörender Lärm; ~ **of contract** Vertragsbruch, *der;* ~ **of promise** Wortbruch, *der;* (*Law Hist.: breaking off an engagement to marry*) Bruch des Eheversprechens; **be in ~ of the regulations** gegen die Verordnungen verstoßen; Ⓑ (*of relations*) Bruch, *der;* ~ **of diplomatic relations** Abbruch der diplomatischen Beziehungen; Ⓒ (*gap*) Bresche, *die;* (*fig.*) Riss, *der;* **stand in the ~** (*fig.*) in der Schusslinie stehen; **step into the ~** (*fig.*) in die Bresche treten *od.* springen.

❷ *v.t.* eine Bresche schlagen in (+ *Akk.*); **the wall/dike was ~ed** in die Mauer wurde eine Bresche geschlagen/der Deich wurde durchbrochen

**bread** /bred/ ❶ *n.* Ⓐ Brot, *das;* **a piece of ~ and butter** ein Butterbrot; [**some**] ~ **and butter** [ein paar] Butterbrote; ~ **and butter** (*fig.*) tägliches Brot; **quarrel with one's ~ and butter** (*fig.*) an dem Ast sägen, auf dem man sitzt; ~ **and circuses** Brot und Spiele; ~ **and milk** heiße Milch mit eingebrocktem Brot; ~ **and water** (*lit. or fig.*) Wasser und Brot; **have one's ~ buttered on both sides** es in jeder Hinsicht gut getroffen haben; **know which side one's ~ is buttered** wissen, wo etwas zu holen ist; ⇒ *also* **water** 1 B; Ⓑ (*necessary food*) [**daily**] ~: [tägliches] Brot; **break ~ [with sb.]** (*arch.*) das Brot [mit jmdm.] brechen; **eat the ~ of idleness** (*literary*) müßig gehen (*geh.*); **take the ~ out of sb.'s mouth** (*fig.*) jmdn. seiner Existenzgrundlage berauben; Ⓒ (*coll.: money*) Kies, *der* (*salopp*).

❷ *v.t.* panieren

**bread:** ~**-and-butter** '**pudding** *n.* Brot-und-Butter-Pudding, *der; Auflauf aus Brot, Butter, Zucker, Rosinen usw.;* ~ **bin** *n.* Brotkasten, *der;* ~**board** *n.* [Brot]brett, *das;* ~**crumb** *n.* Brotkrume, *die;* ~**crumbs** (*for coating e.g. fish*) Paniermehl, *das;* ~**fruit** *n.* Brotfrucht, *die;* ~ **knife** *n.* Brotmesser, *das;* ~**line** *n.* (*Amer.*) *Warteschlange bei der Ausgabe kostenloser Nahrungsmittel an Bedürftige;* **live on/below the ~line** (*fig.*) gerade noch/nicht einmal mehr das Notwendigste zum Leben haben; ~ '**roll** *n.* Brötchen, *das;* ~ '**sauce** *n.* (*Gastr.*) [englische] Brotsauce (*Kochk.*); ~**stick** *n. stangenförmiges Gebäck aus Brotteig*

**breadth** /bredθ/ *n.* **A** ▶**1284** | (*broadness*) Breite, *die;* **what is the ~ of ...?** wie breit ist ...?; **be 20 metres in ~:** 20 Meter breit sein; **B** (*extent*) Weite, *die;* (*range*) **with his ~ of experience/knowledge** bei seiner großen Erfahrung/bei seiner umfassenden Kenntnis; **~ of mind/vision** *etc.* (*fig.*) große Aufgeschlossenheit/Einbildungskraft *usw.*

**bread: ~ tin** Brotbüchse, *die;* **~winner** *n.* Ernährer, *der*/Ernährerin *die*

**break**[1] /breɪk/ ❶ *v.t.*, **broke** /brəʊk/, **broken** /ˈbrəʊkn/ **A** brechen; (*so as to damage*) zerbrechen; kaputtmachen (*ugs.*); aufschlagen ‹Ei zum Kochen›; zerstören ‹Ufer›; zerreißen ‹Seil›; (*fig.: interrupt*) unterbrechen; brechen ‹Bann, Zauber, Schweigen›; **~ sth. in two/in pieces** etw. in zwei Teile/in Stücke brechen; **~ the set** Teile des Satzes einzeln abgeben; **the TV/my watch is broken** der Fernseher/meine Uhr ist kaputt (*ugs.*); **B** (*crack*) zerbrechen; zertrümmern ‹Fundament, Schiffsrumpf›; **C** (*fracture*) sich (*Dat.*) brechen; (*pierce*) verletzen ‹Haut›; **he broke his leg** er hat sich (*Dat.*) das Bein gebrochen; **sth. ~s no bones** (*fig.*) etw. ist nicht so schlimm; **no ~s broken** (*fig.*) es ist nichts passiert; **~ one's/sb.'s back** (*fig.*) sich/jmdn. kaputtmachen (*ugs.*); **~ one's back** (*fig.*) sich abstrampeln (*ugs.*); **~ the back of sth.** (*fig.*) bei etw. das Schwerste hinter sich bringen; **~ a tooth** sich (*Dat.*) ein Stück vom Zahn abbrechen; **~ open** aufbrechen; **D** (*violate*) brechen ‹Vertrag, Versprechen›; verletzen, verstoßen gegen ‹Regel, Tradition›; nicht einhalten ‹Verabredung›; überschreiten ‹Grenze›; **~ the law** gegen das Gesetz verstoßen; **E** (*destroy*) zerstören, ruinieren ‹Freundschaft, Ehe›; **F** (*surpass*) brechen ‹Rekord›; **G** (*abscond from*) **~ jail** [aus dem Gefängnis] ausbrechen; **~ the bounds** ausreißen; **~ ship** sich beim Landgang absetzen (*ugs.*); ⇒ *also* **cover** 1 J; **H** (*weaken*) brechen, beugen ‹Stolz›; (*quash*) niederschlagen ‹Rebellion, Aufstand›; zusammenbrechen lassen ‹Streik›; **~ sb.'s spirit** jmds. Lebensmut brechen; **~ sb.'s heart** jmdm. das Herz brechen; **it broke my heart** es brach mir das Herz; **~ sb.** (*crush*) jmdn. fertig machen (*ugs.*); **~ a horse [to the rein]** ein Pferd zureiten; **~ the habit** es sich (*Dat.*) abgewöhnen; **~ the smoking/drinking habit** sich (*Dat.*) das Rauchen/Trinken abgewöhnen; **~ sb. of the smoking habit** jmdm. das Rauchen abgewöhnen; ⇒ *also* **make** 1 P; **I** (*cushion*) auffangen ‹Schlag, jmds. Fall›; abschwächen ‹Wind›; **J** (*make bankrupt*) ruinieren; **~ the bank** die Bank sprengen; **you mustn't ~ the bank** (*fig. coll.*) (*spend a lot*) du darfst dich nicht in Unkosten stürzen; (*ruin yourself*) du darfst dich nicht finanziell ruinieren; **it won't ~ the bank** (*fig. coll.*) es kostet kein Vermögen; **K** (*reveal*) **~ the news that ...:** melden, dass ...; **~ the glad/bad news to sb. that ...:** jmdm. die frohe Nachricht mitteilen/jmdm. die schlechte Nachricht beibringen, dass ...; **I don't know how to ~ this news to you, but ...:** ich weiß nicht, wie ich dir das sagen soll, aber ...; **L** (*use part of*) anbrechen ‹Banknote›; **M** (*unfurl*) entfalten ‹Fahne›; **N** (*solve*) entschlüsseln, entziffern ‹Kode, Geheimschrift›; **O** (*disprove*) entkräften ‹Alibi›; **P** (*Tennis*) **~ service/sb.'s service** den Aufschlag des Gegners/jmds. Aufschlag durchbrechen. ⇒ *also* **broken** 2; **wind**[1] 1 E.

❷ *v.i.*, **broke, broken** **A** kaputtgehen (*ugs.*); entzweigehen; ‹Faden, Seil:› [zer]reißen; ‹Glas, Tasse, Teller:› zerbrechen; ‹Eis:› brechen; (*fig.: be interrupted*) unterbrochen werden; **sb.'s heart is ~ing** jmdm. bricht das Herz; **~ in two/in pieces** entzweibrechen; **the chocolate ~s easily** die Schokolade bricht sich leicht; **B** (*crack*) ‹Fenster-, Glasscheibe:› zerspringen; **the bows of the ship broke against** *or* **on the rocks** der Bug des Schiffes zerschellte an den Felsen; **my back was nearly ~ing** ich brach mir fast das Kreuz; **C** (*be destroyed*) ‹Freundschaft, Ehe, Bündnis:› zerbrechen; ‹Familienbande:› zerreißen; **D** (*sever links*) **~ with sb./sth.** mit jmdm./etw. brechen; **E** (*weaken*) gebrochen werden; **until he/his will ~s** bis er zusammenbricht/sein Wille gebrochen ist; **F ~ into** einbrechen in (+ *Akk.*) ‹Haus›; aufbrechen ‹Safe›; **~ into laughter/tears** in Gelächter/Tränen ausbrechen; **he broke into a sweat** ihm brach der Schweiß aus; **~ into a trot/run** *etc.* zu traben/laufen *usw.* anfangen; **sb. ~s into acting/industry** (*coll.*) jmdm. gelingt der Durchbruch in der Schauspielerei/in der Industrie; **~ into one's capital** sein Kapital angreifen; **~ into a banknote** eine Banknote anbrechen; **~ out of prison** *etc.* aus dem Gefängnis *usw.* ausbrechen; **G** (*escape*) **~ free** *or* **loose [from sb./sb.'s grip]** sich [von jmdm./aus jmds. Griff] losreißen; **~ free/loose [from prison]** [aus dem Gefängnis] ausbrechen; **some planks had broken loose** einige Planken waren losgebrochen; **H** ‹Welle:› sich brechen **(on/against** an + *Dat.*), branden **(on/against** an + *Akk.*/gegen); **I** ‹Wetter:› umschlagen; **J** ‹Wolkendecke:› aufreißen; **K** ‹Tag:› anbrechen; **L** ‹Sturm:› losbrechen; **M** (*disperse*) ‹Truppen:› auseinander laufen; **N** (*change tone*) **sb.'s voice ~s** jmd. kommt in den Stimmbruch; (*with emotion*) jmdm. bricht die Stimme; **O** (*Boxing*) sich aus dem Clinch lösen; **~!** break!; **P** (*have interval*) **~ for coffee/lunch** [eine] Kaffee-/Mittagspause machen; **we'll ~ for five minutes** wir machen fünf Minuten Pause; **Q** (*Cricket*) die Richtung beim Aufprall ändern; ≈ Drall haben; **R** (*become public*) bekannt werden.

❸ *n.* **A** Bruch, *der;* (*of rope*) Reißen, *das;* **~ [of service]** (*Tennis*) Break, *der od. das;* **a ~ in the weather** ein Wetterumschlag; **a ~ with sb./sth.** ein Bruch mit jmdm./etw.; **~ of day** Tagesanbruch, *der;* **at ~ of day** bei Tagesanbruch; **B** (*gap*) Lücke, *die;* (*in ground*) Riss, *der;* Spalte, *die;* (*Electr.: in circuit*) Unterbrechung, *die;* (*broken place*) Sprung, *der;* **C** (*escape from prison*) Ausbruch, *der;* (*sudden dash*) **they made a sudden ~:** sie stürmten plötzlich davon; **they made a ~ for the gateway** sie stürzten zum Tor; **D** (*interruption*) Unterbrechung, *die;* **E** (*pause, holiday*) Pause, *die;* **during the commercial ~s on TV** während der Werbespots im Fernsehen; **take** *or* **have a ~:** [eine] Pause machen; **work without a ~:** ohne Pause arbeiten; **tea ~** (*Brit.*) Teepause, *die;* **go away for a weekend ~:** übers Wochenende verreisen; **F** (*coll.: fair chance, piece of luck*) Chance, *die;* **lucky ~:** große Chance; **that was a bad ~ for him** das war Pech für ihn; **G [bad] ~** (*coll.*) (*unfortunate remark*) ungeschickte Bemerkung; (*ill-judged action*) Dummheit, *die;* **H** (*Electr.*) Unterbrechen, *das* (**in** *Gen.*); **I** (*Cricket*) Richtungsänderung beim Aufprall; ≈ Drall, *der;* **J** (*Billiards etc.*) Serie, *die;* **K** (*Jazz*) Break, *der od. das*

**~ aˈway** ❶ *v.t.* **~ sth. away [from sth.]** etw. [von etw.] losbrechen *od.* abbrechen. ❷ *v.i.* **A ~ away [from sth.]** [von etw.] losbrechen *od.* abbrechen; (*separate itself/oneself*) sich [von etw.] lösen; (*escape*) [aus etw.] entkommen; **he broke away from them** er distanzierte sich von ihnen; (*escaped*) er entkam ihnen; **B** (*Footb.*) sich freilaufen; **C** (*get out of control*) ‹Auto:› ausbrechen. ⇒ *also* **~away**

**~ ˈdown** ❶ *v.i.* **A** (*fail*) zusammenbrechen; ‹Verhandlungen:› scheitern; **B** (*cease to function*) ‹Auto:› eine Panne haben; ‹Telefonnetz:› zusammenbrechen; **the machine has broken down** die Maschine funktioniert nicht mehr; **C** (*be overcome by emotion*) zusammenbrechen; **D** (*Chem.*) aufspalten. ❷ *v.t.* **A** (*demolish*) aufbrechen ‹Tür›; zum Einsturz bringen ‹Mauer›; umknicken ‹Baum›; **B** (*suppress*) brechen ‹Widerstand›; niederreißen ‹Barriere, Schranke›; **C** (*analyse*) aufgliedern. ⇒ *also* **~down; broken-down**

**~ ˈin** ❶ *v.i.* **A** (*intrude forcibly*) einbrechen; ⇒ *also* **~-in**; **B** (*interrupt*) **~ in [on sb./sth.]** [jmdn./etw.] unterbrechen. ❷ *v.t.* **A** (*accustom to habit*) eingewöhnen; einarbeiten ‹Lehrling etc.›; (*tame*) zureiten ‹Pferd›; abrichten ‹Hund›; (*discipline*) zur Disziplin erziehen; **B** (*wear etc. until comfortable*) einlaufen ‹Schuhe›; sich gewöhnen an (+ *Akk.*) ‹Brille, Gebiss›; **C ~ the door in** die Tür aufbrechen

**~ into** ⇒ **~** 2 F

**~ ˈoff** ❶ *v.t.* abbrechen; abreißen ‹Faden›; auflösen ‹Verlobung›; **~ it off [with sb.]** sich von jmdm. trennen. ❷ *v.i.* **A** abbrechen; **B** (*cease*) aufhören; ‹Gespräch, Gesang:› abbrechen; ‹Diskussion, Verfahren:› abgebrochen werden

**~ ˈout** *v.i.* (*escape, appear*) ausbrechen; ‹Flecken, Pusteln, Schweißtropfen:› sich bilden; **~ out in spots/a rash** *etc.* Pickel/einen Ausschlag *usw.* bekommen; **he broke out in a cold sweat** ihm brach der kalte Schweiß aus

**~ out of** ⇒ **~** 2 F

**~ ˈthrough** *v.t. & i.* durchbrechen; ⇒ *also* **~through**

**~ ˈup** ❶ *v.t.* **A** (**~** *into pieces*) zerkleinern; ausschlachten ‹Auto›; abwracken ‹Schiff›; aufbrechen ‹Erde›; zerbrechen ‹Stuhl›; **B** (*disband*) auflösen; auseinander reißen ‹Familie›; zerstreuen ‹Menge›; **~ it up!** (*coll.*) auseinander!; **C** (*disconcert*) aus der Fassung bringen; **D** (*end*) zerstören ‹Freundschaft, Ehe›. ❷ *v.i.* **A** (**~** *into pieces, lit. or fig.*) zerbrechen; ‹Erde, Straßenoberfläche:› aufbrechen; ‹Eis:› brechen; **B** (*disband*) sich auflösen; ‹Schule:› schließen; ‹Schüler, Lehrer:› in die Ferien gehen; **C** (*be convulsed*) **~ up [with laughter]** in Gelächter ausbrechen; **D** (*cease*) abgebrochen werden; (*end relationship*) **~ up [with sb.]** sich [von jmdm.] trennen; **they broke up last year** sie trennten sich letztes Jahr; **E** ⇒ **~** 2 I; **F** (*mentally*) zusammenbrechen. ⇒ *also* **~-up**

**break**[2] ⇒ **brake**[4]

**breakable** /ˈbreɪkəbl/ ❶ *adj.* zerbrechlich. ❷ *n. in pl.* zerbrechliche Dinge

**breakage** /ˈbreɪkɪdʒ/ *n.* **A** (*breaking*) Zerbrechen, *das;* **B** (*result of breaking*) Bruchschaden, *der;* **~s must be paid for** zerbrochene Ware muss bezahlt werden

**break: ~away** ❶ *n.* **A** Ausbrechen, *das;* **a ~away from tradition** ein Bruch mit der Tradition; **B** (*Sport: false start*) Fehlstart, *der;* **C** (*Rugby*) [*schnelles*] *Lösen aus dem Gedränge.* ❷ *adj.* (*Brit.*) abtrünnig; **~away group** Splittergruppe, *die;* **~-dancing** *n.* Breakdancetanzen, *das;* **~down** *n.* **A** (*fig.: collapse*) **a ~down in the system** (*fig.*) ein Zusammenbruch des Systems; **B** (*mechanical failure*) Panne, *die;* (*in machine*) Störung, *die;* **~down service** Pannendienst, *der;* **~down truck/van** Abschleppwagen, *der;* **C** (*health or mental failure*) Zusammenbruch, *der;* **a ~down in health** ein gesundheitlicher Zusammenbruch; **D** (*analysis*) Aufschlüsselung, *die;* **E** (*Chem.*) Aufspaltung, *die;* **~down product** Spaltprodukt, *das* (*Chemie*)

**breaker** /ˈbreɪkə(r)/ *n.* **A** (*wave*) Brecher, *der;* **B [car] ~** *jmd., der Autos ausschlachtet;* **~'s [yard]** Autoverwertung, *die*

**break ˈeven** *v.i.* die Kosten decken; **~ point** Rentabilitätsschwelle, *die*

**breakfast** /ˈbrekfəst/ ❶ *n.* Frühstück, *das;* **for ~:** zum Frühstück; **have sth. for ~:** etw. zum Frühstück essen/trinken; **eat** *or* **have [one's] ~:** frühstücken; **have a cooked ~:** zum Frühstück etwas Warmes essen; ⇒ *also* **wedding breakfast.** ❷ *v.i.* frühstücken; **we ~ed on bacon and eggs** wir aßen Eier mit Speck zum Frühstück

**breakfast: ~ cereal** *n.* ≈ Frühstücksflocken *Pl.;* **~ television** *n.* Frühstücksfernsehen, *das;* **~ time** *n.* Frühstückszeit, *die*

**ˈbreak-in** *n.* Einbruch, *der;* **there has been a ~ at the bank** in der *od.* die Bank ist eingebrochen worden

**ˈbreaking** *n.* **~ and entering** (*Law*) Einbruch, *der*

**breaking: ~ point** *n.* Belastungsgrenze, *die;* **be at ~ point** (*mentally*) die Grenze der Belastbarkeit erreicht haben; **~-strength** *n.* Belastbarkeit, *die*

**break: ~neck** *adj.* halsbrecherisch; **~out** *n.* Ausbruch, *der;* **~through** *n.* Durchbruch, *der;* **~-up** *n.* **A** (*disintegration*) (*of earth, soil, road surface*) Aufbrechen, *das;* (*fig.*) Zusammenbruch, *der;* (*of weather*) Umschlag, *der;* (*of old structure*) Zerfall, *der;* **B** (*disbanding, dispersal*) Auflösung, *die;* **C** (*ceasing*) Ende, *das;* (*ending of relationship*) Bruch, *der;* **~water** *n.* Wellenbrecher, *der*

b

**bream** /bri:m/ *n., pl. same (Zool.)* Ⓐ Brachsen, *der;* Ⓑ **[sea]** ~ *(Sparidae)* Meerbrassen, *der;* Ⓒ *(Amer.: sunfish)* Sonnenbarsch, *der*

**breast** /brest/ ❶ *n. (lit. or fig.)* Brust, *die;* **make a clean ~ [of sth.]** *(fig.)* [etw.] offen bekennen. ❷ *v.t.* Ⓐ *(oppose, confront)* sich entgegenstellen (+ *Dat.*); Ⓑ *(Brit.: climb)* übersteigen ‹Mauer, Hindernis›; besteigen ‹Berg›; **~ the waves** gegen die Wellen ankämpfen. ⇒ *also* **tape** 1 B

**breast: ~bone** *n.* ▶ **966** Brustbein, *das;* **~ cancer** *n.* ▶ **1232** Brustkrebs, *der;* **~fed** *adj.* **be ~fed** gestillt werden; **~feed** *v.t. & i.* stillen; **~feeding** *n.* das Stillen; **~plate** *n. (armour)* Brustharnisch, *der;* **~ 'pocket** *n.* Brusttasche, *die;* **~stroke** *n. (Swimming)* Brustschwimmen, *das;* **do** *or* **swim [the] ~stroke** brustschwimmen

**breath** /breθ/ *n.* Ⓐ Atem, *der;* **have bad ~:** Mundgeruch haben; **say sth. below** *or* **under one's ~:** etw. vor sich (*Akk.*) hin murmeln; **draw ~:** Atem holen; **as long as I draw ~:** solange ich atme; **a ~ of fresh air** ein wenig frische Luft; **go out for a ~ of fresh air** frische Luft schnappen gehen; **be a ~ of fresh air in sb.'s life** etwas Abwechslung in jmds. Leben bringen; **waste one's ~:** seine Worte verschwenden; **sth. is the ~ of life to sb.** jmd. kann ohne etw. nicht leben; **she caught her ~:** ihr stockte der Atem; **hold one's ~:** den Atem anhalten; **get one's ~ back** wieder zu Atem kommen; **be out of/short of ~:** außer Atem *od.* atemlos sein/kurzatmig sein; **take ~:** [sich] verschnaufen; **pause for ~:** eine Verschnaufpause machen; **take sb.'s ~ away** *(fig.)* jmdm. den Atem verschlagen; ⇒ *also* **save** 1 E; Ⓑ *(one respiration)* Atemzug, *der;* **take** *or* **draw a [deep] ~:** [tief] einatmen; **in the same ~:** im selben Atemzug; Ⓒ *(air movement, whiff)* Hauch, *der;* **there wasn't a ~ of air** es regte sich kein Lüftchen; **a ~ of wind** ein Windhauch; **not a ~ of suspicion/rumour** nicht die Spur eines Verdachts/nicht die leiseste Andeutung eines Gerüchts

**breathalyse** /'breθəlaɪz/ *v.t.* ins Röhrchen *od.* in die Tüte blasen lassen (*ugs.*)

**breathalyser** ® (*Amer.:* **breathalyzer**) /'breθəlaɪzə(r)/ *n.* Alcotest-Röhrchen Ⓦⓩ *das; attrib.* **~ test** Alcotest Ⓦⓩ, *der;* **blow/breathe into a ~:** ins Röhrchen *od.* in die Tüte blasen (*ugs.*)

**breathe** /bri:ð/ ❶ *v.i.* Ⓐ *(lit. or fig.)* atmen; **~ in** einatmen; **~ out** ausatmen; **~ into sth.** [sanft] in etw. (*Akk.*) [hinein]blasen; ⇒ *also* **neck** 1 A; Ⓑ *(take breath)* **stop to ~:** eine Verschnaufpause machen; **give me a chance to ~!** lass mich erst wieder zur Besinnung kommen!; Ⓒ *(blow)* [sanft] wehen. ❷ *v.t.* Ⓐ **~ a breath** einen Atemzug tun; **~ one's last** seinen letzten Atemzug tun; **~ fire** Feuer speien; *(fig.)* Gift und Galle spucken; **~ [in/out]** ein-/ausatmen; **~ new life into sth.** *(fig.)* etw. mit neuem Leben erfüllen; Ⓑ *(utter)* hauchen; **~ a sigh [of relief]/a sigh of regret** [erleichtert] aufatmen/aufseufzen; **don't ~ a word about** *or* **of this to anyone** sag kein Sterbenswörtchen darüber zu irgendjemandem; Ⓒ *(show evidence of)* atmen (*geh.*); ausstrahlen

**breather** /'bri:ðə(r)/ *n.* Ⓐ *(brief pause)* Verschnaufpause, *die; (brief holiday etc.)* Erholungspause, *die;* **take** *or* **have a ~:** eine Verschnaufpause/Erholungspause einlegen; **go out for a ~:** ein wenig frische Luft schöpfen; Ⓑ *(Motor Veh.)* Entlüfter, *der*

**breathing** /'bri:ðɪŋ/ *n.* Atmen, *das*

**breathing: ~ apparatus** *n.* Ⓐ *(Med.)* Beatmungsgerät, *das;* Ⓑ *(of fireman etc.)* Atemschutzgerät, *das;* **~ space** *n. (time to breathe)* Zeit zum Luftholen; *(pause)* Atempause, *die;* **~ tube** *n.* Atemschlauch, *der*

**breathless** /'breθlɪs/ *adj.* atemlos (**with** vor + *Dat.*); **leave sb. ~** *(lit. or fig.)* jmdm. den Atem nehmen; **we stood ~ while ...:** uns (*Dat.*) stockte der Atem, während ...; **we were ~ with amazement** uns (*Dat.*) blieb vor Staunen die Luft weg (*ugs.*)

**breathlessly** /'breθlɪslɪ/ *adv.* atemlos

**breathlessness** /'breθlɪsnɪs/ *n., no pl.* Atemlosigkeit, *die; (caused by smoking or illness)* Kurzatmigkeit, *die*

**breath: ~taking** *adj.* atemberaubend; **~ test** *n.* Alcotest Ⓦⓩ, *der*

**breathy** /'breθɪ/ *adj.* hauchig ‹Stimme›

**Brechtian** /'brektɪən/ *adj.* *(Theatre)* brechtsch

**bred** ⇒ **breed** 1, 2

**breech** /bri:tʃ/ *n.* [Geschütz]verschluss, *der*

**breech: ~ birth** *n. (Med.)* Steißgeburt, *die;* **~block** *n.* Verschlussblock, *der*

**breeches** /'brɪtʃɪz/ *n. pl.* Ⓐ *(short trousers)* **[pair of] ~:** [Knie]bundhose, *die;* **[riding] ~:** Reithose, *die;* Breeches *Pl.;* Ⓑ *(trousers)* Hose, *die; (knickerbockers)* Knickerbocker *Pl.;* **wear the ~** *(fig.)* die Hosen anhaben (*ugs.*); ⇒ *also* **big** 1 G

**'breeches buoy** *n. (Naut.)* Hosenboje, *die*

**breech: ~-loader** *n.* Hinterlader, *der;* **~-loading** *adj.* Hinterlader-

**breed** /bri:d/ ❶ *v.t.*, **bred** /bred/ Ⓐ *(be the cause of)* erzeugen; hervorrufen; Ⓑ *(raise)* züchten ‹Tiere, Pflanzen›; **bred in the bone** angeboren; Ⓒ *(bring up)* erziehen; **be bred and born** *or* **born and bred sth.** etw. durch und durch sein; **he was born and bred in London** er ist in London geboren und aufgewachsen; Ⓓ *(bear)* gebären ‹Nachkommen›; *(generate)* hervorbringen ‹Rasse›. ❷ *v.i.*, **bred** Ⓐ sich vermehren; ‹Vogel:› brüten; ‹Tier:› Junge haben; **they ~ like flies** *or* **rabbits** sie vermehren sich wie die Kaninchen; Ⓑ *(arise)* entstehen; *(spread)* sich ausbreiten.
❸ *n.* Ⓐ Art, *die; (of animals)* Rasse, *die;* **~s of cattle** Rinderrassen; **the Jersey ~ [of cattle]** das Jerseyrind; **what ~ of dog is that?** zu welcher Rasse gehört dieser Hund?; Ⓑ *(lineage)* Rasse, *die;* **a noble ~ of men** ein vornehmer Menschenschlag; Ⓒ *(sort)* Art, *die*

**breeder** /'bri:də(r)/ *n.* ▶ **1261** Züchter, *der;* **be a ~ of sth.** etw. züchten; **dog/horse ~:** Hunde-/Pferdezüchter, *der*

**'breeder reactor** *n. (Nucl. Engin.)* Brutreaktor, *der;* Brüter, *der*

**breeding** /'bri:dɪŋ/ *n.* Erziehung, *die;* **[good] ~:** gute Erziehung; **have ~:** eine gute Erziehung genossen haben

**breeding: ~ ground** *n. (lit. or fig.)* Brutstätte, *die;* **~ season** *n.* Brutzeit, *die*

**breeze**[1] /bri:z/ ❶ *n.* Ⓐ *(gentle wind)* Brise, *die;* **there is a ~:** es weht eine Brise; **night ~:** nächtliche Brise; **sea ~:** Seebrise, *die;* Ⓑ *(Meteorol.)* [leichter] Wind. ❷ *v.i. (coll.)* **~ along** dahinrollen; *(on foot)* dahinschlendern; **~ in** hereingeschneit kommen (*ugs.*)

**breeze**[2] *n. (cinders)* Lösche, *die*

**breeze**[3] *n. (Zool.)* Bremse, *die*

**'breeze block** *n. (Building)* ≈ Leichtstein, *der*

**breezily** /'bri:zɪlɪ/ *adv. (coll.)* [frisch und] unbekümmert; *(carelessly)* leichthin; unbekümmert

**breeziness** /'bri:zɪnɪs/ *n., no pl. (coll.) (carefree nature)* [frische und] unbekümmerte Art; *(carelessness)* Unbekümmertheit, *die*

**breezy** /'bri:zɪ/ *adj.* Ⓐ *(windy)* windig; Ⓑ *(coll.) (brisk and carefree)* [frisch und] unbekümmert; *(careless)* unbekümmert

**brent** /brent/ *n.* **~[ goose]** Ringelgans, *die*

**brethren** ⇒ **brother** D

**Breton** /'bretn/ ▶ **1275** ❶ *adj.* bretonisch; ⇒ *also* **English** 1. ❷ *n.* Ⓐ *(language)* Bretonisch, *das;* ⇒ *also* **English** 2 A; Ⓑ *(person)* Bretone, *der*/Bretonin, *die*

**breve** /bri:v/ *n.* Ⓐ *(Mus.)* Brevis, *die (veralt.);* Doppelganze, *die;* Ⓑ *(of short/unstressed vowel)* Halbkreis, *der (zur Kennzeichnung kurzer/unbetonter Vokale)*

**breviary** /'bri:vɪərɪ/ *n. (Eccl.)* Brevier, *das*

**brevity** /'brevɪtɪ/ *n.* Kürze, *die*

**brew** /bru:/ ❶ *v.t.* Ⓐ brauen ‹Bier›; keltern ‹Apfelwein›; **~ [up]** kochen ‹Kaffee, Tee, Kakao usw.›; aufbrühen ‹Tee, Kaffee›; **~ up** *abs.* Tee kochen; [sich (*Dat.*)] einen Tee kochen *od.* aufbrühen; Ⓑ *(fig.: put together)* **~ [up]** [zusammen]brauen (*ugs.*) ‹Mischung›; *(generate)* hervorrufen ‹Empfindungen›; *(formulate)* ausbrüten (*ugs.*) ‹Plan usw.›.
❷ *v.i.* Ⓐ ‹Bier, Apfelwein:› gären; ‹Kaffee, Tee:› ziehen; Ⓑ *(fig.: gather)* ‹Unwetter:› sich zusammenbrauen; ‹Rebellion, Krieg:› drohen.
❸ *n.* Ⓐ Gebräu, *das (abwertend); (brewed beer/tea)* Bier, *das*/Tee, *der;* **~ [of tea/coffee]** Tee, *der*/Kaffee, *der;* Ⓑ *(amount brewed)* ≈ Abfüllung, *die; (of tea etc.)* **we'll have to make another ~:** wir müssen noch einmal aufbrühen

**brewer** /'bru:ə(r)/ *n.* Ⓐ ▶ **1261** *(person)* Brauer, *der;* Ⓑ *(firm)* Brauerei, *die*

**brewery** /'bru:ərɪ/ *n.* Brauerei, *die*

**briar** ⇒ **brier**[1, 2]

**bribe** /braɪb/ ❶ *n.* Bestechung, *die;* **a ~ [of £100]** ein Bestechungsgeld [in Höhe von 100 Pfund]; **take a ~/~s** sich bestechen lassen; **he won't accept ~s** er ist unbestechlich; **offer sb. a ~:** jmdn. bestechen wollen. ❷ *v.t.* bestechen; **he won't be ~d** er ist unbestechlich; **~ sb. to do/into doing sth.** jmdn. bestechen, damit er etw. tut

**bribery** /'braɪbərɪ/ *n.* Bestechung, *die;* **open to ~:** bestechlich; käuflich; **be involved in ~:** in einen Bestechungsfall verwickelt sein

**bric-à-brac** /'brɪkəbræk/ *n.* Antiquarisches; *(smaller things)* Nippsachen *Pl.;* **~ collector** ≈ Antiquitätensammler, *der*

**brick** /brɪk/ ❶ *n.* Ⓐ *(block)* Ziegelstein, *der;* Backstein, *der; (clay)* Lehmziegel, *der;* **~s and mortar** *(buildings)* Gebäude; *(as investment)* Immobilien *Pl.;* **drop a ~** *(fig. coll.)* ins Fettnäpfchen treten (*ugs. scherzh.*); **be** *or* **come down on sb. like a load** *or* **ton of ~s** *(coll.)* jmdn. unheimlich fertig machen *od.* zusammenstauchen (*ugs.*); Ⓑ *(toy)* Bauklötzchen, *das;* Ⓒ *(of ice cream)* Packung, *die;* Ⓓ *(coll.: person)* feiner Kerl; **you've been a real ~:** du warst ein prima Kumpel (*ugs.*). ❷ *adj.* Ⓐ Ziegelstein-; Backstein-; Ⓑ *(red)* ziegelrot. ❸ *v.t.* **~ up/in** zu-/einmauern

**brick: ~bat** *n.* Ⓐ Backsteinbrocken, *der;* Ⓑ *(fig.: uncomplimentary remark)* schlechte Kritik; **greet sb. with ~bats** jmdn. attackieren; **~-built** *adj.* backsteinern; Backstein ‹haus, -mauer›; **it is ~-built** es ist aus Backstein

**brickie** /'brɪkɪ/ *n. (Brit. coll.)* Maurer, *der*

**brick: ~-kiln** *n.* Ziegelofen, *der;* **~layer** *n.* ▶ **1261** Maurer, *der;* **~laying** *n.* ▶ **1261** Mauern, *das;* **~-red** *adj.* ziegelrot; **~ 'wall** *n.* Backsteinmauer, *die;* **bang one's head against a ~ wall** *(fig.)* mit dem Kopf gegen die Wand rennen (*fig.*); **come up against a ~ wall** *(fig.)* plötzlich vor einer Mauer stehen (*fig.*); **~work** *n.* Ⓐ *(~laying)* Mauern, *das;* Ⓑ *(structure)* [Backstein]mauerwerk, *das;* **~yard** *n.* Ziegelei, *die*

**bridal** /'braɪdl/ *adj. (of bride)* Braut-; *(of wedding)* Hochzeits-; **~ couple/suite** Brautpaar, *das*/Hochzeitssuite, *die*

**bride** /braɪd/ *n.* Braut, *die*

**'bridegroom** *n.* Bräutigam, *der*

**bridesmaid** /'braɪdzmeɪd/ *n.* Brautjungfer, *die;* **chief ~:** erste Brautjungfer

**bridge**[1] /brɪdʒ/ ❶ *n.* Ⓐ *(lit. or fig.)* Brücke, *die;* **cross that ~ when you come to it** *(fig.)* alles zu seiner Zeit; ⇒ *also* **burn**[1] 2 A; Ⓑ *(Naut.)* [Kommando]brücke, *die;* Ⓒ *(of nose)* Nasenbein, *das;* Sattel, *der;* Ⓓ *(of violin, spectacles)* Steg, *der;* Ⓔ *(Dent.)* [Zahn]brücke, *die.* ❷ *v.t.* eine Brücke bauen *od.* errichten *od.* schlagen über (+ *Akk.*); **~ the gap** *(fig.)* die Kluft überbrücken

**bridge**[2] *n. (Cards)* Bridge, *das*

**'bridgehead** *n.* Brückenkopf, *der*

**'bridging loan** *n. (Commerc.)* Überbrückungskredit, *der*

**bridle** /'braɪdl/ ❶ *n.* Zaumzeug, *das;* Zaum, *der.* ❷ *v.t.* Ⓐ aufzäumen ‹Pferd›; Ⓑ *(fig.: restrain)* zügeln ‹Zunge›; im Zaum halten ‹Leidenschaft›. ❸ *v.i.* **~ at sth.** sich gegen etw. sträuben *od.* (*geh.*) stemmen

**'bridle path, 'bridle road** *ns.* Saumpfad, *der;* *(for horses)* Reitweg, *der*

**Brie** /bri:/ *n.* Brie[käse], *der*

**brief¹** /bri:f/ *adj.* A (*of short duration*) kurz; gering, geringfügig ‹Verspätung›; **after a ~ discussion/the ~est of discussions** nach kurzer/ganz kurzer Diskussion; B (*concise*) knapp; **in ~, to be ~:** kurz gesagt; **make** *or* **keep it ~:** es kurz machen; **be ~:** sich kurz fassen; **the news in ~:** die Nachrichten im Überblick

**brief²** ❶ *n.* A (*Law: summary of facts*) Schriftsatz, *der;* **hold a ~ for sb.** jmdn. als Anwalt [vor Gericht] vertreten; **hold no ~ for sb.** (*fig.*) nicht auf jmds. Seite (*Dat.*) stehen; nicht für jmdn. plädieren *od.* eintreten; B (*Brit. Law: piece of work*) Mandat, *das;* C (*Amer. Law: statement of arguments*) Darlegung der Beweisgründe; D (*instructions*) Instruktionen *Pl.;* Anweisungen *Pl.* ❷ *v.t.* A (*Brit. Law*) mit der Vertretung eines Falles betrauen; B (*Mil.: instruct*) Anweisungen *od.* Instruktionen geben (+ *Dat.*); instruieren; unterweisen; C (*inform, instruct*) unterrichten; informieren

**'briefcase** *n.* Aktentasche, *die*

**briefing** /'bri:fɪŋ/ *n.* A Briefing, *das;* (*of reporters or press*) Unterrichtung, *die;* (*before raid etc.*) Einsatzbesprechung, *die;* B (*instructions*) Instruktionen *Pl.;* Anweisungen *Pl.;* (*information*) Informationen *Pl.*

**briefly** /'bri:flɪ/ *adv.* A (*for a short time*) kurz; B (*concisely*) knapp; kurz; **[to put it] ~, ...:** kurz gesagt ...

**briefness** /'bri:fnɪs/ *n., no pl.* A (*shortness*) Kürze, *die;* B (*conciseness*) Knappheit, *die*

**briefs** /bri:fs/ *n. pl.* **[pair of] ~:** Slip, *der*

**brier¹** /'braɪə(r)/ *n.* (*Bot.: rose*) Wilde Rose

**brier²** *n.* A (*pipe*) Bruyèrepfeife, *die;* B (*Bot.: heath*) Baumheide, *die*

**'brier rose** *n.* Hundsrose, *die*

**brig** /brɪg/ *n.* A (*Naut.*) Brigg, *die;* B (*Amer. coll.: prison*) Bau, *der* (*salopp*); Bunker, *der* (*salopp*)

**Brig.** *abbr.* ▶ 1617 **brigadier** Brig.

**brigade** /brɪ'geɪd/ *n.* A (*Mil.*) Brigade, *die;* **the old ~** (*fig.*) die alte Garde; B (*organized or uniformed body*) Einheit, *die*

**brigadier [general]** /brɪgə'dɪə(r) ('dʒenrl)/ *n.* ▶ 1617 (*Mil.*) Brigadegeneral, *der;* Brigadier, *der*

**brigand** /'brɪgənd/ *n.* Bandit, *der;* Brigant, *der* (*geh.*)

**bright** /braɪt/ ❶ *adj.* A hell ‹Licht, Stern, Fleck›; grell ‹Scheinwerfer[licht], Sonnenlicht›; strahlend ‹Sonnenschein, Stern, Augen›; glänzend ‹Metall, Augen›; leuchtend, lebhaft ‹Farbe, Blume›; **~ reflection** starke Reflexion *od.* Spiegelung; **~ blue** *etc.* leuchtend blau *usw.;* **~ yellow/red** leuchtend gelb/rot; knallgelb/-rot (*ugs.*); **a ~ day** ein heiterer *od.* strahlender Tag; **~ intervals/periods** Aufheiterungen; **the one ~ spot** (*fig.*) der Lichtblick; **the ~ lights of the city** (*fig.*) der Glanz der Großstadt; **look on the ~ side** (*fig.*) die Sache positiv sehen; **~-eyed and bushy-tailed** (*joc.*) fidel und munter; B (*cheerful*) fröhlich, heiter ‹Person, Charakter, Stimmung›; strahlend ‹Lächeln›; freundlich ‹Zimmer, Farbe›; C (*clever*) intelligent; **that wasn't very ~ [of you], was it?** das war nicht gerade intelligent [von dir]!; **he is a ~ boy** er ist ein heller *od.* aufgeweckter Junge; D (*hopeful*) viel versprechend ‹Zukunft›; glänzend ‹Aussichten›. ❷ *adv.* A hell; B **~ and early** in aller Frühe

**brighten** /'braɪtn/ ❶ *v.t.* **~ [up]** A aufhellen ‹Farbe›; aufpolieren, zum Glänzen bringen ‹Metall›; B (*make more cheerful*) aufhellen, aufheitern ‹Zimmer›. ❷ *v.i.* **~ [up]** A ‹Himmel:› sich aufhellen; **the weather** *or* **it is ~ing [up]** es klärt sich auf; es klart auf (*Met.*); B (*become more cheerful*) ‹Person:› vergnügter werden; ‹Augen:› [auf]leuchten; ‹Gesicht:› sich aufhellen; ‹Aussichten:› sich verbessern

**brightly** /'braɪtlɪ/ *adv.* A hell ‹scheinen, glänzen›; glänzend ‹poliert›; **~ lit** hell erleuchtet; **~ coloured** leuchtend bunt; B (*cheerfully*) gut gelaunt; strahlend

**brightness** /'braɪtnɪs/ *n., no pl.* A (*of light, star, spot*) Helligkeit, *die;* (*of sunlight*) Grelle, *die;* Grellheit, *die;* (*of sun, eyes, star*) Strahlen, *das;* (*of metal, eyes*) Glanz, *der;* (*of colours*) Leuchtkraft, *die;* (*of eyes*) Leuchten, *das;* **the ~ of the reflection** die Stärke der Reflexion; B (*cheerfulness*) Fröhlichkeit, *die;* Heiterkeit, *die;* C (*cleverness*) Intelligenz, *die;* **the ~ of his ideas** seine glänzenden Ideen

**brill¹** /brɪl/ *n., pl. same* (*Zool.*) Glattbutt, *der*

**brill²** *adj.* (*Brit. coll.*) super (*ugs.*)

**brilliance** /'brɪljəns/, **brilliancy** /'brɪljənsɪ/ *n., no pl.* A (*brightness*) (*of light*) Helligkeit, *die;* (*of star, diamond*) Funkeln, *das;* (*of flash*) Grelle, *die;* Grellheit, *die;* (*of colours*) Leuchten, *das;* B (*of person, invention, idea, move, achievement*) Genialität, *die;* **the ~ of his mind** sein genialer Geist; C (*illustriousness*) Glanz, *der*

**brilliant** /'brɪljənt/ ❶ *adj.* A (*bright*) hell ‹Licht›; strahlend ‹Sonne›; funkelnd ‹Diamant, Stern›; leuchtend ‹Farbe›; B (*highly talented*) genial ‹Person, Erfindung, Gedanke, Schachzug, Leistung›; glänzend ‹Verstand›; brillant, glänzend ‹Aufführung, Vorstellung, Idee›; bestechend ‹Theorie, Argument›; **that was ~** (*iron.*) das war gekonnt *od.* intelligent (*iron.*); C (*illustrious*) glänzend ‹Karriere, Erfolg, Sieg›; großartig ‹[Helden]tat›; **a ~ achievement** eine Glanzleistung. ❷ *n.* Brillant, *der*

**brilliantine** /'brɪljənti:n/ *n.* Brillantine, *die;* Haarpomade, *die*

**brilliantly** /'brɪljəntlɪ/ *adv.* A hell ‹scheinen, funkeln, schimmern›; **it was a ~ sunny day** es war ein strahlender Sonnentag; **~ lit** hell erleuchtet; B (*with great talent*) brillant; **a ~ thought-out scheme** ein genial ausgedachter Plan; C (*illustriously*) glänzend ‹erfolgreich sein, triumphieren›

**brim** /brɪm/ ❶ *n.* A (*of cup, bowl, hollow*) Rand, *der;* **full to the ~:** randvoll; B (*of hat*) [Hut]krempe, *die.* ❷ *v.i.,* **-mm-: be ~ming with sth.** randvoll mit etw. sein; (*fig.*) strotzen vor etw. (*Dat.*); **be ~ming with tears** (*fig.*) ‹Augen:› voller Tränen stehen

**~ 'over** *v.i.* A übervoll sein; B (*fig.*) **he was ~ming over with confidence** er strotzte vor Zuversicht

**brim-'full** *adj.* **be ~ with sth.** randvoll mit etw. sein; **be ~ of energy/curiosity** (*fig.*) vor Energie (*Dat.*) sprühen/vor Neugierde (*Dat.*) platzen; **be ~ of new ideas** (*fig.*) von neuen Ideen übersprudeln

**brimless** /'brɪmlɪs/ *adj.* ‹Hut› ohne Krempe

**brindle** /'brɪndl/, **brindled** /'brɪndld/ *adjs.* gestreift ‹Katze›; gestromt ‹Kuh, Hund›

**brine** /braɪn/ *n.* (*salt water*) Salzwasser, *das;* Sole, *die;* (*for preserving*) Pökellake, *die;* [Salz]lake, *die*

**bring** /brɪŋ/ *v.t.,* **brought** /brɔ:t/ A bringen; (*as a present or favour*) mitbringen; **~ sth. with one** etw. mitbringen; **I haven't brought my towel** ich habe mein Handtuch nicht mitgebracht *od.* dabei; **he brought the chair nearer** er zog den Stuhl näher heran; **~ sb. before sb.** jmdn. vor jmdn. führen; **what ~s you here?** was führt dich hierher?; **who brought you here?** wer hat Sie hergebracht?; **he brought the car to the front door** er fuhr mit dem Wagen vor; **April brought a change in the weather** der April brachte einen Wetterumschwung mit sich; **~ sb. low** jmdn. erniedrigen; **~ sth. [up]on oneself/sb.** sich selbst/jmdm. etw. einbrocken; **~ a business/country through a crisis** ein Unternehmen/ein Land durch eine Krise führen; B (*result in*) [mit sich] bringen; **the television appeal brought thousands of replies** auf den Aufruf im Fernsehen meldeten sich Tausende; **the distress call brought help within a matter of minutes** auf den Notruf kam Hilfe in Minutenschnelle; **this will ~ shame on you** das wird dir Schande bringen; **~ honour to sb.** jmdm. Ehre machen; **~ tears to sb.'s eyes** jmdm. Tränen in die Augen treiben; C (*persuade*) **~ sb. to do sth.** jmdn. dazu bringen *od.* bewegen, etw. zu tun; **I could not ~ myself to do it** ich konnte es nicht über mich bringen, es zu tun; D (*initiate, put forward*) **~ a charge/legal action against sb.** gegen jmdn. [An]klage erheben/einen Prozess anstrengen; **~ a case/matter before a court** einen Fall/eine Sache vor Gericht bringen; **~ a complaint** eine Beschwerde vorbringen; E (*be sold for, earn*) [ein]bringen ‹Geldsumme›; F (*adduce*) vorbringen ‹Argument›

**~ a'bout** *v.t.* A (*cause to happen*) verursachen; herbeiführen; **~ it about that ...:** es zustande bringen, dass ...; B (*Naut.*) **~ the ship about** das Schiff auf Gegenkurs bringen

**~ a'long** *v.t.* A mitbringen; B ⇒ **~ on b**

**~ 'back** *v.t.* A (*return*) zurückbringen; (*from a journey*) mitbringen; B (*recall*) in Erinnerung bringen *od.* rufen; **~ sth. back to sb.** ‹Musik, Foto usw.:› jmdn. an etw. (*Akk.*) erinnern; **~ back memories** Erinnerungen wachrufen *od.* wecken; C (*restore, reintroduce*) wieder einführen ‹Sitten, Todesstrafe›; **~ back the Socialists!** wir wollen die Sozialisten wieder haben; **be brought back to power** wieder an die Macht kommen; **~ sb. back to health** jmdn. wieder gesund machen; **~ sb. back to life** jmdn. wieder beleben; **nothing will ~ him back to life** nichts kann ihn wieder lebendig machen

**~ 'down** *v.t.* A herunterbringen; B (*shoot down out of the air*) abschießen; herunterholen (*ugs.*); C (*land*) herunterbringen ‹Flugzeug, Drachen›; D (*kill, wound*) zur Strecke bringen ‹Person, Tier›; erlegen ‹Tier›; E (*reduce*) senken ‹Preise, Inflationsrate, Fieber›; **~ sb. down to one's own level** jmdn. zu sich *od.* auf sein [eigenes] Niveau herunterziehen; F (*attract*) **that'll ~ a penalty down on you** das wird dir eine Strafe einbringen; **that'll ~ the boss's wrath down on you[r head]** damit werden Sie sich (*Dat.*) den Zorn des Chefs zuziehen; G (*cause to fall*) zu Fall bringen ‹Gegner, Fußballer›; einstürzen lassen ‹Haus, Mauer›; (*fig.*) stürzen, zu Fall bringen ‹Regierung›; ⇒ *also* **house 1 I**

**~ 'forth** *v.t.* A (*produce*) hervorbringen ‹Frucht›; zur Welt bringen ‹Kinder, Junge›; B (*fig.*) vorbringen ‹Vorschlag, Idee›; auslösen ‹Protest, Kritik›

**~ 'forward** *v.t.* A nach vorne bringen; **~ your chairs forward** rücken Sie nach vorn; B (*draw attention to*) vorlegen ‹Beweise›; vorbringen ‹Argument, Beschwerde›; zur Sprache bringen ‹Fall, Angelegenheit, Frage›; C (*move to earlier time*) vorverlegen ‹Termin› (**to** auf + *Akk.*); D (*Bookk.*) übertragen; **the amount brought forward** der Übertrag

**~ 'in** *v.t.* A hereinbringen; auftragen ‹Essen›; einbringen ‹Ernte›; B (*introduce*) anschneiden ‹Thema›; einführen ‹Mode›; einbringen ‹Gesetzesvorlage›; **why ~ all that in?** das gehört hier nicht hin; C (*yield*) einbringen ‹Verdienst, Summe›; bringen ‹Zinsen›; D (*Law*) **~ in a verdict of guilty/not guilty** einen Schuldspruch fällen/auf Freispruch erkennen; E (*call in*) hinzuziehen, einschalten ‹Experten›

**~ 'off** *v.t.* A (*rescue*) retten; in Sicherheit bringen; B (*conduct successfully*) zustande *od.* zuwege bringen; **~ off a coup** einen Coup landen; **we didn't ~ it off** wir haben es nicht geschafft

**~ 'on** *v.t.* A (*cause*) verursachen; **brought on by ...** ‹Krankheit› infolge von ...; B (*advance progress of*) wachsen *od.* sprießen lassen ‹Blumen, Getreide›; weiterbringen, fördern ‹Schüler, Sportler›; C (*on stage etc.*) auftreten lassen; D (*Sport*) bringen (*ugs.*); einsetzen

**~ 'out** *v.t.* A herausbringen; **he put his hand in his pocket and brought out a knife** er griff in die Tasche und zog ein Messer heraus; B (*show clearly*) hervorheben, betonen ‹Unterschied›; verdeutlichen ‹Bedeutung›; herausbringen ‹Farbe›; C (*cause to appear*) herausbringen ‹Pflanzen, Blüte›; **the crisis brought out the best in him** die Krise brachte seine besten Seiten zum Vorschein *od.* ans Licht; **~ sb. out in a rash** bei jmdm. einen Ausschlag verursachen; D (*begin to sell*) einführen ‹Produkt›; herausbringen ‹Buch, Zeitschrift›

b

~ **'over** *v.t.* Ⓐ herüberbringen; Ⓑ (*convert*) ~ **sb. over to sth.** jmdn. von etw. überzeugen; ~ **sb. over to a cause** jmdn. für eine Sache gewinnen
~ **'round** *v.t.* Ⓐ mitbringen ‹Bekannte, Freunde usw.›; vorbeibringen ‹Gegenstände›; Ⓑ (*restore to consciousness*) wieder zu sich bringen ‹Ohnmächtigen›; Ⓒ (*win over*) überreden; herumkriegen (*ugs.*); ~ **sb. round to one's way of thinking** jmdn. von seiner Meinung überzeugen; Ⓓ (*direct*) ~ **a conversation round to sth.** ein Gespräch auf etw. (*Akk.*) bringen *od.* lenken
~ **'through** *v.t.* durchbringen ‹Kranken›
~ **'to** *v.t.* Ⓐ (*restore to consciousness*) wieder zu sich bringen; Ⓑ (*Naut.*) beidrehen
~ **to'gether** *v.t.* zusammenbringen
~ **'up** *v.t.* Ⓐ heraufbringen; Ⓑ (*educate*) erziehen; ~ **sb. up to be economical** jmdn. zur Sparsamkeit erziehen; **I was brought up to believe that ...:** ich wurde in dem Glauben erzogen, dass ...; Ⓒ (*rear*) aufziehen; großziehen; Ⓓ (*call attention to*) zur Sprache bringen ‹Angelegenheit, Thema, Problem›; **did you have to ~ that up?** mussten Sie davon anfangen?; ~ **up the past** die Vergangenheit aufrühren; Ⓔ (*vomit*) erbrechen; wieder von sich geben; Ⓕ (*Law*) ~ **sb. up [before a judge]** jmdn. [einem Richter] vorführen; Ⓖ (*Mil.*) an die Front bringen ‹Truppen, Panzer›; Ⓗ (*cause to stop*) ~ **sb. up short** jmdn. innehalten lassen. ⇒ *also* **rear**[1] 1 B

**bring-and-'buy [sale]** *n.* [Wohltätigkeits]basar, *der*

**brink** /brɪŋk/ *n.* (*lit. or fig.*) Rand, *der*; **shiver on the ~** (*fig.*) mit sich ringen; **be on the ~ of doing sth.** nahe daran sein, etw. zu tun; **be on the ~ of ruin/success** am Rand des Ruins sein *od.* stehen/dem Erfolg greifbar nahe sein; **they were on the ~ of starvation** sie waren kurz vor dem *od.* nahe am Verhungern

**brinkmanship** /'brɪŋkmənʃɪp/ *n., no pl.* gefährlicher Poker; **be playing a game of ~:** sich auf einen gefährlichen Poker eingelassen haben

**briny** /'braɪnɪ/ *n.* (*Brit. coll.*) **the ~:** das Meer

**briquet, briquette** /brɪ'ket/ *n.* Brikett, *das*

**brisk** /brɪsk/ *adj.* flott ‹Gang, Bedienung›; forsch ‹Person, Art›; frisch ‹Wind›; (*fig.*) rege ‹Handel, Nachfrage›; lebhaft ‹Geschäft›; **we set off at a ~ pace** wir marschierten in flottem Tempo los; **we went for a ~ walk** wir machten einen zünftigen Spaziergang; **business was ~:** das Geschäft florierte; **bidding for the lots was ~:** auf die Auktionsstücke wurde eifrig geboten

**brisket** /'brɪskɪt/ *n.* (*Gastr.*) Bruststück, *das*; Brust, *die*; ~ **of beef** Rinderbrust, *die*;

**briskly** /'brɪsklɪ/ *adv.* flott; **the wind blew ~:** es wehte ein frischer Wind; **sell ~:** sich gut verkaufen

**briskness** /'brɪsknɪs/ *n., no pl.* ⇒ **brisk**: Flottheit, *die*; Forschheit, *die*; *die*; Frische, *die*; (*fig.*) Lebhaftigkeit, *die*; **the ~ of trade/demand** der rege Handel/die rege Nachfrage

**bristle** /'brɪsl/ ❶ *n.* Ⓐ Borste, *die*; **be made of ~:** aus Borsten bestehen; Ⓑ **~s** (*of beard*) [Bart]stoppeln. ❷ *v.i.* Ⓐ ~ **[up]** ‹Haare:› sich sträuben; **the dog's hair ~d [up], the dog ~d** dem Hund sträubte sich (*Dat.*) das Fell; Ⓑ ~ **with** (*fig.: have many*) strotzen *od.* starren vor (+ *Dat.*); ~ **with difficulties/obstacles** mit Schwierigkeiten/Hindernissen gespickt sein; Ⓒ ~ **[up]** (*fig.: become angry*) ‹Person:› ungehalten reagieren

**bristly** /'brɪslɪ/ *adj.* borstig; stopp[e]lig ‹Kinn›; ~ **beard** Stoppelbart, *der*

**Brit** /brit/ *n.* (*coll.*) Brite, *der*/Britin, *die*; Engländer, *der*/Engländerin, *die* (*ugs.*)

**Brit.** *abbr.* Ⓐ **Britain** Gr.-Brit.; Gr.-Br.; Ⓑ **British** brit.

**Britain** /'brɪtn/ *pr. n.* Großbritannien (*das*); Britannien *das* (*hist.; auch Zeitungsjargon*)

**Britannia** /brɪ'tænjə/ *pr. n.* (*literary*) Britannia, *die* (*dichter.*)

**Briticism** /'brɪtɪsɪzm/ *n.* Britizismus, *der*

**British** /'brɪtɪʃ/ ▶ 1340 ❶ *adj.* britisch; **he/she is ~:** er ist Brite/sie ist Britin; **sth. is ~:** etw. ist aus Großbritannien; **the best of ~ [luck]** (*coll.*) na, [dann mal] viel Glück!; ⇒ *also* **English** 1. ❷ *n. pl.* **the ~:** die Briten

**British: ~ Columbia** /brɪtɪʃ kə'lʌmbɪə/ *pr. n.* Britisch-Kolumbien (*das*); ~ **'Council** *n. britisches Kulturinstitut im Ausland*

**Britisher** /'brɪtɪʃə(r)/ *n.* Brite, *der*/Britin, *die*

**British 'Isles** *pr. n. pl.* Britische Inseln

**Britishism** /'brɪtɪʃɪzm/ ⇒ **Briticism**

**Briton** /'brɪtn/ *n.* Brite, *der*/Britin, *die*

**Britpop** /'brɪtpɒp/ *n., no pl., no art.* Britpop, *der*

**Brittany** /'brɪtənɪ/ *pr. n.* Bretagne, *die*

**brittle** /'brɪtl/ *adj.* Ⓐ spröde ‹Material›; zerbrechlich ‹Glas›; schwach ‹Knochen›; brüchig ‹Gestein›; Ⓑ (*fig.: insecure*) empfindlich ‹Person›; schwach ‹Nerven›

**brittleness** /'brɪtlnɪs/ *n., no pl.* ⇒ **brittle**: Ⓐ Sprödigkeit, *die*; Zerbrechlichkeit, *die*; Schwäche, *die*; Brüchigkeit, *die*; Ⓑ (*fig.*) Empfindlichkeit, *die*; Schwäche, *die*

**bro.** *abbr.* **brother** Br.

**broach** /brəʊtʃ/ *v.t.* Ⓐ anzapfen; anstechen ‹Fass›; anbrechen ‹Vorräte›; Ⓑ (*fig.*) zur Sprache bringen ‹Vorschlag, Idee›; anschneiden ‹Thema›

**broad** /brɔːd/ ❶ *adj.* Ⓐ breit; (*extensive*) weit ‹Ebene, Meer, Land, Felder›; ausgedehnt ‹Fläche›; **a river sixty feet ~:** ein sechzig Fuß breiter Fluss; **grow ~er** breiter werden; sich verbreitern; **make sth. ~er** etw. verbreitern; **it's as ~ as it is long** (*fig.*) es ist gehupft wie gesprungen (*ugs.*); Ⓑ (*explicit*) deutlich, klar ‹Hinweis›; breit ‹Lächeln›; **a ~ hint** ein Wink mit dem Zaunpfahl (*scherzh.*); Ⓒ (*clear, main*) grob; wesentlich ‹Fakten›; **in ~ outline** in groben *od.* großen Zügen; **give the ~ outlines of a plan** einen Plan in groben Zügen erläutern; **draw a ~ distinction between ...:** grob unterscheiden zwischen (+ *Dat.*) ...; ⇒ *also* **daylight** A; Ⓓ (*generalized*) allgemein; **in the ~est sense** im weitesten Sinne; **as a ~ rule/indication** als Faustregel; Ⓔ (*strongly regional*) stark ‹Akzent›; breit ‹Aussprache›; **he speaks ~ Scots** er spricht breites Schottisch *od.* einen starken schottischen Dialekt; Ⓕ (*coarse*) derb ‹Humor, Geschichte›; Ⓖ (*tolerant*) großzügig; liberal; vielseitig ‹Interessen›; **B~ Church** *liberale Richtung in der Kirche von England*; Broad Church (*fachspr.*). ❷ *n.* Ⓐ (*broad part*) breiter Teil; **the ~ of the back** die Schultergegend; Ⓑ (*Amer.: woman*) Weib, *das* (*abwertend*); Weibsstück, *das* (*salopp abwertend*)

**broad: ~ 'bean** *n.* Saubohne, *die*; dicke Bohne; **~-brimmed** /'brɔːdbrɪmd/ *adj.* breitkrempig

**broadcast** /'brɔːdkɑːst/ ❶ *n.* (*Radio, Telev.*) Sendung, *die*; (*live*) Übertragung, *die*. ❷ *v.t.*, ~ *or* **~ed**, ~ Ⓐ (*Radio, Telev.*) senden; ausstrahlen; übertragen ‹Livesendung, Sportveranstaltung›; Ⓑ (*spread*) aussäen ‹Samen›; (*fig.*) verbreiten ‹Gerücht, Nachricht›; ausposaunen (*ugs.*) ‹Neuigkeit›. ❸ *v.i.*, ~ *or* **~ed** ‹Rundfunk-, Fernsehstation:› senden; ‹Redakteur usw.:› [im Rundfunk/Fernsehen] sprechen. ❹ *adj.* (*Radio, Telev.*) im Rundfunk/Fernsehen gesendet; Rundfunk-/Fernseh-; **a ~ appeal** ein Aufruf im Rundfunk/Fernsehen

**broadcaster** /'brɔːdkɑːstə(r)/ *n.* ▶ 1261 (*Radio, Telev.*) *jmd., der durch häufige Auftritte im Rundfunk und Fernsehen, besonders als Interviewpartner, Diskussionsteilnehmer od. Kommentator, bekannt ist*

**broadcasting** /'brɔːdkɑːstɪŋ/ *n., no pl.* (*Radio, Telev.*) Senden, *das*; (*of live programmes*) Übertragen, *das*; **written for ~:** für den Rundfunk/das Fernsehen geschrieben; **the early days of ~:** die Anfänge des Rundfunks; **work in ~:** beim Funk arbeiten

**broaden** /'brɔːdn/ ❶ *v.t.* Ⓐ verbreitern; Ⓑ (*fig.*) ausweiten ‹Diskussion›; ~ **one's mind** seinen Horizont erweitern; **travel ~s the mind** Reisen bildet. ❷ *v.i.* breiter werden; sich verbreitern; (*fig.*) sich erweitern; **her smile ~ed into a grin** ihr Lächeln verzog sich zu einem breiten Grinsen

**'broad jump** *n.* (*Amer. Sport*) Weitsprung, *der*

**broadly** /'brɔːdlɪ/ *adv.* Ⓐ deutlich ‹hinweisen›; breit ‹grinsen, lächeln›; Ⓑ (*in general*) allgemein ‹beschreiben›; ~ **speaking** allgemein gesprochen; ~ **based** auf breiter Grundlage *nachgestellt*

**broad: ~-'minded** *adj.* tolerant; **have very ~-minded views about sth.** sehr freie Ansichten über etw. (*Akk.*) haben; **~mindedness** /brɔːd'maɪndɪdnɪs/ *n., no pl.* Toleranz, *die*

**broadness** /'brɔːdnɪs/ ⇒ **breadth**

**broad: ~sheet** *n.* Ⓐ (*Printing*) Einblattdruck, *der*; Ⓑ (*pamphlet*) Flugblatt, *das*; **~-'shouldered** *adj.* breitschultrig; **~side** *n.* Ⓐ (*Naut.; also fig.*) Breitseite, *die*; **~side on [to sth.]** mit der Breitseite [nach etw.]; **fire [off] a ~side** (*lit. or fig.*) eine Breitseite abfeuern; Ⓑ ⇒ **~sheet**; **~sword** *n.* breites Schwert; Pallasch, *der*; **~way** *n.* Hauptstraße, *die*; **B~way** (*Amer.*) der Broadway

**brocade** /brə'keɪd/ *n.* Brokat, *der*

**broccoli** /'brɒkəlɪ/ *n.* Ⓐ (*heading ~*) Brokkoli, *der*; Spargelkohl, *der*; Ⓑ (*sprouting ~*) Schößlinge des Spargelkohls

**brochure** /'brəʊʃə(r), brəʊ'ʃʊə(r)/ *n.* Broschüre, *die*; Prospekt, *der*

**broderie anglaise** /'brəʊdrɪ ã'gleɪz/ *n.* Lochstickerei, *die*

**brogue**[1] /brəʊg/ *n.* Ⓐ (*rough shoe*) fester Schuh; Ⓑ (*decorated outdoor shoe*) Budapester, *der*

**brogue**[2] *n.* (*accent*) irischer Akzent

**broil** /brɔɪl/ *v.t.* braten; (*on gridiron*) grillen; **~ing sun** (*fig.*) brennende Sonne

**broiler** /'brɔɪlə(r)/ *n.* Ⓐ (*chicken*) Brathähnchen, *das*; [Gold]broiler, *der* (*DDR*); Ⓑ (*utensil*) Grill, *der*; Bratrost, *der*

**'broiler house** *n.* Hähnchenmästerei, *die*

**broke** /brəʊk/ ❶ ⇒ **break** 1, 2. ❷ *pred. adj.* (*coll.*) pleite (*ugs.*); **go ~:** pleite gehen; **go for ~** (*coll.*) alles auf eine Karte setzen; alles riskieren

**broken** /'brəʊkn/ ❶ ⇒ **break** 1, 2. ❷ *adj.* Ⓐ zerbrochen; gebrochen ‹Bein, Hals›; verletzt ‹Haut›; abgebrochen ‹Zahn›; gerissen ‹Seil›; kaputt (*ugs.*) ‹Uhr, Fernsehen, Fenster›; ~ **glass** Glasscherben; **get ~:** zerbrechen/brechen/reißen/kaputtgehen; **he got a ~ arm** er hat sich (*Dat.*) den Arm gebrochen; Ⓑ (*uneven*) uneben ‹Fläche›; bewegt ‹See, Wasser›; Ⓒ (*imperfect*) gebrochen; **in ~ English** in gebrochenem Englisch; Ⓓ (*fig.*) ruiniert ‹Ehe›; gebrochen ‹Person, Herz, Stimme›; unruhig, gestört ‹Schlaf›; **come from a ~ home** aus zerrütteten Familienverhältnissen kommen; **in a ~ voice** mit gebrochener Stimme

**broken: ~-down** *adj.* baufällig ‹Gebäude›; kaputt (*ugs.*) ‹Wagen, Maschine›; **~-hearted** /brəʊkn'hɑːtɪd/ *adj.* untröstlich; ~ **'line** *n.* gestrichelte Linie

**brokenly** /'brəʊknlɪ/ *adv.* gebrochen

**broker** /'brəʊkə(r)/ *n.* ▶ 1261 Ⓐ (*Commerc.: middleman*) Händler, *der*; Kommissionär, *der*; (*of real estate*) [Immobilien]makler, *der*; (*stock~*) [Börsen]makler, *der*; Ⓑ ⇒ **pawn~**; Ⓒ (*intermediary*) Vermittler, *der*; Unterhändler, *der*; ⇒ *also* **honest** A

**brolly** /'brɒlɪ/ *n.* (*Brit. coll.*) [Regen]schirm, *der*

**bromide** /'brəʊmaɪd/ *n.* Ⓐ (*Chem.*) Bromsalz, *das*; Ⓑ (*fig.*) (*person*) Langweiler, *der*; (*remark*) [All]gemeinplatz, *der*; Plattitüde, *die* (*abwertend*)

**bromine** /'brəʊmiːn/ *n.* (*Chem.*) Brom, *das*

**bronchial** /'brɒŋkɪəl/ *adj.* ▶ 1232 (*Anat., Med.*) bronchial; Bronchial-; ~ **tubes** Bronchien; ~ **pneumonia** Bronchopneumonie, *die*

**bronchitis** /brɒŋ'kaɪtɪs/ *n., no pl.* ▶ 1232 (*Med.*) Bronchitis, *die*

**bronco** /'brɒŋkəʊ/ *n., pl.* **~s** Ⓐ *wildes od. halbwildes Pferd im Westen der USA*; Ⓑ (*any horse*) Gaul, *der* (*ugs.*)

**bronze** /brɒnz/ ❶ *n.* Ⓐ Bronze, *die*; **the B~ Age** die Bronzezeit; **a statuette in ~:** eine Bronzestatuette; Ⓑ (*colour*) Bronze[farbe], *die*; Ⓒ (*work of art*) Bronze, *die*; Ⓓ (*medal*) Bronze, *die*. ❷ *attrib. adj.* Bronze-; (*coloured* *like* ~) bronzefarben; bronzen; ~ **medal** Bronzemedaille, *die.* ❸ *v.t.* bräunen ‹Gesicht, Haut›. ❹ *v.i.* braun werden

**bronzed** /brɒnzd/ *adj.* [sonnen]gebräunt; braun [gebrannt]

**brooch** /brəʊtʃ/ *n.* Brosche, *die*

**brood** /bru:d/ ❶ *n.* Ⓐ Brut, *die;* (*of hen*) Küken *Pl.;* Küchlein *Pl.* (*veralt.*); Ⓑ (*joc./derog.: human family*) Sippe, *die;* Sippschaft, *die;* (*children only*) Brut, *die.* ❷ *v.i.* Ⓐ (*think*) [vor sich (*Akk.*) hin] brüten; ~ **over** *or* **upon sth.** über etw. (*Akk.*) [nach]grübeln; über etw. (*Dat.*) brüten; Ⓑ (*sit*) ‹Vogel:› brüten; Ⓒ (*fig.: hang close*) **thunder clouds ~ed over the valley** Gewitterwolken hingen über dem Tal

'**brood mare** *n.* Zuchtstute, *die*

**broody** /'bru:dɪ/ *adj.* Ⓐ brütig; ~ **hen** Glucke, *die;* Ⓑ (*fig. coll.*) **she is getting** *or* **feeling ~:** in ihr werden Muttergefühle wach; Ⓒ (*fig.: depressed*) grüblerisch; schwermütig

**brook**[1] /brʊk/ *n.* Bach, *der*

**brook**[2] *v.t.* dulden; ~ **no nonsense/delay** keinen Unfug/Aufschub dulden

**broom** /bru:m/ *n.* Ⓐ Besen, *der;* **a new ~** (*fig.*) ein neuer Besen; **a new ~ sweeps clean** (*prov.*) neue Besen kehren gut; Ⓑ (*Bot.*) (*Genista*) Ginster, *der;* (*Cytisus scoparius*) Besenginster, *der*

**broom:** ~ **cupboard** *n.* Besenschrank, *der;* **~stick** *n.* Besenstiel, *der*

**Bros.** *abbr.* **Brothers** Gebr.

**broth** /brɒθ/ *n.* Ⓐ (*unclarified stock*) Brühe, *die;* Ⓑ (*thin soup*) Bouillon, *die;* [Fleisch]brühe, *die*

**brothel** /'brɒθl/ *n.* Bordell, *das*

**brother** /'brʌðə(r)/ *n.* Ⓐ Bruder, *der;* **they are ~ and sister** sie sind Geschwister *od.* Bruder und Schwester; **the ~s Robinson** *or* **Robinson ~s** die Brüder Robinson; **the Marx B~s** die Marx Brothers; Ⓑ (*friend, associate, fellow member*) Bruder, *der;* (*in trade union*) Kollege, *der;* **oh ~!** (*coll.*) Junge, Junge!; **be ~s in arms** Kameraden sein; *attrib.* **his ~ doctors/officers** seine Ärztekollegen/Offizierskameraden; Ⓒ *pl.* (*Commerc.*) **Hedges B~s** Gebrüder Hedges; Ⓓ *pl.* **brethren** /'breðrɪn/ (*Eccl.*) Bruder, *der*

**brotherhood** /'brʌðəhʊd/ *n.* Ⓐ *no pl.* Brüderschaft, *die;* brüderliches Verhältnis; **the ~ of all men** (*fig.*) die Gemeinschaft aller Menschen; Ⓑ (*association*) Bruderschaft, *die;* (*Amer.: trade union*) Gewerkschaft, *die*

'**brother-in-law** *n.*, *pl.* **brothers-in-law** Schwager, *der*

**brotherly** /'brʌðəlɪ/ *adj.* brüderlich; ~ **love** Bruderliebe, *die*

**brought** ⇒ **bring**

**brouhaha** /'bru:hɑ:hɑ:/ *n.* (*coll.*) (*noise*) Spektakel, *der* (*ugs.*); (*fuss*) Getue, *das*

**brow** /braʊ/ *n.* Ⓐ (*eye~*) Braue, *die;* Ⓑ (*forehead*) Stirn, *die;* Ⓒ (*of hill*) [Berg]kuppe, *die*

'**browbeat** *v.t.*, *forms as* **beat** 1 unter Druck setzen; einschüchtern; ~ **sb. into doing sth.** jmdn. so unter Druck setzen, dass er etw. tut; **I refuse to be ~en** ich lasse mich nicht unter Druck setzen

**brown** /braʊn/ ❶ *adj.* braun; **as ~ as berries/a berry** schokoladenbraun. ❷ *n.* Ⓐ Braun, *das;* Ⓑ (*Snooker*) braune Kugel; Ⓒ (~ *clothes*) **dressed in ~:** braun gekleidet. ❸ *v.t.* Ⓐ bräunen ‹Haut, Körper›; Ⓑ (*Cookery*) [an]bräunen; anbraten ‹Fleisch›; Ⓒ (*Brit. coll.*) **be ~ed off with sth./sb.** etw./jmdn. satt haben (*ugs.*); **be ~ed off with doing sth.** es satt haben, etw. zu tun (*ugs.*). ❹ *v.i.* Ⓐ ‹Haut:› bräunen; **I don't ~ easily** ich werde nicht leicht braun; Ⓑ (*Cookery*) ‹Fleisch:› braun werden

**brown:** ~ '**ale** *n.* dunkles Bier; ~ '**bear** *n.* Braunbär, *der;* ~ '**bread** *n.* ≈ Mischbrot, *das;* (*made with wholemeal flour*) Vollkornbrot, *das;* ~ '**coal** *n.* Braunkohle, *die;* **~-eyed** *adj.* braunäugig; **be ~-eyed** braune Augen haben

**brownie** /'braʊnɪ/ *n.* Ⓐ **the B~s** die Wichtel (*Pfadfinderinnen von 7-11 Jahren*); **get ~ points** (*fig. coll.*) Pluspunkte sammeln; Ⓑ (*elf*) Heinzelmännchen, *das;* Kobold, *der;* Wichtel, *der;* Ⓒ (*Amer.: cake*) *kleiner Schokoladenkuchen, oft mit Nüssen*

**browning** /'braʊnɪŋ/ *n.* (*Cookery*) (*sugar*) brauner Zucker; (*flour*) braunes Mehl

**brownish** /'braʊnɪʃ/ *adj.* bräunlich

**brown:** **~-nose** *v.i.* (*Amer. coll.*) hinten reinkriechen (*derb*); ~ '**paper** *n.* Packpapier, *das;* ~ '**rice** *n.* Naturreis, *der;* **B~shirt** *n.* (*Hist.*) Braunhemd, *das;* **~stone** *n.* (*Amer.*) Ⓐ rotbrauner Sandstein; Ⓑ (*house*) Sandsteinhaus, *das;* ~ '**study** *n.* **be in a ~ study** geistesabwesend *od.* in Gedanken verloren sein; ~ '**sugar** *n.* brauner Zucker

**browse** /braʊz/ ❶ *v.t.* Ⓐ abgrasen ‹Weide›; abfressen ‹Blätter›; Ⓑ (*Computing*) ~ **sth** in etw. (*Dat.*) suchen. ❷ *v.i.* Ⓐ ‹Vieh:› weiden; ‹Wild:› äsen; ~ **on sth.** etw. fressen; Ⓑ (*fig.*) ~ **through a book/a magazine** in einem Buch schmökern/in einer Zeitschrift blättern; **I'm just browsing** (*in shop*) ich sehe mich nur mal um. Ⓒ (*Computing*) suchen; ~ **through sth.** etw. durchsuchen. ❸ *n.* (*fig.*) **have a ~:** sich umsehen; **it's worth a ~:** es ist das Reinschauen wert

**browser** /'braʊzə(r)/ *n.* (*Computing*) Browser, *der*

**Bruges** /bru:ʒ/ *pr. n.* ▶ **1626** Brügge (*das*)

**bruise** /bru:z/ ❶ *n.* Ⓐ (*Med.*) blauer Fleck; Ⓑ (*on fruit*) Druckstelle, *die.* ❷ *v.t.* Ⓐ quetschen ‹Obst, Pflanzen›; ~ **oneself/one's leg** sich stoßen/sich am Bein stoßen; **he was badly ~d when he fell off his bike** er hat sich (*Dat.*) starke Prellungen zugezogen, als er vom Rad fiel; **the peaches are ~d/easily ~d** die Pfirsiche haben Druckstellen/bekommen leicht Druckstellen; Ⓑ (*fig.*) mitnehmen. ❸ *v.i.* ‹Person:› blaue Flecken bekommen; ‹Obst:› Druckstellen bekommen

**bruiser** /'bru:zə(r)/ *n.* (*coll.*) Schläger, *der* (*abwertend*)

**brunch** /brʌnʃ/ *n.* (*coll.*) Brunch, *der;* ausgedehntes, spätes Frühstück

**brunette** /bru:'net/ ❶ *n.* Brünette, *die.* ❷ *adj.* brünett

**Brunswick** /'brʌnzwɪk/ ▶ **1626** ❶ *pr. n.* Braunschweig (*das*). ❷ *attrib. adj.* Braunschweiger

**brunt** /brʌnt/ *n.* Hauptlast, *die;* **the main** *or* **full ~ of the attack fell on the French** die Franzosen waren der vollen Wucht des Angriffs ausgesetzt; **the ~ of the financial cuts** die Hauptlast der Einsparungen; **bear the ~:** das meiste abkriegen

**brush** /brʌʃ/ ❶ *n.* Ⓐ Bürste, *die;* (*for sweeping*) Hand-, Kehrbesen, *der;* (*with short handle*) Handfeger, *der;* (*for scrubbing*) [Scheuer]bürste, *die;* (*for painting or writing*) Pinsel, *der;* **flat ~:** Flachpinsel, *der;* Ⓑ (*quarrel, skirmish*) Zusammenstoß, *der;* **his first ~ with the law came at an early age** er kam schon früh mit dem Gesetz in Konflikt; Ⓒ (*light touch*) flüchtige Berührung; Ⓓ (*tail*) (*of squirrel*) Rute, *die;* (*of fox*) Lunte, *die;* Ⓔ **give your hair/teeth a ~:** bürste dir die Haare/putz dir die Zähne; **give your shoes/clothes a ~:** bürste deine Schuhe/Kleider ab; Ⓕ (*Amer., Austral.: undergrowth*) Unterholz, *das;* Ⓖ (*land covered with undergrowth*) Buschland, *das.* ❷ *v.t.* Ⓐ (*sweep*) kehren; fegen; abbürsten ‹Kleidung›; ~ **one's teeth/hair** sich (*Dat.*) die Zähne putzen/die Haare bürsten; ~ **the dust from one's coat/the shelf** den Staub vom Mantel bürsten/vom Regal wischen; Ⓑ (*treat*) bepinseln, bestreichen ‹Teigwaren, Gebäck›; **~ed aluminium/fabric** aufgerautes Aluminium/aufgerauter Stoff; Ⓒ (*touch in passing*) flüchtig berühren; streifen; ~ **one's hand over one's hair/brow** sich (*Dat.*) mit der Hand über das Haar/die Stirn fahren. ❸ *v.i.* ~ **by** *or* **against** *or* **past sb./sth.** jmdn./etw. streifen

~ **a'side** *v.t.* beiseite schieben ‹Personen, Hindernis›; abtun, vom Tisch wischen ‹Einwand, Zweifel, Beschwerde›

~ **a'way** *v.t.* abwischen, wegwischen ‹Staub, Schmutz›; verscheuchen ‹Insekt›

~ **'down** *v.t.* abbürsten ‹Kleidungsstück›; ~ **oneself down** sich abbürsten; (*with hand*) sich abklopfen

~ **'off** *v.t.* Ⓐ abbürsten ‹Schmutz usw.›; (*with hand or cloth*) abwischen; wegwischen; verscheuchen ‹Insekt›; Ⓑ (*fig.: rebuff*) abblitzen lassen (*ugs.*); **she ~ed me off** sie gab mir einen Korb; ⇒ *also* **brush-off**

~ **'up** ❶ *v.t.* Ⓐ zusammenfegen ‹Krümel›; Ⓑ auffrischen ‹Sprache, Kenntnisse›. ❷ *v.i.* ~ **up on** auffrischen. ⇒ *also* **brush-up**

'**brushfire** ❶ *n.* Buschfeuer, *das.* ❷ *adj.* (*fig.*) ~ **warfare** begrenzter Krieg *od.* Konflikt

**brushless** /'brʌʃlɪs/ *adj.* schaumlos ‹Rasiercreme›

**brush:** **~-off** *n.* Abfuhr, *die;* **give sb. the ~-off** jmdm. einen Korb geben (*ugs.*); jmdn. abblitzen lassen (*ugs.*); ~ **stroke** *n.* Pinselstrich, *der;* **~-up** *n.* Ⓐ **I'll have to give my English a ~-up** ich muss meine Englischkenntnisse auffrischen; Ⓑ **have a wash and ~-up** sich frisch machen; **~wood** *n.* Ⓐ Reisig, *das;* Ⓑ (*thicket*) Dickicht, *das;* Unterholz, *das;* **~work** *n.* Pinselführung, *die*

**brusque** /brʊsk, brʌsk/ *adj.*, **brusquely** /'brʊsklɪ, 'brʌsklɪ/ *adv.* schroff

**brusqueness** /'brʊsknɪs, 'brʌsknɪs/ *n.*, *no pl.* Schroffheit, *die*

**Brussels** /'brʌslz/ *pr. n.* ▶ **1626** Brüssel (*das*)

**Brussels:** ~ '**carpet** *n.* Brüsseler Teppich; ~ '**lace** *n.* Brüsseler Spitze[n]; ~ '**sprouts** *n. pl.* Rosenkohl, *der;* Kohlsprossen (*österr.*)

**brutal** /'bru:tl/ *adj.* brutal; (*fig.*) brutal, schonungslos ‹Offenheit›; bitter ‹Wahrheit›

**brutalism** /'bru:təlɪzm/ *n.* Ⓐ Brutalität, *die;* Ⓑ (*Art, Archit.*) Brutalismus, *der*

**brutality** /bru:'tælɪtɪ/ *n.* Brutalität, *die*

**brutalization** /bru:təlaɪ'zeɪʃn/ *n.* (*treating brutally*) brutale Behandlung; (*becoming brutalized*) Verrohung, *die*

**brutalize** /'bru:təlaɪz/ ❶ *v.t.* Ⓐ verrohen lassen; brutalisieren; Ⓑ (*treat brutally*) brutal behandeln. ❷ *v.i.* verrohen

**brutally** /'bru:təlɪ/ *adv.* brutal; **be ~ frank with sb.** (*fig.*) mit jmdm. schonungslos offen sein

**brute** /bru:t/ ❶ *n.* Ⓐ (*animal*) Bestie, *die;* Ⓑ (*brutal person*) Rohling, *der;* brutaler Kerl (*ugs.*); (*thing*) höllische Sache; **a ~ of a problem** (*fig.*) ein höllisches Problem; **a drunken ~:** ein brutaler Trunkenbold; **an unfeeling ~ of a man** eine gefühllose Bestie; Ⓒ (*coll.: person*) Kerl, *der* (*ugs.*). ❷ *attrib. adj.* (*without capacity to reason*) vernunftlos; irrational; (*merely material*) roh ‹Gewalt›; nackt ‹Tatsachen›; bitter ‹Notwendigkeit›; ~ **beasts** wilde Tiere *Pl.;* **by ~ force** mit roher Gewalt

**brutish** /'bru:tɪʃ/ *adj.* brutal ‹Flegel›; tierisch ‹Leidenschaften, Gelüste›; **lead a ~ existence** das Leben eines Tieres führen

**bryony** /'braɪənɪ/ *n.* (*Bot.*) Zaunrübe, *die*

**BS** *abbr.* Ⓐ **British Standard** Britische Norm; Ⓑ **Bachelor of Surgery** „Bachelor" der Chirurgie; ⇒ *also* **B. Sc.**; Ⓒ (*Amer.*) **Bachelor of Science;** ⇒ *also* **B. Sc.**

**B. Sc.** /bi:es'si:/ *abbr.* **Bachelor of Science** Bakkalaureus der Naturwissenschaften; **John Clarke ~** John Clarke, Bakkalaureus der Naturwissenschaften; **he is a** *or* **has a ~** ≈ er hat ein Diplom in Naturwissenschaften; **[study for] one's** *or* **a ~ in physics/chemistry** ≈ ein Diplom in Physik/Chemie [machen wollen]

**BSE** *abbr.* **bovine spongiform encephalopathy** BSE

**BSI** *abbr.* **British Standards Institution** Britischer Normenausschuss

**BST** *abbr.* **British Summer Time** Britische Sommerzeit

**Bt.** *abbr.* **baronet**

**bubble** /'bʌbl/ ❶ *n.* Ⓐ Blase, *die;* (*small*) Perle, *die;* (*fig.*) Seifenblase, *die;* **blow ~s** [Seifen]blasen machen; **the/his ~ has burst** (*fig.*) alles ist wie eine Seifenblase zerplatzt; Ⓑ (*sound or appearance of boiling*)

Brodeln, *das;* Ⓒ (*domed canopy*) [Glas]kuppel, *die.* ❷ *v.i.* Ⓐ (*rise in ~s*) ‹Schlamm:› in Blasen aufsteigen; (*form ~s*) ‹Wasser, Schlamm, Lava:› Blasen bilden; ‹Suppe, Flüssigkeiten:› brodeln; (*make sound of ~s*) ‹Bach, Quelle:› plätschern; ‹Schlamm:› blubbern; Ⓑ (*fig.*) **~ with sth.** vor etw. (*Dat.*) übersprudeln

**~ 'over** *v.i.* überschäumen; **~ over with excitement/joy** (*fig.*) vor Aufregung/übersprudeln/vor Freude überquellen

**~ 'up** *v.i.* ‹Gas:› in Blasen aufsteigen; ‹Wasser:› aufsprudeln

**bubble: ~ and 'squeak** *n.* Pfannengericht aus Gemüse und Kartoffeln [mit Fleischresten]; **~ bath** *n.* Schaumbad, *das;* **~ car** *n.* Kabinenroller, *der;* **~ gum** *n.* Bubble-Gum, *der;* Ballonkaugummi, *der;* **~ pack** *n.* Klarsichtpackung, *die;* **~-wrapped** *adj.* in Luftpolsterfolie verpackt

**bubbly** /'bʌblɪ/ ❶ *adj.* Ⓐ sprudelnd; schäumend ‹Bade-, Spülwasser›; Ⓑ (*fig. coll.*) quirlig (*ugs.*) ‹Person›. ❷ *n.* (*Brit. coll.*) Schampus, *der* (*ugs.*)

**bubonic plague** /bju:bɒnɪk 'pleɪg/ *n.* ▶ 1232 (*Med.*) Beulenpest, *die*

**buccaneer** /bʌkə'nɪə(r)/ *n.* Seeräuber, *der;* Freibeuter, *der* (*auch fig.*)

**Bucharest** /bju:kə'rest/ *pr. n.* ▶ 1626 Bukarest (*das*)

**buck**[1] /bʌk/ ❶ *n.* Ⓐ (*male*) männliches Tier; Männchen, *das;* (*deer, chamois*) Bock, *der;* (*rabbit, hare*) Rammler, *der;* Ⓑ (*arch.: dandy*) Geck, *der* (*abwertend*); Stutzer, *der* (*abwertend*); Ⓒ *attrib.* **~ private** (*Amer. Mil. sl.*) Schütze Arsch (*derb*). ❷ *v.i.* ‹Pferd:› bocken. ❸ *v.t.* Ⓐ **~ [off]** ‹Pferd:› abwerfen; Ⓑ (*Amer.: resist*) sich sträuben gegen; sich widersetzen (+ *Dat.*)

**buck**[2] *n.* (*coll.*) **pass the ~ to sb.** (*fig.*) jmdm. den Schwarzen Peter zuschieben; jmdm. die Verantwortung aufhalsen; **the ~ stops here** (*fig.*) die Verantwortung liegt letzten Endes bei mir

**buck**[3] (*coll.*) ❶ *v.i.* **~ 'up** Ⓐ (*make haste*) sich ranhalten (*ugs.*); **~ up!** los, schnell!; auf, los!; Ⓑ (*cheer up*) ein fröhliches Gesicht machen; **~ up!** Kopf hoch! ❷ *v.t.* **~ 'up** Ⓐ (*cheer up*) aufmuntern; **we were ~ed up by the good news** die gute Nachricht hat uns aufgemuntert; Ⓑ **~ one's ideas up** (*coll.*) sich zusammenreißen

**buck**[4] *n.* ▶ 1328 (*Amer. and Austral. coll.: dollar*) Dollar, *der;* **make a fast ~:** eine schnelle Mark machen (*ugs.*)

**bucked** /bʌkt/ *adj.* (*coll.*) aufgemuntert; **I was** *or* **felt ~ by it** es hat mich aufgemuntert

**bucket** /'bʌkɪt/ ❶ *n.* Ⓐ Eimer, *der;* **a ~ of water** ein Eimer [voll] Wasser; **the rain fell in ~s** (*fig.*) es goss wie aus Kübeln (*ugs.*); es schüttete (*ugs.*); **kick the ~** (*fig. coll.*) abkratzen (*derb*); ins Gras beißen (*salopp*); Ⓑ (*of waterwheel*) Schaufelkammer, *die.* ❷ *v.i.* Ⓐ (*pour down*) **the rain is ~ing down** es gießt wie aus Kübeln (*ugs.*); es schüttet (*ugs.*); Ⓑ (*move jerkily*) ‹Fahrzeug:› holpern; ‹Boot:› schaukeln

**bucketful** /'bʌkɪtfʊl/ *n.* Eimer [voll]; **two ~s of water** zwei Eimer [voll] Wasser

**bucket: ~ seat** *n.* Schalensitz, *der;* **~ shop** *n.* [nicht ganz seriöses] Maklerbüro; (*for air tickets*) Reisebüro (*das vor allem Billigflüge vermittelt*)

**buckle** /'bʌkl/ ❶ *n.* Schnalle, *die.* ❷ *v.t.* Ⓐ zuschnallen; **~ sth. on** etw. anschnallen; **~ sth. up** etw. festschnallen *od.* zuschnallen; Ⓑ (*crumple*) verbiegen ‹Stoßstange, Rad›. ❸ *v.i.* ‹Rad, Metallplatte:› sich verbiegen; **~ under the weight** unter dem Gewicht nachgeben

**~ to** ❶ /'--/ *v.t.* **~ [down] to a task/to work** sich hinter eine Aufgabe klemmen/sich an die Arbeit machen. ❷ /--'-/ *v.i.* sich zusammenreißen (*ugs.*); sich am Riemen reißen (*ugs.*)

**buckler** /'bʌklə(r)/ *n.* (*Hist.*) Rundschild, *der*

**buckram** /'bʌkrəm/ *n.* (*Textiles*) Buckram, *der*

**buck 'rarebit** *n. überbackene Käseschnitte mit pochiertem Ei*

**Buck's Fizz** /bʌks 'fɪz/ *n.* Sekt mit Orangensaft

**buckshee** /'bʌkʃi:/ (*Brit. coll.*) ❶ *adj.* Gratis-; **a ~ trip** eine Reise zum Nulltarif; eine Gratisreise. ❷ *adv.* gratis, umsonst ‹bekommen, reisen›; zum Nulltarif ‹reisen›

**buck: ~shot** *n.* grober Schrot; Rehposten, *der;* **~thorn** *n.* (*Bot.*) Kreuzdorn, *der;* **~-tooth** *n.* vorstehender Zahn; Raffzahn, *der* (*ugs.*)

**buckwheat** /'bʌkwi:t/ *n.* (*Agric.*) Buchweizen, *der*

**bucolic** /bju:'kɒlɪk/ *adj.* bukolisch

**bud** /bʌd/ ❶ *n.* Knospe, *die;* **come into ~/be in ~:** knospen; Knospen treiben; **the trees are in ~:** die Bäume schlagen aus; **nip sth. in the ~** (*fig.*) etw. im Keim ersticken. ❷ *v.i.*, **-dd-** knospen; Knospen treiben; ‹Baum:› ausschlagen; **a ~ding painter/actor** (*fig.*) ein angehender Maler/Schauspieler

**Buddha** /'bʊdə/ *n.* Buddha, *der*

**Buddhism** /'bʊdɪzm/ *n.* Buddhismus, *der*

**Buddhist** /'bʊdɪst/ ❶ *n.* Buddhist, *der*/Buddhistin, *die.* ❷ *adj.* buddhistisch

**buddleia** /'bʌdlɪə/ *n.* (*Bot.*) Schmetterlingsstrauch, *der;* Buddleia, *die* (*fachspr.*)

**buddy** /'bʌdɪ/ (*coll.*) ❶ *n.* Kumpel, *der* (*ugs.*). ❷ *v.i.* **~ up [with sb.]** sich [mit jmdm.] anfreunden

**budge** /bʌdʒ/ ❶ *v.i.* ‹Person, Tier:› sich [von der Stelle] rühren; ‹Gegenstand:› sich bewegen, nachgeben; (*fig.: change opinion*) nachgeben. ❷ *v.t.* Ⓐ bewegen; **I can't ~ this screw** ich kriege diese Schraube nicht los; Ⓑ (*fig.: change opinion*) abbringen; **he refuses to be ~d** er lässt sich nicht umstimmen

**budgerigar** /'bʌdʒərɪgɑ:(r)/ *n.* Wellensittich, *der*

**budget** /'bʌdʒɪt/ ❶ *n.* Budget, *das;* Etat, *der;* Haushalt[splan], *der;* **keep within ~:** seinen Etat nicht überschreiten; **be on a ~:** haushalten *od.* wirtschaften müssen; **~ meal/holiday** preisgünstige Mahlzeit/Ferien. ❷ *v.i.* planen; **~ for sth.** etw. [im Etat] einplanen. ❸ *v.t.* [im Etat] einplanen

**'budget account** *n.* Konto für laufende Zahlungen

**budgetary** /'bʌdʒɪtərɪ/ *adj.* budgetär; Budget- ‹beratung, -betrag, -entwurf, -vorlage›

**budget: ~ day** *n.* Haushaltsdebattentermin, *der;* **~ speech** *n.* Etatrede, *die*

**budgie** /'bʌdʒɪ/ *n.* (*coll.*) Wellensittich, *der*

**budo** /'bu:dəʊ/ *n.* Budo, *das*

**buff** /bʌf/ ❶ *adj.* gelbbraun. ❷ *n.* Ⓐ (*coll.: enthusiast*) Fan, *der* (*ugs.*); Ⓑ **in the ~:** nackt; im Adams-/Evaskostüm (*scherzh.*); **strip down to the ~:** sich bis auf die Haut ausziehen; Ⓒ (*colour*) Gelbbraun, *das.* ❸ *v.t.* Ⓐ (*polish*) polieren, [blank] putzen ‹Metall, Schuhe usw.›; Ⓑ aufrauen ‹Leder›

**buffalo** /'bʌfələʊ/ *n., pl.* **~es** *or same* (*Zool.*) Büffel, *der*

**buffer**[1] /'bʌfə(r)/ ❶ *n.* Ⓐ (*Railw.*) Prellbock, *der;* (*on vehicle; also Chem., fig.*) Puffer, *der;* Ⓑ (*Computing*) Pufferspeicher, *der.* ❷ *v.t.* dämpfen

**buffer**[2] *n.* (*Brit. coll.*) **old ~:** alter Zausel (*ugs.*)

**'buffer state** *n.* Pufferstaat, *der*

**'buffer zone** *n.* Pufferzone, *die*

**buffet**[1] /'bʌfɪt/ ❶ *n.* (*blow, lit. or fig.*) Schlag, *der;* **~s of fate** Schicksalsschläge. ❷ *v.t.* schlagen; **~ed by the wind/waves** vom Wind geschüttelt/von den Wellen hin und her geworfen

**buffet**[2] /'bʊfeɪ/ *n.* Ⓐ (*Brit.: place*) Büfett, *das;* **~ car** (*Railw.*) Büfettwagen, *der;* Ⓑ (*Brit.: meal*) Imbiss, *der;* **~ lunch/supper/meal** Büfettessen, *das;* **a cold ~:** ein kaltes Büfett; Ⓒ (*cupboard*) Büfett, *das;* Geschirrschrank, *der;* (*sideboard*) Anrichte, *die*

**buffeting** /'bʌfɪtɪŋ/ *n.* Schütteln, *das;* (*fig.*) Schläge; **~s of fate** Schicksalsschläge

**buffoon** /bə'fu:n/ ❶ *n.* Kasper, *der;* Clown, *der.* ❷ *v.i.* den Clown *od.* Kasper spielen

**buffoonery** /bə'fu:nərɪ/ *n.* Clownerie, *die;* Possenreißerei, *die*

**bug** /bʌg/ ❶ *n.* Ⓐ Wanze, *die;* Ⓑ (*Amer.: small insect*) Insekt, *das;* Käfer, *der;* Ⓒ (*coll.: virus*) Bazillus, *der;* **don't you breathe your ~s over me** steck mich nicht an; Ⓓ (*coll.: disease*) Infektion, *die;* Krankheit, *die;* **catch a ~:** sich (*Dat.*) eine Krankheit *od.* (*ugs.*) was holen; **I don't want to catch that ~ of yours** ich will mich nicht bei dir anstecken; Ⓔ (*coll.: concealed microphone*) Wanze, *die* (*ugs.*); Ⓕ (*coll.: defect*) Macke, *die* (*salopp*); **we have got all the ~s out of the system** wir haben alle Fehler im System beseitigt; Ⓖ (*coll.: obsession*) Tick, *der* (*ugs.*); **he has a ~ about neatness** er hat einen Ordnungsfimmel (*ugs.*); **then I got the ~:** dann packte es mich; Ⓗ (*coll.: enthusiast*) Fan, *der* (*ugs.*).
❷ *v.t.*, **-gg-:** Ⓐ (*coll.: install microphone in*) verwanzen ‹Zimmer› (*ugs.*); abhören ‹Telefon, Konferenz›; **~ging device** Abhöreinrichtung, *die;* Wanze, *die* (*ugs.*); Ⓑ (*coll.*) (*annoy*) nerven (*salopp*); den Nerv töten (+ *Dat.*) (*ugs.*); (*bother*) beunruhigen; **what's ~ging you?** was ist los mit dir?

**bugbear** /'bʌgbeə(r)/ *n.* Ⓐ (*annoyance, problem*) Problem, *das;* Sorge, *die;* Ⓑ (*object of fear*) Schreckgespenst, *das*

**bugger** /'bʌgə(r)/ ❶ *n.* Ⓐ (*sodomite*) Analverkehr Ausübender; Sodomit, *der;* Ⓑ (*coarse*) (*fellow*) Bursche, *der* (*ugs.*); Macker, *der* (*salopp*); *as insult* Scheißkerl, *der* (*derb*); Arschloch, *das* (*salopp*); **you lucky ~:** du hast vielleicht ein Schwein *od.* Dusel (*ugs.*); **you poor ~:** du kannst einem Leid tun; **play silly ~s** Scheiß machen (*derb*); Ⓒ (*coarse: thing*) Scheißding, *das* (*derb*); **that door is a ~ to open** diese Scheißtür geht immer so schwer auf (*derb*); Ⓓ (*coarse: damn*) **~!** Scheiße! (*derb*); **I don't give a ~ what you think** ich gebe einen Scheiß drauf, was du denkst (*derb*).
❷ *v.t.* Ⓐ anal verkehren mit; Ⓑ (*coarse: damn*) **~ you/him** (*dismissive*) du kannst/der kann mich mal (*derb*); **~ this car/him!** (*angry*) dieses Scheißauto/dieser Scheißkerl! (*derb*); **~ it!** ach du Scheiße (*derb*); (*in surprise*) **well, ~ me** *or* **I'll be ~ed!** ach du Scheiße *od.* meine Fresse! (*derb*); Ⓒ (*coarse: tire*) **be [completely] ~ed** [total] fertig sein (*ugs.*)

**~ a'bout, ~ a'round** (*coarse*) ❶ *v.i.* Scheiß machen (*derb*); rumblödeln (*ugs.*); **~ about with sth.** mit etw. rumfummeln (*ugs.*). ❷ *v.t.* verarschen (*derb*)

**~ 'off** *v.i.* (*coarse*) abhauen (*ugs.*); **~ off!** hau ab! (*ugs.*); verdufte! (*ugs.*); verpiss dich! (*salopp*)

**~ 'up** *v.t.* (*coarse*) verkorksen (*ugs.*)

**bugger-'all** *n.* (*coarse*) rein gar nichts; Null Komma nichts; **be worth ~:** keinen Pfifferling wert sein (*ugs.*); zum Wischen sein (*salopp*)

**buggery** /'bʌgərɪ/ *n.* Analverkehr, *der*

**Buggins's turn** /'bʌgɪnzɪz tɜ:n/ *n.* (*Brit.*) Ernennung aufgrund von Dienstjahren

**buggy** /'bʌgɪ/ *n.* Ⓐ (*horse-drawn or motor vehicle*) Buggy, *der;* Ⓑ (*pushchair*) Sportwagen, *der;* Ⓒ (*Amer.*) ⇒ **baby buggy**

**bugle[-horn]** /'bju:gl(hɔ:n)/ *n.* Bügelhorn, *das*

**bugler** /'bju:glə(r)/ *n.* Hornist, *der*

**build** /bɪld/ ❶ *v.t.*, **built** /bɪlt/ Ⓐ bauen; errichten ‹Gebäude, Damm›; mauern ‹Schornstein, Kamin›; zusammenbauen *od.* -setzen ‹Fahrzeug›; **the house is still being built** das Haus ist noch im Bau; **the house took three years to ~:** der Bau des Hauses dauerte drei Jahre; **he was the man who built the bridge** er war der Erbauer der Brücke; **the house is solidly built** das Haus ist sehr solide; **~ a fire** [ein] Feuer machen; **~ sth. from** *or* **out of sth.** etw. aus etw. machen *od.* bauen; **the dinghy was built from a kit** das Dingi entstand aus einem Bausatz; **be sturdily/strongly built** (*fig.*) ‹Sache:› solide gebaut sein; ‹Person:› stämmig/kräftig gebaut sein; Ⓑ (*fig.*) aufbauen ‹System, Gesellschaft, Reich, Zukunft›; schaffen ‹bessere Zukunft, Bedingungen, Beziehung›; begründen ‹Ruf›; **~ one's hopes upon sb./sth.** seine Hoffnungen auf jmdn./etw. setzen; **~ a new career for oneself** sich (*Dat.*) eine neue Existenz aufbauen.

b

❷ *v.i.*, **built** [A] bauen; [B] (*fig.*) ‹Drama, Musik:› sich steigern (**to** zu); **~ on one's successes** auf seinen Erfolgen aufbauen.
❸ *n.* Bauweise, *die;* (*of person*) Körperbau, *der*

**~ 'in** *v.t.* einbauen; ⇒ *also* **built-in**

**~ into** *v.t.* **~ sth. into sth.** (*to form part*) etw. in etw. (*Akk.*) einbauen; (*fig.*) **~ a clause into a contract** eine Klausel in einen Vertrag aufnehmen

**~ on** *v.t.* [A] aufbauen auf (+ *Dat.*); bebauen ‹Gelände›; [B] (*attach*) **~ sth. on to sth.** etw. an etw. (*Akk.*) anbauen

**~ 'up** ❶ *v.t.* [A] bebauen ‹Land, Gebiet›; [B] (*accumulate*) aufhäufen ‹Reserven, Mittel, Kapital›; **~ up a reputation** sich (*Dat.*) einen Namen machen; **~ up a fine reputation as a speaker** sich (*Dat.*) einen ausgezeichneten Ruf als Redner erwerben; [C] (*strengthen*) stärken ‹Gesundheit, Widerstandskraft›; widerstandsfähig machen, kräftigen ‹Person, Körper›; [D] (*increase*) erhöhen, steigern ‹Produktion, Kapazität›; verstärken ‹Truppen›; stärken ‹[Selbst]vertrauen›; **~ up sb.'s hopes [unduly]** jmdm. [falsche] Hoffnung machen; [E] (*develop*) aufbauen ‹Firma, Geschäft›; (*expand*) ausbauen; **~ sth. up from nothing** etw. aus dem Nichts aufbauen; **~ up one's strength** sich kräftigen; ‹Athlet:› seine Muskelkraft trainieren; [F] (*praise, boost*) aufbauen ‹Star, Schauspieler›; **the film was built up to be something marvellous** der Film wurde großartig herausgebracht *od.* angekündigt; **he wasn't half the performer he was built up to be** seine Vorstellung war nicht mal halb so gut wie angekündigt. ❷ *v.i.* [A] ‹Spannung, Druck:› zunehmen, ansteigen; ‹Musik:› anschwellen; ‹Lärm:› sich steigern (**to** in + *Akk.*); **~ up to a crescendo** sich zu einem Crescendo steigern; [B] ‹Schlange, Rückstau:› sich bilden; ‹Verkehr:› sich verdichten, sich stauen. ⇒ *also* **build-up; built-up, built-up**

**builder** /ˈbɪldə(r)/ *n.* ▶1261 [A] Erbauer, *der;* [B] (*contractor*) Bauunternehmer, *der;* **~'s labourer** Bauarbeiter, *der;* **~'s merchant** (*person*) Baustoffhändler, *der;* (*firm*) Baustoffhandlung, *die*

**building** /ˈbɪldɪŋ/ *n.* [A] Bau, *der;* (*of vehicle*) Zusammenbauen/-setzen, *das;* **~ commenced three years ago** mit dem Bau wurde vor drei Jahren begonnen; *attrib.* **~ materials** Baumaterialien; **~ operations** Baumaßnahmen; **~ land** Bauland, *das;* [B] (*structure*) Gebäude, *das;* (*for living in*) Haus, *das*

**building: ~ contractor** *n.* ▶1261 Bauunternehmer, *der;* **~ line** *n.* (*Archit.*) Bauflucht[linie], *die;* **~-site** *n.* Baustelle, *die;* **~ society** *n.* (*Brit.*) Bausparkasse, *die;* **~ trade** *n.* Baugewerbe, *das*

**'build-up** *n.* [A] (*publicity*) Reklame[rummel], *der;* Werbung, *die;* **give sb./sth. a good ~:** jmdn./etw. groß ankündigen; **give a film a massive ~:** für einen Film kräftig die Werbetrommel rühren; [B] (*approach to climax*) Vorbereitungen *Pl.* (**to** für); [C] (*increase*) Zunahme, *die;* (*of forces*) Verstärkung, *die;* **a ~ of traffic** ein [Verkehrs]stau *od.* eine Stauung

**built** ⇒ **build** 1, 2

**built: ~-in** *adj.* [A] eingebaut; **a ~-in cupboard/bookcase/kitchen** ein Einbauschrank/-regal/eine Einbauküche; [B] (*fig.: instinctive*) angeboren; **the system has ~-in safeguards against accidents** (*fig.*) das System hat eine Art eingebauten Schutz gegen Unfälle; ⇒ *also* **obsolescence**; **~-up** *adj.* [A] bebaut; **a ~-up area** ein Wohngebiet; **the speed limit applies in all ~-up areas** die Geschwindigkeitsbegrenzung gilt für alle geschlossenen Ortschaften; [B] (*prefabricated*) vorgefertigt; [C] **~-up shoulders** [aus]wattierte *od.* gepolsterte Schultern; **a ~-up shoe** ein Schuh mit dickerer Sohle

**bulb** /bʌlb/ *n.* [A] (*Bot., Hort.*) Zwiebel, *die;* [B] (*of lamp*) [Glüh]birne, *die;* [C] (*of thermometer, chemical apparatus*) [Glas]kolben, *der;* [D] (*of syringe, dropper, horn*) Gummiballon, *der*

**bulbous** /ˈbʌlbəs/ *adj.* [A] bauchig ‹Form›; bulbös, bulboid ‹Schwellung›; **~ fingers/nose** Wurstfinger/Knollennase, *die;* [B] (*Bot.*) Zwiebel-; zwiebelartig

**Bulgaria** /bʌlˈgeərɪə/ *pr. n.* Bulgarien (*das*)

**Bulgarian** /bʌlˈgeərɪən/ ▶1275, ▶1340 ❶ *adj.* bulgarisch; **he/she is ~:** er ist Bulgare/sie ist Bulgarin; ⇒ *also* **English** 1. ❷ *n.* [A] (*person*) Bulgare, *der*/Bulgarin, *die;* [B] (*language*) Bulgarisch, *das;* ⇒ *also* **English** 2 A

**bulge** /bʌldʒ/ ❶ *n.* [A] Ausbeulung, *die;* ausgebeulte Stelle; (*in line*) Bogen, *der;* (*in tyre*) Wulst, *der od. die;* [B] (*coll.: increase*) Anstieg, *der* (**in** *Gen.*); [C] (*Mil.*) Frontausbuchtung, *die.* ❷ *v.i.* [A] (*swell outwards*) sich wölben; **her eyes ~d out of her head** (*fig. coll.*) die Augen traten ihr [fast] aus dem Kopf; sie bekam Stielaugen (*ugs.*); [B] (*be full*) voll gestopft sein (**with** mit)

**bulging** /ˈbʌldʒɪŋ/ *adj.* prall gefüllt ‹Einkaufstasche usw.›; voll gestopft ‹Hosentasche, Kiste›; rund ‹Bauch›; **~ eyes** hervortretende Augen; (*in surprise*) staunende Augen

**bulimia (nervosa)** /bʊˈliːmɪə(nɜːˈvəʊsə)/ *n.* Bulimie, *die;* Bulimia nervosa, *die* (*fachspr.*)

**bulimic** /bʊˈlɪmɪk/ ❶ *n.* Bulimiker, *der*/Bulimikerin, *die.* ❷ *adj.* bulimisch

**bulk** /bʌlk/ ❶ *n.* [A] (*large quantity*) **in ~:** in großen Mengen; [B] (*large shape*) massige Gestalt; [C] (*size*) Größe, *die;* **be of great ~:** [sehr] massig sein; [D] (*volume*) Menge, *die;* Umfang, *der;* **sea water is heavier, ~ for ~, than fresh water** Seewasser ist, Quantum für Quantum, schwerer als Süßwasser; [E] (*greater part*) **the ~ of the money/goods** der Groß- *od.* Hauptteil des Geldes/der Waren; **the ~ of the population/votes** die Mehrheit der Bevölkerung/Stimmen; [F] (*Commerc.*) **in ~** (*loose*) lose; unabgefüllt ‹Wein›; (*wholesale*) en gros; **~ transport** Massentransport, *der;* **~ sales** Großverkauf, *der.*
❷ *v.i.* **~ large** eine wichtige Rolle spielen.
❸ *v.t.* [A] (*combine*) zu einer Sendung zusammenstellen; [B] (*make thicker*) anschwellen lassen; an Umfang zunehmen lassen

**bulk: ~ 'buyer** *n.* Großabnehmer, *der;* **~ 'buying** *n.* Großeinkauf, *der;* **~ 'carrier** *n.* Bulkfrachter, *der;* **~ goods** *n. pl.* Schüttgut, *das;* **~head** *n.* Schott, *das*

**bulkiness** /ˈbʌlkɪnɪs/ *n., no pl.* (*unwieldiness*) Unhandlichkeit, *die*

**bulky** /ˈbʌlkɪ/ *adj.* sperrig ‹Gegenstand›; beleibt ‹Person›; massig, wuchtig ‹Gestalt, Körper›; unförmig ‹Kleidungsstück›; (*unwieldy*) unhandlich ‹Gegenstand, Paket›; **~ goods** Sperrgut, *das;* **a ~ book** ein dickes Buch

**bull**[1] /bʊl/ ❶ *n.* [A] Bulle, *der;* (*for ~fight*) Stier, *der;* **like a ~ in a china shop** (*fig.*) wie ein Elefant im Porzellanladen; **like a ~ at a gate** wie ein Wilder; **take the ~ by the horns** (*fig.*) den Stier bei den Hörnern fassen *od.* packen; [B] (*Astrol.*) **the B~:** der Stier; ⇒ *also* **archer** B; [C] (*whale, elephant*) Bulle, *der;* [D] ⇒ **~'s eye a;** [E] (*Amer. coll.: policeman*) Bulle, *der* (*salopp*); [F] (*St. Exch.*) Haussier, *der.* ❷ *adj.* bullig

**bull**[2] *n.* (*RC Ch.*) Bulle, *die*

**bull**[3] ⇒ **Irish bull**

**bull**[4] *n.* (*coll.*) [A] (*routine*) [lästige] Routine; (*Mil.: discipline*) Drill, *der;* [B] (*nonsense*) Geschwafel, *das* (*ugs. abwertend*); Gesülze, *das* (*salopp abwertend*); [C] (*Amer.: blunder*) grober Schnitzer

**bull: ~-at-a-gate** *adj., adv.* wild; rücksichtslos; **~ bar** *n.* Rammschutz, *der;* Rammbügel, *der;* **~ calf** *n.* Bullenkalb, *das;* **~dog** *n.* [A] Bulldogge, *die;* **he's one of the ~dog breed** (*fig.*) er ist hartnäckig und fürchtet sich vor nichts; **~dog clip** Flügelklammer, *die;* [B] (*Brit. Univ.*) Helfer des Proktors; **~doze** *v.t.* [A] planieren ‹Boden›; mit der Planierraupe wegräumen ‹Gebäude›; **~doze a path** mit der Planierraupe einen Weg bahnen; [B] (*fig.: force*) **~doze sb. into doing sth.** jmdn. dazu zwingen, etw. zu tun; **the Bill was ~dozed through Parliament by the government** (*fig.*) das Gesetz wurde von der Regierung im Parlament durchgeboxt; **~dozer** /ˈbʊldəʊzə(r)/ *n.* Planierraupe, *die;* Bulldozer, *der*

**bullet** /ˈbʊlɪt/ *n.* [Gewehr-, Pistolen]kugel, *die;* ⇒ *also* **bite** 2 D

**bullet: ~ head** *n.* [kugel]runder Kopf; Rundkopf, *der;* **~ hole** *n.* Einschuss, *der;* Einschussloch, *das;* **be riddled with ~ holes** von Kugeln durchsiebt sein

**bulletin** /ˈbʊlɪtɪn/ *n.* Bulletin, *das;* **we will bring you further ~s to keep you informed** wir bringen Ihnen weitere Meldungen, um Sie auf dem Laufenden zu halten

**'bulletin board** *n.* [A] (*Amer.*) Anschlagtafel, *die;* (*Sch., Univ.*) Schwarzes Brett; [B] (*Computing*) Schwarzes Brett

**bullet: ~proof** *adj.* kugelsicher; **~proof glass** Panzerglas, *das;* **~ wound** *n.* Schusswunde, *die*

**bull: ~fight** *n.* Stierkampf, *der;* **~fighter** *n.* ▶1261 Stierkämpfer, *der;* **~fighting** *n.* Stierkämpfe; **~finch** *n.* (*Ornith.*) Gimpel, *der;* **~frog** *n.* Ochsenfrosch, *der;* **~horn** *n.* Megaphon, *das;* Flüstertüte, *die* (*ugs. scherzh.*)

**bullion** /ˈbʊljən/ *n., no pl., no indef. art.* Bullion, *das* (*fachspr.*); **gold/silver ~:** ungemünztes Gold/Silber; (*ingots*) Gold-/Silberbarren *Pl.*

**bullish** /ˈbʊlɪʃ/ *adj.* (*St. Exch.*) haussierend; auf Hausse spekulierend ‹Kapitalanleger›; **feel ~:** in Haussestimmung sein; (*fig.*) in optimistischer Stimmung sein

**bull: ~ market** *n.* (*St. Exch.*) Haussemarkt, *der;* **~ neck** *n.* Stiernacken, *der;* **~-necked** *adj.* stiernackig; **~-nose[d]** /ˈbʊlnəʊz(d)/ *adj.* abgerundet

**bullock** /ˈbʊlək/ *n.* Ochse, *der*

**bull: ~ point** *n.* (*coll.*) Vorteil, *der;* **~ring** *n.* Stierkampfarena, *die;* **~ session** *n.* (*esp. Amer.*) zwanglose Diskussionsrunde; (*men only*) Männerrunde, *die* (*ugs.*); **~seye** *n.* [A] (*of target*) Schwarze, *das;* **score a ~seye** (*lit. or fig.*) ins Schwarze treffen; [B] (*boss of glass*) Butzen, *der;* (*Naut.*) Bullauge, *das;* (*Archit.*) Ochsenauge, *das;* [C] (*boiled sweet*) rundes, schwarz-weißes Pfefferminzbonbon; **~shit** (*coarse*) *n.* Scheiße, *die* (*salopp abwertend*); **~ terrier** *n.* Bullterrier, *der*

**bully**[1] /ˈbʊlɪ/ ❶ *n.* [A] *jmd., der gern Schwächere schikaniert bzw. tyrannisiert;* (*esp. schoolboy etc.*) ≈ Rabauke, *der* (*abwertend*); (*boss*) Tyrann, der; [B] (*hired ruffian*) ⇒ **bully-boy**. ❷ *v.t.* (*persecute*) schikanieren; (*frighten*) einschüchtern; **~ sb. into/out of doing sth.** jmdn. so sehr einschüchtern, dass er etw. tut/lässt

**bully**[2] (*coll.*) ❶ *adj.* toll (*ugs.*); prima (*ugs.*). ❷ *int.* **~ for you** (*also iron.*) gratuliere!; **~ for him!** (*also iron.*) da muss man ihm gratulieren!

**bully**[3] (*Hockey*) ❶ *n.* Bully, *das.* ❷ *v.i.* **~ off** das Bully ausführen (*fachspr.*)

**bully: ~ beef** *n.* Cornedbeef, *das;* **~ boy** *n.* [angeheuerter] Schläger; **a gang of ~ boys** ein Schlägertrupp

**bullying** /ˈbʊlɪɪŋ/ ❶ *n.* Schikanieren, *das.* ❷ *adj.* tyrannisch

**'bully-off** *n.* (*Hockey*) Bully, *das* (*fachspr.*)

**bulrush** /ˈbʊlrʌʃ/ *n.* [A] (*Bot.*) Teichsimse, *die;* [B] (*Bibl.*) Rohr, *das*

**bulwark** /ˈbʊlwək/ *n.* [A] (*rampart*) Wall, *der;* Bollwerk, *das* (*auch fig.*); [B] (*breakwater*) Mole, *die;* [C] *usu. in pl.* (*Naut.*) Schanzkleid, *das*

**bum**[1] /bʌm/ *n.* (*Brit. coll.*) Hintern, *der* (*ugs.*); Arsch, *der* (*derb*)

**bum**[2] (*coll.*) ❶ *n.* (*Amer.*) [A] (*tramp*) Penner, *der* (*salopp abwertend*); Berber, *der* (*salopp*); [B] (*lazy dissolute person*) Penner, *der* (*salopp abwertend*); Gammler, *der* (*ugs. abwertend*); [C] **be on the ~** (*be a vagrant*) rumgammeln (*ugs.*); als Berber leben (*salopp*); (*cadge*) schnorren (*ugs.*). ❷ *adj.* mies (*ugs.*); schlimm (*ugs.*) ‹Fuß, Bein usw.›; **a ~ cheque** ein fauler Scheck (*ugs.*). ❸ *v.i.*, **-mm-: ~ [about** *or* **around]** rumgammeln (*ugs.*). ❹ *v.t.*, **-mm-** schnorren (*ugs.*) ‹Zigaretten usw.› (**off** bei); **~ one's way through France** durch Frankreich gammeln (*ugs.*)

**bumble** /ˈbʌmbl/ *v.i.* zockeln (*ugs.*); ~ **about** herumwursteln (*ugs.*)

ˈ**bumble-bee** *n.* Hummel, *die*

**bumbling** /ˈbʌmblɪŋ/ *adj.* stümperhaft

**bumf** /bʌmf/ *n.* (*Brit. coll.*) **A** (*derog.: papers*) Papierkram, *der* (*ugs.*); **B** (*toilet paper*) Klopapier, *das* (*ugs.*)

**bump** /bʌmp/ **1** *n.* **A** (*sound*) Bums, *der;* (*impact*) Stoß, *der;* **this car has had a few ~s** der Wagen hat schon einige Dellen abgekriegt; **B** (*swelling*) Beule, *die;* **C** (*hump*) Buckel, *der* (*ugs.*); Hubbel, *der* (*ugs.*); **D** (*on skull*) Höcker, *der;* **E** (*coll.: dancer's forward thrust of abdomen*) Stoß, *der* [mit dem Bauch]; **~s and grinds** erotische Zuckungen. **2** *adv.* bums; rums, bums; **the car went ~ into the vehicle in front** das Auto bumste gegen das Fahrzeug vor ihm; **be afraid of things that go ~ in the night** Angst vor komischen Geräuschen in der Nacht haben. **3** *v.t.* **A** anstoßen; **I ~ed the chair against the wall** ich stieß mit dem Stuhl an die Wand; **B** (*hurt*) **~ one's head/knee** sich am Kopf/Knie stoßen. **4** *v.i.* **A** **~ against sth.** an etw. (*Akk.*) *od.* gegen etw. stoßen; **~ against sb.** jmdn. anstoßen; **B** (*move with jolts*) rumpeln; **~ down the stairs** die Treppe runterpurzeln (*ugs.*)

**~ into** *v.t.* **A** stoßen an (+ *Akk.*) *od.* gegen; (*with car, shopping trolley, etc.*) fahren gegen ‹Mauer, Baum›; **~ into sb.** jmdn. anstoßen; (*with vehicle*) jmdn. anfahren; **I ~ed into the back of another car** ich hatte einen Auffahrunfall; **B** (*meet by chance*) zufällig [wieder]treffen; **if you ~ into Tom, tell him ...:** wenn dir Tom über den Weg läuft, sag ihm, ...

**~ ˈoff** *v.t.* (*coll.*) kaltmachen (*salopp*); umlegen (*salopp*)

**~ up** *v.t.* (*coll.*) aufschlagen ‹Preise›; aufbessern ‹Gehalt›

**bumper** /ˈbʌmpə(r)/ **1** *n.* **A** (*Motor Veh.*) Stoßstange, *die;* **B** (*Amer. Railw.*) Puffer, *der;* **C** (*brim-full glass*) [rand]volles Glas; **D** (*Cricket*) Schmetterball, *der.* **2** *adj.* Rekord‹ernte, -jahr›; **~ edition** [besonders umfangreiche] Extra- *od.* Sonderausgabe

**bumper:** **~ car** *n.* [Auto]skooter, *der;* **~-to-~** **1** *adj.* **a ~-to-~ traffic jam** ein Stau, bei dem nichts mehr geht/ging; **2** *adv.* Stoßstange an Stoßstange

**bumpkin** /ˈbʌmpkɪn/ *n.* **[country] ~:** [Bauern]tölpel, *der* (*abwertend*)

**bumptious** /ˈbʌmpʃəs/ *adj.*, **bumptiously** /ˈbʌmpʃəslɪ/ *adv.* wichtigtuerisch

**bumptiousness** /ˈbʌmpʃəsnɪs/ *n.*, *no pl.* Wichtigtuerei, *die*

**bumpy** /ˈbʌmpɪ/ *adj.* holp[e]rig ‹Straße, Fahrt, Fahrzeug›; uneben ‹Fläche›; unruhig ‹Flug›

**bum:** **~ ˈrap** *n.* (*Amer. coll.*) Verurteilung unter falscher Anklage; **~'s ˈrush** *n.* (*Amer. coll.*) Rausschmiss, *der* (*ugs.*); **give sb. the ~'s rush** jmdn. rausschmeißen (*ugs.*); **~ ˈsteer** *n.* (*Amer. sl.*) **give sb. a ~ steer** jmdn. in die falsche Richtung lenken

**bun** /bʌn/ *n.* **A** süßes Brötchen; (*currant ~*) Korinthenbrötchen, *das;* **B** (*hair*) [Haar]knoten, *der.* ⇒ *also* **oven**

**bunch** /bʌntʃ/ **1** *n.* **A** (*of flowers*) Strauß, *der;* (*of grapes, bananas*) Traube, *die;* (*of parsley, radishes*) Bund, *das;* **~ of flowers/grapes** Blumenstrauß, *der*/Traube, *die;* **a ~ of roses/parsley** ein Strauß Rosen/Bund Petersilie; **a ~ of keys** ein Schlüsselbund; **B** (*lot*) Anzahl, *die;* **a whole ~ of ...:** ein ganzer Haufen ... (*ugs.*); **the best** *or* **pick of the ~:** der/die/das Beste [von allen]; **C** (*coll.: gang*) Bande, *die* (*ugs.*); (*group*) Haufen, *der* (*ugs.*); **look a real ~ of idiots** wie ein Haufen [von] Idioten dastehen (*ugs.*).
**2** *v.t.* **A** zu einem Strauß/zu Sträußen binden ‹Blumen›; bündeln ‹Radieschen, Spargel›; zusammendrängen ‹Personen›; **the runners were tightly ~ed as they came round the final bend** die Läufer lagen alle dicht beieinander, als sie in die Zielgerade einbogen; **B** (*gather into folds*) [zusammen]raffen ‹Kleid›

**~ ˈup** **1** *v.i.* ‹Personen:› zusammenrücken; ‹Kleid, Stoff:› sich zusammenknüllen. **2** *v.t.* zusammenraffen ‹Kleid›

**bundle** /ˈbʌndl/ **1** *n.* **A** Bündel, *das;* (*of papers*) Packen, *der;* (*of hay*) Bund, *das;* (*of books*) Stapel, *der;* (*of fibres, nerves*) Strang, *der;* **tie sth. up in a ~:** etw. zu einem Bündel zusammenbinden; **in ~s** bündelweise; **she's a ~ of mischief/energy/misery** (*fig.*) sie hat nichts als Unfug im Kopf/ist ein Energiebündel/ist ein Häufchen Unglück *od.* Elend; **B** (*coll.: large amount of money*) Vermögen, *das;* [schöne] Stange Geld (*ugs.*); **C** (*coll.*) **go a ~ on sb./sth.** von jmdm./etw. begeistert sein. ⇒ *also* **nerve** 1 B; **D** (*Computing*) Paket, *das.*
**2** *v.t.* **A** bündeln; **B** (*throw hastily*) **~ sth. into the suitcase/back of the car** etw. in den Koffer stopfen/hinten ins Auto werfen; **C** (*put hastily*) **~ sb. into the car** jmdn. ins Auto verfrachten *od.* packen; **D** (*Computing*) in einem *od.* als Paket verkaufen.

**~ ˈoff** *v.t.* [eilig] schaffen; schicken

**~ ˈup** *v.t.* **A** (*put in ~s*) bündeln; **B** (*dress warmly*) einmummeln (*fam.*)

ˈ**bunfight** *n.* (*Brit. coll. joc.*) Teegesellschaft, *die*

**bung** /bʌŋ/ **1** *n.* Spund[zapfen], *der.* **2** *v.t.* **A** verspunden; spunden; **B** (*coll.: throw*) schmeißen (*ugs.*)

**~ ˈup** *v.t.* **be/get ~ed up** verstopft sein/verstopfen

**bungalow** /ˈbʌŋgələʊ/ *n.* Bungalow, *der*

**bungee jumping** /ˈbʌndʒɪ/ *n.*, *no pl.* Bungeespringen, *das*

ˈ**bunghole** *n.* Spundloch, *das*

**bungle** /ˈbʌŋgl/ **1** *v.t.* stümpern bei; **~ it/the job** alles vermasseln. **2** *n.* Stümperei, *die* (*ugs.*)

**bungler** /ˈbʌŋglə(r)/ *n.* Stümper, *der* (*abwertend*)

**bungling** /ˈbʌŋglɪŋ/ **1** *adj.* stümperhaft ‹Versuch›; **~ person** Stümper, *der;* **you ~ idiot!** du Trottel! **2** *n.* Stümperei, *die*

**bunion** /ˈbʌnjən/ *n.* ▶ 1232 (*Med.*) chronische Bursitis bei Hallux valgus (*fachspr.*); ≈ entzündeter Ballen

**bunk**[1] /bʌŋk/ *n.* (*in ship, aircraft, lorry*) Koje, *die;* (*in room, sleeping car*) Bett, *das;* (*~ bed*) Etagenbett, *das*

**bunk**[2] *n.* (*coll.: nonsense*) Quatsch, *der* (*salopp*); Mist, *der* (*salopp*)

**bunk**[3] *n.* (*Brit. coll.*) **do a ~:** türmen (*salopp*); **the cashier did a ~ with the money** der Kassierer brannte mit dem Geld durch (*ugs.*)

ˈ**bunk bed** *n.* Etagenbett, *das*

**bunker** /ˈbʌŋkə(r)/ **1** *n.* (*fuel ~ also Mil., Golf*) Bunker, *der.* **2** *v.t.* (*Golf*) **be ~ed** im Bunker *od.* Sand liegen; (*fig. coll.*) in der Klemme sitzen (*ugs.*)

**bunkum** /ˈbʌŋkəm/ *n.* Unsinn, *der*

**bunny** /ˈbʌnɪ/ *n.* Häschen, *das*

**Bunsen burner** /bʌnsn ˈbɜːnə(r)/ *n.* Bunsenbrenner, *der*

**bunting**[1] /ˈbʌntɪŋ/ *n.* (*Ornith.*) Ammer, *die*

**bunting**[2] *n.*, *no pl.* **A** (*fabric*) Fahnentuch, *das;* **B** (*flags, decoration*) [bunte] Fähnchen; Wimpel *Pl.*

**buoy** /bɔɪ/ **1** *n.* **A** Boje, *die;* (*buoyant part*) Schwimmkörper, *der;* **B** (*life~*) Rettungsring, *der.* **2** *v.t.* **~ [up]** über Wasser halten; (*fig.: support, sustain*) aufrechterhalten; **I was ~ed [up] by the thought that ...:** der Gedanke, dass ..., hielt mich aufrecht *od.* ließ mich durchhalten

**buoyancy** /ˈbɔɪənsɪ/ *n.* **A** (*of body*) Auftrieb, *der;* **B** (*fig.*) (*of stock market prices*) Aufwärtstendenz, *die;* (*of person*) Schwung, *der;* Elan, *der*

ˈ**buoyancy tank** *n.* (*Naut.*) Trimmtank, *der*

**buoyant** /ˈbɔɪənt/ *adj.* **A** Auftrieb habend; schwimmend; **be [more] ~:** [einen größeren] Auftrieb haben; [besser] schwimmen; **B** (*fig.*) rege, lebhaft ‹Markt›; heiter, munter ‹Person›; federnd ‹Schritt›; **share prices were ~ today** die Kurse sind heute gestiegen *od.* hochgegangen; **in ~ spirits** in Hochstimmung

**bur** /bɜː(r)/ *n.* **A** (*Bot.; also fig.*) Klette, *die;* **B** ⇒ **burr** A; **C** ⇒ **burr** B

**burble** /ˈbɜːbl/ *v.i.* **A** (*speak lengthily*) **~ [on] about sth.** von etw. ständig quasseln (*ugs.*); **~ [on] incessantly to sb.** jmdm. die Ohren voll schwatzen (*ugs.*); **B** (*make a murmuring sound*) brummeln (*ugs.*); ‹Baby:› plappern; ‹Bach:› murmeln

**burbot** /ˈbɜːbət/ *n.* (*Zool.*) Aalquappe, *die*

**burden** /ˈbɜːdn/ **1** *n.* **A** (*load*) Last, *die;* (*fig.*) Last, *die;* Bürde, *die* (*geh.*); **beast of ~:** Lasttier, *das;* **become a ~:** zur Last werden; **be a ~ to sb.** für jmdn. eine Belastung sein; (*less serious*) jmdm. zur Last fallen; **put a fresh ~ upon sb.** ‹Person:› jmdm. eine zusätzliche Last aufladen; ‹Sache:› für jmdn. eine zusätzliche Belastung darstellen; **put too much of a ~ upon sb.** jmdn. überlasten; **the ~ of proof rests with** *or* **on you** Sie tragen die Beweislast; **tax ~:** steuerliche Belastung; Steuerlast, *die;* **B** (*chief theme*) Schwerpunkt, *der;* Kern, *der;* **C** (*of song*) Refrain, *der;* **D** (*Naut.: tonnage*) Tonnage, *die;* Tragfähigkeit, *die.*
**2** *v.t.* belasten; **they were heavily ~ed** sie hatten schwer *od.* eine schwere Last zu tragen; (*fig.*) **~ sb./oneself with sth.** jmdn./sich mit etw. belasten; **~ sb./oneself with too many responsibilities** jmdm./sich zu viel Verantwortung aufladen

**burdensome** /ˈbɜːdnsəm/ *adj.* schwer ‹Last›; (*fig.*) lästig ‹Person, Pflicht, Verantwortung›; **become/be ~ to sb.** jmdm. zur Last werden/fallen

**burdock** /ˈbɜːdɒk/ *n.* (*Bot.*) Klette, *die*

**bureau** /ˈbjʊərəʊ, bjʊəˈrəʊ/ *n.*, *pl.* **~x** /ˈbjʊərəʊz, bjʊəˈrəʊz/ *or* **~s** **A** (*Brit.: writing desk*) Schreibschrank, *der;* Sekretär, *der;* (*Amer.: chest of drawers*) Kommode, *die;* **B** (*office*) Büro, *das;* (*department*) Abteilung, *die;* (*Amer.: government department*) Dienststelle, *die;* Amt, *das*

**bureaucracy** /bjʊəˈrɒkrəsɪ/ *n.* **A** Bürokratie, *die;* **B** (*officials*) Beamte *Pl.;* Bürokraten *Pl.* (*abwertend*)

**bureaucrat** /ˈbjʊərəkræt/ *n.* Bürokrat, *der*/Bürokratin, *die* (*abwertend*)

**bureaucratic** /bjʊərəˈkrætɪk/ *adj.* bürokratisch; **~ mentality** Beamtenmentalität, *die*

**bureaucratically** /bjʊərəˈkrætɪkəlɪ/ *adv.* bürokratisch

**bureau de change** /bjʊərəʊ də ʃɑ̃ʒ/ *n.* Wechselstube, *die*

**burette** (*Amer.:* **buret**) /bjʊəˈret/ *n.* (*Chem.*) Bürette, *die*

**burg** /bɜːg/ *n.* (*Amer. coll.*) Ort, *der*

**burgee** /bɜːˈdʒiː/ *n.* (*Naut.*) [gezackter] Stander; (*triangular*) Wimpel, *der*

**burgeon** /ˈbɜːdʒən/ *v.i.* **A** (*begin to grow rapidly*) blühen; **the arts and sciences ~ed** die Künste und Wissenschaften erlebten eine Blütezeit; **B** (*bud*) ‹Pflanze:› sprießen; ‹Baum:› Knospen treiben, ausschlagen

**burger** /ˈbɜːgə(r)/ *n.* (*coll.*) Hamburger, *der*

ˈ**burger bar** *n.* (*coll.*) Hamburgerlokal, *das*

**burgess** /ˈbɜːdʒɪs/ *n.* **A** (*Brit.*) Bürger, *der*/Bürgerin, *die;* **B** (*Amer.*) Stadtverordnete, *der*/*die*

**burgh** /ˈbʌrə/ *n.* (*Scot. Hist.*) Stadt mit Stadtrechten; freie Stadt

**burgher** /ˈbɜːgə(r)/ *n.* Bürger, *der*/Bürgerin, *die*

**burglar** /ˈbɜːglə(r)/ *n.* Einbrecher, *der*

ˈ**burglar alarm** *n.* Alarmanlage, *die*

**burglarize** /ˈbɜːgləraɪz/ (*Amer.*) ⇒ **burgle** 1

ˈ**burglar-proof** *adj.* einbruch[s]sicher

**burglary** /ˈbɜːglərɪ/ *n.* Einbruch, *der;* (*offence*) [Einbruchs]diebstahl, *der*

**burgle** /ˈbɜːgl/ **1** *v.t.* einbrechen in (+ *Akk.*); **the shop/he was ~d** in dem Laden/bei ihm wurde eingebrochen. **2** *v.i.* einen Einbruch begehen

**burgomaster** /ˈbɜːgəmɑːstə(r)/ *n.* Bürgermeister, *der* (*einer holländ. od. fläm. Stadt*)

**burgundy** *n.* **A** (*wine*) Burgunder[wein], *der;* **B** (*colour*) Burgunderrot, *das*

**Burgundy** /ˈbɜːgəndɪ/ *pr. n.* Burgund (*das*)

**burial** /ˈberɪəl/ *n.* Bestattung, *die;* Begräbnis, *das;* (*funeral*) Beerdigung, *die;* Beisetzung, *die* (*geh.*); **Christian ~:** christliches Begräbnis; **~ at sea** Seebestattung, *die*

**burial:** ~ **ground** *n.* Begräbnisstätte, *die;* ~ **mound** *n.* Grabhügel, *der;* ~ **service** *n.* Trauerfeier, *die*

**burin** /ˈbjʊərɪn/ *n.* [A] Stichel, *der;* Punze, *die;* [B] *(Archaeol.)* Meißel, *der*

**burlap** /ˈbɜːlæp/ *n.* Sackleinen, *das*

**burlesque** /bɜːˈlesk/ ❶ *adj.* burlesk, possenhaft ‹Theaterstück›; parodistisch ‹Literatur, Rede›; ~ **show** Varieteevorstellung, *die.* ❷ *n.* [A] Kabarett, *das;* Varietee, *das;* [B] *(book, play)* Burleske, *die;* *(parody)* Parodie, *die;* [C] *(Amer.: variety show)* Varietee, *das;* Tingeltangel, *das (abwertend).* ❸ *v.t.* parodieren

**burly** /ˈbɜːlɪ/ *adj.* kräftig; stämmig; stramm ‹Soldat›

**Burma** /ˈbɜːmə/ *pr. n.* Birma *(das)*

**Burmese** /bɜːˈmiːz/ ▶ 1275, ▶ 1340 ❶ *adj.* birmanisch; **sb. is** ~: jmd. ist Birmane/Birmanin; ⇒ *also* **English** 1. ❷ *n., pl. same* [A] *(person)* Birmane, *der*/Birmanin, *die;* [B] *(language)* Birmanisch, *das;* ⇒ *also* **English** 2 A

**burn**[1] /bɜːn/ ❶ *n.* ▶ 1232 *(on the skin)* Verbrennung, *die;* *(on material)* Brandfleck, *der;* *(hole)* Brandloch, *das;* **second-degree** ~**s** Verbrennungen zweiten Grades.

❷ *v.t.,* ~**t** /bɜːnt/ *or* ~**ed** [A] verbrennen; ~ **a hole in sth.** ein Loch in etw. *(Akk.)* brennen; **money** ~**s a hole in his pocket** *(fig.)* das Geld rinnt ihm nur so durch die Finger; ~ **one's boats** *or* **bridges** *(fig.)* alle Brücken hinter sich *(Dat.)* abbrechen; [B] *(use as fuel)* als Brennstoff verwenden ‹Gas, Öl usw.›; heizen mit ‹Kohle, Holz, Torf›; verbrauchen ‹Strom›; *(use up)* verbrauchen ‹Treibstoff›; verfeuern ‹Holz, Kohle›; ~ **coal in the stove** den Ofen mit Kohle feuern; **this lamp** ~**s oil** das ist eine Öllampe; **have money to** ~ *(fig.)* Geld wie Heu haben; **I haven't got money to** ~: ich bin doch kein Krösus *(ugs.);* [C] ▶ 1232 *(injure)* verbrennen; ~ **oneself/one's hand** sich verbrennen/sich *(Dat.)* die Hand verbrennen; **he was severely** ~**t in the fire** er erlitt schwere Brandverletzungen; ~ **one's fingers, get one's fingers** ~**t** *(fig.)* sich *(Dat.)* die Finger verbrennen *(fig.);* [D] *(spoil)* anbrennen lassen ‹Fleisch, Kuchen›; **be** ~**t** angebrannt sein; ~**t toast** verbrannter *od.* schwarzer Toast; [E] *(cause burning sensation to)* verbrennen; **this curry is** ~**ing my throat** das Curry verbrennt mir den Hals *od.* brennt mir im Hals; [F] *(put to death)* ~ **sb. [at the stake/alive]** jmdn. [auf dem Scheiterhaufen/bei lebendigem Leibe] verbrennen; [G] *(fire, harden)* brennen; ~ **wood to make** *or* **for charcoal** Holz zu Holzkohle verbrennen; [H] *(corrode)* ätzen; verätzen ‹Haut›; [I] *(parch)* **the earth was** ~**ed brown/dry** die Erde war ganz versengt/ausgedörrt.

❸ *v.i.,* ~**t** *or* ~**ed** [A] brennen; ~ **to death** verbrennen; **five people** ~**ed to death in the fire** fünf Menschen kamen in den Flammen um; **may you** ~ **in hell** in der Hölle sollst du schmoren *(ugs.);* [B] *(blaze)* ‹Feuer:› brennen; ‹Gebäude:› in Flammen stehen, brennen; [C] *(give light)* ‹Lampe, Kerze, Licht:› brennen; ~ **lower** ‹Kerze:› herunterbrennen; ‹Lampe:› schwach brennen; [D] ▶ 1232 *(be injured)* sich verbrennen; **she/her skin** ~**s easily** sie bekommt leicht einen Sonnenbrand; [E] *(be spoiled)* ‹Kuchen, Milch, Essen:› anbrennen; [F] *(feel hot)* brennen; glühen; *(fig.)* [glut]rot sein **(with** vor + *Dat.*); **her cheeks were** ~**ing with embarrassment** sie lief vor Verlegenheit rot an; **I was** ~**ing with shame** ich wurde rot vor Scham; **his ears were** ~**ing** *(fig.)* ihm klangen die Ohren; [G] *(fig.: be passionate)* ~ **with rage/anger** vor Wut/Ärger kochen; ~ **with desire/longing [for sb.]** sich vor Verlangen/Sehnsucht [nach jmdm.] verzehren; **be** ~**ing with curiosity** vor Neugierde sterben; **be** ~**ing to do sth.** darauf brennen, etw. zu tun; [H] *(be corrosive)* ätzen; ätzend sein

~ **a'way** ❶ *v.t.* verbrennen; *(by laser etc.)* wegbrennen. ❷ *v.i.* [A] *(continue to* ~*)* weiterbrennen; vor sich *(Dat.)* hin brennen; [B] *(diminish, be destroyed)* verbrennen; ‹Kerze, Docht:› herunterbrennen

~ **'down** ❶ *v.t.* niederbrennen. ❷ *v.i.* ‹Gebäude:› niederbrennen, abbrennen; *(less brightly)* ‹Feuer, Kerze:› herunterbrennen

~ **'in** *v.t. (lit. or fig.)* einbrennen

~ **into** *v.t.* einbrennen in (+ *Akk.*); **the events were** ~**t into her memory** *(fig.)* die Ereignisse hatten sich ihrem Gedächtnis *od.* in ihr Gedächtnis eingebrannt

~ **'out** ❶ *v.t.* [A] ausbrennen; **the fire** ~**ed itself out** das Feuer brannte aus *od.* nieder; [B] *(fig.)* **feel** ~**ed out** sich erschöpft fühlen; total kaputt sein *(ugs.);* ~ **oneself out** sich völlig verausgaben *od. (ugs.)* kaputtmachen; [C] **the family was** ~**ed out of house and home** Haus und Hof der Familie waren abgebrannt; [D] *(Electr.)* durchbrennen lassen ‹Sicherung›; ausbrennen lassen ‹Motor›. ❷ *v.i.* [A] ‹Kerze, Feuer:› erlöschen, ausgehen; ‹Rakete, Raketenstufe:› ausbrennen; [B] *(Electr.)* durchbrennen

~ **'up** ❶ *v.t.* [A] verbrennen; verbrauchen ‹Energie›; ~ **up the road** *(fig. coll.)* die Straße entlangrasen; [B] *(Amer.: make furious)* in Wut versetzen; zur Weißglut bringen *(fig.);* fuchsteufelswild machen *(ugs.).* ❷ *v.i.* [A] *(begin to blaze)* auflodern; [B] *(be destroyed)* ‹Rakete, Meteor, Satellit:› verglühen

**burn**[2] *n. (Scot.)* Bach, *der*

**'burned-out** *adj. (lit. or fig.)* ausgebrannt

**burner** /ˈbɜːnə(r)/ *n.* Brenner, *der;* ⇒ *also* **back burner; Bunsen burner**

**burning** /ˈbɜːnɪŋ/ ❶ *adj.* [A] brennend; [B] *(fig.)* glühend ‹Leidenschaft, Hass, Wunsch›; brennend ‹Wunsch, Frage, Problem, Ehrgeiz›; **sth. is a** ~ **shame** etw. ist eine wahre Schande *od.* schreit zum Himmel. ❷ *n.* Brennen, *das;* **a smell of** ~: ein Brandgeruch

**'burning glass** *n.* Brennglas, *das*

**burnish** /ˈbɜːnɪʃ/ *v.t.* polieren

**'burn-out** *n.* Burn-out, *das (Med.);* totale Erschöpfung *od.* Entkräftung; **risk** ~: Gefahr laufen, sich zu übernehmen

**burnt** ⇒ **burn**[1] 2, 3

**burnt:** ~ **'offering** *n.* Brandopfer, *das;* *(fig. joc.: burnt food)* angebranntes Essen; ~-**out** ⇒ **burned-out**

**burp** /bɜːp/ *(coll.)* ❶ *n.* Rülpser, *der (ugs.);* *(of baby)* Bäuerchen, *das (fam.);* **emit a loud** ~**/a series of** ~**s** laut/mehrmals rülpsen. ❷ *v.i.* rülpsen *(ugs.);* aufstoßen. ❸ *v.t.* ein Bäuerchen machen lassen *(fam.)* ‹Baby›

**burr** /bɜː(r)/ *n.* [A] *(rough edge)* Grat, *der;* [B] *(drill)* Bohrer, *der;* [C] ⇒ **bur** A

**burrow** /ˈbʌrəʊ/ ❶ *n.* Bau, *der.* ❷ *v.t.* graben, *(ugs.)* buddeln ‹Loch, Höhle, Tunnel›; ~ **one's way under/through sth.** einen Weg *od.* Gang unter etw. *(Dat.)* durch/durch etw. graben. ❸ *v.i.* [sich *(Dat.)*] einen Gang graben; sich durchbuddeln *(ugs.);* ~ **into sth.** *(fig.)* sich in etw. *(Akk.)* einarbeiten; ~ **through sth.** *(fig.)* sich durch etw. hindurchwühlen

**bursar** /ˈbɜːsə(r)/ *n.* ▶ 1261 *Verwalter der geschäftlichen Angelegenheiten einer Schule/Universität*

**bursary** /ˈbɜːsərɪ/ *n.* Kasse, *die;* *(scholarship)* Stipendium, *das*

**burst** /bɜːst/ ❶ *n.* [A] *(split)* Bruch, *der;* **a** ~ **in a pipe** ein Rohrbruch; [B] *(of flame)* Auflodern, *das;* **a sudden** ~ **of flame** eine Stichflamme; [C] *(outbreak of firing)* Feuerstoß, *der;* Salve, *die;* [D] *(fig.)* **a** ~ **of applause/cheering** ein Beifallsausbruch/Beifallsrufe *Pl.;* **there was a** ~ **of laughter** man brach in Lachen aus; ~ **of rage** Wutausbruch, *der;* ~ **of enthusiasm** Begeisterungsausbruch, *der;* **a** ~ **of speed** ein Spurt; [E] *(explosion)* Explosion, *die;* **a bomb** ~: eine Bombenexplosion.

❷ *v.t.,* ~ zum Platzen bringen; platzen lassen ‹Luftballon›; platzen ‹Reifen›; sprengen ‹Kessel›; ~ **pipe** Rohrbruch, *der;* **the river** ~ **its banks** der Fluss trat über die Ufer; **he** ~ **a blood vessel** ihm ist eine Ader geplatzt; **he [almost]** ~ **a blood vessel** *(fig.)* ihn traf [fast] der Schlag; ~ **the door open** die Tür aufbrechen *od.* aufsprengen; ~ **one's sides with laughing** *(fig.)* vor Lachen beinahe platzen.

❸ *v.i.,* ~ [A] platzen; ‹Granate, Bombe, Kessel:› explodieren; ‹Damm:› brechen; ‹Flussufer:› überschwemmt werden; ‹Furunkel, Geschwür:› aufgehen, aufplatzen; ‹Knospe:› aufbrechen; ~ **open** ‹Tür, Deckel, Kiste, Koffer:› aufspringen; [B] *(be full to overflowing)* **be** ~**ing with sth.** zum Bersten voll sein mit etw.; **be full to** ~**ing[-point]** proppenvoll sein *(ugs.);* **be** ~**ing with pride/impatience** *(fig.)* vor Stolz/Ungeduld platzen; **be** ~**ing with health** *(fig.)* vor Gesundheit strotzen; **be** ~**ing with happiness/excitement** *(fig.)* vor Freude/Aufregung außer sich sein; **I can't eat any more. I'm** ~**ing** *(fig.)* Ich kann nichts mehr essen. Ich platze [gleich] *(ugs.);* **be** ~**ing to say/do sth.** *(fig.)* es kaum abwarten können, etw. zu sagen/tun; [C] *(appear, come suddenly)* ~ **from sb.'s lips** ‹Schrei:› jmds. Lippen entfahren; ~ **through sth.** etw. durchbrechen; **the Beatles** ~ **upon the pop scene in the early sixties** die Beatles wurden Anfang der 60er-Jahre in die Popszene katapultiert; **the sun** ~ **through the clouds** die Sonne brach durch die Wolken

~ **'in** *v.i.* hereinplatzen; hereinstürzen; ~ **in [up]on sb./sth.** bei jmdm./etw. hereinplatzen

~ **into** *v.t.* [A] eindringen in; **we** ~ **into the room** wir stürzten ins Zimmer; [B] *(suddenly begin)* ~ **into tears/laughter** in Tränen/Gelächter ausbrechen; ~ **into flower** [plötzlich] aufblühen; ~ **into song** ein Lied anstimmen; ~ **into flames** in Brand geraten

~ **'out** *v.i.* [A] herausstürzen; ~ **out of a room** aus einem Raum [hinaus]stürmen *od.* stürzen; [B] *(exclaim)* losplatzen; [C] *(suddenly begin)* ~ **out laughing/crying** in Lachen/Tränen ausbrechen

**burton** /ˈbɜːtn/ *n. (Brit. coll.)* **go for a** ~ *(be destroyed)* kaputtgehen *(ugs.);* futsch gehen *(salopp);* *(be lost)* hopsgehen *(salopp);* flötengehen *(salopp);* *(be killed)* dran glauben müssen *(salopp)*

**bury** /ˈberɪ/ *v.t.* [A] begraben; beisetzen *(geh.)* ‹Toten›; ~ **sb. at sea** jmdn. auf See bestatten; **be dead and buried** *(lit. or fig.)* tot und begraben sein; schon lange tot sein; **where is Marx buried?** wo ist *od.* liegt Marx begraben?; ~ **sb. alive** jmdn. lebendig begraben; [B] *(hide)* vergraben; verbuddeln *(ugs.);* *(fig.)* begraben; ~ **one's differences** *(fig.)* seinen Streit begraben; ~ **the hatchet** *or (Amer.)* **tomahawk** *(fig.)* das Kriegsbeil begraben; ~ **one's face in one's hands** das Gesicht in den Händen vergraben; [C] *(bring underground)* eingraben; abdecken ‹Wurzeln›; **buried cable** *(Electr.)* Erdkabel; **the houses were buried by a landslide** die Häuser wurden durch einen Erdrutsch verschüttet; [D] *(plunge)* ~ **one's teeth in sth.** seine Zähne in etw. *(Akk.)* graben *od.* schlagen; ~ **one's hands in one's pockets** seine Hände in den Taschen vergraben; **sth. buries itself in sth.** etw. bohrt sich in etw. *(Akk.);* [E] *(involve deeply)* ~ **oneself in one's studies/books** sich in seine Studien vertiefen/in seinen Büchern vergraben

**burying** /ˈberɪɪŋ/: ~-**ground,** ~-**place** *ns.* Friedhof, *der;* Begräbnisstätte, *die*

**bus** /bʌs/ ❶ *n., pl.* ~**es** ((*Amer.*) ~**ses**) [A] [Auto-, Omni]bus, *der;* **go by** ~: mit dem Bus fahren; [B] *(coll.: car, aircraft)* Kiste, *die (ugs.).* ⇒ *also* **miss** 2 D. ❷ *v.i.,* *(Amer.)* -**ss**- mit dem Bus fahren. ❸ *v.t.,* -**ss**- *(Amer.)* mit dem Bus befördern

**bus:** ~**bar** *n. (Electr.)* Stromschiene, *die;* ~**boy** *n. (Amer.)* Bedienungshilfe, *die;* Abräumer, *der*

**busby** /ˈbʌzbɪ/ *n. (Brit.)* Kalpak, *der;* *(worn by guardsmen)* Bärenfellmütze, *die*

**bus:** ~ **company** *n.* ≈ Verkehrsbetrieb, *der;* ~ **conductor** *n.* ▶ 1261 Busschaffner, *der;* ~ **depot** ⇒ ~ **garage;** ~ **driver** *n.* ▶ 1261 Busfahrer, *der;* ~ **fare** *n.* [Bus]fahrpreis, *der;* **how much is the** ~ **fare from A to B?** wieviel kostet die [Bus]fahrt von A nach B?; ~ **garage** *n.* Busdepot, *das*

**bush**[1] /bʊʃ/ *n.* [A] *(shrub)* Strauch, *der;* Busch, *der;* *(collect.: shrubs)* Gebüsch, *das;* Gestrüpp, *das;* ⇒ *also* **beat** 1 H, 2 C; [B] *(woodland)* Busch, *der;* **go** ~ *(Austral.)* *(leave* *usual surroundings*) abhauen (*ugs.*); verschwinden (*ugs.*); (*run wild*) verwildern; (*go berserk*) durchdrehen (*salopp*); Ⓒ ~ **[of hair]** [Haar]schopf, *der*

**bush²** *n.* Ⓐ (*threaded socket*) Gewindeanschluss, *der;* Ⓑ (*metal lining*) Buchse, *die;* Ⓒ (*Electr.*) Durchführung, *die*

**'bushbaby** *n.* (*Zool.*) Galago, *der;* Buschbaby, *das*

**bushed** /bʊʃt/ *adj.* (*Amer. coll.*) erledigt (*ugs.*); groggy (*ugs.*)

**bushel** /'bʊʃl/ *n.* Bushel, *der;* ≈ Scheffel, *der;* **hide one's light under a ~** (*fig.*) sein Licht unter den Scheffel stellen (*Spr.*)

**bushing** /'bʊʃɪŋ/ ⇒ **bush²**

**bush: ~ jacket** *n.* Safarijacke, *die;* **~ league** *n.* (*Amer.*) Provinzliga, *die* (*abwertend*); **B~man** *n.* Ⓐ (*native*) Buschmann, *der;* Ⓑ (*language*) Buschmännisch, *das;* **~ranger** *n.* (*Austral. Hist.*) Strauchdieb, *der* (*veralt.*); Buschklepper, *der* (*veralt.*); **~ 'telegraph** *n.* (*fig.*) Informationssystem, *das;* **the news spread via the ~ telegraph** die Nachricht sprach sich herum; **~whacker** *n.* (*Amer., Austral., NZ: backwoodsman*) Waldsiedler, *der*

**bushy** /'bʊʃɪ/ *adj.* (*covered with bushes*) buschbewachsen; (*growing luxuriantly*) buschig

**busily** /'bɪzɪlɪ/ *adv.* eifrig

**business** /'bɪznɪs/ *n.* Ⓐ (*trading operation*) Geschäft, *das;* (*company, firm*) Betrieb, *der;* (*large*) Unternehmen, *das;* Ⓑ *no pl.* (*buying and selling*) Geschäfte *Pl.;* **on ~:** geschäftlich; **he's in the wool ~:** er ist in der Wollbranche; **~ is brisk** die Geschäfte florieren; **how's ~ with you?** (*lit. or fig.*) was machen die Geschäfte [bei Ihnen]?; **~ is ~** (*fig.*) Geschäft ist Geschäft; **in my ~:** in meiner Branche; **set up in ~:** ein Geschäft *od.* eine Firma gründen; **he's in ~ for himself** er ist selbstständig; **go out of ~:** pleite gehen (*ugs.*); **go into ~:** Geschäftsmann/-frau werden; **do ~ [with sb.]** [mit jmdm.] Geschäfte machen; **I'm glad we were able to do ~:** ich bin froh, dass wir ins Geschäft gekommen sind; **be in ~:** Geschäftsmann/-frau sein; **we're in ~ [again]** (*fig.*) es kann [wieder] losgehen; **it was ~ as usual** die Geschäfte gingen ihren normalen Gang; **'B~ as usual during alterations'** „Während des Umbaus geht der Verkauf/Betrieb weiter"; **do you want to go into ~ or become a lawyer?** wollen Sie in die Wirtschaft gehen oder Anwalt werden?; **go about one's ~:** seinen Geschäften nachgehen; Ⓒ (*task, duty, province*) Aufgabe, *die;* Pflicht, *die;* **that is 'my ~/none of 'your ~:** das ist meine Angelegenheit/nicht deine Sache; **that is 'your ~:** das ist deine Sache; **what ~ is it of yours?** was geht Sie das an?; **send sb. about his ~:** jmdn. abblitzen lassen (*ugs.*); jmdm. eine Abfuhr erteilen; **mind your own ~:** kümmere dich um deine [eigenen] Angelegenheiten!; **he has no ~ to do that** er hat kein Recht, das zu tun; **make it one's ~ to do sth.** es sich (*Dat.*) angelegen sein lassen, etw. zu tun (*geh.*); (*with more effort*) es sich (*Dat.*) zur Aufgabe machen, etw. zu tun; **like nobody's ~** (*coll.*) wie verrückt (*ugs.*); Ⓓ (*matter to be considered*) Angelegenheit, *die;* **'any other ~'** „Sonstiges"; **the [main] ~ of the day** das [Haupt]anliegen des Tages; **get on with the ~ in hand** zur Sache kommen; Ⓔ (*difficult matter*) Problem, *das;* **a lengthy ~:** eine langwierige Angelegenheit; **it's going to be a ~ getting the piano down the stairs** das wird noch ein Problem geben, das Klavier die Treppe hinunterzukriegen; **what a ~ [this is]!** was für ein Theater!; **make a [great] ~ of sth.** ein [großes] Problem aus etw. machen; (*make a fuss*) einen [Riesen]wirbel um etw. machen; Ⓕ (*serious work*) **get down to [serious] ~:** [ernsthaft] zur Sache kommen; (*Commerc.*) an die Arbeit gehen; **mean ~:** es ernst meinen; **~ before pleasure** erst die Arbeit, dann das Vergnügen; **combine ~ and pleasure** das Angenehme mit dem Nützlichen verbinden; Ⓖ (*derog.: affair*) Sache, *die;* Geschichte, *die* (*ugs.*); Ⓗ *no pl.* (*Theatre*) Gestik und Mimik, *die*

**business: ~ address** *n.* Geschäftsadresse, *die;* **~ card** *n.* Geschäftskarte, *die;* **~ class** ❶ *n., no pl.* Businessklasse, *die; attrib.* Businessklasse-; ❷ *adv.* **fly/travel ~ class** in der Businessklasse fliegen/reisen; **~ correspondence** *n.* Geschäftskorrespondenz, *die;* **~ cycle** *n.* Konjunkturzyklus, *der;* **~ end** *n.* (*coll.*) (*of tool*) vorderes Ende; (*of hammer etc.*) Kopf, *der;* (*of rifle etc.*) Lauf, *der;* **~ hours** *n. pl.* Geschäftszeit, *die;* (*in office*) Dienstzeit, *die;* **~ letter** *n.* Geschäftsbrief, *der;* **~like** *adj.* geschäftsmäßig ‹Art›; sachlich, nüchtern ‹Untersuchung›; geschäftstüchtig ‹Person›; **~ lunch** *n.* Arbeitsessen, *das;* **~ machine** *n.* Büromaschine, *die;* **~man** *n.* ▶ **1261** Geschäftsmann, *der;* **~ park** *n.* Gewerbepark, *der;* **~ plan** *n.* Geschäftsplan, *der;* **~ premises** *n. pl.* Geschäftsräume; **~ school** *n.* kaufmännische Fachschule; **~ studies** *n. pl.* Wirtschaftslehre, *die;* **~ suit** *n.* Straßenanzug, *der;* **~ trip** *n.* Geschäftsreise, *die;* **on a ~ trip** auf Geschäftsreise; **~woman** *n.* ▶ **1261** Geschäftsfrau, *die*

**busker** /'bʌskə(r)/ *n.* Straßenmusikant, *der*

**busking** /'bʌskɪŋ/ *n.* Musizieren auf Straßen und Plätzen

**bus: ~ lane** *n.* (*Brit.*) Busspur, *die;* **~load** *n.* Busladung, *die;* **~man** /'bʌsmən/ *n.* **a ~man's holiday** (*fig.*) praktisch gar keine Ferien (*weil man dasselbe wie im Berufsalltag tut*); **~ ride** *n.* Busfahrt, *die;* **B. is only an hour's ~ ride away** B. ist nur eine Busstunde entfernt; **~ route** *n.* Buslinie, *die;* **~ service** *n.* Omnibusverkehr, *der;* (*specific service*) Busverbindung, *die;* **~ shelter** *n.* Wartehäuschen, *das*

**bussing** /'bʌsɪŋ/ *n., no pl.* (*Amer.*) *Busbeförderung von Schulkindern in andere Bezirke zur Förderung der Rassenintegration*

**bus: ~ station** *n.* Omnibusbahnhof, *der;* **~ stop** *n.* Bushaltestelle, *die*

**bust¹** /bʌst/ *n.* Ⓐ (*sculpture*) Büste, *die;* Ⓑ (*upper front of body*) Brust, *die;* (*woman's bosom*) Busen, *der;* **what ~ are you?, what is your ~ [measurement]?** welche Oberweite haben Sie?

**bust²** (*coll.*) ❶ *n.* Ⓐ (*collapse of trade*) Pleite, *die* (*ugs.*); (*general*) Zusammenbruch, *der;* Ⓑ (*police raid*) Razzia, *die;* Ⓒ (*Cards*) schlechtes Blatt; Ⓓ (*drinking bout*) Sauftour, *die* (*salopp*); **go on a ~:** auf Sauftour gehen.

❷ *adj.* Ⓐ (*broken*) kaputt (*ugs.*); Ⓑ (*bankrupt*) bankrott; pleite (*ugs.*); **go ~:** pleite gehen.

❸ *v.t.,* **~** *or* **~ed** Ⓐ (*burst*) aufplatzen lassen ‹Koffer usw.›; (*break*) kaputtmachen (*ugs.*); **~ sth. open** etw. aufbrechen; Ⓑ (*coll.*) (*dismiss*) entlassen; (*demote*) degradieren ‹Unteroffizier usw.›; (*break up*) auffliegen lassen ‹Verbrecherring›; (*arrest*) schnappen (*ugs.*); Ⓒ (*coll.: punch*) schlagen; hauen (*ugs.*); **~ sb. on the chin/jaw** jmdm. einen Kinnhaken geben *od.* verabreichen.

❹ *v.i.,* **~** *or* **~ed** kaputtgehen (*ugs.*); ‹Lineal usw.:› zerbrechen; ‹Bleistiftspitze:› abbrechen; **be laughing fit to ~:** sich halb tot lachen; **~ in half** auseinander brechen

**~ 'up** *v.t.* kaputtmachen (*ugs.*) ‹Ehe, Partnerschaft›; **~ a place up** in einem Laden Kleinholz machen (*salopp*)

**bustard** /'bʌstəd/ *n.* (*Ornith.*) Trappe, *die*

**buster** /'bʌstə(r)/ *n.* (*sl.*) (*as address*) Meister (*der*) (*salopp*); (*threatening*) Freundchen (*das*) (*salopp*)

**bus: ~ terminal** *n.* Busbahnhof, *der;* **~ ticket** *n.* Busfahrkarte, *die;* Busfahrschein, *der*

**bustle¹** /'bʌsl/ ❶ *v.i.* eilig umherlaufen; **~ in/out/about** geschäftig hinein- *od.* herein-/hinaus- *od.* herauseilen/geschäftig hin und her eilen; **the town centre was bustling with activity** im Stadtzentrum herrschte großer Betrieb *od.* ein reges Treiben. ❷ *v.t.* jagen (*ugs.*); treiben (*ugs.*). ❸ *n.* (*activity*) Betrieb, *der;* (*of fair, streets also*) geschäftiges *od.* reges Treiben (**of** auf, in + *Dat.*); (*fuss*) Aufregung, *die*

**bustle²** *n.* (*Fashion Hist.*) Turnüre, *die*

**bustling** /'bʌslɪŋ/ *adj.* belebt ‹Straße, Stadt, Markt usw.›; emsig, geschäftig ‹Person, Art›; rege ‹Tätigkeit›

**'bust-up** *n.* (*coll.*) Krach, *der* (*ugs.*); **have a ~:** Krach haben (*ugs.*); sich verkrachen (*ugs.*); **there's going to be a ~:** es wird Krach geben

**busty** /'bʌstɪ/ *adj.* vollbusig

**busy** /'bɪzɪ/ ❶ *adj.* Ⓐ (*occupied*) beschäftigt; **I'm ~ now** ich habe jetzt zu tun; **keep oneself ~:** sich [selbst] beschäftigen; **keep sb. ~:** jmdn. auf Trab halten; **be ~ at** *or* **with sth.** mit etw. beschäftigt sein; **be ~ in the kitchen** in der Küche zu tun haben; **he was ~ packing** er war mit Packen beschäftigt *od.* war gerade beim Packen; **get ~:** sich an die Arbeit machen; **as ~ as a bee** (*fig.*) bienenfleißig; Ⓑ (*full of activity*) arbeitsreich ‹Leben›; ziemlich hektisch ‹Zeit›; belebt ‹Stadt›; ausgelastet ‹Person›; fleißig ‹Hände›; rege ‹Verkehr›; **a ~ road** eine verkehrsreiche *od.* viel befahrene Straße; **the office was ~ all day** im Büro war den ganzen Tag viel los; **I'm/he's a ~ man** ich habe/er hat viel zu tun; **he leads a very ~ life** er ist immer beschäftigt; **it has been a ~ day/week** heute/diese Woche war viel los; **I had a ~ day/week** ich hatte heute/diese Woche viel zu tun; Ⓒ (*Amer. Teleph.*) besetzt.

❷ *v. refl.* **~ oneself with sth.** sich mit etw. beschäftigen; **~ oneself [in] doing sth.** sich damit beschäftigen, etw. zu tun

**busy: ~body** *n.* G[e]schaftlhuber, *der* (*südd., österr.*); Wichtigtuer, *der;* **don't be such a ~body** misch dich nicht überall ein; **~ Lizzie** /bɪzɪ 'lɪzɪ/ *n.* (*Bot.*) Fleißiges Lieschen; **~ signal** *n.* (*Amer. Teleph.*) Besetztzeichen, *das*

**but** ❶ /bət, *stressed* bʌt/ *conj.* Ⓐ *coordinating* aber; **Sue wasn't there, ~ her sister was** Sue war nicht da, dafür aber ihre Schwester; **I can't come today ~ I can come tomorrow** heute kann ich [zwar] nicht kommen, aber [ich kann dafür] morgen [kommen]; **he might have been able to help, ~ then he isn't here** er hätte vielleicht helfen können, aber er ist ja nicht hier; **we tried to do it ~ couldn't** wir haben es versucht, aber nicht gekonnt; **~ surely you must have noticed ...:** aber du hast doch sicherlich bemerkt, ...; **~ I 'did!** hab ich doch!; **~ then what if the plane is delayed?** aber was ist, wenn das Flugzeug Verspätung hat?; Ⓑ *correcting after a negative* sondern; **not that book ~ this one** nicht das Buch, sondern dieses; **not only ... ~ also** nicht nur ..., sondern auch; **I can't change the way my son acts, not ~ what I've tried** ich kann das Verhalten meines Sohnes nicht ändern, obwohl ich es schon versucht habe; **I don't doubt ~ that it's true** ich bezweifle nicht, dass es wahr ist; **I don't deny ~ that ...:** ich leugne nicht ab, dass ...; Ⓒ *subordinating* ohne dass; **never a week passes ~ he phones** keine Woche vergeht, ohne dass er anruft.

❷ *prep.* außer (+ *Dat.*); **all ~ him** alle außer ihm; **no one ~ you** niemand außer dir; nur du; **anyone ~ Jim** alle mit Ausnahme von *od.* alle außer Jim; **all ~ three** alle außer dreien; **the next ~ one/two** der/die/das über-/überübernächste; **the last ~ one/two** der/die/das vor-/vorvorletzte; **nobody, ~ nobody, may leave the room** niemand, aber auch wirklich niemand darf das Zimmer verlassen; ⇒ *also* **all** 3; **anything** 1 C; **nothing** 1 A.

❸ /bət/ *adv.* nur; bloß; **they are ~ children** sie sind doch noch Kinder; **if I could ~ talk to her ...:** wenn ich [doch] nur mit ihr sprechen könnte ...; **we can ~ try** wir können es immerhin versuchen.

❹ *rel. pron.* der/die/das nicht; **there is no one ~ knows that ...:** es gibt niemanden, der nicht weiß, dass ...

❺ /bʌt/ *n.* Aber, *das;* **no ~s [about it]!** kein Aber!; **there are no ~s about it** da gibt es kein Wenn und kein Aber; ⇒ *also* **if** 2

**butane** /'bju:teɪn/ *n.* (*Chem.*) Butan, *das*

**butch** /bʊtʃ/ ❶ *adj.* betont männlich ‹Frau, Kleidung, Frisur›; betont maskulin, (*salopp*) macho ‹Mann›; ~ **haircut** (*Amer.*) Bürstenschnitt, *der.* ❷ *n.* (*woman*) kesser Vater (*salopp*); (*man*) betont maskuliner Typ; Macho, *der* (*salopp*)

**butcher** /ˈbʊtʃə(r)/ ❶ *n.* Ⓐ ▶1261 Fleischer, *der;* Metzger, *der* (*bes. westmd., südd.*); Schlachter, *der* (*nordd.*); **~'s [shop]** Fleischerei, *die;* Metzgerei, *die* (*bes. westmd., südd.*); **~'s meat** Rind-, Schweine- und Hammelfleisch (*im Gegensatz zu Geflügel, Wild und Speck*); **the ~, the baker, the candlestick-maker** (*fig.*) ehrbare Bürger; **have** *or* **take a ~'s [hook] at sb./sth.** (*coll.*) [sich (*Dat.*)] jmdn./etw. angucken (*ugs.*); ⇒ *also* **baker**; Ⓑ (*fig.: murderer*) [Menschen]schlächter, *der;* Ⓒ (*Amer. coll.: vendor*) Verkäufer in Eisenbahnzügen.
❷ *v.t.* schlachten; (*fig.: murder*) niedermetzeln; abschlachten; (*fig.: ruin*) verhunzen (*ugs.*), verunstalten ‹Text usw.›

**butchery** /ˈbʊtʃərɪ/ *n.* Ⓐ **~ [trade** *or* **business]** Fleischerhandwerk, *das;* Ⓑ (*fig.: needless slaughter*) Metzelei, *die;* Gemetzel, *das;* **it's sheer ~!** das ist [ja] das reinste Gemetzel!; Ⓒ (*slaughterhouse*) Schlachthaus, *das*

**butler** /ˈbʌtlə(r)/ *n.* ▶1261 Butler, *der;* erster Diener

**butt¹** /bʌt/ *n.* (*vessel*) Fass, *das;* (*for rainwater*) Tonne, *die*

**butt²** *n.* Ⓐ (*end*) dickes Ende; (*of rifle*) Kolben, *der;* (*of spear, fishing rod, etc.*) Schaft, *der;* Ⓑ (*of cigarette, cigar*) Stummel, *der;* **cigarette ~:** Zigarettenstummel, *der;* Kippe, *die* (*ugs.*); Ⓒ (*Amer. coll.: buttocks*) Hintern, *der* (*ugs.*)

**butt³** *n.* Ⓐ (*object of teasing or ridicule*) Zielscheibe, *die;* Gegenstand, *der;* **be the ~ of ridicule** Zielscheibe des Spottes sein; **make a ~ of sb.** sich über jmdn. lustig machen; Ⓑ *in pl.* (*shooting range*) Schießstand, *der;* Waffenjustierstand, *der;* Ⓒ (*target*) Schießscheibe, *die;* Ⓓ (*grouse-shooter's stand*) Schießstand (*beim Moorhuhnschießen*)

**butt⁴** ❶ *n.* (*push*) (*by person*) [Kopf]stoß, *der;* (*by animal*) Stoß [mit den Hörnern], *der;* **give sb. a ~ in the stomach** jmdm. mit dem Kopf in den Bauch stoßen. ❷ *v.i.* Ⓐ (*push with head*) ‹Person:› [mit dem Kopf] stoßen; ‹Stier, Widder, Ziege:› [mit den Hörnern] stoßen; Ⓑ (*meet end to end*) **~ against sth.** an etw. (*Akk.*) stoßen. ❸ *v.t.* Ⓐ (*push with head*) ‹Person:› mit dem Kopf stoßen; ‹Widder, Ziege:› mit den Hörnern stoßen; **~ sb. in the stomach** jmdm. mit dem Kopf in den Bauch stoßen; Ⓑ aneinander fügen; zusammenstoßen lassen; **~ sth. against sth.** etw. mit etw. zusammenstoßen lassen *od.* auf etw. (*Akk.*) stoßen lassen

**~ 'in** *v.i.* (*fig. coll.*) dazwischenreden; (*meddle*) sich [ungefragt] einmischen; **may I ~ in?** darf ich mal kurz stören?

**butte** /bju:t/ *n.* (*Amer. Geog.*) Restberg, *der*

**'butt-end** ⇒ **butt²** A, B

**butter** /ˈbʌtə(r)/ ❶ *n.* Butter, *die;* **he looks as if ~ wouldn't melt in his mouth** (*fig.*) er sieht aus, als ob er kein Wässerchen trüben könnte; **melted ~:** zerlassene Butter. ❷ *v.t.* buttern; mit Butter bestreichen; **fine words ~ no parsnips** Worte allein genügen nicht

**~ 'up** *v.t.* **~ sb. up** jmdm. Honig um den Mund *od.* Bart schmieren (*fig.*)

**butter: ~ bean** *n.* Gartenbohne, *die;* (*lima bean*) Mondbohne, *die;* Limabohne, *die;* **~ cream** *n.* Buttercreme, *die;* **~cup** *n.* (*Bot.*) Butterblume, *die;* **~ dish** *n.* Butterdose, *die;* **~fingers** *n. sing.* Tollpatsch, *der* (*beim Fangen usw.*)

**butterfly** /ˈbʌtəflaɪ/ *n.* Ⓐ Schmetterling, *der;* **break a ~ on the wheel** (*fig.*) mit Kanonen nach Spatzen schießen; **have butterflies [in one's stomach]** (*fig. coll.*) ein flaues Gefühl im Magen haben; Ⓑ (*fig.: showy person*) Paradiesvogel, *der;* (*frivolous woman*) Schmetterling, *der* (*abwertend*); Ⓒ ⇒ **butterfly stroke**

**butterfly: ~-nut** *n.* Flügelmutter, *die;* **~ stroke** *n.* (*Swimming*) Delphinstil, *der;* Delphin (*das*); **do** *or* **swim the ~ stroke** delphinschwimmen; **~ valve** *n.* Drosselklappe, *die*

**butter: ~ knife** *n.* Buttermesser, *das;* **~milk** *n.* Buttermilch, *die;* **~scotch** *n.* Buttertoffee, *das*

**buttery** /ˈbʌtərɪ/ *n.* Vorratskammer, *die;* (*Univ.*) ≈ Cafeteria, *die*

**buttock** /ˈbʌtək/ *n.* ▶966 (*of person*) Hinterbacke, *die;* Gesäßhälfte, *die;* (*of animal*) Hinterbacke, *die;* **~s** Gesäß, *das*

**button** /ˈbʌtn/ ❶ *n.* Ⓐ Knopf, *der;* **as bright as a ~:** putzmunter (*ugs.*); **he didn't care** *or* **give a ~ [about it]** (*fig.*) er hat sich den Teufel darum geschert (*ugs.*); Ⓑ (*of electric bell etc., on fencing foil*) Knopf, *der;* **press** *or* **push the ~:** auf den Knopf drücken; Ⓒ (*bud*) Auge, *das;* Knopf, *der* (*südd., österr., schweiz.*); **~ mushroom** Champignon, *der.* ❷ *v.t.* (*fasten*) zuknöpfen; einknöpfen ‹Futter›; **~ one's lip** (*Amer. sl.*) die Klappe halten (*salopp*). ❸ *v.i.* [zu]geknöpft werden; **this dress ~s down the back** dieses Kleid wird hinten geknöpft

**~ 'up** ❶ *v.t.* zuknöpfen; (*fig.*) erledigen ‹Job›; **have the deal [all] ~ed up** das Geschäft unter Dach und Fach haben (*ugs.*); **~ed up** (*fig.: taciturn*) zugeknöpft (*ugs.*); reserviert. ❷ *v.i.* [zu]geknöpft werden

**'button-down** *adj.* Buttondown ‹-Kragen›

**'buttonhole** ❶ *n.* Ⓐ Knopfloch, *das;* **~ stitch** Knopflochstich, *der;* Ⓑ (*Brit.: flowers worn in coat lapel*) Knopflochsträußchen, *das;* (*single flower*) Knopflochblume, *die;* Blume im Knopfloch. ❷ *v.t.* (*detain*) zu fassen kriegen (*ugs.*); **he was ~d by X** X hat sich (*Dat.*) ihn geschnappt (*ugs.*)

**'button-through** *adj.* durchgeknöpft ‹Kleid›

**buttress** /ˈbʌtrɪs/ ❶ *n.* Ⓐ (*Archit.*) Mauerstrebe, *die;* Mauerstütze, *die;* (*not built-on*) Strebepfeiler, *der;* **~es** Strebewerk, *das;* Ⓑ (*support*) Pfeiler, *der;* Ⓒ (*fig.*) Stütze, *die;* [Eck]pfeiler, *der.* ❷ *v.t.* **~ [up]** [durch Strebepfeiler] stützen; (*fig.*) [unter]stützen; stärken; untermauern ‹Argument›

**'butt weld** *n.* Stumpfschweißnaht, *die*

**butty** /ˈbʌtɪ/ *n.* (*coll.*) Butterbrot, *das;* Stulle, *die* (*nordd.*)

**buxom** /ˈbʌksəm/ *adj.* drall

**buy** /baɪ/ ❶ *v.t.,* **bought** /bɔ:t/ Ⓐ kaufen; lösen ‹Fahrkarte›; **~ sb./oneself sth.** jmdm./sich etw. kaufen; **~ and sell goods** Waren an- und verkaufen; **the pound ~s less than it used to** für ein Pfund bekommt man heute weniger als früher; **~ [oneself]/sb. a pint** sich (*Dat.*) einen Halben genehmigen/jmdm. einen Halben ausgeben; **he bought them a round** er spendierte ihnen eine Runde; **money cannot ~ happiness** Glück kann man nicht kaufen; Ⓑ (*fig.*) erkaufen ‹Sieg, Ruhm, Frieden›; einsparen, gewinnen ‹Zeit›; Ⓒ (*bribe*) bestechen; kaufen (*ugs.*); erkaufen ‹Zustimmung›; Ⓓ (*coll.*) (*believe*) schlucken (*ugs.*); glauben; (*accept*) akzeptieren; einverstanden sein mit; **I'll ~ that** (*believe*) das nehm' ich dir ab (*ugs.*); (*agree*) ja, das glaube ich; Ⓔ **~ it** (*sl.: be killed*): **we nearly bought it that time** da hätte es uns beinahe erwischt.
❷ *n.* [Ein]kauf, *der;* **be a good ~:** preiswert sein; **plenty of good ~s** viele preiswerte Artikel; **the best ~:** der/die/das Preiswerteste; der preiswerteste Artikel; **this week's best ~ is ...** der Preisschlager der Woche ist ...

**~ 'in** *v.t.* Ⓐ einkaufen, sich eindecken mit ‹Vorräte, Fleisch usw.›; Ⓑ (*at auction*) [durch höheres Gebot] zurückkaufen

**~ into** *v. refl. & i.* **~ [oneself] into a business** sich in ein Geschäft einkaufen

**~ 'off** *v.t.* auszahlen ‹Forderung›; abfinden ‹Anspruchberechtigten›; (*bribe*) bestechen; kaufen (*ugs.*)

**~ 'out** *v.t.* auszahlen ‹Aktionär, Partner›; aufkaufen ‹Firma›

**~ 'up** *v.t.* aufkaufen

**buyer** /ˈbaɪə(r)/ *n.* Ⓐ Käufer, *der*/Käuferin, *die;* **potential ~:** Kaufinteressent, *der;* Ⓑ ▶1261 (*Commerc.*) Einkäufer, *der*/Einkäuferin, *die;* Ⓒ **a ~'s** *or* **~s' market** ein Käufermarkt

**buying** /ˈbaɪɪŋ/ *n., no pl.* Kaufen, *das*

**'buying power** /ˈbaɪɪŋ/ *n.* Kaufkraft, *die*

**'buyout** *n.* Aufkauf, *der;* Management-Buy-Out, *das* (*Wirtsch.*)

**buzz** /bʌz/ ❶ *n.* Ⓐ (*of insect*) Summen, *das;* (*of large insect*) Brummen, *das;* (*of smaller or agitated insect*) Schwirren, *das;* Ⓑ (*sound of buzzer*) Summen, *das;* **give one's secretary a ~:** über den Summer seine Sekretärin rufen; Ⓒ (*of conversation, movement*) Gemurmel, *das;* Ⓓ (*coll.: telephone call*) [Telefon]anruf, *der;* **give sb. a ~:** jmdn. anrufen; Ⓔ (*coll.: thrill*) Nervenkitzel, *der* (*ugs.*).
❷ *v.i.* Ⓐ ⇒ **1** A: ‹Insekt:› summen/brummen/schwirren; Ⓑ (*signal with buzzer*) [mit dem Summer] rufen; Ⓒ (*sound confusedly*) **the courtroom ~ed as ...:** im Gerichtssaal erhob sich *od.* hörte man ein Raunen, als ...; **~ with excitement** in heller Aufregung sein; **the rumour set the office ~ing** das Gerücht versetzte das Büro in helle Aufregung; **my ears are ~ing** mir sausen die Ohren.
❸ *v.t.* (*Aeronaut.*) dicht vorbeifliegen *od.* (*ugs.*) vorbeizischen an (+ *Dat.*)

**~ a'bout, ~ a'round** ❶ *v.i.* herumschwirren; herumsurren; (*fig.*) ‹Person:› herumsausen, herumschwirren. ❷ *v.t.* **~ around sth.** um etw. [herum]schwirren; **~ around the room** im Zimmer herumschwirren *od.* umherschwirren

**~ 'off** *v.i.* (*coll.*) abhauen (*salopp*); abzischen (*salopp*)

**buzzard** /ˈbʌzəd/ *n.* (*Ornith.*) Ⓐ (*Brit.*) Bussard, *der;* Ⓑ (*Amer.: turkey ~*) Amerikanischer Truthahngeier

**buzzer** /ˈbʌzə(r)/ *n.* Summer, *der*

**buzz: ~-saw** *n.* (*Amer.*) Kreissäge, *die;* **~word** *n.* Schlagwort, *das*

**by¹** /baɪ/ ❶ *prep.* Ⓐ (*near, beside*) an (+ *Dat.*); bei; (*next to*) neben; **by the window/river** am Fenster/Fluss; **the bus stop by the school** die Haltestelle an der Schule; **she sat by me** sie saß neben mir; **come and sit by me** komm, setz dich zu mir!; Ⓑ (*to position beside*) zu; **go over by the table/wall** geh zum Tisch/zur Wand!; **come by the fire** komm ans Feuer!; Ⓒ (*about, in the possession of*) bei; **have sth. by one** etw. bei sich haben; Ⓓ (*slightly inclining to*) auf (+ *Dat.*); **north-east by east** Nordost auf Ost; Ⓔ **by herself** *etc.* ⇒ **herself** A; Ⓕ (*along*) entlang; **by the river** am *od.* den Fluss entlang; Ⓖ (*via*) über (+ *Akk.*); **to Paris by Dover** nach Paris über Dover; **leave by the door/window** zur Tür hinausgehen/zum Fenster hinaussteigen; **they escaped by the back door/a stairway/a ladder** sie flüchteten durch die Hintertür/über eine Treppe/mit[tels] einer Leiter; **we came by the quickest/shortest route** wir sind die schnellste/kürzeste Strecke gefahren; Ⓗ (*passing*) vorbei an (+ *Dat.*); **run/drive by sb./sth.** an jmdn./etw. vorbeilaufen/vorbeifahren; Ⓘ (*during*) bei; **by day/night** bei Tag/Nacht; tagsüber/nachts; **by the light of the moon** im Mondschein; Ⓙ (*through the agency of*) von; **written by ...:** geschrieben von ...; **by sheer good fortune** durch reines Glück; Ⓚ (*through the means of*) durch; **he was killed by lightning/a falling chimney** er ist vom Blitz/von einem umstürzenden Schornstein erschlagen worden; **heated by gas/oil** mit Gas/Öl geheizt; gas-/ölbeheizt; **begin/end by doing sth.** damit beginnen/aufhören, etw. zu tun; **by turning the knob** durch Drehen des Griffs; **grab sb. by the collar** jmdn. am Kragen packen; **I knew him by his voice** ich erkannte ihn an seiner Stimme; **I could tell by his face that ...:** ich erkannte an seinem Gesicht, dass ...; **by bus/ship** *etc.* mit dem Bus/Schiff *usw.;* **by air/sea** mit dem Flugzeug/Schiff; **make a living by sth.** sich (*Dat.*) seinen Lebensunterhalt mit *od.* durch etw. verdienen; **have children by sb.** Kinder von jmdm. haben; Ⓛ ▶1055 (*not later than*) bis; **by now/this time** inzwischen; **by next week she will be in China** nächste Woche ist sie schon in China; **by the time this letter reaches you** bis dich dieser Brief erreicht;

b

**but by that time all the tickets had been sold** aber bis dahin waren schon alle Karten verkauft; **but by that time it was too late** aber da war es schon zu spät; **by the 20th of the month** bis zum 20. des Monats; M *indicating unit of time* pro; *indicating unit of length, weight, etc.* -weise; **by the second/minute/hour** pro Sekunde/Minute/Stunde; **rent a house by the year** ein Haus für jeweils ein Jahr mieten; **you can hire a car by the day or by the week** man kann sich (*Dat.*) ein Auto tageweise oder wochenweise mieten; **pay sb. by the month** jmdn. monatlich bezahlen; **day by day/month by month, by the day/month** (*as each day etc. passes*) Tag für Tag/Monat für Monat; **cloth by the metre** Stoff am Meter; **sell sth. by the packet/ton/dozen** etw. paket-/tonnenweise/im Dutzend verkaufen; **10 ft. by 20 ft.** 10 [Fuß] mal 20 Fuß; N *indicating amount* **by the thousands** zu Tausenden; **one by one** einzeln; **two by two/three by three/four by four** zu zweit/dritt/viert; **little by little** nach und nach; O *indicating factor* durch; **8 divided by 2 is 4** 8 geteilt durch 2 ist 4; P *indicating extent* um; **wider by a foot** um einen Fuß breiter; **win by ten metres** mit zehn Metern Vorsprung gewinnen; **passed by nine votes to two** mit neun zu zwei Stimmen angenommen; Q (*according to*) nach; **by my watch** nach meiner Uhr; **by the left, quick march!** (*Mil.*) im Geschwindschritt — marsch! [Links, zwo, drei, vier!]; R *in oaths* bei; **by [Almighty] God** bei Gott[, dem Allmächtigen].

❷ *adv.* A (*past*) vorbei; **march/drive/run/flow by** vorbeimarschieren/-fahren/-laufen/-fließen; B (*near*) **close/near by** in der Nähe; C (*aside, in reserve*) auf die Seite; D **by and large** im Großen und Ganzen; **by and by** nach und nach; (*in past*) nach einer Weile

**by²** ⇒ **bye²**

**bye¹** /baɪ/ *int.* (*coll.*) tschüs (*ugs.*); **~ [for] now!** bis später!; tschüs! (*ugs.*)

**bye²** *n.* A (*Sport*) **draw a ~ in the first round** spielfrei in die zweite Runde kommen; B **by the ~:** = **by the way** ⇒ **way** 1 G; C (*Cricket*) *Lauf bei einem Ball, der vom Schlagmann nicht getroffen wurde*

**bye-bye¹** /baɪˈbaɪ/ *int.* (*coll.*) Wiedersehen (*ugs.*); **~ [for] now!** [also] tschüs! (*ugs.*)

**bye-bye²** /ˈbaɪbaɪ/, **bye-byes** /ˈbaɪbaɪz/ *n.* (*child lang.*) **go [to] ~:** in die Heia gehen (*Kinderspr.*)

**bye-law** ⇒ **by-law**

**ˈby-election** *n.* Nachwahl, *die*

**ˈbygone** ❶ *n.* **let ~s be ~s** die Vergangenheit ruhen lassen. ❷ *adj.* **[in] ~ days** [in] vergangene[n] Tage[n]

**ˈby-law** *n.* A (*esp. Brit.*) Verordnung, *die;* **the park ~s** die Parkordnung; B (*of company etc.*) Punkt der Richtlinien; *in pl.* Richtlinien *Pl.*

**byline** *n.* A (*source of income*) Nebenerwerb, *der;* B (*in newspaper*) *Zeile mit dem Namen des Verfassers*

**ˈbypass** ❶ *n.* (*road*) Umgehungsstraße, *die;* (*channel; also Electr.*) Nebenleitung, *die;* (*Med.*) Bypass, *der;* **~ surgery** (*Med.*) eine Bypassoperation/Bypassoperationen.

❷ *v.t.* A umleiten ‹Flüssigkeit, Gas›; B **the road ~es the town** die Straße führt um die Stadt herum; C (*avoid*) aus dem Wege gehen (+ *Dat.*); (*fig.: ignore*) übergehen

**by-play** *n., no pl., no indef. art.* (*Theatre*) Nebenhandlung, *die*

**ˈby-product** *n.* Nebenprodukt, *das*

**byre** /ˈbaɪə(r)/ *n.* (*Brit.*) Kuhstall, *der*

**ˈbyroad** *n.* Nebenstraße, *die;* Seitenstraße, *die*

**bystander** /ˈbaɪstændə(r)/ *n.* Zuschauer, *der*/Zuschauerin, *die*

**byte** /baɪt/ *n.* (*Computing*) Byte, *das*

**ˈbyway** *n.* Seitenweg, *der*

**ˈbyword** *n.* (*proverb*) Spruch, *der;* [Sprich]wort, *das;* (*person or thing taken as typical or notable example*) Inbegriff, *der* (**for** *Gen.*)

**Byzantine** /bɪˈzæntaɪn, baɪˈzæntaɪn/ *adj.* A byzantinisch; B (*complicated*) undurchschaubar

**Byzantium** /bɪˈzæntɪəm, baɪˈzæntɪəm/ *pr. n.* Byzanz (*das*)

# C c



**C, c** /si:/ *n., pl.* **Cs** *or* **C's** Ⓐ *(letter)* C, c, *das;* Ⓑ **C** *(Mus.)* C, c, *das;* **middle C** das eingestrichene c; **C sharp** cis, Cis, *das;* Ⓒ *(Roman numeral)* C; Ⓓ *(example)* C, c *(ohne Artikel);* Ⓔ **C** *(Sch., Univ.: mark)* Drei, *die;* **he got a C** er bekam „befriedigend" *od.* eine Drei

**C.** *abbr.* Ⓐ ▶ 1603 **Celsius** C; Ⓑ ▶ 1603 **Centigrade** C; Ⓒ *(Geogr.)* **Cape;** Ⓓ *(Pol.)* **Conservative**

**c.** *abbr.* Ⓐ **circa** ca.; Ⓑ ▶ 1328 **cent[s]** c; Ⓒ **century** Jh.; Ⓓ **chapter** Kap.; Ⓔ **cubic** Kubik-

**©** *symb.* **copyright** ©

**CA** *abbr.* **chartered accountant**

**ca.** *abbr.* **circa** ca.

**cab** /kæb/ *n.* Ⓐ *(taxi)* Taxi, *das;* Taxe, *die (ugs.);* Ⓑ *(Hist.: hackney carriage)* [Pferde]droschke, *die;* Ⓒ *(of lorry, truck)* Fahrerhaus, *das; (of crane)* Fahrerkabine, *die; (of train)* Führerstand, *der*

**CAB** *abbr.* **Citizens' Advice Bureau** ≈ Bürgerbüro, *das*

**cabal** /kəˈbæl/ *n.* Ⓐ *(intrigue)* Intrige, *die;* Kabale, *die (veralt.);* Ⓑ *(clique, faction)* Clique, *die (abwertend)*

**cabaret** /ˈkæbəreɪ/ *n.* Varietee, *das;* Cabaret, *das; (more sophisticated)* Kabarett, *das*

**cabbage** /ˈkæbɪdʒ/ *n.* Ⓐ Kohl, *der;* **red/white ~:** Rot-/Weißkohl, *der;* **a [head of] ~:** ein Kopf Kohl; ein Kohlkopf; **as big as ~s** riesengroß ‹Rosen usw.›; Ⓑ *(coll.: person)* stumpfsinniger Mensch; Trottel, *der (ugs. abwertend);* **become a ~:** stumpfsinnig werden; vertrotteln *(ugs. abwertend);* **after his accident he became a complete ~:** nach seinem Unfall vegetierte er nur noch dahin

**cabbage: ~ lettuce** *n.* Kopfsalat, *der;* **~ ˈwhite** *n. (Zool.)* Kohlweißling, *der*

**cabbalistic** /kæbəˈlɪstɪk/ *adj.* kabbalistisch

**cabby** /ˈkæbɪ/ *(coll.),* **ˈcab-driver** *ns.* Taxifahrer, *der; (of horse-drawn vehicle)* Kutscher, *der*

**caber** /ˈkeɪbə(r)/ *n.* Pfahl, *der;* Stamm, *der;* **tossing the ~:** Baumstammwerfen, *das*

**cabin** /ˈkæbɪn/ *n.* Ⓐ *(in ship) (for passengers)* Kabine, *die; (for crew)* Kajüte, *die; (in aircraft)* Kabine, *die;* Ⓑ *(simple dwelling)* Hütte, *die;* Ⓒ *(driver's)* ⇒ **cab** C

**cabin: ~ boy** *n. (Naut.)* Kabinensteward, *der;* **~ class** *n.* zweite Klasse; **they travelled ~ class** sie reisten zweiter Klasse; **~ cruiser** *n.* Kajütboot, *das*

**cabinet** /ˈkæbɪnɪt/ *n.* Ⓐ Schrank, *der; (in bathroom, for medicines)* Schränkchen, *das; (display ~)* Vitrine, *die; (for radio, TV, etc.)* Gehäuse, *das;* Ⓑ **C~** *(Polit.)* Kabinett, *das*

**cabinet: ~maker** *n.* ▶ 1261 Möbeltischler, *der;* **C~ ˈMinister** *n.* Minister, *der;* Mitglied des Kabinetts

**cable** /ˈkeɪbl/ ❶ *n.* Ⓐ *(rope)* Kabel, *das;* Trosse, *die (Naut.); (of mountain railway)* Seil, *das;* **cut one's ~s** *(fig.)* alle Brücken hinter sich *(Dat.)* abbrechen; Ⓑ *(Electr., Teleph.)* Kabel, *das;* Ⓒ *(cablegram)* Kabel, *das;* Überseetelegramm, *das;* Ⓓ *(Naut.) (chain of anchor)* Ankerkette, *die; (measure)* Kabellänge, *die.* ❷ *v.t.* *(transmit)* telegraphisch durchgeben, kabeln ‹Mitteilung, Nachricht›; *(inform)* **~ sb.** jmdm. kabeln

**cable: ~ car** *n.* Drahtseilbahn, *die; (in street)* gezogene Straßenbahn; **~gram** *n.* Kabel, *das;* Überseetelegramm, *das;* **~-knit** *adj.* **~-knit sweater/cardigan** Pullover/Strickjacke mit Zopfmuster; **~ railway** *n.* Standseilbahn, *die;* **~ stitch** *n.* Zopfmuster, *das;* **~ television, ~ TV** *ns.* Kabelfernsehen, *das;* **~way** *n.* *(double-~ ropeway)* Seilschwebebahn, *die; (gondola type)* Kleinkabinenbahn, *die*

**ˈcabman** /ˈkæbmən/ *n., pl.* **cabmen** /ˈkæbmən/ Taxifahrer, *der*

**caboodle** /kəˈbu:dl/ *n., no pl. (coll.)* **the whole ~** *(things)* der ganze Kram *(ugs.);* das ganze Gelumpe *(ugs.); (people)* die ganze Bande *(salopp) od.* Sippschaft *(ugs.)*

**caboose** /kəˈbu:s/ *n.* Ⓐ *(on ship)* Kombüse, *die;* Ⓑ *(Amer.: on train)* Dienstwagen, *der*

**ˈcab rank** *n. (Brit.)* Taxistand, *der;* Droschken[halte]platz, *der (Amtsspr.)*

**cabriolet** /kæbrɪəˈleɪ/ *n. (Hist.)* Ⓐ *(carriage)* Kabriolett, *das;* Ⓑ *(car)* Kabriolett, *das;* Kabrio, *das (ugs.)*

**cacao** /kəˈkɑ:əʊ, kəˈkeɪəʊ/ *n., pl.* **~s** Ⓐ *(seed)* Kakaobohne, *die;* Ⓑ *(tree)* **~ [tree]** Kakaobaum, *der*

**cache** /kæʃ/ ❶ *n.* Ⓐ *(hiding place)* geheimes [Waffen-/Proviant-]lager; Versteck, *das;* Ⓑ *(things hidden)* Lager, *das;* **make a ~ of sth.** etw. verstecken *od.* in Sicherheit bringen. ❷ *v.t.* verstecken

**cachet** /ˈkæʃeɪ/ *n.* Ⓐ *(mark)* Siegel, *das (fig.);* Stempel, *der (fig.);* Ⓑ *(prestige)* Ansehen, *das;* Distinktion, *die (geh.)*

**cack-handed** /kækˈhændɪd/ *adj. (coll.)* Ⓐ *(left-handed)* linkshändig; Ⓑ *(clumsy)* tollpatschig *(ugs.)*

**cackle** /ˈkækl/ ❶ *n.* Ⓐ *(clucking of hen)* Gackern, *das;* Gegacker, *das;* Ⓑ *(laughter)* [meckerndes] Gelächter; *(of woman)* Gegacker, *das (abwertend); (laugh)* **he gave a loud ~:** er prustete los *(ugs.);* Ⓒ *(talk)* Geschwätz, *das (abwertend);* **cut the ~!** *(coll.)* genug geredet!; Schluss mit dem Geschwätz! *(ugs.).* ❷ *v.i.* Ⓐ ‹Henne:› gackern; Ⓑ *(laugh)* meckernd lachen; ‹Frau auch:› gackern *(ugs.)*

**cacophonous** /kəˈkɒfənəs/ *adj.* kakophon *(geh.);* misstönend *(geh.)*

**cacophony** /kəˈkɒfənɪ/ *n.* Kakophonie, *die (geh.);* Missklang, *der (geh.)*

**cactus** /ˈkæktəs/ *n., pl.* **cacti** /ˈkæktaɪ/ *or* **~es** Kaktus, *der*

**cad** /kæd/ *n. (dated derog.)* Schuft, *der;* Schurke, *der (veralt.)*

**CAD** *abbr.* **computer-aided design** CAD

**cadaver** /kəˈdɑ:və(r)/ *n. (of animal)* Kadaver, *der; (of human)* Leiche, *die*

**cadaverous** /kəˈdævərəs/ *adj.* Ⓐ *(corpse-like)* Kadaver-, Leichen-; Ⓑ *(deathly pale)* leichenfahl; totenblass; Ⓒ *(gaunt)* dürr

**caddie** /ˈkædɪ/ *(Golf)* ❶ *n.* Caddie, *der.* ❷ *v.i.* **~ for sb.** jmds. Caddie sein; für jmdn. Caddie spielen *(ugs.)*

**caddis**/ˈkædɪs/**: ~ fly** *n.* Köcherfliege, *die;* Frühlingsfliege, *die;* **~ worm** *n.* Köcherlarve, *die*

**caddy**[1] /ˈkædɪ/ *n.* Behälter, *der; (tin)* Büchse, *die;* Dose, *die*

**caddy**[2] ⇒ **caddie**

**cadence** /ˈkeɪdəns/ *n.* Ⓐ *(rhythm)* Rhythmus, *der;* **marching/dancing ~:** Marsch-/Tanzrhythmus, *der;* **speech ~:** Sprachmelodie, *die;* Ⓑ *(close of musical phrase, fall of voice)* Kadenz, *die*

**cadenza** /kəˈdenzə/ *n. (Mus.)* [Konzert]kadenz, *die*

**cadet** /kəˈdet/ *n.* Ⓐ *(Mil. etc.)* Offiziersschüler, *der;* Kadett, *der (veralt.);* **naval/police ~:** Marinekadett/Anwärter für den Polizeidienst; **~ corps** Kadettenkorps; Ⓑ *(younger brother/son)* jüngerer Bruder/Sohn

**cadge** /kædʒ/ ❶ *v.t.* schnorren *(ugs.);* [sich *(Dat.)*] erbetteln; **could I ~ a lift with you?** können Sie mich vielleicht [ein Stück] mitnehmen? ❷ *v.i.* schnorren *(ugs.)*

**cadger** /ˈkædʒə(r)/ *n.* Schnorrer, *der (ugs.)*

**cadmium** /ˈkædmɪəm/ *n.* Kadmium, *das*

**cadre** /ˈkɑ:də(r), kɑ:dr/ *(Mil., Polit.)* Kader, *der*

**CAE** *abbr.* **computer-aided engineering** CAE

**caecum** /ˈsi:kəm/ *n., pl.* **caeca** /ˈsi:kə/ *(Anat.)* Blinddarm, *der*

**Caesar** /ˈsi:zə(r)/ *n.* Ⓐ Cäsar, Caesar *(der); (fig.)* Alleinherrscher, *der;* Ⓑ *(Med. coll.)* Kaiserschnitt, *der*

**Caesarean, Caesarian** /sɪˈzeərɪən/ *adj. & n.* **~ [birth** *or* **operation** *or* **section]** Kaiserschnitt, *der*

**caesura** /sɪˈzjuːrə/ *n. (Pros.)* Zäsur, *die*

**café, cafe** /ˈkæfɪ, ˈkæfeɪ/ *n.* Ⓐ Lokal, *das; (tearoom)* Café, *das;* Ⓑ *(Amer.: bar)* Bar, *die*

**café: ~ au lait** /kæfeɪ əʊ ˈleɪ/ *n., no pl.* Kaffee mit Sahne/Milch; Café crème *(schweiz.);* Brauner *(österr.);* **~ society** *n., no pl.* Schickeria, *die*

**cafeteria** /kæfɪˈtɪərɪə/ *n.* Selbstbedienungsrestaurant, *das;* Cafeteria, *die*

**cafetière** /kæfəˈtjeə/ *n.* Kaffeebereiter, *der*

**caff** /kæf/ *n. (Brit. coll.)* Café, *das;* **transport ~:** Fernfahrerimbiss, *der*

**caffeinated** /ˈkæfmeɪtɪd/ *adj.* koffeinhaltig

**caffeine** /ˈkæfi:n/ *n.* Koffein, *das; (in tea)* T[h]ein, *das*

**caftan** /ˈkæftæn/ *n.* Kaftan, *der*

**cage** /keɪdʒ/ ❶ *n.* Ⓐ Käfig, *der; (for small birds)* Bauer, *das;* Ⓑ *(Mining)* Förderkorb, *der;* Ⓒ *(of lift)* Fahrkabine, *die.* ❷ *v.t.* einsperren; käfigen *(fachspr.)* ‹Vögel›

**ˈcage bird** *n.* Käfigvogel, *der*

**cagey** /ˈkeɪdʒɪ/ *adj. (coll.)* Ⓐ *(wary)* vorsichtig; **be ~ about sth.** vorsichtig bei etw. sein; sich mit etw. [sehr] zurückhalten; **a ~ buyer** ein wachsamer *od.* misstrauischer Käufer; Ⓑ *(secretive, uncommunicative)* zugeknöpft *(ugs.);* **be ~ about saying sth.** mit etw. hinterm Berg halten *(ugs.)*

**cagily** /ˈkeɪdʒɪlɪ/ *adv. (coll.)* vorsichtig; *(shrewdly)* clever *(ugs.);* geschickt

**caginess** /ˈkeɪdʒɪnɪs/ *n. (caution)* Vorsicht, *die; (secretiveness)* Zugeknöpftheit, *die*

**cagoule** /kəˈgu:l/ *n.* [leichter, knielanger] Anorak

**cagy** ⇒ **cagey**

**cahoots** /kəˈhu:ts/ *n. pl. (coll.)* Ⓐ *(company, partnership)* **be in ~ with the devil** mit dem Teufel im Bunde stehen; **go into ~ with sb.** sich mit jmdm. verbünden; Ⓑ *(collusion)* **be in ~ with sb.** mit jmdm. unter einer Decke stecken *(ugs.)*

**caiman** ⇒ **cayman**

**Cain** /keɪn/ *pr. n.* Kain *(der);* **raise ~** *(coll.)* Krach schlagen *(ugs.)*

**cairn** /keən/ *n.* Ⓐ *(pyramid of stones)* Steinpyramide, *die;* Cairn, *der (fachspr.);* **a ~ of stones** ein Steinhaufen; Ⓑ *(dog)* **~ [terrier]** Cairn-Terrier, *der; schottischer Zwergterrier*

**Cairo** /ˈkaɪərəʊ/ *pr. n.* ▶ 1626 Kairo *(das)*

**caisson** /ˈkeɪsən, kəˈsu:n/ *n.* Ⓐ *(watertight chamber)* Senkkasten, *der;* Caisson, *der;* Ⓑ *(floating vessel)* Docktor, *das;* Dockponton, *der*

**ˈcaisson disease** *n.* Druckluftkrankheit, *die;* Caissonkrankheit, *die*

**cajole** /kəˈdʒəʊl/ *v.t.* **~ sb. into sth./into doing sth.** jmdm. etw. einreden/jmdm. einreden, etw. zu tun; **~ sb. out of doing sth.**

jmdm. ausreden, etw. zu tun; **~ sth. out of a person** jmdm. etw. entlocken

**cajolery** /kə'dʒəʊlərɪ/ *n.* Überredungskunst, *die*

**cake** /keɪk/ ❶ *n.* Ⓐ Kuchen, *der;* **a piece of ~:** ein Stück Kuchen/Torte; **a slice of ~:** eine Scheibe Kuchen; Ⓑ (*fig.*) **get a slice of the ~:** sein Teil abbekommen; **go** *or* **sell like hot ~s** weggehen wie warme Semmeln (*ugs.*); **a piece of ~** (*coll.*) ein Kinderspiel (*ugs.*); **you cannot have your ~ and eat it** *or* **eat your ~ and have it** beides auf einmal geht nicht; **~s and ale** (*fig.*) reinste Vergnügungen; ⇒ *also* **take** 1 C; Ⓒ (*block*) **a ~ of soap** ein Riegel *od.* Stück Seife; **a ~ of wax** ein Riegel Wachs; **a ~ of tobacco** ein Plättchen Tabak.
❷ *v.t.* Ⓐ (*cover*) verkrusten; **~d with dirt/blood** schmutz-/blutverkrustet; **his suit was ~d with mud** sein Anzug war voll Schlamm; Ⓑ (*form into mass*) **rain ~d the soil** Regen machte die Erde klumpig.
❸ *v.i.* (*form a mass*) verklumpen

**cake: ~ shop** *n.* Konditorei, *die;* **~ slice** *n.* Tortenheber, *der;* **~ stand** *n.* Etagere, *die;* **~ tin** *n.* Kuchenform, *die;* **~walk** *n.* (*dance*) Cakewalk, *der;* (*easy task*) Kinderspiel, *das* (*ugs.*)

**cal.** *abbr.* **calorie[s]** cal.

**CAL** /kæl/ *abbr.* **computer-aided** *or* **computer-assisted learning** computergestütztes Lernen

**calabash** /'kæləbæʃ/ *n.* Ⓐ (*gourd*) Flaschenkürbis, *der;* Ⓑ (*pipe, container*) Kalebasse, *die*

**calaboose** /kælə'bu:s/ *n.* (*Amer.*) Gefängnis, *das;* Kittchen, *das* (*ugs.*)

**calamitous** /kə'læmɪtəs/ *adj.* verhängnisvoll

**calamity** /kə'læmɪtɪ/ *n.* Ⓐ Unheil, *das;* Unglück, *das;* **calamities of nature** Naturkatastrophen; Ⓑ (*adversity*) Schicksalsschlag, *der;* Ⓒ (*distress*) Not, *die;* Elend, *das;* **a ~:** ein Unglück

**Calamity 'Jane** *n.* Schwarzseherin, *die*

**calcification** /kælsɪfɪ'keɪʃn/ *n.* Verkalkung, *die*

**calcify** /'kælsɪfaɪ/ ❶ *v.i.* verkalken. ❷ *v.t.* verkalken lassen

**calcine** /'kælsaɪn, 'kælsɪn/ ❶ *v.t.* kalzinieren. ❷ *v.i.* kalziniert werden

**calcite** /'kælsaɪt/ *n.* (*Min.*) Kalzit, *der*

**calcium** /'kælsɪəm/ *n.* Kalzium, *das;* Calcium, *das* (*fachspr.*)

**calcium: ~ 'carbide** *n.* Kalziumkarbid, *das;* **~ 'carbonate** *n.* Kalziumkarbonat, *das;* kohlensaures Kalzium

**calculable** /'kælkjʊləbl/ *adj.* berechenbar; kalkulierbar ‹Risiko›

**calculate** /'kælkjʊleɪt/ ❶ *v.t.* Ⓐ (*ascertain*) berechnen; (*by estimating*) ausrechnen; errechnen; Ⓑ (*plan*) **be ~d to do sth.** darauf abzielen, etw. zu tun; Ⓒ (*Amer. coll.: suppose, believe*) meinen; schätzen (*ugs.*). ❷ *v.i.* Ⓐ (*Math.*) rechnen; Ⓑ **~ on doing sth.** damit rechnen, etw. zu tun

**calculated** /'kælkjʊleɪtɪd/ *adj.* (*deliberate*) vorsätzlich ‹Handlung, Straftat›; bewusst ‹Zurückhaltung, Affront›; kalkuliert ‹Risiko›; (*apt, suitable*) geeignet

**calculating** /'kælkjʊleɪtɪŋ/ *adj.* berechnend; **with a ~ eye** mit berechnendem Blick

**calculation** /kælkjʊ'leɪʃn/ *n.* Ⓐ (*result*) Rechnung, *die;* **he is out in his ~s** er hat sich verrechnet; Ⓑ (*calculating*) Berechnung, *die;* Ⓒ (*forecast*) Schätzung, *die;* **by my ~s** nach meiner Schätzung

**calculator** /'kælkjʊleɪtə(r)/ *n.* Ⓐ (*person, machine*) Rechner, *der;* Ⓑ (*set of tables*) Rechentabelle, *die*

**calculus** /'kælkjʊləs/ *n., pl.* **calculi** /'kælkjʊlaɪ/ *or* **~es** Ⓐ (*Math. etc.*) -rechnung, *die;* (*infinitesimal ~*) Infinitesimalrechnung, *die;* **[the] differential/infinitesimal/integral ~:** [die] Differenzial-/Infinitesimal-/Integralrechnung; Ⓑ (*Med.*) Stein, *der*

**Calcutta** /kæl'kʌtə/ *pr. n.* ▶**1626** Kalkutta (*das*)

**caldron** ⇒ **cauldron**

**Caledonia** /kælɪ'dəʊnɪə/ *pr. n.* (*Hist./poet.*) Kaledonien (*das*)

**Caledonian** /kælɪ'dəʊnɪən/ ❶ *adj.* kaledonisch. ❷ *n.* (*joc./Hist.*) Kaledonier, *der*/Kaledonierin, *die*

**calendar** /'kælɪndə(r)/ *n.* Ⓐ Kalender, *der; attrib.* Kalender ‹woche, -monat, -jahr›; **[church] ~:** Kirchenkalender, *der;* Ⓑ (*register, list*) Verzeichnis, *das;* (*list of canonized saints*) Heiligenkalender, *der;* (*list of cases for trial*) Prozessregister, *das;* (*Amer.: list of matters for debate*) Tagesordnung, *die*

**calender** /'kælɪndə(r)/ ❶ *n.* Kalander, *der* (*Technik*). ❷ *v.t.* kalandern, kalandrieren (*Technik*)

**calends** /'kælɪndz/ *n. pl.* Kalenden *Pl.*

**calendula** /kə'lendjʊlə/ *n.* (*Bot.*) Ringelblume, *die*

**calf**[1] /kɑ:f/ *n., pl.* **calves** /kɑ:vz/ Ⓐ (*young of bovine animal*) Kalb, *das;* (*leather*) **~[skin]** Kalbsleder, *das;* **a cow in** *or* **with ~:** eine trächtige Kuh; Ⓑ (*of deer*) Kalb, *das;* (*of elephant, whale, rhinoceros*) Junge, *das.* ⇒ *also* **fat** 3; **golden calf**

**calf**[2] *n., pl.* **calves** ▶**966** (*Anat.*) Wade, *die*

**calf: ~ love** *n.* [Jugend]schwärmerei, *die;* **~skin** *n.* Kalbfell, *das;* (*leather*) Kalbsleder, *das*

**caliber** (*Amer.*) ⇒ **calibre**

**calibrate** /'kælɪbreɪt/ *v.t.* kalibrieren; eichen, kalibrieren ‹Messgerät›

**calibration** /kælɪ'breɪʃn/ *n.* Kalibrierung, *die;* (*of gauge*) Eichung, *die;* Kalibrierung, *die*

**calibre** /'kælɪbə(r)/ *n.* (*Brit.*) Ⓐ (*diameter*) Kaliber, *das;* Ⓑ (*fig.*) Format, *das;* Kaliber, *das;* **a man of your ~:** ein Mann Ihres Kalibers *od.* von Ihrem Format

**calico** /'kælɪkəʊ/ ❶ *n., pl.* **~es** *or* (*Amer.*) **~s** Ⓐ Kattun, *der;* Ⓑ (*Amer.: printed cotton fabric*) Druckkattun, *der.* ❷ *adj.* Ⓐ Kattun-; kattunen (*geh.*); Ⓑ (*Amer.: multicoloured*) bunt

**California** /kælɪ'fɔ:nɪə/ *pr. n.* Kalifornien (*das*)

**Californian** /kælɪ'fɔ:nɪən/ ❶ *adj.* kalifornisch. ❷ *n.* Kalifornier, *der*/Kalifornierin, *die*

**caliper** ⇒ **calliper**

**caliph** /'kælɪf, 'keɪlɪf/ *n.* (*Hist.*) Kalif, *der*

**calisthenics** ⇒ **callisthenics**

**calk** ⇒ **caulk**

**call** /kɔ:l/ ❶ *v.i.* Ⓐ (*shout*) rufen; **~ to sb.** jmdm. zurufen; **~ [out] for help** um Hilfe rufen; **~ [out] for sb.** nach jmdm. rufen; **~ [out] for food/drink** nach Essen/zu trinken verlangen; **~ after sb.** jmdm. hinterherrufen; hinter jmdm. herrufen; Ⓑ (*pay brief visit*) [kurz] besuchen (**at** *Akk.*); vorbeikommen (*ugs.*) (**at** bei); ‹Zug:› halten (**at** in + *Dat.*); **~ at a port/station** einen Hafen anlaufen/an einem Bahnhof halten; **~ on sb.** jmdn. besuchen; bei jmdm. vorbeigehen (*ugs.*); **the postman ~ed to deliver a parcel** der Postbote war da und brachte ein Päckchen; **a man has ~ed to read the meter** ein Mann ist da, um den Zähler abzulesen; **~ round** vorbeikommen (*ugs.*); Ⓒ (*communicate by telephone*) **who is ~ing, please?** wer spricht da, bitte?; **thank you for ~ing** vielen Dank für Ihren Anruf!; (*communicate by radio*) **this is London ~ing** hier spricht *od.* ist London.
❷ *v.t.* Ⓐ (*cry out*) rufen; aufrufen ‹Namen, Nummer›; Ⓑ (*cry to*) rufen ‹Person›; Ⓒ (*summon*) rufen; (*into the army*) einberufen; (*to a duty, to do sth.*) aufrufen; **~ him into the room** rufen Sie ihn herein!; **be ~ed home/to arms** nach Hause/zu den Waffen gerufen werden; **he was ~ed to his maker** (*literary*) er ist in die Ewigkeit abberufen worden (*geh. verhüllend*); **~ sth. into being** etw. ins Leben rufen; **~ sb.'s bluff** es darauf ankommen lassen (*ugs.*); **that was ~ed in question** das wurde infrage gestellt *od.* in Zweifel gezogen; **please ~ me a taxi** *or* **~ a taxi for me** bitte rufen Sie mir ein Taxi; Ⓓ (*communicate with by radio/telephone*) rufen/anrufen; (*initially*) Kontakt aufnehmen mit; **don't ~ us, we'll ~ you** wir sagen Ihnen Bescheid; Ⓔ (*rouse*) wecken; Ⓕ (*announce*) einberufen ‹Konferenz›; ausrufen ‹Streik›; anberaumen ‹Gerichtstermin›; **~ a halt to sth.** mit etw. Schluss machen; **time was ~ed by the bartender** der Barmann rief „Feierabend“ *od.* (*veralt., geh.*) bot Feierabend; Ⓖ (*urge*) **duty ~s** die Pflicht ruft; **he was ~ed to preach the Gospel by God** er war von Gott zur Verkündigung des Evangeliums auserwählt; ⇒ *also* **attention** 1 A; Ⓗ (*nominate*) **he was ~ed to the presidency of the university** er wurde zum Präsidenten der Universität berufen; **be ~ed to witness sth.** als Zeuge bei etw. aufgerufen werden; Ⓘ (*name*) nennen; **he is ~ed Bob** er heißt Bob; **he doesn't mind if you simply ~ him Bob** er hat nichts dagegen, wenn du ihn einfach Bob nennst *od.* einfach Bob zu ihm sagst; **you can ~ him by his first name** ihr könnt ihn mit Vornamen anreden; **what is it ~ed in English?** wie heißt das auf Englisch?; **~ it what you will** wie immer man es auch nennen will; **~ sb. names** jmdn. beschimpfen; Ⓙ (*consider*) nennen; **I ~ that selfish** das nenne ich egoistisch; **£1.03 — let's ~ it one pound** ein Pfund drei Pence — sagen wir ein Pfund (*ugs.*); **shall we ~ it ten dollars/even?** sagen wir zehn Dollar/, wir sind quitt? (*ugs.*); **~ sth. one's own** etw. sein Eigen nennen; Ⓚ (*Cards etc.*) ansagen; (*in coin-tossing*) sagen; **he ~ed heads and lost** er setzte auf Kopf und verlor. ⇒ *also* **account** 3 C; **bar**[1] 1 I; **day** A; **spade** A; **tune** 1 A.
❸ *n.* Ⓐ (*shout, cry*) Ruf, *der;* **a ~ for help** ein Hilferuf; **he came at my ~:** er kam, als ich rief; **can you give me a ~ at 6 o'clock?** können Sie mich um 6 Uhr wecken?; **remain/be within ~:** in Rufweite bleiben/sein; **on** *or* **at ~:** dienstbereit; Ⓑ (*of bugle, whistle*) Signal, *das;* (*of drum*) Schlag, *der;* Ⓒ (*instrument*) Lockinstrument, *das;* Locke, *die* (*Jägerspr.*); Ⓓ (*visit*) Besuch, *der;* **make** *or* **pay a ~ on sb., make** *or* **pay sb. a ~:** jmdn. besuchen; jmdm. einen Besuch abstatten (*geh.*); **have to pay a ~** (*coll.: need lavatory*) mal [verschwinden] müssen (*ugs.*); Ⓔ (*telephone ~*) Anruf, *der;* Gespräch, *das;* **give sb. a ~:** jmdn. anrufen; **make a ~:** ein Telefongespräch führen; **receive a ~:** einen Anruf erhalten; Ⓕ (*invitation, summons*) Aufruf, *der;* (*by God*) Berufung, *die;* (*Theatre*) Aufruf, *der;* (*by audience*) Hervorruf, *der;* **the ~ of the sea/the wild** der Ruf des Meeres/der Wildnis; **~ of nature** natürlicher Drang; **answer the ~ of duty** der Pflicht gehorchen; **a ~ for unity** ein Aufruf zur Einheit; **a worldwide ~ for disarmament** ein weltweiter Ruf nach Abrüstung; Ⓖ (*need, occasion*) Anlass, *der;* Veranlassung, *die;* **what ~ is there for you to worry?** aus welchem Anlass *od.* Grund sorgen Sie sich?; Ⓗ (*esp. Commerc.: demand*) Abruf, *der;* (*demand made*) Inanspruchnahme, *die;* **a ~ for capital/money** Abruf von Kapital/Geldern; **have many ~s on one's purse/time** finanziell/zeitlich sehr in Anspruch genommen sein; Ⓘ (*Cards etc.*) Ansage, *die;* **it is your ~ now** du musst ansagen; **was your ~ heads or tails?** hatten Sie Kopf oder Zahl?; Ⓙ (*St. Exch.*) Kaufoption, *die*

**~ a'side** *v.t.* beiseite rufen ‹Person›

**~ a'way** *v.t.* wegrufen; abrufen

**~ 'back** ❶ *v.t.* zurückrufen. ❷ *v.i.* Ⓐ zurückrufen; Ⓑ (*come back*) zurückkommen; noch einmal vorbeikommen (*ugs.*)

**~ 'down** *v.t.* Ⓐ (*invoke*) herabflehen (*geh.*) ‹Segen›; herausfordern ‹Unwillen, Tadel›; **~ down curses on sb.'s head** jmdn. verfluchen; Ⓑ (*reprimand*) ausschimpfen

**~ for** *v.t.* Ⓐ (*send for, order*) [sich (*Dat.*)] kommen lassen, bestellen ‹Taxi, Essen, Getränke, Person›; Ⓑ (*collect*) abholen ‹Person, Gepäck, Güter›; **'to be ~ed for'** „wird abgeholt“; Ⓒ (*require, demand*) erfordern; verlangen; **that remark was not ~ed for** die Bemerkung war unangebracht; **this ~s for a celebration** das muss gefeiert werden

**~ 'forth** *v.t.* hervorrufen ‹Protest, Kritik›; zusammennehmen ‹Mut, Energie›; beschwören, lebendig werden lassen ‹Eindrücke, Erinnerungen, Erlebnisse›

~ 'in ❶ *v.i.* vorbeikommen (*ugs.*); **I'll ~ in on you** ich komme bei dir vorbei (*ugs.*); **I'll ~ in at your office** ich komme bei dir im Büro vorbei (*ugs.*). ❷ *v.t.* Ⓐ aus dem Verkehr ziehen ‹Waren, Münzen›; zurückfordern ‹Bücher›; Ⓑ ~ **in a specialist** einen Fachmann/Facharzt zurate ziehen

~ '**off** *v.t.* (*cancel*) absagen ‹Treffen, Verabredung›; rückgängig machen ‹Geschäft›; lösen ‹Verlobung›; (*stop, end*) abbrechen, (*ugs.*) abblasen ‹Streik›; ~ **off your dogs!** rufen Sie Ihre Hunde zurück!

~ **on** ⇒ ~ **[up]on**

~ '**out** ❶ *v.t.* alarmieren ‹Truppen›; rufen ‹Wache›; zum Streik aufrufen ‹Arbeitnehmer›. ❷ *v.i.* ⇒ ~ 1 A; ~ **out to warn sb.** jmdm. zurufen, um ihn zu warnen

~ '**up** *v.t.* Ⓐ (*imagine, recollect*) wachrufen ‹Erinnerungen, Bilder›; [herauf]beschwören, erwecken ‹böse Erinnerungen, Fantasien›; Ⓑ (*summon*) anrufen, beschwören ‹Teufel, Geister›; Ⓒ (*by telephone*) anrufen; **I'll ~ you up again** ich rufe Sie wieder an; Ⓓ (*Mil.*) einberufen; **they were ~ed up to go to Vietnam** sie wurden nach Vietnam einberufen; ⇒ *also* **call-up**

~ **[up]on** *v.t.* ~ **upon God** Gott anrufen; ~ **[up]on sb.'s generosity/sense of justice** an jmds. Großzügigkeit/Gerechtigkeitssinn (*Akk.*) appellieren; ~ **[up]on sb. to do sth.** jmdn. auffordern, etw. zu tun

**call:** ~ **box** *n.* Telefonzelle, *die;* Fernsprechzelle, *die* (*Amtsspr.*); ~ **boy** *n.* Ⓐ (*in theatre*) Gehilfe des Inspizienten/Souffleurs; Ⓑ (*in hotel*) [Hotel]boy, *der;* ~ **button** *n.* Ruftaste, *die;* ~ **centre** *n* Callcenter, *das*

**caller** /'kɔ:lə(r)/ *n.* Ⓐ Rufende, *der/die;* (*visitor*) Besucher, *der*/Besucherin, *die;* (*on telephone*) Anrufer, *der*/Anruferin, *die;* Ⓑ (*in bingo, square dance*) Ansager, *der*/Ansagerin, *die*

'**call girl** *n.* Callgirl, *das*

**calligrapher** /kə'lɪgrəfə(r)/ *n.* ▶ **1261** Schönschreiber, *der*/Schönschreiberin, *die;* (*professional*) Kalligraph, *der*/Kalligraphin, *die*

**calligraphy** /kə'lɪgrəfɪ/ *n.* Ⓐ (*beautiful handwriting*) Schönschrift, *die;* Kalligraphie, *die;* (*as an art*) Kalligraphie, *die;* Schönschreiben, *das;* Ⓑ (*handwriting*) Handschrift, *die;* Hand, *die* (*geh.*)

**calling** /'kɔ:lɪŋ/ *n.* Ⓐ (*occupation, profession*) Beruf, *der;* Ⓑ (*divine summons*) Berufung, *die*

'**calling card** *n.* (*Amer.*) Visitenkarte, *die*

**calliper** /'kælɪpə(r)/ *n.* Ⓐ *in pl.* **[pair of]** ~**s** Greifzirkel, *der;* Tasterzirkel, *der;* Taster, *der;* Ⓑ ~ **[splint]** (*Med.*) Beinschiene, *die;* Ⓒ **[brake]** ~: Bremssattel, *der*

**callisthenics** /kælɪs'θenɪks/ *n. pl.* Kallisthenie, *die;* leichte Gymnastik

'**call meter** *n.* (*Teleph.*) Gebührenzähler, *der*

**callosity** /kə'lɒsɪtɪ/ *n.* Ⓐ *no pl.* Schwieligkeit, *die;* Ⓑ (*lump*) Schwiele, *die*

**callous** /'kæləs/ ❶ *adj.* (*unfeeling, insensitive*) gefühllos; herzlos ‹Handlung, Verhalten›; lieblos ‹Leben, Welt›. ❷ *n.* ⇒ **callus**

**callously** /'kæləslɪ/ *adv.* herzlos

**callousness** /'kæləsnɪs/ *n., no pl.* (*want of feeling*) Gefühllosigkeit, *die;* (*of act, behaviour*) Herzlosigkeit, *die;* **his ~ towards [the feelings of] other people** seine Gleichgültigkeit den Gefühlen anderer gegenüber

'**call out** *n.* Einsatz, *der;* **the ~ could come at any time** es kann jederzeit eine Einsatzanforderung kommen; **call-out fee/charge** Anfahrtskosten *Pl.*

'**call-over** *n.* Namensruf, *der;* (*of betting-prices*) Verlesen, *das*

**callow** /'kæləʊ/ *adj.* Ⓐ (*raw, inexperienced*) unreif ‹Junge, Student›; grün (*ugs.*) ‹Jüngling›; **in my ~ youth** als ich noch jung und unreif war; Ⓑ (*unfledged*) nackt; kahl

**call:** ~ **sign,** ~ **signal** *ns.* Rufzeichen, *das;* ~**-up** *n.* (*Mil.*) Einberufung, *die*

**callus** /'kæləs/ *n.* Ⓐ (*Physiol.*) Schwiele, *die;* Kallus, *der* (*fachspr.*); Ⓑ (*Med.*) Knochennarbe, *die;* Kallus, *der* (*fachspr.*); Ⓒ (*Bot.*) Wundgewebe, *das;* Kallus, *der* (*fachspr.*)

**calm** /kɑ:m/ ❶ *n.* Ⓐ (*stillness*) Stille, *die;* (*serenity*) Ruhe, *die;* **the peaceful ~ of the night** die friedliche Stille der Nacht; Ⓑ (*windless period*) Windstille, *die;* Kalme, *die* (*Met.*); **a dead ~:** totale Windstille; **the ~ before the storm** (*lit. or fig.*) die Ruhe vor dem Sturm. ❷ *adj.* Ⓐ (*tranquil, quiet, windless*) ruhig; **keep ~:** ruhig bleiben; Ruhe bewahren; **keep one's voice ~:** ruhig sprechen; Ⓑ (*coll.: self-confident*) lässig (*ugs.*); gelassen. ❸ *v.t.* beruhigen ‹Person›; besänftigen ‹Leidenschaften, Zorn›; ~ **sb. down** jmdn. beruhigen. ❹ *v.i.* ~ **[down]** sich beruhigen; ‹Sturm:› abflauen

**calmly** /'kɑ:mlɪ/ *adv.* ruhig; gelassen

**calmness** /'kɑ:mnɪs/ *n., no pl.* Ruhe, *die;* (*of water, sea*) Stille, *die*

**Calor gas** ® /'kælə gæs/ *n.* Butangas, *das*

**calorie** /'kælərɪ/ *n.* Kalorie, *die*

**calorific** /kælə'rɪfɪk/ *adj.* wärmeerzeugend; ~ **value** Heizwert, *der*

**calorimeter** /kælə'rɪmɪtə(r)/ *n.* Kalorimeter, *das*

**calumniate** /kə'lʌmnɪeɪt/ *v.t.* verleumden

**calumny** /'kæləmnɪ/ ❶ *n.* Verleumdung, *die.* ❷ *v.t.* verleumden

**calvados** /'kælvədɒs/ *n.* Calvados, *der*

**Calvary** /'kælvərɪ/ *n.* (*place*) Golgatha (*das*); (*representation*) Kalvarienberg, *der*

**calve** /kɑ:v/ *v.i.* kalben; abkalben (*fachspr.*)

**calves** *pl. of* **calf**[1,2]

**Calvinism** /'kælvɪnɪzm/ *n.* Kalvinismus, *der*

**Calvinist** /'kælvɪnɪst/ *n.* Kalvinist, *der*/Kalvinistin, *die*

**Calvinistic** /kælvɪ'nɪstɪk/, **Calvinistical** /kælvɪ'nɪstɪkl/ *adj.* kalvinistisch

**calypso** /kə'lɪpsəʊ/ *n., pl.* ~**s** Calypso, *der*

**calyx** /'keɪlɪks, 'kælɪks/ *n., pl.* **calyces** /'keɪlɪsi:z, 'kælɪsi:z/ *or* **-es** Ⓐ (*Bot.*) Kelch, *der;* Kalyx, *der* (*fachspr.*); Ⓑ (*Anat.*) Kelch, *der*

**cam** /kæm/ *n.* Nocken, *der*

**CAM** *abbr.* **computer-aided manufacturing** CAM

**camaraderie** /kæmə'rɑ:dərɪ/ *n.* Kameradschaft, *die*

**camber** /'kæmbə(r)/ ❶ *n.* Ⓐ (*convexity*) Wölbung, *die;* Ⓑ (*Motor Veh.*) Achssturz, *der;* Radsturz, *der.* ❷ *v.t.* wölben; **a ~ed road** eine gewölbte Straße

**Cambodia** /kæm'bəʊdɪə/ *pr. n.* (*Hist.*) Kambodscha (*das*)

**Cambodian** /kæm'bəʊdɪən/ ▶ **1340** (*Hist.*) ❶ *adj.* kambodschanisch. ❷ *n.* Kambodschaner, *der*/Kambodschanerin, *die*

**Cambrian** /'kæmbrɪən/ ❶ *adj.* Ⓐ (*Welsh*) walisisch; Waliser *nicht präd.*; Ⓑ (*Geol.*) kambrisch. ❷ *n.* (*Geol.*) Kambrium, *das*

**cambric** /'kæmbrɪk/ *n.* Kambrik[batist], *der*

**Cambridge**/'keɪmbrɪdʒ/: ~ **blue** *n.* Blassblau, *das;* Cambridgeblau, *das*

**camcorder** /'kæmkɔ:də(r)/ *n.* Camcorder, *der;* Kamerarecorder, *der*

**came** ⇒ **come** 1

**camel** /'kæml/ *n.* (*Zool.*) Kamel, *das*

**camellia** /kə'mi:lɪə, kə'melɪə/ *n.* (*Bot.*) Kamelie, *die*

'**camel['s] hair** *n.* Kamelhaar, *das;* ~ **brush** Haarpinsel, *der;* ~ **coat** Kamelhaarmantel, *der*

**cameo** /'kæmɪəʊ/ *n., pl.* ~**s** Ⓐ (*carving*) Kamee, *die;* Ⓑ (*short sketch*) Sketch, *der;* (*minor role*) [winzige] Nebenrolle

**camera** /'kæmərə/ *n.* Ⓐ Kamera, *die;* (*for still pictures*) Fotoapparat, *der;* Kamera, *die;* **be/go on ~:** vor der Kamera sein/vor die Kamera treten; Ⓑ (*Law*) **in ~:** unter Ausschluss der Öffentlichkeit; (*fig.*) hinter verschlossenen Türen

**camera:** ~ **case** *n.* Kameratasche, *die;* ~**man** *n.* ▶ **1261** Kameramann, *der;* ~**-shy** *adj.* kamerascheu; ~**work** *n., no pl., no indef. art.* Kameraführung, *die*

**Cameroon** /'kæməru:n/ *pr. n.* Kamerun (*das*)

**camiknickers** /'kæmɪnɪkəz/ *n. pl.* (*Brit.*) Spitzenhemdhöschen, *das*

**camisole** /'kæmɪsəʊl/ *n.* (*arch.*) Leibchen, *das;* Mieder, *das;* Kamisol, *das* (*veralt.*)

**camomile** /'kæməmaɪl/ *n.* (*Bot.*) Kamille, *die;* ~ **tea** Kamillentee, *der*

**camouflage** /'kæməflɑ:ʒ/ ❶ *n.* (*lit. or fig.*) Tarnung, *die;* Camouflage, *die* (*Milit. veralt./fig. geh.*). ❷ *v.t.* (*lit. or fig.*) tarnen; camouflieren (*veralt./geh.*)

**camp**[1] /kæmp/ ❶ *n.* Lager, *das;* (*Mil.*) Feldlager, *das;* **the world is divided into two opposing ~s** (*fig.*) die Welt teilt sich in zwei entgegengesetzte Lager; ⇒ *also* **foot** 1 A. ❷ *v.i.* ~ **[out]** campen; (*in tent*) zelten; **go ~ing** Campen/Zelten fahren/gehen

**camp**[2] ❶ *adj.* Ⓐ (*affected*) affektiert, geziert ‹Person, Art, Benehmen›; Ⓑ (*exaggerated*) übertrieben, theatralisch ‹Gestik, Ausdrucksform›; Ⓒ (*homosexual*) schwul (*ugs.*); (*effeminate*) tuntenhaft (*ugs.*). ❷ *n.* Manieriertheit, *die.* ❸ *v.t.* ~ **it up** zu dick auftragen (*ugs.*); ~ **up a part** bei einer Rolle zu dick auftragen (*ugs.*)

**campaign** /kæm'peɪn/ ❶ *n.* Ⓐ (*Mil.*) Feldzug, *der;* Kampagne, *die* (*veralt.*); **be on ~:** im Felde stehen (*veralt.*); Ⓑ (*organized course of action*) Kampagne, *die;* Feldzug, *der;* **publicity ~:** Werbekampagne, *die;* ⇒ *also* **presidential**. ❷ *v.i.* ~ **for sth.** sich für etw. einsetzen; ~ **against sth.** gegen etw. etwas unternehmen; **be ~ing** (*for election*) ‹Politiker:› im Wahlkampf stehen; ~ **hard** einen intensiven Wahlkampf führen

**campaigner** /kæm'peɪnə(r)/ *n.* Ⓐ Vorkämpfer, *der*/Vorkämpferin, *die;* Ⓑ (*veteran*) Veteran, *der;* alter Kämpfer; **an old ~:** ein alter Kämpfer *od.* (*veralt.*) Kämpe; Ⓒ ~ **for ...:** Anhänger, *der*/Anhängerin, *die* (+ *Gen.*); ~ **against ...:** Gegner, *der*/Gegnerin, *die* (+ *Gen.*)

**cam'paign trail** *n.* Wahlkampfreise, *die*; **on the ~:** im Wahlkampf

**campanology** /kæmpə'nɒlədʒɪ/ *n.* Kunst des Glockenläutens

**campanula** /kæm'pænjʊlə/ *n.* Glockenblume, *die;* Campanula, *die* (*fachspr.*)

'**camp bed** *n.* Campingliege, *die*

**camper** /'kæmpə(r)/ *n.* Ⓐ Camper, *der*/Camperin, *die;* Ⓑ (*vehicle*) Wohnmobil, *das;* (*adapted minibus*) Campingbus, *der*

**camp:** ~**fire** *n.* Lagerfeuer, *das;* ~ **follower** Marketender, *der*/Marketenderin, *die;* (*fig.: disciple, follower*) Mitläufer, *der*/Mitläuferin, *die*

**camphor** /'kæmfə(r)/ *n.* Kampfer, *der*

**camping** /'kæmpɪŋ/ *n.* Camping, *das;* (*in tent*) Zelten, *das*

**camping:** ~**-ground** (*Amer.*) ⇒ ~ **site**; ~ **holiday** *n.* Campingurlaub, *der;* ~ **site** *n.* Campingplatz, *der*

**camp:** ~**site** *n.* Campingplatz, *der;* ~ **stool** *n.* Campinghocker, *der*

**campus** /'kæmpəs/ *n.* Ⓐ (*grounds of university*) Campus, *der;* Hochschulgelände, *das;* Ⓑ (*university*) Hochschule, *die*

**CAMRA** /'kæmrə/ *abbr.* **Campaign for Real Ale**

'**camshaft** *n.* Nockenwelle, *die*

**can**[1] /kæn/ ❶ *n.* Ⓐ (*milk ~, watering ~*) Kanne, *die;* (*for oil, petrol*) Kanister, *der;* (*Amer.: for refuse*) Eimer, *der;* Tonne, *die;* **a ~ of paint** eine Büchse Farbe; (*with handle*) ein Eimer Farbe; **carry** *or* **take the ~ [back]** (*Brit. fig. coll.*) die Sache ausbaden (*ugs.*); Ⓑ (*container for preserving*) [Konserven]dose, *die;* [Konserven]büchse, *die;* **a ~ of tomatoes/sausages** eine Dose *od.* Büchse Tomaten/Würstchen; ~**s of food** Lebensmittelkonserven; **a ~ of beer** eine Dose Bier; **a ~ of worms** (*fig.*) eine verzwickte Angelegenheit (*ugs.*); Ⓒ (*Amer. sl.: lavatory*) Lokus, *der* (*ugs.*); Ⓓ (*sl.: prison*) Knast, *der* (*salopp*).

❷ *v.t.,* **-nn-** Ⓐ (*preserve*) konservieren; Ⓑ (*put into ~*) eindosen; einmachen ‹Obst›

**can**[2] *v. aux., only in pres.* ~, *neg.* ~**not** /'kænət/, (*coll.*) ~**'t** /kɑ:nt/, *past* **could** /kʊd/, *neg.* (*coll.*) **couldn't** /'kʊdnt/ können; (*have right, be permitted*) dürfen; können; **as much as one ~:** so viel man kann; **as ... as '~ be** wirklich sehr ...; ~ **do** (*coll.*) kein Problem; **he ~'t be more than 40** er kann nicht über 40 sein; **you ~'t smoke in this compartment** in diesem Abteil dürfen Sie nicht rauchen; **what you say ~not be true** was du sagst, kann nicht stimmen; **come nearer, I ~'t hear what you're saying** kommen Sie näher, ich kann Sie nicht verstehen; **could you ring me tomorrow?** könnten Sie mich morgen anrufen?; **how [ever] could you do this to me?** wie konnten Sie mir das bloß antun?; **I could have killed him** ich hätte ihn umbringen können; **[that] could be [so]** das könnte *od.* kann sein

C

**Canada** /'kænədə/ *pr. n.* Kanada (das)

**'Canada goose** *n.* Kanadagans, *die*

**Canadian** /kə'neɪdɪən/ ▶ 1340 ❶ *adj.* kanadisch; **sb. is ~:** jmd. ist Kanadier/Kanadierin. ❷ *n.* Kanadier, *der*/Kanadierin, *die;* **the French/English ~s** die Franko-/Anglokanadier

**canaille** /kə'nɑ:i:/ *n.* Pöbel, *der* (*abwertend*)

**canal** /kə'næl/ *n.* Ⓐ (*watercourse, marking on Mars*) Kanal, *der;* **the Panama C~:** der Panamakanal; Ⓑ (*Zool., Bot.*) Gang, *der;* (*alimentary ~*) [Verdauungs]kanal, *der*

**ca'nal boat** *n. langes, enges Boot zum Befahren der Kanäle;* (*Hist.: towed barge*) Schleppkahn, *der*

**canalization** /kænəlaɪ'zeɪʃn/ *n.* Kanalisierung, *die*

**canalize** /'kænəlaɪz/ *v.t.* kanalisieren ‹Fluss›

**canapé** /'kænəpɪ/ *n.* (*food*) Cocktailhappen, *der;* Kanapee, *das*

**canard** /kə'nɑ:d, 'kænɑ:d/ *n.* (*false report*) Ente, *die* (*ugs.*)

**Canaries** /kə'neərɪz/ *pr. n. pl.* Kanarische Inseln *Pl.;* Kanaren *Pl.*

**canary** /kə'neərɪ/ *n.* Kanarienvogel, *der*

**canary: C~ 'Islands** *pr. n. pl.* Kanarische Inseln *Pl.;* **~-seed** *n.* Kanariensamen, *der;* **~ 'yellow** *n.* Kanariengelb, *das;* **~-yellow** *adj.* kanariengelb

**canasta** /kə'næstə/ *n.* (*Cards*) Canasta, *das*

**cancan** /'kænkæn/ *n.* Cancan, *der*

**cancel** /'kænsl/ ❶ *v.t.*, (*Brit.*) **-ll-:** Ⓐ (*cross out*) streichen ‹Wort, Satz, Absatz›; Ⓑ (*call off*) absagen ‹Besuch, Urlaub, Reise, Sportveranstaltung›; ausfallen lassen ‹Veranstaltung, Vorlesung, Zug, Bus›; fallen lassen ‹Pläne›; (*annul, revoke*) rückgängig machen ‹Einladung, Vertrag›; zurücknehmen ‹Befehl›; stornieren ‹Bestellung, Auftrag›; streichen ‹Schuld[en]›; kündigen ‹Abonnement›; abbestellen ‹Zeitung›; aufheben ‹Klausel, Gesetz, Recht›; **the match had to be ~led** das Spiel musste ausfallen *od.* abgesagt werden; **the boat to Dublin has been ~led** die Fähre nach Dublin fährt *od.* verkehrt nicht; **the lecture has been ~led** die Vorlesung fällt aus; Ⓒ (*balance, neutralize*) aufheben; **the arguments ~ each other out** die Argumente heben sich gegenseitig auf; Ⓓ (*deface*) entwerten ‹Briefmarke, Fahrkarte›; ungültig machen ‹Scheck›; Ⓔ (*Math.*) aufheben; wegkürzen (*ugs.*); Ⓕ (*Amer. Mus.*) auflösen. ❷ *v.i.*, (*Brit.*) **-ll-: ~ [out]** sich [gegenseitig] aufheben

**cancellation** /kænsə'leɪʃn/ *n.* ⇒ **cancel** 1: Ⓐ Streichung, *die;* Ⓑ Absage, *die;* Ausfall, *der;* Ausfallen, *das;* Fallenlassen, *das;* Aufgabe, *die;* Rückgängigmachen, *das;* [Zu]rücknahme, *die;* Stornierung, *die;* Streichung, *die;* Kündigung, *die;* Abbestellung, *die;* Aufhebung, *die;* Ⓒ Aufhebung, *die;* Ⓓ Entwertung, *die;* Ungültigmachen, *das;* Ⓔ Aufhebung, *die;* Wegkürzen, *das* (*ugs.*); Ⓕ Auflösung, *die*

**cancer** /'kænsə(r)/ *n.* Ⓐ ▶ 1232 (*Med.*) Krebs, *der;* (*fig.*) Krebsgeschwür, *das;* **~ of the liver** Leberkrebs, *der;* Ⓑ **C~** (*Astrol., Astron.*) der Krebs; der Cancer; ⇒ *also* **Aries; tropic**

**Cancerian** /kæn'sɪərɪən/ *n.* (*Astrol.*) Krebs, *der*

**cancerous** /'kænsərəs/ *adj.* Krebs‹geschwulst, -geschwür›; krebsartig ‹Wucherung, Wachstum›; kanzerös (*fachspr.*); (*fig.*) bösartig ‹Hass, Einfluss›; **~ growth** krebsartige Wucherung

**candelabra** /kændɪ'lɑ:brə/ *n.*, **candelabrum** /kændɪ'læbrəm, kændɪ'lɑ:brəm/ *n.*, *pl.* **~** or (*Amer.*) **candelabrums** Leuchter, *der;* (*large*) Kandelaber, *der*

**candid** /'kændɪd/ *adj.* offen; ehrlich ‹Ansicht, Bericht›; **let me be ~ with you** ich will ganz offen mit Ihnen sein

**candidacy** /'kændɪdəsɪ/ *n.* Kandidatur, *die*

**candidate** /'kændɪdət, 'kændɪdeɪt/ *n.* Ⓐ Kandidat, *der*/Kandidatin, *die;* Anwärter, *der*/Anwärterin, *die;* **a ~ for Mayor** ein Bürgermeisterkandidat/-kandidatin; **he offered himself as a ~ for the position** er bot sich als Kandidat für den Posten an; **~s for a club/for membership** Anwärter für einen Klub/auf Mitgliedschaft; Ⓑ (*examinee*) Kandidat, *der*/Kandidatin, *die;* **a Ph. D. ~:** ein Promotionskandidat *od.* Promovend; **a ~ for a degree** ein Prüfling *od.* Examinand

**candidature** /'kændɪdətʃə(r)/ *n.* (*esp. Brit.*) Kandidatur, *die*

**candid 'camera** *n.* versteckte Kamera

**candidly** /'kændɪdlɪ/ *adv.* offen; ehrlich; **~, I dislike the whole idea** offen gesagt, gefällt mir die Idee gar nicht

**candle** /kændl/ ❶ *n.* Ⓐ Kerze, *die;* **burn the ~ at both ends** (*fig.*) sich übernehmen; sich (*Dat.*) zu viel aufladen; **she can't** *or* **is not fit to hold a ~ to him** (*fig.*) sie kann ihm nicht das Wasser reichen; **the game is not worth the ~** (*fig.*) die Sache lohnt sich nicht *od.* ist nicht der Mühe (*Gen.*) wert; Ⓑ (*unit*) **~[power]** Kerze, *die* (*veralt.*); Candela, *die.* ⇒ *also* **Roman candle.** ❷ *v.t.* gegen das Licht halten, durchleuchten ‹Eier›

**candle: ~light** *n.* Kerzenlicht, *das;* **by ~light:** bei Kerzenlicht ‹lesen›; im Kerzenschein (*geh.*) ‹feiern, speisen›; **~power** ⇒ **candle** 1 B; **~stick** *n.* Kerzenhalter, *der;* (*elaborate*) Leuchter, *der;* **~wick** *n.* Ⓐ (*of candle*) Kerzendocht, *der;* Ⓑ (*material*) Frottierplüsch, *der*

**candour** (*Brit.; Amer.:* **candor**) /'kændə(r)/ *n.* (*frankness*) Offenheit, *die;* (*honesty*) Ehrlichkeit, *die*

**candy** /'kændɪ/ ❶ *n.* Ⓐ Kandis[zucker], *der;* **a ~:** ein Stück Kandis[zucker]; Ⓑ (*Amer.*) (*sweets*) Süßigkeiten *Pl.;* (*sweet*) Bonbon, *das od. der.* ❷ *v.t.* kandieren ‹Früchte›; **candied lemon/orange peel** Zitronat/Orangeat, *das*

**candy: ~floss** *n.* Zuckerwatte, *die;* **~ store** *n.* (*Amer.*) Süßwarengeschäft, *das;* Bonbonladen, *der* (*ugs.*); **~-stripe** *n.* Muster mit bunten Streifen [auf weißem Hintergrund]; **~-striped** *adj.* bunt gestreift

**'candytuft** (*Bot.*) *n.* Schleifenblume, *die*

**cane** /keɪn/ ❶ *n.* Ⓐ (*stem of bamboo, rattan, etc.*) Rohr, *das;* (*of raspberry, blackberry*) Spross, *der;* ⇒ *also* **sugar cane**; Ⓑ (*material*) Rohr, *das;* Ⓒ (*stick*) [Rohr]stock, *der;* **get the ~:** eine Tracht Prügel bekommen; Ⓓ (*esp. Brit.: walking stick*) Spazierstock, *der.* ❷ *v.t.* Ⓐ (*beat*) [mit dem Stock] schlagen; Ⓑ (*weave*) flechten

**cane: ~ chair** *n.* Rohrstuhl, *der;* **~ sugar** *n.* Rohrzucker, *der*

**canine** /'keɪnaɪn, 'kænaɪn/ ❶ *adj.* Ⓐ (*of dog[s]*) Hunde‹rasse, -gebell, -natur›; Ⓑ **~ tooth** Eck- *od.* Augenzahn, *der.* ❷ *n.* Eckzahn, *der;* Augenzahn, *der*

**caning** /'keɪnɪŋ/ *n.* [Ver]prügeln, *das od.* [Ver]hauen, *das* [mit dem Stock]; **he got a ~:** er kriegte eine Tracht Prügel (*ugs.*) [mit dem Stock]

**canister** /'kænɪstə(r)/ *n.* Büchse, *die;* Dose, *die;* (*for petrol, oil etc.*) Kanister, *der*

**canker** /'kæŋkə(r)/ ❶ *n.* Ⓐ (*disease*) (*of dogs, cats, rabbits, etc.*) Ohrräude, *die;* (*of horses*) Strahlfäule, *die;* Ⓑ (*fig.: corrupting influence*) [Krebs]geschwür, *das.* ❷ *v.t.* Ⓐ (*consume with ~*) verrotten; Ⓑ (*fig.: infect, corrupt*) vergiften ‹Gemüt, Gefühl›

**cannabis** /'kænəbɪs/ *n.* (*Bot.*) Kannabis, *der;* Hanf, *der;* (*drug*) Haschisch, *das;* Marihuana, *das*

**cannabis 'resin** *n.* Haschisch, *das;* Cannabisharz, *das* (*fachspr.*)

**canned** /kænd/ *adj.* Ⓐ Dosen-; in Dosen *nachgestellt;* **~ fish/meat/fruit** Fisch-/Fleisch-/Obstkonserven *Pl.;* Fisch/Fleisch/Obst in Dosen; **~ beer** Dosenbier; **~ food** [Lebensmittel]konserven *Pl.;* Ⓑ (*sl.: drunk*) abgefüllt (*ugs.*); Ⓒ (*recorded*) aufgezeichnet; **~ music/entertainment** Musikkonserve, *die*/Unterhaltungskonserve, *die*

**canner** /'kænə(r)/ *n.* Konservenfabrikant, *der;* (*worker*) Arbeiter/Arbeiterin in einer Konservenfabrik

**cannery** /'kænərɪ/ *n.* Konservenfabrik, *die*

**cannibal** /'kænɪbl/ *n.* Kannibale, *der*/Kannibalin, *die;* Menschenfresser, *der*/-fresserin, *die* (*ugs.*); **these animals are ~s** diese Tiere fressen ihre Artgenossen auf

**cannibalise** ⇒ **cannibalize**

**cannibalism** /'kænɪbəlɪzm/ *n.* Kannibalismus, *der;* Menschenfresserei, *die* (*ugs.*); (*fig.*) Blutdurst, *der*

**cannibalistic** /kænɪbə'lɪstɪk/ *adj.* kannibalisch

**cannibalize** /'kænɪbəlaɪz/ *v.t.* ausschlachten ‹Auto, Flugzeug, Maschine usw.›

**cannily** /'kænɪlɪ/ *adv.* (*cautiously*) vorsichtig; (*shrewdly*) schlau

**cannon** /'kænən/ ❶ *n.* Ⓐ (*gun*) Kanone, *die;* Ⓑ (*Brit. Billiards etc.*) Karambolage, *die.* ❷ *v.i.* (*Brit.*) Ⓐ **~ against sth.** gegen etw. prallen; **~ into sb./sth.** mit etw./jmdm. zusammenprallen; Ⓑ (*Billiards*) karambolieren

**cannonade** /kænə'neɪd/ (*arch.*) ❶ *n.* Kanonade, *die* (*veralt.*). ❷ *v.t.* kanonieren (*veralt.*)

**cannon: ~ ball** *n.* (*Hist.*) Kanonenkugel, *die;* **~ fodder** *n.* Kanonenfutter, *das* (*salopp abwertend*)

**cannot** ⇒ **can²**

**cannula** /'kænjʊlə/ *n.*, *pl.* **~e** /'kænjʊli:/ *or* **~s** (*Med.*) Kanüle, *die*

**canny** /'kænɪ/ *adj.* Ⓐ (*shrewd*) schlau; bauernschlau (*ugs.*); (*thrifty*) sparsam; Ⓑ (*cautious, wary*) vorsichtig; umsichtig; Ⓒ trocken ‹Humor›

**canoe** /kə'nu:/ ❶ *n.* Paddelboot, *das;* (*Indian ~, Sport*) Kanu, *das;* ⇒ *also* **paddle¹** 2. ❷ *v.i.* paddeln; (*in Indian ~, Sport*) Kanu fahren; **~ down the river** flussabwärts paddeln/im Kanu flussabwärts fahren

**canoeing** /kə'nu:ɪŋ/ *n.* Paddeln, *das;* (*Sport*) Kanufahren, *das;* Kanusport, *der*

**canoeist** /kə'nu:ɪst/ *n.* Paddelbootfahrer, *der*/-fahrerin, *die;* (*Sport*) Kanute, *der*/Kanutin, *die;* Kanufahrer, *der*/-fahrerin, *die*

**canon** /'kænən/ *n.* Ⓐ (*general law, criterion*) Grundregel, *die;* Grundprinzip, *das;* **the ~s of conduct** die Grundregeln des Verhaltens; der Verhaltenskodex; Ⓑ ▶ 1617 (*member of cathedral chapter*) Kanoniker, *der;* Kanonikus, *der;* Ⓒ (*church decree*) Kirchengebot, *das;* Ⓓ (*list of sacred books*) Kanon, *der;* (*fig.*) **the Shakespearean ~:** das Gesamtwerk Shakespeares; Ⓔ (*Mus.*) Kanon, *der*

**cañon** ⇒ **canyon**

**canonical** /kə'nɒnɪkl/ ❶ *adj.* Ⓐ kanonisch ‹Gehorsam, Gelübde, Bücher, Schriften›; **~ dress** Priestertracht *od.* -kleidung, *die;* **~ hours** Gebetszeiten *Pl.;* (*Brit.: for weddings*) Trauzeiten *Pl.;* Ⓑ (*authoritative, standard*) verbindlich, kanonisch ‹Urteil, Werte, Vorschriften›; maßgeblich ‹Person›; Ⓒ (*Mus.*) Kanon‹form, -komposition›; ‹Musikstück› in Kanonform; Ⓓ (*of cathedral chapter or member of it*) Kanoniker-; Chorherren-; **a ~ clergyman** ein Kanoniker *od.* Chorherr. ❷ *n. in pl.* Priesterkleidung, *die*

**canonisation, canonise** ⇒ **canoniz-**

**canonization** /kænənaɪ'zeɪʃn/ *n.* Kanonisation, *die;* **~ of saints** Heiligsprechungen

**canonize** /'kænənaɪz/ *v.t.* Ⓐ kanonisieren ‹Heiligen›; heilig sprechen ‹Märtyrer›; **he was ~d [a saint]** er wurde heilig gesprochen; Ⓑ (*regard as saint*) wie einen Heiligen/eine Heilige/Heilige *Pl.* verehren

**canon: ~ law** *n.* kanonisches Recht; **~ 'regular** *n.* regulierter Chorherr

**canoodle** /kə'nu:dl/ (*coll.*) ❶ *v.i.* [rum]knutschen (*salopp*). ❷ *v.t.* abknutschen (*salopp*)

**'can-opener** *n.* Dosen-, Büchsenöffner, *der*

**canopy** /'kænəpɪ/ ❶ *n.* Ⓐ Baldachin, *der* (*auch fig.*); (*over entrance*) Vordach, *das;* **the ~ of the heavens** *or* **celestial ~:** das Himmelszelt *od.* himmlische Zelt (*dichter.*); **a ~ of leaves** ein Blätterdach; Ⓑ (*of parachute*)

[Fall]schirmkappe, *die;* **C** *(of aircraft)* [Kanzel]haube, *die.* ❷ *v.t.* überwölben

**cant**[1] /kænt/ ❶ *v.t.* kippen; ankippen, kanten ‹Fass›; ~ **off** abschrägen; ~ **over** umdrehen; umkippen. ❷ *v.i.* *(take inclined position, lie aslant)* sich neigen. ❸ *n.* *(movement)* Ruck, *der;* *(tilted position)* Schräglage, *die;* *(bevel)* Schräge, *die*

**cant**[2] ❶ *n.* **A** *(derog.: language of class, sect, etc.)* Zunftsprache, *die;* Jargon, *der;* **thieves'/beggars' ~:** Rotwelsch, *das;* Gaunersprache, *die;* **B** *(insincere use of words)* Scheinheiligkeit, *die;* *(talk)* scheinheiliges Gerede; **C** *(ephemeral catchwords)* Phrase, *die* *(abwertend)*; **a ~ phrase** eine [leere] Phrase; **~ phrases/terms/words** [leere] Phrasen. ❷ *v.i.* **A** ⇒ **1** A: *(use, speak in ~)* Jargon/Rotwelsch reden; **B** *(talk with affectation of piety)* [scheinheilig] schwafeln *(abwertend)*

**can't** /kɑːnt/ *(coll.)* = **cannot;** ⇒ **can**[2]

**Cantab.** /ˈkæntæb/ *abbr.* **of Cambridge University** der Universität Cambridge

**cantabile** /kænˈtɑːbɪlɪ/ *(Mus.)* ❶ *adv.* cantabile. ❷ *adj.* Kantabile‹satz, -stil, -ton›; sangbar ‹Stück, Musik›. ❸ *n.* Kantabile, *das*

**cantaloup[e]** /ˈkæntəluːp/ *n.* Zucker-, Gartenmelone, *die*

**cantankerous** /kænˈtæŋkərəs/ *adj.* streitsüchtig; knurrig *(ugs.)* ‹müde od. launische Person›; störrisch ‹Esel, altes Auto usw.›; **don't be so ~ on Monday mornings** sei doch nicht immer so eklig *od.* mufflig am Montagmorgen! *(ugs.)*

**cantankerously** /kænˈtæŋkərəslɪ/ *adv.* ⇒ **cantankerous**: **behave** *or* **act ~:** streitsüchtig/knurrig *(ugs.)*/störrisch/mufflig *od.* eklig *(ugs.)* sein

**cantankerousness** /kænˈtæŋkərəsnɪs/ *n., no pl.* ⇒ **cantankerous**: Streitsucht, *die;* Knurrigkeit, *die* *(ugs.)*; störrisches Benehmen

**cantata** /kænˈtɑːtə/ *n.* *(Mus.)* Kantate, *die*

**canteen** /kænˈtiːn/ *n.* **A** Kantine, *die;* **B** *(case of plate or cutlery)* Besteckkasten, *der*

**canter** /ˈkæntə(r)/ ❶ *n.* Handgalopp, *der;* Kanter, Canter, *der* *(fachspr.)*; **the horse broke into an easy ~:** das Pferd begann leicht zu galoppieren; **win in a ~** *(fig.)* spielend gewinnen. ❷ *v.i.* leicht galoppieren; kantern *(fachspr.)*. ❸ *v.t.* in Handgalopp *od.* Kanter gehen lassen ‹Pferd›

**'Canterbury bell** /ˈkæntəbərɪ bel/ *n.* *(Bot.)* Glockenblume, *die*

**canticle** /ˈkæntɪkl/ *n.* **A** Lobgesang, *der;* Canticum, *das* *(Theol.)*; *(hymn)* Preislied, Hohelied, *das* **B** **the C~ of Solomon** *or* **C~s** das Hohe Lied *od.* Hohelied; das Lied der Lieder

**cantilever** /ˈkæntɪliːvə/ *n.* **A** *(bracket)* Konsole, *die;* Kragplatte, *die;* **B** *(beam, girder)* Träger, *der*

**'cantilever: ~ brake** *n.* Cantileverbremse, *die;* **~ bridge** *n.* Auslegerbrücke, *die*

**canto** /ˈkæntəʊ/ *n., pl.* **~s** Gesang, *der;* Canto, *der* *(fachspr.)*

**canton** /ˈkæntɒn/ *n.* Kanton, *der*

**cantonal** /ˈkæntənl/ *adj.* kantonal; Kantons-

**Cantonese** /kæntəˈniːz/ ▶ **1275**, ▶ **1340** ❶ *adj.* kantonesisch; **sb. is ~:** jmd. ist Kantonese/Kantonesin. ❷ *n., pl. same* **A** *(person)* Kantonese, *der*/Kantonesin, *die;* **B** *(language)* Kantonesisch *(das)*

**cantor** /ˈkæntə(r)/ *n.* Kantor, *der*

**canvas** /ˈkænvəs/ *n.* **A** *(cloth)* Leinwand, *die;* *(for tents, tarpaulins, etc.)* Segeltuch, *das;* **under ~:** im Zelt; *(Naut.)* unter Segel; **under full ~:** mit vollen Segeln; **B** *(Art)* Leinwand, *die;* *(painting)* Gemälde, *das;* *(for tapestry and embroidery)* Kanevas, *der;* Gitterleinwand, *die;* **C** *(of racing boat)* Segeltuchbezug, *der;* **win by a ~:** mit einer Nasenlänge gewinnen

**canvass** /ˈkænvəs/ ❶ *v.t.* **A** *(solicit votes in or from)* Wahlwerbung treiben in ‹einem Wahlkreis, Gebiet›; Wahlwerbung treiben bei ‹Wählern, Bürgern›; **~ customers** Kunden werben; **they were ~ed on their political views** man versuchte, ihre politischen Ansichten herauszufinden; **B** *(Brit.: propose)* vorschlagen ‹Plan, Idee, Handel›; **C** *(Amer.: check validity of)* auszählen ‹Stimmen›. ❷ *v.i.* werben **(on behalf of** für); **~ for votes** um Stimmen werben; **~ for a seat in Parliament** sich um einen Parlamentssitz bewerben; **~ for an applicant** sich für einen Bewerber einsetzen. ❸ *n.* [Wahl]kampagne, *die;* *(Amer.: scrutiny of votes)* Auszählung, *die*

**canvasser** /ˈkænvəsə(r)/ *n.* **A** *(for votes)* Wahlhelfer, *der*/Wahlhelferin, *die;* **B** *(salesperson)* Vertreter, *der*/Vertreterin, *die;* **C** *(Amer.: checker of votes)* Auszähler, *der*/Auszählerin, *die*

**canvassing** /ˈkænvəsɪŋ/ *n.* *(for votes)* Wahlwerbung, *die;* *(Commerc.)* Kundenwerbung, *die;* *(opinion polling)* Meinungsforschung, *die*

**canyon** /ˈkænjən/ *n.* Cañon, *der*

**cap** /kæp/ ❶ *n.* **A** Mütze, *die;* *(nurse's, servant's)* Haube, *die;* *(bathing ~)* Badekappe, *die;* *(with peak)* Schirmmütze, *die;* *(skull~)* Kappe, *die;* Käppchen, *das;* **college ~** *viereckige akademische Kopfbedeckung;* ≈ Barett, *das;* **in ~ and gown** mit Barett und Talar; **if the ~ fits, [he** *etc.* **should] wear it** *(fig.)* wem die Jacke passt, der soll sie sich *(Dat.)* anziehen; **with ~ in hand** *(fig.)* demütig; **she set her ~ at him** *(fig.)* sie hatte es auf ihn abgesehen; **~ and bells** Narren- *od.* Schellenkappe, *die;* ⇒ *also* **feather** 1 A; **B** *(of mushroom)* Hut, *der;* *(of honeycomb)* Deckel, *der;* **C** *(device to seal or close)* [Verschluss]kappe, *die;* *(petrol ~, radiator-~)* Verschluss, *der;* *(on milk bottle)* Deckel, *der;* *(of shoe)* Kappe, *die;* **D** *(Brit. Sport)* *Ziermütze als Zeichen der Aufstellung für die [National]mannschaft;* *(player)* Nationalspieler, *der*/-spielerin, *die;* **get one's ~:** für die [National]mannschaft aufgestellt werden; **E** *(contraceptive)* Pessar, *das;* **F** *(explosive)* Zündhütchen, *das;* *(for toy gun)* Zündplättchen, *das.*

❷ *v.t.,* **-pp-** **A** verschließen ‹Flasche›; zu-, abdecken ‹Brunnen, Bohrloch›; mit einer Schutzkappe versehen ‹Zahn›; **B** *(Brit. Sport: award ~ to)* aufstellen; **he was ~ped ten times for England** er ist zehnmal für die englische Nationalmannschaft aufgestellt worden; **C** *(crown)* *(with clouds, snow, mist)* bedecken; *(fig.)* krönen **(by** durch); **~ped with snow** schneebedeckt; **D** *(follow with sth. even more noteworthy)* überbieten ‹Geschichte, Witz usw.›; **to ~ it all** obendrein; **that ~s the lot!** das ist die Höhe!

**cap.** /kæp/ *abbr.* **A** *(Printing etc.)* **capital** Vers.; **B** **chapter** Kap.

**CAP** *abbr.* **Common Agricultural Policy** gemeinsame Agrarpolitik

**capability** /keɪpəˈbɪlɪtɪ/ *n.* **A** Fähigkeit, *die;* Vermögen, *das* *(geh.)*; **his ~ of understanding difficult texts** sein Verständnis [-vermögen] für schwierige Texte; **this plot of land has the ~ for further development** dieses Grundstück lässt sich noch weiter erschließen; **~ for growth** Wachstumschancen *Pl.*; **B** *in pl.* *(undeveloped faculty)* Entwicklungsmöglichkeiten *Pl.*

**capable** /ˈkeɪpəbl/ *adj.* **A** **be ~ of sth.** ‹Person:› zu etw. imstande sein; **show him what you are ~ of** zeig ihm, wozu du imstande bist *od.* wessen du fähig bist; **he is ~ of any crime** er ist zu jedem Verbrechen fähig; **she is quite ~ of neglecting her duties** sie bringt es durchaus fertig, ihre Pflichten zu vernachlässigen; **be ~ of improvement** verbesserungsfähig sein; **be ~ of misinterpretation** sich leicht falsch interpretieren lassen; leicht falsch interpretiert werden; **it is not ~ of being expressed in a few words** es lässt sich nicht in ein paar Worten ausdrücken; **B** *(gifted, able)* fähig ‹Person, Lehrer usw.›; **~ fingers** geschickte Finger

**capably** /ˈkeɪpəblɪ/ *adv.* gekonnt, kompetent ‹leiten, führen›

**capacious** /kəˈpeɪʃəs/ *adj.* geräumig; groß ‹Gedächtnis, Verstand, Appetit›; weit, groß ‹Schuhe, Taschen›

**capaciousness** /kəˈpeɪʃəsnɪs/ *n., no pl.* *(of room, hall)* Geräumigkeit, *die;* *(of receptacle)* Größe, *die*

**capacitance** /kəˈpæsɪtəns/ *n.* *(Electr.)* Kapazitanz, *die*

**capacitor** /kəˈpæsɪtə(r)/ *n.* *(Electr.)* Kondensator, *der*

**capacity** /kəˈpæsɪtɪ/ *n.* **A** *(power)* Aufnahmefähigkeit, *die;* *(to do things)* Leistungsfähigkeit, *die;* **this book is within the ~ of young readers** junge Leser sind mit diesem Buch nicht überfordert; **some have more ~ for happiness than others** manche sind zu größeren Glücksempfindungen fähig als andere; **B** *no pl.* *(maximum amount)* Fassungsvermögen, *das;* **the machine is working to ~:** die Maschine ist voll ausgelastet; **a seating ~ of 300** 300 Sitzplätze; **filled to ~** ‹Saal, Theater› bis auf den letzten Platz besetzt; **the film drew ~ houses for ten weeks** zehn Wochen lang waren alle Vorstellungen dieses Films ausverkauft; **the star was cheered by a ~ audience** ein volles Haus jubelte dem Star zu; **C** ▶ **1671** *(measure)* Rauminhalt, *der;* Volumen, *das;* **measure of ~:** Hohlmaß, *das;* **D** *(position)* Eigenschaft, *die;* Funktion, *die;* **in his ~ as critic/lawyer** *etc.* in seiner Eigenschaft als Kritiker/Anwalt *usw.*; **in a civil ~:** als Zivilist; **E** *(mental power)* **he has a mind of great ~:** er ist ein äußerst fähiger Kopf; **have a ~ for genuine love** echter Liebe *(Gen.)* fähig sein; **F** *(legal competence)* Geschäftsfähigkeit, *die;* **he does not have any legal ~:** er ist nicht geschäftsfähig; **G** *(Electr.)* Kapazität, *die*

**caparison** /kəˈpærɪsən/ *n., usu. in pl.* *(horse's trappings)* Schabracke, *die*

**cape**[1] /keɪp/ *n.* *(garment)* Umhang, *der;* Cape, *das;* *(part of coat)* Pelerine, *die*

**cape**[2] *n.* *(Geog.)* Kap, *das;* **the C~ [of Good Hope]** das Kap der guten Hoffnung; **C~ Horn** Kap Hoorn *(das)*; **C~ Town** Kapstadt *(das)*; **C~ Verde Islands** Kapverdische Inseln *Pl.*

**caper**[1] /ˈkeɪpə(r)/ ❶ *n.* **A** *(frisky movement)* Luftsprung, *der;* **cut a ~/~s** einen Luftsprung/Luftsprünge machen; **B** *(wild behaviour)* Kapriole, *die;* **C** *(coll.: activity, occupation)* Masche, *die* *(salopp)*. ❷ *v.i.* **~ [about]** [herum]tollen; [umher]tollen

**caper**[2] *n.* **A** *(shrub)* Kapernstrauch, *der;* **B** *in pl.* *(pickled buds)* Kapern *Pl.*

**capercaillie** /kæpəˈkeɪljɪ/, **capercailzie** /kæpəˈkeɪlzɪ/ *ns.* *(Ornith.)* Auerhahn, *der*

**capful** /ˈkæpfʊl/ *n.* **one ~:** der Inhalt einer Verschlusskappe

**capillary** /kəˈpɪlərɪ/ ❶ *adj.* *(of hairlike diameter)* haardünn; haarfein; Kapillar‹gefäß›; *(of hair)* Haar-; **~ tube** Kapillare, *die* *(fachspr.)*. ❷ *n.* Kapillare, *die* *(fachspr.)*

**capital**[1] /ˈkæpɪtl/ ❶ *adj.* **A** Todes ‹strafe, -urteil›; Kapital‹verbrechen›; tödlich ‹Irrtum, Fehler, Laster, Torheit›; **B** *attrib.* groß, Groß-, *(fachspr.)* Versal‹buchstabe›; **~ letters** Großbuchstaben; Versalien *(fachspr.)*; **'I' is written with a ~ letter** „I" wird groß geschrieben *od.* mit großem I geschrieben; **with a ~ A** *etc.* mit großem A *usw. od.* *(fachspr.)* mit Versal-A *usw.*; *(fig.)* im wahrsten Sinne des Wortes; **C** *attrib.* *(principal)* Haupt‹stadt›; **London is the ~ city of Britain** London ist die Hauptstadt *od.* *(geh.)* Kapitale Großbritanniens; **D** *(important, leading)* einmalig ‹Vorteil, Person, Buch, Vorstellung›; *(dated coll.: excellent, first-rate)* einmalig; famos *(veralt.)* ‹Idee›; **~!** tadellos!; famos! *(veralt.)*; **E** *(Commerc.)* **~ funds/stock** Grundkapital, *das;* **~ sum/expenditure/investment** Kapitalbetrag, *der*/-aufwendungen *Pl.*/-anlage, *die.*

❷ *n.* **A** *(letter)* Großbuchstabe, *der;* **[large] ~s** Großbuchstaben; Versalien *(fachspr.)*; **small ~s** Kapitälchen *(fachspr.)*; **write one's name in [block] ~s** seinen Namen in Blockbuchstaben schreiben; **B** *(city, town)* Hauptstadt, *die;* Kapitale, *die* *(geh.)*; **C** *(stock, accumulated wealth, its holders)* Kapital, *das;* **personal** *or* **private ~:** Eigenkapital, *das;* **~ and labour** Kapital und Arbeit; *(in non-socialist terminology)* Arbeitgeber und Arbeitnehmer; **make ~ out of sth.** *(fig.)* aus etw. Kapital schlagen

**capital**[2] *n.* *(Archit.)* Kapitell, *das;* Kapitäl, *das*

C

**capital:** ~ **'gain** *n.* Kapitalgewinn, *der;* Kapitalertrag, *der;* ~ **'gains tax** *n.* (*Brit.*) Steuer auf Kapitalgewinn, *die;* ~ **goods** *n. pl.* Investitionsgüter *Pl.*

**capitalise** ⇒ **capitalize**

**capitalism** /'kæpɪtəlɪzm/ *n.* Kapitalismus, *der;* (*possession of capital*) Kapitalbesitz, *der;* ~ **is ...:** der Kapitalismus ist ...

**capitalist** /'kæpɪtəlɪst/ ❶ *n.* Kapitalist, *der*/Kapitalistin, *die.* ❷ *adj.* kapitalistisch; **the** ~ **class** die Kapitalistenklasse

**capitalistic** /kæpɪtə'lɪstɪk/ *adj.* kapitalistisch

**capitalize** /'kæpɪtəlaɪz/ ❶ *v.t.* Ⓐ großschreiben ‹Buchstabe, Wort›; Ⓑ (*convert, compute*) kapitalisieren ‹Rente, Reserven›. ❷ *v.i.* (*fig.*) ~ **on sth.** von etw. profitieren; aus etw. Kapital schlagen (*ugs.*)

**capital:** ~ **'levy** *n.* Vermögensabgabe, *die;* Kapitalabgabe, *die;* ~ **ship** *n.* Großkampfschiff, *das;* ~ **territory** *n.* Gebiet der/einer Hauptstadt

**capitation** /kæpɪ'teɪʃn/ *n.* Kopfsteuer, *die*

**capi'tation grant** *n.* Zuschuss pro Kopf

**Capitol** /'kæpɪtl/ *n.* Kapitol, *das*

**capitulate** /kə'pɪtjʊleɪt/ *v.i.* kapitulieren

**capitulation** /kəpɪtjʊ'leɪʃn/ *n.* Kapitulation, *die*

**capo** /'kæpəʊ/ *n., pl.* ~**s** (*Mus.*) Kapodaster, *der*

**capon** /'keɪpn/ *n.* Kapaun, *der*

**cappuccino** /kɑːpʊ'tʃiːnəʊ/ *n., pl.* ~**s** Cappuccino, *der*

**Capri** /kə'priː/ *pr. n.* Capri (*das*); ~ **pants,** ~**s** Caprihosen *Pl.*

**caprice** /kə'priːs/ *n.* Ⓐ (*change of mind or conduct*) Laune, *die;* Kaprice, *die* (*geh.*); (*inclination*) Willkür, *die;* **out of sheer** ~**:** aus einer Laune heraus; **the** ~**s of English weather** die Launen[haftigkeit] des englischen Wetters; Ⓑ (*work of art*) Capriccio, *das;* Caprice, *die* (*geh.*)

**capricious** /kə'prɪʃəs/ *adj.* launisch; kapriziös (*geh.*); (*irregular, unpredictable*) wechselhaft, launisch ‹Wetter›; unberechenbar, schwankend ‹System, Markt›

**capriciously** /kə'prɪʃəslɪ/ *adv.* willkürlich

**capriciousness** /kə'prɪʃəsnɪs/ *n., no pl.* Launenhaftigkeit, *die;* (*of actions*) Willkür, *die;* (*of weather*) Wechselhaftigkeit, *die;* Launenhaftigkeit, *die*

**Capricorn** /'kæprɪkɔːn/ *n.* (*Astrol., Astron.*) der Steinbock; der Capricornus; ⇒ *also* **Aries; tropic**

**Capricornian** /kæprɪ'kɔːnɪən/ *n.* (*Astrol.*) Steinbock, *der*

**caps.** /kæps/ *abbr.* **capital letters** Vers.

**capsicum** /'kæpsɪkəm/ *n.* Ⓐ (*pod*) Pfefferschote, *die;* Ⓑ (*plant*) Paprika, *der*

**capsize** /kæp'saɪz/ ❶ *v.t.* zum Kentern bringen. ❷ *v.i.* kentern

**capstan** /'kæpstən/ *n.* Ⓐ (*barrel for cable*) Winde, *die;* Spill, *das* (*Seemannsspr.*); Ⓑ (*in tape recorder*) Tonwelle, *die;* Tonrolle, *die*

**'capstan lathe** *n.* Sattelrevolverdrehmaschine, *die*

**'cap stone** *n.* (*top stone*) Deckstein, *der;* (*coping*) Mauerkrone, *die*

**capsule** /'kæpsjʊl/ *n.* (*Med., Physiol., Bot., of rocket*) Kapsel, *die*

**Capt.** *abbr.* **Captain** Kapt.; Hptm.

**captain** /'kæptɪn/ ❶ *n.* Ⓐ ▶ 1617 Kapitän, *der;* (*in army*) Hauptmann, *der;* (*in navy*) Kapitän [zur See]; ~ **of a ship** Schiffskapitän, *der;* ~ **of industry** (*fig.*) Industriekapitän, *der* (*ugs.*); Ⓑ (*head boy/girl at school*) Schulsprecher, *der*/-sprecherin, *die;* **form** ~**:** Klassensprecher, *der*/-sprecherin, *die;* Ⓒ (*Sport*) Kapitän, *der;* Spielführer, *der*/-führerin, *die;* Ⓓ (*Amer.: police rank*) ≈ Polizeidirektor, *der.* ❷ *v.t.* befehligen ‹Soldaten, Armee›; ~ **a team** Mannschaftskapitän sein; Kapitän einer Mannschaft sein

**captaincy** /'kæptɪnsɪ/ *n.* (*Sport*) Führung, *die*

**caption** /'kæpʃn/ ❶ *n.* Ⓐ (*heading*) Überschrift, *die;* Ⓑ (*wording under photograph/drawing*) Bildunterschrift, *die;* (*Cinemat., Telev.*) Untertitel, *der.* ❷ *v.t.* betiteln; mit Bildunterschrift[en] versehen ‹Foto, Illustration›; mit Untertiteln versehen ‹Film›

**captious** /'kæpʃəs/ *adj.* überkritisch

**captivate** /'kæptɪveɪt/ *v.t.* fesseln (*fig.*); gefangen nehmen (*fig.*); **she was** ~**d by his charm/by Tom** sie war von seinem Charme gefesselt/von Tom fasziniert

**captivating** /'kæptɪveɪtɪŋ/ *adj.* bezaubernd; einnehmend ‹Lächeln›

**captivation** /kæptɪ'veɪʃn/ *n.* Fesselung, *die* (*fig.*); Verzauberung, *die*

**captive** /'kæptɪv/ ❶ *adj.* (*taken prisoner*) gefangen; ‹Zustand, Stunden, Ketten› der Gefangenschaft; **a** ~ **person** ein Gefangener/eine Gefangene; **a** ~ **animal** ein Tier in Gefangenschaft; **be taken** ~**:** gefangen genommen werden; **hold sb.** ~**:** jmdn. gefangen halten; **lead/bring sb.** ~ **somewhere** jmdn. als Gefangenen irgendwohin führen/bringen. ❷ *n.* Gefangener, *der*/Gefangene, *die*

**captive:** ~ **'audience** *n.* unfreiwilliges Publikum; ~ **bal'loon** *n.* Fesselballon, *der*

**captivity** /kæp'tɪvɪtɪ/ *n.* Gefangenschaft, *die;* **in [a state of]** ~**:** in [der] Gefangenschaft; **be held in** ~**:** gefangen gehalten werden

**captor** /'kæptə(r)/ *n.* (*of city, country*) Eroberer, *der;* (*Hist.: of ship*) Kaperer, *der;* **his** ~**:** der/die ihn gefangen nahm

**capture** /'kæptʃə(r)/ ❶ *n.* Ⓐ (*seizing*) (*of thief etc.*) Festnahme, *die;* (*of town*) Einnahme, *die;* Ⓑ (*thing or person captured*) Fang, *der;* Ⓒ (*Chess etc.*) Schlagen, *das.* ❷ *v.t.* Ⓐ ergreifen, festnehmen ‹Person›; [ein]fangen ‹Tier›; einnehmen ‹Stadt›; holen, ergattern ‹Preis›; gefangen nehmen ‹Fantasie›; erregen ‹Aufmerksamkeit›; (*Hist.*) kapern ‹Schiff›; ~ **sb.'s heart** jmds. Herz gewinnen; **they** ~**d the city from the Romans** sie nahmen den Römern die Stadt ab; Ⓑ (*put in permanent form*) einfangen ‹Augenblick, Eindruck›; Ⓒ (*Chess etc.*) schlagen ‹Figur›; Ⓓ (*Computing*) erfassen ‹Daten›

**Capuchin** /'kæpjʊtʃɪn/ *n.* (*Franciscan friar*) Kapuziner[mönch], *der*

**capuchin:** ~ **monkey** *n.* Kapuzineraffe, *der;* ~ **pigeon** *n.* Mönchtaube, *die*

**capybara** /kæpɪ'bɑːrə/ *n.* (*Zool.*) Capybara, *das;* Wasserschwein, *das*

**car** /kɑː(r)/ *n.* Ⓐ (*motor* ~) Auto, *das;* Wagen, *der;* (*official*) Dienstwagen, *der;* **by** ~**:** mit dem Auto *od.* Wagen; Ⓑ (*railway carriage etc.*) Wagen, *der;* Ⓒ (*Amer.: lift cage*) Fahrkabine, *die;* Ⓓ (*of balloon, airship, etc.*) Gondel, *die*

**carafe** /kə'ræf, kə'rɑːf/ *n.* Karaffe, *die*

**caramel** /'kærəmel/ *n.* Ⓐ (*toffee*) Karamelle, *die;* Karamellbonbon, *das;* Ⓑ (*burnt sugar or syrup*) Karamell, *der;* Ⓒ (*colour*) Karamellfarbe, *die;* bräunliches Gelb

**carapace** /'kærəpeɪs/ *n.* (*of turtle, tortoise*) Rückenschild, *der;* (*of other crustacean*) Schale, *die*

**carat** /'kærət/ *n.* Karat, *das;* **a 22-**~ **gold ring, a gold ring of 22** ~**s** ein 22-karätiger Goldring

**caravan** /'kærəvæn/ ❶ *n.* Ⓐ (*Brit.*) Wohnwagen, *der;* (*used for camping*) Wohnwagen, *der;* Caravan, *der;* Ⓑ (*company of merchants, pilgrims, etc.*) Karawane, *die.* ❷ *v.i.,* (*Brit.*) **-nn-: go** ~**ning** Urlaub im Wohnwagen *od.* Caravan machen; ~ **through Ireland** im Wohnwagen *od.* Caravan durch Irland fahren

**caravan:** ~ **park,** ~ **site** *ns.* Campingplatz für Wohnwagen

**caravel** /'kærəvel/ *n.* (*Hist.*) Karavelle, *die*

**caraway** /'kærəweɪ/ *n.* Kümmel, *der*

**'caraway seed** *n.* Kümmelkorn, *das; in pl.* Kümmel, *der*

**carbide** /'kɑːbaɪd/ *n.* Karbid, *das;* Carbid, *das* (*fachspr.*)

**carbine** /'kɑːbaɪn/ *n.* Karabiner, *der*

**carbohydrate** /kɑːbə'haɪdreɪt/ *n.* (*Chem.*) Kohle[n]hydrat, *das*

**carbolic** /kɑː'bɒlɪk/ *adj.* Karbol‹säure›; ~ **soap** Karbolseife, *die*

**'car bomb** *n.* Autobombe, *die*

**carbon** /'kɑːbən/ *n.* Ⓐ Kohlenstoff, *der;* Ⓑ (*copy*) Durchschlag, *der;* (*paper*) Kohlepapier, *das;* Ⓒ (*Electr.*) Kohle, *die;* Kohlestift, *der*

**carbonade** /kɑːbə'neɪd/ *n.* **[beef]** ~ (*mit Bier abgeschmeckter*) Rindfleischeintopf

**carbonate** /'kɑːbəneɪt/ ❶ *n.* Karbonat, (*fachspr.*) Carbonat, *das.* ❷ *v.t.* mit Kohlensäure versetzen ‹Getränke›; **a** ~**d beverage** ein kohlensäurehaltiges Getränk

**carbon:** ~ **'copy** *n.* Durchschlag, *der;* (*fig.*) (*imitation*) Nachahmung, *die;* Abklatsch, *der* (*abwertend*); (*identical counterpart*) Ebenbild, *das;* ~ **dating** *n.* Radiokarbonmethode, *die;* Radiokohlenstoffmethode, *die;* ~ **di'oxide** *n.* (*Chem.*) Kohlendioxid, *das*

**carboniferous** /kɑːbə'nɪfərəs/ ❶ *adj.* Ⓐ (*producing coal*) kohlehaltig; Ⓑ (*Geol.*) Karbon-, Steinkohlen-; **C**~ **period** Karbon*od.* Steinkohlenformation, *die.* ❷ *n.* (*Geol.*) **the C**~**:** das Karbon

**carbonize (carbonise)** /'kɑːbənaɪz/ *v.t.* karbonisieren ‹Diamanten, Graphit›; verkohlen ‹Kohle›; (*to obtain gas*) verkoken ‹Kohle›; verschwelen ‹Torf, Lignit›; [mit der/einer Färbemasse] beschichten ‹Papier, Formulare›

**carbon:** ~ **mo'noxide** *n.* (*Chem.*) Kohlenmonoxid, Kohlenmonoxyd, *das;* ~ **paper** *n.* Kohlepapier, *das;* ~ **'steel** *n.* Kohlenstoffstahl, *der;* ~ **tetra'chloride** *n.* (*Chem.*) Tetrachlorkohlenstoff, *der*

**car 'boot sale** *n. Trödelmarkt, bei dem die Händler ihre Waren aus dem Kofferraum ihrer Autos heraus verkaufen*

**carborundum** /kɑːbə'rʌndəm/ *n.* Karborund, *das*

**carboy** /'kɑːbɔɪ/ *n.* Korbflasche, *die*

**carbuncle** /'kɑːbʌŋkl/ *n.* Ⓐ (*stone*) Karfunkel[stein], *der;* Ⓑ (*abscess*) Karbunkel, *der*

**carburettor** (*Amer.:* **carburetor**) /kɑːbə'retə(r)/ *n.* Vergaser, *der*

**carcass** (*Brit. also:* **carcase**) /'kɑːkəs/ *n.* Ⓐ (*dead body; joc.: live human body*) Kadaver, *der;* (*at butcher's*) Rumpf, *der;* ~ **meat** Frischfleisch, *das;* Ⓑ (*remains*) Überreste *Pl.;* ~**es of old cars/bikes** Schrottautos/-räder *Pl.;* Ⓒ (*of ship, fortification, etc.*) Skelett, *das;* (*of new building*) Rohbau, *der;* Ⓓ (*of tyre*) Karkasse, *die*

**carcinogen** /kɑː'sɪnədʒən/ *n.* (*Med.*) Karzinogen, *das* (*fachspr.*); Krebserreger, *der*

**carcinogenic** /kɑːsɪnə'dʒenɪk/ *adj.* (*Med.*) karzinogen (*fachspr.*); Krebs erregend

**carcinoma** /kɑːsɪ'nəʊmə/ *n., pl.* ~**ta** /kɑːsɪ'nəʊmətə/ *or* ~**s** (*Med.*) Karzinom, *das*

**car:** ~ **coat** *n.* Autocoat, *der;* ~ **crash** *n.* Autounfall, *der*

**card**[1] /kɑːd/ *n.* Ⓐ (*playing* ~) Karte, *die;* **read the** ~**s** Karten lesen; **be on the** ~**s** (*fig.*) zu erwarten sein; **put [all] one's** ~**s on the table** (*fig.*) [alle] seine Karten auf den Tisch legen; **have [yet] another** ~ **up one's sleeve** (*fig.*) noch einen Trumpf in der Hand haben; noch etwas in petto haben (*ugs.*); Ⓑ *in pl.* (*game*) Karten *Pl.;* **play** ~**s** Karten spielen; **lose money at** ~**s** beim Kartenspiel[en] Geld verlieren; Ⓒ (*post*~, *visiting* ~, *greeting* ~, *ticket, invitation*) Karte, *die;* **let me give you my** ~**:** ich gebe Ihnen meine Karte; Ⓓ (*programme at races etc.*) Programm, *das;* Ⓔ *in pl.* (*coll.: employee's documents*) Papiere *Pl.;* **ask for/get one's** ~**s** sich (*Dat.*) seine Papiere geben lassen/seine Papiere kriegen (*ugs.*); Ⓕ (*person*) Type, *die* (*ugs.*); **an odd** ~**:** eine komische Type; Ⓖ (*coll.: eccentric person*) komischer Vogel (*ugs.*)

**card**[2] (*Textiles*) ❶ *n.* (*instrument*) Karde, *die;* Kratze, *die.* ❷ *v.t.* karden

**cardamom, cardamum** /'kɑːdəməm/ *n.* Kardamom, *das od. der*

**card:** ~**board** *n.* Pappe, *die;* Pappkarton, *der;* (*fig. attrib.*) klischeehaft ‹Figur›; ~**board box** Karton, *der;* ~**board 'city** *n.: Platz, an dem Obdachlose (oft in Pappkartons) unter freiem Himmel schlafen;* ~**-carrying** *adj.* **a** ~**-carrying member** ein eingetragenes Mitglied; ~ **file** *n.* Kartei, *die;* (*large*) Kartothek, die; ~ **game** *n.* Kartenspiel, *das;* ~**holder** *n.* Karteninhaber, *der*/-inhaberin, *die*

**cardiac** /'kɑ:dɪæk/ *adj.* (*of heart*) Herz-; (*of stomach*) Magen-

**cardiac ar'rest** *n.* Herzstillstand, *der*

**cardigan** /'kɑ:dɪgən/ *n.* Strickjacke, *die*

**cardinal** /'kɑ:dɪnl/ ❶ *adj.* Ⓐ (*fundamental*) grundlegend ‹Frage, Doktrin, Pflicht›; Kardinal- ‹fehler, -problem›; (*chief*) hauptsächlich, Haupt- ‹argument, -punkt, -merkmal›; Ⓑ (*of deep scarlet*) scharlachfarben; scharlachrot ‹Farbe›; ~ **red** scharlachrot. ❷ *n.* Ⓐ ▶ 1617 (*Eccl.*) Kardinal, *der;* Ⓑ ⇒ **cardinal number**; Ⓒ (*songbird*) Kardinal, *der*

**cardinal:** ~ **number** *n.* ▶ 1352 Grund-, Kardinalzahl, *die;* ~ **points** *n. pl.* Himmelsrichtungen *Pl.;* ~ **'sin** *n.* Todsünde, *die;* ~ **'virtues** *n. pl.* Kardinaltugenden *Pl.;* ~ **'vowel** *n.* (*Phonet.*) Kardinalvokal, *der*

**card:** ~ **'index** *n.* Kartei, *die;* ~-**'index** *v.t.* karteimäßig erfassen *od.* ordnen

**carding machine** /'kɑ:dɪŋməʃi:n/ *n.* Karde, *die*

**cardio-** /kɑ:dɪəʊ/ *in comb.* (*Med.*) kardio-/Kardio-

**'cardiogram** *n.* Kardiogramm, *das* (*Med.*)

**'cardiograph** *n.* Kardiograph, *der* (*Med.*)

**cardiologist** /kɑ:dɪ'ɒlɪgɪst/ *n.* ▶ 1261 Kardiologe, *der*/Kardiologin, *die*

**cardiology** /kɑ:dɪ'ɒlədʒɪ/ *n.* Kardiologie, *die*

**card:** ~**phone** *n.* Kartentelefon, *das;* ~ **playing** *n., no pl.* Kartenspielen, *das;* **all forms of** ~ **playing** alle Formen des Kartenspiels; ~ **room** *n.* Spielzimmer, *das;* ~-**sharp**, ~ **sharper** *ns.* Falschspieler, *der;* ~ **table** *n.* Kartentisch, *der;* ~ **trick** *n.* Kartentrick, *der;* ~ **vote** *n.* Abstimmung durch Wahlmänner (*in Gewerkschaften*)

**care** /keə(r)/ ❶ *n.* Ⓐ (*anxiety*) Sorge, *die;* **a life full of** ~: ein Leben voller Sorgen; **cast** ~ **aside** (*arch./literary*) seine Sorgen vergessen; **she hasn't got a** ~ **in the world** sie hat keinerlei Sorgen; Ⓑ (*pains*) Sorgfalt, *die;* **take** ~: sich bemühen; **he takes great** ~ **over his work** er gibt sich (*Dat.*) große Mühe mit seiner Arbeit; Ⓒ (*caution*) Vorsicht, *die;* **take** ~, **have a** ~: aufpassen; **take** ~ *or* **have a** ~ **to do sth.** darauf achten, etw. zu tun; **take more** ~! paß [doch] besser auf!; **take** ~ **to lock the door** vergiss ja *od.* nur nicht, die Tür abzuschließen; Ⓓ (*attention*) **medical** ~: ärztliche Betreuung; **old people need special** ~: alte Menschen brauchen besondere Fürsorge; Ⓔ (*concern*) ~ **for sb./sth.** die Sorge um jmdn./etw.; Ⓕ ▶ 1191 (*charge*) Obhut, *die* (*geh.*); ~ **of**, (*Amer.*) **in** ~ **of** (*on letter*) per Adresse; bei; **be in** ~: in Pflege sein; **put sb. in** ~/**take sb. into** ~: jmdn. in Pflege geben/nehmen; **take** ~ **of sb./sth.** (*ensure safety of*) auf jmdn./etw. aufpassen; (*attend to, dispose of*) sich um jmdn./etw. kümmern; **take** ~ **of one's appearance** auf sein Äußeres achten; **take** ~ **of oneself** für sich selbst sorgen; (*as to health*) sich schonen; **take** ~ **[of yourself]!** machs gut! (*ugs.*); **that will take** ~ **of itself** das erledigt sich von selbst. ❷ *v.i.* Ⓐ ~ **for** *or* **about sb./sth.** (*heed*) sich um jmdn./etw. kümmern; (*feel interest*) sich für jmdn./etw. interessieren; **he** ~**s only for his own interests** er hat nur seine eigenen Interessen im Sinn; Ⓑ ~ **for** *or* **about sb./sth.** (*like*) jmdn./etw. mögen; **someone he really** ~**s for** *or* **about** jemand, der ihm wirklich etwas bedeutet; **he never shows how much he** ~**s** er zeigt nie die Stärke seiner Zuneigung; **I don't** ~ **about him** er ist mir völlig gleichgültig; **would you** ~ **for a drink?** möchten Sie etwas trinken?; Ⓒ (*feel concern*) **I don't** ~ **[whether/how/what** *etc.***]** es ist mir gleich[, ob/wie/was *usw.*]; **do you** ~ **if ...:** macht es Ihnen etwas aus, wenn ...; **people who** ~: Leute, die nicht nur an sich selbst denken; **she doesn't appear to** ~ **[how she dresses]** es scheint ihr gleich zu sein[, wie sie angezogen ist]; **don't you** ~? ist es dir [denn] gleichgültig?; **for all I** ~ (*coll.*) von mir aus (*ugs.*); **I couldn't** ~ **less** (*coll.*) es ist mir völlig einerlei *od.* (*ugs.*) egal; **I couldn't** ~ **less about money** (*coll.*) Geld ist mir völlig gleichgültig; **I couldn't/don't** ~ **a tinker's cuss** *or* **a hoot** *or* **two hoots** *or* **tuppence about him/it** *etc.* (*coll.*) er/es *usw.* ist mir piepegal *od.* schnuppe (*ugs.*); **what do I** ~? (*coll.*) mir ist es egal (*ugs.*); **not that 'I** ~ (*coll.*) obwohl es mir egal ist (*ugs.*); **who** ~**s?** (*coll.*) was solls (*ugs.*); ⇒ *also* **damn** 2 B; Ⓓ (*wish*) ~ **to do sth.** etw. tun mögen; **would you** ~ **to try some cake?** darf ich Ihnen ein Stückchen Kuchen anbieten?; Ⓔ ~ **for sb./sth.** (*look after*) sich um jmdn./etw. kümmern; **well** ~**d for** gepflegt; gut versorgt ‹Person›; gut erhalten ‹Auto›

**careen** /kə'ri:n/ ❶ *v.t.* (*Naut.*) kielholen. ❷ *v.i.* Ⓐ (*Naut.: be turned over*) gekielholt werden; krängen; (*fig.*) schwanken; torkeln; Ⓑ (*Amer.: career*) rasen

**career** /kə'rɪə(r)/ ❶ *n.* Ⓐ (*way of livelihood*) Beruf, *der;* **a teaching** ~: der Beruf des Lehrers; **take up a** ~ **in journalism** *or* **as a journalist** den Beruf des Journalisten ergreifen; **her modelling** ~ **was finished** sie musste ihren Beruf als Modell aufgeben; **she's not interested in [having] a** ~: sie interessiert sich nicht für eine Berufslaufbahn; Ⓑ (*progress in life*) [berufliche] Laufbahn; (*very successful*) Karriere, *die;* Ⓒ (*swift course*) Rasen, *das;* **in our** ~ **down the slope** als wir den Abhang hinuntersausten; **in full** ~: in rasendem Lauf; ‹Wagen, Rennboot› in voller Fahrt; ‹Pferd› in gestrecktem Galopp; **in mid** ~: mittendrin. ❷ *v.i.* rasen; ‹Pferd, Reiter:› galoppieren; **go** ~**ing down the hill** den Hügel hinunterrasen

**career:** ~ **break** *n.* Karriereknick, *der;* ~ **'diplomat** *n.* ▶ 1261 Berufsdiplomat, *der;* ~ **girl** *n.* Karrierefrau, *die*

**careerist** /kə'rɪərɪst/ *n.* Karrieremacher, *der* (*abwertend*)

**career:** ~**s adviser** *n.* ▶ 1261 Berufsberater, *der*/-beraterin, *die;* ~**s [advisory] service** *n.* Berufsberatung, *die;* ~**s master**/~**s mistress** *n. Lehrer, der/Lehrerin, die die Schüler bei der Wahl des Berufs berät;* ~**s office** *n.* Berufsberatung[sstelle], *die;* ~**s officer** ⇒ ~**s adviser**; ~ **woman** *n.* Karrierefrau, *die*

**'carefree** *adj.* sorgenfrei

**careful** /'keəfl/ *adj.* Ⓐ (*thorough*) sorgfältig; (*watchful, cautious*) vorsichtig; **[be]** ~! Vorsicht!; **be** ~ **to do sth.** darauf achten, etw. zu tun; **he was** ~ **not to mention the subject** er war darum bemüht, das Thema nicht zu erwähnen; **be** ~ **that ...:** darauf achten, dass ...; **be** ~ **for sb./sth.** auf jmdn./etw. achten; **he is** ~ **for his own interests** er achtet darauf, seine eigenen Interessen zu wahren; **be** ~ **of sb./sth.** (*take care of*) mit jmdm./etw. vorsichtig sein; (*be cautious of*) sich vor jmdm./etw. in Acht nehmen; **be** ~ **of the roads!** pass auf, wenn du über die Straße gehst!; **be** ~ **how you word the letter** sei vorsichtig bei der Formulierung des Briefes; **be** ~ **[about] how/what/where** *etc.* darauf achten, wie/was/wo *usw.;* **be** ~ **about sth.** auf etw. (*Akk.*) achten; **be** ~ **about sb.** auf jmdn. aufpassen *od.* achten; **they're so** ~ **about the baby** sie kümmern sich sehr um das Baby; **be** ~ **about saying too much** darauf achten, nicht zu viel zu sagen; **do be** ~ **about drinking and driving** bitte sei vorsichtig mit dem Alkohol, wenn du noch fahren musst; **be** ~ **with sb./sth.** vorsichtig mit jmdm./etw. umgehen; **he's very** ~ **with his words** er wählt seine Worte sehr genau; Ⓑ (*showing care*) sorgfältig; **a** ~ **piece of work** ein sorgfältig gearbeitetes Stück; **after** ~ **consideration** nach reiflicher Überlegung; **pay** ~ **attention to what he says** achte genau auf das, was er sagt

**carefully** /'keəfəlɪ/ *adv.* (*thoroughly*) sorgfältig; gewissenhaft; (*attentively*) aufmerksam; (*cautiously*) vorsichtig; **watch** ~: gut aufpassen

**carefulness** /'keəflnɪs/ *n., no pl.* Sorgfalt, *die;* (*caution*) Vorsicht, *die*

**careless** /'keəlɪs/ *adj.* Ⓐ (*inattentive*) unaufmerksam; (*thoughtless*) gedankenlos; unvorsichtig, leichtsinnig ‹Fahrer›; nachlässig ‹Arbeiter›; **be** ~ **about** *or* **of sb./sth.** wenig auf jmdn./etw. achten; **you oughtn't to be so** ~ **about drinking and driving** du solltest mehr auf deinen Alkoholkonsum achten, wenn du noch fahren musst; ~ **of sb./sth.** (*unconcerned about*) unbekümmert um jmdn./etw.; ~ **with sb./sth.** unvorsichtig mit jmdm./etw.; **be** ~ **[about** *or* **of] how/what/where** *etc.* wenig darauf achten, wie/was/wo *usw.;* Ⓑ (*showing lack of care*) unordentlich, nachlässig ‹Arbeit›; gedankenlos ‹Bemerkung, Handlung›; unachtsam ‹Fahren›; **a [very]** ~ **mistake** ein [grober] Flüchtigkeitsfehler; Ⓒ (*nonchalant*) ungezwungen; lässig ‹Aussehen, Geste›

**carelessly** /'keəlɪslɪ/ *adv.* Ⓐ (*without care*) nachlässig; (*thoughtlessly*) gedankenlos; unvorsichtig, leichtsinnig ‹fahren›; Ⓑ (*nonchalantly*) lässig

**carelessness** /'keəlɪsnɪs/ *n., no pl.* (*lack of care*) Nachlässigkeit, *die;* (*thoughtlessness*) Gedankenlosigkeit, *die*

**carer** /'keərə(r)/ *n.* ▶ 1261 Betreuer, *der*/Betreuerin, *die;* (*for sick person also*) Pfleger, *der*/Pflegerin, *die;* **be a** ~ **for** *or* **of sb.** jmdn. versorgen *od.* betreuen; sich um jmdn. kümmern; (*for sick person*) jmdn. pflegen

**caress** /kə'res/ ❶ *n.* Liebkosung, *die.* ❷ *v.t.* liebkosen; ~ **[each other]** sich *od.* einander liebkosen

**caret** /'kæret/ *n. Korrekturzeichen für fehlende Buchstaben od. Wörter in einem Text*

**care:** ~**taker** *n.* Ⓐ ▶ 1261 Hausmeister, *der*/-meisterin, *die;* (*in private house*) Hausverwalter, *der*/-verwalterin, *die;* Ⓑ ~**taker government** Übergangsregierung, *die;* ~ **worker** *n.* ▶ 1261 in einem Hilfsberuf Tätige, *der/die;* ~**worn** *adj.* von Sorgen gezeichnet; **he looked** ~**worn** sein Gesicht war von Sorgen gezeichnet

**car:** ~**fare** *n.* (*Amer.*) Fahrgeld, *das;* ~ **ferry** *n.* Autofähre, *die*

**cargo** /'kɑ:gəʊ/ *n., pl.* ~**es** *or* (*Amer.*) ~**s** Fracht, *die;* Ladung, *die;* **a** ~ **of spices** eine Ladung Gewürze

**cargo:** ~ **boat**, ~ **ship**, ~**vessel** *ns.* Frachter, *der;* Frachtschiff, *das*

**'car hire** *n.* Autovermietung, *die*

**'carhop** *n.* (*Amer. coll.*) *Kellner/Kellnerin in einem Drive-in-Restaurant*

**Caribbean** /kærɪ'bi:ən/ ❶ *n.* **the** ~: die Karibik. ❷ *adj.* karibisch; **the** ~ **Sea** das Karibische Meer; ~ **holiday** Urlaub in der Karibik

**caribou** /'kærɪbu:/ *n., pl. same* (*Zool.*) Karibu, *der od. das*

**caricature** /'kærɪkətjʊə(r)/ ❶ *n.* Karikatur, *die;* (*in mime*) Parodie, *die;* **do a** ~ **of sb.** jmdn. karikieren/parodieren. ❷ *v.t.* karikieren; (*in mime*) parodieren

**caricaturist** /'kærɪkətjʊərɪst/ *n.* ▶ 1261 Karikaturist, *der*/Karikaturistin, *die;* (*in mime*) Parodist, *der*/Parodistin, *die*

**caries** /'keəri:z/ *n., pl. same* (*Med., Dent.*) Karies, *die*

**carillon** /kə'rɪljən, 'kærɪljən/ *n.* Glockenspiel, *das*

**caring** /'keərɪŋ/ *adj.* sozial ‹Gesellschaft›; fürsorglich ‹Person›

**Carinthia** /kə'rɪnθɪə/ *pr. n.* Kärnten (*das*)

**Carinthian** /kə'rɪnθɪən/ ❶ *n.* Kärntner, *der*/Kärntnerin, *die.* ❷ *adj.* kärntnerisch; **the** ~ **Lakes** die Kärntner Seen

**car:** ~**jacker** /'kɑ:dʒækə(r)/ *n.* Carjacker, *der;* '~**load** *n.* Ⓐ Wagenladung, *die;* **people were arriving by the** ~**load** es trafen ganze Wagenladungen von Menschen ein; Ⓑ (*Amer.*) *Mindestladung für ermäßigten Frachtbrief*

**carman** /'kɑ:mən/ *n., pl.* **carmen** /'kɑ:mən/ [Berufskraft]fahrer, *der*

**'car mat** *n.* Fußmatte, *die* (*im Auto*)

**Carmelite** /'kɑ:mɪlaɪt/ ❶ *n.* (*friar*) Karmelit[er], *der;* (*nun*) Karmelit[er]in, *die.* ❷ *adj.* Karmeliter-

**carmine** /'kɑ:maɪn, 'kɑ:mɪn/ ❶ *n.* Karmin[rot], *das.* ❷ *adj.* karminrot

**carnage** /ˈkɑːnɪdʒ/ *n.* Gemetzel, *das;* **a scene of ~:** ein Schlachtfeld (*fig.*); **the dreadful annual ~ on the roads** das alljährliche schreckliche Blutvergießen auf den Straßen

**carnal** /ˈkɑːnl/ *adj.* Ⓐ (*sensual*) körperlich; sinnlich; fleischlich (*geh.*); **~ desires/sins** sinnliche Begierden/Sünden des Fleisches (*geh.*); **~ lust** Fleischeslust, *die* (*geh.*); Ⓑ (*worldly*) profan

**carnal ˈknowledge** *n.* (*Law*) **have ~ of sb.** mit jmdm. Geschlechtsverkehr haben

**carnation**[1] /kɑːˈneɪʃn/ *n.* (*Bot.*) [Garten]nelke, *die*

**carnation**[2] ❶ *n.* Rosarot, *das.* ❷ *adj.* **~ [pink]** [zart]rosa

**carnet** /ˈkɑːneɪ/ *n.* (*of motorist*) Triptyk, *das;* (*of camper*) Ausweis für Camper

**carnival** /ˈkɑːnɪvl/ *n.* Ⓐ (*festival*) Volksfest, *das;* **~ procession** Festzug, *der;* Ⓑ (*pre-Lent festivities*) Karneval, *der;* Fastnacht, *die;* Fasching, *der* (*bes. südd., österr.*); (*fig.: revelry*) ausgelassenes Fest; **~ procession** Karnevals[um]zug, *der;* Ⓒ (*Amer.*) (*circus*) Zirkus, *der;* (*funfair*) Jahrmarkt, *der*

**carnivore** /ˈkɑːnɪvɔː(r)/ *n.* (*animal*) Fleischfresser, *der;* Karnivore, *der* (*Zool.*); (*plant*) Fleisch fressende Pflanze; Karnivore, *die* (*Bot.*)

**carnivorous** /kɑːˈnɪvərəs/ *adj.* Fleisch fressend; karnivor (*Zool., Bot.*)

**carob** /ˈkærəb/ *n.* Ⓐ (*pod*) Johannisbrot, *das;* Ⓑ (*tree*) Johannisbrotbaum, *der*

**carol** /ˈkærl/ ❶ *n.* Ⓐ **[Christmas] ~:** Weihnachtslied, *das;* **~ concert, ~ singing** weihnachtliches Liedersingen; **~ singers** *Leute, die von Haus zu Haus gehen und Weihnachtslieder vortragen;* ≈ Weihnachtssänger *Pl.;* Ⓑ (*joyous song*) fröhliches Lied. ❷ *v.t.*, (*Brit.*) **-ll-:** Ⓐ (*sing as ~*) singen ‹Weihnachtslied›; Ⓑ (*sing joyfully*) [fröhlich] singen. ❸ *v.i.*, (*Brit.*) **-ll-:** Ⓐ Weihnachtslieder singen; Ⓑ (*sing joyfully*) [fröhlich] singen

**carom** /ˈkærəm/ (*Amer.*) ❶ *n.* Karambolage, *die;* **~ billiards** Karambolagebillard, *das.* ❷ *v.i.* (*Billiards*) karambolieren

**carotid** /kəˈrɒtɪd/ (*Anat.*) ❶ *adj.* Karotis-; **~ artery** ⇒ **2.** ❷ *n.* Halsschlagader, *die;* Karotis, *die* (*fachspr.*)

**carousal** /kəˈraʊzl/ *n.* Zechgelage, *das*

**carouse** /kəˈraʊz/ ❶ *v.i.* zechen (*veralt., noch scherzh.*). ❷ *n.* ⇒ **carousal**

**carousel** /kærʊˈsel, kærʊˈzel/ *n.* Ⓐ (*conveyor system*) Ausgabeband, *das;* Ⓑ (*Amer.: roundabout*) Karussell, *das*

**ˈcar owner** *n.* Autobesitzer, *der*

**carp**[1] /kɑːp/ *n.*, *pl. same* (*Zool.*) Karpfen, *der*

**carp**[2] *v.i.* nörgeln; **~ [on and on] at sb./sth.** an jmdm./etw. [dauernd] herumnörgeln (*ugs.*)

**ˈcar park** *n.* Parkplatz, *der;* (*underground*) Tiefgarage, *die;* (*multi-storey*) Parkhaus, *das*

**ˈcar parking** *n.* Parken, *das;* **~ facilities are available** Parkplätze [sind] vorhanden

**Carpathians** /kɑːˈpeɪθjənz, kɑːˈpeɪðjənz/ *pr. n. pl.* Karpaten *Pl.*

**carpel** /ˈkɑːpl/ *n.* (*Bot.*) Fruchtblatt, *das;* Karpell, *das* (*fachspr.*)

**carpenter** /ˈkɑːpɪntə(r)/ ❶ *n.* ▶ **1261** Zimmermann, *der;* (*for furniture*) Tischler, *der*/Tischlerin, *die;* (*ship's ~*) Schiffszimmermann, *der.* ❷ *v.t.* zimmern; tischlern ‹Regale›

**carpentry** /ˈkɑːpɪntrɪ/ *n.* Ⓐ (*art*) Zimmerhandwerk, *das;* (*in furniture*) Tischlerhandwerk, *das;* Ⓑ (*woodwork*) **[piece of] ~:** Tischlerarbeit, *die;* (*structure*) [Holz]konstruktion, *die*

**carpet** /ˈkɑːpɪt/ ❶ *n.* Ⓐ (*covering*) Teppich, *der;* **[fitted] ~:** Teppichboden, *der;* **stair ~:** [Treppen]läufer, *der;* **be on the ~** (*coll.: be reprimanded*) zusammengestaucht werden (*ugs.*); (*be under discussion*) zur Debatte stehen; **have sb. on the ~** (*coll.: reprimand sb.*) jmdn. zusammenstauchen (*ugs.*); **sweep sth. under the ~** (*fig.*) etw. unter den Teppich kehren (*ugs.*); ⇒ *also* **red carpet;** Ⓑ (*expanse*) **~ of flowers** Blumenteppich, *der;* **~ of grass/snow/leaves** Gras-/Schnee-/Laubdecke, *die.* ❷ *v.t.* Ⓐ (*cover*) [mit Teppich(boden)] auslegen; (*fig.*) bedecken; **snow ~ed the village in [a layer of] white** Schnee bedeckte das Dorf mit einem weißen Teppich; Ⓑ (*coll.: reprimand*) **be ~ed for sth.** wegen etw. zusammengestaucht werden (*ugs.*)

**carpet: ~ bag** *n.* Reisetasche, *die;* **~bagger** /ˈkɑːpɪtbægə(r)/ *n.* Ⓐ politischer Karrieremacher; Ⓑ (*Hist.*) *Politiker aus dem Norden der USA, der in den Südstaaten nach dem Sezessionskrieg rasch Karriere machen wollte;* **~ beater** *n.* Teppichklopfer, *der;* **~ bombing** *n.* Flächenbombardement, *das*

**carpeting** /ˈkɑːpɪtɪŋ/ *n.* Ⓐ Teppich[boden], *der;* **some ~** ein Stück Teppichboden; **wall-to-wall ~:** Teppichboden, *der;* **stair~:** [Treppen]läufer, *der;* Ⓑ (*fig.*) ⇒ **carpet** 1 B

**carpet: ~ slipper** *n.* Hausschuh, *der;* **~ sweeper** *n.* Teppichkehrer, *der;* Teppichkehrmaschine, *die*

**car: ~ phone** *n.* Autotelefon, *das;* **~ pool** *n.* Fahrgemeinschaft, *die;* (*of a firm etc.*) Fahrzeugpark, *der;* **~port** *n.* Einstellplatz, *der*

**ˈcar radio** *n.* Autoradio, *das*

**carrel** /ˈkærl/ *n.* [abgeteilter] Arbeitsplatz (*in einer Bibliothek/hist.: in einem Kloster*)

**car rental** ⇒ **car hire**

**carriage** /ˈkærɪdʒ/ *n.* Ⓐ (*horse-drawn vehicle*) Kutsche, *die;* **~ and pair/four/six** *etc.* Zwei-/Vier-/Sechsspänner *usw.*, *der;* ⇒ *also* **drive** 2 A; Ⓑ (*Railw.*) [Eisenbahn]wagen, *der;* Ⓒ (*Mech.*) Schlitten, *der;* (*of typewriter*) Schlitten, *der;* Wagen, *der;* Ⓓ *no pl.* (*conveying, being conveyed*) Transport, *der;* **use for ~:** für den Transport benutzen; Ⓔ (*cost of conveying*) Frachtkosten *Pl.;* **~ forward** Fracht[kosten] zulasten des Empfängers; **~ paid** frachtfrei; Ⓕ (*bearing*) Haltung, *die.* ⇒ *also* **gun carriage; invalid carriage**

**carriage: ~ clock** *n.* Reiseuhr, *die;* **~way** *n.* Fahrbahn, *die*

**ˈcar ride** *n.* Autofahrt, *die*

**carrier** /ˈkærɪə(r)/ *n.* Ⓐ (*bearer*) Träger, *der;* **~ of good news** Überbringer guter Nachrichten; Ⓑ (*conductor*) **be the ~ of sth.** etw. transportieren *od.* leiten; Ⓒ (*hired conveyor of goods or passengers*) Transportunternehmen, *das;* (*person*) Transportunternehmer, *der;* **firm of ~s** Transportunternehmen, *das;* Ⓓ (*on bicycle etc.*) Gepäckträger, *der;* (*for child passenger*) Kindersitz, *der;* Ⓔ ⇒ **carrier bag;** Ⓕ ⇒ **carrier wave;** Ⓖ ⇒ **aircraft carrier;** Ⓗ (*Med.: of disease*) Ausscheider, *der;* (*Genetics: of characteristic*) Konduktor, *der*

**carrier: ~ bag** *n.* Tragetasche, *die;* Tragetüte, *die;* **~ pigeon** *n.* Brieftaube, *die;* **by ~ pigeon** mit der Taubenpost; **~ wave** *n.* (*Phys.*) Trägerwelle, *die*

**carrion** /ˈkærɪən/ *n.* Ⓐ (*flesh*) Aas, *das;* Ⓑ (*fig.: garbage*) Unflat, *der;* Schmutz, *der*

**ˈcarrion crow** *n.* Rabenkrähe, *die;* (*Corvus corone*) Aaskrähe, *die*

**carrot** /ˈkærət/ *n.* Ⓐ Möhre, *die;* Karotte, *die;* **grated ~[s]** geraspelte Möhren *od.* Karotten; Ⓑ (*fig.*) Köder, *der;* **dangle a ~ in front of sb.'s nose** jmdm. einen Köder vor die Nase halten; **with ~ and stick** mit Zuckerbrot und Peitsche

**carroty** /ˈkærətɪ/ *adj.* rotblond ‹Haare›

**carrousel** (*Amer.*) ⇒ **carousel**

**carry** /ˈkærɪ/ ❶ *v.t.* Ⓐ (*transport*) tragen; (*with emphasis on destination*) bringen; überbringen ‹Nachrichten›; ‹Tornado:› fegen; ‹Strom:› spülen; ‹Verkehrsmittel:› befördern; **~ sth. with one in a bag** etw. in einer Tasche bei sich haben *od.* tragen; **where do you ~ your purse?** wo hast *od.* trägst du dein Portemonnaie?; **~ sth. in one's head** etw. im Kopf haben; **~ sth. round with one** (*lit. or fig.*) etw. mit sich herumtragen (*ugs.*); (*fig.*) etw. nicht vergessen können; **~ all before one** (*fig.*) nicht aufzuhalten sein; Ⓑ (*conduct*) leiten; **~ sth. into effect** etw. in die Tat umsetzen; Ⓒ (*support*) tragen; (*contain*) fassen; **~ responsibility** Verantwortung tragen; Ⓓ (*have with one*) **~ [with one]** bei sich haben *od.* tragen; tragen ‹Waffe, Kennzeichen›; ‹Schiff:› führen ‹Lichter, Segel›; Ⓔ (*possess*) besitzen ‹Autorität, Gewicht›; ⇒ *also* **conviction** B; Ⓕ (*hold*) **he carries his head in a proud way** er trägt den Kopf hoch; **she carries herself well** sie hat eine gute Haltung; **he carries himself very erect** er hält sich sehr aufrecht; Ⓖ (*prolong*) **~ sth. to sth.** etw. zu etw. führen; **~ sth. to a close** *or* **an end** etw. zu Ende führen *od.* bringen; **such plans must be carried to their natural conclusions** solche Pläne müssen [bis zum Ende] durchgezogen werden (*ugs.*); **~ modesty/altruism** *etc.* **to excess** die Bescheidenheit/den Altruismus *usw.* bis zum Exzess treiben; **~ things to extremes** die Dinge auf die Spitze treiben; ⇒ *also* **far** 1 D; Ⓗ (*transmit*) übertragen ‹Krankheit›; Ⓘ (*Math.: transfer*) im Sinn behalten; **~ one** eins im Sinn; Ⓙ (*be pregnant with*) erwarten ‹Kind›; **she was ~ing his child** sie erwartete ein Kind von ihm; Ⓚ (*win*) erringen ‹Sieg›; bekommen, erhalten ‹Belohnung›; gewinnen ‹Preis, Wahl›; durchbringen ‹Antrag, Gesetzentwurf, Vorschlag›; **the motion is carried** der Antrag ist angenommen; **~ one's point [with sb.]** seine Sache [bei jmdm.] durchsetzen; **~ one's hearers/audience with one** die Zuhörer/das Publikum überzeugen; **~ the day** den Sieg davontragen; Ⓛ (*involve*) [mit sich] bringen; bringen ‹Gewinn, Zinsen›; **discipline carries both advantages and disadvantages** Disziplin hat ihre Vor- und Nachteile; Ⓜ (*stock*) führen; Ⓝ (*publish, broadcast*) bringen.

❷ *v.i.* ‹Stimme, Laut:› zu hören sein; ‹Geruch:› zu riechen sein; ‹Geschoss, Ball:› [weit] fliegen

**~ aˈway** *v.t.* forttragen; (*by force*) fortreißen; (*fig.*) **be** *or* **get carried away** (*be inspired*) hingerissen sein (**by** von); (*lose self-control*) sich hinreißen lassen; **don't get carried away!** übertreibs nicht!

**~ ˈback** *v.t.* Ⓐ (*return*) zurückbringen; Ⓑ ⇒ **take back b**

**~ ˈforward** *v.t.* (*Bookk.*) vortragen

**~ ˈoff** *v.t.* Ⓐ (*from place*) davontragen; (*as owner or possessor*) mit sich nehmen; (*cause to die*) dahinraffen (*geh.*); Ⓑ (*abduct*) entführen ‹Person›; Ⓒ (*win*) gewinnen ‹Preis, Medaille›; erringen ‹Sieg›; Ⓓ (*make acceptable*) durchführen; (*cope with*) fertig werden mit; **~ it/sth. off [well]** es/etw. [gut] zustande bringen

**~ ˈon** ❶ *v.t.* (*continue*) fortführen ‹Tradition, Diskussion, Arbeit›; **~ on the firm** die Firma übernehmen; **~ on [doing sth.]** weiterhin etw. tun; **they carried on talking** sie fuhren fort, sich zu unterhalten. ❷ *v.i.* Ⓐ (*continue*) weitermachen; **~ on with a plan/project** einen Plan/ein Projekt weiterverfolgen; Ⓑ (*coll.: behave in unseemly manner*) sich danebenbenehmen (*ugs.*); (*make a fuss*) Theater machen (*ugs.*); Ⓒ **~ on with sb.** (*flirt*) mit jmdm. flirten; (*have affair*) mit jmdm. ein Verhältnis haben. ⇒ *also* **carry-on**

**~ ˈout** *v.t.* (*put into practice*) durchführen ‹Plan, Programm, Versuch›; in die Tat umsetzen ‹Plan, Vorschlag, Absicht, Vorstellung›; ausführen ‹Anweisung, Auftrag›; halten ‹Versprechen›; vornehmen ‹Verbesserungen›; wahr machen ‹Drohung›

**~ ˈover** *v.t.* Ⓐ (*postpone*) vertagen (**to** auf + *Akk.*); Ⓑ (*St. Exch.*) prolongieren; Ⓒ ⇒ **~ forward.** ⇒ *also* **~-over**

**~ ˈthrough** *v.t.* Ⓐ (*bring safely through*) **~ sb. through** jmdm. durchhelfen; Ⓑ (*complete*) durchführen

**ˈcarrycot** *n.* Babytragetasche, *die*

**carryings-on** /kærɪɪŋzˈɒn/ *n. pl.* (*coll.*) Ⓐ (*questionable behaviour*) seltsames Treiben; **there are strange ~ in that house** in diesem Haus geht Seltsames vor; Ⓑ (*love affairs*) Affären

**carry: ~-on** *n.* (*coll.*) Ⓐ Theater, *das* (*ugs.*); Ⓑ (*flirtation*) Flirt, *der;* (*love affair*) [Liebes]affäre, *die;* **~-out** *n.* **~-out [meal]** Essen *od.* Mahlzeit zum Mitnehmen; **~-out [restaurant]** Restaurant mit Straßenverkauf; **get a ~-out** sich (*Dat.*) in einem Restaurant was zu essen holen; (*to drink*) sich (*Dat.*) was zu trinken holen; **~-over** *n.* (*St. Exch.*) Prolongation, *die*

**ˈcarsick** *adj.* **children are often ~:** Kindern wird beim Autofahren oft schlecht

**cart** /kɑːt/ ❶ *n.* Karren, *der;* Wagen, *der;* **horse and ~:** Pferdewagen, *der;* **be [left]**

in the ~ (*Brit. coll.*) in der Tinte sitzen (*ugs.*); **put sb. in the ~** (*Brit. coll.*) jmdn. in die Bredouille bringen (*ugs.*); **put the ~ before the horse** (*fig.*) das Pferd beim Schwanz aufzäumen. ❷ *v.t.* Ⓐ (*carry [as] in ~*) karren; Ⓑ (*fig. coll.: carry with effort*) schleppen; **~ sth. around with one** etw. mit sich herumschleppen

**~ 'off** *v.t.* (*coll.*) abtransportieren

**carte blanche** /kɑːt 'blɑ̃ʃ/ *n.* Carte blanche, *die;* unbeschränkte Vollmacht

**cartel** /kɑː'tel/ *n.* Kartell, *das*

**carter** /'kɑːtə(r)/ *n.* ▶ 1261 Fuhrmann, *der*

**Cartesian** /kɑː'tiːzjən/ *adj.* **~ coordinates** (*Math.*) kartesische Koordinaten

**Carthage** /'kɑːθɪdʒ/ *pr. n.* ▶ 1626 Karthago (*das*)

**'car thief** *n.* Autodieb, *der* /-diebin, *die*

**'carthorse** *n.* Arbeitspferd, *das*

**Carthusian** /kɑː'θjuːzjən/ ❶ *adj.* Kartäuser-. ❷ *n.* Kartäuser, *der*

**cartilage** /'kɑːtɪlɪdʒ/ *n.* Knorpel, *der*

**'cartload** *n.* Ⓐ Wagenladung, *die;* Fuhre, *die;* **by the ~:** fuhrenweise; Ⓑ (*fig.: large quantity*) **a ~ of books** ein Berg von Büchern; **~s of food** Essen in Hülle und Fülle

**cartographer** /kɑː'tɒgrəfə(r)/ *n.* ▶ 1261 Kartograph, *der*/Kartographin, *die*

**cartographic** /kɑːtə'græfɪk/, **cartographical** /kɑːtə'græfɪkl/ *adjs.* kartographisch

**cartography** /kɑː'tɒgrəfɪ/ *n.* Kartographie, *die*

**carton** /'kɑːtn/ *n.* [Papp]karton, *der;* **a ~ of milk** eine Tüte Milch; **a ~ of detergent** ein Paket Waschpulver; **a ~ of cigarettes** eine Stange Zigaretten; **a ~ of yoghurt** ein Becher Joghurt

**cartoon** /kɑː'tuːn/ ❶ *n.* Ⓐ (*amusing drawing*) humoristische Zeichnung; Cartoon, *der;* (*satirical illustration*) Karikatur, *die;* (*sequence of drawings*) [humoristische] Bilderserie; Cartoon, *der;* Ⓑ (*film*) Zeichentrickfilm, *der;* Ⓒ (*Art*) Entwurf, *der;* Karton, *der* (*Kunstwiss.*). ❷ *v.t.* (*draw amusingly*) karikieren

**cartoonist** /kɑː'tuːnɪst/ *n.* ▶ 1261 Cartoonist, *der*/Cartoonistin, *die;* (*satirical ~*) Karikaturist, *der*/Karikaturistin, *die*

**cartridge** /'kɑːtrɪdʒ/ *n.* Ⓐ (*case for explosive*) Patrone, *die;* Ⓑ (*spool of film, cassette*) Kassette, *die;* Ⓒ (*for pickup head*) Tonabnehmer, *der;* Ⓓ (*ink container*) Patrone, *die*

**cartridge: ~ belt** *n.* Patronengurt, *der;* **~ case** *n.* Patronenhülse, *die;* **~ paper** *n.* (*for drawing*) Zeichenpapier, *das;* (*for envelopes, gun cartridges*) *festes, haltbares Papier*

**cart: ~ road, ~ track** *ns.* ≈ Feldweg, *der;* **~wheel** *n.* Ⓐ Wagenrad, *das;* Ⓑ (*Gymnastics*) Rad, *das;* **turn** *or* **do ~wheels** Rad schlagen; **~wright** /'kɑːtraɪt/ *n.* Stellmacher, *der*

**carve** /kɑːv/ ❶ *v.t.* Ⓐ (*cut up*) tranchieren, aufschneiden ‹Fleisch, Braten›; tranchieren ‹Hähnchen›; Ⓑ (*produce by cutting*) (*from wood*) schnitzen; (*from stone*) meißeln; **~ sth. out of wood/stone** etw. aus Holz schnitzen/aus Stein meißeln; **~ sth. in/into/on sth.** etw. in etw. (*Akk.*) [ein]ritzen; **~ a tunnel in the rock** einen Tunnel in den Fels hauen; **~ one's way** sich (*Dat.*) seinen Weg hauen; Ⓒ (*change by cutting*) **he ~d a block of wood/stone into a madonna** er schnitzte aus einem Holzblock/meißelte aus einem Steinblock eine Madonna; Ⓓ (*adorn by cutting*) **the frame was ~d with leaves** der Rahmen war mit geschnitzten/in Stein gehauenen Blättern verziert.

❷ *v.i.* Ⓐ tranchieren; Ⓑ **~ in wood/ivory/stone** in Holz/Elfenbein schnitzen/in Stein meißeln; **~ through sth.** sich (*Dat.*) einen Weg durch etw. hauen

**~ out** *v.t.* heraushauen; **~ out a tunnel in the rock** einen Tunnel in den Fels hauen *od.* treiben; **~ out an existence** (*fig.*) sich (*Dat.*) eine Existenz aufbauen

**~ up** *v.t.* aufschneiden ‹Fleisch›; aufteilen ‹Erbe, Land›; zerstückeln ‹Leiche›

**carver** /'kɑːvə(r)/ *n.* Ⓐ (*in wood*) [Holz]schnitzer, *der;* (*in stone*) Bildhauer, *der;* (*of meat*) Trancheur, *der;* Ⓑ (*knife*) ⇒ **carving knife**; Ⓒ *in pl.* (*knife and fork*) Tranchierbesteck, *das*

**carving** /'kɑːvɪŋ/ *n.* Ⓐ (*in or from wood, ivory*) Schnitzerei, *die;* **a ~ of a madonna in wood** eine holzgeschnitzte Madonna; **an ivory ~ of an elephant** ein aus Elfenbein geschnitzter Elefant; Ⓑ (*in or from stone*) Skulptur, *die;* (*on stone*) eingeritztes Bild; (*ornament*) eingeritztes Muster

**'carving: ~ fork** *n.* Tranchiergabel, *die;* **~ knife** *n.* Tranchiermesser, *das*

**'car wash** *n.* Waschanlage, *die*

**caryatid** /kærɪ'ætɪd/ *n., pl.* **~s** *or* **~es** /kærɪ'ætɪdiːz/ (*Archit.*) Karyatide, *die*

**Casanova** /kæzə'nəʊvə, kæsə'nəʊvə/ *n.* Casanova, *der*

**cascade** /kæs'keɪd/ ❶ (*lit. or fig.*) Kaskade, *die.* ❷ *v.i.* [in Kaskaden] herabstürzen; **her hair ~d down her back** (*fig.*) ihr Haar fiel in Kaskaden über ihren Rücken hinab

**case**[1] /keɪs/ *n.* Ⓐ (*instance, matter*) Fall, *der;* **if there is another ~ of this happening** wenn das noch einmal vorkommt; **several ~s of fire** mehrere Brände; **if it's a ~ of your not being able to get here** wenn es nur daran liegt, dass du nicht herkommen kannst; **it's just a ~ of concentrating** es ist nur eine Sache der Konzentration; **then that's a different ~:** dann ist das was anderes; **if that's the ~:** wenn das so ist; **it is [not] the ~ that ...:** es trifft [nicht] zu *od.* stimmt [nicht], dass ...; **it seems to be the ~ that they have ...:** sie scheinen tatsächlich ... zu haben; **as is generally the ~ with ...:** wie das normalerweise bei ... der Fall ist; **such being the ~:** deshalb; **as the ~ may be** je nachdem; **in ~ ...:** falls ...; für den Fall, dass ... (*geh.*); **[just] in ~** (*to allow for all possibilities*) für alle Fälle; **in ~ of fire/complaints/burst pipes/danger** bei Feuer/Reklamationen/Rohrbrüchen/Gefahr; **in ~ of emergency** im Notfall; **in ~ of the hostages' being released** falls die Geiseln freigelassen werden; **in the ~ of** bei; **in the ~ of New College** was das New College anbelangt; **in any ~** (*regardless of anything else*) jedenfalls; **I don't need it in any ~:** ich brauche es sowieso nicht; **we don't want to go to the party and in any ~ it's raining** wir haben keine Lust, auf die Party zu gehen, und außerdem regnet es ja; **in no ~** (*certainly not*) unter keinen Umständen; auf keinen Fall; **in that ~:** in diesem Fall; **in which ~ he would ...:** in diesem Fall *od.* dann würde er ...; Ⓑ (*Med., Police, Soc. Serv., etc., or coll.: person afflicted*) Fall, *der;* **a murder ~:** ein Mordfall; **he is a mental/psychiatric ~:** er ist ein Fall für den Psychiater; **this man is a dangerous ~:** dieser Mann ist gefährlich; **her son is a problem ~:** ihr Sohn ist ein Problemkind; Ⓒ (*Law*) Fall, *der;* (*action*) Verfahren, *das;* **which was that ~ five years ago?** welcher Fall war das vor fünf Jahren?; **the Dreyfus ~:** der Fall Dreyfus; die Dreyfusaffäre (*hist.*); **the ~ for the prosecution/defence** die Anklage/Verteidigung; **put one's ~:** seinen Fall darlegen; **and that is our ~:** und damit beende ich meine Ausführungen; Ⓓ (*fig.: set of arguments*) Fall, *der;* (*valid set of arguments*) **you have no ~ there** das ist kein Argument; **there's a ~ for doing sth.** es gibt Gründe, die dafür sprechen, dass man etw. tut; **have a [good] ~ for doing sth./for sth.** gute Gründe haben, etw. zu tun/für etw. haben; **make out a ~ for sth.** Argumente für etw. anführen; Ⓔ (*Ling.*) Fall, *der;* Kasus, *der* (*fachspr.*); Ⓕ (*fig. coll.*) (*comical person*) ulkiger Typ (*ugs.*); (*comical woman*) ulkige Nudel (*ugs.*)

**case**[2] ❶ *n.* Ⓐ Koffer, *der;* (*small*) Handkoffer, *der;* (*brief~*) [Akten]tasche, *die;* (*for musical instrument*) Kasten, *der;* **violin ~:** Geigenkasten, *der;* **doctor's ~:** Arzttasche, *die;* **pen and pencil ~:** Federmäppchen, *das;* Ⓑ (*sheath*) Hülle, *die;* (*for spectacles, cigarettes*) Etui, *das;* (*for jewellery*) Schmuckkassette, *die;* Schmuckkästchen, *das;* Ⓒ (*crate*) Kiste, *die;* **~ of oranges** Kiste [mit] Apfelsinen; Ⓓ (*glass box*) Vitrine, *die;* **[display] ~:** Schaukasten, *der;* Ⓔ (*cover*) Gehäuse, *das;* (*seed vessel*) Hülle, *die;* (*of sausage*) Haut, *die;* (*of book*) Buchdeckel, *der;* Ⓕ (*Printing*) Schriftkasten, *der;* ⇒ *also* **lower case**; **upper case**.

❷ *v.t.* Ⓐ (*box*) verpacken; Ⓑ (*sl.: examine*) **~ the joint** sich (*Dat.*) den Laden mal ansehen (*ugs.*)

**case: ~book** *n.* Ⓐ (*Law*) Sammlung von Rechtsfällen; Ⓑ (*Med.*) Sammlung von Krankheitsfällen; Ⓒ (*of social worker etc.; also fig.*) Fallsammlung, *die;* **~-bound** *adj.* mit festem Einband *nachgestellt;* **be ~-bound** einen festen Einband haben; **~ ending** *n.* (*Ling.*) Beugungsendung, *die;* Kasusendung, *die* (*fachspr.*); **~-harden** *v.t.* härten ‹Metall›; **~-hardened** (*fig.*) abgebrüht; **~ history** *n.* Ⓐ (*record*) [Vor]geschichte, *die;* Ⓑ (*Med.*) Krankengeschichte, *die;* **~ knife** *n.* Fahrtenmesser, *das;* **~ law** *n.* (*Law*) Fallrecht, *das;* **~load** *n.* Fälle *Pl.;* **he has a heavy ~load, his ~load is heavy** er hat sehr viele Fälle zu bearbeiten; **the [doctor's] ~load** die Anzahl der Patienten; **share the [doctor's] ~load** einen Teil der Patienten übernehmen

**casement** /'keɪsmənt/ *n.* Ⓐ [Fenster]flügel, *der;* Ⓑ (*poet.: window*) Fenster, *das*

**'casement window** *n.* Flügelfenster, *das*

**case: ~ study** *n.* Fallstudie, *die;* **~work** *n., no pl., no indef. art.* [auf den Einzelfall bezogene] Sozialarbeit; Casework, *das* (*Psychol., Soziol.*); **~worker** *n.* ▶ 1261 [Einzelfälle betreuender] Sozialarbeiter

**cash** /kæʃ/ ❶ *n., no pl., no indef. art.* ▶ 1328 Ⓐ Bargeld, *das;* **payment in ~ only** nur Barzahlung; **pay [in] ~, pay ~ down** bar zahlen; **we haven't got the ~:** wir haben [dafür] kein Geld; **be short of ~:** knapp bei Kasse sein (*ugs.*); **~ on delivery** per Nachnahme; Ⓑ (*Banking etc.*) Geld, *das;* **can I get ~ for these cheques?** kann ich diese Schecks einlösen?; **you may withdraw £50 in ~:** Sie können 50 Pfund in bar abheben; ⇒ *also* **discount** 1.

❷ *v.t.* Ⓐ einlösen ‹Scheck›; Ⓑ (*Bridge*) ausspielen [und den Stich machen]

**~ in** ❶ /'--/ *v.t.* sich (*Dat.*) gutschreiben lassen ‹Scheck›; auf die Bank bringen ‹Geld, Einnahmen›; **~ in one's checks** *or* **chips** (*fig. coll.*) abkratzen (*salopp*). ❷ /-'-/ *v.i.* **~ in on sth.** (*lit. or fig.*) von etw. profitieren

**cash: ~ account** *n.* Kassekonto, *das* (*Buchf.*); **~ and 'carry** *n.: Verkaufssystem, bei dem der Kunde bar bezahlt und die Ware selbst nach Hause transportiert;* cash and carry; **~-and-carry store** Cash-and-carry-Laden, *der;* **~back** *n., no pl., no art.: Barauszahlung eines Differenzbetrages bei Kauf mit Geldkarte;* **~ book** *n.* Kassenbuch, *das;* **~ box** *n.* Geldkassette, *die;* **~ card** *n.* Geldautomatenkarte, *die;* **~ crop** *n.: zum Verkauf bestimmtes landwirtschaftliches Erzeugnis;* **~ desk** *n.* (*Brit.*) Kasse, *die;* **~ dispenser** *n.* Geldautomat, *der*

**cashew** /'kæʃuː/ *n.* Ⓐ (*nut*) ⇒ **cashew nut**; Ⓑ (*tree*) Nierenbaum, *der* (*Bot.*); Cashewbaum, *der* (*Bot.*)

**'cashew nut** *n.* Cashewnuss, *die*

**'cash flow** *n.* (*Econ.*) Cashflow, *der*

**cashier**[1] /kæ'ʃɪə(r)/ *n.* ▶ 1261 Kassierer, *der*/Kassiererin, *die;* **~'s office** Kasse, *die*

**cashier**[2] *v.t.* entlassen; des Amtes entheben (*geh.*); (*Mil.*) [unehrenhaft] entlassen

**'cashless** *adj.* bargeldlos; **the ~ society** die bargeldlose Gesellschaft

**cashmere** /'kæʃmɪə(r)/ *n.* Kaschmir, *der;* **~ wool/sweater** Kaschmirwolle, *die*/Kaschmirpullover, *der*

**cash: ~ payment** *n.* Barzahlung, *die;* **make ~ payment** bar bezahlen; **~point** *n.* Geldautomat, *der;* **~ price** *n.* Barzahlungspreis, *der;* **~ register** *n.* [Registrier]kasse, *die;* (*in shop also*) [Laden]kasse, *die;* **~ sale** *n.* Bargeschäft, *das*

**casing** /'keɪsɪŋ/ *n.* Gehäuse, *das;* (*of projectile, cable, tyre*) Mantel, *der*

**casino** /kə'siːnəʊ/ *n., pl.* **~s** Kasino, *das;* (*for gambling*) [Spiel]kasino, *das;* Spielbank, *die*

C

**cask** /kɑ:sk/ *n.* Fass, *das*

**casket** /'kɑ:skɪt/ *n.* Ⓐ (*box*) Schatulle, *die* (*veralt.*); Kästchen, *das;* Ⓑ (*Amer.: coffin*) Sarg, *der*

**Caspian Sea** /kæspɪən 'si:/ *pr. n.* Kaspische Meer, *das;* Kaspisee, *der*

**Cassandra** /kə'sændrə/ *n.* Kassandra, *die*

**cassata** /kæ'sɑ:tə/ *n.* Cassata, *die od. das*

**cassava** /kə'sɑ:və/ *n.* Ⓐ (*plant*) Maniok, *der;* Ⓑ (*flour*) Tapioka, *die*

**casserole** /'kæsərəʊl/ ❶ *n.* Ⓐ (*vessel*) Schmortopf, *der;* (*oval also*) Bräter, *der;* (*with long handle*) Kasserolle, *die;* Ⓑ (*food*) Schmortopf, *der.* ❷ *v.t.* schmoren

**cassette** /kə'set, kæ'set/ *n.* Kassette, *die;* **miniature film ~:** Kleinbildkassette, *die*

**cassette: ~ deck** Kassettendeck, *das;* **~ player** *n.* Kassettengerät, *das;* **~ recorder** *n.* Kassettenrecorder, *der*

**cassock** /'kæsək/ *n.* (*Eccl.*) Soutane, *die*

**cast** /kɑ:st/ ❶ *v.t.*, **~** Ⓐ (*throw*) werfen; **~ sth. adrift** etw. abtreiben lassen; **~ loose** losmachen; **he ~ loose from his family** (*fig.*) er löste sich von seiner Familie; **~ sth. ashore** etw. an Land spülen; **~ an** *or* **one's eye over sth.** einen Blick auf etw. (*Akk.*) werfen; **~ one's eyes round a room** seine Augen *od.* Blicke durch ein Zimmer schweifen lassen; **~ light on sth.** Licht auf etw. (*Akk.*) werfen; (*fig.*) Licht in etw. (*Akk.*) bringen; **~ the line/net** die Angel[schnur]/das Netz auswerfen; **~ a shadow [on/over sth.]** (*lit. or fig.*) einen Schatten [auf etw. (*Akk.*)] werfen; **~ a spell on sb./sth.** jmdn./etw. verzaubern; **~ a vote** seine Stimme abgeben; **~ one's mind back to sth.** an etw. (*Akk.*) zurückdenken; sich an etw. (*Akk.*) erinnern; **~ sth. to the winds** (*fig.*) etw. über Bord werfen (*fig.*); ⇨ *also* **aspersion**; **lot** G; Ⓑ (*shed*) verlieren ‹Haare, Winterfell›; abwerfen ‹Gehörn, Blätter, Hülle›; **the snake ~s its skin** die Schlange häutet sich; **a horse ~s a shoe** ein Pferd verliert ein Hufeisen; **~ aside** (*fig.*) beiseite schieben ‹Vorschlag›; ablegen ‹Vorurteile, Gewohnheiten›; vergessen ‹Sorgen, Vorstellungen›; fallen lassen ‹Freunde, Hemmungen›; sich (*Dat.*) entgehen lassen ‹günstige Gelegenheit›; **she ~ aside her books and the academic life** sie kehrte den Büchern und dem akademischen Leben den Rücken; Ⓒ (*shape, form*) gießen; Ⓓ (*calculate*) stellen ‹Horoskop›; Ⓔ (*assign role[s] of*) besetzen; **~ Joe as sb./in the role of sb.** jmdn./jmds. Rolle mit Joe besetzen; **~ a play/film** die Rollen [in einem Stück/Film] besetzen.

❷ *n.* Ⓐ (*Med.*) Gipsverband, *der;* Ⓑ (*set of actors*) Besetzung, *die;* Ⓒ (*model*) Abdruck, *der;* Ⓓ (*throwing of missile etc., throw of dice*) Wurf, *der;* (*distance of throw*) **a stone's ~:** einen Steinwurf [weit]; Ⓔ (*Fishing*) (*throw of net*) Auswerfen, *das;* (*throw of line*) Wurf, *der;* Ⓕ (*twist*) **develop a ~:** sich verbiegen; **have a ~ in the** *or* **one's eye** [leicht] schielen; Ⓖ (*tinge*) Schimmer, *der;* Ⓗ (*quality*) Zuschnitt, *der;* **~ of mind** Gesinnung, *die;* **~ of features** *or* **countenance** Gesichtsschnitt, *der*

**~ a'bout** *v.i.* **~ about [to find** *or* **for sth.]** sich [nach etw.] umsehen

**~ a'round** ⇨ **~ about**

**~ a'way** *v.t.* Ⓐ wegwerfen; Ⓑ **be ~ away on an island** auf einer Insel stranden

**~ 'down** *v.t.* **be ~ down [by sth.]** [wegen etw.] niedergeschlagen sein

**~ in** *v.i.* **~ in one's lot with sb.** sich mit jmdm. zusammentun

**~ 'off** ❶ *v.t.* Ⓐ (*abandon*) verlassen ‹Kind›; aufgeben ‹früheres Leben›; ablegen ‹alte Kleider›; (*reject*) den Laufpass geben (+ *Dat.*) (*ugs.*); Ⓑ (*Naut.*) losmachen; Ⓒ (*Knitting*) abketten; Ⓓ (*Printing*) **~ off [the manuscript]** den Umfang [des Manuskripts] berechnen. ❷ *v.i.* Ⓐ (*Knitting*) abketten; Ⓑ (*Naut.*) ablegen. ⇨ *also* **~-off**

**~ 'on** *v.t. & i.* (*Knitting*) anschlagen

**~ 'up** *v.t.* Ⓐ (*add*) zusammenzählen; Ⓑ (*wash up*) an Land spülen

**castanet** /kæstə'net/ *n., usu. in pl.* (*Mus.*) Kastagnette, *die*

**castaway** /'kɑ:stəweɪ/ *n.* Schiffbrüchige, *der/die*

**caste** /kɑ:st/ *n.* (*lit. or fig.*) Ⓐ Kaste, *die;* Ⓑ *no pl., no art.* (*class system*) Kastenwesen, *das;* (*social position*) soziale Stellung; **lose ~:** gesellschaftliches Ansehen einbüßen

**castellated** /'kæstəleɪtɪd/ *adj.* Ⓐ (*castle-like*) schlossartig; Ⓑ (*battlemented*) mit Zinnen bewehrt

**'caste mark** *n.* Kastenzeichen, *das*

**caster** /'kɑ:stə(r)/ *n.* Ⓐ ⇨ **castor**; Ⓑ (*Printing*) [Schrift]gießmaschine, *die*

**castigate** /'kæstɪgeɪt/ *v.t.* (*punish*) züchtigen (*geh.*); (*criticize*) geißeln (*geh.*)

**castigation** /kæstɪ'geɪʃn/ *n.* (*punishment*) Züchtigung, *die* (*geh.*); (*criticism*) Geißelung, *die* (*geh.*)

**Castilian** /kə'stɪlɪən/ ❶ *adj.* kastilisch; ⇨ *also* **English** 1. ❷ *n.* Ⓐ (*person*) Kastilier, *der*/Kastilierin, *die;* Ⓑ (*language*) Kastilisch, *das;* ⇨ *also* **English** 2 A

**casting** /'kɑ:stɪŋ/ *n.* Ⓐ (*Metallurgy: product*) Gussstück, *das;* (*Art*) Abguss, *der;* Ⓑ (*Theatre, Cinemat.*) Rollenbesetzung, *die*

**casting 'vote** *n.* ausschlaggebende Stimme (*des Vorsitzenden bei Stimmengleichheit*); **the ~ rests with the manager** die [letzte] Entscheidung hat der Geschäftsführer

**cast: ~ 'iron** *n.* Gusseisen, *das;* **~-iron** *adj.* gusseisern; (*fig.*) eisern ‹Wille, Konstitution, Magen›; handfest, triftig ‹Grund, Entschuldigung›; hieb- und stichfest ‹Alibi, Beweis›; hundertprozentig ‹Garantie›

**castle** /'kɑ:sl/ ❶ *n.* Ⓐ (*stronghold*) Burg, *die;* (*mansion*) Schloss, *das;* **Windsor C~:** Schloss Windsor; **an Englishman's home is his ~:** für den Engländer ist sein Haus wie eine Burg; **~s in the air** *or* **in Spain** Luftschlösser; Ⓑ (*Chess*) Turm, *der.* ❷ *v.i.* (*Chess*) rochieren

**'cast-off** ❶ *adj.* abgelegt. ❷ *n. in pl.* abgelegte Sachen; **she didn't want her friend's ~s** (*fig. joc.*) sie wollte nicht die abgelegten Liebhaber ihrer Freundin haben (*ugs.*)

**castor** /'kɑ:stə(r)/ *n.* Ⓐ (*sprinkler*) Streuer, *der;* Ⓑ (*wheel*) Rolle, *die;* Laufrolle, *die* (*Technik*)

**castor: ~ 'oil** *n.* Rizinusöl, *das;* Kastoröl, *das* (*Kaufmannsspr.*); **~ sugar** *n.* (*Brit.*) Raffinade, *die;* Kastorzucker, *der* (*selten*)

**castrate** /kæ'streɪt/ *v.t.* Ⓐ kastrieren; (*fig.*) beschneiden ‹Macht›; Ⓑ (*expurgate*) verstümmeln; kastrieren (*ugs. scherzh.*)

**castration** /kæ'streɪʃn/ *n.* Ⓐ Kastration, *die;* (*fig.*) Beschneidung, *die;* Ⓑ (*expurgation*) Verstümmelung, *die*

**castrato** /kæ'strɑ:təʊ/ *n., pl.* **castrati** /kæ'strɑ:ti:/ (*Mus. Hist.*) Kastrat, *der*

**casual** /'kæʒjʊəl, 'kæzjʊəl/ ❶ *adj.* Ⓐ ungezwungen; zwanglos; leger ‹Kleidung›; beiläufig ‹Bemerkung›; flüchtig ‹Bekannter, Bekanntschaft, Blick›; unbekümmert, unbeschwert ‹Haltung, Einstellung›; salopp ‹Ausdrucksweise›; lässig ‹Auftreten›; gemächlich ‹Schritt, Spaziergang›; **I'm just here on a ~ visit** ich habe nur mal vorbeigeschaut (*ugs.*); **be ~ about sth.** etw. auf die leichte Schulter nehmen; **you can't be so ~ about timekeeping** du musst es mit der Pünktlichkeit schon etwas genauer nehmen; **he's so ~ about his work** er nimmt seine Arbeit einfach nicht richtig ernst; **~ sex** Sex ohne feste Bindung; Ⓑ (*accidental*) zufällig; **by some ~ coincidence** durch Zufall.
❷ *n.* Ⓐ *in pl.* (*clothes*) Freizeitkleidung, *die;* Ⓑ ⇨ **casual labourer**; Ⓒ ⇨ **casual shoe**

**casual: ~'earnings** *n. pl.* Nebeneinkünfte *Pl.;* **~ 'labour** *n., no pl.* Gelegenheitsarbeit, *die;* **~ 'labourer** *n.* Gelegenheitsarbeiter, *der*

**casually** /'kæʒjʊəlɪ, 'kæzjʊəlɪ/ *adv.* Ⓐ ungezwungen; zwanglos; beiläufig ‹bemerken›; flüchtig ‹anschauen›; gemächlich ‹wandern, spazieren gehen›; lustlos ‹Problem anpacken›; salopp ‹sich ausdrücken›; leger ‹sich kleiden›; **I glanced ~ at the headlines** ich überflog die Schlagzeilen; **I was ~ reading a book** ich blätterte in einem Buch; **he treats/approaches his work too ~:** er nimmt seine Arbeit zu wenig ernst; Ⓑ (*accidentally*) zufällig

**casualness** /'kæʒjʊəlnɪs, 'kæzjʊəlnɪs/ *n., no pl.* Ungezwungenheit, *die;* Zwanglosigkeit, *die;* (*of remark*) Beiläufigkeit, *die*

**casual 'shoe** *n.* Freizeitschuh, *der*

**casualty** /'kæʒjʊəltɪ, 'kæzjʊəltɪ/ *n.* Ⓐ (*injured person*) Verletzte, *der/die;* (*in battle*) Verwundete, *der/die;* (*dead person*) Tote, *der/die;* Ⓑ (*fig.*) Opfer, *das;* (*failure*) Versager, *der;* Ⓒ *no art.* (*hospital department*) Unfallstation, *die;* **work in ~:** in der Unfallstation arbeiten

**casualty: ~ department** *n.* Unfallstation, *die;* **~ list** *n.* Verletztenliste, *die;* Liste der Getöteten/Gefallenen; **~ ward** *n.* Unfallstation, *die*

**casuist** /'kæʒjʊɪst, 'kæzju:ɪst/ *n.* Kasuist, *der* (*Philos.*)

**casuistry** /'kæʒjʊɪstrɪ, 'kæzju:ɪstrɪ/ *n.* Kasuistik, *die* (*Philos.*)

**cat** /kæt/ *n.* Ⓐ Katze, *die;* **she-~:** Kätzin, *die;* [weibliche] Katze; **tom~:** Kater, *der;* **be as nervous as a ~:** furchtbar ängstlich sein; **play ~ and mouse with sb.** Katz und Maus mit jmdm. spielen (*ugs.*); **when the ~'s away [the mice will play]** (*prov.*) wenn die Katze aus dem Haus ist, tanzen die Mäuse [auf dem Tisch]; **let the ~ out of the bag** (*fig.*) die Katze aus dem Sack lassen; **be like a ~ on hot bricks** wie auf glühenden Kohlen sitzen; **look like something the ~ brought in** (*fig.*) aussehen wie unter die Räuber gefallen; **curiosity killed the ~** (*fig.*) sei nicht so neugierig; **[fight] like ~ and dog** wie Hund und Katze [sein]; **not a ~ in hell's chance** nicht die geringste Chance; **we'll wait and see which way the ~ jumps** (*fig.*) wir warten ab, bis wir sehen, wie der Hase läuft (*ugs.*); **a ~ may look at a king** (*prov.*) das ist doch auch nur ein Mensch; **enough to make a ~ laugh** zum Schreien [komisch] (*ugs.*); **put the ~ among the pigeons** (*fig.*) für Aufregung sorgen; **it would be putting the ~ among the pigeons** es würde einigen Aufruhr verursachen; **rain ~s and dogs** in Strömen regnen; **no room to swing a ~** (*fig.*) kaum Platz zum Umdrehen; **has the ~ got your tongue?** hast du die Sprache verloren?; Ⓑ (*coll. derog.: malicious woman*) Biest, *das;* (*coll.: person*) Typ, *der;* (*coll.: jazz enthusiast*) Jazzfan, *der;* Ⓒ (*Zool.: member of genus Felis*) Katze, *die;* **the [great] Cats** die Großkatzen; **the ~ family** die Familie der Katzen; Ⓓ ⇨ **cat-o'-nine-tails**

**cataclysm** /'kætəklɪzm/ *n.* [Natur]katastrophe, *die;* Kataklysmus, *der* (*Geol.*); (*fig.: upheaval*) Umwälzung, *die*

**cataclysmic** /kætə'klɪzmɪk/ *adj.* katastrophal; verheerend; (*fig.*) umwälzend; dramatisch ‹Umwälzung›

**catacomb** /'kætəku:m, 'kætəkəʊm/ *n.* Ⓐ Katakombe, *die;* Ⓑ (*cellar*) Keller[raum], *der*

**catafalque** /'kætəfælk/ *n.* Katafalk, *der;* (*movable*) Leichenwagen, *der*

**Catalan** /'kætəlæn/ **▶1275**, **▶1340** ❶ *adj.* katalanisch; ⇨ *also* **English** 1. ❷ *n.* Ⓐ (*person*) Katalane, *der*/Katalanin, *die;* Ⓑ (*language*) Katalanisch, *das;* ⇨ *also* **English** 2 A

**catalog, cataloger** (*Amer.*) ⇨ **catalogue, cataloguer**

**catalogue** /'kætəlɒg/ ❶ *n.* Katalog, *der;* **subject ~:** Sachkatalog, *der* (*Buchw.*). ❷ *v.t.* katalogisieren

**cataloguer** /'kætəlɒgə(r)/ *n.* Bearbeiter/Bearbeiterin des Katalogs

**Catalonia** /kætə'ləʊnɪə/ *pr. n.* Katalonien (*das*)

**catalyse** /'kætəlaɪz/ *v.t.* (*Chem.; also fig.*) katalysieren

**catalysis** /kə'tælɪsɪs/ *n., pl.* **catalyses** /kə'tælɪsi:z/ (*Chem.*) Katalyse, *die*

**catalyst** /'kætəlɪst/ *n.* (*Chem.; also fig.*) Katalysator, *der;* **act as a ~:** als Katalysator wirken (**to** bei)

**catalytic** /kætə'lɪtɪk/ *adj.* (*Chem.; also fig.*) katalytisch

**catalytic con'verter** *n.* (*Motor Veh.*) Katalysator, *der*

**catalyze** (*Amer.*) ⇨ **catalyse**

**catamaran** /kætəmə'ræn/ *n.* (*Naut.*) Katamaran, *der*

**cat-and-'dog** *adj.* **lead a ~ life** wie Hund und Katze leben

**catapult** /'kætəpʌlt/ ❶ *n.* Katapult, *das.* ❷ *v.t.* Ⓐ (*fling*) katapultieren; **they were ~ed into action** (*fig.*) sie wurden [plötzlich] zum Handeln gezwungen; **the tragedy ~ed us into the depths of despair** die Tragödie stürzte uns in tiefste Verzweiflung; Ⓑ (*launch*) katapultieren. ❸ *v.i.* (*be flung*) katapultiert werden

**cataract** /'kætərækt/ *n.* Ⓐ Katarakt, *der;* Wasserfall, *der;* (*fig.*) Katarakt, *der;* Ⓑ (*Med.*) grauer Star; Katarakt[a], *die* (*fachspr.*)

**catarrh** /kə'tɑ:(r)/ *n.* ▶ **1232** Ⓐ (*discharge*) Schleimabsonderung, *die;* Ⓑ (*inflammation*) Katarrh, *der* (*Med.*)

**catastrophe** /kə'tæstrəfɪ/ *n.* Katastrophe, *die;* **end in ~:** in einer Katastrophe enden; **mean ~:** eine Katastrophe bedeuten

**catastrophic** /kætə'strɒfɪk/ *adj.*, **catastrophically** /kætə'strɒfɪkəlɪ/ *adv.* katastrophal

**catatonia** /kætə'təʊnɪə/ *n.* (*Psych.*) Katatonie, *die*

**catatonic** /kætə'tɒnɪk/ *adj.* (*Psych.*) katatonisch

**cat:** **~ burglar** *n.* Fassadenkletterer, *der*/Fassadenkletterin, *die;* **~call** ❶ *n.* ≈ Pfiff, *der;* ❷ *v.i.* ≈ pfeifen

**catch** /kætʃ/ ❶ *v.t.*, **caught** /kɔ:t/ Ⓐ (*capture*) fangen; (*lay hold of*) fassen; packen; **~ sb. by the arm** jmdn. am Arm packen *od.* fassen; **~ hold of sb./sth.** jmdn./etw. festhalten; (*to stop oneself falling*) sich an jmdm./etw. festhalten; **he caught hold of me by the throat** er packte mich an der Kehle; Ⓑ (*intercept motion of*) auffangen; fangen ‹Ball›; **he caught the door before it slammed** er hielt die Tür fest, bevor sie zuschlagen konnte; **the brambles kept ~ing our clothes** die Dornenranken verfingen sich immer wieder in unseren Kleidern; **~ a thread** einen Faden vernähen; **get sth. caught** *or* **~ sth. on/in sth.** mit etw. an/in etw. (*Dat.*) hängen bleiben; **I got my finger caught** *or* **caught my finger in the door** ich habe mir den Finger in der Tür eingeklemmt; **get caught on/in sth.** an/in etw. (*Dat.*) hängen bleiben; ⇒ *also* **breath** A; Ⓒ (*travel by*) nehmen; (*manage to see*) sehen; (*manage to hear*) bekommen ‹Sender, Sendung›; (*be in time for*) [noch] erreichen; [noch] kriegen (*ugs.*) ‹Bus, Zug›; [noch] erwischen (*ugs.*) ‹Person›; **did you ~ her in?** hast du sie zu Hause erwischt? (*ugs.*); **did you ~ the post?** bist du noch rechtzeitig zum Briefkasten gekommen?; Ⓓ (*surprise*) **~ sb. at/doing sth.** jmdn. bei etw. erwischen (*ugs.*)/[dabei] erwischen, wie er etw. tut (*ugs.*); **~ sb. unawares** jmdn. überraschen; **caught by a sudden fall of the dollar** vom plötzlichen Sturz des Dollars überrascht; **caught in a mist/thunderstorm** vom Nebel/Sturm überrascht; **I caught myself thinking how old she looked** ich ertappte mich bei dem Gedanken, wie alt sie doch aussah; **~ sb. in sth./somewhere** jmdn. in etw. (*Dat.*)/irgendwo antreffen; **you'll never ~ me in this pub again** in diesem Lokal siehst du mich nicht mehr; **~ me!/him!** das wirst du nicht erleben!; ⇒ *also* **act** 1 B; **bend[1]** 3 B; **hop[2]** 3 C; Ⓔ ▶ **1232** (*become infected with, receive*) sich (*Dat.*) zuziehen *od.* (*ugs.*) holen; **~ sth. from sb.** sich bei jmdm. mit etw. anstecken; **~ [a] cold** sich erkälten/sich (*Dat.*) einen Schnupfen holen; (*fig.*) übel dran sein; **he caught this habit from his wife** (*fig.*) diese Angewohnheit hat er von seiner Frau geerbt (*ugs.*); **he caught that trick from his brother** (*fig.*) diesen Trick hat er von seinem Bruder; **you'll ~ a terrible scolding/beating** *etc.* **from your father** dein Vater wird dich furchtbar ausschimpfen/verprügeln *usw.;* **~ it** (*fig. coll.*) etwas kriegen (*ugs.*); **you'll ~ it from me** du kannst von mir was erleben (*ugs.*); ⇒ *also* **death** A; Ⓕ (*arrest*) **~ sb.'s gaze** jmds. Aufmerksamkeit erregen; **~ sb.'s attention/interest** jmds. Aufmerksamkeit erregen/jmds. Interesse wecken; **~ sb.'s fancy** jmdm. gefallen; jmdn. ansprechen; **~ the Speaker's eye** (*Parl.*) das Wort erhalten; **~ sb.'s eye** jmdm. auffallen; jmdn. auf sich (*Akk.*) aufmerksam machen; ‹Gegenstand:› jmdm. ins Auge fallen; (*be impossible to overlook*) jmdm. ins Auge springen; Ⓖ (*hit*) **~ sb. on/in sth.** jmdn. auf/in etw. (*Akk.*) treffen; **~ sb. a blow [on/in sth.]** jmdm. einen Schlag [auf/in etw. (*Akk.*)] versetzen; Ⓗ (*grasp in thought*) verstehen; mitbekommen; **did you ~ his meaning?** hast du verstanden *od.* mitbekommen, was er meint?; **~ the mood** die Stimmung einfangen; **~ sb.'s likeness** jmdn. treffen; Ⓘ ⇒ **~ out** a.

❷ *v.i.*, **caught** Ⓐ (*begin to burn*) [anfangen zu] brennen; Ⓑ (*become fixed*) hängenbleiben; ‹Haar, Faden:› sich verfangen; **my coat caught on a nail** ich blieb mit meinem Mantel an einem Nagel hängen; Ⓒ **~ at sb.'s sleeve** jmdn. am Ärmel zupfen.

❸ *n.* Ⓐ (*of ball*) **make [several] good ~es** [mehrmals] gut fangen; **make a ~ with one hand** mit einer Hand fangen; Ⓑ (*amount caught, lit. or fig.*) Fang, *der;* **you've made a great ~ as far as your house is concerned** (*fig.*) mit eurem Haus habt ihr das große Los gezogen; **sth. is no [great] ~** (*fig.*) etw. ist kein gutes Geschäft; **he was no ~[, matrimonially]** (*fig.*) er war keine gute Partie; Ⓒ (*trick, unexpected difficulty*) Haken, *der* (**in** an + *Dat.*); **there must be a ~ in it somewhere** da muss irgendwo ein Haken sein; **the ~ is that ...:** der Haken an der Sache ist, dass ...; **~-22** (*coll.*) Dilemma, *das;* **it's ~-22** (*coll.*) es ist ein Teufelskreis; Ⓓ (*fastener*) Verschluss, *der;* (*of door*) Schnapper, *der;* Ⓔ (*Cricket etc.*) ≈ Fang, *der* (*Schlagball*)*; Abfangen des Balles, das den Schlagmann aus dem Spiel bringt;* **miss a ~:** einen Ball nicht abfangen; **he is a good ~:** er kann gut fangen

**~ 'on** *v.i.* (*coll.*) Ⓐ (*become popular*) [gut] ankommen (*ugs.*); sich durchsetzen; Ⓑ (*understand*) begreifen; kapieren (*ugs.*)

**~ 'out** *v.t.* Ⓐ (*Cricket etc.*) *durch Abfangen des Balles aus dem Spiel bringen;* Ⓑ (*detect in mistake etc.*) [bei einem Fehler] ertappen; **it's not easy to ~ him out** man kann ihm nicht leicht etwas am Zeug flicken (*ugs.*); **he was caught out on a point of form** er stolperte über eine Formsache; Ⓒ (*take unawares*) erwischen (*ugs.*)

**~ 'up** ❶ *v.t.* Ⓐ (*reach*) **~ sb. up** jmdn. einholen; (*in quality, skill*) mit jmdm. mitkommen; Ⓑ (*absorb*) **be caught up in sth.** in etw. (*Dat.*) [völlig] aufgehen; **they were completely caught up in each other** sie waren nur mit sich [selbst] beschäftigt; Ⓒ (*snatch*) packen; **sth. gets caught up in sth.** etw. verfängt sich in etw. (*Dat.*). ❷ *v.i.* (*get level*) **~ up** einholen; **~ up with sb.** (*in quality, skill*) mit jmdm. mitkommen; **~ up on sth.** etw. nachholen; **I'm longing to ~ up on your news** ich bin gespannt, was für Neuigkeiten du hast

**catch:** **~-all** *n.* Sammelplatz, *der;* (*fig.*) Auffangbecken, *das;* **~-all term** Allerweltswort, *das;* **~-as-~-'can** *n.* Catch-as-catch-can, *das;* **play ~-as-~-can** keine Rücksicht nehmen; **~ crop** *n.* (*Agric.*) Zwischenfrucht, *die*

**catcher** /'kætʃə(r)/ *n.* Ⓐ Fänger, *der*/Fängerin, *die;* Ⓑ (*Baseball*) Fänger, *der*

**catching** /'kætʃɪŋ/ *adj.* ansteckend

**catchment area** /'kætʃmənt eərɪə/ *n.* (*lit. or fig.*) Einzugsgebiet, *das*

**catch:** **~penny** *adj.* **~penny goods** Ramsch, *der* (*ugs.*); Tinnef, *der* (*ugs.*); **~phrase** *n.* Slogan, *der;* **~ points** *n. pl.* (*Railw.*) Entgleisungsvorrichtung, *die;* **~ question** *n.* Fangfrage, *die;* **~word** *n.* Ⓐ (*headword*) Kolumnentitel, *der;* (*rhyme-word*) Reimwort, *das;* (*cue*) Stichwort, *das;* (*slogan*) Schlagwort, *das;* Ⓑ (*at foot of page*) Kustos, *der*

**catchy** /'kætʃɪ/ *adj.* Ⓐ eingängig; **a ~ song** ein Ohrwurm (*ugs.*); Ⓑ (*attractive*) reizvoll; ansprechend ‹Farbe, Kleidung›

**'cat door** *n.* Katzentür, *die*

**catechise** ⇒ **catechize**

**catechism** /'kætɪkɪzm/ *n.* (*Relig.*) Ⓐ (*book*) Katechismus, *der;* **Church C~:** Katechismus der Anglikanischen Kirche; Ⓑ (*instruction*) [Unterweisung im] Katechismus; (*fig.: questioning*) Befragung, *die;* **put sb. through a ~** (*fig.*) jmdn. ins Kreuzverhör nehmen (*fig.*)

**catechize** /'kætɪkaɪz/ *v.t.* (*Relig.*) (*instruct*) katechisieren; (*fig.: question*) befragen

**categorial** /kætɪ'gɔ:rɪəl/ *adj.* kategorial (*geh.*)

**categorical** /kætɪ'gɒrɪkl/ *adj.* kategorisch; **he was quite ~ about it** er vertrat in dieser Angelegenheit eine recht entschiedene Haltung; **~ imperative** (*Philos.*) kategorischer Imperativ

**categorically** /kætɪ'gɒrɪkəlɪ/ *adv.* kategorisch

**categorize (categorise)** /'kætɪgəraɪz/ *v.t.* kategorisieren

**category** /'kætɪgərɪ/ *n.* (*also Philos.*) Kategorie, *die*

**cater** /'keɪtə(r)/ *v.i.* Ⓐ (*provide or supply food*) **~ [for sb./sth.]** [für jmdn./etw.] [die] Speisen und Getränke liefern; **~ for weddings** Hochzeiten ausrichten; Ⓑ (*provide requisites etc.*) **~ for sb./sth.** auf jmdn./etw. eingestellt sein; **~ for the needs of the individual** den Bedürfnissen des Einzelnen gerecht werden; **~ for all ages** jeder Altersgruppe etwas bieten; Ⓒ **~ to** (*pander*) nachgeben (+ *Dat.*); entgegenkommen (+ *Dat.*)

**catercorner** /'kætəkɔ:nə(r)/, **catercornered** /'kætəkɔ:nəd/ (*Amer.*) *adv., adj.* diagonal

**caterer** /'keɪtərə(r)/ *n.* ▶ **1261** Lieferant von Speisen und Getränken; Caterer, *der* (*fachspr.*); (*for party*) Partyservice, *der*

**catering** /'keɪtərɪŋ/ *n.* Ⓐ (*trade*) **~ [business]** Gastronomie, *die;* **he is interested in ~ as a career** er interessiert sich beruflich für die Gastronomie; Ⓑ (*service*) Lieferung von Speisen und Getränken; Catering, *das* (*fachspr.*); **who's responsible for the ~ in this hotel?** wer hat in diesem Hotel die Küche unter sich (*Dat.*)?; **do the ~:** für Speisen und Getränke sorgen; **~ firm/service** ⇒ **caterer**

**caterpillar** /'kætəpɪlə(r)/ *n.* Ⓐ (*Zool.*) Raupe, *die;* Ⓑ **C~ [tractor]** ® (*Mech.*) Raupenfahrzeug, *das*

**caterpillar:** **~ 'track,** **~ 'tread** *ns.* Raupen-, Gleiskette, *die*

**caterwaul** /'kætəwɔ:l/ ❶ *v.i.* ‹Katze:› schreien, [laut] miauen; ‹Sänger:› jaulen (*abwertend*). ❷ *n.* Katzengeschrei, *das;* (*of singer*) Gejaule, *das* (*abwertend*); ≈ Katzenmusik, *die* (*ugs.*)

**cat:** **~fish** *n.* Wels, *der;* **~ flap** ⇒ **cat-door**; **~gut** *n.* Darm, *der;* (*Med.*) Katgut, *das*

**catharsis** /kə'θɑ:sɪs/ *n.*, *pl.* **catharses** /kə'θɑ:si:z/ (*emotional outlet; also Psych.*) Katharsis, *die*

**cathartic** /kə'θɑ:tɪk/ ❶ *adj.* Ⓐ (*Med.*) abführend; **~ medicine** Abführmittel, *das;* Ⓑ (*effecting catharsis; also Psych.*) kathartisch. ❷ *n.* (*Med.*) Abführmittel, *das*

**Cathay** /kə'θeɪ/ *pr. n.* (*arch./poet.*) China; das Reich der Mitte (*dichter.*)

**cathedral** /kə'θi:drl/ *n.* **~ [church]** Dom, *der;* Kathedrale, *die* (*bes. in England, Frankreich u. Spanien*); **Cologne C~:** der Kölner Dom; **Rheims C~:** die Kathedrale von Reims

**ca'thedral city** *n.* Domstadt, *die*

**Catherine** /'kæθərɪn/ *pr. n.* (*Hist., as name of ruler etc.*) Katharina (*die*)

**'Catherine wheel** *n.* Ⓐ (*firework*) Feuerrad, *das;* Ⓑ ⇒ **cartwheel** B; Ⓒ (*Archit.*) Radfenster, *das;* Katharinenfenster, *das* (*selten*)

**catheter** /'kæθɪtə(r)/ *n.* (*Med.*) Katheter, *der*

**catheterize** /'kæθɪtəraɪz/ *v.t.* (*Med.*) katheterisieren

**cathode** /'kæθəʊd/ *n.* (*Electr.*) Kathode, *die*

**'cathode ray** *n.* Kathodenstrahl, *der;* **cathode-ray tube** Kathodenstrahlröhre, *die;* Braunsche Röhre

**catholic** /'kæθəlɪk, 'kæθlɪk/ ❶ *adj.* Ⓐ (*all-embracing*) umfassend; vielseitig ‹Interessen›; (*universal, universally applicable*) allgemein;

C

universell ‹Lehren›; Ⓑ C~ (*Relig.*) katholisch. ❷ *n.* **C~:** Katholik, *der*/Katholikin, *die*

**Catholicism** /kə'θɒlɪsɪzm/ *n.* (*Relig.*) Katholizismus, *der*

**cation** /'kætaɪən/ *n.* (*Phys.*) Kation, *das*

**catkin** /'kætkɪn/ *n.* (*Bot.*) Kätzchen, *das*

**cat:** **~lick** *n.* Katzenwäsche, *die;* **give oneself a ~lick** Katzenwäsche machen; **~like** *adj.* katzenartig; katzenhaft ‹Art, Bewegung›; **~ lover** *n.* Katzenfreund, *der*/-freundin, *die;* **~mint** *n.* (*Bot.*) Katzenminze, *die;* **~nap** *n.* Nickerchen, *das* (*ugs.*); kurzes Schläfchen; **have** *or* **take a ~nap** ein Nickerchen machen (*ugs.*); **~-nip** *n.* (*Bot.*) Katzenminze, *die;* **~-o'-'nine-tails** *n.* neunschwänzige Katze; **~'s-'cradle** *n.* Ⓐ (*game*) Fadenspiel, *das;* Ⓑ (*string pattern*) *Figur beim Fadenspiel;* Fadenspannbild, *das;* **~'s-eye** *n.* Ⓐ (*stone*) Katzenauge, *das;* Ⓑ (*Brit.: reflector*) Bodenrückstrahler, *der* (*Verkehrsw.*); **~'s-paw** *n.* Ⓐ (*person*) Handlanger, *der;* Werkzeug, *das* (*fig.*); Ⓑ (*Naut.*) leichte Brise; **~'s pyjamas** ⇒ **~'s whiskers**; **~'s-tail** *n.* (*Bot.*) Rohrkolben, *der;* **~suit** *n.* (*woman's*) hautenger einteiliger Hosenanzug; (*infant's*) Overall, *der;* **~'s 'whiskers** *n. pl.* (*coll.: the best*) **sb. is the ~'s whiskers** jmd. ist der/die Größte (*ugs.*); **sth. is the ~'s whiskers** etw. ist spitze (*ugs.*)

**cattery** /'kætərɪ/ *n.* Katzenpension, *die*

**cattily** /'kætɪlɪ/ *adv.* gehässig

**cattish** /'kætɪʃ/ ⇒ **catty**

**cattle** /'kætl/ *n. pl.* Vieh, *das;* Rinder *Pl.;* **sheep and ~:** Schafe und Rinder; **700 head of ~:** 700 Rinder *od.* Stück Vieh

**cattle:** **~ breeding** *n.* Rinderzucht, *die;* Viehzucht, *die;* **~ cake** *n.* (*Brit. Agric.*) *konzentriertes, gepresstes Viehfutter;* ≈ Presskuchen, *der;* **~ grid** *n.* (*Brit.*), **~ guard** *n.* (*Amer.*) *mit einem Gitterrost bedeckte Grube als Durchlass bei Weiden od. Gehegen;* **~man** *n.* Ⓐ (*tender*) Viehhüter, *der;* Ⓑ (*breeder*) Viehzüchter, *der;* **~ market** *n.* Viehmarkt, *der;* (*fig.*) Fleischbeschau, *die* (*ugs. scherzh.*); **~ plague** *n.* Rinderpest, *die;* **~ rustler** *n.* (*Amer.*) Viehdieb, *der;* **~ truck** *n.* Viehtransporter, *der;* (*Railw.*) Viehwagen, *der*

**catty** /'kætɪ/ *adj.* gehässig; **they're so ~ about their colleague** sie sprechen so gehässig über ihre Kollegin

**'catwalk** *n.* Laufsteg, *der*

**Caucasia** /kɔː'keɪzɪə, kɔː'keɪʒə/ *pr. n.* Kaukasien (*das*)

**Caucasian** /kɔː'keɪzɪən, kɔː'keɪʒn/ ❶ *adj.* kaukasisch. ❷ *n.* Kaukasier, *der*/Kaukasierin, *die*

**Caucasus** /'kɔːkəsəs/ *pr. n.* Kaukasus, *der*

**caucus** /'kɔːkəs/ *n.* (*Brit. derog., Amer.*) Ⓐ (*committee*) *den Wahlkampf und die Richtlinien der Politik bestimmendes regionales Gremium einer Partei;* Ⓑ (*party meeting*) *den Wahlkampf und die Richtlinien der Politik bestimmende Sitzung der regionalen Parteiführung*

**caudal** /'kɔːdl/ *adj.* (*Zool.*) Ⓐ (*of tail*) Schwanz-; (*at tail*) kaudal; Ⓑ (*of posterior of body*) Kaudal-

**caught** ⇒ **catch** 1, 2

**cauldron** /'kɔːldrən, 'kɒldrən/ *n.* Kessel, *der*

**cauliflower** /'kɒlɪflaʊə(r)/ *n.* Blumenkohl, *der*

**cauliflower:** **~ 'cheese** *n.* (*mit Käse*) überbackener Blumenkohl; **~ 'ear** *n.* Blumenkohlohr, *das* (*Boxerjargon*)

**caulk** /kɔːk/ *v.t.* kalfatern (*Seemannsspr.*); abdichten

**causal** /'kɔːzl/ *adj.* kausal; **~ connection** Kausalzusammenhang, *der;* **~ sentence** Kausalsatz, *der*

**causality** /kɔː'zælɪtɪ/ *n., no pl.* (*esp. Ling., Philos.*) Kausalität, *die;* **the law[s] of ~:** das Kausalitätsgesetz

**causally** /'kɔːzəlɪ/ *adv.* kausal

**causation** /kɔː'zeɪʃn/ *n.* Ⓐ (*causing*) Verursachung, *die;* Ⓑ (*relation of cause and effect*) Kausalität, *die*

**causative** /'kɔːzətɪv/ *adj.* Ⓐ verursachend; Ⓑ (*Ling.*) kausativ

**cause** /kɔːz/ ❶ *n.* Ⓐ (*what produces effect*) Ursache, *die* (**of** für *od. Gen.*); (*person*) Verursacher, *der*/Verursacherin, *die;* **be the ~ of sth.** etw. verursachen; Ⓑ (*Philos.*) Ursache, *die;* Ⓒ (*reason*) Grund, *der;* Anlass, *der;* **~ for/to do sth.** Grund *od.* Anlass zu etw./, etw. zu tun; **no ~ for concern** kein Grund zur Beunruhigung; **where he saw ~ to do so** wo er es für nötig hielt; **show ~ why ...:** Gründe vorbringen, weshalb ...; **without good ~:** ohne triftigen Grund; Ⓓ (*object of support*) Sache, *die;* **he died in the ~ of peace** er starb für die Sache des Friedens *od.* für den Frieden; **take up sb.'s ~:** sich für jmds. Sache einsetzen; **freedom is our common ~:** Freiheit ist unser gemeinsames Anliegen *od.* Ziel; **be a lost ~:** aussichtslos sein; verlorene Liebesmühe sein (*ugs.*); **make common ~ with sb.** mit jmdm. gemeinsame Sache machen; **[in] a good ~:** [für] eine gute Sache; Ⓔ (*Law*) (*matter*) Sache, *die;* (*case*) Fall, *der;* **he lost his ~ in the courts** er hat seinen Prozess verloren.

❷ *v.t.* Ⓐ (*produce*) verursachen; erregen ‹Aufsehen, Ärgernis›; hervorrufen ‹Verstimmung, Unruhe, Verwirrung›; Ⓑ (*give*) **~ sb. worry/pain** *etc.* jmdm. Sorge/Schmerzen *usw.* bereiten; **~ sb. expense** jmdm. Ausgaben verursachen; **~ sb. trouble/bother** jmdm. Umstände machen; Ⓒ (*induce*) **~ sb. to do sth.** jmdn. veranlassen, etw. zu tun; **~ the alarm to go off** den Alarm auslösen; **~ sb. to lose concentration** jmdm. die Konzentration nehmen; **~ sb. to be miserable** bewirken, dass sich jemand elend fühlt; **~ sth. to be done** dazu führen, dass etw. getan wird

**cause célèbre** /kɔːz seɪ'lebr/ *n., pl.* **causes célèbres** /kɔːz seɪ'lebr/ Cause célèbre, *die* (*geh.*); aufsehenerregender Fall

**causeless** /'kɔːzlɪs/ *adj.* grundlos

**causeway** /'kɔːzweɪ/ *n.* Damm, *der*

**caustic** /'kɔːstɪk/ ❶ *adj.* Ⓐ (*sarcastic*) kaustisch (*geh.*); beißend ‹Spott›; bissig ‹Bemerkung, Worte›; spitz, scharf ‹Zunge›; Ⓑ (*burning*) ätzend; (*Chem.*) kaustisch; **~ potash/soda** Ätzkali, *das*/Ätznatron, *das.* ❷ *n.* (*substance*) Ätzmittel, *das;* Kaustikum, *das* (*Med.*)

**caustically** /'kɔːstɪkəlɪ/ *adv.* (*sarcastically*) bissig

**cauterisation**, **cauterise** ⇒ **cauteriz-**

**cauterization** /kɔːtəraɪ'zeɪʃn/ *n.* (*Med.*) Kauterisation, *die*

**cauterize** /'kɔːtəraɪz/ *v.t.* (*Med.*) kauterisieren; (*fig.*) abstumpfen

**caution** /'kɔːʃn/ ❶ *n.* Ⓐ Vorsicht, *die;* **use ~:** vorsichtig sein; Ⓑ (*warning*) Warnung, *die;* (*warning and reprimand*) Verwarnung, *die;* **by way of a ~:** als Warnung; **act as a ~ to sb.** jmdm. eine Warnung sein; **just a word of ~:** noch ein guter Rat; Ⓒ (*dated coll.: sb. comical*) **be a ~:** ein Kasper sein (*ugs.*). ❷ *v.t.* (*warn*) warnen; (*warn and reprove*) verwarnen (**for** wegen); **~ sb. against sth./doing sth.** jmdn. vor etw. (*Dat.*) warnen/davor warnen, etw. zu tun; **~ sb. to/not to do sth.** jmdn. ermahnen, etw. zu tun/nicht zu tun

**cautionary** /'kɔːʃənərɪ/ *adj.* [er]mahnend; warnend ‹Beispiel›

**'caution money** *n.* Kaution, *die;* **demand/pay ~:** eine Kaution verlangen/zahlen

**cautious** /'kɔːʃəs/ *adj.* vorsichtig; (*circumspect*) umsichtig

**cautiously** /'kɔːʃəslɪ/ *adv.* vorsichtig; (*circumspectly*) umsichtig

**cavalcade** /kævəl'keɪd/ *n.* Kavalkade, *die* (*veralt., auch fig.*); (*convoy of cars*) Konvoi, *der;* (*procession of cars*) Korso, *der*

**cavalier** /kævə'lɪə(r)/ ❶ *n.* Ⓐ Kavalier, *der;* Ⓑ (*Hist.: Royalist*) Kavalier, *der* (*Anhänger König Karls I.*); Ⓒ (*arch.: horseman*) Ritter, *der.* ❷ *adj.* (*offhand*) keck; (*arrogant*) anmaßend

**cavalry** /'kævəlrɪ/ *n. constr. as sing. or pl.* Kavallerie, *die;* (*soldiers in vehicles*) motorisierte Streitkräfte

**cavalry:** **~man** /'kævəlrɪmən/ *n., pl.* **~men** /'kævəlrɪmən/ Kavallerist, *der;* **~ officer** *n.* Kavallerieoffizier, *der;* **~ regiment** *n.* Reiterregiment, *das;* **~ sword** *n.* Säbel, *der;* **~ twill** *n.* Kavallerietwill, *der*

**cave**[1] /keɪv/ ❶ *n.* Höhle, *die.* ❷ *v.t.* aushöhlen. ❸ *v.i.* Höhlen erforschen

**~ 'in** *v.i.* einbrechen; (*fig.*) (*collapse*) zusammenbrechen; (*submit*) nachgeben. ⇒ *also* **cave-in**

**cave**[2] /'keɪvɪ/ *int.* (*Brit. dated sl.*) Achtung!

**caveat** /'kævɪæt/ *n.* (*warning*) Warnung, *die;* (*against repetition*) Mahnung, *die;* **~ emptor** /kævɪæt 'emptɔː(r)/ Ausschluss der Gewährleistung

**cave:** **~ bear** *n.* (*Zool.*) Höhlenbär, *der;* **~ dweller** *n.* Höhlenbewohner, *der;* (*fig.*) Wilde, *der;* **~-in** *n.* Einsturz, *der;* **~man** ⇒ **~ dweller**; **~ painting** *n.* Höhlenmalerei, *die*

**caver** /'keɪvə(r)/ *n.* Höhlenforscher, *der*

**cavern** /'kævən/ *n.* (*cave, lit. or fig.*) Höhle, *die;* (*artificial*) Kaverne, *die*

**cavernous** /'kævənəs/ *adj.* (*like a cavern*) höhlenartig; herzhaft ‹Gähnen›; (*full of caverns*) reich an Höhlen

**caviare** (**caviar**) /'kævɪɑː(r), kævɪ'ɑː(r)/ *n.* Kaviar, *der;* **it is ~ (caviar) to the general** (*fig.*) das ist Perlen vor die Säue geworfen (*ugs.*)

**cavil** /'kævɪl/ ❶ *v.i.,* (*Brit.*) **-ll-** kritteln (*abwertend*); **~ at/about sth.** etw. bekritteln (*abwertend*). ❷ *n.* unsachlicher Anwurf

**caving** /'keɪvɪŋ/ *n.* Höhlenforschung, *die*

**cavity** /'kævɪtɪ/ *n.* Hohlraum, *der;* (*in tooth*) Loch, *das;* **nasal/oral/uterine ~:** Nasen-/Mund-/Gebärmutterhöhle, *die*

**'cavity wall** *n.* (*Building*) Hohlmauer, *die*

**cavort** /kə'vɔːt/ *v.i.* (*coll.*) **~ [about** *or* **around]** herumtollen (*ugs.*)

**caw** /kɔː/ ❶ *n.* Krächzen, *das.* ❷ *v.i.* krächzen

**cay** /keɪ/ *n.* Riff, *das*

**cayenne** /keɪ'en/ *n.* **~ 'pepper** Cayennepfeffer, *der*

**cayman** /'keɪmən/ *n.* (*Zool.*) Kaiman, *der*

**CB** *abbr.* Ⓐ **Companion [of the Order] of the Bath** *Mitglied der 3. Klasse des Bathordens;* Ⓑ **citizens' band** CB

**CBE** *abbr.* **Commander [of the Order] of the British Empire** *Träger des Ordens des British Empire 3. Klasse*

**CBI** *abbr.* **Confederation of British Industry** *britischer Unternehmerverband*

**cc** /siː'siː/ *abbr.* ▶ **1671** **cubic centimetre(s)** $cm^3$

**CCTV** *abbr.* **closed-circuit television** CCTV

**CD** *abbr.* Ⓐ **civil defence;** Ⓑ **Corps Diplomatique** CD; Ⓒ **compact disc** CD; **CD player** CD-Spieler, *der;* **CD burner**, **CD writer** CD-Brenner, *der*

**Cdr.** *abbr.* **commander b** Kdt

**CD-ROM** /siːdiː'rɒm/ *n.* CD-ROM, *die;* **~ drive** CD-ROM-Laufwerk, *das*

**CE** *abbr.* Ⓐ **Church of England;** Ⓑ **civil engineer;** Ⓒ **Common Era**

**cease** /siːs/ ❶ *v.i.* aufhören; **he never ~d in his efforts** er gab seine Bemühungen nie auf; **when the storm ~d** als der Sturm sich legte; **~ from sth./from doing sth.** mit etw. aufhören/aufhören, etw. zu tun; **without ceasing** ununterbrochen.

❷ *v.t.* Ⓐ (*stop*) aufhören; **~ doing** *or* **to do sth.** aufhören, etw. zu tun; **~ to understand** nicht mehr verstehen; **sth. has ~d to exist** etw. existiert *od.* besteht nicht mehr; **we have ~d manufacturing tyres** wir stellen keine Reifen mehr her; **it never ~s to amaze me** ich kann nur immer darüber staunen; Ⓑ (*end*) aufhören mit; einstellen ‹Bemühungen, Versuche›; **~ 'fire** (*Mil.*) das Feuer einstellen.

❸ *n.* **without ~:** ununterbrochen; ohne Unterbrechung

**'ceasefire** *n.* Waffenruhe, *die;* (*signal*) Befehl zur Feuereinstellung

**ceaseless** /'siːslɪs/ *adj.* endlos; unaufhörlich ‹Anstrengung›; ständig ‹Wind, Regen, Lärm›

**ceaselessly** /'siːslɪslɪ/ *adv.* unaufhörlich; endlos ‹streiten›

**cedar** /'si:də(r)/ *n.* **A** Zeder, *die;* **~ of Lebanon** Libanonzeder, *die;* **B** ⇒ **cedarwood**

**'cedarwood** *n.* Zedernholz, *das*

**cede** /si:d/ *v.t.* (*surrender*) abtreten ‹Land, Rechte› (**to** *Dat.*, an + *Akk.*); einräumen ‹Privilegien› (**to** *Dat.*); (*grant*) überlassen ‹Land› (**to** *Dat.*); zugestehen ‹Rechte› (**to** *Dat.*)

**cedilla** /sɪ'dɪlə/ *n.* (*Ling.*) Cedille, *die*

**Ceefax** ® /'si:fæks/ *n.* (*Brit.*) Bildschirmtextdienst der BBC

**ceilidh** /'keɪlɪ/ *n.* (*Scot., Ir.*) *zwangloses Beisammensein zum Musizieren, Tanzen, Singen und Geschichtenerzählen*

**ceiling** /'si:lɪŋ/ *n.* **A** Decke, *die;* ⇒ *also* **hit** 1 B; **B** (*upper limit*) Maximum, *das;* **~ temperature** maximale Temperatur; **C** (*Aeronaut.*) Gipfelhöhe, *die;* **D** (*Meteorol.*) **[cloud] ~:** Wolkenuntergrenze, *die;* (*height*) Wolkenhöhe, *die*

**celandine** /'seləndaɪn/ *n.* (*Bot.*) **A** **[greater] ~:** [Großes] Schöllkraut; **B** **[lesser] ~:** Scharbockskraut, *das*

**celebrant** /'selɪbrənt/ *n.* (*Eccl.*) Zelebrant, *der*

**celebrate** /'selɪbreɪt/ **1** *v.t.* **A** (*observe*) feiern; **B** (*Eccl.*) zelebrieren, lesen ‹Messe›; **the wedding was ~d in St Paul's** die Hochzeit fand in St Paul's statt; **C** (*extol*) verherrlichen. **2** *v.i.* **A** feiern; **B** (*officiate at Eucharist*) die Eucharistie *od.* das Abendmahl feiern

**celebrated** /'selɪbreɪtɪd/ *adj.* gefeiert, berühmt ‹Person›; berühmt ‹Gebäude, Werk usw.›

**celebration** /selɪ'breɪʃn/ *n.* **A** (*observing*) Feiern, *das;* (*party etc.*) Feier, *die;* **in ~ of** aus Anlass (+ *Gen.*); (*with festivities*) zur Feier (+ *Gen.*); **the ~ of Easter** *etc.* das Feiern *od.* Begehen des Osterfestes *usw.;* **the ~ on her birthday** ihre Geburtstagsfeier; **the Coronation ~s** die Feierlichkeiten anlässlich der Krönung; **this calls for a ~!** das muss gefeiert werden!; **B** (*performing*) **the ~ of the wedding/christening** die Trauung[szeremonie]/Taufe; **the ~ of Communion** die Feier der Kommunion; **C** (*extolling*) Verherrlichung, *die*

**celebratory** /'selɪbreɪtərɪ/ *adj.* feierlich; Fest‹programm, -essen, -trunk›

**celebrity** /sɪ'lebrɪtɪ/ *n.* **A** *no pl.* (*fame*) Berühmtheit, *die;* **B** (*person*) Berühmtheit, *die;* **that ~ of stage and cinema** der Star von Bühne und Leinwand

**celeriac** /sɪ'lerɪæk/ *n.* [Wurzel-, Knollen]sellerie, *der od. die*

**celerity** /sɪ'lerɪtɪ/ *n.* (*literary*) Schnelligkeit, *die*

**celery** /'selərɪ/ *n.* [Bleich-, Stangen]sellerie, *der od. die*

**celesta** /sɪ'lestə/ *n.* (*Mus.*) Celesta, *die*

**celestial** /sɪ'lestɪəl/ *adj.* **A** (*heavenly*) himmlisch; **~ realm** Himmelreich, *das;* **B** (*of the sky*) Himmels-

**celibacy** /'selɪbəsɪ/ *n., no art.* Zölibat, *das od. der* (*Rel.*); Ehelosigkeit, *die*

**celibate** /'selɪbət/ **1** *adj.* zölibatär (*Rel.*); ehelos; **remain ~:** im Zölibat leben (*Rel.*); ehelos bleiben. **2** *n.* Zölibatär, *der* (*Rel.*)

**cell** /sel/ *n.* **A** (*also Biol., Electr.*) Zelle, *die;* **B** (*enclosed cavity*) Pore, *die;* (*fig.: compartment of brain*) Gehirnzelle, *die*

**cellar** /'selə(r)/ *n.* Keller, *der;* (*wine storage place, stock of wine*) [Wein]keller, *der;* **they keep a good ~:** sie haben einen guten Weinkeller

**cellist** /'tʃelɪst/ *n.* ▶ **1261** (*Mus.*) Cellist, *der*/Cellistin, *die*

**cello** /'tʃeləʊ/ *n., pl.* **~s** (*Mus.*) Cello, *das*

**Cellophane, cellophane** ® /'seləfeɪn/ *n.* Cellophan Ⓦ, *das*

**cellular** /'seljʊlə(r)/ *adj.* **A** porös ‹Mineral, Gestein, Substanz›; (*Biol.: of cells*) zellular; Zell-; **~ plant** Lagerpflanze, *die;* Zellenpflanze, *die* (*veralt.*); **B** (*with open texture*) luftdurchlässig; atmungsaktiv (*Werbespr.*)

**cellular: ~ 'phone** *n.* Mobiltelefon, *das;* **~ 'radio** *n.* Mobilfunk, *der*

**cellule** /'selju:l/ *n.* (*Anat.*) kleine Zelle; Cellula, *die* (*fachspr.*)

**cellulite** /'seljʊlaɪt/ *n., no pl., no indef. art.: überschüssige Fettdepots an Oberschenkeln und Hüften*

**cellulitis** /seljʊ'laɪtɪs/ *n.* ▶ **1232** (*Med.*) Zellulitis, *die;* Zellgewebsentzündung, *die*

**celluloid** /'seljʊlɔɪd/ *n.* **A** Zelluloid, *das;* **B** (*cinema films*) Kino, *das;* **~ hero** Leinwandheld, *der*

**cellulose** /'seljʊləʊs, 'seljʊləʊz/ *n.* **A** (*Chem.*) Zellulose, *die;* **B** *in popular use* **~ [lacquer]** Lack, *der;* **~ finish** Lackierung, *die*

**Celsius** /'selsɪəs/ *adj.* ▶ **1603** Celsius; **~ scale** Celsiusskala, *die*

**celt** /selt/ *n.* (*Archaeol.*) Kelt, *der*

**Celt** /kelt, selt/ *n.* Kelte, *der*/Keltin, *die*

**Celtic** /'keltɪk, 'seltɪk/ **1** *adj.* keltisch. **2** *n.* Keltisch, *das*

**Celtic: ~ 'cross** *n.* Radkreuz, *das;* **~ 'fringe** *n. keltische Randgebiete [Großbritanniens]*

**cement** /sɪ'ment/ **1** *n.* **A** (*Building*) Zement, *der;* (*mortar*) [Zement]mörtel, *der;* **B** (*sticking substance*) Klebstoff, *der;* (*for mending broken vases etc. also*) Kitt, *der;* (*fig.*) Band, *das;* Kitt, *der.* **2** *v.t.* **A** (*unite with binder*) mit Zement/Mörtel zusammenfügen; (*stick together*) zusammenkleben; (*fig.*) zusammenkitten; zementieren ‹Freundschaft, Beziehung›; **B** (*apply* **~** *to*) zementieren/mörteln

**cemetery** /'semɪtərɪ/ *n.* Friedhof, *der*

**C. Eng.** *abbr.* **chartered engineer**

**cenotaph** /'senətɑ:f, 'senətæf/ *n.* Kenotaph, *das;* Zenotaph, *das;* **the C~** (*Brit.*) *Mahnmal in London für die Gefallenen der beiden Weltkriege*

**censer** /'sensə(r)/ *n.* Rauchfass, *das*

**censor** /'sensə(r)/ **1** *n.* **A** (*also Roman Hist.*) Zensor, *der;* **get past the ~s** durch die Zensur kommen; **B** (*judge*) Kritiker, *der;* **C** (*Psych.*) Zensur, *die.* **2** *v.t.* **A** zensieren; **B** (*make changes in*) abändern

**censorious** /sen'sɔ:rɪəs/ *adj.* [übertrieben] kritisch; [übertrieben] scharf ‹Kritik, Kritiker›; **be ~ of sb./sth.** jmdn./etw. scharf kritisieren

**censorship** /'sensəʃɪp/ *n.* Zensur, *die*

**censure** /'senʃə(r)/ **1** *n.* Tadel, *der;* **~ of sth.** Tadel für etw.; **propose a vote of ~:** einen Tadelsantrag stellen. **2** *v.t.* tadeln

**census** /'sensəs/ *n.* Zählung, *die;* **[national] ~:** Volkszählung, *die;* Zensus, *der*

**cent** /sent/ *n.* ▶ **1328** Cent, *der;* **I don't** *or* **couldn't care a ~ about that** (*coll.*) das ist mir völlig egal (*ugs.*)

**cent.** *abbr.* **century** Jh.

**centaur** /'sentɔ:(r)/ *n.* (*Mythol.*) Zentaur, *der;* Kentaur, *der*

**centenarian** /sentɪ'neərɪən/ **1** *adj.* hundertjährig; (*over 100 years old*) mehr als hundert Jahre alt. **2** *n.* Hundertjährige, *der/die;* (*over 100 years old*) über Hundertjährige, *der/die;* **he/she lived to be a ~:** er/sie wurde hundert Jahre alt/über hundert Jahre alt

**centenary** /sen'ti:nərɪ, sen'tenərɪ/ **1** *adj.* **~ celebrations/festival** Hundertjahrfeier, *die.* **2** *n.* Hundertjahrfeier, *die;* (*birthday*) 100. Geburtstag

**centennial** /sen'tenɪəl/ **1** *adj.* (*100th*) hundertst...; (*lasting 100 years*) hundertjährig; (*occurring every 100 years*) Jahrhundert-. **2** *n.* ⇒ **centenary** 2

**center** (*Amer.*) ⇒ **centre**

**centering** /'sentərɪŋ/ (*Amer.*) ⇒ **centring**

**centi-** /'sentɪ/ *pref.* **A** (*one-hundredth*) Zenti-; **B** (*one hundred*) Hundert-/hundert-

**centigrade** /'sentɪgreɪd/ ▶ **1603** ⇒ **Celsius**

**centime** /'sɑ̃ti:m/ *n.* ▶ **1328** Centime, *der*

**centimetre** (*Brit.; Amer.:* **centimeter**) /'sentɪmi:tə(r)/ *n.* ▶ **928**, ▶ **1210**, ▶ **1284**, ▶ **1671** Zentimeter, *der*

**centipede** /'sentɪpi:d/ *n.* Hundertfüßer, *der* (*Zool.*); ≈ Tausendfüßler, *der*

**central** /'sentrl/ **1** *adj.* zentral; **be ~ to sth.** von zentraler Bedeutung für etw. sein; **in ~ London** im Zentrum von London; **in a ~ situation** in zentraler Lage; **the ~ part** *or* **portion of the apple/the earth** das Innere des Apfels/der Erde; **the ~ part of the town** das Zentrum der Stadt. **2** *n., no art.* (*Amer.*) Vermittlung, *die;* **call ~:** die Vermittlung anrufen

**Central: ~ African Re'public** *pr. n.* Zentralafrikanische Republik; **~ A'merica** *pr. n.* Mittelamerika (*das*); **~ A'merican** **1** *adj.* mittelamerikanisch; **2** *n.* Mittelamerikaner, *der*/-amerikanerin, *die;* **~ 'Europe** *pr. n.* Mitteleuropa (*das*); **~ Euro'pean** **1** *adj.* mitteleuropäisch; **2** *n.* Mitteleuropäer, *der*/-europäerin, *die;* **c~ 'heating** *n.* Zentralheizung, *die*

**centralisation, centralise** ⇒ **centraliz-**

**centralization** /sentrəlaɪ'zeɪʃn/ *n.* Zentralisierung, *die*

**centralize** /'sentrəlaɪz/ *v.t.* zentralisieren; **~ records** Unterlagen zentral erfassen

**central 'locking** *n.* (*Motor Veh.*) Zentralverriegelung, *die*

**centrally** /'sentrəlɪ/ *adv.* **A** (*in centre*) zentral; **B** (*in leading place*) an zentraler Stelle

**central: ~ 'nervous system** *n.* (*Anat., Zool.*) Zentralnervensystem, *das;* **~ processing unit** *n.* (*Computing*) Zentraleinheit, *die;* **~ reser'vation** *n.* Mittelstreifen, *der;* **~ 'station** *n.* (*Railw.*) Hauptbahnhof, *der*

**centre** /'sentə(r)/ (*Brit.*) **1** *n.* **A** Mitte, *die;* (*of circle, globe*) Mitte, *die;* Zentrum, *das;* Mittelpunkt, *der;* **be the ~ of attention** im Mittelpunkt des Interesses stehen; **be in the ~ of things** im Brennpunkt des Geschehens sein; **B** (*town ~*) Innenstadt, *die;* Stadtzentrum, *das;* **C** (*of rotation*) Drehpunkt, *der;* (*in lathe etc.*) Spitzdocke, *die* (*Technik*); **D** (*nucleus*) Zentrum, *das;* **E** (*serving an area*) Zentrum, *das;* **university careers ~:** Studienberatung, *die;* **F** (*filling of chocolate*) Füllung, *die;* **G** (*Polit.*) Mitte, *die;* **left of ~:** links von der Mitte; **H** (*Sport: player*) Mittelfeldspieler, *der*/-spielerin, *die;* (*Basketball*) Center, *der;* (*Football, Hockey: kick or hit*) Flanke, *die;* **he kicked/hit a ~:** er schlug eine Flanke [nach innen]; **I** **~ of attraction** (*Phys.*) Zentrum der Anziehungskraft; **she likes to be the ~ of attraction** (*fig.*) sie steht gern im Mittelpunkt [des Interesses]; **sth. is a [great] ~ of attraction** (*fig.*) etw. ist eine [große] Attraktion; ⇒ *also* **gravity** D; **mass**[2] 1 F; **J** ⇒ **centring.**

**2** *adj.* mittler...; **~ party** (*Polit.*) Partei der Mitte; **the ~ point of the circle/triangle** der Mittelpunkt des Kreises/Dreiecks.

**3** *v.i.* **~ in sth.** seinen Mittelpunkt in etw. (*Dat.*) haben; **~ on sth.** sich auf etw. (*Akk.*) konzentrieren; **the novel ~s on Prague** Prag steht im Mittelpunkt des Romans; **the discussion ~d on pollution** im Mittelpunkt der Diskussion stand die Umweltverschmutzung; **~ [a]round sth.** um etw. kreisen; sich um etw. drehen.

**4** *v.t.* **A** (*place in ~*) in der Mitte anbringen; in der Mitte aufhängen ‹Bild, Lampe›; zentrieren ‹Überschrift›; **B** (*concentrate*) **be ~d/~ sth. in a place** einen Ort zum Mittelpunkt haben/von etw. machen; **~ sth. on sth.** etw. auf etw. (*Akk.*) konzentrieren; **~ a novel [a]round sth.** etw. in den Mittelpunkt eines Romans stellen; **be ~d [a]round sth.** etw. zum Mittelpunkt haben; **C** (*Football, Hockey*) [nach innen] flanken

**centre: ~ bit** *n.* Zentrumbohrer, *der* (*Technik*); **~board** *n.* (*Naut.*) Schwert, *das;* **~ circle** *n.* (*Football, Basketball, Ice Hockey*) Mittelkreis, *der;* **~fold** *n.* Faltblatt in der Mitte; **~ 'forward** *n.* (*Sport*) Mittelstürmer, *der*/-stürmerin, *die;* **~ 'half** *n.* (*Sport*) Mittelläufer, *der*/-läuferin, *die;* (*Football also*) Vorstopper, *der*/-stopperin, *die;* **~piece** *n.* (*ornament*) ≈ Tafelschmuck, *der* (*in der Mitte der Tafel*); (*principal item*) Kernstück, *das;* **~ 'spread** *n.* Doppelseite in der Mitte; **~ three-'quarter** *n.* (*Rugby*) Innendreiviertel[spieler], *der*

**centrifugal** /sen'trɪfjʊgl/ *adj.* zentrifugal; **~ force** Zentrifugalkraft, *die;* Fliehkraft, *die*

**centrifuge** /'sentrɪfju:dʒ/ **1** *n.* Zentrifuge, *die.* **2** *v.t.* zentrifugieren

**centring** /'sentrɪŋ/ *n.* (*Building*) Lehrgerüst, *das*

C

**centripetal** /sen'trɪpɪtl/ *adj.* zentripetal; ~ **force** Zentripetalkraft, *die*

**centrism** /'sentrɪzm/ *n.* (*Polit. etc.*) gemäßigter Kurs; Zentrismus, *der* (*abwertend*)

**centrist** /'sentrɪst/ *n.* (*Polit. etc.*) Vertreter/Vertreterin eines gemäßigten Kurses; Zentrist, *der*/Zentristin, *die* (*abwertend*)

**centurion** /sen'tjʊərɪən/ *n.* (*Roman Hist.*) Zenturio, *der*

**century** /'sentʃərɪ/ *n.* **A** ▶1055 (*hundred-year period from a year ..00*) Jahrhundert, *das;* (*hundred years*) hundert Jahre; **~-old** hundertjährig; **centuries-old** jahrhundertealt; seit Jahrhunderten bestehend ‹Gebäude usw.›; **B** (*Cricket*) hundert Läufe; (*more than a hundred*) über hundert Läufe; **C** (*hundred*) Hundert, *das;* **a ~ of** hundert; **D** (*Roman Hist.*) Zenturie, *die*

**cephalopod** /'sefələpɒd/ *n.* (*Zool.*) Kopffüßer, *der*

**ceramic** /sɪ'ræmɪk/ **1** *adj.* keramisch; Keramik‹vase, -kacheln›. **2** *n.* Keramik, *die*

**ceramics** /sɪ'ræmɪks/ *n., no pl.* Keramik, *die*

**Cerberus** /'sɜːbərəs/ *n.* Zerberus, *der*

**cereal** /'sɪərɪəl/ **1** *n.* **A** (*kind of grain*) Getreide, *das;* **B** (*breakfast dish*) Getreideflocken *Pl.* **2** *adj.* Getreide-; **~ grasses** Getreidepflanzen

**cerebellum** /serɪ'beləm/ *n.* (*Anat.*) Kleinhirn, *das;* Cerebellum, *das* (*fachspr.*)

**cerebral** /'serɪbrl/ *adj.* **A** ▶1232 (*of the brain*) Gehirn‹tumor, -blutung, -schädigung›; zerebral (*Anat.*); **B** (*appealing to intellect, intellectual*) intellektuell

**cerebral 'palsy** *n.* ▶1232 (*Med.*) Zerebralparese, *die;* zerebrale Kinderlähmung

**cerebrate** /'serɪbreɪt/ *v.i.* (*literary*) nachdenken

**cerebration** /serɪ'breɪʃn/ *n.* Gehirntätigkeit, *die*

**cerebrum** /'serɪbrəm/ *n.* (*Anat.*) Großhirn, *das;* Cerebrum, *das* (*Anat.*)

**ceremonial** /serɪ'məʊnɪəl/ **1** *adj.* feierlich; (*prescribed for ceremony*) zeremoniell; **~ clothing** Festkleidung, *die.* **2** *n.* Zeremoniell, *das*

**ceremonially** /serɪ'məʊnɪəlɪ/ *adv.* feierlich; festlich ‹gekleidet›

**ceremonious** /serɪ'məʊnɪəs/ *adj.* formell; förmlich ‹Höflichkeit›; (*according to prescribed ceremony*) zeremoniell

**ceremoniously** /serɪ'məʊnɪəslɪ/ *adv.* formell; förmlich; **he bowed ~:** er verbeugte sich mit aller Förmlichkeit

**ceremoniousness** /serɪ'məʊnɪəsnɪs/ *n., no pl.* Förmlichkeit, *die*

**ceremony** /'serɪmənɪ/ *n.* **A** Feier, *die;* (*formal act*) Zeremonie, *die;* **opening/prize-giving ~:** Eröffnungsfeier, *die*/Preisverleihung, *die;* **Christmas ~:** Weihnachtsfeier, *die;* **B** *no pl., no art.* (*formalities*) Zeremoniell, *das;* **stand on ~:** Wert auf Förmlichkeiten legen; **without [great] ~:** ohne große Förmlichkeit. ⇒ *also* **master** 1 F

**cerise** /sə'riːz, sə'riːs/ **1** *adj.* kirschrot; cerise (*fachspr.*). **2** *n.* Kirschrot, *das;* Cerise, *das* (*fachspr.*)

**cerium** /'sɪərɪəm/ *n.* (*Chem.*) Cer, *das;* Zer, *das*

**cert** /sɜːt/ *n.* (*Brit. coll.*) **A** **that's a ~:** das steht fest; **B** (*as winner*) todsicherer Tipp (*ugs.*); **be tipped as a/look [like] a ~:** als todsicherer Tipp gelten; **C** (*for appointment*) **be a ~ for the job/as the next party leader** die Stelle mit Sicherheit kriegen/mit Sicherheit der nächste Parteiführer werden; **his record makes him a ~ for the team** durch seine Leistung kommt er bestimmt in die Mannschaft

**cert.** /sɜːt/ *abbr.* **certificate**

**certain** /'sɜːtn, 'sɜːtɪn/ *adj.* **A** (*settled*) bestimmt ‹Zeitpunkt›; **B** (*unerring*) sicher; (*sure to happen*) unvermeidlich; sicher ‹Tod›; **the course of the tragedy is ~:** der Verlauf der Tragödie steht fest; **for ~:** bestimmt; **I [don't] know for ~ when ...:** ich weiß [nicht] genau, wann ...; **I can't say for ~ that ...:** ich kann nicht mit Bestimmtheit sagen, dass ...; **make ~ of sth.** (*ensure*) für etw. sorgen; (*examine and establish*) sich einer Sache (*Gen.*) vergewissern; **we made ~ of a seat on the train** wir sicherten uns einen Sitzplatz im Zug; **we made ~ of a timely arrival** wir sorgten dafür, dass wir rechtzeitig ankamen; **the doctor had to make absolutely ~ of his diagnosis** der Arzt musste in seiner Diagnose absolut sichergehen; **C** (*indisputable*) unbestreitbar; **D** (*confident*) sicher; **I'm not ~ of** *or* **about the colour** was die Farbe betrifft, da bin ich mir nicht sicher; **of that I'm quite ~:** dessen bin ich [mir] ganz sicher; **we're not ~ about emigrating** wir wissen nicht [recht], ob wir auswandern sollen/können; **are you ~ of the facts?** sind Sie Ihrer Sache sicher?; **she wasn't ~ about** *or* **of her love for him** sie war [sich (*Dat.*)] nicht sicher, ob sie ihn liebte; **be ~ that ...:** sicher sein, dass ...; **E** **be ~ to do sth.** etw. bestimmt tun; **people were ~ to notice that she'd been crying** die Leute würden bestimmt merken, dass sie geweint hatte; **F** (*particular but as yet unspecified*) bestimmt; **G** (*slight; existing but probably not already known*) gewiss; **to a ~ extent** in gewisser Weise; **a ~ Mr Smith** ein gewisser Herr Smith

**certainly** /'sɜːtnlɪ, 'sɜːtɪnlɪ/ **A** (*admittedly*) sicher[lich]; (*definitely*) bestimmt; (*clearly*) offensichtlich; **B** (*in answer*) [aber] gewiss; [aber] sicher; **[most] ~ 'not!** auf [gar] keinen Fall!

**certainty** /'sɜːtntɪ, 'sɜːtɪntɪ/ *n.* **A** **be a ~:** sicher sein; feststehen; **regard sth. as a ~:** etw. für sicher halten; **it isn't as much of a ~ now as it was** es ist jetzt nicht mehr ganz so sicher; **B** (*absolute conviction, sure fact, assurance*) Gewissheit, *die;* **~ of** *or* **about sth./sb.** Gewissheit über etw./jmdn.; **~ that ...:** Gewissheit [darüber], dass ...; **with some ~:** mit einiger Sicherheit; **with ~, for a ~:** mit Sicherheit *od.* Bestimmtheit; **have the ~ of accommodation/sunshine** die Gewissheit haben, eine Unterkunft zu bekommen/dass die Sonne scheint

**Cert. Ed.** /sɜːt 'ed/ *abbr.* (*Brit.*) **Certificate in Education** ≈ *Berechtigung, an Grund- bzw. Hauptschulen zu unterrichten*

**certifiable** /'sɜːtɪfaɪəbl/ *adj.* **A** nachweislich; überprüfbar ‹Ergebnis›; **what makes a person ~ as dead?** wann kann jemand für tot erklärt werden?; **B** (*as insane*) unzurechnungsfähig ‹Person›; **~ insanity** Unzurechnungsfähigkeit, *die*

**certifiably** /'sɜːtɪfaɪəblɪ/ *adv.* **~ [in]sane** [un]zurechnungsfähig

**certificate** **1** /sə'tɪfɪkət/ *n.* Urkunde, *die;* (*of action performed*) Schein, *der;* (*Cinemat.*) *Einblendung zu Beginn eines Films, die angibt, für welches Publikum der Film freigegeben ist;* **doctor's ~:** ärztliches Attest; **teaching ~** *Zeugnis über eine Ausbildung als Lehrer;* **~ of satisfactory performance** Zeugnis über zufriedenstellende Leistungen; **he gained a ~ of merit in his exam** er bestand die Prüfung mit Auszeichnung. **2** /sə'tɪfɪkeɪt/ *v.t.* zulassen

**Certificate of Secondary Edu'cation** *n.* (*Brit. Hist.*) ≈ Volksschulabschluss, *der*

**certification** /sɜːtɪfɪ'keɪʃn/ *n.* Bestätigung, *die;* (*as teacher etc.*) Zulassung, *die;* (*as insane*) Bescheinigung der Unzurechnungsfähigkeit; (*certificate*) Bescheinigung, *die*

**certified** /'sɜːtɪfaɪd/ *adj.* **A** zugelassen; **~ as unfit for human habitation** für unbewohnbar erklärt; **she's a ~ driving instructor** sie ist als Fahrlehrerin zugelassen; **state-~:** staatlich anerkannt; **this film is ~ as unsuitable for children** dieser Film ist als nicht jugendfrei eingestuft worden; **B** (*declared insane*) unzurechnungsfähig

**certified:** **~ 'cheque** *n.* (*Finance*) bestätigter Scheck; **~ 'mail** *n.* (*Amer.*) **send sth. by ~ mail** etw. per Einschreiben schicken; **an item of ~ mail** eine Einschreibesendung; **~ public ac'countant** *n.* (*Amer.*) Wirtschaftsprüfer, *der*/-prüferin, *die*

**certify** /'sɜːtɪfaɪ/ *v.t.* **A** bescheinigen; bestätigen; (*declare by certificate*) berechtigen; **~ sb. as competent** jmds. Befähigung bescheinigen *od.* bestätigen; **this is to ~ that ...:** hiermit wird bescheinigt *od.* bestätigt, dass ...; **this building has been certified [as] Crown property** dieses Gebäude ist zum Eigentum der Krone erklärt worden; **certified as a true copy** beglaubigt; **B** (*declare insane*) für unzurechnungsfähig erklären; **you ought to be certified** (*coll.*) du bist wohl verrückt (*salopp*)

**certitude** /'sɜːtɪtjuːd/ *n.* Gewissheit, *die*

**cervical** /'sɜːvɪkl, sɜː'vaɪkl/ *adj.* (*Anat.*) **A** (*of neck*) Hals-; zervikal (*Anat.*); **B** (*of cervix*) Gebärmutterhals-; zervikal (*Anat.*); **~ smear test** [Gebärmutterhals]abstrich, *der*

**cervix** /'sɜːvɪks/ *n., pl.* **cervices** /'sɜːvɪsiːz/ (*Anat.: of uterus*) Gebärmutterhals, *der*

**Cesarean, Cesarian** (*Amer.*) ⇒ **Caesarean**

**cessation** /se'seɪʃn/ *n.* Ende, *das;* (*interval*) Nachlassen, *das*

**cession** /'seʃn/ *n.* Abtretung, *die*

**cesspit** /'sespɪt/ *n.* **A** (*refuse pit*) Abfallgrube, *die;* **B** ⇒ **cesspool**

**cesspool** /'sespuːl/ *n.* Senk- *od.* Jauchegrube, *die;* (*fig.*) Sumpf, *der;* **~ of iniquity** Sündenpfuhl, *der*

**cetacean** /sɪ'teɪʃn/ *n.* (*Zool.*) Waltier, *das*

**Ceylon** /sɪ'lɒn/ *pr. n.* (*Hist.*) Ceylon (*das*)

**cf.** *abbr.* **compare** vgl.

**c.f.** *abbr.* **carried forward** Vortrag (*Buchf.*)

**CFC** *abbr.* (*Chem., Ecol.*) **chlorofluorocarbon** FCKW, *das*

**ch.** *abbr.* **A** **chapter** Kap.; **B** **church** K.

**cha** /tʃɑː/ ⇒ **char**[3]

**cha-cha** /'tʃɑːtʃɑː/ **1** *n.* Cha-Cha-Cha, *der.* **2** *v.i.* Cha-Cha-Cha tanzen

**Chad** /tʃæd/ *pr. n.* Tschad, *der*

**chafe** /tʃeɪf/ **1** *v.t.* (*make sore*) aufscheuern; wund scheuern; (*rub*) reiben; (*fig.*) reizen; ärgern. **2** *v.i.* ‹Person, Tier:› sich scheuern; ‹Gegenstand:› scheuern (**[up]on, against** an + *Dat.*); **my skin ~s easily** meine Haut wird leicht wund; **~ at** *or* **under sth.** (*fig.*) sich über etw. (*Akk.*) ärgern

**chafer** /'tʃeɪfə(r)/ *n.* (*Zool.*) [Mai]käfer, *der*

**chaff** /tʃɑːf/ **1** *v.t.* **~ sb. about sth.** jmdn. wegen etw. necken *od.* (*ugs.*) mit etw. aufziehen. **2** *v.i.* scherzen; flachsen (*ugs.*). **3** *n.* **A** (*banter*) Neckerei, *die;* Flachserei, *die* (*ugs.*); **enough of the ~!** genug geflachst! (*ugs.*); **B** (*husks of corn, etc.*) Spreu, *die;* ⇒ *also* **wheat**; **C** (*cattle food*) Häcksel, *das*

**chaffinch** /'tʃæfɪnʃ/ *n.* (*Ornith.*) Buchfink, *der*

**chagrin** /'ʃægrɪn/ **1** *n.* Kummer, *der;* (*annoyance*) Verdruss, *der;* **much to sb.'s ~:** zu jmds. großen Kummer *od.* Verdruss. **2** *v.t.* bekümmern; **be** *or* **feel ~ed at** *or* **by sth.** niedergeschlagen *od.* bekümmert sein wegen etw.

**chain** /tʃeɪn/ **1** *n.* **A** Kette, *die;* (*fig.*) Fessel, *die;* (*of flowers*) Kranz, der; (*to stop skidding*) Schneekette, *die;* (*jewellery*) [Hals]kette, *die;* (*barrier*) Sperrkette, *die;* **~ of office** Amtskette, *die;* **be in ~s** in Ketten sein; **be/put on a ~:** an der Kette sein/an die Kette legen; **door ~:** Tür- *od.* Sicherungskette, *die;* **B** (*series*) Kette, *die;* Reihe, *die;* **~ of events** Reihe *od.* Kette von Ereignissen; **~ of ideas** Gedankenkette, *die;* **~ of mountains** Gebirgskette, *die;* **~ of islands/lakes** Insel-/Seenkette, *die;* **~ of shops/hotels** Laden-/Hotelkette, *die;* **C** (*measurement*) Chain, *das* (≈ *20 m*).
**2** *v.t.* (*lit. or fig.*) **~ sb./sth. to sth.** jmdn./etw. an etw. (*Akk.*) [an]ketten; **the dog must be kept ~ed up** der Hund muss an der Kette bleiben

**chain:** **~ armour** *n.* Kettenpanzer, *der;* **~ gang** *n.* Trupp aneinander geketteter Sträflinge; **~ letter** *n.* Kettenbrief, *der;* **~-link fencing** *n.* Maschendraht, *der;* **~ mail** *n.* Kettenpanzer, *der;* **~ re'action** *n.* (*Chem., Phys.; also fig.*) Kettenreaktion, *die;* **~saw** *n.* Kettensäge, *die;* **~-smoke** *v.t. & i.* Kette rauchen (*ugs.*); **~-smoker** *n.* Kettenraucher, *der*/-raucherin, *die;* **~-smoking** *n.* Kettenrauchen, *das;* **~ stitch** *n.* Kettenstich, *der;*

~ **store** *n.* Kettenladen, *der (Wirtsch.)*; ~ **wheel** *n.* Kettenblatt, *das*

**chair** /tʃeə(r)/ ❶ *n.* **A** Stuhl, *der; (armchair, easy* ~) Sessel, *der;* **take a** ~ **[please]** bitte nehmen Sie Platz; **hairdresser's** ~**:** Frisierstuhl, *der;* **B** *(professorship)* Lehrstuhl, *der; (of authority)* [Thron]sessel, *der;* **C** *(at meeting)* Vorsitz, *der; (*~*man)* Vorsitzende, *der/die;* **be** *or* **preside in/take the** ~**:** den Vorsitz haben *od.* führen/übernehmen; **leave** *or* **vacate the** ~**:** den Vorsitz abgeben; **address the** ~**:** den Vorsitzenden ansprechen. ❷ *v.t.* **A** *(preside over)* den Vorsitz haben *od.* führen bei; ~ **a meeting** den Vorsitz bei einer Versammlung haben *od.* führen; **the meeting was** ~**ed by ...:** den Vorsitz bei der Versammlung hatte *od.* führte...; **B** *(Brit.: carry as victor) im Triumph tragen*

**chair:** ~ **back** *n.* Rückenlehne, *die;* ~**lift** *n.* Sessellift, *der*

**chairman** /ˈtʃeəmən/ *n., pl.* **chairmen** /ˈtʃeəmən/ **A** ▶ **1261**, ▶ **1617** Vorsitzende, *der/die;* Präsident, *der*/Präsidentin, *die;* **Mr/Madam C**~**:** Herr Vorsitzender/Frau Vorsitzende; ~ **of the firm** Firmenleiter, *der;* ~**'s report** Geschäftsbericht, *der;* ⇒ *also* **board** 1 J; **B** *(master of ceremonies)* Conferencier, *der*

**chairmanship** /ˈtʃeəmənʃɪp/ *n.* Vorsitz, *der*

**chair:** ~**person** *n.* Vorsitzende, *der/die;* ~**woman** *n.* Vorsitzende, *die*

**chaise** /ʃeɪz/ *n. (esp. Hist.)* Cab, *das;* **closed** *or* **covered** ~**:** Chaise, *die*

**chaise longue** /ʃeɪz ˈlɒŋg/ *n.* Chaiselongue, *die*

**chalcedony** /kælˈsedənɪ/ *n. (Min.)* Chalzedon, *der*

**chalet** /ˈʃæleɪ/ *n.* Chalet, *das*

**chalet ˈbungalow** *n. einem Chalet ähnliches, aber kleineres Haus mit tief heruntergezogenem Satteldach*

**chalice** /ˈtʃælɪs/ *n. (poet./Eccl.)* Kelch, *der*

**chalk** /tʃɔːk/ ❶ *n.* Kreide, *die; (Geol.)* Oberkreide, *die;* **a drawing in** ~/~**s** eine Kreidezeichnung; **as white as** ~**:** kreidebleich; **by a long** ~ *(Brit. coll.)* bei weitem; mit Abstand; **not by a long** ~ *(Brit. coll.)* bei weitem nicht; **as different as** ~ **and cheese** so verschieden wie Tag und Nacht. ❷ *v.t.* mit Kreide schreiben/malen/zeichnen *usw.*

~ **ˈout** *v.t.* [mit Kreide] zeichnen; **she had her future career** ~**ed out** *(fig.)* ihr künftiger Lebensweg war vorgezeichnet

~ **ˈup** *v.t.* **A** [mit Kreide] an- *od.* aufschreiben; **B** *(fig.: register)* zu verzeichnen haben, für sich verbuchen können ‹Erfolg:› **C** ~ **it up** *(fig.)* es auf die Rechnung setzen; ~ **it up to sb.'s account** *(fig.)* es auf jmds. Rechnung setzen

**chalk:** ~**-pit** *n.* Kalksteinbruch, *der;* ~**-stripe** *n. (Textiles)* Kreidestreifen, *der*

**chalky** /ˈtʃɔːkɪ/ *adj.* kalkig

**challenge** /ˈtʃælɪndʒ/ ❶ *n.* **A** *(to contest or duel; also Sport)* Herausforderung, *die* **(to** *Gen.*); **issue a** ~ **to sb.** jmdn. herausfordern; **B** *(call for a response)* Herausforderung, *die* **(to** an + *Akk.*); **the main** ~ **facing us today** die größte Herausforderung *od.* Aufgabe für uns heute; **rise to a** ~**:** sich einer Herausforderung gewachsen zeigen; **pose a** ~ **to sb.** für jmdn. eine Herausforderung bedeuten; **C** *(of sentry)* Aufforderung, *die; (call for password)* Anruf, *der;* **D** *(person, task)* Herausforderung, *die;* **accept a** ~**:** sich einer Herausforderung *(Dat.)* stellen; **hold a** ~ **for sb.** einen Reiz für jmdn. haben; **E** *(Law: exception taken)* Ablehnung, *die; (Amer.: to a vote)* Anfechtung, *die.*
❷ *v.t.* **A** *(to contest etc.)* herausfordern; ~ **sb. to a duel** jmdn. zum Duell [heraus]fordern; ~ **sb. to a match/fight/debate** jmdn. zu einem Wettkampf/zum Kampf/zu einem Streitgespräch herausfordern; ~ **the world record** versuchen, einen neuen Weltrekord aufzustellen; **B** *(fig.)* auffordern; ~ **sb.'s authority** jmds. Autorität *od.* Befugnis infrage stellen; **C** *(demand password etc. from)* ‹Wachposten:› anrufen; **D** *(Law)* ~ **a juryman** einen Geschworenen ablehnen; ~ **[the] evidence [of a witness]** gegen die Aussage [eines Zeugen] Einspruch erheben; **E** *(question)* infrage stellen; anzweifeln; ~ **sb.'s right to do sth.** jmds. Recht anzweifeln, etw. zu tun; ~ **a belief/principle** eine Glaubenslehre/ein Prinzip infrage stellen; ~ **a verdict** ein Urteil kritisieren; ~ **an opinion** einer Ansicht widersprechen; **F** *(stimulate)* erregen

**ˈchallenge cup** *n.* Wanderpokal, *der*

**challenged** /ˈtʃælɪndʒd/ *adj. (euphem. or joc.)* behindert; **physically/vertically** ~**:** körperbehindert/kleinwüchsig; **mentally** ~**:** geistig behindert

**challenger** /ˈtʃælɪndʒə(r)/ *n.* Herausforderer, *der*/Herausforderin, *die*

**challenging** /ˈtʃælɪndʒɪŋ/ *adj.* herausfordernd; fesselnd, faszinierend ‹Problem›; anspruchsvoll ‹Arbeit›

**chamber** /ˈtʃeɪmbə(r)/ *n.* **A** *(poet./arch.: room)* Gemach, *das (geh.); (bedroom)* [Schlaf]gemach, *das (geh.);* **B** *in pl. (Brit.) (set of rooms)* Geschäftsräume *Pl.; (lawyer's rooms)* ≈ Praxisräume *Pl.; (judge's room)* ≈ Amtszimmer, *das;* **in** ~**s** ≈ im Amtszimmer; **C** *(of deliberative or judicial body)* Sitzungszimmer, *das;* Sitzungssaal, *der;* **Upper/Lower C**~ *(Parl.)* Ober-/Unterhaus, *das;* **D** *(Anat.; in machinery, esp. of gun; artificial compartment)* Kammer, *die;* ~ **of the heart/eye** Herz-/Augenkammer, *die.* ⇒ *also* **cloud chamber**; **horror** 1 C

**ˈchamber concert** *n.* Kammerkonzert, *das*

**chamberlain** /ˈtʃeɪmbəlɪn/ *n.* Kammerherr, *der; (of corporation etc.)* [Stadt]kämmerer, *der;* **Lord Great C**~ **[of England]** *(Brit.) Hofbeamter mit bestimmten zeremoniellen Aufgaben;* **Lord C**~ **[of the Household]** *(Brit.) Vorsteher des königlichen Hofstaates*

**chamber:** ~**maid** *n.* ▶ **1261** Zimmermädchen, *das;* ~ **music** *n.* Kammermusik, *die;* **C**~ **of ˈCommerce** *n.* Industrie- und Handelskammer, *die;* ~ **orchestra** *n.* Kammerorchester, *das;* ~ **pot** *n.* Nachttopf, *der*

**chameleon** /kəˈmiːlɪən/ *n. (Zool.; also fig.)* Chamäleon, *das*

**chamfer** /ˈtʃæmfə(r)/ ❶ *v.t.* abfasen *(Technik).* ❷ *n.* Fase, *die (Technik)*

**chamois** /ˈʃæmwɑː/ *n., pl. same* /ˈʃæmwɑːz/ **A** *(Zool.)* Gämse, *die;* **B** *(leather)* Chamois[leder], *das;* ~ **leather** /ˈʃæmwɑː-, ˈʃæmɪ-/ Chamoisleder, *das*

**chamomile** ⇒ **camomile**

**champ**[1] /tʃæmp/ ❶ *v.t.* ‹Pferd:› [geräuschvoll] kauen ‹Futter›; ‹Pferd:› [geräuschvoll] kauen auf (+ *Dat.*) ‹Gebiss›; ‹Person:› [geräuschvoll] kauen. ❷ *v.i.* [geräuschvoll] kauen **(on, at** an, auf + *Dat.*); **be** ~**ing [at the bit] to do sth.** *(fig.)* voll Ungeduld darauf brennen, etw. zu tun

**champ**[2] *(coll.)* ⇒ **champion** 1 B, C

**champagne** /ʃæmˈpeɪn/ *n.* Sekt, *der; (from C*~*)* Champagner, *der*

**champagne:** ~**-coloured** *adj.* champagnerfarben; ~ **glass** *n.* Sektglas, *das*

**champers** /ˈʃæmpəz/ *n. (Brit. coll.)* Schampus, *der (ugs.)*

**champion** /ˈtʃæmpɪən/ ❶ *n.* **A** *(defender)* Verfechter, *der*/Verfechterin, *die;* **he is a** ~ **of the poor** er ist ein Anwalt der Armen; **B** *(Sport)* Meister, *der*/Meisterin, *die;* Champion, *der;* **the ice skating/discus** ~**:** der Meister/die Meisterin im Eiskunstlauf/Diskuswurf; **world** ~**:** Weltmeister, *der*/-meisterin, *die;* **the world lightweight** ~**:** der Weltmeister im Leichtgewicht; **C** *(animal or plant best in contest)* Sieger, *der;* **be a** ~**:** prämiert *od.* preisgekrönt sein; **D** *attrib.* ~ **dog** preisgekrönter Hund; ~ **boxer** Champion im Boxen.
❷ *v.t.* verfechten ‹Sache›; ~ **a person** sich für eine Person einsetzen.
❸ *adj., adv. (N. Engl. coll.)* klasse *(ugs.)*

**championship** /ˈtʃæmpɪənʃɪp/ *n.* **A** *(Sport)* Meisterschaft, *die;* **defend the** ~**:** den Titel *od.* die Meisterschaft verteidigen; **the world figure skating** ~**s** die Weltmeisterschaften im Eiskunstlauf; *attrib.* ~ **title/match** Titel, *der*/Titelkampf, *der;* **compete for the** ~ **title** um den Titel kämpfen; **B** *(advocacy)* ~ **of a cause** Engagement für eine Sache

**chance** /tʃɑːns/ ❶ *n.* **A** *no art. (fortune)* Zufall, *der; attrib.* Zufalls-; zufällig; ~ **encounter** Zufallsbegegnung, *die;* **as** ~ **would have it** wie der Zufall *od.* das Schicksal es wollte; **leave sth. to** ~, **let** ~ **decide** es dem Zufall *od.* Schicksal überlassen; **trust to** ~**:** auf den Zufall *od.* sein Glück vertrauen; **game of** ~**:** Glücksspiel, *das;* **the result of** ~**:** [reiner] Zufall; **pure** ~**:** reiner Zufall; **by** ~**:** zufällig; durch Zufall; **it's not just** ~**:** es ist kein Zufall; **B** *(trick of fate)* Zufall, *der;* **by [any]** ~, **by some** ~ **or other** zufällig; **could you by any** ~ **give me a lift?** könntest du mich vielleicht mitnehmen?; **C** *(opportunity)* Chance, *die;* Gelegenheit, *die; (possibility)* Chance, *die;* Möglichkeit, *die;* **give sb. a** ~**:** jmdm. eine Chance geben; **give sb. half a** ~**:** jmdm. nur die [geringste] Chance geben; **given the** ~**:** wenn ich *usw.* die Gelegenheit dazu hätte; **give sth. a** ~ **to do sth.** einer Sache *(Dat.)* Gelegenheit geben, etw. zu tun; **offer sb. the** ~ **of doing sth.** jmdm. die Möglichkeit *od.* Gelegenheit bieten, etw. zu tun; **get a/the** ~ **to do sth.** eine/die Gelegenheit haben, etw. zu tun; ~ **would be a fine thing!** *(coll.)* keine Chance! *(ugs.)*; **have a** ~ **to do sth., have the** ~ **of doing sth.** die Gelegenheit *od.* Möglichkeit haben, etw. zu tun; **this is my big** ~**:** das ist die Chance für mich; **now's your** ~**!** das ist deine Chance!; **have no** ~ **of doing** *or* **to do sth.** keine Gelegenheit haben, etw. zu tun; **not have much** ~ **of doing** *or* **to do sth.** kaum eine Gelegenheit haben, etw. zu tun; **on the [off]** ~ **of doing sth./that ...:** in der vagen Hoffnung, etw. zu tun/dass ...; **be in with a** ~ **of doing sth.** [gute] Aussichten haben, etw. zu tun; **stand a** ~ **of doing sth.** die Chance haben, etw. zu tun; **no** ~**!** *(coll.)* unmöglich!; ist nicht drin! *(ugs.)*; **D** *in sing. or pl. (probability)* **have a good/fair** ~ **of doing sth.** gute Aussichten haben, etw. zu tun; **[is there] any** ~ **of your attending?** besteht eine Chance, dass Sie kommen können?; **what** ~ **[of a breakthrough] is there?** wie stehen die Chancen [für einen Durchbruch]? **there is every/not the slightest** ~ **that...** es ist sehr gut möglich/es besteht keine Möglichkeit, dass ...; **there's a good/fair** ~ **of its working out** es besteht eine gute Chance, dass es gelingt; **there's little** ~ **of its being a success** es wird wohl kaum ein Erfolg werden; **the** ~**s are that ...** es ist wahrscheinlich, dass ...; **the** ~**s are against it** es ist unwahrscheinlich; **the** ~**s against its happening are slight** die Chancen, dass es nicht geschieht, sind gering; **the** ~**s are ten to one against its being a success** die Chancen, dass es ein Erfolg sein wird, stehen [nur] 1 zu 10; **sb.'s** ~**s are slim** jmds. Aussichten sind gering; **E** *(risk)* **take one's** ~**:** es darauf ankommen lassen; **take a** ~/~**s** ein Risiko/Risiken eingehen; es riskieren; **take a** ~ **on sth.** es bei etw. auf einen Versuch ankommen lassen.
❷ *v.i.* zufällig geschehen *od.* sich ereignen; **it** ~**d that ...:** es traf *od.* fügte sich, dass ...; ~ **to do sth.** zufällig etw. tun; **she** ~**d to be sitting there** zufällig saß sie gerade da; ~ **[up]on sth./sb.** zufällig auf etw./jmdn. stoßen.
❸ *v.t.* riskieren; ~ **it** es riskieren *od.* darauf ankommen lassen; **we'll have to** ~ **that happening** wir müssen es riskieren; ~ **one's arm** *(Brit. coll.)* es riskieren; ~ **one's luck** sein Glück versuchen

**chancel** /ˈtʃɑːnsl/ *n. (Eccl.)* Altarraum, *der; (choir)* Chor, *der*

**chancellery** /ˈtʃɑːnsələrɪ/ *n. (office)* ≈ Botschaft, *die; (of consul)* Konsulat, *das*

**chancellor** /ˈtʃɑːnsələ(r)/ *n.* **A** *(Polit., Law, Univ.)* Kanzler, *der;* **C**~ **of the Exchequer** *(Brit.)* Schatzkanzler, *der;* **Lord [High] C**~ *(Brit.)* Lordkanzler, *der;* **B** *(chief minister of State)* Kanzler, *der;* **Federal C**~**:** Bundeskanzler, *der*

**chancery** /ˈtʃɑːnsərɪ/ *n.* **A** **C**~ *(Brit. Law)* Gerichtshof des Lordkanzlers; **Court of C**~

(*Hist.*) Kanzleigericht, *das (veralt.)*; **B** (*Brit. Diplom.*) ≈ Botschaft, *die*/Gesandtschaft, *die*; **C** (*public records office*) Archiv, *das*

**chancy** /ˈtʃɑːnsɪ/ *adj.* riskant; gewagt

**chandelier** /ʃændəˈlɪə(r)/ *n.* Kronleuchter, *der*

**chandler** /ˈtʃɑːndlə(r)/ *n.* ▶ 1261 (*arch.*) Krämer, *der*; ⇒ *also* **ship's chandler**

**change** /ˈtʃeɪndʒ/ **1** *n.* **A** (*of name, address, lifestyle, outlook, condition, etc.*) Änderung, *die*; (*of job, surroundings, government, etc.*) Wechsel, *der*; **there has been a ~ of plan** der Plan ist geändert worden; **sth. undergoes a ~:** etw. ändert sich; (*more profoundly*) etw. verändert sich; **How is she, doctor? — No ~:** Wie geht es ihr, Doktor? — Unverändert; **see a ~ in sb.** eine Veränderung an jmdm. bemerken; **this last year has seen many ~s** das vergangene Jahr hat viele Veränderungen [mit sich] gebracht; **there has been a ~ in sb./sth.** eine Veränderung ist in jmdm. vorgegangen/es hat bei etw. eine Änderung gegeben; **make ~s/a ~:** einiges ändern/etwas verändern (**to, in** an + *Dat.*); **make a ~ [of trains/buses]** umsteigen; **a ~ in the weather** ein Witterungs- *od.* Wetterumschlag; **a ~ for the better/worse** eine Verbesserung/Verschlechterung; **a ~ of air would do her good** eine Luftveränderung täte ihr gut; **a ~ of scene/environment** ein positiver Ortswechsel; **the ~ [of life]** die Wechseljahre; **a ~ of drivers every four hours** ein Fahrerwechsel alle vier Stunden; **a ~ of heart** ein Sinneswandel; **B** *no pl., no art.* (*process of changing*) Veränderung, *die*; **be for/against ~:** für/gegen eine Veränderung sein; **~ came slowly** nur allmählich zeigte sich eine Veränderung; **C** (*for the sake of variety*) Abwechslung, *die*; **[just] for a ~:** [nur so] zur Abwechslung; (*iron.*) zur Abwechslung mal; **make a ~** (*be different*) mal etwas anderes sein (**from** als); **that makes a ~** (*iron.*) das ist ja [et]was ganz Neues!; **a ~ is as good as a rest** (*prov.*) Abwechslung wirkt Wunder; **D** ▶ 1328 *no pl., no indef. art.* (*money*) Wechselgeld, *das*; **[loose** *or* **small] ~:** Kleingeld, *das*; **give ~,** (*Amer.*) **make ~:** herausgeben; **give sb. his/her ~:** jmdm. das Wechselgeld [heraus]geben; **give sb. 40p in ~:** jmdm. 40p [Wechselgeld] herausgeben; **can you give me ~ for 50p?** können Sie mir 50p wechseln?; **[here is] 15 marks ~:** 15 Mark zurück; **I haven't got ~ for a pound** ich kann auf ein Pfund nicht herausgeben; **[you can] keep the ~:** behalten Sie den Rest; [es] stimmt so; **get no ~ out of sb.** (*fig. coll.*) nichts aus jmdm. rauskriegen (*ugs.*); **E a ~ [of clothes]** (*fresh clothes*) Kleidung zum Wechseln; **F** (*of moon*) Mondwechsel, *der*; **G** *usu. in pl.* (*Bell-ringing*) Schlagtonfolge, *die* (*Musik*); **ring the ~s** (*fig.*) für Abwechslung sorgen.

**2** *v.t.* **A** (*switch*) wechseln; auswechseln ‹Glühbirne, Batterie, Zündkerzen›; **~ one's clothes** seine Kleider *od.* Kleidung wechseln; sich umziehen; **~ one's address/name** seine Anschrift/seinen Namen ändern; **~ trains/buses** umsteigen; **~ schools/one's doctor** die Schule/den Arzt wechseln; **he's always changing jobs** er wechselt ständig den Job; **~ seats** sich woanders hinsetzen *od.* auf einen anderen Platz setzen (⇒ *also* **c**); **~ the record** eine andere Platte auflegen; **~ the bed** das Bett frisch beziehen; die Bettwäsche wechseln; **~ the baby** das Baby [frisch] wickeln *od.* trockenlegen; **~ ownership** den Besitzer wechseln; ⇒ *also* **gear** 1 A; **hand** 1 A, C; **horse** 1 A; **side** 1 I; **B** (*transform*) verwandeln; (*alter*) ändern; **~ sth./sb. into sth./sb.** etw./jmdn. in etw./jmdn. verwandeln; **she ~d him from a prince into a frog** sie verwandelte den Prinzen in einen Frosch; **marriage ~d his way of life** die Ehe veränderte sein Leben; **you won't be able to ~ him** du kannst ihn nicht ändern; **~ direction** die Richtung ändern; ⇒ *also* **colour** 1 C; **mind** 1 B; **step** 1 E; **tune** 1 A; **C** (*exchange*) eintauschen; **~ seats** die Plätze tauschen (⇒ *also* **a**); **~ seats with sb.** mit jmdm. den Platz tauschen; **~ sth./sb. for sth./sb.** etw./jmdn. für etw./jmdn. eintauschen; **take sth. back to the shop and ~ it for sth.** etw. [zum Laden zurückbringen und] gegen etw. umtauschen; ⇒ *also* **place** 1 F; **D** ▶ 1328 (*in currency or denomination*) wechseln ‹Geld›; **~ one's money into Deutschmarks** sein Geld in DM umtauschen.

**3** *v.i.* **A** (*alter*) sich ändern; ‹Person, Land:› sich verändern; ‹Wetter:› umschlagen, sich ändern; **has she ~d?** hat sie sich verändert?; (*for the better also*) hat sie sich geändert?; **she'll never ~!** sie wird sich nie ändern!; **wait for the lights to ~:** warten, dass es grün/rot wird; **~ for the better** sich verbessern; **conditions ~d for the worse** die Lage verschlechterte sich; **B** (*into something else*) sich verwandeln; **he ~d from a prince into a frog** aus dem Prinzen wurde ein Frosch; **the wind ~s from east to west** der Wind dreht von Ost nach West; **Britain ~d to the metric system** Großbritannien führte das metrische System ein; **almost overnight it seemed to ~ from winter to spring** fast über Nacht schien sich der Winter in den Frühling verwandelt zu haben; **C** (*exchange*) tauschen; **~ with sb.** mit jmdm. tauschen; **D** (*put on other clothes*) sich umziehen; **~ out of/into sth.** etw. ausziehen/anziehen; **E** (*take different train or bus*) umsteigen; **where do I ~?** wo muss ich umsteigen?; **all ~!** Endstation! Alles aussteigen!; **~ at Bristol** in Bristol umsteigen

**~ 'down** *v.i.* (*Motor Veh.*) herunterschalten

**~ 'over** *v.i.* **A** (*to something else*) **~ over from sth. to sth.** von etw. zu etw. übergehen; **the student ~d over to medicine** der Student wechselte zum Fach Medizin über; **they ~d over from one system to another** sie stellten das System auf ein anderes um; **B** (*exchange places*) die Plätze wechseln; (*Sport*) [die Seiten] wechseln. ⇒ *also* **~over**

**~ 'round** **1** *v.i.* wechseln; (*Sport*) [die Seiten] wechseln. **2** *v.t.* umstellen ‹Möbel, Tagesordnung[spunkte]›; umräumen ‹Zimmer›

**~ 'up** *v.i.* (*Motor Veh.*) hochschalten

**changeability** /tʃeɪndʒəˈbɪlɪtɪ/ ⇒ **changeableness**

**changeable** /ˈtʃeɪndʒəbl/ *adj.* veränderlich; (*irregular, inconstant*) unbeständig ‹Charakter, Wetter›; wankelmütig ‹Person›; wechselhaft, veränderlich ‹Wetter›; wechselnd ‹Wind, Stimmung›

**changeableness** /ˈtʃeɪndʒəblnɪs/ *n., no pl.* Veränderlichkeit, *die*; (*inconstancy*) Unbeständigkeit, *die*; (*of person*) Wankelmütigkeit, *die*

**'change[-giving] machine** *n.* Geldwechsler, *der*

**changeless** /ˈtʃeɪndʒlɪs/ *adj.* unveränderlich

**changeling** /ˈtʃeɪndʒlɪŋ/ *n.* Wechselbalg, *der*

**'changeover** *n.* **A** Wechsel, *der*; **~ from sth. to sth.** Umstellung von etw. auf etw. (*Akk.*); **the ~ from one government to the next** der Wechsel von einer Regierung zur nächsten; **the sudden ~ in public opinion** der plötzliche Umschwung der öffentlichen Meinung; **B** (*Sport: of baton in relay race*) Stabwechsel, *der*; (*of teams changing ends*) Seitenwechsel, *der*

**changing** /ˈtʃeɪndʒɪŋ/ **1** *adj.* wechselnd; sich ändernd. **2** *n.* **the C~ of the Guard** die Wachablösung (*der brit. Hofwache*)

**changing: ~ cubicle** *n.* Umkleidekabine, *die*; **~ room** *n.* (*Brit.*) **A** (*Sport*) Umkleideraum, *der*; **B** (*in shop*) Umkleidekabine, *die*

**channel** /ˈtʃænl/ **1** *n.* **A** Kanal, *der*; (*gutter*) Rinnstein, *der*; (*navigable part of waterway*) Fahrrinne, *die*; **the C~** (*Brit.*) der [Ärmel]kanal; **~ of a/the river** Flussbett, *das*; **B** (*fig.*) Kanal, *der*; **your application will go through the usual ~s** Ihre Bewerbung wird auf dem üblichen Weg weitergeleitet; **you must apply through the official ~s** Sie müssen mit Ihrer Bewerbung den Dienstweg einhalten; **direct sb.'s talents into the right ~:** jmds. Talente in die richtige Bahn lenken; **C** (*Telev., Radio*) Kanal, *der*; **D** (*on recording tape etc.*) Spur, *die*; **E** (*groove*) Rille, *die*; (*flute*) Kannelüre, *die*.

**2** *v.t.,* (*Brit.*) **-ll-** (*convey*) übermitteln; (*fig.: guide, direct*) lenken, richten (**into** auf + *Akk.*)

**Channel: c~-hop** *v.i.* (*coll.*) **A** (*Telev.*) zappen (*ugs.*); **B** (*cross the English Channel*) kurz mal über den Kanal fahren; **~ Islands** *pr. n. pl.* Kanalinseln *Pl.*; **~ 'Tunnel** *n.* [Ärmel]kanaltunnel, *der*; **~ Tunnel rail link** *schnelle Bahnverbindung zwischen London und dem Kanaltunnel*

**chant** /tʃɑːnt/ **1** *v.t.* **A** (*Eccl.*) singen; **B** (*utter rhythmically*) skandieren. **2** *v.i.* **A** (*Eccl.*) singen; **B** (*utter slogans etc.*) Sprechchöre anstimmen. **3** *n.* **A** (*Eccl., Mus.*) Gesang, *der*; **B** (*sing-song*) Singsang, *der*; (*slogans*) Sprechchor, *der*

**chanterelle** /ʃɑːntəˈrel/ *n.* (*Bot.*) Pfifferling, *der*

**chaos** /ˈkeɪɒs/ *n., no indef. art.* Chaos, *das*; **be in [a state of] [complete] ~:** ein [einziges] Chaos sein; **it's absolute ~:** es herrscht ein totales Chaos; **cause ~:** zu einem Chaos führen

**'chaos theory** *n.* (*Phys.*) Chaostheorie, *die*

**chaotic** /keɪˈɒtɪk/ *adj.*, **chaotically** /keɪˈɒtɪkəlɪ/ *adv.* chaotisch

**chap**[1] /tʃæp/ *n.* (*Brit. coll.*) Bursche, *der*; Kerl, *der*; **old ~:** alter Knabe (*ugs.*); **my dear ~:** mein lieber Mann (*ugs.*); **would you ~s lend a hand?** könntet ihr mal helfen, Jungs?; **hello, old ~!** hallo, alter Junge!

**chap**[2] **1** *v.t.,* **-pp-** aufplatzen lassen; **my hands are ~ped** meine Hände sind [ganz] aufgesprungen; **~ped skin** aufgesprungene *od.* rissige Haut. **2** *n. usu. in pl.* Riss, *der*

**chap**[3] *n.* (*jaw*) Kinnbacke, *die*; (*Gastr.: of pig*) Schweinebacke, *die*

**chap.** *abbr.* **chapter** Kap.

**chapat[t]i** /tʃəˈpætɪ/ *n.* [indisches] Fladenbrot

**'chap-book** *n.* (*Hist.*) Volksbuch, *das*

**chapel** /ˈtʃæpl/ *n.* **A** Kapelle, *die*; **~ of rest** (*Brit.*) *Raum in einem Bestattungsinstitut, in dem Tote bis zur Beerdigung aufgebahrt werden*; ≈ Kapelle, *die*; **B** (*Brit.: of Nonconformists*) Kirche, *die*; **C** (*subordinate to parish church*) ≈ Filialkirche, *die*

**chaperon** /ˈʃæpərəʊn/ **1** *n.* Anstandsdame, *die*; (*joc.*) Anstandswauwau, *der* (*ugs. scherzh.*). **2** *v.t.* beaufsichtigen; (*escort*) begleiten

**chaplain** /ˈtʃæplɪn/ *n.* Kaplan, *der*

**chaplaincy** /ˈtʃæplɪnsɪ/ *n.* **A** Amt eines Kaplans; **B** (*building*) Haus des/eines Kaplans

**chaplet** /ˈtʃæplɪt/ *n.* **A** (*Hist.: wreath*) Schappel, *das*; Kranz, *der*; **B** (*string of beads*) (*RC Ch.*) Rosenkranz, *der*; (*as necklace*) Perlenkette, *die*

**chappie, chappy** /ˈtʃæpɪ/ *n.* (*coll.*) **a nice ~** ein liebes Kerlchen

**chaps** /tʃæps/ *n. pl.* (*Amer.: overalls*) lederne Beinschützer

**chapter** /ˈtʃæptə(r)/ *n.* **A** (*of book*) Kapitel, *das*; **[quote sth.] ~ and verse** [etw.] mit genauer Quellenangabe [zitieren]; **give ~ and verse for sth.** etw. hieb- und stichfest belegen; **B** (*fig.*) **~ in** *or* **of sb.'s life** Abschnitt in jmds. Leben; **~ of history** Kapitel [in] der Geschichte; ⇒ *also* **accident** D; **C** (*Eccl.*) Kapitel, *das*; **D** (*Amer.: branch of a society*) Sektion, *die*

**chapter: ~ heading** *n.* [Kapitel]überschrift, *die*; **~ house** *n.* **A** Kapitelsaal, *der*; **B** (*Amer.: for student meetings*) ≈ Klubhaus, *das*

**char**[1] /tʃɑː(r)/ *v.t. & i.,* **-rr-** (*burn*) verkohlen

**char**[2] ▶ 1261 **1** *n.* (*Brit.: cleaner*) Putzfrau, *die*. **2** *v.i.,* **-rr-** (*be cleaner*) als Putzfrau arbeiten; putzen; **~ for sb.** bei jmdm. putzen *od.* als Putzfrau arbeiten

**char**[3] *n.* (*Brit. coll.: tea*) Tee, *der*; **a cup of ~:** eine Tasse Tee

**charabanc** /ˈʃærəbæŋ/ *n.* (*Brit. dated*) [*offener*] *Bus für Ausflugsfahrten usw.*

**character** /ˈkærɪktə(r)/ *n.* **A** (*mental or moral qualities, integrity*) Charakter, *der*; (*description of qualities*) Charakterbild, *das*; **be of good ~:** ein guter Mensch sein; einen guten Charakter haben; **a woman of ~:** eine Frau mit Charakter; **strength of ~:** Charakterstärke, *die*; **B** (*reputation*) Ruf, der; (*testimonial*) Zeugnis, *das;* **C** *no pl.* (*individuality, style*) Charakter, *der;* (*characteristic, esp. Biol.*) Charakteristikum, *das;* **the town has a ~ all of its own** die Stadt hat einen ganz eigenen Charakter; **have no ~:** charakterlos *od.* ohne Charakter sein; **his face has ~:** er hat ein charakter- *od.* ausdrucksvolles Gesicht; **D** (*in novel etc.*) Charakter, *der;* (*part played by sb.*) Rolle, *die;* **be in/out of ~** (*fig.*) typisch/untypisch sein; **his behaviour was quite out of ~** (*fig.*) sein Betragen war ganz und gar untypisch für ihn; **act in/out of ~** (*fig.*) sich typisch/untypisch verhalten; **E** (*coll.: extraordinary person*) Original, *das;* **be [quite] a ~/a real ~:** ein [echtes/richtiges] Original sein; **what a ~!** was für ein Mann/eine Frau!; **F** (*personage*) Persönlichkeit, *die;* Gestalt, *die;* (*coll.: individual*) Mensch, *der;* (*derog.*) Individuum, *das;* **a public ~:** eine Persönlichkeit des öffentlichen Lebens; **G** (*graphic symbol; Computing*) Zeichen, *das;* (*set of letters*) Schrift, *die*

**character: ~ actor** *n.* Chargenspieler, *der;* **~ actress** *n.* Chargenspielerin, *die;* **~ assassination** *n.* Rufmord, *der;* **~-building** **1** *n.* Charakterbildung, *die;* **2** *adj.* charakterbildend

**characterisation, characterise** ⇒ **characteriz-**

**characteristic** /kærɪktə'rɪstɪk/ **1** *adj.* charakteristisch (**of** für). **2** *n.* **A** charakteristisches Merkmal; Charakteristikum, *das;* **one of the main ~s** eines der charakteristischsten Merkmale; **B** ⇒ **characteristic curve**

**characteristically** /kærɪktə'rɪstɪkəlɪ/ *adv.* in charakteristischer Weise; **~ American** typisch amerikanisch; **~ enough for him he ...:** es ist/war typisch *od.* bezeichnend für ihn, dass er ...

**characteristic 'curve** *n.* Kennlinie, *die*

**characterization** /kærɪktəraɪ'zeɪʃn/ *n.* Charakterisierung, *die*

**characterize** /'kærɪktəraɪz/ *v.t.* charakterisieren

**characterless** /'kærɪktəlɪs/ *adj.* nichts sagend; charakterlos

**character: ~ part** *n.* (*Theatre*) Charge, *die;* **~ sketch** *n.* Charakterskizze, *die;* **~ study** *n.* Charakterstudie, *die*

**charade** /ʃə'rɑːd/ *n.* Scharade, *die;* (*fig.*) Farce, *die;* **play [a game of] ~s** Scharade spielen; **be an absolute ~** (*fig.*) die reinste Farce sein

**charcoal** /'tʃɑːkəʊl/ *n.* **A** Holzkohle, *die;* (*for drawing*) Kohle, *die;* **B** ⇒ **charcoal grey**

**charcoal: ~ biscuit** *n. Keks mit Holzkohle zur Förderung der Verdauung;* **~-burner** *n.* Köhler, *der;* **~ drawing** *n.* Kohlezeichnung, *die;* **~ 'grey** *n.* [Kohlen]grau, *das;* **~ pencil** *n.* Kohlestift, *der*

**chard** /tʃɑːd/ *n.* (*Bot.*) Mangold, *der*

**charge** /tʃɑːdʒ/ **1** *n.* **A** ▶ **1328** (*price*) Preis, *der;* (*payable to telephone company, bank, authorities, etc., for services*) Gebühr, *die;* **what's your ~?** wie viel verlangen *od.* berechnen Sie?; **what would the ~ be for doing that?** was würde es kosten, das zu tun?; **is there a ~ for it?** kostet das etwas?; **make a ~ of £1/no ~ for sth.** ein Pfund/nichts für etw. berechnen; **at no extra ~:** ohne Extrakosten; **incidental ~s** Nebenkosten; **B** (*care*) Verantwortung, *die;* (*task*) Auftrag, *der;* (*person entrusted*) Schützling, *der;* **be in ~ of a child** ein Kind betreuen; **the boy was placed in his ~:** der Junge wurde in seine Obhut gegeben; der Junge wurde ihm anvertraut; **the patients in** *or* **under her ~:** die ihr anvertrauten Patienten; **be under sb.'s ~:** unter jmds. Obhut stehen; sich in jmds. Obhut befinden; **leave sb. in [full] ~ of sth.** jmdm. die [volle] Verantwortung für etw. übertragen; **the officer/teacher in ~:** der Dienst habende Offizier/der verantwortliche Lehrer; **be in ~:** die Verantwortung haben; **be in ~ of sth.** für etw. die Verantwortung haben; (*be the leader*) etw. leiten; **put sb. in ~ of sth.** jmdn. mit der Verantwortung für etw. betrauen; (*make leader*) jmdm. die Leitung einer Sache (*Gen.*) übertragen; **take ~:** die Verantwortung übernehmen; (*fig. coll.: get out of control*) außer Kontrolle geraten; **take ~ of sth.** (*become responsible for*) etw. übernehmen; (*as deputy*) sich um etw. kümmern; (*for safe keeping*) etw. in Verwahrung nehmen; **the police took ~ of the evidence** die Polizei stellte das Beweisstück sicher; **give sb. in ~** (*Brit.*) jmdn. der Polizei übergeben; **C** (*Law: accusation*) Anklage, *die;* **make a ~ against sb.** jmdn. beschuldigen; **bring a ~ of sth. against sb.** jmdn. wegen etw. beschuldigen/verklagen; ‹Staatsanwalt:› jmdn. wegen etw. anklagen; **press ~s** Anzeige erstatten; **face a ~ [of sth.]** sich [wegen etw.] vor Gericht zu verantworten haben; **on a ~ of** wegen; **[stand] convicted on all six ~s** in allen sechs Anklagepunkten für schuldig befunden [werden]; **what's the ~?** wie lautet die Anklage?; was liegt gegen mich/ihn *usw.* vor?; **lay to sb.'s ~:** jmdm. zur Last legen; **D** (*allegation*) Beschuldigung, *die;* **E** (*attack*) Angriff, *der;* Attacke, *die;* **return to the ~** (*fig.*) es erneut versuchen; **F** (*of explosives etc.*) Ladung, *die;* (*in blast furnace etc.*) Gicht, *die;* **G** (*of electricity*) Ladung, *die;* **put the battery on ~:** die Batterie an das Ladegerät anschließen; **poetry/person with an emotional ~** (*fig.*) von [tiefen] Gefühlen geprägte Dichtung/geprägter Mensch; **H** (*directions*) Anweisung, *die;* (*of judge to jury*) Rechtsbelehrung, *die;* **I** (*Her.*) Wappenbild, *das.*

**2** *v.t.* **A** ▶ **1328** (*demand payment of or from*) **~ sb. sth., ~ sth. to sb.** jmdm. etw. berechnen; etw. von jmdm. verlangen (*ugs.*); **be ~d** bezahlen müssen; **I wasn't ~d for it** ich musste nichts dafür bezahlen; mir wurde nichts dafür berechnet; **~ sb. £1 for sth.** jmdm. ein Pfund für etw. berechnen; **customers are ~d for breakages** Kunden haften für Bruchschäden; **~ sth. [up] to sb.'s account** jmds. Konto mit etw. belasten; jmdm. etw. in Rechnung stellen; **to whom is the dress to be ~d?** auf wessen Rechnung geht das Kleid?; **~ it [up] to the firm** stellen Sie das der Firma in Rechnung; **I'd like to ~ this dress** ich möchte dieses Kleid über mein Kreditkonto bezahlen; **B** (*Law: accuse*) anklagen; **~ sb. with sth.** jmdn. wegen etw. anklagen; **C** (*blame*) beschuldigen; bezichtigen; **~ sb. with doing sth.** jmdn. beschuldigen, etw. getan zu haben; **~ sb. with being lazy** jmdm. vorwerfen, er/sie sei faul; **D** (*formal: entrust*) **~ sb. with sth.** jmdn. mit etw. betrauen; **~ oneself with sth.** etw. übernehmen; **E** (*load*) laden ‹Gewehr›; beschicken ‹Hochofen›; **F** (*Electr.*) laden; [auf]laden ‹Batterie›; **~d with emotion** (*fig.*) voller Gefühl; gefühlsgeladen; **G** (*rush at*) angreifen; **H** (*formal: command*) befehlen; **~ sb. to do sth.** jmdm. befehlen, etw. zu tun; **the judge ~d the jury** der Richter erteilte den Geschworenen Rechtsbelehrung.

**3** *v.i.* **A** (*attack*) angreifen; **~!** Angriff!; Attacke!; **~ at sb./sth.** jmdn./etw. angreifen; **he ~d into a wall** (*fig.*) er krachte gegen eine Mauer; **B** (*coll.: hurry*) sausen

**chargeable** /'tʃɑːdʒəbl/ *adj.* **A** **be ~ to sb.** auf jmds. Kosten gehen; **B** (*Law*) **be ~ with sth.** wegen einer Sache belangt werden können

**charge: ~ account** *n.* (*Amer.*) Kreditkonto, *das;* **~ card** *n.* Kreditkarte, *die*

**chargé d'affaires** /ʃɑːʒeɪ dæ'feə(r)/ *n., pl.* **chargés d'affaires** /ʃɑːʒeɪ dæ'feə(r)/ ▶ **1261** Chargé d'affaires, *der;* [diplomatischer] Geschäftsträger

**charge: ~-hand** *n.* (*Brit.*) Vorarbeiter, *der*/Vorarbeiterin, *die;* **~-nurse** *n.* (*Brit.*) Stationsschwester, *die*

**charger** /'tʃɑːdʒə(r)/ *n.* **A** (*Mil.: cavalry horse*) [Kavallerie]pferd, *das;* (*of knight*) Schlachtross, *das* (*veralt.*); **B** (*poet.: horse*) Ross, *das* (*dichter.*); **C** (*arch.: dish*) Platte, *die;* **D** (*Electr.*) [Batterie]ladegerät, *das*

**'charge sheet** *n.* **A** *Buch, in dem auf einem Polizeirevier Festnahmen und Beschuldigungen registriert werden;* **B** (*Mil.*) Anklageschrift, *die*

**charily** /'tʃeərɪlɪ/ *adv.* vorsichtig

**chariot** /'tʃærɪət/ *n.* (*Hist.*) (*for fighting or racing*) [zweirädriger] Streitwagen; (*carriage*) [leichter, vierrädriger] Wagen

**charioteer** /tʃærɪə'tɪə(r)/ *n.* Wagenlenker, *der*

**charisma** /kə'rɪzmə/ *n., pl.* **~ta** /kə'rɪzmətə/ Charisma, *das*

**charismatic** /kærɪz'mætɪk/ *adj.* charismatisch

**charitable** /'tʃærɪtəbl/ *adj.* **A** (*generous*) großzügig; **B** (*lenient*) nachsichtig; großzügig; **C** (*of or for charity*) karitativ; wohltätig, karitativ ‹Organisation, Werke›

**charity** /'tʃærɪtɪ/ *n.* **A** (*leniency*) Nachsicht, *die;* **B** (*Christian love*) Nächstenliebe, *die;* **faith, hope, and ~:** Glaube, Hoffnung, Liebe; **C** (*kindness*) Güte, *die;* **D** (*beneficence*) Wohltätigkeit, *die;* **live on ~/accept ~:** von Almosen leben/Almosen annehmen; **~ begins at home** (*prov.*) man muss zuerst an die eigenen Leute denken; **give money to ~:** Geld für wohltätige Zwecke spenden; **collect for ~:** für wohltätige Zwecke sammeln; **be in aid of ~:** für einen wohltätigen Zweck sein; **[as] cold as ~:** eiskalt (*fig.*); **E** (*institution*) wohltätige Organisation; **F** (*educational trust*) gemeinnützige Bildungseinrichtung

**'charity: ~ concert** *n.* Benefizkonzert, *das;* **~ match** *n.* Benefizspiel, *das;* **~ performance** *n.* Benefizvorstellung, *die;* Wohltätigkeitsvorstellung, *die;* **~ shop** *n.: Secondhandladen, dessen Erlöse einem wohltätigen Zweck dienen*

**charlady** /'tʃɑːleɪdɪ/ *n.* (*Brit.*) ⇒ **char²** 1

**charlatan** /'ʃɑːlətən/ *n.* Scharlatan, *der*

**Charlemagne** /'ʃɑːləmeɪn/ *pr. n.* Karl der Große

**Charles** /tʃɑːlz/ *pr. n.* (*Hist., as name of ruler etc.*) Karl (*der*)

**Charles's Wain** /'tʃɑːlzɪz weɪn/ *n.* (*Astron.*) der Große Wagen *od.* Bär

**charleston** /'tʃɑːlstən/ *n.* Charleston, *der*

**charley horse** /'tʃɑːlɪ hɔːs/ *n.* (*Amer. coll.*) Muskelkater, *der*

**charlie** /'tʃɑːlɪ/ *n.* **be/look a right ~** (*coll.*) dämlich sein/aussehen (*ugs.*); **feel a proper ~** (*coll.*) sich (*Dat.*) richtig blöd *od.* dämlich vorkommen (*ugs.*)

**charm** /tʃɑːm/ **1** *n.* **A** (*act*) Zauber, *der;* (*thing*) Zaubermittel, *das;* (*words*) Zauberspruch, *der;* Zauberformel, *die;* **lucky ~:** Glücksbringer, *der;* **work like a ~:** Wunder wirken; **B** (*talisman*) Talisman, *der;* **C** (*trinket*) Anhänger, *der;* Berlocke, *die* (*veralt.*); **D** (*attractiveness*) Reiz, *der;* (*of person*) Charme, *der;* **have ~** ‹Person:› Charme haben; ‹Schloss, Buch:› seinen eigenen Reiz haben; **place of great ~:** reizvoller Ort; **person of great ~:** sehr charmanter Mensch; **turn on the ~** (*coll.*) auf charmant machen (*ugs.*).

**2** *v.t.* **A** (*captivate*) bezaubern ; **be ~ed with sth.** von etw. bezaubert *od.* begeistert sein; **she can ~ the birds out of the trees** sie kann mit ihrem Charme alles erreichen; **~ed, I'm sure** (*coll. iron.*) [wie] charmant (*iron.*); **B** (*by magic*) verzaubern; beschwören ‹Schlange›; **~ sth. out of sb.** jmdm. etw. [durch Zauberei] entlocken; **bear** *or* **lead a ~ed life** unter einem Glücksstern geboren sein; ein Glückskind sein

**charmer** /'tʃɑːmə(r)/ *n.* (*man*) Charmeur, *der;* (*woman*) bezauberndes Geschöpf

**charming** /'tʃɑːmɪŋ/ *adj.* bezaubernd; charmant, bezaubernd ‹Person, Lächeln›; **~!** (*iron.*) [wie] charmant! (*iron.*)

**charmingly** /'tʃɑːmɪŋlɪ/ *adv.* bezaubernd; charmant ‹lächeln›

**charnel house** /'tʃɑːnlhaʊs/ *n.* Leichenhalle, *die;* (*for bones*) Beinhaus, *das*

**chart** /tʃɑːt/ **1** *n.* **A** (*map*) Karte, *die;* **naval ~:** Seekarte, *die;* **weather ~:** Wetterkarte, *die;* **B** (*graph etc.*) Schaubild, *das;* (*diagram*) Diagramm, *das;* **C** (*tabulated information*) Tabelle, *die;* **the ~s** (*of pop records*) die Hitliste. **2** *v.t.* grafisch darstellen; (*map*) kartographisch erfassen; kartographieren; (*fig.: describe*) schildern ‹Werdegang, Leben›

**'chart-buster** *n.* Hit, *der*

**charter** /'tʃɑ:tə(r)/ ❶ *n.* Ⓐ Charta, *die;* (*of foundation also*) Gründungs- *od.* Stiftungsurkunde, *die;* (*fig.*) Freibrief, *der;* **grant a ~ to a city** einem Ort das Stadtrecht verleihen; **the Great C~** (*Hist.*) die Magna Charta; Ⓑ (*deed conveying land*) ≈ [Besitz]urkunde, *die;* Ⓒ (*privilege, admitted right*) Privileg, *das;* Vorrecht, *das;* Ⓓ (*Transport*) **be on ~:** gechartert sein. ❷ *v.t.* (*Transport*) chartern ‹Schiff, Flugzeug›; mieten ‹Bus›

**chartered**/'tʃɑ:təd/: **~ ac'countant** *n.* ▶ 1261 (*Brit.*) Wirtschaftsprüfer, *der*/ -prüferin, *die;* **~ 'aircraft** *n.* Charterflugzeug, *das;* Chartermaschine, *die;* **~ engi'neer** *n.* ▶ 1261 (*Brit.*) Ingenieur, *der*/Ingenieurin, *die* (*der/die Mitglied eines Verbands ist*); **~ li'brarian** *n.* ▶ 1261 (*Brit.*) Bibliothekar, *der*/Bibliothekarin, *die* (*der/die Mitglied eines Verbands ist*); **~ sur'veyor** *n.* ▶ 1261 (*Brit.*) Vermessungsingenieur, *der*/ -ingenieurin, *die* (*der/die Mitglied eines Verbands ist*)

**charter: ~ flight** *n.* Charterflug, *der;* **~-party** *n.* (*Transport*) Charterpartie, *die;* **~ plane** ⇒ **chartered aircraft**

**charwoman** /'tʃɑ:wʊmən/ ⇒ **char**[2] 1

**chary** /'tʃeərɪ/ *adj.* Ⓐ (*sparing, ungenerous*) zurückhaltend (**of** mit); **be ~ of doing sth.** zurückhaltend damit sein, etw. zu tun; Ⓑ (*cautious*) vorsichtig; **be ~ of doing sth.** darauf bedacht sein, etw. nicht zu tun

**chase**[1] /tʃeɪs/ ❶ *n.* Ⓐ Verfolgungsjagd, *die;* **car ~:** Verfolgungsjagd im Auto; **give ~ [to the thief]** [dem Dieb] hinterherjagen; Ⓑ (*Hunting*) Jagd, *die;* (*steeple~*) Jagdrennen, *das;* Steeplechase, *die.* ❷ *v.t.* (*pursue*) jagen; **~ sth.** (*fig.*) einer Sache (*Dat.*) nachjagen; hinter etw. (*Dat.*) her sein (*ugs.*); **~ yourself** *imper.* (*fig. coll.*) verschwinde (*ugs.*). ❸ *v.i.* **~ after sb./sth.** hinter jmdm./etw. herjagen; **I've been chasing about all over the place** (*coll.*) ich bin überall herumgerast (*ugs.*)

**~ around** ❶ /--'-/ *v.i.* **~ around after sb.** jmdm. hinterherrennen. ❷ /'---/ *v.t.* **~ around town** in der Stadt herumrennen (*ugs.*)

**~ a'way** *v.t.* wegjagen

**~ 'off** *v.i.* davonjagen

**~ round** ⇒ **~ around**

**~ 'up** *v.t.* (*coll.*) ausfindig machen

**chase**[2] *v.t.* (*Metalw.*) ziselieren

**chaser** /'tʃeɪsə(r)/ *n.* Ⓐ (*horse*) Steepler, *der* (*Reitsport*); Ⓑ **drink sth. as a ~** (*coll.*) etw. zum Nachspülen trinken (*ugs.*); **drink beer with vodka ~s** Bier trinken und mit Wodka nachspülen

**chasm** /'kæzm/ *n.* (*lit. or fig.*) Kluft, *die*

**chassis** /'ʃæsɪ/ *n., pl. same* /'ʃæsɪz/ (*Motor Veh.*) Chassis, *das;* Fahrgestell, *das*

**chaste** /tʃeɪst/ *adj.* Ⓐ keusch; Ⓑ (*decent*) gesittet ‹Worte, Ausdruck, Antwort›; Ⓒ (*restrained*) schlicht ‹Erscheinung, Kleidung›

**chastely** /'tʃeɪstlɪ/ *adv.* ⇒ **chaste**: keusch; gesittet; schlicht

**chasten** /'tʃeɪsn/ *v.t.* Ⓐ züchtigen (*geh.*); strafen; Ⓑ (*fig.*) dämpfen ‹Stimmung›; demütigen ‹Person›

**chastening** /'tʃeɪsənɪŋ/ *adj.* ernüchternd

**chastise** /tʃæ'staɪz/ *v.t.* Ⓐ (*punish*) züchtigen (*geh.*); bestrafen; Ⓑ (*thrash*) züchtigen (*geh.*)

**chastisement** /tʃæ'staɪzmənt/ *n.* Züchtigung, *die* (*geh.*); Strafe, *die*

**chastity** /'tʃæstɪtɪ/ *n., no pl.* Keuschheit, *die;* **vow of ~:** Keuschheitsgelübde, *das*

**'chastity belt** *n.* Keuschheitsgürtel, *der*

**chasuble** /'tʃæzjʊbl/ *n.* (*Eccl.*) Messgewand, *das;* Kasel, *die*

**chat** /tʃæt/ ❶ *n.* Ⓐ Schwätzchen, *das;* Plausch, *der* (*bes. südd., österr.*); **have a ~ about sth.** sich über etw. (*Akk.*) unterhalten; Ⓑ *no pl., no indef. art.* (*~ting*) Geplauder, *das;* Ⓒ (*Computing*) Chat, *der; attrib.* Chat-. ❷ *v.i.*, **-tt-:** Ⓐ plaudern; **~ with** *or* **to sb. about sth.** mit jmdm. von etw. plaudern; sich mit jmdm. über etw. (*Akk.*) unterhalten; Ⓑ (*Computing*) chatten.

**~ 'up** *v.t.* (*Brit. coll.*) sich heranmachen an (+ *Akk.*) (*ugs.*); (*amorously*) anmachen (*ugs.*)

**château** /'ʃætəʊ/ *n., pl.* **~x** /'ʃætəʊz/ Château, *das*

**chat: ~ line** *n.* Chatline, *die;* **~ room** *n.* (*Computing*) Chat-Room, *der;* **~ show** *n.* Talk-Show, *die*

**chattel** /'tʃætl/ *n., usu. in pl.* **~[s]** bewegliche Habe (*geh.*); ⇒ *also* **good** 3 G

**chatter** /'tʃætə(r)/ ❶ *v.i.* Ⓐ schwatzen; ‹Kind:› schwatzen, plappern; ‹Affe:› schnattern; Ⓑ (*rattle*) ‹Zähne:› klappern; **his teeth ~ed** er klapperte mit den Zähnen. ❷ *n.* Ⓐ Schwatzen, *das;* (*of child*) Plappern, *das;* Schwatzen, *das;* (*of monkey*) Schnattern, *das;* Ⓑ (*of teeth*) Klappern, *das*

**chatterbox** /'tʃætəbɒks/ *n.* Quasselstrippe, *die* (*ugs.*); (*child*) Plappermäulchen, *das*

**chattily** /'tʃætɪlɪ/ *adv.* im Plauderton

**chattiness** /'tʃætɪnɪs/ *n., no pl.* Gesprächigkeit, *die;* Schwatzhaftigkeit, *die* (*abwertend*)

**chatty** /'tʃætɪ/ *adj.* gesprächig; schwatzhaft (*abwertend*)

**chauffeur** /'ʃəʊfə(r), ʃəʊ'fɜ:(r)/ ▶ 1261 ❶ *n.* Fahrer, *der;* Chauffeur, *der;* **~-driven car** Wagen mit Chauffeur. ❷ *v.t.* fahren; chauffieren (*veralt.*)

**chauvinism** /'ʃəʊvɪnɪzm/ *n., no pl.* Chauvinismus, *der;* **male ~:** männlicher Chauvinismus

**chauvinist** /'ʃəʊvɪnɪst/ *n.* Chauvinist, *der*/ Chauvinistin, *die;* **male ~/[male] ~ pig** Chauvinist, *der*/Chauvinistenschwein, *das*

**chauvinistic** /ʃəʊvɪ'nɪstɪk/ *adj.* chauvinistisch

**cheap** /tʃi:p/ ❶ *adj.* Ⓐ (*inexpensive*) billig; **~ ticket** (*at reduced rate*) verbilligte Fahrkarte; **be ~ and nasty** billiger Ramsch sein; **be ~ at the price** sehr preiswert sein; (*fig.*) es wert sein; **on the ~** (*coll.*) billig; **do it on the ~** (*coll.*) es billig machen (*ugs.*); Ⓑ (*easily got or made*) billig; Ⓒ (*worthless*) billig ‹Aussehen›; gemein ‹Lügner›; schäbig ‹Verhalten, Betragen›; **feel ~:** sich (*Dat.*) schäbig vorkommen; **hold ~:** gering schätzen; **make oneself ~:** sich [selbst] herabsetzen; Ⓓ (*Finance*) billig ‹Geld›. ❷ *adv.* billig; **I got it ~:** ich habs billig gekriegt (*ugs.*); **be going ~:** besonders günstig sein (*ugs.*)

**cheapen** /'tʃi:pn/ ❶ *v.t.* verbilligen; verringern ‹Kosten›; (*fig.*) herabsetzen; **~ oneself** sich [selbst] herabsetzen; **feel ~ed** sich gedemütigt fühlen. ❷ *v.i.* billiger werden

**'cheapjack** ❶ *n.* Straßenhändler, *der;* billiger Jakob (*ugs.*). ❷ *adj.* Billig-

**cheaply** /'tʃi:plɪ/ *adv.* ⇒ **cheap** 1: billig; gemein; schäbig

**cheapness** /'tʃi:pnɪs/ *n., no pl.* niedriger Preis; (*fig.*) Gewöhnlichkeit, *die*

**cheat** /tʃi:t/ ❶ *n.* Ⓐ (*person*) Schwindler, *der*/Schwindlerin, *die;* Ⓑ (*act*) Schwindel, *der;* **that's a ~!** das ist Betrug! ❷ *v.t.* Ⓐ hintergehen; betrügen; **~ sb./sth. [out] of sth.** jmdn./etw. um etw. betrügen; **~ sb. into doing sth.** jmdn. durch Täuschung dazu bringen, etw. zu tun; Ⓑ (*escape*) **~ sb.** jmdm. entgehen; **~ death** dem Tod entkommen. ❸ *v.i.* betrügen; (*Sch.*) täuschen; **~ at cards** beim Kartenspielen mogeln

**Chechen** /'tʃetʃn/ ❶ *adj.* tschetschenisch; **he/she is ~:** er ist Tschetschene/sie ist Tschetschenin. ❷ *n.* Ⓐ (*Person*) Tschetschene, *der*/Tschetschenin, *die;* Ⓑ (*language*) Tschetschenisch, *das*

**Chechenia, Chechnya** /tʃeʃ'nɪɑ:/ *pr. ns.* Tschetschenien (*das*)

**check**[1] /tʃek/ ❶ *n.* Ⓐ (*stoppage, thing that restrains*) Hindernis, *das;* (*restraint*) Kontrolle, *die;* **[hold** *or* **keep sth.] in ~:** [etw.] unter Kontrolle [halten]; **hold** *or* **keep one's temper in ~:** sich beherrschen; **act as a ~ upon sth.** etw. unter Kontrolle halten; **a ~ must be put on sth.** etw. muss unter Kontrolle gebracht werden; **[a system of] ~s and balances** ein Kontrollsystem; Ⓑ (*for accuracy*) Kontrolle, *die;* **make a ~ on sth./sb.** etw./jmdn. überprüfen *od.* kontrollieren; **give sth. a ~:** etw. überprüfen *od.* kontrollieren; **keep a ~ on** überprüfen; kontrollieren; überwachen ‹Verdächtigen›; Ⓒ (*token*) (*for left luggage*) Gepäckaufbewahrungsschein, *der;* (*Amer.: in theatre*) Garderobenmarke, *die;* (*for seat-holder*) Platzkarte, *die;* (*of verification*) Kontrollzeichen, *das;* (*Amer.: bill in restaurant etc.*) Rechnung, *die;* Ⓓ (*rebuff; also Mil.*) Widerstand, *der;* Ⓔ (*Chess*) Schach, *das;* **be in ~:** im Schach stehen; **put sb. in ~:** jmdm. Schach bieten; Ⓕ (*Hunting*) Stocken [beim Verlieren der Fährte]; Ⓖ (*Amer.: counter at cards*) Spielmarke, *die;* ⇒ *also* **cash in** 1; Ⓗ (*Amer.*) ⇒ **cheque**.
❷ *v.t.* Ⓐ (*restrain*) unter Kontrolle halten; unterdrücken ‹Ärger, Lachen›; **~ oneself** sich beherrschen; Ⓑ (*examine accuracy of*) nachprüfen; nachsehen ‹Hausaufgaben›; kontrollieren ‹Fahrkarte›; (*Amer.: mark with tick*) abhaken; (*Amer.: deposit*) aufgeben ‹Gepäck›; Ⓒ (*stop; also Mil.*) aufhalten; Ⓓ (*Chess*) Schach bieten (+ *Dat.*).
❸ *v.i.* Ⓐ (*test*) **~ on sth.** etw. überprüfen; **~ with sb.** bei jmdm. nachfragen; **just ~ing** (*coll. joc.*) wollte mich nur vergewissern; Ⓑ (*Amer.: agree*) übereinstimmen; Ⓒ (*Hunting*) stocken.
❹ *int.* Ⓐ (*Chess*) Schach; Ⓑ (*Amer.*) einverstanden

**~ 'back** *v.i.* nachsehen

**~ 'in** ❶ *v.t.* eintragen; (*at airport*) **~ in one's luggage** sein Gepäck abfertigen lassen *od.* einchecken. ❷ *v.i.* (*arrive at hotel*) ankommen; (*sign the register*) sich eintragen; (*report one's arrival*) sich melden; (*at airport*) einchecken. ⇒ *also* **check-in**

**~ 'off** *v.t.* abhaken

**~ 'out** ❶ *v.t.* überprüfen. ❷ *v.i.* abreisen; **~ out [of one's hotel]** abreisen; (*pay*) seine Hotelrechnung bezahlen; **~ out of the supermarket** im Supermarkt bezahlen; ⇒ *also* **checkout**

**~ 'over** *v.t.* durchsehen

**~ 'through** *v.t.* kontrollieren; durchsehen ‹Brief, Rechnung›

**~ 'up** *v.i.* überprüfen; **~ up on sb./sth.** jmdn./etw. überprüfen *od.* kontrollieren; **the police will ~ up on you** die Polizei wird Nachforschungen über dich anstellen; ⇒ *also* **check-up**

**check**[2] *n.* (*pattern*) Karo, *das;* **a shirt of red and white ~:** ein rotweiß kariertes Hemd

**checked** /tʃekt/ *adj.* (*patterned*) kariert

**checker** /'tʃekə(r)/ *n.* Prüfer, *der*/Prüferin, *die;* Kontrolleur, *der*

**'checkerboard** *n.* (*Amer.*) Schachbrett, *das*

**checkers** /'tʃekəz/ *n., no pl.* (*Amer.*) ⇒ **draughts**

**'check-in** *n.* Abfertigung, *die; attrib.* Abfertigungs-

**'checking account** *n.* (*Amer.*) Girokonto, *das*

**check: ~list** *n.* Verzeichnis, *das;* Checkliste, *die* (*Technik, Flugw.*); **~mate** /'tʃekmeɪt/ ❶ *n.* [Schach]matt, *das;* ❷ *int.* [schach]matt; ❸ *v.t.* Ⓐ matt setzen; Ⓑ (*fig.*) zunichte machen; **~out** *n.* Abreise, *die;* (*desk*) Kasse, *die; attrib.* **~out desk** *or* **point** *or* **counter** Kasse, *die;* **~point** *n.* Kontrollpunkt, *der;* **~room** *n.* (*Amer.*) Ⓐ (*cloakroom*) Garderobe, *die;* Ⓑ (*for left luggage*) Gepäckaufbewahrung, *die;* **~-up** *n.* (*Med.*) Untersuchung, *die;* **get/have a ~-up** untersucht werden; **go to the doctor for a ~-up** sich beim Arzt untersuchen lassen

**Cheddar** /'tʃedə(r)/ *n.* Cheddar[käse], *der*

**cheek** /tʃi:k/ ❶ *n.* Ⓐ ▶ 966 Backe, *die;* Wange, *die* (*geh.*); **~ by jowl** Seite an Seite; dicht nebeneinander ‹stehen, wohnen›; **dance ~ to ~:** Wange an Wange tanzen; **turn the other ~** (*fig.*) die andere Wange darbieten; Ⓑ (*impertinence*) Frechheit, *die;* **have the ~ to do sth.** die Frechheit *od.* Stirn besitzen, etw. zu tun; **I like your ~** (*iron.*) du hast vielleicht Nerven! (*ugs.*); **none of your ~:** sei nicht so frech; **have plenty of ~:** ziemlich unverschämt sein; Ⓒ ▶ 966 *in pl.* (*coll.: buttocks*) Hinterbacken (*ugs.*). ❷ *v.t.* **~ sb.** zu jmdm. frech sein

**'cheekbone** *n.* Backenknochen, *der*

**cheekily** /'tʃi:kɪlɪ/ *adv.* frech; **behave ~:** frech sein

**cheekiness** /ˈtʃiːkɪnɪs/ *n., no pl.* Frechheit, *die*

**ˈcheek pouch** *n.* (*Zool.*) Backentasche, *die*

**cheeky** /ˈtʃiːkɪ/ *adj.* frech; **~ girl** freches Ding (*ugs.*); **~ boy** frecher Bengel; **~ devil/monkey** (*coll.*) Frechdachs, *der* (*ugs.*)

**cheep** /tʃiːp/ ❶ *v.i.* piep[s]en. ❷ *n.* Piep[s]en, *das;* **not a ~ [out of sb.]** (*fig. coll.*) kein Pieps [von jmdm.] (*ugs.*)

**cheer** /tʃɪə(r)/ ❶ *n.* **A** (*applause*) Beifallsruf, *der;* **give sb. a [big] ~:** jmdm. zujubeln; **give three ~s for sb.** jmdn. [dreimal] hochleben lassen; **two ~s** (*iron.*) ist ja großartig (*iron.*); **B** *in pl.* (*Brit. coll.: as a toast*) prost; **C** *in pl.* (*Brit. coll.: thank you*) danke; **D** *in pl.* (*Brit. coll.: goodbye*) tschüs (*ugs.*); **E** (*arch.: frame of mind*) **be of good ~:** sei/seid guten Mutes (*geh.*). ❷ *v.t.* **A** (*applaud*) **~ sth./sb.** etw. bejubeln/jmdm. zujubeln; **B** (*gladden*) aufmuntern; aufheitern. ❸ *v.i.* jubeln

**~ ˈon** *v.t.* anfeuern ‹Sportler, Wettkämpfer›

**~ ˈup** ❶ *v.t.* aufheitern. ❷ *v.i.* bessere Laune bekommen; **~ up!** Kopf hoch!

**cheerful** /ˈtʃɪəfl/ *adj.* (*in good spirits*) fröhlich; gut gelaunt; (*bright, pleasant*) heiter; erfreulich ‹Aussichten›; lustig ‹Feuer›; (*willing*) bereitwillig; **make sb. ~:** jmdn. heiter stimmen

**cheerfully** /ˈtʃɪəfəlɪ/ *adv.* vergnügt; **the fire blazed ~:** das Feuer brannte lustig; **~ assuming that ...** (*iron.*) in der unbekümmerten Annahme, dass ...

**cheerily** /ˈtʃɪərɪlɪ/ *adv.* fröhlich

**cheering** /ˈtʃɪərɪŋ/ ❶ *adj.* **A** (*gladdening*) fröhlich stimmend; **B** (*applauding*) jubelnd. ❷ *n.* Jubeln, *das*

**cheerio** /tʃɪərɪˈəʊ/ *int.* **A** (*Brit. coll.: goodbye*) tschüs (*ugs.*); **B** (*dated: as a toast*) zum Wohl

**ˈcheerleader** *n. jmd., der andere zu Beifall, Hochrufen usw. anfeuert*

**cheerless** /ˈtʃɪəlɪs/ *adj.* freudlos; düster ‹Aussichten›

**cheery** /ˈtʃɪərɪ/ *adj.* fröhlich

**cheese** /tʃiːz/ *n.* **A** (*food*) Käse, *der;* **~s** Käsesorten; **B** (*whole*) Käselaib, *der;* (*piece*) Stück Käse; **C** **say ~!** (*Photog.*) bitte recht freundlich!; **hard ~!** (*dated coll.*) Pech gehabt! (*ugs.*). ⇒ *also* **lemon cheese**

**cheese: ~board** *n.* Käseplatte, *die;* **~cake** *n.* **A** Käsetorte, *die;* **B** *no pl., no indef. art.* (*coll.*) Pin-up-Girls *Pl.;* **~cloth** *n.* [indischer] Baumwollstoff; **~-cutter** *n. Draht zum Schneiden von Käse;* **~ dish** *n.* ≈ Käseglocke, *die*

**cheesed off** /tʃiːzd ˈɒf/ *adj.* (*Brit. coll.*) angeödet; **I am ~ with school** die Schule ödet mich an (*ugs.*) *od.* stinkt mir (*salopp*); **I'm ~:** mir stinkts! (*salopp*)

**cheese: ~-grater** *n.* Käseraspel, *die;* **~-paring** ❶ *adj.* knauserig; ❷ *n.* Knauserei, *die;* **~ ˈstraw** *n.* Käsestange, *die*

**cheetah** /ˈtʃiːtə/ *n.* (*Zool.*) Gepard, *der*

**chef** /ʃef/ *n.* ▶ **1261** Küchenchef, *der;* (*as profession*) Koch, *der*

**Chelsea**/ˈtʃelsɪ/: **~ ˈbun** *n.* ≈ Rosinenbrötchen, *das;* **~ ˈpensioner** *n. Insasse des Chelsea Royal Hospital für alte und kriegsversehrte Soldaten*

**chemical** /ˈkemɪkl/ ❶ *adj.* chemisch. ❷ *n.* Chemikalie, *die*

**chemical: ~ engiˈneer** *n.* Chemieingenieur, *der*/-ingenieurin, *die;* **~ engiˈneering** *n.* Chemotechnik, *die;* **~ firm** *n.* Chemiebetrieb, *der*

**chemically** /ˈkemɪkəlɪ/ *adv.* chemisch

**chemical: ~ ˈwarfare** *n.* chemische Krieg[s]führung; **~ worker** *n.* Chemiearbeiter, *der*/-arbeiterin, *die*

**chemise** /ʃəˈmiːz/ *n.* Unterkleid, *das*

**chemist** /ˈkemɪst/ *n.* ▶ **1261** **A** (*person skilled in chemistry*) Chemiker, *der*/Chemikerin, *die;* **B** (*Brit.: pharmacist*) Drogist, *der*/Drogistin, *die;* **~'s [shop]** Drogerie, *die;* (*dispensary*) Apotheke, *die;* ⇒ *also* **baker**

**chemistry** /ˈkemɪstrɪ/ *n., no pl.* **A** *no indef. art.* Chemie, *die;* **the ~ of iron** die chemischen Eigenschaften des Eisens; **B** (*fig.*) unerklärliche Wirkungskraft

**chemistry: ~ laboratory** *n.* Chemiesaal, *der;* **~ set** *n.* Chemiebaukasten, *der*

**chemotherapy** /kiːmə(ʊ)ˈθerəpɪ/ *n.* Chemotherapie, *die*

**chenille** /ʃəˈniːl/ *n.* Chenille, *die*

**cheque** /tʃek/ *n.* ▶ **1328** Scheck, *der;* **write a ~:** einen Scheck ausfüllen; **will you take a ~?** kann ich mit Scheck bezahlen?; **pay by ~:** mit [einem] Scheck bezahlen

**cheque: ~book** *n.* Scheckbuch, *das;* **~book journalism** *n.* Scheckbuchjournalismus, *der;* **~ card** *n.* Scheckkarte, *die*

**chequer** /ˈtʃekə(r)/ ❶ *n.* Karomuster, *das.* ❷ *v.t.* karieren

**ˈchequerboard** *n.* Schachbrett, *das*

**chequered** /ˈtʃekəd/ *adj.* **A** kariert; **a lawn ~ with sunlight and shade** ein von Licht und Schatten gefleckter Rasen; **B** (*fig.*) bewegt ‹Geschichte, Leben, Laufbahn›

**cherish** /ˈtʃerɪʃ/ *v.t.* **A** (*value and keep*) hegen ‹Hoffnung, Gefühl›; in Ehren halten ‹[Erinnerungs]gegenstand›; **~ an illusion** sich einer Illusion (*Dat.*) hingeben; **~ sb.'s memory** jmds. Andenken in Ehren bewahren; **B** (*foster*) **~ sb.** [liebevoll] für jmdn. sorgen; **to love and to ~, till death us do part** (*in marriage ceremony*) zu lieben und zu ehren, bis dass der Tod uns scheidet

**cheroot** /ʃəˈruːt/ *n.* Stumpen, *der*

**cherry** /ˈtʃerɪ/ ❶ *n.* **A** (*fruit*) Kirsche, *die;* **it's no use having two bites at a ~** (*fig.*) es hat keinen Sinn, das Ganze zweimal durchzuführen; **we may get two bites at the ~** (*fig.*) wir werden vielleicht eine zweite Chance haben; **B** (*tree*) Kirschbaum, *der.* ❷ *adj.* kirschrot; **a bright ~ red** ein helles Kirschrot

**cherry: ~ blossom** *n.* Kirschblüte, *die;* **~ ˈbrandy** *n.* Cherry Brandy, *der;* ≈ Kirschlikör, *der;* **~-pick** ❶ *v.t.* sich (*Dat.*) [her]aussuchen (**from** aus); ❷ *v.i.* sich (*Dat.*) die Rosinen herauspicken; **~ ˈpie** *n.* **A** Kirschkuchen, *der;* **B** (*Brit.: flower*) Vanillestrauch, *der;* **~ stone** *n.* Kirschkern, *der*

**cherub** /ˈtʃerəb/ *n.* **A** *pl.* **~im** /ˈtʃerəbɪm/ (*Theol., of celestial order*) Cherub, *der;* **B** *pl.* **~s** (*Art*) Putte, *die;* Putto, *der;* (*child*) Engelchen, *das*

**cherubic** /tʃɪˈruːbɪk/ *adj.* cherubinisch; engelhaft; **~ face** Engelsgesicht, *das*

**chervil** /ˈtʃɜːvɪl/ *n.* (*Bot.*) Kerbel, *der*

**Cheshire**/ˈtʃeʃə(r), ˈtʃeʃɪə(r)/: **~ ˈcat** *n.* **grin like a ~ cat** übers ganze Gesicht grinsen; **~ ˈcheese** *n.* Cheshirekäse, *der*

**chess** /tʃes/ *n., no pl., no indef. art.* das Schach[spiel]; **play ~:** Schach spielen; **be good at ~:** gut Schach spielen

**chess: ~board** *n.* Schachbrett, *das;* **~man** *n.* Schachfigur, *die;* **~ player** *n.* Schachspieler, *der*/-spielerin, *die*

**chest** /tʃest/ *n.* **A** Kiste, *die;* (*for clothes or money*) Truhe, die; (*treasury; also fig.*) Kasse, *die;* **B** ▶ **966**, ▶ **1232** (*part of body*) Brust, *die;* (*Anat.*) Brustkorb, *der;* Brustkasten, *der* (*ugs.*); **cold on the ~:** Bronchitis, *die;* **get sth. off one's ~** (*fig. coll.*) sich (*Dat.*) etw. von der Seele reden; **play sth. close to one's ~** (*fig. coll.*) so wenig wie möglich über etw. (*Akk.*) erwähnen

**-chested** /tʃestɪd/ *adj. in comb.* -brüstig; **a broad-~ man** ein Mann mit einem breiten Brustkorb

**chesterfield** /ˈtʃestəfiːld/ *n.* gepolstertes Sofa (*mit hohen Armlehnen*)

**chest: ~ expander** *n.* Expander, *der;* **~ measurement** *n.* Brustumfang, *der;* Brustweite, *die*

**chestnut** /ˈtʃesnʌt/ ❶ *n.* **A** (*tree*) Kastanie, *die;* **Spanish** *or* **sweet ~:** Edelkastanie, *die;* ⇒ *also* **horse chestnut**; **B** (*fruit*) Kastanie, *die;* **pull the ~s out of the fire** (*fig.*) die Kastanien aus dem Feuer holen (*ugs.*); **C** (*colour*) Kastanienbraun, *das;* **D** ⇒ **chestnut wood**; **E** (*stale story or topic*) **[old] ~:** alte *od.* olle Kamelle (*ugs.*); **F** (*horse*) Fuchs, *der.* ❷ *adj.* (*colour*) **~[-brown]** kastanienbraun

**chestnut: ~ tree** ⇒ **chestnut** 1 A; **~ wood** *n.* Kastanienholz, *das*

**chest of ˈdrawers** Kommode, *die*

**chesty** /ˈtʃestɪ/ *adj.* (*coll.*) anfällig (*für Erkältungen*); tief sitzend ‹Husten›; **be ~:** es auf der Brust haben (*ugs.*); **you sound rather ~ today** du klingst heute ziemlich erkältet

**chevron** /ˈʃevrən/ *n.* **A** (*badge*) Winkel, *der;* **B** (*Her.*) Sparren, *der;* Chevron, *der;* **C** (*traffic sign*) Winkel (*auf Richtungstafeln o. Ä.*)

**chew** /tʃuː/ ❶ *v.t.* kauen; **~ one's fingernails** an den [Finger]nägeln kauen; **~ the rag** *or* **the fat [about sth.]** (*fig.*) [über etw. (*Akk.*)] meckern (*ugs.*); ⇒ *also* **bite off**; **cud**. ❷ *v.i.* kauen (**on** auf + *Dat.*); **~ on** *or* **over sth.** (*fig.*) sich (*Dat.*) etw. durch den Kopf gehen lassen. ❸ *n.* Kauen, *das*

**~ ˈout** *v.t.* (*Amer. coll.*) zusammenstauchen (*ugs.*)

**chewing gum** /ˈtʃuːɪŋgʌm/ *n.* Kaugummi, *der od. das*

**chewy** /ˈtʃuːɪ/ *adj.* zäh ‹Fleisch, Bonbon›

**Chianti** /kɪˈæntɪ/ *n.* Chianti[wein], *der*

**chiaroscuro** /kjɑːrəˈskʊərəʊ/ *n., pl.* **~s** (*in painting*) Clair-obscur, *das;* (*fig. also*) Helldunkel, *das*

**chic** /ʃiːk/ ❶ *adj.* schick; elegant. ❷ *n.* Schick, *der*

**chicane** /ʃɪˈkeɪn/ *n.* (*Sport*) Schikane, *die*

**chicanery** /ʃɪˈkeɪnərɪ/ *n.* **A** *no pl.* (*deception*) Täuschungsmanöver, *das;* (*legal trickery*) Rechtsverdrehung, *die;* **B** (*sophistry*) Winkelzug, *der;* Trick, *der*

**chichi** /ˈʃiːʃiː/ ❶ *adj.* überspannt, affektiert ‹Person, Verhalten›; extravagant ‹Gegenstand›. ❷ *n.* Chichi, *das*

**chick** /tʃɪk/ *n.* **A** Küken, *das;* **B** (*coll.: child*) Kleine, *das;* **C** (*sl.: young woman*) Biene, *die* (*ugs.*)

**chickadee** /ˈtʃɪkədiː/ *n.* (*Ornith.*) Chickadee-Meise, *die*

**chicken** /ˈtʃɪkɪn/ ❶ *n.* **A** Huhn, *das;* (*grilled, roasted*) Hähnchen, *das;* **don't count your ~s [before they are hatched]** (*prov.*) man soll den Pelz nicht verkaufen, ehe man den Bären erlegt hat; **B** (*coll.: youthful person*) Küken, *das;* **she's no ~** (*is no longer young*) sie ist nicht mehr die Jüngste; (*is experienced*) sie ist kein [kleines] Kind mehr; **C** (*coll.: game*) **play ~:** eine Mutprobe ablegen; **D** (*coll.: coward*) Angsthase, *der.* ❷ *adj.* (*coll.*) feig[e]. ❸ *v.i.* **~ out** (*coll.*) kneifen; **~ out of sth.** sich vor etw. (*Dat.*) drücken; vor etw. (*Dat.*) kneifen

**chicken: ~-and-ˈegg** *adj.* Huhn-Ei- ‹Frage›; **~-breasted** *adj.* hühnerbrüstig; flachbrüstig; **~ feed** *n.* **A** Hühnerfutter, *das;* **B** (*fig. coll.*) eine lächerliche Summe; **the firm pays them ~ feed** die Firma zahlt ihnen einen Hungerlohn; **~-hearted** *adj.* feige; hasenfüßig; **~ ˈpie** *n.* Hühnerpastete, *die;* **~pox** *n.* ▶ **1232** (*Med.*) Windpocken *Pl.;* **~ run** *n.* Auslauf, *der* (*Landw.*); **~ ˈsalad** *n.* Geflügelsalat, *der;* **~ ˈsoup** *n.* Hühnersuppe, *die;* **~ wire** *n.* Maschendraht, *der*

**chick: ~pea** *n.* Kichererbse, *die;* **~weed** *n.* (*Bot.*) Vogelmiere, *die;* Hühnerdarm, *der*

**chicory** /ˈtʃɪkərɪ/ *n.* **A** (*plant*) Chicorée, *der od. die;* (*for coffee*) Zichorie, *die;* (*flower*) Wegwarte, *die;* **B** (*Amer.: endive*) Endivie, *die*

**chide** /tʃaɪd/, **~d** *or* **chid** /tʃɪd/, **~d** *or* **chid** *or* (*arch./literary*) **chidden** /ˈtʃɪdn/ ❶ *v.t.* schelten (*geh.*) (**for** wegen). ❷ *v.i.* schelten (*geh.*)

**chief** /tʃiːf/ ❶ *n.* **A** (*of state, town, clan*) Oberhaupt, *das;* (*of party*) Vorsitzende, *der;* (*of tribe*) Häuptling, *der;* **~ of state** Staatschef, *der;* **B** (*of department*) Leiter, *der;* (*coll.: one's superior, boss*) Chef, *der;* Boss, *der;* **~ of police** Polizeipräsident, *der;* **~ of staff** (*of a service*) Generalstabschef, *der;* (*commander*) Stabschef, *der;* **C** **in ~** *postpos.* hauptsächlich; **Colonel-in-C~:** Regimentskommandeur, *der;* **D** (*Her.*) Schildhaupt, *das.*

❷ *adj., usu. attrib.* **A** Ober-; **~ priest** Oberpriester, *der;* **~ clerk** Bürochef, *der;* **~ engineer** erster Maschinist (*Seew.*); **[Lord]**

C~ Justice (*Brit.*) [Lord] Oberrichter, *der;* Ⓑ (*first in importance, influence, etc.*) Haupt-; ~ **reason/aim** Hauptgrund, *der*/-ziel, *das;* **his ~ crime** das Schlimmste, was er sich (*Dat.*) geleistet hat; **his ~ hope** seine größte Hoffnung; Ⓒ (*prominent, leading*) führend; ~ **culprit** Hauptschuldige, *der/die;* ~ **offender** Haupttäter, *der*/-täterin, *die*

**chiefly** /'tʃi:flɪ/ *adv.* hauptsächlich; vor allem

**chieftain** /'tʃi:ftən/ *n.* (*of Highland clan*) Oberhaupt, *das;* (*of tribe*) Stammesführer, *der;* (*of band of robbers*) Hauptmann, *der* (*hist.*)

**chiff-chaff** /'tʃɪftʃæf/ *n.* (*Ornith.*) Zilpzalp, *der*

**chiffon** /'ʃɪfɒn/ ❶ *n.* (*Textiles*) Chiffon, *der.* ❷ *adj.* Chiffon-

**chignon** /'ʃi:njɔ̃/ *n.* Chignon, *der;* [Haar]knoten, *der*

**chihuahua** /tʃɪ'wɑ:wə/ *n.* Chihuahua, *der*

**chilblain** /'tʃɪlbleɪn/ *n.* Frostbeule, *die*

**child** /tʃaɪld/ *n., pl.* **~ren** /'tʃɪldrən/ Kind, *das;* **when I was a ~:** als ich klein war; **a ~'s guide to ...** (*fig.*) ...für Kinder; **[be] with ~** (*dated*) schwanger [sein]; **the ~ is the father of the man** (*prov.*) *Einflüsse und Erfahrungen der Kindheit bestimmen den Charakter des Erwachsenen*

**child: ~ abuse** *n.* Kindesmisshandlung, *die;* **~-bearing** ❶ *n.* Schwangerschaften; ❷ *adj.* gebärfähig; **~ 'benefit** *n.* (*Brit.*) Kindergeld, *das;* **~birth** *n.* Geburt, *die;* **die in ~birth** bei der Geburt *od.* im Wochenbett sterben; **~ care** *n.* Ⓐ Betreuung von Kindern; Ⓑ (*social services department*) Kinderfürsorge, *die;* **~ 'guidance** *n.* Erziehungsberatung, *die*

**childhood** /'tʃaɪldhʊd/ *n.* Kindheit, *die;* **in ~:** als Kind; **from** *or* **since ~:** schon als Kind; **be in one's second ~:** an Altersschwachsinn leiden

**childish** /'tʃaɪldɪʃ/ *adj.*, **childishly** /'tʃaɪldɪʃlɪ/ *adv.* kindlich; (*derog.*) kindisch

**childishness** /'tʃaɪldɪʃnɪs/ *n., no pl.* Kindlichkeit, *die;* (*derog.*) kindisches Wesen; (*behaviour*) kindisches Benehmen

**childless** /'tʃaɪldlɪs/ *adj.* kinderlos

**childlike** /'tʃaɪldlaɪk/ *adj.* kindlich

**child: ~minder** *n.* ▶ 1261 (*Brit.*) Tagesmutter, *die;* **~ por'nography** *n.* Kinderpornographie, *die;* **~ 'prodigy** *n.* Wunderkind, *das;* **~proof** *adj.* kindersicher; **~proof (door) lock** (*in car*) Kindersicherung, *die;* **~ psy'chology** *n.* Kinderpsychologie, *die*

**children** *pl. of* **child**

**child: ~'s play** *n., no pl.* (*fig.*) Kinderspiel, *das;* **it's ~'s play!** es ist ein Kinderspiel!; **C~ Sup'port Agency** *n.* (*Brit.*) *staatliche Einrichtung zur Durchsetzung von Unterhaltsansprüche für Kinder;* **~ 'welfare** *n.* Kinderfürsorge, *die*

**Chile** /'tʃɪlɪ/ *pr. n.* Chile (*das*)

**Chilean** /'tʃɪlɪən/ ▶ 1340 ❶ *adj.* chilenisch; **sb. is ~:** jmd. ist Chilene/Chilenin. ❷ *n.* Chilene, *der*/Chilenin, *die*

**Chile: ~ 'pine** *n.* (*Bot.*) Chilefichte, *die;* **~ saltpetre** *n.* Chilesalpeter, *der*

**chili** ⇒ **chilli**

**chill** /tʃɪl/ ❶ *n.* Ⓐ (*cold sensation*) Frösteln, *das;* (*feverish shivering*) Schüttelfrost, *der;* (*illness*) Erkältung, *die;* **catch a ~:** sich verkühlen *od.* erkälten; Ⓑ (*unpleasant coldness*) Kühle, *die;* (*fig.*) Abkühlung, *die;* **take the ~ off [sth.]** etw. leicht erwärmen; **there's a ~ in the air** es ist ziemlich kühl [draußen]; Ⓒ (*depressing influence*) Ernüchterung, *die;* **her presence at the party cast** *or* **spread a ~ over things** durch ihre Anwesenheit bei der Party entstand eine frostige Atmosphäre; Ⓓ (*of manner*) Frostigkeit, *die.*
❷ *v.t.* Ⓐ (*make cold, preserve*) kühlen; **I was ~ed to the marrow** ich war ganz durchgefroren; Ⓑ (*Metallurgy*) abschrecken.
❸ *v.i.* Ⓐ abkühlen; Ⓑ (*Amer.*) ⇒ **~ out.**
❹ *adj.* (*literary; lit. or fig.*) kühl

**~ out** *v.i.* (*Amer. coll.*) (*relax*) sich entspannen; (*calm down*) sich abregen (*ugs.*)

**'chill factor** ⇒ **wind chill factor**

**chilli** /'tʃɪlɪ/ *n., pl.* **~es** Chili, *der;* **~ con carne** /tʃɪlɪ kɒn 'kɑ:nɪ/ (*Gastr.*) Chili con carne

**chilliness** /'tʃɪlɪnɪs/ *n., no pl.* (*lit. or fig.*) Kühle, *die*

**chilling** /'tʃɪlɪŋ/ *adj.* (*fig.*) ernüchternd; frostig ‹Art, Worte, Blick›

**chilly** /'tʃɪlɪ/ *adj.* Ⓐ (*lit. or fig.*) kühl; Ⓑ (*feeling somewhat cold*) **I am rather ~:** mir ist ziemlich kühl; (*sensitive to cold*) **I'm rather a ~ person** ich friere ziemlich leicht

**Chiltern Hundreds** /tʃɪltən 'hʌndrədz/ *n.* (*Brit. Polit.*) *Kronamt, dessen Übernahme Parlamentariern die Aufgabe ihres Parlamentssitzes ermöglicht;* **apply for the ~:** seinen Unterhaussitz aufgeben

**chimaera** ⇒ **chimera**

**chime** /tʃaɪm/ ❶ *n.* Ⓐ Geläute, *das;* **ring the ~s** die Glocken läuten; Ⓑ (*set of bells*) Glockenspiel, *das.* ❷ *v.i.* läuten; ‹Turmuhr:› schlagen; **chiming clock** Schlaguhr, *die.* ❸ *v.t.* erklingen lassen ‹Melodie›; schlagen ‹Stunde, Mitternacht›

**~ 'in** *v.i.* Ⓐ (*Mus.*) einstimmen; (*fig.*) übereinstimmen (**with** mit); Ⓑ (*interject remark*) sich [in die Unterhaltung] einmischen

**chimera** /kaɪ'mɪərə, kɪ'mɪərə/ *n.* Ⓐ (*hybrid*) [bunte, fantastische] Mischung; (*fanciful conception*) Schimäre, *die;* Ⓑ (*bogy*) Schimäre, *die;* Schreckgespenst, *das;* Ⓒ (*Biol.*) Chimäre, *die*

**chimerical** /kaɪ'merɪkl, kɪ'merɪkl/ *adj.* schimärisch (*geh.*); trügerisch

**chimney** /'tʃɪmnɪ/ *n.* Ⓐ (*of house, factory, etc.*) Schornstein, *der;* (*of house also*) Kamin, *der* (*bes. südd.*); (*of factory or ship also*) Schlot, *der;* (*above open fire*) Rauchfang, *der;* **the smoke goes up the ~:** der Rauch zieht durch den Kaminschacht ab; **come down the ~:** durch den Schornstein kommen; **smoke like a ~** (*fig.*) wie ein Schlot rauchen; Ⓑ (*of lamp*) [Lampen]zylinder, *der;* Ⓒ (*vent of volcano etc.*) Schlot, *der;* Ⓓ (*Mountaineering*) Kamin, *der*

**chimney: ~ breast** *n.* Kaminmantel, *der;* **~ corner, ~ nook** *ns.* Sitzecke am Kamin; **~ piece** *n.* Kaminsims, *der;* **~ pot** *n.* ≈ Schornsteinkopf, *der;* **~ stack** ⇒ **stack** 1 D; **~ sweep** *n.* ▶ 1261 Schornsteinfeger, *der*

**chimp** /tʃɪmp/ (*coll.*), **chimpanzee** /tʃɪmpən'zi:/ *ns.* Schimpanse, *der*

**chin** /tʃɪn/ *n.* ▶ 966 Kinn, *das;* **keep one's ~ up** (*fig.*) den Kopf nicht hängen lassen; **~ up!** Kopf hoch!; **take it on the ~** (*suffer severe blow*) einen harten Schlag einstecken müssen; (*endure sth. courageously*) es mit Fassung tragen; ⇒ *also* **stick out** 1 A

**china** *n.* Porzellan, *das;* (*crockery*) Geschirr, *das;* **broken ~:** Scherben *Pl.*

**China** /'tʃaɪnə/ *pr. n.* China (*das*)

**china: ~ cabinet** *n.* Vitrine, *die;* **~ 'clay** *n.* Porzellanerde, *die;* **~ cupboard** *n.* Geschirrschrank, *der*

**China: ~man** /'tʃaɪnəmən/ *n., pl.* **~men** /'tʃaɪnəmən/ (*derog.*) Chinese, *der;* **c~ shop** ⇒ **bull** 1 A; **~ 'tea** *n.* Chinatee, *der;* **~town** *n.* Chinesenviertel, *das;* **c~ware** *n., no pl.* Porzellan, *das*

**chinch [bug]** /'tʃɪntʃ(bʌg)/ *n.* (*Amer.*) Ⓐ Bettwanze, *die;* Ⓑ (*destroying grain*) Getreidewanze, *die*

**chinchilla** /tʃɪn'tʃɪlə/ *n.* Ⓐ (*Zool.*) Chinchilla, *die;* Ⓑ (*fur*) Chinchilla[pelz], *der;* Ⓒ (*cat*) Chinchillaperser, *der;* (*rabbit*) Chinchilla, *das*

**chin-chin** /tʃɪn'tʃɪn/ *int.* (*Brit.*) (*greeting*) hallo! (*ugs.*); (*farewell*) tschüs! (*ugs.*); cheerio!; (*as a toast*) prost!

**chine**[1] /tʃaɪn/ *n.* (*Brit. Geog.: ravine*) ≈ Klamm, *die*

**chine**[2] *n.* Ⓐ (*backbone*) Rückgrat, *das;* (*Cookery: joint of meat*) Rückenstück, *das;* Ⓑ (*Geog.: ridge*) Kamm, *der*

**Chinese** /tʃaɪ'ni:z/ ▶ 1275, ▶ 1340 ❶ *adj.* chinesisch; **sb. is ~:** jmd. ist Chinese/Chinesin; ⇒ *also* **English** 1. ❷ *n.* Ⓐ *pl. same* (*person*) Chinese, *der*/Chinesin, *die;* Ⓑ (*language*) Chinesisch, *das;* ⇒ *also* **English** 2 A

**Chinese: ~ 'boxes** *n. pl.* Satz ineinander passender Schachteln; **~ 'burn** *n.* tausend Stecknadeln; **give sb. a ~ burn** bei jmdm. tausend Stecknadeln machen; **~ 'goose** *n.* Höckergans, *die;* **~ 'lantern** *n.* Ⓐ (*of paper*) Lampion, *der;* Ⓑ (*Bot.*) Judenkirsche, *die;* **~ 'puzzle** *n.* chinesisches Geduldsspiel; **~ 'white** *n.* Zinkweiß, *das*

**chink**[1] *n.* Ⓐ Spalt, *der;* **a ~ in sb.'s armour** (*fig.*) jmds. schwache Stelle; Ⓑ **a ~ of light** ein Lichtspalt

**chink**[2] ❶ *n.* (*sound*) ⇒ **clink**[1] 1. ❷ *v.i. & t.* ⇒ **clink**[1] 2, 3

**Chink** /tʃɪŋk/ *n.* (*sl. derog.*) Schlitzauge, *das* (*abwertend*)

**chinless** /'tʃɪnlɪs/ *adj.* Ⓐ mit fliehendem Kinn *nachgestellt;* **be ~:** ein fliehendes Kinn haben; Ⓑ (*fig.*) **~ wonder** (*Brit. joc.*) *bornierter Vertreter der Oberschicht*

**chinoiserie** /ʃɪn'wɑ:zərɪ/ *n.* Chinoiserie, *die*

**chin: ~ rest** *n.* Kinnstütze, *die;* **~strap** *n.* (*of helmet*) Kinnriemen, *der;* (*of bonnet*) Kinnband, *das*

**chintz** /tʃɪnts/ *n.* Chintz, *der*

**chintzy** /'tʃɪntsɪ/ *adj.* auffällig bunt und billig

**'chinwag** (*coll.*) ❶ *n.* Schwatz, *der.* ❷ *v.i.* schwatzen

**chip** /tʃɪp/ ❶ *n.* Ⓐ Splitter, *der;* **have a ~ on one's shoulder** (*fig.*) einen Komplex haben; ⇒ *also* **block** 1 C; Ⓑ (*of potato*) [Kartoffel]stäbchen, *das;* Ⓒ *in pl.* (*Brit.: fried*) Pommes frites *Pl.;* (*Amer.: crisps*) Kartoffelchips *Pl.;* Ⓓ **there is a ~ on this cup/paintwork** diese Tasse ist angeschlagen/etwas Farbe ist abgeplatzt; Ⓔ (*Gambling*) Chip, *der;* Jeton, *der;* **have had one's ~s** (*Brit. fig. coll.*) erledigt sein (*ugs.*); **when the ~s are down** (*fig. coll.*) wenns ernst wird; ⇒ *also* **cash in** 1; Ⓕ (*Electronics*) Chip, *der;* Ⓖ (*for making baskets*) Span, *der;* **~ [basket]** (*Brit.*) Spankorb, *der;* Ⓗ ⇒ **chip shot.**
❷ *v.t.*, **-pp-:** Ⓐ anschlagen ‹Geschirr›; Späne abschlagen von ‹Holz›; **~ [off]** abschlagen; **the paint is ~ped** der Lack ist abgesprungen; Ⓑ (*cut into ~s*) **~ped potatoes** Kartoffelstäbchen, *das;* Ⓒ **~ the ball** (*Golf*) den Ball mit einem kurzen Annäherungsschlag auf das Grün bringen; (*Football*) den Ball anheben.
❸ *v.i.*, **-pp-: this china ~s easily** von diesem Porzellan platzt leicht etwas ab

**~ 'in** (*coll.*) ❶ *v.i.* Ⓐ (*interrupt*) sich einmischen; **who asked you to ~ in with your opinion?** wer hat dich nach deiner Meinung gefragt?; Ⓑ (*contribute money*) etwas beisteuern; **~ in with £5** sich mit 5 Pfund beteiligen. ❷ *v.t.* (*contribute*) beisteuern

**'chipboard** *n.* Spanplatte, *die*

**chipmunk** /'tʃɪpmʌŋk/ *n.* (*Zool.*) Chipmunk, *das*

**chipolata** /tʃɪpə'lɑ:tə/ *n.* *kleine, scharf gewürzte Wurst;* Chipolata, *die*

**'chip pan** *n.* Fritteuse, *die*

**chipper** /'tʃɪpə(r)/ *adj.* (*Amer.*) fröhlich

**chipping** /'tʃɪpɪŋ/ *n.* Splitter, *der;* (*stone also*) Steinchen, *das;* **~s** (*Road Constr.*) Splitt, *der;* **'loose ~s'** „Rollsplitt“

**chippy** /'tʃɪpɪ/ *n.* (*coll.*) Pommes-frites-Bude, *die;* Frittenbude, *die* (*ugs.*)

**chip: ~ shop** *n.* (*Brit.*) ⇒ **chippy;** **~ shot** *n.* (*Golf*) kurzer Annäherungsschlag; (*Footb.*) kurzer Heber

**chiropodist** /kɪ'rɒpədɪst, ʃɪ'rɒpədɪst/ *n.* ▶ 1261 Fußpfleger, *der*/-pflegerin, *die*

**chiropody** /kɪ'rɒpədɪ, ʃɪ'rɒpədɪ/ *n.* Fußpflege, *die*

**chiropractor** /kaɪərə'præktə(r)/ *n.* ▶ 1261 (*Med.*) Chiropraktiker, *der*/-praktikerin, *die*

**chirp** /tʃɜ:p/ ❶ *v.i.* zwitschern; ‹Sperling:› tschilpen; ‹Grille:› zirpen; (*talk merrily*) jubilieren. ❷ *n.* Zwitschern, *das;* (*of sparrow*) Tschilpen, *das;* (*of grasshopper*) Zirpen, *das*

**~ 'up** *v.i.* munter werden

**chirpily** /'tʃɜ:pɪlɪ/ *adv.*, **chirpy** /'tʃɜ:pɪ/ *adj.* (*coll.*) vergnügt

**chirrup** /'tʃɪrəp/ ❶ *v.i.* zwitschern; ‹Sperling:› tschilpen. ❷ *n.* Zwitschern, *das;* (*of sparrow*) Tschilpen, *das*

**chisel** /ˈtʃɪzl/ ❶ *n.* Meißel, *der;* (*for wood*) Stemmeisen, *das;* Beitel, *der;* ⇒ *also* **cold chisel**. ❷ *v.t.*, (*Brit.*) **-ll-:** A meißeln; (*in wood*) hauen; stemmen; **finely ~led features** fein gemeißelte [Gesichts]züge (*geh.*); B (*coll.: defraud*) hereinlegen (*ugs.*); **~ sb. out of sth.** jmdn. um etw. bringen

**chiseller** (*Amer.:* **chiseler**) /ˈtʃɪzələ(r)/ *n.* (*coll.: swindler*) Betrüger, *der*/Betrügerin, *die*

**chit¹** /tʃɪt/ *n.* A (*young child*) Balg, *das od. der* (*bes. südd.*); Gör, *das* (*nordd.*); **be a mere ~ of a child** nur ein Kind sein; B (*usu. derog.: woman*) junges Ding; **only a ~ of a girl** noch ein halbes Kind

**chit²** *n.* (*note*) Notiz, *die;* (*certificate*) Zeugnis, *das;* (*bill*) Rechnung, *die;* (*receipt*) Quittung, *die;* (*from doctor*) Krankmeldung, *die*

**chit-chat** /ˈtʃɪttʃæt/ ❶ *n.* Plauderei, *die.* ❷ *v.i.*, **-tt-** plaudern

**chitterling** /ˈtʃɪtəlɪŋ/ *n.*, *usu. in pl.* Schweinsdarm, *der*

**chivalric** /ˈʃɪvlrɪk/ *adj.* (*of chivalry*) **the ~ ages** die Ritterzeit

**chivalrous** /ˈʃɪvlrəs/ *adj.* ritterlich; **~ age** Ritterzeit, *die;* **~ deed** ritterliche Tat

**chivalrously** /ˈʃɪvlrəslɪ/ *adv.* ritterlich

**chivalry** /ˈʃɪvlrɪ/ *n.*, *no pl.* A Ritterlichkeit, *die;* B (*medieval knightly system*) Rittertum, *das;* **Age of C~:** Ritterzeit, *die;* **the Age of C~ is not dead** es gibt noch richtige Kavaliere

**chives** /tʃaɪvz/ *n. pl.* Schnittlauch, *der*

**chiv[v]y** /ˈtʃɪvɪ/ *v.t.* hetzen; (*harass*) schikanieren; **~ sb. into doing sth.** jmdn. drängen, etw. zu tun; **~ sb. about sth.** jmdn. wegen etw. drängen

**~ aˈlong** *v.t.* antreiben

**chloride** /ˈklɔːraɪd/ *n.* (*Chem.*) Chlorid, *das;* (*bleaching agent*) chloridhaltiges Bleichmittel

**chlorinate** /ˈklɔːrɪneɪt/ *v.t.* chloren

**chlorination** /klɔːrɪˈneɪʃn/ *n.* Chlorung, *die*

**chlorine** /ˈklɔːriːn/ *n.* Chlor, *das*

**chlorofluorocarbon** /klɔːrəʊflʊərəʊˈkɑːbən/ *n.* Chlorfluorkohlenstoff, *der*

**chloroform** /ˈklɒrəfɔːm/ ❶ *n.* Chloroform, *das.* ❷ *v.t.* chloroformieren

**chlorophyll** /ˈklɒrəfɪl/ *n.* (*Bot.*) Chlorophyll, *das*

**choc** /tʃɒk/ *n.* (*Brit. coll.*) Schokopraline, *die*

**ˈchoc ice** *n.* Eis mit Schokoladenüberzug

**chock** /tʃɒk/ ❶ *n.* Bremsklotz, *der;* (*on rail*) Bremsschuh, *der.* ❷ *v.t.* blockieren

**ˈchock-a-block** *pred. adj.* voll gepfropft

**chocker** /ˈtʃɒkə(r)/ *adj.* (*Brit. sl.*) sauer (*salopp*); **be ~ with** *or* **of sth.** von etw. die Nase gestrichen voll haben (*salopp*)

**ˈchock-full** *pred. adj.* gestopft voll (*ugs.*); **~ with sth.** mit etw. voll gepfropft

**chockie** /ˈtʃɒkɪ/ ⇒ **choc**

**chocolate** /ˈtʃɒkələt, ˈtʃɒklət/ ❶ *n.* A Schokolade, *die;* (*sweetmeat*) Praline, *die;* **drinking ~:** Trinkschokolade, *die;* B (*colour*) Schokoladenbraun, *das.* ❷ *adj.* A (*with flavour of ~*) Schokoladen-; B (*with colour of ~*) **~[-brown]** schokoladenbraun

**chocolate: ~ ˈbiscuit** *n.* Schokoladenkeks, *der;* **~ box** ❶ *n.* Pralinenschachtel, *die;* Bonbonniere, *die;* ❷ *adj.* (*fig.*) kitschig; **~-coated** *adj.* mit Schokoladeüberzug *nachgestellt*

**choice** /tʃɔɪs/ ❶ *n.* A Wahl, *die;* **if the ~ were mine, if I had the ~:** wenn ich die Wahl hätte; **by** *or* **for ~:** am liebsten; **of my/his** *etc.* **~:** meiner/seiner *usw.* Wahl; **take your ~:** suchen Sie sich (*Dat.*) eine/einen/eins aus; wählen Sie; (*truculently*) entscheiden Sie sich; **take one's ~ of sth. from sth.** etw. aus etw. auswählen; **make a [good] ~:** eine [gute] Wahl treffen; **make a careful ~:** sorgfältig [aus]wählen; **give sb. the ~:** jmdm. die Wahl lassen; **the ~ is yours** Sie haben die Wahl; **you have a free ~:** Sie können frei wählen; **do sth. from ~:** etw. freiwillig tun; **if I were given the ~:** wenn man mir die Wahl ließe; **have no ~ but to do sth.** keine andere Wahl haben, als etw. zu tun; **leave sb. no ~:** jmdm. keine [andere] Wahl lassen; **you have several ~s** Sie haben mehrere Möglichkeiten; B (*thing chosen*) **his ~ of wallpaper was ...:** die Tapete, die er sich ausgesucht hatte, war ...; **the curtains were your ~:** die Vorhänge hast du ausgesucht; **this is my ~:** ich habe mich dafür entschieden; ⇒ *also* **Hobson's choice**; C (*variety*) Auswahl, *die;* **there is a ~ of three** es gibt drei zur Auswahl; **be spoilt for ~:** die Qual der Wahl haben; **have a ~:** die Auswahl haben.
❷ *adj.* ausgewählt; auserlesen (*geh.*); **~ wine** erlesener Wein (*geh.*); **~ tomatoes/fruit** Tomaten/Obst erster Wahl

**choir** /ˈkwaɪə(r)/ *n.* (*also Archit.*) Chor, *der*

**choir: ~boy** *n.* Chorknabe, *der;* **~master** *n.* Chorleiter, *der;* **~ practice** *n.* Chorprobe, *die;* **~ school** *n.* [*Konfessions*]*schule für Chorknaben;* **~-screen** *n.* Chorschranke, *die;* **~-stall** ⇒ **stall¹** 1 C

**choke** /tʃəʊk/ ❶ *v.t.* A (*lit. or fig.*) ersticken; **a fish bone was choking him** er drohte an einer Fischgräte zu ersticken; **you'll ~ yourself** du wirst ersticken; **in a voice ~d with emotion** (*fig.*) mit vor Erregung versagender Stimme; **be/get ~d up about sth.** (*fig. coll.*) sich (*Dat.*) etw. sehr zu Herzen nehmen; B (*strangle*) erdrosseln; **~ to death** erdrosseln; **the collar was choking him** der Kragen würgte ihn; C (*fill chock-full*) voll stopfen; (*block up*) verstopfen.
❷ *v.i.* A (*temporarily*) keine Luft [mehr] bekommen; (*permanently*) ersticken (**on** an + *Dat.*); B (*from emotion*) **he almost ~d with rage** er brachte vor Wut fast keinen Ton heraus.
❸ *n.* A (*Motor Veh.*) Choke, *der;* B (*Electr.*) Drosselspule, *die*

**~ ˈback** *v.t.* unterdrücken ‹Wut›; zurückhalten ‹Tränen›; hinunterschlucken (*ugs.*) ‹Wut, Worte›

**~ ˈdown** *v.t.* unterdrücken

**~ ˈoff** *v.t.* (*fig. coll.*) abwimmeln (*ugs.*); (*tell off*) einen Rüffel verpassen (+ *Dat.*)

**choked** /tʃəʊkt/ *adj.* (*coll.: disgusted*) sauer (*salopp*)

**choker** /ˈtʃəʊkə(r)/ *n.* (*high collar*) Stehkragen, *der;* (*necklace*) Halsband, *das*

**choler** /ˈkɒlə(r)/ *n.* A (*Hist.*) Galle, *die;* B (*poet./arch.*) **in ~:** wutentbrannt; **fit of ~:** Zornesausbruch, *der* (*geh.*)

**cholera** /ˈkɒlərə/ *n.* ▶ **1232** (*Med.*) Cholera, *die*

**choleric** /ˈkɒlərɪk/ *adj.* cholerisch

**cholesterol** /kəˈlestərɒl/ *n.* (*Med.*) Cholesterin, *das*

**chomp** /tʃɒmp/ ⇒ **champ¹**

**choo-choo** /ˈtʃuːtʃuː/ *n.* (*child lang./coll.*) Puffpuff, *die* (*Kinderspr.*)

**choose** /tʃuːz/ ❶ *v.t.*, **chose** /tʃəʊz/, **chosen** /ˈtʃəʊzn/ A (*select*) wählen; (*from a group*) auswählen; **~ a career** einen Beruf wählen; **~ sb. as** *or* **to be** *or* **for leader** jmdn. zum Anführer wählen; **~ sb. from among ...:** jmdn. unter (+ *Dat.*) *od.* aus ... auswählen; **carefully chosen words** sorgfältig gewählte Worte; **the chosen [few]** (*Theol.*) die [wenigen] Auserwählten; **the chosen people** *or* **race** (*Theol.*) das auserwählte Volk; B (*decide*) **~/~ not to do sth.** sich dafür/dagegen entscheiden, etw. zu tun; **he chose rather to study** er zog es vor zu lernen; **she did not ~ to wear ˈblack** sie zog es vor, nicht Schwarz zu tragen; **she did not ˈ~ to wear black** sie hat nicht freiwillig Schwarz getragen; **there's nothing/not much/little to ~ between them** sie unterscheiden sich in nichts/nicht sehr/nur wenig voneinander.
❷ *v.i.*, **chose, chosen** wählen; **when I ~:** wenn es mir passt; **do just as you ~:** machen Sie es so, wie Sie möchten; **~ between ...:** zwischen ... wählen; **~ from sth.** aus etw./(*from several*) unter etw. (*Dat.*) [aus]wählen; **there are several to ~ from** es stehen mehrere zur Auswahl; **he cannot ~ but submit** er hat keine andere Wahl, als nachzugeben; **if you/we** *etc.* **so ~:** wenn Sie/wir *usw.* [es] möchten *od.* wollen; **as you ~:** wie Sie möchten

**chooser** /ˈtʃuːzə(r)/ ⇒ **beggar** 1 A

**choos[e]y** /ˈtʃuːzɪ/ *adj.* (*coll.*) wählerisch

**chop¹** /tʃɒp/ ❶ *n.* A Hieb, *der;* B (*of meat*) Kotelett, *das;* C (*coll.*) **get the ~** (*be killed*) abgemurkst werden (*salopp*); (*be dismissed*) rausgeworfen werden (*ugs.*); **sth. gets the ~:** etw. wird abgeschafft; **give sb. the ~** (*dismiss*) jmdn. rauswerfen (*ugs.*); (*kill*) jmdn. abmurksen (*salopp*); **be due for the ~:** die längste Zeit existiert haben (*ugs.*). ⇒ *also* **karate chop**.
❷ *v.t.*, **-pp-:** A hacken ‹Holz›; klein schneiden ‹Fleisch, Obst, Gemüse›; **they ~ped a way through the undergrowth** sie schlugen einen Weg durch das Unterholz; **~ped herbs** gehackte Kräuter; B (*Sport*) schneiden ‹Ball›.
❸ *v.i.*, **-pp-:** **~ [away] at sth.** auf etw. (*Akk.*) einhacken; **~ through the bone** den Knochen durchhacken

**~ ˈdown** *v.t.* fällen ‹Baum›; umhauen ‹Busch, Pfosten›

**~ ˈoff** *v.t.* abhacken

**~ ˈup** *v.t.* klein schneiden ‹Fleisch, Obst, Gemüse›; zerhacken ‹Möbel›; zerkleinern ‹Holz›; **~ped-up parsley** [klein]gehackte Petersilie

**chop²** *n.* A (*jaw*) Kiefer, *der;* B *in pl.* Maul, *das;* (*coll.: person's mouth*) Klappe, *die* (*salopp*); ⇒ *also* **lick** 1 A

**chop³** *v.i.*, **-pp-:** **she's always ~ping and changing** sie überlegt es sich (*Dat.*) dauernd anders; **keep ~ping and changing** ‹Wetter:› [sich] dauernd ändern

**~ aˈbout** *v.i.* (*coll.*) sprunghaft sein; ‹Wind:› umspringen

**ˈchophouse** *n.* (*coll.*) Gaststätte, *die*

**chopper** /ˈtʃɒpə(r)/ *n.* A (*axe*) Beil, *das;* (*cleaver*) Hackbeil, *das;* B (*coll.: helicopter*) Hubschrauber, *der;* C *in pl.* (*coll.: teeth*) Beißerchen (*ugs.*)

**chopping board** /ˈtʃɒpɪŋbɔːd/ *n.* Hackbrett, *das*

**choppy** /ˈtʃɒpɪ/ *adj.* bewegt; kabbelig (*Seemannsspr.*)

**ˈchopstick** *n.* [Ess]stäbchen, *das*

**chop suey** /tʃɒpˈsuːɪ, tʃɒpˈsjuːɪ/ *n.* (*Gastr.*) Chopsuey, *das*

**choral¹** /ˈkɔːrl/ *adj.* Chor-; chorisch; **~ piece** Komposition für Chor

**chorale** (**choral²**) /kɔːˈrɑːl/ *n.* A Choral, *der;* B (*group*) Chor, *der*

**choral**/ˈkɔːrl/: **~ service** *n.* Gottesdienst mit Chorgesang; **~ society** *n.* Gesangverein, *der*

**chord¹** /kɔːd/ *n.* A (*string of harp etc.; also fig.*) Saite, *die;* **strike a [familiar/responsive] ~ with sb.** (*fig.*) bei jmdm. eine Saite zum Erklingen bringen/bei jmdm. Echo finden; **touch the right ~** (*fig.*) den richtigen Ton anschlagen *od.* treffen; B (*Math.*) Sehne, *die;* (*Aeron.: of wing*) Flügeltiefe, *die*

**chord²** *n.* (*Mus.*) Akkord, *der;* **common ~:** Dreiklang [mit reiner Quinte]

**chore** /tʃɔː(r)/ *n.* [lästige] Routinearbeit; **do the [general] household ~s** die üblichen Hausarbeiten erledigen; **writing letters is a ~:** Briefe zu schreiben ist eine lästige Pflicht

**chorea** /kəˈriːə/ *n.* (*Med.*) Chorea, *die* (*fachspr.*); Veitstanz, *der*

**choreograph** /ˈkɒrɪəgrɑːf/ *v.t. & i.* choreographieren

**choreographer** /kɒrɪˈɒgrəfə(r)/ *n.* ▶ **1261** Choreograph, *der*/Choreographin, *die*

**choreographic** /kɒrɪəˈgræfɪk/ *adj.* choreographisch

**choreography** /kɒrɪˈɒgrəfɪ/ *n.* Choreographie, *die*

**chorister** /ˈkɒrɪstə(r)/ *n.* A (*choirboy*) Chorknabe, *der;* B (*Amer.: leader of choir*) Chorleiter, *der*

**chortle** /ˈtʃɔːtl/ ❶ *v.i.* vor Lachen glucksen; (*contemptuously*) [hämisch] kichern. ❷ *n.* Glucksen, *das;* **reply/say with a ~:** glucksend erwidern/sagen

**chorus** /ˈkɔːrəs/ ❶ *n.* A (*utterance*) Chor, *der;* **they broke [out] into a ~ of ...:** sie fingen an, im Chor ... zu singen/rufen; **say sth. in ~:** etw. im Chor sagen; **the football fans kept up a ~ of 'Scotland'** die Fußballfans hörten nicht auf, im Chor „Scotland“

zu rufen; B (*of singers*) Chor, *der;* (*of dancers*) Ballett, *das;* **be in the ~:** zum Chor/zum Ballett gehören; C (*of popular song*) Chorus, *der;* D (*Mus.: composition*) Chor, *der.* **2** *v.t.* im Chor singen/sprechen

**chorus: ~ girl** *n.* Chorsängerin, *die;* (*dancer*) [Revue]girl, *das;* **~ line** *n.* Ballett, *das;* **~-master** *n.* Chorleiter, *der*

**chose, chosen** ⇒ **choose**

**chough** /tʃʌf/ *n.* (*Ornith.*) **[Cornish] ~:** Alpenkrähe, *die;* **[alpine] ~:** Alpendohle, *die*

**choux** /ʃu:/ *n.* **~ [pastry]** Brandteig, *der*

**chow** /tʃaʊ/ *n.* A (*dog*) Chow-Chow, *der;* B (*Amer. sl.: food*) Futterage, *die* (*ugs.*); Futter, *das* (*salopp*)

**chowder** /'tʃaʊdə(r)/ *n.* (*Amer.*) *Suppe od. Eintopf mit Fisch od. Muscheln, Pökelfleisch od. Schinken, Milch, Kartoffeln u. Gemüse*

**Christ** /kraɪst/ **1** *n.* Christus (*der*); ⇒ *also* **before** 2 A. **2** *int.* (*sl.*) **[oh] ~!, ~ almighty!** Herrgott noch mal! (*ugs.*)

**Christadelphian** /krɪstə'delfɪən/ *n.* Christadelphian, *der* (*Mitglied einer chiliastischen Sekte*)

**'Christ-child** *n.* Christkind, *das*

**christen** /'krɪsn/ *v.t.* A taufen; **she was ~ed Martha** sie wurde [auf den Namen] Martha getauft; B (*coll.: use for first time*) einweihen (*ugs. scherzh.*)

**Christendom** /'krɪsndəm/ *n., no pl., no art.* die christliche Welt; (*Christians*) die Christenheit; die Christen

**christening** /'krɪsənɪŋ/ *n.* Taufe, *die;* **her ~ will be next Sunday** sie wird nächsten Sonntag getauft

**Christian** /'krɪstjən/ **1** *adj.* christlich. **2** *n.* Christ, *der*/Christin, *die*

**Christian 'era** *n.* **in the first centuries of the ~:** in den ersten Jahrhunderten christlicher Zeitrechnung

**Christianity** /krɪstɪ'ænɪtɪ/ *n., no pl., no art.* das Christentum

**Christian: ~ name** *n.* Vorname, *der;* **~ 'Science** *n.* Christian Science, *die;* Christliche Wissenschaft; **~ 'Scientist** *n.* Christian Scientist, *der;* Christlicher Wissenschaftler

**Christlike** /'kraɪstlaɪk/ *adj.* christusgleich

**Christmas** /'krɪsməs/ *n.* ▶ **1191** Weihnachten, *das od. Pl.;* **merry** *or* **happy ~:** frohe *od.* fröhliche Weihnachten; **what did you get for ~?** was hast du zu Weihnachten bekommen?; **at ~:** [zu *od.* an] Weihnachten

**Christmas: ~ box** *n.* (*Brit.*) *Geschenk/Trinkgeld zu Weihnachten für den Postboten, Zeitungsjungen usw.;* **~ cake** *n.* Weihnachtskuchen, *der; mit Marzipan und Zuckerguss verzierter, reichhaltiger Gewürzkuchen;* **~ card** *n.* Weihnachtskarte, *die;* **~ 'carol** *n.* Weihnachtslied, *das;* **~ 'Day** *n.* erster Weihnachtsfeiertag; **~ 'Eve** *n.* Heiligabend, *der;* **~ 'holiday** *n.* Weihnachtsurlaub, *der;* **the ~ holidays** die Weihnachtsferien; **~ present** *n.* Weihnachtsgeschenk, *das;* **~ 'pudding** *n.* Plumpudding, *der;* **~ 'rose** *n.* Christrose, *die;* **~ 'stocking** *n. von den Kindern am Heiligabend aufgehängter Strumpf, den der Weihnachtsmann mit Geschenken füllen soll*

**Christmassy** /'krɪsməsɪ/ *adj.* weihnachtlich; **it doesn't feel very ~:** es herrscht keine rechte Weihnachtsstimmung

**Christmas: ~-tide, ~ time** *ns.* Weihnachtszeit, *die;* **at ~-tide** *or* **~ time** in der *od.* zur Weihnachtszeit; **~ tree** *n.* Weihnachtsbaum, *der*

**chromatic** /krə'mætɪk/ *adj.* chromatisch

**chromatic 'scale** *n.* (*Mus.*) chromatische Tonleiter

**chromatography** /krəʊmə'tɒgrəfɪ/ *n.* (*Chem.*) Chromatographie, *die*

**chrome** /krəʊm/ *n.* A (*chromium-plate*) Chrom, *das;* B (*colour*) Chromgelb, *das*

**chrome: ~ 'steel** *n.* Chromstahl, *der;* **~ 'yellow** ⇒ **chrome** A

**chromium** /'krəʊmɪəm/ *n.* Chrom, *das*

**chromium: ~-plate 1** *n.* Chrom, *das;* **2** *v.t.* verchromen; **~-plated** *adj.* verchromt; **~-'plating** *n.* Verchromung, *die*

**chromosome** /'krəʊməsəʊm/ *n.* (*Biol.*) Chromosom, *das*

**chronic** /'krɒnɪk/ *adj.* A chronisch; **~ sufferers from arthritis** Personen, die an chronischer Arthritis leiden; **~ fatigue syndrome** chronisches Müdigkeitssyndrom; **he had been plagued by ~ doubts** ihn hatten ständig Zweifel geplagt; B (*Brit. coll.: bad, intense*) katastrophal (*ugs.*); **be ~:** eine [einzige] Katastrophe sein (*ugs.*); **it hurt something ~:** es hat wahnsinnig weh getan (*ugs.*)

**chronically** /'krɒnɪkəlɪ/ *adv.* chronisch; **she was ~ afraid of ...:** sie hatte [eine] chronische Angst vor ...

**chronicle** /'krɒnɪkl/ **1** *n.* A Chronik, *die;* B (*account*) Schilderung, *die;* C (*Bibl.*) **C~s** Chronik, *die.* **2** *v.t.* [chronologisch] aufzeichnen; **he ~d these events** er verfasste eine Chronik dieser Ereignisse

**chronicler** /'krɒnɪklə(r)/ *n.* ▶ **1261** Chronist, *der*

**chronological** /krɒnə'lɒdʒɪkl/ *adj.*, **chronologically** /krɒnə'lɒdʒɪkəlɪ/ *adv.* chronologisch

**chronology** /krə'nɒlədʒɪ/ *n.* Chronologie, *die;* (*table*) Zeittafel, *die*

**chronometer** /krə'nɒmɪtə(r)/ *n.* Chronometer, *das*

**chrysalis** /'krɪsəlɪs/ *n., pl.* **~es** *or* **chrysalides** /krɪ'sælɪdi:z/ (*Zool.*) A (*pupa*) Chrysalide, *die* (*Zool.*); Puppe, *die;* B (*case enclosing pupa*) Puppenhülle, *die*

**chrysanth** /krɪ'sænθ/ *n.* (*coll.*) ⇒ **chrysanthemum**

**chrysanthemum** /krɪ'sænθɪməm/ *n.* (*Bot.*) A (*flower*) Chrysantheme, *die;* B (*plant*) Chrysanthemum, *das;* Wucherblume, *die*

**chub** /tʃʌb/ *n., pl. same* (*Zool.*) Döbel, *der*

**chubby** /'tʃʌbɪ/ *adj.* A (*plump*) pummelig; rundlich ‹Gesicht›; **~ cheeks** Pausbacken (*fam.*); B (*plump-faced*) pausbäckig

**chuck**[1] /tʃʌk/ **1** *v.t.* A (*coll.: throw*) schmeißen (*ugs.*); B **~ sb. under the chin** jmdm. einen Stups unters Kinn geben; C (*coll.: throw out*) wegschmeißen (*ugs.*); **~ it!** (*coll.*) hör schon auf [damit]!; **~ the whole thing** alles hinschmeißen. **2** *n.* A **give sb. a ~ under the chin** jmdm. einen Stups unters Kinn geben; B (*coll.: dismissal*) **give sb. the ~ [from his/her job]** jmdn. [aus der Firma *usw.*] rausschmeißen (*ugs.*); **get the ~:** rausfliegen (*ugs.*)

**~ a'way** *v.t.* (*coll.*) wegschmeißen (*ugs.*); (*fig.: waste*) zum Fenster rauswerfen (*ugs.*) ‹Geld› (**on** für); vertun ‹Chance, Gelegenheit›

**~ 'out** *v.t.* (*coll.*) wegschmeißen (*ugs.*); (*fig.: eject*) rausschmeißen (*ugs.*)

**chuck**[2] *n.* (*of drill, lathe*) Futter, *das*

**chuck**[3] *n.* (*Amer. coll.: food*) Futter, *das* (*salopp*)

**chucker-out** /tʃʌkə'raʊt/ *n.* (*coll.*) Rausschmeißer, *der* (*ugs.*)

**chuckle** /'tʃʌkl/ **1** *v.i.* A leise [vor sich hin] lachen (**at** über + *Akk.*); B (*exult*) sich (*Dat.*) eins lachen. **2** *n.* leises, glucksendes Lachen; **have a ~ [to oneself] about sth.** leise über etw. (*Akk.*) sich hin lachen

**chuckle: ~-head** *n.* Schwachkopf, *der* (*abwertend*); **~-headed** *adj.* schwachköpfig (*abwertend*)

**'chuck wagon** *n.* (*Amer. coll.*) *Proviantwagen mit Kochvorrichtung (auf einer Ranch usw.)*

**chuff** /tʃʌf/ *v.i.* puffen (*ugs.*)

**chuffed** /tʃʌft/ *pred. adj.* (*Brit. coll.*) zufrieden (**about, at, with** über + *Akk.*); **be ~:** sich freuen

**chug** /tʃʌg/ **1** *v.i.*, **-gg-** ‹Motor:› tuckern. **2** *n.* Tuckern, *das*

**chum** /tʃʌm/ *n.* (*coll.*) A Kumpel, *der* (*salopp*); **be great ~s** dicke Freunde sein (*ugs.*); B (*Austral., NZ*) **new ~:** Neuling, *der*

**~ 'up** *v.i.* (*coll.*) **~ up [with sb.]** sich [mit jmdm.] anfreunden

**chummy** /'tʃʌmɪ/ *adj.* (*coll.*) freundlich; **be ~ with sb.** mit jmdm. dick befreundet sein (*ugs.*)

**chump** /tʃʌmp/ *n.* A (*coll.: foolish person*) Trottel, *der* (*ugs.*); B **be off one's ~** (*coll.*) nicht bei Trost sein (*ugs.*)

**chump 'chop** *n.* ≈ Lammkotelett, *das*

**chunk** /tʃʌŋk/ *n.* dickes Stück; (*broken off*) Brocken, *der;* (*large amount*) guter Brocken; **~ of wood** Holzklotz, *der*

**chunky** /'tʃʌŋkɪ/ *adj.* A (*containing chunks*) ‹Orangenmarmelade, Hundefutter› mit ganzen Stücken; B (*small and sturdy, short and thick*) stämmig; **~ fingers** kurze, dicke Finger; **~ book** kleines, dickes Buch; C (*made of thick, bulky material*) dick ‹Pullover, Strickjacke›

**Chunnel** /'tʃʌnl/ *n.* (*Brit. coll.*) [Ärmel]kanaltunnel, *der*

**chunter** /'tʃʌntə(r)/ *v.i.* (*coll.*) A (*murmur*) brummeln; brabbeln; B (*grumble*) murren

**chupatty** ⇒ **chapat[t]i**

**church** /tʃɜ:tʃ/ *n.* A Kirche, *die;* **in** *or* **at ~:** in der Kirche; **after ~:** nach der Kirche; **go to ~:** in die *od.* zur Kirche gehen; B **C~** (*body*) die Kirche; **go into the C~:** Geistlicher werden; **the C~ of England** die Kirche von England; **the C~ militant/triumphant** Ecclesia militans/triumphans, *die* (*Rel.*)

**church: ~goer** *n.* Kirchgänger, *der*/-gängerin, *die;* **~-going 1** *n., no pl.* Kirchenbesuch, *der;* **2** *attrib. adj.* regelmäßig den Gottesdienst besuchend; **~man** /'tʃɜ:tʃmən/ *n., pl.* **~men** /'tʃɜ:tʃmən/ A (*member of clergy*) Geistliche, *der;* B (*member of church*) Mitglied der Kirche; **~ 'mouse** *n.* **as poor as a ~ mouse** arm wie eine Kirchenmaus (*ugs. scherzh.*); **~ parade** *n.* gemeinsamer Kirchgang (*von Soldaten, Pfadfindern usw.*); **~warden** *n.* A Kirchenvorsteher, *der*/-vorsteherin, *die;* B (*Amer.: ~ administrator*) *[für die Finanzen zuständiger] Beauftragter der Protestantischen Episkopalkirche;* **~woman** *n.* [weibliches] Mitglied der Kirche

**churchy** /'tʃɜ:tʃɪ/ *adj.* streng kirchlich; kirchenfromm (*abwertend*)

**'churchyard** *n.* Kirchhof, *der* (*veralt.*); Friedhof, *der* (*bei einer Kirche*)

**churl** /tʃɜ:l/ *n.* A (*derog.*) (*ill-bred person*) ungehobelter Kerl (*ugs. abwertend*); (*surly person*) Griesgram, *der* (*abwertend*); B (*arch.*) (*peasant*) Bauer, *der;* (*person of low birth*) einfacher *od.* gemeiner Mann

**churlish** /'tʃɜ:lɪʃ/ *adj.* (*derog.*) (*ill-bred*) ungehobelt (*abwertend*); (*surly*) griesgrämig (*abwertend*)

**churlishly** /'tʃɜ:lɪʃlɪ/ *adv.* (*derog.*) ⇒ **churlish**: ungehobelt; griesgrämig

**churlishness** /'tʃɜ:lɪʃnɪs/ *n., no pl.* (*derog.*) ⇒ **churlish**: Ungehobeltheit, *die;* Griesgrämigkeit, *die*

**churn** /tʃɜ:n/ **1** *n.* (*Brit.*) A (*for making butter*) Butterfass, *das;* B (*milk can*) Milchkanne, *die.* **2** *v.t.* A verbuttern; **~ butter** buttern; B aufwühlen ‹Wasser, Schlamm›. **3** *v.i.* ‹Meer:› wallen (*geh.*); ‹Schiffsschraube:› wirbeln; ‹Räder:› durchdrehen; **my stomach was ~ing** mir drehte sich der Magen um

**~ 'out** *v.t.* massenweise produzieren (*ugs.*); **he's been ~ing out three books a year** er hat pro Jahr drei Bücher produziert

**~ 'up** *v.t.* aufwühlen

**chute** /ʃu:t/ *n.* A Schütte, *die;* (*for persons*) Rutsche, *die;* **escape ~** (*in aircraft*) Notrutsche, *die;* B (*coll.: parachute*) [Fall]schirm, *der*

**chutney** /'tʃʌtnɪ/ *n.* Chutney, *das*

**chutzpah** /'hʊtspə/ *n.* (*coll.*) Chuzpe, *die* (*salopp abwertend*)

**CI** *abbr.* (*Brit.*) **Channel Islands**

**CIA** *abbr.* (*Amer.*) **Central Intelligence Agency** CIA, *der od. die*

**ciborium** /sɪ'bɔ:rɪəm/ *n., pl.* **ciboria** /sɪ'bɔ:rɪə/ (*Archit., Eccl.*) Ziborium, *das*

**cicada** /sɪ'kɑ:də/ *n.* (*Zool.*) Zikade, die

**CID** *abbr.* (*Brit.*) **Criminal Investigation Department** C. I. D.; **the ~** die Kripo

**cider** /'saɪdə(r)/ *n.* ≈ Apfelwein, *der;* (*from France*) Cidre, *der*

**cider: ~ apple** *n.* Mostapfel, *der;* **~ press** *n.* Mostpresse, *die*

**cig** /sɪg/ *n.* (*coll.*) Glimmstängel, *der* (*ugs.*)

**cigar** /sɪ'gɑ:(r)/ *n.* Zigarre, *die*

**cigarette** /sɪgə'ret/ *n.* Zigarette, *die*

**cigarette: ~ card** *n.* Zigarettenbild, *das;* **~ case** *n.* Zigarettenetui, *das;* **~ end** *n.* Zigarettenstummel, *der;* **~ holder** *n.* Zigarettenspitze, *die;* **~ lighter** *n.* Feuerzeug, *das;* (*in car*) Zigarettenanzünder, *der;* **~ packet** *n.* Zigarettenschachtel, *die;* **~ paper** *n.* Zigarettenpapier, *das*

**cigar: ~ lighter** ⇒ **cigarette lighter**; **~-shaped** *adj.* zigarrenförmig

**cilium** /'sɪlɪəm/ *n., pl.* **cilia** /'sɪlɪə/ (*Biol., Anat.*) Wimper, *die;* Zilie, *die* (*fachspr.*)

**C.-in-C.** *abbr.* (*Mil.*) **Commander-in-Chief**

**cinch** /sɪntʃ/ **1** *n.* **A** (*coll.*) (*easy thing*) Klacks, *der* (*ugs.*); Kinderspiel, *das;* (*Amer.: sure thing*) todsichere Sache (*ugs.*); **that's a ~:** [das ist] ganz klar! (*ugs.*); klarer Fall! (*ugs.*); **B** (*Amer.: saddle girth*) Sattelgurt, *der.* **2** *v.t.* (*Amer.*) **A** (*coll.: make certain of*) **~ sth. for sb.** jmdm. etw. sichern; **B** (*put girth on*) **~ a horse** den Sattelgurt eines Pferdes schnallen

**cinchona** /sɪŋ'kəʊnə/ *n.* **A** (*Med.*) Chinarinde, *die;* **B** (*Bot.*) Chinarindenbaum, *der*

**cinder** /'sɪndə(r)/ *n.* **A** Zinder, *der;* ausgeglühtes Stück Holz/Kohle; **~s** Asche, *die;* **burnt to a ~:** völlig verkohlt; **B** (*glowing ember*) glühendes Stück Holz/Kohle; **C** (*slag*) Schlacke, *die*

**Cinderella** /sɪndə'relə/ *n.* **A** (*person*) Aschenbrödel, *das;* Aschenputtel, *das;* **B** (*fig.: thing*) Stiefkind, *das*

**cinder: ~-path** *n.* Schlackenweg, *der* (*Bauw.*); **~-track** *n.* Aschenbahn, *die*

**cine** /'sɪnɪ/ *adj.* Schmalfilm-

**cine: ~ camera** *n.* Filmkamera, *die;* **~ film** *n.* Schmalfilm, *der*

**cinema** /'sɪnɪmə/ *n.* **A** (*Brit.: building*) Kino, *das;* **go to the ~:** ins Kino gehen; **what's on at the ~?** was gibts im Kino?; **B** *no pl., no art.* (*cinematography*) Kinematographie, *die;* **C** (*films, film production*) Film, *der;* Kino, *das* (*seltener*)

**cinema: ~ complex** *n.* Kinocenter, *das;* **~-goer** *n.* (*Brit.*) Kinogänger, *der*/-gängerin, *die*

**cinematic** /sɪnɪ'mætɪk/ *adj.* filmisch; **~ art** Filmkunst, *die*

**cinematographic** /sɪnɪmætə'græfɪk/ *adj.* kinematographisch

**cinematography** /sɪnɪmə'tɒgrəfɪ/ *n., no pl.* Kinematographie, *die*

**cineraria** /sɪnə'reərɪə/ *n.* (*Bot.*) Zinerarie, *die;* Aschenpflanze, *die*

**cinnabar** /'sɪnəbɑ:(r)/ *n.* Zinnober, *der*

**cinnamon** /'sɪnəmən/ *n.* Zimt, *der;* (*plant*) Zimtbaum, *der*

**cinquefoil** /'sɪŋkfɔɪl/ *n.* **A** (*Bot.*) Fingerkraut, *das;* **B** (*Archit.*) Fünfpass, *der*

**Cinque Ports** /sɪŋk 'pɔ:ts/ *n. pl.* Cinque Ports *Pl.* (*hist.; südenglischer Städtebund*)

**cipher** /'saɪfə(r)/ **1** *n.* **A** (*code, secret writing*) Chiffre, *die;* Geheimschrift, *die;* (*key*) Kode, *der;* (*method*) Chiffrierung, *die;* Kodierung, *die;* **in ~:** chiffriert; **B** (*symbol for zero*) [Ziffer] Null, *die;* **C** (*fig.: nonentity*) Nummer, *die;* **D** (*monogram*) Monogramm, *das.* **2** *v.t.* (*put into code*) chiffrieren

**circa** /'sɜ:kə/ *prep.* zirka

**circadian** /sɜ:'keɪdɪən/ *adj.* (*Physiol.*) zirkadian

**circle** /'sɜ:kl/ **1** *n.* **A** (*also Geom.*) Kreis, *der;* **great/small ~** (*Geom., Naut., Aeronaut., Astron.*) Groß-/Kleinkreis, *der;* **fly/stand in a ~:** im Kreis fliegen/stehen; (*inside a ~*) in einem Kreis fliegen/stehen; **run round in ~s** (*fig. coll.*) hektisch herumlaufen (*ugs.*); **go round in ~s** im Kreis laufen; (*fig.*) sich im Kreis drehen; **~ of friends** Freundeskreis, *der;* **come full ~** (*fig.*) zum Ausgangspunkt zurückkehren; **things have now come full ~:** der Kreis schließt sich *od.* hat sich geschlossen; **B** ⇒ **vicious circle**; **C** (*seats in theatre or cinema*) Rang, *der;* **D** (*Archaeol.*) [Stein]kreis, *der;* **E** (*Hockey*) Schusskreis, *der.* **2** *v.i.* kreisen; (*walk in a ~*) im Kreis gehen. **3** *v.t.* **A** (*move in a ~ round*) umkreisen; **the aircraft ~d the airport** das Flugzeug kreiste über dem Flughafen; **B** (*draw ~ round*) einkreisen

**~ 'back** *v.i.* auf einem Umweg zurückkehren

**~ 'round** *v.i.* kreisen

**circlet** /'sɜ:klɪt/ *n.* (*of gold etc.*) Reif, *der;* (*of flowers*) Kranz, *der*

**circuit** /'sɜ:kɪt/ *n.* **A** (*Electr.*) Schaltung, *die;* (*path of current*) Stromkreis, *der;* **B** (*Motor racing*) Rundkurs, *der;* **C** (*journey round*) Runde, *die;* (*by car etc.*) Rundfahrt, *die;* **we made a ~ of the lake** wir machten einen Rundgang/eine Rundfahrt um den See; **D** (*judge's itinerary*) *dienstliche Rundreise* (*eines Richters, der in Städten in England und Wales in Zivil- u. Strafsachen Gerichtssitzungen abhält*); (*district visited*) Gerichtsbezirk, *der;* **go on ~:** den Gerichtsbezirk bereisen; **E** (*sequence of sporting events*) **on the professional tennis/golf ~:** bei den Turnieren der professionellen Tennis-/Golfspieler

**circuit: ~ board** *n.* (*Computing*) Schaltbrett, *das;* **~-breaker** *n.* (*Electr.*) Leistungsschalter, *der;* (*as protection*) Leistungsschutzschalter, *der;* **~ diagram** *n.* (*Electr.*) Schaltplan, *der*

**circuitous** /sə'kju:ɪtəs/ *adj.* umständlich; **the path followed a ~ route** der Pfad machte einen weiten Bogen; **reach sb. by a ~ route** jmdn. auf Umwegen erreichen

**circuitry** /'sɜ:kɪtrɪ/ *n.* (*Electr.*) Schaltungen *Pl.*

**circular** /'sɜ:kjʊlə(r)/ **1** *adj.* **A** (*round*) kreisförmig; **~ form** Kreisform, *die;* **B** (*moving in circle*) Kreis‹bahn, -bewegung›; **C** (*Logic*) **that argument is ~:** das ist ein Zirkelschluss *od.* -beweis. **2** *n.* (*letter, notice*) Rundbrief, *der;* Rundschreiben, *das;* (*advertisement*) Werbeprospekt, *der*

**circularize** (**circularise**) /'sɜ:kjʊləraɪz/ *v.t.* **every household was ~d** jeder Haushalt erhielt ein Rundschreiben/einen Werbeprospekt

**circular: ~ 'letter** *n.* ⇒ **circular** 2; **~ 'saw** *n.* Kreissäge, *die;* **~ 'tour** *n.* (*Brit.*) Rundfahrt, *die* (**of** durch)

**circulate** /'sɜ:kjʊleɪt/ **1** *v.i.* ‹Blut, Flüssigkeit:› zirkulieren; ‹Geld, Gerüchte:› zirkulieren, in Umlauf sein, kursieren; ‹Nachrichten:› sich herumsprechen; ‹Verkehr:› fließen; ‹Personen, Wein usw.:› herumgehen (*ugs.*), die Runde machen (*ugs.*). **2** *v.t.* in Umlauf setzen ‹Gerücht›; in Verkehr bringen ‹Falschgeld›; verbreiten ‹Nachricht, Information›; zirkulieren lassen ‹Aktennotiz, Rundschreiben›; herumgehen lassen ‹Buch, Bericht› (**around** in + *Dat.*)

**circulation** /sɜ:kjʊ'leɪʃn/ *n.* **A** (*Physiol.*) Kreislauf, *der;* Zirkulation, *die* (*Med.*); (*of sap, water, atmosphere*) Zirkulation, *die;* **~ trouble, poor ~** (*Physiol.*) schlechte Durchblutung; Kreislaufstörungen *Pl.;* **B** (*of news, rumour, publication*) Verbreitung, *die;* **have a wide ~:** große Verbreitung finden; **that document was not intended for public ~:** das Dokument war nicht für die Öffentlichkeit bestimmt; **C** (*of notes, coins*) Umlauf, *der;* **withdraw from ~:** aus dem Umlauf ziehen; **put/come into ~:** in Umlauf bringen/kommen; **D** (*fig.*) **be back in ~** (*after illness etc.*) wieder auf dem Posten sein; (*after emotional crisis*) wieder am normalen Leben teilnehmen; **be out of ~:** aus dem Verkehr gezogen sein (*ugs. scherzh.*); **E** (*number of copies sold*) verkaufte Auflage

**circulatory** /sɜ:kjʊ'leɪtərɪ, 'sɜ:kjʊleɪtərɪ/ *adj.* (*Physiol., Bot.*) Kreislauf-; **~ system** Kreislauf, *der*

**circumcise** /'sɜ:kəmsaɪz/ *v.t.* beschneiden

**circumcision** /sɜ:kəm'sɪʒn/ *n.* **A** Beschneidung, *die;* **B C~** (*Eccl.*) Beschneidung Christi

**circumference** /sə'kʌmfərəns/ *n.* Umfang, *der;* (*periphery*) Kreislinie, *die;* **be ... in ~:** einen Umfang von ... haben

**circumflex** /'sɜ:kəmfleks/ **1** *adj.* **~ accent** Zirkumflex, *der.* **2** *n.* Zirkumflex, *der*

**circumlocution** /sɜ:kəmlə'kju:ʃn/ *n.* **A** *no pl.* (*use of many words*) Weitschweifigkeit, *die;* (*evasive talk*) Drumherumreden, *das* (*ugs.*); **without ~:** ohne Umschweife; **B** (*roundabout expression*) umständliche Formulierung

**circumnavigate** /sɜ:kəm'nævɪgeɪt/ *v.t.* umfahren; (*by sailing boat*) umsegeln

**circumscribe** /'sɜ:kəmskraɪb/ *v.t.* (*lay down limits of*) eingrenzen; einschränken ‹Macht, Handlungsfreiheit usw.›; **our choice was ~d** unsere Auswahl war begrenzt

**circumspect** /'sɜ:kəmspekt/ *adj.* umsichtig; **we must be ~ about making new investments** neue Investitionen wollen [von uns] genau überlegt sein

**circumspection** /sɜ:kəm'spekʃn/ *n., no pl.* Umsicht, *die*

**circumspectly** /'sɜ:kəmspektlɪ/ *adv.* umsichtig; vorsichtig ‹sich nähern›

**circumstance** /'sɜ:kəmstəns/ *n.* **A** *usu. in pl.* Umstand *der;* **by force of ~[s]** durch den Zwang der Umstände; **in** *or* **under the ~s** unter den gegebenen *od.* diesen Umständen; **in certain ~s** unter [gewissen] Umständen; **under no ~s** unter [gar] keinen Umständen; **B** *in pl.* (*financial state*) Verhältnisse; **C** *no pl.* (*full detail in narrative*) Detailschilderung, *die;* **D** *no pl.* (*ceremony*) Prachtentfaltung, *die;* Gepränge, *das* (*geh.*); **E** (*incident, occurrence, fact*) Umstand, *der.* ⇒ *also* **creature** C

**circumstantial** /sɜ:kəm'stænʃl/ *adj.* **A ~ evidence** Indizienbeweise *Pl.;* **the evidence was purely ~:** der Beweis war nur auf Indizien gegründet; **B** (*detailed*) detailliert; ins Einzelne gehend

**circumvent** /sɜ:kəm'vent/ *v.t.* umgehen; hinters Licht führen ‹Gegner, Feind›

**circumvention** /sɜ:kəm'venʃn/ *n.* Umgehung, *die*

**circus** /'sɜ:kəs/ *n.* **A** Zirkus, *der;* (*arena*) Arena, *die;* **B** (*Brit.: in town*) [runder] Platz

**cirque** /sɜ:k/ *n.* (*Geog.*) Kar, *das*

**cirrhosis** /sɪ'rəʊsɪs/ *n., pl.* **cirrhoses** /sɪ'rəʊsi:z/ ▶ **1232** (*Med.*) Zirrhose, *die;* **~ of the liver** Leberzirrhose, *die*

**cirrus** /'sɪrəs/ *n., pl.* **cirri** /'sɪraɪ/ (*Meteorol.*) Zirrus, *der*

**CIS** *abbr.* **Commonwealth of Independent States**

**cissy** /'sɪsɪ/ ⇒ **sissy**

**cist** /sɪst/ *n.* (*Archaeol.*) (*coffin*) [Stein]kistengrab, *das;* (*burial chamber*) Kammergrab, *das*

**Cistercian** /sɪ'stɜ:ʃn/ **1** *n.* Zisterzienser, *der*/Zisterzienserin, *die.* **2** *adj.* Zisterzienser-

**cistern** /'sɪstən/ *n.* Wasserkasten, *der;* (*in roof*) Wasserbehälter, *der*

**citadel** /'sɪtədəl/ *n.* (*fortress*) Zitadelle, *die*

**citation** /saɪ'teɪʃn/ *n.* **A** *no pl.* (*citing*) Zitieren, *das;* **B** (*quotation*) Zitat, *das;* **C** (*announcement accompanying award*) Text der Verleihungsurkunde; **D** (*Mil.: mention in dispatch*) lobende Erwähnung

**cite** /saɪt/ *v.t.* **A** (*quote*) zitieren; anführen ‹Beispiel›; **B** (*Mil.: mention in dispatch*) lobend erwähnen (**for** wegen); **C** (*Law*) vorladen ‹Person›

**citizen** /'sɪtɪzən/ *n.* **A** (*of town, city*) Bürger, *der*/Bürgerin, *die;* **B** (*of state*) [Staats]bürger, *der*/-bürgerin, *die;* **he is a British ~:** er ist britischer Staatsbürger *od.* Brite; **~ of the world** (*fig.*) Weltbürger, *der*/-bürgerin, *die;* **C~s' Advice Bureau** (*Brit.*) Bürgerberatungsstelle, *die;* **~'s arrest** Festnahme durch eine Zivilperson; **~s' band radio** CB-Funk, *der;* (*radio set*) CB-Funkgerät, *das;* **C** (*Amer.: civilian*) Zivilist, *der*

**citizenry** /'sɪtɪzənrɪ/ *n.* Bürgerschaft, *die*

**citizenship** /'sɪtɪzənʃɪp/ *n.* Staatsbürgerschaft, *die*

**citric acid** /sɪtrɪk 'æsɪd/ *n.* (*Chem.*) Zitronensäure, *die*

**citron** /'sɪtrən/ *n.* **A** (*fruit*) Zitrone, *die;* **B** (*tree*) Zitronenbaum, *der*

**citrus** /'sɪtrəs/ *n.* **A ~ [fruit]** Zitrusfrucht, *die;* **B** (*tree*) Zitrusgewächs, *das*

**city** /'sɪtɪ/ *n.* ▶ **1626** **A** [Groß]stadt, *die;* **the ~ of Birmingham** die Stadt Birmingham; **the C~:** die [Londoner] City; das Londoner Banken- und Börsenviertel; **Heavenly C~,**

**C~ of God** Himmelreich, *das;* **B** *(Brit.: town created ~ by charter)* Stadt, *die (Ehrentitel für bestimmte Städte, meist Bischofssitze);* **C** *(Amer.: municipal corporation)* ≈ Stadtgemeinde, *die;* **D** *attrib.* [Groß]stadt‹leben, -verkehr›; ~ **lights** Lichter der Großstadt; ~ **wall** Stadtmauer, *die;* ~ **workers** Leute, die in der Stadt arbeiten

**city:** ~ **'centre** *n.* Stadtzentrum, *das;* Innenstadt, *die;* ~ **desk** *n. (Amer.)* Lokalredaktion, *die;* **C~ editor** *n. (Brit.)* Wirtschaftsredakteur, *der;* ~ **editor** *n. (Amer.)* Lokalredakteur, *der;* ~ **'fathers** *n. pl.* Stadtväter *Pl. (ugs. scherzh.);* ~ **'hall** *n. (Amer.)* **A** Rathaus, *das;* **B** *no pl., no art. (municipal officers)* die Stadtverwaltung; ~ **'slicker** *n.* **A** *(derog.: plausible rogue)* raffinierter Großstadttyp *(ugs.);* **B** *(sophisticated ~-dweller)* eleganter Großstädter; ~-**state** *n. (Hist.)* Stadtstaat, *der*

**civet** /'sɪvɪt/ *n.* ~[ **cat**] Zibetkatze, *die;*

**civic** /'sɪvɪk/ *adj.* **A** *(of citizens, citizenship)* [Staats]bürger-; [staats]bürgerlich; **my ~ responsibility** meine Verantwortung als Staatsbürger; **B** *(of city)* Stadt-; städtisch; ~ **authorities** Stadtverwaltung, *die;* ~ **centre** Verwaltungszentrum der Stadt

**civics** /'sɪvɪks/ *n., no pl.* Gemeinschaftskunde, *die;* Staatsbürgerkunde, *die (DDR)*

**civies** ⇒ **civvies**

**civil** /'sɪvɪl, 'sɪvl/ *adj.* **A** *(not military)* zivil; **in ~ life** im Zivilleben; **the ~ authorities** die Zivilbehörden; **B** *(polite, obliging)* höflich; **C** *(Law)* Zivil‹gerichtsbarkeit, -prozess, -verfahren›; zivilrechtlich; **D** *(of citizens)* bürgerlich; Bürger‹krieg, -recht, -pflicht›; **E** *(defined by enactment)* bürgerlich ‹Jahr, Zeit›; **F** *(not ecclesiastical)* weltlich

**civil:** ~ **avi'ation** *n.* Zivilluftfahrt, *die;* ~ **de'fence** *n.* Zivilschutz, *der;* ~ **diso'bedience** *n.* ziviler Ungehorsam; ~ **engi'neer** *n.* ▶ **1261** Bauingenieur, *der/*-ingenieurin, *die;* ~ **engi'neering** *n.* Hoch- und Tiefbau, *der*

**civilian** /sɪ'vɪljən/ **1** *n.* Zivilist, *der.* **2** *adj.* Zivil-; **wear ~ clothes** Zivil[kleidung] tragen

**civilisation, civilise** ⇒ **civiliz-**

**civility** /sɪ'vɪlɪtɪ/ *n.* **A** *no pl.* Höflichkeit, *die;* **B** *in pl.* Höflichkeiten; *(remarks also)* Höflichkeitsfloskeln

**civilization** /sɪvɪlaɪ'zeɪʃn/ *n.* Zivilisation, *die*

**civilize** /'sɪvɪlaɪz/ *v.t.* **A** zivilisieren; **B** *(refine)* ~ **sb.** jmdm. Manieren beibringen

**civilized** /'sɪvɪlaɪzd/ *adj.* zivilisiert; *(refined)* kultiviert

**civil:** ~ **'law** *n.* Zivilrecht, *das;* ~ **'liberty** *n., usu. in pl.* bürgerliche Freiheit; ~ **list** *n. (Brit.)* Zivilliste, *die*

**civilly** /'sɪvɪlɪ, 'sɪvəlɪ/ *adv.* höflich

**civil:** ~ **'marriage** *n.* Ziviltrauung, *die;* standesamtliche Trauung; ~ **'rights** *n. pl.* Bürgerrechte; ~ **rights movement** Bürgerrechtsbewegung, *die;* ~ **'servant** *n.* ▶ **1261** ≈ [Staats]beamte, *der/*-beamtin, *die;* **C~ 'Service** *n.* öffentlicher Dienst; ~ **'war** *n.* Bürgerkrieg, *der*

**civvies** /'sɪvɪz/ *n. pl. (Brit. sl.)* Zivil, *das;* Zivilklamotten *Pl. (ugs.)*

**Civvy Street** /'sɪvɪ stri:t/ *n., no pl., no art. (Brit. coll.)* das Zivilleben; **get back to ~:** ins Zivilleben zurückkehren

**CJD** *abbr.* ▶ **1232** **Creutzfeldt-Jakob disease**

**cl.** *abbr.* **class** Kl.

**clad¹** /klæd/ *adj. (arch./literary/joc.)* gekleidet; **walls ~ in ivy** mit Efeu bewachsene Mauern; ⇒ *also* **ironclad; ivy-clad**

**clad²** *v.t.*, **-dd-** verkleiden

**cladding** /'klædɪŋ/ *n.* Verkleidung, *die*

**claim** /kleɪm/ **1** *v.t.* **A** *(demand as one's due property)* Anspruch erheben auf (+ *Akk.*), beanspruchen ‹Thron, Gebiete›; fordern ‹Lohnerhöhung, Schadensersatz›; beantragen ‹Arbeitslosenunterstützung, Sozialhilfe usw.›; abholen ‹Fundsache›; ~ **one's luggage** sein Gepäck [ab]holen; **B** *(represent oneself as having)* für sich beanspruchen, in Anspruch nehmen ‹Sieg›; **C** *(profess, contend)* behaupten; **the new system is ~ed to have many advantages** das neue System soll viele Vorteile bieten; **D** *(need, deserve)* in Anspruch nehmen ‹Interesse, Aufmerksamkeit›; **E** *(result in loss of)* fordern ‹Opfer, Menschenleben›.

**2** *v.i.* **A** *(Insurance)* Ansprüche geltend machen; **B** *(for costs)* ~ **for damages/expenses** Schadenersatz fordern/sich *(Dat.)* Auslagen rückerstatten lassen.

**3** *n.* **A** Anspruch, *der* (**to** auf + *Akk.*); **lay ~ to sth.** auf etw. *(Akk.)* Anspruch erheben; **make too many ~s on sth.** etw. zu sehr in Anspruch nehmen; **B** *(assertion)* **make ~s about sth.** Behauptungen über etw. *(Akk.)* aufstellen; **C** *(pay ~)* Forderung, *die* (**for** nach); **put in a ~ for a pay rise** eine Lohnerhöhung fordern; **D** ~ [**for expenses**] Spesenabrechnung, *die* (**for** über + *Akk.*); ~ **for damages** Schadenersatzforderung, *die;* **E** *(Mining)* Claim, *das;* **stake a ~:** ein Claim abstecken; **stake a ~ to sth.** *(fig.)* ein Anrecht auf etw. *(Akk.)* anmelden; **I staked my ~ to the seat** ich habe mir den Platz gesichert; **F** *(Insurance)* [Versicherungs]anspruch, *der;* **G** *(in patent)* [Patent]anspruch, *der*

~ **'back** *v.t.* zurückfordern; ~ **tax/expenses** *etc.* **back** sich *(Dat.)* Steuern/Spesen *usw.* rückerstatten lassen (**from** von)

**claimant** /'kleɪmənt/ *n. (for rent rebate, social security benefit)* Antragsteller, *der/*-stellerin, *die; (for inheritance)* Erbberechtigte, *der/die;* ~ **to a title** Titelanwärter, *der/*-anwärterin, *die;* ~ **to the throne** Thronanwärter, *der/*-anwärterin, *die*

**'claim form** *n.* **A** *(Insurance)* Antragsformular, *das;* **B** *(for expenses)* Spesenabrechnungsformular, *das*

**clairvoyance** /kleə'vɔɪəns/ *n., no pl.* Hellsehen, *das*

**clairvoyant** /kleə'vɔɪənt/ **1** *n.* Hellseher, *der/*Hellseherin, *die.* **2** *adj.* hellseherisch

**clam** /klæm/ **1** *n.* Klaffmuschel, *die; (Mercenaria mercenaria)* Quahogmuschel, *die;* **shut up like a ~** *(fig.)* ausgesprochen wortkarg werden. **2** *v.i.*, **-mm-:** ~ **up** *(coll.)* den Mund nicht [mehr] aufmachen

**'clambake** *n. (Amer.)* Picknick, *das (bes. am Strand, bei dem Muscheln und Fisch auf heißen Steinen gebacken werden)*

**clamber** /'klæmbə(r)/ **1** *v.i.* klettern; kraxeln *(ugs., bes. südd., österr.);* ‹Baby:› krabbeln; ~ **up a wall** auf eine Mauer klettern; eine Mauer hochklettern. **2** *n.* Kletterei, *die;* Kraxelei, *die (ugs., bes. südd., österr.)*

**clamminess** /'klæmɪnɪs/ *n., no pl.* ⇒ **clammy**: Feuchtigkeit, *die;* Klammheit, *die*

**clammy** /'klæmɪ/ *adj.* feucht; kalt und schweißig ‹Hände, Gesicht, Haut›; klamm ‹Kleidung usw.›; nasskalt ‹Luft usw.›; ~ **with sweat** klebrig von Schweiß

**clamor** *(Amer.)* ⇒ **clamour**

**clamorous** /'klæmərəs/ *adj.* lärmend ‹Menge›; lautstark ‹Protest, Forderung›

**clamour** /'klæmə(r)/ *(Brit.)* **1** *n.* **A** *(noise, shouting)* Lärm, *der;* lautes Geschrei; **B** *(protest)* [lautstarker] Protest; *(appeal, demand)* [lautstarke] Forderung (**for** nach). **2** *v.i.* **A** *(shout)* schreien; **B** *(protest, demand)* ~ **against sth.** gegen etw. [lautstark] protestieren; ~ **for sth.** nach etw. schreien; ~ **to be let out** lautstark fordern, herausgelassen zu werden

**clamp** /klæmp/ **1** *n.* Klammer, *die; (Woodw.)* Schraubzwinge, *die;* ⇒ *also* **wheel clamp**. **2** *v.t.* **A** klemmen; einspannen ‹Werkstück›; *(Med.)* klammern; ~ **two pieces of wood together** zwei Holzstücke miteinander verklammern; **B** ~ **a vehicle** eine Parkkralle an ein Fahrzeug anbringen. **3** *v.i. (fig.)* ~ **down on sb./sth.** gegen jmdn./etw. rigoros vorgehen; ~ **down on expenses** die Ausgaben radikal drosseln

**'clampdown** *n.* rigoroses Vorgehen (**on** gegen); **the credit ~, the ~ on credit** das Anziehen der Kreditbremse

**clan** /klæn/ *n.* **A** Sippe, *die; (of Scottish Highlanders)* Clan, *der;* **B** *(derog.: group, set)* Clan, *der;* Sippschaft, *die (abwertend)*

**clandestine** /klæn'destɪn/ *adj.*, **clandestinely** /klæn'destɪnlɪ/ *adv.* heimlich

**clang** /klæŋ/ **1** *n. (of bell)* Läuten, *das; (of hammer)* Klingen, *das; (of sword)* Klirren, *das.* **2** *v.i.* ‹Glocke:› läuten; ‹Hammer:› klingen; ‹Schwert:› klirren

**clanger** /'klæŋə(r)/ *n. (Brit. coll.)* Schnitzer, *der (ugs.);* **drop a ~:** sich *(Dat.)* einen Schnitzer leisten *(ugs.)*

**clangor** *(Amer.)* ⇒ **clangour**

**clangorous** /'klæŋgərəs/ *adj.* [laut] schallend

**clangour** /'klæŋgə(r)/ *n. (Brit.)* [lauter] Schall

**clank** /klæŋk/ **1** *n.* Klappern, *das; (of sword, chain)* Klirren, *das.* **2** *v.i.* klappern; ‹Schwert, Kette:› klirren; ‹Kette:› rasseln. **3** *v.t.* klirren mit ‹Schwert, Kette›

**clannish** /'klænɪʃ/ *adj. (derog.)* cliquenbewusst; klüngelnd *(ugs.)*

**clap¹** /klæp/ **1** *n.* **A** Klatschen, *das;* **give sb. a ~:** jmdm. applaudieren *od.* Beifall klatschen; **B** *(slap)* Klaps, *der (ugs.);* **give sb. a congratulatory ~ on the back** jmdm. anerkennend auf die Schulter klopfen; **C** ~ **of thunder** Donnerschlag, *der.*

**2** *v.i.*, **-pp-** klatschen.

**3** *v.t.*, **-pp-:** **A** ~ **one's hands** in die Hände klatschen; ~ **sth.** etw. beklatschen; ~ **sb.** jmdm. Beifall klatschen; **B** *(slap)* ~ **sb. on the back** jmdm. auf die Schulter klopfen; **C** *(place)* ~ **sb. in prison** jmdn. ins Gefängnis werfen *od. (ugs.)* stecken; **the prisoner was ~ped in irons** der Gefangene wurde in Ketten gelegt; ~ **one's hand over sb.'s mouth** jmdm. den Mund zuhalten; ~ **eyes on sb./sth.** jmdn./etw. zu Gesicht bekommen; **D** ~**ped out** *(coll.)* schrottreif *(ugs.)* ‹Auto, Flugzeug›; kaputt *(ugs.)* ‹Person, Idee›

~ **on** *v.t.* **A** draufschlagen ‹Steuern usw.›; **the airlines ~ped 25% on the fare** die Fluggesellschaften haben auf den Flugpreis 25% aufgeschlagen; **a preservation order has been ~ped on my house** die haben mein Haus einfach unter Denkmalschutz gestellt *(ugs.);* **B** *(Naut.)* ~ **on sail** mehr Segel setzen *(Seemannsspr.);* **C** *(put on hastily)* aufstülpen ‹Hut›; ~ **handcuffs on sb.** jmdm. Handschellen anlegen

**clap²** *n. (coarse)* Tripper, *der;* **pick up a dose of the ~:** sich *(Dat.)* einen Tripper holen

**clapboard** /'klæpbɔ:d, 'klæbəd/ *n. (Amer.)* Schindel, *die*

**Clapham** /'klæpəm/ *n.* **the man on the ~ omnibus** *(Brit.)* der kleine Mann; der Durchschnittsbürger

**clapper** /'klæpə(r)/ *n.* **A** *(of bell)* Klöppel, *der;* Schwengel, *der;* **B like the ~s** *(Brit. coll.)* mit einem Affenzahn *od.* Affentempo *(salopp)*

**'clapperboard** *n. (Cinemat.)* Synchronklappe, *die*

**clapping** /'klæpɪŋ/ *n., no pl.* Beifall, *der;* Applaus, *der*

**claptrap** /'klæptræp/ *n., no pl.* **A** *(pretentious assertions)* [leere] Phrasen; **B** *(coll.: nonsense)* Geschwafel, *das (ugs. abwertend);* Geschwätz, *das (ugs. abwertend)*

**claque** /klɑ:k, klæk/ *n.* Claque, *die*

**claret** /'klærət/ **1** *n.* roter Bordeauxwein; Claret, *der.* **2** *adj.* weinrot

**clarification** /klærɪfɪ'keɪʃn/ *n.* **A** Klärung, *die; (explanation)* Klarstellung, *die;* **I should like more ~ on several points** zu einigen Punkten hätte ich gern nähere Erläuterungen; **B** *(of liquid)* Klärung, *die;* Klären, *das*

**clarify** /'klærɪfaɪ/ *v.t.* **A** *(make clear)* klären ‹Situation, Problem usw.›; *(by explanation)* klarstellen; erläutern ‹Bedeutung, Gedanken, Aussage, Bemerkung›; **the discussion helped me to ~ my thoughts about the matter** die Diskussion half mir, mir über die Sache klarzuwerden; **B** *(purify, make transparent)* reinigen; klären ‹Abwasser, Flüssigkeit›

**clarinet** /klærɪ'net/ *n. (Mus.)* Klarinette, *die*

**clarinettist** *(Amer.:* **clarinetist)** /klærɪ'netɪst/ *n.* ▶ **1261** *(Mus.)* Klarinettist, *der/*Klarinettistin, *die*

**clarion** /ˈklærɪən/ *attrib. adj.* hell klingend; **like a ~ call** wie ein Fanfarenstoß

**clarity** /ˈklærɪtɪ/ *n., no pl.* Klarheit, *die*

**clash** /klæʃ/ ❶ *v.i.* Ⓐ scheppern (*ugs.*); ‹Gangschaltung:› krachen; ‹Becken:› dröhnen; ‹Schwerter:› aneinander schlagen; Ⓑ (*meet in conflict*) zusammenstoßen; aufeinander stoßen; **~ with sb.** mit jmdm. zusammenstoßen; Ⓒ (*disagree*) sich streiten; **~ with sb.** mit jmdm. eine Auseinandersetzung haben; Ⓓ (*be incompatible*) aufeinander prallen; ‹Interesse, Ereignis:› kollidieren (**with** mit); ‹Persönlichkeit, Stil:› nicht zusammenpassen (**with** mit); ‹Farbe:› sich beißen (*ugs.*) (**with** mit).
❷ *v.t.* gegeneinander schlagen.
❸ *n.* Ⓐ (*of cymbals*) Dröhnen, *das;* (*of swords*) Aneinanderschlagen, *das;* (*of gears*) Krachen, *das;* Ⓑ (*meeting in conflict*) Zusammenstoß, *der;* Ⓒ (*disagreement*) Auseinandersetzung, *die;* Ⓓ (*incompatibility*) Unvereinbarkeit, *die;* (*of personalities, styles, colours*) Unverträglichkeit, *die;* (*of events*) Überschneidung, *die;* **~ of interests** Interessenkonflikt, *der*

**clasp** /klɑːsp/ ❶ *n.* Ⓐ Verschluss, *der;* Schließe, *die;* (*of belt*) Schnalle, *die;* Ⓑ (*embrace*) Umarmung, *die;* Ⓒ (*grasp*) Griff, *der;* Ⓓ (*on medal ribbon*) Ordensspange, *die.*
❷ *v.t.* Ⓐ (*embrace*) drücken (**to** an + *Akk.*); **the lovers lay ~ed in each other's arms** die Liebenden lagen eng umschlungen; Ⓑ (*grasp*) umklammern; **~ hands** sich [gegenseitig] bei den Händen fassen; **~ sth. in one's hand** etw. mit der Hand umklammern; **~ one's hands** die Hände falten; **he stood with his hands ~ed behind his back** er stand da, die Hände auf dem Rücken verschränkt

**ˈclasp knife** *n.* Klappmesser, *das*

**class** /klɑːs/ ❶ *n.* Ⓐ (*in society*) Gesellschaftsschicht, *die;* Klasse, *die* (*Soziol.*); (*system*) Klassensystem, *das;* Ⓑ (*Educ.*) Klasse, *die;* (*Sch.: lesson*) Stunde, *die;* (*Univ.: seminar etc.*) Übung, *die;* **teach a ~** (*Univ.*) eine Übung abhalten; **in ~:** im Unterricht; während des Unterrichts; **a French ~:** eine Französischstunde; **the ~ of 1970** (*Amer.*) der Jahrgang 1970; Ⓒ (*division according to quality*) Klasse, *die;* (*of hotel*) [Hotel]kategorie, *die;* **be in a ~ by itself** *or* **on its own/of one's own** *or* **by oneself** eine Klasse für sich sein; **he's not in the same ~ as ...:** er hat nicht die Klasse von ...; Ⓓ (*coll.: quality*) Klasse, *die* (*ugs.*); **there's not much ~ about her** sie hat keine Klasse; **have [no] ~:** [keine] Klasse haben; *attrib.* **a ~ football player** ein klasse Fußballer (*ugs.*); Ⓔ (*group, set; also Biol.*) Klasse, *die;* Ⓕ (*Univ.: of degree*) Prädikat, *das;* Ⓖ (*Mil.*) Rekrutenjahrgang, *der;* Jahrgang, *der.*
❷ *v.t.* einordnen; **~ sth. as sth.** etw. als etw. einstufen

**class: ~-conscious** *adj.* klassenbewusst; **~ consciousness** *n.* Klassenbewusstsein, *das;* **~ distinction** *n.* Klassenunterschied, *der*

**classic** /ˈklæsɪk/ ❶ *adj.* klassisch. ❷ *n.* Ⓐ *in pl.* (*classical studies*) Altphilologie, *die;* Ⓑ (*writer; follower of ~ models*) Klassiker, *der;* Ⓒ (*garment*) klassisch-zeitlose Kleidung; Ⓓ (*book, play, film*) Klassiker, *der;* Ⓔ (*Brit.: horse race*) Klassiker [unter den Pferderennen]

**classical** /ˈklæsɪkl/ *adj.* klassisch; **~ scholar/studies** Altphilologe, *der*/Altphilologie, *die;* **the ~ period** die Klassik; **the ~ world** die Antike; **~ education** humanistische [Schul]bildung

**classically** /ˈklæsɪkəlɪ/ *adv.* klassisch

**classicism** /ˈklæsɪsɪzm/ *n.* Klassizismus, *der*

**classicist** /ˈklæsɪsɪst/ *n.* Anhänger des Klassizismus; (*classics scholar*) Altphilologe, *der*/-philologin, *die*

**classifiable** /ˈklæsɪfaɪəbl/ *adj.* klassifizierbar; **be ~ into five main types** sich in fünf Hauptgruppen einteilen lassen

**classification** /klæsɪfɪˈkeɪʃn/ *n.* Klassifikation, *die*

**classified** /ˈklæsɪfaɪd/ *adj.* Ⓐ (*arranged in classes*) gegliedert; unterteilt; **~ advertisement** Kleinanzeige, *die;* **~ directory** Branchenverzeichnis, *das;* **~ results** Sportergebnisse; Ⓑ (*officially secret*) geheim

**classify** /ˈklæsɪfaɪ/ *v.t.* Ⓐ klassifizieren; **~ books by subjects** Bücher nach Fachgebieten [ein]ordnen; Ⓑ (*designate as secret*) für geheim erklären

**classless** /ˈklɑːslɪs/ *adj.* klassenlos ‹Gesellschaft›

**class: ~-list** *n.* (*Univ.*) Liste der Prüfungsergebnisse; **~mate** *n.* Klassenkamerad, *der*/-kameradin, *die;* **~room** *n.* (*Sch.*) Klassenzimmer, *das;* Klasse, *die;* **~ ˈstruggle, ~ ˈwar** *ns.* Klassenkampf, *der;* **~work** *n.* Arbeit am Studienplatz

**classy** /ˈklɑːsɪ/ *adj.* (*coll.*) klasse (*ugs.*); nobel ‹Vorort, Hotel›

**clatter** /ˈklætə(r)/ ❶ *n.* Klappern, *das;* **the kettle fell with a ~ to the ground** der Kessel fiel scheppernd zu Boden. ❷ *v.i.* Ⓐ klappern; Ⓑ (*move or fall with a ~*) poltern. ❸ *v.t.* klappern mit

**clause** /klɔːz/ *n.* Ⓐ Klausel, *die;* Ⓑ (*Ling.*) Teilsatz, *der;* **[subordinate] ~:** Nebensatz, *der;* Gliedsatz, *der*

**claustrophobia** /klɔːstrəˈfəʊbɪə/ *n., no pl.* (*Psych.*) Klaustrophobie, *die*

**claustrophobic** /klɔːstrəˈfəʊbɪk/ *adj.* beengend ‹Ort, Atmosphäre›; an Klaustrophobie leidend ‹Person›

**clavicle** /ˈklævɪkl/ *n.* (*Anat.*) Schlüsselbein, *das;* Clavicula, *die* (*fachspr.*)

**claw** /klɔː/ ❶ *n.* Ⓐ (*of bird, animal*) Kralle, *die;* (*of crab, lobster, etc.*) Schere, *die;* (*foot with ~*) Klaue, *die;* **the cat bared its ~s** die Katze zeigte die Krallen; **get one's ~s into sb.** (*fig. coll.*) auf jmdm. herumhacken (*ugs.*); Ⓑ (*of hammer*) Klaue, *die;* (*of cine camera, projector*) Greifer, *der.* ❷ *v.t.* kratzen; **the two women ~ed each other** die beiden Frauen gingen mit den Fingernägeln aufeinander los; **~ one's way to the top** sich zum Gipfel durchkämpfen; (*fig.*) sich nach oben durchboxen (*ugs.*). ❸ *v.i.* **~ at sth.** sich an etw. (*Akk.*) krallen; **she ~ed desperately for the door handle** sie versuchte verzweifelt, die Türklinke zu fassen

**~ ˈback** *v.t.* wieder eintreiben ‹Geld, Unterstützung›; wieder an sich reißen ‹Kontrolle›; wettmachen ‹Defizit›

**ˈclawback** *n.* Wiedereintreiben, *das*

**clay** /kleɪ/ *n.* Lehm, *der;* (*for pottery*) Ton, *der*

**clayey** /ˈkleɪɪ/ *adj.* lehmig

**clay: ~ ˈpigeon** *n.* (*Sport*) Tontaube, *die;* **~ ˈpigeon shooting** *n.* Tontaubenschießen, *das;* **~ ˈpipe** *n.* Tonpfeife, *die*

**clean** /kliːn/ ❶ *adj.* Ⓐ sauber; frisch ‹Wäsche, Hemd›; Ⓑ (*unused, fresh*) sauber; (*free of defects*) einwandfrei; sauber; **start with/have a ~ sheet** (*fig.*) ganz neu beginnen/eine reine Weste haben (*ugs.*); **he has a ~ record** gegen ihn liegt nichts vor; **make a ~ start** noch einmal neu anfangen; **come ~** (*coll.*) (*confess*) auspacken (*ugs.*); (*tell the truth*) mit der Wahrheit [he]rausrücken (*ugs.*); **have ~ hands** *or* **fingers** (*fig.*) eine reine Weste haben (*ugs.*); Ⓒ (*well-formed, shapely*) makellos ‹Glieder, Taille›; **a ship/car with ~ lines** ein Schiff/Auto mit klarer Linienführung; Ⓓ (*regular, complete*) glatt ‹Bruch›; glatt, sauber ‹Schnitt›; **make a ~ break [with** *or* **from sth.]** (*fig.*) einen Schlussstrich [unter etw. (*Akk.*)] ziehen; **make a ~ break with sb.** sich endgültig von jmdm. trennen; **make a ~ job of sth.** (*fig. coll.*) etw. vernünftig machen; etw. sauber hinkriegen (*ugs., auch iron.*); Ⓔ (*cleanly*) sauber; (*house-trained*) stubenrein, sauber; Ⓕ (*free from disease*) gesund; (*Relig.: not prohibited*) rein; Ⓖ (*deft*) sauber; Ⓗ (*not obscene or indecent*) sauber; stubenrein (*scherzh.*) ‹Witz›; **be good ~ fun** völlig harmlos sein; **keep the jokes ~!** bitte nur stubenreine Witze! (*scherzh.*); Ⓘ (*sportsmanlike, fair*) sauber; Ⓙ astrein ‹Holz›.
❷ *adv.* Ⓐ (*completely, outright, simply*) glatt; einfach ‹vergessen›; **we're ~ out of whisky** wir haben überhaupt keinen Whisky mehr; **the fox got ~ away** der Fuchs ist uns/ihnen *usw.* glatt entwischt; Ⓑ (*fairly*) sauber ‹spielen, kämpfen›.
❸ *v.t.* sauber machen; putzen ‹Zimmer, Haus, Fenster, Schuh›; reinigen ‹Teppich, Möbel, Käfig, Kleidung, Wunde›; fegen, kehren ‹Kamin›; ausnehmen ‹Fisch›; (*with cloth*) aufwischen ‹Fußboden›; **~ that dirt off your face** wisch dir den Schmutz aus dem Gesicht!; **~ the house from top to bottom** großen Hausputz halten; **~ one's hands/teeth** sich (*Dat.*) die Hände waschen/sich (*Dat.*) die Zähne putzen; **~ one's plate** (*eat everything*) seinen Teller leer essen.
❹ *v.i.* sich reinigen lassen.
❺ *n.* **this carpet needs/your teeth need a good ~:** dieser Teppich muss gründlich gereinigt werden/du musst dir gründlich die Zähne putzen; **give your shoes/face/jacket a ~:** putz deine Schuhe/wasch dir das Gesicht/mach deine Jacke sauber

**~ ˈdown** *v.t.* waschen ‹Auto›; abwaschen ‹Tür, Wand›

**~ ˈout** *v.t.* Ⓐ (*remove dirt from*) sauber machen; ausmisten ‹Stall›; (*remove rubbish from*) entrümpeln; Ⓑ (*coll.*) **~ sb. out** (*take all sb.'s money*) jmdn. total schröpfen (*ugs.*); **I'm completely ~ed out** ich bin total blank (*ugs.*); **the tobacconist was ~ed out of cigarettes** beim Tabakhändler war alles an Zigaretten aufgekauft worden; **sb. is ~ed out of sherry** jmdm. ist der Sherry ausgegangen. ⇒ *also* **~-out**

**~ ˈup** ❶ *v.t.* Ⓐ aufräumen ‹Zimmer, Schreibtisch›; beseitigen ‹Trümmer, Unordnung›; Ⓑ **~ oneself up** sich sauber machen; (*get washed*) sich waschen; Ⓒ (*coll.: acquire*) absahnen (*ugs.*) ‹Geld›; **~ up a fortune** ein Vermögen machen; Ⓓ (*Mil.*) ausheben ‹Schlupfwinkel des Feindes›; Ⓔ (*fig.*) säubern ‹Stadt›; aufräumen mit ‹Korruption, Laster, Drogenhandel›. ❷ *v.i.* Ⓐ aufräumen; Ⓑ ⇒ **1** B; Ⓒ (*coll.: make money*) absahnen (*ugs.*). ⇒ *also* **~-up**

**ˈclean-cut** *adj.* klar [umrissen]; **his ~ features** seine klar geschnittenen Gesichtszüge

**cleaner** /ˈkliːnə(r)/ *n.* Ⓐ ▶1261 (*person*) Raumpfleger, *der*/-pflegerin, *die;* (*woman also*) Putzfrau, *die;* Rein[e]machefrau, *die;* Ⓑ (*vacuum ~*) Staubsauger, *der;* (*substance*) Reinigungsmittel, *das;* Reiniger, *der;* Ⓒ *usu. in pl.* (*dry-~*) Reinigung, *die;* **take sth. to the ~s** etw. in die Reinigung bringen; **take sb. to the ~s** (*coll.*) jmdn. bis aufs Hemd ausziehen (*ugs.*)

**cleaning**/ˈkliːnɪŋ/: **~-rag** *n.* Putzlappen, *der;* **~-woman** *n.* ▶1261 Putzfrau, *die*

**clean-limbed** /ˈkliːnlɪmd/ *adj.* wohlproportioniert; wohlgeformt

**cleanliness** /ˈklenlɪnɪs/ *n., no pl.* Reinlichkeit, *die;* Sauberkeit, *die;* **~ is next to godliness** (*prov.*) Reinlichkeit ist die erste Tugend nach Gottseligkeit (*veralt.*)

**ˈclean-living** *adj.* von untadeligem Lebenswandel *nachgestellt*

**cleanly**[1] /ˈkliːnlɪ/ *adv.* sauber; **the bone broke ~:** der Knochen ist glatt gebrochen

**cleanly**[2] /ˈklenlɪ/ *adj.* sauber

**cleanness** /ˈkliːnnɪs/ *n., no pl.* Ⓐ Sauberkeit, *die;* Ⓑ (*freshness*) Sauberkeit, *die;* (*freedom from defects*) Makellosigkeit, *die;* Ⓒ (*shapeliness*) Wohlgeformtheit, *die;* **the ~ of the ship's lines** die klare Linienführung des Schiffes; Ⓓ (*regularity of cut or break*) Glätte, *die;* Ⓔ (*cleanliness*) Sauberkeit, *die;* **the ~ of her habits** ihre Sauberkeit; Ⓕ (*deftness*) Sauberkeit, *die;* Ⓖ (*of joke, entertainment, etc.*) Harmlosigkeit, *die;* Ⓗ (*of fight, contest, etc.*) Sauberkeit, *die*

**clean: ~-out** *n.* **give sth. a ~-out:** etw. sauber machen; **sth. needs a [good] ~-out** etw. muss [gründlich] sauber gemacht werden; **~ room** *n.* Rein[st]raum, *der*

**cleanse** /klenz/ *v.t.* Ⓐ (*spiritually purify*) läutern; **~d of** *or* **from sin** von der Sünde befreit; Ⓑ (*clean*) [gründlich] reinigen; Ⓒ (*Bibl.*) heilen ‹Aussatz, Aussätzige›

**cleanser** /ˈklenzə(r)/ *n.* Ⓐ Reinigungsmittel, *das;* Reiniger, *der;* Ⓑ (*for skin*) Reinigungscreme, *die;* (*fluid*) Reinigungsmilch, *die* '**clean-shaven** *adj.* glatt rasiert

**cleansing**/'klenzɪŋ/: ~ **cream** *n.* Reinigungscreme, *die;* ~ **department** *n.* Stadtreinigung, *die;* ~ **tissue** *n.* Papiertuch, *das*

'**clean-up** *n.* **A** **give sth./oneself a ~:** etw./sich sauber machen; **sth. needs a ~:** etw. muss sauber gemacht werden; **B** (*reducing crime or corruption*) Säuberungsaktion, *die*

**clear** /klɪə(r)/ **1** *adj.* **A** klar; rein ‹Haut, Teint›; **as ~ as a bell** glockenhell; **B** (*distinct*) scharf ‹Bild, Foto, Umriss›; deutlich ‹Abbild›; klar ‹Ton›; klar verständlich ‹Wort›; **C** (*obvious, unambiguous*) klar ‹Aussage, Vorteil, Vorsprung, Mehrheit, Sieg, Fall›; **you have a ~ duty to report these thefts** es ist eindeutig Ihre Pflicht, diese Diebstähle zu melden; **make oneself ~:** sich deutlich *od.* klar [genug] ausdrücken; **make sth. ~:** etw. deutlich zum Ausdruck bringen; **make it ~ [to sb.] that ...:** [jmdm.] klar und deutlich sagen, dass ...; **let's get this/one thing ~:** lass uns das klarstellen/eins wollen wir klarstellen; **in ~:** im Klartext; **D** (*free*) frei; (*Horse riding*) fehlerfrei ‹Runde›; **[be] ~ of a place** aus einem Ort heraus[sein]; **~ of debt** schuldenfrei; frei von Schulden; **he is ~ of blame** ihm kann man keinen Vorwurf machen; **be ~ of suspicion** nicht unter Verdacht stehen; **we're in the ~** (*free of suspicion*) auf uns fällt kein Verdacht; (*free of trouble*) wir haben es geschafft; **be three points ~:** drei Punkte Vorsprung haben; **E** (*complete*) **a ~ six inches** volle sechs Zoll; **three ~ days/lines** drei volle *od.* volle drei Tage/Zeilen; **F** (*open, unobstructed*) frei; **keep sth. ~** (*not block*) etw. frei halten; **~ of snow** schneefrei; frei von Schnee; **have a ~ run** freie Fahrt haben; **all ~** (*one will not be detected*) die Luft ist rein (*ugs.*); ⇒ *also* **all-~**; **the way is [now] ~ [for sb.] to do sth.** (*fig.*) es steht [jmdm.] nichts [mehr] im Wege, etw. zu tun; **G** (*discerning*) klar; **keep a ~ head** einen klaren *od.* kühlen Kopf bewahren; **a ~ thinker** jmd., der klar denken kann; **H** (*certain, confident*) **be ~ [on *or* about sth.]** sich (*Dat.*) [über etw. (*Akk.*)] im Klaren sein; **are you ~ in your own mind that ...?** sind Sie ganz sicher, dass ...?; **I** (*without deduction, net*) **~ profit** Reingewinn, *der.* ⇒ *also* **coast** 1 A; **conscience.**

**2** *adv.* **A** (*apart, at a distance*) **keep ~ of sth./sb.** etw./jmdn. meiden; **'keep ~'** (*don't approach*) „Vorsicht [Zug *usw.*]"; **please stand *or* keep ~ of the door** bitte von der Tür zurücktreten; **move sth. ~ of sth.** etw. von etw. wegräumen; **the driver was pulled ~ of the wreckage** man zog den Fahrer aus dem Wrack seines Wagens; **the driver leaped ~ just before the crash** der Fahrer konnte im Moment vor dem Zusammenstoß noch abspringen; **B** (*distinctly*) deutlich ‹sprechen, sehen, hören›; **C** (*completely*) **the prisoners had got ~ away** die Häftlinge waren auf und davon (*ugs.*); **D** (*Amer.: all the way*) ganz; **~ through to Boston** direkt bis Boston.

**3** *v.t.* **A** (*make ~*) klären ‹Flüssigkeit›; reinigen ‹Blut›; **~ the air** lüften; (*fig.*) die Atmosphäre reinigen; **~ one's mind of doubts/anxieties** (*fig.*) seine Zweifel/Ängste loswerden; **he tried to ~ his head** (*fig.*) er versuchte, einen klaren Kopf zu bekommen; **~ one's conscience** sein Gewissen erleichtern; **B** (*free from obstruction*) räumen ‹Straße›; abräumen ‹Regal, Schreibtisch›; reinigen ‹Pfeife›; freimachen ‹Abfluss, Kanal›; **~ the streets of snow** den Schnee von den Straßen räumen; **~ a space for sb./sth.** für jmdn./etw. Platz machen; **~ one's throat** sich räuspern; **~ the ground** (*fig.*) die Bahn frei machen; **~ land [for cultivation]** Land roden [um es urbar zu machen]; ⇒ *also* **deck** 1 A; **way** 1 F; **C** (*make empty*) räumen; leeren ‹Briefkasten›; **~ the room** das Zimmer räumen; **~ the table** den Tisch abräumen; **~ one's desk** seinen Schreibtisch ausräumen; **~ a country of bandits** ein Land von Banditen befreien; **~ the court** den Saal räumen; **~ one's plate** seinen Teller leer essen; **D** (*remove*) wegräumen; beheben ‹Verstopfung›; **~ sth. out of the way** etw. aus dem Weg räumen; **E** (*pass over without touching*) nehmen ‹Hindernis›; überspringen ‹Latte›; (*pass by*) vorbeikommen; **F** (*show to be innocent*) freisprechen; **~ oneself** seine Unschuld beweisen; **~ sb. of sth.** jmdn. von etw. freisprechen; **seek to ~ oneself of a charge** versuchen, eine Anschuldigung zu widerlegen; **~ one's name** seine Unschuld beweisen; **G** (*declare fit to have secret information*) für unbedenklich erklären; **H** (*get permission for*) **~ sth. with sb.** etw. von jmdm. genehmigen lassen; (*give permission for*) **~ a plane for take-off/landing** einem Flugzeug Start-/Landeerlaubnis erteilen; **I** (*at customs*) **~ customs** vom Zoll abgefertigt werden; **~ sth. through customs** etw. [zollamtlich] abfertigen; **J** (*make as gain*) verdienen ‹Geld›; **~ one's expenses** seine Ausgaben wieder hereinbekommen; **K** (*pay off*) begleichen ‹Schuld›; **L** (*pass through bank*) **~ a cheque** einen Scheck verrechnen; **M** (*get rid of*) **~ [old] stock** Lagerbestände räumen; **'reduced to ~'** „reduziertes Einzelstück"; **N** (*Sport: move away*) klären; **the ball was ~ed upfield** der Ball wurde ins Feld hinausgeschlagen.

**4** *v.i.* **A** (*become ~*) klar werden; sich klären; ‹Wetter, Himmel:› aufklaren (*Met.*), sich aufheitern; (*fig.*) ‹Gesicht:› sich aufhellen; **B** (*disperse*) sich verziehen; ‹Nebel:› sich auflösen, sich verziehen; **C** (*Sport*) klären

**~ a'way** **1** *v.t.* wegschaffen; (*from the table*) abräumen ‹Geschirr, Besteck›. **2** *v.i.* **A** abräumen; **B** (*disperse*) ‹Nebel:› sich auflösen, sich verziehen

**~ 'off** **1** *v.t.* begleichen ‹Schulden›; abzahlen, abtragen ‹Hypothek›; aufarbeiten ‹Rückstand›. **2** *v.i.* (*coll.*) abhauen (*salopp*)

**~ 'out** **1** *v.t.* ausräumen. **2** *v.i.* (*coll.*) verschwinden. ⇒ *also* **~-out**

**~ 'up** **1** *v.t.* **A** beseitigen ‹Unordnung›; wegräumen ‹Abfall›; aufräumen ‹Platz, Sachen›; **B** (*explain, solve*) klären. **2** *v.i.* **A** aufräumen; Ordnung machen; **B** (*become ~*) ‹Wetter:› aufklaren (*Met.*), sich aufhellen; **C** (*disappear*) ‹Symptome, Ausschlag:› zurückgehen. ⇒ *also* **~-up**

**clearance** /'klɪərəns/ *n.* **A** (*of obstruction*) Beseitigung, *die;* (*of old building*) Abriss, *der;* (*of forest*) Abholzung, *die;* **make a ~:** gründlich aufräumen; **B** (*of people*) Räumung, *die;* **C** (*of cheque*) Verrechnung, *die;* Clearing, *das* (*Finanzw.*); **D** (*of ship at customs*) Klarierung, *die* (*Seemannsspr.*); (*certificate*) [Zoll]papiere *Pl.;* **E** (*for aircraft to land/take off*) Lande-/Starterlaubnis, *die;* **F** (*security ~*) *Einstufung als unbedenklich* [*im Sinne der Sicherheitsbestimmungen*]; (*document*) ≈ Sonderausweis, *der;* **G** (*clear space*) Spielraum, *der;* (*headroom*) lichte Höhe; **H** (*Sport*) Abwehr, *die;* **make a poor ~:** schlecht abwehren

**clearance:** **~ order** *n.* Räumungsbefehl, *der;* **~ sale** *n.* Räumungsverkauf, *der*

**clear:** **~-cut** *adj.* klar umrissen; klar ‹Sieg, Abgrenzung, Ergebnis, Entscheidung›; [gestochen] scharf ‹Umriss, Raster›; **~-headed** *adj.* besonnen; **remain ~-headed** einen kühlen *od.* klaren Kopf bewahren

**clearing** /'klɪərɪŋ/ *n.* (*land*) Lichtung, *die*

**clearing:** **~ bank** *n.* (*Commerc.*) Clearingbank, *die;* **~ house** *n.* (*Commerc.*) Abrechnungsstelle, *die;* Clearingstelle, *die;* (*fig.*) Zentrale, *die*

**clearly** /'klɪəlɪ/ *adv.* **A** (*distinctly*) klar; deutlich ‹sprechen›; **B** (*obviously, unambiguously*) eindeutig; klar ‹denken›; **please explain yourself more ~:** bitte erklären Sie sich deutlicher; **~, immediate action is called for** ohne Frage ist sofortiges Handeln vonnöten

**clearness** /'klɪənɪs/ *n., no pl.* **A** Klarheit, *die;* (*of skin, complexion*) Reinheit, *die;* **B** (*distinctness*) (*of photograph, outline*) Schärfe, *die;* (*of articulation, words, reflection*) Deutlichkeit, *die;* (*of note, sound, image*) Klarheit, *die;* **C** (*obviousness, unambiguousness*) Eindeutigkeit, *die;* Klarheit, *die;* (*of argument also*) Schärfe, *die*

**clear:** **~-out** *n.* Entrümpelung, *die;* **have a ~-out** eine Aufräum- *od.* Entrümpelungsaktion starten; **sth. needs a good ~-out** etw. muss einmal gründlich entrümpelt werden; **~-sighted** *adj.* weitsichtig; vorausschauend; **~ 'soup** *n.* klare Brühe

**clearstory** (*Amer.*) ⇒ **clerestory**

**clear:** **~-thinking** *adj.* klar denkend; **~-up** *n.* Aufräumen, *das;* **have a [good] ~-up** [gründlich] aufräumen; **~way** *n.* (*Brit.*) Straße mit Halteverbot

**cleat** /kli:t/ *n.* **A** (*to give footing on gangway*) Querleiste, *die;* (*to prevent rope from slipping*) Klampe, *die* (*Seemannsspr.*); **B** (*wedge*) Keil, *der;* **C** (*to strengthen woodwork*) Leiste, *die;* **D** (*on boot, shoe*) Stollen, *der*

**cleavage** /'kli:vɪdʒ/ *n.* **A** (*act of splitting*) Spaltung, *die;* (*tendency*) Spaltbarkeit, *die;* (*fig.*) Kluft, *die;* **the sharp ~ of opinions/interests** das deutliche Auseinandergehen der Meinungen/Interessen; **B** (*between breasts*) Dekolleté, *das;* **C** (*Biol.*) Spaltung, *die*

**cleave**[1] /kli:v/ *v.t.,* **~d** *or* **clove** /kləʊv/ *or* **cleft** /kleft/ , **~d** *or* **cloven** /'kləʊvn/ *or* **cleft** (*literary*) **A** (*split*) spalten; **B** (*make way through*) durchpflügen ‹Wellen, Wasser›; **~ one's way through sth.** sich [mühsam] einen Weg durch etw. bahnen. ⇒ *also* **cleft**[2] 2; **cloven** 2

**cleave**[2] *v.i.* (*literary: adhere*) kleben (**to** an + *Dat.*); **~ to sb./sth.** (*fig.*) jmdm./einer Sache treu bleiben

**cleaver** /'kli:və(r)/ *n.* Hackbeil, *das*

**clef** /klef/ *n.* (*Mus.*) Notenschlüssel, *der*

**cleft**[1] /kleft/ *n.* Spalte, *die;* (*fig.*) Kluft, *die*

**cleft**[2] **1** ⇒ **cleave**[1]. **2** *adj.* gespalten; **~ palate** Gaumenspalte, *die;* **be [caught] in a ~ stick** (*fig.*) in der Klemme sitzen (*ugs.*)

**clematis** /'klemətɪs, klə'meɪtɪs/ *n.* (*Bot.*) Klematis, *die*

**clemency** /'klemənsɪ/ *n., no pl.* **A** (*mercy*) Milde, *die;* Nachsicht, *die;* **show ~ to sb.** jmdm. gegenüber Milde *od.* Nachsicht walten lassen; **B** (*of weather, climate*) Milde, *die*

**clementine** /'kleməntɪ:n, 'kleməntaɪn/ *n.* Klementine, *die*

**clench** /klentʃ/ *v.t.* **A** (*close tightly*) zusammenpressen; **~ one's fist *or* fingers** die Faust ballen; **with one's fist ~ed *or* [one's] ~ed fist** mit geballter Faust; **they gave the ~ed-fist salute** sie hoben die geballte Faust zum Gruß; **~ one's teeth** die Zähne zusammenbeißen; **through ~ed teeth** durch die zusammengebissenen Zähne; **B** (*grasp firmly*) umklammern; **~ sth. between one's teeth** etw. zwischen die Zähne klemmen; **C** (*secure by bending*) umschlagen (*Nagel*)

**clerestory** /'klɪəstɔ:rɪ/ *n.* **A** (*Archit.*) Lichtgaden, *der;* **B** (*Amer. Railw.*) *erhöhter Teil des Daches eines Eisenbahnwagens mit Fenstern od. Luftsaugern*

**clergy** /'klɜ:dʒɪ/ *n. pl.* Geistlichkeit, *die;* Klerus, *der;* **thirty ~:** dreißig Geistliche

**clergyman** /'klɜ:dʒɪmən/ *n., pl.* **clergymen** /'klɜ:dʒɪmən/ ▶ **1261** Geistliche, *der*

**cleric** /'klerɪk/ *n.* Kleriker, *der*

**clerical** /'klerɪkl/ *adj.* **A** (*of clergy*) klerikal; geistlich; **~ collar** Kollar, *das;* **B** (*of or by clerk*) **~ duties/task/occupation/work** Büroarbeit, *die;* **~ error** Schreibfehler, *der;* **~ staff** Büropersonal, *das;* **~ worker** ▶ **1261** Büroangestellte, *der/die;* Bürokraft, *die*

**clerihew** /'klerɪhju:/ *n.* (*Lit.*) Clerihew, *das*

**clerk** /klɑ:k/ *n.* ▶ **1261** **A** Angestellte, *der/die;* (*in bank*) Bankangestellte, *der/die;* (*in office*) Büroangestellte, *der/die;* (*in shop, firm*) kaufmännischer Angestellter/kaufmännische Angestellte; **B** (*in charge of records*) Schriftführer, *der*/Schriftführerin, *die;* **C** **~ of the course** (*Horseracing*) Assistent der Rennleitung; **~ of [the] works** (*Building*) Bauleiter, *der;* **D** (*Eccl.: lay officer*) Küster, *der;* Kirchendiener, *der;* (*arch./Law: clergyman*) **~ [in holy orders]** Geistliche, *der;* **E** (*Brit. Parl.*) Parlamentssekretär, *der;* **F** (*Amer.: assistant in shop*) Verkäufer, *der*/Verkäuferin, *die;* (*in hotel*) Hotelangestellte, *der/die*

**clever** /ˈklevə(r)/ *adj.*, **~er** /ˈklevərə(r) /;/ **~est** /ˈklevərɪst/ **A** gescheit; klug; **be ~ at mathematics/thinking up excuses** gut in Mathematik/findig im Ausdenken von Entschuldigungen sein; **B** (*skilful, dextrous*) geschickt; **be ~ with one's hands** geschickte Hände haben; **C** (*ingenious*) brillant, geistreich ‹Idee, Argument, Rede, Roman, Gedicht›; geschickt ‹Verkleidung, Täuschung, Vorgehen›; glänzend (*ugs.*) ‹Idee, Erfindung, Mittel›; **D** (*smart, cunning*) clever; raffiniert ‹Schritt, Taktik, Täuschung›; schlau, gewitzt, raffiniert ‹Person›

**clever: ~-~** *adj.* (*derog.*) superklug (*iron.*); **~-clogs** *n. sing., pl. same:* ⇒ **~-sticks**; **~ Dick** *n.* (*coll. derog.*) Schlaumeier, *der* (*ugs.*)

**cleverly** /ˈklevəlɪ/ *adv.* **A** klug; **B** (*skilfully, dextrously*) geschickt

**cleverness** /ˈklevənɪs/ *n., no pl.* **A** Klugheit, *die;* (*talent*) Begabung, *die* (**at** für); **B** (*skilfulness, dexterity*) Geschicklichkeit, *die;* **his ~ with his hands** seine handwerkliche Begabung; **C** (*ingenuity*) Brillanz, *die;* **D** (*smartness*) Cleverness, *die;* Raffiniertheit, *die;* (*of person also*) Schläue, *die*

**ˈclever-sticks** *n. sing., pl. same* (*coll. derog.*) Superschlaue, *der/die* (*iron.*)

**clew** /klu:/ (*Naut.*) **1** *n.* (*of hammock*) Schlaufe, *die;* (*of sail*) [Schot]horn, *das* (*Seemannsspr.*). **2** *v.t.* **~ up** aufgeien (*Seemannsspr.*)

**cliché** /ˈkli:ʃeɪ/ *n.* (*also Printing*) Klischee, *das*

**click** /klɪk/ **1** *n.* **A** Klicken, *das;* **B** (*Ling.*) Schnalzlaut, *der.* **2** *v.t.* **A** zuschnappen lassen ‹Schloss, Tür›; **~ the shutter of a camera** den Verschluss einer Kamera auslösen; **~ one's heels/tongue** die Hacken zusammenschlagen/mit der Zunge schnalzen; **~ finger and thumb** mit Daumen und Finger schnalzen; **B** (*Computing*) drücken ‹Maustaste›. **3** *v.i.* **A** klicken; ‹Absätze, Stricknadeln:› klappern; **B** (*coll.: agree*) **~ with sth.** mit etw. übereinstimmen; **C** (*be successful*) [gut] ankommen (*ugs.*); (*coll.: fall into context*) **it's just ~ed** ich hab's (*ugs.*); **the name ~ed** ich konnte mit dem Namen etwas anfangen; **~ with sb.** (*coll.*) mit jmdm. gleich prima auskommen (*ugs.*); **they ~ed immediately** sie kamen gleich prima miteinander aus (*ugs.*)

**~ on** *v.t.* (*Computing*) anklicken

**ˈclick beetle** *n.* Schnellkäfer, *der*

**client** /ˈklaɪənt/ *n.* **A** (*of lawyer, solicitor, barrister, social worker*) Klient, *der*/Klientin, *die;* (*esp. of barrister*) Mandant, *der*/Mandantin, *die;* (*of architect*) Auftraggeber, *der*/-geberin, *die;* **B** (*customer*) Kunde, *der*/Kundin, *die*

**clientele** /kli:ɒnˈtel/ *n.* (*of shop*) Kundenkreis, *der;* Kundschaft, *die;* (*of theatre*) Publikum, *das;* (*of lawyer*) Klientel, *die*

**cliff** /klɪf/ *n.* (*on coast*) Kliff, *das;* (*inland*) Felswand, *die*

**cliff: ~hanger** *n.* Thriller, *der;* **~-hanging** *adj.* äußerst spannend; atemberaubend

**climacteric** /klaɪˈmæktərɪk, klaɪmækˈterɪk/ **1** *adj.* **A** (*critical*) entscheidend; **B** (*Med.*) klimakterisch. **2** *n.* (*Med.*) Klimakterium, *das* (*fachspr.*); Wechseljahre *Pl.;* (*fig.*) Wendepunkt, *der*

**climactic** /klaɪˈmæktɪk/ *adj.* **~ scene/event** Höhepunkt, *der*

**climate** /ˈklaɪmət/ *n.* Klima, *das;* **the ~ of opinion** (*fig.*) die allgemeine Meinung

**ˈclimate control** *n.* Klimatisierung, *die;* **automatic ~:** Klimaautomatik, *die*

**climatic** /klaɪˈmætɪk/ *adj.* klimatisch

**climatology** /klaɪməˈtɒlədʒɪ/ *n., no pl.* Klimatologie, *die;* Klimakunde, *die*

**climax** /ˈklaɪmæks/ **1** *n.* **A** Höhepunkt, *der;* **B** (*orgasm*) Höhepunkt, *der;* Orgasmus, *der.* **2** *v.i.* seinen Höhepunkt erreichen; **~ in sth.** mit etw. seinen Höhepunkt erreichen

**climb** /klaɪm/ **1** *v.t.* hinaufsteigen ‹Treppe, Leiter, Hügel, Berg›; hinaufklettern ‹Mauer, Seil, Mast›; klettern auf ‹Baum›; ‹Auto:› hinaufkommen ‹Hügel›; **this mountain had never been ~ed before** dieser Berg war noch nie zuvor bestiegen worden; **the prisoners escaped by ~ing the wall** die Gefangenen entkamen, indem sie über die Mauer kletterten. **2** *v.i.* **A** klettern (**up** auf + *Akk.*); **~ into/out of** steigen in (+ *Akk.*)/aus ‹Auto, Bett›; **~ aboard** einsteigen; **~ing plants/roses** Kletterpflanzen/-rosen; **B** ‹Flugzeug, Sonne:› aufsteigen; **C** (*slope upwards*) ansteigen; **D** (*in social rank*) aufsteigen. **3** *n.* (*ascent*) Aufstieg, *der;* (*of road*) Steigung, *die;* (*of aeroplane*) Steigflug, *der;* **the pilot put the plane into a steep ~:** der Pilot zog die Maschine steil nach oben; **the first ~ of Everest** die erste Besteigung des Everest

**~ ˈdown** *v.i.* **A** hinunterklettern; (*from horse*) absteigen; **B** (*fig.: retreat, give in*) nachgeben; einlenken; **~ down over an issue** in einer Frage nachgeben; ⇒ *also* **climbdown**

**climbable** /ˈklaɪməbl/ *adj.* besteigbar

**ˈclimbdown** *n.* Rückzieher, *der* (*ugs.*)

**climber** /ˈklaɪmə(r)/ *n.* **A** (*mountaineer*) Bergsteiger, *der;* (*of cliff, rock face*) Kletterer, *der;* **B** (*plant*) Kletterpflanze, *die*

**climbing: ~ boot** *n.* Kletterschuh, *der;* **~ frame** *n.* Klettergerüst, *das;* **~ iron** *n.* Steigeisen, *das*

**clime** /klaɪm/ *n.* (*literary*) **A** *in sing. or pl.* (*region*) Gefilde, *das* (*geh.*); **B** (*climate*) Klima, *das*

**clinch** /klɪntʃ/ **1** *v.t.* **A** (*confirm or settle conclusively*) zum Abschluss bringen ‹Angelegenheit, Meinungsverschiedenheit›; perfekt machen (*ugs.*) ‹Geschäft, Handel›; **that ~es it** damit ist der Fall klar; **B** ⇒ **clench** C. **2** *n.* **A** (*Boxing*) Clinch, *der;* **B** (*coll.: embrace*) Umschlingung, *die;* Clinch, *der* (*ugs. scherzh.*); **go into a ~:** sich eng umschlingen; in den Clinch gehen (*ugs. scherzh.*)

**clincher** /ˈklɪntʃə(r)/ *n.* entscheidender Faktor; **be the ~:** den Ausschlag geben

**cling** /klɪŋ/ *v.i.*, **clung** /klʌŋ/ **A** **~ to sth./sb.** sich an etw./jmdn. klammern; ‹Schmutz:› einer Sache/jmdm. anhaften; ‹Staub:› sich auf etw./jmdn. setzen; ‹Klette:› an etw./jmdm. hängen; ‹Schlamm usw.:› an etw./jmdm. haften bleiben; **the lovers clung to each other** die Liebenden hielten sich umschlungen; **his sweat-soaked shirt clung to his back** das durchgeschwitzte Hemd klebte ihm am Rücken; **her perfume still ~s to the scarf** der Duft ihres Parfüms haftet noch immer an dem Schal; **~ together** aneinander haften; (*Personen:*) sich aneinander klammern; **a ~ing dress** ein eng anliegendes Kleid; **B** (*remain stubbornly faithful*) **~ to sb./sth.** sich an jmdn./etw. klammern

**cling: ~ film** *n.* Klarsichtfolie, *die;* **~[stone] peach** *n.* (*Bot.*) Härtling, *der*

**clinic** /ˈklɪnɪk/ *n.* **A** (*place*) [Abteilung einer] Klinik; (*occasion*) Sprechstunde, *die;* **B** (*private hospital*) Privatklinik, *die;* (*specified hospital*) Klinik, *die;* **dental ~:** Zahnklinik, *die;* **C** (*medical teaching at bedside*) Klinik, *die;* Klinikum, *das;* **D** (*Amer.: conference, short course*) Seminar, *das*

**clinical** /ˈklɪnɪkl/ *adj.* **A** (*Med.*) klinisch ‹Medizin, Tod›; **~ thermometer** Fieberthermometer, *das;* **B** (*objective, dispassionate*) nüchtern; (*coldly detached*) kühl; distanziert ‹Haltung›; klinisch ‹Interesse›; **C** (*bare, functional*) steril

**clinically** /ˈklɪnɪkəlɪ/ *adv.* **A** (*Med.*) klinisch; **B** (*dispassionately*) nüchtern

**clinical: ~ psyˈchologist** *n.* ▶ **1261** klinischer Psychologe/klinische Psychologin; **~ psyˈchology** *n.* klinische Psychologie

**clink**[1] /klɪŋk/ **1** *n.* (*of glasses, bottles*) Klirren, *das;* (*of coins, keys*) Klimpern, *das.* **2** *v.i.* ‹Flaschen, Gläser:› klirren; ‹Münzen, Schlüssel:› klimpern. **3** *v.t.* klirren mit ‹Glas›; klimpern mit ‹Kleingeld, Schlüssel›

**clink**[2] *n.* (*sl.: prison*) Knast, *der* (*salopp*); **be in ~:** im Knast sitzen (*salopp*); **be put in ~:** in den Knast kommen (*salopp*)

**clinker** /ˈklɪŋkə(r)/ *n.* Schlacke, *die*

**ˈclinker-built** *adj.* in Klinkerbauweise [gebaut]; **a ~ boat** ein klinkergebautes Boot *od.* Klinkerboot

**clip**[1] /klɪp/ **1** *n.* **A** Klammer, *die;* (*for paper*) Büroklammer, *die;* (*of pen*) Klipp, *der;* (*hose ~*) Schelle, *die;* (*for wires*) Klemme, *die;* **B** (*piece of jewellery*) Klipp, *der;* Clip, *der;* **C** (*set of cartridges*) Ladestreifen, *der.* **2** *v.t.*, **-pp-:** **~ sth. [on] to sth.** etw. an etw. (*Akk.*) klammern; **~ papers together** Schriftstücke zusammenklammern; **~ the leads to the battery terminals** die Kabel an die Batteriepole klemmen

**~ ˈon** **1** *v.i.* angeklemmt *od.* angesteckt werden; ‹Sonnenbrille:› aufgesteckt werden. **2** *v.t.* anlegen ‹Ohrring›; anstecken ‹Brosche, Mikrofon›; aufstecken ‹Sonnenbrille›. ⇒ *also* **clip-on**

**clip**[2] **1** *v.t.*, **-pp-:** **A** (*cut*) schneiden ‹Fingernägel, Haar, Hecke›; scheren ‹Wolle›; stutzen ‹Flügel›; **~ sb.'s wings** (*fig.*) jmdm. die Flügel stutzen; **~ a second off the record** einen Rekord um eine Sekunde unterbieten; **B** scheren ‹Schaf›; trimmen ‹Hund›; **C** lochen, entwerten ‹Fahrkarte›; **D** (*coll.: hit*) **~ sb.'s ear** jmdm. eins *od.* ein paar hinter die Ohren geben (*ugs.*); **~ sb. on the jaw** jmdm. einen Kinnhaken verpassen (*ugs.*); **~ the crash barrier** die Leitplanke streifen; **E** **~ one's words/letters** abgehackt sprechen; **F** (*Amer.: cut from newspaper*) ausschneiden. **2** *n.* **A** (*of fingernails, hedge*) Schneiden, *das;* (*of dog*) Trimmen, *das;* (*of sheep*) Schur, *die;* **give the hedge a ~:** die Hecke schneiden; **B** (*extract from film*) [Film]ausschnitt, *der;* **C** (*blow with hand*) Schlag, *der;* **~ round** *or* **on** *or* **over the ear** Ohrfeige, *die;* **~ on the jaw** Kinnhaken, *der;* **D** **be going at a good** *or* **fast ~** (*coll.*) einen ziemlichen Zahn draufhaben (*ugs.*); **E** (*quantity of wool*) Schur, *die*

**clip: ~ art** *n.* (*Computing*) Clipart, *die;* **~board** **A** *n.* Klemmbrett, *das;* **B** (*Computing*) Zwischenablage, *die;* **~-clop** /ˈklɪpklɒp/ **1** *n.* Klappern, *das;* Klippklapp, *das;* **2** *v.i.*, **-pp-** klappern; **~ frame** *n.* [rahmenloser] Bilderhalter; **~ joint** *n.* (*coll. derog.*) Nepplokal, *das* (*ugs. abwertend*); **~-on** *adj.* **a ~-on accessory** ein Accessoire zum Anstecken; **~-on sunglasses** eine Sonnenbrille zum Aufstecken; **a ~-on handle** ein Griff zum Feststecken

**clipped** /klɪpt/ *adj.* abgehackt ‹Wörter›

**clipper** /ˈklɪpə(r)/ *n.* **A** *in pl.* (*for hair*) Haarschneidemaschine, *die;* **B** (*Naut.*) Klipper, *der*

**clipping** /ˈklɪpɪŋ/ *n.* **A** (*piece clipped off*) Schnipsel, *der od. das;* **B** (*newspaper cutting*) Ausschnitt, *der*

**clique** /kli:k/ *n.* Clique, *die*

**cliquey** /ˈkli:kɪ/, **cliquish** /ˈkli:kɪʃ/ *adjs.* (*derog.*) **be ~:** zur Cliquenbildung neigen; **a ~ attitude** eine Neigung zur Cliquenbildung

**clitoris** /ˈklɪtərɪs/ *n.* (*Anat.*) Kitzler, *der;* Klitoris, *die* (*fachspr.*)

**cloak** /kləʊk/ **1** *n.* **A** Umhang, *der;* Mantel, *der* (*hist.*); (*fig.*) **~ of snow** Schneedecke, *die;* **under the ~ of darkness** im Schutz der Dunkelheit; **use sth. as a ~ for sth.** etw. als Deckmantel für etw. benutzen; **a ~ of secrecy** ein Mantel des Schweigens; **B** *in pl.* (*Brit. euphem.: lavatory*) Toilette, *die.* **2** *v.t.* **A** [ein]hüllen; **B** (*fig.*) **~ed in mist/darkness** in Nebel/Dunkel gehüllt; **sth. is ~ed in secrecy** über etw. (*Akk.*) wird der Mantel des Schweigens gebreitet

**cloak: ~-and-ˈdagger** *adj.* mysteriös; Spionage‹stück, -tätigkeit›; **~room** *n.* Garderobe, *die;* (*Brit. euphem.: lavatory*) Toilette, *die;* **~room attendant** ▶ **1261** Garderobier, *der*/Garderobiere, *die*/Toilettenmann, *der*/-frau, *die*

**clobber**[1] /ˈklɒbə(r)/ *n.* (*Brit. coll.*) Klamotten *Pl.* (*salopp*)

**clobber**[2] *v.t.* (*coll.*) **A** (*hit*) zusammenschlagen; (*fig.: financially*) zur Ader lassen (*ugs. scherzh.*); schröpfen (*ugs.*); **B** (*defeat, criticize*) in die Pfanne hauen (*salopp*)

**cloche** /klɒʃ/ *n.* **A** (*Agric., Hort.*) [Frühbeet]abdeckung, *die;* (*polythene*) Folientunnel, *der;* **B** **~ [hat]** Glocke, *die;* Glockenhut, *der*

C

# The clock

***What time is it?***
= Wie viel Uhr ist es?, Wie spät ist es?
***Could you tell me the time?***
= Könnten Sie mir sagen, wie spät es ist?
***What time do you make it?***
= Wie viel Uhr hast du?
***By my watch it's five to/ten past nine***
= Nach meiner Uhr ist es fünf vor/zehn nach neun

***My watch is fast/slow***
= Meine Uhr geht vor/nach
***It's just after*** or ***just gone ten***
= Es ist etwas nach zehn
***It's gone eleven***
= Es ist elf Uhr vorbei
***It's coming up to seven***
= Es ist gleich sieben

Unlike English, German uses the twenty-four hour clock most of the time, even sometimes in conversation, and it is certainly the only possibility when quoting times in print or on radio and television. Note that when such times are spoken, the word **Uhr** is never omitted, and it is immediately followed by the number of minutes – these cannot come before with **vor** or **nach**, nor can **Viertel** be used for "quarter" or **halb** for "half". However the twelve hour clock is also used in conversation and letters, followed by **nachmittags, abends** ("in the afternoon", "in the evening"), etc. if it is necessary to make this clear.

| WRITTEN | SPOKEN |
|---|---|
| ***1.00 a.m./0100*** | ***one*** [*a.m.* or ***in the morning***]/***one hundred hours*** |
| = 1 Uhr | eins, ein Uhr [nachts or morgens]/ein Uhr |
| ***1.00 p.m./1300*** | ***one*** [*p.m.* or ***in the afternoon***]/***thirteen hundred hours*** |
| = 13 Uhr | eins, ein Uhr [mittags]/dreizehn Uhr |
| ***2.05 a.m./0205*** | ***five past two [in the morning]/[o] two o five*** |
| = 2.05 Uhr | fünf [Minuten] nach zwei [Uhr nachts *or* morgens]/zwei Uhr fünf |
| ***2.05 p.m./1405*** | ***five past two [in the afternoon]/fourteen o five*** |
| = 14.05 Uhr | fünf [Minuten] nach zwei [Uhr nachmittags]/vierzehn Uhr fünf |
| ***4.15 a.m./0415*** | ***four fifteen [a.m.], a quarter past four [in the morning]/[o] four fifteen*** |
| = 4.15 Uhr | Viertel nach vier [morgens]/vier Uhr fünfzehn |
| ***4.15 p.m./1615*** | ***four fifteen [p.m.], a quarter past four [in the afternoon]*** |
| = 16.15 Uhr | Viertel nach vier [nachmittags]/sechzehn Uhr fünfzehn |
| ***5.30 a.m./0530*** | ***five thirty [a.m.], half past five [in the morning]/[o] five thirty*** |
| = 5.30 Uhr | halb sechs [morgens]/ fünf Uhr dreißig |
| ***5.30 p.m./1730*** | ***five thirty [p.m.], half past five [in the afternoon]/seventeen thirty*** |
| = 17.30 Uhr | halb sechs [abends]/siebzehn Uhr dreißig |
| ***7.45 a.m./0745*** | ***seven forty-five [a.m.], a quarter to eight [in the morning]/[o] seven forty-five*** |
| = 7.45 Uhr | Viertel vor acht [morgens]/sieben Uhr fünfundvierzig |
| ***7.45 p.m./1945*** | ***seven forty-five p.m., a quarter to eight [in the evening]/nineteen forty-five*** |
| = 19.45 Uhr | Viertel vor acht [abends]/neunzehn Uhr fünfundvierzig |
| ***12.00 [midnight]/, 0000, 2400*** | ***twelve [o'clock], [twelve] midnight/oo double o, twenty-four hundred hours*** |
| = 0 Uhr, 24 Uhr | zwölf, zwölf Uhr [nachts]/null Uhr, vierundzwanzig Uhr |
| ***12 [noon]/1200*** | ***twelve [o'clock], [twelve] noon/twelve hundred hours*** |
| = 12 Uhr | zwölf, zwölf Uhr [mittags]/zwölf Uhr |

N.B. When using the twenty-four hour clock, **0000 = null Uhr** indicates the beginning of the day, **2400 = vierundzwanzig Uhr** the end of the day.

## When?

"at" with a time is **um**:
***He came at eight o'clock***
= Er kam um acht Uhr
***[At] what time do you want breakfast?***
= Um wie viel Uhr wollen Sie frühstücken?
***at half past***
= um halb
***at half past eight, at half eight***
= um halb neun
***at six exactly, on the dot of six***
= genau um sechs, [um] Punkt sechs

***at about ten***
= gegen zehn
***at twelve at the latest***
= spätestens um zwölf
***It must be ready by eleven***
= Es muss bis elf fertig sein
***I won't be there until six***
= Ich bin erst um sechs dort
***closed from 1 to 2 p.m.***
= von 13 bis 14 Uhr geschlossen
***every hour on the hour***
= stündlich zur vollen Stunde

**clock** /klɒk/ ❶ *n.* Ⓐ ▶ **1012** Uhr, *die;* **[work] against the ~:** gegen die Zeit [arbeiten]; **beat the ~ [by ten minutes]** [10 Minuten] früher fertig werden; **put** *or* **turn the ~ back** (*fig.*) die Zeit zurückdrehen; **round the ~:** rund um die Uhr; **hold the ~ on sb.** jmds. Zeit stoppen; **watch the ~** (*fig.*) [dauernd] auf die Uhr sehen (*weil man ungeduldig auf den Arbeitsschluss wartet*); Ⓑ (*coll.*) (*speedometer*) Tacho, *der* (*ugs.*); (*milometer*) ≈ Kilometerzähler, *der;* (*taximeter*) Taxameter, *das;* Ⓒ (*coll.: stopwatch*) Uhr, *die;* Ⓓ (*Bot.: seedhead*) Haarkelch, *der* (*Bot.*); Ⓔ (*Brit. sl.: face*) Visage, *die* (*salopp abwertend*). ⇒ *also* **o'clock.**
❷ *v.t.* Ⓐ **~ [up]** zu verzeichnen haben ‹Sieg, Zeit, Erfolg›; erreichen ‹Geschwindigkeit›; zurücklegen ‹Entfernung, Kilometer›; **~ 3.43·7/a personal best** ‹Läufer:› 3:43,7/eine persönliche Bestzeit laufen; Ⓑ (*coll.: time*) stoppen **(at mit)**; Ⓒ (*coll.: hit*) **~ sb. [one]** jmdm. eins überbraten (*ugs.*)
**~ 'in, ~ 'on** *v.i.* [bei Arbeitsantritt] stechen *od.* stempeln; **the night shift ~s in** *or* **on at 8 p.m.** die Nachtschicht beginnt abends um acht
**~ 'off, ~ 'out** *v.i.* [bei Arbeitsschluss] stechen *od.* stempeln; **we ~ off** *or* **out earlier than usual on a Friday** freitags machen wir früher Feierabend
**clock: ~-face** *n.* Zifferblatt, *das;* **~ golf** *n.* Uhrengolf, *das;* **~maker** *n.* ▶ **1261** Uhrmacher, *der*/-macherin, *die;* **~ 'radio** *n.* Radiowecker, *der;* **~ tower** *n.* Uhr[en]turm, *der;* **~-watcher** *n. jmd., der keine Sekunde länger als vorgeschrieben am Arbeitsplatz bleibt;*

**~-watching** *n.* ständiges Auf-die-Uhr-Sehen *weil man ungeduldig auf den Arbeitsschluss wartet*

**'clockwise** ❶ *adv.* im Uhrzeigersinn. ❷ *adj.* im Uhrzeigersinn *nachgestellt;* rechtsläufig (*Technik*); **in a ~ direction** im Uhrzeigersinn

**'clockwork** *n.* Uhrwerk, *das;* **~ [mechanism]** Aufziehmechanismus, *der;* Uhrwerk, *das* (*veralt.*); **a ~ car** ein Aufziehauto; **as regular as ~** (*fig.*) absolut regelmäßig; **with ~ precision/regularity** (*fig.*) absolut genau/regelmäßig; **go like ~** (*fig.*) klappen wie am Schnürchen (*ugs.*)

**clod** /klɒd/ *n.* [A] (*lump*) Klumpen, *der;* (*of earth*) Scholle, *die;* [B] (*derog.: dolt*) Tölpel, *der* (*abwertend*)

**'clodhopper** *n.* [A] ⇒ **clod** B; [B] (*coll.: shoe*) Elbkahn, der (*ugs. scherzh.*); Quadratlatschen, *der* (*salopp scherzh.*)

**clog** /klɒg/ ❶ *n.* Holzschuh, *der;* ([*fashionable*] *wooden-soled shoe*) Clog, *der;* **pop one's ~s** (*Brit. coll.*) den Löffel abgeben (*ugs.*). ❷ *v.t.*, **-gg-:** [A] **~ [up]** verstopfen ‹Rohr, Poren›; blockieren ‹Rad, Maschinerie›; **be ~ged [up] with sth.** mit etw. verstopft/durch etw. blockiert sein; [B] (*impede*) hemmen; (*obstruct*) blockieren; [C] **~ [up]** (*encumber*) belasten

**'clog dance** *n.* Holzschuhtanz, *der*

**cloister** /'klɔɪstə(r)/ ❶ *n.* [A] (*covered walk*) Kreuzgang, *der;* [B] (*convent, monastery; monastic life*) Kloster, *das.* ❷ *v. refl.* **~ oneself in one's study** (*fig.*) sich in sein Studierzimmer einschließen

**cloistered** /'klɔɪstəd/ *adj.* in einem Kloster lebend; (*fig.*) klösterlich ‹Abgeschiedenheit, Dasein›

**clone** /kləʊn/ (*Biol.*) ❶ *n.* Klon, *der;* (*fig.: copy*) [schlechte] Kopie. ❷ *v.t.* klonen

**clonk** /klɒŋk/ *n.* (*coll.*) [A] (*sound*) harter Schlag; [B] **get a ~ on the head** eins gegen die Birne kriegen (*ugs.*)

**close** ❶ /kləʊs/ *adj.* [A] (*near in space*) dicht; nahe; **be ~ to sth.** nahe bei *od.* an etw. (*Dat.*) sein; **how ~ is London to the South coast?** wie weit ist London von der Südküste entfernt?; **you're too ~ to the fire** du bist zu dicht *od.* nah am Feuer; **fly ~ to the ground** dicht über dem Boden fliegen; **I wish we lived ~r to your parents** ich wünschte, wir würden näher bei deinen Eltern wohnen; **be ~ to tears/breaking point** den Tränen/einem Zusammenbruch nahe sein; **be ~ to exhaustion** vor Erschöpfung fast umfallen; **at ~ quarters, the building looked less impressive** aus der Nähe betrachtet, wirkte das Gebäude weniger imposant; **fighting at ~ quarters** der Kampf Mann gegen Mann; **at ~ range** aus kurzer Entfernung; [B] (*near in time*) nahe (**to** an + *Dat.*); **war is ~:** ein Krieg steht unmittelbar bevor; [C] (*in near or intimate relation*) eng ‹Freund, Freundschaft, Beziehung, Zusammenarbeit, Verbindung›; nahe ‹Verwandte, Angehörige, Bekanntschaft›; **be/become ~ to sb.** jmdm. nahe stehen/nahe kommen; [D] (*rigorous, painstaking*) eingehend, genau ‹Untersuchung, Prüfung, Befragung usw.›; streng, verschärft ‹Haft, Arrest›; **pay ~ attention** genau aufpassen; [E] (*stifling*) stickig ‹Luft, Raum›; drückend, schwül ‹Wetter›; [F] (*nearly equal*) hart ‹[Wett]kampf, Spiel›; knapp ‹Ergebnis›; **a ~ race** ein Kopf-an-Kopf-Rennen; **that was too ~ for comfort** das ging gerade noch gut; **I had a ~ call** *or* **shave** *or* **thing** (*coll.*) ich bin gerade noch davongekommen; **that was a ~ call** *or* **shave** *or* **thing** (*coll.*) das war knapp!; [G] (*fitting exactly*) genau passend ‹Kleidungsstück›; (*nearly matching*) wortgetreu ‹Übersetzung›; getreu, genau ‹Imitation, Kopie›; groß ‹Ähnlichkeit›; **be the ~st equivalent to sth.** einer Sache (*Dat.*) am ehesten entsprechen; **bear a ~ resemblance to sb.** jmdm. sehr ähnlich sehen; große Ähnlichkeit mit jmdm. haben; [H] (*narrow, confined*) eng ‹Raum›; [I] (*dense*) dicht, fest (*Gewebe*); dicht, undurchdringlich ‹Dickicht, Gestrüpp›; eng ‹Schrift›; (*fig.*) lückenlos, stichhaltig ‹Beweisführung, Argument›; [J] (*concealed*) verborgen; **keep** *or* **lie ~:** sich verborgen *od.* versteckt halten; (*secret*) **keep sth. ~:** etw. geheim halten; (*secretive*) **be ~ about sth.** in Bezug auf etw. (*Akk.*) verschwiegen sein; [K] (*niggardly*) knauserig (*ugs. abwertend*); [L] (*Phonet.*) geschlossen ‹Vokal›.
❷ /kləʊs/ *adv.* [A] (*near*) nah[e]; **come ~ to the truth** der Wahrheit nahe kommen; **that's the ~st I've ever come to being involved in an accident** so knapp *od.* (*ugs.*) haarscharf bin ich noch nie einem Unfall entgangen; **be ~ at hand** in Reichweite sein; ‹Ereignis:› nahe bevorstehen; **~ by** in der Nähe; **~ by the river** in der Nähe des Flusses; nahe am Fluss; **the lamb stayed ~ by its mother's side** das Lamm blieb dicht an der Seite seiner Mutter; **~ on 60 years** fast 60 Jahre; **~ on 2 o'clock** kurz vor 2 [Uhr]; **~ to sb./sth.** nahe bei jmdm./etw.; **don't stand so ~ to the edge of the cliff** stell dich nicht so nah *od.* dicht an den Rand des Kliffs; **come ~ to tears** den Tränen nahe sein; **she came ~ to being the best/the winner** sie wäre fast *od.* beinah[e] die Beste geworden/sie hätte fast *od.* beinah[e] gewonnen; **~ together** dicht beieinander; **can't you stand ~r together?** könnt ihr nicht etwas mehr zusammenrücken?; **try not to come too ~ together** versucht, einander nicht zu nahe zu kommen; **these deadlines come too ~ together** diese Termine liegen zu nahe zusammen; **it brought them ~r together** (*fig.*) es brachte sie einander näher; **~ behind** dicht dahinter; **leave sth./stand ~ behind sb./sth.** etw. dicht hinter jmdm./etw. lassen/ dicht hinter jmdm./etw. stehen; **see sth. [from] ~ 'to** *or* **'up** etw. aus der Nähe sehen; **go ~:** es beinahe schaffen; [B] (*in ~ manner*) fest ‹schließen›; genau ‹hinsehen›; **on looking ~r** bei genauerem Hinsehen.
❸ /kləʊz/ *v.t.* [A] (*shut*) schließen, (*ugs.*) zumachen ‹Augen, Tür, Fenster, Geschäft›; zuziehen ‹Vorhang›; (*declare shut*) schließen ‹Laden, Geschäft, Fabrik, Betrieb, Werk, Zeche›; stilllegen ‹Betrieb, Werk, Zeche, Bahnlinie›; sperren ‹Straße, Brücke›; **behind ~d doors** hinter verschlossenen Türen; **~ one's eyes to sth.** (*fig.*) die Augen vor etw. (*Dat.*) verschließen; [B] (*conclude*) schließen, beenden ‹Besprechung, Rede, Diskussion›; schließen ‹Versammlung, Sitzung›; abschließen ‹Handel, Geschäft›; **~ an account** ein Konto auflösen; **the matter is ~d** der Fall *od.* die Sache ist abgeschlossen; [C] (*make smaller*) schließen (*auch fig.*) ‹Lücke›; zustopfen ‹Riss›; **~ the gap between rich and poor** die Kluft zwischen Arm und Reich überwinden; [D] (*Electr.*) schließen ‹Stromkreis›.
❹ /kləʊz/ *v.i.* [A] (*shut*) sich schließen; ‹Tür:› zugehen (*ugs.*), sich schließen; **the door/lid doesn't ~ properly** die Tür/der Deckel schließt nicht richtig; **the valve won't ~:** das Ventil schließt nicht; [B] ‹Laden, Geschäft, Fabrik:› schließen, (*ugs.*) zumachen; (*permanently*) ‹Betrieb, Werk, Zeche:› geschlossen *od.* stillgelegt werden; ‹Geschäft:› geschlossen werden, (*ugs.*) zumachen; ‹Theaterstück:› abgesetzt werden; [C] (*come to an end*) zu Ende gehen; enden; (*finish speaking*) schließen; **in closing** abschließend; [D] (*come closer, within striking distance*) sich nähern; aufschließen (*bes. Sport*); (*join battle*) aufeinander treffen; aneinander geraten; **I ~d with him in hand-to-hand fighting** ich fing ein Handgemenge mit ihm an.
❺ *n.* [A] /kləʊz/ *no pl.* Ende, *das;* Schluss, *der;* **come** *or* **draw to a ~:** zu Ende gehen; **bring** *or* **draw sth. to a ~:** einer Sache (*Dat.*) ein Ende bereiten; etw. zu Ende bringen; **at ~ of business** bei Geschäftsschluss; **~ of play** (*Cricket*) Ende des Spieltages; [B] /kləʊz/ (*Mus.*) Kadenz, *die;* [C] /kləʊs/ (*Brit.: precinct of cathedral*) Domhof, *der;* (*cul-de-sac*) Sackgasse, *die;* (*enclosed place*) Hof, *der*

**~ 'down** /kləʊz/ ❶ *v.t.* schließen; zumachen (*ugs.*); stilllegen ‹Werk, Zeche›; einstellen ‹Betrieb, Arbeit›. ❷ *v.i.* geschlossen werden, zugemacht werden (*ugs.*); ‹Werk, Zeche:› stillgelegt werden; (*Brit.*) ‹Rundfunkstation:› Sendeschluss haben

**~ 'in** *v.i.* ‹Nacht, Dunkelheit:› hereinbrechen; ‹Tage:› kürzer werden; **~ in [up]on sb./sth.** (*draw nearer*) sich jmdm./etw. nähern; (*draw around*) jmdn./etw. umzingeln

**~ 'off** *v.t.* [ab]sperren; abriegeln

**~ 'out** *v.t.* (*Amer.*) absetzen, abstoßen ‹Waren›; auflösen ‹Betrieb›

**~ 'up** ❶ *v.i.* [A] aufrücken; [B] ‹Blume:› sich schließen; [C] (*lock up*) abschließen. ❷ *v.t.* abschließen. ⇒ *also* **~-up**

**close-cropped** /'kləʊskrɒpt/ *adj.* kurz geschoren

**closed** /kləʊzd/ *adj.* [A] (*no longer open*) geschlossen ‹Laden, Geschäft, Fabrik›; **we're ~:** wir haben geschlossen; '**~**' „Geschlossen"; **the subject is ~:** das Thema ist [für mich] erledigt; [B] (*restricted*) [der Öffentlichkeit] nicht frei zugänglich; (*Sport*) nur für Teilnehmer einer bestimmten Gruppe/Klasse offen ‹Wettbewerb etc.›; **a women's ~ golf tournament** ein Golfturnier für Damen; ⇒ *also* **scholarship** A; [C] (*Phonet.*) geschlossen ‹Silbe›. ⇒ *also* **book** 1 A

**closed: ~-circuit** *adj.* **~-circuit television** interne Fernsehanlage; (*for supervision*) Videoüberwachungsanlage, *die*

**close-down** /'kləʊzdaʊn/ *n.* [A] (*closing*) Schließung, *die;* (*of works, railway, mine*) Stilllegung, *die;* (*of project, operation*) Einstellung, *die;* [B] (*Radio, Telev.*) Sendeschluss, *der*

**closed: ~ season** (*Amer.*) ⇒ **close season**; **~ 'shop** *n.* Closed Shop, *der;* **we have** *or* **operate a ~ shop in this factory** in unserer Fabrik besteht Gewerkschaftszwang

**close**/kləʊs/: **~-fisted** *adj.* geizig; knauserig (*ugs. abwertend*); **~-fitting** *adj.* eng anliegend; knapp sitzend ‹Anzug›; **~-grained** *adj.* fest ‹Gewebe›; fein gemasert ‹Holz›; feinnarbig ‹Leder›; **~ 'harmony** *n.* (*Mus.*) enge Lage; **~-hauled** *adj.* (*Naut.*) hart am Wind segelnd ‹Schiff›; **~-knit** *adj.* fest zusammengewachsen

**closely** /'kləʊslɪ/ *adv.* [A] dicht; **follow me ~:** bleib *od.* geh dicht hinter mir!; **look ~ at** genau betrachten; **look ~ into** (*fig.*) näher untersuchen; **the first explosion was ~ followed by two more** unmittelbar auf die [erste] Explosion folgten zwei weitere; [B] (*intimately*) eng; **we're not ~ related** wir sind nicht nah miteinander verwandt; [C] (*rigorously, painstakingly*) genau; genau, eingehend ‹befragen, prüfen›; streng, scharf ‹bewachen›; **a ~ guarded secret** ein streng *od.* sorgsam gehütetes Geheimnis; [D] (*nearly equally*) **~ fought/contested** hart umkämpft; **the contest was ~ fought** man kämpfte hart um den Sieg; [E] (*exactly*) genau; **~ resemble sb.** jmdm. sehr ähneln; [F] (*densely*) dicht; **~ printed/written** eng bedruckt/beschrieben; **~ reasoned** (*fig.*) schlüssig

**closeness** /'kləʊsnɪs/ *n., no pl.* [A] (*nearness in space or time*) Nähe, *die;* [B] (*intimacy*) Enge, *die;* **the ~ of their friendship** die Tiefe ihrer Freundschaft; [C] (*rigorousness*) Genauigkeit, *die;* (*of questioning*) Nachdrücklichkeit, *die;* (*of guard, watch*) Strenge, *die;* [D] (*of atmosphere, air*) Schwüle, *die;* [E] (*of contest, election, etc.*) knapper Ausgang; [F] (*exactness*) **the ~ of the fit** der genaue Sitz; **the ~ of a translation** die Worttreue einer Übersetzung; **the ~ of the resemblance** die große Ähnlichkeit

**close**/kləʊs/: **~-range** *adj.* ‹Sicht, Betrachtung› aus nächster Nähe; **~-range weapon** Nahkampfwaffe, *die;* **~-range shots** (*Photog.*) Nahaufnahmen; **~ season** *n.* Schonzeit, *die;* **~-set** *adj.* dicht beieinander liegend ‹Augen›; dicht ‹Hecke›

**closet** /'klɒzɪt/ *n.* [A] (*Amer.: cupboard*) Schrank, *der;* **come out of the ~** (*fig.*) sich nicht länger verstecken; [B] (*water ~*) Klosett, *das*

**closeted** /'klɒzɪtɪd/ *adj.* **be ~ together/with sb.** eine Besprechung/mit jmdm. eine Besprechung hinter verschlossenen Türen haben

**close-up** /'kləʊsʌp/ *n.* (*Cinemat., Telev.*) **~ [picture/shot]** Nahaufnahme *die;* (*of face etc.*) Großaufnahme, *die;* **in ~:** in Nahaufnahme/Großaufnahme

**closing**/'kləʊzɪŋ/: **~ date** *n.* (*for competition*) Einsendeschluss, *der;* (*to take part*) Meldefrist, *die;* **the ~ date for applications**

C

**for the job is ...:** Bewerbungen bitte bis zum ... einreichen; **~ time** *n.* (*of public house*) Polizeistunde, *die;* (*of shop*) Ladenschlusszeit, *die;* **it's nearly ~ time** es wird gleich geschlossen

**closure** /ˈkləʊʒə(r)/ *n.* Ⓐ (*closing*) Schließung, *die;* (*of factory, pit also*) Stilllegung, *die;* (*of road, bridge*) Sperrung, *die;* **a two-year ~:** eine zweijährige Stilllegung; Ⓑ (*Parl.*) Schluss der Debatte; Ⓒ (*cap, stopper*) [Flaschen]verschluss, *der*

**clot** /klɒt/ ❶ *n.* Ⓐ Klumpen, *der;* **a ~ [of blood] had formed over the wound/in the artery** geronnenes Blut hatte die Wunde verschlossen/ein Blutgerinnsel hatte sich in der Arterie gebildet; Ⓑ (*Brit. coll.: stupid person*) Trottel, *der* (*ugs. abwertend*). ❷ *v.i.*, **-tt-** ‹Blut:› gerinnen; ‹Sahne:› klumpen

**cloth** /klɒθ/ *n., pl.* **~s** /klɒθs/ Ⓐ Stoff, *der;* Tuch, *das;* **~ of gold/silver** gold-/silberdurchwirkter Stoff; **bound in ~:** mit Leineneinband *nachgestellt;* **cut one's coat according to one's ~** (*fig.*) sich nach der Decke strecken (*ugs.*); Ⓑ (*piece of ~*) Tuch, *das;* (*dish~*) Spültuch, *das;* (*table~*) Tischtuch, *das;* [Tisch]decke, *die;* (*duster*) Staubtuch, *das;* Ⓒ *no pl.* (*clerical profession*) **a gentleman of the ~:** ein Geistlicher; **the ~** (*clergy*) die Geistlichkeit

**cloth: ~ binding** *n.* Leineneinband, *der;* **~-bound** *adj.* mit Leineneinband *nachgestellt;* **~-cap** *adj.* **he tried to project a ~-cap image** er versuchte, das Image des [typischen] Arbeiters zu vermitteln; **a ~-cap comedian/entertainer** ein Komiker/Entertainer für die Arbeiterklasse

**clothe** /kləʊð/ *v.t.* kleiden; (*fig.*) **~ one's sentiments/ideas in words** seine Gefühle/Gedanken in Worte kleiden; **the cherry trees were ~d in blossom** die Kirschbäume standen in voller Blüte; **the hills were ~d in snow** die Hügel waren mit Schnee bedeckt

ˈ**cloth-eared** *adj.* (*coll. derog.*) schwerhörig

**clothes** /kləʊðz/ *n. pl.* Ⓐ Kleider *Pl.;* (*collectively*) Kleidung, *die;* **with one's ~ on** angezogen; **put one's ~ on** sich anziehen; **without any ~ on** völlig unbekleidet; **take one's ~ off** sich ausziehen; Ⓑ ⇒ **bedclothes**

**clothes: ~ basket** *n.* Wäschekorb, *der;* **~ brush** *n.* Kleiderbürste, *die;* **~ hanger** *n.* Kleiderbügel, *der;* **~ horse** *n.* Wäscheständer, *der;* **~ line** *n.* Wäscheleine, *die;* **~ moth** *n.* Motte, *die;* **~ peg** (*Brit.*), **~pin** (*Amer.*) *ns.* Wäscheklammer, *die*

**clothier** /ˈkləʊðɪə(r)/ *n.* ▶ 1261 (*formal*) Herrenausstatter, *der*

**clothing** /ˈkləʊðɪŋ/ *n., no pl.* Kleidung, *die;* **article of ~:** Kleidungsstück, *das;* **bloodstained ~ was found** blutbefleckte Kleidungsstücke wurden gefunden

**clotted cream** /klɒtɪd ˈkri:m/ ⇒ **Devonshire cream**

**cloture** /ˈkləʊtʃə(r)/ (*Amer.*) ⇒ **closure** B

**cloud** /klaʊd/ ❶ *n.* Ⓐ Wolke, *die;* (*collective*) Bewölkung, *die;* **be** *or* **live in the ~s** (*fig.*) auf Wolken *od.* in den Wolken schweben; **walk** *or* **go round with one's head** *or* **have one's head in the ~s** (*fig.*) (*be unrealistic*) in den Wolken schweben; (*be absent-minded*) mit seinen Gedanken ganz woanders sein; **[be] on ~ seven** *or* **nine** (*fig. coll.*) im sieb[en]ten Himmel [sein] (*ugs.*); **every ~ has a silver lining** (*prov.*) es hat alles sein Gutes; **there wasn't a ~ in the sky** (*lit. or fig.*) es zeigte sich [noch] kein Wölkchen am Himmel; **a ~ on the horizon** (*fig.*) ein Wölkchen am Horizont; Ⓑ **~ of dust/smoke** Staub-/Rauchwolke, *die;* Ⓒ (*fig.: cause of gloom or suspicion*) dunkle Wolke; **the ~ of suspicion hangs over him** der Schatten des Verdachts liegt auf ihm; **he left under a ~:** unter zweifelhaften Umständen schied er aus dem Dienst.

❷ *v.t.* Ⓐ verdunkeln ‹Himmel›; blind machen ‹Fenster[scheibe], Spiegel›; Ⓑ (*fig.: cast gloom or trouble on*) trüben ‹Glück, Freude, Aussicht›; umwölken ‹Gesicht, Stirn›; überschatten ‹Zukunft›; (*make unclear*) trüben ‹Urteilsvermögen, Verstand, Bewusstsein›; verunklaren ‹Problem›

**~** ˈ**over** *v.i.* sich bewölken; ‹Spiegel:› beschlagen; **her face ~ed over** ihr Gesicht verdüsterte sich (*geh.*)

**cloud: ~ bank** *n.* Wolkenbank, *die;* **~berry** *n.* Moltebeere, *die;* **~burst** *n.* Wolkenbruch, *der;* **~-capped** *adj.* wolkenverhangen ‹Gipfel›; **~ chamber** *n.* (*Phys.*) Nebelkammer, *die;* **~ cover** *n.* Wolkendecke, *die;* **~** ˈ**cuckoo land** *n.* Wolkenkuckucksheim, *das* (*geh.*)

**cloudiness** /ˈklaʊdɪnɪs/ *n.* Ⓐ (*of liquid*) Trübheit, *die;* Ⓑ (*of sky*) Bewölkung, *die*

**cloudless** /ˈklaʊdlɪs/ *adj.* wolkenlos

**cloudy** /ˈklaʊdɪ/ *adj.* bewölkt, bedeckt, wolkig ‹Himmel›; trübe ‹Wetter, Flüssigkeit, Glas›; wolkig ‹Edelstein, Mineral›; **it is getting ~:** der Himmel bewölkt sich

**clout** /klaʊt/ ❶ *n.* Ⓐ (*coll.: hit*) Schlag, *der;* **get a ~ round the ears** eins hinter die Ohren kriegen (*ugs.*); Ⓑ (*coll.: power, influence*) Schlagkraft, *die;* Ⓒ **~ [nail]** Pappnagel, *der.* ❷ *v.t.* (*coll.*) hauen (*ugs.*); **~ sb. round the ear/on the head** jmdm. eins hinter die Ohren/auf den Deckel geben (*ugs.*); **~ sb. [one]** jmdm. eine runterhauen (*salopp*)

**clove**[1] /kləʊv/ *n.* Brutzwiebel, *die;* (*of garlic*) [Knoblauch]zehe, *die*

**clove**[2] *n.* Ⓐ (*spice*) [Gewürz]nelke, *die;* (*plant*) Gewürznelkenbaum, *der;* **oil of ~s** Nelkenöl, *das;* Ⓑ **~ [gillyflower]** Gartennelke, *die*

**clove**[3] ⇒ **cleave**[1]

ˈ**clove hitch** *n.* Webeleinenstek, *der*

**cloven** /ˈkləʊvn/ ❶ ⇒ **cleave**[1]. ❷ *adj.* **~ foot/hoof** Spaltfuß, *der* (*veralt.*)/ Spalthuf, *der* (*veralt.*); (*of devil*) Pferdefuß, *der*

**clover** /ˈkləʊvə(r)/ *n.* Klee, *der;* **be/live in ~** (*fig.*) wie Gott in Frankreich leben

ˈ**cloverleaf** *n.* (*also Road Constr.*) Kleeblatt, *das*

**clown** /klaʊn/ ❶ *n.* Ⓐ Clown, *der;* **act** *or* **play the ~:** den Clown spielen; Ⓑ (*ignorant person*) Dummkopf, *der* (*ugs.*); (*ill-bred person*) ungehobelter Klotz. ❷ *v.i.* **~ [about** *or* **around]** den Clown spielen (*abwertend*)

**clownish** /ˈklaʊnɪʃ/ *adj.* (*derog.*) albern (*abwertend*)

**cloy** /klɔɪ/ ❶ *v.t.* übersättigen; überfüttern; **~ the appetite** sich (*Dat.*) den Appetit verderben; **be ~ed with pleasure** des Vergnügens überdrüssig sein. ❷ *v.i.* seinen Reiz verlieren; an Reiz verlieren

**cloying** /ˈklɔɪɪŋ/ *adj.* (*lit. or fig.*) süßlich

**cloze** /kləʊz/ *n.* **~ test** (*Educ.*) Ergänzungstest, *der*

**club** /klʌb/ ❶ *n.* Ⓐ (*weapon*) Keule, *die;* (*Indian ~*) [Gymnastik]keule, *die;* (*golf ~*) Golfschläger, *der;* Ⓑ (*association*) Klub, *der;* Club, *der;* Verein, *der;* **social ~:** ≈ Vereinsgaststätte, *die;* (*of firm*) ≈ Gemeinschaftsräume *Pl.;* **Conservative ~:** Club der Konservativen; **join the ~** (*fig.*) mitmachen; **join the** *or* **welcome to the ~!** (*fig.*) du also auch!; **be in the ~** (*Brit. fig. coll.*) ein Kind kriegen (*ugs.*); **put sb. in the ~** (*Brit. fig. coll.*) jmdm. ein Kind machen (*ugs.*); Ⓒ (*premises*) Klub, *der;* (*buildings/grounds*) Klubhaus/-gelände, *das;* Ⓓ (*Cards*) Kreuz, *das;* Treff, *das;* **the ace/seven of ~s** das Kreuzas/die Kreuzsieben; **~s are trumps** Kreuz ist Trumpf.

❷ *v.t.*, **-bb-** Ⓐ (*beat*) prügeln; (*with ~*) knüppeln; Ⓑ (*contribute*) **~ [together]** zusammenlegen ‹Geld, Ersparnisse›.

❸ *v.i.*, **-bb-: ~ together** sich zusammentun; (*in order to buy something*) zusammenlegen

**clubbable** /ˈklʌbəbl/ *adj.* gesellig

**club: ~ chair** *n.* Klubsessel, *der;* **~ foot** *n.* Klumpfuß, *der;* **~house** *n.* Klubhaus, *das;* **~man** *n.* Klubmensch, *der* (*jmd., der in seinem Klub/in Klubs zu Hause ist*); Vereinsmeier, *der* (*abwertend*); **~moss** *n.* (*Bot.*) Bärlapp, *der;* (*Selaginella*) Moosfarn, *der;* **~root** *n.* (*Bot.*) Kohlhernie, *die;* Knotensucht, *die;* **~** ˈ**sandwich** *n.* (*Amer.*) Club-Sandwich, *das;* Doppeldecker, *der* (*ugs.*)

**cluck** /klʌk/ ❶ *n.* Gackern, *das;* (*to call chicks*) Glucken, *das.* ❷ *v.i.* gackern; (*to call chicks*) glucken

**clue** /klu:/ ❶ *n.* Ⓐ (*fact, principle*) Anhaltspunkt, *der;* (*in criminal investigation*) Spur, *die;* **find a ~ to a mystery/problem** einen Zugang zu einem Geheimnis/einem Problem finden; **the fingerprints are a ~ as to who murdered the man** die Fingerabdrücke können auf die Spur des Mörders führen; Ⓑ (*fig. coll.*) **give sb. a ~:** jmdm. einen Tipp geben; **not have a ~:** keine Ahnung haben (*ugs.*); **he never seems to have a ~ about anything** er hat offenbar nie die geringste Ahnung; Ⓒ (*in crossword*) Frage, *die.*

❷ *v.t.* (*coll.: inform*) **~ sb. up** jmdm. Bescheid sagen; **be ~d up about** *or* **on sth.**, **be ~d in on sth.** über etw. (*Akk.*) Bescheid wissen; **keep sb. ~d up** jmdn. auf dem Laufenden halten

**clueless** /ˈklu:lɪs/ *adj.* (*coll. derog.*) unbedarft (*ugs.*) ‹Person›; **he's completely ~:** er hat absolut keine Ahnung

**clump** /klʌmp/ ❶ *n.* (*of trees, bushes, flowers*) Gruppe, *die;* (*of grass*) Büschel, *das;* **a ~ of shrubs** ein Gebüsch. ❷ *v.i.* Ⓐ (*tread*) stapfen; Ⓑ (*form ~*) klumpen. ❸ *v.t.* Ⓐ (*heap, plant together*) zusammengruppieren; in Gruppen anordnen; Ⓑ (*coll.: hit*) hauen (*ugs.*)

**clumsily** /ˈklʌmzɪlɪ/ *adv.* ⇒ **clumsy**: schwerfällig; unbeholfen; plump

**clumsiness** /ˈklʌmzɪnɪs/ *n., no pl.* ⇒ **clumsy**: Schwerfälligkeit, *die;* Plumpheit, *die*

**clumsy** /ˈklʌmzɪ/ *adj.* Ⓐ (*awkward*) schwerfällig, unbeholfen ‹Person, Bewegungen›; ungeschickt ‹Hände›; plump ‹Form, Figur›; tollpatschig ‹Heranwachsender›; Ⓑ (*ill-contrived*) plump ‹Verse, Nachahmung›; unbeholfen ‹Worte›; primitiv ‹Vorrichtung, Maschine, Erfindung›; Ⓒ (*tactless*) plump

**clung** ⇒ **cling**

**cluster** /ˈklʌstə(r)/ ❶ *n.* Ⓐ (*of grapes, berries*) Traube, *die;* (*of fruit, flowers, curls*) Büschel, *das;* (*of eggs*) Gelege, *das;* (*of trees, shrubs*) Gruppe, *die;* Ⓑ (*of stars, cells*) Haufen, *der;* (*of houses, huts, etc.*) Gruppe, *die;* Haufen, *der;* (*of coral animals, bees, spectators*) Traube, *die;* (*of islands*) Gruppe, *die;* (*of diamonds on brooch*) Kranz, *der;* Besatz, *der;* Ⓒ (*Ling.*) Cluster, *der.* ❷ *v.t.* **be ~ed with sth.** dicht mit etw. bestanden sein. ❸ *v.i.* **~ [a]round sb./sth.** sich um jmdn./etw. scharen *od.* drängen

**clutch**[1] /klʌtʃ/ ❶ *v.t.* umklammern; **the mother ~ed the child to her breast** die Mutter drückte das Kind fest an ihre Brust. ❷ *v.i.* **~ at sth.** nach etw. greifen; (*fig.*) sich an etw. (*Akk.*) klammern; ⇒ *also* **straw** B. ❸ *n.* Ⓐ (*tight grasp*) Umklammerung, *die;* Ⓑ *in pl.* (*fig.: control*) Klauen; **fall into sb.'s ~es** jmdm. in die Klauen fallen; in jmds. Klauen (*Akk.*) fallen; **get out of sb.'s ~es** sich aus jmds. Klauen befreien; Ⓒ (*grasping*) **make a ~ at sth./sb.** nach etw./jmdm. greifen; Ⓓ (*Motor Veh., Mech.*) Kupplung, *die;* **let in the ~, put the ~ in** einkuppeln; **disengage the ~, let the ~ out** auskuppeln; **~ pedal** Kupplungspedal, *das*

**clutch**[2] *n.* (*of eggs*) Gelege, *das;* (*of chicks*) Brut, *die*

ˈ**clutch bag** *n.* Unterarmtasche, *die*

**clutter** /ˈklʌtə(r)/ ❶ *n.* Ⓐ Durcheinander, *das;* **in a ~:** in einem Durcheinander; völlig verkramt (*ugs.*); **he pushed the ~ into a corner** er schob den ganzen Kram in eine Ecke; Ⓑ (*on radar screen*) Störflecke *Pl.* ❷ *v.t.* **~ [up] the table/room** überall auf dem Tisch/im Zimmer herumliegen; **be ~ed [up] with sth.** ‹Zimmer:› mit etw. voll gestopft sein; ‹Tisch:› mit etw. übersät sein; **be ~ed [up] with holidaymakers/cabs** von Urlaubern/Taxis wimmeln; **a ~ed room** ein total voll gestopftes Zimmer

**cm.** *abbr.* ▶ 928, ▶ 1210, ▶ 1284 **centimetre[s]** cm

**CND** *abbr.* (*Brit.*) **Campaign for Nuclear Disarmament** Kampagne für atomare Abrüstung

**c/o** *abbr.* ▶1286 **care of** bei; c/o

**Co.** *abbr.* A **company** Co.; **and Co.** /ənd kəʊ/ (*coll.*) und Co. (*ugs.*); B **county**

**CO** *abbr.* A **Commanding Officer;** B **conscientious objector** KDV

**coach** /kəʊtʃ/ ❶ *n.* A (*road vehicle*) Kutsche, *die;* (*state* ~) [Staats]karosse, *die;* ~ **and four/six** Vier-/Sechsspänner, *der;* ⇒ *also* **drive** 2 A; B (*railway carriage*) Wagen, *der;* C (*bus*) [Reise]bus, *der;* **by** ~: mit dem Bus; D (*tutor*) Privat- *od.* Nachhilfelehrer, *der*/-lehrerin, *die;* (*sport instructor*) Trainer, *der*/Trainerin, *die;* (*baseball* ~) Coach, *der.* ❷ *v.t.* trainieren; ~ **a pupil for an examination** einen Schüler auf eine Prüfung vorbereiten

**coach:** ~**builder** *n.* ▶1261 Karosseriebauer, *der;* ~ **house** *n.* Remise, *die*

**coaching** /ˈkəʊtʃɪŋ/ *n., no pl.* A (*teaching*) Privatunterricht, *der;* B (*Sport*) Training, *das;* C (*travelling*) ~ **days** Postkutschenzeit, *die;* ~ **inn** Herberge einer Poststation (*hist.*)

**coach:** ~**load** *n.* **a** ~**load of football supporters** ein Bus voll Fußballanhänger; ~**man** /ˈkəʊtʃmən/ *n., pl.* ~**men** /ˈkəʊtʃmən/ Kutscher, *der;* ~ **party** *n.* Reisegesellschaft, *die;* ~ **station** *n.* Busbahnhof, *der;* ~ **tour** *n.* Rundreise [im Omnibus], *die;* Omnibusreise, *die;* ~**work** *n.* Karosserie, *die*

**coagulant** /kəʊˈægjʊlənt/ *n.* (*Med.*) blutgerinnungsförderndes Mittel; Koagulans, *das* (*fachspr.*)

**coagulate** /kəʊˈægjʊleɪt/ ❶ *v.t.* gerinnen lassen; koagulieren (*fachspr.*). ❷ *v.i.* gerinnen; koagulieren (*fachspr.*)

**coagulation** /kəʊægjʊˈleɪʃn/ *n.* A (*process*) Gerinnung, *die;* Koagulation, *die* (*fachspr.*); B (*mass*) Gerinnsel, *das;* Koagulat, *das* (*fachspr.*)

**coal** /kəʊl/ *n.* A Kohle, *die;* (*hard* ~) Steinkohle, *die;* B (*piece of* ~) Stück Kohle; **live** ~**s** Glut, *die;* **heap** ~**s of fire on sb.'s head** (*fig.*) feurige Kohlen auf jmds. Haupt (*Akk.*) sammeln (*fig.*); **haul** *or* **call sb. over the** ~**s** (*fig.*) jmdm. die Leviten lesen (*ugs.*); **carry** ~**s to Newcastle** (*fig.*) Eulen nach Athen tragen (*fig.*)

**coal:** ~**bed** *n.* Kohlenflöz, *der;* ~**-black** *adj.* kohlrabenschwarz; ~ **box** *n.* Kohlenkasten, *der;* ~ **bunker** *n.* Kohlenbunker, *der;* ~ **cellar** *n.* Kohlenkeller, *der;* ~ **dust** *n.* Kohlenstaub, *der*

**coalesce** /kəʊəˈles/ *v.i.* A sich verbinden; eine Verbindung eingehen; B (*unite*) sich vereinigen

**coalescence** /kəʊəˈlesəns/ *n.* Verbindung, *die;* (*fig.*) Vereinigung, *die*

**coal:** ~**face** *n.* Streb, *der;* **at the** ~**face** im Streb *od.* vor Ort; ~**field** *n.* Kohlenrevier, *das;* ~ **fire** *n.* Kohlenfeuer, *das;* ~**-fired** *adj.* mit Kohle beheizt; kohlebeheizt; ~**-fired power station** Kohlekraftwerk, *das;* ~ **gas** *n.* Leuchtgas, *das;* Stadtgas, *das;* ~ **heaver** *n.* Kohlenträger, *der;* ~**-hole** *n.* (*Brit.*) A Kohlenbunker, *der;* B (*cellar*) Kohlenkeller, *der;* ~**house** *n.* Kohlenschuppen, *der*

**coalition** /kəʊəˈlɪʃn/ *n.* (*Polit.*) Koalition, *die;* (*union, fusion*) Zusammenschluss, *der* (*von Gruppen, Firmen*); **a** ~ **of plans/projects** eine Planungsgemeinschaft; **a** ~ **of interests** eine Interessenkoalition

**coaˈlition government** *n.* Koalitionsregierung, *die*

**coal:** ~**man** *n.* ▶1261 Kohlenmann, *der* (*ugs.*); ~ **measures** *n. pl.* (*Geol.*) Kohlevorkommen, *das;* ~ **merchant** *n.* ▶1261 Kohlenhändler, *der;* ~ **mine** *n.* [Kohlen]bergwerk, *das;* ~ **miner** *n.* ▶1261 [im Kohlenbergbau tätiger] Grubenarbeiter; ~ **mining** *n.* Kohlenbergbau, *der;* ~ **oil** *n.* (*Amer.*) Paraffin, *das;* ~ **scuttle** *n.* Kohleneimer, *der;* Kohlenschütte, *die;* ~**-seam** *n.* Kohlenflöz, *der;* ~ **shed** ⇒ ~**house;** ~ **shovel** *n.* Kohlenschaufel, *die;* ~ **tar** *n.* Steinkohlenteer, *der;* ~ **tit** *n.* (*Ornith.*) Tannenmeise, *die*

**coaming** /ˈkəʊmɪŋ/ *n.* (*Naut.*) Süllrand, *der*

**coarse** /kɔːs/ *adj.* A (*inferior*) derb, einfach ‹Essen›; B (*in texture*) grob; rau, grob ‹Haut, Teint›; C (*unrefined, rude, obscene*) derb; roh ‹Geschmack, Kraft›; primitiv ‹Person, Geist›; ungehobelt ‹Manieren, Person›; gemein ‹Lachen, Witz, Geräusch›

**coarse:** ~ **ˈfish** *n.* (*esp. Brit.*) Süßwasserfisch, *der* (*außer Lachs und Forelle*); ~**-grained** *adj.* grob gekörnt ‹Sand, Salz, Papier›; grob genarbt ‹Leder›; grob gemasert ‹Holz›

**coarsely** /ˈkɔːslɪ/ *adv.* ⇒ **coarse:** A derb; einfach; B grob; rau; C derb; roh; primitiv; ungehobelt; gemein

**coarsen** /ˈkɔːsn/ ❶ *v.t.* vergröbern. ❷ *v.i.* sich vergröbern

**coarseness** /ˈkɔːsnɪs/ *n., no pl.* ⇒ **coarse:** A Derbheit, *die;* Einfachheit, *die;* B Grobheit, *die;* Rauheit, *die;* C Derbheit, *die;* Rohheit, *die;* Primitivität, *die;* Ungehobeltheit, *die;* Gemeinheit, *die*

**coast** /kəʊst/ ❶ *n.* A Küste, *die;* **on the** ~: an der Küste; **off the** ~: vor der Küste; **the** ~ **is clear** (*fig.: there is no danger*) die Luft ist rein (*fig.*); B (*Amer.*) **the C**~: die Pazifik- *od.* Westküste [der USA]; C (*Amer.: slide*) Rodelbahn, *die;* **go for a** ~: rodeln gehen. ❷ *v.i.* A (*ride*) im Freilauf fahren; B (*fig.: progress*) **they are just** ~**ing along in their work** sie tun bei der Arbeit nur das Nötigste; sie arbeiten nur im Schongang (*ugs.*); **he** ~**s through every examination** er schafft jede Prüfung spielend; C (*sail*) die Küste entlang fahren; D (*Amer.: toboggan*) hinunterfahren

**coastal** /ˈkəʊstl/ *adj.* Küsten-; ~ **traffic** Küstenschifffahrt, *die*

**coaster** /ˈkəʊstə(r)/ *n.* A (*mat*) Untersetzer, *der;* B (*tray*) Tablett, *das;* C (*ship*) Küstenmotorschiff, *das;* Kümo, *das;* D (*Amer.: sledge*) Rodelschlitten, *der*

**coast:** ~**guard** *n.* A ▶1261 (*person*) Angehörige[r] der Küstenwacht; B (*organization*) Küstenwache, -wacht, *die;* ~**line** *n.* Küste, *die*

**coat** /kəʊt/ ❶ *n.* A Mantel, *der;* (*man's jacket*) Jackett, *das;* Rock, *der* (*veralt.*); **turn one's** ~ (*fig.*) sein Mäntelchen nach dem Winde hängen (*ugs. abwertend*); ⇒ *also* **cloth** A; B (*layer*) Schicht, *die;* C (*animal's hair, fur, etc.*) Fell, *das;* (*of bird*) Federkleid, *das;* D ⇒ **coating;** E (*skin, rind, husk*) Schale, *die;* F (*Anat.*) Haut, *die.* ❷ *v.t.* überziehen; (*with paint*) streichen

**ˈcoat dress** *n.* Mantelkleid, *das*

**coated** /ˈkəʊtɪd/ *adj.* gestrichen ‹Papier›; belegt ‹Zunge›; imprägniert ‹Stoff›; getönt ‹Glas, Linsen›; ~ **with dust/sugar** staubbedeckt/mit Zucker überzogen

**coat:** ~ **hanger** *n.* Kleiderbügel, *der;* ~ **hook** *n.* Kleiderhaken, *der*

**coating** /ˈkəʊtɪŋ/ *n.* (*of paint*) Anstrich, *der;* (*of dust, snow, wax, polish, varnish*) Schicht, *die;* (*for ceramic glazes*) Überzug, *der*

**coat:** ~ **of ˈarms** *n.* Wappen, *das;* ~**-tails** *n. pl.* Frackschöße

**co-author** /kəʊˈɔːθə(r)/ ❶ *n.* Mitautor, *der*/-autorin, *die;* **they were** ~**s of the book** sie haben das Buch gemeinsam verfasst. ❷ *v.t.* gemeinsam verfassen ‹Buch, Dokument›

**coax** /kəʊks/ *v.t.* überreden; ~ **sb. to do sth.** jmdn. überreden *od.* dazu bringen, etw. zu tun; ~ **sb. into doing sth.** jmdn. herumkriegen (*ugs.*), etw. zu tun; ~ **a fire to burn/an engine into life** ein Feuer/einen Motor in Gang bringen; ~ **a smile/some money out of sb.** jmdm. ein Lächeln/etw. Geld entlocken; ~ **sb. out of doing sth.** jmdm. ausreden, etw. zu tun

**coaxial** /kəʊˈæksɪəl/ *adj.* koaxial

**coaxing** /ˈkəʊksɪŋ/ *n.* Überredung, *die;* Zureden, *das*

**cob** /kɒb/ *n.* A (*nut*) Haselnuss, *die;* B (*swan*) männlicher Schwan; C (*horse*) Cob, *die; kleines, stämmiges Pferd;* D ⇒ **corn cob;** E (*loaf*) rundes Brot

**cobalt** /ˈkəʊbɔːlt, ˈkəʊbɒlt/ *n.* A (*element*) Kobalt, *das;* B (*pigment, colour*) Kobaltblau, *das*

**cobber** /ˈkɒbə(r)/ *n.* (*Austral. and NZ coll.*) Kumpel, *der* (*ugs.*)

**cobble**[1] /ˈkɒbl/ ❶ *n.* (*stone*) Pflaster-, Kopfstein, *der;* Katzenkopf, *der;* **rumble over the** ~**s** über das Kopfsteinpflaster rumpeln. ❷ *v.t.* pflastern ‹Straße›; ~**d streets** Straßen mit Kopfsteinpflaster

**cobble**[2] *v.t.* (*put together, mend*) flicken; ~ **up plans/verses** [sich (*Dat.*)] Pläne zusammenbasteln (*ugs.*) *od.* zusammenreimen/[sich (*Dat.*)] Gedichte zusammenstoppeln (*ugs.*); ~ **together** zusammenbasteln; zusammenmischen ‹Essen, Mannschaft›

**cobbler** /ˈkɒblə(r)/ *n.* A ▶1261 Schuster, *der;* Flickschuster, *der* (*veralt.*); B *in pl.* (*Brit. sl.: nonsense*) Scheiße, *die* (*derb*); Mist, *der* (*salopp*); **a load of** ~**s** totaler Mist (*salopp*)

**ˈcobblestone** ⇒ **cobble**[1] 1

**Coblenz** /kəʊˈblents/ *pr. n.* Koblenz (*das*)

**ˈcobnut** ⇒ **cob** A

**cobra** /ˈkɒbrə/ *n.* (*Zool.*) Kobra, *die*

**cobweb** /ˈkɒbweb/ *n.* A (*network*) Spinnengewebe, *das;* Spinnennetz, *das;* (*material*) Spinn[en]weben *Pl.;* Spinn[en]fäden *Pl.;* B *in pl.* (*rubbish*) Hirngespinste *Pl.;* **blow away the** ~**s** (*fig.*) für einen klaren Kopf sorgen

**Coca-Cola** ® *n.* /kəʊkəˈkəʊlə/ Coca-Cola Ⓦⓩ, *das od. die*

**cocaine** /kəˈkeɪn/ *n.* Kokain, *das*

**coccyx** /ˈkɒksɪks/ *n.* (*Zool.*) Steiß, *der;* (*Anat.*) Steißbein, *das*

**cochineal** /kɒtʃɪˈniːl/ *n.* Koschenille, *die*

**cochlea** /ˈkɒklɪə/ *n. pl.* ~**e** /ˈkɒkliː/ (*Anat.*) Schnecke, *die;* Cochlea, *die* (*fachspr.*)

**cock**[1] /kɒk/ ❶ *n.* A (*bird, lobster, crab, salmon*) Männchen, *das;* (*domestic fowl*) Hahn, *der;* (*wood*~) Waldschnepfe, *die;* **that** ~ **won't fight** (*fig.*) das hat keinen Zweck; B (*sl.: man*) Bengel, *der* (*ugs.*); Bursche, *der* (*ugs.*); **old** ~: alter Junge (*ugs.*); C (*spout, tap, etc.*) Hahn, *der;* D (*coarse: penis*) Schwanz, *der* (*salopp*); Pimmel, *der* (*salopp*); E (*in gun*) Hahn, *der;* **be/start/go off at half** ~ (*fig.*) danebengehen (*ugs.*); ein Reinfall sein (*ugs.*).
❷ *v.t.* A (*erect, stand up*) aufstellen, (*fig.*) spitzen ‹Ohren›; ~ **one's eye at sb.** zu jmdm. hinblicken; (*wink*) jmdm. zublinzeln; B (*bend*) anwinkeln ‹Knie-, Handgelenk›; **the parrot** ~**ed its head [to one side]** der Papagei legte den Kopf auf die Seite; C (*put on slanting*) schief *od.* schräg aufsetzen ‹Hut›; (*turn up brim of*) hochstülpen ‹Hut›; **a** ~**ed hat** ein Hut mit hoher Krempe; (*triangular hat*) ein Dreispitz; **knock sb./sth. into a** ~**ed hat** (*fig.*) (*destroy*) jmdn./etw. zerschmettern (*fig.*); (*surpass*) jmdn./etw. weit übertreffen; jmdn./etw. in den Sack stecken (*ugs. fig.*); D ~ **a/the gun** den Hahn spannen
~ **ˈup** *v.t.* (*Brit. sl.*) versauen (*salopp*); ⇒ *also* ~**-up**

**cock**[2] *n.* (*heap*) Haufen, *der*

**cockade** /kəˈkeɪd/ *n.* Kokarde, *die*

**cock-a-doodle-doo** /kɒkəduːdlˈduː/ *n.* (*crowing*) Kikeriki, *das;* (*child lang.: cock*) Kikeriki, *der*

**cock-a-hoop** /kɒkəˈhuːp/ ❶ *adj.* überschwänglich; (*boastful*) triumphierend; **be** ~: triumphieren. ❷ *adv.* überschwänglich; (*boastfully*) triumphierend

**cock and ˈbull story** *n.* Lügengeschichte, *die*

**cockatoo** /kɒkəˈtuː/ *n.* (*parrot*) Kakadu, *der*

**cockchafer** /ˈkɒktʃeɪfə(r)/ *n.* Maikäfer, *der*

**ˈcockcrow** *n.* **at** ~: beim ersten Hahnenschrei

**cockerel** /ˈkɒkərəl/ *n.* junger Hahn

**cocker [spaniel]** /ˈkɒkə(ˈspænjəl)/ *n.* Cockerspaniel, *der*

**cock-eyed** /ˈkɒkaɪd/ *adj.* A (*crooked*) schief; B (*absurd*) verrückt; C (*coll.: squinting*) schielend ‹Blick›; **be** ~: schielen

**ˈcockfighting** *n.* Hahnenkampf, *der*

**cockily** /ˈkɒkɪlɪ/ *adv.* anmaßend; frech

**cockiness** /ˈkɒkɪnɪs/ *n., no pl.* Anmaßung, *die;* Frechheit, *die*

**cockle** /kɒkl/ *n.* A (*bivalve, shell*) Herzmuschel, *die;* B **warm the** ~**s of sb.'s heart** es jmdm. warm ums Herz werden lassen

**cockney** /ˈkɒknɪ/ ❶ *adj.* Cockney-. ❷ *n.* **A** (*person*) waschechter Londoner/waschechte Londonerin; Cockney, *der;* **B** (*dialect*) Cockney, *das*

**cock: ~ of the ˈwalk** (*fig.*) **be the ~ of the walk** die Szene beherrschen; (*domineer*) den Ton angeben; **~ of the ˈwood** *n.* **A** (*capercaillie*) Auerhahn, *der;* **B** (*Amer.: woodpecker*) Haubenschwarzspecht, *der;* **~pit** *n.* **A** (*Aeronaut.*) Cockpit, *das;* [Piloten]kanzel, *die;* **B** (*in racing car*) Cockpit, *das;* (*in boat*) Plicht, *die;* Cockpit, *das;* **C** (*for ~fighting*) Hahnenkampfplatz, *der*

**cockroach** /ˈkɒkrəʊtʃ/ *n.* [Küchen-, Haus-]schabe, *die;* Kakerlak, *der*

**cockscomb** /ˈkɒkskəʊm/ *n.* (*Ornith.*, *Bot.*) Hahnenkamm, *der*

**cocksure** /kɒkˈʃʊə(r)/ *adj.* **A** (*convinced*) todsicher; **B** (*self-confident*) selbstsicher; (*dogmatic*) selbstgerecht; **be ~ of oneself** sich (*Dat.*) seiner Sache (*Gen.*) [unberechtigterweise] völlig sicher sein

**cocktail** /ˈkɒkteɪl/ *n.* Cocktail, *der;* ⇒ *also* **fruit cocktail**

**cocktail: ~ cabinet** *n.* Hausbar, *die;* **~ dress** *n.* Cocktailkleid, *das;* **~ glass** *n.* Cocktailglas, *das;* **~ party** *n.* Cocktailparty, *die;* **~ shaker** *n.* Mixbecher, *der;* **~ stick** *n.* Partystick, *der od. das*

**ˈcock-up** *n.* (*Brit. sl.*) Schlamassel, *der* (*ugs.*); **make a ~ of sth.** bei etw. Scheiße bauen (*derb*)

**cocky** /ˈkɒkɪ/ *adj.* anmaßend

**coco** /ˈkəʊkəʊ/ ⇒ **coconut** A

**cocoa** /ˈkəʊkəʊ/ *n.* Kakao, *der*

**ˈcocoa bean** *n.* Kakaobohne, *die*

**coconut** /ˈkəʊkənʌt/ *n.* **A** (*tree*) Kokospalme, *die;* **B** (*nut*) Kokosnuss, *die;* **C** (*coll.: head*) Rübe, *die* (*derb*)

**coconut: ~ ˈbutter** *n.* Kokosfett, *das;* **~ ˈmatting** *n.* Kokosmatten *Pl.;* **~ milk** *n.* Kokosmilch, *die;* **~ palm** ⇒ **coconut** A; **~ shy** *n.* Wurfbude, *die*

**cocoon** /kəˈkuːn/ ❶ *n.* **A** (*Zool.*) Kokon, *der;* **B** (*covering*) Hülle, *die.* ❷ *v.t.* (*wrap as in ~*) einmummen

**cod**[1] /kɒd/ *n.*, *pl. same* Kabeljau, *der;* (*in Baltic*) Dorsch, *der*

**cod**[2] (*coll.*) ❶ *v.t.*, **-dd- A** (*fool*) vergackeiern (*salopp*); verscheißern (*derb*); **B** (*parody*) verulken (*ugs.*). ❷ *v.i.*, **-dd-** rumblödeln (*ugs.*); flachsen (*ugs.*)

**COD** *abbr.* **cash on delivery; collect on delivery** (*Amer.*) p. Nachn.

**coda** /ˈkəʊdə/ *n.* (*Mus.*) Koda, *die*

**coddle** /ˈkɒdl/ *v.t.* **A** [ver]hätscheln ‹Kind›; verwöhnen ‹Kranken›; **B** (*Cookery*) schwach pochieren ‹Eier›

**code** /kəʊd/ ❶ *n.* **A** (*collection of statutes etc.*) Kodex, *der;* Gesetzbuch, *das;* **a ~ of laws** ein Gesetzbuch; eine Gesetzessammlung; **~ of religion/literature/society** religiöse/literarische/gesellschaftliche Normen; **~ of honour** Ehrenkodex, *der;* **~s of behaviour** Verhaltensnormen; Verhaltenskodizes (*geh.*); **B** (*system of signals*) Kode, Code, *der;* (*coded word, etc.*) Chiffre, *die;* **be in ~:** verschlüsselt sein; **put sth. into ~:** etw. verschlüsseln; ⇒ *also* **genetic** A. ❷ *v.t.* chiffrieren, verschlüsseln ‹Nachricht›

**code: ~ book** *n.* Signalbuch, *das;* **~ name** *n.* Deckname, *der;* **~ number** *n.* Kenn-, Tarnzahl, *die;* **~ word** *n.* Kennwort, *das*

**codex** /ˈkəʊdeks/ *n.*, *pl.* **codices** /ˈkəʊdɪsiːz/ **A** (*manuscript volume*) Kodex, *der;* **B** (*of drugs etc.*) *pharmazeutisches Nachschlagewerk*

**ˈcodfish** ⇒ **cod**[1]

**codger** /ˈkɒdʒə(r)/ *n.* (*coll.*) Knacker, *der* (*salopp*)

**codicil** /ˈkəʊdɪsɪl/ *n.* Kodizill, *das*

**codification** /kəʊdɪfɪˈkeɪʃn/ *n.* Kodifizierung, *die;* Kodifikation, *die*

**codify** /ˈkəʊdɪfaɪ/ *v.t.* kodifizieren ‹Gesetze, Rechtsnormen›; festlegen, kodifizieren ‹Rechtschreibung, Grammatik›

**coding** /ˈkəʊdɪŋ/ *n.* **A** (*action*) Chiffrieren, *das;* **B** (*result*) verschlüsselte Informationen

**codling** *n.* (*fish*) Dorsch, *der*

**cod-liver ˈoil** *n.* Lebertran, *der*

**codpiece** /ˈkɒdpiːs/ *n.* (*Hist.*) Hosenlatz, *der*

**co-driver** /ˈkəʊdraɪvə(r)/ *n.* Beifahrer, *der*/-fahrerin, *die*

**cods** /kɒdz/, **codswallop** /ˈkɒdzwɒləp/ *n.* (*Brit. coll.*) Stuss, *der* (*ugs.*); **this is a load of ~:** das ist großer Stuss

**coed** /ˈkəʊed/ (*esp. Amer. coll.*) ❶ *n.* Studentin, *die.* ❷ *adj.* koedukativ; Koedukations-; **~ school** gemischte Schule

**co-edition** /kəʊɪˈdɪʃn/ *n.* gemeinsame Ausgabe

**coeducation** /kəʊedjʊˈkeɪʃn/ *n.* Koedukation, *die*

**coeducational** /kəʊedjʊˈkeɪʃənl/ *adj.* koedukativ; Koedukations-

**coefficient** /kəʊɪˈfɪʃənt/ *n.* (*Math.*, *Phys.*) Koeffizient, *der*

**coelacanth** /ˈsiːləkænθ/ *n.* (*Zool.*) Coelacanthus, *der*

**coequal** /kəʊˈiːkwəl/ (*arch./literary*) *adj.* ebenbürtig (*geh.*)

**coerce** /kəʊˈɜːs/ *v.t.* zwingen; **~ sb. into sth.** jmdn. zu etw. zwingen; **~ sb. into doing sth.** jmdn. dazu zwingen, etw. zu tun

**coercion** /kəʊˈɜːʃn/ *n.* Zwang, *der*

**coercive** /kəʊˈɜːsɪv/ *adj.* Zwangs‹gewalt, -herrschaft, -gesetz, -maßnahmen›

**coexist** /kəʊɪɡˈzɪst/ *v.i.* ‹Ideen, Überzeugungen:› nebeneinander bestehen, koexistieren; **~ [together] with sb./sth.** neben jmdm./etw. bestehen; mit jmdm./etw. koexistieren

**coexistence** /kəʊɪɡˈzɪstəns/ *n.* Koexistenz, *die;* **peaceful ~:** friedliche Koexistenz

**coexistent** /kəʊɪɡˈzɪstənt/ *adj.* (*formal*) nebeneinander bestehend ‹Systeme, Regierungen›

**coextensive** /kəʊɪkˈstensɪv/ *adj.* (*formal*) **be ~:** übereinstimmen; sich decken

**C. of E.** /siːəvˈiː/ *abbr.* **Church of England**

**coffee** /ˈkɒfɪ/ *n.* **A** Kaffee, *der;* **drink** *or* **have a cup of ~:** eine Tasse Kaffee trinken; **three black/white ~s** drei [Tassen] Kaffee ohne/mit Milch; **I was invited to ~:** ich bin zum Kaffee[trinken] eingeladen worden; **wake up and smell the ~!** (*esp. Amer. coll.*) sieh den Tatsachen ins Auge!; **B** (*colour*) Kaffeebraun, *das*

**coffee: ~ bar** *n.* Café, *das;* (*in department store, university, etc.*) Erfrischungsraum, *der;* **~ bean** *n.* Kaffeebohne, *die;* **~ break** *n.* Kaffeepause, *die;* **~ cup** *n.* Kaffeetasse, *die;* **~ ˈessence** *n.* Kaffee-Extrakt, *der;* **~ filter** *n.* Kaffeefilter, *der;* **~ grinder** *n.* Kaffeemühle, *die;* **~ grounds** *n. pl.* Kaffeesatz, *der;* **~ house** *n.* Café, *das;* (*Hist.*) Kaffeehaus, *das;* **~ machine, ~ maker** *ns.* Kaffeeautomat, *der;* **~ mill** *n.* Kaffeemühle, *die;* **~ morning** *n.* Morgenkaffee, *der* (*als Wohltätigkeitsveranstaltung*); **~ percolator** *n.* Kaffeemaschine, *die;* **~ pot** *n.* Kaffeekanne, *die;* **~ shop** *n.* Kaffeestube, *die;* Café, *das;* (*selling ~ beans etc.*) Kaffeegeschäft, *das;* **~ stall** *n.* Kaffeebar, *die;* (*serving other light refreshments also*) Erfrischungsstand, *der;* **~ table** *n.* Couchtisch, *der;* **~ table book** Bildband [in Luxusausstattung]

**coffer** /ˈkɒfə(r)/ *n.* **A** (*box*) Truhe, *die;* **B** *in pl.* (*treasure, funds*) **the household ~s** die Privatschatulle; **the ~s of the government** der Staatssäckel (*scherzh.*); **C** (*Archit.*) Kassette, *die;* **D** **~[dam]** Caisson, *der*

**coffin** /ˈkɒfɪn/ *n.* Sarg, *der;* ⇒ *also* **nail** 1 B

**cog** /kɒɡ/ *n.* (*Mech.*) Zahn, *der;* **be just a ~ [in the wheel/machine]** (*fig.*) bloß ein Rädchen im Getriebe sein

**cogency** /ˈkəʊdʒənsɪ/ *n.* (*of argument, reason*) Stichhaltigkeit, *die;* (*of narration, description, slogan*) Überzeugungskraft, *die*

**cogent** /ˈkəʊdʒənt/ *adj.* (*convincing*) überzeugend ‹Argument, Grund›; zwingend ‹Grund›; (*valid*) stichhaltig ‹Kritik, Analyse›

**cogently** /ˈkəʊdʒəntlɪ/ *adv.* ⇒ **cogent**: überzeugend; zwingend; stichhaltig

**cogitate** /ˈkɒdʒɪteɪt/ (*formal/joc.*) ❶ *v.i.* nachsinnen, nachdenken (**on** über + *Akk.*). ❷ *v.t.* nachsinnen, nachdenken über (+ *Akk.*)

**cogitation** /kɒdʒɪˈteɪʃn/ *n.* (*formal/joc.*) Nachdenken, *das;* Nachsinnen, *das;* **after much ~:** nach langem Grübeln

**cognac** /ˈkɒnjæk/ *n.* Cognac, *der* Ⓦⓩ

**cognate** /ˈkɒɡneɪt/ *adj.* (*Ling.*) verwandt

**cognisance**, **cognisant** ⇒ **cogniz-**

**cognition** /kɒɡˈnɪʃn/ *n.* Erkenntnis, *die*

**cognitive** /ˈkɒɡnɪtɪv/ *adj.* kognitiv ‹Fähigkeiten›; Erkenntnis ‹gehalt, -kräfte›

**cognizance** /ˈkɒɡnɪzəns/ *n.* (*formal*) **A** *no pl.* (*awareness*) Kenntnis, *die;* **have ~ of sth.** von etw. Kenntnis haben; **take ~ of sb./sth.** jmdn./etw. zur Kenntnis nehmen; **B** *no pl.* ([*right of*] *dealing with a matter legally*) Zuständigkeit, *die* (**of** in + *Dat.*)

**cognizant** /ˈkɒɡnɪzənt/ *adj.* (*formal*) **A** (*having knowledge*) in Kenntnis (**of** *Gen.*); **B** (*having jurisdiction*) zuständig (**of** für)

**cognoscenti** /kɒnjəˈʃentiː, kɒnjəˈʃentɪ/ *n. pl.* Kenner

**cog: ~ railway** *n.* (*esp. Amer.*) Zahnradbahn, *die;* **~wheel** *n.* Zahnrad, *das*

**cohabit** /kəʊˈhæbɪt/ *v.i.* zusammenleben; in eheähnlicher Gemeinschaft leben (*Rechtsspr.*)

**cohabitation** /kəʊhæbɪˈteɪʃn/ *n.* Zusammenleben, *das;* eheähnliche Gemeinschaft (*Rechtsspr.*)

**cohere** /kəʊˈhɪə(r)/ *v.i.* **A** ‹Teile, Ganzes, Gruppe:› zusammenhalten; **B** ‹Argumentation, Komposition, Aufsatz:› in sich (*Dat.*) geschlossen sein

**coherence** /kəʊˈhɪərəns/ *n.* **A** Zusammenhang, *der;* Kohärenz, *die* (*geh.*); (*in work, system, form*) Geschlossenheit, *die;* **B** (*Phys.*) Kohärenz, *die*

**coherent** /kəʊˈhɪərənt/ *adj.* **A** (*cohering*) zusammenhängend; **B** (*fig.*) zusammenhängend; kohärent (*geh.*); in sich (*Dat.*) geschlossen ‹System, Ganzes, Werk, Aufsatz, Form›; **a ~ presentation of the facts** eine [in sich (*Dat.*)] stimmige Darlegung der Fakten; **C** (*Phys.*) kohärent

**coherently** /kəʊˈhɪərəntlɪ/ *adv.* zusammenhängend; im Zusammenhang

**cohesion** /kəʊˈhiːʒn/ *n.* **A** (*sticking together*) Zusammenhängen, *das;* (*of substances*) Haften, *das;* **B** (*fig.*) (*of group, state, community*) Zusammenhalt, *der;* Kohäsion, *die* (*geh.*); **C** (*Phys.*) Kohäsion, *die*

**cohesive** /kəʊˈhiːsɪv/ *adj.* geschlossen, in sich (*Dat.*) ruhend ‹Ganzes, Einheit, Form›; stimmig ‹Stil, Argument›; kohäsiv ‹Masse, Mischung›

**cohort** /ˈkəʊhɔːt/ *n.* **A** (*division of Roman army, band of warriors*) Kohorte, *die;* **B** (*group*) Gruppe, *die;* **C** (*Amer.: assistant, colleague*) Helfer, *der*/Helferin, *die*

**coiffure** /kwɑːˈfjʊə(r)/ *n.* Frisur, *die;* Coiffure, *die* (*veralt.*, *geh.*)

**coil** /kɔɪl/ ❶ *v.t.* **A** (*arrange*) aufwickeln; **the snake ~ed itself round a branch** die Schlange wand sich um einen Ast; **B** (*twist*) aufdrehen; **the snake ~ed itself up** die Schlange rollte sich auf. ❷ *v.i.* **A** (*twist*) **~ round sth.** etw. umschlingen; **B** (*move sinuously*) sich winden; ‹Rauch:› sich ringeln. ❸ *n.* **A** **~s of rope/wire/piping** aufgerollte Seile *Pl.*/aufgerollter Draht/aufgerollte Leitungen *Pl.;* **B** (*single turn of ~ed thing*) Windung, *die;* **C** (*length of ~ed rope etc.*) Stück, *das;* **D** (*lock of hair*) Locke, *die;* **E** (*contraceptive device*) Spirale, *die;* **F** (*Electr.*) Spule, *die*

**ˈcoil spring** *n.* Spiralfeder, *die*

**coin** /kɔɪn/ ❶ ▶ **1328** *n.* Münze, *die;* (*metal money*) Münzen *Pl.;* Münzgeld, *das;* **in ~:** in Münzen; **the other side of the ~** (*fig.*) die Kehrseite der Medaille; **pay sb. in his own ~** (*fig.*) jmdm. in *od.* mit gleicher Münze heimzahlen. ❷ *v.t.* **A** (*invent*) prägen ‹Wort, Redewendung›; **..., to ~ a phrase** (*iron.*) ..., um mich ganz originell auszudrücken; **B** (*make*) prägen ‹Geld›; **~ money** (*fig.*) Geld scheffeln; **C** (*make into money*) münzen (*Gold, Silber usw.*)

**coinage** /ˈkɔɪnɪdʒ/ *n.* **A** (*system*) Währung, *die;* **B** (*coins*) Münzen *Pl.;* Hartgeld, *das;* **C** (*coining*) Prägung, *die;* Prägen, *das;* **D** (*invention*) Prägung, *die;* **'astronaut' and 'sputnik' are modern ~s** „Astronaut" und „Sputnik" sind Neuprägungen

**'coin-box telephone** *n.* Münzfernsprecher, *der*

**coincide** /kəʊɪnˈsaɪd/ *v.i.* **A** (*in space*) sich decken; **~ with one another** sich decken; **B** (*in time*) ‹Ereignisse, Veranstaltungen:› zusammenfallen; **C** (*agree together, concur in opinion*) übereinstimmen (**with** mit); **~ in sth.** in etw. (*Dat.*) übereinstimmen

**coincidence** /kəʊˈɪnsɪdəns/ *n.* **A** (*being coincident*) Deckungsgleichheit, *die;* (*of two points*) Zusammenfall, *der;* **B** (*instance*) Zufall, *der;* **by pure** *or* **sheer ~:** rein zufällig; **it was a happy ~:** es traf sich gut; **by a curious ~:** durch einen merkwürdigen Zufall; **C** (*of events*) Duplizität der Ereignisse; Koinzidenz, *die*

**coincident** /kəʊˈɪnsɪdənt/ *adj.* (*formal*) (*in space*) deckungsgleich ‹Figuren›; (*in time or place*) zusammenfallend; (*agreeing*) übereinstimmend; **be ~ with sth.** mit etw. deckungsgleich sein/zusammenfallen/übereinstimmen

**coincidental** /kəʊɪnsɪˈdentl/ *adj.* zufällig; **be ~ with sth.** mit etw. zufällig zusammentreffen

**coincidentally** /kəʊɪnsɪˈdentəlɪ/ *adv.* gleichzeitig; (*by coincidence*) zufälligerweise

**coiner** /ˈkɔɪnə(r)/ *n.* (*esp. Brit.*) Falschmünzer, *der*

**'coin-operated** *adj.* Münz-

**coir** /ˈkɔɪə(r)/ *n.* Coir, *das od. die;* Kokosfaser, *die*

**coition** /kəʊˈɪʃn/, **coitus** /ˈkəʊɪtəs/ *ns.* (*Med.*) Koitus, *der;* Beischlaf, *der*

**coitus interruptus** /kəʊɪtəs ɪntəˈrʌptəs/ *n.* Coitus interruptus, *der*

**coke**[1] /kəʊk/ ❶ *n.* Koks, *der.* ❷ *v.t.* verkoken

**coke**[2] *n.* (*coll.: cocaine*) Koks, *der* (*salopp*)

**Coke** ® /kəʊk/ *n.* (*drink*) Coke, *das* Wz

**col** /kɒl/ *n.* [Berg]sattel, *der*

**col.** *abbr.* **column** Sp.

**Col.** *abbr.* **Colonel** Obst.

**cola** /ˈkəʊlə/ *n.* Cola, *das od. die* (*ugs.*)

**colander** /ˈkʌləndə(r)/ *n.* Sieb, *das;* Durchschlag, *der*

**cold** /kəʊld/ ❶ *adj.* **A** kalt; **I feel ~:** ich friere; mir ist kalt; **her hands/feet were ~:** sie hatte kalte Hände/Füße; **B** (*without ardour etc.*) kalt ‹Intellekt, Herz›; [betont] kühl ‹Person, Ansprache, Aufnahme, Begrüßung›; eiskalt ‹Handlung›; unterdrückt ‹Wut›; **go ~ on sth.** das Interesse an etw. (*Dat.*) verlieren; **leave sb. ~:** jmdn. kalt lassen (*ugs.*); **C** (*dead*) kalt; **D** (*coll.: unconscious*) bewusstlos; k.o. (*ugs.*); **he laid him out ~:** er schlug ihn k.o.; **the punch knocked him out ~:** durch den Schlag ging er bewusstlos zu Boden; **E** (*coll.: at one's mercy*) **have sb. ~:** jmdn. am Kragen haben (*ugs.*); **F** (*sexually frigid*) [gefühls]kalt; **G** (*slow to warm*) kalt ‹Boden›; **H** (*unrehearsed*) ohne Vorbereitung *nachgestellt;* **I** (*chilling, depressing*) kalt ‹Farbe›; nackt ‹Tatsache, Statistik›; **J** (*uninteresting*) fade ‹Geschichte›; **the news is already ~:** für die Sache interessiert sich niemand mehr; **K** (*Hunting*) kalt ‹Fährte›; (*in children's games*) **you're ~ and getting ~er** kalt, noch kälter.

❷ *adv.* **A** (*in ~ state*) kalt; (*without preparation*) ohne Vorbereitung ‹tun›; **B** (*Amer. coll.: completely*) voll (*salopp*).

❸ *n.* **A** Kälte, *die;* **shiver with ~:** vor Kälte (*Dat.*) zittern; **be left out in the ~** (*fig.*) links liegen gelassen werden; **B** ▶ **1232** (*illness*) Erkältung, *die;* **~ [in the head]** Schnupfen, *der.* ⇒ *also* **blood** 1 A, D; **catch** 1 E; **cold turkey; fish** 1 C; **snap** 3 E; **water**

**cold: ~-blooded** /ˈkəʊldblʌdɪd/ *adj.* **A** wechselwarm ‹Tier›; kaltblütig (*selten*); **~-blooded animals** Kaltblüter *Pl.;* wechselwarme Tiere; **B** (*callous*) kaltblütig ‹Person, Mord›; **~ chisel** *n.* (*Metalw.*) Kaltmeißel, *der;* **~ 'comfort** *n.* ein schwacher Trost; **~ cream** *n.* Coldcream, *die od. das;* **~ cuts** *n. pl.* Aufschnitt, *der;* **~ frame** *n.* Frühbeet, *das;* **~ 'front** *n.* (*Meteorol.*) Kaltfront, *die;* **~-hearted** *adj.* kaltherzig

**coldly** /ˈkəʊldlɪ/ *adv.* [betont] kühl; [eis]kalt ‹handeln›

**cold 'meat** *n.* **A** kaltes Fleisch; **~s** Aufschnitt, *der;* **B** (*sl.: corpse*) Kadaver, *der* (*salopp*)

**coldness** /ˈkəʊldnɪs/ *n., no pl.* **A** Kälte, *die;* **the ~ of the weather** die Kälte; das kalte Wetter; **B** (*feeling cold*) Frieren, *das;* (*of hands, feet*) Kälte, *die;* **C** (*lack of ardour etc.*) (*of heart, intellect*) Kälte, *die;* (*of person, attitude, manner, look*) betonte Kühle; **D** (*of dead body, colour*) Kälte, *die*

**cold: ~-pressed** *adj.* kaltgepresst; **~-'shoulder** *v.t.* schneiden (*fig.*); **~ 'steel** *n.* kalter Stahl (*dichter.*); Hieb- und Stichwaffen *Pl.;* **~ 'storage** *n.* Kühllagerung, *die;* **put sth. in ~ storage** (*fig.*) etw. auf Eis legen (*fig.*); **~store** *n.* Kühlhaus, *das;* **~ 'sweat** *n.* kalter Schweiß; **break out in a ~ sweat** in kalten Schweiß ausbrechen; **~ 'turkey** *n.* (*Amer. sl.*) Totalentzug, *der;* Cold turkey, *der* (*Drogenjargon*); *attrib.* **the ~ turkey cure/treatment** Totalentzugstherapie, *die;* **~ 'war** *n.* kalter Krieg: **~ wave** *n.* Kältewelle, *die;* **~-work** *v.t.* kaltformen ‹Metall›

**coleslaw** /ˈkəʊlslɔː/ *n.* Kohl-, Krautsalat, *der*

**coleus** /ˈkəʊlɪəs/ *n.* (*Bot.*) Buntnessel, *die*

**colic** /ˈkɒlɪk/ *n.* Kolik, *die*

**coliseum** /kɒlɪˈsiːəm/ *n.* (*Amer.*) Stadion, *das*

**colitis** /kəˈlaɪtɪs/ *n.* ▶ **1232** (*Med.*) Entzündung des Dickdarms; Kolitis, *die* (*fachspr.*)

**collaborate** /kəˈlæbəreɪt/ *v.i.* **A** (*work jointly*) zusammenarbeiten; **~ [with sb.] on sth.** zusammen [mit jmdm.] an etw. (*Dat.*) arbeiten; **~ [with sb.] on** *or* **in doing sth.** mit jmdm. bei etw. zusammenarbeiten; **B** (*cooperate with enemy*) kollaborieren (*abwertend*); zusammenarbeiten

**collaboration** /kəlæbəˈreɪʃn/ *n.* Zusammenarbeit, *die;* (*with enemy*) Kollaboration, *die* (*abwertend*); **work in ~ with sb.** mit jmdm. zusammenarbeiten

**collaborator** /kəˈlæbəreɪtə(r)/ *n.* Mitarbeiter, *der*/-arbeiterin, *die;* (*with enemy*) Kollaborateur, *der*/Kollaborateurin, *die* (*abwertend*); **they were ~s on this book** sie haben zusammen an diesem Buch gearbeitet

**collage** /ˈkɒlɑːʒ/ *n.* Collage, *die*

**collapse** /kəˈlæps/ ❶ *n.* **A** (*of person*) (*physical, mental breakdown*) Zusammenbruch, *der;* (*heart attack; of lung, blood vessel, circulation*) Kollaps, *der;* (*cerebral haemorrhage*) Gehirnschlag, *der;* **B** (*of tower, bridge, structure, wall, roof*) Einsturz, *der;* (*of tent*) Zusammenfallen, *das;* (*of table, chair*) Zusammenbruch, *der;* **C** (*fig.: failure*) Zusammenbruch, *der;* (*of negotiations, plans, hopes*) Scheitern, *das;* (*of civilization, empire, society, system*) Zerfall, *der;* (*of prices, currency*) Sturz, *der.*

❷ *v.i.* **A** ‹Person:› zusammenbrechen, (*Med.*) kollabieren; ‹Lunge, Gefäß, Kreislauf:› kollabieren; **his circulation ~d** er erlitt einen Kreislaufkollaps; **~ into tears** weinend zusammenbrechen; **~ with laughter** (*fig.*) sich vor Lachen kugeln; **B** ‹Zelt:› in sich zusammenfallen; ‹Tisch, Stuhl:› zusammenbrechen; ‹Turm, Brücke, Gebäude, Mauer, Dach:› einstürzen; **C** (*fig.: fail*) ‹Verhandlungen, Pläne, Hoffnungen:› scheitern; ‹Zivilisation, Reich, Gesellschaft, System:› zerfallen; ‹Geschäft, Unternehmen usw.:› zusammenbrechen, zugrunde gehen; ‹Traum:› zerbrechen; ‹Preise, Währung:› [zusammen]stürzen; **D** (*fold down*) ‹Fernrohr, Spazierstock:› sich zusammenschieben lassen; ‹Regenschirm, Fahrrad, Tisch:› sich zusammenklappen lassen.

❸ *v.t.* zusammenklappen ‹Regenschirm, Fahrrad, Tisch›; zusammenschieben ‹Fernrohr›

**collapsible** /kəˈlæpsɪbl/ *adj.* Klapp-, zusammenklappbar ‹Stuhl, Tisch, Fahrrad›; Falt-, faltbar ‹Boot›; zusammenschiebbar ‹Fernrohr›; **it is ~:** es lässt sich zusammenklappen/falten/zusammenschieben

**collar** /ˈkɒlə(r)/ ❶ *n.* **A** Kragen, *der;* **with ~ and tie** mit Krawatte; **[surgical] ~:** Halsmanschette, *die;* **hot under the ~** (*fig.*) (*embarrassed*) verlegen; (*angry*) wütend; **B** (*for dog*) [Hunde]halsband, *das;* Halsung, *die* (*Jagdw.*); **C** (*for horse*) Kumt, *das;* Kummet, *das;* **D** (*on bolt, pipe, etc.*) Bund, *der.* ❷ *v.t.* **A** (*seize*) am Kragen kriegen (*ugs.*); schnappen (*ugs.*); **B** (*coll.: appropriate*) sich (*Dat.*) unter den Nagel reißen (*salopp*); klemmen (*salopp*)

**collar: ~bone** *n.* (*Anat.*) Schlüsselbein, *das;* **~ button** *n.* **A** (*Brit.*) Hemd[en]knopf, *der;* **B** (*Amer.: stud*) Kragenknopf, *der;* **~ stud** *n.* (*esp. Brit.*) Kragenknopf, *der*

**collate** /kəˈleɪt/ *v.t.* **A** (*Bibliog.: compare*) kollationieren (*Buchw.*) ‹Manuskripte, Druckbögen›; **~ a copy with the original** eine Abschrift mit dem Original vergleichen; **B** (*put together*) zusammenstellen ‹Daten, Beweismaterial›

**collateral** /kəˈlætərl/ ❶ *adj.* **A** (*subordinate*) nebensächlich ‹Dinge, Themen›; (*contributory*) **~ evidence** zusätzliches Beweismaterial; **B** **~ relatives** Verwandte einer Seitenlinie. ❷ *n.* **A** (*person*) Kollateralverwandte, *der/die* (*veralt.*) **B** (*property pledged as guarantee*) **~ [security]** Sicherheiten *Pl.*

**collation** /kəˈleɪʃn/ *n.* **A** Textvergleich, *der;* (*of book or set of sheets*) Kollationierung, *die* (*Buchw.*); **B** (*light meal*) Imbiss, *der;* Kollation, *die* (*veralt., landsch.*); (*in RC Ch.*) Kollation, *die;* **cold ~:** kaltes Büfett

**collator** /kəˈleɪtə(r)/ *n.* (*Computing*) Mischer, *der*

**colleague** /ˈkɒliːg/ *n.* Kollege, *der*/Kollegin, *die*

**collect**[1] /kəˈlekt/ ❶ *v.i.* **A** (*assemble*) sich versammeln; **B** (*accumulate*) ‹Staub, Müll usw.:› sich ansammeln.

❷ *v.t.* **A** (*assemble*) sammeln; aufsammeln ‹Müll, leere Flaschen usw.›; **~ volunteers** Freiwillige zusammenbringen; **~ [up] one's belongings** seine Siebensachen (*ugs.*) zusammensuchen; **she ~ed a lot of praise/good marks** sie hat viel Lob/viele gute Noten eingeheimst (*ugs.*); **~ dust** Staub anziehen; **B** (*fetch, pick up*) abholen ‹Menschen, Dinge›; **~ a parcel from the post office** ein Paket bei *od.* auf der Post abholen; **~ sb. from the station** jmdn. am Bahnhof *od.* von der Bahn abholen; **C** (*get from others*) eintreiben ‹Steuern, Zinsen, Schulden›; [wohltätig] sammeln ‹Geld, Altkleider›; kassieren ‹Miete, Fahrgeld›; beziehen ‹Zahlungen, Sozialhilfe›; einsammeln ‹Fahrkarten›; **~ on delivery** (*Amer.*) per Nachnahme; **D** (*as hobby*) sammeln ‹Münzen, Bücher, Briefmarken, Gemälde usw.›; **E** (*regain control of*) **~ one's wits/thoughts** seine Gedanken sammeln; **F** (*coll. abs.: receive money*) abkassieren (*ugs.*) (**on** bei).

❸ *adj.* (*Amer.*) **a ~ telephone call** ein R-Gespräch; **a ~ telegram** ein Nachnahmetelegramm.

❹ *adv.* (*Amer.*) **send a message ~:** eine vom Empfänger zu bezahlende Nachricht senden; **pay for the goods ~:** die Ware bei Lieferung bezahlen; **he called New York ~:** er führte ein R-Gespräch nach New York

**collect**[2] /ˈkɒlekt/ *n.* (*Eccl.*) Altargebet, *das;* Kollekte, *die* (*veralt.*)

**collected** /kəˈlektɪd/ *adj.* **A** (*gathered*) gesammelt; **B** (*calm*) gesammelt; gelassen

**collectedly** /kəˈlektɪdlɪ/ *adv.* gesammelt; gelassen

**collection** /kəˈlekʃn/ *n.* **A** (*collecting*) Sammeln, *das;* (*of rent, fares*) Kassieren, *das;* (*of taxes, interest, debts*) Eintreiben, *das;* (*of goods, persons*) Abholen, *das;* **make** *or* **hold a ~ of old clothes** eine Altkleidersammlung durchführen; **B** (*amount of money collected*) Sammlung, *die;* (*in church*) Kollekte, *die;* **take the ~:** einsammeln; **C** (*of mail*) Abholung, *die;* (*from postbox*) Leerung, *die;* **D** (*group collected*) (*of coins, books, stamps, paintings, etc.*) Sammlung, *die;* (*of fashionable clothes*) Kollektion, *die;* (*of people*) Ansammlung, *die;* **E** (*accumulated quantity*) Ansammlung, *die*

**collective** /kə'lektɪv/ ❶ *adj.* kollektiv *nicht präd.;* gesamt *nicht präd.;* ~ **interests** gemeinsame Interessen; Gesamt- *od.* Kollektivinteressen; ~ **leadership/responsibility** kollektive Führung/Verantwortung; ~ **guilt** Kollektivschuld, *die;* ~ **agreement** Tarifvertrag, *der.* ❷ *n.* [A] Genossenschaftsbetrieb, *der;* [B] ⇒ **collective noun**

**collective:** ~ **'bargaining** *n.* Tarifverhandlungen *Pl.;* ~ **'farm** *n.* landwirtschaftliche Produktionsgenossenschaft, LPG, *die* (*bes. DDR*); Kolchose, *die*

**collectively** /kə'lektɪvlɪ/ *adj.* gemeinsam; **work/act** ~: gemeinsam arbeiten/handeln

**collective:** ~ **'noun** *n.* (*Ling.*) Kollektivum, *das;* Sammelbegriff, *der;* ~ **'ownership** *n.* Kollektiveigentum, *das* (**of** an + *Dat.*); Gemeineigentum, *das* (**of** an + *Dat.*); ~ **se'curity** *n.* kollektive Sicherheit

**collectivism** /kə'lektɪvɪzm/ *n.* Kollektivwirtschaft, *die;* (*doctrine*) Kollektivismus, *der*

**collector** /kə'lektə(r)/ *n.* [A] (*of stamps, coins, etc.*) Sammler, *der*/Sammlerin, *die;* (*of taxes*) Einnehmer, *der*/Einnehmerin, *die;* (*of rent, cash*) Kassierer, *der*/Kassiererin, *die;* (*of jumble*) Abholer, *der*/Abholerin, *die;* ⇒ *also* **ticket collector**; [B] (*of electric train*) Stromabnehmer, *der*

**collector:** ~**'s item**, ~**'s piece** *ns.* Liebhaberstück, *das;* Sammlerstück, *das*

**colleen** /kɒ'li:n/ *n.* (*Ir.*) [junges] Mädel

**college** /'kɒlɪdʒ/ *n.* [A] (*esp. Brit.: independent corporation in university*) College, *das;* [B] (*small university*) [private] Hochschule; [C] (*place of further education*) Fach[hoch]schule, *die;* **military/naval** ~: Militär-/Marineakademie; **go to** ~ (*esp. Amer.*) studieren; **start** ~ (*esp. Amer.*) sein Studium aufnehmen; [D] (*esp. Brit.: school*) Internatsschule, *die;* Kolleg, *das;* [E] (*of physicians, surgeons*) [Ärzte]kammer, *die;* (*of cardinals*) Kollegium, *das*

**College:** ~ **of 'Arms** *n.* (*esp. Brit.*) Heroldsamt, *das;* ~ **of Edu'cation** Pädagogische Hochschule; (*for graduates*) Studienseminar, *das*

**collegiate** /kə'li:dʒət/ *adj.* College‹leben, -system usw.›; **Oxford has a** ~ **structure/is a** ~ **university** die Universität von Oxford ist nach dem Collegesystem organisiert

**collide** /kə'laɪd/ *v.i.* [A] (*come into collision*) zusammenstoßen (**with** mit); ‹Schiff:› kollidieren; [B] (*be in conflict*) zusammenprallen; kollidieren

**collie** /'kɒlɪ/ *n.* Collie, *der*

**collier** /'kɒlɪə(r)/ *n.* [A] ▶ 1261 ⇒ **coal miner**; [B] (*ship*) Kohlenschiff, *das*

**colliery** /'kɒljərɪ/ *n.* Kohlengrube, *die*

**collision** /kə'lɪʒn/ *n.* [A] (*colliding*) Zusammenstoß, *der;* (*between ships*) Kollision, *die;* **come into** ~: zusammenstoßen; ‹Schiffe:› in Kollision geraten, kollidieren; **a head-on** ~ **of a car with a bus** *or* **between a car and a bus** ein Frontalzusammenstoß eines PKW mit einem Bus; [B] (*fig.*) Konflikt, *der;* Kollision, *die;* **come into** ~ **with the law** in Konflikt mit dem Gesetz geraten

**col'lision course** *n.* (*lit. or fig.*) Kollisionskurs, *der;* **on a** ~: auf Kollisionskurs

**collocate** /'kɒləkeɪt/ ❶ *v.t.* [A] (*place together*) zusammenstellen; [B] (*arrange*) [an]ordnen; [C] (*put in a place*) aufführen; [D] (*Ling.*) kombinieren, (*fachspr.*) kollokieren ‹Wörter›. ❷ *v.i.* (*Ling.*) kollokieren

**collocation** /kɒlə'keɪʃn/ *n.* Zusammenstellung, *die;* (*arrangement*) Anordnung, *die;* (*Ling.: of words*) Kollokation, *die*

**collocator** /'kɒləkeɪtə(r)/ *n.* (*Ling.*) Kollokator, *der*

**colloid** /'kɒlɔɪd/ *n.* (*Chem.*) Kolloid, *das*

**colloidal** /kə'lɔɪdl/ *adj.* (*Chem.*) kolloid[al]

**colloquial** /kə'ləʊkwɪəl/ *adj.* umgangssprachlich; ~ **language** Umgangssprache, *die*

**colloquialism** /kə'ləʊkwɪəlɪzm/ *n.* [A] (*style*) Umgangssprache, *die;* [B] (*a form*) umgangssprachlicher Ausdruck

**colloquially** /kə'ləʊkwɪəlɪ/ *adv.* umgangssprachlich

**colloquium** /kə'ləʊkwɪəm/ *n., pl.* **colloquia** /kə'ləʊkwɪə/ Kolloquium, *das*

**colloquy** /'kɒləkwɪ/ *n.* (*formal*) [A] *no pl.* (*act of conversing*) Konversation, *die;* [B] (*a conversation*) Unterhaltung, *die*

**collusion** /kə'lju:ʒn, kə'lu:ʒn/ *n.* geheime Absprache; **act in** ~ **with sb.** mit jmdm. gemeinsame Sache machen

**collywobbles** /'kɒlɪwɒblz/ *n. pl.* (*coll.*) (*feeling of apprehension*) flaues Gefühl (*ugs.*) [im Magen]; (*stomach ache*) Bauchschmerzen *Pl.*

**cologne** ⇒ **eau-de-Cologne**

**Cologne** /kə'ləʊn/ ▶ 1626 ❶ *pr. n.* Köln (*das*). ❷ *attrib. adj.* Kölner

**Colombia** /kə'lɒmbɪə/ *pr. n.* Kolumbien (*das*)

**Colombian** /kə'lɒmbɪən/ ▶ 1340 ❶ *adj.* kolumbianisch. ❷ *n.* Kolumbianer, *der*/Kolumbianerin, *die*

**colon**[1] /'kəʊlən/ *n.* Doppelpunkt, *der;* Kolon, *das* (*veralt.*)

**colon**[2] /'kəʊlən, 'kəʊlɒn/ *n.* ▶ 966 (*Anat.*) Grimmdarm, *der*

**colonel** /'kɜ:nl/ *n.* ▶ 1617 [A] (*highest regimental officer*) Oberst, *der;* [B] (*member of military junta*) Obrist, *der* (*abwertend*). ⇒ *also* **blimp** A; **chief** 1 C

**colonial** /kə'ləʊnɪəl/ *adj.* [A] (*of colony*) Kolonial-; kolonial; ~ **empire** Kolonialreich, *das;* **C**~ **Office** (*Hist.*) Kolonialministerium, *das;* [B] (*Amer.: of period of British colonies*) kolonial; Kolonial-; ~ **architecture** Kolonialstil, *der*

**colonialism** /kə'ləʊnɪəlɪzm/ *n.* Kolonialismus, *der*

**colonialist** /kə'ləʊnɪəlɪst/ *n.* Kolonialist, *der*/Kolonialistin, *die; attrib.* kolonialistisch

**colonic** /kəʊ'lɒnɪk/ *adj.* (*Med.*) Kolon-; des Grimmdarms *nachgestellt*

**colonisation**, **colonise** ⇒ **coloniz-**

**colonist** /'kɒlənɪst/ *n.* Siedler, *der*/Siedlerin, *die;* Kolonist, *der*/Kolonistin, *die*

**colonization** /kɒlənaɪ'zeɪʃn/ *n.* Kolonisation, *die;* Kolonisierung, *die*

**colonize** /'kɒlənaɪz/ *v.t.* kolonisieren; besiedeln ‹unbewohntes Gebiet›

**colonnade** /kɒlə'neɪd/ *n.* (*Archit.*) Säulengang, *der;* Kolonnade, *die*

**colony** /'kɒlənɪ/ *n.* Kolonie, *die;* **a** ~ **of artists/ants** eine Künstlerkolonie/ein Ameisenstaat

**colophon** /'kɒləfən/ *n.* [A] (*tailpiece*) Kolophon, *der;* [B] (*on title page*) Signet, *das*

**color** (*Amer.*) ⇒ **colour**

**Colorado beetle** /kɒlə'rɑ:dəʊ bi:tl/ *n.* Kartoffelkäfer, *der;* Coloradokäfer, *der* (*fachspr.*)

**coloration** /kʌlə'reɪʃn/ *n.* [A] (*colouring*) Kolorierung, *die;* [B] (*colour*) Färbung, *die*

**coloratura** /kɒlərə'tu:rə, kɒlərə'tju:rə/ *n.* (*Mus.*) Koloratur, *die;* ~ **soprano** Koloratursopran, *der*

**colored** (*Amer.*) ⇒ **coloured**

**colossal** /kə'lɒsl/ *adj.* [A] (*gigantic, huge*) ungeheuer; gewaltig ‹Bauwerk›; [B] (*of or like a colossus*) riesenhaft, kolossal ‹Mann, Statue›; [C] (*coll.: remarkable, splendid*) ungeheuer, (*veralt.*) kolossal ‹Irrtum, Glücksfall›

**colossus** /kə'lɒsəs/ *n., pl.* **colossi** /kə'lɒsaɪ/ *or* ~**es** Koloß, *der*

**colostomy** /kə'lɒstəmɪ/ *n.* (*Med.*) Kolostomie, *die*

**colour** /'kʌlə(r)/ (*Brit.*) ❶ *n.* [A] Farbe, *die;* **primary** ~**s** Grundfarben *Pl.;* Primärfarben *Pl.* (*fachspr.*); **secondary** ~**s** Mischfarben *Pl.;* **what** ~ **is it?** welche Farbe hat es?; **see the** ~ **of sb.'s money** (*fig.*) Geld sehen (*ugs.*); [B] (*Art, Her.*) Farbe, *die;* (*Art: colouring*) Farbe, *die;* Farbgebung, *die;* **a box of** ~**s** ein Mal- *od.* Tuschkasten; [C] (*complexion*) [Gesichts]farbe, *die;* **change** ~: die Farbe ändern; (*go red/pale*) rot/blass werden; **lose/gain** ~: Farbe verlieren/wieder Farbe bekommen; **get one's** ~ **back** wieder etwas Farbe kriegen; **bring the** ~ **back to sb.'s cheeks** jmdm. wieder Farbe geben; **he is/feels/looks a bit off** ~ **today** ihm ist heute nicht besonders gut/er fühlt sich heute nicht besonders gut/er sieht heute nicht besonders gut aus; **have a high** ~: rot im Gesicht sein; ein rotes Gesicht haben; [D] (*racial*) Hautfarbe, *die;* [E] *usu. in pl.* (*appearance, aspect*) Farben *Pl.;* **appear in its true** ~**s** sich so zeigen, wie es wirklich ist; **see sth. in its true** ~**s** etw. so sehen, wie es wirklich ist; [F] (*appearance of reasonableness*) **give** *or* **lend** ~ **to sth.** etw. glaubhaft *od.* glaubwürdig erscheinen lassen; [G] (*character, tone, quality, etc.*) Charakter, *der;* Gepräge, *das;* (*aspect, appearance*) Anstrich, *der;* **add** ~ **to a story** einer Erzählung Farbe *od.* Kolorit geben; **local** ~: Lokalkolorit, *das;* [H] *in pl.* (*ribbon, dress, etc., worn as symbol of party, club, etc.*) Farben *Pl.;* **get** *or* **win one's** ~**s** (*Brit. Sport*) als Vollmitglied aufgenommen werden; **give sb. his** ~**s** (*Brit. Sport*) jmdn. als Vollmitglied aufnehmen; **show one's [true]** ~**s** *or* **oneself in one's true** ~**s** (*fig.*) sein wahres Gesicht zeigen; [I] *in pl.* (*national flag*) Farben *Pl.;* [J] (*flag*) Fahne, *die;* (*of ship*) Flagge, *die;* **Queen's/King's/regimental** ~: Regimentsfahne, *die;* **serve with the** ~**s** (*Hist.*) der Fahne dienen (*veralt.*); **join the** ~**s** (*Hist.*) den bunten Rock anziehen (*veralt.*); **come off/pass with flying** ~**s** (*fig.*) glänzend abschneiden; **nail one's** ~**s to the mast** (*fig.*) Farbe bekennen; sich zu seiner Überzeugung bekennen; **lower one's** ~ (*fig.*) zurückstecken; **sail under false** ~**s** (*fig.*) unter falscher Flagge segeln; [K] (*Mus.*) (*timbre, quality*) Klangfarbe, *die.* ⇒ *also* **troop** 3.
❷ *v.t.* [A] (*give* ~ *to*) Farbe geben (+ *Dat.*); [B] (*paint*) malen; ~ **in** ausmalen ‹Bild, Figur›; ~ **a wall red** eine Wand rot anmalen; [C] (*stain, dye*) färben ‹Material, Stoff›; [D] (*disguise*) verstecken; [E] (*misrepresent*) [schön]färben ‹Nachrichten, Bericht›; [F] (*fig.: influence*) beeinflussen.
❸ *v.i.* [A] ‹Blätter, Trauben:› sich verfärben; [B] (*blush*) ~ **[up]** erröten; rot werden

**colouration** (*Brit.*) ⇒ **coloration**

**colour:** ~ **bar** *n.* Rassenschranke, *die;* ~**-blind** *adj.* farbenblind; **a** ~**-blind person** ein Farbenblinder/eine Farbenblinde; ~**-blindness** *n.* Farbenblindheit, *die;* ~ **code** *n.* Farbkennzeichnung, *die;* ~**-coded** *adj.* mit Farbkennzeichnung *nachgestellt*

**coloured** /'kʌləd/ (*Brit.*) ❶ *adj.* [A] farbig; **yellow-/green-**~: gelb/grün; ~ **paper** (*for printing or wrapping*) farbiges Papier; (*for making designs*) Buntpapier, *das;* ~ **pencil** Farbstift, *der;* [B] (*of non-white descent*) farbig; ~ **people** Farbige *Pl.;* [C] (*S. Afr.: of mixed descent*) gemischtrassig; gemischtrassisch; ~ **people** Mischlinge *Pl.*. ❷ *n.* [A] Farbige, *der/die;* [B] (*S. Afr.: person of mixed descent*) Mischling, *der*

**colour:** ~**-fast** *adj.* farbecht; ~ **film** *n.* Farbfilm, *der*

**colourful** /'kʌləfl/ *adj.* (*Brit.*) bunt; farbenfroh, bunt ‹Bild, Schauspiel›; farbig, anschaulich ‹Sprache, Stil, Bericht›; buntbewegt ‹Zeitepoche, Leben›

**colourfully** /'kʌləfəlɪ/ *adv.* (*Brit.*) bunt; ~ **dressed/striped/painted** bunt gekleidet/-gestreift/-bemalt *attr.*

**colouring** /'kʌlərɪŋ/ *n.* (*Brit.*) [A] (*action*) Malen, *das;* ~ **'in** Ausmalen, *das;* [B] (*colours*) Farben *Pl.;* [C] (*facial complexion*) Teint, *der;* [D] ~ **[matter]** (*in food etc.*) Farbstoff, *der*

**colouring book** *n.* Malbuch, *das*

**colourless** /'kʌləlɪs/ *adj.* (*Brit.*) [A] (*without colour*) farblos ‹Flüssigkeit, Gas›; (*pale*) blass ‹Teint›; (*dull-hued*) grau, düster ‹Bild, Stoff, Himmel, Meer›; [B] (*fig.*) farblos, langweilig ‹Geschichte, Schilderung, Stil›; unauffällig ‹Person›

**colour:** ~ **magazine** ⇒ ~ **supplement**; ~ **photograph** *n.* Farbfotografie, -aufnahme, *die;* ~ **photography** *n.* Farbfotografie, *die;* ~ **printing** *n.* Farbdruck, *der;* ~ **scheme** *n.* Farb[en]zusammenstellung, *die;* ~**-sergeant** *n.* (*Mil.*) ≈ Hauptfeldwebel, *der;* ~ **supplement** *n.* Farbbeilage, *die;* ~ **television** *n.* Farbfernsehen, *das;* (*set*) Farbfernsehgerät, *das;* ~ **transparency** *n.* Farbdia, *das*

**colt** /kəʊlt/ *n.* [A] [Hengst]fohlen, *das;* (*player in junior team*) Fohlen, *das;* [B] (*inexperienced person*) (*girl*) Küken, *das* (*ugs.*); (*boy*) junger Dachs (*ugs.*) *od.* Springer (*ugs.*)

**coltsfoot** /ˈkəʊltsfʊt/ *n.*, *pl.* **~s** (*Bot.*) Huflattich, *der*

**columbine** /ˈkɒləmbaɪn/ *n.* (*Bot.*) Akelei, *die*

**Columbus** /kəˈlʌmbəs/ *pr. n.* Kolumbus (*der*)

**column** /ˈkɒləm/ *n.* A Säule, *die;* B (*in machine*) Ständer, *der;* (*of tripod*) Säule, *die;* C (*of liquid, vapour, etc.*) Säule, *die;* **~ of mercury/smoke** Quecksilber-/Rauchsäule, *die;* D (*division of page, table, etc.*) Spalte, *die;* Kolumne, *die;* **a ~ of figures** eine Zahlenkolonne; **in two ~s** zweispaltig; E (*in newspaper*) Spalte, *die;* Kolumne, *die;* **the sports ~:** der Sportteil; **the gossip ~:** die Klatschspalte (*ugs. abwertend*); F (*of troops, vehicles, ships*) Kolonne, *die;* **dodge the ~** (*fig. coll.*) sich drücken (*ugs.*); G (*Amer.: party, faction*) Lager, *das*

**columnar** /kəˈlʌmnə(r)/ *adj.* säulenförmig

**ˈcolumn inch** *n.* **advertisement of two ~es** ≈ Anzeige von 50 Millimeterzeilen

**columnist** /ˈkɒləmɪst/ *n.* Kolumnist, *der*/Kolumnistin, *die;* **radio ~:** Rundfunkkommentator, *der*/-kommentatorin, *die*

**coma** /ˈkəʊmə/ *n.* A (*Med.*) Koma, *das;* **be in a ~:** im Koma liegen; **go into a ~:** ins Koma fallen; B (*fig.: torpor*) Dämmerzustand, *der*

**comb** /kəʊm/ ❶ *n.* A (*also as tech. term*) Kamm, *der;* (*curry-~*) Striegel, *der;* B (*action*) **give one's hair a ~:** sich (*Dat.*) die Haare kämmen; C (*honey~*) Wabe, *die.* ❷ *v.t.* A kämmen ‹Haare, Flachs, Wolle›; **~ sb.'s/one's hair** jmdm./sich die Haare kämmen; jmdn./sich kämmen; **~ sth. out of sb.'s hair** jmdm. etw. aus den Haaren kämmen; B (*curry*) striegeln ‹Pferd›; C (*search*) durchkämmen ‹Gelände, Wald›

**~ ˈout** *v.t.* A auskämmen ‹Haare›; B (*separate for removal*) aussortieren; C (*search*) durchkämmen; durchforsten

**combat** /ˈkɒmbæt/ ❶ *n.* Kampf, *der;* **single ~:** Einzelkampf, *der;* (*duel*) Zweikampf, *der.* ❷ *v.t.* (*fig.: strive against*) bekämpfen. ❸ *v.i.* (*engage in battle or contest*) kämpfen

**ˈcombat aircraft** *n.* Kampfflugzeug, *das*

**combatant** /ˈkɒmbətənt/ ❶ *adj.* zur Kampftruppe gehörend. ❷ *n.* (*in war*) Kombattant, *der;* (*in duel*) Kämpfer, *der*

**combat: ~ dress** *n.* Kampfanzug, *der;* **~ fatigue** *n.* Frontneurose, *die*

**combative** /ˈkɒmbətɪv/ *adj.*, **combatively** /ˈkɒmbətɪvlɪ/ *adv.* streitlustig

**combativeness** /ˈkɒmbətɪvnɪs/ *n.*, *no pl.* Streitlust, *die*

**combe** (*Brit.*) ⇒ **coomb**

**combed** /kəʊmd/ *adj.* gekämmt

**comber** /ˈkəʊmə(r)/ *n.* (*wave, breaker*) Sturzwelle, *die*

**combination** /kɒmbɪˈneɪʃn/ *n.* A Kombination, *die;* **in ~:** zusammen; B (*Chem.*) Verbindung, *die;* C (*Brit. Motor Veh.*) Motorrad mit Beiwagen; D *in pl.* (*dated Brit.: undergarment*) Kombination, *die* (*veralt.*); Hemdhose, *die* (*veralt.*)

**combiˈnation lock** *n.* Kombinationsschloss, *das*

**combine** ❶ /kəmˈbaɪn/ *v.t.* A (*join together*) kombinieren; zusammenfügen (**into** zu); vereinigen ‹Städte›; B (*possess together*) vereinigen, in sich (*Dat.*) vereinigen ‹Eigenschaften›; C (*cause to coalesce*) verbinden ‹Substanzen›. ❷ *v.i.* A (*join together, coalesce*) ‹Stoffe:› sich verbinden; B (*cooperate*) zusammenwirken; ‹Parteien:› sich zusammentun. ❸ /ˈkɒmbaɪn/ *n.* A Konzern, *der;* (*in socialist economy*) Kombinat, *das;* B (*machine*) **~ [harvester]** Mähdrescher, *der;* Kombine, *die*

**combined** /kəmˈbaɪnd/ *adj.* vereint; **a ~ operation** eine gemeinsame Operation

**combings** /ˈkəʊmɪŋz/ *n. pl.* ausgekämmte Haare

**combining form** /kəmˈbaɪnɪŋ fɔːm/ *n.* (*Ling.*) Wortbildungselement, *das*

**combo** /ˈkɒmbəʊ/ *n.*, *pl.* **~s** Combo, *die*

**combust** /kəmˈbʌst/ *v.t.* verbrennen

**combustible** /kəmˈbʌstɪbl/ *adj.* A brennbar; B (*fig.*) entflammbar; erregbar

**combustion** /kəmˈbʌstʃn/ *n.* Verbrennung, *die;* **~ chamber** (*Mech. Engin.*) (*of jet engine*) Brennkammer, *die;* (*of internal-~ engine*) Verbrennungsraum, *der*

**come** /kʌm/ ❶ *v.i.*, **came** /keɪm/, **~** /kʌm/ A (*start or move towards or to sth. or sb.*) kommen; **~ here!** komm [mal] her!; **[I'm] coming!** [ich] komme schon!; **~ running** angelaufen kommen; **~ running into the room** ins Zimmer gerannt kommen; **~ laughing into the room** lachend ins Zimmer kommen; **not know whether** *or* **if one is coming or going** nicht wissen, wo einem der Kopf steht; **~, ~!** aber ich bitte dich!; **~ [now]!** (*fig.*) (*encouraging*) komm!; (*don't be hasty*) [also] komm! (*ugs.*); B (*arrive at a place*) kommen; **they came to a house/town** sie kamen zu einem Haus/in eine Stadt; **he has just ~ from school/America** er ist gerade aus der Schule/aus Amerika gekommen; **let 'em all ~!, ~ one ~ all** (*coll.*) sollen sie doch alle kommen!; **~ and see me soon** besuchen Sie mich bald einmal!; **the news came as a surprise** die Nachricht kam überraschend; **Christmas/Easter is coming** bald ist Weihnachten/Ostern; C (*traverse*) kommen; **he has ~ a long way** er kommt von weit her; **the project has ~ a long way** (*fig.*) das Projekt ist schon weit gediehen; D (*be brought*) kommen; **~ to sb.'s notice** *or* **attention/knowledge** jmdm. auffallen/zu Ohren kommen; E (*enter*) kommen; **the train came into the station** der Zug fuhr in den Bahnhof ein; F (*occur*) kommen; (*in list etc.*) stehen; **the adjective ~s before the noun** das Adjektiv steht vor dem Substantiv; G (*be~, be*) **the shoelaces have ~ undone** die Schnürsenkel sind aufgegangen; **the handle has ~ loose** der Griff ist lose; **it ~s cheaper to buy things in bulk** es ist *od.* (*ugs.*) kommt billiger, en gros einzukaufen; **it all came right in the end** es ging alles gut aus; **it will all ~ right in the end** es wird schon alles gut gehen; **it ~s easily/naturally to him** das fällt ihm leicht; **what you say ~s to this: ...:** was du sagst, läuft auf Folgendes hinaus: ...; **when it ~s to cooking** wenn es ums Kochen geht; **~ to that, if it ~s to that** wenn es darum geht; **~ to oneself** zu sich selbst kommen; **have ~ to believe/realize that ...:** zu der Überzeugung/Einsicht gelangt sein, dass ...; **we came to know him better** wir lernten ihn allmählich *od.* nach und nach besser kennen; H (*become present*) kommen; **in the coming week/month** kommende Woche/kommenden Monat; **be a coming man** der kommende Mann sein; **this coming Christmas** Weihnachten dieses Jahr; **she had it coming to her** das hat sie sich (*Dat.*) selbst zu verdanken (*iron.*); **you've got it coming to you if you go on behaving like that** du kannst dich auf was gefasst machen, wenn du so weitermachst (*ugs.*); I **to ~** (*future*) künftig; **in years to ~:** in künftigen Jahren; **for some time to ~:** [noch] für einige Zeit; J (*be left or willed*) **he has a lot of money coming to him** er erbt einmal viel Geld; **the farm came to him on his father's death** beim Tod seines Vaters bekam er den Hof; K (*be result*) kommen; **that's what ~s of grumbling** das kommt vom Schimpfen; **nothing came of it** es ist nichts daraus geworden; **~ of noble parents** aus adligem Elternhaus stammen; **the suggestion came from him** der Vorschlag war *od.* stammte von ihm; L (*reach, extend*) **the motorway ~s within 10 miles of us** die Autobahn ist nur zehn Meilen von uns entfernt; M (*happen*) **how ~s it that you ...?** wie kommt es, dass du ...?; **how did you ~ to break your leg?** wie hast du dir denn das Bein gebrochen?; **how ~?** (*coll.*) wieso?; weshalb?; **~ what may** komme, was wolle (*geh.*); ganz gleich, was kommt; N (*be available*) ‹Waren:› erhältlich sein; **this dress ~s in three sizes** dieses Kleid gibt es in drei Größen *od.* ist in drei Größen erhältlich; **as tough/clever/stupid as they ~:** zäh/schlau/dumm wie sonst was (*ugs.*); O (*coll.: play a part*) **~ the bully with sb.** bei jmdm. den starken Mann markieren (*salopp*); **don't ~ the innocent with me** spiel mir nicht den Unschuldsengel vor! (*ugs.*); **don't ~ that game with me** komm mir bloß nicht mit dieser Tour *od.* Masche! (*salopp*); **~ it strong** [es] übertreiben; **~ it too strong** zu dick auftragen (*ugs.*); P **~ [next] Friday/next week** [nächsten] Freitag/nächste Woche; **it's two years ~ Christmas since we were divorced** Weihnachten sind wir zwei Jahre geschieden; Q (*sl.: have orgasm*) kommen (*salopp*).
❷ *n.* (*sl.: semen*) Soße, *die* (*derb*)

**~ aˈbout** *v.i.* A passieren; **how did it ~ about that ...?** wie kam es, dass ...?; B (*Naut.*) wenden

**~ across** ❶ /--ˈ-/ *v.i.* A (*be understood*) ‹Bedeutung:› verstanden werden; ‹Mitteilung, Rede:› ankommen (*ugs.*), rüberkommen (*salopp*); B (*coll.: make an impression*) wirken (**as** wie); **he always wants to ~ across as a tough guy** er will immer den harten Burschen mimen (*ugs.*); C **~ across with** (*coll.: give, hand over*) rausrücken (*ugs.*) ‹Geld, Schlüssel›; rausrücken mit (*ugs.*) ‹Informationen›. ❷ /ˈ---/ *v.t.* **~ across sb./sth.** jmdm./einer Sache begegnen; **have you ~ across my watch?** ist dir meine Uhr begegnet? (*ugs.*)

**~ aˈlong** *v.i.* (*coll.*) A (*hurry up*) **~ along!** komm/kommt!; nun mach/macht schon! (*ugs.*); B (*try harder*) **~ along, now!** nun überleg aber mal!; C (*make progress*) **~ along nicely** gute Fortschritte machen; **her maths is coming along nicely** in Mathematik macht sie recht gute Fortschritte *od.* kommt sie recht gut voran; D (*arrive, present oneself/itself*) ‹Person:› ankommen; ‹Gelegenheit, Stelle:› sich bieten; **he'll take any job that ~s along** er nimmt jeden Job, der sich ihm bietet; E (*to place*) mitkommen (**with** mit)

**~ at** *v.t.* A herausfinden ‹Tatsachen, Wahrheit›; B (*attack*) losgehen auf (+ *Akk.*); **he came at me with a knife** er ging mit einem Messer auf mich los

**~ aˈway** *v.i.* A weggehen; B (*become detached*) sich lösen (**from** von); abgehen (**from** von); C (*be left*) **~ away with the impression/feeling that ...:** mit dem Eindruck/Gefühl gehen, dass ...

**~ ˈback** *v.i.* A (*return*) zurückkommen; ‹Gedächtnis, Vergangenes:› wiederkehren; B (*return to memory*) **it will ~ back [to me]** es wird mir wieder einfallen; C **~ back [into fashion]** wiederkommen; wieder in Mode kommen; D (*retort*) **~ back at sb. with sth.** jmdm. etw. entgegnen; **the team came back strongly** die Mannschaft spielte glänzend auf. ⇒ *also* **~back**

**~ between** *v.t.* treten zwischen (+ *Akk.*)

**~ by** ❶ /ˈ--/ *v.t.* (*obtain, receive*) kriegen (*ugs.*); bekommen; **was the money honestly ~ by?** ist das Geld auf ehrliche Weise erworben worden? ❷ /-ˈ-/ *v.i.* vorbeikommen

**~ ˈdown** *v.i.* A (*collapse*) herunterfallen; runterfallen (*ugs.*); (*fall*) ‹Schnee, Regen, Preis:› fallen; **the beams came down on my head** die Balken fielen mir auf den Kopf; B (*~ to place regarded as lower*) herunterkommen; runterkommen (*ugs.*); (*~ southwards*) runterkommen (*ugs.*); C (*leave university*) **~ down [from Oxford]** sein Studium [in Oxford] abschließen; **when he came down [from Oxford] he got married** als er sein Studium [in Oxford] abgeschlossen hatte, heiratete er; D (*land*) [not]landen; (*crash*) abstürzen; **~ down in a field** auf einem Acker [not]landen/auf einen Acker stürzen; E (*be transmitted*) ‹Sage, Brauch:› überliefert werden; F **~ down to** (*reach*) reichen bis; G **~ down to** (*be reduced to*) hinauslaufen auf (+ *Akk.*); H **~ down to** (*be a question of*) ankommen (**to** auf + *Akk.*); I (*be reduced; suffer change for the worse*) angewiesen sein (**to** auf + *Akk.*); **she has ~ down in the world** sie hat einen Abstieg erlebt; J (*make a decision*) **~ down in favour of sb./sth.** sich zu gunsten jmds./einer Sache entscheiden; **~ down on the side of sb./sth.** sich für jmdn./etw. einsetzen; K **~ down on** (*rebuke, pounce on*) fertig machen (*ugs.*); ~

**down on sb. for sth.** jmdn. wegen etw. rankriegen (*ugs.*); **L** **~ down with** bekommen ‹Krankheit›. ⇒ *also* **~down**; **earth** 1 A

**~ 'forth** *v.i.* herauskommen

**~ 'in** *v.i.* **A** (*enter*) hereinkommen; reinkommen (*ugs.*); **~ in!** herein!; **this is where we came in** (*fig.*) wie gehabt; **B** ‹Flut:› kommen; **C** (*be received*) ‹Nachrichten, Bericht:› hereinkommen; **D** (*in radio communication*) melden; **Come in, Tom, ~ in, Tom. Over** Tom melden, Tom melden. Ende; **E** (*make next contribution to discussion etc.*) sich einschalten; **would you like to ~ in here, Mr Brown?** würden Sie bitte an dieser Stelle fortfahren, Mr. Brown?; **F** (*become fashionable*) in Mode kommen; aufkommen; **G** (*become seasonable or available*) reinkommen (*ugs.*); ⇒ *also* **handy** B; **H** (*gain power, be elected*) an die Regierung kommen; ans Ruder kommen (*ugs.*); rankommen (*ugs.*); **I** (*in race*) einlaufen als *od.* durchs Ziel gehen als ‹Erster usw.›; **J** (*as income*) ‹Geld:› hereinkommen; reinkommen (*ugs.*); **K** (*find a place; have a part to play*) **where do I ~ in?** welche Rolle soll ich spielen?; **~ in on sth.** sich an etw. (*Dat.*) beteiligen; **L** **~ in for** erregen ‹Bewunderung, Aufmerksamkeit›; auf sich (*Akk.*) ziehen, hervorrufen ‹Kritik›

**~ into** *v.t.* **A** (*enter*) hereinkommen in (+ *Akk.*); ‹Zug:› einfahren in ‹Bahnhof›; ‹Schiff:› einlaufen in ‹Hafen›; **B** (*inherit*) erben ‹Vermögen›; **C** (*play a part*) **wealth does not ~ into it** Reichtum spielt dabei keine Rolle; **where do I ~ into it?** welche Rolle soll ich [dabei] spielen?

**~ near** *v.t.* **~ near [to] doing sth.** drauf und dran sein, etw. zu tun (*ugs.*); **he came near [to] committing suicide** er war kurz davor, sich das Leben zu nehmen

**~ off** ❶ /-'-/ *v.i.* **A** (*become detached*) ‹Griff, Knopf:› abgehen; (*be removable*) sich abnehmen lassen; ‹Fleck:› weg-, rausgehen (*ugs.*); **B** (*fall from sth.*) runterfallen; **C** (*emerge from contest etc.*) abschneiden; **D** (*succeed*) ‹Pläne, Versuche:› Erfolg haben, (*ugs.*) klappen; **the play/experiment/wedding/holiday didn't ~ off** das Stück war kein Erfolg/das Experiment war erfolglos/die Ehe/der Urlaub war ein Reinfall (*ugs.*); **E** (*take place*) stattfinden; **their marriage/holiday did not ~ off** aus ihrer Hochzeit/ihrem Urlaub wurde nichts; **F** (*coll.: have orgasm*) kommen (*salopp*).
❷ *v.t.* **~ off a horse/bike** vom Pferd/Fahrrad fallen; **~ 'off it!** (*coll.*) nun mach mal halblang! (*ugs.*)

**~ on** ❶ /-'-/ *v.i.* **A** (*continue coming, follow*) kommen; **~ on!** komm, komm/kommt, kommt!; (*encouraging*) na, komm; (*impatient*) na, komm schon; (*incredulous*) ach komm!; **I'll ~ on later** ich komme später nach; **B** (*make progress*) **my work is coming on very well** meine Arbeit macht gute Fortschritte; mit meiner Arbeit geht es gut voran; **C** (*begin to arrive*) ‹Nacht, Dunkelheit, Winter:› anbrechen; **the rain came on, it came on to rain** es begann zu regnen; **he thought he had a cold coming on** er glaubte, eine Erkältung zu kriegen; **D** (*be heard or seen on television etc.*) gegeben werden; **the film/opera** *etc.* **doesn't ~ on till 8 o'clock** der Film/die Oper *usw.* ist erst um 8 Uhr; **E** (*appear on stage or scene*) auftreten. ⇒ *also* **~-on**.
❷ /'--/ *v.t.* ⇒ **~ upon**

**~ 'out** *v.i.* **A** herauskommen; **~ out [on strike]** in den Streik treten; **B** (*emerge from examination etc.*) **~ out top/second/bottom** am besten/zweitbesten/schlechtesten abschneiden; **C** (*appear, become visible*) ‹Sonne, Knospen, Blumen:› herauskommen, (*ugs.*) rauskommen; ‹Sterne:› zu sehen sein; **D** (*be revealed*) ‹Wahrheit, Nachrichten:› herauskommen, (*ugs.*) rauskommen; **the results came out negative** die Resultate waren negativ; **the answer came out wrong** das Ergebnis war falsch; **E** (*be published, declared, etc.*) herauskommen; rauskommen (*ugs.*); ‹Ergebnisse, Zensuren:› bekannt gegeben werden; **F** (*be solved*) ‹Aufgabe, Rätsel:› sich lösen lassen; **G** (*make début*) debütieren; **H** (*be released from prison*) rauskommen (*ugs.*); herauskommen; **I** (*declare oneself*) **~ out for** *or* **in favour of sth.** sich für etw. aussprechen; etw. befürworten; **~ out against sth.** sich gegen etw. aussprechen; **J** ‹Homosexuelle[r]:› sich öffentlich zu seiner Homosexualität bekennen; **K** (*be satisfactorily visible*) herauskommen; **you have ~ out very well in all of these photos** du bist auf allen Fotos gut getroffen; **the photo has not ~ out** das Foto ist nichts geworden; **L** (*be covered*) **his face came out in pimples** er bekam im ganzen Gesicht Pickel; **she came out in a rash** sie bekam einen Ausschlag; **M** (*be removed*) ‹Fleck, Schmutz:› rausgehen (*ugs.*); **N** **~ out with** herausrücken mit (*ugs.*) ‹Wahrheit, Fakten›; loslassen (*ugs.*) ‹Flüche, Bemerkungen›

**~ 'over** ❶ *v.i.* **A** (**~** *from some distance*) herüberkommen; **B** (*change sides or opinions*) **~ over to sb./sth.** sich jmdm./einer Sache anschließen; **C** ⇒ **~across** 1 B; **D** **she came over funny/dizzy** ihr wurde auf einmal ganz komisch/schwindlig (*ugs.*); **he came over faint** ihm wurde plötzlich schwarz vor [den] Augen. ❷ *v.t.* kommen über (+ *Akk.*); **what has ~ 'over him?** was ist über ihn gekommen?

**~ 'round** *v.i.* **A** (*make informal visit*) vorbeischauen; **B** (*recover*) wieder zu sich kommen; **C** (*be converted*) es sich [anders] (*Dat.*) überlegen; **he came round to my way of thinking** er hat sich meiner Auffassung (*Dat.*) angeschlossen; **D** (*recur*) **Christmas ~s round again** wir haben wieder Weihnachten

**~ 'through** ❶ *v.i.* durchkommen. ❷ *v.t.* (*survive*) überleben

**~ to** ❶ /'--/ *v.t.* **A** (*amount to*) ‹Rechnung, Gehalt, Kosten:› sich belaufen auf (+ *Akk.*); **his plans came to nothing** aus seinen Plänen wurde nichts; **he/it will never ~ to much** aus ihm wird nichts Besonderes werden/daraus wird nicht viel; **B** (*inherit*) erben ‹Vermögen›; **~ to oneself** ⇒ 2; **C** (*arrive at*) **what is the world coming to?** wohin ist es mit der Welt gekommen?; **this is what he has ~ to** so weit ist es also mit ihm gekommen. ❷ /-'-/ *v.i.* wieder zu sich kommen

**~ to'gether** *v.i.* ‹Personen:› zusammenkommen; ‹Ereignisse:› zusammenfallen

**~ under** *v.t.* **A** (*be classed as or among*) kommen unter (+ *Akk.*); **B** (*be subject to*) geraten *od.* kommen unter (+ *Akk.*); **these shops have ~ under new management** diese Läden stehen unter neuer Leitung

**~ 'up** *v.i.* **A** (**~** *to place regarded as higher*) hochkommen; heraufkommen; (**~** *northwards*) raufkommen (*ugs.*); **he ~s up to London every other weekend** er kommt jedes zweite Wochenende nach London; **B** (*join university*) **~ up [to Cambridge]** sein Studium [in Cambridge] beginnen; **C** **~ up to sb.** (*approach for talk*) auf jmdn. zukommen; **D** **~ up with sb.** (*get abreast*) jmdn. einholen; **E** (*arise out of ground*) herauskommen; rauskommen (*ugs.*); **F** (*be discussed*) ‹Frage, Thema:› angeschnitten werden, aufkommen; ‹Name:› genannt werden; ‹Fall:› verhandelt werden; **G** (*present itself*) sich ergeben; **~ up for sale/renewal** zum Kauf angeboten werden/erneuert werden müssen; **coming up** (*coll.: sth. is nearly ready*) kommt gleich; **H** **~ up to** (*reach*) reichen bis an (+ *Akk.*); (*be equal to*) entsprechen (+ *Dat.*) ‹Erwartungen, Anforderungen›; **I** **~ up against sth.** (*fig.*) auf etw. (*Akk.*) stoßen; **J** **~ up with** vorbringen ‹Vorschlag›; wissen ‹Lösung, Antwort›; haben ‹Erklärung, Idee›; geben, liefern ‹Informationen›

**~ upon** *v.t.* **A** (*attack*) kommen über (+ *Akk.*); **disaster/war came upon them** Unheil/Krieg kam über sie (*geh.*) *od.* brach über sie herein (*geh.*); **B** (*meet by chance*) begegnen (+ *Dat.*)

**~ with** *v.t.* (*be supplied together with*) **this model ~s with ...:** zu diesem Modell gehört ...

**'comeback** *n.* **A** (*return to profession etc.*) Comeback, *das;* **B** (*coll.: retort*) Reaktion, *die;* **I got an immediate ~ from him that ...:** er entgegnete mir darauf sofort, dass ...; **C** (*means of redress*) **have no ~:** [etw.] nicht beanstanden können

**comedian** /kə'mi:dɪən/ *n.* ▶ **1261** Komiker, *der*

**comedienne** /kəmi:dɪ'en, kəmedɪ'en/ *n.* ▶ **1261** Komikerin, *die*

**'comedown** *n.* (*loss of prestige etc.*) Abstieg, *der*

**comedy** /'kɒmɪdɪ/ *n.* **A** (*Theatre*) Lustspiel, *das;* Komödie, *die;* **B** (*humorous incident in life*) komischer Vorfall; **a ~ of errors** eine einzige Kette komischer Irrtümer; **C** (*humour*) Witz, *der;* Witzigkeit, *die*

**come-'hither** *attrib. adj.* einladend

**comeliness** /'kʌmlɪnɪs/ *n., no pl.* Ansehnlichkeit, *die*

**comely** /'kʌmlɪ/ *adj.* gut aussehend; ansehnlich

**'come-on** *n.* (*coll.*) (*lure*) **give sb. the ~:** jmdn. anmachen (*salopp*)

**comer** /'kʌmə(r)/ *n.* **the competition is open to all ~s** an dem Wettbewerb kann sich jeder beteiligen; **the first ~:** derjenige, der zuerst kommt

**comestible** /kə'mestɪbl/ *n. usu. in pl.* Nahrungsmittel, *das*

**comet** /'kɒmɪt/ *n.* (*Astron.*) Komet, *der*

**comeuppance** /kʌm'ʌpəns/ *n.* **get one's ~:** die Quittung kriegen (*fig.*)

**comfort** /'kʌmfət/ ❶ *n.* **A** (*consolation*) Trost, *der;* **it is a ~/no ~ to know that ...:** es ist tröstlich/alles andere als tröstlich zu wissen, dass ...; **he takes ~ from the fact that ...:** er tröstet sich mit der Tatsache, dass ...; **B** (*physical well-being*) Behaglichkeit, *die;* **live in great ~:** sehr behaglich *od.* bequem leben; **C** (*person*) Trost, *der;* **be a ~ to sb.** jmdm. *od.* für jmdn. ein Trost sein; **D** (*cause of satisfaction*) Tröstung, *die;* **E** *usu. in pl.* (*things that make life easy*) Komfort, *der o. Pl.;* **with every modern ~** *or* **all modern ~s** mit allem modernen Komfort; **he likes his ~s** er schätzt den Komfort; **creature ~s** leibliches Wohl. ⇒ *also* **cold comfort**.
❷ *v.t.* trösten; (*give help to*) sich annehmen (+ *Gen.*)

**comfortable** /'kʌmfətəbl/ ❶ *adj.* **A** (*giving, having, providing comfort*) bequem ‹Bett, Sessel, Schuhe, Leben›; komfortabel ‹Haus, Hotel, Zimmer›; (*fig.*) ausreichend ‹Einkommen, Rente›; **a ~ victory** ein leichter Sieg; **a ~ majority** eine gute Mehrheit; **B** (*at ease*) **be/feel ~:** sich wohl fühlen; **make yourself ~:** machen Sie es sich (*Dat.*) bequem; **the patient/his condition is ~:** der Patient/er ist schmerzfrei; **C** (*having an easy conscience*) **she didn't feel very ~ about it** ihr war nicht ganz wohl bei der Sache. ❷ *n.* (*Amer.*) Deckbett, *das*

**comfortably** /'kʌmfətəblɪ/ *adv.* bequem; komfortabel ‹eingerichtet›; gut, leicht ‹gewinnen›; **they are ~ off** es geht ihnen gut

**comforter** /'kʌmfətə(r)/ *n.* **A** (*person*) Tröster, *der*/Trösterin, *die;* **B** (*esp. Brit.: baby's dummy*) Schnuller, *der;* **C** (*esp. Brit.: woollen scarf*) Schal, *der;* **D** (*Amer.: warm quilt*) Deckbett, *das*

**comforting** /'kʌmfətɪŋ/ *adj.* beruhigend ‹Gedanke›; tröstend ‹Worte›; wohlig ‹Wärme›; **we gave her a ~ cup of tea** wir gaben ihr zur Beruhigung eine Tasse Tee

**comfortless** /'kʌmfətlɪs/ *adj.* unbequem; ‹Hotel, Zimmer› ohne Komfort; ungemütlich ‹Person, Leben›; unangenehm ‹Gedanke›; unwirtlich ‹Landschaft, Welt›

**comfort: ~ station** *n.* (*Amer.*) öffentliche Toilette; Bedürfnisanstalt, *die* (*veralt.*); **~ zone** *n.* Kuschelecke, *die*

**comfrey** /'kʌmfrɪ/ *n.* (*Bot.*) Beinwell, *der;* Schwarzwurz, *die*

**comfy** /'kʌmfɪ/ *adj.* (*coll.*) bequem; gemütlich ‹Hotel, Zimmer›; **make yourself ~:** machs dir gemütlich; **are you ~?** sitzt/liegst *usw.* du bequem?

**comic** /'kɒmɪk/ ❶ *adj.* **A** (*burlesque, funny*) komisch; belustigend; **B** (*of or in the style of* *comedy*) humoristisch ‹Dichtung, Dichter›; ~ **relief** befreiende Komik. ❷ *n.* [A] ▶ **1261** (*comedian*) Komiker, *der*/Komikerin, *die;* [B] (*periodical*) Comicheft, *das;* [C] (*amusing person*) Witzbold, *der;* ulkiger Vogel (*ugs.*)

**comical** /ˈkɒmɪkl/ *adj.* ulkig; komisch

**comically** /ˈkɒmɪkəlɪ/ *adv.* ulkig; komisch

**comic:** ~ ˈ**opera** *n.* (*lit. or fig.*) komische Oper; ~ **strip** *n.* Comic, *der;* ~ **strips** Comicstrips; Comics

**coming** /ˈkʌmɪŋ/ ❶ *adj.* ⇒ **come.** ❷ *n.* (*of person*) Ankunft, *die;* (*of time*) Beginn, *der;* (*of institution*) Einführung, *die;* ~**s and goings** das Kommen und Gehen

**comma** /ˈkɒmə/ *n.* Komma, *das*

**command** /kəˈmɑːnd/ ❶ *v.t.* [A] (*order, bid*) befehlen (**sb.** jmdm.); **he** ~**ed that the work should be done immediately** er befahl, die Arbeit sofort auszuführen; [B] (*be in* ~ *of*) befehligen ‹Schiff, Armee, Streitkräfte›; (*have authority over or control of*) gebieten über (+ *Akk.*) (*geh.*); beherrschen; [C] (*have at one's disposal*) verfügen über (+ *Akk.*) ‹Gelder, Ressourcen, Wortschatz›; [D] (*restrain*) ~ **oneself/one's temper** sich beherrschen; [E] (*deserve and get*) verdient haben ‹Achtung, Respekt›; **he** ~**s a high fee** er kann ein hohes Honorar verlangen; [F] überragen ‹Küste, Stadt, Bucht, Hafen›; **the hill** ~**s a fine view [of ...]** der Berg bietet eine schöne Aussicht auf (+ *Akk.*).

❷ *v.i.* [A] (*be supreme*) befehlen; Befehle geben; [B] (*be in* ~) das Kommando *od.* die Befehlsgewalt haben.

❸ *n.* [A] Kommando, *das;* (*in writing*) Befehl, *der;* **at** *or* **by sb.'s** ~**:** auf jmds. Befehl (*Akk.*) [hin]; **at the** ~ **'halt'** auf das Kommando „stehen bleiben" [hin]; **word of** ~**:** Befehl, *der;* Kommando, *das;* [B] (*exercise or tenure*) Kommando, *das;* Befehlsgewalt, *die;* **be in** ~ **of an army/ship** eine Armee/ein Schiff befehligen; **the army is under the** ~ **of General X** die Armee steht unter dem Befehl von General X; **have/take** ~ **of ...:** das Kommando über (+ *Akk.*) ... haben/übernehmen; **officer in** ~**:** befehlshabender Offizier; [C] (*control, mastery, possession*) Beherrschung, *die;* **have a good** ~ **of French** das Französische gut beherrschen; **all the money at his** ~**:** das gesamte ihm zur Verfügung stehende Geld; [D] (*body of troops*) Kommando, *das;* (*district under* ~) Abschnitt, *der;* Befehlsbereich, *der;* (*ship*) Schiff, *das;* [E] (*Computing*) Befehl, *der*

**commandant** /kɒmənˈdænt/ *n.* Kommandant, *der;* **C~-in-Chief** Oberbefehlshaber, *der*

**commandeer** /kɒmənˈdɪə(r)/ *v.t.* [A] (*take arbitrary possession of*) sich (*Dat.*) aneignen; requirieren (*scherzh.*); [B] (*seize for military service*) einziehen ‹Männer›; beschlagnahmen, requirieren ‹Pferde, Vorräte, Gebäude›

**commander** /kəˈmɑːndə(r)/ *n.* ▶ **1617** [A] (*one who commands*) Führer, *der;* Leiter, *der;* [B] (*naval officer below captain*) Fregattenkapitän, *der;* [C] (*Police*) Abschnittsleiter, *der;* [D] **C~-in-Chief** Oberbefehlshaber, *der.* ⇒ *also* **wing commander**

**commanding** /kəˈmɑːndɪŋ/ *adj.* [A] gebieterisch ‹Persönlichkeit, Erscheinung, Stimme›; imposant, eindrucksvoll ‹Statur, Gestalt›; **be in a** ~ **position** Befehlsbefugnis haben; (*Sport*) stark in Führung liegen; [B] beherrschend ‹Ausblick, Lage›; ~ **heights** (*fig.*) Kommandohöhen *Pl.*

**commanding** ˈ**officer** *n.* Befehlshaber, *der*/Befehlshaberin, *die*

**commandment** /kəˈmɑːndmənt/ *n.* Gebot, *das;* **the Ten C~s** die Zehn Gebote

**commando** /kəˈmɑːndəʊ/ *n., pl.* ~**s** [A] (*unit*) Kommando, *das;* Kommandotrupp, *der;* [B] (*member of* ~) Angehöriger eines Kommando[trupp]s

**command: C~ Paper** *n.* (*Brit.*) königliche Parlamentsvorlage; ~ **performance** *n.* königliche Galavorstellung; ~ **post** *n.* Kommandozentrale, *die*

**commemorate** /kəˈmeməreɪt/ *v.t.* gedenken (+ *Gen.*); **Easter** ~**s the resurrection of Christ** zu Ostern wird die Wiederauferstehung Christi gefeiert; **in order to** ~ **the victory** zum Gedenken an den Sieg

**commemoration** /kəmeməˈreɪʃn/ *n.* [A] (*act*) Gedenken, *das;* **in** ~ **of** zum Gedenken an (+ *Akk.*); **the** ~ **of sb.'s death** das Gedenken an jmds. Tod (*Akk.*); [B] (*church service*) Gedenkgottesdienst, *der*

**commemorative** /kəˈmemərətɪv/ *adj.* Gedenk-; ~ **of** zum Gedenken an (+ *Akk.*)

**commence** /kəˈmens/ *v.t. & i.* beginnen; **building** ~**d** mit dem Bau wurde begonnen; ~ **to do** *or* ~ **doing sth.** beginnen, etw. zu tun

**commencement** /kəˈmensmənt/ *n.* Beginn, *der*

**commend** /kəˈmend/ *v.t.* [A] (*praise*) loben; ~ **sb. [up]on sth.** jmdn. wegen etw. loben; ~ **sb./sth. to sb.** jmdm. jmdn./etw. empfehlen; **be highly** ~**ed** eine sehr gute Beurteilung bekommen; [B] (*entrust or commit to person's care*) anvertrauen

**commendable** /kəˈmendəbl/ *adj.* lobenswert; löblich

**commendably** /kəˈmendəblɪ/ *adv.* lobenswert

**commendation** /kɒmenˈdeɪʃn/ *n.* [A] (*praise*) Lob, *das;* (*official*) Belobigung, *die;* (*award*) Auszeichnung, *die;* [B] (*act of commending*) Empfehlung, *die*

**commendatory** /kəˈmendətərɪ/ *adj.* lobend

**commensurable** /kəˈmenʃərəbl, kəˈmensjərəbl/ *adj.* [A] vergleichbar (**with, to** mit); [B] (*proportionate*) **be** ~ **with sth.** einer Sache (*Dat.*) entsprechen

**commensurate** /kəˈmenʃərət, kəˈmensjərət/ *adj.* ~ **to** *or* **with** entsprechend (+ *Dat.*); **be** ~ **to** *or* **with sth.** einer Sache (*Dat.*) entsprechen

**comment** /ˈkɒment/ ❶ *n.* [A] (*explanatory note, remark*) Bemerkung, *die* (**on** über + *Akk.*); (*marginal note*) Anmerkung, *die* (**on** über + *Akk.*); **no** ~**!** (*coll.*) kein Kommentar!; [B] (*criticism*) Rederei, *die* (*ugs.*); [C] *no pl.* (*gossip*) Gerede, *das;* [D] (*illustration*) Deutung, *die;* Beschreibung, *die.* ❷ *v.i.* [A] (*make remarks*) ~ **on sth.** über etw. (*Akk.*) Bemerkungen machen; **he** ~**ed that ...:** er bemerkte, dass ...; [B] (*write explanatory notes*) ~ **on a text/manuscript** einen Text/ein Manuskript kommentieren

**commentary** /ˈkɒməntərɪ/ *n.* [A] (*series of comments, expository treatise*) Kommentar, *der* (**on** zu); [B] (*comment*) Erläuterung, *die* (**on** zu); **the sombre factories are a sad** ~ **upon our civilization** die düsteren Fabriken sind traurige Zeugnisse unserer Kultur; [C] (*Radio, Telev.*) **[live** *or* **running]** ~**:** Live-Reportage, *die*

**commentate** /ˈkɒmənteɪt/ *v.i.* ~ **on sth.** etw. kommentieren

**commentator** /ˈkɒmənteɪtə(r)/ *n.* ▶ **1261** Kommentator, *der*/Kommentatorin, *die;* (*Sport*) Reporter, *der*/Reporterin, *die*

**commerce** /ˈkɒmɜːs/ *n.* Handel, *der;* (*between countries*) Handel[sverkehr], *der;* **the world of** ~**:** die Geschäftswelt

**commercial** /kəˈmɜːʃl/ ❶ *adj.* [A] Handels-; kaufmännisch ‹Ausbildung›; **the** ~ **world** die Geschäftswelt; [B] (*interested in financial return*) kommerziell; [C] (*impure*) handelsüblich. ❷ *n.* Werbespot, *der;* **during the** ~**s on TV** während der Fernsehwerbung

**commercial:** ~ ˈ**art** *n.* Gebrauchs-, Werbegrafik, *die;* ~ ˈ**bank** *n.* private Geschäftsbank; ~ ˈ**break** *n.* Werbepause, *die;* ~ ˈ**broadcasting** *n.* Werbefunk und -fernsehen; ~ **college** *n.* Fach[hoch]schule für kaufmännische Berufe; [höhere] Handelsschule; ~ **correspondence** *n.* Handelskorrespondenz, *die*

**commercialise** ⇒ **commercialize**

**commercialism** /kəˈmɜːʃəlɪzm/ *n.* Kommerzialismus, *der*

**commercialize** /kəˈmɜːʃəlaɪz/ *v.t.* kommerzialisieren; vermarkten

**commercially** /kəˈmɜːʃəlɪ/ *adv.* kommerziell

**commercial:** ~ ˈ**radio** *n.* Werbefunk, *der;* ~ ˈ**television** *n.* kommerzielles Fernsehen; Werbefernsehen, *das;* ~ ˈ**traveller** *n.* ▶ **1261** Handelsvertreter, *der*/-vertreterin, *die;* ~ ˈ**vehicle** *n.* Nutzfahrzeug, *das*

**Commie** /ˈkɒmɪ/ *n.* (*coll. derog.*) Rote, *der/die* (*abwertend*)

**commingle** /kəˈmɪŋgl/ (*formal*) ❶ *v.t.* vermischen. ❷ *v.i.* sich vermischen

**commis** /ˈkɒmɪ, ˈkɒmɪs/ *adj.* ~ **chef** Assistenzkoch, *der*

**commiserate** /kəˈmɪzəreɪt/ *v.i.* ~ **with sb.** mit jmdm. mitfühlen; (*express one's commiseration*) jmdm. sein Mitgefühl aussprechen (**on** zu)

**commiseration** /kəmɪzəˈreɪʃn/ *n.* [A] Mitgefühl, *das;* [B] *in sing. or pl.* (*condolence*) Teilnahme, *die;* Beileid, *das*

**commissar** /ˈkɒmɪsɑː(r)/ *n.* (*Hist.*) Kommissar, *der*

**commissariat** /kɒmɪˈseərɪət/ *n.* Intendantur, *die*

**commissary** /ˈkɒmɪsərɪ, kəˈmɪsərɪ/ *n.* [A] (*Mil.*) Verpflegungsoffizier, *der;* [B] (*Amer.: store for supply of food etc.*) Laden, *der* (*auf Baustellen, in Lagern, Bergwerken usw.*)

**commission** /kəˈmɪʃn/ ❶ *n.* [A] (*authority*) Vollmacht, *die;* [B] (*body of persons having authority, department of Commissioner*) Kommission, *die;* [C] (*instruction, piece of work*) Auftrag, *der;* [D] **Royal C~** (*Brit.*) Königliche [Untersuchungs]kommission; [E] (*warrant conferring authority*) Ernennung, *die;* Bestellung, *die;* (*in armed services*) Ernennungsurkunde, *die;* Offizierspatent, *das* (*veralt.*); **get one's** ~**:** zum Offizier ernannt werden; **resign one's** ~**:** aus dem Offiziersdienst ausscheiden; den Dienst quittieren (*veralt.*); [F] (*pay of agent*) Provision, *die;* **sell goods on** ~**:** Waren auf Provisionsbasis verkaufen; [G] (*act of committing crime etc.*) Begehen, *das;* Begehung, *die;* [H] **in/out of** ~ ‹Kriegsschiff› in/außer Dienst; ‹Auto, Maschine, Lift usw.› in/außer Betrieb.

❷ *v.t.* [A] beauftragen ‹Künstler›; in Auftrag geben ‹Gemälde usw.›; [B] (*empower by* ~) bevollmächtigen; ~**ed officer** Offizier, *der;* [C] (*give command of ship to*) zum Kapitän ernennen; [D] (*prepare for service*) in Dienst stellen ‹Schiff›; [E] (*bring into operation*) in Betrieb setzen ‹Kraftwerk, Fabrik›

**commissionaire** /kəmɪʃəˈneə(r)/ *n.* ▶ **1261** (*esp. Brit.*) Portier, *der*

**commissioner** /kəˈmɪʃənə(r)/ *n.* [A] (*person appointed by commission*) Beauftragte, *der/die;* (*of police*) Präsident, *der;* [B] (*member of commission*) Kommissions-, Ausschussmitglied, *das;* [C] (*representative of supreme authority*) Kommissar, *der;* **High C~:** Hochkommissar, *der;* [D] **C~ for Oaths** Notar, *der*/Notarin, *die*

**commit** /kəˈmɪt/ *v.t.,* **-tt-** [A] (*perpetrate*) begehen, verüben ‹Mord, Selbstmord, Verbrechen, Raub›; begehen ‹Dummheit, Bigamie, Fehler, Ehebruch›; **thou shalt not** ~ **adultery** (*Bibl.*) du sollst nicht ehebrechen; [B] (*pledge, bind*) ~ **oneself/sb. to doing sth.** sich/jmdn. verpflichten, etw. zu tun; ~ **oneself to a course of action** sich auf eine Vorgehensweise festlegen; [C] (*entrust*) anvertrauen (**to** *Dat.*); ~ **sth. to a person/a person's care** jmdm. etw. anvertrauen/etw. jmds. Obhut (*Dat.*) anvertrauen; ~ **sth. to the flames/waves** etw. den Flammen/Wellen übergeben (*geh.*); ~ **sth. to writing/paper** etw. zu Papier bringen; ⇒ *also* **memory** A; [D] (*consign to custody*) ~ **sb. for trial** jmdn. dem Gericht überstellen; ~ **sb. to prison** jmdn. ins Gefängnis einliefern

**commitment** /kəˈmɪtmənt/ *n.;* [A] (*to course of action or opinion*) Verpflichtung, *die* (**to** gegenüber); (*by conviction*) Engagement, *das* (**to** für); [B] ⇒ **committal** A

**committal** /kəˈmɪtl/ *n.* [A] (*to prison*) Einlieferung, *die;* (*to hospital*) Einweisung, *die;* [B] (*to grave*) Bestattung, *die;* ~ **service** Bestattungsgottesdienst, *der*

**committed** /kəˈmɪtɪd/ *adj.* [A] verpflichtet (**to** zu); festgelegt (**to** auf + *Akk.*); [B] (*morally dedicated*) engagiert

**committee** /kəˈmɪtɪ/ *n.* Ausschuss, *der* (*auch Parl.*); Komitee, *das*

C

**com'mittee man, com'mittee woman** *ns.* Ausschussmitglied, *das*

**commode** /kə'məʊd/ *n.* **A** (*chest of drawers*) Kommode, *die;* **B** (*chamber pot*) **[night] ~:** Nachtstuhl, *der*

**commodious** /kə'məʊdɪəs/ *adj.* geräumig

**commodity** /kə'mɒdɪtɪ/ *n.* **A** (*utility item*) Gebrauchsgegenstand, *der;* (*not luxury*) Gebrauchsartikel, *der;* **household ~:** Haushaltsartikel, *der;* **a rare/precious ~** (*fig.*) etwas Seltenes/Kostbares; **B** (*St. Exch.*) [vertretbare] Ware; (*raw material*) Rohstoff, *der*

**commodore** /'kɒmədɔ:(r)/ *n.* **A** (*naval officer*) Flottillenadmiral, *der;* **B** (*of squadron*) Kommodore, *der;* **C** (*of yacht club*) Präsident, *der*/Präsidentin, *die;* **D** (*senior captain of shipping line*) Kommodore, *der*

**common** /'kɒmən/ **1** *adj.*, **~er** /'kɒmənə(r)/, **~est** /'kɒmənɪst/ **A** (*belonging equally to all*) gemeinsam ‹Ziel, Interesse, Sache, Unternehmung, Vorteil, Merkmal, Sprache›; **~ to all birds** allen Vögeln gemeinsam; ⇨ *also* **cause** 1 D; **consent** 2 A; **B** (*belonging to the public*) öffentlich; **the ~ good** das Gemeinwohl; **a ~ belief** [ein] allgemeiner Glaube; **a ~ prostitute** *or* **harlot** (*arch.*) eine Straßendirne (*veralt.*); **a ~ criminal** ein gewöhnlicher *od.* gemeiner Verbrecher; **have the ~ touch** volkstümlich sein; **C** (*usual*) gewöhnlich, normal; (*frequent*) häufig ‹Vorgang, Erscheinung, Ereignis, Erlebnis›; allgemein verbreitet ‹Sitte, Wort, Redensart›; allgemein bekannt ‹Marke, Produkt›; (*Bot., Zool.: of the most familiar type*) gemein ‹Farnkraut, Sperling usw.›; **a ~ sight** ein ganz gewöhnlicher *od.* alltäglicher Anblick; **such a thing is ~ nowadays** so etwas ist heutzutage ganz normal; (*is frequent*) kommt heutzutage häufig vor; **a word in ~ usage** ein Wort des allgemeinen Sprachgebrauchs; **drugs are in ~ use today** die Einnahme von Drogen ist heute weit verbreitet; **~ honesty/courtesy** [ganz] normale Ehrlichkeit/Höflichkeit; **~ or garden** (*coll.*) ganz gewöhnlich *od.* normal; **a ~ or garden subject/programme** ein Feld-Wald-und-Wiesen-Thema/-Programm (*ugs.*); **a hotel out of the ~ run** ein Hotel, das über dem Durchschnitt liegt; **no ~ mind** ein außergewöhnlicher Kopf (*fig.*); **D** (*without rank or position*) einfach; gemein (*veralt.*); ⇨ *also* **herd** 1 B; **E** (*vulgar*) gemein; gewöhnlich (*abwertend*), ordinär (*ugs. abwertend*) ‹Ausdrucksweise, Mundart, Aussehen, Benehmen›; **be as ~ as muck** schrecklich ordinär *od.* gewöhnlich sein; **F** (*Math.*) gemeinsam; **G** (*Ling.*) **~ noun** Gattungsbegriff, *der;* **~ gender** doppeltes Geschlecht.

**2** *n.* **A** (*land*) Gemeindeland, *das;* Allmende, *die;* **B** **have sth./nothing/a lot in ~ [with sb.]** etw./nichts/viel [mit jmdm.] gemein[sam] haben; **in ~ with most of his friends he wanted ...:** ebenso wie die meisten seiner Freunde wollte er ...; **C** (*coll.: ~ sense*) Grips, *der* (*ugs.*); **use your ~!** denk doch mal ein bisschen nach! (*ugs.*)

**common: C~ Agri'cultural Policy** *n.* gemeinsame Agrarpolitik [der EU]; **~ 'cold** *n.* ▶ **1232** Erkältung, *die;* **~ de'nominator** *n.* (*Math.*) gemeinsame Nenner, *der;* **the least** *or* **lowest ~ denominator** (*lit. or fig.*) der kleinste gemeinsame Nenner; **~ 'entrance** *n.* (*Brit.*) *Aufnahmeprüfung für eine Privatschule*

**commoner** /'kɒmənə(r)/ *n.* **A** (*one of the people*) Bürgerliche, *der/die;* **B** (*student*) *Student, der kein Stipendium erhält*

**common: ~ 'factor** *n.* (*Math.*) gemeinsamer Teiler; **~ 'ground** *n.* gemeinsame Basis; **~ 'knowledge** *n.* **it's [a matter of] ~ knowledge that ...** es ist allgemein bekannt, dass ...; **~ land** *n.* Gemeindeland, *das;* **~ 'law** *n.* Common Law, *das;* **~ law** *adj.* **~ law marriage** eheähnliche Gemeinschaft; **she's his ~ law wife/he's her ~ law husband** sie lebt mit ihm/er lebt mit ihr in eheähnlicher Gemeinschaft

**commonly** /'kɒmənlɪ/ *adv.* **A** (*generally*) im Allgemeinen; gemeinhin; **B** (*vulgarly*) gewöhnlich (*abwertend*)

**common: C~ 'Market** *n.* Gemeinsamer Markt; **~ 'multiple** *n.* (*Math.*) gemeinsames Vielfaches; **the least** *or* **lowest ~ multiple** das kleinste gemeinsame Vielfache

**commonness** /'kɒmənnɪs/ *n., no pl.* **A** (*usualness*) Gewöhnlichkeit, *die;* Normalität, *die;* (*frequency*) Häufigkeit, *die;* **B** (*vulgarity*) Gewöhnlichkeit, *die* (*abwertend*)

**commonplace** /'kɒmənpleɪs/ **1** *n.* (*platitude*) Gemeinplatz, *der;* (*anything usual or trite*) Alltäglichkeit, *die.* **2** *adj.* nichts sagend, banal ‹Person, Bemerkung, Buch›; alltäglich ‹Angelegenheit, Ereignis›

**common: C~ 'Prayer** *n.* Liturgie, *die* (*der Kirche von England*); **the Book of C~ Prayer** *liturgisches Buch der Kirche von England;* **~ room** *n.* (*Brit.*) Gemeinschaftsraum, *der;* (*for lecturers*) Dozentenzimmer, *das*

**commons** /'kɒmənz/ *n. pl.* **A** **the [House of] C~:** das Unterhaus; **B** (*Brit.: common people*) einfache Volk, *das.* ⇨ *also* **short commons**

**common: ~ 'sense** *n.* gesunder Menschenverstand; **~ sense** *adj.* vernünftig; gesund ‹Ansicht, Standpunkt›; **~ stock** *n.* (*Amer. Finance*) Stammaktien; **~ time** *n.* (*Mus.*) Viervierteltakt, *der*

**commonwealth** /'kɒmənwelθ/ *n.* **A** **the [British] C~ [of Nations]** das Commonwealth; **C~ Day** Commonwealthtag, *der;* **B** (*independent state*) Staat, *der;* Gemeinwesen, *das;* (*republic or democratic state*) Republik, *die;* **C~ of Australia** Australischer Bund; **C** **the C~** (*Brit. Hist.*) *die Republik unter Cromwell*

**commotion** /kə'məʊʃn/ *n.* (*noisy confusion*) Tumult, *der;* (*insurrection*) Aufruhr, *der;* **make a ~:** einen Tumult *od.* einen großen Spektakel veranstalten

**communal** /'kɒmjʊnl/ *adj.* **A** (*of or for the community*) gemeindlich; Gemeinde-, kommunal ‹Verwaltung›; **~ living/life** Gemeinschaftsleben, *das;* **B** (*for the common use*) gemeinsam; Gemeinschafts‹küche, -schüssel, -bad, -grab, -zelle, -ehe›

**communally** /'kɒmjʊnəlɪ/ *adv.* gemeinsam; gemeinschaftlich; **be ~ owned** Gemeinschaftsbesitz sein

**commune**[1] /'kɒmju:n/ *n.* **A** Kommune, *die;* **B** (*territorial division*) Gemeinde, *die;* Kommune, *die*

**commune**[2] /kə'mju:n/ *v.i.* **A** **~ with sb./sth.** mit jmdm./etw. Zwiesprache halten (*geh.*); **~ together** miteinander Zwiesprache halten (*geh.*); **B** (*Amer. Eccl.*) das Abendmahl empfangen; (*RC Ch.*) kommunizieren

**communicable** /kə'mju:nɪkəbl/ *adj.* übertragbar ‹Krankheit›; vermittelbar, kommunizierbar ‹Ideen, Informationen›

**communicant** /kə'mju:nɪkənt/ *n.* (*RC Ch.*) Kommunizierende, *der/die;* (*Protestant Ch.*) Empfänger/Empfängerin des Abendmahls

**communicate** /kə'mju:nɪkeɪt/ **1** *v.t.* (*impart, transmit*) übertragen ‹Wärme, Bewegung, Krankheit›; übermitteln ‹Nachrichten, Informationen›; vermitteln ‹Gefühle, Ideen›; **he ~d the plan to his friends** er teilte seinen Freunden den Plan mit. **2** *v.i.* **A** (*have common door*) verbunden sein; **communicating rooms** Zimmer mit einer Verbindungstür; **B** **~ with sb.** mit jmdm. kommunizieren; **she has difficulty in communicating** sie hat Kommunikationsschwierigkeiten; **C** (*RC Ch.*) kommunizieren; (*Protestant Ch.*) das Abendmahl empfangen

**communication** /kəmju:nɪ'keɪʃn/ *n.* **A** (*imparting of disease, motion, heat, etc.*) Übertragung, *die;* (*imparting of news, information*) Übermittlung, *die;* (*imparting of ideas*) Vermittlung, *die;* **~ with the spacecraft/the mainland** die Verbindung zum Raumschiff/Festland; **~ among the deaf and dumb** die Verständigung unter Taubstummen; **B** (*information given*) Mitteilung, *die* (**to** an + *Akk.*); **C** (*interaction with sb.*) Verbindung, *die;* **lines of ~:** Verbindungslinien; **means/systems of ~:** Kommunikationsmittel/-systeme; **be in ~ with sb.** mit jmdm. in Verbindung stehen; **D** *in pl.* (*conveying information*) Kommunikation, *die;* (*science, practice*) Kommunikationswesen, *das;* (*Mil.*) Nachschublinien *Pl.*

**communication: ~ cord** *n.* Notbremse, *die;* **~ link** *n.* Nachrichtenverbindung, *die;* **~s satellite** *n.* Nachrichten- *od.* Kommunikationssatellit, *der;* **~ theory** *n.* Kommunikationstheorie, *die*

**communicative** /kə'mju:nɪkətɪv/ *adj.* gesprächig; mitteilsam

**communion** /kə'mju:nɪən/ *n.* **A** **[Holy] C~** (*Protestant Ch.*) das [heilige] Abendmahl; (*RC Ch.*) die [heilige] Kommunion; **receive** *or* **take [Holy] C~:** das [heilige] Abendmahl/die [heilige] Kommunion empfangen; **B** (*fellowship*) Gemeinschaft, *die;* **the ~ of saints** die Gemeinschaft der Heiligen; **~ with nature/God** Zwiesprache mit der Natur/mit Gott

**communion: ~ cup** *n.* Abendmahlskelch, *der;* **~ rail** *n.* Kommunionbank, *die;* **~ service** *n.* Abendmahlsgottesdienst, *der*

**communiqué** /kə'mju:nɪkeɪ/ *n.* Kommuniqué, *das*

**communism** /'kɒmjʊnɪzm/ *n.* Kommunismus, *der;* **C~:** der Kommunismus

**communist, Communist** /'kɒmjʊnɪst/ **1** *n.* Kommunist, *der*/Kommunistin, *die.* **2** *adj.* kommunistisch; **the C~ Party/Manifesto** die Kommunistische Partei/das Kommunistische Manifest; **~-led/-dominated** von Kommunisten angeführt/beherrscht

**communistic** /kɒmjʊ'nɪstɪk/ *adj.* kommunistisch

**community** /kə'mju:nɪtɪ/ *n.* **A** (*organized body*) Gemeinwesen, *das;* **B** (*persons living in same place, having common religion, etc.*) **the Jewish ~:** die jüdische Gemeinde; **a ~ of monks** eine Mönchsgemeinde; **C** *no pl.* (*public*) Öffentlichkeit, *die;* **the ~ at large** die breite Öffentlichkeit; **D** (*body of nations*) Gemeinschaft, *die;* **the ~ of nations** die Völkergemeinschaft; **E** *no pl.* (*sharedness*) Gemeinschaft, *die;* **a sense of ~:** ein Gemeinschaftsgefühl

**community: ~ 'care** *n., no pl.* ≈ ambulante Betreuung; **~ centre** *n.* Gemeindezentrum, *das;* Kulturhaus, *das;* **~ 'charge** *n.* (*Brit.*) Gemeindesteuer, *die;* **~ chest** *n.* (*Amer.*) Sozialfonds, *der* (*einer Gemeinde*); **~ council** *n.* (*Brit.*) Gemeinderat, *der;* **~ home** *n.* (*Brit.*) Jugendhof, *der;* **~ 'medicine** *n.* Sozialhygiene, *die;* **~ re'lations** *n. pl.* Verhältnis zwischen den Bevölkerungsgruppen; **~ 'service** *n.* [*freiwilliger od. als Strafe auferlegter*] *sozialer Dienst;* **~ singing** *n.* gemeinsames Singen; **~ spirit** *n.* Gemeinschaftsgeist, *der*

**commutable** /kə'mju:təbl/ *adj.* **A** (*interchangeable*) austauschbar; **B** (*convertible*) umwandelbar

**commutation** /kɒmjʊ'teɪʃn/ *n.* **A** (*of punishment*) Umwandlung, *die;* **B** (*Electr.*) Kommutierung, *die*

**commu'tation ticket** *n.* (*Amer.*) Zeitkarte, *die*

**commutator** /'kɒmjʊteɪtə(r)/ *n.* (*Electr.*) Kommutator, *der;* Stromwender, *der*

**commute** /kə'mju:t/ **1** *v.t.* **A** (*change to sth. milder*) umwandeln ‹Strafe› (**to** in + *Akk.*); **B** (*change to sth. different*) umwandeln; **C** (*interchange*) austauschen ‹Dinge, Begriffe›; **D** (*make payment*) ablösen ‹Verpflichtung, Schulden› (**for, into** durch). **2** *v.i.* **A** (*travel daily*) pendeln; **B** (*Amer.: hold season ticket*) eine Zeitkarte haben

**commuter** /kə'mju:tə(r)/ *n.* Pendler, *der*/Pendlerin, *die*

**com'muter: ~ belt** *n.* großstädtischer Einzugsbereich; **~ train** *n.* Pendlerzug, *der*

**compact**[1] /kəm'pækt/ **1** *adj.* kompakt; komprimiert ‹Stil, Sprache›. **2** *v.t.* **A** (*put firmly together*) zusammenpressen; **B** (*fig.: condense*) zusammenfügen (**into** zu)

**compact**[2] /'kɒmpækt/ *n.* **A** Puderdose [mit Puder(stein)]; **B** (*Amer.: car*) Kompaktauto, *das;* Kompaktwagen, *der*

**compact**[3] *n.* (*agreement*) Vertrag, *der;* **a ~ with the devil** ein Pakt mit dem Teufel

**compact 'disc** *n.* Compactdisc, *die;* Kompaktschallplatte, *die;* **~ player** CD-Spieler, *der*

**compactly** /kəm'pæktlɪ/ *adv.* kompakt; komprimiert ‹ausgedrückt›

**compactness** /kəm'pæktnɪs/ *n., no pl.* Kompaktheit, *die*

**companion**[1] /kəm'pænjən/ *n.* **A** (*one accompanying*) Begleiter, *der*/Begleiterin, *die;* **my travelling ~s** meine Reisebegleiter; **B** (*associate*) Kamerad, *der*/Kameradin, *die;* Gefährte, *der*/Gefährtin, *die* (*geh.*); Genosse, *der*/Genossin, *die* (*veralt.*); **the ~s of his youth** seine Jugendgefährten; **his drinking ~s** seine Zechgenossen (*veralt.*) *od.* (*ugs.*) -brüder; **~ in arms** Kampfgefährte, *der;* **C** (*Brit.: of* [*knightly*] *order*) *unterste Stufe verschiedener* [*Ritter*]*orden, z. B.* **C~ of the Bath,** (*nicht ritterlich*) **C~ of Honour/Literature; D** (*woman living with another*) Gesellschafterin, *die;* **E** (*handbook*) Ratgeber, *der;* **Gardener's C~:** Ratgeber für den Gartenfreund; **C~ to Music/the Theatre** Musik-/Theaterführer, *der;* **F** (*matching thing*) Gegenstück, *das;* Pendant, *das; attrib.;* **the ~ volume to ...:** der Begleitband zu ...; **G** (*Astron.*) Begleiter, *der*

**companion**[2] *n.* (*Naut.*) **A** Kajütskappe, *die;* **B** (*stairs*) ⇒ **companionway**

**companionable** /kəm'pænjənəbl/ *adj.* freundlich

**companion: ~ hatch** *n.* (*Naut.*) Luke, *die;* Luk, *das* (*fachspr.*); **~ ladder** *n.* (*Naut.*) Niedergang, *der;* **~ set** *n.* Kaminbesteck, *das*

**companionship** /kəm'pænjənʃɪp/ *n.* Gesellschaft, *die;* (*fellowship*) Kameradschaft, *die;* Freundschaft, *die*

**com'panionway** *n.* (*Naut.*) Niedergang, *der*

**company** /'kʌmpənɪ/ *n.* **A** (*persons assembled, companionship*) Gesellschaft, *die;* **expect/receive ~:** Besuch *od.* Gäste *Pl.* erwarten/empfangen; **for ~:** zur Gesellschaft; **two is ~, three is a crowd** zu zweit ist es gemütlich, ein Dritter stört; **keep one's own ~:** für sich bleiben; **he likes his own ~:** er ist gern für sich; **in ~ with sb.** in jmds. Gesellschaft (*Dat.*); **be in ~:** in Gesellschaft sein; **bear** *or* **keep sb. ~:** jmdm. Gesellschaft leisten; **keep ~ with sb.** mit jmdm. verkehren; **part ~ with sb./sth.** sich von jmdm./etw. trennen; **B** (*companion*[*s*]) **low ~:** schlechte Gesellschaft; **the ~ he keeps** sein Umgang; seine Gesellschaft; **be good/bad** *etc.* **~:** ein guter/schlechter Gesellschafter sein; **C** (*firm*) Gesellschaft, *die;* Firma, *die; attrib.* **~ car** Firmenwagen, *der;* **~ policy** Unternehmenspolitik, *die;* Firmenpolitik, *die;* **D** (*Commerc.*) **Jones and C~:** Jones & Co.; **E** (*of actors*) Truppe, *die;* Ensemble, *das;* **F** (*of Guides*) Trupp, *der;* **G** (*Mil.*) Kompanie, *die;* **~ sergeant major** Kompaniefeldwebel, *der;* **H** (*Navy*) **ship's ~:** Besatzung, *die*

**comparability** /kɒmpərə'bɪlɪtɪ/ *n., no pl.* Vergleichbarkeit, *die*

**comparable** /'kɒmpərəbl/ *adj.* vergleichbar (**to, with** mit)

**comparably** /'kɒmpərəblɪ/ *adv.* in vergleichbarer Weise; vergleichbar

**comparative** /kəm'pærətɪv/ **1** *adj.* **A** vergleichend ‹Anatomie, Sprachwissenschaft usw.›; **~ religion** vergleichende Religionswissenschaft; **B** (*estimated by comparison*) **the ~ merits/advantages of the proposals** die Vorzüge/Vorteile der Vorschläge im Vergleich; **C** (*relative*) relativ; **in ~ comfort** relativ *od.* verhältnismäßig komfortabel; **with ~ ease** relativ *od.* verhältnismäßig leicht; **D** (*Ling.*) komparativ (*fachspr.*); **the ~ degree** der Komparativ; die erste Steigerungsstufe; **a ~ adjective/adverb** ein Adjektiv/Adverb im Komparativ; ≈ ein gesteigertes Adjektiv/Adverb.

**2** *n.* (*Ling.*) Komparativ, *der;* erste Steigerungsstufe

**comparatively** /kəm'pærətɪvlɪ/ *adv.* **A** (*by means of comparison*) vergleichend; im Vergleich; **B** (*relatively*) relativ; verhältnismäßig

**compare** /kəm'peə(r)/ **1** *v.t.* **A** vergleichen (**to, with** mit); **~ two/three** *etc.* **things** zwei/drei *usw.* Dinge [miteinander] vergleichen; **~d with** *or* **to sb./sth.** verglichen mit *od.* im Vergleich zu jmdm./etw.; **X is not to be ~d to Y** X lässt sich nicht mit Y vergleichen; **~ notes about sth.** Erfahrungen über etw. (*Akk.*) austauschen; **B** (*Ling.*) steigern; komparieren (*fachspr.*). **2** *v.i.* sich vergleichen lassen. **3** *n.* (*literary*) **beyond** *or* **without ~:** unvergleichlich; **lovely beyond ~:** unvergleichlich *od.* einmalig reizvoll

**comparison** /kəm'pærɪsn/ *n.* **A** (*act of comparing, simile*) Vergleich, *der;* **the ~ of X and** *or* **with Y** ein Vergleich von *od.* zwischen X und Y; **in** *or* **by ~ [with sb./sth.]** im Vergleich [zu jmdm./etw.]; **this one is cheaper in** *or* **by ~:** dieser ist vergleichsweise billiger; **beyond [all] ~:** über jeden Vergleich erhaben; **there's no ~ between them** man kann sie einfach nicht vergleichen; **bear** *or* **stand ~:** einem Vergleich standhalten; **~s are odious** Vergleiche sind immer ungerecht; **B** (*Ling.*) Steigerung, *die;* **degrees of ~:** Steigerungsstufen

**compartment** /kəm'pɑ:tmənt/ *n.* (*in drawer, desk, etc.*) Fach, *das;* (*fig.*) Schubfach, *das;* (*of railway carriage*) Abteil, *das;* (*Naut.*) Abteilung, *die*

**compartmentalize** /kɒmpɑ:t'mentəlaɪz/ *v.t.* aufgliedern; (*excessively*) aufsplittern

**compass** /'kʌmpəs/ **1** *n.* **A** *in pl.* **[a pair of] ~es** ein Zirkel; **B** ▶ 1024 (*for navigating*) Kompass, *der;* **mariner's ~:** Magnetkompass, *der;* **the four points of the ~:** die vier Himmelsrichtungen; **C** (*boundary*) Umkreis, *der;* **D** (*extent*) Gebiet, *das;* (*fig.: scope*) Rahmen, *der;* **beyond the ~ of the human mind** jenseits des menschlichen Fassungsvermögens; **in a small ~:** im kleinen Rahmen; **E** (*Mus.*) (*of instrument*) Tonraum, *der;* (*of voice*) Umfang, *der.* **2** *v.t.* (*grasp mentally*) erfassen

**'compass card** *n.* Kompass-, Windrose, *die*

**compassion** /kəm'pæʃn/ *n., no pl.* Mitgefühl, *das* (**for, on** mit)

**compassionate** /kəm'pæʃənət/ *adj.* mitfühlend; **on ~ grounds** aus persönlichen Gründen; (*for family reasons*) aus familiären Gründen

**compassionate 'leave** *n.* (*Brit.*) Sonderurlaub aus familiären Gründen

**compatibility** /kəmpætɪ'bɪlɪtɪ/ *n., no pl.* (*consistency, mutual tolerance*) Vereinbarkeit, *die;* (*of people*) Zueinanderpassen, *das;* (*of equipment etc.*) Aufeinander-Abgestimmtsein, *das;* Zueinanderpassen, *das;* (*Computing*) Kompatibilität, *die;* (*of drugs*) Verträglichkeit, *die*

**compatible** /kəm'pætɪbl/ *adj.* (*consistent, mutually tolerant*) vereinbar; zueinander passend ‹Personen›; aufeinander abgestimmt, zueinander passend, (*Computing*) kompatibel ‹Geräte, Maschinen›; verträglich ‹Medikamente›

**compatriot** /kəm'pætrɪət, kəm'peɪtrɪət/ *n.* Landsmann, *der*/-männin, *die*

**compel** /kəm'pel/ *v.t.,* **-ll-** zwingen; **~ sb. to do sth.** jmdn. [dazu] zwingen, etw. zu tun; **~ sb.'s admiration/respect** jmdm. Bewunderung/Achtung abnötigen; **he felt ~led to tell her** er sah sich gezwungen *od.* genötigt, es ihr zu sagen

**compelling** /kəm'pelɪŋ/ *adj.* bezwingend

**compellingly** /kəm'pelɪŋlɪ/ *adv.* mit bezwingender Überzeugungskraft/Logik

**compendious** /kəm'pendɪəs/ *adj.* kompendiarisch (*veralt.*); kurz gefasst, knapp ‹Buch, Aufzeichnungen›

**compendium** /kəm'pendɪəm/ *n., pl.* **~s** *or* **compendia** /kəm'pendɪə/ Abriss, *der;* Kurzfassung, *die;* (*summary*) Kompendium, *das;* **~ of games** Spielemagazin, *das*

**compensate** /'kɒmpenseɪt/ **1** *v.i.* **A** (*make amends for*) **~ for sth.** etw. ersetzen; **~ for injury** *etc.* für Verletzung *usw.* Schaden[s]ersatz leisten; **B** (*Psych.*) **~ for sth.** etw. kompensieren. **2** *v.t.* **A** **~ sb. for sth.** jmdn. für etw. entschädigen; **B** (*Mech.*) ausgleichen ‹Pendel›

**compensation** /kɒmpen'seɪʃn/ *n.* **A** Ersatz, *der;* (*for damages, injuries, etc.*) Schaden[s]ersatz, *der;* (*for requisitioned property*) Entschädigung, *die;* Ausgleichszahlung, die; **£100 in ~** *or* **by way of ~:** 100 Pfund Schaden[s]ersatz; **but he had the ~ of knowing that ...:** aber er hatte die Genugtuung zu wissen, dass ...; **growing old has its ~s** das Altwerden hat auch seine guten Seiten; **B** (*Psych.*) Kompensation, *die*

**compère** /'kɒmpeə(r)/ (*Brit.*) **1** *n.* Conférencier, *der;* Showmaster, *der.* **2** *v.t.* konferieren ‹Show›

**compete** /kəm'pi:t/ *v.i.* konkurrieren (**for** um); (*Sport*) kämpfen; **~ with sb./sth.** mit jmdm./etw. konkurrieren; **he ~d against** *or* **with his rivals for the title** er kämpfte gegen seine *od.* mit seinen Rivalen um den Titel; **~ in a race** an einem Rennen teilnehmen; **be [un]able to ~:** [nicht] konkurrenzfähig sein; **~ with one another** miteinander wetteifern

**competence** /'kɒmpɪtəns/, **competency** /'kɒmpɪtənsɪ/ *ns.* **A** (*ability*) Fähigkeiten *Pl.;* **a high degree of ~ in French** sehr gute Französischkenntnisse; (*of native speaker*) hohe Sprachkompetenz im Französischen; **B** (*Law*) Zuständigkeit, *die;* **C** (*Ling.*) Kompetenz, *die*

**competent** /'kɒmpɪtənt/ *adj.* **A** (*qualified*) fähig; befähigt; **not ~ to do sth.** nicht kompetent, etw. zu tun; **B** (*effective*) angemessen, adäquat ‹Antwort, Kenntnisse›; **C** (*appropriate*) angemessen; geboten; **D** (*Law*) zuständig ‹Richter, Gericht›; zugelassen ‹Zeuge›; zulässig ‹Beweismaterial›

**competently** /'kɒmpɪtəntlɪ/ *adv.* sachkundig; kompetent

**competition** /kɒmpɪ'tɪʃn/ *n.* **A** (*contest*) Wettbewerb, *der;* (*in magazine etc.*) Preisausschreiben, *das;* **B** (*those competing*) Konkurrenz, *die;* (*Sport*) Gegner *Pl.;* **C** (*act of competing*) Konkurrenz, *die;* **a spirit of ~:** Konkurrenz- *od.* Wettbewerbsdenken, *das;* **be in ~ with sb.** mit jmdm. konkurrieren *od.* im Wettbewerb stehen

**competitive** /kəm'petɪtɪv/ *adj.* **A** Leistungs-; **~ sports** Wettkampf- *od.* Leistungssport, *der;* **~ spirit** Konkurrenz- *od.* Wettbewerbsdenken, *das;* **a ~ examination** eine Auswahlprüfung; **on a ~ basis** nach Leistung; **B** (*comparable with rivals*) leistungs-, wettbewerbsfähig ‹Preis, Unternehmen›; **a very ~ market** ein Markt mit starker Konkurrenz

**competitively** /kəm'petɪtɪvlɪ/ *adv.* **they were bidding ~:** sie boten um die Wette (*ugs.*); **these models are ~ priced** der Preis dieser Modelle ist wettbewerbs- *od.* konkurrenzfähig

**competitor** /kəm'petɪtə(r)/ *n.* Konkurrent, *der*/Konkurrentin, *die;* Mitbewerber, *der*/-bewerberin *die* (*fachspr.*); (*in contest, race*) Teilnehmer, *der*/-nehmerin, *die;* (*for job*) Mitbewerber, *der*/-bewerberin, *die;* **our ~s** unsere Konkurrenz

**compilation** /kɒmpɪ'leɪʃn/ *n.* Zusammenstellung, *die;* Kompilation, *die* (*geh.*); (*of dictionary, guidebook*) Verfassen, *das*

**compile** /kəm'paɪl/ *v.t.* **A** (*put together*) zusammenstellen; kompilieren (*geh.*); verfassen ‹Wörterbuch, Reiseführer›; **B** (*accumulate*) sammeln ‹Punkte›

**compiler** /kəm'paɪlə(r)/ *n.* **A** Verfasser, *der*/Verfasserin, *die;* Kompilator, *der*/Kompilatorin, *die* (*geh.*); **B** (*Computing*) Compiler, *der*

**complacency** /kəm'pleɪsənsɪ/ *n., no pl.* Selbstzufriedenheit, Selbstgefälligkeit, *die*

**complacent** /kəm'pleɪsənt/ *adj.* selbstzufrieden; selbstgefällig

**complain** /kəm'pleɪn/ *v.i.* (*express dissatisfaction*) sich beklagen *od.* beschweren (**about, at** über + *Akk.*); **~ of sth.** über etw. (*Akk.*) klagen; **his continual ~ing** sein ständiges Klagen; **she ~s of [having] toothache** sie klagt über Zahnschmerzen; **I have nothing to ~ about/of** ich habe keine Beanstandungen/ich kann nicht klagen

**complaint** /kəm'pleɪnt/ *n.* **A** (*utterance of grievance*) Beanstandung, *die;* Beschwerde, *die;* Klage, *die;* (*formal accusation, expression of grief*) Klage, *die;* **have/cause grounds for ~:** Grund zur Klage haben/Anlass zu Beschwerden geben; **B** ▶ 1232 (*bodily ailment*) Leiden, *das;* **a heart ~:** ein Herzleiden

C

# Points of the compass

| | COMPASS POINT | DIRECTION, AREA | ABBR | ADJECTIVE, ADVERB, PREPOSITION |
|---|---|---|---|---|
| ***north*** | Nord | Norden | N | nördlich |
| ***south*** | Süd | Süden | S | südlich |
| ***east*** | Ost | Osten | O | östlich |
| ***west*** | West | Westen | W | westlich |
| ***north-east*** | Nordost | Nordosten | NO | nordöstlich |
| ***north-west*** | Nordwest | Nordwesten | NW | nordwestlich |
| ***south-east*** | Südost | Südosten | SO | südöstlich |
| ***south-west*** | Südwest | Südwesten | SW | südwestlich |
| ***north-north-east*** | Nordnordost | Nordnordosten | NNO | nordnordöstlich |
| ***north-north-west*** | Nordnordwest | Nordnordwesten | NNW | nordnordwestlich |
| ***south-south-east*** | Südsüdost | Südsüdosten | SSO | südsüdöstlich |
| ***south-south-west*** | Südsüdwest | Südsüdwesten | SSW | südsüdwestlich |
| ***east-north-east*** | Ostnordost | Ostnordosten | ONO | ostnordöstlich |
| ***west-north-west*** | Westnordwest | Westnordwesten | WNW | westnordwestlich |
| ***east-south-east*** | Ostsüdost | Ostsüdosten | OSO | ostsüdöstlich |
| ***west-south-west*** | Westsüdwest | Westsüdwesten | WSW | westsüdwestlich |

The forms **Nord**, **Süd**, **Ost** and **West** and their derivatives have no gender (except in the nautical sense of a wind) and exist mainly as labels for the points of the compass. They are also used in nautical and meteorological contexts, without an article. The more commonly used forms are **Norden**, **Süden**, **Osten** and **Westen** and their combinations, which are masculine and can be used with the article, indicating either a direction or an area.

## Directions

***The wind is from the north/the north-east***
= Der Wind kommt von Norden/Nordosten *or* (*Meteorol.*, *Naut.*) von Nord/Nordost

***We are going north tomorrow***
= Wir fahren morgen nach Norden

***They were travelling westwards*** or ***in a westerly direction***
= Sie fuhren in Richtung Westen *or* in westliche Richtung

***The road runs due north***
= Die Straße führt genau nach Norden

***the northbound train***
= der Zug in Richtung Norden

***The aircraft/ship is southward bound***
= Das Flugzeug fliegt/Das Schiff fährt nach Süden

***The sitting room faces north***
= Das Wohnzimmer geht nach Norden

## Locations

***the South of England***
= der Süden Englands *or* von England, Südengland

***the Deep South***
= der tiefe Süden

***the far North***
= der hohe Norden

***the Middle/Far East***
= der Nahe/Ferne Osten

***They live in the South-West***
= Sie wohnen im Südwesten

***She comes from the North-East***
= Sie stammt aus dem Nordosten

***It's a few miles to the west***
= Es liegt ein paar Meilen westlich *or* nach Westen

***further [to the] east***
= weiter östlich *or* nach Osten

***25 miles [to the] north of London***
= 40 Kilometer nördlich von London

***just to the south of the island/of Crete***
= etwas südlich der Insel/von Kreta

The terms **nördlich**, **südlich** etc. operate in combination with **von** + dative or as prepositions with the genitive in the sense [*to the*] *north of*, *south of* etc. The use with the genitive is more common where there is an article, i.e. with nouns rather than place names.

## Adjectives

The English adjectives *north/northern*, *south/southern* etc. are frequently translated by the combining forms **Nord-**, **Süd-** etc. rather than the adjectives **nördlich**, **südlich** etc. This is especially the case with countries and other geographical names:

***Northern/Southern Italy***
= Norditalien/Süditalien

***the Southern States***
= die Südstaaten

***North/South America***
= Nordamerika/Südamerika

***the West Coast***
= die Westküste

***West/East Africa***
= Westafrika/Ostafrika

***the north face of the Eiger***
= die Eigernordwand

***the south side***
= die Südseite

**nördlich**, **südlich** etc. are generally used for less specific terms, as is illustrated by the difference between

***South Africa***
= Südafrika

***southern Africa***
= das südliche Afrika

***the north wind***
= der Nordwind

***northerly winds***
= nördliche Winde, Winde aus nördlichen Richtungen

However it would be a mistake to think that the German adjectives are straightforward equivalents for the English northern, southern etc. Consider for instance:

***East*** or ***Eastern Germany***
= Ostdeutschland

***West*** or ***Western Germany***
= Westdeutschland

Cf. also:

***a southern climate***
= ein südliches Klima

***the easternmost*** or ***most easterly point***
= der östlichste Punkt

***Western journalists***
= westliche Journalisten

***the Western countries***
= die westlichen Länder

But:

***the Western Powers***
= die Westmächte

***the Eastern Bloc***
= der Ostblock

**complaisance** /kəm'pleɪzəns/ *n., no pl. (formal)* Entgegenkommen, *das; (deference)* Respekt, *der*

**complaisant** /kəm'pleɪzənt/ *adj. (formal)* entgegenkommend

**complement** ❶ /'kɒmplɪmənt/ *n.* Ⓐ *(what completes)* Vervollständigung, *die;* Komplement, *das (geh.);* Ⓑ *(full number)* **a [full] ~:** die volle Zahl; *(of people)* die volle Stärke; **the ship's ~:** die volle Schiffsbesatzung; Ⓒ *(Ling.)* Ergänzung, *die.* ❷ /'kɒmplɪment/ *v.t.* ergänzen

**complementary** /kɒmplɪ'mentərɪ/ Ⓐ *(completing)* ergänzend; Ⓑ *(completing each other)* einander ergänzend; **they are ~ to one another** sie ergänzen einander

**complementary: ~ 'colour** *n.* Komplementärfarbe, *die;* **~ 'medicine** *n.* Komplementärmedizin, *die*

**complete** /kəm'pli:t/ ❶ *adj.* Ⓐ vollständig; *(in number)* vollzählig; komplett; **a ~ edition** eine Gesamtausgabe; **the ~ works of Schiller** Schillers sämtliche Werke; **make a ~ confession** ein umfassendes Geständnis ablegen; **a house ~ with contents** ein Haus mit allem Inventar; Ⓑ *(finished)* fertig; abgeschlossen ‹Arbeit›; fertig gestellt ‹Gebäude, Bauwerk›; Ⓒ *(absolute)* völlig; total, komplett ‹Idiot, Reinfall, Ignoranz›; absolut ‹Chaos, Katastrophe›; vollkommen ‹Ruhe›; total, *(ugs.)* blutig ‹Anfänger, Amateur›; **a ~ stranger** ein völlig Fremder; **meet with ~ approval** uneingeschränkte Zustimmung finden; Ⓓ *(accomplished)* perfekt ‹Sportler, Reiter, Gentleman usw.›.
❷ *v.t.* Ⓐ *(finish)* beenden; fertig stellen ‹Gebäude, Arbeit›; abschließen ‹Vertrag›; Ⓑ *(make whole)* vervollkommnen, vollkommen machen ‹Glück›; vervollständigen, *(geh.)* komplettieren ‹Sammlung›; Ⓒ *(make whole amount of)* vollzählig machen; voll machen *(ugs.);* Ⓓ ausfüllen ‹Fragebogen, Formular›

**completely** /kəm'pli:tlɪ/ *adv.* völlig; absolut ‹erfolgreich›

**completeness** /kəm'pli:tnɪs/ *n., no pl.* Vollständigkeit, *die; (in numbers)* Vollzähligkeit, *die*

**completion** /kəm'pli:ʃn/ *n.* Beendigung, *die; (of building, work)* Fertigstellung, *die; (of contract)* Abschluss, *der; (of questionnaire, form)* Ausfüllen, *das;* **on ~ of the course** nach Abschluss des Kurses; **on ~ of all the formalities** nach Erledigung aller Formalitäten; **on ~ of the sale** bei Kaufabschluss

**com'pletion date** *n.* Datum der Fertigstellung/des Vertragsabschlusses

**complex** /'kɒmpleks/ ❶ *adj.* Ⓐ *(complicated)* kompliziert; Ⓑ *(composite)* komplex; Ⓒ *(Ling.)* **a ~ sentence** ein Satzgefüge; Ⓓ *(Chem., Math.)* komplex. ❷ *n. (also Psych.)* Komplex, *der;* **a [building] ~:** ein Gebäudekomplex; **have a ~ about sth.** *(coll.)* Komplexe wegen etw. haben

**complexion** /kəm'plekʃn/ *n.* Gesichtsfarbe, *die;* Teint, *der; (fig.)* Gesicht, *das;* **of various political ~s** verschiedener politischer Richtungen; **that puts a different ~ on the matter** dadurch sieht die Sache schon anders aus

**-complexioned** /kəm'plekʃnd/ *adj. in comb.* **sallow-/fair-~:** mit gelblichem Teint/mit hellem Teint

**complexity** /kəm'pleksɪtɪ/ *n.* ⇨ **complex** 1: Komplexität, *die;* Kompliziertheit, *die*

**compliance** /kəm'plaɪəns/ *n.* Ⓐ *(action)* Zustimmung, *die* **(with** zu); **act in ~ with sth.** gemäß etw. handeln; Ⓑ *(unworthy submission)* Unterwürfigkeit, *die;* Willfährigkeit, *die (geh.)*

**compliant** /kəm'plaɪənt/ *adj.* unterwürfig; willfährig *(geh.)*

**complicate** /'kɒmplɪkeɪt/ *v.t.* komplizieren; verkomplizieren

**complicated** /'kɒmplɪkeɪtɪd/ *adj.* kompliziert

**complication** /kɒmplɪ'keɪʃn/ *n.* Ⓐ Kompliziertheit, *die;* Ⓑ *(circumstance; also Med.)* Komplikation, *die*

**complicity** /kəm'plɪsɪtɪ/ *n.* Mittäterschaft, *die;* Komplizenschaft, *die* **(in** bei)

**compliment** ❶ /'kɒmplɪmənt/ *n.* Ⓐ *(polite words)* Kompliment, *das;* **pay sb. a ~ [on sth.]** jmdm. [wegen etw.] ein Kompliment machen; **return the ~:** das Kompliment erwidern; *(fig.)* zurückschlagen; **my ~s to the chef** mein Kompliment dem Küchenchef; Ⓑ *in pl. (formal greetings)* Grüße *Pl.;* Empfehlung, *die;* **my ~s to your parents** eine Empfehlung an Ihre Eltern *(geh.);* **give them my ~s** bitte empfehlen Sie mich ihnen *(geh.);* bitte grüßen Sie sie von mir; **the ~s of the season** Grüße zum Fest; **with the ~s of the management/author** mit den besten Empfehlungen, die Geschäftsleitung/der Verfasser.
❷ /'kɒmplɪment/ *v.t. (say polite words to)* **~ sb. on sth.** jmdm. Komplimente wegen etw. machen

**complimentary** /kɒmplɪ'mentərɪ/ *adj.* Ⓐ *(expressing compliment)* schmeichelhaft; Ⓑ *(given free as compliment)* Frei-; **a ~ ticket/copy** eine Freikarte/ein Freiexemplar

**compline** /'kɒmplɪn, 'kɒmplaɪn/ *n. (Eccl.)* Komplet, *die*

**comply** /kəm'plaɪ/ *v.i.* **~ with sth.** sich nach etw. richten; **~ with a treaty/conditions** einen Vertrag/Bedingungen erfüllen; **he refused to ~:** er wollte sich nicht danach richten

**component** /kəm'pəʊnənt/ ❶ *n.* Ⓐ Bestandteil, *der; (of machine)* [Einzel]teil, *das; (in manufacturing)* Teilfabrikat, *das;* Ⓑ *(Math.)* Komponente, *die.* ❷ *adj.* **a ~ part** ein Bestandteil; **the ~ parts of a car** die [Einzel]teile eines Wagens

**comport** /kəm'pɔ:t/ *v. refl. (formal)* sich verhalten

**compose** /kəm'pəʊz/ *v.t.* Ⓐ *(make up)* bilden; **be ~d of** sich zusammensetzen aus; Ⓑ *(construct)* verfassen ‹Rede, Gedicht, Liedertext, Libretto›; abfassen, aufsetzen ‹Brief›; Ⓒ *(Mus.)* komponieren; Ⓓ *(Printing)* setzen; Ⓔ *(arrange)* in Ordnung bringen ‹Aussehen, Kleider usw.›; **~ oneself to** *or* **for an action** sich auf eine Handlung konzentrieren; **~ one's thoughts** Ordnung in seine Gedanken bringen; Ⓕ *(calm)* **~ oneself** sich zusammennehmen; Ⓖ *(put together)* anordnen, arrangieren ‹Blumen, Sträucher usw.›

**composed** /kəm'pəʊzd/ *adj. (calm)* gefasst

**composer** /kəm'pəʊzə(r)/ *n.* Ⓐ ▶ **1261** *(of music)* Komponist, *der*/Komponistin, *die;* Ⓑ *(of poem etc.)* Verfasser, *der*/Verfasserin, *die*

**composite** /'kɒmpəzɪt/ ❶ *adj.* Ⓐ zusammengesetzt; **a ~ illustration/photograph** eine Bild-/Fotomontage; Ⓑ *(Bot.)* **~ flower/plant** Korbblütler, *der;* Komposite, *die (fachspr.).* ❷ *n.* Ⓐ Gemisch, *das;* Komposition, *die (geh.);* Ⓑ *(Bot.)* Korbblütler, *der;* Komposite, *die (fachspr.)*

**composition** /kɒmpə'zɪʃn/ *n.* Ⓐ *(act)* Zusammenstellung, *die; (construction)* Herstellung, *die; (formation of words)* Wortbildung, *die;* Komposition, *die (fachspr.);* Ⓑ *(constitution) (of soil, etc.)* Zusammensetzung, *die; (mental constitution)* Wesen, *das; (of picture)* Aufbau, *der;* Ⓒ *(composed thing) (mixture)* Gemisch, *das; (piece of writing)* Darstellung, *die; (essay)* Aufsatz, *der; (piece of music)* Komposition, *die;* Ⓓ *(construction in writing) (of sentences)* Konstruktion, *die; (of prose, verse)* Verfassen, *das; (literary production)* Schreiben, *das; (Mus.)* Komposition, *die;* Komponieren, *das; (art of ~)* Komposition, *die;* Kompositionslehre, *die;* Ⓔ *(Printing)* Setzen, *das;* Satz, *der;* Ⓕ *(formal: compromise)* Abmachung, *die; (with creditors etc.)* Vergleich, *der;* Akkord, *der; (sum paid to creditors)* Vergleichssumme, *die;* Ⓖ *(formal: of disagreement)* Beilegung, *die*

**composition 'floor** *n.* Estrich, *der*

**compositor** /kəm'pɒzɪtə(r)/ *n.* ▶ **1261** *(Printing)* Schriftsetzer, *der*/-setzerin, *die*

**compos mentis** /kɒmpɒs 'mentɪs/ *adj.* zurechnungsfähig; bei Trost *(ugs.)*

**compost** /'kɒmpɒst/ ❶ *n.* Kompost, *der; (fig.)* Nährboden, *der.* ❷ *v.t.* kompostieren

**compost: ~ heap, ~ pile** *ns.* Komposthaufen, *der*

**composure** /kəm'pəʊʒə(r)/ *n.* Gleichmut, *der;* **lose/regain one's ~:** die Fassung verlieren/wieder finden; **upset sb.'s ~:** jmdn. aus der Fassung bringen

**compote** /'kɒmpəʊt/ *n.* Kompott, *das*

**compound**[1] ❶ /'kɒmpaʊnd/ *adj.* Ⓐ *(of several ingredients)* zusammengesetzt; **a ~ substance** eine Verbindung; Ⓑ *(of several parts)* kombiniert; **a ~ word** ein zusammengesetztes Wort; eine Zusammensetzung; Ⓒ *(Zool.)* **~ eye** Facettenauge, *das;* Ⓓ *(Bot.)* zusammengesetzt; Ⓔ *(Med.)* **~ fracture** komplizierter Bruch; Ⓕ *(Ling.)* zusammengesetzt ‹Zeit›; **~ sentence** Satzreihe, *die.*
❷ *n.* Ⓐ *(mixture)* Mischung, *die;* Ⓑ *(Ling.)* Kompositum, *das;* Zusammensetzung, *die;* Ⓒ *(Chem.)* Verbindung, *die.*
❸ /kəm'paʊnd/ *v.t.* Ⓐ *(mix)* mischen ‹Bestandteile›; *(fig.)* vereinigen; *(combine)* zusammensetzen ‹Wort›; *(make up)* herstellen ‹Präparat›; **be ~ed of ...:** sich aus ... zusammensetzen; Ⓑ *(increase, complicate)* verschlimmern ‹Schwierigkeiten, Verletzung usw.›; Ⓒ *(formal: settle)* beilegen ‹Affäre, Meinungsverschiedenheit›; begleichen ‹Schulden›.
❹ *v.i. (formal)* **~ with sb. for sth.** sich mit jmdm. auf etw. *(Akk.)* einigen

**compound**[2] /'kɒmpaʊnd/ *n.* Ⓐ *(enclosed space)* umzäuntes Gebiet *od.* Gelände; **prison ~:** Gefängnishof, *der;* Ⓑ *(enclosure round building)* Grundstück, *das;* **embassy ~:** Botschaftsgelände, *das*

**compound interest** /kɒmpaʊnd 'ɪntrɪst/ *n. (Finance)* Zinseszinsen *Pl.;* Zinseszins, *der*

**comprehend** /kɒmprɪ'hend/ *v.t.* Ⓐ *(understand)* begreifen; verstehen; Ⓑ *(include, embrace)* umfassen

**comprehensibility** /kɒmprɪhensɪ'bɪlɪtɪ/ *n., no pl.* Fasslichkeit, *die;* Verständlichkeit, *die*

**comprehensible** /kɒmprɪ'hensɪbl/ *adj.* fassbar; verständlich; **~ only to specialists** nur Fachleuten *od.* für Fachleute verständlich

**comprehensibly** /kɒmprɪ'hensɪblɪ/ *adv.* verständlich

**comprehension** /kɒmprɪ'henʃn/ *n.* Ⓐ *(understanding)* Verständnis, *das;* **her behaviour is beyond my ~:** für ihr Benehmen habe ich kein Verständnis; Ⓑ **~ [exercise/test]** Übung zum Textverständnis

**comprehensive** /kɒmprɪ'hensɪv/ ❶ *adj.* Ⓐ *(inclusive)* umfassend; universal ‹Verstand›; allseitig, universal ‹Begriffsvermögen›; Ⓑ *(Sch.)* **~ school** Gesamtschule, *die;* **go ~** ‹Schule:› zur Gesamtschule [gemacht] werden; ‹Stadt:› die Gesamtschule einführen; Ⓒ *(Insurance)* Vollkasko-; **~ policy** Vollkaskoversicherung, *die;* **have you ~ insurance?** sind Sie vollkaskoversichert?. ❷ *n. (Sch.)* Gesamtschule, *die*

**comprehensively** /kɒmprɪ'hensɪvlɪ/ *adv.* umfassend; **~ beaten** deutlich geschlagen

**comprehensiveness** /kɒmprɪ'hensɪvnɪs/ *n., no pl.* Allseitigkeit, *die;* **the ~ of the book is surprising** das Buch ist überraschend umfassend

**compress** ❶ /kəm'pres/ *v.t.* Ⓐ *(squeeze)* zusammenpressen **(into** zu); Ⓑ komprimieren ‹Luft, Gas, Bericht›; Ⓒ *(Computing)* komprimieren. ❷ /'kɒmpres/ *n. (Med.)* Kompresse, *die*

**compressed air** /kəmprest 'eə(r)/ *adj.* Druck-, Pressluft, *die*

**compressible** /kəm'presɪbl/ *adj.* zusammendrückbar; *(Phys.)* kompressibel

**compression** /kəm'preʃn/ *n.* Kompression, *die;* Verdichtung, *die*

**compressor** /kəm'presə(r)/ *n.* Kompressor, *der;* Verdichter, *der*

**comprise** /kəm'praɪz/ *v.t. (include)* umfassen; *(not exclude)* einschließen; *(consist of)* bestehen aus; *(compose, make up)* bilden

**compromise** /'kɒmprəmaɪz/ ❶ *n.* Kompromiss, *der; attrib.* **~ decision/agreement** Kompromissentscheidung/-vereinbarung, *die.* ❷ *v.i.* Kompromisse/einen Kompromiss schließen; **~ with sb. over sth.** mit jmdm. einen Kompromiss in etw. *(Dat.)* schließen; **agree to ~:** einem Kompromiss zustimmen. ❸ *v.t. (bring under suspicion)* kompromittieren; *(bring into danger)* schaden (+ *Dat.*); ~

oneself sich kompromittieren; ~ **one's reputation** seinem Ruf schaden

**compromising** /ˈkɒmprəmaɪzɪŋ/ *adj.* kompromittierend

**comptroller** /kənˈtrəʊlə(r)/ *n.* ▶ 1261 Controller, *der; Mitarbeiter des betriebswirtschaftlichen Rechnungswesens*

**compulsion** /kəmˈpʌlʃn/ *n.* (*also Psych.*) Zwang, *der;* **be under no ~ to do sth.** keineswegs etw. tun müssen

**compulsive** /kəmˈpʌlsɪv/ *adj.* **A** (*also Psych.*) zwanghaft; pathologisch ‹Lügner›; **he is a ~ eater/gambler** er leidet unter Esszwang/er ist dem Spiel verfallen; **B** (*irresistible*) **this book is ~ reading/this TV programme is ~ viewing** von diesem Buch/dieser Fernsehsendung kann man sich nicht losreißen

**compulsively** /kəmˈpʌlsɪvlɪ/ *adv.* **do sth. ~:** etw. wie unter einem [inneren] Zwang tun

**compulsorily** /kəmˈpʌlsərɪlɪ/ *adv.* zwangsweise

**compulsory** /kəmˈpʌlsərɪ/ *adj.* obligatorisch; **be ~:** obligatorisch *od.* Pflicht sein; **a ~ subject** ein Pflichtfach; ~ **purchase** Enteignung, *die*

**compunction** /kəmˈpʌŋkʃn/ *n.* Schuldgefühle; Gewissensbisse *Pl.*

**computation** /kɒmpjʊˈteɪʃn/ *n.* Berechnung, *die;* **form of ~:** Rechenart, *die*

**compute** /kəmˈpjuːt/ **1** *v.t.* berechnen (**at** auf + *Akk.*). **2** *v.i.* **A** (*make reckoning*) rechnen; **B** (*use computer*) Computer/einen Computer benutzen

**computer** /kəmˈpjuːtə(r)/ *n.* Computer, *der*

**computer: ~-aided, ~-assisted** *adjs.* computergestützt; **~-aided design** computergestütztes Entwerfen; **~-aided engineering** computergestütztes Konstruieren; ~ **aniˈmation** *n.* Computeranimation, *die;* ~ **ˈarchitecture** *n.* Rechnerarchitektur, *die;* ~ **crime** *n.* **A** *no pl.* Computerkriminalität, *die;* **B** (*individual crime*) Computerdelikt, *das;* ~ **ˈdating** *n.* Partnervermittlung per Computer; *attrib.* ~ **dating agency/service** Computer-Partnervermittlung[sagentur], *die;* ~ **game** *n.* Computerspiel, *das;* ~ **ˈgraphics** *n. pl.* Computergrafik, *die*

**computerisation, computerise, computerised** ⇨ **computeriz-**

**computerization** /kəmpjuːtəraɪˈzeɪʃn/ *n.* Computerisierung, *die*

**computerize** /kəmˈpjuːtəraɪz/ *v.t.* computerisieren; auf Computer umstellen ‹Buchhaltung›

**computerized** /kəmˈpjuːtəraɪzd/ *adj.* computerisiert

**computerized toˈmography** /təˈmɒgrəfɪ/ *n.* (*Med.*) Computertomographie, *die*

**computer: ~-ˈliterate** *adj.* mit Computern vertraut; **~-ˈoperated** *adj.* computergesteuert; rechnergesteuert; ~ **ˈprocessing** *n.* elektronische Datenverarbeitung; ~ **program** *n.* Programm, *das;* ~ **programmer** *n.* ▶ 1261 Programmierer, *der*/Programmiererin, *die;* ~ **programming** *n.* Programmieren, *das;* ~ **room** *n.* Computerraum, *der;* ~ **ˈscience** *n.* Computerwissenschaft, *die;* ~ **terminal** *n.* Terminal, *das;* ~ **ˈtypesetting** *n.* Computersatz, *der;* ~ **virus** *n.* [Computer]virus, *das od. der*

**computing** /kəmˈpjuːtɪŋ/*n.* **A** EDV, *die;* elektronische Datenverarbeitung; **personal ~:** PC-Nutzung, *die;* **B** *attrib.* Computer-; ~ **skills** Computerkenntnisse *Pl.;* ~ **time** Rechenzeit, *die*

**comrade** /ˈkɒmreɪd/ *n.* **A** Kamerad, *der*/Kameradin, *die;* **~-in-arms** Kampfgefährte, *der;* Waffenbruder, *der* (*geh.*); **B** (*Polit.*) Genosse, *der*/Genossin, *die*

**comradely** /ˈkɒmreɪdlɪ, ˈkɒmrɪdlɪ/ *adj.* kameradschaftlich

**comradeship** /ˈkɒmreɪdʃɪp, ˈkɒmrɪdʃɪp/ *n., no pl.* Kameradschaft, *die;* **a spirit of ~:** Kameradschaftsgeist

**con**[1] /kɒn/ (*coll.*) **1** *n.* Schwindel, *der.* **2** *v.t.,* **-nn-: A** (*swindle*) reinlegen (*ugs.*); ~ **sb. out of sth.** jmdm. etw. abschwindeln *od.* (*ugs.*) abgaunern; **B** (*persuade*) beschwatzen (*ugs.*); ~ **sb. into sth.** jmdm. etw. aufschwatzen (*ugs.*); ~ **sb. into believing sth.** jmdm. etw. einreden

**con**[2] *n., adv., prep.* ⇨ **pro**[1]

**con**[3] *n.* (*coll.: convict*) Knacki, *der* (*salopp*)

**con**[4] *v.t.,* **-nn-** (*arch.: study*) sorgfältig durchlesen

**concatenation** /kənkætɪˈneɪʃn/ *n.* (*lit. or fig.*) Verkettung, *die*

**concave** /ˈkɒnkeɪv/ *adj.* konkav; ~ **mirror/lens** Konkav- *od.* Hohlspiegel, *der*/Konkavlinse, *die*

**concavity** /kɒnˈkævɪtɪ/ *n.* Konkavität, *die*

**conceal** /kənˈsiːl/ *v.t.* verbergen (**from** vor + *Dat.*); ~ **the true state of affairs from sb.** jmdm. den wirklichen Sachverhalt verheimlichen; ~ **vital facts** entscheidende Tatsachen unterschlagen

**concealed** /kənˈsiːld/ *adj.* verdeckt; ~ **lighting** indirekte Beleuchtung

**concealment** /kənˈsiːlmənt/ *n.* ⇨ **conceal**: Verbergen, *das;* Verheimlichung, *die;* Unterschlagung, *die;* **stay in ~:** sich versteckt halten

**concede** /kənˈsiːd/ *v.t.* (*admit, allow*) zugeben; (*grant*) zugestehen, einräumen ‹Recht, Privileg›; (*Sport*) abgeben ‹Punkte, Spiel› (**to** an + *Akk.*); zulassen ‹Tor›; in Kauf nehmen ‹Elfmeter›; ~ **[defeat]** (*in election etc.*) seine Niederlage eingestehen

**conceit** /kənˈsiːt/ *n.* **A** *no pl.* (*vanity*) Einbildung, *die;* **B** *in pl.* (*Lit.*) Konzetti *Pl.*

**conceited** /kənˈsiːtɪd/ *adj.* eingebildet

**conceitedly** /kənˈsiːtɪdlɪ/ *adv.* eingebildet

**conceitedness** /kənˈsiːtɪdnɪs/ *n.* Einbildung, *die*

**conceivable** /kənˈsiːvəbl/ *adj.* vorstellbar; **it's scarcely ~ that ...:** man kann sich (*Dat.*) kaum vorstellen, dass ...

**conceivably** /kənˈsiːvəblɪ/ *adv.* möglicherweise; **he cannot ~ have done it** er kann es unmöglich getan haben

**conceive** /kənˈsiːv/ **1** *v.t.* **A** empfangen ‹Kind›; **B** (*form in mind*) sich (*Dat.*) vorstellen *od.* denken; haben, kommen auf (+ *Akk.*) ‹Idee, Plan›; ~ **a dislike for sb./sth.** eine Abneigung gegen jmdn./etw. entwickeln; ~ **a liking for sb./sth.** Zuneigung zu jmdm./etw. fassen; **when the idea was first ~d** als man erstmals auf die Idee kam; **C** (*think*) meinen; glauben; **D** (*express*) fassen; ausdrücken. **2** *v.i.* **A** (*become pregnant*) empfangen; **B** ~ **of sth.** sich (*Dat.*) etw. vorstellen

**concentrate** /ˈkɒnsəntreɪt/ **1** *v.t.* konzentrieren, zusammenziehen ‹Truppen, Flotte›; zusammendrängen ‹Wissen, Informationen›; ~ **one's efforts/energies [up]on sth.** seine Bemühungen/Energien auf etw. (*Akk.*) konzentrieren; ~ **one's mind on sth.** sich auf etw. (*Akk.*) konzentrieren; ~ **the mind** jmds. Gedanken ausschließlich beschäftigen. **2** *v.i.* sich konzentrieren (**on** auf + *Akk.*); ~ **on doing sth.** sich darauf konzentrieren, etw. zu tun. **3** *n.* Konzentrat, *das;* (*animal food*) Kraftfutter, *das*

**concentrated** /ˈkɒnsəntreɪtɪd/ *adj.* konzentriert; geballt ‹Hass, Eifersucht›

**concentration** /kɒnsənˈtreɪʃn/ *n.* **A** (*also Chem.*) Konzentration, *die;* **power[s] of ~:** Konzentrationsfähigkeit, *die;* Konzentrationsvermögen, *das;* **lose one's ~:** sich nicht mehr konzentrieren können; **B** (*people brought together*) Ansammlung, *die;* (*of troops etc.*) Konzentration, *die*

**concenˈtration camp** *n.* Konzentrationslager, *das;* KZ, *das*

**concentric** /kənˈsentrɪk/ *adj.* konzentrisch; **the circles were ~ with each other** die Kreise hatten einen gemeinsamen Mittelpunkt

**concept** /ˈkɒnsept/ *n.* **A** (*notion*) Begriff, *der;* (*idea*) Vorstellung, *die;* **B** (*invention*) Idee, *die;* Konzept, *das;* **a new ~ in make-up** eine neue Make-up-Idee; ein neues Make-up-Konzept

**conception** /kənˈsepʃn/ *n.* **A** (*idea*) Vorstellung, *die* (**of** von); **I had no ~ of how ...:** ich hatte keine Vorstellung, wie ...; **the original ~ of a picture** die ursprüngliche Konzeption eines Bildes; **B** (*conceiving*) **great powers of ~:** ein großes Vorstellungsvermögen; **C** (*of child*) Empfängnis, *die*

**conceptual** /kənˈseptjʊəl/ *adj.* begrifflich

**conceptualize** /kənˈseptjʊəlaɪz/ *v.t.* begrifflich fassen

**conceptually** /kənˈseptjʊəlɪ/ *adv.* begrifflich; **the plan is ~ good** in der Vorstellung *od.* als Idee ist der Plan gut

**concern** /kənˈsɜːn/ **1** *v.t.* **A** (*affect*) betreffen; **as ~s ..., so far as ... is ~ed** was ... betrifft; **all that ~s us is whether ...:** uns hat nur zu interessieren, ob ...; **'to whom it may ~'** ≈ „Bestätigung"; (*on certificate, testimonial*) ≈ „Zeugnis"; **B** (*interest*) ~ **oneself with** *or* **about sth.** sich mit etw. befassen; **she does not ~ herself with politics** sie kümmert sich nicht um Politik; **C** (*trouble*) **the news/her health greatly ~s me** ich bin über diese Nachricht tief beunruhigt/ihre Gesundheit bereitet mir große Sorgen.

**2** *n.* **A** (*relation*) **have no ~ with sth.** mit etw. nichts zu tun haben; **have a ~ in sth.** an etw. (*Dat.*) beteiligt sein *od.* einen Anteil haben; **B** (*anxiety*) Besorgnis, *die;* (*interest*) Interesse, *das;* **a matter of general ~:** eine Sache, die alle beunruhigt/eine Sache von allgemeinem Interesse; **an expression of ~ on one's face** ein besorgter Gesichtsausdruck; **express ~:** Sorge ausdrücken; **C** (*matter*) Angelegenheit, *die;* **that's no ~ of mine** das geht mich nichts an; **it's his ~:** das ist seine Sache *od.* seine Angelegenheit; **D** (*firm*) Unternehmen, *das;* ⇨ *also* **going** 2 E

**concerned** /kənˈsɜːnd/ *adj.* **A** (*involved*) betroffen; (*interested*) interessiert; **the people ~:** die Betroffenen; **the firms/countries ~:** die betroffenen Firmen/Länder; **we are not ~ with it** damit haben wir nichts zu tun; **where work/health** *etc.* **is ~:** wenn es um die Arbeit/die Gesundheit *usw.* geht; **as** *or* **so far as I'm ~:** was mich betrifft *od.* anbelangt; **not as far as I'm ~:** von mir aus nicht; **B** (*implicated*) verwickelt (**in** in + *Akk.*); **C** (*troubled*) besorgt; **I am ~ to hear/learn that ...:** ich höre/erfahre mit Sorge, dass ...; **I was ~ at the news** die Nachricht beunruhigte mich; **I am very ~ for** *or* **about him/his health** er/seine Gesundheit macht mir Sorgen

**concerning** /kənˈsɜːnɪŋ/ *prep.* bezüglich

**concernment** /kənˈsɜːnmənt/ *n.* (*formal*) **A** Beteiligung, *die;* **B** (*anxiety*) Sorge, *die*

**concert 1** /ˈkɒnsət/ *n.* **A** (*of music*) Konzert, *das;* **B** (*agreement, union*) Übereinkunft, *die;* **work in ~ with sb.** mit jmdm. zusammenarbeiten; **C** (*combined sounds*) Chor, *der;* Konzert, *das;* **in ~:** im Chor. **2** /kənˈsɜːt/ *v.t.* abstimmen ‹Maßnahmen, Pläne›

**concerted** /kənˈsɜːtɪd/ *adj.* vereint; gemeinsam; ~ **action** eine konzertierte Aktion; **make a ~ effort** mit vereinten Kräften vorgehen

**concert: ~-goer** *n.* Konzertbesucher, *der*/-besucherin, *die;* ~ **ˈgrand** *n.* Konzertflügel, *der;* ~ **hall** *n.* Konzertsaal, *der;* (*building*) Konzerthalle, *die*

**concertina** /kɒnsəˈtiːnə/ **1** *n.* (*Mus.*) Konzertina, *die.* **2** *v.i.* [wie eine Ziehharmonika] zusammengeschoben werden

**ˈconcertmaster** *n.* (*esp. Amer.*) Konzertmeister, *der*

**concerto** /kənˈtʃɜːtəʊ, kənˈtʃeətəʊ/ *n., pl.* **~s** *or* **concerti** /kənˈtʃeətiː/ (*Mus.*) Konzert, *das*

**concert: ~ overture** *n.* (*Mus.*) Konzertouvertüre, *die;* ~ **pianist** *n.* Konzertpianist, *der*/-pianistin, *die;* ~ **pitch** *n.* Kammerton, *der*

**concession** /kənˈseʃn/ *n.* Konzession, *die;* (*act of conceding, yielding*) Zugeständnis, *das*

**concessionaire** /kənseʃəˈneə(r)/ *n.* Konzessionär, *der*/Konzessionärin, *die*

**concessionary** /kənˈseʃənərɪ/ *adj.* Konzessions-; ~ **rate/fare** ermäßigter Tarif

**concessionnaire** ⇨ **concessionaire**

**concessive** /kən'sesɪv/ *adj.* (*Ling.*) konzessiv; einräumend; **a ~ clause** ein Konzessiv- *od.* Einräumungssatz

**conch** /kɒntʃ, kɒŋk/ *n.* (*Zool.*) Meeresschnecke, *die;* (*shell*) Gehäuse einer Meeresschnecke

**concierge** /'kɔ:nsɪeəʒ, 'kɒnsɪeəʒ/ *n.* Concierge, *der/die;* (*in hotel*) Empfangschef, *der*

**conciliate** /kən'sɪlɪeɪt/ ❶ *v.t.* Ⓐ (*reconcile*) in Einklang bringen ‹Gegensätze, Theorien›; Ⓑ (*pacify*) besänftigen; beschwichtigen ❷ *v.i.* vermitteln; (*in industrial dispute*) schlichten

**conciliation** /kənsɪlɪ'eɪʃn/ *n.* Ⓐ (*reconcilement*) Versöhnung, *die;* Ⓑ (*pacification*) Besänftigung, *die;* Beschwichtigung, *die;* Ⓒ (*in industrial relations*) Schlichtung, *die;* **~ board** Schlichtungsausschuss, *der*

**conciliator** /kən'sɪlɪeɪtə(r)/ *n.* Schlichter, *der*/Schlichterin, *die*

**conciliatory** /kən'sɪljətərɪ/ *adj.* versöhnlich; (*pacifying*) beschwichtigend; besänftigend

**concise** /kən'saɪs/ *adj.* kurz und prägnant; knapp, konzis ‹Stil›; **be ~** ‹Person:› sich knapp fassen; **a ~ dictionary** ein Handwörterbuch

**concisely** /kən'saɪslɪ/ *adv.* kurz und prägnant; knapp, konzis ‹schreiben›

**conciseness** /kən'saɪsnɪs/, **concision** /kən'sɪʒn/ *ns., no pl.* Kürze, *die;* Prägnanz, *die*

**conclave** /'kɒnkleɪv/ *n.* Ⓐ (*RC Ch.*) Konklave, *das;* Ⓑ (*private meeting*) Klausurtagung, *die*

**conclude** /kən'klu:d/ ❶ *v.t.* Ⓐ (*end*) beschließen; beenden; Ⓑ (*infer*) schließen; folgern; Ⓒ (*reach decision*) beschließen; **~ from the evidence that ...:** aufgrund des Beweismaterials zu dem Schluss kommen, dass ...; Ⓓ (*agree on*) schließen ‹Bündnis, Vertrag›. ❷ *v.i.* (*end*) schließen

**concluding** /kən'klu:dɪŋ/ *attrib. adj.* abschließend

**conclusion** /kən'klu:ʒn/ *n.* Ⓐ (*end*) Abschluss, *der;* **in ~:** zum Abschluss; Ⓑ (*result*) Ausgang, *der;* Ⓒ (*decision reached*) Beschluss, *der;* **come to a ~:** einen Beschluss fassen; Ⓓ (*inference*) Schluss, *der;* **draw** *or* **reach a ~:** zu einem Schluss kommen; Ⓔ (*Logic*) [Schluss]folgerung, *die;* Konklusion, *die* (*fachspr.*); Ⓕ (*agreement*) Abschluss, *der*

**conclusive** /kən'klu:sɪv/ *adj.* schlüssig

**conclusively** /kən'klu:sɪvlɪ/ *adv.* abschließend ‹regeln›; schlüssig ‹beweisen, belegen›; eindeutig ‹klären›

**conclusiveness** /kən'klu:sɪvnɪs/ *n., no pl.* Schlüssigkeit, *die*

**concoct** /kən'kɒkt/ *v.t.* zubereiten; zusammenbrauen ‹Trank›; (*fig.*) sich (*Dat.*) ausdenken ‹Geschichte›; aushecken ‹Komplott, Intrige usw.›; sich (*Dat.*) zurechtlegen ‹Ausrede, Alibi›

**concoction** /kən'kɒkʃn/ *n.* Ⓐ (*preparing*) Zubereitung, *die;* Ⓑ (*drink*) Gebräu, *das;* (*meal*) Fraß, *der* (*ugs.*)

**concomitant** /kən'kɒmɪtənt/ (*formal*) ❶ *adj.* begleitend; (*simultaneous*) gleichzeitig; **~ circumstances** Begleitumstände. ❷ *n.* Begleiterscheinung, *die*

**concord** /'kɒŋkɔ:d, 'kɒnkɔ:d/ *n.* Ⓐ (*agreement*) Eintracht, *die;* Ⓑ (*treaty*) Freundschaftsvertrag, *der;* Ⓒ (*Mus.*) Harmonie, *die;* Ⓓ (*Ling.*) Kongruenz, *die*

**concordance** /kən'kɔ:dəns/ *n.* Ⓐ (*formal: agreement*) Übereinstimmung, *die;* Ⓑ (*index*) Konkordanz, *die*

**concordant** /kən'kɔ:dənt/ *adj.* (*formal*) übereinstimmend; **be ~ with sth.** mit etw. übereinstimmen

**concordat** /kən'kɔ:dæt/ *n.* Konkordat, *das*

**concourse** /'kɒŋkɔ:s, 'kɒnkɔ:s/ *n.* (*of public building*) Halle, *die;* **station ~:** Bahnhofshalle, *die*

**concrete** /'kɒnkri:t/ ❶ *adj.* (*specific*) konkret; **~ noun** (*Ling.*) Konkretum, *das.* ❷ *n.* Beton, *der; attrib.* Beton-; aus Beton *präd.* ❸ *v.t.* betonieren; (*embed in ~*) **~ [in]** einbetonieren

**concretely** /'kɒnkri:tlɪ/ *adv.* konkret

**concrete**/'kɒnkri:t/: **~ mixer** *n.* Betonmischer, *der;* Betonmischmaschine, *die;* **~ 'poetry** *n.* konkrete Poesie

**concretion** /kən'kri:ʃn/ *n.* Ⓐ *no pl.* (*coalescence*) Verwachsung, *die;* Zusammenwachsen, *das;* Ⓑ (*Med.*) Konkrement, *das;* Ⓒ (*Geol.*) Konkretion, *die*

**concubine** /'kɒŋkjʊbaɪn/ *n.* Ⓐ (*formal: cohabiting mistress*) Konkubine, *die;* Ⓑ (*secondary wife*) Nebenfrau, *die*

**concur** /kən'kɜ:(r)/ *v.i.*, **-rr-** Ⓐ (*agree*) **~ [with sb.] [in sth.]** [jmdm.] [in etw. (*Dat.*)] zustimmen *od.* beipflichten; Ⓑ (*coincide, combine*) zusammenkommen

**concurrence** /kən'kʌrəns/ *n., no pl.* Ⓐ (*general agreement*) Übereinstimmung, *die;* Ⓑ (*coincidence*) Zusammentreffen, *das*

**concurrent** /kən'kʌrənt/ *adj.* Ⓐ gleichzeitig; **be ~ with sth.** gleichzeitig mit etw. stattfinden; **~ sentences** zu einer Gesamtstrafe zusammengefasste Einzelstrafen; Ⓑ (*agreeing*) übereinstimmend; **be ~ with sth.** mit etw. übereinstimmen

**concurrently** /kən'kʌrəntlɪ/ *adv.* Ⓐ (*simultaneously*) gleichzeitig; Ⓑ (*Law*) **run ~** ‹Gefängnisstrafen:› zu einer Gesamtstrafe zusammengefasst sein/werden

**concuss** /kən'kʌs/ *v.t.* **be ~ed** eine Gehirnerschütterung haben

**concussion** /kən'kʌʃn/ *n.* (*Med.*) Gehirnerschütterung, *die;* Konkussion, *die* (*fachspr.*)

**condemn** /kən'dem/ *v.t.* Ⓐ (*censure*) verdammen; Ⓑ (*Law: sentence*) verurteilen; (*fig.*) verdammen; **~ sb. to death/to life imprisonment** jmdn. zum Tode/zu lebenslanger Haft verurteilen; **be ~ed to do sth.** (*fig.*) dazu verdammt sein, etw. zu tun; Ⓒ (*give judgement against*) aburteilen; Ⓓ (*show to be guilty*) überführen; Ⓔ (*declare unfit*) für unbewohnbar erklären ‹Gebäude›; für ungenießbar erklären ‹Fleisch›

**condemnation** /kɒndem'neɪʃn/ *n.* Ⓐ (*censure*) Verdammung, *die;* Ⓑ (*Law: conviction*) Verurteilung, *die*

**condemnatory** /kən'demnətərɪ/ *adj.* verdammend; scharf missbilligend ‹Blick›

**condemned** /kən'demd/ *adj.* Ⓐ verurteilt; **a ~ man** ein zum Tode Verurteilter; ein Todeskandidat; Ⓑ **a ~ house** ein Haus, das auf der Abrissliste steht; Ⓒ **~ cell** Todeszelle, *die*

**condensate** /kən'denseɪt, 'kɒndənseɪt/ *n.* Kondensat, *das*

**condensation** /kɒnden'seɪʃn/ *n.* Ⓐ *no pl.* (*condensing*) Kondensation, *die;* Ⓑ (*what is condensed*) Kondensat, *das;* (*water*) Kondenswasser, *das;* Ⓒ (*abridgement*) [Ver]kürzung, *die;* (*abridged form*) Kurzfassung, *die*

**conden'sation trail** *n.* (*Aeronaut.*) Kondensstreifen, *der*

**condense** /kən'dens/ ❶ *v.t.* Ⓐ komprimieren; **~d milk** Kondensmilch, *die;* Ⓑ (*Phys., Chem.*) kondensieren; Ⓒ (*make concise*) zusammenfassen; **in a ~d form** in verkürzter Form. ❷ *v.i.* kondensieren

**condenser** /kən'densə(r)/ *n.* Ⓐ (*of steam engine*) Kondensator, *der;* Ⓑ (*Electr.*) ⇨ **capacitor**; Ⓒ (*Chem.*) Kühler, *der*

**condescend** /kɒndɪ'send/ *v.i.* **~ to do sth.** geruhen (*geh.*), etw. zu tun; sich dazu herablassen, etw. zu tun; **~ to sb.** jmdn. von oben herab behandeln

**condescending** /kɒndɪ'sendɪŋ/ *adj.* (*derog.*) herablassend

**condescendingly** /kɒndɪ'sendɪŋlɪ/ *adv.* (*derog.*) herablassend; von oben herab

**condescension** /kɒndɪ'senʃn/ *n.* (*derog.: patronizing manner*) Herablassung, *die;* **his air of ~:** sein herablassendes Gebaren

**condiment** /'kɒndɪmənt/ *n.* Gewürz, *das*

**condition** /kən'dɪʃn/ ❶ *n.* Ⓐ (*stipulation*) [Vor]bedingung, *die;* Voraussetzung, *die;* **make it a ~ that ...:** es zur Bedingung machen, dass ...; **on [the] ~ that ...:** unter der Voraussetzung *od.* Bedingung, dass ...; Ⓑ (*in pl.: circumstances*) Umstände *Pl.;* **weather/light ~s** Witterungsverhältnisse/Lichtverhältnisse; **under** *or* **in present ~s** unter den gegenwärtigen Umständen *od.* Bedingungen; **living/working ~s** Unterkunfts-/Arbeitsbedingungen; Ⓒ (*state of being*) (*of athlete, etc.*) Kondition, *die;* Form, *die;* (*of thing*) Zustand, *der;* (*of invalid, patient, etc.*) Verfassung, *die;* **keep sth. in good ~:** etw. in gutem Zustand erhalten; **be out of ~/in [good] ~** ‹Person:› schlecht/gut in Form sein; **sb. is in no ~ to do sth.** jmds. Gesundheitszustand erlaubt ihm nicht, etw. zu tun; **she's in no ~ to travel/drive** sie ist nicht reisefähig/fahrtüchtig; **get into ~** (*Sport*) sich in Form *od.* Kondition bringen; Ⓓ ▶ 1232 (*Med.*) Leiden, *das;* **have a heart/lung** *etc.* **~:** ein Herz-/Lungenleiden *usw.* haben; herz-/lungenleidend sein. ❷ *v.t.* Ⓐ (*determine*) bestimmen; Ⓑ (*make suitable or fit*) in Form bringen ‹Sportler, Tier, Haar›; ⇨ *also* **air-conditioned**; Ⓒ (*accustom*) dressieren ‹Pferd, Hund›; **~ sb. to sth.** jmdn. an etw. (*Akk.*) gewöhnen; **be ~ed to do sth.** gewöhnt sein, etw. zu tun; **be ~ed to respond to a stimulus** konditioniert sein, auf einen Reiz zu reagieren; ⇨ *also* **reflex** 1

**conditional** /kən'dɪʃənl/ ❶ *adj.* Ⓐ bedingt; **be ~ [up]on sth.** von etw. abhängen; Ⓑ (*Ling.*) konditional; bedingend; **~ clause** Konditional- *od.* Bedingungssatz, *der;* **~ mood/tense** Konditional[is], *der.* ❷ *n.* (*Ling.*) Konditional[is], *der*

**conditionally** /kən'dɪʃənəlɪ/ *adv.* mit *od.* unter Vorbehalt

**conditioner** /kən'dɪʃənə(r)/ *n.* Ⓐ ⇨ **air conditioner**; Ⓑ ⇨ **hair conditioner**

**condole** /kən'dəʊl/ *v.i.* (*formal*) **~ with sb. [up]on sth.** jmdm. zu etw. seine Anteilnahme *od.* sein Mitgefühl aussprechen; **~ with sb. on the death of his mother** jmdm. zum Tode seiner Mutter kondolieren

**condolence** /kən'dəʊləns/ *n.* Anteilnahme, *die;* Mitgefühl, *das;* (*on death*) Beileid, *das;* **offer sb. one's ~s** jmdm. sein Mitgefühl/sein Beileid *od.* seine Teilnahme aussprechen; **letter of ~:** Beileidsbrief, *der;* Kondolenzbrief, *der;* **please accept my ~s** darf ich Ihnen mein Beileid *od.* meine [An]teilnahme aussprechen?

**condom** /'kɒndəm/ *n.* Kondom, *das od. der;* Präservativ, *das*

**condominium** /kɒndə'mɪnɪəm/ *n.* Ⓐ (*Polit.*) Kondominium, *das;* Ⓑ (*Amer.: property*) Appartementhaus [mit Eigentumswohnungen]; (*single dwelling*) Eigentumswohnung, *die*

**condone** /kən'dəʊn/ *v.t.* Ⓐ hinwegsehen über (+ *Akk.*); (*approve*) billigen; Ⓑ (*Law*) in Kauf nehmen; stillschweigend billigen

**condor** /'kɒndə(r)/ *n.* (*Ornith.*) Kondor, *der*

**conduce** /kən'dju:s/ *v.i.* (*formal*) **~ to** förderlich sein (+ *Dat.*); beitragen zu

**conducive** /kən'dju:sɪv/ *adj.* **be ~ to sth.** einer Sache (*Dat.*) förderlich sein; zu etw. beitragen

**conduct** ❶ /'kɒndʌkt/ *n.* Ⓐ (*behaviour*) Verhalten, *das;* **good ~:** gute Führung; **rules of ~:** Verhaltensregeln; Ⓑ (*way of ~ing*) Führung, *die;* (*of conference, inquiry, operation*) Leitung, *die;* Durchführung, *die;* **his ~ of the war** seine Kriegsführung; **their ~ of the negotiations** ihre Verhandlungsführung; Ⓒ (*leading, guidance*) Geleit, *das;* ⇨ *also* **safe conduct**.
❷ /kən'dʌkt/ *v.t.* Ⓐ (*Mus.*) dirigieren; Ⓑ (*direct*) führen ‹Geschäfte, Krieg, Gespräch›; durchführen ‹Operation, Untersuchung›; leiten ‹Konferenz›; **~ one's affairs** seine Geschäfte führen; Ⓒ (*Phys.*) leiten ‹Wärme, Elektrizität›; Ⓓ **~ oneself** sich verhalten; Ⓔ (*guide*) führen; **~ sb. away [from]** jmdn. wegführen [von]; **a ~ed tour [of a museum/factory]** eine [Museums-/Werks]führung

**conduction** /kən'dʌkʃn/ *n.* (*Phys.*) Leitung, *die*

**conductivity** /kɒndək'tɪvɪtɪ/ *n.* (*Phys.*) Leitfähigkeit, *die;* Konduktivität, *die* (*fachspr.*)

**conductor** /kən'dʌktə(r)/ *n.* Ⓐ ▶ 1261 (*Mus.*) Dirigent, *der*/Dirigentin, *die;* Ⓑ ▶ 1261 (*of bus, tram*) Schaffner, *der;* (*Amer.: of train*) Zugführer, *der;* Schaffner, *der* (*ugs.*); Ⓒ (*Phys.*) Leiter, *der;* Konduktor, *der* (*fachspr.*); ~ **rail** Strom-, Sammelschiene, *die*

**conductress** /kənˈdʌktrɪs/ *n.* ▶ 1261 Schaffnerin, *die*

**conduit** /ˈkɒndɪt, ˈkɒndjʊɪt/ *n.* **A** Leitung, *die;* Kanal, *der* (*auch fig.*); **B** (*Electr.*) Isolierrohr, *das*

**cone** /kəʊn/ ❶ *n.* **A** Kegel, *der;* Konus, *der* (*fachspr.*); (*traffic* ~) Leitkegel, *der;* Pylon, *der* (*fachspr.*); Pylone, *die* (*fachspr.*); **B** (*Bot.*) Zapfen, *der;* **C** **ice cream** ~: Eistüte, *die;* **D** (*Anat.*) Zapfen, *der.* ❷ *v.t.* ~ **off** [mit Leitkegeln *od.* Pylonen] absperren ‹Fahrbahn›

**confab** /ˈkɒnfæb/ *n.* (*coll.*) Unterhaltung, *die;* Schwätzchen, *das* (*ugs.*); (*discussion*) Besprechung, *die*

**confection** /kənˈfekʃn/ *n.* **A** Konfekt, *das;* **B** (*mixing, compounding*) Anfertigung, *die;* **C** (*article of dress*) [Damen]modeartikel, *der*

**confectioner** /kənˈfekʃənə(r)/ *n.* ▶ 1261 (*maker*) Hersteller von Süßigkeiten; (*retailer*) Süßwarenhändler, *der;* (*cake decorator*) Konditor, *der;* Zuckerbäcker, *der* (*veralt., südd., österr.*); ~**'s [shop]** Süßwarengeschäft, *das;* ~**s' sugar** (*Amer.*) Puderzucker, *der*

**confectionery** /kənˈfekʃənərɪ/ *n.* **A** Süßwaren *Pl.;* (*cakes etc.*) Konditoreiwaren *Pl.;* **B** (*shop*) Süßwarengeschäft, *das;* **C** (*confectioner's art*) Konditorei, *die;* Zuckerbäckerei, *die* (*veralt., südd., österr.*)

**confederacy** /kənˈfedərəsɪ/ *n.* **A** (*league, alliance*) Bündnis, *das;* **B** (*conspiracy*) Verschwörung, *die;* **C** (*body*) Konföderation, *die;* **the [Southern] C**~ (*Amer. Hist.*) die Konföderierten [Staaten]

**confederate** ❶ /kənˈfedərət/ *adj.* **A** (*allied*) verbündet; **B** (*Polit.*) konföderiert; **the C**~ **States** (*Amer. Hist.*) die Konföderierten Staaten von Amerika. ❷ *n.* Verbündete, *der/die;* (*accomplice*) Komplize, *der*/Komplizin, *die;* **C**~ (*Amer. Hist.*) Konföderierte, *der.* ❸ /kənˈfedəreɪt/ *v.t.* vereinigen. ❹ *v.i.* sich verbünden *od.* zusammenschließen

**confederation** /kənfedəˈreɪʃn/ *n.* **A** (*Polit.*) [Staaten]bund, *der;* **the Swiss C**~: die Schweizerische Eidgenossenschaft; **B** (*alliance*) Bund, *der;* **C**~ **of British Industry** *britischer Unternehmerverband*

**confer** /kənˈfɜː(r)/ ❶ *v.t.*, **-rr-:** ~ **a title/degree/knighthood [up]on sb.** jmdm. einen Titel/Grad verleihen/jmdn. zum Ritter schlagen; ~ **a quality [up]on sth.** einer Sache (*Dat.*) eine Eigenschaft verleihen. ❷ *v.i.*, **-rr-:** ~ **with sb.** sich mit jmdm. beraten

**conference** /ˈkɒnfərəns/ *n.* **A** (*meeting*) Konferenz, *die;* Tagung, *die;* **B** (*consultation*) Beratung, *die;* (*business discussion*) Besprechung, *die;* **be in** ~: in einer Besprechung sein

**conference:** ~ **room** *n.* Konferenzraum, *der;* (*smaller*) Besprechungszimmer, *das;* ~ **table** *n.* Konferenztisch, *der;* **get round the** ~ **table** (*fig.*) sich an den Verhandlungstisch setzen

**conferment** /kənˈfɜːmənt/ *n.* Verleihung, *die*

**confess** /kənˈfes/ ❶ *v.t.* **A** zugeben; gestehen; **he** ~**ed himself to be the culprit** er gestand, der Schuldige zu sein; **I** ~ **myself a traditionalist** ich bekenne mich als Traditionalist; **B** (*Eccl.*) beichten; ~ **one's sins to a priest** einem Priester seine Sünden beichten *od.* bekennen; **C** (*Eccl.*) **the priest** ~**ed the penitent** der Priester nahm dem reuigen Sünder die Beichte ab. ❷ *v.i.* **A** ~ **to sth.** etw. gestehen; ~ **to being unable to do sth.** gestehen *od.* zugeben, dass man etw. nicht kann; **B** (*Eccl.*) beichten (**to sb.** jmdm.); ‹Priester:› die Beichte abnehmen

**confessed** /kənˈfest/ *adj.* geständig ‹Verbrecher›; **a** ~ **homosexual** jemand, der sich dazu bekennt, homosexuell zu sein

**confessedly** /kənˈfesɪdlɪ/ *adv.* zugegebenermaßen; (*avowedly*) eingestandenermaßen

**confession** /kənˈfeʃn/ *n.* **A** (*of offence etc.*) Geständnis, *das;* **on** *or* **by one's own** ~: nach eigenem Geständnis; **I have a** ~ **to make** ich muss ein Geständnis ablegen; **B** (*Eccl.: of sins etc.*) Beichte, *die;* ~ **of sins** Sündenbekenntnis, *das;* **hear sb.'s** ~: jmdm. die Beichte abnehmen; **make one's** ~: seine Sünden bekennen; **C** (*thing confessed*) Geständnis, *das;* **D** (*Relig.: denomination*) Konfession, *die;* **what** ~ **is he?** welcher Konfession ist er?; **Roman Catholic** *etc.* **by** ~: römisch-katholischer *usw.* Konfession; **E** (*Eccl.: confessing*) Bekenntnis, *das;* ~ **of faith** Glaubensbekenntnis, *das*

**confessional** /kənˈfeʃənl/ (*Eccl.*) ❶ *adj.* (*of confession*) bekennend; (*denominational*) konfessionell; ~ **schools** Konfessionsschulen. ❷ *n.* **A** (*stall*) Beichtstuhl, *der;* **B** (*act*) Beichte, *die*

**confessor** /kənˈfesə(r)/ *n.* (*Eccl.*) Beichtvater, *der*

**confetti** /kənˈfetɪ/ *n.* Konfetti, *das*

**confidant** /ˈkɒnfɪdænt, kɒnfɪˈdænt/ *n.* Vertraute, *der*

**confidante** /ˈkɒnfɪdænt, kɒnfɪˈdænt/ *n.* Vertraute, *die*

**confide** /kənˈfaɪd/ ❶ *v.i.* ~ **in sb.** sich jmdm. anvertrauen; ~ **to sb. about sth.** jmdm. etw. anvertrauen. ❷ *v.t.* ~ **sth. to sb.** jmdm. etw. anvertrauen; **he** ~**d that he ...:** er gestand, dass er ...

**confidence** /ˈkɒnfɪdəns/ *n.* **A** (*firm trust*) Vertrauen, *das;* **have [complete** *or* **every/no]** ~ **in sb./sth.** [volles/kein] Vertrauen zu jmdm./etw. haben; **have [absolute]** ~ **that ...:** [absolut] sicher sein, dass ...; **place** *or* **put one's** ~ **in sb./sth.** sein Vertrauen in jmdn./etw. setzen; auf jmdn./etw. bauen; **B** (*assured expectation*) Gewissheit, *die;* Sicherheit, *die;* **in full** ~ **of success** voller Erfolgsgewissheit; **C** (*self-reliance*) Selbstvertrauen, *das;* **D** (*boldness*) Dreistigkeit, *die;* **E** (*telling of private matters*) Vertraulichkeit, *die;* **in** ~: im Vertrauen; **this is in [strict]** ~: das ist [streng] vertraulich; **take sb. into one's** ~: jmdn. ins Vertrauen ziehen; **be in sb.'s** ~: jmds. Vertrauen genießen; **F** (*thing told in* ~) Vertraulichkeit, *die*

**confidence:** ~ **game** (*Amer.*) ⇒ ~ **trick;** ~ **man** *n.* Trickbetrüger, *der;* Bauernfänger, *der* (*ugs.*); ~ **trick** *n.* (*Brit.*) Trickbetrug, *der;* Bauernfängerei, *die* (*ugs.*); ~ **trickster** (*Brit.*) ⇒ ~ **man**

**confident** /ˈkɒnfɪdənt/ *adj.* **A** (*trusting, fully assured*) zuversichtlich (**about** in Bezug auf + *Akk.*); **be** ~ **that [sth. will happen]** sicher sein, dass [etw. geschieht]; **be** ~ **of sth.** auf etw. (*Akk.*) vertrauen; **B** (*bold*) dreist; **C** (*self-assured*) selbstbewusst

**confidential** /kɒnfɪˈdenʃl/ *adj.* **A** (*uttered in confidence*) vertraulich; **B** (*entrusted with secrets*) persönlich; privat; ~ **secretary** Privatsekretär, *der*/-sekretärin, *die*

**confidentiality** /kɒnfɪdenʃɪˈælɪtɪ/ *n.*, *no pl.* Vertraulichkeit, *die*

**confidentially** /kɒnfɪˈdenʃəlɪ/ *adv.* vertraulich

**confidently** /ˈkɒnfɪdəntlɪ/ *adv.* zuversichtlich

**confiding** /kənˈfaɪdɪŋ/ *adj.*, **confidingly** /kənˈfaɪdɪŋlɪ/ *adv.* vertrauensvoll

**configuration** /kənfɪgjʊˈreɪʃn/ *n.* **A** (*arrangement, outline*) Gestaltung, *die;* **B** (*Astron., Computing*) Konfiguration, *die*

**configure** /kənˈfɪgə(r)/ *v.t.* (*esp. Computing*) konfigurieren

**confine** /kənˈfaɪn/ *v.t.* **A** einsperren; eindämmen ‹Flut, Feuer usw.›; **be** ~**d to bed/the house** ans Bett/Haus gefesselt sein; **be** ~**d to barracks** keinen Ausgang bekommen; **be** ~**d to a small area** auf ein kleines Gebiet begrenzt sein; **B** (*fig.*) ~ **sb./sth. to sth.** jmdn./etw. auf etw. (*Akk.*) beschränken; ~ **oneself to sth./doing sth.** sich auf etw. (*Akk.*) beschränken/sich darauf beschränken, etw. zu tun **C** (*imprison*) einsperren;

**confined** /kənˈfaɪnd/ *adj.* begrenzt

**confinement** /kənˈfaɪnmənt/ *n.* **A** (*imprisonment*) Einsperrung, *die;* (*in asylum*) Einweisung, *die;* **B** (*being confined*) **put/keep sb. in** ~: jmdn. in Haft nehmen/halten; ~ **in hospital** ein Krankenhausaufenthalt; **animals kept in** ~: gefangen gehaltene Tiere; **C** (*childbirth*) Niederkunft, *die;* **D** (*limitation*) Beschränkung, *die* (**to** auf + *Akk.*)

**confines** /ˈkɒnfaɪnz/ *n. pl.* Grenzen

**confirm** /kənˈfɜːm/ *v.t.* **A** bestätigen; **be** ~**ed in one's suspicions** sich in seinem Verdacht bestätigt sehen; **B** (*Protestant Ch.*) konfirmieren; einsegnen; (*RC Ch.*) firmen

**confirmation** /kɒnfəˈmeɪʃn/ *n.* **A** Bestätigung, *die;* **B** (*Protestant Ch.*) Konfirmation, *die;* Einsegnung, *die;* (*RC Ch.*) Firmung, *die;* ~ **class[es]** Konfirmanden-/Firmunterricht, *der;* **C** (*of Jewish faith*) Konfirmation, *die*

**confirmatory** /kənˈfɜːmətərɪ/ *adj.* bestätigend

**confirmed** /kənˈfɜːmd/ *adj.* **A** (*unlikely to change*) eingefleischt ‹Junggeselle›; überzeugt ‹Atheist, Vegetarier›; unheilbar ‹Trinker, Kranker›; **B** (*Protestant Ch.*) konfirmiert; (*RC Ch.*) gefirmt

**confiscate** /ˈkɒnfɪskeɪt/ *v.t.* beschlagnahmen; konfiszieren; ~ **sth. from sb.** jmdm. etw. wegnehmen

**confiscation** /kɒnfɪsˈkeɪʃn/ *n.* Beschlagnahme, *die;* Konfiskation, *die*

**conflagration** /kɒnfləˈgreɪʃn/ *n.* Feuersbrunst, *die* (*geh.*); Großbrand, *der*

**conflate** /kənˈfleɪt/ *v.t.* verschmelzen

**conflation** /kənˈfleɪʃn/ *n.* Verschmelzung, *die*

**conflict** ❶ /ˈkɒnflɪkt/ *n.* **A** (*fight*) Kampf, *der;* (*prolonged*) Krieg, *der;* **come into** ~ **with sb./sth.** mit jmdm./etw. in Konflikt geraten; **be in** ~ **with sb./sth.** (*fig.*) mit jmdm./etw. im Kampf liegen; **B** (*clashing*) Konflikt, *der;* **a** ~ **of views/interests** ein Meinungs-/Interessenkonflikt; **C** (*Psych.*) Konflikt, *der.* ❷ /kənˈflɪkt/ *v.i.* (*be incompatible*) sich (*Dat.*) widersprechen; ~ **with sth.** einer Sache (*Dat.*) widersprechen; zu einer Sache im Widerspruch stehen

**conflicting** /kənˈflɪktɪŋ/ *adj.* widersprüchlich

**confluence** /ˈkɒnfluəns/ *n.* Zusammenfluss, *der*

**conform** /kənˈfɔːm/ ❶ *v.i.* **A** entsprechen (**to** *Dat.*); ~ **to a pattern** sich mit einem Muster decken; (*fig.*) einem Muster entsprechen; **those who do not** ~ **will be asked to leave the club** wer sich nicht einfügt, wird aufgefordert, den Klub zu verlassen; **B** (*comply*) ~ **to** *or* **with sth./with sb.** sich nach etw./jmdm. richten. ❷ *v.t.* ~ **sth. to sth.** etw. an etw. (*Akk.*) anpassen; etw. auf etw. (*Akk.*) abstimmen (*fig.*)

**conformation** /kɒnfəˈmeɪʃn/ *n.* **A** (*structure*) Gestalt, *die;* **B** (*adaptation*) Anpassung, *die* (**to** an + *Akk.*)

**conformism** /kənˈfɔːmɪzm/ *n.* Konformismus, *der*

**conformist** /kənˈfɔːmɪst/ *n.* Konformist, *der*/Konformistin, *die*

**conformity** /kənˈfɔːmɪtɪ/ *n.* Übereinstimmung, *die* (**with, to** mit)

**confound** /kənˈfaʊnd/ *v.t.* **A** ~ **it!** verflixt noch mal! (*ugs.*); ~ **him** *or* **the man!** der verflixte Kerl! (*ugs.*); **B** (*defeat*) vereiteln ‹Plan, Hoffnung›; **C** (*confuse*) verwirren; **D** (*discomfit*) ins Unrecht setzen; **E** (*make indistinguishable*) durcheinander bringen; verwischen ‹Unterschied›; **F** (*mix up mentally*) verwechseln; **G** (*throw into disorder*) durcheinander werfen

**confounded** /kənˈfaʊndɪd/ *adj.*, **confoundedly** /kənˈfaʊndɪdlɪ/ *adv.* (*coll. derog.*) verdammt

**confront** /kənˈfrʌnt/ *v.t.* **A** gegenüberstellen; konfrontieren; ~ **sb. with sth./sb.** jmdn. mit etw./[mit] jmdm. konfrontieren; **he was** ~**ed with** *or* **by an angry mob** er sah sich [mit] einer wütenden Menge konfrontiert; **B** (*stand facing*) gegenüberstehen (+ *Dat.*); **enemies** ~**ing one another** einander gegenüberstehende Feinde; **find oneself** ~**ed by** *or* **with a problem** sich [mit] einem Problem konfrontiert sehen; **C** (*face in defiance*) ins Auge sehen (+ *Dat.*); **D** (*oppose*) widersprechen (+ *Dat.*); (*make comparison*) gegenüberstellen

**confrontation** /kɒnfrənˈteɪʃn/ *n.* Konfrontation, *die;* (*with witnesses*) Gegenüberstellung, *die*

**Confucianism** /kənˈfjuːʃənɪzm/ *n.*, *no pl.* Konfuzianismus, *der*

C

**confuse** /kən'fju:z/ *v.t.* Ⓐ (*disorder*) durcheinander bringen; verwirren; (*blur*) verwischen; ~ **the issue** den Sachverhalt unklar machen; **it simply ~s matters** das verwirrt die Sache nur; Ⓑ (*mix up mentally*) verwechseln; ~ **two things** zwei Dinge [miteinander] verwechseln; Ⓒ (*perplex*) konfus machen; verwirren

**confused** /kən'fju:zd/ *adj.* konfus; wirr ‹Gedanken, Gerüchte›; verworren ‹Lage, Situation›; (*embarrassed*) verlegen

**confusing** /kən'fju:zɪŋ/ *adj.* verwirrend

**confusion** /kən'fju:ʒn/ *n.* Ⓐ (*disordering*) Verwirrung, *die;* (*mixing up*) Verwechslung, *die;* ~ **of tongues** Sprachverwirrung, *die;* Ⓑ (*state*) Verwirrung, *die;* (*embarrassment*) Verlegenheit, *die;* **throw sb./sth. into ~:** jmdn./etw. [völlig] durcheinander bringen; **reply/blush in ~:** verlegen antworten/erröten; **in [total] ~:** in völligem Durcheinander ‹fliehen›; [völlig *od.* wild] durcheinander ‹daliegen›; **a scene of total ~:** ein totales Chaos

**confutation** /kɒnfjʊ'teɪʃn/ *n.* Widerlegung, *die*

**confute** /kən'fju:t/ *v.t.* widerlegen

**conga** /'kɒŋgə/ *n.* Conga, *die*

**congeal** /kən'dʒi:l/ ❶ *v.i.* Ⓐ (*coagulate*) gerinnen; ~ **into sth.** (*fig.*) zu etw. erstarren; Ⓑ (*freeze*) gefrieren. ❷ *v.t.* Ⓐ (*coagulate*) gerinnen lassen; koagulieren; Ⓑ (*solidify by cooling*) gefrieren lassen

**congenial** /kən'dʒi:nɪəl/ *adj.* Ⓐ (*kindred*) geistesverwandt; ~ **spirits** kongeniale Geister; Ⓑ (*agreeable*) angenehm

**congeniality** /kəndʒi:nɪ'ælɪtɪ/ *n., no pl.* Geistesverwandtschaft, *die*

**congenital** /kən'dʒenɪtl/ *adj.* angeboren; kongenital (*fachspr.*); **a ~ idiot** ein von Geburt an Schwachsinniger; **a ~ defect** ein Geburtsfehler

**congenitally** /kən'dʒenɪtəlɪ/ *adv.* von Geburt an

**conger** /'kɒŋgə(r)/ *n.* (*Zool.*) ~ **[eel]** Meer- *od.* Seeaal, *der*

**congest** /kən'dʒest/ *v.t.* verstopfen

**congested** /kən'dʒestɪd/ *adj.* überfüllt, verstopft ‹Straße›; übervölkert ‹Stadtviertel›; **my nose is ~:** ich habe eine verstopfte Nase

**congestion** /kən'dʒestʃn/ *n.* (*of traffic etc.*) Stauung, *die;* (*overpopulation*) Übervölkerung, *die;* ~ **of the lungs** (*Med.*) Lungenstauung, *die;* **nasal ~:** verstopfte Nase

**conglomerate** ❶ /kən'glɒməreɪt/ *v.t.* (*lit. or fig.*) verschmelzen. ❷ *v.i.* sich zusammenballen; (*fig.*) sich versammeln. ❸ /kən'glɒmərət/ *n.* Ⓐ (*Commerc.*) Großkonzern, *der;* Ⓑ (*Geol.*) Konglomerat, *das*

**conglomeration** /kənglɒmə'reɪʃn/ *n.* Konglomerat, *das;* (*collection*) Ansammlung, *die*

**Congo** /'kɒŋgəʊ/ *pr. n.* ▶ 1480 (*Geog.: river, country*) Kongo, *der*

**Congolese** /kɒŋgə'li:z/ ▶ 1340 ❶ *adj.* kongolesisch. ❷ *n.* Kongolese, *der*/Kongolesin, *die*

**congratulate** /kən'grætjʊleɪt/ *v.t.* gratulieren (+ *Dat.*); ~ **sb./oneself [up]on sth.** jmdm./sich zu etw. gratulieren

**congratulation** /kəngrætjʊ'leɪʃn/ ❶ *int.* **~s!** herzlichen Glückwunsch! (**on** zu). ❷ *n.* Ⓐ *in pl.* Glückwünsche *Pl.;* **offer sb. one's ~s** jmdm. gratulieren; jmdn. beglückwünschen; Ⓑ (*action*) Gratulation, *die*

**congratulatory** /kən'grætjʊlətərɪ/ *adj.* beglückwünschend; ~ **note/letter** Glückwunschschreiben, *das*/-brief, *der*

**congregate** /'kɒŋgrɪgeɪt/ ❶ *v.i.* sich versammeln; zusammenkommen. ❷ *v.t.* versammeln

**congregation** /kɒŋgrɪ'geɪʃn/ *n.* Ⓐ (*Eccl.*) Gemeinde, *die;* Ⓑ (*Brit. Univ.*) ≈ Konzil, *das*

**congress** /'kɒŋgres/ *n.* Ⓐ (*meeting of heads of state etc.*) Kongress, *der;* **the C~ of Vienna** der Wiener Kongress; **a party ~:** ein Parteitag; Ⓑ (*association*) Verband, *der;* Ⓒ **C~** (*Amer.: legislature*) der Kongress

**congressional** /kən'greʃənl/ *adj.* Kongress-; ‹Erlaubnis› des Kongresses; ~ **district** Kongresswahlbezirk, *der*

**Congress:** **~man** /'kɒŋgresmən/ *n., pl.* **~men** /'kɒŋgresmən/ (*Amer.*) Kongressabgeordnete, *der;* **~woman** *n.* (*Amer.*) Kongressabgeordnete, *die*

**congruence** /'kɒŋgrʊəns/, **congruency** /'kɒŋgrʊənsɪ/ *n.* Ⓐ Übereinstimmung, *die;* Ⓑ (*Geom.*) Kongruenz, *die;* Deckungsgleichheit, *die*

**congruent** /'kɒŋgrʊənt/ *adj.* Ⓐ (*formal*) übereinstimmend; Ⓑ (*Geom.*) kongruent; deckungsgleich

**congruity** /kɒŋ'gru:ɪtɪ/ *n.* Übereinstimmung, *die;* Kongruenz, *die* (*geh.*)

**conic** /'kɒnɪk/ *adj.* Kegel-; ~ **section** Kegelschnitt, *der*

**conical** /'kɒnɪkl/ *adj.* konisch; kegelförmig; ⇒ *also* **projection** I

**conifer** /'kɒnɪfə(r), 'kəʊnɪfə(r)/ *n.* Nadelbaum, *der;* Konifere, *die;* **~s** Nadelhölzer

**coniferous** /kə'nɪfərəs/ *adj.* Nadel-; ~ **tree** Nadelbaum, *der;* Konifere, *die;* ~ **forest** Nadelwald, *der*

**conjectural** /kən'dʒektʃərl/ *adj.* auf Mutmaßungen (*geh.*) *od.* Vermutungen beruhend; konjektural (*Literaturw.*); **all this is ~:** all das ist Vermutung; **a ~ emendation of a text** eine Konjektur (*Literaturw.*)

**conjecturally** /kən'dʒektʃərəlɪ/ *adv.* aufgrund von Mutmaßungen (*geh.*) *od.* Vermutungen

**conjecture** /kən'dʒektʃə(r)/ ❶ *n.* Ⓐ Mutmaßung, *die* (*geh.*); Vermutung, *die;* **rely on ~:** sich auf Mutmaßungen (*Akk.*) stützen; Ⓑ (*Lit.*) Konjektur, *die.* ❷ *v.t.* mutmaßen (*geh.*); vermuten. ❸ *v.i.* (*guess*) Mutmaßungen (*geh.*) *od.* Vermutungen anstellen

**conjoin** /kən'dʒɔɪn/ ❶ *v.t.* verbinden. ❷ *v.i.* sich verbinden

**conjoint** /kən'dʒɔɪnt/ *adj.* (*formal*) Ⓐ (*united*) gemeinsam; Ⓑ (*associated*) Mit-

**conjointly** /kən'dʒɔɪntlɪ/ *adv.* gemeinsam

**conjugal** /'kɒndʒʊgl/ *adj.* ehelich; **the ~ state** der Stand der Ehe; ~ **bliss/worries** Eheglück, *das*/Ehesorgen

**conjugate** ❶ /'kɒndʒʊgeɪt/ *v.t.* (*Ling.*) konjugieren. ❷ *v.i.* Ⓐ (*Ling.*) konjugiert werden; Ⓑ (*Biol.*) sich paaren *od.* vereinigen. ❸ /'kɒndʒʊgət/ *adj.* Ⓐ gepaart; Ⓑ (*Ling.*) wurzelverwandt; Ⓒ (*Math.*) konjugiert. ❹ *n.* (*Ling.*) wurzelverwandtes Wort

**conjugation** /'kɒndʒʊ'geɪʃn/ *n.* Ⓐ (*joining together*) Vereinigung, *die;* Ⓑ (*Ling., Biol.*) Konjugation, *die*

**conjunction** /kən'dʒʌŋkʃn/ *n.* Ⓐ Verbindung, *die;* **in ~ with sb./sth.** in Verbindung mit jmdm./etw.; Ⓑ (*formal: of events*) Zusammentreffen, *das;* Ⓒ (*Ling.*) Konjunktion, *die;* Bindewort, *das;* Ⓓ (*Astrol., Astron.*) Konjunktion, *die*

**conjunctivitis** /kəndʒʌŋktɪ'vaɪtɪs/ *n.* ▶ 1232 (*Med.*) Bindehautentzündung, *die;* Konjunktivitis, *die* (*fachspr.*)

**conjure** ❶ *v.t.* Ⓐ /kən'dʒʊə(r)/ (*formal: beseech*) beschwören; anflehen; Ⓑ /'kʌndʒə(r)/ (*by magic*) beschwören ‹Geister›. ❷ /'kʌndʒə(r)/ *v.i.* zaubern; **conjuring trick** Zaubertrick, *der;* Zauberkunststück, *das;* **a name to ~ with** ein exotischer *od.* geheimnisvoller Name; (*because of great importance*) ein klangvoller Name

~ **'away** *v.t.* wegzaubern

~ **'up** *v.t.* beschwören ‹Geister, Teufel›; (*fig.*) heraufbeschwören

**conjurer, conjuror** /'kʌndʒərə(r)/ *n.* Zauberkünstler, *der*/-künstlerin, *die;* Zauberer, *der*/Zauberin, *die*

**conk**[1] /kɒŋk/ *v.i.* ~ **'out** (*coll.*) schlappmachen (*ugs.*); ‹Maschine, Auto usw.:› den Geist aufgeben (*scherzh.*), kaputtgehen (*ugs.*)

**conk**[2] *n.* (*coll.*) Ⓐ (*nose*) Zinken, *der* (*ugs.*); Rüssel, *der* (*salopp*); Ⓑ (*head*) Rübe, *die* (*salopp*); Birne, *die* (*salopp*)

**conker** /'kɒŋkə(r)/ *n.* (*horse chestnut*) [Ross]kastanie, *die;* **play ~s** ein Wettspiel mit Kastanien machen

**'conman** (*coll.*) ⇒ **confidence man**

**connect** /kə'nekt/ ❶ *v.t.* Ⓐ (*join together*) verbinden (**to, with** mit); (*Electr.*) anschließen (**to, with** an + *Akk.*); Ⓑ (*join in sequence*) verbinden; verknüpfen; Ⓒ (*associate*) verbinden; ~ **sth. with sth.** etw. mit etw. verbinden *od.* in Verbindung bringen; **be ~ed with sb./sth.** mit jmdm./etw. in Verbindung stehen. ❷ *v.i.* Ⓐ (*join*) ~ **with sth.** mit etw. zusammenhängen *od.* verbunden sein; ‹Zug, Schiff usw.:› Anschluss haben an etw. (*Akk.*); Ⓑ (*form logical sequence*) einen Zusammenhang/Zusammenhänge darstellen; Ⓒ (*coll.: hit*) einen Haken *usw.* landen (**with** auf, an + *Dat.*)

~ **'up** *v.t.* anschließen

**connected** /kə'nektɪd/ *adj.* Ⓐ (*logically joined*) zusammenhängend; **sth. is ~ with sth.** etw. hängt mit etw. zusammen; etw. hat mit etw. zu tun; Ⓑ (*related*) verwandt; **he is well ~:** er hat einflussreiche Verwandte

**connecting**/kə'nektɪŋ/: ~ **door** *n.* Verbindungstür, *die;* ~ **rod** *n.* (*Mech. Engin.*) Pleuelstange, *die*

**connection** /kə'nekʃn/ *n.* Ⓐ (*act, state*) Verbindung, *die;* (*Electr.; of telephone*) Anschluss, *der;* **cut the ~:** die Verbindung abbrechen; **the Italian ~:** die Beziehungen zu Italien; **run in ~ with sth.** ‹Zug usw.:› Anschluss haben an etw. (*Akk.*); Ⓑ (*fig.: of ideas*) Zusammenhang, *der;* **in this ~:** in diesem Zusammenhang; **in ~ with sth.** im Zusammenhang mit etw.; Ⓒ (*part*) Verbindung, *die;* Verbindungsstück, *das;* Ⓓ (*train, boat, etc.*) Anschluss, *der;* **miss a ~:** einen Anschluss verpassen; **catch** *or* **make a ~:** einen Anschluss erreichen *od.* (*ugs.*) kriegen; Ⓔ (*family relationship*) Verwandtschaft, *die;* Ⓕ (*person*) (*relative*) Verwandte, *der/die;* **business ~s** Geschäftsbeziehungen; **have ~s** Beziehungen haben; Ⓖ (*personal dealings*) **he has no ~ with the firm of this name** er hat keinerlei Verbindung zu dem gleichnamigen Unternehmen; Ⓗ (*sl.: supplier of narcotics*) Dealer, *der* (*Jargon*)

**connective** /kə'nektɪv/ *adj.* Ⓐ verbindend; Ⓑ (*Anat.*) ~ **tissue** Bindegewebe, *das*

**connexion** (*Brit.*) ⇒ **connection**

**conning tower** /'kɒnɪŋtaʊə(r)/ *n.* (*Naut.*) Kommandoturm, *der*

**connivance** /kə'naɪvəns/ *n.* stillschweigende Duldung

**connive** /kə'naɪv/ *v.i.* Ⓐ ~ **at sth.** (*disregard*) über etw. (*Akk.*) hinwegsehen; etw. stillschweigend dulden; Ⓑ (*conspire*) ~ **with sb.** mit jmdm. gemeinsame Sache machen (**in** bei)

**connoisseur** /kɒnə'sɜ:(r)/ *n.* Kenner, *der;* **a ~ of wine** ein Weinkenner

**connotation** /kɒnə'teɪʃn/ *n.* Assoziation, *die;* Konnotation, *die* (*Sprachw.*)

**connote** /kə'nəʊt/ *v.t.* (*formal*) Ⓐ (*suggest*) suggerieren; Ⓑ (*signify*) bezeichnen

**connubial** /kə'nju:bɪəl/ *adj.* ehelich; Ehe-

**conquer** /'kɒŋkə(r)/ *v.t.* besiegen ‹Gegner, Leidenschaft, Gewohnheit›; erobern ‹Land›; bezwingen ‹Berg, Gegner›; **I came, I saw, I ~ed** ich kam, ich sah, ich siegte

**conqueror** /'kɒŋkərə(r)/ *n.* Sieger, *der*/Siegerin, *die* (**of** über + *Akk.*); (*of a mountain*) Bezwinger, *der;* (*of a country*) Eroberer, *der;* **[William] the C~:** Wilhelm der Eroberer

**conquest** /'kɒŋkwest/ *n.* Ⓐ Eroberung, *die;* **the [Norman] C~:** die Eroberung Englands durch die Normannen; Ⓑ (*territory*) Eroberung, *die;* erobertes Gebiet; Ⓒ (*fig.: of mountain*) Bezwingung, *die;* Sieg, *der* (**of** über + *Akk.*)

**'con rod** *n.* (*Motor Veh. coll.*) Pleuelstange, *die*

**conscience** /'kɒnʃəns/ *n.* Gewissen, *das;* **have a good** *or* **clear/bad** *or* **guilty ~:** ein gutes/schlechtes Gewissen haben; **have no ~:** gewissenlos sein; **with a clear** *or* **easy ~:** mit gutem Gewissen; guten Gewissens (*geh.*); **have sth. on one's ~:** wegen etw. ein schlechtes Gewissen haben; **that is still on my ~:** das liegt mir immer noch auf der Seele; **in all ~:** ehrlicherweise; (*without doubt*) zweifellos; **freedom** *or* **liberty of ~:** Gewissensfreiheit, *die;* Freiheit des Gewissens; **a matter of ~:** eine Gewissensfrage

**conscience:** ~ **clause** *n.* (*Law*) Gewissensklausel, *die;* ~ **money** *n.* freiwillige Geldbuße; **~-smitten, ~-stricken, ~-struck** *adjs.* schuldbewusst

**conscientious** /kɒnʃɪ'enʃəs/ *adj.* pflichtbewusst; (*meticulous*) gewissenhaft; **~ objector** Wehrdienstverweigerer [aus Gewissensgründen]

**conscientiously** /kɒnʃɪ'enʃəslɪ/ *adv.* pflichtbewusst; (*meticulously*) gewissenhaft

**conscientiousness** /kɒnʃɪ'enʃəsnɪs/ *n., no pl.* Pflichtbewusstsein, *das;* (*meticulousness*) Gewissenhaftigkeit, *die*

**conscious** /'kɒnʃəs/ ❶ *adj.* Ⓐ **be ~ of sth.** sich (*Dat.*) einer Sache (*Gen.*) bewusst sein; **I was ~ that ...:** mir war bewusst, dass ...; **but he is not ~ of it** aber es ist ihm nicht bewusst; **I suddenly became ~ that ...:** mir wurde plötzlich bewusst, dass ...; Ⓑ *pred.* (*awake*) bei Bewusstsein *präd.;* **become ~:** wach werden; **become ~ again** wieder zu sich kommen; Ⓒ (*realized by doer*) bewusst ‹Handeln, Versuch, Bemühung›; Ⓓ (*self-~*) gewollt ‹Auftreten, Gehabe›. ❷ *n.* Bewusste, *das* (*Psych.*)

**consciously** /'kɒnʃəslɪ/ *adv.* bewusst; **be ~ superior** sich (*Dat.*) seiner Überlegenheit (*Gen.*) bewusst sein

**consciousness** /'kɒnʃəsnɪs/ *n., no pl.* Ⓐ Bewusstsein, *das;* **lose/recover** *or* **regain ~:** das Bewusstsein verlieren/wiedererlangen; bewusstlos werden/wieder zu sich kommen; Ⓑ (*totality of thought*) Bewusstsein, *das;* Ⓒ (*perception*) Bewusstsein, *das;* Bewusstheit, *die*

**conscript** ❶ /kən'skrɪpt/ *v.t.* einberufen ‹Soldaten›; ausheben ‹Armee›; **be ~ed into the army** zum Wehrdienst einberufen werden. ❷ /'kɒnskrɪpt/ *n.* Einberufene, *der/die;* **an army of ~s** eine Armee von Wehrpflichtigen

**conscription** /kən'skrɪpʃn/ *n.* (*action*) Einberufung, *die;* (*compulsory military service*) Wehrpflicht, *die*

**consecrate** /'kɒnsɪkreɪt/ *v.t.* (*Eccl.; also fig.*) weihen; konsekrieren; **~ sb. a bishop** jmdn. zum Bischof weihen

**consecration** /kɒnsɪ'kreɪʃn/ *n.* (*Eccl.; also fig.*) Weihe, *die;* Konsekration, *die*

**consecutive** /kən'sekjʊtɪv/ *adj.* Ⓐ (*following continuously*) aufeinander folgend ‹Monate, Jahre›; fortlaufend ‹Zahlen›; **this is the fifth ~ day that ...:** heute ist schon der fünfte Tag, an dem ...; Ⓑ (*in logical sequence*) folgerichtig; Ⓒ (*Ling.*) konsekutiv; Konsekutiv-; **~ clause** Konsekutiv-/Folgesatz, *der*

**consecutive interpre'tation** *n.* Konsekutivdolmetschen, *das*

**consecutively** /kən'sekjʊtɪvlɪ/ *adv.* hintereinander; fortlaufend ‹nummeriert›

**consensus** /kən'sensəs/ *n.* Einigkeit, *die;* Konsens[us], *der* (*geh.*); *attrib.* ‹Politik, Regierungsstil usw.› des Miteinander *od.* der Gemeinsamkeit; **the general ~ is that ...:** es besteht allgemeiner Konsens (*geh.*) *od.* allgemeine Einigkeit darüber, dass ...; **the ~ of opinion is in favour of the amendment** die allgemeine Mehrheit *od.* die Mehrheitsmeinung ist für den Änderungsantrag

**consent** /kən'sent/ ❶ *v.i.* zustimmen; **~ to sth.** einer Sache (*Dat.*) zustimmen; in eine Sache einwilligen; **~ to do sth.** einwilligen, etw. zu tun; **~ing adult** erwachsene homosexuelle Person. ❷ *n.* Ⓐ (*agreement*) Zustimmung, *die* (**to** zu); Einwilligung, *die* (**to** in + *Akk.*); **by common** *or* **general ~:** nach allgemeiner Auffassung; (*as wished by all*) auf allgemeinen Wunsch; **age of ~** *Alter, in dem man hinsichtlich Heirat und Geschlechtsleben nicht mehr als minderjährig gilt;* ≈ Ehemündigkeitsalter, *das;* Ⓑ (*permission*) Zustimmung, *die;* Erlaubnis, *die;* **give/refuse [sb.] one's ~:** [jmdm.] seine Zustimmung geben/verweigern

**consequence** /'kɒnsɪkwəns/ *n.* Ⓐ (*result*) Folge, *die;* **in ~:** folglich; infolgedessen; **in ~ of** als Folge (+ *Gen.*); **as a ~:** infolgedessen; **as a ~ of** infolge (+ *Gen.*); **with the ~ that ...:** mit dem Ergebnis, dass ...; **accept** *or* **take the ~s** die Folgen tragen; Ⓑ (*importance*) Bedeutung, *die;* **be of no ~:** unerheblich *od.* ohne Bedeutung sein; **nothing of ~:** nichts von Bedeutung; nichts Erhebliches; **persons of [no] ~** (*significant*) [un]bedeutende/(*influential, high-ranking*) [un]wichtige Leute; **he's of no ~:** er ist unbedeutend *od.* unwichtig

**consequent** /'kɒnsɪkwənt/ *adj.* Ⓐ (*resultant*) daraus folgend; sich daraus ergebend; (*following in time*) darauf folgend; **be ~ [up]on sth.** (*formal*) die Folge einer Sache (*Gen.*) sein; Ⓑ (*logically consistent*) folgerichtig

**consequential** /kɒnsɪ'kwenʃl/ *adj.* Ⓐ (*resulting*) daraus folgend; sich daraus ergebend; (*following in time*) darauf folgend; Ⓑ (*indirectly following*) indirekt; sich indirekt ergebend; **~ damage[s]** Folgeschäden *Pl.;* Ⓒ (*self-important*) überheblich ‹Lächeln, Stimme, Person›

**consequentially** /kɒnsɪ'kwenʃəlɪ/ *adv.* Ⓐ (*indirectly*) indirekt; Ⓑ (*self-importantly*) überheblich

**consequently** /'kɒnsɪkwəntlɪ/ *adv.* infolgedessen; folglich

**conservancy** /kən'sɜ:vənsɪ/ *n.* Ⓐ (*Brit.: conserving body*) *Behörde, der der Natur-/Gewässerschutz usw. untersteht;* **the Nature C~:** die Naturschutzbehörde; **the Thames C~:** der Themse-Gewässerschutz; Ⓑ (*preservation*) Naturschutz, *der*

**conservation** /kɒnsə'veɪʃn/ *n.* Ⓐ (*preservation*) Schutz, *der;* Erhaltung, *die;* (*wise utilization*) sparsamer Umgang (**of** mit); **wildlife ~:** Schutz wild lebender Tierarten; Ⓑ (*Phys.*) **~ of energy/momentum** Erhaltung der Energie/des Impulses

**conser'vation area** *n.* (*Brit.*) (*rural*) Landschaftsschutzgebiet, *das;* (*urban*) unter Denkmalschutz stehendes Gebiet

**conservationist** /kɒnsə'veɪʃənɪst/ *n.* Naturschützer, *der*/-schützerin, *die*

**conservatism** /kən'sɜ:vətɪzm/ *n.* Konservati[vi]smus, *der*

**conservative** /kən'sɜ:vətɪv/ ❶ *adj.* Ⓐ (*conserving*) erhaltend; konservierend; **~ surgery** konservative Chirurgie; Ⓑ (*averse to change*) konservativ; Ⓒ (*not too high*) vorsichtig, eher zu niedrig ‹Zahlen, Schätzung›; **at a ~ estimate** nach vorsichtiger *od.* (*Jargon*) konservativer Schätzung; Ⓓ (*avoiding extremes*) konservativ ‹Geschmack, Ansichten, Baustil›; Ⓔ (*Brit. Polit.*) konservativ; **the C~ Party** die Konservative Partei. ❷ *n.* Ⓐ **C~** (*Brit. Polit.*) Konservative, *der/die;* Ⓑ (*~ person*) Konservative, *der/die*

**conservatively** /kən'sɜ:vətɪvlɪ/ *adv.* vorsichtig, eher zu niedrig ‹geschätzt›

**conservatoire** /kən'sɜ:vətwɑ:(r)/ *n.* (*school of music*) Konservatorium, *das;* (*school of other arts*) Kunsthochschule, *die*

**conservatory** /kən'sɜ:vətərɪ/ *n.* Ⓐ (*greenhouse*) Wintergarten, *der;* Ⓑ (*Amer.*) ⇒ **conservatoire**

**conserve** /kən'sɜ:v/ ❶ *v.t.* Ⓐ erhalten ‹Gebäude, Kunstwerk, Wälder›; bewahren ‹Ideale, Prinzipien›; schonen ‹Gesundheit, Kräfte›; Ⓑ *esp. in p. p.* (*Phys.*) erhalten ‹Energie, Impuls›. ❷ *n. often in pl.* Eingemachte, *das;* **~s** Eingemachtes

**consider** /kən'sɪdə(r)/ *v.t.* Ⓐ (*look at*) betrachten; (*think about*) **~ sth.** an etw. (*Akk.*) denken; Ⓑ (*weigh merits of*) denken an (+ *Akk.*); **he's ~ing emigrating** er denkt daran *od.* trägt sich mit dem Gedanken, auszuwandern; **five candidates are being ~ed** fünf Kandidaten sind in der engeren Wahl; Ⓒ (*reflect*) sich (*Dat.*) überlegen; bedenken; **you must ~ that you/whether or not you ...:** du musst bedenken *od.* dir überlegen, dass du/ob du ... oder nicht; **just ~!** (*abs.*) überleg [dir das] doch mal!; Ⓓ (*have opinion*) annehmen; finden; **we ~ that you are not to blame** wir sind der Ansicht *od.* finden, dass Sie nicht schuld sind; Ⓔ (*regard as*) halten für; **I ~ him [to be** *or* **as] a swindler** ich halte ihn für einen Betrüger; **do you ~ yourself educated?** hältst du dich für gebildet?; **~ yourself under arrest** betrachten Sie sich als verhaftet; **she is ~ed a great beauty** sie gilt als große Schönheit; Ⓕ (*allow for*) berücksichtigen; **~ other people's feelings** auf die Gefühle anderer Rücksicht nehmen; **all things ~ed** alles in allem

**considerable** /kən'sɪdərəbl/ *adj.* Ⓐ (*no little*) beträchtlich; erheblich ‹Schwierigkeiten, Ärger›; groß ‹Freude, Charakterstärke›; eingehend ‹Überlegung›; (*Amer.: large*) ansehnlich ‹Gebäude, Edelstein›; Ⓑ (*important*) bedeutend ‹Person, Künstler›

**considerably** /kən'sɪdərəblɪ/ *adv.* erheblich; (*in amount*) beträchtlich

**considerate** /kən'sɪdərət/ *adj.* rücksichtsvoll; (*thoughtfully kind*) entgegenkommend; **be ~ to[wards] sb.** rücksichtsvoll gegenüber jmdm. sein; auf jmdn. Rücksicht nehmen

**considerately** /kən'sɪdərətlɪ/ *adv.* rücksichtsvoll; (*obligingly*) entgegenkommend

**considerateness** /kən'sɪdərətnɪs/ *n.* Rücksichtnahme, *die* (**for** auf + *Akk.*); (*obligingness*) Entgegenkommen, *das*

**consideration** /kənsɪdə'reɪʃn/ *n.* Ⓐ Überlegung, *die;* (*meditation*) Betrachtung, *die;* **take sth. into ~:** etw. berücksichtigen *od.* bedenken; **give sth. one's ~:** etw. in Erwägung ziehen; **the matter is under ~:** die Angelegenheit wird geprüft; **in ~ of** unter Berücksichtigung (+ *Gen.*); **leave sth. out of ~:** etw. unberücksichtigt lassen; etw. außer Betracht lassen; Ⓑ (*thoughtfulness*) Rücksichtnahme, *die* (**for** auf + *Akk.*); **show ~ for sb.** Rücksicht auf jmdn. nehmen; Ⓒ (*sth. as reason*) Umstand, *der;* **an important ~:** ein wichtiger Faktor; Ⓓ (*payment*) Bezahlung, *die;* **for a ~:** gegen Entgelt; Ⓔ (*Law*) Ausgleich, *der;* Ersatz, *der*

**considered** /kən'sɪdəd/ *adj.* Ⓐ **~ opinion** feste *od.* ernsthafte Überzeugung; Ⓑ **be highly ~ [by others]** [bei anderen] in hohem Ansehen stehen

**considering** /kən'sɪdərɪŋ/ *prep.* **~ sth.** wenn man etw. bedenkt; **~ [that] ...:** wenn man bedenkt, dass ...; **that's not so bad, ~** (*coll.*) das ist eigentlich gar nicht mal so schlecht (*ugs.*)

**consign** /kən'saɪn/ *v.t.* Ⓐ anvertrauen (**to** *Dat.*); **~ a child to its uncle's care** ein Kind in die Obhut seines Onkels geben; **~ sth. to the scrap heap** (*lit. or fig.*) etw. auf den Schrotthaufen werfen; **~ a letter to the flames** einen Brief dem Feuer übergeben (*geh.*); Ⓑ (*Commerc.*) übersenden, (*fachspr.*) konsignieren ‹Güter› (**to** an + *Akk.*); senden ‹Brief, Paket› (**to** an + *Akk.*)

**consignment** /kən'saɪnmənt/ *n.* (*Commerc.*) Ⓐ (*consigning*) Übersendung, *die* (**to** an + *Akk.*); Konsignation, *die* (*fachspr.*) (**to** an + *Akk.*); **~ note** Frachtbrief, *der;* Ⓑ (*goods*) Sendung, *die;* (*large*) Ladung, *die*

**consist** /kən'sɪst/ *v.i.* Ⓐ **~ of** bestehen aus; Ⓑ **~ in** bestehen in (+ *Dat.*)

**consistence** /kən'sɪstəns/, **consistency** /kən'sɪstənsɪ/ *ns.* Ⓐ (*density*) Konsistenz, *die;* **mixtures of various consistencies** Mischungen verschiedener Konsistenz; Ⓑ (*being consistent*) Konsequenz, *die;* **~ of style** stilistische Konsistenz

**consistent** /kən'sɪstənt/ *adj.* Ⓐ (*compatible*) [miteinander] vereinbar; **be ~ with sth.** mit etw. übereinstimmen; mit etw. vereinbar sein; Ⓑ (*uniform*) beständig; gleich bleibend ‹Qualität›; einheitlich ‹Verfahren, Vorgehen, Darstellung›; Ⓒ (*adhering to principles*) konsequent

**consistently** /kən'sɪstəntlɪ/ *adv.* (*compatibly, in harmony*) in Übereinstimmung ‹handeln›; (*uniformly*) einheitlich ‹gestalten›; konsistent ‹denken›; (*persistently*) konsequent ‹behaupten, verfolgen, handeln›

**consistory** /kən'sɪstərɪ, 'kɒnsɪstərɪ/ *n.* (*RC Ch.*) Konsistorium, *das*

**consolation** /kɒnsə'leɪʃn/ *n.* Ⓐ (*act*) Tröstung, *die;* Trost, *der;* **words of ~:** Worte des Trostes; tröstende Worte; **a letter of ~:** ein trostvoller Brief; Ⓑ (*consoling circumstance*) Trost, *der;* **that's one ~!** das ist tröstlich *od.* ein Trost!

**conso'lation prize** *n.* Trostpreis, *der*

**consolatory** /kən'sɒlətərɪ, kən'səʊlətərɪ/ *adj.* tröstend, trostvoll (**to** für)

**console**[1] /kən'səʊl/ *v.t.* trösten; **~ sb. for a loss** jmdn. über einen Verlust hinwegtrösten

**console**[2] /'kɒnsəʊl/ *n.* **A** (*Mus.*) Spieltisch, *der;* **B** (*panel*) [Schalt]pult, *das;* **C** (*cabinet*) Truhe, *die*

**consolidate** /kən'sɒlɪdeɪt/ **1** *v.t.* **A** (*strengthen*) festigen ‹Macht, Stellung›; (*fig.*) konsolidieren ‹Stellung, Einfluss, Macht›; **B** (*combine*) zusammenlegen ‹Territorien, Grundstücke, Firmen›; konsolidieren ‹Schulden, Anleihen›. **2** *v.i.* **A** (*become solid*) hart werden; **B** (*merge*) ‹Firmen:› fusionieren

**consolidation** /kənsɒlɪ'deɪʃn/ *n., no pl.* **A** (*strengthening*) Festigung, *die;* (*fig.*) Konsolidierung, *die;* **B** (*combining*) Zusammenlegung, *die;* (*of debts, loans*) Konsolidation, *die*

**consoling** /kən'səʊlɪŋ/ *adj.* tröstlich

**consommé** /kən'sɒmeɪ/ *n.* (*Gastr.*) Kraftbrühe, *die;* Consommé, *die* (*fachspr.*)

**consonance** /'kɒnsənəns/ *n.* **A** (*Mus.*) Harmonie, *die;* (*of two notes*) Konsonanz, *die;* **B** (*fig. formal*) Übereinstimmung, *die;* **C** (*Phonet.*) Konsonanz, *die*

**consonant** /'kɒnsənənt/ **1** *n.* Konsonant, *der;* Mitlaut, *der;* **~ shift** Lautverschiebung, *die.* **2** *adj.* **A** (*formal*) **be ~ with** *or* **to sth.** im Einklang mit etw. stehen; **B** (*Mus.*) konsonant; **C** (*Phonet.*) gleichklingend

**consonantal** /kɒnsə'næntl/ *adj.* (*Phonet.*) konsonantisch

**consort**[1] /'kɒnsɔ:t/ *n.* Gemahl, *der*/Gemahlin, *die;* **queen ~:** Gemahlin des Königs; Königin, *die* (*volkst.*)

**consort**[2] /kən'sɔ:t/ *v.i.* **A** (*keep company*) verkehren (**with** mit); **B** (*arch.: agree*) übereinstimmen (**with, to** mit); **they ~ed ill together** sie passten schlecht zusammen

**consort**[3] /'kɒnsɔ:t/ *n.* (*Mus.*) Consort, *das*

**consortium** /kən'sɔ:tɪəm/ *n., pl.* **consortia** /kən'sɔ:tɪə/ (*association*) Konsortium, *das*

**conspectus** /kən'spektəs/ *n.* Übersicht, *die*

**conspicuous** /kən'spɪkjʊəs/ *adj.* **A** (*clearly visible*) unübersehbar; **make oneself ~:** dafür sorgen, dass man deutlich sichtbar ist; **leave sth. in a ~ position** etw. sichtbar liegen lassen; **B** (*noticeable*) auffallend; **be ~:** sehr auffallen; **make oneself ~ by one's absence** durch Abwesenheit auffallen *od.* (*iron.*) glänzen; **~ expenditure/consumption** Prestigeausgaben/demonstrativer Konsum; **C** (*obvious, noteworthy*) auffallend ‹Schönheit›; herausragend ‹Tapferkeit›; **~ for their loyalty** bekannt für ihre Loyalität; **the most ~ example** das augenfälligste Beispiel; das Paradebeispiel

**conspicuously** /kən'spɪkjʊəslɪ/ *adv.* **A** (*very visibly*) unübersehbar; **B** (*obviously*) auffallend

**conspicuousness** /kən'spɪkjʊəsnɪs/ *n., no pl.* **A** (*being clearly visible*) Unübersehbarkeit, *die;* **B** (*obviousness*) Auffälligkeit, *die*

**conspiracy** /kən'spɪrəsɪ/ *n.* **A** (*conspiring*) Verschwörung, *die;* **be in ~ against sb.** sich gegen jmdn. verschworen haben; **B** (*plot*) Komplott, *das;* **form a ~:** ein Komplott schmieden; **~ of silence** verabredetes Stillschweigen; **C** (*Law*) Verabredung zu einer Straftat; **~ to murder** Mordkomplott, *das*

**conspirator** /kən'spɪrətə(r)/ *n.* Verschwörer, *der*/Verschwörerin, *die*

**conspiratorial** /kənspɪrə'tɔ:rɪəl/ *adj.* verschwörerisch

**conspire** /kən'spaɪə(r)/ *v.i.* (*lit. or fig.*) sich verschwören

**constable** /'kʌnstəbl, 'kɒnstəbl/ *n.* ▶ 1261, ▶ 1617 **A** (*Brit.*) ⇒ **police constable**; **B** (*Brit.*) **Chief C~:** ≈ Polizeipräsident, *der*/-präsidentin, *die*

**constabulary** /kən'stæbjʊlərɪ/ **1** *n.* Polizei, *die;* (*unit*) Polizeieinheit, *die.* **2** *adj.* Polizei-

**Constance** /'kɒnstəns/ *pr. n.* (*Geog.*) Konstanz (*das*); **Lake ~:** der Bodensee

**constancy** /'kɒnstənsɪ/ *n.* **A** (*steadfastness*) Standhaftigkeit, *die;* **B** (*faithfulness*) Treue, *die;* **C** (*unchangingness*) Beständigkeit, *die;* (*uniformity*) Gleichmäßigkeit, *die*

**constant** /'kɒnstənt/ **1** *adj.* **A** (*unceasing*) ständig; anhaltend ‹Regen›; **it's ~ laughter when they're around** es wird ununterbrochen gelacht, wenn sie da sind; **be a ~ reminder of sth./sb.** ständig an etw./jmdn. erinnern; **we had ~ rain** es hat dauernd geregnet; **there was a ~ stream of traffic** der Verkehr floss ununterbrochen; **B** (*unchanging*) gleich bleibend; konstant; **C** (*steadfast*) standhaft; **be ~ in one's determination** stets an seinem Entschluss festhalten; **D** (*faithful*) treu; **be ~ [to sb.]** [jmdm.] treu sein. **2** *n.* (*Phys., Math.*) Konstante, *die*

**constantly** /'kɒnstəntlɪ/ *adv.* **A** (*unceasingly*) ständig; **B** (*unchangingly*) konstant; **C** (*steadfastly*) standhaft; **D** (*faithfully*) treu

**constellation** /kɒnstə'leɪʃn/ *n.* Sternbild, *das;* Konstellation, *die* (*Astron.*)

**consternation** /kɒnstə'neɪʃn/ *n.* Bestürzung, *die;* (*confusion*) Aufregung, *die;* **in ~:** bestürzt/aufgeregt; **be filled with ~:** sehr bestürzt/aufgeregt sein

**constipate** /'kɒnstɪpeɪt/ *v.t.* zu Verstopfung führen bei; **be ~d** an Verstopfung leiden

**constipation** /kɒnstɪ'peɪʃn/ *n.* ▶ 1232 Verstopfung, *die;* Konstipation, *die* (*Med.*)

**constituency** /kən'stɪtjʊənsɪ/ *n.* (*voters*) Wählerschaft, *die* (*eines Wahlkreises*); (*area*) Wahlkreis, *der*

**constituent** /kən'stɪtjʊənt/ **1** *adj.* (*composing a whole*) **~ part** Bestandteil, *der;* **~ member** Mitglied, *das;* **the ~ gases in air/~ parts of water** die Gase, aus denen Luft/die Teile, aus denen Wasser besteht. **2** *n.* **A** (*component part*) Bestandteil, *der;* **B** (*member of constituency*) Wähler, *der* /Wählerin, *die* (*eines Wahlkreises*)

**constitute** /'kɒnstɪtju:t/ *v.t.* **A** (*form*) sein; **~ a threat to** eine Gefahr sein für; **B** (*make up*) bilden; begründen ‹Anspruch›; **be ~d of bricks and mortar** aus Ziegelsteinen und Mörtel bestehen; **C** (*give legal form to*) gründen ‹Partei, Organisation›; konstituieren ‹Versammlung›

**constitution** /kɒnstɪ'tju:ʃn/ *n.* **A** (*of person*) Konstitution, *die;* **B** (*mode of State organization*) Staatsform, *die;* **C** (*body of laws and principles*) Verfassung, *die;* **written ~:** schriftlich festgelegte Verfassung; **D** (*giving legal form*) Gründung, *die*

**constitutional** /kɒnstɪ'tju:ʃənl/ **1** *adj.* **A** (*of bodily or mental constitution*) konstitutionell; **B** (*Polit.*) (*of constitution*) der Verfassung *nachgestellt;* (*authorized by or in harmony with constitution*) verfassungsmäßig; konstitutionell ‹Monarchie›; **~ law** Verfassungsrecht, *das;* **C** (*essential*) wesentlich; grundsätzlich ‹Fähigkeit›. **2** *n.* Spaziergang, *der*

**constitutionality** /kɒnstɪtju:ʃə'nælɪtɪ/ *n., no pl.* Verfassungskonformität, *die*

**constitutionally** /kɒnstɪ'tju:ʃənəlɪ/ *adv.* **A** (*in bodily or mental constitution*) konstitutionell; **B** (*Polit.*) verfassungsmäßig; **C** (*essentially*) wesentlich

**constrain** /kən'streɪn/ *v.t.* **A** zwingen; **B** (*confine*) [auf]halten; (*fig.*) zügeln

**constrained** /kən'streɪnd/ *adj.* gequält; gezwungen ‹Pose›; steif ‹Bewegung, Pose›

**constraint** /kən'streɪnt/ *n.* **A** Zwang, *der;* **he felt himself under some ~ to speak** er fühlte sich gezwungen zu sprechen; **B** (*confinement*) Enge, *die;* (*limitation*) Einschränkung, *die;* **C** (*restraint*) Gezwungenheit, *die;* **the atmosphere was one of ~:** die Atmosphäre war gezwungen *od.* steif

**constrict** /kən'strɪkt/ *v.t.* (*make narrow*) verengen; **roadworks are ~ing the flow of traffic** Straßenarbeiten behindern den Verkehrsfluss

**constriction** /kən'strɪkʃn/ *n.* (*narrowing*) Verengung, *die;* **~ of the neck/throat** Einschnürung des Halses/der Kehle

**construct** **1** /kən'strʌkt/ *v.t.* **A** (*build*) bauen; (*fig.*) aufbauen; erstellen ‹Plan›; entwickeln ‹Idee›; **B** (*Ling.; Geom.: draw*) konstruieren. **2** /'kɒnstrʌkt/ *n.* **A** Konstrukt, *das;* **B** (*Ling.*) Konstruktion, *die*

**construction** /kən'strʌkʃn/ *n.* **A** (*constructing*) Bau, *der;* (*of sentence*) Konstruktion, *die;* (*fig.*) (*of empire, kingdom*) Errichtung, *die;* Aufbau, *der;* (*of plan, syllabus*) Erstellung, *die;* (*of idea*) Entwicklung, *die;* **~ work** Bauarbeiten *Pl.;* **~ worker** ▶ 1261 Bauarbeiter, *der;* **of wooden ~:** aus Holz gebaut; **be under ~:** im Bau sein; **B** (*thing constructed*) Bauwerk, *das;* (*fig.*) Gebilde, *das;* **a wooden ~:** eine Holzkonstruktion; **C** (*Ling.; Geom.: drawing*) Konstruktion, *die;* **D** (*interpretation*) Deutung, *die;* **what ~ would you put upon ...?** wie würden Sie ... interpretieren *od.* auslegen?

**constructional** /kən'strʌkʃənl/ *adj.* Bau‹vorhaben, -plan, -weise›; Konstruktions‹element, -teil, -basis›; **~ kit** Bausatz, *der;* **~ toy** Spielzeug zum Aufbauen

**constructive** /kən'strʌktɪv/ *adj.* **A** (*of construction; of structure of building*) konstruktiv; Bau‹arbeiter, -material, -element, -plan›; **B** (*tending to construct*) konstruktiv ‹Philosophie, Methode›; schöpferisch ‹Talent, Intelligenz›; **C** (*helpful*) konstruktiv; **D** (*inferred*) indirekt

**constructively** /kən'strʌktɪvlɪ/ *adv.* **A** (*in construction*) bautechnisch gesehen; **B** (*helpfully*) konstruktiv

**construe** /kən'stru:/ *v.t.* **A** (*Ling.*) (*combine*) konstruieren; (*analyse*) zerlegen; (*translate*) übersetzen; **B** (*interpret*) auslegen; auffassen; **I ~d his words as meaning that ...:** ich habe ihn so verstanden, dass ...

**consul** /'kɒnsl/ *n.* Konsul, *der*

**consular** /'kɒnsjʊlə(r)/ *adj.* (*of State agent*) konsularisch; **~ rank** Rang eines Konsuls

**consulate** /'kɒnsjʊlət/ *n.* **A** (*period*) Amtszeit [als Konsul]; **B** (*establishment*) Konsulat, *das;* **C** (*Roman & French Hist.*) Konsulat, *das*

**consulship** /'kɒnslʃɪp/ ⇒ **consulate A, C**

**consult** /kən'sʌlt/ **1** *v.i.* sich beraten (**with** mit); **~ together** sich miteinander beraten. **2** *v.t.* **A** (*seek information from*) konsultieren; befragen ‹Orakel›; fragen, konsultieren, zu Rate ziehen ‹Arzt, Fachmann›; **~ a list/book** in einer Liste/einem Buch nachsehen; **~ one's watch** auf die Uhr sehen; **~ a dictionary** in einem Wörterbuch nachschlagen; **B** (*consider*) berücksichtigen; bedenken

**consultancy** /kən'sʌltənsɪ/ *n.* **A** (*of adviser*) Beraterstelle, *die;* **~ fee** Beratungsgebühr, *die;* **B** (*of physician*) ≈ Chefarztstelle, *die*

**consultant** /kən'sʌltənt/ **1** *n.* ▶ 1261 **A** (*adviser*) Berater, *der* /Beraterin, *die;* **B** (*physician*) ≈ Chefarzt, *der*/-ärztin, *die.* **2** *attrib. adj.* ⇒ **consulting**

**consultation** /kɒnsʌl'teɪʃn/ *n.* Beratung, *die* (**on** über + *Akk.*); **have a ~ with sb.** sich mit jmdm. beraten; **by ~ of a dictionary/of an expert** durch Konsultation eines Wörterbuchs/Experten; **they are in ~ with the management about wages** sie stehen mit der Betriebsleitung in Lohnverhandlungen; **act in ~ with sb.** in Absprache mit jmdm. handeln

**consultative** /kən'sʌltətɪv/ *adj.* beratend; konsultativ; **work on a ~ basis** *or* **in a ~ capacity for sb.** als Berater für jmdn. arbeiten; **~ document** ≈ Entwurf als Diskussionsgrundlage; (*governmental*) Regierungsentwurf, *der*

**consulting** /kən'sʌltɪŋ/ *attrib. adj.* beratend ‹Architekt, Chemiker, Ingenieur›; **~ physician** Konsiliararzt, *der*/-ärztin, *die*

**con'sulting room** *n.* Sprechzimmer, *das*

**consumable** /kən'sju:məbl/ *adj.* **A** (*exhaustible*) kurzlebig ‹Konsumgüter›; **B** (*edible, drinkable*) genießbar

**consume** /kən'sju:m/ *v.t.* **A** (*use up*) verbrauchen; ‹Person:› aufwenden, ‹Sache:› kosten ‹Zeit, Energie›; **B** (*destroy*) vernichten; (*eat, drink*) konsumieren; verkonsumieren (*ugs.*); **'nothing is to be ~d on these premises'** „Verzehr von Speisen und Getränken nicht gestattet"; **C** (*fig.*) **be ~d with love/passion** sich in Liebe/Leidenschaft verzehren; **be ~d with fear/jealousy/envy/longing** sich vor Angst/Eifersucht/Neid/Sehnsucht verzehren (*geh.*)

**consumer** /kən'sju:mə(r)/ *n.* (*Econ.*) Verbraucher, *der*/Verbraucherin, *die;* Konsument, *der*/Konsumentin, *die;* ⇒ *also* **durable** 2

**con'sumer goods** *n. pl.* Konsumgüter

**consumerism** /kən'sju:mərɪzm/ *n., no pl., no art.* Konsumerismus, *der*

**consumer:** ~ **pro'tection** *n.* Verbraucherschutz, *der;* ~ **research** *n.* Verbrauchsforschung, *die;* Konsumforschung, *die;* ~ **resistance** ⇒ **sales resistance**

**consuming** /kən'sju:mɪŋ/ *adj.* ganz in Anspruch nehmend, verzehrend (*geh.*) ‹Sehnsucht, Ehrgeiz›; **stamp-collecting is a ~ interest of his** sein Interesse am Briefmarkensammeln nimmt ihn ganz in Anspruch

**consummate** ❶ /kən'sʌmət/ *adj.* [A] (*perfect*) vollkommen; **with ~ ease** mühelos; [B] (*accomplished*) perfekt; **a ~ artist** ein vollendeter Künstler. ❷ /'kɒnsəmeɪt, 'kɒnsjʊmeɪt/ *v.t.* vollenden, zum Abschluss bringen ‹Diskussion, Geschäftsverhandlungen›; vollziehen ‹Ehe›

**consummately** /kən'sʌmətlɪ/ *adj.* (*highly*) höchst; (*perfectly*) vollendet; (*completely*) völlig

**consummation** /kɒnsə'meɪʃn/ *n.* [A] (*completion*) Vollendung, *die;* (*of discussion, business*) Abschluss, *der;* (*of marriage*) Vollzug, *der;* [B] (*goal*) Erfüllung, *die;* (*perfection, perfected thing*) Vollendung, *die*

**consumption** /kən'sʌmpʃn/ *n.* [A] (*using up, eating, drinking*) Verbrauch, *der* (**of** an + *Dat.*); (*act of eating or drinking*) Verzehr, *der* (**of** von); **~ of electricity/fuel/sugar** Strom-/Kraftstoff-/Zuckerverbrauch, *der;* **~ of alcohol** Alkoholkonsum, *der;* **what is our milk ~?** wieviel Milch verbrauchen wir?; [B] (*destruction*) Vernichtung, *die;* (*waste*) Vergeudung, *die;* [C] (*Econ.*) Verbrauch, *der;* Konsum, *der;* [D] ▸ 1232 (*Med. dated*) Schwindsucht, *die* (*veralt.*)

**consumptive** /kən'sʌmptɪv/ ❶ *adj.* (*Med. dated*) schwindsüchtig (*veralt.*). ❷ *n.* Tuberkulosekranke, *der/die;* Schwindsüchtige, *der/die* (*veralt.*)

**cont.** *abbr.* **continued** Forts.

**contact** ❶ /'kɒntækt/ *n.* [A] (*state of touching*) Berührung, *die;* Kontakt, *der;* (*fig.*) Verbindung, *die;* Kontakt, *der;* **point of ~:** Berührungspunkt, *der;* **be in ~ with sth.** etw. berühren; **be in ~ with sb.** (*fig.*) mit jmdm. in Verbindung stehen *od.* Kontakt haben; **come in** *or* **into ~ [with sth.]** [mit etw.] in Berührung kommen; **come into ~ with sb./sth.** (*fig.*) mit jmdm./etw. etwas zu tun haben; **make ~ with sth.** etw. berühren; **make ~ with sb.** (*fig.*) sich mit jmdm. in Verbindung setzen; mit jmdm. Kontakt aufnehmen; **lose ~ with sb.** (*fig.*) den Kontakt mit jmdm. verlieren; **renew ~ [with sb.]** (*fig.*) den Kontakt [mit *od.* zu jmdm.] wieder aufnehmen; [B] (*Electr.*) (*connection*) Kontakt, *der;* **make/break a/the ~:** einen/den Kontakt herstellen/unterbrechen; **when the two wires make ~:** wenn die beiden Drähte sich berühren; [C] (*Med.: person*) Kontaktperson, *die;* [D] (*adviser etc.*) Verbindung, *die;* Kontakt, *der.*
❷ /'kɒntækt, kən'tækt/ *v.t.* [A] (*get into touch with*) sich in Verbindung setzen mit; **can I ~ you by telephone?** sind Sie telefonisch zu erreichen?; **try to ~ sb.** jmdn. zu erreichen versuchen; **~ your bank manager about the loan** wenden Sie sich bezüglich des Darlehens an den Direktor Ihrer Bank; **~ sb. by letter** sich schriftlich mit jmdm. in Verbindung setzen; [B] (*begin dealings with*) Kontakt aufnehmen mit

**contact:** ~ **lens** *n.* Kontaktlinse, *die;* ~ **man** *n.* Kontaktmann, *der;* Mittelsmann, *der;* ~ **print** *n.* (*Photog.*) Kontaktabzug, *der*

**contagion** /kən'teɪdʒn/ *n.* [A] (*communication of disease*) Ansteckung, *die;* [B] (*contagious disease*) ansteckende Krankheit; [C] (*moral corruption*) Seuche, *die* (*fig.*)

**contagious** /kən'teɪdʒəs/ *adj.* (*lit. or fig.*) ansteckend; **~ area/water** verseuchtes Gebiet/Wasser; **he is ~/is no longer ~:** er hat eine ansteckende Krankheit/er steckt niemanden mehr an

**contain** /kən'teɪn/ *v.t.* [A] (*hold as contents, include*) enthalten; (*comprise*) umfassen; **be ~ed within a space/between limits** sich in einem Gebiet/zwischen Grenzen befinden; [B] (*prevent from moving*) halten; (*prevent from spreading; also Mil.*) aufhalten; eindämmen ‹Krankheit›; (*restrain*) unterdrücken; **he could hardly ~ himself for joy** er konnte vor Freude kaum an sich (*Akk.*) halten

**container** /kən'teɪnə(r)/ *n.* Behälter, *der;* (*cargo ~*) Container, *der;* **cardboard/wooden ~:** Pappkarton, *der*/Holzkiste, *die;* **in cylindrical/circular plastic ~s** in Plastiktrommeln/in [runden] Plastikbehältern

**containerize** /kən'teɪnəraɪz/ *v.t.* in Container verpacken; auf Containertransport umstellen ‹Handelsweg, Verfahren›

**con'tainer ship** *n.* Containerschiff, *das*

**containment** /kən'teɪnmənt/ *n.* Eindämmung, *die;* (*Mil.*) Aufhalten, *das*

**contaminant** /kən'tæmɪnənt/ *n.* verunreinigende Substanz

**contaminate** /kən'tæmɪneɪt/ *v.t.* [A] (*pollute*) verunreinigen; (*with radioactivity*) verseuchen; [B] (*infect, lit. or fig.*) infizieren; (*fig.: spoil*) verseuchen

**contamination** /kəntæmɪ'neɪʃn/ *n.* ⇒ **contaminate**: Verunreinigung, *die;* Verseuchung, *die;* Infizierung, *die*

**contango** /kən'tæŋgəʊ/ *n., pl.* **~s** (*Brit. Finance*) Report, *der* (*Bankw.*)

**contemplate** /'kɒntəmpleɪt/ ❶ *v.t.* [A] betrachten; (*mentally*) nachdenken über (+ *Akk.*); ⇒ *also* **navel**; [B] (*expect*) rechnen mit; (*consider*) in Betracht ziehen; **~ sth./doing sth.** an etw. (*Akk.*) denken/daran denken, etw. zu tun; **I wouldn't even ~ the idea** das käme für mich überhaupt nicht in Betracht. ❷ *v.i.* nachdenken

**contemplation** /kɒntəm'pleɪʃn/ *n.* [A] Betrachtung, *die;* (*mental*) Nachdenken, *das* (**of** über + *Akk.*); [B] (*expectation*) Erwartung, *die;* (*consideration*) Erwägung, *die;* **be in ~:** erwogen werden; [C] (*meditation*) Kontemplation, *die*

**contemplative** /kən'templətɪv, 'kɒntəmpleɪtɪv/ *adj.* besinnlich; kontemplativ (*geh.*)

**contemporaneous** /kəntempə'reɪnɪəs/ *adj.* (*formal*) gleichzeitig; (*of the same period*) aus derselben Zeit *nachgestellt*

**contemporary** /kən'tempərərɪ/ ❶ *adj.* [A] zeitgenössisch; (*present-day*) heutig; zeitgenössisch; **A is ~ with B** A und B finden zur gleichen Zeit statt; **the design is highly/very ~:** das Design ist hochmodern; [B] (*equal in age*) gleichaltrig; **A is ~ with B** A und B sind gleichaltrig.
❷ *n.* [A] (*person belonging to same time*) Zeitgenosse, *der*/-genossin, *die* (**to** von); **we were contemporaries** *or* **he was a ~ of mine at university/school** er war ein Studienkollege *od.* Kommilitone/Schulkamerad von mir; [B] (*person of same age*) Altersgenosse, *der*/-genossin, *die;* **they are contemporaries** sie sind gleichaltrig *od.* Altersgenossen; **he is a ~ of hers** er ist [genau]so alt wie sie

**contempt** /kən'tempt/ *n.* [A] Verachtung, *die* (**of, for** für); ⇒ *also* **familiarity** C; [B] (*disregard*) Missachtung, *die;* **in ~ of all rules** unter Missachtung aller Regeln; [C] (*being despised*) **have** *or* **hold sb. in ~:** jmdn. verachten; **bring sb. into ~:** jmdn. in Verruf bringen; **fall into ~:** in Verruf kommen; ⇒ *also* **beneath** 1 A; [D] (*Law*) Ungehorsam, *der;* **~ of court** *Ungehorsam od. Missachtung gegenüber der Justiz;* (*in face of court*) ≈ Ungebühr vor Gericht

**contemptible** /kən'temptɪbl/ *adj.* verachtenswert; **Old C~s** (*coll.*) *1914 nach Frankreich geschicktes britisches Expeditionskorps*

**contemptibly** /kən'temptɪblɪ/ *adv.* verachtenswert

**contemptuous** /kən'temptjʊəs/ *adj.* verächtlich; überheblich ‹Person›; **be ~ of sth./sb.** etw./jmdn. verachten; **~ of danger/warning** die Gefahr verachtend/alle Warnungen missachtend; **with** *or* **in ~ disdain** voller Verachtung

**contemptuously** /kən'temptjʊəslɪ/ *adv.* verächtlich

**contend** /kən'tend/ ❶ *v.i.* [A] (*strive*) **~ [with sb. for sth.]** [mit jmdm. um etw.] kämpfen; [B] (*struggle*) **be able/have to ~ with** fertig werden können/müssen mit; bewältigen können/müssen ‹Post, Hindernis›; ins Reine kommen können/müssen mit ‹Gewissen›; **I've got enough to ~ with at the moment** ich habe schon so genug um die Ohren (*ugs.*); **~ with/against the waves** mit den Wellen kämpfen/gegen die Wellen ankämpfen; [C] (*arch.: argue*) **~ with sb. about sth.** mit jmdm. über etw. streiten. ❷ *v.t.* **~ that ...** behaupten, dass ...

**contender** /kən'tendə(r)/ *n.* Bewerber, *der*/Bewerberin, *die*

**content¹** /'kɒntent/ *n.* [A] *in pl.* Inhalt, *der;* **the ~s of the room had all been damaged** alles im Zimmer war beschädigt worden; **the ~s of this medicine are listed on the packet** die Zusammensetzung dieses Medikaments ist auf der Packung angegeben; **[table of] ~s** Inhaltsverzeichnis, *das;* **something in the ~s of the letter has made her very upset** etwas, was in dem Brief steht, hat sie ganz aus der Fassung gebracht; [B] (*amount contained*) Gehalt, *der* (**of** an + *Dat.*); [C] (*capacity*) Fassungsvermögen, *das;* (*volume*) Volumen, *das;* [D] (*constituent elements, substance*) Gehalt, *der*

**content²** /kən'tent/ ❶ *pred. adj.* zufrieden (**with** mit); **not rest ~ until** nicht zufrieden sein, bis; **not ~ with being late every morning, he also wants a pay rise** nicht genug [damit], dass er jeden Morgen zu spät kommt, er will auch noch eine Gehaltserhöhung; **be ~ to do sth.** bereit sein, etw. zu tun; (*pleased*) etw. gern tun; **I should be well ~ to do so** das würde ich recht gern tun. ❷ *n.* **to one's heart's ~:** nach Herzenslust. ❸ *v.t.* zufriedenstellen; befriedigen; **~ oneself with sth./sb.** sich mit etw./jmdm. zufrieden geben

**contented** /kən'tentɪd/ *adj.* zufrieden (**with** mit); glücklich ‹Kindheit, Ehe, Leben›; **be ~ to do sth.** sich damit abfinden, etw. zu tun

**contentedly** /kən'tentɪdlɪ/ *adv.* zufrieden

**contentedness** /kən'tentɪdnɪs/ *n., no pl.* Zufriedenheit, *die*

**contention** /kən'tenʃn/ *n.* [A] (*dispute*) Streit, *der;* Auseinandersetzung, *die;* (*rivalry*) Kampf, *der;* **the matter in ~:** die Streitfrage; **sth. is the subject of much ~:** etw. wird heftig diskutiert *od.* ist eine sehr strittige Frage; **be in ~ with sb.** sich mit jmdm. streiten; [B] (*point asserted*) Behauptung, *die;* ⇒ *also* **put¹** 1 F

**contentious** /kən'tenʃəs/ *adj.* [A] (*quarrelsome*) streitsüchtig; streitlustig; [B] (*involving contention*) strittig ‹Punkt, Frage, Thema›; umstritten ‹Verhalten, Argument, Angelegenheit›

**contentiously** /kən'tenʃəslɪ/ *adv.* provozierend; **a ~ worded question** eine kontrovers formulierte Frage

**contentment** /kən'tentmənt/ *n.* Zufriedenheit, *die;* **smile with ~:** zufrieden lächeln

**contest** ❶ /'kɒntest/ *n.* [A] (*competition*) Wettbewerb, *der;* (*Sport*) Wettkampf, *der;* [B] *no pl., no art.* (*dated/formal*) **a matter of ~:** eine Streitfrage; **engage in ~:** sich auf einen Kampf einlassen. ❷ /kən'test/ *v.t.* [A] (*dispute*) bestreiten; anfechten ‹Anspruch, Recht›; infrage stellen ‹Behauptung, These›; [B] (*fight for*) kämpfen um; [C] (*Brit.*) (*compete in*) kandidieren bei; (*compete for*) kandidieren für; [D] (*Amer.: dispute result of*) anfechten. ❸ *v.i.* **~ with** *or* **against sb./sth.** sich mit jmdm./etw. auseinander setzen

**contestable** /kən'testəbl/ *adj.* anfechtbar

**contestant** /kən'testənt/ *n.* (*competitor*) Teilnehmer, *der*/Teilnehmerin, *die* (**in** an + *Dat.*, bei); (*in election*) Bewerber, *der*/Bewerberin, *die* (**for** um, für); (*in fight*) Gegner, *der*/Gegnerin, *die*

**contestation** /kɒntes'teɪʃn/ *n.* Ⓐ *(contesting)* Bestreiten, *das;* *(of claim, right)* Anfechtung, *die;* Ⓑ *(disputation)* Streit, *der;* Ⓒ *(assertion)* Behauptung, *die*

**context** /'kɒntekst/ *n.* Ⓐ Kontext, *der;* **in/out of ~:** im/ohne Kontext; **this sentence is quoted out of [its proper] ~:** dieser Satz ist aus dem Zusammenhang gerissen; **in this ~:** in diesem Zusammenhang; Ⓑ *(fig.: ambient conditions)* Umgebung, *die;* **in the ~ of** im Rahmen (+ *Gen.*)

**contextual** /kən'tekstjʊəl/ *adj.* kontextuell

**contextualize** /kən'tekstjʊəlaɪz/ *v.t.* *(place in context)* in einen Kontext einordnen

**contiguity** /kɒntɪ'gju:ɪtɪ/ *n., no pl.* *(formal)* Ⓐ *(contact)* Berührung, *die;* Ⓑ *(proximity)* [unmittelbare] Nähe

**contiguous** /kən'tɪgjʊəs/ *adj.* *(formal)* *(touching)* sich berührend; *(adjoining, neighbouring)* aneinander grenzend; **be ~:** sich berühren/aneinandergrenzen/aufeinanderfolgen; **be ~ to sth.** etw. berühren/an etw. *(Akk.)* grenzen

**continence** /'kɒntɪnəns/ *n.* Ⓐ *(temperance)* Mäßigkeit, *die;* *(chastity)* [sexuelle] Enthaltsamkeit; Ⓑ *(Med.)* Kontinenz, *die*

**continent**[1] /'kɒntɪnənt/ *n.* Kontinent, *der;* Erdteil, *der;* **the ~s of Europe, Asia, Africa** die Erdteile Europa, Asien, Afrika; **the C~:** das europäische Festland; der Kontinent

**continent**[2] *adj.* Ⓐ *(temperate)* maßvoll; *(chaste)* [sexuell] enthaltsam; Ⓑ *(Med.)* **be ~:** Harn und Stuhl zurückhalten können

**continental** /kɒntɪ'nentl/ ❶ *adj.* Ⓐ kontinental; **~ Europe** Kontinentaleuropa *(das);* Ⓑ **C~** *(mainland European)* kontinental[europäisch]. ❷ *n.* **C~:** Kontinentaleuropäer, *der*/-europäerin, *die*

**continental: ~ 'breakfast** *n.* kontinentales Frühstück *(im Unterschied zum englischen Frühstück);* **~ climate** *n. (Geog.)* Kontinentalklima, *das;* **~ quilt** *(Brit.) n.* [Stepp]federbett, *das;* **~ 'shelf** *n. (Geog.)* Festland[s]sockel, *der*

**contingency** /kən'tɪndʒənsɪ/ *n.* Ⓐ *(chance event)* Eventualität, *die;* *(possible event)* Eventualfall, *der;* Ⓑ *(incidental event)* unvorhergesehenes Ereignis; *(incidental expense)* unvorhergesehene Ausgabe

**contingency: ~ fund** *n.* Fonds für unvorhergesehene Ausgaben; **~ plan** *n.* Alternativplan, *der*

**contingent** /kən'tɪndʒənt/ ❶ *adj.* Ⓐ *(fortuitous)* zufällig; Ⓑ *(incidental)* unvorhergesehen; Ⓒ *(Philos.)* kontingent; Ⓓ *(conditional)* abhängig ([**up**]**on** von). ❷ *n.* *(Mil.; also fig.)* Kontingent, *das*

**continual** /kən'tɪnjʊəl/ *adj.* *(frequently happening)* ständig; *(without cessation)* unaufhörlich; **there have been ~ quarrels** es gab ständig *od.* dauernd Streit; **she's a ~ chatterbox** ihr Mundwerk steht nie still *(ugs.)*

**continually** /kən'tɪnjʊəlɪ/ *adv.* *(frequently)* ständig; immer wieder; *(without cessation)* unaufhörlich; **~ tired** immer müde

**continuance** /kən'tɪnjʊəns/ *n.* Ⓐ *(continuing)* Fortbestand, *der;* *(of happiness, noise, rain)* Fortdauer, *die;* *(remaining)* Verbleiben, *das;* Ⓑ *(Amer. Law)* Vertagung, *die* (**until** auf + *Akk.*)

**continuation** /kəntɪnjʊ'eɪʃn/ *n.* Ⓐ Fortsetzung, *die;* **a ~ of these good relations** eine Fortdauer dieser guten Beziehungen; Ⓑ *(St. Exch.)* Reportgeschäft, *das*

**continue** /kən'tɪnju:/ ❶ *v.t.* Ⓐ fortsetzen; **'to be ~d'** „Fortsetzung folgt"; **'~d on page 2'** „Fortsetzung auf S. 2"; **~ doing** *or* **to do sth.** etw. weiter tun; **it ~d to rain** es regnete weiter; **it ~s to be a problem** es ist weiterhin ein Problem; **'...', he ~d** „...", fuhr er fort; **do ~ what you were saying** sprechen Sie nur weiter!; **I'll ~ the story where I left off** ich werde die Geschichte von da an weitererzählen, wo ich aufgehört habe; Ⓑ *(Amer. Law)* vertagen (**until** auf + *Akk.*).

❷ *v.i.* Ⓐ *(persist)* ‹Wetter, Zustand, Krise usw.:› andauern; *(persist in doing sth.)* weitermachen *(ugs.)*; nicht aufhören; *(last)* dauern; **this tradition still ~s** diesen Brauch gibt es immer noch; dieser Brauch lebt weiter; **if the rain ~s** wenn der Regen anhält; **if you ~ like this/in this manner** wenn Sie so weitermachen *(ugs.)*; **how long is his speech likely to ~?** wie lange dauert seine Rede wohl noch?; **~ with sth.** mit etw. fortfahren; **we ~d with the work until midnight** wir arbeiteten weiter bis Mitternacht; **~ with a plan** einen Plan weiterverfolgen; **~ on one's way** seinen Weg fortsetzen; Ⓑ *(stay)* bleiben; **~ in power** an der Macht bleiben; **~ in control** die Kontrolle behalten; **she ~d in mourning for him all her life** sie trauerte ihr ganzes Leben lang um ihn; Ⓒ *(not become other than)* weiterhin sein; **he ~s feverish** er hat immer noch Fieber

**continued** /kən'tɪnju:d/ *adj.* fortgesetzt ‹Bemühungen›; **~ existence** Weiterbestehen, *das*

**continuity** /kɒntɪ'nju:ɪtɪ/ *n., no pl.* Ⓐ *(of path, frontier)* ununterbrochener Verlauf; *(unbroken succession, logical sequence, consistency)* Kontinuität, *die;* Ⓑ *(Cinemat., Telev., Radio)* *(scenario)* Szenario, *das;* *(script)* Skript, *das;* *(linking announcements)* Zwischentext, *der*

**conti'nuity girl** *n.* ▶ 1261 Skriptgirl, *das*

**continuo** /kən'tɪnjʊəʊ/ *n., pl.* **~s** *(Mus.)* Ⓐ *(accompaniment)* Generalbass, *der;* Basso continuo, *der;* Ⓑ *(instruments)* Generalbassinstrumente

**continuous** /kən'tɪnjʊəs/ *adj.* Ⓐ ununterbrochen; anhaltend ‹Regen, Sonnenschein, Anstieg›; ständig ‹Kritik, Streit, Änderung›; fortlaufend ‹Mauer›; durchgezogen ‹Linie›; Ⓑ *(Ling.)* **~ [form]** Verlaufsform, *die;* **present ~** *or* **~ present/past ~** *or* **~ past** Verlaufsform des Präsens/Präteritums

**continuously** /kən'tɪnjʊəslɪ/ *adv.* *(in space)* durchgehend; nahtlos ‹aneinander fügen›; *(in time or sequence)* ununterbrochen; unablässig, anhaltend ‹ansteigen›; ständig ‹sich ändern›

**continuous 'stationery** *n.* Endlosdruck, *der* *(Druckw.)*

**continuum** /kən'tɪnjʊəm/ *n., pl.* **continua** /kən'tɪnjʊə/ Kontinuum, *das*

**contort** /kən'tɔ:t/ *v.t.* verdrehen *(auch fig.)*; verzerren ‹Gesicht, Gesichtszüge›; verrenken, verdrehen ‹Körper›; **his face was ~ed with anger** sein Gesicht war wutverzerrt

**contortion** /kən'tɔ:ʃn/ *n.* Verzerrung, *die;* *(of body)* Verdrehung, *die;* Verrenkung, *die*

**contortionist** /kən'tɔ:ʃənɪst/ *n.* Schlangenmensch, *der*

**contour** /'kɒntʊə(r)/ *n.* Ⓐ *(outline)* Kontur, *die;* Ⓑ ⇒ **contour line**

**contour: ~ line** *n.* *(Geog., Surv.)* Höhen[schicht]linie, *die;* **~ map** *n.* Höhenlinienkarte, *die;* **~ ploughing** *n.* *(Agric.)* Konturpflügen, *das*

**contra** /'kɒntrə/ ❶ *prep. & adv.* **pro and ~:** pro und kontra. ❷ *n.* **the pros and ~s** das Pro und Kontra

**contraband** /'kɒntrəbænd/ ❶ *n.* *(smuggled goods)* Schmuggelware, *die;* **~ of war** Konterbande, *die* *(Völkerrecht)*. ❷ *adj.* geschmuggelt; **~ goods** Schmuggelware, *die*

**contrabassoon** /'kɒntrəbəsu:n/ *n.* Kontrafagott, *das*

**contraception** /kɒntrə'sepʃn/ *n.* Empfängnisverhütung, *die*

**contraceptive** /kɒntrə'septɪv/ ❶ *adj.* empfängnisverhütend; kontrazeptiv *(Med.)*; **~ device/method** Verhütungsmittel, *das*/-methode, *die.* ❷ *n.* Verhütungsmittel, *das*

**contract** ❶ /'kɒntrækt/ *n.* Ⓐ Vertrag, *der;* **~ of employment** Arbeitsvertrag, *der;* **be under ~ to do sth.** vertraglich verpflichtet sein, etw. zu tun; **exchange ~s** *(Law)* die Vertragsurkunden austauschen; **marriage ~:** Ehevertrag, *der;* Ⓑ *(Bridge etc.)* Kontrakt, *der;* Ⓒ ⇒ **contract bridge**.

❷ /kən'trækt/ *v.t.* Ⓐ *(cause to shrink, make smaller)* schrumpfen lassen; *(draw together)* zusammenziehen; verengen ‹Pupillen›; Ⓑ *(form)* **~ marriage** die Ehe eingehen *od.* schließen; **~ a habit** eine Angewohnheit annehmen; Ⓒ *(become infected with)* sich *(Dat.)* zuziehen; **~ sth. from sb.** sich mit etw. bei jmdm. anstecken; **~ sth. from ...:** an etw. *(Dat.)* durch ... erkranken; Ⓓ *(incur)* machen ‹Schulden›; Ⓔ *(Ling.)* zusammenziehen ‹Wort, Silbe›. ❸ *v.i.* Ⓐ *(enter into agreement)* Verträge/einen Vertrag schließen; **~ for sth.** etw. vertraglich zusichern; **~ to do sth.** *or* **that one will do sth.** sich vertraglich verpflichten, etw. zu tun; Ⓑ *(shrink, become smaller, be drawn together)* sich zusammenziehen; ‹Pupillen:› sich verengen

**~ 'out** ❶ *v.i.* **~ out [of sth.]** sich [an etw. *(Dat.)*] nicht beteiligen; *(withdraw)* [aus etw.] aussteigen *(ugs.)*. ❷ *v.t.* **~ work out [to another firm]** Arbeit [an eine andere Firma] vergeben

**contract bridge** /kɒntrækt 'brɪdʒ/ *n.* Kontraktbridge, *das*

**contractile** /kən'træktaɪl/ *adj.* *(Anat.: capable of contracting)* kontraktil

**contraction** /kən'trækʃn/ *n.* Ⓐ *(shrinking)* Kontraktion, *die* *(Physik)*; *(of eye pupils)* Verengung, *die;* Ⓑ *(Physiol.: of muscle)* Zusammenziehung, *die;* Kontraktion, *die* *(Med.)*; Ⓒ *(Ling.)* Kontraktion, *die;* Ⓓ *(catching)* Ansteckung, *die* (**of** mit); Ⓔ *(forming)* Annahme, *die;* *(of marriage)* Schließen, *das;* **~ of debts** Schuldenmachen, *das*

**'contract killer** *n.* Auftragskiller, *der*/Auftragskillerin, *die*

**contractor** /kən'træktə(r)/ *n.* ▶ 1261 Auftragnehmer, *der*/-nehmerin, *die;* ⇒ *also* **building contractor**

**contractual** /kən'træktjʊəl/ *adj.*, **contractually** /kən'træktjʊəlɪ/ *adv.* vertraglich

**contradict** /kɒntrə'dɪkt/ *v.t.* widersprechen (+ *Dat.*)

**contradiction** /kɒntrə'dɪkʃn/ *n.* Widerspruch, *der* (**of** gegen); **in ~ to sth./sb.** im Widerspruch *od.* Gegensatz zu etw./jmdm.; **be a ~ to** *or* **of sth.** im Widerspruch zu etw. stehen; **a ~ in terms** ein Widerspruch in sich selbst; eine Contradictio in adjecto *(Rhet.)*

**contradictory** /kɒntrə'dɪktərɪ/ *adj.* Ⓐ widersprechend; *(mutually opposed)* widersprüchlich; **that is ~ to what was said last week** das widerspricht dem, was letzte Woche gesagt wurde; Ⓑ *(inclined to contradict)* widersetzlich; *(inconsistent)* widersprüchlich

**contradistinction** /kɒntrədɪ'stɪŋkʃn/ *n.* Unterscheidung, *die;* **in ~ to sth.** im Unterschied zu etw.

**'contraflow** *n.* Gegenverkehr auf einem Fahrstreifen; **~ system** Verkehrsführung mit Gegenverkehr

**contralto** /kən'træltəʊ/ *n., pl.* **~s** *(Mus.)* Ⓐ *(voice)* Alt, *der;* *(very low)* Kontraalt, *der;* Ⓑ *(singer)* Altistin, *die;* Alt, *der* *(selten)*; *(with very low voice)* Kontraalt, *der;* Ⓒ *(part)* Alt, *der;* *(for very low voice)* zweiter Alt; Alt II

**contraption** /kən'træpʃn/ *n.* *(coll.)* *(strange machine)* Apparat, *der* *(ugs.)*; *(vehicle)* Vehikel, *das;* *(device)* [komisches] Gerät

**contrapuntal** /kɒntrə'pʌntl/ *adj.* *(Mus.)* kontrapunktisch

**contrarily** *adv.* Ⓐ /'kɒntrərɪlɪ/ *(in a contrary manner)* **I think ~:** ich glaube das Gegenteil; **we've decided ~:** wir haben uns für das Gegenteil entschieden; Ⓑ /kən'treərɪlɪ/ *(coll.: perversely)* widerspenstig; widerborstig

**contrariness** /kən'treərɪnɪs/ *n., no pl.* *(coll.)* Widerspenstigkeit, *die;* Widerborstigkeit, *die*

**contrariwise** /kən'treərɪwaɪz/ *adv.* Ⓐ *(on the other hand)* andererseits; Ⓑ *(in the opposite way)* umgekehrt

**contrary** ❶ *adj.* Ⓐ /'kɒntrərɪ/ entgegengesetzt; **be ~ to sth.** im Gegensatz zu etw. stehen; **the result was ~ to expectation** das Ergebnis entsprach nicht den Erwartungen; Ⓑ *(opposite)* entgegengesetzt; *(adverse)* widrig ‹Wind›; Ⓒ /kən'treərɪ/ *(coll.: perverse)* widerspenstig; widerborstig; **he's ~ by nature** er ist von Natur aus voller Widerspruchsgeist.

❷ /'kɒntrərɪ/ *n.* **the ~:** das Gegenteil; **be/do completely the ~:** das genaue Gegenteil

sein/tun; **go by contraries** anders als erwartet verlaufen; ‹Traum:› das Gegenteil bedeuten; ‹Stimmung:› [grundsätzlich] konträr sein; **on the ~:** im Gegenteil; **appearances to the ~, ...:** dem äußeren Anschein zum Trotz, ...; **quite the ~:** ganz im Gegenteil.
❸ *adv.* **~ to sth.** entgegen einer Sache; **~ to expectation** wider Erwarten

**contrast** ❶ /kən'trɑ:st/ *v.t.* gegenüberstellen; kontrastieren lassen, [deutlich] voneinander abheben ‹Farben›; **~ sth. with sth.** etw. von etw. [deutlich] abheben; **be ~ed with sth.** sich [deutlich] von etw. abheben.
❷ *v.i.* **~ with sth.** mit etw. kontrastieren; sich von etw. abheben.
❸ /'kɒntrɑ:st/ *n.* Ⓐ (*juxtaposition*) Kontrast, *der* (**with** zu); **what a ~!** welch ein Gegensatz!; **in ~, ...:** im Gegensatz dazu, ...; **[be] in ~ with sth.** im Gegensatz *od.* Kontrast zu etw. [stehen]; **by way of ~:** als Kontrast; Ⓑ (*thing*) **a ~ to sth.** ein Gegensatz zu etw.; (*person*) **be a ~ to sb.** [ganz] anders sein als jmd.; Ⓒ (*Photog., Telev., Psych.*) Kontrast, *der;* Ⓓ **~ medium** (*Med.*) Kontrastmittel, *das*

**contrasting** /kən'trɑ:stɪŋ/ *adj.* gegensätzlich; kontrastierend ‹Farbe›; (*very different*) sehr unterschiedlich

**contravene** /kɒntrə'vi:n/ *v.t.* (*infringe*) verstoßen gegen ‹Recht, Gesetz›; zuwiderhandeln (+ *Dat.*) ‹Beschluss, Rat, Empfehlung›; (*conflict with*) widersprechen (+ *Dat.*)

**contravention** /kɒntrə'venʃn/ *n.* **~ of the law/rules/moral standards** Verstoß gegen das Gesetz/die Regeln/die Moral; **be in ~ of sth.** im Widerspruch zu etw. stehen; **act in ~ of sth.** einer Sache (*Dat.*) zuwiderhandeln

**contretemps** /'kɔ̃trətɑ̃/ *n., pl. same* /'kɔ̃trətɑ̃z/ Missgeschick, *das;* Malheur, *das* (*ugs.*)

**contribute** /kən'trɪbju:t/ ❶ *v.t.* **~ sth. [to *or* towards sth.]** etw. [zu etw.] beitragen/(*cooperatively*) beisteuern; **~ money towards sth.** für etw. Geld beisteuern/(*for charity*) spenden; **he regularly ~s articles to the 'Guardian'** er schreibt regelmäßig für den „Guardian".
❷ *v.i.* **~ to *or* towards a jumble sale** etwas zu einem Trödelmarkt beisteuern; **if only the child would ~ more in class** wenn das Kind nur mehr zum Unterricht beitragen würde; **everyone ~d towards the production** jeder trug etwas zur Aufführung bei; **~ to charity** für karitative Zwecke spenden; **~ to sb.'s misery/disappointment** jmds. Kummer/Enttäuschung vergrößern; **~ to a newspaper** für eine Zeitung schreiben; **he ~d to the 'Encyclopaedia Britannica'** er hat an der Encyclopaedia Britannica mitgearbeitet; **~ to the success of sth.** zum Erfolg einer Sache (*Gen.*) beitragen

**contribution** /kɒntrɪ'bju:ʃn/ *n.* Ⓐ (*act of contributing*) **make a ~ to a fund** etw. für einen Fonds spenden; **the ~ of clothing and money to sth.** das Spenden von Kleidern und Geld für etw.; Ⓑ (*thing contributed*) Beitrag, *der;* (*for charity*) Spende, *die* (**to** für); **~s of clothing and money** Kleider- und Geldspenden; **make a ~ to sth.** einen Beitrag zu etw. leisten

**contributor** /kən'trɪbjʊtə(r)/ *n.* Ⓐ (*giver*) Spender, *der*/Spenderin, *die;* Ⓑ (*to encyclopaedia, dictionary, etc.*) Mitarbeiter, *der*/Mitarbeiterin, *die* (**to** *Gen.*); **he is a regular ~ [of articles] to the 'Guardian'** er schreibt regelmäßig [Artikel] für den „Guardian"

**contributory** /kən'trɪbjʊtərɪ/ *adj.* Ⓐ (*that contributes*) **a ~ factor to his state of mind/in the poor state of the economy** ein Faktor, der bei seiner geistigen Verfassung/bei der schlechten Wirtschaftslage eine Rolle spielt; **~ funds** Hilfsfonds; **~ negligence** (*Law*) Mitverschulden, *das;* Ⓑ (*operated by contributions*) **be run on a ~ basis** mit Beiträgen *od.* Spenden finanziert werden; **~ insurance payments** Versicherungspflichtbeiträge

**'con trick** (*coll.*) ⇒ **confidence trick**

**contrite** /'kɒntraɪt/ *adj.* zerknirscht; (*showing contrition*) reuevoll; **~ sigh/tears/words** Seufzer/Tränen/Worte der Reue; **~ apology** zerknirschte Entschuldigung

**contritely** /'kɒntraɪtlɪ/ *adv.* zerknirscht

**contrition** /kən'trɪʃn/ *n.* Reue, *die;* **~ leads to absolution** Kontrition ist die Voraussetzung für die Absolution (*kath. Theol.*); **hang one's head in ~:** den Kopf reumütig senken

**contrivance** /kən'traɪvəns/ *n.* Ⓐ (*contriving*) Plan, *der;* **deceitful ~s** faule Tricks (*ugs. abwertend*); Ⓑ (*invention*) Ersinnen, *das;* (*inventive capacity*) Erfindungsgabe, *die;* Ⓒ (*device*) Gerät, *das*

**contrive** /kən'traɪv/ *v.t.* Ⓐ (*manage*) **~ to do sth.** es fertig bringen *od.* zuwege bringen, etw. zu tun; **can you ~ to be here by 6 a.m.?** können Sie es einrichten, bis 6 Uhr morgens hier zu sein?; **they ~d to meet** es gelang ihnen, sich zu treffen; Ⓑ (*devise*) sich (*Dat.*) ausdenken; ersinnen (*geh.*); **~ ways and means of doing sth.** Mittel und Wege finden, etw. zu tun

**contrived** /kən'traɪvd/ *adj.* künstlich

**control** /kən'trəʊl/ ❶ *n.* Ⓐ (*power of directing, restraint*) Kontrolle, *die* (**of** über + *Akk.*); (*management*) Leitung, *die;* **~ of the economy** Wirtschaftslenkung, *die;* **board of ~:** Aufsichtsbehörde, *die;* **~ over ecclesiastical matters** höchste Gewalt in kirchlichen Dingen; **governmental ~:** Regierungsgewalt, *die;* **~ of the vehicle/machine is totally automatic** das Fahrzeug/die Maschine hat vollautomatische Steuerung; **have ~ of sth.** die Kontrolle über etw. (*Akk.*) haben; etw. kontrollieren; (*take decisions*) für etw. zuständig sein; **take ~ of** die Kontrolle übernehmen über (+ *Akk.*); **keep ~ of sth.** etw. unter Kontrolle halten; **be in ~ [of sth.]** die Kontrolle [über etw. (*Akk.*)] haben; **be in ~ of the situation** die Situation unter Kontrolle haben; **who's in ~ here?** wer hat hier zu bestimmen?; **be in ~ of education** für das Erziehungswesen zuständig sein; **[go *or* get] out of ~ *or* beyond [sb.'s] ~:** außer Kontrolle [geraten]; **circumstances beyond sb.'s ~:** unvorhersehbare, nicht in jmds. Hand liegende Umstände; **[get sth.] under ~:** [etw.] unter Kontrolle [bringen]; **keep oneself/sth. under ~:** sich/etw. in der Gewalt haben; **everything's under ~** (*fig.*) alles in Ordnung; **lose ~ [of sth.]** die Kontrolle [über etw. (*Akk.*)] verlieren; **lose ~ of the situation** die Situation nicht mehr unter Kontrolle haben; **gain ~ of sth.** etw. unter Kontrolle bekommen; **lose/regain ~ of oneself** die Beherrschung verlieren/wiedergewinnen; **have some/complete/no ~ over sth.** eine gewisse/die absolute/keine Kontrolle über etw. (*Akk.*) haben; **have ~ over oneself** sich in der Gewalt haben; **he has no ~ over himself** er hat sich nicht in der Gewalt; ⇒ *also* **flight control**; Ⓑ (*standard of comparison*) Kontrollobjekt, *das;* (*person*) Kontrollperson, *die;* **~ experiment** Kontrollversuch, *der;* Ⓒ (*device*) Regler, *der;* **~s** (*as a group*) Schaltafel, *die;* (*of TV, stereo system*) Bedienungstafel, *die;* **at the ~s** an der Schalttafel; **be at the ~s** an der Schalttafel sitzen; ‹Fahrer, Pilot:› am Steuer sitzen; (*fig.*) das Steuer in der Hand haben; Ⓓ *in pl.* (*means of regulating*) Beschränkung, *die;* Kontrolle, *die;* **impose ~s on imports** Importbeschränkungen einführen; Ⓔ (*Spiritualism*) Kontrolle, *die* (*Parapsych.*); Kontrollgeist, *der* (*Parapsych.*); Ⓕ (*checkpoint for rally cars*) Kontrollpunkt, *der.*
❷ *v.t.*, **-ll-** Ⓐ (*have ~ of*) kontrollieren; steuern, lenken ‹Auto›; leiten ‹Firma›; **you must ~ your dog** Sie müssen Ihren Hund unter Kontrolle halten; **he ~s the financial side of things** er ist für die Finanzen zuständig *od.* hat die Finanzen unter sich; **~ a class** eine Klasse fest im Griff haben; **~ling company** (*Econ.*) Kontrollgesellschaft, *die;* **~ling interest** Mehrheitsbeteiligung, *die* (*Wirtsch.*); Ⓑ (*hold in check*) beherrschen; zügeln ‹Zorn, Ungeduld, Temperament›; im Zaum halten ‹Zunge›; (*regulate*) kontrollieren; regulieren ‹Geschwindigkeit, Temperatur›; einschränken ‹Export, Ausgaben›; regeln ‹Verkehr›; unterdrücken ‹Gefühlsäußerung›; **~ yourselves, children!** nehmt euch zusammen, Kinder!; Ⓒ (*check, verify*) [über]prüfen

**control: ~ centre** *n.* Kontrollzentrum, *das;* **~ desk** *n.* Schaltpult, *das;* **~ freak** *n.* (*coll.*) Kontrollfreak, *der*

**controller** /kən'trəʊlə(r)/ *n.* Ⓐ (*director*) Leiter, *der*/Leiterin, *die;* Chef, *der*/Chefin, *die* (*ugs.*); Ⓑ ⇒ **comptroller**

**control: ~ panel** *n.* Schalttafel, *die;* **~ room** *n.* Kontrollraum, *der;* (*in theatre*) Stellwarte, *die;* (*Radio, Telev.*) Regieraum, *der;* (*in power station*) Schaltwarte, *die;* **~ tower** *n.* Kontrollturm, *der;* Tower, *der*

**controversial** /kɒntrə'vɜ:ʃl/ *adj.* (*causing controversy*) umstritten ‹Mode, Kunstwerk, Gesetz, Idee›; strittig ‹Frage, Punkt, Angelegenheit›; (*given to controversy*) streitsüchtig; (*lacking neutrality*) polemisch

**controversy** /'kɒntrəvɜ:sɪ, kən'trɒvəsɪ/ *n.* Kontroverse, *die;* Auseinandersetzung, *die;* **much ~:** eine längere Kontroverse *od.* Auseinandersetzung

**controvert** /'kɒntrəvɜ:t, kɒntrə'vɜ:t/ *v.t.* (*formal*) bestreiten; ‹Argument, Theorie:› widersprechen (+ *Dat.*)

**contuse** /kən'tju:z/ *v.t.* prellen

**contusion** /kən'tju:ʒn/ *n.* Prellung, *die*

**conundrum** /kə'nʌndrəm/ *n.* (*riddle*) (*auf einem Wortspiel beruhendes*) Rätsel; (*hard question*) Problem, *das;* **pose ~s** Rätsel aufgeben

**conurbation** /kɒnɜ:'beɪʃn/ *n.* Konurbation, *die* (*Soziol.*); ≈ Stadtregion, *die*

**convalesce** /kɒnvə'les/ *v.i.* genesen; rekonvaleszieren (*Med.*)

**convalescence** /kɒnvə'lesəns/ *n.* Genesung, *die;* Rekonvaleszenz, *die* (*Med.*)

**convalescent** /kɒnvə'lesənt/ ❶ *adj.* rekonvaleszent (*Med.*); **you'll be ~ for a few weeks** Ihre Genesung wird ein paar Wochen dauern; **~ patient** Rekonvaleszent, *der*/Rekonvaleszentin, *die* (*Med.*). ❷ *n.* Rekonvaleszent, *der*/Rekonvaleszentin, *die* (*Med.*); Genesende, *der/die*

**convalescent: ~ home, ~ hospital** *ns.* Genesungsheim, *das*

**convection** /kən'vekʃn/ *n.* (*Phys., Meteorol.*) Konvektion, *die;* **~ current** Konvektionsstrom, *der*

**convective** /kən'vektɪv/ *adj.* (*Phys., Meteorol.*) konvektiv

**convector** /kən'vektə(r)/ *n.* Konvektor, *der*

**convene** /kən'vi:n/ ❶ *v.t.* einberufen. ❷ *v.i.* zusammenkommen; ‹Gericht, gewählte Vertreter:› zusammentreten; ‹Konferenz, Versammlung:› beginnen

**convener** /kən'vi:nə(r)/ *n.* (*Brit.*) *jmd., der eine Versammlung einberuft/leitet*

**convenience** /kən'vi:nɪəns/ *n.* Ⓐ *no pl.* (*suitableness, advantageousness*) Annehmlichkeit, *die;* **its ~ to *or* for the city centre** seine günstige Lage zum Stadtzentrum; **marriage of ~:** Vernunftehe, *die;* ⇒ *also* **flag**[1] 1; Ⓑ (*personal satisfaction*) Bequemlichkeit, *die;* Wohlbefinden, *das;* **for sb.'s ~, for ~'s sake** zu jmds. Bequemlichkeit; **is it to your ~?** passt es Ihnen?; **at your ~:** wann es Ihnen passt; **at your earliest ~:** möglichst bald; baldmöglichst (*Papierdt.*); Ⓒ (*advantage*) **be a ~ to sb.** angenehm *od.* praktisch für jmdn. sein; **having a car is such a ~:** ein Auto zu haben ist so angenehm *od.* praktisch; **make a ~ of sb.** jmdn. ausnutzen; Ⓓ (*advantageous thing*) Annehmlichkeit, *die;* **a car is a [great] ~ to have** es ist [sehr] angenehm *od.* praktisch, ein Auto zu haben; Ⓔ (*esp. Admin.: toilet*) Toilette, *die;* **public ~:** öffentliche Toilette *od.* (*Amtsspr.*) Bedürfnisanstalt

**con'venience food** *n.* Fertignahrung, *die*

**convenient** /kən'vi:nɪənt/ *adj.* Ⓐ (*suitable, not troublesome*) günstig; (*useful*) praktisch; angenehm; **be ~ to *or* for sb.** günstig für jmdn. sein; **would it be ~ to you?** würde es Ihnen passen?; wäre es Ihnen recht?; **it's not very ~ at the moment** es passt im Augenblick nicht gut; **if it is not ~ to have**

**us to stay** wenn es ungelegen kommt, dass wir bleiben; **B** (*of easy access*) **be ~ to** *or* **for sth.** günstig zu etw. liegen; **our house is very ~ to** *or* **for the city centre** wir haben es nicht weit zum Stadtzentrum; **C** (*opportunely available or occurring*) **a ~ taxi** ein Taxi, das gerade da steht/angefahren kommt

**conveniently** /kən'vi:nɪəntlɪ/ *adv.* **A** (*suitably, without difficulty, accessibly*) günstig ‹gelegen, angebracht›; leicht ‹gesehen werden›; angenehm ‹ruhig›; **when can you ~ drop round?** wann passt es dir *od.* wann kannst du es einrichten, mal vorbeizukommen?; **we're ~ situated for the shops** wir haben es nicht weit zu den Geschäften; **B** (*opportunely*) angenehmerweise; **very ~, we were only a mile from a garage** glücklicherweise waren wir nur eine Meile von einer Werkstatt entfernt

**convenor** ⇒ **convener**

**convent** /'kɒnvənt/ *n.* Kloster, *das;* **~ of nuns** Nonnenkloster, *das;* **enter a ~:** ins Kloster gehen

**convention** /kən'venʃn/ *n.* **A** (*a practice*) Brauch, *der;* **it is the ~ to do sth.** es ist Brauch, etw. zu tun; **~s of spelling** Rechtschreibregeln; **B** *no art.* (*established customs*) Konvention, *die;* **break with ~:** sich über die Konventionen hinwegsetzen; **C** (*formal assembly*) Konferenz, *die;* **D** (*agreement between parties*) Abkommen, *das;* Übereinkunft, *die;* (*agreement between States*) Konvention, *die* (*bes. Völkerrecht*)

**conventional** /kən'venʃənl/ *adj.* konventionell; (*not spontaneous*) formell; **it is ~ wisdom that ...:** man glaubt allgemein, dass ...; **it is ~ to send flowers** es ist üblich, Blumen zu schicken; **~ weapons** konventionelle Waffen

**conventionally** /kən'venʃənəlɪ/ *adv.* konventionell

**conventioneer** /kənvenʃə'nɪə(r)/ *n.* (*Amer.*) Konferenzteilnehmer, *der*/-teilnehmerin, *die*

**'convent school** *n.* Klosterschule, *die*

**converge** /kən'vɜ:dʒ/ *v.i.* **~ [on each other]** aufeinander zulaufen; ‹Gedanken, Meinungen, Ansichten:› sich [einander] annähern, (*geh.*) konvergieren; **~ on sb.** auf jmdn. zulaufen; **they ~d on the scene of the accident** sie liefen am Unfallort zusammen

**convergence** /kən'vɜ:dʒəns/ *n.* **A** Annäherung, *die;* Konvergenz, *die* (*geh.*); (*of roads, rivers*) Zusammentreffen, *das;* **at the ~ of the roads** an der Stelle, wo die Straßen zusammentreffen; **B** (*Math., Biol., Psych.*) Konvergenz, *die*

**convergent** /kən'vɜ:dʒənt/ *adj.* **A** aufeinander zulaufend; konvergierend (*geh.*), sich einander annähernd ‹Meinungen, Gedanken, Ansichten›; **B** (*Math., Biol., Psych.*) konvergent; **~ lens** (*Optics*) Sammellinse, *die*

**conversant** /kən'vɜ:sənt/ *pred. adj.* vertraut (**with** mit)

**conversation** /kɒnvə'seɪʃn/ *n.* Unterhaltung, *die;* Gespräch, *das;* Konversation, *die* (*geh.*); (*in language-teaching*) Konversation, *die;* **be in ~ [with sb.]** sich [mit jmdm.] unterhalten; **be deep in ~:** in ein Gespräch vertieft sein; **enter into ~ with sb.** mit jmdm. ein Gespräch anfangen *od.* anknüpfen; **make [polite] ~ with sb.** mit jmdm. Konversation machen; **in the course of ~:** im Verlauf des Gesprächs; **come up in ~:** gesprächsweise erwähnt werden; **he hasn't much ~:** man kann sich kaum mit ihm unterhalten; **have a ~ with sb.** mit jmdm. ein Gespräch führen

**conversational** /kɒnvə'seɪʃənl/ *adj.* gesprächig ‹Person›; ungezwungen ‹Art›; **talk in ~ tones/in a ~ manner** im Plauderton/ungezwungen sprechen; **~ English** gesprochenes Englisch; **the discussion remained on a casual, ~ level** die Diskussion blieb auf der Ebene einer zwanglosen Unterhaltung

**conversationalist** /kɒnvə'seɪʃənəlɪst/ *n.* Unterhalter, *der*/Unterhalterin, *die;* **be a/no great ~:** gut/nicht gut Konversation machen können

**conversationally** /kɒnvə'seɪʃənəlɪ/ *adv.* **'Nice day today', he remarked ~:** „Schöner Tag heute", stellte er fest, um ein Gespräch zu beginnen

**conver'sation piece** *n.* (*topic of conversation*) Gesprächsthema, *das*

**converse**[1] /kən'vɜ:s/ *v.i.* (*formal*) **~ [with sb.] [about** *or* **on sth.]** sich [mit jmdm.] [über etw. (*Akk.*)] unterhalten

**converse**[2] /'kɒnvɜ:s/ **1** *adj.* entgegengesetzt; umgekehrt ‹Fall, Situation›. **2** *n.* **A** (*opposite*) Gegenteil, *das;* **B** (*Math.*) Kehrsatz, *der;* **C** (*Logic*) Konversion, *die*

**conversely** /kən'vɜ:slɪ/ *adv.* umgekehrt

**conversion** /kən'vɜ:ʃn/ *n.* **A** (*transforming*) Umwandlung, *die* (**into** in + *Akk.*); **B** (*adaptation, adapted building*) Umbau, *der;* **do a ~ on sth.** etw. umbauen; **C** (*of person*) Bekehrung, *die* (**to** zu); Konversion, *die* (*Rel.*); **D** (*to different units or expression*) Übertragung, *die* (**into** in + *Akk.*); **E** (*Finance, Logic, Theol., Psych., Phys.*) Konversion, *die;* (*calculation*) Umrechnung, *die;* (*Rugby, Amer. Footb.*) Erhöhung, *die*

**con'version table** *n.* Umrechnungstabelle, *die*

**convert** **1** /kən'vɜ:t/ *v.t.* **A** (*transform, change in function*) umwandeln (**into** in + *Akk.*); **B** (*adapt*) **~ sth. [into sth.]** etw. [zu etw.] umbauen; **C** (*bring over*) **~ sb. [to sth.]** (*lit. or fig.*) jmdn. [zu etw.] bekehren; **D** (*to different units or expressions*) übertragen (**into** in + *Akk.*); **E** (*Finance*) konvertieren; (*calculate*) umrechnen (**into** in + *Akk.*); **F** (*Rugby, Amer. Footb.*) erhöhen; **G** **~ to one's own use** sich (*Dat.*) aneignen.

**2** *v.i.* **A** (*be transformable, be changeable in function*) **~ into sth.** sich in etw. (*Akk.*) umwandeln lassen; **B** (*be adaptable*) sich umbauen lassen; **C** (*to new method etc.*) umstellen (**to** auf + *Akk.*).

**3** /'kɒnvɜ:t/ *n.* **A** (*Relig.*) Konvertit, *der*/Konvertitin, *die;* **B** (*fig.*) **the new ~ s to the Party** die neuen Anhänger der Partei; **he became a ~ to Asian philosophy** er wurde ein Anhänger der asiatischen Philosophie

**converter** /kən'vɜ:tə(r)/ *n.* **A** (*Metall.*) Konverter, *der;* **B** (*Electr.*) Umformer, *der*

**convertibility** /kənvɜ:tɪ'bɪlɪtɪ/ *n., no pl.* **A** Umwandelbarkeit, *die;* **B** (*Finance*) Konvertierbarkeit, *die*

**convertible** /kən'vɜ:tɪbl/ **1** *adj.* **A** **be ~ into sth.** sich in etw. (*Akk.*) umwandeln lassen; **~ sofa** Ausziehcouch, *die;* **B** (*able to be altered*) **be ~ [into sth.]** sich zu etw. umbauen lassen; **C** (*Finance*) **be ~ into sth.** in etw. (*Akk.*) konvertierbar sein. **2** *n.* (*car*) Kabrio, *das;* Cabrio, *das*

**convex** /'kɒnveks/ *adj.* konvex; *attrib.* Konvex ‹linse, -spiegel›

**convexity** /kən'veksɪtɪ/ *n.* Wölbung, *die;* Konvexität, *die* (*Optik*)

**convey** /kən'veɪ/ *v.t.* **A** (*transport*) befördern; (*transmit*) übermitteln ‹Nachricht, Grüße›; **the TV pictures are ~ed by satellite** die Fernsehbilder werden per Satellit übertragen; **B** (*impart*) vermitteln; **words cannot ~ it** Worte können es nicht wiedergeben; **the message ~ed nothing whatever to me** die Nachricht sagte mir überhaupt nichts; **~ one's meaning to sb.** jmdm. deutlich machen, was man meint; **C** (*Law*) **~ property [to sb.]** [jmdm.] Eigentum übertragen *od.* überschreiben

**conveyance** /kən'veɪəns/ *n.* **A** (*transportation*) Beförderung, *die;* (*of sound, picture, heat, light*) Übertragung, *die;* (*of message, greetings*) Übermittlung, *die;* **B** (*formal: vehicle*) Beförderungsmittel, *das;* **C** (*Law*) Übertragung, *die;* Überschreibung, *die;* **[deed of] ~:** Übertragungsurkunde, *die*

**conveyancing** /kən'veɪənsɪŋ/ *n.* (*Law*) **~ [of property]** [Eigentums]übertragung, *die*

**conveyer, conveyor** /kən'veɪə(r)/ *n.* Förderer, *der* (*Technik*); **[bucket] ~** Becherwerk, *das;* **[chain] ~** Kettenförderer, *der;* **~ [belt]** (*Industry*) Förderband, *das;* (*in manufacture also*) Fließband, *das*

**convict** **1** /'kɒnvɪkt/ *n.* Strafgefangene, *der/die.* **2** /kən'vɪkt/ *v.t.* **A** (*declare guilty*) für schuldig befinden; verurteilen; **be ~ed** verurteilt werden; **B** (*prove guilty*) **~ sb. of sth.** jmdn. einer Sache (*Gen.*) überführen

**conviction** /kən'vɪkʃn/ *n.* **A** (*Law*) Verurteilung, *die* (**for** wegen); **have you [had] any previous ~s?** sind Sie vorbestraft?; **he has no criminal ~s at all** er hat keinerlei Vorstrafen; **B** (*settled belief*) Überzeugung, *die;* **a vegetarian by ~:** ein überzeugter Vegetarier; **it is their ~ that ...:** sie sind der Überzeugung, dass ...; **her ~ of the existence of God/of his innocence** ihr fester Glaube an die Existenz Gottes/an seine Unschuld; **what are his political ~s?** wie sind seine politischen Anschauungen?; **carry ~:** überzeugend sein; ‹Stimme:› überzeugend klingen

**convince** /kən'vɪns/ *v.t.* überzeugen; **~ sb. that ...:** jmdn. davon überzeugen, dass ...; **be ~d that ...:** davon überzeugt sein, dass ...; **manage to ~ oneself that ...:** sich (*Dat.*) einreden, dass ...; **~ sb. of sth.** jmdn. von etw. überzeugen

**convincing** /kən'vɪnsɪŋ/ *adj.* überzeugend; täuschend ‹Ähnlichkeit›

**convincingly** /kən'vɪnsɪŋlɪ/ *adv.* überzeugend

**convivial** /kən'vɪvɪəl/ *n.* fröhlich

**conviviality** /kənvɪvɪ'ælɪtɪ/ *n., no pl.* Fröhlichkeit, *die*

**convivially** /kən'vɪvɪəlɪ/ *adv.* fröhlich

**convocation** /kɒnvə'keɪʃn/ *n.* **A** (*calling together*) Zusammenrufen, *das;* (*of council, synod*) Einberufung, *die;* **B** (*assembly*) Versammlung, *die;* **C** (*Brit. Eccl.*) Provinzialsynode, *die;* **D** (*Brit. Univ.*) *universitäre gesetzgebende Versammlung;* ≈ Vollversammlung, *die*

**convoke** /kən'vəʊk/ *v.t.* zusammenrufen; einberufen ‹Versammlung, Synode, Rat›

**convoluted** /'kɒnvəlu:tɪd/ *adj.* **A** (*twisted*) verschlungen; verdreht ‹Körperhaltung›; **B** (*complex*) kompliziert

**convolution** /kɒnvə'lu:ʃn/ *n.* Windung, *die;* **the ~s of the winding road** die Biegungen der kurvenreichen Straße

**convolvulus** /kən'vɒlvjʊləs/ *n.* (*Bot.*) Winde, *die*

**convoy** /'kɒnvɔɪ/ **1** *n.* Konvoi, *der;* **in ~:** im Konvoi. **2** *v.t.* Geleitschutz geben (+ *Dat.*)

**convulse** /kən'vʌls/ *v.t.* **A** **be ~d** von Krämpfen geschüttelt werden; (*fig.*) **be ~d with laughter** sich vor Lachen biegen (*ugs.*); **be ~d with rage/fury** sich vor Wut krümmen; **B** (*shake, lit. or fig.*) erschüttern

**convulsion** /kən'vʌlʃn/ *n.* **A** *in pl.* Schüttelkrampf, *der* (*Med.*); Krämpfe; (*fig.*) **~s of laughter** Lachkrampf, *der;* **we were in absolute ~s** wir bogen uns förmlich vor Lachen (*ugs.*); **B** (*shaking, lit. or fig.*) Erschütterung, *die*

**convulsive** /kən'vʌlsɪv/ *adj.*, **convulsively** /kən'vʌlsɪvlɪ/ *adv.* konvulsivisch

**cony** /'kəʊnɪ/ *n.* **A** (*rabbit*) Kaninchen, *das;* **B** (*fur*) Kaninchenfell, *das;* Kanin, *das* (*Kürschnerei, Mode*)

**coo** /ku:/ **1** *int.* (*of person*) oh; (*of dove*) ruckedigu. **2** *n.* (*of dove*) **the ~[s]** das Gurren. **3** *v.i.* gurren; ‹Baby:› gurren (*fig.*). **4** *v.t. & i.* gurren (*auch fig.*)

**cooee** /'ku:i:/ **1** *int.* huhu (*ugs.*). **2** *v.i.* **they ~d to us** sie riefen uns „huhu" zu

**cook** /kʊk/ **1** *n.* ▶ 1261 Koch, *der*/Köchin, *die;* **too many ~s spoil the broth** (*prov.*) viele Köche verderben den Brei (*Spr.*).

**2** *v.t.* **A** garen; zubereiten, kochen ‹Mahlzeit›; (*fry, roast*) braten; (*boil*) kochen; **how would you ~ this piece of meat?** wie würden Sie dieses Stück Fleisch zubereiten?; **~ed in the oven** im Backofen zubereitet *od.* (*Kochk.*) gegart; **~ed meal** warme Mahlzeit; **how long should one ~ this joint?** wie lange sollte man diesen Braten garen lassen? (*Kochk.*); *abs.* **do you ~ with gas or electricity?** kochen Sie mit Gas oder mit Strom?; **she knows how to ~:** sie kann gut kochen *od.* kocht gut; **~ sb.'s goose [for him]** (*fig.*)

jmdm. alles verderben; **he ~ed his own goose** er hat sich (*Dat.*) alles verdorben *od.* (*ugs.*) vermasselt; Ⓑ (*fig. coll.: falsify*) frisieren (*ugs.*); Ⓒ (*Brit. coll.: fatigue*) **be ~ed** fix und fertig sein (*ugs.*).
❸ *v.i.* kochen; garen (*Kochk.*); **the meat was ~ing slowly** das Fleisch garte langsam; **what's ~ing?** (*fig. coll.*) was liegt an? (*ugs.*)
**~ 'up** *v.t.* sich (*Dat.*) ausbrüten, (*ugs.*) aushecken ‹Plan›; erfinden ‹Geschichte›

**cook: ~book** ⇒ **cookery book**; **~-chill 'food** *n. durch rasche Abkühlung haltbar gemachte Fertiggerichte*

**cooker** /'kʊkə(r)/ *n.* Ⓐ (*Brit.: appliance*) Herd, *der*; **electric/gas ~:** Elektroherd/Gasherd, *der*; Ⓑ (*vessel*) Kochgefäß, *das*; Ⓒ (*fruit*) **are those apples eaters or ~s?** sind diese Äpfel zum Essen oder zum Kochen?

**cookery** /'kʊkərɪ/ *n.* Ⓐ Kochen, *das*; Ⓑ (*Amer.: place*) Küche, *die*

**'cookery book** *n.* (*Brit.*) Kochbuch, *das*

**cookhouse** /'kʊkhaʊs/ *n.* (*Mil.*) Feldküche, *die*

**cookie** /'kʊkɪ/ *n.* Ⓐ (*Scot.*) Plätzchen, *das*; Ⓑ (*Amer.: biscuit*) Keks, *der*; **that's the way the ~ crumbles** (*fig. coll.*) es kommt, wie es kommen muss; Ⓒ (*coll.: person*) (*woman*) Person, *die*; (*attractive woman*) Klasseweib, *das* (*ugs.*); (*man*) Typ, *der* (*ugs.*)

**cooking** /'kʊkɪŋ/ *n.* Kochen, *das*; **German ~:** die deutsche Küche; **your ~ is marvellous** du kochst wunderbar; **do one's own ~:** für sich selbst kochen; **do the ~:** kochen

**cooking: ~ apple** *n.* Kochapfel, *der*; **~ fat** *n.* Bratfett, *das*; **~ salt** *n.* Speisesalz, *das*; **~ sherry** *n. Sherry zum Kochen*; **~ utensil** *n.* Küchengerät, *das*; **~ vessel** *n.* Kochgefäß, *das*

**cook: ~out** *n.* (*Amer.*) ≈ Grillparty, *die*; **have a ~out** im Freien kochen; **~ stove** *n.* (*Amer.*) [Koch]herd, *der*

**cool** /ku:l/ ❶ *adj.* Ⓐ kühl; luftig ‹Kleidung›; **I wait until my tea is ~ enough to drink** ich warte, bis mein Tee so weit abgekühlt ist, dass ich ihn trinken kann; **I am/feel ~:** mir ist kühl; **'store in a ~ place'** „kühl aufbewahren"; **bake in a ~ oven** bei schwacher Hitze backen; Ⓑ (*unexcited*) **he kept** *or* **stayed ~:** er blieb ruhig *od.* bewahrte die Ruhe; **play it ~** (*coll.*) ruhig bleiben; cool vorgehen (*salopp*); **she's always so ~ about things** sie ist immer so ruhig und besonnen; **he was ~, calm, and collected** er war ruhig und gelassen; **a ~ customer** ein kühler Kopf; **keep a ~ head** einen kühlen Kopf bewahren; ⇒ *also* **cucumber**; Ⓒ (*unemotional, unfriendly*) kühl; (*calmly audacious*) kaltblütig; unverfroren ‹Forderung›; **be a ~ customer** (*fig.*) ganz schön unverschämt sein; **a ~ £3,000/thousand** (*coll.*) glatt 3 000 Pfund/ein glatter Tausender (*ugs.*); Ⓓ (*Jazz*) *in der Art des Cooljazz*; **~ jazz** Cooljazz, *der*; Ⓔ (*coll.: excellent*) cool (*salopp*); geil (*salopp*).
❷ *n.* Ⓐ (*coolness*) Kühle, *die*; Ⓑ (*~ air, place*) **sit in the ~:** im Kühlen sitzen; **store sth. in the ~:** etw. kühl aufbewahren; Ⓒ (*coll.: composure*) **keep/lose one's ~:** die Ruhe bewahren/verlieren.
❸ *v.i.* abkühlen; **the weather has ~ed** es ist kühler geworden; **wait until your milk ~s a bit** lass deine Milch etwas abkühlen; (*fig.*) **our relationship has ~ed** unsere Beziehung ist kühler geworden; **the first heat of passion had ~ed** die erste Leidenschaft war verflogen; **~ towards sb./sth.** an jmdm./etw. das Interesse verlieren.
❹ *v.t.* kühlen; (*from high temperature*) abkühlen; (*fig.*) abkühlen ‹Leidenschaft, Raserei, Liebe›; **[have to] ~ one's heels** lange warten [müssen]; **~ it!** (*coll.*) reg dich ab! (*ugs.*)
**~ 'down** ❶ *v.i.* Ⓐ ‹Tee:› abkühlen; ‹Luft:› sich abkühlen; Ⓑ (*fig.*) sich beruhigen; **his anger has ~ed down** sein Zorn hat sich gelegt. ❷ *v.t.* abkühlen; (*fig.*) besänftigen; (*disillusion*) ernüchtern
**~ 'off** ❶ *v.i.* Ⓐ abkühlen; **the weather has ~ed off** es ist kühler geworden; **we need a few minutes to ~ off** wir brauchen ein paar Minuten, um uns abzukühlen; Ⓑ (*fig.*) sich beruhigen; ‹Zorn, Begeisterung, Interesse, Leidenschaft:› sich legen, nachlassen; ‹Freundschaft:› sich abkühlen. ❷ *v.t.* abkühlen; (*fig.*) beruhigen; besänftigen; abkühlen ‹Leidenschaft, Begeisterung›

**coolant** /'ku:lənt/ *n.* Kühlmittel, *das*; (*for cutting-tool*) Schneidflüssigkeit, *die* (*Technik*); (*for internal-combustion engine*) Kühlwasser, *das*

**'cool box** *n.* Kühlbox, *die*

**cooler** /'ku:lə(r)/ *n.* Ⓐ (*vessel*) Kühler, *der*; Ⓑ (*Amer.: refrigerator*) Kühlschrank, *der*; Ⓒ (*coll.: prison*) Knast, *der* (*ugs.*)

**'cool-headed** *adj.* kühl; nüchtern

**coolie** /'ku:lɪ/ *n.* Kuli, *der*

**'coolie hat** *flacher Hut* [*der chinesischen Kulis*]; Chinesenhut, *der*

**cooling**/'ku:lɪŋ/: **~ fan** *n.* Kühlgebläse, *das* (*Technik*); **~-'off period** *n.* Rücktrittsfrist, *die*; **~ tower** *n.* Kühlturm, *der*

**coolly** /'ku:llɪ/ *adv.* Ⓐ kühl; Ⓑ (*fig.*) (*calmly*) ruhig; (*unemotionally, in unfriendly manner*) kühl; (*impudently*) kaltblütig; unverfroren ‹verlangen, fordern›

**coolness** /'ku:lnɪs/ *n., no pl.* Kühle, *die*; (*fig.*) (*calmness*) Ruhe, *die*; (*unemotional nature, unfriendliness*) Kühle, *die*; (*impudence*) Kaltblütigkeit, *die*; (*insolence*) Unverfrorenheit, *die*

**coomb** /ku:m/ *n.* (*Brit.*) (*on hill flank*) *Taleinschnitt an der Seite eines Berges*; (*short valley*) Schlucht, *die*

**coon** /ku:n/ *n.* Ⓐ (*Amer.: racoon*) Waschbär, *der*; Ⓑ (*sl. derog.*) (*black person*) Nigger, *der* (*abwertend*); (*black woman*) Niggerweib, *das* (*abwertend*)

**'coonskin** *n.* (*Amer.*) Waschbärfell, *das*; Waschbär[pelz], *der*; (*cap*) Waschbärmütze, *die*; (*jacket*) Waschbärjacke, *die*

**coop** /ku:p/ ❶ *n.* (*cage*) Geflügelkäfig, *der*; (*for poultry*) Hühnerstall, *der*; (*fowl-run*) Auslauf, *der*. ❷ *v.t.* **~ in** *or* **up** einpferchen

**co-op** /'kəʊɒp/ *n.* (*coll.*) Ⓐ (*Brit.*) (*society*) Genossenschaft, *die*; (*shop*) Konsum[laden], *der*; Ⓑ (*Amer.*) ⇒ **cooperative** 2 B

**cooperate** /kəʊ'ɒpəreɪt/ *v.i.* mitarbeiten (**in** bei); (*with each other*) zusammenarbeiten (**in** bei); (*not obstruct*) mitmachen (*ugs.*); ‹Dinge, Ereignisse:› zusammenwirken; (*Polit., Econ. also*) kooperieren (**in** bei); **~ with sb.** mit jmdm. zusammenarbeiten/kooperieren; **the patient refused to ~:** der Patient verweigerte die Mitarbeit *od.* war nicht kooperativ; **~ with the police** die Polizei unterstützen

**cooperation** /kəʊɒpə'reɪʃn/ *n.* Ⓐ ⇒ **cooperate:** Mitarbeit, *die*; Zusammenarbeit, *die*; Kooperation, *die*; **with the ~ of** unter Mitarbeit von; **in ~ with** in Zusammenarbeit mit; Ⓑ (*Econ.*) Genossenschaft, *die*; **the principle of ~:** das genossenschaftliche Prinzip

**cooperative** /kəʊ'ɒpərətɪv/ ❶ *adj.* Ⓐ (*offering cooperation*) kooperativ; (*helpful*) hilfsbereit; Ⓑ (*Econ.*) genossenschaftlich. ❷ *n.* Ⓐ Genossenschaft, *die*; Kooperative, *die* (*DDR*); (*shop*) Genossenschaftsladen, *der*; **workers' ~:** Produktivgenossenschaft, *die*; Ⓑ (*Amer.: dwelling*) *gemeinschaftlich gemieteter/gekaufter Wohnraum*

**cooperative: ~ shop** *n.* ⇒ **~ store**; **~ society** *n.* Genossenschaft, *die*; **~ store** *n.* Genossenschaftsladen, *der*

**co-opt** /kəʊ'ɒpt/ *v.t.* kooptieren; hinzuwählen; **be ~ed [on] to a committee** von einem Komitee kooptiert werden

**co-option** /kəʊ'ɒpʃn/ *n.* Koop[ta]tion, *die*

**coordinate** ❶ /kəʊ'ɔ:dɪnət/ *adj.* Ⓐ (*equal in rank*) gleichrangig; Ⓑ (*Ling.*) nebengeordnet. ❷ *n.* Ⓐ (*Math.*) Koordinate, *die*; Ⓑ *in pl.* (*clothes*) Kombination, *die*. ❸ /kəʊ'ɔ:dɪneɪt/ *v.t.* Ⓐ koordinieren; **~ one's thoughts** seine Gedanken sammeln *od.* ordnen; Ⓑ (*Ling.*) **coordinating conjunction** koordinierende *od.* nebenordnende Konjunktion

**coordination** /kəʊɔ:dɪ'neɪʃn/ *n.* Koordination, *die*; **he lacks ~:** er hat Koordinationsschwierigkeiten

**coordinator** /kəʊ'ɔ:dɪneɪtə(r)/ *n.* Koordinator, *der*/Koordinatorin, *die*

**coot** /ku:t/ *n.* Ⓐ (*Ornith.*) **[bald] ~:** Blässhuhn, *das*; **be [as] bald as a ~:** völlig kahl sein; Ⓑ (*coll.: stupid person*) **[silly] ~:** dummes Huhn

**co-owner** /kəʊ'əʊnə(r)/ *n.* Miteigentümer, *der*/-eigentümerin, *die*; (*of business*) Mitinhaber, *der*/-inhaberin, *die*

**cop**[1] /kɒp/ *n.* (*coll.: police officer*) Bulle, *der* (*salopp*); Polyp, *der* (*salopp*); **she's a ~:** sie ist von der Polente (*salopp*); **~s and robbers** Räuber und Gendarm

**cop**[2] (*coll.*) ❶ *v.t.*, **-pp-:** Ⓐ **when ..., you'll ~ it** (*be punished*) wenn ..., dann kannst du was erleben; Ⓑ **they ~ped it** (*were killed*) sie mussten dran glauben (*salopp*); Ⓒ (*hit*) **he ~ped him one under the chin** er hat ihm eins unters Kinn verpasst (*ugs.*). ❷ *n.* **it's a fair ~!** guter Fang!; **no ~, not much ~:** nichts Besonderes
**~ 'out** *v.i.* (*coll.*) Ⓐ (*escape*) abhauen (*salopp*); **~ out of society** [aus der Gesellschaft] aussteigen (*ugs.*); Ⓑ (*give up*) alles hinwerfen (*ugs.*); Ⓒ (*go back on one's promise*) **you can't ~ out like that** du kannst mich/ihn *usw.* doch nicht so hängen lassen (*ugs.*). ⇒ *also* **cop-out**

**copartner** /kəʊ'pɑ:tnə(r)/ *n.* Partner, *der*/Partnerin, *die*; Teilhaber, *der*/-haberin, *die*

**copartnership** /kəʊ'pɑ:tnəʃɪp/ *n.* (*relationship*) Partnerschaft, *die*; Teilhaberschaft, *die*; (*company*) Sozietät, *die*

**cope**[1] /kəʊp/ *v.i.* Ⓐ (*be able to contend*) **~ with sb./sth.** mit jmdm./etw. fertig werden; **~ with a handicapped child** mit einem behinderten Kind zurechtkommen; Ⓑ (*deal with sth.*) klarkommen (*ugs.*); **we must find someone who will ~:** wir brauchen jemanden, der die Sache in die Hand nimmt

**cope**[2] *n.* (*Eccl.*) Pluviale, *das* (*kath. Kirche*)

**Copenhagen** /kəʊpn'heɪgn/ *pr. n.* ▶ **1626** Kopenhagen (*das*)

**Copernican** /kə'pɜ:nɪkn/ *adj.* kopernikanisch

**copier** /'kɒpɪə(r)/ *n.* (*machine*) Kopiergerät, *das*; Kopierer, *der* (*ugs.*)

**co-pilot** /'kəʊpaɪlət/ *n.* Kopilot, *der*/Kopilotin, *die*

**coping** /'kəʊpɪŋ/ *n.* Mauerabdeckung, *die*

**'coping stone** *n.* Abdeckplatte, *die*

**copious** /'kəʊpɪəs/ *adj.* (*plentiful*) reichhaltig; voll ‹Haar›; (*informative*) umfassend

**copiously** /'kəʊpɪəslɪ/ *adv.* (*plentifully*) reichlich; (*informatively*) umfassend

**copiousness** /'kəʊpɪəsnɪs/ *n., no pl.* (*plentifulness*) Fülle, *die*

**'cop-out** *n.* (*coll.*) Drückebergerei, *die* (*ugs. abwertend*); **that's a ~:** das ist Drückebergerei (*ugs. abwertend*)

**copper**[1] /'kɒpə(r)/ ❶ *n.* Ⓐ Kupfer, *das*; Ⓑ (*coin*) Kupfermünze, *die*; **a few ~s** etwas Kupfergeld; **it only costs a few ~s** es kostet nur ein paar Pfennige; Ⓒ (*boiler*) [Kupfer]kessel, *der*; (*for laundry*) Waschkessel, *der*. ❷ *attrib. adj.* Ⓐ (*made of ~*) kupfern; Kupfer‹münze, -kessel, -rohr›; Ⓑ (*coloured like ~*) kupferfarben; kupfern

**copper**[2] (*Brit. coll.*) ⇒ **cop**[1]

**copper: ~ 'beech** *n.* Blutbuche, *die*; **~-bottomed** *adj.* gekupfert (*Seew.*) ‹Schiff›; ‹Pfanne› mit Kupferboden; (*fig.*) (*authentic*) waschecht; (*financially reliable*) todsicher (*ugs.*); **~-coloured** *adj.* kupferfarben; **~plate** ❶ *n.* Ⓐ (*metal plate*) Kupferplatte, *die*; Ⓑ (*print*) Kupferstich, *der*; ❷ *adj.* **~plate writing** ≈ Schönschrift, *die*; *Schreib- und Druckschrift mit dickem Ab- und dünnem Aufstrich*

**coppery** /'kɒpərɪ/ *adj.* kupferfarben; kupfern

**coppice** /'kɒpɪs/ *n.* Wäldchen, *das*; Niederwald, *der* (*Forstw.*)

**'coppice wood** *n.* Unterholz, *das*

**copra** /'kɒprə/ *n.* Kopra, *die*

**copse** /kɒps/ ⇒ **coppice**

**'cop shop** *n.* (*Brit. coll.*) Wache, *die*; Revier, *das*

**Copt** /kɒpt/ *n.* Kopte, *der*/Koptin, *die*

**Coptic** /ˈkɒptɪk/ ❶ *adj.* koptisch. ❷ *n.* (*language*) Koptisch, *das*

**copula** /ˈkɒpjʊlə/ *n.* (*Ling.*) Kopula, *die*

**copulate** /ˈkɒpjʊleɪt/ *v.i.* kopulieren

**copulation** /kɒpjʊˈleɪʃn/ *n.* Kopulation, *die*

**copy** /ˈkɒpɪ/ ❶ *n.* [A] (*reproduction*) Kopie, *die;* (*imitation*) Nachahmung, *die;* (*with carbon paper etc.*) (*typed*) Durchschlag, *der;* (*written*) Durchschrift, *die;* **write a ~:** eine Abschrift machen; ⇒ *also* **fair²** 1 H; **rough ~**; [B] (*specimen*) Exemplar, *das;* **have you a ~ of today's 'Times'?** haben Sie die „Times" von heute?; **send three copies of the application** die Bewerbung in dreifacher Ausfertigung schicken; **top ~:** Original, *das;* [C] (*manuscript etc. for printing*) Druckvorlage, *die;* **supply ~:** die Druckvorlage liefern; **make good ~** (*Journ. coll.: news*) ein klasse Stoff sein (*ugs.*); **[advertising] ~:** Werbetext, *der.*
❷ *v.t.* [A] (*make ~ of*) kopieren; (*by photocopier*) [foto]kopieren; (*transcribe*) abschreiben; [B] (*imitate*) nachahmen.
❸ *v.i.* [A] kopieren; **~ from sb./sth.** jmdn./etw. kopieren; [B] (*in exam etc.*) abschreiben; **~ from** *or* **off sb./sth.** bei jmdm./aus etw. abschreiben

**~ 'out** *v.t.* abschreiben

**copy: ~book** *n. attrib.* wie im Bilderbuch *nachgestellt;* Bilderbuch‹landschaft, -wetter›; ⇒ *also* **blot** 2 B; **~cat** *n.* (*coll.*) **you're such a ~cat!** du musst immer alles nachmachen!; **~desk** *n.* (*Amer.*) Redaktionstisch, *der;* **~ editor** *n.* Redakteur, *der*/Redakteurin, *die* (*für formale Manuskriptbearbeitung und redaktionelles Korrekturlesen*)

**copyist** /ˈkɒpɪɪst/ *n.* Kopist, *der*

**copy: ~ protection** *n.* (*Computing*) Kopierschutz, *der;* **~right** ❶ *n.* Copyright, *das;* Urheberrecht, *das;* **be out of ~right** gemeinfrei [geworden] sein; **protected by ~right** urheberrechtlich geschützt; ❷ *adj.* urheberrechtlich geschützt; **~right library** (*Brit.*) *Bibliothek, die Anspruch auf ein Freiexemplar jedes in Großbritannien veröffentlichten Buches hat;* ❸ *v.t.* urheberrechtlich schützen; **~ typist** *n.* ▶ **1261** | Schreibkraft (*die nur nach schriftlichen Vorlagen arbeitet*); **~writer** *n.* [Werbe]texter, *der*/-texterin, *die*

**coquetry** /ˈkɒkɪtrɪ, ˈkəʊkɪtrɪ/ *n.* Koketterie, *die;* (*fig.*) Kokettieren, *das*

**coquette** /kəˈket/ ❶ *n.* Kokette, *die.* ❷ *v.i.* kokettieren

**coquettish** /kəˈketɪʃ/ *adj.* kokett

**cor** /kɔː(r)/ *int.* (*Brit. sl.*) Mensch! (*salopp*)

**coracle** /ˈkɒrəkl/ *n.* (*Brit.*) Coracle, *das* (*Fischerboot aus lederüberzogenem Flechtwerk*)

**coral** /ˈkɒrl/ ❶ *n.* Koralle, *die.* ❷ *attrib. adj.* korallen; Korallen‹insel, -riff, -rot›

**cor anglais** /kɔːr ˈɑ̃gleɪ, kɔːr ˈɒŋgleɪ/ *n.* (*Mus.*) [A] (*instrument*) Englischhorn, *das;* Englisch Horn, *das* (*fachspr.*); [B] (*organ stop*) Englisch Horn, *das*

**corbel** /kɔːbl/ *n.* (*Archit.*) (*of stone*) Kragstein, *der;* (*of timber*) Sattelholz, *das*

**'corbel table** *n.* (*Archit.*) Bogenfries, *der*

**cord** /kɔːd/ *n.* [A] Kordel, *die;* [B] (*Anat.*) ⇒ **spermatic cord; spinal cord; umbilical cord; vocal cords;** [C] (*rib*) Rippe, *die;* (*cloth*) Cord, *der;* [D] *in pl.* (*trousers*) **[pair of] ~s** Cordhose, *die;* [E] (*Amer. Electr.: flex*) Kabel, *das*

**cordage** /ˈkɔːdɪdʒ/ *n.* (*Naut.*) Tauwerk, *das*

**cordate** /ˈkɔːdeɪt/ *adj.* (*Biol.*) herzförmig

**cordial** /ˈkɔːdɪəl/ ❶ *adj.* herzlich; **a ~ dislike for sb.** eine tief empfundene Abneigung gegenüber jmdm. ❷ *n.* (*drink*) Sirup, *der*

**cordiality** /kɔːdɪˈælɪtɪ/ *n., no pl.* Herzlichkeit, *die*

**cordially** /ˈkɔːdɪəlɪ/ *adv.* herzlich; **~ dislike sb.** eine tief empfundene Abneigung gegenüber jmdm. haben; **~ yours** mit herzlichen Grüßen

**cordillera** /kɔːdɪˈljeərə/ *n.* (*Geog.*) Kettengebirge, *das*

**cordite** /ˈkɔːdaɪt/ *n.* Kordit, *der*

**cordless** /ˈkɔːdlɪs/ *adj.* [A] (*without cord*) ohne Kordel *nachgestellt;* [B] (*without flex*) ohne Kabel *nachgestellt*

**'cordless phone** *n.* Schnurlostelefon, *das*

**cordon** /ˈkɔːdn/ ❶ *n.* (*line of police; also Mil.*) Kordon, *der;* **a ~ of policemen** ein Polizeikordon; ⇒ *also* **throw around b** ❷ *v.t.* **~ [off]** absperren; abriegeln

**cordon bleu** /kɔːdɔ̃ ˈblɜː/ *n.* Meisterkoch, *der*/-köchin, *die;* **~ cookery** feine Küche

**corduroy** /ˈkɔːdərɔɪ, ˈkɔːdjʊrɔɪ/ *n.* [A] (*material*) Cordsamt, *der;* [B] *in pl.* (*trousers*) Cordsamthose, *die*

**core** /kɔː(r)/ ❶ *n.* [A] (*of fruit*) Kerngehäuse, *das;* [B] (*Geol.*) (*rock sample*) [Bohr]kern, *der;* (*of earth*) [Erd]kern, *der;* [C] (*Electr.: of soft iron*) [Eisen]kern, *der;* [D] (*fig.: innermost part*) **get to the ~ of the matter** zum Kern der Sache kommen; **rotten to the ~:** verdorben bis ins Mark; **English to the ~:** durch und durch englisch; **shake sb. to the ~:** jmdn. zutiefst erschüttern; [E] (*Industry: internal mould*) Kern, *der;* [F] (*Nucl. Engin.*) Core, *das;* Reaktorkern, *der;* [G] (*Computing*) Magnetkern, *der;* [H] (*of rope, electrical cable*) Seele, *die.* ❷ *v.t.* entkernen ‹Apfel, Birne›

**corer** /ˈkɔːrə(r)/ *n.* Entkerner, *der*

**co-respondent** /kəʊrɪˈspɒndənt/ *n.* Mitbeklagte, *der/die* (*im Scheidungsprozess*)

**'core time** *n.* Kernzeit, *die*

**Corfu** /kɔːˈfuː/ *pr. n.* Korfu (*das*)

**corgi** /ˈkɔːgɪ/ *n.* **[Welsh] ~:** Welsh Corgi, *der*

**coriander** /kɒrɪˈændə(r)/ *n.* Koriander, *der*

**cori'ander seed** *n.* Koriander, *der*

**Corinth** /ˈkɒrɪnθ/ *pr. n.* ▶ **1626** | Korinth (*das*)

**cork** /kɔːk/ ❶ *n.* [A] (*bark*) Kork, *der;* [B] (*bottle stopper*) Korken, *der;* [C] (*fishing float*) Schwimmer, *der;* [D] *attrib.* Kork-. ❷ *v.t.* zukorken; verkorken

**~ 'up** *v.t.* zukorken; verkorken; **~ up one's emotions** seine Gefühle unterdrücken

**corked** /kɔːkt/ *adj.* [A] (*stopped with cork*) verkorkt; [B] (*impaired*) korkig ‹Wein›

**corker** /ˈkɔːkə(r)/ *n.* (*coll.*) (*thing*) **that joke was a real ~, that was a ~ of a joke** der Witz war echt Spitze (*ugs.*); (*person*) **she's/he's a real ~:** sie/er ist einsame Spitze (*ugs.*)

**corking** /ˈkɔːkɪŋ/ *adj.* (*coll.*) (*large*) Riesen-; (*excellent*) klasse (*ugs.*)

**cork: ~screw** ❶ *n.* (*bottle opener*) Korkenzieher, *der;* (*spiral*) Spirale, *die;* ❷ *v.i.* ‹Flugzeug:› trudeln; **~'tile** *n.* Korkplatte, *die;* **~-tipped** *adj.* (*Brit.*) ‹Zigarette› mit Korkmundstück; **~wood** *n.* [A] (*wood*) Korkholz, *das;* [B] (*tree*) Korkholzbaum, *der*

**corky** /ˈkɔːkɪ/ *adj.* korkig

**corm** /kɔːm/ *n.* (*Bot.*) Knolle, *die*

**cormorant** /ˈkɔːmərənt/ *n.* (*Ornith.*) Kormoran, *der*

**corn¹** /kɔːn/ *n.* [A] (*cereal*) Getreide, *das;* (*esp. rye, wheat also*) Korn, *das;* **[sweet]~** (*maize*) Mais, *der;* **~ on the cob** [gekochter/gerösteter] Maiskolben; [B] (*seed*) Korn, *das*

**corn²** *n.* (*on foot*) Hühnerauge, *das;* **tread on sb.'s ~s** (*fig.*) jmdm. auf die Hühneraugen treten (*ugs.*)

**corn: ~ cob** *n.* Maiskolben, *der;* **~crake** /ˈkɔːnkreɪk/ *n.* (*Ornith.*) Wachtelkönig, *der;* **~ dolly** *n.* Strohpuppe, *die*

**cornea** /ˈkɔːnɪə/ *n.* (*Anat.*) Hornhaut, *die;* Cornea, *die* (*fachspr.*)

**corneal** /ˈkɔːnɪəl/ *adj.* (*Anat.*) Korneal- (*fachspr.*); Hornhaut-

**corned beef** /kɔːnd ˈbiːf/ *n.* Cornedbeef, *das*

**cornelian 'cherry** *n.* Kornelkirsche, *die*

**corner** /ˈkɔːnə(r)/ ❶ *n.* [A] Ecke, *die;* (*curve*) Kurve, *die;* **on the ~:** an der Ecke/in der Kurve; **at the ~:** an der Ecke; **~ of the street** Straßenecke, *die;* **sharp ~:** scharfe *od.* enge Kurve; **cut [off] a/the ~:** eine/die Kurve schneiden; **cut ~s** (*fig.*) auf die Schnelle arbeiten (*ugs.*); **cut ~s with sth.** (*fig.*) bei etw. pfuschen (*ugs.*); **[sth. is] just [a]round the ~:** [etw. ist] gleich um die Ecke; **Christmas is just round the ~** (*fig. coll.*) Weihnachten steht vor der Tür; **turn the ~:** um die Ecke biegen; **he has turned the ~ now** (*fig.*) er ist jetzt über den Berg (*ugs.*); [B] (*hollow angle between walls*) Ecke, *die;* (*of mouth, eye*) Winkel, *der;* **~ of the mouth/eye** Mund-/Augenwinkel, *der;* **drive sb. into a ~:** jmdn. in die Enge treiben; ⇒ *also* **paint** 2 A; **tight** 1 I; [C] (*Boxing, Wrestling*) Ecke, *die;* [D] (*secluded place*) Eckchen, *das;* Plätzchen, *das;* (*remote region*) Winkel, *der;* **from the four ~s of the earth** aus aller Welt; [E] (*Hockey/Footb.*) Ecke, *die;* **score from a ~:** eine Ecke verwandeln; **take a ~:** eine Ecke schlagen/treten; [F] (*Commerc.*) Corner, *der;* Schwänze, *die.*
❷ *v.t.* [A] (*drive into ~*) in eine Ecke treiben; (*fig.*) in die Enge treiben; **have [got] sb. ~ed** jmdn. in der Falle haben; [B] (*Commerc.*) **~ the market in coffee** die Kaffeevorräte aufkaufen; den Kaffeemarkt aufschwänzen (*fachspr.*).
❸ *v.i.* die Kurven nehmen; **~ well/badly** eine gute/schlechte Kurvenlage haben; **when ~ing** beim Kurvenfahren

**corner: ~ cupboard** *n.* Eckschrank, *der;;* **~ flag** *n.* (*Sport*) Eckfahne, *die;* **~ hit** *n.* (*Hockey*) Eckball, *der;* Eckschlag, *der;* **score [a goal] from a ~ hit** einen Eckball verwandeln; **take a ~ hit** eine Ecke schlagen; **~ kick** *n.* (*Footb.*) Eckball, *der;* Eckstoß, *der;* **score from a ~ kick** einen Eckstoß verwandeln; **take a ~ kick** eine Ecke treten; **~ seat** *n.* Ecksitz, *der;* **~ shop** *n.* Tante-Emma-Laden, *der* (*ugs.*); **~stone** *n.* Eckstein, *der;* (*fig.*) Eckpfeiler, *der*

**cornet** /ˈkɔːnɪt/ *n.* [A] (*Brit.: wafer*) [Eis]tüte, *die;* Eishörnchen, *das;* [B] (*Mus.*) (*instrument*) Kornett, *das*

**corn: ~ exchange** *n.* Getreidebörse, *die;* **~field** *n.* Kornfeld, *das;* (*Amer.*) Maisfeld, *das;* **~flakes** *n. pl.* Cornflakes *Pl.;* **~flour** *n.* [A] (*Brit.: ground maize*) Maismehl, *das;* [B] (*flour of rice etc.*) Stärkemehl, *das;* **~flower** *n.* Kornblume, *die*

**cornice** /ˈkɔːnɪs/ *n.* [A] (*Archit.*) Kranzgesims, *das;* [B] (*moulding*) Fries, *der* (*an der Wand unmittelbar unter der Decke*); [C] (*Mount.*) [Schnee]wächte, *die*

**Cornish** /ˈkɔːnɪʃ/ ❶ *adj.* kornisch. ❷ *n.* Kornisch, *das*

**Cornish: ~ 'cream** ⇒ **Devonshire cream;** **~ pasty** /kɔːnɪʃ ˈpæstɪ/ *n. mit Fleisch, Kartoffeln und Zwiebeln gefülltes Blätterteiggebäck*

**corn: ~ marigold** *n.* Saatwucherblume, *die;* **~starch** (*Amer.*) ⇒ **~flour** A

**cornucopia** /kɔːnjʊˈkəʊpɪə/ *n.* Füllhorn, *das;* **a ~ of information** (*fig.*) Information in Hülle und Fülle

**corny** /ˈkɔːnɪ/ *adj.* (*coll.*) (*old-fashioned*) altmodisch ‹Witz usw.›; (*trite*) abgedroschen (*ugs.*); (*sentimental*) schmalzig (*abwertend*)

**corolla** /kəˈrɒlə/ *n.* (*Bot.*) Krone, *die;* Korolla, *die*

**corollary** /kəˈrɒlərɪ/ *n.* (*proposition*) Korollar[ium], *das* (*Logik*); (*inference*) Schluss, *der;* Folgerung, *die;* (*consequence*) [logische *od.* natürliche] Folge

**corona** /kəˈrəʊnə/ *n., pl.* **~e** /kəˈrəʊniː/ *or* **~s** [A] (*circle of light round sun or moon*) Hof, *der;* (*gaseous envelope of sun*) Korona, *die;* [B] (*Anat.*) Corona, *die*

**coronary** /ˈkɒrənərɪ/ ❶ *adj.* (*Anat.*) koronar. ❷ *n.* (*Med.*) ⇒ **coronary thrombosis**

**coronary: ~ 'artery** *n.* (*Anat.*) Herzkranzarterie, *die;* Koronararterie, *die* (*fachspr.*); **~ throm'bosis** *n.* ▶ **1232** | (*Med.*) Koronarthrombose, *die*

**coronation** /kɒrəˈneɪʃn/ *n.* Krönung, *die*

**coroner** /ˈkɒrənə(r)/ *n.* Coroner, *der;* *Beamter, der gewaltsame od. unnatürliche Todesfälle untersucht*

**coronet** /ˈkɒrənet/ *n.* Krone, *die*

**Corp.** *abbr.* [A] (*Mil.*) **corporal** ≈ Uffz.; [B] (*Amer.*) **corporation**

**corpora** *pl. of* **corpus**

**corporal¹** /ˈkɔːpərl/ *adj.* körperlich

**corporal²** *n.* ▶ **1617** | (*Mil.*) Korporal, *der* (*hist., österr.*); ≈ Hauptgefreite, *der;* ≈ Stabsgefreite, *der* (*DDR*)

**corporate** /'kɔːpərət/ *adj.* A *(forming corporation)* körperschaftlich; **~ body, body ~:** Körperschaft, *die;* juristische Person; B *(of corporation)* körperschaftlich; korporativ

**corporately** /'kɔːpərətlɪ/ *adv.* körperschaftlich; korporativ

**corporation** /kɔːpə'reɪʃn/ *n.* A *(civic authority)* **[municipal] ~:** Gemeindeverwaltung, *die; (of borough, city)* Stadtverwaltung, *die;* B *(united body)* Körperschaft, *die;* Korporation, *die; (artificial person)* juristische Person; **~ tax** Körperschaftssteuer, *die;* C *(coll.: belly)* Schmerbauch, *der (ugs.);* Wampe, *die (ugs. abwertend)*

**corporative** /'kɔːpərətɪv/ *adj.* A *(of civic authorities)* behördlich; *(of united body)* korporativ; *(of artificial body)* körperschaftlich; B *(organized in corporations)* berufsständisch organisiert; korporativ ‹Organisation›; *(governed by corporations)* **~ state** Ständestaat, *der*

**corporeal** /kɔː'pɔːrɪəl/ *adj.* A *(bodily)* körperlich; B *(material)* materiell; stofflich

**corps** /kɔː(r)/ *n., pl. same* /kɔːz/ Korps, *das;* ⇒ *also* **diplomatic corps**

**corps:** ~ **de ballet** /kɔː də 'bæleɪ/ *n.* Corps de ballet, *das;* Ballettkorps, *das;* ~ **diplomatique** /kɔː dɪpləmæ'tiːk/ Corps diplomatique, *das;* diplomatisches Korps

**corpse** /kɔːps/ *n.* Leiche, *die;* Leichnam, *der (geh.)*

**corpulence** /'kɔːpjʊləns/, **corpulency** /'kɔːpjʊlənsɪ/ *n.* Korpulenz, *die*

**corpulent** /'kɔːpjʊlənt/ *adj.* korpulent

**corpus** /'kɔːpəs/ *n., pl.* **corpora** /'kɔːpərə/ *(texts)* Sammlung, *die;* Korpus, *das*

**Corpus Christi** /kɔːpəs 'krɪstɪ/ *n. (Eccl.)* Fronleichnam *(der);* Fronleichnamsfest, *das*

**corpuscle** /'kɔːpəsl/ *n.* A *(Phys.)* Korpuskel, *das od. die;* B *(Anat.)* Corpusculum, *das;* **[blood] ~s** Blutkörperchen

**corral** /kə'rɑːl/ ❶ *n.* A *(Amer.: pen)* Pferch, *der;* B *(Hist.: defensive enclosure)* Wagenburg, *die;* C *(for wild animals)* Korral, *der.* ❷ *v.t.,* **-ll-** A *(Hist.: form into ~)* zu einer Wagenburg formieren; B *(confine in ~)* einpferchen; C *(Amer. coll.: acquire)* einsacken *(ugs.);* mit Beschlag belegen ‹Person›

**correct** /kə'rekt/ ❶ *v.t.* A *(amend)* korrigieren; verbessern, korrigieren ‹Fehler, Formulierung, jmds. Englisch/Deutsch›; **~ a few points** einige Punkte richtig stellen; **~ed for spelling mistakes** auf Rechtschreibfehler hin korrigiert; **these glasses should ~ your eyesight/vision** mit dieser Brille müssten Sie richtig sehen können; **~ the focus** die Bildschärfe richtig einstellen; **~ me if I'm wrong** ich könnte mich natürlich irren; **I stand ~ed** ich nehme das zurück; B *(counteract)* ausgleichen ‹etw. Schädliches›; C *(admonish)* zurechtweisen **(for** wegen); D *(punish)* bestrafen; E *(bring to standard)* korrigieren **(for** hinsichtlich); F *(eliminate aberration from)* korrigieren *(Optik).*
❷ *adj.* richtig; korrekt; *(precise)* korrekt; akkurat; **that is ~:** das stimmt; **have you the ~ time?** haben Sie die genaue Uhrzeit?; **is that clock ~?** geht die Uhr richtig?; **am I ~ in assuming that ...?** gehe ich recht in der Annahme, dass ...?; **the ~ thing for you to do is to speak to the manager** darüber sollten Sie mit dem Abteilungsleiter sprechen; **what is the ~ thing to do in such a situation?** was soll man in so einer Situation korrekterweise tun?; **~ to five decimal places** auf fünf Dezimalstellen genau

**correcting fluid** /kə'rektɪŋ fluːɪd/ *n.* Korrekturflüssigkeit, *die*

**correction** /kə'rekʃn/ *n.* A *(correcting)* Korrektur, *die;* **I speak under ~:** ich sage das mit *od.* unter Vorbehalt; **I'm open to ~:** ich lasse mich korrigieren; B *(corrected version)* **~s to the manuscript** Manuskriptkorrekturen; **the pupils had to write out** *or* **do their ~s** die Schüler mussten die Verbesserung *od.* Berichtigung schreiben; C *(punishment)* Bestrafung, *die;* **house of ~** *(arch.)* Erziehungsheim, *das;* Besserungsanstalt, *die (veralt.)*

**corrective** /kə'rektɪv/ *adj.* korrigierend; **take ~ action** korrigierend eingreifen

**correctly** /kə'rektlɪ/ *adv.* richtig; korrekt; *(precisely)* korrekt; akkurat; **behave very ~:** sich sehr korrekt benehmen

**correctness** /kə'rektnɪs/ *n., no pl.* ⇒ **correct** 2: Richtigkeit, *die;* Korrektheit, *die;* Akkuratesse, *die*

**corrector** /kə'rektə(r)/ *n.* Korrektor, *der*/Korrektorin, *die*

**correlate** /'kɒrɪleɪt/ ❶ *v.i.* einander entsprechen; **~ with** *or* **to sth.** einer Sache *(Dat.)* entsprechen. ❷ *v.t.* **~ sth. with sth.** etw. zu etw. in Beziehung setzen. ❸ *n.* Korrelat, *das*

**correlation** /kɒrɪ'leɪʃn/ *n.* [Wechsel]beziehung, *die;* Korrelation, *die (bes. Math., Naturw.); (connection)* Zusammenhang, *der*

**correlative** /kə'relətɪv/ *adj.* A *(having correlation)* **~ [with** *or* **to sth.]** [mit etw.] korrelierend; **be ~ with** *or* **to sth.** mit etw. korrelieren; B *(Ling.)* korrelativ

**correspond** /kɒrɪ'spɒnd/ *v.i.* A *(be analogous, agree in amount)* **~ [to each other]** einander entsprechen; **~ to sth.** einer Sache *(Dat.)* entsprechen; **do the classes ~ in number?** sind die Klassen gleich stark?; B *(agree in position)* **~ [to sth.]** [mit etw.] übereinstimmen; *(be in harmony)* **~ [with** *or* **to sth.]** [mit etw.] zusammenpassen *od. (geh.)* korrespondieren; C *(communicate)* **~ with sb.** mit jmdm. korrespondieren; **do you still ~ with your old school friends?** hast du noch Briefkontakt mit deinen alten Schulfreunden?

**correspondence** /kɒrɪ'spɒndəns/ *n.* A Übereinstimmung **(with, to** mit, **between** zwischen); **the ~ of form with** *or* **to** *or* **and content** die Übereinstimmung von Form und Inhalt; B *(communication, letters)* Briefwechsel, *der;* Korrespondenz, *die;* **be in ~ with sb.** mit jmdm. im Briefwechsel *od.* in Korrespondenz stehen

**correspondence:** ~ **college** *n.* Fernschule, *die;* ~ **column** *n.* Rubrik „Leserbriefe"; ~ **course** *n.* Fernkurs, *der;* ~ **school** ⇒ ~ **college**

**correspondent** /kɒrɪ'spɒndənt/ *n.* A Briefschreiber, *der*/-schreiberin, *die; (penfriend)* Brieffreund, *der*/-freundin, *die; (to newspaper)* Leserbriefschreiber, *der*/-schreiberin, *die;* **be a good/bad ~:** ein fleißiger/fauler Briefschreiber sein; B ▶ **1261** *(Radio, Telev., Journ., etc.)* Berichterstatter, *der*/-erstatterin, *die;* Korrespondent, *der*/Korrespondentin, *die;* C *(business ~)* Geschäftspartner, *der*/-partnerin, *die;* Korrespondent, *der*/Korrespondentin, *die (Kaufmannsspr.)*

**corresponding** /kɒrɪ'spɒndɪŋ/ *adj.* A entsprechend *(to Dat.);* **the number of calories ~ to the amount of energy** die Anzahl der Kalorien, die der Energiemenge entspricht; B **~ member** korrespondierendes Mitglied

**correspondingly** /kɒrɪ'spɒndɪŋlɪ/ *adv.* entsprechend

**corrida** /kɒ'riːdə/ *n.* Stierkampf, *der;* Corrida, *die*

**corridor** /'kɒrɪdɔː(r)/ *n.* A *(inside passage)* Flur, *der;* Gang, *der;* Korridor, *der; (outside passage)* Galerie, *die;* **in the ~s of power** *(fig.)* in den politischen Schaltstellen; B *(Railw.)* [Seiten]gang, *der*

**corridor:** ~ **coach** *n. (Railw.)* Durchgangswagen, *der;* ~ **train** *n.* Zug mit Durchgangswagen

**corrie** /'kɒrɪ/ *n. (esp. Scot.)* Kar, *das (Geol.)*

**corrigenda** /kɒrɪ'dʒendə/ *n. pl.* zu verbessernde Fehler; *(in book)* Korrigenda *Pl.*

**corroborate** /kə'rɒbəreɪt/ *v.t.* bestätigen; bekräftigen ‹Anspruch, Überzeugung›; *(formally)* [offiziell] bestätigen

**corroboration** /kərɒbə'reɪʃn/ *n.* ⇒ **corroborate**: Bestätigung, *die;* Bekräftigung, *die;* **in ~ of sth.** als *od.* zur Bestätigung *od.* Bekräftigung einer Sache *(Gen.)*

**corroborative** /kə'rɒbərətɪv/ *adj.* bekräftigend; bestätigend ‹Aussage›; erhärtend ‹Beweis›

**corrode** /kə'rəʊd/ ❶ *v.t.* zerfressen; korrodieren, zerfressen ‹Metall, Gestein›; *(fig.)* aushöhlen. ❷ *v.i.* zerfressen werden; ‹Gestein, Metall:› korrodieren, zerfressen werden; *(fig.)* ausgehöhlt werden

**corrosion** /kə'rəʊʒn/ *n.* Zerfall, *der; (of metal, stone)* Korrosion, *die; (fig.)* Aushöhlung, *die*

**cor'rosion-resistant** *adj.* korrosionsbeständig

**corrosive** /kə'rəʊsɪv/ ❶ *adj.* zerstörend; korrosiv *(bes. Chemie, Geol.);* ätzend ‹Chemikalien›; *(fig.)* zerstörerisch. ❷ *n.* Korrosion verursachender Stoff; *(fig.)* zerstörerische Kraft

**corrosiveness** /kə'rəʊsɪvnɪs/ *n., no pl.* zerstörende Wirkung; *(of chemicals)* ätzende Wirkung; *(fig.)* zersetzende Wirkung

**corrugate** /'kɒrʊgeɪt/ *v.t.* zerfurchen; *(bend into ridges)* wellen; **~d cardboard/paper** Wellpappe, *die;* **~d iron** Wellblech, *das*

**corrugation** /kɒrʊ'geɪʃn/ *n.* A Zerfurchung, *die;* B *(wrinkle, ridge mark)* Furche, *die; (ridge made by bending)* Rille, *die*

**corrupt** /kə'rʌpt/ ❶ *adj.* A *(rotten)* verunreinigt; schlecht; verfault ‹Körper›; B *(depraved)* verkommen; verdorben *(geh.); (influenced by bribery)* korrupt; **~ practices** Korruption, *die;* C *(impure)* verdorben, korrumpiert ‹Sprache›; *(vitiated)* verfälscht ‹Text, Buch›. ❷ *v.t.* A *(taint)* verderben; verschmutzen ‹Luft, Wasser›; *(fig.)* zerstören; B *(deprave)* korrumpieren; *(bribe)* bestechen; C *(destroy purity of)* verderben; korrumpieren; *(vitiate)* verfälschen

**corruption** /kə'rʌpʃn/ *n.* A *(decomposition)* Fäulnis, *die;* Verwesung, *die;* B *(moral deterioration)* Verdorbenheit, *die (geh.);* C *(use of corrupt practices)* Korruption, *die;* D *(perversion)* Korrumpierung, *die;* Entstellung, *die; (vitiation)* Verfälschung, die

**corruptness** /kə'rʌptnɪs/ *n., no pl.* ⇒ **corrupt** 1: Verunreinigung, *die;* Verfaultheit, *die;* Verkommenheit, *die;* Verdorbenheit, *die (geh.);* Korruptheit, *die;* Korrumpiertheit, *die;* Verfälschung, *die*

**corsage** /kɔː'sɑːʒ/ *n.* A *(bodice)* Korsage, *die;* Mieder, *das;* B *(bouquet)* [Ansteck]sträußchen, *das*

**corsair** /'kɔːseə(r)/ *n. (Hist.)* Korsar, *der*

**corselette** /'kɔːsəlet/ *n.* Korselett, *das*

**corset** /'kɔːsɪt/ ❶ *n.* A *in sing. or pl. (woman's undergarment)* Korsett, *das;* B *(garment worn for injury etc.)* [Stütz]korsett, *das.* ❷ *v. refl.* sich schnüren. ❸ *v.t. (fig.)* einengen

**Corsica** /'kɔːsɪkə/ *pr. n.* Korsika *(das)*

**Corsican** /'kɔːsɪkən/ ▶ **1275**, ▶ **1340** ❶ *adj.* korsisch; **sb. is ~:** jmd. ist Korse/Korsin. ❷ *n.* A *(person)* Korse, *der*/Korsin, *die;* B *(dialect)* Korsisch, *das*

**cortège** /kɔː'teɪʒ/ *n. (funeral procession)* Trauerzug, *der*

**cortex** /'kɔːteks/ *n., pl.* **cortices** /'kɔːtɪsiːz/ *(Bot., Anat., Zool.)* Rinde, *die;* Kortex, *der (fachspr.)*

**cortical** /'kɔːtɪkl/ *adj. (Bot., Anat., Zool.)* Rinden-; kortikal *(fachspr.)*

**cortisone** /'kɔːtɪzəʊn/ *n.* Kortison, *das (Med.);* Cortison, *das (fachspr.)*

**corundum** /kə'rʌndəm/ *n.* Korund, *der*

**coruscate** /'kɒrəskeɪt/ *v.i.* funkeln; [auf]blitzen; *(fig.)* glänzen; brillieren

**corvette** /kɔː'vet/ *n. (Naut.)* Korvette, *die*

**cos[1]** /kɒs/ *n.* Römischer Salat; Sommerendivie, *die*

**cos[2], 'cos** /kɒz/ *(coll.)* ⇒ **because**

**cos[3]** /kɒs, kɒz/ *abbr. (Math.)* **cosine** cos

**cosecant** /kəʊ'siːkənt/ *n. (Math.)* Kosekans, *der*

**cosh** /kɒʃ/ *(Brit. coll.)* ❶ *n.* Totschläger, *der;* Knüppel, *der.* ❷ *v.t.* niederknüppeln

**co-signatory** /kəʊ'sɪgnətərɪ/ ❶ *adj.* mitunterzeichnend. ❷ *n.* Mitunterzeichner, *der*/-unterzeichnerin, *die*

**cosily** /'kəʊzɪlɪ/ *adv.* bequem; gemütlich, behaglich ‹plaudern, wohnen›

**cosine** /'kəʊsaɪn/ *n. (Math.)* Kosinus, *der*

**cosiness** /'kəʊzɪnɪs/ *n., no pl.* ⇒ **cosy** 1 A: Gemütlichkeit, *die;* Behaglichkeit, *die*

**cosmetic** /kɒzˈmetɪk/ ❶ *adj.* (*lit. or fig.*) kosmetisch; ~ **surgery** Schönheitschirurgie, *die.* ❷ *n.* Kosmetikum, *das*

**cosmetician** /kɒzmeˈtɪʃn/ *n.* ▶ 1261 (*Amer.*) Kosmetiker, *der*/Kosmetikerin, *die*

**cosmic** /ˈkɒzmɪk/ *adj.* (*lit. or fig.*) kosmisch; ~ **radiation** *or* **rays** kosmische Strahlung; Höhenstrahlung, *die*

**cosmology** /kɒzˈmɒlədʒɪ/ *n.* (*Astron., Philos.*) Kosmologie, *die* (*fachspr.*)

**cosmonaut** /ˈkɒzmənɔ:t/ *n.* ▶ 1261 Kosmonaut, *der*/Kosmonautin, *die*

**cosmopolitan** /kɒzməˈpɒlɪtən/ ❶ *adj.* kosmopolitisch; weltbürgerlich. ❷ *n.* Kosmopolit, *der*/Kosmopolitin, *die* (*geh.*); Weltbürger, *der*/-bürgerin, *die*

**cosmos** /ˈkɒzmɒs/ *n.* Ⓐ Kosmos, *der;* Weltall, *das;* Ⓑ (*fig.: system*) Kosmos, *der*

**Cossack** /ˈkɒsæk/ *n.* Kosak, *der*/Kosakin, *die;* ~ **hat** Kosakenmütze, *die;* ~ **trousers** Stiefelhose, *die*

**cosset** /ˈkɒsɪt/ *v.t.* [ver]hätscheln

**cost** /kɒst/ ❶ *n.* Ⓐ ▶ 1328 Kosten *Pl.;* **the ~ of bread/gas/oil** der Brot-/Gas-/Ölpreis; **the ~ of heating a house** die Heizkosten für ein Haus; **the ~ of travelling by public transport** die Kosten für die Benutzung der öffentlichen Verkehrsmittel; **regardless of ~, whatever the ~:** ganz gleich, was es kostet; **bear the ~ of sth.** die Kosten für etw. tragen; **do sth. at great/little ~ to sb./sth.** etw. unter großer/geringer finanzieller Belastung für jmdn./etw. tun; **[sell sth.] at ~:** [etw.] zum Selbstkostenpreis [verkaufen]; Ⓑ (*fig.*) Preis, *der;* **at all ~s, at any ~:** um jeden Preis; **at the ~ of sth.** auf Kosten einer Sache (*Gen.*); **at great ~ in human lives** um den Preis vieler Menschenleben; **whatever the ~:** koste es, was es wolle; **to my/his** *etc.* **~:** zu meinem/seinem *usw.* Nachteil; **as I know to my ~:** wie ich aus bitterer Erfahrung weiß; ⇒ *also* **count**[1] 2 A; Ⓒ *in pl.* (*Law*) [Gerichts]kosten *Pl.;* **which party was ordered to pay ~s?** welche Seite hatte die [Gerichts]kosten zu tragen? **in the case A v. B, A was awarded ~s** in der Sache A gegen B wurden A die Kosten erstattet.
❷ *v.t.* Ⓐ ▶ 1328 *p.t., p.p.* ~ (*lit. or fig.*) kosten; **how much does it ~?** was kostet es?; ~ **money** Geld kosten; ~ **what it may, whatever it may ~:** koste es, was es wolle; ~ **sb. sth.** jmdn. etw. kosten; **it'll ~ you** (*coll.*) das wird ein teures Vergnügen; ~ **sb. dear[ly]** jmdm. *od.* jmdn. teuer zu stehen kommen; ⇒ *also* **arm**[1] A; **earth** 1 F; Ⓑ *p.t., p.p.* **~ed** (*Commerc.: fix price of*) ~ **sth.** den Preis für etw. kalkulieren

**cost:** ~ **accountant** *n.* ▶ 1261 (*Commerc.*) Betriebskalkulator, *der;* ~ **accounting** *n.* (*Commerc.*) Betriebskostenrechnung, *die*

**co-star** /ˈkəʊstɑ:(r)/ (*Cinemat., Theatre*) ❶ *n.* **be a/the ~:** eine der Hauptrollen/die zweite Hauptrolle spielen; **Bogart and Bacall were ~s** Bogart und Bacall spielten die Hauptrollen. ❷ *v.i.*, **-rr-** eine der Hauptrollen spielen. ❸ *v.t.*, **-rr-: the film ~red Robert Redford** der Film zeigte Robert Redford in einer der Hauptrollen

**Costa Rican** /kɒstə ˈri:kən/ ▶ 1340 ❶ *adj.* costa-ricanisch. ❷ *n.* Costa-Ricaner, *der*/Costa-Ricanerin, *die*

**cost:** **~-'benefit** *adj.* Kosten-Nutzen-; **~-effective** *adj.* rentabel

**coster[monger]** /ˈkɒstə(mʌŋgə(r))/ *n.* (*Brit.*) Straßenhändler, *der*/-händlerin, *die*

**costing** /ˈkɒstɪŋ/ *n.* Ⓐ (*estimation of costs*) Kostenberechnung, *die;* Ⓑ (*costs*) Kosten *Pl.*

**costly** /ˈkɒstlɪ/ *adj.* Ⓐ teuer; kostspielig; Ⓑ (*fig.*) **a ~ victory** ein teuer erkaufter Sieg; **a ~ error** ein folgenschwerer Irrtum

**cost:** ~ **of 'living** *n.* Lebenshaltungskosten *Pl;* **~-of-living allowance** Ausgleichszulage, *die;* **~-of-living bonus** Teuerungszulage, *die;* **~-of-living index** Lebenshaltungsindex, *der;* ~ **price** *n.* Selbstkostenpreis, *der*

**costume** /ˈkɒstju:m/ ❶ *n.* Ⓐ Kleidermode, *die;* (*theatrical ~*) Kostüm, *das;* **the ~ of the nation** die Nationaltracht; **historical ~s** historische Kostüme; **Highland ~:** schottische Tracht; Ⓑ (*dated: jacket and skirt*) Kostüm, *das.* ❷ *v.t.* ausstatten

**costume:** ~ **ball** *n.* Kostümfest, *das;* Kostümball, *der;* ~ **designer** *n.* Kostümbildner, *der*/-bildnerin, *die;* ~ **'jewellery** *n.* Modeschmuck, *der;* ~ **piece**, ~ **play** *ns.* Kostümstück, *das*

**costumer** /ˈkɒstjʊmə(r)/, **costumier** /kɒˈstju:mɪə(r)/ *ns.* ▶ 1261 Kostümschneider, *der*/-schneiderin, *die;* (*hirer of costumes*) Kostümverleiher, *der*/-verleiherin, *die*

**cosy** /ˈkəʊzɪ/ ❶ *adj.* Ⓐ gemütlich; behaglich ‹Atmosphäre›; bequem ‹Sessel›; **feel ~:** sich wohl *od.* behaglich fühlen; **be ~:** es gemütlich haben; **a ~ feeling** ein Gefühl der Behaglichkeit; Ⓑ (*derog.: complacent, convenient*) bequem; **they have a very ~ relationship** sie passen zueinander wie ein altes Paar Filzpantoffeln. ❷ *n.* ⇒ **egg cosy; tea cosy**

~ **a'long** *v.t.* (*coll.*) beruhigen

~ **'up to** *v.i.* (*coll.*) ~ **up to the fireplace** es sich (*Dat.*) am Kamin gemütlich machen; ~ **up to sb.** mit jmdm. vertraulich werden; (*ingratiate oneself with sb.*) sich bei jmdm. einschmeicheln

**cot** /kɒt/ *n.* (*Brit.: child's bed*) Kinderbett, *das;* **the baby cried in his ~:** das Baby schrie in seinem Bettchen

**cotangent** /kəʊˈtændʒənt/ *n.* (*Math.*) Kotangens, *der*

**'cot death** *n.* (*Brit.*) plötzlicher Kindstod; Cot-death, *der* (*Med.*)

**cote** /kəʊt/ *n.* Stall, *der;* ⇒ *also* **dovecote**

**coterie** /ˈkəʊtərɪ/ *n.* Zirkel, *der;* **artistic ~:** Künstlerkreis, *der*

**cotoneaster** /kətəʊnɪˈæstə(r)/ *n.* (*Bot.*) Zwergmispel, *die*

**cottage** /ˈkɒtɪdʒ/ *n.* Cottage, *das;* Häuschen, *das*

**cottage:** ~ **'cheese** *n.* Hüttenkäse, *der;* ~ **'hospital** *n. kleines [Land]krankenhaus ohne ständige ärztliche Betreuung;* ~ **industry** *n.* Heimarbeit, *die;* ~ **loaf** *n. eine Art rundes Weißbrot;* ~ **'pie** *n. mit Kartoffelbrei überbackenes Hackfleisch*

**cottager** /ˈkɒtɪdʒə(r)/ *n.* Cottagebewohner, *der*/-bewohnerin, *die*

**cotter** /ˈkɒtə(r)/ *n.* ~[pin] Splint, *der*

**cotton** /ˈkɒtn/ ❶ *n.* (*substance, plant*) Baumwolle, *die;* (*thread*) Baumwollgarn, *das;* (*cloth*) Baumwollstoff, *der.* ❷ *attrib. adj.* Baumwoll-. ❸ *v.i.* ~ **'on** (*coll.*) kapieren (*ugs.*); ~ **'on to** (*coll.*) (*catch on to*) spitzkriegen (*ugs.*); (*understand*) kapieren (*ugs.*); ~ **to sb.** (*Amer.*) sich mit jmdm. anfreunden

**cotton:** ~ **belt** *n.* (*Geog.*) Baumwollgürtel, *der;* ~ **candy** *n.* (*Amer.*) Zuckerwatte, *die;* ~ **gin** *n.* (*machine*) Egreniermaschine, *die* (*fachspr.*); ~ **mill** *n.* Baumwollspinnerei, *die;* **~-picking** *adj.* (*Amer. coll.*) verdammt; verflucht; ~ **plant** *n.* Baumwollpflanze, *die;* ~ **'print** *n.* bedruckter Baumwollstoff; ~ **reel** *n.* [Näh]garnrolle, *die;* ~ **spinner** *n.* Baumwollspinner, *der*/-spinnerin, *die;* ~ **spinning** *n.* Baumwollspinnerei, *die;* **~tail** *n.* (*Amer. Zool.*) Waldkaninchen, *das;* Baumwollschwanzkaninchen, *das;* ~ **'waste** *n.* Putzwolle, *die;* ~ **'wool** *n.* Ⓐ Watte, *die;* **~-wool ball** Wattebausch, *der;* **wrap sb. up** *or* **keep sb. in ~ wool** (*fig.*) jmdn. in Watte packen; Ⓑ (*Amer.: raw ~*) Rohbaumwolle, *die*

**cotyledon** /kɒtɪˈli:dən/ *n.* (*Bot.*) Keimblatt, *das*

**couch**[1] /kaʊtʃ/ ❶ *n.* Ⓐ (*sofa*) Couch, *die;* Ⓑ **doctor's ~:** [Untersuchungs]liege, *die;* **psychiatrist's ~:** Couch [des Psychiaters]; Ⓒ (*arch./literary: bed*) Lager, *das.* ❷ *v.t.* formulieren; **~ed in modest terms** in bescheidener Sprache abgefasst

**couch**[2] /ku:tʃ, kaʊtʃ/ *n.* ~[ **grass**] (*Bot.*) Quecke, *die*

**couchette** /ku:ˈʃet/ *n.* (*Railw.*) Liegewagen, *der;* (*berth*) Liegesitz, *der*

**couch po'tato** *n.* (*coll.*) Couchpotato[e], *der*

**cougar** /ˈku:gə(r)/ *n.* (*Amer. Zool.*) Puma, *der*

**cough** /kɒf/ ❶ *n.* (*act of coughing, condition*) Husten, *der;* **give a ~:** husten; **have a [bad] ~:** [einen schlimmen] Husten haben. ❷ *v.i.* Ⓐ husten; Ⓑ ‹Motor:› stottern; ‹Gewehr usw.:› knattern. ❸ *v.t.* ~ **out** [her]aushusten; (*say with ~*) husten; ~ **up** [her]aushusten; (*coll.: pay*) ausspucken (*ugs.*); **come on, ~ up!** na los, spuck's aus!

**'cough drop** ⇒ **cough sweet**

**coughing** /ˈkɒfɪŋ/ *n.* Husten, *das;* Gehuste, *das;* **there was a lot of ~:** es wurde ständig gehustet; **a bout of ~:** ein Hustenanfall

**cough:** ~ **medicine** *n.* Hustenmittel, *das;* ~ **mixture** *n.* Hustensaft, *der;* ~ **sweet** *n.* Hustenbonbon, *das od. der*

**could** ⇒ **can**[2]

**couldn't** /ˈkʊdnt/ (*coll.*) = **could not;** ⇒ **can**[2]

**coulomb** /ˈku:lɒm/ *n.* (*Electr.*) Coulomb, *das;* Amperesekunde, *die*

**council** /ˈkaʊnsl/ *n.* Ⓐ Ratsversammlung, *die;* **family ~:** Familienrat, *der;* Ⓑ (*administrative/advisory body*) Rat, *der;* **local ~:** Gemeinderat, *der;* **city/town ~:** Stadtrat, *der;* Ⓒ (*Eccl.*) Konzil, *das;* **diocesan ~:** Diözesanrat, *der*

**council:** ~ **chamber** *n.* Sitzungssaal [des Rats]; ~ **estate** *n.* Wohnviertel mit Sozialwohnungen; ~ **flat** *n.* Sozialwohnung, *die;* ~ **house** *n.* Haus des sozialen Wohnungsbaus; ~ **housing** *n.* sozialer Wohnungsbau

**councillor** /ˈkaʊnsələ(r)/ *n.* ▶ 1261, ▶ 1617 Ratsmitglied, *das;* **town ~:** Stadtrat, *der*/-rätin, *die*

**council:** ~ **man** /ˈkaʊnslmən/ *n., pl.* **~men** /ˈkaʊnslmən/ [Gemeinde-/Stadt]ratsmitglied, *das* (*bes. in London und in den USA*); ~ **meeting** *n.* Ratssitzung, *die;* ~ **of 'war** *n.* (*lit. or fig.*) Kriegsrat, *der;* ~ **tax** *n.* (*Brit.*) Gemeindesteuer, *die*

**counsel** /ˈkaʊnsl/ ❶ *n.* Ⓐ (*consultation*) Beratung, *die;* **take/hold ~ with sb. [about sth.]** sich mit jmdm. [über etw. (*Akk.*)] beraten; Ⓑ Rat[schlag], *der;* ~ **of perfection** Vollkommenheitsforderung, *die* (*Rel.*); (*fig.*) ideale Forderung; **keep one's own ~:** seine Meinung für sich behalten; Ⓒ *pl. same* (*Law*) Rechtsanwalt, *der*/-anwältin, *die;* ~ **for the defence** Verteidiger, *der*/Verteidigerin, *die;* ~ **for the prosecution** Anklagevertreter, *der*/-vertreterin, *die;* Staatsanwalt, *der*/-anwältin, *die;* **Queen's/King's C~:** Anwalt/Anwältin der Krone; Kronanwalt, *der*/-anwältin, *die.*
❷ *v.t.*, (*Brit.*) **-ll-:** Ⓐ (*advise*) beraten; ~ **sb. to do sth.** jmdm. raten *od.* den Rat geben, etw. zu tun; Ⓑ (*suggest*) ~ **forbearance** *etc.* zur Nachsicht *usw.* raten

**counselling** (*Amer.:* **counseling**) /ˈkaʊnsəlɪŋ/ *n.* Beratung, *die;* **marriage ~:** Eheberatung, *die*

**counsellor**, (*Amer.*) **counselor** /ˈkaʊnsələ(r)/ *n.* ▶ 1261 Ⓐ Berater, *der*/Beraterin, *die;* **marriage-guidance ~:** Eheberater, *der*/-beraterin, *die;* **[student] ~:** Studienberater, *der*/-beraterin, *die;* Ⓑ (*Diplom.*) Botschaftsrat, *der*/-rätin, *die;* Ⓒ (*Law*) ~ **[-at-law]** (*Amer.: barrister*) Rechtsanwalt, *der*/-anwältin, *die;* Ⓓ (*Brit.*) **C~ of State** Stellvertreter des Königs/der Königin

**count**[1] /kaʊnt/ ❶ *n.* Ⓐ Zählen, *das;* Zählung, *die* ; **keep ~ [of sth.]** [etw.] zählen; **I'm going to keep ~ of the number of times he says 'incredible'** ich werde mitzählen, wie oft er „unglaublich" sagt; **lose ~:** beim Zählen durcheinander geraten; **lose ~ of sth.** etw. gar nicht mehr zählen können; **have/take/make a ~:** zählen; **on the ~ of three** bei „drei"; Ⓑ (*sum total*) Ergebnis, *das;* Ⓒ (*Law*) Anklagepunkt, *der;* **on all ~s** in allen [Anklage]punkten; **on that ~** (*fig.*) in diesem Punkt; Ⓓ (*Boxing*) Auszählen, *das;* **be out for the ~:** ausgezählt werden; (*fig.*) hinüber sein (*ugs.*); Ⓔ (*Phys.*) (*event*) Impuls, *der;* (*total number*) Impulszahl, *die.*
❷ *v.t.* Ⓐ zählen; ~ **ten** bis zehn zählen; ~ **the votes** die Stimmen [aus]zählen; ~ **again** nachzählen; ~ **the pennies** (*fig.*) jeden Pfennig umdrehen; sparsam sein; ~ **the cost** (*fig.*) unter den Folgen zu leiden haben; Ⓑ (*include*) mitzählen; **be ~ed against sb.** gegen jmdn. sprechen; **not ~ing** abgesehen

von; **C** (*consider*) halten für; **~ oneself lucky** sich glücklich schätzen können; **~ sb. as one of us/a friend** jmdn. als einen von uns/als Freund betrachten; **I ~ him [as] one of the family** er gehört für mich zur Familie; **~ sb. among one's friends/clients** jmdn. zu seinen Freunden/Kunden zählen.
**3** *v.i.* **A** zählen; **~ from one to ten** von eins bis zehn zählen; **~ [up] to ten** bis zehn zählen; **B** (*be included*) zählen; **every moment ~s** jede Sekunde zählt; **~ against sb.** gegen jmdn. sprechen; **money ~s/looks ~:** Geld/Aussehen ist wichtig; **money is what ~s** Geld ist das, was zählt; **~ for much/little** viel/wenig zählen; **appearances ~ for a great deal** *or* **a lot** der äußere Schein macht viel aus; **C** (*conduct a reckoning*) zählen; **~ing from now** von jetzt an [gerechnet]; ab jetzt
**~ 'down** **1** *v.i.* rückwärts zählen. **2** *v.t.* **~ sth. down** den *od.* das Count-down für etw. durchführen. ⇒ *also* **count-down**
**~ 'in** *v.t.* mitrechnen; **~ sb. in on a venture** jmdn. bei einem Unternehmen einplanen; **shall I ~ you in?** machst/kommst du mit? **you can ~ me in** ich bin dabei
**~ on** *v.t.* **~ on sb./sth.** sich auf jmdn./etw. verlassen; **you mustn't ~ on winning first prize** du darfst nicht damit rechnen, den ersten Preis zu gewinnen
**~ 'out** *v.t.* **A** (*one by one*) abzählen; **B** (*exclude*) **[you can] ~ me out** ich komme/mache nicht mit; **C** (*Boxing*) auszählen; **D** (*Brit. Parl.*) **~ the House out** die Sitzung wegen Beschlussunfähigkeit vertagen
**~ 'up** *v.t.* zusammenzählen; zusammenrechnen
**~ upon** ⇒ **~ on**

**count²** *n.* ▶ **1617** (*nobleman*) Graf, *der*

**countable** /'kaʊntəbl/ *adj.* (*also Ling.*) zählbar

**'countdown** *n.* Countdown, *der od. das*

**countenance** /'kaʊntɪnəns/ **1** *n.* **A** (*literary: face*) Antlitz, *das* (*dichter.*); **B** (*formal: expression*) Gesichtsausdruck, *der*; **change ~:** den Gesichtsausdruck verändern; **keep ~:** keine Miene verziehen; **C** (*dated/formal: composure*) Haltung, *die*; **keep sb. in ~** (*arch.*) jmdn. ermuntern *od.* aufrichten; **keep one's ~:** Haltung *od.* die Fassung bewahren; **lose ~:** die Fassung verlieren; **put sb. out of ~:** jmdn. aus der Fassung bringen; **D** (*dated/formal: moral support*) Ermutigung, *die*; [moralische] Unterstützung; **give ~ to sb./sth.** jmdn./etw. unterstützen.
**2** *v.t.* (*formal*) (*approve*) billigen; gutheißen; (*support*) unterstützen

**counter¹** /'kaʊntə(r)/ *n.* **A** (*in shop*) Ladentisch, *der*; (*in cafeteria, restaurant, train*) Büfett, *das*; (*in post office, bank*) Schalter, *der*; **~ clerk** ▶ **1261** Schalterbeamte, *der*/-beamtin, *die*; **these medicines/weapons can be bought over the ~:** diese Arzneimittel kann man ohne Rezept kaufen/diese Waffen kann man ohne Waffenschein kaufen; **[buy/sell sth.] under the ~** (*fig.*) [etwas] unter dem Ladentisch [kaufen/verkaufen]; **B** (*small disc for games*) Spielmarke, *die*; (*token representing coin*) Jeton, *der*; **C** (*apparatus for counting*) Zähler, *der*

**counter²** **1** *adj.* entgegengesetzt; Gegen-/gegen-. **2** *v.t.* **A** (*oppose, contradict*) begegnen (+ *Dat.*); **B** (*meet by ~move*) kontern; zurückschlagen. **3** *v.i.* **A** (*make ~move*) antworten; kontern; **B** (*Boxing*) kontern. **4** *adv.* **A** (*in the opposite direction*) in entgegengesetzter Richtung; **go/run ~:** in die falsche Richtung gehen/laufen; **B** (*contrary*) **act ~ to** zuwiderhandeln (+ *Dat.*); **go ~ to** zuwiderlaufen (+ *Dat.*); **run ~ to** im Widerspruch stehen zu. **5** *n.* **A** (*Boxing*) Konter, *der*; **B** (*~move*) Antwort, *die* (**to** auf + *Akk.*)

**counter³** *n.* (*Naut.*) Gilling, *die*

**counter:** **~'act** *v.t.* entgegenwirken (+ *Dat.*); **~'action** *n.* Gegenwirkung, *die*; **~-attack** (*lit. or fig.*) **1** *n.* Gegenangriff, *der*; **2** *v.t.* **~-attack sb.** gegen jmdn. einen Gegenangriff richten; **3** *v.i.* zurückschlagen; **~ attraction** *n.* **A** (*rival*) Konkurrenz, *die*; **B** (*of contrary tendency*) entgegengesetzte Anziehungskraft; **~balance** **1** *v.t.* ein Gegengewicht bilden zu; (*fig.: neutralize*) ausgleichen; **2** *n.* (*lit. or fig.*) Gegengewicht, *das*; **~blast** *n.* Gegenschlag, *der*; **~charge** *n.* Gegenbeschuldigung, *die*; Gegenklage, *die* (*Rechtsspr.*); **~check** *n.* **A** (*double check*) Gegenkontrolle, *die*; **B** (*check that opposes a thing*) Gegenkraft, *die*; **~claim** (*Law*) **1** *n.* Gegenforderung, *die*; **2** *v.t.* eine Gegenforderung erheben auf (+ *Akk.*); **~'clockwise** ⇒ **anticlockwise**; **~-'espionage** *n.* Spionageabwehr, *die*; Gegenspionage, *die*

**counterfeit** /'kaʊntəfɪt, 'kaʊntəfi:t/ **1** *adj.* falsch, unecht ‹Schmuck›; falsch, gefälscht ‹Unterschrift, Münze, Banknote›; (*fig. literary*) vorgetäuscht ‹Emotionen›; **~ money** Falschgeld, *das*. **2** *v.t.* **A** (*forge*) fälschen; **B** (*fig.: simulate*) vortäuschen

**counterfeiter** /'kaʊntəfɪtə(r)/ *n.* (*forger*) Fälscher, *der*/Fälscherin, *die*

**counter:** **~foil** *n.* Kontrollabschnitt, *der*; **~-intelligence** *n.* ⇒ **~-espionage**; **~'irritant** *n.* (*Med.*) Hautreizmittel, *das*

**countermand** /kaʊntə'mɑ:nd/ *v.t.* **A** (*revoke*) widerrufen; **B** (*cancel order for*) abstellen ‹Waren›; **~ an action/payment** die Anweisung für eine Handlung/Zahlung zurücknehmen; **C** (*recall*) zurückrufen

**counter:** **~measure** *n.* Gegenmaßnahme, *die*; **~move** *n.* Gegenzug, *der*; **~offensive** *n.* (*Mil.*) Gegenoffensive, *die*; **~-offer** *n.* Gegenangebot, *das*

**counterpane** /'kaʊntəpeɪn/ *n.* (*dated*) Tagesdecke, *die*

**counter:** **~part** *n.* Gegenstück, *das* (**of** zu); Pendant, *das* (*geh.*) (**of** zu); **~point** *n.* (*Mus.*) Kontrapunkt, *der*; **~poise** *n.* Gegengewicht, *das*; **~pro'ductive** *adj.* das Gegenteil des Gewünschten bewirkend; **sth. is ~-productive** etw. bewirkt das Gegenteil des Gewünschten; **~-proposal** *n.* Gegenvorschlag, *der*; **C~-Reformation** *n.* (*Hist.*) Gegenreformation, *die*; **~-revolution** *n.* Gegenrevolution, *die*; Konterrevolution, *die* (*bes. marx.*); **~-revolutionary** **1** *adj.* gegenrevolutionär; konterrevolutionär (*bes. marx.*); **2** *n.* Konterrevolutionär, *der*/-revolutionärin, *die*; **~shaft** *n.* (*Mech. Engin.*) Transmissionswelle, *die*; (*Amer.: layshaft*) Vorgelegewelle, *die*; **~sign** **1** *v.t.* **A** (*add signature to*) gegenzeichnen; **B** (*ratify*) bestätigen; **2** *n.* (*Mil.: password*) Parole, *die*; **~'signature** *n.* Gegenunterschrift, *die*; **~sink** *v.t.*, **~sunk** /'kaʊntəsʌŋk/ (*Woodw., Metalw.*) **A** (*bevel off*) senken ‹Loch›; **B** (*sink*) versenken ‹Schraube›; **~stroke** *n.* Gegenschlag, *der*; **~-'tenor** *n.* (*Mus.*) Contratenor, *der*; **~weight** *n.* Gegengewicht, *das*

**countess** /'kaʊntɪs/ *n.* ▶ **1617** Gräfin, *die*

**counting house** /'kaʊntɪŋhaʊs/ *n.* (*dated*) Kontor, *das* (*veralt.*)

**countless** /'kaʊntlɪs/ *adj.* zahllos; **~ numbers of** eine zahllose Menge von

**countrified** /'kʌntrɪfaɪd/ *adj.* ländlich

**country** /'kʌntrɪ/ *n.* **A** Land, *das*; (*fatherland*) Heimat, *die*; **sb.'s [home] ~:** jmds. Heimat; **fight/die for one's ~:** für sein [Vater]land kämpfen/sterben; **farming ~:** Ackerland, *das*; **this is excellent bird-watching ~:** das ist eine Gegend, in der man hervorragend Vögel beobachten kann; **densely wooded ~:** dicht bewaldetes Gebiet; **this is unknown ~ to me** (*fig.*) das ist Neuland *od.* unbekanntes Gelände für mich; **[the] Hardy ~:** das Land Hardys; **B** (*rural district*) Land, *das*; (**~side**) Landschaft, *die*; **~ road/air** Landstraße, *die*/Landluft, *die*; **~ inn** [ländlicher] Gasthof; **[be/live** *etc.***] in the ~:** auf dem Land [sein/leben *usw.*]; **to the ~:** aufs Land; **[go/travel** *etc.***] across ~:** über Land [fahren/reisen *usw.*]; **up ~** (*Richtung*) ins Landesinnere; (*Lage*) im Landesinneren; **in the ~** (*Cricket coll.*) weit draußen; **C** (*Brit.: population*) Volk, *das*; **appeal** *or* **go to the ~:** den Wähler entscheiden lassen

**country:** **~-and-'western** *adj.* Countryund-Western-; **~ club** *n.* Country Club, *der*; **~ 'cousin** *n.* Landei, *das* (*ugs. abwertend*); (*woman also*) Landpomeranze, *die* (*ugs. abwertend*); **~ 'dance** *n.* Kontertanz, *der*; **~ 'dancing** *n.* Kontertanz, *der*

**countryfied** ⇒ **countrified**

**country:** **~ folk** *n.* Landbewohner *Pl.*; **~ 'gentleman** *n.* Landbesitzer, *der*; **~ 'house** *n.* Landhaus, *das*; **~ life** *n.* Landleben, *das*; **~man** /'kʌntrɪmən/ *n.*, *pl.* **~men** /'kʌntrɪmən/ **A** (*national*) Landsmann, *der*; **[my/her** *etc.***] fellow ~man** [mein/ihr *usw.*] Landsmann; **B** (*rural*) Landbewohner, *der*; **~ music** *n.* Countrymusic, *die*; **~ 'park** *n.* Naturpark, *der*; **~ people** *n. pl.* Landbewohner *Pl.*; **~ 'seat** *n.* Landsitz, *der*; **~side** *n.* **A** (*rural areas*) Land, *das*; **the preservation of the ~side** die Erhaltung der Landschaft; **B** (*rural scenery*) Landschaft, *die*; **C~side Commission** *n.* (*Brit.*) Landschaftsschutzkommission, *die*; **~wide** *adj.* landesweit; **~woman** *n.* **A** (*national*) Landsmännin, *die*; **my fellow ~woman** meine Landsmännin; **B** (*rural*) Landbewohnerin, *die*

**county** /'kaʊntɪ/ **1** *n.* **A** (*Brit.*) Grafschaft, *die*; (*Amer., Commonwealth*) Verwaltungsbezirk, *der*; **B** (*Brit.: gentry*) Gentry [der/einer Grafschaft]. **2** *adj.* (*Brit.*) *den Lebensstil reicher Grundbesitzer pflegend*; ≈ junkerhaft

**county:** **~ 'borough** *n.* (*Hist./Ir.*) *Stadt mit dem Status einer Grafschaft*; **~ 'council** *n.* Grafschaftsrat, *der*; **~ 'court** *n.* (*Law*) (*Brit.*) Grafschaftsgericht, *das*; (*Amer.*) *Zivil- und Strafgericht*; **~ 'cricket** *n.* (*Brit.*) *Kricketspiele zwischen Grafschaftsauswahlen*; **~ family** *n.* *alteingesessene [Adels]familie*; **~ school** *n.* *von der Grafschaft bezuschusste öffentliche Schule*; **~ 'seat** *n.* (*Amer.*) ≈ Bezirksstadt, *die*; **~ 'town** *n.* (*Brit.*) *Verwaltungssitz einer Grafschaft*

**coup** /ku:/ *n.* **A** Coup, *der*; **pull off** (*coll.*) *or* **make a ~:** einen Coup landen (*ugs.*); **B** ⇒ **coup d'état**

**coup:** **~ de grâce** /ku: də 'grɑ:s/ *n.* Todesstoß, *der*; **~ d'état** /ku: deɪ'tɑ:/ *n.* Staatsstreich, *der*; **~ de théâtre** /ku: də teɪ'ɑ:tr/ *n.* Theatercoup, *der*

**coupé** /'ku:peɪ/ (*Amer.:* **coupe** [ku:p]) *n.* (*car*) Coupé, *das*

**couple** /kʌpl/ **1** *n.* **A** (*pair*) Paar, *das*; (*married*) [Ehe]paar, *das*; (*dancing*) [Tanz]paar, *das*; **in ~s** paarweise; **B a ~ [of]** (*a few*) ein paar; (*two*) zwei; **a ~ of people/things/days/weeks** *etc.* ein paar/zwei Leute/Dinge/Tage/Wochen *usw.*; **a ~ of times** ein paarmal/zweimal; **C** (*Mech.*) Kräftepaar, *das*. **2** *v.t.* **A** (*associate*) verbinden; **be ~d with sth.** mit etw. verbunden sein; **B** (*fasten together*) koppeln. **3** *v.i.* sich paaren
**~ 'on** *v.t.* ankoppeln
**~ to'gether** *v.t.* ankoppeln; (*fig.*) miteinander in Verbindung bringen
**~ 'up** *v.t.* ankoppeln

**coupler** /'kʌplə(r)/ *n.* (*Mus.*) Koppel, *die*

**couplet** /'kʌplɪt/ *n.* (*Pros.*) Verspaar, *das*; (*rhyming*) Reimpaar, *das*

**coupling** /'kʌplɪŋ/ *n.* **A** (*Railw., Mech. Engin.*) Kupplung, *die*; **B** (*arrangement on gramophone record*) Zusammenstellung, *die*; (*recording on reverse side*) B-Seite, *die*

**coupon** /'ku:pɒn/ *n.* (*detachable ticket*) Abschnitt, *der*; (*for rationed goods*) Marke, *die*; (*in advertisement*) Gutschein, *der*; Coupon, *der*; (*entry form for football pool etc.*) Tippschein, *der*; (*voucher*) Gutschein, *der*

**courage** /'kʌrɪdʒ/ *n.* Mut, *der*; **have/lack the ~ to do sth.** den Mut haben/nicht den Mut haben, etw. zu tun; **take one's ~ in both hands** sein Herz in beide Hände nehmen; **sb. takes ~ from sth.** etw. macht jmdm. Mut; **take ~!** nur Mut!; **lose ~:** den Mut verlieren; **have the ~ of one's convictions** zu seiner Überzeugung stehen

**courageous** /kə'reɪdʒəs/ *adj.* mutig

**courageously** /kə'reɪdʒəslɪ/ *adv.* mutig

**courageousness** /kə'reɪdʒəsnɪs/ *n.*, *no pl.* Mut, *der*

**courgette** /kʊə'ʒet/ *n.* (*Brit.*) Zucchino, *der*

**courier** /'kʊrɪə(r)/ *n.* ▶ **1261** **A** (*Tourism*) Reiseleiter, *der*/-leiterin, *die*; **B** (*messenger*) Kurier, *der*

**'courier company** *n.* Kurierdienst, *der*

**course** /kɔːs/ ❶ *n.* Ⓐ (*of ship, plane*) Kurs, *der;* **change [one's] ~** (*lit. or fig.*) den Kurs wechseln; **~ [of action]** Vorgehensweise, *die;* **what are our possible ~s of action?** welche Möglichkeiten haben wir?; **the most sensible ~ would be to …:** das Vernünftigste wäre, zu …; **in the ordinary ~ of things** *or* **events** unter normalen Umständen; **the ~ of nature/history** der Lauf der Dinge/Geschichte; **run** *or* **take its ~:** seinen/ihren Lauf nehmen; **let things take their ~:** den Dingen ihren Lauf lassen; **off/on ~:** vom Kurs abgekommen/auf Kurs; **be on ~ for sth.** (*fig.*) auf etw. (*Akk.*) zusteuern; Ⓑ **of ~:** natürlich; **[do sth.] as a matter of ~:** [etw.] selbstverständlich [tun]; Ⓒ (*progression*) Lauf, *der;* **in due ~:** zu gegebener Zeit; **the road is in ~ of construction** die Straße wird gerade gebaut; **be in the ~ of doing sth.** gerade dabei sein, etw. zu tun; **in the ~ of a few minutes** im Laufe von wenigen Minuten; **in the ~ of the lesson/the day/his life** im Lauf[e] der Stunde/des Tages/seines Lebens; **in the ~ of time/our relationship** im Lauf[e] der Zeit/unserer Beziehung; Ⓓ (*of river etc.*) Lauf, *der;* Ⓔ (*of meal*) Gang, *der;* Ⓕ (*Sport*) Kurs, *der;* (*for race*) Rennstrecke, *die;* **[golf]~:** [Golf]platz, *der;* Ⓖ (*Educ.*) Kurs[us], *der;* (*for employee also*) Lehrgang, *der;* (*book*) Lehrbuch, *das;* **a ~ of lectures** eine Vorlesungsreihe; **go to** *or* **attend/do a ~ in sth.** einen Kurs in etw. (*Dat.*) besuchen/machen; **be/go on a ~:** auf einem Lehrgang sein/zu einem Lehrgang gehen; Ⓗ (*Med.*) **a ~ of treatment** eine Kur; **a ~ of tablets** eine Tablettenkur; Ⓘ (*Building*) Schicht, *die.* ❷ *v.i.* (*rhet.: flow*) strömen

**coursing** /'kɔːsɪŋ/ *n.* (*Sport*) Hetzjagd, *die*

**court** /kɔːt/ ❶ *n.* Ⓐ Hof, *der;* (*Brit.: quadrangle*) [Innen]hof [des/eines Colleges] (*in Cambridge*); (*hall in building*) ≈ Halle, *die;* Ⓑ (*Sport*) Spielfeld, *das;* (*Tennis, Squash also*) Platz, *der;* Ⓒ (*of sovereign*) Hof, *der;* **the C~ of St James's** (*Brit.*) der englische Königshof; **hold ~** (*fig.*) Hof halten (*scherzh.*); Ⓓ (*Law*) Gericht, *das;* (*~room*) Gerichtssaal, *der;* **~ of law** *or* **justice** Gerichtshof, *der;* **go to ~ [over sth.]** [wegen *od.* mit etw.] vor Gericht gehen; **take sb. to ~:** jmdn. vor Gericht bringen *od.* verklagen; **appear in ~:** vor Gericht erscheinen; **the case comes up in ~ today** der Fall wird heute verhandelt; **settle sth. in ~:** etw. gerichtlich klären; **out of ~:** außergerichtlich; (*fig.*) indiskutabel; **rule/laugh sth. out of ~** (*fig.*) etw. verwerfen/auslachen; Ⓔ (*managing body*) Rat, *der;* Ⓕ *no art.* (*dated: attentions*) **pay ~ to sb.** jmdn. hofieren (*veralt.*); **pay ~ to a woman** einer Frau den Hof machen (*veralt.*).
❷ *v.t.* Ⓐ (*woo*) **~ sb.** jmdn. umwerben; **~ing couple** Liebespärchen, *das;* **are they ~ing?** sind sie ein Pärchen?; Ⓑ (*Zool., Ornith.*) umwerben; Ⓒ (*fig.*) suchen ‹Gunst, Ruhm, Gefahr›; **he is ~ing disaster/danger** er wandelt am Rande des Abgrunds (*fig. geh.*); **~ death** sein Leben riskieren

**court: ~ card** *n.* Figurenkarte, *die;* **~ 'circular** *n.* (*Brit.*) Hofnachrichten *Pl.;* **~ dress** *n.* Hofkleid, *das*

**courteous** /'kɜːtɪəs/ *adj.* höflich; **~ manners** gute Manieren

**courteously** /'kɜːtɪəslɪ/ *adv.* höflich; **behave ~:** höflich sein

**courtesan** /kɔːtɪ'zæn/ *n.* Kokotte, *die;* Kurtisane, *die* (*hist.*)

**courtesy** /'kɜːtəsɪ/ *n.* Höflichkeit, *die;* **drinks were [served] by ~ of sb.** die Getränke gingen auf jmds. Kosten; **by ~ of the museum** mit freundlicher Genehmigung des Museums; **by ~** (*with some exaggeration*) mit viel Wohlwollen; (*as mark of politeness*) aus Höflichkeit

**courtesy: ~ call** *n.* Höflichkeitsbesuch, *der;* **~ light** *n.* (*Motor Veh.*) Innenbeleuchtung, *die;* **~ title** *n. Höflichkeitsanrede mit einem höheren Titel, als die betreffende Person besitzt*

**'court house** *n.* (*Law*) Gerichtsgebäude, *das;* (*Amer.*) *Verwaltungsgebäude eines Verwaltungsbezirks [mit Bezirksgefängnis]*

**courtier** /'kɔːtɪə(r)/ *n.* Höfling, *der*

**courtly** /'kɔːtlɪ/ *adj.* vornehm; **~ love** (*Hist.*) Minne, *die*

**court: ~ 'martial** *n., pl.* **~s martial** (*Mil.*) Kriegsgericht, *das;* **be tried by ~ martial** vor das/ein Kriegsgericht kommen; **~-'martial** *v.t.*, (*Brit.*) **-ll-** vor das/ein Kriegsgericht stellen; **C~ of Ap'peal** *n.* (*Brit.*) Berufungsgericht, *das;* **~room** *n.* (*Law*) Gerichtssaal, *der*

**courtship** /'kɔːtʃɪp/ *n.* Werben, *das*

**court: ~ shoe** *n.* Pumps, *der;* **~yard** *n.* Hof, *der*

**cousin** /'kʌzn/ *n.* **[first] ~:** Cousin, *der*/Cousine, *die;* Vetter, *der*/(*veralt.*) Base, *die;* **[second] ~:** Cousin/Cousine zweiten Grades; **they are ~s** sie sind Cousins/Cousinen/Cousin und Cousine; **first ~ once removed** (*first ~'s child*) Kind eines Cousins/einer Cousine; (*parent's ~*) Cousin/Cousine des Vaters/der Mutter; **sth. is first ~ to sth.** (*fig.*) etw. ist fast das gleiche wie etw.

**couture** /kuː'tjʊə(r)/ *n.* Couture, *die;* ⇒ *also* **haute couture**

**couturier** /kuː'tjʊərjeɪ/ *n.* Couturier, *der;* Modeschöpfer, *der*

**couturière** /kuː'tjʊərjeə(r)/ *n.* Modeschöpferin, *die*

**cove**[1] /kəʊv/ *n.* Ⓐ (*Geog.*) [kleine] Bucht; Ⓑ (*sheltered recess*) Einbuchtung, *die*

**cove**[2] *n.* (*dated Brit. coll.*) Kerl, *der*

**coven** /kʌvn/ *n.* ≈ Hexensabbat, *der; Zusammenkunft von [dreizehn] Hexen*

**covenant** /'kʌvənənt/ ❶ *n.* Ⓐ formelle Übereinkunft; Ⓑ (*Law*) [besiegelter] Vertrag; **deed of ~:** Vertragsurkunde, *die;* Ⓒ (*Bibl.*) Bund, *der.* ❷ *v.i.* (*also Law*) **~ [with sb.] [for sth.]** [mit jmdm.] [etw.] vertraglich festlegen. ❸ *v.t.* (*also Law*) [vertraglich] vereinbaren

**Coventry** /'kɒvəntrɪ/ *n.* **send sb. to ~** (*fig.*) jmdn. [demonstrativ] schneiden

**cover** /'kʌvə(r)/ ❶ *n.* Ⓐ (*piece of cloth*) Decke, *die;* (*of cushion, bed*) Bezug, *der;* (*lid*) Deckel, *der;* (*of hole, engine, typewriter, etc.*) Abdeckung, *die;* **put a ~ on** *or* **over** zudecken; abdecken ‹Loch, Fußboden, Grab, Fahrzeug, Maschine›; beziehen ‹Kissen, Bett›; Ⓑ (*of book*) Einband, *der;* (*of magazine*) Umschlag, *der;* (*of record*) [Platten]hülle, *die;* Cover, *das;* **read sth. from ~ to ~:** etw. von vorn bis hinten lesen; **on the [front/back] ~:** auf dem [vorderen/hinteren] Buchdeckel; (*of magazine*) auf der Titelseite/hinteren Umschlagseite; **a removable paper ~:** ein loser Papierumschlag; Ⓒ (*Post: envelope*) [Brief]umschlag, *der;* **under plain ~:** in neutralem Umschlag; **[send sth.] under separate ~:** [etw.] mit getrennter Post [schicken]; Ⓓ *in pl.* (*bedclothes*) Bettzeug, *das;* Ⓔ (*of pneumatic tyre*) Decke, *die;* Ⓕ (*hiding place, shelter*) Schutz, *der;* **take ~ [from sth.]** Schutz [vor etw. (*Dat.*)] suchen; **take ~ from the rain** sich unterstellen; **[be/go] under ~** (*from bullets etc.*) in Deckung [sein/gehen]; **under ~** (*from rain*) überdacht ‹Sitzplatz›; regengeschützt; **keep sth. under ~:** etw. abgedeckt halten; **under ~ of darkness** im Schutz der Dunkelheit; Ⓖ (*Mil.: supporting force*) Deckung, *die;* **fighter ~:** Deckung durch Jagdflugzeuge; ⇒ *also* **air cover**; Ⓗ (*protection*) Deckung, *die;* **give sb./sth. ~:** jmdm. Deckung geben; Ⓘ (*pretence*) Vorwand, *der;* (*false identity, screen*) Tarnung, *die;* **under ~ of charity** unter dem Deckmantel der Barmherzigkeit; **blow sb.'s ~** (*coll.*) jmdn. enttarnen; Ⓙ (*Hunting*) Deckung, *die;* **break ~:** aus der Deckung herauskommen; Ⓚ (*Insurance*) **[insurance] ~:** Versicherung, *die;* **get ~ against sth.** sich gegen etw. versichern; **have adequate ~:** ausreichend versichert sein; Ⓛ (*place laid at table*) Gedeck, *das;* Ⓜ (*~ version*) **~ [version]** Coverversion, *die.*
❷ *v.t.* Ⓐ bedecken; **~ a book with leather** ein Buch in Leder binden; **~ your mouth while coughing** halte die Hand vor den Mund, wenn du hustest; **~ the table with a cloth** ein Tischtuch auf den Tisch legen; **~ a roof with shingles** ein Dach mit Schindeln decken; **~ a chair with chintz** einen Stuhl mit Chintz beziehen; **~ a pan with a lid/a car with plastic sheeting** eine Pfanne mit einem Deckel/ein Auto mit einer Plastikplane zudecken; **she ~ed her face with her hands** sie verbarg das Gesicht in den Händen; **~ed with blood** blutüberströmt; **the roses are ~ed with greenfly** die Rosen sind voller Blattläuse; **cats are ~ed with fur** Katzen haben ein Fell; **floodwaters ~ed the town** die Stadt war überflutet; **the children were ~ed in mud** die Kinder waren von oben bis unten voller Schlamm; **the car ~ed us with mud** das Auto bespritzte uns von oben bis unten mit Schlamm; **sb. is ~ed in** *or* **with confusion/shame** (*fig.*) jmd. ist ganz verlegen/sehr beschämt; ⇒ *also* **glory** 1 B; Ⓑ (*conceal, lit. or fig.*) verbergen; (*for protection*) abdecken; Ⓒ (*travel*) zurücklegen; Ⓓ *in p.p.* (*having roof*) überdacht; **~ed market** Markthalle, *die;* **a ~ed wagon** ein Planwagen; Ⓔ (*deal with*) behandeln; (*include*) abdecken; **~ all possible cases** alle möglichen Fälle abdecken; **an examination ~ing last year's work** eine Prüfung über den Stoff des vergangenen Jahres; **this book does not fully ~ the subject** dieses Buch behandelt das Thema nicht vollständig; Ⓕ (*Journ.*) berichten über (+ *Akk.*); Ⓖ (*suffice to defray*) decken; **~ expenses** die Kosten decken; **£10 will ~ my needs for the journey** 10 Pfund werden für die Reisekosten reichen; Ⓗ (*shield*) decken; **I'll keep you ~ed** ich gebe dir Deckung; Ⓘ **~ oneself** (*fig.*) sich absichern; (*Insurance*) **~ oneself against sth.** sich gegen etw. versichern; Ⓙ (*aim gun at*) in Schach halten (*ugs.*); **I've got you ~ed** ich habe meine Waffe auf dich gerichtet; Ⓚ (*command*) kontrollieren ‹Gelände›; Ⓛ ‹Hengst› decken

**~ for** *v.t.* einspringen für

**~ 'in** *v.t.* überdachen; (*fill in*) zuschütten

**~ 'over** *v.t.* zudecken; (*with gold etc.*) überziehen

**~ 'up** ❶ *v.t.* (*conceal*) zudecken; (*fig.*) vertuschen. ❷ *v.i.* (*fig.: conceal*) es vertuschen; **~ up for sb.** jmdn. decken. ⇒ *also* **cover-up**

**'cover address** *n.* Deckadresse, *die*

**coverage** /'kʌvərɪdʒ/ *n., no pl.* Ⓐ (*Radio, Telev.: area*) Sendebereich, *der;* **provide a greater ~ of the country** den Sendebereich innerhalb des Landes vergrößern; Ⓑ (*Journ., Radio, Telev.: treatment*) Berichterstattung, *die* (**of** über + *Akk.*); **newspaper/broadcast ~:** Berichterstattung in der Presse/in Funk und Fernsehen; **give sth. [full/limited] ~:** [ausführlich/kurz] über etw. (*Akk.*) berichten; Ⓒ (*Advertising*) Abdeckung des Marktes; Ⓓ (*Insurance*) Deckung, *die*

**coverall** /'kʌvərɔːl/ *n. usu. in pl.* (*esp. Amer.*) Overall, *der;* (*for baby*) Strampelanzug, *der*

**cover: ~ charge** *n.* [Preis für das] Gedeck; **~ girl** *n.* Covergirl, *das*

**covering** /'kʌvərɪŋ/ *n.* (*material*) Decke, *die;* (*of billiard table, aircraft wing*) Bespannung, *die;* (*of chair, bed*) Bezug, *der*

**covering: ~ letter** *n.* Begleitbrief, *der;* **~ note** *n.* [kurzes] Begleitschreiben

**coverlet** /'kʌvəlɪt/ *n.* Tagesdecke, *die*

**cover: ~ note** *n.* (*Insurance*) Deckungskarte, *die;* **~ story** *n.* Ⓐ (*Journ.*) Titelgeschichte, *die;* Ⓑ (*espionage*) [zur Tarnung erfundene] Geschichte

**covert** ❶ /'kʌvət/ *adj.* versteckt. ❷ /'kʌvət, 'kʌvə(r)/ *n.* (*shelter*) Schlupfwinkel, *der;* (*thicket*) Dickicht, *das*

**covertly** /'kʌvətlɪ/ *adv.* versteckt; **glance ~ at sb./sth.** jmdn./etw. verstohlen anschauen

**cover: ~-up** *n.* Verschleierung, *die;* **the Watergate ~-up** die Watergate-Affäre; **~ version** *n.* Coverversion, *die*

**covet** /'kʌvɪt/ *v.t.* begehren (*geh.*)

**covetous** /'kʌvɪtəs/ *adj.* (*desirous*) begehrlich (*geh.*); (*avaricious*) habgierig; **be ~ of sth.** etw. begehren (*geh.*)

**covetously** /ˈkʌvɪtəslɪ/ *adv.* begehrlich (*geh.*)

**covetousness** /ˈkʌvɪtəsnɪs/ *n.*, *no pl.* Begehrlichkeit, *die*

**covey** /ˈkʌvɪ/ *n.* (*Hunting*) Kette, *die* (*Jägerspr.*)

**cow**[1] /kaʊ/ *n.* Ⓐ Kuh, *die;* **till the ~s come home** (*fig. coll.*) bis in alle Ewigkeit (*ugs.*); Ⓑ (*female elephant, whale, etc.*) Kuh, *die;* **~ buffalo/elephant** Büffelkuh, *die*/Elefantenkuh, *die;* Ⓒ (*sl. derog.: woman*) Kuh, *die* (*salopp abwertend*)

**cow**[2] *v.t.* einschüchtern; **~ sb. into submission** jmdn. so einschüchtern, dass er sich unterordnet; **have a ~ed look/appearance** verschüchtert aussehen

**coward** /ˈkaʊəd/ *n.* Feigling, *der;* **the ~'s way out** die feige Art, sich aus der Affäre zu ziehen

**cowardice** /ˈkaʊədɪs/ *n.* Feigheit, *die;* ⇒ *also* **moral cowardice**

**cowardly** /ˈkaʊədlɪ/ *adj.* feig[e]

**cow: ~bell** *n.* Kuhglocke, *die;* **~boy** *n.* Cowboy, *der;* (*Brit. coll.: unscrupulous businessman, tradesman, etc.*) Betrüger, *der;* **play Cowboys and Indians** Cowboy und Indianer spielen; **~catcher** *n.* (*Amer. Railw.*) Bahnräumer, *der;* Kuhfänger, *der;* **~ dung** *n.* Kuhmist, *der*

**cower** /ˈkaʊə(r)/ *v.i.* sich ducken; (*squat*) kauern; **~ in fear** sich ängstlich ducken; **stand ~ing in the corner** geduckt in der Ecke stehen

**cow: ~hand** *n.* Cowboy, *der;* **~herd** *n.* ▶ 1261 Kuhhirte, *der;* **~hide** *n.* Rindsleder, *das*

**cowl** /kaʊl/ *n.* Ⓐ (*of monk*) Kutte, *die;* (*hood*) Kapuze, *die;* Ⓑ (*of chimney*) Schornsteinaufsatz, *der*

**ˈcowlick** *n.* [Haar]tolle, *die* (*ugs.*)

**cowling** /ˈkaʊlɪŋ/ *n.* (*Aeronaut., Motor Veh.*) Motorhaube, *die*

**ˈcowman** *n.* ▶ 1261 Stallknecht, *der*

**ˈco-worker** *n.* Kollege, *der*/Kollegin, *die*

**cow: ~ parsley** *n.* (*Bot.*) Wiesenkerbel, *der;* **~pat** *n.* Kuhfladen, *der;* **~pox** *n.* Kuhpocken *Pl.;* **~puncher** /ˈkaʊpʌnʃə(r)/ *n.* (*Amer.*) Cowboy, *der*

**cowrie, cowry** /ˈkaʊrɪ/ *n.* Kaurischnecke, *die;* (*shell*) Kaurimuschel, *die*

**cow: ~shed** *n.* Kuhstall, *der;* **~slip** *n.* Ⓐ Schlüsselblume, *die;* Ⓑ (*Amer.: marsh marigold*) Sumpfdotterblume, *die;* **~'s milk** *n.* Kuhmilch, *die*

**cox** /kɒks/ ❶ *n.* Steuermann, *der.* ❷ *v.t.* (*esp. Rowing*) steuern; **~ a crew** Steuermann einer Mannschaft sein; **~ed four** Vierer mit Steuermann. ❸ *v.i.* steuern

**coxcomb** /ˈkɒkskəʊm/ *n.* (*literary/arch.*) Stutzer, *der* (*veralt.*)

**coxless** /ˈkɒkslɪs/ *adj.* ohne Steuermann

**coxswain** /ˈkɒksweɪn, ˈkɒksn/ ⇒ **cox** 1

**coy** /kɔɪ/ *adj.* gespielt schüchtern; geziert ‹Benehmen, Ausdruck›; **play ~:** auf schüchtern machen

**coyly** /ˈkɔɪlɪ/ *adv.* gespielt schüchtern; geziert ‹sich benehmen›

**coyness** /ˈkɔɪnɪs/ *n.*, *no pl.* Schüchternheit, *die;* (*of behaviour*) Geziertheit, *die*

**coyote** /kəˈjəʊtɪ, ˈkɔɪəʊt/ *n.* (*Zool.*) Kojote, *der*

**coypu** /ˈkɔɪpuː/ *n.* (*Zool.*) Biberratte, *die;* Nutria, *die*

**cozily, coziness, cozy** (*Amer.*) ⇒ **cos-**

**cp.** *abbr.* **compare** vgl.

**Cpl.** *abbr.* **Corporal** Korp.

**c.p.s.** *abbr.* **cycles per second** Hz

**CPU** *abbr.* (*Computing*) **central processing unit** ZE

**Cr.** *abbr.* Ⓐ **creditor** Gl.; Ⓑ **Councillor** ≈ StR

**crab** /kræb/ ❶ *n.* Ⓐ Krabbe, *die;* Ⓑ (*Astrol.*) **the C~:** der Krebs; ⇒ *also* **archer** B; Ⓒ (*Rowing*) **catch a ~:** einen Krebs fangen; Ⓓ (*Bot.*) ⇒ **crab apple**. ❷ *v.i.*, **-bb-** (*coll.*) **~ about sth.** über etw. (*Akk.*) meckern (*ugs.*)

**ˈcrab apple** *n.* Holzapfel, *der*

**crabbed** /kræbd/ *adj.* Ⓐ (*perverse*) starrköpfig; Ⓑ (*morose*) griesgrämig; Ⓒ (*badly formed*) unleserlich ‹Handschrift›

**crabby** /ˈkræbɪ/ ⇒ **crabbed** A, B

**crabwise** /ˈkræbwaɪz/ *adv.* seitwärts [wie eine Krabbe]

**crack** /kræk/ ❶ *n.* Ⓐ (*noise*) Krachen, *das;* **a ~ of the whip** ein Peitschenknall; **give sb./have a fair ~ of the whip** (*fig.*) jmdm. eine Chance geben/eine Chance haben; **the ~ of doom** (*fig.*) die Posaunen des Jüngsten Gerichts; Ⓑ (*in china, glass, eggshell, ice, etc.*) Sprung, *der;* (*in rock*) Spalte, *die;* (*chink*) Spalt, *der;* **there's a ~ in the ceiling** die Decke hat einen Riss; ⇒ *also* **paper over;** Ⓒ (*blow*) Schlag, *der;* Ⓓ (*coll.: try*) Versuch, *der;* **have a ~ at sth./at doing sth.** etw. in Angriff nehmen/versuchen, etw. zu tun; Ⓔ **the/at the ~ of dawn** *or* **day** der/bei Tagesanbruch; Ⓕ (*coll.: wisecrack*) [geistreicher] Witz; Ⓖ (*sl.: drug*) **~ [cocaine]** Crack, *das.* ❷ *adj.* (*coll.*) erstklassig.
❸ *v.t.* Ⓐ (*break, lit. or fig.*) knacken ‹Nuss, Problem›; knacken (*salopp*) ‹Safe, Kode›; **~ a bottle** (*fig.*) einer Flasche den Hals brechen (*ugs. scherzh.*); **~ sth. open** etw. aufbrechen; Ⓑ (*make a ~ in*) anschlagen ‹Porzellan, Glas›; **~ one's head/skull** sich (*Dat.*) den Kopf/Schädel aufschlagen; Ⓒ **~ a whip** mit einer Peitsche knallen; **~ the whip** (*fig.*) Druck machen (*ugs.*); **~ one's knuckles** mit den Knöcheln knacken; Ⓓ **~ a joke** einen Witz machen; Ⓔ (*Chem.: decompose*) kracken.
❹ *v.i.* Ⓐ ‹Porzellan, Glas:› einen Sprung/Sprünge bekommen; ‹Haut:› aufspringen, rissig werden; ‹Eis:› Risse bekommen; Ⓑ (*make sound*) ‹Peitsche:› knallen; ‹Gelenk:› knacken; ‹Gewehr:› krachen; Ⓒ (*change*) ‹Stimme:› brechen (*geh.*), versagen (**with** vor + *Dat.*); **his voice is ~ing** (*at age of puberty*) er ist im Stimmbruch; Ⓓ (*yield under torture etc.*) zusammenbrechen; Ⓔ (*coll.*) **get ~ing!** mach los! (*ugs.*); **let's get ~ing** fangen wir endlich an; **get ~ing [with sth.]** [mit etw.] loslegen (*ugs.*)

**~ ˈdown** *v.i.* (*coll.*) **~ down [on sb./sth.]** [gegen jmdn./etw.] [hart] vorgehen; ⇒ *also* **~-down**

**~ ˈup** (*coll.*) ❶ *v.i.* ‹Flugzeug:› auseinander brechen; ‹Gesellschaft, Person:› zusammenbrechen; **~ up [laughing]** einen Lachkrampf kriegen. ❷ *v.t.* **he/it** *etc.* **is not all he/it** *etc.* **is ~ed up to be** so toll ist er/es *usw.* nun auch wieder nicht[, wie er/es dargestellt wird]; **she is ~ed up to be brilliant** sie soll brillant sein (*ugs.*). ⇒ *also* **~-up**

**crack: ~-brained** *adj.* (*coll.*) bescheuert (*salopp abwertend*) ‹Person›; hirnrissig (*abwertend*) ‹Idee usw.›; **~-down** *n.* (*coll.*) **there will be a ~-down** man wird hart durchgreifen; **have/order a ~-down on sb./sth.** drastische Maßnahmen gegen jmdn./etw. ergreifen/anordnen

**cracked** /krækt/ *adj.* Ⓐ gesprungen ‹Porzellan, Ziegel, Glas›; rissig, aufgesprungen ‹Haut, Erdboden›; rissig ‹Verputz›; brüchig ‹Stimme›; Ⓑ (*coll.: crazy*) übergeschnappt (*ugs.*)

**cracker** /ˈkrækə(r)/ *n.* Ⓐ (*paper toy*) **[Christmas] ~:** ≈ Knallbonbon, *der od. das;* Ⓑ (*firework*) Knallkörper, *der;* Ⓒ (*thin dry biscuit*) Cracker, *der;* (*Amer.: biscuit*) Keks, *der;* Ⓓ ⇒ **crackerjack** 2

**ˈcrackerjack** (*Amer. coll.*) ❶ *adj.* fantastisch (*ugs.*). ❷ *n.* (*person*) Ass, *das* (*ugs.*); (*thing*) Knüller, *der* (*ugs.*)

**crackers** /ˈkrækəz/ *pred. adj.* (*Brit. coll.*) übergeschnappt (*ugs.*); **go ~:** überschnappen (*ugs.*)

**crackle** /ˈkrækl/ ❶ *v.i.* knistern; ‹Maschinengewehr:› knattern; ‹Feuer:› prasseln; ‹Blätter:› rascheln; **the telephone line/the radio ~s** in der Telefonleitung/im Radio knackt es. ❷ *n.* Knistern, *das;* (*of leaves*) Rascheln, *das;* (*of telephone line*) Knacken, *das;* (*of machine gun*) Knattern, *das;* (*of fire*) Prasseln, *das*

**crackling** /ˈkræklɪŋ/ *n.*, *no pl.*, *no indef. art.* (*Cookery*) Kruste, *die*

**crackly** /ˈkræklɪ/ *adj.* knisternd

**ˈcrackpot** *n.* (*coll.*) Spinner, *der*/Spinnerin, *die* (*ugs.*); *attrib.* **~ ideas/schemes** hirnrissige Ideen/Pläne (*abwertend*)

**cracksman** /ˈkræksmən/ *n.*, *pl.* **cracksmen** /ˈkræksmən/ Einbrecher, *der*

**ˈcrack-up** *n.* (*coll.*) Zusammenbruch, *der*

**Cracow** /ˈkrækaʊ/ *pr. n.* ▶ 1626 Krakau (*das*)

**cradle** /ˈkreɪdl/ ❶ *n.* Ⓐ (*cot, lit. or fig.*) Wiege, *die;* **from the ~:** von der Wiege an; von Kindesbeinen an; **from the ~ to the grave** von der Wiege bis zur Bahre; Ⓑ (*Building*) Hängebühne, *die;* (*to support ship*) Stapel, *der;* Ⓒ (*Teleph.*) Gabel, *die.* ❷ *v.t.* wiegen; **~ sb./sth. in one's arms** jmdn. in den Armen halten/etw. im Arm halten

**cradle: ~-snatch** *v.i.* (*coll.*) **Your boyfriend/girlfriend is much younger than you. You're ~-snatching** Dein Freund/deine Freundin ist viel jünger als du. Du vergreifst dich ja an kleinen Kindern (*ugs. scherzh.*); **~-snatcher** (*coll.*) ⇒ **babysnatcher** B; **~-snatching** (*coll.*) ⇒ **babysnatching** B; **~ song** *n.* Wiegenlied, *das*

**craft** /krɑːft/ *n.* Ⓐ (*trade*) Handwerk, *das;* (*art*) Kunsthandwerk, *das;* (*in school*) **~[s]** Werken, *das;* Ⓑ *no pl.* (*skill*) Kunstfertigkeit, *die;* Ⓒ *no pl.* (*cunning*) List, *die;* **be full of ~:** sehr gewitzt sein; Ⓓ *pl. same* (*boat*) Boot, *das;* (*air~*) Flugzeug, *das;* (*space~*) Raumfahrzeug, *das*

**craftily** /ˈkrɑːftɪlɪ/ *adv.* listig

**craftiness** /ˈkrɑːftɪnɪs/ *n.*, *no pl.* Schläue, *die*

**craftsman** /ˈkrɑːftsmən/ *n.*, *pl.* **craftsmen** /ˈkrɑːftsmən/ Handwerker, *der;* (*skilled person*) **a real ~:** ein wahrer Künstler

**craftsmanship** /ˈkrɑːftsmənʃɪp/ *n.*, *no pl.* (*skilled workmanship*) handwerkliches Können; (*performance*) **shoddy ~:** schludrige Arbeit

**ˈcraftwork** *n.*, *no pl.* Kunsthandwerk, *das*

**crafty** /ˈkrɑːftɪ/ *adj.* listig; **as ~ as a fox** schlau wie ein Fuchs

**crag** /kræg/ *n.* Felsspitze, *die*

**craggy** /ˈkrægɪ/ *adj.* (*rugged*) zerklüftet; zerfurcht ‹Gesicht›; (*rocky*) felsig; (*steep*) schroff

**crake** /kreɪk/ *n.* (*Ornith.*) Ralle, *die*

**cram** /kræm/ ❶ *v.t.*, **-mm-:** Ⓐ (*overfill*) voll stopfen (*ugs.*); (*force*) stopfen; **~med with information** voll gepackt mit Informationen; **~ people into a bus** Leute in einen Bus zwängen; **the bus was ~med** der Bus war gerammelt voll (*ugs.*) *od.* war überfüllt; ⇒ *also* **throat** A; Ⓑ (*for examination*) **~ pupils** mit Schülern pauken (*ugs.*); **~ up maths** Mathe pauken *od.* büffeln (*ugs.*); Ⓒ (*feed to excess*) mästen; **~ poultry** *etc.* Geflügel *usw.* mästen *od.* (*bes. südd.*) stopfen. ❷ *v.i.*, **-mm-** (*for examination*) büffeln (*ugs.*); pauken (*ugs.*)

**~ ˈin** ❶ *v.i.* [sich] herein-/hineindrängen. ❷ *v.t.* hineinstopfen

**ˈcram-full** ⇒ **chock-full**

**crammer** /ˈkræmə(r)/ *n.* (*place*) Presse, *die* (*ugs. abwertend*); (*person*) [Ein]pauker, *der* (*ugs.*)

**cramp** /kræmp/ ❶ *n.* Ⓐ (*Med.*) Krampf, *der;* **suffer an attack of ~:** einen Krampf bekommen; **have ~ [in one's leg/arm]** einen Krampf [im Bein/Arm] haben; ⇒ *also* **writer's cramp;** Ⓑ (*Woodw.*) Schraubzwinge, *die;* Ⓒ (*Building*) **~ [iron]** [Bau]klammer, *die.* ❷ *v.t.* Ⓐ (*confine*) einengen; **~ [up]** zusammenpferchen; **~ sb.'s style** jmdn. einengen; Ⓑ (*restrict*) lähmen ‹Willen, Eifer, Fleiß, Handel›

**cramped** /kræmpt/ *adj.* eng ‹Raum›; gedrängt ‹Handschrift›

**crampon** /ˈkræmpən/ (*Amer.:* **crampoon** /kræmˈpuːn/) *n.* Ⓐ (*metal hook*) Kanthaken, *der;* Ⓑ (*on boot*) Steigeisen, *das*

**cranberry** /ˈkrænbərɪ/ *n.* Preiselbeere, *die;* (*Vaccinium oxycoccos*) Moosbeere, *die* (*Bot.*); (*Vaccinium macrocarpon*) Großfrüchtige Moosbeere (*Bot.*); **~ sauce** Preiselbeersoße, *die*

**crane** /kreɪn/ ❶ *n.* Ⓐ (*machine*) Kran, *der;* Ⓑ (*Ornith.*) Kranich, *der.* ❷ *v.t.* **~ one's neck** den Hals recken. ❸ *v.i.* den Hals recken; ~ forward den Hals [nach vorn] recken

**crane:** ~ **driver** *n.* ▶ 1261 | Kranführer, *der;* ~ **fly** *n.* (*Zool.*) Schnake, *die;* ~**sbill** *n.* (*Bot.*) Storch[en]schnabel, *der*

**crania** *pl. of* **cranium**

**cranial** /'kreɪnɪəl/ *adj.* (*Anat.*) Schädel-; kranial (*fachspr.*)

**cranium** /'kreɪnɪəm/ *n., pl.* **crania** /'kreɪnɪə/ *or* ~**s** (*Anat.*) Schädel, *der;* Kranium, *das* (*fachspr.*); (*bones enclosing the brain*) Hirnschädel, *der*

**crank**[1] /kræŋk/ ❶ *n.* Ⓐ (*Mech. Engin.*) [Hand]kurbel, *die;* Ⓑ (*of bicycle*) ~ **[arm]** Tretkurbel, *die.* ❷ *v.t.* (*turn with* ~) ankurbeln

~ **'up** *v.t.* (*Motor Veh.*) ankurbeln

**crank**[2] *n.* Irre, *der/die* (*salopp*); **health** ~: Gesundheitsfanatiker, *der/*-fanatikerin, *die* (*ugs.*)

**crank:** ~ **arm** *n.* (*of bicycle*) Tretkurbel, *die;* ~**case** *n.* (*Mech. Engin.*) Kurbelwellengehäuse, *das;* ~**pin** *n.* (*Mech. Engin.*) Kurbelzapfen, *der;* ~**shaft** *n.* (*Mech. Engin.*) Kurbelwelle, *die*

**cranky** /'kræŋkɪ/ *adj.* Ⓐ (*eccentric*) schrullig; verschroben; Ⓑ (*esp. Amer.: ill-tempered*) griesgrämig

**cranny** /'krænɪ/ *n.* Ritze, *die;* ⇒ *also* **nook**

**crap**[1] /kræp/ (*coarse*) ❶ *n.* Ⓐ (*faeces*) Scheiße, *die* (*derb*); **have a** ~: scheißen (*derb*); Ⓑ (*nonsense*) Scheiß, *der* (*salopp abwertend*); **a load of** ~: ein Haufen Scheiß (*salopp abwertend*). ❷ *v.i.*, **-pp-** scheißen (*derb*)

**crap**[2] *n.* (*Amer.: throw in craps*) Fehlwurf, *der;* Crap, *der;* ~ **game** Craps, *das*

**crape** /kreɪp/ *n.* [schwarzer] Krepp; (*ribbon*) Trauerflor, *der*

**crappy** /'kræpɪ/ *adj.* (*coarse*) beschissen (*derb*); ~ **film/café** Scheißfilm, *der*/Scheißcafé, *das* (*derb*)

**craps** /kræps/ *n. pl.* (*Amer.: dice game*) Craps, *das;* **shoot** ~: Craps spielen

**crash** /kræʃ/ ❶ *n.* Ⓐ (*noise*) Krachen, *das;* **fall with a** ~: mit einem lauten Krach fallen; **a sudden** ~ **of thunder** ein plötzlicher Donnerschlag; Ⓑ (*collision*) Zusammenstoß, *der;* **plane/train** ~: Flugzeugunglück, *das*/Eisenbahnunglück, *das;* **have a** ~: einen Unfall haben; **in a [car]** ~: bei einem [Auto]unfall; **be in a [car]** ~: in einen [Auto]unfall verwickelt sein; Ⓒ (*Finance etc.*) Zusammenbruch, *der;* **the great** ~ **on Wall Street** der große Börsenkrach in der Wall Street; Ⓓ *attrib.* (*intensive*) ~ **job** Noteinsatz, *der;* ~ **measures** Sofortmaßnahmen *Pl.*
❷ *adv.* krachend; ~, **bang, wallop** (*coll.*) holterdiepolter (*ugs.*).
❸ *v.i.* Ⓐ (*make a noise*) krachen; Ⓑ (*go noisily*) krachen; ~ **down** herunterkrachen; ~ **about one's ears** (*fig.*) zusammenbrechen; Ⓒ (*have a collision*) einen Unfall haben; ‹Flugzeug, Flieger:› abstürzen; ~ **into sth.** gegen etw. krachen; Ⓓ (*Finance etc., Computing*) zusammenbrechen.
❹ *v.t.* Ⓐ (*smash*) schmettern; Ⓑ (*cause to have collision*) einen Unfall haben mit; ~ **a plane** mit dem Flugzeug abstürzen; Ⓒ (*pass illegally*) überfahren; **he** ~**ed the lights** er fuhr bei Rot über die Ampel; Ⓓ ⇒ **gatecrash 1**

~ **a'bout** *v.i.* laut herumtollen

~ **'out** *v.i.* (*coll.*) pennen (*salopp*); (*go to sleep*) einpennen (*salopp*)

**crash:** ~ **barrier** *n.* Leitplanke, *die;* ~ **course** *n.* Intensivkurs, *der;* ~ **diet** *n.* radikale Diät; ≈ Nulldiät, *die;* ~**-dive** ❶ *v.t.* schnell untertauchen lassen ‹U-Boot›; abstürzen lassen ‹Flugzeug›; ❷ *v.i.* ‹Unterseeboot:› schnell untertauchen; ~**-dive on sth.** im Sturzflug auf etw. (*Akk.*) herabstoßen; ❸ *n.* (*of submarine*) schnelles Untertauchen; (*of aircraft*) Sturzflug, *der;* ~ **helmet** *n.* Sturzhelm, *der*

**crashing** /'kræʃɪŋ/ *adj.* (*coll.*) **be a** ~ **bore** wahnsinnig langweilig sein (*ugs.*)

**crash:** ~**-land** ❶ *v.t.* ~**-land a plane** mit einem Flugzeug bruchlanden; ❷ *v.i.* bruchlanden; ~**-landing** *n.* Bruchlandung, *die;* ~ **pad** *n.* (*youth sl.*) Schlafplatz, *der;* Penne, *die* (*salopp*); ~ **programme** *n.* Sofortprogramm, *das*

**crass** /kræs/ *adj.* krass; grob ‹Benehmen›; haarsträubend ‹Dummheit, Unwissenheit›; (*grossly stupid*) strohdumm

**crassly** /'kræslɪ/ *adv.* grob, unfein ‹sich benehmen›; grob, krass ‹fehldeuten›

**crassness** /'kræsnɪs/ *n., no pl.* Krassheit, *die;* (*of person*) Grobheit, *die;* (*stupidity*) Dummheit, *die*

**crate** /kreɪt/ ❶ *n.* Ⓐ (*case*) Kiste, *die;* **a** ~ **of beer/lemonade** ein Kasten Bier/Limonade; Ⓑ (*coll.: vehicle*) Kiste, *die* (*ugs.*). ❷ *v.t.* ~ **[up]** in eine Kiste/in Kisten packen

**crater** /'kreɪtə(r)/ *n.* Krater, *der*

**crater 'lake** *n.* Kratersee, *der*

**cravat** /krə'væt/ *n.* Schalkrawatte, *die;* (*Hist.: necktie*) Krawatte, *die*

**crave** /kreɪv/ ❶ *v.t.* Ⓐ (*beg*) erbitten; erflehen ‹Gnade›; Ⓑ (*long for*) sich sehnen nach. ❷ *v.i.* ~ **for** *or* **after** ⇒ **1**

**craven** /'kreɪvn/ ❶ *adj.* feige; **a** ~ **coward** ein elender *od.* erbärmlicher Feigling. ❷ *n.* Feigling, *der*

**cravenly** /'kreɪvnlɪ/ *adv.* feige

**craving** /'kreɪvɪŋ/ *n.* Verlangen, *das;* **have a** ~ **for sth.** ein [dringendes] Verlangen nach etw. haben

**craw** /krɔ:/ *n.* Kropf, *der;* **stick in sb.'s** ~ (*fig.*) jmdm. gegen den Strich gehen

**crawfish** /'krɔ:fɪʃ/ *n., pl. same* Languste, *die*

**crawl** /krɔ:l/ ❶ *v.i.* Ⓐ kriechen; **the baby/insect** ~**s along the ground** das Baby/Insekt krabbelt über den Boden; Ⓑ (*coll.: behave abjectly*) kriechen (*abwertend*); ~ **to sb.** vor jmdm. buckeln *od.* kriechen; **don't you come** ~**ing back to me** du brauchst nicht wieder angekrochen zu kommen; Ⓒ **be** ~**ing** (*be covered or filled*) wimmeln (**with** von); Ⓓ ⇒ **creep 1 B.** ❷ *n.* Ⓐ Kriechen, *das;* (*of insect, baby also*) Krabbeln, *das;* (*slow speed*) Schneckentempo, *das;* **move/go at a** ~: sich im Schneckentempo bewegen/im Schneckentempo fahren; Ⓑ (*swimming stroke*) Kraulen, *das;* **do** *or* **swim the** ~: kraulen

**crawler** /'krɔ:lə(r)/ *n.* Ⓐ *usu. in pl.* (*baby's overall*) Spielanzug, *der;* Ⓑ (*coll. derog.: abject person*) Kriecher, *der* (*abwertend*)

**'crawler lane** *n.* Kriechspur, *die*

**crayfish** /'kreɪfɪʃ/ *n., pl. same* Ⓐ Flusskrebs, *der;* Ⓑ (*crawfish*) Languste, *die*

**crayon** /'kreɪən/ *n.* Ⓐ (*pencil*) **[coloured]** ~: Buntstift, *der;* (*of wax*) Wachsmalstift, *der;* (*of chalk*) Kreidestift, *der;* Ⓑ (*drawing*) [Kreide]zeichnung, *die*

**craze** /kreɪz/ ❶ *n.* Ⓐ (*temporary enthusiasm*) Begeisterung, *die;* Fimmel, *der* (*ugs. abwertend*); **there's a** ~ **for doing sth.** es ist gerade große Mode, etw. zu tun; Ⓑ (*mania*) Manie, *die.* ❷ *v.t. usu. in p. p.* (*make insane*) zum Wahnsinn treiben; **be [half]** ~**d with pain/grief** *etc.* [halb] wahnsinnig vor Schmerz/Kummer *usw.* sein; **a** ~**d look/expression [on sb.'s face]** ein vom Wahnsinn verzerrtes Gesicht

**crazily** /'kreɪzɪlɪ/ *adv.* verrückt; (*of motion*) wie verrückt

**craziness** /'kreɪzɪnɪs/ *n., no pl.* Verrücktheit, *die;* **sheer** ~: heller Wahnsinn

**crazy** /'kreɪzɪ/ *adj.* Ⓐ (*mad*) verrückt; wahnsinnig; **go** ~: verrückt *od.* wahnsinnig werden; **drive** *or* **send sb.** ~: jmdn. verrückt *od.* wahnsinnig machen (*ugs.*); **like** ~ (*coll.*) wie verrückt (*ugs.*); Ⓑ (*coll.: enthusiastic*) **be** ~ **about sb./sth.** nach jmdm./etw. verrückt sein (*ugs.*); **she's** ~ **about dancing** sie ist ganz wild aufs Tanzen (*ugs.*); **football/pop music** ~: verrückt nach Fußball/Popmusik (*ugs.*); Ⓒ (*coll.: exciting*) irre (*salopp*); Ⓓ (*of irregular pieces*) ~ **paving** gestückeltes Pflaster; ~ **quilt** Flickendecke, *die;* Ⓔ **lean [over] at a** ~ **angle** gefährlich schief stehen

**'crazy bone** *n.* (*Amer.*) Musikantenknochen, *der*

**creak** /kri:k/ ❶ *n.* (*of gate, door*) Quietschen, *das;* (*of floorboard, door, chair*) Knarren, *das.* ❷ *v.i.* ‹Tor, Tür:› quietschen; ‹Diele, Tür, Stuhl:› knarren; ‹Gelenke:› knacken; **the old car** ~**ed to a halt** der alte Wagen kam quietschend zum Stehen

**creaky** /'kri:kɪ/ *adj.* quietschend ‹Tor, Tür›; knarrend ‹Stuhl, Treppe, Stiefel, Tür›

**cream** /kri:m/ ❶ *n.* Ⓐ Sahne, *die;* Ⓑ (*Cookery*) (*sauce*) Sahnesoße, *die;* (*dessert*) Creme, *die;* (*chocolate*) gefülltes Bonbon; (*biscuit*) gefüllter Keks; ~ **of mushroom soup** Champignoncremesuppe, *die;* **custard** ~**s** Kekse mit Vanillecremefüllung; Ⓒ (*cosmetic preparation*) Creme, *die;* Ⓓ (*fig.: best*) Beste, *das;* **the** ~ **of society** die Creme der Gesellschaft; **the** ~ **of the applicants** die besten Bewerber; Ⓔ (*colour*) Creme, *das.* ❷ *adj.* Ⓐ ~**[-coloured]** creme[farben]; Ⓑ (*Cookery*) ~ **soup/sauce** Cremesuppe, *die*/Sahnesoße, *die.* ❸ *v.t.* cremig rühren *od.* schlagen; schaumig rühren ‹Butter›; ~**ed potatoes** Kartoffelpüree, *das*

~ **'off** *v.t.* ~ **off the best players** die besten Spieler wegschnappen (*ugs.*)

**cream:** ~ **'bun** *n.* ≈ Eclair, *das;* ~ **cake** *n.* Cremetorte, *die;* (*small*) Cremetörtchen, *das;* (*with whipped* ~) Sahnetorte, *die*/Sahnetörtchen, *das;* ~ **'cheese** *n.* ≈ Frischkäse, *der;* ~ **'cracker** *n.* ≈ Cracker, *der*

**creamer** /'kri:mə(r)/ *n.* (*Amer.: jug*) Sahnekännchen, *das*

**creamery** /'kri:mərɪ/ *n.* (*butter factory*) Molkerei, *die;* (*shop*) Milchgeschäft, *das*

**cream:** ~**jug** *n.* Sahnekännchen, *das;* ~ **of 'tartar** *n.* Weinstein, *der;* ~ **'puff** *n.* Windbeutel, *der;* ~ **'tea** *n.* Tee mit Marmeladetörtchen und Sahne

**creamy** /'kri:mɪ/ *adj.* Ⓐ (*with cream*) sahnig; (*like cream*) cremig; Ⓑ ~**[-coloured]** creme[farben]

**crease** /kri:s/ ❶ *n.* Ⓐ (*pressed*) Bügelfalte, *die;* (*accidental; in skin*) Falte, *die;* (*in fabric*) Falte, *die;* Knitter, *der;* (*in paper*) Kniff, *der;* Knick, *der;* **put a** ~ **in trousers** Bügelfalten in Hosen bügeln; Ⓑ (*Cricket*) Linie, *die.* ❷ *v.t.* (*press*) eine Falte/Falten bügeln in (+ *Akk.*); (*accidentally*) knittern; (*extensively*) zerknittern. ❸ *v.i.* Falten bekommen; knittern

~ **'up** *v.i.* (*coll.: in amusement*) sich [vor Lachen] kringeln (*ugs.*)

**'crease-resistant** *adj.* knitterfrei

**create** /krɪ'eɪt/ ❶ *v.t.* Ⓐ schaffen; erschaffen (*geh.*); verursachen ‹Verwirrung›; machen ‹Eindruck›; ‹Sache:› mit sich bringen, ‹Person:› machen ‹Schwierigkeiten›; ~ **a scene** eine Szene machen; ~ **a sensation** für eine Sensation sorgen; Ⓑ (*design*) schaffen; kreieren ‹Mode, Stil›; Ⓒ (*invest with rank*) ernennen; ~ **sb. a peer** jmdn. zum Peer erheben *od.* ernennen. ❷ *v.i.* (*Brit. coll.: make a fuss*) Theater machen (*ugs.*)

**creation** /krɪ'eɪʃn/ *n.* Ⓐ *no pl.* (*act of creating*) Schaffung, *die;* (*of the world*) Erschaffung, *die;* Schöpfung, *die* (*geh.*); Ⓑ *no pl.* (*all created things*) Schöpfung, *die;* **the wonders of C**~: die Wunder der Schöpfung; **all [of]** ~, **the whole of** ~: alle Kreatur (*geh.*); alle Geschöpfe; Ⓒ *no pl.* (*investing with title, rank, etc.*) Ernennung, *die;* Ⓓ (*Fashion*) Kreation, *die*

**creationism** /krɪ'eɪʃənɪzm/ *n.* Kreatianismus, *der*

**creationist** /krɪ'eɪʃənɪst/ *n.* Anhänger des Kreatianismus

**creative** /krɪ'eɪtɪv/ *adj.*, **creatively** /krɪ'eɪtɪvlɪ/ *adv.* schöpferisch; kreativ

**creativeness** /krɪ'eɪtɪvnɪs/, **creativity** /krɪeɪ'tɪvɪtɪ/ *ns., no pl.* Kreativität, *die*

**creator** /krɪ'eɪtə(r)/ *n.* Schöpfer, *der*/Schöpferin, *die;* **the C**~: der Schöpfer

**creature** /'kri:tʃə(r)/ *n.* Ⓐ (*created being*) Geschöpf, *das;* Kreatur, *die* (*geh.*); **all living** ~**s** alle Lebewesen; alle Kreatur (*geh.*); Ⓑ (*human being*) Geschöpf, *das;* (*derog.*) Kerl, *der* (*abwertend*); (*woman*) **the** ~ **with the red hair** die mit den roten Haaren (*ugs.*); **lovely** ~: reizendes Geschöpf; **wicked/deserving** ~: böser/verdienstvoller Mensch; ~ **of habit** Gewohnheitsmensch, *der;* Gewohnheitstier, *das* (*scherzh.*); Ⓒ (*minion, lit.*

*or fig.*) Kreatur, *die* (*abwertend*); **~s of circumstance** Opfer der Umstände. ⇒ *also* **comfort** 1 E

**crèche** /kreʃ/ *n.* [Kinder]krippe, *die*

**credence** /'kri:dəns/ *n.* Ⓐ (*belief*) Glaube, *der;* **give** *or* **attach ~ to sth./sb.** einer Sache (*Dat.*) /jmdm. Glauben schenken; **lend ~ to sth.** etw. glaubwürdig machen *od.* erscheinen lassen; **gain ~:** an Glaubwürdigkeit gewinnen; **worthy of ~:** glaubwürdig; Ⓑ (*Eccl.*) **~ [table]** Kredenz, *die*

**credential** /krɪ'denʃl/ *n. usu. in pl.* (*testimonial*) Zeugnis, *das;* (*of ambassador*) Beglaubigungsschreiben, *das;* (*letter[s] of introduction*) Referenzen *Pl.;* **present one's ~s** seine Referenzen vorlegen

**credibility** /kredɪ'bɪlɪtɪ/ *n.* Glaubwürdigkeit, *die;* **~ gap** Mangel an Glaubwürdigkeit

**credible** /'kredɪbl/ *adj.* glaubwürdig ‹Mensch, Aussage›; glaubhaft ‹Aussage›

**credibly** /'kredɪblɪ/ *adv.* glaubwürdig; glaubhaft

**credit** /'kredɪt/ ❶ *n.* Ⓐ *no pl.* (*commendation*) Anerkennung, *die;* (*honour*) Ehre, *die;* (*good reputation*) Ansehen, *das* (**with** bei); **give sb. [the] ~ for sth.** jmdm. für etw. Anerkennung zollen (*geh.*); **get [the] ~ for sth.** Anerkennung für etw. finden; **take the ~ for sth.** die Anerkennung für etw. einstecken; **all ~ to her/them for not giving in** alle Achtung, dass sie nicht nachgegeben hat/haben; **[we must give] ~ where ~ is due** Ehre, wem Ehre gebührt; **it is [much** *or* **greatly/little] to sb.'s/sth.'s ~ that ...:** es macht jmdm./einer Sache [große/wenig] Ehre, dass ...; **it is to his ~ that ...:** es ehrt ihn, dass ...; **do ~ to sb./sth., do sb./sth. ~, be a ~ to sb./sth.** jmdm./einer Sache Ehre machen; **reflect [great/little] ~ on sb./sth.** jmdm./einer Sache [große/wenig] Ehre machen; Ⓑ *in pl.* (*in book*) Liste der Mitarbeiter und sonstigen Beteiligten; (*in film, play, etc.*) Liste der Mitwirkenden und sonstigen Beteiligten; **~s, ~ titles** (*at beginning of film*) Vorspann, *der;* (*at end*) Nachspann, *der;* Ⓒ *no pl., no art.* (*belief*) Glaube, *der;* **give ~ to sth.** einer Sache (*Dat.*) Glauben schenken; **gain ~:** an Glaubwürdigkeit gewinnen; Ⓓ *no pl.* (*Commerc.*) Kredit, *der;* **give [sb.] ~:** [jmdm.] Kredit geben; **deal on ~:** Kredit geben; **buy [sth.] on ~:** [etw.] auf Kredit kaufen; **six months' ~:** Kredit mit sechsmonatiger Laufzeit; **their ~ is excellent** sie sind unbedingt kreditwürdig; Ⓔ *no pl.* (*Finance, Bookk.*) Guthaben, *das;* **be in ~** ‹Konto:› im Haben sein; ‹Person:› mit seinem Konto im Haben sein; **get a ~ line** Kredit bekommen; **she has sth. to her ~:** ihr ist etw. gutzuschreiben; **letter of ~:** Kreditbrief, *der;* Akkreditiv, *das* (*Bankw.*); Ⓕ (*fig.*) **have sth. to one's ~:** etw. vorzuweisen haben; **we must give him ~ for being able to finish it by tomorrow** wir dürfen annehmen, dass er es bis morgen erledigen kann; **he's cleverer than I gave him ~ for** er ist klüger, als ich dachte; **I gave you ~ for being a kind man** ich habe dich für einen netten Menschen gehalten; **I gave her ~ for better taste** ich hatte ihr einen besseren Geschmack zugetraut; Ⓖ (*Amer. Educ.*) Schein, *der.*
❷ *v.t.* Ⓐ (*believe*) glauben; Ⓑ (*accredit*) **~ sb. with sth.** jmdm. etw. zutrauen; **~ sth. with sth.** einer Sache (*Dat.*) etw. zuschreiben; Ⓒ (*Finance, Bookk.*) gutschreiben; **~ £10 to sb./sb.'s account** jmdm./jmds. Konto 10 Pfund gutschreiben; **be ~ed with £10** 10 Pfund gutgeschrieben bekommen

**creditable** /'kredɪtəbl/ *adj.* anerkennenswert

**creditably** /'kredɪtəblɪ/ *adv.* achtbar

**credit: ~ account** *n.* Kreditkonto, *das;* **~ balance** *n.* Guthaben, *das;* **~ card** *n.* ▶ 1328 Kreditkarte, *die;* **~ facilities** *n. pl.* [Kredit]fazilität, *die* (*fachspr.*); **~ limit** *n.* Kreditlinie, *die;* **~ note** *n.* Gutschein, *der*

**creditor** /'kredɪtə(r)/ *n.* Ⓐ (*one to whom debt is owing*) Gläubiger, *der*/Gläubigerin, *die;* Ⓑ (*one who gives credit for money or goods*) Kreditgeber, *der*/-geberin, *die*

**credit: ~ rating** *n.* [Einschätzung der] Kreditwürdigkeit; **have a good/bad ~ rating** als kreditwürdig/kreditunwürdig eingeschätzt werden; **~ sale** *n.* Kreditkauf, *der;* **~ side** *n.* (*Finance*) Habenseite, *die;* (*fig.*) **on the ~ side she has experience** für sie spricht ihre Erfahrung; **~ squeeze** *n.* Kreditrestriktion, *die;* **~ 'transfer** *n.* (*Finance*) Banküberweisung, *die;* **~worthiness** *n.* Kreditwürdigkeit, *die;* **~ worthy** *adj.* kreditwürdig

**credo** /'kri:dəʊ, 'kreɪdəʊ/ *n., pl.* **~s** Glaubensbekenntnis, *das;* Kredo, *das*

**credulity** /krɪ'dju:lɪtɪ/ *n., no pl.* Leichtgläubigkeit, *die*

**credulous** /'kredjʊləs/ *adj.* leichtgläubig; naiv ‹Erstaunen, Verhalten›

**credulously** /'kredjʊləslɪ/ *adv.* leichtgläubig; **believe sth. too ~:** etw. allzu arglos glauben

**creed** /kri:d/ *n.* (*lit. or fig.*) Glaubensbekenntnis, *das*

**creek** /kri:k/ *n.* Ⓐ (*Brit.*) (*inlet on sea coast*) [kleine] Bucht; (*small harbour*) [kleiner] Hafen; Ⓑ (*short arm of river*) [kurzer] Flussarm; Ⓒ (*Amer.: tributary of river*) Nebenfluss, *der;* (*Austral., NZ: stream*) Bach, *der;* Ⓓ **be up the ~** (*coll.: be in difficulties or trouble*) in der Klemme *od.* Tinte sitzen (*ugs.*); (*be wrong*) ‹Antwort usw.:› völlig falsch sein; ‹Person:› auf dem Holzweg sein

**creel** /kri:l/ *n.* Fischkorb, *der*

**creep** /kri:p/ ❶ *v.i.,* **crept** /krept/ Ⓐ kriechen; (*move timidly, slowly, stealthily*) schleichen; **~ and crawl** (*fig.*) kriechen; **~ing Jesus** (*sl.*) Scheinheilige, *der/die;* (*fig.: develop gradually*) **~ing inflation/sickness** schleichende Inflation/Krankheit; (*insinuate oneself/itself unobserved*) **~ into sth.** sich in etw. (*Akk.*) einschleichen; Ⓑ **make sb.'s flesh ~:** jmdm. eine Gänsehaut über den Rücken jagen; **the thought made my flesh ~:** bei dem Gedanken lief mir eine Gänsehaut über den Rücken.
❷ *n.* Ⓐ *in pl.* (*coll.*) **give sb. the ~s** jmdm. nicht [ganz] geheuer sein; Ⓑ (*coll.: person*) Fiesling, *der* (*salopp abwertend*); Ⓒ (*Metallurgy*) Kriechen, *das*

**~ 'in** *v.i.* [sich] hinein-/hereinschleichen; (*fig.*) ‹Irrtum, Enttäuschung usw.:› sich einschleichen

**~ 'on** *v.i.* **time is ~ing on** die Zeit verrinnt [unaufhaltsam]

**~ 'up** *v.i.* (*approach*) sich anschleichen; **~ up on sb.** sich an jmdn. anschleichen; (*fig.*) für jmdn. langsam näher rücken

**creeper** /'kri:pə(r)/ *n.* Ⓐ (*Bot.*) (*growing along ground*) Kriechpflanze, *die;* (*growing up wall etc.*) Kletterpflanze, *die;* Rankengewächs, *das;* Ⓑ (*Ornith.*) [Wald]baumläufer, *der;* Ⓒ (*coll.: soft-soled shoe*) *Schuh mit dicker, weicher Sohle;* Leisetreter, *der* (*scherzh.*)

**creepy** /'kri:pɪ/ *adj.* unheimlich; gruselig, schaurig ‹Geschichte, Film›

**creepy-crawly** /kri:pɪ 'krɔ:lɪ/ (*coll./child lang.*) ❶ *n.* **she's got a horror of creepy-crawlies** sie hat eine Heidenangst vor allem, was krabbelt; **there's a ~ in the bathtub** da krabbelt was in der Badewanne (*ugs.*). ❷ *adj.* krabbelnd ‹Insekt›

**cremate** /krɪ'meɪt/ *v.t.* einäschern; kremieren (*schweiz.*)

**cremation** /krɪ'meɪʃn/ *n.* Einäscherung, *die;* Kremation, *die*

**crematorium** /kremə'tɔ:rɪəm/ *n., pl.* **crematoria** /kremə'tɔ:rɪə/ *or* **~s** Krematorium, *das*

**crematory** /'kremətərɪ/ *n.* (*Amer.*) Krematorium, *das*

**crème: ~ de la ~** /kreɪm dlɑ:'kreɪm/ *n.* Crème de la crème, *die* (*geh.*); **~ de menthe** /kreɪm də 'mɑ̃t/ *n.* Pfefferminzlikör, *der*

**crenellated** /'krenəleɪtɪd/ *adj.* kreneliert (*veralt.*); mit Zinnen versehen

**Creole** /'kri:əʊl/ ▶ 1275 ❶ *n.* Ⓐ (*person*) Kreole, *der*/Kreolin, *die;* (*of mixed European and Black African descent*) Mulatte, *der*/Mulattin, *die;* Ⓑ (*language*) Kreolisch, *das.* ❷ *adj.* kreolisch

**creosote** /'kri:əsəʊt/ ❶ *n.* Kreosot, *das.* ❷ *v.t.* mit Kreosot behandeln

**crêpe** /kreɪp/ *n.* Ⓐ Krepp, *der;* Ⓑ (**~ rubber**) Kreppgummi, *der;* **~ soles** Kreppsohlen *Pl.;* Ⓒ (*pancake*) dünner Eierkuchen

**crêpe: ~ de Chine** /kreɪp də 'ʃi:n/ *n.* Crêpe de Chine, *der;* **~ 'paper** *n.* Krepppapier, *das;* **~ 'rubber** *n.* Kreppgummi, *der;* **~ Suzette** /kreɪp su:'zet/ *n.* (*Cookery*) Crêpe Suzette, *die*

**crept** ⇒ **creep** 1

**crescendo** /krɪ'ʃendəʊ/ *n., pl.* **~s** (*Mus.*) Crescendo, *das;* (*fig.*) Zunahme, *die;* **a ~ of cheers** immer lauter werdende Jubelrufe; **reach a ~** (*fig. coll.*) einen Höhepunkt erreichen

**crescent** /'kresənt/ ❶ *n.* Ⓐ Mondsichel, *die;* (*as emblem*) Halbmond, *der;* **~-shaped** halbmondförmig; Ⓑ (*Brit.: street*) [kleinere] halbkreisförmige Straße; Ⓒ (*~-shaped object*) Bogen, *der.* ❷ *adj.* halbmondförmig; **the ~ moon** die Mondsichel

**cress** /kres/ *n.* Kresse, *die;* **garden ~:** Gartenkresse, *die;* ⇒ *also* **watercress**

**crest** /krest/ *n.* Ⓐ (*on bird's or animal's head*) Kamm, *der;* (*neck of horse*) Genick, *das;* (*plume of feathers*) Federschopf, *der;* Ⓑ (*top of mountain or wave*) Kamm, *der;* (*top of roof*) Dachfirst, *der;* **[be/ride] on the ~ of a** *or* **the wave** (*fig.*) ganz oben [sein/schwimmen]; Ⓒ (*Her.*) Helmzier, *die;* (*emblem*) Emblem, *das*

**crested** /'krestɪd/ *adj.* Ⓐ ‹Vogel, Tier› mit einem Kamm; **~ tit/lark** Haubenmeise/-lerche, *die;* Ⓑ ‹Siegel, Briefpapier usw.› mit einem Emblem versehen

**'crestfallen** *adj.* (*fig.*) niedergeschlagen

**Cretaceous** /krɪ'teɪʃəs/ ❶ *adj.* (*Geol.*) Kreide-; kretazeisch (*fachspr.*); **the ~ period** die Kreidezeit. ❷ *n.* (*Geol.*) Kreide, *die*

**Cretan** /'kri:tn/ ❶ *adj.* kretisch. ❷ *n.* Kreter, *der*/Kreterin, *die*

**Crete** /kri:t/ *pr. n.* Kreta (*das*)

**cretin** /'kretɪn/ *n.* Ⓐ (*Med.*) Kretin, *der;* Ⓑ (*coll.: fool*) Trottel, *der* (*ugs. abwertend*)

**cretinous** /'kretɪnəs/ *adj.* Ⓐ (*Med.*) kretinoid; Ⓑ (*coll.: stupid*) schwachsinnig (*abwertend*)

**cretonne** /krɪ'tɒn, 'kretɒn/ *n.* (*Textiles*) Cretonne, *die od. der*

**Creutzfeldt-Jakob disease** /'krɔɪtsfelt 'jækɒb/ *n.* ▶ 1232 (*Med.*) Creutzfeldt-Jakob-Krankheit, *die*

**crevasse** /krɪ'væs/ *n.* Gletscherspalte, *die*

**crevice** /'krevɪs/ *n.* Spalt, *der;* (*of skin*) Riss, *der*

**crew** /kru:/ ❶ *n.* Ⓐ (*of ship, aircraft, etc.*) Besatzung, *die;* Crew, *die;* (*excluding officers*) Mannschaft, *die;* Crew, *die;* (*of train*) Personal, *das;* (*Sport*) Mannschaft, *die;* Crew, *die;* Ⓑ (*associated body*) Gruppe, *die;* (*gang of workers*) Kolonne, *die;* (*often derog.: set*) Haufen, *der;* **a motley ~:** ein bunt zusammengewürfelter Haufen. ❷ *v.i.* die Mannschaft/Mitglied der Mannschaft sein; **he ~s on my boat** er gehört zu meiner Mannschaft. ❸ *v.t.* **~ a boat** Mitglied der Mannschaft eines Bootes sein

**crew: ~ cut** *n.* Bürstenschnitt, *der;* **~-man** /'kru:mən/ *n., pl.* **~-men** /'kru:mən/ Besatzungsmitglied, *das;* **~ neck** *n.* enger, runder Halsausschnitt; **a ~-neck pullover** ein Pullover mit engem, rundem Halsausschnitt

**crib** /krɪb/ ❶ *n.* Ⓐ (*cot*) Gitterbett, *das;* Ⓑ (*model of manger scene; manger*) Krippe, *die;* Ⓒ (*coll.*) (*translation*) Klatsche, *die* (*Schülerspr.*); (*plagiarism*) **that's a ~:** das ist abgekupfert (*salopp*). ❷ *v.t.,* **-bb-** (*coll.*) (*plagiarize*) abkupfern (*salopp*)

**cribbage** /'krɪbɪdʒ/ *n.* (*Cards*) Cribbage, *das*

**'crib death** (*Amer.*) ⇒ **cot death**

**crick** /krɪk/ ❶ *n.* **a ~ [in one's neck/back]** ein steifer Hals/Rücken. ❷ *v.t.* **~ one's neck/back** einen steifen Hals/Rücken bekommen

**cricket**[1] /'krɪkɪt/ *n.* (*Sport*) Kricket, *das;* **it's/that's not ~** (*Brit. dated coll.*) das ist nicht die feine Art (*ugs.*)

**cricket**[2] *n.* (*Zool.*) Grille, *die;* **as lively as a ~:** putzmunter (*ugs.*)

**cricket: ~ bag** *n. Tasche für das Schlagholz usw.;* **~ ball** *n.* Kricketball, *der;* **~ bat** Schlagholz, *das*

**cricketer** /'krɪkɪtə(r)/ *n.* Kricketspieler, *der*/-spielerin, *die*

**cricket: ~ match** *n.* Kricketspiel, *das;* **~ pitch** *n.* Kricketfeld, *das* (*zwischen den Toren*)

**cri de cœur** /kri: də 'kɜ(r)/ *n., pl.* **cris de cœur** /kri: də 'kɜ(r)/ (*complaint*) Stoßseufzer, *der;* (*appeal*) [verzweifelter] Hilferuf

**crier** /'kraɪə(r)/ *n.* (*in lawcourt*) Gerichtsdiener, *der* (*veralt.*); (*in a town*) Ausrufer, *der*

**crikey** /'kraɪkɪ/ *int.* (*coll.*) Jesses (*ugs.*)

**crime** /kraɪm/ *n.* **A** Verbrechen, *das;* **B** *collect., no pl.* **a wave of ~:** eine Welle von Straftaten; **juvenile ~ is on the increase** die Jugendkriminalität nimmt zu; **lead a life of ~:** ein Krimineller sein; **~ doesn't pay** Verbrechen lohnen sich nicht; **C** (*fig. coll.: shameful action*) Sünde, *die*

**Crimea** /kraɪ'mi:ə/ *pr. n.* Krim, *die*

**Crimean** /kraɪ'mi:ən/ *adj.* **the ~ War** der Krimkrieg

**crime: ~ prevention** *n.* Verbrechensverhütung, *die;* **C~ Prevention Officer** *Polizeibeamter, dessen/-beamtin, deren Aufgabe aktive, vorbeugende Verbrechensbekämpfung ist;* **~ rate** *n.* Kriminalitätsrate, *die;* **~-sheet** *n.* (*Mil.*) Strafregister, *das;* **~ story** *n.* Kriminalgeschichte, *die;* **~ wave** *n.* Welle von Straftaten; **~-writer** *n.* Kriminalschriftsteller, *der*/-schriftstellerin, *die*

**criminal** /'krɪmɪnl/ **1** *adj.* **A** (*illegal*) kriminell; strafbar; (*concerned with criminals and crime*) Straf-; **~ act** *or* **deed/offence** Straftat, *die;* **take ~ proceedings against sb.** strafrechtlich gegen jmdn. vorgehen; **~ judge** Strafrichter, *der;* **B** (*guilty of crime*) kriminell; straffällig; **~ gang** Verbrecherbande, *die;* **C** (*tending to be guilty of crime*) kriminell; **D** (*fig. coll.*) kriminell (*ugs.*); **it's ~ to do that** es ist eine Schande, das zu tun; **it's a ~ shame** es ist einfach ungeheuerlich; **it's a ~ waste** es ist eine sträfliche Verschwendung. **2** *n.* Kriminelle, *der/die*

**criminal: ~ charge** *n.* Anklage, *die;* **face ~ charges [for sth.]** sich [wegen etw.] vor Gericht zu verantworten haben; **there are ~ charges against him** er steht unter Anklage; **~ 'code** *n.* Strafgesetzbuch, *das;* **~ 'court** *n.* Strafgericht, *das;* Kriminalgericht, *das* (*veralt.*); **C~ Investi'gation Department** *n.* (*Brit.*) Kriminalpolizei, *die*

**criminality** /krɪmɪ'nælɪtɪ/ *n.* Kriminalität, *die*

**criminal: ~ 'law** *n.* Strafrecht, *das;* **~ 'lawyer** *n.* Anwalt/Anwältin für Strafsachen; **~ 'libel** *n.* [schriftliche] Verleumdung

**criminally** /'krɪmɪnəlɪ/ *adv.* kriminell; (*according to criminal law*) strafrechtlich

**criminal 'record** *n.* Strafregister, *das;* **have a ~:** vorbestraft sein

**criminologist** /krɪmɪ'nɒlədʒɪst/ *n.* ▶ 1261 Kriminologe, *der*/Kriminologin, *die*

**criminology** /krɪmɪ'nɒlədʒɪ/ *n.* Kriminologie, *die*

**crimp** /krɪmp/ *v.t.* kräuseln; **~ed hair** onduliertes Haar

**Crimplene** ® /'krɪmpli:n/ *n.* Crimplene, *das* (Wz); *knitterfreier Stoff*

**crimson** /'krɪmzn/ **1** *adj.* purpurrot; **turn ~** ‹Himmel:› sich blutrot färben; (*with anger*) ‹Mensch:› rot anlaufen; (*blush*) puterrot werden. **2** *n.* Purpurrot, *das.* **3** *v.i.* purpurrot werden

**cringe** /krɪndʒ/ *v.i.* **A** (*cower*) zusammenzucken; ‹Hund:› sich ducken, kuschen; **~ at sth.** bei etw. zusammenzucken; **~ away** *or* **back [from sb./sth.]** [vor jmdm./etw.] zurückschrecken; **it makes me ~:** es lässt mich zusammenzucken; (*in disgust*) da wird mir schlecht; **B** (*behave obsequiously*) kriechen (*abwertend*); kuschen; **~ before sb.** vor jmdm. kriechen *od.* kuschen; **go cringing to sb.** zu jmdm. gekrochen kommen

**cringing** /'krɪndʒɪŋ/ *adj.* kriecherisch (*abwertend*); **a ~ person** ein Kriecher (*abwertend*)

**crinkle** /krɪŋkl/ **1** *n.* Knick, *der;* (*in fabric*) Knitterfalte, *die;* (*in hair*) Kräusel, *die;* (*in skin*) Fältchen, *das.* **2** *v.t.* knicken; zerknittern ‹Stoff, Papier›; kräuseln ‹Haar›. **3** *v.i.* ‹Stoff, Papier:› knittern; ‹Haar:› sich kräuseln; ‹Haut:› Fältchen bekommen; ‹Papierrand:› sich wellen

**crinkly** /'krɪŋklɪ/ *adj.* zerknittert ‹Stoff, Papier›; gekräuselt ‹Haar›; faltig ‹Haut›

**crinoline** /'krɪnəlɪn, 'krɪnəli:n/ *n.* (*Hist.*) Krinoline, *die*

**cripes** /kraɪps/ *int.* (*dated coll.*) Jesses (*ugs.*)

**cripple** /krɪpl/ **1** *n.* (*lit. or fig.*) Krüppel, *der.* **2** *v.t.* zum Krüppel machen; (*fig.*) lähmen

**crippled** /krɪpld/ *adj.* verkrüppelt ‹Arm, Baum, Bettler›; **be ~ with rheumatism** durch Rheuma gelähmt sein; **industry was ~ by the strikes** die Streiks haben die ganze Industrie lahmgelegt; **small firms, ~ by inflation** kleine, durch [die] Inflation geschwächte Firmen; **a ~ ship/plane** ein schwer beschädigtes Schiff/Flugzeug

**crippling** /'krɪplɪŋ/ *adj.* zur Verkrüppelung führend ‹Krankheit, Verletzung›; (*fig.*) erdrückend ‹Preise, Inflationsrate, Steuern, Mieten›; lähmend ‹Streik, Schmerzen›; **deal sb. a ~ blow** (*fig.*) jmdm. einen vernichtenden Schlag versetzen

**crisis** /'kraɪsɪs/ *n., pl.* **crises** /'kraɪsi:z/ Krise, *die;* **reach ~ point** einen kritischen Punkt erreichen; **a time of ~:** eine kritische Zeit; **at times of ~:** in Krisenzeiten; **suffer a ~:** eine Krise durchmachen

**crisis 'management** *n.* Krisenmanagement, *das*

**crisp** /krɪsp/ **1** *adj.* knusprig ‹Brot, Keks, Kruste, Speck›; knackig ‹Apfel, Gemüse›; steif ‹Papier›; trocken ‹Herbstblätter, Zweige›; frisch [gebügelt/gestärkt] ‹Wäsche›; [druck]frisch ‹Banknote›; verharscht ‹Schnee›; (*clearly defined*) scharf ‹Züge, Umrisse, Kanten›; (*bracing*) frisch ‹Brise, Seeluft›; (*brisk*) knapp [und klar] ‹Stil›; frisch [und flott (*ugs.*)] ‹Auftreten, Erscheinung›; **~ intonation/speech** klare Intonation/Sprache. **2** *n.* **A** *usu. in pl.* (*Brit.: potato ~*) [Kartoffel]chip, *der;* **B** (*sth. overcooked*) **be burned to a ~:** verbrannt sein. **3** *v.t.* (*make ~*) **~ [up]** aufbacken ‹Brot›; knusprig backen ‹Speck›; knackig machen ‹Gemüse›

**'crispbread** *n.* Knäckebrot, *das*

**crisper** /'krɪspə(r)/ *n.* Gemüsefach, *das*

**crisply** /'krɪsplɪ/ *adv.* knusprig ‹gebacken›; klar ‹sprechen›; frisch ‹gebügelt, gestärkt›

**crispness** /'krɪspnɪs/ *n., no pl.* (*of bread, biscuit, bacon*) Knusprigkeit, *die;* (*of apple, vegetable*) Knackigkeit, *die;* (*of style*) Knappheit [und Klarheit], *die;* (*of manner*) Frische [und Knappheit], *die*

**crispy** /'krɪspɪ/ *adj.* knusprig ‹Brot, Keks, Speck›; knackig ‹Apfel, Gemüse›

**crispy 'noodles** *n. pl.* gebratene Nudeln

**criss-cross** /'krɪskrɒs/ **1** *n.* Gewirr, *das.* **2** *adj.* **~ pattern** Muster aus gekreuzten Linien. **3** *adv.* kreuz und quer. **4** *v.t.* (*intersect repeatedly*) wiederholt schneiden. **5** *v.i.* (*move crosswise*) kreuz und quer laufen/fahren/fliegen *usw.;* (*intersect repeatedly*) kreuz und quer verlaufen

**criterion** /kraɪ'tɪərɪən/ *n., pl.* **criteria** /kraɪ'tɪərɪə/ Kriterium, *das;* **by what ~ will the issue be judged?** nach welchen Kriterien wird man die Angelegenheit beurteilen?

**critic** /'krɪtɪk/ *n.* ▶ 1261 Kritiker, *der*/Kritikerin, *die;* **literary ~:** Literaturkritiker, *der*/-kritikerin, *die*

**critical** /'krɪtɪkl/ *adj.* **A** kritisch; **be ~ of sb./sth.** jmdn./etw. kritisieren; **cast a ~ eye over sth.** etw. mit kritischen Augen betrachten; **the play received ~ acclaim** das Stück fand die Anerkennung der Kritik; **~ skills/ability** Kritikfähigkeit, *die;* **~ edition** kritische Ausgabe; **B** (*involving risk, crucial*) kritisch ‹Zustand, Punkt, Phase›; entscheidend ‹Faktor, Test›; gefährlich ‹Operation›

**critically** /'krɪtɪkəlɪ/ *adv.* kritisch; **be ~ important** von entscheidender Bedeutung sein; **be ~ ill** ernstlich krank sein

**critical: ~ 'mass** *n.* (*Phys.*) kritische Masse; **~ 'path** *n.* (*Managem.*) kritischer Pfad *od.* Weg

**criticise** ⇨ **criticize**

**criticism** /'krɪtɪsɪzm/ *n.* Kritik, *die* (**of** an + *Dat.*); **come in for a lot of ~:** heftig kritisiert werden; **be open to ~:** (*receptive*) für Kritik offen sein; (*liable to be criticized*) der Kritik ausgesetzt sein; **literary ~:** Literaturkritik, *die*

**criticize** /'krɪtɪsaɪz/ *v.t.* kritisieren (**for** wegen); (*review*) besprechen; rezensieren; **~ sb. for sth.** jmdn. wegen etw. kritisieren

**critique** /krɪ'ti:k/ *n.* Kritik, *die*

**critter** /'krɪtə(r)/ *n.* (*coll. joc.*) Viech, *das* (*ugs.*); (*derog.: person*) Kerl, *der* (*ugs. abwertend*); (*female*) Person, *die* (*abwertend*)

**croak** /krəʊk/ **1** *n.* (*of frog*) Quaken, *das;* (*of raven, person*) Krächzen, *das.* **2** *v.i.* **A** ‹Frosch:› quaken; ‹Rabe, Person:› krächzen; **B** (*sl.: die*) abkratzen (*salopp*). **3** *v.t.* krächzen

**croaky** /'krəʊkɪ/ *adj.* krächzend

**Croat** /'krəʊæt/ *n.* **A** (*person*) Kroate, *der*/Kroatin, *die;* **B** (*language*) Kroatisch, *das*

**Croatia** /krəʊ'eɪʃə/ *pr. n.* Kroatien (*das*)

**Croatian** /krəʊ'eɪʃən/ ▶ 1340 **1** *adj.* kroatisch; **sb. is ~:** jmd. ist Kroate/Kroatin. **2** *n.* ⇨ **Croat**

**croc** /krɒk/ *n.* (*coll.: crocodile*) Krokodil, *das*

**crochet** /'krəʊʃeɪ, 'krəʊʃɪ/ **1** *n.* Häkelarbeit, *die;* **~ hook** Häkelhaken, *der.* **2** *v.t., p. t. and p. p.* **~ed** /'krəʊʃeɪd, 'krəʊʃɪd/ häkeln

**crocheting** /'krəʊʃeɪɪŋ, 'krəʊʃɪɪŋ/ *n.* Häkeln, *das;* (*product*) Häkelarbeit, *die*

**crock**[1] /krɒk/ *n.* **A** (*pot*) Topf, *der* (*aus Ton*); (*jar*) Krug, *der* (*aus Ton*); ⇨ *also* **gold** 1 B; **B** (*broken piece of earthenware*) [Ton]scherbe, *die*

**crock**[2] (*coll.*) **1** *n.* (*person*) Wrack, *das* (*fig.*); (*vehicle*) [Klapper]kiste, *die* (*ugs.*). **2** *v.i.* **~ up** zusammenklappen. **3** *v.t.* **~ [up]** den Rest geben (+ *Dat.*) (*ugs.*)

**crockery** /'krɒkərɪ/ *n.* Geschirr, *das*

**crocodile** /'krɒkədaɪl/ *n.* **A** Krokodil, *das;* (*skin*) Krokodilleder, *das;* Kroko, *das;* **B** (*Brit. coll.: line of schoolchildren*) Schulkinder in Zweierreihen; **walk in a ~:** zwei und zwei [hintereinander] gehen

**crocodile: ~ clip** *n.* (*Electr.*) Krokodilklemme, *die;* **~ tears** *n. pl.* Krokodilstränen *Pl.* (*ugs.*)

**crocus** /'krəʊkəs/ *n.* Krokus, *der*

**Croesus** /'kri:səs/ *n.* Krösus, *der;* **be as rich as ~:** ein [wahrer] Krösus sein

**croft** /krɒft/ *n.* (*Brit.*) **A** [kleines] Stück Acker-/Weideland; **B** (*smallholding*) [kleines] Pachtgut

**crofter** /'krɒftə(r)/ *n.* (*Brit.*) Pächter, *der*/Pächterin, *die*

**crofting** /'krɒftɪŋ/ *n., no pl., no art.* (*Brit.*) *Bewirtschaftung kleiner Pachtgüter*

**croissant** /'krwɑ:sɑ̃/ *n.* Hörnchen, *das*

**cromlech** /'krɒmlek/ *n.* **A** ⇨ **dolmen;** **B** (*stone circle*) Kromlech, *der*

**crone** /krəʊn/ *n.* **a[n old] ~:** ein altes Weib

**crony** /'krəʊnɪ/ *n.* Kumpel, *der;* (*female*) Freundin, (*die;*) (*drinking companion*) Kumpan, *der;* **they were old cronies** sie waren gute, alte Freunde

**crook** /krʊk/ **1** *n.* **A** (*coll.: rogue*) Gauner, *der;* **B** (*staff*) Hirtenstab, *der;* (*of bishop*) [Krumm]stab, *der;* **C** (*hook*) Haken, *der;* **D** (*of arm*) [Arm]beuge, *die;* **E** (*curve in river, road, etc.*) Biegung, *die.* **2** *adj.* (*Austral. and NZ coll.*) mies (*ugs.*); (*ill*) krank; (*bad-tempered*) sauer (*ugs.*); **go ~:** sauer werden (**at, on** + *Akk.*). **3** *v.t.* biegen; **~ one's finger** seinen Finger krümmen; **she has only to ~ her little finger** (*fig.*) sie braucht nur mit dem kleinen Finger zu winken

**crooked** **1** /krʊkt/ *p.t. and p.p. of* **crook** 3. **2** *adj.* **A** /'krʊkɪd/ krumm; schief ‹Lächeln›; (*fig.: dishonest*) betrügerisch; **this coin is ~:** diese Münze ist verbogen; **the picture on the wall is ~:** das Bild an der Wand hängt schief; **you've got your hat on ~:** dein Hut sitzt schief; **a ~ person** (*fig.*) ein Gauner; **~ dealings** krumme Geschäfte; **B** /krʊkt/ (*having a transverse handle*) **a ~ stick** ein Krückstock

**crookedly** /'krʊkɪdlɪ/ *adv.* schief; **a tree that has grown ~:** ein krumm gewachsener Baum; (*fig.: dishonestly*) **deal ~:** krumme Geschäfte machen; **~ acquired** unrechtmäßig erworben

C

**crookedness** /ˈkrʊkɪdnɪs/ *n., no pl.* Verkrümmung, *die; (fig.: dishonesty)* Unehrlichkeit, *die*

**croon** /kru:n/ ❶ *v.t. & i.* [leise] singen; ‹Popsänger:› schmachtend singen; schnulzen *(ugs. abwertend).* ❷ *n.* [leises] Singen

**crooner** /ˈkru:nə(r)/ *n. Sänger mit schmachtender Stimme;* Schnulzensänger, *der (ugs. abwertend)*

**crop** /krɒp/ ❶ *n.* **A** *(Agric.)* [Feld]frucht, *die; (season's total yield)* Ernte, *die; (fig.)* [An]zahl, *die;* **cereal ~:** Getreide, *das;* **get the ~s in** die Ernte einbringen; **arable ~s** Feldfrüchte *Pl.;* **~ of apples** Apfelernte, *die;* **B** *(of bird)* Kropf, *der;* **C** *(of whip)* [Peitschen]stiel, *der;* **[hunting] ~:** Jagdpeitsche, *die;* **D** *(of hair)* kurzer Haarschnitt; *(style)* Kurzhaarfrisur, *die.* ❷ *v.t.,* **-pp-** **A** *(cut off)* abschneiden; *(cut short)* stutzen ‹Bart, Haare, Hecken, Flügel›; kupieren ‹Ohren, Schwanz (bei Hunden od. Pferden)›; abschneiden ‹Kante›; ‹Tier:› abweiden ‹Gras›; **have one's hair ~ped** sich *(Dat.)* das Haar kurz schneiden lassen; **B** *(reap)* ernten. ❸ *v.i.,* **-pp-** tragen

**~ 'out** ⇒ **~ up b**

**~ 'up** *v.i.* **A** *(occur)* auftauchen; *(be mentioned)* erwähnt werden; **B** *(Geol.)* ausbeißen

**crop: ~-dusting** *n. (Agric.)* Schädlingsbekämpfung aus der Luft; **~-eared** *adj.* ‹Tier› mit gestutzten *od.* kupierten Ohren

**cropper** /ˈkrɒpə(r)/ *n. (coll.: heavy fall)* [schwerer] Sturz; **come a ~:** einen Sturz bauen *(ugs.); (fig.)* auf die Nase fallen *(ugs.)*

**crop: ~ rotation** *n. (Agric.)* Fruchtfolge, *die;* **~-spraying** *n. (Agric.)* Schädlingsbekämpfung *(mit Sprühmitteln);* **~ top** *n.* bauch- *od.* nabelfreies Top

**croquet** /ˈkrəʊkeɪ, ˈkrəʊkɪ/ *n.* Krocket[spiel], *das*

**croquette** /krəˈket/ *n. (Cookery)* Krokette, *die*

**crosier** /ˈkrəʊzɪə(r)/ *n.* Krummstab, *der*

**cross** /krɒs/ ❶ *n.* **A** Kreuz, *das; (monument)* [Gedenk]kreuz, *das; (sign)* Kreuzzeichen, *das;* **the C~:** das Kreuz [Christi]; **make the sign of the C~:** das Kreuzzeichen machen; ein Kreuz schlagen; **B** *(~-shaped thing or mark)* Kreuz[zeichen], *das;* **mark with a ~:** ankreuzen; **C** *(mixture, compromise)* Mittelding, *das* (**between** zwischen + *Dat.*); Mischung, *die* (**between** aus); **D** *(trial, affliction, cause of trouble)* Kreuz, *das;* Leid, *das;* **take [up] one's ~:** sein Kreuz auf sich nehmen; **we all have our [little] ~es to bear** wir haben alle unser Kreuz zu tragen; **E** *(intermixture of breeds)* Kreuzung, *die;* **F** *(Astron.)* **[Southern] C~:** Kreuz des Südens; Südliches Kreuz; **G** *(decoration)* Kreuz, *das;* **Grand C~:** Großkreuz, *das;* **H** *(Footb.)* Querpass, *der; (Boxing)* Cross, *der;* **I on the ~:** quer; **J** *(Dressmaking)* **cut on the ~:** schräg [zum Fadenlauf] zugeschnitten.
❷ *v.t.* **A** *(place crosswise)* [über]kreuzen; **~ one's arms/legs** die Arme verschränken/die Beine übereinander schlagen; **~ one's fingers** *or* **keep one's fingers ~ed [for sb.]** *(fig.)* [jmdm.] die *od.* den Daumen drücken/halten; **~ swords [with sb.]** *(fig.)* [mit jmdm.] die Schwerter kreuzen *od.* sich streiten (**on** über + *Akk.*); **I got a ~ed line** *(Teleph.)* es war jemand in der Leitung; **you've got your** *or* **the lines** *or* **wires ~ed** *(fig. coll.)* du hast da etwas falsch verstanden; **~ a fortune teller's hand** *or* **palm with silver** einer Wahrsagerin Geld in die Hand drücken; **B** *(go across)* kreuzen; überqueren ‹Straße, Gewässer, Gebirge›; durchqueren ‹Land, Wüste, Zimmer›; **~ the picket line** die Streikpostenkette durchbrechen; **~ the road** über die Straße gehen; **we can ~** *abs.* die Straße ist frei; wir können gehen/fahren; '**~ now'** „Gehen"; **the bridge ~es the river** die Brücke führt über den Fluss; **the lines ~ each other** die Linien schneiden sich; **a train ~ed the river** ein Zug fuhr über den Fluss; **a plane ~es the desert** ein Flugzeug fliegt über *od.* überfliegt die Wüste; **~ sb.'s mind** *(fig.)* jmdm. einfallen; **it seems never to have ~ed his mind to do it** es scheint ihm nie in den Sinn gekommen zu sein *od.* es scheint ihm nie der Gedanke gekommen zu sein, es zu tun; **~ sb.'s path** *(fig.)* jmdm. über den Weg laufen *(ugs.);* jmdm. begegnen; **C** *(Brit.)* **~ a cheque** einen Scheck zur Verrechnung ausstellen; **a ~ed cheque** ein Verrechnungsscheck; **D** *(make sign of ~ on)* **~ oneself** sich bekreuzigen; **~ my heart** Ehrenwort!; **E** *(thwart)* durchkreuzen ‹Plan›; zerstören ‹Hoffnung›; vereiteln ‹Wunsch, Hoffnung›; **be ~ed in love** Unglück in der Liebe haben; **he ~es me in everything I do** er kommt mir bei allem in die Quere; **F** *(cause to interbreed)* kreuzen; *(~-fertilize)* kreuzbefruchten. ⇒ *also* **bridge**[1] 1 A; **T** A.
❸ *v.i. (meet and pass)* aneinander vorbeigehen; **~ [in the post]** ‹Briefe:› sich kreuzen; **our paths have ~ed several times** *(fig.)* unsere Wege haben sich öfters gekreuzt.
❹ *adj.* **A** *(transverse)* Quer-; **~ traffic** kreuzender Verkehr; **B** *(peevish)* verärgert; ärgerlich ‹Worte›; **sb. will be ~:** jmd. wird ärgerlich *od.* böse werden; **be ~ with sb.** böse auf jmdn. *od.* mit jmdm. sein; **as ~ as two sticks** *(coll.)* unleidlich; **C** *(Cricket)* **~ bat** *schräg gehaltenes Schlagholz*

**~ 'off** *v.t.* streichen; **~ a name off a list** einen Namen von einer Liste streichen

**~ 'out** *v.t.* ausstreichen

**~ 'over** *v.t.* überqueren; *abs.* hinübergehen

**cross-** *in comb.* **A** ⇒ **cross** 1 A Kreuz-; **B** ⇒ **cross** 4 Quer-; **C** = **across** quer durch

**cross: ~bar** *n.* **A** [Fahrrad]stange, *die;* **B** *(Footb.)* Querlatte, *die;* **~-beam** *n.* Querbalken, *der;* **~-bench** *n. (Brit. Parl.) quergestellte Bank, auf der die „cross-benchers" sitzen;* **~-bencher** *n.* Abgeordnete, *der/die weder der Regierungspartei noch der Opposition angehört;* **~bill** *n. (Ornith.)* Kreuzschnabel, *der;* **~bones** *n. pl.* gekreuzte Knochen *Pl. (unter Totenkopf);* **~bow** *n.* Armbrust, *die;* **~-bred** *adj.* gekreuzt; **~-breed** ❶ *n.* Hybride, *die; (animal)* Bastard, *der;* ❷ *v.t.* kreuzen; **~-Channel** *adj.* **~-Channel traffic/ferry** Verkehr/Fähre über den Kanal; **~-check** ❶ *n.* Gegenprobe, *die;* ❷ *v.t.* [nochmals] nachprüfen; nachkontrollieren; **~-country** ❶ *adj.* Querfeldein-; **~-country running** Crosslauf, *der;* Querfeldeinlauf, *der;* **~-country skiing** Skilanglauf, *der;* ❷ *adv.* querfeldein; **~-cultural** *adj.* interkulturell; **~-current** *n. (lit. or fig.)* Gegenströmung, *die;* **~-dressing** *n.* Crossdressing, *das;* **~-examination** *n.* Kreuzverhör, *das;* **undergo** *or* **be under ~-examination** ins Kreuzverhör genommen werden; **~-examine** *v.t.* ins Kreuzverhör nehmen; einem Kreuzverhör unterziehen; **~-eyed** *adj.* [nach innen] schielend; **be ~-eyed** schielen; **~-fertili'zation** *n.* Fremdbestäubung, *die;* Kreuzbefruchtung, *die; (fig.)* gegenseitige Befruchtung; **~-'fertilize** *v.t.* fremdbestäuben; kreuzbefruchten; *(fig.)* sich gegenseitig befruchten; **~fire** *n. (lit. or fig.)* Kreuzfeuer, *das;* **~-grained** *adj. (fig.)* verquer, vertrackt ‹Situation, Problem›; querköpfig ‹Person›; **~-head[ing]** *n.* Überschrift, *die*

**crossing** /ˈkrɒsɪŋ/ *n.* **A** *(act of going across)* Überquerung, *die;* **a Channel ~:** eine Überfahrt über den Kanal; **B** *(road or rail intersection)* Kreuzung, *die;* **C** *(pedestrian ~)* Überweg, *der;* **[railway] ~:** Bahnübergang, *der;* **D** *(in church)* Vierung, *die*

**cross-legged** /ˈkrɒslegd/ *adv.* mit gekreuzten Beinen; *(with feet across thighs)* im Schneidersitz

**crossly** /ˈkrɒslɪ/ *adv.* verärgert

**crossness** /ˈkrɒsnɪs, ˈkrɔ:snɪs/ *n., no pl.* Verärgerung, *die*

**cross: ~-over** *n.* Übergang, *der; (Railw.)* Gleiskreuzung, *die;* **~patch** *n.* Griesgram, *der;* Miesepeter, *der;* **~piece** *n.* Querbalken, *der;* **~-ply tyre** *n.* Diagonalreifen, *der;* **~ 'purposes** *n. pl.* **talk at ~ purposes** aneinander vorbeireden; **be at ~ purposes [with sb.]** *(have different aims)* gegensätzliche Vorstellungen haben; *(misunderstand)* [jmdn.] missverstehen; **~-'question** *v.t.* ins Kreuzverhör nehmen; **~-refer** *v.i.* einen Querverweis machen; **~ 'reference** *n.* Querverweis, *der;* **~-reference** *v.t.* verweisen ‹Person, Stichwort› (**to** auf + *Akk.*); mit Querverweisen versehen ‹Eintrag, Werk›; **~roads** *n. sing.* Kreuzung, *die; (fig.)* Wendepunkt, *der;* **be at a/the ~roads** *(fig.)* am Scheideweg stehen; **~ section** *n.* Querschnitt, *der; (fig.)* repräsentative Auswahl; **in ~ section** im Querschnitt; **a ~ section of the population** ein Querschnitt durch die Bevölkerung; **~ stitch** *n.* Kreuzstichstickerei, *die; (stitch)* Kreuzstich, *der;* **~talk** *n. (Communications)* Übersprechen, *das;* **~-town** ❶ *adj.* **a ~-town route/road** eine Strecke/Straße, die quer durch die Stadt führt; **a ~-town bus** ein Bus, der quer durch die Stadt fährt; ❷ *adv. (Amer.)* quer durch die Stadt ‹gehen, fahren›; **~-voting** *n. Stimmabgabe für eine andere als die eigene Partei;* **~walk** *n. (Amer.)* Fußgängerüberweg, *der*

**crossways** /ˈkrɒsweɪz/ ⇒ **crosswise** 2

**'crosswind** *n.* Seitenwind, *der*

**crosswise** /ˈkrɒswaɪz/ ❶ *adj.* Quer-. ❷ *adv.* kreuzweise; *(of one in relation to another)* quer

**crossword** /ˈkrɒswɜ:d/ *n.* **~ [puzzle]** Kreuzworträtsel, *das*

**crotch** /krɒtʃ/ *n.* **A** *(of tree)* Gabelung, *die;* **B** *(of trousers, body)* Schritt, *der;* **kick sb. in the ~:** jmdn. zwischen die Beine treten

**crotchet** /ˈkrɒtʃɪt/ *n. (Brit. Mus.)* Viertelnote, *die*

**crotchety** /ˈkrɒtʃɪtɪ/ *adj.* launisch; quengelig ‹Kind›

**crouch** /kraʊtʃ/ *v.i.* [sich zusammen]kauern; **~ down** sich niederkauern; ‹Person:› sich hinhocken

**croup**[1] /kru:p/ *n. (of horse)* Kruppe, *die*

**croup**[2] *n. (Med.)* Krupp, *der*

**croupier** /ˈkru:pɪə(r), ˈkru:pɪeɪ/ *n.* ▶ 1261 Croupier, *der*

**crouton** /ˈkru:tɔ̃/ *n. (Gastr.)* Croûton, *der*

**crow** /krəʊ/ ❶ *n.* **A** *(bird)* Krähe, *die;* **as the ~ flies** Luftlinie; **eat ~** *(Amer. fig.)* zu Kreuze kriechen; **B** *(cry of cock or infant)* Krähen, *das;* **C** ⇒ **crowbar.** ❷ *v.i.* **A** ‹Hahn, Baby:› krähen; **B** *(exult)* **~ over** [hämisch] frohlocken über (+ *Akk.*)

**crow: ~bar** *n.* Brechstange, *die;* **~berry** *n. (Bot.)* Krähenbeere, *die*

**crowd** /kraʊd/ ❶ *n.* **A** *(large number of persons)* Menschenmenge, *die;* **~[s] of people** Menschenmassen *Pl.;* **he would pass in a ~:** er ist passabel; **stand out from the ~:** aus der Menge herausragen; **B** *(mass of spectators, audience)* Zuschauermenge, *die;* **C** *(multitude)* breite Masse; **follow the ~** *(fig.)* mit der Herde laufen; **be just one of the ~** *(fig.)* in der Masse untergehen; **D** *(coll.: company, set)* Clique, *die;* **a strange ~:** ein komischer Haufen; **E** *(large number of things)* Menge, *die;* **a ~ of thoughts/new ideas** eine Menge Gedanken/ein Haufen neuer Ideen.
❷ *v.t.* **A** *(collect in a ~)* **be ~ed at a place** sich an einem Ort drängen; **B** *(fill, occupy, cram)* füllen; **~ people into a bus/room** Leute in einen Bus/ein Zimmer pferchen; **~ sth. with sth.** etw. mit etw. voll stopfen; **the port was ~ed with ships** im Hafen lagen die Schiffe dicht an dicht; **the streets were ~ed with people** die Straßen waren voll mit Leuten; **C** *(fig.: fill)* ausfüllen; **the year was ~ed with incidents** es war ein sehr ereignisreiches Jahr; **D** *(come close to)* [absichtlich] fast berühren; **E** *(force)* drängen; **~ sb. into doing sth.** jmdn. drängen, etw. zu tun; **F** *(Amer. coll.: approach)* **he's ~ing thirty** er geht auf die Dreißig zu.
❸ *v.i.* **A** *(collect)* sich sammeln; **~ around sb./sth.** sich um jmdn./etw. drängen *od.* scharen; **B** *(force itself)* strömen; **memories were ~ing in [on him]** Erinnerungen stürmten auf ihn ein; **~ into/through sth.** in (+ *Akk.*)/durch etw. strömen *od.* drängen

**~ 'out** *v.t.* herausdrängen; **be ~ed out by sth.** von etw. verdrängt werden

**'crowd control** *n. Ordnungsdienst bei Großveranstaltungen*

**crowded** /'kraʊdɪd/ *adj.* überfüllt; voll ‹Programm›; ereignisreich ‹Tag, Leben, Karriere›; ~ **'out** (*coll.*) proppenvoll (*ugs.*); gerammelt voll (*ugs.*)

**'crowd-puller** *n.* (*coll.*) Publikumsmagnet, *der*

**'crowfoot** *n.* (*Bot.*) Hahnenfuß, *der*

**crown** /kraʊn/ **1** *n.* **A** (*of monarch; device, ornament*) Krone, *die;* **the C~:** die Krone; **succeed to the C~:** die Thronfolge antreten; **be heir to the C~:** Thronfolger/-folgerin sein; **the world heavyweight ~:** der Weltmeisterschaftstitel im Schwergewicht; **B** (*wreath of flowers etc.*) Sieger-, Ehrenkranz, *der;* **C** (*bird's crest*) Kamm, *der;* **D** (*of head*) Scheitel, *der;* (*of arched structure*) Scheitelpunkt, *der;* (*of arch*) Kappe, *die;* (*of tree, tooth*) Krone, *die;* (*of hat*) Kopfteil, *das;* (*thing that forms the summit*) Gipfel, *der;* (*fig.*) Krönung, *die;* **E** (*coin*) Krone, *die.* **2** *v.t.* **A** krönen; ~ **sb. king/queen** jmdn. zum König/zur Königin krönen; **B** (*surmount*) krönen; **the hill was ~ed with trees** die Kuppe des Hügels war mit Bäumen bewachsen; **C** (*put finishing touch to*) krönen; **to ~ [it] all** zur Krönung des Ganzen; (*to make things even worse*) um das Maß voll zu machen; **D** (*bring to happy ending*) krönen; **success ~ed his efforts** seine Anstrengungen waren von Erfolg gekrönt; **E** (*coll.: hit on the head*) einen überbraten (*salopp*) (+ *Dat.*); **F** (*Draughts*) zur Dame machen; eine Dame bekommen mit; **G** (*Dent.*) überkronen; eine Krone machen für

**crown:** ~ **'cap** *n.* Kron[en]korken, *der;* **C~ 'Colony** *n.* Kronkolonie, *die;* **C~ 'Court** *n.* (*Brit. Law*) Krongericht, *das*

**crowned** /kraʊnd/ *adj.* **A** (*invested with royal crown*) gekrönt; **B** (*provided with a crown*) mit einer Krone; ⇒ *also* **head¹** 1 A

**'crown green** *n. Bowlingrasen, der in der Mitte höher ist als an den Seiten*

**crowning** /'kraʊnɪŋ/ **1** *n.* Krönung, *die.* **2** *adj.* krönend; **her ~ glory is her hair** ihr Haar ist ihre größte Zier

**crown:** ~ **'jewels** *n. pl.* Kronjuwelen; ~ **land** *n.* Ländereien *Pl.* der Krone; ~ **of 'thorns** *n.* (*Zool., Relig.*) Dornenkrone, *die;* **C~ 'prince** *n.* (*lit. or fig.*) Kronprinz, *der;* **C~ 'princess** *n.* Kronprinzessin, *die*

**crow:** **~'s-foot** *n., usu. in pl.* Krähenfuß, *der;* **~'s-nest** *n.* (*Naut.*) Krähennest, *das;* Mastkorb, *der*

**crozier** ⇒ **crosier**

**crucial** /'kru:ʃl/ *adj.* entscheidend (**to** für)

**crucially** /'kru:ʃəlɪ/ *adv.* entscheidend; **be ~ important** von entscheidender Wichtigkeit sein

**crucible** /'kru:sɪbl/ *n.* [Schmelz]tiegel, *der*

**crucifix** /'kru:sɪfɪks/ *n.* Kruzifix, *das*

**crucifixion** /kru:sɪ'fɪkʃn/ *n.* Kreuzigung, *die*

**cruciform** /'kru:sɪfɔ:m/ *adj.* kreuzförmig

**crucify** /'kru:sɪfaɪ/ *v.t.* **A** kreuzigen; **B** (*torment, persecute*) peinigen; verfolgen; (*severely criticize*) verreißen

**crud** /krʌd/ *n.* (*sl.*) **A** (*impurity etc.*) Verunreinigung, *die;* Fremdstoff, *der;* **B** (*nonsense*) Schrott, *der* (*salopp*); Mist, *der* (*ugs.*)

**crude** /kru:d/ **1** *adj.* **A** (*in natural or raw state*) roh; Roh-; ~ **oil/ore** Rohöl, *das*/Roherz, *das;* **B** (*fig.: rough, unpolished*) primitiv; simpel; grob ‹Entwurf, Skizze›; **C** (*rude, blunt*) ungehobelt, ungeschliffen ‹Person, Benehmen›; grob, derb ‹Worte›; ordinär ‹Witz›; **D** (*not adjusted or corrected*) unbereinigt ‹Statistik›; roh ‹Ziffer›. **2** *n.* Rohöl, *das;* Erdöl, *das*

**crudely** /'kru:dlɪ/ *adv.* (*roughly*) grob ‹skizzieren, schätzen, entwerfen›; (*rudely, bluntly*) ungehobelt, ungeschliffen ‹sich benehmen›; derb, plump ‹sagen›; ordinär ‹reden›

**crudeness** /'kru:dnɪs/ *n. no pl.* **A** (*roughness*) Primitivität, *die;* (*of theory, design, plan*) Skizzenhaftigkeit, *die;* **B** (*rudeness, bluntness*) (*of person, behaviour, manners*) Ungeschliffenheit, *die;* (*of words*) Derbheit, *die;* (*of joke*) Geschmacklosigkeit, *die*

**crudity** /'kru:dɪtɪ/ *n.* **A** *no pl.* ⇒ **crudeness;** **B** (*crude remark*) Grobheit, *die*

**cruel** /'kru:əl/ *adj.,* (*Brit.*) **-ll-** **A** grausam; **be ~ to sb.** grausam zu jmdm. sein; **be ~ to animals** ein Tierquäler sein; **be ~ to one's dog** seinen Hund quälen; **B** (*causing pain or suffering*) grausam; unbarmherzig; **be ~ to be kind** in jmds. Interesse unbarmherzig sein müssen

**cruelly** /'kru:əlɪ/ *adv.* grausam; unbarmherzig ‹kritisieren›; **life treated him ~:** das Leben spielte ihm grausam mit

**cruelty** /'kru:əltɪ/ *n.* ⇒ **cruel**: Grausamkeit, *die;* Unbarmherzigkeit, *die;* ~ **to animals** Tierquälerei, *die;* ~ **to children** Kindesmisshandlung, *die*

**cruet** /'kru:ɪt/ *n.* **A** Essig-/Ölfläschchen, *das;* **B** ⇒ **cruet-stand**

**'cruet stand** *n.* Menage, *die*

**cruise** /kru:z/ **1** *v.i.* **A** (*sail for pleasure*) eine Kreuzfahrt machen; **B** (*at random*) ‹Fahrzeug, Fahrer:› herumfahren; **C** (*at economical speed*) ‹Fahrzeug:› mit Dauergeschwindigkeit fahren; ‹Flugzeug:› mit Reisegeschwindigkeit fliegen; **cruising speed** Reisegeschwindigkeit, *die;* **we are now cruising at a height/speed of ...:** wir fliegen nun in einer Flughöhe/mit einer Reisegeschwindigkeit von ...; **D** (*for protection of shipping*) kreuzen. **2** *n.* Kreuzfahrt, *die;* **go on** *or* **for a ~:** eine Kreuzfahrt machen

**'cruise missile** *n.* Marschflugkörper, *der*

**cruiser** /'kru:zə(r)/ *n.* Kreuzer, *der*

**'cruiserweight** *n.* (*Boxing etc.*) Halbschwergewicht, *das;* (*person also*) Halbschwergewichtler, *der*

**crumb** /krʌm/ **1** *n.* **A** Krümel, *der;* Brösel, *der;* (*fig.*) Brocken, *der;* **~s of wisdom** ein bisschen Weisheit; **~s from the rich man's table** (*fig.*) Brosamen, die von des Reichen Tische fallen; **~[s] of comfort** kleiner Trost; **B** (*soft part of bread*) Krume, *die.* **2** *v.t.* (*cover with ~s*) panieren

**crumble** /'krʌmbl/ **1** *v.t.* zerbröckeln ‹Brot›; zerkrümeln ‹Keks, Kuchen›; ~ **sth. into/onto sth.** etw. in/auf etw. (*Akk.*) bröckeln *od.* krümeln. **2** *v.i.* ‹Brot, Kuchen:› krümeln; ‹Gestein:› [zer]bröckeln; ‹Mauer:› zusammenfallen; (*fig.*) ‹Hoffnung:› sich zerschlagen; ‹Reich, Gesellschaft:› zerfallen, zugrunde gehen. **3** *n.* (*Cookery*) **A** (*dish*) *mit Streuseln bestreutes und überbackenes [Apfel-, Rhabarber- usw.]dessert;* **B** (*substance*) Streusel *Pl.*

**crumbly** /'krʌmblɪ/ *adj.* krümelig ‹Keks, Kuchen, Brot›; bröckelig ‹Gestein, Erde›

**crumbs** /krʌmz/ *int.* (*Brit. coll.*) Mensch (*ugs.*); verflixt (*ugs.*)

**crummy** /'krʌmɪ/ *adj.* (*coll.*) **A** (*dirty, unpleasant*) schmuddelig (*ugs.*); verdreckt (*ugs.*); **B** (*inferior, worthless*) mies (*ugs.*)

**crumpet** /'krʌmpɪt/ *n.* **A** (*cake*) *weiches Hefeküchlein zum Toasten;* **B** (*sl.: women*) Weiber *Pl.* (*salopp*); Miezen *Pl.* (*salopp*); **a bit/piece of ~:** ein Weib; **C** (*arch. coll.: head*) Birne, *die* (*salopp*); Rübe, *die* (*salopp*); **off one's ~:** übergeschnappt

**crumple** /'krʌmpl/ **1** *v.t.* **A** (*crush*) zerdrücken; zerquetschen; **B** (*ruffle, wrinkle*) zerknittern ‹Kleider, Papier, Stoff›; ~ **[up] a piece of paper** ein Stück Papier zerknüllen. **2** *v.i.* ‹Kleider, Stoff, Papier:› knittern; ~ **[up]** (*fig.*) ‹Person:› zusammensinken

**'crumple zone** *n.* (*Motor Veh.*) Knautschzone, *die*

**crunch** /krʌnʃ/ **1** *v.t.* [geräuschvoll] knabbern ‹Keks, Zwieback›; [geräuschvoll] nagen an (+ *Dat.*) ‹Knochen›. **2** *v.i.* **A** ~ **away [at sth.]** [an etw. (*Dat.*)] herumknabbern *od.* -nagen; **B** ‹Schnee, Kies:› knirschen; ‹Eis:› [zer]splittern; **the wheels ~ed on the gravel** der Kies knirschte unter den Rädern; **he ~ed through the snow** er ging durch den knirschenden Schnee. **3** *n.* **A** (*crunching noise*) Knirschen, *das;* **B** (*decisive event*) **when it comes to the ~, when the ~ comes** wenn es hart auf hart geht

**crunchy** /'krʌnʃɪ/ *adj.* knusprig ‹Gebäck, Nüsse›; knackig ‹Apfel›

**crupper** /'krʌpə(r)/ *n.* **A** (*strap*) Schweifriemen, *der;* **B** (*of horse*) Kruppe, *die*

**crusade** /kru:'seɪd/ **1** *n.* (*Hist.*) Kreuzzug, *der;* **a ~ against sth.** (*fig.*) ein Feldzug *od.* Kreuzzug gegen etw. **2** *v.i.* einen Kreuzzug unternehmen; (*fig.*) zu Felde ziehen

**crusader** /kru:'seɪdə(r)/ *n.* (*Hist.*) Kreuzfahrer, *der;* Kreuzritter, *der*

**crush** /krʌʃ/ **1** *v.t.* **A** (*compress with violence*) quetschen; auspressen ‹Trauben, Obst›; (*kill, destroy*) zerquetschen; zermalmen; ~ **to death** zu Tode quetschen; **~ed strawberry** (*colour*) Erdbeerrot, *das;* **B** (*reduce to powder*) zerstampfen; zermahlen; zerstoßen ‹Gewürze, Tabletten›; **C** (*fig.: subdue, overwhelm*) niederwerfen, niederschlagen ‹Aufstand›; vernichten ‹Feind›; zunichte machen ‹Hoffnungen, Wünsche›; **her angry look ~ed him** vernichtend traf ihn ihr zorniger Blick; **D** (*crumple, crease*) zerknittern ‹Kleid, Stoff›; zerdrücken, verbeulen ‹Hut›.
**2** *n.* **A** (*crowded mass*) Gedränge, *das;* Gewühl, *das;* **B** (*coll.*) (*infatuation*) Schwärmerei, *die;* (*person*) Schwarm, *der* (*ugs.*); **have/get a ~ on sb.** in jmdn. verknallt sein/sich in jmdn. verknallen (*ugs.*); **C** (*drink*) Saftgetränk, *das;* **D** (*coll.: crowded gathering*) Rummel, *der* (*ugs.*)

**crush:** ~ **bar** *n.* Bar, *die* (*im Foyer eines Theaters*); **~-barrier** *n.* Absperrgitter, *das*

**crushing** /'krʌʃɪŋ/ *adj.* niederschmetternd ‹Antwort›; vernichtend ‹Niederlage, Schlag›

**crust** /krʌst/ *n.* **A** (*of bread*) Kruste, *die;* Rinde, *die;* **B** (*hard surface, coating, deposit*) Kruste, *die;* **the earth's ~:** die Erdkruste; **C** (*of pie*) Teigdeckel, *der;* **D** (*scab*) Kruste, *die;* Schorf, *der;* **E** (*fig.: superficial hardness*) Panzer, *der;* **F** (*in wine bottle*) Depot, *das.* ⇒ *also* **last¹** 1; **upper** 1 B

**crustacean** /krʌ'steɪʃn/ *n.* Krustentier *od.* Krebstier, *das;* Krustazee, *die* (*fachspr.*)

**crusted** /'krʌstɪd/ *adj.* (*having a crust*) verkrustet; abgelagert ‹Wein›; ~ **snow** Harsch, *der*

**crusty** /'krʌstɪ/ *adj.* **A** (*crisp*) knusprig; **B** (*hard*) hart; **C** (*irritable, curt*) barsch

**crutch** /krʌtʃ/ *n.* **A** (*lit. or fig.*) Krücke, *die;* **go about on ~es** an Krücken gehen; **B** ⇒ **crotch** B

**crux** /krʌks/ *n., pl.* **~es** *or* **cruces** /'kru:si:z/ **A** (*difficult matter, puzzle*) Rätsel, *das;* harte Nuss (*ugs.*); **the ~ of the matter** der Haken bei der Sache; **B** (*decisive point*) Kern[punkt], *der;* **the ~ of the matter** der springende Punkt bei der Sache

**cry** /kraɪ/ **1** *n.* **A** (*loud utterance of grief*) Schrei, *der;* (*loud utterance of words*) Schreien, *das;* Geschrei, *das;* (*of hounds or wolves*) Heulen, *das;* Geheul, *das;* (*of birds*) Schreien, *das;* Geschrei, *das;* **a ~ of pain/rage/happiness** ein Schmerzens-/Wut-/Freudenschrei; **a far ~ from ...** (*fig.*) etwas ganz anderes als ...; **be in full ~** ‹Hundemeute:› laut bellend hinter der Beute herhetzen; **be in full ~ after sb.** (*fig.*) jmdn. mit großem Geheul verfolgen; **B** (*appeal, entreaty*) Appell, *der;* **a ~ for freedom/independence/justice** ein Ruf nach Freiheit/Unabhängigkeit/Gerechtigkeit; **a ~ for mercy** eine flehentliche Bitte um Gnade; **a ~ for help** ein Hilferuf; **C** (*proclamation of goods or business*) Ausrufen, *das;* **D** (*public demand*) Ruf, *der;* **E** (*watchword*) Losung, *die;* Parole, *die;* (*in battle*) Schlachtruf, *der;* **F** (*fit or spell of weeping*) **have a good ~:** sich ausweinen; **it will do her good to have a ~:** es wird ihr gut tun, sich einmal richtig auszuweinen. **2** *v.t.* **A** rufen; (*loudly*) schreien; **B** (*weep*) weinen; ~ **bitter tears over sth.** bittere Tränen wegen etw. weinen *od.* über etw. (*Akk.*) vergießen; ~ **one's eyes out** sich (*Dat.*) die Augen ausweinen *od.* aus dem Kopf weinen; ~ **oneself to sleep** sich in den Schlaf weinen; **C** ~ **one's wares** (*lit. or fig.*) seine Waren anpreisen.
**3** *v.i.* **A** rufen; (*loudly*) schreien; ~ **[out] for sth./sb.** nach etw./jmdm. rufen *od.* schreien; ~ **[out] for mercy** um Gnade flehen; ~ **[out] for help** um Hilfe schreien; ~ **to sb. [to come]** jmdm. zurufen[, er solle kommen *od.* dass er kommen soll]; ~ **with pain** vor Schmerz[en] schreien; **sth. cries out for sth.** (*fig.*) etw. schreit nach etw.; **[well,] for ~ing out loud** (*coll.*) das darf doch wohl nicht wahr sein! (*ugs.*); **what's**

C

the matter, for **~ing out loud?** was ist los, um Himmels willen?; **~ for the moon** (*fig.*) Unmögliches verlangen; **B** (*weep*) weinen (**over** wegen); **~ for sth.** nach etw. weinen; (*fig.*) einer Sache (*Dat.*) nachweinen; ⇒ *also* **milk** 1; **C** ‹Möwe:› schreien; ‹Hund:› bellen

**~ 'down** *v.t.* **~ sb./sth. down** jmdn./etw. herabsetzen *od.* (*ugs.*) mies machen

**~ 'off** *v.i.* absagen; einen Rückzieher machen (*ugs.*)

**~ 'out** *v.i.* aufschreien; ⇒ *also* **~** 3 A

**~ 'up** *v.t.* **~ sth./sb. up** etw./jmdn. hochjubeln (*ugs.*) *od.* in den Himmel heben (*ugs.*); **it/he wasn't all it/he was cried up to be** so großartig war es/er nun auch wieder nicht

**'cry-baby** *n.* Heulsuse, *die* (*ugs.*)

**cryer** ⇒ **crier**

**crying** /'kraɪɪŋ/ *adj.* weinend ‹Kind›; schreiend ‹Unrecht›; dringend ‹Bedürfnis, Notwendigkeit›; dringlich ‹Forderung›; krass ‹Missverhältnis›; **it is a ~ shame** es ist eine wahre Schande

**cryo-** /kraɪəʊ/ *in comb.* Kryo-/kryo-

**cryogenic** /kraɪəʊ'dʒenɪk/ *adj.* **~ laboratory** Tieftemperaturlabor, *das*

**crypt** /krɪpt/ *n.* Krypta, *die*

**cryptic** /'krɪptɪk/ *adj.* **A** (*secret, mystical*) geheimnisvoll; **B** (*obscure in meaning*) undurchschaubar; kryptisch

**cryptically** /'krɪptɪkəlɪ/ *adv.* ⇒ **cryptic**: geheimnisvoll; undurchschaubar; kryptisch

**crypto-** /krɪptəʊ/ *in comb.* Krypto-

**cryptogram** /'krɪptəgræm/ *n.* verschlüsselter Text; Geheimtext, *der*

**cryptographic** /krɪptə'græfɪk/ *adj.* verschlüsselt; (*employing cryptography*) Verschlüsselungs-

**cryptography** /krɪp'tɒgrəfɪ/ *n.* Kryptographie, *die*

**crystal** /'krɪstl/ **1** *n.* **A** (*Chem., Min., etc.*) Kristall, *der;* **B** ⇒ **crystal glass**. **2** *adj.* (*made of ~ glass*) kristallen; **~ bowl/vase** Kristallschale, *die*/-vase, *die*

**crystal: ~ 'ball** *n.* Kristallkugel, *die;* **I haven't got a ~ ball!** ich bin [doch] kein Hellseher!; **~ clear** *adj.* kristallklar; kristallen (*geh.*); (*fig.*) glasklar; **make sth. ~ clear** (*fig.*) etw. ganz klar machen; **~-gazing** *n.* Hellseherei, *die;* Kristallomantie, *die* (*fachspr.*); **~ 'glass** *n.* Bleikristall, *das;* Kristallglas, *das*

**crystalline** /'krɪstəlaɪn/ *adj.* **A** (*made of crystal*) Kristall-; kristallen; **B** (*Chem., Min.*) kristallin[isch]

**crystallisation, crystallise** ⇒ **crystalliz-**

**crystallization** /krɪstəlaɪ'zeɪʃn/ *n.* Kristallbildung, *die;* Kristallisation, *die;* (*fig.*) Kristallisierung, *die*

**crystallize** /'krɪstəlaɪz/ **1** *v.t.* auskristallisieren ‹Salze›; kandieren ‹Früchte›; **~ one's thoughts** (*fig.*) seinen Gedanken feste Form geben. **2** *v.i.* kristallisieren; (*fig.*) feste Form annehmen

**crystallographer** /krɪstə'lɒgrəfə(r)/ *n.* Kristallograph, *der*/-graphin, *die*

**crystallography** /krɪstə'lɒgrəfɪ/ *n.* Kristallographie, *die*

**c/s** *abbr.* **cycle[s] per second** Hz

**CSA** *abbr.* (*Brit.*) **Child Support Agency**

**CSCE** *abbr.* **Conference on Security and Cooperation in Europe** KSZE

**CSE** *abbr.* (*Brit. Hist.*) **Certificate of Secondary Education**

**CS 'gas** *n.* CS, *das* (*fachspr.*); ≈ Tränengas, *das*

**ct** *abbr.* **A** **carat** Kt.; **B** **cent** ct., Ct.

**CT** *abbr.* **computerized tomography** CT

**cu.** *abbr.* **cubic** Kubik-

**cub** /kʌb/ *n.* **A** Junge, *das;* (*of wolf, fox, dog*) Welpe, *der;* Junge, *das;* **B** **Cub** ⇒ **Cub Scout**; **C** (*Amer.: apprentice*) Lehrling, *der*

**Cuba** /'kju:bə/ *n.* Kuba (*das*)

**Cuban** /'kju:bn/ ▶ **1340** **1** *adj.* kubanisch; **sb. is ~:** jmd. ist Kubaner/Kubanerin. **2** *n.* Kubaner, *der*/Kubanerin, *die*

**Cuban 'heel** *n.* Blockabsatz, *der*

**cubby[hole]** /'kʌbɪ(-həʊl)/ *n.* Kämmerchen, *das;* (*snug place*) Kuschelecke, *die*

**cube** /kju:b/ **1** *n.* **A** Würfel, *der;* Kubus, *der* (*fachspr.*); **B** (*Math.*) dritte Potenz; Kubus, *der* (*fachspr.*). **2** *v.t.* in die dritte Potenz erheben ‹Zahl›; hoch drei nehmen; **2 ~d is 8** 2 hoch 3 ist 8; die dritte Potenz von 2 ist 8

**cube: ~ 'root** *n.* Kubikwurzel, *die;* **the ~ root of 8 is 2** die dritte Wurzel aus 8 ist 2; **~ sugar** *n.* Würfelzucker, *der*

**cubic** /'kju:bɪk/ *adj.* **A** würfelförmig; **have a ~ form** würfelförmig sein; die Form eines Würfels haben; **B** ▶ **1671** (*of three dimensions*) Kubik-; Raum-; **~ content** Rauminhalt, *der;* **~ metre/centimetre/foot/yard** Kubikmeter/-zentimeter/-fuß/-yard, *der;* **C** (*Math.*) kubisch; **~ equation** Gleichung dritten Grades

**cubical** /'kju:bɪkl/ ⇒ **cubic** A

**cubicle** /'kju:bɪkl/ *n.* **A** (*sleeping compartment*) Alkoven, *der;* **B** (*for dressing, private discussion, etc.*) Kabine, *die*

**cubism** /'kju:bɪzm/ *n.* (*Art*) Kubismus, *der*

**cubist** /'kju:bɪst/ *n.* (*Art*) Kubist, *der*/Kubistin, *die*

**cubit** /'kju:bɪt/ *n.* (*Hist.*) Elle, *die*

**'cub reporter** *n.* (*coll.*) unerfahrener [junger] Reporter/unerfahrene [junge] Reporterin

**'Cub Scout** *n.* Wölfling, *der*

**cuckold** /'kʌkəld/ (*arch.*) **1** *n.* Hahnrei, *der* (*veralt.*); gehörnter Ehemann (*scherzh.*). **2** *v.t.* Hörner aufsetzen (+ *Dat.*) (*scherzh.*); hörnen (*scherzh.*)

**cuckoo** /'kʊku:/ **1** *n.* **A** Kuckuck, *der;* **~ in the nest** (*fig.*) Fremdkörper, *der;* **B** (*simpleton*) Einfaltspinsel, *der* (*ugs.*); Heini, *der* (*ugs.*). **2** *adj.* (*coll.*) meschugge *nicht attr.* (*salopp*); **a ~ notion/idea** eine bekloppte Idee (*salopp*)

**cuckoo: ~ clock** *n.* Kuckucksuhr, *die;* **~ flower** *n.* (*Bot.*) **A** (*lady's smock*) Wiesenschaumkraut, *das;* **B** (*ragged robin*) Kuckuckslichtnelke, *die;* **~-pint** /'kʊku:pɪnt/ *n.* (*Bot.*) Aron[s]stab, *der*

**cucumber** /'kju:kʌmbə(r)/ *n.* [Salat]gurke, *die;* **be as cool as a ~:** taufrisch sein; (*fig.: remain calm*) einen kühlen Kopf behalten

**cud** /kʌd/ *n.* wiedergekäutes Futter; **chew the ~:** wiederkäuen; (*fig.*) vor sich hin grübeln

**cuddle** /'kʌdl/ **1** *n.* Liebkosung, *die;* enge Umarmung; **give sb. a ~:** jmdn. drücken *od.* in den Arm nehmen; **have a ~:** schmusen. **2** *v.t.* schmusen mit; hätscheln ‹kleines Kind›. **3** *v.i.* schmusen; **~ up** sich zusammenkuscheln; (*in bed*) sich einmummeln; **he ~d up beside her** er kuschelte sich an ihre Seite

**cuddlesome** /'kʌdlsəm/ *adj.* zum Liebhaben *od.* Schmusen *nachgestellt*

**cuddly** /'kʌdlɪ/ *adj.* **A** (*given to cuddling*) verschmust; **B** ⇒ **cuddlesome**

**cuddly 'toy** *n.* Plüschtier, *das*

**cudgel** /'kʌdʒl/ **1** *n.* Knüppel, *der;* **take up the ~s for sb./sth.** (*fig.*) [energisch] für jmdn./etw. eintreten. **2** *v.t.*, (*Brit.*) **-ll-** knüppeln; **~ one's brains** (*fig.*) sich (*Dat.*) das [Ge]hirn zermartern

**cue**[1] /kju:/ *n.* (*Billiards etc.*) Queue, *das;* Billardstock, *der*

**cue**[2] **1** *n.* **A** (*Theatre*) Stichwort, *das;* (*Music*) Stichnoten *Pl.;* (*Cinemat., Broadcasting*) Zeichen zum Aufnahmebeginn; **be/speak/play on ~:** rechtzeitig einsetzen; **enter on ~:** auf das Stichwort hin auftreten; **B** (*sign when or how to act*) Wink, *der;* Zeichen, *das;* **take one's ~ from sb.** (*lit. or fig.*) sich nach jmdm. richten. **2** *v.t.* (*label*) kennzeichnen

**cuff**[1] /kʌf/ *n.* **A** Manschette, *die;* **off the ~** (*fig.*) aus dem Stegreif; **B** (*Amer.: trouser turn-up*) [Hosen]aufschlag, *der;* **C** *in pl.* (*coll.: handcuffs*) Handschellen *Pl.*

**cuff**[2] **1** *v.t.* **~ sb.'s ears, ~ sb. over the ears** jmdm. eins hinter die Ohren geben (*ugs.*); **~ sb.** jmdm. einen Klaps geben. **2** *n.* Klaps, *der;* **give sb. a ~ on the ears** jmdm. eins hinter die Ohren geben (*ugs.*)

**'cuff link** *n.* Manschettenknopf, *der*

**cuirass** /kwɪ'ræs/ *n.* (*armour*) Küraß, *der;* Brustharnisch, *der*

**cuisine** /kwɪ'zi:n/ *n.* Küche, *die;* **French/Italian** *etc.* **~:** französische/italienische *usw.* Küche

**cul-de-sac** /'kʌldəsæk/ *n., pl.* **culs-de-sac** /'kʌldəsæk/ Sackgasse, *die*

**culinary** /'kʌlɪnərɪ/ *adj.* kulinarisch; **the ~ arts** die Kochkunst; **~ herbs/plants** *etc.* Küchenkräuter/-gewächse *usw.*

**cull** /kʌl/ **1** *v.t.* **A** (*select*) auswählen; **B** (*select and kill*) erlegen; (*shoot*) abschießen; **C** (*literary: pick*) pflücken; **2** *n.* **A** (*act of ~ing*) Erlegung, *die;* (*shooting*) Abschuss, *der;* **~ of seals** Robbenschlag, *der;* **B** (*~ed animal*) Merztier, *das*

**cullet** /'kʌlɪt/ *n.* (*Glass-making*) Glasscherben; Glasbruch, *der*

**culm** /kʌlm/ *n.* (*Bot.*) Halm, *der*

**culminate** /'kʌlmɪneɪt/ *v.i.* (*reach highest point, lit. or fig.*) gipfeln; kulminieren; **~ in sth.** in etw. (*Dat.*) seinen Höchststand erreichen

**culmination** /kʌlmɪ'neɪʃn/ *n.* Höhepunkt, *der;* Kulmination, *die* (*geh.*)

**culottes** /kju:'lɒt/ *n. pl.* Hosenrock, *der*

**culpable** /'kʌlpəbl/ *adj.* schuldig ‹Person›; strafbar ‹Handlung›; **hold sb. ~:** jmdn. für schuldig halten; **~ negligence** grobe Fahrlässigkeit

**culprit** /'kʌlprɪt/ *n.* (*guilty of crime*) Schuldige, *der/die;* Täter, *der*/Täterin, *die;* (*guilty of wrong*) Übeltäter, *der*/-täterin, *die;* Missetäter, *der*/-täterin, *die*

**cult** /kʌlt/ *n.* Kult, *der;* **the ~ of the dead** der Totenkult; *attrib.* Kult‹film, -figur usw.›

**cultivate** /'kʌltɪveɪt/ *v.t.* **A** (*prepare and use for crops*) kultivieren; bestellen, bebauen ‹Feld, Land›; (*prepare with cultivator*) mit dem Kultivator bearbeiten; **B** (*produce by culture*) anbauen, züchten ‹Pflanzen›; züchten ‹Tiere›; **C** (*fig.*) (*improve, develop*) kultivieren ‹Stimme, Sprache›; kultivieren, entwickeln ‹Geschmack›; kultivieren, verfeinern ‹Manieren›; (*pay attention to, cherish*) kultivieren ‹Freundschaft, Gefühl, Gewohnheit›; pflegen ‹Freundschaft, Verbindung›; entwickeln ‹Kunst, Fertigkeit›; betreiben ‹Wissenschaft›; **~ sb.** die Verbindung mit jmdm. pflegen; sich (*Dat.*) jmdn. warm halten (*ugs.*); **~ one's mind** sich bilden; **D** züchten ‹Bakterien›

**cultivated** /'kʌltɪveɪtɪd/ *adj.* **A** kultiviert; gezüchtet ‹Pflanzen›; bebaut ‹Land, Feld›; **~ plant** Zuchtpflanze, *die;* **B** (*fig.*) kultiviert ‹Manieren, Sprache, Geschmack›; kultiviert, gebildet ‹Person›

**cultivation** /kʌltɪ'veɪʃn/ *n.* (*lit. or fig.*) Kultivierung, *die;* (*of a skill*) Entwicklung, *die;* **~ of plants** Anbau von Pflanzen; **~ of land** Landbau, *der;* Pflanzenbau, *der;* **land that is under ~:** Boden, der landwirtschaftlich genutzt wird; **bring land into ~:** Land urbar machen; (*fig.*) **~ of the mind** Bildung, *die*

**cultivator** /'kʌltɪveɪtə(r)/ *n.* **A** (*person*) Ackerbauer, *der;* **B** (*implement*) Handkultivator, *der;* (*machine*) Kultivator, *der;* Grubber, *der*

**cultural** /'kʌltʃərl/ *adj.* kulturell ‹Entwicklung, Ereignis, Interessen, Beziehungen›; **~ revolution/anthropology** Kulturrevolution/-anthropologie, *die;* **there are ~ activities** es wird kulturell etwas geboten

**culture** /'kʌltʃə(r)/ **1** *n.* **A** Kultur, *die;* **the two ~s** die entgegengesetzten Bereiche Geisteswissenschaft und Naturwissenschaft; **B** (*intellectual development*) [Geistes]bildung, *die;* Kultur, *die;* **C** **physical ~:** Fitnesstraining, *das;* **beauty ~:** Schönheitspflege, *die;* **D** (*Agric.*) Kultur, *die;* (*tillage of the soil*) Landbau, *der;* (*rearing, production*) Zucht, *die;* **methods of ~:** Anbaumethoden *Pl.;* **E** (*of bacteria*) Kultur, *die*. **2** *v.t.* züchten ‹Bakterien›

**cultured** /'kʌltʃəd/ *adj.* **A** (*cultivated, refined*) kultiviert; gebildet; **B** **~ pearl** Zuchtperle, *die*

**culture: ~ shock** *n.* Kulturschock, *der;* **~ vulture** *n.* (*joc.*) Kulturfanatiker, *der*/-fanatikerin, *die* (*ugs.*)

**culvert** /'kʌlvət/ *n.* **A** (*for water*) [unterirdischer] Kanal, *der;* **B** (*for electric cable*) Kabelkanal, *der*

**cum** /kʌm/ *prep.* Ⓐ *(Finance)* ~ **dividend** mit Dividende; Ⓑ *(indicating combined nature or function)* **dining-~-sitting room** Wohn- und Speisezimmer, *das;* **dinner-~-cocktail dress** Abend- und Cocktailkleid, *das*

**cumbersome** /ˈkʌmbəsəm/ *adj.* lästig, hinderlich ‹Kleider›; sperrig ‹Gepäck, Pakete›; unhandlich ‹Paket›; schwerfällig ‹Bewegung, Stil, Arbeitsweise, Ausdruck›; umständlich ‹Methode›

**cumin** /ˈkʌmɪn/ *n. (Bot.)* Kreuzkümmel, *der*

**cummerbund** /ˈkʌməbʌnd/ *n.* Kummerbund, *der*

**cummin** ⇒ **cumin**

**cumulate** /ˈkjuːmjʊleɪt/, **cumulation** /kjuːmjʊˈleɪʃn/ ⇒ **accumul-**

**cumulative** /ˈkjuːmjʊlətɪv/ *adj.* Ⓐ *(increased by successive additions)* kumulativ *(geh.)*; ~ **strength/effect** Gesamtstärke/-wirkung, *die;* ~ **evidence** Häufung von Beweismaterial; Ⓑ *(formed by successive additions)* zusätzlich; Zusatz-; kumulierend, kumuliert ‹Bibliographie›

**cumulatively** /ˈkjuːmjʊlətɪvlɪ/ *adv.* kumulativ

**cumulus** /ˈkjuːmjʊləs/ *n., pl.* **cumuli** /ˈkjuːmjʊlaɪ/ *(Meteorol.)* Kumuluswolke, *die*

**cuneiform** /ˈkjuːnɪɪfɔːm, ˈkjuːnɪfɔːm/ *adj.* keilförmig; ‹Text, Dokument, Inschrift› in Keilschrift; ~ **writing** Keilschrift, *die*

**cunnilingus** /kʌnɪˈlɪŋgəs/ *n., no pl., no art.* Cunnilingus, *der*

**cunning** /ˈkʌnɪŋ/ ❶ *n.* Ⓐ Schläue, *die;* Gerissenheit, *die;* Ⓑ *(arch.: skill)* Geschicklichkeit, *die;* Geschick, *das.* ❷ *adj.* Ⓐ schlau; gerissen; Ⓑ *(arch.: skilful)* geschickt; Ⓒ *(Amer.: quaint, small)* niedlich

**cunningly** /ˈkʌnɪŋlɪ/ *adv.* schlau ‹reden, denken›; listig ‹täuschen›; gerissen ‹handeln›; *as sentence modifier* schlauerweise

**cunt** /kʌnt/ *n. (coarse)* Ⓐ *(female genitals)* Fotze, *die (vulg.)*; Möse, *die (vulg.)*; Ⓑ *(derog.) (woman)* Fotze, *die (vulg.)*; Schlampe, *die (derb)*; *(man)* Arschloch, *das (derb)*

**cup** /kʌp/ ❶ *n.* Ⓐ *(drinking vessel)* Tasse, *die;* **there's many a slip between the ~ and the lip** *(fig.)* da kann immer noch etwas dazwischenkommen; **in one's ~s** *(fig.)* in angetrunkenem Zustand; Ⓑ *(prize, competition)* Pokal, *der;* Ⓒ *(cupful)* Tasse, *die;* **a ~ of coffee/tea** eine Tasse Kaffee/Tee; **another ~ of tea** *(fig.)* etwas ganz anderes; **a nasty/nice ~ of tea** *(fig. coll.)* ein fieses Stück *(ugs. abwertend)* /ein netter Typ *(ugs.)*; **it's [not] my ~ of tea** *(fig. coll.)* das ist [nicht] mein Fall *(ugs.)*; Ⓓ *(flavoured wine etc.)* Bowle, *die;* Ⓔ *(Eccl.)* Kelch, *der;* Ⓕ *(fig.: fate, experience)* **his ~ [of happiness/sorrow] was full** er war überglücklich/das Maß seiner Leiden war voll; Ⓖ *(of brassière)* Körbchen, *das;* **A/B** *etc.* **~:** A-/B-Körbchen *usw.*
❷ *v.t.*, **-pp-** Ⓐ *(take or hold as in ~)* ~ **one's chin in one's hand** das Kinn in die Hand stützen; ~ **water** Wasser [mit der hohlen Hand] schöpfen; Ⓑ *(make ~-shaped)* hohl machen; ~ **one's hand to one's ear** die Hand ans Ohr halten

**cupboard** /ˈkʌbəd/ *n.* Schrank, *der*

ˈ**cupboard love** *n.* geheuchelte Zuneigung; **it's just ~:** es ist nur Getue *(ugs.)*

ˈ**cupcake** *n. kleiner [Rühr]kuchen in einem Förmchen aus Papier*

**Cup** ˈ**Final** *n. (Footb.)* Pokalendspiel, *das*

**cupful** /ˈkʌpfʊl/ *n.* Tasse, *die;* **a ~ of water** eine Tasse Wasser

**Cupid** /ˈkjuːpɪd/ *n. (god)* Amor, *der;* Cupido, *der;* *(representation)* Amorette, *die;* **~'s bow** Amors Bogen

**cupidity** /kjuːˈpɪdɪtɪ/ *n., no pl.* Begierde, *die* **(for** nach); Gier, *die* **(for** nach)

**cupola** /ˈkjuːpələ/ *n.* Kuppel, *die;* *(ceiling of dome)* Kuppel, *die;* Kuppelgewölbe, *das*

**cuppa** /ˈkʌpə/, **cupper** /ˈkʌpə(r)/ *n. (Brit. coll.)* Tasse Tee

ˈ**cup tie** *n.* Pokalspiel, *das*

**cur** /kɜː(r)/ *n. (derog.)* Ⓐ *(dog)* Köter, *der (ugs. abwertend)*; Ⓑ *(fig.: person)* [Schweine]hund, *der (derb abwertend)*

**curable** /ˈkjʊərəbl/ *adj.* heilbar; **the patient is ~:** der Patient kann geheilt werden; **not ~** *(lit. or fig.)* unheilbar

**curaçao** /ˈkjʊərəsəʊ/ *n.* Curaçao, *der*

**curare** /kjʊəˈrɑːrɪ/ *n.* Curare, *das*

**curate** /ˈkjʊərət/ *n.* Ⓐ *(Eccl.)* Kurat, *der;* Hilfsgeistliche, *der;* Ⓑ **sth. is a** *or* **like the ~'s egg** *(fig.)* etw. hat seine guten und seine schlechten Seiten

**curative** /ˈkjʊərətɪv/ *adj.* heilend; Heil-; **be ~:** heilend wirken; heilen

**curator** /kjʊəˈreɪtə(r)/ *n.* ▶ **1261** Ⓐ *(of museum)* Direktor, *der*/Direktorin, *die;* Ⓑ *(person in charge)* Verwalter, *der*/Verwalterin, *die*

**curb** /kɜːb/ ❶ *v.t. (lit. or fig.)* zügeln. ❷ *n.* Ⓐ *(chain or strap for horse)* Kandare, *die;* **put a ~ on** *(fig.)* an die Kandare nehmen ‹Person›; zügeln ‹Gefühle›; einschränken ‹Ausgaben, Einfuhr›; Ⓑ ⇒ **kerb**

ˈ**curd cheese** *n.* ≈ Quark, *der*

**curdle** /ˈkɜːdl/ ❶ *v.t. (lit. or fig.)* gerinnen lassen; ⇒ *also* **blood-curdling**. ❷ *v.i. (lit. or fig.)* gerinnen

**curds** /kɜːdz/ *n. pl.* ≈ Quark, *der;* ~ **and whey** Quark [mit Molke]

**cure** /kjʊə(r)/ ▶ **1232** ❶ *n.* Ⓐ *(thing that ~s)* [Heil]mittel, *das* **(for** gegen); *(fig.)* Mittel, *das;* Ⓑ *(restoration to health)* Heilung, *die;* Ⓒ *(treatment)* Behandlung, *die;* **take a ~ at a spa** in *od.* zur Kur gehen; Ⓓ *(spiritual charge)* ~ **of souls** Seelsorge, *die.*
❷ *v.t.* Ⓐ heilen; kurieren; ~ **sb. of a disease** jmdn. von einer Krankheit heilen; Ⓑ *(fig.)* kurieren; **he was ~d of his bad habits** er wurde von seinen schlechten Gewohnheiten kuriert; ihm wurden seine schlechten Gewohnheiten ausgetrieben; Ⓒ *(preserve)* haltbar machen ‹Nahrungsmittel›; [ein]pökeln ‹Fleisch›; räuchern ‹Fisch›; trocknen ‹Häute, Tabak›; Ⓓ *(harden)* aushärten ‹Beton, Kunststoffe›

ˈ**cure-all** *n.* Allheilmittel, *das*

**curfew** /ˈkɜːfjuː/ *n.* Ⓐ Ausgangssperre, *die;* Ⓑ *(Hist.: bell)* Abendglocke, *die*

**Curia** /ˈkjʊərɪə/ *n.* Kurie, *die*

**curio** /ˈkjʊərɪəʊ/ *n., pl.* **~s** Kuriosität, *die*

**curiosity** /kjʊərɪˈɒsɪtɪ/ *n.* Ⓐ *(desire to know)* Neugier[de], *die* **(about** in Bezug auf + *Akk.*); **~ killed the cat** *(fig.)* die Neugier ist schon manchem zum Verhängnis geworden; Ⓑ *(strange object, matter)* Kuriosität, *die;* Ⓒ *no pl. (strangeness)* Fremdartigkeit, *die*

**curious** /ˈkjʊərɪəs/ *adj.* Ⓐ *(inquisitive)* neugierig; *(eager to learn)* wissbegierig; **be ~ about sth.** *(eagerly awaiting)* auf etw. *(Akk.)* neugierig sein; **be ~ about sb.** in Bezug auf jmdn. neugierig sein; **be ~ to know sth.** etw. gern wissen wollen; **he was ~ to know what ...:** er wollte zu gerne wissen, was ...; Ⓑ *(strange, odd)* merkwürdig; seltsam; **how [very] ~!** [sehr] seltsam!; **~er and ~er** *(coll.)* es wird immer geheimnisvoller

**curiously** /ˈkjʊərɪəslɪ/ *adv.* ⇒ **curious**: neugierig ‹fragen, gucken›; seltsam, merkwürdig ‹sprechen, sich verhalten›; **it was ~ quiet** es war merkwürdig still; **~ [enough]** *(as sentence-modifier)* merkwürdigerweise; seltsamerweise

**curiousness** /ˈkjʊərɪəsnɪs/ *n., no pl. (inquisitiveness)* Neugier[de], *die;* *(oddness)* Merkwürdigkeit, *die;* Sonderbarkeit, *die*

**curl** /kɜːl/ ❶ *n.* Ⓐ *(of hair)* Locke, *die;* **put one's/sb.'s hair in ~s** sich/jmdm. das Haar locken; **hair in ~s** gelocktes Haar; **hair in tight ~s** Kraushaar, *das;* Ⓑ *(sth. spiral or curved inwards)* **the ~ of a leaf/wave** ein gekräuseltes Blatt/eine gekräuselte Welle; **a ~ of smoke** ein Rauchkringel; Ⓒ *(act of curling)* Kräuseln, *das;* **with a ~ of the lip** mit gekräuselten Lippen.
❷ *v.t.* Ⓐ *(cause to form coils)* locken; *(tightly)* kräuseln; **she ~ed her hair** sie legte ihr Haar in Locken *(Akk.)*; Ⓑ *(bend, twist)* kräuseln ‹Blätter, Lippen›; **the animal ~ed itself into a ball** das Tier rollte sich zu einer Kugel zusammen; **it's enough to ~ your hair** *(fig.)* da stehen einem ja die Haare zu Berge!
❸ *v.i.* Ⓐ *(grow in coils)* sich locken; *(tightly)* sich kräuseln; **her hair ~s naturally** sie hat Naturlocken; *(tightly)* sie hat eine Naturkrause; **it's enough to make your hair ~** *(fig.)* da stehen einem ja die Haare zu Berge!; Ⓑ *(move in spiral form)* ‹Straße, Fluss› sich winden, sich schlängeln; **the smoke ~ed upwards** der Rauch stieg in Kringeln hoch

~ ˈ**up** ❶ *v.t.* hochbiegen; ~ **oneself up** *(roll into shape of ball)* sich zusammenrollen; sich einrollen. ❷ *v.i. (roll into curved shape)*; sich zusammenrollen; sich einrollen; *(fig.: writhe with horror)* erschauern; **he ~ed up on the sofa** er machte es sich *(Dat.)* auf dem Sofa bequem *od. (ugs.)* fläzte sich auf das Sofa; **she ~ed up with a book** sie machte es sich *(Dat.)* mit einem Buch gemütlich

**curler** /ˈkɜːlə(r)/ *n.* Lockenwickler, *der;* **in ~s** mit Lockenwicklern

**curlew** /ˈkɜːljuː/ *n. (Ornith.)* Brachvogel, *der*

**curlicue** /ˈkɜːlɪkjuː/ *n.* Schnörkel, *der*

**curling** /ˈkɜːlɪŋ/ *n. (game)* Curling, *das;* ≈ Eisschießen, *das*

**curling: ~-iron** *n.*, *(Brit.)* **~-tongs** *n. pl.* Brennschere, *die;* *(electrical appliance)* Lockenstab, *der*

**curly** /ˈkɜːlɪ/ *adj.* lockig, *(tightly)* kraus ‹Haar›; kraus ‹Salat›; gewellt, gekräuselt ‹Blatt›; Schnörkel‹schrift, -muster,› verschnörkelt ‹Schrift, Muster›

**curly: ~-haired** *adj.* lockenköpfig; mit lockigem Haar; **~-head** *n.* Lockenkopf, *der;* *(with tight curls)* Krauskopf, *der;* **~-headed** ⇒ **~-haired**

**currant** /ˈkʌrənt/ *n.* Ⓐ *(dried fruit)* Korinthe, *die;* Ⓑ *(fruit)* Johannisbeere, *die;* *(plant)* Johannisbeerstrauch, *der;* ⇒ *also* **black currant; flowering; redcurrant**

**currency** /ˈkʌrənsɪ/ *n.* Ⓐ ▶ **1328** *(money)* Währung, *die;* *(circulation)* Umlauf, *der;* **foreign currencies** Devisen *Pl.;* **withdraw from ~:** aus dem Verkehr ziehen; Ⓑ *(other commodity)* [Tausch]ware, *die;* Zahlungsmittel, *das;* Ⓒ *(prevalence) (of word, idea, story, rumour)* Verbreitung, *die;* *(of expression)* Gebräuchlichkeit, *die;* **gain wide ~:** weite Verbreitung finden; **give ~ to a rumour** ein Gerücht in Umlauf bringen

**current** /ˈkʌrənt/ ❶ *adj.* Ⓐ *(in general circulation or use)* kursierend, umlaufend ‹Geld, Geschichte, Gerücht›; verbreitet ‹Meinung›; gebräuchlich ‹Wort›; gängig ‹Redensart›; **these coins are no longer ~:** diese Münzen sind nicht mehr in Umlauf; Ⓑ laufend ‹Jahr, Monat›; **in the ~ year** in diesem Jahr; Ⓒ *(belonging to the present time)* aktuell ‹Ereignis, Mode›; Tages‹politik, -preis›; derzeitig ‹Politik, Preis›; gegenwärtig ‹Krise, Aufregung›; **~ issue/edition** letzte Ausgabe/neueste Auflage; **~ affairs** Tagespolitik, *die;* aktuelle Fragen.
❷ *n.* Ⓐ ▶ **1480** *(of water, air)* Strömung, *die;* **air/ocean ~:** Luft-/Meeresströmung, *die;* **swim against/with the ~:** gegen den/mit dem Strom schwimmen; **upward/downward ~ of air** *(in atmosphere)* Aufwind/Abwind, *der;* Ⓑ *(Electr.)* Strom, *der;* *(intensity)* Stromstärke, *die;* Ⓒ *(running stream)* Strömung, *die;* Ⓓ *(tendency of events, opinions, etc.)* Tendenz, *die;* Trend, *der;* **the ~ of public opinion** der Trend in der öffentlichen Meinung; **go against/with the ~:** gegen den/mit dem Strom schwimmen

ˈ**current account** *n.* Girokonto, *das;* *(in balance of payments)* Leistungsbilanz, *die*

**currently** /ˈkʌrəntlɪ/ *adv.* gegenwärtig; momentan; zur Zeit; **he is ~ writing a book** er schreibt gerade *od.* zur Zeit an einem Buch; **it is ~ thought** *or* **believed that ...:** heute glaubt man, dass ...

**curriculum** /kəˈrɪkjʊləm/ *n., pl.* **curricula** /kəˈrɪkjʊlə/ Lehrplan, *der;* Curriculum, *das;* **be on the ~:** auf dem Lehrplan stehen

**curriculum vitae** /kərɪkjʊləm ˈviːtaɪ/ *n.* Lebenslauf, *der*

**curry**[1] /ˈkʌrɪ/ *(Cookery)* ❶ *n.* Curry[gericht], *das.* ❷ *v.t.* mit Curry würzen

**curry**[2] *v.t.* Ⓐ striegeln ‹Pferd›; Ⓑ zurichten ‹Leder›; Ⓒ ~ **favour [with sb.]** sich [bei jmdm.] einschmeicheln *od.* lieb Kind machen *(ugs.)*

**curry: ~-comb** *n.* Striegel, *der;* **~ powder** *n.* Currypulver, *das;* Curry, *das od. der*

**curse** /kɜːs/ ❶ *n.* Ⓐ Fluch, *der;* **be under a ~:** unter einem Fluch stehen; **put a ~ on sb./sth.** einen Fluch über jmdn./etw. aussprechen; jmdn./etw. mit einem Fluch belegen; **call down ~s [from Heaven] upon sb.** jmdn. verfluchen; Ⓑ (*profane oath*) Fluch, *der,* Verwünschung, *die;* **bawl ~s at sb.** Flüche gegen jmdn. ausstoßen; **a thousand ~s on this old car** (*joc.*) zum Teufel mit diesem verfluchten alten Auto!; **~s! he's diddled me again** (*joc. coll.*) verflucht! der Kerl hat mich wieder reingelegt (*ugs.*); Ⓒ (*great evil*) Geißel, *die;* Plage, *die;* Ⓓ (*coll.: menstruation*) **the ~:** die Tage (*ugs.*).
❷ *v.t.* Ⓐ (*utter ~ against*) verfluchen; Ⓑ (*as oath*) **~ it/you!** verflucht!; verdammt!; Ⓒ (*afflict*) strafen; **~d with poverty** mit Armut geschlagen *od.* gestraft.
❸ *v.i.* fluchen (**at** über + *Akk.*); **he started cursing and swearing** er fing an, heftig zu fluchen

**cursed** /ˈkɜːsɪd/ *adj.* Ⓐ (*under a curse*) verflucht; verwünscht; Ⓑ (*damnable*) verdammt

**cursive** /ˈkɜːsɪv/ *adj.* kursiv; **~ writing** Schreibschrift, *die*

**cursor** /ˈkɜːsə(r)/ *n.* Läufer, *der;* (*on screen*) Cursor, *der;* Schreibmarke, *die*

**cursorily** /ˈkɜːsərɪlɪ/ *adv.* flüchtig ‹lesen›; oberflächlich ‹untersuchen›

**cursory** /ˈkɜːsərɪ/ *adj.* flüchtig ‹Blick›; oberflächlich ‹Untersuchung, Bericht, Studium›

**curt** /kɜːt/ *adj.* (*discourteously brief*) kurz und schroff ‹Brief, Mitteilung›; kurz angebunden ‹Person, Art›; **he gave a ~ nod and left** er nickte kurz und ging

**curtail** /kɜːˈteɪl/ *v.t.* kürzen; abkürzen ‹Urlaub›; beschneiden ‹Macht›

**curtailment** /kɜːˈteɪlmənt/ *n.* Kürzung, *die;* (*of power*) Beschneidung, *die*

**curtain** /ˈkɜːtən/ ❶ *n.* Ⓐ Vorhang, *der;* (*with net ~s*) Übergardine, *die;* **draw** *or* **pull the ~s** (*open*) die Vorhänge aufziehen; (*close*) die Vorhänge zuziehen; **draw** *or* **pull back the ~s** die Vorhänge aufziehen; Ⓑ (*fig.*) **a ~ of fog/mist** ein Nebelschleier; **a ~ of smoke/flames/rain** eine Rauch-/Flammen-/Regenwand; Ⓒ (*Theatre*) Vorhang, *der;* (*end of play*) Schlussszene, *die;* (*rise of ~ at start of play*) Aufgehen des Vorhanges; Aktbeginn, *der;* (*fall of ~ at end of scene*) Fallen des Vorhanges; Aktschluss, *der;* **the ~ rises/falls** der Vorhang hebt sich/fällt; Ⓓ ⇒ **curtain call**; Ⓔ ⇒ **Iron Curtain**; Ⓕ *in pl.* (*coll.: the end*) Ende, *das;* **that's ~s for him** jetzt ist er erledigt (*ugs.*). ⇒ *also* **safety curtain**.
❷ *v.t.* **~ a window** an einem Fenster Vorhänge/einen Vorhang aufhängen *od.* anbringen; **~ off** mit einem Vorhang abteilen; durch einen Vorhang abtrennen

**curtain: ~ call** *n.* Vorhang, *der;* **get/take a ~ call** einen Vorhang bekommen/vor den Vorhang treten; **~ hook** *n.* Gardinenhaken, *der;* **~ lecture** *n.* Gardinenpredigt, *die;* **~ rail** *n.* Gardinenstange, *die;* **~-raiser** *n.* [kurzes] Vorspiel; (*fig.*) Auftakt, *der;* **~ ring** *n.* Gardinenring, *der;* **~ rod** *n.* Gardinenstange, *die;* **~ runner** *n.* Gardinenröllchen, *das;* **~ track** Gardinenleiste, *die*

**curtly** /ˈkɜːtlɪ/ *adv.* kurz ‹sprechen›; knapp ‹schreiben, antworten›

**curtsy (curtsey)** /ˈkɜːtsɪ/ ❶ *n.* Knicks, *der;* **make** *or* **drop a ~ to sb.** vor jmdm. einen Knicks machen. ❷ *v.i.* **~ to sb.** vor jmdm. knicksen *od.* einen Knicks machen

**curvaceous** /kɜːˈveɪʃəs/ *adj.* kurvenreich (*ugs.*); **a ~ figure** eine üppige Figur

**curvature** /ˈkɜːvətʃə(r)/ *n.* Krümmung, *die;* **~ of the spine** Rückgratverkrümmung, *die*

**curve** /kɜːv/ ❶ *v.t.* krümmen. ❷ *v.i.* ‹Straße, Fluss:› (*once*) eine Biegung machen; (*repeatedly*) sich winden; ‹Horizont:› sich krümmen; ‹Linie:› einen Bogen machen *od.* beschreiben; **the road ~s round the town** die Straße macht einen Bogen um die Stadt. ❸ *n.* Ⓐ Kurve, *die;* Ⓑ (*surface; ~d form or thing*) (*of vase, figure*) Rundung, *die;* **there's a ~ in the road/river** die Straße/der Fluss macht einen Bogen *od.* eine Biegung

**curved** /kɜːvd/ *adj.* krumm; gebogen; gekrümmt ‹Horizont, Raum, Linie›

**cushion** /ˈkʊʃn/ ❶ *n.* Ⓐ Kissen, *das;* Ⓑ (*for protection*) Kissen, *das;* Polster, *das;* Ⓒ (*of billiard table*) Bande, *die;* Ⓓ (*of hovercraft*) Luftkissen, *das.* ❷ *v.t.* Ⓐ [aus]polstern ‹Stuhl›; **~ sb. against sth.** (*fig.*) jmdn. gegen etw. schützen; **~ed seats** Polsterstühle; Ⓑ (*absorb*) dämpfen ‹Aufprall, Stoß›

**cushy** /ˈkʊʃɪ/ *adj.* (*coll.*) bequem; gemütlich; **a ~ job** *or* **number** ein ruhiger Job

**cuss** /kʌs/ (*coll.*) ❶ *n.* Ⓐ (*curse*) Fluch, *der;* Beschimpfung, *die;* **sb. does not give** *or* **care a ~:** jmdm. ist es vollkommen schnuppe (*ugs.*); **he/it is not worth a tinker's ~:** er/es ist keinen Pfifferling *od.* roten Heller wert (*ugs.*); Ⓑ (*usu. derog.: person*) Kerl, *der* (*ugs.*). ❷ *v.i.* fluchen; schimpfen. ❸ *v.t.* verfluchen; beschimpfen

**cussed** /ˈkʌsɪd/ *adj.* (*coll.*) Ⓐ (*perverse, obstinate*) stur (*ugs.*); Ⓑ (*cursed*) verdammt (*ugs.*); verflixt (*ugs.*)

**cussedness** /ˈkʌsɪdnɪs/ *n., no pl.* Sturheit, *die;* **from sheer ~:** aus reiner Sturheit

**ˈcuss word** *n.* (*Amer.*) Fluch, *der;* Verwünschung, *die*

**custard** /ˈkʌstəd/ *n.* Ⓐ **~ [pudding]** ≈ Vanillepudding, *der;* Ⓑ (*sauce*) ≈ Vanillesoße, *die*

**custard: ~ apple** *n.* Zimt-, Rahmapfel, *der;* **~ ˈpie** *n.* (*pie*) *Kuchen mit einer Füllung aus Vanillepudding;* (*in comedy*) Sahnetorte, *die;* **~ pie comedy** Slapstickkomödie, *die;* **~ powder** *n.* Vanillesoßenpulver, *das*

**custodial** /kʌsˈtəʊdɪəl/ *adj.* **~ sentence** Freiheitsstrafe, *die*

**custodian** /kʌsˈtəʊdɪən/ *n.* ▶ **1261** (*of public building, of prisoner*) Wärter, *der*/Wärterin, *die;* Aufseher, *der*/Aufseherin, *die;* (*of park, museum*) Wächter, *der*/Wächterin, *die;* (*of valuables, traditions, culture, place*) Hüter, *der*/Hüterin, *die;* (*of child*) Vormund, *der*

**custody** /ˈkʌstədɪ/ *n.* Ⓐ (*guardianship, care*) Obhut, *die;* **be in the ~ of sb.** unter jmds. Obhut (*Dat.*) stehen; **put** *or* **place sb./sth. in sb.'s ~:** jmdn./etw. in jmds. Obhut (*Akk.*) geben; **the child is in the ~ of his uncle** sein Onkel hat die Vormundschaft über *od.* für das Kind; **in safe ~:** in sicherer Obhut; **the mother was given** *or* **awarded [the] ~ of the children** die Kinder wurden der Mutter zugesprochen; Ⓑ (*imprisonment*) **[be] in ~:** in Haft [sein]; **take sb. into ~:** jmdn. verhaften *od.* festnehmen

**custom** /ˈkʌstəm/ *n.* Ⓐ Brauch, *der;* Sitte, *die;* **it was his ~ to smoke a cigar after dinner** er pflegte nach dem Essen eine Zigarre zu rauchen; er rauchte gewöhnlich eine Zigarre nach dem Essen; Ⓑ *in pl.* (*duty on imports*) Zoll, *der;* **[the] Customs** (*government department*) der Zoll; **go through C~s** durch den Zoll gehen (*ugs.*); Ⓒ (*Law*) Gewohnheitsrecht, *das;* Ⓓ (*business patronage, regular dealings*) Kundschaft, *die* (*veralt.*); **I shall withdraw my ~ from that shop** ich werde in dem Laden nichts mehr kaufen; **we should like to have your ~:** wir hätten Sie gern zum/zur *od.* als Kunden/Kundin; Ⓔ (*regular ~ers*) Kundschaft, *die*

**customarily** /ˈkʌstəmərɪlɪ/ *adv.* in der Regel; üblicherweise

**customary** /ˈkʌstəmərɪ/ *adj.* Ⓐ üblich; Ⓑ (*Law*) gewohnheitsmäßig; Gewohnheits-

**custom: ~-built** *adj.* spezial[an]gefertigt; **~-built clothes** (*Amer.*) maßgeschneiderte Kleidung; **~ clothes** *n.* (*Amer.*) maßgeschneiderte Kleidung

**customer** /ˈkʌstəmə(r)/ *n.* Ⓐ Kunde, *der*/Kundin, *die;* (*of restaurant*) Gast, *der;* (*of theatre*) Besucher, *der*/Besucherin, *die;* (*of library*) Benutzer, *der*/Benutzerin, *die;* Ⓑ (*coll.: person*) Kerl, *der* (*ugs.*); **a queer/an awkward ~:** ein schwieriger Kunde (*ugs.*)

**ˈcustom house** *n.* Zollamt, *das*

**customize (customise)** /ˈkʌstəmaɪz/ *v.t.* speziell anfertigen; (*alter*) umbauen

**ˈcustom-made** *adj.* spezial[an]gefertigt; maßgeschneidert ‹Kleidung›

**customs: ~ clearance** *n.* Zollabfertigung, *die;* **get ~ clearance for sth.** etw. zollamtlich abfertigen lassen; **~ declaration** *n.* Zollerklärung, *die;* **~ duty** *n.* Zoll, *der;* **~ inspection** *n.* Zollkontrolle, *die;* **~ officer** *n.* ▶ **1261** Zollbeamter, *der*/-beamtin, *die;* **~ union** *n.* Zollunion, *die*

**cut** /kʌt/ ❶ *v.t.,* **-tt-, ~:** Ⓐ (*penetrate, wound*) schneiden; **~ one's finger/leg** sich (*Dat. od. Akk.*) in den Finger/ins Bein schneiden; **he ~ himself on broken glass** er hat sich an einer Glasscherbe geschnitten; **he ~ his head open** er schlug sich (*Dat.*) den Kopf auf; **the icy blasts that ~ one to the marrow** (*fig.*) die eisigen Winde, die einem durch und durch *od.* durch Mark und Bein gehen; **the remark ~ him to the quick** (*fig.*) die Bemerkung traf ihn ins Mark; Ⓑ (*divide*) (*with knife*) schneiden; durchschneiden ‹Seil›; (*with axe*) durchhacken; **~ sth. in half/two/three** etw. halbieren/zweiteilen/dreiteilen; **~ sth. [in]to pieces** etw. in Stücke schneiden/hacken; **~ one's ties** *or* **links** alle Verbindungen abbrechen; alle Brücken hinter sich (*Dat.*) abbrechen; **~ no ice with sb.** (*fig. coll.*) keinen Eindruck auf jmdn. machen; jmdm. nicht imponieren (*ugs.*); **~ the knot** (*fig.*) das Problem lösen; Ⓒ (*detach, reduce*) abschneiden; schneiden, stutzen ‹Hecke›; mähen ‹Getreide, Gras›; **~** (*p.p.*) **flowers** Schnittblumen; **~ one's nails** sich (*Dat.*) die Nägel schneiden; Ⓓ (*shape, fashion*) schleifen ‹Glas, Edelstein, Kristall›; hauen, schlagen ‹Stufen›; treiben ‹Tunnel›; einhauen ‹Inschrift›; **~ a key** einen Schlüssel feilen *od.* anfertigen; **~ figures in wood/stone** Figuren aus Holz schnitzen/aus Stein hauen; **~ a record** eine Schallplatte schneiden; Ⓔ (*meet and cross*) ‹Straße, Linie, Kreis:› schneiden; **the two lines ~ one another at right angles** die beiden Linien schneiden sich im rechten Winkel; Ⓕ (*fig.: renounce, refuse to recognize*) schneiden; **~ sb. dead** jmdn. wie Luft behandeln; Ⓖ (*carve*) [auf]schneiden ‹Fleisch, Geflügel›; abschneiden ‹Scheibe›; **~** (*p.p.*) **loaf** (*Brit. dated*) Schnittbrot, *das;* Ⓗ (*reduce*) senken ‹Preise›; verringern, einschränken ‹Menge, Produktion›; mindern ‹Qualität›; drosseln ‹Tempo, Produktion›; kürzen ‹Ausgaben, Lohn›; verkürzen ‹Arbeitszeit, Urlaub›; (*cease, stop*) einstellen ‹Dienstleistungen, Lieferungen›; abstellen ‹Strom›; (*coll.*) aufhören mit ‹Tätigkeit›; **these scenes were ~ by the censor** diese Szenen hat die Zensur herausgeschnitten; Ⓘ ⇒ **figure** 1 D; Ⓙ (*absent oneself from*) schwänzen ‹Schule, Unterricht›; Ⓚ **~ a loss** der Sache (*Dat.*) ein Ende machen (*ehe der Schaden noch größer wird*); **~ one's losses** höherem Verlust vorbeugen; Ⓛ **~ sth. short** (*lit. or fig.: interrupt, terminate*) etwas abbrechen; **the war ~ short his career** der Krieg hat seine Karriere vorzeitig beendet; **~ sb. short** jmdn. unterbrechen; (*impatiently*) jmdm. ins Wort fallen; **to ~ a long story short** der langen Rede kurzer Sinn; Ⓜ (*Cards*) abheben; **~ the pack [of cards]** [die Karten] abheben; Ⓝ **~ a tooth** einen Zahn bekommen; **~ one's teeth on sth.** (*fig.*) sich (*Dat.*) die ersten Sporen an etw. (*Dat.*) *od.* mit etw. verdienen; Ⓞ **be ~ and dried** genau festgelegt *od.* abgesprochen sein; **her opinions are ~ and dried** ihre Ansichten sind unverrückbar; Ⓟ (*Cricket, Tennis*) [an]schneiden ‹Ball›; Ⓠ (*Cinemat.*) schneiden; cutten; Ⓡ **half ~** (*coll.*) angetrunken. ⇒ *also* **cloth** A; **corner** 1 A; **eye tooth**; **fine**[2] 1 G; Ⓢ (*Computing*) **~ and paste** ausschneiden und einfügen.
❷ *v.i.,* **-tt-, ~:** Ⓐ ‹Messer, Schwert usw.:› schneiden; ‹Papier, Tuch, Käse:› sich schneiden lassen; **~ into a cake** einen Kuchen anschneiden; **~ both ways** (*fig.*) ein zweischneidiges Schwert sein (*fig.*); Ⓑ (*cross, intersect*) sich schneiden; Ⓒ (*pass*) **~ through** *or* **across the field/park** [quer] über das Feld/durch den Park gehen; **~ across sth.** (*fig.*) sich über etw. (*Akk.*) hinwegsetzen; Ⓓ (*Cinemat.*) (*stop the cameras*) abbrechen; (*go quickly to another shot*) überblenden (**to** zu); **the film director cried '~!'** der Regisseur rief: „Schnitt!" *od.* „Aus!"; Ⓔ (*coll.: run*) **~ along** sich auf die Socken machen (*ugs.*); **~**

**and run** abhauen (*ugs.*). ⇒ *also* **loose** 1 A. ❸ *n.* **A** (*act of* ~*ting*) Schnitt, *der;* **B** (*stroke, blow*) (*with knife*) Schnitt, *der;* (*with sword, whip*) Hieb, *der;* (*injury*) Schnittwunde, *die;* **the ~ and thrust of politics** (*fig.*) das Spannungsfeld der Politik; **the ~ and thrust of debate** (*fig.*) die Hitze der Debatte; **C** (*reduction*) (*in wages*) Kürzung, *die;* (*in expenditure, budget*) Kürzung, *die;* Einsparung, *die;* (*in prices*) Senkung, *die;* (*in time, working hours, holiday, etc.*) Verkürzung, *die;* (*in services*) Verringerung, *die;* (*in production, output, etc.*) Einschränkung, *die;* (*in quality*) Minderung, *die;* **make the ~** (*Sport, esp. Golf*) sich für den weiteren Wettkampf qualifizieren; **D** (*wounding act or utterance*) Seitenhieb, *der* (**at** gegen); Affront, *der* (*geh.*); **the unkindest ~ of all** der schlimmste Schlag; **E** (*of meat*) Stück, *das;* **F** ⇒ **wood~**; **G** (*coll.: commission, share*) Anteil, *der;* **H** (*way thing is* ~) (*of gem*) Schliff, *der;* (*of hair: style*) [Haar]schnitt, *der;* Frisur, *die;* (*of clothes*) Schnitt, *der;* **be a ~ above [the rest]** [den anderen] um einiges überlegen sein; **I** (*in play, book, etc.*) Streichung, *die;* (*in film*) Schnitt, *der;* **make ~s** Streichungen/Schnitte vornehmen; **J** (*channel made for river*) Rinne, *die;* Einschnitt, *der.* ⇒ *also* **jib**[1] A; **short ~**

**~ 'away** ⇒ **~ off a**

**~ 'back** ❶ *v.t.* **A** (*reduce*) einschränken ‹Produktion›; verringern ‹Investitionen›; **B** (*prune*) stutzen. ❷ *v.i.* **A** (*reduce*) **~ back on sth.** etw. einschränken; **B** (*Cinemat.*) zurückblenden. ⇒ *also* **~-back**

**~ 'down** ❶ *v.t.* **A** (*fell*) fällen; **B** (*kill*) töten; **~ sb. down with a sword** jmdn. mit dem Schwert erschlagen *od.* (*geh.*) niederstrecken; **C** (*reduce*) einschränken; **~ an article down** einen Artikel zusammenstreichen *od.* kürzen; **~ sb. down to size** (*fig.*) jmdn. auf seinen Platz verweisen. ❷ *v.i.* (*reduce*) **~ down on sth.** etw. einschränken; **~ down on tobacco** den Tabakverbrauch einschränken; **~ down on clothes** die Ausgaben für die Garderobe einschränken

**~ 'in** ❶ *v.i.* **A** (*come in abruptly, interpose*) sich einschalten; unterbrechen; **~ in on sb./sth.** jmdn./etw. unterbrechen; **B** (*after overtaking*) schneiden; **~ in in front of sb.** jmdn. schneiden; **C** (*take dance partner from another*) **~ in [on sb.]** [jmdn.] abklatschen; **D** (*switch itself on*) ‹Motor usw.:› sich einschalten. ❷ *v.t.* (*give share of profit to*) beteiligen ‹Komplizen›

**~ 'off** *v.t.* **A** (*remove by cutting*) abschneiden; abtrennen; (*with axe etc.*) abschlagen; **B** (*interrupt, make unavailable*) abschneiden ‹Zufuhr›; streichen ‹Zuschuss›; abstellen ‹Strom, Gas, Wasser›; unterbrechen ‹Telefongespräch, Sprecher am Telefon›; **C** (*isolate*) abschneiden; **be ~ off by the snow/tide** durch den Schnee/die Flut [von der Außenwelt] abgeschnitten sein; **D** (*prevent, block*) abschneiden; **their retreat was ~ off** ihnen wurde der Rückzug abgeschnitten; **E** (*exclude from contact with others*) **~ sb. off from friends/the outside world** jmdn. von seinen Freunden trennen/von der Außenwelt abschneiden; **~ oneself off** sich absondern; **F** (*disinherit*) enterben; **~ sb. off with a shilling** jmdn. mit einem Apfel und einem Ei abspeisen (*ugs.*). ⇒ *also* **~-off**

**~ 'out** ❶ *v.t.* **A** (*remove by cutting*) ausschneiden; **~ sth. out of sth.** etw. aus etw. ausschneiden; **B** (*omit*) [heraus]streichen; **C** (*stop doing or using*) aufhören mit; **~ out cigarettes/alcohol/drugs** aufhören, Zigaretten zu rauchen/Alkohol zu trinken/Drogen zu nehmen; **~ it** *or* **that out** (*coll.*) hör/hört auf damit!; lass/lasst das sein!; **D** (*defeat*) ausstechen (*ugs.*) ‹Rivalen, Konkurrenten, Gegner›; **E** (*shape*) zuschneiden ‹Stoff, Kleid, Leder›; **F** (*disconnect electrically*) ausschalten ‹Motor, Licht›; abstellen ‹Motor›; abschalten ‹Strom›; **G** (*make suitable*) **be ~ out for sth.** für etw. geeignet sein; **he was not ~ out to be a teacher** er war nicht zum Lehrer gemacht; er taugte nicht zum Lehrer; **Peter and Susan seem to be ~ out for each other** Peter und Susan sind füreinander wie geschaffen. ❷ *v.i.* (*cease functioning*) ‹Motor:› aussetzen; ‹Gerät:› sich abschalten. ⇒ *also* **~-out**

**~ 'up** ❶ *v.t.* **A** (~ *in pieces*) zerschneiden; in Stücke schneiden ‹Fleisch, Gemüse›; (*chop*) zerhacken; **B** (*injure*) verletzen; (*fig.: criticize*) zerreißen; **~ up the enemy** den Feind vernichten; **be ~ up about sth.** (*fig.*) zutiefst betroffen über etw. (*Akk.*) sein. ❷ *v.i.* **~ up rough** Krach schlagen (*ugs.*); Radau machen (*ugs.*)

**cutaneous** /kju:'teɪnɪəs/ *adj.* Haut-; kutan (*fachspr.*)

**cut: ~away** *adj.* Schnitt-; **~away model** Schnittmodell, *das;* **~-back** *n.* (*reduction*) Kürzung, *die;* (*Cinemat.*) Rückblende, *die*

**cute** /kju:t/ *adj.* (*coll.*) **A** (*attractive*) süß, niedlich ‹Kind, Mädchen›; entzückend ‹Stadt, Haus›; **B** (*shrewd*) schlau; gerissen; (*ingenious*) raffiniert ‹Gerät›; einfallsreich ‹Person›; pfiffig ‹Erklärung›

**cut 'glass** *n.* Kristall[glas], *das*

**'cut-glass** *adj.* Kristall-

**cuticle** /'kju:tɪkl/ *n.* Epidermis, *die* (*fachspr.*); Oberhaut, *die;* (*of nail*) Nagelhaut, *die*

**'cuticle remover** *n.* Nagelhautentferner, *der*

**cutie** /'kju:tɪ/ *n.* (*coll.*) **A** (*woman*) Süße, *die;* **B** (*usu. joc. : man*) irrer Typ (*ugs.*)

**cutlass** /'kʌtləs/ *n.* **A** (*Hist.*) Entersäbel, *der;* **B** ⇒ **machete**

**cutler** /'kʌtlə(r)/ *n.* ▶ **1261** Messerschmied, *der*

**cutlery** /'kʌtlərɪ/ *n.* Besteck, *das*

**cutlet** /'kʌtlɪt/ *n.* **A** (*of mutton or lamb*) Kotelett, *das;* **B** **veal ~:** Frikandeau, *das;* **C** (*minced meat etc. in shape of* ~) Hacksteak, *das;* **nut/cheese/potato ~** *aus Nüssen/Käse/Kartoffeln hergestelltes Gericht in Form eines Schnitzels od. Koteletts*

**cut: ~-off** *n.* **A** Trennung, *die;* **~-off point** Trennungslinie, *die;* **B** *as tech. term* Ausschaltmechanismus, *der;* Ausschaltung, *die;* **~-out** *n.* (*Electr.*) Unterbrecher, *der;* (*figure ~ out of material*) Ausschneidefigur, *die;* **~-out box** (*Amer.*) ⇒ **fuse box**; **~-price** *adj.* herabgesetzt; **~-price goods** Waren zu herabgesetzten Preisen; **~-price offer** Billigangebot, *das;* **~-rate** *adj.* verbilligt; herabgesetzt

**cutter** /'kʌtə(r)/ *n.* **A** (*person*) (*of cloth*) Zuschneider, *der*/-schneiderin, *die;* (*of stones*) Steinmetz, *der;* (*of glass, gems*) Schleifer, *der*/Schleiferin, *die;* (*of films*) Cutter, *der*/Cutterin, *die;* Schnittmeister, *der*/-meisterin, *die;* (*miner*) Hauer, *der;* **B** (*machine*) Schneidmaschine, *die;* Schneidwerkzeug, *das;* (*rotary cutting tool*) Bohrkrone, *die;* Bohrkopf, *der;* (*cutting stylus*) Cutter, *der;* **C** (*Naut.*) Kutter, *der*

**'cutthroat** ❶ *n.* **A** Strolch, *der;* (*murderer*) Killer, *der* (*ugs.*); **B** (*Amer.: trout*) Purpurforelle, *die.* ❷ *adj.* **A** mörderisch, gnadenlos ‹Wettbewerb›; **B** **~ razor** Rasiermesser, *das*

**cutting** /'kʌtɪŋ/ ❶ *adj.* beißend ‹Bemerkung, Antwort›; schneidend ‹Wind›; **~ edge** Schneide, *die;* **~ tool** Schneidewerkzeug, *das.* ❷ *n.* **A** (*esp. Brit.: from newspaper*) Ausschnitt, *der;* **B** (*esp. Brit.: excavation for railway, road etc.*) Einschnitt, *der;* **C** (*of plant*) Ableger, *der*

**'cutting edge** *n.* **be at the ~ of technology** auf dem Gebiet der Technologie führend sein; die Speerspitze der Technologie sein; **be at the ~ of fashion** auf dem Gebiet der Mode führend sein

**cuttle[fish]** /'kʌtl(fɪʃ)/ *n.* Tintenfisch, *der;* Sepia, *die* (*fachspr.*)

**c.v.** *abbr.* **curriculum vitae**

**c.w.o.** *abbr.* **cash with order** Barzahlung *od.* Kasse bei Auftragserteilung

**cwt.** *abbr.* **hundredweight** ≈ Ztr.

**cyan** /'saɪən/ ❶ *adj.* grünstichig blau. ❷ *n.* Cyanblau, *das*

**cyanide** /'saɪənaɪd/ *n.* Cyanid, *das*

**cyanogen** /saɪ'ænədʒən/ *n.* (*Chem.*) Cyan, *das*

**cybernetics** /saɪbə'netɪks/ *n., no pl.* Kybernetik, *die*

**cyber: ~sex** /'saɪbəseks/ *n., no pl., no art.* Cybersex, *der;* **~space** /'saɪbəspeɪs/ *n., no pl., no art.* Cyberspace, *der*

**cyclamen** /'sɪkləmən/ *n.* (*Bot.*) Alpenveilchen, *das;* Zyklamen, *das* (*fachspr.*)

**cycle** /'saɪkl/ ❶ *n.* **A** (*recurrent period*) Zyklus, *der;* (*period of completion*) Turnus, *der;* **~ of the seasons** Jahreszyklus, *der;* **~ per second** (*Phys., Electr.*) Schwingung pro Sekunde; Hertz, *das;* **B** (*recurring series*) Kreislauf, *der;* (*complete set or series*) Zyklus, *der;* **C** (*bicycle*) Rad, *das.* ❷ *v.i.* Rad fahren; mit dem [Fahr]rad fahren

**cycle: ~ computer** *n.* Fahrradcomputer, *der;* **~ lane** *n.* Fahrradspur, *die;* **~ race** *n.* Radrennen, *das;* **~ track** *n.* Rad[fahr]weg, *der;* (*for racing*) Radrennbahn, *die;* **~way** ⇒ **~ track**

**cyclic** /'saɪklɪk/, **cyclical** /'saɪklɪkl/ *adj.*, **cyclically** /'saɪklɪkəlɪ/ *adv.* zyklisch

**cycling** /'saɪklɪŋ/ *n.* (*activity*) Radfahren, *das;* (*sport*) Radsport, *der;* **amateur ~:** Amateur-Radrennsport, *der; attrib.* **~ enthusiast** Radsportfan, *der;* **~ shorts** Radlerhose, *die*

**cyclist** /'saɪklɪst/ *n.* Radfahrer, *der*/-fahrerin, *die*

**cyclo-cross** *n.* Querfeldeinrennen, *das*

**cyclone** /'saɪkləʊn/ *n.* (*system of winds*) Tiefdruckgebiet, *das;* Zyklon, *die* (*fachspr.*); (*violent hurricane*) Zyklon, *der*

**cyclonic** /'saɪklɒnɪk/ *adj.* Zyklon‹wind, -stärke›; **~ storm** Zyklon, *der*

**Cyclops** /'saɪklɒps/ *n., pl. same or* **~es** *or* **Cyclopes** /saɪ'kləʊpi:z/ (*Mythol.*) Zyklop, *der*

**cyclotron** /'saɪklətrɒn/ *n.* (*Phys.*) Zyklotron, *das*

**cygnet** /'sɪgnɪt/ *n.* junger Schwan

**cylinder** /'sɪlɪndə(r)/ *n.* (*also Geom., Motor Veh.*) Zylinder, *der;* (*of revolver, carding machine*) Trommel, *die;* (*for compressed or liquefied gas*) Gasflasche, *die;* (*of diving apparatus*) [Sauerstoff]flasche, *die;* (*of platen press, typewriter, mower*) Walze, *die*

**cylinder: ~ block** *n.* Motorblock, *der;* **~ head** *n.* Zylinderkopf, *der*

**cylindrical** /sɪ'lɪndrɪkl/ *adj.* zylindrisch; ⇒ *also* **projection** I

**cymbal** /'sɪmbl/ *n.* (*Mus.*) Beckenteller, *der;* **~s** Becken *Pl.*

**cyme** /saɪm/ *n.* (*Bot.*) Trugdolde, *die*

**cynic** /'sɪnɪk/ *n.* **A** Zyniker, *der;* **B** **C~** (*Greek philosopher*) Kyniker, *der*

**cynical** /'sɪnɪkl/ *adj.* zynisch; bissig ‹Artikel, Bemerkung, Worte›; **be ~ about sth.** sich zynisch zu etw. äußern

**cynically** /'sɪnɪkəlɪ/ *adv.* zynisch

**cynicism** /'sɪnɪsɪzm/ *n.* Zynismus, *der*

**cypher** ⇒ **cipher**

**cypress** /'saɪprɪs/ *n.* Zypresse, *die*

**Cyprian** /'sɪprɪən/, **Cypriot** /'sɪprɪət/ ▶ **1340** ❶ *adjs.* zyprisch; zypriotisch. ❷ *ns.* Zypriot, *der*/Zypriotin, *die;* Zyprer, *der*/Zyprerin, *die*

**Cyprus** /'saɪprəs/ *pr. n.* Zypern (*das*)

**Cyrillic** /sɪ'rɪlɪk/ *adj.* kyrillisch

**cyst** /sɪst/ *n.* ▶ **1232** (*Biol., Med.*) Zyste, *die*

**cystitis** /sɪs'taɪtɪs/ *n.* ▶ **1232** (*Med.*) Zystitis, *die* (*Med.*); Blasenentzündung, *die*

**cytology** /saɪ'tɒlədʒɪ/ *n.* Zytologie, *die*

**cytoplasm** /'saɪtəplæzm/ *n.* (*Biol.*) Zytoplasma, *das*

**czar** *etc.* ⇒ **tsar** *etc.*

**Czech** /tʃek/ ▶ **1275**, ▶ **1340** ❶ *adj.* tschechisch; **sb. is ~:** jmd. ist Tscheche/Tschechin; ⇒ *also* **English** 1. ❷ *n.* **A** (*language*) Tschechisch, *das;* ⇒ *also* **English** 2 A; **B** (*person*) Tscheche, *der*/Tschechin, *die*

**Czechoslovak** /tʃekəʊ'sləʊvæk/ (*Hist.*) ⇒ **Czechoslovakian**

**Czechoslovakia** /tʃekəʊslə'vækɪə/ *pr. n.* (*Hist.*) die Tschechoslowakei

**Czechoslovakian** /tʃekəʊslə'vækɪən/ ▶ **1340** (*Hist.*) ❶ *adj.* tschechoslowakisch. ❷ *n.* Tschechoslowake, *der*/Tschechoslowakin, *die*

**Czech Republic** *n.* Tschechische Republik; Tschechien (*das*)

C

# Dd

d

**D, d** /diː/ *n., pl.* **Ds** *or* **D's** Ⓐ (*letter*) D, d, *das;* Ⓑ **D** (*Mus.*) D, d, *das;* **D sharp** dis, Dis, *das;* **D flat** des, Des, *das;* Ⓒ (*Roman numeral*) D; Ⓓ **D** (*Sch., Univ.: mark*) Vier, *die;* **he got a D** er bekam „ausreichend" *od.* eine Vier

**D.** *abbr.* Ⓐ (*Amer.*) **Democrat;** Ⓑ **dimensional**

**d.** *abbr.* Ⓐ **daughter** T.; Ⓑ **deci-** d; Ⓒ **delete** d.; Ⓓ **died** gest.; Ⓔ (*Brit. Hist.*) **penny/pence** d.

**'d** /d/ (*coll.*) = **would, had, should**

**DA** *abbr.* ▶ **1261** (*Amer.*) **District Attorney**

**dab¹** /dæb/ ❶ *n.* Ⓐ Tupfer, *der;* Ⓑ (*slight blow, tap*) Klaps, *der;* (*bird's peck*) Picken, *das;* Ⓒ *in pl.* (*Brit. coll.: fingerprints*) Fingerabdrücke *Pl.* ❷ *v.t.*, **-bb-:** Ⓐ (*press with sponge etc.*) abtupfen; (*press on surface*) ~ **sth. on** *or* **against sth.** etw. auf etw. (*Akk.*) tupfen; Ⓑ (*strike lightly, tap*) ~ **sb.** jmdm. einen Klaps geben; Ⓒ ‹Vogel:› picken. ❸ *v.i.*, **-bb-:** ~ **at sth.** etw. ab- *od.* betupfen

**dab²** *n.* (*Zool.*) Kliesche, *die;* Scharbe, *die*

**dab³** (*Brit. coll.: expert*) ❶ *n.* Könner, *der;* Ass, *das* (*ugs.*) (**at** in + *Dat.*). ❷ *adj.* geschickt; **be a ~ hand at cricket/making omelettes** ein Ass im Kricket/Eierkuchenbacken sein (*ugs.*)

**dabble** /'dæbl/ ❶ *v.t.* Ⓐ (*wet slightly*) befeuchten; (*move in water*) ~ **one's feet in the water** mit den Füßen im Wasser planschen; Ⓑ (*soil, splash*) bespritzen. ❷ *v.i.* (*engage in*) ~ **at/in sth.** sich in etw. (*Dat.*) versuchen; in etw. (*Dat.*) dilettieren

**dabbler** /'dæblə(r)/ *n.* Amateur, *der;* Dilettant, *der* (*abwertend*)

**dabchick** /'dæbtʃɪk/ *n.* (*Ornith.*) Lappentaucher, *der;* Steißfuß, *der*

**dace** /deɪs/ *n., pl. same* (*Zool.*) Hasel, *der;* Häsling, *der*

**dacha** /'dætʃə/ *n.* Datscha, *die;* (*bes. DDR:*) Datsche, *die*

**dachshund** /'dækshʊnd/ *n.* Dackel, *der;* Dachshund, *der* (*fachspr.*)

**dactyl** /'dæktɪl/ *n.* (*Pros.*) Daktylus, *der*

**dad** /dæd/ *n.* (*coll.*) Vater, *der*

**Dadaism** /'dɑːdɑːɪzm/ *n.* (*Art Hist.*) Dadaismus, *der*

**daddy** /'dædɪ/ *n.* (*coll.*) Ⓐ Vati, *der* (*fam.*); Papi, *der* (*fam.*); Papa, *der* (*fam.*); Ⓑ (*man*) Alte, *der* (*ugs.*); Ⓒ (*oldest/most important person*) König, *der* (*ugs.*); **the ~ of them all** der/die/das Allergrößte (*ugs.*)

**daddy-'long-legs** *n. sing.* (*Zool.*) Ⓐ (*crane-fly*) Schnake, *die;* Ⓑ (*Amer.: harvestman*) Weberknecht, *der;* Kanker, *der*

**dado** /'deɪdəʊ/ *n., pl.* **~s** *or* (*Amer.*) **~es** Ⓐ (*of room wall*) Sockel, *der;* Ⓑ (*of column*) Kehle, *die*

**daemon** /'diːmən/ *n.* Dämon, *der*

**daffodil** /'dæfədɪl/ *n.* Gelbe Narzisse; Osterglocke, *die*

**daffy** /'dæfɪ/ *adj.* (*coll.*) blöd[e] (*ugs.*); dämlich (*ugs.*)

**daft** /dɑːft/ *adj.* Ⓐ (*foolish, wild*) doof (*ugs.*); blöd[e] (*ugs.*); **what a ~ thing to do!** so was Doofes (*ugs.*) *od.* Blödes (*ugs.*)!; Ⓑ (*crazy*) verrückt (*ugs.*); übergeschnappt (*ugs.*); **be ~ about sth./sb.** verrückt nach etw./jmdm. sein

**dagger** /'dægə(r)/ *n.* Ⓐ Dolch, *der;* **be at ~s drawn with sb.** (*fig.*) mit jmdm. auf Kriegsfuß stehen; **look ~s at sb.** jmdn. finster anblicken; jmdm. finstere Blicke zuwerfen; Ⓑ (*Printing*) Kreuz, *das*

**dago** /'deɪgəʊ/ *n., pl.* **~s** *or* **~es** (*sl. derog.*) Ⓐ (*Spaniard, Portuguese, Italian*) Welsche, *der* (*veralt. abwertend*); Kanake, *der* (*derb abwertend*); Ⓑ (*any foreigner*) Kanake, *der* (*derb abwertend*)

**daguerreotype** /də'gerətaɪp/ *n.* Daguerreotypie, *die*

**dahlia** /'deɪlɪə/ *n.* Dahlie, *die*

**daily** /'deɪlɪ/ ❶ *adj.* täglich; **~ [news]paper** Tageszeitung, *die;* **the ~ grind [of life]** der Alltagstrott; **on a ~ basis** tageweise. ❷ *adv.* täglich; jeden Tag; (*constantly*) Tag für Tag; täglich. ❸ *n.* Ⓐ (*newspaper*) Tageszeitung, *die;* Ⓑ (*Brit. coll.: charwoman*) Reinemachefrau, *die.* ⇒ *also* **bread** 1 B; **dozen** B

**daintily** /'deɪntɪlɪ/ *adv.* zierlich; anmutig ‹gehen, sich bewegen›

**daintiness** /'deɪntɪnɪs/ *n., no pl.* Zierlichkeit, *die;* (*of movement, manner, etc.*) Anmut, *die*

**dainty** /'deɪntɪ/ ❶ *adj.* Ⓐ (*of delicate beauty*) zierlich; anmutig ‹Bewegung, Person›; zart, fein ‹Gesichtszüge›; Ⓑ (*choice*) delikat, köstlich ‹Essen›; Ⓒ (*having delicate tastes*) empfindsam; feinfühlig. ❷ *n.* (*lit. or fig.*) Delikatesse, *die;* Leckerbissen, *der*

**dairy** /'deərɪ/ *n.* Ⓐ Molkerei, *die;* Ⓑ (*shop*) Milchladen, *der*

**dairy: ~ cattle** *n.* Milchvieh, *das;* **~ cream** *n.* [echter] Rahm; [echte] Sahne; **~ farm** *n.* Milchbetrieb, *der;* **~ farmer** *n.* Milchbauer, *der*

**dairying** /'deərɪɪŋ/ *n.* Milchwirtschaft, *die*

**dairy: ~maid** *n.* Molkereiangestellte, *die;* **~man** /'deərɪmən/ *n., pl.* **~men** /'deərɪmən/ Milchmann, *der;* **~ produce** *n.*, **~ products** *n. pl.* Molkereiprodukte

**dais** /'deɪɪs, 'deɪs/ *n.* Podium, *das*

**daisy** /'deɪzɪ/ *n.* Gänseblümchen, *das;* (*ox-eye*) Margerite, *die;* **be pushing up [the] daisies** (*fig. coll.*) sich (*Dat.*) die Radieschen von unten ansehen (*salopp*); ⇒ *also* **fresh** 1 E

**daisy: ~ chain** *n.* Kranz aus Gänseblümchen; **~ wheel** *n.* Typenrad, *das*

**dale** /deɪl/ *n.* (*literary/N. Engl.*) Tal, *das;* ⇒ *also* **up** 2 A

**dalliance** /'dælɪəns/ *n.* (*literary*) Tändelei, *die* (*veralt. geh.*)

**dally** /'dælɪ/ *v.i.* Ⓐ (*amuse oneself, sport*) **~ with sb.** mit jmdm. spielen *od.* leichtfertig umgehen; (*flirt*) mit jmdm. schäkern (*ugs.*) *od.* flirten; **~ with an idea** mit einem Gedanken spielen; Ⓑ (*idle, loiter*) [herum]trödeln (*ugs.*); **~ [over sth.]** mit etw. trödeln (*ugs.*)

**Dalmatian** /dæl'meɪʃn/ *n.* Dalmatiner, *der*

**dam¹** /dæm/ ❶ *n.* Ⓐ [Stau]damm, *der;* Ⓑ (*barrier made by beavers*) Damm, *der.* ❷ *v.t.*, **-mm-:** Ⓐ (*lit. or fig.*) **~ [up/back] sth.** etw. abblocken; **~ [up/back] the flow of words** dem Wortschwall Einhalt gebieten; **~ [up/back] one's feelings** seine Gefühle zurückhalten; Ⓑ (*furnish or confine with ~*) eindämmen; aufstauen

**dam²** *n.* (*Zool.*) Muttertier, *das*

**damage** /'dæmɪdʒ/ ❶ *n.* Ⓐ *no pl.* Schaden, *der;* **do a lot of ~ to sb./sth.** jmdm./einer Sache großen Schaden zufügen; jmdm. sehr schaden/etw. stark beschädigen; **the ~ is done now** es ist nun einmal passiert; Ⓑ *no pl.* (*loss of what is desirable*) **to sb.'s great ~:** zu jmds. großem Leidwesen; Ⓒ *in pl.* (*Law*) Schaden[s]ersatz, *der;* Ⓓ *no pl.* (*Brit. coll.: cost*) **what's the ~?** was kostet der Spaß? (*ugs.*).
❷ *v.t.* Ⓐ beschädigen; **smoking can ~ one's health** Rauchen gefährdet die Gesundheit; Ⓑ (*detract from*) schädigen; **the article ~d his good reputation** der Artikel hat seinem guten Ruf geschadet; **that ~d his chances [of promotion]/his pride** das hat seine [Aufstiegs]chancen geschmälert/seinen Stolz verletzt

**damaging** /'dæmɪdʒɪŋ/ *adj.* schädlich (**to** für)

**damask** /'dæməsk/ ❶ *n.* Ⓐ (*material*) Damast, *der;* Ⓑ (*twilled table linen*) Damastdecke, *die.* ❷ *adj.* damasten

**damask 'rose** *n.* Damaszenerrose, *die*

**dame** /deɪm/ *n.* Ⓐ **D~** (*Brit.*) Dame (*Titel der weiblichen Träger verschiedener Orden im Ritterstand*); Ⓑ **D~** (*literary/poet.: title of woman of rank*) Dame, *die;* (*title of thing personified as woman*) **D~ Nature** Mutter Natur; **D~ Fortune** Frau Fortuna; Ⓒ (*arch./poet./joc./Amer. sl.*) Weib, *das;* Ⓓ (*in pantomime*) komische Alte

**damfool** /'dæmfuːl/ (*coll.*) ❶ *adj.* idiotisch (*ugs.*); blöd (*ugs.*); **~ action/remark** *etc.* Blödsinn, *der* (*ugs.*); **that was a ~ thing to do!** das war saublöd! (*ugs.*) ❷ *n.* Idiot, *der* (*ugs.*); Blödmann, *der* (*salopp*)

**dammit** /'dæmɪt/ *int.* (*coll.*) verdammt noch mal! (*ugs.*); **as ... as ~:** verdammt ... (*ugs.*); **as near as ~:** jedenfalls so gut wie (*ugs.*)

**damn** /dæm/ ❶ *v.t.* Ⓐ (*condemn, censure*) verreißen ‹Buch, Film, Theaterstück›; **~ with faint praise** durch kühles Lob ablehnen; Ⓑ (*doom to hell, curse*) verdammen; Ⓒ (*coll.*) **~ [it]!, ~ and blast [it]!** verflucht [noch mal]! (*ugs.*); zum Teufel [noch mal]! (*ugs.*); **~ it all!** verdammt noch mal! (*ugs.*); zum Donnerwetter! (*ugs.*); **~ all** (*Brit. coll.*) nicht die Bohne (*ugs.*); **~ you/him!** hol dich/ihn der Teufel! (*salopp*); **[well,] I'll be** *or* **I'm ~ed** ich werd verrückt (*ugs.*) *od.* dreh durch (*salopp*); **[I'll be** *or* **I'm] ~ed if I know** ich habe nicht die leiseste Ahnung; **[I'll be** *or* **I'm] ~ed if I'll go to meet him** ich werde ihn auf gar keinen Fall *od.* garantiert nicht treffen; **I'm ~ed if I can find it** ich kann es beim besten Willen nicht finden; ⇒ *also* **God;** Ⓓ (*be the ruin of*) zu Fall bringen.
❷ *n.* Ⓐ (*curse*) Fluch, *der;* Ⓑ **he didn't give** *or* **care a ~ [about it]** ihm war es völlig Wurscht (*ugs.*) *od.* scheißegal (*salopp*); **I don't give a ~ for that girl** das Mädchen ist mir völlig schnuppe *od.* Wurscht (*ugs.*).
❸ *adj.* verdammt (*ugs.*); Scheiß- (*salopp*).
❹ *adv.* verdammt

**damnable** /'dæmnəbl/ *adj.* grässlich, scheußlich ‹Wetter›; ungeheuerlich ‹Lüge, Anschuldigung›; **~ luck** entsetzliches Pech

**damnably** /'dæmnəblɪ/ *adv.* verdammt

**damnation** /dæm'neɪʃn/ ❶ *n.* Verdammnis, *die.* ❷ *int.* verdammt [noch mal]! (*ugs.*)

**damned** /dæmd/ ❶ *adj.* Ⓐ (*doomed*) verdammt; Ⓑ (*infernal, unwelcome*) verdammt (*ugs.*); **I can't see a ~ thing in this fog** so'n Mist, ich sehe überhaupt nichts [mehr] bei diesem Nebel (*ugs.*); **I have to walk back in this rain. What a ~ nuisance!** Verdammter Mist! Jetzt muss ich bei dem Regen zurücklaufen! (*ugs.*); Ⓒ **do/try one's ~est** sein Möglichstes tun. ❷ *adv.* verdammt (*ugs.*); **I should ~ well hope so/think so** das will ich aber [auch] schwer hoffen (*ugs.*) / stark annehmen. ❸ *n. pl.* **the ~:** die Verdammten

**damning** /'dæmɪŋ/ *adj.* Ⓐ (*expressing severe criticism*) vernichtend ‹Urteil, Kritik, Worte›; Ⓑ (*that proves guilt*) belastend ‹Beweise›

**Damocles** /'dæməkliːz/ *pr. n.* Damokles (*der*); **sword of ~:** Damoklesschwert, *das*

**damp** /dæmp/ ❶ *adj.* feucht; **a ~ squib** (*fig.*) ein Reinfall. ❷ *v.t.* Ⓐ befeuchten; [ein]sprengen ‹Wäsche›; Ⓑ (*stifle, extinguish*) dämpfen ‹Lärm›; **~ [down] a fire** ein Feuer ersticken; Ⓒ (*Mus., Phys.*) dämpfen; Ⓓ (*discourage, depress*) dämpfen ‹Eifer, Begeisterung›; **~ sb.'s spirits** jmdm. den Mut nehmen. ❸ *n.* (*moisture*) Feuchtigkeit, *die*

**'damp course** ⇒ **damp-proof**

**dampen** /'dæmpn/ ⇒ **damp** 2 A, D

**damper** /'dæmpə(r)/ *n.* Ⓐ (*sth. that checks or depresses*) **put a ~ on sth.** einer Sache (*Dat.*) einen Dämpfer aufsetzen; **his presence put a ~ on us** seine Anwesenheit dämpfte unsere Stimmung; Ⓑ (*Mus.*) Dämpfer, *der;* Ⓒ (*in vehicle*) Stoßdämpfer, *der;* Ⓓ (*in flue*) Luftklappe, *die*

**dampness** /'dæmpnɪs/ *n. no pl.* Feuchtigkeit, *die;* **~ in the air** Luftfeuchtigkeit, *die*

**'damp-proof** *adj.* feuchtigkeitsbeständig; **~ course** Sperrschicht, *die* (*gegen aufsteigende Bodenfeuchtigkeit*)

**damsel** /'dæmzl/ *n.* (*arch./literary*) Maid, *die* (*veralt.*); **a ~ in distress** (*joc.*) eine hilflose junge Dame

**damson** /'dæmzn/ *n.* Ⓐ (*fruit*) Haferpflaume, *die;* Ⓑ (*tree*) Haferpflaumenbaum, *der*

**damson 'plum** *n.* große Haferpflaume

**dance** /dɑ:ns/ ❶ *v.i.* Ⓐ tanzen; **~ to sb.'s tune** (*fig.*) nach jmds. Pfeife tanzen; Ⓑ (*jump about, skip*) herumtanzen; **~ about in agony/with rage** vor Schmerzen/Zorn rasen; **~ for joy** vor Freude an die Decke springen; einen Freudentanz aufführen; Ⓒ (*bob up and down*) tanzen; **the boat was dancing on the waves** das Boot tanzte *od.* schaukelte auf den Wellen.
❷ *v.t.* Ⓐ tanzen; **~ attendance on sb.** (*fig.*) jmdn. vorn und hinten bedienen (*ugs.*); um jmdn. herumscharwenzeln (*ugs. abwertend*); Ⓑ (*move up and down, dandle*) schaukeln.
❸ *n.* Ⓐ Tanz, *der;* **lead sb. a [merry] ~** (*fig.*) jmdn. [schön] an der Nase herumführen; Ⓑ (*party*) Tanzveranstaltung, *die;* (*private*) Tanzparty, *die;* Ⓒ (*tune in ~ rhythm*) Tanz, *der;* **light ~ music** leichte Tanzmusik; Ⓓ ▶1232 (*Med.*) **St. Vitus's ~:** Veitstanz, *der*

**dance: ~ band** *n.* Tanzkapelle, *die;* **~ floor** *n.* Tanzfläche, *die;* **~ hall** *n.* Tanzsaal, *der*

**dancer** /'dɑ:nsə(r)/ *n.* Tänzer, *der*/Tänzerin, *die*

**'dance step** *n.* Tanzschritt, *der*

**dancing**/'dɑ:nsɪŋ/: **~ girl** *n.* Tänzerin, *die;* **~ master** *n.* Tanzlehrer, *der;* **~ partner** *n.* Tanzpartner, *der*/-partnerin, *die;* **~ step** *n.* Tanzschritt, *der*

**dandelion** /'dændɪlaɪən/ *n.* Löwenzahn, *der;* (*with seedhead*) Pusteblume, *die* (*Kinderspr.*)

**dander** /'dændə(r)/ *n.* (*coll.*) Rage, *die* (*ugs.*); **get one's/sb.' ~ up** in Rage kommen (*ugs.*)/jmdn. in Rage bringen (*ugs.*)

**dandify** /'dændɪfaɪ/ *v.t.* herausputzen

**dandle** /'dændl/ *v.t.* schaukeln

**dandruff** /'dændrʌf/ *n.* [Kopf]schuppen *Pl.*

**dandy** /'dændɪ/ ❶ *n.* (*person*) Dandy, *der* (*geh.*); Geck, *der* (*abwertend*); Stutzer, *der* (*veralt. abwertend*). ❷ *adj.* (*coll.*) **[fine and] ~:** prima (*ugs.*)

**Dane** /deɪn/ *n.* ▶1340 Däne, *der*/Dänin, *die*

**danger** /'deɪndʒə(r)/ *n.* Gefahr, *die;* **a ~ to sb./sth.** eine Gefahr für jmdn./etw.; **'~!'** „Vorsicht!"; (*stronger*) „Lebensgefahr!"; **there is [a/the] ~ of war/disease** es besteht Kriegs-/Seuchengefahr; **[a] ~ of invasion** die Gefahr einer Invasion; **in ~:** in Gefahr; **put sb. in ~:** jmdn. in Gefahr bringen; **in ~ of one's life/of death** in Lebensgefahr/Todesgefahr; **be in ~ of doing sth.** ‹Person:› Gefahr laufen, etw. zu tun; ‹Sache:› drohen, etw. zu tun; **out of ~:** außer Gefahr

**danger: ~ area** *n.* Gefahrzone, *die;* **~ level** *n.* Gefahrengrenze, *die;* **~ list** *n.* **be on/off the ~ list** in/außer Lebensgefahr sein; **~ money** *n.* Gefahrenzulage, *die*

**dangerous** /'deɪndʒərəs/ *adj.* gefährlich; **~ to health** gesundheitsgefährdend

**dangerously** /'deɪndʒərəslɪ/ *adv.* gefährlich; **he drives ~:** er hat einen gefährlichen Fahrstil; **he's ~ overweight** er hat gefährliches Übergewicht

**danger: ~ signal** *n.* Warnzeichen, *das;* **~ zone** *n.* Gefahrenzone, *die*

**dangle** /'dæŋgl/ ❶ *v.i.* baumeln (**from** an + *Dat.*). ❷ *v.t.* baumeln lassen; **~ [the prospect of] sth. in front of sb.** (*fig.*) jmdm. etw. [als Anreiz] in Aussicht stellen

**Danish** /'deɪnɪʃ/ ▶1275, ▶1340 ❶ *adj.* dänisch; **sb. is ~:** jmd. ist Däne/Dänin; ⇒ *also* **English** 1. ❷ *n.* Dänisch, *das;* ⇒ *also* **English** 2 A

**Danish: ~ 'blue** *n.* dänischer Blauschimmelkäse; Danablu ⓦⓩ, *der;* **~ 'pastry** *n.* Plunderstück, *das*

**dank** /dæŋk/ *adj.* feucht

**Danube** /'dænju:b/ *pr. n.* ▶1480 Donau, *die*

**daphne** /'dæfnɪ/ *n.* (*Bot.*) Seidelbast, *der*

**dapper** /'dæpə(r)/ *adj.* (*neat*) adrett; schmuck (*veralt.*); (*sprightly*) munter

**dapple** /'dæpl/ *v.t.* [be]sprenkeln

**dappled** /'dæpld/ *adj.* gesprenkelt; gefleckt ‹Pferd, Kuh›

**dapple-'grey** ❶ *adj.* **~ mare** Apfelschimmelstute, *die.* ❷ *n.* Apfelschimmel, *der*

**Darby and Joan** /dɑ:bɪ ən 'dʒəʊn/ *n., pl.* **Darbies and Joans** *treues, altes Ehepaar;* ≈ Philemon und Baucis (*geh.*)

**Darby and 'Joan club** *n.* (*Brit.*) Seniorenklub, *der*

**dare** /deə(r)/ ❶ *v.t., pres.* **he ~** *or* **~s,** *neg.* **~ not,** (*coll.*) **~n't** /deənt/ Ⓐ (*venture*) [es] wagen; sich (*Akk.*) trauen; **if you ~ [to] give away the secret** wenn du es wagst, das Geheimnis zu verraten; **we didn't ~ [to] go any further** wir wagten [es] nicht *od.* trauten uns nicht, noch weiter zu gehen; **we ~ not/~d not** *or* (*coll.*) **didn't ~ tell him the truth** wir wagen/wagten [es] nicht *od.* trauen/trauten uns nicht, ihm die Wahrheit zu sagen; **you wouldn't ~:** das wagst du nicht; du traust dich nicht; **just you ~!** untersteh dich!; das versuch mal! (*ugs.*); **don't you ~!** untersteh dich!; wehe!; **how ~ you [do ...]?** wie kannst du es wagen[, ... zu tun]?; **how ~ you!** was fällt dir ein!; (*formal*) was erlauben Sie sich!; **I ~ say** (*supposing*) ich nehme an; (*confirming*) das glaube ich gern; Ⓑ (*attempt*) wagen ‹Aufstieg, Flucht›; sich wagen an (+ *Akk.*) ‹Projekt, Berg›; (*take the risk of*) riskieren; herausfordern ‹Zorn der Götter›; Ⓒ (*challenge*) herausfordern; **~ sb. to do sth.** jmdn. dazu aufstacheln, etw. zu tun; **I ~ you!** trau dich!; **I ~ you to** *or* **I bet you ~n't call the boss by his first name** wetten, dass du dich nicht traust, den Chef beim Vornamen zu rufen?
❷ *n.* (*act of daring*) **do sth. for/as a ~:** etw. als Mutprobe tun; (*challenge*) **Go on! It's a ~!** Los! Sei kein Frosch!

**'daredevil** *n.* Draufgänger, *der*/-gängerin, *die*

**daren't** /deənt/ (*coll.*) = **dare not**

**daring** /'deərɪŋ/ ❶ *adj.* (*bold*) kühn; waghalsig ‹Kunststück, Tat›; (*fearless*) wagemutig. ❷ *n.* Kühnheit, *die*

**daringly** /'deərɪŋlɪ/ *adv.* (*boldly*) kühn; (*fearlessly*) wagemutig

**dark** /dɑ:k/ ❶ *adj.* Ⓐ (*without light*) dunkel; dunkel, finster ‹Nacht, Haus, Straße›; (*gloomy*) düster; dunkel, finster ‹Wolke›; Ⓑ dunkel ‹Farbe›; (*brown-complexioned*) dunkelhäutig; (*~-haired*) dunkelhaarig; **~-blue/-brown/-green** *etc.* dunkelblau/-braun/-grün *usw.;* ⇒ *also* **blue**[1] 2 E; Ⓒ (*evil*) finster; übel ‹Zauber, Ruf, Fluch›; düster ‹Drohung, Bedeutung›; furchtbar ‹Grausamkeiten›; Ⓓ (*cheerless*) finster; düster ‹Bild›; (*sad*) düster ‹Stimmung, Gedanke›; (*frowning*) finster; **don't always look on the ~ side of things** sieh doch nicht immer alles so schwarz *od.* düster; Ⓔ (*obscure*) dunkel; schwierig ‹Frage›; **he's a ~ one as far as his plans are concerned** er ist so verschwiegen, was seine Pläne anbelangt; **keep sth./it ~:** etw./es geheim halten (**from** vor + *Dat.*); **be in ~est Africa** im tiefsten *od.* finstersten Afrika sein.
❷ *n.* Ⓐ (*absence of light*) Dunkel, *das;* **in the ~:** im Dunkeln; Ⓑ *no art.* (*nightfall*) Einbruch der Dunkelheit; Ⓒ **the ~** (*fig.: lack of knowledge*) **keep sb./be [kept] in the ~ about/as to sth.** jmdn. über etw. (*Akk.*) im Dunkeln lassen/über etw. (*Akk.*) im Dunkeln gelassen werden; **a leap in the ~:** ein Sprung ins Ungewisse; **it was a shot in the ~:** es war aufs Geratewohl geraten/versucht

**'Dark Ages** *n. pl.* [frühes] Mittelalter

**darken** /'dɑ:kn/ ❶ *v.t.* Ⓐ verdunkeln; **the sun had ~ed her skin** die Sonne hatte ihre Haut gebräunt; Ⓑ (*fig.*) verdüstern; verfinstern ‹Miene›; **never ~ my door again!** du betrittst mir meine Schwelle nicht mehr! ❷ *v.i.* Ⓐ ‹Zimmer:› dunkel werden; ‹Wolken, Himmel:› sich verfinstern; **the day ~ed** es wurde dunkel; Ⓑ (*fig.*) sich verfinstern

**dark: ~ 'glasses** *n. pl.* dunkle Brille; **~-haired** *adj.* dunkelhaarig; **~ 'horse** *n.* unbekanntes Pferd; (*fig.: little-known yet successful person*) [erfolgreicher] Außenseiter; (*fig.: secretive person*) **be a ~ horse** ein stilles Wasser sein

**darkie** ⇒ **darky**

**darkish** /'dɑ:kɪʃ/ *adj.* ziemlich dunkel

**darkly** /'dɑ:klɪ/ *adv.* Ⓐ dunkel; Ⓑ (*ominously*) finster; (*obscurely, dimly*) dunkel

**darkness** /'dɑ:knɪs/ *n., no pl.* Ⓐ (*dark*) Dunkelheit, *die;* Ⓑ (*wickedness, ominousness*) Finsterkeit, *die;* **the powers of ~:** die Mächte der Finsternis; Ⓒ (*obscurity*) Dunkelheit, *die*

**'darkroom** *n.* Dunkelkammer, *die*

**darky** /'dɑ:kɪ/ *n.* (*coll.*) Schwarze, *der/die*

**darling** /'dɑ:lɪŋ/ ❶ *n.* Liebling, *der;* **she was his ~:** sie war seine Liebste *od.* sein Schatz; **her little ~s** ihre Lieblinge; **you 'are a ~** (*coll.*) du bist ein Schatz. ❷ *adj.* geliebt; (*coll.: delightful*) reizend

**darn**[1] /dɑ:n/ ❶ *v.t.* stopfen. ❷ *n.* gestopfte Stelle

**darn**[2] (*coll.: damn*) ❶ *v.t.* **~ you** *etc.* **!** zum Kuckuck mit dir *usw.* ! (*salopp*); **~ [it]!** verflixt [und zugenäht]! (*ugs.*); **~ it all!** verflixt noch mal! (*ugs.*); **I'll be ~ed** ich werd nicht mehr (*salopp*); **I'm** *or* **I'll be ~ed if I'll help you** ich werde dir auf gar keinen Fall helfen; **I'm** *or* **I'll be ~ed if I know** ich habe nicht die leiseste Ahnung (*ugs.*). ❷ *n.* ⇒ **damn** 2 B. ❸ *adj.* verflixt (*ugs.*). ❹ *adv.* verflixt (*ugs.*); **~ stupid** schrecklich dumm

**darned** /dɑ:nd/ (*coll.*) ❶ *adj.* verflixt (*ugs.*); **you ~ fool!** du verdammter Narr!; ⇒ *also* **damned** 1 B, C. ❷ *adv.* verflixt; **don't be so ~ stubborn!** sei nicht so verdammt *od.* furchtbar stur!; ⇒ *also* **damned** 2

**darning** /'dɑ:nɪŋ/ *n.* Stopfen, *das;* **there's a lot of ~ to be done** es sind eine Menge Sachen zu stopfen

**'darning needle** *n.* Stopfnadel, *die*

**dart** /dɑ:t/ ❶ *n.* Ⓐ (*missile*) Pfeil, *der;* Ⓑ (*Sport*) Wurfpfeil, *der;* **~s** *sing.* (*game*) Darts, *das;* Ⓒ (*Zool.*) Stachel, *der;* Ⓓ (*rapid motion*) Satz, *der;* **the child made a sudden ~ into the road** das Kind rannte plötzlich auf die Fahrbahn; Ⓔ (*Dressmaking: tapering tuck*) Abnäher, *der.* ❷ *v.t.* **~ a look at sb.** jmdm. einen Blick zuwerfen; **the toad ~ed its tongue out** die Kröte ließ ihre Zunge herausschnellen. ❸ *v.i.* (*start rapidly*) sausen; **~ towards sth.** auf etw. (*Akk.*) zustürzen; **her eyes ~ed towards the staircase** sie warf einen raschen Blick zur Treppe; **the fish ~ed through the water** der Fisch schnellte durch das Wasser

**'dartboard** *n.* Dartsscheibe, *die*

**dash** /dæʃ/ ❶ *v.i.* (*move quickly*) sausen; (*coll.: hurry*) sich eilen; **~ along behind sb./sth.** hinter jmdm./etw. herrasen; **~ away from sb./sth.** von jmdm./etw. wegrasen; **~ down/up [the stairs]** [die Treppe] hinunter-/hinaufstürzen; **~ up to sb./sth.** auf jmdn./etw. zustürzen; **I must just ~ to the loo** ich muss noch [eben] schnell aufs Klo; **~ against sth.** ‹Wellen usw.:› gegen etw. peitschen *od.* schlagen.
❷ *v.t.* Ⓐ (*shatter*) **~ sth. [to pieces]** etw.

[in tausend Stücke] zerschlagen *od.* zerschmettern; Ⓑ (*fling*) schleudern; schmettern; (*splash*) schütten; (*bespatter*) bespritzen (**with** mit); Ⓒ (*frustrate*) **sb.'s hopes are ~ed** jmds. Hoffnungen haben sich zerschlagen; Ⓓ (*coll.*) ⇒ **darn²** 1.

❸ *n.* Ⓐ **make a ~ for sth.** zu etw. rasen (*ugs.*); **make a ~ at sb.** auf jmdn. losstürzen (*ugs.*); **make a ~ for shelter** rasch Schutz suchen; **make a ~ for freedom** plötzlich versuchen, wegzulaufen; Ⓑ (*horizontal stroke*) Gedankenstrich, *der;* Ⓒ (*Morse signal*) Strich, *der;* Ⓓ (*slight admixture*) Schuss, *der;* **a ~ of salt** eine Prise Salz; **add a ~ of colour to sth.** einer Sache (*Dat.*) etwas Farbe geben; **beige with a ~ of brown** beige mit einem Stich ins Braune; Ⓔ (*vigorous action*) Schwung, *der;* (*showy appearance etc.*) **cut a ~:** Aufsehen erregen; Ⓕ ⇒ **dashboard**

**~ a'way** ❶ *v.i.* (*rush*) davonjagen; (*coll.: hurry*) **they had to ~ away** sie mussten schnell weg; **you're not going to ~ away so soon, surely** du willst doch nicht schon wieder weg. ❷ *v.t.* wegstoßen

**~ 'off** ❶ *v.i.* ⇒ **~ away** 1. ❷ *v.t.* rasch schreiben

**~ 'out** *v.t.* **~ sb.'s brains out** jmdm. den Schädel einschlagen

**'dashboard** *n.* (*Motor Veh.*) Armaturenbrett, *das*

**dashed** /dæʃt/ ⇒ **darned**

**dashing** /'dæʃɪŋ/ *adj.* schneidig

**dastardly** /'dæstədlɪ/ *adj.* feige; (*malicious*) hinterhältig

**data** /'deɪtə, 'dɑ:tə/ *n. pl., constr. as pl. or sing.* Daten *Pl.;* ⇒ *also* **datum**

**data: ~ bank** *n.* Datenbank, *die;* **~base** *n.* Datenbank, *die;* **~base management system** Datenbank-Managementsystem, *das;* **~ capture** *n.* Datenerfassung, *die;* **~ communications** *n. pl.* (*Computing*) Datenaustausch, *der;* **~ entry** *n., no. pl., no art.* (*Computing*) Dateneingabe, *die;* **~ file** *n.* (*Computing*) Datei, *die;* **~glove** *n.* (*Computing*) Datenhandschuh, *der;* **~ handling** ⇒ **~ processing; ~ highway** *n.* (*Computing*) Datenautobahn, *die;* **~ link** *n.* (*Computing*) Datenleitung, *die;* **~ processing** *n.* (*Computing*) Datenverarbeitung, *die;* **~ processor** *n.* (*Computing*) Datenverarbeitungsanlage, *die;* **~ pro'tection** *n.* (*Computing*) Datenschutz, *der;* **~ retrieval** *n.* (*Computing*) Retrieval, *das;* Datenabruf, *der;* **~ retrieval system** Retrievalsystem, *das;* **~ security** *n.* (*Computing*) Datensicherung, *die;* **~ sheet** *n.* Informationsblatt, *das;* **~ storage** *n.* (*Computing*) Datenspeicherung, *die;* (*capacity*) Speicherkapazität, *die;* Speicherplatz, *der;* **~ transmission** *n.* (*Computing*) Datenübertragung, *die*

**date¹** /deɪt/ *n.* (*Bot.*) Ⓐ (*fruit*) Dattel, *die;* Ⓑ (*tree*) ⇒ **date palm**

**date²** ❶ *n.* Ⓐ ▶ **1055** Datum, *das;* (*on coin etc.*) Jahreszahl, *die;* **~ of birth** Geburtsdatum, *das;* **what are his ~s?** von wann bis wann hat er gelebt?; **the last ~ for payment** der letzte Termin für die Zahlung; Ⓑ (*coll.: appointment*) Verabredung, *die;* **have/make a ~ with sb.** mit jmdm. verabredet sein/sich mit jmdm. verabreden; **go [out] on a ~ with sb.** mit jmdm. ausgehen; ⇒ *also* **blind ~;** Ⓒ (*Amer. coll.: person*) Freund, *der*/Freundin, *die;* Ⓓ (*period*) [Entstehungs]zeit, *die;* Ⓔ **be out of ~:** altmodisch sein; (*expired*) nicht mehr gültig sein; **to ~:** bis heute. ⇒ *also* **up to date.**

❷ *v.t.* Ⓐ (*mark with ~, refer to a time*) datieren; **~ sth. to a time** etw. einer Zeit zuordnen; Ⓑ (*coll: make seem old*) alt machen; Ⓒ (*coll.: make ~ with*) **~ [each other]/sb.** miteinander/mit jmdm. gehen (*ugs.*).

❸ *v.i.* Ⓐ **~ back to/~ from a certain time** aus einer bestimmten Zeit stammen; Ⓑ (*coll.: become out of ~*) aus der Mode kommen

**dated** /'deɪtɪd/ *adj.* altmodisch; **a ~ fashion** eine Mode von gestern

**date: ~ line** *n.* Ⓐ (*Geog.*) Datumsgrenze, *die;* Ⓑ (*in newspaper etc.*) *Zeile, in der das Datum steht;* ≈ Kopf, *der;* **~ palm** *n.* Dattelpalme, *die;* **~ rape** *n.: Vergewaltigung der eigenen Freundin oder Vergewaltigung einer Frau während einer Verabredung mit ihr;* **~ stamp** *n.* Datumsstempel, *der;* **~-stamp** *v.t.* abstempeln; mit einem Datumsstempel versehen

**'dating agency** /'deɪtɪŋ/ *n.* Partnervermittlung, *die*

**dative** /'deɪtɪv/ (*Ling.*) ❶ *adj.* Dativ-; dativisch; **~ case** Dativ, *der.* ❷ *n.* Dativ, *der*

**datum** /'deɪtəm, 'dɑ:təm/ *n., pl.* **data** /'deɪtə, 'dɑ:tə/ Ⓐ (*premiss*) Datum, *das;* Faktum, *das;* Ⓑ (*fixed starting point*) Nullpunkt, *der*

**'datum line** *n.* (*Surv.*) Normalnull, *das*

**daub** /dɔ:b/ ❶ *v.t.* Ⓐ (*coat*) bewerfen; verschmieren ‹Geflecht›; (*smear, soil*) beschmieren; Ⓑ (*lay crudely*) schmieren. ❷ *v.i.* ‹Künstler:› die Leinwand voll schmieren (*abwertend*). ❸ *n.* Ⓐ (*plaster etc.*) Bewurf, *der;* Ⓑ (*crude painting*) Kleckserei, *die* (*ugs. abwertend*); (*large*) Schinken, *der* (*ugs. abwertend*); Ⓒ (*smear*) Fleck, *der;* **covered with great ~s of sth.** reichlich mit etw. beschmiert

**daughter** /'dɔ:tə(r)/ *n.* (*lit. or fig.*) Tochter, *die*

**'daughter-in-law** *n., pl.* **daughters-in-law** Schwiegertochter, *die*

**daunt** /dɔ:nt/ *v.t.* entmutigen; schrecken (*geh.*); **nothing ~ed** unverzagt

**dauntless** /'dɔ:ntlɪs/ *adj.* unerschrocken

**dauphin** /'dɔ:fɪn/ *n.* (*Hist.*) Dauphin, *der*

**davenport** /'dævnpɔ:t/ *n.* Ⓐ (*Brit.: writing desk*) Sekretär, *der;* Ⓑ (*Amer.: sofa*) Sofa, *das*

**davit** /'dævɪt/ *n.* [Boots]davit, *der*

**Davy [lamp]** /'deɪvɪ (læmp)/ *n.* Wetterlampe, *die;* Davy-Lampe, *die*

**dawdle** /'dɔ:dl/ ❶ *v.i.* bummeln (*ugs.*). ❷ *v.t.* **~ away** verbummeln (*ugs.*). ❸ *n.* (*dawdling*) Bummelei, *die* (*ugs.*); (*stroll*) Bummel, *der* (*ugs.*)

**dawn** /dɔ:n/ ❶ *v.i.* Ⓐ dämmern; **day[light] ~ed** der Morgen dämmerte; der Tag brach an; Ⓑ (*fig.*) ‹Zeitalter:› anbrechen; ‹Idee:› aufkommen; ‹Liebe, Hoffnung:› erwachen; **until the meaning finally ~ed** bis schließlich der Sinn klar wurde; **sth. ~s on** *or* **upon sb.** etw. dämmert jmdm.; **hasn't it ~ed on you that ...?** ist dir nicht langsam klar geworden, dass ...?; **the idea ~ed on her that ...:** ihr kam die Idee, dass ...

❷ *n.* Ⓐ [Morgen]dämmerung, *die;* **from ~ to dusk** von früh bis spät; **it is ~:** die Dämmerung bricht an; es wird hell; **at ~:** im Morgengrauen; **[the] ~ breaks** der Tag bricht an; **in the ~:** in der Morgendämmerung; **into the ~:** gen Sonnenaufgang (*geh.*); Ⓑ (*fig.*) Morgenröte, *die* (*geh.*); (*of idea, love, hope*) Keimen, *das* (*geh.*); **at the ~ of civilization** in der Morgenröte der Zivilisation (*geh.*)

**dawn 'chorus** *n.* morgendlicher Gesang der Vögel

**dawning** /'dɔ:nɪŋ/ *n.* Ⓐ Anbruch, *der;* **at the ~ of the day** bei Tagesanbruch; Ⓑ (*fig.*) Anfänge *Pl.;* **at the ~ of a new era/civilization** bei Anbruch eines neuen Zeitalters/in den Anfängen der Zivilisation

**'dawn raid** *n.* (*St. Exch.*) *frühzeitiges, heimliches Aufkaufen von Aktien (um überraschend eine Aktienmehrheit zu erlangen)*

**day** /deɪ/ *n.* Ⓐ ▶ **1012**, ▶ **1056** Tag, *der;* **on a ~ like today:** an einem Tag wie heute; **all ~ [long]** den ganzen Tag [lang]; **take all ~** (*fig.*) eine Ewigkeit brauchen; **as happy as the ~ is long** äußerst glücklich; **the ~ of ~s** der Tag der Tage; **all ~ and every ~:** tagaus, tagein; **not for many a long ~:** schon lange nicht mehr; **to this ~, from that ~ to this** bis zum heutigen Tag; **as clear as ~:** augenfällig; **for two ~s** zwei Tage [lang]; **what's the ~** *or* **what ~ is it today?** welcher Tag ist heute?; **twice a ~:** zweimal täglich *od.* am Tag; **in a ~/two ~s** (*within*) in *od.* an einem Tag/in zwei Tagen; **in a ~['s time]/a few ~s[' time]** in einem Tag/in ein paar Tagen; **in six ~s[' time]** in sechs Tagen; **in eight ~s** in genau acht Tagen; **[on] the ~ after/before** am Tag danach/davor; **[on] the ~ after/before sth.** am Tag nach/vor etw. (*Dat.*); **[on] the ~ after/before we met** am Tag, nach dem/bevor wir uns trafen; **[the] next/[on] the following/[on] the previous ~:** am nächsten/folgenden/vorhergehenden Tag; **the ~ before yesterday/after tomorrow** vorgestern/übermorgen; **the other ~:** neulich; **only the other ~:** erst vor ein paar Tagen; **every other ~:** alle zwei Tage; **from this/that ~ [on]** von heute an/von diesem Tag an; **one ~ he came** eines Tages kam er; **come and see us one ~:** komm irgendwann einmal vorbei; **one ~ ..., the next ...:** heute ..., morgen ...; **one of these [fine] ~s** eines [schönen] Tages; **two ~s ago** vor zwei Tagen; **some ~:** eines Tages; irgendwann einmal; **for the ~:** für einen Tag; **to the ~:** auf den Tag genau; **~ after ~:** Tag für Tag; **~ by ~, from ~ to ~:** von Tag zu Tag; **from one ~ to the next** von einem Tag zum andern; **~ in ~ out** tagaus, tagein; **it's all in the/a ~'s work** das gehört dazu (*ugs.*); **call it a ~** (*end work*) Feierabend machen; (*more generally*) Schluss machen; (*fig.*) es gut sein lassen (*ugs.*); **at the end of the ~** (*fig.*) letzten Endes; **early in the ~** (*fig.*) früh; **he's 65 if he's a ~:** er ist mindestens 65; **it's not my ~:** ich habe [heute] einen schlechten Tag; **it's my ~:** ich habe [heute] einen guten Tag; **on his ~:** wenn er seinen guten Tag hat; **that will be the ~** (*iron.*) das möchte ich sehen/erleben (*ugs.*); **it's been one of those ~s** das war vielleicht ein Tag (*ugs.*); **soup/dish of the ~:** Tagessuppe, *die*/Stammessen, *das;* ⇒ *also* **any** 1 E; **good** 1 M; **late** 2 E; **make** 1 P; **off** 1 E; Ⓑ (*daylight*) **before/at ~:** vor/bei Tagesanbruch; Ⓒ *in sing. or pl.* (*period*) **in the ~s when ...:** zu der Zeit, als ...; **in his/that/Queen Anne's ~:** zu seiner/jener Zeit/zur Zeit der Königin Anne; **in former/earlier ~s** in früheren Zeiten; **these ~s** heutzutage; **in those ~s** damals; zu jener Zeit; **in this ~ and age, at the present ~:** heutzutage; **this ~ and age, the [present] ~:** die heutige Zeit; **have seen/known better ~s** bessere Tage gesehen/gekannt haben; **I have seen the ~ when ...:** zu meiner Zeit ...; **those were the ~s** das waren noch Zeiten; (*iron.*) schöne Zeiten waren das; ⇒ *also* **bad** 1 A; **good** 1 D; Ⓓ *in sing. or pl.* (*lifetime*) **in our ~[s]** zu unserer Zeit; **end one's ~s** seine Tage beenden; Ⓔ (*time of prosperity*) **in one's ~:** zu seiner Zeit; (*during lifetime*) in seinem Leben; **sth.'s ~ is over** die Zeiten einer Sache (*Gen.*) sind vorbei; **every dog has its ~:** jeder hat einmal seine Chance; **it has had its ~:** es hat ausgedient (*ugs.*); Ⓕ (*victory*) **win** *or* **carry the ~:** den Sieg davontragen; Ⓖ (*~ for regular event*) **Monday is my ~:** montags bin ich an der Reihe (*ugs.*); **it's my ~ [for doing** *or* **to do sth.]** ich bin an der Reihe[, etw. zu tun]; **whose ~ is it?** wer ist an der Reihe?

**-day** *adj. suf.* -tägig; **three-~[s]-old** drei Tage alt; **five-~ week** Fünftagewoche, *die*

**day: ~bed** *n.* Liegesofa, *das;* **~book** *n.* (*Commerc.*) Journal, *das;* **~ boy** *n.* (*Brit.*) externer Schüler; **~break** *n.* Tagesanbruch, *der;* **at ~break** bei Tagesanbruch; **~ care** *n.* Ganztagsbetreuung, *die; attrib.* **~-care centre** Tagesstätte, *die;* (*for children*) Kindertagesstätte, *die;* [Kinder]krippe, *die;* (*for the elderly*) Altenzentrum, *das;* Altentagesstätte, *die;* (*for invalids or the disabled*) Tagesbetreuungsstätte, *die;* **~dream** ❶ *n.* Tagtraum, *der;* **lost in a ~dream** traumverloren; ❷ *v.i.* träumen; **~dreamer** *n.* Tagträumer, *der*/-träumerin, *die;* **~ girl** *n.* (*Brit.*) externe Schülerin; **~light** *n.* Ⓐ (*light of ~*) Tageslicht, *das;* **by ~light** bei Tageslicht; **go on working while it's still ~light** weiterarbeiten, solange es noch hell ist; **~light comes** es wird hell; der Tag bricht an; **it's [already] ~light** es ist [schon] hell; **during the hours of ~light, in ~light** bei Tag[eslicht]; **in broad ~light** am hellichten Tag[e]; **~light saving [time]** Sommerzeit, *die;* Ⓑ (*dawn*) **at** *or* **by/before ~light** bei/vor Tagesanbruch; Ⓒ (*fig.*) **bring sth. into the ~light** etw. ans Tageslicht bringen; **I see ~light** ich denke, die Situation lichtet sich; (*understand*) mir geht

d

# Dates

Unlike English which has several variations (May 10, 10 May, May 10th, 10th May etc.), dates in German are always written in the same way:

der 10. Mai

The accusative form is used at the head of letters, preceded by the name of the place:

Amstetten, den 25. August 1997

Dates written all in numbers are found in German as in English, particularly in business letters:

Frankfurt a.M., den 15.1.1997

***With reference to your letter of the 4.1.1997*** or (*Amer.*) ***1.4.1997***
= Bezug nehmend auf Ihr Schreiben vom 4.1.1997 (*spoken*: vom vierten Ersten neunzehnhundertsiebenundneunzig)

## Saying dates

***What's the date?***
= Welches Datum haben wir heute?, Der Wievielte ist heute?

***It's May the tenth***
= Es ist der zehnte Mai

***What date is the wedding?***
= Wann ist die Hochzeit?; (*if the month is known*) Am Wievielten ist die Hochzeit?

***The wedding is on the 22nd (twenty-second)***
= Die Hochzeit ist am 22. (Zweiundzwanzigsten)

| | WRITTEN | SPOKEN |
|---|---|---|
| ***May 1st, May 1*** | der 1. Mai | der erste Mai |
| ***May 21st, May 21*** | der 21. Mai | der einundzwanzigste Mai |
| ***May 30th, May 30*** | der 30. Mai | der dreißigste Mai |
| ***Monday May 3rd 1994*** | Montag, der 3. Mai 1994 | Montag, der dritte Mai neunzehnhundertvierund-neunzig |
| ***21.5.66*** or (*Amer.*) ***5.21.66*** | 21.5.66 | der einundzwanzigste Fünfte sechsundsechzig |
| ***1900*** | 1900 | neunzehnhundert |
| ***the year 2000*** | das Jahr 2000 | das Jahr zweitausend |
| ***2001*** | 2001 | zweitausend[und]eins |
| ***230 AD*** | 230 n.Chr. | zweihundertdreißig nach Christus |
| ***55 BC*** | 55 v.Chr. | fünfundfünfzig vor Christus |
| ***the 16th century*** | das 16. Jahrhundert *or* Jh. | das sechzehnte Jahrhundert |

## Saying when

*on* with days and dates is translated by **an** with the definite article, conflated to **am**, whether there is a definite article in English or not:

***on Friday***
= am Freitag*

***on March 6th***
= am 6. März (*spoken* am sechsten März)

***on Friday March 6th***
= am Freitag, den *or* dem 6. März

***on the first of next month***
= am nächsten Ersten

An exception is not unnaturally:

***It happened on a Tuesday***
= Es geschah an einem Dienstag

If an adjective follows *a* or *one*, the genitive construction can be used:

***on a fine Sunday, one fine Sunday***
= eines schönen Sonntags

*in* with months is **in** plus the definite article, conflated to **im**:

***in June***
= im Juni

***next June***
= im Juni nächsten Jahres

***last June***
= voriges Jahr im Juni

But note:

***at the end/beginning of June***
= Ende/Anfang Juni

***in the middle of July***
= Mitte Juli

When giving the year when something happened in German, the year is usually given on its own without any preposition, although "im Jahre" can be added in more formal language or when "v.Chr." or "n.Chr" follow:

***He died in 1945***
= Er starb 1945

***in 27 AD***
= im Jahre 27 n.Chr.

***in 55 BC***
= im Jahre 55 v.Chr.

Other phrases:

***from November/November 5th [onwards]***
= ab November/ab dem 5. November, vom November an/vom 5 November an

***from next Tuesday***
= ab kommendem Dienstag

***from the 21st to the 30th***
= vom 21. bis zum 30.

***It will be ready by Friday/by the 14th***
= Es wird bis Freitag/bis zum 14. fertig

***It won't be ready until Friday***
= Es wird erst [am] Freitag fertig

***around May 16th***
= um den 16. Mai [herum]

***in the sixties*** or ***60s***
= in den Sechzigerjahren *or* 60er-Jahren

***in the 1880s***
= in den Achtzigerjahren des 19. Jahrhunderts, in den 1880er-Jahren

***the 1912 uprising***
= der Aufstand von 1912

***the 19th century novel***
= der Roman des 19. Jahrhunderts

***a 17th century composer***
= ein Komponist des 17. Jahrhunderts

***a 14th century building***
= ein Gebäude aus dem 14. Jahrhundert

*With days of the week the **am** can be omitted colloquially:

***She's coming on Friday***
= Sie kommt Freitag

ein Licht auf (*ugs.*); **scare/beat the [living] ~lights out of sb.** (*coll.*) jmdn. zu Tode erschrecken/(*ugs.*) windelweich schlagen; **it's ~light robbery** es ist der reine Wucher; **D** (*visible interval*) Luft, *die;* **~-long** *attrib. adj.* den ganzen Tag dauernd; **~ nursery** *n.* **A** (*room*) Kinderzimmer, *das;* **B** (*school*) Kindergarten, *der;* **~ release** *n.* (*Brit.*) [tageweise] Freistellung zur Fortbildung; **on ~ release** unter Inanspruchnahme von tageweiser Freistellung; *attrib.* **~-release course** Fortbildungskurs, *der;* Fortbildung, *die;* **~ return** **1** *attrib. adj.* **~ return ticket** ⇒ 2; **2** *n.* Tagesrückfahrkarte, *die;* **~ school** *n.* Tagesschule, *die;* **~ shift** *n.* Tagschicht, *die;* **be on [the] ~ shift** Tagschicht haben; **~time** *n.* Tag, *der;* **in** *or* **during the ~time** während des Tages; tagsüber; **~-to-~** *adj.* [tag]täglich; **~-to-~ life** Alltagsleben, *das;* **~ trip** *n.* Tagesausflug, *der;* **~ tripper** *n.* Tagesausflügler, *der*/-ausflüglerin, *die*

**daze** /deɪz/ **1** *v.t.* benommen machen; **be ~d** benommen sein (**at** von). **2** *n.* Benommen-

d

# Days of the week

| ENGLISH | GERMAN | ABBREVIATION |
|---|---|---|
| Monday | **Montag** | **Mo** |
| Tuesday | **Dienstag** | **Di** |
| Wednesday | **Mittwoch** | **Mi** |
| Thursday | **Donnerstag** | **Do** |
| Friday | **Freitag** | **Fr** |
| Saturday | **Samstag*** | **Sa** |
| Sunday | **Sonntag** | **So** |

Note that the week is considered as beginning on Monday. The abbreviations given are used mainly in printed matter, such as calendars, diaries, timetables and notices giving opening times, rather than in private or business correspondence. All the days of the week are masculine.

*An alternative for **Samstag** used mainly in North Germany is **Sonnabend**.

## Saying when

As with dates, the English *on* is translated by **am**:

***I am leaving on Wednesday***
= Ich fahre am Mittwoch

Sometimes this is omitted in speech or a letter, especially where there are further details in the sentence:

***I am leaving on Wednesday for Cairo***
= Ich fahre Mittwoch nach Kairo

One exception to the use of **am** is naturally enough when the indefinite article *a* or *one* is used for a particular occasion:

***Her birthday is on a Tuesday***
= Ihr Geburtstag ist an einem Dienstag

***It happened one wet Sunday***
= Es geschah an einem verregneten Sonntag

***One Saturday I met him at the zoo***
= Eines Samstags traf ich ihn im Zoo

Repeated events are another exception to the use of **am**:

***I go home on Fridays/every Friday***
= Ich fahre freitags/jeden Freitag nach Hause

***Her evening class is on Mondays*** or ***on a Monday***
= Ihr Abendkurs ist montags

Notice that the adverbial forms **montags, dienstags** etc. are written with a small letter.

Some more expressions for less frequent or regular events:

***every other Thursday***
= jeden zweiten Donnerstag

***every third Monday***
= jeden dritten Montag

***most Saturdays***
= fast jeden Samstag

***some Wednesdays***
= manchmal am Mittwoch

***on the occasional*** or ***odd Friday***
= ab und zu am Freitag

### ■ LOOKING BACKWARDS AND FORWARDS

***last Thursday***
= letzten Donnerstag

***[on] the preceding Thursday***
= am vorangehenden Donnerstag

***[on] the Thursday before last***
= vorletzten Donnerstag

***a week ago on Thursday***
= Donnerstag vor einer Woche

***I shall see her next Monday*** or ***this [coming] Monday***
= Ich werde sie [am] nächsten *or* kommenden Montag sehen

***I saw her the next*** or ***the following Monday***
= Ich habe sie am [darauf] folgenden Montag gesehen

***the Monday after next***
= übernächsten Montag

***a week on Monday***
= Montag in einer Woche

***from Saturday [on]***
= ab Samstag, von Samstag an

***It has to be ready by Friday***
= Es muss bis Freitag fertig sein

### ■ TIMES OF DAY

***on Monday morning***
= [am] Montagmorgen

***on Wednesday afternoon***
= [am] Mittwochnachmittag

***on Thursday evening***
= [am] Donnerstagabend

***on Friday night***
= (*early*) [am] Freitagabend; (*late*) Freitagnacht

And if it's habitual:

***on Monday mornings***
= montagmorgens

***on Wednesday afternoons***
= mittwochnachmittags

***on Thursday evenings***
= donnerstagabends

***on Friday nights***
= (*early*) freitagabends; (*late*) freitagnachts

### ■ TODAY

***What day is it [today]?***
= Welchen Tag haben wir heute?

***It's Tuesday [today]***
= Heute ist Dienstag

### ■ BELONGING TO A CERTAIN DAY

German has more than one way of expressing this, where in English we have simply the name of the day with or without an apostrophe s; there are adjectives for all the days of the week except Wednesday (**Mittwoch**) which relate to a habitual occurrence, or a compound can be formed, especially for a particular institution:

***his [regular] Sunday walk***
= sein sonntäglicher Spaziergang

***the Sunday papers***
= die Sonntagszeitungen

***a Sunday driver***
= ein Sonntagsfahrer

***Monday's trains***
= die Züge am Montag

***Wednesday's classes***
= die Schulstunden am Mittwoch

***Tuesday's paper***
= die Zeitung von Dienstag

***There will be a Saturday [train] service***
= Die Züge werden wie an einem Samstag verkehren

***Wednesday's sailing is cancelled***
= Das Schiff am Mittwoch fällt aus

····➤ Dates

heit, *die;* **in a [complete/bit of a] ~:** [völlig/ein wenig] benommen

**dazzle** /'dæzl/ *v.t.* (*lit., or fig.: delude*) blenden; (*fig.: confuse, impress*) überwältigen

**dB** *abbr.* **decibel[s]** dB

**DBMS** *abbr.* (*Computing*) **database management system** DBMS

**DC** *abbr.* Ⓐ (*Electr.*) **direct current** GS; Ⓑ (*Geog.*) **District of Columbia** Bundesdistrikt Columbia; Ⓒ (*Mus.*) **da capo** d.c.

**DD** *abbr.* **Doctor of Divinity** ≈ Dr. theol.; ⇒ *also* **B. Sc.**

**D-Day** /'di:deɪ/ *n.* Ⓐ (*6 June 1944*) *Tag der Landung der Alliierten in der Normandie;* Ⓑ (*starting day*) der Tag X

**DDT** /di:di:'ti:/ *n.* DDT, *das*

**deacon** /'di:kn/ *n.* Diakon, *der*

**deaconess** /'di:kənɪs/ *n.* Diakonin, *die*

**deactivate** /di:'æktɪveɪt/ *v.t.* entschärfen ‹Bombe›; desaktivieren ‹Chemikalie›; abschalten ‹Maschine, Motor›

**dead** /ded/ ❶ *adj.* Ⓐ tot; tot, abgestorben ‹Gewebe, Pflanze›; **[as] ~ as a doornail/as mutton** mausetot (*ugs.*); **be ~ from the neck up** (*coll.*) gehirnamputiert sein (*salopp*); **I wouldn't be seen ~ doing sth./in that dress** (*coll.*) ich würde nie im Leben etw. tun/dieses Kleid anziehen (*ugs.*); **I wouldn't be seen ~ in a place like that** (*coll.*) keine zehn Pferde würden mich an solch einen Ort bringen (*ugs.*); **~ men tell no tales** (*prov.*) Tote reden nicht; ⇒ *also* **body** 1 B; **bury** A; **go**[1] 1 J; Ⓑ (*inanimate, extinct*) tot ‹Materie›; erloschen ‹Vulkan, Gefühl, Interesse›; ausgestorben ‹Spezies›; (*without power*) verbraucht, leer ‹Batterie›; ausgebrannt ‹Glühbirne›; (*extinguished*) ausgegangen ‹Zigarette›; erloschen ‹Feuer›; (*not glowing*) ausgeglüht ‹Kohle, Asche›; **the fire is ~:** das Feuer ist aus (*ugs.*); ⇒ *also* **dodo**; Ⓒ (*dull, lustreless*) stumpf ‹Haar, Farbe›; (*without force*) wirkungslos ‹Gesetz, Politik›; (*without warmth*) kalt ‹Stimme, Ton›; ausgestorben, tot ‹Stadt›; (*quiet*) [toten]still ‹Nacht, Wald, Straße›; unbelebt, tot ‹Straße›; (*unexciting*) öde ‹Party, Geschmack›; (*flat*) schal, abgestanden ‹Getränk›; Ⓓ (*inactive, unproductive*) tot ‹Telefon, Leitung, Saison, Kapital, Ball›; unfruchtbar ‹Land, Erde›; **go ~:** zusammenbrechen; (*lose interest*) Interesse verlieren (**on** an + *Dat.*); **the phone has gone ~:** die Leitung ist tot; **the motor is ~:** der Motor läuft nicht; **a ~ engine** eine Maschine, die/ein Motor, der nicht läuft; Ⓔ *expr. completeness* plötzlich ‹Halt›; völlig ‹Stillstand›; genau ‹Mitte›; (*coll.: absolute*) absolut; **~ silence** *or* **quiet** Totenstille, *die;* **~ calm** Flaute, *die;* Windstille, *die;* **~ faint** [totenähnliche] Ohnmacht; **~ trouble** große Schwierigkeiten *Pl.;* **a ~ shot** ein unfehlbarer Schütze; Ⓕ (*benumbed*) taub; (*sleeping*) schlafend; **be ~ to sth.** (*lit. or fig.*) etw. nicht mehr empfinden; **be ~ to shame** gar kein Schamgefühl haben; **be ~ to the world** (*unconscious*) bewusstlos sein; weggetreten sein (*ugs.*); (*asleep*) tief und fest schlafen; Ⓖ (*exhausted*) erschöpft; kaputt (*ugs.*); **I feel absolutely ~:** ich bin völlig erschöpft.

❷ *adv.* Ⓐ (*completely*) völlig; **~ silent** totenstill; **~ straight** schnurgerade; **~ tired** todmüde; **~ easy** *or* **simple/slow** kinderleicht/ganz langsam; '**~ slow**' „besonders langsam fahren"; **~ drunk** stockbetrunken (*ugs.*); **~ level** völlig eben; **~ still** regungslos; (*without wind*) windstill; **make ~ certain** *or* **sure of sth.** etw. todsicher machen; **be ~ against sth.** absolut gegen etw. sein; Ⓑ (*exactly*) **~ on the target** genau im Ziel; **~ on time** auf die Minute; **~ on two [o'clock]** Punkt zwei [Uhr].

❸ *n.* Ⓐ **in the ~ of winter/night** mitten im Winter/in der Nacht; **it was the ~ of winter** es war mitten im Winter; Ⓑ *pl.* **the ~:** die Toten *Pl.*

**dead: ~-[and-]a'live** *adj.* langweilig; öde ‹Ort, Leben›; **~ beat** /-'-/ *adj.* (*exhausted*) völlig zerschlagen; (*without money*) bettelarm; **~beat** /'--/ *n.* (*coll.*) (*sponger*) Nassauer, *der* (*ugs.*); (*penniless person*) **he is a ~beat** er ist bettelarm; **~ 'duck** *n.* (*coll.*) Ⓐ (*person*) Null, *die* (*ugs.*); Ⓑ (*thing*) **it is a ~ duck** das kann man vergessen

**deaden** /'dedn/ *v.t.* dämpfen; abstumpfen ‹Gefühl›; betäuben ‹Nerv, Körperteil, Schmerz›; **~ sb./sth. to sth.** jmdn./etw. gegen etw. unempfindlich machen

**dead: ~ 'end** *n.* (*closed end*) Absperrung, *die;* (*street; also fig.*) Sackgasse, *die;* **~-end** *attrib. adj.* Ⓐ **~-end street/road** Sackgasse, *die;* Ⓑ (*fig.*) aussichtslos; **she's in a ~-end job** in ihrem Job hat sie keine Aufstiegschancen; **he is a ~-end kid** er ist in ärmlichen Verhältnissen aufgewachsen; **~eye** *n.* (*Naut.*) Jungfer, *die;* **~ head** *n.* (*flower head*) verblühte Blüte; **~ 'heat** *n.* totes Rennen; **finish** *or* **end in a ~ heat** unentschieden ausgehen; **~ 'language** *n.* tote Sprache; **~ 'letter** *n.* Ⓐ (*law*) Gesetz, das nicht angewendet wird; **be a ~ letter** nur noch auf dem Papier bestehen; Ⓑ (*letter*) unzustellbarer Brief; **~ 'lift** *n.* Gewaltleistung, *die;* **~light** *n.* (*Naut.*) [Seeschlag]blende, *die;* **~line** *n.* Ⓐ (*line of limit*) *Linie um ein Gefängnis o. Ä., die von den Gefangenen nicht überschritten werden darf;* Ⓑ (*time limit*) [letzter] Termin; **meet the ~line** den Termin einhalten; **set a ~line for sth.** eine Frist für etw. setzen

**deadliness** /'dedlɪnɪs/ *n., no pl.* (*fatal quality*) tödliche Wirkung

**dead: ~lock** ❶ *n.* Ⓐ (*standstill*) völliger Stillstand; **come to a** *or* **reach [a] ~lock/be at ~lock** an einem toten Punkt anlangen/angelangt sein; **the negotiations had reached ~lock** die Verhandlungen waren festgefahren; Ⓑ (*lock*) einfaches Schloss ohne Feder; ❷ *v.t.* blockieren; **~ 'loss** *n.* Ⓐ (*complete loss*) [totaler] Verlust; Ⓑ (*coll.*) (*worthless thing*) totaler Reinfall (*ugs.*); (*person*) hoffnungsloser Fall (*ugs.*)

**deadly** /'dedlɪ/ ❶ *adj.* Ⓐ tödlich; (*fig. coll.: awful*) fürchterlich; (*very boring*) todlangweilig; (*very dangerous*) lebensgefährlich; **~ enemy** Todfeind, *der;* **~ fear** Todesangst, *die;* **he looked ~** (*dangerous*) er sah furchterregend aus; **I'm in ~ earnest about this** es ist mir todernst damit; Ⓑ (*accurate*) [absolut] exakt; Ⓒ (*Theol.*) **~ sin** Todsünde, *die.* ❷ *adv.* tod-; (*extremely*) äußerst; **~ pale** totenblass; **~ dull** todlangweilig

**deadly 'nightshade** *n.* (*Bot.*) Tollkirsche, *die*

**dead: ~ man's 'handle** *n.* (*Transport*) Sicherheitsfahrschalter, *der;* **~ march** *n.* Trauermarsch, *der;* **~ men** *n. pl.* (*coll.: bottles*) leere Flaschen; tote Marine (*salopp scherzh.*)

**deadness** /'dednɪs/ *n., no pl.* (*numbness*) Gefühllosigkeit, *die;* (*inactivity*) Öde, *die;* Trostlosigkeit, *die*

**dead: ~ 'on** ❶ *adj.* [ganz] genau; **he was ~ on with his shot** er hat mit seinem Schuss genau getroffen; **you were ~ on when you said that** du hattest vollkommen Recht, als du das sagtest; ❷ *adv.* [ganz] genau; **~pan** *adj.* unbewegt; **he looked ~pan** *or* **had a ~pan expression** er verzog keine Miene; **~ 'reckoning** *n.* (*Naut.*) Koppeln, *das;* Besteckrechnung, *die;* **~ ringer** /ded 'rɪŋə(r)/ *n.* (*coll.*) Doppelgänger, *der*/-gängerin, *die;* **a ~ ringer for Trotski** ein Doppelgänger *od.* Double Trotskis; **a ~ ringer for his father** ein Ebenbild seines Vaters; **be a ~ ringer for sb.** jmdm. zum Verwechseln ähnlich sehen; **D~ 'Sea** *pr. n.* Tote Meer, *das;* **D~ Sea Scrolls** *pr. n. pl.* Schriftrollen von Kumran *od.* vom Toten Meer; **~ weight** *n.* Ⓐ (*inert mass*) Eigengewicht, *das;* Totgewicht, *das* (*Technik*); (*fig.*) schwere Bürde; Ⓑ (*Naut.: weight of cargo etc.*) Tragfähigkeit, *die;* Deadweight, *das;* **~ 'wood** *n.* Ⓐ totes Holz; Ⓑ (*fig.*) **be just ~ wood** völlig überflüssig sein; **get rid of much of the ~ wood** (*persons*) viele Nieten loswerden (*ugs.*); (*things*) viel Überflüssiges loswerden

**deaf** /def/ ❶ *adj.* Ⓐ (*without hearing*) taub; **~ and dumb** taubstumm; **~ in one ear** auf einem Ohr taub; **go** *or* **become ~:** taub werden; Ⓑ (*insensitive*) **musically ~:** unmusikalisch; **be ~ to sth.** kein Ohr für etw. haben; (*fig.*) taub gegenüber etw. sein; **turn a ~ ear [to sth./sb.]** sich [gegenüber etw./jmdm.] taub stellen; **fall on ~ ears** kein Gehör finden. ❷ *n. pl.* **the ~:** die Gehörlosen *Pl.*

**deaf: ~ aid** *n.* Hörgerät, *das;* **~-and-'dumb alphabet** *or* **language** *n.* Taubstummensprache, *die*

**deafen** /'defn/ *v.t.* **~ sb.** bei jmdm. zur Taubheit führen; **I was ~ed by the noise** (*fig.*) ich war von dem Lärm wie betäubt

**deafening** /'defənɪŋ/ *adj.* ohrenbetäubend ‹Lärm, Musik, Geschrei›

**deaf 'mute** *n.* Taubstumme, *der/die*

**deafness** /'defnɪs/ *n., no pl.* Taubheit, *die;* **cause ~ in sb.** bei jmdm. zur Taubheit führen

**deal**[1] /di:l/ ❶ *v.t.,* **dealt** /delt/ Ⓐ (*Cards*) austeilen; **who ~t the cards?** wer hat gegeben?; **he was ~t four aces** er bekam vier Asse; Ⓑ (*deliver as share*) **~ sb. sth.** jmdm. etw. zuteil werden lassen (*geh.*); Ⓒ (*administer*) versetzen; **~ sb. a blow** (*lit. or fig.*) jmdm. einen Schlag versetzen; Ⓓ (*distribute*) verteilen.

❷ *v.i.,* **dealt** Ⓐ (*do business*) **~ with sb.** mit jmdm. Geschäfte machen; **~ in sth.** mit etw. handeln; Ⓑ (*occupy oneself*) **~ with sth.** sich mit etw. befassen; (*manage*) mit etw. fertig werden; **this point must be ~t with** dieser Punkt muss behandelt werden; **I'll ~ with the washing-up** ich kümmere mich um den Abwasch; **the play ~s with the Civil War** das Stück handelt vom Bürgerkrieg; Ⓒ (*associate*) **~ with sb.** mit jmdm. zu tun haben; Ⓓ (*behave*) **~ gently/circumspectly with sb./sth.** mit jmdm./etw. sanft/vorsichtig umgehen; Ⓔ (*take measures*) **~ with sb.** mit jmdm. fertig werden.

❸ *n.* Ⓐ (*arrangement, bargain*) Geschäft, *das;* **new ~:** neue Bedingungen; (*Polit.*) Reformprogramm, *das;* **make a ~ with sb.** mit jmdm. ein Geschäft abschließen; **you've got a good ~ there** da hast du ein gutes Geschäft gemacht; **it's a ~!** abgemacht!; **big ~!** (*iron.*) na und?; **fair ~** (*bargain*) gutes Geschäft; (*treatment*) faire *od.* gerechte Behandlung; **raw** *or* **rough ~** (*treatment*) ungerechte Behandlung; (*bad luck*) Pech, *das;* Ⓑ (*agreement*) **make** *or* **do a ~ with sb.** mit jmdm. eine Vereinbarung treffen; **let's stick to our ~:** lass uns bei unserer Abmachung bleiben; Ⓒ (*Cards*) **it's your ~:** du gibst

**~ 'out** *v.t.* verteilen; **~ sth. out to sb.** etw. an jmdn. verteilen

**deal**[2] *n.* **a great** *or* **good ~,** (*coll.*) **a ~:** viel; (*often*) ziemlich viel; **a great** *or* **good ~ of,** (*coll.*) **a ~ of** eine [ganze] Menge, viel; **we resent it a [great/good] ~ that ...** (*coll.*) es ärgert uns ganz schön, dass ... (*ugs.*)

**deal**[3] *n.* (*fir/pine timber*) [Tannen-/Kiefern]holz, *das*

**dealer** /'di:lə(r)/ *n.* Ⓐ ▶ 1261 (*trader*) Händler, *der;* **he's a ~ in antiques** er ist Antiquitätenhändler *od.* handelt mit Antiquitäten; Ⓑ (*Cards*) Geber, *der;* **he's the ~:** er gibt; Ⓒ ▶ 1261 (*Stock Exch.*) Börsenmakler, *der*

**dealership** /'di:ləʃɪp/ *n.* (*Commerc.*) Vertretung, *die;* **a network of Ford ~s** ein Netz von Fordvertragshändlern

**dealing** /'di:lɪŋ/ *n.* **have ~s with sb.** mit jmdm. zu tun haben

**dealt** ⇒ **deal**[1] 1, 2

**dean** /di:n/ *n.* Ⓐ (*Eccl.*) Dechant, *der;* Dekan, *der;* Ⓑ (*in college, university, etc.*) (*resident fellow*) *Fellow mit Aufsichts- und Beratungsfunktion;* (*head of faculty*) Dekan, *der*

**deanery** /'di:nərɪ/ *n.* Ⓐ (*office*) Dekanat, *das;* Ⓑ (*house*) Dekanei, *die;* Ⓒ (*Brit.: group of parishes*) Dekanat, *das*

**dear** /dɪə(r)/ ❶ *adj.* Ⓐ (*beloved; also iron.*) lieb; geliebt; (*sweet; also iron.*) entzückend; reizend; **my ~ sir/madam** [mein] lieber Herr/[meine] liebe Dame; **my ~ man/woman** guter Mann/gute Frau; **my ~ Jones/child/girl** [mein] lieber Jones/liebes Kind/liebes Mädchen; **sb./sth. is [very] ~ to sb.['s heart]** jmd. liebt jmdn./etw. [über alles]; **sb. holds sb./sth. ~ [to him/to his**

heart] jmd./etw. liegt jmdm. [sehr] am Herzen; **run for ~ life** um sein Leben rennen; **my ~est wish** mein innigster *od.* sehnlichster Wunsch; **his ~est ambition** sein höchstes Ziel; Ⓑ ▶1286 (*beginning letter*) **D~ Sir/Madam** Sehr geehrter Herr/Sehr verehrte gnädige Frau; **D~ Mr Jones/Mrs Jones** Sehr geehrter Herr Jones/Sehr verehrte Frau Jones; **D~ Malcolm/Emily** Lieber Malcolm/Liebe Emily; **Dearest Auntie Minnie** Liebste Tante Minnie; **My ~ Smith** (*Brit.: less formal*) Lieber Herr Smith; (*between old schoolfellows etc.*) Lieber Smith; (*Amer.: more formal*) Sehr geehrter Herr Smith; Ⓒ (*in addressing sb.*) lieb; (*in exclamation*) **~ God!** ach du lieber Gott! ⇒ *also* **madam** A; **sir** B; Ⓓ (*expensive*) teuer.
❷ *int.* **~, ~!, ~ me!, oh ~!** [ach] du liebe *od.* meine Güte!
❸ *n.* Ⓐ **you 'are a ~** (*coll.*) du bist wirklich lieb; **she is a ~:** sie ist ein Schatz; Ⓑ **[my] ~** (*to wife, husband, younger relative*) [mein] Liebling; [mein] Schatz; (*to aunt*) Tantchen; (*to little girl/boy*) [meine] Kleine/[mein] Kleiner; (*to man/woman*) guter Mann/gute Frau; **~est** Liebling (*der*).
❹ *adv.* teuer; ⇒ *also* **cost** 2 A

**dearie** /ˈdɪərɪ/ *n.* Kleine, *der/die;* **~ me!** [ach] du liebe *od.* meine Güte!

**dearly** /ˈdɪəlɪ/ *adv.* Ⓐ (*very fondly, earnestly*) von ganzem Herzen; **I'd ~ love to do that** ich würde das liebend gern tun; Ⓑ (*at high price*) teuer; **you'll pay ~ for it** (*fig.*) du wirst teuer dafür bezahlen müssen

**dearth** /dɜːθ/ *n.* Mangel, *der* (**of** an + *Dat.*); **there is a ~ of sth.** es besteht *od.* herrscht Mangel an etw. (*Dat.*); **there is no ~ of sth.** es fehlt nicht an etw. (*Dat.*)

**death** /deθ/ *n.* Ⓐ Tod, *der;* **end in/mean ~:** zum Tod führen; **be afraid of ~:** Angst vor dem Tod haben; **after ~:** nach dem Tod; **[as] sure as ~:** todsicher; **meet one's ~:** den Tod finden (*geh.*); **catch one's ~ [of cold]** (*coll.*) sich (*Dat.*) den Tod holen (*ugs.*); **drink will be the ~ of him** er trinkt sich noch zu Tode; **... to ~:** zu Tode ...; **bleed to ~:** verbluten; **freeze to ~:** erfrieren; **beat sb. to ~:** jmdn. totschlagen; **burn [sb.] to ~:** [jmdn.] verbrennen; **he worked/drank himself to ~:** er hat sich totgearbeitet/totgetrunken (*ugs.*); **I'm scared to ~** (*fig.*) mir ist angst und bange (**about** vor + *Dat.*); **be sick** *or* **tired to ~ of sth.** (*fig.*) etw. gründlich satt haben; **be tickled to ~ by sth.** (*fig.*) sich über etw. totlachen; **be done to ~:** getötet werden; (*fig.*) zu Tode geritten werden; **be worked to ~:** zu Tode geschunden werden; (*fig.*) zu Tode geritten werden; **[fight] to the ~:** auf Leben und Tod [kämpfen]; **be in at the ~** (*in fox-hunting*) dabei sein, wenn der Fuchs getötet wird; (*fig.*) das Ende miterleben; **a fate worse than ~** (*joc.*) das Allerschlimmste; **~ or glory!** Ruhm oder Untergang!; **~ to fascism!** Tod dem Faschismus!; **D~** (*personified*) der Tod; **be at ~'s door** an der Schwelle des Todes stehen; **feel/look like ~ [warmed up]** (*coll.*) sich wie eine Leiche auf Urlaub fühlen/wie eine Leiche auf Urlaub aussehen (*salopp*); Ⓑ (*instance*) Todesfall, *der;* **how many ~s were there?** wie viele Tote gab es?

**death: ~bed** *n.* Totenbett, *das;* Sterbebett, *das; attrib.* auf dem Sterbebett *nachgestellt;* **on one's ~bed** auf dem Sterbebett; **~ blow** *n.* (*lit. or fig.*) Todesstoß, *der* (**to** für); **~ cell** *n.* Todeszelle, *die;* **~ certificate** *n.* (*from authorities*) Sterbeurkunde, *die;* (*from doctor*) Totenschein, *der;* **~-dealing** *attrib. adj.* todbringend; **~-defying** *adj.* todesmutig; **~ duty** *n.* (*Brit. Hist.*) Erbschaftssteuer, *die;* **~ knell** *n.* (*lit. or fig.*) Totengeläut, *das*

**deathless** /ˈdeθlɪs/ *adj.* unsterblich; (*fig.*) unvergänglich; **~ prose** (*iron.*) hochgestochene Prosa

**deathly** /ˈdeθlɪ/ ❶ *adj.* tödlich; **~ stillness/hush** Totenstille, *die;* **~ pallor** Totenblässe, *die.* ❷ *adv.* tödlich; **~ pale** totenblass; **~ still/quiet** totenstill

**death: ~ mask** *n.* Totenmaske, *die;* **~ penalty** *n.* Todesstrafe, *die;* **~ rate** *n.* Sterblichkeitsziffer, *die;* **~ rattle** *n.* Todesröcheln, *das;* **~ ray** *n.* tödlicher Strahl; **~ roll** *n.* Verlustliste, *die;* (*after battle*) Gefallenenliste, *die;* **~ row** /deθ ˈrəʊ/ *n.* [Reihe von] Todeszellen; **~ sentence** *n.* Todesurteil, *das;* **~'s head** *n.* Totenkopf, *der;* **~ squad** *n.* Todesschwadron, *die;* Killerkommando, *das;* **~ tax** (*Amer.*) Erbschaftssteuer, *die;* **~ threat** *n.* Morddrohung, *die;* **~ throes** *n. pl.* Todeskampf, *der;* Agonie, *die* (*geh.*); **be in one's [last] ~ throes** mit dem Tode[e] ringen; in Agonie liegen (*geh.*); **be in its [last] ~ throes** ‹Tier:› am Verenden sein; (*fig.*) ‹politisches System:› in Agonie liegen (*geh.*); **~ toll** *n.* Zahl der Todesopfer; Blutzoll, *der* (*geh.*); **~ trap** *n.* lebensgefährliche Sache; **this corner/house/car is a ~ trap** diese Kurve/dieses Haus/Auto ist lebensgefährlich; **~ warrant** *n.* Exekutionsbefehl, *der;* (*fig.*) Todesurteil, *das;* **~-watch [beetle]** *n.* (*Zool.*) Totenuhr, *die;* **~ wish** *n.* (*Psych.*) Todeswunsch, *der*

**deb** /deb/ *n.* (*coll.*) Debütantin, *die*

**débâcle** /deɪˈbɑːkl/ *n.* Debakel, *das* (*geh.*)

**debar** /dɪˈbɑː(r)/ *v.t.*, **-rr-** ausschließen; **~ sb. from doing sth.** jmdn. davon ausschließen, etw. zu tun

**debase** /dɪˈbeɪs/ *v.t.* Ⓐ verschlechtern; herabsetzen, entwürdigen ‹Person›; **~ oneself** sich erniedrigen; Ⓑ **~ the coinage** den Wert der Währung mindern

**debatable** /dɪˈbeɪtəbl/ *adj.* Ⓐ (*questionable*) fraglich; Ⓑ **~ ground** umstrittenes Gebiet

**debate** /dɪˈbeɪt/ ❶ *v.t.* debattieren über (+ *Akk.*); **be ~d** diskutiert *od.* debattiert werden. ❷ *v.i.* **~ [up]on sth.** etw. debattieren; **~ about sth.** über etw. (*Akk.*) debattieren *od.* streiten. ❸ *n.* Debatte, *die;* **there was much ~ about whether ...:** es wurde viel darüber debattiert, ob ...

**debating** /dɪˈbeɪtɪŋ/: **~ point** *n.* (*für die Sache unerheblicher, nur aus rhetorischen Gründen vorgebrachter*) Diskussionspunkt; **~ society** *n.* (*regelmäßig zusammentretende*) Diskussionsrunde

**debauch** /dɪˈbɔːtʃ/ (*literary*) ❶ *v.t.* Ⓐ verderben; Ⓑ (*seduce*) verführen. ❷ *n.* Gelage, *das*

**debauched** /dɪˈbɔːtʃt/ *adj.* verderbt (*geh.*)

**debauchery** /dɪˈbɔːtʃərɪ/ *n.* (*literary*) Ausschweifung, *die*

**debenture** /dɪˈbentʃə(r)/ *n.* (*Finance*) Schuldverschreibung, *die*

**debilitate** /dɪˈbɪlɪteɪt/ *v.t.* schwächen

**debilitating** /dɪˈbɪlɪteɪtɪŋ/ *adj.* anstrengend ‹Klima›; schwächend ‹Krankheit›

**debility** /dɪˈbɪlɪtɪ/ *n.* Schwäche, *die*

**debit** /ˈdebɪt/ ❶ *n.* (*Bookk.*) Soll, *das;* (**~ side**) Soll, *das;* Debet, *das;* **~ balance** Lastschrift, *die;* **~ side** (*Finance*) Sollseite, *die.* ❷ *v.t.* belasten; **~ a sum against** *or* **to sb./sb.'s account, ~ sb./sb.'s account with a sum** jmdn./jmds. Konto mit einer Summe belasten

**debonair** /debəˈneə(r)/ *adj.* frohgemut

**debrief** /diːˈbriːf/ *v.t.* (*coll.*) befragen (*bei Rückkehr von einem Einsatz usw.*)

**debriefing** /diːˈbriːfɪŋ/ *n.* (*coll.*) Befragung, *die;* **hold a ~ session** sich Bericht erstatten lassen

**debris** /ˈdebriː, ˈdeɪbriː/ *n., no pl.* Trümmer *Pl.*

**debt** /det/ *n.* Schuld, *die;* **owe sb. a ~ of gratitude** *or* **thanks** jmdm. Dank schulden; [tief] in jmds. Schuld stehen; **~ of honour** Ehrenschuld, *die;* **National D~:** Staatsverschuldung, *die;* **be in ~:** Schulden haben; verschuldet sein; **get** *or* **run into ~:** in Schulden geraten; sich verschulden; **get out of ~:** aus den Schulden herauskommen; **be in sb.'s ~:** in jmds. Schuld stehen

**'debt collector** *n.* Inkassobevollmächtigte, *der/die;* Schuldeneintreiber, *der* (*veralt.*)

**debtor** /ˈdetə(r)/ *n.* Schuldner, *der*/Schuldnerin, *die*

**debug** /diːˈbʌg/ *v.t.*, **-gg-** Ⓐ entwanzen; Ⓑ (*fig. coll.*) (*remove microphones from*) von Wanzen befreien; (*remove defects from*) von Fehlern befreien

**debunk** /diːˈbʌŋk/ *v.t.* (*coll.*) (*remove false reputation from*) entlarven; (*expose falseness of*) bloßstellen

**début** (*Amer.:* **debut**) /ˈdeɪbjuː, ˈdeɪbuː/ *n.* Debüt, *das;* **make one's ~:** debütieren

**débutante** (*Amer.:* **debutante**) /ˈdebjuːtɑːnt, ˈdeɪbjuːtɑːnt/ *n.* Debütantin, *die*

**Dec.** *abbr.* **December** Dez.

**decade** /ˈdekeɪd/ *n.* Jahrzehnt, *das;* Dekade, *die*

**decadence** /ˈdekədəns/ *n.* Dekadenz, *die*

**decadent** /ˈdekədənt/ *adj.* dekadent

**decaf, decaff** /ˈdiːkæf/*n.* (*coll.*) *or* ® koffeinfreier Kaffee; ≈ Kaffee Hag ⓌⓏ, *der*

**decaffeinated** /diːˈkæfɪneɪtɪd/ *adj.* entkoffeiniert; koffeinfrei (*veralt.*)

**Decalogue** /ˈdekəlɒg/ *n.* **the ~:** der Dekalog; die Zehn Gebote

**decamp** /dɪˈkæmp/ *v.i.* Ⓐ (*abscond*) verschwinden (*ugs.*); Ⓑ (*leave camp*) das Lager abbrechen

**decant** /dɪˈkænt/ *v.t.* abgießen; dekantieren ‹Wein›; (*fig.*) abladen

**decanter** /dɪˈkæntə(r)/ *n.* Karaffe, *die*

**decapitate** /dɪˈkæpɪteɪt/ *v.t.* Ⓐ köpfen ‹Person, Blume›; enthaupten (*geh.*); Ⓑ (*Amer.: dismiss*) entlassen

**decathlete** /dɪˈkæθliːt/ *n.* (*Sport*) Zehnkämpfer, *der*

**decathlon** /dɪˈkæθlən/ *n.* (*Sport*) Zehnkampf, *der*

**decay** /dɪˈkeɪ/ ❶ *v.i.* Ⓐ (*become rotten*) verrotten; [ver]faulen; ‹Zahn:› faul *od.* (*fachspr.*) kariös werden; ‹Gebäude, Tuch:› zerfallen; Ⓑ (*decline*) verfallen; Ⓒ (*Phys.: decrease*) zerfallen. ❷ *n.* Ⓐ (*rotting*) Verrotten, *das;* (*of tooth*) Fäule, *die;* (*of building*) Zerfall, *der;* Verfall, *der;* Ⓑ (*decline*) Verfall, *der;* (*of nation*) Verfall, *der;* Niedergang, *der;* Ⓒ (*decayed tissue etc.*) Zersetzung, *die;* Fäulnis, *die;* Ⓓ (*Phys.: decrease*) Zerfall, *der*

**decease** /dɪˈsiːs/ (*Law/formal*) ❶ *n.* Ableben, *das* (*geh.*). ❷ *v.i.* versterben (*geh.*); sterben

**deceased** /dɪˈsiːst/ (*Law/formal*) ❶ *adj.* verstorben; **the ~ man** der Tote *od.* Verstorbene; **Jim Fox ~:** der verstorbene Jim Fox. ❷ *n.* Verstorbene, *der/die*

**decedent** /dɪˈsiːdənt/ *n.* (*Amer.*) Verstorbene, *der/die*

**deceit** /dɪˈsiːt/ *n.* (*misrepresentation*) Täuschung, *die;* Betrug, *der;* (*trick*) Täuschungsmanöver, *das;* Betrügerei, *die;* (*being deceitful*) Falschheit, *die*

**deceitful** /dɪˈsiːtfl/ *adj.* falsch ‹Person, Art, Charakter›; hinterlistig ‹Trick›; **that was a ~ thing to say** es war hinterlistig, das zu sagen

**deceitfully** /dɪˈsiːtfəlɪ/ *adv.* ⇒ **deceitful**: falsch; hinterlistig

**deceitfulness** /dɪˈsiːtflnɪs/ *n., no pl.* ⇒ **deceitful**: Falschheit, *die;* Hinterlistigkeit, *die*

**deceive** /dɪˈsiːv/ *v.t.* täuschen; (*be unfaithful to*) betrügen; **if my eyes/ears do not ~ me** wenn ich richtig sehe/höre; **~ sb. into doing sth.** jmdn. [durch Täuschung] dazu bringen, etw. zu tun; **~ oneself** sich täuschen; (*delude oneself*) sich (*Dat.*) etwas vormachen (*ugs.*); **[let oneself] be ~d** sich täuschen lassen; **[let oneself] be ~d into doing sth.** sich dazu bringen lassen, etw. zu tun

**deceiver** /dɪˈsiːvə(r)/ *n.* Betrüger, *der*/Betrügerin, *die*

**decelerate** /diːˈseləreɪt/ ❶ *v.t.* verlangsamen. ❷ *v.i.* ‹Fahrzeug, Fahrer:› die Fahrt verlangsamen

**deceleration** /diːseləˈreɪʃn/ *n.* Verlangsamung, *die*

**December** /dɪˈsembə(r)/ *n.* ▶1055 Dezember, *der;* ⇒ *also* **August**

**decency** /ˈdiːsənsɪ/ *n.* Ⓐ (*modesty, propriety*) Anstand, *der;* (*of manners, literature, language*) Schicklichkeit, *die* (*geh.*); (*fairness, respectability*) Anständigkeit, *die;* **it is [a matter of] common ~:** es ist eine Frage des Anstands; es gehört sich; Ⓑ *in pl.* (*requirements of propriety*) Anstandsregeln *Pl.*

**decent** /ˈdiːsənt/ *adj.* Ⓐ (*seemly*) schicklich (*geh.*); anständig ‹Person›; **are you ~?** (*coll.*) hast du was an? (*ugs.*); Ⓑ (*passable, respectable*) annehmbar; anständig ‹Person, ugs. auch Preis, Gehalt›; **do the ~ thing** das einzig Richtige tun; Ⓒ (*Brit.: kind*) nett; **that is very ~ of you** das ist sehr liebenswürdig von Ihnen; **be ~ about sth.** auf etw. (*Akk.*) nett reagieren

**decently** /ˈdiːsəntlɪ/ *adv.* Ⓐ (*in seemly manner*) anständig; geziemend (*geh.*); schicklich (*geh.*); Ⓑ (*passably, respectably*) annehmbar; Ⓒ (*Brit.: kindly*) netterweise (*ugs.*); **behave ~:** sich nett verhalten

**decentralisation**, **decentralise** ⇒ **decentraliz-**

**decentralization** /diːsentrəlaɪˈzeɪʃn/ *n.* Dezentralisierung, *die*

**decentralize** /diːˈsentrəlaɪz/ *v.t.* dezentralisieren

**deception** /dɪˈsepʃn/ *n.* Ⓐ (*deceiving, trickery*) Betrug, *der;* (*being deceived*) Täuschung, *die;* **use ~:** betrügen; Ⓑ (*trick*) Betrügerei, *die*

**deceptive** /dɪˈseptɪv/ *adj.* trügerisch

**deceptively** /dɪˈseptɪvlɪ/ *adv.* täuschend

**decibel** /ˈdesɪbel/ *n.* Dezibel, *das*

**decide** /dɪˈsaɪd/ ❶ *v.t.* Ⓐ (*settle, judge*) entscheiden über (+ *Akk.*); **~ sth. by tossing a coin** etw. durch Werfen einer Münze entscheiden; **~ the winner** entscheiden, wer gewonnen hat; **~ that …:** entscheiden, dass …; Ⓑ (*resolve*) **be ~d** sich entschieden haben; **~ that …:** beschließen, dass …; **~ to do sth.** sich entschließen, etw. zu tun. ❷ *v.i.* sich entscheiden (**between** zwischen + *Dat.*, **in favour of** zugunsten von, **against** gegen, **on** für); **~ against/on doing sth.** sich dagegen/dafür entscheiden, etw. zu tun

**decided** /dɪˈsaɪdɪd/ *adj.* Ⓐ (*unquestionable*) entschieden; eindeutig; **he made a ~ effort** er hat sich deutlich *od.* entschieden bemüht; Ⓑ (*not hesitant*) bestimmt; entschlossen, entschieden ‹Haltung, Ansicht›

**decidedly** /dɪˈsaɪdɪdlɪ/ *adv.* Ⓐ (*unquestionably*) entschieden; deutlich; Ⓑ (*firmly*) bestimmt

**decider** /dɪˈsaɪdə(r)/ *n.* (*game*) Entscheidungsspiel, *das*

**deciduous** /dɪˈsɪdjʊəs/ *adj.* (*Bot.*) **~ leaves** Blätter, die abgeworfen werden; **~ tree** laubwerfender Baum; ≈ Laubbaum, *der*

**decimal** /ˈdesɪml/ ▶ **1352** ❶ *adj.* Dezimal-; dezimal; **go ~:** sich auf das Dezimalsystem umstellen. ❷ *n.* Dezimalbruch, *der*

**decimal: ~ ˈcoinage**, **~ ˈcurrency** *ns.* Dezimalwährung, *die;* **~ ˈfraction** *n.* Dezimalbruch, *der*

**decimalize** (**decimalise**) /ˈdesɪməlaɪz/ *v.t.* (*express as decimal*) als Dezimalzahl schreiben; (*convert to decimal system*) dezimalisieren

**decimal: ~ ˈplace** *n.* Dezimale, *die;* **calculate sth. to five ~ places** etw. auf fünf Stellen nach dem Komma ausrechnen; **~ ˈpoint** *n.* Komma, *das;* **~ system** *n.* Dezimalsystem, *das*

**decimate** /ˈdesɪmeɪt/ *v.t.* dezimieren ‹Bevölkerung, Truppe›; drastisch verringern ‹Zahl›

**decimetre** /ˈdesɪmiːtə(r)/ *n.* Dezimeter, *der*

**decipher** /dɪˈsaɪfə(r)/ *v.t.* entziffern

**decipherable** /dɪˈsaɪfərəbl/ *adj.* entzifferbar

**decision** /dɪˈsɪʒn/ *n.* Ⓐ (*settlement, judgement, conclusion*) Entscheidung, *die* (**on** über + *Akk.*); (*resolve*) Entschluss, *der;* **it's ˈyour ~:** die Entscheidung liegt ganz bei dir; **come to** *or* **arrive at** *or* **reach a ~:** zu einer Entscheidung kommen; **has there been a ~?** ist eine Entscheidung gefallen?; **make** *or* **take a ~:** eine Entscheidung treffen; **make a firm ~ to do sth.** den festen Entschluss fassen, etw. zu tun; **leave the ~ to sb.** jmdm. die Entscheidung überlassen; **~s, ~s!** immer diese Entscheidungen!; Ⓑ *no pl.* (*resoluteness*) Entschlossenheit, *die*

**deˈcision-making** *n.* Beschlussfassung, *die*

**decisive** /dɪˈsaɪsɪv/ *adj.* Ⓐ (*conclusive*) entscheidend; Ⓑ (*decided*) entschlussfreudig ‹Person›; bestimmt ‹Charakter, Art›

**decisively** /dɪˈsaɪsɪvlɪ/ *adv.* Ⓐ (*conclusively*) entscheidend; Ⓑ (*decidedly*) entschlossen

**decisiveness** /dɪˈsaɪsɪvnɪs/ *n., no pl.* Ⓐ (*conclusiveness*) entscheidende Bedeutung; Ⓑ (*decidedness*) Entschlossenheit, *die*

**deck** /dek/ ❶ *n.* Ⓐ (*of ship*) Deck, *das;* **above ~:** auf Deck; **below ~[s]** unter Deck; **clear the ~s [for action** *etc.***]** das Schiff klarmachen [zum Gefecht *usw.*]; (*fig.*) alles startklar machen; **on ~:** an Deck; **all hands on ~!** alle Mann an Deck!; **it was all hands on ~** (*fig.*) alle packten mit an; Ⓑ (*of bus etc.*) Deck, *das;* **the upper ~:** das Oberdeck; Ⓒ (*sunbathing platform*) ≈ Sonnenterrasse, *die;* Ⓓ (*tape ~*) Tapedeck, *das;* (*record ~*) Plattenspieler, *der;* Ⓔ (*coll.: ground*) Boden, *der;* **hit the ~:** auf den Boden schlagen; Ⓕ (*Amer.: pack*) **a ~ of cards** ein Spiel Karten; **split/shuffle the ~:** die Karten austeilen/mischen. ❷ *v.t.* **~ sth. [with sth.]** etw. [mit etw.] schmücken; **they were ~ed in all their finery** sie waren prächtig herausgeputzt

**~ ˈout** *v.t.* herausputzen ‹Person›; [aus]schmücken ‹Raum›

**deck: ~chair** *n.* Liegestuhl, *der;* (*on ship*) Liege- *od.* Deckstuhl, *der;* **~hand** *n.* (*Naut.*) Decksmann, *der*

**deckle** /ˈdekl/: **~-ˈedge** *n.* Büttenrand, *der;* **~-ˈedged** *adj.* mit Büttenrand

**declaim** /dɪˈkleɪm/ ❶ *v.i.* Ⓐ **~ against sb./sth.** gegen jmdn./etw. eifern *od.* (*ugs.*) wettern; Ⓑ (*deliver impassioned speech*) eifern; deklamieren (*veralt.*). ❷ *v.t.* deklamieren ‹Gedicht›; verkünden (*geh.*) ‹Botschaft›

**declamatory** /dɪˈklæmətərɪ/ *adj.* deklamatorisch ‹Stil, Rede, Art›; leidenschaftlich ‹Kritik, Worte›

**declaration** /dekləˈreɪʃn/ *n.* Erklärung, *die;* (*at customs*) Deklaration, *die;* Zollerklärung, *die;* (*of the truth, one's errors*) Eingeständnis, *das;* **~ of love** Liebeserklärung, *die;* **income tax ~:** Einkommensteuererklärung, *die;* **~ of the poll** *or* **election results** Bekanntgabe der Wahlergebnisse; **~ of war** Kriegserklärung, *die;* **make a ~:** eine Erklärung abgeben; (*of guilt*) ein Geständnis ablegen; **D~ of Human Rights** Menschenrechtserklärung, *die*

**declare** /dɪˈkleə(r)/ ❶ *v.t.* Ⓐ (*announce*) erklären; zugeben ‹Schuld, Wissen›; (*state explicitly*) kundtun (*geh.*) ‹Wunsch, Absicht›; Ausdruck verleihen (+ *Dat.*) (*geh.*) ‹Erwartung, Hoffnung›; (*prove*) bezeugen; **[well,] I [do] ~!** (*dated*) das darf [doch] nicht wahr sein! (*ugs.*); Ⓑ (*pronounce*) **~ sth./sb. [to be] sth.** etw./jmdn. für etw. erklären; **~ oneself** sich zu erkennen geben; Ⓒ (*acknowledge*) deklarieren; angeben ‹Einkünfte›; ⇒ *also* **interest** 1 F. ❷ *v.i.* **~ for/against sb./sth.** sich für/gegen jmdn./etw. erklären

**declassify** /diːˈklæsɪfaɪ/ *v.t.* freigeben

**declension** /dɪˈklenʃn/ *n.* (*Ling.*) Deklination, *die*

**declination** /deklɪˈneɪʃn/ *n.* Ⓐ (*downward bend*) Neigung, *die;* Ⓑ (*Amer.: refusal*) Ablehnung, *die*

**decline** /dɪˈklaɪn/ ❶ *v.i.* Ⓐ (*fall off*) nachlassen; ‹Moral:› sinken, nachlassen; ‹Preis, Anzahl:› sinken, zurückgehen; ‹Gesundheitszustand:› sich verschlechtern; ‹Reich, Kultur:› verfallen; **~ in popularity** an Beliebtheit verlieren; **his strength ~d rapidly** seine Kräfte nahmen rasch ab; Ⓑ (*slope downwards*) abfallen; (*droop*) sich neigen; Ⓒ **his declining years** die letzten Jahre seines Lebens; Ⓓ (*refuse*) **~ with thanks** (*also iron.*) dankend ablehnen. ❷ *v.t.* Ⓐ (*refuse*) ablehnen; **~ to do sth.** *or* **doing sth.** [es] ablehnen, etw. zu tun; **they ~d to make any comment** sie lehnten jede Stellungnahme ab; Ⓑ (*Ling.*) deklinieren. ❸ *n.* Nachlassen, *das* (**in** *Gen.*); **a ~ in prices/numbers** ein Sinken der Preise/Anzahl; **the ~ of the empire** der Verfall des Reiches; **~ and fall** Verfall und Untergang; **a ~ in wealth/poverty/the birth rate** eine Abnahme des Wohlstands/ein Rückgang der Armut/der Geburten; **be on the ~:** nachlassen; **he is on the ~:** er ist auf dem absteigenden Ast (*ugs.*); **be in ~:** rückläufig sein

**declutch** /diːˈklʌtʃ/ *v.i.* (*Motor Veh.*) auskuppeln; **double-~:** Zwischengas geben

**decoction** /dɪˈkɒkʃn/ *n.* (*product*) Dekokt, *das* (*Pharm.*); Abkochung, *die*

**decode** /diːˈkəʊd/ *v.t.* dekodieren, dechiffrieren ‹Mitteilung, Signal›; entschlüsseln ‹Schrift, Hieroglyphen›

**decoder** /diːˈkəʊdə(r)/ *n.* (*Electronics*) Decoder, *der*

**décolleté** /deɪˈkɒlteɪ/ ❶ *adj.* dekolletiert ‹Kleid, Dame›. ❷ *n.* Dekolleté, *das*

**decolonize** (**decolonise**) /diːˈkɒlənaɪz/ *v.t.* dekolonisieren

**decommission** /diːkəˈmɪʃən/ *v.t.* stilllegen; außer Dienst stellen ‹Schiff›

**decompose** /diːkəmˈpəʊz/ *v.i.* sich zersetzen

**decomposition** /diːkɒmpəˈzɪʃn/ *n.* Zersetzung, *die;* (*rotting also*) Verrottung, *die*

**decompress** /diːkəmˈpres/ *v.t.* (*Computing*) dekomprimieren

**decompression** /diːkəmˈpreʃn/ *n.* Dekompression, *die*

**decomˈpression: ~ chamber** *n.* Dekompressionskammer, *die;* **~ sickness** *n., no pl.* Dekompressionskrankheit, *die*

**decongestant** /diːkənˈdʒestənt/ *n.* (*Med.*) Abschwellung bewirkendes Mittel; **bronchial ~:** ≈ Hustensaft, *der;* **nasal ~:** Nasenspray, *das;* (*drops*) Nasentropfen *Pl.*

**decontaminate** /diːkənˈtæmɪneɪt/ *v.t.* dekontaminieren (*fachspr.*); entseuchen

**decontamination** /diːkəntæmɪˈneɪʃn/ *n.* Dekontamination, *die* (*fachspr.*); Entseuchung, *die*

**decontrol** /diːkənˈtrəʊl/ *v.t.*, **-ll-** (*Admin.*) freigeben

**décor** /ˈdeɪkɔː(r)/ *n.* Ausstattung, *die;* Dekor, *der od. das*

**decorate** /ˈdekəreɪt/ *v.t.* Ⓐ (*adorn*) schmücken ‹Raum, Straße, Baum›; verzieren ‹Kuchen, Kleid›; dekorieren ‹Schaufenster›; (*with wallpaper*) tapezieren; (*with paint*) streichen; Ⓑ (*invest with order etc.*) auszeichnen; dekorieren

**decorated** /ˈdekəreɪtɪd/ *adj.* Ⓐ geschmückt ‹Zimmer›; verziert ‹Kuchen›; Ⓑ (*Archit.*) **D~ style** Decorated style, *der* (*fachspr.*) (*Stil der englischen Hochgotik*)

**decoration** /dekəˈreɪʃn/ *n.* Ⓐ ⇒ **decorate** A: Schmücken, *das;* Verzieren, *das;* Dekoration, *die;* Tapezieren, *das;* Streichen, *das;* Ⓑ (*adornment*) (*thing*) Schmuck, *der;* (*in shop window*) Dekoration, *die;* Ⓒ (*medal etc.*) Auszeichnung, *die;* Dekoration, *die;* **D~ Day** (*Amer.*) *amerikanischer Heldengedenktag* (*30. Mai*); Ⓓ *in pl.* **Christmas ~s** Weihnachtsschmuck, *der*

**decorative** /ˈdekərətɪv/ *adj.* dekorativ

**decorator** /ˈdekəreɪtə(r)/ *n.* Maler, *der*/Malerin, *die;* (*paperhanger*) Tapezierer, *der*/Tapeziererin, *die;* **[firm of] ~s** Malerbetrieb, *der*

**decorous** /ˈdekərəs/ *adj.*, **decorously** /ˈdekərəslɪ/ *adv.* schicklich (*geh.*)

**decorousness** /ˈdekərəsnɪs/ *n., no pl.* Schicklichkeit, *die* (*geh.*)

**decorum** /dɪˈkɔːrəm/ *n.* Dekorum, *das* (*geh. veralt.*); (*seemliness also*) Schicklichkeit, *die* (*geh.*); **behave with ~:** sich schicklich benehmen

**decoy** ❶ /dɪˈkɔɪ/ *v.t.* Ⓐ (*allure*) locken; (*ensnare*) betören; **~ sb./sth. into sth.** jmdn./etw. in etw. (*Akk.*) locken; **~ sb./sth. into doing sth.** jmdn./etw. dazu verleiten, etw. zu tun; Ⓑ (*Hunting*) locken. ❷ /dɪˈkɔɪ, ˈdiːkɔɪ/ *n.* Ⓐ (*Hunting*) Lockvogel, *der;* Ⓑ (*person*) Lockvogel, *der;* Ⓒ (*bait*) Verlockung, *die*

**decrease** ❶ /dɪˈkriːs/ *v.i.* abnehmen; ‹Anzahl, Einfuhr, Produktivität:› abnehmen, zurückgehen; ‹Stärke, Gesundheit:› nachlassen; **~ in value/size/weight/popularity** an Wert/Größe/Gewicht/Popularität verlieren; **~ in price** im Preis fallen; billiger werden. ❷ *v.t.* reduzieren; [ver]mindern ‹Wert, Lärm, Körperkraft›; schmälern ‹Popularität, Macht›; senken ‹Standard,

Kaufkraft›. ❸ /ˈdiːkriːs/ *n.* Rückgang, *der;* (*in weight, knowledge, stocks*) Abnahme, *die;* (*in strength, power, energy*) Nachlassen, *das;* (*in value, noise*) Minderung, *die;* (*in standards*) Senkung, *die;* **a ~ in inflation/strength/speed** ein Rückgang der Inflation/ein Nachlassen der Kräfte/eine Minderung der Geschwindigkeit; **be on the ~** ⇒ **1**

**decreasingly** /dɪˈkriːsɪŋlɪ/ *adv.* immer weniger

**decree** /dɪˈkriː/ ❶ *n.* [A] (*ordinance*) Dekret, *das;* Erlass, *der;* [B] (*Law*) Urteil, *das;* **~ nisi/absolute** vorläufiges/endgültiges Scheidungsurteil. ❷ *v.t.* (*ordain*) verfügen

**decrepit** /dɪˈkrepɪt/ *adj.* altersschwach; (*dilapidated*) heruntergekommen ‹Haus, Stadt›; schrottreif ‹Auto, Maschine›

**decrepitude** /dɪˈkrepɪtjuːd/ *n., no pl.* Altersschwäche, *die;* (*of house*) heruntergekommener Zustand; (*of car, machine*) schrottreifer Zustand

**decriminalize** /diːˈkrɪmɪnəlaɪz/ *v.t.* entkriminalisieren

**decry** /dɪˈkraɪ/ *v.t.* verwerfen

**dedicate** /ˈdedɪkeɪt/ *v.t.* [A] (*with name of honoured person*) **~ sth. to sb.** jmdm. etw. widmen; **a statue ~d to the memory of ...**: eine Statue zum Gedenken an ...; [B] (*give up*) **~ one's life to sth.** sein Leben einer Sache (*Dat.*) weihen; [C] (*devote solemnly*) weihen

**dedicated** /ˈdedɪkeɪtɪd/ *adj.* [A] (*devoted*) **be ~ to sth./sb.** nur für etw./jmdn. leben; [B] (*devoted to vocation*) hingebungsvoll; **a ~ teacher/politician** ein Lehrer/Politiker mit Leib und Seele

**dedication** /dedɪˈkeɪʃn/ *n.* [A] (*act, inscription*) Widmung, *die* (**to** *Dat.*); (*in book*) Widmung, *die;* Zueignung, *die;* (*on building, monument*) Inschrift, *die;* [B] (*devotion*) Hingabe, *die;* [C] (*ceremony*) Weihe, *die*

**deduce** /dɪˈdjuːs/ *v.t.* **~ sth. [from sth.]** etw. [aus etw.] ableiten; auf etw. (*Akk.*) [aus etw.] schließen; **~ from sth. that ...**: aus etw. schließen, dass ...

**deducible** /dɪˈdjuːsɪbl/ *adj.* ableitbar, (*Philos.*) deduzierbar (**from** aus)

**deduct** /dɪˈdʌkt/ *v.t.* **~ sth. [from sth.]** etw. [von etw.] abziehen

**deductible** /dɪˈdʌktɪbl/ *adj.* **be ~**: einbehalten werden [können]

**deduction** /dɪˈdʌkʃn/ *n.* [A] (*deducting*) Abzug, *der;* [B] (*deducing, thing deduced*) Ableitung, *die;* [C] (*amount*) Abzüge *Pl.;* **a ~ from the price** ein Preisnachlass

**deductive** /dɪˈdʌktɪv/ *adj.* deduktiv

**deductively** /dɪˈdʌktɪvlɪ/ *adv.* deduktiv

**deed** /diːd/ ❶ *n.* [A] Tat, *die;* [B] (*Law*) [gesiegelte] Urkunde; **~ of transfer** Übertragungsurkunde, *die;* ⇒ *also* **covenant** 1 B. ❷ *v.t.* (*Amer.*) **~ sth. to sb.** jmdm. etw. [urkundlich] übertragen

**deed: ~ box** *n.: Kasten zur Aufbewahrung von Urkunden;* ≈ Dokumentenbox, *die;* **~ poll** /ˈdiːd pəʊl/ *n.* (*Law*) einseitiges Rechtsgeschäft (*Rechtsw.*)

**deejay** /ˈdiːdʒeɪ/ *n.* (*coll.*) Diskjockey, *der*

**deem** /diːm/ *v.t.* erachten für; **[as] I ~ed** wie mir schien; **she is ~ed to be the best singer** sie gilt als die beste Sängerin; **he shall be ~ed to have given his assent** man wird annehmen, dass er seine Zustimmung gegeben hat

**deep** /diːp/ ❶ *adj.* [A] ▶ **1210** (*extending far down, going far in, lit. or fig.*) tief; **water ten feet ~**: drei Meter tiefes Wasser; **take a ~ breath/drink** tief Atem holen/einen tiefen Schluck nehmen; [B] (*lying far down or back or inwards*) tief; **ten feet ~ in water** drei Meter tief unter Wasser; **be ~ in thought/prayer** in Gedanken/im Gebet versunken sein; **be ~ in discussion** mitten in einer Diskussion sein; **be ~ in debt** hoch verschuldet sein; **be standing three ~**: drei hintereinander stehen; [C] (*profound*) tief ‹Grund›; ernst ‹Problem, Sache›; gründlich ‹Studium, Forschung›; tiefgründig ‹Bemerkung›; **give sth. ~ thought** über etw. (*Akk.*) gründlich nachdenken; **he's a ~ one** (*coll.*) er ist ein stilles Wasser (*ugs.*); **in ~ space** [tief] im Weltraum; [D] (*heartfelt*) tief; aufrichtig ‹Interesse, Dank›; [E] (*low-pitched, intense*) tief; (*full-toned*) volltönend; **the ~-blue sea** das tiefblaue Meer; [F] (*Cricket*) *weit vom Schlagmann entfernt.* ⇒ *also* **end** 1 F.

❷ *adv.* tief; **still waters run ~** (*prov.*) stille Wasser sind tief (*Spr.*); **~ down** (*fig.*) im Innersten.

❸ *n.* [A] (**~ part**) **~s** Tiefen *Pl.;* **the ~** (*poet.*) der Ozean; [B] (*abyss, lit. or fig.*) Tiefe, *die;* [C] (*Cricket*) **the ~**: *äußerer Rand des Spielfeldes*

**deep ˈbreathing** *n.* tiefes Atmen; **~ [exercise]** Atemübung, *die*

**deepen** /ˈdiːpn/ ❶ *v.t.* [A] tiefer machen; vertiefen; [B] (*make lower*) tiefer werden lassen ‹Stimme›; [C] (*increase, intensify*) vertiefen; intensivieren ‹Farbe›. ❷ *v.i.* [A] tiefer werden; [B] (*intensify*) sich vertiefen

**deep: ~-ˈfreeze** ❶ *n.* (*Amer.:* ®) Tiefkühltruhe, *die;* (*in shop also*) Tiefkühlbox, *die;* (*upright*) Gefrierschrank, *der;* ❷ *v.t.* tiefgefrieren; **~-fried** *adj.* frittiert; **~-laid** *adj.* ausgeklügelt; ausgetüftelt

**deeply** /ˈdiːplɪ/ *adv.* [A] (*to great depth, lit. or fig.*) tief; **drink ~**: einen kräftigen Zug *od.* Schluck nehmen; [B] tief ‹beeindruckt, gerührt, verletzt, getroffen›; äußerst ‹interessiert, dankbar, engagiert, selbstbewusst›; **be ~ in love** sehr verliebt sein; **be ~ indebted to sb.** jmdm. sehr zu Dank verpflichtet sein; **sleep ~**: tief *od.* fest schlafen; **read/study ~**: sehr aufmerksam lesen/studieren

**deepness** /ˈdiːpnɪs/ *n., no pl.* Tiefe, *die;* (*of interest, gratitude*) Ausmaß, *das*

**deep: ~-rooted** *adj.* tief ‹Abneigung›; tief verwurzelt ‹Tradition›; **~-sea** *adj.* Tiefsee-; **~-ˈseated** *adj.* tief sitzend; **D~ ˈSouth** *n.* (*Amer.*) tiefer Süden (*die Staaten der USA am Golf von Mexiko*); **~ space** *n.* [erdferne] Weltraum, *der;* All, *das*

**deer** /dɪə(r)/ *n., pl. same* Hirsch, *der;* (*roe ~*) Reh, *das*

**deer: ~ forest** *n.* Jagdgehege, *das;* **~ park** *n.* Wildpark, *der;* **~skin** *n.* Rehleder, *das;* **~stalker** *n.* [A] (*person*) Jäger (*auf der Pirsch*); [B] (*hat*) Mütze (*aus Stoff mit einem Schild vorn und hinten*); ≈ Sherlock-Holmes-Mütze, *die*

**de-escalate** /diːˈeskəleɪt/ *v.t.* deeskalieren

**de-escalation** /diːeskəˈleɪʃn/ *n., no pl.* Deeskalation, *die* (*geh.*); (*of a conflict*) Entschärfung, *die*

**deface** /dɪˈfeɪs/ *v.t.* verunstalten; verschandeln ‹Gebäude›

**defacement** /dɪˈfeɪsmənt/ *n.* Verunstaltung, *die;* (*of building*) Verschandelung, *die*

**de facto** /diː ˈfæktəʊ, deɪ ˈfæktəʊ/ ❶ *adj.* de facto; **a ~ government** eine De-facto-Regierung. ❷ *adv.* de facto

**defamation** /defəˈmeɪʃn, diːfəˈmeɪʃn/ *n.* Diffamierung, *die*

**defamatory** /dɪˈfæmətərɪ/ *adj.* diffamierend; **be ~ about sb.** jmdn. diffamieren

**defame** /dɪˈfeɪm/ *v.t.* diffamieren; beschmutzen ‹Name, Ansehen›

**default** /dɪˈfɔːlt, dɪˈfɒlt/ ❶ *n.* [A] (*lack*) Mangel, *der;* **in ~ of** mangels (+ *Gen.*); in Ermangelung (*geh.*) (+ *Gen.*); [B] (*Law*) (*failure to act*) Versäumnis, *das;* (*failure to appear*) Säumnis, *die od. das;* **judgement by ~**: Versäumnisurteil, *das;* [C] (*failure to pay*) Verzug, *der;* (*failure to act or appear*) Ausbleiben, *das;* (*Sport*) Nichterscheinen, *das;* **~ of payment** Zahlungsverzug, *der;* **lose/go by ~**: durch Abwesenheit verlieren/nicht zur Geltung kommen; **win by ~**: durch Nichterscheinen des Gegners gewinnen; [D] (*Computing*) Voreinstellung, *die.*

❷ *v.i.* versagen; **~ on one's payments/debts** seinen Zahlungsverpflichtungen nicht nachkommen

**defaulter** /dɪˈfɔːltə(r), dɪˈfɒltə(r)/ *n.* [A] (*Brit. Mil.*) Straffällige, *der;* [B] (*who fails to pay*) säumiger Schuldner/säumige Schuldnerin

**defeat** /dɪˈfiːt/ ❶ *v.t.* [A] (*overcome*) besiegen; (*in battle or match also*) schlagen; ablehnen, zu Fall bringen ‹Antrag, Vorschlag›; [B] (*baffle*) **sth. ~s me** ich kann etw. nicht begreifen; **it ~s me why ...**: ich verstehe einfach nicht, warum ...; (*frustrate*) **the task has ~ed us** diese Aufgabe hat uns überfordert; **~ the object/purpose of sth.** etw. völlig sinnlos machen; **~ one's own object** seine eigenen Pläne durchkreuzen. ❷ *n.* (*being defeated*) Niederlage, *die;* (*defeating*) Sieg, *der* (**of** über + *Akk.*); **the ~ of a motion/bill** das Scheitern eines Antrags/Gesetzentwurfs; **admit ~**: seine Niederlage eingestehen

**defeatism** /dɪˈfiːtɪzm/ *n.* Defätismus, *der*

**defeatist** /dɪˈfiːtɪst/ ❶ *n.* Defätist, *der.* ❷ *adj.* defätistisch; **you're so ~ about things** du siehst die Dinge immer so schwarz

**defecate** /ˈdefəkeɪt/ *v.i.* Kot ausscheiden; defäkieren (*Med.*)

**defecation** /defəˈkeɪʃn/ *n.* Ausscheidung, *die;* Defäkation, *die* (*Med.*)

**defect** ❶ /ˈdiːfekt, dɪˈfekt/ *n.* [A] (*lack*) Mangel, *der;* [B] (*shortcoming*) Fehler, *der;* (*in construction, body, mind, etc. also*) Defekt, *der;* **the ~s in his character, his character ~s** seine Charakterfehler; **he has the ~s of his qualities** er hat die für seine guten Eigenschaften typischen Charakterfehler. ❷ /dɪˈfekt/ *v.i.* überlaufen (**to** zu); **~ from the cause** sich von der Sache lossagen

**defection** /dɪˈfekʃn/ *n.* Abfall, *der;* (*desertion*) Flucht, *die;* **~ from the army** Desertion aus der Armee

**defective** /dɪˈfektɪv/ *adj.* [A] (*faulty*) defekt ‹Maschine›; gestört ‹Gehirn›; fehlerhaft ‹Sprache, Material, Arbeiten, Methode, Plan›; mangelhaft, gestört ‹Verdauung, Kreislauf, Wachstum, Entwicklung›; **sb./sth. is ~ in sth.** es mangelt jmdm./einer Sache an etw. (*Dat.*); **have a ~ heart** einen Herzfehler haben; [B] (*mentally deficient*) geistig gestört; [C] (*Ling.*) defektiv

**defectiveness** /dɪˈfektɪvnɪs/ *n., no pl.* Fehlerhaftigkeit, *die*

**defector** /dɪˈfektə(r)/ *n.* Überläufer, *der*/-läuferin, *die;* (*from a cause or party*) Abtrünnige, *der/die;* (*from army*) Deserteur, *der*

**defence** /dɪˈfens/ *n.* (*Brit.*) [A] (*defending*) Verteidigung, *die;* (*of body against disease*) Schutz, *der;* **in ~ of** zur Verteidigung (+ *Gen.*); [B] (*thing that protects, means of resisting attack*) Schutz, *der;* [C] (*justification*) Rechtfertigung, *die;* **in sb.'s ~**: zu jmds. Verteidigung; **come to sb.'s ~**: jmdm. zur Seite springen; [D] (*military resources*) Verteidigung, *die;* [E] *in pl.* (*fortification*) Befestigungsanlagen *Pl.;* (*fig.*) Widerstandskraft, *die;* **sb.'s ~s are down** (*fig.*) jmds. Widerstandskraft ist erschöpft; [F] (*Law*) Verteidigung, *die;* **the case for the ~**: die Verteidigung; **~ witness** Zeuge/Zeugin der Verteidigung; [G] (*Sport*) Verteidigung, *die*

**deˈfence budget** *n.* Verteidigungshaushalt, *der*

**defenceless** /dɪˈfenslɪs/ *adj.* (*Brit.*) wehrlos; **look ~**: hilflos dreinschauen

**deˈfence mechanism** *n.* (*Physiol., Psych.*) Abwehrmechanismus, *der*

**defend** /dɪˈfend/ ❶ *v.t.* [A] (*protect*) schützen (**from** vor + *Dat.*); (*by fighting*) verteidigen; [B] (*uphold by argument, vindicate, speak or write in favour of*) verteidigen; verteidigen, rechtfertigen ‹Politik, Handeln›; [C] (*Sport*) verteidigen ‹Titel, Tor›; [D] (*Law*) verteidigen; **~ oneself** sich selbst verteidigen. ❷ *v.i.* (*Sport*) verteidigen

**defendant** /dɪˈfendənt/ *n.* (*Law*) (*accused*) Angeklagte, *der/die;* (*sued*) Beklagte, *der/die*

**defender** /dɪˈfendə(r)/ *n.* [A] (*one who defends*) Verteidiger, *der;* (*of principle, method, etc.*) Verfechter, *der;* [B] (*Sport*) (*of championship*) Titelverteidiger, *der*/-verteidigerin, *die;* (*of goal*) Verteidiger, *der*/Verteidigerin, *die*

**defense, defenseless** (*Amer.*) ⇒ **defence, defenceless**

**defensible** /dɪˈfensɪbl/ *adj.* [A] (*easily defended*) wehrhaft; [B] (*justifiable*) vertretbar

**defensive** /dɪˈfensɪv/ ❶ *adj.* [A] (*protective*) defensiv ‹Strategie, Handlung›; **~ player** Defensivspieler, *der;* **~ wall** Schutzwall, *der;* **~ fortification** Verteidigungsanlage, *die;* [B] (*by argument*) rechtfertigend; [C] (*excessively self-justifying*) **he's always so ~ when he's**

**criticized** er will sich immer um jeden Preis rechtfertigen, wenn er kritisiert wird. ❷ *n.* Defensive, *die;* **be/act on the ~:** in der Defensive sein; **she's always so much on the ~:** sie geht immer gleich in die Defensive

**defensively** /dɪˈfensɪvlɪ/ *adv.* **act ~:** sich in übertriebener Weise rechtfertigen

**defer¹** /dɪˈfɜː(r)/ *v.t.*, **-rr-:** Ⓐ (*postpone*) aufschieben; **~red annuity** aufgeschobene Rente; **~red payment** Ratenzahlung, *die;* **~red shares/stock** Nachzugsaktien *Pl.;* Ⓑ (*Amer.: postpone call-up of*) zurückstellen

**defer²** *v.i.*, **-rr-: ~ [to sb.]** sich [jmdm.] beugen; **~ to sb.'s wishes** sich jmds. Wünschen fügen

**deference** /ˈdefərəns/ *n.* Respekt, *der;* Ehrerbietung, *die* (*geh.*); **in ~ to sb./sth.** aus Achtung vor jmdm./etw.; **in ~ to your wishes** Ihren Wünschen entsprechend

**deferential** /defəˈrenʃl/ *adj.* respektvoll; groß ‹Respekt›; **be ~ to sb./sth.** jmdm./einer Sache mit Respekt begegnen

**deferentially** /defəˈrenʃəlɪ/ *adv.* respektvoll

**deferment** /dɪˈfɜːmənt/ *n.* Ⓐ (*deferring*) Aufschub, *der;* Ⓑ (*Amer.: postponement of call-up*) **have a ~:** zurückgestellt sein

**defiance** /dɪˈfaɪəns/ *n.* Aufsässigkeit, *die;* (*open disobedience*) Missachtung, *die;* **act of ~:** Herausforderung, *die;* **in ~ of sb./sth.** jmdm./einer Sache zum Trotz

**defiant** /dɪˈfaɪənt/ *adj.* aufsässig ‹Tonfall, Kind, Benehmen›

**defiantly** /dɪˈfaɪəntlɪ/ *adv.* aufsässig

**deficiency** /dɪˈfɪʃənsɪ/ *n.* Ⓐ (*lack*) Mangel, *der* (**of,** in an + *Dat.*); **mental ~:** geistige Behinderung; **nutritional ~:** Ernährungsmangel, *der;* Ⓑ (*inadequacy*) Unzulänglichkeit, *die;* Ⓒ (*deficit*) Defizit, *das*

**deˈficiency disease** *n.* Mangelkrankheit, *die*

**deficient** /dɪˈfɪʃənt/ *adj.* Ⓐ (*not having enough*) **sb./sth. is ~ in sth.** jmdm./einer Sache mangelt es an etw. (*Dat.*); **be [mentally] ~:** geistig behindert sein; Ⓑ (*not being enough*) nicht ausreichend; (*in quality also*) unzulänglich

**deficit** /ˈdefɪsɪt/ *n.* Defizit, *das* (**of** an + *Dat.*); **a ~ of manpower** ein Mangel an Arbeitskräften

**ˈdeficit spending** *n.* (*Finance*) Defizitfinanzierung, *die*

**defile¹** ❶ /dɪˈfaɪl/ *v.i.* [hintereinander] marschieren; defilieren (*geh.*). ❷ /ˈdiːfaɪl/ *n.* Ⓐ (*narrow way*) Engpass, *der;* Ⓑ (*gorge*) Hohlweg, *der*

**defile²** /dɪˈfaɪl/ *v.t.* Ⓐ (*pollute*) verpesten ‹Luft›; verseuchen ‹Wasser›; Ⓑ (*desecrate*) beflecken ‹Unschuld, Reinheit›

**defilement** /dɪˈfaɪlmənt/ *n.* Ⓐ Verschandelung, *die;* (*of air*) Verpestung, *die;* Ⓑ (*desecration*) Befleckung, *die*

**definable** /dɪˈfaɪnəbl/ *adj.* (*able to be set forth*) definierbar; erklärbar; **love is not ~ in words** Liebe kann man nicht mit Worten erklären

**define** /dɪˈfaɪn/ *v.t.* Ⓐ (*mark out limits of, make clear*) definieren; festlegen; **be ~d [against sth.]** sich [gegen etw.] abzeichnen; **~ one's position** (*fig.*) Stellung beziehen (**on** zu); Ⓑ (*set forth essence or meaning of*) definieren; Ⓒ (*characterize*) charakterisieren

**definite** /ˈdefɪnɪt/ *adj.* (*having exact limits*) bestimmt; (*precise*) eindeutig, definitiv ‹Antwort, Entscheidung›; eindeutig ‹Beschluss, Verbesserung, Standpunkt›; eindeutig, klar ‹Vorteil›; klar *od.* scharf umrissen ‹Ziel, Plan, Thema›; klar ‹Konzept, Linie, Vorstellung›; deutlich ‹Konturen, Umrisse›; genau ‹Zeitpunkt›; entschlossen ‹Schritte, Stimme, Person›; **..., but that is not yet ~:** ..., aber das ist noch nicht endgültig; **you don't seem to be very ~:** Sie scheinen sich nicht ganz sicher zu sein; **she was so ~ about marrying him** sie war so fest entschlossen, ihn zu heiraten

**definitely** /ˈdefɪnɪtlɪ/ ❶ *adv.* bestimmt; eindeutig ‹festlegen, größer sein, verbessert, erklären›; endgültig ‹entscheiden, annehmen›; fest ‹vereinbaren›; **she's ~ going to America** sie fährt auf jeden Fall nach Amerika. ❷ *int.* (*coll.*) na klar (*ugs.*)

**definition** /defɪˈnɪʃn/ *n.* Ⓐ Definition, *die;* **by ~:** per definitionem (*geh.*); Ⓑ (*making or being distinct, degree of distinctness*) Schärfe, *die;* **improve the ~ on the TV** den Fernseher schärfer einstellen

**definitive** /dɪˈfɪnɪtɪv/ *adj.* Ⓐ (*decisive*) endgültig, definitiv ‹Beschluss, Antwort, Urteil›; entschieden ‹Ton, Art›; entscheidend ‹Vorsprung›; Ⓑ (*most authoritative*) maßgeblich; Ⓒ (*Philat.*) **~ stamp** Dauermarke, *die*

**definitively** /dɪˈfɪnɪtɪvlɪ/ *adv.* endgültig; definitiv; mit Entschiedenheit ‹beanspruchen, behaupten›

**deflate** /dɪˈfleɪt/ ❶ *v.t.* Ⓐ (*release air etc. from*) **~ a tyre/balloon** die Luft aus einem Reifen/Ballon ablassen; Ⓑ (*cause to lose conceitedness*) ernüchtern; **~ sb.'s opinion of himself** jmds. Selbsteinschätzung (*Dat.*) einen Dämpfer versetzen (*ugs.*); Ⓒ (*Econ.*) deflationieren. ❷ *v.i.* Ⓐ ‹Reifen:› Luftdruck verlieren; Ⓑ (*Econ.*) deflationieren

**deflation** /dɪˈfleɪʃn/ *n.* (*Econ., Geol.*) Deflation, *die*

**deflationary** /dɪˈfleɪʃənərɪ/ *adj.* (*Econ.*) deflationär

**deflect** /dɪˈflekt/ ❶ *v.t.* (*bend*) umleiten ‹Fluss›; brechen, beugen ‹Licht›; (*cause to deviate*) **~ sb./sth. [from sb./sth.]** jmdn./etw. [von jmdm./einer Sache] ablenken. ❷ *v.i.* (*bend*) einen Bogen machen; (*deviate*) abbiegen; (*fig.*) abweichen

**deflection** ⇒ **deflexion**

**deflector** /dɪˈflektə(r)/ *n.* Deflektor, *der*

**deflexion** /dɪˈflekʃn/ *n.* (*Brit.*) Ⓐ (*bending*) Umleitung, *die;* (*deviation*) Ablenkung, *die;* (*turn*) Abweichung, *die;* (*fig.*) Ablenkung, *die;* Ⓑ (*Phys.*) Ausschlag, *der*

**deflower** /diːˈflaʊə(r)/ *v.t.* deflorieren

**defocus** /diːˈfəʊkəs/ *v.t.*, **-s-** *or* **-ss-** unscharf machen; (*Phys.*) defokussieren ‹Strahl›

**defoliant** /diːˈfəʊlɪənt/ *n.* Entlaubungsmittel, *das*

**defoliate** /diːˈfəʊlɪeɪt/ *v.t.* entlauben

**defoliation** /diːfəʊlɪˈeɪʃn/ *n.* Entlaubung, *die*

**deforestation** /diːfɒrɪˈsteɪʃn/ *n.* Entwaldung, *die;* Abholzung, *die*

**deform** /dɪˈfɔːm/ ❶ *v.t.* Ⓐ (*deface*) deformieren; verunstalten; Ⓑ (*misshape*) verformen. ❷ *v.i.* Ⓐ (*become disfigured*) entstellt werden; Ⓑ (*Phys.*) sich verformen

**deformation** /diːfɔːˈmeɪʃn/ *n.* Ⓐ (*disfigurement*) Deformation, *die;* Entstellung, *die;* Ⓑ (*Phys.*) Verformung, *die*

**deformed** /dɪˈfɔːmd/ *adj.* entstellt ‹Gesicht›; verunstaltet ‹Person, Körperteil›

**deformity** /dɪˈfɔːmɪtɪ/ *n.* (*being deformed*) Missgestalt, *die;* (*malformation*) Verunstaltung, *die*

**defraud** /dɪˈfrɔːd/ *v.t.* **~ sb. [of sth.]** jmdn. [um etw.] betrügen

**defray** /dɪˈfreɪ/ *v.t.* bestreiten ‹Kosten›

**defrayal** /dɪˈfreɪəl/, **defrayment** /dɪˈfreɪmənt/ *ns.* Bestreitung, *die*

**defrock** /diːˈfrɒk/ ⇒ **unfrock**

**defrost** /diːˈfrɒst/ *v.t.* auftauen ‹Speisen›; abtauen ‹Kühlschrank›; enteisen ‹Windschutzscheibe, Fenster›

**deft** /deft/ *adj.* sicher und geschickt

**deftly** /ˈdeftlɪ/ *adv.* sicher und geschickt

**deftness** /ˈdeftnɪs/ *n.*, *no pl.* Geschicklichkeit, *die*

**defunct** /dɪˈfʌŋkt/ *adj.* tot, verstorben ‹Person›; (*extinct*) ausgestorben; (*fig.*) defekt ‹Maschine›; veraltet ‹Gesetz›; eingegangen ‹Zeitung›; stillgelegt ‹Betrieb, Bahnlinie›; überholt, vergessen ‹Brauch, Idee, Mode›

**defuse** /diːˈfjuːz/ *v.t.* (*lit. or fig.*) entschärfen

**defy** /dɪˈfaɪ/ *v.t.* Ⓐ auffordern; **~ sb. to do sth.** jmdn. auffordern, etw. zu tun; Ⓑ (*resist openly*) **~ sb.** jmdm. trotzen *od.* Trotz bieten; (*refuse to obey*) **~ sb./sth.** sich jmdm./einer Sache widersetzen; Ⓒ (*present insuperable obstacles to*) widerstehen; **it defies explanation** das spottet jeder Erklärung

**degeneracy** /dɪˈdʒenərəsɪ/ *n.* (*also Biol.*) Degeneration, *die*

**degenerate** ❶ /dɪˈdʒenəreɪt/ *v.i.* Ⓐ **~ [into sth.]** [zu etw.] verkommen *od.* degenerieren; Ⓑ (*Biol.*) **~ [into sth.]** [zu etw.] verkümmern *od.* degenerieren. ❷ /dɪˈdʒenərət/ *adj.* (*also Biol.*) degeneriert; **become ~:** degenerieren

**degeneration** /dɪdʒenəˈreɪʃn/ *n.* (*also Biol., Med.*) Degeneration, *die*

**degradation** /degrəˈdeɪʃn/ *n.* Ⓐ (*abasement*) Erniedrigung, *die;* Ⓑ (*demotion; also Geol.*) Degradierung, *die;* Ⓒ (*Biol.*) Degeneration, *die;* Ⓓ (*Chem.*) Abbau, *der*

**degrade** /dɪˈgreɪd/ *v.t.* Ⓐ (*abase*) erniedrigen; herabsetzen ‹Ansehen, Maßstab›; Ⓑ (*demote*) degradieren; Ⓒ (*Chem.*) abbauen; Ⓓ (*Geol.*) zerfallen lassen; erodieren

**degrading** /dɪˈgreɪdɪŋ/ *adj.* entwürdigend; erniedrigend

**degree** /dɪˈgriː/ *n.* Ⓐ ▶ 1603 (*Math., Phys.*) Grad, *der;* **an angle/a temperature of 45 ~s** ein Winkel/eine Temperatur von 45 Grad; Ⓑ (*stage in scale or extent*) Grad, *der;* **by ~s** allmählich; **a certain ~ of imagination** ein gewisses Maß an Phantasie; **to a high ~:** in hohem Grade *od.* Maße; **to some** *or* **a certain ~:** [bis] zu einem gewissen Grad; **to the last ~:** in höchstem Grade; **obstinate to a ~:** reichlich widerspenstig (*ugs.*); **to what ~?** [in]wieweit?; Ⓒ (*relative condition*) Art, *die;* **in its ~:** auf seine Art; Ⓓ (*step in genealogical descent*) [Verwandtschafts]grad, *der;* Ⓔ **forbidden** *or* **prohibited ~s** *Verwandtschaftsgrade, die eine Heirat ausschließen;* Ⓕ (*rank*) Stand, *der;* Ⓖ (*academic rank*) [akademischer] Grad; **take/receive a ~ in sth.** einen akademischen Grad in etw. (*Dat.*) erwerben/verliehen bekommen; **have a ~ in physics/maths** einen Hochschulabschluss in Physik/Mathematik haben; Ⓗ (*Ling.*) **~s of comparison** Steigerungsstufen *Pl.;* **positive/comparative/superlative ~:** Positiv, *der*/Komparativ, *der*/Superlativ, *der;* Ⓘ (*Amer.*) **give sb. the third ~:** jmdn. schonungslos ins Verhör nehmen

**degree: ~ ceremony** *n.* Feierstunde zur Verleihung der akademischen Würde; **~ course** *n.* Studium, *das;* **~ day** *n.* Tag der Verleihung der akademischen Würde

**dehumanize (dehumanise)** /diːˈhjuːmənaɪz/ *v.t.* entmenschlichen; dehumanisieren

**dehydrate** /diˈhaɪdreɪt/ *v.t.* Ⓐ (*remove water from*) das Wasser entziehen (+ *Dat.*), austrocknen ‹Körper›; **~d** dehydratisiert (*fachspr.*); getrocknet; Ⓑ (*make dry*) austrocknen

**dehydration** /diːhaɪˈdreɪʃn/ *n.* ⇒ **dehydrate:** Dehydration, *die* (*fachspr.*); Austrocknung, *die*

**de-ice** /diːˈaɪs/ *v.t.* enteisen

**de-icer** /diːˈaɪsə(r)/ *n.* Defroster, *der*

**deify** /ˈdiːɪfaɪ/ *v.t.* (*make a god of*) vergotten; deifizieren; (*worship*) vergöttern

**deign** /deɪn/ *v.t.* **~ to do sth.** sich [dazu] herablassen, etw. zu tun

**deism** /ˈdiːɪzm/ *n.* Deismus, *der*

**deist** /ˈdiːɪst/ *n.* Deist, *der*/Deistin, *die*

**deity** /ˈdiːɪtɪ/ *n.* Ⓐ (*god*) Gottheit, *die;* **the D~:** Gott; die Gottheit (*geh.*); Ⓑ (*divine status*) Göttlichkeit, *die;* Gottheit, *die* (*geh.*)

**déjà vu** /deɪʒɑː ˈvuː/ *n.*, *no pl.*, *no art.* Déjà-vu, *das;* **a sense of ~:** ein Déjà-vu-Gefühl

**dejected** /dɪˈdʒektɪd/ *adj.* niedergeschlagen

**dejection** /dɪˈdʒekʃn/ *n.* Niedergeschlagenheit, *die*

**delay** /dɪˈleɪ/ ❶ *v.t.* Ⓐ (*postpone*) verschieben; **he ~ed his visit for a few weeks** er verschob seinen Besuch einige Wochen; Ⓑ (*make late*) aufhalten; verzögern ‹Ankunft, Abfahrt›; **the train has been seriously ~ed** der Zug hat beträchtliche Verspätung; Ⓒ (*hinder*) aufhalten; (*retard*) **be ~ed** ‹Veranstaltung:› verspätet *od.* später erfolgen. ❷ *v.i.* (*wait*) warten; (*loiter*) trödeln (*ugs.*); **don't ~:** warte nicht damit; **~ in doing sth.** zögern, etw. zu tun. ❸ *n.* Ⓐ Verzögerung, *die* (**to** bei); **what's the ~ now?** weshalb geht es jetzt nicht weiter?; **without ~:** unverzüglich; **without**

d

further ~: ohne weitere Verzögerung; Ⓑ (*Transport*) Verspätung, *die;* **trains are subject to ~:** es ist mit Zugverspätungen zu rechnen

**delayed-action** /dɪleɪdˈækʃn/ *adj.* **~ bomb** Bombe mit Zeitzünder; **~ mechanism** (*Photog.*) Selbstauslöser, *der;* **~ drug** Medikament mit Depotwirkung

**delectable** /dɪˈlektəbl/ *adj.* köstlich; **she looked ~:** sie sah reizend aus

**delectation** /diːlekˈteɪʃn/ *n.* Ergötzen, *das* (*geh.*); Vergnügen, *das*

**delegate** ❶ /ˈdelɪgət/ *n.* Ⓐ (*elected representative*) Delegierte, *der/die;* (*of firm*) Beauftragte, *der/die;* Ⓑ (*deputy*) Vertreter, *der/* Vertreterin, *die;* Ⓒ (*member of deputation*) Delegierte, *der/die.* ❷ /ˈdelɪgeɪt/ *v.t.* Ⓐ (*depute*) delegieren; Ⓑ (*commit*) **~ power/responsibility/a task [to sb.]** Macht/Verantwortlichkeit/eine Aufgabe [an jmdn.] delegieren; **he does not know how to ~:** er will alles selbst erledigen

**delegation** /delɪˈgeɪʃn/ *n.* Ⓐ (*body of delegates*) Delegation, *die;* Ⓑ (*deputation*) Abordnung, *die;* Delegation, *die;* Ⓒ (*entrusting of authority to deputy*) Delegation, *die* (**to** an + *Akk.*)

**delete** /dɪˈliːt/ *v.t.* streichen (**from** in + *Dat.*); (*Computing*) löschen; **~ where inapplicable** Nichtzutreffendes streichen

**deˈlete key** *n.* (*Computing*) Löschtaste, *die*

**deleterious** /delɪˈtɪərɪəs/ *adj.* schädlich (**to** für); **~ [to health]** gesundheitsschädlich

**deletion** /dɪˈliːʃn/ *n.* Streichung, *die;* (*Computing*) Löschung, *die*

**delft** /delft/ (**delf** /delf/) *n.* **~ [pottery]/tiles** *etc.* Delfter Keramik/Kacheln *usw.*

**deli** /ˈdelɪ/ (*coll.*) ⇒ **delicatessen**

**deliberate** ❶ /dɪˈlɪbərət/ *adj.* Ⓐ (*intentional*) absichtlich; bewusst ‹Lüge, Irreführung›; vorsätzlich ‹Verbrechen›; Ⓑ (*fully considered*) wohlerwogen; [sorgfältig] überlegt; Ⓒ (*cautious*) behutsam; Ⓓ (*unhurried and considered*) bedächtig. ❷ /dɪˈlɪbəreɪt/ *v.i.* Ⓐ (*think carefully*) **~ on sth.** über etw. (*Akk.*) [sorgfältig] nachdenken; Ⓑ (*debate*) **~ over** *or* **on** *or* **about sth.** über etw. (*Akk.*) beraten. ❸ *v.t.* ‹Gruppe:› beraten; ‹Einzelner:› überlegen

**deliberately** /dɪˈlɪbərətlɪ/ *adv.* Ⓐ (*intentionally*) absichtlich; mit Absicht; vorsätzlich ‹ein Verbrechen begehen›; Ⓑ (*with full consideration*) **[very] ~:** [ganz] bewusst; Ⓒ (*in unhurried manner*) bedächtig

**deliberation** /dɪlɪbəˈreɪʃn/ *n.* Ⓐ (*care*) Sorgfalt, *die;* Ⓑ (*unhurried nature*) Bedächtigkeit, *die;* Ⓒ (*careful consideration*) Überlegung, *die;* **after much ~:** nach reiflicher Überlegung; Ⓓ (*discussion*) Beratung, *die*

**deliberative** /dɪˈlɪbərətɪv/ *adj.* beratend

**delicacy** /ˈdelɪkəsɪ/ *n.* Ⓐ (*tactfulness and care*) Feingefühl, *das;* Delikatesse, *die* (*geh.*); Ⓑ (*fineness*) Zartheit, *die;* Feinheit, *die;* Ⓒ (*weakliness*) Zartheit, *die;* Ⓓ (*need of discretion etc.*) Delikatheit, *die;* Ⓔ (*food*) Delikatesse, *die*

**delicate** /ˈdelɪkət/ *adj.* Ⓐ (*easily injured*) empfindlich ‹Organ›; zart ‹Gesundheit, Konstitution›; (*sensitive*) sensibel, empfindlich ‹Person, Natur›; empfindlich ‹Waage, Instrument, Verfassung›; Ⓑ (*requiring careful handling*) empfindlich; (*fig.*) delikat, heikel ‹Frage, Angelegenheit, Problem›; Ⓒ (*fine, of exquisite quality, subdued*) zart; fein; delikat; (*dainty*) delikat; Ⓓ (*subtle*) fein; Ⓔ (*deft, light*) geschickt; zart; Ⓕ (*tactful*) taktvoll; behutsam

**delicately** /ˈdelɪkətlɪ/ *adv.* fein; **~ put** taktvoll ausgedrückt

**delicatessen** /delɪkəˈtesən/ *n.* Feinkostgeschäft, *das;* Delikatessengeschäft, *das*

**delicious** /dɪˈlɪʃəs/ *adj.* köstlich, lecker ‹Speise, Geschmack›; köstlich ‹Anblick, Spaß, Humor›

**deliciously** /dɪˈlɪʃəslɪ/ *adv.* köstlich; herrlich ‹kühl, lustig›

**deliciousness** /dɪˈlɪʃəsnɪs/ *n., no pl.* Köstlichkeit, *die*

**delight** /dɪˈlaɪt/ ❶ *v.t.* erfreuen. ❷ *v.i.* **sb. ~s in doing sth.** es macht jmdm. Freude, etw. zu tun; **~ to do sth.** etw. gern tun. ❸ *n.* Ⓐ (*great pleasure*) Freude, *die;* **~ at sth./at doing sth.** Freude über etw. (*Akk.*) /darüber, etw. zu tun; **~ in sth./in doing sth.** Freude an etw. (*Dat.*) /daran, etw. zu tun; **to my/our ~:** zu meiner/unserer Freude; **sb. takes ~ in doing sth.** es macht jmdm. Freude, etw. zu tun; Ⓑ (*cause of pleasure*) Vergnügen, *das;* **these cakes are a ~ to eat** diese Kuchen schmecken köstlich

**delighted** /dɪˈlaɪtɪd/ *adj.* freudig ‹Schrei›; **be ~** ‹Person:› hocherfreut sein; **be ~ by** *or* **with sth.** sich über etw. (*Akk.*) freuen; **be ~ to do sth.** sich freuen, etw. zu tun; **we shall be ~ to accept your invitation** wir werden Ihre Einladung gern annehmen

**delightedly** /dɪˈlaɪtɪdlɪ/ *adv.* erfreut

**delightful** /dɪˈlaɪtfl/ *adj.* wunderbar; köstlich ‹Geschmack, Klang›; reizend ‹Person, Landschaft›

**delightfully** /dɪˈlaɪtfəlɪ/ *adv.* wunderbar; bezaubernd ‹singen, tanzen, hübsch›; angenehm ‹hell, luftig›

**delimit** /dɪˈlɪmɪt/ *v.t.* begrenzen ‹Gebiet, Region›; (*fig.*) eingrenzen

**delimitation** /dɪlɪmɪˈteɪʃn/ *n.* Begrenzung, *die;* (*fig.*) Eingrenzung, *die*

**delineate** /dɪˈlɪnɪeɪt/ *v.t.* (*draw*) zeichnen; (*describe*) darstellen; **sharply ~d** sich scharf abzeichnend

**delinquency** /dɪˈlɪŋkwənsɪ/ *n.* Ⓐ *no pl.* Kriminalität, *die;* Ⓑ (*misdeed*) Straftat, *die*

**delinquent** /dɪˈlɪŋkwənt/ ❶ *n.* (*bes. jugendlicher*) Randalierer, *der.* ❷ *adj.* Ⓐ (*offending*) kriminell; Ⓑ (*Amer.: in arrears*) säumig

**delirious** /dɪˈlɪrɪəs/ *adj.* Ⓐ delirant (*Med.*); **be ~:** im Delirium sein; ≈ fantasieren; Ⓑ (*wildly excited*) **be ~ [with sth.]** außer sich (*Dat.*) [vor etw. (*Dat.*)] sein; Ⓒ (*ecstatic, wild*) wahnsinnig; rasend ‹Zorn, Wut›

**deliriously** /dɪˈlɪrɪəslɪ/ *adv.* Ⓐ wie im Delirium; Ⓑ (*ecstatically*) wahnsinnig

**delirium** /dɪˈlɪrɪəm/ *n.* Delirium, *das*

**delirium tremens** /dɪlɪrɪəm ˈtriːmenz/ *n., no pl.* Delirium tremens, *das* (*Med.*); Säuferwahn, *der* (*veralt.*)

**deliver** /dɪˈlɪvə(r)/ *v.t.* Ⓐ (*utter*) halten ‹Rede, Vorlesung, Predigt›; vorbringen ‹Worte›; vortragen ‹Verse›; (*pronounce*) verkünden ‹Urteil, Meinung, Botschaft›; Ⓑ (*launch*) werfen ‹Ball›; versetzen ‹Stoß, Schlag, Tritt›; vortragen ‹Angriff›; Ⓒ (*hand over*) bringen; liefern ‹Ware›; zustellen ‹Post, Telegramm›; überbringen ‹Botschaft›; **~ sth. to the door** etw. ins Haus liefern; **~ [the goods]** (*fig.*) es schaffen (*ugs.*); (*fulfil promise*) halten, was man versprochen hat; Ⓓ (*give up*) aushändigen; **stand and ~!** halt, Geld her!; Ⓔ (*render*) erzählen ‹Geschichte›; geben, liefern ‹Bericht, Beschreibung›; stellen ‹Ultimatum›; geben ‹Versprechen›; ablegen ‹Gelübde›; Ⓕ (*Law*) aushändigen ‹Dokument›; Ⓖ (*assist in giving birth, aid in being born*) entbinden; (*give birth to*) gebären; **be ~ed [of a child]** [von einem Kind] entbunden werden; Ⓗ (*formal: unburden*) **~ oneself of one's opinion** seine Meinung loswerden; Ⓘ (*save*) **~ sb./sth. from sb./sth.** jmdn./etw. von jmdm./etw. erlösen; **~ us from evil** (*Relig.*) erlöse uns von dem Übel *od.* Bösen (*bibl.*)

**~ ˈup** *v.t.* aushändigen; übergeben

**deliverance** /dɪˈlɪvərəns/ *n.* Erlösung, *die* (**from** von); **~ from captivity** Befreiung aus der Gefangenschaft

**delivery** /dɪˈlɪvərɪ/ *n.* Ⓐ (*handing over*) Lieferung, *die;* (*of letters, parcels*) Zustellung, *die;* **there is no charge for ~:** Lieferung frei Haus; **there are no deliveries on Sunday** sonntags wird keine Post zugestellt *od.* ausgetragen; **take ~ of sth.** etw. annehmen; **pay on ~:** bei Lieferung bezahlen; (*Post*) per Nachnahme bezahlen; Ⓑ (*Sport*) Wurf, *der;* **~ of a blow/punch** Schlag, *der;* Ⓒ (*uttering*) Vortragen, *das;* (*manner of uttering*) Vortragsweise, *die;* Vortrag, *der;* Ⓓ (*childbirth*) Entbindung, *die*

**delivery:** **~ boy** *n.* Austräger, *der;* **~ date** *n.* Liefertermin, *der;* **~ girl** *n.* Austrägerin, *die;* **~ man** *n.* Lieferant, *der;* Ausfahrer, *der* (*landsch.*); **~ note** *n.* Lieferschein, *der;* **~ room** *n.* (*Med.*) Kreißsaal, *der;* **~ service** *n.* Zustelldienst, *der;* **~ van** *n.* Lieferwagen, *der*

**dell** /del/ *n.* [bewaldetes] Tal; Grund, *der* (*veralt.*)

**delouse** /diːˈlaʊs/ *v.t.* entlausen

**delphinium** /delˈfɪnɪəm/ *n.* (*Bot.*) Rittersporn, *der*

**delta** /ˈdeltə/ *n.* Ⓐ (*of river; Greek letter*) Delta, *das;* Ⓑ (*Sch., Univ.: mark*) Vier, *die*

**delta ˈwing** *n.* Deltaflügel, *der;* **~ aircraft** Deltaflugzeug, *das*

**delude** /dɪˈljuːd, dɪˈluːd/ *v.t.* täuschen; **~ sb. into believing that ...:** jmdm. weismachen, dass ...; **stop deluding yourself!** machen Sie sich doch nichts vor!

**deluge** /ˈdeljuːdʒ/ ❶ *n.* Ⓐ (*rain*) sintflutartiger Regen; Ⓑ (*Bibl.*) **the D~:** die Sintflut; Ⓒ **~ of complaints/letters** Flut von Beschwerden/Briefen. ❷ *v.t.* (*lit. or fig.*) überschwemmen; **~ sb. with questions** jmdn. mit Fragen überschütten

**delusion** /dɪˈljuːʒn, dɪˈluːʒn/ *n.* Illusion, *die;* (*as symptom or form of madness*) Wahnvorstellung, *die;* **be under a ~:** einer Täuschung unterliegen; **be under the ~ that ...:** sich (*Dat.*) der Täuschung hingeben, dass ...; **have ~s of grandeur** größenwahnsinnig sein

**delusive** /dɪˈljuːsɪv, dɪˈluːsɪv/ *adj.*, **delusively** /dɪˈljuːsɪvlɪ, dɪˈluːsɪvlɪ/ *adv.* trügerisch

**de luxe** /dəˈlʌks, dəˈluːks/ *adj.* Luxus-; **~ trade** Handel mit Luxusartikeln

**delve** /delv/ *v.i.* Ⓐ (*arch./poet.: dig*) graben (**for** nach); Ⓑ (*search*) **~ into sth. [for sth.]** tief in etw. (*Akk.*) greifen[, um etw. herauszuholen]; Ⓒ (*research*) **~ into sth.** sich in etw. (*Akk.*) vertiefen; **~ into sb.'s past** in jmds. Vergangenheit nachforschen

**Dem.** *abbr.* (*Amer.*) **Democrat** Dem.

**demagogue** (*Amer.:* **demagog**) /ˈdeməgɒg/ *n.* Demagoge, *der*/Demagogin, *die*

**demagoguery** /ˈdeməgɒgərɪ/, **demagogy** /ˈdeməgɒgɪ/ *ns.* Demagogie, *die*

**demand** /dɪˈmɑːnd/ ❶ *n.* Ⓐ (*request*) Forderung, *die* (**for** nach); **a ~ for sb. to do sth.** eine Forderung, dass jmd. etw. tun soll; **payable on ~:** zahlbar bei Sicht (*Kaufmannsspr.*); **final ~:** letzte Mahnung; Ⓑ (*desire for commodity*) Nachfrage, *die* (**for** nach); **by popular ~:** auf vielfachen Wunsch; **sth./sb. is in [great] ~:** etw. ist [sehr] gefragt/jmd. ist [sehr] begehrt; **~ for teachers/clerks** Bedarf an Lehrern/Büroangestellten; Ⓒ (*claim*) **make ~s on sb.** jmdn. beanspruchen; **make too many ~s on sb.'s patience/time** jmds. Geduld/Zeit zu sehr beanspruchen; **I have many ~s on my time** ich bin zeitlich sehr beansprucht. ⇒ *also* **supply** 2 A.
❷ *v.t.* Ⓐ (*ask for, require, need*) verlangen (**of, from** von); fordern ‹Recht, Genugtuung›; **~ to know/see sth.** etw. zu wissen/zu sehen verlangen; **he ~ed to be told everything** er wollte unbedingt alles wissen; **~ money with menaces** Geld erpressen; Ⓑ (*insist on being told*) unbedingt wissen wollen; **he ~ed my business** er fragte mich nachdrücklich, was ich wünschte

**demanding** /dɪˈmɑːndɪŋ/ *adj.* anspruchsvoll; (*taxing*) anstrengend ‹Kind›; **physically [very] ~:** körperlich [sehr] anstrengend

**deˈmand note** *n.* Ⓐ (*Brit.: request for payment*) Zahlungsaufforderung, *die;* Ⓑ (*Amer.: bill payable at sight*) Sichtwechsel, *der*

**demarcate** /ˈdiːmɑːkeɪt/ *v.t.* festlegen ‹Grenze›; demarkieren (*geh.*); **~ sth. from sth.** etw. von etw. abgrenzen

**demarcation** /diːmɑːˈkeɪʃn/ *n.* (*of frontier*) Demarkation, *die* (*geh.*); (*of topics*) Abgrenzung, *die;* **line of ~** (*frontier*) Demarkationslinie, *die;* (*of topics*) Trennungslinie, *die*

**demarˈcation dispute** *n.* Streit um die Abgrenzung der Zuständigkeitsbereiche

**démarche** /ˈdeɪmɑːʃ/ *n.* (*Diplom.*) Demarche, *die*

**demean** /dɪˈmiːn/ *v. refl.* (*lower one's dignity*) **~ oneself [to do sth.]** sich [dazu] erniedrigen[, etw. zu tun]; **~ oneself by sth./doing**

**sth.** sich durch etw. erniedrigen/sich dadurch erniedrigen, dass man etw. tut

**demeaning** /dɪˈmiːnɪŋ/ *adj.* erniedrigend

**demeanour** (*Brit.; Amer.:* **demeanor**) /dɪˈmiːnə(r)/ *n.* Benehmen, *das*

**demented** /dɪˈmentɪd/ *adj.* wahnsinnig; **be ~ with worry** verrückt vor Angst sein (*ugs.*); **like somebody ~:** wie ein Wahnsinniger/eine Wahnsinnige

**dementedly** /dɪˈmentɪdlɪ/ *adv.* wie von Sinnen

**dementia** /dɪˈmenʃə/ (*Med.*) Demenz, *die*

**demerara** /deməˈreərə/ *n.* **~ [sugar]** brauner Zucker; Farin, *der*

**demerit** /diːˈmerɪt/ *n.* Ⓐ Schwäche, *die;* Ⓑ (*quality deserving blame*) [Charakter]fehler, *der;* (*action*) Fehlverhalten, *das;* Ⓒ (*Amer.: mark*) Strafpunkt, *der*

**demesne** /dɪˈmiːn, dɪˈmeɪn/ *n.* (*land attached to mansion etc.*) Grundstück des Landsitzes

**demi-** /ˈdemɪ/ *pref.* Halb-

ˈ**demigod** *n.* Halbgott, *der*

**demijohn** /ˈdemɪdʒɒn/ *n.* Demijohn, *der* (*fachspr.*); Korbflasche, *die*

**demilitarisation**, **demilitarise** ⇒ **demilitariz-**

**demilitarization** /diːmɪlɪtəraɪˈzeɪʃn/ *n.* Entmilitarisierung, *die*

**demilitarize** /diːˈmɪlɪtəraɪz/ *v.t.* entmilitarisieren

**demi-monde** /ˈdemɪmɔ̃d/ *n.* Demimonde, *die* (*geh.*); Halbwelt, *die*

**demise** /dɪˈmaɪz/ *n.* (*death*) Ableben, *das* (*geh.*); (*fig.*) Verschwinden, *das;* (*of firm, party, creed, etc.*) Untergang, *der*

**demisemiquaver** /demɪˈsemɪkweɪvə(r), ˈdemɪsemɪkweɪvə(r)/ *n.* (*Brit. Mus.*) Zweiunddreißigstelnote, *die*

**demist** /diːˈmɪst/ *v.t.* (*Brit.*) trockenblasen; (*with cloth etc.*) trockenreiben

**demister** /diːˈmɪstə(r)/ *n.* (*Brit.*) Defroster, *der;* Gebläse, *das*

**demo** /ˈdeməʊ/ *n., pl.* **~s** (*coll.*) Demo, *die* (*ugs.*)

**demob** /diːˈmɒb/ (*Brit. coll.*) ❶ *v.t.*, **-bb-** aus dem Kriegsdienst entlassen. ❷ *n.* Entlassung aus dem Kriegsdienst

**demobilisation**, **demobilise** ⇒ **demobiliz-**

**demobilization** /diːməʊbɪlaɪˈzeɪʃn/ *n.* Demobilisation, *die;* (*of soldier*) Entlassung aus dem Kriegsdienst

**demobilize** /diːˈməʊbɪlaɪz/ *v.t.* demobilisieren ‹Armee, Kriegsschiff›; aus dem Kriegsdienst entlassen ‹Soldat›

**democracy** /dɪˈmɒkrəsɪ/ *n.* Demokratie, *die*

**democrat** /ˈdeməkræt/ *n.* Ⓐ (*advocate of democracy*) Demokrat, *der*/Demokratin, *die;* Ⓑ **D~** (*Amer. Polit.*) Demokrat, *der*/Demokratin, *die*

**democratic** /deməˈkrætɪk/ *adj.* Ⓐ demokratisch; Ⓑ (*Amer. Polit.*) **D~ Party** Demokratische Partei

**democratically** /deməˈkrætɪkəlɪ/ *adv.* demokratisch

**democratize** /dɪˈmɒkrətaɪz/ *v.t.* demokratisieren

**demographic** /diːməˈgræfɪk, deməˈgræfɪk/, **demographical** /diːməˈgræfɪkl, deməˈgræfɪkl/ *adj.* demographisch

**demolish** /dɪˈmɒlɪʃ/ *v.t.* Ⓐ (*pull down*) abreißen; (*break to pieces*) zerstören; demolieren; schleifen, niederreißen ‹Festungsanlagen›; **~ by bombing** zerbomben; Ⓑ (*overthrow*) auflösen ‹Institution›; abschaffen ‹System, Privilegien›; widerlegen, umstoßen ‹Theorie›; entkräften ‹Einwand›; zerstören ‹Legende, Mythos›; Ⓒ (*joc.: eat up*) verschlingen

**demolition** /deməˈlɪʃn, diːməˈlɪʃn/ *n.* Ⓐ ⇒ **demolish** A: Abriss, *der;* Zerstörung, *die;* Demolierung, *die;* Schleifung, *die;* **~ contractors** Abbruchunternehmen, *das;* **due for ~:** abbruchreif; **~ work** Abbrucharbeit, *die;* Ⓑ ⇒ **demolish** B: Auflösung, *die;* Abschaffung, *die;* Widerlegung, *die;* Entkräftung, *die;* Zerstörung, *die*

**demon** /ˈdiːmən/ *n.* Ⓐ Dämon, *der;* Ⓑ (*person, animal*) Teufel, *der;* **~ bowler** (*Cricket*) sehr schneller Werfer; **he is a ~ for work** er arbeitet wie ein Besessener

**demonetize** (**demonetise**) /diːˈmʌnɪtaɪz/ *v.t.* (*Finance*) demonetisieren (*Bankw.*); aus dem Umlauf ziehen

**demoniac** /dɪˈməʊnɪæk/ ❶ *adj.* dämonisch; (*possessed*) besessen. ❷ *n.* Besessene, *der/die*

**demoniacal** /diːməˈnaɪəkl, deməˈnaɪəkl/ *adj.* dämonisch

**demonic** /diːˈmɒnɪk/ ⇒ **demoniac** 1

**demonstrability** /demənstrəˈbɪlɪtɪ, dɪmɒnstrəˈbɪlɪtɪ/ *n., no pl.* Beweisbarkeit, *die*

**demonstrable** /ˈdemənstrəbl, dɪˈmɒnstrəbl/ *adj.* beweisbar; nachweislich ‹Schaden›; **it is ~ that ...:** man kann beweisen, dass ...; es lässt sich nachweisen, dass ...

**demonstrably** /ˈdemənstrəblɪ, dɪˈmɒnstrəblɪ/ *adv.* nachweislich

**demonstrate** /ˈdemənstreɪt/ ❶ *v.t.* Ⓐ (*by examples, experiments, etc.*) zeigen; demonstrieren; (*show, explain*) vorführen ‹Vorrichtung, Gerät›; Ⓑ (*be proof of*) zeigen; beweisen; Ⓒ (*logically prove the truth of*) beweisen; nachweisen; Ⓓ (*prove the existence of*) zeigen ‹Gefühl, Bedürfnis, Gutwilligkeit›. ❷ *v.i.* Ⓐ (*make, take part in, a meeting or procession*) demonstrieren; Ⓑ (*give a demonstration*) **~ on sth./sb.** etw./jmdn. als Demonstrationsobjekt benutzen

**demonstration** /demənˈstreɪʃn/ *n.* Ⓐ (*as way of teaching*) Demonstration, *die;* praktische Vorführung; **cookery ~s** Anschauungsunterricht im Kochen; Ⓑ (*showing of appliances etc.*) Vorführung, *die;* **give sb. a ~ of sth.** jmdm. etw. vorführen; Ⓒ (*meeting, procession*) Demonstration, *die;* Ⓓ (*exhibition of feeling etc.*) Ausdruck, *der;* **make a ~ of sth.** etw. zeigen; Ⓔ (*proof*) Beweis, *der*

**demonstrative** /dɪˈmɒnstrətɪv/ *adj.* Ⓐ (*with open expression*) offen; unverhohlen ‹Freude›; Ⓑ (*serving to point out or to exhibit*) anschaulich; Ⓒ (*logically conclusive*) schlüssig ‹Beweis, Argument›; Ⓓ (*Ling.*) Demonstrativ-; hinweisend

**demonstrator** /ˈdemənstreɪtə(r)/ *n.* Ⓐ (*in a meeting or procession*) Demonstrant, *der*/Demonstrantin, *die;* Ⓑ (*Commerc.*) Vorführer, *der*/Vorführerin, *die*

**demoralisation**, **demoralise** ⇒ **demoraliz-**

**demoralization** /dɪmɒrəlaɪˈzeɪʃn/ *n.* Demoralisierung, *die*

**demoralize** /dɪˈmɒrəlaɪz/ *v.t.* demoralisieren

**demote** /diːˈməʊt/ *v.t.* degradieren (**to** zu); zurückstufen ‹Schüler›

**demotic** /dɪˈmɒtɪk/ *adj.* Ⓐ (*popular*) volkstümlich; Ⓑ **~ Greek** Demotike, *die*

**demotion** /diːˈməʊʃn/ *n.* Degradierung, *die* (**to** zu); (*Sch.*) Zurückstufung, *die*

**demur** /dɪˈmɜː(r)/ *v.i.*, **-rr-** Einwände erheben; **~ to sth.** gegen etw. Einwände erheben; **~ at doing sth.** Einwände dagegen erheben, etw. zu tun

**demure** /dɪˈmjʊə(r)/ *adj.* Ⓐ (*affectedly quiet and serious*) betont zurückhaltend; Ⓑ (*sober*) nüchtern; (*grave, composed*) ernst; gesetzt ‹Benehmen›; Ⓒ (*decorous*) sittsam (*veralt.*); gesittet ‹Rede›

**demurely** /dɪˈmjʊəlɪ/ *adv.* zurückhaltend; **~ dressed** sittsam (*veralt.*) gekleidet

**demythologize** (**demythologise**) /diːmɪˈθɒlədʒaɪz/ *v.t.* entmythologisieren

**den** /den/ *n.* Ⓐ (*of wild beast*) Höhle, *die;* **fox's ~:** Fuchsbau, *der;* **Daniel in the lions' ~** (*Bibl.*) Daniel in der Löwengrube; Ⓑ (*resort of criminals etc.*) **~ of thieves, thieves' ~:** Diebeshöhle, *die;* Diebesnest, *das;* **~ of vice or iniquity** Lasterhöhle, *die* (*ugs. abwertend*); **robbers' ~:** Räuberhöhle, *die* (*veralt.*); Ⓒ (*small room*) Bude, *die* (*ugs.*)

**denationalisation**, **denationalise** ⇒ **denationaliz-**

**denationalization** /diːnæʃənəlaɪˈzeɪʃn/ *n., no pl.* Privatisierung, *die*

**denationalize** /diːˈnæʃənəlaɪz/ *v.t.* privatisieren

**denaturalize** (**denaturalise**) /diːˈnætʃərəlaɪz/ *v.t.* Ⓐ (*make unnatural*) denaturieren; (*make unfit for drinking etc.*) denaturieren (*Chemie, Physik*); ungenießbar machen; vergällen (*Chemie*) ‹Alkohol›; **~d** denaturiert (*Chemie, Physik*); ungenießbar; Ⓑ (*deprive of citizenship*) denaturalisieren

**denature** /diːˈneɪtʃə(r)/ *v.t.* denaturieren

**denazification** /diːnɑːtsɪfɪˈkeɪʃn/ *n.* Entnazifizierung, *die*

**denazify** /diːˈnɑːtsɪfaɪ/ *v.t.* entnazifizieren

**dendrochronology** /dendrəʊkrəˈnɒlədʒɪ/ *n.* Dendrochronologie, *die;* Jahresringforschung, *die*

**deniable** /dɪˈnaɪəbl/ *adj.* bestreitbar; (*refutable*) widerlegbar

**denial** /dɪˈnaɪəl/ *n.* Ⓐ (*refusal*) Verweigerung, *die;* (*of request, wish*) Ablehnung, *die;* Ⓑ (*contradiction*) Leugnen, *das;* **an official ~:** ein offizielles Dementi; **~ of [the existence of] God** Gottesleugnung, *die;* Ⓒ (*disavowal of person*) Verleugnung, *die*

**denier** /ˈdenjə(r)/ *n.* Denier, *das* (*Textilw.*); **20 ~ stockings** 20-den-Strümpfe

**denigrate** /ˈdenɪgreɪt/ *v.t.* verunglimpfen; **~ sb.'s character** jmdn. verunglimpfen *od.* (*ugs.*) schlecht machen

**denigration** /denɪˈgreɪʃn/ *n.* Verunglimpfung, *die*

**denigratory** /ˈdenɪgreɪtərɪ/ *adj.* verunglimpfend

**denim** /ˈdenɪm/ *n.* Ⓐ (*fabric*) Denim (Wz), *der;* Jeansstoff, *der;* **~ jacket** Jeansjacke, *die;* Ⓑ *in pl.* (*garment*) Bluejeans *Pl.;* (*for workman*) Arbeitsanzug, *der*/-hose, *die*

**denizen** /ˈdenɪzən/ *n.* (*inhabitant, occupant*) Bewohner, *der*/Bewohnerin, *die*

**Denmark** /ˈdenmɑːk/ *pr. n.* Dänemark (*das*)

**denominate** /dɪˈnɒmɪneɪt/ *v.t.* bezeichnen

**denomination** /dɪnɒmɪˈneɪʃn/ *n.* Ⓐ (*class of units*) Einheit, *die;* **coins/paper money of the smallest ~:** Münzen/Papiergeld mit dem geringsten Nennwert; Ⓑ (*Relig.*) Glaubensgemeinschaft, *die;* Konfession, *die;* Ⓒ (*name, designation*) Bezeichnung, *die;* Ⓓ (*class, kind*) Art, *die*

**denominational** /dɪnɒmɪˈneɪʃənl/ *adj.* (*Relig.*) konfessionell; **~ school** Konfessions- *od.* Bekenntnisschule, *die*

**denominator** /dɪˈnɒmɪneɪtə(r)/ *n.* (*Math.*) Nenner, *der;* ⇒ *also* **common denominator**

**denotation** /diːnəˈteɪʃn/ *n.* Ⓐ (*marking*) Kennzeichnung, *die;* Ⓑ (*sign, indication*) Zeichen, *das;* Ⓒ (*designation*) Bezeichnung, *die;* Ⓓ (*meaning*) Bedeutung, *die;* (*esp. Ling.*) Denotation, *die*

**denote** /dɪˈnəʊt/ *v.t.* Ⓐ (*indicate*) hindeuten auf (+ *Akk.*); **~ that ...:** darauf hindeuten, dass ...; Ⓑ (*designate*) bedeuten; (*by specified symbol*) bezeichnen; Ⓒ (*signify*) symbolisieren; bedeuten

**dénouement**, **denouement** /deɪˈnuːmɑ̃/ *n.* Ausgang, *der;* Auflösung, *die*

**denounce** /dɪˈnaʊns/ *v.t.* Ⓐ (*inform against*) denunzieren (*abwertend*); (*accuse publicly*) beschuldigen; (*openly attack*) anprangern; **~ sb. to sb.** jmdn. bei jmdm. denunzieren; **~ sb. as a spy** jmdn. beschuldigen, ein Spion zu sein; Ⓑ (*terminate*) [auf]kündigen

**denouncement** /dɪˈnaʊnsmənt/ ⇒ **denunciation**

**dense** /dens/ *adj.* Ⓐ (*compacted in substance*) dicht; massiv ‹Körper›; (*Photog.*) undurchlässig ‹Negativ›; Ⓑ (*crowded together*) dicht gedrängt; eng ‹Schrift›; **the population is very ~:** die Bevölkerungsdichte ist sehr hoch; Ⓒ (*stupid*) dumm; **he's pretty ~:** er ist ziemlich schwer von Begriff

**densely** /ˈdenslɪ/ *adv.* dicht; **~ packed** dicht gedrängt

**denseness** /ˈdensnɪs/ *n., no pl.* Ⓐ Dichte, *die;* Ⓑ (*stupidity*) Begriffsstutzigkeit, *die*

**density** /ˈdensɪtɪ/ *n.* Ⓐ (*also Phys.*) Dichte, *die;* **population ~:** Bevölkerungsdichte, *die;* Ⓑ (*Photog.*) Schwärzung, *die;* Dichte, *die*

**dent** /dent/ ❶ *n.* Beule, *die;* Delle, *die* (*landsch.*); (*fig. coll.*) Loch, *das;* **make a ~**

**in production/in sb.'s savings** ein Loch in die Produktion/in jmds. Ersparnisse reißen; **make a bit of a ~ in sb.'s pride** jmds. Stolz leicht anknacksen (*ugs.*). ❷ *v.t.* einbeulen; verbeulen; eindellen ‹Holz, Tisch› (*ugs.*); (*fig.*) anknacksen (*ugs.*); **he ~ed his car in a collision** sein Auto wurde bei einem Zusammenstoß verbeult *od.* eingebeult

**dental** /ˈdentl/ ❶ *adj.* **A** Zahn-; **~ care** Zahnpflege, *die;* **~ treatment** zahnärztliche Behandlung; **~ training** Ausbildung in der Zahnheilkunde; **B** (*Phonet.*) Dental-; **~ consonant** ⇒ 2. ❷ *n.* (*Phonet.*) Dental, *der;* Zahnlaut, *der*

**dental: ~ floss** *n.* Zahnseide, *die;* **~ mechanic** *n.* ▶ 1261 Zahntechniker, *der*/-technikerin, *die;* **~ surgeon** *n.* ▶ 1261 Zahnarzt, *der*/-ärztin, *die*

**dentate** /ˈdenteɪt/ *adj.* (*Bot., Zool.*) gezähnt

**dentine** /ˈdentiːn/ (*Amer.:* **dentin** /ˈdentɪn/) *n.* (*Med.*) Dentin, *das* (*fachspr.*); Zahnbein, *das*

**dentist** /ˈdentɪst/ *n.* ▶ 1261 Zahnarzt, *der*/-ärztin, *die;* **at the ~['s]** beim Zahnarzt; **~'s chair** Zahnarztstuhl, *der*

**dentistry** /ˈdentɪstrɪ/ *n., no pl.* Zahnheilkunde, *die*

**denture** /ˈdentʃə(r)/ *n.* **~[s]** Zahnprothese, *die;* [künstliches] Gebiss; **partial ~:** Teilprothese, *die*

**denuclearize (denuclearise)** /diːˈnjuːklɪəraɪz/ *v.t.* atomwaffenfrei machen

**denudation** /diːnjuːˈdeɪʃn/ *n.* (*of valley, slope*) Abholzung, *die;* (*of tree*) Entlaubung, *die;* (*fig.*) Entzug, *der;* (*Geol.*) Denudation, *die* (*fachspr.*); Abtragung, *die*

**denude** /dɪˈnjuːd/ *v.t.* **A** abholzen, kahl schlagen ‹Tal, Hang›; **~ a tree [of its leaves]** einen Baum entlauben; **~d of trees** abgeholzt; **~ sb. of sth.** (*fig.*) jmdm. etw. entziehen; **B** (*Geol.*) erodieren (*fachspr.*)

**denunciation** /dɪmʌnsɪˈeɪʃn/ *n.* **A** Denunziation, *die* (*abwertend*); (*public accusation*) Beschuldigung, *die;* (*act of attacking*) Anprangerung, *die;* **B** (*of treaty etc.*) [Auf]kündigung, *die*

**deny** /dɪˈnaɪ/ *v.t.* **A** (*declare untrue*) bestreiten; zurückweisen ‹Beschuldigung›; **he denied knowing it** er bestritt, es zu wissen; **it cannot be denied** *or* **there is no ~ing the fact that ...:** es lässt sich nicht bestreiten *od.* leugnen, dass ...; **he denied this to be the case** er bestritt, dass dies der Fall sei; **~ all knowledge of sth.** bestreiten, irgendetwas von etw. zu wissen; **B** (*refuse*) verweigern; **~ sb. sth.** jmdm. etw. verweigern; **he can't ~ her anything** er kann ihr nichts abschlagen; **recognition was denied [to] him** die Anerkennung blieb ihm versagt; **C** (*disavow, repudiate; refuse access to*) verleugnen; ablehnen ‹Verantwortung›; **D** (*Relig.*) **~ oneself** *or* **the flesh** sich kasteien

**deodorant** /diːˈəʊdərənt/ ❶ *adj.* desodorierend; **~ spray** Deo[dorant]spray, *der od. das.* ❷ *n.* Deodorant, *das*

**deodorisation, deodorise** ⇒ **deodoriz-**

**deodorization** /diːəʊdəraɪˈzeɪʃn/ *n.* Desodorierung, *die*

**deodorize** /diːˈəʊdəraɪz/ *v.t.* desodorieren

**dep.** *abbr.* **A** **departs** (*Railw.*) Abf.; (*Aeronaut.*) Abfl.; **B** **deputy** stellv.

**depart** /dɪˈpɑːt/ ❶ *v.i.* **A** (*go away, take one's leave*) weggehen; fortgehen; sich entfernen (*geh.*); **B** (*set out, start, leave*) abfahren; ‹Schiff auch:› auslaufen, ablegen; ‹Flugzeug:› abfliegen; (*on one's journey*) abreisen; **ready to ~:** abfahrbereit; **C** (*fig.: deviate*) **~ from sth.** von etw. abweichen; **D** (*literary: die*) **~ from this life** aus dem Leben *od.* von hinnen scheiden (*geh.*); **he has ~ed from us** er ist von uns gegangen (*verhüll.*). ❷ *v.t.* (*literary*) **~ this life/world** aus dem Leben/aus dieser Welt scheiden (*geh.*)

**departed** /dɪˈpɑːtɪd/ ❶ *adj.* **A** (*bygone*) vergangen; **B** (*deceased*) dahingeschieden (*geh. verhüll.*). ❷ *n.* **the ~:** der/die Dahingeschiedene; die Dahingeschiedenen (*geh. verhüll.*)

**department** /dɪˈpɑːtmənt/ *n.* **A** (*of municipal administration*) Amt, *das;* (*of State administration*) Ministerium, *das;* (*of university*) Seminar, *das;* (*of shop*) Abteilung, *die;* **D~ of Employment/Education** Arbeits-/Erziehungsministerium, *das;* **the shipping ~/personnel ~:** die Versand-/Personalabteilung; **D~ for Education and Employment** (*Brit.*) Ministerium für Erziehung und Arbeit; **D~ of Trade and Industry** (*Brit.*) Ministerium für Handel und Industrie; ≈ Wirtschaftsministerium, *das;* **D~ of Social Security** (*Brit.*) Sozialversicherungsministerium, *das;* **English ~:** anglistisches *od.* englisches Seminar; **history ~:** Seminar *od.* Institut für Geschichte; **~ of pathology** Pathologie, *die;* pathologisches Institut; (*in hospital*) pathologische Abteilung; **B** (*administrative district in France*) Departement, *das;* **C** (*fig.: area of activity*) Ressort, *das;* **it's not my ~:** da kenne ich mich nicht aus; (*not my responsibility*) dafür bin ich nicht zuständig

**departmental** /diːpɑːˈtmentl/ *adj.* **A** ⇒ **department** A, B: Amts-; Ministerial-; Seminar-; Abteilungs-; Departement-; **B** **be ~:** die Abteilung betreffen

**departmentally** /diːpɑːˈtmentəlɪ/ *adv.* ⇒ **departmental** A: auf Amts-/Ministerial-/Seminar-/Abteilungsebene

**deˈpartment store** *n.* Kaufhaus, *das*

**departure** /dɪˈpɑːtʃə(r)/ *n.* **A** (*going away*) Abreise, *die;* **take one's ~:** sich entfernen (*geh.*); **after sb.'s ~:** nachdem jmd. weggegangen war/ist; **make a hasty ~:** sich rasch entfernen; **B** (*deviation*) **~ from sth.** Abweichen von etw.; **C** (*of train, bus, ship*) Abfahrt, *die;* (*of aircraft*) Abflug, *der;* **two ~s a day** täglich zwei Abfahrtszeiten; **D** (*of action or thought*) Ansatz, *der;* **point of ~:** Ansatzpunkt, *der;* **this product is a new ~ for us** mit diesem Produkt schlagen wir einen neuen Weg ein

**departure: ~ gate** *n.* Flugsteig, *der;* **~ lounge** *n.* Abflughalle, *die;* **~ platform** *n.* [Abfahrt]gleis, *das;* **~ time** *n.* (*of train, bus*) Abfahrtzeit, *die;* (*of aircraft*) Abflugzeit, *die*

**depend** /dɪˈpend/ *v.i.* **A** **~ [up]on** abhängen von; **it [all] ~s on whether/what/how ...:** das hängt [ganz] davon ab *od.* kommt ganz darauf an, ob/was/wie ...; **that ~s** es kommt darauf an; **~ing on how ...:** je nachdem, wie ...; **B** (*rely, trust*) **~ [up]on** sich verlassen auf (+ *Akk.*); (*have to rely on*) angewiesen sein auf (+ *Akk.*); **~ on sb. for help** sich auf jmds. Hilfe verlassen/auf jmds. Hilfe angewiesen sein

**dependability** /dɪpendəˈbɪlɪtɪ/ *n., no pl.* Verlässlichkeit, *die;* Zuverlässigkeit, *die*

**dependable** /dɪˈpendəbl/ *adj.* verlässlich; zuverlässig

**dependably** /dɪˈpendəblɪ/ *adv.* zuverlässig

**dependant** /dɪˈpendənt/ *n.* **A** Abhängige, *der/die;* **~s** (*Taxation*) abhängige Angehörige; **B** (*servant*) Bedienstete, *der/die*

**dependence** /dɪˈpendəns/ *n.* **A** Abhängigkeit, *die;* **~ [up]on sb./sth.** Abhängigkeit von jmdm./etw.; **B** (*reliance*) **put** *or* **place ~ [up]on sb.** sich auf jmdn. verlassen

**dependency** /dɪˈpendənsɪ/ *n.* **A** (*country*) Territorium, *das;* **B** (*condition of being dependent*) Abhängigkeit, *die* (**on** von); **~ culture** (*Sociol.*) Kultur der Abhängigkeit [vom Staat]

**dependent** /dɪˈpendənt/ ❶ *n.* ⇒ **dependant.** ❷ *adj.* **A** (*also Ling., Math.*) abhängig; **be ~ on sth.** von etw. abhängen *od.* abhängig sein; **B** **be ~ on** (*be unable to do without*) angewiesen sein auf (+ *Akk.*); abhängig sein von ‹Droge, Ursache›; **be ~ on heroin** heroinabhängig sein

**depict** /dɪˈpɪkt/ *v.t.* darstellen

**depiction** /dɪˈpɪkʃn/ *n.* Darstellung, *die*

**depilate** /ˈdepɪleɪt/ *v.t.* enthaaren; depilieren (*Med.*)

**depilatory** /dɪˈpɪlətərɪ/ ❶ *adj.* Enthaarungs-. ❷ *n.* Enthaarungsmittel, *das*

**deplete** /dɪˈpliːt/ *v.t.* **A** (*reduce in number or amount*) erheblich verringern; **the audience is ~d** die Zuschauerzahl hat sich deutlich verringert; **our stores are ~d** unser Vorrat ist zusammengeschrumpft; **air ~d of oxygen** Luft mit wenig Sauerstoff; **B** (*empty*) entleeren; (*exhaust*) erschöpfen

**depletion** /dɪˈpliːʃn/ *n.* **A** Verringerung, *die;* **B** (*emptying*) Entleerung, *die;* (*exhausting*) Erschöpfung, *die*

**deplorable** /dɪˈplɔːrəbl/ *adj.* beklagenswert; erbärmlich ‹Essen, Leistung›

**deplorably** /dɪˈplɔːrəblɪ/ *adv.* erbärmlich; **~ neglected** schändlich verwahrlost

**deplore** /dɪˈplɔː(r)/ *v.t.* **A** (*disapprove of*) verurteilen; **B** (*bewail, regret*) beklagen; **sth. is to be ~d** etw. ist beklagenswert

**deploy** /dɪˈplɔɪ/ ❶ *v.t.* **A** (*bring into effective action*) einsetzen; **B** (*Mil.*) einsetzen; (*extend*) ausschwärmen lassen. ❷ *v.i.* (*Mil.*) eingesetzt werden

**deployment** /dɪˈplɔɪmənt/ *n.* Einsatz, *der*

**deponent** /dɪˈpəʊnənt/ ❶ *adj.* (*Ling.*) **~ verb** Deponens, *das.* ❷ *n.* **A** (*Law*) ≈ Zeuge, *der*/Zeugin, *die;* **B** (*Ling.*) Deponens, *das*

**depopulate** /diːˈpɒpjʊleɪt/ *v.t.* entvölkern

**depopulation** /diːpɒpjʊˈleɪʃn/ *n.* Entvölkerung, *die*

**deport** /dɪˈpɔːt/ ❶ *v.t.* deportieren; (*from country*) ausweisen. ❷ *v. refl.* sich benehmen

**deportation** /diːpɔːˈteɪʃn/ *n.* Deportation, *die;* (*from country*) Ausweisung, *die*

**deportee** /diːpɔːˈtiː/ *n.* Deportierte, *der/die;* (*from country*) Ausgewiesene, *der/die*

**deportment** /dɪˈpɔːtmənt/ *n.* Benehmen, *das*

**depose** /dɪˈpəʊz/ ❶ *v.t.* absetzen; **~ sb. from an office** jmdn. eines Amtes entheben. ❷ *v.i. & t.* (*Law*) [unter Eid] aussagen

**deposit** /dɪˈpɒzɪt/ ❶ *n.* **A** (*in bank*) Depot, *das;* (*credit*) Guthaben, *das;* (*Brit.: at interest*) Sparguthaben, *das;* **make a ~:** etwas einzahlen; **have £70 on ~:** ein [Spar]guthaben von 70 Pfund haben; **B** (*payment as pledge*) Kaution, *die;* (*first instalment*) Anzahlung, *die;* **pay** *or* **make** *or* **leave a ~:** eine Kaution zahlen *od.* hinterlegen/eine Anzahlung leisten; **there is a five pence ~ on the bottle** auf der Flasche sind fünf Pence Pfand; **put down a ~ on sth.** eine Anzahlung für etw. leisten; **lose one's ~** (*Polit.*) die Kaution verlieren; **C** (*for safe keeping*) anvertrautes Gut; **D** (*natural accumulation*) (*of sand, mud, lime, etc.; also Med.*) Ablagerung, *die;* (*of ore, coal, oil*) Lagerstätte, *die;* (*in glass, bottle*) Bodensatz, *der.* ❷ *v.t.* **A** (*lay down in a place*) ablegen; abstellen ‹etw. Senkrechtes, auch Tablett, Teller usw.›; absetzen ‹Mitfahrer›; **B** (*leave lying*) ‹Wasser usw.:› ablagern; **be ~ed** sich ablagern; **~ a layer of sand/dust over sth.** etw. mit einer Schicht Sand/Staub überziehen; **C** (*in bank*) deponieren, [auf ein Konto] einzahlen ‹Geld›; (*Brit.: at interest*) [auf ein Sparkonto] einzahlen; **~ money in a bank** Geld bei einer Bank einzahlen; **D** (*pay as pledge*) anzahlen

**deˈposit account** *n.* (*Brit.*) Sparkonto, *das*

**deposition** /depəˈzɪʃn, diːpəˈzɪʃn/ *n.* **A** (*depositing*) (*of papers, money, etc.*) Hinterlegung, *die* (**with** bei); (*of mud, coal, ore, etc.*) Ablagerung, *die;* **B** (*from office*) Absetzung, *die;* **C** (*Law: giving of evidence, allegation*) [eidliche Zeugen]aussage

**depositor** /dɪˈpɒzɪtə(r)/ *n.* (*Banking*) Einleger, *der*/Einlegerin, *die*

**depository** /dɪˈpɒzɪtərɪ/ *n.* (*storehouse*) Lagerhaus, *das;* (*place for safe keeping*) Aufbewahrungsort, *der;* (*fig.*) Fundgrube, *die*

**depot** /ˈdepəʊ/ *n.* **A** Depot, *das;* **B** (*storehouse*) Lager, *das;* **grain ~:** Getreidespeicher, *der;* **C** **[bus] ~** (*Brit.*) Depot, *das;* Omnibusgarage, *die;* (*Amer.: bus station*) Omnibusbahnhof, *der;* (*Amer.: railway station*) Bahnhof, *der*

**deprave** /dɪˈpreɪv/ *v.t.* verderben

**depraved** /dɪˈpreɪvd/ *adj.* verdorben; lasterhaft ‹Gewohnheit›

**depravity** /dɪˈprævɪtɪ/ *n.* Lasterhaftigkeit, *die;* Verderbtheit, *die (geh.);* Verdorbenheit, *die*

**deprecate** /ˈdeprɪkeɪt/ *v.t.* **A** *(disapprove of)* missbilligen; **B** *(plead against)* abzuwenden suchen

**deprecation** /deprɪˈkeɪʃn/ *n.* Missbilligung, *die*

**depreciate** /dɪˈpri:ʃɪeɪt, dɪˈpri:sɪeɪt/ **1** *v.t.* **A** *(diminish in value)* abwerten; herabsetzen; abwerten ‹Währung›; **B** *(disparage)* herabsetzen. **2** *v.i.* an Wert verlieren

**depreciation** /dɪpri:ʃɪˈeɪʃn, dɪpri:sɪˈeɪʃn/ *n.* *(of money, currency, property)* Wertverlust, *der;* *(of person)* Herabsetzung, *die;* **allowance for ~:** Abschreibung, *die*

**depreciatory** /dɪˈpri:ʃətərɪ/ *adj.* verächtlich; abfällig

**depredation** /deprɪˈdeɪʃn/ *n.* **A** Verwüstung, *die;* **B** *(ravages of disease etc.)* verheerende Wirkung

**depress** /dɪˈpres/ *v.t.* **A** *(deject)* deprimieren; **B** *(push or pull down)* herunterdrücken; *(cause to move to a lower level)* absenken; **C** *(reduce activity of)* unterdrücken; sich nicht entfalten lassen ‹Handel, Wirtschaftswachstum›

**depressant** /dɪˈpresənt/ **1** *adj.* *(Med.)* beruhigend; sedativ *(fachspr.)*. **2** *n.* **A** *(influence)* Hemmnis, *das;* **B** *(Med.)* Beruhigungsmittel, *das;* Sedativ[um], *das (fachspr.)*

**depressed** /dɪˈprest/ *adj.* deprimiert ‹Person, Stimmung›; abgesenkt ‹Gelände, Ebene›; geschwächt ‹Industrie›; **~ area** unter [wirtschaftlicher] Depression leidendes Gebiet

**depressing** /dɪˈpresɪŋ/ *adj.* deprimierend

**depressingly** /dɪˈpresɪŋlɪ/ *adv.* deprimierend

**depression** /dɪˈpreʃn/ *n.* **A** Depression, *die;* **B** *(sunk place)* Vertiefung, *die;* **C** *(Meteorol.)* Tief[druckgebiet], *das;* Depression, *die (fachspr.);* **D** *(reduction in vigour, vitality)* Schwächung, *die;* **E** *(Econ.)* **the D~:** die Weltwirtschaftskrise; **economic ~:** Wirtschaftskrise, *die;* Depression, *die;* **F** *(lowering, sinking)* Senkung, *die;* *(pressing down)* Herunterdrücken, *das*

**depressive** /dɪˈpresɪv/ **1** *adj.* **A** *(tending to depress)* bedrückend; deprimierend; **B** *(Psych.)* depressiv. **2** *n.* *(Psych.)* Depressive, *der/die*

**depressurize** (**depressurise**) /di:ˈpreʃəraɪz/ *v.t.* dekomprimieren

**deprival** /dɪˈpraɪvl/ ⇒ **deprivation A**

**deprivation** /deprɪˈveɪʃn, di:praɪˈveɪʃn/ *n.* **A** *(being deprived)* Entzug, *der;* *(of one's rights, liberties, or title)* Aberkennung, *die;* **B** *(loss of desired thing)* Entbehrung, *die;* **that is a great ~:** das ist ein großer Verlust; **oxygen ~:** Sauerstoffmangel, *der*

**deprive** /dɪˈpraɪv/ *v.t.* **A** *(strip, bereave)* **~ sb. of sth.** jmdm. etw. nehmen; *(debar from having)* jmdm. etw. vorenthalten; **trees that ~ a house of light** Bäume, die einem Haus das Licht nehmen; **the village was ~d of electricity** das Dorf war ohne Stromversorgung; **he will be ~d of his right to vote** ihm wird das Wahlrecht entzogen werden; **~ sb. of citizenship** jmdm. die Staatsbürgerschaft aberkennen; **~ sb. of his command** jmdm. das Kommando entziehen; **am I depriving you of it?** brauchen Sie das gerade?; **be ~d of one's car/books** auf sein Auto/seine Bücher verzichten müssen; **be ~d of light** nicht genug Licht haben; **~ sb. of a pleasure** jmdm. ein Vergnügen vorenthalten; jmdn. eines Vergnügens berauben *(geh.);* **B** *(depose)* absetzen; **C** *(prevent from having normal life)* benachteiligen

**deprived** /dɪˈpraɪvd/ *adj.* benachteiligt ‹Kind, Familie usw.›

**Dept.** *abbr.* **Department** Amt/Min./Seminar/Abt.

**depth** /depθ/ *n.* **A** ▶ **1210** *(lit. or fig.)* Tiefe, *die;* **at a ~ of 3 metres** in einer Tiefe von 3 Metern; **3 feet in ~:** 3 Fuß tief; **what is the ~ of the pond?** wie tief ist der Teich?; **~ of thought/meaning** Gedankentiefe, *die*/Bedeutungsgehalt, *der;* **from/in the ~s of the forest/ocean** aus/in der Tiefe des Waldes/des Ozeans; **from the ~s of his soul** aus tiefster Seele; **sink** *or* **fall into the ~s of oblivion/despair** völlig in Vergessenheit/in tiefste Verzweiflung geraten; **sink** *or* **fall to such ~s that ...** *(fig.)* so tief sinken, dass ...; **in the ~s of winter** im tiefen Winter; **great ~ of feeling** große Gefühls- *od.* Ausdruckstiefe; **B** *(mental profundity)* geistige Tiefe; **C** **in ~:** gründlich, intensiv ‹studieren›; **an in-~ study/analysis** *etc.* eine gründliche Untersuchung/Analyse *usw.;* **defence in ~:** tief gestaffelte Verteidigung; **D** **be out of one's ~:** nicht mehr stehen können; keinen Grund mehr unter den Füßen haben; *(fig.)* ins Schwimmen kommen *(ugs.);* überfordert sein; **go/get out of one's ~** *(lit. or fig.)* den Grund unter den Füßen verlieren; **don't go out of your ~:** geh nicht zu tief hinein

**depth: ~ bomb, ~ charge** *ns.* Wasserbombe, *die;* **~-charge** *v.t.* mit Wasserbomben angreifen; **~ of field** *n.* *(Photog.)* Schärfentiefe, *die;* **~ psychology** *n.* Tiefenpsychologie, *die*

**deputation** /depjʊˈteɪʃn/ *n.* Abordnung, *die;* Delegation, *die*

**depute** **1** /dɪˈpju:t/ *v.t.* **A** *(commit task or authority to)* **~ sb. to do sth.** jmdn. beauftragen, etw. zu tun; **~ sth. to sb.** etw. auf jmdn. übertragen; **B** *(appoint as deputy)* **~ sb. to do sth.** jmdn. [als Stellvertreter] damit betrauen, etw. zu tun. **2** /ˈdepju:t/ *n.* *(Scot.: deputy)* Stellvertreter, *der*/-vertreterin, *die*

**deputize** (**deputise**) /ˈdepjʊtaɪz/ *v.i.* als Stellvertreter einspringen; **~ for sb.** jmdn. vertreten

**deputy** /ˈdepjʊtɪ/ *n.* **A** *attrib.* stellvertretend; **~ sheriff** ▶ **1261** *(Amer.)* Hilfssheriff, *der;* **B** *(person appointed to act for another)* [Stell]vertreter, *der*/-vertreterin, *die;* **act as ~ for sb.** jmdn. vertreten; **C** *(parliamentary representative)* Abgeordnete, *der/die;* Deputierte, *der/die;* **Chamber of Deputies** Abgeordnetenkammer, *die;* **D** *(Brit.: coalmine overseer)* Steiger, *der*

**derail** /dɪˈreɪl, di:ˈreɪl/ *v.t. usu. in pass.* zum Entgleisen bringen; **be ~ed** entgleisen

**derailleur** /di:ˈreɪlə(r), di:ˈreɪljə(r)/ *n.* **~ [gear]** Kettenschaltung, *die*

**derailment** /dɪˈreɪlmənt, di:ˈreɪlmənt/ *n.* Entgleisung, *die;* **cause the ~ of sth.** etw. zum Entgleisen bringen

**derange** /dɪˈreɪndʒ/ *v.t.* **A** *(throw into confusion, put out of order)* durcheinander bringen; *(make insane)* geistig verwirren; **B** *(disturb, interrupt)* stören

**deranged** /dɪˈreɪndʒd/ *adj.* **[mentally] ~:** geistesgestört

**derangement** /dɪˈreɪndʒmənt/ *n.* **A** Unordnung, *die;* **cause ~ of** durcheinander bringen; **B** **[mental] ~:** Geistesgestörtheit, *die*

**Derby** /ˈdɑ:bɪ/ *n.* **A** *(annual horse race at Epsom)* Derby [in Epsom], *das;* *(other race or contest)* Derby, *das;* **~ Day** Tag des Derbys [in Epsom]; **local ~:** Lokalderby, *das;* **B** **d~** *(Amer.: bowler hat)* Melone, *die*

**deregulate** /di:ˈregjʊleɪt/ *v.t.* deregulieren *(fachspr.);* dem freien Wettbewerb überlassen

**deregulation** /di:regjʊˈleɪʃn/ *n.* Deregulation, *die (fachspr.);* Deregulierung, *die (fachspr.)*

**derelict** /ˈderɪlɪkt/ **1** *adj.* **A** *(abandoned)* verlassen und verfallen; aufgegeben ‹Schiff›; **B** *(Amer.: negligent)* nachlässig. **2** *n.* **A** *(abandoned property)* herrenloses Gut; *(ship)* aufgegebenes Schiff; *(wreck)* [treibendes] Wrack; **B** *(person)* Ausgestoßene, *der/die*

**dereliction** /derɪˈlɪkʃn/ *n.* **A** *(abandoning)* Vernachlässigung, *die;* *(state)* verkommener Zustand; **the building is in a state of ~:** das Gebäude ist verkommen; **B** *(neglect)* **~ of duty** Pflichtverletzung, *die*

**derestrict** /di:rɪˈstrɪkt/ *v.t.* [wieder] freigeben; **~ed road** Straße ohne Geschwindigkeitsbeschränkung

**derestriction** /di:rɪˈstrɪkʃn/ *n.* Freigabe, *die*

**deride** /dɪˈraɪd/ *v.t.* *(treat with scorn)* sich lustig machen über (+ *Akk.*); *(laugh scornfully at)* verlachen

**de rigueur** /də rɪˈgɜ:(r)/ *pred. adj.* de rigueur *nicht attr. (veralt.);* unerlässlich

**derision** /dɪˈrɪʒn/ *n.* Spott, *der;* **be an object of ~:** Zielscheibe des Spottes sein; **bring sb./sth. into ~:** jmdn./etw. zum Gespött *od.* lächerlich machen

**derisive** /dɪˈraɪsɪv/ *adj.* *(ironical)* spöttisch; *(scoffing)* verächtlich

**derisively** /dɪˈraɪsɪvlɪ/ *adv.* ⇒ **derisive**: spöttisch; verächtlich

**derisory** /dɪˈraɪsərɪ, dɪˈraɪzərɪ/ *adj.* **A** *(ridiculously inadequate)* lächerlich; **B** *(scoffing)* verächtlich; *(ironical)* spöttisch

**derivation** /derɪˈveɪʃn/ *n.* **A** *(obtaining from a source)* Herleitung, *die;* **B** *(extraction, origin)* Herkunft, *die;* *(descent)* Abstammung, *die;* **C** *(Ling.)* Ableitung, *die;* Derivation, *die (fachspr.);* *(origin)* Ursprung, *der;* Herkunft, *die*

**derivative** /dɪˈrɪvətɪv/ **1** *adj.* abgeleitet; *(lacking originality)* nachahmend; epigonal; *(secondary)* indirekt. **2** *n.* **A** Abkömmling, *der;* *(word)* Ableitung, *die;* Derivat[iv], *das (Sprachw.);* *(chemical substance)* Derivat, *das;* **B** *(Finance)* **~s** Derivate *Pl.*, **~s market** Derivatenmarkt, *der;* **~s trader** Derivatenhändler, *der;* **C** *(Math.)* Ableitung, *die*

**derive** /dɪˈraɪv/ **1** *v.t.* **A** *(get, obtain, form)* **~ sth. from sth.** etw. aus etw. gewinnen; **he ~s much of his earnings from freelance work** er bezieht einen großen Teil seines Einkommens aus freiberuflicher Tätigkeit; **the river ~s its name** *or* **the name of the river is ~d from a Greek god** der Name des Flusses geht auf eine griechische Gottheit zurück; **he ~s pleasure from his studies** er hat Freude an seinem Studium; **~ profit/advantage from sth.** aus etw. Nutzen/seinen Vorteil ziehen; **B** *(deduce)* ableiten; herleiten; **C** **~ one's origin/ancestry/pedigree from sth.** aus etw. stammen. **2** *v.i.* **~ from** beruhen auf (+ *Dat.*); **the word ~s from Latin** das Wort stammt *od.* kommt aus dem Lateinischen

**dermatitis** /dɜ:məˈtaɪtɪs/ *n.* ▶ **1232** *(Med.)* Hautentzündung, *die;* Dermatitis, *die (fachspr.)*

**dermatologist** /dɜ:məˈtɒlədʒɪst/ *n.* ▶ **1261** *(Med.)* Hautarzt, *der*/-ärztin, *die;* Dermatologe, *der*/Dermatologin, *die*

**dermatology** /dɜ:məˈtɒlədʒɪ/ *n.* *(Med.)* Dermatologie, *die*

**dern** /dɜ:n/, **derned** /dɜ:nd/ *(Amer.)* ⇒ **darn²**, **darned**

**derogate** /ˈderəgeɪt/ *v.i.* *(formal)* **~ from sth.** etw. schmälern

**derogation** /derəˈgeɪʃn/ *n.* *(formal)* Schmälerung, *die* (**from** *Gen.*)

**derogatory** /dɪˈrɒgətərɪ/ *adj.* **A** *(depreciatory)* abfällig; abschätzig; **~ sense [of a word]** abwertende Bedeutung [eines Wortes]; **B** *(tending to detract)* **be ~ to sth.** einer Sache *(Dat.)* abträglich sein; **be regarded as ~:** als etwas Ehrenrühriges angesehen werden

**derrick** /ˈderɪk/ *n.* **A** *(for moving or hoisting)* [Derrick]kran, *der;* **B** *(over oil well)* Bohrturm, *der*

**derring-do** /derɪŋˈdu:/ *n.* *(literary)* Wagemut, *der;* **a deed of ~:** eine wagemutige Tat

**derv** /dɜ:v/ *n.* *(Brit. Motor Veh.)* Diesel[kraftstoff], *der*

**dervish** /ˈdɜ:vɪʃ/ *n.* Derwisch, *der*

**desalination** /di:sælɪˈneɪʃn/ *n.* Entsalzung, *die*

**descale** /di:ˈskeɪl/ *v.t.* entkalken

**descant** **1** /ˈdeskænt/ *n.* **A** *(Mus.)* Diskant, *der;* **B** *(poet.: melody)* Weise, *die;* Melodie, *die.* **2** /dɪˈskænt/ *v.i.* **A** *(formal: talk lengthily)* **~ upon sth.** sich über etw. *(Akk.)* verbreiten; **B** *(sing ~)* Diskant singen

**ˈdescant recorder** *n.* *(Mus.)* Sopranflöte, *die*

**descend** /dɪˈsend/ **1** *v.i.* **A** *(go down)* hinuntergehen/-steigen/-klettern/-fahren; *(come down)* herunterkommen; *(sink)* niedergehen

d

(**on** auf + *Dat.*); **the lift ~ed** der Aufzug fuhr nach unten; **~ in the lift** mit dem Aufzug nach unten fahren; **~ into hell** zur Hölle hinabsteigen *od.* niederfahren; **~ on sb.** (*fig.*) über jmdn. hereinbrechen; **night ~ed upon the village** die Nacht senkte sich auf das Dorf herab; **(B)** (*slope downwards*) abfallen; **the hill ~s into/towards the sea** der Hügel fällt zum Meer hin ab; **(C)** (*in quality, thought, etc.*) herabsinken; **~ from the general to the particular** vom Allgemeinen zum Besonderen gehen *od.* kommen; **(D)** (*in pitch*) fallen; sinken; tiefer werden; **~ to a low note** auf einen tiefen Ton hinuntergehen; **(E)** (*make sudden attack*) **~ on sth.** über etw. (*Akk.*) herfallen; **~ on sb.** (*lit., or fig.: arrive unexpectedly*) jmdn. überfallen; **~ on a country** in ein Land einfallen; **(F)** (*fig.: lower oneself*) **~ to sth.** sich zu etw. erniedrigen; **(G)** (*pass by inheritance*) vererbt werden (**to** an + *Akk.*); **(H)** (*derive*) abstammen (**from** von); (*have origin*) zurückgehen (**from** auf + *Akk.*); **(I)** (*go forward in time*) weitergehen.

**(2)** *v.t.* **(A)** (*go/come down*) hinunter- / heruntergehen / -steigen / -klettern /-fahren; hinab-/herabsteigen (*geh.*); **(B)** (*go along*) hinuntergehen/-fahren ‹Straße›

**descendant** /dɪˈsendənt/ *n.* Nachkomme, *der;* **be ~s/a ~ of** abstammen von

**descended** /dɪˈsendɪd/ *adj.* **be ~ from sb.** von jmdm. abstammen

**descent** /dɪˈsent/ *n.* **(A)** (*going or coming down*) (*of person*) Abstieg, *der;* (*of parachute, plane, bird, avalanche*) Niedergehen, *das;* **the ~ of the mountain took us a few hours** für den Abstieg vom Berg brauchten wir einige Stunden; **the D~ from the Cross** die Kreuzabnahme; **(B)** (*way*) Abstieg, *der;* **the ~ leading to the river** der Weg hinunter zum Fluss; **(C)** (*slope*) Abfall, *der;* **the road made a sharp ~ into the valley** die Straße fiel zum Tal hin steil ab; **the ~ was very steep** das Gefälle war sehr stark; **(D)** (*sudden attack*) **the Danes made numerous ~s upon the English coast** die Dänen fielen mehrfach an der englischen Küste ein; **(E)** (*decline, fall*) Abstieg, *der;* **(F)** (*lineage*) Abstammung, *die;* Herkunft, *die;* **be of Russian/noble ~:** russischer/adliger Abstammung sein; **(G)** (*transmission by inheritance*) Herkunft, *die;* **jazz traces its ~ from African music** der Jazz hat seine Ursprünge in afrikanischer Musik

**describable** /dɪˈskraɪbəbl/ *adj.* beschreibbar; **be ~:** zu beschreiben sein; **it's not ~ in words** es ist unbeschreiblich *od.* nicht mit Worten zu beschreiben

**describe** /dɪˈskraɪb/ *v.t.* **(A)** (*set forth in words*) beschreiben; schildern; (*distinguish*) bezeichnen; **it can't be ~d in words** es ist unbeschreiblich *od.* nicht mit Worten zu beschreiben; **~ [oneself] as ...:** [sich] als ... bezeichnen; **sth. can hardly be ~d as ...:** etw. ist kaum ... zu nennen; **(B)** (*move in, draw*) beschreiben ‹Kreis, Bogen, Kurve›

**description** /dɪˈskrɪpʃn/ *n.* **(A)** (*describing, verbal portrait*) Beschreibung, *die;* Schilderung, *die;* **she is beautiful beyond ~:** sie ist unbeschreiblich schön; **he answers [to]** *or* **fits the ~:** er entspricht der Beschreibung (*Dat.*); **(B)** (*sort, class*) Art, *die;* **cars of every ~:** Autos aller Art; **(C)** (*more or less complete definition*) Beschreibung, *die;* (*designation*) Bezeichnung, *die*

**descriptive** /dɪˈskrɪptɪv/ *adj.* **(A)** anschaulich; beschreibend ‹Lyrik›; deskriptiv ‹Analyse›; **a purely ~ report** ein reiner Tatsachenbericht; **(B)** (*not expressing feelings or judgements; also Ling.*) deskriptiv

**descriptively** /dɪˈskrɪptɪvlɪ/ *adv.* anschaulich ‹schreiben, sprechen›; deskriptiv ‹analysieren›

**descry** /dɪˈskraɪ/ *v.t.* (*catch sight of*) erblicken; erspähen; (*fig.: perceive*) erkennen

**desecrate** /ˈdesɪkreɪt/ *v.t.* entweihen; schänden

**desecration** /desɪˈkreɪʃn/ *n.* Entweihung, *die;* Schändung, *die*

**desegregate** /diːˈsegrɪgeɪt/ *v.t.* die Rassentrennung aufheben an (+ *Dat.*)

**desegregation** /diːsegrɪˈgeɪʃn/ *n.* Aufhebung der Rassentrennung (**of** an + *Dat.*)

**deselect** /diːsɪˈlekt/ *v.t.* (*Brit. Polit.*) nicht mehr als Wahlkandidat vorsehen

**desensitize (desensitise)** /diːˈsensɪtaɪz/ *v.t.* (*Med., Phot., Psych.*) desensibilisieren

**desert**[1] /dɪˈzɜːt/ *n.* **(A)** *in pl.* (*what is deserved*) Verdienste *Pl.;* **meet with** *or* **get one's [just] ~s** das bekommen, was man verdient hat; **(B)** (*deserving*) Verdienst, *das*

**desert**[2] /ˈdezət/ **(1)** *n.* Wüste, *die;* (*fig.*) Einöde, *die;* **the Sahara D~:** die Wüste Sahara; **a cultural ~** (*fig.*) kulturelles Ödland. **(2)** *adj.* öde; Wüsten‹klima, -stamm›

**desert**[3] /dɪˈzɜːt/ **(1)** *v.t.* verlassen; im Stich lassen ‹Frau, Familie usw.›. **(2)** *v.i.* (*run away*) davonlaufen; ‹Soldat:› desertieren; **~ to sb.** zu jmdm. überlaufen

**deserted** /dɪˈzɜːtɪd/ *adj.* verlassen; **the streets were ~:** die Straßen waren wie ausgestorben

**deserter** /dɪˈzɜːtə(r)/ *n.* Deserteur, *der;* Fahnenflüchtige, *der/die*

**desertion** /dɪˈzɜːʃn/ *n.* Verlassen, *das;* (*of one's duty*) Vernachlässigen, *das;* (*Mil.*) Desertion, *die;* Fahnenflucht, *die;* **~ to the enemy** Überlaufen zum Feind

**desert island** /dezət ˈaɪlənd/ *n.* einsame Insel

**deserve** /dɪˈzɜːv/ **(1)** *v.t.* verdienen; **he ~s to win** er verdient [es] zu gewinnen; **he ~s to be punished** er verdient [es], bestraft zu werden; er verdient Strafe; **what have I done to ~ this?** womit habe ich das verdient?; **he got what he ~d** er hat es nicht besser verdient. **(2)** *v.i.* (*formal*) **~ well of** sich verdient gemacht haben um

**deservedly** /dɪˈzɜːvɪdlɪ/ *adv.* verdientermaßen; **and ~ so** und das zu Recht; **be ~ punished** zu Recht bestraft werden

**deserving** /dɪˈzɜːvɪŋ/ *adj.* **(A)** (*worthy*) verdienstvoll; **donate money to a ~ cause** Geld für einen guten Zweck geben; **the ~ poor** die unverschuldet Bedürftigen; **(B)** (*meritorious*) **be ~ of sth.** etw. verdienen; **people most ~ of help** Leute, die am ehesten Hilfe verdienen

**déshabillé** /deɪzæˈbiːeɪ/ *n.* Nachlässigkeit in der Kleidung; **in ~:** nachlässig gekleidet; (*partly undressed*) halb bekleidet

**desiccated** /ˈdesɪkeɪtɪd/ *adj.* getrocknet; (*fig.*) vertrocknet ‹Person›; **~ fruit** Dörr- *od.* Backobst, *das*

**desideratum** /dɪzɪdəˈreɪtəm/ *n., pl.* **desiderata** /dɪzɪdəˈreɪtə/ (*literary*) Desiderat, *das* (*geh.*); Desideratum, *das* (*geh.*)

**design** /dɪˈzaɪn/ **(1)** *n.* **(A)** (*preliminary sketch*) Entwurf, *der;* **~s of costumes** Kostümentwürfe; **a technical ~:** eine technische Zeichnung; **(B)** (*pattern*) Muster, *das;* **(C)** *no art.* (*art*) Design, *das;* Gestaltung, *die* (*geh.*); **(D)** (*established form of a product*) Entwurf, *der;* (*of machine, engine, etc.*) Bauweise, *die;* **(E)** (*general idea, construction from parts*) Konstruktion, *die;* **a machine of faulty/good ~:** eine schlecht/gut konstruierte Maschine; **(F)** (*mental plan*) Planung, *die;* **argument from ~** (*Theol.*) theologischer Gottesbeweis; **(G)** *in pl.* (*scheme of attack*) **have ~s on sb./sth.** es auf jmdn./etw. abgesehen haben; **(H)** (*purpose*) Absicht, *die;* **by ~:** mit Absicht; absichtlich

**(2)** *v.t.* **(A)** (*draw plan of*) entwerfen; konstruieren, entwerfen ‹Maschine, Fahrzeug, Flugzeug›; **(B)** (*make preliminary sketch of*) entwerfen; **(C)** (*contrive, plan*) planen; aufstellen ‹Lehrplan›; **(D)** (*intend*) beabsichtigen; **be ~ed to do sth.** ‹Maschine, Werkzeug, Gerät:› etw. tun sollen; **the book is ~ed as an aid to beginners** das Buch ist als Hilfe für Anfänger konzipiert; **(E)** (*set apart*) vorsehen; **be ~ed for sb./sth.** für jmdn./etw. gedacht *od.* vorgesehen sein; **(F)** (*destine*) bestimmen.

**(3)** *v.i.* Entwürfe machen

**designate** **(1)** /ˈdezɪgnət/ *postpos. adj.* designiert. **(2)** /ˈdezɪgneɪt/ *v.t.* **(A)** (*serve as name of, describe*) bezeichnen; (*serve as distinctive mark of*) kennzeichnen; **~ sth. A** etw. als A bezeichnen/kennzeichnen; **(B)** (*specify, particularize*) angeben; aufzeigen ‹Fehler, Mängel›; **(C)** (*appoint to office*) designieren (*geh.*); **be ~d as sb.'s successor** zu jmds. Nachfolger ernannt werden

**designation** /dezɪgˈneɪʃn/ *n.* **(A)** Bezeichnung, *die;* **(B)** (*appointing to office*) Designation, *die*

**designedly** /dɪˈzaɪnɪdlɪ/ *adv.* absichtlich

**designer** /dɪˈzaɪnə(r)/ *n.* ▶ 1261 Designer, *der*/Designerin, *die;* (*of machines, buildings*) Konstrukteur, *der*/Konstrukteurin, *die;* (*of clothes*) Modedesigner, *der*/-designerin, *die;* (*Theatre: stage ~*) Bühnenbildner, *der*/-bildnerin, *die; attrib.* Modell‹kleidung, -jeans›; **~ drug** Designerdroge, *die*

**designing** /dɪˈzaɪnɪŋ/ *adj.* (*crafty, artful, scheming*) ränkevoll; intrigant

**desirability** /dɪzaɪərəˈbɪlɪtɪ/ *n., no pl.* Wünschbarkeit, *die* (*bes. schweiz.*); **consider the ~ of sth.** erwägen, ob etw. wünschenswert ist

**desirable** /dɪˈzaɪərəbl/ *adj.* **(A)** (*worth having or wishing for*) wünschenswert; **'knowledge of French ~'** „Französischkenntnisse erwünscht“; **(B)** (*causing desire*) attraktiv; begehrenswert ‹Frau›

**desire** /dɪˈzaɪə(r)/ **(1)** *n.* **(A)** (*wish*) Wunsch, *der* (**for** nach); (*longing*) Sehnsucht, *die* (**for** nach); **~ to do sth.** Wunsch, etw. zu tun; **~ for wealth** Verlangen nach Reichtum; **~ for freedom/peace** Freiheits-/Friedenswille, *der;* **his ~ for adventure** seine Abenteuerlust; **I have no ~ to see him** ich habe nicht den Wunsch, ihn zu sehen; **I have no ~ to cause you any trouble** ich möchte Ihnen keine Unannehmlichkeiten bereiten; **(B)** (*request*) Wunsch, *der;* **at your ~:** auf Ihren Wunsch; **(C)** (*thing desired*) **she is my heart's ~:** sie ist die Frau meines Herzens; **(D)** (*lust*) Verlangen, *das;* **fleshly ~s** fleischliche Begierden.

**(2)** *v.t.* **(A)** (*wish*) sich (*Dat.*) wünschen; (*long for*) sich sehnen nach; **he only ~d her happiness** er wollte nur ihr Glück; **(B)** (*request*) wünschen; **as ~d, the door has been painted red** die Tür ist, wie gewünscht, rot gestrichen worden; **the furniture can be arranged as ~d** die Einrichtung kann ganz nach Wunsch gestaltet werden; **what do you ~ me to do?** was habe ich zu tun?; **(C)** (*ask for*) **leave much to be ~d** viel zu wünschen übrig lassen; **(D)** (*sexually*) begehren ‹Mann, Frau›; **(E)** (*arch.: pray, entreat*) ersuchen (*geh.*)

**desirous** /dɪˈzaɪərəs/ *pred. adj.* (*formal*) **be ~ to do sth.** den Wunsch haben, etw. zu tun; **be ~ of sth.** etw. wünschen

**desist** /dɪˈzɪst, dɪˈsɪst/ *v.i.* (*literary*) einhalten (*geh.*); **~ from sth.** von etw. ablassen (*geh.*); **~ in one's efforts to do sth.** von seinen Bemühungen ablassen, etw. zu tun

**desk** /desk/ *n.* **(A)** Schreibtisch, *der;* (*in school*) Tisch, *der;* (*teacher's raised ~*) Pult, *das;* **~ unit** Schreibplatz, *der;* **~ copy** Arbeitsexemplar, *das;* **~ dictionary** Wörterbuch für den Schreibtisch; **(B)** (*compartment*) (*for cashier*) Kasse, *die;* (*for receptionist*) Rezeption, *die;* **information ~:** Auskunft, *die;* **sales ~:** Verkauf, *der;* **(C)** (*music stand*) Notenpult, *das;* **(D)** (*section of newspaper office*) Ressort, *das*

**desk: ~-bound** *adj.* an den Schreibtisch gefesselt (*fig.*); **~ calendar, ~ diary** *ns.* Tischkalender, *der;* **~ editor** *n.* Manuskriptbearbeiter, *der*/-bearbeiterin, *die;* Lektor, *der*/Lektorin, *die;* **~ lamp** *n.* Schreibtischlampe, *die;* **~top** *adj.* **~top publishing** Desktoppublishing, *das;* **~top computer** Tischcomputer, *der*

**desolate** **(1)** /ˈdesələt/ *adj.* **(A)** (*ruinous, neglected, barren*) trostlos ‹Haus, Ort›; desolat ‹Zustand›; **(B)** (*solitary*) einsam; **(C)** (*uninhabited*) öde; verlassen; **(D)** (*forlorn, wretched*) trostlos ‹Leben›; arm ‹Seele›; verzweifelt ‹Schrei›. **(2)** /ˈdesəleɪt/ *v.t.* **(A)** (*depopulate*) entvölkern; **(B)** (*devastate*) verwüsten ‹Land›; **(C)** (*make wretched*) in Verzweiflung stürzen

**desolation** /desəˈleɪʃn/ *n.* **(A)** (*desolating*) Verwüstung, *die;* **(B)** (*neglected, solitary, or barren state*) Öde, *die;* (*state of ruin*) Verwüstung, *die;* **(C)** (*loneliness, being forsaken*) Verlassenheit, *die;* **(D)** (*grief, wretchedness*) Verzweiflung, *die*

**despair** /dɪ'speə(r)/ ❶ *n.* Ⓐ Verzweiflung, *die;* **commit suicide in ~:** aus Verzweiflung Selbstmord begehen; **a cry of ~:** ein Verzweiflungsschrei; **his ~ of ever seeing her again** seine aufgegebene Hoffnung, sie je wiederzusehen; Ⓑ *(cause)* **be the ~ of sb.** jmdn. zur Verzweiflung bringen *od.* verzweifeln lassen. ❷ *v.i.* Ⓐ verzweifeln; Ⓑ **~ of doing sth.** die Hoffnung aufgeben, etw. zu tun; **~ of sth.** die Hoffnung auf etw. *(Akk.)* aufgeben

**despatch** *(Brit.)* ⇒ **dispatch**

**desperado** /despə'rɑːdəʊ/ *n., pl.* **~es** *(Amer.:* **~s)** Desperado, *der*

**desperate** /'despərət/ *adj.* Ⓐ verzweifelt; *(coll.: urgent)* dringend; **get** *or* **become ~:** verzweifeln; **feel ~:** verzweifelt sein; **be ~ for sth.** etw. dringend brauchen; **he was ~ for a beer** *(coll.)* er lechzte nach einem Bier; **be ~ to do sth.** verzweifelt versuchen, etw. zu tun; **don't do anything ~:** tun Sie nur nichts Unüberlegtes!; Ⓑ *(staking all on a small chance)* extrem ‹Maßnahmen, Lösung›; **a ~ disease must have a ~ remedy** *(fig.)* extreme Situationen erfordern extreme Maßnahmen; Ⓒ *(extremely dangerous or serious)* verzweifelt ‹Lage, Situation›; **things are getting ~:** die Lage wird immer verzweifelter; Ⓓ *(extremely bad)* schrecklich; **be in ~ need of sth.** etw. äußerst dringend brauchen

**desperately** /'despərətlɪ/ *adv.* Ⓐ verzweifelt; hoffnungslos ‹verliebt›; *(urgently)* dringend; *(recklessly, with extreme energy)* verzweifelt; **be ~ ill** *or* **sick** todkrank sein; Ⓑ *(appallingly, shockingly, extremely)* schrecklich *(ugs.)*

**desperation** /despə'reɪʃn/ *n.* Verzweiflung, *die;* **out of** *or* **in [sheer] ~:** aus [lauter] Verzweiflung; **be in ~:** verzweifelt sein; **act** *or* **deed of ~:** Verzweiflungstat, *die;* **fight with ~:** verzweifelt kämpfen

**despicable** /'despɪkəbl/ *adj.*, **despicably** /'despɪkəblɪ/ *adv.* verabscheuungswürdig

**despise** /dɪ'spaɪz/ *v.t.* verachten; verschmähen *(geh.)* ‹Geschenke›; **this is not to be ~d** das ist nicht zu verachten

**despite** /dɪ'spaɪt/ *prep.* trotz; **~ what she said** ungeachtet dessen, was sie sagte; **~ his warning** trotz seiner Warnung

**despoil** /dɪ'spɔɪl/ *v.t. (literary)* berauben **(of** *Gen.*); ausplündern

**despoliation** /dɪspəʊlɪ'eɪʃn/ *n.* Plünderung, *die*

**despond** /dɪ'spɒnd/ *n. (arch.)* **Slough of D~** *(literary)* Pfuhl der Verzweiflung *(dichter.)*

**despondency** /dɪ'spɒndənsɪ/ *n., no pl.* Niedergeschlagenheit, *die;* **view a situation with ~:** einer Lage sehr mutlos gegenüberstehen; **fall into ~:** den Mut verlieren; **answer in a tone of ~:** bedrückt antworten

**despondent** /dɪ'spɒndənt/ *adj.* niedergeschlagen; bedrückt; **be ~ about sth.** wegen etw. *od.* über etw. *(Akk.)* bedrückt sein; **feel ~:** niedergeschlagen sein; **grow** *or* **get ~:** mutlos werden; **don't become ~!** nur Mut!

**despondently** /dɪ'spɒndəntlɪ/ *adv.* niedergeschlagen

**despot** /'despɒt/ *n.* Despot, *der*

**despotic** /dɪ'spɒtɪk/ *adj.*, **despotically** /dɪ'spɒtɪkəlɪ/ *adv.* despotisch

**despotism** /'despətɪzm/ *n. (tyranny)* Despotie, *die;* Gewaltherrschaft, *die; (political system)* Despotismus, *der; (fig.: absolute power)* Tyrannei, *die*

**dessert** /dɪ'zɜːt/ *n.* Ⓐ süße Nachspeise; Ⓑ *(Brit.: after dinner)* Dessert, *das;* Nachtisch, *der*

**dessert: ~ apple** *n.* Dessertapfel, *der;* **~spoon** *n.* Esslöffel, *der;* **~spoonful** *n.* Esslöffel, *der;* **a ~spoonful** ein Esslöffel; **~ wine** *n.* Dessertwein, *der*

**destabilize** /diː'steɪbɪlaɪz/ *v.t. (Polit.)* destabilisieren

**destination** /destɪ'neɪʃn/ *n. (of person)* Reiseziel, *das; (of goods)* Bestimmungsort, *der; (of train, bus)* Zielort, *der;* **arrive at one's ~:** am Ziel ankommen; **place/port of ~:** Bestimmungsort, *der*/-hafen, *der*

**destine** /'destɪn/ *v.t.* bestimmen; **~ sb. for sth.** jmdn. für etw. bestimmen; ‹Schicksal:› jmdn. für etw. vorbestimmen; **be ~d to do sth.** dazu ausersehen *od.* bestimmt sein, etw. zu tun; **we were ~d [never] to meet again** wir sollten uns [nie] wieder sehen; **be ~d for sth.** für etw. bestimmt sein; **qualities which ~d him for leadership** Eigenschaften, die ihn für Führungsaufgaben prädestinierten

**destiny** /'destɪnɪ/ *n.* Ⓐ Schicksal, *das;* Los, *das;* **find one's ~:** seine Bestimmung finden; Ⓑ *no art. (power)* das Schicksal

**destitute** /'destɪtjuːt/ *adj.* Ⓐ *(without resources)* mittellos; **the ~ [poor]** die Mittellosen; Ⓑ *(devoid)* **be ~ of sth.** *(formal)* einer Sache *(Gen.)* bar sein *(geh.)*

**destitution** /destɪ'tjuːʃn/ *n., no pl.* Armut, *die;* Not, *die*

**destroy** /dɪ'strɔɪ/ *v.t.* Ⓐ *(demolish)* zerstören; kaputtmachen *(ugs.)* ‹Tisch, Stuhl, Uhr, Schachtel›; **the paintings were ~ed by fire** die Gemälde wurden durch einen Brand vernichtet; Ⓑ *(make useless)* vernichten ‹Ernte, Papiere, Dokumente›; Ⓒ *(kill, annihilate)* vernichten ‹Feind, Insekten›; **the dog will have to be ~ed** der Hund muss eingeschläfert werden; Ⓓ *(fig.)* zunichte machen ‹Hoffnungen, Chancen›; ruinieren ‹Zukunft›; zerstören ‹Glück, Freundschaft, Schönheit, Macht›

**destroyer** /dɪ'strɔɪə(r)/ *n. (also Naut.)* Zerstörer, *der*

**destruct** /dɪ'strʌkt/ *(Amer.)* ❶ *v.t. & i.* zerstören. ❷ *n.* Zerstörung, *die*

**destruction** /dɪ'strʌkʃn/ *n.* Ⓐ Zerstörung, *die; (of documents, mankind, a regime, an enemy)* Vernichtung, *die; (of toys, small objects)* Kaputtmachen, *das (ugs.); (of hopes)* Zunichtemachen, *das;* **bring about one's own ~:** sich selbst zugrunde richten; Ⓑ *(cause of ruin)* Untergang, *der*

**destructive** /dɪ'strʌktɪv/ *adj.* Ⓐ *(destroying, tending to destroy)* zerstörerisch; verheerend ‹Sturm, Feuer, Krieg›; zersetzend ‹Einfluss, Haltung, Tendenz›; destruktiv ‹Mensch›; **~ urge** Destruktionstrieb, *der (Psych.);* Zerstörungswut, *die;* Ⓑ *(negative)* destruktiv ‹Kritik, Vorstellung, Kommentar, Einfluss, Ziel›

**destructively** /dɪ'strʌktɪvlɪ/ *adv.* zerstörerisch; **behave ~:** sich destruktiv aufführen

**destructor** /dɪ'strʌktə(r)/ *n. (Brit.)* Müllverbrennungsanlage, *die*

**desuetude** /dɪ'sjuːɪtjuːd, 'deswɪtjuːd/ *n. (literary)* **fall into ~:** in Vergessenheit geraten; ‹Wort, Sitte:› außer Gebrauch kommen

**desultory** /'desəltərɪ/ *adj.* Ⓐ *(going from one subject to another, disconnected)* sprunghaft; zwanglos, ungezwungen ‹Gespräch›; Ⓑ *(unmethodical)* planlos

**detach** /dɪ'tætʃ/ *v.t.* Ⓐ *(unfasten)* entfernen; ablösen ‹Aufgeklebtes›; abbrechen ‹Angewachsenes›; abtrennen ‹zu Entfernendes›; abnehmen ‹wieder zu Befestigendes›; abhängen ‹Angekuppeltes›; herausnehmen ‹innen Befindliches›; **a couple of pages of the book have become ~ed** einige Seiten des Buches sind lose; **~ oneself from sb.** sich von jmdm. lösen; Ⓑ *(Mil., Navy)* abkommandieren **(from** aus); detachieren *(veralt.)*

**detachable** /dɪ'tætʃəbl/ *adj.* abnehmbar; herausnehmbar ‹Futter›

**detached** /dɪ'tætʃt/ *adj.* Ⓐ *(impartial)* unvoreingenommen; *(unemotional)* unbeteiligt; **~ garage** freistehende Garage; Ⓑ *(separate)* **~ house** Einzelhaus, *das;* **~ retina** abgelöste Netzhaut

**detachment** /dɪ'tætʃmənt/ *n.* Ⓐ *(detaching)* ⇒ **detach** A: Entfernen, *das;* Ablösen, *das;* Abbrechen, *das;* Abtrennen, *das;* Abnehmen, *das;* Abhängen, *das;* Herausnehmen, *das;* Ⓑ *(Mil., Navy)* Abteilung, *die;* Detachement, *das (veralt.);* Ⓒ *(being aloof)* Abstand, *der;* Distanz, *die;* Ⓓ *(independence of judgement)* Unvoreingenommenheit, *die*

**detail** /'diːteɪl/ ❶ *n.* Ⓐ *(item)* Einzelheit, *die;* Detail, *das;* **enter** *or* **go into ~s** ins Detail gehen; auf Einzelheiten eingehen; **a minor ~:** eine Kleinigkeit; **leave the ~s to sb. else** die Kleinarbeit [einem] anderen überlassen; **our correspondent will be giving you the ~s** unser Korrespondent wird [Ihnen] im Einzelnen darüber berichten; **plan sth. down to the last ~:** etw. bis ins letzte Detail planen; **but that is a ~** *(iron.)* aber was macht das schon?; Ⓑ *(dealing with things item by item)* **in ~:** Punkt für Punkt; **have too much ~:** zu sehr ins Einzelne *od.* Detail gehen; **we haven't discussed anything in ~ yet** wir haben bisher noch nicht im Einzelnen darüber gesprochen; **in great** *or* **much ~:** in allen Einzelheiten; **in greater ~:** [noch] näher; **in minute ~:** haarklein; **go into ~:** ins Detail gehen; auf Einzelheiten eingehen; **attention to ~:** Sorgfalt in den Details; Ⓒ *(account)* Aufstellung, *die;* Ⓓ *(in building, picture, etc.)* Detail, *das;* Ⓔ *(part of picture)* Ausschnitt, *der;* Ⓕ *(Mil.)* Dienstplan, *der;* Ⓖ *(body for special duty)* Kommando, *das.*
❷ *v.t.* Ⓐ *(list)* einzeln aufführen; **be fully ~ed** *(stated, described)* im Detail ausgeführt werden; Ⓑ *(Mil.)* abkommandieren

**detailed** /'diːteɪld/ *adj.* detailliert; eingehend ‹Studie›

**detain** /dɪ'teɪn/ *v.t.* Ⓐ *(keep in confinement)* festhalten; *(take into confinement)* verhaften; Ⓑ *(delay)* aufhalten; **do not let me ~ you** lassen Sie sich durch mich nicht aufhalten

**detainee** /dɪteɪ'niː/ *n.* Verhaftete, *der/die*

**detect** /dɪ'tekt/ *v.t.* Ⓐ *(discover presence of)* entdecken; bemerken ‹Trauer, Verärgerung›; wahrnehmen ‹Bewegung›; aufdecken ‹Irrtum, Verbrechen›; durchschauen ‹Beweggrund›; feststellen ‹Strahlung›; **~ a note of anger in sb.'s voice** eine gewisse Verärgerung aus jmds. Stimme heraushören; Ⓑ *(reveal guilt of)* **~ sb. in doing sth.** jmdn. bei etw. ertappen

**detectable** /dɪ'tektəbl/ *adj.* feststellbar; wahrnehmbar ‹Bewegung›

**detection** /dɪ'tekʃn/ *n.* Ⓐ ⇒ **detect** A: Entdeckung, *die;* Bemerken, *das;* Wahrnehmung, *die;* Aufdeckung, *die;* Durchschauen, *das;* Feststellung, *die;* **in order to escape ~:** um nicht entdeckt zu werden; **try to escape ~:** versuchen, unentdeckt zu bleiben; Ⓑ *(work of detective)* Ermittlungsarbeit, *die*

**detective** /dɪ'tektɪv/ ❶ *n.* ▶ **1261** Detektiv, *der; (policeman)* Kriminalbeamte, *der*/Kriminalbeamtin, *die;* **private ~:** Privatdetektiv, *der.* ❷ *attrib. adj.* Kriminal-; **~ novel** Kriminalroman, *der;* **~ work** Ermittlungsarbeit, *die;* **~ story** Detektivgeschichte, *die*

**detector** /dɪ'tektə(r)/ *n.* Ⓐ *(device)* Detektor, *der; (indicator)* Anzeiger, *der;* Ⓑ *(Electr.)* [Kristall]detektor, *der*

**détente** /deɪ'tɑ̃t/ *n. (Polit.)* Entspannung, *die*

**detention** /dɪ'tenʃn/ *n.* Ⓐ Festnahme, *die; (confinement)* Haft, *die;* Ⓑ *(Sch.)* Nachsitzen, *das; (Mil.)* Arrest, *der (veralt.);* **give sb. two hours' ~:** jmdn. zwei Stunden nachsitzen lassen; Ⓒ *(delay)* [unfreiwilliger] Aufenthalt

**de'tention: ~ camp** *n. (prison camp)* [Gefangenen]lager, *das; (internment camp)* [Internierungs]lager, *das;* **~ centre** *n. (Brit.)* Jugendstrafanstalt, *die*

**deter** /dɪ'tɜː(r)/ *v.t.*, **-rr-** abschrecken; **~ sb. from sth.** jmdn. von etw. abhalten; **~ sb. from doing sth.** jmdn. davon abhalten, etw. zu tun; **the danger did not ~ him** er ließ sich durch die Gefahr nicht abschrecken; die Gefahr schreckte ihn nicht *(geh.);* **be ~red by sth.** sich durch etw. abschrecken lassen

**detergent** /dɪ'tɜːdʒənt/ ❶ *adj.* reinigend. ❷ *n.* Reinigungsmittel, *das; (for washing)* Waschmittel, *das;* Detergens, *das (Chemie)*

**deteriorate** /dɪ'tɪərɪəreɪt/ ❶ *v.t.* verschlechtern; verringern, mindern ‹Wert›. ❷ *v.i.* sich verschlechtern; ‹Haus:› verfallen, verkommen; ‹Holz, Leder:› verrotten; **his condition** *or* **he has ~d** sein Zustand hat sich verschlechtert; **his work has ~d** seine Arbeit hat nachgelassen; **~ in value** an Wert verlieren

**deterioration** /dɪtɪərɪə'reɪʃn/ *n.* ⇒ **deteriorate** 2: Verschlechterung, *die;* Verfall, *der;* Verrottung, *die;* **preserve paintings from ~:** Gemälde vor Schädigungen schützen

**determinable** /dɪ'tɜːmɪnəbl/ *adj. (capable of being fixed or ascertained)* bestimmbar; **sth. is ~:** etw. lässt sich bestimmen

d

**determinate** /dɪ'tɜ:mɪnət/ *adj.* **A** (*limited, finite*) begrenzt; **B** (*distinct*) bestimmt; **C** (*definitive*) eindeutig; fest ‹Begriff›

**determination** /dɪtɜ:mɪ'neɪʃn/ *n.* **A** (*ascertainment, definition*) Bestimmung, *die;* **B** (*resoluteness*) Entschlossenheit, *die;* **with [sudden] ~:** [kurz] entschlossen; **he had an air of ~ about him** er wirkte fest entschlossen; **C** (*intention*) [feste] Absicht; **D** (*Law: ending*) Ablauf, *der;* **E** (*judicial decision*) Entscheidung, *die;* **F** (*fixing beforehand*) Festlegung, *die*

**determine** /dɪ'tɜ:mɪn/ ❶ *v.t.* **A** (*decide*) beschließen; **~ to do sth.** beschließen, etw. zu tun; sich entschließen, etw. zu tun; **B** (*make decide*) veranlassen; **~ sb. to do sth.** jmdn. dazu veranlassen, etw. zu tun; **C** (*be a decisive factor for*) bestimmen; entscheiden über (+ *Akk.*); **D** (*ascertain, define*) feststellen; bestimmen; **E** (*fix beforehand*) festlegen; **F** (*Law: end*) beenden. ❷ *v.i.* (*decide*) **~ on doing sth.** beschließen, etw. zu tun; **~ on sth.** sich für etw. entscheiden

**determined** /dɪ'tɜ:mɪnd/ *adj.* **A** (*resolved*) **be ~ to do** *or* **on doing sth.** etw. unbedingt tun wollen; fest entschlossen sein, etw. zu tun; **sb. is ~ that ...:** es ist für jmdn. beschlossene Sache, dass ...; **I am ~ that he shall win** ich werde alles Mögliche tun, dass er siegt; **B** (*resolute*) entschlossen; resolut ‹Person›; **C** (*fixed*) bestimmt

**determinedly** /dɪ'tɜ:mɪndlɪ/ *adv.* entschlossen

**determinism** /dɪ'tɜ:mɪnɪzm/ *n.* Determinismus, *der*

**deterrence** /dɪ'terəns/ *n.* Abschreckung, *die*

**deterrent** /dɪ'terənt/ ❶ *adj.* abschreckend. ❷ *n.* Abschreckungsmittel, *das* (**to** für); **~ strategy** Strategie der Abschreckung

**detest** /dɪ'test/ *v.t.* verabscheuen; **~ doing sth.** es verabscheuen, etw. zu tun

**detestable** /dɪ'testəbl/ *adj.* verabscheuenswert; verabscheuungswürdig

**detestably** /dɪ'testəblɪ/ *adv.* abscheulich

**detestation** /di:te'steɪʃn/ *n., no pl.* Abscheu, *der* (**of** vor + *Dat.*)

**dethrone** /di:'θrəʊn/ *v.t.* (*lit. or fig.*) entthronen

**dethronement** /di:'θrəʊnmənt/ *n.* (*lit. or fig.*) Entthronung, *die*

**detonate** /'detəneɪt/ ❶ *v.i.* detonieren. ❷ *v.t.* zur Explosion bringen; zünden

**detonation** /detə'neɪʃn/ *n.* **A** (*detonating*) Detonation, *die;* **B** (*Motor Veh.*) Klopfen, *das*

**detonator** /'detəneɪtə(r)/ *n.* **A** (*part of bomb or shell*) Sprengkapsel, *die;* Detonator, *der;* **B** (*Railw.*) Knallkapsel, *die*

**detour** /'di:tʊə(r)/ ❶ *n.* Umweg, *der;* (*in a road, river*) Bogen, *der;* Schleife, *die;* (*diversion*) Umleitung, *die;* **make a ~:** einen Umweg machen. ❷ *v.t.* umleiten

**detox** (*coll.*) ❶ /'di:tɒks/ *n.* Entzug, *der;* **be in ~:** auf Entzug sein. ❷ /di:'tɒks/ *v.t.* entziehen (*ugs.*) ‹Drogensüchtigen, Alkoholiker›. ❸ /di:'tɒks/ *v.i.* einen Entzug machen.

**detoxification** /di:tɒksɪfɪ'keɪʃn/ *n., no pl.* Entgiftung, *die;* Detoxikation, *die* (*fachspr.*)

**detoxify** /di:'tɒksɪfaɪ/ ❶ *v.t.* entgiften; unschädlich machen ‹Gift usw.›. ❷ *v.i* sich entgiften

**detract** /dɪ'trækt/ *v.i.* **~ from sth.** etw. beeinträchtigen; **~ from sb.'s merits** jmds. Verdienste schmälern

**detraction** /dɪ'trækʃn/ *n.* Beeinträchtigung, *die* (**from** *Gen.*); (*defamation*) Schmähung, *die*

**detractor** /dɪ'træktə(r)/ *n.* Verleumder, *der*/Verleumderin, *die*

**detriment** /'detrɪmənt/ *n.* Schaden, *der;* **to the ~ of sth.** zum Nachteil *od.* Schaden einer Sache (*Gen.*); **without ~ to** ohne Schaden für; **I know nothing to his ~:** mir ist nichts Nachteiliges über ihn bekannt

**detrimental** /detrɪ'mentl/ *adj.* schädlich; **be ~ to sth.** einer Sache (*Dat.*) schaden *od.* (*geh.*) abträglich sein

**detrimentally** /detrɪ'mentəlɪ/ *adv.* auf schädliche Weise

**detritus** /dɪ'traɪtəs/ *n., no pl.* **A** (*debris*) Überbleibsel, *das;* **B** (*Geol.*) Geröll, *das;* Detritus, *der*

**de trop** /də 'trəʊ/ *pred. adj.* fehl am Platz; überflüssig

**deuce**[1] /dju:s/ *n.* **A** (*on dice; arch. Cards*) Zwei, *die;* **B** (*Tennis*) Einstand, *der*

**deuce**[2] (*coll.*) ⇒ **devil** 1 C

**deuced** /dju:sɪd, dju:st/ *adj., adv.* (*arch.*) ⇒ **damned** 1 B, C, 2

**deus ex machina** /deɪəs eks 'mɑ:kɪnə, di:əs eks 'mɑ:kɪnə/ *n.* Deus ex Machina, *der*

**deuterium** /dju:'tɪərɪəm/ *n.* Deuterium, *das*

**Deuteronomy** /dju:tə'rɒnəmɪ/ *n.* (*Bibl.*) das fünfte Buch Mose

**Deutschmark** /'dɔɪtʃmɑ:k/ *n.* Deutsche Mark

**devaluation** /di:vælju:'eɪʃn/ *n.* **A** Abwertung, *die;* **B** (*Econ.*) Abwertung, *die;* Devalvation, *die*

**devalue** /di:'vælju:/ *v.t.* **A** (*reduce value of*) abwerten; **B** (*Econ.*) abwerten; devalvieren

**devastate** /'devəsteɪt/ *v.t.* verwüsten; verheeren; (*fig.*) niederschmettern

**devastating** /'devəsteɪtɪŋ/ *adj.* verheerend; niederschmetternd ‹Nachricht, Analyse›; vernichtend ‹Spielweise, Kritik›

**devastation** /devə'steɪʃn/ *n., no pl.* Verwüstung, *die;* Verheerung, *die*

**develop** /dɪ'veləp/ ❶ *v.t.* **A** (*bring into existence*) entwickeln; aufbauen ‹Handel, Handelszentrum›; **the girl had ~ed a mature figure** die Figur des Mädchens war voll entwickelt; **the machine was ~ed from their plans** die Maschine wurde nach ihren Plänen entwickelt; **~ a business from scratch** ein Geschäft neu aufziehen; **B** (*bring to more evident form*) entwickeln ‹Instinkt, Fähigkeiten, Kräfte›; entfalten ‹Persönlichkeit, Individualität›; erschließen ‹natürliche Ressourcen›; **C** (*bring to fuller form*) entwickeln; (*expand; make more sophisticated*) weiterentwickeln; ausbauen ‹Verkehrsnetz, System, Handel, Verkehr, Position›; wachsen lassen ‹Pflanze, Korn›; **~ sth. further** etw. weiterentwickeln; **~ an essay into a book** einen Essay zu einem Buch ausbauen; **a highly ~ed civilization** eine hoch entwickelte Zivilisation; **D** (*begin to exhibit, begin to suffer from*) annehmen ‹Gewohnheit›; bei sich entdecken ‹Vorliebe›; bekommen ‹Krankheit, Fieber, Lust›; entwickeln ‹Talent, Stärke›; erkranken an (+ *Dat.*) ‹Krebs, Tumor›; **~ a taste for sth.** Geschmack an etw. (*Akk.*) finden; **the car ~ed a fault** an dem Wagen ist ein Defekt aufgetreten; **E** (*Photog.*) entwickeln; **F** (*construct buildings etc. on, convert to new use*) erschließen; sanieren ‹Altstadt›; aufschließen ‹Schacht›; **G** (*Mus.*) durchführen ‹Thema›; **H** (*Chess*) entwickeln; **I** (*Amer.: make known*) an den Tag bringen.
❷ *v.i.* **A** (*come into existence, become evident*) sich entwickeln (**from** aus; **into** zu); ‹Defekt, Symptome, Erkrankungen:› auftreten; **B** (*become fuller*) sich [weiter]entwickeln (**into** zu); **C** (*Amer.: become known*) an den Tag kommen; **it ~ed that ...:** es stellte sich heraus, dass ...

**developable** /dɪ'veləpəbl/ *adj.* entwicklungsfähig; erschließungsfähig ‹Gebiet›

**developer** /dɪ'veləpə(r)/ *n.* **A** (*Photog.*) (*chemical agent*) Entwickler, *der;* **B** (*person who develops real estate*) ≈ Bauunternehmer, *der;* **C** (*person who matures*) **late** *or* **slow ~:** Spätentwickler, *der*

**developing:** **~ country** *n.* Entwicklungsland, *das;* **~ world** *n.* Entwicklungsländer *Pl.*

**development** /dɪ'veləpmənt/ *n.* **A** (*bringing into existence*) Entwicklung, *die* (**from** aus, **into** zu); **B** (*bringing into more evident form*) (*of individuality*) Entfaltung, *die;* (*of heat, gas, vapour*) Entwicklung, *die;* (*of natural resources etc.*) Erschließung, *die;* **sth. is in the course of ~:** etw. befindet sich in der Entwicklung; **C** (*bringing into fuller form*) Entwicklung, *die;* (*expansion*) Ausbau, *der;* Weiterentwicklung, *die;* **be capable of [further] ~:** noch weiter entwicklungsfähig sein; **D** (*beginning to exhibit*) Entwicklung, die; (*of a talent also*) Entfaltung, *die;* (*beginning to suffer from*) Beginn, *der;* **E** (*of land etc.*) Erschließung, *die;* **regional ~:** Regionalplanung, *die;* **F** (*evolution*) Entwicklung, *die;* **G** (*full-grown state*) Vollendung, *die;* **H** (*developed product or form*) **a ~ of sth.** eine Fortentwicklung *od.* Weiterentwicklung einer Sache; **at that time tea bags were a new ~:** damals waren Teebeutel eine Neuerung; **I** (*Photog.*) Entwickeln, *das;* Entwicklung, *die;* **J** (*Mus.*) Durchführung, *die;* **K** (*Chess*) Entwicklung, *die;* **L** (*developed land*) **[new] ~:** Neubaugebiet, *das*

**developmental** /dɪveləp'mentl/ *adj.* Entwicklungs-

**de'velopment area** *n.* (*Brit.*) Entwicklungsgebiet, *das*

**deviance** /'di:vɪəns/, **deviancy** /'di:vɪənsɪ/ *n.* abweichendes Verhalten; Devianz, *die* (*Soziol.*)

**deviant** /'di:vɪənt/ ❶ *adj.* [von der Norm] abweichend; deviant (*Soziol.*). ❷ *n.* [von der Norm] Abweichende, *der/die/das;* **a sexual ~:** jmd. mit [von der Norm] abweichendem Sexualverhalten; sexuell devianter Mensch (*Soziol.*)

**deviate** /'di:vɪeɪt/ *v.i.* (*lit. or fig.*) abweichen

**deviation** /di:vɪ'eɪʃn/ *n.* **A** (*deviating*) Abweichung, *die;* **B** (*of compass needle*) Ablenkung, *die;* Deviation, *die;* **C** (*Statistics*) **[standard] ~:** [Standard]abweichung, *die*

**deviationism** /di:vɪ'eɪʃənɪzm/ *n.* (*Polit.*) Abweichlertum, *das*

**deviationist** /di:vɪ'eɪʃənɪst/ *n.* (*Polit.*) Abweichler, *der*/Abweichlerin, *die*

**device** /dɪ'vaɪs/ *n.* **A** (*contrivance*) Gerät, *das;* (*as part of sth.*) Vorrichtung, *die;* **nuclear ~:** atomarer Sprengkörper; **B** (*plan, scheme*) List, *die;* **rhetorical ~s** rhetorische Kunstgriffe; **C** (*drawing, design, figure*) Verzierung, *die;* **D** (*emblematic or heraldic design*) Emblem, *das;* **E** (*motto*) Motto, *das;* Devise, *die;* **F** *in pl.* (*fancy, will*) **leave sb. to his own ~s** jmdn. sich (*Dat.*) selbst überlassen; **be left to one's own ~s** sich (*Dat.*) selbst überlassen sein

**devil** /'devl/ ❶ *n.* **A** (*Satan*) **the D~:** der Teufel; **B** (*heathen god*) Götze, *der;* (*evil spirit, Satan's follower*) Teufel, *der;* **the ~ of greed** der Dämon Habgier; **C** *or* **D~** (*coll.*) **who/where/what** *etc.* **the ~?** wer/wo/was *usw.* zum Teufel? (*salopp*); **the ~ take him!** hol ihn der Teufel! (*salopp*); **he's got the ~ in him** er hat den Teufel im Leib (*ugs.*); **the ~!** Teufel auch! (*salopp*); **the ~ knows** weiß der Teufel (*salopp*); **there will be the ~ to pay** da ist der Teufel los (*ugs.*); **go to the ~:** zum Teufel gehen (*salopp*); sich zum Teufel scheren (*salopp*); **[you can] go to the ~!** scher dich zum Teufel! (*salopp*); **work/shout like the ~:** wie ein Besessener arbeiten/schreien; **run/fight like the ~:** wie der Teufel rennen/kämpfen (*ugs.*); **between the ~ and the deep [blue] sea** in einer Zwickmühle (*ugs.*); **~ take it!** verdammt noch mal!; **it was ~ take the hindmost** es galt nur noch: Rette sich, wer kann!; **play the ~ with sb./sth.** jmdm./einer Sache übel mitspielen; **better the ~ one knows** lieber das bekannte Übel; **speak** *or* **talk of the ~ [and he will appear]** wenn man vom Teufel spricht[, kommt er]; ⇒ *also* **idle** 1 F; **needs; D a** *or* **the ~ of a mess** ein verteufelter Schlamassel (*ugs.*); **be in a ~ of a mess** im dicksten Schlamassel sitzen (*ugs.*); **a** *or* **the ~ of a problem** ein verteufelt schwieriges Problem; **have a ~ of a temper** verteufelt jähzornig sein (*ugs.*); **have the ~ of a time** es verteufelt schwer haben; **be a ~!** sei kein Frosch!; **he is a ~ of a [good] teacher** er ist ein verdammt guter Lehrer (*ugs.*); **this car is the [very] ~ to start** dieses Auto lässt sich verteufelt schwer starten (*ugs.*); **the crossword is a real ~:** das Kreuzworträtsel ist verteufelt schwer (*ugs.*); **E** (*wicked or cruel person, vicious animal*) Teufel, *der* (*fig.*); (*mischievously energetic or self-willed person*) Teufel, *der* (*fig. ugs.*); Teufelsbraten, *der* (*ugs. scherzh.*); (*able, clever person*) Ass, *das* (*ugs.*); **he's a ~ with the women** er spielt mit den Frauen; **he's a clever ~:** er ist ein schlauer Hund (*ugs.*); **you ~!** (*ugs.*) du Schlingel!; **a poor**

**~:** ein armer Teufel; **lucky ~:** Glückspilz, *der* (*ugs.*); **unlucky ~:** Unglücksrabe, *der* (*ugs.*); **cheeky/naughty ~:** Frechdachs, *der* (*fam., meist scherzh.*); **queer** *or* **odd ~:** komischer Kauz; **F** (*fighting spirit*) Kampfgeist, *der;* **G** (*Law*) [*unbezahlter*] *Gehilfe eines Anwalts;* **H** (*literary hack*) *Zuarbeiter eines Schriftstellers;* **I** (*S.Afr.*) **[dust] ~:** Sandsturm, *der.* **2** *v.t.*, (*Brit.*) **-ll-** **A** (*Cookery*) *klein geschnitten und scharf gewürzt braten;* **B** (*Amer. coll.: harass, worry*) piesacken (*ugs.*)

**'devilfish** *n.* **A** (*anglerfish*) Seeteufel, *der;* **B** (*Amer.: ray*) Teufelsrochen, *der*

**devilish** /'devəlɪʃ/ **1** *adj.* **A** (*of the Devil*) teuflisch ‹Künste, Zauberei›; ‹Erfindung, Lehre› des Teufels; **B** (*damnable*) teuflisch. **2** *adv.* (*arch. coll.*) verteufelt (*ugs.*)

**devilishly** /'devəlɪʃlɪ/ *adv.* (*diabolically*) teuflisch; (*exceedingly*) verteufelt (*ugs.*)

**'devil-may-care** *adj.* sorglos-unbekümmert

**devilment** /'devlmənt/ *n.* **A** (*mischief*) Unfug, *der;* (*wild spirits*) Übermut, *der;* **be up to some ~:** Unfug treiben *od.* anstellen; **B** (*devilish phenomenon*) Teufelei, *die*

**devilry** /'devlrɪ/ *n.* **A** (*black magic*) Teufelskunst, *die;* **B** (*wickedness, cruelty*) teuflische Bosheit; (*action*) Teufelei, *die;* **C** (*mischief*) Unfug, *der;* (*hilarity*) Schabernack, *der;* **out of sheer ~:** aus purem Schabernack

**devil: ~'s 'advocate** *n.* (*RC Ch.; also fig.*) Advocatus Diaboli, *der;* **~'s 'coach-horse** *n.* (*Brit. Zool.*) Schwarzer *od.* Stinkender Moderkäfer; **~s-on-'horseback** *n.* (*Gastr.*) Austern in Röllchen aus Frühstücksspeck; Austern auf englische Art; **~'s 'own** *attrib. adj.* **the ~'s own** ein/eine verteufelt... (*ugs.*); **[take] the ~'s own time** eine verteufelt lange Zeit [dauern] (*ugs.*); **he has the ~'s own luck** er hat verteufeltes Glück (*ugs.*)

**devious** /'di:vɪəs/ *adj.* **A** (*winding*) verschlungen; **take a ~ route** einen Umweg fahren; **B** (*unscrupulous, insincere*) verschlagen ‹Person›; hinterhältig ‹Person, Methode, Tat›

**deviously** /'di:vɪəslɪ/ *adv.* hinterhältigerweise; **behave ~:** sich hinterhältig verhalten

**deviousness** /'di:vɪəsnɪs/ *n., no pl.* Hinterhältigkeit, *die;* Verschlagenheit, *die*

**devise** /dɪ'vaɪz/ *v.t.* (*plan*) entwerfen; schmieden ‹Pläne›; kreieren ‹Mode, Stil›; ausarbeiten ‹Programm›

**devoid** /dɪ'vɔɪd/ *adj.* **~ of sth.** (*lacking*) ohne etw.; bar einer Sache (*Gen.*) (*geh.*); (*free from*) frei von etw.

**devolution** /di:və'lu:ʃn/ *n.* **A** (*deputing, delegation*) Übertragung, *die;* Delegieren, *das;* (*Polit.*) Dezentralisierung, *die;* **B** (*descent of property, power, etc.*) Übergang, *der* (**on [to]** auf + *Akk.*); **C** (*Biol.*) Degeneration, *die;* **D** (*Brit. Polit.*) *Übertragung von administrativer Unabhängigkeit;* Devolution, *die* (*fachspr.*)

**devolve** /dɪ'vɒlv/ *v.i.* **A** (*be transferred*) **~ [up]on sb.** ‹Pflicht, Verantwortung, Aufgabe:› jmdm. zufallen; **B** (*descend*) vererbt werden; **~ to sb.** auf jmdn. übergehen

**Devonian** /dɪ'vəʊnɪən/ **1** *adj.* (*Geol.*) devonisch. **2** *n.* (*Geol.*) Devon, *das*

**Devonshire cream** /devnʃɪə 'kri:m/ *n.: sehr fetter Rahm;* Dickrahm, *der*

**devote** /dɪ'vəʊt/ *v.t.* (*consecrate*) widmen; **~ one's thoughts/energy to sth.** sein Denken/seine Energie auf etw. (*Akk.*) verwenden; **~ sums of money to sth.** Geldsummen für etw. bestimmen

**devoted** /dɪ'vəʊtɪd/ *adj.* treu; ergeben ‹Diener›; aufrichtig ‹Freundschaft, Liebe, Verehrung›; **he is very ~ to his work/his wife** er geht in seiner Arbeit völlig auf/liebt seine Frau innig

**devotedly** /dɪ'vəʊtɪdlɪ/ *adv.* [treu] ergeben; innig ‹lieben›

**devotee** /devə'ti:/ *n.* **A** (*enthusiast*) Anhänger, *der*/Anhängerin, *die;* (*of music, art*) Liebhaber, *der*/Liebhaberin, *die;* (*of a person*) Verehrer, *der*/Verehrerin, *die;* **B** (*pious person*) [fanatischer/glühender] Anhänger/[fanatische/glühende] Anhängerin

**devotion** /dɪ'vəʊʃn/ *n.* **A** (*addiction, loyalty, devoutness*) **~ to sb./sth.** Hingabe an jmdn./etw.; **~ to music/the arts** Liebe zur Musik/Kunst; **~ to duty** Pflichteifer, *der;* **B** (*devoting*) Weihung, *die;* **C** (*divine worship*) Anbetung, *die* (**to** *Gen.*); **D** *in pl.* (*prayers*) Gebet, *das;* **be at one's ~s** seine Andacht halten; **book of ~s** Andachtsbuch, *das*

**devotional** /dɪ'vəʊʃənl/ *adj.* fromm; andächtig ‹Gebet›; religiös ‹Literatur, Lied›; Andachts‹buch, -übung›

**devour** /dɪ'vaʊə(r)/ *v.t.* **A** verschlingen; ‹Pest:› dahinraffen (*geh.*); **B** (*absorb the attention of*) verzehren; **he was ~ed by anxiety** er verzehrte sich vor Angst

**devouring** /dɪ'vaʊərɪŋ/ *adj.* verzehrend ‹Hunger, Leidenschaft, Feuer›; verschlingend ‹Fluten›; Menschen fressend, alles verschlingend ‹Ungeheuer, Tier›

**devout** /dɪ'vaʊt/ *adj.* fromm; sehnlich ‹Wunsch›; inständig ‹Hoffnung›

**devoutly** /dɪ'vaʊtlɪ/ *adv.* in [frommer] Andacht ‹knien, beten, bekennen›; inständig ‹hoffen, wünschen›

**dew** /dju:/ **1** *n.* Tau, *der.* **2** *v.t.* (*poet./literary*) betauen (*geh.*)

**dew: ~berry** *n.* Brombeere, *die;* **~claw** *n.* Afterklaue, *die;* **~drop** *n.* Tautropfen, *der*

**Dewey system** /'dju:ɪ sɪstəm/ *n.* (*Bibliog.*) Dezimalklassifikation, *die*

**dewlap** /'dju:læp/ *n.* (*of animal*) Wamme, *die;* (*of person*) Doppelkinn, *das*

**dew: ~ point** *n.* (*Phys.*) Taupunkt, *der;* **~ pond** *n.* (*Brit.*) *flacher, künstlich angelegter Teich, in dem sich Tau- und Regenwasser sammelt*

**dewy** /'dju:ɪ/ *adj.* taufeucht; tauig (*geh.*)

**'dewy-eyed** *adj.* naiv; **go all ~:** ganz feuchte Augen bekommen

**dexter** /'dekstə(r)/ *adj.* (*Her.*) recht...; dexter (*fachspr.*)

**dexterity** /dek'sterɪtɪ/ *n., no pl.* (*skill*) Geschicklichkeit, *die;* **~ in argument** Redegewandtheit, *die*

**dexterous[ly]** ⇒ **dextr-**

**dextrose** /'dekstrəʊs/ *n.* (*Chem.*) Traubenzucker, *der;* Dextrose, *die* (*fachspr.*)

**dextrous** /'dekstrəs/ *adj.* **A** (*nimble of hand, skilful, clever*) geschickt; **B** (*using right hand*) rechtshändig

**dextrously** /'dekstrəslɪ/ *adv.* geschickt; mit großem Geschick

**DFE** *abbr.* (*Brit.*) **Department for Education and Employment**

**dhow** /daʊ/ *n.* (*Naut.*) D[h]au, *die*

**DHSS** *abbr.* (*Brit. Hist.*) **Department of Health and Social Security** *Amt für Gesundheit und Sozialwesen*

**dia.** *abbr.* **diameter** D.; Durchm.

**diabetes** /daɪə'bi:ti:z/ *n., pl. same* ▶ **1232** (*Med.*) Zuckerkrankheit, *die;* Diabetes, *der* (*fachspr.*)

**diabetic** /daɪə'betɪk, daɪə'bi:tɪk/ (*Med.*) **1** *adj.* **A** (*of diabetes*) diabetisch; **B** (*having diabetes*) diabetisch (*Med.*); zuckerkrank; **C** (*for diabetics*) Diabetiker‹nahrung, -schokolade usw.›. **2** *n.* Diabetiker, *der*/Diabetikerin, *die*

**diabolic** /daɪə'bɒlɪk/, **diabolical** /daɪə'bɒlɪkl/ *adj.* **A** (*cruel, wicked*) teuflisch; diabolisch; (*coll.: extremely bad*) mörderisch (*ugs.*) ‹Hitze›; teuflisch (*ugs.*) ‹Kälte, Wetter›; **this child is a ~ nuisance!** (*coll.*) dieses Kind kann einen zur Weißglut treiben! (*ugs.*); **shopping today was ~** (*coll.*) das Einkaufen heute war die reinste Hölle (*ugs.*); **B** (*of the Devil*) diabolisch; teuflisch

**diabolically** /daɪə'bɒlɪkəlɪ/ *adv.* (*coll.*) teuflisch (*ugs.*) ‹kalt, grausam›; mörderisch (*ugs.*) ‹heiß›

**diachronic** /daɪə'krɒnɪk/ *adj.*, **diachronically** /daɪə'krɒnɪkəlɪ/ *adv.* (*Ling.*) diachronisch

**diacritic** /daɪə'krɪtɪk/, **diacritical** /daɪə'krɪtɪkl/ **1** *adj.* **A** (*distinctive*) distinktiv (*geh.*); **B** (*Ling.*) **~ mark** *or* **sign** diakritisches Zeichen. **2** *n.* (*Ling.*) diakritisches Zeichen

**diadem** /'daɪədem/ *n.* Diadem, *das*

**diagnose** /daɪəg'nəʊz/ ▶ **1232** *v.t.* diagnostizieren ‹Krankheit›; feststellen ‹Fehler›

**diagnosis** /daɪəg'nəʊsɪs/ *n., pl.* **diagnoses** /daɪəg'nəʊsi:z/ **A** ▶ **1232** (*of disease*) Diagnose, *die;* **make a ~:** eine Diagnose stellen; **B** (*of difficulty, fault*) Feststellung, *die*

**diagnostic** /daɪəg'nɒstɪk/ **1** *adj.* diagnostisch; **~ sign** (*Med.*) Symptom, *das.* **2** *n.* (*Med.*) Symptom, *das*

**diagnostics** /daɪəg'nɒstɪks/ *n. sing.* Diagnostik, *die*

**diagonal** /daɪ'ægənl/ **1** *adj.* diagonal. **2** *n.* Diagonale, *die*

**diagonally** /daɪ'ægənəlɪ/ *adv.* diagonal

**diagram** /'daɪəgræm/ **1** *n.* **A** (*sketch*) schematische Darstellung; **I'll make a ~ to show you how to get there** ich zeichne Ihnen auf, wie Sie dorthin kommen; **B** (*graphic or symbolic representation*) Diagramm, *das;* **C** (*Geom.*) Diagramm, *das.* **2** *v.t.*, (*Brit.*) **-mm-** [in einem Diagramm] grafisch darstellen; (*make sketch of*) aufzeichnen

**diagrammatic** /daɪəgrə'mætɪk/ *adj.*, **diagrammatically** /daɪəgrə'mætɪkəlɪ/ *adv.* diagrammatisch

**dial** /'daɪəl/ **1** *n.* **A** (*of clock or watch*) Zifferblatt, *das;* **B** (*of gauge, meter, etc., on radio or television*) Skala, *die;* **C** **[sun]~:** Sonnenuhr, *die;* **D** (*Teleph.*) Wählscheibe, *die;* **E** (*Brit. coll.: face*) Visage, *die* (*salopp abwertend*). **2** *v.t.*, (*Brit.*) **-ll-** (*Teleph.*) wählen; **~ [London] direct** [nach London] durchwählen; **~ a call to somewhere/to sb.** irgendwo/bei jmdm. anrufen. **3** *v.i.*, (*Brit.*) **-ll-** (*Teleph.*) wählen

**dialect** /'daɪəlekt/ *n.* Dialekt, *der;* Mundart, *die;* (*of class*) Ausdrucksweise, *die; attrib.* **~ expression** mundartlicher *od.* dialektaler Ausdruck

**dialectal** /daɪə'lektl/ *adj.* dialektal; mundartlich

**dialectic** /daɪə'lektɪk/ **1** *n. in sing. or pl. constr. as sing.* Dialektik, *die.* **2** *adj.* **A** dialektisch; **B** (*dialectal*) dialektal; dialektisch

**dialectical** /daɪə'lektɪkl/ *adj.* **A** ⇒ **dialectic** 2 A; **B** **~ materialism** dialektischer Materialismus

**'dialling tone** *n.* (*Brit.*) Wählton, *der*

**dialogue** (*Amer.:* **dialog**) /'daɪəlɒg/ *n.* Dialog, *der;* **written in ~ [form]** in der Form eines Dialogs geschrieben

**'dialogue box** *n.* (*Computing*) Dialogbox, *die;* Dialogfenster, *das*

**'dial tone** (*Amer.*) ⇒ **dialling tone**

**dialysis** /daɪ'ælɪsɪs/ *n., pl.* **dialyses** /daɪ'ælɪsi:z/ **A** (*Chem.*) Dialyse, *die;* **B** (*Med.*) [Hämo]dialyse, *die* (*fachspr.*); Blutwäsche, *die; attrib.* **~ machine** Dialyseapparat, *der*

**diameter** /daɪ'æmɪtə(r)/ *n.* **A** Durchmesser, *der;* Diameter, *der* (*Geom.*); **B** **a magnification of eight ~s** eine achtfache Vergrößerung; **magnify 2,000 ~s** zweitausendfach vergrößern

**diametrical** /daɪə'metrɪkl/ *adj.* diametral; **I hold opinions in ~ opposition to his** meine Ansichten sind seinen diametral entgegengesetzt

**diametrically** /daɪə'metrɪkəlɪ/ *adv.* **A** (*in direct opposition*) diametral ‹entgegengesetzt, widersprechen›; **B** (*straight through*) diametrisch

**diamond** /'daɪəmənd/ **1** *n.* **A** Diamant, *der;* **it was [a case of] ~ cut ~** (*fig.*) da sind die Richtigen aneinander geraten; **B** (*figure*) Raute, *die;* Rhombus, *der;* **C** (*Cards*) Karo, *das;* ⇒ *also* **club** 1 D; **D** (*tool*) [Glaser]diamant, *der;* **E** (*Baseball*) (*space enclosed by bases*) Innenfeld, *das;* (*entire field*) Spielfeld, *das.* ⇒ *also* **rough diamond**. **2** *adj.* **A** (*made of ~[s]*) diamanten; (*set with ~[s]*) diamantenbesetzt; Diamant‹ring, -staub, -schmuck›; **B** (*rhomb-shaped*) rautenförmig

**diamond: ~-drill** *n.* Diamantbohrer, *der;* **~-field** *n.* Diamantlagerstätte, *die;* **~ 'jubilee** *n.* 60-jähriges/75-jähriges Jubiläum; **~-merchant** *n.* Diamantenhändler, *der*/-händlerin,

d

die; ~ **mine** *n.* Diamantenbergwerk, *das;* **~-shaped** *adj.* rautenförmig; ~ **'wedding** *n.* diamantene Hochzeit

**dianthus** /daɪ'ænθəs/ *n.* (*Bot.*) Nelke, *die*

**diaper** /'daɪəpə(r)/ *n.* Ⓐ (*Amer.: nappy*) Windel, *die;* Ⓑ (*fabric*) *mit kleinen Rauten o. Ä. gemustertes* [*Jacquard*]*gewebe*

**diaphanous** /daɪ'æfənəs/ *adj.* durchsichtig

**diaphragm** /'daɪəfræm/ *n.* Diaphragma, *das* (*fachspr.*); (*Anat. also*) Zwerchfell, *das;* (*Zool., Bot. also*) Scheidewand, *die;* (*Photog. also*) Blende, *die;* (*contraceptive also*) Pessar, *das;* (*Mech., Teleph. also*) Membran, *die*

**diapositive** /daɪə'pɒzɪtɪv/ *n.* (*Photog.*) Diapositiv, *das*

**diarist** /'daɪərɪst/ *n.* Tagebuchautor, *der*/-autorin, *die*

**diarrhoea** (*Amer.:* **diarrhea**) /daɪə'ri:ə/ *n.* Durchfall, *der;* Diarrhö[e], *die* (*Med.*)

**diary** /'daɪərɪ/ *n.* Ⓐ Tagebuch, *das;* **keep a ~:** [ein] Tagebuch führen; Ⓑ (*for appointments*) Terminkalender, *der;* **pocket/desk ~:** Taschen-/Tischkalender, *der*

**Diaspora** /daɪ'æspərə/ *n.* Zerstreuung der Juden; (*persons*) Diaspora, *die*

**diastolic** /daɪə'stɒlɪk/ *adj.* (*Physiol.*) diastolisch

**diatonic** /daɪə'tɒnɪk/ *adj.* (*Mus.*) diatonisch

**diatribe** /'daɪətraɪb/ *n.* (*speech*) Schmährede, *die;* (*piece of writing*) Schmähschrift, *die*

**dibber** /'dɪbə(r)/ ⇒ **dibble** 1

**dibble** /'dɪbl/ ❶ *n.* Pflanzholz, *das.* ❷ *v.t.* [mit dem Pflanzholz] pflanzen

**dice** /daɪs/ ❶ *n., pl. same* Ⓐ (*cube*) Würfel, *der;* **throw ~:** würfeln; **throw ~ for sth.** etw. auswürfeln; **no ~!** (*fig. coll.*) kommt nicht infrage!; Ⓑ *in sing.* (*game*) Würfelspiel, *das;* **play ~:** würfeln; Ⓒ *in pl.* (*Cookery*) Würfel *Pl.;* **cut into ~:** würfeln. ❷ *v.i.* würfeln (**for** um); **~ with death** mit seinem Leben spielen. ❸ *v.t.* (*Cookery*) würfeln

**dicey** /'daɪsɪ/ *adj.* (*coll.*) riskant; (*unreliable*) unzuverlässig

**dichotomy** /daɪ'kɒtəmɪ, dɪ'kɒtəmɪ/ *n.* Dichotomie, *die*

**dick** /dɪk/ *n.* Ⓐ (*coll.: detective*) Schnüffler, *der* (*ugs. abwertend*); Ⓑ (*coarse: penis*) Schwanz, *der* (*derb*); Riemen, *der* (*derb*). ⇒ *also* **clever Dick**; **Tom** A

**dickens** /'dɪkɪnz/ *n.* (*coll.*) **what/why/who** *etc.* **the ~ ...:** was/warum/wer *usw.* zum Kuckuck ... (*salopp*)

**Dickensian** /dɪ'kenzɪən/ ❶ *n.* Dickensianer. ❷ *adj.* dickenssch; **~ conditions** Zustände, wie man sie aus Dickens' Romanen kennt

**dicky**[1] (**dickey**) /'dɪkɪ/ *n.* Ⓐ ⇒ **dicky bird**; Ⓑ (*Brit. Hist.: seat*) Klappsitz (*im Fond eines Zweisitzers*); Ⓒ (*shirt front*) Vorhemd, *das*

**dicky**[2] *adj.* (*coll.*) mies (*ugs. abwertend*); klapprig (*ugs.*) ‹Herz›

**'dicky bird** *n.* (*child lang./coll.*) Piepvogel, *der* (*Kinderspr.*); (*coll.: word*) **not a ~:** kein Sterbenswörtchen

**dicta** *pl. of* **dictum**

**Dictaphone** ® /'dɪktəfəʊn/ *n.* Diktaphon, *das* (*fachspr.*); Diktiergerät, *das*

**dictate** ❶ /dɪk'teɪt/ *v.t. & i.* diktieren; (*prescribe*) vorschreiben; **~ to** Vorschriften machen (+ *Dat.*); **I will not be ~d to** ich lasse mir keine Vorschriften machen. ❷ /'dɪkteɪt/ *n., usu. in pl.* Diktat, *das*

**dic'tating machine** *n.* Diktiergerät, *das*

**dictation** /dɪk'teɪʃn/ *n.* Diktat, *das;* **take a ~:** ein Diktat aufnehmen

**dictator** /dɪk'teɪtə(r)/ *n.* (*lit. or fig.*) Diktator, *der;* **be a ~** (*fig.*) diktatorisch sein

**dictatorial** /dɪktə'tɔ:rɪəl/ *adj.*, **dictatorially** /dɪktə'tɔ:rɪəlɪ/ *adv.* (*lit. or fig.*) diktatorisch

**dictatorship** /dɪk'teɪtəʃɪp/ *n.* (*lit. or fig.*) Diktatur, *die*

**diction** /'dɪkʃn/ *n.* Diktion, *die* (*geh.*)

**dictionary** /'dɪkʃənərɪ/ *n.* Wörterbuch, *das;* ⇒ *also* **walking** 1

**dictum** /'dɪktəm/ *n., pl.* **~s** *or* **dicta** /'dɪktə/ Ⓐ (*pronouncement, maxim*) Spruch, *der;* Diktum, *das* (*geh.*); Ⓑ (*Law*) richterliche Meinung

**did** ⇒ **do**[1]

**didactic** /dɪ'dæktɪk, daɪ'dæktɪk/ *adj.* Ⓐ didaktisch; Ⓑ (*authoritarian*) schulmeisterlich (*abwertend*)

**diddle** /'dɪdl/ *v.t.* (*coll.*) übers Ohr hauen (*ugs.*); **~ sb. out of sth.** jmdm. etw. abluchsen (*salopp*); **~ sb. into doing sth.** jmdn. so verschaukeln, dass er etw. tut (*ugs.*)

**diddums** /'dɪdəmz/ *n.* (*child lang./coll.*) der/die arme Kleine; **[poor little] ~!** armes Kleines!

**didn't** /'dɪdnt/ (*coll.*) = **did not;** ⇒ **do**[1]

**dido** /'daɪdəʊ/ *n., pl.* **~s** *or* **~es** (*Amer. coll.*) Mätzchen, *das* (*ugs.*)

**die**[1] /daɪ/ ❶ *v.i.*, **dying** /'daɪɪŋ/ Ⓐ sterben; ‹Tier, Pflanze:› eingehen, (*geh.*) sterben; ‹Körperteil:› absterben; **be dying** sterben; **~ from** *or* **of sth.** an etw. (*Dat.*) sterben; **~ of grief** vor Kummer sterben; **~ of a heart attack/a brain tumour** einem Herzanfall/Hirntumor erliegen; **~ from one's injuries** seinen Verletzungen erliegen; **~ a rich man** als reicher Mann sterben; **~ by one's own hand** (*literary*) Hand an sich (*Akk.*) legen (*geh.*); **~ in one's bed** im Bett sterben; **~ in one's boots** (*working*) in den Sielen sterben; ‹Soldat:› im Kampf fallen; **sb. would ~ rather than do sth.** um nichts in der Welt würde jmd. etw. tun; **never say ~** (*fig.*) nur nicht den Mut verlieren; Ⓑ (*fig.*) **be dying for sth.** etw. unbedingt brauchen; **be dying for a cup of tea** nach einer Tasse Tee lechzen; **be dying to do sth.** darauf brennen, etw. zu tun; **I'm dying to know how she ...:** ich möchte zu gerne wissen, wie sie ...; **be dying of boredom/curiosity** vor Langeweile sterben/vor Neugier platzen; **~ [laughing]** sich totlachen (*ugs.*); **I [nearly] ~d with** *or* **of embarrassment** es war mir furchtbar peinlich; **~ with** *or* **of shame** sich zu Tode schämen; Ⓒ (*disappear*) in Vergessenheit geraten; ‹Gefühl, Liebe, Ruhm:› vergehen; ‹Ton:› verklingen; ‹Flamme:› verlöschen; ‹Worte, Lächeln:› ersterben (*geh.*); **the secret ~d with them** sie haben das Geheimnis mit ins Grab genommen; Ⓓ (*coll.: cease to function*) ‹Zeitschrift, Firma:› eingehen (*ugs.*); **the engine ~d on me** der Motor ist mir abgestorben

❷ *v.t.*, **dying: ~ a natural/violent death** eines natürlichen/gewaltsamen Todes sterben; **let the matter ~ a natural death** die Sache langsam einschlafen lassen; **sth. ~s the death** (*coll.*) mit etw. ist nichts mehr (*ugs.*)

**~ a'way** *v.i.* ‹Laut, Geräusch:› schwächer werden; ‹Wind, Zorn:› sich legen

**~ 'back** *v.i.* absterben

**~ 'down** *v.i.* ‹Sturm, Wind, Protest, Aufruhr:› sich legen; ‹Flammen:› kleiner werden; ‹Feuer:› herunterbrennen; ‹Lärm:› leiser werden; ‹Kämpfe:› nachlassen; ‹Epidemie:› abklingen

**~ 'off** *v.i.* ‹Pflanzen, Tiere:› [nacheinander] eingehen; ‹Blätter:› [nacheinander] absterben; ‹Menschen:› [nacheinander] sterben

**~ 'out** *v.i.* aussterben

**die**[2] *n.* Ⓐ *pl.* **dice** /daɪs/ (*formal*) Würfel, *der;* **the ~ is cast** die Würfel sind gefallen; **as straight** *or* **true as a ~:** schnurgerade ‹Weg, Linie›; (*fig.*) grundehrlich; Ⓑ *pl.* **~s** (*engraved stamp*) Stempel, *der;* Ⓒ *pl.* **~s** (*Metalw.*) Gussform, *die;* (*in drop-forging*) Gesenk, *das;* Ⓓ (*for cutting threads*) [Gewinde]schneideisen, *das*

**die: ~-casting** *n.* Ⓐ (*process*) [Kokillen]guss, *der;* Ⓑ (*product*) Gussstück, *das;* **~hard** ❶ *n.* hartnäckiger Typ; (*reactionary*) Ewiggestrige, *der/die;* ❷ *adj.* hartnäckig; (*dyed-in-the-wool*) eingefleischt; (*reactionary*) ewiggestrig

**diesel** /'di:zl/ *n.* **~ [engine]** Diesel[motor], *der;* **~ [lorry/car]** Diesel, *der;* **~ [train]** (*Railw.*) Dieseltriebwagen, *der;* **~ [fuel]** Diesel[kraftstoff], *der*

**diesel-e'lectric** *adj.* dieselelektrisch

**'diesel oil** *n.* Dieseltreibstoff, *der*

**diet**[1] /'daɪət/ ❶ *n.* Ⓐ (*for slimming*) Diät, *die;* Schlankheitskur, *die;* **be/go on a ~:** eine Schlankheitskur *od.* Diät machen; Ⓑ (*Med.*) Diät, *die;* Schonkost, *die;* Ⓒ (*habitual food*) Kost, *die.* ❷ *v.i.* eine Schlankheitskur *od.* Diät machen

**diet**[2] *n.* (*Polit.*) Reichstag, *der*

**dietary** /'daɪɪtərɪ/ *adj.* **~ rules** Diätvorschriften; **~ habits** Essgewohnheiten; **~ deficiencies** mangelhafte Ernährung

**dietetic** /daɪə'tetɪk/ *adj.* Diät-; diätetisch

**dietetics** /daɪə'tetɪks/ *n., no pl.* Ernährungslehre, *die;* Diätetik, *die* (*fachspr.*)

**dietitian** (**dietician**) /daɪə'tɪʃn/ *n.* ▶ 1261 Diätassistent, *der*/-assistentin, *die*

**'diet sheet** *n.* Diätplan, *der*

**differ** /'dɪfə(r)/ *v.i.* Ⓐ (*vary, be different*) sich unterscheiden; **the two accounts of what happened ~ed greatly** die beiden Berichte von den Ereignissen wichen stark voneinander ab; **opinions/ideas ~:** die Meinungen/Vorstellungen gehen auseinander; **tastes/temperaments ~:** die Geschmäcker (*ugs.*) / Temperamente sind verschieden; **people ~:** es sind nicht alle Menschen gleich; **~ from sb./sth. in that ...:** sich von jmdm./etw. dadurch *od.* darin unterscheiden, dass ...; Ⓑ (*disagree*) anderer Meinung sein; **~ with sb. over** *or* **on sth.** über etw. (*Akk.*) anderer Meinung sein als jmd.; ⇒ *also* **agree** 1 A; **beg** 1 B

**difference** /'dɪfərəns/ *n.* Ⓐ Unterschied, *der;* **~ in age** Altersunterschied, *der;* **have a ~ of opinion [with sb.]** eine Meinungsverschiedenheit [mit jmdm.] haben; **there is a ~ in her now** (*in appearance*) sie sieht jetzt anders aus; (*in character*) sie hat sich geändert; **it makes a ~:** es ist ein *od.* (*ugs.*) macht einen Unterschied; **what ~ would it make if ...?** was würde es schon ausmachen, wenn ...?; **the new curtains make a big ~ to the room** mit den neuen Vorhängen sieht das Zimmer schon ganz anders aus; **it makes a ~:** es ist ein *od.* (*ugs.*) macht einen Unterschied; **as if that made any ~:** als ob das etwas ändern würde; **make all the ~ [in the world]** ungeheuer viel ausmachen; **I could [as well] have stayed at home for all the ~ it made** da hätte ich auch gleich zu Hause bleiben können; **make no ~ [to sb.]** [jmdm.] nichts ausmachen; **a holiday with a ~:** Urlaub — einmal anders; **same ~** (*coll.*) ein und dasselbe; Ⓑ (*between amounts*) Differenz, *die;* **pay the ~:** den Rest[betrag] bezahlen; **split the ~:** sich (*Dat.*) den Rest[betrag] teilen; (*fig.*) einen Kompromiss machen; Ⓒ (*dispute*) **have a ~ with sb.** mit jmdm. eine Auseinandersetzung haben; **resolve** *or* **settle one's ~s** seine Differenzen beilegen

**different** /'dɪfrənt/ *adj.* verschieden; (*pred. also*) anders; (*attrib. also*) ander...; **be ~ from** *or* (*esp. Brit.*) **to** *or* (*Amer.*) **than ...:** anders sein als ...; **the two sisters are very ~ from each other** die beiden Schwestern sind sehr verschieden; **she was totally ~ from** *or* **to what I'd expected** sie war ganz anders, als ich erwartet hatte; **~ viewpoints/cultures** unterschiedliche Standpunkte/Kulturen; **how are they ~?** worin *od.* wodurch unterscheiden sie sich?; **I feel a ~ person** ich fühle mich wie neugeboren; **I asked several ~ people** ich habe mehrere *od.* verschiedene Leute gefragt; **wear a ~ dress on every occasion** zu jedem Anlass ein anderes Kleid tragen; **oh, that's ~:** ach so, das ist was anderes; **a holiday that is ~:** Urlaub — einmal anders; **the same, only ~** (*coll.*) fast der-/die-/dasselbe

**differential** /dɪfə'renʃl/ ❶ *adj.* Ⓐ unterschiedlich; ungleich ‹Behandlung›; gestaffelt ‹Lohn, Kosten›; unterscheidend ‹Merkmal›; **~ tariffs/duties** (*Commerc.*) Differenzialtarife/-zölle; Ⓑ (*Math.*) **~ calculus** Differenzialrechnung, *die;* **~ equation** Differenzialgleichung, *die;* **~ coefficient** ⇒ **derivative** 2 B. ❷ *n.* Ⓐ (*Commerc.*) **[wage] ~:** [Einkommens]unterschied, *der;* **price ~s** Preisunterschiede; Ⓑ (*Motor Veh.*) Differenzial[getriebe], *das;* Ausgleichsgetriebe, *das*

**differentiate** /dɪfə'renʃɪeɪt/ ❶ *v.t.* Ⓐ unterscheiden; Ⓑ (*Biol.*) herausbilden; Ⓒ (*Math.*) differenzieren. ❷ *v.i.* Ⓐ (*recognize the difference*) unterscheiden; differenzieren; Ⓑ (*treat sth. differently*) einen Unterschied machen; differenzieren

**differentiation** /dɪfərenʃɪ'eɪʃn/ *n.* **A** Unterscheidung, *die;* Differenzierung, *die;* **B** (*Biol., Math.*) Differenzierung, *die*

**differently** /'dɪfərəntlɪ/ *adv.* anders (**from,** *esp. Brit.* **to** als); **~ [to** *or* **from each other]** verschieden; (*with different result, at various times*) unterschiedlich; **they reacted ~ to the news** sie reagierten unterschiedlich auf die Nachricht

**differing** /'dɪfərɪŋ/ *adj.* unterschiedlich

**difficult** /'dɪfɪkəlt/ *adj.* **A** schwer; schwierig; **a ~ writer** ein schwieriger Schriftsteller; **he finds it ~ to do sth.** ihm fällt es schwer, etw. zu tun; **make things ~ for sb.** es jmdm. nicht leicht machen; **the ~ thing is ...:** die Schwierigkeit ist ...; **B** (*unaccommodating*) schwierig; **he is being ~:** er macht Schwierigkeiten; **he is ~ to get on with** es ist schwer, mit ihm auszukommen

**difficulty** /'dɪfɪkəltɪ/ *n.* **A** Schwierigkeit, *die;* **with [great] ~:** [sehr] mühsam; **with the greatest ~:** unter größten Schwierigkeiten; **without [great] ~:** ohne große Probleme; mühelos; **have ~ [in] doing sth.** Schwierigkeiten haben, etw. zu tun; **experience** *or* **have [some] ~ in walking** Beschwerden beim Gehen haben; **B** *usu. in pl.* (*trouble*) **be in ~** *or* **difficulties** in Schwierigkeiten sein; **under great difficulties** unter großen Schwierigkeiten; **fall** *or* **get into difficulties** in Schwierigkeiten kommen *od.* geraten

**diffidence** /'dɪfɪdəns/ *n., no pl.* Zaghaftigkeit, *die;* (*modesty*) Zurückhaltung, *die*

**diffident** /'dɪfɪdənt/ *adj.* zaghaft; (*modest*) zurückhaltend

**diffraction** /dɪ'frækʃn/ *n.* (*Phys.*) Beugung, *die;* Diffraktion, *die* (*veralt.*)

**diffuse** ❶ /dɪ'fju:z/ *v.t.* verbreiten; diffundieren (*fachspr.*); **~d lighting/traces** diffuse Beleuchtung/Spuren. ❷ *v.i.* sich ausbreiten (**through** in + *Dat.*); diffundieren (*fachspr.*). ❸ /dɪ'fju:s/ *adj.* **A** (*dispersed*) diffus; **B** (*verbose*) weitschweifig; diffus (*fig.*)

**diffusion** /dɪ'fju:ʒn/ *n.* **A** (*also Anthrop.*) Verbreitung, *die;* **B** (*Phys.*) Diffusion, *die*

**dig** /dɪg/ ❶ *v.i.*, **-gg-, dug** /dʌg/ **A** graben (**for** nach); **B** (*Archaeol.: excavate*) Ausgrabungen machen; graben; (*fig.: search*) **~ for information** versuchen, Informationen zu bekommen; **C ~ at sb.** eine [spitze] Bemerkung über jmdn. machen.
❷ *v.t.*, **-gg-, dug** **A** graben; **~ a hole [in sth.]** ein Loch [in etw. (*Akk.*)] graben; **B** (*turn up with spade etc.*) umgraben; (*obtain by digging*) **~ potatoes/peat** Kartoffeln ernten *od.* (*landsch.*) ausmachen/Torf stechen; **C** (*Archaeol.*) ausgraben; **D** (*coll.: appreciate*) stark finden (*Jugendspr.*); (*understand*) schnallen (*salopp*).
❸ *n.* **A** Grabung, *die;* **B** (*Archaeol. coll.*) Ausgrabung, *die;* (*site*) Ausgrabungsort, *der;* **C** (*fig.*) Anspielung, *die* (**at** auf + *Akk.*); **have** *or* **make a ~ at sb./sth.** eine [spitze] Bemerkung über jmdn./etw. machen; **D** ⇒ **rib** 1A

**~ 'in** ❶ *v.i.* **A** (*Mil.*) sich eingraben; (*fig.*) sich festsetzen; **B** (*coll.: begin eating, eat*) zulangen (*ugs.*). ❷ *v.t.* **A** (*Mil.*) eingraben; **~ oneself in** sich eingraben; (*fig.*) sich etablieren; **B** (*thrust*) **the cat dug its claws in** die Katze krallte sich fest; **~ one's heels** *or* **toes in** (*fig.*) sich auf die Hinterbeine stellen (*ugs.*); **C** (*mix with soil*) eingraben

**~ into** *v.t.* **A** wühlen in (+ *Akk.*) ‹Tasche›; eindringen in (+ *Akk.*) ‹Materie›; vordringen in (+ *Akk.*) ‹Vergangenheit, Geschichte›; **B** (*coll.: begin eating*) zulangen bei (*ugs.*); **C** (*take from*) **~ into one's savings** seine Ersparnisse angreifen; **have to ~ into one's pocket** in die Tasche greifen müssen; **D** (*mix with*) **~ compost into the soil** Kompost untergraben; **E** (*embed itself in*) sich graben in (+ *Akk.*)

**~ 'out** *v.t.* (*lit. or fig.*) ausgraben; **~ sb. out from underneath the debris/out of the wreckage** jmdn. aus den Trümmern bergen

**~ 'up** *v.t.* **A** umgraben ‹Garten, Rasen, Erde›; ausgraben ‹Pflanzen, Knochen, Leiche, Schatz›; aufreißen ‹Straße›; **B** (*fig.: find*) ausgraben ‹Fakten, Informationen›; (*coll. derog.: obtain*) aufgabeln (*ugs.*)

**digest** ❶ /dɪ'dʒest, daɪ'dʒest/ *v.t.* **A** (*assimilate, lit or fig.*) verdauen; **B** (*consider*) durchdenken. ❷ /'daɪdʒest/ *n.* **A** (*periodical*) Digest, *der od. das* (*Zeitschrift mit Auszügen aus Büchern od. anderen Zeitschriften*); **B** (*summary*) Zusammenfassung, *die*

**digestible** /dɪ'dʒestɪbl, daɪ'dʒestɪbl/ *adj.* verdaulich; (*fig.*) verständlich

**digestion** /dɪ'dʒestʃn, daɪ'dʒestʃn/ *n.* Verdauung, *die;* Digestion, *die* (*Physiol.*); (*fig.*) [geistige] Verarbeitung

**digestive** /dɪ'dʒestɪv, daɪ'dʒestɪv/ ❶ *adj.* Verdauungs-; **~ biscuit** (*Brit.*) ⇒ **2.** ❷ *n.* (*Brit.: biscuit*) Keks (*aus Vollkornmehl*)

**digger** /'dɪgə(r)/ *n.* **A** (*Archaeol.*) Ausgräber, *der*/Ausgräberin, *die;* (*miner*) Bergmann, *der;* (*gold-~*) Goldgräber, *der;* **B** (*Mech.*) Bagger, *der;* (*garden tool*) Grabschaufel, *die;* **C** (*fig. coll.*) (*Australian*) Australier, *der*/Australierin, *die;* (*New Zealander*) Neuseeländer, *der*/Neuseeländerin, *die*

**diggings** /'dɪgɪŋz/ *n. pl.* **A** (*Mining*) [Gold]lagerstätte, *die;* **B** (*Archaeol.*) Ausgrabungsort, *der*

**digit** /'dɪdʒɪt/ *n.* **A** (*numeral*) Ziffer, *die;* **a six-~ number** eine sechsstellige Zahl; **B** (*finger*) Finger, *der;* (*toe*) Zehe, *die*

**digital** /'dɪdʒɪtl/ *adj.* **A** (*numerical*) digital; **~ clock/watch** Digitaluhr, *die;* **~ computer** Digitalrechner, *der;* **~ recording** Digitalaufnahme, *die;* **~ audio tape** Digitaltonband, *das;* **~ camera** Digitalkamera, *die;* **~ video disc** DVD, *die;* Digital Video Disc, *die;* **B** (*Zool., Anat.*) digital

**digitize (digitise)** /'dɪdʒɪtaɪz/ *v.t.* (*Computing*) digitalisieren

**dignified** /'dɪgnɪfaɪd/ *adj.* würdig; (*self-respecting, stately*) würdevoll

**dignify** /'dɪgnɪfaɪ/ *v.t.* **A** (*make stately*) Würde verleihen (+ *Dat.*); **B** (*give distinction to*) Glanz verleihen (+ *Dat.*); auszeichnen ‹Person›; **C** (*give grand title to*) aufwerten (*fig.*)

**dignitary** /'dɪgnɪtərɪ/ *n.* Würdenträger, *der;* **dignitaries** (*notabilities*) Honoratioren; **church ~:** kirchlicher Würdenträger

**dignity** /'dɪgnɪtɪ/ *n.* Würde, *die;* **speak with quiet ~:** ruhig und würdevoll sprechen; **he is not one to stand on his ~:** er hat keine Angst, sich (*Dat.*) etwas zu vergeben; **be beneath one's ~:** unter seiner Würde sein

**digress** /daɪ'gres, dɪ'gres/ *v.i.* abschweifen (**from** von, **on** zu)

**digression** /daɪ'greʃn, dɪ'greʃn/ *n.* Abschweifung, *die;* (*passage*) Exkurs, *der*

**digs** /dɪgz/ *n. pl.* (*Brit. coll.*) Bude, *die* (*ugs.*); **he's in ~:** er hat eine [eigene] Bude (*ugs.*)

**dike** /daɪk/ *n.* **A** (*flood wall*) Deich, *der;* **B** (*ditch*) Graben, *der;* **C** (*causeway*) Damm, *der;* **D** (*Mining, Geol.*) Gang, *der;* (*of igneous rock*) Eruptivgang, *der*

**diktat** /'dɪktæt/ *n.* **A** (*decree*) Anordnung, *die;* **B** (*severe settlement*) Diktat, *das*

**dilapidated** /dɪ'læpɪdeɪtɪd/ *adj.* verfallen ‹Gebäude›; verwahrlost ‹Äußeres, Erscheinung›

**dilapidation** /dɪlæpɪ'deɪʃn/ *n., no pl.* Verfall, *der;* **in a state of ~:** in verwahrlostem Zustand

**dilatation** /daɪlə'teɪʃn, dɪlə'teɪʃn/ *n.* **A** ⇒ **dilation;** **B** (*Med.*) Dilatation, *die* (*fachspr.*); Erweiterung, *die*

**dilate** /daɪ'leɪt, dɪ'leɪt/ ❶ *v.i.* **A** sich weiten; **B** (*discourse*) **~ [up]on sth.** sich über etw. (*Akk.*) verbreiten. ❷ *v.t.* ausdehnen; blähen ‹Nüstern›

**dilation** /daɪ'leɪʃn, dɪ'leɪʃn/ *n.* Dilatation, *die;* (*Phys. also*) Ausdehnung, *die;* (*Med. also*) Erweiterung, *die*

**dilatory** /'dɪlətərɪ/ *adj.* langsam; saumselig (*geh.*); zögernd ‹Antwort, Reaktion›; (*causing delay*) **be ~ in** sich (*Dat.*) [viel] Zeit lassen bei

**dildo** /'dɪldəʊ/ *n., pl.* **~s** Godemiché, *der*

**dilemma** /dɪ'lemə, daɪ'lemə/ *n.* (*also Logic*) Dilemma, *das;* **be on the horns of** *or* **faced with a ~:** vor einem Dilemma stehen

**dilettante** /dɪlɪ'tæntɪ/ ❶ *n., pl.* **dilettanti** /dɪlɪ'tænti:/ *or* **~s** Dilettant, *der*/Dilettantin, *die;* Laie, *der.* ❷ *adj.* dilettantisch; laienhaft ‹Interesse›

**diligence** /'dɪlɪdʒəns/ *n.* Fleiß, *der;* (*purposefulness*) Eifer, *der*

**diligent** /'dɪlɪdʒənt/ *adj.* fleißig; (*purposeful*) eifrig; sorgfältig, gewissenhaft ‹Arbeit, Suche›

**diligently** /'dɪlɪdʒəntlɪ/ *adv.* fleißig; (*purposefully*) eifrig; **execute one's duties ~:** seine Pflichten gewissenhaft erfüllen

**dill** /dɪl/ *n.* (*Bot.*) Dill, *der*

**dill: ~ pickle** *n.: mit Dill eingelegte Gurke usw.;* **~-water** *n.* Dillöl, *das* (*Pharm.*)

**dilly** /'dɪlɪ/ *n.* (*coll.*) irre Type (*ugs.*); (*thing*) irres Ding (*ugs.*)

**dilly-dally** /'dɪlɪdælɪ/ *v.i.* (*coll.*) **A** (*dawdle*) trödeln; **B** (*vacillate*) **~ over the choice of sth.** sich nicht für etw. entscheiden können; **stop ~ing!** entscheide dich endlich!

**diluent** /'dɪljʊənt/ *n.* Verdünnungsmittel, *das*

**dilute** ❶ /daɪ'lju:t, 'daɪlju:t/ *adj.* **A** verdünnt; **B** (*washed out*) verwaschen ‹Farbe›; (*faded*) verblasst, ausgebleicht ‹Farbe›; **C** (*fig.*) blass (*geh.*). ❷ /daɪ'lju:t/ *v.t.* **A** verdünnen; **B** ausbleichen ‹Farbe›; **C** (*fig.*) abschwächen; entschärfen

**dilution** /daɪ'lju:ʃn, daɪ'lu:ʃn/ *n.* **A** (*act*) Verdünnen, *das;* **B** (*state, substance*) Verdünnung, *die;* **C** (*fig.*) Abschwächung, *die*

**dim** /dɪm/ ❶ *adj.* **A** schwach, trüb ‹Licht, Flackern›; matt, gedeckt ‹Farbe›; dämmrig, dunkel ‹Zimmer›; undeutlich, verschwommen ‹Gestalt›; **grow ~:** schwächer werden; **B** (*fig.*) blass; verschwommen; **in the ~ and distant past** in ferner Vergangenheit; **have a ~ suspicion that ...:** den leisen Verdacht haben, dass ...; **have only a ~ understanding of sth.** nur eine ungefähre *od.* vage Vorstellung von etw. haben; **C** (*indistinct*) schwach, getrübt ‹Seh-, Hörvermögen›; **his eyesight/hearing had grown ~:** seine Augen hatten/sein Gehör hatte nachgelassen; **D** (*coll.*) (*stupid*) beschränkt; (*clumsy*) ungeschickt; **E take a ~ view of sth.** (*coll.*) von etw. nicht erbaut sein.
❷ *v.i.*, **-mm-** (*lit. or fig.*) schwächer werden.
❸ *v.t.*, **-mm-** **A** verdunkeln; verdüstern; (*fig.*) trüben; dämpfen; **~ the lights** (*Theatre, Cinemat.*) die Lichter langsam verlöschen lassen; **B** (*Amer. Motor Veh.*) abblenden

**~ 'out** *v.t.* **A** verdunkeln; **B** (*Theatre*) **~ out the lights on stage** die Bühne abblenden. ⇒ *also* **dim-out**

**dime** /daɪm/ *n.* (*Amer.*) Zehncentstück, *das;* ≈ Groschen, *der* (*ugs.*); **be a ~ a dozen** (*fig.*) Dutzendware sein (*fig. abwertend*); **it's not worth a ~** (*fig.*) es ist keinen Pfifferling wert (*ugs.*); **~ novel** Groschenroman, *der* (*abwertend*)

**dimension** /dɪ'menʃn, daɪ'menʃn/ ❶ *n.* (*lit. or fig.*) Dimension, *die;* (*measurement*) Abmessung, *die.* ❷ *v.t.* dimensionieren

**-dimensional** /dɪ'menʃənl, daɪ'menʃənl/ *adj. in comb.* -dimensional

**diminish** /dɪ'mɪnɪʃ/ ❶ *v.i.* nachlassen; ‹Zahl:› sich verringern; ‹Vorräte, Autorität, Einfluss:› abnehmen; ‹Wert, Bedeutung, Ansehen:› geringer werden; **~ in value/number** an Wert verlieren/an Zahl od. zahlenmäßig abnehmen. ❷ *v.t.* vermindern; verringern; (*fig.*) herabwürdigen ‹Person›; schmälern ‹Ansehen, Ruf›

**diminished** /dɪ'mɪnɪʃt/ *adj.* geringer ‹Wert, Anzahl, Einfluss, Popularität›; vermindert ‹Stärke, Fähigkeit›; verringert ‹Belegschaft›; verkleinert ‹Reich›; **[plead] ~ responsibility** (*Law*) [auf] verminderte Zurechnungsfähigkeit [plädieren]; **~ interval** (*Mus.*) vermindertes Intervall

**diminishing** /dɪ'mɪnɪʃɪŋ/ *adj.* sinkend; abnehmend ‹Vorräte›; schwindend ‹Kraft, Einfluss, Macht›; **law of ~ returns** (*Econ.*) Gesetz vom abnehmenden Ertragszuwachs; Ertragsgesetz, *das*

**diminuendo** /dɪmɪnjʊ'endəʊ/ (*Mus.*) *n., pl.* **~s** Diminuendo, *das*

**diminution** /dɪmɪ'nju:ʃn/ *n.* (*of number, supplies*) Verringerung, *die;* (*of value*) Minderung, *die;* (*of strength, influence*) Schwinden, *das;* (*of reputation, fame*) Schmälerung, *die;* (*Mus.*) Diminution, *die*

**diminutive** /dɪˈmɪnjʊtɪv/ ❶ *adj.* Ⓐ winzig; Ⓑ (*Ling.*) diminutiv. ❷ *n.* (*Ling.*) Diminutiv[um], *das*

**dimly** /ˈdɪmlɪ/ *adv.* schwach; undeutlich ‹sehen›; ungefähr ‹begreifen›; **I ~ remember it** ich erinnere mich noch dunkel daran

**dimmer** /ˈdɪmə(r)/ *n.* Ⓐ Dimmer, *der;* Helligkeitsregler, *der;* Ⓑ (*Amer. Motor Veh.: switch*) Abblendschalter, *der*

**dimness** /ˈdɪmnɪs/ *n., no pl.* Ⓐ Trübheit, *die;* (*almost darkness*) Halbdunkel, *das;* Ⓑ (*fig.*) Undeutlichkeit, *die;* Unklarheit, *die*

**dimorphic** /daɪˈmɔːfɪk/ *adj.* (*Biol., Chem., Min.*) dimorph

**dimorphism** /daɪˈmɔːfɪzm/ *n.* (*Biol., Chem., Min.*) Dimorphie, *die*

**ˈdim-out** *n.* Ⓐ Verdunk[e]lung, *die;* Ⓑ (*Theatre*) Abblendung, *die*

**dimple** /ˈdɪmpl/ *n.* Grübchen, *das;* (*on golf ball etc.*) kleine Vertiefung

**dim: ~wit** *n.* (*coll.*) Dummkopf, *der* (*ugs.*); **~-witted** /ˈdɪmwɪtɪd/ *adj.* (*coll.*) dusselig (*salopp*); dämlich (*ugs. abwertend*)

**din** /dɪn/ ❶ *n.* Lärm, *der.* ❷ *v.t.*, **-nn-: ~ sth. into sb.** jmdm. etw. einhämmern *od.* einbläuen

**din-din[s]** /ˈdɪndɪn(z)/ *n.* (*child lang.*) Fresschen, *das* (*ugs.*)

**dine** /daɪn/ ❶ *v.i.* (*at midday/in the evening*) [zu Mittag/zu Abend] essen *od.* (*geh.*) speisen; dinieren (*geh.*); **~ off/on sth.** etw. [zum Mittag-/Abendessen] verzehren; **~ off sth.** (*eat from*) von etw. speisen. ❷ *v.t.* bewirten; ⇒ *also* **wine and dine**

**~ ˈout** *v.i.* Ⓐ auswärts [zu Mittag/Abend] essen; Ⓑ **~ out on sth.** wegen etw. zum Essen eingeladen werden

**diner** /ˈdaɪnə(r)/ *n.* Ⓐ Gast, *der* (*zum Abendessen*); Ⓑ (*Railw.*) Speisewagen, *der;* Ⓒ (*Amer.: restaurant*) Restaurant, *das*

**ding-a-ling** /ˈdɪŋəlɪŋ/ ⇒ **ting-a-ling**

**ding-dong** /ˈdɪŋdɒŋ/ ❶ *n.* Ⓐ Bimbam, *das;* Ⓑ (*coll.: argument*) Krach, *der* (*ugs.*). ❷ *adj.* hin- und herwogend. ❸ *adv.* mit Feuereifer

**dinghy** /ˈdɪŋgɪ, ˈdɪŋɪ/ *n.* Ding[h]i, *das;* (*inflatable*) Schlauchboot, *das*

**dingle** /ˈdɪŋgl/ *n.* waldiges kleines Tal

**dingo** /ˈdɪŋgəʊ/ *n., pl.* **~es** Ⓐ (*dog*) Dingo, *der;* Ⓑ (*Austral. coll.: rogue*) [gemeiner] Hund (*salopp*)

**dingy** /ˈdɪndʒɪ/ *adj.* schmuddelig

**dining**/ˈdaɪnɪŋ/**: ~ area** *n.* ≈ Essecke, *die;* **~ car** *n.* (*Railw.*) Speisewagen, *der;* **~ chair** *n.* Esszimmerstuhl, *der;* **~ hall** *n.* Speisesaal, *der;* **~ room** *n.* (*in private house*) Esszimmer, *das;* (*in hotel etc.*) Speisesaal, *der;* **~ table** *n.* Esstisch, *der*

**dinkel** /ˈdɪŋkl/ ⇒ **spelt²**

**dinkum** /ˈdɪŋkəm/ (*Austral. and NZ coll.*) *adj.* astrein (*ugs.*); **fair ~:** echt (*ugs.*); **[the] ~ oil** die Wahrheit

**dinky** /ˈdɪŋkɪ/ *adj.* (*coll.*) Ⓐ (*Brit.: pretty*) niedlich; Ⓑ (*Amer.: trifling*) kümmerlich

**dinner** /ˈdɪnə(r)/ *n.* Essen, *das;* (*at midday also*) Mittagessen, *das;* (*in the evening also*) Abendessen, *das;* (*formal event*) Diner, *das;* **have** *or* **eat [one's] ~:** zu Mittag/Abend essen; **go out to ~:** [abends] essen gehen; (*to friends*) zum [Abend]essen eingeladen sein; **~'s ready!** [das] Essen ist fertig!; **be at** *or* **having** *or* **eating [one's] ~:** gerade beim Essen sein; **have people [in] to** *or* **for ~:** Gäste zum Essen haben

**dinner: ~ dance** *n.: Abendessen mit anschließendem Tanz;* **~ gong** *n.* Gong, *der;* **~ jacket** *n.* (*Brit.*) Dinnerjacket, *das;* **~ lady** *n.* ▶ **1261** (*Brit.*) *Serviererin beim Mittagessen in der Schule;* **~ party** *n.* Abendeinladung, *die* (*mit Essen*); (*more formal*) Abendgesellschaft, *die;* **~ plate** *n.* flacher Teller; Essteller, *der;* **~ service** *n.* Essgeschirr, *das;* **~ table** *n.* Esstisch, *der;* **be at** *or* **seated round the ~ table** bei Tisch sitzen; **~ time** *n.* Essenszeit, *die;* **at ~ time** zur Essenszeit; (*12-2 p.m.*) mittags

**dinosaur** /ˈdaɪnəsɔː(r)/ *n.* Dinosaurier, *der*

**dint** /dɪnt/ *n.* Ⓐ **by ~ of** durch; **by ~ of doing sth.** indem jmd. etw. tut; Ⓑ ⇒ **dent** 1

**diocesan** /daɪˈɒsɪsən/ *adj.* (*Eccl.*) diözesan; **~ synod** Diözesansynode, *die*

**diocese** /ˈdaɪəsɪs/ *n.* (*Eccl.*) Diözese, *die*

**dioxide** /daɪˈɒksaɪd/ *n.* (*Chem.*) Dioxid, *das* (*fachspr.*); Dioxyd, *das*

**dioxin** /daɪˈɒksɪn/ *n.* (*Chem.*) Dioxin, *das*

**dip** /dɪp/ ❶ *v.t.*, **-pp-** Ⓐ [ein]tauchen (**in** in + *Akk.*); **she ~ped her hand into the sack** sie griff in den Sack; Ⓑ (*dye*) in ein Färbemittel tauchen; Ⓒ (*Agric.*) dippen ‹Schaf›; Ⓓ (*Brit. Motor Veh.*) **~ one's [head-]lights** abblenden; **[drive with** *or* **on] ~ped headlights** [mit] Abblendlicht [fahren].

❷ *v.i.*, **-pp-** Ⓐ (*go down*) sinken; **the sun ~ped below the horizon** die Sonne versank hinter dem Horizont; Ⓑ (*Aeronaut.*) vor dem Steigen plötzlich absacken; Ⓒ (*incline downwards, lit. or fig.*) abfallen; **the magnetic needle ~s** die Magnetnadel neigt sich; Ⓓ (*go under water*) [ein]tauchen; **~ under** untertauchen; Ⓔ (*Brit. Motor Veh.*) abblenden.

❸ *n.* Ⓐ (*dipping*) [kurzes] Eintauchen; **give sb./sth. a ~ in sth.** jmdn./etw. in etw. (*Akk.*) [kurz] eintauchen; ⇒ *also* **lucky ~;** Ⓑ (*bathe*) [kurzes] Bad; Ⓒ (*of stratum*) Fallen, *das* (*Geol.*); (*of road*) Senke, *die;* (*hollow, depression in landscape*) Mulde, *die;* Ⓓ (*Gastr.*) Dip, *der;* Ⓔ (*for sheep*) Räudebad, *das;* Ⓕ (*underworld sl.: pickpocket*) Krebs, *der* (*Gaunerspr.*)

**~ ˈinto** *v.t.* Ⓐ greifen in (+ *Akk.*); (*put ladle into*) den Löffel tauchen in (+ *Akk.*); (*fig.*) **~ into one's pocket** *or* **purse** tief in die Tasche greifen; **~ into one's reserves/savings** seine Reserven antasten/Ersparnisse angreifen; Ⓑ (*look cursorily at*) einen flüchtigen Blick werfen in (+ *Akk.*); **the book is good for ~ping into** man kann das Buch gut in kurzen Abschnitten lesen

**Dip.** *abbr.* **Diploma** Dipl.

**Dip. Ed.** /dɪp ˈed/ *abbr.* **Diploma in Education** Pädagogikdiplom, *das;* ⇒ *also* **B.Sc.**

**diphtheria** /dɪfˈθɪərɪə/ *n.* ▶ **1232** (*Med.*) Diphtherie, *die*

**diphthong** /ˈdɪfθɒŋ/ *n.* (*Phonet.*) Diphthong, *der* (*fachspr.*); Doppellaut, *der*

**diploma** /dɪˈpləʊmə/ *n.* Ⓐ (*Educ.*) Diplom, *das;* Ⓑ (*conferring honour*) [Ehren]urkunde, *die;* Ⓒ (*charter*) Charte, *die*

**diplomacy** /dɪˈpləʊməsɪ/ *n.* (*Polit.; also fig.*) Diplomatie, *die;* **use ~** (*fig.*) diplomatisch vorgehen

**diplomat** /ˈdɪpləmæt/ *n.* ▶ **1261** (*Polit.; also fig.*) Diplomat, *der*/Diplomatin, *die*

**diplomatic** /dɪpləˈmætɪk/ *adj.*, **diplomatically** /dɪpləˈmætɪkəlɪ/ *adv.* (*Polit.; also fig.*) diplomatisch

**diplomatic: ~ ˈbag** *n.* **~ bags** Kuriergepäck, *das;* **~ corps** *n.* diplomatisches Korps; **~ imˈmunity** *n.* diplomatische Immunität; **~ ˈpassport** *n.* Diplomatenpass, *der;* **~ service** *n.* diplomatischer Dienst

**diplomatist** /dɪˈpləʊmətɪst/ ⇒ **diplomat**

**dipole** /ˈdaɪpəʊl/ *n.* (*Electr., Magn., Chem., Radio*) Dipol, *der*

**dipper** /ˈdɪpə(r)/ *n.* Ⓐ (*excavating machine*) Löffelbagger, *der;* Ⓑ (*Ornith.*) Wasseramsel, *die;* Ⓒ (*ladle*) Schöpfkelle, *die;* Ⓓ (*Amer. Astron.*) **Big/Little D~:** Großer/Kleiner Wagen *od.* Bär; Ⓔ ⇒ **big dipper a**

**dippy** /ˈdɪpɪ/ *adj.* (*coll.*) übergeschnappt (*ugs.*); **go ~:** überschnappen (*ugs.*); **be ~ about sb./sth.** verrückt nach jmdm./etw. sein

**dip: ~stick** *n.* [Öl-/Benzin]messstab, *der;* **~ switch** *n.* (*Brit. Motor Veh.*) Abblendschalter, *der*

**dire** /daɪə(r)/ *adj.* Ⓐ (*dreadful*) entsetzlich; furchtbar; Ⓑ (*ominous*) unheilvoll; Ⓒ (*extreme*) **~ necessity** dringende Notwendigkeit; **be in ~ need of sth.** etw. dringend benötigen *od.* brauchen; **in cases of ~ emergency** im äußersten Notfall; **be in ~ [financial] straits** in einer ernsten [finanziellen] Notlage sein

**direct** /dɪˈrekt, daɪˈrekt/ ❶ *v.t.* Ⓐ ▶ **1679** (*turn*) richten (**to[wards]** auf + *Akk.*); **~ one's steps towards sth.** seine Schritte nach etw. lenken; **~ sb.'s attention to sth.** jmds. Aufmerksamkeit auf etw. (*Akk.*) lenken; **the remark/wink was ~ed at you** die Bemerkung/das Zwinkern galt dir; **~ a blow at sb.** nach jmdm. schlagen; **the bomb/missile was ~ed at** die Bombe/das Geschoss galt (+ *Dat.*); **government policy is ~ed at reducing inflation** die Regierungspolitik ist darauf ausgerichtet, die Inflation einzudämmen; **~ sb. to a place** jmdm. den Weg zu einem Ort weisen *od.* sagen; **~ a parcel to sb./an address in L.** ein Paket an jmdn. adressieren/an eine Adresse in L. senden *od.* schicken; Ⓑ (*control*) leiten; beaufsichtigen ‹Arbeitskräfte, Arbeitsablauf›; lenken ‹Volksmassen›; regeln, dirigieren ‹Verkehr›; **does fate ~ our actions?** lenkt das Schicksal unser Tun?; Ⓒ (*order*) anweisen; **~ sb. to do sth.** jmdn. anweisen, etw. zu tun; **~ sth. to be done** *or* **that sth. [should] be done** anordnen, dass etw. zu tun sei; **as ~ed [by the doctor]** wie [vom Arzt] verordnet; nach [ärztlicher] Verordnung; Ⓓ (*Theatre, Cinemat., Telev., Radio*) Regie führen bei; inszenieren; **~ed by Orson Welles** unter der Regie von Orson Welles.

❷ *adj.* Ⓐ (*straight, without intermediaries; also Geneal., Logic*) direkt; durchgehend ‹Zug›; unmittelbar ‹Ursache, Gefahr, Auswirkung›; (*immediate*) unmittelbar, persönlich ‹Erfahrung, Verantwortung, Beteiligung›; **be in the ~ line of fire** genau in der Schusslinie stehen; **'keep away from ~ heat'** „nicht unmittelbar der Hitze aussetzen!“; Ⓑ (*diametrical*) genau ‹Gegenteil›; direkt ‹Widerspruch›; diametral ‹Gegensatz›; Ⓒ (*frank*) direkt; offen; glatt ‹Absage›; **he's a very ~ person** er ist immer sehr direkt *od.* geradeheraus; **be ~ with sb.** offen zu jmdm. sein.

❸ *adv.* direkt

**direct: ~ ˈaccess** *n.* (*Computing*) direkter Zugriff; Direktzugriff, *der;* **~ ˈaction** *n.* direkte Aktion; **~ ˈcurrent** *n.* (*Electr.*) Gleichstrom, *der;* **~ ˈdebit** *n.* (*Brit.*) Lastschriftverfahren, *das;* **~ ˈdialling** *n.* Durchwahl, *die;* **we will soon have ~ dialling** wir werden bald ein Durchwahlsystem haben; **~ ˈflight** *n.* Direktflug, *der;* **~-ˈgrant school** *n.* (*Brit. Hist.*) *staatlich unterstützte Privatschule;* **~ ˈhit** *n.* Volltreffer, *der*

**direction** /dɪˈrekʃn, daɪˈrekʃn/ *n.* Ⓐ (*guidance*) Führung, *die;* (*of firm, orchestra*) Leitung, *die;* (*of play, film, TV or radio programme*) Regie, *die;* (*of play also*) Spielleitung, *die;* Ⓑ *usu. in pl.* (*order*) Anordnung, *die;* (*instruction*) **~s [for use]** Gebrauchsanweisung, *die;* **~s for use** (*of machine*) Bedienungsanleitung, *die;* **on** *or* **by sb.'s ~:** auf jmds. Anordnung (*Akk.*) [hin]; **give sb. ~s to the museum/to York** jmdm. den Weg zum Museum/nach York beschreiben; Ⓒ ▶ **1679** (*point moved towards or from, lit. or fig.*) Richtung, *die;* **from which ~?** aus welcher Richtung?; **travel in a southerly ~/in the ~ of London** in südliche[r] Richtung/in Richtung London reisen; **go in the ~ of the tower** in Richtung des Turms gehen; **in the ~ of** (*fig.*) in Richtung auf (+ *Akk.*); **sense of ~:** Orientierungssinn, *der;* (*fig.*) Orientierung, *die;* **lose all sense of ~** (*lit. or fig.*) jede Orientierung verlieren; **complaints poured in from all ~s** (*fig.*) von allen Seiten hagelte es Beschwerden

**directional** /dɪˈrekʃənl, daɪˈrekʃənl/ *adj.* Ⓐ (*spatial*) Richtungs-; **~ gyro** Kurskreisel, *der;* Ⓑ (*directorial*) führend ‹Rolle›; steuernd ‹Kontrolle›; Ⓒ (*Communications*) Richt-

**direction: ~ finder** *n.* (*Communications*) Peilgerät, *das;* **~ indicator** *n.* (*Motor Veh.*) [Fahrt]richtungsanzeiger, *der*

**directive** /dɪˈrektɪv, daɪˈrektɪv/ *n.* Weisung, *die;* Direktive, *die*

**direct ˈlabour** *n.* **do the work by ~:** die Arbeit mit eigenen Arbeitskräften ausführen

**directly** /dɪˈrektlɪ, daɪˈrektlɪ/ ❶ *adv.* Ⓐ (*in direct manner*) direkt; unmittelbar ‹folgen, verantwortlich sein›; Ⓑ (*exactly*) direkt; genau; wörtlich ‹zitieren, abschreiben›; Ⓒ (*at once*) direkt; umgehend; Ⓓ (*shortly*) gleich; sofort. ❷ *conj.* (*Brit. coll.*) sowie

**directness** /dɪˈrektnɪs, daɪˈrektnɪs/ *n., no pl.* Ⓐ (*of route, course*) Geradheit, *die;* **~ of aim** Zielgenauigkeit, *die;* Ⓑ (*fig.*) Direktheit, *die;* **he replied with ~ and honesty** er antwortete offen und ehrlich

**di'rect object** *n.* (*Ling.*) direktes Objekt

**director** /dɪˈrektə(r), daɪˈrektə(r)/ *n.* ▶ **1261** Ⓐ (*Commerc.*) Direktor, *der*/Direktorin, *die;* (*of project*) Leiter, *der*/Leiterin, *die;* **board of ~s** Aufsichtsrat, *der;* Ⓑ (*Theatre, Cinemat., Telev., Radio*) Regisseur, *der*/Regisseurin, *die;* (*Mus., esp. Amer.*) Dirigent, *der*/Dirigentin, *die*

**directorate** /dɪˈrektərət, daɪˈrektərət/ *n.* Ⓐ (*position, period of service*) Direktorat, *das;* (*of project*) Leitung, *die;* Ⓑ (*board of directors*) Direktorium, *das*

**director 'general** *n., pl.* **directors general** Generaldirektor, *der*/-direktorin, *die;* (*Telev., Radio*) ≈ Intendant, *der*/Intendantin, *die*

**directorial** /dɪrekˈtɔːrɪəl, daɪrekˈtɔːrɪəl/ *adj.* Ⓐ direktorial; Ⓑ (*Theatre, Cinemat., Telev., Radio*) als Regisseur/Regisseurin *nachgestellt*

**directorship** /dɪˈrektəʃɪp, daɪˈrektəʃɪp/ *n.* (*Commerc.*) Leitung, *die;* **hold two ~s** in zwei Aufsichtsräten sein

**directory** /dɪˈrektərɪ, daɪˈrektərɪ/ Ⓐ *n.* (*of local residents*) Adressbuch, *das;* (*telephone ~*) Telefonbuch, *das;* Fernsprechbuch, *das* (*postamtl.*); (*of tradesmen etc.*) Branchenverzeichnis, *das;* **~ enquiries** (*Brit.*), **~ information** (*Amer.*) [Fernsprech]auskunft, *die;* Ⓑ (*Computing*) Verzeichnis, *das*

**direct: ~ pro'portion** *n.* direkte Proportionalität; **~ question** *n.* (*Ling.*) direkter Fragesatz; **~ speech** *n.* (*Ling.*) direkte Rede; **~ tax** *n.* direkte Steuer; **~ taxation** *n.* direkte Besteuerung

**direly** /ˈdaɪəlɪ/ *adv.* **be ~ in need of sth.** etw. dringend brauchen

**dirge** /dɜːdʒ/ *n.* Ⓐ (*for the dead*) Grabgesang, *der;* Ⓑ (*mournful song*) Klagegesang, *der;* Klage, *die* (*dichter.*)

**dirigible** /ˈdɪrɪdʒɪbl, dɪˈrɪdʒɪbl/ ❶ *adj.* lenkbar. ❷ *n.* Luftschiff, *das*

**dirk** /dɜːk/ *n.* [längerer] Dolch

**dirndl** /ˈdɜːndl/ *n.* Dirndl[kleid], *das;* **~ [skirt]** Dirndlrock, *der*

**dirt** /dɜːt/ *n., no pl.* Ⓐ Schmutz, *der;* Dreck, *der* (*ugs.*); **be covered in ~:** ganz schmutzig sein; (*stronger*) vor Schmutz starren; **~ cheap** spottbillig; **treat sb. like ~:** jmdn. wie [den letzten] Dreck behandeln (*salopp*); **do sb. ~** (*fig. coll.*) jmdm. eins auswischen (*ugs.*); Ⓑ (*soil*) Erde, *die;* Ⓒ (*fig.*) (*lewdness*) Schmutz, *der;* (*worthless thing*) Dreck, *der* (*salopp abwertend*); Schund, *der* (*ugs.*); (*person*) Abschaum, *der;* **give me the ~ on him** (*coll.*) sag mir, wo er Dreck am Stecken hat (*ugs.*)

**'dirt farmer** *n.* (*Amer.*) [richtiger] Farmer (*der selbst sein Land bestellt*)

**dirtiness** /ˈdɜːtɪnɪs/ *n., no pl.* Schmutzigkeit, *die*

**dirt: ~ road** *n.* (*Amer.*) unbefestigte Straße; **~-track** *n.* (*Sport*) Aschenbahn, *die;* (*made of earth*) ≈ Sandbahn, *die*

**dirty** /ˈdɜːtɪ/ ❶ *adj.* Ⓐ schmutzig; dreckig (*ugs.*); **get one's shoes/hands ~:** sich (*Dat.*) die Schuhe/Hände schmutzig machen; **get sth. ~:** etw. schmutzig machen; **~ money** Schmutzzulage, *die;* Ⓑ (*with dark tinge*) schmutzig ‹Farbe›; **~ grey colour** schmutzig graue Farbe; Ⓒ **~ weather** stürmisches Wetter; Dreckwetter, *das* (*ugs. abwertend*); Ⓓ (*coll.: causing fallout*) ‹Kernwaffe:› mit starkem Fallout; schmutzig (*fig.*); Ⓔ **~ look** (*coll.*) giftiger Blick; **give sb. a ~ look** jmdn. giftig ansehen; Ⓕ (*ill-gotten*) schmutzig ‹Geld›; Ⓖ (*fig.: obscene*) schmutzig; schlüpfrig; (*sexually illicit*) **spend a ~ weekend together** ein Liebeswochenende zusammen verbringen; (*lascivious*) **have a ~ mind** eine schmutzige Fantasie haben; **~ old man** alter Lustmolch (*ugs. abwertend*); geiler alter Bock (*salopp abwertend*); Ⓗ (*despicable, sordid*) schmutzig ‹Lüge, Gerücht, Geschäft›; dreckig (*salopp abwertend*), gemein ‹Lügner, Betrüger›; (*unsportsmanlike*) unfair; **do the ~ on sb.** (*coll.*) jmdn. [he]reinlegen (*ugs.*); **~ dog** (*fig. coll.*) Schwein, *das* (*ugs. abwertend*); **~ trick** gemeiner Trick; **play sb. a ~ trick** jmdn. ganz gemein übers Ohr hauen (*ugs.*); **~ work [at the crossroads]** (*coll.*) schmutziges Geschäft; **do sb.'s/the ~ work** sich (*Dat.*) für jmdn./sich (*Dat.*) die Finger schmutzig machen; **get the ~ end of the stick** (*coll.*) der Dumme sein (*ugs.*). ❷ *adv.* (*coll.*) **~ great** riesig (*ugs.*). ❸ *v.t.* schmutzig machen; beschmutzen

**dirty 'word** *n.* unanständiges Wort; (*fig.*) Schimpfwort, *das*

**disability** /dɪsəˈbɪlɪtɪ/ *n.* Ⓐ Behinderung, *die;* (*inability to be gainfully employed*) Invalidität, *die;* Erwerbsunfähigkeit, *die;* **suffer from** *or* **have a ~:** behindert/erwerbsunfähig sein; Ⓑ (*cause of inability*) Behinderung, *die*

**disability: ~ allowance** *n.* Erwerbsunfähigkeitsentschädigung, *die;* **~ pension** *n.* Erwerbsunfähigkeitsrente, *die*

**disable** /dɪˈseɪbl/ *v.t.* Ⓐ **~ sb. [physically]** jmdn. zum Invaliden machen; **be ~d by sth.** durch etw. behindert sein; **be permanently ~d by sth.** eine bleibende Behinderung bei etw. davontragen; **strikes which ~ the economy** Streiks, die die Wirtschaft lahm legen; Ⓑ (*make unable to fight*) kampfunfähig machen ‹Feind, Schiff, Panzer, Flugzeug›; kampfunfähig schlagen ‹Boxer›; unbrauchbar machen ‹Gewehr, Kanone›

**disabled** /dɪˈseɪbld/ ❶ *adj.* Ⓐ behindert; **~ ex-serviceman** Kriegsinvalide, *der;* **physically/mentally ~:** körperbehindert/geistig behindert; Ⓑ (*unable to fight*) kampfunfähig ‹Schiff, Panzer, Flugzeug, Boxer›; unbrauchbar ‹Kanone, Gewehr›. ❷ *n. pl.* **the [physically/mentally] ~:** die [Körper]behinderten/[geistig] Behinderten

**disablement** /dɪˈseɪblmənt/ *n., no pl.* Behinderung, *die*

**disabuse** /dɪsəˈbjuːz/ *v.t.* **~ sb. of sth.** jmdn. von etw. abbringen

**disadvantage** /dɪsədˈvɑːntɪdʒ/ ❶ *n.* Ⓐ Nachteil, *der;* (*state of being disadvantaged*) Benachteiligung, *die;* **be at a ~:** im Nachteil sein; benachteiligt sein; **his inexperience put him at a ~:** er war durch seine mangelnde Erfahrung benachteiligt; Ⓑ *no pl.* (*damage*) Schaden, *der;* **be to sb.'s/sth.'s ~:** sich zu jmds. Nachteil/zum Nachteil einer Sache auswirken. ❷ *v.t.* benachteiligen

**disadvantaged** /dɪsədˈvɑːntɪdʒd/ *adj.* benachteiligt

**disadvantageous** /dɪsædvənˈteɪdʒəs/ *adj.* Ⓐ nachteilig; ungünstig ‹Zeitpunkt›; **be ~ to sb./sth.** für jmdn./etw. von Nachteil sein; Ⓑ (*unflattering*) unvorteilhaft

**disaffected** /dɪsəˈfektɪd/ *adj.* Ⓐ (*disloyal*) illoyal (**to gegenüber**); Ⓑ (*estranged*) entfremdet (**from** *Dat.*)

**disaffection** /dɪsəˈfekʃn/ *n., no pl.* Entfremdung, *die* (**from** von)

**disagree** /dɪsəˈgriː/ *v.i.* Ⓐ anderer Meinung sein; **~ with sb.** mit jmdm. nicht übereinstimmen; anderer Meinung als jmd. sein; **~ with sth.** mit etw. nicht übereinstimmen; **~ [with sb.] about** *or* **over sth.** sich [mit jmdm.] über etw. (*Akk.*) nicht einig sein; ⇒ *also* **agree** 1 A; Ⓑ (*quarrel*) eine Auseinandersetzung haben; Ⓒ (*be mutually inconsistent*) nicht übereinstimmen; Ⓓ **~ with sb.** (*have bad effects on*) jmdm. nicht bekommen

**disagreeable** /dɪsəˈgrɪəbl/ *adj.* unangenehm; unappetitlich ‹Nahrungsmittel›

**disagreeably** /dɪsəˈgrɪəblɪ/ *adv.* Ⓐ unangenehm; Ⓑ (*bad-temperedly*) übellaunig

**disagreement** /dɪsəˈgriːmənt/ *n.* Ⓐ (*difference of opinion*) Uneinigkeit, *die;* (*refusal to agree*) **be in ~:** geteilter Meinung sein; **be in ~ with sb./sth.** mit jmdm./etw. nicht übereinstimmen; Ⓑ (*strife, quarrel*) Meinungsverschiedenheit, *die;* Ⓒ (*discrepancy*) Diskrepanz, *die*

**disallow** /dɪsəˈlaʊ/ *v.t.* nicht gestatten; abweisen ‹Antrag, Anspruch, Klage›; (*refuse to admit*) nicht anerkennen; nicht gelten lassen; (*Sport*) nicht geben ‹Tor›

**disambiguate** /dɪsæmˈbɪgjʊeɪt/ *v.t.* eindeutig machen; disambiguieren (*Sprachw.*)

**disappear** /dɪsəˈpɪə(r)/ *v.i.* verschwinden; ‹Brauch, Kunst, Tierart:› aussterben; ‹Angst, Ärger, Laune:› verfliegen; **do a ~ing act** *or* **trick** (*fig.*) spurlos verschwinden

**disappearance** /dɪsəˈpɪərəns/ *n.* Verschwinden, *das;* (*of customs; extinction*) Aussterben, *das*

**disappoint** /dɪsəˈpɔɪnt/ *v.t.* enttäuschen; **be ~ed in** *or* **by** *or* **with sb./sth.** von jmdm./etw. enttäuscht sein; **he was ~ed at** *or* **by** *or* **with having failed/the way things had changed** er war enttäuscht [darüber], dass er durchgefallen war/darüber, wie sich die Dinge verändert hatten

**disappointing** /dɪsəˈpɔɪntɪŋ/ *adj.* enttäuschend; **how ~!** so eine Enttäuschung!

**disappointingly** /dɪsəˈpɔɪntɪŋlɪ/ *adv.* enttäuschend; **~, he only came fourth** enttäuschenderweise wurde er nur Vierter

**disappointment** /dɪsəˈpɔɪntmənt/ *n.* Enttäuschung, *die;* **come as a ~ to sb.** eine Enttäuschung für jmdn. sein

**disapprobation** /dɪsæprəˈbeɪʃn/, **disapproval** /dɪsəˈpruːvl/ *ns.* Missbilligung, *die;* **show one's/cause disapproval** sein Missfallen zeigen/Missfallen erregen; **with disapproval** missbilligend; mit Missbilligung

**disapprove** /dɪsəˈpruːv/ ❶ *v.i.* dagegen sein; **~ of sb./sth.** jmdn. ablehnen/etw. missbilligen; **~ of sb. doing sth.** es missbilligen, wenn jmd. etw. tut. ❷ *v.t.* missbilligen

**disapproving** /dɪsəˈpruːvɪŋ/ *adj.*, **disapprovingly** /dɪsəˈpruːvɪŋlɪ/ *adv.* missbilligend

**disarm** /dɪsˈɑːm/ ❶ *v.t.* Ⓐ entwaffnen; entschärfen ‹Bombe›; Ⓑ (*fig.*) entwaffnen; verstummen lassen ‹Kritik›; abbauen ‹Feindseligkeit›. ❷ *v.i.* abrüsten

**disarmament** /dɪsˈɑːməmənt/ *n.* Abrüstung, *die;* **~ talks** Abrüstungsgespräche

**disarming** /dɪsˈɑːmɪŋ/ *adj.* entwaffnend

**disarmingly** /dɪsˈɑːmɪŋlɪ/ *adv.* entwaffnend

**disarrange** /dɪsəˈreɪndʒ/ *v.t.* durcheinander bringen; zerzausen ‹Haar›

**disarray** /dɪsəˈreɪ/ ❶ *n.* Unordnung, *die;* (*confusion*) Wirrwarr, *der;* **fall into ~:** durcheinander geraten; **be in ~:** in Unordnung sein. ❷ *v.t.* in Unordnung bringen

**disassemble** /dɪsəˈsembl/ *v.t.* auseinander nehmen ‹Maschine›; abbauen ‹Gebäude, Anlage›

**disassembly** /dɪsəˈsemblɪ/ *n.* (*of machine*) Auseinandernehmen, *das;* (*of structure*) Abbau, *der*

**disassociation** /dɪsəsəʊsɪˈeɪʃn/ ⇒ **dissociation** A

**disaster** /dɪˈzɑːstə(r)/ *n.* Ⓐ Katastrophe, *die;* **air ~:** Flugzeugunglück, *das;* (*with many deaths also*) Flugzeugkatastrophe, *die;* **a railway/mining ~:** ein Eisenbahn-/Grubenunglück; **natural ~:** Naturkatastrophe, *die;* **motorway ~:** schwerer Unfall auf der Autobahn; **end in ~:** in einer Katastrophe enden; Ⓑ (*complete failure*) Fiasko, *das;* Katastrophe, *die;* **lead to ~:** zu einem Fiasko *od.* einer Katastrophe führen; **prove a ~:** sich als katastrophal erweisen

**disaster: ~ area** *n.* Katastrophengebiet, *das;* **he/she is a [walking] ~ area** (*fig. coll.*) er/sie ist eine wandelnde Katastrophe (*fig.*); **~ fund** *n.* Nothilfefonds, *der*

**disastrous** /dɪˈzɑːstrəs/ *adj.* katastrophal; verhängnisvoll ‹Irrtum, Entscheidung, Politik›; verheerend ‹Überschwemmung, Wirbelsturm, Feuer›

**disastrously** /dɪˈzɑːstrəslɪ/ *adv.* katastrophal

**disavow** /dɪsəˈvaʊ/ *v.t.* verleugnen; nicht anerkennen ‹Rechtsprechung, Vereinbarung›; **~ responsibility for sth.** die Verantwortung für etw. von sich weisen

d

**disavowal** /dɪsə'vaʊəl/ *n.* Verleugnung, *die*

**disband** /dɪs'bænd/ ❶ *v.t.* auflösen; **the ~ed soldiers** die entlassenen Soldaten. ❷ *v.i.* sich auflösen

**disbar** /dɪs'bɑː(r)/ *v.t.* **-rr-** (*Law*) die Zulassung entziehen (+ *Dat.*)

**disbelief** /dɪsbɪ'liːf/ *n.* Unglaube, *der;* **be met with ~:** auf Unglauben stoßen; **in ~:** ungläubig

**disbelieve** /dɪsbɪ'liːv/ ❶ *v.t.* **~ sb./sth.** jmdm. nicht glauben *od.* (*geh.*) keinen Glauben schenken/etw. nicht glauben. ❷ *v.i.* nicht glauben; **~ in sth.** nicht an etw. (*Akk.*) glauben

**disbeliever** /dɪsbɪ'liːvə(r)/ *n.* Ungläubige, *der/die;* **be a ~ in sth.** nicht an etw. (*Akk.*) glauben

**disburden** /dɪs'bɜːdn/ ⇒ **unburden**

**disburse** /dɪs'bɜːs/ *v.t.* ausgeben

**disbursement** /dɪs'bɜːsmənt/ *n.* Auszahlung, *die;* (*expenditure*) Ausgabe, *die*

**disc** /dɪsk/ *n.* Ⓐ Scheibe, *die;* Ⓑ (*gramophone record*) [Schall]platte, *die;* ⇒ *also* **compact disc**; Ⓒ (*Computing*) ⇒ **disk**; Ⓓ (*Anat.*) Bandscheibe, *die;* ⇒ *also* **slipped disc**; Ⓔ (*Bot.*) Körbchen, das

**discard** ❶ /dɪ'skɑːd/ *v.t.* Ⓐ wegwerfen; ablegen ‹Kleidung›; fallen lassen ‹Vorschlag, Idee, Mensch›; Ⓑ (*Cards*) abwerfen. ❷ /'dɪskɑːd/ *n.* Ausschuss, *der;* (*person*) Ausgestoßene, *der/die*

**'disc brake** *n.* Scheibenbremse, *die*

**discern** /dɪ'sɜːn/ *v.t.* wahrnehmen; **sth. can be ~ed** etw. ist zu erkennen; **~ from sth. whether ...:** an etw. (*Dat.*) erkennen, ob ...

**discernible** /dɪ'sɜːnɪbl/ *adj.* erkennbar; wahrnehmbar ‹Stimme, Geruch›; **a ~ pattern has emerged** ein Schema ist erkennbar geworden

**discerning** /dɪ'sɜːnɪŋ/ *adj.* fein ‹Gaumen, Ohr, Geschmack›; scharf ‹Auge›; urteilsfähig ‹Richter, Kritiker›; kritisch ‹Leser, Kunde, Zuschauer, Kommentar›; scharfsichtig ‹Kritik›

**discernment** /dɪ'sɛːnmənt/ *n., no pl.* (*act of discerning*) Wahrnehmung, *die;* (*faculty of discerning*) Urteilsfähigkeit, *die*

**discharge** ❶ /dɪs'tʃɑːdʒ/ *v.t.* Ⓐ (*dismiss, allow to leave*) entlassen (**from** aus); freisprechen ‹Angeklagte›; (*exempt from liabilities*) befreien (**from** von); **the patient ~d himself from hospital** der Patient verließ eigenmächtig das Krankenhaus; Ⓑ (*send out*) abschießen ‹Pfeil, Torpedo›; ablassen ‹Flüssigkeit, Gas›; absondern ‹Eiter›; (*unload from ship*) ausschiffen; löschen ‹Ladung›; (*Electr.*) entladen; Ⓒ (*relieve of load*) entladen; löschen ‹Schiff›; (*fire*) abfeuern ‹Gewehr, Kanone›; Ⓓ (*acquit oneself of, pay*) erfüllen ‹Pflicht, Verbindlichkeiten, Versprechen›; bezahlen ‹Schulden›.
❷ *v.i.* Ⓐ entladen werden; ‹Schiff auch:› gelöscht werden; ‹Batterie:› sich entladen; ‹Gewehr:› losgehen; Ⓑ (*flow*) münden (**into** in + *Akk.*); Ⓒ ‹Wunde, Geschwür:› eitern.
❸ /dɪs'tʃɑːdʒ, 'dɪstʃɑːdʒ/ *n.* Ⓐ (*dismissal*) Entlassung, *die* (**from** aus); (*of defendant*) Freispruch, *der;* (*exemption from liabilities*) Befreiung, *die;* (*written certificate of release*) Entlassungsschein, *der;* (*written certificate of exemption*) Entlastungsschein, *der;* **be granted a full ~ [by the court]** [vom Gericht] in allen Punkten freigesprochen werden; Ⓑ (*emission*) Ausfluss, *der;* (*of gas*) Austritt, *der;* (*of pus*) Absonderung, *die;* (*Electr.*) Entladung, *die;* (*of gun*) Abfeuern, *das;* **vaginal ~:** [Scheiden]ausfluss, *der;* Ⓒ (*of debt*) Begleichung, *die;* (*of duty*) Erfüllung, *die*

**'disc harrow** *n.* (*Agric.*) Scheibenegge, *die*

**disciple** /dɪ'saɪpl/ *n.* Ⓐ (*Relig.*) Jünger, *der;* Ⓑ (*follower*) Anhänger, *der*/Anhängerin, *die;* Jünger, *der* (*geh., oft scherzh.*)

**disciplinarian** /dɪsɪplɪ'neərɪən/ *n.* Zuchtmeister, *der*/-meisterin, *die* (*veralt., noch scherzh.*); (*in school, family also*) [strenger] Erzieher; **he is a poor ~:** er kann nicht für Disziplin sorgen

**disciplinary** /'dɪsɪplɪnərɪ, dɪsɪ'plɪnərɪ/ *adj.* Disziplinar-; disziplinarisch; **~ action** Disziplinarmaßnahmen *Pl.;* **~ proceedings** Disziplinarverfahren, *das*

**discipline** /'dɪsɪplɪn/ ❶ *n.* Ⓐ (*order, branch*) Disziplin, *die;* **maintain ~:** die Disziplin aufrechterhalten; **lack of ~:** Mangel an Disziplin; **change ~s** die Disziplin *od.* das Fach wechseln; Ⓑ (*mental training*) Schulung, *die;* **the ~ of adversity** die strenge Schule der Not; Ⓒ (*system of rules*) Kanon, *der;* Ⓓ (*punishment*) Strafe, *die;* (*physical also*) Züchtigung, *die* (*geh.*); (*Relig.*) Kasteiung, *die.*
❷ *v.t.* Ⓐ disziplinieren; (*train in military exercises*) ausbilden; **you must ~ yourself to eat less** Sie müssen sich zwingen, weniger zu essen; **~ one's emotions/feelings** *etc.* seine Emotionen/Gefühle *usw.* unter Kontrolle halten; Ⓑ (*punish*) bestrafen; (*physically also*) züchtigen (*geh.*); (*Relig.*) kasteien

**disciplined** /'dɪsɪplɪnd/ *adj.* diszipliniert; **highly/well ~:** sehr diszipliniert; **badly ~:** undiszipliniert

**'disc jockey** *n.* Diskjockey, *der*

**disclaim** /dɪs'kleɪm/ *v.t.* Ⓐ abstreiten; Ⓑ (*Law*) verzichten auf (+ *Akk.*)

**disclaimer** /dɪs'kleɪmə(r)/ *n.* Gegenerklärung, *die;* (*Law*) Verzichterklärung, *die*

**disclose** /dɪs'kləʊz/ *v.t.* Ⓐ (*expose to view*) den Blick freigeben auf (+ *Akk.*); Ⓑ (*make known*) enthüllen; bekannt geben ‹Information, Nachricht›; **research ~d that ...:** Nachforschungen ergaben, dass ...; **he didn't ~ why he'd come** er verriet nicht, warum er gekommen war

**disclosure** /dɪs'kləʊʒə(r)/ *n.* Enthüllung, *die;* (*of information, news*) Bekanntgabe, *die;* **for fear of possible ~:** aus Furcht vor einer möglichen Enthüllung; **the newspaper's ~ of bribery** die Enthüllungen der Zeitung über Bestechung

**disco** /'dɪskəʊ/ *n., pl.* **~s** (*coll.*) Ⓐ (*discothèque, party*) Disko, *die;* Ⓑ (*equipment*) **travelling ~:** rollende Disko

**'disco dancing** *n.* Diskotanz, *der*

**discolor** (*Amer.*) ⇒ **discolour**

**discoloration** /dɪskʌlə'reɪʃn/ *n.* Verfärbung, *die*

**discolour** /dɪs'kʌlə(r)/ (*Brit.*) ❶ *v.t.* verfärben; (*fade*) ausbleichen. ❷ *v.i.* sich verfärben; (*fade*) ausbleichen

**discolouration** (*Brit.*) ⇒ **discoloration**

**discombobulate** /dɪskəm'bɒbjʊleɪt/ *v.t.* (*Amer. joc.*) durcheinander bringen

**discomfit** /dɪs'kʌmfɪt/ *v.t.* Ⓐ (*baffle, disconcert*) verunsichern; Ⓑ (*arch.: overwhelm, thwart*) schlagen

**discomfiture** /dɪs'kʌmfɪtʃə(r)/ *n.* Verunsicherung, *die*

**discomfort** /dɪs'kʌmfət/ ❶ *n.* Ⓐ *no pl.* (*uneasiness of body*) Beschwerden *Pl.;* **cause/give sb. ~:** jmdm. Beschwerden machen; Ⓑ *no pl.* (*uneasiness of mind*) Unbehagen, *das;* Ⓒ (*hardship*) Unannehmlichkeit, *die.* ❷ *v.t.* zu schaffen machen (+ *Dat.*)

**discompose** /dɪskəm'pəʊz/ *v.t.* aus der Fassung bringen; **appear ~d** einen verstörten Eindruck machen

**discomposure** /dɪskəm'pəʊʒə(r)/ *n., no pl.* Verstörtheit, *die*

**'disco music** *n.* Diskomusik, *die*

**disconcert** /dɪskən'sɜːt/ *v.t.* irritieren; **I was ~ed to find the gates locked** ich war verwirrt, als ich vor verschlossenen Toren stand

**disconcerted** /dɪskən'sɜːtɪd/ *adj.* verstört; irritiert

**disconcerting** /dɪskən'sɜːtɪŋ/ *adj.*, **disconcertingly** /dɪskən'sɜːtɪŋlɪ/ *adv.* irritierend

**disconnect** /dɪskə'nekt/ *v.t.* Ⓐ abtrennen; abhängen ‹Wagen›; Ⓑ (*Electr., Teleph.*) **~ the electricity from a house** ein Haus von der Stromversorgung abtrennen; **~ the TV** den Stecker des Fernsehers herausziehen; **the loudspeakers have become ~ed** die Lautsprecher sind nicht mehr angeschlossen; **if you don't pay your telephone bill you will be ~ed** wenn Sie Ihre Telefonrechnung nicht bezahlen, wird Ihr Telefon abgestellt; **operator, I've been ~ed** hallo, Vermittlung, die Verbindung ist unterbrochen; **~ a call** ein Gespräch unterbrechen

**disconnected** /dɪskə'nektɪd/ *adj.* Ⓐ abgetrennt; abgestellt ‹Telefon›; **is the cooker/TV ~?** ist der Stecker beim Herd/Fernseher herausgezogen?; Ⓑ (*incoherent*) unzusammenhängend ‹Rede, Worte›

**disconnectedly** /dɪskə'nektɪdlɪ/ *adv.* unzusammenhängend

**disconnection**, (*Brit.*) **disconnexion** /dɪskə'nekʃn/ *n.* Abtrennung, *die*

**disconsolate** /dɪs'kɒnsələt/ *adj.* Ⓐ (*unhappy*) unglücklich; Ⓑ (*inconsolable*) untröstlich

**disconsolately** /dɪs'kɒnsələtlɪ/ *adj.* Ⓐ (*unhappily*) unglücklich; Ⓑ (*inconsolably*) untröstlich

**discontent** /dɪskən'tent/ ❶ *n.* Unzufriedenheit, *die.* ❷ *v.t.* unzufrieden machen

**discontented** /dɪskən'tentɪd/ *adj.* unzufrieden (**with, about** mit)

**discontentment** /dɪskən'tentmənt/ *n., no pl.* Unzufriedenheit, *die*

**discontinuance** /dɪskənt'tɪnjʊəns/, **discontinuation** /dɪskəntɪnjʊ'eɪʃn/ *ns.* Einstellung, *die;* (*of subscription*) Abbestellung, *die;* (*of treatment*) Abbruch, *der;* (*of habit*) Aufgabe, *die*

**discontinue** /dɪskən'tɪnjuː/ *v.t.* Ⓐ einstellen; abbestellen ‹Abonnement›; abbrechen ‹Behandlung›; aufgeben ‹Gewohnheit›; Ⓑ (*Commerc.*) **a ~d range** *or* **line** eine auslaufende Serie

**discontinuity** /dɪskɒntɪ'njuːɪtɪ/ *n.* Bruch, *der;* **a ~ of style** ein stilistischer Bruch

**discontinuous** /dɪskən'tɪnjʊəs/ *adj.* nicht kontinuierlich; diskontinuierlich (*geh.*)

**discontinuously** /dɪskən'tɪnjʊəslɪ/ *adv.* mit Unterbrechungen; nicht kontinuierlich

**discord** /'dɪskɔːd/ *n.* Ⓐ Zwietracht, *die;* (*quarrelling*) Streit, *der;* Ⓑ (*Mus.*) (*chord*) Dissonanz, *die;* (*interval*) Disharmonie, *die;* (*single note*) Misston, *der;* Ⓒ (*harsh noise*) Missklang, *der*

**discordant** /dɪ'skɔːdənt/ *adj.* Ⓐ gegensätzlich; Ⓑ (*dissonant*) misstönend

**discordantly** /dɪ'skɔːdəntlɪ/ *adv.* Ⓐ gegensätzlich; Ⓑ (*dissonantly*) misstönend

**discothèque** /'dɪskətek/ *n.* Diskothek, *die*

**discount** ❶ /'dɪskaʊnt/ *n.* (*Commerc.*) Rabatt, *der;* (*on bill of exchange*) Diskont, *der;* (*discounting*) Diskontierung, *die;* **give** *or* **offer [sb.] a ~ on sth.** [jmdm.] Rabatt auf etw. (*Akk.*) geben *od.* gewähren; **~ for cash** Skonto, *der od. das;* Rabatt bei Barzahlung; **at a ~:** mit Rabatt; (*St. Exch.*) unter dem Nennwert; (*fig.*) nicht gefragt; **the books were sold at a [big] ~:** die Bücher wurden [weit] unter dem normalen Preis verkauft.
❷ /dɪ'skaʊnt/ *v.t.* Ⓐ (*disbelieve*) unberücksichtigt lassen; (*discredit*) widerlegen ‹Beweis, Theorie›; (*underrate*) zu gering einschätzen; (*lessen*) schmälern ‹Wert›; (*reduce effect of*) einkalkulieren; Ⓑ (*Commerc.*) diskontieren ‹Wechsel›

**'discount broker** *n.* (*Commerc.*) Wechselmakler, *der*

**'discount: ~ house** *n.* (*Commerc.*) Diskontbank, *die;* **~ shop**, **~ store** *ns.* Discountladen, *der;* Discountgeschäft, *das*

**discourage** /dɪ'skʌrɪdʒ/ *v.t.* Ⓐ (*dispirit*) entmutigen; **be** *or* **become ~d [by sth.** *or* **because of sth.]** sich [durch etw.] entmutigen lassen; **be ~d because ...:** sich entmutigt fühlen, weil ...; Ⓑ (*advise against*) abraten; **~ sb. from sth.** jmdm. von etw. abraten; **~ sb. from doing sth.** jmdm. davon abraten, etw. zu tun; Ⓒ (*act against*) zu unterbinden suchen; Ⓓ (*disapprove of*) nicht gutheißen; **sth. must be ~d** man darf etw. nicht gutheißen; Ⓔ (*stop*) abhalten ‹Person›; verhindern ‹Handlung›; **~ sb. from doing sth.** jmdn. davon abhalten, etw. zu tun; **not ~d by fear of reprisals** ohne Furcht vor Vergeltungsmaßnahmen

**discouragement** /dɪ'skʌrɪdʒmənt/ *n.* Ⓐ Entmutigung, *die;* Ⓑ (*deterrent*) Abschreckung, *die;* **act as a ~ to sb.** eine abschreckende Wirkung auf jmdn. haben; Ⓒ (*depression*) Mutlosigkeit, *die*

**discouraging** /dɪ'skʌrɪdʒɪŋ/ *adj.* Ⓐ (*dispiriting*) entmutigend; **paint a ~ picture of**

**sth.** ein düsteres Bild von etw. malen; **he was rather ~:** er hat mir/ihm/ihr *usw.* wenig Mut gemacht; **the article makes ~ reading** die Lektüre des Artikels ist entmutigend; Ⓑ (*deterring*) abschreckend

**discouragingly** /dɪ'skʌrɪdʒɪŋlɪ/ *adv.* entmutigend

**discourse** ❶ /'dɪskɔ:s/ *n.* Diskurs, *der;* **hold a ~** *or* **be in ~ with sb.** einen Diskurs mit jmdm. haben *od.* führen. ❷ /dɪ'skɔ:s/ *v.i.* **~ [upon sth.]** sich [über etw. (*Akk.*)] ausführlich äußern; (*converse*) [über etw.] ausführlich reden

**discourteous** /dɪs'kɜ:tɪəs/ *adj.*, **discourteously** /dɪs'kɜ:tɪəslɪ/ *adv.* unhöflich

**discourtesy** /dɪs'kɜ:təsɪ/ *n.* Unhöflichkeit, *die;* **he did her a ~:** er beging ihr gegenüber eine Unhöflichkeit

**discover** /dɪ'skʌvə(r)/ *v.t.* Ⓐ (*find, notice, get knowledge of, realize*) entdecken; Ⓑ (*by search*) herausfinden; **~ a meaning in life** entdecken, dass das Leben einen Sinn hat; **it was never ~ed how ...:** es kam nie heraus, wie ...; **~ sb.'s identity** herausfinden, wer jmd. ist; **as far as I can ~:** soweit ich feststellen kann; Ⓒ (*Chess*) **~ed check** Abzugsschach, *das*

**discoverable** /dɪ'skʌvərəbl/ *adj.* auffindbar

**discoverer** /dɪ'skʌvərə(r)/ *n.* Entdecker, *der*/Entdeckerin, *die*

**discovery** /dɪ'skʌvərɪ/ *n.* Entdeckung, *die;* **voyage of ~:** Entdeckungsreise, *die;* **for fear of ~:** aus Angst, entdeckt zu werden

**'disc parking** *n.* (*Brit.*) Parken mit Parkscheibe

**discredit** /dɪs'kredɪt/ ❶ *n.* Ⓐ *no pl.* Misskredit, *der;* **bring ~ on sb./sth., bring sb./sth. into ~:** jmdn./etw. in Misskredit (*Akk.*) bringen; **be to the ~ of sb.** jmdm. keine Ehre machen; **without any ~ to the firm** ohne die Firma in Misskredit zu bringen; Ⓑ (*sb. or sth. that ~s*) **be a ~ to sb./sth.** jmdm./einer Sache keine Ehre machen; Ⓒ *no pl.* (*doubt*) **throw ~ on sth.** etw. unglaubwürdig erscheinen lassen; **fall into ~:** ins Zwielicht geraten.
❷ *v.t.* Ⓐ (*disbelieve*) keinen Glauben schenken (+ *Dat.*); (*discount as unreliable*) anzweifeln; (*cause to be disbelieved*) unglaubwürdig machen; **careful research has ~ed this theory** sorgfältige Untersuchungen haben diese Theorie zweifelhaft werden lassen; Ⓑ (*disgrace*) diskreditieren (*geh.*); in Verruf bringen; **be ~ed** diskreditiert werden (*geh.*); in Verruf geraten

**discreditable** /dɪs'kredɪtəbl/ *adj.* unehrenhaft

**discreditably** /dɪs'kredɪtəblɪ/ *adv.* unehrenhaft; **perform ~ in the examination** bei der Prüfung unrühmlich abschneiden

**discreet** /dɪ'skri:t/ *adj.*, **~er** /dɪ'skri:tə(r)/, **~est** /dɪ'skri:tɪst/ diskret; taktvoll; (*unobtrusive*) diskret; dezent ‹Parfüm, Kleidung›

**discreetly** /dɪ'skri:tlɪ/ *adv.* diskret; dezent ‹gekleidet›

**discreetness** /dɪ'skri:tnɪs/ *n., no pl.* Diskretheit, *die*

**discrepancy** /dɪ'skrepənsɪ/ *n.* Diskrepanz, *die;* **there is wide ~ between the statements of the two witnesses** die beiden Zeugenaussagen stimmen bei weitem nicht überein

**discrepant** /dɪ'skrepənt/ *adj.* [voneinander] abweichend

**discrete** /dɪ'skri:t/ *adj.* eigenständig; (*Math., Phys.*) diskret; **a ~ whole** ein Ganzes aus eigenständigen Teilen

**discreteness** /dɪ'skri:tnɪs/ *n., no pl.* Eigenständigkeit, *die*

**discretion** /dɪ'skreʃn/ *n.* Ⓐ (*prudence*) Umsicht, *die;* (*reservedness*) Diskretion, *die;* **use ~:** diskret sein; **reach years** *or* **the age of ~:** mündig werden; **~ is the better part of valour** (*prov.*) Vorsicht ist besser als Nachsicht (*ugs. scherzh.*); Vorsicht ist die Mutter der Weisheit; Ⓑ (*liberty to decide*) Ermessen, *das;* **leave sth. to sb.'s ~:** etw. in jmds. Ermessen (*Akk.*) stellen; etw. jmds. Entscheidung (*Dat.*) überlassen; **at sb.'s ~:** nach jmds. Ermessen; **be within** *or* **at** *or* **left to sb.'s ~:** in jmds. Ermessen (*Dat.*) liegen; **use one's ~:** nach eigenem Ermessen *od.* Gutdünken handeln

**discretionary** /dɪ'skreʃənərɪ/ *adj.* nach freiem Ermessen gewährt ‹Leistung, Zuschuss usw.›; Ermessens‹leistung›; **~ powers** Entscheidungsgewalt, *die*

**discriminate** /dɪ'skrɪmɪneɪt/ ❶ *v.t.* unterscheiden. ❷ *v.i.* Ⓐ (*distinguish, use discernment*) unterscheiden; **~ between [two things]** unterscheiden zwischen [zwei Dingen]; Ⓑ **~ against sb.** jmdn. diskriminieren; **~ in favour of sb.** jmdn. bevorzugen

**discriminating** /dɪ'skrɪmɪneɪtɪŋ/ *adj.* kritisch ‹Urteil, Auge, Kunde, Kunstsammler›; fein ‹Geschmack, Gaumen, Ohr›

**discriminatingly** /dɪ'skrɪmɪneɪtɪŋlɪ/ *adv.* kritisch; scharfsichtig ‹kritisieren›

**discrimination** /dɪskrɪmɪ'neɪʃn/ *n.* Ⓐ (*act of discriminating*) Unterscheidung, *die;* Ⓑ (*discernment*) [kritisches] Urteilsvermögen; Ⓒ (*differential treatment*) Diskriminierung, *die* (**against** *Gen.*); **~ against Blacks/women** Diskriminierung von Schwarzen/Frauen; **~ against foreign imports** die Erschwerung von ausländischen Importen; **~ in favour of** Bevorzugung (+ *Gen.*); **racial ~:** Rassendiskriminierung, *die*

**discriminatory** /dɪ'skrɪmɪnətərɪ/ *adj.* diskriminierend

**discursive** /dɪ'skɜ:sɪv/ *adj.*, **discursively** /dɪ'skɜ:sɪvlɪ/ *adv.* weitschweifig

**discursiveness** /dɪ'skɜ:sɪvnɪs/ *n., no pl.* Weitschweifigkeit, *die*

**discus** /'dɪskəs/ *n.* (*Sport*) Ⓐ Diskus, *der;* Ⓑ (*event*) Diskuswerfen, *das*

**discuss** /dɪ'skʌs/ *v.t.* Ⓐ (*talk about*) besprechen; **~ sth. with sb.** etw. mit jmdm. besprechen; **the children were ~ing the wedding** die Kinder sprachen über die Hochzeit; **I'm not willing to ~ this matter at present** ich möchte jetzt nicht darüber sprechen; Ⓑ (*debate*) diskutieren über (+ *Akk.*); (*examine*) erörtern; diskutieren

**discussion** /dɪ'skʌʃn/ *n.* Ⓐ (*conversation*) Gespräch, *das;* (*more formal*) Unterredung, *die;* **after much ~:** nach langen Gesprächen/Unterredungen; **let's have a ~ about it** wir wollen darüber reden *od.* sprechen; **there was some ~ before they ...:** sie besprachen sich miteinander, bevor sie ...; Ⓑ (*debate*) Diskussion, *die;* (*examination*) Erörterung, *die;* **come up for ~:** zur Diskussion gestellt werden; **be under ~:** zur Diskussion stehen; **matter** *or* **topic for ~:** Thema *od.* Gegenstand der Diskussion; **hold** *or* **have a ~ with sb.** mit jmdm. diskutieren

**discussion: ~ group** *n.* Diskussionsrunde, *die;* **~ programme** *n.* (*Radio, Telev.*) Diskussionssendung, *die*

**disdain** /dɪs'deɪn/ ❶ *n.* Verachtung, *die;* **with ~:** verächtlich; **a look of ~:** ein verächtlicher *od.* geringschätziger Blick. ❷ *v.t.* verachten; verächtlich ablehnen ‹Rat, Hilfe›; **~ to do sth.** zu stolz sein, etw. zu tun

**disdainful** /dɪs'deɪnfl/ *adj.* verächtlich, geringschätzig ‹Lachen, Ton, Blick, Kommentar›; **look ~:** verächtlich dreinblicken; **be ~ of advice/simple pleasures** Ratschläge verächtlich ablehnen/einfache Freuden verachten

**disdainfully** /dɪs'deɪnfəlɪ/ *adv.* verächtlich; geringschätzig; voll Verachtung ‹ignorieren›; **look ~ at sb./sth.** jmdn./etw. verächtlich *od.* geringschätzig ansehen

**disease** /dɪ'zi:z/ *n.* ▶ **1232** (*lit. or fig.*) Krankheit, *die;* **suffer from a ~:** an einer Krankheit leiden; **the spreading of ~:** die Ausbreitung von Krankheiten

**diseased** /dɪ'zi:zd/ *adj.* (*lit. or fig.*) krank

**disembark** /dɪsɪm'bɑ:k/ ❶ *v.t.* ausschiffen. ❷ *v.i.* von Bord gehen; **wait a long time to ~:** lange auf die Ausschiffung warten

**disembarkation** /dɪsembɑ:'keɪʃn/ *n.* (*of troops*) Landung, *die;* (*of cargo, passengers*) Ausschiffung, *die*

**disembodied** /dɪsɪm'bɒdɪd/ *adj.* körperlos ‹Seele, Geist›; geisterhaft ‹Stimme›

**disembowel** /dɪsɪm'baʊəl/ *v.t.*, (*Brit.*) **-ll-** die Eingeweide herausnehmen (+ *Dat.*); (*by violence*) den Bauch aufschlitzen (+ *Dat.*)

**disenchant** /dɪsɪn'tʃɑ:nt/ *v.t.* Ⓐ entzaubern (*geh.*); Ⓑ (*disillusion*) ernüchtern; **he became ~ed with sb./sth.** jmd./etw. hat ihn desillusioniert

**disenchantment** /dɪsɪn'tʃɑ:ntmənt/ *n.* ⇒ **disenchant**: Entzauberung, *die* (*geh.*); Ernüchterung, *die* (**with** in Bezug auf)

**disenfranchise** /dɪsɪn'fræntʃaɪz/ ⇒ **disfranchise**

**disengage** /dɪsɪn'geɪdʒ/ ❶ *v.t.* Ⓐ lösen (**from** aus, von); **~ one's hand** seine Hand freibekommen; Ⓑ (*Mech.*) **~ the clutch** auskuppeln; **~ the gear** den Gang herausnehmen; Ⓒ (*Mil.*) abziehen. ❷ *v.i.* Ⓐ sich zurückziehen (**from** aus); ‹Kupplung:› sich lösen; Ⓑ (*Mil.*) sich zurückziehen (**from** aus); Ⓒ (*Fencing*) sich [aus der gegnerischen Bindung] lösen

**disengaged** /dɪsɪn'geɪdʒd/ *adj.* Ⓐ frei; Ⓑ (*uncommitted*) nicht [politisch] engagiert

**disentangle** /dɪsɪn'tæŋgl/ ❶ *v.t.* Ⓐ (*extricate*) befreien (**from** aus); (*fig.*) herauslösen (**from** aus); Ⓑ (*unravel*) entwirren; (*fig.*) ordnen ‹Gedanken›; entwirren ‹Handlung, Hinweise›. ❷ *v.i.* sich entwirren

**disentanglement** /dɪsɪn'tæŋglmənt/ *n.* (*lit. or fig.*) Entwirrung, *die*

**disentomb** /dɪsɪn'tu:m/ *v.t.* ausgraben; freilegen

**disequilibrium** /dɪsi:kwɪ'lɪbrɪəm/ *n., no pl.* gestörtes Gleichgewicht; Ungleichgewicht, *das*

**disestablishment** /dɪsɪ'stæblɪʃmənt/ *n.* **the ~ of the Church** die Trennung der Kirche vom Staat

**disfavour** (*Brit.;* *Amer.:* **disfavor**) /dɪs'feɪvə(r)/ ❶ *n.* Ⓐ (*displeasure, disapproval*) Missfallen, *das;* (*condition of being out of favour*) Ungnade, *die;* **incur sb.'s ~:** jmds. Unwillen erregen; Ⓑ (*disadvantage*) **in sb.'s ~:** zu jmds. Ungunsten. ❷ *v.t.* missbilligen

**disfigure** /dɪs'fɪgə(r)/ *v.t.* entstellen; verunstalten ‹Landschaft›

**disfigurement** /dɪs'fɪgəmənt/ *n.* Entstellung, *die;* (*of countryside*) Verunstaltung, *die*

**disfranchise** /dɪs'fræntʃaɪz/ *v.t.* die Privilegien entziehen (+ *Dat.*); (*of right to vote*) das Wahlrecht entziehen (+ *Dat.*)

**disgorge** /dɪs'gɔ:dʒ/ *v.t.* Ⓐ ausspucken; ausspeien (*geh.*); (*fig.*) ausspeien (*geh.*); herausgeben ‹Gefangene, Beute, Eigentum›; Ⓑ (*discharge*) ergießen ‹Wasser›

**disgrace** /dɪs'greɪs/ ❶ *n., no pl.* Ⓐ (*ignominy*) Schande, *die;* Schmach, *die* (*geh.*); (*deep disfavour*) Ungnade, *die;* **bring ~ on sb./sth.** Schande über jmdn./etw. bringen; **send sb. home in ~:** jmdn. wegen ungebührlichen Verhaltens nach Hause schicken; **he had to resign in ~:** er musste unehrenhaft zurücktreten; Ⓑ **be a ~ [to sb./sth.]** [für jmdn./etw.] eine Schande sein. ❷ *v.t.* Ⓐ (*bring shame on*) ‹Person:› Schande machen (+ *Dat.*); ‹Person, Handlung:› Schande bringen über (+ *Akk.*); sich blamieren; ‹Kind, Hund:› **~ oneself** sich danebenbenehmen (*ugs.*); Ⓑ **be ~d** (*be put out of favour*) in Ungnade fallen; (*be held up to reproach*) bloßgestellt werden

**disgraceful** /dɪs'greɪsfl/ *adj.* erbärmlich; miserabel ‹Handschrift›; skandalös ‹Benehmen, Enthüllung, Bedingungen, Verstoß, Behandlung, Tat›; **what a ~ thing to say/do!** wie kann man nur so etwas Schändliches sagen/tun!; **it's [absolutely** *or* **really** *or* **quite] ~:** es ist [wirklich] ein Skandal; **how ~!** was für eine Schande!; **you look ~:** du siehst ja furchtbar aus! (*ugs.*)

**disgracefully** /dɪs'greɪsfəlɪ/ *adv.* erbärmlich; schändlich ‹verraten, betrügen, behandeln›; **behave ~:** sich schändlich *od.* (*geh.*) schimpflich benehmen; **arrive ~ late** (*coll.*) furchtbar spät eintreffen; **she neglected her duties quite ~:** sie vernachlässigte ihre Pflichten geradezu sträflich

**disgruntled** /dɪs'grʌntld/ *adj.* verstimmt; **be in a ~ mood** verstimmt sein

**disguise** /dɪsˈgaɪz/ ❶ *v.t.* A verkleiden ‹Person›; verstellen ‹Stimme›; tarnen ‹Gegenstand›; ~ **oneself** sich verkleiden; **he ~d himself with a false beard** er tarnte sich mit einem falschen Bart; B (*misrepresent*) verschleiern; **there is no disguising the fact that ...:** es lässt sich nicht verheimlichen, dass ...; **a ~d tax** eine versteckte Steuer; C (*conceal*) verbergen; hinter dem Berg halten mit ‹Ansichten, Missbilligung›; **the herbs ~ the taste of the meat** die Kräuter überdecken den Geschmack des Fleisches.
❷ *n.* Verkleidung, *die;* (*fig.*) Maske, *die;* **adopt/wear a ~:** eine Verkleidung wählen/verkleidet sein; **wear sth. as a ~:** etw. zur Tarnung tragen; **in the ~ of** verkleidet als; **in ~:** verkleidet; **without any attempt at ~:** ohne irgendeinen Versuch, sich zu tarnen; ⇒ *also* **blessing** C

**disgust** /dɪsˈgʌst/ ❶ *n.* (*nausea*) Ekel, *der* (**at** vor + *Dat.*); (*revulsion*) Abscheu, *der* (**at** vor + *Dat.*); (*indignation*) Empörung, *die* (**at** über + *Akk.*); **in/with ~:** angewidert; (*with indignation*) empört. ❷ *v.t.* anwidern; (*fill with nausea*) anwidern; ekeln; (*fill with indignation*) empören

**disgusted** /dɪsˈgʌstɪd/ *adj.* angewidert; (*nauseated*) angewidert; angeekelt; (*indignant*) empört; **feel ~ at sth./with sb.** angewidert/angeekelt von etw./empört über etw./jmdn. sein

**disgustedly** /dɪsˈgʌstɪdlɪ/ *adv.* voller Ekel; angewidert; (*with nausea*) angewidert, angeekelt; (*indignantly*) empört

**disgusting** /dɪsˈgʌstɪŋ/ *adj.* widerlich; widerwärtig; (*nauseating also*) ekelhaft; miserabel (*ugs. abwertend*) ‹Prüfungsergebnis, schulische Leistungen›; **don't be ~:** sei nicht so geschmacklos

**disgustingly** /dɪsˈgʌstɪŋlɪ/ *adv.* widerlich; (*causing nausea also*) ekelhaft; unmöglich (*ugs.*) ‹sich kleiden›; (*iron.*) unverschämt ‹gut aussehen, reich›

**dish** /dɪʃ/ ❶ *n.* A (*for food*) Schale, *die;* (*flatter*) Platte, *die;* (*deeper*) Schüssel, *die;* B *in pl.* (*crockery*) Geschirr, *das;* **wash** *or* (*coll.*) **do the ~es** Geschirr spülen; abwaschen; C (*type of food*) Gericht, *das;* **it is [not] my/everybody's ~** (*fig. coll.*) darauf steh ich [nicht]/darauf steht [nicht] jeder (*ugs.*); D (*coll.: person*) (*woman, girl*) klasse Frau (*ugs.*); (*man*) klasse Typ (*ugs.*); **be quite a ~:** eine Wucht sein (*salopp*); E (*receptacle*) Schale, *die;* (*concavity*) Mulde, *die;* F (*Radio, Telev.*) Parabolantenne, *die.*
❷ *v.t.* A anrichten ‹Essen›; B (*coll.*) (*outmanœuvre*) austricksen (*ugs.*); (*ruin*) kleinkriegen (*ugs.*); zunichte machen ‹Hoffnung, Chancen›

~ **'out** *v.t.* A austeilen ‹Essen›; B (*coll.: distribute*) verteilen

~ **'up** *v.t.* auftragen, servieren ‹Essen›; (*fig.*) auftischen (*ugs. abwertend*)

**dishabille** /dɪsəˈbiːl/ ⇒ **déshabillé**

**disharmony** /dɪsˈhɑːmənɪ/ *n.* (*lit. or fig.*) Disharmonie, *die*

**dish: ~cloth** *n.* A (*for washing*) Abwaschlappen, *der;* Spültuch, *das;* B (*Brit.: for drying*) Geschirrtuch, *das;* ~ **cover** *n.* Cloche, *die* (*Gastr.*); (*against flies etc.*) Fliegenglocke, *die*

**dishearten** /dɪsˈhɑːtn/ *v.t.* entmutigen; **be ~ed** den Mut verlieren/verloren haben

**disheartening** /dɪsˈhɑːtənɪŋ/ *adj.*, **dishearteningly** /dɪsˈhɑːtənɪŋlɪ/ *adv.* entmutigend

**dished** /dɪʃt/ *adj.* konkav

**dishevelled** (*Amer.:* **disheveled**) /dɪˈʃevld/ *adj.* unordentlich ‹Kleidung›; zerzaust ‹Haar, Bart›; ungepflegt ‹Erscheinung›

**'dishmop** *n.* ≈ Spülbürste, *die*

**dishonest** /dɪsˈɒnɪst/ *adj.* unehrlich ‹Person›; unaufrichtig ‹Person, Antwort›; unlauter (*geh.*) ‹Geschäftsgebaren, Vorhaben›; unredlich ‹Geschäftsmann›; unreell ‹Geschäft, Gewinn›; ~ **goings-on** undurchsichtige Vorgänge; **be ~ with sb.** unehrlich *od.* unaufrichtig gegen jmdn. sein

**dishonestly** /dɪsˈɒnɪstlɪ/ *adv.* unehrlich; unaufrichtig; unlauter (*geh.*) ‹handeln›; unredlich ‹sich verhalten›

**dishonesty** /dɪsˈɒnɪstɪ/ *n.* Unehrlichkeit, *die;* Unaufrichtigkeit, *die;* (*of methods*) Unlauterkeit, *die* (*geh.*)

**dishonor** *etc.* (*Amer.*) ⇒ **dishonour** *etc.*

**dishonour** /dɪsˈɒnə(r)/ ❶ *n.* Schande, *die;* **bring ~ [up]on the nation/sb.** Schande über die Nation/jmdn. bringen. ❷ *v.t.* A beleidigen; B (*disgrace*) entehren; ~ **one's family** seiner Familie (*Dat.*) Schande machen; C (*Commerc.*) nicht honorieren ‹Wechsel›; nicht einlösen, zurückgehen lassen ‹Scheck›; nicht bezahlen ‹Schulden›

**dishonourable** /dɪsˈɒnərəbl/ *adj.* unehrenhaft

**dishonourably** /dɪsˈɒnərəblɪ/ *adv.* in unehrenhafter Weise

**dish: ~ rack** *n.* Abtropfgestell, *das;* (*in dishwasher*) Geschirrwagen, *der;* ~ **towel** *n.* Geschirrtuch, *das;* **~washer** *n.* A Geschirrspülmaschine, *die;* Geschirrspüler, *der* (*ugs.*); *attrib.* **~washer detergent** Geschirreiniger, *der;* B (*person*) Geschirrspüler, *der*/-spülerin, *die;* **~-washing** *n.* Geschirrspülen, *das;* **~-washing machine** ⇒ **~washer** A; **~water** *n.* Abwaschwasser, *das;* Spülwasser, *das;* **this tea's like ~water** der Tee schmeckt wie Spülwasser

**dishy** /ˈdɪʃɪ/ *adj.* (*Brit. coll.*) klasse (*ugs.*)

**disillusion** /dɪsɪˈljuːʒn, dɪsɪˈluːʒn/ ❶ *n., no pl.* Desillusion, *die* (**with** über + *Akk.*). ❷ *v.t.* ernüchtern; **I don't want to ~ you, but ...:** ich möchte dir nicht deine Illusionen rauben, aber ...

**disillusioned** /dɪsɪˈljuːʒnd, dɪsɪˈluːʒnd/ *adj.* desillusioniert; **become ~ with sth.** seine Illusionen über etw. (*Akk.*) verlieren

**disillusionment** /dɪsɪˈljuːʒnmənt, dɪsɪˈluːʒnmənt/ *n.* Desillusionierung, *die*

**disincentive** /dɪsɪnˈsentɪv/ *n.* Hemmnis, *das;* **act as** *or* **be a ~ to sb. to do sth.** jmdn. davon abhalten, etw. zu tun

**disinclination** /dɪsɪnklɪˈneɪʃn/ *n.* Abneigung, *die* (**for, to** gegen)

**disincline** /dɪsɪnˈklaɪn/ *v.t.* abgeneigt machen (**for, to** gegen)

**disinclined** /dɪsɪnˈklaɪnd/ *adj.* abgeneigt

**disinfect** /dɪsɪnˈfekt/ *v.t.* desinfizieren

**disinfectant** /dɪsɪnˈfektənt/ ❶ *adj.* desinfizierend. ❷ *n.* Desinfektionsmittel, *das*

**disinfection** /dɪsɪnˈfekʃn/ *n.* Desinfektion, *die;* Desinfizierung, *die*

**disinfest** /dɪsɪnˈfest/ *v.t.* von Ungeziefer befreien; entwesen (*fachspr.*)

**disinformation** /dɪsɪnfəˈmeɪʃn/ *n.* Desinformation, *die*

**disingenuous** /dɪsɪnˈdʒenjʊəs/ *adj.* unaufrichtig

**disingenuously** /dɪsɪnˈdʒenjʊəslɪ/ *adv.* in unaufrichtiger Weise

**disinherit** /dɪsɪnˈherɪt/ *v.t.* enterben; (*fig.*) entrechten

**disinheritance** /dɪsɪnˈherɪtəns/ *n.* Enterbung, *die*

**disintegrate** /dɪsˈɪntɪgreɪt/ ❶ *v.i.* A zerfallen; ‹Straßenbelag:› aufbrechen; ‹Gestein:› zerbröckeln, zerfallen; (*shatter suddenly*) zerbersten; (*fig.*) sich auflösen; B (*Phys.*) zerfallen. ❷ *v.t.* A zerstören; (*by weathering also*) zerfressen; (*by exploding*) sprengen; (*fig.*) auflösen; B (*Phys.*) spalten

**disintegration** /dɪsɪntɪˈgreɪʃn/ *n.* A Zerfall, *der;* (*of road surface*) Aufbrechen, *das;* (*fig.*) Auflösung, *die;* (*of personality*) [allmähliche] Zerstörung; (*of hopes*) Zusammenbruch, *der;* B (*Phys.*) Zerfall, *der*

**disinter** /dɪsɪnˈtɜː(r)/ *v.t.*, **-rr-** A ausgraben; B (*fig.*) ans Licht bringen

**disinterest** /dɪsˈɪntrəst, dɪsˈɪntrɪst/ ⇒ **disinterestedness**

**disinterested** /dɪsˈɪntrəstɪd, dɪsˈɪntrɪstɪd/ *adj.* A (*impartial*) unvoreingenommen; unparteiisch; (*free from selfish motive*) selbstlos; uneigennützig; B (*coll.: uninterested*) desinteressiert

**disinterestedly** /dɪsˈɪntrəstɪdlɪ, dɪsˈɪntrɪstɪdlɪ/ *adv.* ⇒ **disinterested**: unvoreingenommen; unparteiisch; selbstlos; uneigennützig; desinteressiert

**disinterestedness** /dɪsˈɪntrəstɪdnɪs, dɪsˈɪntrɪstɪdnɪs/ *n., no pl.* ⇒ **disinterested**: Unvoreingenommenheit, *die;* Selbstlosigkeit, *die;* Uneigennützigkeit, *die;* Desinteresse, *das* (**in** an + *Dat.*)

**disinterment** /dɪsɪnˈtɜːmənt/ *n.* A Ausgrabung, *die;* B (*fig.*) Ausgraben, *das*

**disinvestment** /dɪsɪnˈvestmənt/ *n.* (*Econ.*) Desinvestition, *die*

**disjoin** /dɪsˈdʒɔɪn/ *v.t.* [voneinander] trennen

**disjointed** /dɪsˈdʒɔɪntɪd/ *adj.*, **disjointedly** /dɪsˈdʒɔɪntɪdlɪ/ *adv.* unzusammenhängend; zusammenhanglos

**disjunctive** /dɪsˈdʒʌŋktɪv/ *adj.* A trennend; B (*Ling., Logic*) disjunktiv

**disk** A (*Computing*) **[magnetic] ~:** Magnetplatte, *die;* **[floppy] ~:** Floppy Disk, *die;* Diskette, *die;* **[hard] ~** (*exchangeable*) [harte] Magnetplatte; (*fixed*) Festplatte, *die;* B ⇒ **disc** A, B, D, E

**'disk drive** *n.* (*Computing*) Diskettenlaufwerk, *das*

**diskette** /dɪsˈket/ *n.* (*Computing*) Diskette, *die*

**dislike** /dɪsˈlaɪk/ ❶ *v.t.* nicht mögen; (*a little stronger*) nicht leiden können; ~ **sb./sth. greatly** *or* **intensely** jmdn./etw. ganz und gar nicht leiden können; **I don't ~ it** ich finde es nicht schlecht; ~ **doing sth.** es nicht mögen/nicht leiden können, etw. zu tun; etw. ungern tun; **I ~ your having to stay late** ich sehe es nicht gern, dass du lange bleiben musst.
❷ *n.* A *no pl.* Abneigung, *die* (**of, for** gegen); **she took an instant ~ to him/the house** sie empfand sofort eine Abneigung gegen ihn/das Haus; **have a ~ for sb./sth.** eine Abneigung gegen jmdn./etw. haben *od.* (*geh.*) hegen; **feel ~ for sb./sth.** jmdn./etw. nicht leiden können; B (*object*) **one of my greatest ~s is ...:** zu den Dingen, die ich am wenigsten leiden kann, gehört ...

**dislocate** /ˈdɪsləkeɪt/ *v.t.* A (*Med.*) luxieren (*fachspr.*); ausrenken; auskugeln ‹Schulter, Hüfte›; B (*fig.*) beeinträchtigen

**dislocation** /dɪsləˈkeɪʃn/ *n.* A (*Med.*) Luxation, *die* (*fachspr.*); Ausrenkung, *die;* (*of shoulder, hip*) Auskugelung, *die;* B (*fig.*) Beeinträchtigung, *die*

**dislodge** /dɪsˈlɒdʒ/ *v.t.* entfernen (**from** aus); (*detach*) lösen (**from** von); (*Mil.: drive out*) vertreiben (**from** aus)

**disloyal** /dɪsˈlɔɪəl/ *adj.* illoyal (**to** gegenüber); treulos ‹Freund, Ehepartner›; **be ~:** nicht loyal sein

**disloyalty** /dɪsˈlɔɪəltɪ/ *n.* Illoyalität, *die* (**to** gegenüber); (*to spouse, friend*) Treulosigkeit, *die*

**dismal** /ˈdɪzməl/ *adj.* trist; düster; trostlos ‹Landschaft, Ort›; bedrückend ‹Niedergang›; (*coll.: feeble*) kläglich ‹Zustand, Leistung, Versuch›; **in a ~ manner/tone of voice** düster/mit bedrückter Stimme; **a ~ failure** ein völliger Reinfall (*ugs.*)

**dismally** /ˈdɪzməlɪ/ *adv.* trostlos; trübe ‹beleuchtet›; kläglich ‹fehlschlagen, jammern›

**dismantle** /dɪsˈmæntl/ *v.t.* zerlegen; demontieren; (*fig.*) demontieren; abbauen ‹Schuppen, Gerüst›; (*permanently*) abreißen, niederreißen ‹Gebäude›; schleifen ‹Befestigungsanlage›; abwracken ‹Schiff›

**dismast** /dɪsˈmɑːst/ *v.t.* (*Naut.*) entmasten

**dismay** /dɪsˈmeɪ/ ❶ *v.t.* bestürzen; **he was ~ed to hear that ...:** mit Bestürzung hörte er, dass ...; **he was ~ed at the news** er war bestürzt über die Nachricht. ❷ *n.* Bestürzung, *die* (**at** über + *Akk.*); **he was filled with ~ at the news** die Nachricht erfüllte ihn mit Bestürzung; **watch in** *or* **with ~:** bestürzt zusehen

**dismember** /dɪsˈmembə(r)/ *v.t.* A verstümmeln; B (*partition*) zersplittern

**dismemberment** /dɪsˈmembəmənt/ *n.* A Verstümmelung, *die;* B (*partitioning*) Zersplitterung, *die*

**dismiss** /dɪsˈmɪs/ *v.t.* A (*send away, ask to leave or disperse*) entlassen; auflösen, aufheben ‹Versammlung›; **~!** (*Mil.*) weggetreten!; B (*from employment*) entlassen; C (*from the mind*) verwerfen; (*treat very briefly*) abtun; Ⓓ (*Law*) abweisen ‹Klage›; entlassen ‹Geschworene›; **~ with costs** kostenpflichtig abweisen; Ⓔ (*Cricket*) ausscheiden lassen

**dismissal** /dɪsˈmɪsl/ *n.* Ⓐ Entlassung, *die;* (*of committee, gathering, etc.*) Auflösung, *die;* Aufhebung, *die;* **she made a gesture of ~ to the servant** sie entließ den Diener mit einer Handbewegung; Ⓑ (*from employment*) Entlassung, *die;* **give sb. his/her ~:** jmdn. entlassen; Ⓒ (*from the mind*) Aufgabe, *die;* (*rejection*) Ablehnung, *die;* (*very brief treatment*) Abtun, *das;* Ⓓ (*Law*) (*of a case*) Abweisung, *die;* (*of jury*) Entlassung, *die;* Ⓔ (*Cricket*) Ausscheiden, *das*

**dismissive** /dɪsˈmɪsɪv/ *adj.* abweisend; (*disdainful*) abschätzig; **be ~ about sth.** etw. abtun *od.* nicht würdigen

**dismissively** /dɪsˈmɪsɪvlɪ/ *adv.* abweisend; (*disdainfully*) abschätzig

**dismount** /dɪsˈmaʊnt/ ❶ *v.i.* absteigen. ❷ *v.t.* abwerfen ‹Reiter›

**disobedience** /dɪsəˈbiːdɪəns/ *n.* Ungehorsam, *der;* **act of ~:** ungehorsames Verhalten; Ungehorsam, *der;* **~ to orders** Nichtbefolgen der Anordnungen

**disobedient** /dɪsəˈbiːdɪənt/ *adj.* ungehorsam; **be ~ to orders/to sb.** Anordnungen nicht befolgen/jmdm. nicht gehorchen

**disobediently** /dɪsəˈbiːdɪəntlɪ/ *adv.* ungehorsam; **act/behave ~:** ungehorsam sein

**disobey** /dɪsəˈbeɪ/ *v.t.* nicht gehorchen (+ *Dat.*); nicht befolgen, missachten ‹Befehl, Vorschrift usw.›; übertreten ‹Gesetz›; (*Mil.*) den Gehorsam verweigern (+ *Dat.*)

**disoblige** /dɪsəˈblaɪdʒ/ *v.t.* **~ sb.** jmds. Wunsch nicht nachkommen

**disobliging** /dɪsəˈblaɪdʒɪŋ/ *adj.* ungefällig; **be very/most ~:** wenig/kein bisschen entgegenkommend sein

**disorder** /dɪsˈɔːdə(r)/ ❶ *n.* Ⓐ Unordnung, *die;* Durcheinander, *das;* **everything was in [complete] ~:** alles war ein einziges[, heilloses] Durcheinander; **the meeting broke up in ~:** die Versammlung endete in einem heillosen Durcheinander; **throw sth. into ~:** etw. in Unordnung bringen; **the marchers were thrown into ~:** die Marschierenden gerieten aus der Reihe; **the troops fled in ~:** die Soldaten flohen in ungeordneten Haufen; **leave the house in a state of ~:** das Haus in großer Unordnung hinterlassen; Ⓑ (*rioting, disturbance*) Unruhen *Pl.;* Ⓒ (*Med.*) [Funktions]störung, *die;* **suffer from a mental ~:** geisteskrank sein; **a stomach/liver ~:** ein Magen-/Leberleiden; **a blood ~:** eine Blutkrankheit. ❷ *v.t.* Ⓐ in Unordnung bringen; durcheinander bringen; Ⓑ verwirren ‹Geist›

**disordered** /dɪsˈɔːdəd/ *adj.* Ⓐ unordentlich; ungeordnet ‹Wortschwall, Gedanken[gang]›; wirr ‹Fantasie›; Ⓑ (*Med.*) gestört; angegriffen ‹Organ›; (*mentally unbalanced*) geistesgestört

**disorderly** /dɪsˈɔːdəlɪ/ *adj.* Ⓐ (*untidy*) unordentlich; ungeordnet ‹Denkweise, Ansammlung›; Ⓑ (*unruly*) undiszipliniert; disziplinlos; zügellos, unsolide ‹Lebensweise›; aufrührerisch ‹Mob›; **~ conduct** ungebührliches *od.* ungehöriges Benehmen

**disˈorderly house** *n.* (*brothel*) öffentliches Haus (*verhüll.*); (*gambling-den*) Spielhölle, *die* (*abwertend*)

**disorganization** /dɪsɔːgənaɪˈzeɪʃn/ *n., no pl.* Desorganisation, *die;* (*muddle*) Durcheinander, *das;* **cause ~ of sth.** etw. durcheinander bringen

**disorganize** /dɪsˈɔːgənaɪz/ *v.t.* durcheinander bringen; desorganisieren (*geh.*)

**disorganized** /dɪsˈɔːgənaɪzd/ *adj.* chaotisch; unsystematisch, chaotisch ‹Arbeiter, Person›; **he's completely ~:** er geht völlig unsystematisch vor

**disorient** /dɪsˈɔːrɪənt, dɪsˈɒrɪənt/, **disorientate** /dɪsˈɒrɪənteɪt, dɪsˈɔːrɪənteɪt/ *v.t.* die Orientierung nehmen (+ *Dat.*); (*fig.*) verwirren

**disorientated** /dɪsˈɒrɪənteɪtɪd, dɪsˈɔːrɪənteɪtɪd/ *adj.* verwirrt; desorientiert

**disorientation** /dɪsɒrɪənˈteɪʃn, dɪsɔːrɪənˈteɪʃn/ *n.* (*lit. or fig.*) Verwirrung, *die;* Desorientiertheit, *die*

**disoriented** /dɪsˈɔːrɪəntɪd, dɪsˈɒrɪəntɪd/ ⇒ **disorientated**

**disown** /dɪsˈəʊn/ *v.t.* Ⓐ (*repudiate*) verleugnen; **if you do that I'll ~ you** (*joc.*) wenn du das tust, sind wir geschiedene Leute; Ⓑ (*renounce allegiance to*) nicht anerkennen

**disparage** /dɪˈspærɪdʒ/ *v.t.* Ⓐ herabsetzen; Ⓑ (*discredit*) in Verruf bringen; diskreditieren (*geh.*)

**disparagement** /dɪˈspærɪdʒmənt/ *n.* Herabsetzung, *die;* **speak with ~ of sth./sb.** sich verächtlich über etw./jmdn. äußern

**disparaging** /dɪˈspærɪdʒɪŋ/ *adj.* abschätzig

**disparagingly** /dɪˈspærɪdʒɪŋlɪ/ *adv.* abschätzig

**disparate** /ˈdɪspərət/ *adj.* [völlig] verschieden; disparat (*geh.*)

**disparity** /dɪˈspærɪtɪ/ *n.* Disparität, *die* (*geh.*); (*difference also*) Unterschied, *der;* (*lack of parity*) Ungleichheit, *die*

**dispassionate** /dɪˈspæʃənət/ *adj.* leidenschaftslos; (*impartial*) unvoreingenommen

**dispassionately** /dɪˈspæʃənətlɪ/ *adv.* leidenschaftslos; (*impartially*) unvoreingenommen

**dispatch** /dɪˈspætʃ/ ❶ *v.t.* Ⓐ (*send off*) schicken; **~ sb. [to do sth.]** jmdn. entsenden (*geh.*) [um etw. zu tun]; Ⓑ (*get through*) erledigen; abschließen ‹Geschäft›; erfüllen ‹Pflicht›; Ⓒ (*kill*) töten; Ⓓ (*eat*) verschlingen; verputzen (*ugs.*). ❷ *n.* Ⓐ (*official report, Journ.*) Bericht, *der;* Depesche, *die* (*veralt.*); **they were mentioned in ~es** (*Mil.*) ≈ ihnen wurde förmliche Anerkennung ausgesprochen; Ⓑ (*sending off*) Absenden, *das;* (*of troops, messenger, delegation*) Entsendung, *die* (*geh.*); Ⓒ (*killing*) Tötung, *die;* Ⓓ (*prompt execution*) Erledigung, *die;* Ⓔ **act with ~:** prompt handeln

**dispatch: ~ box, ~ case** *ns.* Aktenkoffer, *der*

**dispatcher** /dɪˈspætʃə(r)/ *n.* Verkehrsbetriebsregler, *der*

**dispatch: ~ note** *n.* Versandanzeige, *die;* **~ rider** *n.* Bote, *der;* (*Mil.*) Meldefahrer, *der*

**dispel** /dɪˈspel/ *v.t.*, **-ll-** vertreiben; zerstreuen ‹Besorgnis, Befürchtung›; verdrängen, unterdrücken ‹Gefühl, Erinnerung, Vorahnung›

**dispensable** /dɪˈspensəbl/ *adj.* entbehrlich

**dispensary** /dɪˈspensərɪ/ *n.* (*Pharm.*) Apotheke, *die;* (*in hospital*) [Krankenhaus]apotheke, *die*

**dispensation** /dɪspenˈseɪʃn/ *n.* Ⓐ (*distribution*) Verteilung, *die* (**to** an + *Akk.*); (*of grace*) Zuteil-werden-Lassen, *das;* (*of favours*) Gewährung, *die;* **~ of justice** Rechtsprechung, *die;* Ⓑ (*management*) Verfügung, *die;* (*Theol.: by Providence*) **divine ~:** göttliche Fügung; Ⓒ (*exemption*) Sonderregelung, *die;* **~ from the examination** Erlass der Prüfung; Ⓓ (*Eccl.*) Dispens, *die*

**dispense** /dɪˈspens/ ❶ *v.i.* **~ with** verzichten auf (+ *Akk.*); (*set aside*) außer Acht lassen; (*do away with*) überflüssig machen. ❷ *v.t.* Ⓐ (*distribute, administer*) verteilen (**to** an + *Akk.*); gewähren ‹Gastfreundschaft›; zuteil werden lassen ‹Gnade›; spenden ‹Sakrament›; **~ justice** Recht sprechen; **the machine ~s hot drinks** der Automat gibt heiße Getränke aus; **the device ~s liquid soap/toilet paper** aus der Vorrichtung kommt flüssige Seife/Toilettenpapier; Ⓑ (*Pharm.*) dispensieren (*fachspr.*); bereiten und abgeben

**dispenser** /dɪˈspensə(r)/ *n.* Ⓐ (*Pharm.*) Apotheker, *der*/Apothekerin, *die;* Ⓑ (*vending machine*) Automat, *der;* (*container*) Spender, *der*

**dispensing ˈchemist** *n.* ▶ 1261 Apotheker, *der*/Apothekerin, *die*

**dispersal** /dɪˈspɜːsl/ *n.* Ⓐ (*scattering*) Zerstreuung, *die;* (*diffusion*) Ausbreitung, *die;* (*of mist, oil slick*) Auflösung, *die;* (*Mil.*) Auseinanderziehen, *das;* Ⓑ (*Bot., Zool.*) Verbreitung, *die;* Ⓒ (*Phys.*) Dispersion, *die*

**disperse** /dɪˈspɜːs/ ❶ *v.t.* Ⓐ (*scatter*) zerstreuen; (*dispel*) auflösen ‹Dunst, Öl›; vertreiben ‹Wolken, Gase›; (*Mil.*) auseinander ziehen; Ⓑ (*Phys.*) dispergieren (*fachspr.*); verteilen; zerlegen ‹Lichtstrahl›. ❷ *v.i.* sich zerstreuen; (*Phys.*) sich verteilen

**dispersion** /dɪˈspɜːʃn/ *n.* Ⓐ (*scattering*) Zerstreuung, *die;* (*diffusion*) Ausbreitung, *die;* (*Mil.*) Auseinanderziehen, *das;* Ⓑ **D~** (*Jewish Hist.*) ⇒ **Diaspora**; Ⓒ (*Phys.*) Dispersion, *die;* (*system*) Dispersoid, *das;* Ⓓ (*Statistics*) Streuung, *die;* Dispersion, *die* (*fachspr.*)

**dispirit** /dɪˈspɪrɪt/ *v.t.* entmutigen

**dispirited** /dɪˈspɪrɪtɪd/ *adj.* entmutigt; mutlos ‹Gesichtsausdruck›; halbherzig ‹Versuch›

**dispiritedly** /dɪˈspɪrɪtɪdlɪ/ *adv.* entmutigt

**dispiriting** /dɪˈspɪrɪtɪŋ/ *adj.* entmutigend

**displace** /dɪsˈpleɪs/ *v.t.* Ⓐ (*move from place*) verschieben; (*force to flee*) vertreiben; (*remove from office*) entlassen; Ⓑ (*supplant*) ersetzen; (*crowd out*) verdrängen; Ⓒ (*Phys.: take the place of*) verdrängen

**displaced ˈperson** *n.* Vertriebene, *der/die*

**displacement** /dɪsˈpleɪsmənt/ *n.* Ⓐ (*moving*) Verschiebung, *die;* (*removal from office*) Entlassung, *die;* Ⓑ (*supplanting*) Ersetzung, *die;* Ⓒ (*Phys.: [amount] taking the place of sth.*) Verdrängung, *die;* Ⓓ (*Naut.: weight displaced*) [Wasser]verdrängung, *die;* Ⓔ (*Psych.*) Verschiebung, *die;* Ⓕ (*Motor Veh.*) Hubraum, *der*

**display** /dɪˈspleɪ/ ❶ *v.t.* Ⓐ tragen ‹Abzeichen›; vorzeigen ‹Fahrkarte, Einladung›; aufstellen ‹Trophäe›; (*to public view*) ausstellen; (*on noticeboard*) aushängen; (*standing*) aufstellen ‹Schild›; (*attached*) aufhängen ‹Schild, Fahne›; (*make manifest*) zeigen; (*depict*) zeigen, darstellen; Ⓑ (*flaunt*) zur Schau stellen; Ⓒ (*Commerc.*) ausstellen; Ⓓ (*reveal involuntarily*) zeigen; Ⓔ (*Printing*) hervorheben. ❷ *n.* Ⓐ Aufstellung, *die;* (*to public view*) Ausstellung, *die;* (*manifestation*) Demonstration, *die;* **a ~ of ill will/courage** eine Demonstration von jmds. Übelwollen/Mut; Ⓑ (*exhibition*) Ausstellung, *die;* (*Commerc.*) Auslage, *die;* Display, *das* (*Werbespr.*); **a military ~:** eine öffentliche militärische Veranstaltung; **a fashion ~:** eine Modenschau; **a ~ of flowers** ein Blumenarrangement; **an air ~:** eine Flugschau; **be on ~:** ausgestellt werden; **[be] for ~:** zur Ansicht [sein]; **put a house on ~:** ein Haus als Musterhaus herrichten; Ⓒ (*ostentatious show*) Zurschaustellung, *die;* **make a ~ of one's knowledge/affection** sein Wissen/seine Gefühle zur Schau stellen; Ⓓ (*Computing etc.*) Display, *das;* Anzeige, *die;* Ⓔ (*Printing*) Hervorhebung, *die;* **~ advertising** [größere] Zeitungsanzeige; Ⓕ (*Ornith.*) Imponiergehabe, *das;* (*courtship ~*) Balzverhalten, *das*

**display: ~ cabinet, ~ case** ⇒ **case²** 1 D; **~ window** *n.* Schaufenster, *das*

**displease** /dɪsˈpliːz/ *v.t.* Ⓐ (*earn disapproval of*) **~ sb./the authorities** jmds. Missfallen/das Missfallen der Behörden erregen; Ⓑ (*annoy*) verärgern; **be ~d [with sb./at sth.]** [über jmdn./etw.] verärgert sein; **she was most ~d to see that ...:** sie war sehr ärgerlich, als sie sah, dass ...

**displeasing** /dɪsˈpliːzɪŋ/ *adj.* unangenehm; unerfreulich ‹Anblick, Aussicht›; unschön ‹Akzent›; **be ~ to sb./to the eye/ear** jmdm. missfallen/keine Freude für das Auge/das Ohr sein

**displeasure** /dɪsˈpleʒə(r)/ *n., no pl.* Missfallen, *das* (**at** über + *Akk.*); **arouse/cause ~:** Missfallen erregen

**disport** /dɪˈspɔːt/ *v. refl. & i.* (*literary*) sich vergnügen

**disposable** /dɪˈspəʊzəbl/ ❶ *adj.* Ⓐ (*to be thrown away after use*) Wegwerf-; **~ bottle/container/syringe** Einwegflasche/-behälter/-spritze; **be ~:** nach Gebrauch weggeworfen werden; Ⓑ (*available*) verfügbar; (*Finance also*) disponibel (*fachspr.*). ❷ *n.* Wegwerfartikel, *der*

**disposable: ~ ˈassets** *n. pl.* (*Finance*) frei verfügbares *od.* disponibles Vermögen; **~ ˈincome** *n.* (*Finance*) verfügbares Einkommen

**disposal** /dɪˈspəʊzl/ *n.* Ⓐ (*getting rid of, killing*) Beseitigung, *die;* (*of waste*) Entsorgung, *die;* **~ of sewage** Abwasserbeseitigung, *die;* Ⓑ (*putting away*) Forträumen, *das;* Ⓒ

d

(*eating up*) Aufessen, *das;* **D** (*settling*) Erledigung, *die;* (*of argument*) Beilegung, *die;* **E** (*treating*) Abhandlung, *die;* **F** (*bestowal*) Übertragung, *die* (**to** auf + *Akk.*); **G** (*sale*) Veräußerung, *die;* **H** (*control*) Verfügung, *die;* **place** *or* **put sth./sb. at sb.'s [complete] ~:** jmdm. etw./jmdn. [ganz] zur Verfügung stellen; **have sth./sb. at one's ~:** etw./jmdn. zur Verfügung haben; **be at sb.'s ~:** jmdm. zur Verfügung *od.* zu jmds. Verfügung stehen; **I** ⇒ **disposition A**

**dispose** /dɪ'spəʊz/ **1** *v.t.* **A** (*make inclined*) **~ sb. to sth.** jmdn. zu etw. veranlassen; **~ sb. to do sth.** jmdn. dazu veranlassen, etw. zu tun; **B** (*arrange*) anordnen; (*Mil.*) aufstellen ‹Truppen›. **2** *v.i.* (*determine course of events*) entscheiden; Entscheidungen treffen; **man proposes, God ~s** (*prov.*) der Mensch denkt, Gott lenkt (*Spr.*)

**~ of** *v.t.* **A** (*do as one wishes with*) **~ of sth./sb.** über etw./jmdn. frei verfügen; **B** (*kill, get rid of*) beseitigen ‹Rivalen, Leiche, Abfall›; erlegen, töten ‹Gegner, Drachen›; **she ~d of the tea leaves down the sink** sie hat die Teeblätter in den Ausguss getan *od.* den Ausguss hinuntergespült; **C** (*put away*) wegräumen; **D** (*eat up*) aufessen; verputzen (*ugs.*); **E** (*settle, finish*) erledigen; **~ of the business** das Geschäftliche erledigen *od.* regeln; **F** (*disprove*) widerlegen

**disposed** /dɪ'spəʊzd/ *adj.* **be ~ to sth.** zu etw. neigen; **be ~ to do sth.** dazu neigen, etw. zu tun; **be ~ to anger** leicht zornig werden; **I'm not ~/don't feel ~ to help that lazy fellow** ich bin nicht geneigt/fühle mich nicht veranlasst, diesem Faulpelz zu helfen; **feel ~ to make a complaint** meinen, dass man sich beschweren muss; **be well/ill ~ towards sb.** jmdm. wohlgesinnt/übel gesinnt sein; **be well/ill ~ towards sth.** einer Sache (*Dat.*) positiv/ablehnend gegenüberstehen

**disposition** /dɪspə'zɪʃn/ *n.* **A** (*arrangement; also Mil.: attack plan*) Aufstellung, *die;* (*of guards etc.*) Aufstellung, *die;* Postierung, *die;* (*of seating, figures*) Anordnung, *die;* **~ of troops** Truppenaufstellung, *die;* **B** *in pl.* (*preparations; also Mil.*) Vorbereitungen *Pl.;* **C** (*ordinance of Providence, fate, or God*) Fügung, *die;* **D** (*temperament*) Veranlagung, *die;* Disposition, *die;* **his boastful ~:** seine prahlerische Art; **she has a/is of a rather irritable ~:** sie ist ziemlich reizbar; **E** (*inclination*) Hang, *der;* Neigung, *die* (**towards** zu); **have a ~ to do sth./to[wards] sth.** dazu neigen, etw. zu tun/zu etw. neigen

**dispossess** /dɪspə'zes/ *v.t.* **A** (*oust*) verdrängen; entthronen ‹Monarchen›; stürzen ‹Diktator›; enterben ‹Kind›; **B** (*deprive*) **~ sb. of sth.** jmdm. etw. entziehen; (*fig.*) jmdm. etw. rauben

**disproportion** /dɪsprə'pɔːʃn/ *n.* Missverhältnis, *das*

**disproportionate** /dɪsprə'pɔːʃənət/ *adj.* **A** (*relatively too large/small*) vom Normalen abweichend; unangemessen; **be [totally] ~ to sth.** in einem [völligen] Missverhältnis *od.* in [gar] keinem Verhältnis zu etw. stehen; **B** (*lacking proportion*) unproportioniert

**disproportionately** /dɪsprə'pɔːʃənətlɪ/ *adv.* unverhältnismäßig

**disprove** /dɪs'pruːv/ *v.t.* widerlegen; **~ sb.'s innocence** jmds. Schuld beweisen

**disputable** /dɪ'spjuːtəbl, 'dɪspjʊtəbl/ *adj.* strittig; disputabel (*geh.*)

**disputant** /dɪ'spjuːtənt/ *n.* Disputant, *der/* Disputantin, *die*

**disputation** /dɪspjʊ'teɪʃn/ *n.* **A** *no pl.* (*argument*) Meinungsverschiedenheiten *Pl.;* Streit, *der;* **B** (*arch.: academic debate*) Disputation, *die*

**disputatious** /dɪspjʊ'teɪʃəs/ *adj.* streitlustig; streitbar

**dispute** /dɪ'spjuːt/ **1** *n.* **A** *no pl.* (*controversy*) Streit, *der;* **there has been some ~ as to what ...:** es hat Streit darüber gegeben, was ...; **be a matter/subject of much ~:** eine sehr umstrittene Frage/ein sehr umstrittenes Thema sein; **it is a matter of ~ whether ...:** man kann darüber streiten, ob ...; **that is [not] in ~:** darüber wird [nicht] gestritten; **be beyond ~:** außer Frage stehen; **B** (*argument*) Streit, *der* (**over** um); **a ~ arose as to whether ...:** wegen der Frage, ob ..., kam es zum *od.* zu einem Streit **2** *v.t.* **A** (*discuss*) sich streiten über (+ *Akk.*); **~ whether .../how ...:** sich darüber streiten, ob .../wie ...; **B** (*oppose*) bestreiten; anfechten ‹Rechtsanspruch›; angreifen ‹Entscheidung›; **C** (*resist*) [an]kämpfen gegen; **D** (*contend for*) streiten um; **they are disputing the leadership of the party** sie machen sich (*Dat.*) gegenseitig die Parteiführung streitig. **3** *v.i.* (*argue*) streiten; **~ with sb. on** *or* **about sth.** mit jmdm. über etw. (*Akk.*) diskutieren

**disqualification** /dɪskwɒlɪfɪ'keɪʃn/ *n.* **A** (*disqualifying*) Ausschluss, *der* (**from** von); (*Sport*) Disqualifikation, *die;* **B** (*thing that disqualifies*) Grund zum Ausschluss

**disqualify** /dɪs'kwɒlɪfaɪ/ *v.t.* **A** (*debar*) ausschließen (**from** von); (*Sport*) disqualifizieren; **B** (*make unfit*) ungeeignet machen; **~ sb./sth. for sth.** jmdn./etw. für etw. ungeeignet machen; **C** (*incapacitate*) verbieten (+ *Dat.*)

**disquiet** /dɪs'kwaɪət/ *n.* Unruhe, *die*

**disquieting** /dɪs'kwaɪətɪŋ/ *adj.* beunruhigend

**disquisition** /dɪskwɪ'zɪʃn/ *n.* Abhandlung, *die;* (*long speech*) Vortrag, *der;* Sermon, *der* (*abwertend*)

**disregard** /dɪsrɪ'gɑːd/ **1** *v.t.* ignorieren; nicht berücksichtigen ‹Tatsache›; **~ a request** einer Bitte (*Dat.*) nicht nachkommen. **2** *n.* Missachtung, *die* (**of, for** *Gen.*); (*of wishes, feelings*) Gleichgültigkeit, *die* (**for, of** gegenüber); **he shows a total ~ of** *or* **for other people/others' feelings/wishes** ihm sind andere/die Gefühle anderer/die Wünsche anderer völlig gleichgültig

**disrepair** /dɪsrɪ'peə(r)/ *n.* (*of building*) schlechter [baulicher] Zustand; Baufälligkeit, *die;* (*of furniture etc.*) schlechter Zustand; **the house is in a state of/has fallen into ~:** das Haus ist baufällig

**disreputable** /dɪs'repjʊtəbl/ *adj.* zwielichtig; übel beleumdet ‹Person›; verrufen ‹Etablissement, Gegend›; schäbig ‹Aussehen, Kleidung›

**disrepute** /dɪsrɪ'pjuːt/ *n.* Verruf, *der;* (*of area*) Verrufenheit, *die;* **bring sb./sth. into ~:** jmdn./etw. in Verruf bringen; **fall into ~:** in Verruf kommen *od.* geraten

**disrespect** /dɪsrɪ'spekt/ *n.* Missachtung, *die;* **show [only] ~ for sb./sth.** [überhaupt] keine Achtung *od.* keinen Respekt vor jmdm./etw. haben; **I meant no ~ [to you]** ich wollte [Ihnen gegenüber] nicht respektlos sein

**disrespectful** /dɪsrɪ'spektfl/ *adj.* respektlos; **be ~ towards sb.** vor jmdm. keinen Respekt *od.* keine Achtung haben

**disrespectfully** /dɪsrɪ'spektfəlɪ/ *adv.* respektlos

**disrobe** /dɪs'rəʊb/ (*formal*) **1** *v.t.* **A** (*divest of robe*) das Gewand abnehmen (+ *Dat.*); **B** (*undress*) ausziehen; entkleiden (*geh.*). **2** *v.i.* **A** (*divest oneself of robe, coat, etc.*) ablegen; **B** (*undress*) sich ausziehen; sich entkleiden (*geh.*)

**disrupt** /dɪs'rʌpt/ *v.t.* **A** (*break up*) zerschlagen ‹Regierung, Partei, System›; **B** (*interrupt*) unterbrechen; stören ‹Klasse, Sitzung›

**disruption** /dɪs'rʌpʃn/ *n.* **A** (*break-up*) Zerschlagung, *die;* **B** (*interruption*) Unterbrechung; (*of class, meeting*) Störung, *die*

**disruptive** /dɪs'rʌptɪv/ *adj.* **A** (*breaking up*) zerstörerisch; **B** (*violently interrupting*) störend

**dissatisfaction** /dɪsætɪs'fækʃn/ *n., no pl.* Unzufriedenheit, *die* (**with, at** mit)

**dissatisfied** /dɪ'sætɪsfaɪd/ *adj.* **be ~ with** *or* **at sb./sth.** mit jmdm./etw. unzufrieden sein

**dissect** /dɪ'sekt/ *v.t.* **A** (*cut into pieces*) zerschneiden, zerlegen (**into** in + *Akk.*); **B** (*Med., Biol.*) präparieren; sezieren, präparieren ‹Leiche›; **C** (*analyse*) zergliedern; sezieren

**dissection** /dɪ'sekʃn/ *n.* **A** (*cutting into pieces*) Zerlegung, *die;* **B** (*Med., Biol.*) Präparation, *die;* (*of body*) Sektion, *die;* Präparation, *die;* **C** (*Med.: thing cut up*) Präparat, *das;* **D** (*analysis*) Zergliederung, *die;* Sezierung, *die*

**dissemble** /dɪ'sembl/ **1** *v.t.* (*disguise*) verbergen ‹Gefühle, Absichten›; verheimlichen ‹Liebe›. **2** *v.i.* **A** (*conceal one's motives*) sich verstellen; **B** (*talk or act hypocritically*) heucheln

**disseminate** /dɪ'semɪneɪt/ *v.t.* (*lit. or fig.*) verbreiten; verstreuen ‹Samen, Truppen, Flüchtlinge›; ⇒ *also* **sclerosis A**

**dissemination** /dɪsemɪ'neɪʃn/ *n.* Verbreitung, *die*

**dissension** /dɪ'senʃn/ *n.* Dissens, *der;* Streit, *der* (**on** über + *Akk.*); **~s** Streitigkeiten; Meinungsverschiedenheiten

**dissent** /dɪ'sent/ **1** *v.i.* **A** (*refuse to assent*) nicht zustimmen; **~ from sth.** mit etw. nicht übereinstimmen; **B** (*disagree*) **~ from sth.** von etw. abweichen. **2** *n.* **A** (*difference of opinion*) Ablehnung, *die;* (*from majority*) Abweichung, *die;* **B** (*refusal to accept*) Ablehnung, *die*

**dissenter** /dɪ'sentə(r)/ *n.* Andersdenkende, *der/die;* **be a ~ from sth.** etw. ablehnen

**dissentient** /dɪ'senʃɪənt, dɪ'senʃənt/ **1** *adj.* anders denkend ‹Person, Minderheit›; abweichend ‹Meinung, Vorstellung, Standpunkt›. **2** *n.* Andersdenkende, *der/die*

**dissertation** /dɪsə'teɪʃn/ *n.* (*spoken*) Vortrag, *der;* (*written*) Abhandlung, *die;* (*for bachelor's degree*) Diplomarbeit, *die;* (*for master's degree*) Magisterarbeit, *die;* (*for Ph. D.*) Dissertation, *die*

**disservice** /dɪ'sɜːvɪs/ *n.* **do sb. a ~:** jmdm. einen schlechten Dienst erweisen

**dissidence** /'dɪsɪdəns/ *n., no pl.* Uneinigkeit, *die;* Meinungsverschiedenheit, *die*

**dissident** /'dɪsɪdənt/ **1** *adj.* **A** (*disagreeing*) anders denkend; **a ~ person** ein Andersdenkender; **a ~ group/faction** eine Dissidentengruppe; **B** (*dissentient*) **hold a ~ view** *or* **opinion** eine abweichende Meinung vertreten. **2** *n.* Dissident, *der*/Dissidentin, *die;* Regimekritiker, *der*/-kritikerin, *die*

**dissimilar** /dɪ'sɪmɪlə(r)/ *adj.* unähnlich; unterschiedlich, verschieden ‹Ideen, Ansichten, Geschmäcker›; **be [highly] ~ to sth./sb.** [ganz] anders als etw./jmd. sein

**dissimilarity** /dɪsɪmɪ'lærɪtɪ/ *n.* Unähnlichkeit, *die*

**dissimulate** /dɪ'sɪmjʊleɪt/ *v.t.* verbergen ‹Gefühle›; verheimlichen ‹Tatsache, Wahrheit, Ideale›; verleugnen ‹Identität›.

**dissipate** /'dɪsɪpeɪt/ **1** *v.t.* **A** (*dispel*) auflösen ‹Nebel, Dunst›; vertreiben ‹Angst, Sorgen, Wolken›; zerstreuen ‹Befürchtungen, Zweifel›; zunichte machen ‹Begeisterung, Illusion›; aufhellen, heben ‹düstere Stimmung›; **B** (*bring to nothing*) zerstören; **C** (*break up*) auseinander treiben ‹Gruppe, Truppen, Menge›; auseinander brechen lassen ‹Familie, Gemeinde, Volk›; **D** (*fritter away*) vergeuden; (*squander*) durchbringen ‹Vermögen, Erbschaft›; verschwenden ‹Geld›; **~ sb.'s energy** jmdn. entkräften; jmds. Energien aufzehren.
**2** *v.i.* ‹Nebel, Dunst:› sich auflösen

**dissipated** /'dɪsɪpeɪtɪd/ *adj.* ausschweifend; zügellos; **~ morals** lockere Moral

**dissipation** /dɪsɪ'peɪʃn/ *n.* **A** (*scattering*) Auflösung, *die;* **B** (*intemperate living*) Ausschweifung, *die;* **C** (*wasteful expenditure*) Verschwendung, *die;* (*of fortune, inheritance*) Vergeudung, *die;* **~ of money/energy** Geld-/Energieverschwendung, *die;* **D** (*frivolous amusement*) Amüsement, *das*

**dissociate** /dɪ'səʊʃɪeɪt, dɪ'səʊsɪeɪt/ *v.t.* **A** (*disconnect*) trennen; **~ oneself from sth./sb.** sich von etw./jmdm. distanzieren; **~ oneself from all responsibility** alle Verantwortung ablehnen; **B** (*Chem.*) dissoziieren

**dissociation** /dɪsəʊsɪ'eɪʃn/ *n.* **A** Distanzierung, *die* (**of** von); (*of ideas*) Abgrenzung, *die;* **B** (*Chem.*) Dissoziation, *die*

# Distance

***1 yard*** = 0,914 m (null Komma neun eins vier Meter)
***1 mile*** = 1,61 km (eins Komma sechs eins Kilometer)

***How far is it*** or ***What's the distance from London to Edinburgh?***
= Wie weit ist es von London nach Edinburgh?

***It's/The distance is 365 miles***
= Es sind/Die Entfernung beträgt 588 Kilometer

***It's quite a long way [away]***
= Es ist ziemlich weit [entfernt]

***The house is just a few hundred yards from here***
= Das Haus liegt nur ein paar hundert Meter von hier [entfernt]

***Manchester is further from the sea than Chester***
= Manchester liegt *or* ist weiter vom Meer entfernt als Chester

***Reading is nearer to London than Oxford***
= Reading liegt näher an London als Oxford

***A and B are the same distance away***
= A und B sind gleich weit entfernt

***He hit the target from a distance of 50 metres***
= Er traf das Ziel aus einer Entfernung von 50 Metern

***a fifty mile drive***
= eine Autofahrt von achtzig Kilometern

***an hour's drive***
= eine Stunde Fahrt [mit dem Auto], eine Autostunde

***It's only a ten minute walk***
= Es sind nur zehn Minuten zu Fuß

**dissolute** /'dɪsəlu:t, 'dɪsəlju:t/ *adj.* (*licentious*) ausschweifend; (*against morality*) lasterhaft; freizügig ‹Mode›; zügellos ‹Benehmen›

**dissolutely** /'dɪsəlu:tlɪ, 'dɪsəlju:tlɪ/ *adv.* lasterhaft ‹leben›; zügellos ‹sich benehmen›

**dissolution** /dɪsə'lu:ʃn, dɪsə'lju:ʃn/ *n.* Ⓐ (*disintegration*) Zersetzung, *die;* Ⓑ (*undoing, dispersal*) Auflösung, *die;* **~ of a bond** Lösung einer Bindung

**dissolve** /dɪ'zɒlv/ ❶ *v.t.* auflösen; abbrechen ‹Freundschaft›; **acid ~s protein** Säure zersetzt Eiweiß. ❷ *v.i.* Ⓐ sich auflösen; (*in acid*) sich zersetzen; ‹Vorstellung:› vorbeigehen; **~ into tears/laughter** in Tränen/Gelächter ausbrechen; **~ into thin air** sich in Luft auflösen; Ⓑ (*Cinemat.*) überblenden. ❸ *n.* (*Cinemat.*) Überblendung, *die*

**dissonance** /'dɪsənəns/ *n.* (*Mus.*) Dissonanz, *die;* (*fig.*) Disharmonie, *die*

**dissonant** /'dɪsənənt/ *adj.* (*Mus.*) dissonant; (*fig.*) disharmonisch; voneinander abweichend ‹Meinungen›

**dissuade** /dɪ'sweɪd/ *v.t.* **~ sb. from sth.** jmdn. von etw. abbringen; **~ sb. from doing sth.** jmdn. davon abbringen, etw. zu tun

**dissuasion** /dɪ'sweɪʒn/ *n.* Abbringen, *das*

**distance** /'dɪstəns/ ▶ 1079 ❶ *n.* Ⓐ Entfernung, *die* (**from** zu); **their ~ from each other** die räumliche Entfernung zwischen ihnen; **keep [at] a [safe] ~ [from sb./sth.]** jmdm./einer Sache nicht zu nahe kommen; **maintain a safe ~ from the car in front** einen Sicherheitsabstand zum Vordermann einhalten; Ⓑ (*fig.: aloofness*) Abstand, *der;* **keep one's ~** *or* **at a ~ [from sb./sth.]** Abstand [zu jmdm./etw.] wahren; Ⓒ (*way to cover*) Strecke, *die;* Weg, *der;* (*gap*) Abstand, *der;* **accompany sb. for part of the ~:** jmdn. einen Teil des Weges *od.* ein Stück begleiten; **from this ~:** aus dieser Entfernung; von hier aus; **at a ~ of ... [from sb./sth.]** in einer Entfernung von ... [von jmdm./etw.]; **a short ~ away** ganz in der Nähe; **fall a ~ of one metre** einen Meter tief fallen; **that's no [great] ~:** das ist nicht weit; das ist keine Entfernung; Ⓓ (*remoter field of vision*) Ferne, *die;* **in/into the ~:** in der/die Ferne; **run off into the ~:** weit weglaufen; **the car vanished into the ~:** das Auto verschwand in der Ferne; **middle ~** (*Art*) Mittelgrund, *der;* Ⓔ (*distant point*) Entfernung, *die;* **at a ~/[viewed] from a ~:** von weitem; (*fig.*) oberflächlich betrachtet; **they remained at a ~:** sie blieben in einiger Entfernung stehen; Ⓕ (*space of time*) Abstand, *der;* **at a ~ of 20 years** aus einem Abstand von 20 Jahren; nach [einem Zeitraum von] 20 Jahren; Ⓖ (*Racing, Boxing*) Distanz, *die;* **go** *or* **stay the ~:** über die volle Distanz gehen; (*fig.*) [bis zum Schluss] durchhalten
❷ *v.t.* Ⓐ (*leave behind in race*) hinter sich (*Dat.*) lassen; Ⓑ (*fig.*) entfremden; **~ oneself from sb./sth.** sich von jmdm./etw. distanzieren

**distance: ~ learning** *n.* Fernstudium, *das;* **~ runner** *n.* Langstreckenläufer, *der*/-läuferin, *die*

**distant** /'dɪstənt/ *adj.* Ⓐ (*far*) fern; **from nearby and ~ parts** von *od.* aus nah und fern; **be ~ [from sb.]** weit [von jmdm.] weg sein; **about three miles ~ from here** ungefähr drei Meilen von hier [entfernt]; Ⓑ (*fig.: remote*) entfernt ‹Ähnlichkeit, Verwandtschaft, Verwandte, Beziehung›; **it's a ~ prospect/possibility** das ist Zukunftsmusik; **~ memories/recollections** weit zurückreichende Erinnerungen; **have a ~ memory of sth.** sich an etw. (*Akk.*) vage erinnern; Ⓒ (*in time*) fern; **in the ~ past/future** in ferner Vergangenheit/Zukunft; **in some ~ era** in fernen Zeiten; Ⓓ (*cool*) reserviert, distanziert ‹Mensch, Haltung›; **be ~ with sb.** jmdm. gegenüber reserviert sein

**distantly** /'dɪstəntlɪ/ *adv.* Ⓐ (*far*) fern; Ⓑ (*fig.: remotely*) entfernt; **~ resemble each other** eine entfernte Ähnlichkeit aufweisen; Ⓒ (*coolly*) reserviert

**distaste** /dɪs'teɪst/ *n.* Abneigung, *die;* **[have] a ~ for sb./sth.** eine Abneigung gegen jmdn./etw. [haben]; **in ~:** aus Abneigung; **turn away in ~:** sich angewidert abwenden

**distasteful** /dɪs'teɪstfl/ *adj.* unangenehm; **be ~ to sb.** jmdm. zuwider sein

**distastefully** /dɪs'teɪstfəlɪ/ *adv.* geschmacklos; **look ~ at sth.** etw. angewidert betrachten

**distastefulness** /dɪs'teɪstflnɪs/ *n., no pl.* Widerwärtigkeit, *die*

**distemper**[1] /dɪ'stempə(r)/ ❶ *n.* Ⓐ (*paint*) Temperafarbe, *die;* Ⓑ (*method*) Temperamalerei, *die.* ❷ *v.t.* mit Temperafarbe bemalen

**distemper**[2] *n.* (*animal disease*) Staupe, *die*

**distend** /dɪ'stend/ *v.t.* aufblähen, auftreiben ‹Leib, Bauch›; blähen ‹Nüstern›; aufblasen ‹Backen, Ballon›; erweitern ‹Gefäße, Darm, Ader›; aufschwellen ‹Euter›

**distension** /dɪ'stenʃn/ *n.* Aufblähung, *die;* Auftreiben, *das;* (*of blood vessel, intestine*) Erweiterung, *die*

**distich** /'dɪstɪk/ *n.* (*Pros.*) Distichon, *das*

**distil,** (*Amer.:*) **distill** /dɪ'stɪl/ *v.t.,* **-ll-** (*lit. or fig.*) destillieren; brennen ‹Branntwein›; **~ sth. from sth.** (*fig.*) etw. aus etw. [heraus]destillieren;

**distillate** /'dɪstɪleɪt/ *n.* Destillat, *das*

**distillation** /dɪstɪ'leɪʃn/ *n.* Destillation, *die;* (*fig.*) Herausdestillieren, *das;* (*result*) Destillat, *das*

**distiller** /dɪ'stɪlə(r)/ *n.* Destillateur, *der;* Branntweinbrenner, *der*

**distillery** /dɪ'stɪlərɪ/ *n.* [Branntwein]brennerei, -destillation, *die;* Destille, *die*

**distinct** /dɪ'stɪŋkt/ *adj.* Ⓐ (*different*) verschieden; **keep two things ~:** zwei Dinge auseinander halten; **as ~ from** im Unterschied zu; Ⓑ (*clearly perceptible, decided*) deutlich; klar ‹Stimme, Sicht›; ausgeprägt ‹Falten, Charme›; Ⓒ (*separate*) unterschiedlich; Ⓓ (*particular*) bestimmt ‹Gegend, Gebiet›

**distinction** /dɪ'stɪŋkʃn/ *n.* Ⓐ (*making a difference*) Unterscheidung, *die;* **by way of ~, for ~:** zur Unterscheidung; Ⓑ (*difference*) Unterschied, *der;* **there is a clear ~ between A and B** es besteht ein deutlicher Unterschied zwischen A und B; **make** *or* **draw a ~ between A and B** einen Unterschied zwischen A und B machen; **draw a sharp/clear ~ between A and B** streng/klar zwischen A und B trennen; **a ~ without a difference** ein nomineller Unterschied; Ⓒ (*being different*) Andersartigkeit, *die;* Ⓓ (*distinctive feature*) besonderes Merkmal; **have the ~ of being ...:** sich dadurch auszeichnen, dass man ... ist; Ⓔ (*showing of special consideration*) Ehrung, *die;* **be mentioned with special ~:** besonders lobend erwähnt werden; **a mark of ~:** eine Ehre *od.* Auszeichnung; Ⓕ (*mark of honour*) Auszeichnung, *die;* **gain** *or* **get a ~ in one's examination** das Examen mit Auszeichnung bestehen; Ⓖ (*excellence*) hoher Rang; **a scientist of ~:** ein Wissenschaftler von Rang [und Namen]

**distinctive** /dɪ'stɪŋktɪv/ *adj.* unverwechselbar; **be ~ of sth.** für etw. typisch *od.* charakteristisch sein

**distinctively** /dɪ'stɪŋktɪvlɪ/ *adv.* unverwechselbar

**distinctly** /dɪ'stɪŋktlɪ/ *adv.* Ⓐ (*clearly*) deutlich; **we couldn't see ~ in the mist** in dem Nebel konnten wir nichts deutlich erkennen; Ⓑ (*decidedly*) merklich; **be ~ aware of sth.** etw. deutlich spüren; Ⓒ (*markedly*) ausgeprägt

**distinctness** /dɪ'stɪŋktnɪs/ *n., no pl.* Ⓐ (*difference*) Verschiedenheit, *die;* Ⓑ (*separateness*) Getrenntheit, *die*

**distinguish** /dɪ'stɪŋgwɪʃ/ ❶ *v.t.* Ⓐ (*make out*) erkennen; (*hear*) verstehen; (*read*) lesen; entziffern; Ⓑ (*differentiate*) unterscheiden; (*characterize*) kennzeichnen; **~ sth./sb. from sth./sb.** etw./jmdn. von etw./jmdm. unterscheiden; Ⓒ (*divide*) einteilen; **~ things/persons into ...:** Dinge/Personen einteilen in (+ *Akk.*); Ⓓ (*make prominent*) **~ oneself [by sth.]** sich [durch etw.] hervortun; **~ oneself by doing sth.** sich dadurch hervortun, dass man etw. tut; **~ oneself in an exam** in einem Examen glänzen (*ugs.*); **you've really ~ed yourself, haven't you?** (*iron.*) na, da hast du vielleicht 'ne Glanzleistung vollbracht!
❷ *v.i.* unterscheiden; **~ between persons/things** Personen/Dinge auseinander halten *od.* voneinander unterscheiden; **one can barely ~ between the original and the**

copy man kann das Original kaum von der Kopie unterscheiden

**distinguishable** /dɪ'stɪŋgwɪʃəbl/ *adj.* A (*able to be made out*) erkennbar; (*audible*) hörbar; (*readable*) lesbar; (*decipherable*) entzifferbar; B (*able to be differentiated*) erkennbar; unterscheidbar; C (*able to be divided*) einteilbar

**distinguished** /dɪ'stɪŋgwɪʃt/ *adj.* A (*eminent*) namhaft, angesehen ‹Persönlichkeit, Schule, Firma›; glänzend ‹Laufbahn›; hervorragend ‹Qualität›; **a ~ politician** ein Politiker von Rang [und Namen]; B (*looking eminent*) vornehm, (*geh.*) distinguiert ‹Aussehen, Mensch›; C (*remarkable*) **~ [for/by sth.]** sich [durch etw.] auszeichnend *attr.*

**distort** /dɪ'stɔːt/ *v.t.* A verzerren ‹Gesicht, Stimme, Musik›; verformen ‹Gegenstand›; ‹Schmerz, Krankheit:› entstellen; B (*misrepresent*) entstellt *od.* verzerrt wiedergeben; verdrehen ‹Worte, Wahrheit›

**distortion** /dɪ'stɔːʃn/ *n.* A Verzerrung, *die;* (*by disease*) Entstellung, *die;* B (*misrepresentation*) Entstellung, *die;* (*of words, truth*) Verdrehung, *die*

**distract** /dɪ'strækt/ *v.t.* A (*divert*) ablenken; **~ sb.['s attention/concentration/mind from sth.]** jmdn. [von etw.] ablenken; B *usu. in pass.* (*make mad or angry*) wahnsinnig machen; **grow ~ed** außer sich geraten; **~ed with joy/worry** außer sich vor Freude/Sorge; C (*bewilder*) irritieren

**distracted** /dɪ'stræktɪd/ *adj.* A (*mad*) von Sinnen *nachgestellt;* außer sich *nachgestellt;* (*worried*) besorgt; beunruhigt; **run round like one ~:** wie von Sinnen umherlaufen; B (*mentally far away*) abwesend

**distraction** /dɪ'strækʃn/ *n.* A (*frenzy*) Wahnsinn, *der;* **love sb. to ~:** jmdn. wahnsinnig *od.* bis zur Raserei lieben; **drive sb. to ~:** jmdn. wahnsinnig machen *od.* zum Wahnsinn treiben; **be worried to ~ by sth.** sich (*Dat.*) wegen etw. wahnsinnige (*ugs.*) Sorgen machen; B (*confusion*) Unruhe, *die;* C (*diversion*) Ablenkung, *die;* D (*interruption*) Störung, *die;* **I don't want any ~s** ich möchte nicht gestört werden; **be a ~:** ein Störfaktor sein; E (*amusement*) Zerstreuung, *die;* (*pastime*) Zeitvertreib, *der*

**distrain** /dɪ'streɪn/ *v.i.* (*Law*) **~ [upon sb./sth.]** [jmdn. *od.* bei jmdm./etw.] pfänden

**distraint** /dɪ'streɪnt/ *n.* (*Law*) Pfändung, *die*

**distraught** /dɪ'strɔːt/ *adj.* aufgelöst (**with** vor + *Dat.*); verstört ‹Blick, Gesichtsausdruck›; **tearful and ~:** in Tränen aufgelöst

**distress** /dɪ'stres/ **1** *n.* A (*anguish*) Kummer, *der* (**at** über + *Akk.*); **suffer ~:** Leid erdulden; Kummer ertragen; **be in [a state of] ~:** in Sorge sein; **cause sb. much ~:** jmdm. viel Kummer zufügen *od.* bereiten; B (*suffering caused by want*) Not, *die;* Elend, *das;* C (*danger*) Not, *die;* Gefahr, *die;* **an aircraft/a ship in ~:** ein Flugzeug in Not/ein Schiff in Seenot; D (*exhaustion*) Erschöpfung, *die;* (*severe pain*) Qualen *Pl.;* **be in ~:** Qualen leiden; E (*misfortune*) Unglück, *das;* F (*Law*) ⇒ **distraint**.
**2** *v.t.* A (*worry*) bedrücken; bekümmern; (*cause anguish to*) ängstigen; (*upset*) nahe gehen (+ *Dat.*); mitnehmen; **don't ~ yourself/try not to ~ yourself** ängstigen Sie sich nicht; **we were most ~ed** wir waren zutiefst betroffen *od.* bestürzt; B (*exhaust*) erschöpfen; C (*afflict*) plagen; heimsuchen

**distressed** /dɪ'strest/ *adj.* A (*anguished*) leidvoll; betrübt; (*desperate*) gequält; verzweifelt; B (*impoverished*) Not leidend ‹Volkswirtschaft, Dritte Welt›; verarmt ‹Adel›; armselig ‹Verhältnisse›

**distressed 'area** *n.* (*Brit.*) Notstandsgebiet (*mit hoher Arbeitslosigkeit*)

**distressing** /dɪ'stresɪŋ/ *adj.* A (*upsetting*) erschütternd; **be ~ to sb.** jmdn. sehr belasten; B (*regrettable*) beklagenswert

**di'stress signal** *n.* Notsignal, *das*

**distribute** /dɪ'strɪbjuːt/ *v.t.* A verteilen (**to** an + *Akk.*, **among** unter + *Akk.*); austeilen ‹Sakramente›; B (*divide, classify*) aufteilen; **~ sth. into parts/categories/groups** etw. in Absätze/Kategorien unterteilen/in Gruppen aufteilen; C (*Printing*) ablegen

**distribution** /dɪstrɪ'bjuːʃn/ *n.* A Verteilung, *die* (**to** an + *Akk.*, **among** unter + *Akk.*); (*of seeds*) [Aus]streuen, *das;* (*Econ.: of goods*) Distribution, *die* (*fachspr.*); Vertrieb, *der;* (*of films*) Verleih, *der;* **~ of weight** Gewichtverteilung, *die;* **the ~ of wealth** die Vermögensverteilung; B (*division*) Aufteilung, *die;* (*classification*) Einteilung, *die*

**distributive** /dɪ'strɪbjʊtɪv/ (*Ling.*) **1** *n.* Distributivum, *das.* **2** *adj.* ⇒ **pronoun**

**distributor** /dɪ'strɪbjʊtə(r)/ *n.* A Verteiler, *der*/Verteilerin, *die;* (*Econ.*) Vertreiber, *der;* (*firm*) Vertrieb, *der;* (*of films*) Verleih[er], *der* B (*Motor Veh.*) [Zünd]verteiler, *der*

**district** /'dɪstrɪkt/ *n.* A (*administrative area*) Bezirk, *der;* B (*Brit.: part of county*) Distrikt, *der;* C (*Amer.: political division*) Wahlkreis, *der;* D (*tract of country, area*) Gegend, *die;* **country ~s** ländliche Gegenden; **residential ~:** Wohngebiet, *das*

**district: ~ at'torney** *n.* ▶ 1261 (*Amer. Law*) [Bezirks]staatsanwalt, *der*/-anwältin, *die;* **~ 'council** *n.* (*Brit.*) Rat des Distrikts; **Newbury D~ Council** der Rat des Distrikts Newbury; **~ 'court** *n.* (*Amer. Law*) [Bundes]bezirksgericht, *das;* **~ 'heating** *n.* Fernheizung, *die;* **~ 'nurse** *n.* ▶ 1261 (*Brit.*) Gemeindeschwester, *die*

**distrust** /dɪs'trʌst/ **1** *n.* Misstrauen, *das* (**of** gegen); **show ~ of sb.** jmdm. Misstrauen entgegenbringen. **2** *v.t.* misstrauen (+ *Dat.*); (*because of bad experiences*) mit Argwohn *od.* Misstrauen begegnen (+ *Dat.*); **I rather ~ his driving ability/his motives** ich traue seinen Fahrkünsten nicht so recht/ich bezweifle seine Motive

**distrustful** /dɪs'trʌstfl/ *adj.* misstrauisch; **be ~ of sb./sth.** jmdm./einer Sache nicht trauen

**disturb** /dɪ'stɜːb/ *v.t.* A (*break calm of*) stören; aufscheuchen ‹Vögel›; aufhalten, behindern ‹Fortschritt›; **'do not ~!'** „bitte nicht stören!"; **~ing the peace** Ruhestörung, *die;* **sorry to ~ you at this late hour** entschuldigen Sie bitte die späte Störung; **if you find that the noise ~s you** wenn Sie sich durch den Lärm gestört fühlen; **~ sb.'s sleep** jmdn. im Schlaf stören; **don't let us ~ you** lassen Sie sich [durch uns] nicht stören; **they hoped they would not be ~ed** sie hofften, ungestört zu sein; B (*move from settled position*) durcheinander bringen; bewegen ‹Blätter›; **could I ~ you for a minute?** dürfte ich Sie einen Augenblick stören?; C (*worry*) beunruhigen; (*agitate*) nervös machen; **be greatly ~ed by the fact that ...:** sehr darüber beunruhigt sein, dass ...; **don't be ~ed** beunruhigen Sie sich nicht

**disturbance** /dɪ'stɜːbəns/ *n.* A (*interruption*) Störung, *die;* (*nuisance*) Belästigung, *die;* **be a ~ to sth.** etw. stören; **I don't want any ~s** ich möchte nicht gestört werden; B (*agitation, tumult*) Unruhe, *die;* **social/political ~s** soziale/politische Unruhen; **racial ~[s]** Rassenunruhen

**disturbed** /dɪ'stɜːbd/ *adj.* A (*worried*) besorgt ‹Eindruck, Ausdruck›; (*restless*) unruhig ‹Nacht›; B (*Psych.*) **be [mentally] ~:** geistig gestört sein; **a ~ person** ein Geistesgestörter/eine Geistesgestörte

**disturbing** /dɪs'tɜːbɪŋ/ *adj.* bestürzend

**disunity** /dɪs'juːnɪtɪ/ *n.* Uneinigkeit, *die*

**disuse** /dɪs'juːs/ *n.* A (*discontinuance*) Außer-Gebrauch-Kommen, *das;* (*disappearance*) Verschwinden, *das;* (*abolition*) Abschaffung, *die;* **the bicycle was rusty from ~:** das Fahrrad war rostig, weil es nicht benutzt wurde; B (*disused state*) **fall into ~:** außer Gebrauch kommen

**disused** /dɪs'juːzd/ *adj.* stillgelegt ‹Bergwerk, Eisenbahnlinie›; leer stehend ‹Gebäude›; ausrangiert (*ugs.*) ‹Fahrzeug, Möbel›

**disyllabic** /dɪsɪ'læbɪk, daɪsɪ'læbɪk/ *adj.* (*Ling.*) zweisilbig

**ditch** /dɪtʃ/ **1** *n.* Graben, *der;* (*at side of road*) Straßengraben, *der;* **be driven to the last ~** (*fig.*) in die Enge getrieben werden; **die in a ~** (*lit. or fig.*) im Straßengraben sterben. **2** *v.t.* (*coll.*) A (*abandon*) sitzen lassen ‹Familie, Freunde›; sausen lassen (*ugs.*) ‹Plan›; B (*make forced sea-landing with*) im Bach landen mit (*salopp*)

**'ditchwater** *n.* stehendes, fauliges Wasser; **[as] dull as ~:** sterbenslangweilig

**dither** /'dɪðə(r)/ **1** *v.i.* schwanken; **I'm ~ing** ich bin noch am Schwanken; **~ about doing sth.** lange hin und her überlegen, ob man etw. tun soll [oder nicht]. **2** *n.* (*coll.*) **be all of a ~** *or* **in a ~:** am Rotieren (*ugs.*) sein

**dithery** /'dɪðərɪ/ *adj.* unentschlossen

**ditto** /'dɪtəʊ/ *n., pl.* **~s: p. 5 is missing, p. 19 ~:** S. 5 fehlt, ebenso S. 19; **~ marks** Unterführungszeichen, *das;* **I'm hungry. — D~:** Ich habe Hunger. — Ich auch

**ditty** /'dɪtɪ/ *n.* Weise, *die*

**'ditty bag** *n.* (*Naut.*) *Segeltuchtasche für Werkzeug, Nähzeug, Rasierzeug usw. des Seemanns*

**diuretic** /daɪjʊə'retɪk/ (*Med.*) **1** *adj.* diuretisch (*fachspr.*); harntreibend; **~ drug/substance/remedy** ⇒ **2**. **2** *n.* Diuretikum, *das* (*fachspr.*); harntreibendes Mittel

**diurnal** /daɪ'ɜːnl/ *adj.* A (*of the day*) Tages-; B (*daily*) täglich

**diva** /'diːvə/ *n.* Primadonna, *die;* Göttin, *die* (*fig. geh.*)

**divan** /dɪ'væn/ *n.* A (*couch, bed*) [Polster]liege, *die;* B (*long seat*) Chaiselongue, *die*

**di'van bed** ⇒ **divan** A

**dive** /daɪv/ **1** *v.i.*, **~d** *or* (*Amer.*) **dove** /dəʊv/ A einen Kopfsprung machen; springen; (*when already in water*) [unter]tauchen; B (*plunge downwards*) ‹Vogel, Flugzeug usw.:› einen Sturzflug machen; ‹Unterseeboot usw.:› abtauchen (*Seemannsspr.*), tauchen; ‹Achterbahn usw.:› hinunterschießen; C (*dart down*) sich hinwerfen; **~ under the table for protection** schnell unter dem Tisch Schutz suchen; D (*dart*) **~ [out of sight]** sich schnell verstecken; (*when frightened*) sich flüchten *od.* verkriechen; sich schnell verstecken; E (*rush*) hechten; springen; **~ into the nearest pub** gleich in die nächste Kneipe stürzen; **~ into bed** ins Bett springen; F (*plunge with hand*) **~ into sth.** in etw. (*Akk.*) mit der Hand greifen *od.* fassen; (*fig.: begin to eat*) über etw. (*Akk.*) herfallen; G (*begin to work*) **~ into a job** sich auf eine Arbeit stürzen.
**2** *n.* A (*plunge*) Kopfsprung, *der;* (*of bird, aircraft, etc.*) Sturzflug, *der* (**towards** auf + *Akk.*); (*of submarine etc.*) [Unter]tauchen; B (*sudden darting movement*) Sprung, *der;* Satz, *der;* **make a ~ for cover** schnell in Deckung gehen; C (*coll.: disreputable place*) Spelunke, *die* (*abwertend*)

**~ 'in** *v.i.* [mit dem Kopf voraus] hineinspringen; (*fig.: help oneself*) zulangen

**dive: ~-bomb** *v.t.* (*Mil.*) im Sturzflug bombardieren; **~-bomber** *n.* (*Mil.*) Sturzkampfflugzeug, *das*

**diver** /'daɪvə(r)/ *n.* A (*Sport*) Kunstspringer, *der*/-springerin, *die;* B ▶ 1261 (*as profession*) Taucher, *der*/Taucherin, *die;* C (*diving bird*) Taucher, *der*

**diverge** /daɪ'vɜːdʒ, dɪ'vɜːdʒ/ *v.i.* A auseinander gehen; **here the road ~s from the river** hier entfernt die Straße sich vom Fluss; B (*fig.*) ‹Berufswege, Pfade:› sich trennen; (*from norm etc.*) abweichen; C (*differ*) ‹Meinungen, Ansichten:› voneinander abweichen, (*geh.*) divergieren

**divergence** /daɪ'vɜːdʒəns, dɪ'vɜːdʒəns/ *n.* A Divergenz, *die* (*fachspr.*); Auseinandergehen, *das;* B (*fig.*) Abweichung, *die;* (*of careers, lifestyles*) Auseinanderstreben, *das;* **~ of opinions/views** Meinungsverschiedenheit, *die* (**over** über + *Akk.*)

**divergent** /daɪ'vɜːdʒənt, dɪ'vɜːdʒənt/ *adj.* A divergent (*fachspr.*); auseinander gehend, auseinander laufend ‹Routen, Wege›; (*fig.*) auseinander strebend ‹Berufswege›; **~ lens** (*Optics*) Zerstreuungslinse, *die;* B (*differing*) unterschiedlich, voneinander abweichend ‹Ansichten, Methoden›

**diverse** /daɪ'vɜːs, dɪ'vɜːs/ *adj.* A (*unlike*) verschieden[artig]; unterschiedlich; **be [very] ~ from sth.** [ganz] anders sein als etw.; **B** (*varied*) vielseitig, breit gefächert ‹[Aus]bildung, Interessen, Kenntnisse›; umfassend ‹Wissen›; vielfältig ‹Arbeitsgebiet›; bunt [gewürfelt] ‹Mischung›

**diversification** /daɪvɜːsɪfɪˈkeɪʃn, dɪvɜːsɪfɪˈkeɪʃn/ *n.* **A** (*varying*) [Auf]fächerung, *die;* breite Fächerung; **B** (*Econ.*) Streuung, *die;* ~ **[of production]** Diversifikation, *die*

**diversify** /daɪˈvɜːsɪfaɪ, dɪˈvɜːsɪfaɪ/ ❶ *v.t.* **A** (*vary*) abwechslungsreich[er] gestalten; Abwechslung bringen in (+ *Akk.*); **B** (*Econ.*) diversifizieren (*fachspr.*). ❷ *v.i.* sich auf neue Produktions-/Produktbereiche umstellen

**diversion** /daɪˈvɜːʃn, dɪˈvɜːʃn/ *n.* **A** (*diverting of attention*) Ablenkung, *die;* **B** (*feint*) Ablenkungsmanöver, *das;* **create a ~:** ein Ablenkungsmanöver durchführen; **C** *no pl.* (*recreation*) Unterhaltung, *die;* (*distraction*) Zerstreuung, *die;* Abwechslung, *die;* **D** (*amusement*) [Möglichkeit der] Freizeitbeschäftigung; **the ~s of the big city** das Unterhaltungsangebot der Großstadt; **E** (*deviating*) (*of river, traffic*) Ableitung, *die;* **F** (*Brit.: alternative route*) Umleitung, *die;* **there is a traffic ~ on the road** der Verkehr auf der Straße wird umgeleitet

**diversionary** /daɪˈvɜːʃənərɪ, dɪˈvɜːʃənərɪ/ *adj.* Ablenkungs‹angriff, -bombardement, -manöver›

**diversity** /daɪˈvɜːsɪtɪ, dɪˈvɜːsɪtɪ/ *n.* Vielfalt, *die;* **~ of opinion, ~ in opinions** *or* **views** Meinungsvielfalt, *die*

**divert** /daɪˈvɜːt, dɪˈvɜːt/ *v.t.* **A** umleiten ‹Verkehr, Fluss, Fahrzeug›; ablenken ‹Aufmerksamkeit, Gedankengang, Blick›; ableiten ‹Lavastrom, Blitz›; lenken ‹Energien, Aggressionen›; **~ sb.'s attention/gaze from sth. to sth. else** jmds. Aufmerksamkeit/Blick von etw. auf etw. anderes lenken; **B** (*distract*) ablenken; **C** (*entertain*) unterhalten

**diverting** /daɪˈvɜːtɪŋ, dɪˈvɜːtɪŋ/ *adj.* (*entertaining*) unterhaltsam

**divest** /daɪˈvest, dɪˈvest/ *v.t.* **A** (*formal: unclothe*) entkleiden (*geh.*); **~ sb. of sth.** jmdm. etw. abnehmen; **~ sth. of sth.** etw. einer Sache (*Gen.*) entkleiden; **~ oneself of one's clothing/jewellery** seine Kleidung/seinen Schmuck ablegen; **B ~ sb./sth. of sth.** (*deprive*) jmdn./etw. einer Sache (*Gen.*) berauben; (*rid*) jmdn./etw. von einer Sache befreien; **~ sb. of a responsibility** jmdn. einer Verantwortung (*Gen.*) entheben; **~ oneself of sth.** sich einer Sache (*Gen.*) entledigen

**divide** /dɪˈvaɪd/ ❶ *v.t.* **A** teilen; (*subdivide*) aufteilen; (*with precision*) einteilen; (*into separated pieces*) zerteilen; **~ sth. in[to] parts** (*separate*) etw. [in Stücke (*Akk.*)] aufteilen; **~ sth. into halves/quarters** etw. halbieren/vierteln; **~ sth. in two** etw. [in zwei Teile] zerteilen; **B** (*by marking out*) **~ sth. into sth.** etw. in etw. (*Akk.*) unterteilen; **C** (*part by marking*) trennen; **~ sth./sb. from** *or* **and sth./sb.** etw./jmdn. von etw./jmdm. trennen; **D** (*mark off*) **~ sth. from sth. else** etw. von etw. anderem abgrenzen; **dividing line** Trennungslinie, *die;* **E** (*distinguish*) unterscheiden; **F** (*classify*) einteilen ‹Lebewesen, Gegenstände, Gesellschaft›; **G** (*cause to disagree*) entzweien; **be ~d over an issue** in einer Angelegenheit nicht einig sein; **opinion is ~d** die Meinungen sind geteilt; **be ~d against itself** zerstritten sein; **H** (*distribute*) aufteilen; **~ sth. among/between persons/groups** etw. unter Personen/Gruppen (*Akk. od. Dat.*) aufteilen; **I** (*share*) teilen; **J** (*Math.*) dividieren (*fachspr.*), teilen (**by** durch); **~ three into nine** neun durch drei dividieren *od.* teilen; **K** (*part for voting*) [durch Hammelsprung] abstimmen lassen.
❷ *v.i.* **A** (*separate*) **~ [in** *or* **into parts]** sich [in Teile] teilen; ‹Buch, Urkunde usw.:› sich [in Teile] gliedern *od.* [in Teile] gegliedert sein; **we ~d into groups for discussion** wir bildeten Diskussionsgruppen; **~ into two** sich in zwei Teile teilen; **B ~ [from sth.]** von etw. abzweigen; **C** (*Math.*) **~ [by a number/amount]** sich [durch eine Zahl/einen Betrag] dividieren (*fachspr.*) *od.* teilen lassen; **3 ~s into 36 to give 12** 3 geht zwölfmal in 36; **D** (*be parted in voting*) **the council ~d and a vote was taken** der Rat stimmte [durch Hammelsprung] ab.
❸ *n.* **A** (*Geog.*) Wasserscheide, *die;* **B** (*fig.*) (*line*) Grenze, *die;* (*gulf*) Kluft, *die;* (*rift*) Riss, *der;* **the Great D~:** die Scheidelinie; (*euphem.*) die Schwelle des Todes (*geh.*)

**~ ˈoff** ❶ *v.t.* trennen; **~ off an area** einen Bereich abtrennen *od.* abteilen. ❷ *v.i.* **~ off from sth.** sich von etw. trennen

**~ ˈout** *v.t.* **~ sth. out [among/between persons]** etw. unter Personen (*Akk. od. Dat.*) aufteilen; (*distribute*) etw. an Personen (*Akk.*) verteilen

**~ ˈup** ❶ *v.t.* aufteilen; **~ persons up into groups** Personen in Gruppen einteilen. ❷ *v.i.* **~ up into sth.** sich in etw. (*Akk.*) aufteilen lassen

**divided** /dɪˈvaɪdɪd/: **~ ˈhighway** (*Amer.*) ⇒ **dual carriageway**; **~ ˈskirt** *n.* Hosenrock, *der*

**dividend** /ˈdɪvɪdend/ *n.* **A** (*Commerc., Finance*) Dividende, *die;* **B** *in pl.* (*fig.: benefit*) Vorteil, *der;* **your studying will pay ~s** Ihr Studium wird sich auszahlen *od.* rentieren; **reap the ~s** die Früchte ernten *od.* den Nutzen daraus ziehen

**dividend: ~ stripping** *n.* (*Finance*) Rosinenpickerei, *die* (*abwertend*); **~-warrant** *n.* (*Brit. Finance*) Dividendenschein, *der*

**divider** /dɪˈvaɪdə(r)/ *n.* **A** (*screen*) Trennwand, *die;* (*other means*) Abgrenzung, *die;* **B ~s** *pl.* Stechzirkel, *der*

**divination** /dɪvɪˈneɪʃn/ *n.* **A** (*foreseeing*) Ahnung, *die;* **powers of ~:** Gabe der Weissagung; **B** (*discovering*) Deutung, *die*

**divine** /dɪˈvaɪn/ ❶ *adj.*, **~r** /dɪˈvaɪnə(r)/, **~st** /dɪˈvaɪnɪst/ **A** göttlich; (*devoted to God*) gottgeweiht; **~ service** Gottesdienst, *der;* **the ~ right of kings** das Gottesgnadentum; **have no ~ right to do sth.** kein gottgewolltes Recht haben, etw. zu tun; **B** (*superhumanly excellent*) überragend ‹Begabung›; göttlich ‹Schönheit, Musik›; (*superhumanly gifted*) gottbegnadet; **C** (*coll.: delightful*) traumhaft. ❷ *n.* Geistliche, *der/die.* ❸ *v.t.* **A** (*discover*) deuten; (*guess*) erraten; **~ what sb. is thinking** *or* **sb.'s thoughts** jmds. Gedanken lesen; **B** (*locate*) aufspüren; **C** (*foresee*) vorhersehen; (*foretell*) weissagen; **~ the future** in die Zukunft sehen

**divinely** /dɪˈvaɪnlɪ/ *adv.* **A** (*by God/a god*) von Gott/von einem Gott; **B** (*with superhuman excellence*) genial; virtuos; (*with superhuman giftedness*) gottbegnadet; **C** (*coll.: excellently, extremely well*) traumhaft

**diving** /ˈdaɪvɪŋ/ *n.* (*Sport*) Kunstspringen, *das*

**diving: ~ bell** *n.* Taucherglocke, *die;* **~ board** *n.* Sprungbrett, *das;* **~ suit** *n.* Taucheranzug, *der*

**divining rod** /dɪˈvaɪnɪŋrɒd/ ⇒ **dowsing rod**

**divinity** /dɪˈvɪnɪtɪ/ *n.* **A** (*god*) Gottheit, *die;* **B** *no pl.* (*being a god*) Göttlichkeit, *die;* **C** *no pl.* (*theology*) Theologie, *die*

**divisible** /dɪˈvɪzɪbl/ *adj.* **A** (*separable*) aufteilbar; (*capable of being marked out*) [unter-, ein]teilbar; **be ~ into …:** sich in … aufteilen lassen; **B** (*Math.*) **be ~ [by a number/an amount]** [durch eine Zahl/einen Betrag] teilbar sein

**division** /dɪˈvɪʒn/ *n.* **A** ⇒ **divide** 1 A: Teilung/Auf-/Ein-/Zerteilung, *die;* **B** (*parting*) (*of things*) Abtrennung, *die;* (*of persons*) Trennung, *die;* (*marking off*) Abgrenzung, *die;* **C** (*distinguishing*) Unterscheidung, *die;* Abgrenzung, *die* (**from** gegenüber); **D** (*classifying*) Einteilung, *die;* **E** (*distributing*) Verteilung, *die* (**between/among** an + *Akk.*); (*sharing*) Teilen, *das;* **~ of labour** Arbeitsteilung, *die;* **F** (*disagreement*) Unstimmigkeit, *die;* **G** (*Math.*) Teilen, *das;* Dividieren, *das;* Division, *die* (*fachspr.*); **do ~:** dividieren; **long ~:** ausführliche Division (*mit Aufschreiben der Zwischenprodukte*); **short ~:** verkürzte Division (*ohne Aufschreiben der Zwischenprodukte*); **H** (*separation in voting*) Abstimmung [durch Hammelsprung]; **I** (*dividing line*) Trennungslinie, *die;* (*between states*) Grenze, *die;* (*partition*) Trennwand, *die;* **J** (*part*) Unterteilung, *die;* Abschnitt, *der;* (*of drawer*) Fach, *das;* **K** (*section*) Abteilung, *die;* **L** (*group*) Gruppe, *die;* **M** (*Mil. etc.*) Division, *die;* (*of police*) Einheit, *die;* **N** (*of High Court*) Kammer, *die;* **O** (*Footb. etc.*) Liga, *die;* Spielklasse, *die;* (*in British football*) Division, *die;* **P** (*administrative district*) [Verwaltungs]bezirk, *der*

**divisional** /dɪˈvɪʒənl/ *adj.* (*of section*) Abteilungs-

**division: ~ bell** *n.* (*Parl.*) Abstimmungsklingel, *die;* **~ sign** *n.* Divisionszeichen, *das*

**divisive** /dɪˈvaɪsɪv/ *adj.* **A** (*dividing in opinion etc.*) strittig; umstritten ‹Vorschlag›; **B** (*dividing*) spalterisch; **have a ~ effect on sth.** etw. spalten

**divisor** /dɪˈvaɪzə(r)/ *n.* (*Math.*) Divisor, *der;* Teiler, *der*

**divorce** /dɪˈvɔːs/ ❶ *n.* **A** [Ehe]scheidung, *die; attrib.* **~ court** Scheidungsgericht, *das;* **~ proceedings** [Ehe]scheidungsverfahren, *das;* **want a ~:** sich scheiden lassen wollen; **get** *or* **obtain a ~:** sich scheiden lassen; geschieden werden; **grounds for ~:** Scheidungsgründe; **B** (*fig.*) Trennung, *die.* ❷ *v.t.* **A** (*dissolve marriage of*) scheiden ‹Ehepartner›; **they were ~d last year** sie wurden letztes Jahr geschieden *od.* ließen sich letztes Jahr scheiden; **B ~ one's husband/wife** sich von seinem Mann/seiner Frau scheiden lassen; **her husband refused to ~ her** ihr Mann willigte nicht in die Scheidung ein; **C** (*fig.*) **~ sth./sb. from sth.** etw./jmdn. von etw. loslösen; **keep sth. ~d from sth.** etw. von etw. getrennt halten

**divorcee** /dɪvɔːˈsiː/ *n.* Geschiedene, *der/die;* **be a ~:** geschieden sein

**divot** /ˈdɪvət/ *n.* (*Golf*) ausgehacktes Rasenstück

**divulge** /daɪˈvʌldʒ, dɪˈvʌldʒ/ *v.t.* preisgeben; enthüllen ‹Identität›; bekannt geben ‹Nachrichten›; lüften ‹Geheimnis›; verraten ‹Alter›

**divvy** /ˈdɪvɪ/ (*coll.*) *n.* **A** (*share*) Anteil, *der;* **B** (*distribution*) Verteilung, *die*

**dixie** *n.* (*Brit.*) Kochkessel, *der*

**Dixie** /ˈdɪksɪ/ *n.* **A** die Südstaaten [der USA]; **B** (*Mus.*) Dixie, *der*

**ˈDixieland** *n.* **A** (*Mus.*) Dixie[land], *der;* **B** ⇒ **Dixie** A

**DIY** *abbr.* **do-it-yourself**

**dizzily** /ˈdɪzɪlɪ/ *adv.* **A** (*giddily*) taumelnd; schwankend; (*fig.*) benommen; **B** (*so as to cause giddiness*) auf Schwindel erregende Weise

**dizziness** /ˈdɪzɪnɪs/ *n., no pl.* Schwindelgefühl, *das*

**dizzy** /ˈdɪzɪ/ *adj.* **A** (*giddy*) schwind[e]lig; **I feel ~:** mir ist schwindlig; **he felt ~:** ihm wurde schwindlig; **B** (*making giddy*) Schwindel erregend; **the ~ heights of fame** die Schwindel erregenden Höhen des Ruhms

**DJ** /diːˈdʒeɪ/ *abbr.* **A disc jockey** Diskjockey, *der;* **B** (*Brit.*) **dinner jacket** Smokingjacke, *die*

**D. Litt.** /diː ˈlɪt/ *abbr.* **Doctor of Letters** ≈ Dr. habil.; ⇒ *also* **B. Sc.**

**DM, D-mark** /ˈdiːmɑːk/ *abbr.* **Deutschmark** DM; D-Mark, *die*

**D. Mus.** /diː ˈmʌz/ *abbr.* **Doctor of Music** Doktor der Musikwissenschaften; ⇒ *also* **B.Sc.**

**DNA** *abbr.* **deoxyribonucleic acid** DNS

**D-notice** /ˈdiː nəʊtɪs/ *n.* (*Brit.*) **the government had issued a ~ to the media** die Regierung hatte den Medien die Veröffentlichung [aus Sicherheitsgründen] untersagt

**do**[1] /də, *stressed* duː/ ❶ *v.t., neg. coll.* **don't** /dəʊnt/, *pres. t.* **he does** /dʌz/, *neg.* (*coll.*) **doesn't** /ˈdʌznt/, *p. t.* **did** /dɪd/, *neg.* (*coll.*) **didn't** /ˈdɪdnt/, *pres. p.* **doing** /ˈduːɪŋ/, *p.p.* **done** /dʌn/ **A** (*impart*) tun; **do sb. a favour** jmdm. einen Gefallen tun; **B** (*perform*) machen ‹Hausaufgaben, Hausarbeit, Examen, Striptease, Handstand›; vollbringen ‹Tat›; tun, erfüllen ‹Pflicht›; tun, verrichten ‹Arbeit›; ausführen ‹Malerarbeiten›; vorführen ‹Trick, Nummer, Tanz›; durchführen ‹Test›; aufführen ‹Stück›; singen ‹Lied›; mitmachen ‹Rennen, Wettbewerb›;

d

spielen ‹Musikstück, Rolle›; tun ‹Buße›; **do the shopping / washing-up / cleaning / gardening** einkaufen [gehen]/abwaschen/sauber machen/die Gartenarbeit erledigen; **do a test on sb.** jmdn. einem Test unterziehen; **do a lot of reading/walking** *etc.* viel lesen/spazieren gehen *usw.*; **do a dance/the foxtrot** tanzen/Foxtrott tanzen; **do one's round** seine Runde machen; **is there anything we can do to help?** können wir [Ihnen] irgendwie helfen *od.* behilflich sein?; **have nothing to do** nichts zu tun haben; **what are you going/planning to do?** was hast du vor?; **what does he do for a living?** was macht er beruflich?; **what is 'he/'that doing here?** was hat er/das hier zu suchen?; **Don't just sit there! Do something!** Sitz nicht so tatenlos herum! Tu *od.* Unternimm doch etwas!; **have sth. [already] done** etw. fertig haben *od.* mit etw. fertig sein; **what are you doing this evening?** was machst du heute Abend?; **what am I going to do?** (*baffled*) was mach ich bloß?; **do sth. to sth./sb.** etw. mit etw./jmdm. machen; **what have you done to yourself/the cake?** was hast du bloß mit dir/dem Kuchen gemacht?; **do one or two things to the car** noch ein oder zwei Dinge am Wagen in Ordnung bringen; **how could you do this to me?** wie konntest du mir das nur antun!; **he/it does something or things to me** (*fig. coll.*) er/das macht mich an (*salopp*); **do sth. for sb./sth.** etw. für jmdn./etw. tun; **what can I do for you?** was kann ich für Sie tun?; (*in shop*) was darfs sein?; **this dress does something/nothing for you** (*coll.*) dieses Kleid steht dir gut/nicht [gut]; **do sth. about sth./sb.** etw. gegen etw./jmdn. unternehmen; **there's nothing we can do about the noise** wir können nichts gegen den Lärm tun *od.* machen; **why don't you do something about your hair?** tu doch mal was für dein Haar!; **what are you going to do about money while you're on holiday?** wie machst du das mit dem Geld, wenn du im Urlaub bist?; **what shall we do for food?** was machen wir mit dem Essen?; **can you do anything with these apples?** kannst du etwas mit diesen Äpfeln anfangen?; **what's to do?** was ist zu tun?; **not know what to do with oneself** nicht wissen, was man machen soll; **that does it** jetzt reichts (*ugs.*); **that's done it** das war der ausschlaggebende Faktor; (*caused a change for the worse*) das hat das Fass zum Überlaufen gebracht; (*caused a change for the better*) das hätten wir; **that will/should do it** so müsste es gehen; (*is enough*) das müsste genügen; **he's [really] done it** (*ruined things*) er hat es [wahrlich] geschafft; (*achieved something*) er hat es [wirklich] geschafft; **do a Garbo** (*coll.*) es der Garbo (*Dat.*) gleichtun; **how many miles has this car done?** wie viele Kilometer hat der Wagen gefahren?; **the car does or can do/was doing about 100 m.p.h./does 45 miles to the gallon** das Auto schafft/fuhr mit ungefähr 160 Stundenkilometer/frisst (*ugs.*) *od.* braucht sechs Liter pro 100 Kilometer; **C** (*spend*) **do a spell in the armed forces** eine Zeit lang bei der Armee sein; **how much longer have you to do at college?** wie lange musst du noch aufs College gehen?; **D** (*produce*) machen ‹Übersetzung, Kopie›; schreiben ‹Gedicht, Roman, Brief›; anfertigen ‹Bild, Skulptur›; herstellen ‹Artikel, Produkte›; schaffen ‹Pensum›; **E** (*provide*) haben ‹Vollpension, Mittagstisch›; (*coll.: offer for sale*) führen; (*effect*) erreichen; **F** (*deal with*) (*prepare*) machen ‹Bett, Frühstück›; (*work on*) machen (*ugs.*), fertig machen ‹Garten, Hecke›; (*clean*) sauber machen; putzen ‹Schuhe, Fenster›; machen (*ugs.*) ‹Treppe›; (*arrange*) [zurecht]machen ‹Haare›; fertig machen ‹Korrespondenz, Akten, Zimmer›; (*make up*) schminken ‹Lippen, Augen, Gesicht›; machen (*ugs.*) ‹Nägel›; (*cut*) schneiden ‹Nägel›; schneiden ‹Gras, Hecke, Blumen›; (*paint*) machen (*ugs.*) ‹Zimmer›; streichen ‹Haus, Möbel›; (*attend to*) sich kümmern um ‹Bücher, Rechnungen, Korrespondenz›; abfertigen ‹Patienten›; (*repair*) in Ordnung bringen; machen ‹Garten›; (*wash*) abwaschen ‹Geschirr›; **a living room done in blue** ein blau gestrichenes Wohnzimmer; **G** (*cook*) braten; **how do you like your meat done?** wie hätten Sie gern das Fleisch?; **well done** durch[gebraten]; **the meat isn't/the potatoes aren't done [enough] yet** das Fleisch ist/die Kartoffeln sind noch nicht richtig durch *od.* gar; **H** (*solve*) lösen ‹Problem, Rätsel›; machen ‹Puzzle, Kreuzworträtsel›; **I** (*translate*) übersetzen; **J** (*study, work at*) machen; haben ‹Abiturfach›; durchnehmen ‹Wissensgebiet›; **do history at university** Geschichte studieren; **K** (*play the part of*) spielen; (*impersonate*) imitieren; nachmachen; (*act like*) spielen; mimen (*ugs.*); **L** (*coll.: rob*) einsteigen in (+ *Akk.*) ‹Haus› (*ugs.*); **M** (*coll.: prosecute*) **do sb. [for sth.]** jmdn. wegen etw. rankriegen (*ugs.*); **N** (*sl.: with sexual intercourse*) **do sb.** jmdn. bumsen (*salopp*); **do it [with sb.]** es [mit jmdm.] machen (*salopp*); **O** (*coll.: swindle*) reinlegen (*ugs.*); **do sb. out of sth.** jmdn. um etw. bringen; **P** (*sl.*) (*defeat, kill*) fertig machen (*ugs.*); (*ruin*) erledigen (*ugs.*); **Q** (*coll.: exhaust*) schaffen (*ugs.*); fertig machen (*ugs.*); **we were completely done [in or up]** wir waren total geschafft (*ugs.*) *od.* fix und fertig (*ugs.*); **R** (*traverse*) schaffen ‹Entfernung›; **S** (*sl.: undergo*) absitzen, (*salopp*) abreißen ‹Strafe›; **T** (*coll.: visit*) besuchen; **do Europe in three weeks** Europa in drei Wochen absolvieren *od.* abhaken (*ugs.*); **U** (*Brit. coll.: provide sth. for*) versorgen; **do oneself well** es sich (*Dat.*) gut gehen lassen; **V** (*satisfy*) zusagen (+ *Dat.*); (*suffice for, last*) reichen (+ *Dat.*); **do sb. very nicely/better** jmdm. voll und ganz/mehr zusagen; **we've got enough food here to do us for a week** wir haben genug Essen für eine Woche hier.

❷ *v.i., forms as* 1 **A** (*act*) tun; (*perform*) spielen; **you can do just as you like** du kannst machen, was du willst; **do as they do** mach es wie sie; **B** (*perform deeds*) **do or die** kämpfen oder untergehen; **do-or-die** verzweifelt ‹Versuch, Angriff›; wild entschlossen ‹Gesichtsausdruck›; **C** (*fare*) **how are you doing?** wie gehts dir?; **D** (*get on*) vorankommen; (*in exams*) abschneiden; **how are you doing at school?** wie geht es in der Schule?; was macht die Schule?; **do well/badly at school** gut/schlecht in der Schule sein; **E how do you do?** (*formal*) guten Tag/Morgen/Abend!; **F** (*coll.: manage*) **how are we doing for time or as regards time?** wie steht es mit der Zeit *od.* (*ugs.*) sieht es mit der Zeit aus?; **G** (*finish*) **have done with** ⇒ **done** E; **H** (*serve purpose*) es tun; (*suffice*) [aus]reichen; (*be suitable*) gehen; **would that do?** tuts das [auch]?; **that won't do** das geht nicht; **that will never do** das geht einfach nicht; **you won't do, Peter** du bist nicht gut genug, Peter; **nothing but the best will do for her** das Beste ist gerade gut genug für sie; **that will do!** jetzt aber genug!; **it doesn't/wouldn't do to tell lies/be late for work/believe all that one is told** es ist/wäre nicht gut zu lügen/zu spät zur Arbeit zu kommen/alles zu glauben, was einem gesagt wird; **I** (*be usable*) **do for or as sth.** als etw. benutzt werden können; **make do** ⇒ **make** 1 T; **J** (*happen*) **what's doing?** was ist los?; **what's doing at your place?** was ist bei euch los?; was läuft bei euch? (*ugs.*); **there's nothing doing on the job market** es tut sich nichts auf dem Arbeitsmarkt (*ugs.*); **Nothing doing. He's not interested** Nichts zu machen (*ugs.*). Er ist nicht interessiert; **what's to do?** was ist los? ⇒ *also* **doing**; **done**.

❸ *v. substitute, forms as* 1 **A** *replacing v.: usually not translated;* **you mustn't act as he does** du darfst nicht so wie er handeln; **if you drank as much water as you do coffee** wenn du so viel Wasser trinken würdest, wie du Kaffee trinkst; **B** *replacing v. and obj. etc.* **he read the Bible every day as his father did before him** er las täglich in der Bibel, wie es schon sein Vater vor ihm getan hatte *od.* wie schon vor ihm sein Vater; **as they did in the Middle Ages** wie sie es im Mittelalter taten; wie im Mittelalter; **if I ate as much chocolate as you do** wenn ich so viel Schokolade äße wie du; **you might not want to ..., but if you do, ...:** du willst vielleicht nicht ..., falls aber doch, ...; **C** *as ellipt. aux.* **You went to Paris, didn't you? — Yes, I did** Du warst doch in Paris, oder *od.* nicht wahr? — Ja[, stimmt *od.* war ich]; **D** *with 'so', 'it', 'which', etc.* **I knew John Lennon. — So did I** Ich kannte John Lennon. — Ich auch; **if you want to go abroad then do so** wenn du ins Ausland reisen willst, tu es [ruhig]; **go ahead and do it** nur zu; **then please do so within 10 days** dann [tun Sie das] bitte innerhalb von 10 Tagen; **E** *in emphatic repetition* **come in, do!** komm doch herein!; **take a seat, do!** nehmen Sie doch Platz!; **F** *in tag questions* **I know you from somewhere, don't I?** wir kennen uns doch irgendwoher, nicht?; **he doesn't by any chance play the guitar, does he?** er spielt nicht zufällig Gitarre, oder?; **so you enjoyed yourself in Spain, did you?** es hat Ihnen also in Spanien gefallen, ja?

❹ *v. aux. + inf. as pres. or past, forms as* 1 **A** *for special emphasis* **I do love Greece** Griechenland gefällt mir wirklich gut; ich liebe Griechenland ganz einfach; **I do apologize** es tut mir wirklich Leid; **you do look glum** du siehst ja so bedrückt aus; **you do smoke a lot** du rauchst ja wirklich viel; **so we did go after all** also gingen wir schließlich doch; **but I tell you, I did see him** aber ich sage dir doch, dass ich ihn gesehen habe; **B** *for inversion* **little did he know that ...** er hatte keine Ahnung, dass ...; **rarely do such things happen** so etwas passiert nur selten; **did he but realize it** wenn ihm das bloß klar wäre!; **C** *in questions* **do you know him?** kennst du ihn?; **what does he want?** was will er?; **doesn't/didn't he want or does/did he not want to accompany us?** will/wollte er uns nicht begleiten?; **didn't they look wonderful?** haben sie nicht wunderhübsch ausgesehen?; **D** *in negation* **I don't or do not wish to take part** ich möchte nicht teilnehmen; **E** *in neg. commands* **don't or do not expect to find him in a good mood** erwarten Sie nicht, dass Sie ihn in guter Stimmung antreffen; **children, do not forget ...:** Kinder, vergesst [ja] nicht ...; **don't be so noisy!** seid [doch] nicht so laut!; **don't worry yourselves** macht euch keine Sorgen; **don't!** tus/tuts/tun Sies nicht!; **F** + *inf. as imper. for emphasis etc.* **do sit down, won't you?** bitte setzen Sie sich doch!; wollen Sie sich nicht setzen?; **do let us know how you ...:** sag uns aber Bescheid, wie du ...; **do be quiet, Paul!** Paul, sei doch mal ruhig!; **do look here** schau doch mal her!; **do hurry up** beeil dich doch!; **do cheer up!** Kopf hoch!

**do a'way with** *v.t.* abschaffen

**'do by** *v.t.* **do well by sb.** jmdn. gut behandeln; **he felt hard done by** er fühlte sich zurückgesetzt *od.* schlecht behandelt; **do as you would be done by** handle so, wie du behandelt werden möchtest

**do 'down** *v.t.* (*coll.*) **A** (*get the better of*) ausstechen; **B** (*speak ill of*) schlecht machen; heruntermachen (*ugs.*)

**'do for** *v.t.* **A** ⇒ **do**[1] 2 I; **B** (*coll.: destroy*) **do for sb.** jmdn. fertig machen *od.* schaffen (*ugs.*); **do for sth.** etw. kaputtmachen (*ugs.*); **be done for** (*exhausted*) fix und fertig (*ugs.*) *od.* ganz geschafft (*ugs.*) sein; **if we don't do better next time we're done for** wenn wir das nächste Mal nicht besser sind, sind wir erledigt; **C** (*Brit. coll.: keep house for*) **do for sb.** für jmdn. sorgen; ‹Putzfrau:› für *od.* bei jmdm. putzen

**do 'in** *v.t.* (*sl.*) kaltmachen (*salopp*); alle machen (*derb*); ⇒ *also* **do**[1] 1 Q

**do 'out** *v.t.* (*clean*) sauber machen; (*redecorate*) streichen; (*in wallpaper*) tapezieren; (*decorate, furnish*) herrichten

**do 'over** *v.t.* **A** (*sl.: beat*) zusammenschlagen; **B** (*Amer. coll.: do again*) noch einmal machen

**do 'up** ❶ *v.t.* **A** (*fasten*) zumachen; binden ‹Schnürsenkel, Fliege›; **B** (*wrap*) einpacken; verpacken; (*arrange*) zurechtmachen; **she did her hair up in a bun** sie machte sich (*Dat.*)

einen Knoten; **C** (*adorn*) zurechtmachen ‹Menschen›; schmücken ‹Kutsche, Pferd, Haus›; dekorieren ‹Haus›. **2** *v.i.* ‹Kleid, Reißverschluss, Knopf usw.:› zugehen

**'do with** *v.t.* **A** (*get by with*) auskommen mit; (*get benefit from*) **I could do with a glass of orange juice** ich könnte ein Glas Orangensaft vertragen (*ugs.*); **he could do with a good hiding** eine Tracht Prügel würde ihm nicht schaden; **B have to do with** zu tun haben mit; **have something/nothing/little to do with sth./sb.** etwas/nichts/wenig mit etw./jmdm. zu tun haben; **it's to do with that job I applied for** es geht um die Stelle, für die ich mich beworben habe

**'do without** *v.t.* **do without sth.** ohne etw. auskommen; auf etw. (*Akk.*) verzichten; **he could not do without her** er konnte nicht ohne sie leben; **he can't do without drink** er kann das Trinken nicht lassen; *abs.* **you've never had to do with'out** du hast nie auf etwas verzichten müssen

**do²** /du:/ *n., pl.* **dos** *or* **do's** /du:z/ **A** (*coll.: swindle*) Schwindel, *der;* krumme Sache (*ugs.*); **B** (*Brit. coll.: festivity*) Feier, *die;* Fete, *die* (*ugs.*); **C** *in pl.* **the dos and don'ts** die Ge- und Verbote (**of** *Gen.*); **the dos and don'ts of bringing up children** was man bei der Kindererziehung tun und lassen sollte; **D** *in pl.* (*Brit. coll.*) **fair dos!** gleiches Recht für alle

**do³** ⇒ **doh**

**do.** *abbr.* **ditto** do.; dto.

**doc** /dɒk/ *n.* (*coll.*) Doktor, *der* (*ugs.*); *as address* Herr/Frau Doktor

**docile** /'dəʊsaɪl/ *adj.* sanft; (*submissive*) unterwürfig

**docilely** /'dəʊsaɪllɪ/ *adv.* unterwürfig

**docility** /də'sɪlɪtɪ/ *n., no pl.* Sanftmut, *die;* (*submissiveness*) Unterwürfigkeit, *die*

**dock¹** /dɒk/ **1** *n.* **A** Dock, *das;* **the ship came into ~:** das Schiff ging in[s] Dock; **be in ~:** im Dock liegen; (*coll.: in hospital*) im Krankenhaus liegen; **B** *usu. in pl.* (*area*) Hafen, *der;* **at the ~s in Hull** im Hafen von Hull; **down by the ~[s]** unten im Hafen; **C** (*Amer.*) (*ship's berth*) Kai, *der;* (*for trucks etc.*) Laderampe, *die.* **2** *v.t.* **A** (*bring into ~*) [ein]docken; **B** (*Astronaut.*) docken. **3** *v.i.* **A** (*come into ~*) anlegen; **B** (*Astronaut.*) docken

**dock²** *n.* (*in lawcourt*) Anklagebank, *die;* **stand/be in the ~** (*lit. or fig.*) ≈ auf der Anklagebank sitzen; **put sb. in the ~** (*lit. or fig.*) ≈ jmdn. auf die Anklagebank bringen

**dock³** *n.* (*Bot.*) Ampfer, *der*

**dock⁴** *v.t.* **A** (*cut short*) kupieren ‹Hund, Pferd, Schwanz›; **B** (*lessen*) kürzen ‹Lohn, Stipendium usw.›; **he had his pay ~ed by £14, he had £14 ~ed from his pay** sein Lohn wurde um 14 Pfund gekürzt

**docker** /'dɒkə(r)/ *n.* ▶ **1261** Hafenarbeiter, *der;* Schauermann, *der;* Docker, *der*

**docket** /'dɒkɪt/ **1** *n.* **A** (*Brit. Commerc.: list*) Liste, *die;* **B** (*Brit.: custom-house warrant*) Zollquittung, *die;* **C** (*voucher*) Bestellschein, *der;* (*delivery note*) Lieferschein, *der;* **D** (*endorsement on documents etc.*) [Register mit] Inhaltsangabe. **2** *v.t.* (*endorse*) mit Inhaltsangabe versehen; (*label*) etikettieren

**dock: ~land** *n.* das Hafenviertel; **~yard** *n.* Schiffswerft, *die*

**doctor** /'dɒktə(r)/ **1** *n.* ▶ **1261**, ▶ **1617** **A** (*physician*) Arzt, *der*/Ärztin, *die;* Doktor, *der* (*ugs.*); *as title* Doktor, *der; as address* Herr/Frau Doktor; **~'s orders** ärztliche Anweisung; **just what the ~ ordered** [ganz] genau das Richtige!; **an apple a day keeps the ~ away** (*prov.*) [iss] täglich einen Apfel, und du bleibst gesund; **you're the ~** (*coll.*) Sie sind der Fachmann; **works ~:** Werksarzt, *der;* **B** (*Amer.: dentist*) Zahnarzt, *der*/-ärztin, *die;* **C** (*Amer.: veterinary surgeon*) Tierarzt, *der*/-ärztin, *die;* **D** (*holder of degree*) Doktor, *der;* **D~ of Medicine/Divinity** Doktor der Medizin/Theologie; **graduate as ~, do one's ~'s degree** promovieren; seinen Doktor machen (*ugs.*).

**2** *v.t.* (*coll.*) **A** (*falsify*) verfälschen ‹Dokumente, Tonbänder›; frisieren (*ugs.*) ‹Bilanzen, Bücher›; (*adulterate*) panschen (*ugs.*) ‹Wein›; verwürzen ‹Gericht›; (*improve by altering*) verfeinern ‹Gericht›; verschönern ‹Aussehen›; **her punch had been ~ed with something** ihrem Punsch war etwas beigemischt worden; **B** (*treat*) behandeln ‹Patienten›; **~ oneself** sein eigener Arzt sein; **C** (*patch up*) zusammenflicken (*ugs.*); **D** (*sterilize*) sterilisieren ‹Tier›

**doctoral** /'dɒktərl/ *adj.* Doktor-; **~ thesis** Dissertation, *die;* Doktorarbeit, *die*

**doctorate** /'dɒktərət/ *n.* Doktorwürde, *die;* **do a ~:** seinen Doktor machen (*ugs.*); promovieren

**doctrinaire** /dɒktrɪ'neə(r)/ *adj.* doktrinär

**doctrinal** /dɒk'traɪnl, 'dɒktrɪnl/ *adj.*, **doctrinally** /dɒk'traɪnəlɪ, 'dɒktrɪnəlɪ/ *adv.* doktrinell

**doctrine** /'dɒktrɪn/ *n.* **A** (*principle*) Lehre, *die;* **the ~ of free speech/equality** der Grundsatz der Redefreiheit/der Gleichheitsgrundsatz; **educational ~s** pädagogische Grundsätze; **B** (*body of instruction*) Doktrin, *die;* Lehrmeinung, *die*

**document** **1** /'dɒkjʊmənt/ *n.* Dokument, *das;* Urkunde, *die;* **all the necessary ~s** alle erforderlichen Unterlagen. **2** /'dɒkjʊment/ *v.t.* **A** (*prove by document[s]*) dokumentieren; [mit Dokumenten] belegen; **B** (*furnish with document[s]*) **be well ~ed** ‹Leben, Zeit usw.:› gut belegt sein

**documentary** /dɒkjʊ'mentərɪ/ **1** *adj.* **A** (*pertaining to documents*) dokumentarisch, urkundlich ‹Beweis›; **B** (*factual*) dokumentarisch; **~ film** Dokumentarfilm, *der.* **2** *n.* (*film*) Dokumentarfilm, *der*

**documentation** /dɒkjʊmen'teɪʃn/ *n.* **A** (*documenting*) Dokumentation, *die;* **B** (*material*) beweiskräftige Dokumente *Pl.;* Beweisstücke *Pl.*

**document: ~ case** *n.* Kollegmappe, *die;* **~ holder** *n.* Konzepthalter, *der*

**dodder** /'dɒdə(r)/ *v.i.* **A** (*totter*) wacklig gehen; **B** (*tremble*) zittern

**dodderer** /'dɒdərə(r)/ *n.* Tattergreis, *der* (*ugs.*)

**doddery** /'dɒdərɪ/ *adj.* tatterig (*ugs.*) ‹alter Mann›; zittrig ‹Beine, Bewegungen›

**doddle** /'dɒdl/ *n.* (*Brit. coll.*) Kinderspiel, *das* (*fig.*)

**dodecaphonic** /dəʊdekə'fɒnɪk/ *adj.* (*Mus.*) Zwölfton-

**dodge** /dɒdʒ/ **1** *v.i.* **A** (*move quickly*) ausweichen; **~ [out of sight]** schnell verschwinden; **~ behind the hedge/the trees** hinter die Hecke/die Bäume springen *od.* schlüpfen; **~ out of the way/to the side** zur Seite springen; **B** (*move to and fro*) ständig in Bewegung sein; **~ through the traffic** sich durch den Verkehr schlängeln. **2** *v.t.* (*elude by movement*) ausweichen (+ *Dat.*) ‹Schlag, Hindernis usw.›; entkommen (+ *Dat.*) ‹Polizei, Verfolger›; (*avoid*) sich drücken vor (+ *Dat.*) ‹Wehrdienst›; umgehen ‹Steuer›; aus dem Weg gehen (+ *Dat.*) ‹Frage, Problem›; (*evade by trickery*) austricksen (*ugs.*); **~ doing sth.** es umgehen, etw. zu tun; sich davor drücken, etw. zu tun; ⇒ *also* **column**. **3** *n.* **A** (*move*) Sprung zur Seite; **B** (*trick*) Trick, *der;* **he's up to all the ~s** er ist mit allen Wassern gewaschen

**dodgem** /'dɒdʒəm/ *n.* [Auto]skooter, *der; in pl.* [Auto]skooterbahn, *die;* **have a ride/go on the ~s** Autoskooter fahren

**dodger** /'dɒdʒə(r)/ *n.* Drückeberger, *der* (*ugs. abwertend*)

**dodgy** /'dɒdʒɪ/ *adj.* **A** (*cunning*) gerissen (*ugs.*); ausgekocht (*ugs.*); **B** (*Brit. coll.*) (*unreliable*) unsicher; schwach ‹Knie, Herz usw.›; (*awkward*) verzwickt; vertrackt; (*tricky*) knifflig; (*risky*) gewagt; heikel; **the car's a bit ~ sometimes** das Auto hat hin und wieder seine Mucken (*ugs.*)

**dodo** /'dəʊdəʊ/ *n., pl.* **~s** *or* **~es** Dodo, *der;* Dronte, *die;* **[as] dead as the** *or* **a ~:** völlig ausgestorben

**doe** /dəʊ/ *n.* (*Zool.*) **A** (*deer*) Damtier, *das;* Damgeiß, *die;* **B** (*hare*) Häsin, *die;* **C** (*rabbit*) [Kaninchen]weibchen, *das*

**DOE** *abbr.* (*Brit.*) **Department of the Environment** Umweltministerium, *das*

**does** /dʌz/ ⇒ **do¹**

**'doeskin** *n.* **A** Rehfell, *das;* **B** (*leather*) Rehleder, *das;* **C** (*fine cloth*) Doeskin, *der*

**doesn't** /'dʌznt/ (*coll.*) = **does not;** ⇒ **do¹**

**doff** /dɒf/ *v.t.* (*dated*) sich entledigen (+ *Gen.*) ‹Kleidung›; lüften, ziehen ‹Hut›

**dog** /dɒg/ **1** *n.* **A** Hund, *der;* **not [stand** *or* **have] a ~'s chance** nicht die geringste Chance [haben]; **I was as sick as a ~:** mir war hundeelend; (*fig.*) ich hätte heulen können; **it shouldn't happen to a ~:** das würde man seinem ärgsten Feind nicht wünschen; **dressed up/done up like a ~'s dinner** (*coll.*) aufgeputzt wie ein Pfau (*ugs.*); ‹Frau:› aufgetakelt wie eine Fregatte (*ugs.*); **a hair of the ~ [that bit one]** ein Schluck gegen den Kater; **give a ~ a bad name [and hang him]** einmal in Verruf gekommen, bleibt man immer verdächtig; **go to the ~s** vor die Hunde gehen (*ugs.*); **help a lame ~ over a stile** einem Bedürftigen unter die Arme greifen; **love me, love my ~:** man muss mich so nehmen, wie ich bin; **a ~ in the manger** ein Biest, das keinem was gönnt; **~-in-the-manger** missgünstig ‹Benehmen›; **put on ~** (*coll.*) angeben (*ugs.*); **be like a ~ with two tails** sich freuen wie ein Schneekönig (*ugs.*); **see a man about a ~:** etwas erledigen; (*visit lavatory*) hingehen, wo auch der Kaiser zu Fuß hingeht (*scherzh.*); **there's life in the old ~ yet** er ist noch ganz schön fit für sein Alter (*ugs.*); er gehört noch nicht zum alten Eisen (*ugs.*); **you can't teach an old ~ new tricks** alte Menschen können sich nicht mehr umstellen; **the ~s** (*Brit. coll.: greyhound racing*) das Windhundrennen; **try it on the ~:** ihn/sie *usw.* als Versuchskaninchen benutzen; ⇒ *also* **cat A; day E; hot; sleeping; B** (*Hunting*) [Jagd]hund, *der;* **[you must] let the ~ see the rabbit** (*fig.*) lass mich mal ran (*ugs.*); (*sb. must be given a fair chance*) du musst ihn *usw.* ranlassen; **C** (*male ~*) Rüde, *der;* **D** (*despicable person; coll.: fellow*) Hund, *der* (*derb*); **you ~!** du Hund[esohn]! (*derb*); **wise old ~/clever old ~/sly ~/cunning ~:** schlauer Fuchs (*ugs.*).

**2** *v.t.*, **-gg-** (*follow*) verfolgen; (*fig.*) heimsuchen; verfolgen; **~ sb.'s steps** jmdm. hart auf den Fersen bleiben

**dog: ~ biscuit** *n.* Hundekuchen, *der;* **~ breeder** ⇒ **breeder**; **~cart** *n.* Dogcart, *der;* **~ collar** *n.* **A** [Hunde]halsband, *das;* **B** (*joc.: clerical collar*) Kollar, *das;* **~ days** *n. pl.* Hundstage *Pl.;* **~ dirt** *n.* (*coll.*) Hundedreck, *der* (*ugs.*)

**doge** /dəʊdʒ/ *n.* (*Hist.*) Doge, *der*

**dog: ~-eared** *adj.* **a ~-eared book** ein Buch mit Eselsohren; **~-eat-'~** *adj.* gnadenlos; **~-end** *n.* (*coll.*) Kippe, *die* (*ugs.*); **~fight** *n.* **A** Hundekampf, *der;* (*fig.*) Handgemenge, *das;* **B** (*between aircraft*) Luftkampf, *der;* **~fish** *n.* **[spotted/spiny] ~:** Katzen-/Dornhai, *der*

**dogged** /'dɒgɪd/ *adj.* hartnäckig ‹Weigerung, Verurteilung›; zäh ‹Durchhaltevermögen, Ausdauer›; beharrlich ‹Haltung, Kritik›

**doggedly** /'dɒgɪdlɪ/ *adv.* ⇒ **dogged**: hartnäckig; zäh; beharrlich

**doggerel** /'dɒgərəl/ **1** *adj.* holp[e]rig, unbeholfen ‹Übersetzung, Geschreibsel›; **~ verse** *or* **rhyme** Knittelvers, *der.* **2** *n.* Knittelvers, *der*

**doggie** /'dɒgɪ/ ⇒ **doggy**

**doggo** /'dɒgəʊ/ *adv.* (*coll.*) **lie ~:** sich nicht mucksen (*ugs.*) *od.* rühren

**doggone** /'dɒgɒn/ *adj., adv.* (*Amer. coll.*) verdammt

**doggy** *n.* (*coll.*) Hündchen, *das*

**'doggy bag** *n.* (*coll.*) Tüte, *in der man Essensreste [bes. von einer Mahlzeit im Restaurant] mit nach Hause nimmt*

**dog: ~house** *n.* **A** (*Amer.*) Hundehütte, *die;* **B be in the ~house** (*coll.: in disgrace*) in Ungnade sein; verschissen haben (*derb*); **he is in the ~house** (*in family life*) bei ihm hängt der Haussegen schief; **~-leg** *n.* Knick, *der;* **~ licence** *n.* Hundesteuerbescheinigung, *die;* **~like** *adj.* hundeähnlich ‹Aussehen›; hündisch ‹Ergebenheit›

**dogma** /'dɒgmə/ *n.* Dogma, *das*

**dogmatic** /dɒg'mætɪk/ *adj.* dogmatisch; **~ theology** Dogmatik, *die;* **be ~ about sth.** in etw. (*Dat.*) dogmatisch sein

**dogmatically** /dɒg'mætɪkəlɪ/ *adv.* dogmatisch

**dogmatism** /'dɒgmətɪzm/ *n.* Dogmatismus, *der*

**do-gooder** /du:'gʊdə(r)/ *n.* Wohltäter, *der* (*iron.*); (*reformer*) Weltverbesserer, *der* (*iron.*)

**dog: ~-paddle** *v.i.* Hundepaddeln machen; **~rose** *n.* (*Bot.*) Hundsrose, *die;* **~sbody** *n.* (*Brit. coll.*) Mädchen für alles; **~'s 'breakfast** *n.* (*coll.*) Bockmist, *der* (*salopp*); **make a ~'s breakfast of sth.** etw. verbocken (*ugs.*); **~'s life** *n.* **a ~'s life** ein Hundeleben; **give** *or* **lead sb. a ~'s life** jmdn. schäbig behandeln; **~ star** *n.* Sirius, *der;* Hundsstern, *der;* **~ tag** *n.* (*lit. or fig.*) Hundemarke, *die;* **~-'tired** *adj.* hundemüde; **~-tooth** *n.* (*Archit.*) Hundszahnornament, *das;* **~trot** *n.* gemächlicher Trott; **~ violet** *n.* (*Bot.*) Hundsveilchen, *das;* **~watch** *n.* (*Naut.*) (*from 4 p.m. to 6 p.m./from 6 p.m. to 8 p.m.*) 1./2. Plattfuß, *der* (*Seemannsspr.*); **~wood** *n.* (*Bot.*) Hartriegel, *der;* Hornstrauch, *der*

**doh** /dəʊ/ *n.* (*Mus.*) do

**doily** /'dɔɪlɪ/ *n.* [Spitzen-, Zier]deckchen, *das*

**doing** /'du:ɪŋ/ ❶ *pres. p. of* **do**[1]. ❷ *n.* Ⓐ *vbl. n. of* **do;**[1] Ⓑ *no pl.* Tun, *das;* **be [of] sb.'s ~:** jmds. Werk sein; **it was not [of]** *or* **none of his ~:** er hatte nichts damit zu tun; **that takes a lot of/some ~:** da gehört sehr viel/schon etwas dazu; Ⓒ *in pl.* **sb.'s ~s** (*actions*) jmds. Tun und Treiben; **the ~s** (*coll.*) die Dinger (*ugs.*); (*thing with unknown name*) das Dings (*ugs.*)

**do-it-yourself** /du:ɪtjə'self/ ❶ *adj.* Do-it-yourself-; **~ equipment** Heimwerkerausrüstung, *die.* ❷ *n.* Heimwerken, *das;* Do-it-yourself, *das*

**doldrums** /'dɒldrəmz/ *n. pl.* Ⓐ (*low spirits*) Niedergeschlagenheit, *die;* Trübsinn, *der;* **in the ~:** niedergeschlagen; Ⓑ (*Naut.*) **in the ~:** ohne Wind; (*fig.*) in einer Flaute

**dole** /dəʊl/ ❶ *n.* (*coll.*) **the ~:** Stempelgeld, *das* (*ugs.*); Stütze, *die* (*ugs.*); **draw the ~:** Stempelgeld *od.* Stütze kriegen; **be/go on the ~:** stempeln gehen (*ugs.*). ❷ *v.t.* **~ out** [in kleinen Mengen] verteilen

**doleful** /'dəʊlfl/ *adj.* traurig ‹Augen, Blick, Gesichtsausdruck›

**dolefully** /'dəʊlfəlɪ/ *adv.* (*sadly*) traurig; trübselig

**doll** /dɒl/ ❶ *n.* Ⓐ (*small model of person, dummy*) Puppe, *die;* Ⓑ (*pretty but silly woman*) Dummchen, *das* (*ugs.*); Püppchen, *das* (*ugs.*); (*sl.: young woman*) Mieze, *die* (*ugs.*). ❷ *v.t.* **~ up** herausputzen; herausstaffieren (*abwertend*); auftakeln ‹Frau› (*abwertend*); **she was all ~ed up** sie war so richtig aufgedonnert (*abwertend*)

**dollar** /'dɒlə(r)/ *n.* ▶ **1328** Dollar, *der;* **feel/look like a million ~s** (*coll.*) sich pudelwohl fühlen (*ugs.*)/tipptopp aussehen (*ugs.*); **sixty-four [thousand] ~ question** (*lit. or fig.*) Preisfrage, *die;* ⇒ *also* **bottom** 2 B

**dollar: ~ 'bill** *n.* ▶ **1328** Dollarnote, *die;* Dollarschein, *der;* **~ sign** *n.* Dollarzeichen, *das*

**'dollhouse** (*Amer.*) ⇒ **doll's house**

**dollop** /'dɒləp/ ❶ *n.* (*coll.*) Klacks, *der* (*ugs.*). ❷ *v.t.* (*coll.*) klatschen (*ugs.*)

**doll's house** *n.* Puppenhaus, *das*

**dolly** /'dɒlɪ/ *n.* Ⓐ Puppe, *die;* Püppchen, *das;* (*child language*) Püppi, *die* (*Kinderspr.*); Ⓑ ⇒ **dolly-bird**

**'dolly bird** *n.* (*coll.*) Mieze, *die* (*ugs.*)

**dolmen** /'dɒlmən/ *n.* (*Archaeol.*) Dolmen, *der*

**Dolomites** /'dɒləmaɪts/ *pr. n. pl.* **the ~:** die Dolomiten

**dolorous** /'dɒlərəs/ *adj.* (*literary/dated*) Ⓐ (*dismal*) düster; trist; schwermütig ‹Klang›; (*distressing*) bedrückend ‹Nachricht, Vorstellung›; Ⓑ (*distressed*) gequält ‹Blick, Ausdruck, Seufzer›

**dolphin** /'dɒlfɪn/ *n.* Delphin, *der*

**dolt** /dəʊlt/ *n.* Tölpel, *der;* Tollpatsch, *der*

**domain** /də'meɪn/ *n.* Ⓐ (*estate*) Gut, *das;* Ländereien *Pl.;* (*of the State; also fig.*) Domäne, *die;* ⇒ *also* **public domain**; Ⓑ (*field*) Domäne, *die* (*geh.*); [Arbeits-, Wissens-, Aufgaben]gebiet, *das;* Ⓒ (*Computing*) Domäne, *die;* Domain, *die;* **~ name** Domänenname, *der*

**dome** /dəʊm/ *n.* Kuppel, *die;* (*fig.*) Gewölbe, *das*

**Domesday [Book]** /'du:mzdeɪ (bʊk)/ *n.: das Reichsgrundbuch Englands aus dem Jahre 1086*

**domestic** /də'mestɪk/ ❶ *adj.* Ⓐ (*household*) häuslich ‹Verhältnisse, Umstände›; (*family*) familiär ‹Atmosphäre, Angelegenheit, Reibereien›; ‹Wasserversorgung, Ölverbrauch› der privaten Haushalte; **~ servant** Hausgehilfe, *der/-gehilfin, die;* **~ help** Haushaltshilfe, *die;* **~ waste** Hausmüll, *der;* **~ life** Familienleben, *das;* Ⓑ (*of one's own country*) inländisch; einheimisch ‹Produkt, Tier-/Pflanzenart›; innenpolitisch ‹Problem, Auseinandersetzungen›; (*home-produced*) im Inland hergestellt; **~ economy/trade** Binnenwirtschaft, *die*/Binnenhandel, *der;* Ⓒ (*kept by man*) **~ animal** Haustier, *das;* **~ rabbit/cat** Hauskaninchen, *das*/Hauskatze, *die;* Ⓓ (*fond of home life*) häuslich [veranlagt]. ❷ *n.* Domestik, *der* (*veralt.*); Hausangestellte, *der/die*

**domesticate** /də'mestɪkeɪt/ *v.t.* Ⓐ (*make fond of home life or work*) fürs häusliche Leben begeistern; (*accustom to home life or work*) an häusliches Leben gewöhnen; Ⓑ (*naturalize*) einbürgern ‹Tier, Pflanze›; Ⓒ (*tame*) zähmen; domestizieren (*fachspr.*)

**domesticated** /də'mestɪkeɪtɪd/ *adj.* Ⓐ (*fond of home life or work*) häuslich; Ⓑ (*naturalized*) eingebürgert; Ⓒ (*tamed*) domestiziert (*fachspr.*); gezähmt

**domesticity** /dəʊmes'tɪsɪtɪ, dɒmes'tɪsɪtɪ/ *n., no pl.* (*being domestic*) Häuslichkeit, *die*

**domestic 'science** *n., no pl.* Hauswirtschaftslehre, *die*

**domicile** /'dɒmɪsaɪl, 'dɒmɪsɪl/ (**domicil** /'dɒmɪsɪl/) ❶ *n.* Ⓐ (*home*) Heimat, *die;* Ⓑ (*Law*) (*place of residence*) [ständiger] Wohnsitz; (*fact of residing*) Aufenthalt, *der.* ❷ *v.t.* ansiedeln

**dominance** /'dɒmɪnəns/ *n., no pl.* Dominanz, *die;* Vorherrschaft, *die* (**over** über + *Akk.*); (*of colours etc.*) Vorherrschen, *das*

**dominant** /'dɒmɪnənt/ ❶ *adj.* Ⓐ dominierend (*geh.*); beherrschend; hervorstechend, herausragend ‹[Wesens]merkmal, Eigenschaft›; vorherrschend ‹Kultur, Farbe, Geschmack›; **have a ~ position** eine beherrschende Stellung einnehmen; **be ~ over** dominieren über (+ *Akk.*); Ⓑ (*imposing*) beherrschend ‹Gebäude, Berg usw.›; Ⓒ (*Mus.*) dominant; **~ seventh** Dominantseptakkord, *der;* Ⓓ (*Genetics*) dominant. ❷ *n.* (*Mus.*) Dominante, *die*

**dominate** /'dɒmɪneɪt/ ❶ *v.t.* beherrschen. ❷ *v.i.* Ⓐ **~ over sb./sth.** jmdn./etw. beherrschen; ‹großer Mensch, Turm:› jmdn./etw. überragen; Ⓑ (*be the most influential*) dominieren

**domination** /dɒmɪ'neɪʃn/ *n., no pl.* [Vor]herrschaft, *die* (**over** über + *Akk.*); **under Roman ~:** unter römischer Herrschaft; **X's ~ of the car market** die Vorherrschaft von X auf dem Automarkt

**domineer** /dɒmɪ'nɪə(r)/ *v.i.* despotisch herrschen; **~ over sb./sth.** jmdn./etw. tyrannisieren

**domineering** /dɒmɪ'nɪərɪŋ/ *adj.* herrisch, herrschsüchtig ‹Person›

**Dominican** /də'mɪnɪkən/ ▶ **1340** ❶ *adj.* dominikanisch. ❷ *n.* Dominikaner[mönch], *der*

**Dominican Re'public** *pr. n.* **the ~:** die Dominikanische Republik

**dominion** /də'mɪnjən/ *n.* Ⓐ (*control*) Herrschaft, *die* (**over** über + *Akk.*); **[be] under Roman ~:** unter römischer Herrschaft [stehen]; **have ~ over sb./a country** Macht über jmdn. haben/ein Land beherrschen; Ⓑ *usu. in pl.* (*feudal domains*) Ländereien *Pl.;* (*territory of sovereign or government*) Reich, *das;* Ⓒ (*Commonwealth Hist.*) Dominion, *das;* **the D~ of Canada** das Dominion Kanada

**domino** /'dɒmɪnəʊ/ *n., pl.* **~es** Ⓐ (*piece for game*) Domino[stein], *der;* Ⓑ **~es** *sing.* (*game*) Domino[spiel], *das;* **play ~es** Domino spielen; Ⓒ (*cloak*) Domino, *der*

**'domino effect** *n.* Dominoeffekt, *der*

**don**[1] /dɒn/ *n.* Ⓐ **D~** (*Spanish title*) Don; Ⓑ (*Spanish gentleman*) spanischer Edelmann; Ⓒ ▶ **1261** (*Univ.*) [Universitäts]dozent, *der* (*bes. in Oxford und Cambridge*)

**don**[2] *v.t.,* **-nn-** anlegen (*geh.*); anziehen ‹Mantel usw.›; aufsetzen ‹Hut›

**donate** /də'neɪt/ *v.t.* spenden ‹Organe›; stiften, spenden ‹Geld, Kleidung›; stiften ‹Land›; **~ money to charity** Geld für wohltätige Zwecke stiften; **he ~d his body to science** er stellte seinen Körper der Wissenschaft zur Verfügung

**donation** /də'neɪʃn/ *n.* Spende, *die* (**to[wards]** für); Schenkung, *die* (*Rechtsspr.*); (*large-scale*) Stiftung, *die;* **a ~ of money/clothes** eine Geld-/Kleiderspende; **make a ~ of £1,000 [to charity]** 1000 Pfund [für wohltätige Zwecke] spenden *od.* stiften

**done** /dʌn/ *adj.* Ⓐ *p.p. of* **do;**[1] **what's ~ is ~** geschehen ist geschehen; **well ~!** großartig!; Ⓑ (*coll.: acceptable*) **it's not ~ [in this country]** das macht man [hierzulande] nicht; **it's [not] the ~ thing** es ist [nicht] üblich; Ⓒ *as int.* (*accepted*) abgemacht!; einverstanden!; Ⓓ (*finished*) **be ~:** vorbei sein; **be ~ with sth.** mit etw. fertig sein; (*fed up*) etw. satt haben; **she's ~ with him** sie ist fertig mit ihm (*ugs.*); **be ~ with alcohol/cigarettes** das Trinken/Zigarettenrauchen aufgegeben haben; **is your plate ~ with?** brauchen Sie Ihren Teller noch?; **when the operation was ~ with** als die Operation vorbei *od.* beendet war; Ⓔ **have ~ [doing sth.]** aufgehört haben, etw. zu tun; **have ~ with sth./doing sth.** mit etw. aufhören/aufhören, etw. zu tun

**donjon** /'dɒndʒən, 'dʌndʒən/ *n.* Hauptturm, *der;* Wachtturm, *der*

**donkey** /'dɒŋkɪ/ *n.* (*lit. or fig.*) Esel, *der;* **she could talk the hind leg[s] off a ~!** (*fig.*) die kann einem die Ohren abreden! (*ugs.*)

**donkey: ~ jacket** *n.* dicke, wasserundurchlässige Jacke; **~'s years** *n. pl.* (*coll.*) eine Ewigkeit (*ugs.*); **for** *or* **in ~'s years** eine Ewigkeit (*ugs.*); **~ work** *n.* Schwerarbeit, *die*

**donnish** /'dɒnɪʃ/ *adj.* Ⓐ (*of college don*) akademisch; professoral (*oft abwertend*); Ⓑ (*pedantic*) oberlehrerhaft (*abwertend*); professoral (*abwertend*)

**donor** /'dəʊnə(r)/ *n.* Ⓐ (*of gift*) Schenker, *der*/Schenkerin, *die;* (*to institution etc.*) Stifter, *der*/Stifterin, *die;* Ⓑ (*of blood, organ, etc.*) Spender, *der*/Spenderin, *die;* **be a ~ of sth.** etw. spenden; **blood ~:** Blutspender, *der/-*spenderin, *die*

**Don Quixote** /dɒn 'kwɪksət/ *pr. n.* Don Quichotte

**don't** /dəʊnt/ ❶ *v.i.* (*coll.*) = **do not;** ⇒ **do**[1]. ❷ *n.* Nein, *das;* Verbot, *das;* **dos and ~s** ⇒ **do**[2] C

**don't: ~-'care** *n.* Gleichgültige, *der/die;* **~-'know** *n.* jmd., der keine Meinung hat; **be a ~-know** zu etw. unentschieden sein

**doodad** /'du:dæd/ *n.* (*Amer.*) Ⓐ (*fancy article, trivial ornament*) Spielerei, *die;* *in pl.* Kinkerlitzchen *Pl.* (*ugs.*); Firlefanz, *der* (*ugs.*); Ⓑ (*gadget*) Dingsbums, *das* (*ugs.*); Apparillo, *der* (*ugs.*)

**doodah** /'du:dɑ:/ *n.* (*coll.*) Ⓐ (*gadget*) ⇒ **doodad** B; Ⓑ (*thingamy*) (*thing*) Dings, *das* (*ugs.*); Dingsbums, *das* (*ugs.*); (*person*) Dingsbums, *der/die;* Dingsda, *der/die;* Ⓒ **be all of a ~:** ganz aus dem Häuschen sein (*ugs.*)

**doodle** /'du:dl/ ❶ *v.i.* ≈ Männchen malen; [herum]kritzeln; doodeln. ❷ *n.* Kritzelei, *die;* *in pl.* Gekritzel, *das;* Kritzeleien *Pl.*

**'doodlebug** *n.* Ⓐ (*Amer. Zool.*) (*tiger beetle*) Ameisenjungfer, *die;* (*larva*) Ameisenlöwe, *der;* Ⓑ *(Hist. coll.: flying bomb)* V1-Rakete, *die*

**doom** /duːm/ ❶ *n.* Ⓐ *(fate)* Schicksal, *das;* *(ruin)* Verhängnis, *das;* **meet one's ~:** vom Schicksal heimgesucht *od.* *(geh.)* ereilt werden; Ⓑ *no pl., no art.* *(Last Judgement)* das Jüngste Gericht; ⇒ *also* **crack**. ❷ *v.t.* verurteilen; verdammen; **~ sb./sth. to sth.** jmdn./eine Sache zu etw. verdammen *od.* verurteilen; **~ sb. to die** jmdn. dem Tode weihen *(geh.)*; **be ~ed to fail** *or* **failure** zum Scheitern verurteilt sein; **be ~ed to exile** ins Exil verbannt werden; **be ~ed** verloren sein

**doomsday** /ˈduːmzdeɪ/ *n.* der Jüngste Tag; **till ~** *(fig.)* bis zum Jüngsten Tag; noch Ewigkeiten

**door** /dɔː(r)/ *n.* Ⓐ Tür, *die;* *(of castle, barn)* Tor, *das;* *(of car, coach)* Tür, *die;* [Wagen]schlag, *der;* '**~s open at 7**' „Einlass ab 7 Uhr"; **he popped** *(coll.)* *or* **put his head round the ~:** er streckte den Kopf durch die Tür; **just pop a note through the ~** *(coll.)* wirf einfach einen Zettel durch den Briefschlitz; **walk sb. right to the ~:** jmdn. bis vor die *od.* bis zur Haustür begleiten; **I'll drop you at the ~:** ich bringe dich vorbei; **milk is delivered to the ~:** Milch wird an die Haustür geliefert; **lay sth. at sb.'s ~** *(fig.)* jmdm. etw. anlasten *od.* zur Last legen; **next ~:** nebenan; **the boy/girl next ~:** der Junge/das Mädchen von nebenan; **two/three ~s away [from ...]** zwei/drei Türen *od.* Häuser entfernt [von ...]; **live next ~ to sb.** neben jmdm. *od.* nebenan wohnen; **next ~ to** *(fig.)* *(beside)* neben (+ *Dat.*); *(almost)* fast; beinahe; **from ~ to ~:** von Haus zu Haus; von Tür zu Tür; **go from ~ to ~:** von Tür zu Tür gehen; Klinken putzen *(ugs. abwertend)*; Ⓑ *(fig.: entrance)* Zugang, *der* **(to** zu); **all ~s are open/closed to him** ihm stehen alle Türen offen/sind alle Türen verschlossen; **close the ~ to sth.** etw. unmöglich machen; **have/get one's foot/keep a foot in the ~:** mit einem Fuß *od.* Bein drin sein/hineinkommen/drinbleiben; **leave the ~ open for sth.** die Tür für *od.* zu etw. offen halten; **leave the ~ open for sb. to do sth.** jmdm. die Tür offen halten, etw. zu tun; **open the ~ to** *or* **for sth.** etw. möglich machen; **packed to the ~s** voll [besetzt]; gerammelt voll *(ugs.)*; **show sb. the ~:** jmdm. die Tür weisen; jmdn. vor die Tür setzen *(ugs.)*; Ⓒ *(~way)* [Tür]eingang, *der;* **walk through the ~:** zur Tür hineingehen/hereinkommen; **shop ~:** Geschäftseingang, *der;* Ⓓ **out of ~s** im Freien; draußen; **go out of ~s** nach draußen gehen; ins Freie gehen. ⇒ *also* **darken** 1 B; **indoors**

**door: ~bell** *n.* Türklingel, *die;* **~ chimes** *n. pl.* Türglocke, *die;* **~frame** *n.* Türrahmen, *der;* **~ handle** *n.* Türklinke, *die;* **~keeper** *n.* Pförtner, *der;* Portier, *der;* **~knob** *n.* Türknopf, -knauf, *der;* **~ knocker** ⇒ **knocker** A; **~man** *n.* Portier, *der;* **~mat** *n.* Fußmatte, *die;* *(fig.)* Fußabtreter, *der;* Putzlappen, *der;* **~nail** *n.* Türnagel, *der;* Tornagel, *der;* ⇒ *also* **dead** 1 A; **~post** *n.* Türpfosten, *der;* **~step** *n.* Eingangsstufe, *die;* Türstufe, *die;* *(coll.: slice)* dicke Scheibe Brot; **on one's/the ~step** *(fig.)* vor jmds./der Tür; **have sth. right on the ~step** *(fig.)* etw. direkt vor der [Haus]tür haben; **~stop** *n.* Türanschlag, *der;* *(stone, wedge, etc.)* Türstopper, *der;* **~-to-~** *adj.* **~-to-~ collection** Haussammlung, *die;* **~-to-~ journey** Fahrt von Haus zu Haus; **~-to-~ selling** Hausverkauf, *der;* **~-to-~ salesman** Vertreter, *der;* Hausierer, *der* *(abwertend)*; **~way** *n.* Eingang, *der;* **~yard** *n.* *(Amer.)* *(garden patch)* Vorgarten, *der;* *(yard)* Vorhof, *der*

**dope** /dəʊp/ ❶ *n.* Ⓐ *(stimulant)* Aufputschmittel, *das;* *(sl.: narcotic)* Stoff, *der* *(salopp)*; **~ test** Dopingkontrolle, *die;* Ⓑ *(sl.)* *(information)* Informationen *Pl.;* *(misleading information)* Märchen *Pl.* *(ugs.)*; Ⓒ *(coll.: fool)* Dussel, *der* *(ugs.)*; **I felt such a ~:** ich kam mir ziemlich dusslig vor *(ugs.)*. ❷ *v.t.* *(administer stimulant to)* dopen ‹Pferd, Athleten›; *(administer narcotic to)* Rauschgift verabreichen (+ *Dat.*); *(stupefy)* betäuben. ❸ *v.i.* Rauschgift *od.* Drogen nehmen

**~ 'out** *v.t.* *(sl.)* rauskriegen *(ugs.)*

**dopey** /ˈdəʊpɪ/ *adj.* *(coll.)* Ⓐ benebelt *(ugs.)*; Ⓑ *(stupid)* blöd; dämlich; bekloppt

**dorm** /dɔːm/ *(coll.)* ⇒ **dormitory** A, C

**dormant** /ˈdɔːmənt/ *adj.* untätig ‹Vulkan›; ruhend ‹Tier, Pflanze›; verborgen, schlummernd ‹Talent, Fähigkeiten›; **lie ~** ‹Tier:› schlafen; ‹Pflanze, Ei:› ruhen; ‹Talent, Fähigkeiten:› schlummern; **be** *or* **lie ~** ‹Regel, Gesetz, Anspruch:› ruhen

**dormer** /ˈdɔːmə(r)/ *n.* **~ [window]** Mansardenfenster, *das*

**dormitory** /ˈdɔːmɪtərɪ/ *n.* Ⓐ Schlafsaal, *der;* Ⓑ *(commuter area)* **~ suburb** *or* **town** Schlafstadt, *die;* Ⓒ *(Amer.: student hostel)* Studentenwohnheim, *das*

**dormouse** /ˈdɔːmaʊs/ *n., pl.* **dormice** /ˈdɔːmaɪs/ Haselmaus, *die*

**dorsal** /ˈdɔːsəl/ *adj.* *(Anat., Zool., Bot.)* dorsal *(fachspr.)*; Rücken-

**dory** *n.* *(Naut.)* Dory, *das* *(fachspr.)*

**dos** *pl. of* **do**[2]

**DOS** /dɒs/ *abbr.* *(Computing)* **disk operating system** DOS

**dosage** /ˈdəʊsɪdʒ/ *n.* Ⓐ *(giving of medicine)* Dosierung, *die;* Ⓑ *(size of dose)* Dosis, *die*

**dose** /dəʊs/ ❶ *n.* Ⓐ *(amount of medicine)* Dosis, *die;* *(fig.)* Dosis, *die;* Quantum, *das;* **take a ~ of medicine** Medizin [ein]nehmen; **in small ~s** *(fig.)* in kleinen Mengen; **like a ~ of salts** *(coll.)* in null Komma nichts *(ugs.)*; Ⓑ *(amount of radiation)* Strahlen-, Bestrahlungsdosis, *die;* Ⓒ *(sl.: venereal infection)* Tripper, *der.* ❷ *v.t.* *(give medicine to)* Arznei geben (+ *Dat.*); **~ sb. with sth.** jmdm. etw. geben *od.* verabreichen

**doss** /dɒs/ *(Brit. coll.)* ❶ *n.* *(bed)* was zum Pennen *(salopp)*; *(of down-and-out)* Platte, *die* *(salopp)*. ❷ *v.i.* Ⓐ pennen *(salopp)*; Ⓑ **~ down** sich hinhauen *(salopp)*

**dosshouse** *n.* *(Brit. coll.)* Nachtasyl, *das*

**dossier** /ˈdɒsɪə(r), ˈdɒsjeɪ/ *n.* Akte, *die;* *(bundle of papers)* Dossier, *das;* **compile a ~ of information** ein Dossier anlegen

**dot** /dɒt/ ❶ *n.* Ⓐ Punkt, *der;* *(smaller)* Pünktchen, *das;* Ⓑ **on the ~:** auf den Punkt genau; **at 5 on the ~, on the ~ of 5** Punkt 5 Uhr; **[in] the year ~** *(Brit. coll.)* Anno dunnemals *(ugs. scherzh.)*. ❷ *v.t.*, **-tt-** Ⓐ *(mark with ~)* mit Punkten/einem Punkt markieren; **~ted with white** weiß gepunktet; Ⓑ *(place [diacritical] ~ over)* **~ one's i's/j's** i-/j-Punkte machen; **~ the i's and cross the t's** *(fig.)* peinlich genau sein; Ⓒ *(Mus.)* punktieren; Ⓓ *(mark as with ~s)* [be]sprenkeln; **the sky was ~ted with stars** der Himmel war von Sternen übersät; Ⓔ *(scatter)* verteilen; **be ~ted about the place** über den ganzen Ort verstreut sein

**dotage** /ˈdəʊtɪdʒ/ *n.* Senilität, *die* *(abwertend)*; Altersblödsinn, *der* *(fachspr.)*; **be in one's ~:** senil sein

**dot-com** /ˈdɒtkɒm/ ❶ *adj.* Dot-com-. ❷ *n.* Dot-com-Firma, *die*

**dote** /dəʊt/ *v.i.* **[absolutely] ~ on sb./sth.** jmdn./etw. abgöttisch lieben

**doting** /ˈdəʊtɪŋ/ *adj.* vernarrt; **her ~ father/husband** ihr in sie vernarrter Vater/Mann

'**dot matrix** *n.* *(Computing)* Punktmatrix, *die;* **~ printer** Nadeldrucker, *der*

**dotted** /ˈdɒtɪd/ *adj.* gepunktet ‹Kleid, Linie›; *(Mus.)* punktiert ‹Note usw.›; **sign on the ~ line** *(fig.)* unterschreiben

**dotty** /ˈdɒtɪ/ *adj.* *(coll.)* Ⓐ *(silly)* dümmlich; **a ~ female** ein Dumm[er]chen *(ugs.)*; **be ~ over** *or* **about sb./sth.** in jmdn./etw. vernarrt sein; **go ~ over** *or* **about sb./sth.** für jmdn./etw. schwärmen; Ⓑ *(feeble-minded)* schrullig *(ugs. abwertend)*; vertrottelt *(ugs. abwertend)*; **go ~:** vertrotteln; Ⓒ *(absurd)* blödsinnig *(ugs.)*; verrückt ‹Idee›; **that was a ~ thing to do** das war Blödsinn *(ugs.)*

**double** /ˈdʌbl/ ❶ *adj.* Ⓐ *(consisting of two parts etc.)* doppelt ‹Anstrich, Stofflage, Sohle›; **~ wall** Doppelwand, *die;* Ⓑ *(twofold)* doppelt ‹Sandwich, Futter, Fenster, Boden›; **win a ~ gold** zwei Goldmedaillen gewinnen; **give a ~ ring on the phone** das Telefon zweimal klingeln lassen; **underline sth. with a ~ line** etw. doppelt unterstreichen; **~ sink** Doppelspüle, *die;* **sleep with a ~ layer of blankets** unter zwei Bettdecken schlafen; Ⓒ *(with pl.: two)* zwei ‹Punkte, Klingen›; Ⓓ *(for two persons)* Doppel-; **~ seat** Doppelsitz, *der;* **~ bed/room/cabin** Doppelbett, *das*/-zimmer, *das*/-kabine, *die;* Ⓔ **folded ~:** einmal *od.* einfach gefaltet; **be bent ~ with pain** sich vor Schmerzen krümmen; Ⓕ *(having some part ~)* Doppel- ‹adler, -heft, -stecker›; **~ flower** *(Bot.)* gefüllte *od.* doppelte Blüte; **~ domino/six** Pasch/Sechserpasch, *der;* Ⓖ *(dual)* doppelt ‹Sinn, [Verwendungs]zweck›; **have a ~ meaning** einen doppelten Sinn haben; doppeldeutig sein; Ⓗ *(twice as much)* doppelt ‹Anzahl›; **a room ~ the size of this** ein doppelt so großes Zimmer wie dieses; **that's ~ what I usually eat** das ist doppelt so viel, wie ich sonst esse; **be ~ the height/width/length/area/time** doppelt so hoch/breit/lang/groß/lang sein; **be ~ the breadth/weight/cost** doppelt so breit/schwer/teuer sein; **~ the heat/strength** doppelt so heiß/stark; **at ~ the cost** zum doppelten Preis; **have ~ the responsibility** doppelt so große Verantwortung haben; Ⓘ *(twice as many)* doppelt so viele wie; Ⓙ *(of twofold size etc.)* doppelt ‹Portion, Lautstärke, Kognak, Whisky›; Ⓚ *(of extra size etc.)* doppelt so groß ‹Anstrengung, Mühe, Schwierigkeit, Problem, Anreiz›; Ⓛ *(deceitful)* falsch ‹Spiel›.

❷ *adv.* *(to twice the amount)* doppelt.

❸ *n.* Ⓐ *(~ quantity)* Doppelte, *das;* Ⓑ *(~ measure of whisky etc.)* Doppelte, *der;* *(~ room)* Doppelzimmer, *das;* Ⓒ *(twice as much)* das Doppelte; doppelt so viel; *(twice as many)* doppelt so viele; **~ or quits** doppelt oder nichts; Ⓓ *(duplicate person)* Doppelgänger, *der*/-gängerin, *die;* **I saw somebody today who was your ~:** ich habe heute jemanden gesehen, der Ihnen zum Verwechseln ähnlich sah; Ⓔ *(duplicate thing)* Gegenstück, *das* **(of** zu); Ⓕ **at the ~:** unverzüglich; *(Mil.)* aufs Schnellste; Ⓖ *(pair of victories)* Doppelerfolg, *der;* Ⓗ *(pair of championships)* Double, *das;* Doppel, *das;* Ⓘ *(Bridge)* Verdoppelung, *die;* Ⓙ *in pl.* *(Tennis etc.)* Doppel, *das;* **women's** *or* **ladies'/men's/mixed ~s** Damen-/Herrendoppel, *das*/gemischtes Doppel; Ⓚ *(Darts)* Wurf mit doppeltem Punktwert; Ⓛ *(Racing)* Doppelwette, *die.*

❹ *v.t.* Ⓐ verdoppeln; *(make ~)* doppelt nehmen ‹Decke›; Ⓑ *(Bridge, Mus.)* verdoppeln; Ⓒ *(Naut.)* umschiffen ‹Kap usw.›; Ⓓ *(clench)* ballen ‹Faust›; Ⓔ *(bend over upon itself)* **~ [over]** doppelt nehmen.

❺ *v.i.* Ⓐ sich verdoppeln; Ⓑ *(run)* laufen; *(turn sharply)* einen Haken schlagen; Ⓒ *(have two functions)* doppelt verwendbar sein; **the sofa ~s as a bed** man kann das Sofa auch als Bett benutzen

**~ 'back** *v.i.* kehrtmachen *(ugs.)*

**~ 'up** ❶ *v.i.* Ⓐ sich krümmen; **~ up with pain** sich vor Schmerzen *(Dat.)* krümmen; Ⓑ *(fig.)* **~ up with laughter/mirth** sich vor Lachen/Heiterkeit krümmen; Ⓒ *(share quarters)* sich *(Dat.)* eine Unterkunft teilen; *(in hotel etc.)* sich *(Dat.)* ein Zimmer teilen. ❷ *v.t.* Ⓐ in die Knie zwingen; *(fig.)* **the sight ~d us up with laughter/mirth** bei dem Anblick krümmten wir uns vor Lachen/Heiterkeit; **be ~d up with laughter/pain** *etc.* sich vor Lachen/Schmerzen *usw.* krümmen; Ⓑ *(fold)* einmal falten

**double: ~-'acting** *adj.* doppelt wirkend; **~ 'agent** *n.* Doppelagent, *der*/-agentin, *die;* **~-barrelled** *(Amer.:* **~-barreled)** /ˈdʌblbærəld/ *adj.* Ⓐ doppelläufig; **~-barrelled [shot]gun/rifle** Doppelflinte/-büchse, *die;* Ⓑ *(fig.: twofold)* doppelt; Doppel-; zweifach; Ⓒ *(fig.: with two parts)* Doppel-; **~-barrelled surname** *(Brit.)* Doppelname, *der;* **~ bass** /dʌblˈbeɪs/ *n.* *(Mus.)* Kontrabass, *der;* **~-bedded** /dʌblˈbedɪd/ *adj.* ‹Zimmer› mit Doppelbett/mit zwei Einzelbetten; **~ 'bend** *n.* S-Kurve, *die;* **~ 'bill** *n.* Doppelprogramm, *das;* **~ 'bind** *n.* Zwickmühle, *die;* **be in a ~ bind** in einer Zwickmühle stecken; **~-'blind** *(Med., Psych.)* ❶ *adj.* Doppelblind-; ❷ *n.* Doppelblindversuch, *der;* **~ 'boiler** *n.* *(Cookery)* Wasserbadtopf, *der;* **~-'book** *v.t.*

doppelt reservieren; doppelt buchen ‹Flug›; (*fig.*) sich zweierlei vornehmen für; **~-breasted** /dʌbl'brestɪd/ *adj.* (*Tailoring*) zwei- *od.* doppelreihig; **~-breasted jacket** Zweireiher, *der;* **~-'check** *v.t.* [A] (*verify twice*) zweimal kontrollieren; **~-check sb.'s statements** jmds. Aussagen zweimal überprüfen; [B] (*verify in two ways*) zweifach überprüfen; **~ 'chin** *n.* Doppelkinn, *das;* **~-click** (*Computing*) ❶ *v.i.* doppelklicken; ❷ *v.t.* **~click sth.** auf etw. (*Dat.*) doppelklicken; **~ 'cream** *n.* Sahne mit hohem Fettgehalt; **~-'cross** ❶ *n.* Doppelspiel, *das;* ❷ *v.t.* ein Doppelspiel treiben mit; reinlegen (*ugs.*); **~-'dealer** *n.* Betrüger, *der;* **~-dealing** ❶ /--'--/ *n.* Betrügerei, *die;* ❷ /'----/ *adj.* betrügerisch; **~-decker** /dʌbldekə(r)/ ❶ /'---/ *adj.* Doppeldecker-; Doppelstock- (*Amtsspr.*); **~-decker bus** Doppeldeckerbus, *der;* Doppelstockomnibus, *der* (*Amtsspr.*); **~-decker train** Doppelstockzug, *der;* **a ~-decker sandwich** ein doppelter Sandwich; ein Doppeldecker (*ugs.*); ❷ /--'--/ *n.* Doppeldecker, *der;* (*train*) Doppelstockzug, *der;* **~-de'clutch** ⇨ **declutch**; **~ 'door** *n.* (*door with two parts*) Flügeltür, *die;* (*twofold door*) Doppeltür, *die;* **~ 'Dutch** ⇨ **Dutch** 2 C; **~-dyed** *adj.* (*Textiles*) doppelt gefärbt; (*fig.*) Erz- ‹Schurke, -ganove›; unverbesserlich ‹Heuchler›; **~-edged** *adj.* (*lit. or fig.*) zweischneidig

**double entendre** /du:bl ɑ̃'tɑ̃dr/ *n.* Zweideutigkeit, *die*

**double: ~ 'entry** ⇨ **entry** H; **~ ex'posure** *n.* (*Photog.*) Doppelbelichtung, *die;* (*result*) doppelt belichtetes Foto; **~ 'fault** ⇨ **fault** 1 D; **~ 'feature** *n.* Doppelprogramm, *das;* **~ 'figures** ⇨ **figure** 1 L; **~-'glazed** *adj.* Doppel‹fenster›; **~ 'glazing** *n.* Doppelverglasung, *die;* **~ 'harness** *n.* [A] (*fig.: matrimony*) Ehe, *die;* [B] (*fig.: close partnership*) enge Zusammenarbeit; **~ 'header** *n.* (*Amer.*) *zwei Spiele zwischen denselben Gegnern an einem Tag;* **~-'jointed** *adj.* sehr gelenkig; **~ 'life** *n.* Doppelleben, *das;* **~-'lock** *v.t.* zweimal abschließen; **~ 'meaning** ⇨ **double entendre**; **~ 'negative** *n.* doppelte Verneinung; **~-page 'spread** ⇨ **spread** 3 K; **~-park** *v.t. & i.* in der zweiten Reihe parken; **~-'parking** *n.* Parken in der zweiten Reihe; **~ 'play** *n.* (*Baseball*) doppeltes Ausmachen; **~-quick** ❶ /'---/ *adj.* [A] **in ~-quick time/at a ~-quick pace** im Laufschritt; [B] (*fig.*) ganz schnell; ❷ /--'-/ *adv.* (*Mil.*) im Laufschritt; (*fig.*) ganz schnell; **~ 'room** *n.* Doppelzimmer, *das;* **~ 'saucepan** ⇨ **double boiler**; **~-'spaced** *adj.* mit doppeltem Zeilenabstand *nachgestellt;* **~ 'spread** ⇨ **spread** 3 K; **~ 'standard** *n.* (*rule*) Doppelmoral, *die;* **apply** *or* **operate a ~ standard** *or* **~ standards** mit zweierlei Maß messen; **~ star** *n.* (*Astron.*) Doppelstern, *der;* **~-stop** *v.i.* (*Mus.*) mit Doppelgriff spielen

**doublet** /'dʌblɪt/ *n.* [A] (*Hist.: garment*) Wams, *das;* [B] (*one of pair*) Dublette, *die*

**double: ~ 'take** *n.* **he did a ~ take a moment after he saw her walk by** nachdem sie vorbeigegangen war, stutzte er und sah er ihr nach; **~-talk** *n.* Doppeldeutigkeiten; **~-think** *n.* zwiespältiges Denken; **~ 'time** *n.* [A] (*Econ.*) doppelter Stundenlohn; **be on ~ time** 100% Zuschlag bekommen; [B] (*Mil.: running pace*) Laufschritt, *der;* **~ 'track** ⇨ **track** 1 E; **~ 'vision** *n.* (*Med.*) Doppeltsehen, *das;* **~ 'wedding** *n.* Doppelhochzeit, *die;* **~ whammy** /dʌbl 'wæmɪ/ *n.* (*coll.*) doppelter Schlag; **be hit by a ~ whammy** doppelt *od.* in zweifacher Weise getroffen werden; **~ yellow 'lines** *n. pl.: am Fahrbahnrand verlaufende gelbe Doppellinie, die ein Halteverbot signalisiert*

**doubloon** /dʌ'blu:n, də'blu:n/ *n.* (*Hist.*) Dublone, *die*

**doubly** /'dʌblɪ/ *adv.* doppelt; **make ~ sure that ...:** [ganz] besonders darauf achten, dass ...; **this response made him ~ angry/upset** diese Antwort hat ihn sehr *od.* besonders geärgert/bestürzt

**doubt** /daʊt/ ❶ *n.* [A] Zweifel, *der;* **~[s] [about** *or* **as to sth./as to whether ...]** (*as to future*) Ungewissheit, (*as to fact*) Unsicherheit [über etw. (*Akk.*)/darüber, ob ...]; **there was no ~** *or* **there were no ~s in our minds about** *or* **as to ...:** uns war ... klar; wir waren uns über ... (*Akk.*) im Klaren; **~[s] about** *or* **as to sth., ~ of sth.** (*inclination to disbelieve*) Zweifel an etw. (*Dat.*); **there's no ~ that ...:** es besteht kein Zweifel daran, dass ...; **~[s]** (*hesitations*) Bedenken *Pl.;* **have ~ about doing sth., have [one's] ~s about doing sth.** [seine] Bedenken haben, ob man etw. tun soll [oder nicht]; **he's now having ~s [about whether ...]** ihm kommen jetzt Bedenken[, ob ...]; **have one's ~s [about sb./sth.]** seine Bedenken [gegen jmdn./etw.] haben; **have one's ~s about whether ...:** bezweifeln *od.* daran zweifeln, dass ...; **be in ~ about** *or* **as to sth.** (*disbelieve*) über etw. (*Akk.*) im Zweifel sein; **be in no ~ about** *or* **as to sth.** nicht an etw. (*Dat.*) zweifeln; **be in ~ about** *or* **as to whether to do sth.** (*have reservations*) Bedenken haben, ob man etw. tun soll; **when** *or* **if in ~:** im Zweifelsfall; **no ~** (*certainly*) gewiss; (*probably*) sicherlich; (*admittedly*) wohl; **there's no ~ about it** daran besteht kein Zweifel; das steht fest; **cast ~ on sth.** etw. in Zweifel ziehen; [B] *no pl.* (*uncertain state of things*) Ungewissheit, *die;* **be in ~:** ungewiss sein; **beyond [all] ~, without [a] ~:** ohne [jeden] Zweifel; **it is beyond [all] ~ that ...:** es steht [völlig] außer Zweifel, dass ...; **without a shadow of [a] ~:** ohne den geringsten Zweifel.

❷ *v.i.* zweifeln; **~ of sth./sb.** an etw./jmdm. zweifeln.

❸ *v.t.* anzweifeln; zweifeln an (+ *Dat.*); **she ~ed him** sie zweifelte an ihm; **I don't ~ that** *or* **it** ich zweifle nicht daran; ich bezweifle das nicht; **I ~ whether** *or* **if** *or* **that ...:** ich bezweifle, dass ...; ich zweifle daran, dass ...; **not ~ that** *or* **but that** *or* **but** nicht daran zweifeln, dass ...; nicht bezweifeln, dass ...

**doubter** /'daʊtə(r)/ *n.* Zweifler, *der*/Zweiflerin, *die*

**doubtful** /'daʊtfl/ *adj.* [A] (*sceptical*) skeptisch ‹Mensch, Wesen›; **a ~ person** ein Skeptiker/eine Skeptikerin; [B] (*showing doubt*) ungläubig ‹Gesicht, Blick, Stirnrunzeln›; [C] (*uncertain*) zweifelnd; **be ~ as to** *or* **about sth.** an etw. (*Dat.*) zweifeln; **be ~ whether ...:** daran zweifeln, dass ...; (*be unsure*) sich (*Dat.*) nicht sicher sein, ob ...; **be ~ about sth.** hinsichtlich einer Sache unsicher sein; [D] (*causing doubt*) fraglich; **the situation looks ~:** die Lage ist unsicher; [E] (*uncertain in meaning etc.*) ungewiss ‹Ergebnis, Ausgang, Herkunft, Aussicht›; (*questionable*) zweifelhaft ‹Ruf, Charakter, Organisation, Wert, Tugend, Autorität, Kräfte, Potenzial›; (*ambiguous*) unklar ‹Bedeutung›; [F] (*unreliable*) zweifelhaft ‹Person, Maßstab, Stütze›; [G] (*giving reason to suspect evil*) bedenklich ‹Gewohnheit, Spiel, Botschaft›

**doubtfully** /'daʊtfəlɪ/ *adv.* [A] (*with doubt*) skeptisch; [B] (*ambiguously*) missverständlich

**doubting Thomas** /daʊtɪŋ 'tɒməs/ *n.* ungläubiger Thomas

**doubtless** /'daʊtlɪs/ *adv.* [A] (*certainly*) gewiss; [B] (*probably*) sicherlich; [C] (*admittedly*) wohl

**douche** /du:ʃ/ *n.* [A] (*jet*) Dusche, *die;* (*Med.*) Spülung, *die;* [B] (*device*) Dusche, *die;* (*Med.*) Spülapparat, *der*

**dough** /dəʊ/ *n.* [A] Teig, *der;* **yeast ~:** Hefeteig, *der;* [B] (*coll.: money*) Knete, *die* (*salopp*)

**'doughnut** *n.* [Berliner] Pfannkuchen, *der;* Berliner, *der* (*landsch.*)

**doughtily** /'daʊtɪlɪ/ *adv.*, **doughty** /'daʊtɪ/ *adj.* (*arch./joc.*) kühn; wacker (*veralt./scherzh.*)

**doughy** /'dəʊɪ/ *adj.* teigig ‹Konsistenz, Finger, Schüssel, Masse›

**dour** /dʊə(r)/ *adj.* hartnäckig ‹Person, Charakter, Arbeiten›; düster ‹Blick, Gesicht›; finster ‹Miene, Stirnrunzeln›

**douse** /daʊs/ *v.t.* [A] (*extinguish*) ausmachen ‹Licht, Laterne, Kerze, Feuer›; [B] (*throw water on*) übergießen ‹Feuer, Flamme, Menschen›; **~ sth. with water** etw. mit Wasser übergießen

**dove**[1] /dʌv/ *n.* (*Ornith., Polit., Relig.*) Taube, *die*

**dove**[2] /dəʊv/ ⇨ **dive** 1

**dove: ~-coloured** *adj.* taubengrau; **~cot, ~cote** *n.* Taubenschlag, *der;* **flutter the ~cots** (*fig.*) für einige Aufregung sorgen; **~-grey** ⇨ **~-coloured**; **~tail** ❶ *n.* (*Carpentry*) [A] (*joint*) Schwalbenschwanzverbindung, *die;* [B] (*tenon*) Schwalbenschwanz, *der;* ❷ *v.t.* [A] (*fig.: fit together*) aufeinander abstimmen ‹Pläne, Verabredungen, Termine›; [B] (*put together with ~tails*) verschwalben (**into, with** mit); ❸ *v.i.* (*fig.: fit together*) ‹Vorbereitungen, Zeitpläne:› aufeinander abgestimmt sein

**dovish** /'dʌvɪʃ/ *adj.* gemäßigt; kompromissbereit

**dowager** /'daʊədʒə(r)/ *n.* [A] ▶ 1617 (*widow with title or property*) Witwe von Stand; **Queen ~/~ duchess** Königin-/Herzoginwitwe, *die;* [B] (*coll.: dignified elderly lady*) Matrone, *die*

**dowdily** /'daʊdɪlɪ/ *adv.* schäbig

**dowdiness** /'daʊdɪnɪs/ *n.* Unansehnlichkeit, *die;* (*shabbiness*) Schäbigkeit, *die*

**dowdy** /'daʊdɪ/ *adj.* (*unattractively dull*) unansehnlich; (*shabby*) schäbig

**dowel** /'daʊəl/ (*Carpentry*) ❶ *n.* [Holz]dübel, *der.* ❷ *v.t.*, (*Brit.*) **-ll-: ~ [together]** zusammendübeln

**doweling**, (*Brit.*) **dowelling** /'daʊəlɪŋ/ *n.* Verdübelung, *die*

**'dower house** *n.* (*Brit.*) Haus einer Witwe (*Teil des Wittums*)

**Dow Jones index** /daʊ'dʒəʊnz ɪndeks/ *n.* (*Econ.*) Dow-Jones-Index, *der*

**down**[1] /daʊn/ *n.* (*Geog.*) [baumloser] Höhenzug; *in pl.* Downs *Pl.* (*an der Süd- und Südostküste Englands*); **the North/South D~s** die North/South Downs

**down**[2] *n.* [A] (*of bird*) Daunen *Pl.;* Flaum, *der;* **chicks covered in ~:** Vogeljunge im Daunenkleid; [B] (*hair*) Flaum, *der;* **have a covering of ~:** mit Flaum bedeckt sein; [C] (*fluffy substance*) Flausch, *der;* (*of thistle, dandelion*) Flaum, *der*

**down**[3] ❶ *adv.* [A] (*to lower place*) runter (*bes. ugs.*); herunter/hinunter (*bes. schriftsprachlich*); (*in lift*) abwärts; (*in crossword puzzle*) senkrecht; **[right] ~ to sth.** [ganz] bis zu etw. her-/hinunter; **come on ~!** komm [hier/weiter] herunter!; [B] (*to ~stairs*) runter (*bes. ugs.*); herunter/hinunter (*bes. schriftsprachlich*); [C] (*of money: at once*) sofort; **pay ~ for sth., pay for sth. cash ~:** etw. [in] bar bezahlen; [D] (*into prostration*) nieder‹fallen, -geschlagen werden›; **shout the place/house ~** (*fig.*) schreien, dass die Wände zittern; [E] (*on to paper*) **copy sth. ~ from the board** etw. von der Tafel abschreiben; [F] (*on programme*) **put a meeting ~ for 2 p.m.** ein Treffen für *od.* auf 14 Uhr ansetzen; **put oneself ~ for a dental appointment** sich (*Dat.*) einen Termin beim *od.* vom Zahnarzt geben lassen; [G] (*to place regarded as lower*) runter (*bes. ugs.*); herunter/hinunter (*bes. schriftsprachlich*); **go ~ to the shops/the end of the road** zu den Läden/zum Ende der Straße hinuntergehen; [H] (*with current*) stromab[wärts]; (*with wind*) mit/vor dem Wind; **brought ~ by river** flussabwärts befördert; [I] (*to place regarded as less important*) **go ~ to one's cottage in the country for the weekend** zum Wochenende in sein Ferienhaus auf dem Land *od.* (*DDR*) seine Datsche fahren; [J] (*southwards*) runter (*bes. ugs.*); herunter/hinunter (*bes. schriftsprachlich*); **come ~ from Edinburgh to London** von Edinburgh nach London [he]runterkommen; [K] (*Brit.: from capital*) raus (*bes. ugs.*); heraus/hinaus (*bes. schriftsprachlich*); **get ~ to Reading from London** von London nach Reading raus-/hinausfahren; [L] (*Brit.: from university*) **come ~ [from Oxford]** das Studium [in Oxford] abschließen; [M] (*Naut.: with rudder to windward*) in Lee; **put the helm ~:** das Ruder in Lee legen; [N] *as int.* runter! (*bes. ugs.*); (*to dog*) leg dich!; nieder!; (*Mil.*) hinlegen!; **~ with imperialism/the**

**president!** nieder mit dem Imperialismus/dem Präsidenten!; **O** (*in lower place*) unten; **~ on the floor** auf dem Fußboden; **low/lower ~:** tief/tiefer unten; **~ at the bottom of the hill** [unten] am Fuß des Berges; **~ under the table** unter dem Tisch; **wear one's hair ~:** sein Haar offen tragen; **~ below the horizon** hinter *od.* unter dem Horizont; **~ at the bottom of the sea/pool** [tief] auf dem Meeresgrund/Grund des Schwimmbeckens; **~ there/here** da/hier unten; **X metres ~:** x Meter tief; **his flat is on the next floor ~:** seine Wohnung ist ein Stockwerk tiefer; **P** (*facing ~wards, bowed*) zu Boden; **keep one's eyes ~:** zu Boden sehen; **Q** (*~stairs*) unten; **R** (*in fallen position*) unten; **~ [on the floor]** (*Boxing*) am Boden; auf den Brettern; **~ and out** (*Boxing*) k. o.; (*fig.*) fertig (*ugs.*); ⇒ *also* **down-and-out**; **S** (*prostrate*) auf dem Fußboden/der Erde; **be ~ with an illness** eine Krankheit haben; **T** ausgefallen ‹Computer›; **U** (*on paper*) nieder-; **be ~ in writing/on paper/in print** niedergeschrieben/zu Papier gebracht/gedruckt sein; **V** (*on programme*) angesetzt ‹Termin, Treffen›; **be ~ for an appointment** einen Termin haben; **be ~ to speak** als Redner vorgesehen sein; **be ~ to run in a race** für ein Rennen gemeldet sein; **W** (*in place regarded as lower*) unten; **~ at the bottom of the garden** am unteren Ende des Gartens; **~ at the doctor's/social security office** beim Arzt/Sozialamt; **X** (*brought to the ground*) **be ~:** am Boden liegen; **Y** (*in place regarded as less important*) **~ in Wales/in the country** weit weg in Wales/draußen auf dem Lande; **~ on the farm** auf dem Bauernhof; **Z** **~ [south]** unten [im Süden] (*ugs.*); **AA** (*Brit.: not in capital*) draußen; **BB** (*Brit.: not in university*) nicht mehr im Studium; (*for vacation*) nicht an der Universität; **how long have you been ~ from Oxford?** seit wann sind Sie nicht mehr an der Universität Oxford?; **CC** (*Amer.*) **~ south/east** in den Südstaaten/im Osten; **DD** (*in depression*) **~ [in the mouth]** niedergeschlagen; **are you [feeling] ~ about something?** bedrückt Sie etwas?; **EE** **be ~ on sb./sth.** (*dislike*) etwas gegen jmdn./etw. haben; **be very ~ on sb./sth.** jmdm./einer Sache gegenüber sehr kritisch eingestellt sein; **FF** **~ to the ground** ⇒ **ground**[1] 1 B; **GG** (*now cheaper*) [jetzt] billiger; **prices have gone/are ~:** die Preise sind gesunken; **HH** **be ~ to ...** (*have only ... left*) nichts mehr haben außer ...; **we're ~ to our last £100** wir haben nur noch 100 Pfund; **strip off ~ to one's underwear** sich bis auf die Unterwäsche ausziehen; **be [left] ~ to sb.** an jmdm. hängen bleiben; **now it's ~ to him to do something** nun liegt es bei *od.* an ihm, etwas zu tun; **II** (*to reduced consistency or size*) **thin gravy ~:** Soße verdünnen; **the water had boiled right ~:** das Wasser war fast verdampft; **wear the soles ~:** die Sohlen ablaufen; **JJ** (*to smoother state*) **sand sth. ~:** etw. abschmirgeln; **KK** (*including lower limit*) **from ... ~ to ...:** von ... bis zu ... hinunter; **LL** (*from earlier time*) weiter-; **last ~ to the present day/our time** bis zum heutigen Tag/bis in unsere Zeit weitergegeben werden; **MM** (*more quietly*) leiser; **put the sound/TV ~:** den Ton/Fernseher leiser stellen; **NN** (*in position of lagging or loss*) weniger; **be three points/games ~:** mit drei Punkten/Spielen zurückliegen; **start the second half 1-0 ~:** mit einem 1:0-Rückstand in die zweite Halbzeit gehen; **we're £3,000 ~ on last year, in terms of profit** was unseren Gewinn angeht, so liegt er um 3 000 Pfund unter dem des letzten Jahres; **be ~ on one's earnings of the previous year** weniger verdienen als im Vorjahr; **be ~ on one's luck** eine Pechsträhne haben. ⇒ *also* **heel**[1] 1 B; **up** 1 AA.

❷ *prep.* **A** (*~wards along*) runter (*bes. ugs.*); herunter/hinunter (*bes. schriftsprachlich*); **lower ~ the river** weiter unten am Fluss; **fall ~ the stairs/steps** die Treppe/Stufen herunterstürzen; **fall ~ the ladder** die Leiter runter-/herunterrutschen; **walk ~ the hill/road** den Hügel/die Straße heruntergehen; **lower sb. ~ a cliff** jmdn. an einem Felsen herunterlassen; **B** (*~wards through*) durch; **C** (*~wards into*) rein in (+ *Akk.*) (*bes. ugs.*); hinein in (+ *Akk.*) (*bes. schriftsprachlich*); **fall ~ a hole/well/ditch** in ein Loch/einen Brunnen/einen Graben fallen; **trickle ~ the plughole** ins Abflussloch tröpfeln; **D** (*~wards over*) über (+ *Akk.*); **ivy grew ~ the wall** Efeu wuchs an der Mauer herunter; **spill water all ~ one's skirt** sich (*Dat.*) Wasser über den Rock gießen; **condensation running ~ the windows** an den Fenstern herunterlaufendes Kondenswasser; **E** (*from top to bottom of*) runter (*bes. ugs.*); herunter/hinunter (*bes. schriftsprachlich*); **his eye travelled ~ the list** sein Auge wanderte über die Liste; **draw a line ~ the page** eine Linie längs über die Seite ziehen; **F** (*~wards in time*) weiter-; **the tradition has continued ~ the ages** die Tradition ist von Generation zu Generation weitergegeben worden; **G** (*along*) **go ~ the road/corridor/track** die Straße/den Korridor/den Weg hinunter- *od.* entlang- *od.* (*ugs.*) langgehen; **come ~ the street** die Straße herunter- *od.* entlangkommen; **turn ~ a side street** in eine Seitenstraße einbiegen; **part one's hair ~ the middle** einen Mittelscheitel tragen; **H** (*Brit. coll.: to*) **go ~ the pub/disco** in die Kneipe/Disko gehen; **I** (*at or in a lower position in or on*) [weiter] unten; **further ~ the ladder/coast** weiter unten auf der Leiter/an der Küste; **live in a hut ~ the mountain/hill** in einer Hütte weiter unten am Berg wohnen; **live just ~ the road** ein Stück weiter unten in der Straße wohnen; **a place just ~ the river** eine Stelle etwas weiter flussabwärts; ⇒ *also* **downtown**; **J** (*from top to bottom along*) an (+ *Dat.*); **~ the stem of a plant/the side of a house** am Stiel einer Pflanze/an der Seite eines Hauses; **the lines ~ the page** die senkrechten Linien auf der Seite; **the buttons ~ the back of the dress** die senkrechte Knopfreihe auf dem Rücken des Kleides; **there were festivities ~ every road** auf allen Straßen wurde gefeiert; **K** (*all over*) überall auf (+ *Dat.*); **I've got coffee [all] ~ my skirt** mein ganzer Rock ist voll Kaffee; **leave marks ~ sb.'s face** in jmds. ganzem Gesicht Spuren hinterlassen; **L** (*Brit. coll.: in, at*) **~ the pub/café/town** in der Kneipe/im Café/in der Stadt; **be ~ the shops** einkaufen sein (*ugs.*).

❸ *adj.* (*directed ~wards*) nach unten führend ‹Rohr, Kabel›; ‹Rolltreppe› nach unten; nach unten gerichtet ‹Kolbenhub, Sog›; **~ train/line/journey** (*Railw.*) Zug/Gleis/Fahrt stadtauswärts

❹ *v.t.* (*coll.*) **A** (*knock ~*) auf die Bretter schicken ‹Boxer›; **B** (*fig.: defeat*) fertig machen (*ugs.*) ‹Gegner›; **C** (*drink ~*) leer machen (*ugs.*) ‹Flasche, Glas›; schlucken (*ugs.*) ‹Getränk›; **D** (*throw ~*) ‹Tier:› abschmeißen (*ugs.*) ‹Reiter, Last›; **~ tools** (*cease work*) zu arbeiten aufhören; (*make a break*) die Arbeit unterbrechen; (*finish work*) Feierabend machen; (*go on strike*) die Arbeit niederlegen; **E** (*shoot ~*) abschießen, runterholen (*ugs.*) ‹Flugzeug›; **F** (*stop by shot etc.*) zusammenschießen (*ugs.*); **G** (*Footb.*) legen (*Sportjargon*) ‹Gegenspieler›.

❺ *n.* **A** (*Wrestling*) Wurf, *der;* **B** (*Amer. and Can. Footb.*) Versuch, *der;* **C** **ups and ~s** ⇒ **up** 4; **D** (*coll.*) **have a ~ on sb./sth.** jmdn./etw. auf dem Kieker haben (*ugs.*)

**down: ~-and-out** *n.* Stadtstreicher, *der*/Stadtstreicherin, *die;* Penner, *der*/Pennerin, *die* (*ugs.*); **~beat** ❶ *n.* (*Mus.*) erster/betonter Taktteil; ❷ *adj.* (*coll.*) **A** (*relaxed*) ungezwungen; **B** (*pessimistic*) düster ‹Film usw.›; **~cast** *adj.* **A** (*dejected*) niedergeschlagen ‹Blick, Gesicht›; **B** (*directed ~wards*) gesenkt ‹Blick, Kopf›; **with one's head ~cast** mit gesenktem Kopf; **~ draught** *n.* [Luft]zug von oben; **~fall** *n.* (*ruin*) Untergang, *der;* **be** *or* **mean sb.'s ~fall** jmds. Untergang *od.* Ruin sein; **~ grade** *n.* Gefällstrecke, *die;* **he was on the ~ grade** (*fig.*) es ging bergab mit ihm; **~grade** *v.t.* niedriger einstufen; **~'hearted** *adj.* niedergeschlagen ‹Blick, Gesicht›; **~hill** ❶ /'--/ *adj.* bergab führend ‹Fahrt›; ‹Strecke, Weg› bergab; **the journey was ~hill** die Reise führte bergab; **he's on the ~hill path** (*fig.*) es geht bergab mit ihm; **a ~hill trend** (*fig.*) ein Abwärtstrend; **the ~hill course of the economy** (*fig.*) die Talfahrt der Wirtschaft; **be ~hill all the way** (*fig.*) ganz einfach sein; ❷ /-'-/ *adv.* bergab; **come ~hill** den Berg herunterkommen; **sb./sth. is going ~hill** (*fig.*) es geht bergab mit jmdm./etw.; ❸ /'--/ *n.* **A** (*~ward slope*) Gefällstrecke, *die;* **B** (*Skiing*) Abfahrtslauf, *der;* **~land** *n.* [baumloses] Hügelland; **~'load** *v.t.* (*Computing*) herunterladen; **~market** *adj.* weniger anspruchsvoll; **~ payment** *n.* Anzahlung, *die;* **~pipe** *n.* [Regenab]fallrohr, *das;* **~pour** *n.* Regenguss, *der;* **~right** ❶ *adj.* **A** (*utter*) ausgemacht ‹Frechheit, Dummheit, Idiot, Lügner›; glatt ‹Lüge›; **B** (*straightforward*) ehrlich ‹Rat, Darstellung, Person›; offen ‹Wort›; ❷ *adv.* geradezu; ausgesprochen; **it would be ~right stupid to do that** es wäre eine ausgemachte Dummheit, das zu versuchen; **~size** ❶ *v.t.* verschlanken; ❷ *v.i.* abspecken; **~stage** (*Theatre*) ❶ *adv.* im Vordergrund der Bühne; **move ~stage** sich zum Vordergrund der Bühne bewegen; ❷ *adj.* **a ~stage door/entrance** eine Vordertür/ein Vordereingang zur Bühne; **~stairs** ❶ /-'-/ *adv.* die Treppe hinunter‹gehen, -fallen, -kommen›; unten ‹wohnen, sein›; ❷ /'--/ *adj.* im Parterre *od.* Erdgeschoss *nachgestellt;* Parterre‹wohnung›; ❸ /-'-/ *n.* Untergeschoss, *das;* **~stream** ▶ **1480** ❶ /-'-/ *adv.* flussabwärts; ❷ /'--/ *adj.* flussabwärts gelegen ‹Ort›; **the ~stream voyage** die Reise flussabwärts; **~stroke** *n.* **A** (*in writing*) Abstrich, *der;* **B** (*Mech.: of piston*) Abwärtshub, *der;* **~swing** *n.* (*Golf, Commerc.*) Abschwung, *der;* **~ time** *n.* (*Computing*) Ausfallzeit, *die;* **~-to-earth** *adj.* praktisch, nüchtern ‹Person›; realistisch ‹Plan, Vorschlag›; sachlich ‹Bemerkung, Antwort›; **~town** (*Amer.*) ❶ *adj.* im Stadtzentrum *nachgestellt;* in der Innenstadt *nachgestellt;* **~town Manhattan** das Zentrum von Manhattan; ❷ *adv.* ins Stadtzentrum, in die Innenstadt ‹gehen, fahren›; im Stadtzentrum, in der Innenstadt ‹leben, liegen, sein›; ❸ *n.* Stadtzentrum, *das;* Innenstadt, *die;* **~trodden** *adj.* geknechtet; unterdrückt; **~turn** *n.* (*Econ., Commerc.*) Abschwung, *der;* **~ 'under** (*coll.*) ❶ *adv.* in/(*to*) nach Australien/Neuseeland; ❷ *n.* (*Australia*) Australien (*das*); (*New Zealand*) Neuseeland (*das*)

**downward** /'daʊnwəd/ ❶ *adj.* nach unten *nachgestellt;* nach unten gerichtet; **~ movement/trend** (*lit. or fig.*) Abwärtsbewegung, *die*/-trend, *der;* **~ gradient** *or* **slope** Gefälle, *das;* **move in a ~ direction** sich abwärts *od.* nach unten bewegen; **he was on a/the ~ path** (*fig.*) mit ihm ging es bergab. ❷ *adv.* abwärts ‹sich bewegen›; nach unten ‹sehen, gehen›; ⇒ *also* **face down[ward]**

**downwards** /'daʊnwədz/ ⇒ **downward** 2

**'downwind** ❶ *adv.* mit dem Wind; vor dem Wind ‹segeln›; **be ~ of sb./sth.** in jmds. Windschatten/im Windschatten einer Sache (*Gen.*) sein. ❷ *adj.* in Windrichtung liegend; **the ~ side** die windabgewandte Seite

**downy** /'daʊnɪ/ *adj.* flaumig; flaumweich ‹Haar, Haut›; Flaum‹haar, -bart›

**dowry** /'daʊrɪ/ *n.* Mitgift, *die* (*veralt.*); Aussteuer, *die*

**dowse**[1] ⇒ **douse**

**dowse**[2] /daʊz/ *v.i.* mit der Wünschelrute suchen (**for** nach)

**dowser** /'daʊzə(r)/ *n.* (*person*) Wünschelrutengänger, *der*/-gängerin, *die*

**dowsing rod** /'daʊzɪŋrɒd/ *n.* Wünschelrute, *die*

**doxology** /dɒk'sɒlədʒɪ/ *n.* (*Eccl.*) Doxologie, *die*

**doyen** /'dɔɪən, 'dwɑːjæ̃/ *n.* Doyen, *der*

**doyenne** /dɔɪ'en, dwɑː'jen/ *n.* Doyenne, *die*

**doyley** ⇒ **doily**

**doz.** *abbr.* **dozen** Dtzd.

**doze** /dəʊz/ ❶ *v.i.* dösen (*ugs.*); [nicht tief] schlafen; **lie dozing** im Halbschlaf liegen. ❷ *n.* Nickerchen, *das* (*ugs.*); **fall into a ~:** eindösen (*ugs.*)

**~ 'off** *v.i.* eindösen (*ugs.*)

**dozen** /'dʌzn/ *n.* **A** *pl. same (twelve)* Dutzend, *das;* **six ~ bottles of wine** sechsmal zwölf Flaschen Wein; **there were several/a few ~ [people] there** Dutzende von Leuten/ein paar Dutzend Leute waren da; **a ~ times/reasons** *(fig. coll.: many)* dutzend Mal/Dutzende von Gründen; **half a ~:** sechs; ein halbes Dutzend *(veralt.)*; **B** *pl.* **~s** *(set of twelve)* Dutzend, *das;* **by the ~** *(in twelves)* im Dutzend; *(fig. coll.: in great numbers)* in großen Scharen; **do one's daily ~** *(coll.)* Frühsport machen; **C** *in pl. (coll.: many)* Dutzende *Pl.;* **in [their] ~s** *(in great numbers)* in großen Scharen; **~s of times** dutzendmal

**dozy** /'dəʊzɪ/ *adj. (drowsy)* dösig *(ugs.)*; schläfrig

**DP** *abbr.* **data processing** DV

**D. Phil.** /diː'fɪl/ *abbr.* **Doctor of Philosophy** Dr. phil.; ⇒ *also* **B. Sc.**

**DPP** *abbr. (Brit.)* **Director of Public Prosecutions** ≈ Generalstaatsanwalt, *der*

**Dr** *abbr.* **A** ▶1617 **doctor** *(as prefix to name)* Dr.; **B debtor** Sch.

**drab** /dræb/ *adj.* **A** *(dull brown)* gelblich braun; sandfarben; *(dull-coloured)* matt; **B** *(dull, monotonous)* langweilig ‹Ort, Gebäude›; trostlos, öde ‹Landschaft, Umgebung›; grau, trist ‹Stadt›; farblos ‹Person›; **C** *(fig.)* eintönig, trist ‹Leben›

**drabness** /'dræbnɪs/ *n., no pl.* **A** *(of surroundings)* Trostlosigkeit, *die;* Ödheit, *die;* **B** *(fig.: of life, existence)* Eintönigkeit, *die*

**drachma** /'drækmə/ *n. pl.* **~s** *or* **drachmae** /'drækmiː/ Drachme, *die*

**Draconian** /drə'kəʊnɪən/ *adj.* drakonisch

**draft** /drɑːft/ ❶ *n.* **A** *(rough copy) (of speech)* Konzept, *das; (of treaty, parliamentary bill)* Entwurf, *der;* **~ copy/version** Konzept, *das;* **~ letter** Entwurf eines Briefes; **B** *(plan of work)* Skizze, *die;* [Bau-, Riss-]zeichnung, *die;* **C** *(Mil.: detaching for special duty)* Sonderkommando, *das; (Brit.: those detached)* Abkommandierte *Pl.;* Sonderkommando, *das;* **D** *(Amer. Mil.: conscription)* Einberufung, *die; (those conscripted)* Wehrpflichtige *Pl.;* Einberufene *Pl.;* **E** *(Commerc.)* Abhebung, *die;* Abheben, *das; (cheque drawn)* Wechsel, *der;* Tratte, *die;* **F** *(Amer.)* ⇒ **draught**.
❷ *v.t.* **A** *(make rough copy of)* entwerfen; **B** *(Mil.)* abkommandieren; **C** *(Amer. Mil.: conscript)* einberufen; **be ~ed** eingezogen *od.* einberufen werden; **D** *(fig.) (call upon)* berufen; *(select)* auswählen

**'draft dodger** *n. (Amer. Mil.) jmd., der sich dem Wehrdienst entzieht*

**draftee** /drɑːf'tiː/ *n. (Amer. Mil.)* Wehrpflichtige, *der*

**draftsman** /'drɑːftsmən/ *n., pl.* **draftsmen** /'drɑːftsmən/ **A** *jemand, der Gesetzesvorlagen usw. verfasst;* ≈ Schreiber, *der;* **B** ⇒ **draughtsman**

**drafty** *(Amer.)* ⇒ **draughty**

**drag** /dræg/ ❶ *n.* **A** *(dredging apparatus)* Suchanker, *der;* **B** ⇒ **dragnet**; **C** *(Hunting) (artificial scent)* Fuchs, *der; (club)* Schleppjagd, *die;* Reitjagd, *die;* **D** *(difficult progress)* **it was a long ~ up the hill** der Aufstieg auf den Hügel war ein ganz schöner Schlauch *(ugs.)*; **E** *(Aeronaut.)* Strömungswiderstand, *der;* **~ coefficient** *or* **factor** [Luft]widerstandszahl, *die;* **F** *(obstruction)* Hindernis, *das* (**on** für); Hemmnis, *das* (**on** für); **be a ~ on sb./sth.** jmdm./für etw. eine Last sein; **G** *(boring thing)* langweilige Sache *od.* Angelegenheit; **be a ~:** langweilig sein; **H** *(coll.: at cigarette)* Zug, *der;* **I** *no pl. (coll.: women's dress worn by men)* Frauenkleider *Pl.;* **in ~:** in Frauenkleidung; **J** *(Amer. coll.: road)* **the main ~:** die Hauptstraße; **K** *(Amer. coll.: influence)* Einfluss, *der.*
❷ *v.t.,* **-gg-:** **A** [herum]schleppen; **~ one's feet** *or* **heels** *(fig.)* sich *(Dat.)* Zeit lassen (**over, in** mit); **B** *(move with effort)* **~ oneself** sich schleppen; **~ one's feet** [mit den Füßen] schlurfen; **I could scarcely ~ myself out of bed** ich konnte mich kaum aufraffen aufzustehen; **C** *(fig. coll.: take despite resistance)* **he ~ged me to a dance** er schleifte mich *(ugs.)* zu einer Tanzveranstaltung; **~ the children away from the television** die Kinder [mit Gewalt] vom Fernsehen losreißen; **he ~s her about with him everywhere** er schleppt sie überall mit sich herum; **~ sb. into sth.** jmdn. in etw. *(Akk.)* hineinziehen; **~ sb. into doing sth.** jmdn. dazu drängen, etw. zu tun; **D** *(search)* [mit einem Schleppnetz] absuchen ‹Fluss-, Seegrund›; **E** *(Naut.)* **the ship ~s her anchor** das Schiff treibt vor Anker; **F** *(Computing)* ziehen; **~ and drop** ziehen und ablegen.
❸ *v.i.,* **-gg-:** **A** schleifen; **~ on** *or* **at a cigarette** *(coll.)* an einer Zigarette ziehen; **B** *(fig.: pass slowly)* sich [hin]schleppen

**~ 'down** *v.t.* nach unten ziehen; **~ sb. down to one's own level** *(fig.)* jmdn. auf sein Niveau herabziehen

**~ 'in** *v.t.* hineinziehen

**~ 'on** *v.i. (continue)* sich [da]hinschleppen; **time ~ged on** die Zeit verstrich; **~ on for months** sich über Monate hinziehen

**~ 'out** *v.t. (protract unduly)* hinausziehen; in die Länge ziehen; **~ out [one's days/existence]** [sein Leben/Dasein] fristen

**~ 'up** *v.t. (coll.)* wieder ausgraben ‹alte Geschichte, Skandal›

**drag: ~ hounds** *n. pl.* Hunde für die Schleppjagd; **~net** *n. (lit. or fig.)* Schleppnetz, *das; (fig.)* Netz, *das*

**dragon** /'drægn/ *n.* Drache, *der; (fig.: fearsome person)* Drachen, *der*

**'dragonfly** *n. (Zool.)* Libelle, *die*

**dragoon** /drə'guːn/ ❶ *n. (Mil.)* Dragoner, *der.* ❷ *v.t.* zwingen; **~ sb. into doing sth.** jmdn. zwingen, etw. zu tun

**'drag racing** *n.* Beschleunigungsrennen *Pl.*

**dragster** /'drægstə(r)/ *n.* Dragster, *der; für Beschleunigungsrennen gebautes Fahrzeug*

**drain** /dreɪn/ ❶ *n.* **A** Abflussrohr, *das; (underground)* Kanalisationsrohr, *das; (grating at roadside)* Gully, *der;* **open ~:** Abflussrinne, *die;* **down the ~** *(fig. coll.)* für die Katz *(ugs.)*; **go down the ~** *(fig. coll.)* umsonst *od.* vergeblich *od. (ugs.)* für die Katz sein; **that was money [thrown] down the ~** *(fig. coll.)* das Geld war zum Teufel *(salopp) od.* zum Fenster hinausgeworfen *(ugs.)*; **be going down the ~:** vor die Hunde gehen *(geh.)*; **laugh like a ~** *(fig. coll.)* schallend lachen; sich vor Lachen ausschütten wollen; **B** *(fig.: constant demand)* Belastung, *die* (**on** *Gen.*); **be a ~ on sb.'s strength** an jmds. Kräften zehren.
❷ *v.t.* **A** trockenlegen ‹Teich›; entwässern ‹Land›; ableiten ‹Wasser›; **B** *(Cookery)* abgießen ‹Wasser, Kartoffeln, Gemüse›; **C** *(Geog.)* **the river ~s the valley** der Fluss nimmt das Wasser des ganzen Tales auf; **D** *(drink all contents of)* austrinken; **E** *(fig.: deprive)* **~ a country of its manpower/wealth** *or* **resources** ein Land ausbluten/auslaugen; **~ sb. of his energy** jmdn. auslaugen.
❸ *v.i.* **A** ‹Geschirr, Gemüse:› abtropfen; ‹Flüssigkeit:› ablaufen; **B the colour ~ed from her face** *(fig.)* die Farbe wich aus ihrem Gesicht

**drainage** /'dreɪnɪdʒ/ *n.* **A** *(draining)* Entwässerung, *die;* Trockenlegung, *die; (fig.)* Ausbeutung, *die;* **B** *(Geog.: natural ~)* [natürliche] Entwässerung; *(artificial ~ of fields etc.)* Entwässerung, *die;* Dränung *od.* Dränage, *die (fachspr.)*; *(system)* Entwässerungssystem, *das; (of city, house, etc.)* Kanalisation, *die*

**draining board** /'dreɪnɪŋ bɔːd/ *(Brit.; Amer.:* **'drainboard**) *n.* Abtropfbrett, *das*

**drain: ~pipe** *n.* **A** *(to carry off rainwater)* Regen[abfall]rohr, *das;* **B** *(to carry off sewage)* Abwasserleitung, *die; (underground)* Kanalisationsleitung, *die;* **~pipes, ~pipe 'trousers** *ns. pl. (Fashion)* Röhrenhosen

**drake** /dreɪk/ *n.* Enterich, *der;* Erpel, *der;* ⇒ *also* **duck**[1] 1 A

**dram** /dræm/ *n.* **A** *(Pharm.) (weight)* Drachme, *die;* **fluid ~** *(Brit.)* 3,5515 $cm^3$; *(Amer.)* 3,6967 $cm^3$; **B** *(small drink)* Schlückchen, *das (ugs.)*

**drama** /'drɑːmə/ *n.* **A** *(play, lit. or fig.)* Drama, *das;* **B** *no pl. (genre)* Drama, *das; (dramatic art)* Schauspielkunst, *die;* Dramatik, *die; (fig.: episode as in play)* Schauspiel, *das; attrib.* **~ critic** Theaterkritiker, *der;* **~ school** Schauspielschule, *die*

**dramatic** /drə'mætɪk/ *adj.* **A** *(Theatre)* dramatisch; **~ art** Dramatik, *die;* **a ~ critic** ein Theaterkritiker; **B** *(fig.)* dramatisch; *(exaggerated)* theatralisch; bühnenreif

**dramatically** /drə'mætɪkəlɪ/ *adv.* dramatisch; *(in exaggerated way)* theatralisch

**dramatic 'irony** *n.* tragische Ironie *(Literaturwiss.)*

**dramatics** /drə'mætɪks/ *n., no pl.* **A** Theater[spiel], *das;* **amateur ~:** Laientheater, *das;* **B** *(fig. derog.)* Theatralik, *die (geh. abwertend)*

**dramatisation, dramatise** ⇒ **dramatiz-**

**dramatis personae** /dræmətɪs pə'səʊniː, dræmətɪs pə'səʊnaɪ/ *n. pl., often constr. as sing.* dramatis personae; die Personen; *(fig.)* Hauptpersonen *Pl.*

**dramatist** /'dræmətɪst/ *n.* Dramatiker, *der/*Dramatikerin, *die*

**dramatization** /dræmətaɪ'zeɪʃn/ *n.* **A** Dramatisierung, *die;* **a television/stage ~:** eine Fernseh-/Bühnenbearbeitung; **B** *(fig.)* Dramatisieren, *das*

**dramatize** /'dræmətaɪz/ *v.t.* **A** dramatisieren; [für die Bühne/das Fernsehen *usw.*] bearbeiten; **B** *(fig.)* dramatisieren; [künstlich] hochspielen; *(emphasize)* betonen

**drank** ⇒ **drink** 2, 3

**drape** /dreɪp/ ❶ *v.t.* **A** *(cover, adorn)* **~ oneself/sb. in sth.** sich/jmdn. in etw. *(Akk.)* hüllen; **~ an altar/walls with sth.** einen Altar/Wände mit etw. behängen; **B** *(put loosely)* **~ sth. over/round sth.** etw. über etw. *(Akk.)*/um etw. legen *od.* drapieren; **C** *(rest casually)* legen; hängen. ❷ *n.* **A** *(cloth)* Tuch, *das;* **B** *usu. in pl. (Amer.: curtain)* Vorhang, *der*

**draper** /'dreɪpə(r)/ *n.* ▶1261 *(Brit.)* Textilkaufmann, *der;* **the ~'s [shop]** das Textilgeschäft; ⇒ *also* **baker**

**drapery** /'dreɪpərɪ/ *n.* **A** *(Brit.: cloth)* Stoffe; Textilien *Pl.;* **B** *(Brit.: trade)* Textilgewerbe, *das;* **~ shop** Textilgeschäft, *das;* **C** *(arrangement of cloth)* Draperie, *die;* **D** *(cloth artistically arranged)* Faltenwurf, *der;* **E** *usu. in pl. (Amer.: curtain)* Vorhang, *der*

**drastic** /'dræstɪk, 'drɑːstɪk/ *adj.* drastisch; erheblich ‹Wandel, Verbesserung›; durchgreifend, rigoros ‹Mittel›; dringend ‹Bedarf›; einschneidend ‹Veränderung›; erschreckend ‹Mangel›; bedrohlich ‹Lage›; **something ~ will have to be done** drastische Maßnahmen müssen ergriffen werden

**drastically** /'dræstɪkəlɪ, 'drɑːstɪkəlɪ/ *adv.* drastisch; erheblich; rigoros, hart ‹durchgreifen›; **be ~ in need of sth.** dringenden Bedarf an etw. *(Dat.)* haben

**drat** /dræt/ *v.t. (coll.)* **~ [it]/him/the weather!** verflucht!/verfluchter Kerl!/verfluchtes Wetter! *(salopp)*

**dratted** /'drætɪd/ *adj. (coll.)* verflucht

**draught** /drɑːft/ *n.* **A** *(of air)* [Luft]zug, *der;* **where is the ~ coming from?** woher zieht es?; **be [sitting] in a ~:** im Zug sitzen; **there's a ~ [in here]** es zieht [hier]; **feel the ~** *(fig. coll.)* [finanziell] in der Klemme sitzen *(ugs.)*; **B [beer] on ~:** [Bier] vom Fass; **C** *(swallowing) (act)* Zug, *der; (amount)* Schluck, *der;* **D** *(Naut.)* Tiefgang, *der*

**draught: ~ animal** *n.* Zugtier, *das;* **~ 'beer** *n.* Fassbier, *das;* **~ board** *n. (Brit.)* Damebrett, *das;* **~ excluder** *n.* Abdichtvorrichtung, *die;* Zugluftverhinderer, *der;* **~horse** *n.* Zugpferd, *das;* **~proof** ❶ *adj.* winddicht; ❷ *v.t.* winddicht machen

**draughts** /drɑːfts/ *n., no pl. (Brit.)* Damespiel, *das;* **have a game of ~:** eine Partie Dame spielen; **play ~:** Dame spielen

**draughtsman** /'drɑːftsmən/ *n., pl.* **draughtsmen** /'drɑːftsmən/ *(Brit.)* **A** ▶1261 Zeichner, *der/*Zeichnerin, *die;* **B** *(in game)* Damestein, *der*

**draughtsmanship** /ˈdrɑːftsmənʃɪp/ *n.* (*art and practice*) Zeichenkunst, *die;* (*skill*) zeichnerisches Können

**draughty** /ˈdrɑːftɪ/ *adj.* zugig

**Dravidian** /drəˈvɪdɪən/ (*Ethnol.*) ❶ *adj.* drawidisch. ❷ *n.* Ⓐ (*person*) Drawide, *der*/Drawidin, *die;* Ⓑ (*language*) Drawidisch, *das*

**draw** /drɔː/ ❶ *v.t.*, **drew** /druː/, **drawn** /drɔːn/ Ⓐ (*pull*) ziehen; einholen ‹Fangnetz›; spannen ‹Bogen›; **~ the curtains/blinds** (*open*) die Vorhänge aufziehen/die Jalousien hochziehen; (*close*) die Vorhänge zuziehen/die Jalousien herunterlassen; **~ the bolt** (*fasten*) den Riegel vorschieben; (*unfasten*) den Riegel zurückschieben; **~ sth. towards one** etw. zu sich heran- *od.* hinziehen; Ⓑ (*attract, take in*) anlocken ‹Publikum, Menge, Kunden›; **all eyes were ~n to him** alle Blicke waren auf ihn gerichtet; **~ the fresh air into one's lungs** die frische Luft tief einatmen; **~ criticism upon oneself** Kritik auf sich (*Akk.*) ziehen; **be ~n to sb.** von jmdm. angezogen werden; **feel ~n to sb.** sich von jmdm. angezogen *od.* zu jmdm. hingezogen fühlen; **~ sb. into sth.** jmdn. in etw. (*Akk.*) mit hineinziehen; **he refused to be ~n** (*be provoked*) er ließ sich nichts entlocken; **~ sb. out of himself** jmdn. aus sich herauslocken; **~ the enemy's/(*fig.*) sb.'s fire** das feindliche Feuer/jmds. Kritik auf sich (*Akk.*) ziehen; ⇒ *also* **breath** A, B; Ⓒ (*take out*) herausziehen; ziehen (**from** aus); aufstöbern, aufjagen ‹Fuchs, Dachs› (**from** aus); **~ money from the bank/one's account** Geld bei der Bank holen/von seinem Konto abheben; **~ a pistol on sb.** eine Pistole auf jmdn. richten; **~ the cork from the bottle** die Flasche entkorken; **~ water from a well** Wasser an einem Brunnen holen *od.* schöpfen; **~ beer from a barrel** Bier vom Fass zapfen; ⇒ *also* **blood** 1 A; **~ trumps** Trümpfe ziehen; **~ cards from a pack** Karten von einem Haufen abheben; Ⓓ (*derive, elicit*) finden; **~ an example from a book** ein Beispiel einem Buch entnehmen; **~ a response from sb.** von jmdm. eine Antwort bekommen; (*interested*) Echo bei jmdm. finden; **~ comfort/sustenance from sth.** Trost/Halt in etw. (*Dat.*) finden; **~ reassurance/encouragement from sth.** Zuversicht/Mut aus etw. schöpfen; **~ inspiration from sth.** sich von etw. inspirieren lassen; Anregungen bei *od.* in etw. (*Dat.*) finden; **~ applause/a smile [from sb.]** Applaus/ein Lächeln [bei jmdm.] hervorrufen; ⇒ *also* **conclusion** D; Ⓔ (*get as one's due*) erhalten; bekommen; beziehen ‹Gehalt, Rente, Arbeitslosenunterstützung›; Ⓕ (*select at random*) **~ [straws]** [Lose] ziehen; losen; **~ [for partners]** [die Partner] auslosen; **Italy has been ~n against Spain in the World Cup** Italien ist als Gegner für Spanien im Weltmeisterschaftsspiel ausgelost worden; **~ a winner** ein Gewinnlos ziehen; Ⓖ (*trace*) ziehen ‹Strich›; zeichnen ‹geometrische Figur, Bild›; (*fig.: represent in words*) darstellen; **do you ~?** kannst du zeichnen?; **~ the line at sth.** (*fig.*) bei etw. nicht mehr mitmachen; **the line has to be ~n somewhere** *or* **at some point** (*fig.*) irgendwo muss Schluss sein; **it's difficult to ~ the line** (*fig.*) es ist schwierig, die Grenze zu ziehen; Ⓗ (*Commerc.: write out*) ziehen ‹Wechsel› (**on** auf + *Akk.*); **~ a cheque on one's bank for £100** einen Scheck über 100 Pfund auf seine Bank ausstellen; Ⓘ (*formulate*) ziehen ‹Parallele, Vergleich›; herstellen ‹Analogie›; herausstellen ‹Unterschied›; ⇒ *also* **distinction** B; Ⓙ (*end with neither side winner*) unentschieden beenden ‹Spiel›; **the match was ~n** das Spiel ging unentschieden aus; *abs.* **they drew three-all** sie spielten 3:3 unentschieden; Ⓚ (*disembowel*) ausnehmen ‹Geflügel, Fisch›; ausweiden ‹Wild›; Ⓛ (*extend*) [aus]dehnen; ziehen ‹Draht›; **long ~n death agony** lang dauernder Todeskampf; Ⓜ (*Naut.*) **~ 3 m. [of water]** 3 m Tiefgang haben; Ⓝ (*Hunting*) **~ a covert** [ein Tier aus seinem Versteck] aufjagen. ⇒ *also* **blank** 2 C; **hang** 1 F; **lot** G. ❷ *v.i.*, **drew, drawn** Ⓐ (*make one's way, move*) ‹Person:› gehen; ‹Fahrzeug:› fahren; ‹Flugzeug:› fliegen; **~ into sth.** ‹Zug:› in etw. (*Akk.*) einfahren; ‹Schiff:› in etw. (*Akk.*) einlaufen; **~ towards sth.** sich einer Sache (*Dat.*) nähern; **~ together** zusammenkommen; **~ closer together** enger zusammenrücken; **~ to an end** zu Ende gehen; Ⓑ (*allow draught*) ‹Kamin, Zigarette:› ziehen; **~ well/badly** einen guten/schlechten Zug haben; Ⓒ (*infuse*) ‹Tee:› ziehen.
❸ *n.* Ⓐ (*raffle*) Tombola, *die;* (*for matches, contests*) Auslosung, *die;* **be the luck of the ~** (*fig.*) Glück[s]sache sein; Ⓑ ([*result of*] *drawn game*) Unentschieden, *das;* (*Chess*) Remis, *das;* **end in a ~:** mit einem Unentschieden enden; Ⓒ Attraktion, *die;* (*film, play*) Publikumserfolg, *der;* Ⓓ **be quick/slow on the ~:** den Finger schnell/zu langsam am Abzug haben; (*fig.*) sich geistesgegenwärtig zeigen/nicht geistesgegenwärtig genug sein; ‹Quizteilnehmer:› schlagfertig sein/nicht schlagfertig genug sein; Ⓔ (*Amer.: in smoking*) Zug, *der*

**~ a'side** *v.t.* zur Seite ziehen; **~ sb. aside** jmdn. beiseite nehmen

**~ a'way** ❶ *v.i.* Ⓐ (*move ahead*) **~ away from sth./sb.** sich von etw. entfernen/jmdm. davonziehen; Ⓑ (*set off*) losfahren; Ⓒ (*recoil*) zurückweichen (**from** vor + *Dat.*). ❷ *v.t.* wegnehmen; wegziehen; weglocken ‹Person›

**~ 'back** ❶ *v.t.* zurückziehen; aufziehen ‹Vorhang›. ❷ *v.i.* zurückweichen; (*fig.*) sich zurückziehen

**~ 'in** ❶ *v.i.* Ⓐ (*move in and stop*) einfahren; **the car drew in to the side of the road** das Auto fuhr an den Straßenrand heran; Ⓑ ‹Tage:› kürzer werden; ‹Abende, Nächte:› länger werden. ❷ *v.t.* (*fig.*) hineinziehen ‹Person›; zum Mitmachen überreden; **I refuse to be ~n in** ich will nicht mit hineingezogen werden

**~ 'off** *v.t.* ausziehen ‹Kleidung›; ablassen ‹Flüssigkeit›

**~ on** ❶ /ˈ-ˈ-/ *v.i.* ‹Zeit:› vergehen, (*geh.*) fortschreiten; (*approach*) ‹Winter, Nacht:› nahen. ❷ *v.t.* Ⓐ /ˈ--/ anziehen ‹Kleidung›; Ⓑ /ˈ-ˈ-/ (*induce*) anziehen (*fig.*) ‹Person›; Ⓒ /ˈ--/ zurückgreifen auf (+ *Akk.*) ‹Ersparnisse, Vorräte›; schöpfen aus ‹Wissen, Erfahrungen›; **you may ~ on my account** du kannst von meinem Konto abheben

**~ 'out** ❶ *v.t.* (*extend*) ausdehnen; in die Länge ziehen; **long ~n out** ausgedehnt; in die Länge gezogen. ❷ *v.i.* Ⓐ abfahren; **the train/bus drew out of the station** der Zug fuhr aus dem Bahnhof aus/der Bus verließ den Busbahnhof; Ⓑ ‹Tage:› länger werden; ‹Abende:› kürzer werden

**~ 'up** ❶ *v.t.* Ⓐ (*formulate*) abfassen; aufsetzen ‹Vertrag›; aufstellen ‹Liste›; entwerfen ‹Plan, Budget›; Ⓑ heranziehen; **~ up a chair!** holen Sie sich doch einen Stuhl!; Ⓒ **~ oneself up [to one's full height]** sich [zu seiner vollen Größe] aufrichten; Ⓓ aufstellen ‹Truppen, Fahrzeuge›. ❷ *v.i.* [an]halten

**~ upon** ⇒ **~ on** 2 C

**draw: ~back** *n.* (*snag*) Nachteil, *der;* **~bridge** *n.* Zugbrücke, *die*

**drawee** /drɔːˈiː/ *n.* (*Commerc.*) Bezogene, *der;* Trassat, *der* (*fachspr.*)

**drawer** *n.* Ⓐ /drɔː(r), ˈdrɔːə(r)/ (*in furniture*) Schublade, *die;* Ⓑ /ˈdrɔːə(r)/ (*maker of drawings*) Zeichner, *der*/Zeichnerin, *die;* Ⓒ (*Commerc.*) Aussteller, *der;* Trassant, *der* (*fachspr.*); Ⓓ *in pl.* /drɔːz, ˈdrɔːəz/ (*dated/joc.: underpants*) Unterhosen *Pl.;* (*for women*) Schlüpfer *Pl.*

**drawing** /ˈdrɔːɪŋ/ *n.* Ⓐ (*activity*) Zeichnen, *das;* **be good at ~:** gut zeichnen können; Ⓑ (*sketch*) Zeichnung, *die*

**drawing: ~ board** *n.* Zeichenbrett, *das;* **so it's back to the ~ board, I'm afraid** dann müssen wir wohl wieder von vorne beginnen, fürchte ich; **~ office** *n.* Konstruktionsbüro, *das;* **~ paper** *n.* Zeichenpapier, *das;* **~ pin** *n.* (*Brit.*) Reißzwecke, *die;* **~ room** *n.* Salon, *der*

**'drawknife** *n.* Zugmesser, *das*

**drawl** /drɔːl/ ❶ *v.i.* gedehnt *od.* (*ugs.*) breit sprechen. ❷ *v.t.* dehnen; gedehnt *od.* (*ugs.*) breit aussprechen. ❸ *n.* gedehntes *od.* (*ugs.*) breites Sprechen; **speak with a ~:** gedehnt sprechen

**drawn** /drɔːn/ ❶ *p.p. of* **draw.** ❷ *adj.* Ⓐ verzogen ‹Gesicht›; **look ~** (*from tiredness*) abgespannt aussehen; (*from worries*) abgehärmt aussehen; Ⓑ (*Sport*) unentschieden; **~ game** Unentschieden, *das;* (*Chess*) Remis, *das*

**'drawstring** *n.* Durchziehband, *das*

**dray** /dreɪ/ *n.* Tafelwagen, *der;* Rollwagen, *der*

**dread** /dred/ ❶ *v.t.* sich sehr fürchten vor (+ *Dat.*); große Angst haben vor (+ *Dat.*); **the ~ed day/moment** der gefürchtete *od.* mit Schrecken erwartete Tag/Augenblick; **I ~ the moment when ...:** ich fürchte mich vor dem Augenblick, wenn ...; **I ~ to think [what may have happened]** ich mag gar nicht daran denken[, was passiert sein könnte]; **I ~ the thought of ...:** mich schreckt der Gedanke an (+ *Akk.*) ... ❷ *n., no pl.* (*terror*) Angst, *die;* **be** *or* **live** *or* **stand in ~ of sth./sb.** in [ständiger] Furcht vor etw./jmdm. leben. ❸ *adj.* (*literary*) fürchterlich

**dreadful** /ˈdredfl/ *adj.* schrecklich; furchtbar; (*coll.: very bad*) fürchterlich; **I feel ~** (*unwell*) ich fühle mich scheußlich (*ugs.*); (*embarrassed*) es ist mir furchtbar peinlich

**dreadfully** /ˈdredfəlɪ/ *adv.* Ⓐ schrecklich; entsetzlich, furchtbar ‹leiden›; (*coll.: very badly*) grauenhaft; fürchterlich; Ⓑ (*coll.: extremely*) schrecklich; furchtbar

**dream** /driːm/ ❶ *n.* Ⓐ Traum, *der;* **sweet ~s!** träume süß!; **have a ~ about sb./sth.** von jmdm./etw. träumen; **I had a bad ~ last night** letzte Nacht habe ich schlecht geträumt; **it was all a bad ~:** das Ganze war wie ein böser Traum; **in a ~:** im Traum; **go/work like a ~** (*coll.*) wie eine Eins fahren/funktionieren (*ugs.*); Ⓑ (*fig.: reverie*) **go** *or* **walk around/be/live in a [complete] ~:** in einer [perfekten] Traumwelt leben; Ⓒ (*ambition, vision*) Traum, *der;* **have ~s of doing sth.** davon träumen, etw. zu tun; **never in one's wildest ~s** nicht in seinen kühnsten Träumen; Ⓓ (*perfect person*) **~ [man/woman]** Traummann, *der*/-frau, *die;* (*perfect thing*) Traum, *der; attrib.* traumhaft; Traum‹haus, -auto, -urlaub›. ⇒ *also* **wet dream.** ❷ *v.i.*, **~t** /dremt/ *or* **~ed** träumen; (*while awake*) vor sich (*Akk.*) hin träumen; **~ about** *or* **of sb./sth.** von jmdm./etw. träumen; **~ of doing sth.** (*fig.*) davon träumen, etw. zu tun; **he wouldn't ~ of doing it** (*fig.*) er würde nicht im Traum daran denken, das zu tun.
❸ *v.t.*, **~t** *or* **~ed** träumen; **she never** *or* **little ~t that she'd win** sie hätte sich (*Dat.*) nie träumen lassen, dass sie gewinnen würde

**~ 'up** *v.t.* sich (*Dat.*) ausdenken; sich (*Dat.*) einfallen lassen

**dreamer** /ˈdriːmə(r)/ *n.* (*in sleep*) Träumende, *der/die;* (*day~*) Träumer, *der*/Träumerin, *die*

**dreamily** /ˈdriːmɪlɪ/ *adv.* verträumt

**'dreamland** *n.* Traumland, *das;* Reich der Träume, *das*

**dreamless** /ˈdriːmlɪs/ *adj.* traumlos

**dreamlike** /ˈdriːmlaɪk/ *adj.* traumhaft

**dreamt** ⇒ **dream** 2, 3

**dreamy** /ˈdriːmɪ/ *adj.* Ⓐ verträumt ‹Person, Blick›; träumerisch ‹Stimmung›; Ⓑ (*dreamlike*) traumähnlich; Ⓒ (*coll.: delightful*) traumhaft [schön]

**'dreamy-eyed** *adj.* ‹Verliebte, Mädchen, Kind› mit verträumten Augen

**drearily** /ˈdrɪərɪlɪ/ *adv.* ⇒ **dreary**: monoton; düster

**dreary** /ˈdrɪərɪ/ *adj.* trostlos; monoton ‹Musik›; langweilig ‹Unterricht, Lehrbuch›; düster ‹Gemüt, Gedanken›

**dredge** /dredʒ/ *v.t.* ausbaggern; (*fig.*) ausgraben; **~ up** (*fig.*) ausgraben

**dredger** /ˈdredʒə(r)/ *n.* Bagger, *der;* (*boat*) Schwimmbagger, *der;* Nassbagger, *der*

**dregs** /dregz/ *n. pl.* Ⓐ [Boden]satz, *der;* **drain one's glass to the ~:** sein Glas bis zur Neige *od.* bis zum letzten Tropfen leeren; Ⓑ (*fig.*) Abschaum, *der*

**drench** /drenʃ/ *v.t.* durchnässen; **get completely ~ed, get ~ed to the skin** nass bis auf die Haut werden

**drenching** /'drenʃɪŋ/ ❶ *n.* **get a ~:** bis auf die Haut nass werden. ❷ *adj.* **~ rain** strömender Regen

**Dresden** /'drezdn/ *pr. n.* Dresden *(das)*; **~ china** *or* **porcelain** Meißner Porzellan

**dress** /dres/ ❶ *n.* [A] *(woman's or girl's frock)* Kleid, *das;* [B] *no pl.* *(clothing)* Kleidung, *die;* **be in native/formal ~:** nach Art der Einheimischen/formell gekleidet sein; **articles of ~:** Kleidungsstücke; [C] *no pl.* *(manner of dressing)* Kleidung, *die;* **she's rather slovenly in her ~:** sie kleidet sich sehr nachlässig; [D] *(external covering)* Kleid, *das.* ⇒ *also* **evening ~; full ~; morning ~.** ❷ *v.t.* [A] *(clothe)* anziehen; **be ~ed** angezogen sein; **be well ~ed** gut gekleidet sein; **the bride was ~ed in white** die Braut trug Weiß; **get ~ed** sich anziehen; [B] *(provide clothes for)* einkleiden ‹Familie›; [C] *(deck, adorn)* schmücken; beflaggen ‹Schiff›; dekorieren ‹Schaufenster›; [D] *(arrange)* frisieren ‹Haare›; [E] *(Med.)* verbinden, versorgen ‹Wunde›; [F] *(Cookery)* zubereiten; [G] *(treat, prepare)* hobeln ‹Holz›; gerben ‹tierische Häute, Felle›; schleifen ‹Tontöpfe, Metall, Stein›; *(put finish on)* appretieren ‹Gewebe, Holz, Leder›; polieren ‹Tontöpfe, Metall, Stein›; [H] *(Mil.)* **~ ranks** die Front ausrichten; [I] *(Agric.: manure)* düngen.
❸ *v.i.* *(wear clothes)* sich anziehen; sich kleiden; *(get dressed)* sich anziehen; sich ankleiden *(geh.)*; **I like to ~ in dark colours** ich trage gerne dunkle Farben; **~ for dinner** sich zum Abendessen umziehen

**~ 'down** *v.t. (fig.)* zurechtweisen

**~ 'up** ❶ *v.t.* [A] *(in formal clothes)* fein machen; fein anziehen; **sb. is all ~ed up and nowhere to go** *(fig.)* jmds. ganzer Aufwand ist umsonst *(ugs.)*; [B] *(disguise)* verkleiden; *(elaborately as a game)* herausputzen; [C] *(smarten)* verschönern. ❷ *v.i.* [A] *(wear formal clothes)* sich fein machen; [B] *(disguise oneself)* sich verkleiden; *(elaborately as a game)* sich herausputzen

**dressage** /'dresɑːʒ/ *n.* Dressurreiten, *das*

**dress: ~ circle** *n. (Theatre)* erster Rang; **~ coat** *n.* Frack, *der;* **~-conscious** *adj.* modebewusst; **~ designer** *n.* Modeschöpfer, *der*/-schöpferin, *die;* Modedesigner, *der*/ -designerin, *die*

**dresser[1]** /'dresə(r)/ *n.* [A] *(sideboard)* Anrichte, *die;* Büfett, *das;* [B] *(Amer.)* ⇒ **dressing table**

**dresser[2]** *n.* [A] **he's a careless/elegant/ tasteful ~:** er kleidet sich nachlässig/elegant/geschmackvoll; [B] ▶ **1261** *(Theatre)* Garderobier, *der*/Garderobiere, *die;* [C] ▶ **1261** *(Med.)* Operationsassistent, *der*/ -assistentin, *die*

**dressing** /'dresɪŋ/ *n.* [A] *no pl.* Anziehen, *das;* Ankleiden, *das (geh.)*; [B] *(Cookery)* Dressing, *das;* [C] *(Med.)* Verband, *der;* [D] *(Agric.)* Dünger, *der*

**dressing: ~ case** *n.* Kosmetikkoffer, *der;* **~ 'down** *n.* **give sb. a ~ down** jmdm. einen Rüffel verpassen *od.* eine Standpauke halten *(ugs.)*; **get a ~ down** zurechtgewiesen *od.* *(ugs.)* heruntergemacht werden; **~ gown** *n.* Bademantel, *der;* **~ room** *n.* [A] *(of actor or actress)* [Schauspieler]garderobe, *die;* [Künstler]garderobe, *die;* [B] *(for games players)* Umkleidekabine, *die;* [C] *(in house)* Ankleideraum, *der;* Ankleidezimmer, *das;* **~ table** *n.* Frisierkommode, *die; (with kneehole)* Frisiertoilette, *die*

**dress: ~ length** *n. Stoffstück, das für ein Kleid ausreicht;* **~maker** *n.* ▶ **1261** Damenschneider, *der*/-schneiderin, *die;* **~making** *n.* Damenschneiderei, *die;* **~ rehearsal** *n.* *(lit. or fig.)* Generalprobe, *die;* **~ sense** *n.* **she hasn't much ~ sense** sie hat nicht viel Sinn für Mode; **~ 'shirt** *n.* Smokinghemd, *das;* **~ shop** *n.* Geschäft für Damenbekleidung; Kleiderladen, *der (ugs.)*; **~ 'suit** *n.* Abendanzug, *der;* **~ uniform** *n. (Mil.)* Paradeuniform, *die*

**dressy** /'dresɪ/ *adj.* [A] **be ~** ‹Person:› immer schick angezogen sein; [B] *(smart)* fein, elegant ‹Kleidung›; [C] *(grand, formal)* vornehm ‹Veranstaltung›

**drew** ⇒ **draw** 1, 2

**dribble** /'drɪbl/ ❶ *v.i.* [A] *(trickle)* tropfen; [B] *(slobber)* ‹Baby:› sabbern; [C] *(Sport)* dribbeln. ❷ *v.t.* [A] ‹Baby:› kleckern; [B] *(Sport)* dribbeln mit ‹Ball›. ❸ *n.* *(trickle)* Tröpfeln, *das*

**driblet** /'drɪblɪt/ *n.* Tropfen, *der;* **in** *or* **by ~s** in kleinen Mengen; kleckerweise *(ugs.)*

**dribs** *n. pl.* **~ and drabs** /drɪbz n 'dræbz/ kleine Mengen; **in ~ and drabs** kleckerweise *(ugs.)*

**dried** /draɪd/ *adj.* getrocknet; **~ fruit[s]** Dörr- *od.* Backobst, *das;* **~ milk/egg/meat** Trockenmilch, *die od.* Milchpulver, *das*/Trockenei *od.* Eipulver, *das*/Trockenfleisch, *das*

**drier[1]** ⇒ **dry** 1

**drier[2]** /'draɪə(r)/ *n. (for hair)* Trockenhaube, *die; (hand-held)* Föhn, *der;* Haartrockner, *der;* *(for laundry)* [Wäsche]trockner, *der*

**driest** ⇒ **dry** 1

**drift** /drɪft/ ❶ *n.* [A] *(flow, steady movement)* Wanderung, *die;* [B] *(fig.: trend, shift, tendency)* Tendenz, *die;* [C] *(flow of air or water)* Strömung, *die;* **the North Atlantic D~:** der Nordatlantische Strom; [D] *(Naut., Aeronaut.: deviation from course)* Abdrift, *die (fachspr.)*; Abweichung vom Sollkurs; [E] *(Motor Veh.: controlled slide)* Driften, *das;* [F] *(wind-propelled mass)* *(of snow or sand)* Verwehung, *die;* *(of leaves)* zusammengewehter Haufen; [G] *(fig.: gist, import)* das Wesentliche; **get** *or* **catch the ~ of sth.** etw. im Wesentlichen verstehen; **I don't get your ~:** ich kann Ihnen nicht ganz folgen *od.* verstehe nicht ganz, worauf Sie hinauswollen; [H] *(Geol.: deposits)* Geschiebe, *das;* **glacial ~:** [Glazial]geschiebe, *das.*
❷ *v.i.* [A] *(be borne by current; fig.: move passively or aimlessly)* treiben; ‹Wolke:› ziehen; **~ out to sea** aufs Meer hinaustreiben; **~ off course** abtreiben; vom Kurs abgelenkt werden; **come ~ing along** angetrieben kommen; **the mist ~ed away** der Nebel verwehte; **the smoke ~ed to the east** der Rauch zog nach Osten ab; **his thoughts ~ed** er schweifte mit seinen Gedanken ab; **let things ~:** die Dinge treiben lassen; den Dingen ihren Lauf lassen; **~ along** *(fig.)* sich treiben lassen; **~ into crime** in die Kriminalität [ab]driften; **~ into unconsciousness** in Bewusstlosigkeit versinken; **months ~ed by** die Monate vergingen; [B] *(coll.: come or go casually)* **~ in** hereinschneien *(ugs.)*; **~ out** abziehen *(ugs.)*; **~ in at 1 a. m.** um ein Uhr nachts eintrudeln *(ugs.)*; [C] *(form ~s)* zusammengeweht werden; **~ing sand** Treibsand, *der*

**~ a'part** *v.i.* sich *(Dat.)* fremd werden; *(in marriage)* sich auseinander leben

**drifter** /'drɪftə(r)/ *n.* [A] *(Naut.)* Drifter, *der;* [B] *(person)* jmd., der sich treiben lässt; *(vagrant)* Gammler, *der (ugs.)*; **be a ~:** sich treiben lassen

**drift: ~ ice** *n.* Treibeis, *das;* **~ net** *n.* Treibnetz, *das;* **~wood** *n.* Treibholz, *das*

**drill[1]** /drɪl/ ❶ *n.* [A] *(tool)* Bohrer, *der;* *(Dent.)* Bohrinstrument, *das;* *(Metalw.)* Drillbohrer, *der;* *(Carpentry, Building)* Bohrmaschine, *die;* [B] *(Mil.: training)* Drill, *der;* [C] *(Educ.; also fig.)* Übung, *die;* **lifeboat ~:** Rettungsbootübung, *die;* [D] *(Brit. coll.: agreed procedure)* Prozedur, *die;* **know the ~:** wissen, wie es gemacht wird; **what's the ~?** wie wird das gemacht? ❷ *v.t.* [A] *(bore)* bohren ‹Loch, Brunnen›; an-, ausbohren ‹Zahn›; **~ sth.** *(right through)* etw. durchbohren; [B] *(Mil.: instruct)* drillen; [C] *(Educ.; also fig.)* **~ sb. in sth., ~ sth. into sb.** mit jmdm. etw. systematisch einüben; jmdm. etw. eindrillen *(ugs.)* *od.* *(abwertend)* einpauken. ❸ *v.i.* [A] *(bore)* bohren **(for** nach); **~ deep/50 ft. into the ground** tief/15 m tief bohren; **finish ~ing** die Bohrung/Bohrungen beenden; **~ down a long way** tief bohren; **~ through sth.** etw. durchbohren; [B] *(Mil.)* exerzieren

**drill[2]** *n.* *(Agric.)* [A] *(furrow)* Saatrille, *die;* [B] *(machine)* Drillmaschine, *die*

**drill[3]** *n.* *(Textiles)* Drillich, *der*

**drill: ~ bit** *n.* Bohrer, *der;* **~ chuck** *n.* Bohrfutter, *das* **~ core** *n.* Bohrkern, *der*

**drilling**/'drɪlɪŋ/: **~ platform** *n.* Bohrturmplattform, *die;* **~ rig** *n.* Bohrturm, *der;* *(in offshore ~)* Bohrinsel, *die*

**drily** ⇒ **dryly**

**drink** /drɪŋk/ ❶ *n.* [A] *(type of liquid)* Getränk; *das;* *(class of liquids)* Getränke *Pl.;* **many different sorts of ~s** viele verschiedene Getränke; [B] *(quantity of liquid)* Getränk, *das;* **have a ~** [etwas] trinken; **would you like a ~ of milk?** möchten Sie etwas Milch [trinken]?; **take a long ~ from sth.** einen großen Schluck aus etwas nehmen; **give sb. a ~ [of fruit juice]** jmdm. etwas [Fruchtsaft] zu trinken geben; [C] *(glass of alcoholic liquor)* Glas, *das;* *(not with food)* Drink, *der;* Glas, *das;* Gläschen, *das;* **have a ~** ein Glas trinken; **let's have a ~!** trinken wir einen!; **she likes a ~ now and then** hin und wieder trinkt sie ganz gern einen *od.* ein Glas; **I think we all need a ~!** ich glaube, wir können alle einen vertragen *(ugs.)*; **he has had a few ~s** er hat einige getrunken *(ugs.)*; [D] *no pl., no art.* *(intoxicating liquor)* Alkohol, *der;* **[strong] ~** scharfe *od.* hochprozentige Getränke; **in ~, the worse for ~** betrunken; **take to ~** zu trinken anfangen; **~ was his ruin** der Alkohol war sein Verderben; **the ~ problem** der Alkoholismus *od.* Alkoholmissbrauch; **have a ~ problem** Probleme mit [dem] Alkohol haben; **drive sb. to ~** jmdn. zum Trinker werden lassen; [E] *(coll.: sea)* **the drink** der große Bach *(Flieger-, Seemannsspr.)*.
❷ *v.t.,* **drank** /dræŋk/, **drunk** /drʌŋk/ [A] trinken ‹Kaffee, Glas Milch, Flasche Whisky›; **~ down** *or* **off [in one gulp]** [in einem *od.* auf einen Zug] austrinken; [B] *(absorb)* ‹Pflanze, poröses Material:› aufsaugen; **the car ~s petrol** *(fig.)* das Auto schluckt viel Benzin; [C] **~ oneself to death** sich zu Tode trinken; **~ sb. under the table** jmdn. unter den Tisch trinken.
❸ *v.i.,* **drank, drunk** trinken; **~ from a bottle** aus einer Flasche trinken; **~ of sth.** *(literary)* von etw. trinken; **~[ing and] driving** Alkohol am Steuer; **~ and drive** unter Alkoholeinfluss fahren; **~ to sb./sth.** auf jmdn./etw. trinken; **I'll ~ to that** *(coll.)* dem kann ich nur zustimmen; ⇒ *also* **fish** 1 A

**~ 'in** *v.t.* [A] *(readily take in)* einsaugen ‹Luft, *fig.:* Schönheit›; ‹Pflanze:› aufsaugen ‹Wasser›; [B] *(absorb eagerly)* begierig aufnehmen ‹Worte, Geschichten›

**~ 'up** *v.t. & i.* austrinken; ‹Pflanze:› aufsaugen

**drinkable** /'drɪŋkəbl/ *adj.* [A] *(suitable for drinking)* trinkbar ‹Wasser›; [B] *(pleasant to drink)* trinkbar *(ugs.)* ‹Wein›

**'drink-driving** *n.* Fahren unter Alkoholeinfluss; Alkohol am Steuer; **~ offence** Alkoholdelikt, *das*

**drinker** /'drɪŋkə(r)/ *n.* Trinker, *der*/Trinkerin, *die*

**drinkie** /'drɪŋkɪ/ *n.* *(coll.)* was zu trinken *(ugs.)*; **have ~s** trinken

**drinking**/'drɪŋkɪŋ/: **~ bout** *n.* Trinkgelage, *das;* **~ fountain** *n.* Trinkbrunnen, *der;* **~ glass** *n.* Glas, *das;* **~ song** *n.* Trinklied, *das;* **~-'up time** *n.* *(Brit.) Zeit zwischen Ende des Ausschanks und der Schließung der Gaststätte (meist 10 Minuten)*; **~ vessel** ⇒ **vessel** A; **~ water** *n.* Trinkwasser, *das*

**drip** /drɪp/ ❶ *v.i.,* **-pp-** [A] tropfen; *(overflow in drops)* triefen; **be ~ping with water/ moisture** triefend nass sein; **the windows were ~ping with condensation** an den Fenstern lief Kondenswasser herunter; **~ off/down sth.** von etw. [herunter]tropfen; [B] *(fig.)* **be ~ping with** überladen sein mit ‹Schmuck›; überlaufen vor (+ *Dat.*) ‹Gefühlen›; triefen von *od.* vor ‹Ironie, Sentimentalität usw.›. ❷ *v.t.,* **-pp-** tropfen lassen. ❸ *n.* [A] *(act)* Tropfen, *das;* [B] *(liquid)* Tropfen, *der;* [C] *(Med.)* Tropfinfusion, *die;* **the patient was on a ~:** der Patient hing am

Tropf; **D** (*coll.: feeble, spineless person*) Schlappschwanz, *der* (*salopp abwertend*)

**drip: ~-dry** (*Textiles*) **1** /'-·-/ *v.i.* knitterfrei trocknen; **2** /'--/ *adj.* bügelfrei; schnell trocknend; **~-feed** *v.t.* (*Med.*) durch parenterale Tropfinfusion ernähren

**dripping** /'drɪpɪŋ/ **1** *adj.* tropfend ‹Wasserhahn›; **~ bathing costumes** tropfnasse Badeanzüge. **2** *adv.* **~ wet** tropf- *od.* (*ugs.*) patsch- *od.* (*ugs.*) klitschnass. **3** *n.* **A** Tropfen, *das;* **B** (*Cookery*) Schmalz, *das;* **bread and ~:** Schmalzbrot, *das*

**drive** /draɪv/ **1** *n.* **A** (*trip*) Fahrt, *die;* **take sb. for a ~:** jmdn. *od.* mit jmdm. spazieren fahren; **B** (*distance travelled*) [Auto]fahrt, *die;* **a ~ of 40 kilometres, a 40-kilometre ~:** eine [Auto]fahrt von 40 Kilometern; **a nine-hour ~, a ~ of nine hours** eine neunstündige Autofahrt; **within an hour's ~ of sth.** keine Autostunde von etw. entfernt; **be an hour's ~ from sth.** eine Autostunde von etw. entfernt sein; **have a long ~ to work** eine lange Anfahrt zur Arbeit haben; **C** (*street*) Straße, *die;* **D** (*private road*) Zufahrt, *die;* (*entrance*) (*to small building*) Einfahrt, *die;* (*to large building*) Auffahrt, *die;* **E** (*energy to achieve*) Tatkraft, *die;* **a salesman with ~:** ein dynamischer Vertreter; **F** (*Commerc., Polit., etc.: vigorous campaign*) Aktion, *die;* Kampagne, *die;* **export/sales/recruiting/charity ~:** Export-/Verkaufs-/Anwerbe-/Wohltätigkeitskampagne, *die;* **G** (*Mil.: offensive*) Vorstoß, *der;* **H** (*Psych.*) Trieb, *der;* **I** (*Motor Veh.: position of steering wheel*) **left-hand/right-hand ~:** Links-/Rechtssteuerung *od.* -lenkung, *die;* **be left-hand ~:** Linkssteuerung haben; ein Linkslenker sein (*Kfz-W.*); **J** (*Motor Veh., Mech. Engin.: transmission of power*) Antrieb, *der;* **belt/front-wheel/rear-wheel ~:** Riemen-/Front-/Heckantrieb, *der;* **fluid ~:** hydraulische Kupplung; **K** (*Cards etc.*) **whist/bridge ~:** Whist-/Bridgerunde mit vielen Teilnehmern; **L** (*Sport*) Drive, *der* (*fachspr.*); Treibschlag, *der.*

**2** *v.t.,* **drove** /drəʊv/, **driven** /'drɪvn/ **A** fahren ‹Auto, Lkw, Route, Strecke, Fahrgast›; lenken ‹Kutsche, Streitwagen›; treiben ‹Tier›; führen ‹Pflug›; **this is a nice car to ~/this car is easy to ~:** dieses Auto fährt sich gut/leicht; **~ a carriage** *or* **coach and four through** (*fig.*) zerfetzen (*fig.*); zunichte machen ‹Argumentation›; **B** (*as job*) **~ a lorry/train** Lkw-Fahrer/Lokomotivführer sein; **C** (*compel to move*) vertreiben; **~ sb. out of** *or* **from a place/country** jmdn. von einem Ort/aus einem Land vertreiben; **~ sb. out of** *or* **from the house** jmdn. aus dem Haus jagen; **D** (*chase, urge on*) treiben ‹Vieh, Wild›; **E** (*fig.*) **~ sb. to sth.** jmdn. zu etw. treiben; **~ sb. to do sth.** *or* **into doing sth.** jmdn. dazu treiben, etw. zu tun; **~ sb. to suicide** jmdn. zum *od.* in den Selbstmord treiben; **~ sb. out of his mind** *or* **wits** jmdn. in den Wahnsinn treiben *od.* um den Verstand bringen; **F** ‹Wind, Wasser:› treiben; **be ~n off course** abgetrieben werden; **G** (*cause to penetrate*) **~ sth. into sth.** etw. in etw. (*Akk.*) treiben; **~ sth. into sb.'s head** (*fig.*) jmdm. etw. einbläuen *od.* einhämmern (*ugs.*); **H** (*power*) antreiben ‹Mühle, Maschine›; **be steam-~n** *or* **~n by steam** dampfgetrieben sein; **be ~n by electricity** [einen] Elektroantrieb haben; **I** (*incite to action*) antreiben; **he was hard ~n** er wurde hart herangenommen; **be ~n by ambition** von Ehrgeiz getrieben werden; **J** (*overwork*) **~ oneself [too] hard** sich [zu sehr] schinden; **K** (*transact*) **~ a good bargain** ein gutes Geschäft machen; ⇒ *also* **hard** 1 A.

**3** *v.i.,* **drove, driven** **A** (*conduct motor vehicle*) fahren; **in Great Britain we ~ on the left** bei uns in Großbritannien ist Linksverkehr; **he ~s to see her every weekend** er besucht sie jedes Wochenende mit dem Auto; **~ at 30 m.p.h.** mit 50 km/h fahren; **learn to ~:** [Auto]fahren lernen; den Führerschein machen (*ugs.*); **can you ~?** kannst du Auto fahren?; **~ past** vorbeifahren; **~ into a bollard/the back of a lorry** gegen einen Poller fahren/auf einen Lastwagen fahren; **B** (*travel*) mit dem [eigenen] Auto fahren; **C** (*rush, dash violently*) ‹Hagelkörner, Wellen:› schlagen; **clouds were driving across the sky** Wolken jagten über den Himmel

**~ at** *v.t.* hinauswollen auf (+ *Akk.*); **what are you driving at?** worauf wollen Sie hinaus?

**~ a'way** **1** *v.i.* wegfahren. **2** *v.t.* **A** wegfahren, wegbringen ‹Ladung, Fahrzeug›; (*chase away*) wegjagen; **B** (*fig.*) zerstreuen ‹Bedenken, Befürchtungen, Verdacht›

**~ 'back** *v.t.* (*force to retreat*) zurückschlagen ‹Eindringlinge›; **be ~n back on doing sth.** (*fig.*) keine andere Wahl haben, als etw. zu tun

**~ 'off** **1** *v.i.* **A** wegfahren; **B** (*Golf*) abschlagen. **2** *v.t.* (*repel*) zurückschlagen ‹Angreifer›

**~ 'on** **1** *v.i.* weiterfahren. **2** *v.t.* (*impel*) treiben (**to** zu)

**~ 'out** *v.t.* **A** hinauswerfen ‹Person›; hinausjagen ‹Hund›; hinausblasen ‹Luft›; **B** (*fig.*) vertreiben ‹Sorgen›; austreiben ‹bösen Geist›

**~ 'up** **1** *v.i.* vorfahren (**to** vor + *Dat.*); **she drove up to the starting line** sie fuhr an die Startlinie heran. **2** *v.t.* hochtreiben ‹Kosten›

**drive: ~ belt** *n.* (*Mech. Engin.*) Treibriemen, *der;* **~-in** *adj.* Drive-in-; **~-in bank** Bank mit Autoschalter; **~-in cinema** *or* (*Amer.*) **movie [theater]** Autokino, *das*

**drivel** /'drɪvl/ **1** *n.* Gefasel, *das* (*ugs. abwertend*); **talk ~:** faseln (*ugs. abwertend*). **2** *v.i.,* (*Brit.*) **-ll-** **A** (*talk stupidly*) faseln (*ugs. abwertend*); **B** (*slaver*) geifern

**driven** ⇒ **drive** 2, 3

**'drive-on** *adj.* **~ car ferry** Autofährschiff, *das*

**driver** /'draɪvə(r)/ *n.* **A** Fahrer, *der*/Fahrerin, *die;* Führer, *der* (*Amtsspr.*); (*of locomotive*) Führer, *der*/Führerin, *die;* (*of horse-drawn carriage*) Kutscher, *der*/Kutscherin, *die;* **be in the ~'s seat** (*fig.*) das Steuer *od.* die Zügel in der Hand haben (*fig.*); **B** (*Golf*) Driver, *der* (*fachspr.*); Holz 1, *das*

**driverless** /'draɪvəlɪs/ *adj.* führerlos

**'driver's license** (*Amer.*) ⇒ **driving licence**

**drive: ~shaft** *n.* Antriebswelle, *die;* **~-time** *n. attrib.* ‹Sender, Sendung› für Autofahrer im Berufsverkehr; **~way** ⇒ **drive** 1 D

**driving** /'draɪvɪŋ/ **1** *n., no pl.* Fahren, *das;* **his ~ is awful** er fährt furchtbar. **2** *adj.* **A** **~ rain** peitschender Regen; **B** (*fig.*) treibend; **~ ambition** brennender Ehrgeiz

**driving: ~ force** *n.* treibende Kraft; Triebfeder, *die;* **the ~ force behind sth.** die treibende Kraft hinter etw.; **~ gloves** *n. pl.* Autohandschuhe; **~ instructor** *n.* ▶ 1261 Fahrlehrer, *der*/-lehrerin, *die;* **~ lesson** *n.* Fahrstunde, *die;* **[take] ~ lessons** Fahrunterricht [nehmen]; **~ licence** *n.* Führerschein, *der;* **~ mirror** *n.* Rückspiegel, *der;* **~ range** *n.* (*Golf*) Drivingrange, *das;* **~ school** *n.* Fahrschule, *die;* **~ seat** *n.* **A** Fahrersitz, *der;* **B** **be in the ~ seat** = **be in the driver's seat** ⇒ **driver** A; **~ test** *n.* Fahrprüfung, *die;* **take/pass/fail one's ~ test** die Fahrprüfung ablegen/bestehen/nicht bestehen; **~ wheel** *n.* Treibrad, *das*

**drizzle** /'drɪzl/ **1** *n.* Sprühregen, *der;* Nieseln, *das;* **there was light ~:** es hat leicht genieselt. **2** *v.i.* **it's drizzling** es nieselt; **drizzling rain** Nieselregen, *der*

**droll** /drəʊl/ *adj.* **A** (*amusing*) drollig; **B** (*odd*) komisch

**dromedary** /'drɒmɪdərɪ, 'drʌmɪdərɪ/ *n.* (*Zool.*) Dromedar, *das*

**drone** /drəʊn/ **1** *n.* **A** (*of bees, flies*) Summen, *das;* (*of machine*) Brummen, *das;* **B** (*derog.: monotonous tone of speech*) Geleier, *das;* **C** (*Zool.: bee; Aeronaut.*) Drohne, *die;* (*fig.: idler*) Müßiggänger, *der;* **D** (*of bagpipe*) Bordunpfeife, *die.* **2** *v.i.* **A** (*buzz, hum*) ‹Biene:› summen; ‹Maschine:› brummen; **B** (*derog.: monotonously*) ‹Rezitator:› leiern; ‹Rede, Predigt:› in einförmigem Tonfall vorgetragen werden. **3** *v.t.* leiern

**drool** /dru:l/ *v.i.* **A** (*show excessive delight*) **~ over sb./sth.** eine kindische Freude an jmdm./etw. haben; **B** (*slaver*) geifern

**droop** /dru:p/ **1** *v.i.* **A** herunterhängen; ‹Blume:› den Kopf hängen lassen; ‹Stiel:› sich beugen, sich biegen; **his shoulders ~:** seine Schultern hängen; **her head ~ed forwards** ihr Kopf sank nach vorn; **his eyelids were ~ing** ihm fielen die Augen zu; **the dog's tail ~ed** der Hund ließ den Schwanz hängen; **B** (*fig.: flag*) ‹Mut, Moral:› sinken; ‹Mensch:› ermatten. **2** *v.t.* [herunter]hängen lassen

**drop** /drɒp/ **1** *n.* **A** (*of liquid*) Tropfen, *der;* **~s of rain/dew/blood/sweat** Regen-/Tau-/Bluts-/Schweißtropfen; **~ by ~, in ~s** tropfenweise; **be a ~ in the ocean** *or* **in the** *or* **a bucket** (*fig.*) ein Tropfen auf einen heißen Stein sein; **B** (*fig.: small amount*) **[just] a ~:** [nur] ein kleiner Tropfen; **a ~ too much** (*of flavouring etc.*) eine Idee zu viel; **C** (*fig. coll.: of alcohol*) Gläschen, *das;* **have had a ~ too much** ein Glas über den Durst getrunken haben (*ugs.*); **take a ~:** sich (*Dat.*) einen genehmigen (*ugs.*); **that's a nice ~ of beer/wine** das ist ein feines Bierchen/Weinchen (*ugs.*); **D** *in pl.* (*Med.*) Tropfen *Pl.;* **E** (*sweet*) Drops, *der;* **F** (*vertical distance*) **there was a ~ of 50 metres from the roof to the ground below** vom Dach bis zum Boden waren es 50 Meter; **G** (*abrupt descent of land*) plötzlicher Abfall; Absturz, *der;* **there was a sheer** *or* **steep ~ of some 500 ft.** das Gelände fiel etwa 150 m steil ab; **H** (*Aeronaut.*) (*of men*) Absetzen, *das;* (*of supplies*) Abwurf, *der;* **I** (*fig.: decrease*) Rückgang, *der;* **~ in temperature/prices/outgoings** Temperatur-/ Preis-/ Ausgabenrückgang, *der;* **a ~ in the price of coffee/in house prices** ein Preisrückgang bei Kaffee/bei Häusern; **a ~ in the cost of living** ein Sinken der Lebenshaltungskosten; **a ~ in salary/wages/income** eine Gehalts-/Lohn-/Einkommensminderung; **a ~ in value** eine Wertminderung; ein Wertverlust; **a ~ in atmospheric pressure/the voltage/power output** (*Phys.*) ein Druck-/Spannungs-/Leistungsabfall; **a ~ in crime** ein Rückgang der Kriminalität; **a ~ in turnover/sales/production** ein Umsatz-/Absatz-/Produktionsrückgang; **J** (*coll.: advantage*) **get** *or* **have the ~ on sb.** jmdm. zuvorkommen; **K** (*pendant, hanging ornament*) Gehänge, *das;* (*of earring*) Ohrgehänge, *das;* **L** (*underworld sl.: hiding place*) Versteck, *das.* ⇒ *also* **hat** B.

**2** *v.i.,* **-pp-:** **A** (*fall*) (*accidentally*) [herunter]fallen; (*deliberately*) sich [hinunter]fallen lassen; (*have abrupt descent*) abstürzen (**to** zu); **~ out of** *or* **from sb.'s hand** jmdm. aus der Hand fallen; **let sth. ~:** etw. fallen lassen; **B** (*sink to ground*) ‹Person:› fallen; **~ to the ground** umfallen; zu Boden fallen; **~ like flies** wie die Fliegen umfallen; **~ [down] dead** tot umfallen; **~ dead!** (*coll.*) scher dich zum Teufel!; **~ into bed/an armchair** ins Bett/in einen Sessel sinken; **be fit** *or* **ready to ~** (*coll.*) zum Umfallen *od.* Umsinken müde sein; **~ on** *or* **to one's knees** auf die Knie fallen; **C** (*in amount etc.*) sinken; ‹[An]zahl:› abnehmen, sinken; ‹Preis, Wert, Verkaufsziffern:› sinken, fallen; ‹Wind:› abflauen, sich legen; ‹Stimme:› sich senken; ‹Kinnlade:› herunterfallen *od.* -klappen; **the record has ~ped a place/to third place** die Schallplatte ist um einen Platz/auf Platz drei gefallen; **D** (*move, go*) **~ down stream** [sich] stromabwärts treiben [lassen]; **~ back** (*Sport*) zurückfallen; **~ behind in one's work** mit seiner Arbeit in Rückstand geraten; **~ behind schedule** hinter dem Zeitplan zurückbleiben; **~ astern** (*Naut.*) achteraus sacken; **E** (*fall in ~s*) ‹Flüssigkeit:› tropfen (**from** aus); **F** (*pass into some condition*) **~ [back] into one's old routine** in den alten Trott verfallen *od.* zurückfallen; **~ into the habit** *or* **way of doing sth.** die Gewohnheit annehmen *od.* sich (*Dat.*) angewöhnen, etw. zu tun; **~ into a dialect** in einen Dialekt fallen; **G** (*cease*) **the affair was allowed to ~:** man ließ die Angelegenheit auf sich (*Dat.*) beruhen; **and there the matter ~ped** und dabei blieb es; **H** **let ~:** beiläufig erwähnen ‹Termin, Tatsache, Absicht›; fallen lassen ‹Bemerkung›; **let [it] ~ that/when …:** beiläufig erwähnen, dass/wann …

❸ *v.t.*, **-pp-** A (*let fall*) fallen lassen; abwerfen ‹Bomben, Flugblätter, Nachschub›; absetzen ‹Fallschirmjäger, Truppen›; **~ a letter in the letter box** einen Brief einwerfen *od.* in den Briefkasten stecken; **~ the curtain** (*Theatre*) den Vorhang herablassen; **~ the latch on the door** den Türriegel vorlegen; B (*by mistake*) fallen lassen; **she ~ped crumbs on the floor/juice on the table** ihr fielen Krümel auf den Boden/tropfte Saft auf den Tisch; **he ~ped the glass/ball** ihm fiel das Glas/der Ball herunter; C (*let fall in drops*) tropfen; D (*utter casually*) fallen lassen ‹Namen›; **~ a hint** eine Anspielung machen; **~ a word in sb.'s ear [about sth.]** einmal mit jmdm. [über etw.] sprechen; E (*send casually*) **~ sb. a note** *or* **line** jmdm. [ein paar Zeilen] schreiben; **~ sb. a postcard** jmdm. eine Karte schreiben; F (*set down, unload from car*) absetzen ‹Mitfahrer, Fahrgast›; (*from ship*) an Land gehen lassen; (*from aircraft*) von Bord gehen lassen; G (*omit*) (*in writing*) auslassen; (*in speech*) nicht aussprechen; **~ one's h's** das h [im Anlaut] nicht aussprechen; **~ a subject from the syllabus/a name from a list** ein Fach aus dem Lehrplan/einen Namen von einer Liste streichen; H (*discontinue, abandon*) fallen lassen ‹Plan, Thema, Schlagzeile, Anklage›; einstellen ‹Untersuchung, Ermittlungen›; ablegen ‹Titel›; absetzen ‹Fernsehsendung›; beiseite lassen ‹Formalitäten›; aufgeben, Schluss machen mit ‹Verstellung, Heuchelei›; **~ it!** lass das!; **~ everything!, ~ whatever you're doing!** lass alles stehen und liegen!; **shall we ~ the subject?** lassen Sie uns [lieber] das Thema wechseln; **~ a case** (*Law*) einen Fall zu den Akten legen; I (*stop associating with*) fallen lassen ‹Freund, Freundin›; (*exclude*) **~ sb. from a team** jmdn. aus einer Mannschaft nehmen; **~ sb. from a committee** jmdn. aus einem Ausschuss entlassen; J **~ one's voice** die Stimme senken; K (*lower*) tiefer hängen ‹Lampe›; auslassen ‹Rocksaum›; **~ped handlebars** Rennlenker, *der;* L (*knock down, fell*) zu Boden strecken; M (*lose by gambling or in business*) verlieren

**~ a'way** *v.i.* ‹Mitgliedschaft, Einnahmen:› sinken; ‹Gelände:› abfallen

**~ by** ❶ /ˈ-ˈ-/ *v.i.* vorbeikommen. ❷ /ˈ--/ *v.t.* **~ by sb.'s house** bei jmdm. vorbeigehen *od.* hereinschauen

**~ 'in** ❶ *v.t.* (*deliver*) vorbeibringen. ❷ *v.i.* A hineinfallen; B (*visit*) hereinschauen; vorbeikommen; **~ in on sb.** *or* **at sb.'s house** bei jmdm. hereinschauen; **~ in for a pint** auf ein Bier vorbeikommen

**~ 'off** ❶ *v.i.* A (*fall off*) abfallen; (*become detached*) abgehen; B (*fall asleep*) einnicken; C (*decrease*) ‹Teilnahme, Geschäft:› zurückgehen; ‹Unterstützung, Interesse:› nachlassen; ‹Absatz:› rückläufig sein. ❷ *v.t.* A (*fall off*) abfallen von; **~ off a truck** von einem Lkw herunterfallen; B (*set down*) absetzen ‹Fahrgast›; **the ship ~ped off the cargo** das Schiff hat seine Ladung gelöscht; **~ a package/the shopping off at sb.'s house** ein Paket/die Einkäufe bei jmdm. vorbeibringen

**~ 'out** *v.i.* A (*fall out*) herausfallen (**of** aus); **your teeth will ~ out** Ihnen werden die Zähne ausfallen; B (*withdraw beforehand*) seine Teilnahme absagen; (*withdraw while in progress*) aussteigen (*ugs.*) (**of** aus); (*abandon sth.*) ausscheiden (**of** aus); (*disappear from one's place in a series or group*) ausfallen; **~ out of the bidding** aussteigen (*ugs.*); nicht mehr mitbieten; C (*cease to take part*) aussteigen (*ugs.*) (**of** aus); ‹Student:› das Studium abbrechen *od.* aufgeben; **~ out of university/the course** das Studium abbrechen *od.* aufgeben; **~ out [of society]** aussteigen (*ugs.*); D (*be omitted*) aus-, weggelassen werden (**of** aus). ⇒ *also* **~out**

**~ 'round** *v.i.* vorbeikommen

**drop: ~-dead** *adv.* (*coll.*) umwerfend (*ugs.*) ‹schön›; unverschämt (*ugs.*) ‹gut aussehen›; **~-down menu** *n.* (*Computing*) Dropdown-Menü, *das;* **~-forging** *n.* (*Metalw.*) Gesenkschmieden, *das;* **~ handlebars** *n. pl.* Rennlenker, *der;* **~head** *n.* (*Brit. Motor Veh.*) Klappverdeck, *das;* (*vehicle*) Kabriolett, *das;* **~-in centre** *n.* (*jedermann zugängliche, auch Rat und Hilfe anbietende*) Begegnungsstätte; **~ kick** *n.* (*Football*) Dropkick, *der;* (*Rugby*) Sprungtritt, *der;* **~-leaf table** *n.* Klapptisch, *der*

**droplet** /ˈdrɒplɪt/ *n.* Tröpfchen, *das*

**'dropout** *n.* (*coll.*) A (*act of withdrawing*) Aussteigen, *das* (*ugs.*); (*from expedition or trip*) Ausfall, *der;* Rücktritt, *der;* **the ~ rate** die Aussteigerquote; (*among students or trainees*) die Zahl der Abbrecher; B (*person*) (*from college etc.*) Abbrecher, *der*/Abbrecherin, *die;* (*from society*) Aussteiger, *der*/Aussteigerin, *die* (*ugs.*)

**dropper** /ˈdrɒpə(r)/ *n.* (*esp. Med.*) Tropfer, *der;* Guttiole, *die* (*fachspr.*)

**droppings** /ˈdrɒpɪŋz/ *n. pl.* Mist, *der;* (*of horse*) Pferdeäpfel *Pl.;* (*of cattle*) Kuhfladen *Pl.*

**'drop shot** *n.* (*Tennis etc.*) Stoppball, *der*

**dropsy** /ˈdrɒpsɪ/ *n.* Wassersucht, *die*

**dross** /drɒs/ *n.* A Abfall, *der;* B (*Metallurgy*) Gekrätz, *das;* C (*fig.*) Tand, *der* (*geh. veralt.*); **human ~** (*derog.*) Abschaum, *der* (*abwertend*)

**drought** /draʊt/ (*Amer., Scot., Ir./poet.:* **drouth** /draʊθ/) *n.* A Dürre, *die;* **a period of ~:** eine Dürreperiode; B (*fig.: shortage*) Mangel, *der* (**of** an + *Dat.*)

**drove**[1] ⇒ **drive** 2, 3

**drove**[2] /drəʊv/ *n.* A (*herd*) Herde, *die;* B *usu. in pl.* (*fig.: of people*) Schar, *die;* **in ~s** scharenweise; in Scharen

**drover** /ˈdrəʊvə(r)/ *n.* Viehtreiber, *der*

**drown** /draʊn/ ❶ *v.i.* ertrinken. ❷ *v.t.* A ertränken; **be ~ed** ertrinken; B (*fig.*) **~ one's sorrows [in liquor]** seine Sorgen [im Alkohol] ertränken; C (*submerge, flood*) überfluten; überschwemmen; verwässern ‹Whisky, Brandy›; **~ed valley** (*Geog.*) überflutetes Tal; Ria[s]tal, *das;* D (*make inaudible*) übertönen ‹Geräusch, Musik›. ⇒ *also* **rat** 1 A

**~ 'out** *v.t.* (*make inaudible*) übertönen; niederschreien ‹Redner›

**drowse** /draʊz/ *v.i.* [vor sich hin]dösen; **~ off** eindösen; einnicken

**drowsily** /ˈdraʊzɪlɪ/ *adv.* (*while falling asleep*) schläfrig; (*on just waking*) verschlafen

**drowsiness** /ˈdraʊzɪnɪs/ *n., no pl.* Schläfrigkeit, *die;* **cause ~:** müde *od.* schläfrig machen

**drowsy** /ˈdraʊzɪ/ *adj.* A (*half asleep*) schläfrig; (*on just waking*) verschlafen; **feel ~:** sich schläfrig fühlen; B (*soporific*) einschläfernd

**drub** /drʌb/ *v.t.*, **-bb-** (*thrash*) verprügeln; verdreschen (*ugs.*); (*beat in fight*) schlagen

**drubbing** /ˈdrʌbɪŋ/ *n.* A (*thrashing*) Tracht Prügel, *die;* B (*fig.*) Niederlage, *die*

**drudge** /drʌdʒ/ ❶ *n.* Schwerarbeiter, *der* (*fig.*); Kuli, *der* (*ugs. abwertend*). ❷ *v.i.* schuften; sich abplacken

**drudgery** /ˈdrʌdʒərɪ/ *n.* Schufterei, *die;* Plackerei, *die*

**drug** /drʌg/ ❶ *n.* A (*Med., Pharm.*) Medikament, *das;* [Arznei]mittel, *das;* (*as ingredient*) Mittel, *das;* **this patient is on ~s** dieser Patient muss Medikamente nehmen; B (*narcotic, opiate, etc.*) Droge, *die;* Rauschgift, *das;* **take ~s** Drogen *od.* Rauschgift nehmen; **be on ~s** [regelmäßig] Drogen *od.* Rauschgift nehmen; C (*Commerc. fig.*) **a ~ on the market** unverkäufliche Ware; ein Ladenhüter (*ugs.*). ❷ *v.t.*, **-gg-:** A (*administer ~ to*) **he was ~ged and kidnapped** er wurde betäubt und entführt; B (*add ~ to*) **~ sb.'s food/drink** jmds. Essen/Getränk (*Dat.*) ein Betäubungsmittel beimischen

**drug: ~ abuse** *n.* Drogenmissbrauch, *der;* **~ abuser** *n.* Drogenmissbrauch Treibender/Treibende; **~ addict** *n.* Drogen- *od.* Rauschgiftsüchtige, *der/die;* **~ addiction** *n.;* Drogen- *od.* Rauschgiftsucht, *die;* **~ dealer** *n.* Drogenhändler, *der*/-händlerin, *die;* Dealer, *der*/Dealerin, *die* (*Drogenjargon*)

**druggist** /ˈdrʌgɪst/ *n.* ▶ 1261 Drogist, *der*/Drogistin, *die*

**drug: ~ peddler** ⇒ **drug dealer; ~ pusher** Pusher, *der* (*Drogenjargon*); Drogen- *od.* Rauschgifthändler, *der;* **~-related** *adj.* Drogen‹tote, -kriminalität, -delikt, -probleme›; **~ scene** *n.* Drogenszene, *die;* **~store** *n.* (*Amer.*) Drugstore, *der;* **~-taking** *n., no pl.* Drogeneinnahme, *die;* **~ trafficking** *n.* Drogenhandel, *der*

**Druid** /ˈdruːɪd/ *n.* Druide, *der*

**drum** /drʌm/ ❶ *n.* A Trommel, *die;* B *in pl.* (*in jazz or pop*) Schlagzeug, *das;* (*section of band etc.*) Trommeln *Pl.;* C (*sound*) Trommeln, *das;* D (*Anat.*) ⇒ **eardrum;** E (*container for oil etc.*) Fass, *das;* **~ of paint** Farbenhobbock, *der.* ❷ *v.i.*, **-mm-** trommeln. ❸ *v.t.*, **-mm-: ~ one's fingers on the desk** mit den Fingern auf den Tisch trommeln

**~ into** *v.t.* **~ sth. into sb.** jmdm. etw. einhämmern (*ugs.*) *od.* einbläuen (*ugs.*)

**~ 'out** *v.t.* (*Mil.*) **~ sb. out** jmdn. austrommeln (*veralt.*); (*fig.*) jmdn. [mit Schimpf und Schande] ausstoßen; **he was ~med out of town** er wurde aus der Stadt gejagt

**~ 'up** *v.t.* (*Mil.*) zusammentrommeln; (*fig.*) auftreiben ‹Kunden, Unterstützung›; erwecken ‹Enthusiasmus›; zusammentrommeln (*ugs.*) ‹Helfer, Anhänger›; anbahnen ‹Geschäfte›

**drum: ~beat** *n.* Trommelschlag, *der;* **~ brake** *n.* Trommelbremse, *die;* **~fire** *n.* (*Mil.; also fig.*) Trommelfeuer, *das;* **~head** *n.* (*Mus.*) [Trommel]fell, *das*

**drum: ~ 'major** *n.* (*Mil.*) Tambourmajor, *der;* **~ majo'rette** *n.* Tambourmajorette, *die*

**drummer** /ˈdrʌmə(r)/ *n.* ▶ 1261 A Schlagzeuger, *der;* B (*Amer.: representative*) Vertreter, *der*/Vertreterin, *die*

**'drumstick** *n.* A (*Mus.*) Trommelschlägel, *der;* B (*of fowl*) Keule, *die;* Schlegel, *der* (*südd., österr., schweiz.*)

**drunk** /drʌŋk/ ❶ ⇒ **drink** 2, 3. ❷ *adj.* **be ~:** betrunken sein; **be half ~:** angetrunken sein; **get ~ [on gin]** [von Gin] betrunken werden; (*intentionally*) sich [mit Gin] betrinken; **get sb. ~:** jmdn. betrunken machen; **be ~ as a lord** (*coll.*) voll wie eine Haubitze sein (*ugs.*); **~ in charge [of a vehicle]** betrunken am Steuer. ❸ *n.* Betrunkene, *der/die*

**drunkard** /ˈdrʌŋkəd/ *n.* Trinker, *der*/Trinkerin, *die;* Säufer, *der*/Säuferin, *die* (*derb abwertend*)

**drunken** /ˈdrʌŋkn/ *attrib. adj.* A betrunken; besoffen (*derb*); (*habitually drunk*) ständig besoffen; B **a ~ brawl** *or* **fight** eine Schlägerei zwischen Betrunkenen; **in a ~ stupor** im Vollrausch; **~ driving** Trunkenheit am Steuer

**drunkenness** /ˈdrʌŋknnɪs/ *n., no pl.* A (*temporary*) Betrunkenheit, *die;* B (*habitual*) Trunksucht, *die*

**drupe** /druːp/ *n.* (*Bot.*) Steinfrucht, *die*

**Druze** /druːz/ *n.* Druse, *der*/Drusin, *die*

**dry** /draɪ/ ❶ *adj.*, **drier** /ˈdraɪə(r)/, **driest** /ˈdraɪɪst/ A trocken; trocken, (*very dry*) herb ‹Wein›; ausgetrocknet ‹Fluss, Flussbett›; **get** *or* **become ~:** trocken werden; trocknen; **~ bread** trocken[es] Brot; **go ~:** austrocknen; **my throat is** *or* **feels ~:** meine Kehle ist wie ausgetrocknet; **~ work** Arbeit, die durstig macht; **as ~ as a bone** völlig trocken; **there wasn't a ~ eye in the house** da blieb kein Auge trocken; **store sth. in a ~ place** etw. trocken lagern; B (*not using liquid*) Trocken-; **~ shave/shampoo** Trockenrasur, *die*/-shampoo, *das;* C (*not rainy*) trocken ‹Wetter, Klima›; D (*coll.: thirsty*) durstig; **I'm a bit ~:** ich habe eine trockene Kehle; E **go ~** ‹Flüssigkeit:› verdunsten; ‹Suppe usw.:› verkochen; F (*not yielding*) ausgetrocknet, versiegt ‹Brunnen›; G (*teetotal*) **go ~:** das Alkoholverbot *od.* die Prohibition einführen; H (*fig.*) trocken ‹Humor›; (*impassive, cold*) kühl ‹Art, Bemerkung usw.›; I (*fig.: meagre, bare*) nüchtern ‹Fakten, Dankesworte›; nackt ‹Tatsachen›; (*dull*) trocken ‹Stoff, Bericht, Vorlesung›; **be as ~ as dust** sterbenslangweilig *od.* (*ugs.*) stinklangweilig sein.

❷ *n.* A **give it a good ~:** trockne es gut ab; B (*place*) **in the ~:** im Trock[e]nen.

❸ *v.t.* A trocknen ‹Haare, Wäsche›; abtrocknen ‹Geschirr, Baby›; **~ oneself** sich abtrocknen; **~ one's eyes** *or* **tears/hands** sich (*Dat.*) die

Tränen abwischen/die Hände abtrocknen; Ⓑ (*preserve*) trocknen ‹Kräuter, Holz, Blumen›; dörren ‹Obst, Fleisch›.
❹ *v.i.* trocknen; trocken werden; **~ hard on sth.** ‹Schlamm:› an etw. (*Dat.*) an- *od.* festtrocknen

**~ 'out** ❶ *v.t.* Ⓐ trocknen; Ⓑ einer Entziehungskur unterziehen ‹Alkoholiker, Drogenabhängigen›; trockenlegen (*ugs.*) ‹Alkoholiker›; ausnüchtern ‹Betrunkenen›. ❷ *v.i.* Ⓐ trocknen; Ⓑ ‹Alkoholiker, Drogenabhängiger:› eine Entziehung[skur] machen; ‹Alkoholiker:› trocken werden (*ugs.*); ‹Betrunkener:› ausnüchtern

**~ 'up** ❶ *v.t.* Ⓐ abtrocknen ‹Geschirr›; Ⓑ austrocknen ‹Fluss, Teich›; versiegen lassen ‹Brunnen›. ❷ *v.i.* Ⓐ (*~ the dishes*) abtrocknen; ⇒ *also* **drying-up**; Ⓑ ‹Brunnen, Quelle:› versiegen; ‹Fluss, Teich:› austrocknen; **a dried-up person** ein vertrockneter Typ; Ⓒ (*fig.*) ‹Initiative, Ideen, Erfindergeist:› versiegen; ‹Renten, Ersparnisse:› schrumpfen; Ⓓ (*be unable to continue*) stecken bleiben; Ⓔ (*coll.: stop talking*) **~ up!** halt die Klappe! (*ugs.*); hör auf zu sülzen! (*salopp*)

**dryad** /'draɪæd/ *n.* (*Mythol.*) Dryade, *die*

**dry: ~ 'battery** *n.* (*Electr.*) Trockenbatterie, *die;* **~ 'cell** *n.* (*Electr.*) Trockenelement, *das;* **~-'clean** *v.t.* chemisch reinigen; **have sth. ~-cleaned** etw. in die Reinigung geben; '**~-clean only**' „chemisch reinigen"; **~-'cleaners** *n. pl.* chemische Reinigung; **~-'cleaning** *n.* chemische Reinigung; **~ 'dock** *n.* Trockendock, *das*

**dryer** ⇒ **drier²**

**dry: ~-eyed** *adj.* ohne Rührung; **~ goods** *n. pl.* (*Commerc.*) Textilwaren *Pl.;* Kurzwaren *Pl.;* **~ 'ice** *n.* Trockeneis, *das*

**drying**/'draɪɪŋ/: **~ cupboard** *n.* Wäschetrockenschrank, *der;* **~-'up** *n.* Abtrocknen, *das;* **do the ~-up** abtrocknen; *attrib.* **~-up cloth** Geschirrtuch, *das*

**dry 'land** *n.* Festland, *das;* **be back on ~:** wieder festen Boden unter den Füßen haben

**dryly** /'draɪlɪ/ *adv.* (*fig.*) Ⓐ (*coldly*) kühl; Ⓑ (*with dry humour*) trocken; **sb. is ~ humorous** jmd. hat einen trockenen Humor

**'dry measure** *n.* Trocken[hohl]maß, *das*

**dryness** /'draɪnɪs/ *n., no pl.* Ⓐ Trockenheit, *die;* Ⓑ (*fig.: coldness*) Kühle, *die;* Ⓒ (*fig.: of humour*) Trockenheit, *die;* Ⓓ (*fig.: dullness*) Trockenheit, *die;* Langweiligkeit, *die*

**dry: ~ 'rot** *n.* Ⓐ Trockenfäule, *die;* Ⓑ (*fungi*) Polyparus, *der* (*fachspr.*); Hausschwamm, *der;* Holzschwamm, *der;* **~ 'run** *n.* (*coll.*) Probelauf, *der;* **~stone** *adj.* **~stone wall** Trockensteinmauer, *die*

**D. Sc.** /di:es'si:/ *abbr.* **Doctor of Science** Dr. rer. nat.; ⇒ *also* **B. Sc.**

**DSS** *abbr.* (*Brit.*) **Department of Social Security** Amt für Sozialwesen

**DTI** *abbr.* (*Brit.*) **Department of Trade and Industry**

**DTs** /di: 'ti:z/ *n. pl.* (*coll.*) Delirium, *das;* **have the ~:** [vom Trinken] das Zittern haben (*ugs.*)

**dual** /'dju:əl/ *adj.* Ⓐ doppelt; Doppel-; **~ status/role/function** Doppelstatus, *der*/-rolle, *die*/-funktion, *die;* Ⓑ (*Psych.*) **~ personality** gespaltene Persönlichkeit

**dual: ~ 'carriageway** *n.* (*Brit.*) Straße mit Mittelstreifen; **~ con'trol** *n.* (*Aeronaut.*) Doppelsteuerung, *die;* (*Motor Veh.*) doppelte Bedienungselemente *Pl.*

**dualism** /'dju:əlɪzm/ *n.* (*Philos., Theol.*) Dualismus, *der*

**duality** /dju:'ælɪtɪ/ *n.* Dualität, *die*

**dual-'purpose** *adj.* zweifach verwendbar

**dub¹** /dʌb/ *v.t.,* **-bb-** (*Cinemat.*) synchronisieren

**dub²** *v.t.,* **-bb-** Ⓐ **~ sb. [a] knight** jmdn. zum Ritter schlagen; Ⓑ (*call, nickname*) titulieren

**dub³** *n.* (*coll.: novice*) Flasche, *die* (*ugs.*)

**dubbin** /'dʌbɪn/ *n.* Lederfett, *das*

**dubious** /'dju:bɪəs/ *adj.* Ⓐ (*doubting*) unschlüssig; **feel ~ of sb.'s honesty** an jmds. Ehrlichkeit (*Dat.*) zweifeln; **I'm ~ about accepting the invitation** ich weiß nicht recht, ob ich die Einladung annehmen soll; Ⓑ (*suspicious*) dubios; zweifelhaft; Ⓒ (*questionable*) zweifelhaft; fragwürdig; Ⓓ (*of doubtful result*) ungewiss; Ⓔ (*unreliable*) zweifelhaft

**dubiously** /'dju:bɪəslɪ/ *adv.* Ⓐ (*doubtingly*) unschlüssig; Ⓑ (*suspiciously*) dubios

**ducal** /'dju:kl/ *adj.* herzoglich; Herzogs‹titel, -krone›

**duchess** /'dʌtʃɪs/ *n.* ▶ **1617** Herzogin, *die*

**duchy** /'dʌtʃɪ/ *n.* Herzogtum, *das*

**duck¹** /dʌk/ ❶ *n.* Ⓐ *pl.* **~s** *or* (*collect.*) *same* (*Ornith.; as food*) Ente, *die;* **wild ~:** Wildente, *die;* **toy ~:** Schwimmente, *die;* Spielzeugente, *die;* **can a ~ swim?** (*iron.*) und ob!; **it was [like] water off a ~'s back** (*fig.*) das lief alles an ihm/ihr *usw.* ab; **take to sth. like a ~ to water** bei etw. gleich in seinem Element sein; **fine weather for ~s** (*joc./iron.*) bei dem Wetter könnte man Flossen gebrauchen (*scherzh.*); **play [at] ~s and drakes** [flache] Steine über die Wasseroberfläche springen lassen; titschern; **play ~s and drakes with, make ~s and drakes of** (*fig.*) verschwenden; durchbringen ‹Ersparnisse, Vermögen›; zum Fenster hinauswerfen ‹Geld›; Ⓑ (*Brit. coll.: dear*) **[my] ~:** Schätzchen; Ⓒ (*Cricket*) **be out for a ~:** ohne einen Punkt zu machen aus sein; **break one's ~:** den ersten Punkt holen. ⇒ *also* **dead duck**; **lame duck**.
❷ *v.i.* Ⓐ (*bend down*) sich [schnell] ducken; **~ [down] [out of sight]** sich ducken, um nicht gesehen zu werden; Ⓑ (*under water*) tauchen; Ⓒ (*coll.: move hastily*) türmen (*ugs.*).
❸ *v.t.* Ⓐ **~ sb. [in water]** jmdn. untertauchen; jmdn. tunken (*landsch.*); Ⓑ **~ one's head** den Kopf einziehen; Ⓒ (*fig. coll.: evade*) ausweichen ‹einer Frage, einem Problem›

**~ 'out** *v.i.* (*coll.*) **~ out [of sth.]** sich [vor etw. (*Dat.*)] drücken (*ugs.*); [vor etw. (*Dat.*)] kneifen (*ugs. abwertend*)

**duck²** *n.* (*Textiles*) Segeltuch, *das*

**duck: ~bill, ~-billed 'platypus** ⇒ **platypus**; **~boards** *n. pl.* Lattenrost, *der;* **~ egg** *n.* Entenei, *das;* **~-egg 'blue** *n.* zartes Blaugrau

**duckie** /'dʌkɪ/ ⇒ **duck¹** 1 B

**ducking** /'dʌkɪŋ/ *n.* (*immersion*) [Ein-, Unter]tauchen, *das;* **give sb. a ~:** jmdn. untertauchen; jmdn. tunken (*landsch.*)

**'ducking stool** *n.* (*Hist.*) Tauchstuhl, *der*

**duckling** /'dʌklɪŋ/ *n.* Entenküken, *das;* (*as food*) junge Ente; ⇒ *also* **ugly** A

**'duck pond** *n.* Ententeich, *der*

**ducks** /dʌks/ ⇒ **duck¹** 1 B

**'duckweed** *n.* (*Bot.*) Wasserlinse, *die;* Entengrütze, *die*

**duct** /dʌkt/ ❶ *n.* Ⓐ (*for fluid, gas, cable*) [Rohr]leitung, *die;* Rohr, *das;* (*for air*) Ventil, *das;* Ⓑ (*Anat.*) Gang, *der;* **hepatic/cystic/acoustic ~:** Leber-/Gallenblasen-/Gehörgang, *der;* **spermatic ~:** Samenleiter, *der;* **tear ~:** Tränenkanal, *der;* Ⓒ (*Bot.*) Gang, *der;* Kanal, *der.* ❷ *v.t.* leiten

**ductile** /'dʌktaɪl/ *adj.* dehnbar, (*fachspr.*) duktil ‹Metall›

**ducting** /'dʌktɪŋ/ *n.* Leitungssystem, *das*

**dud** /dʌd/ (*coll.*) ❶ *n.* Ⓐ (*useless thing*) Niete, *die* (*ugs.*); (*counterfeit*) Fälschung, *die;* (*banknote*) Blüte, *die* (*ugs.*); (*failure*) Reinfall, *der* (*ugs.*); (*Cards*) Lusche, *die* (*ugs.*); **this battery/lightbulb/watch/ballpoint is a ~:** diese Batterie/Glühlampe/Uhr/dieser Kugelschreiber taugt nichts; **that cheque was a ~:** der Scheck war faul (*ugs.*); Ⓑ (*bomb etc.*) Blindgänger, *der;* Ⓒ (*ineffectual person*) Niete, *die* (*ugs.*); Versager, *der.*
❷ *adj.* Ⓐ mies (*ugs.*); schlecht; (*fake*) gefälscht; geplatzt ‹Scheck›; **a ~ banknote** eine Blüte (*ugs.*); Ⓑ **a ~ bullet/shell/bomb** ein Blindgänger

**dude** /dju:d, du:d/ *n.* (*esp. Amer. coll.*) Ⓐ (*dandy*) feiner Pinkel aus der Stadt (*ugs.*); Ⓑ (*fellow, guy*) Typ, *der* (*ugs.*)

**'dude ranch** *n.* (*Amer.*) Ferienranch, *die*

**dudgeon** /'dʌdʒn/ *n.* **in high ~:** äußerst empört

**due** /dju:/ ❶ *adj.* Ⓐ (*owed*) geschuldet; zustehend ‹Eigentum, Recht usw.›; **the share/reward ~ to him** der ihm zustehende Anteil/die ihm zustehende Belohnung; der Anteil, der/die Belohnung, die ihm zusteht; **the amount ~:** der zu zahlende Betrag; **there's sth. ~ to me, I've got sth. ~, I'm ~ for sth.** mir steht etw. zu; Ⓑ (*immediately payable, lit. or fig.*) fällig; **be more than ~** (*fig.*) überfällig sein; Ⓒ (*that it is proper to give*) gebührend, geziemend (*geh.*); erforderlich ‹Hilfe›; entsprechend ‹Ermutigung›; angemessen ‹Belohnung›; **be ~ to sb.** jmdm. gebühren; **recognition ~ to sb.** Anerkennung, die jmdm. gebührt; **respect ~ from sb. to sb.** Respekt, den jmd. jmdm. schuldet; **with all ~ respect, madam** bei allem gebotenen Respekt, meine Dame; **with ~ allowance** *or* **regard** unter gebührender Berücksichtigung (**for** *Gen.*); Ⓓ (*that it is proper to use*) gebührend, geziemend (*geh.*); reiflich ‹Überlegung›; **with ~ caution/care** mit der nötigen Vorsicht/Sorgfalt; **they were given ~ warning** sie wurden hinreichend gewarnt; **in ~ time** rechtzeitig; **~ process of law** ordentliches Gerichtsverfahren; Ⓔ (*attributable*) **~ to negligence** aufgrund von Nachlässigkeit; **the mistake was ~ to negligence** der Fehler war durch Nachlässigkeit verursacht; **the discovery is ~ to Newton** die Entdeckung ist Newton (*Dat.*) zu verdanken; **it's ~ to her that we missed the train** ihretwegen verpassten wir den Zug; es lag an ihr, dass wir den Zug verpassten; **his death was ~ to a heart attack** Ursache seines Todes war ein Herzanfall; **the difficulty is ~ to our ignorance** die Schwierigkeit ergibt sich aus unserer Unwissenheit; **be ~ to the fact that ...:** darauf zurückzuführen sein, dass ...; Ⓕ (*scheduled, expected, under engagement or instructions*) **be ~ to do sth.** etw. tun sollen; **I'm ~** (*my plan is*) **to leave tomorrow** ich werde morgen abfahren; **be ~ [to arrive]** ankommen sollen; **the train is now ~:** der Zug müsste jetzt planmäßig ankommen; **when are we ~ to land/dock?** wann landen wir/laufen wir ein?; **I'm ~ in Paris tonight** ich muss heute Abend in Paris sein; **the baby is ~ in two weeks' time** das Baby kommt in zwei Wochen; Ⓖ (*likely to get, deserving*) **be ~ for sth.** etw. verdienen; **he is ~ for promotion** seine Beförderung ist fällig. ⇒ *also* **course** 1 C.
❷ *adv.* Ⓐ ▶ **1024** **~ north** genau nach Norden; **~ north wind** Wind direkt von Norden; **the town is ~ north of us** die Stadt liegt genau nördlich von uns; Ⓑ **~ to** aufgrund (+ *Gen.*).
❸ *n.* Ⓐ *in pl.* (*debt*) Schulden *Pl.;* **pay one's ~s** seine Schulden bezahlen; Ⓑ *no pl.* (*fig.: just deserts, reward*) **sb.'s ~:** das, was jmdm. zusteht; das, was jmdm. gebührt (*geh.*); **that was no more than his ~:** das hatte er auch verdient; das stand ihm auch zu; **give sb. his ~:** jmdm. Gerechtigkeit widerfahren lassen; **but to give him** *or* **the Devil his ~ he ...:** aber das muss man ihm lassen, er ...; Ⓒ *usu. in pl.* (*fee*) Gebühr, *die;* (*toll*) Zoll, *der;* **membership ~s** Mitgliedsbeiträge *Pl.*

**duel** /'dju:əl/ ❶ *n.* Ⓐ Duell, *das;* (*Univ.*) Mensur, *die;* **fight a ~:** ein Duell/eine Mensur austragen; Ⓑ (*fig.: contest*) Kampf, *der;* **~ of wits** geistiger Wettstreit; **~ of words** Wortgefecht, *das;* Rededuell, *das;* **propaganda ~:** Propagandagefecht, *das.* ❷ *v.i.,* (*Brit.*) **-ll-** sich duellieren; (*Univ.*) eine Mensur austragen *od.* schlagen

**duet** /dju:'et/ *n.* (*Mus.*) (*for voices*) Duett, *das;* (*instrumental*) Duo, *das*

**duettist** /dju:'etɪst/ *n.* [Duett]partner, *der*/[Duett]partnerin, *die*

**duff** /dʌf/ *adj.* (*Brit. coll.*) mies (*ugs.*)

**duffel bag, duffel coat** ⇒ **duffle bag, duffle coat**

**duffer** /'dʌfə(r)/ *n.* Trottel, *der* (*ugs. abwertend*); **be a ~ at football/school** im Fußball/in der Schule eine Niete sein (*ugs.*)

**duffle**/'dʌfl/: **~ bag** *n.* Matchbeutel, *der;* (*waterproof, also*) Seesack, *der;* **~ coat** *n.* Dufflecoat, *der*

**dug** ⇨ **dig** 1, 2

**'dugout** *n.* Ⓐ(*canoe*) Einbaum, *der;* Ⓑ(*Mil.: shelter*) Unterstand, *der*

**duke** /dju:k/ *n.* Ⓐ ▶1617 Herzog, *der;* **royal ~:** Herzog und Mitglied des Königshauses; Ⓑ*in pl.* (*coll.: fists*) Flossen *Pl.* (*salopp*); **put up your ~s** Fäuste hoch! (*salopp*)

**dukedom** /'dju:kdəm/ *n.* Ⓐ(*territory*) Herzogtum, *das;* Ⓑ(*rank*) Herzogwürde, *die*

**dulcet** /'dʌlsɪt/ *adj.* lieblich; **sb.'s ~ tones** (*iron.*) jmds. zarte Stimme (*iron.*)

**dulcimer** /'dʌlsɪmə(r)/ *n.* (*Mus.*) Hackbrett, *das;* Zimbal, *das*

**dull** /dʌl/ ❶*adj.* Ⓐ(*stupid*) beschränkt; (*slow to understand*) begriffsstutzig (*abwertend*); Ⓑ(*boring*) langweilig; stumpfsinnig ‹Arbeit, Routine›; nichts sagend ‹Eindruck›; Ⓒ(*gloomy*) trübe ‹Wetter, Tag›; Ⓓ(*not bright*) matt, stumpf ‹Farbe, Glanz, Licht, Metall›; trübe ‹Augen›; blind ‹Spiegel›; (*not sharp*) dumpf ‹Geräusch, Aufprall, Schmerz, Gefühl›; Ⓔ(*not keen*) unscharf; schwach ‹Augen, Gehör›; **grow ~** ‹Geisteskräfte:› nachlassen; Ⓕ(*sluggish*) träge; Ⓖ(*listless*) lustlos; (*dejected*) niedergeschlagen; bedrückt; Ⓗ(*blunt*) stumpf; Ⓘ(*Commerc.*) flau. ⇨ *also* **ditchwater**.
❷*v.t.* Ⓐ(*make less acute*) schwächen; trüben; betäuben ‹Schmerz›; Ⓑ(*make less bright or sharp*) stumpf werden lassen; verblassen lassen ‹Farbe›; Ⓒ(*blunt*) stumpf machen; Ⓓ(*fig.*) dämpfen ‹Freude, Enthusiasmus›; abstumpfen ‹Geist, Sinne, Verstand, Vorstellungskraft›; lindern ‹Kummer, Hass›; **~ the edge of sth.** (*fig.*) einer Sache (*Dat.*) ihren Reiz nehmen

**dullard** /'dʌləd/ *n.* Dummkopf, *der* (*ugs.*)

**dullness** /'dʌlnɪs/ *n., no pl.* Ⓐ(*stupidity*) Beschränktheit, *die;* (*slow-wittedness*) Begriffsstutzigkeit, *die* (*abwertend*); [geistige] Trägheit; Ⓑ(*boringness*) Langweiligkeit, *die;* (*of work, life, routine*) Stumpfsinn, *der;* Ⓒ(*of weather*) Trübheit, *die;* Ⓓ(*of colour, light, metal*) Stumpfheit, *die;* Mattheit, *die;* Ⓔ(*of sight, hearing etc.*) Schwächung, *die;* (*of sight, mind, senses*) Trübung, *die;* Ⓕ(*sluggishness*) Trägheit, *die*

**dull-witted** /dʌl'wɪtɪd/ ⇨ **dull** 1 A

**dully** /'dʌllɪ/ *adv.* Ⓐ(*dimly, indistinctly*) trübe ‹scheinen›; dumpf ‹fühlen, aufprallen, tönen, schmerzen›; **his arm was aching ~:** er spürte einen dumpfen Schmerz im Arm; Ⓑ(*sluggishly*) träge; Ⓒ(*listlessly*) lustlos; (*dejectedly*) niedergeschlagen; bedrückt

**duly** /'dju:lɪ/ *adv.* Ⓐ(*rightly, properly*) ordnungsgemäß; Ⓑ(*sufficiently*) ausreichend; hinreichend; **he was ~ punished** er wurde gehörig bestraft; Ⓒ(*punctually*) pünktlich

**dumb** /dʌm/ ❶*adj.*, **~er** /'dʌmə(r)/, **~est** /'dʌmɪst/ Ⓐ stumm; **a ~ person** ein Stummer/eine Stumme; **~ animals** *or* **creatures** die Tiere; die stumme Kreatur (*dichter.*); **~ friend** vierbeiniger Freund; Ⓑ(*temporarily speechless*) stumm; **he was [struck] ~ with fright/amazement** vor Furcht/Staunen verschlug es ihm die Sprache; Ⓒ(*inarticulate*) sprachlos ‹Massen, Millionen›; (*saying nothing*) stumm; schweigend; Ⓓ(*coll.: stupid*) doof (*ugs.*); **act ~:** sich dumm stellen (*ugs.*); **a ~ blonde** eine dümmliche Blondine (*ugs.*).
❷*n. pl.* **the ~:** die Stummen; **the deaf and ~:** die Taubstummen

**~ down** *v.t. & i.* (*coll.*) verflachen

**'dumb-bell** *n.* Ⓐ Hantel, *die;* Ⓑ(*coll.: stupid person*) Dummkopf, *der* (*ugs.*); Dümmling, *der* (*ugs.*)

**dumbfound** /dʌm'faʊnd/ *v.t.* sprachlos machen; verblüffen

**dumbfounded** /dʌm'faʊndɪd/ *adj.* sprachlos; verblüfft; **be ~:** sprachlos sein

**dumbly** /'dʌmlɪ/ *adv.* stumm

**dumb: ~ show** *n.* **in ~ show** durch Mimik; **~ 'waiter** *n.* Ⓐ(*trolley*) stummer Diener; Ⓑ(*lift*) Speisenaufzug, *der*

**dumdum** /'dʌmdʌm/ *n.* **~ [bullet]** Dumdum[geschoss], *das*

**dummy** /'dʌmɪ/ ❶*n.* Ⓐ(*of tailor*) Schneiderpuppe, *die;* (*in shop*) Modepuppe, *die;* Schaufensterpuppe, *die;* (*of ventriloquist*) Puppe, *die;* (*figurehead, person acting for another*) Strohmann, *der;* (*stupid person*) Dummkopf, *der* (*ugs.*); Doofi, *der* (*ugs.*); **like a stuffed ~:** wie ein Ölgötze (*ugs.*); Ⓑ(*imitation*) Attrappe, *die;* Dummy, *der;* (*Commerc.*) Schaupackung, *die;* Ⓒ(*esp. Brit.: for baby*) Schnuller, *der;* Ⓓ(*Bridge etc.*) (*person*) Strohmann, *der;* (*hand*) Tisch, *der;* Ⓔ(*Rugby coll.*) **sell sb. the** *or* **a ~:** jmdn. antäuschen.
❷*attrib. adj.* unecht; blind ‹Tür, Fenster›; Übungs- (*Mil.*); **~ gun** Gewehrattrappe, *die;* **~ run** Probelauf, *der*

**dump** /dʌmp/ ❶*n.* Ⓐ(*place*) Müllkippe, *die;* (*heap*) Müllhaufen, *der;* (*permanent*) Müllhalde, *die;* Ⓑ(*Mil.*) Depot, *das;* Lager, *das;* Ⓒ(*coll. derog.: unpleasant place*) Schweinestall, *der* (*derb abwertend*); Dreckloch, *das* (*salopp abwertend*); (*boring town*) Kaff, *das* (*ugs. abwertend*); Nest, *das* (*ugs. abwertend*). ❷*v.t.* Ⓐ(*dispose of*) werfen; (*deposit*) abladen, kippen ‹Sand, Müll usw.›; (*leave*) lassen; (*place*) abstellen; Ⓑ(*Commerc.: send abroad*) zu Dumpingpreisen verkaufen; Ⓒ(*fig. coll.: abandon*) abladen (*ugs.*)

**dumper** /'dʌmpə(r)/ *n.* Kipper, *der*

**dumping** /'dʌmpɪŋ/ *n.* Ⓐ[Schutt]abladen, *das;* **'no ~ [of refuse]'** „Schuttabladen verboten"; Ⓑ(*Commerc.: sending abroad*) Dumping, *das*

**'dumping ground** *n.* Müllkippe, *die;* Schuttabladeplatz, *der;* (*fig.*) Abstellplatz, *der*

**dumpling** /'dʌmplɪŋ/ *n.* Ⓐ(*Gastr.*) Kloß, *der;* **apple ~:** Apfel im Schlafrock; Ⓑ(*coll.: short, plump person*) Tönnchen, *das* (*ugs.*)

**dumps** /dʌmps/ *n. pl.* (*coll.*) **be** *or* **feel [down] in the ~:** ganz down sein (*ugs.*)

**'dump truck** *n.* Kipper, *der*

**dumpy** /'dʌmpɪ/ *adj.* pummelig (*ugs.*)

**dun**[1] /dʌn/ ❶*adj.* graubraun. ❷*n.* Graubraun, *das*

**dun**[2] *v.t.*, **-nn-** (*demand money due from*) [Geld] anmahnen bei; **~ sb. for sth.** bei jmdm. etw. anmahnen

**dunce** /dʌns/ *n.* Null, *die* (*ugs. abwertend*); Niete, *die* (*ugs. abwertend*); **the ~ of the class** das Schlusslicht der Klasse (*ugs.*); **~'s cap** (*Hist.*) Spotthut, *der* (*für schlechte Schüler*)

**dunderhead** /'dʌndəhed/ *n.* Schwachkopf, *der* (*ugs. abwertend*)

**dune** /dju:n/ *n.* Düne, *die*

**dung** /dʌŋ/ ❶*n.* Dung, *der;* Mist, *der.* ❷*v.t.* mit Mist düngen

**dungaree** /dʌŋgə'ri:/ *n.* Ⓐ(*fabric*) grober Kattun; Ⓑ*in pl.* (*garment*) Latzhose, *die;* **a pair of ~s** eine Latzhose

**'dung beetle** *n.* Mistkäfer, *der*

**dungeon** /'dʌndʒn/ *n.* Kerker, *der;* Verlies, *das*

**'dunghill** *n.* Misthaufen, *der*

**dunk** /dʌŋk/ *v.t.* Ⓐ tunken; stippen (*bes. nordd.*); Ⓑ(*immerse*) tauchen

**Dunkirk** /dʌn'kɜ:k/ *pr. n.* ▶1626 Dünkirchen (*das*); **~ spirit** Durchhaltevermögen, *das*

**dunlin** /'dʌnlɪn/ *n.* (*Ornith.*) Alpenstrandläufer, *der*

**duo** /'dju:əʊ/ *n., pl.* **~s** Ⓐ(*Theatre*) Paar, *das;* **comedy ~:** Komikerpaar, *das;* Ⓑ(*Mus.*) Duo, *das;* Ⓒ(*coll.: couple*) Duo, *das* (*oft iron.*); **an odd ~:** ein komisches Gespann (*ugs.*)

**duodenal** /dju:ə'di:nl/ *adj.* (*Anat.*) duodenal (*fachspr.*); Zwölffingerdarm-

**duodenal 'ulcer** *n.* ▶1232 (*Med.*) Zwölffingerdarmgeschwür, *das*

**duodenum** /dju:ə'di:nəm/ *n.* (*Anat.*) Duodenum, *das* (*fachspr.*); Zwölffingerdarm, *der*

**dupe** /dju:p/ ❶*v.t.* düpieren (*geh.*); übertölpeln; **be ~d [into doing sth.]** sich übertölpeln lassen [und etw. tun]; **be ~d into believing sth.** auf etw. (*Akk.*) hereinfallen. ❷*n.* Düpierte, *der/die* (*geh.*); Dumme, *der/die;* Gelackmeierte, *der/die* (*salopp scherzh.*)

**duple** /'dju:pl/ *adj.* **~ time** (*Mus.*) gerader Takt

**duplex** /'dju:pleks/ ❶*adj.* Ⓐ(*twofold*) doppelt; zweifach; Ⓑ(*esp. Amer.: two-storey*) zweistöckig ‹Wohnung›; Ⓒ(*esp. Amer.: two-family*) Zweifamilien‹haus›. ❷*n.* (*esp. Amer.*) zweistöckige Wohnung

**duplicate** ❶/'dju:plɪkət/ *adj.* Ⓐ(*identical*) Zweit-; **~ key** Nach- *od.* Zweitschlüssel, *der;* **~ copy** Zweit- *od.* Abschrift, *die;* Doppel, *das;* Ⓑ(*twofold*) doppelt; Ⓒ(*Cards*) **~ bridge/whist** *Form des Bridge/Whists, bei der das Spiel mit derselben Verteilung der Karten, aber mit anderen Spielern wiederholt wird.* ❷*n.* Ⓐ Kopie, *die;* (*second copy of letter/document/key*) Duplikat, *das;* Ⓑ**prepare/complete sth. in ~:** etw. in doppelter Ausfertigung machen/ausfüllen; **make sth. in ~:** etw. doppelt anfertigen; Ⓒ(*Cards*) = **~ bridge** *etc.*; ⇨ 1 C. ❸/'dju:plɪkeɪt/ *v.t.* Ⓐ(*make a copy of, make in ~*) **~ sth.** eine zweite Anfertigung von etw. machen; etw. nachmachen (*ugs.*); **they have tried to ~ his results** sie haben versucht, zu denselben Ergebnissen wie er zu kommen; Ⓑ(*be exact copy of*) genau gleichen (+ *Dat.*); Ⓒ(*on machine*) vervielfältigen; Ⓓ(*unnecessarily*) [unnötigerweise] noch einmal tun

**duplicating**/'dju:plɪkeɪtɪŋ/: **~ machine** ⇨ **duplicator**; **~ paper** *n.* (*Printing*) Vervielfältigungspapier, *das*

**duplication** /dju:plɪ'keɪʃn/ *n.* Ⓐ Wiederholung, *die;* Ⓑ(*on machine*) Vervielfältigung, *die;* Ⓒ(*unnecessary*) [unnötige] Wiederholung; **avoid unnecessary ~!** vermeiden Sie unnötige Wiederholungen!; **~ of effort** doppelte Arbeit

**duplicator** /'dju:plɪkeɪtə(r)/ *n.* (*Printing*) Vervielfältigungsgerät, *das*

**duplicity** /dju:'plɪsɪtɪ/ *n.* Falschheit, *die*

**durability** /djʊərə'bɪlɪtɪ/ *n., no pl.* Ⓐ(*permanence*) (*of friendship, peace, etc.*) Dauerhaftigkeit, *die;* (*of person*) Unverwüstlichkeit, *die;* Ⓑ(*resistance to wear or decay*) (*of garment, material*) Haltbarkeit, die; Strapazierfähigkeit, *die;* (*of metal, rock, component*) Widerstandsfähigkeit, *die*

**durable** /'djʊərəbl/ ❶*adj.* Ⓐ(*lasting*) dauerhaft ‹Friede, Freundschaft usw.›; Ⓑ(*resisting wear or decay*) solide; strapazierfähig, haltbar ‹Kleidung, Stoff›; widerstandsfähig ‹Metall, Fels, Bauelement›; **~ goods** ⇨ 2. ❷*n. in pl.* (*Econ.*) **consumer ~s** langlebige *od.* dauerhafte Konsumgüter

**duration** /djʊə'reɪʃn/ *n.* Dauer, *die;* **be of short/long ~:** von kurzer/langer Dauer sein; **the courses are of three years' ~:** die Kurse dauern drei Jahre; **for the ~ of sth.** für die Dauer *od.* während [der Dauer] einer Sache (*Gen.*); **for the ~** (*of war*) auf Kriegsdauer; **I'm afraid we're here for the ~** (*fig. coll.*) wir werden wohl bis zum Ende ausharren müssen, fürchte ich

**duress** /djʊə'res, 'djʊəres/ *n., no pl.* Zwang, *der;* **under ~:** unter Zwang

**during** /'djʊərɪŋ/ *prep.* während; (*at a point in*) in (+ *Dat.*); **~ the rehearsal/wedding ceremony** während *od.* bei der Probe/Trauung; **~ the night** während *od.* in der Nacht; **~ the journey** während *od.* auf der Reise

**dusk** /dʌsk/ *n.* (*twilight*) [Abend]dämmerung, *die;* Einbruch der Dunkelheit; **at/after/until ~:** bei/nach/bis zum Einbruch der Dunkelheit

**dusky** /'dʌskɪ/ *adj.* (*dark-coloured*) dunkel; dunkelhäutig ‹Person, Schönheit›; **a ~ blue/red** ein dunkles Blau/Rot

**dust** /dʌst/ ❶*n., no pl.* Ⓐ Staub, *der;* (*pollen*) Blütenstaub, *der;* **be covered in ~** ‹Erde:› staubbedeckt sein; ‹Gegenstände:› eingestaubt *od.* verstaubt sein; **the ~ of ages** der Staub der Jahrhunderte; **make a great deal of ~:** sehr stauben; **throw ~ in sb.'s eyes** (*fig.*) jmdm. Sand in die Augen streuen; **shake the ~ off one's feet** (*fig.*) den Staub von den Füßen schütteln (*geh.*); **turn to ~ and ashes** Staub werden; (*fig.*) zunichte werden; **wait till the ~ has settled** (*fig.*) warten, bis sich die Wogen geglättet haben; **you couldn't see him for ~** (*fig.*) man konnte nur noch seine Staubwolke sehen; Ⓑ(*~ing*) Staubwischen, *das;* **give sth. a ~** den Staub von etw. abwischen; etw. abstauben. ⇨ *also*

bite 1; raise 1 B.
❷ *v.t.* Ⓐ (*clear of* ∼) abstauben ‹Möbel›; ∼ **a room/house** in einem Zimmer/Haus Staub wischen; **the house/the furniture needs ∼ing** *or* **to be ∼ed** in dem Haus muss Staub gewischt werden/die Möbel müssen abgestaubt werden; Ⓑ (*sprinkle; also Cookery*) ∼ **sth. with sth.** etw. mit etw. bestäuben; (*with talc etc.*) etw. mit etw. pudern; (*with grated material*) etw. mit etw. bestreuen; ∼ **sth. over** *or* **on [to] sth.** (*using powder*) etw. auf etw. (*Akk.*) stäuben; (*using grated material*) etw. auf etw. (*Akk.*) streuen.
❸ *v.i.* Staub wischen
∼ **'off** *v.t.* abstauben; (*fig. derog.*) aus der Mottenkiste hervorholen

**dust:** ∼**bin** *n.* (*Brit.*) Mülltonne, *die;* Abfalltonne, *die;* **relegate sth. to the ∼bin** (*fig.*) etw. in *od.* auf den Müll wandern lassen (*ugs.*); ∼ **bowl** *n.* (*Geog.*) Trockengebiet, *das* (*mit häufigen Staubstürmen*); ∼**cart** *n.* (*Brit.*) Müllwagen, *der;* ∼**cloth** *n.* Schonbezug, *der;* (*duster*) Staubtuch, *das;* ∼**coat** *n.* (*Brit.*) Staubmantel, *der;* ∼ **cover** *n.* (*on record player*) Abdeckhaube, *die;* (*for clothes*) Staubschutz, *der;* (*on book*) ⇒ **dust jacket**; ∼ **devil** ⇒ **devil** 1 I

**duster** /'dʌstə(r)/ *n.* Ⓐ (*cloth*) Staubtuch, *das;* Ⓑ (*coat*) Staubmantel, *der*

**dusting** /'dʌstɪŋ/ *n.* Ⓐ (*removal of dust*) ⇒ **dust** 2 A: Abstauben, *das;* Staubwischen, *das;* **give a room a ∼:** in einem Zimmer Staub wischen; Ⓑ (*sprinkling*) Bestreuen, *das*

**dust:** ∼ **jacket** *n.* Schutzumschlag, *der;* ∼**man** /'dʌstmən/ *n., pl.* ∼**men** /'dʌstmən/ ▶ **1261** (*Brit.*) Müllwerker, *der;* Müllmann, *der;* ∼**pan** *n.* Kehrschaufel, *die;* ∼**proof** *adj.* staubdicht; ∼ **sheet** *n.* Staubdecke, *die;* ∼ **storm** *n.* Staubsturm, *der;* ∼ **trap** *n.* Staubfänger, *der* (*abwertend*); ∼**-up** *n.* (*coll.*) Krach, *der* (*ugs.*); ∼ **wrapper** ⇒ ∼ **jacket**

**dusty** /'dʌstɪ/ *adj.* Ⓐ staubig ‹Straße, Stadt, Zimmer›; verstaubt ‹Bücher, Möbel›; **the house is/has got very ∼:** das Haus ist sehr verstaubt; im Haus hat sich viel Staub angesammelt; Ⓑ (*dull*) schmutzig ‹Rosa, Blau, Grün›; Ⓒ (*vague*) vage; Ⓓ (*bad-tempered*) schroff ‹Antwort›; Ⓔ **not so** ∼ (*Brit. dated coll.*) gar nicht so übel (*ugs.*)

**dutch** *n.* (*Brit. coll.*) **my old ∼:** meine gute Alte

**Dutch** /dʌtʃ/ ❶ *adj.* Ⓐ ▶ **1275**, ▶ **1340** holländisch; niederländisch; Ⓑ (*coll.*) **go ∼ [with sb.] [on sth.]** getrennte Kasse [mit jmdm.] [bei etw.] machen; **talk to sb. like a ∼ uncle** jmdm. ernstlich ins Gewissen reden. ⇒ *also* **English** 1. ❷ *n.* Ⓐ ▶ **1340** *constr. as pl.* **the ∼:** die Holländer *od.* Niederländer; Ⓑ (*language*) ▶ **1275** Holländisch, *das;* Niederländisch, *das;* **[Cape] ∼:** Kapholländisch, *das;* Ⓒ **it was all double ∼ to him** das waren alles böhmische Dörfer für ihn. ⇒ *also* **English** 2 A

**Dutch:** ∼ **'auction** ⇒ **auction** 1 A; ∼ **'barn** *n.* offene Scheune; ∼ **'courage** *n.* angetrunkener Mut; **give oneself** *or* **get ∼ courage** sich (*Dat.*) Mut antrinken; ∼ **'doll** *n.* holländische Gliederpuppe; ∼ **'door** *n.* (*Amer.*) quer geteilte Tür; ∼ **'elm disease** *n.* (*Bot.*) Ulmensterben, *das;* ∼ **'hoe** *n.* (*Agric.*) Schuffel, *die;* ∼**man** /'dʌtʃmən/ *n., pl.* ∼**men** /'dʌtʃmən/ Ⓐ Holländer, *der;* Niederländer, *der;* Ⓑ (*fig. coll.*) **or I'm a ∼man** oder ich will Emil heißen; Ⓒ (*ship*) holländisches Schiff; **The Flying ∼man** Der Fliegende Holländer; ∼ **'oven** *n.* (*Cookery*) Ⓐ (*box*) *Backgefäß mit mehreren Fächern;* Ⓑ (*pot*) Schmortopf, *der;* ∼ **'treat** *n. gemeinsames Vergnügen, bei dem jeder für sich selbst bezahlt;* ∼**woman** *n.* Holländerin, *die;* Niederländerin, *die*

**dutiable** /'dju:tɪəbl/ *adj.* (*Customs*) zollpflichtig; abgabenpflichtig

**dutiful** /'dju:tɪfl/ *adj.* pflichtbewusst ‹Ehefrau, Arbeiter, Bürger›; gehorsam ‹Tochter, Sklave›

**dutifully** /'dju:tɪfəlɪ/ *adv.* pflichtbewusst ‹handeln›; treu ‹dienen›

**duty** /'dju:tɪ/ *n.* Ⓐ *no pl.* (*moral or legal obligation*) Pflicht, *die;* Verpflichtung, *die;* ∼ **calls** die Pflicht ruft; **have a ∼ to do sth.** die Pflicht haben, etw. zu tun; **have a ∼ to sb.** jmdm. gegenüber eine Verpflichtung haben; **one's ∼ to** *or* **towards sb./sth.** seine Pflicht gegenüber jmdm./einer Sache; **do one's ∼ [by sb.]** [jmdm. gegenüber] seine Pflicht [und Schuldigkeit] tun; **make it one's ∼ to do sth.** es sich (*Dat.*) zur Pflicht machen, etw. zu tun; **be/feel in ∼ bound to do sth.** verpflichtet sein/sich verpflichtet fühlen, etw. zu tun; **in ∼ bound** pflichtschuldigst; Ⓑ (*specific task, esp. professional*) Aufgabe, *die;* Pflicht, *die;* **do one's ∼:** seine Pflicht tun; **take up one's duties** seinen Dienst antreten; **your duties will consist of ...:** zu Ihren Aufgaben gehören ...; **[purely] in [the] line of ∼:** [rein] dienstlich; **the ∼ nurse/∼ porter** die Dienst habende Schwester/der Dienst habende Pförtner; **on ∼:** im Dienst; **be on ∼:** Dienst haben; **while on ∼:** während des Dienstes; im Dienst; **go/come on ∼ at seven p.m.** um 19 Uhr seinen Dienst antreten; **off ∼:** nicht im Dienst; **be off ∼:** keinen Dienst haben; ‹ab ... Uhr› dienstfrei sein; **go/come off ∼ at eight a.m.** seinen Dienst um acht Uhr beenden; **Dr Smith is off ∼ tomorrow** Dr. Smith hat morgen dienstfrei; ⇒ *also* **off-duty**; *attrib.* ∼ **chemist** Apotheke, die Nachtdienst hat; **which is the ∼ chemist tonight?** welche Apotheke hat heute Nachtdienst?; Ⓒ (*Econ.: tax*) Zoll, *der;* **pay ∼ on sth.** Zoll für etw. bezahlen; etw. verzollen; **be liable to ∼:** zollpflichtig sein; ∼ **on alcohol** Branntweinsteuer, *die;* **free of ∼:** zollfrei ‹Ware, Preis›; Ⓓ **do ∼ as/for sth.** (*serve as*) als/zu etw. dienen

**duty:** ∼**-bound** *adj.* **be/feel [oneself] ∼-bound to do sth.** verpflichtet sein/sich verpflichtet fühlen, etw. zu tun; ⇒ *also* **duty** A; ∼**-free** *adj.* zollfrei ‹Ware, Preis›; ∼**-frees** *n. pl.* (*coll.*) zollfreie Waren; ∼**-free 'shop** *n.* Duty-free-Shop, *der;* ∼ **officer** *n.* (*Mil.*) Offizier vom Dienst; ∼**-paid** *adj.* (*Econ.*) verzollt ‹Ware›; ∼ **visit** *n.* Pflichtbesuch, *der*

**duvet** /'du:veɪ/ *n.* Federbett, *das;* (*quilted*) Steppdecke, *die; attrib.* ∼ **cover** Bettbezug, *der*

**DVD** *abbr.* **digital video disc** DVD

**dwarf** /dwɔ:f/ ❶ *n., pl.* ∼**s** *or* **dwarves** /dwɔ:vz/ Ⓐ (*person*) Liliputaner, *der*/Liliputanerin, *die;* Zwerg, *der*/Zwergin, *die* (*auch abwertend*); Ⓑ (*tree*) Zwergbaum, *der;* (*plant*) Zwergpflanze, *die;* (*animal*) Zwergtier, *das;* Ⓒ (*Mythol.*) Zwerg, *der*/Zwergin, *die;* Ⓓ (*Astron.*) Zwerg[stern], *der.* ❷ *adj.* Ⓐ Zwerg‹baum, -stern›; Ⓑ (*stunted*) winzig. ❸ *v.t.* Ⓐ (*stunt in growth*) verkümmern lassen; Ⓑ (*cause to look small*) klein erscheinen lassen; verzwergen (*geh.*); Ⓒ (*fig.*) in den Schatten stellen

**dwarves** *pl. of* **dwarf**

**dweeb** /dwi:b/ *n.* (*esp. Amer. coll.*) trübe Tasse (*ugs. abwertend*)

**dwell** /dwel/ *v.i.*, **dwelt** /dwelt/ (*literary; lit. or fig.*) wohnen; weilen (*geh.*)
∼ **[up]on** *v.t.* Ⓐ (*in discussion*) sich länger *od.* ausführlich befassen mit; (*in thought*) in Gedanken verweilen bei; **don't ∼ upon the past** halten Sie sich nicht bei *od.* mit der Vergangenheit auf; Ⓑ (*prolong*) gedehnt aussprechen ‹Wort, Silbe›

**dweller** /'dwelə(r)/ *n., esp. in comb.* Bewohner, *der*/Bewohnerin, *die;* **city-∼s** Großstädter *Pl.*

**dwelling** /'dwelɪŋ/ *n.* (*Admin. lang./literary*) Wohnung, *die;* **council ∼:** Sozialwohnung, *die*

**dwelling:** ∼ **house** *n.* Wohnhaus, *das;* ∼ **place** *n.* Wohnsitz, *der*

**dwelt** ⇒ **dwell**

**dwindle** /'dwɪndl/ *v.i.* Ⓐ ∼ **[away]** abnehmen; ‹Unterstützung, Interesse:› nachlassen; ‹Güter, Vermögen:› zusammenschrumpfen; ‹Vorräte, Handel, Hoheitsgebiet:› schrumpfen; ‹Macht, Einfluss, Tageslicht:› schwinden (*geh.*); ‹Gewinn, Umsatz:› rückläufig sein; ‹Bodenschätze:› zur Neige gehen (*geh.*); ‹Ruhm:› verblassen (*geh.*); ∼ **in importance** an Bedeutung abnehmen *od.* verlieren; ∼ **away to nothing** dahinschwinden; Ⓑ (*fig.: degenerate*) herunterkommen **(into** zu)

**dye** /daɪ/ ❶ *n.* Ⓐ (*substance*) Färbemittel, *das;* **eyelash ∼:** Wimperntusche, *die;* Ⓑ (*colour*) Farbe, *die.* ❷ *v.t.*, ∼**ing** /'daɪɪŋ/ färben; ∼**d blond hair** blond gefärbtes Haar; ∼**d-in-the-wool** (*fig.*) eingefleischt, (*ugs.*) in der Wolle gefärbt ‹Konservativer, Gewerkschaftler, Reaktionär›. ❸ *v.i.*, ∼**ing** sich färben lassen

**dyer** /'daɪə(r)/ *n.* Färber, *der*/Färberin, *die*

**'dyestuff** ⇒ **dye** 1 A

**dying** /'daɪɪŋ/ ❶ *adj.* Ⓐ sterbend ‹Person, Tier›; eingehend ‹Pflanze›; absterbend ‹Baum›; verendend ‹Tier›; aussterbend ‹Kunst, Kultur, Tradition, [Tier]art, Menschenschlag›; zu Ende gehend ‹Jahr›; erlöschend ‹Glut, Leidenschaft›; **he's a ∼ man** (*will not recover*) er lebt nicht mehr lange; Ⓑ (*related to time of death*) letzt...; **to my ∼ day** bis an mein Lebensende. ❷ *n. pl.* **the ∼:** die Sterbenden. ⇒ *also* **die**[1]

**dyke** ⇒ **dike**

**dynamic** /daɪ'næmɪk/ *adj.*, **dynamically** /daɪ'næmɪkəlɪ/ *adv.* (*lit. or fig.; also Mus.*) dynamisch

**dynamics** /daɪ'næmɪks/ *n., no pl.* Ⓐ (*Mech.*) Dynamik, *die* (*fachspr.*); Kräftelehre, *die;* Ⓑ (*in other sciences*) -dynamik, *die*

**dynamism** /'daɪnəmɪzm/ *n.* Dynamik, *die*

**dynamite** /'daɪnəmaɪt/ ❶ *n.* Ⓐ (*explosive*) Dynamit, *das;* Ⓑ (*fig.: politically dangerous person or thing*) Sprengstoff, *der;* **these revelations are ∼:** diese Enthüllungen sind [politisch] brisant; Ⓒ (*fig.: sensational person or thing*) **be ∼** ‹Person:› eine Wucht sein (*salopp*); ‹Sache:› eine Sensation sein. ❷ *v.t.* mit Dynamit sprengen

**dynamo** /'daɪnəməʊ/ *n., pl.* ∼**s** Ⓐ Dynamomaschine, *die;* (*of car*) Lichtmaschine, *die;* (*of bicycle*) Dynamo, *der;* Ⓑ (*fig.*) **[human] ∼:** Energiebündel, *das* (*ugs.*)

**dynastic** /dɪ'næstɪk/ *adj.* dynastisch; ‹Regierung, Herrschaft, Diktatur› einer Dynastie; ∼ **families** Familiendynastien *Pl.*

**dynasty** /'dɪnəstɪ/ *n.* (*lit. or fig.*) Dynastie, *die*

**dyne** /daɪn/ *n.* (*Phys.*) Dyn, *das*

**dysentery** /'dɪsəntərɪ/ *n.* (*Med.*) Ruhr, *die;* Dysenterie, *die* (*fachspr.*)

**dysfunctional** /dɪs'fʌŋkʃənl/ *adj.* [funktions]gestört ‹Modem, Telefonleitung›; **a ∼ family** eine nicht [mehr] intakte Familie

**dyslexia** /dɪs'leksɪə/ *n.* (*Med., Psych.*) Dyslexie, *die* (*fachspr.*); Lesestörung, *die*

**dyslexic** /dɪs'leksɪk/ (*Med., Psych.*) ❶ *adj.* dyslektisch (*fachspr.*); **a ∼ child** ein Kind mit einer Lesestörung. ❷ *n.* Dyslektiker, *der*/Dyslektikerin, *die* (*fachspr.*); Mensch mit einer Lesestörung

**dyspepsia** /dɪs'pepsɪə/ *n.* ▶ **1232** (*Med.*) Dyspepsie, *die* (*fachspr.*); Verdauungsstörung, *die*

**dystrophy** /'dɪstrəfɪ/ *n.* ▶ **1232** (*Med.*) Dystrophie, *die* (*fachspr.*); Ernährungsstörung, *die;* **muscular ∼:** Muskeldystrophie, *die;* (*fortschreitender*) Muskelschwund

# E e

**E**[1], **e** /iː/ *n., pl.* **Es** *or* **E's** A (*letter*) E, e, *das;* B E (*Mus.*) E, e, *das;* **E flat** es, Es, *das;* C E (*Sch., Univ.: mark*) Fünf, *die;* **he got an E** er bekam „mangelhaft" *od.* eine Fünf

**E**[2] *abbr.* A ▶ 1024 **east** O; B ▶ 1024 **eastern** ö.; C (*sl.*) **Ecstasy** E; XTC

**each** /iːtʃ/ ❶ *adj.* jeder/jede/jedes; **there's cream between ~ layer** zwischen den einzelnen Schichten ist Sahne; **we have two votes ~, we ~ have two votes** jeder von uns hat zwei Stimmen; **they cost** *or* **are a pound ~:** sie kosten ein Pfund pro Stück *od.* je[weils] ein Pfund; **they ~ have ...:** sie haben jeder ...; jeder von ihnen hat ...; **books at £1 ~:** Bücher zu je einem Pfund *od.* für je ein Pfund; **two teams with 10 players ~:** zwei Mannschaften mit je 10 Spielern; **I gave them a book ~** *or* **~ a book** ich habe jedem von ihnen ein Buch *od.* ihnen je ein Buch gegeben; **~ one of them** jeder/jede/jedes Einzelne von ihnen; **~ and every employee** jeder einzelne Mitarbeiter; **I travelled 10 miles ~ way every day** ich habe jeden Tag 16 km pro Weg zurückgelegt; **back a horse ~ way** (*Brit. Racing*) auf Sieg oder Platz eines Pferdes wetten; **the houses ~ have their own garage[s]** die Häuser haben alle ihre eigene Garage.
❷ *pron.* A jeder/jede/jedes; **they are ~ of them ...** jeder *usw.* von ihnen ist ...; **~ despises the other** jeder verachtet den anderen; sie verachten sich [gegenseitig]; **have some of ~:** von jedem etwas nehmen/haben *usw.;* B **~ other** sich [gegenseitig]; einander (*meist geh.*); **they are cross with ~ other** sie sind böse aufeinander; **we have not seen ~ other in years** wir haben uns jahrelang nicht gesehen; **they wore ~ other's hats** jeder trug den Hut des anderen; **be in love with ~ other** ineinander verliebt sein; **live next door to ~ other** Tür an Tür wohnen

**eager** /ˈiːgə(r)/ *adj.* eifrig ‹Person, Arbeiter, Art›; rege, lebhaft ‹Interesse›; brennend, sehnlich ‹Wunsch›; erwartungsvoll ‹Ton, Gesichtsausdruck, Lächeln›; begeistert ‹Anhänger einer Partei›; **be ~ to do sth.** etw. unbedingt tun wollen; **be ~ to make a good impression** eifrig bemüht sein, einen guten Eindruck zu machen; **be ~ to learn** lernbegierig *od.* -eifrig sein; **be ~ for sth.** etw. unbedingt haben wollen; ⇒ *also* **beaver** 1 A

**eagerly** /ˈiːgəlɪ/ *adv.* eifrig ‹Ja sagen, zustimmen›; bereitwillig ‹Auskunft geben›; gespannt, ungeduldig ‹warten, Ausschau halten, aufblicken›; erwartungsvoll ‹lächeln›; begierig ‹ergreifen›; **look forward ~ to sth.** sich sehr auf etw. (*Akk.*) freuen; **~ seize an opportunity** eine Gelegenheit beim Schopf ergreifen

**eagerness** /ˈiːgənɪs/ *n., no pl.* Eifer, *der;* **~ to learn** Lerneifer, *der;* Lernbegier[de], *die;* **~ to succeed** Erfolgshunger, *der;* **~ to assist** Hilfsbereitschaft, *die*

**eagle** /ˈiːgl/ *n.* A Adler, *der;* B (*Golf*) Eagle, *das*

**eagle: ~ 'eye** *n.* Falkenauge, *das* (*geh.*); **have/keep/fix one's ~ eye on sb./sth.** ein wachsames Auge *od.* einen wachsamen Blick auf jmdn./etw. haben; **~-eyed** *adj.* adleräugig

**eaglet** /ˈiːglɪt/ *n.* (*Ornith.*) Adlerjunge, *das*

**ear**[1] /ɪə(r)/ *n.* A ▶ 966 Ohr, *das;* (*of red deer*) Lauscher, *der;* (*of red fox*) Gehör, *das;* (*of rabbit, hare*) Löffel, *der;* (*of hound*) Behang, *der* (*Jägerspr.*); **his good/bad ~:** sein besseres/schlechteres Ohr; **~, nose, and throat hospital/specialist** Hals-Nasen-Ohren-Klinik, *die/*-Arzt, *der/*-Ärztin, *die;* **smile from ~ to ~:** von einem Ohr zum anderen strahlen (*ugs.*); **have nothing between one's ~s** (*fig. coll.*) nichts im Kopf haben (*ugs.*); **be out on one's ~** (*fig. coll.*) auf der Straße stehen (*ugs.*); **this brought a storm of criticism about his ~s** das setzte ihn einem Sturm der Kritik aus; **sb. would give his/her ~s to do sth.** jmd. würde alles darum geben, etw. zu tun; **over head and ~s, head over ~s** (*fig. coll.*) bis über die *od.* beide Ohren; **up to one's ~s in work/debt** bis zum Hals in Arbeit/Schulden; **be pleasing to the ~[s]** sich angenehm anhören; **come to** *or* **reach sb.'s ~s** jmdm. zu Ohren kommen; **have a word in sb.'s ~:** jmdm. ein Wort im Vertrauen sagen; **listen with half an ~:** [nur] mit halbem Ohr zuhören; **keep one's ~s open** (*fig.*) die Ohren offen halten; **have/keep an ~ to the ground** sein Ohr ständig am Puls der Masse haben (*ugs. scherzh.*); **be[come] all ~s** [plötzlich] ganz Ohr sein; **go in [at] one ~ and out [at] the other** (*coll.*) zum einen Ohr herein-, zum anderen wieder hinausgehen; **lend an ~ to sb.** jmdm. Gehör schenken; **give ~ to** ein geneigtes Ohr haben für (*geh.*); **have sb.'s ~/get** *or* **win the ~ of sb.** bei jmdm. Gehör *od.* ein offenes Ohr finden; B *no pl.* (*sense*) Gehör, *das;* **have an ~** *or* **a good ~/no ~ for music** ein [gutes]/kein Gehör für Musik haben; **play by ~** (*Mus.*) nach dem Gehör spielen; **play it by ~** (*fig.*) es dem Augenblick/der Situation überlassen

**ear**[2] *n.* (*Bot.*) Ähre, *die;* **~ of corn** Kornähre, *die*

**ear: ~ache** *n.* ▶ 1232 (*Med.*) Ohrenschmerzen *Pl.;* **~ clip** *n.* Ohr[en]klipp, *der;* **~ drops** *n. pl.* A (*Med.*) Ohrentropfen *Pl.;* B (*earrings*) Ohrgehänge, *das;* **~drum** *n.* (*Anat.*) Trommelfell, *das*

**-eared** /ɪəd/ *adj. in comb.* **long-/short-~:** lang-/kurzohrig

**'ear flap** *n.* Ohrenklappe, *die*

**earful** /ˈɪəfʊl/ *n.* (*coll.*) **get an ~:** ordentlich was zu hören bekommen (*ugs.*); **give sb. an ~ about sth.** jmdm. ein paar Takte [über etw.] erzählen (*ugs.*)

**earl** /ɜːl/ *n.* ▶ 1617 Graf, *der*

**earldom** /ˈɜːldəm/ *n.* A (*territory*) Grafschaft, *die;* B (*rank*) Grafenwürde, *die*

**'earlobe** *n.* Ohrläppchen, *das*

**early** /ˈɜːlɪ/ ❶ *adj.* ▶ 912 A früh; **they had an ~ lunch** sie aßen früh zu Mittag; **I am a bit ~:** ich bin etwas zu früh gekommen *od.* (*ugs.*) dran; **the train was 10 minutes ~:** der Zug kam 10 Minuten zu früh; **an ~ train** (*earlier than one usually takes*) ein früherer Zug; **have an ~ night** früh ins Bett gehen; **~ riser** Frühaufsteher, *der/*-aufsteherin, *die;* **~ to bed, ~ to rise [makes a man healthy, wealthy, and wise]** (*prov.*) früh zu Bette und auf zu früher Stund, macht den Menschen glücklich, reich, gesund (*Spr.*); **an ~ reply** eine baldige Antwort; **at the earliest** frühestens; **the ~ part of** der Anfang (+ *Gen.*); **in the ~ afternoon/evening** am frühen Nachmittag/Abend; **into the ~ hours** bis in die frühen Morgenstunden; **at/from an ~ age** in jungen Jahren/von klein auf; **from one's earliest years** von frühester Kindheit an; **at an ~ stage, in its ~ stages** im Frühstadium; **~ Gothic** Frühgotik, *die;* **an ~ work/the ~ writings of an author** ein Frühwerk/die Frühschriften eines Autors; **~ Christian times** die frühchristliche Zeit; B (*of the distant past*) vorgeschichtlich ‹Fund, Fossilien›; (*prehistoric*) frühgeschichtlich ‹Fund, Fossilien›; **the earliest records of a civilization** die frühesten Spuren einer Zivilisation; **at a very ~ date** schon sehr früh; C (*forward in flowering, ripening, etc.*) früh blühend ‹Pflanze›; Früh‹gemüse, -obst›.
❷ *adv.* früh; **~ next week** Anfang der nächsten Woche; **~ next Wednesday** nächsten Mittwoch früh; **~ in June** Anfang Juni; **the earliest I can come is Friday** ich kann frühestens Freitag kommen; **I cannot come earlier than Thursday** ich kann nicht vor Donnerstag kommen; **from ~ in the morning till late at night** von früh [morgens] bis spät [nachts]; **~ on** schon früh; **earlier on this week/year** früher in der Woche/im Jahr

**early: ~ bird** *n.* (*joc.*) *jmd., der etw. frühzeitig tut;* (*getting up*) Frühaufsteher, *der/*-aufsteherin, *die;* **the ~ bird catches the worm** (*prov.*) Morgenstunde hat Gold im Munde (*Spr.*); **~ 'closing** *n.* **it is ~ closing** die Geschäfte haben nachmittags geschlossen; **~-'closing day** *n. Tag, an dem die Geschäfte nachmittags geschlossen haben;* **~ 'days** *n. pl.* **in the ~ days** am Anfang (**of** *Gen.*); **it is ~ days [yet]** es ist noch zu früh; **~-'warning** *attrib. adj.* Frühwarn-

**ear: ~mark** ❶ *n.* Ohrmarke, *die;* (*fig.*) Kennzeichen, *das;* ❷ *v.t.* A (*mark, lit. or fig.*) [kenn]zeichnen; B (*assign to definite purpose*) bestimmen; vorsehen; **~muffs** *n. pl.* Ohrenschützer *Pl.*

**earn** /ɜːn/ *v.t.* A ‹Person, Tat, Benehmen:› verdienen; **~ed income** Einkommen aus Arbeit; **it ~ed him much respect** es trug ihm viel Respekt ein; B (*bring in as income or interest*) einbringen; C (*incur*) eintragen; einbringen; **he ~ed nothing but ingratitude** er erntete nur Undank

**earner** /ˈɜːnə(r)/ *n.* **be a nice little ~** (*coll.*) ganz schön was einbringen (*ugs.*)

**earnest**[1] /ˈɜːnɪst/ ❶ *adj.* A (*serious, zealous*) ernsthaft; **be ~ in one's endeavour to do sth.** sich ernsthaft bemühen, etw. zu tun; B (*ardent*) innig ‹Wunsch, Gebet, Hoffnung›; leidenschaftlich ‹Appell›. ❷ *n.* **in ~:** mit vollem Ernst; **this time I'm in ~ [about it]** diesmal ist es mir Ernst *od.* meine ich es ernst [damit]; **it's raining in ~ now** jetzt regnet es richtig

**earnest**[2] *n.* A (*money*) Handgeld, *das;* B (*foretaste*) Vorgeschmack, *der* (**of** von)

**earnestly** /ˈɜːnɪstlɪ/ *adv.* ernsthaft

**earning** /ˈɜːnɪŋ/ *n.* A Erreichen, *das;* (*of money*) Verdienen, *das;* B *in pl.* (*money earned*) Verdienst, *der;* (*of business etc.*) Ertrag, *der*

**ear: ~phones** *n. pl.* Kopfhörer, *der;* **~piece** *n.* Hörmuschel, *die;* **~-piercing** ❶ *adj.* durch Mark und Bein gehend ‹Lärm›; ❷ *n.* Durchstechen der Ohrläppchen; **~plug** *n.* Ohropax, *das* (Wz); **~ring** *n.* Ohrring, *der;* **~shot** *n.* **out of/within ~shot** außer/in Hörweite; **~-splitting** *adj.* ohrenbetäubend

**earth** /ɜːθ/ ❶ *n.* A (*land, soil*) Erde, *die;* (*ground*) Boden, *der;* **be brought/come down** *or* **back to ~ [with a bump]** (*fig.*) [schnell] wieder auf den Boden der Tatsachen zurückgeholt werden/zurückkommen; B *or* **E~** (*planet*) Erde, *die;* C (*world*) Erde, *die;* **on ~** (*existing anywhere*) auf der Welt; auf Erden (*geh.*); **nothing on ~ will stop me** keine Macht der Welt kann mich aufhalten; **how/what** *etc.* **on ~ ...?** wie/was *usw.* in

aller Welt ...?; **who on ~ is that?** wer ist das bloß?; **what on ~ do you mean?** was meinst du denn nur?; **where on ~ has she got to?** wo ist sie denn bloß hingegangen?; **look like nothing on ~** (*be unrecognizable*) nicht zu erkennen sein; (*look repellent*) furchtbar aussehen; **be like nothing on ~:** unvergleichlich sein; **feel like nothing on ~:** sich ganz mies fühlen (*ugs.*); **on ~** (*Relig.*) auf Erden; Ⓓ (*land and sea together*) Erde, *die;* Welt, *die;* Ⓔ (*of animal*) Bau, *der;* **run to ~:** in seinen Unterschlupf hetzen ‹Tier›; (*fig.*) aufspüren; **have gone to ~** (*fig.*) untergetaucht sein; Ⓕ (*coll.*) **charge/cost/pay the ~:** ein Vermögen *od.* (*ugs.*) eine ganze Stange Geld verlangen/kosten/bezahlen; **it won't cost the ~:** das kostet nicht die Welt (*ugs.*); **promise sb. the ~:** jmdm. das Blaue vom Himmel versprechen (*ugs.*); Ⓖ (*Chem.*) Erde, *die;* Ⓗ (*Brit. Electr.*) Erde, *die;* Erdung, *die.*
❷ *v.t.* (*Brit. Electr.*) erden
**~ 'up** *v.t.* mit Erde bedecken

**'earth closet** *n.* (*Brit.*) Humustoilette, *die*

**earthen** /'ɜːθn/ *adj.* (*made of clay*) irden; Ton-

**earthenware** /'ɜːθnweə(r)/ ❶ *n.*, *no pl.* Ⓐ (*vessels etc.*) Tonwaren *Pl.;* Irdenware, *die* (*selten*); Ⓑ (*clay*) Ton, *der.* ❷ *adj.* Ton-; tönern

**earthiness** /'ɜːθɪnɪs/ *n.*, *no pl.* Ⓐ Erdigkeit, *die;* Ⓑ (*of person*) Derbheit, *die*

**earthly** /'ɜːθlɪ/ *adj.* irdisch; **no ~ use** *etc.* (*coll.*) nicht der geringste Nutzen *usw.;* **this is no ~ use to me** (*coll.*) das nützt mir nicht im Geringsten *od.* überhaupt nicht; **not an ~** (*sl.*) nicht die geringste Chance

**earth: ~-moving** ❶ *n.* Erdarbeiten *Pl.;* ❷ *adj.* **~-moving vehicle** Fahrzeug für Erdarbeiten; **~quake** *n.* Erdbeben, *das;* **~ sciences** *n. pl.* Geowissenschaften *Pl.;* **~-shaking, ~-shattering** *adjs.* (*fig.*) weltbewegend; **not of ~-shattering importance** nicht weltbewegend; **~ tremor** *n.* Erdstoß, *der;* leichtes Erdbeben; **~work** *n.* Ⓐ (*bank*) Wall, *der;* Ⓑ (*raising of bank*) Erdarbeiten *Pl.;* **~worm** *n.* Regenwurm, *der*

**earthy** /'ɜːθɪ/ *adj.* Ⓐ erdig; Ⓑ derb ‹Person›

**ear: ~ trumpet** *n.* Hörrohr, *das;* **~wax** *n.* Ohrenschmalz, *das*

**earwig** /'ɪəwɪg/ *n.* Ohrwurm, *der*

**ease** /iːz/ ❶ *n.* Ⓐ (*freedom from pain or trouble*) Ruhe, *die;* **set sb. at ~:** jmdn. beruhigen; Ⓑ (*leisure*) Muße, *die;* (*idleness*) Müßiggang, *der;* **a life of ~:** ein Leben der Muße; Ⓒ (*freedom from constraint*) Entspanntheit, *die;* **at [one's] ~:** entspannt; behaglich; **she sat there taking her ~:** sie machte es sich (*Dat.*) gemütlich *od.* behaglich; **be *or* feel at [one's] ~:** sich wohl fühlen; **put *or* set sb. at his ~:** jmdm. die Befangenheit nehmen; **he is always at his ~** (*never embarrassed*) er ist immer unbefangen *od.* ungezwungen; Ⓓ **with ~** (*without difficulty*) mit Leichtigkeit; Ⓔ (*relief from pain*) Linderung, *die;* Ⓕ (*Mil.*) **[stand] at ~!** rührt euch! ⇒ *also* **ill** 3 C.
❷ *v.t.* Ⓐ (*relieve*) lindern ‹Schmerz, Kummer›; (*make lighter, easier*) erleichtern ‹Last, Arbeit›; entspannen ‹Lage, Person›; verringern ‹Belastung›; **~ sb. of a burden** jmdm. eine Last abnehmen; Ⓑ (*give mental ~ to*) erleichtern; **~ sb.'s mind** jmdn. beruhigen; Ⓒ (*relax, adjust*) lockern ‹Griff, Knoten›; verringern ‹Druck, Spannung, Geschwindigkeit›; beruhigen ‹Verkehr›; Ⓓ (*joc.: rob*) erleichtern (*ugs. scherzh.*); **~ sb. of sth.** jmdn. um etw. erleichtern; Ⓔ (*cause to move*) behutsam bewegen; **~ the clutch in** die Kupplung langsam kommen lassen; **~ the cap off a bottle** eine Flasche vorsichtig öffnen.
❸ *v.i.* Ⓐ ‹Belastung, Druck, Wind, Sturm:› nachlassen; Ⓑ **~ off *or* up** (*begin to take it easy*) sich entspannen; **~ off, you're going much too fast** fahre ein bisschen langsamer, du bist viel zu schnell; Ⓒ ‹Aktien usw.:› nachgeben

**easel** /'iːzl/ *n.* Staffelei, *die*

**easily** /'iːzɪlɪ/ *adv.* Ⓐ (*without difficulty*) leicht; **more ~ said than done** leichter gesagt als getan; Ⓑ (*without doubt*) zweifelsohne; **it is ~ a hundred metres deep** es ist gut und gerne hundert Meter tief; Ⓒ (*quite possibly*) leicht; **that may ~ be** das kann gut sein

**easiness** /'iːzɪnɪs/ *n.* Leichtigkeit, *die*

**east** /iːst/ ▶ 1024 ❶ *n.* Ⓐ Osten, *der;* **the ~:** Ost (*Met., Seew.*); **in/to[wards]/from the ~:** im/nach *od.* (*geh.*) gen/von Osten; **to the ~ of** östlich von; östlich (+ *Gen.*); **~, west, home's best** (*prov.*) ob Osten oder Westen, zu Hause ists zum Besten; Ⓑ *usu.* **E~** (*part lying to the ~*) Osten, *der;* (*Geog., Polit.: world lying ~ of Europe*) Osten, *der;* Orient, *der;* Morgenland, *das* (*dichter.*); **from the E~:** aus dem Osten; **the E~** (*Amer.: NE part of US*) der Osten; ⇒ *also* **Far East**; **Middle East**; **Near East**; Ⓒ (*Cards*) Ost.
❷ *adj.* östlich; Ost‹küste, -wind, -grenze, -tor›.
❸ *adv.* ostwärts; nach Osten; **~ of** östlich von; östlich (+ *Gen.*); **~ and west** nach Osten und Westen ‹verlaufen, sich erstrecken›; **~ by north/south** ⇒ **by**[1] 1 D

**East: ~ 'Africa** *pr. n.* Ostafrika (*das*); **~ Anglia** /iːst 'æŋglɪə/ *pr. n. die beiden englischen Grafschaften Norfolk und Suffolk;* **~ Ber'lin** *pr. n.* (*Hist.*) Ost-Berlin (*das*); Berlin, *das* (*DDR*); **e~bound** *adj.* ▶ 1024 ‹Zug, Verkehr usw.› in Richtung Osten; **~ 'End** *n.* (*Brit.*) Londoner Osten; **~-Ender** /iːst'endə(r)/ *n.* (*Brit.*) Bewohner/Bewohnerin des Londoner Ostens

**Easter** /'iːstə(r)/ *n.* ▶ 1191 Ostern, *das od. Pl.;* **at ~:** [zu *od.* an] Ostern; **next/last ~:** nächste/letzte Ostern

**Easter: ~ 'Day** *n.* Ostersonntag, *der;* **~ egg** *n.* Osterei, *das*

**easterly** /'iːstəlɪ/ ▶ 1024 ❶ *adj.* Ⓐ (*in position or direction*) östlich; **in an ~ direction** nach Osten; Ⓑ (*from the east*) ‹Wind› aus östlichen Richtungen; **the wind was ~:** der Wind kam aus östlichen Richtungen. ❷ *adv.* Ⓐ (*in position*) östlich; (*in direction*) ostwärts; Ⓑ (*from the east*) aus *od.* von Ost[en]. ❸ *n.* Ost[wind], *der*

**eastern** /'iːstən/ *adj.* ▶ 1024 östlich; Ost‹grenze, -hälfte, -seite, -wind›; **~ Germany** Ostdeutschland; ⇒ *also* **bloc**; **Far Eastern**; **Middle Eastern**; **Near Eastern**

**Eastern: ~ 'Europe** *pr. n.* Osteuropa (*das*); **~ Euro'pean** ❶ *adj.* osteuropäisch; ❷ *n.* Osteuropäer, *der*/-europäerin, *die;* **~ Germany** *pr. n.* Ostdeutschland (*das*)

**easternmost** /'iːstənməʊst/ *adj.* ▶ 1024 östlichst...

**Easter: ~ 'Sunday** ⇒ **Easter Day**; **~ term** *n.* (*Brit.*) Ⓐ (*Univ.*) ⇒ **Trinity term**; Ⓑ (*Law*) Sitzungsperiode von Ostern bis Pfingsten; **~tide** *n.* (*arch.*) [Tage *Pl.* nach] Ostern; **~ week** *n.* Osterwoche, *die*

**East: ~ 'German** (*Hist.*) ❶ *adj.* ostdeutsch; ❷ *n.* Ostdeutsche, *der/die;* **~ 'Germany** *pr. n.* (*Hist.*) Ostdeutschland (*das*); **~ 'Indies** ⇒ **Indies** B; **e~-north-'~** ▶ 1024 ❶ *n.* Ostnordost[en], *der;* ❷ *adj.* ostnordöstlich; ❸ *adv.* nach Ostnordost[en]; **~ 'Prussia** *pr. n.* Ostpreußen (*das*); **~ Side** *n.* (*Amer.*) *Ostteil von Manhattan;* **e~-south-'~** ▶ 1024 ❶ *n.* Ostsüdost[en], *der;* ❷ *adj.* ostsüdöstlich; ❸ *adv.* nach Ostsüdost[en]

**eastward** /'iːstwəd/ ▶ 1024 ❶ *adj.* nach Osten gerichtet; (*situated towards the east*) östlich; **in an ~ direction** nach Osten; [in] Richtung Osten. ❷ *adv.* ostwärts; **they are ~ bound** sie fahren nach *od.* [in] Richtung Osten. ❸ *n.* Osten, *der*

**eastwards** /'iːstwədz/ ▶ 1024 ⇒ **eastward** 2

**easy** /'iːzɪ/ ❶ *adj.* Ⓐ (*not difficult*) leicht; **~ to clean/learn/see** *etc.* leicht zu reinigen/lernen/sehen *usw.;* **it is ~ to see that ...:** es ist offensichtlich, dass ...; man sieht sofort, dass ...; **it's as ~ as falling off a log *or* as ~ as pie *or* as ~ as anything** (*coll.*) es ist kinderleicht; **be an ~ winner** mit Leichtigkeit siegen; **the ~ fit of a coat** *etc.* der bequeme Sitz eines Mantels *usw.;* **it is ~ for him to talk** er hat leicht *od.* gut reden; **it's ~ for him to complain** er kann sich gut beklagen; **on ~ terms** auf Raten ‹kaufen›; Ⓑ (*free from pain, anxiety, etc.*) sorglos, angenehm ‹Leben, Zeit›; **make life ~ for oneself** sich (*Dat.*) das Leben leicht machen; **make it *or* things ~ for sb.** es jmdm. leicht machen; **[not] ~ in one's mind** be[un]ruhigt; **I do not feel altogether ~ about it/her** ich mache mir deswegen/ihretwegen doch Sorgen; **~ circumstances** (*coll.*) Wohlstand, *der;* ⇒ *also* **conscience**; Ⓒ (*free from constraint, strictness, etc.*) ungezwungen; unbefangen ‹Art›; **at an ~ pace** in einem gemütlichen *od.* gemächlichen Tempo; **he is an ~ person *or* is ~ to get on with/work with** mit ihm kann man gut auskommen/zusammenarbeiten; **I'm ~** (*coll.*) es ist mir egal; **be ~ on the eye** (*coll.*) ansprechend aussehen; **woman *or* lady of ~ virtue** (*euphem.*) Freudenmädchen, *das* (*verhüll.*).
❷ *adv.* leicht; **easier said than done** leichter gesagt als getan; **~ come ~ go** (*coll.*) wie gewonnen, so zerronnen (*Spr.*); **~ does it** immer langsam *od.* sachte; **go ~:** vorsichtig sein; **go ~ on *or* with** sparsam sein *od.* umgehen mit; **be *or* go ~ on *or* with sb.** mit jmdm. nachsichtig sein; **take it ~!** beruhige dich!; **take it *or* things *or* life ~:** sich nicht übernehmen; **stand ~!** (*Brit. Mil.*) rührt euch!

**easy: ~-care** *attrib. adj.* pflegeleicht; **~ 'chair** *n.* Sessel, *der;* **~going** *adj.* (*calm, placid*) gelassen; (*casually pleasant*) gemütlich; (*informal*) ungezwungen; (*lax*) nachlässig; (*careless*) unbekümmert; **~ 'meat** *n.* (*coll.*) leichte Beute; **sth./sb. is ~ meat** man hat [ein] leichtes Spiel mit etw./jmdm.; **~ 'money** *n.* leicht verdientes Geld; **~ 'option** *n.* leichter Weg; **E~ Street** *n.* **be on E~ Street** im Wohlstand leben

**eat** /iːt/ ❶ *v.t.*, **ate** /et, eɪt/, **eaten** /'iːtn/ Ⓐ ‹Mensch:› essen; ‹Tier:› fressen; **I've had enough to ~:** ich habe genug gegessen; ich bin satt *od.* gesättigt; **I could ~ a horse!** ich habe einen Bärenhunger! (*ugs.*); **you should ~ regular meals** du solltest regelmäßig essen; **don't be afraid — he won't ~ you!** (*fig.*) keine Angst, er wird dich schon nicht fressen (*ugs.*); **I could ~ you** du siehst zum Fressen aus (*ugs.*); **she looks nice enough to ~:** sie sieht zum Anbeißen aus (*ugs.*); **~ sb. out of house and home** jmdn. arm essen; jmdm. die Haare vom Kopf fressen (*ugs.*); **what's ~ing you?** (*coll.*) was hast du denn?; **~ one's words** seine Worte zurücknehmen; Ⓑ (*destroy, consume, make hole in*) fressen; **~ its way into/through sth.** sich in etw.(*Akk.*)/durch etw. hindurchfressen. ⇒ *also* **bread** 1 B; **dirt** A; **hat** B; **heart** 1 A; **humble** 1 A.
❷ *v.i.*, **ate, eaten** Ⓐ ‹Person:› essen; ‹Tier:› fressen; **~ out of sb.'s hand** (*lit. or fig.*) jmdm. aus der Hand fressen (*ugs.*); Ⓑ (*make a way by gnawing or corrosion*) **~ into** sich hineinfressen in (+ *Akk.*); **~ through sth.** sich durch etw. durchfressen
**~ a'way** *v.t.* ‹Rost, Säure:› zerfressen.
**~ 'out** *v.i.* essen gehen
**~ 'up** ❶ *v.t.* Ⓐ (*consume*) ‹Person:› aufessen; ‹Tier:› auffressen; **the chickens were ~en up by the fox** die Hühner wurden vom Fuchs gefressen; **the car ~s up a lot of petrol** das Auto verbraucht *od.* (*ugs.*) frisst viel Benzin; **be ~en up by sth.** (*fig.*) vor etw. [fast] vergehen; Ⓑ (*traverse rapidly*) **our car ~s up the miles** unser Auto frisst die Meilen nur so (*ugs.*). ❷ *v.i.* aufessen

**eatable** /'iːtəbl/ ❶ *adj.* genießbar; essbar. ❷ *n. in pl.* Lebensmittel *Pl.;* **have no ~s with one** nichts zu essen dabeihaben

**'eat-by date** *n.* Verfallsdatum, *das*

**eaten** ⇒ **eat**

**eater** /'iːtə(r)/ *n.* Ⓐ (*person*) Esser, *der*/Esserin, *die;* **a big ~:** ein guter Esser; Ⓑ (*apple*) Essapfel, *der*

**eating** /'iːtɪŋ/ *n.* Essen, *das;* **make good ~:** ein gutes Essen sein; **not for ~:** nicht zum Essen [geeignet]

**eating: ~ apple** *n.* Essapfel, *der;* **~ disorder** *n.* Essstörung, *die* (*meist Pl.*); **~ habits** *n. pl.* Essgewohnheiten *Pl.;* **~ house** *n.* Restaurant, *das;* Speisehaus, *das;* **~ place** *n.* Essgelegenheit, *die*

**eats** /iːts/ *n. pl.* (*coll.*) Fressalien *Pl.* (*ugs.*); **what's for ~?** was gibts zu essen? (*ugs.*)

**eau-de-Cologne** /əʊdəkə'ləʊn/ *n.* Eau de Cologne, *das;* Kölnisch Wasser, *das*

**eaves** /i:vz/ *n. pl.* Dachgesims, *das*

**eaves: ~drop** *v.i.* lauschen; **~drop on sth./sb.** etw./jmdn. belauschen; **~dropper** *n.* Lauscher, *der*/Lauscherin, *die*

**ebb** /eb/ ❶ *n.* Ⓐ (*of tide*) Ebbe, *die;* **the tide is on the ~:** es ist Ebbe; Ⓑ (*decline, decay*) Niedergang, *der;* **be at a low ~** (*fig.*) ‹Person, Stimmung, Moral:› auf dem Nullpunkt sein; **my funds are at a low ~:** in meinem Geldbeutel ist Ebbe (*ugs.*); **the ~ and flow** das Auf und Ab; **the ~ and flow of life** die Höhen und Tiefen des Lebens. ❷ *v.i.* Ⓐ (*flow back*) zurückgehen; Ⓑ (*recede, decline*) schwinden; **~ away** dahinschwinden; **his life is ~ing out** mit ihm geht es zu Ende

'**ebb tide** *n.* Ebbe, *die*

**ebony** /'ebənɪ/ ❶ *n.* Ebenholz, *das.* ❷ *adj.* Ebenholz‹baum›; ebenholzfarben ‹Haar, Haut›; **~ box** *etc.* Kiste *usw.* aus Ebenholz

**ebullience** /ɪ'bʌlɪəns, ɪ'bʊlɪəns/ *n.* Überschwänglichkeit, *die;* **~ of youth** jugendlicher Überschwang

**ebullient** /ɪ'bʌlɪənt, ɪ'bʊlɪənt/ *adj.* (*exuberant*) überschwänglich; übersprudelnd, überschäumend ‹Temperament, Laune›

**EC** *abbr.* **European Community** EG

**eccentric** /ɪk'sentrɪk/ ❶ *adj.* Ⓐ (*odd, whimsical*) exzentrisch ‹Person›; (*differing from the usual*) ausgefallen, ungewöhnlich ‹Person›; Ⓑ (*not placed centrally, irregular*) exzentrisch; einseitig ‹Belastung›. ❷ *n.* Exzentriker, *der*/Exzentrikerin, *die*

**eccentrically** /ɪk'sentrɪkəlɪ/ *adv.* exzentrisch

**eccentricity** /eksən'trɪsɪtɪ/ *n.* Exzentrizität, *die*

**Eccles cake** /'eklz keɪk/ *n.* (*Brit.*) *rundes Rosinengebäck*

**Ecclesiastes** /ɪkli:zɪ'æsti:z/ *n.* (*Bibl.*) Ekklesiastes, *der;* Prediger Salomo

**ecclesiastic** /ɪkli:zɪ'æstɪk/ *n.* Kleriker, *der*/Klerikerin, *die;* Geistliche, *der/die*

**ecclesiastical** /ɪkli:zɪ'æstɪkl/ *adj.* kirchlich; Kirchen‹recht, -amt, -jahr›; **~ music** geistliche Musik; Kirchenmusik, *die*

**ECG** *abbr.* **electrocardiogram** EKG

**echelon** /'eʃəlɒn, 'eɪʃəlɒn/ *n.* Ⓐ (*of troops*) Echelon, *der;* Staffelstellung, *die;* **in ~:** in Staffelstellung; Ⓑ (*of ships, aircraft, etc.*) Staffel, *die;* **in ~:** in staffelförmiger Formation; Ⓒ (*group in an organization*) Stab, *der;* **the lower ~s** die niedrigeren Ränge; ⇒ *also* **upper** 1 B

**echinoderm** /ɪ'kaɪnədɜ:m, 'ekɪnədɜ:m/ *n.* (*Zool.*) Echinoderme, *der* (*fachspr.*); Stachelhäuter, *der*

**echo** /'ekəʊ/ ❶ *n., pl.* **~es** Ⓐ Echo, *das;* **cheer sb. to the ~:** jmdn. begeistert *od.* stürmisch feiern; Ⓑ (*fig.*) Anklang, *der* (**of** an + *Akk.*). ❷ *v.i.* Ⓐ ‹Ort:› hallen (**with** von); **it ~es in here** hier gibt es ein Echo; Ⓑ (*Geräusch:*) widerhallen. ❸ *v.t.* Ⓐ (*repeat*) zurückwerfen; Ⓑ (*repeat words of*) echoen; wiederholen; (*imitate words or opinions of*) widerspiegeln

**éclair** /'eɪkleə(r), eɪ'kleə(r)/ *n.* Eclair, *das*

**eclectic** /ɪ'klektɪk/ ❶ *adj.* eklektisch. ❷ *n.* Eklektiker, *der*

**eclipse** /ɪ'klɪps/ ❶ *n.* Ⓐ (*Astron.*) Eklipse, *die* (*fachspr.*); Finsternis, *die;* **~ of the sun, solar ~:** Sonnenfinsternis, *die;* **~ of the moon, lunar ~:** Mondfinsternis, *die;* **in ~:** verfinstert; Ⓑ (*deprivation of light*) Dunkelheit, *die;* Finsternis, *die;* Ⓒ (*fig.*) Niedergang, *der;* **his fame suffered a total ~:** sein Ruhm verblasste völlig; **in ~:** im Dunkel. ❷ *v.t.* Ⓐ verfinstern ‹Sonne, Mond›; Ⓑ (*fig.: outshine, surpass*) in den Schatten stellen

**ecliptic** /ɪ'klɪptɪk/ *n.* (*Astron.*) Ekliptik, *die*

**eco-** /'i:kəʊ/ *in comb.* öko-/Öko-

'**eco-audit** *n.* Ökoaudit, *das*

'**eco-friendly** *adj.* umweltfreundlich

**ecological** /i:kə'lɒdʒɪkl/ *adj.* ökologisch

**ecologist** /i:'kɒlədʒɪst/ *n.* Ökologe, *der*/Ökologin, *die*

**ecology** /i:'kɒlədʒɪ/ *n.* Ökologie, *die*

**e-commerce** /i:'kɒmɜ:s/ *n.* (*Computing*) elektronischer Handel; E-Commerce, *der*

**economic** /i:kə'nɒmɪk, ekə'nɒmɪk/ *adj.* Ⓐ (*of economics*) Wirtschafts‹politik, -abkommen, -system, -modell›; ökonomisch, wirtschaftlich ‹Entwicklung, Zusammenbruch›; **~ cycle** Konjunkturzyklus, *der;* Konjunkturablauf, *der;* Ⓑ (*giving adequate return*) wirtschaftlich ‹Miete›; Ⓒ (*maintained for profit*) wirtschaftlich; Gewinn bringend

**economical** /i:kə'nɒmɪkl, ekə'nɒmɪkl/ *adj.* wirtschaftlich; ökonomisch; sparsam ‹Person›; **be ~ with sth.** mit etw. haushalten; **the car is ~ to run** das Auto ist wirtschaftlich; **~ use of words** knappe Ausdrucksweise

**economically** /i:kə'nɒmɪkəlɪ, ekə'nɒmɪkəlɪ/ *adv.* Ⓐ (*with reference to economics*) wirtschaftlich; Ⓑ (*not wastefully*) sparsam; **be ~ minded** wirtschaftlich denken

**economics** /i:kə'nɒmɪks, ekə'nɒmɪks/ *n., no pl.* Ⓐ Wirtschaftswissenschaft, *die* (*meist Pl.*); [politische] Ökonomie; Ⓑ (*economic considerations*) wirtschaftlicher Aspekt; **the ~ of the situation** die wirtschaftliche *od.* finanzielle Seite der Situation; Ⓒ (*condition of a country*) Wirtschaft, *die*

**economise** ⇒ **economize**

**economist** /ɪ'kɒnəmɪst/ *n.* ▶ **1261** Wirtschaftswissenschaftler, *der*/-wissenschaftlerin, *die;* **political ~:** Wirtschaftspolitiker, *der*/-politikerin, *die*

**economize** /ɪ'kɒnəmaɪz/ *v.i.* sparen; **~ on sth.** etw. sparen

**economy** /ɪ'kɒnəmɪ/ *n.* Ⓐ (*frugality*) Sparsamkeit, *die;* (*of effort, motion*) Wirtschaftlichkeit, *die;* (*of style*) Kürze, *die;* Knappheit, *die;* Ⓑ (*instance*) Einsparung, *die;* **make economies** zu Sparmaßnahmen greifen; Ⓒ (*of country etc.*) Wirtschaft, *die*

**economy: ~ class** *n.* Touristenklasse, *die;* Economyklasse, *die;* **~ size** *n.* Haushaltspackung, *die;* Sparpackung, *die;* **an ~-size packet of salt** eine Haushaltspackung Salz

**eco: ~system** *n.* Ökosystem, *das;* **~-tax** *n.* Ökosteuer, *die*

**ecstasy** /'ekstəsɪ/ Ⓐ *n.* Ekstase, *die;* Verzückung, *die;* **be in/go into ecstasies [over sth.]** in Ekstase [über etw. (*Akk.*)] sein/geraten; Ⓑ **E~** (*drug*) Ecstasy, *das*

**ecstatic** /ɪk'stætɪk/ *adj.*, **ecstatically** /ɪk'stætɪkəlɪ/ *adv.* ekstatisch; verzückt

**ECT** *abbr.* **electroconvulsive therapy** EKT

**ectopic** /ek'tɒpɪk/ *adj.* (*Med.*) **~ pregnancy** ektopische Schwangerschaft; (*tubal pregnancy*) Eileiterschwangerschaft, *die*

**ECU, ecu** /'eɪkju:/ *abbr.* ▶ **1328** **European currency unit** Ecu, *der od. die*

**Ecuador** /ekwa'dɔ:(r)/ *pr. n.* Ekuador (*das*)

**Ecuadorean** /ekwə'dɔ:rɪən/ ▶ **1340** ❶ *adj.* ecuadorianisch; **sb. is ~:** jmd. ist Ecuadorianer/Ecuadorianerin. ❷ *n.* Ecuadorianer, *der*/Ecuadorianerin, *die*

**ecumenical** /i:kjʊ'menɪkl, ekjʊ'menɪkl/ *adj.* Ⓐ (*Relig.*) ökumenisch; **E~ Council** ökumenisches Konzil; Ⓑ (*worldwide*) [welt]umfassend; [welt]umspannend

**ecumenicalism** /i:kjʊ'menɪkəlɪzm, ekjʊ'menɪkəlɪzm/ *n.* (*Relig.*) ökumenische Bewegung; Ökumenismus, *der* (*kath. Kirche*)

**eczema** /'eksɪmə, 'ekzɪmə/ *n.* ▶ **1232** (*Med.*) Ekzem, *das* (*fachspr.*); Hautausschlag, *der*

**ed.** *abbr.* Ⓐ **edited [by]** hg.; hrsg.; Ⓑ **edition** Ausg.; Ⓒ **editor** Hrsg.; Ⓓ **editor's note** Anm. d. Hrsg.; (*in newspaper*) Anm. d. Red.

**Edam** /'i:dæm/ *n.* Edamer [Käse], *der*

**eddy** /'edɪ/ ❶ *n.* Ⓐ (*whirlpool*) Strudel, *der;* Ⓑ (*of wind, fog, smoke*) Wirbel, *der;* **eddies of dust** Staubwirbel *Pl.* ❷ *v.i.* ‹Blätter:› wirbeln; ‹Wasser:› sprudeln

**edelweiss** /'eɪdlvaɪs/ *n.* Edelweiß, *das*

**edema** (*Amer.*) ⇒ **oedema**

**Eden** /'i:dn/ *n.* Eden (*das*); (*fig.*) Paradies, *das;* **the Garden of ~:** der Garten Eden

**edge** /edʒ/ ❶ *n.* Ⓐ (*of knife, razor, weapon*) Schneide, *die;* (*sharpness*) Schärfe, *die;* (*fig.: effectiveness*) Schärfe, *die;* Beißende, *das;* Schneidende, *das;* **the knife has lost its ~/has no ~:** das Messer ist stumpf geworden *od.* ist nicht mehr scharf/ist stumpf *od.* schneidet nicht; **take the ~ off sth.** etw. stumpf machen; (*fig.*) etw. abschwächen; **that took the ~ off our hunger** das nahm uns erst einmal den Hunger; **be on ~ [about sth.]** [wegen etw.] nervös *od.* gereizt sein; **her nerves have been all on ~ lately** in letzter Zeit ist sie schrecklich nervös; **set sb.'s teeth on ~:** jmdn. nervös machen; **give sb. the rough** *or* **sharp ~ of one's tongue** jmdm. gehörig Bescheid sagen (*ugs.*); **have/get the ~ [on sb./sth.]** (*coll.*) jmdm./einer Sache überlegen *od.* (*ugs.*) über sein/jmdn./etw. übertreffen; Ⓑ (*of solid, bed, brick, record, piece of cloth*) Kante, *die;* (*of dress*) Saum, *der;* **~ of a table** Tischkante, *die;* **roll off the ~ of the table** vom Tisch hinunterrollen; **a book with gilt ~s** ein Buch mit Goldschnitt; Ⓒ (*boundary*) (*of sheet of paper, road, forest, desert, cliff*) Rand, *der;* (*of sea, lake, river*) Ufer, *das;* (*of estate*) Grenze, *die;* **~ of the paper/of a road** Papierrand, *der*/Straßenrand, *der;* **platform ~:** Bahnsteigkante, *die;* **the ~ of the kerb** die Bordsteinkante; **at the ~ of a precipice** am Rande eines Abgrundes; **fall off the ~ of the cliff** die Klippe hinunterfallen; **on the ~ of sth.** (*fig.*) am Rande einer Sache (*Gen.*); **be on the ~ of disaster/bankruptcy** am Rande des Untergangs/Bankrotts stehen; **go over the ~** (*fig. coll.*) verrückt werden (*salopp*).
❷ *v.i.* (*move cautiously*) sich schieben; **~ along sth.** sich an etw. (*Dat.*) entlangschieben; **~ away** sich davonstehlen; sich wegschleichen; **~ away from sb./sth.** sich allmählich von jmdm./etw. entfernen; **~ up to sb.** sich an jmdn. heranmachen (*ugs.*); **~ out of the room** sich aus dem Zimmer stehlen.
❸ *v.t.* Ⓐ (*furnish with border*) säumen ‹Straße, Platz›; besetzen ‹Kleid, Hut›; einfassen ‹Garten, Straße›; **~ with fur** mit Pelz verbrämen ‹Kragen›; Ⓑ (*push gradually*) [langsam] schieben; **~ oneself** *or* **one's way through a crowd** sich [langsam] durch eine Menschenmenge schieben *od.* drängen; **he ~d his chair nearer to the fire** er rückte mit seinem Stuhl etwas näher ans Feuer; Ⓒ (*Cricket*) mit der Kante des Schlägers schlagen ‹Ball›

**edged** /edʒd/ *adj.* mit einer Schneide versehen; **an ~ blade/tool** eine scharfe Klinge/ein Werkzeug mit einer Schneide; **double-** *or* **two-~ blade** zweischneidige Klinge; **sharp-/dull-~:** scharf/stumpf; **black-/rough-~:** schwarzrandig/mit einem unebenen Rand

**edgeways** /'edʒweɪz/, **edgewise** /'edʒwaɪz/ *adv.* Ⓐ (*with edge uppermost or foremost*) mit der Schmalseite voran; **stand sth. ~:** etw. hochkant stellen; Ⓑ (*edge to edge*) Kante an Kante; Ⓒ (*fig.*) **I can't get a word in ~!** ich komme überhaupt nicht zu Wort!

**edging** /'edʒɪŋ/ *n.* (*border, fringe*) (*of dress*) Borte, *die;* (*of lawn, garden, flower bed*) Einfassung, *die;* (*lace, ribbon*) Paspel, *die;* **fur ~:** Pelzbesatz, *der*

'**edging shears** *n. pl.* Kantenschneider, *der*

**edgy** /'edʒɪ/ *adj.* nervös

**edible** /'edɪbl/ ❶ *adj.* essbar; genießbar. ❷ *n. in pl.* Nahrungsmittel *Pl.;* Lebensmittel *Pl.*

**edict** /'i:dɪkt/ *n.* Erlass, *der;* Edikt, *das* (*hist.*)

**edification** /edɪfɪ'keɪʃn/ *n.* Erbauung, *die;* **for the ~ of ...:** zur Erbauung (+ *Gen.*)

**edifice** /'edɪfɪs/ *n.* Gebäude, *das;* (*fig.*) Gefüge, *das;* Gebäude, *das*

**edifying** /'edɪfaɪɪŋ/ *adj.* erbaulich

**Edinburgh** /'edɪnbərə/ ▶ **1626** ❶ *pr. n.* Edinburgh (*das*); Edinburg (*das*). ❷ *attrib. adj.* Edinburger

**edit** /'edɪt/ *v.t.* Ⓐ (*act as editor of*) herausgeben ‹Zeitung›; Ⓑ (*prepare for publication*) redigieren ‹Buch, Artikel, Manuskript›; Ⓒ (*prepare an edition of*) bearbeiten; **~ the works of Homer** die Werke Homers neu herausgeben; Ⓓ (*take extracts from and collate*)

schneiden, cutten, montieren ‹Film, Bandaufnahme›; Ⓔ ~ sth. **out** etw. weglassen
**edition** /ɪ'dɪʃn/ *n.* Ⓐ (*form of work, one copy; also fig.*) Ausgabe, *die;* **paperback** ~: Taschenbuchausgabe, *die;* **first** ~: Erstausgabe, *die;* **he is a second** ~ **of his father** er gleicht seinem Vater aufs Haar; Ⓑ (*from same types or at one time*) Auflage, *die;* **the book is in its fourth** ~: das Buch erscheint in seiner vierten Auflage; **the work has already gone through six** ~**s** das Werk erscheint schon in der sechsten Auflage; **morning/evening** ~ **of a newspaper** Morgen-/Abendausgabe einer Zeitung
**editor** /'edɪtə(r)/ *n.* ▶ 1261 Ⓐ (*who prepares the work of others*) Redakteur, *der*/Redakteurin, *die;* (*of particular work*) Bearbeiter, *der*/Bearbeiterin, *die;* (*scholarly*) Herausgeber, *der*/-geberin, *die;* Ⓑ (*who conducts a newspaper or periodical*) Herausgeber, *der*/-geberin, *die;* **chief/sports/business** ~: Chef-/Sport-/Wirtschaftsredakteur, *der;* Ⓒ (*of films etc.*) Cutter, *der*/Cutterin, *die*
**editorial** /edɪ'tɔ:rɪəl/ ❶ *n.* Leitartikel, *der.* ❷ *adj.* (*of an editor*) redaktionell; Redaktions‹assistent›; ~ **staff** Redaktion[sangestellte *Pl.*], *die;* ~ **department** Redaktion, *die;* ~ **job/work** Lektorenstelle, *die*/Lektorentätigkeit, *die;* ~ **article** Leitartikel, *der*
**editorship** /'edɪtəʃɪp/ *n.* Chefredaktion, *die;* Schriftleitung, *die;* **under the [general]** ~ **of Mr X** unter Herrn X als Herausgeber
**EDP** *abbr.* **electronic data processing** EDV
**EDT** *abbr.* (*Amer.*) **Eastern Daylight Time** östliche Sommerzeit
**educable** /'edjʊkəbl/ *adj.* erziehbar
**educate** /'edjʊkeɪt/ *v.t.* Ⓐ (*bring up*) erziehen; ~ **sb. in sth.** jmdm. etw. beibringen; Ⓑ (*provide schooling for*) **he was** ~**d at Eton and Cambridge** er hat seine Ausbildung in Eton und Cambridge erhalten; Ⓒ (*give intellectual and moral training to*) bilden; ~ **oneself** sich [weiter]bilden; **the public must be** ~**d how to save energy** die Öffentlichkeit muss aufgeklärt werden, wie man Energie spart; Ⓓ (*train*) schulen ‹Geist, Körper›; [aus]bilden ‹Geschmack›; dressieren, abrichten ‹Tier›; ~ **oneself to do sth.** sich dazu erziehen, etw. zu tun
**educated** /'edjʊkeɪtɪd/ *adj.* gebildet; **make an** ~ **guess** eine wohl begründete Vermutung anstellen
**education** /edjʊ'keɪʃn/ *n.* Ⓐ (*instruction*) Erziehung, *die;* (*course of instruction*) Ausbildung, *die;* (*system*) Erziehungs[- und Ausbildungs]wesen, *das;* (*science*) Erziehungswissenschaften *Pl.;* Pädagogik, *die;* ~ **is free** die Schulausbildung ist kostenlos; **Ministry of E**~: Ministerium für Erziehung und Unterricht; Kultusministerium, *das;* **be a man of** ~: ein gebildeter Mensch sein; **receive a good** ~: eine gute Ausbildung genießen; **sb. with school/a higher/university** ~: jmd. mit Schulbildung/mit einer höheren Schulbildung/Universitätsausbildung; **literary/scientific** ~: literarische/naturwissenschaftliche Bildung; **lecturer in** ~: Dozent/Dozentin für Pädagogik; **science/methods of** ~: Erziehungswissenschaften *Pl.*/-methoden *Pl.;* Ⓑ (*development of character or mental powers*) Schulung, *die.* ⇒ *also* **College of Education**
**educational** /edjʊ'keɪʃənl/ *adj.* pädagogisch; erzieherisch; Lehr‹film, -spiele, -anstalt›; Erziehungs‹methoden, -arbeit›; ~ **equipment** Unterrichtsmittel *Pl.;* **for** ~ **purposes** zu Lehr- *od.* Unterrichtszwecken
**educationalist** /edjʊ'keɪʃənəlɪst/ *n.* Pädagoge, *der*/Pädagogin, *die;* Erziehungswissenschaftler, *der*/-wissenschaftlerin, *die*
**educationally** /edjʊ'keɪʃənəlɪ/ *adv.* pädagogisch; ~ **subnormal** lernbehindert; **be** ~ **backward** ein niedriges Bildungsniveau haben
**educationist** /edjʊ'keɪʃənɪst/ ⇒ **educationalist**
**educative** /'edjʊkətɪv/ *adj.* (*educational*) erzieherisch, pädagogisch ‹Fragen, Gründe›; (*instructive*) erzieherisch; Erziehungs-; lehrreich ‹Film, Buch›
**educator** /'edjʊkeɪtə(r)/ *n.* Pädagoge, *der*/Pädagogin, *die;* Erzieher, *der*/Erzieherin, *die;* (*fig.*) Erzieher, *der*
**Edward** /'edwəd/ *pr. n.* (*Hist., as name of ruler etc.*) Eduard (*der*)
**Edwardian** /ed'wɔ:dɪən/ ❶ *adj.* edwardianisch. ❷ *n.* Edwardianer, *der*
**EEC** *abbr.* **European Economic Community** EWG
**eel** /i:l/ *n.* Aal, *der;* **be as slippery as an** ~: aalglatt sein
**e'en** /i:n/ (*arch./poet.*) ⇒ **even**[1,2]
**e'er** /eə(r)/ (*poet.*) ⇒ **ever**
**eerie** /'ɪərɪ/ *adj.* unheimlich ‹Ort, Gebäude, Form›; schaurig ‹Klang›; schauerlich ‹Schrei›; **give sb. an** ~ **feeling** jmdn. schaudern lassen
**eerily** /'ɪərɪlɪ/ *adv.* ⇒ **eerie**: unheimlich; schaurig
**eff** /ef/ *v.i.* (*sl.*) ~ **and blind** fluchen
**efface** /ɪ'feɪs/ ❶ *v.t.* Ⓐ (*rub out*) beseitigen ‹Inschrift›; Ⓑ (*fig.: obliterate*) auslöschen; tilgen (*geh.*). ❷ *v. refl.* sich im Hintergrund halten
**effect** /ɪ'fekt/ ❶ *n.* Ⓐ (*result*) Wirkung, *die* (**on** auf + *Akk.*); **her words had little** ~ **on him** ihre Worte erzielten bei ihm nur eine geringe Wirkung; **the** ~**s of sth. on sth.** die Auswirkungen einer Sache (*Gen.*) auf etw. (*Akk.*); die Folgen einer Sache (*Gen.*) für etw.; **the** ~ **of this was that ...:** das hatte zur Folge, dass ...; **be of no** *or* **to no** ~: erfolglos *od.* ergebnislos sein; **with the** ~ **that ...:** mit der Folge *od.* dem Resultat, dass ...; **take** ~: wirken; die erwünschte Wirkung erzielen; **in** ~: in Wirklichkeit; praktisch; Ⓑ *no art.* (*impression*) Wirkung, *die;* Effekt, *der;* **solely** *or* **only for** ~: nur des Effekts wegen; aus reiner Effekthascherei (*abwertend*); Ⓒ (*meaning*) Inhalt, *der;* Sinn, *der;* **or words to that** ~: oder etwas in diesem Sinne; **a letter to the following** ~: ein Brief folgenden Inhalts; **we received a letter to the** ~ **that ...:** wir erhielten ein Schreiben des Inhalts, dass ...; **all families received instructions to that** ~: alle Familien bekamen entsprechende Anweisungen; **to the same** ~: desselben Inhalts; Ⓓ (*operativeness*) Kraft, *die;* Gültigkeit, *die;* **be in** ~: gültig *od.* in Kraft sein; **come into** ~: gültig *od.* wirksam werden; ‹bes. Gesetz:› in Kraft treten; **bring** *or* **carry** *or* **put into** ~: in Kraft setzen ‹Gesetz›; verwirklichen ‹Plan›; verwerten ‹Erfahrung, Kenntnisse›; **give** ~ **to sth.** etw. in Kraft treten lassen; **take** ~: in Kraft treten; **with** ~ **from 2 November/Monday** mit Wirkung vom 2. November/von Montag; Ⓔ *in pl.* (*in play, film, broadcast*) **light** ~**s** Lichteffekte *Pl.;* Ⓕ *in pl.* (*property*) Vermögenswerte *Pl.;* Eigentum, *das;* **personal** ~**s** persönliches Eigentum; Privateigentum, *das;* **household** ~**s** Hausrat, *der.*
❷ *v.t.* durchführen; herbeiführen ‹Einigung›; erzielen ‹Übereinstimmung, Übereinkommen›; tätigen ‹Umsatz, Kauf›; abschließen ‹Versicherung›; leisten ‹Zahlung›; ~ **one's purpose** *or* **intention/desire** seine Absicht verwirklichen *od.* in die Tat umsetzen/sich (*Dat.*) einen Wunsch erfüllen; **payment was** ~**ed in dollars** die Zahlung erfolgte in Dollar
**effective** /ɪ'fektɪv/ *adj.* Ⓐ (*having an effect*) wirksam ‹Mittel›; effektiv ‹Maßnahmen›; gleichwertig ‹Ersatz›; **the measures have not been** ~: die Maßnahmen blieben ohne Wirkung *od.* waren wirkungslos; **be** ~ ‹Arzneimittel:› wirken; Ⓑ (*having come into operation*) gültig; ~ **from/as of** mit Wirkung von; **the law is no longer** ~**/is** ~ **as from 1 September** das Gesetz hat keine Gültigkeit mehr *od.* ist außer Kraft/tritt ab 1. September in Kraft *od.* wird ab 1. September wirksam; Ⓒ (*powerful in effect*) überzeugend ‹Rede, Redner, Worte›; kraftvoll ‹Stimme›; Ⓓ (*striking*) wirkungsvoll; effektvoll; Ⓔ (*existing*) wirklich, tatsächlich ‹Hilfe›; effektiv ‹Gewinn, Umsatz›; **the** ~ **strength of the army** die Iststärke der Armee
**effectively** /ɪ'fektɪvlɪ/ *adv.* (*in fact*) effektiv; (*with effect*) wirkungsvoll; effektvoll; **they are** ~ **the same** effektiv sind sie gleich
**effectiveness** /ɪ'fektɪvnɪs/ *n., no pl.* Wirksamkeit, *die;* Effektivität, *die*
**effectual** /ɪ'fektjʊəl/ *adj.* Ⓐ (*sufficient*) wirksam ‹Mittel, Maßnahmen›; Ⓑ (*valid*) [rechts]gültig, bindend ‹Vertrag, Dokument›
**effectually** /ɪ'fektjʊəlɪ/ *adv.* erfolgreich
**effectuate** /ɪ'fektjʊeɪt/ *v.t.* bewirken; herbeiführen ‹Änderung›; erzielen ‹Übereinstimmung›
**effeminate** /ɪ'femɪnət/ *adj.* unmännlich, (*geh.*) effeminiert ‹Mann›
**effervesce** /efə'ves/ *v.i.* sprudeln; effervészieren (*fachspr.*); (*fig.*) übersprudeln; überschäumen; **be effervescing with sth.** vor etw. übersprudeln *od.* überschäumen
**effervescence** /efə'vesəns/ *n., no pl.* Sprudeln, *das;* (*fig.*) Übersprudeln, *das;* Überschäumen, *das*
**effervescent** /efə'vesənt/ *adj.* sprudelnd; (*fig.*) übersprudelnd, überschäumend ‹Freude, Verhalten›; überschwänglich ‹Stimme›; ~ **tablets** Brausetabletten
**effete** /e'fi:t/ *adj.* (*exhausted, worn out*) verbraucht; saft- und kraftlos ‹Person›; überlebt ‹System›; (*soft, decadent*) verweichlicht
**efficacious** /efɪ'keɪʃəs/ *adj.* wirksam ‹Methode, Mittel, Medizin›
**efficaciousness** /efɪ'keɪʃəsnɪs/, **efficacy** /'efɪkəsɪ/ *ns., no pl.* Wirksamkeit, *die*
**efficiency** /ɪ'fɪʃənsɪ/ *n.* Ⓐ (*of person*) Fähigkeit, *die;* Tüchtigkeit, *die;* (*of machine, engine, factory*) Leistungsfähigkeit, *die;* (*of organization, method*) gutes Funktionieren; Ⓑ (*Mech., Phys.*) Wirkungsgrad, *der*
**efficient** /ɪ'fɪʃənt/ *adj.* fähig ‹Person›; tüchtig ‹Arbeiter, Sekretärin›; leistungsfähig ‹Maschine, Motor, Fabrik›; gut funktionierend ‹Methode, Organisation›
**efficiently** /ɪ'fɪʃəntlɪ/ *adv.* gut; effizient (*geh.*)
**effigy** /'efɪdʒɪ/ *n.* Bildnis, *das;* **hang/burn sb. in** ~: jmdn. in effigie hängen/verbrennen (*geh.*)
**effing** /'efɪŋ/ *adj.* (*sl.*) Scheiß- (*salopp*)
**effluent** /'eflʊənt/ ❶ *adj.* abfließend ‹Fluss, Wasser›; ~ **drain** Abfluss, *der.* ❷ *n.* Ⓐ (*stream*) Abfluss, *der;* Ⓑ (*outflow from sewage tank, waste etc.*) Abwässer *Pl.*
**effluvium** /e'flu:vɪəm/ *n., pl.* **effluvia** /e'flu:vɪə/ Ausdünstung, *die*
**effort** /'efət/ *n.* Ⓐ (*exertion*) Anstrengung, *die;* Mühe, *die;* **make an/every** ~ (*physically*) sich anstrengen; (*mentally*) sich bemühen; **without [any]/only with the greatest** ~: ohne Anstrengung *od.* mühelos/nur mit äußerster Anstrengung *od.* größter Mühe; **for all his** ~**s** trotz all seiner Bemühungen; **vain** ~**s** vergebliche Bemühungen; **it is an** ~ **[for me] to get up in the mornings** es kostet [mich] einige Mühe *od.* Anstrengung, morgens aufzustehen; **[a] waste of time and** ~: verlorene *od.* vergebliche Liebesmüh; **make every possible** ~ **to do sth.** jede nur mögliche Anstrengung unternehmen *od.* machen, etw. zu tun; **he makes no** ~ **at all** er bemüht sich überhaupt nicht; er gibt sich überhaupt keine Mühe; Ⓑ (*attempt*) Versuch, *der;* **in an** ~ **to do sth.** beim Versuch, etw. zu tun; **make no** ~ **to be polite** sich (*Dat.*) nicht die Mühe machen, höflich zu sein; **make one last** ~**s**: einen letzten Versuch unternehmen; ~**s are being made to do sth.** es sind Bestrebungen im Gange, etw. zu tun; Ⓒ (*activity*) **research** ~**[s]** Einsatz in der Forschungsarbeit; **business** ~**s** geschäftliche Unternehmungen; Ⓓ (*coll.: result*) Leistung, *die;* **that was a pretty poor** ~: das war ein ziemlich schwaches Bild (*ugs.*); **whose is this rather poor** ~**?** welcher Stümper hat das denn verbrochen? (*ugs.*); **the book was one of his first** ~**s** das Buch war einer seiner ersten Versuche
**effortless** /'efətlɪs/ *adj.* mühelos; leicht; flüssig, leicht ‹Stil›
**effortlessly** /'efətlɪslɪ/ *adv.* mühelos; ohne Anstrengung; flüssig ‹schreiben›
**effrontery** /ɪ'frʌntərɪ/ *n.* Dreistigkeit, *die;* **have the** ~ **to do sth.** die Frechheit *od.* (*geh.*) Stirn besitzen, etw. zu tun
**effusion** /ɪ'fju:ʒn/ *n.* Ⓐ (*pouring forth*) (*of light, sound*) Ausströmen, *das;* Entströmen,

e

e

das; (*of the Holy Spirit*) Ausgießung, *die;* Ⓑ (*utterance*) Überschwang, *der;* **literary/romantic ~s** literarische/romantische Ergüsse

**effusive** /ɪˈfjuːsɪv/ *adj.* überschwänglich; exaltiert (*geh.*) ‹Person, Stil, Charakter›

**effusively** /ɪˈfjuːsɪvlɪ/ *adv.* ⇒ **effusive**: überschwänglich; exaltiert (*geh.*)

**effusiveness** /ɪˈfjuːsɪvnɪs/ *n., no pl.* (*of speech, action, greeting*) Überschwänglichkeit, *die;* (*of style*) Exaltiertheit, *die* (*geh.*)

**EFL** *abbr.* **English as a foreign language**

**Efta, EFTA** /ˈeftə/ *n. abbr.* **European Free Trade Association** EFTA

**e.g.** /iːˈdʒiː/ *abbr.* **for example** z. B.

**egalitarian** /ɪgælɪˈteərɪən/ ❶ *adj.* egalitär (*geh.*) ‹Person, Einstellung, Gruppe›; Gleichheits‹prinzipien›. ❷ *n.* Verfechter/Verfechterin des Egalitarismus

**egg**[1] /eg/ *n.* Ei, *das;* **a bad ~** (*fig. coll.*) (*person*) eine üble Person; **a good/tough ~** (*coll.*) (*person*) ein feiner *od.* (*veralt.*) famoser/harter Kerl (*ugs.*); **good ~!** (*dated coll.*) famos! (*veralt.*); **have** *or* **put all one's ~s in one basket** (*fig. coll.*) alles auf eine Karte setzen; **it's like teaching your grandmother to suck ~s** da will das Ei wieder klüger sein als die Henne; **as sure as ~s is** *or* **are ~s** (*coll.*) so sicher wie das Amen in der Kirche (*ugs.*); **have ~ on** *or* **all over one's face** (*fig.*) dumm *od.* blöd dastehen (*ugs.*); dumm aus der Wäsche gucken (*salopp*)

**egg**[2] *v.t.* **~ sb. on [to do sth.]** jmdn. anstacheln *od.* aufhetzen[, etw. zu tun]

**egg: ~-and-ˈspoon race** Eierlaufen, *das;* **~ beater** *n.* Ⓐ (*device*) Rührbesen, *der;* Ⓑ (*Amer. coll.: helicopter*) Hubschrauber, *der;* **~ cosy** *n.* (*Brit.*) Eierwärmer, *der;* **~cup** *n.* Eierbecher, *der;* **~ ˈcustard** *n.* Eierkrem, *die;* **~ ˈflip** *n.* Eierlikör, *der;* **~head** *n.* (*coll.*) Eierkopf, *der* (*abwertend*); Egghead, *der* (*geh. oft scherzhaft od. abwertend*); **~ ˈnog** ⇒ **~ flip**; **~plant** *n.* Aubergine, *die;* (*fruit also*) Eierfrucht, *die;* (*plant also*) Eierpflanze, *die;* **~ powder** *n.* Eipulver, *das;* **~-shaped** *adj.* eiförmig; **~shell** *n.* Ⓐ Eierschale, *die;* Ⓑ *attrib.* (*fragile*) **~shell china** Eierschalenporzellan, *das;* **~shell glaze** Mittelglanzglasur, *die;* **~ slice** *n.* ≈ Wender, *der;* **~ spoon** *n.* Eierlöffel, *der;* **~ timer** *n.* Eieruhr, *die;* **~ whisk** *n.* Schneebesen, *der;* **~ white** *n.* Eiweiß, *das;* **~ yolk** *n.* Eigelb, *das;* Eidotter, *der od. das*

**EGM** *abbr.* **extraordinary general meeting** aoHV, ao.HV (*außerordentliche Hauptversammlung*); (*of club*) aoMV, ao.MV (*außerordentliche Mitgliederversammlung*)

**ego** /ˈegəʊ, ˈiːgəʊ/ *n., pl.* **~s** Ⓐ (*Psych.*) Ego, *das;* (*Metaphys.*) Ich, *das;* Ⓑ (*self-esteem*) Selbstbewusstsein, *das;* **inflated ~:** übersteigertes Selbstbewusstsein; **boost sb.'s ~:** jmds. Selbstbewusstsein stärken; jmdm. Auftrieb geben

**egocentric** /egəʊˈsentrɪk/ *adj.* egozentrisch; ichbezogen

**egoism** /ˈegəʊɪzm/ *n., no pl.* Ⓐ (*systematic selfishness*) Egoismus, *der;* Selbstsucht, *die* (*abwertend*); Ⓑ (*self-opinionatedness*) Selbstherrlichkeit, *die;* Ⓒ ⇒ **egotism** A

**egoist** /ˈegəʊɪst/ *n.* Egoist, *der*/Egoistin, *die*

**egoistic** /egəʊˈɪstɪk/, **egoistical** /egəʊˈɪstɪkl/ *adj.* Ⓐ (*self-regarding, selfish*) egoistisch; selbstsüchtig; eigennützig; Ⓑ ⇒ **egotistic** A

**egomania** /iːgəʊˈmeɪnɪə/ *n.* Egomanie, *die*

**egomaniac** /iːgəʊˈmeɪnɪæk/ *n.* Egomane, *der*/Egomanin, *die*

**egotism** /ˈegətɪzm/ *n., no pl.* Ⓐ Egotismus, *der* (*fachspr.*); Ichbezogenheit, *die;* Ⓑ (*self-conceit*) Egotismus, *der;* Selbstgefälligkeit, *die;* Ⓒ ⇒ **egoism** A

**egotist** /ˈegətɪst/ *n.* Egotist, *der*/Egotistin, *die* (*fachspr.*); (*self-centred person*) Egozentriker, *der*/Egozentrikerin, *die*

**egotistic** /egəˈtɪstɪk/, **egotistical** /egəˈtɪstɪkl/ *adj.* Ⓐ ichbezogen ‹Rede, Gespräch›; Ⓑ selbstsüchtig, selbstgefällig (*abwertend*) ‹Person›

**egregious** /ɪˈgriːdʒəs/ *adj.* ungeheuer[lich]; ausgemacht ‹Trottel›

**egress** /ˈiːgres/ *n.* (*formal*) Ausgang, *der* (**to, into** zu)

**egret** /ˈiːgrɪt, ˈegrɪt/ *n.* (*Ornith.*) Reiher, *der*

**Egypt** /ˈiːdʒɪpt/ *pr. n.* Ägypten (*das*)

**Egyptian** /ɪˈdʒɪpʃn/ ▶1275, ▶1340 ❶ *adj.* ägyptisch; **sb. is ~:** jmd. ist Ägypter/Ägypterin; ⇒ *also* **English** 1. ❷ *n.* Ⓐ (*person*) Ägypter, *der*/Ägypterin, *die;* Ⓑ (*language*) Ägyptisch, *das;* ⇒ *also* **English** 2 A

**Egyptologist** /iːdʒɪpˈtɒlədʒɪst/ *n.* Ägyptologe, *der*/Ägyptologin, *die*

**Egyptology** /iːdʒɪpˈtɒlədʒɪ/ *n., no pl.* Ägyptologie, *die*

**eh** /eɪ/ *int.* (*coll.*) *expr. inquiry or surprise* wie?; wie bitte?; *inviting assent* nicht [wahr]?; *asking for sth. to be repeated or explained* was?; hä? (*salopp*); **wasn't that good, eh?** war das nicht gut?; **let's not have any more fuss, eh?** Schluss mit dem Theater, ja? (*ugs.*)

**eider**/ˈaɪdə(r)/: **~ [duck]** *n.* Eiderente, *die;* **~ [down]** *n.* [Eider]daunen *Pl.;* Flaumfedern *Pl.*

**eiderdown** /ˈaɪdədaʊn/ *n.* Daunenbett, *das;* Federbett, *das*

**eight** /eɪt/ ▶912, ▶1012, ▶1352 ❶ *adj.* acht; **at ~:** um acht; **it's ~ [o'clock]** es ist acht [Uhr]; **half past ~:** halb neun; **~ thirty** acht Uhr dreißig; **~ ten/fifty** zehn nach acht/vor neun; (*esp. in timetable*) acht Uhr zehn/fünfzig; **around ~ at about ~:** gegen acht [Uhr]; **half ~** (*coll.*) halb neun; **girl of ~:** Mädchen von acht Jahren; **~-year-old boy** achtjähriger Junge; **an ~-year-old** ein Achtjähriger/eine Achtjährige; **be ~ [years old]** acht [Jahre alt] sein; **at [the age of] ~, aged ~:** mit acht Jahren; im Alter von acht Jahren; **he won ~-six** er hat acht zu sechs gewonnen; **Book/Volume/Part/Chapter E~:** Buch/Band/Teil/Kapitel acht; achtes Buch/achter Band/achter Teil/achtes Kapitel; **~-figure number** achtstellige Zahl; **~-page** achtseitig; **~-storey[ed] building** achtstöckiges *od.* achtgeschossiges Gebäude; **~-sided polygon** achtseitiges Vieleck; **bet at ~ to one** acht zu eins wetten; **~ times** achtmal.
❷ *n.* Ⓐ (*number, symbol*) Acht, *die;* **the first/last ~:** die ersten/letzten acht; **there were ~ of us present** wir waren [zu] acht; **~ of us attended the lecture** wir waren [zu] acht bei der Vorlesung; **come ~ at a time/in ~s** acht auf einmal kommen/zu je acht kommen; **arabic/Roman ~:** arabische/römische Acht; **stack the boxes in ~s** die Kisten zu achten stapeln; **the [number] ~ [bus]** die Buslinie Nr. 8; der Achter (*ugs.*); **two-~ time** (*Mus.*) Zweiachteltakt, *der;* **behind the ~ ball** (*Amer.*) (*at a disadvantage*) im Nachteil; (*in a baffling situation*) in einer misslichen Lage; Ⓑ (*8-shaped figure*) **[figure of] ~:** Achter, *der* (*ugs.*); Acht, *die;* Ⓒ (*Cards*) **~ of hearts/trumps** Herz-/Trumpfacht, *die;* Ⓓ (*size*) **a size ~ dress** ein Kleid [in] Größe 8; **wear size ~ shoes** Schuhgröße 8 haben *od.* tragen; **wear an ~, be size ~:** Größe 8 tragen *od.* haben; Ⓔ (*Rowing*) (*crew*) Achtermannschaft, *die;* (*boat*) Achter, *der;* **the Eights** (*boat races*) Achterrennen, *das;* Ⓕ **have had one over the ~** (*coll.*) einen über den Durst getrunken haben (*ugs.*)

**eighteen** /eɪˈtiːn/ ❶ *adj.* ▶912, ▶1012, ▶1352 achtzehn; ⇒ *also* **eight** 1. ❷ *n.* Achtzehn, *die;* **~ seventy** achtzehnhundertsiebzig; **in the ~ seventies** in den siebziger Jahren des neunzehnten Jahrhunderts; **~ hundred hours** ⇒ **hundred** 1 A; ⇒ *also* **eight** 2 A, D

**eighteenth** /eɪˈtiːnθ/ ▶1055 ❶ *adj.* ▶1352 achtzehnt...; ⇒ *also* **eighth** 1. ❷ *n.* (*fraction*) Achtzehntel, *das;* ⇒ *also* **eighth** 2

**eightfold** /ˈeɪtfəʊld/ ❶ *adj.* achtfach; **an ~ increase** ein Anstieg auf das Achtfache. ❷ *adv.* achtfach; **multiply ~:** sich verachtfachen; **increase ~:** sich auf das Achtfache erhöhen

**eighth** /eɪtθ/ ❶ *adj.* ▶1352 acht...; **be/come ~:** Achter sein/als Achter ankommen; **an ~ part/share** ein Achtel; **~ largest** achtgrößt... ❷ *n.* ▶1055 (*in sequence, rank*) Achte, *der/die/das;* (*fraction*) Achtel, *das;* **be the ~ to do sth.** der/die/das Achte sein, der/die/das etw. tut; (*day*) **the ~ of May** der achte Mai; **the ~ [of the month]** der Achte [des Monats]

**ˈeighth note** *n.* (*Amer. Mus.*) Achtel, *das;* Achtelnote, *die*

**eightieth** /ˈeɪtɪɪθ/ ❶ *adj.* ▶1352 achtzigst...; ⇒ *also* **eighth** 1. ❷ *n.* (*fraction*) Achtzigstel, *das;* ⇒ *also* **eighth** 2

**eighty** /ˈeɪtɪ/ ▶912, ▶1352 ❶ *adj.* achtzig; **one-and-~** (*arch.*) ⇒ **~-one** 1; ⇒ *also* **eight** 1. ❷ *n.* Achtzig, *die;* **be in one's eighties** in den Achtzigern sein; **be in one's early/late eighties** Anfang/Ende achtzig sein; **the eighties** (*years*) die Achtzigerjahre; **the temperature will be rising [well] into the eighties** die Temperatur steigt auf [gut] über 80 Grad Fahrenheit; **one-and-~** (*arch.*) ⇒ **eighty-one** 2; ⇒ *also* **eight** 2 A

**eighty: ~-ˈfirst** *etc. adj.* ▶1352 einundachtzigst... *usw.;* ⇒ *also* **eighth** 1; **~-ˈone** *etc.* ❶ *adj.* einundachtzig *usw.;* ⇒ *also* **eight** 1; ❷ *n.* ▶1352 Einundachtzig *usw., die;* ⇒ *also* **eight** 2 A

**Eire** /ˈeərə/ *pr. n.* Irland (*das*); Eire (*das*)

**eisteddfod** /aɪˈsteðvəd/ *n., pl.* **~s** *or* **~au** /aɪˈsteðvədaɪ/ Ⓐ (*of Welsh bards*) Eisteddfod, *das;* Ⓑ (*gathering for competitions*) Dichter- und Sängerfest, *das*

**either** /ˈaɪðə(r), ˈiːðə(r)/ ❶ *adj.* Ⓐ (*each*) **at ~ end of the table** an beiden Enden des Tisches; **on ~ side of the road** auf beiden Seiten der Straße; **~ way** ⇒ **way** 1 C; Ⓑ (*one or other*) [irgend]ein ... [von beiden]; **take ~ one** nimm einen/eine/eins von [den] beiden.
❷ *pron.* Ⓐ (*each*) beide *Pl.;* **~ is possible** beides ist möglich; **I can't cope with ~:** ich kann mit keinem von beiden fertig werden; **I don't like ~ [of them** *or* **of the two]** ich mag beide nicht *od.* keinen von beiden; Ⓑ (*one or other*) einer/eine/ein[e]s [von beiden]; **~ of the buses** jeder der beiden Busse; beide Busse.
❸ *adv.* Ⓐ (*any more than the other*) auch [nicht]; **'I don't like that ~:** ich mag es auch nicht; **I don't like 'that ~:** auch das mag ich nicht; **she plays the piano badly and she can't sing ~:** sie spielt schlecht Klavier, und singen kann sie auch nicht; Ⓑ (*moreover, furthermore*) noch nicht einmal; **there was a time, and not so long ago ~:** früher, noch gar nicht einmal so lange her.
❹ *conj.* **~ ... or ...** entweder ... oder ...; (*after negation*) weder ... noch ...; **I've never been to ~ Berlin or Munich** ich bin weder in Berlin noch in München gewesen

**ˈeither-or** ❶ *adj.* Entweder-Oder-‹Problem›. ❷ *n.* Entweder-Oder, *das*

**ejaculate** /ɪˈdʒækjʊleɪt/ ❶ *v.t.* Ⓐ (*utter suddenly*) ausstoßen ‹Fluch, Gebet›; Ⓑ (*eject*) ausstoßen; ejakulieren ‹Samen›. ❷ *v.i.* (*eject semen*) ejakulieren

**ejaculation** /ɪdʒækjʊˈleɪʃn/ *n.* Ⓐ (*utterance*) Ausbruch, *der;* (*cry*) Ausruf, *der;* Ⓑ (*ejection*) Ausstoß, *der;* (*of semen*) Ejakulation, *die;* Samenerguss, *der*

**eject** /ɪˈdʒekt/ ❶ *v.t.* Ⓐ (*expel*) (*from committee, hall, meeting*) hinauswerfen (**from** aus); Ⓑ (*from machine gun*) auswerfen; (*from aircraft*) hinausschleudern; (*from video player etc.*) ‹Gerät:› auswerfen, ‹Person:› herausholen ‹Kassette›; Ⓒ (*dispossess*) hinauswerfen; exmittieren (*Amtsspr.*). ❷ *v.i.* sich hinauskatapultieren

**ejection** /ɪˈdʒekʃn/ *n.* (*of intruder etc.*) Vertreibung, *die;* (*of heckler, troublesome drunk*) Hinauswurf, *der;* (*of empty cartridge*) Ausstoß, *der;* Auswerfen, *das;* (*of pilot*) Hinausschleudern, *das*

**ejector** /ɪˈdʒektə(r)/ *n.* (*of firearm*) Auswerfer, *der*

**eˈjector seat** *n.* Schleudersitz, *der*

**eke** /iːk/ *v.t.* **~ out** strecken ‹Vorräte, Essen, Einkommen›; **~ out a living** *or* **an existence** sich (*Dat.*) seinen Lebensunterhalt [notdürftig *od.* mühsam] verdienen

**elaborate** ❶ /ɪ'læbərət/ *adj.* kompliziert; ausgefeilt ‹Stil›; durchorganisiert ‹Studium, Forschung›; kunstvoll [gearbeitet] ‹Arrangement, Stickerei, Verzierung, Kleidungsstück›; üppig, umfangreich ‹Menü›. ❷ /ɪ'læbəreɪt/ *v.t.* weiter ausarbeiten; weiter ausführen ‹Arbeit, Plan, Thema›. ❸ *v.i.* mehr ins Detail gehen; **could you ~?** könnten Sie das näher ausführen?; **~ on sth.** etw. ausführlicher erklären *od.* näher ausführen

**elaborately** /ɪ'læbərətlɪ/ *adv.* anspruchsvoll ‹sich kleiden›; kompliziert ‹ausarbeiten, planen›; kunstvoll ‹entwerfen, verzieren›; umfangreich ‹vorbereiten›

**elaboration** /ɪlæbə'reɪʃn/ *n.* (*of plan, theory, etc.*) Ausarbeitung, *die* (*meist Pl.*); (*of style*) Ausfeilung, *die;* (*that which elaborates*) Elaborat, *das* (*abwertend*)

**élan** /'eɪlɑ̃/ *n., no pl.* Energie, *die;* Schwung, *der*

**eland** /'i:lənd/ *n.* (*Zool.*) Elenantilope, *die*

**elapse** /ɪ'læps/ *v.i.* ‹Zeit:› vergehen, ins Land gehen

**elastic** /ɪ'læstɪk, ɪ'lɑ:stɪk/ ❶ *adj.* [A] elastisch; [B] (*springy*) geschmeidig ‹Bewegung›; federnd ‹Gang›; elastisch ‹Muskel›; [C] (*fig.: flexible*) flexibel; weit ‹Gewissen›; weit auslegbar ‹Klausel, Bestimmung›; Gummi‹begriff, -paragraph› (*ugs.*). ❷ *n.* (**~ band**) Gummiband, *das;* (*fabric*) elastisches Material

**elasticated** /ɪ'læstɪkeɪtɪd, ɪ'lɑ:stɪkeɪtɪd/ *adj.* elastisch

**elastic 'band** *n.* Gummiband, *das*

**elasticity** /elæs'tɪsɪtɪ, i:læs'tɪsɪtɪ/ *n., no pl.* [A] (*of material etc.*) Elastizität, *die;* [B] (*springiness*) Geschmeidigkeit, *die;* [C] (*fig.: flexibility*) Flexibilität, *die;* (*of rules, laws*) [weite] Auslegbarkeit; [D] (*Econ.*) Anpassungsfähigkeit, *die*

**elastic 'stocking** *n.* Gummistrumpf, *der*

**elate** /ɪ'leɪt/ *v.t.* erfreuen; erbauen (*geh.*); **be ~d by/over sth.** aufgrund einer Sache (*Gen.*)/über etw. (*Akk.*) hocherfreut *od.* in Hochstimmung sein

**elated** /ɪ'leɪtɪd/ *adj.* freudig erregt; **~ mood** *or* **state of mind** Hochstimmung, *die;* **be** *or* **feel ~:** in Hochstimmung sein

**elation** /ɪ'leɪʃn/ *n., no pl.* freudige Erregung; **feel ~ at one's success** über seinen Erfolg hocherfreut sein

**elbow** /'elbəʊ/ ❶ *n.* [A] ▶ 966 Ell[en]bogen, *der;* [B] (*of piping*) Knie, *das;* [C] (*bend, corner*) Knick, *der;* (*of river*) Biegung, *die;* Knie, *das;* (*of road*) Biegung, *die;* [D] (*of garment*) Ellbogen, *der;* [E] **at one's ~:** bei sich; in Reichweite; **sth./sb. is at sb.'s ~:** etw. ist in Reichweite/jmd. ist in jmds. Nähe; **bend** *or* **lift one's ~** (*coll.: drink*) einen heben (*ugs.*); **give sb. the ~** (*coll.*) jmdm. den Laufpass geben (*ugs.*); **out at ~s** an den Ellbogen abgetragen *od.* durchgewetzt ‹Mantel›; heruntergekommen ‹Person›; **be up to one's** *or* **the ~s in sth./work** mit etw. alle Hände voll zu tun haben/bis über die Ohren in Arbeit stecken.

❷ *v.t.* **~ one's way** sich mit den Ellenbogen einen Weg bahnen; sich drängeln (*ugs.*); **~ sb. aside** jmdn. mit den Ellenbogen zur Seite stoßen; **~ sb. out** (*fig.*) jmdn. hinausdrängeln

**elbow: ~ grease** *n., no pl.* (*joc.*) Muskelkraft, *die;* **~ patch** *n.* [Ellbogen]flicken, *der;* Ellbogenverstärkung, *die* (*Textilw.*); **~ room** *n.* (*lit. or fig.*) Ell[en]bogenfreiheit, *die;* (*fig.*) Spielraum, *der*

**elder**[1] /'eldə(r)/ ❶ *attrib. adj.* älter...; **Pliny the E~, the ~ Pliny** Plinius der Ältere. ❷ *n.* [A] (*senior*) Ältere, *der/die;* **he is my ~ by several years** er ist mehrere Jahre älter als ich; [B] *in pl.* Alten *Pl.;* **our ~s and betters** die Älteren mit mehr Lebenserfahrung; **the village ~s** die Dorfältesten; **the ~s of the tribe** die Stammesältesten; [C] (*official in Church*) [Kirchen]älteste, *der/die*

**elder**[2] *n.* (*Bot.*) Holunder, *der*

**elder: ~berry** *n.* Holunderbeere, *die;* **~berry 'wine** *n.* Holunderbeerwein, *der;* **~flower** *n.* Holunderblüte, *die;* **~flower 'wine** *n.* Holunderblütenwein, *der*

**elderly** /'eldəlɪ/ ❶ *adj.* älter; **my parents are both quite ~ now** meine Eltern sind beide inzwischen ziemlich alt geworden. ❷ *n. pl.* **the ~:** ältere Menschen

**elder: ~ 'statesman** *n.* Elder statesman, *der* (*Politik*); **~ 'wine** ⇒ **elderberry wine**

**eldest** /'eldɪst/ *adj.* ältest...

**eldorado** /eldə'rɑ:dəʊ/ *n., pl.* **~s** Eldorado, *das*

**elect** /ɪ'lekt/ ❶ *adj.* [A] *postpos.* (*chosen but not installed*) gewählt; **the President ~:** der gewählte *od.* designierte Präsident; [B] (*choice*) auserlesen, exklusiv ‹Gruppe›; (*chosen*) [aus]erwählt. ❷ *v.t.* [A] (*choose by vote*) wählen; **~ sb. chairman/MP** *etc.* jmdn. zum Vorsitzenden/Abgeordneten *usw.* wählen; **~ sb. to the chair/to the Senate** jmdn. zum Vorsitzenden/in den Senat wählen; [B] (*choose*) **~ to do sth.** sich dafür entscheiden, etw. zu tun

**election** /ɪ'lekʃn/ *n.* Wahl, *die;* **presidential ~s** (*Amer.*) Präsidentschaftswahlen *Pl.;* **general/local ~:** allgemeine/kommunale Wahlen; **~ as chairman** Wahl zum Vorsitzenden; **~ results** Wahlergebnisse *Pl.;* **~ day** Wahltag, *der;* ⇒ *also* **by-election**

**e'lection campaign** *n.* Wahlkampf, *der;* (*in US presidential election*) Wahlkampagne, *die*

**electioneer** /ɪlekʃə'nɪə(r)/ *v.i.* **be/go ~ing** Wahlkampf machen

**electioneering** /ɪlekʃə'nɪərɪŋ/ *n.* Agitation, *die* (**for/against** für/gegen)

**elective** /ɪ'lektɪv/ *adj.* [A] (*chosen or filled by election*) gewählt; **an ~ office** ein Amt, das durch Wahl besetzt wird/wurde; [B] (*having the power to elect*) wahlberechtigt; [C] (*optional*) wahlfrei, fakultativ ‹Kursus, Fach›

**elector** /ɪ'lektə(r)/ *n.* [A] Wähler, *der*/Wählerin, *die;* Wahlberechtigte, *der/die;* [B] **E~** (*Hist.: prince*) Kurfürst, *der*

**electoral** /ɪ'lektərl/ *adj.* Wahl‹liste, -zettel, -system, -bezirk, -berechtigung›; Wähler‹liste, -verzeichnis, -wille, -gruppe›

**electoral 'college** *n.* Wahlmännergremium, *das;* Wahlausschuss, *der*

**electorate** /ɪ'lektərət/ *n.* Wähler *Pl.;* Wählerschaft, *die*

**electric** /ɪ'lektrɪk/ ❶ *adj.* elektrisch ‹Strom, Feld, Licht, Orgel usw.›; Elektro‹kabel, -motor, -karren, -herd, -kessel›; Elektrizitäts‹lehre, -erzeuger, -werk›; Strom‹versorgung›; (*fig.*) spannungsgeladen ‹Atmosphäre›; elektrisierend ‹Wirkung›. ❷ *n. in pl.* elektrische Geräte; Elektrogeräte *Pl.;* (*whole system*) Elektrik, *die*

**electrical** /ɪ'lektrɪkl/ *adj.* elektrisch ‹Defekt, Kontakt›; Elektro‹abteilung, -handel, -geräte›

**electrical: ~ engi'neer** *n.* ▶ 1261 Elektroingenieur, *der*/-ingenieurin, *die;* **~ engi'neering** *n.* Elektrotechnik, *die*

**electrically** /ɪ'lektrɪkəlɪ/ *adv.* elektrisch; (*fig.*) [wie] elektrisiert

**electric: ~ 'blanket** *n.* Heizdecke, *die;* **~ 'blue** *n.* Stahlblau, *das;* **~ 'chair** *n.* elektrischer Stuhl; **~ cooker** *n.* Elektroherd, *der;* **~ 'eel** *n.* Zitteraal, *der;* **~ 'eye** *n.* Photozelle, *die;* **~ 'fan** *n.* Ventilator, *der;* **~ 'fence** *n.* elektrischer Zaun; Elektrozaun, *der;* **~ 'fire** *n.* [elektrischer] Heizofen; Heizstrahler, *der;* **~ gui'tar** *n.* elektrische Gitarre; E-Gitarre, *die*

**electrician** /ɪlek'trɪʃn/ *n.* ▶ 1261 Elektriker, *der*/Elektrikerin, *die;* (*who sets up electrical apparatus*) Elektromechaniker, *der*/-mechanikerin, *die*

**electricity** /ɪlek'trɪsɪtɪ, elek'trɪsɪtɪ/ *n., no pl.* [A] Elektrizität, *die;* [B] (*supply*) Strom, *der;* **install ~:** Stromanschlüsse legen; [C] (*fig.*) Spannung, *die*

**electricity: ~ bill** *n.* Stromrechnung, *die;* **~ man** *n.* (*fitter*) Elektroinstallateur, *der;* (*meter-reader, collector*) Stromableser, *der;* Strommann, *der* (*ugs.*); **~ meter** *n.* Stromzähler, *der*

**electric: ~ 'shock** *n.* Stromschlag, *der;* [elektrischer] Schlag; (*Med.*) Elektroschock, *der;* **~ 'storm** *n.* Gewitter, *das;* Gewittersturm, *der*

**electrification** /ɪlektrɪfɪ'keɪʃn/ *n.* [A] (*charging*) Unter-Strom-Setzen, *das;* [B] (*conversion*) Elektrifizierung, *die;* [C] (*fig.*) Elektrisierung, *die*

**electrify** /ɪ'lektrɪfaɪ/ *v.t.* [A] (*charge*) an das Stromnetz anschließen ‹Maschine›; unter Strom setzen ‹Kabel, Leiter›; [B] (*convert*) elektrifizieren ‹Eisenbahnstrecke›; [C] (*fig.*) elektrisieren

**electro-** /ɪlektrəʊ/ *in comb.* elektro-/Elektro-

**electro'cardiogram** *n.* Elektrokardiogramm, *das*

**electro'chemical** *adj.* elektrochemisch

**electrocon'vulsive** *adj.* Elektrokrampf-; **~ shock/treatment** *or* **therapy** Elektroschock, *der*/Elektroschockbehandlung, *die*

**electrocute** /ɪ'lektrəkju:t/ *v.t.* durch Stromschlag töten

**electrocution** /ɪlektrə'kju:ʃn/ *n.* [A] (*execution*) Hinrichtung auf dem elektrischen Stuhl; [B] (*death*) Tod durch Stromschlag

**electrode** /ɪ'lektrəʊd/ *n.* Elektrode, *die*

**electrolyse** /ɪ'lektrəlaɪz/ *v.t.* [A] (*Chem.*) elektrolysieren; [B] (*Med.*) elektroresezieren

**electrolysis** /ɪlek'trɒlɪsɪs, elek'trɒlɪsɪs/ *n., pl.* **electrolyses** /ɪlek'trɒlɪsi:z, elek'trɒlɪsi:z/ [A] (*Chem.*) Elektrolyse, *die;* [B] (*Med.*) Elektroresektion, *die*

**electrolyte** /ɪ'lektrəlaɪt/ *n.* Elektrolyt, *der*

**electrolytic** /ɪlektrə'lɪtɪk/ *adj.* (*Chem.*) elektrolytisch

**electrolyze** (*Amer.*) ⇒ **electrolyse**

**electro'magnet** *n.* Elektromagnet, *der*

**electromag'netic** *adj.* elektromagnetisch

**electro'magnetism** *n.* Elektromagnetismus, *der*

**electron** /ɪ'lektrɒn/ *n.* Elektron, *das*

**electron: ~ 'beam** *n.* Elektronenstrahl, *der;* **~ 'gun** *n.* Elektronenkanone, *die*

**electronic** /ɪlek'trɒnɪk, elek'trɒnɪk/ *adj.* elektronisch; Elektronen‹uhr, -orgel›

**electronic: ~ 'brain** *n.* (*coll.*) Elektronen[ge]hirn, *das* (*ugs.*); **~ 'cash** *n.* elektronisches Geld; **~ com'puter** *n.* Computer, *der;* Elektronenrechner, *der;* **~ 'flash** *n.* Elektronenblitz, *der;* **~ 'mail** *n.* elektronische Post; **~ 'publishing** *n.* elektronisches Publizieren

**electronics** /ɪlek'trɒnɪks, elek'trɒnɪks/ *n., no pl.* Elektronik, *die*

**electron: ~ 'microscope** *n.* Elektronenmikroskop, *das;* **~ 'optics** *n.* Elektronenoptik, *die*

**e'lectroplate** *v.t.* galvanisieren

**electro'static** *adj.* elektrostatisch

**elegance** /'elɪgəns/ *n., no pl.* Eleganz, *die;* (*of lifestyle*) Kultiviertheit, *die*

**elegant** /'elɪgənt/ *adj.* elegant; kultiviert ‹Lebensstil›

**elegantly** /'elɪgəntlɪ/ *adv.* elegant

**elegiac** /elɪ'dʒaɪək/ ❶ *adj.* elegisch. ❷ *n. in pl.* elegische Verse

**elegy** /'elɪdʒɪ/ *n.* Elegie, *die*

**element** /'elɪmənt/ *n.* [A] (*component part*) Element, *das;* **a novel with a strong ~ of religion** ein Roman mit einem stark religiösen Element; **have all the ~s of a real scandal** alle Voraussetzungen für einen richtigen Skandal tragen; **an ~ of truth** ein Körnchen Wahrheit; **an ~ of chance/danger in sth.** eine gewisse Zufälligkeit/Gefahr bei etw.; **when reduced to its ~s** im Grunde [genommen]; [B] (*Chem.*) Element, *das;* Grundstoff, *der;* [C] *in pl.* (*atmospheric agencies*) Elemente *Pl.;* [D] (*Philos.*) **the four ~s** die vier Elemente; **be in one's ~** (*fig.*) in seinem Element sein; **be out of one's ~** (*fig.*) sich fehl am Platz fühlen; [E] (*Electr.*) (*wire*) Heizelement, *das;* (*electrode*) Elektrode, *die;* [F] *in pl.* (*rudiments of learning*) Grundlagen *Pl.;* Elemente *Pl.;* [G] *in pl.* (*Relig.*) Brot und Wein; [H] (*Math., Logic*) Element, *das*

**elemental** /elɪ'mentl/ *adj.* [A] (*of the four elements*) urgewaltig; elementar; [B] Natur‹gottheit, -religion›; Elementar‹geist›; [C] (*fig.*) elementar; natürlich ‹Größe›; urwüchsig, ursprünglich ‹Leben, Fantasie›; [D] (*essential*) grundlegend

e

**elementary** /elɪˈmentərɪ/ *adj.* **A** elementar; grundlegend ‹Fakten, Wissen›; schlicht ‹Fabel, Stil›; Grundschul‹lehrer, -bildung›; Grund‹stufe, -kurs, -ausbildung, -rechnen, -kenntnisse›; Ausgangs‹text, -thema›; Anfangs‹stadium›; **course in ~ German** Grundkurs in Deutsch; **my knowledge is ~:** ich habe nur Anfängerkenntnisse; **be still in its ~ stages** noch in den Anfängen stecken; **an ~ mistake** ein grober Fehler; **B** *(Chem.)* elementar; Elementar-

**elementary: ~ 'particle** *n. (Phys.)* Elementarteilchen, *das;* **~ school** *n.* Grundschule, *die*

**elephant** /ˈelɪfənt/ *n.* Elefant, *der;* **see pink ~s** weiße Mäuse sehen; **white ~** *(fig.)* nutzloser Besitz; **be a ~ elephant** ‹Gebäude, Einkaufszentrum usw.:› reine Geldverschwendung sein; *attrib.* **a white ~ stall** *eine Bude, an der Sachen angeboten werden, die deren ehemalige Besitzer gern loswerden wollen*

**elephantine** /elɪˈfæntaɪn/ *adj.* **A** *(of elephants)* Elefanten-; **B** *(huge)* massig ‹Körper, Person, Ringer, Boxer›; gigantisch ‹Masse›; **C** *(clumsy)* schwerfällig

**elevate** /ˈelɪveɪt/ *v.t.* **A** *(bring higher)* erhöhen ‹Temperatur›; aufschütten ‹Boden›; [empor]heben ‹Gerät, Gegenstand›; *(fig.)* aufwerten ‹Stellung› **(into** zu); **B** *(Eccl.)* emporheben, zeigen ‹Hostie›; **C** *(raise)* heben ‹Stimme, Blick›; aufrichten ‹Blick, Geschützrohr›; auf einer Hochtrasse führen ‹Bahn›; **D** *(in rank)* befördern; **~ sb. to top management/a professorship/the peerage** jmdn. in die Unternehmensspitze berufen/auf einen Lehrstuhl berufen/in den Adelsstand erheben; **E** *(morally, intellectually)* erbauen ‹Geist, Person›; aufrichten ‹Mut›; erheben ‹Seele, Gemüt›

**elevated** /ˈelɪveɪtɪd/ *adj.* **A** *(raised)* gehoben ‹Stellung›; erhöht ‹Lage, Platzierung›; hoch gelegen ‹Land›; aufgeschüttet ‹Damm, Straße›; erhoben ‹Stimme, Blick, Bein, Arm›; **keep one's arm in an ~ position** den Arm erhoben halten; **B** *(above ground level)* Hoch‹bahn, -straße›; **C** *(noble, refined)* erhaben; edel; **feel ~:** sich aufgerichtet fühlen; **D** *(formal, dignified)* gehoben ‹Stil, Rede, Wortwahl›

**elevation** /elɪˈveɪʃn/ *n.* **A** *(position of house, building, land)* erhöhte Lage; **B** *(Eccl.: of the Host)* Elevation, *die;* **C** *(of temperature)* Ansteigen, *das;* Anstieg, *der;* **D** *(of voice)* Heben, *das;* Hebung, *die;* **E** *(in rank)* Beförderung, *die; (to the peerage)* Erhebung, *die; (to top management, professorship)* Berufung, *die;* **F** *(of mind, thought)* Erhebung, *die; (state)* Erhabenheit, *die;* **the ~ of his style** sein gehobener Stil; **G** *(height)* Höhe, *die;* **~ of the ground** Bodenerhebung *od.* Anhöhe, *die;* **H** *(angle)* Elevation, *die;* **angle of ~:** Elevationswinkel, *der;* Erhöhungswinkel, *der;* **I** *(drawing, diagram)* Aufriss, *der*

**elevator** /ˈelɪveɪtə(r)/ *n.* **A** *(machine)* Förderwerk, *das;* Elevator, *der;* **B** *(storehouse)* Getreidesilo, *der od. das;* **C** *(Amer.)* ⇒ **lift** 3 B; **D** *(Aeron.)* Höhenruder, *das*

**eleven** /ɪˈlevn/ ▶ **912**, ▶ **1012**, ▶ **1352** **1** *adj.* elf; ⇒ *also* **eight** 1. **2** *n. (number, symbol; also Sport)* Elf, *die;* ⇒ *also* **eight** 2 A, D

**eleven-'plus** *n. (Brit. Educ. Hist.)* **~ [examination]** *Prüfung der elf- bis zwölfjährigen Schüler [vor Fortsetzung der schulischen Laufbahn an höherer Schule]*

**elevenses** /ɪˈlevnzɪz/ *n. sing. or pl. (Brit. coll.)* ≈ zweites Frühstück [gegen elf Uhr]

**eleventh** /ɪˈlevnθ/ ▶ **1055** **1** *adj.* ▶ **1352** elft...; **at the ~ hour** im letzten Augenblick; in letzter Minute; **an ~-hour change of plan** eine Planungsänderung in letzter Minute; ⇒ *also* **eighth** 1. **2** *n. (fraction)* Elftel, *das;* ⇒ *also* **eighth** 2

**elf** /elf/ *n., pl.* **elves** /elvz/ **A** *(Mythol.)* Elf, *der*/Elfe, *die;* **B** *(mischievous creature)* [boshafter] Schelm; Kobold, *der*

**elfin** /ˈelfɪn/ *adj.* elfenhaft

**elfish** /ˈelfɪʃ/ *adj.* elfenhaft; *(mischievous)* schalkhaft; koboldhaft

**elicit** /ɪˈlɪsɪt/ *v.t.* entlocken ‹Antwort, Auskunft, Wahrheit, Geheimnis› **(from** *Dat.*); hervorrufen ‹Begeisterung, Zustimmung›; gewinnen ‹Unterstützung› **(amongst** bei); **the discussion has ~ed some important facts** die Diskussion brachte einige interessante Einzelheiten ans Tageslicht

**elide** /ɪˈlaɪd/ *v.t. (Ling.)* elidieren *(fachspr.)*; auslassen

**eligibility** /elɪdʒɪˈbɪlɪtɪ/ *n., no pl. (fitness)* Qualifikation, *die; (for a job)* Eignung, *die; (entitlement)* Berechtigung, *die* **(for** zu)

**eligible** /ˈelɪdʒɪbl/ *adj.* **A be ~ for sth.** *(fit)* für etw. qualifiziert *od.* geeignet sein; *(entitled)* zu etw. berechtigt sein; **be ~ for membership/a pension/an office** mitglieds-/pensionsberechtigt sein/für ein Amt infrage kommen; **be ~ to do sth.** etw. tun dürfen; **become ~ to vote** das Wahlrecht erhalten; **B** *(marriageable)* begehrt ‹Junggeselle›

**eliminate** /ɪˈlɪmɪneɪt/ *v.t.* **A** *(remove)* beseitigen ‹Zweifel, Fehler›; ausschließen ‹Möglichkeit›; eliminieren, beseitigen ‹Gegner›; **B** *(exclude)* ausschließen; *(Sport)* aus dem Wettbewerb werfen; **the team was ~d at the end of the third round** die Mannschaft schied nach der dritten Runde aus; **C** *(Physiol.)* ausscheiden

**elimination** /ɪlɪmɪˈneɪʃn/ *n.* **A** *(removal) (of doubt, error)* Beseitigung, *die; (of opponent)* Eliminierung, *die;* Beseitigung, *die;* **process of ~:** Ausleseverfahren, *das;* **B** *(exclusion)* Ausschluss, *der; (Sport)* Ausscheiden, *das;* **C** *(Physiol.)* Ausscheidung, *die*

**elision** /ɪˈlɪʒn/ *n. (Ling.)* Elision, *die (fachspr.)*; Auslassung, *die*

**élite** /eɪˈliːt/ *n. (the best)* Elite, *die; (of society, club)* Spitze, *die;* Creme, *die; (group, class)* Elite, *die;* **the ~** *(high society)* die oberen Zehntausend *(ugs.)*

**élitism** /eɪˈliːtɪzm/ *n.* Elitedenken, *das*

**élitist** /eɪˈliːtɪst/ **1** *adj.* elitär; Elite‹denken›. **2** *n.* Anhänger/Anhängerin des Elitedenkens; elitär Denkender/Denkende

**elixir** /ɪˈlɪksə(r)/ *n.* Heilmittel, *das;* **~ [of life]** [Lebens]elixier, *das*

**Elizabeth** /ɪˈlɪzəbəθ/ *pr. n. (Hist., as name of ruler etc.)* Elisabeth

**Elizabethan** /ɪlɪzəˈbiːθn/ **1** *adj.* elisabethanisch. **2** *n.* elisabethanischer Zeitgenosse

**elk** /elk/ *n., pl.* **~s** *or same* **A** *(deer)* Elch, *der;* **B** *(moose)* Riesenelch, *der*

**elk: ~ hound** *n.* Jämthund, *der;* **~ test** *n.* Elchtest, *der*

**ellipse**[1] /ɪˈlɪps/ *n. (Math.)* Ellipse, *die*

**ellipsis** /ɪˈlɪpsɪs/ (**[2]ellipse**) *n., pl.* **ellipses** /ɪˈlɪpsiːz/ **A** *(Ling., Lit.)* Ellipse, *die;* **B** *(set of dots etc.)* Auslassungszeichen *Pl.*

**elliptic** /ɪˈlɪptɪk/, **elliptical** /ɪˈlɪptɪkl/ *adj.* **A** *(of ellipses; also Ling.)* elliptisch; Ellipsen‹bogen, -bahn›; **B** *(Lit.)* kryptisch *(geh.)*; **C** *(brief, concise)* komprimiert

**elliptically** /ɪˈlɪptɪkəlɪ/ *adv. (Ling., Lit.)* in elliptischen Sätzen

**elm** /elm/ *n.* Ulme, *die*

**'elmwood** *n.* Ulmen- *od.* Rüsternholz, *das*

**elocution** /eləˈkjuːʃn/ *n.* **A** *no pl. (art)* Sprechkunst, *die;* Vortragskunst, *die;* **teacher of ~:** Sprecherzieher, *der*/-erzieherin, *die;* **give lessons in ~:** Sprechunterricht geben; **B** *(style of speaking)* Redeweise, *die;* Diktion, *die*

**elocutionary** /eləˈkjuːʃənərɪ/ *adj.* deklamatorisch ‹Sprechweise, Fertigkeit, Effekt›

**elocutionist** /eləˈkjuːʃənɪst/ *n.* Vortragskünstler, *der*/-künstlerin, *die*

**elongate** /ˈiːlɒŋgeɪt/ *v.t.* länger werden lassen ‹Schatten›; strecken ‹Körper›; recken ‹Hals›

**elongated** /ˈiːlɒŋgeɪtɪd/ *adj.* lang gestreckt ‹Gestalt, Gliedmaße›; lang gereckt ‹Hals›

**elongation** /iːlɒŋˈgeɪʃn/ *n.* Verlängerung, *die; (of limbs, neck)* [Aus]recken, *das; (of forms, shapes)* Strecken, *das*

**elope** /ɪˈləʊp/ *v.i.* weglaufen; durchbrennen *(ugs.)*

**elopement** /ɪˈləʊpmənt/ *n.* Weglaufen, *das;* Durchbrennen, *das (ugs.)*

**eloquence** /ˈeləkwəns/ *n.* Beredtheit, *die;* Eloquenz, *die (geh.)*; **he is a man of great ~:** er ist ein sehr beredter Mann

**eloquent** /ˈeləkwənt/ *adj.* **A** eloquent *(geh.)*; gewandt ‹Sprechweise, Ausdruck, Stil, Redner›; beredt ‹Person›; **B** *(fig.)* beredt ‹Blick, Schweigen›

**eloquently** /ˈeləkwəntlɪ/ *adv.* **A** gewandt ‹sprechen, schreiben, sich ausdrücken, formulieren›; **B** *(fig.)* beredt ‹schauen›

**else** /els/ *adv.* **A** *(besides, in addition)* sonst [noch]; **anybody/anything ~?** sonst noch jemand/etwas?; **don't mention it to anybody ~:** erwähnen Sie es gegenüber niemandem sonst; **somebody/something ~:** [noch] jemand anders/noch etwas; **everybody/everything ~:** alle anderen/alles andere; **nobody ~:** niemand sonst; **nothing ~:** sonst *od.* weiter nichts; **will there be anything ~, sir?** *(asked by salesperson)* darf es sonst noch etwas sein[, der Herr]?; *(asked by butler)* haben Sie sonst noch einen Wunsch, Herr ...?; **nothing ~, thank you** das ist alles, danke; **that is something ~ again** das ist wieder etwas anderes; **be something ~** *(Amer. coll.: very good)* schon was Besonderes sein *(ugs.)*; **anywhere ~?** anderswo? *(ugs.)*; woanders?; **not anywhere ~:** sonst nirgendwo; **somewhere ~:** anderswo *(ugs.)*; woanders; **go somewhere ~:** anderswohin *(ugs.) od.* woandershin gehen; **everywhere ~:** auch sonst überall; **go everywhere ~:** sonst überallhin gehen; **nowhere ~:** sonst nirgendwo; **go nowhere ~:** sonst nirgendwohin gehen; **little ~:** kaum noch etwas; nur noch wenig; **much ~:** [noch] vieles andere *od.* mehr; **not much ~:** nicht mehr viel; nur noch wenig; **who/what/when/how ~?** wer/was/wann/wie sonst noch?; **where ~?** wo/wohin sonst noch?; **why ~?** warum sonst?; **B** *(instead)* ander...; **sb. ~'s hat** der Hut von jmd. anders *od.* jmd. anderem *(ugs.)*; **anybody/anything ~?** [irgend]jemand anders/etwas anderes?; **anyone ~ but Joe would have realized that** jeder [andere] außer Joe hätte das bemerkt; **somebody/something ~:** jemand anders/etwas anderes; **everybody/everything ~:** alle anderen/alles andere; **nobody/nothing ~:** niemand anders/nichts anderes; **no one ~ but he** nur er; niemand außer ihm; **nothing ~ but the best** nur das Beste; **there's nothing ~ for it** es hilft nichts; **anywhere ~?** anderswo? *(ugs.)*; woanders?; **somewhere ~:** anderswo *(ugs.)*; woanders; **go somewhere ~:** woandershin gehen; **his mind was/his thoughts were somewhere ~:** im Geist/mit seinen Gedanken war er woanders; **everywhere ~:** überall anders; überall sonst; **nowhere ~:** nirgendwo sonst; **go nowhere ~:** nirgendwo sonst hingehen; **there's not much ~ we can do but ...:** wir können kaum etwas anderes tun, als ...; **who ~ [but]?** wer anders [als]?; **it was John — who ~?** es war John — wer [denn] sonst? **what ~ can I do?** was kann ich anderes machen?; **why ~ would I have done it?** warum hätte ich es sonst getan?; **when/where ~ can we meet?** wann/wo können wir uns stattdessen treffen?; **where ~ could we go?** wohin könnten wir stattdessen gehen?; **how ~ would you do it?** wie würden Sie es anders *od.* sonst machen?; **C** *(otherwise)* sonst; anderenfalls; **or ~:** oder aber; **do it or ~ ...!** tun Sie es, sonst ...!; **do it or ~!** *(coll.)* tu es gefälligst!

**'elsewhere** *adv.* woanders; **go ~:** woandershin gehen; **his mind was/his thoughts were ~:** im Geist/mit seinen Gedanken war er woanders

**elucidate** /ɪˈljuːsɪdeɪt, ɪˈluːsɪdeɪt/ *v.t.* erläutern; aufklären ‹Geheimnis›

**elucidation** /ɪljuːsɪˈdeɪʃn, ɪluːsɪˈdeɪʃn/ *n.* Erläuterung, *die; (of mystery)* Aufklärung, *die*

**elude** /ɪˈljuːd, ɪˈluːd/ *v.t.* sich entziehen (+ *Dat.*); missachten ‹Befehl, Gesetz, Forderung›; umgehen ‹Verpflichtung›; *(avoid)* ausweichen (+ *Dat.*) ‹Person, Schlag, Angriff, Blick, Frage, Gefahr›; *(escape from)* entkommen (+ *Dat.*); **the causes of this disease have so far ~d medical science** die Mediziner konnten die Ursachen dieser Krankheit noch nicht herausfinden; **~ the police** sich dem Zugriff der Polizei entziehen; **sleep ~s me** der

Schlaf flieht mich (*veralt. geh.*); ich kann keinen Schlaf finden; **the name ~s me at the moment** der Name ist mir im Moment entfallen *od.* fällt mir im Moment nicht ein; **the significance of his remark ~s me** die Bedeutung seiner Bemerkung ist mir nicht klar

**elusive** /ɪ'lju:sɪv, ɪ'lu:sɪv/ *adj.* **A** (*avoiding grasp or pursuit*) schwer zu erreichen ‹Person›; schwer zu fassen ‹Straftäter›; scheu ‹Fuchs, Waldbewohner›; **I have phoned every day but she has been very ~:** ich habe jeden Tag angerufen, aber sie ist sehr schwer zu erreichen; **B** (*short-lived*) flüchtig ‹Freude, Glück›; **C** (*tending to escape from memory*) schwer zu behaltend, (*präd.*) schwer zu behalten ‹Gedanke, Wort›; **~ memory** schwache Erinnerung; **D** (*avoiding definition*) schwer definierbar ‹Begriff, Sinn›; **E** (*hard to pin down or identify*) schwer zu bestimmend, (*präd.*) schwer zu bestimmen ‹Geruch›; schwer durchschaubar ‹Person›; **F** (*evasive*) ausweichend ‹Antwort›

**elver** /'elvə(r)/ *n.* (*Zool.*) Glasaal, *der*

**elves** *pl. of* **elf**

**elvish** /'elvɪʃ/ ⇒ **elfish**

**Elysium** /ɪ'lɪzɪəm/ *n.* **A** (*Greek Mythol.*) Elysium, *das;* **B** (*fig.: place of ideal happiness*) Paradies, *das;* Elysium, *das* (*dichter.*)

**em** /em/ *n.* (*Printing*) Cicero, *das*

**'em** /əm/ *pron.* (*coll.*) se (*Akk.*) (*ugs.*); ihnen (*Dat.*)

**emaciated** /ɪ'meɪsɪeɪtɪd, ɪ'meɪʃɪeɪtɪd/ *adj.* ausgemergelt; abgezehrt; **become ~:** abmagern

**emaciation** /ɪmeɪsɪ'eɪʃn/ *n., no pl.* Ausmergelung, *die;* Abzehrung, *die*

**e-mail** /'i:meɪl/ **1** *n.* E-Mail, *die; attrib.* **~ address** E-Mail-Adresse, *die;* **~ message** E-Mail, *die.* **2** *v.t.* per E-Mail übermitteln ‹Ergebnisse, Datei usw.›; **~ sb.** jmdm. eine E-Mail schicken; **~ sb. with sth.** jmdm. etw. per E-Mail mitteilen

**emanate** /'eməneɪt/ *v.i.* **A** (*originate*) ausgehen (**from** von); **B** (*proceed, issue*) ausgestrahlt werden (**from** von); ausstrahlen; **C** (*formal: be sent out*) ‹Befehle:› erteilt *od.* erlassen werden; ‹Briefe, Urkunden:› ausgestellt *od.* ausgefertigt werden

**emanation** /emə'neɪʃn/ *n.* **A** (*Theol.*) Emanation, *die* (**from** aus); **B** *no pl.* (*issuing*) Ausstrahlen, *das;* **C** (*sth. proceeding from source*) Ausströmung, *die;* **D** (*fig.*) Ausfluss, *der;* **be an ~ of** *or* **from sth.** von etw. ausgehen; **~ of grace/love from God** Ausgehen von Gnade/Liebe von Gott

**emancipate** /ɪ'mænsɪpeɪt/ *v.t.* emanzipieren; unabhängig machen; **~ sb. from slavery** jmdn. aus der Sklaverei befreien; **~ oneself from sth./sb.** sich von etw. emanzipieren *od.* frei machen/sich von jmdm. frei machen

**emancipated** /ɪ'mænsɪpeɪtɪd/ *adj.* emanzipiert ‹Frau, Vorstellung, Einstellung›; **become ~:** sich emanzipieren; **~ slave** freigelassener Sklave

**emancipation** /ɪmænsɪ'peɪʃn/ *n.* Emanzipation, *die;* (*of slave*) Freilassung, *die;* **~ from servitude/superstition** Befreiung aus der Knechtschaft/vom Aberglauben

**emasculate** /ɪ'mæskjʊleɪt/ *v.t.* **A** (*Med.: castrate*) entmannen; emaskulieren (*fachspr.*); kastrieren ‹Tier›; **B** (*weaken*) schwächen; kastrieren (*ugs. scherzh.*); verwässern ‹Plan, Vorschlag, Gesetzentwurf›

**emasculation** /ɪmæskjʊ'leɪʃn/ *n.* **A** (*Med.: castration*) Entmannung, *die;* Emaskulation, *die* (*fachspr.*); (*of animal*) Kastration, *die;* **B** (*weakening*) Schwächung, *die;* Kastration, *die;* (*of plan, proposal*) Verwässerung, *die*

**embalm** /ɪm'bɑ:m/ *v.t.* einbalsamieren

**embankment** /ɪm'bæŋkmənt/ *n.* Damm, *der;* **~ of a river** Uferdamm, *der;* **~ of earth/stone** Erd-/Steindamm, *der;* **~ of a road** Straßendamm, *der;* Böschung, *die;* **~ of a track/railway** Bahndamm, *der;* **the Thames E~:** die Themse-Uferstraße (*in London*)

**embargo** /em'bɑ:gəʊ, ɪm'bɑ:gəʊ/ **1** *n., pl.* **~es** **A** Embargo, *das;* **be under an ~:** mit einem Embargo belegt sein; **put** *or* **lay an ~ on sth., place** *or* **lay sth. under an ~:** etw. mit einem Embargo belegen; **lift** *or* **raise** *or* **remove an ~ [from sth.]** ein Embargo [für etw.] aufheben; **B** (*impediment*) Stopp, *der;* **~ on new appointments** Einstellungsstopp, *der;* Einstellungssperre, *die;* **~ on further spending** Ausgabenstopp, *der.* **2** *v.t.* mit einem Embargo belegen

**embark** /ɪm'bɑ:k/ **1** *v.t.* einschiffen ‹Passagiere, Waren›. **2** *v.i.* **A** sich einschiffen (**for** nach); **the troops ~ed at night** die Truppen wurden nachts eingeschifft; **B** (*engage*) **~ [up]on sth.** etw. in Angriff nehmen; **~ [up]on a war** einen Krieg anfangen *od.* beginnen

**embarkation** /embɑ:'keɪʃn/ *n.* Einschiffung, *die;* **port of ~:** Einschiffungshafen, *der;* **~ leave** Einschiffungsurlaub, *der*

**embarrass** /ɪm'bærəs/ *v.t.* **A** (*make feel awkward*) in Verlegenheit bringen; **become seriously ~ed** in ernste Verlegenheit kommen; **be ~ed by lack of money** in Geldverlegenheit sein; **B** (*arch.: encumber*) behindern

**embarrassed** /ɪm'bærəst/ *adj.* verlegen ‹Person, Blick, Lächeln, Benehmen, Schweigen›; **be** *or* **feel/look/get ~:** verlegen sein/aussehen/werden; **now don't be ~!** geniere dich nicht!; **make sb. feel ~:** jmdn. verlegen machen

**embarrassing** /ɪm'bærəsɪŋ/ *adj.* peinlich ‹Benehmen, Schweigen, Situation, Augenblick, Frage, Thema›; beschämend ‹Großzügigkeit›; verwirrend ‹Auswahl›; **~ person** jmd., der andere blamiert; **I find it very ~ to have to say this, but ...:** es ist mir sehr peinlich, so etwas sagen zu müssen, aber ...

**embarrassingly** /ɪm'bærəsɪŋlɪ/ *adv.* peinlich; irritierend ‹freimütig›; unerhört ‹grob›; beschämend ‹großzügig›

**embarrassment** /ɪm'bærəsmənt/ *n.* Verlegenheit, *die;* (*instance*) Peinlichkeit, *die;* **much to his ~:** zu seiner großen Verlegenheit; **cause sb. ~:** jmdn. verlegen machen; **cause sb. a great deal of ~:** jmdn. in große Verlegenheit bringen; **he was a source of ~ to his family** seine Familie musste sich seinetwegen schämen; **financial ~[s]** Geldverlegenheit, *die;* **~ of riches** verwirrende [Über]fülle

**embassy** /'embəsɪ/ *n.* Botschaft, *die*

**embattled** /ɪm'bætld/ *adj.* kampfbereit ‹Armee›; befestigt ‹Turm, Wall, Gebäude›

**embed** /ɪm'bed/ *v.t.*, **-dd-:** **A** (*fix*) einlassen; **stones ~ded in rock** in Fels eingelagerte Steine; **a brick firmly ~ded in mortar** ein fest in Mörtel gefügter Ziegelstein; **~ sth. in cement/concrete** etw. einzementieren/einbetonieren; **the bullet ~ded itself in the ground** die Kugel bohrte sich in den Boden; **~ded in the mud** im Schlamm versunken; **~ded sentences** (*Ling.*) eingeschobene Sätze; **B** (*fig.*) **be firmly ~ded in sth.** fest in etw. (*Dat.*) verankert sein

**embellish** /ɪm'belɪʃ/ *v.t.* **A** (*beautify*) schmücken; beschönigen ‹Wahrheit›; **B** ausschmücken ‹Geschichte, Bericht›

**embellishment** /ɪm'belɪʃmənt/ *n.* **A** *no pl.* (*ornamentation*) (*of church, room*) Verschönerung, *die;* (*of story*) Ausschmückung, *die;* (*of truth*) Beschönigung, *die;* **B** (*sth. that embellishes*) Verzierung, *die;* (*in narrative*) Mittel der Ausschmückung; **C** (*Mus.*) Verzierung, *die;* Ornament, *das* (*fachspr.*)

**ember** /'embə(r)/ *n., usu. in pl.* (*lit. or fig.*) Glut, *die;* **dying ~s** verlöschende Glut; ⇒ *also* **fan**[1] 2

**'ember day** *n.* (*Eccl.*) Quatember, *der*

**embezzle** /ɪm'bezl/ *v.t.* unterschlagen; veruntreuen

**embezzlement** /ɪm'bezlmənt/ *n.* Unterschlagung, *die;* Veruntreuung, *die*

**embitter** /ɪm'bɪtə(r)/ *v.t.* vergiften ‹Beziehungen›; verschärfen ‹Auseinandersetzung›; verbittern ‹Person›

**emblazon** /ɪm'bleɪzn/ *v.t.* **A** (*Her.*) verzieren; blasonieren (*fachspr.*); **B** (*mark boldly*) **the book covers were ~ed with his name** sein Name prangte auf den Einbänden

**emblem** /'embləm/ *n.* **A** (*Her.*) Wappenbild, *das;* **B** (*symbol*) Emblem, *das;* Wahrzeichen, *das;* (*on national flag etc.*) Hoheitszeichen, *das;* **~ of peace** Friedenssymbol, *das*

**emblematic** /emblɪ'mætɪk/, **emblematical** /emblɪ'mætɪkl/ *adj.* emblematisch; sinnbildlich; **be ~ of sth.** das Sinnbild einer Sache (*Gen.*) sein

**embodiment** /ɪm'bɒdɪmənt/ *n.* **A** (*act, state*) Verkörperung, *die;* **B** (*incarnation*) Inbegriff, *der;* **C** (*incorporation*) Eingliederung, *die;* Integration, *die* (*geh.*)

**embody** /ɪm'bɒdɪ/ *v.t.* **A** (*express tangibly*) Ausdruck verleihen (+ *Dat.*); **his ideas are embodied in this letter** seine Vorstellungen kommen in diesem Brief zum Ausdruck *od.* erhalten in diesem Brief Form und Gestalt; **B** (*give concrete form to*) verkörpern ‹Vorstellungen, Gefühle, Ideale›; **C** (*be incarnation of*) personifizieren; verkörpern; der Inbegriff (+ *Gen.*) sein; **D** (*include*) enthalten

**embolden** /ɪm'bəʊldn/ *v.t.* ermutigen; **~ sb. to do sth.** jmdn. [dazu] ermutigen, etw. zu tun

**embolism** /'embəlɪzm/ *n.* (*Med.*) Embolie, *die*

**emboss** /ɪm'bɒs/ *v.t.* prägen ‹Metall, Papier, Leder usw.›; (*with heat*) gaufrieren ‹Papier, Gewebe usw.›; **an ~ed design** ein erhabenes Muster; **~ed notepaper** geprägtes Briefpapier; **~ed stamp** im Prägedruck hergestellte Brief-/Wertmarke

**embrace** /ɪm'breɪs/ **1** *v.t.* **A** (*hold in arms*) umarmen; **they ~d [each other]** sie umarmten sich *od.* (*geh.*) einander; **B** (*fig.: surround*) umgeben; **C** (*accept*) wahrnehmen, ergreifen ‹Gelegenheit›; annehmen ‹Angebot›; **D** (*adopt*) annehmen; **~ a cause** eine Sache zu seiner eigenen machen; **~ Catholicism** sich zum Katholizismus bekennen; **E** (*include*) umfassen. **2** *n.* Umarmung, *die;* **he held her to him in a close ~:** er hielt sie eng umschlungen

**embrasure** /ɪm'breɪʒə(r)/ *n.* **A** (*of door, window*) [abgeschrägte] Laibung; **B** (*in parapet*) Schießscharte, *die*

**embrocation** /embrə'keɪʃn/ *n.* Einreibemittel, *das;* Liniment, *das* (*fachspr.*)

**embroider** /ɪm'brɔɪdə(r)/ *v.t.* sticken ‹Blumen, Muster›; besticken ‹Tuch, Kleid›; (*fig.*) ausschmücken ‹Erzählung, Wahrheit›

**embroiderer** /ɪm'brɔɪdərə(r)/ *n.* Sticker, *der*/Stickerin, *die*

**embroidery** /ɪm'brɔɪdərɪ/ *n.* **A** Stickerei, *die;* **B** *no pl.* (*embroidering*) Sticken, *das;* **C** (*fig.: ornament*) Ausschmückungen *Pl.;* schmückendes Beiwerk

**embroil** /ɪm'brɔɪl/ *v.t.* **~ sb. in sth.** jmdn. in etw. (*Akk.*) hineinziehen; **become/be ~ed in a war** in einen Krieg verwickelt werden/sein; **~ oneself in a dispute** sich in einen Streit einmischen

**embryo** /'embrɪəʊ/ *n., pl.* **~s** Embryo, *der;* **in ~** (*fig.*) im Keim; in nuce (*geh.*); **the plans are as yet in ~:** die Planungen befinden sich erst im Anfangsstadium

**embryology** /embrɪ'ɒlədʒɪ/ *n.* (*Biol.*) Embryologie, *die*

**embryonic** /embrɪ'ɒnɪk/ *adj.* (*Biol., fig.*) Embryonal‹entwicklung, -struktur, -zustand, -stadium›; unausgereift ‹Vorstellung›; **~ membrane** Eihülle, *die;* **~ plant** Pflanzenembryo, *der;* **~ plan** Plan im Embryonalstadium

**'em dash** *n.* (*Printing*) Geviertstrich, *der*

**emend** /ɪ'mend/ *v.t.* (*Lit.*) emendieren (*fachspr.*); berichtigen

**emendation** /i:men'deɪʃn/ *n.* (*Lit.*) Emendation, *die* (*fachspr.*); Berichtigung, *die*

**emerald** /'emərəld/ **1** *n.* **A** Smaragd, *der;* **B** ⇒ **emerald green**. **2** *adj.* **A** smaragdgrün; **B** **~ ring** Smaragdring, *der;* **C** **the E~ Isle** die Grüne Insel

**emerald 'green** *n.* Smaragdgrün, *das*

**emerge** /ɪ'mɜ:dʒ/ *v.i.* **A** (*come up out of liquid, come into view, crop up*) auftauchen (**from** aus, **from behind** hinter + *Dat.*, **from beneath** *or* **under** unter + *Dat.* hervor); **the sun ~d from behind the clouds** die Sonne trat hinter den Wolken hervor; **~ from the shadow into bright daylight**

aus dem Schatten ans helle Tageslicht treten *od.* kommen; **the river ~s from the mountains** der Fluss tritt aus dem Gebirge heraus; **the caterpillar ~d from the egg/ as a beautiful butterfly** die Raupe schlüpfte aus dem Ei/wurde zu einem wunderschönen Schmetterling; **difficulties may ~ in this venture** bei diesem Unterfangen können Schwierigkeiten auftreten; Ⓑ (*come out, become known, arise by evolution*) hervorgehen (**from** aus); ‹Leben:› entstammen (**from** + *Dat.*); ‹Wahrheit:› an den Tag kommen; ‹Virus usw.:› entstehen; **it ~s that ...:** es zeigt sich *od.* stellt sich heraus, dass ...; **it ~s from this that ...:** hieraus geht hervor, dass ...; **two essential points ~d from the discussion** aus der Diskussion haben sich zwei wesentliche Punkte ergeben

**emergence** /ɪˈmɜːdʒəns/ *n.* Ⓐ (*rising out of liquid*) Auftauchen, *das;* Ⓑ (*coming forth*) Hervortreten, *das;* (*of mode, school of thought, new ideas*) Aufkommen, *das*

**emergency** /ɪˈmɜːdʒənsɪ/ ❶ *n.* Ⓐ (*serious happening*) Notfall, *der;* **in an** *or* **in case of ~:** im Notfall; **be prepared for any ~:** auf den Notfall vorbereitet sein; **~ [case]** (*Med.*) Notfall, *der;* **be called out on an ~:** zu einem Notfall gerufen werden; Ⓑ (*Polit.*) Ausnahmezustand, *der;* **declare a state of ~:** den Ausnahmezustand ausrufen *od.* erklären. ❷ *adj.* Not‹bremse, -ruf, -ausgang, -landung›; **~ ward** Unfallstation, *die*

**e'mergency services** *n. pl.* Hilfsdienste *Pl.*

**emergent** /ɪˈmɜːdʒənt/ *adj.* Ⓐ (*rising out*) aufragend ‹Insel, Felsen, Baum› (**from** aus); jung, sprießend ‹Vegetation›; Ⓑ jung, aufstrebend ‹Volk›

**emeritus** /ɪˈmerɪtəs/ *adj.* emeritiert ‹Professor›; **professor ~:** Professor emeritus

**emery** /ˈemərɪ/ *n.* Schmirgel, *der*

**emery: ~ board** *n.* Schleifbrett, *das;* (*strip for fingernails*) Sandblattfeile, *die;* **~ paper** *n.* Schmirgelpapier, *das*

**emetic** /ɪˈmetɪk/ (*Med.*) ❶ *adj.* emetisch (*fachspr.*); Brechreiz erregend; **be ~:** Brechreiz erregen. ❷ *n.* Emetikum, *das* (*fachspr.*); Brechmittel, *das*

**EMF** *abbr.* **electromotive force** EMK

**emigrant** /ˈemɪgrənt/ ❶ *adj.* auswandernd; emigrierend; **~ birds** Zugvögel *Pl;* **the ~ population in the USA** die Einwanderer in den USA. ❷ *n.* (*person*) Auswanderer, *der*/ Auswanderin, *die;* Emigrant, *der*/Emigrantin, *die;* (*plant*) Wanderpflanze, *die*

**emigrate** /ˈemɪgreɪt/ *v.i.* auswandern, emigrieren (**to** nach, **from** aus)

**emigration** /emɪˈgreɪʃn/ *n.* Auswanderung, Emigration, *die* (**to** nach, **from** aus)

**émigré** /ˈemɪgreɪ/ *n.* Emigrant, *der*/Emigrantin, *die*

**eminence** /ˈemɪnəns/ *n.* Ⓐ *no pl.* (*distinguished superiority*) hohes Ansehen; **person of great ~:** bedeutender *od.* hoch angesehener Mensch; **win/reach/attain ~:** hohes Ansehen erwerben/erreichen/erlangen; **rise to** *or* **reach ~:** zu hohem Ansehen gelangen; Ⓑ (*person*) angesehener Mensch; Ⓒ (*rising ground*) Erhebung, *die;* Ⓓ **E~** (*Eccl.*) Eminenz, *die*

**éminence grise** /eɪmiːnɑ̃s ˈgriːz/ *n.* graue Eminenz

**eminent** /ˈemɪnənt/ *adj.* Ⓐ (*exalted, distinguished*) bedeutend, hoch angesehen ‹Redner, Gelehrter, Künstler›; **~ guest** hoher Gast; **the most ~ citizens** die angesehensten Bürger; **be ~ in one's field** eine Koryphäe auf seinem Gebiet sein; Ⓑ (*remarkable*) ausnehmend ‹Eigenschaft›

**eminently** /ˈemɪnəntlɪ/ *adv.* ausnehmend; vorzüglich ‹geeignet›; überaus ‹erfolgreich›; **~ respectable** hoch angesehen

**emir** /eˈmɪə(r)/ *n.* Emir, *der*

**emirate** /ˈemɪərət/ *n.* Emirat, *das*

**emissary** /ˈemɪsərɪ/ *n.* Emissär, *der*/Emissärin, *die;* Abgesandte, *der/die;* **special ~:** Sonderbotschafter, *der*/-botschafterin, *die*

**emission** /ɪˈmɪʃn/ *n.* Ⓐ (*giving off or out*) Aussendung, *die;* (*of vapour*) Ablassen, *das;* (*of liquid*) Ausscheidung, *die;* (*of sparks*) Versprühen, *das;* **~ of light/heat** Licht-/Wärmeausstrahlung, *die;* **~ of fumes** Abgasemission, *die;* **~ of smell/gas** Geruchs-/ Gasausströmung, *die;* **~ of rays** Strahlenaussendung, *die;* **~ of sound** Geräuschabgabe, *die;* **~ of smoke/lava** Rauch-/Lavaausstoß, *der;* Ⓑ (*thing given off*) Abstrahlung, *die;* (*effluvium*) Ausdünstung, *die;* (*of semen*) Samenerguss, *der*

**emit** /ɪˈmɪt/ *v.t.*, **-tt-** aussenden ‹Strahlen›; ausstrahlen ‹Wärme, Licht›; ausstoßen ‹Lava, Asche, Rauch, Schrei›; ausscheiden ‹Flüssigkeit›; abgeben ‹Geräusch›; versprühen ‹Funken›; ausströmen ‹Geruch, Gas›; ablassen ‹Dampf›

**emolument** /ɪˈmɒljʊmənt/ *n., usu. in pl.* Vergütung, *die;* Bezüge *Pl.*

**emoticon** /ɪˈmɒtɪkɒn/ *n.* (*Computing*) Emoticon, *das*

**emotion** /ɪˈməʊʃn/ *n.* Ⓐ (*state*) Ergriffenheit, *die;* Bewegtheit, *die;* **speak with deep ~:** tief ergriffen *od.* bewegt sprechen; **charged with ~:** gefühlsgeladen; **be overcome with ~:** von Gefühl übermannt sein; **be touched with/full of ~:** ergriffen/bewegt sein; **show no ~:** keine Gefühlsregung *od.* Emotionen zeigen; Ⓑ (*feeling*) Gefühl, *das;* **conflicting ~s** widerstrebende Gefühle

**emotional** /ɪˈməʊʃənl/ *adj.* Ⓐ (*of emotions*) emotional; Gefühls‹ausdruck, -leben, -erlebnis, -reaktion›; Gemüts‹zustand, -störung›; seelisch ‹Belastung›; psychologisch ‹Erpressung›; gefühlsgeladen ‹Worte, Musik, Geschichte, Film›; gefühlsbetont, emotional ‹Verhalten›; gefühlsmäßig ‹Einschätzung, Entscheidung›; gefühlvoll ‹Stimme, Ton›; **~ appeal** Appell an die Gefühle *od.* Emotionen; Ⓑ (*liable to excessive emotion*) emotiv (*geh.*); leicht erregbar ‹Person›; **~ character** *or* **nature** *or* **disposition** leichte Erregbarkeit; **get ~ over sth.** sich über etw. (*Akk.*) erregen

**emotionalism** /ɪˈməʊʃənəlɪzm/ *n., no pl.* Gefühlsbetontheit, *die;* Rührseligkeit, *die* (*abwertend*)

**emotionally** /ɪˈməʊʃənəlɪ/ *adv.* emotional; gefühlvoll ‹sprechen, sich verhalten›; gefühlsmäßig, emotional ‹reagieren›; gefühlsbetont ‹denken›; **thank sb. ~:** [sich bei] jmdm. von Herzen [be]danken; **be ~ exhausted/worn out/ disturbed** seelisch erschöpft/ausgelaugt/gestört sein; **get ~ involved with sb.** eine gefühlsmäßige Bindung mit jmdm. eingehen

**emotionless** /ɪˈməʊʃnlɪs/ *adj.* emotionslos; emotionsfrei; gefühllos; ausdruckslos ‹Gesicht›; gleichgültig ‹Stimme›

**emotive** /ɪˈməʊtɪv/ *adj.* emotional; gefühlsbetont; emotiv (*Psych., Sprachw.*)

**empathize** /ˈempəθaɪz/ *v.i.* **~ with sb.** sich in jmdn. hineinversetzen; **~ with sth.** etw. nachempfinden

**empathy** /ˈempəθɪ/ *n.* Empathie, *die* (*Psych.*); Einfühlung, *die*

**emperor** /ˈempərə(r)/ *n.* ▶ **1617** Kaiser, *der;* **~ penguin** Kaiserpinguin, *der*

**emphasis** /ˈemfəsɪs/ *n., pl.* **emphases** /ˈemfəsiːz/ Ⓐ (*in speech etc.*) Betonung, *die;* **the ~ is on sth.** die Betonung liegt auf etw. (*Dat.*); **lay** *or* **place** *or* **put ~ on sth.** etw. betonen; Ⓑ (*intensity*) Nachdruck, *der;* **do sth. with ~:** etw. nachdrücklich tun; Ⓒ (*importance attached*) Gewicht, *das;* **lay** *or* **place** *or* **put [considerable] ~ on sth.** [großes] Gewicht auf etw. (*Akk.*) legen; **the school's ~ is on languages** die Schule legt das Schwergewicht auf die [Fremd]sprachen; **the ~ has shifted** der Akzent hat sich verlagert; **with particular** *or* **special ~ on sth.** unter besonderer Berücksichtigung einer Sache (*Gen.*)

**emphasize** (**emphasise**) /ˈemfəsaɪz/ *v.t.* (*lit. or fig.*) betonen; (*attach importance to*) Gewicht auf etw. (*Akk.*) legen; **sth. cannot be too strongly ~d** etw. kann nicht genug betont werden

**emphatic** /ɪmˈfætɪk/ *adj.* nachdrücklich; emphatisch (*geh.*); eindringlich, emphatisch (*geh.*) ‹Redner›; (*forcible*) demonstrativ ‹Rückzug, Ablehnung›; eindringlich ‹Demonstration›; **make sth. more ~:** einer Sache (*Dat.*) Nachdruck verleihen; **be quite ~ that ...:** durchaus darauf bestehen, dass ...

**emphatically** /ɪmˈfætɪkəlɪ/ *adv.* nachdrücklich; emphatisch (*geh.*); eindringlich ‹sprechen›; (*decisively*) entschieden ‹bestreiten usw.›

**emphysema** /emfɪˈsiːmə/ *n.* ▶ **1232** (*Med.*) Emphysem, *das*

**empire** /ˈempaɪə(r)/ *n.* Ⓐ Reich, *das;* **the E~** (*Hist.*) (*British*) das Empire; das britische Weltreich; (*Holy Roman*) das Heilige Römische Reich; Ⓑ (*commercial organization*) Imperium, *das* (*fig.*)

**empire: ~ builder** *n.* (*fig.*) **be an ~ builder** seinen Einflussbereich ausweiten wollen; **~-building** *n.* (*fig.*) **it is just ~-building** es geht dabei nur um den Aufbau eines kleinen Imperiums

**empirical** /ɪmˈpɪrɪkl/ *adj.* empirisch; empirisch begründet ‹Entscheidung, Argument, Wissen, Schlussfolgerung›

**empirically** /ɪmˈpɪrɪkəlɪ/ *adv.* empirisch

**empiricism** /ɪmˈpɪrɪsɪzm/ *n., no pl.* Ⓐ (*method*) Empirie, *die;* Ⓑ (*Philos.*) Empirismus, *der*

**emplacement** /ɪmˈpleɪsmənt/ *n.* (*Mil.*) Geschützstand, *der*

**employ** /ɪmˈplɔɪ/ ❶ *v.t.* Ⓐ (*take into one's service*) einstellen; (*keep in one's service*) beschäftigen; **are you ~ed in London/as a teacher?** arbeiten Sie in London/als Lehrer?; **be ~ed by** *or* **with a company** bei einer Firma arbeiten; Ⓑ (*use services of*) **~ sb. in** *or* **on sth.** jmdn. für etw. einsetzen; **~ sb. in** *or* **on doing sth., ~ sb. to do sth.** jmdn. dafür einsetzen, etw. zu tun; Ⓒ (*use*) einsetzen (**for, in, on** für); unternehmen ‹Anstrengungen›; anwenden ‹Methode, List› (**for, in, on** bei); **~ sth. to do sth.** etw. anwenden, um etwas zu tun; **~ [one's] time on sth./ [on] doing sth.** [seine] Zeit mit etw. verbringen/damit verbringen, etw. zu tun; Ⓓ (*busy*) **~ oneself/sb. doing sth./in sth.** sich/jmdn. damit beschäftigen, etw. zu tun/mit etw. beschäftigen.
❷ *n., no pl., no indef. art.* Arbeit, *die;* Beschäftigung, *die;* **be in the ~ of sb.** bei jmdm. beschäftigt sein; in jmds. Diensten stehen (*veralt.*); **the firm has 500 people in its ~:** bei der Firma sind 500 Leute beschäftigt

**employable** /ɪmˈplɔɪəbl/ *adj.* Ⓐ (*fit to be taken into service*) **be ~:** zu beschäftigen sein; Ⓑ (*usable*) verwendbar; **be ~ as/for sth.** als/für etw. verwendet werden können

**employee** (*Amer.:* **employe**) /emplɔɪˈiː, emˈplɔɪiː/ *n.* Angestellte, *der/die;* (*in contrast to employer*) Arbeitnehmer, *der*/-nehmerin, *die;* **the firm's ~s** die Belegschaft der Firma

**employer** /ɪmˈplɔɪə(r)/ *n.* Arbeitgeber, *der*/ -geberin, *die;* **the firm is only a small ~:** die Firma hat nur wenige Beschäftigte

**employment** /ɪmˈplɔɪmənt/ *n., no pl.* Ⓐ (*work*) Arbeit, *die;* **there's no ~ available** es gibt keine freien Stellen *od.* keine Arbeit; **be in gainful ~:** erwerbstätig sein; **be in ~ with sb.** bei jmdm. arbeiten; **be in/without regular ~:** eine/keine feste Anstellung haben; Ⓑ (*regular trade or profession*) Beschäftigung, *die;* **what is your ~?** welchen Beruf üben Sie aus?; Ⓒ *no art.* (*amount of work available*) **full ~:** Vollbeschäftigung, *die;* Ⓓ **Secretary for E~** (*Brit.*) Arbeitsminister, *der*/-ministerin, *die*

**employment: ~ agency** *n.* Stellenvermittlung, *die;* **~ exchange, ~ office** *ns.* (*Brit.*) Arbeitsamt, *das*

**emporium** /emˈpɔːrɪəm/ *n., pl.* **~s** *or* **emporia** /emˈpɔːrɪə/ Ⓐ (*market*) Handelszentrum, *das;* Ⓑ (*shop*) Kaufhaus, *das*

**empower** /ɪmˈpaʊə(r)/ *v.t.* (*authorize*) ermächtigen; (*enable*) befähigen

**empress** /ˈemprɪs/ *n.* Kaiserin, *die*

**emptiness** /ˈemptɪnɪs/ *n., no pl.* (*lit. or fig.*) Leere, *die*

**empty** /ˈemptɪ/ ❶ *adj.* Ⓐ leer; **find an ~ seat/parking place** einen freien Sitz-/Parkplatz finden; **~ of sth.** ohne etw.; **~ of people** menschenleer; **the street is ~ of traffic** in der Straße herrscht kein Verkehr; ⇒ *also* **stomach** 1 A; Ⓑ (*coll.: hungry*) **I feel a bit ~:** ich bin ein bisschen hungrig;

an hour later you feel quite ~: eine Stunde später hat man schon wieder Hunger; **C** (*fig.*) (*foolish*) dumm; hohl ‹Kopf›; (*meaningless*) leer. **2** *n.* (*vehicle*) Leerfahrzeug, *das;* (*bottle*) leere Flasche; (*container*) leerer Behälter; **sb. is running on ~:** jmdm. geht der Sprit aus: (*fig.*) jmd. ist am Ende. **3** *v.t.* **A** (*remove contents of*) leeren; [aus]leeren ‹Tasche›; (*finish using contents of*) aufbrauchen; (*remove people from*) räumen; (*eat/drink whole contents of*) leer essen ‹Teller›/leeren ‹Glas›; **~ one's bladder/bowels** die Blase/den Darm entleeren; **B** (*transfer*) umfüllen (**into** in + *Akk.*); (*pour*) schütten (**over** über + *Akk.*); **~ sth. into/down the sink** etw. in den Ausguss schütten. **4** *v.i.* **A** (*become* ~) sich leeren; **B** (*discharge*) **~ into** ‹Fluss, Abwasserkanal:› münden in (+ *Akk.*)

**empty: ~-'handed** *pred. adj.* mit leeren Händen; **~-headed** *adj.* hohlköpfig (*abwertend*)

**EMS** *abbr.* **European Monetary System** EWS

**emu** /'iːmjuː/ *n.* (*Ornith.*) Emu, *der*

**EMU** *abbr.* **Economic and Monetary Union** WWU

**emulate** /'emjʊleɪt/ *v.t.* **A** (*try to equal or excel*) nacheifern (+ *Dat.*); **B** (*imitate zealously*) nachahmen

**emulation** /emjʊ'leɪʃn/ *n.* **A** (*attempt at equalling or excelling*) **~ of sb.** Bestreben, es jmdm. gleichzutun; **B** (*zealous imitation*) Nachahmung, *die*

**emulsifier** /ɪ'mʌlsɪfaɪə(r)/ *n.* Emulgator, *der*

**emulsify** /ɪ'mʌlsɪfaɪ/ *v.t.* emulgieren

**emulsion** /ɪ'mʌlʃn/ *n.* **A** Emulsion, *die;* **B** ⇒ **emulsion paint**

**e'mulsion paint** *n.* Dispersionsfarbe, *die*

**en** /en/ *n.* (*Printing*) Halbgeviert, *das*

**enable** /ɪ'neɪbl/ *v.t.* **~ sb. to do sth.** es jmdm. ermöglichen, etw. zu tun; **~ sth. [to be done]** etw. ermöglichen; **~ an investigation to be made** eine Untersuchung ermöglichen; **enabling act** (*Law*) Ermächtigungsgesetz, *das;* (*Amer. Law: legalizing*) gesetzliche Sonderregelung

**enact** /ɪ'nækt/ *v.t.* **A** (*ordain, make law*) erlassen; **~ that ...:** verfügen, dass ...; **B** (*act out*) aufführen ‹Theaterstück›; spielen ‹Rolle›; mitwirken bei ‹Feier›; **be ~ed** ‹Geschehen, Szene:› sich abspielen

**enamel** /ɪ'næml/ **1** *n.* **A** Emaille, *die;* Email, *das;* (*paint*) Lack, *der;* (*on pottery*) Glasur, *die;* **B** (~ *painting*) Email[le]malerei, *die;* **C** (*Anat.*) [Zahn]schmelz, *der.* **2** *attrib. adj.* **A** (*containing* ~) Email[le]-; **B** (*with ~ coating and/or design*) emailliert; Email[le]‹geschirr›. **3** *v.t.,* (*Brit.*) **-ll-** emaillieren; glasieren ‹Ton, Steinzeug›

**enamoured** (*Brit.; Amer.:* **enamored**) /ɪ'næməd/ *adj.* **~ of sb.** (*in love with*) in jmdn. verliebt; (*liking*) von jmdm. angetan; **[not exactly** *or* **particularly] ~ of sth.** von etw. [nicht gerade] begeistert

**en bloc** /ɑ̃ 'blɒk/ *adv.* en bloc

**encamp** /ɪn'kæmp/ (*Mil.*) **1** *v.t.* **the troops were ~ed near the border** die Truppen bezogen ein Lager nahe der Grenze. **2** *v.i.* ein Lager aufschlagen

**encampment** /ɪn'kæmpmənt/ *n.* **A** *no pl.* Lagern, *das;* **B** (*place*) Lager, *das*

**encapsulate** /ɪn'kæpsjʊleɪt/ *v.t.* **A** (*in capsule*) einkapseln ‹Medikament›; in eine[r] Kapsel einschließen; (*as in capsule*) einschließen; **B** (*fig.*) festhalten; einfangen (*geh.*)

**encase** /ɪn'keɪs/ *v.t.* einschließen; fassen ‹Edelstein›; **the watch was ~d in metal** die Armbanduhr hatte ein Metallgehäuse; **~ in plaster** eingipsen ‹Bein, Arm›

**encash** /ɪn'kæʃ/ *v.t.* (*Brit.*) (*realize*) [in bar] einnehmen; sich (*Dat.*) [bar] auszahlen lassen ‹Gewinn›; (*convert into cash*) [bar] einlösen

**encephalitis** /ensefə'laɪtɪs/ *n.* (*Med.*) Enzephalitis, *die* (*fachspr.*); Gehirnentzündung, *die*

**enchant** /ɪn'tʃɑːnt/ *v.t.* **A** (*bewitch*) verzaubern; **she ~s men with her beauty** (*fig.*) sie bezaubert die Männer mit ihrer Schönheit; **B** (*delight*) entzücken; **be ~ed by sth.** von etw. entzückt sein; **we were ~ed by the place** wir waren von dem Ort bezaubert

**enchanted** /ɪn'tʃɑːntɪd/ *adj.* **A** (*bewitched*) verzaubert; **~ forest** Zauberwald, *der;* **~ evening** (*fig.*) zauberischer Abend (*geh.*); **B** (*delighted*) entzückt

**enchanting** /ɪn'tʃɑːntɪŋ/ *adj.* **A** zauberisch (*veralt.*); **~ power** Zauberkraft, *die;* **B** (*delightful*) entzückend; bezaubernd

**enchantingly** /ɪn'tʃɑːntɪŋlɪ/ *adv.* bezaubernd

**enchantment** /ɪn'tʃɑːntmənt/ *n.* **A** Verzauberung, *die;* (*fig.*) Zauber, *der;* **world of ~:** Zauberwelt, *die;* **B** (*delight*) Entzücken, *das* (**with** über + *Akk.*)

**enchantress** /ɪn'tʃɑːntrɪs/ *n.* (*lit. or fig.*) Zauberin, *die*

**encipher** /ɪn'saɪfə(r)/ *v.t.* verschlüsseln; chiffrieren

**encircle** /ɪn'sɜːkl/ *v.t.* **A** umgeben; **the enemy ~d us** der Feind kreiste uns ein *od.* umstellte uns; **~d with** *or* **by bodyguards** von Leibwächtern umringt; **his arms ~d her waist** seine Arme umschlangen ihre Taille; **B** (*mark with circle*) einkreisen ‹Buchstabe, Antwort›

**encirclement** /ɪn'sɜːklmənt/ *n.* (*Mil.*) Einkreisung, *die*

**encl.** *abbr.* **enclosed a, enclosure[s]** Anl.

**enclave** /'enkleɪv/ *n.* (*lit. or fig.*) Enklave, *die*

**enclitic** /en'klɪtɪk/ (*Ling.*) **1** *adj.* enklitisch. **2** *n.* Enklitikon, *das*

**enclose** /ɪn'kləʊz/ *v.t.* **A** (*surround*) umgeben; (*shut up or in*) einschließen; **be ~d in a cell/tomb/coffin** in einer Zelle/einem Grab/Sarg eingeschlossen sein; **~d in this casing is ...:** in diesem Gehäuse befindet sich ...; **~ land in** *or* **with barbed wire** Land mit Stacheldraht einzäunen; **B** (*put in envelope with letter*) beilegen (**with, in** *Dat.*); **I [herewith] ~ the completed application form** anbei der ausgefüllte Bewerbungsbogen; **your passport is ~d herewith** Ihr Pass liegt als Anlage bei; **please find ~d, ~d please find** als Anlage übersenden wir Ihnen; anbei erhalten Sie; **a cheque for £10 is ~d** beiliegend finden Sie einen Scheck über 10 Pfund; **C** (*Math.*) einschließen; **D** (*Hist.: make private*) zur privaten Nutzung einfrieden

**enclosed** /ɪn'kləʊzd/ *adj.* **A** (*in a container*) darin enthalten; (*included with letter*) beigelegt; beigefügt; **from the ~ you will see that ...:** aus der Anlage werden Sie ersehen, dass ...; **B** (*closed off*) eingefriedet; (*by fence*) eingezäunt

**enclosure** /ɪn'kləʊʒə(r)/ *n.* **A** (*action*) Einfriedung, *die;* (*with fence*) Einzäunung, *die;* **B** (*place*) eingefriedeter/eingezäunter Bereich; (*in zoo*) Gehege, *das;* (*paddock*) Koppel, *die;* **C** (*fence*) Umzäunung, *die;* (*wall etc.*) Einfriedung, *die;* **D** (*with letter in envelope*) Anlage, *die*

**encode** /ɪn'kəʊd/ *v.t.* verschlüsseln; chiffrieren

**encomium** /en'kəʊmɪəm/ *n., pl.* **~s** *or* **encomia** /en'kəʊmɪə/ Lobpreisung, *die* (*geh.*); **give sb. an ~:** jmdn. lobpreisen (*geh.*)

**encompass** /ɪn'kʌmpəs/ *v.t.* **A** (*encircle*) umgeben; (*surround*) umringen; **B** (*take in*) umfassen; **C** (*contain*) einhüllen

**encore** /'ɒŋkɔː(r), 'ɒŋkɔː(r)/ **1** *int.* Zugabe! **2** *n.* Zugabe, *die;* **receive three ~s** drei Zugaben geben müssen; **give an ~** ‹Band, Orchester:› eine Zugabe spielen. **3** *v.t.* als Zugabe verlangen ‹Lied, Tanz usw.›; um eine Zugabe bitten ‹Sänger, Tänzer, Künstler›

**encounter** /ɪn'kaʊntə(r)/ **1** *v.t.* **A** (*as adversary*) treffen auf (+ *Akk.*); **B** (*by chance*) begegnen (+ *Dat.*); **C** (*meet with, come across*) stoßen auf (+ *Akk.*) ‹Problem, Schwierigkeit, Kritik, Widerstand usw.›. **2** *n.* **A** (*in combat*) Zusammenstoß, *der;* **have an ~ with the authorities over a matter** mit den Behörden wegen einer Angelegenheit aneinander geraten; **I had a slight ~ with another car yesterday** (*coll. iron.*) ich hatte gestern eine etwas heftige Begegnung mit einem anderen Auto (*iron.*); **verbal ~:** Wortgefecht, *das;* **this was not his first ~ with the law** das war nicht das erste Mal, dass er mit dem Gesetz in Konflikt kam; **B** (*chance meeting, introduction*) Begegnung, *die;* **have a chance ~ with sb.** jmdm. zufällig begegnen

**en'counter group** *n.* Encountergruppe, *die* (*Psych.*)

**encourage** /ɪn'kʌrɪdʒ/ *v.t.* **A** (*stimulate, incite*) ermutigen; **bread ~s rats and mice** Brot lockt Ratten und Mäuse an; **B** (*promote*) fördern; beleben ‹Verkauf›; **~ a smile/a response from sb.** jmdm. ein Lächeln/eine Reaktion entlocken; **~ bad habits** schlechte Angewohnheiten unterstützen; **we do not ~ smoking in this office** wir unterstützen es nicht, dass in diesem Büro geraucht wird; **C** (*urge*) **~ sb. to do sth.** jmdn. dazu ermuntern, etw. zu tun; **D** (*cheer*) **be [much] ~d by sth.** durch etw. neuen Mut schöpfen; **we were ~d to hear** *or* **felt ~d when we heard ...:** wir schöpften neuen Mut, als wir hörten ...

**encouragement** /ɪn'kʌrɪdʒmənt/ *n.* **A** (*support, incitement*) Ermutigung, *die* (**from** durch); **give sb. ~:** jmdn. ermutigen; **get** *or* **receive ~ from sth.** durch etw. ermutigt werden; **B** (*urging*) Ermunterung, *die;* **C** (*stimulus*) Ansporn, *der;* **be an ~ to rats/moths** *etc.* Ratten/Motten *usw.* anlocken

**encouraging** /ɪn'kʌrɪdʒɪŋ/ *adj.* ermutigend; **the teacher is very ~** (*by nature*) der Lehrer hat eine sehr ermutigende Art

**encouragingly** /ɪn'kʌrɪdʒɪŋlɪ/ *adv.* ermutigend

**encroach** /ɪn'krəʊtʃ/ *v.i.* (*lit. or fig.*) **~ [on sth.]** [in etw. (*Akk.*)] eindringen; **the shadows began ~ing on the lawn** die Schatten drangen allmählich auf den Rasen vor; **the sea is ~ing [on the land]** das Meer dringt vor; **~ on sb.'s time** jmds. Zeit immer mehr in Anspruch nehmen

**encroachment** /ɪn'krəʊtʃmənt/ *n.* (*lit. or fig.*) Eindringen, *das* (**on** in + *Akk.*); **make ~s** eindringen; **make ~s on sb.'s time** jmds. Zeit immer mehr in Anspruch nehmen

**encrust** /ɪn'krʌst/ *v.t.* überkrusten; **be ~ed with diamonds/beads/gold** über und über mit Diamanten/Perlen besetzt/mit Gold überzogen sein

**encumber** /ɪn'kʌmbə(r)/ *v.t.* **A** (*hamper*) behindern; **~ oneself/sb. with sth.** sich/jmdn. mit etw. belasten; **B** (*burden*) **~ sb. with debt** jmdn. mit Schulden belasten

**encumbrance** /ɪn'kʌmbrəns/ *n.* **A** (*burden*) Last, *die;* (*nuisance*) Belastung, *die;* **B** (*impediment*) Hindernis, *das* (**to** für); **be without ~** (*without family*) ohne Anhang sein; **C** (*on property*) Belastung, *die*

**encyclic** /en'sɪklɪk/, **encyclical** /en'sɪklɪkl/ **1** *adj.* **~ letter** Enzyklika, *die.* **2** *n.* Enzyklika, *die*

**encyclopaedia** /ensaɪklə'piːdɪə, ɪnsaɪklə'piːdɪə/ *n.* **A** Lexikon, *das;* Enzyklopädie, *die;* **B** (*Hist.*) **the E~:** die Enzyklopädie. ⇒ *also* **walking 1**

**encyclopaedic** /ensaɪklə'piːdɪk, ɪnsaɪklə'piːdɪk/ *adj.* enzyklopädisch

**encyclopedia** *etc.* ⇒ **encyclopaedia** *etc.*

**end** /end/ **1** *n.* **A** (*extremity, farthest point, limit*) Ende, *das;* (*of nose, hair, tail, branch, finger*) Spitze, *die;* **go to the ~s of the earth** bis ans Ende der Welt gehen; **that was the ~** (*coll.*) (*no longer tolerable*) da war Schluss (*ugs.*); (*very bad*) das war das Letzte (*ugs.*); **you are the ~** (*coll.*) du bist [einfach] unmöglich; **he beat him all ~s up** er hat ihn vernichtend geschlagen; **at an ~:** zu Ende; **come to an ~:** enden (⇒ *also* **1 G**); **my patience has come to** *or* **is now at an ~:** meine Geduld ist jetzt am Ende; **our supplies have come to an ~:** unsere Vorräte sind erschöpft; **come to/be coming to the ~ of sth.** etw. aufbrauchen/fast aufgebraucht haben; **turn sth. ~ for ~:** etw. umdrehen; **look at a building/a pencil ~ on** ein Gebäude von der Schmalseite/einen Bleistift von der Spitze her betrachten; **~ on against** *or* **to sth.** mit dem Ende gegen etw.; **from ~ to ~:** von einem Ende zum anderen; **~ to ~:** längs hintereinander; **lay ~ to ~:** aneinander reihen; **keep one's ~ up**

e

(*fig.*) seinen Mann stehen; **make an ~ of sth.** etw. abschaffen; **make [both] ~s meet** (*fig.*) [mit seinem Geld] zurechtkommen; **no ~** (*coll.*) unendlich viel; **it's been criticized no ~:** es ist über die Maßen kritisiert worden; **have no ~ of trouble/a surprise** nichts als Ärger haben/maßlos überrascht sein; **no ~ of a fuss** ein wahnsinniges Theater (*ugs.*); **there is no ~ to sth.** (*coll.*) etw. nimmt kein Ende; **there's no ~ to what you can achieve/learn** du kannst unendlich viel erreichen/lernen; **put an ~ to sth.** einer Sache (*Dat.*) ein Ende machen; **not know** *or* **not be able to tell one ~ of sth. from the other** bei etw. nicht wissen, wo hinten und vorne ist (*ugs.*); **B** (*of box, packet, tube, etc.*) Schmalseite, *die;* (*top/bottom surface*) Ober-/Unterseite, *die;* **on ~** (*upright*) hochkant; **sb.'s hair stands on ~** (*fig.*) jmdm. stehen die Haare zu Berge (*ugs.*); ⇒ *also* **g**; **C** (*remnant*) Rest, *der;* (*of cigarette, candle*) Stummel, *der;* **tie up the/a few [loose] ~s** (*fig.*) die/ein paar Einzelheiten erledigen; **D** (*side*) Seite, *die;* **how are things at the business/social/at your ~?** wie sieht es geschäftlich/mit den sozialen Kontakten/bei dir aus?; **be on the receiving ~ of sth.** etw. abbekommen *od.* einstecken müssen; **he was on the receiving ~ in the fight** er musste in dem Kampf einiges einstecken; **E** (*half of sports pitch or court*) Spielfeldhälfte, *die;* **change ~s** die Seiten wechseln; **choice of ~s** Seitenwahl, *die;* **F** (*of swimming pool*) **deep/shallow ~ [of the pool]** tiefer/flacher Teil [des Schwimmbeckens]; **go in/be thrown in at the deep ~** (*fig.*) ins kalte Wasser springen/geworfen werden; **go [in] off the deep ~** (*fig. coll.*) aus der Haut fahren (*ugs.*); **G** ▶ **1055** (*conclusion, lit. or fig.*) Ende, *das;* (*of lesson, speech, story, discussion, meeting, argument, play, film, book, sentence*) Schluss, *der;* Ende, *das;* **the ~ is not yet** ein Ende ist noch nicht abzusehen; (*there is still hope*) es ist noch nicht aller Tage Abend; **by the ~ of the hour/day/week** *etc.* **we were exhausted** als die Stunde/der Tag/die Woche *usw.* herum war, waren wir erschöpft; **at the ~ of 1987/March** Ende 1987/März; **by the ~ of the meeting** als die Versammlung zu Ende war; **until** *or* **till the ~ of time** bis ans Ende aller Tage; **read to the ~ of the page** die Seite zu Ende lesen; **leave before the ~ of the film** gehen, ehe der Film zu Ende ist; **that's the ~ of sth.** (*coll.: sth. is used up*) etw. ist alle (*ugs.*); **that's the ~ of 'that** (*fig.*) damit ist die Sache erledigt; **will there never be an ~ to all this?** wird das alles nie ein Ende nehmen?; **want [to see] an ~ to sth.** das Ende einer Sache (*Gen.*) wollen; **I shall never hear the ~ of it** (*joc.*) das werde ich noch lange zu hören bekommen; **I wonder if there's an ~ to it all** ich frage mich, ob das denn gar kein Ende nimmt; **be at an ~:** zu Ende sein; **bring a meeting/discussion/lesson to an ~:** eine Versammlung/Diskussion/Unterrichtsstunde beenden; **his education/journey was brought to an abrupt ~:** seine Ausbildung/Reise fand ein plötzliches Ende; **come to an ~:** ein Ende nehmen (⇒ *also* **1 A**); **have come to the ~ of sth.** mit etw. fertig sein; **be coming to the ~ of sth.** mit etw. fast fertig sein; **when you come to the ~ of the page** wenn Sie mit der Seite fertig sind; **in the ~:** schließlich; **on ~:** ununterbrochen; ⇒ *also* **b**; **H** (*downfall, destruction*) Ende, *das;* (*death*) Ende, *das* (*geh. verhüll.*); **meet one's ~:** den Tod finden (*geh.*); **meet its ~** ‹Sache:› sein Ende finden (*fig.*); **sb. is nearing his ~:** mit jmdm. geht es zu Ende (*verhüll.*); **this will be the ~ of him** das bedeutet das Ende für ihn; **drink will be the ~ of him** der Alkohol wird ihn noch ins Grab bringen; **sb. comes to a bad** *or* **sticky ~:** es nimmt ein böses *od.* schlimmes Ende mit jmdm.; **I** (*purpose, object*) Ziel, *das;* Zweck, *der;* **~ in itself** Selbstzweck, *der;* **be an ~ in itself** (*likewise a purpose*) auch ein lohnendes Ziel sein; (*the only purpose*) das eigentliche Ziel sein; **the ~ justifies the means** der Zweck heiligt die Mittel; **with this ~ in view** mit diesem Ziel vor Augen; **as a means to an ~:** als Mittel zum Zweck; **for material ~s** aus materiellen Gründen; **gain** *or* **win** *or* **achieve one's ~s** seine Ziele erreichen; **to** *or* **for this ~:** zu diesem Zweck *od.* (*veralt.*) Ende; **to** *or* **for what ~[s]** zu welchem Zweck *od.* (*veralt.*) Ende; **to no ~:** vergebens; ohne Erfolg. ⇒ *also* **bitter 1 B**; **East End**; **tether 1 B**; **West End**; **without 1 A**; **world A**.

**2** *v.t.* **A** (*bring to an end*) beenden; kündigen ‹Abonnement›; **~ one's life/days** (*spend last part of life*) sein Leben/seine Tage beschließen; **B** (*put an end to, destroy*) ein Ende setzen (+ *Dat.*); **~ it [all]** (*coll.: kill oneself*) [mit dem Leben] Schluss machen (*ugs.*); **C** (*stand as supreme example of*) **a car/feast/race** *etc.* **to ~ all cars/feasts/races** *etc.* ein Auto/Fest/Rennen *usw.*, das alles [bisher Dagewesene] in den Schatten stellt.

**3** *v.i.* enden; **where will it all ~?** wo soll das noch hinführen?; **~ by doing sth.** schließlich etw. tun; **the project ~ed in chaos/disaster** das Vorhaben endete im Chaos/in einer Katastrophe; **the discussion ~ed in a quarrel** die Diskussion endete mit einem Streit; **the match ~ed in a draw** das Spiel ging unentschieden aus

**~ 'up** *v.i.* enden; **we ~ed up in a ditch** (*coll.*) wir landeten in einem Graben (*ugs.*); **he'll ~ up in prison** (*coll.*) er wird im Gefängnis landen (*ugs.*); **we ~ed up at his place** (*coll.*) wir landeten schließlich bei ihm zu Hause (*ugs.*); **~ up [as] a teacher/an alcoholic** (*coll.*) schließlich Lehrer/zum Alkoholiker werden; **I always ~ up doing all the work** (*coll.*) am Ende bleibt die ganze Arbeit immer an mir hängen

**'end-all** ⇒ **be 4**

**endanger** /ɪn'deɪndʒə(r)/ *v.t.* gefährden

**endangered** /ɪn'deɪndʒəd/ *adj.* gefährdet; **an ~ species** eine vom Aussterben bedrohte Art

**'en dash** *n.* (*Printing*) Halbgeviertstrich, *der*

**endear** /ɪn'dɪə(r)/ *v.t.* **~ sb./sth./oneself to sb.** jmdn./etw./sich bei jmdm. beliebt machen

**endearing** /ɪn'dɪərɪŋ/ *adj.* reizend; gewinnend ‹Lächeln, Art›

**endearingly** /ɪn'dɪərɪŋlɪ/ *adv.* reizend; gewinnend ‹lächeln›

**endearment** /ɪn'dɪəmənt/ *n.* Zärtlichkeit, *die;* **term of ~:** Kosename, *der*

**endeavour** (*Brit.; Amer.:* **endeavor**) /ɪn'devə(r)/ **1** *v.i.* **~ to do sth.** sich bemühen, etw. zu tun. **2** *n.* Bemühung, *die;* (*attempt*) Versuch, *der;* **~ to do sth.** Bemühen, etw. zu tun (*geh.*); **make every ~ to do sth.** alle Anstrengungen unternehmen, um etw. zu tun; **make an ~** *or* **make ~s to do sth.** *or* **at doing sth.** sich bemühen, etw. zu tun; **despite his best ~s** obwohl er sich nach Kräften bemühte; **human ~:** das Streben des Menschen

**endemic** /en'demɪk/ *adj.* (*Biol., Med.*) endemisch; einheimisch ‹Pflanze, Tier›; örtlich begrenzt auftretend ‹Infektionskrankheit›; (*regularly found*) verbreitet ‹Krankheit›; [allgemein] verbreitet ‹Gewalt, Alkoholismus, Rastlosigkeit›

**endemically** /en'demɪkəlɪ/ *adv.* endemisch

**'endgame** *n.* Endspiel, *das*

**ending** /'endɪŋ/ *n.* Schluss, *der;* (*of word*) Endung, *die;* ⇒ *also* **happy ending**

**endive** /'endɪv/ *n.* **A** Endivie, *die;* **B** (*Amer.: chicory crown*) Brüsseler Endivie; Chicorée, *der od. die*

**endless** /'endlɪs/ *adj.* **A** endlos; (*coll.: innumerable*) unzählig; (*eternal*) unendlich; **have an ~ wait, wait an ~ time** endlos lange warten; **the journey seemed ~:** die Reise schien kein Ende zu nehmen; **B** (*infinite*) unendlich; endlos ‹Straße›; unbegrenzt ‹Auswahl›; unendlich lang ‹Straße, Liste›

**endless 'cable** *n.* Umlaufseil, *das*

**endlessly** /'endlɪslɪ/ *adv.* **A** (*incessantly*) unaufhörlich ‹streiten, schwatzen›; (*interminably*) endlos lange ‹warten›; **B** (*infinitely*) endlos ‹sich erstrecken, lang›

**endmost** /'endməʊst/ *adj.* letzt...; **the ~ leaves on the branches** die Blätter an den Spitzen der Zweige/Äste

**endocrine** /'endəʊkrɪn/ *adj.* (*Physiol.*) endokrin

**endorse** /ɪn'dɔ:s/ *v.t.* **A** (*write on back of*) auf der Rückseite beschriften; **~ sth. with one's signature** etw. auf der Rückseite signieren; **~ sth. on the [back of the] document** etw. auf die Rückseite des Dokuments schreiben; **B** (*sign one's name on back of*) indossieren ‹Scheck, Wechsel›; **~ a cheque** *etc.* **[over] to sb.** einen Scheck *usw.* durch Indossament auf jmdn. übertragen; **C** (*support, declare approval of*) beipflichten (+ *Dat.*) ‹Meinung, Aussage›; billigen, gutheißen ‹Entscheidung, Handlung, Einstellung›; unterstützen ‹Antrag, Vorschlag, Kandidaten, Kandidatur›; **D** (*Brit.: make entry regarding offence on*) einen Strafvermerk machen auf (+ *Akk. od. Dat.*)

**endorsement** /ɪn'dɔ:smənt/ *n.* **A** (*writing on back*) Beschriftung auf der Rückseite; **the ~ of a document with one's signature** das Unterzeichnen eines Dokuments auf der Rückseite; **B** (*of cheque*) Indossament, *das;* **~ to sb.** Übertragung durch Indossament auf jmdn.; **C** (*support, declaration of approval*) Billigung, *die;* (*of proposal, move, candidate*) Unterstützung, *die;* **D** (*Brit.: entry regarding offence*) Strafvermerk, *der* (**of** auf + *Akk. od. Dat.*)

**endow** /ɪn'daʊ/ *v.t.* **A** (*give permanent income to*) [über Stiftungen/eine Stiftung] finanzieren ‹Einrichtung, Krankenhaus usw.›; mit Geld ausstatten ‹Person›; stiften ‹Preis, Lehrstuhl›; **~ed school** durch Stiftungen finanzierte Schule; **B** (*fig.*) **nature has ~ed her with great beauty** die Natur hat sie mit großer Schönheit ausgestattet; **be ~ed with charm/a talent for music** *etc.* Charme/musikalisches Talent *usw.* besitzen; **be well ~ed** ‹Frau:› Holz vor der Hütte haben (*ugs.*); ‹Mann:› stark gebaut sein (*verhüll.*)

**endowment** /ɪn'daʊmənt/ *n.* **A** (*endowing, property, fund, etc.*) Stiftung, *die;* **B** (*talent etc.*) Begabung, *die*

**endowment: ~ assurance** *n.* abgekürzte *od.* gemischte Lebensversicherung; **~ mortgage** *n.* ≈ Tilgungslebensversicherung, *die;* **~ policy** ⇒ **~ assurance**

**end: ~paper** *n.* Vorsatz, *der;* Vorsatzblatt, *das;* **~ point** *n.* **A** (*Chem.*) Umschlagspunkt, *der;* **B** (*fig.*) Endpunkt, *der;* **~ product** *n.* (*lit. or fig.; also Chem.*) Endprodukt, *das;* (*fig.*) Resultat, *das;* **~ re'sult** *n.* Ergebnis, *das;* (*consequence*) Folge, *die*

**endue** /ɪn'dju:/ *v.t.* (*literary*) **A** (*clothe*) bekleiden (**with** mit); **B** (*furnish*) ⇒ **endow B**

**endurable** /ɪn'djʊərəbl/ *adj.* erträglich

**endurance** /ɪn'djʊərəns/ *n.* **A** Widerstandskraft, *die* (**of** gegen); (*ability to withstand strain*) Ausdauer, *die;* (*patience*) Geduld, *die;* **the material's ~ [of wear and tear]** die Strapazierfähigkeit des Materials; **past** *or* **beyond ~:** unerträglich; **B** (*lastingness*) Dauerhaftigkeit, *die*

**en'durance test** *n.* Belastungsprobe, *die*

**endure** /ɪn'djʊə(r)/ **1** *v.t.* (*undergo, tolerate*) ertragen; (*submit to*) über sich ergehen lassen; (*suffer*) erleiden ‹Verlust, Unrecht›; **~ to do sth.** es ertragen, etw. zu tun; **I can't ~ the thought of** *or* **to think of him alone there** der Gedanke, dass er allein dort ist, ist mir unerträglich. **2** *v.i.* fortdauern; **Shakespeare is a name which will ~:** der Name Shakespeares wird die Zeit überdauern

**enduring** /ɪn'djʊərɪŋ/ *adj.* (*lasting*) dauerhaft; beständig ‹Glaube, Tradition›

**'end user** **A** *n.* (*Econ.*) Endverbraucher, *der;* **B** (*Computing*) Endbenutzer, *der*/-benutzerin, *die*

**endways** /'endweɪz/, **endwise** /'endwaɪz/ *advs.* **A** (*with end towards spectator*) **turn sth. ~ towards sb.** jmdm. die Schmalseite einer Sache (*Gen.*) zuwenden; **B** (*with end foremost*) **~ [on]** längs; **let's have the bed facing that wall ~ [on]** lass uns das Bett mit der Schmalseite zu der Wand aufstellen!; **C** (*with end uppermost*) **~ [on]** hochkant; **D** (*end to end*) der Länge nach hintereinander; längs hintereinander

**ENE** /iːstnɔːθ'iːst/ *abbr.* ▶1024 **east-north-east** ONO

**enema** /'enɪmə/ *n., pl.* **~s** *or* **enemata** /enɪ'mɑːtə/ *(Med.)* **A** *(injection, substance)* Einlauf, *der;* Klistier, *das (Med.);* **B** *(syringe)* Klistierspritze, *die (Med.)*

**enemy** /'enəmɪ/ **1** *n.* **A** *(lit. or fig.)* Feind, *der* **(of, to** *Gen.*); **make enemies** sich *(Dat.)* Feinde machen *od.* schaffen; **make an ~ of sb.** sich *(Dat.)* jmdn. zum Feind machen; **~ of the people/state** Volks-/Staatsfeind, *der;* **the ~ at the gate/within** der Feind vor den Toren/in den eigenen Reihen; **the E~:** der böse Feind *(verhüll.)*; **how goes the ~?** *(dated fig. coll.: the time)* wie spät ist es?; **be one's own worst ~, be nobody's ~ but one's own** niemandem schaden als sich *(Dat.)* selbst; **B** *(member of hostile army or nation, hostile force)* Feind, *der; (ship)* feindliches Schiff.
**2** *adj.* feindlich; **destroyed by ~ action** durch Feindeinwirkung zerstört

**energetic** /enə'dʒetɪk/ *adj.* **A** *(strenuously active)* energiegeladen; schwungvoll ‹Redner›; tatkräftig ‹Mitarbeiter›; lebhaft ‹Kind›; **be an ~ person** sehr tatkräftig sein; **I don't feel ~ enough** ich habe nicht genug Energie; **B** *(vigorous)* schwungvoll; entschieden, energisch ‹Zustimmung, Ablehnung›; kräftig ‹Rühren, Schlag, Beifall›

**energetically** /enə'dʒetɪkəlɪ/ *adv.* schwungvoll; entschieden ‹sich äußern›

**energize (energise)** /'enədʒaɪz/ *v.t.* **A** *(infuse energy into)* in Schwung bringen *(ugs.)*; **B** *(Electr.)* mit Strom versorgen

**energy** /'enədʒɪ/ *n.* **A** *(vigour)* Energie, *die; (active operation)* Kraft, *die;* **save your ~:** schone deine Kräfte!; **I've no ~ left** ich habe keine Energie mehr; **build up one's ~:** Kräfte sammeln; **B** *in pl. (individual's powers)* Kraft, *die;* **C** *(Phys.)* Energie, *die;* **sources of ~:** Energiequellen; ⇒ *also* **conservation** B; **potential** 1

**energy: ~ crisis** *n.* Energiekrise, *die;* **~-giving** *adj.* Energie spendend; **~ resources** *n. pl.* Energieressourcen *Pl.;* **~-saving** *adj.* Energie sparend; **~-saving lamp** Energiesparlampe, *die;* **~ value** *n.* Nährwert, *der*

**enervate** /'enəveɪt/ *v.t.* schwächen

**enervating** /'enəveɪtɪŋ/ *adj.* enervierend *(geh.)*, ermüdend ‹Auseinandersetzung, Streben›; schlapp machend ‹Klima, Feuchtigkeit›; kräftezehrend ‹Krankheit›; lähmend ‹Hitze›

**enervation** /enə'veɪʃn/ *n.* Schwächung, *die; (state)* Schwäche, *die*

**enfant terrible** /ɑ̃fɑ̃ te'riːbl/ *n., pl.* **enfants terribles** /ɑ̃fɑ̃ te'riːbl/ Enfant terrible, *das*

**enfeeble** /ɪn'fiːbl/ *v.t.* schwächen

**enfeeblement** /ɪn'fiːblmənt/ *n.* Schwächung, *die; (state)* Schwäche, *die*

**enfold** /ɪn'fəʊld/ *v.t.* **A** *(wrap up)* **~ sb. in** *or* **with sth.** jmdn. in etw. *(Akk.)* einhüllen *od.* mit etw. umhüllen; **B** *(clasp)* umschließen; **he ~ed her in his arms** er schloss sie in die Arme

**enforce** /ɪn'fɔːs/ *v.t.* **A** durchsetzen; sorgen für ‹Disziplin›; **~ sth. [up]on sb.** jmdm. etw. aufzwingen; **~ the law** dem Gesetz Geltung verschaffen; das Gesetz durchsetzen; **B** *(give more force to)* Nachdruck verleihen (+ *Dat.*)

**enforceable** /ɪn'fɔːsəbl/ *adj.* durchsetzbar

**enforcement** /ɪn'fɔːsmənt/ *n.* Erzwingung, *die; (of law)* Durchsetzung, *die*

**enfranchise** /ɪn'fræntʃaɪz/ *v.t.* **A** *(give vote to)* das Wahlrecht verleihen (+ *Dat.*); **be ~d** das Wahlrecht erhalten; **B** *(invest with municipal rights)* einen Parlamentssitz verleihen (+ *Dat.*)

**enfranchisement** /ɪn'fræntʃɪzmənt/ *n.* **A** *(giving of vote to)* Verleihung des Wahlrechts **(of** an + *Akk.*); **B** *(investing with municipal rights)* Verleihung eines Parlamentssitzes **(of** an + *Akk.*)

**ENG** *abbr.* **electronic news-gathering** elektronische Berichterstattung; EB

**Engadine** /'eŋgədiːn/ *pr. n.* **the ~:** das Engadin

**engage** /ɪn'geɪdʒ/ **1** *v.t.* **A** engagieren; **a singer was ~d to sing at the wedding** ein Sänger/eine Sängerin wurde engagiert *od.* verpflichtet, der/die bei der Hochzeit singen sollte; **B** *(hire)* einstellen; **we have ~d his services** er arbeitet für uns; wir nehmen seine Dienste in Anspruch; **C** *(employ busily)* beschäftigen **(in** mit); *(involve)* verwickeln **(in** in + *Akk.*); **~ oneself in sth.** sich mit etw. befassen *od.* beschäftigen; **~ sb. in conversation** jmdn. ins Gespräch ziehen; *(more absorbingly)* jmdn. in ein Gespräch verwickeln; **D** *(attract and hold fast)* wecken [und wach halten] ‹Interesse›; auf sich *(Akk.)* ziehen ‹Aufmerksamkeit›; fesseln ‹Person›; in Anspruch nehmen ‹Konzentration›; gewinnen ‹Sympathie, Unterstützung›; **E** *(arrange to occupy)* mieten; **F** *(enter into conflict with)* angreifen; *(bring into conflict)* **~ sb. in a duel** jmdn. in einen Zweikampf verwickeln; **G** *(Mech.)* **~ one cog with another** die Zahnräder ineinander greifen lassen; **~ the clutch/gears** einkuppeln/einen Gang einlegen; **H** *(Fencing)* **~ [foils]** [die Klingen] kreuzen.
**2** *v.i.* **A ~ in sth.** sich an etw. *(Dat.)* beteiligen; **~ in politics** sich politisch engagieren; **~ in various sports** verschiedene Sportarten betreiben; **B** *(pledge)* **~ to do sth.** sich verpflichten, etw. zu tun; *(vow)* geloben, etw. zu tun; **~ that ...:** versprechen, dass ...; **C** *(Mech.)* ineinander greifen; **the clutch would not ~:** die Kupplung ließ sich nicht einrücken *od.* fasste nicht; **D** *(come into conflict)* **~ with the enemy** den Feind angreifen

**engaged** /ɪn'geɪdʒd/ *adj.* **A** *(to be married)* verlobt; **be ~ [to be married] [to sb.]** [mit jmdm.] verlobt sein; **become** *or* **get ~ [to be married] [to sb.]** sich [mit jmdm.] verloben; **B** *(bound by promise)* verabredet; **be otherwise ~:** etwas anderes vorhaben; **are you ~ this evening?** bist du für heute Abend verabredet?; hast du [für] heute Abend etwas vor?; **C** *(occupied with business)* beschäftigt; **be** *or* **have become ~ in sth./in doing sth.** mit etw. befasst *od.* beschäftigt sein/damit befasst *od.* beschäftigt sein, etw. zu tun; **D** *(occupied or used by person)* besetzt ‹Toilette, Taxi›; **the telephone [line]/number is ~:** der [Telefon]anschluss/die Nummer ist besetzt; **you're always ~:** bei dir ist immer besetzt; **~ signal** *or* **tone** *(Brit. Teleph.)* Besetztzeichen, *das*

**engagement** /ɪn'geɪdʒmənt/ *n.* **A** *(to be married)* Verlobung, *die* **(to** mit); **have a long ~:** lange verlobt sein; **B** *(appointment made with another)* Verabredung, *die;* **have a previous** *or* **prior ~:** schon anderweitig festgelegt sein; **social ~:** gesellschaftliche Verpflichtung; **lunch/dinner ~:** Verabredung zum Mittag-/Abendessen; **C** *(booked appearance)* Engagement, *das;* **D** *(hiring, appointment)* Einstellung, *die;* **E** *(Mil.)* Kampfhandlung, *die*

**en'gagement ring** *n.* Verlobungsring, *der*

**engaging** /ɪn'geɪdʒɪŋ/ *adj.* bezaubernd; gewinnend ‹Lächeln›; einnehmend ‹Persönlichkeit, Art›

**engagingly** /ɪn'geɪdʒɪŋlɪ/ *adv.* gewinnend ‹lächeln›

**engender** /ɪn'dʒendə(r)/ *v.t.* zur Folge haben; erzeugen; ‹Person:› hervorrufen

**engine** /'endʒɪn/ *n.* **A** *(mechanical contrivance)* Motor, *der; (of spacecraft, jet aircraft)* Triebwerk, *das;* **B** *(locomotive)* Lok[omotive], *die*

**'engine driver** *n.* ▶1261 *(Brit.)* Lok[omotiv]führer, *der*

**engineer** /endʒɪ'nɪə(r)/ **1** *n.* ▶1261 **A** Ingenieur, *der*/Ingenieurin, *die; (service ~, installation ~)* Techniker, *der*/Technikerin, *die;* ⇒ *also* **chemical engineer; civil engineer; electrical engineer; mechanical engineer; sound engineer; B** *(maker or designer of engines)* Maschinenbauingenieur, *der;* **C [ship's] ~:** Maschinist, *der;* **D** *(Amer.: engine driver)* Lok[omotiv]führer, *der;* **E** *(Mil.) (designer and constructor of military works)* technischer Offizier; *(soldier)* Pionier, *der;* ⇒ *also* **Royal Engineers.**
**2** *v.t.* **A** *(contrive)* arrangieren; entwickeln ‹Plan›; **B** *(manage construction of)* konstruieren

**engineering** /endʒɪ'nɪərɪŋ/ *n., no pl.* **A** Technik, *die;* **career in ~:** Ingenieurlaufbahn, *die;* **B** *attrib.* technisch ‹Arbeiten, Fähigkeiten›; **~ science** Ingenieurwesen, *das;* **~ company** *or* **firm** Maschinenbaufirma, *die*

**'engine room** *n.* Maschinenhaus, *das;* Maschinenraum, *der*

**England** /'ɪŋglənd/ *pr. n.* England *(das)*

**Englander** /'ɪŋgləndə(r)/ *n. (Hist.)* **Little ~** *Gegner der imperialistischen Politik Englands*

**English** /'ɪŋglɪʃ/ **1** *adj.* ▶1275, ▶1340 englisch; **he/she is ~:** er ist Engländer/sie ist Engländerin; ⇒ *also* **bond** 1 H.
**2** *n.* **A** *(language)* ▶1275 Englisch, *das;* **grammar of ~:** englische Grammatik; Grammatik der englischen Sprache; **say sth. in ~:** etw. auf Englisch sagen; **speak ~:** Englisch sprechen; **be speaking ~:** englisch sprechen; **I [can] speak/read ~:** ich spreche Englisch/kann Englisch lesen; **I cannot** *or* **do not speak/read ~:** ich spreche kein Englisch/kann Englisch nicht lesen; **translate into/from [the] ~:** ins Englische/aus dem Englischen übersetzen; **speak a very pure [form of] ~:** ein sehr reines Englisch sprechen; **write sth. in ~:** etw. englisch schreiben; etw. auf *od.* in Englisch schreiben; **is that [good** *or* **correct] ~?** ist das gutes Englisch?; **what you've written is just not ~!** was du da geschrieben hast, ist einfach kein Englisch!; **her ~ is very good** sie schreibt/spricht ein sehr gutes Englisch; **the King's/Queen's ~:** die englische Hochsprache; **British/American ~:** britisches/amerikanisches Englisch; **Northern/Southern ~:** in Nordengland/Südengland gesprochenes Englisch; **Middle ~:** Mittelenglisch, *das;* **Old ~:** Altenglisch, *das;* **in plain ~:** in einfachen Worten; **say sth. in plain ~:** etw. frei heraussagen; **now put it into plain ~:** ≈ nun sag es noch mal auf Deutsch; **B** ▶1340 *pl.* **the ~:** die Engländer; **C** *(Amer. Billiards)* ⇒ **side** 1 K. ⇒ *also* **pidgin English**

**English: ~ 'breakfast** *n.* englisches Frühstück; **~ 'Channel** *pr. n.* **the ~ Channel** der [Ärmel]kanal; **~ 'horn** *n. (Mus.)* Englischhorn, *das;* Englisch Horn, *das (fachspr.)*; **~man** /'ɪŋglɪʃmən/ *n., pl.* **~men** /'ɪŋglɪʃmən/ Engländer, *der;* ⇒ *also* **castle** 1 A

**Englishness** /'ɪŋglɪʃnɪs/ *n., no pl.* englische Eigenart

**'Englishwoman** *n.* Engländerin, *die*

**engrave** /ɪn'greɪv/ *v.t.* **A** gravieren ‹Platte, Porträt, Illustration›; **the brass plate had been ~d with his name** sein Name war in die Messingplatte eingraviert worden; **B** *(carve)* **~ figures** *etc.* **[up]on a surface** Figuren *usw.* in eine Oberfläche eingravieren; **~ sth. [up]on a stone** etw. in einen Stein meißeln; **~ one's name on a tree** seinen Namen in einen Baum schnitzen; **the memory of that day has been** *or* **is ~d indelibly on my mind** *(fig.)* die Erinnerung an einen Tag hat sich mir unauslöschlich eingeprägt *od.* eingegraben

**engraver** /ɪn'greɪvə(r)/ *n.* ▶1261 *(of metal)* Graveur, *der;* Stecher, *der; (of wood)* Holzschneider, *der; (of stone)* Steinschneider, *der;* Graveur, *der*

**engraving** /ɪn'greɪvɪŋ/ *n.* **A** *(action)* Gravieren, *das;* **B** *(design, marks)* Gravur, *die;* Gravierung, *die;* **C** *(Art) (form)* Gravierkunst, *die;* Kupferstich, *der; (print)* Stich, *der; (print from wood)* Holzschnitt, *der*

**engross** /ɪn'grəʊs/ *v.t.* *(fully occupy)* fesseln; völlig in Anspruch nehmen ‹Zeit, Kraft usw.›; **be ~ed in sth.** in etw. *(Akk.)* vertieft sein; **become** *or* **get ~ed in sth.** sich in etw. *(Akk.)* vertiefen

**engrossing** /ɪn'grəʊsɪŋ/ *adj.* fesselnd

**engulf** /ɪn'gʌlf/ *v.t.* verschlingen *(auch fig.)*; *(wrap up)* einhüllen; **the house was ~ed in flames** das Haus stand in hellen Flammen

**enhance** /ɪn'hɑːns/ *v.t.* erhöhen ‹Wert, [An]reiz, Macht, Aussichten, Schönheit›; verstärken ‹Wirkung›; steigern ‹Qualität, Wirkung›; heben ‹Stimmung, Aussehen›; betonen ‹Augen›

e

**enhancement** /ɪn'hɑ:nsmənt/ *n.* ⇒ **enhance**: Erhöhung, *die;* Verstärkung, *die;* Steigerung, *die;* Hebung, *die;* Betonung, *die*

**enigma** /ɪ'nɪgmə/ *n.* Rätsel, *das*

**enigmatic** /enɪg'mætɪk/, **enigmatical** /enɪg'mætɪkl/ *adj.* rätselhaft

**enjambment** (**enjambement**) /en'dʒæmmənt/ *n.* (*Pros.*) Enjambement, *das*

**enjoin** /ɪn'dʒɔɪn/ *v.t.* **~ a duty/restriction on sb.** jmdm. eine Pflicht/Einschränkung auferlegen; **~ silence/obedience [on sb.]** [jmdn.] zum Schweigen ermahnen/Gehorsam [von jmdm.] fordern; **notices on the wall ~ed silence** Schilder an der Wand mahnten zur Ruhe; **~ caution on sb.** jmdn. zur Vorsicht ermahnen; **~ sb. [not] to do sth.** jmdn. eindringlich ermahnen, etw. [nicht] zu tun; **~ that sth. should be done** nachdrücklich fordern, dass etw. getan wird

**enjoy** /ɪn'dʒɔɪ/ ❶ *v.t.* **A** **I ~ed the book/film/work** das Buch/der Film/die Arbeit hat mir gefallen; **are you ~ing your meal?** schmeckt dir das Essen?; **he ~s reading/travelling** er liest/reist gern; **he ~s music and drama** er mag Musik und Theater; **we really ~ed seeing you again** wir haben uns wirklich gefreut, euch wiederzusehen; **as a rule, people don't actually ~ going to the dentist** im Allgemeinen geht man nicht gerade gern zum Zahnarzt; **B** (*have use of*) genießen ‹Recht, Privileg, Vorteil›; sich erfreuen (+ *Gen.*) ‹hohen Einkommens›; **~ the right to vote** das Wahlrecht ausüben können; **C** (*experience*) sich erfreuen (+ *Gen.*) ‹Respekts, guter Gesundheit›; genießen ‹Achtung›.
❷ *v. refl.* sich amüsieren; **you look as if you're ~ing yourself** du siehst ganz vergnügt aus; **we thoroughly ~ed ourselves in Spain** wir hatten viel Spaß in Spanien; **~ yourself at the theatre** viel Spaß im Theater!; **the children ~ed themselves making sandcastles** die Kinder vergnügten sich damit, Sandburgen zu bauen

**enjoyable** /ɪn'dʒɔɪəbl/ *adj.* schön; angenehm ‹Empfindung, Unterhaltung, Arbeit›; unterhaltsam ‹Buch, Film, Stück›

**enjoyably** /ɪn'dʒɔɪəblɪ/ *adv.* angenehm

**enjoyment** /ɪn'dʒɔɪmənt/ *n.* (*delight*) Vergnügen, *das* (**of** an + *Dat.*); **don't spoil other people's ~:** verdirb anderen nicht die Freude

**enlarge** /ɪn'lɑ:dʒ/ ❶ *v.t.* vergrößern; (*widen*) verbreitern ‹Straße, Durchgang›; weiter machen ‹Kleidungsstück›; erweitern ‹Wissen›; **the tumour had become ~d** der Tumor war größer geworden. ❷ *v.i.* **A** sich vergrößern; größer werden; (*widen*) sich verbreitern; **B** **~ [up]on sth.** etw. weiter ausführen

**enlargement** /ɪn'lɑ:dʒmənt/ *n.* **A** Vergrößerung, *die;* (*making or becoming wider*) Verbreiterung, *die;* **B** (*further explanation*) weitere Ausführung

**enlarger** /ɪn'lɑ:dʒə(r)/ *n.* (*Photog.*) Vergrößerungsapparat, *der*

**enlighten** /ɪn'laɪtn/ *v.t.* aufklären (**on, as to** über + *Akk.*); **let me ~ you on the matter** lass mich dir die Sache erklären; **be ~ing** erhellend sein

**enlightened** /ɪn'laɪtnd/ *adj.* aufgeklärt

**enlightenment** /ɪn'laɪtnmənt/ *n., no pl.* Aufklärung, *die;* **[spiritual] ~:** [geistige] Erleuchtung; **the E~** (*Hist.*) die Aufklärung; **the Age of E~:** das Zeitalter der Aufklärung

**enlist** /ɪn'lɪst/ ❶ *v.t.* **A** (*Mil.*) anwerben; **~ed person** (*Amer.*) (*soldier*) Soldat, *der;* (*sailor*) Matrose, *der;* **B** (*secure as means of help*) gewinnen. ❷ *v.i.* **~ [for the army/navy]** in die Armee/Marine eintreten; **~ [as a soldier]** Soldat werden

**enlistment** /ɪn'lɪstmənt/ *n.* **A** (*Mil.*) Anwerbung, *die;* **B** (*securing as means of help*) Gewinnung, *die*

**enliven** /ɪn'laɪvn/ *v.t.* beleben; anregen ‹Fantasie›; in Schwung bringen (*ugs.*) ‹Person, Schulklasse usw.›; lebhafter gestalten ‹Tanz, Unterricht›

**en masse** /ɑ̃ 'mæs/ *adv.* **A** (*all together*) alle zusammen; **taken ~:** alles in allem; **B** (*in a crowd*) in Massen

**enmesh** /ɪn'meʃ/ *v.t.* **~ sb./sth. [in sth.]** jmdn./etw. [mit etw.] fangen; (*fig.*) jmdn./etw. [in etw. (*Akk.*)] verstricken; **a fly had become ~ed in the spider's web** eine Fliege hatte sich in dem Spinnennetz verfangen

**enmity** /'enmɪtɪ/ *n.* Feindschaft, *die*

**ennoble** /ɪ'nəʊbl/ *v.t.* **A** adeln; **B** (*elevate*) erheben

**ennui** /'ɒnwi:/ *n.* Ennui, *der* (*geh.*)

**enormity** /ɪ'nɔ:mɪtɪ/ *n.* **A** (*atrocity*) Ungeheuerlichkeit, *die* (*abwertend*); **B** ⇒ **enormousness**

**enormous** /ɪ'nɔ:məs/ *adj.* **A** enorm; riesig, gewaltig ‹Figur, Tier, Meer, Kathedrale, Fluss, Wüste, Menge›; gewaltig, enorm ‹Veränderung, Unterschied, Liebe, Hass, Widerspruch, Größe, Ausgabe, Kraft›; ungeheuer ‹Mut, Charme, Schmerz, Problem, Gefahr›; **B** (*fat*) ungeheuer dick

**enormously** /ɪ'nɔ:məslɪ/ *adv.* ungeheuer; enorm, ungeheuer ‹groß, hoch, sich ändern, wachsen, sich bessern›

**enormousness** /ɪ'nɔ:məsnɪs/ *n., no pl.* ungeheure Größe; Riesenhaftigkeit, *die;* (*of size, length, height*) ungeheures Ausmaß

**enough** /ɪ'nʌf/ ❶ *adj.* genug; genügend; **that's ~ arguing for one evening** für heute [Abend] haben wir uns genug gestritten; **there's ~ room** *or* **room ~:** es ist Platz genug *od.* genügend Platz; **be man/fool/miser** *etc.* **~ to do sth.** Manns/dumm/geizig *usw.* genug sein, etw. zu tun; **he made ~ fuss about getting it/having got it** (*iron.*) er hat so einen Wirbel darum gemacht, dass er es haben wollte/er hat großen Wirbel darum gemacht, dass er es bekommen hatte; **more than ~:** mehr als genug; **~ noise to wake the dead** ein Lärm, um Tote aufzuwecken.
❷ *n., no pl., no art.* genug; **be ~ to do sth.** genügen, etw. zu tun; **she says she's not getting ~ out of her marriage** sie sagt, ihre Ehe gebe ihr nicht genug *od.* fülle sie nicht aus; **are there ~ of us to lift this heavy weight?** sind wir genug [Leute], um diese schwere Last zu heben?; **four people are quite ~:** vier Leute genügen völlig; **he's had quite ~** (*is drunk*) er hat genug; **that [amount] will be ~ to go round** das reicht für alle; **you [already] have ~ to do looking after the baby** du hast schon genug damit zu tun, auf das Baby aufzupassen; **~ of ...:** genug von ...; **have you had ~ of the meat dish?** hast du genug Fleisch gehabt?; **I've seen ~ of Bergman's films** ich habe genug Bergman-Filme gesehen; **are there ~ of these books to go round?** reichen diese Bücher für alle?; **~ of that!** genug davon!; **[that's] ~ [of that]!** [jetzt ist es] genug!; **~ of your nonsense!** Schluss mit dem Unsinn!; **have had ~ [of sb./sth.]** genug [von jmdm./etw.] haben; **I've had ~:** jetzt reichts mir aber!; jetzt habe ich aber genug!; **haven't you had ~ of travelling?** hast du nicht langsam genug vom Reisen?; **more than ~, ~ and to spare** mehr als genug; **[that's] ~ about ...:** genug über ... (*Akk.*) geredet; **but ~ about politics** aber Schluss mit der Politik; **~ about that** genug davon!; Schluss damit!; **~ said** mehr braucht man dazu nicht zu sagen; **~ is ~:** mal muss es auch genug sein (*ugs.*); **it's ~ to make you weep** es ist zum Weinen; **it's ~ to make you sick** da wird einem ganz schlecht; **~ is as good as a feast** allzu viel ist ungesund (*Spr.*); **cry '~'** (*fig.*) aufgeben; **as if that were not ~:** als ob das noch nicht genügte; **be ~ of a man/fool/miser** *etc.* **to do sth.** Manns/dumm/geizig *usw.* genug sein, etw. zu tun.
❸ *adv.* genug; **the meat is not cooked ~:** das Fleisch ist nicht genügend durch; **you don't express your views ~:** du sagst zu wenig über deine Ansichten; **he is not trying hard ~:** er gibt sich nicht genug *od.* genügend Mühe; **they were friendly ~ towards us** sie waren so weit recht nett zu uns; **she's a pretty ~ girl** sie ist doch ein recht hübsches Mädchen; **you know well ~ what we're referring to** ihr wisst recht gut, was wir meinen; **oddly/strangely/funnily ~:** merkwürdiger-/seltsamer-/(*ugs.*) komischerweise; **sure ~:** natürlich; **be good/kind ~ to do sth.** so gut sein, etw. zu tun; ⇒ *also* **fair**[2] 1 A; **right** 1 B; **true** 1 A

**en passant** /ɑ̃ 'pæsɑ̃/ *adv.* en passant (*geh.*); beiläufig; **just ~:** ganz nebenbei

**enquire** *etc.* ⇒ **inquir-**

**enrage** /ɪn'reɪdʒ/ *v.t.* wütend machen; reizen ‹wildes Tier›; **be ~d by sth.** über etw. (*Akk.*) wütend werden/von etw. gereizt werden; **be ~d at** *or* **with sb./sth.** auf jmdn./etw. wütend sein; **become** *or* **get ~d** wütend werden (**at, with** über, auf + *Akk.*); **I was ~d to hear that ...:** ich war wütend, als ich erfuhr, dass ...

**enrapture** /ɪn'ræptʃə(r)/ *v.t.* entzücken; ‹Gesang, Musik:› bezaubern; **be ~d by sth./sb.** von etw./jmdm. entzückt sein

**enraptured** /ɪn'ræptʃəd/ *adj.* entzückt; verzückt

**enrich** /ɪn'rɪtʃ/ *v.t.* **A** (*make wealthy*) reich machen; bereichern (*veralt.*); **B** (*fig.*) bereichern; anreichern ‹Nahrungsmittel, Boden, Uran›; verbessern ‹Haut, Qualität, Gewebe›; erweitern ‹Kenntnisse›; **we were greatly ~ed by the experience** diese Erfahrung hat uns sehr bereichert

**enrichment** /ɪn'rɪtʃmənt/ *n.* (*lit. or fig.*) Bereicherung, *die;* (*of soil, food, uranium*) Anreicherung, *die*

**enrol** (*Amer.:* **enroll**) /ɪn'rəʊl/ ❶ *v.i.*, **-ll-** sich anmelden; sich einschreiben *od.* eintragen [lassen]; (*Univ.*) sich einschreiben; sich immatrikulieren; **~ in sth.** in etw. (*Akk.*) eintreten; **~ for a course/test** sich zu einem Kurs/einer Prüfung anmelden. ❷ *v.t.*, **-ll-** einschreiben ‹Studenten, Kursteilnehmer›; anwerben ‹Rekruten›; aufnehmen ‹Schüler, Mitglied, Rekruten›; **~ sb. in sth.** jmdn. in etw. (*Akk.*) aufnehmen; **~ sb. for a course/the army** jmdn. für einen Kurs annehmen/in die Armee aufnehmen; **State E~led Nurse** (*Brit.*) ≈ Krankenpflegehelfer, *der*/-helferin, *die*

**enrolment** (*Amer.:* **enrollment**) /ɪn'rəʊlmənt/ *n.* **A** Anmeldung, *die;* (*Univ.*) Immatrikulation, *die;* Einschreibung, *die;* (*in army*) Eintritt, *der;* **B** (*Amer.: number of students*) Studentenzahl, *die*

**en route** /ɑ̃ 'ru:t/ *adv.* unterwegs; auf dem Weg; **~ to Scotland/for Edinburgh** unterwegs *od.* auf dem Weg nach Schottland/Edinburgh; **~ [for] home/to school** auf dem Heim-/Schulweg

**ensconce** /ɪn'skɒns/ *v.t.* **~ oneself in sth.** sich in etw. (*Dat.*) niederlassen; (*hide*) sich in etw. (*Dat.*) verbergen; **be ~d in/behind sth.** sich in/hinter etw. (*Dat.*) niedergelassen haben

**ensemble** /ɑ̃'sɑ̃bl/ *n.* Ensemble, *das*

**enshrine** /ɪn'ʃraɪn/ *v.t.* (*lit. or fig.*) bewahren

**ensign** /'ensaɪn, 'ensn/ *n.* **A** (*banner*) Hoheitszeichen, *das;* **B** (*Brit.*) **blue/red/white ~:** Flagge der britischen Marinereserve/britischen Handelsschiffe/britischen Marine; **C** (*standard-bearer*) Fähnrich, *der;* (*Hist.: infantry officer*) Fahnenjunker, *der;* **D** (*Amer.: naval officer*) Fähnrich zur See

**enslave** /ɪn'sleɪv/ *v.t.* **A** versklaven; **B** (*fig.*) **marriage had ~d her to the kitchen sink** die Ehe hatte sie an den Spülstein gekettet; **become ~d to a habit** zum Sklaven einer Gewohnheit werden

**ensnare** /ɪn'sneə(r)/ *v.t.* (*lit. or fig.*) fangen; **the questions were designed to ~ him** (*fig.*) die Fragen waren als Falle für ihn gedacht

**ensue** /ɪn'sju:/ *v.i.* **A** (*follow*) sich daran anschließen; **the discussion which ~d** die anschließende *od.* folgende Diskussion; **B** (*result*) sich daraus ergeben; **~ from sth.** sich aus etw. ergeben

**ensuing** /ɪn'sju:ɪŋ/ *adj.* darauf folgend

**en suite** /ɑ̃ 'swi:t/ *adv.* daran anschließend; **rooms arranged ~:** miteinander verbundene Zimmer; **with ... ~:** mit sich [daran] anschließendem / anschließender / anschließenden ...

**ensure** /ɪn'ʃʊə(r)/ *v.t.* **A** **~ that ...** (*satisfy oneself that*) sich vergewissern, dass ...; (*see *to it that*) gewährleisten, dass ...; Ⓑ (*secure*) **~ sth.** etw. gewährleisten; **this will ~ victory for the Labour Party** dies wird der Labour Party den Sieg sichern; **I cannot ~ you a good seat** ich kann nicht dafür garantieren, dass Sie einen guten Platz bekommen; Ⓒ (*make safe*) **~ sb./sth. against sth.** jmdn./etw. vor etw. (*Dat.*) *od.* gegen etw. schützen; **they ~d themselves against possible disappointment/criticism/hostility** sie sicherten sich gegen eine eventuelle Enttäuschung/Kritik/Anfeindung ab; *abs.* **proper insulation will ~ against loss of heat** sorgfältige Isolierung schützt gegen Wärmeverlust

**ENT** *abbr.* (*Med.*) **ear, nose, and throat** HNO

**entablature** /ɪnˈtæblətʃə(r)/ *n.* (*Archit.*) Gebälk, *das*

**entail** /ɪnˈteɪl/ ❶ *v.t.* Ⓐ (*involve*) mit sich bringen; **what exactly does your job ~?** worin besteht Ihre Arbeit ganz genau?; **sth. ~s doing sth.** etw. bedeutet, dass man etw. tun muss; Ⓑ (*impose*) **~ sth. [on sb.]** etw. [für jmdn.] mit sich bringen; ‹Person:› [jmdm.] etw. aufbürden; **~ disgrace on sb./one's family** jmdm./seiner Familie Schande machen; Ⓒ (*Law*) in ein Fideikommiss umwandeln; (*leave*) als Fideikommiss vererben. ❷ *n.* (*Law*) Fideikommiss, *das*

**entailment** /ɪnˈteɪlmənt/ *n.* (*Law*) Umwandlung in ein Fideikommiss

**entangle** /ɪnˈtæŋgl/ *v.t.* Ⓐ (*catch*) einfangen; sich verfangen lassen; **he got bits of straw ~d in his hair** Strohhalme verfingen sich in seinem Haar; **he got his trouser leg ~d in his bicycle chain** sein Hosenbein hat sich in der Fahrradkette verfangen; **get [oneself]** *or* **become ~d in** *or* **with sth.** sich in etw. (*Dat.*) verfangen; **get [oneself]** *or* **become ~d in a mass of details** (*fig.*) sich in einer Unmenge von Einzelheiten verlieren; **be ~d in sth.** sich in etw. (*Dat.*) verfangen haben; Ⓑ (*fig.: involve*) verwickeln; **don't ~ yourself in obligations you cannot meet** lass dich nicht auf Verpflichtungen (*Akk.*) ein, die du nicht erfüllen kannst; **get [oneself] ~d in sth.** sich in etw. (*Akk.*) verwickeln lassen; **be/become ~d in sth.** in etw. (*Akk.*) verwickelt sein/werden; **get [oneself]/be ~d with** sich einlassen/eingelassen haben auf (+ *Akk.*) ‹Probleme›; in Konflikt geraten/sein mit ‹Gesetz›; sich einlassen/eingelassen haben mit ‹Frau, Mann, politischer Gruppe›; Ⓒ (*make tangled*) völlig durcheinander bringen; **get sth. ~d [with sth.]** etw. [mit etw.] durcheinander bringen; **the threads have become** *or* **are ~d [with each other]** die Fäden haben sich verwirrt

**entanglement** /ɪnˈtæŋglmənt/ *n.* Ⓐ Verwicklung, *die;* Verfangen, *das;* Ⓑ (*fig.: involvement*) **his ~ in a divorce case** seine Verwicklung in eine Scheidungsaffäre; **get oneself into an ~ with sb.** sich mit jmdm. einlassen; Ⓒ (*thing that entangles*) Verwicklung, *die;* (*entangled things*) Durcheinander, *das;* (*Mil.*) [Draht]verhau, *der*

**entente** /ɑ̃ˈtɑ̃t/ *n.* Entente, *die;* **~ cordiale** /ɑ̃tɑ̃t kɔːdɪˈɑːl/ (*Hist.*) Entente cordiale, *die*

**enter** /ˈentə(r)/ ❶ *v.i.* Ⓐ (*go in*) hineingehen; ‹Fahrzeug:› hineinfahren; (*come in*) hereinkommen; (*walk into room*) eintreten; (*cross border into country*) einreisen; (*drive into tunnel etc.*) hineinfahren; (*come on stage*) auftreten; **~ Macbeth** (*Theatre*) Auftritt Macbeth; **~ into a building/another world** ein Gebäude/eine andere Welt betreten; **~ into the world of entertainment** in die Unterhaltungsbranche einsteigen (*ugs.*); **someone called 'E~!'** jemand rief: „Herein!"; **only a small amount of light ~ed through the windows** durch die Fenster fiel *od.* kam nur wenig Licht; Ⓑ (*penetrate*) eindringen; Ⓒ (*announce oneself as competitor in race etc.*) sich zur Teilnahme anmelden (**for** an + *Dat.*). ❷ *v.t.* Ⓐ (*go into*) [hinein]gehen in (+ *Akk.*); ‹Fahrzeug:› [hinein]fahren in (+ *Akk.*); ‹Flugzeug:› [hinein]fliegen in (+ *Akk.*); betreten ‹Gebäude, Zimmer›; eintreten in (+ *Akk.*) ‹Zimmer›; einlaufen in (+ *Akk.*) ‹Hafen›; einreisen in (+ *Akk.*) ‹Land›; (*drive into*) hineinfahren in (+ *Akk.*); (*come into*) [herein]kommen in (+ *Akk.*); **~ a bus/train** in einen Bus/Zug [ein]steigen; **~ the ship/plane** (*go/come into*) an Bord [des Schiffes/Flugzeugs] gehen/kommen; **a small amount of light ~ed the room** in den Raum fiel *od.* kam wenig Licht; **the poison ~ed the blood** das Gift gelangte ins Blut; **it would never ~ his mind** *or* **head to cheat you** es käme ihm nie in den Sinn, dich zu betrügen; **has it ever ~ed your mind** *or* **head that ...?** ist dir nie der Gedanke gekommen, dass ...?; **~ sb.'s heart/soul** von jmdm. Besitz ergreifen (*geh.*); Ⓑ (*penetrate*) eindringen in (+ *Akk.*); Ⓒ (*become a member of*) beitreten (+ *Dat.*) ‹Verein, Klub, Organisation, Partei›; eintreten in (+ *Akk.*) ‹Kirche›; ergreifen ‹Beruf›; **~ the army/[the] university** zum Militär/auf die *od.* zur Universität gehen; **~ school** in die *od.* zur Schule kommen; **~ the legal profession/the medical profession/teaching** die juristische Laufbahn einschlagen/den Arztberuf ergreifen/den Lehrberuf ergreifen; Jurist/Arzt/Lehrer werden; **~ a monastery/nunnery** Mönch/Nonne werden; in ein Kloster eintreten; **~ the House of Commons** Mitglied *od.* Abgeordneter des Unterhauses werden; Ⓓ (*participate in*) sich beteiligen an (+ *Dat.*) ‹Diskussion, Unterhaltung›; teilnehmen an (+ *Dat.*) ‹Rennen, Wettbewerb›; Ⓔ (*write*) **~ sth. in a book/register** *etc.* etw. in ein Buch/Register *usw.* eintragen; **~ a name in** *or* **on a list** einen Namen in eine Liste eintragen *od.* auf eine Liste setzen; **~ sth. in a dictionary/an index** etw. in ein Wörterbuch/ein Register aufnehmen; Ⓕ (*record*) **~ an action against sb.** gegen jmdn. Klage einreichen *od.* erheben; **~ a caveat** Einspruch einlegen *od.* erheben; **~ a judgement** ein Urteil fällen; **~ one's protest** Protest *od.* Widerspruch erheben; **~ a bid** ein Gebot abgeben; Ⓖ **~ sb./sth./one's name for** jmdn./etw./sich anmelden für ‹Rennen, Wettbewerb, Prüfung›; Ⓗ (*Computing*) eingeben ‹Daten usw.›; **press ~:** 'Enter' drücken

**~ into** *v.t.* Ⓐ (*engage in*) anknüpfen ‹Gespräch›; sich beteiligen an (+ *Dat.*) ‹Diskussion, Debatte, Wettbewerb›; aufnehmen ‹Beziehung, Verhandlungen›; (*bind oneself by*) eingehen ‹Verpflichtung, Ehe, Beziehung›; schließen ‹Vertrag›; **~ into details/long-drawn-out explanations** ins Detail gehen/sich in langatmigen Erklärungen ergehen; **it's not worth ~ing into a discussion about it** es lohnt sich nicht, eine Diskussion darüber anzufangen; **~ into an understanding with sb.** mit jmdm. eine Vereinbarung treffen *od.* eingehen; **~ into the pros and cons** auf das Für und Wider eingehen; Ⓑ (*sympathize with*) nachempfinden ‹jmds. Gefühle›; nachvollziehen ‹jmds. Gedanken›; sich hineinversetzen, einfühlen in (+ *Akk.*) ‹Person, Rolle, Stimmung›; **~ into the spirit of Christmas** in Weihnachtsstimmung kommen; **she really ~s into anything she does** sie ist bei allem, was sie tut, ganz bei der Sache; Ⓒ (*form part of*) Bestandteil sein von; **~ into sb.'s considerations** bei jmds. Überlegungen eine Rolle spielen; **having children doesn't ~ into our plans** Kinder sind [bei uns] nicht geplant; **that doesn't ~ into it at all** das hat damit gar nichts zu tun

**~ on** *v.t.* Ⓐ (*Law: assume possession of*) in Besitz nehmen; Ⓑ (*begin*) beginnen ‹Karriere, Laufbahn, Amtsperiode›; aufnehmen ‹Studium›; in Angriff nehmen ‹Aufgabe, Projekt›

**~ 'up** *v.t.* eintragen; **~ up the books** die Bücher auf den letzten Stand bringen

**~ upon** ⇒ **~ on**

**enteric** /enˈterɪk/ *adj.* Ⓐ (*Anat.*) Darm-; Ⓑ ▶ **1232** **~ fever** (*Med.*) Typhus, *der;* Typhus abdominalis, *der* (*fachspr.*)

**enteritis** /entəˈraɪtɪs/ *n.* ▶ **1232** (*Med.*) Enteritis, *die* (*fachspr.*); Dünndarmentzündung, *die*

**ˈenter key** *n.* (*Computing*) Entertaste, *die;* Eingabetaste, *die*

**enterprise** /ˈentəpraɪz/ *n.* Ⓐ (*undertaking*) Unternehmen, *das;* **commercial ~:** Handelsunternehmen, *das;* **free/private ~:** freies/privates Unternehmertum; Ⓑ *no indef. art.* (*readiness to undertake new ventures*) Unternehmungsgeist, *der*

**ˈenterprise zone** *n.* wirtschaftliches Fördergebiet

**enterprising** /ˈentəpraɪzɪŋ/ *adj.* unternehmungslustig; rührig ‹Geschäftsmann›; kühn ‹Reise, Gedanke, Idee›

**entertain** /entəˈteɪn/ *v.t.* Ⓐ (*amuse*) unterhalten; **we were greatly ~ed by ...:** wir haben uns köstlich über ... (*Akk.*) amüsiert; Ⓑ (*receive as guest*) bewirten; **they enjoy ~ing** sie haben gern Gäste; **do some** *or* **a bit of/a lot of ~ing** manchmal/sehr oft Gäste einladen; **~ sb. to lunch/dinner** (*Brit.*) jmdn. zum Mittag-/Abendessen einladen; Ⓒ (*have in the mind*) haben ‹Meinung, Vorstellung›; hegen (*geh.*) ‹Gefühl, Vorurteil, Verdacht, Zweifel, Groll›; (*consider*) in Erwägung ziehen; **he would never ~ the idea of doing that** er würde es nie ernstlich erwägen, das zu tun; **~ ambitions/ideas** *or* **thoughts of doing sth.** den Ehrgeiz haben/sich mit dem Gedanken tragen, etw. zu tun; **~ hopes of achieving sth.** sich (*Dat.*) Hoffnungen machen, etw. zu erreichen

**entertainer** /entəˈteɪnə(r)/ *n.* ▶ **1261** Entertainer, *der*/Entertainerin, *die;* Unterhalter, *der*/Unterhalterin, *die*

**entertaining** /entəˈteɪnɪŋ/ ❶ *adj.* unterhaltsam. ❷ *n., no pl., no indef. art.* **she does a lot of ~:** sie bewirtet häufig Gäste; **she's not very good at ~:** sie ist keine sehr gute Gastgeberin

**entertainment** /entəˈteɪnmənt/ *n.* Ⓐ (*amusement*) Unterhaltung, *die;* **much to our ~, to our great ~:** zu unserem großen Vergnügen; **get ~ from sth.** etw. unterhaltsam finden; **the world of ~:** die Welt des Showbusiness; **~ value** Unterhaltungswert, *der;* **have [great] ~ value** [sehr] unterhaltsam sein; **provide ~ for the children** für die Unterhaltung der Kinder sorgen; Ⓑ (*public performance, show*) Veranstaltung, *die*

**enthral** (*Amer.:* **enthrall**) /ɪnˈθrɔːl/ *v.t.*, **-ll-** Ⓐ (*captivate*) gefangen nehmen (*fig.*); Ⓑ (*delight*) begeistern; entzücken

**enthrone** /ɪnˈθrəʊn/ *v.t.* inthronisieren; **he was ~d [as] King** er bestieg den Königsthron

**enthronement** /ɪnˈθrəʊnmənt/ *n.* Inthronisation, *die;* Thronbesteigung, *die*

**enthuse** /ɪnˈθjuːz, ɪnˈθuːz/ (*coll.*) ❶ *v.i.* **~ [about** *or* **over sth./sb.]** [über etw./jmdn.] in Begeisterung ausbrechen. ❷ *v.t.* begeistern

**enthusiasm** /ɪnˈθjuːzɪæzəm, ɪnˈθuːzɪæzəm/ *n.* Ⓐ *no pl.* Begeisterung, *die;* Enthusiasmus, *der;* **~ for** *or* **about sth.** Begeisterung für *od.* über etw. (*Akk.*); **for this job we want someone with ~:** wir brauchen einen begeisterungsfähigen Menschen für diese Arbeit; **I've no ~ about going out shopping** ich habe keine Lust, einkaufen zu gehen; Ⓑ (*thing about which sb. is enthusiastic*) Leidenschaft, *die*

**enthusiast** /ɪnˈθjuːzɪæst, ɪnˈθuːzɪæst/ *n.* Enthusiast, *der;* (*for sport, pop music*) Fan, *der;* **a DIY/cookery ~:** ein begeisterter Heimwerker/Koch; **be a great ~ for sth.** sich sehr für etw. begeistern

**enthusiastic** /ɪnθjuːzɪˈæstɪk, ɪnθuːzɪˈæstɪk/ *adj.* begeistert; enthusiastisch, begeistert ‹Applaus, Empfang, Lob›; **be ~ about sth.** von etw. begeistert sein; **not be very ~ about doing sth.** keine große Lust haben, etw. zu tun; **become ~ about sth.** sich für etw. begeistern

**enthusiastically** /ɪnθjuːzɪˈæstɪkəlɪ, ɪnθuːzɪˈæstɪkəlɪ/ *adv.* begeistert; enthusiastisch, begeistert ‹empfangen, applaudieren, loben›

**entice** /ɪnˈtaɪs/ *v.t.* locken (**into** in + *Akk.*); **~ sb./sth. [away] from sb./sth.** jmdn./etw. von jmdm./etw. fortlocken; **~ mice from their holes** Mäuse aus ihren Mauselöchern [heraus]locken; **~ sb. into doing** *or* **to do sth.** jmdn. dazu verleiten, etw. zu tun

**enticement** /ɪnˈtaɪsmənt/ *n.* Ⓐ *no pl.* Lockung, *die;* (*into depravity, immorality*) Verleitung, *die* (**into** zu); **~ from sth.** Fortlockung von etw.; Ⓑ (*thing*) Lockmittel, *das*

**enticing** /ɪn'taɪsɪŋ/ *adj.*, **enticingly** /ɪn'taɪsɪŋlɪ/ *adv.* verlockend

**entire** /ɪn'taɪə(r)/ *adj.* **A** (*whole*) ganz; **take an ~ fortnight for one's holiday** volle vierzehn Tage Urlaub machen; **B** (*intact*) vollständig ‹Buch, Manuskript, Service, Ausgabe›; **remain ~:** unversehrt bleiben

**entirely** /ɪn'taɪəlɪ/ *adv.* **A** (*wholly*) völlig; ganz ‹wach›; **not ~ suitable for the occasion** dem Anlass nicht ganz angemessen; **B** (*solely*) ganz ‹für sich behalten›; allein, voll ‹verantwortlich sein›; **it's up to you ~:** es liegt ganz bei dir; **it's your responsibility ~:** du allein hast die Verantwortung

**entirety** /ɪn'taɪərətɪ/ *n.*, *no pl.* (*completeness*) Uneingeschränktheit, *die;* **in its ~:** als Ganzes; in seiner Gesamtheit

**entitle** /ɪn'taɪtl/ *v.t.* **A** (*give title of*) **~ a book/film ...:** einem Buch/Film den Titel ... geben; **B** (*give rightful claim*) berechtigen (**to** zu); **~ sb. to do sth.** jmdn. berechtigen *od.* jmdm. das Recht geben, etw. zu tun; **your degree does not ~ you to more pay** aufgrund Ihres akademischen Grades haben Sie noch keinen Anspruch auf höhere Bezahlung; **she is ~d to a bit of respect from you** sie kann ein wenig Respekt von dir verlangen; **be ~d to [claim] sth.** Anspruch auf etw. (*Akk.*) haben; **be ~d to do sth.** das Recht haben, etw. zu tun

**entitlement** /ɪn'taɪtlmənt/ *n.* (*rightful claim*) Anspruch, *der* (**to** auf + *Akk.*); **your leave ~ is four weeks** Sie haben Anspruch auf vier Wochen Urlaub

**entity** /'entɪtɪ/ *n.* **A** *no pl.* (*existence*) Entität, *die* (*Philos.*); Existenz, *die;* (*independence*) Eigenständigkeit, *die;* **B** (*thing that exists*) **[separate] ~:** eigenständiges Gebilde

**entomb** /ɪn'tu:m/ *v.t.* (*place in tomb*) beisetzen (*geh.*); (*fig.*) einkerkern

**entombment** /ɪn'tu:mmənt/ *n.* Beisetzung, *die* (*geh.*); (*fig.*) Einkerkerung, *die*

**entomological** /entəmə'lɒdʒɪkl/ *adj.* entomologisch

**entomologist** /entə'mɒlədʒɪst/ *n.* ▶ **1261** Entomologe, *der*/Entomologin, *die*

**entomology** /entə'mɒlədʒɪ/ *n.* Entomologie, *die;* Insektenkunde, *die*

**entourage** /ɒntʊ'rɑ:ʒ/ *n.* Gefolge, *das;* **have a permanent ~ of beautiful women** ständig von schönen Frauen umgeben sein

**entr'acte** /'ɒntrækt/ *n.* (*Theatre*) **A** (*interval*) Zwischenakt, *der;* **B** (*performance in interval*) Entreakt, *der*

**entrails** /'entreɪlz/ *n. pl.* Eingeweide; Gedärm, *das;* (*fig.*) Innere, *das;* **read the ~** (*fig.*) die Zukunft deuten

**entrain**[1] /ɪn'treɪn/ *v.t.* **A** (*result in*) nach sich ziehen; **B** (*carry along in flow*) mitführen ‹Tröpfchen, Dampf›

**entrain**[2] **1** *v.t.* [in einen/den Zug] verladen. **2** *v.i.* [in einen/den Zug] einsteigen; **~ for London** in den Zug nach London einsteigen

**entrance**[1] /'entrəns/ *n.* **A** (*entering*) Eintritt, *der* (**into** in + *Akk.*); (*of troops*) Einzug, *der;* (*of vehicle*) Einfahrt, *die;* (*into office, position*) Antritt, *der* (**into, upon** *Gen.*); **before his ~ into the room** bevor er das Zimmer betrat *od.* ins Zimmer trat; **[ceremonial] ~:** [feierlicher] Einzug; **B** (*on to stage, lit. or fig.*) Auftritt, *der;* **make an** *or* **one's ~:** seinen Auftritt haben; **she likes to make a dramatic ~** (*fig.*) sie setzt sich gern in Szene; **C** (*way in*) Eingang, *der* (**to** *Gen. od.* zu); (*for vehicle*) Einfahrt, *die;* **factory ~:** Fabrik- *od.* Werk[s]tor, *das;* **the ~ to the cellar/city is through a trapdoor/large gates** man gelangt durch eine Falltür/große Tore in den Keller/die Stadt; **D** *no pl.*, *no art.* (*right of admission*) Aufnahme, *die* (**to** in + *Akk.*); **gain ~ to/apply for ~ at a school/university** an einer Schule/Universität aufgenommen werden/sich um die Aufnahme an einer Schule/Universität bewerben; **~ to the concert is by ticket only** man kommt nur mit einer Eintrittskarte in das Konzert; ⇨ *also* **common entrance**; **E** (*fee*) Eintritt, *der*

**entrance**[2] /ɪn'trɑ:ns/ *v.t.* **A** (*throw into trance*) in Trance versetzen; **B** (*carry away as in trance*) hinreißen; bezaubern; **become ~d** verzaubert werden; **be ~d by** *or* **with sth.** von etw. hingerissen *od.* bezaubert sein

**entrance**/'entrəns/**: ~ examination** *n.* Aufnahmeprüfung, *die;* **~ fee** *n.* Eintrittsgeld, *das;* (*for competition*) Teilnahmegebühr, *die;* (*on joining club*) Aufnahmegebühr, *die;* **~ hall** *n.* Eingangshalle, *die;* **~ money** ⇨ **~ fee;** **~ requirement** *n.* Aufnahmebedingung, *die*

**entrancing** /ɪn'trɑ:nsɪŋ/ *adj.* bezaubernd; hinreißend

**entrant** /'entrənt/ *n.* **A** Eintretende, *der/die;* (*into country*) Einreisende, *der/die;* **B** (*immigrant*) Einwanderer, *der;* **illegal ~s into the country** illegale Einwanderer; **C** (*into a profession etc.*) Anfänger, *der*/Anfängerin, *die;* **D** (*for competition, race, etc.*) Teilnehmer, *der*/Teilnehmerin, *die* (**for** *Gen.*, an + *Dat.*)

**entrap** /ɪn'træp/ *v.t.*, **-pp-** **A** (*catch in trap*) fangen; **be ~ped** gefangen sein; in der Falle sitzen; **B** (*enclose and retain*) einschließen; **C** (*trick*) locken (**to** in + *Akk.*); **~ sb. into doing sth./into sth.** jmdn. verlocken (*geh.*) *od.* verleiten, etw. zu tun/jmdn. zu etw. verlocken (*geh.*) *od.* verleiten

**entreat** /ɪn'tri:t/ *v.t.* (*ask*) inständig bitten; (*beseech*) anflehen; **~ sb. to do sth.** jmdn. inständig bitten/jmdn. anflehen, etw. zu tun

**entreating** /ɪn'tri:tɪŋ/ *adj.*, **entreatingly** /ɪn'tri:tɪŋlɪ/ *adv.* flehentlich

**entreaty** /ɪn'tri:tɪ/ *n.* ⇨ **entreat**: inständige/flehentliche Bitte; **make an ~ to sb. to do sth.** jmdn. inständig/flehentlich bitten, etw. zu tun

**entrecôte** /'ɒntrəkəʊt/ *n.* (*Gastr.*) **~ [steak]** Entrecote, *das*

**entrée** /'ɒntreɪ, 'ãtreɪ/ *n.* **A** (*right of admission*) Zutritt, *der* (**of, to, into** zu); **give sb. an/the ~ to sth.** jmdm. Zutritt zu etw. verschaffen; **B** (*Gastr.*) (*Brit.*) Entree, *das;* Zwischengericht, *das;* (*Amer.: main dish*) Hauptgericht, *das*

**entrench** /ɪn'trenʃ/ *v.t.* **A** in Sicherheit bringen ‹Person, Besitz›; **~ oneself in/behind sth.** (*lit. or fig.*) sich in/hinter etw. (*Dat.*) verschanzen; **become ~ed** (*fig.*) ‹Vorurteil, Gedanke:› sich festsetzen; ‹Tradition:› sich verwurzeln; **B** (*apply extra safeguards to*) verankern ‹Rechte, Privilegien›

**entrenchment** /ɪn'trenʃmənt/ *n.* (*lit. or fig.*) Verschanzung, *die*

**entre nous** /ɒntrə 'nu:/ *adv.* unter uns; **well, ~, what really happened was ...:** nun, unter uns gesagt, was wirklich geschah, war ...

**entrepôt** /'ɒntrəpəʊ/ *n.* **A** (*commercial centre*) Umschlagplatz, *der;* **B** (*storehouse*) Speicher, *der*

**entrepreneur** /ɒntrəprə'nɜ:(r)/ *n.* **A** Unternehmer, *der*/Unternehmerin, *die;* **B** (*middleman*) Vermittler, *der*

**entrepreneurial** /ɒntrəprə'nɜ:rɪəl/ *adj.* unternehmerisch

**entropy** /'entrəpɪ/ *n.* (*Phys.*) Entropie, *die*

**entrust** /ɪn'trʌst/ *v.t.* **~ sb. with sth.** jmdm. etw. anvertrauen; **he could not be ~ed with such responsibility** man konnte ihm keine solche Verantwortung übertragen; **~ sb./sth. to sb./sth.** jmdn./etw. jmdm./einer Sache anvertrauen; **~ a task to sb., ~ sb. with a task** jmdn. mit einer Aufgabe betrauen; **~ sth. to sb.'s safe keeping** jmdm. etw. zur Aufbewahrung anvertrauen

**entry** /'entrɪ/ *n.* **A** Eintritt, *der* (**into** in + *Akk.*); (*of troops*) Einzug, *der;* (*of foreign matter into wound etc.*) Eindringen, *das;* (*into organization, cartel*) Beitritt, *der* (**into** zu); (*into country*) Einreise, *die;* (*ceremonial entrance*) [feierlicher] Einzug; **upon ~ into Britain** bei der Einreise nach Großbritannien; **gain ~ to the house** ins Haus gelangen; **gain ~ to the EU** der EU beitreten; **force an ~:** sich (*Dat.*) [gewaltsam] Zutritt *od.* Zugang verschaffen; ⇨ *also* **port**[1] 1 A; **B** (*on to stage*) Auftritt, *der;* **C** *no pl.*, *no art.* (*liberty to enter*) (*into car park*) Einfahrt, *die* (**into** in + *Akk.*); (*into building*) Zutritt, *der* (**into** zu); (*into country*) Einreise, *die* (**to** in + *Akk.*); ⇨ *also* **'no entry'**; **D** (*Law: taking possession*) Inbesitznahme, *die;* **make ~ of** *or* **on** in Besitz nehmen; **E** (*way in*) Eingang, *der;* (*for vehicle*) Einfahrt, *die;* **F** (*passage between buildings*) Durchgang, *der;* **G** (*Mus.*) Einsatz, *der;* **H** (*registration, item registered*) Eintragung, *die* (**in, into** in + *Akk. od. Dat.*); (*in dictionary, encyclopaedia, yearbook, index*) Eintrag, *der;* **make an ~:** eine Eintragung vornehmen; **double/single ~** (*Bookk.*) doppelte/einfache Buchführung; **I** (*body of entrants*) (*for race etc.*) Teilnehmerfeld, *das;* (*for university/school*) [Zahl der] Studienanfänger/Schulanfänger; **J** (*person or thing in competition*) Nennung, *die;* (*set of answers etc.*) Lösung, *die;* **latest date for entries** Einsendeschluss, *der;* (*for sporting event*) Meldeschluss, *der*

**entry: ~ fee** ⇨ **entrance fee**; **~ form** *n.* Anmeldeformular, *das;* (*for competition*) Teilnahmeschein, *der;* **~ permit** *n.* Einreiseerlaubnis, *die;* Einreisegenehmigung, *die;* **E~phone** ® *n.* Sprechanlage, *die;* **~ visa** *n.* Einreisevisum, *das*

**entwine** /ɪn'twaɪn/ *v.t.* **A** (*interweave, lit. or fig.*) verflechten (**with** mit); **~ one's hair with ribbons** sich (*Dat.*) Bänder ins Haar flechten; **B** (*wreathe*) **~ sth. about** *or* **round sb./sth.** etw. um jmdn./etw. schlingen *od.* (*geh.*) winden; **~ sth. with sth.** etw. mit etw. umschlingen *od.* (*geh.*) umwinden

**'E number** *n.* (*Commerc.*) E-Nummer, *die*

**enumerable** /ɪ'nju:mərəbl/ *adj.* zählbar

**enumerate** /ɪ'nju:məreɪt/ *v.t.* **A** (*count*) zählen; **B** (*mention one by one*) [einzeln] aufzählen *od.* aufführen

**enumeration** /ɪnju:mə'reɪʃn/ *n.* **A** (*counting*) Zählung, *die;* **B** (*mentioning one by one*) Aufzählung, *die;* Auflistung, *die;* **C** (*list*) Auflistung, *die*

**enunciate** /ɪ'nʌnsɪeɪt/ *v.t.* **A** (*pronounce*) artikulieren; **B** (*express*) formulieren ‹Idee, Theorie›; zum Ausdruck bringen ‹Überzeugung, Wahrheit›

**enunciation** /ɪnʌnsɪ'eɪʃn/ *n.* **A** (*pronunciation*) Artikulation, *die;* [deutliche] Aussprache; **B** (*expression*) Formulierung, *die*

**enure** ⇨ **inure**

**envelop** /ɪn'veləp/ *v.t.* [ein]hüllen (**in** in + *Akk.*); **we were ~ed in mist** Nebel hüllte uns ein; **be ~ed in flames** ganz von Flammen umgeben sein; **he ~ed her in his arms** er schloss sie in die Arme

**envelope** /'envələʊp, 'ɒnvələʊp/ *n.* **A** ▶ **1286** (*for letter*) [Brief]umschlag, *der;* **B** (*Aeronaut.: gas container*) Hülle, *die*

**enviable** /'envɪəbl/ *adj.* beneidenswert; **be ~ for sth.** um etw. zu beneiden sein

**envious** /'envɪəs/ *adj.* neidisch (**of** auf + *Akk.*); **speak in ~ tones** in neiderfülltem Ton sprechen; **I'm so ~ of you!** wie ich dich beneide!

**enviously** /'envɪəslɪ/ *adv.* neidisch; neiderfüllt

**environment** /ɪn'vaɪərənmənt/ *n.* **A** (*natural surroundings*) **the ~:** die Umwelt; **the Department of the E~** (*Brit.*) das Umweltministerium; **B** (*surrounding objects, region*) Umgebung, *die;* (*surrounding circumstances*) Umwelt, *die;* Umfeld, *das* (*bes. Psych., Soziol.*); (*social surroundings*) Milieu, *das;* **physical/working/metropolitan ~:** Umwelt, *die*/Arbeitswelt, *die*/Großstadtmilieu, *das;* **home/family ~:** häusliches Milieu/Familienverhältnisse *Pl.*

**environmental** /ɪnvaɪərən'mentl/ *adj.* Umwelt‹verschmutzung, -schutz, -einflüsse›; **for ~ reasons** aus Gründen des Umweltschutzes; **~ group** Umweltschutzorganisation, *die*

**environmental: ~ 'audit** *n.* Ökoaudit, *das;* **~ 'health** *n.* Umwelthygiene, *die;* **~ health officer** Umwelthygienebeauftragte, *der;* **~ health department** Umwelthygieneamt, *das*

**environmentalism** /ɪnvaɪrən'mentəlɪzm/ *n.*, *no pl.*, *no art.* Engagement für die Umwelt; (*as political movement*) Ökologismus, *der*

**environmentalist** /ɪnvaɪərən'mentəlɪst/ *n.* Umweltschützer, *der*/-schützerin, *die*

**environmentally** /ɪnvaɪrən'mentəlɪ/ *adv.* ökologisch; **~ friendly** umweltfreundlich;

~ **sensitive** ökologisch sensibel; ~ **sound** umweltverträglich; umweltgerecht

**environs** /ɪn'vaɪərənz, 'envɪrənz/ *n. pl.* Umgebung, *die;* **Oxford and its ~:** Oxford und Umgebung

**envisage** /ɪn'vɪzɪdʒ/, **envision** /ɪn'vɪʒn/ *v.t.* (*imagine, contemplate*) sich (*Dat.*) vorstellen; **what do you ~ for the future of the department?** wie siehst du die Zukunft der Abteilung?; **what do you ~ doing [about it]?** was gedenkst du [in der Sache] zu tun?; **she doesn't ~ staying in London for much longer** sie hat nicht vor, noch länger in London zu bleiben

**envoy** /'envɔɪ/ *n.* (*messenger*) Bote, *der*/Botin, *die;* (*Diplom. etc.*) Gesandte, *der*/Gesandtin, *die*

**envy** /'envɪ/ ❶ *n.* Ⓐ Neid, *der;* **feelings of ~:** Neidgefühle; **they could not conceal their ~ of her** sie konnten nicht verbergen, dass sie neidisch auf sie waren; Ⓑ (*object*) **his new sports car was the ~ of all his friends** alle seine Freunde beneideten ihn um seinen neuen Sportwagen; **you'll be the ~ of all your friends** alle deine Freunde werden dich beneiden. ❷ *v.t.* beneiden; **~ sb. sth.** jmdn. um etw. beneiden; **I don't ~ you** dich kann ich nicht beneiden; **I don't ~ you your job** ich beneide dich nicht um deine Tätigkeit

**enwrap** /ɪn'ræp/ *v.t.*, **-pp-:** **~ sb./sth. in sth.** jmdn./etw. in etw. (*Akk.*) [ein]hüllen *od.* [ein]wickeln

**enzyme** /'enzaɪm/ *n.* (*Chem.*) Enzym, *das*

**EOC** *abbr.* (*Brit.*) **Equal Opportunities Commission**

**Eocene** /'i:əsi:n/ (*Geol.*) ❶ *adj.* eozän; Eozän-. ❷ *n.* Eozän, *das*

**eon** ⇒ **aeon**

**EP** *abbr.* **extended-play [record]** EP

**epaulette** (*Amer.:* **epaulet**) /'epɔ:let, 'epəʊlet, epə'let/ *n.* Ⓐ Epaulette, *die;* Ⓑ (*shoulder strap*) Schulterklappe, *die*

**épée** /'epeɪ/ *n.* [Fecht]degen, *der*

**ephemeral** /ɪ'fi:mərl, ɪ'femərl/ *adj.* Ⓐ (*short-lived*) ephemer[isch] (*geh.*); kurzlebig; Ⓑ (*lasting only a day*) eintägig

**epic** /'epɪk/ ❶ *adj.* Ⓐ episch; **~ poet** epischer Dichter; Epiker, *der;* **~ subject** Stoff für ein Epos; Ⓑ (*of heroic type or scale, lit. or fig.*) monumental; **~ film** Filmepos, *das;* **~ book** monumentaler Roman; Epos, *das* (*fig.*); **an ~ voyage** eine waghalsige Reise. ❷ *n.* Epos, *das;* (*film*) [Film]epos, *das;* (*book*) monumentaler Roman; Epos, *das* (*fig.*); **folk/national ~:** Volks-/Nationalepos, *das*

**epicentre** (*Brit.; Amer.:* **epicenter**) /'epɪsentə(r)/ *n.* Epizentrum, *das*

**epicure** /'epɪkjʊə(r)/ *n.* Feinschmecker, *der;* Gourmet, *der*

**epicurean** /epɪkjʊə'ri:ən/ ❶ *adj.* (*devoted to pleasure*) epikureisch (*geh.*); **~ person** ⇒ **2**. ❷ *n.* (*person devoted to pleasure*) Epikureer, *der* (*geh.*); Genussmensch, *der*

**epidemic** /epɪ'demɪk/ (*Med.; also fig.*) ❶ *adj.* epidemisch. ❷ *n.* Epidemie, *die*

**epidermal** /epɪ'dɜ:ml/ *adj.* (*Anat., Biol.*) epidermal

**epidermis** /epɪ'dɜ:mɪs/ *n.* (*Anat., Biol.*) Epidermis, *die* (*fachspr.*); Oberhaut, *die*

**epidiascope** /epɪ'daɪəskəʊp/ *n.* Epidiaskop, *das*

**epidural** /epɪ'djʊərəl/ *n.* (*Med.*) Epiduralanästhesie, *die*

**epiglottis** /epɪ'glɒtɪs/ *n.* (*Anat.*) Epiglottis, *die* (*fachspr.*); Kehldeckel, *der*

**epigram** /'epɪgræm/ *n.* (*Lit.*) Ⓐ (*short poem*) Epigramm, *das;* Sinngedicht, *das;* Ⓑ (*pointed saying*) Sinnspruch, *der;* Ⓒ (*mode of expression*) epigrammatischer Ausdruck

**epigrammatic** /epɪgrə'mætɪk/ *adj.* (*Lit.*) epigrammatisch

**epigraph** /'epɪgrɑ:f/ *n.* Ⓐ (*inscription*) Epigraph, *das;* Ⓑ (*motto*) Motto, *das*

**epilepsy** /'epɪlepsɪ/ *n.* ▶ **1232** (*Med.*) Epilepsie, *die*

**epileptic** /epɪ'leptɪk/ (*Med.*) ❶ *adj.* epileptisch; ⇒ *also* **fit[1]** A. ❷ *n.* Epileptiker, *der*/Epileptikerin, *die*

**epilogue** (*Amer.:* **epilog**) /'epɪlɒg/ *n.* (*Lit.*) Epilog, *der;* (*concluding part of literary work also*) Nachwort, *das*

**Epiphany** /ɪ'pɪfənɪ/ *n.* (*Relig.*) Epiphanie, die; **[Feast of the] ~:** Epiphanias, *das;* Dreikönigsfest, *das;* **at ~:** am Dreikönigstag

**episcopal** /ɪ'pɪskəpl/ *adj.* episkopal; bischöflich; Episkopal‹system, -kirche›; Bischofs‹ornat, -mütze›

**episcopalian** /ɪpɪskə'peɪlɪən/ ❶ *adj.* (*of episcopal church*) der Episkopalkirche *nachgestellt*. ❷ *n.* Ⓐ (*member of episcopal church*) Episkopale, *der/die;* Ⓑ (*adherent of episcopacy*) Episkopalist, *der*/Episkopalistin, *die*

**episcopate** /ɪ'pɪskəpət/ ⇒ **bishopric** A

**episode** /'epɪsəʊd/ *n.* Ⓐ (*also Mus.*) Episode, *die;* Ⓑ (*instalment of serial*) Folge, *die;* **read next week's exciting ~:** lesen Sie die spannende Fortsetzung in der nächsten Woche!

**episodic** /epɪ'sɒdɪk/, **episodical** /epɪ'sɒdɪkl/ *adj.* episodisch; episodenhaft ‹Szene, Ereignis›

**epistemology** /epɪstɪ'mɒlədʒɪ/ *n.* (*Philos.*) Epistemologie, *die* (*fachspr.*); Erkenntnislehre, *die*

**epistle** /ɪ'pɪsl/ *n.* (*Bibl., Lit., or usu. joc.: letter*) Epistel, *die*

**epistolary** /ɪ'pɪstələrɪ/ *adj.* epistolarisch (*veralt.*); **~ style** Briefstil, *der*

**epitaph** /'epɪtɑ:f/ *n.* Epitaph, *das;* Grab[in]schrift, *die*

**epithet** /'epɪθet/ *n.* Ⓐ (*expressing quality or characteristic*) Beiname, *der;* (*as term of abuse*) Schimpfname, *der;* Ⓑ (*Ling.*) Epitheton, *das* (*fachspr.*); Beiwort, *das*

**epitome** /ɪ'pɪtəmɪ/ *n.* Ⓐ (*of quality, type, etc.*) Inbegriff, *der;* Ⓑ (*thing representing another in miniature*) Widerspiegelung im Kleinen; **be the ~ of sth.** etw. im Kleinen widerspiegeln

**epitomize** /ɪ'pɪtəmaɪz/ *v.t.* Ⓐ (*fig.: represent in miniature*) im Kleinen widerspiegeln; Ⓑ (*fig.: embody*) **~ sth.** der Inbegriff einer Sache (*Gen.*) sein

**epoch** /'i:pɒk, 'epɒk/ *n.* (*also Geol.*) Epoche, *die;* **a new ~ in British politics** eine neue Ära in der britischen Politik

**epochal** /'i:pɒkl, 'epɒkl/ *adj.* Ⓐ (*of epoch[s]*) der Epoche[n] *nachgestellt;* Ⓑ ⇒ **epoch-making**

**'epoch-making** *adj.* epochal ‹Bedeutung›; Epoche machend ‹Entdeckung›

**eponymous** /ɪ'pɒnɪməs/ *adj.* namengebend

**epoxy** /ɪ'pɒksɪ/ (*Chem.*) ❶ *adj.* Epoxid-; Epoxid- (*fachspr.*); **~ resin** ⇒ **2**. ❷ *n.* Epoxidharz, *das;* Epoxidharz, *das* (*fachspr.*)

**epsilon** /ep'saɪlən/ *n.* Epsilon, *das*

**Epsom salt** /epsəm 'sɔ:lt, epsəm 'sɒlt/ *n.* **~[s]** (*Med.*) Bittersalz, *das*

**equable** /'ekwəbl/ *adj.* Ⓐ (*uniform*) gleichförmig ‹Stil›; Ⓑ (*balanced*) ausgeglichen ‹Wesen, Person, Klima›; Ⓒ (*equally proportioned*) ausgewogen ‹Maße, System, Proportionen›; Ⓓ (*fair-minded*) sachlich ‹Einstellung, Art›

**equably** /'ekwəblɪ/ *adv.* Ⓐ (*in uniform style*) gleichförmig; Ⓑ (*in balanced manner*) **~ [disposed** *or* **tempered]** ausgeglichen; Ⓒ (*in equal proportions*) gleichmäßig; Ⓓ (*in fair-minded manner*) sachlich

**equal** /'i:kwl/ ❶ *adj.* Ⓐ gleich; **~ in** *or* **of ~ height/weight/size/importance/strength** *etc.* gleich hoch/schwer/groß/wichtig/stark *usw.;* **add flour and cornflour in ~ measure** *or* **amounts** gleich viel Mehl und Stärkemehl hinzufügen; **marry sb. of ~ rank** standesgemäß heiraten; **not ~ in length** verschieden lang; **~ rights** gleiche Rechte; Gleichberechtigung, *die;* **divide a cake into ~ parts/portions** einen Kuchen in gleich große Stücke/Portionen aufteilen; **~ amounts of milk and water** gleich viel Milch und Wasser; **she had ~ success with her second novel** mit ihrem zweiten Roman hatte sie ebenso großen Erfolg; **she does both jobs with ~ pleasure/enjoyment** beide Tätigkeiten machen ihr gleich viel Spaß; **all men were created ~:** alle Menschen sind gleich geschaffen; **some are more ~ than others** (*joc.*) einige sind gleicher; **his salary is ~ to mine** er verdient genauso viel wie ich; **be ~ in size to sth.** ebenso groß wie etw. sein; **three times four is ~ to twelve** drei mal vier ist [gleich] zwölf; **none was ~ to her in beauty/elegance** keine kam ihr an Schönheit/Eleganz gleich; **Britain is now ~ with France in terms of medals won** Großbritannien ist *od.* liegt jetzt im Medaillenspiegel gleichauf mit Frankreich; **Michael came ~ third** *or* **third ~ with Richard in the class exams** bei den Klassenprüfungen kam Michael zusammen mit Richard auf den dritten Platz; **~ pay [for ~ work]** gleicher Lohn für gleiche Arbeit; **have ~ standing [with sb.]** [jmdm.] gleichgestellt sein; **be on ~ terms [with sb.]** [mit jmdm.] gleichgestellt sein; **meet each other/discuss matters on ~ terms** als Gleichgestellte zusammenkommen/Angelegenheiten als Gleichgestellte erörtern; **all/other things being ~:** wenn nichts dazwischen kommt; ⇒ *also* **~ opportunity;** Ⓑ **~ to** (*adequate for*): **be ~ to sth./sb.** (*strong, clever, etc. enough*) einer Sache/jmdm. gewachsen sein; **a job ~ to sb.'s abilities** eine Arbeit, die jmds. Fähigkeiten entspricht; **be ~ to doing sth.** imstande sein, etw. zu tun; Ⓒ (*impartial*) gerecht; **they were all given ~ treatment** sie wurden alle gleich behandelt; Ⓓ (*evenly balanced*) ausgeglichen; **the battle was not ~:** es war ein ungleicher Kampf.

❷ *n.* Gleichgestellte, *der/die;* **be among [one's] ~s** unter seinesgleichen sein; **talk to sb. as [if he were] one's ~:** mit jmdm. wie mit seinesgleichen sprechen; **be sb.'s/sth.'s ~:** jmdm. ebenbürtig sein/einer Sache (*Dat.*) gleichkommen; **he/she/it has no** *or* **is without ~:** er/sie/es hat nicht seines-/ihresgleichen; **he has met an** *or* **his ~ in her** in ihr hat er jemanden gefunden, der ihm ebenbürtig ist.

❸ *v.t.*, (*Brit.*) **-ll-:** Ⓐ (*be equal to*) **~ sb./sth. [in sth.]** jmdm./einer Sache [in etw. (*Dat.*)] entsprechen; **three times four ~s twelve** drei mal vier ist [gleich] zwölf; **she easily ~s him in intelligence** so intelligent wie er ist sie allemal; **the square on the hypotenuse ~s the sum of the squares on the other two sides** das Quadrat über der Hypotenuse ist gleich der Summe der Quadrate über den Katheten; **no pop group has ~led the Beatles in terms of success** keine Popgruppe ist je an den Erfolg der Beatles herangekommen; Ⓑ (*do sth. equal to*) **~ sb.** es jmdm. gleichtun; **I don't know if I could ever ~ such a high score/your success/such an achievement** ich weiß nicht, ob ich je eine so hohe Punktzahl erreichen könnte/so erfolgreich sein könnte wie Sie/eine solche Leistung vollbringen könnte

**equalisation**, **equalise**, **equaliser** ⇒ **equaliz-**

**equality** /ɪ'kwɒlɪtɪ/ *n.* Gleichheit, *die;* (*equal rights*) Gleichberechtigung, *die;* **~ between the races/the religions, racial/religious ~:** Gleichberechtigung der Rassen/Konfessionen; **~ between the sexes** Gleichheit von Mann und Frau; **women are campaigning for ~ with men** die Frauen kämpfen für ihre Gleichstellung den Männern gegenüber

**equalization** /i:kwəlaɪ'zeɪʃn/ *n.* Angleichung, *die* (**to, with** an + *Akk.*)

**equalize** /'i:kwəlaɪz/ ❶ *v.t.* ausgleichen ‹Druck, Temperatur›; angleichen ‹Maßstäbe, Einkommen, Chancen› (**with** *Dat.*); gleichstellen ‹Personen, gesellschaftliche Gruppen› (**to, with** *Dat. od.* mit). ❷ *v.i.* Ⓐ (*become equal*) sich ausgleichen; **~ with sth.** sich einer Sache (*Dat.*) angleichen; Ⓑ (*Footb. etc.*) den Ausgleich[streffer] erzielen

**equalizer** /'i:kwəlaɪzə(r)/ *n.* (*Footb. etc.*) Ausgleich[streffer], *der*

**equally** /'i:kwəlɪ/ *adv.* Ⓐ ebenso; **rank ~ [with one another]** den gleichen Rang einnehmen; **be ~ close to a and b** von a und b gleich weit entfernt sein; **the two are ~ gifted** die beiden sind gleich begabt; Ⓑ (*in*

e

*equal shares*) in gleiche Teile ‹aufteilen›; gleichmäßig ‹verteilen›; **consist ~ of A and B** zu gleichen Teilen aus A und B bestehen; **C** (*according to the same rule and measurement*) in gleicher Weise; gleich ‹behandeln›

**Equal Opportunities Commission** *n.* (*Brit.*) *Ausschuss für Chancengleichheit;* ≈ Gleichstellungsausschuss, *der*

**equal oppor'tunity** *n.* Chancengleichheit, *die;* **an ~** *or* **equal opportunities employer** ein Arbeitgeber, der jedem die gleiche Chance gibt (*unabhängig von Geschlecht, Rasse usw.*)

**'equals sign** *n.* (*Math.*) Gleichheitszeichen, *das*

**equanimity** /ekwəˈnɪmɪtɪ, iːkwəˈnɪmɪtɪ/ *n., no pl.* **A** (*composure, resignation*) Gelassenheit, *die;* **B** (*evenness of mind, temper*) Gleichmut, *der*

**equate** /ɪˈkweɪt/ *v.t.* **~ sth. [to** *or* **with sth.]** etw. [einer Sache (*Dat.*) *od.* mit etw.] gleichsetzen

**equation** /ɪˈkweɪʒn/ *n.* **A** (*Math.*) Gleichung, *die;* **B** (*Chem.*) [chemische] Gleichung; [Reaktions]gleichung, *die*

**equator** /ɪˈkweɪtə(r)/ *n.* (*Geog., Astron.*) Äquator, *der*

**equatorial** /ekwəˈtɔːrɪəl, iːkwəˈtɔːrɪəl/ *adj.* (*Geog., Astron.*) äquatorial ‹Hitze, Klima›; Äquatorial‹gegend, -strom›; Äquator‹linie, -durchmesser, -gürtel, -sonne›; **~ telescope** (*Astron.*) Äquatoreal, *das*

**equerry** /ˈekwərɪ/ *n.* **A** (*in charge of horses*) königlicher Stallmeister; **B** (*of royal household*) Kammerherr, *der*

**equestrian** /ɪˈkwestrɪən/ ❶ *adj.* **A** (*of horse riding*) reiterlich; Reit‹turnier, -talent›; **B** (*on horseback*) Reiter‹standbild, -bildnis›; **C** (*of knights*) Ritter-. ❷ *n.* Reiter, *der*/Reiterin, *die;* **circus ~s** Zirkusreiter

**equestrianism** /ɪˈkwestrɪənɪzm/ ⇒ **horsemanship**

**equidistant** /iːkwɪˈdɪstənt/ *adj.* gleich weit entfernt (**from** von)

**equilateral** /iːkwɪˈlætərl/ *adj.* (*Math.*) gleichseitig ‹Dreieck, Rechteck, Hyperbel›

**equilibrium** /iːkwɪˈlɪbrɪəm/ *n., pl.* **equilibria** /iːkwɪˈlɪbrɪə/ *or* **~s** Gleichgewicht, *das;* (*sense of balance*) Gleichgewichtssinn, *der;* **lose/keep one's ~:** das Gleichgewicht verlieren/nicht verlieren; **mental/emotional ~:** geistige/emotionale Ausgeglichenheit; **in ~:** im Gleichgewicht; **maintain/restore ~:** das Gleichgewicht halten/wieder finden; **~ of power** (*fig.*) Gleichgewicht der Kräfte; **stable/unstable/neutral ~** (*Phys.*) stabiles/labiles/indifferentes Gleichgewicht

**equine** /ˈekwaɪn, ˈiːkwaɪn/ *adj.* **A** (*of horse*) Pferde‹körper›; **B** (*like horse*) pferdeähnlich ‹Gang, Haltung, Gesichtszüge, Augen›

**equinoctial** /iːkwɪˈnɒkʃl, ekwɪˈnɒkʃl/ *adj.* (*Astron., Geog.*) Äquinoktial‹punkt, -kreis, -stürme›; **~ line** Himmelsäquator, *der*

**equinox** /ˈiːkwɪnɒks, ˈekwɪnɒks/ *n.* **A** Tagundnachtgleiche, *die;* Äquinoktium, *das* (*fachspr.*); **spring** *or* **vernal ~:** Frühjahrs-Tagundnachtgleiche, *die;* **autumn** *or* **autumnal ~:** Herbst-Tagundnachtgleiche, *die;* **B** (*Astron.: equinoctial point*) Äquinoktialpunkt, *der;* ⇒ *also* **precession**

**equip** /ɪˈkwɪp/ *v.t.,* **-pp-** ausrüsten ‹Fahrzeug, Armee›; ausstatten ‹Zimmer, Küche›; **fully ~ped** komplett ausgerüstet/ausgestattet; **~ sb./oneself [with sth.] [for a journey** *etc.*] jmdn./sich [für eine Reise *usw.*] [mit etw.] ausrüsten; **be ~ped with sth.** (*fig.*) über etw. (*Akk.*) verfügen; **he is well ~ped for the job** (*fig.*) er bringt gute Voraussetzungen für den Job mit

**equipment** /ɪˈkwɪpmənt/ *n.* **A** Ausrüstung, *die;* (*of kitchen, laboratory, etc.*) Ausstattung, *die;* (*sth. needed for activity*) Geräte *Pl.*; **breathing ~:** Sauerstoffgerät, *das;* **climbing/diving ~:** Bergsteiger-/Taucherausrüstung, *die;* **fighting/skiing ~:** Kampf-/Skiausrüstung, *die;* **gardening/gymnastics/recording ~:** Garten-/Turn-/Aufnahmegeräte; **mining ~:** Bergbauausrüstung, *die;* **playground ~:** Spielgeräte (*auf einem Spielplatz*); **riding ~:** Reitzeug, *das* (*ugs.*); **writing ~:** Schreibutensilien *Pl.*; **B** (*fig.: intellectual resources*) **mental/intellectual ~:** geistiges Rüstzeug

**equitable** /ˈekwɪtəbl/ *adj.* **A** (*fair*) gerecht; **in an ~ manner** gerecht; **B** (*valid*) billig; **~ jurisdiction** Rechtsprechung nach dem Billigkeitsrecht

**equitably** /ˈekwɪtəblɪ/ *adv.* gerecht

**equity** /ˈekwɪtɪ/ *n.* **A** (*Law*) billiges *od.* natürliches Recht; **in ~:** billigermaßen; **acknowledge a claim in ~:** einen Anspruch billigerweise anerkennen; **B** (*fairness*) Gerechtigkeit, *die;* **with ~:** gerecht; **C** (*use of justice as well as law*) Billigkeit, *die;* **on the basis of ~:** auf der Grundlage der Billigkeit; **D** **E~** (*Brit. Theatre*) *britische Schauspielergewerkschaft;* **E** *in pl.* (*stocks and shares without fixed interest*) [Stamm]aktien; **F** (*value of shares*) Eigenkapital, *das;* **G** (*net value of mortgaged property*) *Wert eines Besitzes nach Abzug der Belastungen*

**equity: ~ 'capital** *n.* (*Commerc.*) Eigenkapital, *das;* **~ market** *n.* (*Commerc.*) Aktienmarkt, *der*

**equivalence** /ɪˈkwɪvələns/, **equivalency** /ɪˈkwɪvələnsɪ/ *n.* **A** (*being equivalent*) **~ [of value]** Gleichwertigkeit, *die;* (*of two amounts*) Wertgleichheit, *die;* **B** (*having equivalent meaning*) **~ [in meaning]** Äquivalenz, *die* (*bes. Logik*); Bedeutungsgleichheit, *die;* **C** (*correspondence*) Entsprechung, *die;* **D** (*Chem.*) Äquivalenz, *die*

**equivalent** /ɪˈkwɪvələnt/ ❶ *adj.* **A** (*equal, having same result*) gleichwertig; **be ~ to sth.** einer Sache (*Dat.*) entsprechen; **be ~ to doing sth.** dasselbe sein, wie wenn man etw. tut; **something of ~ value** etwas Gleichwertiges; **an ~ amount [of money]** ein entsprechender *od.* gleich hoher Betrag; **an ~ amount of flour** gleich viel Mehl; **B** (*meaning the same*) äquivalent (*Sprachw.*); entsprechend; **these two words are [not] ~ in meaning** diese beiden Wörter sind [nicht] bedeutungsgleich; **C** (*corresponding*) entsprechend; **be ~ to sth.** einer Sache (*Dat.*) entsprechen; **D** (*Chem.*) äquivalent. ❷ *n.* **A** (*~ or corresponding thing or person*) Pendant, *das;* Gegenstück, *das;* **be the ~ of sb./sth.** das Pendant *od.* Gegenstück zu jmdm./einer Sache sein; **B** (*word etc. having same meaning*) Entsprechung, *die* (**of** zu); Äquivalent, *das* (**of** für); **C** (*thing having same result*) **be the ~ of sth.** einer Sache (*Dat.*) entsprechen; **D** (*Chem.*) Äquivalent, *das*

**equivocal** /ɪˈkwɪvəkl/ *adj.* **A** (*ambiguous*) zweideutig; **~ meaning** Zweideutigkeit, *die;* **B** (*questionable*) zweifelhaft ‹Person, Erfolg, Glück, Ruf›

**equivocally** /ɪˈkwɪvəkəlɪ/ *adv.* (*ambiguously*) zweideutig

**equivocate** /ɪˈkwɪvəkeɪt/ *v.i.* zweideutige Aussagen machen; ausweichen

**equivocation** /ɪkwɪvəˈkeɪʃn/ *n.* zweideutige Formulierungen

**ER** *abbr.* **King Edward/Queen Elizabeth**

**er** /ɜː(r)/ *int.* äh

**era** /ˈɪərə/ *n.* **A** (*system of chronology*) Ära, *die;* **B** (*period*) Zeit; **the Adenauer ~:** die Ära Adenauer; **Byzantine/computer ~:** byzantinische Zeit/(*ugs.*) Computerzeitalter, *das;* **the Renaissance/Beatles ~:** die Zeit der Renaissance/Beatles; **Roman/Viking ~:** Römer-/Wikingerzeit, *die;* **a new ~ in fashion began** in der Mode begann eine neue Ära; **C** (*Geol.*) Ära, *die* (*fachspr.*); Erdzeitalter, *das*

**eradicate** /ɪˈrædɪkeɪt/ *v.t.* (*remove*) ausrotten; gründlich beseitigen ‹Ursache›

**eradication** /ɪrædɪˈkeɪʃn/ *n.* Ausrottung, *die*

**eradicator** /ɪˈrædɪkeɪtə(r)/ *n.* Tintenentferner, *der*

**erase** /ɪˈreɪz/ *v.t.* **A** (*rub out*) auslöschen; (*with rubber, knife*) ausradieren; **B** (*obliterate*) tilgen (*geh.*) (**from** aus); **C** (*remove recorded signal from; also Computing*) löschen

**eraser** /ɪˈreɪzə(r)/ *n.* **[pencil] ~:** Radiergummi, *der;* **[blackboard] ~** *Block mit Filzbelag o. Ä. zum Löschen von Kreideschrift;* (*sponge*) Tafelschwamm, *der*

**erasure** /ɪˈreɪʒə(r)/ *n.* **A** (*rubbing out*) Auslöschen, *das;* (*with rubber*) Ausradieren, *das;* **B** (*obliteration*) Tilgung, *die* (**from** aus); **C** (*removal of recorded signal*) Löschen, *das;* (*place*) gelöschte Stelle

**ere** /eə(r)/ (*poet./arch.*) ❶ *prep.* vor (+ *Dat.*) **~ long** binnen kurzem; **~ now** bereits; **~ then** bis dann. ❷ *conj.* ehe

**erect** /ɪˈrekt/ ❶ *adj.* **A** (*upright, vertical; also fig.*) aufrecht; gerade ‹Rücken, Wuchs›; **stand ~** ‹Soldat:› strammstehen; **with head ~:** mit hoch erhobenem Kopf; **B** (*Physiol.: enlarged and rigid*) erigiert; **C** (*raised*) aufgestellt ‹Ohren›. ❷ *v.t.* **A** (*build*) errichten; aufbauen ‹Gerüst›; aufstellen ‹Standbild, Mast, Verkehrsschild›; aufschlagen, aufstellen ‹Zelt›; konstruieren ‹Theorie›; **B** (*raise*) aufrichten ‹Körper, Ohren, Stacheln›

**erectile** /ɪˈrektaɪl/ *adj.* (*Physiol.*) schwellfähig; erektil (*fachspr.*)

**erection** /ɪˈrekʃn/ *n.* **A** (*building*) ⇒ **erect** 2 A: Errichtung, *die;* Aufbau, *der;* Aufstellen, *das;* Aufschlagen, *das;* Konstruieren, *das;* **B** (*structure*) Bauwerk, *das;* (*other than a building*) Konstruktion, *die;* **C** (*raising*) Aufstellen, *das;* **D** (*Physiol.*) Anschwellen, *das;* (*of penis*) Erektion, *die*

**erectly** /ɪˈrektlɪ/ *adv.* (*in upright manner, vertically; also fig.*) aufrecht

**erectness** /ɪˈrektnɪs/ *n., no pl.* (*uprightness*) **~ [of stance** *or* **bearing** *or* **posture]** aufrechte Haltung

**erg** /ɜːg/ *n.* (*Phys.*) Erg, *das*

**ergo** /ˈɜːgəʊ/ *adv.* (*literary*) ergo

**ergonomic** /ɜːgəˈnɒmɪk/ *adj.,* **ergonomically** /ɜːgəˈnɒmɪklɪ/ *adv.* ergonomisch

**ergonomics** /ɜːgəˈnɒmɪks/ *n., no pl.* Ergonomie, *die;* Ergonomik, *die*

**ergot** /ˈɜːgət/ *n.* **A** (*disease*) Mutterkornbefall, *der;* **B** (*fungus*) Mutterkornpilz, *der;* **C** (*dried mycelium*) Mutterkorn, *das*

**erica** /ˈerɪkə, ɪˈriːkə/ *n.* (*Bot.*) Erika, *die*

**ERM** *abbr.* **exchange rate mechanism** ⇒ **exchange** 3 D

**ermine** /ˈɜːmɪn/ *n.* **A** (*fur; also Her.*) Hermelin, *der;* **B** (*Zool.*) Hermelin, *das*

**Ernie** /ˈɜːnɪ/ *n.* (*Brit. coll.; abbr. of Electronic Random Number Indicator Equipment*) *Gerät zur Ziehung der Gewinnzahlen für Prämienanleihen;* **have you ever won anything on ~?** haben Sie je etwas mit Prämienanleihen gewonnen?

**erode** /ɪˈrəʊd/ ❶ *v.t.* **A** ‹Säure, Rost:› angreifen; ‹Wasser, Regen, Meer:› auswaschen; ‹Wind:› verwittern lassen; ‹Wasser, Regen, Meer, Wind:› erodieren (*Geol.*); **B** (*fig.*) unterminieren ‹Grundlage, Fundament, Beziehung›. ❷ *v.i.* **A** verwittern; **B** (*fig.*) unterminiert werden

**erogenous** /ɪˈrɒdʒɪnəs/ *adj.* erogen ‹Zone›; **~ stimulation** sexuelle Stimulation

**erosion** /ɪˈrəʊʒn/ *n.* **A** ⇒ **erode** 1 A: Angreifen, *das;* Auswaschung, *die;* Verwitterung, *die;* Erosion, *die* (*Geol.*); **B** (*fig.*) Unterminierung, *die*

**erosive** /ɪˈrəʊsɪv/ *adj.* (*Geol.*) erodierend

**erotic** /ɪˈrɒtɪk/ *adj.* erotisch

**erotica** /ɪˈrɒtɪkə/ *n. pl.* Erotika

**erotically** /ɪˈrɒtɪkəlɪ/ *adv.* erotisch

**eroticism** /ɪˈrɒtɪsɪzm/ *n.* Erotik, *die*

**err** /ɜː(r)/ *v.i.* sich irren; **to ~ is human** (*prov.*) Irren ist menschlich; **you ~ in your opinion of him** Sie schätzen ihn falsch ein; **let's ~ on the right** *or* **safe side and ...:** um sicherzugehen, wollen wir ...

**errand** /ˈerənd/ *n.* **A** Botengang, *der;* (*shopping*) Besorgung, *die;* **go on** *or* **run an ~:** einen Botengang/eine Besorgung machen; **go** *or* **run ~s** Botengänge/Besorgungen machen; **send sb. on an ~:** jmdn. auf einen Botengang schicken/jmdn. etwas besorgen lassen; **go on an ~ of mercy [for sb.]** Hilfe für jmdn. holen; **send sb. on an ~ of mercy** jmdn. auf eine Rettungsmission entsenden; ⇒ *also* **fool's errand**; **B** (*object of* *journey*) Auftrag, *der;* **C** (*purpose*) Zweck, *der*

**errand:** ~ **boy** *n.* Laufbursche, *der;* Bote[n-junge], *der;* ~ **girl** *n.* Laufmädchen, *das;* Botin, *die*

**errant** /'erənt/ *adj.* irrig, falsch ‹Prinzip, Maßstab, Meinung, Vorstellung›; fehlgeleitet ‹Person, Verhalten›; untreu ‹Ehemann, Ehefrau›; ⇒ *also* **knight errant**

**errata** *pl. of* **erratum**

**erratic** /ɪ'rætɪk/ **1** *adj.* unregelmäßig; sprunghaft ‹Wesen, Person, Art›; unbeständig ‹Charakter, Leistung, Wetter›; launenhaft ‹Verhalten›; ungleichmäßig ‹Bewegung, Verlauf›; **the ~ moods of the weather** die wechselnden Launen des Wetters; **he is rather ~ in the standard of work he produces** das Niveau seiner Arbeiten ist recht unterschiedlich. **2** *n.* ⇒ **erratic block**

**erratically** /ɪ'rætɪkəlɪ/ *adv.* unregelmäßig; launenhaft ‹sich verhalten›; ungleichmäßig ‹sich bewegen, verlaufen›

**erratic 'block** *n.* (*Geol.*) erratischer Block (*fachspr.*); Findling, *der*

**erratum** /e'reɪtəm, e'rɑːtəm/ *n.*, *pl.* **errata** /e'reɪtə, e'rɑːtə/ (*Bibliog.*, *Printing*) Erratum, *das* (*fachspr.*); Druckfehler, *der*

**erroneous** /ɪ'rəʊnɪəs/ *adj.* falsch; irrig ‹Schlussfolgerung, Eindruck, Ansicht, Auffassung, Annahme›

**erroneously** /ɪ'rəʊnɪəslɪ/ *adv.* fälschlich; irrigerweise

**error** /'erə(r)/ *n.* **A** (*mistake*) Fehler, *der;* **gross ~ of judgement** grobe Fehleinschätzung; **printing/typographical ~:** Druck-/Setzfehler, *der;* **B** (*wrong opinion*) Irrtum, *der;* **lead sb. into ~:** jmdn. irreleiten; **realize the ~ of one's ways** seine Fehler einsehen; **in ~:** irrtümlich[erweise]; **be in ~ in one's calculations** sich verrechnen; **C** (*Math. etc.*) Abweichung, *die*

**'error message** *n.* (*Computing*) Fehlermeldung, *die*

**erstwhile** /'ɜːstwaɪl/ *adj.* einstig; einstmalig (*veralt.*)

**erudite** /'eruːdaɪt/ *adj.* gelehrt ‹Abhandlung, Vortrag›; gebildet, gelehrt ‹Person›

**erudition** /eruː'dɪʃn/ *n.*, *no pl.* Gelehrsamkeit, *die* (*geh.*)

**erupt** /ɪ'rʌpt/ *v.i.* **A** ‹Vulkan, Geysir:› ausbrechen; **ashes and lava ~ed from the volcano** Asche und Lava wurden aus dem Vulkan geschleudert; **~ with anger/into a fit of rage** (*fig.*) einen Wutanfall bekommen; **B** (*appear*) ‹Hautausschlag:› ausbrechen

**eruption** /ɪ'rʌpʃn/ *n.* **A** (*of volcano, geyser*) Ausbruch, *der;* Eruption, *die* (*Geol.*); **B** (*rash*) Eruption, *die* (*Med.*); Hautausschlag, *der;* **C** (*fig.*) Ausbruch, *der*

**eruptive** /ɪ'rʌptɪv/ *adj.* eruptiv; **~ rocks** (*Geol.*) Eruptivgestein, *das*

**erythema** /erɪ'θiːmə/ *n.* (*Med.*) Erythem, *das* (*fachspr.*); Hautrötung, *die*

**erythrocyte** /ɪ'rɪθrəsaɪt/ *n.* (*Anat.*) Erythrozyt, *der* (*fachspr.*); rotes Blutkörperchen

**escalate** /'eskəleɪt/ **1** *v.i.* sich ausweiten (**into** zu); eskalieren (*geh.*) (**into** zu); ‹Löhne, Preise, Kosten:› [ständig] steigen. **2** *v.t.* ausweiten (**into** zu); eskalieren (*geh.*) (**into** zu); beschleunigen ‹Anstieg›

**escalation** /eskə'leɪʃn/ *n.* (*of rioting, war*) Ausweitung, *die;* Eskalation, *die* (*geh.*); (*of wages, prices, costs*) Anstieg, *der*

**escalator** /'eskəleɪtə(r)/ *n.* **A** Rolltreppe, *die;* **B** (*Commerc.*) **~ clause** Gleitklausel, *die*

**escalope** /'eskələʊp/ *n.* (*Gastr.*) Schnitzel, *das*

**escapade** /eskə'peɪd/ *n.* Eskapade, *die* (*geh.*)

**escape** /ɪ'skeɪp/ **1** *n.* **A** (*lit. or fig.*) Flucht, *die* (**from** aus); (*from prison or mental hospital also*) Ausbruch, *der* (**from** aus); (*of large wild animal*) Ausbruch, *der;* (*of small animal*) Entlaufen, *das;* (*of bird*) Entfliegen, *das;* **there is no ~** (*lit. or fig.*) es gibt kein Entkommen; **~ vehicle** Fluchtfahrzeug, *das;* **~ route** (*lit. or fig.*) Fluchtweg, *der;* **make one's ~ [from sth.]** [aus etw.] entkommen; **have a narrow/miraculous ~:** gerade noch einmal/wie durch ein Wunder davonkommen; **have a lucky ~:** glücklich davonkommen; noch einmal Glück haben; **that was a narrow ~** (*joc.*) gerade noch mal davongekommen; **you had a lucky ~** (*joc.*) da haben Sie aber noch mal Glück gehabt; **~ from reality** Flucht vor der Realität; **B** (*leakage of gas etc.*) Austritt, *der;* Entweichen, *das;* **C** (*plant*) verwilderte Pflanze. ⇒ *also* **fire escape**.
**2** *v.i.* **A** (*lit. or fig.*) fliehen (**from** aus); entfliehen (*geh.*) (**from** *Dat.*); (*successfully*) entkommen (**from** *Dat.*); (*from prison or mental hospital also*) ausbrechen (**from** aus); ‹Großtier:› ausbrechen; ‹Kleintier:› entlaufen (**from** *Dat.*); ‹Vogel:› entfliegen (**from** *Dat.*); **~ to freedom** in die Freiheit entkommen; **while trying to ~:** auf der Flucht; **~d prisoner/convict** entflohener Gefangener/Sträfling; **~ to one's room** sich in sein Zimmer zurückziehen; **~ into a dream world** (*fig.*) in eine Traumwelt flüchten; **B** (*leak*) ‹Gas:› ausströmen; ‹Flüssigkeit:› auslaufen; **C** (*avoid harm*) davonkommen; **~ alive** mit dem Leben davonkommen; **he ~d, but she was killed** er überlebte, während sie getötet wurde; **D** (*Computing*) **press ~:** 'Escape' drücken.
**3** *v.t.* **A** entkommen (+ *Dat.*) ‹Verfolger, Angreifer, Feind›; entgehen (+ *Dat.*) ‹Bestrafung, Gefangennahme, Tod, Entdeckung, Schicksal›; verschont bleiben von ‹Katastrophe, Krankheit, Zerstörung, Reduzierung, Auswirkungen›; **~ observation/a duty** sich der Beobachtung/einer Pflicht entziehen; **he ~d the consequences** ihm blieben die Konsequenzen erspart; **~ being seen** nicht gesehen werden; **she narrowly ~d being killed** sie wäre fast getötet worden; **the car ~d damage** der Wagen blieb unbeschädigt; **one can't ~ the fact that …:** es lässt sich nicht leugnen, dass …; **B** (*not be remembered by*) entfallen sein (+ *Dat.*); **C** **~ sb.['s notice]** (*not be seen*) jmdm. entgehen; **~ notice** nicht bemerkt werden; **~ sb.'s attention** jmds. Aufmerksamkeit (*Dat.*) entgehen; ⇒ *also* **memory** B; **D** (*not be understood by*) **~ sb.** sich jmds. Verständnis (*Dat.*) entziehen; **E** (*be uttered involuntarily by*) entfahren (+ *Dat.*)

**escape:** **~ artist** ⇒ **escapologist**; **~ attempt**, **~ bid** *ns.* Fluchtversuch, *der;* (*from prison*) Ausbruchsversuch, *der;* **~ clause** *n.* (*Law*) Ausweichklausel, *die*

**escapee** /ɪskeɪ'piː, eskeɪ'piː/ *n.* Entflohene, *der/die*

**escape:** **~-hatch** *n.* (*Naut.*, *Aeronaut.*) Notausstieg, *der;* (*fig.*) Rettungsanker, *der;* **~ key** *n.* (*Computing*) Escapetaste, *die;* **~ mechanism** *n.* (*Psych.*) Abwehrmechanismus, *der*

**escapement** /ɪ'skeɪpmənt/ *n.* (*Horol.*) Hemmung, *die*

**e'scape-proof** *adj.* ausbruchsicher

**escaper** /ɪ'skeɪpə(r)/ *n.* Entflohene, *der/die*

**escape:** **~ road** *n.* Auslaufstrecke, *die;* **~ route** *n.* Fluchtweg, *der;* **~ valve** *n.* Sicherheitsventil, *das*

**escapism** /ɪ'skeɪpɪzm/ *n.* (*Psych.*) Eskapismus, *der* (*fachspr.*); Realitätsflucht, *die*

**escapist** /ɪ'skeɪpɪst/ (*Psych.*) **1** *n.* Eskapist, *der* (*fachspr.*); Aussteiger, *der*/Aussteigerin, *die* (*ugs.*). **2** *adj.* eskapistisch (*fachspr.*); Aussteiger- (*ugs.*)

**escapologist** /eskə'pɒlədʒɪst/ *n.* (*Brit.*) Entfesselungskünstler, *der*

**escarpment** /ɪ'skɑːpmənt/ *n.* (*Geog.*) Steilhang, *der*

**eschatology** /eskə'tɒlədʒɪ/ *n.* (*Theol.*) Eschatologie, *die*

**eschew** /ɪs'tʃuː/ *v.t.* (*literary*) meiden (*geh.*)

**escort** **1** /'eskɔːt/ *n.* **A** (*armed guard*) Eskorte, *die;* Geleitschutz, *der* (*Milit.*); **police ~:** Polizeieskorte, *die;* **with an ~, under ~:** mit einer Eskorte; **fighter ~:** Jagdschutz, *der;* **B** (*person[s] protecting or guiding*) Begleitung, *die;* **be sb.'s ~:** jmdn. begleiten; **C** (*man accompanying woman socially*) Begleiter, *der;* **D** (*hired companion*) Begleiter, *der*/Begleiterin, *die;* (*woman also*) ≈ Hostess, *die.* **2** /ɪ'skɔːt/ *v.t.* **A** begleiten; (*lead*) führen; geleiten (*geh.*); (*as guard of honour; also Mil.*) eskortieren; **~ sb. to safety** jmdn. in Sicherheit bringen; **B** (*take forcibly*) bringen

**escort**/'eskɔːt/**:** **~ agency** *n. Agentur für Begleiter/Begleiterinnen;* **~ carrier** *n.* (*Navy*) Geleitflugzeugträger, *der;* **~ duty** *n.* **be on ~ duty** als Geleitschutz eingesetzt sein; **~ vessel** *n.* (*Navy*) Geleitschiff, *das*

**escritoire** /eskrɪ'twɑː(r)/ *n.* Sekretär, *der*

**escutcheon** /ɪ'skʌtʃn/ *n.* (*Her.*) Schild, *der;* **be a blot on sb.'s ~** (*fig.*) jmds. Ehre beflecken

**ESE** /iːstsaʊθ'iːst/ *abbr.* **east-south-east** OSO

**Eskimo** /'eskɪməʊ/ ▶ **1275** **1** *adj.* Eskimo-; ⇒ *also* **English** 1. **2** *n.* **A** *no pl.* (*language*) Eskimoisch, *das;* ⇒ *also* **English** 2 A; **B** *pl.* **~s** *or same* Eskimo, *der*/Eskimofrau, *die;* **the ~[s]** die Eskimos

**'Eskimo dog** *n.* Eskimohund, *der*

**ESN** *abbr.* **educationally subnormal**

**esophagus** (*Amer.*) ⇒ **oesophagus**

**esoteric** /esə'terɪk, iːsə'terɪk/ *adj.* esoterisch (*geh.*)

**ESP** *abbr.* (*Psych.*) **extra-sensory perception** ASW

**espalier** /ɪ'spælɪə(r)/ *n.* **A** (*trellis*) Spalier, *das;* **B** (*tree*) Spalierbaum, *der*

**esparto** /ɪ'spɑːtəʊ/ *n.* **~ [grass]** (*Bot.*) Esparto, *der;* Espartogras, *das*

**especial** /ɪ'speʃl/ *attrib. adj.* [ganz] besonder...; **have ~ talent** besonders begabt sein; **for your ~ benefit** gerade um deinetwillen

**especially** /ɪ'speʃəlɪ/ *adv.* besonders; **more ~ because …:** umso eher, als …; **what ~ do you want to see?** was möchten Sie insbesondere sehen?; **~ as** zumal; **more ~:** ganz besonders

**Esperanto** /espə'ræntəʊ/ *n.*, *no pl.* ▶ **1275** Esperanto, *das;* ⇒ *also* **English** 2 A

**espionage** /'espɪənɑːʒ/ *n.* Spionage, *die;* **carry out ~ for sb.** für jmdn. spionieren; ⇒ *also* **industrial espionage**

**esplanade** /esplə'neɪd, esplə'nɑːd/ *n.* Esplanade, *die* (*geh.*)

**espousal** /ɪ'spaʊzl/ *n.* Eintreten, *das* (**of** für)

**espouse** /ɪ'spaʊz/ *v.t.* **A** eintreten für; **B** (*arch.*) (*marry*) ehelichen (*veralt.*); (*give in marriage*) vermählen (*veralt.*) (**to** mit)

**espresso** /e'spresəʊ/ *n.*, *pl.* **~s** (*coffee*) Espresso, *der*

**e'spresso bar** *n.* Espressobar, *die;* Espresso, *das*

**esprit de corps** /espriː də 'kɔː/ *n.* Korpsgeist, *der* (*geh.*); Gemeinschaftsgeist, *der*

**espy** /ɪ'spaɪ/ *v.t.* (*dated/joc.*) entdecken

**Esq.** *abbr.* ▶ **1617** **Esquire** ≈ Hr.; (*on letter*) ≈ Hrn.; **Jim Smith, ~** Hr./Hrn. Jim Smith

**essay** **1** /'eseɪ/ *n.* Essay, *der;* Aufsatz, *der* (*bes. Schulw.*). **2** /ɪ'seɪ/ *v.t.* sich versuchen an (+ *Dat.*); **~ to do sth.** sich bemühen, etw. zu tun

**essayist** /'eseɪɪst/ *n.* ▶ **1261** Essayist, *der*/Essayistin, *die*

**essence** /'esəns/ *n.* **A** Wesen, *das;* (*gist*) Wesentliche, *das;* (*of problem, message, teaching*) Kern, *der;* **she is the [very] ~ of grace/kindness** sie ist der Inbegriff der Anmut/der Liebenswürdigkeit; **in ~:** im Wesentlichen; **be of the ~:** von entscheidender Bedeutung sein; **B** (*Cookery*) Essenz, *die*

**essential** /ɪ'senʃl/ **1** *adj.* **A** (*fundamental*) wesentlich ‹Unterschied, Merkmal, Aspekt›; entscheidend ‹Frage›; zentral ‹Thema›; **B** (*indispensable*) unentbehrlich; lebenswichtig ‹Versorgungseinrichtungen, Nahrungsmittel, Güter, Organe›; unabdingbar ‹Erfordernis, Qualifikation, Voraussetzung›; unbedingt notwendig ‹Bestandteile, Maßnahmen, Ausrüstung›; wesentlich, entscheidend ‹Rolle›; **the ~ thing is for her to be happy** die Hauptsache ist, dass sie glücklich ist; **~ to life** lebensnotwendig *od.* -wichtig; **it is [absolutely *or* most] ~ that …:** es ist unbedingt notwendig, dass …; **these measures are ~:** diese Maßnahmen sind unbedingt erforderlich; **~ oil** ⇒ **ethereal oil**.
**2** *n.*, *esp. in pl.* **A** (*indispensable element*) Notwendigste, *das;* **be an ~ for sth.** für etw.

e

unentbehrlich sein; **the ~s of life** die lebensnotwendigsten Güter; **the bare ~s** das Allernotwendigste; (B) (*fundamental element*) Wesentliche, *das;* **confine oneself to the ~:** sich auf das Wesentliche beschränken; **the ~s of French grammar** die Grundzüge der französischen Grammatik

**essentially** /ɪˈsenʃəlɪ/ *adv.* im Grunde; **my opinion does not ~ differ from yours** ich bin nicht grundsätzlich anderer Meinung als Sie

**establish** /ɪˈstæblɪʃ/ **1** *v.t.* (A) (*set up, create, found*) schaffen ‹Einrichtung, Frieden, Präzedenzfall, Ministerposten›; gründen ‹Organisation, Institut›; stiften ‹Krankenhaus, Frieden›; errichten ‹Reich, Geschäft, Lehrstuhl, System›; einsetzen, bilden ‹Regierung, Ausschuss›; einsetzen ‹Sakrament›; herstellen ‹Kontakt, Beziehungen› (**with** zu); aufschlagen ‹Hauptquartier›; aufstellen ‹Rekord›; erlassen ‹Gesetz›; einführen ‹Mode, Steuer, neue Methoden›; ins Leben rufen, begründen ‹Bewegung›; **~ a routine** Routine entwickeln; **~ one's authority** sich (*Dat.*) Autorität verschaffen; **~ law and order** Recht und Ordnung herstellen; (B) (*settle, place*) unterbringen; **be ~ed in one's new home** sich in seinem neuen Heim eingerichtet haben; **~ sb. in business** jmdm. zum Start im Geschäftsleben verhelfen; **~ sb. in a business of his/her own** jmdm. zur Gründung eines eigenen Geschäfts verhelfen; (C) (*appoint*) einsetzen; (D) (*secure acceptance for*) etablieren; **become ~ed** sich einbürgern; **be firmly ~ed** einen festen Platz haben; **~ one's reputation** sich (*Dat.*) einen Namen machen; (E) (*prove*) beweisen ‹Schuld, Unschuld, Tatsache›; unter Beweis stellen ‹Können›; nachweisen ‹Anspruch›; **an inspection ~ed that ...:** eine Prüfung ergab, dass ...; (F) (*discover*) feststellen; ermitteln ‹Umstände, Aufenthaltsort›.

**2** *v. refl.* (*take up one's quarters*) **~ oneself [at *or* in a place]** sich [an einem Ort] niederlassen; **the practice has ~ed itself** der Brauch hat sich eingebürgert; **~ oneself as a carpenter** sich (*Dat.*) als Tischler einen festen Kundenkreis gewinnen

**established** /ɪˈstæblɪʃt/ *adj.* (A) (*entrenched*) eingeführt ‹Geschäft usw.›; bestehend ‹Ordnung›; etabliert ‹Schriftsteller›; **long-~ company** alteingeführte *od.* -eingesessene Firma; **this firm has an ~ reputation** diese Firma ist sehr renommiert; **~ civil servant** ≈ Beamter auf Lebenszeit; (B) (*accepted*) üblich; etabliert ‹Stilrichtung, Gesellschaftsordnung›; geltend ‹Norm›; fest ‹Brauch›; feststehend ‹Tatsache›; überkommen ‹Glaube›; **become ~:** sich durchsetzen; (C) (*Eccl.*) **~ church/religion** Staatskirche/-religion, *die*

**establishment** /ɪˈstæblɪʃmənt/ *n.* (A) (*setting up, creation, foundation*) Gründung, *die;* (*of government, committee*) Einsetzung, *die;* (*of democracy, empire*) Errichtung, *die;* (*of movement*) Begründung, *die;* (*of peace, relations*) Schaffung, *die;* (B) (*settlement, placement*) Unterbringung, *die;* (C) (*appointment*) Einsetzung, *die;* (D) (*proving*) Nachweis, *der;* (E) (*institution*) **[business] ~:** Unternehmen, *das;* **commercial/industrial ~:** Handels-/Industrieunternehmen, *das;* **educational ~:** Schule, *die;* (F) (*household, residence*) Haus, *das;* (G) (*organized body*) Truppe, *die;* (*quota*) Personalbestand, *der;* **peace[time]/war ~** (*Mil.*) Friedens-/Kriegsstärke, *die;* (H) (*Brit.*) **the E~** (*social group*) das Establishment

**estate** /ɪˈsteɪt/ *n.* (A) (*landed property*) Gut, *das;* **family/private ~:** Familien-/Privatbesitz, *der;* **~ in the country** Landgut, *das;* (B) (*Brit.: area with buildings*) (*housing ~*) [Wohn]siedlung, *die;* (*industrial ~*) Industriegebiet, *das;* (*trading ~*) Gewerbegebiet, *das;* **live on an ~:** in einer Wohnsiedlung leben; **on the industrial/trading ~:** im Industrie-/Gewerbegebiet; (C) (*plantation*) Plantage, *die;* (D) (*total assets*) (*of deceased person*) Erbmasse, *die* (*Rechtsspr.*); Nachlass, *der;* (*of bankrupt*) Konkursmasse, *die* (*Wirtsch., Rechtsspr.*); (E) (*Law: person's interest in landed property*) Eigentumsrecht, *das;* ⇒ *also* **personal ~**; **real ~**; (F) (*political class*) Stand, *der;* **the Three Estates [of the Realm]** die drei [Reichs]stände; **the fourth ~** (*joc.*) die Zunft der Journalisten (*scherzh.*); (G) (*arch.: condition*) Stand, *der;* **reach man's ~:** in den Mannesstand treten (*veralt.*); **the [holy] ~ of matrimony** der heilige Stand der Ehe (*geh.*); (H) (*Brit.*) ⇒ **~ car**

**estate: ~ agent** *n.* ▶ 1261 (*Brit.*) (A) Grundstücksmakler, *der;* Immobilienmakler, *der;* (B) (*steward*) Gutsverwalter, *der;* **~ car** *n.* (*Brit.*) Kombiwagen, *der;* **~ duty** (*Brit.*), **~ tax** (*Amer.*) *ns.* Erbschaftssteuer, *die*

**esteem** /ɪˈstiːm/ **1** *n., no pl.* Achtung, *die* (**for** vor + *Dat.*); Wertschätzung, *die* (*geh.*) (**for** *Gen.*, für); **hold sb./sth. in [high *or* great] ~:** [hohe *od.* große] Achtung vor jmdm./etw. haben; **go up *or* rise/go down *or* sink in sb.'s ~:** in jmds. Achtung steigen/sinken; **[as a] token *or* mark of my ~:** [als] Zeichen meiner Hochachtung *od.* (*geh.*) Wertschätzung. **2** *v.t.* (A) (*think favourably of*) schätzen; **highly *or* much *or* greatly ~ed** hoch geschätzt (*geh.*); sehr geschätzt; (B) (*consider*) **~ [as]** erachten für (*geh.*); ansehen als; **~ sth. an honour** sich (*Dat.*) etw. zur Ehre anrechnen (*geh.*)

**ester** /ˈestə(r)/ *n.* (*Chem.*) Ester, *der*

**esthetic** *etc.* (*Amer.*) ⇒ **aesthetic** *etc.*

**estimable** /ˈestɪməbl/ *adj.* schätzenswert

**estimate** **1** /ˈestɪmət/ *n.* (A) (*of number, amount, etc.*) Schätzung, *die;* **at a rough ~:** grob geschätzt; (B) (*of character, qualities, etc.*) Einschätzung, *die;* **form an ~ of sb.'s abilities** jmds. Fähigkeiten beurteilen; (C) (*Commerc.*) Kostenvoranschlag, *der;* **give an ~ of £50** die Kosten auf 50 Pfund veranschlagen; (D) (*Brit. Parl.*) **the E~s** der Etat. **2** /ˈestɪmeɪt/ *v.t.* schätzen ‹Größe, Entfernung, Zahl, Umsatz› (**at** auf + *Akk.*); einschätzen ‹Fähigkeiten, Durchführbarkeit, Aussichten›; **how far would you ~ the distance to be?** wie groß ist nach Ihrer Schätzung die Entfernung?

**estimation** /estɪˈmeɪʃn/ *n.* Schätzung, *die;* (*of situation etc.*) Einschätzung, *die;* Beurteilung, *die;* (*esteem*) Wertschätzung, *die* (*geh.*); **in sb.'s ~:** nach jmds. Schätzung; **go up/down in sb.'s ~:** in jmds. Achtung steigen/sinken

**estimator** /ˈestɪmeɪtə(r)/ *n.* Kalkulator, *der*

**Estonia** /eˈstəʊnɪə/ *pr. n.* Estland (*das*)

**Estonian** /eˈstəʊnɪən/, ▶ 1275, ▶ 1340 **1** *adj.* estländisch; estnisch; ⇒ *also* **English** 1. **2** *n.* (A) (*language*) Estnisch[e], *das;* Estländisch[e], *das;* ⇒ *also* **English** 2 A; (B) (*person*) Este, *der*/Estin, *die;* Estländer, *der*/Estländerin, *die*

**estrange** /ɪˈstreɪndʒ/ *v.t.* entfremden (**from** *Dat.*); **be/become ~d from sb.** jmdm. entfremdet sein/sich jmdm. entfremden; **they are ~d** sie sind einander fremd geworden; (*married couple also*) sie haben sich auseinander gelebt; **her ~d husband/his ~d wife** ihr ihr fremd gewordener Mann/seine ihm fremd gewordene Frau; **the ~d couple** die einander fremd gewordenen Ehepartner

**estrangement** /ɪˈstreɪndʒmənt/ *n.* Entfremdung, *die* (**from** von); **since their ~:** seit sie sich fremd geworden sind; (*of married couple also*) seit sie sich auseinander gelebt haben

**estrogen** (*Amer.*) ⇒ **oestrogen**

**estuary** /ˈestjʊərɪ/ *n.* ▶ 1480 (*Geog.*) Ästuar, *das* (*fachspr.*); [Trichter]mündung, *die;* **the Thames ~:** die Mündung der Themse

**ETA** *abbr.* **estimated time of arrival** voraussichtliche Ankunftszeit

**et al.** /et ˈæl/ *abbr.* **and others** et al.

**etc.** *abbr.* **et cetera** usw.

**et cetera, etcetera** /etˈsetərə, ɪtˈsetərə/ und so weiter; et cetera

**etch** /etʃ/ **1** *v.t.* (A) ätzen (**on** auf *od.* in + *Akk.*); (*on metal also*) ‹bes. Künstler:› radieren; (B) (*fig.*) einprägen (**in, on** *Dat.*); **be ~ed in *or* on sb.'s mind/memory** sich jmdm. eingeprägt haben/ins Gedächtnis eingegraben haben. **2** *v.i.* ätzen; (*on metal also*) ‹bes. Künstler:› radieren

**etching** /ˈetʃɪŋ/ *n.* Ätzung, *die;* (*piece of art*) Radierung, *die;* **come up and see my ~s** (*joc.*) komm mit rauf, ich zeig dir meine Briefmarkensammlung (*ugs. scherzh.*)

**eternal** /ɪˈtɜːnl, iːˈtɜːnl/ *adj.* (A) ewig; **be called to one's ~ rest** in die Ewigkeit abberufen werden (*geh. verhüll.*); **life ~:** das ewige Leben; **~ triangle** Dreiecksverhältnis, *das;* (B) (*coll.: unceasing*) ewig (*ugs.*); **you'll have my ~ thanks *or* gratitude** ich werde Ihnen ewig dankbar sein

**eternally** /ɪˈtɜːnəlɪ, iːˈtɜːnəlɪ/ *adv.* (A) ewig; **be ~ damned** auf ewig verdammt sein; (B) (*coll.: unceasingly*) ewig (*ugs.*)

**eternity** /ɪˈtɜːnɪtɪ, iːˈtɜːnɪtɪ/ *n.* (A) Ewigkeit, *die;* **for *or* in all *or* throughout ~, from here to ~:** [bis] in alle Ewigkeit; (B) (*coll.: long time*) Ewigkeit, *die* (*ugs.*); **wait for [what seemed] an ~:** [scheinbar] eine Ewigkeit warten

**ether** /ˈiːθə(r)/ *n.* (A) (*Chem.*) Äther, *der;* (B) (*Phys.; also fig.*) Äther, *der*

**ethereal** /ɪˈθɪərɪəl/ *adj.* (A) (*delicate, light, airy; also Phys., Chem.*) ätherisch; (B) (*poet.: heavenly*) ätherisch (*veralt.*); himmlisch

**ethereal ˈoil** *n.* (*Chem.*) ätherisches Öl

**ethic** /ˈeθɪk/ **1** *n.* Ethik, *die* (*geh.*); Ethos, *das* (*geh.*). **2** *adj.* ⇒ **ethical** A, B, D

**ethical** /ˈeθɪkl/ *adj.* (A) (*relating to morals*) ethisch; **~ philosophy** Ethik, *die;* **~ philosopher** Ethiker, *der*/Ethikerin, *die;* (B) (*morally correct*) moralisch einwandfrei; **it is not ~ for a doctor ...:** es entspricht nicht dem Berufsethos eines Arztes ...; (C) (*Med.*) verschreibungspflichtig ‹Medikament›; (D) (*Ling.*) **~ dative** Dativus ethicus, *der*

**ethicality** /eθɪˈkælɪtɪ/ *n., no pl.* (*moral correctness*) Sittlichkeit, *die*

**ethically** /ˈeθɪkəlɪ/ *adv.* (A) (*according to ethical rules*) ethisch; **be ~ obliged *or* bound to do sth.** die moralische Verpflichtung haben, etw. zu tun; (B) (*in a morally correct way*) moralisch einwandfrei

**ethics** /ˈeθɪks/ *n., no pl.* (A) Moral, *die;* (*moral philosophy*) Ethik, *die;* (B) *usu. constr. as pl.* (*moral code of person, group, etc.*) Ethik, *die* (*geh.*); Ethos, *das* (*geh.*); **medical ~:** ärztliche Ethik; **professional ~:** Berufsethos, *das;* **legal ~:** Standespflichten der Juristen; (C) *constr. as pl.* (*moral correctness*) ethische Berechtigung

**Ethiopia** /iːθɪˈəʊpɪə/ *pr. n.* Äthiopien (*das*)

**Ethiopian** /iːθɪˈəʊpɪən/ ▶ 1275, ▶ 1340 **1** *adj.* äthiopisch; **sb. is ~:** jmd. ist Äthiopier/Äthiopierin. **2** *n.* Äthiopier, *der*/Äthiopierin, *die*

**ethnic** /ˈeθnɪk/ *adj.* (A) (*ethnological*) ethnisch; Volks‹gruppe, -musik, -tanz›; **~ mix** Völkergemisch, *das;* **~ minority** ethnische Minderheit; (B) (*from specified group*) Volks‹chinesen, -deutsche›

**ethnic ˈcleansing** *n.* ethnische Säuberung

**ethnology** /eθˈnɒlədʒɪ/ *n.* Ethnologie, *die;* vergleichende Völkerkunde

**ethology** /iːˈθɒlədʒɪ/ *n.* (A) (*science of animal behaviour*) Verhaltensforschung, *die;* Ethologie, *die;* (B) (*science of character-formation*) Charakterkunde, *die;* Charakterologie, *die*

**ethos** /ˈiːθɒs/ *n.* (*guiding beliefs*) Gesinnung, *die;* (*fundamental values*) Ethos, *das* (*geh.*); (*characteristic spirit*) Geist, *der*

**ethyl** /ˈeθɪl, ˈiːθaɪl/ *n.* (*Chem.*) Äthyl, *das*

**ethyl ˈalcohol** *n.* (*Chem.*) Äthylalkohol, *der*

**ethylene** /ˈeθɪliːn/ *n.* (*Chem.*) Äthylen, *das;* **~ ˈglycol** Äthylenglykol, *das*

**etiology** (*Amer.*) ⇒ **aetiology**

**etiquette** /etɪˈket, ˈetɪket/ *n.* (A) (*social convention, court ceremonial*) Etikette, *die;* **breach of ~:** Verstoß gegen die Etikette; **book of ~:** Buch mit Verhaltensregeln; **that's ~:** das gehört sich so; **it's not ~:** das gehört sich nicht; (B) (*professional code*) **professional ~ [of the law]** Berufspraxis [der Juristen]; **medical/legal ~:** Berufspraxis der Ärzte/Juristen

**Etna** /ˈetnə/ *pr. n.* **[Mount] ~:** der Ätna

**Etonian** /iːˈtəʊnɪən/ *n.* Etonschüler, *der*

**Etruscan** /ɪˈtrʌskn/ (*Ethnol.*) ▶ 1275, ▶ 1340 **1** *adj.* etruskisch. **2** *n.* (A) (*language*) Etruskisch, *das;* (B) (*person*) Etrusker, *der*/Etruskerin, *die*

**étude** /'eɪtju:d, eɪ'tju:d/ *n.* (*Mus.*) Etüde, *die*

**etymological** /etɪmə'lɒdʒɪkl/ *adj.*, **etymologically** /etɪmə'lɒdʒɪkəlɪ/ *adv.* (*Ling.*) etymologisch

**etymologist** /etɪ'mɒlədʒɪst/ *n.* (*Ling.*) Etymologe, *der*/Etymologin, *die*

**etymology** /etɪ'mɒlədʒɪ/ *n.* (*Ling.*) Etymologie, *die;* ⇨ *also* **folk etymology**

**EU** *abbr.* **European Union** EU

**eucalyptus** /ju:kə'lɪptəs/ *n., pl.* **~es** *or* **eucalypti** Ⓐ **~ [oil]** (*Pharm.*) Eukalyptusöl, *das;* Ⓑ (*Bot.*) Eukalyptus[baum], *der*

**Eucharist** /'ju:kərɪst/ *n.* (*Eccl.*) Eucharistie, *die*

**eugenics** /ju:'dʒenɪks/ *n., no pl.* Eugenik, *die* (*fachspr.*); Erbgesundheitslehre, *die*

**eulogise** ⇨ **eulogize**

**eulogistic** /ju:lə'dʒɪstɪk/ *adj.* lobrednerisch

**eulogize** /'ju:lədʒaɪz/ *v.t.* preisen (*geh.*); rühmen

**eulogy** /'ju:lədʒɪ/ *n.* Ⓐ (*speech, writing*) Lobrede, *die;* Eloge, *die* (*geh.*); (*Amer.: funeral oration*) Grabrede, *die;* Ⓑ (*praise*) Lobspruch, *der*

**eunuch** /'ju:nək/ *n.* Eunuch, *der;* (*fig. derog.*) Schwächling, *der* (*abwertend*)

**euonymus** /ju:'ɒnɪməs/ *n.* (*Bot.*) Spindelstrauch, *der;* Evonymus, *der od. die;* (*Euonymus europaeus*) Pfaffenhütchen, *das*

**euphemism** /'ju:fəmɪzm/ *n.* Euphemismus, *der* (*bes. Sprachw.*); verhüllende Umschreibung; **resort to ~:** zu Euphemismen greifen

**euphemistic** /ju:fə'mɪstɪk/ *adj.*, **euphemistically** /ju:fə'mɪstɪkəlɪ/ *adv.* euphemistisch (*bes. Sprachw.*); verhüllend

**euphonious** /ju:'fəʊnɪəs/ *adj.* Ⓐ (*pleasant-sounding*) wohlklingend (*geh.*); Ⓑ (*Ling., Phonet.*) euphonisch

**euphonium** /ju:'fəʊnɪəm/ *n.* (*Mus.*) Euphonium, *das*

**euphony** /'ju:fənɪ/ *n.* Ⓐ (*pleasing sound*) Wohlklang, *der* (*geh.*); Ⓑ (*Ling., Phonet.*) Euphonie, *die*

**euphorbia** /ju:'fɔ:bɪə/ *n.* (*Bot.*) Euphorbia[pflanze], *die* (*fachspr.*); Wolfsmilch, *die*

**euphoria** /ju:'fɔ:rɪə/ *n., no pl.* Euphorie, *die* (*geh.*); (*elation also*) Hochstimmung, *die*

**euphoric** /ju:'fɔ:rɪk/ *adj.* euphorisch (*geh.*)

**Euphrates** /ju:'freɪti:z/ *pr. n.* ▶ **1480** Euphrat, *der*

**Eurasia** /jʊə'reɪʒə/ *pr. n.* Eurasien (*das*)

**Eurasian** /jʊə'reɪʒn/ ❶ *adj.* eurasisch. ❷ *n.* Eurasier, *der*/Eurasierin, *die*

**eureka** /jʊə'ri:kə/ *int.* heureka (*geh.*); ich habs (*ugs.*)

**Euro** /'jʊərəʊ/ *n.* Euro, *der*

**Euro-** /'jʊərəʊ/ *in comb.* euro-/Euro-

**Eurobond** *n.* (*Commerc.*) Eurobond, *der;* Euroanleihe, *die*

**Eurocentric** /jʊərəʊ'sentrɪk/ *adj.* eurozentrisch

**Eurocentrism** /jʊərəʊ'sentrɪzm/ *n.* Eurozentrismus, *der*

**Euro: ~cheque** *n.* (*Commerc.*) Euroscheck, *der;* **~crat** /'jʊərəkræt/ *n.* Eurokrat, *der*/Eurokratin, *die* **~currency** *n.* Eurowährung, *die;* **~dollar** *n.* (*Econ.*) Eurodollar, *der;* **~land** *n.* Euroland (*das*); **~market** *n.* Ⓐ (*Commerc.*) Euro[geld]markt, *der;* Ⓑ (*European Community*) europäischer Markt; [EU-]Binnenmarkt, *der;* **~-MP** *n.* Europaabgeordnete, *der/die*

**Europe** /'jʊərəp/ *pr. n.* Ⓐ Europa (*das*); **the continent of ~:** der europäische Kontinent; Ⓑ (*Brit.: EC*) EG, *die;* **go into ~:** der EG beitreten; Ⓒ (*Brit. coll.: mainland ~*) Kontinent, *der*

**European** /jʊərə'pi:ən/ ▶ **1340** ❶ *adj.* europäisch; **sb. is ~:** jmd. ist Europäer/Europäerin; **win ~ recognition** in ganz Europa Anerkennung finden. ❷ *n.* Europäer, *der*/Europäerin, *die*

**European: ~ Com'mission** *n.* Europäische Kommission; **~ 'Cup** *n.* (*Footb.*) Europacup, *der;* Europapokal, *der;* **~ currency unit** *n.* Europäische Währungseinheit; **~ Economic Com'munity** *n.* Europäische Wirtschaftsgemeinschaft; **~ Free 'Trade Association** *n.* Europäische Freihandelsassoziation

**Europeanise** ⇨ **Europeanize**

**Europeanism** /jʊərə'pi:ənɪzm/ *n.* Europäertum, *das;* (*ideal of the unification of Europe*) europäischer Gedanke

**Europeanize** /jʊərə'pi:ənaɪz/ *v.t.* europäisieren

**European: ~ 'Monetary System** *n.* Europäisches Währungssystem; **~ Monetary 'Union** *n.* Europäische Währungsunion; **~ 'Parliament** *n.* Europäisches Parlament; **~ plan** *n.* (*Amer. Hotel Managem.*) Unterkunft ohne Verpflegung; **~ 'Union** *n.* Europäische Union

**Euro: ~-rebel** *n.* (*esp. Brit.*) [innerparteilicher] Europagegner/[innerparteiliche] Europagegnerin; **~sceptic** *n.* Euroskeptiker, *der*/-skeptikerin, *die;* **~star** ® *n.* Eurostar, *der;* **go by ~star** mit dem Eurostar fahren

**'Eurovision** *n.* (*Telev.*) Eurovision, *die*

**Eustachian tube** /ju:s'teɪʃn tju:b/ *n.* (*Anat.*) eustachische Röhre

**euthanasia** /ju:θə'neɪzɪə/ *n.* Euthanasie, *die;* Sterbehilfe, *die*

**evacuate** /ɪ'vækjʊeɪt/ *v.t.* Ⓐ (*remove from danger, clear of occupants*) evakuieren (**from** aus); Ⓑ (*esp. Mil.: cease to occupy*) räumen; Ⓒ (*Physiol.*) entleeren ‹Darm›

**evacuation** /ɪvækjʊ'eɪʃn/ *n.* Ⓐ (*removal of people or things, clearance of place*) Evakuierung, *die* (**from** aus); Ⓑ (*esp. Mil.: withdrawal from occupation*) **the ~ of a territory** die Räumung eines Gebietes; **the ~ of the army** der Abzug der Armee; Ⓒ (*Physiol.*) Entleerung, *die*

**evacuee** /ɪvækjʊ'i:/ *n.* Evakuierte, *der/die;* *attrib.* **~ children** evakuierte Kinder

**evade** /ɪ'veɪd/ *v.t.* Ⓐ ausweichen (+ *Dat.*) ‹Angriff, Angreifer, Schlag, Blick, Problem, Schwierigkeit, Tatsache, Frage, Hindernis, Thema›; sich entziehen (+ *Dat.*) ‹Verhaftung, Ergreifung, Wehrdienst, Einberufung, Gerechtigkeit, Pflicht, Verantwortung, Liebkosung›; entkommen (+ *Dat.*) ‹Polizei, Verfolger, Verfolgung, Gegner›; hinterziehen ‹Steuern, Zölle›; umgehen ‹Zahlungsverpflichtung›; **~ recognition** nicht erkannt werden; **~ doing sth.** vermeiden, etw. zu tun; **~ giving an answer** der Beantwortung einer Frage ausweichen; Ⓑ (*circumvent*) umgehen ‹Gesetz, Vorschrift›; Ⓒ (*elude*) **the significance of his remark ~s me** die Bedeutung seiner Bemerkung ist mir nicht klar; **~ definition** sich einer Definition entziehen

**evaluate** /ɪ'væljʊeɪt/ *v.t.* Ⓐ (*value*) schätzen ‹Wert, Preis, Schaden, Kosten›; Ⓑ (*quantify, express numerically*) in Zahlen ausdrücken; quantifizieren; Ⓒ (*appraise*) einschätzen; auswerten ‹Daten›; (*judge*) beurteilen

**evaluation** /ɪvæljʊ'eɪʃn/ *n.* Ⓐ Schätzung, *die;* (*quantification*) Berechnung, *die;* Quantifizierung, *die;* Ⓑ (*appraisal*) Einschätzung, *die;* (*of data*) Auswertung, *die*

**evanescent** /i:və'nesənt, evə'nesənt/ *adj.* flüchtig ‹Erscheinung, Vision, Glück›; vergänglich ‹Reiz›

**evangelical** /i:væn'dʒelɪkl/ *adj.* Ⓐ (*of the Gospels*) **~ texts/preaching** Texte/Verkündigung des Evangeliums; Ⓑ (*Protestant*) evangelikal; Ⓒ (*evangelizing, crusading*) missionarisch (*fig.*)

**evangelicalism** /i:væn'dʒelɪkəlɪzm/ *n., no pl.* evangelikale Lehre

**evangelise** ⇨ **evangelize**

**evangelism** /ɪ'vændʒəlɪzm/ *n.* Ⓐ (*preaching the Gospel*) Evangelisation, *die;* Ⓑ (*evangelicalism*) evangelikale Lehre; Ⓒ (*crusading zeal*) Bekehrungseifer, *der*

**evangelist** /ɪ'vændʒəlɪst/ *n.* Ⓐ (*Gospel-writer*) Evangelist, *der;* Ⓑ (*Gospel-preacher*) Evangelist, *der;* Prediger, *der;* (*itinerant preacher*) Wanderprediger, *der*

**evangelize** /ɪ'vændʒəlaɪz/ *v.t.* evangelisieren

**evaporate** /ɪ'væpəreɪt/ ❶ *v.i.* Ⓐ (*become vapour*) verdunsten; Ⓑ (*lose liquid*) eindicken; (*completely*) eintrocknen; Ⓒ (*fig.*) sich in Luft auflösen; dahinschwinden (*geh.*); ‹Furcht, Begeisterung:› verfliegen. ❷ *v.t.* Ⓐ (*turn into vapour*) verdunsten lassen; Ⓑ (*cause to lose liquid*) evaporieren (*Chem.*); eindampfen (*Chem.*)

**evaporated 'milk** *n.* Kondensmilch, *die*

**evaporation** /ɪvæpə'reɪʃn/ *n.* Ⓐ (*changing into vapour*) Verdunstung, *die;* Ⓑ (*losing liquid*) Eindickung, *die;* (*completely*) Eintrocknung, *die*

**evasion** /ɪ'veɪʒn/ *n.* Ⓐ (*avoidance*) Umgehung, *die;* (*of duty*) Vernachlässigung, *die;* (*of responsibility, question*) Ausweichen, *das* (**of** vor + *Dat.*); Ⓑ (*evasive statement*) Ausrede, *die;* **~s** Ausflüchte *Pl.;* Ⓒ (*prevarication*) Ausflüchte *Pl.*

**evasive** /ɪ'veɪsɪv/ *adj.* Ⓐ **be/become [very] ~:** [ständig] ausweichen; **be ~ about sth.** um etw. herumreden; Ⓑ (*aimed at evasion*) ausweichend ‹Antwort›; **take ~ action** ein Ausweichmanöver machen

**evasively** /ɪ'veɪsɪvlɪ/ *adv.* ausweichend

**eve** *n.* Ⓐ Vorabend, *der;* (*day*) Vortag, *der;* **the ~ of** der Abend/Tag vor (+ *Dat.*); der Vorabend/Vortag (+ *Gen.*); ⇨ *also* **Christmas Eve; New Year's Eve;** Ⓑ (*fig.*) **[be] on the ~ of sth.** kurz vor etw. (*Dat.*) [stehen]; Ⓒ (*arch.: evening*) Abend, *der*

**Eve** /i:v/ *pr. n.* (*Bibl.*) Eva (*die*)

**even**[1] /'i:vn/ ❶ *adj.*, **~er** /'i:vənə(r)/, **~est** /'i:vənɪst/ Ⓐ (*smooth, flat*) eben ‹Boden, Fläche›; glatt ‹Faser, Gewebe›; **make sth. ~:** etw. ebnen/glätten; Ⓑ (*level*) gleich hoch ‹Stapel, Stuhl-, Tischbein›; gleich lang ‹Vorhang, Stuhl-, Tischbein usw.›; **be of ~ height/length** gleich hoch/lang sein; **~ with** genauso hoch/lang wie; **on an ~ keel** (*Naut., Aeronaut.*) auf ebenem Kiel (*Seemannsspr.*); ≈ ausgetrimmt (*Seemannsspr., Fliegerspr.*); (*fig.*) ausgeglichen; **keep the firm on an ~ keel** die Firma über Wasser halten; Ⓒ (*straight*) gerade ‹Saum, Kante›; Ⓓ (*parallel*) parallel (**with** zu); Ⓔ (*regular*) regelmäßig ‹Zähne›; ebenmäßig ‹Gesichtszüge›; (*steady*) gleichmäßig ‹Schrift, Rhythmus, Atmen, Schlagen›; stetig ‹Fortschritt›; Ⓕ (*equal*) gleich [groß] ‹Menge, Abstand›; ausgewogen ‹Kräfteverhältnis›; gleichmäßig ‹Verteilung, Aufteilung›; ausgeglichen ‹Punktestand›; **start out ~:** mit den gleichen Voraussetzungen beginnen; **the teams are/the score is ~:** die Mannschaften sind punktgleich/die Punktzahl ist dieselbe *od.* gleich; **we need another goal to make it ~:** wir brauchen noch ein Tor zum Ausgleich; **the match is still ~:** die Begegnung steht noch unentschieden; **~s** (*Brit.*), **~ money** (*Betting*) eins zu eins; **an ~s** *or* **~ money favourite [to win]** ein 1 : 1-Favorit; **I have an ~ chance of getting there on time** meine Chancen, pünktlich anzukommen, stehen fünfzig zu fünfzig *od.* (*ugs.*) fifty-fifty; **the odds are ~, it's ~ odds** *or* **an ~ bet** die Chancen stehen fünfzig zu fünfzig *od.* (*ugs.*) fifty-fifty; **~ Stephen** /i:vn 'sti:vn/ (*coll.*) ≈ fifty-fifty (*ugs.*); Ⓖ (*balanced*) im Gleichgewicht; **with an ~ hand** (*fig.*) gerecht; Ⓗ (*quits, fully revenged*) **be** *or* **get ~ with sb.** es jmdm. heimzahlen; Ⓘ (*uniform*) gleichmäßig; Ⓙ (*calm*) ausgeglichen; **have an ~ temper** ausgeglichen sein; Ⓚ (*divisible by two, so numbered*) gerade ‹Zahl, Seite, Hausnummer›; **the ~ syllables** die zweite, vierte usw. Silbe; Ⓛ (*exact*) **an ~ dozen** ein rundes Dutzend (*ugs.*); **let's make it an ~ ten** sagen wir rund zehn (*ugs.*). ⇨ *also* **break even.**

❷ *adv.* Ⓐ sogar; selbst; **~ perhaps ...:** vielleicht sogar ...; **hard, unbearable ~:** hart, sogar *od.* wenn nicht gar unerträglich; **does he ~ suspect the danger?** ahnt er überhaupt die Gefahr?; **do sth. ~ without being told** etw. auch ohne Aufforderung tun; **~ afterwards** selbst *od.* sogar danach; **~ before[hand]** auch schon vorher; **~ today** selbst *od.* sogar heute noch; Ⓑ *with negative* **not** *or* **never ~ ...** [noch] nicht einmal ...; **without ~ saying goodbye** ohne wenigstens Auf Wiedersehen zu sagen; Ⓒ *with compar. adj. or adv.* sogar noch ‹komplizierter, weniger, schlimmer usw.›; Ⓓ **~ if** *or* **though Arsenal win** selbst wenn Arsenal gewinnt; **~ if Arsenal won** selbst wenn Arsenal gewinnen

würde; (*fact*) obgleich Arsenal gewann; ~ **supposing we had been present** selbst wenn wir dabei gewesen wären; ~ **were she to appear** selbst wenn sie auftauchen sollte; ~ **as** (*just when*) gerade als; (*in just the way that*) geradeso wie; (*during the period that*) während ... noch; ~ **so** [aber] trotzdem *od.* dennoch; (*arch.: that is correct*) so ist es; ~ **now/then** (*as well as previously*) selbst *od.* sogar jetzt/dann; (*at this/that very moment*) gerade in diesem Augenblick.
❸ *v.t.* ebnen; (*smooth*) glätten

~ **'out** ❶ *v.t.* Ⓐ (*make smooth*) glätten; Ⓑ (*distribute more equally*) gleich verteilen; ausgleichen ‹Unterschiede›. ❷ *v.i.* Ⓐ (*become smooth*) ‹Boden:› sich einebnen; Ⓑ (*become more equal*) sich ausgleichen

~ **'up** ❶ *v.t.* ausgleichen; **so as to ~ things up** zum Ausgleich. ❷ *v.i.* (*settle debt, get revenge*) abrechnen

**even²** *n.* (*poet.*) Abend, *der*

**even-'handed** *adj.* gerecht

**evening** /'i:vnɪŋ/ *n.* Ⓐ ▶ 1012, ▶ 1056 Abend, *der; attrib.* Abend‹vorstellung, -ausgabe, -messe›; **this/tomorrow ~:** heute/morgen Abend; **during the ~:** am Abend; **[early/late] in the ~:** am [frühen/späten] Abend; (*regularly*) [früh/spät] abends; **at eight in the ~:** um acht Uhr abends; **on the ~ of 2 May** am Abend des 2. Mai; **on Wednesday ~s/~:** Mittwoch abends/am Mittwochabend; **one ~:** eines Abends; **every ~:** jeden Abend; **~ came** es wurde Abend; **one ~:** eines Abends; **~s, of an ~:** abends; **two ~s ago** vorgestern Abend; **the other ~:** neulich abends; **a good ~'s viewing** ein gutes Abendprogramm [im Fernsehen]; **the cool of the ~:** die Abendkühle; **an ~ of cards** ein Abend beim Kartenspiel; ⇒ *also* **good** 1 M; Ⓑ ▶ 1191 (*coll: greeting*) 'n Abend! (*ugs.*); Ⓒ (*soirée*) Abend, *der;* **discussion ~:** Diskussionsabend, *der;* Ⓓ (*fig.*) Abend, *der* (*geh.*); (*of life*) Lebensabend, *der* (*geh.*)

**evening:** ~ **class** *n.* Abendkurs, *der;* **take** *or* **do ~ classes in pottery** *etc.* Abendkurse im Töpfern *usw.* besuchen; ~ **'dress** *n.* Abendkleidung, *die;* **in [full] ~ dress** in Abendkleidung; ~ **dress,** ~ **gown** *ns.* Abendkleid, *das;* ~ **'meal** *n.* Abendessen, *das;* ~ **'paper** *n.* Abendzeitung, *die;* ~ **'primrose** *n.* Nachtkerze, *die;* ~ **school** *n.* Abendschule, *die;* ~ **'service** *n.* (*Eccl.*) Abendandacht, *die;* (*mass*) Abendgottesdienst, *der;* ~ **'star** *n.* Abendstern, *der*

**evenly** /'i:vnlɪ/ *adv.* gleichmäßig; **say sth. ~:** etw. in ruhigem Ton sagen; **be ~ spaced** den gleichen Abstand voneinander haben; **the runners are ~ matched** die Läufer sind einander ebenbürtig

**even-numbered** /'i:vnnʌmbəd/ *adj.* gerade; **the houses are ~:** die Häuser haben gerade Hausnummern

**'evensong** *n.* (*Eccl.*) Abendandacht, *die*

**event** /ɪ'vent/ *n.* Ⓐ **in the ~ of his dying** *or* **death** im Falle seines Todes; falls er stirbt; **in the ~ of rain** bei Regenwetter; **in the ~ of sickness/war** im Falle einer Krankheit/im Kriegsfalle; **in that ~:** in dem Falle; **in such an ~:** in solch einem Falle; **in the unlikely ~ of sb. doing sth.** falls, was nicht sehr wahrscheinlich ist, jmd. etw. tut; **in the ~ that** (*Amer.*) im Falle, dass; Ⓑ (*outcome*) **in any/either ~ = in any case** ⇒ **case¹** A; **at all ~s** auf jeden Fall; **in the ~:** letzten Endes; Ⓒ (*occurrence*) Ereignis, *das;* **~s have proved ...:** die Ereignisse haben gezeigt ...; **the dramatic ~s in Rome** das dramatische Geschehen in Rom; **~s are taking place in Argentina which ...:** es geschehen Dinge in Argentinien, die ...; **sth. is [quite] an ~:** etw. ist schon ein Ereignis; ⇒ *also* **course** 1 A; **wise;** Ⓓ (*Sport*) Wettkampf, *der;* **showjumping ~:** Jagdspringen, *das;* Springprüfung, *die;* **three-day ~:** Military, *die;* Vielseitigkeitsprüfung, *die*

**even-'tempered** *adj.* ausgeglichen

**eventful** /ɪ'ventfl/ *adj.* ereignisreich ‹Tag, Zeiten›; bewegt ‹Leben, Jugend, Zeiten›

**'eventide** *n.* (*arch.*) Abendzeit, *die* (*geh.*)

**eventual** /ɪ'ventjʊəl/ *adj.* **predict sb.'s ~ downfall** vorhersagen, dass jmd. schließlich zu Fall kommen wird; **lead to sb.'s ~ downfall** schließlich zu jmds. Sturz führen; **the career of Napoleon and his ~ defeat** der Aufstieg Napoleons und schließlich seine Niederlage; **we are heading towards ~ destruction** wir steuern letztlich auf den Untergang zu

**eventuality** /ɪventjʊ'ælɪtɪ/ *n.* Eventualität, *die;* **the ~ of war** der mögliche Kriegsfall; **in certain eventualities** in bestimmten [möglichen] Fällen; **be ready for all eventualities** auf alle Eventualitäten gefasst sein

**eventually** /ɪ'ventjʊəlɪ/ *adv.* schließlich; **she'll ~ get married** sie wird irgendwann *od.* eines Tages heiraten; **I'll do that ~:** ich mache das irgendwann [noch]

**eve-of-'poll** *adj.* ~ **[survey]** [Umfrage] kurz vor der Wahl

**ever** /'evə(r)/ *adv.* Ⓐ (*always, at all times*) immer; stets; **for ~:** für immer ‹weggehen, gelten›; ewig ‹lieben, da sein, leben›; auf ewig (*dichter.*) ‹unerreichbar›; **go on for ~:** immer so bleiben; (*derog.*) ewig dauern; **it is for ~ changing** es ändert sich dauernd; **the traffic lights took for ~ to change** (*coll.*) die Ampeln schalteten erst nach einer Ewigkeit um; **Arsenal for ~!** es lebe Arsenal!; **for ~ and ~:** immer und ewig; (*in the Lord's Prayer*) in Ewigkeit; **for ~ and a day** eine Ewigkeit; **~ since [then]** seit [dieser Zeit]; **~ after[wards]** seitdem; **I've been frightened of dogs ~ 'since** *or* **'after** seitdem *od.* seit diesem Tag habe ich Angst vor Hunden; **~ since he inherited it** von dem Tag an, an dem er das geerbt hat; **~ since I've known her** solange ich sie kenne; **~ since I can remember** soweit ich zurückdenken kann; **~ since she was a child** von Kindheit an; **~ yours** *or* **yours ~, Ethel** deine/eure Ethel; immer die deine/eure, Ethel (*veralt.*); Ⓑ *in comb. with compar. adj. or adv.* noch; immer; **get ~ deeper into debt** sich noch *od.* immer mehr verschulden; **~ further** noch immer weiter; Ⓒ *in comb. with participles etc.* **~-increasing** ständig zunehmend; **~-recurring** immer wiederkehrend; **~-present** allgegenwärtig; **~-youthful** ewig jugendlich; **~-changing rules** sich ständig ändernde Vorschriften; **an ~-patient mother** eine Mutter, die nie die Geduld verliert; **go round in ~-decreasing circles** (*fig. coll.*) [mit immer größeren Anstrengungen] immer weniger erreichen; Ⓓ (*at any time*) je[mals]; **not ~:** noch nie; **~ before** je zuvor; **never ~:** nie im Leben; **never ~ before** noch nie zuvor; **nothing ~ happens** es passiert nie etwas; **his best performance ~:** seine beste Vorstellung überhaupt; **it hardly ~ rains** es regnet so gut wie nie; **don't you ~ do that again!** mach das bloß nicht noch mal!; **did you ~?** (*coll.*) hast du Töne? (*salopp*); **he's a devil if ~ there was one** (*coll.*) er ist ein Teufel, alles, was recht ist (*ugs.*); **better than ~:** besser denn je; **more frequently than ~:** häufiger als je zuvor; **the same as ~** *or* **as it ~ was** das Gleiche wie immer; **as ~:** wie gewöhnlich; (*iron.*) wie gehabt; **yours as ~, Bob** (*in letter*) wie immer, dein Bob; **as ... as ~:** unverändert ...; **I'm as stupid as ~:** ich bin immer noch nicht schlauer; **he's as kind a man as ~ lived** er ist der freundlichste Mensch, den es je gegeben hat; **if I ~ catch you doing that again** wenn ich dich dabei noch einmal erwische; **seldom, if ~,** (*coll.*) **seldom ~:** so gut wie nie; **as if I ~ would!** ich doch nicht!; **a fool if ~ there was one** der größte Narr, den man sich (*Dat.*) vorstellen kann; **is he ~ conceited** (*Amer. coll.*) ist der vielleicht eingebildet! (*ugs.*); **the first men ~** *or* **the first ~ men to reach the moon** die Ersten, die je auf dem Mond waren; **you're the first ~:** du bist der/die Allererste; **the greatest tennis player ~:** der größte Tennisspieler, den es je gegeben hat; **the hottest day ~:** der heißeste Tag seit Menschengedenken; Ⓔ *emphasizing question* **what ~ does he want?** was will er nur?; **who/which ~ could it be?** wer/welcher könnte das nur sein?; **how ~ did I drop it?/could I have dropped it?** wie konnte ich es nur fallen lassen?; **when ~ did he do it?** wann hat er es nur getan?; **where ~ in the world have you been?** wo in aller Welt hast du bloß gesteckt?; **why ~ not?** warum denn nicht?; Ⓕ *intensifier* **before ~ he opened his mouth** noch bevor er seinen Mund aufmachte; **as soon as ~ I can** so bald wie irgend möglich; **I'm ~ so sorry** (*coll.*) mir tut es ja so Leid; **~ so nice** (*coll.*) so ungemein schön; **~ so slightly drunk** (*coll.*) ein ganz klein wenig betrunken; **thanks ~ so [much]** (*coll.*) vielen herzlichen Dank; **he liked her ~ so** (*coll.*) er mochte sie so sehr; **it was ~ such a shame** (*coll.*) es war so schade; Ⓖ (*arch.: always*) all[e]zeit (*veralt.*); **it was ~ thus** so ist es immer; Ⓗ **~ and again** *or* (*literary*) **anon** dann und wann

**'everglade** *n.* (*Amer. Geog.*) Sumpfgebiet, *das;* **the E~s** die Everglades

**'evergreen** ❶ *adj.* Ⓐ immergrün ‹Baum, Strauch, Landschaft›; Ⓑ (*fig.*) immer wieder aktuell ‹Problem, Thema›; immer wieder gern gehört ‹Lied, Schlager, Sänger›; **~ song** Evergreen, *der.* ❷ *n.* immergrüne Pflanze/immergrüner Baum

**ever'lasting** *adj.* Ⓐ (*eternal*) immer während; ewig ‹Leben, Gesetz, Höllenqualen, Gott, Gedenken, Berge, Fels›; unvergänglich ‹Ruhm, Ehre›; Ⓑ (*incessant*) ewig (*ugs.*); endlos

**everlastingly** /evə'lɑ:stɪŋlɪ/ *adv.* Ⓐ (*eternally*) ewig ‹leben, leiden›; Ⓑ (*incessantly*) ewig (*ugs.*); ständig

**'ever-loving** *adj.* **your ~ wife/husband** (*in letter*) deine dich ewig liebende Frau/dein dich ewig liebender Mann

**ever'more** *adv.* auf ewig; **for ~:** in [alle] Ewigkeit

**every** /'evrɪ/ *adj.* Ⓐ (*each single*) jeder/jede/jedes; **~ man will do his duty** jeder [Einzelne] wird seine Pflicht tun; **have ~ reason** allen Grund haben; **~ [single] time/on ~ [single] occasion** [aber auch] jedes Mal; **~ [single] time we ...:** [aber auch] jedes Mal, wenn wir ...; **there was one man for ~ three women** auf einen Mann kamen drei Frauen; **he ate ~ last** *or* **single biscuit** (*coll.*) er hat die ganzen Kekse aufgegessen (*ugs.*); **she's spent ~ last penny** (*coll.*) sie hat das ganze Geld ausgegeben; **~ one** jeder/jede/jedes [Einzelne]; **~ time** (*coll.: without any hesitation*) jederzeit; **give me** *or* **I prefer Switzerland ~ time** (*coll.*) es geht doch nichts über die Schweiz; **~ which way** (*Amer.*) in alle Richtungen; Ⓑ *after possessive adj.* **your ~ wish** all[e] deine Wünsche; **his ~ thought** all[e] seine Gedanken; Ⓒ (*indicating recurrence*) **she comes [once] ~ day** sie kommt jeden Tag [einmal]; **~ three/few days** alle drei/paar Tage; **~ third day** jeder dritte/jeden dritten Tag; **~ other** (*every second, or fig.: almost every*) jeder/jede/jedes Zweite; **~ now and then** *or* **again, ~ so often, ~ once in a while** hin und wieder; Ⓓ ▶ 1191 (*the greatest possible*) unbedingt, uneingeschränkt ‹Vertrauen›; voll ‹Beachtung›; all ‹Respekt, Aussicht›; **there's ~ prospect of a victory for England** alles deutet auf einen Sieg Englands hin; **I wish you ~ happiness/success** ich wünsche dir alles Gute/viel Erfolg

**'everybody** *n. & pron.* jeder; **has ~ seen it?** haben es alle *od.* hat es jeder gesehen?; **~ else** alle anderen; **~ knows ~ else round here** hier kennt jeder jeden; **he asked ~ to be quiet** er bat alle um Ruhe; **hello, ~!** (*coll.*) Tag, zusammen! (*ugs.*); **would ~ be quiet please?** würden Sie bitte alle ruhig sein?; **it's not ~ who can ...:** nicht jeder kann ...; **it's ~'s duty** es ist jedermanns Pflicht; jeder[mann] ist verpflichtet; **opera isn't [to] ~'s taste** Oper ist nicht jedermanns Sache; **holidays to suit ~'s purse** Urlaub für jeden Geldbeutel; ⇒ *also* **anybody** C

**'everyday** *attrib. adj.* alltäglich; Alltags‹kleidung, -sprache›; routinemäßig ‹Geschäftsführung›; **in ~ life** im Alltag; im täglichen Leben; **an ~ story of country folk** eine Geschichte über den Alltag der Leute vom Lande; **~ reality** Alltag, *der;* **~ expressions** Ausdrücke der Alltagssprache; **it is a matter of ~**

knowledge that ... jedermann weiß, dass ...

**'Everyman** *n., no pl.* der Durchschnittsbürger; [Herr] Jedermann (*veralt.*)

**everyone** /'evrɪwʌn, 'evrɪwən/ ⇒ **everybody**

**'everyplace** (*Amer.*) ⇒ **everywhere**

**'everything** *n. & pron.* Ⓐ alles; **~ [that] you have** alles, was du hast; **~ else** alles andere; **some pupils are good at ~:** manche Schüler sind in allen Fächern gut; **~ comes to him who waits** (*prov.*) mit Geduld und Spucke fängt man eine Mucke (*ugs.*); **the man who has ~:** der Mann, der schon alles hat; **~ interesting/valuable** alles Interessante/Wertvolle; **there's a [right] time for ~:** alles zu seiner Zeit; **they bought the house and ~ in it** sie kauften das Haus mit allem Inventar; **he is ~ a man should be** er hat alle Qualitäten, die ein Mann besitzen sollte; Ⓑ (*coll.: all that matters*) alles; **looks aren't ~:** das Aussehen [allein] ist nicht alles; **her child is ~ to her** das Kind ist ihr Ein und Alles; **have ~:** [einfach] alles haben

**'everyway** *adv.* in jeder Beziehung

**'everywhere** ❶ *adv.* Ⓐ (*in every place*) überall; Ⓑ (*to every place*) **go ~:** überall hingehen/-fahren; **~ you go/look** wohin man auch geht/sieht. ❷ *n.* **from ~:** überallher; von überall [her]; **~ is quiet in Holland on a Sunday** überall in Holland ist es sonntags ruhig

**evict** /ɪ'vɪkt/ *v.t.* exmittieren (*Rechtsspr.*); **~ a family [from the house]** eine Familie zur Räumung [des Hauses] zwingen

**eviction** /ɪ'vɪkʃn/ *n.* Zwangsräumung, *die;* Exmission, *die* (*Rechtsspr.*); **the ~ of the tenant** die zwangsweise Vertreibung des Mieters [aus seiner Wohnung]; **action for ~** (*Law*) Räumungsklage, *die;* **~ order** (*Law*) Räumungsbefehl, *der*

**evidence** /'evɪdəns/ ❶ *n.* Ⓐ Beweis, *der;* (*indication*) Anzeichen, *das;* Beweis, *der;* **be ~ of sth.** etw. beweisen; **provide ~ of sth.** den Beweis *od.* Beweise für etw. liefern; **as ~ of sth.** als *od.* zum Beweis für etw.; **we do not have any ~ for this** wir haben nicht einen einzigen Beweis *od.* keinerlei Anhaltspunkte dafür; **there was no ~ of a fight** nichts deutete auf einen Kampf hin; **give ~ of having been damaged** offensichtlich beschädigt worden sein; **hard ~:** durchschlagende Beweise; ⇒ *also* **external** 1 F; **internal evidence**; Ⓑ (*Law*) Beweismaterial, *das;* (*object*) Beweisstück, *das;* (*testimony*) [Zeugen]aussage, *die;* **give ~:** [als Zeuge] aussagen; **give ~ under oath/for sb./against sb.** unter Eid/für jmdn./gegen jmdn. aussagen; **refuse to give ~:** die Aussage verweigern; **hear** *or* **take ~:** Zeugen vernehmen; **hearing** *or* **taking of ~:** Beweisaufnahme, *die;* **because of insufficient ~:** aus Mangel an Beweisen; mangels Beweisen (*Amtsspr.*); **piece of ~:** Beweisstück, *das;* (*statement*) Beweis, *der;* **incriminating ~:** Belastungsmaterial, *das;* **[turn] King's/Queen's ~** (*Brit.*) *or* (*Amer.*) **State's ~:** [als] Kronzeuge [auftreten]; **the witness said in ~ that ...:** der Zeuge sagte aus, dass ...; **call sb. in ~:** jmdn. als Zeugen benennen *od.* anrufen; **submit sth. in ~:** etw. als Beweis vorlegen; ⇒ *also* **circumstantial** A; **presumptive**; Ⓒ **be [much] in ~:** [stark] in Erscheinung treten; **he was nowhere in ~:** er war nirgends zu sehen; **sth. is very much in ~:** überall sieht man etw.
❷ *v.t.* zeugen von

**evident** /'evɪdənt/ *adj.* offensichtlich; deutlich ‹Verbesserung›; **the effect is still ~:** die Wirkung ist [immer] noch deutlich sichtbar; **be ~ to sb.** jmdm. klar sein; **it soon became ~ that ...:** es stellte sich bald heraus, dass ...

**evidently** /'evɪdəntlɪ/ *adv.* offensichtlich

**evil** /'i:vl, 'i:vɪl/ ❶ *adj.* Ⓐ böse; schlecht ‹Charakter, Beispiel, Einfluss, System›; übel, verwerflich ‹Praktiken›; **with ~ intent** in *od.* aus böser Absicht; **the E~ One** der Böse; **~ doings** Missetaten *Pl.;* **~ tongue** böse Zunge; Lästerzunge, *die* (*abwertend*); **the ~ eye** der böse Blick; Ⓑ (*unlucky*) verhängnisvoll, unglückselig ‹Tag, Stunde›; böse, schlecht ‹Zeichen›; schwer, schlimm ‹Schicksal›; **~ days** *or* **times** schlechte *od.* schlimme Zeiten; **put off** *or* **postpone the ~ hour** das Unvermeidliche hinauszögern; **fall on ~ days** ins Unglück geraten; Ⓒ (*disagreeable*) übel ‹Geruch, Geschmack›; (*coll.: unattractive*) mies (*ugs.*) ‹Kneipe, Wetter›.
❷ *n.* Ⓐ *no pl.* (*literary*) Böse, *das;* **the root of all ~:** die Wurzel allen Übels; **deliver us from ~** (*Relig.*) erlöse uns von dem Übel (*bibl.*); **he saw the ~ of his ways** er erkannte, dass er auf dem Pfad der Sünde wandelte (*geh.*); **speak ~ of sb.** schlecht über jmdn. reden; **do ~:** Böses tun; sündigen; Ⓑ (*bad thing*) Übel, *das;* **necessary** *or* **inescapable ~:** notwendiges Übel; **social ~s** soziale Missstände; **the lesser ~:** das kleinere Übel; **choose the lesser of two ~s** von zwei Übeln das kleinere wählen

**evil: ~doer** /'i:vldu:ə(ɹ)/ *n.* Übeltäter, *der*/-täterin, *die;* **~-'minded** *adj.* bösartig; böswillig; **~-smelling** *adj.* übel riechend; **~-tasting** *adj.* widerlich schmeckend

**evince** /ɪ'vɪns/ *v.t.* ‹Person:› an den Tag legen; ‹Äußerung, Handlung:› zeugen von

**eviscerate** /ɪ'vɪsəreɪt/ *v.t.* ausweiden ‹Wild›; ausnehmen ‹Geflügel, Fisch›; (*fig.*) der Substanz berauben

**evocation** /evə'keɪʃn/ *n.* Heraufbeschwören, *das;* Evokation, *die* (*geh.*); **the film is an ~ of Edwardian England** in dem Film lebt das England unter Edward VII noch einmal auf

**evocative** /ɪ'vɒkətɪv/ *adj.* evokativ (*geh.*); (*thought-provoking*) aufrüttelnd (*fig.*); **be ~ of sth.** an etw. (*Akk.*) erinnern; etw. heraufbeschwören; **an ~ scent** ein Duft, der Erinnerungen weckt

**evoke** /ɪ'vəʊk/ *v.t.* Ⓐ evozieren (*geh.*); heraufbeschwören; Ⓑ (*elicit, provoke*) hervorrufen ‹Bewunderung, Überraschung, Wirkung›; erregen ‹Interesse›

**evolution** /i:və'lu:ʃn, evə'lu:ʃn/ *n.* Ⓐ (*development*) Entwicklung, *die;* Ⓑ (*Biol.: of species etc.*) Evolution, *die;* **theory of ~:** Evolutionstheorie, *die;* Ⓒ (*Mil., Naut.*) Formierung, *die;* Evolution, *die* (*veralt.*); (*Dancing etc.*) Figur, *die;* Evolution, *die* (*veralt.*); Ⓓ (*of heat, gas, etc.*) Entstehung, *die*

**evolutionary** /i:və'lu:ʃənərɪ, evə'lu:ʃənərɪ/ *adj.* Ⓐ evolutionär; sich [langsam] entwickelnd; **the ~ process** der Entwicklungsprozess; Ⓑ (*Biol.*) evolutionär; **~ theory** Evolutionstheorie, *die*

**evolutionism** /i:və'lu:ʃənɪzm, evə'lu:ʃənɪzm/ *n., no pl.* Evolutionismus, *der*

**evolutionist** /i:və'lu:ʃənɪst, evə'lu:ʃənɪst/ *n.* Evolutionist, *der*/Evolutionistin, *die*

**evolve** /ɪ'vɒlv/ ❶ *v.i.* Ⓐ (*develop*) sich entwickeln (**from** aus); Ⓑ (*Biol.*) sich entwickeln (**into** zu); **~ out of** entstehen aus; sich entwickeln aus. ❷ *v.t.* Ⓐ entwickeln; Ⓑ (*Biol.*) entwickeln ‹Art usw.› (**from** aus)

**ewe** /ju:/ *n.* Mutterschaf, *das*

**ewer** /'ju:ə(r)/ *n.* [Wasch]krug, *der*

**ex**[1] /eks/ *n.* (*coll.*) Verflossene, *der/die* (*ugs.*)

**ex**[2] *prep.* Ⓐ (*Commerc.*) **ex works/store** ‹Güter› ab Werk/Lager; Ⓑ (*Finance*) ohne

**ex-** *pref.* Ex-‹Freundin, Präsident, Champion›; Alt-‹[bundes]kanzler, -bundespräsident, -bürgermeister›; ehemalig

**exacerbate** /ek'sæsəbeɪt/ *v.t.* verschlimmern ‹Schmerz, Krankheit, Wut›; steigern ‹Unzufriedenheit, Feindschaft›; verschlechtern ‹Zustand›; verschärfen ‹Lage›

**exact** /ɪg'zækt/ ❶ *adj.* Ⓐ genau; exakt, genau ‹Daten, Berechnung›; **those were his ~ words** das waren genau seine Worte; **an ~ copy of the painting/inscription** eine perfekte Kopie des Gemäldes/eine wortgetreue Wiedergabe der Inschrift; **on the ~ spot where ...:** genau an der Stelle, wo ...; **could you give me the ~ money?** könnten Sie mir das Geld passend geben?; **11 to be ~:** 11, um genau zu sein; **be ~ in one's work** es mit der Arbeit genau nehmen; Ⓑ (*rigorous*) streng; Ⓒ **~ science** exakte Wissenschaft.
❷ *v.t.* Ⓐ fordern, verlangen; erheben ‹Gebühr, Zoll›; **~ from sb. a promise of sth.** von jmdm. verlangen, dass er etw. verspricht; Ⓑ (*call for*) ‹Sache:› erfordern, verlangen

**exacting** /ɪg'zæktɪŋ/ *adj.* anspruchsvoll; streng ‹Prüfer, Lehrer, Maßstab›; hoch ‹Anforderung, Maßstab›; **be very ~ about punctuality** großen Wert auf Pünktlichkeit legen

**exaction** /ɪg'zækʃn/ *n.* Forderung, *die* (**of** nach)

**exactitude** /ɪg'zæktɪtju:d/ *n., no pl.* Genauigkeit, *die;* **with complete ~:** mit letzter Genauigkeit

**exactly** /ɪg'zæktlɪ/ *adv.* Ⓐ genau; **when ~** *or* **~ when did he leave?** wann genau ging er?; wann ging er genau?; **~ what happened we'll never know** was genau geschehen ist, werden wir nie erfahren; **at ~ the right moment** genau im richtigen Moment; **~! genau!**; **~ a year ago today** heute vor genau einem Jahr; **I'm not ~ sure** ich bin nicht ganz sicher; **at four o'clock ~:** Punkt vier Uhr; **~ as** genau[so] wie; **~ as you wish** ganz wie du willst; **not ~** (*coll. iron.*) nicht gerade; **I'll tell her ~ what I think of her** ich werde ihr ganz genau sagen, was ich von ihr halte; Ⓑ (*with perfect accuracy*) [ganz] genau; **so ~:** mit solcher Genauigkeit

**exactness** /ɪg'zæktnɪs/ *n., no pl.* Genauigkeit, *die;* **doubt the ~ of the figure** bezweifeln, dass die Zahl genau stimmt

**exaggerate** /ɪg'zædʒəreɪt/ *v.t.* Ⓐ übertreiben; **you are exaggerating his importance/its worth** du machst ihn wichtiger, als er ist/so wertvoll ist/war es nun auch wieder nicht; **the story had been grossly ~d** die Sache war gewaltig aufgebauscht worden (*abwertend*); **you always ~:** du musst immer übertreiben; Ⓑ (*accentuate*) unterstreichen; betonen

**exaggerated** /ɪg'zædʒəreɪtɪd/ *adj.* übertrieben; **grossly** *or* **highly ~:** stark übertrieben; **he has an ~ opinion of himself** er hat eine übertrieben hohe Meinung von sich selbst

**exaggeratedly** /ɪg'zædʒəreɪtɪdlɪ/ *adv.* übertrieben

**exaggeration** /ɪgzædʒə'reɪʃn/ *n.* Übertreibung, *die;* **it is a wild/is no ~ to say that ...:** es ist stark/nicht übertrieben, wenn man sagt, dass ...; **no ~!** ohne Übertreibung!; **he's prone to ~:** er übertreibt gern; **that, of course, is an ~:** das ist natürlich übertrieben; **that's a bit of an** *or* **a slight ~:** das ist leicht übertrieben

**exalt** /ɪg'zɔ:lt/ *v.t.* Ⓐ (*praise*) [lob]preisen; **~ sb. to the skies** jmdn. in den Himmel heben (*ugs.*); Ⓑ (*raise in rank or power*) erheben; (*raise in estimation*) hoch achten

**exaltation** /egzɔ:l'teɪʃn, eksɔ:l'teɪʃn/ *n.* Ⓐ (*fig.: elevation*) Erhebung, *die;* Ⓑ (*elation*) Begeisterung, *die*

**exalted** /ɪg'zɔ:ltɪd/ *adj.* Ⓐ (*high-ranking*) hoch; **those in ~ positions** hoch gestellte Persönlichkeiten; Ⓑ (*lofty, sublime*) hoch ‹Ideal›; erhaben ‹Thema, Stil, Stimmung, Gedanke›

**exam** /ɪg'zæm/ (*coll.*) ⇒ **examination** C

**examination** /ɪgzæmɪ'neɪʃn/ *n.* Ⓐ (*inspection*) Untersuchung, *die;* (*of accounts*) [Über]prüfung, *die;* **on ~ it was found to contain drugs** die Untersuchung ergab, dass es Drogen enthielt; **on closer** *or* **further ~:** bei genauerer *od.* näherer Untersuchung *od.* Überprüfung; **be under ~:** untersucht *od.* überprüft werden; **give sth. a thorough ~:** etw. gründlich untersuchen *od.* überprüfen; **carry out an ~ of sth./into sth.** etw. untersuchen *od.* überprüfen/eine Untersuchung über etw. (*Akk.*) anstellen *od.* durchführen; Ⓑ (*Med.*) Untersuchung, *die;* **give sb. a thorough ~:** jmdn. gründlich untersuchen; **undergo an ~:** sich untersuchen lassen; Ⓒ (*test of knowledge or ability*) Prüfung, *die;* (*final ~ at university*) Examen, *das; attrib.* Prüfungs-/Examens-; **~ nerves** Prüfungsangst, *die;* Ⓓ (*Law*) (*of witness, accused*) Verhör, *das;* Vernehmung, *die;* (*of case*) Untersuchung, *die;* **he is still under ~:** er wird noch verhört *od.* vernommen; **be subjected to ~:** einem Verhör *od.* einer Vernehmung unterzogen werden

e

**exami'nation paper** *n.* **A** ~[s] schriftliche Prüfungsaufgaben; **B** (*with candidate's answers*) ≈ Klausurarbeit, *die*

**examine** /ɪg'zæmɪn/ *v.t.* **A** (*inspect*) untersuchen (**for** auf + *Akk.*); prüfen ‹Dokument, Gewissen, Gefühle, Geschäftsbücher›; kontrollieren ‹Ausweis, Gepäck›; **B** (*Med.*) untersuchen; **C** (*test knowledge or ability of*) prüfen (**in** in + *Dat.*); **~ sb. on his knowledge of French** jmds. Französischkenntnisse prüfen; **D** (*Law*) verhören; vernehmen

**examinee** /ɪgzæmɪ'ni:/ *n.* Prüfungskandidat, *der*/-kandidatin, *die;* Prüfling, *der;* (*Univ. also*) Examenskandidat, *der*/-kandidatin, *die;* (*to qualify for higher education also*) Abiturient, *der*/Abiturientin, *die*

**examiner** /ɪg'zæmɪnə(r)/ *n.* Prüfer, *der*/Prüferin, *die;* **board of ~s** Prüfungsausschuss, *der*

**examining body** /ɪg'zæmɪnɪŋ bɒdɪ/ *n.* ≈ Prüfungsamt, *das*

**example** /ɪg'zɑ:mpl/ *n.* **A** Beispiel, *das;* **by way of [an] ~:** als Beispiel; **she is a perfect ~ of how ...:** sie ist das beste Beispiel dafür, wie ...; **take sth. as an ~:** etw. zum Beispiel nehmen; **just to give [you] an** *or* **one ~:** um [dir] nur ein Beispiel zu nennen; **for ~:** zum Beispiel; **she's an ~ to us all** sie gibt uns (*Dat.*) allen ein Beispiel; **set an ~** *or* **a good ~ to sb.** jmdm. ein Beispiel geben; **follow sb.'s ~ [in doing sth.]** sich (*Dat.*) an jmdm. ein Beispiel nehmen [und etw. tun]; (*in a particular action*) jmds. Beispiel folgen; **B** (*as warning*) [abschreckendes] Beispiel; **make an ~ of sb.** ein Exempel an jmdm. statuieren; **punish sb. as an ~ to others** jmdn. exemplarisch bestrafen; **let that be an ~ to you** lass dir das eine Lehre sein

**exasperate** /ɪg'zæspəreɪt, ɪg'zɑ:spəreɪt/ *v.t.* (*irritate*) verärgern; (*infuriate*) zur Verzweiflung bringen; **be ~d at** *or* **by sb./sth.** über jmdn./etw. verärgert/verzweifelt sein; **feel ~d** verärgert/verzweifelt sein; **become** *or* **get ~d [with sb.]** sich [über jmdn.] ärgern

**exasperating** /ɪg'zæspəreɪtɪŋ, ɪg'zɑ:spəreɪtɪŋ/ *adj.* ärgerlich; ‹Aufgabe› die einen zur Verzweiflung bringt; **be ~:** einen zur Verzweiflung bringen

**exasperatingly** /ɪg'zæspəreɪtɪŋlɪ, ɪg'zɑ:spəreɪtɪŋlɪ/ *adv.* zum Verzweifeln

**exasperation** /ɪgzæspə'reɪʃn, ɪgzɑ:spə'reɪʃn/ *n.* ⇒ **exasperate**: Ärger, *der*/Verzweiflung, *die* (**with** über + *Akk.*); **in ~:** verärgert/verzweifelt

**excavate** /'ekskəveɪt/ *v.t.* **A** ausschachten; (*with machine*) ausbaggern; fördern, abbauen ‹Erz, Metall›; **B** (*Archaeol.*) ausgraben; *abs.* Ausgrabungen vornehmen

**excavation** /ekskə'veɪʃn/ *n.* **A** Ausschachtung, *die;* (*with machine*) Ausbaggerung, *die;* (*of ore, metals*) Förderung, *die;* Abbau, *der;* **B** (*Archaeol.*) Ausgrabung, *die;* **~ work** Ausgrabungsarbeiten *Pl.;* **C** (*place*) [Bau]grube, *die;* (*Archaeol.*) Ausgrabungsstätte, *die*

**excavator** /'ekskəveɪtə(r)/ *n.* **A** (*machine*) Bagger, *der;* **B** (*Archaeol.: person*) Ausgräber, *der*/Ausgräberin, *die*

**exceed** /ɪk'si:d/ *v.t.* **A** (*be greater than*) übertreffen (**in** an + *Dat.*); ‹Kosten, Summe, Anzahl:› übersteigen (**by** um); **not ~ing** bis zu; **B** (*go beyond*) überschreiten; hinausgehen über (+ *Akk.*) ‹Auftrag, Befehl›; (*surpass*) übertreffen (**in** an + *Dat.*)

**exceedingly** /ɪk'si:dɪŋlɪ/ *adv.* äußerst; ausgesprochen ‹hässlich, dumm›; **fit ~ well** ausgezeichnet passen; **a joke in ~ bad taste** ein ausgesprochen geschmackloser Witz; **it was ~ obvious that she was pregnant** es war überdeutlich zu sehen, dass sie schwanger war

**excel** /ɪk'sel/ **1** *v.t.*, **-ll-** übertreffen; **~ oneself** (*lit. or iron.*) sich selbst übertreffen. **2** *v.i.*, **-ll-** sich hervortun (**at, in** in + *Dat.*); **~ as an orator** ein hervorragender Redner sein; **she ~s at cookery** sie ist eine glänzende Köchin

**excellence** /'eksələns/ *n.* hervorragende Qualität; (*merit*) hervorragende Leistung; **an unusual degree of ~:** eine außergewöhnlich hohe Qualitätsstufe/ein außergewöhnlich hohes Leistungsniveau; **moral/academic ~:** höchster moralischer/wissenschaftlicher Rang; **this school is known for its standards of ~:** diese Schule ist für ihr außerordentlich hohes Niveau bekannt

**excellency** /'eksələnsɪ/ *n.* Exzellenz, *die*

**excellent** /'eksələnt/ *adj.* ausgezeichnet; hervorragend; exzellent (*geh.*); vorzüglich ‹Wein, Koch, Speise›; **be in an ~ mood** bester Laune sein; **he's an ~ chap** er ist ein Prachtkerl (*ugs.*)

**excellently** /'eksələntlɪ/ *adv.* ausgezeichnet; hervorragend; exzellent (*geh.*)

**except** /ɪk'sept/ **1** *prep.* **~ [for]** außer (+ *Dat.*); **~ for** (*in all respects other than*) bis auf (+ *Akk.*); abgesehen von; **~ [for the fact] that ...,** (*coll.*) **~ ...:** abgesehen davon, dass ...; **I know little of her ~ that she ...** *or* (*coll.*) **~ she ...:** ich weiß wenig über sie, nur dass sie ...; **I should buy a new car ~ that** *or* (*coll.*) **~ I've no money** ich würde mir ein neues Auto kaufen, ich habe nur kein Geld; **I'd come, ~ that** *or* (*coll.*) **~ I have no time** ich würde kommen, doch ich habe keine Zeit; **there was nothing to be done ~ [to] stay there** man konnte nichts anderes tun als dableiben; **where could he be ~ in the house?** wo könnte er [denn] sonst sein, wenn nicht im Haus?; **she's everywhere ~ where she ought to be** sie ist überall, nur nicht da, wo sie sein soll.

**2** *v.t.* ausnehmen (**from** bei); **~ed** ausgenommen; **nobody ~ed** alle ohne Ausnahme; **errors ~ed** Irrtümer vorbehalten; **present company ~ed** Anwesende ausgenommen

**excepting** /ɪk'septɪŋ/ *prep.* außer (+ *Dat.*); **not ~ Peter** Peter nicht ausgenommen; **~ that ...,** (*coll.*) **~ ...:** abgesehen davon, dass ...

**exception** /ɪk'sepʃn/ *n.* **A** Ausnahme, *die;* **with the ~ of** mit Ausnahme (+ *Gen.*); **with the ~ of her/myself** mit Ausnahme von ihr/mir; **the ~ proves the rule** (*prov.*) Ausnahmen bestätigen die Regel; **this case is an ~ to the rule** dieser Fall ist die Ausnahme von der Regel; **be no ~ [to the rule]** durchaus keine Ausnahme sein; **there's an ~ to every rule** keine Regel ohne Ausnahme; **make an ~ [of/for sb.]** [bei jmdm.] eine Ausnahme machen; **by way of an ~:** ausnahmsweise; **B** *no pl., no art.* **take ~ to sth.** (*be offended by sth., object to sth.*) an etw. (*Dat.*) Anstoß nehmen; **great ~ is taken to sth.** etw. erregt großen Unwillen

**exceptional** /ɪk'sepʃənl/ *adj.* außergewöhnlich; **in ~ cases** in Ausnahmefällen

**exceptionally** /ɪk'sepʃənəlɪ/ *adv.* **A** (*as an exception*) ausnahmsweise; **B** (*remarkably*) ungewöhnlich; außergewöhnlich

**excerpt** **1** /'eksɜ:pt/ *n.* Auszug, *der* (**from, of** aus); (*from book also*) Exzerpt, *das* (*geh.*); (*from film, speech*) Ausschnitt, *der;* (*from record*) Stück, *das.* **2** /ɪk'sɜ:pt/ *v.t.* exzerpieren (*geh.*) (**from** aus)

**excess** /ɪk'ses/ *n.* **A** (*inordinate degree or amount*) Übermaß, *das* (**of** an + *Dat.*); **such ~ of detail** ein solches Übermaß an Details; **eat/drink/be generous to ~:** übermäßig essen/trinken/großzügig sein; **don't do anything to ~:** man soll nichts übertreiben; **carry sth. to ~:** etw. bis zum Exzess treiben; **in ~:** im Übermaß; **B** *esp. in pl.* (*act of immoderation, over-indulgence*) Exzess, *der;* (*sexual or gluttonous also*) Ausschweifung, *die;* (*savage also*) Ausschreitung, *die;* **C** **be in ~ of sth.** etw. übersteigen; **a figure in ~ of a million** eine Zahl von über einer Million; **a speed in ~ of ...:** eine Geschwindigkeit von mehr als ...; **D** (*surplus*) Überschuss, *der;* **produce an ~ of sth.** einen Überschuss an etw. (*Dat.*) produzieren; **~ weight** Übergewicht, *das;* **E** (*esp. Brit. Insurance*) Selbstbeteiligung, *die;* Selbstbehalt, *der* (*fachspr.*)

**excess** /'ekses/**: ~ 'baggage** *n.* Mehrgepäck, *das;* **~ 'fare** *n.* Mehrpreis, *der;* **pay the ~ fare** nachlösen

**excessive** /ɪk'sesɪv/ *adj.* übermäßig; exzessiv; übertrieben ‹Forderung, Lob, Ansprüche›; zu stark ‹Schmerz, Belastung›; unmäßig ‹Esser, Trinker›; **~ drinking of alcohol** übermäßiger Alkoholgenuss; **an ~ talker/eater** ein Schwätzer (*abwertend*)/Vielfraß (*ugs.*); **sb. is being rather ~:** jmd. ist ziemlich extrem

**excessively** /ɪk'sesɪvlɪ/ *adv.* **A** (*immoderately*) übertrieben; exzessiv; unmäßig ‹essen, trinken›; **~ cautious** übervorsichtig; **talk/spend ~:** [all]zu viel reden/ausgeben; **B** (*exceedingly*) ausgesprochen

**excess** /'ekses/**: ~ 'luggage** ⇒ **~ baggage**; **~ 'postage** *n.* Nachgebühr, *die*

**exchange** /ɪks'tʃeɪndʒ/ **1** *v.t.* **A** tauschen ‹Plätze, Zimmer, Ringe, Küsse›; umtauschen, wechseln ‹Geld›; austauschen ‹Adressen, [Kriegs]gefangene, Erinnerungen, Gedanken, Erfahrungen›; wechseln ‹Blicke, Worte, Ringe›; **[no] shots were ~d** es fand [k]ein Schusswechsel statt; **the two men ~d letters** die beiden Männer führten einen Briefwechsel; **~ blows/insults** sich schlagen/sich gegenseitig beleidigen; **B** (*give in place of another*) eintauschen (**for** für, gegen); umtauschen ‹[gekaufte] Ware› (**for** gegen); austauschen ‹Spion› (**for** gegen); (*interchange*) austauschen (**for** gegen).

**2** *v.i.* tauschen.

**3** *n.* **A** Tausch, *der;* (*of prisoners, spies, compliments, greetings, insults*) Austausch, *der;* **an ~ of ideas/blows** ein Meinungsaustausch/Handgreiflichkeiten *Pl.;* **in ~:** dafür; **in ~ for sth.** für etw.; **fair ~ is no robbery** (*prov.; joc./iron.*) so kann jeder zufrieden sein (*scherzh./iron.*); **B** (*Educ.*) Austausch, *der;* **an ~ of pupils** ein Schüleraustausch; **an ~ student** ein Austauschstudent/eine Austauschstudentin; **the pupils are going on [an] ~ to Paris** die Schüler fahren im Rahmen eines Austauschprogramms nach Paris; **C** (*quarrel*) Wortwechsel, *der;* **D** (*of money*) Umtausch, *der;* **bill of ~:** Wechsel, *der;* Tratte, *die* (*Bankw.*); **~ [rate], rate of ~:** Wechsel- *od.* Umrechnungskurs, *der;* **E** ⇒ **telephone exchange**; **F** (*Commerc.: building*) Börse, *die*

**exchangeable** /ɪks'tʃeɪndʒəbl/ *adj.* austauschbar (**for** gegen); **these goods are not ~:** diese Waren sind vom Umtausch ausgeschlossen

**exchequer** /ɪks'tʃekə(r)/ *n.* **A** (*Brit.*) Schatzamt, *das;* Finanzministerium, *das;* ⇒ *also* **chancellor** A; **B** (*royal or national treasury*) Staatsschatz, *der*

**excise**[1] /'eksaɪz/ *n.* Verbrauchsteuer, *die;* **Customs and E~ Department** (*Brit.*) *Amt für Zölle und Verbrauchsteuern*

**excise**[2] /ɪk'saɪz/ *v.t.* **A** (*from book, article*) entfernen (**from** aus); (*from film also*) herausschneiden (**from** aus); **B** (*Med.*) entfernen; exzidieren (*fachspr.*)

**excision** /ɪk'sɪʒn/ *n.* **A** Entfernung, *die* (**from** aus); **B** (*Med.*) Entfernung, *die;* Exzision, *die* (*fachspr.*)

**excitable** /ɪk'saɪtəbl/ *adj.* leicht erregbar; **have an ~ temper** reizbar sein

**excite** /ɪk'saɪt/ *v.t.* **A** (*thrill*) begeistern; **she was/became ~d by the idea** die Idee begeisterte sie; **it greatly ~d the children** es machte die Kinder ganz aufgeregt; **B** (*agitate*) aufregen; **be/become ~d by sth.** sich über etw. (*Akk.*) aufregen *od.* erregen; **C** (*elicit*) erregen; **D** (*stimulate; also Physiol.*) anregen; (*sexually*) erregen; **E** (*provoke*) aufstacheln (**to** zu)

**excited** /ɪk'saɪtɪd/ *adj.* **A** (*thrilled*) aufgeregt (**at** über + *Akk.*); **you don't seem very ~ [about it]** du scheinst [davon] nicht sehr begeistert zu sein; **I'm ~ to see what happens next** ich bin gespannt, was als Nächstes geschieht; **it's nothing to get ~ about** es ist nichts Besonderes; **don't get ~:** sei nicht gleich so aufgeregt; **B** (*agitated*) erregt; aufgeregt; **it's nothing to get ~ about** es besteht kein Grund zur Aufregung; **don't get ~, it's only Tom** keine Panik, es ist nur Tom; **don't get so ~:** reg dich nicht so auf; **get all ~** (*coll.*) sich furchtbar aufregen (*ugs.*); **C** (*Physiol.*) angeregt; (*sexually*) erregt

**excitedly** /ɪk'saɪtɪdlɪ/ *adv.* aufgeregt; gespannt ‹warten›; **look forward ~ to the holidays** den Ferien entgegenfiebern

**excitement** /ɪk'saɪtmənt/ *n.* Ⓐ *no pl.* Aufregung, *die;* (*enthusiasm*) Begeisterung, *die;* (*suspense*) Spannung, *die;* **in [a state of] ~:** aufgeregt; **in all the ~/in his ~ he forgot to say thank you** in der Aufregung vergaß er, sich zu bedanken; **full of ~:** ganz aufgeregt; **wild with ~:** wie toll vor Aufregung *od.* Erregung; Ⓑ (*incident*) Aufregung, *die;* Ⓒ (*Physiol.: sexual*) Erregung, *die*

**exciting** /ɪk'saɪtɪŋ/ *adj.* aufregend; (*full of suspense*) spannend; **it isn't exactly ~:** es ist nicht gerade berauschend (*ugs.*)

**exclaim** /ɪk'skleɪm/ ❶ *v.t.* ausrufen; **~ that ...:** rufen, dass ... ❷ *v.i.* aufschreien; **~ in delight** vor Freude aufschreien

**exclamation** /ekskləˈmeɪʃn/ *n.* Ausruf, *der;* **utter an ~ of pain/delight** vor Schmerz aufschreien/einen Freudenschrei ausstoßen

**exclamation: ~ mark,** (*Amer.*) **~ point** *ns.* Ausrufezeichen, *das*

**exclude** /ɪk'sklu:d/ *v.t.* Ⓐ (*keep out, debar*) ausschließen (**from** von); **sb. is ~d from a profession/the Church/a room** jmdm. ist die Ausübung eines Berufes/die Zugehörigkeit zur Kirche/der Zutritt zu einem Raum verwehrt; **the public were ~d from the courtroom** die Verhandlung fand unter Ausschluss der Öffentlichkeit statt; **~ noise/draughts from a room** Lärm von einem Zimmer fernhalten/ein Zimmer gegen Zugluft abdichten; **~ sb. from one's will/the Party** jmdn. im Testament nicht bedenken/aus der Partei ausschließen; Ⓑ (*make impossible, preclude*) ausschließen; **this ~s any [further] question of sth.** damit ist etw. völlig ausgeschlossen; Ⓒ (*leave out of account*) nicht berücksichtigen (**from** bei)

**excluding** /ɪk'sklu:dɪŋ/ *prep.* **~ drinks/VAT** Getränke ausgenommen/ohne Mehrwertsteuer

**exclusion** /ɪk'sklu:ʒn/ *n.* Ausschluss, *der;* **[talk about sth.] to the ~ of everything else** ausschließlich [über etw. (*Akk.*) sprechen]

**exclusive** /ɪk'sklu:sɪv/ ❶ *adj.* Ⓐ (*not shared*) alleinig ‹Besitzer, Kontrolle›; ungeteilt ‹Aufmerksamkeit›; einzig ‹Beschäftigung›; Allein‹eigentum›; (*Journ.*) Exklusiv‹bericht, -interview›; (*Fashion*) Modell‹kleid usw.›; **~ right** Alleinrecht, *das;* (*Journ.*) Exklusivrecht, *das;* **have ~ rights** die Alleinrechte/Exklusivrechte haben; Ⓑ (*select, privileged*) exklusiv; (*unwilling to mix*) unnahbar; distanziert; Ⓒ (*excluding*) ausschließlich; **~ of** ohne; **~ of drinks** Getränke ausgenommen; **the price is ~ of postage** Versandkosten sind im Preis nicht inbegriffen; **be mutually ~:** sich gegenseitig ausschließen.
❷ *n.* (*Journ.*) Exklusivbericht, *der*

**exclusively** /ɪk'sklu:sɪvlɪ/ *adv.* ausschließlich; (*Journ.*) exklusiv

**exclusiveness** /ɪk'sklu:sɪvnɪs/ *n., no pl.* Exklusivität, *die*

**excommunicate** /ekskəˈmju:nɪkeɪt/ *v.t.* (*Eccl.*) exkommunizieren

**excommunication** /ekskəmju:nɪ'keɪʃn/ *n.* (*Eccl.*) Exkommunikation, *die*

**excoriate** /eks'kɔ:rɪeɪt/ *v.t.* (*fig.: censure*) vernichtend kritisieren

**excrement** /'ekskrɪmənt/ *n. in sing. or pl.* Exkremente *Pl.* (*bes. Med.*); Kot, *der* (*geh.*)

**excrescence** /ɪk'skresəns/ *n.* Ⓐ Auswuchs, *der;* Wucherung, *die;* Exkreszenz, *die* (*fachspr.*); Ⓑ (*fig.*) Auswuchs, *der*

**excreta** /ɪk'skri:tə/ *n. pl.* Ausscheidungen *Pl.*

**excrete** /ɪk'skri:t/ *v.t.* ausscheiden

**excretion** /ɪk'skri:ʃn/ *n.* Ausscheidung, *die*

**excretory** /ɪk'skri:tərɪ/ *adj.* Ausscheidungs-

**excruciating** /ɪk'skru:ʃɪeɪtɪŋ/ *adj.* unerträglich; qualvoll ‹Tod›; quälend ‹Frage›; **it is ~:** es ist unerträglich *od.* nicht auszuhalten; **be in ~ pain** unerträgliche Schmerzen haben; **an ~ pun** ≈ ein schlimmer Kalauer

**excruciatingly** /ɪk'skru:ʃɪeɪtɪŋlɪ/ *adv.* entsetzlich; furchtbar; wahnsinnig ‹lustig›

**exculpate** /'ekskəlpeɪt/ *v.t.* freisprechen; **he was ~d** seine Unschuld wurde festgestellt; **~ oneself** sich rechtfertigen (**from** gegenüber)

**exculpation** /ekskəl'peɪʃn/ *n., no pl.* Entlastung, *die;* (*vindication*) Rechtfertigung, *die*

**excursion** /ɪk'skɜ:ʃn/ *n.* Ⓐ Ausflug, *der;* **day ~:** Tagesausflug, *der;* **go on/make an ~:** einen Ausflug machen; **~ rates/fares** Sonderpreis [für Ausflüge]; Ⓑ (*fig.: digression*) Ausflug, *der;* Exkurs, *der* (*geh.*)

**excursionist** /ɪk'skɜ:ʃənɪst/ *n.* Ausflügler, *der*/Ausflüglerin, *die*

**excursion: ~ ticket** *n.* Ausflugskarte, *die;* **~ train** *n.* (*Amer.*) Sonderzug, *der*

**excusable** /ɪk'skju:zəbl/ *adj.* entschuldbar; verzeihlich

**excusably** /ɪk'sku:zəblɪ/ *adv.* verständlicherweise

**excuse** ❶ /ɪk'skju:z/ *v.t.* Ⓐ ▸ 924 (*forgive, exonerate*) entschuldigen; **~ oneself** (*apologize*) sich entschuldigen; **~ me** Entschuldigung; Verzeihung; **please ~ me** bitte entschuldigen Sie; **~ me[, what did you say]?** (*Amer.*) Verzeihung[, was haben Sie gesagt]?; **~ me if I don't get up** entschuldigen Sie, wenn ich nicht aufstehe; **~ sth. in sb., ~ sb. sth.** etw. bei jmdm. entschuldigen; **I can be ~d for confusing them** es ist verzeihlich, dass ich sie verwechselt habe; **sb. can be ~d for that** das ist verzeihlich; **acts which nothing can ~:** Taten, die durch nichts zu entschuldigen sind; Ⓑ (*release, exempt*) befreien; **~ sb. [from] sth.** jmdn. von etw. befreien; **they were ~d payment of all taxes** ihnen wurden alle Steuern erlassen; **~ oneself from doing sth.** sich erlauben, etw. nicht zu tun; Ⓒ (*allow to leave*) entschuldigen; **~ oneself** sich entschuldigen; **and now, if I may be ~d** *or* **if you will ~ me** wenn Sie mich jetzt bitte entschuldigen wollen; **you are ~d** ihr könnt gehen; **may I be ~d?** (*wishing to leave the table*) darf ich aufstehen?; (*euphem.: wishing to go to the toilet*) darf ich mal verschwinden *od.* austreten?
❷ /ɪk'skju:s/ *n.* Ⓐ Entschuldigung, *die;* **give** *or* **offer an ~ for sth.** sich für etw. entschuldigen; **there is no ~ for what I did** was ich getan habe, ist nicht zu entschuldigen; **what did he give as his ~ this time?** welche Entschuldigung hatte er diesmal?; **I'm not trying to make ~s, but ...:** das soll keine Entschuldigung sein, aber ...; **make one's/sb.'s ~s to sb.** sich/jmdn. bei jmdm. entschuldigen; **any ~ for a drink!** zum Trinken gibt es immer einen Grund; **be as good an ~ as any** ein willkommener Anlass sein; Ⓑ (*evasive statement*) Ausrede, *die;* **make ~s** sich herausreden; Ⓒ (*pathetic specimen*) **this is an ~ for a pencil/letter** *etc.*, **isn't it!** das kann man wohl kaum als Bleistift/Brief *usw.* bezeichnen

**ex-di'rectory** *adj.* (*Brit. Teleph.*) Geheim‹nummer, -anschluss›; **famous people are usually ~:** berühmte Leute stehen gewöhnlich nicht im Telefonbuch

**ex 'dividend** (*Finance*) *adv.* abzüglich Dividende

**exec** /ɪg'zek/ *n.* (*coll.*) ⇒ **executive** 1 A

**execrable** /'eksɪkrəbl/ *adj.*, **execrably** /'eksɪkrəblɪ/ *adv.* abscheulich

**execration** /eksɪ'kreɪʃn/ *n.* Ⓐ (*act*) Fluchen, *das;* Ⓑ (*curse*) Fluch, *der;* Verwünschung, *die;* Ⓒ *no pl.* (*abhorrence*) Abscheu, *der;* **hold sth. in ~:** etw. verabscheuen

**execute** /'eksɪkju:t/ *v.t.* Ⓐ (*kill*) hinrichten; exekutieren (*Milit.*); Ⓑ (*put into effect, perform*) ausführen; durchführen ‹Vorschrift, Gesetz›; Ⓒ (*Law: give effect to*) vollstrecken; (*make legally valid*) rechtsgültig machen; unterzeichnen ‹Urkunde›

**execution** /eksɪ'kju:ʃn/ *n.* Ⓐ (*killing*) Hinrichtung, *die;* Exekution, *die* (*Milit.*); Ⓑ (*putting into effect, performance*) Ausführung, *die;* (*of instruction, law*) Durchführung, *die;* (*of will, verdict*) Vollstreckung, *die;* **put sth. into ~:** etw. aus- *od.* durchführen/vollstrecken; **in the ~ of one's duty/duties** bei Erfüllung seiner Pflicht; in [treuer] Pflichterfüllung; Ⓒ (*Mus.*) Vortrag, *der;* Ⓓ (*Law: seizure of property, carrying out*) Vollstreckung, *die;* (*rendering legally valid*) [rechtsgültige] Unterzeichnung

**executioner** /eksɪ'kju:ʃənə(r)/ *n.* Scharfrichter, *der*

**executive** /ɪg'zekjʊtɪv/ ❶ *n.* Ⓐ (*person*) leitender Angestellter/leitende Angestellte; Ⓑ (*administrative body*) **the ~** (*of government*) die Exekutive; (*of political organization, trade union*) der Vorstand. ❷ *adj.* Ⓐ (*Commerc.*) leitend ‹Stellung, Funktion›; geschäftsführend ‹Vorsitzende[r]›; **~ powers** Vollmacht, *die;* (*Commerc. Law*) Prokura, *die;* **~ ability** Führungsqualitäten *Pl.;* Ⓑ (*relating to government*) exekutiv; **~ powers** Exekutivgewalt, *die*

**executive: ~ com'mittee** *n.* [geschäftsführender] Vorstand; **~ 'council** *n.* Ministerrat, *der;* **~ 'stress** *n.* Managerstress, *der;* **~ 'toy** *n.* Managerspielzeug, *das*

**executor** /ɪg'zekjʊtə(r)/ *n.* (*Law*) Testamentsvollstrecker, *der;* **the ~ of his will** sein Testamentsvollstrecker; **literary ~:** Verwalter/Verwalterin des literarischen Nachlasses

**exegesis** /eksɪ'dʒi:sɪs/ *n., pl.* **exegeses** /eksɪ'dʒi:si:z/ Auslegung, *die;* Exegese, *die* (*auch Theol.*)

**exemplary** /ɪg'zemplərɪ/ *adj.* Ⓐ (*model*) vorbildlich; Ⓑ (*deterrent*) exemplarisch; **~ damages** (*Law*) Buße, *die;* Ⓒ (*illustrative*) beispielhaft; exemplarisch

**exemplification** /ɪgzemplɪfɪ'keɪʃn/ *n.* Veranschaulichung, *die;* Exemplifikation, *die* (*geh.*)

**exemplify** /ɪg'zemplɪfaɪ/ *v.t.* veranschaulichen; exemplifizieren (*geh.*); (*serve as example of*) als Beispiel dienen für

**exempt** /ɪg'zempt/ ❶ *adj.* **[be] ~ [from sth.]** [von etw.] befreit [sein]; **make sb. ~ from sth.** jmdn. von etw. befreien. ❷ *v.t.* befreien; **be ~ed from sth.** von etw. befreit werden

**exemption** /ɪg'zempʃn/ *n.* Befreiung, *die;* **~ from payment of a fine** Erlass einer Geldstrafe

**exercise** /'eksəsaɪz/ ❶ *n.* Ⓐ *no pl., no indef. art.* (*physical exertion*) Bewegung, *die;* (*of dog also*) Auslauf, *der;* (*fig.*) Training, *das;* **get ~:** Bewegung haben; **take ~:** sich (*Dat.*) Bewegung verschaffen; **provide ~ for sth.** etw. trainieren; eine gute Übung für etw. sein; Ⓑ (*task set, activity; also Mus., Sch.*) Übung, *die;* **the object of the ~:** der Sinn der Übung; Ⓒ (*to improve fitness*) [Gymnastik]übung, *die;* **morning ~s** Morgengymnastik, *die;* Ⓓ *no pl.* (*employment, application*) Ausübung, *die;* **the ~ of tolerance is essential** Toleranz zu üben ist sehr wichtig; Ⓔ *usu. in pl.* (*Mil.*) Übung, *die;* **go on ~s** eine Übung machen; Ⓕ *in pl.* (*Amer.: ceremony*) Feierlichkeiten *Pl.*
❷ *v.t.* Ⓐ ausüben ‹Recht, Macht, Einfluss›; walten lassen ‹Vorsicht›; **~ restraint/discretion/patience** sich in Zurückhaltung/Diskretion/Geduld üben; **~ one's right of veto** von seinem Vetorecht Gebrauch machen; **~ tact** taktvoll sein; **~ great care** sehr vorsichtig sein; Ⓑ (*tax the powers of*) in Anspruch nehmen; (*perplex, worry*) beschäftigen; **~ the mind** die geistigen Fähigkeiten herausfordern; Ⓒ (*physically*) trainieren ‹Körper, Muskeln›; bewegen ‹Pferd›; Ⓓ (*Mil.*) drillen.
❸ *v.i.* sich (*Dat.*) Bewegung verschaffen

**exercise: ~ bicycle,** (*coll.*) **~ bike** *ns.* Heimtrainer, *der;* **~ book** *n.* [Schul]heft, *das*

**exerciser** /'eksəsaɪzə(r)/ *n.* (*device*) Trainingsgerät, *das*

**exert** /ɪg'zɜ:t/ ❶ *v.t.* aufbieten ‹Kraft, Beredsamkeit›; ausüben ‹Einfluss, Druck, Macht›; **~ all one's force on the door** sich mit aller Kraft gegen die Tür stemmen. ❷ *v. refl.* sich anstrengen; **don't ~ yourself** (*iron.*) überanstrenge dich nur nicht

**exertion** /ɪg'zɜ:ʃn/ *n.* Ⓐ *no pl.* (*exerting*) (*of strength, force*) Aufwendung, *die;* (*of influence, pressure, force*) Ausübung, *die;* **by the ~ of all sb.'s strength** unter Aufbietung aller Kräfte; Ⓑ (*effort*) Anstrengung, *die;* **by**

**her own ~s she managed ...:** durch eigene Anstrengung gelang es ihr, ...

**exeunt** /'eksɪənt/ *v.i.* (*Theatre: as stage direction*) ab; **~ omnes** /eksɪənt 'ɒmni:z/ alle ab

**ex gratia** /eks 'greɪʃə/ *adj.* freiwillig; ohne Anerkennung einer Rechtspflicht

**exhalation** /ekshə'leɪʃn/ *n.* Ⓐ (*breathing out*) Ausatmung, *die;* (*of smoke, gas; also Med.*) Exhalation, *die;* Ⓑ (*puff of breath*) Atemzug, *der;* Ⓒ (*gas etc. emitted*) exhalierte Dämpfe/Gase

**exhale** /eks'heɪl/ ❶ *v.t.* Ⓐ (*from lungs*) ausatmen; exhalieren (*Med.*); Ⓑ (*emit*) verströmen ‹Duft›; ausstoßen ‹Rauch, Gas›. ❷ *v.i.* ausatmen; exhalieren (*Med.*)

**exhaust** /ɪg'zɔ:st/ ❶ *v.t.* Ⓐ (*use up*) erschöpfen; erschöpfend behandeln ‹Thema›; (*try out fully*) ausschöpfen; **she ~ed her ideas in her first novel** sie hat den Vorrat ihrer Ideen bereits in ihrem ersten Roman erschöpft; Ⓑ (*drain of strength, resources, etc.*) erschöpfen; **have been ~ed by sth.** von etw. erschöpft sein; **have ~ed oneself** sich völlig verausgabt haben; **this work is ~ing me** diese Arbeit strengt mich sehr an; Ⓒ (*draw off*) herauspumpen; **~ sth. from sth.** etw. aus etw. [heraus]pumpen; Ⓓ (*empty*) auspumpen.
❷ *n.* Ⓐ **~ [system]** Abgasrohr, *das;* (*Motor Veh.*) Auspuff, *der;* (*of train*) Abgasleitung, *die;* Ⓑ (*what is expelled*) Abgase *Pl.;* (*of car*) Auspuffgase *Pl.;* **~ emissions** Auspuffabgase *Pl.;* **~ emissions test** Abgasuntersuchung, *die*

**exhausted** /ɪg'zɔ:stɪd/ *adj.* erschöpft

**exhausting** /ɪg'zɔ:stɪŋ/ *adj.* anstrengend; beschwerlich ‹Husten›; ermüdend ‹Wetter›; **he is ~ company** *or* **~ to be with** er ist sehr anstrengend

**exhaustion** /ɪg'zɔ:stʃn/ *n., no pl.* Erschöpfung, *die*

**exhaustive** /ɪg'zɔ:stɪv/ *adj.* umfassend

**exhaustively** /ɪg'zɔ:stɪvlɪ/ *adv.* umfassend; **treat a subject ~:** ein Thema erschöpfend *od.* umfassend behandeln

**ex'haust pipe** *n.* Abzugsrohr, *das;* (*of car*) Auspuffrohr, *das*

**exhibit** /ɪg'zɪbɪt/ ❶ *v.t.* Ⓐ (*display*) vorzeigen; (*show publicly*) ausstellen; **he has ~ed in London** er hat in London ausgestellt; **~ in court** (*Law*) dem Gericht vorlegen; Ⓑ (*manifest*) zeigen ‹Mut, Verachtung, Symptome, Neigung, Angst›; beweisen ‹Mut, Können›. ❷ *n.* Ⓐ Ausstellungsstück, *das;* Ⓑ (*Law: in court; also fig.*) Beweisstück, *das*

**exhibition** /eksɪ'bɪʃn/ *n.* Ⓐ (*public display*) Ausstellung, *die;* **~ catalogue** Ausstellungskatalog, *der;* Ⓑ (*act*) Vorführung, *die;* (*manifestation*) **give an ~ of one's skills** sein Können demonstrieren; **her ~ of grief** die Zurschaustellung ihrer Trauer; Ⓒ (*derog.*) **make an ~ of oneself** sich unmöglich aufführen; **what an ~!** ein unmögliches Benehmen!; Ⓓ (*Brit. Univ.: scholarship*) Stipendium, *das*

**exhibitioner** /eksɪ'bɪʃənə(r)/ *n.* (*Brit. Univ.*) Stipendiat, *der*

**exhibitionism** /eksɪ'bɪʃənɪzm/ *n.* Exhibitionismus, *der*

**exhibitionist** /eksɪ'bɪʃənɪst/ *n.* Exhibitionist, *der*/Exhibitionistin, *die*

**exhibitor** /ɪg'zɪbɪtə(r)/ *n.* Aussteller, *der*/Ausstellerin, *die*

**exhilarate** /ɪg'zɪləreɪt/ *v.t.* erfrischen, beleben; (*gladden*) fröhlich stimmen; (*stimulate*) anregen

**exhilarated** /ɪg'zɪləreɪtɪd/ *adj.* erfrischt; belebt; (*gladdened*) fröhlich gestimmt; (*stimulated*) angeregt; **feel ~:** sich erfrischt/angeregt fühlen/fröhlich gestimmt sein

**exhilarating** /ɪg'zɪləreɪtɪŋ/ *adj.* belebend; fröhlich stimmend ‹Nachricht, Musik, Anblick›; **~ feeling** erhebendes Gefühl

**exhilaration** /ɪgzɪlə'reɪʃn/ *n.* **[feeling of] ~:** Hochgefühl, *das;* **the ~ of hang-gliding** das Hochgefühl beim Drachenfliegen

**exhort** /ɪg'zɔ:t/ *v.t.* **~ sb. to do sth.** jmdn. [ernsthaft] ermahnen, etw. zu tun

**exhortation** /eksɔ:'teɪʃn/ *n.* Ⓐ (*exhorting*) Ermahnung, *die;* Ⓑ (*formal address*) Appell, *der;* Exhortation, *die* (*kath. Rel.*)

**exhumation** /eksjʊ'meɪʃn/ *n.* Exhumierung, *die*

**exhume** /ɪg'zju:m/ *v.t.* exhumieren; (*fig.*) ausgraben

**exigence** /'eksɪdʒəns/, **exigency** /'eksɪdʒənsɪ/ *n.* Ⓐ *usu. in pl.* (*urgent demand*) Erfordernis, *das;* Ⓑ (*emergency*) Notlage, *die;* (*Polit. also*) Krisensituation, *die;* Ⓒ (*urgency*) Dringlichkeit, *die*

**exigent** /'eksɪdʒənt/ *adj.* Ⓐ (*exacting*) anspruchsvoll; Ⓑ (*urgent*) dringend ‹Fall, Lage›; zwingend ‹Grund, Notwendigkeit, Umstand›

**exiguous** /eg'zɪgjʊəs/ *adj.* gering; schmal (*geh.*) ‹Gehalt, Budget›; dürftig ‹Kost›

**exile** /'eksaɪl, 'egzaɪl/ ❶ *n.* Ⓐ Exil, *das;* (*forcible also*) Verbannung, *die* (**from** aus); **order sb.'s ~:** jmdn. ins Exil schicken; **live/be in ~:** im Exil leben/sein; **go into ~:** ins Exil gehen; **internal ~:** Verbannung, *die* (*an einen Ort innerhalb des eigenen Landes*); **the E~** (*Jewish Hist.*) die Babylonische Gefangenschaft; Ⓑ (*exiled person, lit. or fig.*) Verbannte, *der/die;* Exilierte, *der/die* (*geh.*). ❷ *v.t.* verbannen; exilieren (*geh.*); **~d Russian** Exilrusse, *der/*-russin, *die*

**exist** /ɪg'zɪst/ *v.i.* Ⓐ (*be in existence*) existieren; ‹Zweifel, Gefahr, Problem, Zusammenarbeit, Brauch, Einrichtung:› bestehen; **ever since records have ~ed ...:** seit es Aufzeichnungen gibt, ...; **fairies do ~:** es gibt Feen; **the biggest book that has ever ~ed** das größte Buch aller Zeiten; **the conditions that ~ in the Third World** die Bedingungen, die man in der Dritten Welt vorfindet; **does life ~ on Venus?** gibt es Leben auf der Venus?; Ⓑ (*survive*) existieren; überleben; **~ on sth.** von etw. leben; Ⓒ (*be found*) **sth. ~s only in Europe** es gibt etw. nur in Europa

**existence** /ɪg'zɪstəns/ *n.* Ⓐ (*existing*) Existenz, *die;* **doubt sb.'s ~/the ~ of sth.** bezweifeln, dass es jmdn./etw. gibt; **the continued ~ of this tradition** das Fortbestehen dieser Tradition; **be in ~:** existieren; **the only such plant [which is] in ~:** die einzige Pflanze dieser Art, die es gibt; **come into ~:** entstehen; **bring sth. into ~:** etw. einführen; **go out of ~:** verschwinden; Ⓑ (*mode of living*) Dasein, *das;* (*survival*) Existenz, *die;* **struggle for ~:** Existenzkampf, *der;* **means of ~:** Existenzgrundlage, *die*

**existent** /ɪg'zɪstənt/ ⇒ **existing**

**existential** /egzɪ'stenʃl/ *adj.* existenziell

**existentialism** /egzɪ'stenʃəlɪzm/ *n., no pl.* (*Philos.*) Existenzialismus, *der*

**existentialist** /egzɪ'stenʃəlɪst/ *n.* (*Philos.*) Existenzialist, *der*/Existenzialistin, *die; attrib.* existenzialistisch

**existing** /ɪg'zɪstɪŋ/ *adj.* existierend; (*present*) bestehend ‹Ordnung, Schwierigkeiten›; gegenwärtig ‹Lage, Führung, Stand der Dinge›

**exit** /'eksɪt/ ❶ *n.* Ⓐ (*way out*) Ausgang, *der* (**from** aus); (*from drive, motorway*) Ausfahrt, *die;* Ⓑ (*from stage*) Abgang, *der;* **make one's ~:** abgehen; Ⓒ (*from room*) Hinausgehen, *das;* (*from group*) Weggehen, *das;* **make a speedy ~:** schnell hinausgehen/weggehen; **she made a dramatic ~:** ihr Abgang war dramatisch; Ⓓ (*departure*) **right of ~ from a country** Recht, ein Land zu verlassen. ❷ *v.i.* Ⓐ (*make one's ~*) hinausgehen (**from** aus); (*from stage*) abgehen (**from** von); Ⓑ (*Theatre: as stage direction*) ab; **~ Hamlet** Hamlet ab

**exit: ~ permit** *n.* Ausreiseerlaubnis, *die;* **~ poll** *n. Befragung der ein Wahllokal verlassenden Wähler;* **~ visa** *n.* Ausreisevisum, *das*

**exodus** /'eksədəs/ *n.* Auszug, *der;* Exodus, *der* (*geh.*); **general ~:** allgemeiner Aufbruch; **[the Book of] E~:** das zweite Buch Mose

**ex officio** /eks ə'fɪʃɪəʊ/ ❶ *adv.* ex officio (*geh.*); von Amts wegen. ❷ *adj.* **~ chairman** Vorsitzender von Amts wegen *od.* ex officio (*geh.*); **be an ~ member** kraft seines Amtes Mitglied sein

**exonerate** /ɪg'zɒnəreɪt/ *v.t.* entlasten; **~ sb. from a duty/task** jmdn. von einer Pflicht/Aufgabe befreien; **~ sb. from blame** jmdn. von der Schuld freisprechen

**exoneration** /ɪgzɒnə'reɪʃn/ *n.* Entlastung, *die;* (*from task, obligation*) Befreiung, *die*

**exorbitance** /ɪg'zɔ:bɪtəns/ *n., no pl.* Maßlosigkeit, *die;* Exorbitanz, *die* (*geh.*)

**exorbitant** /ɪg'zɔ:bɪtənt/ *adj.* [maßlos] überhöht ‹Preis, Miete, Gewinn, Anforderung, Rechnung›; maßlos ‹Ehrgeiz, Forderung›; **£10 — that's ~!** 10 Pfund — das ist unverschämt viel! (*ugs.*); **be ~ in one's demands** [maßlos] überhöhte Ansprüche stellen

**exorcise** ⇒ **exorcize**

**exorcism** /'eksɔ:sɪzm/ *n.* Exorzismus, *der;* Teufelsaustreibung, *die*

**exorcist** /'eksɔ:sɪst/ *n.* Exorzist, *der*

**exorcize** /'eksɔ:saɪz/ *v.t.* austreiben; exorzieren; **be ~d from** *or* **out of sb./sth.** jmdm./einer Sache ausgetrieben werden

**exotic** /ɪg'zɒtɪk/ ❶ *adj.* exotisch. ❷ *n.* Exot[e], *der*/Exotin, *die*

**exotica** /ɪg'zɒtɪkə/ *n. pl.* Exotika *Pl.*

**exotically** /ɪg'zɒtɪkəlɪ/ *adv.* exotisch; **~ named ...:** mit dem exotischen Namen ...

**expand** /ɪk'spænd/ ❶ *v.i.* Ⓐ (*get bigger*) sich ausdehnen; ‹Unternehmen, Stadt, Staat:› expandieren; ‹Verkehrsaufkommen, Wissen:› zunehmen; ‹Institution:› erweitert werden; ‹geistiger Horizont:› sich erweitern; **~ into sth.** zu etw. anwachsen; **~ing watch strap** elastisches Gliederband; Ⓑ (*Commerc.*) expandieren; **~ into a large organization** zu einer großen Organisation heranwachsen; **~ into other areas of production** die Produktion um andere Sektoren erweitern; Ⓒ **~ on a subject** ein Thema weiter ausführen; Ⓓ (*spread out*) sich öffnen; Ⓔ (*become genial*) freundlich werden.
❷ *v.t.* Ⓐ (*enlarge*) ausdehnen; erweitern ‹Horizont, Wissen›; dehnen ‹Körper›; aufblasen ‹Ballon›; aufpumpen ‹Reifen›; **~ sth. into sth.** etw. zu etw. erweitern; **~ed metal** Streckmetall, *das* (*Bauw.*); Ⓑ (*Commerc.: develop*) erweitern; **~ the economy** das Wirtschaftswachstum fördern; Ⓒ (*amplify*) weiter ausführen ‹Gedanken, Notiz, Idee›

**expandable** /ɪk'spændəbl/ *adj.* [aus]dehnbar; (*Commerc.*) entwicklungsfähig

**expanse** /ɪk'spæns/ *n.* [weite] Fläche; **~ of water** Wasserfläche, *die;* **surrounded by a huge ~ of desert** umgeben von einer sich weithin erstreckenden Wüste; **she was swathed in an ~ of red silk** sie war in weite Bahnen roter Seide gehüllt

**expansion** /ɪk'spænʃn/ *n.* Ⓐ Ausdehnung, *die;* (*of territorial rule also*) Expansion, *die;* (*of sphere of influence*) Ausweitung, *die;* (*of knowledge, building*) Erweiterung, *die;* **the ~ of the volume of traffic on the roads** die zunehmende Verkehrsdichte auf den Straßen; Ⓑ (*Commerc.*) Expansion, *die;* **the ~ of this small business into a huge organization** die Erweiterung dieses kleinen Betriebes zu einer großen Firma; Ⓒ (*amplification*) Erweiterung, *die;* **further ~ of the ideas** weitere Ausführung der Ideen

**expansionary** /ɪk'spænʃənərɪ/ *adj.* (*also Commerc.*) expansionistisch

**ex'pansion joint** *n.* Dehnungsfuge, *die*

**expansive** /ɪk'spænsɪv/ *adj.* (*effusive*) offen; (*responsive*) zugänglich; **be ~:** aus sich herausgehen

**expatiate** /ɪk'speɪʃɪeɪt/ *v.i.* **~ [up]on sth.** etw. ausführlich erörtern; sich über etw. (*Akk.*) verbreiten (*oft abwertend*)

**expatiation** /ɪkspeɪʃɪ'eɪʃn/ *n.* [ausführliche] Erörterung (**[up]on** *Gen.*)

**expatriate** ❶ /eks'pætrɪeɪt, eks'peɪtrɪeɪt/ *v.t.* (*exile*) ausbürgern; expatriieren. ❷ /eks'pætrɪət, eks'peɪtrɪət/ *attrib. adj.* im Ausland lebend; **~ community** Kolonie, *die.* ❸ *n.* (*exile*) Exilant, *der*/Exilantin, *die;* (*foreigner*) Ausländer, *der*/Ausländerin, *die;* (*emigrant*) Auswanderer, *der*/Auswanderin, *die*

**expatriation** /ekspætrɪ'eɪʃn, ekspeɪtrɪ'eɪʃn/ *n.* (*forcible*) Ausbürgerung, *die;* Expatriation, *die;* (*voluntary*) [freiwilliges] Exil

**expect** /ɪk'spekt/ *v.t.* Ⓐ (*regard as likely, anticipate*) erwarten; **~ to do sth.** damit rechnen, etw. zu tun; ~ **sth. from sb.** etw. von jmdm. erwarten; ~ **sb. to do sth.** damit rechnen, dass jmd. etw. tut; **I ~ you'd like something to eat** ich nehme an, dass du gern etwas essen möchtest ; **don't ~ me to help you out** von mir hast du keine Hilfe zu erwarten; **it is ~ed that ...:** man erwartet, dass ...; **that was [not] to be ~ed** das war [auch nicht] zu erwarten; **I ~ed as much** das habe ich erwartet; **it is everything one ~s** es erfüllt alle Erwartungen; **it is all one can ~:** mehr kann man [auch] nicht erwarten; ~ **the worst** mit dem Schlimmsten rechnen; **be ~ing a baby/child** ein Baby/Kind erwarten; **be ~ing** *abs.* schwanger sein; **is he/she ~ing you?** werden Sie erwartet?; **I/we shall not ~ you till I/we see you** wenn du kommst, bist du da (*ugs.*); ~ **me when you see me** (*coll.*) wenn ich komme, bin ich da (*ugs.*); **B** (*require*) erwarten; ~ **sb. to do sth.** von jmdm. erwarten, dass er etw. tut; ~ **sth. from** *or* **of sb.** etw. von jmdm. erwarten; **they are ~ed to be present** man erwartet [von ihnen], dass sie da sind; **C** (*coll.: think, suppose*) glauben; **I ~ so** ich glaube schon; **I rather ~ not** ich glaube kaum; **I don't ~ so** ich glaube nicht; **I ~ it was/he did** *etc.* das glaube ich gern

**expectancy** /ɪk'spektənsɪ/ *n.* **A** *no pl.* Erwartung, *die;* **with an air** *or* **a look of ~:** mit erwartungsvoller Miene; **mood of ~:** erwartungsvolle Stimmung; **B** (*prospective chance*) **an ~ of another 28 years of life** eine Lebenserwartung von noch 28 Jahren; ⇒ *also* **life expectancy**

**expectant** /ɪk'spektənt/ *adj.* **A** erwartungsvoll; **B** ~ **mother** werdende Mutter

**expectantly** /ɪk'spektəntlɪ/ *adv.* erwartungsvoll; gespannt ‹warten›

**expectation** /ekspek'teɪʃn/ *n.* **A** *no pl.* (*expecting*) Erwartung, *die;* **in the ~ of sth.** in Erwartung einer Sache (*Gen.*); **B** *usu. in pl.* (*thing expected*) Erwartung, *die;* **have great ~s for sb./sth.** große Erwartungen in jmdn./etw. setzen; **come up to ~[s]/sb.'s ~s** den/jmds. Erwartungen entsprechen; **contrary to ~** *or* **to all ~s** wider Erwarten; **be a success beyond all ~s** über alles Erwarten erfolgreich sein; **C** ~ **of life** ⇒ **life** E; **D** *in pl.* (*prospects of inheritance*) **have great ~s** ein großes Erbe in Aussicht haben

**expectorate** /ɪk'spektəreɪt/ *v.t.* & *i.* aushusten; (*spit*) [aus]spucken

**expedience** /ɪk'spi:dɪəns/, **expediency** /ɪk'spi:dɪənsɪ/ *n.* Zweckmäßigkeit, *die;* **he has sacrificed his integrity for ~:** er hat seine Integrität den so genannten Sachzwängen geopfert

**expedient** /ɪk'spi:dɪənt/ **1** *adj., usu. pred.* **A** (*appropriate, advantageous*) angebracht; **B** (*politic*) zweckmäßig. **2** *n.* Mittel, *das*

**expediently** /ɪk'spi:dɪəntlɪ/ *adv.* zweckmäßigerweise; **act ~:** handeln, wie man es für zweckmäßig hält

**expedite** /'ekspɪdaɪt/ *v.t.* (*hasten*) beschleunigen; vorantreiben; (*execute promptly*) umgehend ausführen

**expedition** /ekspɪ'dɪʃn/ *n.* **A** Expedition, *die;* **B** (*Mil.*) Feldzug, *der;* Expedition, *die* (*veralt.*); **send an ~ to Egypt** Truppen nach Ägypten schicken; **C** (*excursion*) Ausflug, *der;* **go on a hunting/shopping ~:** einen Jagdausflug/eine Einkaufstour machen; **D** *no pl.* (*speed*) Eile, *die*

**expeditionary** /ekspɪ'dɪʃənərɪ/ *adj.* ~ **force** (*Mil.*) Expeditionskorps, *das*

**expeditious** /ekspɪ'dɪʃəs/ *adj.* (*doing or done speedily*) schnell; (*suited for speedy performance*) schnell durchführbar

**expeditiously** /ekspɪ'dɪʃəslɪ/ *adv.* schnell

**expel** /ɪk'spel/ *v.t.*, **-ll- A** ausweisen; ~ **sb. from school [for misconduct]** jmdn. [wegen schlechten Betragens] von der Schule verweisen; ~ **sb. from a country** jmdn. aus einem Land ausweisen; ~ **from a club** aus einem Verein ausschließen; **B** (*with force*) vertreiben (**from** aus); auswerfen ‹Patrone›; absaugen ‹Küchendunst›; **C** (*from substance; also Med.*) austreiben ‹Gas, Wasser usw.›

**expend** /ɪk'spend/ *v.t.* **A** aufwenden ([**up**]**on** für); ~ **much care in doing sth.** etw. mit viel Sorgfalt tun; **B** (*use up*) aufbrauchen ([**up**]**on** für)

**expendable** /ɪk'spendəbl/ *adj.* **A** (*inessential*) entbehrlich; **be ~** (*Mil.; also fig.*) geopfert werden können; **B** (*used up in service*) zum Verbrauch bestimmt

**expenditure** /ɪk'spendɪtʃə(r)/ *n.* **A** (*amount spent*) Ausgaben *Pl.* (**on** für); (*of fuel, effort, etc.*) Aufwand, *der;* **B** (*spending*) Ausgabe, *die;* (*using up of fuel or effort*) Aufwand, *der* (**of** an + *Dat.*); ~ **of money/time** Geldausgabe, *die*/Zeitaufwand, *der*

**expense** /ɪk'spens/ *n.* **A** Kosten *Pl.;* **regardless of ~:** ungeachtet der Kosten; **those who can afford the ~:** diejenigen, die es sich leisten können; **at little ~:** preiswert; **at great ~ to sb./sth.** unter großen Kosten für jmdn./etw.; **living ~s** Lebenshaltungskosten *Pl.;* **at sb.'s ~:** auf jmds. Kosten (*Akk.*); **at one's own ~:** auf eigene Kosten; **go to the ~ of travelling first-class** sogar noch das Geld für die erste Klasse ausgeben; **go to some/great ~:** sich in Unkosten/große Unkosten stürzen; **put sb. to ~:** jmdm. Kosten verursachen; **put sb. to the ~ of sth./of doing sth.** jmdm. die Kosten für etw. zumuten/dafür zumuten, etw. zu tun; **B** (*expensive item*) teure Angelegenheit; **be** *or* **prove a great** *or* **big ~:** mit großen Ausgaben verbunden sein; **C** *usu. in pl.* (*Commerc. etc.: amount spent [and repaid]*) Spesen *Pl.;* **with [all] ~s paid** auf Spesen; **the ~s incurred** die anfallenden Spesen; **he is able to claim ~s** er kann sich (*Dat.*) seine Spesen erstatten lassen; **put sth. on ~s** etw. auf die Spesenabrechnung setzen; **it all goes on to ~s** das geht alles auf Spesen; **D** (*fig.*) Preis, *der;* **[be] at the ~ of sth.** auf Kosten von etw. [gehen]; **at considerable ~ in terms of human lives** unter großem Verlust an Menschenleben; **he achieved it, but at the ~ of his life** er erreichte es, aber es kostete ihn das Leben; **at sb.'s ~:** auf jmds. Kosten (*Akk.*)

**ex'pense account** *n.* Spesenabrechnung, *die; attrib.* ‹Essen, Leben› auf Spesen

**expensive** /ɪk'spensɪv/ *adj.* teuer; **prove ~ to sb.** jmdn. teuer zu stehen kommen

**expensively** /ɪk'spensɪvlɪ/ *adv.* teuer; ~ **priced** teuer

**experience** /ɪk'spɪərɪəns/ **1** *n.* **A** *no pl., no indef. art.* Erfahrung, *die;* **have ~ of sth./sb.** Erfahrung in etw. (*Dat.*) /mit jmdm. haben; **have ~ of doing sth.** Erfahrung darin haben, etw. zu tun; **several years' ~:** mehrjährige Erfahrung; **learn by** *or* **through** *or* **from ~:** durch eigene *od.* aus eigener Erfahrung lernen; **he learnt through** *or* **by ~ that ...:** die Erfahrung hat ihn gelehrt, dass ...; **his first ~ of war/freedom** seine erste Begegnung mit dem Krieg/der Freiheit; **a man of your ~:** ein Mann mit deiner Erfahrung; **in/from my [own] [previous] ~:** nach meiner/aus eigener Erfahrung; **know from** *or* **by ~ that ...:** aus Erfahrung wissen, dass ...; **~ has shown that ...:** die Erfahrung hat gezeigt, dass ...; **chalk** *or* **charge it up** *or* **put it down to ~:** durch Schaden wird man klug; **~ of life** Lebenserfahrung, *die;* **B** (*event*) Erfahrung, *die;* Erlebnis, *das;* **have an [unpleasant/odd] ~:** eine [unangenehme/merkwürdige] Erfahrung machen; **he went through some terrible wartime ~s** er hat im Krieg Schreckliches mitgemacht; **it's quite an ~!** das ist [schon] ein Erlebnis!; **C the American ~ shows how ...:** das Beispiel Amerika zeigt, wie ...

**2** *v.t.* erleben; stoßen auf (+ *Akk.*), haben ‹Schwierigkeiten›; kennen lernen ‹Lebensweise›; verspüren, empfinden ‹Hunger, Kälte, Schmerz, Freude, Trauer, Gefühl›; **he is unable to ~ things deeply** er ist nicht fähig, etwas tief zu empfinden; **only he who has himself ~d poverty** nur wer Armut selbst erfahren hat

**experienced** /ɪk'spɪərɪənst/ *adj.* erfahren; **be ~ in sth.** in etw. (*Dat.*) erfahren sein; mit etw. Erfahrung haben; **an ~ eye** ein geschulter Blick

**experiment 1** /ɪk'sperɪmənt/ *n.* **A** Experiment, *das* (**on** an + *Dat.*); Versuch, *der* (**on** an + *Dat.*); **do an ~:** ein Experiment machen; **series of ~s** Versuchsreihe, *die;* **B** (*fig.*) Experiment, *das;* **by ~:** experimentell; **as an ~:** versuchsweise. **2** /ɪk'sperɪment/ *v.i.* experimentieren; Versuche anstellen; ~ **on sb./sth.** an jmdm./etw. experimentieren *od.* Versuche anstellen; ~ **with sth.** mit etw. experimentieren

**experimental** /ɪksperɪ'mentl/ *adj.* **A** experimentell; (*based on experiment*) Experimental‹physik, -psychologie›; (*used for experiments*) Experimentier‹theater, -kino›; Versuchs‹labor, -bedingungen›; (*used in experiment*) Versuchs‹tier›; **at the/an ~ stage** im Versuchsstadium; im Experimentierstadium; **B** (*fig.: tentative*) vorläufig; **~ drilling/flight** Probebohrung, *die*/-flug, *der;* **on an ~ basis** versuchsweise

**experimentalist** /ɪksperɪ'mentəlɪst/ *n.* Experimentator, *der*

**experimentally** /ɪksperɪ'mentəlɪ/ *adv.* **A** (*as an experiment*) versuchsweise; **B** (*by experiment*) experimentell

**experimentation** /ɪksperɪmen'teɪʃn/ *n.* Experimentieren, *das*

**experimenter** /ɪk'sperɪmentə(r)/ *n.* Experimentator, *der*

**expert** /'ekspɜ:t/ **1** *adj.* **A** ausgezeichnet; **be ~ in** *or* **at sth.** Fachmann *od.* Experte in etw. (*Dat.*) sein; sich in etw. (*Dat.*) sehr gut auskennen; **be ~ in** *or* **at doing sth.** etw. ausgezeichnet können; **B** (*of an ~*) fachmännisch; **~ witness** sachverständiger Zeuge; **an ~ opinion** die Meinung eines Fachmanns; **~ knowledge** Fachkenntnis, *die;* **cast one's ~ eye over sth.** etw. fachmännisch begutachten; **do an ~ job** fachmännisch arbeiten.

**2** *n.* Fachmann, *der;* Experte, *der*/Expertin, *die;* (*Law*) Sachverständige, *der/die;* **among ~s** unter Fachleuten; in Fachkreisen; **be an ~ in** *or* **at/on sth.** Fachmann *od.* Experte in etw. (*Dat.*)/für etw. sein; **an ~ on the subject** ein Fachmann *od.* Experte auf dem Gebiet; **she's an ~ at solving riddles** sie ist eine Expertin im Rätsellösen; **forensic/mining ~:** Gerichts-/Bergbausachverständige, *der/die*

**expertise** /ekspɜ:'ti:z/ *n.* Fachkenntnisse *Pl.;* (*skill*) Können, *das;* **area of ~:** Fachgebiet, *das*

**expertly** /'ekspɜ:tlɪ/ *adv.* meisterhaft; fachmännisch ‹reparieren, beraten, beurteilen›

**expert: ~ system** *n.* (*Computing*) Expertensystem, *das;* **~ 'witness** *n.* sachverständiger Zeuge

**expiate** /'ekspɪeɪt/ *v.t.* sühnen (*geh.*)

**expiation** /ekspɪ'eɪʃn/ *n.* Sühne, *die* (*geh.*); Buße, *die;* **in ~ of** zur *od.* als Buße für

**expiatory** /'ekspɪeɪtərɪ/ *adj.* **an ~ act** ein Akt der Sühne; **~ sacrifice** Sühneopfer, *das*

**expiration** /ekspɪ'reɪʃn/ *n.* **A** ⇒ **expiry**; **B** (*of air*) Ausatmung, *die*

**expire** /ɪk'spaɪə(r)/ **1** *v.i.* **A** (*become invalid*) ablaufen; ‹Patent, Titel:› erlöschen; ‹Gesetz, Statut:› außer Kraft treten; ‹Gutschein:› verfallen; ‹Vertrag, Amtszeit:› auslaufen; **B** (*literary: die*) versterben (*geh.*). **2** *v.t.* (*exhale*) ausatmen

**expiry** /ɪk'spaɪərɪ/ *n.* ⇒ **expire** 1 A: Ablauf, *der;* Erlöschen, *das;* Außerkrafttreten, *das;* Verfall, *der;* **before/at** *or* **on the ~ of sth.** vor/nach Ablauf einer Sache (*Gen.*); **~ date, date of ~** (*of contract, credit card, etc.*) Ablaufdatum, *das;* (*of voucher, medicine, etc.*) Verfallsdatum, *das*

**explain** /ɪk'spleɪn/ **1** *v.t., also abs.* erklären; erläutern ‹Grund, Motiv, Gedanken›; darlegen ‹Absicht, Beweggrund›; aufklären ‹Geheimnis›; **I need to have it ~ed [to me]** ich brauche eine Erklärung; **be good at ~ing [things]** gut erklären können; **how do you ~ that?** wie erklären Sie sich (*Dat.*) das? **2** *v. refl.* **A** *often abs.* (*justify one's conduct*) **please ~**

**[yourself]** bitte erklären Sie mir das; **he refused to ~:** er wollte mir keine Erklärung dafür geben; **let me ~ [myself]** lassen Sie mich Ihnen das erklären; **I'd better ~ [myself]** ich sollte Ihnen das erklären; **you've got some ~ing to do** Sie müssen mir da einiges erklären; Ⓑ *(make one's meaning clear)* **please ~ yourself** bitte erklären Sie das [näher]

**~ a'way** *v.t.* eine [plausible] Erklärung finden für

**explainable** /ɪk'spleɪnəbl/ *adj.* zu erklärend *nicht präd.*; **be ~:** sich erklären lassen

**explanation** /eksplə'neɪʃn/ *n.* Erklärung, *die;* **need ~:** einer Erklärung *(Gen.)* bedürfen; **in ~ [of sth.]** zur Erklärung [einer Sache *(Gen.)*]; **what is the ~ of this?** wie soll ich mir das erklären?; **some ~ is called for** es bedarf einer Erklärung *(Gen.)*

**explanatory** /ɪk'splænətərɪ/ *adj.* erklärend; erläuternd ‹Bemerkung›

**expletive** /ɪk'spli:tɪv, ek'spli:tɪv/ ❶ *n.* Ⓐ *(oath)* Kraftausdruck, *der;* Ⓑ *(Ling.)* Füllwort, *das;* Expletiv, *das (fachspr.).* ❷ *adj. (Ling.)* füllend; **~ word** Füllwort, *das*

**explicable** /ɪk'splɪkəbl/ *adj.* erklärbar

**explicate** /'eksplɪkeɪt/ *v.t.* Ⓐ *(explain)* erläutern; explizieren *(geh.)*; aufklären ‹Geheimnis›; Ⓑ *(develop meaning of)* ausführen

**explicit** /ɪk'splɪsɪt/ *adj.* Ⓐ *(stated in detail)* ausführlich; *(openly expressed)* offen; unverhüllt; *(definite)* klar; ausdrücklich ‹Zustimmung, Erwähnung›; **please would you be more ~:** bitte drücken Sie sich etwas deutlicher aus; **he did not make his meaning very ~:** er wurde nicht sehr deutlich; **make ~ mention of sth.** etw. ausdrücklich erwähnen; Ⓑ *(Theol.)* **~ faith** Fides explicita, *die*

**explicitly** /ɪk'splɪsɪtlɪ/ *adv.* ausdrücklich; deutlich ‹beschreiben, ausdrücken›; *(in openly expressed manner)* unverhüllt

**explicitness** /ɪk'splɪsɪtnɪs/ *n., no pl.* Deutlichkeit, *die; (open expression)* **with less ~:** weniger deutlich

**explode** /ɪk'spləʊd/ ❶ *v.i.* Ⓐ explodieren; Ⓑ *(fig.)* explodieren; ‹Bevölkerung:› rapide zunehmen; **~ with laughter** in Gelächter ausbrechen. ❷ *v.t.* Ⓐ zur Explosion bringen; Ⓑ *(fig.)* widerlegen ‹Vorstellung, Doktrin, Theorie›

**exploded 'view** *n.* Explosionsdarstellung, *die;* auseinander gezogene Darstellung

**exploit** ❶ /'eksplɔɪt/ *n. (feat; also joc.: deed)* Heldentat, *die.* ❷ /ɪk'splɔɪt/ *v.t.* Ⓐ *(derog.)* ausbeuten ‹Arbeiter, Kolonie usw.›; ausnutzen ‹Gutmütigkeit, Freund, Unwissenheit›; Ⓑ *(utilize)* nutzen; nützen; ausnutzen ‹Gelegenheit, Situation›; ausbeuten ‹Grube›

**exploitation** /eksplɔɪ'teɪʃn/ *n.* Ⓐ *(derog.)* *(of the working classes)* Ausbeutung, *die; (of genius, good nature)* Ausnutzung, *die;* Ⓑ *(utilization)* Nutzung, *die*

**exploitative** /ɪk'splɔɪtətɪv/, **exploitive** /ɪk'splɔɪtɪv/ *adj. (derog.)* ausbeuterisch

**exploration** /eksplə'reɪʃn/ *n.* Ⓐ Erforschung, *die; (of town, house)* Erkundung, *die;* **in the course of his ~s** im Verlauf seiner Erforschung/Erkundung; **voyage of ~:** Entdeckungsreise, *die;* Ⓑ *(fig.)* Untersuchung, *die;* Ⓒ *(Med.)* Untersuchung, *die;* Exploration, *die (fachspr.)*

**explorative** /ɪk'splɒrətɪv/, **exploratory** /ɪk'splɒrətərɪ/ *adjs.* Forschungs-; **~ talks** Sondierungsgespräche; **~ drilling** Suchbohrung, *die;* **~ operation** *(Med.)* explorative Operation; Operation zu diagnostischen Zwecken

**explore** /ɪk'splɔ:(r)/ *v.t.* Ⓐ erforschen; erkunden ‹Stadt, Haus›; **go exploring/out to ~:** auf Entdeckungsreise gehen; Ⓑ *(fig.)* untersuchen; **~ every avenue** alle möglichen Wege prüfen; **~ how the land lies** das Terrain sondieren

**explorer** /ɪk'splɔ:rə(r)/ *n.* Ⓐ Entdeckungsreisende, *der/die;* **Arctic ~:** Arktisforscher, *der/*-forscherin, *die;* **~s of the Nile** Erforscher des Nils; Ⓑ *(Amer.: Scout)* Pfadfinder, *der*

**explosion** /ɪk'spləʊʒn/ *n.* Ⓐ Explosion, *die; (noise)* [Explosions]knall, *der;* Ⓑ *(fig.: of anger etc.)* Ausbruch, *der;* **if the boss gets to hear of this there will be an ~:** wenn das der Chef erfährt, explodiert er; Ⓒ *(rapid increase)* Explosion, *die;* explosionsartiger Anstieg; **~ of population** Bevölkerungsexplosion, *die*

**explosive** /ɪk'spləʊsɪv, ɪk'spləʊzɪv/ ❶ *adj.* Ⓐ explosiv; **highly ~:** hochexplosiv; **~ substance** Explosivstoff, *der;* **~ device** Sprengkörper, *der;* Ⓑ *(fig.)* explosiv; brisant ‹Thema›. ❷ *n.* Sprengstoff, *der;* **high ~:** hochexplosiver Stoff; **~s expert** Sprengstoffexperte, *der/*-expertin, *die*

**explosively** /ɪk'spləʊsɪvlɪ, ɪk'spləʊzɪvlɪ/ *adv. (lit. or fig.)* explosionsartig

**exponent** /ɪk'spəʊnənt/ *n.* Ⓐ *(of doctrine)* Vertreter, *der/*Vertreterin, *die; (representative also)* Exponent, *der/*Exponentin, *die; (of cause)* Verfechter, *der/*Verfechterin, *die;* Ⓑ *(Math.)* Exponent, *der;* Hochzahl, *die;* Ⓒ *(Mus.)* Interpret, *der/*Interpretin, *die*

**exponential** /ekspə'nenʃl/ *adj.* exponentiell; Exponential-; **~ function** *(Math.)* Exponentialfunktion, *die*

**exponentially** /ekspə'nenʃəlɪ/ *adv.* exponentiell

**export** ❶ /ɪk'spɔ:t, 'ekspɔ:t/ *v.t.* exportieren; ausführen; **~ing country** Ausfuhrland, *das;* **~ to other nations/to South Africa** in andere Länder/nach Südafrika exportieren; **oil-~ing countries** [Erd]öl exportierende Länder. ❷ /'ekspɔ:t/ *n.* Ⓐ *(process, amount exported)* Export, *der;* Ausfuhr, *die; (exported articles)* Exportgut, *das;* Ausfuhrgut, *das;* **boost ~s** den Export *od.* die Ausfuhr ankurbeln; **ban on the ~ of grain** Ausfuhrverbot für Getreide; **~s of sugar** Zuckerexporte *od.* -ausfuhren; Ⓑ *attrib.* Export‹leiter, -handel, -markt, -kaufmann›

**exportation** /ekspɔ:'teɪʃn/ *n.* Export, *der;* Ausfuhr, *die*

**export** /'ekspɔ:t/**: ~ drive** *n.* Exportkampagne, *die;* **~ duty** *n.* Exportzoll, *der;* Ausfuhrzoll, *der*

**exporter** /ɪk'spɔ:tə(r), 'ekspɔ:tə(r)/ *n.* Exporteur, *der; (person also)* Exporthändler, *der; (firm also)* Exportfirma, *die; (country)* **be an ~ of coal** Kohle exportieren

**export**/'ekspɔ:t/**: ~ licence** *n.* Ausfuhrlizenz, *die;* **~ permit** *n.* Exporterlaubnis, *die;* Ausfuhrerlaubnis, *die;* **~ 'reject** *n.* [wegen ungenügender Qualität] nicht exportfähige Ware; **~ surplus** *n.* Exportüberschuss, *der*

**expose** /ɪk'spəʊz/ ❶ *v.t.* Ⓐ *(uncover)* freilegen; bloßlegen ‹Draht, Nerv›; entblößen ‹Haut, Körper, Knie›; **~ to view** freilegen; sichtbar machen; Ⓑ *(make known)* offenbaren ‹Schwäche, Tatsache, Geheimnis, Plan›; aufdecken ‹Irrtum, Missstände, Verbrechen, Verrat›; entlarven ‹Täter, Verräter, Spion›; Ⓒ *(subject)* **~ to sth.** einer Sache *(Dat.)* aussetzen; *(acquaint with sth.)* mit etw. vertraut machen; **~ to ridicule** der Lächerlichkeit *(Dat.)* preisgeben; Ⓓ *(Photog.)* belichten; Ⓔ *(leave out of doors to die)* aussetzen.
❷ *v. refl.* sich [unsittlich] entblößen

**exposé** /ek'spəʊzeɪ/ *n.* Ⓐ *(of facts)* Exposé, *das;* Ⓑ *(of sth. discreditable)* Enthüllung, *die; (of crime)* Aufdeckung, *die*

**exposed** /ɪk'spəʊzd/ *adj.* Ⓐ *(unprotected)* ungeschützt; **~ to the wind/elements** dem Wind/den Elementen ausgesetzt; **~ position** *(lit. or fig.)* exponierte Stellung; Ⓑ *(visible)* freigelegt; sichtbar ‹Körperteil›; Ⓒ *(Photog.)* belichtet

**exposition** /ekspə'zɪʃn/ *n.* Ⓐ *(statement, presentation)* Darstellung, *die; (commentary)* Kommentar, *der* **(of** zu); *(explanation)* Erläuterung, *die* **(of** zu); *(act of expounding)* **~ of heretical views** Verbreitung ketzerischer Ansichten; Ⓑ *(Mus., Lit.: of principal themes)* Exposition, *die;* Ⓒ *(exhibition)* Ausstellung, *die*

**expostulate** /ɪk'spɒstjʊleɪt/ *v.i.* protestieren; **~ with sb. about** *or* **on sth.** mit jmdm. über etw. *(Akk.)* debattieren

**expostulation** /ɪkspɒstjʊ'leɪʃn/ *n.* Protest, *der*

**exposure** /ɪk'spəʊʒə(r)/ *n.* Ⓐ *(to air, cold, etc.)* *(being exposed)* Ausgesetztsein, *das; (exposing)* Aussetzen, *das; (of goods etc.)* Ausstellung, *die; (of children)* Aussetzung, *die;* **die of/suffer from ~ [to cold]** an Unterkühlung *(Dat.)* sterben/leiden; **~ to infection** Kontakt mit Krankheitserregern; **indecent ~:** Entblößung in schamverletzender Weise; **media ~:** Publicity, *die;* Ⓑ *(unmasking) (of fraud etc.)* Enthüllung, *die; (of criminal)* Entlarvung, *die; (of hypocrite or hypocrisy)* Bloßstellung, *die;* Ⓒ *(Photog.) (exposing time)* Belichtung, *die; (picture)* Aufnahme, *die*

**ex'posure meter** *n. (Photog.)* Belichtungsmesser, *der*

**expound** /ɪk'spaʊnd/ *v.t.* Ⓐ darlegen ‹These, Theorie, Doktrin› **(to** *Dat.***)**; Ⓑ *(explain)* auslegen ‹Schriften, Gesetz› **(to** *Dat.***)**

**express** /ɪk'spres/ ❶ *v.t.* Ⓐ *(indicate)* ausdrücken; Ⓑ *(put into words)* äußern, zum Ausdruck bringen ‹Meinung, Wunsch, Dank, Bedauern, Liebe›; **~ sth. in another language** etw. in einer anderen Sprache ausdrücken; **~ oneself** sich ausdrücken; **he ~ed himself strongly on that subject** er äußerte sich sehr entschieden zu diesem Thema; **~ one's willingness** *or* **readiness to do sth.** sich bereit erklären, etw. zu tun; Ⓒ *(represent by symbols)* ausdrücken ‹Zahl, Wert›; Ⓓ *(squeeze)* [heraus]drücken; [heraus]pressen; Ⓔ *(send by ~ delivery)* als Schnellsendung schicken.
❷ *attrib. adj.* Ⓐ Eil‹brief, -bote usw.›; Schnell‹paket, -sendung›; ⇒ *also* **~ train;** Ⓑ *(particular)* besonder...; bestimmt; ausdrücklich ‹Absicht›; Ⓒ *(stated)* ausdrücklich ‹Wunsch, Befehl usw.›.
❸ *adv.* als Eilsache ‹senden›.
❹ *n.* Ⓐ *(train)* Schnellzug, *der;* D-Zug, *der; (messenger)* Eilbote, *der;* **by ~:** durch Eilboten, Ⓑ *(Amer.: company)* Transportunternehmen, *das*

**express: ~ company** *n. (Amer.)* Transportunternehmen, *das;* **~ de'livery** *n.* Eilzustellung, *die*

**expression** /ɪk'spreʃn/ *n.* Ⓐ Ausdruck, *der;* **find ~ in sth.** in etw. *(Dat.)* Ausdruck finden *od.* zum Ausdruck kommen; **give ~ to one's gratitude** seine Dankbarkeit zum Ausdruck bringen; seiner Dankbarkeit *(Dat.)* Ausdruck verleihen *(geh.)*; **manner** *or* **mode of ~:** Ausdrucksweise, *die;* **profuse ~s of gratitude** überschwängliche Dankesbezeugungen; **the ~ on his face** *or* **his facial ~ was one of deepest hatred** sein Gesichtsausdruck zeugte von tiefstem Hass; tiefster Hass stand ihm im Gesicht geschrieben; **full of/without ~:** ausdrucksvoll/-los; **devoid of all ~:** völlig ausdruckslos; **she put a martyred ~ on her face** sie setzte ihre Duldermiene auf; Ⓑ *(Art, Mus., Math.)* Ausdruck, *der;* **play/sing with ~:** ausdrucksvoll *od.* -stark spielen/singen

**expressionism** /ɪk'spreʃənɪzm/ *n., no pl.* Expressionismus, *der*

**expressionist** /ɪk'spreʃənɪst/ *n.* Expressionist, *der/*Expressionistin, *die; attrib.* expressionistisch ‹Kunst usw.›

**expressionistic** /ɪkspreʃə'nɪstɪk/ *adj.* expressionistisch

**expressionless** /ɪk'spreʃnlɪs/ *adj.* ausdruckslos

**ex'pression mark** *n. (Mus.)* Vortragsbezeichnung, *die*

**expressive** /ɪk'spresɪv/ *adj.* Ⓐ **be ~ of sth.** etw. ausdrücken; Ⓑ *(significant)* ausdrucksvoll; viel sagend ‹Schweigen›; expressiv *(geh.)*, ausdrucksvoll ‹Geste›

**expressively** /ɪk'spresɪvlɪ/ *adv.* ausdrucksvoll

**express: ~ 'letter** *n.* Eilbrief, *der;* **~ 'lift** *n.* Schnellaufzug, *der*

**expressly** /ɪk'spreslɪ/ *adv.* Ⓐ *(particularly)* ausdrücklich; Ⓑ *(definitely)* eindeutig; ausdrücklich

**express: ~ 'train** *n.* Schnellzug, *der;* D-Zug, *der;* **~way** *n. (Amer.)* Schnell[verkehrs]straße, *die*

**expropriate** /eks'prəʊprɪeɪt/ *v.t.* enteignen; ‹Staat usw.:› verstaatlichen

**expropriation** /ekspraʊprɪˈeɪʃn/ *n.* Enteignung, *die;* Expropriation, *die* (*veralt.*); (*esp. by State*) Verstaatlichung, *die*

**expulsion** /ɪkˈspʌlʃn/ *n.* (*from school, college*) Verweisung, *die* (**from** von); Relegation, *die* (**from** von); (*from home, homeland*) Vertreibung, *die* (**from** aus); (*from country*) Ausweisung, *die* (**from** aus); (*from club*) Ausschluss, *der* (**from** aus); (*Med.: from the body*) Austreibung, *die* (**from** aus); (*of gas, water, etc. from substance*) Austreiben, *das* (**from** aus)

**expunge** /ɪkˈspʌndʒ/ *v.t.* [aus]streichen (**from** aus); (*fig.*) tilgen (**from** aus)

**expurgate** /ˈekspəgeɪt/ *v.t.* (*purify*) zensieren, (*verhüll.*) säubern ‹Text, Buch, Theaterstück›; **~d version/edition** zensierte *od.* (*verhüll.*) bereinigte Fassung/Ausgabe

**exquisite** /ˈekskwɪzɪt, ɪkˈskwɪzɪt/ *adj.* **A** erlesen; exquisit, bezaubernd ‹Aussicht, Landschaft, Muster, Melodie, Frau, Anmut›; ausgesucht ‹Höflichkeit›; **B** (*acute*) heftig ‹Schmerz, Freude›; riesig ‹Triumph›; unerträglich ‹Leiden, Schmerzen›

**exquisitely** /ˈekskwɪzɪtlɪ, ɪkˈskwɪzɪtlɪ/ *adv.* **A** (*excellently, beautifully*) vorzüglich; kunstvoll ‹verziert, geschnitzt›; **B** (*acutely*) äußerst; außerordentlich

**ex-ˈservice** *adj.* (*Brit.*) Veteranen-; **~man** ehemaliger Soldat

**ext.** *abbr.* **A exterior; B external; C [telephone] extension** App.

**extant** /ekˈstænt, ˈekstənt/ *adj.* [noch] vorhanden *od.* existent

**extemporaneous** /ɪkstempəˈreɪnɪəs/ *adj.* improvisiert; **~ translation** Stegreifübersetzung, *die*

**extempore** /ɪkˈstempərɪ/ **1** *adv.* aus dem Stegreif; ex tempore (*Theater, geh.*); **speak ~:** frei sprechen; extemporieren. **2** *adj.* improvisiert ‹Gedicht, Lied›; **give an ~ speech** eine Rede aus dem Stegreif *od.* eine Stegreifrede halten

**extemporisation, extemporise** ⇒ **extemporiz-**

**extemporization** /ɪkstempəraɪˈzeɪʃn/ *n.* Improvisation, *die;* Extempore, *das*

**extemporize** /ɪkˈstempəraɪz/ *v.t. & i.* improvisieren; extemporieren

**extend** /ɪkˈstend/ **1** *v.t.* **A** (*stretch out*) ausstrecken ‹Arm, Bein, Hand›; ausziehen ‹Leiter, Teleskop›; spannen ‹Seil›; ausbreiten ‹Flügel›; **~ one's hand to sb.** jmdm. die Hand reichen *od.* entgegenstrecken; **the table can be ~ed** der Tisch ist ausziehbar; **B** (*make longer*) (*in space*) verlängern; ausdehnen ‹Grenze›; ausbauen ‹Bahnlinie, Straße›; (*in time*) verlängern; verlängern lassen ‹Leihbuch, Visum›; **~ a credit** Kreditverlängerung gewähren; **~ the time limit** den Termin hinausschieben; **C** (*enlarge*) ausdehnen ‹Einfluss, Macht, Forschung[sgebiet]›; erweitern ‹Wissen, Wortschatz, Bedeutung, Freundeskreis, Besitz, Geschäft›; verlängern ‹Aufsatz, Referat›; ausbauen, vergrößern ‹Haus, Geschäft, Fabrik, Unternehmen›; **D** (*offer*) gewähren, zuteil werden lassen ‹[Gast]freundschaft, Schutz, Gunst, Hilfe, Kredit› (**to** *Dat.*); erweisen ‹Freundlichkeit, Gefallen› (**to** *Dat.*); (*accord*) aussprechen ‹Dank, Einladung, Glückwunsch› (**to** *Dat.*); ausrichten ‹Gruß› (**to** *Dat.*); **~ a welcome to sb.** jmdn. willkommen heißen; **E** (*tax*) fordern; **~ oneself** sich verausgaben.

**2** *v.i.* sich erstrecken; **the wall ~s for miles** die Mauer zieht sich meilenweit hin; **the bridge ~s over the river** die Brücke führt über den Fluss; **the road ~s from X to Y** die Straße führt von X nach Y; **the winter season ~s from November to March** die Wintersaison währt von November bis März; **negotiations ~ed over weeks** die Verhandlungen zogen sich über Wochen *od.* wochenlang hin; **the problem ~s to other fields as well** das Problem berührt auch andere Bereiche

**extended** /ɪkˈstendɪd/: **~ ˈfamily** *n.* Großfamilie, *die;* **~-play** *adj.* EP-‹Platte, Band›

**extendible** /ɪkˈstendɪbl/, **extensible** /ɪkˈstensɪbl/ *adjs.* [aus]dehnbar ‹Stoff›; ausziehbar ‹Fernrohr, Leiter›; erweiterungsfähig ‹Gebäude, Gewerbe, Firma, Industrie›

**extension** /ɪkˈstenʃn/ *n.* **A** (*stretching out*) (*of arm, leg, hand*) [Aus]strecken, *das;* (*of wings*) Ausbreiten, *das;* (*of muscle*) Streckung, *die;* **B** (*extent*) Umfang, *der;* (*range*) Reichweite, *die;* **C** (*prolonging*) Verlängerung, *die;* (*of road, railway*) Ausbau, *der;* **~ of time** Fristverlängerung, *die;* **ask for an ~:** um Verlängerung bitten; Verlängerung beantragen; **be granted** *or* **get an ~:** Verlängerung bekommen; **D** (*enlargement*) (*of power, influence, research, frontier*) Ausdehnung, *die;* (*of enterprise, trade, knowledge*) Erweiterung, *die;* (*of house, estate*) Ausbau, *der;* **E** (*additional part*) (*of house*) Anbau, *der;* (*of office, university, hospital, etc.*) Erweiterungsbau, *der;* **build an ~ to a hospital** einen Erweiterungsbau zu einem Krankenhaus errichten; ein Krankenhaus ausbauen; **two ~s** zwei Anbauten; **F** (*telephone*) Nebenanschluss, *der;* Fernsprechnebenstelle, *die* (*fachspr.*); (*number*) Apparat, *der;* **G ~ course** (*correspondence course*) Fernstudium, *das*

**extension: ~ cord** (*Amer.*) ⇒ **~ lead; ~ ladder** *n.* Ausziehleiter, *die;* **~ lead** *n.* (*Brit.*) Verlängerungsschnur, *die*

**extensive** /ɪkˈstensɪv/ *adj.* ausgedehnt ‹Ländereien, Reisen, Stadt, Wald, Besitz[tümer], Handel, Forschungen›; extensiv ‹Wirtschaft›; weit ‹Land[strich], Meer[esfläche], Blick›; umfangreich ‹Reparatur, Investitionen, Wissen, Nachforschungen, Studien, Auswahl, Angebot, Sammlung›; beträchtlich ‹Schäden, Geldmittel, Anstrengungen›; weit reichend ‹Änderungen, Reformen, Einfluss, Machtbefugnis, Unterstützung›; langwierig ‹Operation, Unternehmung, Suche›; ausführlich ‹Bericht, Einleitung›; **make ~ use of sth.** von etw. ausgiebig Gebrauch machen

**extensively** /ɪkˈstensɪvlɪ/ *adv.* beträchtlich ‹ändern, beschädigen›; gründlich ‹reparieren›; ausführlich ‹berichten, schreiben›; **they used these rooms ~:** sie machten ausgiebig von diesen Räumen Gebrauch

**extent** /ɪkˈstent/ *n.* **A** (*space over which sth. extends*) Ausdehnung, *die;* (*of wings*) Spannweite, *die;* **B** (*scope*) (*of damage, debt, knowledge, power, authority*) Umfang, *der;* (*of influence, genius*) Größe, *die;* (*of damage, loss, disaster, power, authority*) Ausmaß, *das;* **losses to the ~ of £100** Verluste in Höhe von 100 Pfund; **to what ~?** inwieweit?; in welchem Maße?; **the full ~ of his power** seine ganze Machtfülle; **to a great** *or* **large/small** *or* **slight ~:** in hohem/geringem Maße; **to some** *or* **a certain ~:** in gewissem Maße; **to the same ~ as ...:** im selben Maße wie ...; **to a greater/lesser ~:** in höherem/geringerem Maße; **to a greater or lesser ~:** mehr oder weniger; **to such an ~ that ...:** in solchem Maße, dass ...; **her condition has not improved to any [great] ~:** ihr Zustand hat sich [fast] überhaupt nicht gebessert; **C** (*area of sea, land*) Weite, *die;* **you can see the whole ~ of the park** man kann den Park in seiner ganzen Ausdehnung sehen

**extenuate** /ɪkˈstenjʊeɪt/ *v.t.* verharmlosen, beschönigen ‹Vergehen, Verbrechen, Fehler, Schuld›; entschuldigen ‹Benehmen›; **extenuating circumstances** mildernde Umstände

**extenuation** /ɪkstenjʊˈeɪʃn/ *n.* (*of crime, offence, fault, guilt*) Verharmlosung, *die;* Beschönigung, *die;* **in ~ of sth./sb.** als Entschuldigung für etw./jmdn.

**exterior** /ɪkˈstɪərɪə(r)/ **1** *adj.* **A** äußer...; Außen‹fläche, -wand, -anstrich›; **~ varnish** Lack für Außenanstriche; **B** ([*coming from*] *outside*) äußer...; außerhalb gelegen; **C** (*Cinemat.*) **~ scene** Außenaufnahme, *die.* **2** *n.* **A** Äußere, *das;* (*of house*) Außenwände *Pl.;* **B** (*appearance*) Äußere, *das;* **a man with a pleasant/rough ~:** ein Mann von angenehmem/ungeschlachtem Äußerem; **judge people by their ~:** Menschen nach ihrem Äußeren beurteilen; **C** (*Cinemat.*) Außenaufnahme, *die*

**exterminate** /ɪkˈstɜːmɪneɪt/ *v.t.* ausrotten; vertilgen, vernichten ‹Ungeziefer›

**extermination** /ɪkstɜːmɪˈneɪʃn/ *n.* Ausrottung, *die;* (*of pests*) Vertilgung, *die;* Vernichtung, *die*

**external** /ɪkˈstɜːnl/ **1** *adj.* **A** äußer...; Außen‹fläche, -wirkung, -druck, -winkel, -durchmesser, -abmessungen›; **give the ~ appearance of ease** äußerlich einen ungezwungenen Eindruck machen; **purely ~:** nur *od.* rein äußerlich; **B** (*applied to outside*) äußerlich ‹Heilmittel›; **for ~ use only** nur äußerlich anzuwenden; nur zur äußerlichen Anwendung; **C** (*of foreign affairs*) Außen‹minister, -handel, -wirtschaft, -politik›; **Ministry of E~ Affairs** Außenministerium, *das;* Ministerium für auswärtige Angelegenheiten *od.* des Auswärtigen; **D** (*Univ.*) extern; **~ student** Externe, *der/die;* **do ~ studies/an ~ degree** ein Fernstudium absolvieren; **E** (*of world of phenomena*) äußer...; **the ~ world** die Welt der Erscheinungen; **F ~ evidence** sich auf äußere Umstände gründender Beweis.

**2** *n. in pl.* Äußerlichkeiten *Pl.*

**externalize (externalise)** /ɪkˈstɜːnəlaɪz/ *v.t.* nach außen projizieren; (*Philos.*) veräußerlichen; (*Psych.*) externalisieren

**externally** /ɪkˈstɜːnəlɪ/ *adv.* äußerlich; **the medicine is only to be used ~:** die Medizin ist nur zur äußerlichen Anwendung [bestimmt]; **be ~ calm** äußerlich *od.* nach außen hin ruhig sein; **the work is done ~:** die Arbeit wird außer Haus[e] erledigt

**extinct** /ɪkˈstɪŋkt/ *adj.* erloschen ‹Vulkan, Feuer, Leidenschaft, Liebe, Hoffnung›; ausgestorben ‹Art, Rasse, Volk, Gattung, Leben›; untergegangen ‹Volk, Dynastie, Reich, Kultur, Sitte, Brauch›; abgeschafft ‹Einrichtung, Amt, Posten, System, Gesetz›; tot ‹Sprache›; **become ~** ‹Art, Rasse, Volk, Gattung:› aussterben; ‹Vulkan, Hoffnung, Adelstitel:› erlöschen

**extinction** /ɪkˈstɪŋkʃn/ *n., no pl.* (*of fire, light*) (*extinguishing*) Löschen, *das;* (*being extinguished*) Erlöschen, *das;* Verlöschen, *das;* (*abolition*) (*of religion, system, institution, law, custom*) Abschaffung, *die;* (*of debt*) Tilgung, *die;* (*of independence etc.*) Aufhebung, *die;* **threatened with ~:** vom Aussterben bedroht

**extinguish** /ɪkˈstɪŋgwɪʃ/ *v.t.* **A** löschen; erlöschen lassen ‹Leidenschaft, Hoffnung›; auslöschen ‹Leben›; **B** (*destroy*) beseitigen

**extinguisher** /ɪkˈstɪŋgwɪʃə(r)/ *n.* **A** (*for fire*) Feuerlöscher, *der;* **B** (*for candle*) Löschhütchen, *das*

**extirpate** /ˈekstɜːpeɪt/ *v.t.* [mit der Wurzel] ausreißen ‹Pflanze, Haare›; entfernen ‹Tumor›; ausrotten ‹Rasse, Volk, Sekte, Gattung›; aufräumen mit, ausmerzen ‹Ketzerei, Unsitten, Vorurteil›

**extol** /ɪkˈstəʊl, ɪkˈstɒl/ *v.t.*, **-ll-** rühmen; preisen

**extort** /ɪkˈstɔːt/ *v.t.* erpressen (**out of, from** von); **~ a secret/confession from sb.** ein Geheimnis/Geständnis aus jmdm. herauspressen

**extortion** /ɪkˈstɔːʃn/ *n.* **A** (*of money, taxes*) Erpressung, *die;* **£50? This is sheer ~!** 50 Pfund? Das ist ja Wucher!; **B** (*illegal exaction*) Erpressung im Amt

**extortionate** /ɪkˈstɔːʃənət/ *adj.* **A** (*excessive, exorbitant*) Wucher‹preis, -zinsen usw.›; horrend ‹Gebühr, Steuer›; maßlos überzogen ‹Forderung›; **B** (*using extortion*) erpresserisch ‹Methode›

**extortioner** /ɪkˈstɔːʃənə(r)/ *n.* Erpresser, *der*/Erpresserin, *die*

**extra** /ˈekstrə/ **1** *adj.* **A** (*additional*) zusätzlich; Mehr‹arbeit, -kosten, -ausgaben, -aufwendungen›; Sonder‹bus, -zug›; **~ hours of work** Überstunden; **all we need is an ~ hour/three pounds** wir brauchen nur noch eine Stunde/drei Pfund [zusätzlich]; **~ charge** Aufpreis, *der;* **drinks are ~:** Getränke werden extra bezahlt *od.* (*ugs.*) gehen extra; **make an ~ effort** sich besonders anstrengen; **take ~ care** besonders vorsichtig sein; **for ~ safety** als zusätzliche *od.* besondere Sicherheitsvorkehrung; **can I have an ~ helping?** kann ich noch eine Portion haben?; **B** (*more than is necessary*) überzählig ‹Exemplar, Portion›; **an ~ pair of gloves** noch ein *od.* ein zweites Paar Handschuhe; **have an ~ bed** noch ein Bett frei *od.* ein unbenutztes Bett haben; **we have an ~ ten minutes to kill** wir müssen noch zehn Minuten mehr totschlagen.

**2** *adv.* **A** (*more than usually*) besonders; extra‹lang, -stark, -fein›; überaus ‹froh›; **an ~ large blouse** eine Bluse in Übergröße; **an ~**

**special occasion** eine ganz besondere Gelegenheit; B (*additionally*) extra; **packing and postage ~:** zuzüglich Verpackung und Porto.

❸ *n.* A (*added to services, salary, etc.*) zusätzliche Leistung; (*on car etc. offered for sale*) Extra, *das;* (*adornment on dress etc.*) besondere Note; (*outside normal school curriculum*) zusätzliches Angebot; B (*sth. with ~ charge*) **be an ~:** zusätzlich berechnet werden; C (*in play, film, etc.*) Statist, *der*/Statistin, *die;* Komparse, *der*/Komparsin, *die;* D (*Cricket*) *Lauf, der nicht durch Schlag erzielt wird*

**extra-** /ekstrə/ *pref.* außer-; extra- (*mit Fremdwörtern lateinischen Ursprungs*)

**extract** ❶ /ˈekstrækt/ *n.* A Extrakt, *der* (*fachspr. auch: das*); **an ~ of certain plants** ein Auszug *od.* Extrakt aus bestimmten Pflanzen; B (*from book, music, etc.*) Auszug, *der;* Extrakt, *der* (*geh.*); **in ~s** auszugsweise; im Extrakt (*geh.*). ❷ /ɪkˈstrækt/ *v.t.* A ziehen, (*fachspr.*) extrahieren ‹Zahn›; herausziehen ‹Dorn, Splitter usw.›; **~ a bullet from a wound** eine Kugel aus einer Wunde entfernen; **she ~ed herself from his embrace** sie befreite *od.* löste sich aus seiner Umarmung; **~ sth. from sb.** (*fig.*) etw. aus jmdm. herausholen; **~ a promise/confession from sb.** jmdm. ein Versprechen/Geständnis abpressen; **~ papers from a folder** einem Aktenordner Unterlagen entnehmen; B (*obtain*) extrahieren; **~ the juice of apples** Äpfel entsaften; **~ sugar from beet** aus Rüben Zucker gewinnen; **~ oil from the earth** Erdöl fördern; **~ metal from ore/honey from the honeycomb** Metall aus Erz/Honig aus der Wabe gewinnen; C (*derive*) erfassen ‹Bedeutung, Hauptpunkte›; **~ happiness/pleasure/comfort from sth.** Fröhlichkeit/Freude/Trost aus etw. schöpfen; **~ much pleasure from life** dem Leben viel Freude abgewinnen; D (*Math.*) ziehen ‹Wurzel›

**extraction** /ɪkˈstrækʃn/ *n.* A (*of tooth; also Chem.*) Extraktion, *die;* (*of thorn, splinter, etc.*) Herausziehen, *das;* (*of bullet*) Entfernen, *das;* (*of juice, honey, metal*) Gewinnung, *die;* (*of oil*) Förderung, *die;* B (*descent*) Abstammung, *die;* Herkunft, *die;* **be of German ~:** deutscher Abstammung *od.* Herkunft sein

**extractive** /ɪkˈstræktɪv/ *adj.* **~ industries** Rohstoffindustrie, *die;* **~ processes** Extraktionsverfahren *Pl.*

**extractor** /ɪkˈstræktə(r)/ *n.* (*for extracting juice*) Entsafter, *der*

**exˈtractor fan** *n.* Entlüfter, *der;* Exhaustor, *der*

**extra-curricular** /ekstrəkəˈrɪkjʊlə(r)/ *adj.* extracurricular (*fachspr.*); ‹Aktivität› außerhalb des Lehrplans

**extraditable** /ekstrəˈdaɪtəbl/ *adj.* **this is an ~ offence** für dieses Vergehen kann man ausgeliefert werden

**extradite** /ˈekstrədaɪt/ *v.t.* A ausliefern ‹Verbrecher›; B (*obtain extradition of*) **~ sb.** jmds. Auslieferung erwirken

**extradition** /ekstrəˈdɪʃn/ *n.* Auslieferung, *die;* **~ treaty** Auslieferungsvertrag, *der*

**extraˈmarital** *adj.* außerehelich

**extraˈmural** *adj.* (*Univ.*) außerhalb der Universität *nachgestellt;* außeruniversitär; **~ courses** *or* **classes** Hochschulkurse außerhalb der Universität; Fernkurse

**extraneous** /ɪkˈstreɪnɪəs/ *adj.* A (*from outside*) von außen; (*Med.*) körperfremd; **free from ~ matter** frei von Fremdstoffen; B (*irrelevant*) belanglos; **be ~ to sth.** für etw. ohne Belang sein

**extraordinarily** /ɪkˈstrɔːdɪnərɪlɪ, ekstrəˈɔːdɪnərəlɪ/ *adv.* außergewöhnlich; überaus, ungemein ‹merkwürdig›

**extraordinary** /ɪkˈstrɔːdɪnərɪ, ekstrəˈɔːdɪnərɪ/ *adj.* A (*exceptional*) außergewöhnlich; (*unusual, peculiar*) ungewöhnlich ‹Gabe›; merkwürdig, eigenartig ‹Zeichen, Benehmen, Angewohnheit›; außerordentlich ‹Verdienste, Einfluss›; (*additional*) außerordentlich ‹Versammlung›; **how ~!** wie seltsam!; B (*more than ordinary*) ungewöhnlich; **~ powers** außerordentliche Vollmachten; C (*specially employed*) außerordentlich ‹Gesandte[r], Professor[in]›; **ambassador ~:** Sonderbotschafter, *der*

**extraˈordinary general meeting** *n.* (*of shareholders*) außerordentliche Hauptversammlung; (*of club*) außerordentliche Mitgliederversammlung

**extrapolate** /ɪkˈstræpəleɪt/ (*Math. etc.*) ❶ *v.t.* extrapolieren (**to** auf + *Akk.*, **from** aus); (*fig.*) ableiten; extrapolieren (*geh.*). ❷ *v.i.* extrapolieren

**extra: ~-ˈsensory** *adj.* außersinnlich; **~-sensory perception** außersinnliche Wahrnehmung; **~terˈrestrial** *adj.* außerirdisch; ex[tra]terrestrisch (*fachspr.*); **~terriˈtorial** *adj.* exterritorial

**extra ˈtime** *n.* (*Sport*) **after ~:** nach einer Verlängerung; **the match went to ~:** das Spiel wurde verlängert; **play ~:** in die Verlängerung gehen

**extravagance** /ɪkˈstrævəgəns/ *n.* A *no pl.* (*being extravagant*) Extravaganz, *die;* (*of claim, wish, order, demand*) Übertriebenheit, *die;* (*of words, thoughts, ideas, etc.*) Verstiegenheit, *die;* (*with money*) Verschwendungssucht, *die;* **the ~ of her tastes** ihr teurer Geschmack; B (*extravagant thing*) Luxus, *der*

**extravagancy** /ɪkˈstrævəgənsɪ/ ⇒ **extravagance A**

**extravagant** /ɪkˈstrævəgənt/ *adj.* A (*wasteful*) verschwenderisch; aufwendig ‹Lebensstil›; teuer ‹Geschmack›; B (*immoderate*) übertrieben ‹Benehmen, Lob, Eifer, Begeisterung usw.›; maßlos ‹Gebrauch, Begeisterung›; C (*beyond bounds of reason*) abwegig ‹Theorie, Frage, Einfall›; **it is not ~ to suppose that …:** die Vermutung liegt nahe, dass …; D (*exorbitant*) überhöht ‹Preis›

**extravagantly** /ɪkˈstrævəgəntlɪ/ *adv.* extravagant ‹einrichten, ausstatten, sich kleiden›; verschwenderisch ‹benutzen, verbrauchen›; luxuriös, aufwendig ‹leben›; außergewöhnlich ‹sich benehmen›; überschwänglich ‹loben›; **spend money ~:** mit vollen Händen Geld ausgeben

**extravaganza** /ɪkstrævəˈgænzə/ *n.* (*composition*) (*Lit.*) fantastische Dichtung; (*Mus.*) fantastische Komposition; (*Theatre*) Ausstattungsstück, *das*

**ˈextra-virgin** *adj.* [extra]nativ ‹Olivenöl›

**extreme** /ɪkˈstriːm/ ❶ *adj.* A (*outermost, utmost*) äußerst… ‹Spitze, Rand, Ende›; extrem, krass ‹Gegensätze›; **the ~ end of the finger** die Fingerspitze *od.* -kuppe; **the ~ points of a line/scale** die Endpunkte einer Linie/Skala; **at the ~ edge/left** ganz am Rand/ganz links; **in the ~ North** im äußersten Norden; B (*reaching high degree*) extrem; gewaltig ‹Entfernung, Unterschied›; höchst… ‹Gefahr›; äußerst… ‹Notfall, Grenzen, Höflichkeit, Bescheidenheit›; stärkst… ‹Schmerzen›; heftigst… ‹Zorn›; tiefst… ‹Hass, Dankbarkeit›; größt… ‹Überraschung, Wichtigkeit, Wunsch›; stürmisch ‹Begeisterung›; C (*not moderate*) extrem ‹Person, Einstellung, Gesinnung, Forderungen, Ideen, Tendenzen, Kritik›; **~ right-wing views** rechtsextreme Ansichten; D (*RC & Orthodox Ch.*) **~ unction** die Letzte Ölung; E (*severe*) drastisch ‹Maßnahme›; **take ~ action against sb.** rigoros gegen jmdn. vorgehen.

❷ *n.* Extrem, *das;* [krasser] Gegensatz; **~s of heat and cold** extreme Hitze und Kälte; **the ~s of wealth and poverty** größter Reichtum und äußerste Armut; **~s of passion** extreme Pole der Leidenschaft; **~s of temperature** extreme Temperaturunterschiede; **go to the ~ of doing sth.** bis zum Äußersten gehen und etw. tun; **go to ~s** *or* **to any ~** *or* **to the last ~:** vor nichts zurückschrecken; **go to the other ~:** ins andere Extrem verfallen; **go from one ~ to another** von *od.* aus einem Extrem ins andere fallen; **annoying/monotonous in the ~:** äußerst unangenehm/extrem *od.* äußerst eintönig; **run to ~s** einen Hang zum Extremen haben; ⇒ *also* **carry 1 G**

**extremely** /ɪkˈstriːmlɪ/ *adv.* äußerst; **Did you enjoy the party? — Yes, ~:** Hat dir die Party gefallen? — Ja, sehr sogar!

**extremeness** /ɪkˈstriːmnɪs/ *n., no pl.* (*of views, actions, policies*) Extremität, *die;* (*of measures*) Härte, *die*

**extremism** /ɪkˈstriːmɪzm/ *n., no pl.* Extremismus, *der*

**extremist** /ɪkˈstriːmɪst/ *n.* A Extremist, *der*/Extremistin, *die;* **right-wing ~:** Rechtsextremist, *der*/-extremistin, *die;* B *attrib.* extremistisch

**extremity** /ɪkˈstremɪtɪ/ *n.* A (*of branch, path, road*) äußerstes Ende; (*of region*) Rand, *der;* **the southernmost ~ of a continent** die Südspitze eines Kontinents; B *in pl.* (*hands and feet*) Extremitäten *Pl.;* C (*adversity*) äußerste *od.* höchste Not; (*intensity*) Heftigkeit, *die;* **be reduced to ~:** in eine Notlage geraten

**extricate** /ˈekstrɪkeɪt/ *v.t.* **~ sth. from sth.** etw. aus etw. herausziehen; **~ oneself/sb. from sth.** sich/jmdn. aus etw. befreien

**extrinsic** /ekˈstrɪnsɪk/ *adj.* A äußer…; äußerlich ‹Wert›; extrinsisch (*Philos.*); **be ~ to sth.** einer Sache (*Dat.*) fremd sein; B (*not essential*) irrelevant (**to** für)

**extrovert** /ˈekstrəvɜːt/ ❶ *n.* extravertierter Mensch; Extravertierte, *der/die;* **be an ~:** extravertiert sein. ❷ *adj.* extravertiert; **have ~ tendencies** zur Extravertiertheit neigen

**extroverted** /ˈekstrəvɜːtɪd/ *adj.* extravertiert

**extrude** /ɪkˈstruːd/ *v.t.* ausstoßen; ausstrecken ‹Fühler›; extrudieren (*fachspr.*) ‹Metall, Kunststoff›; (*Geol.*) auswerfen ‹Gestein›; (*fig.: expel*) ausschließen (**from** aus)

**extrusion** /ɪkˈstruːʒn/ *n.* (*of metal, plastic, etc.*) Extrudieren, *das* (*fachspr.*); (*article extruded*) Formstück, *das*

**exuberance** /ɪgˈzjuːbərəns/ *n.* A (*vigour*) Überschwang, *der;* (*of health*) Robustheit, *die;* **~ of joy/spirits** überschwängliche Freude/Stimmung; **~ of youth** jugendlicher Überschwang; B (*of language, style*) Lebendigkeit, *die*

**exuberant** /ɪgˈzjuːbərənt/ *adj.* A (*overflowing, abounding*) strotzend ‹Gesundheit›; überschäumend ‹Kraft, Freude, Eifer, Heiterkeit›; B (*effusive*) überschwänglich; sehr lebhaft ‹Farbe›; **he was ~ when …:** er freute sich überschwänglich, als …

**exuberantly** /ɪgˈzjuːbərəntlɪ/ *adv.* überschwänglich ‹begrüßen, beschreiben›; **~ happy** überglücklich

**exude** /ɪgˈzjuːd/ ❶ *v.i.* abgesondert werden (**from** aus); ‹Blut:› fließen (**from** aus); (*fig.*) ausgehen (**from** von). ❷ *v.t.* absondern ‹Flüssigkeit, Harz›; ausströmen ‹Geruch›; (*fig.*) ausstrahlen ‹Charme, Zuversicht›

**exult** /ɪgˈzʌlt/ *v.i.* A (*literary: rejoice*) jubeln; frohlocken (*geh.*) (**in, at, over** über + *Akk.*); **~ to find that …:** darüber frohlocken, dass …; **~ with joy** vor Freude jubeln; B (*triumph*) triumphieren (**over** über + *Akk.*)

**exultant** /ɪgˈzʌltənt/ *adj.* A (*literary: exulting*) jubelnd ‹Person, Menge, Lachen›; unbändig ‹Freude›; **be ~:** jubeln; **be in an ~ mood** in Hochstimmung sein; B (*triumphant*) triumphierend ‹Sieger›

**exultantly** /ɪgˈzʌltəntlɪ/ *adv.* überglücklich

**exultation** /egzʌlˈteɪʃn/ *n.* Jubel, *der*

**eye** /aɪ/ ❶ *n.* A ▸ **966** Auge, *das;* **as far as the ~ can see** so weit das Auge reicht; **~s** (*look, glance, gaze*) Blick, *der;* **a pair of blue ~s** zwei blaue Augen; **close** *or* **shut/open one's ~s** die Augen schließen/öffnen; **that will make him open his ~s** (*fig.*) da wird er Augen machen; **open sb.'s ~s to sth.** (*fig.*) jmdm. die Augen über etw. (*Akk.*) öffnen; **shut** *or* **close one's ~s to sth.** (*fig.*) die Augen vor etw. (*Dat.*) verschließen; **the sun/light is [shining] in my ~s** die Sonne/das Licht blendet mich; **I've got the sun in my ~s** die Sonne blendet mich; **out of the corner of one's ~:** aus den Augenwinkeln; **lift up one's ~s** die Augen erheben; aufblicken; **drop** *or* **lower one's ~s** die Augen niederschlagen; den Blick senken; **with one's own** *or* **very ~s** mit eigenen Augen; **under/before sb.'s very ~s** unter/vor jmds. Augen (*Dat.*); **measure a distance by ~** *or* **with one's ~[s]** einen Abstand nach Augenmaß schätzen; **judge sth. by ~:**

etw. nach dem Augenschein beurteilen (*geh.*); **paint/draw sth. by ~:** etw. nach der Natur malen/zeichnen; **with the ~ of an artist, with an artist's ~:** mit den Augen eines Künstlers; **look sb. in the ~:** jmdm. gerade in die Augen sehen; **not be able to look sb. in the ~:** jmdm. nicht ins Gesicht sehen können; **have ~s [only] for sb.** sich [nur] für jmdn. interessieren; **be unable to take one's ~s off sb./sth.** die Augen *od.* den Blick nicht von jmdm./etw. abwenden können; **make [sheep's] ~s at sb.** jmdm. [schöne] Augen machen; **keep an ~ on sb./sth.** auf jmdn./etw. aufpassen; ein Auge auf jmdn./etw. haben; **keep a sharp** *or* **close** *or* **strict ~ on sb./sth.** scharf auf jmdn./etw. aufpassen; streng auf jmdn./etw. achten; **keep one's ~[s] on sb./sth.** jmdn./etw. im Auge behalten; **have [got] an** *or* **one's ~[s] on sb./sth.** ein Auge auf jmdn./etw. geworfen haben; **I've got my ~ on you!** ich lasse dich nicht aus den Augen!; **keep an ~ open** *or* **out [for sb./sth.]** [nach jmdm./etw.] Ausschau halten; **keep one's ~s open** die Augen offen halten; **keep one's ~s skinned** *or* **peeled** (*coll.*) wie ein Schießhund aufpassen (*ugs.*); **keep one's ~s open** *or* (*coll.*) **peeled** *or* (*coll.*) **skinned for sth.** nach etw. Ausschau halten; **keep one's ~s and ears open** Augen und Ohren offen halten; **with one's ~s open** (*fig.*) mit offenen Augen; bewusst; **with one's ~s shut** (*fig.*) (*without full awareness*) blind; (*with great ease*) im Schlaf; **with a friendly/jealous/eager/critical ~:** freundlich / eifersüchtig / erwartungsvoll / kritisch; **have you no ~s in your head?** hast du keine Augen im Kopf? (*ugs.*); bist du blind?; **where are your ~s?, use your ~s!** wo hast du deine Augen?; **I haven't [got] ~s at** *or* **in the back of my head** ich habe hinten keine Augen; **in the ~s of God/the law** vor Gott/nach dem Gesetz; **in sb.'s ~s** in jmds. Augen (*Dat.*); **see sb./sth. through sb.'s ~s** jmdn./etw. mit jmds. Augen sehen; **look at sth. through the ~s of sb.** etw. mit jmds. Augen betrachten; **pore one's ~s out over a book** über einem Buch sitzen, bis die Augen ermüden; **tire one's ~s out** seine Augen ermüden; **be all ~s** gespannt zusehen; **[all] my ~** (*coll.*) [alles] Schnickschnack (*ugs. abwertend*); **do sb. in the ~** (*coll.*) jmdn. übers Ohr hauen (*ugs.*); **[an] ~ for [an] ~:** Auge um Auge; **~s front!/right!/left!** (*Mil.*) Augen geradeaus/rechts/links!; **have an ~ to sth./doing sth.** auf etw. (*Akk.*) bedacht sein/darauf bedacht sein, etw. zu tun; **with an ~ to sth.** im Hinblick auf etw. (*Akk.*); **with an ~ to doing sth.** mit dem Gedanken, etw. zu tun; **hit sb. in the ~** (*fig.*) jmdm. ins Auge springen *od.* fallen; **that was one in the ~ for him** (*coll.*) das war ein Schlag ins Kontor (*ugs.*) für ihn; **see ~ to ~ [on sth. with sb.]** [mit jmdm.] einer Meinung [über etw. (*Akk.*)] sein; **not see ~ to ~ with sb. on sth.** über etw. (*Akk.*) anderer Meinung als jmd. sein; **be up to one's ~s** (*fig.*) bis über beide Ohren drinstecken (*ugs.*); **be up to one's ~s in work/debt** bis über beide Ohren in der Arbeit/in Schulden stecken (*ugs.*); **have an ~ for sth.** ein Auge *od.* einen Blick für etw. haben; **have an ~ for sb.** jmdn. gern haben; **a man with an ~ for the ladies** ein Mann, der die Frauen gern hat; **have a keen/good ~ for sth.** einen geschärften/einen sicheren *od.* den richtigen Blick für etw. haben; **make ~s at sb.** jmdm. [schöne] Augen machen; **see with half an ~ that ...:** auf den ersten Blick sehen, dass ...; **get one's ~ in at shooting/tennis** sich einschießen/sich einspielen; **B** (*sth. like an ~*) Auge, *das;* (*of peacock's tail*) Pfauenauge, *das;* (*on butterfly's wing*) Augenfleck, *der;* (*of needle, fish-hook*) Öhr, *das;* (*metal loop*) Öse, *die.*

**2** *v.t.*, **~ing** *or* **eying** /ˈaɪɪŋ/ beäugen; **~ sb. up and down/from head to foot** jmdn. von oben bis unten/von Kopf bis Fuß mustern

**eye: ~ball** *n.* Augapfel, *der;* **~ball to ~ball** (*coll.*) hautnah ‹Konfrontation›; **be** *or* **meet ~ball to ~ball** sich (*Dat.*) Auge in Auge gegenüberstehen; **~bath** *n.* Augenbadewanne, *die;* **~black** *n.* (*dated*) schwarze Wimperntusche; **~bright** *n.* (*Bot.*) Augentrost, *der;* **~brow** *n.* Augenbraue, *die;* **raise** *or* **lift an ~brow** *or* **one's ~brows [at sth.]** die [Augen]brauen [wegen etw.] hochziehen; (*fig.*) (*in surprise*) die Stirn runzeln (**at** über + *Akk.*); (*superciliously*) die Nase rümpfen (**at** über + *Akk.*); **it will raise a few ~brows** das wird einiges Stirnrunzeln hervorrufen; **up to the** *or* **one's ~brows [in sth.]** bis über beide Ohren [in etw. (*Dat.*)]; **~brow pencil** Augenbrauenstift, *der;* **~-catching** *adj.* ins Auge springend *od.* fallend ‹Inserat, Plakat, Buchhülle usw.›; **be [very] ~-catching** ein [wirkungsvoller] Blickfang sein; **she is very ~-catching** sie zieht die Augen aller auf sich (*Akk.*); **~ contact** *n.* Blickkontakt, *der*

**-eyed** /aɪd/ *adj. in comb.* ▶ 966 -äugig; **big-~/bright-~:** groß-/helläugig; **fierce-~/sad-~:** mit grimmigen/traurigen Augen *od.* grimmigem/traurigem Blick *nachgestellt;* **be sad-~:** traurige Augen haben

**eye: ~ dropper** *n.* (*Med.*) Augentropfer, *der;* **~ drops** *n. pl.* (*Med.*) Augentropfen *Pl.*

**eyeful** /ˈaɪfʊl/ *n.* (*coll.*) (*woman*) Klassefrau, *die* (*ugs.*); (*sight*) **get an ~ [of sth.]** einiges [von etw.] zu sehen bekommen

**eye: ~glass** *n.* (*dated*) Augenglas, *das* (*veralt.*); **~ hospital** *n.* Augenklinik, *die;* **~lash** *n.* Augenwimper, *die*

**eyeless** /ˈaɪlɪs/ *adj.* blind ‹Person, Tier›

**eyelet** /ˈaɪlɪt/ *n.* **A** Öse, *die;* (*Naut.*) Auge, *das;* **B** (*to look through*) Guckloch, *das*

**eye: ~ level** *n.* Augenhöhe, *die; attrib.* in Augenhöhe *nachgestellt;* **~lid** *n.* Augenlid, *das;* **~liner** *n.* Eyeliner, *der;* Lidstrich, *der;* **~ make-up** *n.* Augen-Make-up, *das;* **~-opener** *n.* (*surprise, revelation*) Überraschung, *die;* **the book was an ~-opener to the public** das Buch hat der Öffentlichkeit die Augen geöffnet; **~patch** *n.* Augenklappe, *die;* **~piece** *n.* (*Optics*) Okular, *das;* **~shade** *n.* Augenschirm, *der;* **~shadow** *n.* Lidschatten, *der;* **~sight** *n.* Sehkraft, *die;* **have good ~sight** gute Augen haben; gut sehen können; **his ~sight is poor** er hat schlechte Augen; **~sore** *n.* Schandfleck, *der* (*abwertend*); **the building is an ~sore** das Gebäude beleidigt das Auge; **~ strain** *n.* Überanstrengung der Augen; **be a cause of ~ strain** die Augen überanstrengen; **~ test** *n.* Sehtest, *der;* **~ tooth** *n.* Eckzahn, *der;* **cut one's ~ teeth** (*fig.*) Erfahrungen sammeln; **she would give her ~ teeth for it/to do it** sie würde alles dafür geben/darum geben, es zu tun; **~wash** *n.* **A** (*Med.: lotion*) Augenwasser, *das;* **B** (*coll.*) (*nonsense*) Gewäsch, *das* (*ugs. abwertend*); (*concealment*) Augen[aus]wischerei, *die* (*ugs.*); **~witness** *n.* Augenzeuge, *der*/-zeugin, *die;* **be an ~witness of sth.** Augenzeuge einer Sache (*Gen.*) sein; *attrib.* **~witness account** *or* **report** Augenzeugenbericht, *der*

**eyrie** /ˈɪərɪ/ *n.* (*nest*) Horst, *der*

# Ff

**F, f** /ef/ *n., pl.* **Fs** *or* **F's** A (*letter*) F, f, *das;* B F (*Mus.*) F, f, *das;* **F sharp** fis, Fis, *das;* C F (*Sch., Univ.: mark*) Sechs, *die;* **he got an F** er bekam „ungenügend" *od.* eine Sechs

**F.** *abbr.* A **Fahrenheit** F; B **Fellow;** C (*on pencil*) **firm** F; D ▶1328 **franc** F; E (*Phys.*) **farad[s]** F

**f.** *abbr.* A **female** weibl.; B **feminine** f.; C **focal length** f; **f/8** (*Photog.*) Blende 8; D **following [page]** f.; E **forte** f; F **folio** F.

**FA** *abbr.* (*Brit.*) **Football Association** (*Britischer Fußballverband*)

**fa** ⇒ **fah**

**fab** /fæb/ *adj.* (*Brit. coll.*) fabelhaft (*ugs.*); dufte, toll (*salopp*)

**Fabian** /ˈfeɪbɪən/ *adj.* Hinhalte-; Verzögerungs‹taktik, -manöver›

**fable** /ˈfeɪbl/ *n.* A (*story of the supernatural, myth, lie*) Märchen, *das;* **land of ~:** Märchen- *od.* Fabelland, *das;* **separate fact from ~:** Dichtung und Wahrheit unterscheiden; B (*thing that does not really exist, brief story*) Fabel, *die*

**fabled** /ˈfeɪbld/ *adj.* A (*told as in fable*) **it is ~ that ...:** es heißt, dass ...; B (*mythical*) Fabel‹land, -wesen, -tier›; C (*celebrated*) berühmt (**for** für)

**fabric** /ˈfæbrɪk/ *n.* A (*material, construction, texture*) Gewebe, *das;* **woven/knitted/ribbed/coarse/mixed ~:** Web-/Strickware, *die*/Rips, *der*/Grob-/Mischgewebe, *das;* B (*thing put together*) Gebilde, *das;* C (*fig.: frame*) Gefüge, *das;* **the ~ of society** die Struktur der Gesellschaft; **destroy the ~ of sb.'s life** jmds. Welt zerstören; D (*of building*) bauliche Substanz; Bausubstanz, *die*

**fabricate** /ˈfæbrɪkeɪt/ *v.t.* A (*invent*) erfinden; (*forge*) fälschen; B (*construct, manufacture*) herstellen

**fabrication** /fæbrɪˈkeɪʃn/ *n.* A (*of story etc., falsehood*) Erfindung, *die;* **the story is [a] pure ~:** die Geschichte ist frei erfunden; B (*construction, manufacture*) Herstellung, *die*

**ˈfabric softener** *n.* Weichspülmittel, *das;* Weichspüler, *der*

**fabulous** /ˈfæbjʊləs/ *adj.* A (*unhistorical, legendary, celebrated*) sagenhaft; **~ animal/creature** *or* **being** Fabeltier/-wesen, *das;* B (*exaggerated*) fantastisch ‹Geschichte›; C (*coll.: marvellous*) fabelhaft (*ugs.*)

**façade** /fəˈsɑːd/ *n.* (*lit. or fig.*) Fassade, *die;* **that's just a ~ade** (*fig.*) das ist alles nur Fassade

**face** /feɪs/ **1** *n.* A ▶966 Gesicht, *das;* **wash one's ~:** sich (*Dat.*) das Gesicht waschen; **blush/be smiling all over one's ~:** bis über die Ohren rot werden/über das ganze Gesicht strahlen; **go purple** *or* **black in the ~** (*with strangulation*), **go blue in the ~** (*with cold*) blau im Gesicht werden; **go red** *or* **purple in the ~** (*with exertion or passion or shame*) rot im Gesicht werden; **the stone struck me on my ~** *or* **in the ~:** der Stein traf mich ins Gesicht; **the ~ of an angel/a devil/a criminal** ein Engels-/Teufels-/Verbrechergesicht; **bring A and B ~ to ~:** A und B einander (*Dat.*) gegenüberstellen; **stand ~ to ~:** sich (*Dat.*) gegenüberstehen; **meet sb. ~ to ~:** jmdn. persönlich kennen lernen; **come** *or* **be brought ~ to ~ with sb.** mit jmdm. konfrontiert werden; **come ~ to ~ with the fact that ...:** vor der Tatsache stehen, dass ...; **fly in the ~ of sb./sth.** jmdn. mit Verachtung strafen/sich über etw. (*Akk.*) hinwegsetzen; **in [the] ~ of sth.** (*despite*) trotz; (*confronted with*) vor (+ *Dat.*); **cowardice in the ~ of the enemy** Feigheit vor dem Feind; **slam the door in sb.'s ~:** jmdm. die Tür vor der Nase zuknallen (*ugs.*); **shine in sb.'s ~:** jmdm. ins Gesicht scheinen; **fall [flat] on one's ~** (*lit. or fig.*) auf die Nase fallen (*ugs.*); **look sb./sth. in the ~:** jmdm./einer Sache ins Gesicht sehen; **put one's ~ on** (*coll.*) sich anmalen (*ugs.*); **set one's ~ against sb./sth.** sich jmdm./einer Sache entgegenstellen; **show one's ~:** sich sehen *od.* blicken lassen; **tell sb. to his ~ what ...:** jmdm. [offen] ins Gesicht sagen, was ...; **use sb.'s nickname to his ~:** jmds. Spitznamen in seiner Gegenwart benutzen; **talk/scream/complain** *etc.* **till one is blue in the ~:** reden/schreien/klagen *usw.* bis man verrückt wird (*ugs.*); **shut one's ~** (*sl.*) die *od.* seine Klappe halten (*salopp*); **have the ~ to do sth.** die Stirn haben, etw. zu tun; **save one's ~:** das Gesicht wahren *od.* retten; **lose ~ [with sb.] [over sth.]** das Gesicht [vor jmdm.] [wegen etw.] verlieren; **sth. makes sb. lose ~:** etw. kostet jmdn. das Gesicht *od.* Ansehen; **see by sb.'s ~ that ...:** es jmdm. [am Gesicht] *od.* es jmds. Gesicht (*Dat.*) ansehen, dass ...; **make** *or* **pull a ~/~s [at sb.]** (*to show dislike*) ein Gesicht/Gesichter machen *od.* ziehen; (*to amuse or frighten*) eine Grimasse/Grimassen schneiden; **don't make a ~!** mach nicht so ein Gesicht!; **with a ~ like thunder** *or* **as black as thunder** schwarz vor Ärger; **on the ~ of it** dem Anschein nach; **change the ~ of sth.** einer Sache (*Dat.*) ein neues Gesicht geben; **put a brave** *or* **good** *or* **bold ~ on it/the matter/the affair** *etc.* gute Miene zum bösen Spiel machen; B (*front*) (*of mountain, cliff*) Wand, *die;* (*of building*) Stirnseite, *die;* (*of clock, watch*) Zifferblatt, *das;* (*of dice*) Seite, *die;* (*of coin, medal, banknote, playing card*) Vorderseite, *die;* (*of tool*) Bahn, *die;* (*of golf club, cricket bat, hockey stick, tennis racket*) Schlagfläche, *die;* C (*surface*) **the ~ of the earth** die Erde; **disappear off** *or* **from the ~ of the earth** spurlos verschwinden; **be wiped off the ~ of the earth** ausradiert werden; D (*Geom.; also of crystal, gem*) Fläche, *die;* E ⇒ **typeface;** F ⇒ **coalface.** ⇒ *also* **face down[ward]; face up[ward]; fall** 2 N; **laugh** 2; **long**[1] 1 B; **smack**[2] 1 B; **straight face.**

**2** *v.t.* A ▶1024 (*look towards*) sich wenden zu; **sb. ~s the front** jmd. sieht nach vorne; **[stand] facing one another** sich (*Dat.*) *od.* (*meist geh.*) einander gegenüber[stehen]; **the house facing the church** das Haus gegenüber der Kirche; **the window ~s the garden/front** das Fenster geht zum Garten/zur Straße hinaus *od.* liegt zum Garten/zur Straße; **travel/sit facing the engine** mit dem Gesicht in Fahrtrichtung fahren/in Fahrtrichtung sitzen; **sit facing the stage** vor der Bühne *od.* mit dem Gesicht zur Bühne sitzen; B (*fig.: have to deal with*) ins Auge sehen (+ *Dat.*) ‹Tod, Vorstellung›; gegenübertreten (+ *Dat.*) ‹Kläger›; sich stellen (+ *Dat.*) ‹Anschuldigung, Kritik›; stehen vor (+ *Dat.*) ‹Ruin, Entscheidung›; eingehen ‹Risiko›; **~ trial for murder, ~ a charge of murder** sich wegen Mordes vor Gericht verantworten müssen; C (*not shrink from*) ins Auge sehen (+ *Dat.*) ‹Tatsache, Wahrheit›; mit Fassung gegenübertreten (+ *Dat.*) ‹Kläger›; **~ sth. out** etw. durchstehen; **~ sb. down** jmdn. demoralisieren *od.* (*ugs.*) kleinkriegen; **refuse to be ~d down by threats** sich von Drohungen nicht kleinkriegen lassen (*ugs.*); **~ the music** (*fig.*) die Suppe auslöffeln (*ugs.*); **let's ~ it** (*coll.*) machen wir uns (*Dat.*) doch nichts vor (*ugs.*); D **be ~d with sth.** sich einer Sache (*Dat.*) gegenübersehen; **~d with these facts** mit diesen Sachen konfrontiert; **he was ~d with the possibility** für ihn ergab sich die Möglichkeit; **he is ~d with a lawsuit** gegen ihn wird ein Prozess eingeleitet; **the problems/questions that we are ~d with** die Probleme/Fragen, vor denen wir stehen; E (*coll.: bear*) verkraften; abkönnen (*nordd. salopp, meist verneint*); F (*dress, trim*) besetzen ‹Kleidungsstück›; verkleiden, verblenden ‹Wand›; **a cloak ~d with white** ein Umhang mit weißem Besatz.

**3** *v.i.* A ▶1024 (*look*) **~ backwards/forwards** ‹Person/Bank, Sitz:› entgegen der/in Fahrtrichtung sitzen/aufgestellt sein; **in which direction was he facing?** in welche Richtung blickte er?; **~ away [from sb.]** das Gesicht [von jmdm.] abwenden; **stand facing away from sb.** mit dem Rücken zu jmdm. stehen; **~ away from the road/on to the road/east[wards]** *or* **to[wards] the east** ‹Fenster, Zimmer:› nach hinten/vorn/Osten liegen; **the side of the house ~s to[wards] the sea** die Seite des Hauses liegt zum Meer; B (*Amer. Mil.*) eine Wendung machen; **~ about/to the right/left** eine Kehrt-/Rechts-/Linkswendung machen; **left/right ~!** ganze Abteilung links/rechts um!

**~ ˈup to** *v.t.* ins Auge sehen (+ *Dat.*); sich abfinden mit ‹Möglichkeit›; auf sich nehmen ‹Verantwortung›

**face: ~ card** ⇒ **court card; ~cloth** *n.* (*cloth for ~*) Waschlappen [für das Gesicht]; **~ cream** *n.* Gesichtscreme, *die*

**-faced** /feɪst/ *adj. in comb.* -gesichtig

**face: ~ ˈdown[ward]** *adv.* mit der Vorderseite nach unten; **put one's cards ~ down on the table** seine Karten verdeckt auf den Tisch legen; **lie ~ down[ward]** ‹Person:› auf dem Bauch liegen; ‹Buch:› auf dem Gesicht liegen; ⇒ *also* **face** 2 C; **~ flannel** (*Brit.*) ⇒ **~cloth**

**faceless** /ˈfeɪslɪs/ *adj.* A (*without face*) gesichtslos; B (*anonymous*) anonym (*fig.*)

**face: ~lift** *n.* A Facelifting, *das;* **have** *or* **get a ~lift** sich liften lassen; B (*fig.: improvement in appearance*) Verschönerung, *die;* **~-off** *n.* (*Ice Hockey*) Bully, *das;* **~ pack** *n.* [Gesichts]maske, *die;* **~ powder** *n.* Gesichtspuder, *das;* **~-saving** **1** *adj.* zur Wahrung des Gesichts *nachgestellt;* **as a ~-saving gesture** um das Gesicht zu wahren *od.* retten; **2** *n.* Wahrung des Gesichts

**facet** /ˈfæsɪt/ *n.* A (*of many-sided body, esp. of cut stone*) Facette, *die;* B (*aspect*) Seite, *die;* **every ~:** alle Seiten *od.* (*geh.*) Facetten

**faceted** /ˈfæsɪtɪd/ *adj.* facettiert ‹Edelstein, Diamant, Linse›

**facetious** /fəˈsiːʃəs/ *adj.* [gewollt] witzig; (*impudently*) frech; **[not] be ~ [about sth.]** [keine] Witze [über etw. (*Akk.*)] machen (*ugs.*)

**facetiously** /fəˈsiːʃəslɪ/ *adv.* [gewollt] witzig

**face: ~-to-~** *adj.* unmittelbar ‹Gegenüberstellung›; **~ ˈup[ward]** *adv.* mit der Vorderseite nach oben; **lie ~ up[ward]** ‹Karte:› offen *od.* aufgedeckt liegen; ‹Person:› auf dem Rücken liegen; (*open*) ‹Buch:› aufgeschlagen liegen; **~ value** *n.* (*Finance*) Nominalwert, *der* (*fachspr.*); Nennwert, *der;* **accept sth. at [its] ~ value** (*fig.*) etw. für bare Münze nehmen; **take sb. at [his/her] ~ value** (*fig.*) jmdn. nach seinem Äußeren beurteilen; **~worker** *n.* (*Mining*) Untertagearbeiter, *der*

**facia** /ˈfeɪʃə/ *n.* **A** (*plate*) **~ [board]** Firmenschild, *das;* **B** (*Motor Veh.*) **~ [board** *or* **panel]** Armaturenbrett, *das*

**facial** /ˈfeɪʃl/ **1** *adj.* Gesichts-. **2** *n.* Gesichtsmassage, *die;* **have a ~:** sich (*Dat.*) das Gesicht massieren lassen

**facile** /ˈfæsaɪl, ˈfæsɪl/ *adj.* (*often derog.*) leicht ‹Sieg, Arbeit, Aufgabe›; einfach ‹Art, Methode, Technik›; gewandt ‹Lügner, Schriftsteller›; nichts sagend, banal ‹Bemerkung›; oberflächlich, (*abwertend*) flach ‹Person, Einstellung›

**facilitate** /fəˈsɪlɪteɪt/ *v.t.* erleichtern

**facility** /fəˈsɪlɪtɪ/ *n.* **A** *esp. in pl.* Einrichtung, *die;* **cooking/washing facilities** Koch-/Waschgelegenheit, *die;* **sports facilities** Sportanlagen; **drying facilities** (*indoor*) Trockenraum, *der;* (*outdoor*) Trockenplatz, *der;* **postal facilities** Postdienste; **shopping facilities** Einkaufsmöglichkeiten; **banking facilities** Banken; **travel facilities** Verkehrsmittel; **B** (*unimpeded opportunity*) Möglichkeit, *die;* **C** (*ease, aptitude, freedom from difficulty*) Leichtigkeit, *die;* (*dexterity*) Gewandtheit, *die;* **~ in speech/writing** Rede-/Schreibgewandtheit, *die*

**facing** /ˈfeɪsɪŋ/ *n.* **A** (*on garment*) Aufschlag, *der;* Besatz, *der;* **B** *in pl.* (*cuffs, collar, etc. of jacket*) [Uniform]aufschläge *Pl.;* **C** (*covering*) Verblendung, *die;* Verkleidung, *die*

**facsimile** /fækˈsɪmɪlɪ/ *n.* **A** Faksimile, *das;* **B** (*Telecommunications*) ⇒ **fax** 1

**fact** /fækt/ *n.* **A** (*true thing*) Tatsache, *die;* **~s and figures** Fakten und Zahlen; **the ~ remains that ...:** Tatsache bleibt: ...; **the true ~s of the case** *or* **matter** der wahre Sachverhalt; **know for a ~ that ...:** genau *od.* sicher wissen, dass ...; **is that a ~?** (*coll.*) Tatsache? (*ugs.*); **and that's a ~:** und daran gibts nichts zu zweifeln (*ugs.*); **the value/reason lies in the ~ that ...:** der Nutzen/Grund besteht darin, dass ...; **look the ~s in the face, face [the] ~s** den Tatsachen ins Gesicht sehen; **it is a proven/an established/an undisputed/an accepted ~ that ...:** es ist erwiesen/steht fest/ist unbestritten/man geht davon aus, dass ...; **the ~ [of the matter] is that ...:** die Sache ist die, dass ...; **[it is a] ~ of life** [das ist die] harte *od.* rauhe Wirklichkeit; **tell** *or* **teach sb. the ~s of life** (*coll. euphem.*) jmdn. [sexuell] aufklären; **B** (*reality*) Wahrheit, *die;* Tatsachen *Pl.;* **distinguish ~ from fiction** Fakten und Fiktion (*geh.*) *od.* Dichtung und Wahrheit unterscheiden; **in ~:** tatsächlich; **I don't suppose you did/would do it? — In ~, I did/would** Ich nehme an, Sie haben es nicht getan/würden es nicht tun. — Doch[, ich habe es tatsächlich getan/würde es tatsächlich tun]; **I was planning to go to your party and had in ~ bought a bottle of wine** ich wollte zu deiner Party kommen und hatte sogar *od.* auch schon eine Flasche Wein gekauft; **he was supposed to arrive before eight, but he didn't in ~ get here till after twelve** er sollte vor acht Uhr ankommen, ist dann aber doch erst nach 12 Uhr hier eingetroffen; **he has left us; in ~ he is not coming back** er hat uns verlassen, und er kommt auch nicht mehr zurück; **I don't think he'll come back; in ~ I know he won't** ich glaube nicht, dass er zurückkommt, ich weiß es sogar; **C** (*thing assumed to be ~*) Faktum, *das;* **deny the ~ that ...:** [die Tatsache] abstreiten, dass ...; **D** (*Law: crime*) [Straf]tat, *die;* **be an accessory before/after the ~:** jmdm. Beihilfe leisten/Begünstigung gewähren. ⇒ *also* **matter** 1 D

**ˈfact-finding** *attrib. adj.* Erkundungs‹fahrt, -flug, -trupp›; **~ committee/trip/study** Untersuchungsausschuss, *der*/Informationsreise, *die*/Ermittlungsarbeit, *die*

**faction** /ˈfækʃn/ *n.* **A** (*party or group*) Splittergruppe, *die;* Faktion, *die* (*veralt.*); **B** *no pl.* (*party strife*) Parteihader, *der*

**factional** /ˈfækʃənl/ *adj.* parteiintern ‹Konflikt, Uneinigkeit, Streit›; **a ~ group/splinter group** eine Gruppierung/Splittergruppe

**factious** /ˈfækʃəs/ *adj.* faktiös; parteisüchtig ‹Absicht›

**factitious** /fækˈtɪʃəs/ *adj.*, **factitiously** /fækˈtɪʃəslɪ/ *adv.* künstlich

**factor** /ˈfæktə(r)/ **1** *n.* **A** (*Math.; also fact, circumstance*) Faktor, *der;* **B** (*Biol.*) Erbfaktor, *der;* **C** (*merchant*) Kommissionär, *der;* **D** (*Scot.: land agent, steward*) Gutsverwalter, *der;* **E** (*agent, deputy*) Vertreter, *der.* ⇒ *also* **common factor**. **2** *v.t.* **A** (*Math.*) in Faktoren zerlegen; **B** (*resolve into components*) zerlegen

**factoring** /ˈfæktərɪŋ/ *n.* (*Commerc.*) Factoring, *das*

**factorize (factorise)** /ˈfæktəraɪz/ (*Math.*) **1** *v.t.* in Faktoren zerlegen. **2** *v.i.* sich in Faktoren zerlegen lassen

**factory** /ˈfæktərɪ/ *n.* Fabrik, *die;* Werk, *das;* **a ~ for assembling cars/machines** ein Kraftfahrzeug[montage]werk/eine Maschinenfabrik

**factory: ~ ˈfarm** *n.* (*Agric.*) [voll]automatisierter landwirtschaftlicher Betrieb; **~ ˈfarming** *n.* [fabrikmäßige] Massentierhaltung; **the ~ farming of salmon** die massenweise Lachsproduktion; **~-made** *adj.* fabrik- *od.* serienmäßig hergestellt; **~-made clothes/furniture** Konfektion[skleidung], *die*/Serienmöbel *Pl.;* **~ ship** *n.* Fabrikschiff, *das;* **~ work** *n.* Fabrikarbeit, *die;* **~ worker** *n.* ▶ **1261** Fabrikarbeiter, *der*/-arbeiterin, *die*

**factotum** /fækˈtəʊtəm/ *n.* Faktotum, *das*

**ˈfact sheet** *n.* Infoblatt, *das*

**factual** /ˈfæktʃʊəl/ *adj.* sachlich ‹Bericht, Darlegung, Stil›; auf Tatsachen beruhend ‹Aspekt, Punkt, Beweis›; wahr ‹Geschichte›; **~ error** Sachfehler, *der*

**factually** /ˈfæktʃʊəlɪ/ *adv.* sachlich; mit Tatsachen *od.* Fakten ‹beweisen›

**faculty** /ˈfækəltɪ/ *n.* **A** (*physical capability*) Fähigkeit, *die;* Vermögen, *das;* **~ of sight/speech/hearing/thought** Seh-/Sprach-/Hör-/Denkvermögen, *das;* **B** (*mental power*) **mental ~, ~ of the mind** geistige Kraft; Geisteskraft, *die;* **in [full] possession of [all] one's faculties** im [Voll]besitz [all] seiner [geistigen] Kräfte; **all one's creative faculties** seine ganze Kreativität *od.* schöpferische Kraft; **C** (*aptitude*) Begabung, *die;* Fähigkeit, *die;* **have a ~ for doing sth.** die Fähigkeit *od.* das Talent haben, etw. zu tun; **D** (*Univ.: department*) Fakultät, *die;* Fachbereich, *der;* **~ of arts/sciences/medicine** philosophische/naturwissenschaftliche/medizinische Fakultät; **E** (*Amer. Sch., Univ.: staff*) Lehrkörper, *der;* **F** (*members of particular profession*) Berufsstand, *der;* **the [medical] ~:** die Ärzteschaft; der Ärztestand

**fad** /fæd/ *n.* Marotte, *die;* Spleen, *der* (*ugs.*); **the latest fashion ~:** die neueste Modetorheit; **a ~ for doing sth.** die Marotte *od.* der Spleen, etw. zu tun

**faddish** /ˈfædɪʃ/, **faddy** /ˈfædɪ/ *adjs.* heikel ‹Person, Geschmack›

**fade** /feɪd/ **1** *v.i.* **A** (*droop, wither*) ‹Blätter, Blumen, Kränze:› [ver]welken, welk werden; **B** (*lose freshness, vigour*) verblassen; [v]erlöschen; ‹Läufer:› langsamer werden; ‹Frau, Schönheit:› verblühen; **C** (*lose colour*) bleichen; **~ [in colour]** [ver]bleichen; verschießen; **guaranteed not to ~:** garantiert farbecht; **D** (*grow pale, dim*) **the light ~d [into darkness]** es dunkelte; **the fading light of evening** das dämmrige Abendlicht (*dichter.*); die Abenddämmerung; **E** (*fig.: lose strength*) ‹Erinnerung:› verblassen; ‹Eingebung, Kreativität, Optimismus:› nachlassen; ‹Freude, Lust, Liebe:› erlöschen; ‹Ruhm:› verblassen; ‹Traum, Hoffnung:› zerrinnen; schwinden; **~ from sb.'s mind** jmds. Gedächtnis (*Dat.*) entfallen; **F** (*disappear, depart, leave*) weichen; ‹Metapher, Bedeutung, Stern:› verschwinden; (*blend*) übergehen (**into** in + *Akk.*); (*grow faint*) ‹Laut:› verklingen; **~ into the distance** in der Ferne entschwinden; ‹Laut, Stimme:› in der Ferne verklingen; **~ from sight** *or* **sb.'s eyes** dem Blick entschwinden (*geh.*); **his smile ~d from his face** das Lächeln schwand aus seinem Gesicht; **G** (*lose power*) ‹Bremskraft, Bremse:› nachlassen; **H** (*Radio, Telev., Cinemat.*) **~ [down]** ausgeblendet werden; **~ up** eingeblendet werden; **I** (*deviate*) ‹Golfball usw.:› einen Bogen beschreiben.

**2** *v.t.* **A** (*cause to ~*) ausbleichen ‹Vorhang, Gobelin, Teppich, Farbe›; **B** (*Radio, Telev., Cinemat.*) einblenden (**into** in + *Akk.*); **~ one scene into another** eine Szene in eine andere überblenden; **~ a sound down/up** ein Geräusch aus-/einblenden.

**3** *n.* (*Radio, Telev., Cinemat., Motor Veh.*) Fading, *das* (*fachspr.*)

**~ aˈway** *v.i.* **A** schwinden; ‹Farbe:› verblassen; ‹Laut:› verklingen (**into** in + *Dat.*); ‹Erinnerung, Augenlicht, Kraft:› nachlassen; ‹Kranke[r]:› immer schwächer werden; ‹Interesse, Hoffnung:› erlöschen; (*joc.*) ‹dünne Person:› immer weniger werden (*scherzh.*); **the daylight ~d away** es dämmerte; **B** (*depart, leave*) gehen

**~ ˈin** (*Radio, Telev., Cinemat.*) **1** *v.i.* eingeblendet werden. **2** *v.t.* einblenden. ⇒ *also* **fade-in**

**~ ˈout 1** *v.i.* **A** (*Radio, Telev., Cinemat.*) ausgeblendet werden; **B** (*disappear, depart*) **~ out of sb.'s life/mind** aus jmds. Leben/Bewusstsein verschwinden. **2** *v.t.* (*Radio, Telev., Cinemat.*) ausblenden. ⇒ *also* **fade-out**

**faded** /ˈfeɪdɪd/ *adj.* welk ‹Blume, Blatt, Laub›; verblichen ‹Stoff, Jeans, Farbe, Gemälde, Ruhm, Teppich›; verblüht ‹Schönheit›; verblasst ‹Erinnerung›

**ˈfade-in** *n.* (*Radio, Telev., Cinemat.*) Einblendung, *die*

**fadeless** /ˈfeɪdlɪs/ *adj.* farbecht ‹Stoff›; echt ‹Farbe›

**ˈfade-out** *n.* **A** (*Radio, Telev., Cinemat.*) Ausblendung, *die;* **B** (*Radio: by ionospheric disturbances*) Fading, *das* (*fachspr.*); Schwund, *der;* **C** (*fig.: disappearance*) Niedergang, *der*

**fading** /ˈfeɪdɪŋ/ *n.* (*Radio*) Fading, *das* (*fachspr.*); Schwund, *der*

**faecal** /ˈfiːkl/ *adj.* (*Physiol.*) Kot-; kotig; fäkal (*fachspr.*)

**faeces** /ˈfiːsiːz/ *n. pl.* Fäkalien *Pl.*

**faff about** /fæf əˈbaʊt/ *v.i.* (*Brit. coll.*) herummachen (*ugs.*); **stop faffing about!** reg dich ab! (*ugs.*)

**fag¹** /fæg/ **1** *v.i.*, **-gg-:** **A** (*toil*) sich [ab]schinden (*ugs.*), sich abrackern (*salopp*) (**[away] at** mit); **B** (*Brit. Sch.*) **~ for a senior** einen älteren Schüler bedienen. **2** *v.t.*, **-gg-:** **~ sb. [out]** jmdn. schlauchen (*ugs.*); **~ oneself out** sich [ab]schinden (*ugs.*); **be ~ged out** geschlaucht sein (*ugs.*). **3** *n.* **A** (*Brit. coll.*) Schinderei, *die* (*ugs. abwertend*); **B** (*Brit. Sch.*) Diener, *der; Internatsschüler, der einem älteren bestimmte Dienste leistet;* **C** (*coll.: cigarette*) Glimmstängel, *der* (*ugs. scherzh.*)

**fag²** *n.* (*sl. derog.: homosexual*) Schwule, *der* (*ugs.*)

**ˈfag end** *n.* **A** (*remnant*) Schluss, *der;* Ende, *das;* **B** (*coll.: cigarette end*) Kippe, *die* (*ugs.*)

**faggot** (*Amer.:* **fagot**) /ˈfægət/ *n.* **A** (*sticks, twigs*) Reisigbündel, *das;* **B** *usu. in pl.* (*Gastr.*) Leberknödel, *der;* **C** (*woman*) Weib, *das* (*abwertend*); **D** (*sl. derog.: homosexual*) Schwule, *der*

**fah** /fɑː/ *n.* (*Mus.*) fa

**Fahr.** *abbr.* **Fahrenheit** F

**Fahrenheit** /ˈfærənhaɪt/ *adj.* ▶ **1603** Fahrenheit; **~ scale** Fahrenheitskala, *die*

**fail** /feɪl/ **1** *v.i.* **A** (*not succeed*) scheitern; **~ in sth.** mit etw. scheitern; **he ~ed in doing it** es gelang ihm nicht, es zu tun; **~ in one's duty** seine Pflicht versäumen; **~ as a human being/a doctor** als Mensch/Arzt versagen; **he ~ed in his attempts to escape** seine Fluchtversuche schlugen fehl *od.* misslangen; **B** (*miscarry, come to nothing*) scheitern; fehlschlagen; **if all else ~s** wenn alle Stricke *od.* Stränge reißen (*ugs.*); **C** (*become bankrupt*) Bankrott machen; Bankrott gehen; **D** (*in examination*) nicht bestehen (**in** in + *Dat.*); durchfallen (*ugs.*) (**in** in + *Dat.*); **E** (*be rejected*) ‹Bewerber, Kandidat, Bewerbung:› abgelehnt werden; **F** (*become weaker*) ‹Augenlicht, Gehör, Gedächtnis, Stärke, Eifer, Entschlossenheit:› nachlassen; ‹Atem:› schwächer werden; ‹Mut:› sinken; **his voice ~ed** ihm versagte die Stimme; **he** *or* **his health is ~ing** sein

f

Gesundheitszustand verschlechtert sich; **the light was ~ing** (*fig. literary*) es dämmerte; **G** (*break down, stop*) ‹Versorgung:› zusammenbrechen; ‹Motor, Radio:› aussetzen; ‹Generator, Batterie, Pumpe:› ausfallen; ‹Bremse, Herz:› versagen; **H** (*prove misleading*) ‹Prophezeiung, Vorhersage:› sich nicht bewahrheiten; **I** (*be insufficient*) ‹Ernte:› schlecht ausfallen; **J** (*formal: fall short*) **sth. ~s of its intended effect** etw. erreicht die beabsichtigte Wirkung nicht.

❷ *v.t.* **A** **~ to do sth.** (*not succeed in doing*) etw. nicht tun [können]; **~ to reach a decision** zu keinem Entschluss kommen; **~ to achieve one's purpose/aim** seine Absicht/sein Ziel verfehlen; **~ to pass an exam** eine Prüfung nicht bestehen; in einer Prüfung durchfallen (*ugs.*); **~ to remember sth.** etw. vergessen; **his hopes ~ed to materialize** seine Hoffnungen haben sich nicht verwirklicht; **the letter ~ed to reach its destination** der Brief ist nicht an seinem Bestimmungsort eingetroffen; **B** (*be unsuccessful in*) nicht bestehen ‹Prüfung›; durchfallen in (+ *Dat.*) (*ugs.*) ‹Prüfung›; **C** (*reject*) durchfallen lassen (*ugs.*) ‹Prüfling›; **D** **~ to do sth.** (*not do*) etw. nicht tun; (*neglect to do*) [es] versäumen, etw. zu tun; **not ~ to do sth.** etw. tun; **he never ~s to send me a card** er schreibt mir immer eine Karte *od.* versäumt es nie, mir eine Karte zu schreiben; **I ~ to see the reason why ...:** ich sehe nicht ein, warum ...; **E** (*not suffice for*) im Stich lassen; **his legs ~ed him** seine Beine ließen ihn im Stich *od.* (*geh.*) versagten ihm den Dienst; **his heart** *or* **courage ~ed him** ihn verließ der Mut; **words ~ sb.** jmdm. fehlen die Worte; jmd. findet keine Worte; **F** **the wind ~ed us** (*did not blow*) wir hatten keinen Wind; (*was blowing the wrong way*) die Windrichtung war ungünstig..

❸ *n.* **without ~:** auf jeden Fall; garantiert

**failed** /feɪld/ *attrib. adj.* nicht bestanden ‹Prüfung›; durchgefallen (*ugs.*) ‹Prüfling›; gescheitert ‹Person, Geschäft, Ehe, Versuch›

**failing** /ˈfeɪlɪŋ/ ❶ *n.* Schwäche, *die.* ❷ *prep.* **~ that** *or* **this** andernfalls; wenn nicht; **~ which** widrigenfalls (*Papierdt.*); **..., ~ which you can ...:** ..., ansonsten können Sie ... ❸ *adj.* sich verschlechternd ‹Gesundheitszustand›; nachlassend ‹Kraft›; sinkend ‹Mut›; dämmrig ‹Licht›

**'fail-safe** *adj.* ausfallsicher; abgesichert ‹Methode›; Failsafe-‹Vorkehrung, Prinzip› (*fachspr.*)

**failure** /ˈfeɪljə(r)/ *n.* **A** (*omission, neglect*) Versäumnis, *das;* **~ to do sth.** das Versäumnis, etw. zu tun; **~ to observe** *or* **follow the rule** Nichtbeachtung *od.* Übertretung der Regel; **~ to appear in court** Nichterscheinen (*Amtsspr.*) vor Gericht; **~ to deliver goods** Nichtlieferung von Waren; **~ to pass an exam** Nichtbestehen einer *od.* (*ugs.*) Durchfallen bei einer Prüfung; **B** (*lack of success*) Scheitern, *das;* (*of an application*) Ablehnung, *die;* **be doomed to ~, be bound to end in ~:** zum Scheitern verurteilt sein; **end in ~:** scheitern; **C** (*unsuccessful person or thing*) Versager, *der;* **the party/play/film was a ~:** das Fest/Stück/der Film war ein Misserfolg; **our plan/attempt was a ~:** unser Plan/Versuch war fehlgeschlagen; **the cake/dish turned out a ~:** der Kuchen/das Gericht misslang; **be a ~ as a doctor/teacher** als Arzt/Lehrer versagen; **be a ~ at doing sth.** keine glückliche Hand bei etw. haben; **D** (*non-occurrence of a process*) **the ~ of the medicine to have the desired effect** das Ausbleiben der Wirkung der Arznei; **my ~ to understand his motives** mein fehlendes Verständnis für seine Motive; **his ~ to keep in touch/to contact us was ...:** dass er es unterlassen hat, von sich hören zu lassen/mit uns Kontakt aufzunehmen, war ...; **E** (*running short, breaking down*) (*of supply*) Zusammenbruch, *der;* (*of engine, generator*) Ausfall, *der;* **signal/pump/engine/generator ~:** Ausfall des Signals/der Pumpe/des Motors/des Generators; **power** *or* **electricity ~:** Stromausfall, *der;* **brake ~:** Versagen der Bremsen; **crop ~, ~ of crops** Missernte, *die;* **F** (*Med.*) Versagen, *das;* Insuffizienz, *die* (*fachspr.*); **G** (*deterioration, weakening*) (*of health*) Verschlechterung, *die;* (*of hearing, eyesight, strength*) Nachlassen, *das;* (*of energy*) Erlahmen, *das;* (*of courage*) Sinken, *das;* **H** (*absence, non-existence*) Fehlen, *das;* **~ of justice** Versagen der Justiz; **I** (*bankruptcy*) Zusammenbruch, *der;* **a bank ~:** der Zusammenbruch einer Bank

**fain** /feɪn/ (*arch.*) ❶ *adv.* [zu] gern. ❷ *pred. adj.* bereit; geneigt; **be ~ to do** *or* **of doing sth.** geneigt sein, etw. zu tun

**faint** /feɪnt/ ❶ *adj.* **A** (*dim, indistinct, pale*) matt ‹Licht, Farbe, Stimme, Lächeln›; schwach ‹Geruch, Duft›; leise ‹Flüstern, Geräusch, Stimme, Ton, Ruf, Schritt›; entfernt ‹Ähnlichkeit›; undeutlich ‹Umriss, Linie, Gestalt, Spur, Stimme, Fotokopie›; **B** (*weak, vague*) leise ‹Wunsch, Hoffnung, Verdacht, Ahnung›; gering ‹Chance›; **not have the ~est idea** *or* **notion** nicht die geringste *od.* blasseste Ahnung haben; **Where is he? — I haven't the ~est idea** *or* (*coll.*) **~est** Wo ist er? — Keine Ahnung! (*ugs.*); **C** (*giddy, weak*) matt; schwach; **she felt/looked ~:** sie fühlte sich/schien einer Ohnmacht nahe; ihr war schwindelig/ihr schien schwindelig zu sein; **be ~ with** *or* **feel ~ from hunger** *etc.* vor Hunger *usw.* matt *od.* schwach sein; **his breathing grew ~:** sein Atem wurde schwächer; **D** (*timid*) gering, schwach ‹Mut›; **~ heart never won fair lady** (*prov.*) wer nicht wagt, der nicht gewinnt (*Spr.*); **E** (*feeble*) schwach ‹Lob, Widerstand›; zaghaft ‹Versuch, Bemühung›; ⇒ *also* **damn** 1 A; **F** ⇒ **feint²**.

❷ *v.i.* ohnmächtig werden, in Ohnmacht fallen (**from** vor + *Dat.*).

❸ *n.* Ohnmacht, *die;* **in a [dead] ~:** ohnmächtig; **go off in** *or* **fall into a ~:** ohnmächtig werden; in Ohnmacht fallen

**faint: ~-heart** *n.* Hasenherz, *das* (*abwertend*); **~-hearted** *adj.* hasenherzig (*abwertend*); zaghaft ‹Versuch›; **~-heartedly** hasenherzig (*abwertend*)

**faintly** /ˈfeɪntlɪ/ *adv.* **A** (*indistinctly*) undeutlich ‹markieren, hören›; kaum ‹sichtbar›; schwach ‹riechen, scheinen›; entfernt ‹sich ähneln›; **B** (*slightly*) leise ‹hoffen, verdächtigen›; wenig ‹interessieren›; leicht ‹enttäuschen, herablassend›; **C** (*feebly*) zaghaft ‹versuchen, lächeln›

**faintness** /ˈfeɪntnɪs/ *n., no pl.* **A** (*dimness, feebleness*) (*of marking, outline, voice*) Undeutlichkeit, *die;* (*of resemblance*) Entferntheit, *die;* (*of colour*) Mattheit, *die;* (*of old photograph*) Verblasstheit, *die;* **the ~ of the smell/light** der schwache Geruch/das schwache Licht; **the ~ of his smile/recollection** sein schwaches Lächeln/seine schwache Erinnerung; **B** (*dizziness*) Schwäche, *die;* Mattigkeit, *die;* **feeling of ~:** Schwächegefühl, *das;* **C** (*cowardice*) **~ of spirits** Verzagtheit, *die;* **~ of heart** (*literary*) Zagheit, *die* (*geh.*)

**fair¹** /feə(r)/ *n.* **A** (*gathering*) Markt, *der;* (*with shows, merry-go-rounds*) Jahrmarkt, *der;* **village/cattle ~:** Dorf-/Viehmarkt, *der;* **a day after the ~** (*fig.*) zu spät; **B** ⇒ **fun-fair**; **C** (*exhibition*) Ausstellung, *die;* Messe, *die;* **agricultural/world/industries ~:** Landwirtschafts-/Welt-/Industrieausstellung, *die;* **book/antiques/trade ~:** Buch-/Antiquitäten-/Handelsmesse, *die*

**fair²** ❶ *adj.* **A** (*just*) gerecht; begründet ‹Beschwerde, Annahme›; berechtigt ‹Frage›; fair ‹Spiel, Kampf, Prozess, Preis, Beurteilung, Handel›; (*representative, typical*) typisch, markant ‹Beispiel, Kostprobe›; **be ~ with** *or* **to sb.** gerecht gegen jmdn. *od.* zu jmdm. sein; **it's only ~ to do sth./for sb. to do sth.** es ist nur recht und billig, etw. zu tun/dass jmd. etw. tut; **strict but ~:** streng, aber gerecht; **a ~ day's wages for a ~ day's work** anständiger Lohn für anständige Arbeit; **that's not ~, you're not ~:** das ist ungerecht *od.* unfair; **[well, that's] ~ enough!** (*coll.*) dagegen ist nichts einzuwenden; (*OK*) na gut; **by ~ means or foul** egal wie (*ugs.*); auf ehrliche oder unehrliche Weise; **all's ~ in love and war** in der Liebe und im Krieg ist alles erlaubt; **~ play** Fairness, *die;* Fair play, *das;* **~ play in business** anständiges Geschäftsgebaren; **~ and square** ehrlich; ⇒ *also* **crack** 1 A; **deal¹** 3 A; **do²** D; **field** 1 E; **game¹** 1 G; **share** 1 A; **B** (*not bad, pretty good*) ganz gut ‹Bilanz, Vorstellung, Anzahl, Menge, Kenntnisse, Chance›; ziemlich ‹Maß, Geschwindigkeit›; **a ~ amount of work** ein schönes Stück Arbeit; **she has a ~ amount of sense** sie ist ganz vernünftig; **not all, but a ~ number** nicht alle, aber doch recht viele; **be a ~ judge of character** ein recht guter Menschenkenner sein; ⇒ *also* **middling** 1 B; **C** (*favourable*) schön ‹Wetter, Tag, Abend›; günstig ‹Wetterlage, Wind›; heiter ‹Wetter, Tag, Himmel, Morgen›; **the barometer/weather is set ~:** das Barometer steht auf Schönwetter/das schöne Wetter hält an; **be in a ~ way to doing sth.** gute Aussichten haben, etw. zu tun; **be in a ~ way to succeed/winning** gute Erfolgs-/Gewinnchancen haben; **D** (*considerable, satisfactory*) ansehnlich ‹Erbe, Vermögen›; **E** (*specious*) groß ‹Rede, Worte, Versprechung›; schön ‹Geschichte›; **F** (*complimentary*) schön ‹Rede, Worte›; **G** (*blond*) blond ‹Haar, Person›; (*not dark*) hell ‹Teint, Haut›; hellhäutig ‹Person›; **very ~:** hellblond; **a ~ head** ein Blondkopf; **H** (*poet. or literary: beautiful*) hold (*dichter. veralt.*) ‹Kind, Mädchen, Maid, Prinz, Gesicht›; schön ‹Stadt›; (*pure, unsullied*) gut, unbescholten ‹Name, Ruf›; **the ~ sex** das schöne Geschlecht; **with her own ~ hands** (*iron.*) mit ihren zarten Händen; **I** (*clean, clear*) rein (*meist geh.*) ‹Wasser›; sauber ‹Handschrift›; **~ copy** Reinschrift, *die;* **make a ~ copy of sth.** etw. ins Reine schreiben.

❷ *adv.* **A** (*in a ~ manner*) fair ‹kämpfen, spielen›; gerecht ‹behandeln›; **B** (*coll.: completely*) völlig; **the sight ~ took my breath away** der Anblick hat mir glatt (*ugs.*) den Atem verschlagen; **C** **~ and square** (*honestly*) offen und ehrlich; (*accurately*) voll, genau ‹schlagen, treffen›. ⇒ *also* **bid** 2 A; **dinkum**; **play** 2 A.

❸ *n.* **~'s ~** (*coll.*) Gerechtigkeit muss sein

**fair: ~ 'copy** *n.* Reinschrift, *die;* **make a ~ copy of sth.** etw. ins Reine schreiben; **~-faced** *adj.* (*having light complexion*) hellhäutig; **~ground** *n.* Festplatz, *der;* **~-haired** *adj.* blond; **~-haired boy** (*Amer. fig.*) Liebling, *der;* Favorit, *der*

**fairing** *n.* (*structure*) Verkleidung, *die*

**fairish** /ˈfeərɪʃ/ *adj.* passabel

**'Fair Isle** *attrib. adj.* (*Textiles*) *für die Insel Fair Isle typisch;* ≈ Shetland‹pullover, -muster›

**fairly** /ˈfeəlɪ/ *adv.* **A** fair ‹kämpfen, spielen›; gerecht ‹bestrafen, beurteilen, behandeln›; **come by sth. ~:** auf ehrliche Weise zu etw. kommen; **B** (*tolerably*) ziemlich; **C** (*completely*) völlig; heftig, sehr ‹bestürmen, bedrängen›; **it ~ took my breath away** es hat mir glatt (*ugs.*) den Atem verschlagen; **D** (*actually*) richtig; **I ~ jumped for joy** ich habe einen regelrechten Freudensprung gemacht; **E** **~ and squarely** (*honestly*) offen und ehrlich; (*accurately*) voll, genau ‹schlagen, treffen›; **look at a situation ~ and squarely** eine Lage nüchtern betrachten; **beat sb. ~ and squarely** jmdn. nach allen Regeln der Kunst (*ugs.*) besiegen

**'fair-minded** *adj.* unvoreingenommen

**fairness** /ˈfeənɪs/ *n., no pl.* Gerechtigkeit, *die;* **sense of ~:** Gerechtigkeitsgefühl, *das;* **in all ~ [to sb.]** fairerweise; um fair [gegen jmdn.] zu sein

**fair: ~-sized** /ˈfeəsaɪzd/ *adj.* recht ansehnlich; **~way** *n.* **A** (*channel*) Fahrrinne, *die;* **B** (*Golf*) Fairway, *das;* **~-weather friend** *n.* Freund, der/Freundin, die nur in guten Zeiten treu ist

**fairy** /ˈfeərɪ/ ❶ *n.* **A** (*Mythol.*) Fee, *die;* (*in a household*) Kobold, *der;* **B** (*sl. derog.: homosexual*) Tunte, *die* (*salopp*); Warme, *der* (*salopp*). ❷ *attrib. adj.* feenhaft ‹Stimme, Wesen›; Feen‹reigen, -reich›

**fairy: ~ 'godmother** *n.* (*lit. or fig.*) gute Fee; **F~land** *n.* (*land of fairies*) Feenland, *das;* (*enchanted region*) Märchenland, *das;* **winter ~land** winterliche Märchenlandschaft; **~ lights** *n. pl.* kleine farbige Lichter; **~ 'ring** *n.* (*Bot.*) Hexenring, *der;* **~ story** ⇒ **~ tale** 1; **~ tale** ❶ *n.* (*lit. or fig.*) Märchen, *das;* ❷ *adj.* Märchen‹landschaft›; märchenhaft schön ‹Szene, Wirkung, Kleid, Ball›; märchenhaft ‹Schönheit›

**fait accompli** /feɪt əˈkɒmplɪ/ *n., pl.* **faits accomplis** /feɪt əˈkɒmplɪ/ vollendete Tatsache; Fait accompli, *das (geh.)*

**faith** /feɪθ/ *n.* **A** *(reliance, trust)* Vertrauen, *das;* **have ~ in sb./sth.** Vertrauen zu jmdm./etw. haben; auf jmdn./etw. vertrauen; **have ~ in oneself** Selbstvertrauen haben; **lose ~ in sb./sth.** das Vertrauen zu jmdm./etw. verlieren; **pin one's ~ on** *or* **put one's ~ in sb./sth.** sein Vertrauen auf *od.* in jmdn./etw. setzen; **B** *(belief)* Glaube, *der;* **on ~:** in gutem Glauben; **C** *(religious belief)* Glaube, *der;* **the ~:** der [christliche] Glaube; **different Christian ~s** verschiedene christliche Glaubensrichtungen; **a matter of ~:** eine Glaubenssache; **D** *(promise)* [Ehren]wort, *das; (pledge of fidelity)* Treue, *die;* **pledge one's ~ to sb.** jmdm. Treue geloben; **to do that would be breaking ~:** das zu tun, wäre [ein] Wortbruch; **break ~ with an ally** an einem Verbündeten treubrüchig werden; **keep ~ with sb.** jmdm. treu bleiben *od.* die Treue halten; **E** *(loyalty)* Redlichkeit, *die;* **good/bad ~:** Vertrauen/Misstrauen, *das;* **in good ~:** ohne Hintergedanken; *(unsuspectingly)* in gutem Glauben; guten Glaubens; **in all good ~:** auf Treu und Glauben; **in bad ~:** in böser Absicht

**faithful** /ˈfeɪθfl/ **1** *adj.* **A** *(showing faith, loyal)* treu; **remain ~ to sb./sth.** jmdm./einer Sache treu bleiben; **remain ~ to one's promise** [sein] Wort halten; sein Versprechen halten; **B** *(conscientious)* pflichttreu; treu ‹Briefschreiber›; [ge]treu ‹Diener›; **C** *(accurate)* [wahrheits]getreu; originalgetreu ‹Wiedergabe, Kopie›. **2** *n. pl.* **the ~:** die Gläubigen; **the party ~:** treue Anhänger der Partei

**faithfully** /ˈfeɪθfəlɪ/ *adv.* **A** *(loyally)* treu ‹dienen›; pflichttreu ‹überbringen, zustellen›; gewissenhaft ‹hüten, halten›; hoch und heilig, fest ‹versprechen›; **promise [me] ~ that ...** *(coll.: emphatically)* versprich mir ganz fest, dass ...; **B** *(accurately)* wahrheitsgetreu ‹erzählen›; originalgetreu ‹wiedergeben›; genau ‹befolgen›; **C** ▶ **1286** **yours ~** *(in letter)* mit freundlichen Grüßen; *(more formally)* hochachtungsvoll

**faith:** **~ healer** *n.* Gesundbeter, *der*/-beterin, *die;* **~ healing** *n.* Gesundbeten, *das*

**faithless** /ˈfeɪθlɪs/ *adj.* **A** *(perfidious, unreliable)* untreu ‹Geliebte[r], Mann, Frau›; treulos ‹Untertan, Diener, Freund, Handeln, Verhalten›; **be ~ to sb./sth.** jmdm./einer Sache untreu sein; **B** *(unbelieving)* ungläubig

**fake** /feɪk/ **1** *adj.* unecht; gefälscht ‹Dokument, Banknote, Münze›; **~ money** Falschgeld, *das.* **2** *n.* **A** *(thing ~d up)* Imitation, *die; (painting)* Fälschung, *die;* **B** *(trick)* Finte, *die; (fig.)* Schwindel, *der (abwertend);* **C** *(spurious person)* Schwindler, *der*/Schwindlerin, *die.* **3** *v.t.* **A** *(feign, contrive)* nachahmen ‹Akzent›; fälschen ‹Unterschrift›; vortäuschen ‹Krankheit, Einbruch, Unfall›; **B** *(make plausible)* **~ [up]** imitieren ‹Diamanten›; fälschen ‹Gemälde›; erfinden ‹Geschichte›; **C** *(alter so as to deceive)* frisieren *(ugs.);* verfälschen. **4** *v.i.* simulieren

**faker** /ˈfeɪkə(r)/ *n. (swindler)* Schwindler, *der*/Schwindlerin, *die; (pretender)* Heuchler, *der*/Heuchlerin, *die*

**fakir** /ˈfeɪkɪə(r), fəˈkɪə(r)/ *n.* Fakir, *der*

**falcon** /ˈfɔːlkn, ˈfɔːkn/ *n. (Ornith.)* Falke, *der*

**falconer** /ˈfɔːlkənə(r), ˈfɔːkənə(r)/ *n. (Hunting)* Falkner, *der*/Falknerin, *die*

**falconry** /ˈfɔːlknrɪ, ˈfɔːknrɪ/ *n., no pl., no indef. art.* Falknerei, *die*

**fall** /fɔːl/ **1** *n.* **A** *(act or manner of falling)* Fallen, *das; (of person)* Sturz, *der;* **~ of leaves/snow/rain** Blatt- *od.* Laub-/Schnee-/Regenfall, *der;* **in a ~:** bei einem Sturz; **have a ~:** stürzen; **a ten-inch ~ of rain/snow** eine Niederschlagsmenge von 254 mm/25 cm Schnee[fall]; **B** *(collapse, defeat)* Fall, *der; (of culture, dynasty, empire)* Untergang, *der; (of government)* Sturz, *der;* **~ from power** Entmachtung, *die;* **C** *(lapse into sin)* [Sünden]fall, *der;* **the F~ [of man]** *(Theol.)* der Sündenfall; **D** *(slope)* Abfall, *der* **(to** zu, nach); **E** *usu. in pl. (waterfall)* [Wasser]fall, *der;* **Niagara F~s** Niagarafälle; der Niagarafall; **F** *(fig.: decrease)* ⇒ **drop** 1 I; **G** *(of night etc.)* Einbruch, *der;* **H** ▶ **1504** *(Amer.: autumn)* Herbst, *der;* **I** *(Wrestling) (throw)* Schulterwurf, *der; (wrestling-bout)* Ringkampf, *der; (fig.)* **try a** *or* **one's ~ with sb.** es auf eine Kraftprobe mit jmdm. ankommen lassen. ⇒ *also* **ride** 2 C.

**2** *v.i.*, **fell** /fel/, **~en** /ˈfɔːln/ **A** *(drop)* fallen; **~ off sth., ~ down from sth.** von etw. [herunter]fallen; **~ down [into] sth.** in etw. *(Akk.)* [hinein]fallen; **~ out of sth.** aus etw. [heraus]fallen; **~ to the ground** zu Boden *od.* auf den Boden fallen; **she let sth. ~ [from her hand]** *(deliberately)* sie hat etw. [aus der Hand] fallen lassen; *(by mistake)* ihr ist etw. aus der Hand gefallen; **~ down dead** tot umfallen; **~ down the stairs** *or* **downstairs** die Treppe herunter-/hinunterfallen; **~ into the trap** in die Falle gehen; **always ~ on one's feet** *(fig.)* immer [wieder] auf die Beine *(ugs.) od.* Füße fallen; **nearly** *or* **almost ~ off one's chair** *(lit. or fig.)* fast vom Stuhl fallen *(ugs.);* **~ to earth** auf die Erde *od.* zur Erde fallen; **the blossom ~s** die Blüte fällt ab; **the land ~s to sea level** das Gelände fällt auf Meeresspiegelhöhe ab; **~ from a great height** aus großer Höhe abstürzen; **~ing star** *(Astron.)* Sternschnuppe, *die;* **rain/snow is ~ing** es regnet/schneit; **B** *(fig.)* ‹Nacht, Dunkelheit:› hereinbrechen; ‹Abend:› anbrechen; ‹Stille:› eintreten; **night began to ~:** die Nacht brach herein; **C** *(fig.: swoop)* **~ upon** ‹Katastrophe, Unglück, Seuche:› hereinbrechen über (+ *Akk.*) *(geh.);* ‹Rache:› treffen; ‹Furcht:› befallen; **D** *(fig.: be uttered)* ‹Worte, Bemerkungen:› fallen; **~ from sb.'s lips** *or* **mouth** über jmds. Lippen *(Akk.)* kommen; **let ~ a remark** eine Bemerkung fallen lassen; **E** *(lose high position)* fallen; **~ from power** entmachtet werden; **~ from one's high estate** seinen hohen Rang einbüßen; **~en angel** gefallener Engel; **~en arch** *(Med.)* Senkfuß, *der;* **F** *(lose chastity)* fallen; *(become pregnant)* **~ [with child]** schwanger werden; **a ~en woman** ein gefallenes Mädchen; **G** *(become detached)* ‹Blätter:› [ab]fallen; **~ out** ‹Haare, Federn:› ausfallen; **H** *(hang down)* fallen; **a lock fell over her face** eine Locke fiel *od.* hing ihr ins Gesicht; **I** *(be born)* ‹Lamm, Kalb usw.:› geworfen werden; **J** *(sink to lower level)* sinken; ‹Barometer:› fallen; ‹Absatz, Verkauf:› zurückgehen; *(in pitch)* ‹Musik:› [in der Tonhöhe] fallen; **~ by 10 per cent/from 10 [°C] to 0 [°C]** um 10%/von 10 [°C] auf 0 [°C] sinken; **[make sb.] ~ in sb.'s esteem** *or* **estimation/eyes** *(fig.)* [jmdn.] in jmds. Achtung/Augen *(Dat.)* sinken [lassen]; **~ into error/sin/temptation** einen Fehler/eine Sünde begehen/der Versuchung er- *od.* unterliegen; **K** ⇒ **~ away b;** **L** *(issue)* ‹Fluss:› münden **(into** in + *Akk.*); **M** *(subside)* ‹Wasserspiegel, Gezeitenhöhe:› fallen; ‹Wind, Sturm:› sich legen; **N** *(show dismay)* **his/her face** *or* **countenance fell** er/sie machte ein langes Gesicht *(ugs.);* **O** *(look down)* **his/her glance/eyes fell** er/sie senkte den Blick/die Augen; **P** *(no longer stand)* fallen; ‹Baum:› umstürzen; ‹Pferd:› stürzen; **~ to the ground** zu Boden fallen; *(fig.)* ‹Plan, Verabredung usw.:› ins Wasser fallen; ‹Argument, These:› in sich zusammenfallen; **~ into one another's arms** einander in die Arme fallen *od.* sinken; **~ on one's knees** auf die Knie fallen; sich auf die Knie werfen; **~ at sb.'s feet** *or* **down before sb.** jmdm. zu Füßen fallen; **~ [flat] on one's face** *(lit. or fig.)* auf die Nase fallen *(ugs.);* **Q** *(be defeated)* ‹Festung, Stadt:› fallen; ‹Monarchie, Regierung:› gestürzt werden; ‹Reich:› untergehen; **the fortress fell to the enemy** die Festung fiel dem Feind in die Hände; **R** *(fail)* untergehen; **united we stand, divided we ~:** Einigkeit macht stark *(Spr.);* **S** *(perish)* ‹Soldat:› fallen; **the ~en [soldiers]** die Gefallenen; **T** *(collapse, break)* einstürzen; **cause a building to ~:** ein Gebäude zum Einsturz bringen; **~ to pieces, ~ apart** ‹Buch, Wagen:› auseinander fallen; *(fig.)* ‹Unternehmen, jmds. Welt:› zusammenbrechen; **~ in two** entzweigehen; **~ apart at the seams** an den Nähten aufplatzen; *(fig.)* ‹Plan:› ins Wasser fallen *(ugs.);* **U** *(Cricket)* **a wicket ~s** ein Schlagmann wird ausgeschlagen; **V** *(come by chance, duty, etc.)* fallen **(to** an + *Akk.*); **it fell to me** *or* **to my lot to do it** das Los, es tun zu müssen, hat mich getroffen; **~ [in] sb.'s way** jmdm. zufallen; **~ among thieves** unter die Räuber fallen; **~ into an ambush** in einen Hinterhalt fallen; **he has ~en into the role of a mere spectator** er ist in die Rolle des Zuschauers gedrängt worden; **~ into bad company** in schlechte Gesellschaft geraten; **~ into conversation with sb.** mit jmdm. ins Gespräch kommen; **~ into decay** ‹Gebäude:› verfallen; *(fig.)* ‹Monarchie, Reich, Institution:› zerfallen; ‹Gesetz:› seine Bedeutung verlieren; **~ into parts/sections** in Teile/Abschnitte zerfallen; ‹Roman:› sich in Teile/Abschnitte gliedern; **~ into different categories** in *od.* unter verschiedene Kategorien fallen; **~ to doing sth.** anfangen *od.* beginnen, etw. zu tun; **they fell to fighting among themselves** es kam zu einer Schlägerei zwischen ihnen; *abs.* **~ to** beginnen, drauflos zu essen/arbeiten *usw.;* ⇒ *also* **fall on;** **W** *(take specified direction)* ‹Auge, Strahl, Licht, Schatten:› fallen **(upon** auf + *Akk.*); **X** *(have specified place)* liegen **(on, to** auf + *Dat.*, **within** in + *Dat.*); **~ into** *or* **under a category** in *od.* unter eine Kategorie fallen; **Y** *(pass into specified state)* **~ into a rage** einen Wutanfall bekommen; **~ into despair** verzweifeln; **~ into a deep sleep** in tiefen Schlaf fallen *od. (geh.)* versinken; **~ ill** krank werden; **~ into a swoon** *or* **faint** in Ohnmacht fallen; **Z** *(occur)* fallen **(on** auf + *Akk.*) ‹Datum›; **Easter ~s late this year** Ostern fällt dieses Jahr spät. ⇒ *also* **asleep** A; **astern; flat**[2] 1 A, B; **foul** 1 F; **grace** 1 E; **hand** 1 C; **line**[1] 1 F; **love** 1 A; **place** 1 J; **prey** 1 B; **push** 1 A; **short** 2 C; **silent** A; **victim** A; **wayside**

**~ aˈbout** *v.i.* **~ about [laughing** *or* **with laughter]** sich [vor Lachen] kringeln *(ugs.)*

**~ aˈway** *v.i.* **A** abfallen **(from** von); *(from allegiance)* sich lösen **(from** aus); ‹Mitgliedschaft, Einnahmen:› sinken; *(from friend, truth)* sich abwenden **(from** von); **B** *(have slope)* abfallen **(to** zu)

**~ ˈback** *v.i.* zurückweichen; ‹Armee:› sich zurückziehen; *(lag)* zurückbleiben; ⇒ *also* **fall-back**

**~ ˈback on** *v.t.* zurückgreifen auf (+ *Akk.*)

**~ behind** **1** /ˈ---/ *v.t.* zurückfallen hinter (+ *Akk.*). **2** /--ˈ-/ *v.i.* zurückbleiben; **~ behind with sth.** mit etw. in Rückstand *(Akk.)* geraten

**~ ˈdown** *v.i.* **A** ⇒ **~** 2 A; **B** *(collapse)* ‹Brücke, Gebäude:› einstürzen; ‹Person:› hinfallen; **~ down [on sth.]** *(fig. coll.)* [bei etw.] versagen; **the argument ~s down on one point** das Argument sticht in einem Punkt nicht; **the theory fell down for** *or* **on lack of evidence** die Theorie war nicht haltbar, weil es an Beweisen fehlte; **~ down on a job** einer Aufgabe nicht gewachsen sein

**~ for** *v.t. (coll.)* **A** *(~ in love with)* sich verknallen in *(ugs.);* **B** *(be persuaded by)* hereinfallen auf (+ *Akk.*) *(ugs.)*

**~ ˈin** *v.i.* **A** hineinfallen; **B** *(Mil.)* antreten **(for** zu); **~ in!** angetreten!; **C** *(collapse)* ‹Gebäude, Wand usw.:› einstürzen

**~ ˈin with** *v.t.* **A** *(meet and join)* stoßen zu; **B** *(agree)* beipflichten (+ *Dat.*) ‹Person, Meinung, Vorschlag usw.›; eingehen auf (+ *Akk.*) ‹Plan, Person, Bitte, Forderung›; entsprechen (+ *Dat.*) ‹Forderung, Bitte›; einstimmen in (+ *Akk.*) ‹Ton›

**~ ˈoff** *v.i.* **A** ⇒ **~** 2 A; **B** ‹Nachfrage, Produktion, Aufträge, Anzahl:› zurückgehen; **C** ‹Mut, Niveau:› sinken; ‹Dienstleistungen, Gesundheit, Geschäft:› sich verschlechtern; ‹Begeisterung, Eifer, Interesse:› nachlassen. ⇒ *also* **fall-off**

**~ on** *v.t.* **A** *(lit., or fig.: attack)* herfallen über; **B** *(be borne by)* **~ on sb.** jmdm. zufallen; ‹Verdacht, Schuld, Los:› auf jmdn. fallen

**~ ˈout** *v.i.* **A** herausfallen; **B** ⇒ **~** 2 G; **C** *(quarrel)* **~ out [with sb. over sth.]** sich [mit jmdm. über etw. *(Akk.)*] [zer]streiten; **D** *(come to happen)* vonstatten gehen; **see how things ~ out** abwarten, wie sich die Dinge entwickeln; **it [so] fell out that ...** *(literary)* es begab sich *(geh.)*, dass ...; **E** *(Mil.)* wegtreten; **~ out!** weggetreten! ⇒ *also* **fallout**

f

~ **over** ❶ /'---/ *v.t.* Ⓐ (*stumble over*) fallen über (+ *Akk.*); **they were ~ing over each other to get the sweets** sie drängelten sich, um die Süßigkeiten zu bekommen; **~ over oneself** *or* **one's own feet** über seine eigenen Füße stolpern; Ⓑ **~ over oneself to do sth.** (*fig. coll.*) sich vor Eifer überschlagen, um etw. zu tun (*ugs.*). ❷ /-'--/ *v.i.* umfallen; (*in faint*) hinfallen; **~ over on to sth.** auf etw. (*Akk.*) fallen; ⇒ *also* **backwards** A

~ **'through** *v.i.* (*fig.*) ins Wasser fallen (*ugs.*); ‹Einigungsversuch:› fehlschlagen

~ **upon** Ⓐ ⇒ ~ **on**; Ⓑ ⇒ ~ 2 C, W

**fallacious** /fə'leɪʃəs/ *adj.* Ⓐ (*containing a fallacy*) irrig; **~ conclusion/syllogism** Fehl- *od.* Trugschluss, *der;* Ⓑ (*deceptive, delusive*) irreführend ‹Methode, Bericht›; trügerisch ‹Hoffnung, Friede›

**fallacy** /'fæləsɪ/ *n.* Ⓐ (*delusion, error*) Irrtum, *der;* Ⓑ (*unsoundness, delusiveness*) Irrigkeit, *die;* Ⓒ (*Logic*) Trugschluss, *der*

**'fallback** *adj.* **~ pay** Überbrückungsgeld, *das;* **~ job** (*for seasonal worker*) Nebenerwerb, *der* (*zur Überbrückung außerhalb der Saison*)

**fallen** ⇒ **fall** 2

**'fall guy** *n.* (*coll.*) Ⓐ (*victim*) Lackierte, *der/die* (*salopp*); Ⓑ (*scapegoat*) Prügelknabe, *der* (*ugs.*); **be the ~ for sb.** den Prügelknaben für jmdn. abgeben

**fallibility** /fælɪ'bɪlɪtɪ/ *n., no pl.* Fehlbarkeit, *die*

**fallible** /'fælɪbl/ *adj.* Ⓐ (*liable to err*) fehlbar ‹Person›; **~ human nature** die Fehlbarkeit des Menschen; Ⓑ (*liable to be erroneous*) nicht unfehlbar

**'fall-off** *n.* (*in quality*) [Ver]minderung, *die* (**in** *Gen.*); (*in quantity*) Rückgang, *der* (**in** *Gen.*); **~ in quality/exports** Qualitäts[ver]minderung, *die*/Exportrückgang, *der*

**Fallopian tube** /fə'ləʊpɪən tju:b/ *n.* (*Anat.*) Eileiter, *der*

**'fallout** *n.* radioaktiver Niederschlag; (*fig.: side effects*) Abfallprodukte *Pl.;* **~ shelter** Atombunker, *der*

**fallow**[1] /'fæləʊ/ ❶ *n.* (*Agric.*) Brache, *die.* ❷ *adj.* (*lit. or fig.*) brach liegend; **~ ground** *or* **field/land** Brache, *die*/Brachland, *das;* **lie ~** (*lit. or fig.*) brach liegen

**fallow**[2] *adj.* (*in colour*) rotbraun

**'fallow deer** *n.* Damhirsch, *der*

**false** /fɔ:ls, fɒls/ ❶ *adj.* Ⓐ falsch; Fehl‹deutung, -urteil›; Falsch‹meldung. -eid, -aussage, -geld›; treulos ‹Geliebte[r]›; gefälscht ‹Urkunde, Dokument›; **~ doctrine** Irrlehre, *die;* **be ~ to one's wife** seine Frau betrügen; seiner Frau (*Dat.*) untreu sein; Ⓑ (*sham*) falsch ‹Scham, Bescheidenheit, Stolz›; künstlich ‹Wimpern, Auge›; (*deliberate*) geheuchelt ‹Bescheidenheit›; gekünstelt ‹Tränen, Lächeln›; **distinguish the real from the ~:** zwischen Richtigem und Falschem *od.* Echtem und Unechtem unterscheiden; **under a ~ name** unter falschem Namen; Ⓒ (*deceptive*) falsch ‹Hoffnung, Sparsamkeit›; unberechtigt ‹Furcht›; trügerisch ‹Wärme, Licht›.

❷ *adv.* unehrlich; **play sb. ~:** mit jmdm. ein falsches Spiel treiben

**false: ~ a'larm** *n.* blinder Alarm; **~ 'bottom** *n.* doppelter Boden; **~ 'card** *n. zwecks Irreführung des Gegners gespielte Karte;* **~ 'colours** *n. pl.* **sail under ~ colours** (*fig.*) unter falscher Flagge segeln; **~ 'dawn** *n.* (*Astron.*) ≈ Zodiakallicht, *das;* (*fig.*) Täuschung, *die;* **~ 'hair** *n.* falsches Haar

**falsehood** /'fɔ:lshʊd, 'fɒlshʊd/ *n.* Ⓐ *no pl.* (*falseness*) Unrichtigkeit, *die;* Ⓑ (*untrue thing*) Unwahrheit, *die;* **tell a ~:** die Unwahrheit sagen

**false 'keel** *n.* (*Naut.*) Schutzkiel, *der*

**falsely** /'fɔ:lslɪ, 'fɒlslɪ/ *adv.* Ⓐ (*dishonestly*) unaufrichtig ‹sprechen›; falsch ‹schwören›; Ⓑ (*incorrectly, unjustly*) falsch ‹auslegen, verstehen›; fälschlich[erweise] ‹annehmen, glauben, behaupten, anklagen, beschuldigen, verurteilen›; Ⓒ (*insincerely*) gekünstelt ‹lächeln›

**false 'move** ⇒ **false step**

**falseness** /'fɔ:lsnɪs, 'fɒlsnɪs/ *n., no pl.* Ⓐ (*incorrectness*) Unrichtigkeit, *die;* Falschheit, *die;* Ⓑ (*faithlessness*) Treulosigkeit, *die* (**to** gegenüber); Ⓒ (*insincerity*) Unaufrichtigkeit, *die*

**false: ~ po'sition** *n. Lage, in der man scheinbar entgegen seinen Prinzipien handeln muss;* **he was put in a ~ position** er wurde in ein schiefes Licht gerückt; **~ pre'tences** *n. pl.* Vorspiegelung falscher Tatsachen; **~ 'start** *n.* (*Sport; also fig.*) Fehlstart, *der;* **~ 'step** *n.* (*lit. or fig.*) falscher Schritt; **make a ~ step** einen falschen Schritt tun; **~ 'teeth** *n. pl.* [künstliches] Gebiss; Prothese, *die*

**falsetto** /fɔ:l'setəʊ, fɒl'setəʊ/ *n., pl.* **~s** (*voice*) Kopfstimme, *die;* (*Mus.: of man*) Falsett, *das;* Fistelstimme, *die*

**falsies** /'fɔ:lsɪz, 'fɒlsɪz/ *n. pl.* (*coll.*) Gummibusen, *der* (*salopp*)

**falsification** /fɔ:lsɪfɪ'keɪʃn, fɒlsɪfɪ'keɪʃn/ *n.* Ⓐ (*alteration*) Fälschung, *die;* (*of fact, event, truth, history*) Verfälschung, *die;* **lies and ~s** Lügen und Unwahrheiten; Ⓑ (*showing that sth. is false*) Widerlegung, *die*

**falsify** /'fɔ:lsɪfaɪ, 'fɒlsɪfaɪ/ *v.t.* Ⓐ (*alter*) fälschen; (*misrepresent*) verfälschen ‹Tatsache, Geschichte, Ereignis, Wahrheit›; Ⓑ (*show to be false*) widerlegen; falsifizieren (*geh.*)

**falsity** /'fɔ:lsɪtɪ, 'fɒlsɪtɪ/ *n., no pl.* Ⓐ (*incorrectness*) Falschheit, *die;* Ⓑ (*falsehood*) Unwahrheit, *die;* (*error*) Unrichtigkeit, *die;* Ⓒ (*deceitfulness, unfaithfulness*) Treulosigkeit, *die;* Ⓓ (*artificiality*) Unnatürlichkeit, *die*

**falter** /'fɔ:ltə(r), 'fɒltə(r)/ ❶ *v.i.* Ⓐ (*waver*) stocken; ‹Mut, Hoffnung:› sinken; **~ in one's resolve/desire/determination** in seinem Entschluss/Wunsch/seiner Entschlossenheit schwankend werden; **their courage/hopes did not ~:** sie verloren nicht den Mut/die Hoffnung; Ⓑ (*stumble, stagger*) wanken; **with ~ing steps** mit [sch]wankenden Schritten. ❷ *v.t.* **~ [out] sth.** etw. stammeln

**fame** /feɪm/ *n., no pl.* Ruhm, *der;* **rise to ~:** zu Ruhm kommen *od.* gelangen; **win ~ for oneself** Ruhm gewinnen; **a man of [great] literary/political ~:** ein [sehr] berühmter Literat/Politiker; **is that Erich Segal of 'Love Story' ~?** ist das der Erich Segal, der mit „Love Story" berühmt geworden ist?; **ill ~:** schlechter Ruf; ⇒ *also* **house** 1 E

**famed** /feɪmd/ *adj.* berühmt (**for** für, wegen); ⇒ *also* **far-famed**

**familiar** /fə'mɪljə(r)/ ❶ *adj.* Ⓐ (*well acquainted*) bekannt; **be ~ with sb.** jmdn. näher kennen; **we never really got ~:** wir lernten uns (*Akk.*) nie richtig kennen *od.* (*ugs.*) wurden nie so richtig warm miteinander; Ⓑ (*having knowledge*) vertraut; **are you ~ with Ancient Greek?** können Sie Altgriechisch?; Ⓒ (*well known*) vertraut; bekannt ‹Gesicht, Name, Lied›; gewohnt ‹Geruch›; (*common, usual*) geläufig ‹Ausdruck›; gängig ‹Vorstellung›; **be on ~ ground** (*fig.*) Bescheid wissen; **he looks ~:** er kommt mir bekannt vor; **his name seems ~ [to me]** sein Name kommt mir bekannt vor; **the word is ~ to me** das Wort ist mir geläufig; Ⓓ (*informal*) familiär, freundschaftlich ‹Ton, Begrüßung›; ungezwungen ‹Sprache, Art, Stil›; **are you on ~ terms with him?** kennt ihr euch gut?; **a ~ term of address** eine vertrauliche Anrede; Ⓔ (*presumptuous*) plump-vertraulich (*abwertend*); Ⓕ (*intimate*) intim; **make oneself** *or* **become** *or* **get too ~ with sb.** mit jmdm. zu vertraulich werden; **be on ~ terms with sb.** enge Beziehungen zu jmdm. unterhalten.

❷ *n.* (*literary: friend, associate*) Vertraute, *der/die* (*geh.*)

**familiarity** /fəmɪlɪ'ærɪtɪ/ *n.* Ⓐ *no pl.* (*acquaintance*) Vertrautheit, *die;* Ⓑ *no pl.* (*relationship*) ungezwungenes Verhältnis; familiäres Verhältnis; Ⓒ (*of action, behaviour*) Vertraulichkeit, *die;* **the ~ of their greeting** ihre freundschaftliche Begrüßung; **~ breeds contempt** (*prov.*) zu große Vertraulichkeit erzeugt Verachtung; Ⓓ *no pl.* (*sexual intimacy*) Intimität, *die;* Vertraulichkeiten *Pl.;* **attempts at ~:** plumpe Annäherungsversuche; Ⓔ *in pl.* (*caresses*) Intimitäten *Pl.;* Vertraulichkeiten *Pl.*

**familiarize (familiarise)** /fə'mɪljəraɪz/ *v.t.* vertraut machen; einweisen ‹neuen Mitarbeiter›; **~ (familiarise) oneself with a/one's new job** sich einarbeiten

**familiarly** /fə'mɪljəlɪ/ *adv.* Ⓐ (*informally*) ungezwungen; Ⓑ (*intimately*) näher ‹kennen›; Ⓒ (*presumptuously*) plump-vertraulich (*abwertend*); Ⓓ (*commonly*) **~ known as ...:** allgemein ... genannt; **more ~ known as** besser bekannt als

**family** /'fæməlɪ/ *n.* Ⓐ Familie, *die;* **be one of the ~:** zur Familie gehören; **with just the immediate ~:** im engsten Familienkreis; **start a ~:** eine Familie gründen; **give my regards to Mr and Mrs Brown and ~:** grüßen Sie Familie Brown von mir; **run in the ~:** in der Familie liegen; **be in the** *or* **a ~ way** (*coll.*) in anderen Umständen sein (*verhüll.*); Ⓑ (*ancestry*) **of [good] ~:** aus guter Familie; Ⓒ (*group, race*) Geschlecht, *das;* **the ~ of human beings** das Menschengeschlecht; Ⓓ (*brotherhood*) [große] Familie; **the ~ of Christians/of man** die Christenheit/die Menschheit; **the ~ of nations** die Völkerfamilie (*geh.*); Ⓔ (*group of things; also Biol.*) Familie, *die;* (*Ling.*) [Sprach]familie, *die;* Ⓕ *attrib.* Familien-; familiär ‹Hintergrund›; **in the ~ circle** im Kreis der Familie; ⇒ *also* **council** A

**family: ~ al'lowance** *n.* Kindergeld, *das;* **~ 'Bible** *n.* Familienbibel, *die;* **F~ Division** *n.* (*Brit. Law*) *Abteilung für Familienrecht im obersten Gericht;* **~ 'doctor** *n.* Hausarzt, *der;* **~ 'income supplement** *n.* (*Brit.*) ≈ Familienzulage, *die;* **~ man** *n.* Familienvater, *der;* (*home-loving man*) häuslich veranlagter Mann; **~ name** *n.* Familienname, *der;* Nachname, *der;* **~ 'planning** *n.* Familienplanung, *die;* **~ 'planning clinic** *n.* ≈ Familienberatung[sstelle], *die;* **~ room** *n.* Ⓐ (*in a house*) Familienzimmer, *das;* Ⓑ (*Brit.: in a pub*) Familienraum, *der;* **~ 'tree** *n.* Stammbaum, *der;* **~ viewing** *n.* **be ~ viewing/suitable for ~ viewing** ‹Film usw.:› für die ganze Familie geeignet sein; **this programme is ~ viewing** dies ist eine Familiensendung

**famine** /'fæmɪn/ *n.* Ⓐ Hungersnot, *die;* Ⓑ (*shortage*) Knappheit, *die;* **~-stricken** von Hunger betroffen

**famish** /'fæmɪʃ/ *v.i.* hungern; **I'm ~ing!** (*coll.*) ich sterbe vor Hunger (*ugs.*)

**famished** /'fæmɪʃt/ *adj.* ausgehungert; halb verhungert; **I'm absolutely ~** (*coll.*) ich sterbe vor Hunger (*ugs.*)

**famous** /'feɪməs/ *adj.* Ⓐ (*well-known*) berühmt; **a ~ victory** ein rühmlicher Sieg; Ⓑ (*coll.: excellent*) prima (*ugs.*); famos (*ugs. veralt.*)

**famously** /'feɪməslɪ/ *adv.* (*coll.*) prima (*ugs.*); famos (*ugs. veralt.*)

**fan**[1] /fæn/ ❶ *n.* Ⓐ Fächer, *der;* Ⓑ (*sth. spread out*) Fächer, *der;* (*of peacock*) Rad, *das;* Ⓒ (*apparatus*) Ventilator, *der.* ❷ *v.t.,* **-nn-** fächeln ‹Gesicht›; anfachen ‹Feuer›; **~ oneself/sb.** sich/jmdm. Luft zufächeln; **~ one's face** sich (*Dat.*) das Gesicht fächeln; **~ the fire into a brisk blaze** das Feuer anfachen, bis es hell lodert; **~ the flame[s]** *or* **embers** (*fig.*) das Feuer schüren; Öl ins Feuer gießen; **~ dissatisfaction/hate** Unzufriedenheit/Hass schüren

~ **'out** ❶ *v.t.* fächern; auffächern ‹Spielkarten›. ❷ *v.i.* fächern; ‹Soldaten:› ausfächern

**fan**[2] *n.* (*devotee*) Fan, *der;* **she is a Garbo ~:** sie ist ein Garbo-Fan; **I'm quite a ~ of yours!** ich bewundere Sie!

**fanatic** /fə'nætɪk/ ❶ *adj.* fanatisch. ❷ *n.* Fanatiker, *der*/Fanatikerin, *die*

**fanatical** /fə'nætɪkl/ ⇒ **fanatic** 1

**fanatically** /fə'nætɪkəlɪ/ *adv.* fanatisch

**fanaticism** /fə'nætɪsɪzm/ *n.* Fanatismus, *der*

**'fan belt** *n.* (*Motor Veh.*) Keilriemen, *der*

**fancier** /'fænsɪə(r)/ *n.* Liebhaber, *der*/Liebhaberin, *die;* **be a rose/pigeon ~:** Rosen/Tauben züchten

**fanciful** /'fænsɪfl/ *adj.* Ⓐ (*whimsical*) versponnen ‹Person›; abstrus, überspannt ‹Vorstellung, Gedanke›; Ⓑ (*fantastically designed*) fantastisch ‹Gemälde, Design›; reich verziert ‹Kleid, Kostüm›

**fancifully** /'fænsɪfəlɪ/ *adv.* fantasievoll ‹erzählen›; fantastisch ‹[aus]geschmückt›

**fan: ~ club** *n.* Fanklub, *der;* **~-cooled** *adj.* gebläsegekühlt

**fancy** /ˈfænsɪ/ ❶ *n.* (A) (*taste, inclination*) **have a ~ for sth.** eine augenblickliche Schwäche für etw. haben; **have a ~ for a drink/some ice cream** Lust auf einen Drink/ein Eis haben; **he has taken a ~ to our plan/a new car/her** unser Plan/ein neues Auto/sie hat es ihm angetan; **take** *or* **catch sb.'s ~:** jmdm. gefallen; jmdn. ansprechen; (B) (*whim*) Laune, *die;* **I just go where the ~ takes me** ich fahre einfach drauflos *od.* ins Blaue; **just as the ~ takes me** ganz nach Lust und Laune; **he only paints when the ~ takes him** er malt nur, wenn ihm [gerade] danach ist; **a passing ~:** eine [vorübergehende] Laune; nur so eine Laune; **tickle sb.'s ~:** jmdn. reizen; (C) (*notion*) merkwürdiges Gefühl; (*delusion, belief*) Vorstellung, *die;* **a mere ~:** bloße Einbildung; **have a ~ that something is wrong** so ein Gefühl haben, dass etwas nicht stimmt; (D) (*faculty of imagining*) Fantasie, *die;* **let one's ~ roam** seine Fantasie schweifen lassen (*geh.*); seiner Fantasie (*Dat.*) freien Lauf lassen; **in ~ he saw himself as ...:** in Gedanken sah er sich als ...; (E) (*mental image*) Fantasievorstellung, *die;* **just a ~:** nur Einbildung; (F) (*cake*) fein[st]es Gebäck; (G) *constr. as pl.* (*fanciers*) Liebhaber *Pl.;* Kreis der Kenner. ❷ *attrib. adj.* (A) (*ornamental*) kunstvoll ‹Arbeit, Muster, Dribbling›; ausgefallen ‹Artikel, Design›; schick ‹Auto, Laden›; raffiniert ‹Gerät›; fein[st...] ‹Kuchen, Spitzen›; **~ jewellery** Modeschmuck, *der;* **nothing ~:** etwas ganz Schlichtes; **the meal will be nothing ~:** es gibt nichts Besonderes *od.* nur etwas ganz Einfaches zu essen; (B) (*whimsical*) überspannt; (C) (*extravagant*) stolz (*ugs.*); **~ prices** Fantasiepreise (*ugs.*); gepfefferte Preise (*ugs.*); (D) (*based on imagination*) fantasievoll; (E) (*specially bred*) speziell gezüchtet ‹Tier›; (F) (*Amer.: high-quality*) feinst... ‹Lebensmittel›; Delikatess‹gurke, -senf›. ❸ *v.t.* (A) (*imagine*) sich (*Dat.*) einbilden; **~ oneself [to be] clever** sich einbilden, klug zu sein; sich für klug halten; **a fancied resemblance** eine eingebildete Ähnlichkeit; (B) (*coll.*) *in imper. as excl. of surprise* **~ meeting you here!** na, so etwas, Sie hier zu treffen!; **~ his still being so naïve** nicht zu fassen, dass er noch immer so naiv ist; **~ that!** sieh mal einer an!; also so etwas!; **just ~, she's run off with ...:** stell dir vor, sie ist mit ... durchgebrannt!; (C) (*suppose*) glauben; denken; **..., I ~:** ..., möchte ich meinen; (D) (*wish to have*) mögen; **what do you ~ for dinner?** was hättest du gern zum Abendessen?; **I don't ~ this house at all** mir gefällt dieses Haus überhaupt nicht; **he fancies [the idea of] doing sth.** er würde gern etw. tun; er hätte Lust, etw. zu tun; **I don't ~ a secretarial job** eine Sekretärinnenstelle reizt mich überhaupt nicht; **~ a walk?** hast du Lust zu einem Spaziergang?; **do you think she fancies him?** glaubst du, sie mag ihn?; (E) (*coll.: have high opinion of*) **~ oneself** von sich eingenommen sein; **~ oneself as a singer** sich für einen [großen] Sänger halten; **~ one's/sb.'s chances** seine/jmds. Chancen hoch einschätzen; **he fancies his chances with her** er glaubt, bei ihr landen zu können (*ugs.*)

**fancy: ~ 'dress** *n.* [Masken]kostüm, *das;* **in ~ dress** kostümiert; **~-dress party** Kostümfest, *das;* **~-dress ball** *or* **dance** Maskenball, *der;* **~-'free** *adj.* frei und ungebunden; ⇒ *also* **footloose**; **~ goods** *n. pl.* Geschenkartikel; **~ man** *n.* (*coll. derog.*) (A) (*woman's lover*) Liebhaber, *der;* (B) (*pimp*) Zuhälter, *der;* **~ woman** *n.* (*coll. derog.*) Geliebte, *die;* **~-work** *n.* feine Handarbeit

**fanfare** /ˈfænfeə(r)/ *n.* Fanfare, *die;* **a ~ of trumpets** Trompetenstöße *Pl.*

**fang** /fæŋ/ *n.* (A) (*canine tooth*) Reißzahn, *der;* Fang[zahn], *der;* (*of boar; joc.: of person*) Hauer, *der;* (*of vampire*) Vampirzahn, *der;* **draw sb.'s/sth.'s ~s** (*fig.*) jmdn./etw. unschädlich machen; (B) (*of snake*) Giftzahn, *der;* (C) (*root of tooth*) Zahnwurzel, *die*

**fan: ~ heater** *n.* Heizlüfter, *der;* **~light** *n.* Oberlicht, *das;* (*fan-shaped*) Fächerfenster, *das* (*Archit.*); **~ mail** *n.* Fanpost, *die;* Verehrerpost, *die*

**fanny** /ˈfænɪ/ *n.* (A) (*Amer. sl.: buttocks*) Po, *der* (*fam.*); (B) (*Brit. coarse: vulva*) Möse, *die* (*vulg.*)

**fan: ~ oven** *n.* Heißluftofen, *der;* **~ palm** *n.* Fächerpalme, *die;* **~-shaped** *adj.* fächerförmig; **~tail** *n.* Fächerschwanz, *der;* (*pigeon*) Pfautaube, *die*

**fantasia** /fænˈteɪzɪə, fæntəˈziːə/ *n.* (*Mus.*) Fantasia, *die* (*fachspr.*); Fantasie, *die*

**fantastic** /fænˈtæstɪk/ *adj.* (A) (*grotesque, quaint*) bizarr; skurril; (*fanciful*) fantastisch; (*eccentric*) absurd ‹Gerücht, Plan, Geschichte›; (B) (*coll.: magnificent, excellent, extraordinary*) fantastisch (*ugs.*)

**fantastically** /fænˈtæstɪkəlɪ/ *adv.* (A) fantastisch; (B) (*coll.: excellently, extraordinarily*) fantastisch (*ugs.*)

**fantasy** /ˈfæntəzɪ/ *n.* (A) Fantasie, *die;* (*mental image, daydream*) Fantasiegebilde, *das;* (B) (*Lit.*) Fantasie, *die;* (C) (*Mus.*) ⇒ **fantasia**

**fan: ~ 'tracery** *n.* (*Archit.*) fächerförmiges Maßwerk; **~ 'vaulting** *n.* (*Archit.*) Fächergewölbe, *das*

**FAQ** /fæk/ *abbr.* (*Computing*) FAQ

**far** /fɑː(r)/ ❶ *adv.*, **farther, further; farthest, furthest** (A) ▶ 1079, ▶ 1679 (*in space*) weit; **~ away** weit entfernt (⇒ *also* **d**); **~ [away] from** weit entfernt von (⇒ *also* **d**); **see sth. from ~ away** etw. aus der Ferne sehen; **have you come [from] ~** *or* **from ~ off** *or* **away?** hatten Sie einen weiten Weg?; kommen Sie von weit her?; **how ~ have you come?** wie viel Kilometer mussten Sie zurücklegen?; **he travelled ~ into Russia/the desert/the jungle** er reiste bis tief ins Innere Russlands/in die Wüste/in den Dschungel; **I won't be ~ off** *or* **away** ich werde ganz in der Nähe sein; **~ above/below** hoch über/tief unter (+ *Dat.*); *adv.* hoch oben/tief unten; **so ~:** bis hierher (⇒ *also* **d**); **fly as ~ as Munich** bis [nach] München fliegen; **~ and near** fern und nah; **~ and wide** weit und breit; **from ~ and near** *or* **wide** von fern und nah; (B) (*in time*) weit; **~ into the night** bis spät *od.* tief in die Nacht; **the day** *or* **time is not ~ off** *or* **distant when ...:** es dauert nicht mehr lange, bis ...; **as ~ back as I can remember** soweit ich zurückdenken kann; (C) (*by much*) weit; **~ too** viel zu; **~ different from** ganz *od.* völlig anders als; **~ longer/better** weit[aus] länger/besser; **the rent is ~ beyond what I can afford to pay** die Miete übersteigt bei weitem meine Mittel; **they were not ~ wrong** sie hatten gar nicht so Unrecht; **you were/I was not ~ out** du lagst/ich lag gar nicht so falsch (*ugs.*); **your guess wasn't ~ out** deine Vermutung war gar nicht so abwegig; **your shot/guess wasn't ~ off** du hast fast getroffen/richtig vermutet; (D) (*fig.*) **as ~ as** (*to whatever extent, to the extent of*) so weit [wie]; **I haven't got as ~ as phoning her** ich bin noch nicht dazu gekommen, sie anzurufen; **not as ~ as I know** nicht, dass ich wüsste; **your plans are all right as ~ as they go** Ihre Pläne sind so weit gut; **as ~ as I remember/know** soweit ich mich erinnere/weiß; **go so ~ as to do sth.** so weit gehen und etw. tun; **he's gone so ~ as to collect the material** er sammelt immerhin schon Material; **in so ~ as** insofern *od.* insoweit als; **so ~** (*until now*) bisher; bis jetzt; **so ~ so good** so weit, so gut; **~ away** (*in thought*) weit weg; **~ and away** bei weitem; weitaus; **by ~:** bei weitem; **better by ~:** weitaus besser; **by ~ the best** der/die/das weitaus Beste; **~ from easy/good** alles andere als leicht/gut; **~ from admiring his paintings, I dislike them intensely** nicht nur, dass ich seine Gemälde nicht bewundere, sie gefallen mir ganz und gar nicht; **~ from it!** ganz im Gegenteil!; **~ be it from me/us** *etc.* **to do that** es liegt mir/uns *usw.* fern, das zu tun; **go ~:** weit kommen; **I am ~ from doing sth.** ich bin weit davon entfernt, etw. zu tun; **he will go ~ in life** er wird es im Leben weit bringen; **go ~ to** *or* **towards sth./doing sth.** viel zu etw. beitragen/dazu beitragen, etw. zu tun; **not go ~:** nicht weit *od.* lange reichen; **one pound won't go ~:** ein Pfund ist schnell alle *od.* (*ugs.*) weg; **go too ~:** zu weit gehen; **this has gone ~ enough** damit ist jetzt Schluss; **carry** *or* **take sth. too ~:** etw. zu weit treiben; **that's carrying the joke too ~:** da hört der Spaß auf; **you are carrying things too ~ by saying that ...:** du übertreibst, wenn du sagst, dass ...; **how ~ [can she be trusted]?** inwieweit [kann man ihr trauen]?; **he's too ~ gone** er ist nicht mehr in der Lage, etw. zu tun; (*drunk*) er hat zu viel intus (*ugs.*); (*delirious*) er ist nicht mehr ganz bei Sinnen *od.* klar im Kopf. ⇒ *also* **few** 1 A; **further** 2; **furthest** 2.
❷ *adj.*, **farther, further; farthest, furthest** (A) (*remote*) weit entfernt; (*remote in time*) fern; **in the ~ distance** in weiter Ferne; (B) (*more remote*) weiter entfernt; **the ~ bank of the river/side of the road** das andere Flussufer/die andere Straßenseite; **the ~ door/wall** *etc.* die hintere Tür/Wand *usw.* ⇒ *also* **cry** 1 A; **further** 1; **furthest** 1

**'faraway** *attrib. adj.* (A) (*remote in space*) entlegen; abgelegen; (*remote in time*) fern; (B) (*dreamy*) verträumt ‹Stimme, Blick, Augen›

**farce** /fɑːs/ *n.* (A) Farce, *die;* **become nothing but a ~:** zur reinen Farce werden; (B) (*Theatre*) Posse, *die;* Farce, *die*

**farcical** /ˈfɑːsɪkl/ *adj.* (A) (*absurd*) farcenhaft; absurd; (B) (*Theatre*) possenhaft ‹Stück, Element›

**farcically** /ˈfɑːsɪkəlɪ/ *adv.* (*absurdly*) absurd

**fare** /feə(r)/ ❶ *n.* (A) (*price*) Fahrpreis, *der;* (*money*) Fahrgeld, *das;* **train/boat ~:** Bahnpreis/Preis für die Überfahrt; **what** *or* **how much is the ~?** was kostet die Fahrt/(*by air*) der Flug/(*by boat*) die Überfahrt?; **have the exact ~:** das Fahrgeld passend haben; **have one's ~ ready** das Fahrgeld bereithalten; **[all] ~s, please, any more ~s?** noch jemand zugestiegen? noch jemand ohne [Fahrschein]?; (B) (*passenger*) Fahrgast, *der;* (C) (*food*) Kost, *die;* ⇒ *also* **bill**[3] 1 D.
❷ *v.i.* (*get on*) **I don't know how he is faring/how he ~d on his travels** ich weiß nicht, wie es ihm geht/wie es ihm auf seinen Reisen ergangen ist; **~ thee well** (*arch.*) leb[e] wohl (*veralt.*)

**Far: ~ 'East** *n.* **the ~ East** der Ferne Osten; Fernost *o. Art.;* **~ 'Eastern** *adj.* fernöstlich; des Fernen Ostens *nachgestellt;* ‹Person› aus dem Fernen Osten

**'fare stage** *n.* Teilstrecke, *die;* (*end of section*) Zahlgrenze, *die* (*Verkehrsw.*)

**farewell** /feəˈwel/ ❶ *int.* leb[e] wohl (*veralt.*); **say ~ to sth.** von etw. Abschied nehmen. ❷ *n.* (A) **a few words of ~:** ein paar Worte des Abschieds *od.* (*veralt.*) Lebewohls; **make one's ~s** sich verabschieden; (*by visiting*) Abschiedsbesuche machen; ⇒ *also* **bid** 1 E; (B) *attrib.* **~ speech/gift** *etc.* Abschiedsrede, *die*/-geschenk, *das usw.*

**far: ~-famed** *adj.* weithin berühmt; **~-fetched** *adj.* weit hergeholt; an *od.* bei den Haaren herbeigezogen (*ugs.*); **~-flung** *adj.* (*widely spread*) weit ausgedehnt; (*distant*) weit entfernt; abgelegen

**farm** /fɑːm/ ❶ *n.* (A) [Bauern]hof, *der;* [Land]wirtschaft, *die;* (*larger*) Gut, *das;* Gutshof, *der;* (*in English-speaking countries outside Europe*) Farm, *die;* **poultry/chicken ~:** Geflügel-/Hühnerfarm, *die;* **~ bread/eggs** Landbrot, *das*/Landeier *Pl.;* **~ animals** Nutzvieh, *das;* ⇒ *also* **dairy farm**; (B) ⇒ **farmhouse**; (C) (*place for breeding animals*) Zucht, *die;* **trout ~:** Forellenzucht, *die.* ❷ *v.t.* (A) bebauen, bewirtschaften ‹Land›; züchten ‹Lachs, Forellen›; **be engaged in sheep ~ing** Schafzucht betreiben; (B) (*take proceeds of*) pachten; (C) ⇒ **~ out**. ❸ *v.i.* Landwirtschaft betreiben; **he ~s in Africa** er ist Landwirt in Afrika; er hat eine Farm in Afrika

**~ 'out** *v.t.* (A) verpachten ‹Land›; (B) vergeben ‹Arbeit› (**to** an + *Akk.*); (C) (*hire out*) verdingen (*veralt.*) ‹Arbeitskräfte›; in Lohnarbeit geben ‹Arbeitskräfte›; (D) in Pflege geben ‹Kinder› (**to** *Dat.*, bei)

**farmer** /ˈfɑːmə(r)/ *n.* ▶ 1261 Landwirt, *der*/-wirtin, *die;* Bauer, *der*/Bäuerin, *die;* **poultry ~:** Geflügelzüchter, *der*/-züchterin, *die*

**farm: ~hand** *n.* ▶ 1261 Landarbeiter, *der*/-arbeiterin, *die;* (*on a small farm*) Knecht, *der*/Magd, *die* (*veralt.*); **~house** *n.* Bauernhaus, *das;* (*larger*) Gutshaus, *das*

**farming** /ˈfɑːmɪŋ/ *n, no pl., no indef. art.* Landwirtschaft, *die;* **~ of crops** Ackerbau, *der;* **~ of animals** Viehzucht, *die;* **~ community** Landwirtschaft betreibende Gemeinde; **~ implement** Ackergerät, *das;* landwirtschaftliches Gerät; **go into ~:** Landwirt *od.* Bauer werden

**farm: ~stead** *n.* Bauernhof, *der;* Gehöft, *das;* **~worker** *n.* ▶ 1261 Landarbeiter, *der*/-arbeiterin, *die;* **~yard** *n.* Hof, *der*

**Faroes** /ˈfeərəʊz/ *pr. n. pl.* Färöer *Pl.*

**ˈfar-off** *adj.* (*in space*) [weit] entfernt; (*in time*) fern

**ˈfar out** *adj.* Ⓐ (*distant*) [weit] entfernt; Ⓑ (*fig. coll.: excellent*) toll (*ugs.*); super (*ugs.*)

**farrago** /fəˈrɑːgəʊ/ *n., pl.* **~s** ((*Amer.:*) **~es**) (*mixture*) Gemisch, *das;* (*disordered assemblage*) Allerlei, *das*

**ˈfar-reaching** *adj.* ausgedehnt ‹Wälder, Felder›; weit reichend ‹Konsequenzen, Bedeutung, Wirkung›

**farrier** /ˈfærɪə(r)/ *n.* (*Brit.: smith*) Hufschmied, *der*

**farrow** /ˈfærəʊ/ ❶ *n.* Wurf, *der* (*von Ferkeln, Frischlingen*). ❷ *v.t.* werfen ‹Ferkel, Frischling›. ❸ *v.i.* ‹Sau:› ferkeln; ‹Bache:› frischen

**far: ~-seeing** *adj.* weitblickend; **~sighted** *adj.* Ⓐ (*able to see a great distance*) scharfsichtig; Ⓑ (*having foresight*) weitblickend

**fart** /fɑːt/ (*coarse*) ❶ *v.i.* Ⓐ furzen (*derb*); Ⓑ (*fool*) **~ about** *or* **around** sich mit jedem Scheißdreck aufhalten (*derb*). ❷ *n.* Ⓐ Furz, *der* (*derb*); Ⓑ (*person*) Scheißer, *der* (*derb*)

**farther** /ˈfɑːðə(r)/ ⇒ **further** 1 A, 2 A

**farthermost** /ˈfɑːðəməʊst/ ⇒ **furthermost**

**farthest** /ˈfɑːðɪst/ ⇒ **furthest**

**farthing** /ˈfɑːðɪŋ/ *n.* Ⓐ (*Brit. Hist.*) Farthing, *der;* **that old bike isn't worth a ~:** das alte Fahrrad ist keinen [roten] Heller wert; **to the last ~:** auf Heller und Pfennig; Ⓑ (*fig.*) **it doesn't matter a ~:** es macht nicht das Geringste *od.* (*ugs.*) nicht die Bohne was aus; **he doesn't care a ~ for her** er kümmert sich keinen Deut um sie; sie ist ihm völlig schnuppe (*ugs. abwertend*); ⇒ *also* **brass farthing**

**Far ˈWest** *n.* (*Amer.*) **the ~:** der Westen der USA

**fascia** /ˈfeɪʃɪə, ˈfeɪʃə/ *n.* Ⓐ (*Archit.*) Faszie, *die;* Ⓑ ⇒ **facia**

**fascicle** /ˈfæsɪkl/ *n.* Lieferung, *die;* Faszikel, *der* (*Buchw.*)

**fascinate** /ˈfæsɪneɪt/ *v.t.* Ⓐ fesseln; bezaubern; faszinieren (*geh.*); **it ~s me how ...:** ich finde es erstaunlich *od.* faszinierend, wie ...; Ⓑ (*deprive of power*) hypnotisieren ‹Beute›

**fascinated** /ˈfæsɪneɪtɪd/ *adj.* (*enchanted*) fasziniert; **the audience watched ~:** das Publikum sah gebannt zu

**fascinating** /ˈfæsɪneɪtɪŋ/ *adj.* faszinierend (*geh.*); bezaubernd; hochinteressant ‹Thema, Faktum, Meinung›; spannend, fesselnd ‹Buch›; **there is something ~ about her** sie hat etwas Faszinierendes [an sich (*Dat.*)]

**fascinatingly** /ˈfæsɪneɪtɪŋlɪ/ *adv.* faszinierend (*geh.*); hochinteressant, fesselnd ‹erzählen, beschreiben›; berauschend, hinreißend ‹schön›

**fascination** /fæsɪˈneɪʃn/ *n., no pl.* Faszination, *die* (*geh.*); (*quality of fascinating*) Zauber, *der;* Reiz, *der;* **find a certain ~ in sth.** einen gewissen Reiz an einer Sache verspüren; **have a ~ for sb.** einen besonderen Reiz auf jmdn. ausüben

**fascism** /ˈfæʃɪzm/ *n.* Faschismus, *der;* **Italian ~:** der italienische Faschismus

**fascist** /ˈfæʃɪst/ ❶ *n.* Faschist, *der*/Faschistin, *die.* ❷ *adj.* faschistisch

**fashion** /ˈfæʃn/ ❶ *n.* Ⓐ Art [und Weise]; **talk/behave in a peculiar ~:** merkwürdig sprechen/sich merkwürdig verhalten; **dress in a similar ~:** sich ähnlich kleiden; **she will do it in her own ~:** sie wird es auf ihre [eigene] Art [und Weise] tun; **in the Japanese ~:** im japanischen Stil; **in the usual ~:** in der üblichen Art; *as sentence-modifier* wie üblich; **in this ~:** auf diese Weise; so; **he expresses himself in a striking ~:** er hat eine bemerkenswerte Ausdrucksweise *od.* einen bemerkenswerten Ausdruck; **walk crab-~/in a zigzag ~:** im Krebsgang/Zickzack gehen; **German-~:** nach deutscher Sitte; nach Art der Deutschen; **after** *or* **in the ~ of** im Stil *od.* nach Art von; **in best British ~:** nach guter, alter britischer Art; **after** *or* **in a ~:** schlecht und recht; einigermaßen; **after** *or* **in one's/its ~:** auf seine/ihre Art; **Were you successful? — Well yes, after** *or* **in a ~:** Hast du Erfolg gehabt? — Na ja, so einigermaßen *od.* es geht (*ugs.*); Ⓑ (*custom, esp. in dress*) Mode, *die;* **be dressed in the height of** *or* **the latest ~:** hochmodern *od.* nach der neuesten Mode gekleidet sein; **the latest summer/autumn ~s** die neusten Sommer-/Wintermodelle; **~s for men's clothes/women's clothes** die Herrenmode/Damenmode; **the Paris ~s** die Pariser Mode; **it is the ~:** es ist Mode *od.* modern; **hats are the ~ this summer** in diesem Sommer sind Hüte in Mode; **be all the ~:** große Mode *od.* groß in Mode sein; **in ~:** in Mode; modern; **she always follows the/every ~:** sie geht immer nach *od.* mit der Mode/sie macht immer jede Mode mit; **be out of ~:** nicht mehr modern *od.* in Mode sein; **come into/go out of ~:** in Mode/aus der Mode kommen; **bring sth. into ~:** etw. in Mode bringen; **lead** *or* **set the ~:** die Mode vorschreiben; **the ~s in literature/music/art** die Literatur-/Musik-/Kunstrichtungen; Ⓒ (*usages of society*) Sitte, *die;* Brauch, *der;* **it was the ~ in those days** das war damals Sitte *od.* Brauch; **men/women of ~:** Herren/Damen der Gesellschaft. ⇒ *also* **old-fashioned**.
❷ *v.t.* Ⓐ formen, gestalten (**after, according to** nach; **out of, from** aus; **[in]to** zu); **~ sth. after sth.** etw. einer Sache (*Dat.*) nachbilden; Ⓑ (*shape to leg*) in Passform bringen ‹Strümpfe›

**fashionable** /ˈfæʃənəbl/ *adj.* modisch ‹Kleider, Person, Design›; modern ‹Sitte›; vornehm ‹Gegend, Hotel, Restaurant›; zur Zeit bevorzugt ‹Tätigkeit›; Mode‹farbe, -krankheit, -wort, -autor›; **it isn't ~ any more** es ist nicht mehr modern *od.* in Mode; **all the ~ people** die Schickeria

**fashionably** /ˈfæʃənəblɪ/ *adv.* modisch ‹sich kleiden›; modern ‹leben›

**fashion: ~-conscious** *adj.* modebewusst; **~ designer** *n.* ▶ 1261 Modeschöpfer, *der*/-schöpferin, *die;* **~ magazine** *n.* Modezeitschrift, *die;* Modemagazin, *das;* **~ parade** *n.* Mode[n]schau, *die;* **~-plate** *n.* Ⓐ (*picture*) Modezeichnung, *die;* Ⓑ (*fig.: man/woman*) Modegeck, *der*/-puppe, *die* (*abwertend*); **~ show** *n.* Mode[n]schau, *die*

**fast[1]** /fɑːst/ ❶ *v.i.* fasten; **a day of ~ing** ein Fast[en]tag. ❷ *n.* (*going without food*) Fasten, *das;* (*hunger strike*) Hungerstreik, *der;* (*day*) Fast[en]tag, *der;* (*season*) Fastenzeit, *die;* **break one's ~:** das Fasten brechen; **a 40-day ~:** eine Fastenzeit von 40 Tagen

**fast[2]** ❶ *adj.* Ⓐ (*fixed, attached*) fest; **the rope is ~:** das Tau ist fest[gemacht]; **make [the boat] ~:** das Boot festmachen *od.* vertäuen; **hard and ~:** fest; bindend, verbindlich ‹Regeln›; klar ‹Entscheidung›; Ⓑ (*steady, close*) fest ‹Freundschaft›; unzertrennlich, treu ‹Freunde›; Ⓒ (*not fading*) farbecht ‹Stoff›; echt, beständig ‹Farbe›; (*against light*) lichtecht; (*against washing*) waschecht; Ⓓ (*rapid*) schnell; tempogeladen, aktionsreich ‹Krimi, Film›; **~ train** Schnellzug, *der;* D-Zug, *der;* **~ speed** hohe Geschwindigkeit; **he is a ~ worker** (*lit. or fig.*) er arbeitet schnell; (*in amorous activities*) er geht mächtig ran (*ugs.*); **I say, that was ~ work** na, das ging ja sehr schnell; **pull a ~ one [on sb.]** (*coll.*) jmdn. übers Ohr hauen *od.* reinlegen (*ugs.*); Ⓔ ▶ 1012 **be ~ [by ten minutes], be [ten minutes] ~** ‹Uhr:› [zehn Minuten] vorgehen; Ⓕ schnell ‹Tennisplatz, Billardtisch usw.›; **~ road** Straße, auf der man schnell vorankommt; **~ line** (*Railw.*) Schnellverkehrsgleis, *das;* Ⓖ (*immoral*) flott ‹Person, Leben›; locker ‹Lebenswandel›; leichtlebig ‹Frau›; Ⓗ (*Photog.*) hoch empfindlich ‹Film›; lichtstark ‹Objektiv›. ⇒ *also* **furious**.
❷ *adv.* Ⓐ (*lit. or fig.*) fest; **the wall stood ~:** die Mauer blieb stehen; **hold ~ to sth.** sich an etw. (*Dat.*) festhalten; (*fig.*) an etw. (*Dat.*) festhalten; **stand ~ in one's belief** an seiner Meinung festhalten; **stand ~ by sth./sb.** zu etw./jmdm. stehen; Ⓑ (*soundly*) **be ~ asleep** fest schlafen; (*when one should be awake*) fest eingeschlafen sein; Ⓒ ▶ 1552 (*quickly*) schnell; **not so ~!** nicht so hastig!; Ⓓ (*ahead*) **that clock is running ~:** diese Uhr geht vor; **play ~ and loose with sb.** mit jmdm. ein falsches *od.* doppeltes Spiel treiben

**fast: ~back** *n.* (*back of car*) Fließheck, *das;* Fastback, *das;* (*car*) Wagen mit Fließheck; Fastback, *das;* **~ ˈbowler** *n.* (*Cricket*) schneller Werfer; **~ ˈbreeder [reactor]** *n.* schneller Brüter; **~ ˈbuck** ⇒ **buck[4]**; **~ day** *n.* Fast[en]tag, *der*

**fasten** /ˈfɑːsn/ ❶ *v.t.* Ⓐ festmachen, befestigen (**on, to** an + *Dat.*); festmachen, vertäuen (**to** an + *Dat.*) ‹Boot›; festziehen, anziehen ‹Schraube›; zumachen ‹Kleid, Spange, Knöpfe, Jacke›; [ab]schließen, [ver]schließen ‹Tür›; schließen ‹Fenster›; anstecken ‹Brosche› (**to** an + *Akk.*); **~ sth. together with a clip** etw. zusammenheften; **~ the rope to a post** das Tau an einem Pfosten anbinden *od.* festmachen; **~ sth. up with string** etw. zu- *od.* verschnüren; **~ one's safety belt** sich anschnallen; seinen Sicherheitsgurt anlegen; **~ up one's shoes** seine Schuhe binden *od.* schnüren; **she ~ed her hair back** sie band ihre Haare zurück; **~ off a thread** einen Faden vernähen; Ⓑ heften ‹Blick› (**[up]on** auf + *Akk.*); richten ‹Aufmerksamkeit, Gedanken› (**[up]on** auf + *Akk.*); setzen ‹Erwartungen, Hoffnungen› (**[up]on** auf + *Akk.*); **~ one's attention/affections on sb.** jmdm. seine Aufmerksamkeit zuwenden/Zuneigung schenken; Ⓒ (*assign*) anhängen, beilegen ‹Spottnamen› (**[up]on** + *Dat.*); **~ the blame/charge [up]on sb.** die Schuld auf jmdn. schieben; jmdm. die Schuld in die Schuhe schieben (*ugs.*).
❷ *v.i.* Ⓐ sich schließen lassen; **the skirt ~s at the back** der Rock wird hinten zugemacht; **the hook and the eye ~ together** der Haken und die Öse werden miteinander verbunden; Ⓑ **~ [up]on sth.** (*single out*) etw. herausgreifen; (*seize upon*) etw. aufs Korn nehmen (*ugs.*)

**fastener** /ˈfɑːsnə(r)/ *n.* Verschluss, *der*

**fastening** /ˈfɑːsnɪŋ/ *n.* (*device*) Verschluss, *der*

**fast: ~ ˈfood** *n. im Schnellrestaurant angebotenes Essen;* Fastfood, *das; attrib.* **~food restaurant** Schnellrestaurant, *das;* **~ ˈforward** *n.* schneller Vorlauf; (*playback*) Zeitrafferwiedergabe, *die;* **watch sth. on ~ forward** etw. im Zeitraffer ansehen; **~-forward** ❶ *attrib. adj.* Vorspul‹taste, -funktion›; ❷ *v.t. & i.* vorspulen; **~-growing** *adj.* schnell wachsend

**fastidious** /fæˈstɪdɪəs/ *adj.* (*hard to please*) heikel, (*ugs.*) pingelig (**about** in Bezug auf + *Akk.*); (*carefully selective*) wählerisch (**about** in Bezug auf + *Akk.*)

**fastidiously** /fæˈstɪdɪəslɪ/ *adv.* **behave ~:** pingelig (*ugs.*)/wählerisch sein; **dress ~:** in seiner/ihrer Kleidung untadelig sein; **~ clean** peinlich sauber

**fast: ~ lane** *n.* Überholspur, *die;* **life in the ~ lane** (*fig.*) schnelles, lockeres Leben; Leben auf vollen Touren (*ugs.*); **~-moving** *adj.* schnell; spannend, tempogeladen ‹Film, Drama›; **a ~-moving train** ein schnell fahrender Zug

**fastness** /ˈfɑːstnɪs/ *n.* Ⓐ *no pl.* (*of colour, dye*) [Farb]echtheit, *die;* (*against light*) Lichtechtheit, *die;* (*against washing*) Waschechtheit, *die;* Ⓑ *no pl.* (*of vehicle, person, etc.*) Schnelligkeit, *die;* Ⓒ (*stronghold*) Feste, *die*

**ˈfast track** *n.* Überholspur, *die;* **a career on the ~:** eine Blitzkarriere; **the ~ to success**

der schnelle Weg zum Erfolg; **be on the ~:** eine Blitzkarriere machen

**'fast-track** ❶ *v.t.* beschleunigen ‹Projekt›. ❷ *attrib. adj.* Schnell-; **~ procedure** Schnellverfahren, *das;* Fast-Track-Verfahren, *das* (*Politik*)

**fat** /fæt/ ❶ *adj.* [A] dick; fett (*abwertend*); rund ‹Wangen, Gesicht›; fett ‹Schwein›; **grow** *or* **get ~:** dick werden; **grow ~** (*fig.*) reich werden; **you won't get ~ on that** (*fig. coll.*) das wird dir nicht viel einbringen; [B] **~ cattle** Mast- *od.* Schlachtvieh, *das;* [C] (*containing much* ~) fett ‹Essen, Fleisch, Brühe›; [D] (*fig.*) dick ‹Bündel, Buch, Brieftasche, Zigarre›; umfangreich ‹Filmrolle, Band›; üppig, fett ‹Gewinn, Gehalt, Bankkonto, Scheck›; [E] (*coll. iron.*) **~ lot of good 'you are** du bist mir 'ne schöne Hilfe (*iron.*); **a ~ lot [of good it would do me]** [das würde mir] herzlich wenig [helfen]; **~ lot he knows** was der nicht alles weiß (*iron.*); **a ~ chance** herzlich wenig Aussicht; **~ chance 'he's got** da hat er ja Mordschancen (*iron.*).
❷ *n.* Fett, *das;* **low in ~:** fettarm ‹Nahrungsmittel›; **put on ~:** Fett ansetzen; **lose ~:** abnehmen; **the ~ is in the fire** (*fig.*) der Teufel ist los (*ugs.*); **live off** *or* **on the ~ of the land** (*fig.*) wie die Made im Speck leben (*ugs.*). ⇒ *also* **chew** 1.
❸ *v.t.*, **-tt-** mästen; herausfüttern; **~ted cattle** Schlacht- *od.* Mastvieh, *das;* **kill the ~ted calf [for sb.]** [jmdm.] ein Festessen zum Empfang geben

**fatal** /'feɪtl/ *adj.* [A] (*ruinous, disastrous*) verheerend (**to** für); fatal; schicksalsschwer ‹Tag, Moment›; **it would be ~:** das wäre das Ende; **it is ~ to assume that ...:** es ist ein verhängnisvoller Irrtum anzunehmen, dass ...; [B] (*deadly*) tödlich ‹Unfall, Verletzung›; **that sort of thing in her present state would be ~:** das würde in ihrem augenblicklichen Zustand den sicheren Tod für sie bedeuten; **deal sb. a ~ blow** jmdm. einen vernichtenden Schlag versetzen; **be** *or* **come as a ~ blow to sb.** (*fig.*) ein schwerer Schlag für jmdn. sein; [C] (*inevitable*) unabwendbar; unvermeidlich; schicksalhaft ‹Tag›; [D] (*of destiny*) schicksalhaft; Schicksals-

**fatalism** /'feɪtəlɪzm/ *n., no pl.* Fatalismus, *der* (*geh.*); Schicksalsergebenheit, *die*

**fatalist** /'feɪtəlɪst/ *n.* Fatalist, *der*/Fatalistin, *die*

**fatalistic** /feɪtə'lɪstɪk/ *adj.* fatalistisch; schicksalsergeben ‹Person›

**fatality** /fə'tælɪtɪ/ *n.* (*death*) Todesfall, *der;* (*in car crash, war, etc.*) [Todes]opfer, *das*

**fatally** /'feɪtəlɪ/ *adv.* tödlich ‹verwunden, enden›; (*disastrously*) verhängnisvoll; auf verhängnisvolle Weise ‹beeinflusst›; unwiderstehlich ‹attraktiv›; **be ~ wrong** *or* **mistaken** einem verhängnisvollen Irrtum unterliegen; **be ~ ill** todkrank sein

**'fat cat** *n.* (*Amer. coll.*) Geldsack, *der* (*ugs.*) (*mit politischem Einfluss*)

**fate** /feɪt/ *n.* [A] Schicksal, *das;* **an accident** *or* **stroke of ~:** eine Fügung des Schicksals; **~ decided otherwise** das Schicksal hat es anders bestimmt *od.* wollte es anders; **as sure as ~:** todsicher; [B] (*Mythol.*) **the F~s** die Parzen. ⇒ *also* **death** A

**fated** /'feɪtɪd/ *adj.* (*doomed*) zum Scheitern verurteilt ‹Plan, Projekt›; **be ~ to fail** *or* **to be unsuccessful** zum Scheitern verurteilt sein; **it was ~ that we should never meet again** es war uns (*Dat.*) bestimmt, uns nie wieder zu sehen; **be ~:** unter einem ungünstigen Stern stehen

**fateful** /'feɪtfl/ *adj.* [A] (*important, decisive*) schicksalsschwer ‹Tag, Stunde, Entscheidung›; entscheidend ‹Worte›; [B] (*controlled by fate*) schicksalhaft ‹Begegnung, Treffen, Ereignis›; [C] (*prophetic*) prophetisch; (*of misfortune*) unheilverkündend

**fat: ~-free** *adj.* fettfrei; **~head** *n.* Dummkopf, *der* (*ugs.*); Schafskopf, *der* (*ugs. abwertend*); **~-headed** *adj.* dumm; blöd (*ugs.*)

**father** /'fɑːðə(r)/ ❶ *n.* ▶ **1617** [A] Vater, *der;* **become a ~:** Vater werden; **he is a** *or* **the ~ of six** er hat sechs Kinder; **be ~ to sb.** jmds. Vater sein; **be [like] a ~ to sb.** wie ein Vater zu jmdm. sein; **he is his ~'s son** er ist ganz der Vater; **like ~ like son** der Apfel fällt nicht weit vom Stamm (*ugs. scherzhaft, Spr.*); **the wish is ~ to the thought** der Wunsch ist der Vater des Gedankens; **the ~ and mother of a row/beating** (*coll.*) ein furchtbarer Krach/eine furchtbare Tracht Prügel (*ugs.*); ⇒ *also* **child**; [B] *in pl.* (*forefathers*) Väter *Pl.;* [C] (*originator*) Vater, *der;* Urheber, *der;* **F~s [of the Church]** Kirchenväter *Pl.;* [D] (*revered person*) Vater, *der;* **the ~ of his country** der Landesvater; [E] (*God*) **[our heavenly] F~:** [unser himmlischer] Vater; **God the F~, the Son, and the Holy Ghost** der Vater, der Sohn und der Heilige Geist; **the Our F~:** das Vaterunser; [F] (*confessor*) Beichtvater, *der;* (*priest*) Pfarrer, *der;* (*monk*) Pater, *der;* **F~** (*as title: priest*) Herr Pfarrer; (*as title: monk*) Pater; **the Holy F~:** der Heilige Vater; **Right/Most Reverend F~ [in God]** Ehrwürdiger Vater; **F~ Superior** Prior, *der;* [G] **F~** (*venerable person, god*) Vater, *der;* **F~ Thames** die Themse; **[Old] F~ Time** der Chronos (*geh.*); [H] (*oldest member*) [Dienst]älteste, *der;* **F~ of the House of Commons** (*Brit. Polit.*) der Alterspräsident des Unterhauses. ⇒ *also* **city fathers**; **Pilgrim Fathers**.
❷ *v.t.* [A] (*beget*) zeugen; [B] (*originate*) ins Leben rufen

**father: F~ 'Christmas** *n.* der Weihnachtsmann; **~ figure** *n.* Vaterfigur, *die*

**fatherhood** /'fɑːðəhʊd/ *n., no pl.* Vaterschaft, *die*

**father: ~-in-law** *n., pl.* **~s-in-law** Schwiegervater, *der;* **~land** *n.* Vaterland, *das*

**fatherless** /'fɑːðəlɪs/ *adj.* vaterlos; **be ~:** keinen Vater haben

**fatherly** /'fɑːðəlɪ/ ❶ *adj.* väterlich; **~ responsibilities** Vaterpflichten *Pl.;* **~ words of advice** väterliche Ratschläge. ❷ *adv.* wie ein Vater; väterlich ‹belehren›

**'Father's Day** *n.* Vatertag, *der*

**fathom** /'fæðəm/ ❶ *n.* (*Naut.*) Fathom, *das* (*geh.*); Faden, *der.* ❷ *v.t.* [A] (*measure*) mit dem Lot messen; [B] (*fig.: comprehend*) verstehen; **~ sb./sth. out** jmdn./etw. ergründen; **I just cannot ~ him out** er ist mir ein Rätsel

**fathomless** /'fæðəmlɪs/ *adj.* (*immeasurable*) unermesslich; grenzenlos, unendlich ‹Liebe Gottes›; bodenlos ‹Abgrund›

**fatigue** /fə'tiːg/ ❶ *n.* [A] Ermüdung, *die;* Erschöpfung, *die;* **fight against ~:** gegen die Müdigkeit ankämpfen; **extreme ~:** Übermüdung, *die;* [B] (*of metal etc.*) Ermüdung, *die;* [C] (*of muscle, organ, etc.*) Übermüdung, *die;* Überanstrengung, *die;* [D] (*task*) mühselige Arbeit; Mühsal, *die* (*geh.*); [E] (*Mil.*) Arbeitsdienst, *der;* **be put on ~ duty** zum Arbeitsdienst eingeteilt werden; **~s** ⇒ **fatigue-dress**. ❷ *v.t.* ermüden; **with a ~d look** mit müdem Blick; **feel ~d** sich müde *od.* abgespannt fühlen; **look ~d** erschöpft aussehen; **too ~d to do sth.** zu erschöpft, etw. zu tun

**fatigue: ~-dress** *n.* (*Mil.*) Arbeitsanzug, *der;* **~-party** *n.* (*Mil.*) Arbeitskommando, *das*

**fatless** /'fætlɪs/ *adj.* ohne Fett *nachgestellt;* mager ‹Fleisch›

**fatness** /'fætnɪs/ *n., no pl.* (*corpulence*) Dicke, *die;* Beleibtheit, *die* (*verhüll.*); Fettheit, *die* (*abwertend*)

**'fatstock** *n., no pl.* Mastvieh, *das*

**fatted** /'fætɪd/ ⇒ **fat** 3

**fatten** /'fætn/ ❶ *v.t.* herausfüttern ‹Person›; mästen ‹Tier›; **~ oneself on sth.** (*fig.*) sich an etw. (*Akk.*) bereichern. ❷ *v.i.* ‹Tier:› fett werden; ‹Person:› dick werden; fett werden (*abwertend*); **~ on sth.** sich mästen mit etw.; (*fig.*) profitieren von etw.; Nutzen ziehen aus etw.

**fattening** /'fætnɪŋ/ *adj.* dick machend ‹Nahrungsmittel›; **~ foods** Dickmacher *Pl.* (*ugs.*); **be ~:** dick machen

**fatty** /'fætɪ/ ❶ *adj.* [A] fett ‹Fleisch, Soße›; fetthaltig ‹Speise, Nahrungsmittel›; fettig ‹Substanz›; [B] (*consisting of fat*) Fett-; **~ tissue/tumour** Fettgewebe, *das*/Fettgeschwulst, *die.* ❷ *n.* (*coll.*) Dicke, *der/die;* Dickerchen, *das* (*scherzh.*)

**fatty 'acid** *n.* (*Chem.*) Fettsäure, *die*

**fatuous** /'fætjʊəs/ *adj.* albern; töricht; einfältig ‹Grinsen›

**fatuously** /'fætjʊəslɪ/ *adv.* albern; töricht ‹handeln›; einfältig ‹bewundern›

**faucet** /'fɔːsɪt/ *n.* [A] (*for barrel*) Fasszapfen, *der;* [B] (*Amer.: tap*) Wasserhahn, *der*

**fault** /fɔːlt, fɒlt/ ❶ *n.* [A] (*defect*) Fehler, *der;* **we all have our little ~s** wir alle haben unsere Schwächen; **confess one's ~s** seine Sünden bekennen; **to a ~:** allzu übertrieben; übermäßig; **meticulous to a ~:** peinlich genau; **find ~ [with sb./sth.]** etw. [an jmdm./etw.] auszusetzen haben; **find ~ with goods** Mängel an Waren feststellen; **[sold] with all ~s** ohne Mängelgewähr [verkauft]; **free from** *or* **without ~:** mangelfrei; [B] (*responsibility*) Schuld, *die;* Verschulden, *das;* **whose ~ was it?** wer war schuld [daran]?; **it's all your own ~!** das ist deine eigene Schuld!; du bist selbst schuld!; **it isn't my ~:** ich habe keine Schuld; es ist nicht meine Schuld; **not through any ~ of mine** nicht durch meine Schuld; **the ~ lies with him** die Schuld liegt bei ihm; **be at ~:** im Unrecht sein (⇒ *also* **g**); **my memory was at ~:** mein Gedächtnis hat mich getrogen (*geh.*); **it is difficult to determine who is at ~:** es ist schwierig zu sagen, wer die Schuld daran trägt *od.* wer dafür verantwortlich ist; [C] (*thing wrongly done*) Fehler, *der;* **commit a ~:** einen Fehler begehen; [D] (*Tennis etc.*) Fehler, *der;* **double ~:** Doppelfehler, *der;* [E] (*in gas or water supply; also Electr.*) Defekt, *der;* [F] (*Geol.*) Verwerfung, *die;* [G] (*Hunting*) Verlieren der Fährte; **be at ~:** die Fährte verloren haben; (*fig.*) vor einem Rätsel stehen; nicht mehr weiter wissen (⇒ *also* **b**).
❷ *v.t.* [A] Fehler finden an (+ *Dat.*); etwas auszusetzen haben an (+ *Dat.*); **he/his argument had been ~ed** er/seine Argumentation war bemängelt *od.* kritisiert worden; [B] (*declare faulty*) bemängeln

**fault: ~finder** *n.* Krittler, *der*/Krittlerin, *die* (*abwertend*); **~finding** ❶ *n.* Krittelei, *die* (*abwertend*); ❷ *adj.* krittelig (*abwertend*); **~finding critic/criticism** Krittler, *der*/Krittelei, *die*

**faultily** /'fɔːltɪlɪ, 'fɒltɪlɪ/ *adv.* fehlerhaft; mangelhaft

**faultless** /'fɔːltlɪs, 'fɒltlɪs/ *adj.* einwandfrei; tadellos ‹Erscheinung›; fehlerlos, fehlerfrei ‹Übersetzung, Englisch›; untadelig ‹Betragen›; ausgezeichnet ‹Ruf›

**faultlessly** /'fɔːltlɪslɪ, 'fɒltlɪslɪ/ *adv.* fehlerfrei; fehlerlos; makellos ‹schön›; **the dress fits ~:** das Kleid hat einen tadellosen Sitz

**faulty** /'fɔːltɪ, 'fɒltɪ/ *adj.* fehlerhaft; unzutreffend ‹Argument›; defekt ‹Gerät usw.›; **~ design/calculation** Fehlkonstruktion, *die*/Fehlkalkulation, *die*

**faun** /fɔːn/ *n.* (*Mythol.*) Faun, *der*

**fauna** /'fɔːnə/ *n., pl.* **~e** /'fɔːniː/ *or* **~s** (*Zool.*) Fauna, *die*

**faute de mieux** /fəʊt də 'mjɜː/ *adv.* faute de mieux (*geh.*); in Ermangelung eines Besseren; im Notfall

**faux pas** /fəʊ 'pɑː/ *n., pl. same* /fəʊ 'pɑːz/ Fauxpas, *der*

**favor** *etc.* (*Amer.*) ⇒ **favour** *etc.*

**favour** /'feɪvə(r)/ (*Brit.*) ❶ *n.* [A] Gunst, *die;* Wohlwollen, *das;* **look with ~ on** mit Wohlwollen betrachten; wohlwollend gegenüberstehen (+ *Dat.*) ‹Person, Plan, Idee usw.›; **find ~ in the eyes of sb.** *or* **in sb.'s eyes** (*literary*) vor jmds. Augen (*Dat.*) Gnade finden; **find/lose ~ with sb.** ‹Sache:› bei jmdm. Anklang finden/jmdm. nicht mehr gefallen; ‹Person:› jmds. Wohlwollen gewinnen/verlieren; **as a mark of her ~:** als *od.* zum Zeichen ihrer Wertschätzung *od.* Anerkennung; **be in ~ [with sb.]** [bei jmdm.] beliebt *od.* (*ugs.*) gut angeschrieben sein; ‹Idee, Kleidung usw.:› [bei jmdm.] in Mode sein; **be out of ~ [with sb.]** [bei jmdm.] unbeliebt *od.* (*ugs.*) schlecht angeschrieben sein; [bei jmdm.] in Ungnade sein (*oft spött.*); ‹Idee, Kleidung usw.:› [bei jmdm.]

f

nicht mehr in Mode sein; **get back in[to] sb.'s ~:** jmds. Gunst *od.* Wohlwollen wiedergewinnen; **B** (*kindness*) Gefallen, *der;* Gefälligkeit, *die;* **sb. requests the ~ of your company** (*formal*) jmd. gibt sich (*Dat.*) die Ehre, Sie einzuladen; **ask a ~ of sb.** jmdn. um einen Gefallen bitten; **do sb. a ~, do a ~ for sb.** jmdm. einen Gefallen tun; **do me the ~ of shutting up** (*iron.*) tu mir den Gefallen und halt den Mund; **as a ~:** aus Gefälligkeit; **as a ~ to sb.** jmdm. zuliebe; **get special ~s** besondere Vergünstigungen genießen; **C** (*aid, support*) **be in ~ of sth.** für etw. sein; **in ~ of** zugunsten (+ *Gen.*); **all those in ~:** alle, die dafür sind; **in sb.'s ~:** zu jmds. Gunsten; **the exchange rate is in our ~:** der Wechselkurs steht *od.* ist günstig für uns; **D** (*partiality*) Begünstigung, *die;* **show ~ to[wards] sb.** jmdn. begünstigen; **E** (*ornament, badge*) Andenken, *das;* (*ribbon, cockade*) Schleife, *die;* Kokarde, *die;* (*party-badge*) Abzeichen, *das;* Plakette, *die.* ⇒ *also* **fear** 1 A.
❷ *v.t.* **A** (*approve*) für gut halten, gutheißen ‹Plan, Idee, Vorschlag›; (*think preferable*) bevorzugen; **I ~ the first proposal** ich bin für den ersten Vorschlag; **B ~ sb.** (*treat sb. kindly*) jmdm. günstig gesinnt sein; jmdm. wohl wollen; (*encourage or sponsor sb.*) jmdn. unterstützen; jmdn. fördern; **C** (*oblige*) beehren (**with** mit) (*geh.*); **~ sb. with a smile/glance/an interview** jmdm. ein Lächeln/einen Blick schenken/ein Interview gewähren (*geh.*); **he ~ed me with a visit** (*iron.*) er beglückte mich mit einem Besuch; **D** (*treat with partiality*) bevorzugen; **E** (*aid, support*) helfen (+ *Dat.*); **F** (*confirm*) bekräftigen, bestätigen ‹Ansicht, Meinung, Theorie›; **G** (*prove advantageous to*) begünstigen; **the weather ~ed our journey** das Wetter trug zum Gelingen unserer Reise [wesentlich] bei

**favourable** /ˈfeɪvərəbl/ *adj.* (*Brit.*) **A** günstig ‹Eindruck, Licht›; gewogen ‹Haltung, Einstellung›; wohlmeinend ‹Blick, Urteil›; **~ attitude towards sth.** positive Einstellung einer Sache gegenüber; **be ~ to[wards] sth.** einer Sache (*Dat.*) positiv gegenüberstehen; **B** (*praising*) freundlich ‹Erwähnung, Empfehlung›; positiv, günstig ‹Bericht[erstattung], Bemerkung›; **C** (*promising*) vielversprechend; gut ‹Omen, Zeichen›; **D** (*helpful*) günstig (**to** für) ‹Wetter, Wind, Umstand›; **be ~ for doing sth.** günstig sein, um etw. zu tun; **E** (*giving consent*) zustimmend; **give sb. a ~ answer** jmdm. eine Zusage geben

**favourably** /ˈfeɪvərəblɪ/ *adv.* (*Brit.*) **A** wohlwollend ‹ansehen, anhören, denken, urteilen›; günstig ‹stimmen›; **be ~ impressed with sb./sb.'s ideas** von jmdm./jmds. Ideen sehr angetan sein; **be ~ disposed towards sb./sth.** jmdm./einer Sache positiv gegenüberstehen; **B** (*in praising manner*) lobend ‹erwähnen›; positiv ‹vermerken›; **C** (*promisingly*) vielversprechend; **D** (*helpfully*) günstig; **E** (*with consent*) **answer ~:** eine positive Antwort geben

**favoured** /ˈfeɪvəd/ *adj.* (*Brit.*) (*privileged*) bevorzugt; (*well-liked*) Lieblings‹platz, -buch, -gericht›; **the ~ few** die kleine Gruppe der Auserwählten (*iron.*); **most-~ nation** meistbegünstigter Staat; **most-~-nation treatment** Meistbegünstigung, *die* (*Wirtsch.*)

**favourite** /ˈfeɪvərɪt/ (*Brit.*) ❶ *adj.* Lieblings-; **~ son** (*Amer. Polit.*) Favorit, *der;* Spitzenkandidat, *der;* **sb.'s ~ person** jmds. Liebling. ❷ *n.* **A** (*film/food/country/pupil etc.*) Lieblingsfilm, *der*/-essen, *das*/-land, *das*/-schüler, *der usw.;* (*person in general*) Liebling, *der;* **this/he is my ~:** das/ihn mag ich am liebsten; **she's a great ~ with the children** sie wird von den Kindern sehr geliebt; **B** (*Sport*) Favorit, *der*/Favoritin, *die;* **start ~:** als Favorit an den Start gehen; **C** (*unduly favoured intimate*) Günstling, *der*

**favouritism** /ˈfeɪvərɪtɪzm/ *n., no pl.* (*Brit.*) Begünstigung, *die;* (*when selecting sb. for a post etc.*) Günstlingswirtschaft, *die*

**fawn¹** /fɔːn/ ❶ *n.* **A** (*fallow deer*) [Dam]kitz, *das;* (*buck*) Bockkitz, *das;* (*doe*) Geißkitz, *das;* **B** (*colour*) Rehbraun, *das.* ❷ *adj.* rehfarben; **~ colour** Rehbraun, *das*

**fawn²** *v.i.* **A** (*show affection*) seine Freude zeigen; ‹Hund:› [bellen und] mit dem Schwanz wedeln; **~ [up]on sb.** um jmdn. herumstreichen; **B** (*behave servilely*) **~ [on *or* upon sb.]** sich [bei jmdm.] einschmeicheln; [vor jmdm.] katzbuckeln (*abwertend*)

**'fawn-coloured** *adj.* rehfarben

**fawning** /ˈfɔːnɪŋ/ *adj.* (*showing affection*) schwanzwedelnd [und bellend] ‹Hund›; (*cringing*) sich einschmeichelnd; katzbuckelnd (*abwertend*)

**fax** /fæks/ ❶ *n.* Fax, *das;* Fernkopie, *die.* ❷ *v.t.* faxen; fernkopieren; **I'll ~ it [through] to you** ich faxe sie/ihn/es dir zu

**fax: ~ machine** *n.* Faxgerät, *das;* Fernkopierer, *der;* **~ modem** *n.* (*Computing*) Faxmodem, *das;* **~ number** *n.* Faxnummer, *die*

**FBI** *abbr.* (*Amer.*) **Federal Bureau of Investigation** FBI, *das*

**FC** *abbr.* **Football Club** FC, *der*

**FCO** *abbr.* (*Brit.*) **Foreign and Commonwealth Office** [Britisches] Außen- und Commonwealthministerium; ≈ AA

**fealty** /ˈfiːəltɪ/ *n.* (*Hist.*) Lehnstreue, *die;* (*fig.*) Treue, *die*

**fear** /fɪər/ ❶ *n.* **A** Furcht, Angst, *die* (**of** vor + *Dat.*); (*instance*) Befürchtung, *die;* **out of ~:** aus Angst; **~ of death *or* dying/heights/open spaces** Todes-/Höhen-/Platzangst, *die;* **~ of flying** Flugangst, *die;* Angst vorm Fliegen (*ugs.*); **~ of doing sth.** Angst *od.* Furcht davor, etw. zu tun; **have a [terrible] ~ of sth./sb.** [furchtbare] Angst vor etw./jmdm. haben; **have a ~ *or* have ~s of doing sth.** Angst davor haben, etw. zu tun; **in ~:** angstvoll; angsterfüllt; **be in ~:** Angst haben; **in ~ of being caught** in der Angst, gefasst zu werden; **in ~ and trembling** zitternd und zagend (*geh.*); mit schlotternden Knien (*ugs.*); **for ~ of waking *or* [that] we should wake *or* lest we [should] wake the others** aus Angst [davor], die anderen zu wecken *od.* dass wir die anderen wecken könnten; **without ~ or favour** völlig unparteiisch *od.* unvoreingenommen; **B** (*object of ~*) Furcht, *die;* *in pl.* Befürchtungen *Pl.;* **what are your main ~s?** wovor haben Sie am meisten Angst?; **C** (*dread and reverence*) [Ehr]furcht, *die* (**of** vor + *Dat.*); **put the ~ of God into sb.** (*fig.*) jmdn. fürchterlich erschrecken; jmdm. gehörig Angst einjagen; **D** (*anxiety for sb.'s/sth.'s safety*) Sorge, *die* (**for** um); **go *or* be in ~ of one's life** Angst um sein Leben haben; in Todesangst sein; **E** (*risk*) Gefahr, *die;* **no *or* not any ~ of sth./'that happening** keine Gefahr, dass etw./dies geschieht; **there's no ~ of 'that [ever happening]!** (*iron.*) die Gefahr besteht bestimmt nicht! (*iron.*); **no ~!** (*coll.*) keine Bange! (*ugs.*).
❷ *v.t.* **A** (*be afraid of*) **~ sb./sth.** vor jmdm./etw. Angst haben; sich vor jmdm./etw. fürchten; **~ to do *or* doing sth.** Angst haben *od.* sich fürchten, etw. zu tun; **you have nothing to ~:** Sie haben nichts zu befürchten; **~ the worst** das Schlimmste befürchten; **B** (*be worried about*) befürchten; **~ [that ...]** fürchten[, dass ...]; **it is to be ~ed that ...:** es steht zu befürchten, dass ...; **we need not ~ that/but [that] he will come** wir brauchen uns keine Sorgen zu machen, dass er kommt/nicht kommt.
❸ *v.i.* sich fürchten; **~ for sb./sth.** um jmdn./etw. bangen (*geh.*) *od.* fürchten; **never ~** (*also joc. iron.*) keine Bange (*ugs.*)

**fearful** /ˈfɪəfl/ *adj.* **A** (*terrible*) furchtbar; grauenhaft ‹Erfahrung, Anblick, Tod, Untier›; (*coll.: extreme*) fürchterlich; scheußlich ‹Farbe, Wetter›; **we had a ~ wait** wir mussten furchtbar lange warten; **B** (*frightened*) ängstlich; (*apprehensive*) **~ of sth./sb.** erfüllt von Angst vor etw./jmdm.; **be ~ of sth./sb.** vor etw./jmdm. Angst haben; **be ~ of doing sth.** Angst [davor] haben, etw. zu tun; **be ~ [that *or* lest] ...:** Angst haben, dass ...

**fearfully** /ˈfɪəfəlɪ/ *adv.* **A** (*terribly*) furchtbar; (*coll.: extremely*) fürchterlich; schrecklich; furchtbar ‹nett, gut, laut, heiß›; **B** (*in frightened manner*) ängstlich

**fearless** /ˈfɪəlɪs/ *adj.* furchtlos; (*through skill*) kühn; **be ~ [of sth./sb.]** keine Angst [vor etw./jmdm.] haben *od.* kennen

**fearlessly** /ˈfɪəlɪslɪ/ *adv.* furchtlos; ohne Angst

**fearsome** /ˈfɪəsəm/ *adj.* furchteinflößend; furchterregend; grässlich ‹Anblick›; **he/it is a ~-looking man/weapon** er/die Waffe sieht furchterregend aus

**feasibility** /fiːzɪˈbɪlɪtɪ/ *n., no pl.* **A** (*practicability*) Durchführbarkeit, *die;* (*of method*) Tauglichkeit, *die;* Anwendbarkeit, *die;* (*possibility*) Möglichkeit, *die;* **B** (*coll.*) (*manageability*) Machbarkeit, *die;* (*convenience*) Annehmlichkeit, *die*

**feasi'bility study** *n.* Durchführbarkeitsstudie, *die;*

**feasible** /ˈfiːzɪbl/ *adj.* **A** (*practicable*) durchführbar ‹Plan, Vorschlag›; anwendbar ‹Methode›; erreichbar ‹Ziel›; gangbar ‹Weg, Lösung›; (*possible*) möglich; **B** (*manageable*) machbar; (*convenient*) möglich

**feast** /fiːst/ ❶ *n.* **A** (*Relig.*) Fest, *das;* **the ~ of Christmas/Easter/Epiphany** das Weihnachts-/Oster-/Erscheinungsfest; **movable/immovable ~:** beweglicher/unbeweglicher Feiertag; **breakfast is a movable ~ in our family** (*joc.*) wir frühstücken nicht zu festen Zeiten; **B** (*banquet*) Festessen, *das;* Bankett, *das* (*geh.*); (*fig.*) Labsal, *das* (*geh.*); **a ~ for the eyes/ears** eine Augenweide/ein Ohrenschmaus; ⇒ *also* **enough** 2. ❷ *v.i.* **A** schlemmen; schwelgen; **~ on sth.** sich an etw. (*Dat.*) gütlich tun; (*fig.*) sich an etw. (*Dat.*) laben (*geh.*); sich an etw. (*Dat.*) weiden (*geh.*); **B** (*celebrate with festivities*) Feste/ein Fest begehen; feiern. ❸ *v.t.* festlich bewirten; **he ~ed his eyes on her beauty** seine Augen labten *od.* weideten sich an ihrer Schönheit (*geh.*)

**'feast day** *n.* [kirchlicher] Feiertag

**feat** /fiːt/ *n.* (*action*) Meisterleistung, *die;* Bravourleistung, *die;* (*thing*) Meisterwerk, *das;* **a ~ of intellect/strength** eine intellektuelle/physische Meisterleistung; **no mean *or* small ~:** eine beachtliche Leistung

**feather** /ˈfeðə(r)/ ❶ *n.* **A** Feder, *die;* (*on arrow*) [Pfeil]feder, *die;* (*for hat*) [Hut]feder, *die;* **as light as a ~:** federleicht; herrlich locker ‹Kuchen›; **show the white ~** (*fig.*) es mit der Angst [zu tun] kriegen (*ugs.*); kneifen (*ugs.*); **fine ~s make fine birds** (*prov.*) Kleider machen Leute (*Spr.*); **a ~ in sb.'s cap** (*fig.*) ein Grund für jmdn., stolz zu sein; **ruffle sb.'s ~s** jmdn. reizen *od.* aufregen; **you could have knocked me down with a ~:** ich war völlig von den Socken (*ugs.*); **make the ~s fly** = **make the fur fly** ⇒ **fur** 1 A; **B** *collect.* (*plumage*) Gefieder, *das;* Federkleid, *das* (*geh.*); **in high *or* full *or* fine ~** (*fig.*) in guter Form. ⇒ *also* **bird** A.
❷ *v.t.* **A** (*furnish with ~s*) mit Federn versehen; befiedern; **~ one's nest** (*fig.*) auf seinen finanziellen Vorteil bedacht sein; **B** (*turn edgeways*) aufdrehen ‹Paddel, Ruder›. ⇒ *also* **tar¹** 2

**feather: ~ 'bed** *n.* mit Federn gefüllte Matratze; **~-bed** *v.t.* [ver]hätscheln; **~ 'boa** *n.* Federboa, *die;* **~-brain** *n.* Schwachkopf, *der* (*ugs.*); **~-brained** /ˈfeðəbreɪnd/ *adj.* schwachköpfig (*ugs.*); **~ 'duster** *n.* Flederwisch, *der*

**feathered** /ˈfeðəd/ *adj.* gefiedert

**feather: ~-stitch** *n.* Federstich, *der;* **~weight** *n.* **A** (*very light thing/person*) Fliegengewicht, *das;* **be a ~weight** federleicht sein; **B** (*Boxing etc.*) Federgewicht, *das;* (*person also*) Federgewichtler, *der*

**feathery** /ˈfeðərɪ/ *adj.* **A** (*covered with feathers*) befiedert; gefiedert; **B** (*adorned with feathers*) federngeschmückt; Feder‹hut, -schmuck›; **C** (*feather-like*) (*in quality*) federartig; gefiedert ‹Blatt›; (*in weight*) federleicht; locker ‹Kuchenteig›

**feature** /ˈfiːtʃə(r)/ ❶ *n.* **A** *usu. in pl.* (*part of face*) Gesichtszug, *der;* **facial ~s** Gesichtszüge; **B** (*distinctive characteristic*) Charakteristische, *das;* [charakteristisches] Merkmal; Charakteristikum, *das;* **be a ~ of sth.** charakteristisch für etw. sein; **which ~s of**

city life attract you most? was zieht dich am Stadtleben besonders an?; **a/one particular ~:** ein besonderes Merkmal; **make a ~ of sth.** etw. [sehr] betonen *od.* herausstellen; **C** (*Journ. etc.*) Reportage, *die;* Dokumentarbericht, *der;* Feature, *das;* **D** (*Cinemat.*) **~ [film]** Hauptfilm, *der;* Spielfilm *der;* **E** (*Radio, Telev.*) **~ [programme]** Feature, *das.*
**2** *v.t.* (*make attraction of*) vorrangig vorstellen; den Vorrang geben (+ *Dat.*); (*give special prominence to*) (*in film*) in der Hauptrolle zeigen; (*in show*) als Stargast präsentieren.
**3** *v.i.* **A** (*be ~*) vorkommen; **B** (*be [important] participant*) **~ in sth.** eine [bedeutende] Rolle bei etw. spielen; **~ in a film** die Hauptrolle in einem Film spielen

**featureless** /'fi:tʃəlɪs/ *adj.* eintönig; ereignislos ‹Zeit›

**Feb.** *abbr.* **February** Febr.

**febrile** /'fi:braɪl/ *adj.* fiebrig; Fieber‹schweiß, -schlaf, -zustand›

**February** /'februərɪ/ *n.* ▶ **1055** Februar, *der;* ⇒ *also* **August**

**feces** (*Amer.*) ⇒ **faeces**

**feckless** /'feklɪs/ *adj.* (*feeble*) schwächlich ‹Person›; (*futile*) vergeblich ‹Versuch, Anstrengung›; nutzlos, vertan ‹Leben›; (*inefficient*) untauglich; (*aimless*) ziellos

**fecund** /'fi:kənd, 'fekənd/ *adj.* (*fertile, fertilizing, lit. or fig.*) fruchtbar

**fecundity** /fɪ'kʌndɪtɪ/ *n., no pl.* (*fertility, fertilizing power, lit. or fig.*) Fruchtbarkeit, *die*

**fed** /fed/ **1** ⇒ **feed** 1, 2. **2** *pred. adj.* (*coll.*) **be/get ~ up with sb./sth.** jmdn./etw. satt haben (*ugs.*); **you're looking rather ~ up** du siehst aus, als hättest du die Nase voll (*ugs.*); **be/get ~ up with doing sth.** es satt haben, etw. zu tun (*ugs.*); **be/get ~ up to the [back] teeth with sb./sth.** jmdn./etw. zum Kotzen finden (*derb*)

**federal** /'fedərl/ *adj.* **A** Bundes-; föderativ ‹System›; bundesweit ‹Feiertag›; bundeseigen ‹Betrieb›; **~ district/territory** *etc.* Bundesdistrikt, *der*/-territorium, *das usw.;* **~ legislation/representative** Gesetzgebung/Abgeordneter des Bundes; **B** (*relating to or favouring the central government*) föderalistisch ‹Partei usw.›; **~ supporter/tendency** Anhänger des/Neigung zum Föderalismus; **C** **F~** (*Amer. Hist.: of Northern States in Civil War*) der Unionisten *nachgestellt;* **D** (*having largely independent units*) föderiert

**federalism** /'fedərəlɪzəm/ *n., no pl.* Föderalismus, *der*

**federalist** /'fedərəlɪst/ **1** *adj.* föderalistisch. **2** *n.* Föderalist, *der*/Föderalistin, *die*

**federate** /'fedəreɪt/ **1** *v.t.* **A** (*organize on federal basis*) föderalistisch organisieren; föderalisieren; **B** (*band together in league*) zu einem Bund zusammenschließen; föderieren. **2** *v.i.* sich [zu einem Bund] zusammenschließen

**federation** /fedə'reɪʃn/ *n.* **A** (*federating*) Zusammenschluss, *der;* **B** (*group of states*) Bündnis, *das;* Föderation, *die;* (*society*) Bund, *der;* Verband, *der*

**fee** /fi:/ *n.* **A** Gebühr, *die;* **B** (*of doctor, lawyer, etc.*) Honorar, *das;* (*of performer*) Gage, *die;* **what ~ do you charge?** was verlangen Sie als Honorar/Gage?; **C** *in pl.* (*of company director etc.*) Bezüge *Pl.;* **D** ⇒ **transfer fee**; **E** (*entrance money*) Gebühr, *die;* **matriculation/registration ~:** Einschreibe-/Aufnahmegebühr, *die;* **F** (*administrative charge*) Bearbeitungsgebühr, *die;* **G** *in pl.* (*regular payment for instruction*) **school ~s** Schulgeld, *das;* **tuition ~s** ⇒ **tuition** B

**feeble** /'fi:bl/ *adj.*, **~r** /'fi:blə(r)/, **~st** /'fi:blɪst/ **A** (*weak*) schwach; **B** (*deficient*) schwächlich; (*in resolve, argument, commitment*) halbherzig; **C** (*lacking energy*) schwach ‹Leistung, Kampf, Stimme, Applaus›; wenig überzeugend ‹Argument, Entschuldigung, Erklärung, Vorstellung›; zaghaft, kläglich ‹Versuch, Bemühung›; kraftlos ‹Drohung›; lahm (*ugs.*) ‹Witz›; **D** (*indistinct*) schwach ‹[Licht]schein, Herzschlag›

**'feeble-minded** *adj.* **A** töricht; **B** (*Psych.*) geistesschwach; **~ person** Schwachsinnige, *der/die*

**feebly** /'fi:blɪ/ *adv.* **A** (*weakly*) mühsam ‹gehen, sich bewegen›; **B** (*deficiently*) schwach; kaum ‹reagieren›; **C** (*without energy*) schwach ‹widerstehen, unterstützen, applaudieren›; zaghaft ‹versuchen, ablehnen, widersprechen, behaupten›

**feed** /fi:d/ **1** *v.t.*, **fed** /fed/ **A** (*give food to*) füttern; **~ sb./an animal with sth.** jmdm. etw. zu essen/einem Tier [etw.] zu fressen geben; **~ a baby/an animal/an invalid on or with sth.** ein Baby/Tier/einen Invaliden mit etw. füttern; **the dog is fed every evening at 6 o'clock** der Hund bekommt jeden Abend um 6 Uhr sein Fressen; **~ intravenously** intravenös ernähren; **~ [at the breast]** stillen; **B** (*provide food for*) ernähren; satt machen; **~ sb./an animal on or with sth.** jmdn./ein Tier mit etw. ernähren; **C** (*put food into mouth of*) füttern; **~ oneself** allein *od.* ohne Hilfe essen; **can the child ~ herself with a spoon yet?** kann das Kind schon mit dem Löffel essen?; **be ~ing one's face** (*coll. derog.*) fressen (*abwertend*); **D** (*graze*) weiden lassen; weiden; **E** (*produce food for*) **~ sb. [with sth.]** jmdn. [mit etw.] versorgen; **F** (*nourish*) mit Nährstoffen versorgen; (*fig.*) verstärken; **G** ⇒ **feed up**; **H** (*give out*) verfüttern ‹Viehfutter› (**to** an + *Akk.*); **I** (*keep supplied*) speisen ‹Wasserreservoir›; unterhalten ‹Feuer›; am Brennen halten ‹Ofen›; (*supply with material*) versorgen; (*supply*) **~ a film into the projector** einen Film in das Vorführgerät einlegen; **~ data into the computer** Daten in den Computer eingeben; den Computer mit Daten füttern; **~ sth. to sb., ~ sb. sth.** (*fig.*) jmdn. mit etw. füttern; **~ sth. to the flames** etw. den Flammen übergeben; ⇒ *also* **meter**[1] 1 B; **J** (*lead*) **~ sth. through sth.** etw. durch etw. hindurchführen; **K** (*Theatre coll.*) **~ the actor [with] his cues or the cues to the actor** dem Schauspieler das Stichwort geben; **L** (*Football etc.*) zuspielen (**to** *Dat.*). ⇒ *also* **fed** 2.
**2** *v.i.*, **fed** ‹Tier:› fressen (**from** aus); ‹Person:› essen (**off** von); **~ on sth.** ‹Tier:› etw. fressen, mit etw. gefüttert werden; ‹Person:› sich von etw. [er]nähren, etw. essen, etw. futtern (*ugs.*); (*fig.*) von etw. leben; **~ off sth.** sich von etw. ernähren; (*fig.*) von etw. leben.
**3** *n.* **A** (*instance of eating*) (*of animals*) Fressen, *das;* (*of baby*) Mahlzeit, *die;* **when is the baby's next ~ due?** wann muss das Baby wieder gefüttert werden?; **on the ~** (**~ing**) am *od.* beim Fressen; bei der Nahrungsaufnahme; (*looking out for food*) auf Nahrungssuche; **B** (*pasture*) Viehfutter, *das;* **out at ~:** auf der Weide; **C** (*horse's oats etc.*) [Futter]ration, *die;* (*fodder*) **[cattle/sheep/pig] ~:** [Vieh-/Schaf-/Schweine]futter, *das;* **be off its ~** ‹Tier:› schlecht fressen; **be off one's ~** ‹Person:› schlecht essen; keinen Appetit haben; **D** (*coll.*) (*meal*) Mahlzeit, *die;* (*feast*) Mahl, *das;* **have [quite] a ~:** [ordentlich] futtern (*ugs.*); [kräftig] zulangen; **E** (*of machine*) Versorgung, *die;* (*of furnace*) Begichtung, *die;* (*supplying of material*) Einspeisung, *die;* **F** (*material supplied to machine*) Nachschub, *der;* (*amount supplied*) Nachschub, *der;* Nachfüllmenge, *die;* (*into computer*) Einspeisung, *die;* **G** (*hopper*) Trichter, *der*

**~ 'back** **1** *v.t.* **A** zurückleiten; weiterleiten, -geben ‹Informationen›; **be fed back** zurückfließen; **B** (*Electr.*) rückkoppeln.
**2** *v.i.* **~ back into sth.** in etw. (*Akk.*) zurückfließen; **~ back to sth./sb.** an etw./jmdn. weitergeleitet werden. ⇒ *also* **feedback**

**~ 'up** *v.t.* (*fatten*) mästen; (*fill up with food*) voll stopfen (*ugs.*); ⇒ *also* **fed** 2

**'feedback** *n.* **A** (*information about result, response*) Reaktion, *die;* Feedback, *das* (*fachspr.*); **B** (*Electr.*) **[positive/negative] ~:** [positive/negative] Rückkopplung; **C** (*Biol., Psych., etc.*) Reafferenz, *die* (*fachspr.*); Rückkopplung, *die*

**feeder** /'fi:də(r)/ *n.* **A** (*animal*) Fresser, *der;* **plankton ~** Planktonfresser, *der;* **the larvae are voracious ~s** die Larven sind gefräßig; **B** (*dispenser*) Futterspender, *der*

**'feeder road** *n.* Zubringer, *der;* Zubringerstraße, *die*

**feeding**/'fi:dɪŋ/: **~ bottle** *n.* [Saug]flasche, *die;* **~ time** *n.* **A** Fütterungszeit, *die;* **B** (*fig. joc.*) Essenszeit, *die;* **~ time!** Essen!

**feed: ~lot** *n.* Weide, *die;* **~-pipe** *n.* Zuleitungsrohr, *das;* Füllrohr, *das;* **~stock** *n.* Einsatz- *od.* Ausgangsmaterial, *das*

**feel** /fi:l/ **1** *v.t.*, **felt** /felt/ **A** (*explore by touch*) befühlen; **~ sb.'s pulse** jmdm. den Puls fühlen; (*fig.*) bei jmdm. vorfühlen; jmdm. auf den Zahn fühlen (*ugs.*) (**on, about** hinsichtlich); **~ one's way** sich (*Dat.*) seinen Weg ertasten; (*fig.: try sth. out*) vorsichtig vorgehen; sich vorsichtig vor[an]tasten; **be ~ing one's way** versuchen, sich zurechtzufinden; **~ one's way along the corridor/towards the door** sich den Flur entlangtasten/sich zur Tür tasten; **B** (*perceive by touch*) fühlen; (*become aware of*) bemerken; (*be aware of*) merken; (*have sensation of*) spüren; **~ sb.'s temperature** fühlen, ob jmd. Fieber hat; **C** ⇒ **feel up**; **D** (*be conscious of*) empfinden ‹Mitleid, Dank, Eifersucht›; verspüren ‹Drang, Wunsch›; spüren ‹Gefühle anderer›; **~ the cold/heat** unter der Kälte/Hitze leiden; **~ one's age** sein Alter spüren; **~ pride in sb./sth.** stolz auf jmdn./etw. sein; **~ bitterness/amazement** verbittert/erstaunt sein; **~ the temptation** sich versucht fühlen; **make itself felt** zu spüren sein; (*have effect*) sich bemerkbar machen; **make one's presence felt** sich bemerkbar machen; **E** (*experience*) empfinden; (*be affected by*) zu spüren bekommen; **F** (*be emotionally affected by*) leiden unter (+ *Dat.*); **he felt it terribly when his dog died** er litt ganz furchtbar, als sein Hund starb; **G** (*have vague or emotional conviction*) **~ [that] ...:** das Gefühl haben, dass ...; **H** (*think*) **if that's what you ~ about the matter** wenn du so darüber denkst; **~ it to be one's duty to ...:** es für seine Pflicht halten, zu ...; **~ oneself hard done by** sich schlecht behandelt fühlen; **~ [that] ...:** glauben, dass ...; **if you ~ [that] you would like to know more** wenn Sie gern mehr wissen möchten. ⇒ *also* **bone** 1 A; **draught** A.
**2** *v.i.*, **felt** **A** (*search with hand etc.*) **~ [about] in sth. [for sth.]** in etw. (*Dat.*) [nach etw.] [herum]suchen; **~ [about] in one's bag/pocket [to see whether ...]** in seiner Tasche [herum]kramen[, um festzustellen, ob ...] (*ugs.*); **~ [about] [after or for sth.] with sth.** mit etw. [nach etw.] [umher]tasten; **B** (*have sense of touch*) fühlen; **C** (*be conscious that one is*) sich ... fühlen; **~ angry/enthusiastic/sure/delighted/disappointed** böse/begeistert/sicher/froh/enttäuscht sein; **she felt quite sick/horrified at the idea** der Gedanke machte sie ganz krank/widerte sie an; **I felt such a fool** ich kam mir wie ein Idiot vor; **~ [the] better for sth.** (*in mind*) sich erleichtert fühlen; (*in body*) sich besser fühlen; **~ inclined to do sth.** dazu neigen, etw. zu tun; **~ committed to sth.** sich einer Sache (*Dat.*) verschrieben haben; **the child did not ~ loved/wanted/needed** das Kind hatte das Gefühl, ungeliebt/unerwünscht/überflüssig zu sein; **I ~ dubious about doing that** ich weiß nicht recht, ob ich das machen soll; **~ quite hopeful** guter Hoffnung sein; **I felt sorry for him** er tat mir leid; **~ hard done by** sich schlecht behandelt fühlen; **~ like sth.** sich (*Dat.*) vorkommen wie etw.; **he makes you ~ like a fool/lady** bei ihm kommt man sich (*Dat.*) wie ein Idiot vor/er gibt einem das Gefühl, eine Dame zu sein; **~ like a new man/woman** sich wie neugeboren fühlen; **what do you ~ like or how do you ~ today?** wie fühlst du dich *od.* wie geht es dir heute?; **what would you ~ like or how would you ~ if someone said such a thing to you?** was würdest du empfinden *od.* denken, wenn jemand so etwas zu dir sagte?; **let's see what we ~ like or how we ~ when ...:** warten wir ab, in welcher Verfassung wir sind *od.* (*what we should like to do*) wie uns der Sinn steht, wenn ...; **~ like sth./doing sth.** (*coll.: wish to have/do*) Lust haben/Lust haben, etw. zu tun; **do you ~ like a cup of tea?** möchtest du eine Tasse Tee?; **I ~ like a new**

hairdo ich könnte eine neue Frisur gebrauchen; **we ~ as if** *or* **as though ...:** es kommt uns vor, als ob ...; (*have the impression that*) wir haben das Gefühl, dass ...; **how do you ~ about him now/the idea?** was empfindest du jetzt für ihn/was hältst du von der Idee?; **if that's how** *or* **the way you ~ about it** wenn du so darüber denkst; **she just didn't ~ that way about him** sie hatte nun einmal nicht solche Gefühle für ihn; **~ the same [way] about each other** dasselbe füreinander empfinden; **~ [quite] one'self** sich wohl fühlen; **D** (*be emotionally affected*) **~ passionately/bitterly about sth.** sich für etw. begeistern/über etw. (*Akk.*) verbittert sein; **~ kindly towards sb.** jmdm. wohlgesonnen sein; **E** (*be consciously perceived as*) sich ... anfühlen; **~ like sth.** sich wie etw. anfühlen; **it ~s funny/strange/nice/uncomfortable** es ist ein komisches / seltsames / angenehmes / unangenehmes Gefühl; **it ~s so good to be away from the hustle** es tut gut, der Hetze entronnen zu sein; **it all ~s so strange here** es kommt einem hier alles so seltsam vor. ⇒ *also* **cheap** 1 C.

**3** *n.* **A** (*sense of touch*) [Be]tasten, *das;* **be dry/soft** *etc.* **to the ~:** sich trocken/weich *usw.* anfühlen; **B** (*act of ~ing*) Abtasten, *das;* **let me have a ~:** lass mich mal fühlen; **C** (*sensation when touched*) Gefühl, *das;* **have a silky ~:** sich seidig anfühlen; **D** (*sensation characterizing a situation, place, etc.*) Atmosphäre, *die;* **there is a mysterious/ghostly ~ about the place** der Ort hat etwas Mysteriöses/Gespenstisches [an sich]; **get a [real]/the ~ of sth.** ein [wirkliches] Gespür für etw. bekommen; **get the ~ of things in a firm/of a new job** sich in einer Firma zurechtfinden/sich in eine neue Arbeit hineinfinden; **have a ~ for sth.** (*fig.*) ein Gespür *od.* einen Blick für etw. haben; (*talent*) eine Ader für etw. haben

**~ for** *v.t.* **~ for sb.** mit jmdm. Mitleid haben

**~ 'out** *v.t.* **A** (*sound out*) **~ sb. out** jmds. Ansichten feststellen; **B** (*test practicability of*) zur Diskussion stellen; austesten

**~ 'up** *v.t.* (*sl.*) befummeln (*salopp*)

**~ with** *v.t.* Mitgefühl haben mit; mitfühlen; **I ~ with you** Sie haben mein Mitgefühl

**feeler** /ˈfiːlə(r)/ *n.* Fühler, *der;* **put out ~s** (*fig.*) seine Fühler ausstrecken

**feeling** /ˈfiːlɪŋ/ **1** *n.* **A** (*sense of touch*) **[sense of] ~:** Tastsinn, *der;* **have no ~ in one's legs** kein Gefühl in den Beinen haben; **B** (*physical sensation*) Gefühl, *das;* **you'll have a painful ~:** es wird weh tun; **C** (*emotion*) Gefühl, *das;* **what are your ~s for each other?** was empfindet ihr füreinander?; **say sth. with ~:** etw. mit Nachdruck sagen; **~s were running high** Emotionen wurden geweckt; **there were strong ~s about it** es gab sehr entschiedene Ansichten darüber; **bad ~** (*jealousy*) Neid, *der;* (*annoyance*) Verstimmung, *die;* **D** *in pl.* (*sensibilities*) Gefühle; **hurt sb.'s ~s** jmdn. verletzen; **E** (*sympathy*) Mitgefühl, *das;* Einfühlungsvermögen, *das;* **F** (*consciousness*) **a ~ of hopelessness/harmony** *etc.* ein Gefühl der Hoffnungslosigkeit/Harmonie *usw.;* **there was a ~ of mystery/peace about the place** der Ort hatte etwas Mysteriöses/Friedvolles [an sich (*Dat.*)] *od.* mutete mysteriös/friedvoll an; **I have a funny ~ that ...:** ich habe das komische Gefühl, dass ... (*ugs.*); **G** (*belief*) Gefühl, *das;* **have a/the ~ [that] ...:** das Gefühl haben, dass ...; **H** (*sentiment*) Ansicht, *die;* **air one's ~s** seinem Herzen Luft machen; seine Ansicht äußern; **the general ~ was that ...:** man war allgemein der Ansicht, dass ...; ⇒ *also* **mixed** A; **I** (*general emotional effect*) Eindruck, *der.*

**2** *adj.* **A** (*sensitive*) empfindlich; **B** (*sympathetic*) einfühlsam; **be ~ about other people** sich in andere Leute einfühlen können; **C** (*showing emotion*) gefühlvoll

**feelingly** /ˈfiːlɪŋlɪ/ *adv.* **A** (*sympathetically*) mitfühlend ‹reagieren›; **B** (*in manner showing emotion*) gefühlvoll; **say sth. ~:** etw. mit Nachdruck sagen

**'fee-paying** *adj.* **~ school** schulgeldpflichtige Schule; **~ pupil/student** Schulgeld/Studiengebühren zahlender Schüler/Student

**feet** *pl. of* **foot**

**feign** /feɪn/ *v.t.* vorspiegeln; vortäuschen; **~ ignorance** sich dumm stellen; **~ that one is ...:** vorgeben, ... zu sein; **~ to do sth.** vorgeben, etw. zu tun

**feint**[1] /feɪnt/ **1** *n.* **A** (*Boxing, Fencing*) Finte, *die;* **make a ~:** eine Finte ausführen; fintieren; **B** (*Mil.*) Scheinangriff, *der;* **make a ~ [at** *or* **of attacking sb./sth.]** einen Scheinangriff [auf jmdn./etw.] ausführen. **2** *v.i.* **A** (*Boxing, Fencing*) **~ at sb./sth.** eine Finte gegen jmdn./etw. ausführen; **B** (*Mil.*) **~ at** *or* **[up]on sb./sth.** einen Scheinangriff auf jmdn./etw. durchführen

**feint**[2] *adj.* (*Commerc.*) **~ lines** feine Linierung; **ruled ~:** fein liniert

**feldspar** /ˈfeldspɑː(r)/ ⇒ **felspar**

**felicitate** /fɪˈlɪsɪteɪt/ *v.t.* (*literary*) **~ sb. [on sth.]** jmdn. [zu etw.] beglückwünschen

**felicitation** /fɪlɪsɪˈteɪʃn/ *n.* Glückwunsch, *der;* Gratulation, *die;* **give sb. one's ~s on sth.** jmdn. zu etw. beglückwünschen; jmdm. zu etw. gratulieren

**felicitous** /fɪˈlɪsɪtəs/ *adj.* glücklich ‹Zufall, Nachricht, Umstand, Wahl›; nett ‹Bemerkung, Art›; gelungen ‹Formulierung, Kommentar, Anspielung›; geeignet, passend ‹Worte›

**felicitously** /fɪˈlɪsɪtəslɪ/ *adv.* glücklich

**felicity** /fɪˈlɪsɪtɪ/ *n.* **A** *no pl.* (*happiness*) Glück, *das;* **B** (*thing or person causing happiness*) Glück, *das;* **C** (*fortunate trait*) glückliche Gabe; **D** (*in choice of words*) Formulierungskunst, *die;* **~ of expression** glückliche Wahl des Ausdrucks

**feline** /ˈfiːlaɪn/ **1** *adj.* (*of cat[s]*) Katzen-; (*catlike*) katzenartig; katzenhaft. **2** *n.* Katze, *die;* **the ~s** die Katzen *od.* (*fachspr.*) Feliden

**fell**[1] ⇒ **fall** 2

**fell**[2] /fel/ *v.t.* **A** (*cut down*) fällen ‹Baum›; **B** (*strike down*) niederstrecken ‹Gegner›

**fell**[3] *n.* (*Brit.*) **A** (*in names: hill*) Berg, *der;* **B** (*stretch of high moorland*) Hochmoor, *das*

**fell**[4] *adj.* **A** **at** *or* **in one ~ swoop** auf einen Schlag; **B** (*poet./rhet.*) (*fierce*) wild; grimmig ‹Drohung, Feind›; (*destructive*) vernichtend

**fellatio** /fəˈlɑːtɪəʊ/ *n.* Fellatio, *die*

**fellow** /ˈfeləʊ/ **1** *n.* **A** *usu. in pl.* (*comrade*) Kamerad, *der;* **~s at school/work** Schulkameraden/Arbeitskollegen; **a good ~:** ein guter Kumpel (*ugs.*); **B** *usu. in pl.* (*equal*) Gleichgestellte, *der/die;* **be among one's ~s** unter seinesgleichen sein; **C** (*contemporary*) Zeitgenosse, *der*/-genossin, *die;* **D** (*counterpart*) Gegenstück, *das;* **E** (*Brit. Univ.*) Fellow, *der;* (*elected graduate*) graduierter Stipendiat/graduierte Stipendiatin; (*member of governing body*) Mitglied des Verwaltungsrats; **F** (*member of academy or society*) Fellow, *der;* Mitglied, *das;* **G** (*coll.: man, boy*) Bursche, *der* (*ugs.*); Kerl, *der* (*ugs.*); (*boyfriend*) Freund, *der;* **the ~s** die Jungs (*ugs.*); **well, young ~:** nun, junger Mann; **old** *or* **dear ~:** alter Junge *od.* Knabe (*ugs.*); **a ~** (*anyone*) ein Mann; **young ~-my-lad** junger Mann; **I'm not the sort of ~ who ...:** ich bin nicht der Typ, der ...; **a devil of a ~:** ein Teufelskerl; **the other ~** (*fig.*) der andere; **H** (*derog.: despised person*) Kerl, *der* (*abwertend*). ⇒ *also* **hail**[2] 4; **stout** 1 C.

**2** *attrib. adj.* Mit-; **~ lodger/worker** Mitbewohner/Kollege, *der*/Mitbewohnerin/Kollegin, *die;* **~ man** *or* **human being** Mitmensch, *der;* **~ sufferer** Leidensgenosse, *der*/-genossin, *die;* **my ~ teachers/workers** *etc.* meine Lehrer-/Arbeitskollegen *usw.;* **~ member of the party** Parteigenosse, *der*/-genossin, *die;* **~ member of the club** Klubkamerad, *der*/-kameradin, *die;* **~ student** Kommilitone, *der*/Kommilitonin, *die*

**fellow: ~ 'countryman** ⇒ **countryman** A; **~ 'feeling** *n.* **A** (*sympathy*) Mitgefühl, *das;* **have a ~ feeling for sb.** mit jmdm. fühlen; **B** (*mutual understanding*) Zusammengehörigkeitsgefühl, *das*

**fellowship** /ˈfeləʊʃɪp/ *n.* **A** *no pl.* (*companionship*) Gesellschaft, *die;* **in a spirit of good ~:** von Gemeinschaftsgeist erfüllt; **B** *no pl.* (*community of interest*) Zusammengehörigkeit, *die;* **C** (*association*) Verbundenheit, *die;* **D** (*brotherhood*) [Glaubens]gemeinschaft, *die;* **E** (*Univ. etc.*) Status eines Fellows; Fellowship, *die*

**fellow-'traveller** *n.* **A** (*who travels with another*) Mitreisende, *der/die;* **B** (*with Communist sympathies*) Sympathisant, *der*/Sympathisantin, *die*

**felonious** /fəˈləʊnɪəs/ *adj.* verbrecherisch

**felony** /ˈfelənɪ/ *n.* Kapitalverbrechen, *das*

**felspar** /ˈfelspɑː(r)/ *n.* (*Min.*) Feldspat, *der*

**felt**[1] /felt/ *n.* (*cloth*) Filz, *der;* **~ hat/slippers/mat** Filzhut, *der*/-pantoffeln *Pl.*/-matte, *die*

**felt**[2] ⇒ **feel** 1, 2

**felt[-tipped] 'pen** *n.* Filzstift, *der*

**female** /ˈfiːmeɪl/ **1** *adj.* **A** weiblich; Frauen‹stimme, -station, -chor, -verein›; **~ animal/bird/fish/insect** Weibchen, *das;* **~ child/doctor** Mädchen, *das*/Ärztin, *die;* **~ elephant/whale** [Elefanten-/Wal]kuh, *die;* **a ~ engineer/student/slave** eine Ingenieurin/Studentin/Sklavin; **~ impersonator** Frauendarsteller, *der;* **B** **~ screw/thread** [Schrauben]mutter, *die*/Innengewinde, *das.* **2** *n.* **A** (*person*) Frau, *die;* (*foetus, child*) Mädchen, *das;* (*animal*) Weibchen, *das;* **B** (*derog.: woman*) Weib[sbild], *das* (*ugs. abwertend*)

**feminine** /ˈfemɪnɪn/ **1** *adj.* **A** (*of women*) weiblich; Frauen‹angelegenheit, -problem, -leiden›; Damen‹mode›; (*womanly*) fraulich; feminin; feminin, (*abwertend*) weibisch ‹Mann›; **she is so very ~ [in her ways]** sie gibt sich so betont fraulich; **B** (*Ling.*) weiblich; feminin (*fachspr.*). **2** *n.* (*Ling.*) Femininum, *das*

**feminine 'rhyme** *n.* (*Pros.*) weiblicher Reim

**femininity** /femɪˈnɪnɪtɪ/ *n.*, *no pl.* Weiblichkeit, *die;* (*more mature*) Fraulichkeit, *die*

**feminism** /ˈfemɪnɪzm/ *n.*, *no pl.* Feminismus, *der*

**feminist** /ˈfemɪnɪst/ **1** *n.* Feministin, *die*/Feminist, *der;* Frauenrechtlerin, *die*/-rechtler, *der.* **2** *adj.* feministisch; Frauen‹bewegung, -blatt, -gruppe›

**femme fatale** /fæm fæˈtɑl/ *n.* Femme fatale, *die* (*geh.*)

**femoral** /ˈfemərl/ *adj.* (*Anat.*) femoral (*fachspr.*); Oberschenkel[knochen]-

**femur** /ˈfiːmə(r)/ *n.*, *pl.* **~s** *or* **femora** /ˈfemərə/ **A** (*Anat.*) Oberschenkelknochen, *der;* Femur, *der* (*fachspr.*); **B** (*Zool.*) Femur, *der*

**fen** /fen/ *n.* Sumpfland, *das;* Fenn, *das;* Fehn, *das* (*nordd.*); **the Fens** die Fens

**fence** /fens/ **1** *n.* **A** Zaun, *der;* **sunk ~:** Sicherungsgraben, *der;* **mend one's ~s** (*fig.*) das Kriegsbeil begraben (*ugs.*); **sit on the ~** (*fig.*) sich nicht einmischen; sich neutral verhalten; **B** (*for horses to jump*) Hindernis, *das;* **C** (*sl.: receiver*) Hehler, *der*/Hehlerin, *die.* **2** *v.i.* (*Sport*) fechten. **3** *v.t.* (*surround with fence*) einzäunen; (*surround*) umgeben; (*fig.*) absichern **(with** durch)

**~ 'in** *v.t.* einzäunen; (*fig.*) einengen **(with** durch)

**~ 'off** *v.t.* abzäunen; (*fig.*) absperren

**fencer** /ˈfensə(r)/ *n.* Fechter, *der*/Fechterin, *die*

**fencing** /ˈfensɪŋ/ *n.*, *no pl.* **A** Einzäunen, *das;* **B** (*Sport/Hist.*) Fechten, *das; attrib.* Fecht-; **C** (*enclosure*) Zaun, *der;* Einzäunung, *die;* **D** (*fences*) Zäune *Pl.;* Umfriedung, *die* (*geh.*); **E** (*material for fences*) Zaun, *der*

**fend** /fend/ *v.i.* **~ for sb.** für jmdn. sorgen; **~ for oneself** für sich selbst sorgen; (*in hostile surroundings*) sich allein durchschlagen

**~ 'off** *v.t.* abwehren; von sich fern halten; **~ off these criticisms/the flies/fans** sich gegen diese Kritik wehren/sich (*Dat.*) die Fliegen/Fans vom Leib halten

**fender** /ˈfendə(r)/ *n.* **A** Schutz, *der, o. Pl.;* Schutzvorrichtung, *die;* **B** (*for fire*) Kaminschutz, *der;* **C** (*for dock wall etc.*) Fender, *der;* Dalbe, *die* (*Seemannsspr.*); **D** (*on ship*) Fender, *der;* **E** (*Brit.: car bumper*) Stoßstange, *die;* **F** (*Amer.*) (*train bumper*) Rammbohle, *die;* (*car mudguard or wing*)

Kotflügel, *der;* (*bicycle mudguard*) Schutzblech, *das*

**fenland** /ˈfenlənd/ *n.* Marschland, *das*

**fennel** /ˈfenl/ *n.* (*Bot.*) Fenchel, *der*

**fenugreek** /ˈfenjʊgriːk/ *n.* (*Bot.*) Griechisch-Heu, *das;* Bockshornklee, *der*

**feral** /ˈfɪərl, ˈferl/ *adj.* **A** (*wild*) wild; wild wachsend ‹Pflanze›; **B** (*after escape*) verwildert; **become ~:** verwildern

**ferment** ❶ /fəˈment/ *v.i.* **A** (*undergo fermentation*) gären; **cause to ~:** in *od.* zur Gärung bringen; **begin to ~:** in Gärung übergehen; **B** (*be in state of agitation*) gären; ‹Plan, Idee:› reifen; ‹Wut, Frustration:› rumoren, brodeln. ❷ *v.t.* **A** (*subject to fermentation*) zur Gärung bringen; **B** (*excite*) heraufbeschwören ‹Gewalt, Unzufriedenheit, Unruhe›. ❸ /ˈfɜːment/ *n.* **A** (*fermenting agent*) Enzym, *das;* **B** (*fermentation*) Gärung, *die;* Fermentation, *die* (*fachspr.*); **C** (*agitation*) Unruhe, *die;* Aufruhr, *der;* **in [a] ~:** in Unruhe *od.* Aufruhr

**fermentation** /fɜːmenˈteɪʃn/ *n.* **A** Gärung, *die;* Fermentation, *die* (*fachspr.*); **be under** *or* **undergo ~:** gären; sich in Gärung befinden; **B** (*agitation*) (*political*) Unruhe, *die;* (*of ideas*) Reifen, *das*

**fern** /fɜːn/ *n.* Farnkraut, *das; collect.* Farn, *der*

**ferocious** /fəˈrəʊʃəs/ *adj.* wild ‹Tier, Person, Aussehen, Blick, Lachen›; grimmig ‹Stimme›; heftig ‹Schlag, Kampf, Stoß›; (*fig.*) scharf ‹Kritik, Angriff›; heftig ‹Bemerkung, Äußerung, Streit, Auseinandersetzung›; **~-looking** Furcht erregend

**ferociously** /fəˈrəʊʃəslɪ/ *adv.* wütend ‹bellen, knurren›; grimmig ‹blicken, lachen, sagen›; heftig ‹kämpfen, streiten›; (*fig.*) scharf, heftig ‹angreifen, kritisieren›

**ferociousness** /fəˈrəʊʃəsnɪs/, **ferocity** /fəˈrɒsɪtɪ/ *ns., no pl.* ⇒ **ferocious**: Wildheit, *die;* Grimmigkeit, *die;* Heftigkeit, *die;* Schärfe, *die*

**ferrel** /ˈferl/ ⇒ **ferrule**

**ferret** /ˈferɪt/ ❶ *n.* Frettchen, *das.* ❷ *v.i.* **~ [about** *or* **around]** herumstöbern (*ugs.*); herumschnüffeln (*abwertend*); **~ for sth.** nach etw. stöbern (*ugs.*) *od.* (*abwertend*) schnüffeln
**~ ˈout** *v.t.* aufspüren; aufstöbern (*ugs.*)

**Ferris wheel** /ˈferɪs wiːl/ *n.* Riesenrad, *das*

**ferro-** /ferəʊ/ *in comb.* Ferro-

**ferroˈconcrete** *n.* Stahlbeton, *der*

**ferrous** /ˈferəs/ *adj.* (*containing iron*) eisenhaltig; Eisen-

**ferrule** /ˈferuːl, ˈferl/ *n.* Zwinge, *die*

**ferry** /ˈferɪ/ ❶ *n.* **A** Fähre, *die;* **B** (*service*) Fährverbindung, *die;* Fähre, *die* (*ugs.*). ❷ *v.t.* **A** (*convey in boat*) **~ [across** *or* **over]** übersetzen; **B** (*transport*) befördern, bringen ‹Güter, Personen›; **~ the children back and forth to school** die Kinder zur Schule und wieder nach Hause fahren

**ferry: ~ boat** *n.* Fährboot, *das;* (*punt*) Stakfähre, *die;* Kahnfähre, *die;* **~man** /ˈferɪmən/ *n., pl.* **~men** /ˈferɪmən/ Fährmann, *der;* **~ service** *n.* **A** Fährverbindung, *die;* **B** (*business*) Fährbetrieb, *der*

**fertile** /ˈfɜːtaɪl/ *adj.* **A** (*fruitful*) fruchtbar (**in** an + *Dat.*); (*fig.*) produktiv; schöpferisch; **have a ~ imagination** viel Fantasie haben; **B** (*capable of developing*) befruchtet; **C** (*able to become parent*) fortpflanzungsfähig

**fertilisation**, **fertilise**, **fertiliser** ⇒ **fertiliz-**

**fertility** /fɜːˈtɪlɪtɪ/ *n., no pl.* **A** Fruchtbarkeit, *die* (*auch fig.*); Fertilität, *die;* **B** (*ability to become parent*) Fortpflanzungsfähigkeit, *die*

**fertility: ~ drug** *n.* (*Med.*) Hormonpräparat, *das* (*zur Steigerung der Fruchtbarkeit*); **~ symbol** *n.* (*Anthrop.*) Fruchtbarkeitssymbol, *das*

**fertilization** /fɜːtɪlaɪˈzeɪʃn/ *n.* **A** (*Biol.*) Befruchtung, *die;* **B** (*Agric.*) Düngung, *die*

**fertilize** /ˈfɜːtɪlaɪz/ *v.t.* **A** (*Biol.*) befruchten; **B** (*Agric.*) düngen

**fertilizer** /ˈfɜːtɪlaɪzə(r)/ *n.* Dünger, *der*

**fervency** /ˈfɜːvənsɪ/ *n., no pl.* ⇒ **fervent**: Leidenschaftlichkeit, *die;* Inbrunst, *die;* Glut, *die*

**fervent** /ˈfɜːvənt/ *adj.* leidenschaftlich; inbrünstig ‹Gebet, Wunsch, Hoffnung›; glühend ‹Leidenschaft, Verehrer, Liebe, Hass›

**fervently** /ˈfɜːvəntlɪ/ *adv.* ⇒ **fervent**: leidenschaftlich; inbrünstig; glühend

**fervour** (*Brit.; Amer.:* **fervor**) /ˈfɜːvə(r)/ *n.* (*of discussion, feeling, person, campaign*) Leidenschaftlichkeit, *die;* (*of love, belief*) Inbrunst, *die;* (*of passion*) Glut, *die*

**fess[e]** /fes/ *n.* (*Her.*) Balken, *der*

**fest** /fest/ *n.* (*Amer.*) Fest, *das*

**fester** /ˈfestə(r)/ *v.i.* **A** (*lit. or fig.*) eitern; schwären (*geh.*); **B** (*putrefy*) verfaulen

**festival** /ˈfestɪvl/ ❶ *n.* **A** (*feast day*) Fest, *das;* **the ~ of Christmas/Easter** das Weihnachts-/Osterfest; **B** (*performances, plays, etc.*) Festival, *das;* Festspiele *Pl.;* **the Bayreuth F~:** die Bayreuther Festspiele; **the Edinburgh F~:** das Edinburgh-Festival. ❷ *attrib. adj.* Fest-

**festive** /ˈfestɪv/ *adj.* **A** (*joyous*) festlich; fröhlich; **B** (*of a feast*) Fest-; **the ~ season** die Weihnachtszeit; **C** (*convivial*) gesellig

**festivity** /feˈstɪvɪtɪ/ *n.* **A** *no pl.* (*gaiety*) Feststimmung, *die;* **B** (*festive celebration*) Feier, *die;* **festivities** Feierlichkeiten *Pl.*

**festoon** /feˈstuːn/ ❶ *n.* **A** (*chain of flowers*) Girlande, *die;* **B** (*carved ornament*) Feston, *das.* ❷ *v.t.* schmücken (**with** mit)

**fetal** (*Amer.*) ⇒ **foetal**

**fetch** /fetʃ/ ❶ *v.t.* **A** holen; (*collect*) abholen (**from** von); **~ sb. sth.**, **~ sth. for sb.** jmdm. etw. holen; **B** (*be sold for*) erzielen ‹Preis›; **my car ~ed £500** ich habe für den Wagen 500 Pfund bekommen; **C ~ a sigh** aufseufzen; **~ a deep breath** tief Atem *od.* Luft holen; **just give me time to ~ my breath** lass mich erst mal wieder zu Atem kommen; **D** (*deal*) **~ sb. a blow/punch** jmdm. einen Schlag versetzen; **E** (*draw forth*) erregen ‹Bewunderung, Ärger›; entlocken ‹Tränen, Lachen› (**from** + *Dat.*).
❷ *v.i.* **~ and carry [for sb.]** [bei jmdm.] Mädchen für alles sein (*ugs.*); **he is always there to ~ and carry for her** (*does every little thing*) er bedient sie vorn und hinten (*ugs.*)
**~ ˈup** (*coll.*) ❶ *v.t.* erbrechen; wieder von sich geben; (*fig.*) speien. ❷ *v.i.* landen (*ugs.*)

**fetching** /ˈfetʃɪŋ/ *adj.* einnehmend, gewinnend ‹Lächeln, Stimme, Wesen, Benehmen›; schick ‹Kleidung›; **that suit looks very ~ on you** das Kostüm steht dir ausgezeichnet

**fetchingly** /ˈfetʃɪŋlɪ/ *adv.* einnehmend ‹lächeln, sich benehmen›; ausgesprochen ‹hübsch›; schick, geschmackvoll ‹gekleidet, eingerichtet›

**fête** /feɪt/ ❶ *n.* **A** [Wohltätigkeits]basar, *der;* **B** (*festival*) Fest, *das;* Feier, *die.* ❷ *v.t.* feiern

**fetid** /ˈfetɪd/ *adj.* stinkend; übel riechend; **~ smell/odour/stench** Gestank, *der*

**fetish** /ˈfetɪʃ/ *n.* **A** Manie, *die* (*geh.*); Fetisch, *der* (*geh.*); Fimmel, *der* (*ugs.*); **she makes something of a ~ of** *or* **has a ~ about tidiness** Sauberkeit ist bei ihr zur Manie geworden; sie hat einen richtigen Sauberkeitsfimmel (*ugs.*); **B** (*inanimate object of worship; also Psych.*) Fetisch, *der*

**fetishism** /ˈfetɪʃɪzm/ *n.* Fetischismus, *der*

**fetishist** /ˈfetɪʃɪst/ *n.* Fetischist, *der*/Fetischistin, *die*

**fetlock** /ˈfetlɒk/ *n.* Köte, *die*

**fetter** /ˈfetə(r)/ ❶ *n.* **A** (*shackle*) Fußfessel, *die;* **B** *usu. in pl.* (*bond*) Fesseln *Pl.; in pl.* (*fig.: captivity*) Gefangenschaft, *die;* Fesseln *Pl.;* **C** *in pl.* (*restraint*) Fesseln *Pl.*. ❷ *v.t.* **A** (*bind* [*as*] *with* **~s**) fesseln; **be ~ed to sth./sb.** (*fig.*) an etw./jmdn. gekettet sein; **B** (*impede*) einengen ‹Freiheit, Rechte, Souveränität, Personen›; hemmen ‹Fortschritt, Entwicklung, Wachstum, Entfaltung›; lähmen ‹Fantasie›

**fettle** /ˈfetl/ *n.* **be in good** *or* **fine/poor ~:** sich in guter/schlechter Verfassung befinden; ‹Sache:› sich in gutem/schlechtem Zustand befinden

**fetus** (*Amer.*) ⇒ **foetus**

**feud** /fjuːd/ ❶ *n.* Zwist, *der;* Zwistigkeiten *Pl.;* (*Hist./fig.*) Fehde, *die;* **carry on a ~ with sb.** eine Fehde mit jmdm. ausfechten *od.* austragen. ❷ *v.i.* **~ [with sb./each other]** [mit jmdm./miteinander] im Streit liegen

**feudal** /ˈfjuːdl/ *adj.* **A** (*of* [*holding of*] *fief*) Leh[e]ns-; **B** (*of or according to feudal system*) Feudal-; feudalistisch; **~ overlord** Feudal- *od.* Lehnsherr, *der;* **~ rights** Lehnsherrlichkeit, *die;* **in ~ Britain** im feudalistischen England

**feudalism** /ˈfjuːdəlɪzm/ *n., no pl.* Feudalismus, *der*

**ˈfeudal system** *n.* (*Hist.*) Feudalsystem, *das*

**fever** /ˈfiːvə(r)/ *n.* ▶ **1232** **A** *no pl.* (*Med.: high temperature*) Fieber, *das;* **have a** *or* **suffer from a [high] ~:** [hohes] Fieber haben; **a ~ of 105 °F** 40,5 °C Fieber; **B** (*Med.: disease*) Fieberkrankheit, *die;* **C** (*nervous excitement*) Erregung, *die;* Aufregung, *die;* **the crowd was in a ~ of excitement** die Menge befand sich in heller Aufregung; **in a ~ of anticipation** im Fieber der Erwartung

**fevered** /ˈfiːvəd/ *adj.* fiebrig ‹Stirn, Gesicht, Haut usw.›

**fever: ~ heat** *n.* **A** (*high temperature*) Fieberhitze, *die;* **B** (*fig.*) ⇒ **fever pitch**; **~ hospital** *n.* Seuchenkrankenhaus, *das*

**feverish** /ˈfiːvərɪʃ/ *adj.* ▶ **1232** **A** (*Med.: having symptoms of fever*) fiebrig; Fieber‹zustand, -schweiß, -traum›; **be ~:** fiebern; Fieber haben; **spend a ~ night** eine Nacht im Fieber verbringen; **B** (*excited*) erregt, aufgeregt ‹Geschrei, Lachen›; fiebrig ‹Erwartung, Nervosität›; heftig ‹Andrang›; fieberhaft ‹Aufregung, Eifer, Kampf, Eile›; **make ~ attempts to do sth.** fieberhaft versuchen, etw. zu tun

**feverishly** /ˈfiːvərɪʃlɪ/ *adv.* **A** (*Med.*) im Fieber; **toss and turn ~:** sich im Fieber hin und her wälzen; **B** (*excitedly*) fieberhaft ‹kämpfen, gestikulieren›

**ˈfever pitch** *n.* Siedepunkt, *der* (*fig.*); **reach ~:** auf den Siedepunkt angelangt sein; **at ~:** auf dem Siedepunkt

**few** /fjuː/ ❶ *adj.* **A** (*not many*) wenige; **~ people** [nur] wenige [Leute]; **these ~ marks** die paar Mark; **openings for sociologists are ~:** freie Stellen für Soziologen sind knapp *od.* rar; **trees were ~ in that barren region** es gab nur wenige Bäume in dieser kargen Gegend; **the responsibility of these ~ men** die Verantwortung dieser wenigen; **with very ~ exceptions** mit ganz wenigen Ausnahmen; **very ~ housewives know that** das wissen die wenigsten Hausfrauen; **his ~ belongings** seine paar Habseligkeiten; seine wenige Habe; **how could those ~ people have achieved such a thing?** wie konnten so wenige [Leute] das nur erreicht haben?; **[all] too ~ people** [viel] zu wenig Leute; **~ and far between** rar; **they were ~ in number** sie waren nur sehr wenige *od.* nur ein kleines Häuflein; **these stamps are ~ in number** diese Briefmarken sind selten; **a ~ …:** wenige …; **not a ~ …:** eine ganze Reihe …; **they made not a ~ criticisms of the idea** sie übten nicht wenig Kritik an der Idee; **[just** *or* **only] a ~ troublemakers** einige [wenige] Störenfriede; **just a ~ words from you** nur ein paar Worte von dir; **B** (*some*) wenige; **he said his ~ words** er sagte nur ein paar Worte; **a ~ …:** einige *od.* ein paar …; **a very ~:** nur wenige; **a ~ more …:** noch einige *od.* ein paar …; **some ~ […]** einige wenige […]; **every ~ minutes** alle paar Minuten; **a good ~ […]/quite a ~ […]** (*coll.*) eine ganze Menge […]/ziemlich viele […]; **there are a ~ which …:** es gibt welche *od.* ein paar, die …
❷ *n.* **A** (*not many*) wenige; **these are the beliefs of ~:** das glauben nur wenige; **a ~:** wenige; **the ~:** die wenigen; **the wealthy ~:** die wenigen Reichen; **~ of us/them** nur wenige von uns/nur wenige [von ihnen]; **~ of the people** nur wenige [Leute]; **~ of the words meant anything to him** er konnte mit nur wenigen Wörtern etwas anfangen; **they are among** *or* **some of the very ~ who …:** sie gehören zu den wenigen, die …; **only a ~ of them/the applicants** nur wenige [von ihnen]/[der] Bewerber; **just a ~ of**

**you/her friends** nur ein paar von euch/ihrer Freunde; **the privilege of [only] a ~:** das Vorrecht von nur wenigen *od.* einiger weniger; **not a ~ of them** eine ganze Reihe von ihnen; **not a ~:** nicht wenige; ziemlich viele; Ⓑ (*some*) **the/these/those ~ who** diejenigen, die; **there were a ~ of us who ...:** es gab einige unter uns, die ...; **with a ~ of our friends** mit einigen *od.* ein paar unserer Freunde; **a ~ [more] of these biscuits** [noch] ein paar von diesen Keksen; **a ~ [who]** einige[, die]; **some ~:** einige wenige [Leute]; **some ~ of us/the members** einige wenige von uns/[der] Mitglieder; **a good ~/quite a ~** (*coll.*) eine ganze Menge/ziemlich viele [Leute]; **a good ~ of us/quite a ~ of us** (*coll.*) eine ganze Menge von uns/ziemlich viele von uns; **have had a ~** (*coll.: be drunk*) einen sitzen haben (*salopp*). ⇒ *also* **fewer**; **fewest**

**fewer** /ˈfju:ə(r)/ ❶ *adj.* weniger; **become ~ and ~:** immer weniger werden; **smokers are ~ in number than twenty years ago** es gibt weniger Raucher als vor zwanzig Jahren. ❷ *n.* **~ of the apples/of us** weniger Äpfel/von uns

**fewest** /ˈfju:ɪst/ ❶ *adj.* **[the] ~ [...]** die wenigsten [...]. ❷ *n.* **the ~ [of us/them]** die wenigsten [von uns/ihnen]; **at [the] ~:** mindestens

**fey** /feɪ/ *adj.* Ⓐ (*disordered in mind*) versponnen; Ⓑ (*clairvoyant*) hellseherisch; (*otherworldly*) entrückt

**fez** /fez/ *n., pl.* **~zes** Fes, *der*

**ff** *abbr.* **fortissimo** ff

**ff.** *abbr.* Ⓐ **and following pages** ff.; Ⓑ **folios** Bl.

**fiancé** /fɪˈɑ̃seɪ/ *n.* Verlobte, *der*

**fiancée** /fɪˈɑ̃seɪ/ *n.* Verlobte, *die*

**fiasco** /fɪˈæskəʊ/ *n., pl.* **~s** Fiasko, *das*

**fiat** /ˈfi:æt, ˈfi:ət/ *n.* Ⓐ (*authorization*) Genehmigung, *die;* Ⓑ (*decree*) Anordnung, *die*

**fib** /fɪb/ ❶ *n.* Flunkerei, *die* (*ugs.*); **tell ~s** flunkern (*ugs.*); schwindeln; **that was a ~:** das war geschwindelt. ❷ *v.i.*, **-bb-** schwindeln; flunkern (*ugs.*). ❸ *v.t.*, **-bb-: ~ one's way out [of sth.]** sich [aus etw.] herausschwindeln

**fibber** /ˈfɪbə(r)/ *n.* Flunkerer, *der* (*ugs.*); Schwindler, *der*/Schwindlerin, *die*

**fibre** (*Brit.; Amer.:* **fiber**) /ˈfaɪbə(r)/ *n.* Ⓐ Faser, *die;* **with every ~ of his being** (*fig.*) mit jeder Faser seines Herzens; Ⓑ (*substance consisting of fibres*) [Faser]gewebe, *das;* Ⓒ (*substance that can be felted*) Faserstoff, *der;* Ⓓ (*roughage*) Ballaststoffe *Pl.;* Ⓔ (*fibrous structure*) Fasergefüge, *das;* Faserstruktur, *die;* Ⓕ (*character*) Wesensart, *die;* (*strength*) Festigkeit, *die;* (*essence*) Grundstruktur, *die;* **moral ~:** Charakterstärke, *die.* ⇒ *also* **optical fibre**

**fibre: ~board** *n.* Holzfaserplatte, *die;* **~glass** (*Amer.:* **fiber glass**) *n.* (*fibrous glass*) Glasfaser, *die;* (*plastic*) glasfaserverstärkter Kunststoff; *attrib.* **~glass boat** Kunststoffboot, *das;* **~ optic ˈcable** *n.* Glasfaserkabel, *das;* **~ ˈoptics** *n.* Faseroptik, *die*

**fibrillation** /fɪbrɪˈleɪʃn/ *n.* (*Med.*) Zucken, *das;* (*esp. of heart muscle*) Flimmern, *das*

**fibrin** /ˈfaɪbrɪn/ *n.* (*Med.*) Fibrin, *das*

**fibrositis** /faɪbrəˈsaɪtɪs/ *n.* ▶ **1232** (*Med.*) Rheumatismus der Weichteile; Fibrositis, *die* (*fachspr.*)

**fibrous** /ˈfaɪbrəs/ *adj.* faserig ‹Aufbau, Beschaffenheit, Eigenschaft›; Faser‹gewebe, -holz, -stoff›

**fibula** /ˈfɪbjʊlə/ *n., pl.* **~e** /ˈfɪbjʊli:/ *or* **~s** Ⓐ (*Anat.*) Wadenbein, *das;* Ⓑ (*Hist.: brooch*) Fibel, *die*

**fiche** /fi:ʃ/ *n., pl. same or* **~s** ⇒ **microfiche**

**fickle** /ˈfɪkl/ *adj.* unberechenbar, launisch ‹Glück, Schicksal, Person›

**fiction** /ˈfɪkʃn/ *n.* Ⓐ (*literature*) erzählende Literatur; Ⓑ (*thing feigned or imagined*) **a ~/~s** eine Erfindung; **be pure ~** *or* **a mere ~:** [eine] reine Erfindung sein; Ⓒ (*conventionally accepted falsehood*) kleine Unaufrichtigkeit. ⇒ *also* **fact** B; **legal fiction**

**fictional** /ˈfɪkʃənl/ *adj.* belletristisch; fiktional (*fachspr.*); erfunden ‹Inhalt, Geschichte›; **~ literature** erzählende Literatur; Belletristik, *die* (*ohne Lyrik*); **~ characters** fiktive Figuren

**fictionalize** /ˈfɪkʃənəlaɪz/ *v.t.* als Fiktion darstellen

**ˈfiction writer** *n.* ▶ **1261** Belletrist, *der*/Belletristin, *die*

**fictitious** /fɪkˈtɪʃəs/ *adj.* Ⓐ (*counterfeit*) fingiert; vorgetäuscht ‹Ohnmacht, Verletzung›; Schein‹schwangerschaft›; unwahr ‹Behauptung, Darstellung›; Ⓑ (*assumed*) falsch ‹Name, Identität›; angenommen ‹Rolle›; Ⓒ (*imaginary*) [frei] erfunden ‹Person, Figur, Geschichte›; Ⓓ (*regarded as what it is called by legal or conventional fiction*) Schein-; fiktiv; **~ character** *or* **person** erfundene *od.* fiktive Person; **~ person** (*legal entity*) juristische Person; Ⓔ (*of or in novels*) fiktiv

**fiddle** /ˈfɪdl/ ❶ *n.* Ⓐ (*Mus.*) (*coll./derog.*) Fiedel, *die;* (*violin for traditional or folk music*) Geige, *die;* Fiedel, *die;* **[as] fit as a ~:** kerngesund; **a face as long as a ~** (*fig.*) ein Gesicht wie drei *od.* sieben Tage Regenwetter (*ugs.*); **play first/second ~** (*fig.*) die erste/zweite Geige spielen (*ugs.*); **play second ~ to sb.** in jmds. Schatten (*Dat.*) stehen; Ⓑ (*coll.: swindle*) Gaunerei, *die;* **it's some sort of ~:** an der Sache ist was faul (*ugs.*); **it's all a ~:** das ist alles Schiebung (*ugs.*); **get sth. by a ~:** sich (*Dat.*) etw. ergaunern; **be on the ~:** krumme Dinger machen (*ugs.*). ❷ *v.i.* Ⓐ (*coll.: play the ~*) Geige spielen; Ⓑ **~ about** (*coll.: waste time*) herumtrödeln (*ugs.*); (*be frivolous*) [herum]schludern (*ugs.*); **~ about with** *or* **away at sth.** (*work on to adjust etc.*) an etw. (*Dat.*) herumfummeln (*ugs.*); (*tinker with*) an etw. (*Dat.*) herumbasteln (*ugs.*); **~ at sth.** an etw. (*Dat.*) herumspielen *od.* herumfingern; **~ with sth.** (*play with*) mit etw. herumspielen; Ⓒ (*coll.: deceive*) krumme Dinger drehen (*ugs.*); **he ~d, lied, and cheated** er hat geschoben, gelogen und betrogen. ❸ *v.t.* (*coll.*) (*falsify*) frisieren (*ugs.*) ‹Bücher, Rechnungen›; (*get by cheating*) [sich (*Dat.*)] ergaunern (*ugs.*); **~ one's way into sth. [by lying/cheating]** sich [mit Lügen/Betrügereien] in etw. (*Akk.*) einschleichen

**fiddle-de-dee** /fɪdldɪˈdi:/ ❶ *int.* Schnickschnack. ❷ *n.* Schnickschnack, *der* (*ugs.*)

**fiddle-faddle** /ˈfɪdlfædl/ *n.* Unsinn, *der;* Unfug, *der*

**fiddler** /ˈfɪdlə(r)/ *n.* Ⓐ ▶ **1261** (*player*) Geiger, *der*/Geigerin, *die;* Ⓑ (*coll.: swindler etc.*) Gauner, *der*/Gaunerin, *die* (*abwertend*)

**ˈfiddler crab** *n.* Winkerkrabbe, *die*

**ˈfiddlestick** (*coll.*) ❶ *n.* Geigenbogen, *der.* ❷ *int.* **~s** dummes Zeug (*ugs.*); Schnickschnack (*ugs.*)

**fiddling** /ˈfɪdlɪŋ/ *adj.* Ⓐ (*petty*) belanglos; Ⓑ ⇒ **fiddly**

**fiddly** /ˈfɪdlɪ/ *adj.* Ⓐ (*awkward to do*) knifflig; Ⓑ (*awkward to use*) umständlich

**fidelity** /fɪˈdelɪtɪ/ *n.* Ⓐ (*faithfulness*) Treue, *die* (**to** zu); **oath of ~:** Treueid, *der;* **breach of ~:** Treubruch, *der;* Ⓑ (*conformity to truth or fact*) Glaubwürdigkeit, *die;* Ⓒ (*exact correspondence to the original*) (*of photograph, imitation*) Naturtreue, *die;* (*of translation*) [Wort]treue, *die;* Ⓓ (*Radio, Telev., etc.*) Wiedergabetreue, *die;* [original]getreue Wiedergabe; (*of sound*) Klangtreue, *die;* (*of picture*) Bildtreue, *die*

**fidget** /ˈfɪdʒɪt/ ❶ *n.* Ⓐ **[be] in a [terrible] ~:** [ganz] zappelig [sein] (*ugs.*); **put sb. in a ~:** jmdn. unruhig machen; **have/get the ~s** zappelig sein/werden (*ugs.*); **give sb. the ~s** jmdn. zappelig *od.* kribbelig machen (*ugs.*); Ⓑ (*restless mood*) Unrast, *die;* **be [all] in a ~:** [sehr] unruhig sein; **have/get the ~s** ruhelos sein/werden; Ⓒ (*person*) Zappelphilipp, *der* (*ugs.*). ❷ *v.i.* Ⓐ **~ [about]** [herum]zappeln (*ugs.*); herumrutschen; Ⓑ (*be uneasy*) nervös sein; **make sb. ~:** jmdn. unruhig machen

**fidgety** /ˈfɪdʒɪtɪ/ *adj.* unruhig ‹Person, Pferd, Stimmung›; nervös ‹Bewegungen, Zuckungen›

**fiduciary** /fɪˈdju:ʃərɪ/ *adj.* Ⓐ treuhänderisch; **~ money** Giralgeld, *das;* Ⓑ (*Finance: depending on public confidence or securities*) ungedeckt ‹Papiergeld›

**fief** /fi:f/ *n.* Ⓐ (*feudal benefice*) Lehen, *das;* Ⓑ (*sphere of control*) Machtbereich, *der*

**field** /fi:ld/ ❶ *n.* Ⓐ (*cultivated*) Feld, *das;* Acker, *der;* (*for grazing*) Weide, *die;* (*meadow*) Wiese, *die;* **wheat/tobacco/poppy ~:** Weizen-/Tabak-/Mohnfeld, *das;* **work in the ~s** auf dem Feld arbeiten; **~s of rye** Roggenfelder; Ⓑ (*area rich in minerals etc.*) Lagerstätte, *die;* **gas ~:** Gasfeld, *das;* Ⓒ (*battlefield*) Schlachtfeld, *das;* (*fig.*) Feld, *das;* **leave sb. a clear** *or* **the ~** (*fig.*) jmdm. das Feld überlassen; **hold the ~:** das Feld beherrschen; Ⓓ (*scene of campaign*) [Kriegs]schauplatz, *der;* **enter the ~** (*fig.*) eingreifen; auf der Bildfläche erscheinen (*ugs.*); **in the ~:** im Feld; an der Front; (*fig.*) ‹Vertreter› im Außendienst; ‹Student› in der Praxis; **be sent out into the ~:** [hin]ausgeschickt werden; **keep the ~:** weiterkämpfen; **take the ~:** in den Kampf ziehen (⇒ *also* **f**); Ⓔ (*battle*) **a hard-fought/hard-won ~:** eine erbitterte Schlacht/ein schwer erkämpfter Sieg; **win/lose the ~:** siegreich sein/die Schlacht verlieren; Ⓕ (*playing ~*) Sportplatz, *der;* (*ground marked out for game*) Platz, *der;* [Spiel]feld, *das;* **send sb. off the ~:** jmdn. vom Platz stellen; **take the ~:** das Spielfeld betreten (⇒ *also* **d**); Ⓖ (*Sport: area for defence or attack*) [Spiel]feld, *das;* Ⓗ (*competitors in sports event*) Feld, *das;* (*fig.*) Teilnehmerkreis, *der;* **play the ~** (*fig. coll.*) sich nicht festlegen [wollen]; alles nehmen, wie es kommt; (*take advantage of all chances offered*) alle gebotenen Chancen wahrnehmen; Ⓘ (*Hunting*) Feld, *das;* Gruppe, *die;* **lead the ~** (*lit. or fig.*) das Feld anführen; Ⓙ (*airfield*) Flugplatz, *der;* Flugfeld, *das* (*veralt.*); Ⓚ (*expanse*) Fläche, *die;* (*fig.*) Gebiet, *das;* Ⓛ (*Her.*) Feld, *das;* Grund, *der;* Ⓜ (*of picture etc.*) Grund, *der;* Ⓝ (*area of operation, subject areas, etc.*) Fach, *das;* [Fach]gebiet, *das;* (*range of vision or view*) Sichtfeld, *das;* **his researches range over a wide ~:** seine Forschungen, die sich über ein großes Gebiet erstrecken; **in the ~ of medicine** auf dem Gebiet der Medizin; **workers in the ~:** die Leute vom Fach; **he's working in his own ~:** er arbeitet in seinem [erlernten] Beruf; **that is outside my ~:** das fällt nicht in mein Fach; **~ of vision** *or* **view** Blickfeld, *das;* Ⓞ (*Phys.*) **magnetic/gravitational ~:** Magnet-/Gravitationsfeld, *das;* Ⓟ *attrib.* (*found in open country*) Feld-; **~ marigold** [Saat]wucherblume, *die;* **~ mushroom** Wiesenchampignon, *der;* **~ poppy** Klatschmohn, *der;* Ⓠ *attrib.* (*carried out in natural environment; light and mobile*) Feld‹studie, -forschung, -artillerie, -ausrüstung›. ⇒ *also* **airfield**; **coalfield**; **goldfield**; **minefield**; **oilfield**. ❷ *v.i.* (*Cricket, Baseball, etc.*) als Fänger spielen; **he ~s well** er ist ein guter Fänger. ❸ *v.t.* Ⓐ (*Cricket, Baseball, etc.*) (*stop*) fangen ‹Ball›; (*stop and return*) auffangen und zurückwerfen; Ⓑ (*put into ~*) aufstellen, aufs Feld schicken ‹Mannschaft, Spieler›; Ⓒ (*fig.: deal with*) fertig werden mit; parieren ‹Fragen›

**ˈfield day** *n.* Ⓐ (*Mil.*) Feldübung, *die;* Manöver, *das;* Ⓑ (*fig.*) großer Tag; **have a ~** seinen großen Tag haben

**fielder** /ˈfi:ldə(r)/ *n.* (*Cricket, Baseball, etc.*) Feldspieler, *der*

**ˈfield events** *n. pl.* (*Sport*) technische Disziplinen

**fieldfare** /ˈfi:ldfeə(r)/ *n.* (*Ornith.*) Wacholderdrossel, *die*

**field: ~ glasses** *n. pl.* Feldstecher, *der;* **~ hockey** (*Amer.*) ⇒ **hockey** A; **~ hospital** *n.* (*Mil.*) Feldlazarett, *das;* **F~ ˈMarshal** *n.* ▶ **1617** (*Brit. Mil.*) Feldmarschall, *der;* **~ mouse** *n.* Brandmaus, *die;* **~ officer** *n.* (*Mil.*) Stabsoffizier, *der;* **~sman** /ˈfi:ldzmən/ *n., pl.* **~smen** /ˈfi:ldzmən/ ⇒ **fielder**; **~ sports** *n. pl.* Sport im Freien (*bes. Jagen und Fischen*); **~ test** ❶ *n.* ⇒ **~ trial**; ❷ *v.t.* in der Praxis erproben; **~ trial** *n.* Feldversuch, *der;* **~ trip** *n.* Exkursion, *die;* **~work** *n.* Ⓐ (*Mil.: temporary fortification*) Feldbefestigung, *die;* Ⓑ (*outdoor work*) (*of surveyor etc.*) Arbeit im Gelände; (*of sociologist, collector of scientific data, etc.*) Feldforschung, *die;*

**~worker** *n.* ▶ 1261 Feldforscher, *der*/-forscherin, *die*

**fiend** /fi:nd/ *n.* **A** (*very wicked person*) Scheusal, *das;* Unmensch, *der;* **B** **the F~:** der Teufel *od.* Satan; **C** (*evil spirit*) böser Geist; **D** (*coll.*) (*mischievous or tiresome person*) Plagegeist, *der;* (*artful person*) Schlaufuchs, *der;* **E** (*devotee*) Fan, *der;* **travel/theatre ~:** Reise-/Theaternarr, *der*/-närrin, *die;* **motorbike/health food ~:** Motorrad-/Naturkostfreak, *der;* **fresh-air ~:** Frischluftfanatiker, *der*/-fanatikerin, *die*

**fiendish** /'fi:ndɪʃ/ *adj.* **A** (*fiendlike*) teuflisch; **B** (*extremely awkward*) höllisch

**fiendishly** /'fi:ndɪʃlɪ/ *adv.* **A** (*in fiendlike manner*) teuflisch **B** (*extremely awkwardly*) höllisch;

**fierce** /fɪəs/ *adj.* **A** (*violently hostile*) wild; erbittert ‹Widerstand, Kampf›; wuchtig ‹Schlag›; heftig ‹[Bomben]angriff›; feindselig ‹Benehmen›; **B** (*raging*) wütend; tobend ‹Wind›; grimmig ‹Hass, Wut›; grausam ‹Krankheit, Tyrannei›; scharf ‹Kritik, Verurteilung›; wild ‹Tier›; **C** (*ardent*) ungestüm ‹Leidenschaft, Verlangen›; heftig ‹Andrang, Streit›; heiß ‹Wettbewerb›; hitzig ‹Kampagne›; leidenschaftlich ‹Ehrgeiz, Stolz, Wille›; wild ‹Entschlossenheit, Jagd›; **D** (*unpleasantly strong or intense*) unerträglich; **the heat is a bit ~:** die Hitze ist ein bisschen zu stark; **E** (*violent in action*) hart ‹Bremsen, Ruck›

**fiercely** /'fɪəslɪ/ *adv.* **A** (*with violent hostility*) heftig ‹angreifen, Widerstand leisten›; wütend, grimmig ‹brüllen›; **B** (*with raging force*) wütend ‹toben›; aufs Heftigste ‹kritisieren, bekämpfen›; **the fire burnt ~ for several hours** der Brand wütete mehrere Stunden; **C** (*ardently*) äußerst ‹stolz, unabhängig sein›; wild ‹entschlossen, kämpfen›; **D** (*with unpleasant strength or intensity*) unerträglich; **E** (*with violent action*) heftig; scharf ‹bremsen›

**fiery** /'faɪərɪ/ *adj.* **A** (*consisting of or flaming with fire*) glühend; feurig ‹Atem›; **B** (*looking like fire*) feurig; (*blazing red*) feuerrot; glutrot; **C** (*hot as fire*) glühend heiß; **~ temperature** Gluthitze, *die;* **D** (*producing burning sensation*) brennend, juckend ‹Ausschlag›; feurig ‹Geschmack, Gewürz›; scharf ‹Getränk›; **E** (*fervent, full of spirit*) feurig ‹Liebhaber, Pferd›; (*irascible, impassioned*) hitzig ‹Temperament, Debatte›; feurig ‹Rede, Redner›; **~ zeal** Feuereifer, *der;* **have a ~ temper** ein Hitzkopf sein

**fiery 'cross** *n.* **A** (*Hist.: rallying-signal of Scottish Highlanders*) Feuerkreuz, *das;* **B** (*Amer.: of Ku Klux Klan*) Flammenkreuz, *das*

**fiesta** /fi:'estə/ *n.* Fest, *das*

**FIFA** /'fi:fə/ *abbr.* **International Football Federation** FIFA, *die;* Fifa, *die*

**fife** /faɪf/ *n.* Pfeife, *die*

**fifteen** /fɪf'ti:n/ ▶ 912, ▶ 1012, ▶ 1352 **1** *adj.* fünfzehn; ⇨ *also* **eight** 1. **2** *n.* **A** Fünfzehn, *die;* ⇨ *also* **eight** 2 A, D; **eighteen** 2; **B** (*Rugby Football*) [Rugby]mannschaft, *die*

**fifteenth** /fɪf'ti:nθ/ ▶ 1055 **1** *adj.* ▶ 1352 fünfzehnt...; ⇨ *also* **eighth** 1. **2** *n.* (*fraction*) Fünfzehntel, *das;* ⇨ *also* **eighth** 2

**fifth** /fɪfθ/ **1** *adj.* ▶ 1352 fünft...; ⇨ *also* **eighth** 1. **2** *n.* **A** (*in sequence, rank*) Fünfte, *der/die/das;* (*fraction*) Fünftel, *das;* **B** (*~ form*) fünfte [Schul]klasse; Fünfte, *die* (*Schuljargon*); **C** (*Mus.*) Quinte, *die;* **D** ▶ 1055 (*day*) **the ~ of May** der fünfte Mai; **the ~ [of the month]** der Fünfte [des Monats]; **E** (*Amer. coll.*) (*bottle*) ≈ Dreiviertelliterflasche, *die;* (*of a gallon*) *ca. dreiviertel Liter.* ⇨ *also* **eighth** 2

**fifth: ~ 'column** *n.* fünfte Kolonne; **~-'columnist** *n.* Mitglied der fünften Kolonne; **~ form** ⇨ **form** 1 D

**fiftieth** /'fɪftɪɪθ/ **1** *adj.* ▶ 1352 fünfzigst...; ⇨ *also* **eighth** 1. **2** *n.* (*fraction*) Fünfzigstel, *das;* ⇨ *also* **eighth** 2

**fifty** /'fɪftɪ/ ▶ 912, ▶ 1012, ▶ 1352 **1** *adj.* **A** fünfzig; **one-and-~** (*arch.*) ⇨ **fifty-one** 1; **B** (*large indefinite number*) **~ times** hundertmal; zigmal (*ugs.*). ⇨ *also* **eight** 1. **2** *n.* Fünfzig, *die;* **one-and-~** (*arch.*) ⇨ **fifty-one** 2; ⇨ *also* **eight** 2 A; **eighty** 2

**fifty: ~-~** *adv., adj.* fifty-fifty (*ugs.*); halbe-halbe (*ugs.*); **go ~-~:** fifty-fifty *od.* halbpart machen; **on a ~-~ basis** auf der Basis, dass fifty-fifty geteilt wird; **~-'first** *etc. adj.* ▶ 1352 einundfünfzigst... *usw.;* ⇨ *also* **eighth** 1; **~fold** /'fɪftɪfəʊld/ *adj., adv.* fünfzigfach; ⇨ *also* **eightfold; ~-'one** *etc.* **1** *adj.* einundfünfzig *usw.;* ⇨ *also* **eight** 1; **2** *n.* ▶ 1352 Einundfünfzig *usw., die;* ⇨ *also* **eight** 2 A

**fig**[1] /fɪg/ *n.* **A** Feige, *die;* **B** (*valueless thing*) **it's not worth a ~:** das ist keinen Pfifferling *od.* keine müde Mark wert (*ugs.*); **not care** *or* **give a ~ about** *or* **for sth.** sich nicht die Bohne (*ugs.*) *od.* keinen Deut für etw. interessieren

**fig**[2] *n.* (*attire*) Staat, *der;* (*legal, academic, etc.*) Ornat, *der;* **in full ~:** in vollem Staat

**fig.** *abbr.* **figure** Abb.

**fight** /faɪt/ **1** *v.i.*, **fought** /fɔ:t/ **A** (*lit. or fig.*) kämpfen; (*with fists*) sich schlagen; **~ to do sth.** darum kämpfen, etw. zu tun; **~ to save sb.'s life** um jmds. Leben kämpfen; **watch animals/people ~ing** Tieren/Menschen beim Kampf zusehen; **~ shy of sb./sth.** jmdm./einer Sache aus dem Weg gehen; **~ shy of doing sth.** sich davor drücken, etw. zu tun (*ugs.*); es vermeiden, etw. zu tun; **B** (*squabble*) [sich] streiten, [sich] zanken (**about** wegen). ⇨ *also* **cat** A; **cock**[1] 1 A; **hand** 1 A; **tooth** A.

**2** *v.t.*, **fought** **A** (*in battle*) **~ sb./sth.** gegen jmdn./etw. kämpfen; (*using fists*) **~ sb.** sich mit jmdm. schlagen; ‹Boxer:› gegen jmdn. boxen; **B** (*seek to overcome*) bekämpfen; (*resist*) **~ sb./sth.** gegen jmdn./etw. ankämpfen; **C** (*contend in*) durchfechten; durchkämpfen; **~ a battle** einen Kampf austragen; **be ~ing a losing battle** (*fig.*) auf verlorenem Posten stehen *od.* kämpfen; **~ sb.'s battles for him** (*fig.*) jmdm. alle Schwierigkeiten aus dem Weg räumen; **~ the good fight** (*fig.*) für die gute *od.* gerechte Sache kämpfen; **D** ausfechten ‹Problem›; führen ‹Kampagne›; kandidieren bei ‹Wahl›; **E** **~ one's way** sich (*Dat.*) den Weg freikämpfen; (*fig.*) sich (*Dat.*) seinen Weg bahnen; **~ one's way to the top** (*fig.*) sich an die Spitze kämpfen; **~ one's way up** (*fig.*) sich nach oben kämpfen; sich hochkämpfen.

**3** *n.* **A** (*combat, campaign, boxing match*) Kampf, *der* (**for** um); (*brawl*) Schlägerei, *die;* (*literary: battle*) Schlacht, *die;* **their ~ for freedom** ihr Freiheitskampf; **make a ~ of it, put up a ~:** sich wehren; (*fig.*) sich zur Wehr setzen; **give in without a ~** (*fig.*) klein beigeben; **aren't you going to make a ~ of it?** (*fig.*) willst du dir das etwa gefallen lassen?; **world championship title ~:** Titelkampf um die Weltmeisterschaft; **B** (*squabble*) Streit, *der;* **they are always having ~s** zwischen ihnen gibt es dauernd Streit; **he likes a good ~:** er hat nichts gegen einen guten Streit; **C** (*ability to ~*) Kampffähigkeit, *die;* (*appetite for ~ing*) Kampfgeist, *der;* **have no ~ left in one** nicht mehr zum Kampf fähig sein; (*fig.*) erledigt *od.* fertig sein; **all the ~ had gone out of him** (*fig.*) sein Kampfgeist war erloschen; **show ~** (*lit. or fig.*) Stärke demonstrieren

**~ against** *v.t.* **A** (*in war*) kämpfen gegen; (*in boxing match*) antreten gegen; **B** (*resist*) kämpfen gegen; ankämpfen gegen ‹Wellen, Wind, Gefühle›; bekämpfen ‹Krankheit, Analphabetentum›

**~ 'back** **1** *v.i.* zurückschlagen; sich zur Wehr setzen. **2** *v.t.* **A** (*suppress*) zurückhalten; **B** (*resist*) zurückdrängen; aufhalten ‹Vormarsch›

**~ 'down** *v.t.* zurückhalten

**~ for** *v.t.* (*lit. or fig.*) kämpfen für; **~ for one's life** um sein Leben kämpfen

**~ 'off** *v.t.* (*lit. or fig.*) abwehren; abwimmeln (*ugs.*) ‹Reporter, Fans, Bewunderer›; widerstehen (+ *Dat.*) ‹Versuchung›; bekämpfen ‹Erkältung›; **~ off the desire** dem Wunsch widerstehen

**~ 'out** *v.t.* (*lit. or fig.*) ausfechten; **~ it out amongst yourselves** macht das unter euch (*Dat.*) aus

**~ over** *v.t.* **A** (**~ with regard to**) [sich] streiten über (+ *Akk.*); **B** (**~ to gain possession of**) kämpfen um; (*squabble to gain possession of*) [sich] streiten um; [sich] zanken um

**~ with** *v.t.* **A** kämpfen mit; **B** (*squabble with*) [sich] streiten mit; [sich] zanken mit; **C** (**~ on the side of**) kämpfen [zusammen] mit

**fighter** /'faɪtə(r)/ *n.* **A** Kämpfer, *der*/Kämpferin, *die;* (*warrior*) Krieger, *der;* (*boxer*) Fighter, *der;* **B** (*aircraft*) Kampfflugzeug, *das;* **~ pilot** ▶ 1261 Jagdflieger, *der*

**fighting** /'faɪtɪŋ/ **1** *adj.* Kampf‹truppen, -schiff, -flugzeug›; ⇨ *also* **cock**[1] 1 A. **2** *n.* Kämpfe *Pl.;* **be in a ~ mood** kämpferisch gestimmt sein

**fighting: ~ 'chance** *n.* **have a ~ chance of succeeding/of doing sth.** Aussicht auf Erfolg haben/gute Chancen haben, etw. zu tun; **~ 'drunk** *adj.* (*coll.*) betrunken und streitsüchtig; **~ fish** *n.* Kampffisch, *der;* **~ 'fit** *adj.* topfit (*ugs.*); **~ fund** *n.* *Geldmittel [aus einer Spendenaktion] zur Durchführung einer Kampagne;* **raise a ~ fund** eine Spendenaktion durchführen; **~ 'mad** *adj.* [vor Wut] rasend; **~ 'words** *n. pl.* (*coll.*) Kampfparolen

**'fig leaf** *n.* (*lit. or fig.*) Feigenblatt, *das*

**figment** /'fɪgmənt/ *n.* (*imagined thing*) Hirngespinst, *das;* **a ~ of one's** *or* **the imagination** pure Einbildung

**'fig tree** *n.* Feigenbaum, *der*

**figurative** /'fɪgjʊrətɪv, 'fɪgərətɪv/ *adj.* **A** (*metaphorical*) bildlich; übertragen; figurativ (*Sprachw.*); **B** (*metaphorically so called*) im übertragenen Sinne; **C** (*with many figures of speech*) bilderreich; **D** (*emblematic*) symbolisch; **be ~ of sth.** symbolisch für etw. stehen

**figuratively** /'fɪgjʊrətɪvlɪ, 'fɪgərətɪvlɪ/ *adv.* **A** (*metaphorically*) bildlich; übertragen; im übertragenen Sinne; figurativ (*Sprachw.*); **B** (*with many figures of speech*) bilderreich; **C** (*emblematically*) symbolisch

**figure** /'fɪgə(r)/ **1** *n.* **A** (*shape*) Form, *die;* **B** (*Geom.*) Figur, *die;* **C** (*one's bodily shape*) Figur, *die;* **have to worry about one's ~:** auf seine Figur achten müssen; **keep one's ~:** sich (*Dat.*) seine Figur bewahren; schlank bleiben; **lose one's ~:** dick werden; **D** (*person as seen*) Gestalt, *die;* (*literary ~*) Figur, *die;* (*historical etc.* **~**) Persönlichkeit, *die;* **a fine ~ of a man/woman** eine stattliche Erscheinung; **a ~ of fun** eine Spottfigur; **make** *or* **cut a brilliant/poor** *etc.* **~:** eine glänzende/erbärmliche *usw.* Figur machen *od.* abgeben; **E** (*image*) Bild, *das;* **she looked a ~ of misery** sie bot ein Bild des Jammers; **F** (*three-dimensional representation*) Figur, *die;* (*two-dimensional representation*) Gestalt, *die;* **G** (*emblem*) Symbol, *das;* **a ~ of peace** ein Friedenssymbol; **H** (*simile etc.*) **~ [of speech]** Redewendung, *die;* (*Rhet.*) Redefigur, *die;* **it's just a ~ of speech** das habe ich nicht wirklich gemeint; **I** (*illustration*) Abbildung, *die;* **J** (*decorative pattern*) Muster, *das;* **K** (*Dancing, Skating*) Figur, *die;* **L** (*numerical symbol*) Ziffer, *die;* (*number so expressed*) Zahl, *die;* (*amount of money*) Betrag, *der;* (*amount paid for sth.*) Erlös, *der;* (*value*) [Zahlen]wert, *der;* **double ~s** zweistellige Zahlen; **membership is in double ~s** die Mitgliederzahl ist zweistellig; **three/four** *etc.* **~s** drei-/vierstellige *usw.* Zahlen; **go** *or* **run into three ~s** sich auf dreistellige Zahlen belaufen; **three-/four-** *etc.* **~:** drei-/vierstellig *usw.;* **M** *in pl.* (*arithmetical calculations*) Rechnen, *das;* (*accounts, result of calculations*) Zahlen *Pl.;* **can you check my ~s?** kannst du mal nachrechnen?; **do the ~s** den [Jahres-, Rechnungs]abschluss durchführen; **last month's ~s** die Zahlen/Werte des Vormonats; **he is good at ~s** er kann gut rechnen; ⇨ *also* **head** 1 B; **N** (*Ling.*) [grammatische] Figur. ⇨ *also* **eight** 2 B; **father figure**.

**2** *v.t.* **A** (*represent pictorially*) darstellen; **B** (*picture mentally*) sich (*Dat.*) vorstellen; **~ oneself as sth.** sich selbst als etw. [an]sehen; **C** (*be symbol of*) versinnbildlichen; **D** (*embellish*) verzieren; **E** (*Mus.*) beziffern; **F** (*mark with number[s]*) mit einer Zahl versehen; **G** (*calculate*) schätzen; sagen; **H** (*Amer.: understand*) verstehen; **I**

f

(*Amer.: ascertain*) herausfinden. ⇒ *also* **bass³** 2 C.
❸ *v.i.* Ⓐ (*make appearance*) vorkommen; erscheinen; (*in play*) auftreten; **children don't ~ in her plans for the future** Kinder spielen in ihren Zukunftsplänen keine Rolle; **this image often ~d in her dreams** dieses Bild tauchte in ihren Träumen häufig auf; **~ prominently on the music scene/in world politics** in der Musikszene/Weltpolitik eine bedeutende Rolle spielen; Ⓑ (*do arithmetic*) rechnen; Ⓒ (*coll.: be likely, understandable*) **it ~s that ...:** es kann gut sein, dass ...; **that ~s** das kann gut sein *od.* stimmt sicher

**~ on** *v.t.* rechnen mit; **~ on doing sth.** damit rechnen, etw. zu tun

**~ 'out** *v.t.* Ⓐ (*work out by arithmetic*) ausrechnen; Ⓑ (*Amer.: estimate*) **~ out that ...:** damit rechnen, dass ...; Ⓒ (*understand*) verstehen; **I can't ~ him out** ich werde nicht schlau aus ihm; Ⓓ (*ascertain*) herausfinden; **it's difficult to ~ out whether ...:** es ist schwer zu sagen, ob ...; **I can't ~ out where we've met before** ich weiß nicht, wo wir uns schon gesehen haben

**figure: ~head** *n.* (*lit. or fig.*) Galionsfigur, *die;* **~ skating** *n.* Eiskunstlauf, *der;* **~work** *n., no pl.* **do some ~work** ein paar Berechnungen anstellen

**Fiji** /ˈfiːdʒiː/ *pr. n.* Fidschi (*das*); Fidschiinseln *Pl.*

**filament** /ˈfɪləmənt/ *n.* Ⓐ Faden, *der;* (*Chem.*) Filament, *das* (*fachspr.*); Faser, *die;* Ⓑ (*conducting wire or thread*) Glühfaden, *der;* Ⓒ (*Bot.*) Staubfaden, *der;* Filament, *das* (*fachspr.*)

**filbert** /ˈfɪlbət/ *n.* Ⓐ (*cultivated hazel*) Haselnussstrauch, *der;* Ⓑ (*nut*) Haselnuss, *die*

**filch** /fɪltʃ/ *v.t.* stibitzen (*ugs.*)

**file¹** /faɪl/ ❶ *n.* Feile, *die;* (*nail ~*) [Nagel]feile, *die.* ❷ *v.t.* feilen ‹Fingernägel›; mit der Feile bearbeiten ‹Holz, Eisen›; **~ sth. to make it smooth** etw. glatt feilen

**~ a'way** *v.t.* abfeilen

**~ 'down** *v.t.* abfeilen

**file²** ❶ *n.* Ⓐ (*holder*) Ordner, *der;* (*box*) Kassette, *die;* [Dokumenten]schachtel, *die;* **on ~:** in der Kartei/in *od.* bei den Akten; **on** *or* **in sb.'s ~s** in jmds. Kartei/in *od.* bei jmds. Akten; **put sth. on ~:** etw. in die Akten/Kartei aufnehmen; Ⓑ (*set of papers*) Ablage, *die;* (*as cards*) Kartei, *die;* **open/keep a ~ on sb./sth.** eine Akte über jmdn./etw. anlegen/führen; Ⓒ (*series of issues of newspaper etc.*) [Zeitungs]bündel, *das* (*von aufeinander folgenden Nummern*); Ⓓ (*Computing*) Datei, *die;* Ⓔ (*stiff wire*) Zettelspieß, *der;* Ⓕ (*Law*) Akten *Pl.;* **reopen/close the ~ on a case** einen Fall wieder aufnehmen/abschließen.
❷ *v.t.* Ⓐ (*place on a ~*) [in die Kartei] einordnen/[in die Akten] aufnehmen; ablegen (*Bürow.*); (*place among public records*) archivieren; **~ sth. in drawers** etw. [geordnet] in Schubladen aufbewahren; Ⓑ (*submit*) einreichen ‹Antrag›; Ⓒ ‹Journalist:› einsenden ‹Bericht›

**~ a'way** *v.t.* ablegen (*Bürow.*)

**file³** ❶ *n.* Ⓐ (*Mil. etc.*) Reihe, *die;* **stand in ~:** in Reih und Glied stehen; **[in] single** *or* **Indian ~:** [im] Gänsemarsch; Ⓑ (*row of persons or things*) Reihe, *die.* ❷ *v.i.* in einer Reihe gehen; nacheinander gehen

**~ a'way** *v.i.* [einer nach dem anderen] weggehen; [nacheinander] fortgehen

**~ 'off** ⇒ **~ away**

**file: ~ card** *n.* Karteikarte, *die;* **~ copy** *n.* Belegexemplar, *das;* (*of letter*) Kopie für die Akten

**filet** /ˈfileɪ/ *n.* (*Gastr.*) Filet, *das*

**filial** /ˈfɪlɪəl/ *adj.* Ⓐ (*of or due from son or daughter*) kindlich ‹Gehorsam, Achtung, Treue›; Kindes-, Sohnes-/Tochter‹liebe, -pflicht›; Ⓑ (*Biol.*) **~ generation** Filialgeneration, *die*

**filibuster** /ˈfɪlɪbʌstə(r)/ ❶ *n.* (*obstructionist*) Verschleppungstaktiker, *der;* (*obstruction*) Verschleppungstaktik, *die;* Filibuster, *das.* ❷ *v.i.* obstruieren; Dauerreden halten

**filigree** /ˈfɪlɪɡriː/ *n.* (*lit. or fig.*) Filigran, *das*

**filing¹** /ˈfaɪlɪŋ/ *n.* **~s** (*particles*) Späne *Pl.;* **iron ~s** Eisen[feil]späne *Pl.*

**filing²** *n.* (*action of* **file** 2 A) Ablage, *die*

**filing: ~ cabinet** *n.* Aktenschrank, *der;* **~ clerk** *n.* **▶ 1261** Archivkraft, *die;* **~ system** *n.* Ablagesystem, *das*

**Filipino** /fɪlɪˈpiːnəʊ/ **▶ 1340** ❶ *adj.* philippinisch. ❷ *n., pl.* **~s** Filipino, *der*/Filipina, *die*

**fill** /fɪl/ ❶ *v.t.* Ⓐ (*make full*) **~ sth. [with sth.]** etw. [mit etw.] füllen; **the room was ~ed** (*with people*) der Raum war fast voll besetzt; **~ the walls with photos** die Wände mit Fotos vollhängen; **~ sb./sb.'s heart with fear** jmdm. Furcht einflößen; **~ed with** voller ‹Reue, Bewunderung, Neid, Verzweiflung› (**at** über + *Akk.*); **be ~ed with envy at sb.'s success** auf jmds. Erfolg (*Akk.*) neidisch sein; Ⓑ (*distend*) blähen ‹Segel›; Ⓒ (*stock abundantly*) füllen; (*fig.*) anfüllen; **be ~ed with people/flowers/fish** *etc.* voller Menschen/Blumen/Fische *usw.* sein; **the journey had ~ed his mind with new ideas** die Reise hatte ihm zahlreiche neue Anregungen gegeben; Ⓓ (*occupy whole capacity of, spread over*) füllen; besetzen ‹Sitzplätze›; (*fig.*) ausfüllen ‹Gedanken, Zeit›; **the room was ~ed to capacity** der Raum war voll besetzt *od.* (*ugs.*) [proppen]voll; **tears suddenly ~ed her eyes** plötzlich standen ihr Tränen in den Augen; **when you've ~ed this notebook ...:** wenn dein Heft voll ist ...; **the fat lady ~ed two seats** die dicke Dame brauchte zwei Plätze; **enough cake to ~ three large plates** genug Kuchen für drei große Teller; **~ the bill** (*fig.*) den Erwartungen entsprechen; (*be appropriate*) angemessen sein; Ⓔ (*pervade*) erfüllen; **light/silence ~ed the room** Licht strömte in das Zimmer/Schweigen breitete sich im Zimmer aus; Ⓕ (*block up*) füllen ‹Lücke›; füllen, (*veralt.*) plombieren ‹Zahn›; Ⓖ (*Cookery*) (*stuff*) füllen; (*put layer of sth. solid in*) belegen; (*put layer of sth. spreadable in*) bestreichen; Ⓗ (*satisfy*) sättigen; satt machen; Ⓘ (*hold*) innehaben ‹Posten›; versehen ‹Amt›; (*take up*) ausfüllen ‹Position›; Ⓙ (*execute*) ausführen ‹Auftrag›; Ⓚ (*appoint sb. to*) besetzen ‹Posten, Lehrstuhl›.
❷ *v.i.* Ⓐ (*become full*) **~ [with sth.]** sich [mit etw.] füllen; (*fig.*) sich [mit etw.] erfüllen; Ⓑ (*be distended by wind*) sich blähen.
❸ *n.* Ⓐ (*as much as one wants*) **eat/drink one's ~:** sich satt essen/trinken; **have had one's ~ [of food and drink]** seinen Hunger und Durst gestillt haben; **weep one's ~:** sich ausweinen; **have had one's ~ of sth./doing sth.** genug von etw. haben/etw. zur Genüge getan haben; Ⓑ (*enough to ~ sth.*) **he needs a ~ of tobacco for his pipe/of petrol/of ink** er muss seine Pfeife stopfen/tanken/Tinte nachfüllen

**~ 'in** ❶ *v.t.* Ⓐ füllen; zuschütten, auffüllen ‹Erdloch›; Ⓑ (*complete*) ausfüllen; ergänzen ‹Auslassungen›; Ⓒ (*insert*) einsetzen; Ⓓ (*find occupation during*) überbrücken ‹Zeit›; **how did you ~ in your evenings?** was hast du abends unternommen?; Ⓔ (*coll.: inform*) **~ sb. in [on sth.]** jmdn. [über etw. (*Akk.*)] unterrichten *od.* ins Bild setzen. ❷ *v.i.* **~ in for sb.** für jmdn. einspringen

**~ 'out** ❶ *v.t.* Ⓐ (*enlarge to proper size or extent*) ausfüllen; vervollständigen ‹Essay, Aufsatz›; Ⓑ (*Amer.: complete*) ausfüllen ‹Formular usw.›. ❷ *v.i.* Ⓐ (*become enlarged*) sich ausdehnen; Ⓑ (*become plumper*) [Fett] ansetzen; voller werden

**~ 'up** ❶ *v.t.* Ⓐ (*make full*) **~ sth. up [with sth.]** etw. [mit etw.] füllen; **put a little milk into the cup and then ~ it up with water** gießen Sie etwas Milch in die Tasse und füllen Sie mit Wasser auf; **~ oneself/sb. up [with sth.]** sich/jmdn. [mit etw.] voll stopfen; **their mother tried to ~ them up** ihre Mutter versuchte, sie satt zu kriegen; **that will ~ you up!** davon wirst du satt!; Ⓑ (*put petrol into*) **~ up [the tank]** tanken; **~ her up!** (*coll.*) voll [tanken]!; Ⓒ auffüllen ‹Loch›; zuschmieren ‹Riss›; Ⓓ (*complete*) ausfüllen ‹Formular usw.›.
❷ *v.i.* ‹Theater, Zimmer, Zug usw.:› sich füllen; ‹Becken, Spülkasten:› voll laufen

**filled** /fɪld/ *adj.* gefüllt; **a cream-~ cake** ein Kuchen mit Cremefüllung

**filler** /ˈfɪlə(r)/ *n.* Ⓐ (*to fill cavity*) Füllmasse, *die;* Spachtelmasse, *die;* Ⓑ (*to increase bulk*) Sattmacher, *der*

**'filler cap** *n.* Tankverschluss, *der*

**fillet** /ˈfɪlɪt/ ❶ *n.* Ⓐ (*Gastr.*) Filet, *das;* **~ [steak]** (*slice*) Filetsteak, *das;* (*cut*) Filet, *das;* **~ of pork/beef/cod/halibut** Schweine-/Rinder-/Kabeljau-/Heilbuttfilet, *das;* Ⓑ (*Archit.*) (*narrow flat band*) Leiste, *die;* (*between flutes of column*) Kannelüre, *die;* Ⓒ (*headband*) Haarband, *das.* ❷ *v.t.* Ⓐ (*divide into fillets*) filetieren; Ⓑ (*remove bones from*) entgräten ‹Fisch›; ausbeinen ‹Fleisch›

**filling** /ˈfɪlɪŋ/ ❶ *n.* Ⓐ (*for teeth*) Füllung, *die;* Plombe, *die* (*veralt.*); Ⓑ (*for pancakes etc.*) Füllung, *die;* (*for sandwiches etc.*) Belag, *der;* (*for spreading*) Aufstrich, *der.* ❷ *adj.* sättigend

**'filling station** *n.* Tankstelle, *die*

**fillip** /ˈfɪlɪp/ *n.* Anreiz, *der;* Ansporn, *der;* **give sb. a ~:** jmdn. anspornen; **give** *or* **be a ~ to the economy** die Wirtschaft beleben;

**filly** /ˈfɪlɪ/ *n.* Ⓐ junge Stute; Stutfohlen, *das;* Ⓑ (*coll. dated: young woman*) Käfer, *der* (*ugs. veralt.*); Biene, *die* (*ugs. veralt.*)

**film** /fɪlm/ ❶ *n.* Ⓐ (*thin layer*) Schicht, *die;* **~ [of varnish/dust]** [Lack-/Staub]schicht, *die;* **~ [of oil/slime]** [Öl-/Schmier]film, *der;* Ⓑ (*Photog.*) Film, *der;* **put sth. on ~:** etw. ablichten; **the events are all on ~:** die Vorgänge sind alle gefilmt worden; Ⓒ (*Cinemat.: story etc.*) Film, *der;* Streifen, *der* (*ugs.*); **make/direct a ~:** einen Film drehen/bei einem Film Regie führen; Ⓓ *in pl.* (*cinema industry*) Kino, *das;* Film, *der;* **go into ~s** zum Kino *od.* Film gehen; **she is in ~s** sie ist beim Film; Ⓔ *no pl.* (*as art form*) der Film; **are you interested in ~?** interessieren Sie sich für [den] Film?
❷ *v.t.* (*Cinemat. etc.*) Ⓐ (*record on motion ~*) filmen; (*for motion picture*) drehen ‹Kinofilm, Szene›; Ⓑ (*make cinema etc. ~ of*) verfilmen ‹Buch usw.›.
❸ *v.i.* ‹Szene:› sich filmen lassen; ‹Buch, Geschichte:› sich verfilmen lassen

**~ 'over** *v.i.* ‹Spiegel, Glas:› anlaufen; **her eyes ~ed over with tears** Tränen traten ihr in die Augen

**film: ~ clip** ⇒ **clip²** 2 B; **~ crew** *n.* Kamerateam, *das;* **~ director** *n.* **▶ 1261** Filmregisseur, *der*/-regisseurin, *die;* **~ editor** *n.* **▶ 1261** Cutter, *der*/Cutterin, *die;* **~-goer** *n.* Kinogänger, *der*/-gängerin, *die;* **~ industry** *n.* Filmindustrie, *die;* **~ library** *n.* Filmarchiv, *das;* **~ projector** *n.* Projektor, *der;* **~ script** *n.* Drehbuch, *das;* **~ set** *n.* Dekoration, *die;* **~setting** *n.* (*Printing*) Lichtsatz, *der;* **~ show** *n.* Filmvorführung, *die;* **~ star** *n.* **▶ 1261** Filmstar, *der;* **~strip** *n.* Filmstreifen, *der;* **~ studio** *n.* Filmstudio, *das*

**Filofax** ® /ˈfaɪləʊfæks/ *n.* ≈ Terminplaner, *der*

**filter** /ˈfɪltə(r)/ ❶ *n.* Ⓐ Filter, *der;* Ⓑ (*Brit.*) (*route*) Abbiegespur, *die;* (*light*) grünes Licht für Abbieger. ❷ *v.t.* filtern. ❸ *v.i.* Ⓐ (*flow through filter*) ‹Flüssigkeiten:› sickern; ‹Luft usw.:› durch einen Filter strömen; Ⓑ (*make way gradually*) **~ through/into/down sth.** durch etw. hindurch-/in etw. (*Akk.*) hinein-/etw. hinuntersickern; Ⓒ (*at road junction*) sich einfädeln; **~ off** sich ausfädeln

**~ 'out** ❶ *v.t.* (*lit. or fig.*) herausfiltern. ❷ *v.i.* durchsickern

**~ 'through** ⇒ **~ out** 2

**filter: ~ bed** *n.* Filterkies, *der;* Filtersand, *der;* **~ ciga'rette** *n.* Filterzigarette, *die;* **~ coffee** *n.* Filterkaffee, *der;* **~ lane** *n.* Abbiegespur, *die;* **~ paper** *n.* Filterpapier, *das* **~ tip** *n.* Ⓐ Filter, *der;* Ⓑ **~ tip [cigarette]** Filterzigarette, *die*

**filth** /fɪlθ/ *n., no pl.* Ⓐ (*disgusting dirt*) Dreck, *der;* (*pollution*) Schmutzigkeit, *die;* Ⓑ (*moral corruption*) Verderbtheit, *die;* (*vileness*) Abscheulichkeit, *die;* Ⓒ (*obscenity*) Schmutz [und Schund]; Ⓓ (*foul language*) unflätige Sprache; Schweinereien *Pl.* (*ugs.*)

**filthiness** /ˈfɪlθɪnɪs/ *n., no pl.* Ⓐ Schmutzigkeit, *die;* Verdrecktheit, *die* (*ugs.*); Ⓑ (*obscenity*) Unzüchtigkeit, *die*

**filthy** /ˈfɪlθɪ/ ❶ *adj.* [A] (*disgustingly dirty*) dreckig (*ugs.*); schmutzig; (*fig.*) widerlich ‹Angewohnheit›; (*fond of filth*) im Dreck lebend ‹Tiere›; [B] (*vile*) widerlich; gemein ‹Lügner, Trick›; schmutzig ‹Fantasie, Gedanken›; **~ lucre** schnöder Mammon (*abwertend, auch scherzh.*); [C] (*very unpleasant*) ekelhaft; scheußlich; **~ weather** scheußliches Wetter; Dreckwetter, *das* (*ugs.*); [D] (*obscene*) schweinisch (*ugs.*); obszön, unflätig ‹Sprache›; **he is ~, he is a ~ devil** er ist ein Schweinigel (*ugs.*); **a ~-minded person** ein Mensch mit einer schmutzigen Fantasie.
❷ *adv.* **~ dirty** völlig verdreckt (*ugs.*); **~ rich** (*coll.*) stinkreich (*ugs.*)

**filtrate** /ˈfɪltreɪt/ *n.* Filtrat, *das*

**filtration** /fɪlˈtreɪʃn/ *n.* Filtrierung, *die;* (*percolation*) Durchsickern, *das*

**fin** /fɪn/ *n.* [A] (*Zool.; on boat*) Flosse, *die;* (*flipper*) [Schwimm]flosse, *die;* (*on car*) Heckflosse, *die;* [B] (*in internal-combustion engine*) Kühlrippe, *die;* (*on radiator etc.*) Rippe, *die.* ⇒ *also* **tail fin**

**final** /ˈfaɪnl/ ❶ *adj.* [A] (*ultimate*) letzt...; End‹spiel, -stadium, -stufe, -ergebnis›; Schluss‹bericht, -szene, -etappe, -phase›; **~ examination** Abschlussprüfung, *die;* **have a ~ swim** ein letztes Mal schwimmen gehen; **give a ~ wave** noch einmal *od.* ein letztes Mal winken; **what will be the ~ outcome of this crisis?** wie wird diese Krise letztendlich ausgehen?; [B] (*conclusive*) endgültig ‹Urteil, Entscheidung›; **have the ~ word** das letzte Wort haben; **is this your ~ decision/word/verdict?** ist das Ihr letztes Wort?; **the ~ solution** (*euphem.*) die Endlösung; **I'm not coming with you, and that's ~!** ich komme nicht mit, und damit basta! (*ugs.*); [C] (*concerned with goal*) **~ cause** Endziel, *das;* **~ clause** (*Ling.*) Finalsatz, *der.*
❷ *n.* [A] (*Sport etc.*) Finale, *das;* (*of ball game also*) Endspiel, *das;* (*of quiz game*) Endrunde, *die;* [B] *in sing. or pl.* (*examination*) Abschlussprüfung, *die;* (*at university*) Examen, *das;* [C] (*newspaper*) Spätausgabe, *die*

**final 'drive** *n.* (*Motor Veh.*) Achsantrieb [mit Gelenkwelle]

**finale** /fɪˈnɑːlɪ/ *n.* [A] (*Mus.*) Finale, *das;* [B] (*close of drama*) Schlussszene, *die;* [C] (*conclusion*) Abschluss, *der*

**finalise** ⇒ **finalize**

**finalist** /ˈfaɪnəlɪst/ *n.* Teilnehmer/Teilnehmerin in der Endausscheidung; (*Sport*) Finalist, *der*/Finalistin, *die*

**finality** /faɪˈnælɪtɪ/ *n., no pl.* Endgültigkeit, *die;* (*of tone of voice*) Entschiedenheit, *die*

**finalize** /ˈfaɪnəlaɪz/ *v.t.* [endgültig] beschließen; unter Dach und Fach bringen ‹Geschäft, Vertrag›; (*complete*) zum Abschluss bringen; **~ sth. with sb.** etw. mit jmdm. [endgültig] absprechen

**finally** /ˈfaɪnəlɪ/ *adv.* [A] (*in the end*) schließlich; (*expressing impatience etc.*) endlich; [B] (*in conclusion*) abschließend; zum Schluss; [C] (*conclusively*) bestimmt, entschieden ‹sagen›; (*once for all*) ein für alle Mal

**finance** /faɪˈnæns, fɪˈnæns, ˈfaɪnæns/ ❶ *n.* [A] *in pl.* (*resources*) Finanzen *Pl.;* [B] (*management of money*) Geldwesen, *das;* **high ~:** Hochfinanz, *die;* **be in ~:** im Finanz- und Geldwesen tätig sein; [C] (*support*) Gelder *Pl.* (*ugs.*); Geldmittel *Pl.* ❷ *v.t.* finanzieren; finanziell unterstützen ‹Person›; **how are you going to ~ yourself at university?** wie willst du dein Studium finanzieren?

**finance: ~ company** *n.* Finanzierungsgesellschaft, *die;* **~ director** *n.* Leiter der Finanzabteilung; **~ house** ⇒ **~ company**

**financial** /faɪˈnænʃl, fɪˈnænʃl/ *adj.* finanziell; Finanz‹mittel, -quelle, -experte, -lage›; Geld‹mittel, -geber, -sorgen›; Finanzierungs‹last, -geschäft›; Wirtschafts‹nachrichten, -bericht›

**financially** /faɪˈnænʃəlɪ, fɪˈnænʃəlɪ/ *adv.* finanziell; **be ~ rewarded for sth.** für etw. mit Geld entlohnt werden

**financial 'year** *n.* Geschäftsjahr, *das;* (*im öffentlichen Haushalt*) Rechnungsjahr, *das*

**financier** /faɪˈnænsɪə(r), fɪˈnænsɪə(r)/ *n.* [A] (*expert*) Finanzexperte, *der*/-expertin, *die;* [B] (*capitalist*) Finanzier, *der*

**fin-back 'whale** ⇒ **rorqual**

**finch** /fɪnʃ/ *n.* (*Ornith.*) Fink[envogel], *der*

**find** /faɪnd/ ❶ *v.t.*, **found** /faʊnd/ [A] (*get possession of by chance*) finden; (*come across unexpectedly*) entdecken; **~ that ...:** herausfinden *od.* entdecken, dass ...; **hope this letter ~s you well** [ich] hoffe, dass dieser Brief dich gesund antreffen wird; **he was found dead/injured** er wurde tot/verletzt aufgefunden; [B] (*obtain*) finden ‹Zustimmung, Erleichterung, Rückendeckung, Trost, Gegenliebe›; stoßen auf (+ *Akk.*) ‹Kritik, Ablehnung›; erlangen ‹Popularität›; **have found one's feet** (*be able to walk*) laufen können; (*be able to act by oneself*) selbstständig sein; auf eigenen Füßen stehen; [C] (*recognize as present*) sehen ‹Veranlassung, Schwierigkeit›; feststellen ‹Züge, Ähnlichkeit›; (*acknowledge or discover to be*) finden; **~ no difficulty in doing sth.** etw. nicht schwierig finden; **these plants are found nowhere else** diese Pflanzen findet man sonst nirgendwo; **you don't ~ many flowers here** es gibt hier nicht viele Blumen; **~ sb. in/out** jmdn. antreffen/nicht antreffen; **~ sb./sth. to be ...:** feststellen, dass jmd./etw. ... ist/war; **~ oneself somewhere** sich irgendwo wieder finden; **when I came in, I found him opening his/my letters** als ich hineinkam, war er gerade dabei, seine Briefe zu öffnen/ertappte ich ihn dabei, wie er meine Briefe öffnete; **~ oneself doing sth.** sich dabei ertappen, wie man etw. tut; **you must** *or* **will have to take us as you ~ us** du darfst dich nicht daran stören, wie es bei uns aussieht/zugeht *usw.;* **you won't ~ me doing 'that** das wirst du nicht erleben, dass ich das tue; [D] (*discover by trial or experience to be or do*) für ... halten; **do you ~ him easy to get on with?** finden Sie, dass sich gut mit ihm auskommen lässt?; **she ~s it hard to come to terms with his death** es fällt ihr schwer, sich mit seinem Tod abzufinden; **she ~s it impossible to discuss the subject** es ist ihr unmöglich, das Thema zu erörtern; **~ sth. necessary** etw. für nötig befinden *od.* erachten; **~ sth./sb. to be ...:** herausfinden, dass etw./jmd. ... ist/war; **sth. has been found to be ...:** man hat herausgefunden, dass etw. ... ist; **I found that it was already noon** ich stellte fest, dass es [nach] zwölf war; **we ~ [that] we are struggling all the time** wir sehen, wie wir uns die ganze Zeit abmühen; **you will ~ [that] ...:** Sie werden sehen *od.* feststellen, dass ...; [E] (*discover by search*) finden; **want to ~ sth.** etw. suchen; **~ [again]** wieder finden; [F] (*Hunting*) aufstöbern; *abs.* Wild aufstöbern; [G] (*reach by natural or normal process*) [heraus]finden; **~ one's place in society** seinen Platz in der Gesellschaft finden; [H] (*succeed in obtaining*) finden ‹Zeit, Mittel und Wege, Worte›; auftreiben ‹Geld, Gegenstand›; aufbringen ‹Kraft, Energie›; **when I ~ the opportunity** bei passender Gelegenheit; **~ it in oneself** *or* **one's heart to do sth.** es über sich *od.* übers Herz bringen, etw. zu tun; **~ its mark** sein Ziel finden *od.* treffen; [I] (*ascertain by study or calculation or inquiry*) finden; **love will ~ a way** der Liebe ist kein Ding unmöglich (*veralt.*); **~ what time the train leaves** herausfinden, wann der Zug [ab]fährt; **~ one's way [to/into sth.]** [zu etw.] hinfinden/[in etw. (*Akk.*)] hineinfinden; (*accidentally*) [zu etw.] hingelangen/[in etw. (*Akk.*)] hineingeraten; **~ one's way home** nach Hause zurückfinden; **~ one's way into journalism/films** zum Journalismus/Film kommen; **she found her way into teaching quite by accident** eher zufällig war sie Lehrerin geworden; **~ its way [into sth.]** [in etw. (*Akk.*)] gelangen; **the disease found its way into other organs** die Krankheit griff auf andere Organe über; [J] (*Law*) **~ sb. guilty/not guilty [of sth.]** jmdn. [an etw. (*Dat.*)] schuldig sprechen/[von etw.] freisprechen; **~ a verdict of guilty/innocent** [im Urteil] auf schuldig/nicht schuldig erkennen; **the jury found him not guilty of murder** die Geschworenen entschieden, dass er des Mordes nicht schuldig war; [K] (*supply*) besorgen; **~ sb. sth.** *or* **sth. for sb.** jmdn. mit etw. versorgen; **~ sb. in sth.** jmdn. mit etw. versehen; jmdm. etw. verschaffen; **all found** bei freier Kost und Logis; bei freier Station (*veralt.*).
❷ *v. refl.*, **found** [A] (*provide for one's own needs*) **~ oneself [in sth.]** sich selbst [mit etw.] versorgen; [B] (*discover one's vocation*) zu sich selbst finden; seine wahre Bestimmung finden.
❸ *n.* [A] Fund, *der;* **make a ~/two ~s** fündig/zweimal fündig werden; [B] (*person*) Entdeckung, *die*

**~ for** *v.t.* (*Law*) **~ for the defendant/plaintiff** zugunsten der Verteidigung/des Klägers entscheiden; **~ for the accused** auf Freispruch erkennen

**~ 'out** *v.t.* [A] (*discover, devise*) herausfinden; bekommen ‹Informationen›; **~ out new ways** einen neuen Weg finden; **manage to ~ out how ...:** herausbekommen, wie ...; **~ out about** (*get information on*) sich informieren über (+ *Akk.*); (*learn of*) erfahren von; [B] (*detect in offence, act of deceit, etc.*) erwischen, ertappen ‹Dieb usw.›; **~ out a liar** einem Lügner auf die Schliche kommen; einen Lügner durchschauen; **your sins will ~ you out** deine Sünden werden an den Tag kommen

**findable** /ˈfaɪndəbl/ *pred. adj.* **be [easily] ~:** [leicht] zu finden sein

**finder** /ˈfaɪndə(r)/ *n.* [A] (*of sth. lost*) Finder, *der*/Finderin, *die;* (*of sth. unknown*) Entdecker, *der*/Entdeckerin, *die;* **~s keepers** (*coll.*) wers findet, dem gehörts (*ugs.*); [B] (*Photog.*) Sucher, *der*

**fin de siècle** /fæ̃ də ˈsjekl/ *adj.* Fin-de-siècle-‹Architektur, Atmosphäre usw.›

**finding** /ˈfaɪndɪŋ/ *n.* [A] Finden, *das;* **~ is keeping** wer's findet, dem gehört's (*ugs.*); [B] *usu. in pl.* (*conclusion[s]*) Ergebnis, *das;* (*verdict*) Urteil, *das;* **what were the ~s of the investigations?** was haben die Ermittlungen ergeben?; [C] *in pl.* (*Amer.*) (*small parts or tools*) Handwerkszeug, *das;* (*sewing essentials*) Nähzeug, *das*

**fine**[1] /faɪn/ ❶ *n.* [A] Geldstrafe, *die;* (*for minor offence*) Bußgeld, *das;* [B] (*literary*) **in ~** (*finally*) zu guter Letzt; (*to sum up*) kurzum; (*in short*) kurz und gut. ❷ *v.t.* mit einer Geldstrafe belegen; **we were ~d £10** wir mussten ein Bußgeld von 10 Pfund bezahlen; **be ~d for speeding** ein Bußgeld wegen überhöhter Geschwindigkeit zahlen müssen

**fine**[2] ❶ *adj.* [A] (*of high quality*) gut; hochwertig ‹Qualität, Lebensmittel›; fein ‹Besteck, Gewebe, Spitze›; edel ‹Pferd, Holz, Wein›; [B] (*pure*) rein ‹Öl, Metall, Wein›; [C] (*containing specified proportion of pure metal*) fein; **gold 18 carats ~:** 18-karätiges Gold; [D] (*delicately beautiful*) zart ‹Porzellan, Spitze›; ansprechend ‹Beleuchtung, Manuskript›; fein ‹Muster, Kristall, Stickerei, Gesichtszüge›; [E] (*refined*) edel ‹Empfindungen›; fein ‹Taktgefühl, Geschmack›; **a man of ~ feelings** ein Mann mit viel Feingefühl; **sb.'s ~r feelings** das Gute in jmdm.; [F] (*delicate in structure or texture*) fein; [G] (*thin*) fein; hauchdünn; **cut** *or* **run it ~:** knapp kalkulieren; **we'd be cutting it ~ if there are only three minutes to spare** es wird etwas knapp werden, wenn wir nur drei Minuten Zeit haben; [H] (*in small particles*) [hauch]fein ‹Sand, Staub›; **~ rain** Nieselregen, *der;* [I] (*sharp, narrow-pointed*) scharf ‹Spitze, Klinge›; spitz ‹Nadel, Schreibfeder›; [J] **~ print** ⇒ **small print**; [K] (*capable of delicate perception, discrimination*) fein ‹Gehör›; scharf ‹Auge›; genau ‹Waage, Werkzeug›; empfindlich ‹Messgerät›; [L] (*perceptible only with difficulty*) fein ‹Unterschied, Nuancen›; (*precise*) klein ‹Detail›; **the ~r points** die Feinheiten; [M] (*excellent*) schön; gut ‹Ruf, Charakter, Stimmung, Hotel›; edel ‹Gesinnung›; ausgezeichnet ‹Sänger, Schauspieler›; nett ‹Person›; **a ~ time to do sth.** (*iron.*) ein passender Zeitpunkt, etw. zu tun (*iron.*); **well, that's a ~ thing to say** (*iron.*) das ist wirklich nett *od.* reizend, so was zu sagen (*iron.*); **that's a ~ excuse/way to treat your father** (*iron.*) das ist ja eine schöne Entschuldigung/feine Art, seinen Vater zu behandeln (*iron.*); **you 'are a ~ one!** (*iron.*)

du bist mir vielleicht einer! (*ugs.*); **[this/that is] all very ~, but ...:** [das ist ja] alles schön und gut, aber ...; Ⓝ (*satisfactory*) schön; gut; **that's ~ with** *or* **by me** ja, ist mir recht; **everything is ~:** es ist alles in Ordnung; Ⓞ (*well conceived or expressed*) schön ‹Worte, Ausdruck usw.›; gelungen ‹Rede, Übersetzung usw.›; Ⓟ (*of handsome appearance or size*) schön; stattlich ‹Mann, Baum, Tier›; **~-looking** gut aussehend; **a ~ body of men** eine vortreffliche Gruppe; Ⓠ (*in good health or state*) gut; **feel ~:** sich wohl fühlen; **she is ~ there now** sie fühlt sich jetzt wohl dort; **they had a few problems, but they're ~ now** es gab Probleme zwischen ihnen, aber jetzt kommen sie klar; **How are you? — F~, thanks. And you?** Wie geht es Ihnen? — Gut, danke. Und Ihnen?; **the car is ~ now** das Auto ist jetzt wieder in Ordnung *od.* läuft wieder; Ⓡ (*bright and clear*) schön ‹Wetter, Sommerabend›; **~ and sunny** heiter und sonnig; **one ~ day ...:** eines schönen Tages ...; **one of these ~ days ...:** eines [schönen] Tages; Ⓢ (*ornate*) prächtig ‹Kleidung›; **~ feathers** prächtiges Gefieder; (*fig.*) prächtige Gewänder; ⇨ *also* **feather** 1 A; Ⓣ (*fastidious*) vornehm, fein ‹Dame, Herr, Art, Manieren›; (*affectedly ornate*) geziert; schön klingend ‹Worte›; gewählt ‹Ausdrucksweise›; **his ~ sensibilities** sein Feingefühl; **she's too ~ to associate with us** sie ist sich (*Dat.*) zu fein für uns. ⇨ *also* **dandy** 2; **point** 1 B.

❷ *n.* (*fine weather*) schönes Wetter; **in rain or ~:** bei Regen oder Sonnenschein; **in the ~:** bei schönem Wetter.

❸ *adv.* Ⓐ (*into small particles*) fein ‹mahlen, raspeln, hacken›; Ⓑ (*elegantly*) gewählt ‹sich ausdrücken›; Ⓒ (*delicately*) fein ‹gewebt, gesponnen usw.›; Ⓓ (*coll.: well*) gut

**fine: ~ 'art** *n.* Ⓐ (*subject*) bildende Kunst; Ⓑ (*skill*) **get sth. [down] to a ~ art** etw. zu einer richtigen Kunst entwickeln; **have got sth. [down] to a ~ art** etw. aus dem Effeff beherrschen (*ugs.*); Ⓒ **the ~ arts** die Schönen Künste; **~-drawn** *adj.* sehnig, hager ‹Gestalt›; fein geschnitten ‹Gesichtszüge›; (*subtle*) feinsinnig; **~-grained** *adj.* fein gekörnt ‹Sand, Salz, Papier›; fein genarbt ‹Leder›; fein gemasert ‹Holz›

**finely** /'faɪnlɪ/ *adv.* Ⓐ (*exquisitely*) **~ executed** *or* **crafted jewellery** fein gearbeiteter Schmuck; Ⓑ (*delicately*) fein ‹gewebt, gehäkelt usw.›; genau ‹ausbalanciert›; Ⓒ (*to a fine point or edge*) **a ~-sharpened blade** eine sorgfältig geschärfte Klinge; **a ~-pointed needle** eine feinspitzige Nadel; eine Nadel mit feiner Spitze; **a ~-drawn line** eine fein *od.* dünn [aus]gezogene Linie; Ⓓ (*into small particles*) fein ‹mahlen›; Ⓔ (*subtly*) fein[sinnig]

**fine 'print** ⇨ **small print**

**finery** /'faɪnərɪ/ *n., no pl.* Pracht, *die;* (*garments etc.*) Staat, *der;* **in all her wedding ~:** in ihrem Hochzeitsstaat

**finesse** /fɪ'nes/ ❶ *n.* Ⓐ (*refinement*) Feinheit, *die;* (*of diplomat*) Gewandtheit, *die;* (*delicate manipulation*) Finesse, *die;* Ⓑ (*artfulness*) Raffinesse, *die;* **the ~ of the negotiators** das Geschick der Verhandlungspartner; Ⓒ (*Cards*) Schneiden, *das.* ❷ *v.i.* Ⓐ mit aller Raffinesse vorgehen; Ⓑ (*Cards*) schneiden. ❸ *v.t.* (*Cards*) schneiden mit

**fine-tooth 'comb** *n.* fein gezähnter Kamm; **go through a manuscript** *etc.*/**house** *etc.* **with a ~** (*fig.*) ein Manuskript *usw.* Punkt für Punkt durchgehen/ein Haus *usw.* durchkämmen

**finger** /'fɪŋgə(r)/ ❶ *n.* Ⓐ ▶ 966 Finger, *der;* **sb.'s ~s itch [to do sth.]** es juckt jmdm. in den Fingern[, etw. zu tun] (*ugs.*); **lay a ~ on sb.** (*fig.*) jmdm. ein Härchen krümmen (*ugs.*); **they never lift** *or* **move** *or* **raise a ~ to help her** (*fig.*) sie rühren keinen Finger, um ihr zu helfen; **they didn't lift** *or* **move** *or* **raise a ~** (*fig.*) sie haben keinen Finger krumm gemacht; **get** *or* **pull** *or* **take one's ~ out** (*fig. coll.*) Dampf dahinter machen (*ugs.*); **point a** *or* **one's ~ at sb./sth.** mit dem Finger/(*fig. ugs.*) mit Fingern auf jmdn./etw. zeigen; **put the ~ on sb.** (*fig. coll.*) jmdn. verpfeifen (*ugs. abwertend*); **have a ~ in sth.** (*fig.*) die Finger in etw. (*Dat.*) haben; **put** *or* **lay one's ~ on sth.** (*fig.*) etw. genau ausmachen; **I can't put my ~ on it** (*fig.*) ich kann es nicht genau ausmachen; **sth. slips through sb.'s ~s** etw. gleitet jmdm. durch die Finger; (*fig.*) etw. geht jmdm. durch die Lappen (*ugs.*); **let sth. slip through one's ~s** (*fig.*) sich (*Dat.*) etw. entgehen *od.* (*ugs.*) durch die Lappen gehen lassen; **his ~s are [all] thumbs, he is all ~s and thumbs** er hat zwei linke Hände (*ugs.*); **count the things/people on the ~s of one hand** die Dinge/Menschen an einer Hand abzählen; Ⓑ (*of glove etc.*) Finger, *der;* Ⓒ (*finger-like object*) **chocolate ~:** Löffelbiskuit mit Schokoladeüberzug; **a ~ of toast** ein Streifen Toast; **sponge ~s** schmale Stücke Rührkuchen; Ⓓ (*coll.: amount of liquor*) Fingerbreit, *der;* **a ~ of whisky** ein Fingerbreit Whisky. ⇨ *also* **bone** 1 A; **burn**[1] 2 C; **cross** 2 A; **fish finger**; **forefinger**; **green** 1 A; **index finger**; **little finger**; **middle finger**; **pie**; **ring finger**.

❷ *v.t.* Ⓐ (*touch with ~s*) berühren ‹Ware›; greifen ‹Akkord›; (*turn about with ~s*) anfassen; (*toy or meddle with*) befingern; herumfingern an (+ *Dat.*); Ⓑ (*Amer. coll.: indicate*) **~ sb./sth. to the police** jmdn. bei der Polizei verpfeifen/etw. der Polizei stecken (*ugs. abwertend*)

**finger: ~board** *n.* Griffbrett, *das;* **~ bowl** *n.* Fingerschale, *die;* **~-end** Fingerspitze, *die;* **~ glass** ⇨ **~ bowl**

**fingering** /'fɪŋgərɪŋ/ *n.* (*Mus.*) Fingersatz, *der;* (*proper method*) Fingertechnik, *die*

**finger: ~mark** *n.* Fingerabdruck, *der;* **~nail** *n.* Fingernagel, *der;* **~ paint** *n.* Fingerfarbe, *die;* **~post** *n.* Wegweiser, *der;* **~print** ❶ *n.* Fingerabdruck, *der;* **leave one's ~prints** (*fig.*) seine Fingerabdrücke hinterlassen; ⇨ *also* **take** 1 I; ❷ *v.t.* einen Fingerabdruck nehmen von; **~print sb.** jmdm. die Fingerabdrücke abnehmen; **~stall** *n.* Fingerling, *der;* **~tip** *n.* Fingerspitze, *die;* **have sth. at one's ~tips** (*fig.*) etw. aus dem Effeff können *od.* im kleinen Finger haben (*ugs.*); **to the ~tips** (*fig.*) durch und durch; **he's a Spaniard to the very ~tips** er ist durch und durch Spanier

**finial** /'fɪnɪəl/ *n.* (*Archit.*) Kreuzblume, *die*

**finical** /'fɪnɪkl/, **finicking** /'fɪnɪkɪŋ/ *adjs.* heikel; **she's so ~ about her appearance** sie ist so heikel, wenn es um ihr Äußeres geht; **she's so ~ about what she eats** in puncto Essen ist sie sehr wählerisch

**finicky** /'fɪnɪkɪ/ *adj.* Ⓐ ⇨ **finical**; Ⓑ (*needing much attention to detail*) kniff[e]lig ‹Arbeit, Stickerei›

**finish** /'fɪnɪʃ/ ❶ *v.t.* Ⓐ (*bring to an end*) beenden ‹Unterhaltung›; erledigen ‹Arbeit›; abschließen ‹Kurs, Ausbildung›; **have you ~ed the letter/book?** hast du den Brief/das Buch fertig [geschrieben]?; **have ~ed sth.** etw. fertig haben; mit etw. fertig sein; **have ~ed doing one's homework** seine Hausaufgaben fertig haben; mit seinen Hausaufgaben fertig sein; **~ writing/reading sth.** etw. zu Ende schreiben/lesen; **haven't you ~ed eating yet?** hast du noch nicht zu Ende gegessen *od.* fertig gegessen?; *abs.* **please let me ~ [speaking]** bitte lassen Sie mich ausreden; **have you quite ~ed?** sind Sie fertig?; (*iron.*) nun, bist du jetzt endlich fertig?; Ⓑ (*get through*) aufessen ‹Mahlzeit›; auslesen ‹Buch, Zeitung›; austrinken ‹Flasche, Glas›; **I should ~ the book by this evening** ich müsste das Buch bis heute Abend durchhaben (*ugs.*); Ⓒ (*kill*) umbringen; (*destroy*) vernichten ‹Ernte›; (*coll.: overcome*) schaffen (*ugs.*); (*overcome completely*) bezwingen ‹Feind›; (*ruin*) zugrunde richten; **any more stress would ~ him** noch mehr Stress würde ihn kaputtmachen (*ugs.*); **a cold would ~ her** eine Erkältung würde das Ende für sie bedeuten; **it almost ~ed me!** das hat mich fast geschafft! (*ugs.*); **this scandal ~ed her as an actress** dieser Skandal bedeutete das Ende ihrer Schauspielerkarriere; Ⓓ (*perfect*) vervollkommnen; den letzten Schliff geben (+ *Dat.*); **~ a seam** einen Saum vernähen; Ⓔ (*complete education of*) ausbilden; (*make highly accomplished*) mit allen Fertigkeiten ausstatten; (*make polished*) verfeinern ‹Umgangsformen›; ausfeilen ‹Sprechweise›; Ⓕ (*complete manufacture of by surface treatment*) eine schöne Oberfläche geben (+ *Dat.*); glätten ‹Papier, Holz›; appretieren ‹Gewebe, Leder›; glasieren ‹Tonwaren›; polieren ‹Metall›; verputzen ‹Mauerwerk›; **~ sth. with a coat of varnish/waterproof coating/by polishing it** etw. zum Schluss lackieren/imprägnieren/polieren; **the ~ed article** *or* **product** das fertige Produkt.

❷ *v.i.* Ⓐ (*reach the end*) aufhören; ‹Geschichte, Episode:› enden; ‹Sturm, Unwetter:› sich legen; **when does the concert ~?** wann ist das Konzert aus?; **coffee to ~:** Kaffee zum Abschluss; Ⓑ (*come to end of race*) das Ziel erreichen; **~ first** als Erster durchs Ziel gehen; Erster werden; **~ badly/well** nicht durchhalten/einen guten Endspurt haben; Ⓒ **~ in sth.** mit etw. enden; **~ by doing sth.** zum Schluss etw. tun.

❸ *n.* Ⓐ (*termination, cause of ruin*) Ende, *das;* **fight to a ~:** bis zur Entscheidung kämpfen; **it would be the ~ of him as a politician** das würde das Ende seiner Karriere als Politiker bedeuten; Ⓑ (*Hunting*) Ende der Jagd; **be in at the ~:** beim Halali dabei sein; (*fig.*) das Ende *od.* den Schluss miterleben; Ⓒ (*point at which race etc. ends*) Ziel, *das;* **arrive at the ~:** das Ziel erreichen; durchs Ziel gehen; Ⓓ (*what serves to give completeness*) letzter Schliff; **a ~ to sth.** die Vervollkommnung *od.* Vollendung einer Sache; **form a perfect ~ to a memorable evening** einen krönenden Abschluss eines unvergesslichen Abends bilden; Ⓔ (*accomplished or completed state*) Schliff, *der;* **have ~:** Schliff haben; Ⓕ (*mode of finishing*) [technische] Ausführung; Finish, *das;* (*of paper*) Oberflächenfinish, *das;* (*of material, fabric*) Appretur, *die;* (*of metal*) Politur, *die;* **paintwork with a matt/gloss ~:** Matt-/Hochglanzlack, *der;* **kitchen furniture with a vinyl ~:** vinylbeschichtete Küchenmöbel

**~ 'off** *v.t.* Ⓐ ⇨ **finish** 1 C, D; Ⓑ (*provide with ending*) abschließen; beenden; **~ off a story** eine Geschichte zu Ende schreiben/erzählen; Ⓒ (**~** *or trim neatly*) sauber verarbeiten

**~ 'up** *v.i.* Ⓐ ⇨ **~** 2 C; Ⓑ = **end up;** Ⓒ (*complete all outstanding work*) alles erledigen

**~ with** *v.t.* Ⓐ (*complete one's use of*) **have you ~ed with the sugar?** brauchen Sie den Zucker noch?; **have ~ed with a book** ein Buch aus- *od.* fertig gelesen *od.* zu Ende gelesen haben; **are you ~ed with your plate?** hast du deinen Teller leer gegessen?; **if these clothes are ~ed with, then throw them away** wenn du diese Sachen nicht mehr brauchst, wirf sie weg; Ⓑ (*end association with*) brechen mit; **she ~ed with her boyfriend** sie hat mit ihrem Freund Schluss gemacht; Ⓒ **have ~ed with doing sth.** es aufgegeben haben, etw. zu tun

**finisher** /'fɪnɪʃə(r)/ *n.* Ⓐ (*person*) Fertigbearbeiter, *der*/-bearbeiterin, *die;* **metal-~:** Polierer, *der*/Poliererin, *die;* **cloth-~:** Appretierer, *der*/Appretiererin, *die;* Ⓑ (*coll.*) (*crushing blow*) vernichtender Schlag; **be a ~ to sb.** jmdn. schaffen *od.* jmdn. den Rest geben (*ugs.*)

**finishing: ~ post** *n.* Zielpfosten, *der;* **~ school** *n.* Mädchenpensionat, *das* (*veralt.*) (*besonders zur Vorbereitung auf das gesellschaftliche Leben*); **~ 'touch** *n.* **as a ~ touch to sth.** zur Vollendung *od.* Vervollkommnung einer Sache; um eine Sache abzurunden; **put the ~ touches to sth.** einer Sache (*Dat.*) den letzten Schliff geben

**finite** /'faɪnaɪt/ Ⓐ (*bounded*) begrenzt; **~ number** (*Math.*) endliche Zahl; Ⓑ (*Ling.*) finit

**Finland** /'fɪnlənd/ *pr. n.* Finnland (*das*)

**Finn** /fɪn/ *n.* ▶ 1340 Finne, *der*/Finnin, *die*

**Finnish** /'fɪnɪʃ/ ▶ 1275, ▶ 1340 ❶ *adj.* finnisch; **sb. is ~:** jmd. ist Finne/Finnin; **the ~ language** das Finnische; ⇨ *also* **English** 1. ❷ *n.* Finnisch, *das;* ⇨ *also* **English** 2 A

**'fin whale** ⇒ **rorqual**

**fiord** /fjɔ:d/ *n.* Fjord, *der*

**fir** /fɜ:(r)/ *n.* [A] *(tree)* Tanne, *die;* [B] *(wood)* Tanne, *die;* Tannenholz, *das.* ⇒ *also* **Scotch fir**; **silver fir**

**'fir cone** *n.* Tannenzapfen, *der*

**fire** /'faɪə(r)/ ❶ *n.* [A] Feuer, *das;* **set ~ to sth.** ‹Person:› etw. anzünden; **set ~ to oneself** sich anzünden; **strike ~ from sth.** Funken aus etw. schlagen; **be on ~:** brennen *(auch fig.)*; in Flammen stehen; **catch** *or* **take ~,** *(Scot., Ir.)* **go on ~** *(lit. or fig.)* Feuer fangen; ‹Wald, Gebäude:› in Brand geraten; **set sth. on ~:** etw. anzünden; *(in order to destroy)* etw. in Brand stecken; *(deliberately)* Feuer an etw. *(Akk.)* legen; **he won't/it's not going to set the Thames** *(Brit.)* *or (Amer.)* **the world on ~:** er hat das Pulver nicht erfunden *(ugs.)*/es ist nichts Weltbewegendes *od.* Welterschütterndes; [B] *(in grate)* [offenes] Feuer; *(electric or gas ~)* Heizofen, *der;* *(in the open air)* Lagerfeuer, *das;* **open ~:** Kaminfeuer, *das;* **round** *or* **by the ~:** am warmen Ofen; **over a low ~:** auf kleinem Feuer; **make up the ~:** nachlegen; **turn up the ~** *(electric)* die Heizung/*(gas)* das Gas höher drehen *od.* aufdrehen; **switch on another bar of the ~:** einen weiteren Heizstab einschalten; **have ~ in one's belly** *(ambition)* Ehrgeiz haben; *(enthusiasm)* begeisterungsfähig sein; **play with ~** *(lit. or fig.)* mit dem Feuer spielen; **light the ~:** den Ofen anstecken; *(in grate)* das [Kamin]feuer anmachen; **lay a ~:** ein Feuer anlegen; **make a ~:** ein Feuer [an]machen; [C] *(destructive burning)* Brand, *der;* **in case of ~, follow these instructions** bei Feuer *od.* im Brandfall ist diesen Anweisungen Folge zu leisten; **insure sth. against ~:** etw. gegen Feuer versichern; **where's the ~?** *(coll. iron.)* wo brennts denn? *(ugs.)*; **F~!** Feuer!; es brennt!; **go through ~ and water [to help sb.]** *(fig.)* [für jmdn.] durchs Feuer gehen; [D] *(fervour)* Feuer, *das;* **the ~ with which he speaks** die Leidenschaft, mit der er spricht; **his speech was full of ~:** er hielt eine glühende *od.* feurige *od.* *(geh.)* flammende Rede; [E] *(firing of guns)* Schießen, *das;* Schießerei, *die;* **pistol ~:** [Pistolen]schüsse; **cannon ~:** Kanonenfeuer, *das;* **be exposed to the ~ of critics** *(fig.)* im Kreuzfeuer der Kritik stehen; von den Kritikern unter Beschuss genommen werden; **line of ~** *(lit. or fig.)* Schusslinie, *die;* **running ~** *(lit. or fig.)* Trommelfeuer, *das;* **between two ~s** *(lit. or fig.)* zwischen zwei Feuern; **be/come under ~:** beschossen werden/unter Beschuss geraten; *(fig.)* heftig angegriffen werden/unter Beschuss geraten. ⇒ *also* **cease** 2 B; **coal** B; **draw** 1 B; **fat** 2; **frying pan**; **fuel** 1; **hang** 1 I; **hold** 1 T; **iron** 1 B; **open** 3 C; **smoke** 1 A.

❷ *v.t.* [A] *(set fire to)* anzünden; in Brand stecken; [B] *(kindle)* zünden ‹Sprengladung›; [C] *(fig.: stimulate)* beflügeln ‹Fantasie›; anregen ‹Ehrgeiz›; erregen ‹Interesse›; inspirieren, anregen ‹Person›; *(fill with enthusiasm)* begeistern, in Begeisterung versetzen ‹Person›; [D] *(bake)* brennen ‹Tonwaren, Ziegel›; [E] *(supply with fuel)* befeuern ‹Ofen›; [be]heizen ‹Lokomotive›; [F] *(cause to explode)* zünden ‹Sprengladung›; [in die Luft] sprengen ‹Mine›; [G] *(discharge)* abschießen ‹Gewehr›; abfeuern ‹Kanone›; **~ one's gun/pistol/rifle at sb.** auf jmdn. schießen; [H] *(produce with guns)* **~ a 21-gun salute** 21 Salutschüsse abgeben; [I] *(propel from gun etc.)* abgeben, abfeuern ‹Schuss›; *(fig.)* vom Stapel lassen *(ugs.)* ‹Kritik, Bemerkungen›; **~ a bullet/cartridge** einen Schuss abgeben; **~ blank cartridges** mit Platzpatronen schießen; **two shots were ~d/~d by sb.** es fielen zwei Schüsse/zwei Schüsse wurden von jmdm. abgegeben; **~ questions at sb.** jmdn. mit Fragen bombardieren; Fragen auf jmdn. abfeuern; [J] *(coll.: dismiss)* feuern *(ugs.)* ‹Angestellten›.

❸ *v.i.* [A] *(shoot)* schießen; feuern; **~!** [gebt] Feuer!; **be the first to ~:** das Feuer eröffnen; **~ at/on sth./sb.** auf etw./jmdn. schießen; **~ into the air/at the ground/into the crowd** in die Luft/in den Boden/in die Menge schießen; **~ on sth. from above** etw. aus der Luft beschießen; [B] ‹Motor:› zünden; **the engine is not firing properly** der Motor läuft nicht richtig

**~ a'way** *v.i.* *(fig. coll.)* losschießen *(fig. ugs.)*; **~ away!** schieß los!; fang an!

**~ 'out** *(Amer.)* ⇒ **~** 2 J

**fire: ~ alarm** *n.* Feuermelder, *der;* **~arm** *n.* Schusswaffe, *die;* **~ axe** *n.* Feuerwehraxt, *die;* **~ ball** *n.* [A] *(large meteor)* Feuerkugel, *die;* [B] *(ball of flame)* Feuerball, *der;* [C] *(globular lightning)* Kugelblitz, *der;* [D] *(energetic person)* Energiebündel, *das (ugs.)*; **~ bell** *n.* Feuerglocke, *die;* **~bomb** ❶ *n.* Brandsatz, *der;* *(aerial bomb)* Brandbombe, *die;* **~ bomb attack** Brandanschlag, *der;* ❷ *v.t.* **~bomb sth.** einen Brandanschlag auf etw. *(Akk.)* verüben; **~brand** *n.* Brandfackel, *die;* *(fig.)* Unruhestifter, *der/*-stifterin, *die;* Aufwiegler, *der/*Aufwieglerin, *die;* **~break** *n.* Brandschneise, *die;* **~-breathing** *adj.* Feuer speiend; **~brick** *n.* Schamottestein, *der;* **~ brigade** *n.* *(Brit.)* Feuerwehr, *die;* **~ bucket** *n.* Löscheimer, *der;* **~ chief** *n.* *(Amer.)* Branddirektor, *der;* **~clay** *n.* Schamotte, *die;* **~-damaged** *adj.* durch Brand beschädigt; **~damp** *n.* Grubengas, *das;* **~ department** *(Amer.)* ⇒ **~ brigade**; **~ door** *n.* Feuerschutztür, *die;* **~ drill** *n.* *(for firemen)* Feuerwehrübung, *die;* *(for others)* Probe[feuer]alarm, *der;* **~-eater** *n.* [A] *(conjurer)* Feuerschlucker, *der;* [B] *(fond of fighting)* Kampfhahn, *der (ugs.)*; *(fond of quarrelling)* Streithahn, *der (ugs.)*; **~ engine** *n.* Löschfahrzeug, *das;* **~ escape** *n.* *(staircase)* Feuertreppe, *die;* *(ladder)* Feuerleiter, *die;* **~ exit** *n.* Notausgang, *der;* **~ extinguisher** *n.* Feuerlöscher, *der;* **portable ~ extinguisher** Handfeuerlöscher, *der;* **~fighter** *n.* ▶ **1261** Feuerwehrmann, *der/*-frau, *die;* **~fighting** *n.* Feuerbekämpfung, *die;* Brandbekämpfung, *die;* **~fighting equipment** Feuerlöscheinrichtung, *die;* **~fly** *n.* Leuchtkäfer, *der;* Glühwürmchen, *das (ugs.)*; **~guard** *n.* Schutzgitter, *das;* Kamingitter, *das;* **~ hazard** *n.* Brandrisiko, *das;* **~ hose** *n.* Feuerwehrschlauch, *der;* **~ insurance** *n.* Feuerversicherung, *die;* Brandversicherung, *die;* **~ irons** *n. pl.* Kaminbesteck, *das;* **~light** *n.* Schein des Feuers; Schein der Flammen; **~lighter** *n.* *(Brit.)* Feueranzünder, *der;* **~man** /'faɪəmən/ *n., pl.* **~men** /'faɪəmən/ ▶ **1261** [A] *(member of fire brigade)* Feuerwehrmann, *der;* **~man's lift** Feuerwehrgriff, *der;* [B] *(Railw.)* Heizer, *der;* **~place** *n.* Kamin, *der;* **~power** *n.* Feuerkraft, *die;* **~ practice** ⇒ **~ drill**; **~ precautions** *n. pl.* Feuerschutz, *der;* **~proof** ❶ *adj.* feuerfest; ❷ *v.t.* feuerfest machen; **~-raiser** *n.* *(Brit.)* Brandstifter, *der/*-stifterin, *die;* **~-raising** *n.* *(Brit.)* Brandstiftung, *die;* **~-resistant** *adj.* feuerbeständig; **~ risk** ⇒ **~ hazard**; **~ screen** *n.* Ofenschirm, *der;* **F~ Service** *n.* Feuerwehr, *die;* **~side** *n.* Kaminecke, *die;* **at** *or* **by the ~side** am Kamin; **at** *or* **by one's own ~side** am heimischen Herde; **~side chat** Plauderei am Kamin; **~ station** *n.* Feuerwache, *die;* **~ tender** *n.* Gerätewagen *(der Feuerwehr)*; **~ tongs** *n. pl.* Feuerzange, *die;* **a pair of ~ tongs** eine Feuerzange; **~ trap** *n.* Feuerfalle, *die;* **~-walker** *n. jmd., der barfüßig über glühende Steine läuft;* Feuerläufer, *der/*-läuferin, *die;* **~wall** *n.* [A] Feuer[schutz]wand, *die;* [B] *(Computing)* Firewall, *die od. der;* **~-watcher** *n.* Feuerposten, *der;* Brandwart, *der;* *(in war)* Luftschutzwart, *der;* **~water** *n.* *(coll.)* Feuerwasser, *das (ugs.)*; **~wood** *n.* Brennholz, *das;* **~work** *n.* [A] Feuerwerkskörper, *der;* **~work display** Feuerwerk, *das;* [B] *in pl.* *(display)* Feuerwerk, *das;* *(fig.: display of wit)* Feuerwerk des Geistes; **intellectual ~works** ein geistiges *od.* intellektuelles Feuerwerk; **there were** *or* **it caused ~works** *(fig.)* da war was los *od.* flogen die Funken *(ugs.)*

**firing** /'faɪərɪŋ/ *n.* [A] *(of houses)* Anzünden, *das;* *(of pottery)* Brennen, *das;* [B] *(fuel)* Feuerung, *die;* **the ~ for these furnaces was coal** diese Öfen wurden mit Kohle befeuert; [C] *no pl.* *(of guns)* Abfeuern, *das;* **we could hear ~ in the distance** in der Ferne konnten wir Schüsse hören; **the ~ in the streets** die Schießerei in den Straßen

**firing: ~ line** *n.* *(lit. or fig.)* Feuerlinie, *die;* **~ party, ~ squad** *ns.* *(at military funeral)* Ehrensalutkommando, *das;* *(at military execution)* Exekutionskommando, *das*

**firm**[1] /fɜ:m/ *n.* [A] *(carrying on a business)* Firma, *die;* **~ of architects/decorators** Architektenbüro, *das/*Malerbetrieb, *der;* [B] *(group working together)* Team, *das;* Arbeitsgemeinschaft, *die*

**firm**[2] ❶ *adj.* [A] fest; stabil ‹Verhältnis, Konstruktion, Stuhl›; straff ‹Busen›; stramm ‹Bäckchen›; verbindlich ‹Angebot›; **be on ~ ground again** *(lit. or fig.)* wieder festen Boden unter den Füßen haben; **do sth. to make a chair/bench ~:** etw. tun, damit ein Stuhl/eine Bank fest steht; **as ~ as a rock** felsenfest; **they are ~ friends** sie sind gut befreundet; **have a ~ grip on sth.** etw. fest in der Hand haben; **the chair is not ~:** der Stuhl wackelt *od.* ist wacklig; **make a ~ date** eine feste Zeit vereinbaren; [B] *(resolute)* entschlossen ‹Blick›; bestimmt, entschieden ‹Ton›; stark ‹Widerstand›; **in ~ pursuit of his goal** in energischer *od.* entschiedener Verfolgung seines Ziels; **be a ~ believer in sth.** fest an etw. *(Akk.)* glauben; **be ~ when you speak to him** sei bestimmt, wenn du mit ihm sprichst; **be ~ in one's beliefs** fest auf seiner Überzeugung beharren; an seiner Überzeugung festhalten; **~ insistence** Beharrlichkeit, *die;* **she has a ~ character** sie besitzt Charakterstärke; [C] *(insisting on obedience etc.)* bestimmt; **be ~ with sb.** jmdm. gegenüber bestimmt auftreten; **a ~ hand** eine feste Hand; **with a ~ hand** mit fester *od.* starker Hand; [D] *(Commerc.)* fest; stabil ‹Markt›; **oil is not ~:** der Ölmarkt ist nicht stabil.

❷ *adv.* **stand ~!** *(fig.)* sei standhaft!; lass dich nicht davon abbringen!; **stand ~ in sth.** *(fig.)* fest *od.* unerschütterlich bei etw. bleiben; **hold ~ to sth.** *(fig.)* an einer Sache festhalten.

❸ *v.t.* [A] *(make firm or solid)* fest werden lassen; festigen, straffen ‹Muskulatur, Körper›; [B] fest [ein]pflanzen ‹Pflanzen›

**~ 'up** ❶ *v.t.* konkretisieren ‹Plan, Geschäft, Vereinbarung›. ❷ *v.i.* ‹Plan, Geschäft, Vereinbarung:› sich konkretisieren

**firmament** /'fɜ:məmənt/ *n.* *(literary)* Firmament, *das*

**firmly** /'fɜ:mlɪ/ *adv.* [A] fest; **the jelly has set ~:** der Gelee ist fest geworden; **a ~-built structure** eine stabile Konstruktion; **sth. is ~ under lock and key** etw. ist sicher weggeschlossen; [B] *(resolutely)* beharrlich ‹unterstützen, sich widersetzen›; bestimmt, energisch ‹reden›; **deal with** *or* **treat sb. ~:** jmdm. gegenüber bestimmt auftreten

**firmness** /'fɜ:mnɪs/ *n., no pl.* [A] *(solidity)* Festigkeit, *die;* *(of foundations, building)* Stabilität, *die;* *(of offer)* Verbindlichkeit, *die;* [B] *(resoluteness)* Entschlossenheit, *die;* *(of voice)* Bestimmtheit, *die;* *(of support, belief)* Beständigkeit, *die;* Beharrlichkeit, *die;* **the ~ of his resolve** seine feste Entschlossenheit; [C] *(insistence on obedience etc.)* Bestimmtheit, *die;* **use ~ with sb., treat sb. with ~:** jmdm. gegenüber bestimmt auftreten

**'firmware** *n., no pl., no indef. art.* *(Computing)* Firmware, *die*

**first** /fɜ:st/ ❶ *adj.* ▶ **1352** erst...; *(for the ~ time ever)* Erst‹aufführung, -besteigung›; *(of an artist's ~ achievement)* Erstlings‹film, -roman, -stück, -werk›; **he was ~ to arrive** er kam als Erster an; **who was ~?** wer war Erster?; **for the [very] ~ time** zum [aller]ersten Mal; **there's always a ~ time** *(coll.)* irgendwann passierts dann eben doch *(ugs.)*; **~ thing you know** *(coll.)* ehe du dich's versiehst; **just buy the ~ thing one sees** das erste Beste kaufen; **I'll do it at the ~ opportunity** ich tue es bei der erstbesten Gelegenheit; **say the ~ thing that comes into one's head** das sagen, was einem zuerst einfällt; **the ~ two** die ersten beiden *od.* zwei; **come in ~** *(win race)* [das Rennen] gewinnen; **head/feet ~:** mit dem Kopf/den Füßen zuerst *od.* voran; **~ thing after breakfast**

(*coll.*) gleich nach dem Frühstück; **~ thing in the morning** gleich frühmorgens; (*coll.: tomorrow*) gleich morgen früh; **~ thing on arrival** (*coll.*) gleich nach der Ankunft; **the ~ thing [to do]** (*coll.*) das Erste [, was man tun muss]; **~ things ~** (*coll.*) eins nach dem anderen; immer [hübsch] der Reihe nach; **have [the] ~ claim to sth.** eine Option auf etw. (*Akk.*) haben; **she is ~ in the class** sie ist Klassenbeste *od.* die Beste in der Klasse; **he's always [the] ~ to help** er ist immer als Erster zur Stelle, wenn Hilfe benötigt wird; **not know the ~ thing about sth.** von einer Sache nicht das Geringste verstehen; **~ soprano/cello** (*Mus.*) erster Sopran/Cellist; ⇒ *also* **eighth** 1.

❷ *adv.* Ⓐ (*before anyone else*) zuerst; als Erster/Erste ‹sprechen, ankommen›; (*before anything else*) an erster Stelle ‹stehen, kommen›; (*when listing: firstly*) zuerst; als Erstes; **women and children ~!** Frauen und Kinder zuerst; **ladies ~!** Ladys first!; den Damen der Vortritt!; **you [go] ~** (*as invitation*) Sie haben den Vortritt; bitte nach Ihnen; **~ come ~ served** wer zuerst kommt, mahlt zuerst (*Spr.*); **we must put our children's education ~:** die Schulbildung unserer Kinder muss für uns an erster Stelle stehen; **this matter is** *or* **comes ~ on the agenda** diese Angelegenheit ist der erste Punkt unserer Tagesordnung; **come ~ with sb.** (*fig.*) bei jmdm. zuerst kommen; **say ~ one thing and then another** erst so und dann wieder so sagen (*ugs.*); Ⓑ (*beforehand*) vorher; **... but ~ we must ...:** ... aber zuerst *od.* erst müssen wir ...; Ⓒ (*for the ~ time*) zum ersten Mal; das erste Mal; erstmals ‹bekannt geben, sich durchsetzen›; Ⓓ (*in preference*) eher; lieber; **I'd [rather] die ~:** eher *od.* lieber würde ich sterben; **I wouldn't give him a penny. I'd see him damned ~:** ich würde ihm keinen Pfennig geben, soll er zum Teufel gehen! (*ugs.*); Ⓔ **~ of all** zuerst; (*in importance*) vor allem; **~ of all let me express my gratitude to you** zu[aller]erst *od.* als Erstes möchte ich Ihnen meinen Dank aussprechen; **~ and foremost** (*basically*) zunächst einmal; (*in importance*) vor allem; **~ and last** (*almost entirely*) in erster Linie; (*reckoned altogether*) im Ganzen; insgesamt; Ⓕ (*~-class*) **travel ~:** erster Klasse reisen.

❸ *n.* Ⓐ **the ~** (*in sequence, rank*) der/die/das Erste; **the ~ shall be last** (*Bibl.*) die Ersten werden die Letzten sein; **be the ~ to arrive** als Erster/Erste ankommen; **she is the ~ in the class** sie ist Klassenbeste *od.* die Beste in der Klasse; **~ among equals** Primus inter pares (*geh.*); **this is the ~ I've heard of it** das höre ich zum ersten Mal; Ⓑ **at ~:** zuerst; anfangs; **from the ~:** von Anfang an; **from ~ to last** von Anfang bis Ende; **I've always said from ~ to last that ...:** ich habe schon immer gesagt, dass ...; **it took five years, from ~ to last** es hat alles in allem fünf Jahre gedauert; Ⓒ ▶ 1055 (*day*) **the ~ of May** der erste Mai; **the ~ [of the month]** der Erste [des Monats]; Ⓓ (*Brit. Univ.*) Eins, *die;* (*person*) **he's a ~ [in History]** er hat eine Eins [in Geschichte] bekommen; **get** *or* **take** *or* **be awarded a ~ in one's finals** sein Examen mit [der Note] Eins bestehen; Ⓔ (*~ form*) erste [Schul]klasse; Erste, *die* (*Schuljargon*); Ⓕ (*Motor Veh.*) erster Gang; **in ~:** im ersten [Gang]; **change down to ~:** in den ersten [Gang] runterschalten; Ⓖ (*pioneering feat*) Pioniertat, *die;* Ⓗ *in pl.* (*best-quality goods*) erstklassige Ware; Ware von erster *od.* bester Qualität. ⇒ *also* **eighth** 2

**first: ~ 'aid** *n.* erste Hilfe; **give [sb.] ~ aid** [jmdm.] erste Hilfe leisten; **~-aid tent/post** *or* **station** Sanitätszelt, *das*/-wache, *die;* **~-aid box/kit** Verbandskasten, *der*/Erste-Hilfe-Ausrüstung, *die;* **~ 'base** ⇒ **base**[1] 1 C; **~ 'blood** ⇒ **blood** 1 A; **~-born** ❶ *adj.* erstgeboren; ❷ *n.* Erstgeborene, *der/die;* **~ 'class** *n.* Ⓐ erste Kategorie; (*for produce*) Klasse A; Ⓑ (*Transport*) erste Klasse; **travel in the ~ class** erster Klasse reisen; Ⓒ (*Brit. Univ.*) ⇒ **first** 3 D; Ⓓ (*Post*) *bevorzugt beförderte Post;* **~-class** ❶ /ˈ--/ *adj.* Ⓐ (*of the ~ class*) **~-class carriage** Erste[r]-Klasse-Wagen, *der;* **~-class ticket** Fahrkarte erster Klasse; **~-class compartment** Erste[r]-Klasse-Abteil, *das;* Abteil erster Klasse; **~-class honours degree** (*Brit. Univ.*) Prädikatsexamen, *das;* **~-class mail** *or* **post** *bevorzugt beförderte Post;* **~-class stamp** *Briefmarke für bevorzugt beförderte Post;* Ⓑ (*excellent*) erstklassig; **a ~-class idiot** (*iron.*) ein Vollidiot; ❷ /-ˈ-/ *adv.* Ⓐ (*by the ~ class*) erster Klasse ‹reisen›; **send a letter ~-class** *einen Brief bevorzugt befördern lassen;* Ⓑ (*coll.: excellently*) prima (*ugs.*); großartig; **~ 'coat** *n.* (*of paint*) erster Anstrich; **~ 'cousin** ⇒ **cousin**; **~ e'dition** *n.* Erstausgabe, *die;* **~ 'floor** ⇒ **floor** 1 B; **~ form** ⇒ **form** 1 D; **~ 'fruits** *n. pl.* Erstlinge *Pl.;* (*fig.*) erste Ergebnisse; **~ 'gear** *n., no pl.* (*Motor Veh.*) erster Gang; ⇒ *also* **gear** 1 A; **~hand** *adj.* aus erster Hand *nachgestellt;* **from ~hand experience** aus eigener Erfahrung; **have ~hand knowledge of sth.** etw. aus erster Hand wissen; **have ~hand acquaintance with suffering** viel Leid erfahren haben; ⇒ *also* **hand** 1 J; **F~ 'Lady** *n.* First Lady, *die;* **~ lieu'tenant** ⇒ **lieutenant** A; **~ 'light** *n.* **at ~ light** im *od.* beim Morgengrauen

**firstly** /ˈfɜːstlɪ/ *adv.* zunächst [einmal]; (*followed by 'secondly'*) erstens

**first: ~ name** *n.* Vorname, *der;* **be on ~-name terms with sb.** jmdn. mit Vornamen anreden; **~-named** *attrib. adj.* erstgenannt...; **~ 'night** *n.* (*Theatre*) Premiere, *die;* **~-night nerves/audience** Premierenfieber, *das*/-publikum, *das;* **~ off** *adv.* (*coll.*) zuerst; **~ of'fender** *n.* Ersttäter, *der;* **~ 'officer** *n.* (*Naut.*) Erster Offizier; **~ 'person** ⇒ **person** D; **~ 'proof** ⇒ **proof** 1 F; **~-rate** ❶ /ˈ--/ *adj.* Ⓐ (*excellent*) erstklassig; Ⓑ (*coll.*) **feel a ~-rate fool** (*iron.*) sich (*Dat.*) wie ein Dummkopf ersten Ranges vorkommen; ❷ /-ˈ-/ *adv.* (*coll.*) prima (*ugs.*); großartig; **~ 'reading** ⇒ **reading** G; **~ refusal** ⇒ **refusal**; **~ school** *n.* (*Brit.*) ≈ Grundschule, *die;* **F~ 'Secretary** *n.* Erster Sekretär; **~ 'strike** *n.* (*Mil.*) Erstschlag, *der;* Präventivschlag, *der;* **~-strike capability** Präventivschlagkapazität, *die;* **~ 'string** ⇒ **string** 1 B; **~-time** *attrib. adj.* **~-time voter** Erstwähler, *der;* **~-time buyer** *jmd., der zum ersten Mal ein eigenes Haus/eine Eigentumswohnung kauft;* **~ 'water** ⇒ **water** 1 D

**firth** /fɜːθ/ *n.* Förde, *die*

**'fir tree** ⇒ **fir** A

**fiscal** /ˈfɪskl/ *adj.* fiskalisch; finanzpolitisch; **~ policy** Fiskal- *od.* Finanzpolitik, *die;* **~ year** (*Brit.*) Geschäftsjahr, *das;* Rechnungsjahr, *das;* (*Amer.*) Finanzjahr, *das;* Etatjahr, *das;* **~ autonomy** Finanzhoheit, *die*

**fiscally** /ˈfɪskəlɪ/ *adv.* fiskalisch; finanzpolitisch

**fish** /fɪʃ/ ❶ *n., pl. same or* (*esp. child lang./poet.*) **~es** Ⓐ Fisch, *der;* **~ and chips** Fisch mit Pommes frites; **~ and chip shop** ≈ Fischbraterei, *die;* **a big ~ in a little pond** (*fig.*) ein Großer bei den Kleinen; **a little ~ in a big pond** (*fig.*) nur einer von vielen; **[be] like a ~ out of water** [sich] wie ein Fisch auf dem Trockenen [fühlen]; **drink like a ~** (*coll.*) wie ein Loch saufen (*derb*); **have other ~ to fry** (*fig. coll.*) Wichtigeres zu tun haben; **neither ~ nor fowl** (*fig.*) weder Fisch noch Fleisch (*ugs.*); **there are plenty more ~ in the sea** (*fig. coll.*) es gibt noch andere auf der Welt; Ⓑ (*Astrol.*) **the F~[es]** die Fische; ⇒ *also* **archer** B; Ⓒ (*coll.: person*) **queer ~:** komischer Kauz; **big ~:** großes Tier; großer *od.* dicker Fisch (*ugs., scherzh.*); **cold ~:** kalter Fisch (*ugs.*); **the poor ~!** der arme Tropf!

❷ *v.i.* Ⓐ fischen; (*with rod*) angeln; **go ~ing** fischen/angeln gehen; **go trout-~ing** auf Forellenfang gehen; **~ in troubled waters** (*fig.*) im Trüben fischen; Ⓑ (*fig. coll.*) (*try to get information*) auf Informationen aus sein; (*delve*) **~ around in one's bag** in der Tasche herumsuchen.

❸ *v.t.* Ⓐ fischen; fangen ‹Fisch›; (*with rod*) angeln; **~ a river/lake** in einem Fluss/See fischen/angeln; Ⓑ (*fig.: take, pull*) [heraus]fischen (*ugs.*) (**out of** aus)

**~ for** *v.t.* Ⓐ fischen/angeln; fischen/angeln auf (+ *Akk.*) (*Anglerjargon*); Ⓑ (*fig. coll.*) suchen nach; **be ~ing for sth.** auf etw. (*Akk.*) aus sein (*ugs.*)

**~ 'out** *v.t.* (*fig. coll.*) herausfischen (*ugs.*); **~ sb./a dead body out of the river** jmdn./eine Leiche aus dem Fluss fischen (*ugs.*)

**~ 'up** *v.t.* herausfischen

**fish: ~ bone** *n.* [Fisch]gräte, *die;* **~bowl** *n.* Fischglas, *das;* **~ cake** *n.* (*Cookery*) Fischfrikadelle, *die;* **~ course** *n.* Fischgang, *der*

**fisherman** /ˈfɪʃəmən/ *n., pl.* **fishermen** /ˈfɪʃəmən/ ▶ 1261 Fischer, *der;* (*angler*) Angler, *der;* **~'s story** Seemannsgarn, *das*

**fishery** /ˈfɪʃərɪ/ *n.* Ⓐ *no pl., no indef. art.* (*fishing*) Fischfang, *der;* Fischerei, *die;* Ⓑ (*fishing grounds*) Fischfanggebiet, *das;* Fischereigewässer, *das;* **in-shore fisheries** Küstenfischerei, *die;* **deep-sea fisheries** Hochseefischerei, *die*

**fishery pro'tection vessel** *n.* (*Naut.*) Fischereischutzboot, *das*

**fish: ~eye lens** *n.* (*Photog.*) Fischaugenobjektiv, *das;* **~ farm** *n.* Fischzucht[anlage], *die;* **~ farming** *n.* Fischzucht, *die;* **~ 'finger** *n.* Fischstäbchen, *das;* **~ fork** *n.* Fischgabel, *die;* **~-glue** *n.* Fischleim, *der;* **~-hook** *n.* Angelhaken, *der*

**fishing** /ˈfɪʃɪŋ/ *n.* (*occupation*) Fischen, *das;* (*with rod*) Angeln, *das; attrib.* Fischerei-; **freshwater ~:** Süßwasserfischerei, *die;* **~ craft** *pl.* Fischereifahrzeuge *Pl.*

**fishing: ~ boat** *n.* Fischerboot, *das;* **~ expedition** *n.* Ⓐ Fangfahrt, *die;* **go on a ~ expedition** auf Fischfang gehen; Ⓑ (*fig.*) Schnüffeltour, *die* (*ugs.*); **~ fleet** *n.* Fischereiflotte, *die;* **~ grounds** *n. pl.* Fischgründe *Pl.;* **~ limits** *n. pl.* Fischereigrenze, *die;* **~line** *n.* Angelschnur, *die;* **~ net** *n.* Fischernetz, *das;* **~ rights** *n. pl.* Fischereirecht, *das;* **~ rod** *n.* Angelrute, *die;* **~ smack** *n.* Fischkutter, *der;* **~ story** *n.* Seemannsgarn, *das;* **~ tackle** *n.* Angelgeräte *Pl.;* **~ vessel** *n.* Fischereifahrzeug, *das;* **~ village** *n.* Fischerdorf, *das*

**fish: ~ kettle** *n.* Fischkessel, *der;* **~ knife** *n.* Fischmesser, *das;* **~ knife and -fork** Fischbesteck, *das;* **~ ladder** *n.* Fischleiter, *die;* Fischpass, *der;* **~like** *adj.* fischartig; **~meal** *n.* Fischmehl, *das;* **~monger** /ˈfɪʃmʌŋɡə(r)/ *n.* ▶ 1261 (*Brit.*) Fischhändler, *der*/-händlerin, *die;* **a ~monger's** ein Fischgeschäft; ⇒ *also* **baker**; **~net** *n.* Fischnetz, *das;* **~net stockings** Netzstrümpfe; **~ paste** *n.* Fischpaste, *die;* **~ pond** *n.* Fischteich, *der;* **~ shop** *n.* Fischgeschäft, *das;* **~ slice** *n.* Wender, *der;* (*carving knife*) Fischvorlegemesser, *das;* **~ tank** *n.* Fischkasten, *der;* Fischbehälter, *der;* **~wife** *n.* (*derog.*) Fischweib, *das* (*veralt.*)

**fishy** /ˈfɪʃɪ/ *adj.* Ⓐ fischartig; **~ smell/taste** Fischgeruch/-geschmack, *der;* Ⓑ (*coll.: questionable*) verdächtig; zweifelhaft, fragwürdig ‹Umstände›; nicht ganz astrein (*ugs.*) ‹Sache›; **there's something ~ about this whole business** an der ganzen Sache ist was faul (*ugs.*)

**fissile** /ˈfɪsaɪl/ *adj.* (*Nucl. Phys.*) fissil (*fachspr.*); spaltbar

**fission** /ˈfɪʃn/ *n.* Ⓐ (*Nucl. Phys.*) [Kern]spaltung, *die;* Fission, *die* (*fachspr.*); Ⓑ (*Biol.*) [Zell]teilung, *die;* Fission, *die* (*fachspr.*)

**fissionable** /ˈfɪʃənəbl/ *adj.* (*Nucl. Phys.*) spaltbar; fissil (*fachspr.*)

**fissure** /ˈfɪʃə(r)/ *n.* Riss, *der;* (*Geol.*) Erdspalte, *die;* Bodenriss, *der*

**fist** /fɪst/ *n.* Ⓐ Faust, *die;* Ⓑ (*coll.: hand*) Hand, *die;* Pfote, *die* (*salopp*); (*joc.: handwriting*) Handschrift, *die;* Klaue, *die* (*ugs. abwertend*)

**'fist fight** *n.* Schlägerei, *die*

**fistful** /ˈfɪstfʊl/ *n.* Handvoll, *die;* **a ~ of coins** eine Hand voll Münzen

**fisticuffs** /ˈfɪstɪkʌfs/ *n. pl.* Handgreiflichkeiten *Pl.;* **the quarrel ended in ~:** der Streit endete mit einer Schlägerei

**fistula** /ˈfɪstjʊlə/ *n.* (*Med., Zool.*) Fistel, *die*

**fit¹** /fɪt/ *n.* **A** Anfall, *der;* **~ of coughing** Hustenanfall, *der;* **fainting ~:** Ohnmachtsanfall, *der;* **collapse in a ~:** einen Kollaps *od.* Anfall erleiden; zusammenbrechen; **epileptic ~:** epileptischer Anfall; **B** (*fig.*) [plötzliche] Anwandlung; **give sb. a ~** (*startle sb.*) jmdm. einen Schrecken einjagen; (*outrage sb.*) jmdn. aus der Haut fahren lassen (*ugs.*); **[almost] have** *or* **throw a ~:** [fast] Zustände kriegen (*ugs.*); **she'll have a ~ when she hears that** (*fig. coll.*) sie kriegt einen Anfall, wenn sie das erfährt (*ugs.*); **have forty ~s** (*coll.*) Zustände kriegen (*ugs.*); einen Anfall bekommen (*ugs.*); **be in ~s of laughter** sich vor Lachen biegen; **sb./sth. has sb. in ~s [of laughter]** jmd. ruft dröhnendes Gelächter bei jmdm. hervor/etw. löst dröhnendes Gelächter bei jmdm. aus; **in a ~ of ...:** in einem Anfall *od.* einer Anwandlung von ...; **in** *or* **by ~s [and starts]** mit [häufigen] Unterbrechungen

**fit²** **1** *adj.* **A** (*suitable*) geeignet; **~ to eat** *or* **to be eaten/for human consumption** essbar/zum Verzehr geeignet; **be ~ to be seen** sich sehen lassen können; ⇒ *also* **survival** A; **B** (*worthy*) würdig; wert; **a man not ~ to hold high office** ein Mann, der eines hohen Amtes nicht würdig ist; ⇒ *also* **candle** 1 A; **C** (*right and proper*) richtig; **as is only ~ [and proper]** wie es sich gehört *od.* (*geh.*) gebührt; **see** *or* **think ~ [to do sth.]** es für richtig *od.* angebracht halten[, etw. zu tun]; **do as you see** *or* **think ~:** tu, was du für richtig hältst; **D** (*ready*) **be ~ to drop** zum Umfallen müde sein; **E** (*healthy*) gesund; fit (*ugs.*); in Form (*ugs.*); **keep** *or* **stay ~:** sich fit halten; fit bleiben; **get ~ again after an illness** nach einer Krankheit wieder zu Kräften kommen; **be ~ and well** in guter körperlicher Verfassung sein; **~ for duty** *or* **service** dienstfähig *od.* -tauglich; **~ for work/travel** arbeits-/reisefähig; ⇒ *also* **fiddle** 1 A.
**2** *n.* Passform, *die;* **it is a good/bad ~:** es sitzt *od.* passt gut/nicht gut; **be an excellent ~:** einen tadellosen Sitz haben; wie angegossen sitzen *od.* passen; **the coat is a tight ~:** das Jackett sitzt stramm *od.* ist eng; **three in the back seat is a tight ~:** drei auf dem Rücksitz ist sehr eng; **I can just get it in the suitcase, but it's a tight ~** (*fig.*) ich kriege es noch in den Koffer, aber nur gerade so (*ugs.*).
**3** *v.t.*, **-tt-** **A** ‹Kleider:› passen (+ *Dat.*); ‹Schlüssel:› passen in (+ *Akk.*); ‹Deckel, Bezug:› passen auf (+ *Akk.*); **the suit ~s him properly** der Anzug passt ihm gut *od.* sitzt gut; **make sth. to ~:** etw. passend machen; **B** (*Dressm. etc.*) anpassen ‹Kleidungsstück, Brille›; **when may I come to be ~ted?** wann kann ich zur Anprobe kommen?; **C** (*correspond to, suit*) entsprechen (+ *Dat.*); (*make correspond*) abstimmen (**to** auf + *Akk.*); anpassen (**to** an + *Akk.*); **the description ~s this man** die Beschreibung passt auf diesen Mann *od.* trifft auf diesen Mann zu; **the translation ~s the context** die Übersetzung wird dem Kontext gerecht; **~ the bill** = **fill the bill** ⇒ **fill** 1 D; **D** (*put into place*) anbringen (**to** an + *Dat. od. Akk.*); einbauen ‹Motor, Ersatzteil›; einsetzen ‹Scheibe, Tür, Schloss›; (*equip*) ausstatten; **E** (*make competent*) befähigen (**for** zu); **the experience helped to ~ her for the task** die Erfahrung trug dazu bei, dass sie für die Aufgabe gerüstet war.
**4** *v.i.*, **-tt-** passen; (*agree*) zusammenpassen; übereinstimmen; **~ well** ‹Kleidungsstück:› gut sitzen; **the two pieces ~ together to form a screwdriver** die beiden Teile zusammen ergeben einen Schraubenzieher; **we must find a lid that ~s** wir müssen einen passenden Deckel finden; ⇒ *also* **cap** 1 A; **glove** A

**~ 'in** **1** *v.t.* **A** unterbringen; **B** (*install*) einbauen; **C** (*to a schedule*) einen Termin geben (+ *Dat.*); unterbringen, einschieben ‹Treffen, Besuch, Sitzung›; **I could ~ you in just before lunch** so kurz vor Mittag hätte ich Zeit für Sie; **the hairdresser usually manages to ~ me in** gewöhnlich kann mich der Friseur zwischendurch drannehmen (*ugs.*); **~ sth. in with sth.** etw. mit etw. abstimmen.
**2** *v.i.* **A** hineinpassen; **B** (*be in accordance*) **~ in with sth.** mit etw. übereinstimmen; **~ in with sb.'s plan/ideas** in jmds. Plan/Konzept (*Akk.*) passen; **how does that ~ in?** wie passt das dazu *od.* ins Ganze?; **it didn't ~ in with our plans** es ließ sich nicht mit unseren Plänen vereinbaren; **I'll just ~ in with you/your arrangements** ich richte mich ganz nach dir/deinen Plänen; **C** (*settle harmoniously*) ‹Person:› sich anpassen (**with** an + *Akk.*); **~ in easily with a group** sich leicht in eine Gruppe einfügen; **he ~s in well here/with the others** er passt gut hierher/mit den anderen zusammen

**~ 'out** *v.t.* ausstatten; (*for expedition etc.*) ausrüsten

**~ 'up** *v.t.* (*fix*) anbringen ‹Lampe, Waschbecken›; (*install, mount*) aufstellen ‹Arbeitsbank usw.›; **~ sb./sth. up with sth.** jmdn./etw. mit einer Sache versehen *od.* ausstatten; **~ a room up as an office** ein Zimmer als Büro einrichten

**fitful** /ˈfɪtfl/ *adj.* unbeständig; unruhig ‹Schlaf›; vereinzelt ‹Schüsse›; ungleichmäßig ‹Fortgang, Arbeitsweise›; launisch ‹Brise›

**fitfully** /ˈfɪtfəlɪ/ *adv.* unregelmäßig; sporadisch ‹arbeiten›; unruhig ‹schlafen›; **the sun shone ~:** die Sonne kam vereinzelt durch

**fitfulness** /ˈfɪtflnɪs/ *n., no pl.* Unbeständigkeit, *die;* (*of sleep*) Unregelmäßigkeit, *die*

**fitment** /ˈfɪtmənt/ *n.* (*piece of furniture*) Einrichtungsgegenstand, *der;* (*piece of equipment*) Zubehörteil, *das;* **~s** Ausstattung, *die*

**fitness** /ˈfɪtnɪs/ *n., no pl.* **A** (*physical*) Fitness, *die;* **~ for active service** (*Mil.*) Wehrdiensttauglichkeit, *die;* **B** (*suitability*) Eignung, *die;* (*appropriateness*) Angemessenheit, *die;* **have a sense of the ~ of things** ein Gefühl dafür haben, was angebracht *od.* angemessen ist

**'fitness studio** *n.* Fitnessstudio, *das*

**fitted** /ˈfɪtɪd/ *adj.* **A** (*suited*) geeignet (**for** für, zu); **B** (*shaped*) tailliert, auf Taille gearbeitet ‹Kleider›; **~ carpet** Teppichboden, *der;* **~ sheet** Spannbettuch, *das;* **~ kitchen/cupboards** Einbauküche, *die*/Einbauschränke

**fitter** /ˈfɪtə(r)/ *n.* ▶ 1261 **A** Monteur, *der;* (*of pipes*) Installateur, *der;* (*of machines*) Maschinenschlosser, *der;* **electrical ~:** Elektriker, *der;* Elektroinstallateur, *der;* **B** (*of clothes*) Schneider, *der*/Schneiderin, *die* (*als Zuschneider u. für Änderungen*)

**fitting** /ˈfɪtɪŋ/ **1** *adj.* (*appropriate*) passend; angemessen; geeignet ‹Moment, Zeitpunkt›; günstig, passend ‹Gelegenheit›; (*becoming*) schicklich (*geh.*) ‹Benehmen›; **I thought it ~ to inform him** ich hielt es für angebracht, ihn zu informieren; **it is not ~ for a young woman ...:** es schickt sich nicht für eine junge Dame, ... **2** *n.* **A** *usu. in pl.* (*fixture*) Anschluss, *der;* (*connecting piece used for installations*) Fitting, *das* (*Technik*); **~s** (*furniture*) Ausstattung, *die;* **a car with luxurious ~s** ein Wagen mit Luxusausstattung; **electrical ~s** Elektroinstallationen *Pl.;* ⇒ *also* **fixture** A; **B** (*of clothes*) Anprobe, *die;* **go to the tailor's for a ~:** zur Anprobe gehen; **C** (*Brit.: size*) Größe, *die;* **shoes of a wide/narrow ~:** weite/enge Schuhe

**fittingly** /ˈfɪtɪŋlɪ/ *adv.* passend ‹sich kleiden›; angemessen ‹enden›; schicklich ‹sich benehmen›

**fitting:** **~-room** *n.* Anprobe, *die;* **~-shop** *n.* Montagehalle, *die*

**five** /faɪv/ ▶ 912, ▶ 1012, ▶ 1352 **1** *adj.* **A** fünf; ⇒ *also* **eight** 1; **B** **~-finger exercise** (*Mus.: also fig.*) Fingerübung, *die;* **~ o'clock shadow** [nachmittäglicher] Stoppelbart (*ugs.*); ⇒ *also* **week**. **2** *n.* (*number, symbol*) Fünf, *die;* ⇒ *also* **eight** 2 A, C, D

**five-and-'dime, five-and-'ten** *n.* (*Amer.*) Billigkaufhaus, *das*

**fivefold** /ˈfaɪvfəʊld/ *adj., adv.* fünffach; ⇒ *also* **eightfold**

**fiver** /ˈfaɪvə(r)/ *n.* ▶ 1328 (*coll.*) (*Brit.*) Fünfpfundschein, *der;* (*Amer.*) Fünfdollarschein, *der*

**fives** /faɪvz/ *n. sing.: ein Wandballspiel;* **Eton** /ˈiːtn/ **~** *Wandballspiel mit drei Wänden;* **Rugby ~** *Wandballspiel mit vier Wänden*

**five:** **~-star** *adj.* Fünf-Sterne-‹Hotel, General›; (*fig.*) ausgezeichnet; **~-'year plan** *n.* Fünfjahresplan, *der*

**fix** /fɪks/ **1** *v.t.* **A** (*place firmly, attach, prevent from moving*) befestigen; festmachen; (*fig.: imprint*) einprägen; **~ a post in[to] the ground** einen Pfosten im Boden verankern; **~ a stone firmly into position** einen Stein an der vorgesehenen Stelle einsetzen; **~ sth. to/on sth.** etw. an/auf etw. (*Dat.*) befestigen *od.* festmachen; **~ shelves to the wall/a handle on the door** Regale an der Wand/eine Klinke an der Tür anbringen; **~ bayonets** Bajonette aufpflanzen; **~ sth. in one's mind** sich (*Dat.*) etw. fest einprägen; **B** (*direct steadily*) richten ‹Blick, Gedanken, Augen› (**[up]on** auf + *Akk.*); setzen ‹Hoffnung› (**[up]on** auf + *Akk.*); **her mind was [firmly] ~ed on her work** sie war ganz auf ihre Arbeit fixiert; **his thoughts were ~ed elsewhere** er war mit seinen Gedanken [ganz] woanders; **C** (*decide, specify*) festsetzen, festlegen ‹Termin, Preis, Strafe, Grenze›; (*settle, agree on*) ausmachen; (*allocate*) übertragen ‹Verantwortung›; zuschieben ‹Schuld› (**[up]on** + *Dat.*); **~ the price at £50** den Preis auf 50 Pfund festsetzen; **nothing's been ~ed yet** es ist noch nichts fest [ausgemacht *od.* beschlossen]; **it was ~ed that ...:** es wurde beschlossen *od.* vereinbart, dass ...; **D** (*repair*) in Ordnung bringen; reparieren; **need ~ing** repariert werden müssen; **E** (*arrange*) arrangieren; **~ a rehearsal for Friday** eine Probe für *od.* auf Freitag (*Akk.*) ansetzen; **they tried to ~ things so that ...:** sie versuchten es so zu arrangieren, dass ...; **have you anything ~ed for Saturday evening?** hast du [für] Samstagabend schon etwas vor?; **nothing definite has been ~ed yet** es ist noch nichts Endgültiges vereinbart *od.* ausgemacht; **F** (*manipulate fraudulently*) manipulieren ‹Rennen, Kampf›; bestechen ‹Zeugen›; **the whole thing was ~ed** das war eine abgekartete Sache (*ugs.*) **G** (*Amer. coll.: prepare*) machen ‹Essen, Kaffee, Drink›; **~ one's hair** sich frisieren; **~ one's face** sich schminken; **H** (*coll.: deal with*) in Ordnung bringen; regeln; **~ sb.** (*get even with*) es jmdm. heimzahlen; (*kill*) jmdn. kaltmachen (*salopp*); **Don't bother about that. I'll ~ things with her** Mach dir deswegen keine Sorgen. Ich regle das mit ihr *od.* bringe das mit ihr in Ordnung; **I'll soon ~ that** (*prevent*) das werd ich zu verhindern wissen; **that'll ~ her** dann kann sie nichts mehr machen; **I** (*make permanent*) fixieren ‹Farben, Foto, Gewebe›; **J** (*coll.: castrate*) kastrieren; **K** (*Bot.: assimilate*) ‹Pflanze:› binden.
**2** *v.i.* **A** (*coll.: arrange*) **~ for sb. to do sth.** es arrangieren, dass jmd. etw. tun kann; **B** (*Amer. coll.: intend*) vorhaben; **be ~ing to do sth.** vorhaben, etw. zu tun; **C** (*sl.: inject narcotics*) fixen (*Drogenjargon*).
**3** *v. refl.* ⇒ 2 C.
**4** *n.* **A** (*coll.: predicament*) Patsche, *die* (*ugs.*); Klemme, *die* (*ugs.*); **be in a ~:** in der Klemme sein (*ugs.*); **get oneself in[to] a ~:** sich (*Dat.*) eine schöne Suppe einbrocken (*ugs.*); **B** (*Naut.*) Standort, *der;* Position, *die;* **radio ~:** Funkortung, *die;* **C** (*sl.: of narcotics*) Fix, *der* (*Drogenjargon*); **D** (*Amer. coll.: bribery*) Bestechung, *die;* (*illicit arrangement*) abgekartete Sache (*ugs.*)

**~ on** *v.t.* **A** /'-'/ anbringen; **B** /'--/ (*decide on*) sich entscheiden für; (*determine*) festsetzen, festlegen ‹Termin›; **~ on doing sth.** beschließen, etw. zu tun

**~ 'up** *v.t.* **A** (*arrange*) arrangieren; festsetzen, ausmachen ‹Termin, Treffpunkt›; **we've nothing ~ed up for tonight** wir haben noch nichts vor [für] heute Abend; **let's ~ up when and where we'll next meet** machen wir aus, wann und wo wir uns das nächste Mal treffen; **we ~ed up that ...:** wir vereinbarten, dass ...; **I'll ~ up for you to accompany me** ich werde es arrangieren, dass du mich begleiten kannst; **B** (*provide*) versorgen; (*provide with accommodation*) unterbringen; **~ sb. up with sth.** jmdm. etw. verschaffen *od.* besorgen; **~ sb. up [with a bed] for the night**

f

jmdn. für die Nacht unterbringen; (C) (*establish*) **get oneself ~ed up** sich etablieren; **you can stay with us until you get yourself ~ed up** du kannst bei uns wohnen, bis du ein Zimmer/eine Wohnung *usw.* hast; **~ sb. up in the spare room** jmdn. im Gästezimmer unterbringen; (D) (*furnish*) einrichten

**fixate** /fɪk'seɪt/ *v.t.* (*Psych.*) fixieren (**upon** auf + *Akk.*)

**fixation** /fɪk'seɪʃn/ *n.* (*fixing, being fixed, obsession, Psych.*) Fixierung, *die;* **he has a ~ about his mother** er ist zu stark auf seine Mutter fixiert

**fixed** /fɪkst/ *adj.* (A) *pred.* (*coll.: placed*) **how are you/is he** *etc.* **~ for cash/fuel?** wie siehts bei dir/ihm *usw.* mit dem Geld/Treibstoff aus? (*ugs.*); **they are better ~ financially than we are** sie stehen finanziell besser da als wir; **how are you ~ for this evening?** was hast du [für] heute Abend vor?; (B) (*not variable*) fest; starr ‹Lächeln, Gesichtsausdruck›; **~ assets** Anlagevermögen, *das;* **~ cost** Fixkosten *Pl.;* **~ price** Festpreis, *der;* **~-interest stocks** festverzinsliche Wertpapiere; **~ capital** Anlagekapital, *das;* **~ focus** (*Photog.*) Fixfokus, *der;* **~ idea** fixe Idee; **have no ~ ideas on sth.** keine feste Vorstellung von etw. haben; **~ income** festes Einkommen; **~-income investments** Festgeldanlagen *Pl.;* **~ odds** feste *od.* gleich bleibende Gewinnchancen; **~ salary** Fixum, *das;* **~ star** Fixstern, *der;* **~-wing aircraft** Starrflügelflugzeug, *das;* Starrflügler, *der;* ⇒ *also* **abode**[1]; **address** 2 A; (C) (*firm, resolute*) fest ‹Absicht›; **be ~ in one's determination** fest entschlossen sein; **with the ~ intention of doing sth.** in *od.* mit der festen Absicht, etw. zu tun

**fixedly** /'fɪksɪdlɪ/ *adv.* starr, unverwandt ‹blicken, lächeln›; **stare ~ out of the window** aus dem Fenster starren

**fixed: ~ 'point** *n.* (A) (*Phys.*) Fixpunkt, *der;* Festpunkt, *der;* (B) (*Computing*) Festkomma, *das;* **~ price** Festpreis, *der;* **~-rate** *attrib. adj.* Festzins-; mit festem Zins *nachgestellt*

**fixer** /'fɪksə(r)/ *n.* (A) (*Photog.*) Fixiermittel, *das;* (B) (*coll.: person*) Organisator, *der;* (*derog.*) *Mittelsmann, der durch Schmiergeldzahlungen unlautere geschäftliche Transaktionen ermöglicht*

**fixings** /'fɪksɪŋz/ *n. pl.* (*Amer. Cookery: trimmings*) Beilagen *Pl.*

**fixity** /'fɪksɪtɪ/ *n., no pl.* Beständigkeit, *die;* **~ of purpose** Zielstrebigkeit, *die*

**fixture** /'fɪkstʃə(r)/ *n.* (A) (*furnishing*) eingebautes Teil; (*pipe etc.*) fest verlegtes Rohr *usw.;* (*accessory*) festes Zubehörteil; **~s** (*Law*) unbewegliches Inventar; **~s and fittings** Ausstattung und Installationen; **lighting ~s** Beleuchtungskörper *Pl.;* (B) (*Sport*) Veranstaltung, *die;* **the Derby is an annual ~:** das Derby findet jedes Jahr statt; **~ list** Spielplan, *der;* (C) (*fig. joc.: established person or thing*) [lebendes] Inventar (*scherzh.*); **be a ~:** zum Inventar gehören (*scherzh.*)

**fizz** /fɪz/ ❶ *v.i.* [zischend] sprudeln. ❷ *n.* (A) (*effervescence*) Sprudeln, *das;* **the lemonade has lost its ~:** die Limonade sprudelt nicht mehr; (B) (*coll.: effervescent drink*) Sprudel, *der;* (*flavoured*) Brause[limonade], *die* (*ugs.*); **gin ~:** Ginfizz, *der*

**fizzle** /'fɪzl/ *v.i.* zischen

**~ 'out** *v.i.* ‹Feuerwerk:› zischend verlöschen; ‹Begeisterung:› sich legen; ‹Kampagne:› im Sande verlaufen

**fizzy** /'fɪzɪ/ *adj.* sprudelnd; **~ lemonade** Brause[limonade], *die;* **~ drinks** kohlensäurehaltige Getränke; **be ~:** sprudeln

**fjord** ⇒ **fiord**

**fl.** *abbr.* (A) **floor** OG; (B) **fluid** fl.

**flab** /flæb/ *n.* (*coll.*) Fett, *das;* Speck, *der* (*ugs.*)

**flabbergast** /'flæbəgɑːst/ *v.t.* verblüffen; umhauen (*ugs.*); **I was [absolutely] ~ed** ich war [völlig] verblüfft; es hat mich [einfach] umgehauen (*ugs.*); **she looked at them, ~ed** sie sah sie völlig verblüfft an

**flabby** /'flæbɪ/ *adj.* schlaff ‹Muskeln, Bauch, Fleisch, Hände, Wangen, Brüste›; wabbelig (*ugs.*), schwammig ‹Bauch, Fleisch›; (*fig.*) schwammig; schwach ‹Willenskraft›

**flaccid** /'flæksɪd/ *adj.* schlaff; (*fig.*) lasch

**flag**[1] /flæg/ ❶ *n.* Fahne, *die;* (*small paper etc. device*) Fähnchen, *das;* (*national ~, ~ on ship*) Flagge, *die;* **red/white ~:** rote/weiße Fahne; **yellow ~:** Quarantäneflagge, *die;* **~ of convenience** billige Flagge (*Seew.*); **~ of truce** Parlamentärflagge, *die;* **keep the ~ flying** (*fig.*) die Fahne hochhalten; **show the ~** (*fig.*) seiner Repräsentationspflicht nachkommen; **put the ~[s] out** (*fig. coll.*) drei Kreuze machen (*ugs.*). ❷ *v.t.*, **-gg-** (A) beflaggen ‹Gebäude›; (*mark with ~s*) [mit Fähnchen] markieren; (*Computing*) markieren; kennzeichnen; (B) (*communicate by ~ signals*) [mit Fahne *od.* Fähnchen] signalisieren; (C) ⇒ **~ down**

**~ 'down** *v.t.* [durch Winken] anhalten

**flag**[2] *v.i.*, **-gg-** (A) (*lose vigour*) erlahmen; **business is ~ging** die Geschäfte lassen nach; (B) ‹Blume:› den Kopf hängen lassen; ‹Pflanze:› schlappen (*ugs.*), die Blätter hängen lassen

**flag**[3] ❶ *n.* ⇒ **flagstone**. ❷ *v.t.*, **-gg-** mit Fliesen/Steinplatten belegen; fliesen ‹Fußboden›

**flag: ~ captain** *n.* (*Navy*) Kommandant des Flaggschiffs; **~ day** *n.* (A) (*Brit.*) *Tag der Straßensammlung für wohltätige Zwecke;* (B) **F~ Day** (*Amer.*) *14. Juni als Gedenktag der Einführung der amerikanischen Nationalflagge*

**flagella** *pl. of* **flagellum**

**flagellate**[1] /'flædʒəleɪt/ *v.t.* geißeln

**flagellate**[2] /'flædʒələt/ (*Zool.*) ❶ *adj.* geißelförmig; **~ organism** ⇒ **2**. ❷ *n.* Flagellat, *der* (*fachspr.*); Geißeltierchen, *das*

**flagellation** /flædʒə'leɪʃn/ *n.* Flagellation, *die;* Geißelung, *die*

**flagellum** /flə'dʒeləm/ *n., pl.* **flagella** /flə'dʒelə/ (A) (*Bot.: runner*) Ausläufer, *der;* (B) (*Biol.*) Flagellum, *das;* Geißel, *die*

**flageolet** /flædʒə'let, 'flædʒəlet/ *n.* (*Mus.*) Flageolett, *das*

**flag: ~ lieutenant** *n.* (*Navy*) Flaggleutnant, *der;* **~ officer** *n.* (*Navy*) Flaggoffizier, *der*

**flagon** /'flægən/ *n.* (A) (*with handle and spout; for Eucharist*) Kanne, *die;* (B) (*big bottle*) [bauchige] Weinflasche (*in Bocksbeutelform*)

**'flagpole** ⇒ **flagstaff**

**flagrancy** /'fleɪgrənsɪ/ *n., no pl.* Schändlichkeit, *die;* (*of disregard, defiance*) Schamlosigkeit, *die*

**'flag rank** *n.* (*Navy*) Rang eines Flaggoffiziers; ≈ Admiralsrang, *der*

**flagrant** /'fleɪgrənt/ *adj.* eklatant; flagrant ‹Verstoß›; (*scandalous*) ungeheuerlich; himmelschreiend ‹Unrecht›; schamlos ‹Verbrecher, Sünder›

**flagrante delicto** ⇒ **in flagrante [delicto]**

**flagrantly** /'fleɪgrəntlɪ/ *adv.* eklatant; flagrant ‹verstoßen›; unverhohlen ‹beleidigen›; **a ~ criminal act** ein ungeheuerliches Verbrechen

**flag: ~ship** *n.* (*Navy*) Flaggschiff, *das;* (*fig. attrib.*) führend...; **~staff** *n.* Flaggenmast, *der;* Fahnenmast, *der;* (*horizontal*) Fahnenstange, *die;* (*on ship*) Flaggenstock, *der* (*Seemannsspr.*); **~stone** *n.* Steinplatte, *die;* (*for floor*) Fliese, *die;* *in pl.* (*pavement*) Straßenpflaster, *das;* **~ stop** (*Amer.*) ⇒ **request stop**

**flail** /fleɪl/ ❶ *v.i.* [wild] um sich schlagen; ‹Propeller:› sich rasend drehen; **with arms ~ing he tried to keep his balance** mit den Armen fuchtelnd, versuchte er, das Gleichgewicht zu halten. ❷ *v.t.* (*strike with ~*) dreschen; (*strike as if with ~*) [wild] einschlagen auf (+ *Akk.*). ❸ *n.* Dreschflegel, *der*

**flair** /fleə(r)/ *n.* Gespür, *das;* (*special ability*) Talent, *das;* [natürliche] Begabung; **have ~** (*talent*) Talent haben; talentiert sein; (*for dress*) Stil *od.* Geschmack haben; **have a ~ for sth.** (*talent*) ein Talent *od.* eine Begabung für etw. haben; (*instinct*) ein [feines] Gespür für etw. haben; **have [quite] a ~ for writing/[learning] languages** schriftstellerisch [recht] begabt sein/[recht] sprachbegabt sein; **he has a ~ for making money** er weiß, wie man zu Geld kommt

**flak** /flæk/ *n.* Flakfeuer, *das* (*Milit.*); (*gun*) Flak, *die* (*Milit.*); **get a lot of ~ for sth.** (*fig.*) wegen etw. [schwer] unter Beschuss geraten; **give sb. a lot of ~ for sth.** (*fig.*) jmdn. wegen etw. [schwer] unter Beschuss nehmen

**flake** /fleɪk/ ❶ *n.* (A) (*of snow, soap, cereals*) Flocke, *die;* (*of dry skin*) Schuppe, *die;* (*of plaster*) ≈ Bröckchen, *das;* (*of metal*) ≈ Span, *der;* (*of enamel, paint*) ≈ Splitter, *der;* (*of pastry, rust*) ≈ Krümel, *der;* (*of chocolate, coconut*) Raspel, *die;* (B) (*of fish's flesh*) ≈ Stück, *das;* (C) (*shark as food*) Seeaal, *der.* ❷ *v.i.* ‹Stuck, Verputz, Stein:› abbröckeln; ‹Farbe, Rost, Emaille:› abblättern; ‹Haut:› sich schuppen

**~ 'off** *v.i.* ‹Farbe, Rost, Emaille:› abblättern; ‹Stuck, Verputz, Stein:› abbröckeln

**~ 'out** *v.i.* (*coll.*) umkippen (*ugs.*); **be ~d out** total erschöpft sein

**'flak jacket** *n.* kugelsichere Weste

**flaky** /'fleɪkɪ/ *adj.* bröcklig ‹Farbe, Gips, Rost›; blättrig ‹Kruste›; schuppig ‹Haut›; **~ pastry** Blätterteig, *der*

**flambé** /'flɑ̃beɪ/ (*Cookery*) ❶ *adj.* flambiert. ❷ *v.t.* flambieren

**flamboyance** /flæm'bɔɪəns/, **flamboyancy** /flæm'bɔɪənsɪ/ *n.* Extravaganz, *die;* (*of plumage*) Pracht, *die;* (*of clothes, lifestyle*) Pracht, *die;* Pomp, *der* (*abwertend*)

**flamboyant** /flæm'bɔɪənt/ *adj.* (A) extravagant; prächtig ‹Farben, Federkleid›; (*derog.*) großspurig ‹Wesen, Verhalten, Geste›; (B) (*Archit.*) **~ style** Flamboyantstil, *der*

**flamboyantly** /flæm'bɔɪəntlɪ/ *adv.* extravagant; prächtig, extravagant ‹schmücken, kleiden›

**flame** /fleɪm/ ❶ *n.* (A) Flamme, *die;* **be in ~s** in Flammen stehen; **burst into ~:** in Brand geraten; **go up in ~s** in Flammen aufgehen; (B) (*colour*) ≈ Rotorange, *das;* (C) (*joc.: sweetheart*) Flamme, *die* (*ugs.*); **old ~:** alte Flamme (*ugs. veralt.*). ⇒ *also* **fan**[1] 2; **feed** 1 I; (C) (*Computing*) Flame, *die.* ❷ *v.i.* (A) brennen; (B) (*glow*) glühen. ❸ *v.t.* (*Computing*) **~ sb.** jmdm. eine Flame/Flames schicken; **the PC was ~d** die PC wurde mit Flames überzogen

**~ 'up** *v.i.* (*lit. or fig.*) aufflammen; ‹Fett:› anfangen zu brennen

**flame: ~-coloured** *adj.* feuerfarben; **~ gun** *n.* Flämmgerät, *das*

**flameless** /'fleɪmlɪs/ *adj.* ohne offene Flamme *nachgestellt*

**flamenco** /flə'meŋkəʊ/ *n., pl.* **~s** Flamenco, *der*

**flame: ~-proof** nicht entflammbar; flammfest; **~-thrower** *n.* Flammenwerfer, *der*

**flaming** /'fleɪmɪŋ/ ❶ *adj.* (A) (*bright-coloured*) feuerrot; flammend ‹Rot, Abendhimmel›; hochrot ‹Wangen›; (B) (*very hot*) glühend heiß; (*coll.: passionate*) heftig, leidenschaftlich ‹Auseinandersetzung›; **be in a ~ temper** (*coll.*) geladen sein (*salopp*); kochen (*ugs.*); **~ June** der heiße Juni; (C) (*coll.: damned*) verdammt. ❷ *adv.* (A) **~ red** feuerrot; (B) (*coll.: damned*) **he is too ~ idle or lazy** er ist, verdammt noch mal, einfach zu faul (*ugs.*); **who does he ~ well think he is?** verdammt noch mal, für wen hält der sich eigentlich? (*ugs.*)

**flamingo** /flə'mɪŋgəʊ/ *n., pl.* **~s** *or* **~es** (*Ornith.*) Flamingo, *der*

**flammability** /flæmə'bɪlɪtɪ/ ⇒ **inflammability**

**flammable** /'flæməbl/ ⇒ **inflammable** A

**flan** /flæn/ *n.* **[fruit] ~:** [Obst]torte, *die;* **[cheese] ~** *flache Pastete mit [Käse]füllung oder -belag*

**'flan case** *n.* Tortenboden, *der*

**Flanders** /'flɑːndəz/ *pr. n.* Flandern (*das*)

**flange** /flændʒ/ *n.* Flansch, *der;* (*of wheel*) Spurkranz, *der*

**flanged** /flændʒd/ *adj.* mit Flansch/Spurkranz versehen

**flank** /flæŋk/ ❶ *n.* (*of person*) Seite, *die;* (*of animal; also Mil.*) Flanke, *die;* (*of mountain, building*) Seite, *die;* Flanke, *die* (*selten*); (*of beef*) Dünnung, *die;* **attack sb.'s ~** (*Mil.*) jmdn. von der Flanke her angreifen; **~ forward** (*Rugby*) Außenstürmer, *der.* ❷ *v.t.* (A) flankieren; **a road ~ed by** *or* **with trees** eine von Bäumen flankierte Straße; (B) **~ing movement** Flankenangriff, *der*

**flannel** /'flænl/ **1** *n.* (A) *(fabric)* Flanell, *der;* (B) *in pl.* *(trousers)* Flanellhose, *die; (garments)* Flanellsachen *Pl.;* **cricketing ~s** Kricketkleidung [aus Flanell]; (C) *(Brit.)* *(for washing oneself)* Waschlappen, *der;* *(for washing the floor)* Aufwischlappen, *der;* (D) *(Brit. coll.)* *(verbose nonsense)* Geschwafel, *das (ugs. abwertend);* *(flattery)* Schmeicheleien *Pl.* **2** *attrib. adj.* Flanell-

**flannelette** /flænə'let/ *n.* [Baumwoll]flanell, *der*

**flap** /flæp/ **1** *v.t.*, **-pp-** schlagen; **~ its wings** mit den Flügeln schlagen; *(at short intervals)* [mit den Flügeln] flattern. **2** *v.i.*, **-pp-** (A) ‹Flügel:› schlagen; ‹Segel, Fahne, Vorhang:› flattern; (B) **sb.'s ears were ~ping** *(fig. coll.)* jmd. hat mitgehört; *(was very interested)* jmd. spitzte die Ohren; (C) *(fig. coll.: panic)* die Nerven verlieren; **stop ~ping** reg dich ab *(ugs.).* **3** *n.* (A) Klappe, *die; (of leather shorts)* Hosenlatz, *der;* *(of saddle)* Seitenblatt, *das;* *(envelope seal, tongue of shoe)* Lasche, *die;* *(of table)* klappbarer Teil; (B) *(fig. coll.: panic)* **be in a ~:** furchtbar aufgeregt sein; **get [oneself] in[to] a ~:** sich furchtbar aufregen; durchdrehen *(ugs.);* **there's a ~ on** es herrscht große Aufregung

**flapjack** /'flæpdʒæk/ *n.* (A) *(oatcake)* süßer Haferkeks; (B) *(pancake)* Pfannkuchen, *der*

**flare** /fleə(r)/ **1** *v.i.* (A) *(blaze)* flackern; *(fig.)* ausbrechen; **tempers ~d** die Gemüter erhitzten sich; (B) *(widen)* sich erweitern; *(Dressm., Tailoring)* ausgestellt sein; (C) *(billow)* sich bauschen. **2** *n.* (A) *(as signal; also Naut.)* Leuchtsignal, *das;* *(from pistol)* Leuchtkugel, *die;* *(Aeronaut.: to illuminate target)* Leuchtbombe, *die;* (B) *(blaze of light)* Lichtschein, *der;* (C) *(widening)* **skirt/trousers with ~s** ausgestellter Rock/ausgestellte Hose; (D) *in pl.* *(trousers)* ausgestellte Hose

**~ 'up** *v.i.* (A) *(burn more fiercely)* aufflackern; auflodern; (B) *(break out)* [wieder] ausbrechen; **~ up again** ‹Kampf, Streit:› wieder aufflackern; (C) *(become angry)* aufbrausen; aus der Haut fahren *(ugs.).* ⇒ *also* **flare-up**

**flared** /fleəd/ *adj.* *(Dressm., Tailoring)* ausgestellt

**flare: ~-path** *n.* *(Aeronaut.)* Anflugbefeuerung, *die;* **~-up** *n.* (A) *(of fire)* Aufflackern, *das;* Auflodern, *das;* (B) *(of violence, rioting)* Ausbruch, *der;* **a new ~-up** ein erneutes Aufflackern; (C) *(of rage)* Aufregung, *die*

**flash** /flæʃ/ **1** *n.* (A) *(of light)* Aufleuchten, *das;* Aufblinken, *das;* *(as signal)* Lichtsignal, *das;* Blinkzeichen, *das;* **~es from a gun** Mündungsfeuer eines Gewehrs; **did you see the ~?** hast du es aufblitzen *od.* aufleuchten sehen?; **~ of lightning** Blitz, *der;* **[as] quick as a ~** *(coll.)* schnell wie ein Blitz *(ugs.);* **reply as quick as a ~** *(coll.)* wie aus der Pistole geschossen antworten *(ugs.);* **give a ~ of the headlamps** *(Motor Veh.)* aufblenden; die Lichthupe betätigen; **~ in the pan** *(fig. coll.)* Zufallstreffer, *der;* (B) *(Photog.)* Blitzlicht, *das;* **use [a] ~:** mit Blitzlicht fotografieren; **~ photo** Blitzlichtaufnahme, *die;* (C) *(fig.)* **~ of genius** *or* **inspiration** *or* **brilliance** Geistesblitz, *der;* **~ of wit** geistreicher Einfall; **~ of insight** *or* **intuition** Eingebung, *die;* **~ of temper** *or* **anger** Wutausbruch, *der;* (D) *(instant)* **be over in a ~:** gleich *od.* im Nu vorbei sein; **the answer came to me in a ~:** blitzartig kam mir die Antwort; **it all happened in a ~:** es geschah alles blitzschnell; (E) *(Radio, Telev.)* ⇒ **news flash**; (F) *(Cinemat.)* [kurze] Einblendung; (G) *(Brit. Mil.: insignia)* Abzeichen, *das.*

**2** *v.t.* (A) aufleuchten lassen; **~ a torch in sb.'s face** jmdm. mit einer Taschenlampe ins Gesicht leuchten; **~ a signal/warning** blinken/zur Warnung blinken; **~ a message** eine Botschaft blinken; **~ the/one's headlights** aufblenden; die Lichthupe betätigen; **~ sb. with one's headlamps** jmdn. anblinken *od.* mit der Lichthupe anblenden; (B) *(fig.)* **her eyes ~ed fire** ihre Augen sprühten Feuer *od.* funkelten böse; **her eyes ~ed back defiance** ihre Augen funkelten trotzig; (C) *(give briefly and suddenly)* **~ sb. a smile/glance** jmdm. ein Lächeln/einen Blick zuwerfen; (D) *(display briefly)* kurz zeigen; *(flaunt)* zur Schau tragen ‹Reichtum›; funkeln lassen ‹Diamanten›; **~ one's money about** *or* **around** mit [dem] Geld um sich werfen *(ugs.);* (E) *(Communications)* durchgeben; **~ news across the world** Nachrichten in die ganze Welt ausstrahlen.

**3** *v.i.* (A) aufleuchten; **the lightning ~ed** es blitzte; **a signal was ~ing** ein Lichtsignal blitzte; **the lighthouse ~es once a minute** der Leuchtturm blinkt einmal in der Minute ein Signal; **~ing light** Blinklicht, *das;* *(device)* *(Naut.)* Blinkfeuer, *das;* *(Motor Veh.)* Blinkleuchte, *die;* **~ at sb. with one's headlamps** jmdn. anblinken *od.* mit der Lichthupe anblenden; (B) *(fig.)* **her eyes ~ed in anger** ihre Augen blitzten vor Zorn; (C) *(move swiftly)* **~ by** *or* **past** vorbeiflitzen *(ugs.);* *(fig.)* ‹Zeit, Ferien:› wie im Fluge vergehen; (D) *(burst suddenly into perception)* **sth. ~ed through my mind** etw. schoss mir durch den Kopf; **the truth ~ed upon me** die Wahrheit kam über mich; **his whole life ~ed before his eyes** sein ganzes Leben rollte noch einmal vor seinen Augen ab; (E) *(Brit. coll.: expose oneself)* sich [unsittlich] entblößen.

**4** *adj.* *(coll.)* protzig *(ugs. abwertend);* **~ Harry** *(Brit.)* Stenz, *der (ugs. abwertend)*

**~ 'over** *v.i.* *(Electr.)* überspringen

**flash: ~back** *n.* *(Cinemat. etc.)* Rückblende, *die* (**to** auf + *Akk.*); **~ bulb** *n.* *(Photog.)* Blitzbirnchen, *das;* **~ card** *n. als Lernhilfe verwendete Karte, mit der dem Schüler ein Wort, Buchstabe oder sonstiges Zeichen kurz gezeigt wird;* **~cube** *n.* *(Photog.)* Blitzwürfel, *der;* Würfelblitz, *der*

**flasher** /'flæʃə(r)/ *n.* (A) *(in advertising)* blinkende Leuchtreklame; *(Motor Veh.)* Blinker, *der;* **headlamp ~:** Lichthupe, *die;* (B) *(Brit. coll.: who exposes himself)* Exhibitionist, *der*

**flash: ~ flood** *n.* Überschwemmung, *die (durch heftige Regenfälle);* **~gun** *n.* *(Photog.)* Blitz[licht]gerät, *das*

**flashily** /'flæʃɪlɪ/ *adv.* auffällig; protzig *(ugs. abwertend)*

**flashing** /'flæʃɪŋ/ *n.* *(Building)* Dichtungsblech, *das*

**flash: ~ lamp** *n.* Blinklampe, *die;* **~light** *n.* (A) *(for signals)* Blinklicht, *das;* *(in lighthouse)* Leuchtfeuer, *das;* (B) *(Photog.)* Blitzlicht, *das;* (C) *(Amer.)* Taschenlampe, *die;* **~point** *n.* Flammpunkt, *der;* *(fig.)* Siedepunkt, *der*

**flashy** /'flæʃɪ/ *adj.* auffällig; protzig *(ugs. abwertend);* **he's a ~ dresser** er kleidet sich [sehr] auffällig; **~ young men** großspurige junge Männer

**flask** /flɑːsk/ *n.* (A) ⇒ **Thermos**; **vacuum flask**; (B) *(for wine, oil)* [bauchige] Flasche; *(Chem.)* Kolben, *der;* (C) *(hip flask)* Taschenflasche, *die;* Flachmann, *der (ugs. scherzh.)*

**flat**[1] /flæt/ *n.* *(Brit.: dwelling)* Wohnung, *die*

**flat**[2] **1** *adj.* (A) flach; eben ‹Fläche›; platt ‹Nase, Reifen›; *(uniform)* gleichmäßig ‹Tönung, Farbton›; **knock sb. ~:** jmdn. niederstrecken; **the rug is not ~:** der Teppich liegt nicht glatt; **spread the blanket ~ on the ground** die Decke glatt auf dem Boden ausbreiten; **fall ~ on the ground** der Länge nach hinfallen; **fall ~ on one's back** auf den Rücken fallen; **lie ~ on one's stomach** flach auf dem Bauch liegen; (B) *(fig.)* *(monotonous)* eintönig; *(dull)* lahm *(ugs.);* fade; *(stale)* schal, abgestanden ‹Bier, Sekt›; *(Electr.)* leer ‹Batterie›; *(Commerc.: inactive)* flau; **fall ~:** nicht ankommen *(ugs.);* seine Wirkung verfehlen; **go ~:** schal werden; **feel ~:** erschöpft sein; (C) *(downright)* glatt *(ugs.)* ‹Absage, Weigerung, Widerspruch›; **[and] that's ~:** und damit basta *(ugs.);* (D) *(Mus.)* [um einen Halbton] erniedrigt ‹Note›; (E) *(Phonet.)* kurz und offen ‹Vokal›.

**2** *adv.* (A) flach; (B) *(outright)* rundweg; glattweg *(ugs.);* (C) *(Mus.)* zu tief ‹spielen, singen›; (D) *(coll.: completely)* **~ broke** total pleite; (E) *(coll.: exactly)* **in two hours ~:** in genau zwei Stunden; **in no time ~:** in null Komma nichts *(ugs.).*

**3** *n.* (A) flache Seite; **~ of the hand** Handfläche, *die;* (B) *(level ground)* Ebene, *die;* *(shoal)* Untiefe, *die;* **walk on the ~:** auf ebener Strecke gehen; (C) *(Mus.)* erniedrigter Ton; *(symbol)* Erniedrigungszeichen, *das;* (D) *(Horseracing)* **the ~:** das Flachrennen; *(season)* die Saison für Flachrennen; **on the ~:** bei Flachrennen; (E) *(coll.: flat tyre)* Platte, *der (ugs.);* Plattfuß, *der (ugs.);* (F) *(Theatre)* Kulisse, *die*

**flat: ~-bottomed** /'flætbɒtəmd/ *adj.* flach; **~car** *n.* *(Amer. Railw.)* Flachwagen, *der;* **~-chested** /flæt'tʃestɪd/ *adj.* flachbrüstig; flachbusig; **~ 'feet** *n. pl.* Plattfüße *Pl.* **~fish** *n.* Plattfisch, *der;* **~-footed** /flæt'fʊtɪd/ *adj.* plattfüßig; *(fig. coll.)* *(uninspired)* fantasielos; platt *(abwertend);* *(unprepared)* unvorbereitet; **~-heeled** *adj.* ‹Schuh› mit flachem Absatz; flach ‹Schuh›; **~-hunting** *n.* *(Brit.)* Wohnungssuche, *die;* **~ iron** *n.* Bügeleisen, *das;* Plätteisen, *das*

**flatlet** /'flætlɪt/ *n.* *(Brit.)* Appartement, *das*

**flatly** /'flætlɪ/ *adv.* rundweg; glatt *(ugs.)*

**'flat mate** *n.* *(Brit.)* Mitbewohner, *der*/Mitbewohnerin, *die;* **they were ~s** sie haben zusammen gewohnt

**flatness** /'flætnɪs/ *n., no pl.* (A) Flachheit, *die;* *(of nose)* Plattheit, *die;* (B) *(uniformity)* Gleichmäßigkeit, *die;* (C) *(fig.: monotony)* Eintönigkeit, *die;* *(dullness)* Fadheit, *die*

**flat: ~ 'out** *adv.* (A) ▶ **1552** *(at top speed)* **he ran/worked ~ out** er rannte/arbeitete, so schnell er konnte; **drive ~ out** mit Vollgas fahren; **go ~ out** ‹Fahrzeug:› mit Höchstgeschwindigkeit fahren; (B) *(exhausted)* total erledigt; total erschöpft; **~-pack** *adj.* ‹Möbel› zum Selbstbauen; **~ race** *n.* Flachrennen, *das;* **~ racing** *n., no pl., no indef. art.* Flachrennen, *das;* **~ rate** *n.* Einheitstarif, *der;* **~ 'spin** *n.* *(Aeronaut.)* Flachtrudeln, *das;* **go into a ~ spin** ins Flachtrudeln kommen; *(fig. coll.)* durchdrehen *(ugs.)*

**flatten** /'flætn/ **1** *v.t.* (A) flach *od.* platt drücken ‹Schachtel›; dem Erdboden gleichmachen ‹Stadt, Gebäude›; umknicken ‹Bäume, Kornähren›; **~ed against the door** flach *od.* platt gegen die Tür gedrückt; (B) *(humiliate)* **feel ~ed** sich niedergedrückt *od.* niedergeschlagen fühlen; (C) *(Mus.)* erniedrigen. **2** *v. refl.* **~ oneself against sth.** sich flach *od.* platt gegen etw. drücken

**~ 'out** **1** *v.i.* (A) flacher werden; (B) *(Aeronaut.)* in die Waagerechte gehen. **2** *v.t.* ganz flach drücken

**flatter** /'flætə(r)/ **1** *v.t.* (A) schmeicheln (+ *Dat.*); **I'm not just ~ing [you]** das ist keine bloße Schmeichelei; **feel ~ed** sich geschmeichelt fühlen; **be ~ed [by sth.]** sich [durch etw.] geschmeichelt fühlen; **the portrait ~s her/him** das Porträt ist geschmeichelt; (B) *(falsely encourage)* **sth. ~s sb. into doing sth.** etw. verleitet jmdn. dazu, etw. zu tun. **2** *v. refl.* **~ oneself [on being/having sth.]** sich *(Dat.)* einbilden[, etw. zu sein/haben]

**flatterer** /'flætərə(r)/ *n.* Schmeichler, *der*/Schmeichlerin, *die*

**flattering** /'flætərɪŋ/ *adj.* schmeichelhaft; schmeichelnd, schmeichlerisch ‹Person›; vorteilhaft ‹Kleid, Licht, Frisur›

**flattery** /'flætərɪ/ *n.* Schmeichelei, *die;* **~ will get you nowhere** mit Schmeicheleien erreichst du gar nichts

**flat 'tyre** *n.* Reifenpanne, *die;* *(the tyre itself)* platter Reifen

**flatulence** /'flætjʊləns/ *n.* Blähungen *Pl.;* Flatulenz, *die (Med.);* **suffer from ~:** Blähungen haben

**flat: ~ware** *n., no pl.* *(dishes)* Geschirr, *das;* *(Amer.: cutlery)* Besteck, *das;* **~worm** *n.* Plattwurm, *der*

**flaunt** /flɔːnt/ **1** *v.t.* zur Schau stellen. **2** *v.i.* ‹Fahne:› [stolz] flattern; ‹Blume:› sich wiegen, prangen

**flautist** /'flɔːtɪst/ *n.* ▶ **1261** Flötist, *der*/Flötistin, *die*

f

**flavor** *etc.* (*Amer.*) ⇒ **flavour** *etc.*

**flavour** /ˈfleɪvə(r)/ (*Brit.*) ❶ *n.* Ⓐ Aroma, *das;* (*taste*) Geschmack, *der;* **the dish lacks ~:** das Gericht schmeckt fade; **add ~ to sth.** einer Sache (*Dat.*) Geschmack geben; **different ~s** verschiedene Geschmacksrichtungen; **be ~ of the month** (*fig.*) hoch im Kurs stehen; **I'm not ~ of the month with him at the moment** er ist zur Zeit nicht gut auf mich zu sprechen; Ⓑ (*fig.*) Touch, *der* (*ugs.*); Anflug, *der;* **nostalgic ~:** nostalgischer Touch; Anflug von Nostalgie.
❷ *v.t.* Ⓐ abschmecken; würzen; **orange-~ed sweets** Bonbons mit Orangengeschmack; Ⓑ (*fig.*) Würze verleihen (+ *Dat.*)

**flavour enhancer** /ˈfleɪvər ɪnhɑːnsə(r)/ *n.* Geschmacksverstärker, *der*

**flavouring** /ˈfleɪvərɪŋ/ *n.* (*Brit.*) Aroma, *das;* **add [more] ~ to sth.** etw. [stärker] würzen

**flavourless** /ˈfleɪvəlɪs/ *adj.* (*Brit.*) fade

**flavoursome** /ˈfleɪvəsəm/ *adj.* (*Brit.*) schmackhaft

**flaw** /flɔː/ ❶ *n.* Ⓐ (*imperfection*) Makel, *der;* (*in plan, argument, character, or logic; crack in china, glass, or jewel*) Fehler, *der;* (*in workmanship, or goods*) Mangel, *der;* Ⓑ (*Law*) Formfehler, *der.* ❷ *v.t.* entstellen ‹Gesicht, Schönheit›; beschädigen ‹Porzellan, Glas›

**flawed** /flɔːd/ *adj.* fehlerhaft

**flawless** /ˈflɔːlɪs/ *adj.* Ⓐ makellos ‹Schönheit›; untadelig ‹Verhalten›; einwandfrei, fehlerlos ‹Aussprache, Verarbeitung›; Ⓑ (*masterly*) vollendet ‹Aufführung, Wiedergabe›; Ⓒ lupenrein ‹Edelstein›

**flawlessly** /ˈflɔːlɪslɪ/ *adv.* ⇒ **flawless** A, B: makellos; untadelig; einwandfrei; fehlerlos; vollendet

**flax** /flæks/ *n.* Ⓐ (*Bot.*) Flachs, *der;* Ⓑ (*Textiles: fibre*) Flachsfaser, *die;* Flachs, *der*

**flaxen** /ˈflæksn/ *adj.* flachsfarben; (*made of flax*) flächsern; **she's a ~ blonde** sie ist flachsblond

ˈ**flaxen-haired** *adj.* flachsblond

**flay** /fleɪ/ *v.t.* Ⓐ häuten; abziehen ‹Haut›; abschälen ‹Rinde›; **~ sb. alive** jmdm. bei lebendigem Leibe die Haut abziehen; (*fig. coll.*) jmdm. das Fell gerben (*salopp*); Ⓑ (*fig.: criticize*) heruntermachen (*ugs.*); **he was ~ed by them** sie ließen kein gutes Haar an ihm (*ugs.*)

**flea** /fliː/ *n.* Floh, *der;* **send sb. away** *or* **off with a ~ in his/her ear** (*fig. coll.*) jmdn. abblitzen lassen (*ugs.*); **as fit as a ~** (*coll.*) kerngesund

**flea: ~ bite** *n.* Flohbiss, *der;* **it's just a ~ bite** (*fig.*) es ist nur eine Kleinigkeit *od.* (*ugs.*) ein Klacks; **~ circus** *n.* Flohzirkus, *der;* **~ market** *n.* Flohmarkt, *der;* **~pit** *n.* (*Brit. coll. derog.*) Flohkino, *das* (*ugs.*)

**fleck** /flek/ ❶ *n.* Ⓐ Tupfen, *der;* (*small*) Punkt, *der;* (*blemish on skin*) Fleck, *der;* Ⓑ (*speck*) Flocke, *die.* ❷ *v.t.* sprenkeln; **the sky is ~ed with wispy clouds** der Himmel ist mit Wölkchen übersät; **green eyes ~ed with brown** braun gesprenkelte grüne Augen

**fled** ⇒ **flee**

**fledg[e]ling** /ˈfledʒlɪŋ/ *n.* Jungvogel, *der;* (*fig.*) Anfänger, *der;* Grünschnabel, *der* (*abwertend*); **~ writer** Jungautor, *der*/-autorin, *die;* **~ actor** Nachwuchsschauspieler, *der*/-schauspielerin, *die*

**flee** /fliː/ ❶ *v.i.*, **fled** /fled/ Ⓐ fliehen; **~ from sth./sb.** aus etw./vor jmdm. flüchten *od.* fliehen; **~ abroad** [sich] ins Ausland flüchten; **~ before** *or* **from the storm** vor dem Sturm flüchten *od.* fliehen; **~ from sth.** (*fig.*) einer Sache (*Dat.*) entfliehen; **the police arrived and the thieves fled** als die Polizei kam, ergriffen die Diebe die Flucht; **be ~ing from justice** auf der Flucht vor den Richtern sein; Ⓑ (*vanish*) sich verflüchtigen; ‹Jugend, Zeit:› vergehen.
❷ *v.t.*, **fled** Ⓐ fliehen aus; **~ the country** aus dem Land fliehen *od.* flüchten; Ⓑ (*avoid, shun*) sich entziehen (+ *Dat.*); fliehen (*geh.*) ‹Gesellschaft, Personen›

**fleece** /fliːs/ ❶ *n.* Vlies, *das;* [Schaf]fell, *das;* (*quantity shorn*) Schur, *die;* (*woollen fabric*) Flausch, *der;* (*artificial fabric*) Webpelz, *der;* ⇒ *also* **Golden Fleece**. ❷ *v.t.* (*fig.*) ausplündern; (*charge excessively*) neppen (*ugs. abwertend*); **be ~d of one's money** um sein Geld gebracht werden

**fleecy** /ˈfliːsɪ/ *adj.* flauschig; **~ cloud** Schäfchenwolke, *die*

**fleet**[1] /fliːt/ *n.* Ⓐ (*Navy*) Flotte, *die;* **the F~:** die Marine; ⇒ *also* **admiral** A; Ⓑ (*in operation together*) (*vessels*) Flotte, *die;* (*aircraft*) Geschwader, *das;* (*vehicles*) ≈ Kolonne, *die;* **a fishing ~:** eine Fischfangflotte; ⇒ *also* **merchant fleet**; Ⓒ (*under same ownership*) Flotte, *die* (*fig.*); **he owns a ~ of cars** ihm gehört ein ganzer Wagenpark

**fleet**[2] *adj.* (*poet./literary*) flink; **~ of foot, ~-footed** leichtfüßig; schnellfüßig

**fleeting** /ˈfliːtɪŋ/ *adj.* flüchtig; vergänglich ‹Natur, Schönheit›; **~ visit** Stippvisite, *die* (*ugs.*)

**fleetingly** /ˈfliːtɪŋlɪ/ *adv.* flüchtig; **she was here ~:** sie war kurz hier

ˈ**Fleet Street** *pr. n.* (*Brit. fig.*) die [überregionale britische] Presse

**Fleming** /ˈflemɪŋ/ *n.* Flame, *der*/Flämin, *die*

**Flemish** /ˈflemɪʃ/ ▶ 1275, ▶ 1340 ❶ *adj.* flämisch; ⇒ *also* **English** 1. ❷ *n.* Flämisch, *das;* ⇒ *also* **English** 2 A

**flesh** /fleʃ/ ❶ *n., no pl., no indef. art.* Ⓐ Fleisch, *das;* **he's got no ~ on him** er hat kein Fleisch auf den Rippen; **~ and blood** Fleisch und Blut; **it's more than ~ and blood can stand** das ist mehr, als ein Mensch ertragen kann; **one's own ~ and blood** sein eigen[es] Fleisch und Blut (*geh.*); ⇒ *also* **creep** 1 B; Ⓑ (*of fruit, plant*) [Frucht]fleisch, *das;* Ⓒ (*fig.: body*) Fleisch, *das* (*geh.*); **and the Word was made ~** (*Bibl.*) und das Wort ist Fleisch geworden; **go the way of all ~:** den Weg allen Fleisches gehen (*geh.*); **in the ~:** in natura; **one ~:** ein Leib und eine Seele; **sins of the ~:** fleischliche Sünden; ⇒ *also* **spirit** 1 D; Ⓓ (*as food*) Fleisch, *das;* **human ~:** Menschenfleisch, *das.*
❷ *v.t.* **~ out** ausstatten; untermauern ‹Plan›.
❸ *v.i.* **~ out** Fleisch ansetzen

**flesh: ~ colour** *n.* Fleischfarbe, *die;* **~-coloured** *adj.* fleischfarben; **~-eating** *adj.* Fleisch fressend

**fleshly** /ˈfleʃlɪ/ *adj.* (*carnal*) fleischlich; (*mortal, worldly*) irdisch

**flesh: ~pots** *n. pl.* Ⓐ (*high living*) **wallow in the ~pots** wie die Made im Speck leben; Ⓑ (*striptease clubs etc.*) einschlägige Lokale; **~ tints** *n. pl.* (*Art*) Fleischtöne *Pl.;* **~ wound** *n.* Fleischwunde, *die*

**fleshy** /ˈfleʃɪ/ *adj.* Ⓐ (*fat, boneless*) fett; fleischig ‹Hände›; **the ~ parts of a fish** die grätenlosen Stücke eines Fisches; Ⓑ (*Bot.*) fleischig; Ⓒ (*like flesh*) fleischartig

**fleur-de-lis** /flɜːdəˈliː/ *n., pl.* **fleurs-de-lis** /flɜːdəˈliː/ Ⓐ (*Her.*) Lilie, *die;* Ⓑ *in sing. or pl.* (*Hist.: arms of France*) bourbonische Lilie; Ⓒ (*Bot.*) Lilie, *die*

**flew** ⇒ **fly**[2] 1, 2

**flex**[1] /fleks/ *n.* (*Brit. Electr.*) Kabel, *das*

**flex**[2] *v.t.* Ⓐ (*Anat.*) beugen ‹Arm, Knie›; Ⓑ **~ one's muscles** (*lit. or fig.*) seine Muskeln spielen lassen

**flexibility** /fleksɪˈbɪlɪtɪ/ *n., no pl.* Ⓐ Biegsamkeit, *die;* Elastizität, *die;* Ⓑ (*fig.*) Flexibilität, *die*

**flexible** /ˈfleksɪbl/ *adj.* Ⓐ biegsam; elastisch; Ⓑ (*fig.*) flexibel; dehnbar ‹Vorschriften›; schwach ‹Wille›; **~ working hours** *or* **time** gleitende Arbeitszeit

**flexibly** /ˈfleksɪblɪ/ *adv.* Ⓐ elastisch; Ⓑ (*fig.*) flexibel

**flexitime** /ˈfleksɪtaɪm/ (*Brit.*), **flextime** /ˈflekstaɪm/ (*Amer.*) *ns.* (*Office Managem.*) Gleitzeit, *die;* **be on** *or* **work ~:** gleitende Arbeitszeit haben

**flibbertigibbet** /flɪbətɪˈdʒɪbɪt/ *n.* Leichtfuß, *der* (*ugs.*); (*gossipy person*) Klatschbase, *die* (*ugs.*)

**flick** /flɪk/ ❶ *n.* Ⓐ **~ of the wrist** kurze, schnelle Drehung des Handgelenks; **a ~ of the switch** ein einfaches Klicken des Schalters; **a ~ with the whip** ein Schnalzen mit der Peitsche; **with a ~ of its tongue/tail** mit vorschnellender Zunge/mit einem Schlag des Schwanzes; **he removed the piece of dirt with a ~ of his finger[s]** er schnippte den Schmutz mit den Fingern weg; **give the room a quick ~ with the duster** (*coll.*) kurz mit dem Staubtuch durchs Zimmer gehen; Ⓑ (*sound*) (*of switch*) Klicken, *das;* (*of whip*) Schnalzen, *das;* (*of fingers*) Schnippen, *das.* ⇒ *also* **flicks**.
❷ *v.t.* schnippen; anknipsen ‹Schalter›; verspritzen ‹Tinte›; **~ one's fingers/whip** mit den Fingern schnipsen/mit der Peitsche schnalzen; **~ sth. from** *or* **off sth.** (*with fingers*) etw. von etw. schnippen; (*with duster*) etw. von etw. wischen; **the cow ~ed her tail** die Kuh schlug mit dem Schwanz; **would you just ~ the duster round the room?** (*coll.*) würdest du bitte eben mit dem Staubtuch durchs Zimmer gehen? (*ugs.*).
❸ *v.i.* **the lizard's tongue ~ed out** die Eidechse ließ die Zunge hervorschnellen

**~ through** *v.t.* durchblättern

**flicker** /ˈflɪkə(r)/ ❶ *v.i.* Ⓐ flackern; ‹Fernsehapparat:› flimmern; **shadows ~ed on the wall** Schatten huschten über die Wand; **a smile ~ed round her lips** ein Lächeln spielte um ihre Lippen; Ⓑ (*quiver*) ‹Zunge:› züngeln; ‹Fahne, Lid:› flattern; ‹Blatt:› zittern. ❷ *n.* Ⓐ Flackern, *das;* (*of TV*) Flimmern, *das;* (*of shadow*) Huschen, *das;* (*fig.*) Aufflackern, *das;* (*of smile*) Anflug, *der;* (*of hope, life*) Funke, *der;* Ⓑ (*of bird's tail*) Wippen, *das;* (*of eyelid*) Flattern, *das*

**~ ˈout** *v.i.* (*lit. or fig.*) verlöschen

ˈ**flick knife** *n.* (*Brit.*) Schnappmesser, *das*

**flicks** /flɪks/ *n. pl.* (*coll.*) **the ~:** das Kino; **what's on at the ~?** was gibts im Kino?

**flier** ⇒ **flyer**

**flight**[1] /flaɪt/ ❶ *n.* Ⓐ (*flying*) Flug, *der;* **in ~:** im Flug; **whilst in ~:** während des Fluges; Ⓑ (*journey, passage*) Flug, *der;* (*migration of birds*) Zug, *der;* **the six o'clock ~ to ...:** die 6-Uhr-Maschine nach ...; **on [board] a ~ to ...:** an Bord eines Flugzeugs nach ...; **the ~ from Paris to Rome takes about two hours** die Flugzeit von Paris nach Rom beträgt etwa zwei Stunden; Ⓒ (*fig.: of thought*) Höhenflug, *der;* Ⓓ (*set of stairs*) **~ [of stairs** *or* **steps]** Treppe, *die;* **live two ~s up** zwei Treppen hoch wohnen; Ⓔ (*flock of birds*) Schwarm, *der;* Flug, *der* (*Jägerspr.*); (*volley of arrows*) [Pfeil]hagel, *der;* (*Air Force*) ≈ Staffel, *die;* **in the first** *or* **top ~** (*fig.*) in der Spitzengruppe; **the first** *or* **top ~ of actors** die besten Schauspieler; die Spitzenschauspieler; Ⓕ (*tail of dart*) Befiederung, *die.*
❷ *v.t.* (*Cricket etc.*) **~ the ball** den Ball mit unberechenbarer Flugbahn werfen

**flight**[2] *n.* Ⓐ (*fleeing*) Flucht, *die;* **take [to] ~:** die Flucht ergreifen; **put to ~:** in die Flucht schlagen; Ⓑ (*Econ.*) **the ~ from the dollar** die Flucht aus dem Dollar

**flight: ~ attendant** *n.* ▶ 1261 Flugbegleiter, *der*/-begleiterin, *die;* **~ bag** *n.* ≈ Reisetasche, *die;* **~ control** *n.* Ⓐ (*Aeronaut.*) ≈ Flugsicherung, *die;* Ⓑ (*system of levers, cables, etc.*) Steuerung, *die;* **~ controller** *n.* (*Aeronaut.*) Fluglotse, *der;* **~ deck** *n.* Ⓐ (*of aircraft carrier*) Flugdeck, *das;* Ⓑ (*of aircraft*) Cockpit, *das;* **~ engineer** *n.* Flugingenieur, *der*

**flightless** /ˈflaɪtlɪs/ *adj.* flugunfähig

**flight: ~ lieutenant** *n.* ▶ 1617 (*Air Force*) Hauptmann [der Luftwaffe]; **~ mechanic** *n.* Bordmechaniker, *der;* Bordwart, *der;* **~ number** *n.* Flugnummer, *die;* **~ officer** *n.* Ⓐ (*Brit. Air Force*) [weiblicher] Hauptmann; Ⓑ (*Amer. Air Force*) Stabsfeldwebel, *der;* **~ path** *n.* (*Aeronaut.*) Flugweg, *der;* (*Astronaut.*) Flugbahn, *die;* **~ plan** *n.* Flugplan, *der;* **~ recorder** *n.* Flugschreiber, *der;* **~ simulator** *n.* Flugsimulator, *der;* **~-test** *v.t.* [im Flug] testen

**flighty** /ˈflaɪtɪ/ *adj.* Ⓐ (*fickle*) flatterhaft; Ⓑ (*capricious*) kapriziös

**flimsily** /ˈflɪmzɪlɪ/ *adv.* dünn; hastig ‹errichtet›; schlecht ‹gebunden, verpackt›; **a ~ built** *or* **constructed raft** ein flüchtig zusammengezimmertes Floß

**flimsy** /'flɪmzɪ/ ❶ *adj.* Ⓐ dünn; (*very thin*) hauchdünn ‹Seide, Papier›; fadenscheinig ‹Kleidung, Vorhang›; (*of inadequate material or workmanship*) nicht [sehr] haltbar ‹Verpackung›; nicht [sehr] stabil ‹Konstruktion, Haus, Schiff›; Ⓑ (*fig.*) fadenscheinig (*abwertend*) ‹Entschuldigung, Argument›; dürftig (*abwertend*) ‹Entwurf, Handlung›. ❷ *n.* (*thin paper*) Durchschlagpapier, *das;* (*document*) Durchschlag, *der*

**flinch** /flɪnʃ/ *v.i.* Ⓐ zurückschrecken; **~ from sth./doing sth.** vor einer Sache zurückschrecken/davor zurückschrecken, etw. zu tun; **~ from one's responsibilities** sich seinen Pflichten entziehen; **don't ~ from the facts** man muss den Tatsachen ins Auge sehen; Ⓑ (*wince*) zusammenzucken

**fling** /flɪŋ/ ❶ *n.* Ⓐ (*throw*) **give sth. a ~:** etw. werfen; Ⓑ (*fig.: attempt*) **have a ~ at sth., give sth. a ~:** es mit etw. versuchen; **have a ~ at doing sth.** es damit versuchen, etw. zu tun; Ⓒ (*fig.: indulgence*) **have one's ~:** sich ausleben; **youth must have its ~:** die Jugend muss sich austoben [können]; **have one last ~:** sein Leben noch einmal richtig genießen; (*by going on a drinking spree*) noch einmal einen draufmachen (*ugs.*). ❷ *v.t.*, **flung** /flʌŋ/ Ⓐ werfen; **~ open/shut** aufreißen/zuwerfen; **~ back one's head** den Kopf zurückwerfen; **~ one's arms round sb.'s neck** jmdm. die Arme um den Hals werfen; **~ sth. away** (*lit. or fig.*) etw. fortwerfen; **~ down the money** das Geld hinschmeißen (*ugs.*); **~ off one's attacker** seinen Angreifer wegstoßen; **~ off one's clothes** die Kleider von sich werfen; **~ on one's jacket** [sich (*Dat.*)] die Jacke überwerfen; **the horse flung him off** das Pferd warf ihn ab; Ⓑ (*fig.*) **~ sb. into jail** jmdn. ins Gefängnis werfen; **~ sb. into confusion** jmdn. in Verwirrung stürzen; **~ sb. a despairing look** jmdm. einen verzweifelten Blick zuwerfen; **~ down a challenge to sb.** jmdn. herausfordern; **~ caution/prudence to the winds/~ aside one's scruples** alle Vorsicht/alle Umsicht/seine Skrupel über Bord werfen; **~ off restraints** Fesseln abwerfen.
❸ *v. refl.*, **flung** Ⓐ **~ oneself at sb.** sich auf jmdn. stürzen; **~ oneself in front of/upon** *or* **on to sth.** sich vor/auf etw. (*Akk.*) werfen; **~ oneself at sb.'s feet** sich jmdm. zu Füßen werfen; **~ oneself into a chair** sich in einen Sessel fallen lassen *od.* werfen; **~ oneself into sb.'s arms** in jmds. Arme stürzen; Ⓑ (*fig.*) **~ oneself into sth.** sich in etw. (*Akk.*) stürzen; **~ oneself at sb.** sich jmdm. an den Hals werfen (*ugs.*)

**flint** /flɪnt/ *n.* Feuerstein, *der;* Flint, *der* (*veralt.*); **as hard as ~:** hart wie Stein

**flint: ~ glass** *n.* Flintglas, *das;* **~lock** *n.* (*Hist.*) Steinschlossgewehr, *das*

**flinty** /'flɪntɪ/ *adj.* Ⓐ (*containing flint*) feuersteinhaltig; (*resembling flint*) feuersteinartig; Ⓑ (*fig.*) unbeugsam; **have a ~ heart** ein Herz aus Stein haben

**flip¹** /flɪp/ ❶ *n.* Ⓐ Schnipsen, *das;* **give sth. a ~:** etw. hochschnipsen; Ⓑ (*coll.: outing*) [kurzer] Ausflug. ❷ *adj.* (*coll.*) schnodderig (*ugs.*). ❸ *v.t.*, **-pp-** schnipsen; **~ [over]** (*turn over*) umdrehen; **~ one's lid** (*fig. coll.*) ausflippen (*ugs.*). ❹ *v.i.*, **-pp-** Ⓐ (*coll.*) ausflippen; Ⓑ (*turn over*) **the plane ~ped [over] on to its back** das Flugzeug drehte sich auf den Rücken

**~ through** ⇒ **flick through**

**flip²** *n.* (*drink*) Flip, *der;* ⇒ *also* **egg flip**

**'flip chart** *n.* Flipchart, *das*

**'flip-flops** *n. pl.* [Plastik-/Gummi]sandalen *Pl.*

**flippancy** /'flɪpənsɪ/ *n.*, *no pl.* Unernst, *der;* Leichtfertigkeit, *die*

**flippant** /'flɪpənt/ *adj.*, **flippantly** /'flɪpəntlɪ/ *adv.* unernst; leichtfertig

**flipper** /'flɪpə(r)/ *n.* Ⓐ (*Zool.*) Flosse, *die;* Ⓑ (*of swimmer*) [Schwimm]flosse, *die*

**flipping** /'flɪpɪŋ/ (*Brit. coll.*) ❶ *adj.* **it's a ~ nuisance/waste of time** das ist schon verflixt ärgerlich/eine blöde Zeitvergeudung (*ugs.*); **you're a ~ idiot** du bist wirklich ein Idiot!; **~ heck!** Scheibe! (*ugs. verhüll.*). ❷ *adv.* verflixt (*ugs.*) ‹lästig, ärgerlich, kalt›; ganz schön (*ugs.*) ‹schlimm, wütend›

**'flip side** *n.* B-Seite, *die*

**flirt** /flɜːt/ ❶ *n.* **he/she is just a ~:** er/sie will nur flirten; **she looks a bit of a ~:** sie scheint einem Flirt nicht abgeneigt zu sein. ❷ *v.i.* Ⓐ **~ [with sb.]** [mit jmdm.] flirten; Ⓑ (*fig.*) **~ with sth.** mit etw. liebäugeln; **~ with the idea of doing sth.** mit dem Gedanken spielen *od.* liebäugeln, etw. zu tun; **~ with danger/death** die Gefahr [leichtfertig] herausfordern/mit dem Leben spielen

**flirtation** /flɜː'teɪʃn/ *n.* Flirt, *der;* **there's a lot of ~ between the two of them** die beiden flirten ganz schön miteinander; **it was merely innocent ~:** es war nur ein unschuldiger Flirt

**flirtatious** /flɜː'teɪʃəs/ *adj.* kokett ‹Blick, Art›; **their ~ involvement** ihr Flirt; **she's a ~ woman** sie flirtet gern

**flirtatiousness** /flɜː'teɪʃəsnɪs/ *n.*, *no pl.* Koketterie, *die*

**flit** /flɪt/ ❶ *v.i.*, **-tt-** Ⓐ huschen; **thoughts/recollections ~ted through his mind** Gedanken/Erinnerungen schossen ihm durch den Kopf; **his mind ~ted from one thing to another** seine Gedanken eilten von einem Thema zum anderen; Ⓑ (*depart*) **~ northward** nach Norden ziehen; **~ away** verschwinden; Ⓒ (*esp. Scot., N. Engl.: move house*) umziehen. ❷ *n.* **do a ~** (*coll.*) sich absetzen (*ugs.*); ⇒ *also* **moonlight** 2

**flitch** /flɪtʃ/ *n.* **~ [of bacon]** Speckseite, *die*

**float** /fləʊt/ ❶ *v.i.* Ⓐ (*on water*) treiben; ‹gestrandetes Schiff:› flott werden; **~ away** wegtreiben; **she just ~ed for some time** sie ließ sich eine Weile treiben; **~ to the surface** an die Oberfläche treiben; Ⓑ (*through air*) schweben; **~ across sth.** ‹Wolke, Nebel:› über etw. (*Akk.*) ziehen; **~ away** fortschweben; Ⓒ (*fig.*) **~ about** *or* **[a]round** umgehen; im Umlauf sein; **thoughts ~ through my mind** Gedanken gehen mir durch den Kopf; Ⓓ (*sl.: move casually*) **~ [around** *or* **about]** herumziehen (*ugs.*); **~ in and out** rein- und rausgehen (*ugs.*); **~ about the area** sich in der Gegend herumtreiben; Ⓔ (*Finance*) floaten.
❷ *v.t.* Ⓐ (*convey by water, on rafts*) flößen; (*set afloat*) flottmachen ‹Schiff›; (*through air*) schweben lassen; **the ship was ~ed by the tide** das Schiff kam bei Flut wieder flott; **~ the cream on top of the soup** die Sahne [vorsichtig] auf die Suppe geben; Ⓑ (*fig.: circulate*) in Umlauf bringen; Ⓒ (*Finance*) floaten lassen; freigeben; Ⓓ (*Commerc.*) ausgeben, auf den Markt bringen ‹Aktien›; gründen ‹Unternehmen›; lancieren ‹Plan, Idee›; lancieren, auflegen ‹Anleihe›.
❸ *n.* Ⓐ (*for carnival*) Festwagen, *der;* (*Brit.: delivery cart*) Wagen, *der;* ⇒ *also* **milk float;** Ⓑ (*petty cash*) Bargeld, *das;* (*to provide change*) Wechselgeld, *das;* Ⓒ (*Angling*) Floß, *das* (*fachspr.*); Schwimmer, *der;* (*on net*) Schwimmkörper, *der;* Ⓓ (*in cistern, carburettor; also Aeronaut.*) Schwimmer, *der;* Ⓔ (*of fish*) Schwimmblase, *die;* Ⓕ *in sing. or pl.* (*Theatre: footlights*) Rampenlicht, *das;* Ⓖ (*of plasterer*) Reibebrett, *das*

**floating** /'fləʊtɪŋ/ *adj.* treibend; schwimmend ‹Hotel›; **the ~ population** (*fig.*) die mobile Bevölkerung; **~ exchange rate** flexibler *od.* frei schwankender Wechselkurs

**floating: ~ 'bridge** *n.* (*bridge*) Pontonbrücke, *die;* (*ferry*) Kettenfähre, *die;* **~ 'capital** *n.* frei verfügbares Kapital; **~ 'debt** *n.* (*Finance*) schwebende Schuld; **~ 'dock** *n.* Schwimmdock, *das;* **~ 'kidney** *n.* (*Med.*) Wanderniere, *die;* **~ 'point** *n.* (*Computing*) Fließkomma, *das;* **~ 'rib** *n.* (*Anat.*) freie Rippe; **~ 'voter** *n.* Wechselwähler, *der*/-wählerin, *die*

**flock¹** /flɒk/ ❶ *n.* Ⓐ (*of sheep, goats; also Eccl.*) Herde, *die;* (*of birds*) Schwarm, *der;* Ⓑ (*of people*) Schar, *die;* **in ~s** in [großen *od.* hellen] Scharen; scharenweise; Ⓒ (*of things*) Reihe, *die.* ❷ *v.i.* strömen; **~ round sb.** sich um jmdn. scharen; **~ in/out/together** [in Scharen] hinein-/heraus-/zusammenströmen; **~ to Mecca/the seaside** [in Scharen] nach Mekka/ans Meer strömen; **~/come ~ing to hear sb. speak** herbeiströmen/herbeigeströmt kommen, um jmdn. reden zu hören

**flock²** *n.* Ⓐ (*of wool, cotton, etc.*) Flocke, *die;* Ⓑ *in pl.* (*material*) Reißwolle, *die*

**flock: ~-mattress** *n. mit Reißwolle gefüllte Matratze;* **~ 'wallpaper** *n.* Velourstapete, *die;* Flocktapete, *die* (*fachspr.*)

**floe** /fləʊ/ *n.* Eisscholle, *die*

**flog** /flɒg/ *v.t.*, **-gg-** Ⓐ (*beat as punishment*) auspeitschen; (*urge on*) [mit der Peitsche] antreiben; **~ a dead horse** (*fig.*) seine Kraft und Zeit verschwenden; **~ sth. to death** (*fig.*) etw. zu Tode reiten; **~ oneself to death** (*fig.*) sich fast zu Tode arbeiten; Ⓑ (*Brit. coll.: sell*) verscheuern (*salopp*)

**flood** /flʌd/ ❶ *n.* Ⓐ ▶ **1480** Überschwemmung, *die;* **the river is in ~:** der Fluss führt Hochwasser; **the F~** (*Bibl.*) die Sintflut; *attrib.* **~ area** Überschwemmungsgebiet, *das;* Ⓑ (*fig.*) Flut, *die;* **in full ~:** in voller Stärke; **in ~s of tears** tränenüberströmt; Ⓒ (*Theatre coll.*) ⇒ **floodlight** 1; Ⓓ (*of tide*) Flut, *die;* (*poet.: river*) Strom, *der;* **~ and field** (*literary*) Wasser und Land; **the tide is at the ~:** es ist Flut. ❷ *v.i.* Ⓐ ‹Fluss:› über die Ufer treten; **there's danger of ~ing** es besteht Überschwemmungsgefahr; **there's been a lot of ~ing in the area** es ist in dem Gebiet schon zu zahlreichen Überschwemmungen gekommen; Ⓑ (*fig.*) strömen; **~ through sb.** jmdn. durchströmen *od.* -fluten; **light ~ed into the room** Licht flutete ins Zimmer; **applications for the job ~ed in** eine Flut von Bewerbungen ging ein. ❸ *v.t.* Ⓐ überschwemmen; (*with moving liquid*) überfluten; (*deluge, irrigate*) unter Wasser setzen; **the cellar was ~ed** der Keller stand unter Wasser; **be ~ed out** durch eine Überschwemmung obdachlos werden; Ⓑ (*fig.*) überschwemmen; **~ed with light** lichtdurchflutet

**flood: ~ control** *n.* Hochwasserschutz, *der;* **~ damage** *n.* Hochwasserschaden, *der;* **the area suffered extensive ~ damage** in dem Gebiet gab es beträchtliche Hochwasserschäden; **~gate** *n.* (*Hydraulic Engin.*) Schütze, *die;* **open the ~gates to sth.** (*fig.*) einer Sache (*Dat.*) Tür und Tor öffnen; **~light** ❶ *n.* Scheinwerfer, *der;* (*illumination in a broad beam*) Flutlicht, *das;* ❷ *v.t.*, **~lit** /'flʌdlɪt/ anstrahlen ‹Bauwerk›; beleuchten ‹Weg, Straße›; mit Flutlicht erhellen ‹Stadion›; **~lighting** *n.*, *no indef. art.* (*lights*) Flutlichtanlage, *die;* **~-tide** *n.* Flut, *die;* **~ warning** *n.* Hochwasserwarnung, *die;* (*at the seaside*) Flutwarnung, *die;* **~ water** *n.* Hochwasser, *das;* (*in motion*) anflutendes Wasser

**floor** /flɔː(r)/ ❶ *n.* Ⓐ Boden, *der;* (*of room*) [Fuß]boden, *der;* **built-in ~-to-ceiling cupboards** raumhohe Einbauschränke; **wipe the ~ with sb.** (*fig. coll.*) jmdn. auseinander nehmen (*salopp*); **take the ~** (*dance*) sich aufs Parkett begeben; ⇒ *also* **c**; Ⓑ (*storey*) Stockwerk, *das;* **first ~** (*Amer.*) Erdgeschoss, *das;* **first ~** (*Brit.*), **second ~** (*Amer.*) erster Stock; **on the top ~:** im obersten Stock; **ground ~:** Erdgeschoss, *das;* Parterre, *das;* **get in on the ground ~ [of sth.]** (*fig. coll.*) [bei etw.] von Anfang an dabei sein; Ⓒ (*in debate, meeting*) Sitzungssaal, *der;* (*Parl.*) Plenarsaal, *der;* **cross the ~** (*Brit.*) mit der Gegenpartei stimmen; **from the ~:** seitens der Anwesenden; (*Parl.*) seitens des Plenums; **be given** *or* **have the ~:** das Wort haben; **take the ~** (*Amer.: speak*) das Wort ergreifen; ⇒ *also* **a**; **hold²** 1 N; Ⓓ (*fig.: of prices/wages*) Mindestpreis/-lohn, *der.*
❷ *v.t.* Ⓐ (*confound*) überfordern; (*overcome, defeat*) besiegen; **her rejoinder ~ed him completely** mit ihrer Antwort hat sie es ihm ganz schön gegeben (*ugs.*); Ⓑ (*knock down*) zu Boden schlagen *od.* strecken; Ⓒ (*pave*) **~ [with sth.]** mit einem Boden [aus etw.] versehen

**floor: ~ area** *n.* Grundfläche, *die;* **~board** *n.* Dielenbrett, *das;* **~cloth** *n.* (*Brit.*) Scheuertuch, *das;* **~ covering** *n.* Fußbodenbelag, *der*

**flooring** /ˈflɔːrɪŋ/ *n.* Fußboden[belag], *der;* **parquet ~:** Parkettfußboden, *der*

**floor: ~ lamp** *n.* (*Amer.*) Stehlampe, *die;* **~ manager** *n.* (A) (*Telev.*) Aufnahmeleiter, *der;* (B) (*in shop*) ≈ Abteilungsleiter, *der;* **~ plan** *n.* Grundriss eines/des Stockwerks; **~ polish** *n.* Bohnerwachs, *das;* **~ polisher** *n.* Bohnermaschine, *die;* Bohner, *der* (*DDR*); **~ show** *n.* ≈ Unterhaltungsprogramm, *das;* **~ space** *n.* Grundfläche, *die;* **~ tile** *n.* Fliese, *die;* **~walker** *n.* (*Amer.*) ≈ Abteilungsleiter, *der*

**floozie (floosie)** /ˈfluːzɪ/ *n.* (*coll.*) Flittchen, *das* (*ugs. abwertend*)

**flop** /flɒp/ ❶ *v.i.*, **-pp-** (A) plumpsen; (*flap*) flattern; **she ~ped into a chair** sie ließ sich in einen Sessel plumpsen; **the fish ~ped about in the boat** der Fisch zappelte im Boot; **he ~ped down on his knees** er ließ sich auf die Knie fallen; (B) (*coll.: fail*) fehlschlagen; ein Reinfall sein (*ugs.*); ‹Theaterstück, Show:› durchfallen. ❷ *n.* (A) (*coll.: failure*) Reinfall, *der* (*ugs.*); Flop, *der* (*ugs.*); (B) (*motion, sound*) Plumps, *der*

**floppy** /ˈflɒpɪ/ *adj.* weich und biegsam; **~ disk** ⇒ **disk**; **~ ears/hat** Schlappohren/ Schlapphut, *der*

**flora** /ˈflɔːrə/ *n., pl.* **~e** /ˈflɔːriː/ *or* **~s** Flora, *die;* (*list, treatise*) **a ~ of North America** eine Übersicht/Abhandlung über die Flora Nordamerikas

**floral** /ˈflɔːrl, ˈflɒrl/ *adj.* geblümt ‹Kleid, Stoff, Tapete›; Blumen‹gesteck, -arrangement, -muster›; **~ perfumes** nach Blumen duftende Parfüms; **a ~ tribute to sb.** ein Blumengruß für jmdn.

**Florence** /ˈflɒrəns/ *pr. n.* ▶ 1626 Florenz (*das*)

**Florentine** /ˈflɒrəntaɪn/ ❶ *adj.* florentinisch. ❷ *n.* Florentiner, *der*/Florentinerin, *die*

**floret** /ˈflɔːrɪt/ *n.* (*Bot.*) *Einzelblüte eines Blütenstandes*

**florid** /ˈflɒrɪd/ *adj.* (A) (*over-ornate*) schwülstig (*abwertend*); blumig ‹Stil, Redeweise›; überladen ‹Architektur, Stil, Ornament›; (B) (*high-coloured*) gerötet ‹Teint›

**florist** /ˈflɒrɪst/ *n.* ▶ 1261 Florist, *der*/Floristin, *die;* (*grower of flowers*) ≈ Gärtner, *der*/ Gärtnerin, *die;* **~'s [shop]** Blumenladen, *der*

**floss** /flɒs/ *n.* (A) (*silk, thread*) Rohseide, *die;* (*loosely twisted, of silk or cotton*) ≈ Sticktwist, *der;* (B) (*on cocoon*) Flockseide, *die.* ⇒ *also* **candyfloss**; **dental floss**

**flotation** /fləʊˈteɪʃn/ *n.* (A) (*Phys.*) Auftrieb, *der;* (B) (*Metall.*) Schwimmaufbereitung, *die;* Flotation, *die;* (C) (*Commerc.*) ⇒ **float** 2 D: Ausgabe, *die;* Gründung, *die;* Lancierung, *die*

**flotilla** /fləˈtɪlə/ *n.* Flottille, *die*

**flotsam** /ˈflɒtsəm/ *n.* **~ [and jetsam]** Treibgut, *das;* **~ and jetsam** (*fig.: of society*) menschliches Treibgut

**flounce**[1] /flaʊns/ *v.i.* stolzieren

**flounce**[2] (*Dressm.*) ❶ *n.* Volant, *der.* ❷ *v.t.* mit einem Volant besetzen

**flounder**[1] /ˈflaʊndə(r)/ *v.i.* taumeln; (*stumble, lit. or fig.*) stolpern; (*struggle*) sich quälen; **~ through a speech** eine Rede zusammenstottern

**flounder**[2] *n.* (*Zool.*) Flunder, *die*

**flour** /flaʊə(r)/ ❶ *n.* Mehl, *das;* ⇒ *also* **cornflour.** ❷ *v.t.* (*Cookery*) mit Mehl bestäuben; bemehlen (*fachspr.*)

**flourish** /ˈflʌrɪʃ/ ❶ *v.i.* (A) gedeihen; ‹Handel, Geschäft:› florieren, gut gehen; ‹Kunst, Musik, Kirche:› eine Blütezeit erleben *od.* haben; ‹Zeitung, Firma:› sich gut entwickeln; (B) (*be active*) seine Blütezeit erleben *od.* haben; ‹Künstler:› seine beste Schaffensperiode haben. ❷ *v.t.* schwingen; **~ one's cane at sb.** vor jmdm. mit dem Stock herumfuchteln (*ugs.*). ❸ *n.* (A) **do sth. with a ~:** etw. schwungvoll *od.* mit einer schwungvollen Bewegung tun; **with a ~ of his stick/hand** seinen Stock schwenkend/mit einer schwungvollen Handbewegung; (B) (*in writing*) Schnörkel, *der;* (C) (*ornate language*) Ausschmückung, *die;* **a ~ of fine words** ein Feuerwerk von schönen Worten; (D) (*Mus.: fanfare*) Fanfare, *die;* (*florid passage*) Verzierung, *die;* **~ of trumpets** Fanfarenstoß, *der*

**floury** /ˈflaʊərɪ/ *adj.* mehlig

**flout** /flaʊt/ *v.t.* missachten; sich hinwegsetzen über (+ *Akk.*) ‹Ratschlag, Wunsch, öffentliche Meinung›

**flow** /fləʊ/ ❶ *v.i.* (A) ▶ 1480 fließen; ‹Körner, Sand:› rinnen, rieseln; ‹Gas:› strömen; **two rivers ~ into each other/into the sea** zwei Flüsse fließen zusammen/münden ins Meer; **the river ~ed over its banks** der Fluss trat über die Ufer; **the oil has ~ed out** das Öl ist ausgelaufen; **lava ~ed across the valley** Lava ergoss sich *od.* strömte ins Tal; **blood will ~** (*fig.*) es wird Blut fließen; (B) (*fig.*) fließen; ‹Personen:› strömen; **keep the traffic ~ing smoothly** den Verkehr fließend halten; **keep the conversation ~ing** das Gespräch in Fluss halten; **the writing does not ~:** der Text ist nicht flüssig geschrieben; **talk ~ed freely** das Gespräch war sehr lebhaft; **is the work ~ing smoothly?** geht die Arbeit gut von der Hand?; (C) (*abound*) **~ freely** *or* **like water** reichlich *od.* in Strömen fließen; (D) **~ from** (*be derived from*) sich ergeben aus; (*be produced from*) fließen aus ‹Feder›; fließen von ‹Lippen›; (E) (*rise*) ‹Flut, Wasser:› steigen; **the tide ~s twice a day** die Flut kommt zweimal am Tag.
❷ *n.* (A) Fließen, *das;* (*progress*) Fluss, *der;* (*volume*) Durchflussmenge, *die;* **~ of water/ blood/air/gas/lava/money/people** Wasser-/Blut-/Luft-/Gas-/Lava-/Geld-/Menschenstrom, *der;* **~ of electricity/traffic/capital/conversation** Strom-/Verkehrs-/Kapital-/Gesprächsfluss, *der;* **~ of information/ news/ideas/thoughts/words** Informations-/Nachrichten-/Ideen-/Gedanken-/Redefluss, *der;* **the elegant ~ of his prose** der elegante Fluss seiner Prosa; **improve the work ~:** den Arbeitsablauf verbessern; ⇒ *also* **cash flow**; (B) (*of tide, river*) Flut, *die;* **the tide is on the ~:** die Flut kommt; es ist Flut; (C) (*Phys.: of solid*) Fließen, *das*

**~ aˈway** *v.i.* abfließen

**ˈflow chart** *n.* Flussdiagramm, *das*

**flower** /flaʊə(r)/ ❶ *n.* (A) (*blossom*) Blüte, *die;* (*plant*) Blume, *die;* **send sb. ~s** jmdm. Blumen schicken; **'no ~s [by request]'** „es wird gebeten, von Blumenspenden abzusehen"; **say it with ~s** es mit Blumen sagen; Blumen sprechen lassen; **[be] in [full] ~:** in [voller] Blüte [stehen]; **come into ~:** zu blühen beginnen; (B) *no pl.* (*fig.: best part*) Zierde, *die;* (*prime*) Blüte, *die;* **in the ~ of youth/her age** in der Blüte der Jugend/ ihrer Jahre.
❷ *v.i.* blühen; (*fig.*) erblühen (**into** zu)

**flower: ~ arrangement** *n.* (A) ⇒ **flower arranging**; (B) (*result*) Blumenarrangement, *das;* (*smaller also*) Gesteck, *das;* **~ arranging** *n.* Blumenstecken, *das;* **~ bed** *n.* Blumenbeet, *das*

**flowered** /flaʊəd/ *adj.* geblümt ‹Stoff, Teppich, Tapete›; **purple-~:** purpur blühend ‹Pflanze›

**flower: ~ garden** *n.* Blumengarten, *der;* **~ girl** *n.* Blumenverkäuferin, *die;* **~ head** *n.* Köpfchen, *das* (*Bot.*); (*of composite*) Körbchen, *das* (*Bot.*)

**flowering** /ˈflaʊərɪŋ/ *adj.* **~ cherry/shrub/ currant** Zierkirsche, *die*/Blütenstrauch, *der*/ Goldjohannisbeere, *die*

**flowerless** /ˈflaʊəlɪs/ *adj.* blütenlos ‹Pflanze›; **~ gardens** Gärten ohne Blumen

**flower: ~ people** *n. pl.* Blumenkinder; **~pot** *n.* Blumentopf, *der;* **~ shop** *n.* Blumenladen, *der;* **~ show** *n.* Blumenschau, *die*

**flowery** /ˈflaʊərɪ/ *adj.* ‹Wiese› voller Blumen; ‹Garten› voller Blumen/Blüten; geblümt ‹Stoff, Muster›; blumig ‹Duft, Wein›; (*fig.*) blumig ‹Sprache, Ausdruck›

**flowing** /ˈfləʊɪŋ/ *adj.* fließend; wallend ‹Haar, Bart, Gewand›; flüssig ‹Handschrift›

**ˈflow meter** *n.* Durchflussmessgerät, *das*

**flown** ⇒ **fly**[2] 1, 2

**flow: ~ rate** *n.* Durchflussmenge, *die;* **~sheet** ⇒ **flow chart**

**fl oz** *abbr.* ▶ 1671 **fluid ounce**

**flu** /fluː/ *n.* ▶ 1232 (*coll.*) Grippe, *die;* **get** *or* **catch [the] ~:** Grippe bekommen

**fluctuate** /ˈflʌktjʊeɪt/ *v.i.* schwanken; fluktuieren (*bes. Wirtsch., Soziol.*); **the level of attendance ~s** die Teilnehmerzahl schwankt *od.* ist schwankend

**fluctuation** /flʌktjʊˈeɪʃn/ *n.* Schwankung, *die;* Fluktuation, *die* (*bes. Wirtsch., Soziol.*)

**flue** /fluː/ *n.* (A) (*in chimney*) Rauchabzug, *der;* Feuerzug, *der* (*Technik*); (B) (*for passage of hot air*) Luftkanal, *der;* (C) (*in boiler*) Flammrohr, *das* (*Technik*)

**fluency** /ˈfluːənsɪ/ *n.* Gewandtheit, *die;* (*in speaking*) Redegewandtheit, *die;* **I was complimented on the ~ of my Greek** mein flüssiges *od.* gutes Griechisch wurde gelobt

**fluent** /ˈfluːənt/ *adj.* ▶ 1275 gewandt ‹Stil, Redeweise, Redner, Schreiber, Erzähler›; **be ~ in Russian, speak ~ Russian, be a ~ speaker of Russian** fließend Russisch sprechen; **you'll soon become ~:** du wirst bald fließend sprechen [können]; **my Arabic is ~:** ich spreche fließend Arabisch

**fluently** /ˈfluːəntlɪ/ *adv.* fließend ‹sprechen, lesen›; flüssig ‹schreiben›; gewandt ‹sich ausdrücken›; ununterbrochen ‹fluchen›

**fluff** /flʌf/ ❶ *n.* (A) Flusen *Pl.;* Fusseln *Pl.;* (*on birds, rabbits, etc.*) Flaum, *der;* **there are pieces of ~ all over my trousers** meine Hose ist voller Fusseln; **the carpet is covered in ~:** der Teppich ist mit Flusen bedeckt; **bit of ~** (*coll.: young woman*) Mieze, *die* (*ugs.*); (B) (*coll.: mistake*) Patzer, *der* (*ugs.*). ❷ *v.t.* (A) **~ out** *or* **up** aufschütteln ‹Kissen›; **the bird ~ed itself/its feathers** der Vogel plusterte sich/seine Federn auf; (B) (*coll.: bungle*) verpatzen (*ugs.*); **~ one's lines** seinen Text verpatzen

**fluffy** /ˈflʌfɪ/ *adj.* [flaum]weich ‹Kissen, Küken, Haar›; flauschig ‹Spielzeug, Stoff, Decke›; locker ‹Haar, Omelett, Brot›; flockig ‹Schnee›; schaumig ‹Eiweiß›

**flugelhorn** /ˈfluːglhɔːn/ *n.* (*Mus.*) Flügelhorn, *das*

**fluid** /ˈfluːɪd/ ❶ *n.* (A) (*liquid*) Flüssigkeit, *die;* (B) (*liquid or gas*) Fluid, *das* (*Technik, Chemie*). ❷ *adj.* (A) (*liquid*) flüssig; ⇒ *also* **dram** A; (B) (*liquid or gaseous*) fluid (*Technik, Chemie*); (C) (*flowing*) flüssig ‹Stil›; fließend ‹Linie, Form›; (D) (*fig.*) ungewiss, unklar ‹Lage›; [noch] nicht fest umrissen ‹Plan›

**fluid: ~ ˈclutch** *n.* (*Motor Veh.*), **~ ˈcoupling** *n.* (*Mech. Engin.*) hydraulische Kupplung; Flüssigkeitskupplung, *die*

**fluidity** /fluːˈɪdɪtɪ/ *n., no pl.* Flüssigkeit, *die;* Fluidität, *die* (*Technik, Chemie*)

**fluid: ~ ˈounce** *n.* ▶ 1671 (*Brit.*) 28,41 $cm^3$; **~ˈounce** *n.* (*Amer.*) 29,57 $cm^3$; **~ pressure** *n.* hydrostatischer Druck (*Physik*)

**fluke**[1] /fluːk/ *n.* (*piece of luck*) Glücksfall, *der;* **by a** *or* **some [pure] ~:** [nur] durch einen glücklichen Zufall; **by some extraordinary ~:** durch außergewöhnliches Glück; **it was a bit of a ~:** es war ein bisschen Glück dabei

**fluke**[2] *n.* (A) (*Vet. Med.: flatworm*) Saugwurm, *der;* Trematode, *die* (*fachspr.*); **liver ~:** Leberegel, *der;* (B) (*fish*) Flunder, *die*

**fluke**[3] *n.* (A) (*of whale's tail*) Fluke, *die* (*Zool.*); Schwanzflosse, *die;* (B) (*of anchor*) Flunke, *die* (*Seemannsspr.*); Ankerarm, *der;* (C) (*of lance, harpoon, etc.*) Widerhaken, *der*

**fluky** /ˈfluːkɪ/ *adj.* glücklich ‹Zufall, Zusammentreffen, Sieg›; zufällig ‹Ergebnis, Relikt›; Zufalls‹treffer, -ergebnis›

**flummox** /ˈflʌməks/ *v.t.* (*coll.*) aus der Fassung bringen; durcheinander bringen; **be ~ed by sth.** durch etw. verwirrt sein

**flung** ⇒ **fling** 2, 3

**flunk** /flʌŋk/ (*Amer. coll.*) ❶ *v.i.* durchfallen (*ugs.*). ❷ *v.t.* verhauen (*ugs.*) ‹Prüfung, Examen›; durchfallen lassen (*ugs.*) ‹Kandidaten›; **~ the exam** im Examen *od.* bei der Prüfung durchfallen (*ugs.*); **get ~ed** durchfallen (*ugs.*)

**~ ˈout** *v.i.* rausfliegen (*salopp*); [hinaus]fliegen (*ugs.*); **~ out of school** von der Schule fliegen (*ugs.*)

**flunkey, flunky** /ˈflʌŋkɪ/ *n.* (*usu. derog.*) Lakai, *der* (*abwertend*)

**fluoresce** /fluːəˈres/ *v.i.* fluoreszieren

**fluorescence** /fluːəˈresəns/ *n.* Fluoreszenz, *die*

**fluorescent** /flʊəˈresənt/ *adj.* fluoreszierend; **~ material** Leuchtstoff, *der;* **~ display** Leuchtanzeige, *die*

**fluorescent: ~ ˈlamp, ~ ˈlight** *ns.* Leuchtstofflampe, *die* (*Elektrot.*); ≈ Neonlampe, *die;* **~ ˈlighting** *n.* Neonbeleuchtung, *die;* Neonlicht, *das;* **~ ˈscreen** *n.* Leuchtschirm, *der;* **~ ˈtube** *n.* Leucht[stoff]röhre, *die*

**fluoridate** /ˈfluːərɪdeɪt/ *v.t.* fluori[si]eren

**fluoridation** /fluːərɪˈdeɪʃn/ *n.* Fluori[si]erung, *die*

**fluoride** /ˈfluːəraɪd/ *n.* Fluorid, *das;* **~ toothpaste** fluorhaltige Zahnpasta

**fluorine** /ˈfluːəriːn/ *n.* (*Chem.*) Fluor, *das*

**fluorspar** /ˈfluːəspɑː(r)/ *n.* (*Min.*) Flussspat, *der;* Fluorit, *der*

**flurried** /ˈflʌrɪd/ *adj.* nervös

**flurry** /ˈflʌrɪ/ ❶ *n.* Ⓐ Aufregung, *die;* **there was a sudden ~ of activity** es herrschte plötzlich rege Betriebsamkeit; **a ~ of excitement** helle *od.* große Aufregung; Ⓑ (*of rain/snow*) [Regen-/Schnee]schauer, *der;* **~ [of wind]** Windstoß, *der.* ❷ *v.t.* durcheinander bringen; **don't let yourself be flurried** lass dich nicht nervös *od.* (*ugs.*) verrückt machen

**flush¹** /flʌʃ/ ❶ *v.i.* (*blush*) rot werden; erröten (**with** vor + *Dat.*); **~ hotly/bright red** puter-/knallrot anlaufen *od.* werden.

❷ *v.t.* ausspülen ‹Becken›; durch-, ausspülen ‹Rohr›; **~ the toilet** *or* **lavatory** spülen; **~ sth. down the toilet** etw. die Toilette hinunterspülen.

❸ *n.* Ⓐ (*blush*) Erröten, *das;* (*in fever, menopause*) Flush, *der* (*Med.*); fliegende Hitze; (*glow of light or colour*) Glühen, *das;* **hot ~es** Hitzewallungen; Ⓑ (*elation*) **in the [first] ~ of victory** *or* **conquest** im [ersten] Siegestaumel; **~ of excitement** Woge der Begeisterung; **~ of enthusiasm** Begeisterungstaumel, *der;* Ⓒ (*bloom, vigour*) Blüte, *die* (*geh.*); **in the first ~ of youth/romance** in der ersten Blüte der Jugend/in der ersten Liebesglut; Ⓓ (*of lavatory, drain, etc.*) Spülung, *die;* Ⓔ (*sudden abundance*) Flut, *die*

**flush²** *adj.* Ⓐ (*level*) bündig; **be ~ with sth.** mit etw. bündig abschließen; (*horizontally*) auf gleicher Ebene mit etw. liegen; Ⓑ *usu. pred.* (*plentiful*) reichlich vorhanden *od.* im Umlauf ‹Geld›; **be ~ [with money]** gut bei Kasse sein (*ugs.*)

**flush³** *v.t.* aufscheuchen ‹Vögel, Wild›

**~ ˈout** *v.t.* aufscheuchen (*fig.*) ‹Spion, Verbrecher›

**flush⁴** *n.* (*Cards*) *Karten derselben Farbe;* (*Poker*) Flush, *der;* **straight ~:** Straight Flush, *der;* Farbsequenz, *die;* **royal ~:** Royal Flush, *der;* höchste Farbsequenz

**flushed** /flʌʃt/ *adj.* gerötet ‹Wangen, Gesicht›; **you're extremely ~:** du bist ganz rot [im Gesicht]; **~ with pride** vor Stolz glühend

**flush ˈtoilet** *n.* Toilette mit Wasserspülung

**fluster** /ˈflʌstə(r)/ ❶ *v.t.* aus der Fassung bringen; **she is not easily ~ed** sie ist nicht leicht aus der Fassung zu bringen. ❷ *n.* **be [all] in a ~:** [völlig] durcheinander *od.* verstört sein

**flustered** /ˈflʌstəd/ *adj.* **be/become ~:** nervös sein/werden

**flute** /fluːt/ *n.* Ⓐ (*Mus.*) Flöte, *die;* Ⓑ (*Archit.*) Kannelüre, *die;* **~s** Kannelierung, *die;* Ⓒ (*wineglass*) [Sekt]flöte, *die*

**fluted** /ˈfluːtɪd/ *adj.* gerüscht ‹Stoff, Manschette›; gerillt ‹Griff, Tischbein, Stiel›; (*Archit.*) kanneliert

**flutist** /ˈfluːtɪst/ ⇒ **flautist**

**flutter** /ˈflʌtə(r)/ ❶ *v.i.* Ⓐ ‹Vogel, Motte, Papier usw.:› flattern; **~ down** hinunter-/herunterflattern; **a leaf ~ed down** ein Blatt taumelte zur Erde; **~ about** umherflattern; **she was ~ing about** (*fig.*) sie lief unruhig hin und her; Ⓑ (*flap*) ‹Vorhang, Fahne, Segel, Drachen, Flügel:› flattern; ‹Blumen, Gräser usw.:› schaukeln; Ⓒ (*beat abnormally*) ‹Herz:› schneller *od.* höher schlagen; (*Med.*) ‹Puls, Herz:› flattern. ❷ *v.t.* Ⓐ flattern mit ‹Flügel›; **~ one's eyelashes** mit den Wimpern klimpern; **~ one's eyelashes at sb.** jmdm. mit den Wimpern zuklimpern; Ⓑ (*agitate*) erregen; ⇒ *also* **dovecot.**

❸ *n.* Ⓐ Flattern, *das;* Ⓑ (*fig.*) (*stir*) [leichte] Unruhe; (*nervous state*) Aufregung, *die;* **put sb. in a ~:** jmdn. in Aufregung versetzen; **be in a [great] ~:** ganz aufgelöst sein; **be all of a ~:** vor Aufregung fast vergehen; Ⓒ (*Brit. coll.: bet*) Wette, *die;* (*small speculative venture*) kleine Spekulation; **have a ~:** ein paar Scheinchen riskieren (*ugs.*); **I enjoy an occasional ~:** hin und wieder riskiere ich ganz gern ein paar Scheinchen (*ugs.*); Ⓓ (*Med.*) **heart/ventricular ~:** Herz-/Kammerflattern, *das;* Ⓔ (*Mus.*) Flatterzunge, *die;* Ⓕ (*Electronics*) (*in pitch*) rasches Schwanken der Tonhöhe; (*in loudness*) rasches Schwanken der Tonstärke

**flux** /flʌks/ *n.* Ⓐ (*change*) **be in a state of ~:** im Fluss sein; sich verändern; Ⓑ (*Metalw.*) Flussmittel, *das;* Ⓒ (*Phys.*) Fluss, *der;* (*amount of radiation or particles*) Fluss, *der;* Flux, *der*

**fly¹** /flaɪ/ *n.* Ⓐ (*Zool.*) Fliege, *die;* **the only ~ in the ointment** (*fig.*) der einzige Haken [bei der Sache] (*ugs.*); **he wouldn't hurt a ~** (*fig.*) er kann keiner Fliege etwas zuleide tun; **[die** *or* **drop** *or* **fall] like flies** (*fig.*) [sterben *od.* umfallen] wie die Fliegen; **I'd like to be a ~ on the wall of his classroom** in seiner Klasse möchte ich gern Mäuschen sein *od.* spielen (*ugs.*); **[there are] no flies on him** (*fig. coll.*) ihm kann man nichts vormachen (*ugs.*); ⇒ *also* **breed** 2 A; Ⓑ (*Angling*) Fliege, *die*

**fly²** ❶ *v.i.*, **flew** /fluː/, **flown** /fləʊn/ Ⓐ fliegen; **~ about/away** *or* **off** umher-/weg- *od.* davonfliegen; **~ high** (*fig.*) (*be ambitious*) hoch hinauswollen; (*prosper*) Karriere machen; ⇒ *also* **crow** 1 A; **high-flown;** Ⓑ (*as or in aircraft or spacecraft*) fliegen; (*in balloon*) fliegen; fahren; **~ into Heathrow** in Heathrow landen; **~ under a bridge** unter einer Brücke hindurchfliegen; **~ past [sth.]** [an etw. (*Dat.*)] vorbeifliegen; Ⓒ (*float, flutter*) fliegen; **rumours are ~ing about** (*fig.*) es gehen Gerüchte um; Ⓓ (*move quickly*) fliegen; **glass was ~ing everywhere** überall flogen Glassplitter herum; **come ~ing towards sb.** jmdm. entgegengeflogen kommen; **~ to sb.'s assistance** jmdm. zu Hilfe eilen; **~ open** auffliegen; (*be opened*) aufgerissen werden; **knock** *or* **send sb./sth. ~ing** jmdn./etw. umstoßen; **send sth. ~ing to the other side of the room** etw. quer durchs Zimmer schleudern; **~ to arms** (*arch.*) zu den Waffen eilen; Ⓔ (*fig.*) **~ [by** *or* **past]** wie im Fluge vergehen; dahinfliegen (*dichter.*); **how time flies!, doesn't time ~!** wie die Zeit vergeht!; Ⓕ (*wave in the air*) ‹Fahne:› gehisst sein; ⇒ *also* **flag¹** 1; Ⓖ (*attack angrily, react violently*) **~ at sb.** (*lit. or fig.*) über jmdn. herfallen; **let ~:** zuschlagen; (*fig.: become angry*) außer sich geraten; (*fig.: use strong language*) losschimpfen; **let ~ with** abschießen ‹Pfeil, Rakete, Gewehr›; werfen ‹Stein›; **let ~ at sb. with a gun/hammer** auf jmdn. schießen/mit einem Hammer auf jmdn. losgehen; **~ into a temper** *or* **rage** *or* **tantrum** einen Wutanfall bekommen; ⇒ *also* **face** 1 A; **handle** 1 A; Ⓗ (*flee*) fliehen; (*coll.: depart hastily*) eilig aufbrechen; **~ for one's life** um sein Leben rennen/fahren *usw.;* **I really must ~** (*coll.*) jetzt muss ich aber schnell los.

❷ *v.t.*, **flew, flown** Ⓐ (*operate, transport or perform by ~ing*) fliegen ‹Flugzeug, Fracht, Einsatz›; fliegen über (+ *Akk.*) ‹Strecke›; (*travel over*) überfliegen; überqueren; **~ sb./sth. to and from Berlin** jmdn./etw. nach Berlin fliegen und aus Berlin ausfliegen; **~ sth. into Gatwick** etw. nach Gatwick fliegen; **~ Concorde/Lufthansa** mit der Concorde/Lufthansa fliegen; Ⓑ (*cause to ~*) gehisst haben, (*as mark of nationality etc.*) führen ‹Flagge›; fliegen lassen ‹Taube, Falke›; **~ a kite** einen Drachen steigen lassen; (*fig.*) einen Versuchsballon steigen lassen; **go ~ a kite!** (*coll.*) hau ab! (*salopp*); Ⓒ (*flee*) **~ the country** aus dem Land fliehen; **~ one's pursuers** vor seinen Verfolgern fliehen; **the bird has flown its cage** der Vogel ist aus seinem Käfig entflogen; **~ the coop** (*Amer. fig. coll.*) sich aus dem Staube machen (*ugs.*); (*leave home*) durchbrennen (*ugs.*).

❸ *n.* Ⓐ *in sing. or pl.* (*on trousers*) Hosenschlitz, *der;* Ⓑ (*of flag*) Flugseite, *die;* fliegendes Ende; Ⓒ *in pl.* (*Theatre*) Schnürboden, *der*

**~ ˈin** ❶ *v.i.* (*arrive in aircraft*) [mit dem Flugzeug] eintreffen (**from** aus); (*come in to land*) landen. ❷ *v.t.* (*cause to land*) landen; (*bring by aircraft*) einfliegen

**~ ˈoff** *v.i.* Ⓐ abfliegen; Ⓑ (*become detached*) abgehen; ‹Hut:› wegfliegen

**~ ˈout** ❶ *v.i.* abfliegen (**of** von); **~ out there** dort hinfliegen. ❷ *v.t.* ausfliegen; **~ troops out to the disaster area** Truppen in das Katastrophengebiet fliegen

**fly³** *adj.* (*esp. Brit. coll.*) clever

**fly: ~ ˈagaric** *n.* Fliegenpilz, *der;* **~-away** *adj.* widerspenstig ‹Haar›; **~-blown** *adj.* (*infested with flies' eggs*) ≈ von Fliegenlarven befallen; (*fig.*) befleckt; **~-by** *n.* (*Astronaut.*) Vorbeiflug, *der;* **~-by-night** ❶ *adj.* zwielichtig; ❷ *n.: jmd., der sich nachts heimlich aus dem Staub macht;* **~-by-wire** *n.* (*Aeronaut.*) elektronische Flugsteuerung; *attrib.* **a ~-by-wire aircraft** ein Flugzeug mit elektronischer Flugsteuerung; **~catcher** *n.* (*Ornith.*) Schnäpper, *der;* **~-drive** ❶ *attrib. adj.* Fly-drive-‹Paket, Vereinbarung, Urlaub›; ❷ *n.* Fly-drive-Paket, *das;* Fly-drive-Urlaub, *der*

**flyer** /ˈflaɪə(r)/ *n.* Ⓐ (*bird*) Flieger, *der;* Ⓑ (*pilot*) Flieger, *der*/Fliegerin, *die;* Ⓒ (*fast-moving vehicle or animal*) Flitzer, *der* (*ugs.*); (*train*) Express, *der;* **the horse is a ~:** das Pferd ist pfeilschnell; Ⓓ ⇒ **high-flyer;** Ⓔ (*handbill*) Handzettel, *der;* (*Police*) Steckbrief, *der;* Ⓕ (*Amer.: investment*) Spekulation, *die;* **take a ~:** spekulieren

**fly: ~fish** *v.i.* mit [künstlichen] Fliegen fischen; **~-fishing** *n.* Fliegenfischerei, *die;* **~ ˈhalf** *n.* (*Rugby*) Halbspieler, *der*

**flying** /ˈflaɪɪŋ/ ❶ *adj.* Kurz-; (*designed for rapid action*) fliegend ‹Verband, Kolonne, Ambulanz›; **~ visit** Stippvisite, *die* (*ugs.*). ❷ *n.* Fliegen, *das; attrib.* Flug‹wetter, -zeit, -geschwindigkeit, -erfahrung›; **an hour's ~ time** eine Flugstunde; **be frightened of ~:** Angst vor dem Fliegen haben

**flying: ~ ˈbomb** *n.* V-Waffe, *die;* **~ ˈbuttress** *n.* (*Archit.*) Strebebogen, *der;* Schwibbogen, *der;* **~ ˈdoctor** *n.* ▶ **1261** *Arzt, der seine Patienten mit dem Flugzeug besucht;* **F~ Dutchman** ⇒ **Dutchman** C; **~ field** *n.* Flugfeld, *das;* **~ ˈfish** *n.* fliegender Fisch; **~ ˈfox** *n.* (*Zool.*) Flugfuchs, *der;* Fliegender Hund; **~ instructor** *n.* ▶ **1261** Fluglehrer, *der;* **~ ˈjump, ~ ˈleap** *ns.* Sprung mit Anlauf; großer Satz (*ugs.*); **take a ~ jump** *or* **leap** Anlauf nehmen; **~ machine** *n.* Luftfahrzeug, *das;* Flugmaschine, *die* (*veralt.*); **~ ˈmare** *n.* (*Wrestling*) Schulterschwung, *der;* **~ officer** *n.* (*Brit. Air Force*) Oberleutnant, *der;* **~ ˈpicket** *n.* mobiler Streikposten; **~ ˈsaucer** *n.* fliegende Untertasse; **~ school** *n.* Fliegerschule, *die;* **~ squad** *n.* (*Police*) Überfallkommando, *das;* **~ ˈstart** *n.* (*Sport*) fliegender Start; **get off to** *or* **have a ~ start** (*fig.*) (*begin successfully*) einen glänzenden Start haben; (*have an advantage*) die besten Voraussetzungen haben (*fig.*); **have got a ~ start over others** anderen gegenüber im Vorteil sein; **~-suit** *n.* Fliegerkombination, *die;* **~ ˈtackle** *n.* (*Rugby, Amer. Footb.*) Fassen, *das* (*im Lauf oder Sprung*)

**fly: ~leaf** *n.* Vorsatzblatt, *das;* Vorsatz, *der;* **~-on-the-wall** *attrib. adj.* von einer bewusst im Hintergrund gehaltenen Kamera aufgenommen ‹Dokumentarfilm›; die Kamera bewusst möglichst im Hintergrund haltend ‹Aufnahmetechnik, -stil›; **~over** *n.* (*Brit.*) [Straßen]überführung, *die;* Fly-over, *der;* **~paper** *n.* Fliegenfänger, *der;* **~-past** *n.* Luftparade, *die;* **~-post** ❶ *v.t.* illegal Plakate kleben für; ❷ *v.i.* illegal Plakate kleben; **~ screen** *n.* Fliegengitter, *das;* **~sheet** *n.* Ⓐ (*of tent*) Überzelt, *das;* Ⓑ (*circular*) Prospekt, *der;* **~ spray** *n.* Insektenspray, *der od. das;* **~ swatter** *n.* Fliegenklappe, *die;* Fliegenklatsche, *die;* **~-tipping** *n., no pl., no indef. art.* illegales Deponieren von Bauschutt; **~trap** *n.* (*trap*) Fliegenfänger, *der;* (*plant*) [Venus]fliegenfalle, *die;* **~weight** *n.* (*Boxing etc.*)

Fliegengewicht, *das;* (*person also*) Fliegengewichtler, *der;* **~wheel** *n.* Schwungrad, *das;* **fluid ~wheel** (*Motor Veh.*) Flüssigkeitskupplung, *die;* **~ whisk** *n.* Fliegenwedel, *der*

**FM** *abbr.* A **Field Marshal** FM; B **frequency modulation** FM

**f-number** /'efnʌmbə(r)/ *n.* (*Photog.*) Blende[nzahl], *die*

**FO** *abbr.* (*Brit. Hist.*) **Foreign Office** ≈ AA

**foal** /fəʊl/ ❶ *n.* Fohlen, *das;* **in** *or* **with ~:** trächtig. ❷ *v.i.* fohlen

**foam** /fəʊm/ ❶ *n.* A Schaum, *der;* B ⇒ **foam plastic;** C ⇒ **foam rubber.** ❷ *v.i.* (*lit. or fig.*) schäumen (**with** vor + *Dat.*); **~ at the mouth** Schaum vorm Mund haben; (*fig. coll.*) [vor Wut] schäumen

**foam: ~-backed** *adj.* schaumstoffverstärkt; **~ bath** *n.* Schaumbad, *das;* **~ extinguisher** *n.* Schaumlöscher, *der;* Schaumlöschgerät, *das;* **~ 'mattress** *n.* Schaumgummimatratze, *die;* **~ 'plastic** *n.* Schaumstoff, *der;* **~ 'rubber** *n.* Schaumgummi, *der*

**foamy** /'fəʊmɪ/ *adj.* schaumig; schäumend ‹Brandung›

**fob**[1] /fɒb/ *v.t.*, **-bb-: ~ sb. off with sth.** jmdn. mit etw. abspeisen (*ugs.*); **~ sth. off on [to] sb.** jmdm. etw. andrehen (*ugs.*)

**fob**[2] *n.* Uhrtasche, *die*

**f. o. b.** *abbr.* **free on board** fob

**focal**/'fəʊkl/: **~ 'distance, ~ 'length** *ns.* Brennweite, *die;* **~ plane** *n.* Brennebene, *die;* **~ point** *n.* Brennpunkt, *der* (*auch fig.*); Fokus, *der;* **become the ~ point of interest** *or* **attention** in den Brennpunkt des Interesses rücken

**foc's'le** /'fəʊksl/ ⇒ **forecastle**

**focus** /'fəʊkəs/ ❶ *n.*, *pl.* **~es** *or* **foci** /'fəʊsaɪ/ A (*Optics, Photog.*) Brennpunkt, *der;* (*focal length*) Brennweite, *die;* (*adjustment of eye or lens*) Scharfeinstellung, *die;* **depth of ~** (*adjustment*) Schärfentiefe, *die;* (*focal length*) Brennweite, *die;* **out of/in ~:** unscharf/scharf eingestellt ‹Kamera, Teleskop›; unscharf/scharf ‹Foto, Film, Vordergrund usw.›; (*fig.*) unklar *od.* verschwommen/klar; **see things in ~** (*fig.*) die Gegebenheiten klar erkennen; **get sth. in ~** (*fig.*) etw. klarer erkennen; **bring into ~:** scharf einstellen; (*fig.*) deutlich machen; **come into ~:** scharf werden; (*fig.*) sich herauskristallisieren; B (*fig.: centre, central object*) Mittelpunkt, *der;* (*of storm*) Zentrum, *das;* (*of earthquake*) Herd, *der;* Hypozentrum, *das* (*Geol.*); (*Med.: of disease*) Herd, *der;* **be the ~ of attention** im Brennpunkt des Interesses stehen; **the principal ~ of research is ...:** im Mittelpunkt der Forschung steht ...; C (*Geom.*) Brennpunkt, *der.*

❷ *v.t.*, **-s-** *or* **-ss-** A (*Optics, Photog.*) einstellen (**on** auf + *Akk.*); fokussieren (*fachspr.*); **~ a camera properly** *or* **correctly** eine Kamera auf die richtige Entfernung einstellen; **badly ~ed picture** unscharfes Bild; **~ one's eyes on sth./sb.** die Augen auf etw./jmdn. richten; B (*concentrate*) bündeln ‹Licht, Strahlen›; (*fig.*) konzentrieren (**on** auf + *Akk.*).

❸ *v.i.*, **-s-** *or* **-ss-** A **the camera ~es automatically** die Kamera hat automatische Scharfeinstellung; **he can't** *or* **his eyes don't ~ properly** er sieht nicht klar *od.* nur verschwommen; **I can't ~ on print at that distance** ich kann Gedrucktes auf diese Entfernung nicht klar erkennen; **his eyes ~ed [up]on the window** sein Blick war auf das Fenster gerichtet; B ‹Licht, Strahlen:› sich bündeln; (*fig.*) sich konzentrieren (**on** auf + *Akk.*)

**'focus group** *n.* Fokusgruppe, *die*

**fodder** /'fɒdə(r)/ *n.* [Vieh]futter, *das;* (*fig.*) Futter, *das;* **~ plant** Futterpflanze, *die;* ⇒ *also* **cannon fodder**

**foe** /fəʊ/ *n.* (*poet./rhet.*) Feind, *der*

**FoE** *abbr.* **Friends of the Earth**

**'foeman** /'fəʊmən/ *n.*, *pl.* **~men** /'fəʊmən/ (*arch./literary*) Widersacher, *der* (*geh.*)

**foetal** /'fi:tl/ *adj.* fötal; fetal; **the ~ position** die Fötuslage

**foetid** /'fi:tɪd/ ⇒ **fetid**

**foetus** /'fi:təs/ *n.* Fötus, *der;* Fetus, *der*

**fog** /fɒg/ ❶ *n.* A Nebel, *der;* **there are ~s in winter** es herrscht oft dichter Nebel im Winter; **drive in ~:** bei *od.* im Nebel fahren; **London was blanketed in ~:** über London lag eine Nebeldecke; **be in a [complete] ~** (*fig.*) [völlig] verunsichert sein; **be in a ~ about sth./as to what to do** sich (*Dat.*) im Unklaren über etw. (*Akk.*) sein/darüber sein, was zu tun ist; B (*Photog.*) Schleier, *der.* ❷ *v.t.*, **-gg-** A in Nebel hüllen; (*bewilder*) verwirren; **~ [up]** (*obscure as if with ~, make confusing*) vernebeln ‹Aussicht, Straße, Sachverhalt›; B (*Photog.*) **the negative is ~ged** das Negativ hat einen Schleier. ❸ *v.i.*, **-gg-** A **~ [up]** (*become blurred*) beschlagen; B (*Photog.*) einen Schleier bekommen

**fog: ~ bank** *n.* Nebelbank, *die;* **~bound** *adj.* A (*surrounded*) in Nebel gehüllt; B (*immobilized*) durch Nebel festgehalten

**fogey** ⇒ **fogy;** ⇒ *also* **young fogey**

**foggy** /'fɒgɪ/ *adj.* A neblig; B (*fig.*) nebelhaft ‹Vorstellung, Sprache, Bewusstsein›; **[I] haven't the foggiest [idea** *or* **notion]** (*coll.*) [ich] hab keinen blassen Schimmer (*ugs.*)

**fog: ~horn** *n.* (*Naut.*) Nebelhorn, *das;* **a voice like a ~horn** (*fig.*) eine dröhnende *od.* durchdringende Stimme; **~ lamp, ~light** *ns.* (*Motor Veh.*) Nebelscheinwerfer, *der;* **~ signal** *n.* A (*Railw.*) Knallsignal, *das;* B (*Naut.*) Nebelsignal, *das*

**fogy** /'fəʊgɪ/ *n.* **[old] ~:** [alter *od.* rückständiger] Opa (*salopp*)/[alte *od.* rückständige] Oma (*salopp*)

**föhn** /fɜ:n/ *n.* (*Meteorol.*) Föhn, *der*

**foible** /'fɔɪbl/ *n.* A Eigenheit, *die;* B (*Fencing*) ≈ Klingenschwäche, *die*

**foil**[1] /fɔɪl/ *n.* A (*metal as thin sheet*) Folie, *die;* **tin ~:** Stanniol[papier], *das;* **aluminium ~:** Alu[minium]folie, *die;* B (*to wrap or cover food etc.*) Folie, *die;* C (*behind mirror-glass*) Spiegelbelag, *der* (*Technik*); D (*sb./sth. contrasting*) ≈ Kontrast, *der*

**foil**[2] *v.t.* A (*frustrate*) vereiteln ‹Versuch, Plan, Flucht›; durchkreuzen ‹Vorhaben, Plan›; **they were ~ed in their attempts to escape** ihre Fluchtversuche wurden zunichte gemacht *od.* vereitelt; **[I've been] ~ed again** es war wieder nichts; B (*parry*) parieren (*auch fig.*); abwehren

**foil**[3] *n.* (*sword*) Florett, *das*

**foil**[4] *n.* (*hydrofoil*) Tragflächenboot, *das;* Gleitboot, *das*

**foist** /fɔɪst/ *v.t.* A (*introduce surreptitiously*) **~ sth./sb. into sth.** etw./jmdn. in etw. (*Akk.*) einschmuggeln; B (*palm*) **~ [off] on to** *or* **[up]on sb.** jmdm. andrehen (*ugs.*) ‹schlechte Waren›; jmdm. zuschieben ‹Schuld, Verantwortung›; auf jmdn. abwälzen ‹Probleme, Verantwortung›; **~ oneself on [to] sb.** sich jmdm. aufdrängen

**fold**[1] /fəʊld/ ❶ *v.t.* A (*double over on itself*) [zusammen]falten; zusammenlegen ‹Laken, Wäsche›; B (*collapse*) zusammenklappen; C (*embrace*) **~ sb. in one's arms** jmdn. in die Arme schließen; D (*wind*) **~ one's arms about** *or* **[a]round sb.** die Arme um jmdn. schlingen *od.* legen; E **~ one's arms** die Arme verschränken; **~ one's hands** die Hände falten; **the crow ~ed its wings** die Krähe legte die Flügel an; F (*envelop*) **~ sth./sb. in sth.** etw./jmdn. in etw. (*Akk.*) einhüllen; **~ed in a handkerchief** in ein Taschentuch eingewickelt.

❷ *v.i.* A (*become ~ed*) sich zusammenlegen; sich zusammenfalten; B (*collapse*) zusammenklappen; (*fig.*) (*cease to function*) eingehen (*ugs.*); (*go bankrupt*) Konkurs *od.* Bankrott machen; C (*be able to be ~ed*) sich falten lassen; **it ~s easily** es ist leicht zu falten; es lässt sich leicht falten; D (*be collapsible*) sich zusammenklappen lassen.

❸ *n.* A (*doubling*) Falte, *die;* **the baggy ~s of skin under his eyes** die Tränensäcke unter seinen Augen; **~s of flesh** Fettwülste; B (*hollow, nook in mountain, etc.*) Falte, *die* (*Geol.*); [Tal]mulde, *die;* C (*coil of serpent, string, etc.*) Windung, *die;* D (*act of ~ing*) Faltung, *die;* E (*line made by ~ing*) Kniff, *der;* F (*Geol.*) [Gebirgs]faltung, *die*

**~ a'way** ❶ *v.t.* zusammenklappen. ❷ *v.i.* zusammenklappbar sein; sich zusammenklappen lassen. ⇒ *also* **foldaway**

**~ 'back** ❶ *v.t.* zurückschlagen, aufschlagen ‹Laken›; zurückklappen ‹Rücksitz›; umknicken ‹Papier›. ❷ *v.i.* sich zurückschlagen lassen

**~ 'down** ❶ *v.t.* A (*make more compact*) zusammenklappen; B (*bend back part of*) ⇒ **~ back** 1; C (*open out*) ausklappen. ❷ *v.i.* ⇒ **1:** sich zusammenklappen lassen; sich zurückschlagen lassen

**~ 'in** *v.t.* A (*double over and inwards*) nach innen umlegen; B (*Cookery*) unterrühren; unterheben, unterziehen ‹Eischnee›

**~ into** *v.t.* (*Cookery*) unterrühren unter (+ *Akk.*); unterheben unter (+ *Akk.*), unterziehen ‹Eischnee› unter (+ *Akk.*)

**~ 'out** *v.i.* ‹Landkarte:› sich auseinander falten lassen; ‹Tisch:› sich hochklappen lassen; **the settee ~s out to become a double bed** das Sofa lässt sich zu einem Doppelbett ausklappen; ⇒ *also* **fold-out**

**~ 'over** *v.t.* umlegen ‹Saum›; umknicken ‹Seiten›

**~ 'up** ❶ *v.t.* A (*make more compact by ~ing*) zusammenfalten; zusammenlegen ‹Laken, Wäsche›; B (*collapse*) zusammenklappen. ❷ *v.i.* A (*be able to be ~ed up*) sich zusammenfalten lassen; B (*collapse*) sich zusammenklappen lassen; **how does this table ~ up?** wie wird dieser Tisch zusammengeklappt?; (*fig.*) ⇒ **fold**[1] 2 B (*fig.*)

**fold**[2] *n.* A ⇒ **sheepfold;** B (*fig.: body of believers*) Gemeinde, *die;* Herde, *die* (*geh.*); **he has left the ~:** er hat den Schoß der Kirche verlassen (*geh.*)

**-fold** ❶ *adj. in comb.* A (*times*) -fach; B (*having so many parts etc.*) -fältig. ❷ *adv. in comb.* -fach

**'foldaway** *adj.* zusammenklappbar; Klapp‹tisch, -stuhl, -fahrrad, -bett›

**folder** /'fəʊldə(r)/ *n.* A (*cover, holder for loose papers*) Mappe, *die;* B (*folded circular etc.*) Faltblatt, *das;* (*map also*) Faltkarte, *die;* C (*Computing*) Ordner, *der*

**folding** /'fəʊldɪŋ/ ⇒ **foldaway**

**folding: ~ 'door** *n.* Falttür, *die;* **~ 'doors** *n. pl.* Falttür, *die;* (*of hangar, barn, etc.*) Falttor, *das*

**'fold-out** *n.* ausfaltbare Seite

**foliage** /'fəʊlɪɪdʒ/ *n., no pl.* A (*leaves*) Blätter *Pl.;* (*of tree also*) Laub, *das;* B (*Art*) Laubwerk, *das*

**foliage: ~ leaf** *n.* [Laub]blatt, *das;* **~ plant** *n.* Blattpflanze, *die*

**folio** /'fəʊlɪəʊ/ ❶ *n.*, *pl.* **~s** A (*leaf of paper etc.*) [nur auf der Vorderseite nummeriertes] Blatt; B (*leaf- or page number of printed book*) Seitenzahl, *die;* C (*sheet folded once*) Doppelbogen, *der;* **in ~:** in Folio; im Folioformat; D (*book*) Foliant, *der;* **First F~:** erste Folioausgabe. ❷ *adj.* Folio-

**folk** /fəʊk/ *n.*, *pl. same or* **~s** A (*a people*) Volk, *das;* B *in pl.* **~[s]** (*people*) Leute *Pl.;* (*people in general*) die Leute; **some ~[s]** manche [Leute]; C *in pl.* **~s** (*coll., as address: people, friends*) Leute *Pl.* (*ugs.*); D *in pl.* (*people of a particular class*) **[the] rich/poor ~:** die Reichen/Armen; **old ~[s]** alte Leute; **old ~'s home** ⇒ **old people's home;** E *in pl.* **~s** (*coll.*) (*one's relatives*) Verwandte *Pl.;* Leute *Pl.* (*ugs.*); (*one's parents*) Alte Herrschaften (*ugs.*); F ⇒ **folk music;** G *attrib.* (*of the people, traditional*) Volks-; **~ handicrafts** Volkskunst, *die;* **~ museum** Heimatmuseum, *das*

**folk: ~ dance** *n.* Volkstanz, *der;* **~ dancing** *n.* Volkstanz, *der;* **~ etymology** *n.* Volksetymologie, *die;* **~ hero** *n.* Volksheld, *der;* **~lore** *n.* A (*traditional beliefs*) [volkstümliche] Überlieferung; Folklore, *die;* B (*study*) Volkskunde, *die;* Folklore, *die;* **~ memory** *n.* mündliche Überlieferung, *die;* **~ music** *n.* Volksmusik, *die;* **~ singer** *n.* Sänger/Sängerin von Volksliedern; (*modern*) Folksänger, *der*/-sängerin, *die;* **~ singing** *n.* Singen von Volksliedern *od.* (*modern*) Folksongs; **~ song** *n.* Volkslied, *das;* (*modern*) Folksong, *der*

**folksy** /ˈfəʊksɪ/ *adj.* A (*sociable, informal*) gesellig; B (*having characteristics of folk art*) volkstümlich

**folk:** ~ **tale** *n.* Volksmärchen, *das;* ~**ways** *n. pl.* traditionelle Lebensweise; ~**weave** *n.* grob gewebter Stoff

**folky** /ˈfəʊkɪ/ ⇒ **folksy** B

**follicle** /ˈfɒlɪkl/ *n.* Follikel, *der* (*Biol., Med.*)

**follow** /ˈfɒləʊ/ **1** *v.t.* A folgen (+ *Dat.*); **you're being ~ed** Sie werden verfolgt; B (*go along*) folgen (+ *Dat.*); entlanggehen/-fahren ‹Straße usw.›; C (*come after in order or time*) folgen (+ *Dat.*); folgen auf (+ *Akk.*); **A is ~ed by B** auf A folgt B; D (*accompany*) [nach]folgen (+ *Dat.*); E (*provide with sequel*) ~ **sth. with sth.** einer Sache (*Dat.*) etw. folgen lassen; ~ **your meal with a brandy** schließen Sie Ihr Essen mit einem Kognak ab; **his first novel was ~ed by a string of best-sellers** auf seinen ersten Roman folgte eine ganze Reihe von Bestsellern; **that's a hard act to ~** (*fig.*) das macht ihm/ihr keiner so leicht nach; ~ **that!** (*coll.*) das mach mir erst mal nach!; F (*go after as admirer or suitor*) verehren; anhängen (*geh.*) (+ *Dat.*); G (*result from*) die Folge sein von; hervorgehen aus; **a stroke is often ~ed by permanent paralysis** die Folge eines Schlaganfalls ist oft eine dauernde Lähmung; H (*treat or take as guide or leader*) folgen (+ *Dat.*); sich orientieren an (+ *Dat.*); (*adhere to*) anhängen (+ *Dat.*); sich bekennen zu; I (*act according to*) folgen (+ *Dat.*) ‹Prinzip, Instinkt, Trend›; verfolgen ‹Politik›; befolgen ‹Vorschrift, Regel, Anweisung, Rat, Warnung›; handeln nach ‹Gefühl, Wunsch›; sich halten an (+ *Akk.*) ‹Konventionen, Diät, Maßstab›; ~ **one's heart** der Stimme des Herzens folgen; ⇒ *also* **example** A; **fashion** 1 B; **lead**[2] 3 A; **nose** 1 A; J (*practise*) ausüben ‹Beruf, Handwerk, eine Kunst›; ~ **the teaching/medical profession/the arts** Lehrer/Arzt/Künstler sein; K (*keep up with mentally, grasp meaning of*) folgen (+ *Dat.*); **I can't ~ what he says** ich kann ihm nicht folgen; **do you ~ me?, are you ~ing me?** verstehst du, was ich meine?; **I don't ~ you/your meaning** ich verstehe Sie nicht/verstehe nicht, was Sie meinen; ~ **the music from the score** die Partitur mitlesen; L (*be aware of the present state or progress of*) verfolgen ‹Ereignisse, Nachrichten, Prozess›; ~ **a TV serial** eine Fernsehserie regelmäßig sehen.

**2** *v.i.* A (*go, come*) ~ **after sb./sth.** jmdm./einer Sache folgen; B (*go or come after person or thing*) folgen; **you go ahead in the car and I'll ~ on my bike** du fährst mit dem Auto voraus, und ich komme mit dem Fahrrad nach; ~ **in the wake of sth.** etw. ablösen; auf etw. (*Akk.*) folgen; C (*come next in order or time*) folgen; **in the years that ~ed** in den darauf folgenden Jahren; **as ~s** wie folgt; **the details are as ~s** die Einzelheiten lauten folgendermaßen; **there are two options, as ~s: ...:** es gibt zwei Möglichkeiten, und zwar folgende: ...; **would you like coffee to ~?** hätten Sie danach *od.* anschließend gerne [einen] Kaffee?; **what ~s next?** was kommt danach?; D (*ensue*) folgen; E ~ **from sth.** (*result*) die Folge von etw. sein; (*be deducible*) aus etw. folgen; **it ~s [from this] that ...:** daraus folgt, dass ...; das heißt, dass ...

~ **ˈon** *v.i.* A (*continue*) ~ **on from sth.** die Fortsetzung von etw. sein; B (*Cricket*) sofort zum zweiten Mal schlagen; ⇒ *also* **follow-on**

~ **ˈout** *v.t.* A (*pursue to the end*) durchführen ‹Plan, Projekt›; sich (*Dat.*) erfüllen ‹Wunsch›; zu Ende verfolgen ‹Ziel, Politik, Idee›; B (*carry out*) [genau] befolgen ‹Regel, Anweisung›

~ **ˈthrough** **1** *v.t.* zu Ende verfolgen; durchziehen (*ugs.*). **2** *v.i.* (*Sport*) durchschwingen; ⇒ *also* **follow-through**

~ **ˈup** *v.t.* A (*pursue steadily*) stetig verfolgen; B (*add further action etc. to*) ausbauen ‹Erfolg, Sieg›; C (*investigate further*) nachgehen (+ *Dat.*) ‹Hinweis›; (*consider further*) berücksichtigen ‹Bitte, Angebot›. ⇒ *also* **follow-up**

**follower** /ˈfɒləʊə(r)/ *n.* Anhänger, *der*/Anhängerin, *die;* **be a dedicated ~ of fashion** immer mit der Mode gehen

**following** /ˈfɒləʊɪŋ/ **1** *adj.* A *pres. p. of* **follow; on the ~ day** am Tag danach *od.* darauf; **on the ~ Monday** am nächsten Montag; B (*now to be mentioned*) folgend; **the ~ items** folgende Gegenstände; **in the ~ way** folgendermaßen; **for the ~ reasons** aus folgenden Gründen; **the ~:** Folgendes; (*persons*) Folgende; C (*blowing in one's direction of travel*) ~ **wind** Rückenwind, *der.* **2** *prep.* nach. **3** *n.* Anhängerschaft, *die*

**follow:** ~**-my-ˈleader** (*Amer.:* ~**-the-ˈleader**) *n. Spiel, bei dem alle Mitspieler das nachmachen, was einer vormacht;* ~**-on** *n.* (*Cricket*) ≈ sofortiger zweiter Durchgang (*nachdem man im ersten nicht nahe genug an die Punktzahl des Gegners herangekommen ist*); ~**-through** *n.* (*Sport*) Durchschwung, *der;* ~**-up** *n.* Fortsetzung, *die;* (*Med.*) Nachuntersuchung, *die;* **there's never any ~-up to his promises** er erfüllt *od.* hält seine Versprechen nie; **as a ~-up** im Anschluss (**to** an + *Akk.*); ~**-up letter/visit** Nachfassbrief, *der*/-besuch, *der* (*Werbespr.*)

**folly** /ˈfɒlɪ/ *n.* A Torheit, *die* (*geh.*); **it would be [sheer] ~:** es wäre [äußerst] töricht (*geh.*); **an act of ~:** eine Torheit (*geh.*); B (*costly structure considered useless*) nutzloser Prunkbau; C *in pl.* (*Theatre*) Revue mit Glamourgirls

**foment** /fəˈment, fəʊˈment/ *v.t.* A (*foster*) schüren; B (*bathe*) mit feuchter Wärme behandeln

**fomentation** /fəʊmenˈteɪʃn/ *n.* A (*fostering*) Schüren, *das;* B (*warm cloth[s]*) heißer Umschlag; C (*application of warm cloth[s]*) Behandlung mit feuchter Wärme *od.* mit heißen Umschlägen

**fond** /fɒnd/ *adj.* A (*tender*) zärtlich; (*affectionate*) liebevoll ‹Blick›; lieb ‹Erinnerung›; (*in letters*) ~**[est] love** mit lieben Grüßen; alles Liebe; **say a ~ farewell** sich überschwänglich verabschieden; **be ~ of sb.** jmdn. mögen *od.* gern haben; **be ~ of sth.** etw. mögen; **be ~ of doing sth.** etw. gern tun; **she's very ~ of Greece/the theatre** sie liebt Griechenland/das Theater; **I'm not very ~ of sweets** ich mache mir nicht viel aus Süßigkeiten; **he's become very ~ of living in Spain** er lebt mittlerweile sehr gern in Spanien; B (*foolishly credulous or hopeful*) kühn ‹Hoffnung, Traum›; gutgläubig ‹Person›; allzu zuversichtlich ‹Glaube›; voreingenommen ‹Eltern›; **he had ~ hopes of becoming an ambassador one day** er glaubte allen Ernstes daran, einmal Botschafter zu werden; C (*over-affectionate*) übertrieben liebevoll

**fondant** /ˈfɒndənt/ *n.* Fondant, *der od. das*

**fondle** /ˈfɒndl/ *v.t.* streicheln

**fondly** /ˈfɒndlɪ/ *adv.* A (*tenderly*) zärtlich; (*with affection*) liebevoll; **he looks ~ back upon his days at university** er erinnert sich gern an seine Studentenzeit; B (*with foolish credulousness or hopefulness*) allzu zuversichtlich

**fondness** /ˈfɒndnɪs/ *n., no pl.* A (*tenderness*) Zärtlichkeit, *die;* (*affection*) Liebe, *die;* **look back with great ~ on sth.** sich sehr gern an etw. (*Akk.*) erinnern; ~ **for sth./doing sth.** (*special liking*) Vorliebe für etw./dafür, etw. zu tun; ~ **for sb./art/the sea** Liebe zu jmdm./zur Kunst/zum Meer; B (*foolish credulousness or hopefulness*) allzu große Gutgläubigkeit; törichte Zuversicht

**fondue** /ˈfɒndjuː, ˈfɒnduː/ *n.* (*Gastr.*) Fondue, *das od. die*

**font**[1] /fɒnt/ *n.* Taufstein, *der*

**font**[2] (*Amer.*) ⇒ **fount**[1]

**food** /fuːd/ *n.* A *no pl., no art.* Nahrung, *die;* (*for animals*) Futter, *das;* **take ~:** Nahrung zu sich nehmen; **lack of ~:** Nahrungsmangel, *der;* **nutritious ~:** nahrhafte Kost; **be ~ for [the] worms** tot sein; B *no pl., no art.* (*as commodity*) Lebensmittel *Pl.;* **one's week's shopping for ~** *or* ~ **shopping** der wöchentliche Lebensmitteleinkauf; C *no pl.* (*in solid form*) Essen, *das;* **some ~:** etwas zu essen; **there was plenty of ~ and drink** es gab reichlich zu essen und zu trinken; **she had prepared some delicious ~ for the party** für die Party hatte sie einige leckere Sachen vorbereitet; **he likes his ~ too much for that!** dazu isst er viel zu gern!; **he's very keen on Italian ~:** er mag die italienische Küche; er isst gern italienisch; D (*particular kind*) Nahrungsmittel, *das;* Kost, *die;* (*for animals*) Futter, *das;* **nuts are a very nutritious ~:** Nüsse sind sehr nahrhaft; **canned ~s** Konserven *Pl.;* **preserved/imported ~s** eingemachte/importierte Nahrungsmittel; E (*nutriment*) Nahrung, *die;* F (*fig.: material for mental work*) Stoff, *der;* ~ **for thought** Stoff zum Nachdenken; ~ **for discussion** Diskussionsstoff, *der*

**food:** ~ **chain** *n.* (*Ecol.*) Nahrungskette, *die;* ~ **fish** *n.* Speisefisch, *der*

**foodie** /ˈfuːdɪ/ *n.* (*Brit. coll.*) ≈ Feinschmecker, *der*/-schmeckerin, *die*

**food:** ~ **parcel** *n.* Lebensmittelpaket, *das;* ~ **poisoning** *n.* Lebensmittelvergiftung, *die;* ~ **processor** *n.* Küchenmaschine, *die;* ~ **rationing** *n.* Rationierung [von Lebensmitteln]; ~ **shop** ⇒ ~ **store;** ~ **stamps** *n. pl.* (*Amer.*) Lebensmittelgutscheine *Pl.;* ~ **store** *n.* Lebensmittelgeschäft, *das;* ~**stuff** *n.* Nahrungsmittel, *das;* **perishable ~stuffs** leicht verderbliche Lebensmittel; ~ **supplies** *n. pl.* Vorräte *Pl.;* ~ **value** *n.* Nährwert, *der*

**fool**[1] /fuːl/ **1** *n.* A Dummkopf, *der* (*ugs.*); **look a ~:** unmöglich (*ugs.*) aussehen; (*as regards behaviour*) dumm dastehen (*ugs.*); **he's a ~ to believe stories like that** er ist ein Narr *od.* (*ugs.*) er ist schön dumm, wenn er solche Geschichten glaubt; **what a ~ I am!** wie dumm von mir!; **oh, you ˈare a ~!** wie kannst du nur so dumm sein!; **he makes you feel like a ~:** bei ihm kommt man sich (*Dat.*) wie ein Narr vor; **be no** *or* **nobody's ~:** nicht dumm *od.* (*ugs.*) nicht auf den Kopf gefallen sein; **I would never be such a ~:** so dumm wäre ich nie; **be ~ enough to do sth.** so dumm *od.* (*ugs.*) so blöd sein *od.* dumm genug sein, etw. zu tun; **make a ~ of oneself** sich lächerlich machen; **there's no ~ like an old ~:** Alter schützt vor Torheit nicht[, ganz im Gegenteil]; **a ~ and his money are soon parted** ein Dummkopf ist sein Geld bald wieder los; **a ~'s bolt is soon shot** ein Dummkopf hat sein Pulver bald verschossen (*ugs.*); **not suffer ~s gladly** Dummheit nicht ertragen können; **~s rush in where angels fear to tread** blinder Eifer schadet nur (*Spr.*); B (*Hist.: jester, clown*) Narr, *der;* **act** *or* **play the ~:** herumalbern (*ugs.*); den Clown spielen (*abwertend*); C (*dupe*) **make a ~ of sb.** jmdn. blamieren. ⇒ *also* **all** 1 B; **April.**

**2** *v.i.* herumalbern (*ugs.*); **you're ~ing!** mach keine Witze! (*ugs.*).

**3** *v.t.* A (*cheat*) ~ **sb. out of sth.** jmdn. um etw. betrügen; ~ **sb. into doing sth.** jmdn. [durch Tricks] dazu bringen, etw. zu tun; B (*dupe*) täuschen; hereinlegen (*ugs.*); (*play tricks on*) foppen; **don't be ~ed by him** lass dich von ihm nicht täuschen *od.* (*ugs.*) hereinlegen; **you could have ~ed me** (*iron.*) ach, was du nicht sagst!

~ **aˈbout,** ~ **aˈround** *v.i.* (*play the ~*) herumalbern (*ugs.*); Unsinn machen; (*idle*) herumtrödeln (*ugs.*); (*trifle*) Zeit vergeuden; ~ **about** *or* **around with sth./sb.** mit etw./jmdm. herumspielen

~ **aˈway** *v.t.* verschwenden; vergeuden

~ **with** *v.t.* [herum]spielen mit

**fool**[2] *n.* (*Gastr.*) *Süßspeise aus Kompott, das mit Sahne o. Ä. verrührt ist*

**foolery** /ˈfuːlərɪ/ *n., no pl.* Alberei, *die*

**foolhardy** /ˈfuːlhɑːdɪ/ *adj.* tollkühn ‹Handlung, Behauptung, Person›; draufgängerisch ‹Person›; **that was a ~ thing to say** es war sehr riskant, das zu sagen

**foolish** /ˈfuːlɪʃ/ *adj.* A töricht; verrückt (*ugs.*) ‹Idee, Vorschlag›; **we were ~ to expect miracles** es war töricht von uns, Wunder zu erwarten; ~ **minds** Dummköpfe *Pl.* (*ugs.*); **don't do anything ~:** mach keinen Unsinn; **what a ~ thing to do/say** wie kann man nur so etwas Dummes tun/sagen; B (*ridiculous*) albern (*ugs.*) ‹Verhalten›; blöd, dumm (*ugs.*) ‹Grinsen, Bemerkung›; lächerlich ‹Aussehen›

**foolishly** /'fu:lɪʃlɪ/ *adv.* **A** (*in foolish manner*) törichterweise; **B** (*in ridiculous manner*) lächerlich ‹sich benehmen›; blöd, dumm (*ugs.*) ‹grinsen›

**fool: ~proof** *adj.* (*not open to misuse*) wasserdicht (*fig.*); (*not open to misinterpretation*) unmissverständlich; (*infallible*) absolut sicher; (*that cannot break down*) narrensicher (*ugs.*); **~scap** /'fu:lskæp, 'fu:lzkæp/ *n.* **A** (*size of paper*) Kanzleiformat, *das;* **B** (*paper of this size*) Kanzleipapier, *das;* **~'s 'errand** *n.* nutzloses Unternehmen; **go on a ~'s errand** sich vergeblich bemühen; **I was sent on a ~'s errand** man hat mich völlig umsonst losgeschickt; **~'s 'paradise** *n.* Traumwelt, *die;* **be** *or* **live in a ~'s paradise** in einer Traumwelt leben; sich (*Dat.*) Illusionen machen; **~'s 'parsley** *n.* (*Bot.*) Hundspetersilie, *die*

**foot** /fʊt/ **1** *n., pl.* **feet** /fi:t/ **A** ▶ 966 Fuß, *der;* **at sb.'s feet** zu jmds. Füßen; **be at sb.'s feet** (*fig.*) jmdm. zu Füßen liegen (*geh.*); **fall/sit at sb.'s feet** jmdm. zu Füßen fallen/sitzen; **sit at sb.'s feet** (*fig.*) jmds. Jünger sein; **lay the blame for sth. at sb.'s feet** jmdm. etw. anlasten *od.* zur Last legen; **put one's best ~ forward** (*fig.*) (*hurry*) sich beeilen; (*do one's best*) sein Bestes tun; **please wipe your feet** bitte Schuhe abtreten; **do sth. with both feet** (*fig.*) sich voll in etw. (*Akk.*) reinknien (*ugs.*); **feet of clay** (*fig.*) eine Schwachstelle; **feet first** mit den Füßen zuerst *od.* voran; **go into sth. feet first** (*fig.*) sich Hals über Kopf (*ugs.*) in etw. hineinstürzen; **have one ~ in the grave** (*fig.*) mit einem Fuß im Grabe stehen; **have both [one's] feet on the ground** (*fig.*) mit beiden Beinen [fest] auf der Erde stehen; **keep one's feet** (*fig.*) nicht hinfallen; **have a ~ in both camps** (*fig.*) auf beiden Schultern Wasser tragen; **my ~!** (*coll.*) beileibe nicht!; **on ~:** zu Fuß; **set sth. on ~:** etw. in Gang bringen *od.* setzen; **on one's/its feet** (*lit. or fig.*) auf den Beinen; **you'll be back on your feet again before long** (*fig.*) bald wirst du wieder auf die Beine kommen; **put** *or* **get sb. [back] on his feet** (*fig.*) jmdn. auf die Beine bringen; **put** *or* **get** *or* **set sth. [back] on its feet** (*fig.*) etw. [wieder] auf die Beine bringen *od.* stellen; **get on one's feet** sich erheben; aufstehen; **put one's ~ down** (*fig.*) (*be firmly insistent or repressive*) energisch werden; (*accelerate motor vehicle*) [Voll]gas geben; **put one's ~ in it** (*fig. coll.*) ins Fettnäpfchen treten (*ugs.*); einen Fauxpas begehen; **put one's feet up** die Beine hochlegen; **start [off]** *or* **get off** *or* **begin on the right/wrong ~** (*fig.*) einen guten/schlechten Start haben; **set ~ in/on sth.** etw. betreten; **go away and never set ~ in here** *or* **in this place again** geh fort und setze keinen Fuß mehr über diese Schwelle; **he had never set ~ in Britain/outside London** er hatte noch nie einen Fuß auf britischen Boden gesetzt/er war noch nie aus London herausgekommen; **be rushed off one's feet** (*fig.*) in Trab gehalten werden (*ugs.*); **stand on one's own [two] feet** (*fig.*) auf eigenen Füßen stehen; **sweep sb. off his/her feet** (*fig.*) jmdn. *od.* jmds. Herz im Sturm erobern; **rise** *or* **get to one's feet** sich erheben; aufstehen; **help sb. to his feet** jmdm. aufhelfen; **it's a bit muddy under ~:** der Boden ist ein bisschen matschig; **tread sth./sb. under ~:** auf etw./jmdn. treten; (*fig.*) etw./jmdn. unterdrücken; **get under sb.'s feet** (*fig.*) jmdm. vor die Füße laufen; **with four children under her feet** mit vier Kindern, die ihr vor den Füßen herumlaufen; **get one's feet wet** (*fig.*) sich hineinfinden; **never put a ~ wrong** (*fig.*) nie etwas falsch machen; **get/have cold feet** kalte Füße kriegen (*ugs.*)/gekriegt haben (*ugs.*); **catch sb. on the wrong ~** (*fig.*) jmdn. auf dem falschen Fuß erwischen; **have two left feet** (*fig.*) zwei linke Füße haben (*ugs.*); **B** (*step*) **swift/light of ~:** schnell-/leichtfüßig; **C** *pl. same* (*Brit. Hist.*) Infanterie, *die* (*Milit.*); **five hundred ~:** fünfhundert Infanteristen (*Milit.*) *od.* Fußsoldaten; **D** (*far end*) unteres Ende; (*of bed*) Fußende, *das;* (*lowest part*) Fuß, *der;* (*of sail*) Unterliek, *das;* **at the ~ of the list/page** unten auf der Liste/Seite; **the compost heap is at the ~ of the garden** der Komposthaufen ist im hinteren Teil des Gartens; **E** (*of stocking etc.*) Fuß, *der;* Füßling, *der;* **F** (*Pros.: metrical unit*) [Vers]fuß, *der;* **G** (*Phonet.: unit of speech*) ≈ Akzentgruppe, *die;* **H** *pl.* **feet** *or same* ▶ 928, ▶ 1210, ▶ 1284 (*linear measure*) Fuß, *der* (*30,48 cm*); 7 **~** *or* **feet** 7 Fuß; **I** (*base*) Fuß, *der;* (*of statue, pillar*) Sockel, *der;* Basis, *die;* **J** (*Zool.: of invertebrate*) Fuß, *der;* **K** (*Bot.*) Ansatzstelle, *die.* ⇒ *also* **ball**[1] 1 B; **cold feet**; **cubic** B; **door** B; **drag** 2 A; **fall** 2 A, P; **find** 1 B; **hand** 1 A; **square** 2 B; **walk** 2 B.
**2** *v.t.* **A** **~ it** (*dance*) tanzen; (*walk*) zu Fuß gehen; **B** (*pay*) **~ the bill** die Rechnung bezahlen

**footage** /'fʊtɪdʒ/ *n., no pl., no indef. art.* Filmmaterial, *das;* **documentary ~:** Dokumentaraufnahmen *Pl.*

**foot-and-'mouth [disease]** *n.* Maul- und Klauenseuche, *die*

**football** /'fʊtbɔ:l/ *n.* **A** Fußball, *der;* (*elongated*) [ovaler] Ball; (*fig.*) Spielball, *der;* **B** (*Brit.: soccer*) Fußball, *der;* (*Amer.: American ~*) Football, *der.* ⇒ *also* **American football**; **Rugby football**

**'football boot** *n.* Fußballschuh, *der*

**footballer** /'fʊtbɔ:lə(r)/ *n.* ▶ 1261 **A** (*Brit.: soccer player*) Fußballspieler, *der;* Fußballer, *der* (*ugs.*); **B** (*Amer.: American football player*) Footballspieler, *der*

**football: ~ pitch** *n.* Fußballplatz, *der;* **~ pools** *n. pl.* **the ~ pools** das Fußballtoto; ⇒ *also* **pool**[2] 1 A

**foot: ~bath** *n.* **A** (*washing of feet*) Fußbad, *das;* **B** (*small bath*) Fußwanne, *die;* **~ brake** *n.* Fußbremse, *die;* **~ bridge** *n.* Steg, *der;* (*across road, railway, etc.*) Fußgängerbrücke, *die*

**-footed** /fʊtɪd/ *adj. in comb.* -füßig; **nimble-~:** leichtfüßig; **large-/small-~:** mit großen/kleinen Füßen *nachgestellt*

**footer** /'fʊtə(r)/ (*Brit. coll.*) ⇒ **football** 1 B

**-footer** /fʊtə(r)/ *n. in comb.* **she is a six-~:** sie ist sechs Fuß groß; **the boat was a nine-~:** das Boot war neun Fuß lang

**foot: ~fall** *n.* Schritt, *der;* **~ fault** (*Lawn Tennis*) **1** *n.* Fußfehler, *der;* **2** *v.i.* einen Fußfehler machen; **~hill** *n., usu. pl.* [Gebirgs]ausläufer, *der;* **~hold** *n.* Halt, *der;* (*fig.*) Stützpunkt, *der;* **get a ~hold** (*fig.*) Fuß fassen

**footing** /'fʊtɪŋ/ *n.* **A** (*fig.: status*) Stellung, *die;* **be on an equal ~ [with sb.]** [jmdm.] gleichgestellt sein; **put A on an equal ~ with B** A mit B auf die gleiche Stufe stellen; **place sth. on a firm ~:** etw. auf eine feste Basis stellen; **be on a friendly ~ with sb.** ein freundschaftliches Verhältnis zu jmdm. haben; **be on a war ~:** sich im Kriegszustand befinden; **B** (*foothold*) Halt, *der;* **lose/miss/keep one's ~:** den Halt verlieren/keinen Halt finden/sich halten; **C** (*surface for standing on*) Grund, *der;* (*fig.*) Stellung, *die;* **gain a ~ as a journalist** sich (*Dat.*) eine Position als Journalist schaffen; als Journalist Fuß fassen; **D** (*Building*) Bankett, *das*

**footle** /'fu:tl/ *v.i.* (*coll.*) **~ about** (*trifle*) herumtrödeln (*ugs.*); (*play the fool*) Unfug treiben

**'footlights** *n. pl.* (*Theatre*) Rampenlicht, *das*

**footling** /'fu:tlɪŋ/ *adj.* läppisch (*abwertend*); albern (*ugs.*)

**foot: ~loose** *adj.* ungebunden; **~loose and fancy-free** frei und ledig; **~man** /'fʊtmən/ *n., pl.* **~men** /'fʊtmən/ (*servant*) Lakai, *der;* Diener, *der;* **~mark** ⇒ **~print**; **~muff** *n.* Fußsack, *der;* **~note** *n.* Fußnote, *die;* **~ passenger** *n.* Fußpassagier, *der;* **~path** *n.* (*path*) Fußweg, *der;* (*Brit.: pavement*) Gehsteig, *der;* Bürgersteig, *der;* **~plate** *n.* (*Brit. Railw.*) Führerstand, *der;* **~plate workers** Lokomotivführer und Heizer; **~print** *n.* Fußabdruck, *der;* **~prints in the snow** Fußspuren im Schnee; **~ race** *n.* Wettlauf, *der;* Wettrennen, *das;* **~rest** *n.* Fußstütze, *die;* (*on bicycle or motorcycle*) Fußraste, *die;* **~ rot** *n.* (*Vet. Med.*) Stoppellähme, *die;* **~ rule** *n.* [einen Fuß langes] Lineal; **~ scraper** *n.* Fußabstreifer, *der;* Abtreter, *der*

**footsie** /'fʊtsɪ/ *n.* (*coll.*) **play ~ [with sb.]** [mit jmdm.] füßeln (*landsch.*)

**foot: ~slog** (*coll.*) **1** *v.i.* latschen (*salopp*); **2** *n.* Gelaufe, *das* (*ugs.*); **~ soldier** *n.* Infanterist, *der* (*Milit.*); Fußsoldat, *der;* **~sore** *pred. adj.* **be ~sore** wunde Füße haben; **~step** *n.* Schritt, *der;* **follow** *or* **tread in sb.'s ~steps** (*fig.*) in jmds. Fußstapfen (*Akk.*) treten; **~stool** *n.* Fußbank, *die;* Fußschemel, *der;* **~way** *n.* Fußweg, *der;* **~wear** *n., no pl.* Schuhe *Pl.;* Schuhwerk, *das;* Fußbekleidung, *die* (*Kaufmannsspr.*); **~work** *n., no pl.* (*Sport, Dancing*) Beinarbeit, *die*

**fop** /fɒp/ Dandy, *der;* Geck, *der*

**foppish** /'fɒpɪʃ/ *adj.* dandyhaft (*geh.*); geckenhaft (*abwertend*)

**for** /fə(r), *stressed* fɔ:(r)/ ▶ 1155 **1** *prep.* **A** (*representing, on behalf of, in exchange against*) für; (*in place of*) für; anstelle von; **what is the German ~ 'buzz'?** wie heißt „buzz" auf Deutsch?; **I. Smith ~ B. Jones** (*as signature*) B. Jones, i. A. I. Smith; ⇒ *also* **eye** 1 A; **B** (*in defence, support, or favour of*) für; **be ~ doing sth.** dafür sein, etw. zu tun; **the voting was 5 ~ and 10 against** es stimmten 5 dafür und 10 dagegen; **it's each [man]** *or* **every man ~ himself** jeder ist auf sich selbst gestellt; **C** (*to the benefit of*) für; **do sth. ~ sb.** für jmdn. etw. tun; **die ~ one's country** für sein Land sterben; **D** (*with a view to*) für; (*conducive[ly] to*) zu; **they invited me ~ Christmas/Monday/supper** sie haben mich zu Weihnachten/für Montag/zum Abendessen eingeladen; **meet ~ a discussion** sich zu einer Besprechung treffen; **what is it ~?** wofür/wozu ist das?; **that's what I'm there ~:** dafür/dazu bin ich ja da; **be saving up ~ sth.** auf etw. (*Akk.*) sparen; **he did everything ~ his family's well-being** er tat alles für das Wohlergehen der Familie; **E** (*being the motive of*) für; (*having as purpose*) zu; **reason ~ living** Grund zu leben; **a dish ~ holding nuts** eine Schale für Nüsse; **F** (*to obtain, win, save*) **a request ~ help** eine Bitte um Hilfe; **study ~ a university degree** auf einen Hochschulabschluss hin studieren; **go/run ~ a doctor** gehen/laufen, um einen Arzt zu holen; **phone ~ a doctor** nach einem Arzt telefonieren; **take sb. ~ a ride in the car/a walk** jmdn. im Auto spazieren fahren/mit jmdm. einen Spaziergang machen; **work ~ a living** für den Lebensunterhalt arbeiten; **draw on sb. ~ money** jmdn. um Geld angehen; **oh ~ a few minutes' peace!** wäre hier doch *od.* hätte ich doch einmal ein paar Minuten Ruhe!; **run/jump** *etc.* **~ it** loslaufen/-springen *usw.;* ⇒ *also* **life** A; **G** (*to reach*) nach; **set out ~ England/the north/an island** nach England/Norden/zu einer Insel aufbrechen; **7.30 ~ 8** zwischen halb acht und acht; **H** (*to be received by*) für; **there's** *or* **that's gratitude** *etc.* **~ you!** (*iron.*) und so was nennt sich Dankbarkeit *usw.!;* **that's Jim ~ you** das sieht Jim mal wieder ähnlich; **I** (*as regards*) **checked ~ accuracy** auf Richtigkeit geprüft; **be dressed/ready ~ dinner** zum Dinner angezogen/fertig sein; **open ~ business** eröffnet; **open ~ lunch [from ... to ...]** Mittagstisch [von ... bis ...]; **have sth. ~ breakfast/pudding** etw. zum Frühstück/Nachtisch essen; **whether you should do it is not ~ me to say** ob du es tun sollst, kann ich dir nicht sagen; **enough ... ~:** genug ... für; **that's quite enough ~ me** das reicht mir völlig; **too ... ~:** zu ... für; **sb. is not long ~ this world** jmd. wird nicht mehr lange unter uns (*Dat.*) weilen; **there is nothing ~ it but to do sth.** es gibt keine andere Möglichkeit, als etw. zu tun; **J** (*Cricket*) **be out ~ a duck/59** ohne Punktgewinn/mit 59 Punkten aus sein; **65 ~ 3 [wickets]** 65 Punkte mit drei Schlägern ausgeschlagen; **K** (*to the amount of*) **cheque/bill ~ £5** Scheck/Rechnung über *od.* in Höhe von 5 Pfund; **the voucher is good ~ 50p** der Gutschein ist 50 p wert; **L** (*to affect, as if affecting*) für; **things don't look very promising ~ the business** was die Geschäfte angeht, sieht das alles

# For

The most frequent translation of the preposition *for*, with the related senses *on behalf of*, *in place of*, *in favour of*, *for the benefit* or *use of* etc., is **für**:

***a bed for two***
= ein Bett für zwei

***I did it for him***
= Ich habe es für ihn gemacht*

*This translation works whether the stress is on *him*, meaning "for his benefit", or on *for*, meaning "in his place", which could also be "an seiner Stelle".

## Expressing purpose

Where purpose is involved and where a verbal noun or other noun describing action follows, the translation is **zu**:

***a device for removing stones from cherries***
= ein Gerät zum Entkernen von Kirschen

***We met for a discussion***
= Wir trafen uns zu einer Besprechung

***She did it for pleasure***
= Sie machte es zum Vergnügen *or* zum Zeitvertreib

***What's that for?***
= Wozu dient denn das?

This also applies to meals:

***We had meat for lunch/a mousse for dessert***
= Bei uns gab es zum Mittagessen Fleisch/zum Nachtisch eine Mousse

But on the other hand:

***a dish for nuts***
= eine Schale für Nüsse

The construction *for sb.* + infinitive expressing purpose can be rendered by a clause with **damit**:

***For him to be able to come we will have to change the date***
= Wir werden den Termin ändern müssen, damit er mitkommen kann

***I took a piece for her to try***
= Ich nahm ein Stück mit, damit sie es probieren konnte, Ich nahm ihr ein Stück zum Probieren mit

## Expressing reasons

With the sense *because of*, **wegen** can be used, although **für** is also found with some adjectives:

***The area is well known/famous for its wines***
= Die Gegend ist bekannt/berühmt für ihre Weine *or* wegen ihrer Weine

***He was sentenced to death for murder***
= Er wurde wegen Mordes zum Tode verurteilt

**aus** also occurs with a governing emotion:

***for fear of waking her***
= aus Angst, sie zu wecken

***for love of his country***
= aus Liebe zum Vaterland

## Expressing direction

Where the sense is simply *going to*, the translation is **nach**:

***the train for Bath***
= der Zug nach Bath

***We left for Scotland***
= Wir sind nach Schottland abgefahren

But with a more general indication of direction rather than destination (meaning *towards*), **auf ... zu** or **in Richtung** can be used in German:

***The ship was heading for the rocks***
= Das Schiff steuerte auf die Felsen zu

***They were making for London***
= Sie fuhren in Richtung London

## Expressing time

The translation will depend on the tense, which is not always the same in German:

- **PERFECT CONTINUOUS**

***I have been living here for two years*** (*and am still living here*)
= Ich wohne seit zwei Jahren hier

- **PAST CONTINUOUS**

***I had been living here for two years*** (*and was still living here at the time*)
= Ich wohnte seit zwei Jahren hier

- **PAST**

***I lived here for two years*** (*and no longer live here*)
= Ich habe zwei Jahre [lang] hier gewohnt

- **FUTURE**

***You will have to wait for an hour***
= Sie werden eine Stunde warten müssen

***I am going to the USA for two weeks***
= Ich fahre für zwei Wochen in die USA

Note that **lang** is placed after the noun, and is often omitted in speech, especially referring to short periods:

***I was in Paris for a few days***
= Ich war ein paar Tage in Paris

However the translation of the phrase *for hours* is **stundenlang**:

***I had to wait for hours***
= Ich musste stundenlang warten

Similarly

***for weeks***
= wochenlang

***for months***
= monatelang

***for years***
= jahrelang

## With personal pronouns

In most cases **für** can be used, but the dative of the personal pronoun is often found with adjectives and nouns expressing difficulty, impossibility, unpleasantness etc. and also more positive feelings:

***It's good for you***
= Es ist gut für dich, Es tut dir gut

***This makes it impossible for me***
= Das macht es mir unmöglich

***Your visit is inconvenient for her***
= Dein Besuch ist *or* kommt ihr ungelegen

***The whole business is very embarrassing for them***
= Die ganze Sache ist ihnen sehr peinlich

***It's a great pleasure/honour for me***
= Es ist mir eine große Freude/Ehre

nicht sehr vielversprechend aus; **learn to do things ~ oneself** lernen, die Dinge selbstständig zu erledigen; **I think it would work out ~ us to meet some time** ich glaube, es lässt sich machen, dass wir uns einmal treffen; **it is wise/advisable ~ sb. to do sth.** es ist vernünftig/ratsam, dass jmd. etw. tut; **it's always nice ~ us to know that you're well** wir hören immer wieder gern, dass es dir gut geht; **it's hopeless ~ me to try and explain the system** es ist sinnlos, dir das System erklären zu wollen; M (*as being*) für; **what do you take me ~?** wofür hältst du mich?; **I/you** *etc.* **~ one** ich/du *usw.* für mein[en]/dein[en] *usw.* Teil; **see sb. ~ what he really is** jmdn. als das erkennen, was er wirklich ist *od.* so sehen, wie er wirklich ist; N (*on account of*, *as penalty of*) wegen; **famous/well-known ~ sth.** berühmt/bekannt wegen *od.* für etw.; **live ~ one's work** für seine *od.* die Arbeit leben; **~ love of his wife** aus Liebe zu seiner Frau; **jump/shout ~ joy** vor Freude in die Luft springen/schreien; **this is ~ being good** das kriegst du, weil du so artig warst; **had it not been ~ him** wäre er nicht gewesen; **but ~ you/your kindness we might not be here today** nur deinetwegen/nur dank deiner Güte sind wir heute hier; **were it not ~ you/your help, I should not be**

**able to do it** ohne dich/deine Hilfe wäre ich nicht dazu in der Lage; **O** (*on the occasion of*) ~ **the first time** zum ersten Mal; **why can't you help ~ once?** warum kannst du nicht einmal helfen?; **you are mistaken ~ once** nun hast du dich aber mal geirrt; **what shall I give him ~ his birthday?** was soll ich ihm zum Geburtstag schenken?; **P** (*in spite of*) ~ **all ...:** trotz ...; ~ **all that, ...:** trotzdem ...; ~ **all that he ...:** obwohl er ...; **Q** (*on account of the hindrance of*) vor (+ *Dat.*); ~ **fear of ...:** aus Angst vor (+ *Dat.*); **he couldn't see the ring ~ looking at it** (*iron.*) er sah den Ring einfach nicht, obwohl er doch gerade auf ihn blickte; **but ~ ..., except ~ ...:** wenn nicht ... gewesen wäre, [dann] ...; **but ~ the captain's carelessness** wenn der Kapitän nicht so leichtfertig gewesen wäre; **were it not ~ the children** wenn die Kinder nicht wären; ⇒ *also* **wood** A; **R** (*corresponding to*) für; ~ **every cigarette you smoke you are reducing your life expectancy by one day** jede Zigarette, die du rauchst, verkürzt deine Lebenserwartung um einen Tag; ~ **fifty fish eggs that die, a hundred survive** auf fünfzig Fischeier, die absterben, kommen hundert, die sich weiterentwickeln; **man ~ man** Mann für Mann; **S** (*so far as concerns*) ~ **all I know/care ...:** möglicherweise/was mich betrifft, ...; ~ **my part** *or* ~ **myself, I ...:** ich für mein[en] Teil ...; ~ **one thing, ...:** zunächst einmal ...; **T** (*considering the usual nature of*) für; **not bad ~ a first attempt** nicht schlecht für den ersten Versuch; **very active ~ a man of eighty** sehr rege für einen Achtziger; **U** (*during*) seit; **we've/we haven't been here ~ three years** wir sind seit drei Jahren hier/nicht mehr hier gewesen; **we waited ~ hours/three hours** wir warteten stundenlang/drei Stunden lang; **we have been waiting ~ hours [on end]** wir warten schon seit Stunden; **how long are you here ~?** (*coll.*) wie lange bleiben Sie hier?; **stay here ~ a week/some time** eine Woche/einige Zeit hier bleiben; **sit here ~ now** *or* ~ **the moment** *or* ~ **the present** bleiben Sie im Augenblick hier sitzen; ⇒ *also* **ever** A; **V** (*to the extent of*) **walk ~ 20 miles/~ another 20 miles** 20 Meilen [weit] gehen/weiter gehen; **W be ~ it** (*coll.: face trouble*) dran sein (*ugs.*); sich auf was gefasst machen können (*ugs.*).
**2** *conj.* (*since, as proof*) denn

**forage** /ˈfɒrɪdʒ/ **1** *n.* **A** (*food for horses or cattle*) Futter, *das;* **B** (*search for ~*) Nahrungssuche, *die;* Futtersuche, *die;* **on the ~:** auf Nahrungssuche; **C** (*fig.: search for thing*) **on the ~ for sth.** auf der Jagd nach etw. (*ugs.*). **2** *v.i.* auf Nahrungssuche sein; ~ **for sth.** auf der Suche nach etw. sein; (*fig.: rummage*) nach etw. stöbern; ~ **in sb.'s suitcase/among sb.'s papers** jmds. Koffer/Papiere durchstöbern *od.* -wühlen

**'forage cap** *n.* Käppi, *das*

**forasmuch** /fɒrəzˈmʌtʃ/ *adv.* (*Law/arch.*) ~ **as** insofern [als]

**foray** /ˈfɒreɪ/ **1** *n.* Streifzug, *der;* (*Mil.*) Ausfall, *der;* (*brief trip*) kurzer Besuch (*iron.*) (**to** bei); (*fig.: venture*) Ausflug, *der* (*scherzh.*); **go on** *or* **make a ~:** einen Streifzug unternehmen; (*Mil.*) einen Ausfall machen. **2** *v.i.* plündernd einfallen

**forbad, forbade** ⇒ **forbid**

**forbear¹** /ˈfɔːbeə(r)/ *n., usu. in pl.* Vorfahr, *der*

**forbear²** /fɔːˈbeə(r)/ **1** *v.i.,* **forbore** /fɔːˈbɔː(r)/, **forborne** /fɔːˈbɔːn/ **A** (*refrain*) ~ **from doing sth.** davon Abstand nehmen, etw. zu tun; **B** (*be patient*) sich gedulden; ~ **with sth.** etw. geduldig ertragen; **be ~ing** Geduld haben. **2** *v.t.,* **forbore, forborne:** ~ **sth./to do** *or* **doing sth.** auf etw. (*Akk.*) verzichten/darauf verzichten, etw. zu tun

**forbearance** /fɔːˈbeərəns/ *n., no pl.* Nachsicht, *die;* (*forbearing nature*) Nachsichtigkeit, *die;* **show ~:** sich nachsichtig zeigen; Nachsicht üben

**forbid** /fəˈbɪd/ *v.t.,* **-dd-, forbade** /fəˈbæd, fəˈbeɪd/ *or* **forbad** /fəˈbæd/, **forbidden** /fəˈbɪdn/ **A** ~ **sb. to do sth.** jmdm. verbieten, etw. zu tun; ~ **[sb.] sth.** [jmdm.] etw. verbieten; **it is ~den [to do sth.]** es ist verboten *od.* nicht gestattet[, etw. zu tun]; **'the taking of photographs is ~den'** „Fotografieren nicht gestattet"; **B** (*make impossible*) nicht zulassen; nicht erlauben; **I'd like to do it but time ~s** ich würde es gern tun, finde aber nicht die Zeit dazu; **but decency ~s** aber das verbietet [mir] der Anstand; **God/Heaven ~ [that ...]!** Gott/der Himmel bewahre[, dass ...]!; (*future*) der Himmel verhüte[, dass ...]!

**forbidden** /fəˈbɪdn/ **1** ⇒ **forbid. 2** *adj.* verboten; ~ **fruit** (*fig.*) verbotene Früchte; ~ **ground** Gebiet, das nicht betreten werden darf; (*fig.*) **be ~ ground** tabu sein; ⇒ *also* **degree** E

**forbidding** /fəˈbɪdɪŋ/ *adj.* Furcht einflößend ‹Aussehen, Stimme›; unwirtlich ‹Landschaft›; (*fig.*) düster ‹Aussicht›

**forbiddingly** /fəˈbɪdɪŋlɪ/ *adv.* drohend ‹sich abzeichnen›; entmutigend ‹lang, steil, teuer, schwer›

**forbore, forborne** ⇒ **forbear²**

**force¹** /fɔːs/ **1** *n.* **A** *no pl.* (*strength, power*) Stärke, *die;* (*of bomb, explosion, attack, storm*) Wucht, *die;* (*physical strength*) Kraft, *die;* **[a wind of] ~ 12** (*Meteorol.*) Windstärke 12; **destructive ~ of a bomb** Zerstörungskraft einer Bombe; **achieve sth. by brute ~:** etw. mit roher Gewalt erreichen; **in ~** (*in large numbers*) mit einem großen Aufgebot; (⇒ *also* **b**); **B** *no pl.* (*fig.: power, validity*) Kraft, *die;* (*power to convince*) Überzeugungskraft, *die;* **by ~ of** aufgrund (+ *Gen.*); kraft (+ *Gen.*) (*Papierdt.*); **achieve a victory by ~ of numbers** einen Sieg durch zahlenmäßige Überlegenheit erringen; ~ **of conviction/will** Überzeugungs-/Willenskraft, *die;* ~ **of arms** Waffengewalt, *die;* ~ **of character** Charakterstärke, *die;* ~ **of evidence** Beweiskraft, *die;* **have the ~ of law** Gesetzeskraft haben; **argue with much ~:** sehr überzeugend argumentieren; **his dramatic sense comes out with great ~:** seine dramatische Begabung zeigt sich [hier] in voller Stärke; **in ~** (*in effect*) in Kraft; **come into ~** ‹Gesetz usw.:› in Kraft treten; **put in[to] ~:** in Kraft setzen; **the methods currently in ~:** die zur Zeit gängigen Methoden; (⇒ *also* **a**); **C** (*coercion, violence*) Gewalt, *die;* **use** *or* **employ ~ [against sb.]** Gewalt [gegen jmdn.] anwenden; **use of ~:** Gewaltanwendung, *die;* **by ~:** gewaltsam; mit Gewalt; **resort to ~:** zur Gewalt greifen; **with the threat of ~:** unter Androhung von Gewalt; **D** (*organized group*) (*of workers*) Kolonne, *die;* Trupp, *der;* (*of police*) Einheit, *die;* (*Mil.*) Armee, *die;* Streitmacht, *die* (*veralt.*); **the ~s** die Armee; **be in the ~s** beim Militär sein; **the ~** (*Police*) die Polizei; **a large ~ of infantry/naval ~:** starke Infanterie-/Marineverbände; **join ~s [with sb.]** (*fig.*) sich [mit jmdm.] zusammentun; ⇒ *also* **armed; labour force; police force; sales force; task force; workforce; E** (*forceful agency or person*) Kraft, *die;* Macht, *die;* **a ~ for evil** ein Handlanger *od.* Werkzeug des Bösen; **the ~s of destiny/evil** die Macht des Schicksals/Bösen; **there are ~s in action/at work here ...:** hier walten Kräfte/sind Kräfte am Werk ...; **he is a ~ in the land** (*fig.*)/**a ~ to be reckoned with** er ist ein einflussreicher Mann im Land/eine Macht, die nicht zu unterschätzen ist; ⇒ *also* **life force; spent** B; **F** (*meaning*) Bedeutung, *die;* **G** (*Phys.*) Kraft, *die.*
**2** *v.t.* **A** (*coerce by violent means*) ~ **sb. to do sth.** jmdn. zwingen, etw. zu tun; ~ **sb. into marriage/compliance** jmdn. zur Heirat zwingen/jmds. Einverständnis erzwingen; **be ~d into war** sich zum Krieg gezwungen sehen; **be ~d to do sth.** gezwungen sein *od.* sich gezwungen sehen, etw. zu tun; ~ **sb. out of the room [at gunpoint]** jmdn. [mit vorgehaltener Waffe] zwingen, das Zimmer zu verlassen; **B** (*compel by non-violent means*) ~ **sb./oneself [to do sth.]** jmdn./sich zwingen[, etw. zu tun]; ~ **sb./oneself into sth.** (*fig.*) jmdn./sich zu etw. zwingen; **I was ~d to accept/into accepting the offer** ich fühlte mich verpflichtet/ich war *od.* sah mich gezwungen, das Angebot anzunehmen; **I was ~d to the conclusion** *or* **to conclude that ...** (*fig.*) ich musste zu dem Schluss gelangen, dass ...; ~ **sb.'s hand** (*fig.*) jmdn. zwingen zu handeln; ⇒ *also* **issue** 1 F; **C** (*take by ~*) ~ **sth. from sb.** jmdm. etw. entreißen; **he ~d it out of her hands** er riss es ihr aus der Hand; ~ **a promise out of sb.** (*fig.*) jmdm. ein Versprechen abringen; ~ **a confession from sb.** (*fig.*) jmdn. zu einem Geständnis zwingen; ~ **a smile from sb.** (*fig.*) jmdm. ein Lächeln entlocken; **D** (*push*) ~ **sth. into sth.** etw. in etw. *Akk.* [hinein]zwängen; ~ **sth. [up] through an opening** etw. [nach oben und] durch eine Öffnung pressen; ~ **one's way** sich (*Dat.*) [gewaltsam] einen Weg bahnen; **E** (*impose, inflict*) ~ **sth. [up]on sb.** jmdm. etw. aufzwingen *od.* aufnötigen; **he ~d his attentions on her** er drängte sich ihr mit seinen Aufmerksamkeiten auf; **F** (*break open*) ~ **[open]** aufbrechen; **G** (*storm*) stürmen ‹Festung›; **H** (*effect by violent means*) sich (*Dat.*) erzwingen ‹Zutritt›; ~ **one's way in[to a building]** sich (*Dat.*) mit Gewalt Zutritt [zu einem Gebäude] verschaffen; **I had to ~ my way out** ich musste Gewalt anwenden, um herauszukommen; **I** ~ **the pace** (*lit. or fig.*) das Tempo forcieren; ~ **the bidding** das Gebot in die Höhe treiben; **J** (*produce with effort*) sich zwingen zu; ~ **a smile** sich zu einem Lächeln zwingen; **K** (*put strained sense upon*) Gewalt antun (+ *Dat.*); vergewaltigen ‹Sprache›; überstrapazieren ‹Vergleich›; **L** treiben ‹Pflanzen›; **M** (*rape*) ~ **a woman** einer Frau (*Dat.*) Gewalt antun (*veralt.*)

~ **'down** *v.t.* **A** drücken ‹Preis›; **B** (*compel to land*) zur Landung zwingen ‹Flugzeug›; **C** (*make oneself eat*) herunterwürgen (*ugs.*) ‹Nahrung›

~ **'up** *v.t.* hochtreiben ‹Preis›

**force²** *n.* (*N. Engl.*) Wasserfall, *der*

**forced** /fɔːst/ *adj.* **A** (*contrived, unnatural*) gezwungen; gewollt ‹Geste, Vergleich, Metapher›; gekünstelt ‹Benehmen›; **B** (*compelled by force*) erzwungen; Zwangs‹arbeit, -anleihe›; **~-labour camp** Arbeitslager, *das;* **C** (*produced artificially*) ~ **vibration** (*Phys.*) unfreie *od.* erzwungene Schwingung; **~-air ventilation** Zwangslüftung, *die* (*Technik*)

**forced:** ~ **'landing** *n.* Notlandung, *die;* ~ **'march** *n.* (*Mil.*) Gewaltmarsch, *der;* ~ **'marriage** *n.* erzwungene Ehe

**'force-feed** *v.t.* zwangsernähren; (*fig.*) voll stopfen (**on** mit)

**forceful** /ˈfɔːsfl/ *adj.* stark ‹Persönlichkeit, Charakter›; energisch ‹Person, Art, Stimme, Maßnahme›; überzeugend ‹Darlegung›; schwungvoll ‹Rede-, Schreibweise›; eindrucksvoll ‹Sprache›; eindringlich ‹Worte›

**forcefully** /ˈfɔːsfəlɪ/ *adv.* eindringlich ‹reden, darlegen›; energisch ‹verfolgen, umgehen›; nachdrücklich ‹erinnern›

**force majeure** /fɔːs mɑˈʒɜː(r)/ *n.* höhere Gewalt

**'forcemeat** *n.* (*Cookery*) Farce, *die*

**forceps** /ˈfɔːseps/ *n., pl. same* **[pair of] ~:** Zange, *die;* **obstetrical ~:** Geburtszange, *die;* ~ **baby/delivery** Zangengeburt, *die*

**forcible** /ˈfɔːsɪbl/ *adj.* **A** (*done by force*) gewaltsam; **B** ⇒ **forceful**

**forcibly** /ˈfɔːsɪblɪ/ *adv.* **A** (*by force*) gewaltsam; mit Gewalt; **B** ⇒ **forcefully**

**forcing house** /ˈfɔːsɪŋhaʊs/ *n.* (*lit. or fig.*) Treibhaus, *das*

**ford** /fɔːd/ **1** *n.* Furt, *die.* **2** *v.t.* durchqueren; (*wade through*) durchwaten

**fore** /fɔː(r)/ **1** *adj., esp. in comb.* vorder...; Vorder‹teil, -front usw.›. **2** *n.* **[be/come] to the ~** im Vordergrund [stehen]/in den Vordergrund [rücken]. **3** *int.* (*Golf*) Achtung. **4** *adv.* (*Naut.*) vorn; ~ **and aft** längs[schiffs]

**fore-and-'aft** (*Naut.*) **1** *adj.* Längs-; ~ **sail** Schratsegel, *das.* **2** *adv.* längs[schiffs]; ~ **rigged** längsschiffs getakelt

**'forearm¹** *n.* Unterarm, *der*

**fore'arm²** *v.t.* rüsten; (*fig.*) **be ~ed** gerüstet *od.* vorbereitet sein; ⇒ *also* **forewarn**

**forebear** ⇒ **forbear**[1]

**fore'bode** *v.t.* (*portend*) ankündigen; **these clouds ~ a storm** die Wolken bedeuten *od.* deuten auf Sturm

**foreboding** /fɔ:'bəʊdɪŋ/ *n.* Vorahnung, *die;* (*unease caused by premonition*) ungutes Gefühl; (*omen*) Vorzeichen, *das;* Omen, *das*

**'forecast** ❶ *v.t.*, **~** *or* **~ed** vorhersagen. ❷ *n.* Voraussage, *die;* Prognose, *die;* (*Meteorol.*) [Wetter]vorhersage, *die;* Wetterbericht, *der;* **the ~ is for rain** laut Wettervorhersage wird es regnen

**'forecaster** *n.* Meteorologe, *der*/Meteorologin, *die*

**forecastle** /'fəʊksl/ *n.* (*Naut.*) Back, *die;* (*Hist.: deck*) [Vorder]kastell, *das*

**foreclose** /fɔ:'kləʊz/ (*Law*) ❶ *v.t.* kündigen; **~ a mortgage** eine Hypothekenforderung geltend machen. ❷ *v.i.* **~ on sb./a mortgage** eine Hypothekenforderung gegenüber jmdm./eine Hypothekenforderung geltend machen

**'forecourt** *n.* Vorhof, *der;* **~ attendant** ≈ Tankwart, *der;* **~ service** Service an der Tankstelle

**'foredeck** *n.* (*Naut.*) Vordeck, *das*

**fore'doom** *v.t.* vorherbestimmen; **be ~ed to failure** zum Scheitern verurteilt sein

**'forefather** *n.*, *usu. in pl.* Vorfahr, *der;* **our ~s** unsere Vorväter

**'forefinger** *n.* Zeigefinger, *der*

**'forefoot** *n.* Vorderfuß, *der*

**'forefront** *n.* **[be] in the ~ of** in vorderster Linie (+ *Gen.*) [stehen]

**foregather** ⇒ **forgather**

**forego** ⇒ **forgo**

**foregoing** /'fɔ:gəʊɪŋ, fɔ:'gəʊɪŋ/ *adj.* vorhergehend

**'foregone** *adj.* **be a ~ conclusion** (*be predetermined*) von vornherein feststehen; (*be certain*) so gut wie sicher sein

**'foreground** *n.* Vordergrund, *der*

**'forehand** (*Tennis etc.*) ❶ *adj.* Vorhand-. ❷ *n.* (*also part of horse*) Vorhand, *die*

**forehead** /'fɒrɪd, 'fɔ:hed/ *n.* ▶ **966** Stirn, *die*

**foreign** /'fɒrɪn/ *adj.* Ⓐ (*from abroad*) ausländisch; Fremd‹herrschaft, -kapital, -sprache›; fremdartig ‹Gebräuche›; fremdländisch ‹Aussehen›; **~ word** fremdsprachliches Wort; (*used in English*) Fremdwort, *das;* **talk ~** (*coll.*) auswärts reden *od.* sprechen (*ugs. scherzh.*); **~ worker** Gastarbeiter, *der*/-arbeiterin, *die;* **he is ~:** er ist Ausländer; Ⓑ (*abroad*) fremd; Auslands‹reise, -niederlassung, -markt›; **~ countries** Ausland, *das;* **from a ~ country** aus einem anderen Land; aus dem Ausland; **~ travel** Reisen ins Ausland; ⇒ *also* **part** 1 G; Ⓒ (*related to countries abroad*) außenpolitisch; Außen‹politik, -handel›; **~ affairs** auswärtige Angelegenheiten; **spokesman on ~ affairs** außenpolitischer Sprecher; **~ news** Nachrichten aus dem Ausland; Ⓓ (*from outside*) fremd; **~ body** Fremdkörper, *der;* Ⓔ (*alien, unfamiliar*) fremd; **be ~ to sb./sb.'s nature** jmdm. fremd sein/nicht jmds. Art sein; **be ~ to sth.** (*unrelated*) in keiner Beziehung zu etw. stehen

**foreign: ~ 'aid** *n.* Entwicklungshilfe, *die;* **F~ and 'Commonwealth Office** *n.* (*Brit.*) Außenministerium, *das;* **~ corre'spondent** *n.* ▶ **1261** (*Journ.*) Auslandskorrespondent, *der*/-korrespondentin, *die*

**foreigner** /'fɒrɪnə(r)/ *n.* Ausländer, *der*/Ausländerin, *die*

**foreign: ~ ex'change** *n.* (*dealings*) Devisenhandel, *der;* (*currency*) fremde Währung; Devisen *Pl.;* **~ exchange market** Devisenmarkt, *der;* **~ 'language** *n.* Fremdsprache, *die; attrib.* **~-language newspaper/broadcast** fremdsprachige Zeitung/Rundfunksendung; **~-language teaching** Fremdsprachenunterricht, *der;* **~ 'legion** *n.* Fremdenlegion, *die;* **F~ 'Minister** *n.* Außenminister, *der;* **F~ 'Ministry** *n.* Außenministerium, *das;* **F~ Office** *n.* (*Brit. Hist./coll.*) Außenministerium, *das;* Auswärtiges Amt; **~-owned** *adj.* **~-owned subsidiaries** Tochtergesellschaften in ausländischem Besitz; **F~ 'Secretary** *n.* ▶ **1261** (*Brit.*) Außenminister, *der;* **~ service** ⇒ **diplomatic service**

**fore'knowledge** *n.* vorherige Kenntnis; **with the ~ that ...:** im Wissen, dass ...

**'forelady** (*Amer.*) ⇒ **forewoman** A

**foreland** /'fɔ:lənd/ *n.* (*Geog.*) Kap, *das*

**'foreleg** *n.* Vorderbein, *das;* Vorderlauf, *der* (*Jägerspr.*)

**'forelimb** *n.* Vordergliedmaße, *die*

**'forelock** *n.* Stirnlocke, *die;* **take time** *etc.* **by the ~** (*fig.*) die Gelegenheit beim Schopf ergreifen; **touch one's ~** (*joc.*) einen Diener machen (*iron.*)

**foreman** /'fɔ:mən/ *n.*, *pl.* **foremen** /'fɔ:mən/ Ⓐ ▶ **1261** (*chief workman*) Vorarbeiter, *der;* Werkmeister, *der;* Ⓑ (*Law*) Sprecher [der Geschworenen/(*in Germany*) der Schöffen]

**'foremast** *n.* (*Naut.*) Fockmast, *der*

**foremost** /'fɔ:məʊst, 'fɔ:məst/ ❶ *adj.* Ⓐ vorderst...; **the two ~ runners** die beiden Läufer an der Spitze; **fall downstairs head ~:** mit dem Kopf zuerst die Treppe hinunterfallen; Ⓑ (*fig.*) führend; **be in the ~ rank** zur Spitze zählen. ❷ *adv.* ⇒ **first** 2 E

**'forename** *n.* Vorname, *der*

**'forenoon** *n.* (*Naut.*, *Law/arch.*) Vormittag, *der;* **in the ~:** am Vormittag

**forensic** /fə'rensɪk/ *adj.* gerichtlich; forensisch (*fachspr.*); **~ medicine** Gerichtsmedizin, *die;* **~ science** Kriminaltechnik, *die;* **~ laboratory** kriminaltechnisches Labor

**'forepaw** *n.* Vorderpfote, *die*

**'foreplay** *n.* Vorspiel, *das*

**'forerunner** *n.* Ⓐ (*predecessor*) Vorläufer, *der*/Vorläuferin, *die;* Ⓑ (*harbinger, sign*) Vorbote, *der*

**foresail** /'fɔ:seɪl, 'fɔ:sl/ *n.* (*Naut.*) Focksegel, *das*

**foresaw** ⇒ **foresee**

**foresee** /fɔ:'si:/ *v.t.*, *forms as* **see**[1] voraussehen; **trouble which had not been ~n** unvorhergesehener Ärger; **as far as one can ~** *or* **as can be ~n** aller Voraussicht nach

**foreseeable** /fɔ:'si:əbl/ *adj.* Ⓐ vorhersehbar; Ⓑ **in the ~ future** in nächster Zukunft; in absehbarer Zeit

**foreseen** ⇒ **foresee**

**fore'shadow** *v.t.* vorausahnen lassen; vorausdeuten auf (+ *Akk.*)

**'foreshore** *n.* Vorland, *das;* (*between high water and low-water marks*) ≈ Strand, *der*

**fore'shorten** *v.t.* Ⓐ (*Art, Photog.*) [perspektivisch] verkürzen; Ⓑ (*shorten, condense*) verkürzen; verdichten (*fig.*) ‹Ereignisse›

**'foresight** *n.*, *no pl.* Weitblick, *der;* Voraussicht, *die;* **act with ~:** vorausschauend handeln; **use ~:** vorausschauend sein; Weitblick zeigen; **have the ~ to do sth.** so vorausschauend sein, etw. zu tun

**'foreskin** *n.* (*Anat.*) Vorhaut, *die*

**forest** /'fɒrɪst/ *n.* Ⓐ Wald, *der;* (*commercially exploited*) Forst, *der; attrib.* Wald‹brand, -land›; **covered in ~s** bewaldet; **~ law** Forstrecht, *das;* **~ warden** *or* (*Amer.*) **ranger** Förster, *der;* ⇒ *also* **deer forest**; Ⓑ (*fig.*) Wald, *der* (**of** von); (*of ideas etc.*) Gewirr, *das;* Wust, *der* (*abwertend*)

**fore'stall** *v.t.* zuvorkommen (+ *Dat.*); (*prevent by prior action*) vermeiden; (*anticipate*) vorhersehen

**'forestay** *n.* (*Naut.*) Vorstag, *das*

**forested** /'fɒrɪstɪd/ *adj.* bewaldet

**forester** /'fɒrɪstə(r)/ *n.* Ⓐ ▶ **1261** (*warden*) Förster, *der;* Ⓑ (*dweller*) Waldbewohner, *der*

**forestry** /'fɒrɪstrɪ/ *n.* Forstwirtschaft, *die;* (*science*) Forstwissenschaft, *die;* **F~ Commission** (*Brit.*) *britische Forstbehörde*

**'forest tree** *n.* Waldbaum, *der;* Forstbaum, *der*

**'foretaste** *n.* Vorgeschmack, *der;* **have a ~ of sth.** einen Vorgeschmack von etw. bekommen

**fore'tell** *v.t.*, **foretold** vorhersagen; voraussagen

**'forethought** *n.* (*prior deliberation*) [vorherige] Überlegung; (*care for the future*) Vorausdenken, *das;* (*premeditation*) Vorausplanung, *die*

**foretold** ⇒ **foretell**

**forever** /fə'revə(r)/ (*Amer.*) = **for ever;** ⇒ **ever** A

**fore'warn** *v.t.* vorwarnen; **we were ~ed of the difficulties** man hatte uns vor den Schwierigkeiten gewarnt; **~ed is forearmed** (*prov.*) wer gewarnt ist, ist gewappnet

**fore'warning** *n.* Vorwarnung, *die;* **be given adequate ~:** hinreichend vorgewarnt sein

**'forewoman** *n.* Ⓐ (*chief workwoman*) Vorarbeiterin, *die;* Ⓑ (*Law*) Sprecherin [der Geschworenen/(*in Germany*) der Schöffen]

**'foreword** *n.* Vorwort, *das*

**forfeit** /'fɔ:fɪt/ ❶ *v.t.* verlieren (*auch fig.*); einbüßen (*geh.*, *auch fig.*); verlustig gehen (+ *Gen.*) (*Amtsspr.*); verwirken (*geh.*) ‹Recht, jmds. Gunst›; **he ~ed the good opinion of his friends** er verscherzte sich (*Dat.*) die Sympathien seiner Freunde. ❷ *n.* Ⓐ (*penalty*) Strafe, *die;* (*fig.*) Preis, *der;* Ⓑ (*Games*) Pfand, *das;* **pay/redeem a ~:** ein Pfand geben/einlösen; Ⓒ (*~ing*) Verlust, *der;* Einbuße, *die.* ❸ *adj.* **be ~:** verfallen (**to** *Dat.*); ‹Leben, Recht:› verwirkt sein (*geh.*)

**forfeiture** /'fɔ:fɪtʃə(r)/ *n.* Verlust, *der;* Einbuße, *die*

**forgather** /fɔ:'gæðə(r)/ *v.i.* sich treffen; zusammenkommen

**forgave** ⇒ **forgive**

**forge**[1] /fɔ:dʒ/ ❶ *n.* Ⓐ (*workshop*) Schmiede, *die;* Ⓑ (*blacksmith's hearth*) Esse, *die;* (*furnace for melting or refining metal*) Schmiedeofen, *der.* ❷ *v.t.* Ⓐ schmieden (**into** zu); Ⓑ (*fig.*) schmieden ‹Plan, Verbindung›; schließen ‹Vereinbarung, Freundschaft, Frieden›; prägen ‹Charakter›; (*fabricate*) erfinden; sich (*Dat.*) ausdenken; Ⓒ (*counterfeit*) fälschen; **~d money** Falschgeld, *das*

**forge**[2] *v.i.* Ⓐ (*advance rapidly*) **~ into the lead** die Führung übernehmen; in Führung gehen; **~ ahead** [das Tempo] beschleunigen; ‹Wettläufer:› vorstoßen; (*fig.*) vorankommen; Fortschritte machen; (*take lead*) sich an die Spitze setzen; die Führung übernehmen; Ⓑ (*progress steadily*) **~ on** (*lit. or fig.*) [stetig] vorankommen

**forger** /'fɔ:dʒə(r)/ *n.* Fälscher, *der*/Fälscherin, *die*

**forgery** /'fɔ:dʒərɪ/ *n.* Fälschung, *die;* **commit an act of ~:** eine Fälschung begehen

**forget** /fə'get/ ❶ *v.t.*, **-tt-**, **forgot** /fə'gɒt/, **forgotten** /fə'gɒtn/ *or* (*Amer./arch./poet.*) **forgot** Ⓐ vergessen; (*~ learned ability*) verlernen; vergessen; **these names are easy to ~** *or* **easily forgotten** diese Namen vergisst man leicht; **gone but not forgotten** in bleibender Erinnerung; (*iron.*) aus den Augen, aber schwerlich aus dem Sinn; **never-to-be-forgotten** unvergesslich; **I was quite ~ting you know her** ich habe ganz vergessen, dass du sie ja kennst; **I ~ his name** (*have forgotten*) ich habe seinen Namen vergessen; **~ doing sth./having done sth.** vergessen, dass man etw. getan hat; **~ to do sth.** vergessen, etw. zu tun; **don't ~ that ...:** vergiss nicht *od.* denk[e] daran, dass ...; **~ how to dance** das Tanzen verlernen; **a thrashing he won't ~ in a hurry** eine Tracht Prügel, die er nicht so schnell vergessen wird; Ⓑ (*leave*) vergessen; Ⓒ **and don't you ~ it** (*coll.*) vergiss das ja nicht; **~ sth.** (*decide to ignore*) etw. beiseite lassen; **~ it!** (*coll.*) schon gut!; vergiss es!
❷ *v.i.*, **-tt-**, **forgot**, **forgotten** es vergessen; **I almost forgot** fast hätte ich es vergessen; **I quite forgot** ich habe es ganz vergessen; **~ about sth.** etw. vergessen; **~ about it!** (*coll.*) schon gut!; **I had forgotten all about his** *or* **him coming today** ich hatte ganz vergessen, dass er heute kommt; **I forgot about Joe** ich habe gar nicht an Joe gedacht.
❸ *v. refl.*, **-tt-**, **forgot**, **forgotten** Ⓐ (*act unbecomingly or unworthily*) sich vergessen; Ⓑ (*neglect one's own interests*) sich selbst vergessen; nicht an sich (*Akk.*) denken

**forgetful** /fəˈgetfl/ *adj.* Ⓐ (*absent-minded*) vergesslich; Ⓑ ~ **of sth.** ohne an etw. (*Akk.*) zu denken; **be ~ of sth.** etw. vergessen; **be ~ of one's duty** seine Pflicht vernachlässigen

**forgetfully** /fəˈgetfəlɪ/ *adv.* in Gedanken

**forgetfulness** /fəˈgetflnɪs/ *n., no pl.* Vergesslichkeit, *die;* Zerstreutheit, *die;* **in a moment of ~:** in einem Moment von Geistesabwesenheit

**for'get-me-not** *n.* (*Bot.*) Vergissmeinnicht, *das; attrib.* **~ blue** vergissmeinnichtblau

**forgettable** /fəˈgetəbl/ *adj.* **easily ~:** leicht zu vergessen

**forging** /ˈfɔːdʒɪŋ/ *n.* (*object*) Schmiedestück, *das*

**forgivable** /fəˈgɪvəbl/ *adj.* verständlich; verzeihlich

**forgivably** /fəˈgɪvəblɪ/ *adv.* verständlicherweise

**forgive** /fəˈgɪv/ *v.t.*, **forgave** /fəˈgeɪv/, **forgiven** /fəˈgɪvn/ Ⓐ ▶ 924 vergeben ‹Sünden›; verzeihen ‹Unrecht›; entschuldigen, verzeihen ‹Unterbrechung, Neugier, Ausdrucksweise›; **~ sb. [sth. *or* for sth.]** jmdm. [etw.] verzeihen *od.* (*geh.*) vergeben; **~ sb. for doing sth.** jmdm. verzeihen, dass er/sie etw. getan hat; **God ~ me** möge Gott mir vergeben; **am I ~n?** verzeihst du mir?; **you are ~n** ich verzeihe dir; **~ us [for] our sins** vergib uns unsere Sünden; **I'll never ~ myself for not having offered to help** ich werde es mir nie verzeihen, nicht wenigstens meine Hilfe angeboten zu haben; **~ me for saying so, but …:** entschuldigen *od.* verzeihen Sie[, dass ich es sage], [aber] …; **she doesn't ~ easily** es fällt ihr schwer zu verzeihen; **~ and forget** vergeben und vergessen; Ⓑ (*remit, let off*) erlassen; **~ sb. a debt** jmdm. eine Schuld erlassen

**forgiveness** /fəˈgɪvnɪs/ *n., no pl.* Verzeihung, *die;* (*esp. of sins*) Vergebung, *die* (*geh.*); **ask/beg [sb.'s] ~:** [jmdn.] um Verzeihung/(*geh.*) Vergebung bitten; **grant sb. [one's] ~:** jmdm. verzeihen; **~ of sins** Vergebung der Sünden; Sündenvergebung, *die*

**forgiving** /fəˈgɪvɪŋ/ *adj.*, **forgivingly** /fəˈgɪvɪŋlɪ/ *adv.* versöhnlich

**forgo** /fɔːˈgəʊ/ *v.t., forms as* **go**[1] verzichten auf (+ *Akk.*)

**forgone** ⇒ **forgo**

**forgot, forgotten** ⇒ **forget**

**fork** /fɔːk/ ❶ *n.* Ⓐ (*for eating with*) Gabel, *die;* **knife and ~:** Messer und Gabel; Besteck, *das;* **the knives and ~s** das Besteck; **~ lunch** Gabelfrühstück, *das* (*veralt.*); ≈ kaltes Büfett; **~ supper** ≈ kaltes Büfett; Ⓑ (*Agric.*) Gabel, *die;* Forke, *die* (*bes. nordd.*); Ⓒ *in sing. or pl.* (*on bicycle*) Gabel, *die;* Ⓓ ([*point of*] *division into branches*) Gabelung, *die;* (*one branch*) Abzweigung, *die;* (*of tree*) Astgabel, *die.* ❷ *v.i.* Ⓐ (*divide*) sich gabeln; Ⓑ (*turn*) abbiegen; **~ [to the] left [for]** [nach] links abbiegen [nach]. ❸ *v.t.* gabeln; **~ in manure** Mist [mit einer Gabel] untergraben

**~ 'out** (*coll.*) ❶ *v.t.* lockermachen (*ugs.*); **~ out money** blechen (*ugs.*). ❷ *v.i.* **~ out [for sth.]** [für etw.] blechen (*ugs.*)

**~ 'over** *v.t.* lockern ‹Boden›

**~ 'up** ⇒ **~ out**

**forked** /fɔːkt/ *adj.* gegabelt; **speak with ~ tongue** (*fig.*) mit gespaltener *od.* doppelter Zunge sprechen (*geh.*)

**forked 'lightning** *n., no pl., no indef. art.* Linienblitz, *der*

**'forklift truck** *n.* Gabelstapler, *der*

**forlorn** /fəˈlɔːn/ *adj.* Ⓐ (*desperate*) verzweifelt; **~ hope** (*faint hope*) verzweifelte Hoffnung; (*desperate enterprise*) aussichtsloses Unterfangen; Ⓑ (*forsaken*) [einsam und] verlassen; (*wretched*) erbärmlich (*auch fig.*); desolat ‹Anblick, Zustand›

**form** /fɔːm/ ❶ *n.* Ⓐ (*type, guise, style*) Form, *die;* **~ of address** [Form der] Anrede; **~ of life/government** Lebens-/Regierungsform, *die;* **the reward will take the ~ of a holiday** die Belohnung wird eine Urlaubsreise sein; **malaria takes various ~s** Malaria äußert sich in verschiedenen Formen; **in human ~:** in menschlicher Gestalt; in Menschengestalt; **in the ~ of** in Form von *od.* + *Gen.;* **in book ~:** in Buchform; als Buch; Ⓑ *no pl.* (*shape, visible aspect*) Form, *die;* Gestalt, *die;* (*Lit., Mus., Art*) Form, *die;* **~ without substance** Form ohne Inhalt; **take ~** (*lit. or fig.*) Gestalt annehmen *od.* gewinnen; **give ~ to sth.** einer Sache (*Dat.*) Gestalt geben *od.* verleihen; **the ~ and content of a novel** Form und Inhalt eines Romans; Ⓒ (*printed sheet*) Formular, *das;* Ⓓ (*Brit. Sch.*) Klasse, *die;* **first/second** *etc.* **~:** erste/zweite *usw.* Klasse (*an einer weiterführenden Schule*); ⇒ *also* **sixth form;** Ⓔ (*bench*) Bank, *die;* Ⓕ *no pl., no indef. art.* (*Sport: physical condition*) Form, *die;* **peak ~:** Bestform, *die;* **improvement in ~:** Formanstieg, *der;* **out of ~:** außer Form; nicht in Form; **in [good] ~** (*lit. or fig.*) [gut] in Form; **in top ~/at the top of his** *etc.* **~** (*lit. or fig.*) in Höchstform; **she was in great ~ at the party** (*fig.*) bei der Party war sie groß in Form; **on/off ~** (*lit. or fig.*) in/nicht in Form; **be slightly off ~:** nicht ganz in Form sein; Ⓖ (*Sport: previous record*) bisherige Leistungen; **on/judging by [past/present] ~** (*fig.*) nach der Papierform; **true to ~** (*fig.*) wie üblich *od.* zu erwarten; Ⓗ (*set procedure*) **in due/proper ~:** in angemessener/richtiger Form; **matter of ~:** Routineangelegenheit *od.* -sache, *die;* **as a matter of ~:** der Form halber; **common ~:** übliches Verfahren; **what's the ~?** was ist das übliche Verfahren?; **tell me the ~:** wie wird üblicherweise verfahren?; Ⓘ (*etiquette*) **for the sake of ~:** der Form halber; um der Form zu genügen; **good/bad ~:** gutes/schlechtes Benehmen; **it's bad *or* not good ~ to do this** so etwas gehört sich nicht; Ⓙ (*figure*) Gestalt, *die;* Ⓚ (*Ling.*) Form, *die;* **plural ~:** Pluralform, *die;* Plural, *der;* **feminine ~:** Femininum, *das;* **negative ~:** Verneinung, *die;* Negation, *die;* Ⓛ (*Philos.*) Form, *die;* Ⓜ *no pl.* (*coll.: criminal record*) Vorstrafe, *die;* **have ~:** vorbestraft sein; Ⓝ (*hare's lair*) Lager, *das;* Sasse, *die* (*Jägerspr.*); Ⓞ ⇒ **formwork**.
❷ *v.t.* Ⓐ (*make; also Ling.*) bilden; **be ~ed from sth.** aus etw. entstehen; Ⓑ (*shape, mould*) formen, gestalten (**into** zu); (*fig.*) formen ‹Charakter usw.›; Ⓒ (*construct in the mind*) sich (*Dat.*) bilden ‹Meinung, Urteil›; gewinnen ‹Eindruck›; fassen ‹Entschluss, Plan›; kommen zu ‹Schluss›; vornehmen ‹Schätzung›; (*acquire, develop*) entwickeln ‹Vorliebe, Gewohnheit, Wunsch›; schließen ‹Freundschaft›; Ⓓ (*constitute, compose, be, become*) bilden; **Schleswig once ~ed [a] part of Denmark** Schleswig war einmal ein Teil von Dänemark; **Joe ~ed one of our party** Joe war einer von uns; **young people ~ed the bulk of the protesters** das Gros der Protestierenden bestand aus jungen Leuten; Ⓔ (*establish, set up*) bilden ‹Regierung›; gründen ‹Bund, Verein, Firma, Partei, Gruppe›; **the men ~ed themselves into a committee** die Männer gründeten ein Komitee; Ⓕ (*take formation as*) bilden; **the dancers ~ed [themselves into] a circle** die Tänzer bildeten einen Kreis.
❸ *v.i.* Ⓐ (*come into being*) sich bilden; ‹Idee:› sich formen, Gestalt annehmen; Ⓑ (*fully develop*) sich ausformen; Ⓒ (*Mil.*) sich aufstellen (**in[to]** in + *Dat.*); sich formieren (**in[to]** zu); **~ [up]** sich formieren

**formal** /ˈfɔːml/ ❶ *adj.* Ⓐ formell; förmlich ‹Person, Art, Einladung, Begrüßung›; steif ‹Person, Begrüßung›; (*official*) offiziell; (*regular*) regelmäßig angelegt ‹Garten›; **wear ~ dress *or* clothes** Gesellschaftskleidung tragen; **~ call** Höflichkeitsbesuch, *der;* Ⓑ (*explicit*) formell; (*in recognized form*) traditionell; herkömmlich; **a ~ 'yes'/'no'** eine bindende Zusage/endgültige Absage; **~ education/knowledge** ordentliche Schulbildung/reales Wissen; **make a ~ apology** sich in aller Form entschuldigen; Ⓒ (*of the outward form*) formal; äußerlich; (*Philos., Logic*) formal.
❷ *n.* (*Amer.*) Ⓐ (*event*) gesellschaftliches Ereignis; Ⓑ (*dress*) Gesellschaftskleidung, *die*

**formaldehyde** /fɔːˈmældɪhaɪd/ *n.* (*Chem.*) Formaldehyd, *der*

**formalise** ⇒ **formalize**

**formalism** /ˈfɔːməlɪzm/ *n.* Formalismus, *der*

**formality** /fɔːˈmælɪtɪ/ *n.* Ⓐ (*requirement*) Formalität, *die;* **drop the *or* dispense with the formalities** sich nicht mit Formalitäten aufhalten; Ⓑ *no pl.* (*being formal, ceremony*) Förmlichkeit, *die*

**formalize** /ˈfɔːməlaɪz/ *v.t.* Ⓐ (*specify and systematize*) formalisieren; Ⓑ (*make official*) formell bekräftigen

**formally** /ˈfɔːməlɪ/ *adv.* Ⓐ (*ceremoniously*) formell; förmlich; feierlich ‹empfangen›; (*officially*) offiziell; (*regularly*) regelmäßig; Ⓑ (*explicitly*) ausdrücklich ‹formulieren, wünschen›; in aller Form ‹sich entschuldigen›; Ⓒ (*in form*) formal; äußerlich

**format** /ˈfɔːmæt/ ❶ *n.* Ⓐ (*of book*) (*general appearance, layout*) Aufmachung, *die;* (*shape and size*) Format, *das;* Ⓑ (*Telev., Radio: of programme*) Aufbau, *der;* Ⓒ (*Computing*) Format, *das.* ❷ *v.t.*, **-tt-** (*Computing*) formatieren

**formation** /fɔːˈmeɪʃn/ *n.* Ⓐ *no pl.* (*forming*) (*of substance, object*) Bildung, *die;* (*of character*) Formung, *die;* (*of handwriting*) Ausbildung, *die;* Ausformung, *die;* (*of plan*) Entstehung, *die;* (*Ling.*) Bildung, *die;* (*establishing*) Gründung, *die;* Ⓑ (*thing formed; also Ling.*) Bildung, *die;* Ⓒ (*Mil., Aeronaut., Dancing*) Formation, *die;* (*Footb.*) Aufstellung, *die;* **battle ~:** Gefechtsordnung, *die;* **in close ~:** in geschlossener Formation; **~ flying** Formationsflug, *der;* **~ dancing** Formationstanz, *der;* Ⓓ (*Geol.*) Formation, *die;* **rock ~s** Gesteinsformationen *Pl.;* Ⓔ (*structure*) Aufbau, *der;* Struktur, *die*

**formative** /ˈfɔːmətɪv/ *adj.* Ⓐ formend, prägend ‹Einfluss›; **the ~ years of life** die entscheidenden Lebensjahre; Ⓑ (*Ling.*) wortbildend; **~ element** Wortbildungselement, *das;* Formativ, *das*

**former** /ˈfɔːmə(r)/ *attrib. adj.* Ⓐ (*earlier*) früher; (*ex-*) ehemalig; Ex-; **in ~ times** früher; Ⓑ (*first-mentioned*) **the ~ …:** der/die/das erstere …; *pl.* die ersteren …; (*as noun*) *der/die/das* Erstere: *pl. die* Ersteren; **in the ~ case** im ersteren Fall

**-former** /fɔːmə(r)/ *n. in comb.* (*Brit. Sch.*) -klässler, *der*/-klässlerin, *die;* **third-~:** Drittklässler, *der*/-klässlerin, *die;* ⇒ *also* **sixth-former**

**formerly** /ˈfɔːməlɪ/ *adv.* früher; **Mrs Bloggs, ~ Miss Smith** Frau Bloggs, früher Fräulein Smith

**Formica** ® /fɔːˈmaɪkə/ *n.* ≈ Resopal, *das* Ⓦⓩ; **surfaced with ~:** kunststoffbeschichtet

**formidable** /ˈfɔːmɪdəbl, fɔːˈmɪdəbl/ *adj.* gewaltig; ungeheuer; bedrohlich, gefährlich ‹Herausforderung, Gegner›; (*arousing dread*) Furcht erregend; (*awe-inspiring*) formidabel; beeindruckend

**formless** /ˈfɔːmlɪs/ *adj.* formlos; (*having no physical existence*) immateriell; körperlos

**form:** **~ letter** *n.* vorgedruckter Brief; **~-master** *n.* (*Brit. Sch.*) Klassenlehrer, *der;* **~-mate** *n.* (*Brit. Sch.*) Klassenkamerad, *der*/-kameradin, *die;* Mitschüler, *der*/-schülerin, *die;* **~-mistress** *n.* (*Brit. Sch.*) Klassenlehrerin, *die;* **~-room** *n.* (*Brit. Sch.*) Klassenraum, *der*

**formula** /ˈfɔːmjʊlə/ *n., pl.* **~s** *or* (*esp. as tech. term*) **~e** /ˈfɔːmjʊliː/ Ⓐ (*Math., Chem., Phys.*) Formel, *die;* Ⓑ (*fixed form of words*) Formel, *die;* **trite ~s** nichtssagende Floskeln; **find a ~** (*to reconcile differences*) einen gemeinsamen Nenner finden; Ⓒ (*set form*) Schema, *das;* Ⓓ (*prescription, recipe*) Rezeptur, *die;* Formel, *die;* (*fig.*) Rezept, *das;* Formel, *die;* **no sure ~ exists** es gibt kein Patentrezept; Ⓔ (*Motor racing*) Formel, *die;* Ⓕ (*Amer.: infant's food*) Säuglingsmilchpräparat, *das*

**formulate** /ˈfɔːmjʊleɪt/ *v.t.* formulieren; (*devise*) entwickeln; **~ in words/writing** in Worte fassen/schriftlich formulieren

**formulation** /fɔːmjʊˈleɪʃn/ *n.* Formulierung, *die;* **the ~ of a question** eine Fragestellung

**'formwork** *n.* Schalung, *die*

**fornicate** /ˈfɔːnɪkeɪt/ *v.i.* Unzucht treiben; huren (*abwertend*)

**fornication** /fɔːnɪˈkeɪʃn/ *n.* Unzucht, *die;* Hurerei, *die* (*abwertend*)

**for-ˈprofit** *attrib. adj.* gewinnorientiert ‹Organisation›

**forsake** /fəˈseɪk/ *v.t.*, **forsook** /fəˈsʊk/, **~n** /fəˈseɪkn/ [A] (*give up*) entsagen (*geh.*) (+ *Dat.*); verzichten auf (+ *Akk.*); [B] (*desert*) verlassen

**forsaken** /fəˈseɪkn/ *adj.* verlassen

**forsook** ⇒ **forsake**

**forsooth** /fəˈsuːθ/ *adv.* (*arch.*/*iron.*/*derog.*) fürwahr (*geh.*)

**forswear** /fɔːˈsweə(r)/ *v.t.*, *forms as* **swear** abschwören (+ *Dat.*); (*deny*) ableugnen; abschwören (*veralt.*)

**forswore**, **forsworn** ⇒ **forswear**

**forsythia** /fɔːˈsaɪθɪə/ *n.* (*Bot.*) Forsythie, *die*

**fort** /fɔːt/ *n.* (*Mil.*) Fort, *das;* **hold the ~** (*fig.*) die Stellung halten (*fig.*)

**forte**[1] /ˈfɔːteɪ, fɔːt/ *n.* Stärke, *die;* starke Seite (*ugs.*)

**forte**[2] /ˈfɔːtɪ/ (*Mus.*) ❶ *adj.* laut; forte *nicht attr.;* forte gespielt/gesungen; forte. ❷ *adv.* forte. ❸ *n.* Forte, *das*

**fortepiano** /fɔːtɪpɪˈænəʊ/ *n.*, *pl.* **~s** (*Mus.*) Fortepiano, *das*

**forth** /fɔːθ/ *adv.* [A] **and so ~:** und so weiter; [B] **from this/that day** *etc.* **~:** von diesem/jenem Tag *usw.* an; von Stund an (*geh.*); [C] (*literary*) **stretch ~:** ausstrecken; **give ~:** von sich geben; **go ~:** hinausgehen; ‹Befehl:› ausgehen; (*emerge*) hervorgehen; **ride ~:** losreiten; **show ~:** zeigen

**Forth Bridge** /fɔːθ ˈbrɪdʒ/ *n.* **it's like [painting] the ~** (*fig.*) es ist eine Arbeit, mit der man nie zum Ende kommt

**forthcoming** /ˈfɔːθkʌmɪŋ, fɔːθˈkʌmɪŋ/ *adj.* [A] (*approaching*) bevorstehend; (*about to appear*) in Kürze zu erwartend; in Kürze anlaufend ‹Film›; in Kürze erscheinend ‹Ausgabe, Buch usw.›; **be ~:** bevorstehen; (*about to appear*) in Kürze zu erwarten sein/anlaufen/erscheinen; **~ events'** (*Journ.*) „Veranstaltungskalender"; [B] *pred.* (*made available*) **be ~** ‹Geld, Antwort:› kommen; ‹Ware:› geliefert werden; ‹Hilfe:› geleistet werden; **not be ~:** ausbleiben; [C] (*responsive*) mitteilsam, gesprächig ‹Person›; **she wasn't very ~ with hard facts** mit der Mitteilung von Tatsachen hielt sie sich ziemlich zurück

**forthright** /ˈfɔːθraɪt/ *adj.* direkt; offen ‹Blick›

**forthwith** /fɔːθˈwɪθ, fɔːθˈwɪð/ *adv.* unverzüglich

**fortieth** /ˈfɔːtɪɪθ/ ❶ *adj.* ▸ 1352 vierzigst...; ⇒ *also* **eighth** 1. ❷ *n.* (*fraction*) Vierzigstel, *das;* ⇒ *also* **eighth** 2

**fortification** /fɔːtɪfɪˈkeɪʃn/ *n.* [A] *no pl.* (*Mil.: fortifying*) Befestigung, *die;* [B] *usu. in pl.* (*Mil.: defensive works*) Befestigung, *die;* Festungsanlage, *die;* [C] (*of wine*) Aufspriten, *das*

**fortify** /ˈfɔːtɪfaɪ/ *v.t.* [A] (*Mil.*) befestigen; [B] (*strengthen, lit. or fig.*) stärken; [C] aufspriten ‹Wein›; anreichern ‹Nahrungsmittel›

**fortissimo** /fɔːˈtɪsɪməʊ/ (*Mus.*) ❶ *adj.* fortissimo *nicht attr.;* fortissimo gespielt/gesungen; Fortissimo-. ❷ *adv.* fortissimo. ❸ *n.*, *pl.* **~s** *or* **fortissimi** /fɔːˈtɪsɪmiː/ Fortissimo, *das*

**fortitude** /ˈfɔːtɪtjuːd/ *n.*, *no pl.* innere Stärke

**fortnight** /ˈfɔːtnaɪt/ *n.* vierzehn Tage; zwei Wochen; **a ~ [from] today** heute in vierzehn Tagen; **a ~ on Monday** *etc.* Montag *usw.* in vierzehn Tagen; **a ~ ago today** heute vor vierzehn Tagen; **in a ~['s time]** in vierzehn Tagen; **stay/go away for a ~:** vierzehn Tage [lang] bleiben/[für] vierzehn Tage verreisen; **take a ~'s leave** [sich (*Dat.*)] vierzehn Tage Urlaub nehmen; **once a ~, every ~:** alle vierzehn Tage *od.* zwei Wochen

**fortnightly** /ˈfɔːtnaɪtlɪ/ ❶ *adj.* vierzehntäglich; zweiwöchentlich; **~ magazine** ⇒ 3; **at ~ intervals** in Abständen von zwei Wochen; alle zwei Wochen. ❷ *adv.* alle vierzehn Tage; alle zwei Wochen. ❸ *n.* Halbmonatsschrift, *die*

**fortress** /ˈfɔːtrɪs/ *n.* (*lit. or fig.*) Festung, *die*

**fortuitous** /fɔːˈtjuːɪtəs/ *adj.*, **fortuitously** /fɔːˈtjuːɪtəslɪ/ *adv.* zufällig

**fortunate** /ˈfɔːtʃʊnət, ˈfɔːtʃənət/ *adj.* glücklich; **it is ~ for sb. [that ...]** es ist jmds. Glück[, dass ...]; **sb. is ~ to be alive** jmd. kann von Glück sagen *od.* reden, dass er noch lebt; **it was very ~ that ...:** es war ein Glück, dass ...; **how ~!, this is ~!** welch ein Glück!

**fortunately** /ˈfɔːtʃʊnətlɪ, ˈfɔːtʃənətlɪ/ *adv.* [A] (*luckily*) glücklicherweise; zum Glück; **~ for everybody/me** zum Glück [aller]/zu meinem Glück; [B] (*favourably, advantageously*) gut ‹dastehen, gestellt sein›

**fortune** /ˈfɔːtʃən, ˈfɔːtʃuːn/ *n.* [A] (*private wealth*) Vermögen, *das;* **family/private ~:** Familien-/Privatvermögen, *das;* **make one's ~:** sein Glück machen; **come into a ~:** ein Vermögen erben; **his brains are his/her face is her ~** (*fig. joc.*) sein Verstand ist sein/ihr Gesicht ist ihr Kapital; **a [small] ~:** ein [kleines] Vermögen; **make a ~:** ein Vermögen machen; [B] (*prosperous condition*) Glück, *das;* (*of country*) Wohl, *das;* **seek one's ~:** sein Glück suchen; [C] (*luck, destiny*) Schicksal, *das;* **bad/good ~:** Pech/Glück, *das;* **that was a piece of good ~:** das war Glück; **by sheer good ~ there was ...:** es war reines Glück, dass ... war; **he's had a change of ~:** das Blatt hat sich [für ihn] gewendet (*ugs.*); **thank one's good ~ that ...:** dem Glück dafür danken, dass ...; **F~** (*personified*) das Glück; Fortuna (*die*); **~ favours the brave** (*prov.*) das Glück ist auf der Seite der Mutigen; **~ smiles on sb.** das Glück lächelt *od.* lacht jmdm.; **tell sb.'s ~:** jmdm. wahrsagen *od.* sein Schicksal vorhersagen; **tell ~s** wahrsagen; ⇒ *also* **soldier** 1; [D] *in pl.* (*ups and downs, good or bad luck befalling sb., sth.*) Schicksal, *das;* **the ~s of war** das Kriegsglück (*geh.*); **the changing ~s of the combatants** der wechselnde Erfolg der Kämpfer

**fortune: ~ cookie** *n.* (*Amer. Cookery*) *Plätzchen mit einer eingebackenen Weissagung;* **~ hunter** *n.* (*derog.*) Mitgiftjäger, *der* (*abwertend*); **~ teller** *n.* Wahrsager, *der*/Wahrsagerin, *die;* **~ telling** *n.*, *no pl.* Wahrsagerei, *die*

**forty** /ˈfɔːtɪ/ ▸ 912, ▸ 1012, ▸ 1352 ❶ *adj.* vierzig; **have ~ˈwinks** ein Nickerchen (*fam.*) machen *od.* halten; **one-and-~** (*arch.*) ⇒ **~-one** 1; ⇒ *also* **eight** 1. ❷ *n.* Vierzig, *die;* **the roaring forties** (*Geog.*) *stürmisches Ozeangebiet zwischen dem 40. und 50. Breitengrad;* Roaring forties *Pl.;* **the Forties** (*Brit. Geog.*) *Seegebiet zwischen der Nordostküste Schottlands und der Südwestküste Norwegens;* **one-and-~** (*arch.*) ⇒ **~-one** 2; ⇒ *also* **eight** 2 A; **eighty** 2

**forty: ~-ˈfirst** *etc. adj.* ▸ 1352 einundvierzigst... *usw.;* ⇒ *also* **eighth** 1; **~-ˈfive** *n.* ▸ 1352 (*record*) Single[platte], *die;* **~fold** *adj.*, *adv.* vierzigfach; ⇒ *also* **eightfold**; **~-ˈone** *etc.* ❶ *adj.* einundvierzig *usw.;* ⇒ *also* **eight** 1; ❷ *n.* ▸ 1352 Einundvierzig *usw.*, *die;* ⇒ *also* **eight** 2 A

**forum** /ˈfɔːrəm/ *n.* (*also Roman Hist.*) Forum, *das;* **~ for discussion** [Diskussions]forum, *das;* **the ~ of public opinion** das Forum der Öffentlichkeit

**forward** /ˈfɔːwəd/ ❶ *adv.* [A] (*in direction faced, onwards in progress*) vorwärts; **bend ~:** sich vorbeugen; **take three steps ~:** drei Schritte vortreten; **~ march!** (*Mil.*) vorwärts marsch!; [B] (*towards end of room etc. faced*) nach vorn; vor‹laufen, -rücken, -schieben›; **work one's way ~:** sich nach vorn durcharbeiten; **the seat is too far ~:** der Sitz ist zu weit vorn; [C] (*closer*) heran; **rush ~ to help sb.** jmdm. zu Hilfe eilen; **he came ~ to greet me** er kam auf mich zu, um mich zu begrüßen; [D] (*ahead, in advance*) voraus‹schicken, -gehen›; [E] (*into better state*) **the country began to move ~:** mit dem Land ging es allmählich aufwärts; [F] (*into future*) voraus‹schauen, -denken›; **from that day/time ~:** von dem *od.* jenem Tag an/von da an; **from this day/time ~:** von heute/jetzt an; **date ~** (*Commerc.*) vordatieren; [G] (*into prominence*) in den Vordergrund; **come ~** (*present oneself*) ‹Zeuge, Helfer:› sich melden; [H] (*indicating motion*) (*Naut.*) nach vorn [zum Bug]; (*Aeronaut.*) nach vorn [in den Bug]; [I] (*Naut., Aeronaut.: indicating position*) (*inside*) vorn [im Bug]; (*outside*) vorn [am Bug]; [J] (*Cricket*) **play ~:** nach vorn treten, um zu schlagen. ⇒ *also* **backward** 1 B; **bring forward**; **carry forward**; **go forward**; **go forward with**; **look forward to**; **push forward**; **put forward**; **set forward**. ❷ *adj.* [A] (*directed ahead*) vorwärts gerichtet; nach vorn *nachgestellt;* **~ movement** Vorwärtsbewegung, *die;* **~ pass** (*Rugby*) Vorpass, *der;* **~ somersault** Salto vorwärts; [B] (*at or to the front*) Vorder-; vorder...; [C] (*lying in one's line of motion*) vor einem *nachgestellt;* **the ~ horizon** der vor einem liegende Horizont; [D] (*advanced*) frühreif ‹Kind, Pflanze, Getreide›; fortschrittlich ‹Vorstellung, Ansicht, Maßnahme›; [früh]zeitig, verfrüht ‹Frühling, Blüte›; **be well ~ with one's work/in one's plans** mit seiner Arbeit/seinen Plänen gut vorangekommen *od.* weit gediehen sein; [E] (*bold*) dreist; [F] (*Commerc.*) Termin‹geschäft, -verkauf›; Zukunfts‹planung›; [G] (*Naut.*) zum Vor[der]schiff gehörend. ❸ *n.* (*Sport*) Stürmer, *der*/Stürmerin, *die.* ❹ *v.t.* [A] (*send on*) nachschicken ‹Brief, Paket, Post› (**to** an + *Akk.*); (*dispatch*) abschicken ‹Waren› (**to** an + *Akk.*); **'please ~', 'to be ~ed'** „bitte nachsenden"; [B] (*pass on*) weiterreichen, weiterleiten ‹Vorschlag, Plan› (**to** an + *Akk.*); [C] (*promote*) voranbringen ‹Karriere, Vorbereitung›; **~ one's own interests** seine eigenen Interessen verfolgen; [D] (*accelerate*) beschleunigen ‹Wachstum›

**forwarding**/ˈfɔːwədɪŋ/**: ~ address** *n.* Nachsendeanschrift, *die;* **~ agent** *n.* Spediteur, *der;* **~ instructions** *n. pl.* Anweisung über die Nachsendung/(*for dispatch*) den Versand

**forward: ~ line** *n.* (*Sport*) Sturm, *der;* **~-looking** *adj.* vorausschauend

**forwardly** /ˈfɔːwədlɪ/ *adv.* dreist

**forwardness** /ˈfɔːwədnɪs/ *n.*, *no pl.* [A] (*boldness*) Dreistigkeit, *die;* [B] (*advanced state*) (*of child, crop*) Frühreife, *die;* (*of season*) verfrühter *od.* [früh]zeitiger Beginn

**forward ˈplanning** *n.* Vorausplanung, *die*

**forwards** /ˈfɔːwədz/ ⇒ **forward** 1 A, B, C

**forwent** ⇒ **forgo**

**fossil** /ˈfɒsɪl/ ❶ *n.* [A] Fossil, *das;* [B] (*fig. derog.*) (*antiquated person*) Fossil, *das;* (*antiquated thing*) verstaubtes Relikt; [C] (*Ling.*) **[linguistic] ~:** Sprachrelikt, *das.* ❷ *attrib. adj.* fossil (*Paläont.*); **~ fuel** fossiler Brennstoff

**fossilisation**, **fossilise** ⇒ **fossiliz-**

**fossilization** /fɒsɪlaɪˈzeɪʃn/ *n.* Fossilisation, *die* (*Paläont.*)

**fossilize** /ˈfɒsɪlaɪz/ ❶ *v.t.* fossilisieren lassen (*Paläont.*); versteinern lassen (*auch fig.*); **become ~d** ⇒ 2; **~d** fossil (*Paläont.*); (*fig.*) antiquiert; verstaubt (*abwertend*); **~d remains** Fossilien *Pl.* ❷ *v.i.* fossilisieren (*Paläont.*); versteinern (*auch fig.*)

**foster** /ˈfɒstə(r)/ ❶ *v.t.* [A] (*encourage*) fördern; pflegen ‹Freundschaft›; (*harbour*) hegen (*geh.*); [B] (*rear as ~-child*) in Pflege haben ‹Kind›; **the child was ~ed from the age of two** das Kind war seit seinem dritten Lebensjahr in Pflege *od.* bei Pflegeeltern. ❷ *adj.* **~-** Pflege‹bruder, -eltern, -sohn usw.›; **~ home** Pflegestelle, *die;* **put a child into ~ care** ein Kind in Pflege geben; **be in ~ care** in Pflege sein

**ˈfoster-child** *n.* Pflegekind, *das*

**ˈfoster-mother** *n.* [A] Pflegemutter, *die;* [B] (*Brit.: for chickens*) künstliche Glucke

**fought** ⇒ **fight** 1, 2

**foul** /faʊl/ ❶ *adj.* [A] (*offensive to the senses, loathsome*) abscheulich; übel ‹Geruch, Geschmack›; [B] (*polluted*) verschmutzt ‹Wasser, Luft›; (*putrid*) faulig ‹Wasser›; stickig ‹Luft›; [C] (*coll.: awful*) scheußlich (*ugs.*); mies (*ugs. abwertend*); [D] (*morally vile*) anstößig, unanständig ‹Sprache, Gerede›; lose ‹Maul, Mundwerk›; schmutzig ‹Fantasie, Gedanke, Gewerbe›; niederträchtig ‹Verleumdung, Tat›; feige, abscheulich ‹Mord›; gemein, schäbig ‹Behandlung›; böse, (*geh.*) übel ‹Streich›; **~ deed** Schandtat, *die;* [E] (*unfair*) unerlaubt, unredlich ‹Mittel›; (*Sport*) regelwidrig, verboten ‹Schlag, Hieb›; **~**

**play** (*Sport*) Foulspiel, *das;* (*fig.: unfair dealing*) Betrug, *der;* **the police do not suspect ~ play** die Polizei vermutet kein Verbrechen; **there was a lot of ~ play** (*Sport*) es ging recht unfair zu; ⇒ *also* **fair**[2] 1 A; Ⓕ **fall** *or* **run ~ of** (*Naut.*) zusammenstoßen *od.* kollidieren mit; (*fig.*) kollidieren *od.* in Konflikt geraten mit ‹Vorschrift, Gesetz, Polizei›; aneinander geraten mit ‹Person›; Ⓖ (*Naut.: entangled*) unklar; Ⓗ (*clogged up*) verstopft. ❷ *n.* (*Sport*) Foul, *das;* Regelverstoß, *der;* **commit a ~:** foulen; ein Foul *od.* einen Regelverstoß begehen. ❸ *v.t.* Ⓐ (*make ~*) beschmutzen (*auch fig.*); verunreinigen (*abwertend*); verpesten ‹Luft›; ⇒ *also* **nest** 1 A; Ⓑ (*be entangled with*) sich verfangen in (+ *Dat.*); Ⓒ ⇒ **foul up** b; Ⓓ (*Sport*) foulen

**~ 'up** *v.t.* Ⓐ (*coll.: spoil*) vermasseln (*salopp*); verderben ‹Atmosphäre, Beziehung›; Ⓑ (*block*) blockieren. ⇒ *also* **foul-up**

**foully** /'faʊllɪ/ *adv.* (*wickedly*) skrupellos ‹ermorden, verurteilen›; schlecht ‹behandeln›; böswillig ‹verleumden›

**foul-mouthed** /'faʊlmaʊðd/ *adj.* unanständig; unflätig

**foulness** /'faʊlnɪs/ *n., no pl.* Ⓐ Abscheulichkeit, *die;* Ⓑ (*state of being polluted*) Verschmutzung, *die;* (*putridness*) Fauligkeit, *die*

**foul: ~-smelling** *adj.* übel riechend; **~-up** *n.* Durcheinander, *das;* Schlamassel, *der* (*ugs.*)

**found**[1] /faʊnd/ *v.t.* Ⓐ (*establish*) gründen; stiften ‹Krankenhaus, Kloster›; begründen ‹Wissenschaft, Religion, Glauben, Kirche›; **F~ing Fathers** *Mitglieder der verfassunggebenden Versammlung der USA von 1787;* Gründerväter *Pl.;* Ⓑ (*fig.: base*) begründen; **~ sth. [up]on sth.** etw. auf etw. (*Akk.*) gründen; **be ~ed [up]on sth.** [sich] auf etw. (*Akk.*) gründen; auf etw. (*Dat.*) beruhen; ⇒ *also* **ill-founded**; **well-founded**

**found**[2] ⇒ **find** 1, 2

**found**[3] *v.t.* (*Metallurgy*) gießen; (*Glassmaking*) gießen; (*melt*) schmelzen

**foundation** /faʊn'deɪʃn/ *n.* Ⓐ (*establishing*) Gründung, *die;* (*of hospital, monastery*) Stiftung, *die;* (*of school of painting, of religion*) Begründung, *die;* Ⓑ (*institution*) Stiftung, *die;* **be on the ~** (*Brit.*) ein Stipendium erhalten; Ⓒ *usu. in pl.* **~[s]** (*underlying part, lit. or fig.*) (*of building*) Fundament, *das;* (*of road*) Unterbau, *der;* **lay the ~s** das Fundament legen; (*for road*) den Unterbau legen; **be without** *or* **have no ~** (*fig.*) unbegründet sein; der Grundlage entbehren; **lay the ~ of/for sth.** (*fig.*) das Fundament *od.* die Grundlage zu etw. legen; **shake sth. to its ~s** (*fig.*) etw. in seinen Grundfesten erschüttern; Ⓓ (*cosmetic*) Grundierung, *die;* Ⓔ ⇒ **foundation garment**

**foundation: ~ course** *n.* (*Univ. etc.*) Grundkurs, *der;* **~ cream** *n.* Grundierungscreme, *die;* **~ garment** *n.* Mieder, *das;* **~ stone** *n.* (*lit. or fig.*) Grundstein, *der*

**founder**[1] /'faʊndə(r)/ *n.* Gründer, *der*/Gründerin, *die;* (*of hospital, or with an endowment*) Stifter, *der*/Stifterin, *die;* (*of sect, science, school, religion*) Begründer, *der*/Begründerin, *die;* **~ member** Gründungsmitglied, *das*

**founder**[2] *v.i.* Ⓐ ‹Schiff:› sinken, untergehen; ‹Pferd:› straucheln, stürzen; ‹Erdboden, Gebäude:› einstürzen; Ⓑ (*fig.: fail*) sich zerschlagen

**foundling** /'faʊndlɪŋ/ *n.* Findelkind, *das;* Findling, *der*

**foundry** /'faʊndrɪ/ *n.* (*Metallurgy*) Gießerei, *die;* (*Glass-making*) Glashütte, *die*

**fount**[1] /faʊnt, fɒnt/ *n.* (*Printing*) Schrift, *die*

**fount**[2] /faʊnt/ *n.* (*poet./rhet.: fountain*) Born, *der* (*dichter., auch fig. geh.*)

**fountain** /'faʊntɪn/ *n.* Ⓐ ⇒ **drinking fountain**; Ⓑ (*jet[s] of water*) Fontäne, *die;* (*structure*) Springbrunnen, *der;* Ⓒ (*fig.: source*) Quelle, *die;* **~ of youth** Jungbrunnen, *der.* ⇒ *also* **soda-fountain**

**fountain: ~head** *n.* Quelle, *die;* **~ pen** *n.* Füllfederhalter, *der;* Füller, *der* (*ugs.*)

**four** /fɔ:(r)/ **▶ 912**, **▶ 1012**, **▶ 1352** ❶ *adj.* vier; ⇒ *also* **eight** 1. ❷ *n.* Ⓐ (*number, symbol*) Vier, *die;* Ⓑ (*set of ~ people*) Vierergruppe, *die;* (*Rowing*) Vierer, *der;* **the ~:** die Vier; **make up a ~ at tennis/bridge** im Doppel Tennis spielen/der vierte Mitspieler beim Bridge sein; Ⓒ **on all ~s** auf allen vieren (*ugs.*); **be/crawl/move on all ~s** auf allen vieren kriechen (*ugs.*); **get down on all ~s** sich auf alle viere begeben (*ugs.*). ⇒ *also* **eight** 2 A, C, D

**four: ~-ball** *n.* (*Golf*) Vierball, *der;* **~-door** *attrib. adj.* viertürig ‹Auto›; **~fold** /'fɔ:fəʊld/ *adj., adv.* vierfach; ⇒ *also* **eightfold**; **~-footed** /'fɔ:fʊtɪd/ *adj.* vierfüßig; **~-handed** /'fɔ:hændɪd/ *adj.* Ⓐ ‹Spiel› mit vier Mitspielern; Ⓑ (*Mus.*) zu vier Händen *nachgestellt;* vierhändig; **~-in-hand** *adj.* vierspännig; **~-in-hand tie** (*Amer.*) Schlips, *der;* Krawatte, *die;* **~-leaf clover**, **~-leaved clover** *n.* vierblättriges Kleeblatt; **~-legged** /'fɔ:legɪd, 'fɔ:legd/ *adj.* vierbeinig; **~-letter 'word** *n.* vulgärer Ausdruck; (*expressing anger*) ≈ Kraftausdruck, *der;* **~pence** /'fɔ:pəns/ *n.* (*Brit.*) vier Pence; **~penny** /'fɔ:pənɪ/ *adj.* (*Brit.*) (*costing 4p or 4d*) Vier-Pence-; **~-poster** *n.* Himmelbett, *das;* **~score** *adj.* (*arch.*) achtzig; **~some** /'fɔ:səm/ *n.* Ⓐ Quartett, *das;* **go in** *or* **as a ~some** zu viert gehen; Ⓑ (*Golf*) Vierer, *der;* **~-square** *adj.* Ⓐ (*square*) quadratisch; Ⓑ (*fig.: resolute*) unerschütterlich; tatkräftig ‹Unterstützung›; (*forthright*) direkt ‹Inangriffnahme›; unverblümt ‹Schilderung›; **~-stroke** *adj.* (*Mech. Engin.*) Viertakt‹motor, -verfahren›

**fourteen** /fɔ:'ti:n/ **▶ 912**, **▶ 1012**, **▶ 1352** ❶ *adj.* vierzehn; ⇒ *also* **eight** 1. ❷ *n.* Vierzehn, *die;* ⇒ *also* **eight** 2 A, D; **eighteen** 2

**fourteenth** /fɔ:'ti:nθ/ **▶ 1055** ❶ *adj.* **▶ 1352** vierzehnt...; ⇒ *also* **eighth** 1. ❷ *n.* (*fraction*) Vierzehntel, *das;* ⇒ *also* **eighth** 2

**fourth** /fɔ:θ/ ❶ *adj.* Ⓐ **▶ 1352** viert...; **the ~ finger** der kleine Finger; ⇒ *also* **eighth** 1; Ⓑ **~ dimension** vierte Dimension; ⇒ *also* **estate** F. ❷ *n.* Ⓐ (*in sequence, rank*) Vierte, *der/die/das;* (*fraction*) Viertel, *das;* Ⓑ (*~ form*) vierte [Schul]klasse; Vierte, *die* (*Schuljargon*); Ⓒ (*Motor Veh.*) vierter Gang; **in ~:** im vierten [Gang]; **change up [in]to ~:** in den vierten Gang schalten; Ⓓ (*Mus.*) Quarte, *die;* Ⓔ (*person*) vierter Teilnehmer/vierte Teilnehmerin; (*in a game*) vierter Mitspieler/vierte Mitspielerin; **make a ~:** als Vierter/Vierte mitmachen; Ⓕ **▶ 1055** (*day*) **the ~ of May** der vierte Mai; **the ~ [of the month]** der Vierte [des Monats]; **F~ of July** (*Amer.*) *Unabhängigkeitstag der USA;* **F~ of June** (*Brit.*) *jährliche Feier in Eton.* ⇒ *also* **eighth** 2

**fourth: ~ form** ⇒ **form** 1 D; **~ 'gear** *n., no pl.* (*Motor Veh.*) vierter Gang; ⇒ *also* **gear** 1 D

**fourthly** /'fɔ:θlɪ/ *adv.* viertens

**four-wheel 'drive** *n.* (*Motor Veh.*) Vier- *od.* Allradantrieb, *der*

**fowl** /faʊl/ ❶ *n. pl.* **~s** *or same* Ⓐ Haushuhn, *das;* (*collectively*) Geflügel, *das;* Ⓑ (*Gastr.*) Huhn, *das;* **boiling ~:** Suppenhuhn, *das;* Ⓒ (*literary: bird*) Vogel, *der;* ⇒ *also* **waterfowl**; **wildfowl**. ❷ *v.i.* **go ~ing** auf die Vogeljagd gehen

**fowler** /'faʊlə(r)/ *n.* Vogeljäger, *der*

**fox** /fɒks/ ❶ *n., pl.* **~es** *or* (*esp. Hunting*) *same;* Ⓐ Fuchs, *der* (*auch fig. ugs.*); **as cunning as a ~:** schlau wie ein Fuchs; Ⓑ (*fur*) Fuchs[pelz], *der.* ❷ *v.t.* verwirren; **that's got you ~ed** *or* **that's ~ed you, hasn't it?** jetzt bist du verblüfft, was?

**fox: ~ cub** *n.* Fuchswelpe, *der;* **~ fur** *n.* Fuchspelz, *der;* **~glove** *n.* (*Bot.*) Fingerhut, *der;* **~hole** *n.* Ⓐ Fuchsbau, *der;* Ⓑ (*Mil.*) Schützenloch, *das;* (*fig.*) Versteck, *das;* **~hound** *n.* Foxhound, *der;* **~ hunt** ❶ *n.* Fuchsjagd, *die;* ❷ *v.i.* **go ~-hunting** auf die Fuchsjagd gehen; **~-hunter** *n.* Fuchsjäger, *der;* **~-hunting** *n.* Fuchsjagd, *die;* **~tail** *n.* Ⓐ Fuchsschwanz, *der;* Ⓑ (*Bot.*) (*Alopecurus*) Fuchsschwanz, *der;* (*Hordeum*) Gerste, *die;* (*Setaria*) Borstenhirse, *die;* **~ 'terrier** *n.* Foxterrier, *der;* **~trot** ❶ *n.* Foxtrott, *der;* ❷ *v.i.* Foxtrott tanzen

**foxy** /'fɒksɪ/ *adj.* Ⓐ [fuchs]schlau ‹Augen, Manöver›; Ⓑ (*Amer. coll.: attractive*) dufte (*salopp*)

**'foxy-looking** *adj.* fuchsgesichtig

**foyer** /'fɔɪeɪ, 'fwɑjeɪ/ *n.* Foyer, *das*

**fr.** *abbr.* **franc[s]** fr

**Fr.** *abbr.* Ⓐ (*Eccl.*) **Father** P.; Ⓑ **French** frz.; fr.; franz.

**fracas** /'frækɑ:/ *n., pl. same* /'frækɑ:z/ [lautstarke] Auseinandersetzung; Krawall, *der*

**fractal** /'fræktl/ *adj.* (*Math.*) fraktal

**fraction** /'frækʃn/ *n.* **▶ 1352** Ⓐ (*Math.*) Bruch, *der;* **do ~s** bruchrechnen; ⇒ *also* **decimal fraction**; **improper** D; **proper fraction**; **vulgar** C; Ⓑ (*small part*) Bruchteil, *der;* (*tiny bit*) Kleinigkeit, *die* (*ugs.*); Stückchen, *das;* Idee, *die;* **the car missed the pedestrian by a ~ of an inch** das Auto hätte den Fußgänger um Haaresbreite überfahren; Ⓒ (*Chem.*) Fraktion, *die*

**fractional** /'frækʃənl/ *adj.* Ⓐ (*Math.*) Bruch‹zahl, -rechnen›; (*fig.: very slight*) geringfügig; **~ part** Bruchteil, *der;* Ⓑ (*Chem.*) **~ crystallization/distillation** fraktionierte Kristallisation/Destillation

**fractionally** /'frækʃənəlɪ/ *adv.* (*fig.: very slightly*) geringfügig

**fractious** /'frækʃəs/ *adj.* (*unruly*) aufsässig; ungebärdig (*geh.*); störrisch ‹Pferd›; (*peevish*) quengelig ‹Kind›

**fracture** /'fræktʃə(r)/ **▶ 1232** ❶ *n.* (*also Med., Min.*) Bruch, *der;* **nose ~:** Nasenbeinbruch, *der.* ❷ *v.t.* (*also Med.*) brechen; (*break up*) aufspalten; **~ one's jaw** *etc.* sich (*Dat.*) den Kiefer *usw.* brechen; **~ one's skull** sich (*Dat.*) einen Schädelbruch zuziehen; **have a ~d jaw** *etc.* sich (*Dat.*) den Kiefer *usw.* gebrochen haben. ❸ *v.i.* (*Med.*) brechen

**fragile** /'frædʒaɪl/ *adj.* Ⓐ zerbrechlich; zart ‹Teint, Hand›; '**~ — handle with care**' „Vorsicht, zerbrechlich!"; **feel ~** (*coll.: ill, esp. because of hangover*) sich ganz zerschlagen fühlen; Ⓑ (*fig.*) fadenscheinig ‹Entschuldigung, Grund›; heikel ‹Situation›; unsicher ‹Frieden›; zart ‹Glück, Gesundheit, Konstitution›; gebrechlich ‹alte Frau›; schwach ‹Selbstvertrauen›

**fragility** /frə'dʒɪlɪtɪ/ *n., no pl.* Zerbrechlichkeit, *die;* (*of health, constitution, frame, beauty*) Zartheit, *die;* (*fig.: of peace, situation*) Unsicherheit, *die*

**fragment** ❶ /'frægmənt/ *n.* Bruchstück, *das;* (*of document, conversation*) Fetzen, *der;* (*of china*) Scherbe, *die;* (*of rock*) Brocken, *der;* (*Lit., Mus.*) Fragment, *das;* Bruchstück, *das;* **it was in ~s** es war zerbrochen. ❷ /fræg'ment/ *v.t. & i.* zersplittern

**fragmentary** /'frægməntərɪ/ *adj.* bruchstückhaft; fragmentarisch

**fragmentation** /frægmən'teɪʃn/ *n.* Zersplitterung, *die*

**fragmen'tation bomb** *n.* (*Mil.*) Splitterbombe, *die*

**fragmented** /fræg'mentɪd/ *adj.* bruchstückhaft

**fragrance** /'freɪgrəns/ *n.* Duft, *der*

**fragrant** /'freɪgrənt/ *adj.* duftend; (*fig.*) angenehm ‹Erinnerung, Gefühl›; **~ odour** *or* **smell** *or* **aroma** Wohlgeruch, *der;* **be ~ with sth.** nach etw. duften

**frail** /freɪl/ *adj.* zerbrechlich; zart ‹Gesundheit›; gebrechlich ‹Greis, Greisin›; (*lacking force*) schwach ‹Stimme›; (*morally weak*) schwach, labil ‹Person, Natur, Charakter›; (*transient*) vergänglich ‹Leben, Glück›; (*slender*) schwach ‹Hoffnung›; gering ‹Verständnis›

**frailty** /'freɪltɪ/ *n.* Ⓐ *no pl.* Zerbrechlichkeit, *die;* (*of health*) Zartheit, *die;* (*moral weakness*) Schwachheit, *die;* (*transience*) Vergänglichkeit, *die;* Ⓑ *esp. in pl.* (*fault*) Schwäche, *die*

**frame** /freɪm/ ❶ *n.* Ⓐ (*of vehicle, bicycle*) Rahmen, *der;* (*of easel, rucksack, bed, umbrella*) Gestell, *das;* (*of ship, aircraft*) Gerüst, *das;* (*of building*) Tragwerk, *das* (*Bauw.*); **timber ~:** Fachwerk, *das;* Gebälk, *das;* ⇒ *also* **climbing frame**; Ⓑ (*border*) Rahmen, *der;* **[spectacle] ~s** [Brillen]gestell, *das;* Ⓒ (*fig.: established order*) Struktur, *die;* **~ of government/society** Regierungs-/Gesellschaftsform, *die;* **~ of reference** (*Phys., Sociol.*) Bezugssystem, *das;* Ⓓ (*of person, animal*) Körper, *der;* **a man of gigantic ~:**

ein Mann von hünenhafter Gestalt; Ⓔ (*Photog., Cinemat.*) [Einzel]bild, *das;* (*Telev.*) [einzelnes Fernseh]bild; Ⓕ (*of comic strip*) [Einzel]bild, *das;* Ⓖ (*Hort.*) Frühbeet, *das;* Ⓗ (*Snooker*) (*triangle*) [dreieckiger] Rahmen; (*round of play*) Spiel, *das;* [Spiel]runde, *die.* ⇨ *also* **mind** 1 E.

❷ *v.t.* Ⓐ rahmen ‹Bild, Spiegel›; umrahmen ‹Text usw. mit Verzierungen›; **a face ~d in curls** ein von Locken umrahmtes Gesicht; Ⓑ (*compose*) formulieren ‹Frage, Antwort, Satz›; aufbauen ‹Rede, Aufsatz›; (*devise*) entwerfen ‹Gesetz, Politik, Plan›; ausarbeiten ‹Plan, Methode, Denksystem›; aufstellen ‹Regel, Theorie›; (*shape*) konstruieren; schaffen ‹Bau[werk]›; gestalten ‹[Um]welt, Leben›; **~ one's words** sich ausdrücken; **her lips ~d a curse** ihre Lippen formten einen Fluch; Ⓒ (*coll.: incriminate unjustly*) **~ sb.** jmdm. etwas anhängen (*ugs.*)

**~ 'up** *v.t.* (*Amer. coll.*) manipulieren; türken (*ugs.*); ⇨ *also* **frame-up**

**'frame house** *n.* Haus mit Holzgerüst

**framer** /ˈfreɪmə(r)/ *n.* Rahmenschreiner, *der;* **picture-~:** Bildereinrahmer, *der*

**frame: ~-up** *n.* (*coll.*) abgekartetes Spiel (*ugs.*); **~work** *n.* (*of ship etc.*) Gerüst, *das;* (*of building*) Fachwerk, *das;* Gebälk, *das;* (*fig.: of project*) Gerüst, *das;* (*of novel*) Rahmen, *der;* (*of essay, lecture, etc.*) Aufbau, *der;* Gliederung, *die;* (*of society, government, system*) [Grund]struktur, *die;* Grundlagen *Pl.;* **[with]in the ~work of** (*as part of*) im Rahmen (+ *Gen.*); (*in relation to*) im Zusammenhang mit; **outside the ~work of** (*not as part of*) außerhalb (+ *Gen.*)

**framing** /ˈfreɪmɪŋ/ *n.* (*Building*) Fachwerk, *das*

**franc** /fræŋk/ *n.* ▶ **1328** (*Swiss*) Franken, *der;* (*French, Belgian, Luxemburg*) Franc, *der*

**France** /frɑːns/ *pr. n.* Frankreich (*das*)

**franchise** /ˈfræntʃaɪz/ ❶ *n.* Ⓐ Stimmrecht, *das;* (*esp. for Parliament*) Wahlrecht, *das;* Ⓑ (*Commerc.*) Lizenz, *die.* ❷ *v.t.* (*Commerc.*) [die] Lizenz erteilen (+ *Dat.*)

**Francis** /ˈfrɑːnsɪs/ *pr. n.* (*Hist., as name of ruler etc.*) Franz (*der*); **St ~:** der hl. Franziskus

**Franciscan** /frænˈsɪskn/ ❶ *n.* Franziskaner, *der*/Franziskanerin, *die.* ❷ *adj.* franziskanisch/Franziskaner‹mönch, -kloster›

**Franco-** /ˈfræŋkəʊ/ *in comb.* französisch-; franko‹kanadisch›; Franko‹kanadier›; **~German** deutsch-französisch; **the ~Prussian War** der Deutsch-Französische Krieg

**Franconia** /fræŋˈkəʊnɪə/ *pr. n.* Franken, *das*

**Franconian** /fræŋˈkəʊnɪən/ ❶ *adj.* fränkisch. ❷ *n.* (*person*) Franke, *der*/Fränkin, *die;* (*dialect*) Fränkisch, *das*

**francophone** /ˈfræŋkəfəʊn/ ❶ *adj.* frankophon. ❷ *n.* Frankophone, *der/die*

**franglais** /ˈfrɑ̃gleɪ/ *n.* von englischen Ausdrücken durchsetztes Französisch; Franglais, *das*

**frank¹** *adj.* Ⓐ (*candid*) offen ‹Bekenntnis, Aussprache, Blick, Gesicht, Person›; freimütig ‹Geständnis, Äußerung›; (*undisguised*) offen ‹Abneigung, Widerwille›; unverhohlen ‹Bewunderung, Neugier, Verlangen›; (*uninhibited*) unbefangen; **give me your ~ opinion** sag mir offen deine Meinung; **be ~ with sb.** zu jmdm. offen sein; jmdm. offen seine Meinung sagen; **to be [quite] ~** (*as sentence-modifier*) offen gesagt; **~ and open** offen und ehrlich ‹Gesicht›; frei und ungezwungen ‹Benehmen›; Ⓑ (*Med.*) eindeutig; manifest (*fachspr.*)

**frank²** ❶ *v.t.* (*Post*) Ⓐ (*in lieu of postage stamp*) freistempeln; Ⓑ (*put postage stamp on*) frankieren. ❷ *n. Vermerk über Gebührenfreiheit*

**frank³** *n.* (*Amer. coll.: frankfurter*) Frankfurter [Würstchen]

**Frank** /fræŋk/ *n.* (*Hist.*) Franke, *der*/Fränkin, *die*

**Frankenstein['s 'monster]** /ˈfræŋknstaɪn/ *n. seinen Schöpfer vernichtendes Ungeheuer;* ≈ Monster, *das*

**frankfurter** /ˈfræŋkfɜːtə(r)/ (*Amer.:* **frankfurt** /ˈfræŋkfɜːt/) *n.* Frankfurter [Würstchen]

**frankincense** /ˈfræŋkɪnsens/ *n.* Weihrauch, *der;* (*turpentine*) Terpentin, *das*

**franking machine** /ˈfræŋkɪŋməʃiːn/ *n.* (*Brit. Post*) Frankiermaschine, *die;* Freistempler, *der*

**Frankish** /ˈfræŋkɪʃ/ *adj.* (*Hist.*) fränkisch

**frankly** /ˈfræŋklɪ/ *adv.* (*candidly*) offen; frank und frei; (*honestly*) offen *od.* ehrlich gesagt; (*openly, undisguisedly*) unverhohlen ‹kritisch, materialistisch usw.›; (*uninhibitedly*) unbefangen

**frankness** /ˈfræŋknɪs/ *n., no pl.* Offenheit, *die;* Freimütigkeit, *die;* (*uninhibitedness*) Unbefangenheit, *die*

**frantic** /ˈfræntɪk/ *adj.* Ⓐ (*nearly mad*) **be ~ with fear/rage** *etc.* außer sich (*Dat.*) sein vor Angst/Wut *usw.;* **drive sb. ~:** jmdn. in den Wahnsinn treiben *od.* wahnsinnig machen; **she was getting ~:** sie war am Durchdrehen (*ugs.*); sie geriet außer sich; Ⓑ (*very anxious, noisy, uncontrolled*) hektisch ‹Aktivität, Suche, Getriebe›; heftig ‹Protest›; tosend, stürmisch, (*geh.*) frenetisch ‹Beifall›; Ⓒ (*showing that sb. is ~*) erregt ‹Schrei, Wort, Gebärde›

**frantically** /ˈfræntɪkəlɪ/, **franticly** /ˈfræntɪklɪ/ *adv.* verzweifelt ‹schreien, suchen, protestieren›; stürmisch, (*geh.*) frenetisch ‹applaudieren›; wie angestochen, wie wild (*ugs.*) ‹herumrennen›; **the shops are ~ busy** in den Läden herrscht hektische Betriebsamkeit

**frappé** /ˈfræpeɪ/ *adj.* geeist

**fraternal** /frəˈtɜːnl/ *adj.* brüderlich; **~ twins** zweieiige Zwillinge

**fraternisation, fraternise** ⇨ **fraterniz-**

**fraternity** /frəˈtɜːnɪtɪ/ *n.* Ⓐ (*set of men with common interest*) Vereinigung, *die;* (*guild*) Gilde, *die* (*hist.*); Zunft, *die* (*hist.*); **the teaching/medical/legal ~:** die Lehrer-/Ärzte-/Juristenzunft; die Zunft der Lehrer/Ärzte/Juristen; Ⓑ (*Relig.*) Bruderschaft, *die;* Fraternität, *die* (*kath. Kirche*); Ⓒ (*Amer. Univ.: society*) [studentische] Verbindung; Ⓓ *no pl.* (*brotherliness*) Brüderlichkeit, *die*

**fraternization** /frætənaɪˈzeɪʃn/ *n.* Verbrüderung, *die;* **~ [with sb.]** (*Mil.*) Fraternisierung [mit jmdm.]

**fraternize** /ˈfrætənaɪz/ *v.i.* **~ [with sb.]** sich verbrüdern [mit jmdm.]; (*Mil.*) fraternisieren [mit jmdm.]

**Frau** /fraʊ/ *n.* Deutsche, *die;* deutsche Frau

**fraud** /frɔːd/ *n.* Ⓐ *no pl.* (*cheating, deceit*) Betrug, *der;* Täuschung, *die;* (*Law*) [arglistige] Täuschung; Ⓑ (*trick, false thing*) Schwindel, *der;* (*Law*) Betrug, *der;* **~s** Betrügereien *Pl.;* **pious ~:** frommer Betrug; Ⓒ (*person*) (*impostor, sham*) Betrüger, *der*/Betrügerin, *die;* Schwindler, *der*/Schwindlerin, *die;* (*hypocrite*) Heuchler, *der*/Heuchlerin, *die;* **you [old] ~!** (*coll.*) du alter Schlawiner! (*ugs.*)

**fraudulent** /ˈfrɔːdjʊlənt/ *adj.* betrügerisch; **with ~ intent** in betrügerischer Absicht; **~ name** falscher Name

**fraudulently** /ˈfrɔːdjʊləntlɪ/ *adv.* in betrügerischer Weise

**fraught** /frɔːt/ *adj.* Ⓐ **be ~ with danger** voller Gefahren *od.* sehr gefahrvoll sein; **~ with tension** spannungsgeladen; **~ with meaning/memories** bedeutungsschwer/mit Erinnerungen befrachtet; **~ with obstacles/difficulties** voller Hindernisse/Schwierigkeiten; **silence ~ with menace** bedrohliche Stille; Ⓑ (*coll.: distressingly tense*) stressig (*ugs.*) ‹Atmosphäre, Situation, Diskussion›; gestresst (*ugs.*) ‹Person›

**Fräulein** /ˈfrɔɪlaɪn/ *n.* [junge] Deutsche; deutsche [junge] Frau

**fray¹** /freɪ/ *n.* (*fight*) [Kampf]getümmel, *das;* (*noisy quarrel*) Streit, *der;* **in the thick of the ~:** mitten im dicksten Getümmel; **plunge into the ~:** sich ins [Kampf]getümmel stürzen; **in the heat of the ~** (*fig.*) in der Hitze des Gefechts (*fig.*); **be eager/ready for the ~** (*lit. or fig.*) kampflustig/kampfbereit sein; **enter** *or* **join the ~** (*lit. or fig.*) sich in den Kampf *od.* ins Getümmel stürzen

**fray²** ❶ *v.i.* [sich] durchscheuern; ‹Hosenbein, Teppich, Seilende:› ausfransen; **our nerves/tempers began to ~** (*fig.*) wir verloren langsam die Nerven/unsere Gemüter erhitzten sich. ❷ *v.t.* durchscheuern; ausfransen ‹Hosenbein, Teppich, Seilende›; (*fig.*) belasten; strapazieren

**frayed** /freɪd/ *adj.* durchgescheuert; ausgefranst ‹Hosenbein, Teppich, Seilende›; (*fig.*) strapaziert ‹Nerven, Geduld›; erregt, erhitzt ‹Gemüt›; **his politeness was by now somewhat ~:** seine Höflichkeit war inzwischen etwas verkrampft

**frazzle** /ˈfræzl/ *n.* (*coll.*) **to a ~:** völlig; total (*ugs.*); **my nerves were worn to a ~:** ich war mit den Nerven völlig am Ende

**freak** /friːk/ ❶ *n.* Ⓐ (*monstrosity*) (*person, animal*) Missgeburt, *die;* (*plant*) missgebildete Pflanze; Mutation, *die;* **~ of nature** Laune der Natur; Ⓑ (*freakish thing or occurrence*) Laune, *die;* (*attrib.*) ungewöhnlich ‹Wetter, Ereignis›; völlig überraschend ‹Sieg, Ergebnis›; Ⓒ (*coll.: fanatic*) Freak, *der;* **health ~:** Gesundheitsfanatiker, *der;* **health food ~:** Reformköstler, *der* (*ugs.*); Körnerfresser, *der* (*salopp*); Ⓓ (*coll.: eccentric person*) Freak, *der;* Ausgeflippte, *der/die* (*salopp*); (*derog.*) komischer Vogel (*ugs.*); Ⓔ (*caprice*) Laune, *die.*

❷ *v.i.* **~ [out]** (*coll.*) (*with fury*) die Nerven verlieren; durchdrehen (*ugs.*); (*with ecstasy*) vor Freude [ganz] außer sich (*Dat.*) sein

**freakish** /ˈfriːkɪʃ/ *adj.* (*capricious*) launisch; verrückt (*ugs.*); (*abnormal*) absonderlich; **~ trick of fortune** Laune des Schicksals

**freaky** /ˈfriːkɪ/ *adj.* Ⓐ ⇨ **freakish**; Ⓑ (*coll.: bizarre*) irre (*salopp*); verrückt (*ugs.*)

**freckle** /ˈfrekl/ *n.* Sommersprosse, *die*

**freckled** /ˈfrekld/, **freckle-faced** /ˈfreklfeɪst/, **freckly** /ˈfreklɪ/ *adjs.* sommersprossig

**Frederick** /ˈfredrɪk/ *pr. n.* (*Hist., as name of ruler etc.*) Friedrich

**free** /friː/ ❶ *adj.*, **freer** /ˈfriːə(r)/, **freest** /ˈfriːɪst/ Ⓐ frei; **get ~:** freikommen; sich befreien; **her heart is ~** (*fig.*) ihr Herz ist noch frei; **go ~** (*escape unpunished*) straffrei ausgehen; **let sb. go ~** (*leave captivity*) jmdn. freilassen; (*unpunished*) jmdn. freisprechen; **set ~:** freilassen; (*fig.*) erlösen; **as ~ as air** *or* **a bird** *or* **the wind** frei wie ein Vogel; Ⓑ (*Polit.*) frei; **it's a ~ country** (*coll.*) wir leben in einem freien Land; Ⓒ (*unrestricted, unconstrained, unrepressed*) frei; (*untrammelled*) frei; ungebunden; (*frank, open*) offen; freimütig; (*improper*) freizügig; (*forward, familiar*) ungezwungen; **~ of sth.** (*outside*) außerhalb etw.; (*without*) frei von etw.; **~ of prejudice/imperfections** vorurteils-/fehlerfrei; **~ of debts/tax/charge/cost** schulden-/steuer-/gebührenfrei/kostenlos; **be glad to be ~ of sth./sb.** froh sein, etw./jmdn. los zu sein; **~ and easy** ungezwungen; locker (*ugs.*); **give sb. a ~ rein to do sth.** jmdm. freie Hand lassen, etw. zu tun; **give ~ rein to sth.** einer Sache (*Dat.*) freien Lauf lassen; **make ~ with sth.** mit etw. sehr großzügig umgehen; (*help oneself*) etw. ungeniert benutzen; **make [rather too] ~ with sb.** sich (*Dat.*) jmdm. gegenüber etwas [zu viel] herausnehmen; **be ~ with one's hands** (*hitting*) eine lockere Hand haben; (*stroking*) sich (*Dat.*) Freiheiten herausnehmen; Ⓓ (*Commerc., Econ.*) frei ‹Wirtschaft, Wettbewerb›; Ⓔ (*not fixed, untied*) frei; lose; **work ~** ‹Teil:› sich lösen; **she wrenched herself ~ from his arms** sie entwand sich seinen Armen; **get one hand ~:** eine Hand freibekommen; Ⓕ (*having liberty*) **sb. is ~ to do sth.** es steht jmdm. frei, etw. zu tun; **you're ~ to choose** du kannst frei [aus]wählen; **leave sb. ~ to do sth.** es jmdm. ermöglichen, etw. zu tun; **he's not ~ to marry** er kann/darf nicht heiraten; **our thoughts are ~ to roam** die Gedanken sind frei; **feel ~!** nur zu! (*ugs.*); **Do you mind if I smoke? — Feel ~!** Stört es Sie, wenn ich rauche? — Nein, ganz und gar nicht!; **feel ~ to correct me** du darfst mich gerne korrigieren; **make sb. ~ of sth.** jmdm. etw. zur Verfügung stellen; **~ from sth.** frei von etw.; **~ from pain/troubles** schmerz-/sorgenfrei; Ⓖ (*provided without payment*) kostenlos; frei ‹Überfahrt, Unterkunft, Versand, Verpflegung›; Frei‹karte, -exemplar, -fahrt›; Gratis‹probe, -vorstellung›; **they get ~ lunches**

sie haben freies Mittagessen; **'admission ~'** „Eintritt frei"; **have a ~ ride on the train** umsonst mit der Bahn fahren; **have a ~ ride at sb.'s expense** (*fig. coll.*) auf jmds. Kosten faulenzen; **be out for a ~ ride** (*fig. coll.*) Trittbrettfahrer sein (*abwertend*); **for ~** (*coll.*) umsonst; **publicity for ~** (*coll.*) kostenlose Werbung; **H** (*not occupied, not reserved, not being used*) frei; **~ time** Freizeit, *die;* **when would you be ~ to start work?** wann könnten Sie mit der Arbeit anfangen?; **have a ~ period** (*Sch.*) eine Freistunde haben; **he's ~ in the mornings** er hat morgens Zeit; **when can you arrange to be ~?** wann können Sie sich freimachen?; **I** (*generous*) **be ~ with sth.** mit etw. großzügig umgehen; **be a ~ spender** sein Geld mit vollen Händen ausgeben; **J** (*not strict*) frei ‹Übersetzung, Interpretation, Bearbeitung usw.›; **draw a ~ likeness of sb.** jmdn. mit künstlerischer Freiheit zeichnen; **K** (*Chem., Phys.*) frei ‹Elektron, Energie›.
❷ *adv.* **A** (*without cost or payment*) gratis; umsonst; **he gets his accommodation ~:** er hat freies Logis; **B** (*freely*) frei; **C** (*Naut.*) auf raumem Kurs.
❸ *v.t.* (*set at liberty*) freilassen; (*disentangle*) befreien (**of, from** von); **~ sb./oneself from** jmdn./sich befreien von ‹Tyrannei, Unterdrückung, Tradition›; jmdn./sich befreien aus ‹Gefängnis, Sklaverei, Umklammerung›; (*make secure*) jmdn./sich schützen vor (+ *Dat.*) ‹Gefahr, Infektion›; **~ oneself from debt/obligations** sich seiner Schulden/Verpflichtungen entledigen; **~ sb./oneself of** jmdn./sich befreien *od.* freimachen von

**-free** /fri:/ *in comb.* -frei

**free 'agent** *n.* **be a ~** sein eigener Herr sein

**freebie** /'fri:bɪ/ (*coll.*) ❶ *n.* Gratisgeschenk, *das.* ❷ *adj.* Gratis‹essen, -getränk›; **~ ticket** Freikarte, *die*

**'freeboard** *n.* (*Naut.*) Freibord, *der*

**freebooter** /'fri:bu:tə(r)/ *n.* Freibeuter, *der* (*hist.*)

**free: ~-born** *adj.* frei (*hist.*); **F~ 'Church** *n.* Freikirche, *die*

**freedom** /'fri:dəm/ *n.* **A** Freiheit, *die;* **give sb. his ~:** jmdn. freigeben; (*from prison, slavery*) jmdn. freilassen; **~ of the press** Pressefreiheit, *die;* **~ of action/speech/movement** Handlungs-/Rede-/Bewegungsfreiheit, *die;* **~ from taxes/pain** Steuer-/Schmerzfreiheit, *die;* **B** (*frankness*) Ungezwungenheit, *die;* (*over-familiarity*) Vertraulichkeit, *die;* **C** (*ease*) **~ of operation of the mechanism** Leichtgängigkeit des Mechanismus; **D** (*privilege*) **[give sb.** *or* **present sb. with] the ~ of the city** [jmdm.] die Ehrenbürgerrechte [verleihen]; **E** (*use*) **give sb. the ~ of sth.** jmdm. etw. zur freien Verfügung überlassen. ⇒ *also* **conscience**

**'freedom fighter** *n.* Freiheitskämpfer, *der*/-kämpferin, *die*

**free: ~ 'enterprise** *n.* freies Unternehmertum; **~ 'fall** *n.* freier Fall; **~-fall parachuting** Fallschirmspringen mit freiem Fall; **~ 'fight** *n.* Kampf jeder gegen jeden; **F~fone** ® /'fri:fəʊn/ *n., no pl.* ≈ Service 130; **F~phone line** *or* **number/hotline** gebührenfreie Servicenummer/Hotline; **phone us on F~fone 0800 343 027** rufen Sie uns unter 0800 343 027 zum Nulltarif an; **~-for-all** ❶ *n.* [allgemeine] Schlägerei; (*less violent*) [allgemeines] Gerangel; **the discussion soon became a ~-for-all** bei der Diskussion redeten bald alle wild durcheinander; ❷ *adj.* **A** allgemein ‹Schlägerei, Gerangel›; **B** (*observing no rules*) wild ‹Diskussion, Schlägerei›; ‹Spiel› ohne [feste] Regeln; **~ 'gift** *n.* Gratisgabe, *die;* **~ 'hand** *n.* **A** **I picked it up with my ~ hand** ich hob es mit der freien Hand auf; **B** (*fig.*) freier [Handlungs]spielraum; **give sb. a ~ hand** jmdm. freie Hand lassen; **C** **with a ~ hand** (*generously*) großzügig; **~hand** *adj.* freihändig; **~ 'hit** *n.* (*Hockey, Polo*) Freischlag, *der;* **~hold** ❶ *n.* Besitzrecht, *das;* ❷ *adj.* Eigentums-; **~hold land** freier Grundbesitz; **~holder** *n.* Grundeigentümer, *der;* **~ house** *n.* (*Brit.*) *braureiunabhängiges Wirtshaus;* **~ 'kick** *n.* (*Footb.*) Freistoß, *der;* **~lance** ❶ *n.* **A** freier Mitarbeiter/freie Mitarbeiterin; **B** (*Hist.: mercenary*) Söldner, *der;* ❷ *adj.* freiberuflich; **~lance translating** freiberufliche Arbeit als Übersetzer; ❸ *v.i.* freiberuflich arbeiten; **~lancer** /'fri:lɑ:nsə(r)/ ⇒ **~lance** 1; **~'loader** *n.* (*coll.*) Nassauer, *der* (*ugs., meist abwertend*); **~ 'love** *n.* freie Liebe

**freely** /'fri:lɪ/ *adv.* **A** (*willingly*) großzügig; freimütig ‹eingestehen›; **B** (*without restriction, loosely*) frei; **C** (*frankly*) offen; **D** (*abundantly*) reichlich

**free: ~man** /'fri:mən/ *n., pl.* **~men** /'fri:mən/ **A** Freie, *der* (*hist.*); **B** (*who has freedom of city etc.*) Ehrenbürger, *der;* **~ 'market** *n.* (*Econ.*) freier Markt; **F~mason** *n.* Freimaurer, *der;* **~masonry** *n.* **A** **F~masonry** Freimaurerei, *die;* **B** (*fig.: corporate feeling*) Zusammengehörigkeitsgefühl, *das;* **~ on 'board** ❶ *adv.* frei Schiff; ❷ *adj.* frei Schiff geliefert; **~ 'pass** *n.* Freikarte, *die;* (*Railw.*) Freifahrschein, *der;* **F~phone** ⇒ **Freefone**; **~ 'play** *n.* **A** (*Mech.*) Spiel, *das;* **B** (*fig.*) **give ~ play to sth.** etw. sich frei entfalten lassen; **allow one's imagination ~ play** der Fantasie freien Lauf lassen; **~ port** *n.* Freihafen, *der;* **~post** *n.* (*Brit.*) **'~post'** „Gebühr zahlt Empfänger"

**freer** ⇒ **free** 1

**'free radical** *n.* freies Radikal

**'free-range** *adj.* frei laufend ‹Huhn›; **~ eggs** Eier von frei laufenden Hühnern

**freesia** /'fri:zɪə/ *n.* (*Bot.*) Freesie, *die*

**free: ~ 'speech** *n.* Redefreiheit, *die;* **~-spoken** *adj.* freimütig

**freest** ⇒ **free** 1

**free: ~-standing** *adj.* frei stehend; **~style** *n.* (*Sport*) Freistil, *der;* **~thinker** *n.* Freidenker, *der;* **~-thinking** ❶ *n.* Freidenkertum, *das;* ❷ *adj.* freidenkerisch; **~ 'trade** *n.* Freihandel, *der;* **~ 'verse** *n.* (*Lit.*) freie Verse; **~ 'vote** *n.* (*Brit. Parl.*) [dem Fraktionszwang nicht unterworfene] freie Stimmabgabe; **~ware** /'fri:weə(r)/ *n., no pl., no indef. art.* (*Computing*) Freeware, *die;* kostenlose Software; **~way** *n.* (*Amer.*) Autobahn, *die;* **~ 'wheel** *n.* Freilauf, *der;* **~-wheel** *v.i.* im Freilauf fahren; (*fig.: drift*) sich treiben lassen; **~ 'will** *n.* **A** *no art.* (*power*) Willensfreiheit, *die;* **B** (*choice*) **do sth. of one's own ~ will** etw. aus freiem Willen tun; **be left to sb.'s own ~ will** jmds. freier Entscheidung (*Dat.*) überlassen sein; **~ 'world** *n.* freie Welt

**freeze** /fri:z/ ❶ *v.i.*, **froze** /frəʊz/, **frozen** /'frəʊzn/ **A** frieren; **it will ~** (*Meteorol.*) es wird Frost geben; **it froze hard last night** heute Nacht war starker Frost; **B** (*become covered with ice*) ‹See, Fluss, Teich:› zufrieren; ‹Straße:› vereisen; **C** (*solidify*) ‹Flüssigkeit:› gefrieren; ‹Rohr, Schloss:› einfrieren; **the pond has frozen solid** der Teich ist ganz zugefroren; **D** (*become rigid*) steif frieren; (*fig.*) ‹Lächeln:› gefrieren (*geh.*); **E** (*become fastened*) festfrieren (**to** an + *Dat.*); **~ together** aneinander festfrieren; **F** (*be or feel cold*) sehr frieren; (*fig.*) erstarren (**with** vor + *Dat.*); ‹Blut:› gefrieren (*geh.*); **he is freezing** er *od.* ihn friert sehr; **my hands are freezing** meine Hände sind eiskalt; **~ to death** erfrieren; (*fig.*) bitterlich frieren; **G** (*make oneself motionless*) erstarren; **~!** keine Bewegung!
❷ *v.t.*, **froze, frozen** **A** zufrieren lassen ‹Teich, Fluss›; gefrieren lassen ‹Rohr›; (*fig.*) erstarren lassen; **~ sb.'s blood** (*fig.*) jmdm. das Blut in den Adern gefrieren lassen (*geh.*); **you look absolutely frozen** (*fig.*) du siehst ganz durchgefroren aus; **we were frozen stiff** (*fig.*) wir waren steif gefroren; **B** (*preserve*) tiefkühlen, tiefgefrieren ‹Lebensmittel›; **C** (*make unrealizable or unchangeable*) einfrieren ‹Kredit, Guthaben, Gelder, Löhne, Preise usw.›; **D** (*Cinemat.*) in einem Stehkader festhalten; **E** (*stiffen*) gefrieren lassen ‹Erdboden›; festfrieren lassen ‹Wäsche› (**to** an + *Dat.*); **F** (*deaden*) ‹Spritze:› taub machen; ‹Spray:› vereisen; **G** (*kill*) erfrieren lassen ‹Pflanzen›; **H** (*fig.*) erstarren lassen ‹Lächeln›.
❸ *n.* **A** ⇒ **freeze-up** A; **B** (*fixing*) Einfrieren, *das* (**on** *Gen.*); **price/wage/nuclear ~:** Preis-/Lohn-/Atomwaffenstopp, *der;* **C** (*Cinemat.*) **~[-frame]** Stehkader, *der*

**~ 'out** *v.t.* (*socially*) hinausekeln

**~ 'over** *v.i.* ‹Teich, Fluss:› zufrieren; ‹Fenster-, Windschutzscheibe, Straße:› vereisen

**~ 'up** ❶ *v.i.* ‹Fluss, Teich:› zufrieren; ‹Schloss, Rohr:› einfrieren; ‹Fenster:› vereisen. ❷ *v.t.* ⇒ **1**: zufrieren/einfrieren/vereisen lassen. ⇒ *also* **freeze-up**

**'freeze-dry** *v.t.* gefriertrocknen

**freezer** /'fri:zə(r)/ *n.* (*deep-freeze*) Tiefkühltruhe, *die;* Gefriertruhe, *die;* **[upright] ~:** Tiefkühlschrank, *der;* Gefrierschrank, *der;* **~ compartment** Tiefkühlfach, *das;* Gefrierfach, *das;* **~ [room]** Kühlraum, *der;* **[ice cream] ~:** Eismaschine, *die*

**'freeze-up** *n.* **A** (*period*) Dauerfrost, *der;* Frostperiode, *die;* **B** (*fig.*) Stillstand, *der*

**freezing** /'fri:zɪŋ/ ▶ **1603** ❶ *adj.* (*lit. or fig.*) frostig; **~ temperatures** Temperaturen unter null Grad; **it is ~ in here** es ist eiskalt hier drinnen. ❷ *n.* **A** *no pl.* (**~ point**) **above/below ~:** über/unter dem/den Gefrierpunkt; **B** (*of food*) Einfrieren, *das.* ❸ *adv.* **~ cold** eiskalt

**freezing: ~ 'fog** *n.* gefrierender Nebel; **~ point** *n.* ▶ **1603** Gefrierpunkt, *der*

**freight** /freɪt/ ❶ *n.* **A** Fracht, *die;* **~ charges** Frachtgeld, *das;* Frachtkosten *Pl.;* **B** (*transport*) Frachtsendung, *die;* **send goods ~:** Waren als Frachtgut senden; **C** (*hire*) Charter, *die.* ❷ *v.t.* **A** befrachten; **B** (*hire*) chartern; (*hire out*) vermieten

**freightage** /'freɪtɪdʒ/ *n., no pl.* Frachtkosten *Pl.*

**'freight car** *n.* (*Amer. Railw.*) Güterwagen, *der*

**freighter** /'freɪtə(r)/ *n.* **A** (*ship*) Frachter, *der;* Frachtschiff, *das;* (*aircraft*) Frachtflugzeug, *das;* **B** (*Amer. Railw.*) Güterwagen, *der*

**freight: ~-liner** *n.* (*Railw.*) [Container]güterzug, *der;* **~ train** *n.* (*Railw.*) Güterzug, *der*

**French** /frentʃ/ ▶ **1275**, ▶ **1340** ❶ *adj.* französisch; **he/she is ~:** er ist Franzose/sie ist Französin; **the ~ people** die Franzosen; **~ lessons** (*lit. or euphem.*) Französischstunden *Pl.;* ⇒ *also* **English** 1. ❷ *n.* **A** Französisch, *das;* **B** (*euphem.: bad language*) **pardon** *or* **excuse my ~:** entschuldigen Sie die Ausdrucksweise!; **C** *constr. as pl.* **the ~:** die Franzosen. ⇒ *also* **English** 2 A

**French: ~ 'bean** *n.* (*Brit.*) Gartenbohne, *die;* [grüne] Bohne; **~ 'bread** *n.* französisches [Stangen]weißbrot; **~ Ca'nadian** *n.* ▶ **1340** Frankokanadier, *der*/-kanadierin, *die;* **~-Ca'nadian** *adj.* frankokanadisch; **~ 'chalk** *n.* Schneiderkreide, *die;* **~ 'door** ⇒ **window**; **~ 'dressing** *n.* Vinaigrette, *die;* **~ fried po'tatoes, ~ 'fries** *ns. pl.* Pommes frites *Pl.;* **~ 'horn** *n.* (*Mus.*) [Wald]horn, *das*

**Frenchified** /'frentʃɪfaɪd/ *adj.* französiert

**French: ~ 'kiss** *n.* französischer Kuss (*ugs.*); Zungenkuss, *der;* **~ 'leave** *n.* **take ~ leave** (*without giving notice*) sich auf Französisch empfehlen *od.* verabschieden (*ugs.*); (*without permission*) sich heimlich davonstehlen; **~ 'letter** *n.* (*Brit. coll.*) Pariser, *der* (*salopp*); **~man** /'frentʃmən/ *n., pl.* **~men** /'frentʃmən/ Franzose, *der;* **~ 'mustard** *n.* (*Brit.*) französischer Senf; **~ 'polish** *n.* Schellackpolitur, *die;* **~-'polish** *v.t.* [mit Schellackpolitur] polieren; **~ Revo'lution** *n.* (*Hist.*) Französische Revolution; **~ 'toast** *n.* **A** (*toasted*) einseitig gerösteter Toastscheibe; **B** (*fried*) arme Ritter; **~ 'vermouth** *n.* trockener Wermut; **~ 'window** *n., in sing. or pl.* französisches Fenster; **~woman** *n.* Französin, *die*

**Frenchy** /'frentʃɪ/ (*coll.*) ❶ *adj.* [betont] französisch. ❷ *n.* Franzose, *der;* Franzmann, *der* (*ugs. veraltend*)

**frenetic** /frɪ'netɪk/ *adj.* **A** (*frantic*) verzweifelt ‹Hilferuf, Versuch›; **B** (*fanatic*) frenetisch, rasend ‹Beifall›; fanatisch ‹Sekte›

**frenzied** /'frenzɪd/ *adj.* rasend; wahnsinnig ‹Tat›

**frenzy** /'frenzɪ/ *n.* **A** (*derangement*) Wahnsinn, *der;* **B** (*fury, agitation*) Raserei, *die;* **in a ~ of despair/passion** in einem Anfall von Verzweiflung/von wilder Leidenschaft übermannt

**frequency** /'fri:kwənsɪ/ *n.* **A** Häufigkeit, *die;* **B** (*of pulse*) Puls, *der;* [Puls]frequenz, *die* (*Med.*); C (*Phys.*, *Statistics*) Frequenz, *die*

**'frequency:** ~ **band** *n.* (*Radio*, *Telev.*, *Phys.*) Frequenzband, *das;* ~ **modulation** *n.* (*Radio*, *Telev.*) Frequenzmodulation, *die*

**frequent** ❶ /'fri:kwənt/ *adj.* A häufig; **it's a ~ practice/occurrence** es ist üblich/kommt häufig vor; **become less ~:** seltener werden; B (*habitual*, *constant*) eifrig ‹[Kino-, Theater]besucher, Briefschreiber›; **he is a ~ visitor to our restaurant** er ist Stammgast in unserem Restaurant; C (*abundant*) zahlreich. ❷ /frɪ'kwent/ *v.t.* frequentieren (*geh.*); häufig besuchen ‹Café, Klub usw.›; häufig aufsuchen ‹Futterplatz›; **much ~ed** stark frequentiert (*geh.*); viel befahren ‹Straße›

**frequently** /'fri:kwəntlɪ/ *adv.* häufig

**fresco** /'freskəʊ/ *n.*, *pl.* **~es** *or* **~s** A *no pl.*, *no art.* (*method*) Freskomalerei, *die;* B (*a painting*) Fresko, *das*

**fresh** /freʃ/ ❶ *adj.* A neu; frisch, ausgeruht ‹Truppen›; frisch, neu ‹Energie, Mut›; (*lately made or arrived*) frisch; (*raw*, *inexperienced*) [jung und] unerfahren; **a ~ series of attacks** eine neuerliche Serie von Angriffen; **make a ~ start** noch einmal von vorn anfangen; (*fig.*) neu beginnen; **~ from school/India** frisch von der Schule/gerade aus Indien gekommen; **~ from** *or* **off the press** druckfrisch; frisch aus der Presse; **~ from the oven** ofenfrisch; frisch aus dem Ofen; B (*not preserved or stale or faded*) frisch ‹Obst, Fisch, Gemüse, Fleisch, Eier, Tee, Blumen usw.›; C (*clean*, *bright*) frisch ‹Aussehen, Gesichtsfarbe, Hemd, Wäsche›; D (*pure*, *cool*) frisch ‹Luft, Wasser, Wind›; **go out for some ~ air** nach draußen gehen, um Luft zu schöpfen (*geh.*); **the wind became ~:** der Wind frischte auf; E (*vigorous*, *fit*) frisch; (*refreshed*) erfrischt; **as ~ as a daisy/as paint** ganz frisch; (*in appearance*) frisch wie der junge Morgen (*meist scherzh.*); F (*cheeky*) keck; **get ~ with sb.** jmdm. frech kommen (*ugs.*). ⇒ *also* **ground**[1] 1 B.
❷ *adv.* frisch; **we're ~ out of eggs** (*coll.*) uns sind gerade die Eier ausgegangen; **~-ground/-painted** frisch gemahlen/gestrichen

**freshen** /'freʃn/ ❶ *v.i.* A frisch[er] werden; (*increase*) ‹Wind:› auffrischen; B (*brighten*) ein frisch[er]es Aussehen bekommen. ❷ *v.t.* (*ventilate*) durchlüften ‹Zimmer›

**~ 'up** ❶ *v.i.* sich frisch machen. ❷ *v.t.* erfrischen; **~ oneself/sb. up** sich/jmdn. frisch machen

**fresher** /'freʃə(r)/ (*Brit. Univ. coll.*) ⇒ **freshman** A

**freshly** /'freʃlɪ/ *adv.* frisch

**freshman** /'freʃmən/ *n.*, *pl.* **freshmen** /'freʃmən/ A Erstsemester, *das;* Frischling, *der* (*scherzh.*); B (*Amer.*) (*in school*) Anfänger, *der*/Anfängerin, *die;* (*person beginning*) Neuling, *der*

**freshness** /'freʃnɪs/ *n.*, *no pl.* Frische, *die;* (*of idea*, *metaphor*, *etc.*) Neuartigkeit, *die;* (*originality*) Originalität, *die*

**'freshwater** *adj.* Süßwasser-; **~ sailor** Binnenschiffer, *der*

**fresh 'water** *n.* Süßwasser, *das*

**fret**[1] /fret/ ❶ *v.i.*, **-tt-** (*worry*) sich (*Dat.*) Sorgen machen; **don't ~:** keine Sorge!; **~ at** *or* **about** *or* **over sth.** sich über etw. (*Akk.*) *od.* wegen etw. aufregen; **~ and fume** (*anxiously/impatiently*) voller Unruhe/Ungeduld sein. ❷ *v.t.*, **-tt-:** A (*distress*) beunruhigen; quälen; **~ oneself** sich beunruhigen; sich (*Dat.*) Sorgen machen (**about** wegen); B (*chafe*) [wund] scheuern. ❸ *n.* Ärger, *der;* **be in a ~:** voll Verdruss sein

**fret**[2] *n.* (*Mus.*) Bund, *der*

**fretful** /'fretfl/ *adj.* (*peevish*) verdrießlich; mürrisch; quengelig (*ugs.*) ‹Kleinkind›; (*restless*) unruhig; (*impatient*) ungeduldig; (*ill-humoured*) übellaunig

**fret:** **~saw** *n.* Laubsäge, *die;* **~work** *n.* A (*Archit.*) durchbrochene Arbeit; B (*wood*) Laubsägearbeit, *die*

**Freudian** /'frɔɪdɪən/ *adj.* freudianisch; **~ interpretation** freudsche Interpretation; **~ slip** freudsche Fehlleistung; freudscher Versprecher (*ugs.*)

**Fri.** *abbr.* ▶ 1056 **Friday** Fr.

**friable** /'fraɪəbl/ *adj.* bröck[e]lig

**friar** /'fraɪə(r)/ *n.* Ordensbruder, *der;* **Black/Grey/White F~:** Dominikaner/Franziskaner/Karmeliter, *der;* **F~ Peter** Bruder Peter

**fricassee** /'frɪkəsi:, frɪkə'si:/ (*Cookery*) ❶ *n.* Frikassee, *das.* ❷ *v.t.* frikassieren

**fricative** /'frɪkətɪv/ (*Phonet.*) ❶ *adj.* frikativ. ❷ *n.* Frikativ, *der* (*fachspr.*); Reibelaut, *der*

**friction** /'frɪkʃn/ *n.* A Reibung, *die; attrib.* Reibungs-; B (*fig.: between persons*) Reibereien *Pl.;* C (*of body or scalp*) Einreibung, *die;* Friktion, *die* (*Med.*)

**Friday** /'fraɪdeɪ, 'fraɪdɪ/ ▶ 1056 ❶ *n.* Freitag, *der;* **on ~:** [am] Freitag; **on a ~, on ~s** freitags; **we got married on a ~:** wir haben an einem Freitag geheiratet; **~ 13 August** Freitag, der 13. August; (*at top of letter etc.*) Freitag, den 13. August; **on ~ 13 August** am Freitag, den *od.* dem 13. August; **next/last ~:** [am] nächsten/letzten *od.* vergangenen Freitag; **[on] ~ next/last** kommenden/vergangenen Freitag; **we were married a year [ago] last/next ~:** vergangenen/kommenden Freitag vor einem Jahr haben wir geheiratet; **[last] ~'s mail/newspaper** die Post/Zeitung vom [letzten] Freitag; **our ~ session** unsere Freitagssitzung; (*this ~*) unsere Sitzung am Freitag; **Good ~:** Karfreitag, *der;* **man/girl ~:** Mädchen für alles (*ugs.*).
❷ *adv.* (*coll.*) A **~ [week]** Freitag [in einer Woche]; B **~s** freitags; Freitag (*ugs.*); **she comes ~s** sie kommt freitags

**fridge** /frɪdʒ/ *n.* (*Brit. coll.*) Kühlschrank, *der;* **~-freezer** Kühl-und-Gefrierkombination, *die*

**fried** ⇒ **fry**[1] 2, 3

**friend** /frend/ *n.* A Freund, *der*/Freundin, *die;* **~s and relations** Verwandte und Freunde; **be ~s with sb.** mit jmdm. befreundet sein; **I'm not ~s with you any more!** (*joc. or child language*) du bist nicht mehr mein Freund!; **let's be ~s again** wir wollen uns wieder vertragen; **make ~s [with sb.]** [mit jmdm.] Freundschaft schließen; **he makes ~s easily** er findet leicht Anschluss; **make a ~ of sb.** sich mit jmdm. anfreunden; **a ~ in need is a ~ indeed** (*prov.*) Freunde in der Not gehn hundert *od.* tausend auf ein Lot (*Spr.*); **between ~s** unter Freunden; B (*helper*, *patron*) Freund, *der* (**of, to** *Gen.*); **~s in high places** *or* **at court** einflussreiche Freunde; Freunde höheren Orts; **the F~s of Covent Garden** der Freundes- *od.* Förderkreis des Covent Garden; C (*Quaker*) **the Society of F~s** die Quäker; die Gesellschaft der Freunde; D **my honourable/noble ~** (*Brit. Parl.*) mein verehrter Freund; **my learned ~** (*Law*) mein verehrter *od.* werter Kollege

**friendless** /'frendlɪs/ *adj.* ohne Freund[e] *nachgestellt*

**friendliness** /'frendlɪnɪs/ *n.*, *no pl.* Freundlichkeit, *die*

**friendly** /'frendlɪ/ ❶ *adj.* A freundlich (**to** zu); freundschaftlich ‹Rat, Beziehungen, Wettkampf, Gespräch›; **be on ~ terms** *or* **be ~ with sb.** mit jmdm. auf freundschaftlichem Fuße stehen; **we're very ~ with our neighbours** wir sind mit unseren Nachbarn sehr gut befreundet; ⇒ *also* **neighbourhood** D; B (*not hostile*) freundlich [gesinnt] ‹Bewohner›; befreundet ‹Staat›; zutraulich ‹Tier›; **~ game** (*Sport*) Freundschaftsspiel, *das;* C (*well-wishing*) wohlwollend ‹Erwähnung›; günstig gestimmt ‹Götter›.
❷ *n.* (*Sport*) Freundschaftsspiel, *das*

**friendly 'fire** *n.* (*Milit.*) eigenes Feuer

**'Friendly Society** *n.* (*Brit.*) Versicherungsverein auf Gegenseitigkeit

**friendship** /'frendʃɪp/ *n.* Freundschaft, *die;* **[feelings of] ~:** freundschaftliche Gefühle; **strike up a ~ with sb.** sich mit jmdm. anfreunden

**Friends of the Earth** *pr. n. sing. or pl.* Friends of the Earth (*Umweltschutzvereinigung*)

**frier** ⇒ **fryer**

**fries** /fraɪz/ *n. pl.* (*Amer.*) Pommes frites *Pl.*

**Friesian** /'fri:zɪən, 'fri:ʒən/ (*Agric.*) ❶ *adj.* schwarzbunt. ❷ *n.* Schwarzbunte, *die*

**frieze**[1] /fri:z/ *n.* (*Textiles*) Fries, *der;* Friese, *die* (*fachspr.*)

**frieze**[2] *n.* (*Archit.*) Fries, *der*

**frigate** /'frɪgət/ *n.* (*Naut.*) Fregatte, *die*

**fright** /fraɪt/ *n.* A Schreck, *der;* Schrecken, *der;* **in his ~:** vor Schreck; **take ~:** erschrecken; **the ~ of one's life** der Schock seines Lebens; **give sb. a ~:** jmdm. einen Schreck[en] einjagen; **get** *or* **have a ~:** einen Schreck[en] bekommen; B (*grotesque person or thing*) **be** *or* **look a ~:** zum Fürchten aussehen (*ugs.*)

**frighten** /'fraɪtn/ *v.t.* ‹Explosion, Schuss:› erschrecken; ‹Gedanke, Drohung:› Angst machen (+ *Dat.*); **be ~ed at** *or* **by sth.** vor etw. (*Dat.*) erschrecken; **she is not easily ~ed** sie fürchtet sich nicht so schnell; **~ sb. out of his wits/life** jmdn. furchtbar/zu Tode erschrecken; **~ sb. to death** (*fig.*) jmdn. zu Tode erschrecken; **be ~ed to death** (*fig.*) zu Tode erschrocken sein; **~ sb. into doing sth.** jmdm. solche Angst machen, dass er etw. tut

**~ a'way, ~ 'off** *v.t.* vertreiben; (*put off*) abschrecken

**frightened** /'fraɪtnd/ *adj.* verängstigt; angsterfüllt ‹Stimme›; **be ~ [of sth.]** [vor etw. (*Dat.*)] Angst haben

**frightening** /'fraɪtnɪŋ/ *adj.* Furcht erregend

**frightful** /'fraɪtfl/ *adj.* furchtbar; schrecklich; (*coll.: terrible*) furchtbar (*ugs.*)

**frightfully** /'fraɪtfəlɪ/ *adv.* furchtbar; schrecklich; (*coll.: extremely*) furchtbar (*ugs.*)

**frigid** /'frɪdʒɪd/ *adj.* A (*very cold*) eisig kalt; B (*formal*, *unfriendly*) frostig; (*sexually unresponsive*) frigid[e] ‹Frau›

**frigidity** /frɪ'dʒɪdɪtɪ/ *n.*, *no pl.* A (*coldness*) eisige Kälte; B (*formality*, *unfriendliness*) Frostigkeit, *die;* (*of woman*) Frigidität, *die*

**frill** /frɪl/ *n.* A (*ruffled edge*) Rüsche, *die;* B (*on animal*, *plant*) Kragen, *der;* (*on bird*) Halskrause, *die;* C *in pl.* (*embellishments*) Beiwerk, *das;* Ausschmückungen *Pl.* (*fig.*); **with no ~s** ‹Ferienhaus, Auto› ohne besondere Ausstattung

**frilly** /'frɪlɪ/ ❶ *adj.* mit Rüschen besetzt; Rüschen‹kleid, -bluse›. ❷ *n. in pl.* (*coll.*) Rüschenunterwäsche, *die*

**fringe** /frɪndʒ/ ❶ *n.* A (*bordering*) Fransen *Pl.;* Fransenkante, *die* (**on an** + *Dat.*); B (*hair*) [Pony]fransen *Pl.* (*ugs.*); Pony, *der;* C (*edge*) Rand, *der; attrib.* Rand‹geschehen, -gruppe, -gebiet›; **~ benefits** zusätzliche Leistungen; **live on the ~[s] of the city** am Stadtrand *od.* in den Randgebieten der Stadt wohnen; **lunatic ~:** Extremisten *Pl.* ❷ *v.t.* säumen (*auch fig. geh.*)

**frippery** /'frɪpərɪ/ *n.* Putz, *der;* Zierrat, *der* (*geh.*); (*knick-knacks*, *trifles*) Tand, *der* (*geh.*); Kinkerlitzchen *Pl.* (*ugs.*)

**Frisco** /'frɪskəʊ/ *pr. n.* (*Amer. coll.*) San Francisco (*das*)

**Frisian** /'frɪzɪən/ ▶ 1275, ▶ 1340 ❶ *adj.* friesisch; ⇒ *also* **English** 1. ❷ *n.* A (*language*) Friesisch, *das;* B (*person*) Friese, *der*/Friesin, *die.* ⇒ *also* **English** 2 A

**frisk** /frɪsk/ ❶ *v.i.* **~ [about]** [herum]springen; **~ away** davonspringen. ❷ *v.t.* (*coll.*) filzen (*ugs.*). ❸ *n.* A (*frolic*) Hüpfer, *der;* B (*coll.: body search*) Filzung, *die* (*ugs.*)

**frisky** /'frɪskɪ/ *adj.* munter; **as ~ as a kitten** so ausgelassen wie ein Füllen (*geh.*)

**frisson** /'fri:sɔ̃/ *n.* Schauer, *der*

**fritillary** /frɪ'tɪlərɪ/ *n.* A (*Bot.*) Fritillaria, *die* (*fachspr.*); Kaiserkrone, *die;* B (*Zool.*) Fleckenfalter, *der*

**fritter**[1] /'frɪtə(r)/ *n.* (*Cookery*) **apple/sausage ~s** Apfelstücke/Würstchen in Pfannkuchenteig

**fritter**[2] *v.t.* **~ away** vergeuden; verplempern (*ugs.*)

**frivolity** /frɪ'vɒlɪtɪ/ *n.* A *no pl.* Oberflächlichkeit, *die;* Leichtfertigkeit, *die;* B (*thing*) Tand, *der* (*geh.*); (*act*) **he watched these**

**frivolities with contempt** er beobachtete dieses leichtfertige Treiben mit Verachtung

**frivolous** /ˈfrɪvələs/ *adj.* Ⓐ (*not serious*) frivol; extravagant ‹Kleidung›; Ⓑ (*trifling, futile*) belanglos

**frivolously** /ˈfrɪvələslɪ/ *adv.* frivol; extravagant ‹gekleidet›

**frizzle** /ˈfrɪzl/ ❶ *v.i.* brutzeln; braten. ❷ *v.t.* brutzeln (*ugs.*); braten

**frizzy** /ˈfrɪzɪ/ *adj.* kraus

**fro** /frəʊ/ ⇒ **to** 2 B

**frock** /frɒk/ *n.* Ⓐ Kleid, *das;* Ⓑ (*Mil.*) Uniformrock, *der*

ˈ**frock coat** *n.* Gehrock, *der*

**frog**[1] /frɒg/ *n.* Ⓐ Frosch, *der;* **have a ~ in the** *or* **one's throat** (*coll.*) einen Frosch im Hals haben (*ugs.*); Ⓑ (*sl. derog.: Frenchman*) Franzmann, *der* (*ugs., veralt.*)

**frog**[2] *n.* Ⓐ (*coat fastening*) Posamentenverschluss, *der;* Ⓑ (*on belt*) Schlaufe, *die*

**froggy** /ˈfrɒgɪ/ ❶ *adj.* Frosch‹gesicht, -stimme›. ❷ *n.* (*sl. derog.*) ⇒ **frog**[1] B

**frog: ~man** /ˈfrɒgmən/ *n., pl.* **~men** /ˈfrɒgmən/ Froschmann, *der;* **~march** *v.t.* (*carry*) zu viert an Händen und Füßen [mit dem Gesicht nach unten] tragen; (*hustle*) ≈ im Polizeigriff abführen; **~spawn** *n.* Froschlaich, *der*

**frolic** /ˈfrɒlɪk/ ❶ *v.i.*, **-ck-: ~ [about** *or* **around]** [herum]springen. ❷ *n.* (*prank, lark*) Spaß, *der;* (*fun, merriment*) Ausgelassenheit, *die*

**frolicsome** /ˈfrɒlɪksəm/ *adj.* (*dated*) ausgelassen

**from** /frəm, *stressed* frɒm/ *prep.* Ⓐ *expr. starting point* von; (**~** *within*) aus; **[come] ~ Paris/Munich** aus Paris/München [kommen]; **~ Paris to Munich** von Paris nach München; **where have you come ~?** woher kommen Sie?; wo kommen Sie her?; Ⓑ ▶ **1055** *expr. beginning* von; **~ the year 1972 we never saw him again** seit 1972 haben wir ihn nie mehr [wieder] gesehen; **~ tomorrow [until …]** von morgen an [bis …]; **start work ~ 2 August** am 2. August anfangen zu arbeiten; vom 2. August an arbeiten; **~ now on** von jetzt an; ab jetzt; **~ then on** seitdem; (*relating to a place*) von da an; ⇒ *also* **as** 4; Ⓒ *expr. lower limit* von; **blouses [ranging] ~ £2 to £5** Blusen [im Preis] zwischen 2 und 5 Pfund; **dresses ~ £20 [upwards]** Kleider von 20 Pfund aufwärts *od.* ab 20 Pfund; **~ 4 to 6 eggs** 4 bis 6 Eier; **~ the age of 18 [upwards]** ab 18 Jahre *od.* Jahren; **~ a child** (*since childhood*) schon als Kind; Ⓓ *expr. distance* von; **be a mile ~ sth.** eine Meile von etw. entfernt sein; **away ~ home** von zu Hause weg; Ⓔ *expr. removal, avoidance* von; *expr. escape* vor (+ *Dat.*); **release the bomb ~ the aircraft** die Bombe aus dem Flugzeug ausklinken; Ⓕ *expr. change* von; **~ … to …:** von … zu …; (*relating to price*) von … auf …; **~ crisis to crisis, ~ one crisis to another** von einer Krise zur anderen; Ⓖ *expr. source, origin* aus; **pick apples ~ a tree** Äpfel vom Baum pflücken; **buy everything ~ Harrods/the same shop** alles bei Harrods/im selben Laden kaufen; **where do you come ~?, where are you ~?** woher kommen Sie?; **~ the country/another planet** vom Land/von einem anderen Planeten; Ⓗ *expr. viewpoint* von [… aus]; Ⓘ *expr. giver, sender* von; **take it ~ me that …:** lass dir gesagt sein, dass …; Ⓙ (*after the model of*) **painted ~ life/nature** nach dem Leben/nach der Natur gemalt; Ⓚ *expr. reason, cause* **she was weak ~ hunger/tired ~ so much work** sie war schwach vor Hunger/müde von der vielen Arbeit; **~ his looks you might think …:** so wie er aussieht, könnte man denken …; **~ what I can see/have heard …:** wie ich das sehe/wie ich gehört habe, …; **~ the look of things …:** wie es aussieht, …; Ⓛ *with adv.* von ‹unten, oben, innen, außen›; Ⓜ *with prep.* **~ behind/under[neath] sth.** hinter/unter etw. (*Dat.*) hervor; **~ amidst the trees** zwischen den Bäumen hervor; **~ before the marriage** aus der Zeit vor der Heirat; **the cries came ~ inside/outside the house** die Schreie kamen aus dem Inneren des Hauses/von draußen

**frond** /frɒnd/ *n.* (*Bot.*) Wedel, *der;* Blatt, *das*

**front** /frʌnt/ ❶ *n.* Ⓐ Vorderseite, *die;* (*of door*) Außenseite, *die;* (*of house*) Vorderfront, *die;* Frontseite, *die;* (*of dress*) Vorderteil, *das;* (*of queue*) vorderes Ende; (*of procession*) Spitze, *die;* (*of book*) vorderer Deckel; (*of cloth*) rechte Seite; **in** *or* **at the ~ [of sth.]** vorn [in etw. *position: Dat., movement: Akk.*]; **sit in the ~ of the car** vorne sitzen; **the index is at the ~:** das Register ist vorn; **to the ~:** nach vorn; **the living room is at** *or* **in the ~ of the house** das Wohnzimmer liegt zur Straße hin *od.* (*ugs.*) nach vorn[e] raus; **lie on one's ~:** auf dem Bauch liegen; **a spot on the ~ of her dress** ein Fleck vorne am Kleid; **in ~:** vorn[e]; **be in ~ of sth./sb.** vor etw./jmdm. sein; **walk in ~ of sb.** (*preceding*) vor jmdm. gehen; (*to position*) vor jmdn. gehen; **look in ~ of one** nach vorn sehen; **he was murdered in ~ of his wife** er wurde vor den Augen seiner Frau ermordet; Ⓑ (*Mil.; also fig.*) Front, *die;* **on the Western ~:** an der Westfront; **send sb. to the ~:** jmdn. an die Front schicken; **be attacked on all ~s** an allen Fronten/(*fig.*) von allen Seiten angegriffen werden; **change of ~** (*fig.*) Gesinnungswandel, *der;* Frontwechsel, *der* (*Politik*); **on the international/home ~:** im Ausland/Inland; **on the sports ~:** im sportlichen Bereich; **on the entertainment ~:** auf dem Unterhaltungssektor; **the workers'/people's ~:** die Arbeiter-/Volksfront; Ⓒ (*promenade*) (*at seaside*) Strandpromenade, *die;* (*inland*) Uferpromenade, *die;* Ⓓ (*Theatre*) **~ of [the] house** Foyer und Zuschauerraum; Ⓔ (*Archit.*) ‹West-, Garten- usw.›seite, *die;* Ⓕ (*Meteorol.*) Front, *die;* **cold/warm ~:** Kalt-/Warmluftfront, *die;* Ⓖ ⇒ **shirt front**; Ⓗ (*outward appearance*) Aussehen, *das;* (*bluff*) Fassade, *die* (*oft abwertend*); (*pretext, façade*) Tarnung, *die;* **put on** *or* **show** *or* **present a bold/brave ~:** sich nach außen unerschrocken zeigen/nach außen hin gefasst bleiben; **preserve a calm ~:** nach außen hin ruhig bleiben; **it's all a ~:** das ist alles nur Fassade (*abwertend*); Ⓘ (*used as cover*) (*person*) Strohmann, *der;* (*organization*) Tarnorganisation, *die.*

❷ *adj.* Ⓐ vorder…; Vorder‹rad, -zimmer, -zahn, -eingang, -ansicht›; **~ garden** Vorgarten, *der;* **the ~ four coaches of a train** die ersten vier *od.* vier vorderen Wagen eines Zuges; **~ row** erste Reihe; Ⓑ (*Phonet.*) **~ vowel** Vorderzungenvokal, *der.*

❸ *v.i.* Ⓐ **~ on to the street/upon the lake** zur Straße/zum See hin liegen; Ⓑ (*coll.: act as cover*) **~ for sb.** für jmdn. den Strohmann spielen.

❹ *v.t.* (*furnish with façade*) **~ a building with stone** ein Gebäude mit einer Fassade aus Stein versehen

**frontage** /ˈfrʌntɪdʒ/ *n.* Ⓐ (*land*) Grundstück[steil] zwischen Gebäude und Straße; **river/street ~:** an den Fluss/die Straße grenzender Teil des Grundstücks; Ⓑ (*extent*) Frontbreite, *die;* Ⓒ (*façade*) Fassade, *die*

**frontal** /ˈfrʌntl/ *adj.* Ⓐ Frontal-; Ⓑ (*Art*) frontal ‹Darstellung›; **[full] ~:** frontal dargestellt ‹Akt›; Ⓒ (*Anat.*) Stirn‹bein, -hirn, -höhle, -lappen›

**frontally** /ˈfrʌntəlɪ/ *adv.* frontal

**front: ~ ˈbench** *n.* (*Brit. Parl.*) vorderste Bank; **~-bencher** /frʌntˈbentʃə(r)/ *n.* (*Brit. Parl.*) führender Politiker; **~ ˈdoor** *n.* (*of flat*) Wohnungstür, *die;* (*of house; also fig.*) Haustür, *die*

**frontier** /ˈfrʌntɪə(r)/ *n.* Ⓐ (*lit. or fig.*) Grenze, *die; attrib.* Grenz‹stadt, -posten, -streitigkeiten›; **at** *or* **on the ~:** an der Grenze; **push the ~s of science forward** (*fig.*) wissenschaftliches Neuland erobern; Ⓑ (*Amer.: borders of civilization*) Grenzland, *das*

**frontispiece** /ˈfrʌntɪspiːs/ *n.* Frontispiz, *das;* Titelbild, *das*

**front: ~ ˈline** *n.* Front[linie], *die;* **~ man** *n.* Ⓐ (*of criminal organization*) [An]führer, *der;* Ⓑ (*of television programme*) Moderator, *der;* Ⓒ (*of rock group etc.*) Frontmann, *der;* **~ ˈpage** *n.* Titelseite, *die;* **make the ~ page** auf die Titelseite kommen; **~-page** *adj.* ‹Artikel› auf der ersten Seite; **~ passage** *n.* (*Anat. coll.*) Scheide, *die;* **~-rank** *adj.* (*fig.*) herausragend; **~ runner** *n.* Ⓐ (*in race*) *Läufer, der gern an der Spitze läuft;* Ⓑ (*in any competition*) Spitzenkandidat, *der;* **~ ˈseat** *n.* (*in theatre*) Platz in den ersten Reihen; (*in car*) Vordersitz, *der;* (*in bus, coach*) vorderer Sitzplatz; **~-wheel drive** ❶ *n.* Vorderradantrieb, *der;* Frontantrieb, *der;* ❷ *adj.* **a ~-wheel drive vehicle** ein Fahrzeug mit Vorderrad- *od.* Frontantrieb; **the car is ~-wheel drive** das Auto hat Vorderrad- *od.* Frontantrieb

**frost** /frɒst/ ❶ *n.* Ⓐ Frost, *der;* (*frozen dew or vapour*) Reif, *der;* **windows covered with ~:** vereiste Fensterscheiben; **white/black ~:** Frost mit/ohne Reif; **early/late ~s** Herbst-/Frühlingsfröste; **ten degrees of ~** (*Brit.*) zehn Grad minus; **there is still ~ in the ground** der Boden ist noch gefroren; Ⓑ (*fig.: hostility*) Frostigkeit, *die;* Ⓒ (*dated coll.: failure*) Reinfall, *der* (*ugs.*); Pleite, *die* (*salopp*). ❷ *v.t.* Ⓐ (*esp. Amer. Cookery*) mit Zucker bestreuen; (*ice*) glasieren; Ⓑ (*give ~like surface to*) mattieren ‹Glas, Metall›; **~ed glass** Mattglas, *das*

**~ ˈover** ❶ *v.t.* **be ~ed over** vereist sein. ❷ *v.i.* vereisen

**frost: ~bite** *n.* Erfrierung, *die;* **~bitten** *adj.* durch Frost geschädigt; **sb. is ~bitten** jmd. hat Erfrierungen; **his toes are ~bitten** er hat Frost *od.* Erfrierungen in den Zehen

**frostily** /ˈfrɒstɪlɪ/ *adv.* frostig

**frosting** /ˈfrɒstɪŋ/ *n.* (*esp. Amer. Cookery*) Zucker, *der;* (*icing*) Glasur, *die*

**frosty** /ˈfrɒstɪ/ *adj.* (*lit. or fig.*) frostig; (*covered with hoar frost*) bereift; (*fig.: white*) schneeweiß

**froth** /frɒθ/ ❶ *n.* Ⓐ (*foam*) Schaum, *der;* Ⓑ (*worthless matter*) Tand, *der* (*geh.*). ❷ *v.i.* schäumen; **~ at the mouth** Schaum vor dem Mund haben; **~ at the mouth with rage** (*fig.*) vor Wut schäumen (*geh.*). ❸ *v.t.* (*Cookery*) **[beat and] ~ the eggs** die Eier schaumig schlagen

**frothy** /ˈfrɒθɪ/ *adj.* schaumig; schäumend ‹Bier, Brandung, Maul›; (*fig.: empty, shallow*) oberflächlich ‹Person›; seicht (*abwertend*) ‹Unterhaltung, Roman›

**frown** /fraʊn/ ❶ *v.i.* Ⓐ die Stirn runzeln; **~ at sth./sb.** etw./jmdn. stirnrunzelnd ansehen; Ⓑ (*express disapproval*) die Stirn runzeln **(at, [up]on** über + *Akk.*); **~ [up]on a suggestion** über einen Vorschlag die Nase rümpfen; **gambling is very much ~ed upon here** das Glücksspiel ist hier streng verpönt; Ⓒ (*present gloomy aspect*) **~ [down]** düster herabblicken **(upon** auf + *Akk.*). ❷ *n.* Stirnrunzeln, *das;* **with a [deep/worried/puzzled] ~:** mit [stark/sorgenvoll/verwirrt] gerunzelter Stirn; **a ~ of disapproval** ein missbilligender Blick

**froze** ⇒ **freeze** 1, 2

**frozen** /ˈfrəʊzn/ ❶ ⇒ **freeze** 1, 2. ❷ *adj.* Ⓐ gefroren, zugefroren ‹Fluss, See›; erfroren ‹Tier, Person, Pflanze›; eingefroren ‹Wasserleitung›; **I am ~ stiff/through** (*fig.*) ich bin ganz steif gefroren/völlig durchgefroren; **my hands are ~** (*fig.*) meine Hände sind eiskalt; Ⓑ (*to preserve*) tiefgekühlt; **~ food** Tiefkühlkost, *die*

**FRS** *abbr.* **Fellow of the Royal Society**

**fructose** /ˈfrʌktəʊs/ *n.* (*Chem.*) Fructose, *die* (*fachspr.*); Fruchtzucker, *der*

**frugal** /ˈfruːgl/ *adj.* Ⓐ (*careful, economical*) sparsam ‹Hausfrau›; genügsam ‹Lebensweise, Person, Wesen›; Ⓑ (*costing little*) frugal, karg ‹Mahl›; einfach, karg ‹Zimmer, Einrichtung›

**frugally** /ˈfruːgəlɪ/ *adv.* frugal, genügsam ‹leben, essen›; einfach ‹eingerichtet›

**fruit** /fruːt/ ❶ *n.* Ⓐ Frucht, *die;* (*collectively*) Obst, *das;* Früchte; **~s of the earth** Früchte des Feldes; **bear ~** (*lit. or fig.*) Früchte tragen; Ⓑ (*Bot.: seed with envelope*) Frucht, *die;* Ⓒ (*fig.*) (*product of action*) Frucht, *die* (*geh.*); Früchte (*geh.*); **~s** (*revenues produced*) Früchte (*geh.*); **this book is the ~**

**of long study** dieses Buch ist die Frucht langjähriger Arbeit (*geh.*); Ⓓ (*Bibl.: offspring*) Frucht, *die* (*geh.*); **the ~ of her womb/his loins** die Frucht ihres Leibes/seiner Lenden (*geh.*).
❷ *v.i.* [Früchte] tragen; (*fig.*) Früchte tragen

**fruit: ~ cake** *n.* englischer Teekuchen; **he is as nutty as a ~ cake** (*coll.*) (*eccentric*) er ist ein verrücktes Huhn (*ugs.*); (*insane*) er ist völlig übergeschnappt (*ugs.*); **~ 'cocktail** *n.* Früchtecocktail, *der*

**fruiterer** /ˈfruːtərə(r)/ *n.* ▶ 1261 Obsthändler, *der*/-händlerin, *die*

**fruitful** /ˈfruːtfl/ *adj.* Ⓐ fruchtbar; (*fig.*) fruchtbar ‹Diskussion, Lebensabschnitt, Anregung›; erfolgreich ‹Karriere, Leben, Bemühungen›; **be ~ and multiply** (*Bibl.*) seid fruchtbar und mehret euch; Ⓑ (*beneficial*) ertragreich ‹Beschäftigung›; nützlich ‹Entdeckung›

**fruitfully** /ˈfruːtfəlɪ/ *adv.* nutzbringend

**fruition** /fruːˈɪʃn/ *n.* (*of plan, aim*) Verwirklichung, *die;* (*of hope*) Erfüllung, *die;* **bring to ~:** verwirklichen ‹Plan, Ziel›; **come to ~** ‹Plan:› Wirklichkeit werden; ‹Hoffnung:› sich erfüllen

**fruit: ~ juice** *n.* Fruchtsaft, *der;* **~ knife** *n.* Obstmesser, *das*

**fruitless** /ˈfruːtlɪs/ *adj.* (*unprofitable*) nutzlos ‹Versuch, Gespräch›; fruchtlos ‹Verhandlung, Bemühung, Suche›; **the investigation was ~:** die Untersuchung verlief ergebnislos; **it is ~ to ...:** es ist nutzlos zu ...

**fruitlessly** /ˈfruːtlɪslɪ/ *adv.* umsonst ‹versuchen, sich bemühen, suchen›; fruchtlos, ergebnislos ‹verhandeln, diskutieren›

**fruit: ~ machine** *n.* (*Brit.*) Spielautomat, *der;* **~ 'salad** *n.* Obstsalat, *der;* **~ salts** *n. pl.* Magenpulver, *das;* **~ tree** *n.* Obstbaum, *der*

**fruity** /ˈfruːtɪ/ *adj.* Ⓐ fruchtig ‹Duft, Geschmack, Wein›; Ⓑ (*coll.*) (*rich in tone*) volltönend ‹Stimme›; herzhaft ‹Lachen›; (*full of scandalous interest*) saftig (*ugs.*) ‹Geschichte, Buch, Witz›

**frump** /frʌmp/ *n.* (*derog.*) Vogelscheuche, *die* (*ugs.*)

**frumpy** /ˈfrʌmpɪ/ *adj.* (*derog.*) ohne jeden Schick *nachgestellt*

**frustrate** /frʌˈstreɪt, ˈfrʌstreɪt/ *v.t.* vereiteln, durchkreuzen ‹Plan, Vorhaben, Versuch›; zunichte machen ‹Hoffnung, Bemühungen›; enttäuschen ‹Erwartung, Hoffnung›; **he was ~d in his attempts/efforts** seine Versuche/Bemühungen waren vergebens

**frustrated** /frʌˈstreɪtɪd, ˈfrʌstreɪtɪd/ *adj.* frustriert

**frustrating** /frʌˈstreɪtɪŋ, ˈfrʌstreɪtɪŋ/ *adj.* frustrierend; ärgerlich ‹Angewohnheit›; **he is a ~ person to deal with** es ist frustrierend, mit ihm zu tun zu haben

**frustration** /frʌˈstreɪʃn/ *n.* Frustration, *die;* (*defeat*) Enttäuschung, *die;* (*of plans, efforts*) Scheitern, *das*

**fry¹** /fraɪ/ ❶ *n.* Ⓐ Pfannengericht, *das;* Ⓑ (*internal parts of animals*) [gebratene] Innereien *Pl.*; ⇒ *also* **lamb's fry**; Ⓒ (*Amer.: social gathering*) Grillparty, *die.* ❷ *v.t.* braten; **fried eggs/potatoes** Spiegeleier/Bratkartoffeln *Pl.;* ⇒ *also* **fish** 1 A. ❸ *v.i.* braten; (*coll.: burn*) **~ in the sun** in der Sonne schmoren (*ugs.*)

**~ 'up** *v.t.* aufbraten ‹Reste›; **let's ~ up something** lass uns schnell was brutzeln (*ugs.*); ⇒ *also* **fry-up**

**fry²** *n.* (*young fishes etc.*) Brut, *die;* **'small ~** (*fig.*) unbedeutende Leute; (*children*) junges Gemüse (*ugs.*); **compared with him all the others are 'small ~** (*fig.*) im Vergleich mit ihm sind alle anderen unbedeutend

**fryer** /ˈfraɪə(r)/ *n.* Ⓐ (*vessel*) Fritteuse, *die;* Ⓑ (*Amer.: chicken*) Brathühnchen, *das;* Brathähnchen, *das*

**frying pan** /ˈfraɪɪŋpæn/ *n.* Bratpfanne, *die;* **[fall/jump] out of the ~ into the fire** vom Regen in die Traufe [kommen] (*ugs.*)

**fry: ~pan** (*Amer.*) ⇒ **frying pan**; **~-up** *n.* Pfannengericht, *das*

**ft.** *abbr.* ▶ 928, ▶ 1210, ▶ 1284 **feet, foot** ft.

**fuchsia** /ˈfjuːʃə/ *n.* (*Bot.*) Fuchsie, *die*

**fuck** /fʌk/ (*coarse*) ❶ *v.t.* Ⓐ ficken (*vulg.*); Ⓑ (*damn*) **~ ...:** zum Teufel mit ... (*derb*); **~ you!** leck mich am Arsch! (*derb*); **[oh,] ~!**, **[oh,] ~ it!** [au,] Scheiße! (*derb*). ❷ *v.i.* ficken (*vulg.*) ❸ *n.* Ⓐ (*act*) Fick, *der* (*vulg.*); Ⓑ (*person*) **be a good ~:** gut ficken (*vulg.*); Ⓒ (*damn*) **I don't give/care a ~:** es ist mir scheißegal (*derb*)

**~ about, ~ around** (*coarse*) ❶ *v.i.* rumgammeln (*ugs.*); **~ about** *or* **around with sth.** an etw. (*Dat.*) rumfummeln (*ugs.*). ❷ *v.t.* verarschen (*derb*)

**~ 'off** *v.i.* (*coarse*) **~ off!** verpiss dich! (*salopp*)

**~ 'up** (*coarse*) *v.t.* versauen (*derb*)

**fucking** /ˈfʌkɪŋ/ (*coarse*) ❶ *adj.* Scheiß- (*salopp*); **what the ~ hell's that for?** wofür ist das denn, verdammte Scheiße? (*derb*). ❷ *adv.* verdammt (*ugs.*)

**fuddle** /ˈfʌdl/ *v.t.* Ⓐ (*intoxicate*) benebeln ‹Sinne›; **they were slightly ~d** sie waren [leicht] beschwipst *od.* angesäuselt (*ugs.*); Ⓑ (*confuse*) verwirren

**fuddy-duddy** /ˈfʌdɪdʌdɪ/ (*coll.*) ❶ *adj.* verkalkt (*ugs.*). ❷ *n.* Fossil, *das* (*fig.*)

**fudge¹** /fʌdʒ/ *n.* (*sweet*) Karamellbonbon, *der od. das;* [weiche] Karamelle, *die*

**fudge²** ❶ *v.t.* frisieren (*ugs.*) ‹Geschäftsbücher›; ausweichen (+ *Dat.*) ‹Problem›; sich (*Dat.*) aus den Fingern saugen ‹Ausrede, Geschichte, Entschuldigung›. ❷ *v.i.* ausweichen. ❸ *n.* Schwindel, *der*

**fuel** /ˈfjuːəl/ ❶ *n.* Brennstoff, *der;* (*for vehicle*) Kraftstoff, *der;* (*for ship, aircraft, spacecraft*) Treibstoff, *der;* (*for cigarette lighter*) Gas, *das;* (*petrol*) Benzin, *das;* (*Nucl. Engin.*) Kernbrennstoff, *der;* Spaltstoff, *der;* **add ~ to the flames** *or* **fire** (*fig.*) Öl ins Feuer gießen. ❷ *v.t.*, (*Brit.*) **-ll-** heizen ‹Ofen›; beschicken ‹Hochofen›; auftanken ‹Schiff, Flugzeug›; betreiben ‹Kraftwerk, Motor›; (*fig.: stimulate*) Nahrung geben (+ *Dat.*) ‹Verdacht, Hoffnung, Spekulationen›; anheizen ‹Inflation›; fördern ‹Entwicklung›. ❸ *v.i.*, (*Brit.*) **-ll-** auftanken

**fuel: ~ cell** *n.* Brennstoffzelle, *die;* **~ consumption** *n.* Brennstoffverbrauch, *der;* (*of vehicle*) Kraftstoffverbrauch, *der;* (*of aircraft, rocket*) Treibstoffverbrauch, *der;* **~-efficient** *adj.* sparsam ‹Motor, Auto usw.›; **~ element** *n.* (*Nucl. Engin.*) Brenn[stoff]element, *das;* **~ gauge** *n.* Kraftstoffanzeiger, *der;* **~ injection** *n.* Treibstoffeinspritzung, *die;* (*in vehicle*) Benzineinspritzung, *die;* **~ oil** *n.* Heizöl, *das;* **~ pump** *n.* Kraftstoffpumpe, *die;* **~ tank** *n.* (*of motorcycle, vehicle*) Kraftstofftank, *der;* (*of aircraft, spacecraft*) Treibstofftank, *der;* (*of ship*) Treiböltank, *der;* (*for storage*) Kraftstoffbehälter, *der*

**fug** /fʌg/ *n.* (*coll.*) Mief, *der* (*salopp*)

**fugitive** /ˈfjuːdʒɪtɪv/ ❶ *adj.* Ⓐ (*lit. or fig.*) flüchtig; Ⓑ (*flitting, shifting*) unstet ‹Wesen, Charakter›. ❷ *n.* Ⓐ Flüchtige, *der/die;* **be a ~ from justice/from the law** auf der Flucht vor der Justiz/dem Gesetz sein; Ⓑ (*exile*) Flüchtling, *der*

**fugue** /fjuːg/ *n.* (*Mus.*) Fuge, *die*

**fulcrum** /ˈfʊlkrəm/ *n.*, *pl.* **fulcra** /ˈfʊlkrə/ Ⓐ (*Mech.*) Drehpunkt, *der;* Ⓑ (*fig.: factor*) [Dreh- und] Angelpunkt, *der*

**fulfil** (*Amer.:* **fulfill**) /fʊlˈfɪl/ *v.t.*, **-ll-** erfüllen; stillen ‹Verlangen, Bedürfnisse›; entsprechen (+ *Dat.*) ‹Erwartungen›; erhören ‹Gebet›; ausführen ‹Befehl›; beenden ‹Arbeit, Werk›; halten ‹Versprechen›; **be fulfilled** ‹Traum:› in Erfüllung gehen; ‹Wunsch, Hoffnung, Prophezeiung:› sich erfüllen; **~ oneself** sich selbst verwirklichen; **be** *or* **feel fulfilled [in one's job]** [in seinem Beruf] Erfüllung finden

**fulfilling** /fʊlˈfɪlɪŋ/ *adj.* (*giving satisfaction*) befriedigend

**fulfilment** (*Amer.:* **fulfillment**) /fʊlˈfɪlmənt/ *n.* ⇒ **fulfil**: Erfüllung, *die;* Erhörung, *die;* Ausführung, *die;* Beendigung, *die;* **bring sth. to ~:** etw. erfüllen; **sth. reaches ~:** etw. erfüllt sich; **find ~ in one's work** Erfüllung in seiner Arbeit finden

**full¹** /fʊl/ ❶ *adj.* Ⓐ voll; **the jug is ~ of water** der Krug ist voll Wasser; **his pockets are ~ of money** er hat die Taschen voller Geld; **the bus was completely ~:** der Bus war voll besetzt; **~ of hatred/holes** voller Hass/Löcher; **my heart is too ~ for words** mir ist das Herz so voll, dass ich keine Worte finde; **be ~ up** voll [besetzt] sein; ‹Behälter:› randvoll sein; ‹Liste:› voll sein; ‹Flug:› völlig ausgebucht sein; Ⓑ **~ of** (*engrossed with*): **be ~ of oneself/one's own importance** sehr von sich eingenommen sein/sich sehr wichtig nehmen; **ever since this event she's been ~ of it** seit diesem Ereignis spricht sie von nichts anderem [mehr]; **the newspapers are ~ of the crisis** die Zeitungen sind voll von Berichten über die Krise; **he is ~ of his subject** er geht völlig in seinem Fachgebiet auf; Ⓒ (*replete with food*) voll ‹Magen›; satt ‹Person›; **I'm ~ [up]** (*coll.*) ich bin voll [bis obenhin] (*ugs.*); Ⓓ (*comprehensive*) ausführlich, umfassend ‹Bericht, Beschreibung›; (*abundant, satisfying*) vollwertig ‹Mahlzeit›; erfüllt ‹Leben›; (*complete*) geschlagen (*ugs.*), ganz ‹Stunde›; ganz ‹Jahr, Monat, Semester, Seite›; voll ‹Gehalt, Bezahlung, Unterstützung, Mitgefühl, Verständnis›; **weigh a ~ ten tons** volle zehn Tonnen wiegen; **the event received ~ TV coverage** das Fernsehen berichtete in aller Ausführlichkeit über das Ereignis; **with illustrations in ~ colour throughout** durchgehend farbig illustriert; **the ~ details of the case** alle Einzelheiten des Falls; **in ~ daylight** am helllichten Tag; **the moon is ~:** es ist Vollmond; **in ~ bloom** in voller Blüte; **they were in ~ flight** (*fleeing*) sie flohen, so schnell sie konnten; (*impressive*) sie waren in Hochform; **this will require a ~ day's work** dazu braucht man einen ganzen Tag; **~ member** Vollmitglied, *das;* **~ membership** Vollmitgliedschaft, *die;* **in ~ possession of one's faculties** im Vollbesitz seiner Kräfte; **in ~ view of sb.** [direkt] vor jmds. Augen; **we were in ~ view of the house** wir konnten vom Haus aus ohne weiteres gesehen werden; **the ship came into ~ view** man konnte das Schiff allmählich richtig sehen; **at ~ speed** mit Höchstgeschwindigkeit; **~ speed** *or* **steam ahead!** (*lit. or fig.*) volle Kraft *od.* Volldampf voraus!; **the machine was operating at ~ capacity** die Maschine lief auf Hochtouren; **the team/cabinet was at ~ strength** die Mannschaft spielte in ihrer besten Besetzung/das Kabinett war vollzählig; **bound in ~ leather** in Ganzleder gebunden; **pay the ~ fare** voll bezahlen; den vollen Fahrpreis bezahlen; **~ name** voller Name; **~ sister/brother** leibliche Schwester/leiblicher Bruder; Ⓔ (*intense in quality*) hell, voll ‹Licht›; satt ‹Farbe›; voll ‹Klang, Stimme, Aroma›; Ⓕ (*rounded, plump*) voll ‹Gesicht, Busen, Lippen, Mund, Segel›; füllig ‹Figur›; weit geschnitten ‹Rock›; **be ~ in the face** ein volles Gesicht haben.
❷ *n.* Ⓐ **in ~:** vollständig; **write your name [out] in ~:** schreiben Sie Ihren Namen aus; Ⓑ **satisfy sb./enjoy sth. to the ~:** jmdn. vollauf zufrieden stellen/etw. in vollen Zügen genießen; Ⓒ **the moon is at/past the ~:** es ist Vollmond/abnehmender Mond.
❸ *adv.* Ⓐ (*very*) **know ~ well that ...:** ganz genau *od.* sehr wohl wissen, dass ...; Ⓑ (*exactly, directly*) genau; voll (*ugs.*); **~ in the face** direkt ins Gesicht ‹schlagen, scheinen›; **look sb. ~ in the face** jmdn. voll ansehen

**full²** *v.t.* (*Textiles*) walken ‹Tuche›

**full: ~ 'age** *n.* Volljährigkeit, *die;* **~ back** *n.* (*Sport*) Verteidiger, *der*/Verteidigerin, *die;* **~-blooded** /ˈfʊlblʌdɪd/ *adj.* Ⓐ (*pure-bred*) reinrassig ‹Tier›; reinblütig ‹Mensch›; Ⓑ (*vigorous, hearty, sensual*) vollblütig; **~-blown** *adj.* Ⓐ (*at height of bloom*) voll aufgeblüht; Ⓑ (*fig.*) ausgewachsen ‹Skandal›; ausgereift ‹Theorie, Plan, Gedanke›; umfassend ‹Bericht›; **~-blown AIDS** Vollbild-Aids, *das;* **~ 'board** *n.* Vollpension, *die;* **~-bodied** *adj.* vollmundig, (*fachspr.*) körperreich ‹Wein›; voll ‹Ton, Klang›; **~-cream** *adj.* **~-cream milk/cheese** Vollmilch, *die*/Vollfettkäse, *der;* **~ 'dress** *n.* Gesellschaftsanzug, *der;* **~-dress** *adj.* Gala‹uniform, -diner›; (*fig.*) groß angelegt; **~-dress occasion** feierliche Veranstaltung; **~ em'ployment** *n.* Vollbeschäftigung, *die*

f

**fuller's earth** /fʊləz 'ɜ:θ/ *n.* (*Min.*) Fullererde, *die;* Walkerde, *die*

**full:** ~ **'face** *n.* (*Art, Photog.*) **in ~ face** en face; **~-face** ❶ *adv.* (*Art, Photog.*) en face; ❷ *adj.* [A] (*Art, Photog.*) En-face-; [B] **~-face helmet** Integralhelm, *der;* **~-faced** *adj.* mit vollem Gesicht *nachgestellt;* **~-grown** *adj.* ausgewachsen ‹Mensch, Tier›; **~ 'house** *n.* [A] (*Theatre*) ausverkauftes *od.* volles Haus; **play to ~ houses every night** jeden Abend vor ausverkauftem Haus spielen; [B] (*Poker*) Fullhouse, *das;* (*Bingo*) Voll, *das;* **~ 'length** ❶ *n.* **at ~ length** (*in ~ detail*) in aller Ausführlichkeit; (*unabridged*) ungekürzt; **[stretched out] at ~ length** der Länge nach *od.* (*ugs.*) längelang ausgestreckt; ❷ *adv.* längelang (*ugs.*), der Länge nach ‹hinfallen, liegen›; **~-length** *adj.* abendfüllend ‹Film, Theaterstück›; **~-length novel** größerer Roman; **~-length mirror** großer Spiegel (*in dem man sich ganz sehen kann*); **~-length portrait** Ganzporträt, *das;* **~-length dress** langes Kleid; **~ 'marks** *n. pl., no art.* die höchste Bewertung; (*Sch., Univ.*) die beste Note; **~ marks!** (*fig. coll.*) ausgezeichnet!; **you get ~ marks for observation** das hast du ausgezeichnet beobachtet; **give sb. ~ marks** (*fig.*) jmdm. höchstes Lob zollen; **~ 'moon** *n.* Vollmond, *der*

**fullness** /'fʊlnɪs/ *n., no pl.* (*of skirt*) weiter Schnitt; (*of figure*) Fülligkeit, *die;* (*of face*) Rundheit, *die;* **a feeling of ~:** ein Völlegefühl; **in the ~ of time** (*literary*) wenn die Zeit dafür gekommen ist/als die Zeit dafür gekommen war

**full:** **~-page** *adj.* ganzseitig; **~ pitch** ⇒ **~ toss;** **~ 'play** *n.* **give sth. ~ play** einer Sache (*Dat.*) freien Lauf lassen; **give sb. ~ play** jmdm. völlig freie Hand lassen; **~ 'point** Punkt, *der;* **~ pro'fessor** *n.* ordentlicher Professor; **~-scale** *adj.* [A] in Originalgröße *nachgestellt;* [B] groß angelegt ‹Werbekampagne, Untersuchung, Suchaktion›; umfassend ‹Umarbeitung, Revision›; **a ~-scale war/novel** ein richtiger Krieg/größerer Roman; **~ 'score** *n.* (*Mus.*) Partitur, *die;* **~-size, ~-sized** *adjs.* [A] (*standard-size*) normal groß; **~-size trees** ausgewachsene *od.* große Bäume; **~-size bottle** große Flasche; [B] (*not scaled down*) in Originalgröße *postpos.;* **~-size portrait** lebensgroßes Porträt; Porträt in Lebensgröße; **~ 'stop** *n.* [A] Punkt, *der;* [B] (*fig. coll.*) **come to a ~ stop** zum Stillstand kommen; **I'm not going, ~ stop** ich gehe nicht, [und damit] basta! (*ugs.*); **~ 'time** ❶ *adv.* ganztags ‹arbeiten›; ❷ *n.* (*Sport*) Spielende, *das;* **~-time** *adj.* ganztägig; Ganztags‹arbeit, -beschäftigung›; **sb. is ~-time** jmd. arbeitet ganztags; **~-time teacher** Lehrer mit vollem Deputat; **this is a ~-time job** (*fig.*) das hält einen den ganzen Tag auf Trab (*ugs.*); **~-'timer** *n.* Ganztagsbeschäftigte, *der/die;* **become a ~-timer** anfangen, ganztags zu arbeiten; **~ 'toss** (*Cricket*) *n.: Ball, der den Schlagmann erreicht, ohne den Boden zu berühren*

**fully** /'fʊlɪ/ *adv.* [A] voll [und ganz]; fest ‹entschlossen›; reich ‹belohnt›; ausführlich ‹erklären usw.›; **~ convinced** restlos überzeugt; [B] (*at least*) **~ two hours** volle zwei Stunden; **~ three weeks ago** vor gut drei Wochen

**fully:** **~-fledged** *attrib. adj.* flügge ‹Vogel›; (*fig.*) [ganz] selbstständig; **~-qualified** *attrib. adj.* vollqualifiziert

**fulmar** /'fʊlmə(r)/ *n.* (*Ornith.*) Eissturmvogel, *der*

**fulminate** /'fʌlmɪneɪt/ *v.i.* (*protest*) **~ against sb./sth.** gegen jmdn./etw. Sturm laufen

**fulsome** /'fʊlsəm/ *adj.* übertrieben, (*ugs. abwertend*) dick aufgetragen ‹Lob, Kompliment, Schmeichelei›

**fulsomely** /'fʊlsəmlɪ/ *adv.* übertrieben ‹loben, schmeicheln›

**fumble** /'fʌmbl/ ❶ *v.i.* **~ at** *or* **with** [herum]fingern an (+ *Dat.*); **~ with one's papers** in seinen Papieren kramen (*ugs.*); **~ in one's pockets for sth.** in seinen Taschen nach etw. fingern *od.* (*ugs.*) kramen; **~ for the light switch** nach dem Lichtschalter tasten; **~ [about** *or* **around] in the dark** im Dunkeln herumtasten; **~ [about] for the right words** (*fig.*) nach den richtigen Worten suchen. ❷ *v.t.* [A] nesteln an (+ *Dat.*); [B] (*Games*) nicht sicher fangen ‹Ball›

**fume** /fju:m/ ❶ *n.* [A] *in pl.* (*from car exhaust*) Abgase *Pl.;* **petrol/ammonia ~s** Benzin-/Ammoniakdämpfe *Pl.;* **~s of wine/whisky** Alkohol-/Whiskydunst, *der;* **[cigarette/cigar] ~s** [Zigaretten-/Zigarren]rauch, *der;* [B] (*fit of anger*); **be in a ~:** vor Wut schäumen. ❷ *v.i.* [A] ‹Feuer, Ofen:› rauchen; [B] (*be angry*) vor Wut schäumen; **~ at** *or* **over sb.** auf *od.* über jmdn. wütend sein; **~ at** *or* **over** *or* **about sth.** wegen etw. wütend sein. ❸ *v.t.* **~d oak** geräuchertes Eichenholz (*Holzverarb.*)

**fumigate** /'fju:mɪgeɪt/ *v.t.* [A] ausräuchern; [B] (*apply fumes to*) begasen ‹Pflanzen›

**fumigation** /fju:mɪ'geɪʃn/ *n.* ⇒ **fumigate**: Ausräucherung, *die;* Begasung, *die*

**fun** /fʌn/ ❶ *n.* Spaß, *der;* **be half the ~:** [mit] das Schönste sein; **have ~ doing sth.** Spaß daran haben, etw. zu tun; **I/we had great ~ playing with the dog** es hat [mir/uns] viel Spaß gemacht, mit dem Hund zu spielen; **have ~!** viel Spaß!; **[are you] having ~?** (*iron.*) macht Spaß, was? (*ugs. iron.*); **we'll have great ~:** es wird bestimmt sehr lustig; **I was just having a bit of ~:** ich habe nur Spaß gemacht; **be full of ~:** ein fröhliches Wesen haben; ‹Tier:› sehr verspielt sein; **make ~ of** *or* **poke ~ at sb./sth.** sich über jmdn./etw. lustig machen; **in ~:** im Spaß; **the things he said were only in ~:** was er gesagt hat, war nur Spaß; **for ~, for the ~ of it** zum Spaß; **what ~!** toll!; wie schön!; **spoil the** *or* **sb.'s ~:** jmdm. den Spaß verderben; **sounds like ~!** das wird sicher toll werden!; **like ~** (*very much*) wie verrückt (*salopp*); (*iron.: not at all*) von wegen!; **sth. is [good** *or* **great/no] ~:** etw. macht [großen/keinen] Spaß; **he is [good** *or* **great] ~ to have at a party** eine Party mit ihm ist immer sehr lustig; **sb. is [great] ~/no ~ to be with** es macht [großen] Spaß/keinen Spaß, mit jmdm. zusammen zu sein; **it's no ~ being unemployed** es ist kein Vergnügen, arbeitslos zu sein; **~ and games** (*coll.*) Vergnügungen *Pl.;* **we had the usual ~ and games with him** (*iron.: trouble*) wir hatten wieder das übliche Theater mit ihm (*ugs.*); **enjoy** *or* **have the ~ of the fair** (*fig.*) sich vergnügen; ⇒ *also* **figure** 1 D. ❷ *adj.* (*coll.*) lustig; amüsant; **have a ~ time at a party** sich auf einer Party gut amüsieren

**function** /'fʌŋkʃn/ ❶ *n.* [A] (*role*) Aufgabe, *die;* **in his ~ as surgeon** in seiner Funktion *od.* Eigenschaft als Chirurg; [B] (*mode of action*) Funktion, *die;* [C] (*formal event*) Veranstaltung, *die;* (*reception*) Empfang, *der;* (*official ceremony*) Feierlichkeit, *die;* [D] (*Math.*) Funktion, *die.* ❷ *v.i.* ‹Maschine, System, Organisation:› funktionieren; ‹Organ:› arbeiten; **~ as** (*have the ~ of*) fungieren als; (*serve as*) dienen als; **I just don't ~ early in the morning** (*coll.*) am frühen Morgen bin ich zu nichts zu gebrauchen

**functional** /'fʌŋkʃənl/ *adj.* [A] (*useful, practical*) funktionell; funktional ‹Erziehung›; **~ building** Zweckbau, *der;* [B] (*working*) funktionsfähig; **be ~ again** wieder funktionieren; [C] (*Physiol.*) **~ disease** Funktionsstörung eines Organs

**functionalism** /'fʌŋkʃənəlɪzm/ *n.* Funktionalismus, *der*

**functionally** /'fʌŋkʃənəlɪ/ *adv.* funktionell

**functionary** /'fʌŋkʃənərɪ/ *n.* Funktionär, *der*/Funktionärin, *die*

**function:** **~ key** *n.* (*Computing*) Funktionstaste, *die;* **~ word** *n.* Funktionswort, *das*

**fund** /fʌnd/ ❶ *n.* [A] (*collection of money*) Fonds, *der;* [B] (*fig.: stock, store*) Fundus, *der* (**of** von, an + *Dat.*); [C] *in pl.* (*resources*) Mittel *Pl.;* Gelder *Pl.;* **public ~s** öffentliche Mittel; **be in ~s** bei Kasse sein (*ugs.*); **be pressed for** *or* **short of ~s** knapp *od.* schlecht bei Kasse sein (*ugs.*). ❷ *v.t.* [A] finanzieren; [B] (*invest*) anlegen; investieren

**fundamental** /fʌndə'mentl/ ❶ *adj.* [A] grundlegend (**to** für); fundamental, grundlegend ‹Unterschied, Bedeutung, Bestandteil›; elementar ‹Bedürfnisse›; (*primary, original*) Grund‹struktur, -form, -typus›; [B] (*Mus.*) **~ note** Grundton, *der;* (*Acoustics*) **~ tone** Grundton, *der.* ❷ *n.* [A] *in pl.* Grundlage, *die;* Fundament, *das;* [B] (*Mus.*) (*note*) Grundton, *der;* (*tone*) Fundamentalbass, *der*

**fundamentalism** /fʌndə'mentəlɪzm/ *n.* Fundamentalismus, *der*

**fundamentalist** /fʌndə'mentəlɪst/ *n.* Fundamentalist, *der*/Fundamentalistin, *die*

**fundamentally** /fʌndə'mentəlɪ/ *adv.* grundlegend; von Grund auf ‹verschieden, ehrlich›; völlig ‹abhängig›; **I am ~ opposed to this** ich bin grundsätzlich dagegen; **man is ~ good/evil** der Mensch ist von Natur aus gut/böse

**fundamental 'particle** ⇒ **elementary particle**

**fund:** **~holder** *n.* (*Brit.*) *praktischer Arzt mit eigenständig verwaltetem Budget;* **~holding** (*Brit.*) ❶ *adj.* **~ practitioner** praktischer Arzt mit eigenständig verwaltetem Budget; **~ practice** [Arzt]praxis mit eigenständig verwaltetem Budget; ❷ *n.* Eigenbudgetierung, *die*

**funding** /'fʌndɪŋ/ *n., no pl., no indef. art.* [A] (*providing funds*) Finanzierung, *die;* [B] (*resources*) Finanzierungsmittel *Pl.*

**fund:** **~ manager** *n.* Fondsverwalter, *der*/-verwalterin, *die;* Fondsmanager, *der*/-managerin, *die* (*fachspr.*); **~-raiser** /'fʌndreɪzə(r)/ *n.* [A] (*person*) Geldbeschaffer, *der*/-beschafferin, *die;* [B] (*event*) Benefizveranstaltung, *die;* **~-raising** /'fʌndreɪzɪŋ/ *n., no pl.* Geldbeschaffung, *die; attrib.* zur Geldbeschaffung *nachgestellt*

**funeral** /'fju:nərl/ *n.* [A] Beerdigung, *die;* Beisetzung, *die* (*geh.*); [B] (*procession*) Leichenzug, *der* (*geh.*); Trauerzug, *der;* [C] *attrib.* **~ director** ▶ 1261 Bestattungsunternehmer, *der;* **~ home** (*Amer.*) *or* **parlour** Bestattungsunternehmen, *das;* **~ march** Trauermarsch, *der;* **~ procession** Leichenzug, *der* (*geh.*) Trauerzug, *der;* **~ service** Trauerfeier, *die;* **~ pile** *or* **pyre** Scheiterhaufen, *der;* **~ expenses** Bestattungskosten *Pl.;* [D] (*coll.: one's concern*) **that's his/not my ~:** das ist sein/nicht mein Problem; [E] (*Amer.: service*) Trauerfeier, *die;* **preach sb.'s ~:** die Trauerfeier für jmdn. abhalten

**funereal** /fju:'nɪərɪəl/ *adj.* [A] (*of funeral*) Trauer-; [B] (*gloomy*) düster; **~ voice** Grabesstimme, *die* (*ugs.*); **~ expression** Trauermiene, *die* (*ugs.*); trauervolle Miene; **~ pace** Geschwindigkeit eines Trauerzuges

**'funfair** *n.* (*Brit.*) Jahrmarkt, *der*

**fungal** /'fʌŋgl/ ⇒ **fungous**

**fungicide** /'fʌndʒɪsaɪd/ *n.* (*Hort.*) Fungizid, *das;* (*Pharm.*) Antimykotikum, *das*

**fungous** /'fʌŋgəs/ *adj.* pilzartig; (*Med.*) Hautpilz-; **~ infection** Pilzinfektion, *die*

**fungus** /'fʌŋgəs/ *n., pl.* **fungi** /'fʌŋgaɪ, 'fʌndʒaɪ/ *or* **~es** [A] Pilz, *der;* [B] (*Med.*) Hautpilz, *der;* [C] (*disease of fish*) Fischschimmel, *der;* [D] (*coll.: beard*) **[face] ~:** Sauerkohl, *der* (*salopp scherzh.*)

**funicular [railway]** /fju:'nɪkjʊlə(r) (reɪlweɪ)/ *n.* [Stand]seilbahn, *die*

**funk** /fʌŋk/ (*coll.*) ❶ *n.* Bammel, *der* (*salopp*); Schiss, *der* (*salopp*); **be in/go into a [blue] ~:** [mächtig] Bammel *od.* Schiss haben/kriegen (*salopp*); **put sb. in a [blue] ~:** jmdm. Angst einjagen. ❷ *v.t.* kneifen vor (+ *Dat.*) (*ugs.*); **he ~ed it** er hat gekniffen (*ugs.*)

**funky** /'fʌŋkɪ/ *adj.* (*coll.*) irre (*salopp*) ‹Musik›

**'fun-loving** *adj.* lebenslustig

**funnel** /'fʌnl/ ❶ *n.* [A] (*cone*) Trichter, *der;* [B] (*of ship etc.*) Schornstein, *der.* ❷ *v.t.,* (*Brit.*) **-ll-** konzentrieren ‹Aufmerksamkeit, Anstrengung, Bemühungen›; schleusen ‹Daten, Verkehr›; lenken ‹Verkehr›. ❸ *v.i.,* (*Brit.*) **-ll-** strömen

**funnily** /'fʌnɪlɪ/ *adv.* komisch; **~ enough** komischerweise (*ugs.*)

**funny** /'fʌnɪ/ ❶ *adj.* [A] (*comical*) komisch; lustig; witzig ‹Person, Einfall, Bemerkung›; **are you being** *or* **trying to be ~?** das soll wohl ein Witz sein?; [B] (*strange*) komisch; seltsam;

**don't get any ~ ideas** (*coll.*) komm bloß nicht auf komische Gedanken! (*ugs.*); **be ~ about money** in Gelddingen komisch *od.* eigen sein; **that's ~, he's gone** komisch, er ist weg; **the ~ thing 'is that ...:** das Komische [daran] ist, dass ...; **have a ~ feeling that ...:** das komische Gefühl haben, dass ...; **there's something ~ going on here** hier ist doch was faul (*ugs.*); [C] (*coll.: unwell*) **I feel ~:** mir ist komisch *od.* (*ugs.*) blümerant; **he's a bit ~ in the head** er ist nicht ganz richtig im Kopf (*ugs.*).
❷ *n.* (*coll.*) [A] *in pl.* (*comic section*) Comicseite, *die;* [B] (*joke*) Witz, *der*

**funny: ~ bone** *n.* (*Anat.*) Musikantenknochen, *der;* **~ business** *n.* [A] (*comic behaviour*) Alberei, *die;* [B] (*coll.: misbehaviour, deception*) krumme Touren (*ugs.*); **~-face** *n.* (*joc./coll.*) Krümel, *der* (*fam.*); **~-ha-'ha** *adj.* (*coll.*) [zum Lachen] komisch; **~ man** *n.* Komiker, *der;* **~-pe'culiar** *adj.* (*coll.*) seltsam

**fur** /fɜː(r)/ ❶ *n.* [A] (*coat of animal*) Fell, *das;* (*for or as garment*) Pelz, *der;* **trimmed/lined with ~:** mit Pelz besetzt *od.* verbrämt/gefüttert; **make the ~ fly** (*fig.*) hohe Wellen schlagen; *attrib.* **~ coat/hat** Pelzmantel, *der*/-mütze, *die;* **~ rug** Fell, *das* (*als Vorleger*); [B] (*coating*) Belag, *der;* (*formed by hard water*) Wasserstein, *der;* (*in kettle*) Kesselstein, *der.* ❷ *v.t.*, **-rr-: hard water will ~ [up] the kettle/pipes** bei hartem Wasser bildet sich Kesselstein im Kessel/Wasserstein in den Rohren. ❸ *v.i.*, **-rr-: the kettle has/pipes have ~red [up]** im Kessel hat sich Kesselstein/in den Rohren hat sich Wasserstein gebildet

**furbelow** /ˈfɜːbɪləʊ/ *n.* **frills and ~s** (*lit. or fig.*) Kinkerlitzchen *Pl.* (*ugs. abwertend*)

**furbish** /ˈfɜːbɪʃ/ *v.t.* blank reiben; polieren

**'fur-clad** *adj.* in Pelz gekleidet

**furious** /ˈfjʊərɪəs/ *adj.* wütend; heftig ‹Streit, Kampf, Sturm, Lärm›; wild ‹Tanz, Sturm, Tempo, Kampf›; **be ~ with sb./at sth.** wütend auf jmdn./über etw. (*Akk.*) sein; **the fun was fast and ~:** der Spaß war in vollem Gange

**furiously** /ˈfjʊərɪəslɪ/ *adv.* wütend; wild ‹kämpfen, tanzen›; wie wild (*ugs.*) ‹arbeiten, in die Pedale treten›; heftig ‹erröten, kämpfen›

**furl** /fɜːl/ *v.t.* einrollen ‹Segel, Flagge›; zusammenrollen ‹Schirm›

**furlong** /ˈfɜːlɒŋ/ *n.* Achtelmeile, *die*

**furlough** /ˈfɜːləʊ/ *n.* (*Mil.*) Urlaub, *der;* **be/go on ~:** Urlaub haben/in Urlaub gehen

**furnace** /ˈfɜːnɪs/ *n.* Ofen, *der;* (*blast-~*) Hochofen, *der;* (*smelting ~*) Schmelzofen, *der;* (*pottery-kiln*) Brennofen, *der;* **this room is like a ~:** hier ist eine Hitze wie im Treibhaus *od.* Backofen

**furnish** /ˈfɜːnɪʃ/ *v.t.* [A] möblieren; **live in ~ed accommodation** möbliert wohnen; **~ing fabrics** Möbel- und Vorhangstoffe *Pl.;* [B] (*provide, supply*) liefern ‹Vorräte›; **~ sb. with sth.** jmdm. etw. liefern; **the army was ~ed with supplies** die Armee wurde mit Vorräten versorgt *od.* beliefert

**furnishings** /ˈfɜːnɪʃɪŋz/ *n. pl.* Einrichtungsgegenstände *Pl.;* **including ~ and fittings** mit kompletter Einrichtung

**furniture** /ˈfɜːnɪtʃə(r)/ *n., no pl.* Möbel *Pl.;* **piece of ~:** Möbel[stück], *das;* **the house has hardly any ~:** das Haus ist kaum eingerichtet; **a bed and a chair were all the ~:** ein Bett und ein Stuhl waren das ganze Mobiliar; **be [a] part of the ~** (*fig. coll.*) zum lebenden Inventar gehören (*scherzh.*)

**furniture: ~ beetle** *n.* Totenuhr, *die;* **~ polish** *n.* Möbelpolitur, *die;* **~ van** *n.* Möbelwagen, *der*

**furore** /fjʊəˈrɔːrɪ/ (*Amer.:* **furor** /ˈfjʊərɔː(r)/) *n.* **create** *or* **cause a ~:** Furore machen; (*cause a scandal*) einen Skandal verursachen; **when the ~ died down** als allmählich Gras über die Sache gewachsen war

**furred** /fɜːd/ *adj.* (*Med.*) belegt ‹Zunge›

**furrier** /ˈfʌrɪə(r)/ *n.* ▶ **1261** (*dresser*) Kürschner, *der*/Kürschnerin, *die;* (*dealer*) Pelzhändler, *der*/-händlerin, *die*

**furrow** /ˈfʌrəʊ/ ❶ *n.* (*lit. or fig.*) Furche, *die;* **cut a ~ through the waves** ‹Schiff:› die Wellen durchpflügen; ⇒ *also* **plough** 2 C. ❷ *v.t.* [A] (*plough*) pflügen; [B] (*make ~s in*) durchpflügen; [C] (*mark with wrinkles*) **~ed face** zerfurchtes Gesicht

**furry** /ˈfɜːrɪ/ *adj.* haarig; flauschig ‹Mantel, Stofftier›; belegt ‹Zunge›; **~ animal** (*toy*) Plüschtier, *das;* **it has a ~ feel** es fühlt sich weich und flauschig an

**further** /ˈfɜːðə(r)/ ❶ *adj. compar. of* **far** [A] ▶ **1079** (*of two*) ander...; (*in space*) weiter entfernt; **on the ~ bank of the river/side of town** am anderen Ufer/Ende der Stadt; [B] (*additional*) weiter...; **till ~ notice/orders** bis auf weiteres; **I could eat this until ~ orders** (*fig. joc.*) ich könnte das bis in alle Ewigkeit essen (*ugs.*); **will there be anything ~?** darf es noch etwas sein?; haben Sie sonst noch einen Wunsch?; **~ details** *or* **particulars** weitere *od.* nähere Einzelheiten.
❷ *adv. compar. of* **far** [A] weiter; **before it goes any ~:** bevor es sich weiter ausbreitet; **not let it go any ~:** es nicht weitersagen; **one could go ~ and fare worse** es gibt Schlimmeres; **he never got ~ than secondary school** er ist über die Hauptschule nicht hinausgekommen; **until you hear ~ from us** bis Sie wieder von uns hören; **nothing was ~ from his thoughts** nichts lag ihm ferner; [B] (*moreover*) außerdem; [C] (*euphem.: in hell*) **I'll see you/him *etc.* ~ first!** ich denke nicht im Traum daran!
❸ *v.t.* fördern; **in order to ~ one's career** um beruflich voranzukommen

**furtherance** /ˈfɜːðərəns/ *n., no pl.* Förderung, *die;* Unterstützung, *die;* **in ~ of sth.** zur Förderung *od.* Unterstützung einer Sache (*Gen.*)

**further edu'cation** *n.* Weiterbildung, *die;* (*for adults also*) Erwachsenenbildung, *die*

**furthermore** /fɜːðəˈmɔː(r)/ *adv.* außerdem; überdies

**furthermost** /ˈfɜːðəməʊst/ *adj.* äußerst...; entlegenst...; **to the ~ ends of the earth** bis ans Ende der Welt

**furthest** /ˈfɜːðɪst/ ❶ *adj. superl. of* **far** am weitesten entfernt; **take sb. to ~ Siberia** jmdn. ins hinterste Sibirien bringen; **to the ~ limits of the kingdom** bis in die entlegensten *od.* entferntesten Winkel des Königreichs; **ten miles at the ~:** höchstens zehn Meilen. ❷ *adv. superl. of* **far** am weitesten ‹springen, laufen›; am weitesten entfernt ‹sein, wohnen›

**furtive** /ˈfɜːtɪv/ *adj.* verstohlen; **the fox is ~ in its movements** der Fuchs bewegt sich unauffällig; **he is a ~ person** er wirkt schuldbewusst und bemüht, nicht aufzufallen

**furtively** /ˈfɜːtɪvlɪ/ *adv.* verstohlen

**fury** /ˈfjʊərɪ/ *n.* [A] Wut, *die;* (*of storm, sea, battle, war*) Wüten, *das;* **in a ~:** wütend; **in a terrible ~:** in heller Wut; **in a blind ~:** blindwütig; **fly into a/be in a ~:** einen Wutanfall bekommen/haben; **exposed to the ~ of the elements** dem Wüten der Elemente ausgeliefert; [B] **like ~** (*coll.*) wie wild (*ugs.*); [C] **Furies** (*Mythol.*) Furien *Pl.;* **[avenging] furies** Rachegeister *Pl.*

**furze** /fɜːz/ *n.* (*Brit. Bot.*) Stechginster, *der*

**fuse[1]** /fjuːz/ ❶ *v.t.* [A] (*blend*) verschmelzen (**into** zu); [B] (*melt*) schmelzen. ❷ *v.i.* [A] (*blend*) **~ together** miteinander verschmelzen; **~ with sth.** (*fig.*) sich mit etw. verbinden; [B] (*melt*) schmelzen

**fuse[2]** ❶ *n.* **[time] ~:** [Zeit]zünder, *der;* (*cord*) Zündschnur, *die;* **be on a short ~** (*fig.*) leicht explodieren (*fig.*). ❷ *v.t.* **~ a bomb** *etc.* einen Zünder an einer Bombe *usw.* anbringen

**fuse[3]** (*Electr.*) ❶ *n.* Sicherung, *die.* ❷ *v.t.* [A] **~ the lights** die Sicherung [für die Lampen] durchbrennen lassen; [B] (*provide with ~*) mit einer Sicherung versehen; absichern. ❸ *v.i.* **the lights have ~d** die Sicherung [für die Lampen] ist durchgebrannt

**'fuse box** *n.* (*Electr.*) Sicherungskasten, *der*

**fuselage** /ˈfjuːzəlɑːʒ/ *n.* (*Aeronaut.*) [Flugzeug]rumpf, *der*

**fusible** /ˈfjuːzɪbl/ *adj.* schmelzbar

**fusillade** /fjuːzɪˈleɪd/ *n.* Gewehrfeuer, *das*

**fusion** /ˈfjuːʒn/ *n.* [A] (*blending*) Verschmelzung, *die;* (*fig.*) (*of political groups, enterprises*) Verbindung, *die;* Fusion, *die;* (*of ideas, ideologies, races*) Verschmelzung, *die;* [B] (*melting*) Schmelzen, *das;* [C] (*Phys.*) Fusion, *die*

**fuss** /fʌs/ ❶ *n.* Theater, *das* (*ugs.*); **stop this silly ~:** hör mit dem Theater auf! (*ugs.*); **~ and bother** Rummel, *der* (*ugs.*); **without any ~:** ohne großes Theater (*ugs.*); **kick up a ~:** ein großes Theater machen; **make a ~ [about sth.]** Aufhebens [von etw.] *od.* einen Wirbel [um etw.] machen; **make a ~ of** *or* **over** [einen] Wirbel machen um ‹Person, Tier›; **he is made a ~ of** um ihn wird Wirbel gemacht. ❷ *v.i.* Wirbel machen; (*get agitated*) sich [unnötig] aufregen; **she is always ~ing over sb./sth.** sie macht immer ein Theater mit jmdm./etw. (*ugs.*). ❸ *v.t.* **don't ~ me!** mach mich nicht verrückt! (*ugs.*)

**fussily** /ˈfʌsɪlɪ/ *adv.* [A] (*bustlingly*) übereifrig; rührig; [B] (*fastidiously*) mäklig (*ugs.*); [C] (*with undue detail*) überladen

**'fusspot** *n.* (*coll.*) **be a ~:** Theater machen (*ugs.*); **don't be a ~:** mach kein Theater! (*ugs.*)

**fussy** /ˈfʌsɪ/ *adj.* [A] (*bustling*) übereifrig; rührig; (*easily flustered*) reizbar; überempfindlich; **don't be so ~!** mach nicht so ein Theater! (*ugs.*); [B] (*fastidious*) eigen; penibel; **be ~ about one's food** *or* **what one eats** mäklig im Essen sein (*ugs.*); **I'm not ~** (*in answer: I don't mind*) ich bin nicht wählerisch; [C] (*full of undue detail*) überladen; (*full of unnecessary decoration*) verspielt

**fusty** /ˈfʌstɪ/ *adj.* [A] (*mouldy*) schimmelig; [B] (*stuffy*) muffig; [C] (*old-fashioned*) verstaubt

**futile** /ˈfjuːtaɪl/ *adj.* vergeblich ‹Versuch, Bemühungen, Vorschlag usw.›; zum Scheitern verurteilt ‹Plan, Vorgehen usw.›

**futilely** /ˈfjuːtaɪllɪ/ *adv.* vergeblich

**futility** /fjuːˈtɪlɪtɪ/ *n., no pl.* (*of effort, attempt, etc.*) Vergeblichkeit, *die;* (*of plan*) Zwecklosigkeit, *die;* (*of war*) Sinnlosigkeit, *die*

**futon** /ˈfuːtɒn/ *n.* Futon, *der*

**future** /ˈfjuːtʃə(r)/ ❶ *adj.* [A] [zu]künftig; **at some ~ date** zu einem späteren Zeitpunkt; [B] (*Ling.*) futurisch; **~ tense** Futur, *das;* Zukunft, *die;* ⇒ *also* **perfect** 1 H; [C] **the ~ life** das Leben im Jenseits; das Leben nach dem Tod.
❷ *n.* [A] Zukunft, *die;* **sth. is a thing of the ~:** etw. ist Zukunftsmusik; **what will her ~ be?** wie wird ihre Zukunft aussehen?; **a man with a ~:** ein Mann mit Zukunft; **in ~:** in Zukunft; künftig; **in the distant ~:** in ferner Zukunft; **sth. is still very much in the ~:** etw. liegt noch in weiter Ferne; **see sb. in the near ~:** jmdn. demnächst sehen; **there's no/little ~ in it** das hat keine/wenig Zukunft; [B] (*Ling.*) Futur, *das;* Zukunft, *die;* [C] *in pl.* (*Commerc.*) Terminware, *die;* (*contracts*) Lieferungsverträge *Pl.*

**future 'shock** *n.* Zukunftsschock, *der*

**futurism** /ˈfjuːtʃərɪzm/ *n.* Futurismus, *der*

**futuristic** /fjuːtʃəˈrɪstɪk/ *adj.* futuristisch

**futurology** /fjuːtʃəˈrɒlədʒɪ/ *n.* Futurologie, *die*

**fuze** (*Amer.*) ⇒ **fuse[2]**

**fuzz** /fʌz/ *n.* [A] (*fluff*) Flaum, *der;* [B] (*frizzy hair*) Kraushaar, *das;* **a ~ of black curls** schwarzes Kraushaar; [C] *no pl.* (*sl.*) (*police*) Polente, *die* (*salopp*); (*policeman*) Polyp, *der* (*salopp*)

**fuzzy** /ˈfʌzɪ/ *adj.* [A] (*like fuzz*) flaumig; [B] (*frizzy*) kraus; wuschelig (*ugs.*); [C] (*blurred*) verschwommen; unscharf

**fuzzy-wuzzy** /ˈfʌzɪwʌzɪ/ *n.* (*sl. derog.*) Krauskopf, *der*

f

# G g

g

**G, g** /dʒiː/ *n., pl.* **Gs** *or* **G's** Ⓐ (*letter*) G, g, *das;* Ⓑ **G** (*Mus.*) G, g, *das;* **G sharp** gis, Gis, *das;* **G flat** ges, Ges, *das*

**g.** *abbr.* Ⓐ ▶ 1683 **gram[s]** g; Ⓑ **gravity** *g*

**gab** /gæb/ (*coll.*) ❶ *n.* Gequatsche, *das* (*ugs. abwertend*); **have the gift of the ~:** reden können. ❷ *v.i.*, **-bb-** quatschen (*salopp*)

**gabardine** /ˈgæbədiːn/ *n.* Gabardine, *der;* **~ [coat/suit]** Gabardinemantel/-anzug, *der*

**gabble** /ˈgæbl/ ❶ *v.i.* (*inarticulately*) brabbeln (*ugs.*); (*volubly*) schnattern (*fig.*). ❷ *v.t.* herunterschnurren (*salopp*) ‹Gebet, Gedicht›; herunterhaspeln (*ugs.*) ‹Entschuldigung›. ❸ *n.* Gebrabbel, *das* (*ugs.*)

**gable** /ˈgeɪbl/ *n.* Ⓐ Giebel, *der;* Ⓑ ⇒ **gable-end**

**gabled** /ˈgeɪbld/ *adj.* gegiebelt; Giebel‹dach, -haus›

**ˈgable end** *n.* Giebelseite, *die*

**Gabon** /gəˈbɒn/ *pr. n.* Gabun (*das*)

**gad[1]** /gæd/ *int.* **[by] ~!** bei Gott!

**gad[2]** *v.i.*, **-dd-** (*coll.*) **~ about** *or* **around** herumziehen; sich herumtreiben (*ugs. abwertend*); **~ about** *or* **around the country** im Land herumreisen

**ˈgadabout** (*coll.*) *n.* Herumtreiber, *der*/ -treiberin, *die* (*ugs. abwertend*)

**ˈgadfly** *n.* Bremse, *die*

**gadget** /ˈgædʒɪt/ *n.* Gerät, *das;* (*larger*) Apparat, *der;* **~s** (*derog.: knick-knack*) [technischer] Krimskrams (*ugs.*)

**gadgetry** /ˈgædʒɪtrɪ/ *n., no pl.* [hoch technisierte] Ausstattung

**Gael** /geɪl/ *n.* Gäle, *der*/Gälin, *die*

**Gaelic** /ˈgeɪlɪk, ˈgælɪk/ ▶ 1275 ❶ *adj.* gälisch; ⇒ *also* **English** 1. ❷ *n.* Gälisch, *das;* ⇒ *also* **English** 2 A

**Gaelic ˈcoffee** *n.* Irish coffee, *der*

**gaff[1]** /gæf/ ❶ *n.* Ⓐ (*Fishing*) Speer, *der;* (*stick with iron hook*) Gaff, *das;* Ⓑ (*Naut.*) Gaffel, *die.* ❷ *v.t.* mit dem Speer/Gaff erlegen

**gaff[2]** *n.* (*coll.*) **blow the ~:** plaudern (**on** über + *Akk.*); **I'm not going to blow the ~:** ich werde dichthalten (*ugs.*); **stand the ~** (*Amer.*) durchhalten; **stand the ~ for sth.** etw. büßen

**gaffe** /gæf/ *n.* Fauxpas, *der;* Fehler, *der;* **make** *or* **commit a ~:** einen Fauxpas begehen; ins Fettnäpfchen treten (*ugs. scherzh.*)

**gaffer** /ˈgæfə(r)/ *n.* (*coll.*) Ⓐ (*old fellow*) Alte, *der;* **some old ~:** so'n alter Typ (*ugs.*); Ⓑ (*Brit.: boss*) Boss *der* (*ugs.*)

**gag** /gæg/ ❶ *n.* Ⓐ Knebel, *der;* (*Med.*) Mundsperrer, *der;* Ⓑ (*joke*) Gag, *der.* ❷ *v.t.*, **-gg-** Ⓐ **~ sb.** jmdn. knebeln; (*Med.*) jmdm. einen Mundsperrer anlegen; (*fig.: silence sb.*) jmdn. zum Schweigen bringen; Ⓑ (*cause to choke or retch*) **~ sb.** jmdn. würgen. ❸ *v.i.*, **-gg-** Ⓐ Späße machen; witzeln; Ⓑ (*choke, retch*) würgen

**gaga** /ˈgɑːgɑː/ *adj.* (*coll.*) übergeschnappt (*ugs.*); (*senile*) senil, (*ugs.*) verkalkt; **be [a bit] ~:** nicht mehr ganz dicht sein (*ugs.*); **go ~:** überschnappen (*ugs.*); (*become senile*) senil werden, (*ugs.*) verkalken; **she is really ~ about him** sie ist total vernarrt in ihn (*ugs.*)

**gage** (*Amer./Naut.*) ⇒ **gauge**

**gaggle** /ˈgægl/ *n.* Ⓐ **~ [of geese]** Schar [Gänse], *die;* Ⓑ (*fig.: disorderly group*) Schwarm, *der;* Pulk, *der*

**gaiety** /ˈgeɪətɪ/ *n., no pl.* Ⓐ Fröhlichkeit, *die;* Ⓑ (*merrymaking*) Festivität, *die;* Vergnügung, *die*

**gaily** /ˈgeɪlɪ/ *adv.* Ⓐ (*merrily*) fröhlich; Ⓑ (*brightly, showily*) in leuchtenden Farben ‹gekleidet, bemalt, geschmückt›; **~ coloured** farbenfroh; Ⓒ (*airily, without thinking*) fröhlich; unbekümmert

**gain** /geɪn/ ❶ *n.* Ⓐ Gewinn, *der;* **be to sb.'s ~:** für jmdn. von Vorteil sein; **ill-gotten ~s** unrechtmäßig erworbener Besitz; ⇒ *also* **capital gain**; Ⓑ (*increase*) Zunahme, *die* (**in** an + *Dat.*); **a ~ of ten kilograms in weight** eine Gewichtszunahme von zehn Kilogramm; **a ~ in efficiency/value** eine Effektivitäts-/Wertsteigerung; Ⓒ (*Electronics*) Verstärkung, *die.*
❷ *v.t.* Ⓐ (*obtain*) gewinnen; finden ‹Zugang, Zutritt›; sich (*Dat.*) schaffen ‹Feind›; erwerben ‹Wissen, Ruf›; erlangen ‹Freiheit, Ruhm›; erzielen ‹Vorteil, Punkte›; verdienen ‹Lebensunterhalt, Geldsumme›; erreichen ‹Ziel›; **~ possession of sth.** in den Besitz einer Sache (*Gen.*) kommen; **~ nothing** nichts erreichen; **~ time** Zeit gewinnen; Ⓑ (*win*) gewinnen ‹Preis, Schlacht›; erringen ‹Sieg›; Ⓒ (*obtain as increase*) **~ weight/five pounds [in weight]** zunehmen/fünf Pfund zunehmen; **~ speed** schneller werden; Ⓓ (*reach*) gewinnen (*geh.*), erreichen ‹Gipfel, Ufer›; Ⓔ (*become fast by*) **my watch ~s two minutes a day** meine Uhr geht pro Tag zwei Minuten vor. ⇒ *also* **ground[1]** 1 B; **upper** 1 A.
❸ *v.i.* Ⓐ (*make a profit*) **~ by sth.** von etw. profitieren; bei etw. gewinnen; Ⓑ (*obtain increase*) **~ in influence/prestige** an Einfluss/Prestige gewinnen; **~ in health/speed/wealth/wisdom** gesünder/schneller/reicher/weiser werden; **~ in knowledge** sein Wissen vergrößern; **~ in weight** zunehmen; Ⓒ (*be improved*) gewinnen; **~ by comparison** durch einen Vergleich gewinnen; Ⓓ (*become fast*) ‹Uhr:› vorgehen; Ⓔ **~ [up]on sb.** (*come closer*) jmdm. [immer] näher kommen; (*increase lead*) den Vorsprung zu jmdm. vergrößern

**gainful** /ˈgeɪnfl/ *adj.* bezahlt; (*profitable*) Gewinn bringend; **~ employment** Erwerbstätigkeit, *die*

**gainfully** /ˈgeɪnfəlɪ/ *adv.* **~ employed** erwerbstätig

**gainsay** /geɪnˈseɪ/ *v.t.*, **gainsaid** /geɪnˈseɪd, geɪnˈsed/ (*arch./literary*) leugnen

**gait** /geɪt/ *n.* Ⓐ Gang, *der;* **with a slow ~:** mit langsamen Schritten; Ⓑ (*of horse*) Gangart, *die*

**gaiter** /ˈgeɪtə(r)/ *n.* Ⓐ Gamasche, *die;* Ⓑ (*Amer.*) ⇒ **galosh**

**gal** /gæl/ *n.* (*coll.*) Mädchen, *das;* **you're a nice ~:** du bist ein netter Käfer (*ugs.*)

**gal.** *abbr.* ▶ 1671 **gallon[s]** gal.; gall.

**gala** /ˈgɑːlə, ˈgeɪlə/ *n.* Ⓐ (*fête*) Festveranstaltung, *die; attrib.* Gala‹abend, -diner, -vorstellung›; Ⓑ (*Brit.: sports festival*) Sportfest, *das;* **swimming ~:** Schwimmfest, *das*

**galactic** /gəˈlæktɪk/ *adj.* (*of a galaxy*) galaktisch; (*of the Galaxy*) Milchstraßen-

**Galahad** /ˈgæləhæd/ *n.* edler Ritter

**galantine** /ˈgælәntiːn/ *n.* (*Cookery*) Galantine, *die*

**galaxy** /ˈgæləksɪ/ *n.* Ⓐ (*Milky Way*) **the G~:** die Galaxis (*Astron.*); die Milchstraße; Ⓑ (*independent system of stars*) Galaxie, *die;* Ⓒ (*fig.: outstanding group*) illustre Schar (*geh.*)

**gale** /geɪl/ *n.* Ⓐ Sturm, *der;* **it's blowing a ~ outside** draußen stürmt es *od.* tobt ein Sturm; **~ force** Sturmstärke, *die;* **~ warning** Sturmwarnung, *die;* Ⓑ (*fig.: outburst*) Sturm, *der;* **~s of laughter** Lachsalven *Pl.*

**Galicia[1]** /gəˈlɪʃə/ *pr. n.* (*in Spain*) Galicien (*das*)

**Galicia[2]** *pr. n.* (*in SW Poland and W. Russia*) Galizien (*das*)

**Galilee** /ˈgælɪliː/ *pr. n.* Galiläa (*das*); **Sea of ~:** See Genezareth, *der*

**gall[1]** /gɔːl/ *n.* Ⓐ (*Physiol.*) Galle, *die;* Ⓑ (*fig.: bitterness*) Bitternis, *die* (*geh.*); **be ~ and wormwood** [bitter wie] Galle und Wermut sein; Ⓒ (*impudence*) Unverschämtheit, *die;* Frechheit, *die*

**gall[2]** ❶ *n.* (*sore*) Schürfwunde, *die.* ❷ *v.t.* wund scheuern; (*fig.*) (*annoy*) ärgern; (*vex*) schmerzen; **be ~ed by sth.** unter etw. (*Dat.*) leiden

**gall[3]** ⇒ **gall-nut**

**gallant** /ˈgælənt/ ❶ *adj.* Ⓐ (*brave*) tapfer; (*chivalrous*) ritterlich; Ⓑ (*grand, stately*) stattlich ‹Schiff›; Ⓒ /ˈgælənt, gəˈlænt/ (*attentive to women, amatory*) galant; **say ~ things** Galanterien *od.* Artigkeiten sagen (*geh.*). ❷ /ˈgælənt, gəˈlænt/ *n.* (*dated: ladies' man*) Kavalier, *der* (*veralt.*)

**gallantly** /ˈgæləntlɪ/ *adv.* Ⓐ (*bravely*) tapfer; Ⓑ (*grandly*) stattlich; Ⓒ /ˈgæləntlɪ, gəˈlæntlɪ/ (*with courtesy*) galant

**gallantry** /ˈgæləntrɪ/ *n.* Ⓐ (*bravery*) Tapferkeit, *die;* Ⓑ (*courtliness, polite act or speech*) Galanterie, *die* (*geh.*)

**ˈgall bladder** *n.* ▶ 966 (*Anat.*) Gallenblase, *die*

**galleon** /ˈgælɪən/ *n.* (*Hist.*) Galeone, *die*

**gallery** /ˈgælərɪ/ *n.* Ⓐ (*Archit.*) Galerie, *die;* ⇒ *also* **shooting gallery**; Ⓑ (*Theatre*) dritter Rang; Olymp, *der* (*ugs. scherzh.*); (*esp. Golf: group of spectators*) Zuschauer *Pl.;* **play to the ~** (*fig.*) für die Galerie spielen; Ⓒ (*art ~*) (*building*) Galerie, *die;* (*room*) Ausstellungsraum, *der;* Ⓓ (*Mining*) Stollen, *der*

**ˈgallery tray** *n.* Galerietablett, *das*

**galley** /ˈgælɪ/ *n.* Ⓐ (*Hist.*) Galeere, *die;* Ⓑ (*kitchen*) (*of ship*) Kombüse, *die;* (*of aircraft*) Bordküche, *die;* Ⓒ (*Printing*) Satzschiff, *das;* **~ [proof]** [Druck]fahne, *die*

**ˈgalley slave** *n.* Galeerensklave, *der*

**Gallic** /ˈgælɪk/ *adj.* Ⓐ (*of the Gauls*) gallisch; Ⓑ (*often joc.: French*) französisch; gallisch ‹Witz›

**Gallicism** /ˈgælɪsɪzm/ *n.* Ⓐ (*word or idiom*) Gallizismus, *der;* Ⓑ (*characteristic*) französische Eigenart

**galling** /ˈgɔːlɪŋ/ *adj.* äußerst unangenehm

**gallivant** /gælɪˈvænt/ *v.i.* (*coll.*) herumziehen (*ugs.*); **~ about** *or* **around the country/Europe** im Lande/in Europa herumziehen

**ˈgall nut** *n.* (*Bot.*) Gallapfel, *der*

**gallon** /ˈgælən/ *n.* ▶ 1671 Gallone, *die;* **[imperial] ~** (*Brit.*) britische Gallone (4,546 l); **wine ~** (*Brit.*), **~** (*Amer.*) amerikanische Gallone (3,785 l); **drink ~s of water** *etc.* (*fig. coll.*) literweise *od.* eimerweise Wasser *usw.* trinken

**galloon** /gəˈluːn/ *n.* Galone, *die;* Galon, *der*

**gallop** /ˈgæləp/ ❶ *n.* Ⓐ Galopp, *der;* **at a ~/at full ~:** im Galopp/in vollem Galopp; Ⓑ (*ride*) Galoppritt, *der;* Ⓒ (*track*) Galopp[renn]bahn, *die.* ❷ *v.i.* Ⓐ ‹Pferd, Reiter:› galoppieren; Ⓑ (*fig.*) **~ through** im Galopp (*ugs.*) durchlesen ‹Buch›; rasch herunterspielen ‹Musikstück›; im Galopp (*ugs.*) erledigen ‹Arbeit›; **~ing consumption/inflation** (*fig.*) galoppierende Schwindsucht/Inflation

**gallows** /ˈgæləʊz/ *n. sing.* Galgen, *der;* **be sent to the ~:** zum [Tod am] Galgen verurteilt werden

**gallows: ~-bird** *n.* Galgenvogel, *der* (*ugs. abwertend*); **~ humour** *n.* Galgenhumor, *der*

**'gallstone** *n.* ▶1232 (*Med.*) Gallenstein, *der*

**Gallup poll** ® /'gæləp pəʊl/ *n.* Meinungsumfrage, *die*

**galop** /'gæləp/ *n.* (*Mus.*) Galopp, *der*

**galore** /gə'lɔ:(r)/ *adv.* im Überfluss; in Hülle und Fülle

**galosh** /gə'lɒʃ/ *n.* [Gummi]überschuh, *der;* [Gummi]galosche, *die*

**galumph** /gə'lʌmf/ *v.i.* (*coll.*) **A** (*in triumph*) stolzieren; **B** (*noisily, clumsily*) stapfen

**galvanic** /gæl'vænɪk/ *adj.* (*fig.*) (*sudden remarkable*) elektrisierend; Blitz‹wirkung, -reaktion›; (*stimulating, full of energy*) mitreißend ‹Aufführung, Rede, Persönlichkeit›

**galvanize (galvanise)** /'gælvənaɪz/ *v.t.* **A** (*fig.: rouse*) wachrütteln ‹Volk, Partei usw.›; **~ sb. into action/activity** jmdn. veranlassen, sofort aktiv zu werden; **~ sb. into life** jmdn. aufrütteln; **B** (*coat with zinc*) verzinken

**Gambia** /'gæmbɪə/ *pr. n.* **[the] ~:** Gambia (*das*)

**gambit** /'gæmbɪt/ *n.* (*Chess*) Gambit, *das;* (*fig.: trick, device*) Schachzug, *der;* **[opening] ~** (*fig.*) einleitender Schachzug; (*in a conversation*) einleitende Bemerkung; **conversational ~** (*fig.*) Gesprächseinstieg *od.* -aufhänger, *der*

**gamble** /'gæmbl/ **1** *v.i.* **A** [um Geld] spielen; **~ at cards/on horses** um Geld Karten spielen/auf Pferde wetten; **B** (*fig.*) spekulieren; **~ on the Stock Exchange/in oil shares** an der Börse/in Öl[aktien] spekulieren; **~ on sth.** sich auf etw. (*Akk.*) verlassen; auf etw. (*Akk.*) spekulieren (*ugs.*). **2** *v.t.* **A** verspielen; **~ money on horses** Geld für Pferdewetten einsetzen; **B** (*fig.*) riskieren, aufs Spiel setzen ‹Vermögen›. **3** *n.* (*lit. or fig.*) Glücksspiel, *das;* **he likes the occasional ~:** er spielt gelegentlich ganz gern; **take a ~:** ein Wagnis eingehen *od.* auf sich (*Akk.*) nehmen

**~ a'way** *v.t.* verspielen ‹Vermögen, Geld, Geschäft, Haus›; (*on the Stock Exchange*) verspekulieren ‹Vermögen›

**gambler** /'gæmblə(r)/ *n.* Glücksspieler, *der;* (*risk-taker*) Glücksritter, *der;* **born ~:** Spieler- *od.* Abenteurernatur, *die*

**gambling** /'gæmblɪŋ/ *n.* Spiel[en], *das;* Glücksspiel, *das;* (*on horses, dogs*) Wetten, *das*

**gambling: ~ debts** *n. pl.* Spielschulden *Pl.;* **~ den** *n.* Spielhölle, *die* (*abwertend*); **~ machine** *n.* Spielautomat, *der*

**gambol** /'gæmbl/ **1** *n.* **~[s]** Herumspringen, *das.* **2** *v.i.,* (*Brit.*) **-ll-** ‹Kind, Lamm:› herumspringen

**game¹** /geɪm/ **1** *n.* **A** (*form of contest*) Spiel, *das;* (*contest*) (*with ball*) Spiel, *das;* (*at [table] tennis, chess, cards, billiards, cricket*) Partie, *die;* **have** *or* **play a ~ of tennis/chess** *etc.* **[with sb.]** eine Partie Tennis/Schach *usw.* [mit jmdm.] spielen; **give sb. a ~ of tennis/chess** *etc.* eine Partie Tennis/Schach *usw.* mit jmdm. spielen; **have** *or* **play a ~ of football [with sb.]** Fußball [mit jmdm.] spielen; **play a good/poor ~ [of cards** *etc.*] gut/schlecht [Karten *usw.*] spielen; ein guter [Karten- *usw.*]spieler sein; **be back in/get back into the ~ again** (*have a chance of winning*) wieder Gewinnchancen haben/bekommen; **it's all in the ~:** das ist alles dabei möglich; das kann alles dazugehören; **be on/off one's ~:** gut in Form/nicht in Form sein; **beat sb. at his own ~** (*fig.*) jmdn. mit seinen eigenen Waffen schlagen (*geh.*); **play the ~** (*fig.*) sich an die Spielregeln halten (*fig.*); **I'll show her that two can play [at] that ~** *or* **that it's a ~ that two can play** (*fig.*) was sie kann, kann ich auch; ⇒ *also* **name** 1 A; **B** (*fig.: scheme, undertaking*) Vorhaben, *das;* **sb.'s ~ is to do sth.** jmd. führt etw. im Schilde; (*policy*) jmds. Taktik ist es, etw. zu tun; **play a [double] ~:** ein [falsches] Spiel treiben; **play sb.'s ~:** jmdm. in die Hände arbeiten; (*for one's own benefit*) jmds. Spiel mitspielen; **the ~ is up** (*coll.*) das Spiel ist aus; **give the ~ away** alles verraten; **so that's your little ~!** ach, das führst du im Schilde!; **what's his ~?** (*coll.*) was hat er vor?; **what's the ~?** (*coll.*) was soll das?; **C** (*business, activity*) Gewerbe, *das;* Branche, *die;* **the ~ of politics** die Politik; **the publishing/newspaper ~:** das Verlags-/Zeitungs- *od.* Pressewesen; **be new to the ~** (*fig.*) neu im Geschäft sein (*auch fig. ugs.*); **go [out]/be on the ~** (*Brit. coll.*) ‹Dieb, Prostituierte:› anschaffen *od.* auf die Anschaffe gehen (*salopp*); ⇒ *also* **candle** 1 A; **D** (*diversion*) Spiel, *das;* (*piece of fun*) Scherz, *der;* Spaß, *der;* **don't play ~s with me** versuch nicht, mich auf den Arm zu nehmen (*ugs.*); **make ~ of sb./sth.** (*dated*) sich über jmdn./etw. lustig machen; jmdn./etw. zum Gelächter machen (*geh. veralt.*); **E** *in pl.* (*athletic contests*) Spiele *Pl.;* (*in school*) (*sports*) Schulsport, *der;* (*athletics*) Leichtathletik, *die;* **good at ~s** gut im Sport; **F** (*portion of play*) Spiel, *das;* (*winning score*) **21 points is ~:** zum Gewinn eines Spiels sind 21 Punkte erforderlich; **~ all** eins beide; eins zu eins; **two ~s all** zwei beide; zwei zu zwei; **~ to Graf** (*Tennis*) Spiel Graf; **~, set, and match** (*Tennis*) Spiel, Satz und Sieg; (*fig.: complete and decisive victory*) voller Erfolg (**to** für); Sieg auf der ganzen Linie (**to** für); **G** *no pl.* (*Hunting, Cookery*) Wild, *das;* **fair ~:** jagdbares Wild; (*fig.*) Freiwild, *das;* **easy ~** (*fig. coll.*) leichte Beute; **big ~:** Großwild, *das.* **2** *v.i.* [um Geld] spielen

**game²** *adj.* mutig; **~ spirit/manner** Unverzagtheit, *die;* **remain ~:** sich nicht entmutigen lassen; **be ~ to do sth.** (*be willing*) bereit sein, etw. zu tun; **are you ~?** machst du mit?; **be ~ for sth./anything** zu etw./allem bereit sein

**game³** *adj.* (*crippled*) lahm ‹Arm, Bein›

**game: ~ bag** *n.* Tragetasche, *die;* **~ bird** *n.* **the pheasant is a ~ bird** Fasane sind Federwild; **~ birds** Federwild, *das;* **~cock** *n.* Kampfhahn, *der;* **~keeper** *n.* ▶1261 Wildheger, *der*

**gamely** /'geɪmlɪ/ *adv.* mutig ‹kämpfen›

**game: ~ park** *n.* Wildreservat, *das;* **~ plan** *n.* (*Sport*) Taktik, *die;* (*fig.*) Strategie, *die;* **~ point** *n.* (*Sport*) Spielpunkt, *der;* **~ reserve** *n.* Wildreservat, *das*

**gamesmanship** /'geɪmzmənʃɪp/ *n., no pl.* Gerissen- *od.* Gewieftheit (*ugs.*) beim Spiel

**gamete** /'gæmi:t/ *n.* (*Biol.*) Gamet, *der;* Geschlechtszelle, *die*

**'game warden** *n.* ▶1261 Wildhüter, *der*

**gamin** /'gæmɪn, 'gæmæ̃/ *n.* Gamin, *der* (*veralt.*); Gassenjunge, *der* (*abwertend*)

**gamine** /gə'mi:n/ *n.* (*small mischievous young woman*) schelmisches Mädchen; kesse Motte (*salopp*)

**gaming**/'geɪmɪŋ/: **~ house** *n.* Spielbank, *die;* **~ machine** *n.* Münzspielgerät, *das;* **~ table** *n.* Spieltisch, *der*

**gamma** /'gæmə/ *n.* **A** (*letter*) Gamma, *das;* **B** (*Sch., Univ.: mark*) Drei, *die*

**gamma: ~ radiation** *n.* (*Phys.*) Gammastrahlung, *die;* **~ rays** *n. pl.* (*Phys.*) Gammastrahlen *Pl.*

**gammon** /'gæmən/ *n.* (*ham cured like bacon*) Räucherschinken, *der*

**gammy** /'gæmɪ/ *adj.* (*coll.*) lahm ‹Arm, Bein, Fuß›

**gamut** /'gæmət/ *n.* **A** (*Mus.*) (*series of notes, compass*) Tonumfang, *der;* (*recognized scale*) Skala, *die;* Tonleiter, *die;* **B** (*fig.: range*) Skala, *die;* **run the whole ~ of ...:** die ganze Skala von ... durchgehen

**gamy** /'geɪmɪ/ *adj.* **A** (*having flavour or scent of game*) nach Wild ‹schmecken›; **~ taste** Wildgeschmack, *der;* **B** (*spirited*) mutig; **C** (*Amer.: scandalous*) pikant

**gander** /'gændə(r)/ *n.* **A** (*Ornith.*) Gänserich, *der;* **what's sauce for the goose is sauce for the ~** (*prov.*) was dem einen recht ist, ist dem andern billig (*Spr.*); **B** (*coll.: look, glance*) Blick, *der;* **take** *or* **have a ~ at/round sth.** sich (*Dat.*) etw. ansehen

**gang¹** /gæŋ/ **1** *n.* **A** (*of workmen, slaves, prisoners*) Trupp, *der;* **B** (*of criminals*) Bande, *die;* Gang, *die;* **~ of thieves/criminals/terrorists** Diebes-/Verbrecher-/Terroristenbande, *die;* **C** (*coll.: band causing any kind of disapproval*) Gang, *die;* Bande, *die* (*abwertend, oft scherzh.*); **D** (*coll.: group of friends etc.*) Haufen, *der;* Bande, *die* (*scherzh.*). **2** *v.i.* **A** **~ up [with sb.]** (*join*) sich [mit jmdm.] zusammentun (*ugs.*); **B** **~ up against** *or* **on** (*coll.: combine against*) sich verbünden *od.* zusammenschließen gegen

**gang²** *v.i.* (*Scot.: go*) gehen; **~ agley** /ə'gleɪ/ ‹Plan:› scheitern

**'gang-bang** *n.* (*sl.*) Bandenfick, *der* (*derb*)

**ganger** /'gæŋə(r)/ *n.* (*Brit.*) Vorarbeiter, *der*

**gangling** /'gæŋglɪŋ/ *adj.* schlaksig (*ugs.*) ‹Person, Gang, Gestalt›

**ganglion** /'gæŋglɪən/ *n., pl.* **ganglia** /'gæŋglɪə/ *or* **~s** (*Anat.*) Ganglion, *das* (*fachspr.*); Nervenknoten, *der*

**gangly** /'gæŋglɪ/ ⇒ **gangling**

**gang: ~plank** *n.* (*Naut.*) Laufplanke, *die;* **~ rape** *n.* Vergewaltigung durch eine Gruppe

**gangrene** /'gæŋgri:n/ *n.* **A** ▶1232 (*Med.*) Gangrän, *die od. fachspr. das;* [Faul]brand, *der;* **B** (*fig.: corruption*) Krebsgeschwür, *das* (*fig.*)

**gangrenous** /'gæŋgrɪnəs/ *adj.* (*Med.*) gangränös (*fachspr.*); brandig

**gangster** /'gæŋstə(r)/ *n.* Gangster, *der* (*abwertend*); *attrib.* Gangster‹film›

**'gang warfare** *n.* Bandenkrieg, *der*

**'gangway** **1** *n.* **A** (*Naut.: for boarding ship*) Gangway, *die;* **B** (*Brit.: between rows of seats*) Gang, *der;* **leave a ~** (*fig.*) einen Durchgang freilassen. **2** *int.* Platz

**ganja** /'gændʒə/ *n.* (*Bot.*) Indischer Hanf

**gannet** /'gænɪt/ *n.* **A** (*Ornith.*) Tölpel, *der;* **B** (*coll.: greedy person*) Raffke, *der* (*salopp abwertend*)

**gantlet** /'gæntlɪt/ (*Amer.*) ⇒ **gauntlet²**

**gantry** /'gæntrɪ/ *n.* (*crane*) Portal, *das;* (*on road*) Schilderbrücke, *die;* (*Railw.*) Signalbrücke, *die;* (*Astronaut.*) Startrampe, *die*

**gaol** /dʒeɪl/ (*Brit. in official use*) ⇒ **jail** 1, 2

**gaoler** /'dʒeɪlə(r)/ (*Brit. in official use*) ⇒ **jailer**

**gap** /gæp/ *n.* **A** Lücke, *die;* (*in sparking plug*) Elektrodenabstand, *der;* **a ~ in the curtains** ein Spalt im Vorhang; **B** (*Geog.: gorge, pass*) Joch, *das;* **C** (*fig.: contrast, divergence in views etc.*) Kluft, *die;* **that is a ~ in his education/knowledge** er hat hier eine Bildungs-/Wissenslücke; **fill a ~:** eine Lücke füllen *od.* schließen; **stop** *or* **close** *or* **bridge a ~:** eine Kluft überbrücken *od.* überwinden; **close the ~ [on sb.]** den Abstand [zu jmdm.] aufholen

**gape** /geɪp/ **1** *v.i.* **A** (*open mouth*) den Mund aufsperren; ([*be*] *open wide*) ‹Schnabel, Mund:› aufgesperrt sein; ‹Loch, Abgrund, Wunde:› klaffen; **gaping** klaffend ‹Wunde›; gähnend ‹Loch›; **~ at the seams** ‹Kleid:› in den Nähten aufgeplatzt sein; **B** (*stare*) Mund und Nase aufsperren (*ugs.*); **~ at sb./sth.** jmdn./etw. mit offenem Mund anstarren *od.* anstieren; **what are you gaping at?** worauf stierst du so?; **gaping** erstaunt starrend ‹Person›. **2** *n.* stierer Blick

**gap-toothed** /'gæptu:θt/ *adj.* ‹Person› mit Zahnlücken

**gar** /gɑ:(r)/ ⇒ **garfish**

**garage** /'gærɑ:ʒ, 'gærɪdʒ/ **1** *n.* **A** (*for parking*) Garage, *die;* **bus ~:** Busdepot, *das;* **B** (*for selling petrol*) Tankstelle, *die;* (*for repairing cars*) [Kfz-]Werkstatt, *die;* (*for selling cars*) Autohandlung, *die.* **2** *v.t.* in die Garage stellen ‹Fahrzeug›; **be kept ~d** in der Garage stehen; **where do you ~ your car?** wo parken Sie Ihr Auto?

**garb** /gɑ:b/ **1** *n.* Tracht, *die;* **strange ~:** seltsame Kleidung; **official ~:** Amtstracht, *die.* **2** *v.t.* kleiden; (*fig.: invest*) verleihen (*Dat.*); **~ed in white robes** in Weiß gekleidet

**garbage** /'gɑ:bɪdʒ/ *n.* **A** Abfall, *der;* Müll, *der;* **B** (*fig.: foul or rubbishy literature*) Schund, *der;* **C** (*coll.: nonsense*) Quatsch, *der* (*salopp*); **~ in, ~ out** (*Computing fig. coll.*) wenn der Input nichts taugt, ist auch der Output entsprechend

**garbage: ~ can** (*Amer.*) ⇒ **dustbin**; **~ collection** *n.* (*Amer.*) Müllabfuhr, *die;* **~ collector** (*Amer.*) ⇒ **dustman**; **~ dis'posal unit, ~ disposer** *ns.* Abfallvernichter, *der;* Müllwolf, *der;* **~ truck** *n.* (*Amer.*) Müllwagen, *der*

**garble** /'gɑːbl/ *v.t.* **A** verstümmeln, entstellen ‹Bericht, Korrespondenz, Tatsache›; **B** (*confuse*) durcheinander bringen; durcheinander werfen; **get ~d** durcheinander geraten

**garden** /gɑːdn/ **1** *n.* **A** Garten, *der;* **everything in the ~ is lovely** (*fig. coll.*) es ist alles in Butter (*ugs.*); **lead sb. up the ~ [path]** (*fig. coll.*) jmdn. an der Nase herumführen (*ugs.*); **tea ~:** Gartencafé, *das;* **a small amount of ~:** ein kleines Stück Garten; **B** *usu. in pl., with name prefixed* (*Brit.*) (*park*) -park, *der;* (*street, square*) -garten, *der;* **C** (*land for raising crops*) Plantage, *die;* **D** (*Amer.: large hall*) Halle, *die;* **E** *attrib.* (*Bot.: cultivated*) Garten‹pflanze, -kresse, -gemüse›. ⇒ *also* **kitchen garden; market garden; zoological garden[s]**.
**2** *v.i.* gärtnern

**garden: ~ centre** *n.* Gartencenter, *das;* **~ chair** *n.* Gartenstuhl, *der;* **~ 'city** *n.* Gartenstadt, *die*

**gardener** /'gɑːdnə(r)/ *n.* ▶ **1261** Gärtner, *der*/Gärtnerin, *die*

**garden 'gnome** *n.* Gartenzwerg, *der*

**gardenia** /gɑː'diːnɪə/ *n.* (*Bot.*) **A** (*tree, shrub*) Gardenie, *die;* **B** (*flower*) Gardenienblüte, *die*

**gardening** /'gɑːdnɪŋ/ *n.* Gartenarbeit, *die; attrib.* Garten‹gerät, -buch, -handschuh›; **he likes ~:** er gärtnert gern

**garden: ~ party** *n.* Gartenfest, *das;* **~ 'shed** *n.* Geräteschuppen, *der;* **~ 'suburb** *n.* (*Brit.*) Gartenstadt, *die*

**garfish** /'gɑːfɪʃ/ *n., pl. same* (*Zool.*) (*needlefish*) Hornhecht, *der;* (*gar*) Knochenhecht, *der;* (*halfbeak*) Halbschnabelhecht, *der*

**gargantuan** /gɑː'gæntjʊən/ *adj.* gigantisch; riesig ‹Person, Hunger, Gelächter›; Riesen‹größe, -hunger, -gebrüll›

**gargle** /'gɑːgl/ **1** *v.i.* gurgeln. **2** *n.* **A** (*liquid*) Gurgelmittel, *das;* Gargarisma, *das* (*fachspr.*); **B** (*act*) Gurgeln, *das;* **have a ~:** gurgeln

**gargoyle** /'gɑːgɔɪl/ *n.* (*Archit.*) Wasserspeier, *der*

**garish** /'geərɪʃ/ *adj.* **A** (*bright, showy*) grell ‹Farbe, Licht, Beleuchtung›; knallbunt ‹Kleidung, Verzierung›; protzig (*abwertend*) ‹Lebensstil›; **B** (*over-decorated*) protzig (*abwertend*) ‹Gebäude, Baustil, Aussehen›; grellbunt, knallbunt ‹Muster›

**garishly** /'geərɪʃlɪ/ *adv.* grell ‹beleuchten›; protzig (*abwertend*) ‹einrichten›; grellbunt, knallbunt ‹kleiden, tapezieren›; grell-, knall‹bunt›

**garland** /'gɑːlənd/ **1** *n.* (*wreath of flowers etc.; Art: festoon*) Girlande, *die;* (*of laurel*) Kranz, *der;* **~ of flowers/laurel/oak leaves** Blumen-/Lorbeer-/Eichenkranz, *der.* **2** *v.t.* bekränzen

**garlic** /'gɑːlɪk/ *n.* Knoblauch, *der*

**garlicky** /'gɑːlɪkɪ/ *adj.* nach Knoblauch riechend ‹Atem›; nach Knoblauch ‹riechen, schmecken›

**garment** /'gɑːmənt/ *n.* **A** Kleidungsstück, *das; in pl.* (*clothes*) Kleidung, *die;* Kleider *Pl.;* **B** (*fig.: covering*) Gewand, *das* (*geh.*)

**garner** /'gɑːnə(r)/ *v.t.* speichern ‹Getreide›; (*fig.: collect*) sammeln ‹Kenntnisse usw.›

**garnet** /'gɑːnɪt/ *n.* (*Min.*) Granat, *der*

**garnish** /'gɑːnɪʃ/ **1** *v.t.* (*lit. or fig.*) garnieren. **2** *n.* (*Cookery*) Garnierung, *die*

**garotte** ⇒ **garrotte**

**garret** /'gærɪt/ *n.* (*room on top floor*) Dachkammer, *die;* Mansarde, *die;* (*attic*) [Dach]boden, *der*

**garrison** /'gærɪsn/ **1** *n.* Garnison, *die.* **2** *v.t.* (*furnish with ~*) in Garnison legen; garnisonieren (*fachspr.*); (*occupy as ~*) mit einer Garnison belegen; garnisonieren (*fachspr.*)

**garrison: ~ duty** *n.* Garnison[s]dienst, *der;* **~ town** *n.* Garnison[s]stadt, *die*

**garrotte** /gə'rɒt/ *v.t.* **A** garrottieren; **B** (*throttle to rob*) [er]würgen [und ausrauben]

**garrulous** /'gærʊləs/ *adj.* **A** (*talkative*) gesprächig; geschwätzig; **B** (*wordy*) wortreich; weitschweifig, langatmig ‹Rede, Kommentar›

**garrulously** /'gærʊləslɪ/ *adv.* geschwätzig

**garter** /'gɑːtə(r)/ *n.* **A** Strumpfband, *das;* **B** **the [Order of the] G~** (*Brit.*) der Hosenbandorden; **C** (*Amer.: suspender*) Sockenhalter, *der*

**'garter stitch** *n.* Kraus[gestrick], *das;* **knit in ~:** kraus rechts stricken

**gas** /gæs/ **1** *n., pl.* **~es** /'gæsɪz/ **A** Gas, *das;* **natural ~:** Erdgas, *das;* **cook by** *or* **with ~:** mit Gas kochen; **on a low/high ~:** auf kleiner/großer Flamme; **B** (*Amer. coll.: petrol*) Benzin, *das;* **step on the ~:** Gas geben; (*fig.: hurry*) einen Zahn zulegen (*salopp*); **C** (*anaesthetic*) Narkotikum, *das;* Lachgas, *das;* **D** (*for lighting*) Leuchtgas, *das;* **E** (*to fill balloon*) [Trag]gas, *das;* **F** (*Mining*) Grubengas, *das;* **G** (*coll.: idle talk*) leeres Geschwätz (*abwertend*); Blabla, *das* (*salopp*); **H** (*coll.: sb./sth. attractive and impressive*) Wucht, *die* (*salopp*).
**2** *v.t.*, **-ss-** mit Gas vergiften; (*in Third Reich*) vergasen; **~ oneself** den Gashahn aufdrehen (*ugs. verhüll.*).
**3** *v.i.*, **-ss-** (*coll.*) schwatzen (*abwertend*), schwafeln (*ugs. abwertend*) (**about** von)

**gas: ~bag** *n.* **A** Gaszelle, *die;* **B** (*coll. derog.: talker*) Schwätzer, *der*/Schwätzerin, *die* (*abwertend*); Schwafler, *der*/Schwaflerin, *die* (*ugs. abwertend*); **~ chamber** *n.* Gaskammer, *die;* **~-cooled** *adj.* gasgekühlt; **~ cylinder** *n.* Gasflasche, *die*

**gaseous** /'gæsɪəs, 'geɪsɪəs/ *adj.* gasförmig

**gas: ~ 'fire** *n.* Gasofen, *der;* **~-fired** /'gæs faɪəd/ *adj.* mit Gas betrieben; Gas‹boiler, -ofen usw.›; **~ fitter** *n.* Gasinstallateur, *der*

**gash** /gæʃ/ **1** *n.* (*wound*) Schnittwunde, *die;* (*cleft*) [klaffende] Spalte; (*in sack etc.*) Schlitz, *der.* **2** *v.t.* eine Schnittwunde beibringen (+ *Dat.*); aufritzen ‹Haut›; aufschlitzen ‹Sack›; **~ one's finger/knee** sich (*Dat. od. Akk.*) in den Finger schneiden/sich (*Dat.*) das Knie aufschlagen

**gas: ~ heater** *n.* Gasofen, *der;* **~holder** *n.* Gasometer, *der;* Gasbehälter, *der;* **~ jet** *n.* Gasflamme, *die;* (*burner*) Gasbrenner, *der*

**gasket** /'gæskɪt/ *n.* **A** (*sheet, ring*) Dichtung, *die;* **B** (*packing*) Packung, *die*

**gas: ~ lamp** *n.* Gaslampe, *die;* (*in street etc.*) Gaslaterne, *die;* **~light** *n.* **A** ⇒ **~ lamp;** **B** *no pl.* (*illumination*) Gaslicht, *das;* Gasbeleuchtung, *die;* **~ lighter** *n.* **A** [Gas]anzünder, *der;* **B** (*cigarette lighter*) Gasfeuerzeug, *das;* **~ main** *n.* Hauptgasleitung, *die;* **~man** *n.* ▶ **1261** (*fitter*) Gasinstallateur, *der;* (*meter-reader, collector*) Gasableser, *der;* Gasmann, *der* (*ugs.*); **~-mantle** *n.* Glühstrumpf, *der;* **~ mask** *n.* Gasmaske, *die;* **~ meter** *n.* Gaszähler, *der*

**gasoline** (**gasolene**) /'gæsəliːn/ *n.* (*Amer.*) Benzin, *das*

**gasometer** /gæ'sɒmɪtə(r)/ *n.* Gasometer, *der*

**'gas oven** *n.* **A** ⇒ **gas stove a;** **B** ⇒ **gas chamber**

**gasp** /gɑːsp/ **1** *v.i.* nach Luft schnappen (**with** vor); **make sb. ~** (*fig.*) jmdn. den Atem nehmen; **leave sb. ~ing [with sth.]** jmdm. [vor etw.] den Atem verschlagen *od.* rauben; **he was ~ing for air** *or* **breath/ under the heavy load** er rang nach Luft/ keuchte unter der schweren Last.
**2** *v.t.* **~ out** hervorstoßen ‹Bitte, Worte›; **~ [one's] life away, ~ [one's] breath away** sein Leben aushauchen (*geh.*).
**3** *n.* Keuchen, *das;* **give a ~ of fear/surprise** vor Furcht/Überraschung die Luft einziehen; **she gave a ~ of joy** es verschlug ihr vor Freude den Atem; **be at one's last ~:** in den letzten Zügen liegen (*ugs.*); **sth. is at its last ~:** etw. tut's nicht mehr lange (*ugs.*); **fight** *etc.* **to the last ~** (*fig.*) bis zum letzten Atemzug kämpfen *usw.*

**gas: ~ pipe** *n.* Gasleitung, *die;* **~ pistol** *n.* Gasanzünder, *der;* **~ poker** *n.* Gasanzünder, *der* (*für Kohle*); **~-proof** *adj.* gasdicht; **~ ring** *n.* Gasbrenner, *der;* **~ station** *n.* (*Amer.*) Tankstelle, *die;* **~ stove** *n.* **A** Gasherd, *der;* **B** (*portable*) Gaskocher, *der*

**gassy** /'gæsɪ/ *adj.* **A** gasig; (*containing gas*) gashaltig; **B** (*fizzy*) sprudelnd; schäumend ‹Bier›; **be ~:** sprudeln

**gas: ~ tank** *n.* **A** Gastank, *der;* **B** (*Amer.: petrol tank*) Benzintank, *der;* **~ tap** *n.* Gashahn, *der;* **~-tight** *adj.* gasdicht

**gastric** /'gæstrɪk/ *adj.* gastrisch (*fachspr.*); Magen‹beschwerden, -wand, -säfte usw.›

**gastric: ~ 'flu** (*coll.*), **~ influ'enza** *ns.* ▶ **1232** Darmgrippe, *die;* **~ 'ulcer** *n.* ▶ **1232** Magengeschwür, *das*

**gastritis** /'gæ'straɪtɪs/ *n.* ▶ **1232** (*Med.*) Magenschleimhautentzündung, *die;* Gastritis, *die* (*fachspr.*)

**gastro-enteritis** /gæstrəʊentə'raɪtɪs/ *n.* ▶ **1232** (*Med.*) Gastroenteritis, *die* (*fachspr.*); Magen-Darm-Katarrh, *der*

**gastronomic** /gæstrə'nɒmɪk/ *adj.* gastronomisch; kulinarisch ‹Genüsse›

**gastronomy** /gæ'strɒnəmɪ/ *n.* Gastronomie, *die;* **French ~:** französische Küche

**gastropod** /'gæstrəpɒd/ *n.* (*Zool.*) Gastropode, *der*

**gas: ~ turbine** *n.* Gasturbine, *die;* **~works** *n. sing., pl. same* Gaswerk, *das*

**gate** /geɪt/ *n.* **A** (*lit. or fig.*) Tor, *das;* (*barrier*) Sperre, *die;* (*of animal pen*) Gatter, *das;* (*in garden fence*) [Garten]pforte, *die;* (*of lift*) [Scheren]gitter, *das;* (*Railw.: of level crossing*) [Bahn]schranke, *die;* (*in airport*) Flugsteig, *der;* **the ~s of heaven/hell** die Himmelspforte (*dichter.*)/die Pforten der Hölle (*geh.*); **pay at the ~:** am Eingang bezahlen; **B** (*Sport*) (*number to see match*) Besucher[zahl], *die;* (*money*) ⇒ **gate money**; **C** (*Amer. coll.: dismissal*) **give sb. the ~:** jmdn. vor die Tür setzen (*ugs.*); jmdn. rausschmeißen (*salopp*); **get the ~:** vor die Tür gesetzt werden (*ugs.*); rausgeschmissen werden (*salopp*); **D** (*of gear in vehicle*) Kulisse, *die;* **E** (*Cinemat.*) Bildfenster, *das*

**gateau** /'gætəʊ/ *n., pl.* **~s** *or* **~x** /'gætəʊz/ Torte, *die*

**gate: ~crash** **1** *v.t.* ohne Einladung einfach hingehen zu; **2** *v.i.* ohne Einladung einfach hingehen; **~crasher** *n.* Eindringling, *der;* (*at party*) ungeladener Gast; **~house** *n.* Torhaus, *das;* **~keeper** *n.* (*attendant*) Torwächter, *der;* Pförtner, *der;* **~leg[ged]** /'geɪtleg(d)/ *adj.* **~leg[ged] table** Klapptisch, *der;* **~man** ⇒ **~keeper**; **~ money** *n.* Eintrittsgelder *Pl.;* Einnahmen *Pl.;* **~post** *n.* Torpfosten, *der;* **between you and me and the ~post** (*coll.*) unter uns (*Dat.*) gesagt; **~way** *n.* **A** (*gate*) Tor, *das;* **B** (*Archit.*) (*structure*) Torbau, *der;* (*frame*) Torbogen, *der;* **C** (*fig.*) Tor, *das* (**to** zu)

**gather** /'gæðə(r)/ **1** *v.t.* **A** (*bring together*) sammeln; zusammentragen ‹Informationen›; pflücken ‹Obst, Blumen›; **~ sth. [together]** etw. zusammensuchen *od.* -sammeln; **~ [in] potatoes/the harvest** Kartoffeln ernten/die Ernte einbringen; **be ~ed to one's fathers** zu seinen Vätern versammelt werden (*veralt., scherzh.*); **B** (*infer, deduce*) schließen (**from** aus); **~ from sb. that ...:** von jmdm. erfahren, dass ...; **I ~ he's doing a good job** ich höre, dass er gute Arbeit leistet; **not much can be ~ed from the facts/his statement** aus den Fakten/seiner Erklärung lässt sich nicht viel entnehmen; **as far as I can ~:** soweit ich weiß; **as you will have ~ed** wie Sie sicherlich vermutet haben; **C** **it is just ~ing dust** das ist bloß ein Staubfänger; **~ speed/force/strength** schneller/stärker werden/zu Kräften kommen; **D** (*summon up*) **~ [together]** zusammennehmen ‹Kräfte, Mut›; **~ oneself [together]** sich zusammennehmen; **~ one's thoughts** seine Gedanken ordnen; **~ one's breath/strength** [wieder] zu Atem kommen/Kräfte sammeln; **E** (*draw*) **~ sb. into one's arms** jmdn. in die Arme nehmen *od.* (*geh.*) schließen; **she ~ed her shawl round her neck** sie schlang den Schal um den Hals; **~ oneself for a jump** sich zum Sprung sammeln; **F** (*Sewing*) ankrausen.
**2** *v.i.* **A** sich versammeln; ‹Wolken:› sich zusammenziehen; ‹Staub:› sich ansammeln;

‹Schweißperlen:› sich sammeln; **be ~ed [together]** versammelt sein; **~ round** zusammenkommen; **~ round sb./sth.** sich um jmdn./etw. versammeln; **tears/beads of perspiration ~ed in her eyes/on her forehead** Tränen/Schweißperlen traten ihr in die Augen/auf die Stirn; **B** (*increase*) zunehmen; **~ing dangers** wachsende Gefahren; **darkness was ~ing round him** es wurde dunkler um ihn [herum]; **C** (*Sewing*) angekraust sein; **D** (*Med.*) ‹Furunkel:› reif werden.
❸ *n. in pl.* (*Sewing*) Kräusel[falten] *Pl.*
**~ 'up** *v.t.* **A** (*bring together and pick up*) aufsammeln; auflesen; zusammenpacken ‹Habseligkeiten, Werkzeug›; **be left to ~ up the pieces of one's life** (*fig.*) vor dem Scherbenhaufen seines Lebens stehen; **B** (*draw*) hochraffen ‹Rock›; **~ oneself up to one's full height** sich zu seiner vollen Größe aufrichten; **C** (*sum up*) zusammentragen ‹Fakten›; **D** (*summon*) sammeln ‹Kräfte, Gedanken usw.›

**gathering** /'gæðərɪŋ/ *n.* **A** (*group*) Gruppe, *die;* **B** (*assembly, meeting*) Versammlung, *die;* (*in Scottish Highlands*) Volksfest, *das;* **social ~:** gesellschaftliches Ereignis; **C** (*Sewing*) Kräusel[falten] *Pl.*

**GATT** /gæt/ *abbr.* **General Agreement on Tariffs and Trade** GATT, *das*

**gauche** /gəʊʃ/ *adj.* linkisch; (*clumsy*) schwerfällig; (*tactless*) plump

**gaucheness** /'gəʊʃnɪs/ *n., no pl.* ⇒ **gauche**: Linkische, *das;* Schwerfälligkeit, *die;* Plumpheit, *die;* **~ of manner** linkische Art

**gaucherie** /'gəʊʃəri:/ *n.* **A** *no pl.* (*manner*) linkische Art; **B** (*action*) Plumpheit, *die*

**gaucho** /'gaʊtʃəʊ/ *n., pl.* **~s** Gaucho, *der*

**gaudily** /'gɔ:dɪlɪ/ *adv.* prunkvoll ‹dekoriert›; übertrieben aufwendig; protzig (*abwertend*); **~ coloured** knallbunt

**gaudy**[1] /'gɔ:dɪ/ *adj.* protzig (*abwertend*); grell, (*ugs.*) knallig ‹Farben›

**gaudy**[2] *n.* (*Brit. Univ.*) (*jährliches*) [College]fest

**gauge** /geɪdʒ/ ❶ *n.* **A** (*standard measure*) [Normal]maß, *das;* (*of textile*) Gauge, das (*fachspr.*); (*of bullet*) Kaliber, *das;* (*of rail*) Spurweite, *die;* **standard/broad/narrow ~:** Normal- *od.* Regel-/Breit-/Schmalspur, *die;* **B** (*instrument*) Messgerät, *das;* (*to measure water level*) Pegel, *der;* Wasserstandsanzeiger, *der;* (*for dimensions of tools or wire*) Lehre, *die;* ⇒ *also* **oil gauge**; **petrol gauge**; **C** (*Naut.*) *Schiffsposition in Bezug auf den Wind;* **have the weather ~ [of sb.]** in Luv [von jmdm.] liegen; (*fig.*) die Oberhand [über jmdn.] haben; **D** (*fig.: criterion, test*) Kriterium, *das;* Maßstab, *der.*
❷ *v.t.* **A** (*measure*) messen; **B** (*fig.*) beurteilen (**by** nach)

**Gaul** /gɔ:l/ *n.* (*Hist.*) **A** (*country*) Gallien, *das;* **B** (*person*) Gallier, *der*/Gallierin, *die*

**gauleiter** /'gaʊlaɪtə(r)/ *n.* **A** (*Hist.*) Gauleiter, *der;* **B** (*fig.: local or petty tyrant*) Ortstyrann, *der*

**gaunt** /gɔ:nt/ *adj.* **A** (*haggard*) hager; (*from suffering*) verhärmt; **B** (*grim, desolate*) öde; kahl ‹Baum›; karg ‹Landschaft›

**gauntlet**[1] /'gɔ:ntlɪt/ *n.* **A** Stulpenhandschuh, *der;* **B** (*wrist part of glove*) Stulpe, *die;* **C** (*Hist.: armoured glove*) Panzerhandschuh, *der;* **D** **fling** *or* **throw down the ~** (*fig.*) jmdm. den Fehdehandschuh hinwerfen *od.* vor die Füße werfen; **pick** *or* **take up the ~** (*fig.*) den Fehdehandschuh aufnehmen *od.* aufheben

**gauntlet**[2] *n.* **run the ~:** Spießruten laufen

**gauss** /gaʊs/ *n., pl. same or* **~es** (*Phys.*) Gauß, *das*

**gauze** /gɔ:z/ *n.* **A** Gaze, *die;* **B** (*of wire etc.*) Drahtgeflecht, *das;* Gaze, *die*

**gave** ⇒ **give** 1, 2

**gavel** /'gævl/ *n.* Hammer, *der*

**gavotte** /gə'vɒt/ *n.* (*Mus.*) Gavotte, *die*

**gawk** /gɔ:k/ *v.i.* (*coll.*) gaffen (*abwertend*); **~ at sth./sb.** etw./jmdn. begaffen

**gawky** /'gɔ:kɪ/ *adj.* linkisch; unbeholfen; (*with disproportionately long limbs*) schlaksig (*ugs.*)

**gawp** /gɔ:p/ ⇒ **gawk**

**gay** /geɪ/ ❶ *adj.* **A** fröhlich; fidel (*ugs.*) ‹Person, Gesellschaft›; **B** (*showy, bright-coloured*) farbenfroh ‹Stoff, Ausstattung›; fröhlich, lebhaft ‹Farbe›; **~ with flowers/flags** mit Blumen/Fahnen fröhlich geschmückt; **C** (*coll.: homosexual*) schwul (*ugs.*); Schwulen‹lokal, -blatt›; **D** (*euphem.: immoral*) locker; **a ~ dog** ein lockerer Vogel (*salopp, oft scherzh.*). ❷ *n.* (*coll.*) Schwule, *der* (*ugs.*)

**gayety** (*Amer.*) ⇒ **gaiety**

**gay libe'ration** *n.* Schwulenemanzipation, *die;* **~ movement** Schwulenbewegung, *die*

**gayness** /'geɪnɪs/ ⇒ **gaiety**

**gay 'rights** *n. pl.* Schwulenrechte *Pl.;* **~ group/demonstration** Schwulengruppe, *die*/-demonstration, *die*

**Gaza [strip]** /'gɑ:zə (strɪp)/ *pr. n.* Gazastreifen, *der*

**gaze** /geɪz/ ❶ *v.i.* blicken; (*more fixedly*) starren; **~ at sb./sth.** jmdn./etw. anstarren *od.* ansehen; **~ after sb./sth.** jmdm./einer Sache hinterhersehen; **~ around** *or* **about** um sich blicken. ❷ *n.* Blick, *der*

**gazelle** /gə'zel/ *n.* Gazelle, *die*

**gazette** /gə'zet/ ❶ *n.* **A** (*Brit.: official journal*) **London G~:** Londoner Amtsblatt; **B** (*newspaper*) Anzeiger, *der.* ❷ *v.t.* (*Brit.: announce*) [amtlich] bekannt geben

**gazetteer** /gæzɪ'tɪə(r)/ *n.* alphabetisches [Orts]verzeichnis

**gazump** /gə'zʌmp/ *v.t.* (*coll.*) *durch nachträgliches Überbieten um die Chance bringen, ein Haus zu kaufen*

**GB** *abbr.* **Great Britain** GB

**GBH** *abbr.* (*Brit. Law*) **grievous bodily harm**

**GC** *abbr.* (*Brit.*) **George Cross**

**GCE** *abbr.* (*Brit. Hist.*) **General Certificate of Education**

**GCSE** *abbr.* (*Brit.*) **General Certificate of Secondary Education**

**GDP** *abbr.* **gross domestic product** BIP

**GDR** *abbr.* (*Hist.*) **German Democratic Republic** DDR, *die*

**gear** /gɪə(r)/ ❶ *n.* **A** (*Motor Veh.*) Gang, *der;* (*transmission*) Übersetzung, *die;* **first/second** *etc.* **~** (*Brit.*) der erste/zweite *usw.* Gang; **top/bottom ~** (*Brit.*) der höchste/erste Gang; **high/low ~:** hoher/niedriger Gang; **change** *or* **shift ~:** schalten; **change** *or* **shift [up] a ~** (*fig.*) einen Gang zulegen (*ugs.*); **change into second/a higher/lower ~:** in den zweiten Gang/in einen höheren/niedrigeren Gang schalten; **a bicycle with ten-speed ~s** ein Fahrrad mit Zehngangschaltung; **put** *or* **get** *or* **shift the car into ~:** den Wagen in Gang setzen; einen Gang einlegen; **in ~** (*fig.*) in Ordnung; im Gleis; **out of ~:** im Leerlauf; (*fig.*) in Unordnung; aus dem Gleis [geraten]; **the car is in/out of ~:** es ist ein/kein Gang eingelegt; **leave the car in ~:** den Gang drin lassen; **B** (*combination of wheels, levers, etc.*) Getriebe, *das;* **C** (*clothes*) Aufmachung, *die;* **travelling ~:** Reisekleidung, *die;* ⇒ *also* **headgear**; **D** (*equipment, tools*) Gerät, *das;* Ausrüstung, *die;* **E** (*apparatus*) Vorrichtung, *die;* **F** (*harness*) [Sielen]geschirr, *das.* ❷ *v.t.* (*adjust, adapt*) anpassen (**to** *Dat.*); abstimmen, ausrichten (**to** auf + *Akk.*)

**gear: ~box, ~case** *ns.* Getriebekasten, *der;* **five-speed ~box** Fünfganggetriebe, *das;* **~ cable** *n.* Schaltzug, *der;* **~ change** *n.* (*Brit.*) **an upward/a downward ~ change** ein Hoch-/Herunterschalten; **have a smooth/awkward ~ change** ‹Fahrrad, Auto:› sich leicht/schlecht schalten

**gearing** /'gɪərɪŋ/ *n.* **A** Getriebe, *das;* **B** (*Brit. Finance*) *Verhältnis von Ausschüttung auf Vorzugsaktien zu Ausschüttung auf Stammaktien*

**gear: ~ lever,** (*Amer.*) **~ shift, ~stick** *ns.* Schalthebel, *der;* Schaltknüppel, *der;* **~wheel** *n.* Zahnrad, *das*

**gecko** /'gekəʊ/ *n., pl.* **~s** (*Zool.*) Gecko, *der*

**geddit** /'gedɪt/ *v.i.* (*coll.*) **~?** verstanden? (*ugs.*); kapiert? (*salopp*)

**gee**[1] /dʒi:/ *int.* (*to horse*) hü

**gee**[2] *int.* (*coll.*) Mann (*salopp*); Mensch [Meier] (*salopp*)

**'gee-gee** *n.* (*Brit. coll.: horse*) Hottehü, *das* (*Kinderspr.*)

**geese** *pl. of* **goose**

**'gee-up** *int.* ⇒ **gee**[1]

**gee 'whiz** *int.* (*coll.*) ⇒ **gee**[2]

**geezer** /'gi:zə(r)/ *n.* **A** (*coll.: old man*) Opa, *der* (*ugs. scherzh. od. abwertend*); **B** (*coll.: fellow*) Typ, *der* (*ugs.*)

**Geiger counter** /'gaɪgə kaʊntə(r)/ *n.* (*Phys.*) Geigerzähler, *der*

**geisha** /'geɪʃə/ *n., pl.* **~s** *or same* Geisha, *die*

**gel** /dʒel/ ❶ *n.* Gel, *das.* ❷ *v.i.,* **-ll-** **A** gelatinieren; gelieren; **B** (*fig.*) Gestalt annehmen

**gelatin** /'dʒelətɪn/, (*esp. Brit.*) **gelatine** /'dʒeləti:n/ *n.* Gelatine, *die;* **blasting ~e** Sprenggelatine, *die*

**gelatinous** /dʒɪ'lætɪnəs/ *adj.* **A** (*resembling gelatin*) gelatineartig; **B** (*consisting of gelatin*) gelatinös

**geld** /geld/ *v.t.* kastrieren; (*spay*) sterilisieren

**gelding** /'geldɪŋ/ *n.* kastriertes Tier; (*male horse*) Wallach, *der*

**gelignite** /'dʒelɪgnaɪt/ *n.* Gelatinedynamit, *das*

**gem** /dʒem/ *n.* **A** Edelstein, *der;* (*cut also*) Juwel, *das od. der;* ([*semi-*]*precious stone with engraved design*) Gemme, *die;* **B** (*fig.*) Juwel, *das;* Perle, *die;* (*choicest part*) Glanzstück, *das*

**Geminean** /dʒəmɪ'ni:ən/ *n.* (*Astrol.*) Zwilling, *der*

**Gemini** /'dʒemɪnaɪ, 'dʒemɪnɪ/ *n.* (*Astrol., Astron.*) Zwillinge *Pl.;* Gemini *Pl.;* ⇒ *also* **Aries**

**'gemstone** *n.* Edelstein, *der*

**gen** /dʒen/ (*Brit. coll.*) ❶ *n.* notwendige Angaben; **give sb. the ~ on** *or* **about sth.** jmdn. über etw. (*Akk.*) informieren. ❷ *v.t.,* **-nn-: ~ oneself/sb. up on** *or* **about sth.** sich/jmdn. über etw. (*Akk.*) informieren. ❸ *v.i.,* **-nn-: ~ up on** *or* **about sth.** sich über etw. (*Akk.*) informieren

**Gen.** *abbr.* ▶ **1617** **General** Gen.

**gendarme** /'ʒɒndɑ:m/ *n.* Gendarm, *der*

**gender** /'dʒendə(r)/ *n.* **A** (*Ling.*) [grammatisches] Geschlecht; Genus, *das;* **B** (*one's sex*) Geschlecht, *das;* **~ gap** Unterschied zwischen den Geschlechtern

**gene** /dʒi:n/ *n.* (*Biol.*) Gen, *das; attrib.* **~ pool** Genpool, *der*

**genealogical** /dʒi:nɪə'lɒdʒɪkl, dʒenɪə'lɒdʒɪkl/ *adj.* genealogisch; **~ tree** Stammbaum, *der*

**genealogist** /dʒi:nɪ'ælədʒɪst, dʒenɪ'ælədʒɪst/ *n.* ▶ **1261** Genealoge, *der*/Genealogin, *die;* Ahnenforscher, *der*/-forscherin, *die*

**genealogy** /dʒi:nɪ'ælədʒɪ, dʒenɪ'ælədʒɪ/ *n.* **A** Genealogie, *die* (*fachspr.*); (*pedigree*) Ahnentafel, *die* (*geh.*); (*investigation*) Ahnenforschung, *die;* **B** (*Zool., Bot.*) Stammbaum, *der*

**genera** *pl. of* **genus**

**general** /'dʒenrl/ ❶ *adj.* **A** allgemein; **the ~ public** weite Kreise der Öffentlichkeit *od.* Bevölkerung; **in ~ use** allgemein verbreitet; **be in ~ use as sth.** allgemein als etw. benutzt werden; **not for ~ use** (*not to be used by everybody*) nicht für den allgemeinen Gebrauch bestimmt; **his ~ health/manner** sein Allgemeinbefinden/sein Benehmen im Allgemeinen; **he has had a good ~ education** er hat eine gute Allgemeinbildung; **a ~ view of the building** eine Gesamtansicht des Gebäudes; **come to a ~ agreement** sich grundsätzlich einigen; **reach a ~ decision** eine grundsätzliche Entscheidung treffen; **in a ~ state of decay** in einem Zustand allgemeinen Verfalls; **~ matters** allgemeine Angelegenheiten; **the cold weather has been ~ in England** es ist in ganz England kalt gewesen; **B** (*prevalent, widespread, usual*) allgemein; weit verbreitet ‹Übel, Vorurteil, Aberglaube, Ansicht›; häufig ‹Leiden›; **it is the ~ custom** *or* **rule** es ist allgemein üblich *od.* ist Sitte *od.* Brauch; **C** (*not limited in application*) allgemein; (*true of* [*nearly*] *all cases*)

allgemein gültig; generell; **as a ~ rule** im Allgemeinen; **in the ~ way [of things]** normalerweise; **in ~:** im Allgemeinen; **'G~ Enquiries'** „Auskunft"; **D** (*not detailed, vague*) allgemein; ungefähr, vage ‹Vorstellung, Beschreibung, Ähnlichkeit usw.›; allgemein gehalten ‹Übersetzung, Bestimmung, Vertrag›; oberflächlich ‹Ähnlichkeit›; **in its ~ form** im Großen und Ganzen; **in the most ~ terms, in a very ~ way** nur ganz allgemein; **the ~ idea** *or* **plan is that we ...:** wir haben uns das so vorgestellt, dass wir ...; **yes, that was the ~ idea** ja, so war es gedacht; **E** (*Mil.*) Generals‹rang, -streifen usw.›; **~ officer** General, *der;* **F** (*chief, head*) General‹direktor, -vertretung›.
❷ *n.* ▶ 1617 (*Mil.*) General, *der;* (*tactician, strategist*) Stratege, *der;* **~ of the army/air force** (*Amer.*) Fünfsternegeneral, *der*

**general: G~ A'merican** *n.* General American, *das;* amerikanische Standardsprache; **~ anaes'thetic** ⇒ **anaesthetic** 2; **G~ As'sembly** *n.* Generalversammlung, *die;* Vollversammlung, *die;* **G~ Certificate of Edu'cation** *n.* (*Brit. Hist.*) (*ordinary level*) ≈ mittlere Reife; (*advanced level*) ≈ Abitur, *das;* **G~ Certificate of Secondary Edu'cation** *n.* (*Brit.*) *Abschluss der Sekundarstufe;* **~ 'dealer** *n.* Gemischtwarenhändler, *der;* **~ de'livery** *n.* (*Amer.*) Schalter für postlagernde Sendungen; *written in address* postlagernd; **~ e'lection** ⇒ **election**; **~ head'quarters** *n. sing. or pl.* Generalkommando, *das;* **~ hospital** *n.* Allgemeinkrankenhaus, *das;* (*Mil.*) Lazarett, *das*

**generalisation, generalise** ⇒ **generaliz-**

**generalist** /'dʒenrəlɪst/ *n.* Generalist, *der*

**generality** /dʒenə'rælɪtɪ/ *n.* **A** (*applicability*) allgemeine Anwendbarkeit; (*of conclusion*) Allgemeingültigkeit, *die;* **a method of great ~:** eine vielseitig anwendbare Methode; **B** (*vagueness*) Allgemeinheit, *die;* **C talk in/of generalities** verallgemeinern/über Allgemeines sprechen; **D** (*main, body, bulk, majority*) (*of mankind, electorate, etc.*) Großteil, *der;* (*of voters, individuals, etc.*) Mehrheit, *die*

**generalization** /dʒenrəlaɪ'zeɪʃn/ *n.* Generalisierung, *die;* Verallgemeinerung, *die;* **hasty ~:** voreilige Verallgemeinerung

**generalize** /'dʒenrəlaɪz/ ❶ *v.t.* **A** generalisieren; verallgemeinern; **B** (*infer*) ableiten; **C** (*base general statement on*) eine allgemein gültige Feststellung treffen anhand von; **D** (*Math., Philos.*) generalisieren; **E** (*bring into use*) verbreiten. ❷ *v.i.* **~ [about sth.]** [etw.] verallgemeinern; **~ about the French** die Franzosen alle in einen Topf werfen (*ugs.*) *od.* über einen Kamm scheren; **you can't ~; each one is different** man soll nicht verallgemeinern — jeder Einzelne ist wieder anders

**general 'knowledge** *n.* Allgemeinwissen, *das;* **it is ~ that ...:** es ist allgemein bekannt, dass ...; **~ exam/questions** das Allgemeinwissen betreffende Prüfung/Fragen

**generally** /'dʒenrəlɪ/ *adv.* **A** (*extensively*) allgemein; **~ available** überall erhältlich; **B ~ speaking** im Allgemeinen; **C** (*usually*) im Allgemeinen; normalerweise; **D** (*summarizing the situation*) ganz allgemein

**general: ~ 'manager** *n.* ▶ 1261 [leitender] Direktor/[leitende] Direktorin; **~ 'meeting** *n.* Generalversammlung, *die;* Hauptversammlung, *die;* **G~ 'Post Office** *n.* (*Brit.*) Hauptpost[amt, *das*], *die;* **~ 'practice** *n.* (*Med.*) Allgemeinmedizin, *die;* **~ prac'titioner** *n.* ▶ 1261 (*Med.*) Arzt/Ärztin für Allgemeinmedizin; **~ 'public** *n.* Öffentlichkeit, *die;* Allgemeinheit, *die;* **the lecture is open to the ~ public** die Vorlesung *od.* der Vortrag ist öffentlich; **~ reader** *n.* Durchschnittsleser, *der*/-leserin, *die*

**generalship** /'dʒenrlʃɪp/ *n., no pl.* (*strategy*) Führung, *die;* Kommando, *das;* (*fig.*) Leitung, *die*

**general: ~ shop** ⇒ **~ store**; **~ 'staff** *n.* Generalstab, *der;* **~ store** *n.* Gemischtwarenhandlung, *die* (*veralt.*); **~ 'strike** *n.* Generalstreik, *der*

**generate** /'dʒenəreɪt/ *v.t.* (*produce*) erzeugen (**from** aus); (*result in*) führen zu

**generating station** /'dʒenəreɪtɪŋ steɪʃn/ *n.* Elektrizitätswerk, *das*

**generation** /dʒenə'reɪʃn/ *n.* **A** Generation, *die;* **the present/rising ~:** die heutige/heranwachsende *od.* junge Generation; **~ gap** Generationsunterschied, *der;* **first-/second-~ computers** *etc.* Computer *usw.* der ersten/zweiten Generation; **B** (*production*) Erzeugung, *die;* **~ of electricity** Stromerzeugung, *die;* **C** (*procreation*) **organs of ~:** Geschlechtsorgane *Pl.;* Fortpflanzungsorgane *Pl.*

**generative** /'dʒenərətɪv/ *adj.* generativ; Zeugungs‹fähigkeit, -kraft usw.›

**generator** /'dʒenəreɪtə(r)/ *n.* **A** Generator, *der;* (*in motor car also*) Lichtmaschine, *die;* **B** (*originator*) Schöpfer, *der;* **be a ~ of new ideas** neue Ideen entwickeln

**generic** /dʒɪ'nerɪk/ *adj.* **A** gattungsmäßig; generisch (*fachspr.*); **~ term** *or* **name** *or* **heading** Ober- *od.* Gattungsbegriff, *der;* **B** (*Biol.*) Gattungs‹name, -bezeichnung›

**generic 'drug** *n.* Generikum, *das*

**generosity** /dʒenə'rɒsɪtɪ/ *n.* Großzügigkeit, *die;* Generosität, *die* (*geh.*); (*magnanimity*) Großmut, *die;* Generosität, *die* (*geh.*)

**generous** /'dʒenərəs/ *adj.* **A** großzügig; generös (*geh.*); (*noble-minded*) edel (*geh.*); großmütig; **he is ~ with compliments** er spart nicht mit Komplimenten; **B** (*ample, abundant*) großzügig; reichhaltig ‹Mahl›; reichlich ‹Nachschub, Vorrat, Portion›; üppig ‹Figur, Formen, Mahl›; weit ‹Ärmel, Kleidungsstück›; breit ‹Saum›; **~ size 12** groß ausgefallene Größe 12

**generously** /'dʒenərəslɪ/ *adv.* großzügig; generös (*geh.*); (*magnanimously*) großmütig; **'please give ~'** „wir bitten um großzügige Spenden"

**genesis** /'dʒenɪsɪs/ *n., pl.* **geneses** /'dʒenɪsi:z/ **A G~** *no pl.* das erste Buch Mose; Schöpfungsgeschichte, *die;* **B** (*origin*) Ursprung, *der;* Herkunft, *die;* (*development into being*) Entstehung, *die*

**genetic** /dʒɪ'netɪk/ *adj.* **A** genetisch; **~ code** genetischer Code; **B** (*concerning origin*) entwicklungsgeschichtlich; **~ development** Entwicklungsgeschichte, *die*

**genetically** /dʒɪ'netɪkəlɪ/ *adv.* **A** (*according to genetics*) genetisch; **~ modified** gentechnisch verändert; genmanipuliert; **~ engineered** gentechnisch verändert ‹Organismen, Pflanzen, Tiere, Nahrungsmittel›; gentechnisch hergestellt ‹Medikament, Enzym›; **B** (*according to origin*) entwicklungsgeschichtlich

**genetic: ~ engi'neering** *n.* Gentechnologie, *die;* **~ 'fingerprinting, ~ profiling** /'prəʊfaɪlɪŋ/ *ns., no pl.* DNA-Fingerprintmethode, *die*

**geneticist** /dʒɪ'netɪsɪst/ *n.* ▶ 1261 Genetiker, *der*/Genetikerin, *die*

**genetics** /dʒɪ'netɪks/ *n., no pl.* Genetik, *die;* Erbbiologie, *die*

**genetic 'testing** *n., no pl.* Gentests *Pl.*

**Geneva** /dʒɪ'ni:və/ ▶ 1626 ❶ *pr. n.* Genf (*das*); **Lake ~:** der Genfer See. ❷ *attrib. adj.* Genfer

**genial** /'dʒi:nɪəl/ *adj.* (*mild*) angenehm; mild ‹Klima, Luft›; (*jovial, kindly*) freundlich; (*sociable*) jovial, leutselig ‹Person, Art›; (*amiable*) liebenswürdig; (*cheering, enlivening*) anregend; belebend

**geniality** /dʒi:nɪ'ælɪtɪ/ *n., no pl.* Freundlichkeit, *die;* **hearty ~:** Herzlichkeit, *die*

**genially** /'dʒi:nɪəlɪ/ *adv.* freundlich; **be ~ disposed towards sb.** jmdm. freundlich gesinnt sein

**genie** /'dʒi:nɪ/ *n., pl.* **genii** /'dʒi:nɪaɪ/ Flaschenteufel, *der*

**genital** /'dʒenɪtl/ ❶ *n. in pl.* ▶ 966 Geschlechtsorgane *Pl.;* Genitalien *Pl.* ❷ *adj.* Geschlechts‹teile, -organe, -drüse›

**genitalia** /dʒenɪ'teɪlɪə/ *n. pl.* Geschlechtsorgane *Pl.;* Genitalia *Pl.*

**genitival** /dʒenɪ'taɪvl/ *adj.* (*Ling.*) genitivisch; Genitiv-

**genitive** /'dʒenɪtɪv/ (*Ling.*) ❶ *adj.* Genitiv-; genitivisch; **~ case** Genitiv, *der.* ❷ *n.* Genitiv, *der;* ⇒ *also* **absolute** C

**genius** /'dʒi:nɪəs/ *n., pl.* **~es** *or* **genii** /'dʒi:nɪaɪ/ **A** *pl.* **~es** (*person*) Genie, *das;* **B** (*natural ability; also iron.*) Talent, *das;* Begabung, *die;* (*extremely great*) Genius, *der* (*geh.*); Genie, *das;* **a man of ~:** ein genialer Mensch; ein Genie; **~ for languages** Sprachbegabung, *die;* **C** (*special character; prevalent feeling, opinions, or taste*) Geist, *der;* (*of people*) Charakter, *der;* Wesen, *das;* **D** (*spirit*) [Schutz]geist, *der;* Genius, *der;* (*of place, country*) Geist, *der;* Genius, *der;* **good/evil ~:** guter/böser Geist

**Genoa** /'dʒenəʊə/ *pr. n.* ▶ 1626 Genua (*das*)

**genocide** /'dʒenəsaɪd/ *n.* Völkermord, *der;* Genozid, *der* (*geh.*)

**genome** /'dʒi:nəʊm/ *n.* (*Biol.*) Genom, *das*

**genre** /ʒɑ̃r/ *n.* **A** Genre, *das;* Gattung, *die;* **B** ⇒ **~-painting** A

**'genre painting** *n.* **A** Genremalerei, *die;* **B** (*picture*) Genrebild, *das*

**gent** /dʒent/ *n.* **A** (*coll./joc.*) Gent, der (*iron.*); **B** (*in shops etc.*) **~s'** Herren‹friseur, -ausstatter›; **C the G~s** (*Brit. coll.*) die Herrentoilette

**genteel** /dʒen'ti:l/ *adj.* vornehm; fein; **they lived in ~ poverty** sie lebten in vornehmer Armut

**genteelly** /dʒen'ti:llɪ/ *adv.* vornehm

**gentian** /'dʒenʃn, 'dʒenʃɪən/ *n.* (*Bot.*) Enzian, *der*

**Gentile** /'dʒentaɪl/ ❶ *n.* Nichtjude, *der*/-jüdin, *die;* (*Bibl.*) Heide, *der*/Heidin, *die.* ❷ *adj.* nichtjüdisch; (*Bibl.*) heidnisch

**gentility** /dʒen'tɪlɪtɪ/ *n., no pl.* **A** (*condition*) Zugehörigkeit zum niederen Adel; **B** (*members*) niederer Adel; **C** (*genteel behaviour*) Vornehmheit, *die;* **appearance of ~:** vornehme Erscheinung

**gentle** /'dʒentl/ *adj.*, **~r** /'dʒentlə(r)/, **~st** /'dʒentlɪst/ **A** sanft; sanftmütig ‹Wesen›; liebenswürdig, freundlich ‹Person, Verhalten, Ausdrucksweise›; (*not stormy, rough, or violent*) leicht, schwach ‹Brise›; ruhig ‹Fluss, Wesen›; (*not loud*) leise ‹Geräusch›; (*moderate*) gemäßigt ‹Tempo›; mäßig ‹Hitze›; gemächlich ‹Tempo, Schritte, Spaziergang›; (*gradual*) sanft ‹Abhang usw.›; (*mild, not drastic*) mild ‹Reinigungsmittel, Shampoo usw.›; wohlig ‹Wärme›; (*easily managed*) zahm, lammfromm ‹Tier›; **be ~ with sb./sth.** sanft mit jmdm./etw. umgehen; **with ~ care** äußerst vorsichtig *od.* behutsam; **a ~ reminder/hint** ein zarter Wink/eine zarte Andeutung; **the ~ sex** das zarte Geschlecht (*ugs. scherzh.*); **the ~ art** *or* **craft** die edle Kunst; **B** (*dated: honourable, wellborn*) edel (*veralt.*); **of ~ birth** von hoher *od.* edler Geburt; **C ~ reader** (*arch.*) lieber *od.* geneigter Leser

**'gentlefolk[s]** *n. pl.* feine Leute; vornehme Leute

**gentleman** /'dʒentlmən/ *n., pl.* **gentlemen** /'dʒentlmən/ **A** (*man of good manners and breeding*) Herr, *der;* Gentleman, *der;* **~ scholar** Privatgelehrter; **a country ~:** ein Landedelmann; **B** (*man*) Herr, *der;* **Gentlemen!** meine Herren!; **Ladies and Gentlemen!** meine Damen und Herren!; **Gentlemen, ...** (*in formal, business letter*) Sehr geehrte Herren!; **the gentlemen of the jury/press** die Herren Geschworenen/von der Presse; **gentlemen's** Herren‹schneider, -friseur›; **C** (*man attached to household of sovereign etc.*) Höfling, *der;* **D** *in pl., constr. as sing.* **the Gentlemen['s]** (*Brit.*) die Herrentoilette; **'Gentlemen'** „Herren"

**gentleman 'farmer** *n.* Gutsherr, *der*

**gentlemanly** /'dʒentlmənlɪ/ *adj.* gentlemanlike *nicht attrib.;* eines Gentlemans *nachgestellt;* **~ person** Gentleman, *der*

**'gentleman's** *or* **'gentlemen's agreement** *n.* Gentleman's *od.* Gentlemen's Agreement, *das;* Vereinbarung auf Treu und Glauben

**gentleness** /'dʒentlnɪs/ *n., no pl.* Sanftheit, *die;* (*of nature*) Sanftmütigkeit, *die;* (*of nurse, words, action*) Behutsamkeit, *die;* (*of shampoo, cleanser, etc.*) Milde, *die;* (*of animal*) Zahmheit, *die*

**'gentlepeople** ⇒ **gentlefolk[s]**

**'gentlewoman** *n.* (*arch.*) Ⓐ (*woman of good birth or breeding*) Dame von Stand; Ⓑ (*lady*) Dame, *die*

**gently** /'dʒentlɪ/ *adv.* (*tenderly*) zart; zärtlich; (*mildly*) sanft; (*carefully*) vorsichtig; behutsam; (*quietly, softly*) leise; (*moderately*) sanft; (*slowly*) langsam; **she broke the news to him ~:** sie brachte ihm die Nachricht schonend bei; **a ~ teasing/sarcastic manner** eine leicht neckende/sarkastische Art; **she took things very ~:** sie ließ es langsam angehen (*ugs.*); **~ does it!** immer sachte! (*ugs.*); **~!** [sachte] sachte!

**gentrification** /dʒentrɪfɪ'keɪʃn/ *n.* *Einzug von sozial Höherstehenden in heruntergekommene Wohnviertel*

**gentry** /'dʒentrɪ/ *n. pl.* Ⓐ niederer Adel; Gentry, *die;* Ⓑ (*derog.: people*) Leute *Pl.;* **light-fingered ~:** Taschendiebe *Pl.*

**genuflect** /'dʒenju:flekt/ *v.i.* niederknien; das Knie *od.* die Knie beugen

**genuflection, genuflexion** /dʒenju:'flekʃn/ *n.* Kniefall, *der;* [Nieder]knien, *das*

**genuine** /'dʒenjʊɪn/ *adj.* Ⓐ (*actually from reputed source or author*) echt; authentisch ‹Text›; **the ~ article** die echte Ausgabe (*fig.*); Ⓑ (*true*) aufrichtig; wahr ‹Zuneigung, Grund, Not›; echt ‹Tränen›; ernsthaft, ernst gemeint ‹Angebot›; echt, überzeugt ‹Skeptiker, Kommunist usw.›

**genuinely** /'dʒenjʊɪnlɪ/ *adv.* wirklich; **it is ~ antique** es ist echt antik

**genus** /'dʒi:nəs, 'dʒenəs/ *n., pl.* **genera** /'dʒenərə/ Ⓐ (*Biol., Logic*) Gattung, die; Ⓑ (*in popular use*) Gattung, *die;* Art, *die*

**geodesic** /dʒi:ə'desɪk, dʒi:ə'di:sɪk/ *adj.* geodätisch

**geodesy** /dʒi:'ɒdɪsɪ/ *n.* Geodäsie, *die*

**geodetic** /dʒi:ə'detɪk, dʒi:ə'di:tɪk/ ⇒ **geodesic**

**geographer** /dʒɪ'ɒgrəfə(r)/ *n.* ▶ **1261** Geograph, *der*/Geographin, *die*

**geographic** /dʒi:ə'græfɪk/, **geographical** /dʒi:ə'græfɪkl/ *adj.* geographisch; **~ latitude** [geographische] Breite

**geographically** /dʒi:ə'græfɪkəlɪ/ *adv.* geographisch

**geography** /dʒɪ'ɒgrəfɪ/ *n.* Geographie, *die;* Erdkunde, *die* (*Schulw.*); **physical/political/regional ~:** physische Geographie *od.* Naturgeographie, *die*/politische Geographie *od.* Staatengeographie, *die*/Landeskunde, *die;* **show sb. the ~ of the house** (*coll.*) jmdm. zeigen, wo sich die einzelnen Räume befinden; (*location of WC*) jmdm. zeigen, wo das [gewisse] Örtchen ist (*fam. verhüll.*)

**geological** /dʒi:ə'lɒdʒɪkl/ *adj.*, **geologically** /dʒi:ə'lɒdʒɪkəlɪ/ *adv.* geologisch

**geologist** /dʒɪ'ɒlədʒɪst/ *n.* ▶ **1261** Geologe, *der*/Geologin, *die*

**geology** /dʒɪ'ɒlədʒɪ/ *n.* Geologie, *die;* (*features*) geologische Beschaffenheit

**geometric** /dʒi:ə'metrɪk/, **geometrical** /dʒi:ə'metrɪkl/ *adj.* geometrisch; **~ mean** geometrisches Mittel; **geometrical progression** *or* **series** geometrische Reihe

**geometrically** /dʒi:ə'metrɪkəlɪ/ *adv.* geometrisch

**geometry** /dʒɪ'ɒmɪtrɪ/ *n.* Geometrie, *die*

**ge'ometry set** *n.* Reißzeug, *das*

**geophysical** /dʒi:ə'fɪzɪkl/ *adj.* geophysikalisch

**geophysics** /dʒi:ə'fɪzɪks/ *n., no pl.* Geophysik, *die*

**Geordie** /'dʒɔ:dɪ/ *n.* (*Brit.*) Geordie, *der;* *Einwohner von Tyneside*

**George** /dʒɔ:dʒ/ *n.* Ⓐ (*Hist., as name of ruler etc.*) Georg; Ⓑ **by ~!** (*Brit. dated coll.*) potz Blitz!; bei Gott!

**George: ~ 'Cross** *n.* (*Brit.*) Georgskreuz, *das;* **~ 'Medal** *n.* (*Brit.*) Georgsmedaille, *die*

**georgette** /dʒɔ:'dʒet/ *n.* (*Textiles*) [Crêpe] Georgette, *der*

**Georgia** /'dʒɔ:dʒɪə/ *pr. n.* (*in USSR*) Georgien (*das*); (*in US*) Georgia (*das*)

**Georgian**[1] /'dʒɔ:dʒɪən/ *adj.* (*Brit. Hist.*) georgianisch

**Georgian**[2] *adj.* ▶ **1340** (*USSR*) georgisch; (*US*) aus/in/von Georgia *nachgestellt*

**geostationary** /dʒi:ə'steɪʃənərɪ/ *adj.* geostationär

**Ger.** *abbr.* **German** dt.

**geranium** /dʒə'reɪnɪəm/ *n.* Ⓐ (*in popular use*) Geranie, *die;* Pelargonie, *die;* Ⓑ (*herb or shrub Geranium*) Storchschnabel, *der;* Geranie, *die;* Geranium, *das*

**gerbil** /'dʒɜ:bɪl/ *n.* (*Zool.*) Wüstenmaus, *die;* Rennmaus, *die*

**gerfalcon** ⇒ **gyrfalcon**

**geriatric** /dʒerɪ'ætrɪk/ ❶ *adj.* geriatrisch. ❷ *n.* (*also joc.*) Greis, *der*/Greisin, *die*

**geriatrician** /dʒerɪə'trɪʃn/ *n.* ▶ **1261** Geriater, *der*/Geriaterin, *die*

**geriatrics** /dʒerɪ'ætrɪks/ *n., no pl.* Geriatrie, *die;* Altersheilkunde, *die*

**germ** /dʒɜ:m/ *n.* (*lit. or fig.*) Keim, *der;* **I don't want to catch your ~s** ich möchte mich nicht bei dir anstecken; **I don't want you to spread your ~s around** behalte deine Bazillen für dich!; **wheat ~:** Weizenkeim, *der;* **a ~ of truth is contained in this legend** (*fig.*) diese Legende enthält einen wahren Kern

**german** *adj. postpos.* leiblich

**German** /'dʒɜ:mən/ ▶ **1275**, ▶ **1340** ❶ *adj.* deutsch; **a ~ person** ein Deutscher/eine Deutsche; **the ~ people** die Deutschen; **he/she is ~:** er ist Deutscher/sie ist Deutsche; **have a ~ degree** (*in subject*) einen Universitätsabschluss in Germanistik haben; (*from country*) einen akademischen Grad von einer deutschen Universität haben; **he is a native ~ speaker** seine Muttersprache ist Deutsch; **he is a '~ translator** (*translator from ~*) er ist Übersetzer für Deutsch; **'~ teacher/student** Deutschlehrer/-student, *der;* **~ 'teacher/student** deutscher Lehrer/Student; **~ studies** Germanistik, *die;* **~ department** Germanistisches Institut. ⇒ *also* **East German** 1; **English** 1; **West German** 1. ❷ *n.* Ⓐ (*person*) Deutsche, *der/die;* **he/she is a ~:** er ist Deutscher/sie ist Deutsche; Ⓑ (*language*) Deutsch, *das;* **High ~:** Hochdeutsch, *das;* **Low ~:** Niederdeutsch, *das.* ⇒ *also* **East German** 2; **English** 2 A; **West German** 2

**German Democratic Re'public** *pr. n.* (*Hist.*) Deutsche Demokratische Republik

**germane** /dʒɜ:'meɪn/ *adj.* **~ to** von Bedeutung für

**Germanic** /dʒɜ:'mænɪk/ ❶ *adj.* germanisch; (*having German characteristics*) deutsch; **~ Confederation/Empire** (*Hist.*) Deutscher Bund/Deutsches Reich; **~ people** Germanen *Pl.* ❷ *n.* (*Ling.*) **East/North/West ~:** Ost-/Nord-/Westgermanisch, *das*

**Germanise** ⇒ **Germanize**

**Germanism** /'dʒɜ:mənɪzm/ *n.* Ⓐ (*word or idiom*) Germanismus, *der;* Ⓑ (*German ideas or actions*) deutsche Eigenart *od.* Sitte

**Germanist** /'dʒɜ:mənɪst/ *n.* Germanist, *der*/Germanistin, *die*

**germanium** /dʒɜ:'meɪnɪəm/ *n.* (*Chem.*) Germanium, *das*

**Germanize** /'dʒɜ:mənaɪz/ ❶ *v.t.* eindeutschen; germanisieren (*abwertend*). ❷ *v.i.* deutsch werden

**German: ~ 'measles** *n. sing.* ▶ **1232** Röteln *Pl.;* **~ 'sausage** *n.* ≈ Fleischwurst, *die;* **~ 'shepherd [dog]** *n.* [deutscher] Schäferhund; **~ 'silver** *n.* Neusilber, *das*

**Germany** /'dʒɜ:mənɪ/ *pr. n.* Deutschland (*das*); **Federal Republic of ~:** Bundesrepublik Deutschland, *die;* ⇒ *also* **East Germany**; **West Germany**

**'germ cell** *n.* Keimzelle, *die*

**germicide** /'dʒɜ:mɪsaɪd/ *n.* keimtötendes Mittel; Bakterizid, *das* (*fachspr.*)

**germinal** /'dʒɜ:mɪnl/ *adj.* Ⓐ (*in earliest stage of development*) noch unentwickelt; **~ form** Anfangsstadium, *das;* Ⓑ (*of germ*) germinal (*Bot.*); Keim-

**germinate** /'dʒɜ:mɪneɪt/ ❶ *v.i.* keimen; (*fig.*) entstehen. ❷ *v.t.* zum Keimen bringen; (*fig.*) hervorbringen

**germination** /dʒɜ:mɪ'neɪʃn/ *n.* Keimung, *die;* Keimen, *das;* (*fig.*) Entstehung, *die*

**'germ line** *n.* (*Biol.*) Keimbahn, *die*

**germ 'warfare** *n.* Bakterienkrieg, *der;* biologische Kriegführung

**gerrymander** /dʒerɪ'mændə(r)/ ❶ *v.t.* *willkürlich in Wahlbezirke aufteilen, um einer politischen Partei Vorteile zu verschaffen.* ❷ *n.* Wahlkreisschiebungen *Pl.* (*ugs.*)

**gerund** /'dʒerənd/ *n.* (*Ling.*) Gerundium, *das*

**Gestapo** /ge'stɑ:pəʊ/ *n.* Gestapo, *die*

**gestation** /dʒe'steɪʃn/ *n.* Ⓐ (*of animal*) Trächtigkeit, *die;* (*of woman*) Schwangerschaft, *die;* **~ period** Tragezeit, *die*/Zeit der Schwangerschaft; Ⓑ (*fig.*) Reifung, *die;* Heranreifen, *das*

**gesticulate** /dʒe'stɪkjʊleɪt/ *v.i.* gestikulieren; **he ~d to the lorry driver to stop reversing** er signalisierte dem Lkw-Fahrer, nicht weiter rückwärts zu fahren

**gesticulation** /dʒestɪkjʊ'leɪʃn/ *n.* Gesten *Pl.;* **wild ~:** wildes Gestikulieren

**gesture** /'dʒestʃə(r)/ ❶ *n.* Geste, *die* (*auch fig.*); Gebärde, *die* (*geh.*); **a ~ of resignation** eine resignierte Geste. ❷ *v.i.* gestikulieren; **~ to sb. to do sth.** jmdm. zu verstehen geben *od.* (*geh.*) jmdm. bedeuten, etw. zu tun. ❸ *v.t.* zu verstehen geben; **~ sb. to do sth.** jmdm. zu verstehen geben *od.* (*geh.*) jmdm. bedeuten, etw. zu tun

**get** /get/ ❶ *v.t.*, **-tt-**, *p. t.* **got** /gɒt/, *p. p.* **got** *or* (*in comb./arch./Amer. except in sense* M) **gotten** /'gɒtn/ (**got** *also coll. abbr. of* **has got** *or* **have got**) Ⓐ (*obtain*) bekommen; kriegen (*ugs.*); (*by buying*) kaufen; sich (*Dat.*) anschaffen ‹Auto usw.›; (*by one's own effort for special purpose*) sich (*Dat.*) besorgen ‹Visum, Genehmigung, Arbeitskräfte›; sich (*Dat.*) beschaffen ‹Geld›; einholen ‹Gutachten›; (*by contrivance*) kommen zu; (*find*) finden ‹Zeit›; (*extract*) fördern ‹Kohle, Öl›; **~ an income from sth.** ein Einkommen aus etw. beziehen; **where did you ~ that?** wo hast du das her?; **the bogy man will come and ~ you** der schwarze Mann kommt und holt dich; **he got him by the leg/arm** er kriegte ihn am Bein/Arm zu fassen; **~ sb. a job/taxi, ~ a job/taxi for sb.** jmdm. einen Job verschaffen/ein Taxi besorgen *od.* rufen; **~ oneself sth./a rich man/a job** sich (*Dat.*) etw. zulegen/einen reichen Mann finden/einen Job finden; **I need to ~ some bread** ich muss Brot besorgen *od.* holen; **you can't ~ this kind of fruit in the winter months** dieses Obst gibt es im Winter nicht zu kaufen; **~ water from a well** das Wasser vom Brunnen holen; ⇒ *also* **best** 3 C; **better** 3 A; **kick** 1 C; **upper** 1 A; **wind**[1] 1 F; **worst** 3 A; Ⓑ (*fetch*) holen; **what can I ~ you?** was kann ich Ihnen anbieten?; **is there anything I can ~ you in town?** soll ich dir etwas aus der Stadt mitbringen?; **~ sb. from the station** jmdn. vom Bahnhof abholen; Ⓒ **~ the bus** *etc.* (*be in time for, catch*) den Bus *usw.* erreichen *od.* (*ugs.*) kriegen; (*travel by*) den Bus nehmen; Ⓓ (*prepare*) machen (*ugs.*), zubereiten ‹Essen›; Ⓔ (*coll.: eat*) essen; zu sich nehmen ‹Imbiss›; **~ something to eat** etwas zu essen holen; (*be given*) etwas zu essen bekommen; Ⓕ (*gain*) erreichen; **what do I ~ out of it?** was habe ich davon?; Ⓖ (*by calculation*) erhalten; Ⓗ (*receive*) bekommen; erhalten, (*ugs.*) kriegen ‹Geldsumme, Belohnung›; ernten ‹Lob›; **the country ~s very little sun/rain** die Sonne scheint/es regnet nur sehr wenig in dem Land; **he got the full force of the blow** er bekam die volle Wucht des Schlages ab; **she got some bruises from the fall** sie hat sich (*Dat.*) mehrere Prellungen bei dem Sturz zugezogen; **he got his jaw broken in a fight** bei einer Schlägerei wurde ihm der Kiefer gebrochen; **~ nothing but ingratitude** nichts als Undank ernten; Ⓘ (*receive as penalty*) bekommen, (*ugs.*) kriegen ‹6 Monate Gefängnis, lebenslänglich, Geldstrafe, Tracht Prügel›; **that's what I ~ for trying to be helpful** (*iron.*) das hat man nun davon, dass man helfen will; **you'll ~ it** (*coll.*) du kriegst Prügel (*ugs.*); es setzt was (*ugs.*); (*be scolded*) du kriegst was zu hören (*ugs.*); **you'll really ~**

**it this time** diesmal wirst du nicht ungeschoren davonkommen; ⇒ *also* **best** 3 D; **boot** 1 A; **neck** 1 A; **sack**[1] 1 B; **J** (*kill*) töten; erlegen ‹Wild›; (*hit, injure*) treffen; erwischen; **I'll ~ you for that** das wirst du mir büßen; **they've got me** jetzt haben sie mich; ich bin getroffen (*Milit.*); **~ him, boy!** (*to dog*) fass!; **K** (*win*) bekommen; finden ‹Anerkennung›; sich (*Dat.*) verschaffen ‹Ansehen›; erzielen ‹Tor, Punkt, Treffer›; gewinnen ‹Spiel, Preis, Belohnung›; belegen ‹ersten usw. Platz›; **~ fame** berühmt werden; **~ permission** die Erlaubnis erhalten; **he got his fare paid by the firm** seine Firma hat [ihm] die Fahrt bezahlt; **L** (*come to have*) finden ‹Schlaf, Ruhe›; bekommen ‹Einfall, Vorstellung, Gefühl›; gewinnen ‹Eindruck›; (*contract*) bekommen ‹Kopfschmerzen, Grippe, Malaria›; **~ some rest** sich ausruhen; **~ one's freedom** seine Freiheit wiederhaben; **~ an idea/a habit from sb.** von jmdm. eine Idee/Angewohnheit übernehmen; **I hope I don't ~ the flu from you** hoffentlich steckst du mich nicht mit deiner Grippe an; ⇒ *also* **brain** 1 A; **religion** B; **M** **have got** (*coll.: have*) haben; **give it all you've got** gib dein Bestes; **have got a toothache/a cold** Zahnschmerzen/eine Erkältung haben *od.* erkältet sein; **have got to do sth.** etw. tun müssen; **something has got to be done [about it]** dagegen muss etwas unternommen werden; **N** (*succeed in bringing, placing, etc.*) bringen; kriegen (*ugs.*); **~ sth. through the door** *etc.* etw. durch die Tür *usw.* bekommen; **she could hardly ~ herself out of bed** sie kam kaum aus dem Bett hoch; **that bike won't ~ you very far** mit dem Fahrrad wirst du nicht weit kommen; **I must ~ a message to her** ich muss ihr eine Nachricht zukommen lassen; **he's got you where he wants you** er hat dich genau da[hin] gekriegt, wo er dich hin haben wollte (*ugs.*); **O** (*bring into some state*) **this music will ~ the party going** diese Musik wird Schwung in die Party bringen; **~ a project going** ein Projekt in Gang bringen; **~ a machine going** eine Maschine in Gang setzen *od.* bringen; **~ things going** *or* **started** die Dinge in Gang bringen; **~ everything packed/prepared** alles [ein]packen/vorbereiten; **~ sth. ready/done** etw. fertig machen; **~ oneself talked about** sich ins Gerede bringen; **~ one's feet wet** nasse Füße kriegen; **~ one's hands dirty** sich (*Dat.*) die Hände schmutzig machen; **I want to ~ the work done** ich möchte die Arbeit fertig haben; **I didn't ~ much done today** ich habe heute nicht viel geschafft; **~ with child** (*dated*) schwängern; **he's got his sums right** er hat richtig gerechnet; **I need to ~ my house painted** ich muss mein Haus streichen lassen; **you'll ~ yourself thrown out/arrested** du schaffst es noch, dass du rausgeworfen/verhaftet wirst; **I got myself lost** ich habe mich verlaufen; **~ sb. talking/drunk/interested** jmdn. zum Reden bringen/betrunken machen/jmds. Interesse wecken; **~ one's hair cut/clothes dry-cleaned** sich (*Dat.*) die Haare schneiden lassen/seine Sachen reinigen lassen; **P** (*induce*) **~ sb. to do sth.** jmdn. dazu bringen, etw. zu tun; **~ sth. to do sth.** es schaffen, dass etw. etw. tut; **I can never ~ you to listen to me** nie hörst du mir zu!; **I can't ~ the car to start/the door to shut** ich kriege das Auto nicht in Gang/die Tür nicht zu; **Q** (*bring in*) einbringen ‹Ernte›; **R** (*Radio, Telev.: pick up*) empfangen ‹Sender›; **he's trying to ~ BBC 2** er versucht, BBC 2 reinzukriegen (*ugs.*); **S** (*get in touch with by telephone*) **~ sb. [on the phone]** jmdn. [telefonisch] erreichen; **please ~ me this number** bitte verbinden Sie mich mit dieser Nummer; **T** (*answer*) **I'll ~ it!** ich geh schon!; (*answer doorbell*) ich mach auf; (*answer the phone*) ich gehe ran (*ugs.*) *od.* nehme ab; **U** (*coll.: perplex*) in Verwirrung bringen; **this question will ~ him** mit dieser Frage kriegen wir ihn (*ugs.*); **you've got me there; I don't know** da bin ich überfragt — ich weiß es nicht; **V** (*coll.*) (*understand*) kapieren (*ugs.*); verstehen ‹Personen›; (*hear*) mitkriegen (*ugs.*); **~ it?** alles klar? (*ugs.*); **W** (*coll.: annoy*) aufregen (*ugs.*); **X** (*coll.: attract, involve emotionally*) packen.

❷ *v.i.*, **-tt-**, **got**, **got** *or* (*Amer.*) **gotten** **A** (*succeed in coming or going*) kommen; **~ to London/the top before dark** London/den Gipfel vor Einbruch der Dunkelheit erreichen; **we got as far as Oxford** wir kamen bis Oxford; **we have got as far as quadratic equations** wir sind bis zu quadratischen Gleichungen gekommen; **how did that ~ here?** wie ist das hierher gekommen?; **B** (*come to be*) **~ working** sich an die Arbeit machen; **~ talking [to sb.]** [mit jmdm.] ins Gespräch kommen; **~ to talking about sth./sb.** auf etw./jmdn. zu sprechen kommen; **I got [to] thinking how nice ...:** ich habe mir überlegt, wie nett ...; **~ going** *or* **started** (*leave*) losgehen; aufbrechen; (*start talking*) loslegen (*ugs.*); (*become lively or operative*) in Schwung kommen; **once he ~s going** wenn er einmal anfängt; **~ going on** *or* **with sth.** mit etw. anfangen; sich hinter etw. (*Akk.*) klemmen (*ugs.*); **~ going on sb.** jmdn. bearbeiten; **I can't ~ started in the mornings** ich komme morgens nicht in Gang; ⇒ *also* **way** 1 F; **C** **~ to know sb.** jmdn. kennen lernen; **he got to like/hate her** mit der Zeit mochte er sie/begann er, sie zu hassen; **~ to hear of sth.** von etw. erfahren; **I never ~ to see you any more** dich sieht man ja gar nicht mehr *od.* bekommt man ja gar nicht mehr zu Gesicht; **~ to do sth.** (*succeed in doing*) etw. tun können; dazu kommen, etw. zu tun; **D** (*become*) werden; **~ ready/washed** sich fertig machen/waschen; **~ frightened/hungry** Angst/Hunger kriegen; **the time is ~ting near** die Zeit naht; **~ excited about sth.** sich auf etw. (*Akk.*) freuen; **~ interested in sth.** sich für etw. interessieren; **~ caught in the rain** vom Regen überrascht werden; **~ well soon!** gute Besserung!; ⇒ *also* **better** 1; **E** (*coll.: be off, clear out*) verschwinden (*ugs.*)

**~ a'bout** *v.i.* **A** (*move*) sich bewegen; (*travel*) herumkommen; **B** (*spread*) sich herumsprechen; ‹Gerücht:› sich verbreiten

**~ across** ❶ /-ˈ-/ *v.i.* **A** (*to/from other side*) rüberkommen (*ugs.*); **B** (*be communicated*) rüberkommen (*ugs.*); **~ across [to sb.]** ‹Person:› sich [jmdm.] verständlich machen; ‹Witz, Idee:› [bei jmdm.] ankommen. ❷ [*stress varies*] *v.t.* **A** (*cross*) überqueren; **~ sb./sth. across [sth.]** (*transport to/from other side*) jmdn./etw. [über etw. (*Akk.*)] hin-/herüberbringen; **B** (*communicate*) vermitteln, klarmachen (**to** *Dat.*); **~ a joke across to sb.** mit einem Witz bei jmdm. ankommen

**~ a'long** *v.i.* **A** (*advance, progress*) **~ along well** [gute] Fortschritte machen; **how is he ~ting along with his work/is his work ~ting along?** wie kommt er mit seiner Arbeit voran/kommt seine *od.* geht es mit seiner Arbeit voran?; **the patient is ~ting along very well** mit dem Patienten geht es aufwärts; **B** (*manage*) zurechtkommen; **C** (*agree or live sociably*) auskommen; **~ along with each other** *or* **together** miteinander auskommen; **D** (*leave*) sich auf den Weg machen; **~ along with you!** (*fig. coll.*) ach, geh *od.* komm! (*ugs.*); ach, erzähl mir doch nichts! (*ugs.*)

**~ a'round** ❶ *v.i.* **A** ⇒ **~ round** 1 B; **B** ⇒ **~ about** A. ❷ *v.t.* ⇒ **~ round** 2 A, B, D

**~ at** *v.t.* **A** herankommen an (+ *Akk.*); **let sb. ~ at sth.** jmdn. an etw. (*Akk.*) [heran]lassen; **woodworm has got at the wardrobe** in dem Schrank ist der Holzwurm; **B** (*coll.: start work on*) sich machen an (+ *Akk.*); **C** (*get hold of; ascertain*) [he]rausfinden ‹Wahrheit, Ursache usw.›; **D** (*coll.*) **what are you/is he ~ting at?** worauf wollen Sie/will er hinaus?; (*referring to*) worauf spielen Sie/spielt er jetzt an?; **E** (*coll.: tamper with*) sich zu schaffen machen an (+ *Dat.*); (*bribe*) bestechen; (*influence*) unter Druck setzen; **F** (*coll.: attack, taunt*) anmachen (*salopp*); **I have the feeling that I'm being got at** ich habe das Gefühl, dass man mich anpflaumen will (*ugs.*)

**~ a'way** ❶ *v.i.* **A** wegkommen; (*stand back*) zurücktreten; **you need to ~ away [from here]** du müsstest einmal [von hier] fort; **I can't ~ away from work** ich kann nicht von der Arbeit weg; **~ away from the field** (*Racing*) sich vom Feld absetzen; **there is no ~ting away from the fact that ...:** man kommt nicht um die Tatsache *od.* darum herum, dass ...; **~ away from it all** ⇒ **all** 1 A; **B** (*escape*) entkommen; entwischen (*ugs.*); **that's the one that got away** (*fig.*) das/der/die ist mir/dir *usw.* durch die Lappen gegangen (*ugs.*); **C** (*start*) aufbrechen; ‹Läufer:› losrennen; ‹Schwimmer:› losschwimmen; **D** *in imper.* (*coll.*) **~ away [with you]!** ach, geh *od.* komm! (*ugs.*); ach, erzähl mir doch nichts! (*ugs.*).

❷ *v.t.* **A** (*remove, move*) wegnehmen; entfernen, (*ugs.*) wegkriegen ‹Fleck›; wegräumen ‹Besteck, Geschirr›; **~ sth. away from sb.** jmdm. etw. wegnehmen; **we've got to ~ her away from here/his influence/her boyfriend** wir müssen sie von hier fortbringen/seinem Einfluss entziehen/von ihrem Freund fernhalten; **B** (*post*) zur Post bringen; abschicken; wegkriegen (*ugs.*). ⇒ *also* **~away**

**~ a'way with** *v.t.* **A** (*steal and escape with*) entkommen mit; **B** (*as punishment*) davonkommen mit; **C** (*go unpunished for*) ungestraft davonkommen mit; **the things he ~s away with!** was der sich (*Dat.*) alles erlauben kann!; **~ away with it** es sich (*Dat.*) erlauben können; (*succeed*) damit durchkommen; **he can ~ away with anything** *or* (*fig.*) **murder** er kann sich (*Dat.*) alles erlauben

**~ 'back** ❶ *v.i.* **A** (*return*) zurückkommen; **~ back home** nach Hause kommen; **B** (*stand away*) zurücktreten. ❷ *v.t.* **A** (*recover*) wieder- *od.* zurückbekommen; wieder- *od.* zurückkriegen (*ugs.*); zurückgewinnen ‹Kraft, Ehefrau, Freund usw.›; **~ one's strength back** wieder zu Kräften kommen; **B** (*return*) zurücktun; **I can't ~ the lid back on it** ich kriege den Deckel nicht wieder drauf (*ugs.*); **~ the children back home** die Kinder nach Hause zurückbringen; **C** **~ one's 'own back [on sb.]** (*coll.*) sich [an jmdm.] rächen

**~ 'back at** *v.t.* (*coll.*) **~ back at sb. for sth.** jmdm. etw. heimzahlen

**~ 'back to** *v.t.* **~ back to sb./sb.'s question** auf jmdn./jmds. Frage zurückkommen; **I'll ~ back to you on that** ich komme darauf noch zurück; **~ back to one's work/to work/to the office** wieder an seine Arbeit/an die Arbeit/ins Büro gehen; **~ting back to what I was saying ...:** um [noch einmal] auf das, was ich gesagt habe, zurückzukommen

**~ behind** ❶ /-ˈ-/ *v.i.* zurückbleiben; ins Hintertreffen geraten (*ugs.*); (*with payments*) in Rückstand geraten. ❷ [*stress varies*] *v.t.* **A** **~ behind sb./sth.** sich hinter jmdn./etw. stellen; **B** (*not progress as fast as*) **~ behind sb./sth.** hinter jmdm./etw. zurückbleiben

**~ 'by** ❶ *v.i.* **A** (*move past*) passieren; vorbeikommen; **let sb. ~ by** jmdn. vorbeilassen; **B** (*coll.: be acceptable, adequate*) **she should [just about] ~ by in the exam** sie müsste die Prüfung [gerade so] schaffen; **his essay isn't very good but it will ~ by** sein Aufsatz ist nicht sehr gut, aber es reicht noch; **C** (*coll.: survive, manage*) über die Runden kommen (*ugs.*) (**on** mit). ❷ *v.t.* **A** (*move past*) **~ by sb./sth.** an jmdm./etw. vorbeikommen; **he got by the car in front** er überholte den vorderen Wagen; **B** (*pass unnoticed*) entgehen (+ *Dat.*); unbemerkt vorbeikommen an (+ *Dat.*)

**~ down** ❶ /-ˈ-/ *v.i.* **A** (*come down*) heruntersteigen; (*go down*) hinuntersteigen; (*from bus etc.*) aussteigen (**from** aus); (*from horse*) absteigen (**from** von); **help sb. ~ down from the horse/bus** jmdm. vom Pferd/aus dem Bus helfen; **B** (*leave table*) aufstehen; **C** (*bend down*) sich bücken; **~ down on one's knees** niederknien; sich hinknien. ❷ [*stress varies*] *v.t.* **A** (*come down*) heruntersteigen; herunterkommen; (*go down*) hinuntersteigen; hinuntergehen; **B** **~ sb./sth. down** (*manage to bring down*) jmdn./etw. hin-/herunterbringen; (*with some difficulty*) jmdn./etw. hin-/herunterbekommen; (*take down *from above*) jmdn./etw. hin-/herunterholen; C ~ **one's trousers down** die Hose herunterziehen; D (*swallow*) hinunterschlucken; E (*write, record*) ~ **sth. down [on paper]** etw. schriftlich festhalten *od.* zu Papier bringen; F (*depress*) fertig machen (*ugs.*); G (*reduce*) kürzen ‹Aufsatz› (**to** auf + *Akk.*); senken ‹Fieber, Preis›; (*by bargaining*) herunterdrücken ‹Preis›; **I got him down [to £40]** ich habe ihn [auf 40 Pfund] heruntergehandelt

~ **'down to** *v.t.* ~ **down to sth.** sich an etw. (*Akk.*) machen; ~ **down to writing a letter** sich hinsetzen und einen Brief schreiben; **let's ~ down to the facts now** wenden wir uns nun den Fakten zu; ⇒ *also* **brass tacks**; **business** F

~ **'in** ❶ *v.i.* A (*enter*) (*into bus etc.*) einsteigen; (*into bath*) hineinsteigen; (*into bed*) sich hinlegen; (*into room, house, etc.*) eintreten; (*intrude*) eindringen; B (*arrive*) ankommen; (~ *home*) heimkommen; C (*be elected*) gewählt werden; ~ **in for Islington** als Abgeordneter für Islington ins Unterhaus einziehen; D (*obtain place*) (*at institution etc.*) angenommen werden; (*at university*) einen Studienplatz bekommen; (*as employee*) genommen werden; E (*coll.: gain an advantage*) ~ **in first/before sb.** die Nase vorn haben (*ugs.*)/schneller als jmd. sein.
❷ *v.t.* A (*bring in*) einbringen ‹Ernte›; hineinbringen, ins Haus bringen ‹Einkäufe, Kind›; einlagern ‹Kohlen, Kartoffeln›; hineinfahren, in die Garage fahren ‹Auto›; reinholen ‹Wäsche›; einholen ‹Netze, Hummerkörbe›; (*Brit.: fetch and pay for*) holen ‹Getränke›; B (*enter*) einsteigen in (+ *Akk.*) ‹Auto, Zug›; C (*submit*) abgeben ‹Artikel, Hausarbeit›; einreichen ‹Bewerbung, Bericht›; D (*receive*) erhalten; reinkriegen (*ugs.*); E (*send for*) holen; rufen ‹Arzt, Polizei›; hinzuziehen ‹Spezialist›; F (*plant, sow*) in die Erde kriegen (*ugs.*); auspflanzen ‹Blumenzwiebeln›; aussäen ‹Samen›; G (*fit in*) reinkriegen (*ugs.*); einschieben ‹Unterrichtsstunde›; **try to ~ in a word about sth.** sich zu etw. äußern wollen; ⇒ *also* **edgeways** C; H (*cause to be admitted*) ~ **sb. in** (*as member, pupil, etc.*) jmdm. die Aufnahme ermöglichen; jmdn. reinbringen (*ugs.*); **his good results should ~ him in** mit seinen guten Noten müsste er reinkommen; **you can ~ him in as a guest** du kannst ihn als Gast mitbringen; I (*Boxing*) ~ **a blow/punch in** einen Schlag *od.* Treffer landen; (*fig.: coll.*) einen Schlag versetzen. ⇒ *also* **eye** 1 A; **hand** 1 K

~ **'in on** *v.t.* (*coll.*) sich beteiligen an (+ *Dat.*); ⇒ *also* **act** 1 E

~ **into** *v.t.* A (*bring into*) fahren ‹Auto usw.› in (+ *Akk.*) ‹Garage›; bringen in (+ *Akk.*) ‹Haus, Bett, Hafen›; B (*enter*) gehen/(*as intruder*) eindringen in (+ *Akk.*) ‹Haus›; [ein]steigen in (+ *Akk.*) ‹Auto usw.›; [ein]treten in (+ *Akk.*) ‹Zimmer›; steigen in (+ *Akk.*) ‹Wasser›; **the coach ~s into the station at 9 p.m.** der Bus kommt um 21.00 Uhr am Busbahnhof an; **it's ~ting into the hundreds** das geht schon in die Hunderte; C (*gain admission to*) eingelassen werden in (+ *Akk.*); angenommen werden in (+ *Dat.*) ‹Schule›; einen Studienplatz erhalten an (+ *Dat.*) ‹Universität›; genommen werden von ‹Firma›; ~ **sb. into a school/firm/club** dafür sorgen, dass jmd. von einer Schule angenommen/einer Firma genommen/einem Verein aufgenommen wird; ~ **into Parliament** ins Parlament einziehen; D (*coll.: make put on*) hineinkriegen in (+ *Akk.*); ~ **into one's clothes** sich anziehen; **I can't ~ into these trousers** ich komme in diese Hose nicht mehr rein (*ugs.*); E (*penetrate*) [ein]dringen in (+ *Akk.*); **sand got into my eyes** ich habe Sand in die Augen bekommen; **how did the fly ~ into the jam?** wie ist die Fliege in die Marmelade gekommen?; F (*begin to undergo*) geraten in (+ *Akk.*); kommen in (+ *Akk.*) ‹Schwierigkeiten›; (*cause to undergo*) stürzen in (+ *Akk.*) ‹Schulden, Unglück›; bringen in (+ *Akk.*) ‹Schwierigkeiten›; G (*accustom to, become accustomed to*) annehmen ‹Gewohnheit›; ~ **into the job/work** sich einarbeiten; **once you've got into the book, ...:** wenn man sich einmal eingelesen hat, ...; ⇒ *also* **habit** 1 A; **way** 1 L, O; H (*change in mood to*) geraten in (+ *Akk.*) ‹Wut, Panik›; (*cause to change in mood to*) bringen in (+ *Akk.*) ‹Wut›; stürzen in (+ *Akk.*) ‹Verzweiflung, Panik›; I **what's got into him?** was ist nur in ihn gefahren?; **something must have got into him** irgendetwas muss in ihn gefahren sein. ⇒ *also* **act** 1 E

~ **'in with** *v.t.* (*coll.*) ~ **in [well] with sb.** sich mit jmdm. gut stellen; **he got in with a bad crowd** er geriet in schlechte Gesellschaft; **he got in with a pretty girl** er bändelte mit einem hübschen Mädchen an

~ **off** ❶ /-'-/ *v.i.* A (*alight*) aussteigen; (*dismount*) absteigen; **tell sb. where he ~s off** *or* **where to ~ off** (*fig. coll.*) jmdn. in seine Grenzen verweisen; **she told him where to ~ off in no uncertain terms** sie machte ihm unmissverständlich klar, dass er zu weit gegangen war; B (*not remain on sb./sth.*) runtergehen; (*from chair*) aufstehen; (*from ladder, tree, table, lawn, carpet*) herunterkommen; (*let go*) loslassen; ~ **off, you filthy dog!** verschwinde, du dreckiger Köter!; C (*start*) aufbrechen; ~ **off to school/to work** zur Schule/Arbeit losgehen/-fahren; **we hope to ~ off before seven** wir hoffen, noch vor sieben wegzukommen; ~ **off to an early start** früh aufbrechen *od.* wegkommen; ~ **off to a good** *etc.* **start** einen guten *usw.* Start haben; ⇒ *also* **foot** 1 A; D (*be sent*) ‹Brief:› abgeschickt werden; ‹Paket, Telegramm:› aufgegeben werden; E (*escape punishment or injury*) davonkommen; ~ **off lightly** glimpflich davonkommen; F (*fall asleep*) einschlafen; G (*leave*) [weg]gehen; ~ **off early** [schon] früh [weg]gehen.
❷ [*stress varies*] *v.t.* A (*dismount from*) [ab]steigen von ‹Fahrrad›; steigen von ‹Pferd›; (*alight from*) aussteigen aus ‹Bus, Zug usw.›; steigen aus ‹Boot›; B (*not remain on*) herunterkommen von ‹Rasen, Teppich, Mauer, Leiter, Tisch›; aufstehen von ‹Stuhl›; verschwinden von, verlassen ‹Gelände›; ~ **off my toes!** geh von meinem Fuß runter! (*ugs.*); ~ **off the subject** vom Thema abkommen; C (*cause to start*) [los]schicken; **it takes ages to ~ the children off to school** es dauert eine Ewigkeit, die Kinder für die Schule fertig zu machen; ~ **sth. off to a good** *etc.* **start** einer Sache (*Dat.*) zu einem guten *usw.* Start verhelfen; D (*remove*) ausziehen ‹Kleidung usw.›; entfernen ‹Fleck, Farbe usw.›; abbekommen ‹Deckel, Ring›; ~ **sth. off sth.** etw. von etw. entfernen/abbekommen; ~ **sb./an animal off [sth.]** jmdn./ein Tier [von etw.] wegjagen; **I can't ~ my shoes off** ich kriege die Schuhe nicht aus (*ugs.*); ~ **that cat off my desk/me!** schaff mir die Katze vom Tisch/Leib!; ~ **sb. off a subject** jmdn. von einem Thema abbringen; E (*send, dispatch*) abschicken; aufgeben ‹Telegramm, Paket›; F (*cause to escape punishment*) davonkommen lassen; **the lawyer got his client off with a small fine** der Rechtsanwalt konnte für seinen Klienten ein niedriges Bußgeld durchsetzen; G (*not have to do, go to, etc.*) frei haben; ~ **off school/doing one's homework** nicht zur Schule zu gehen/keine Hausaufgaben zu machen brauchen; ~ **time/a day off [work]** frei/einen Tag frei bekommen; ~ **off work [early]** [früher] Feierabend machen; **I have got the afternoon off** ich habe den Nachmittag frei; H (*cause to fall asleep*) zum Einschlafen bringen; I (*coll.: obtain from*) bekommen von; kriegen von (*ugs.*); **I got that recipe off my mother** das Rezept habe ich von meiner Mutter

~ **'off with** *v.t.* (*Brit. coll.*) aufreißen (*salopp*); anbändeln mit (*ugs.*); ~ **sb. off with sb.** jmdn. mit jmdm. zusammenbringen *od.* verkuppeln

~ **on** ❶ /-'-/ *v.i.* A (*climb on*) (*on bicycle*) aufsteigen; (*on horse etc.*) aufsitzen; (*enter vehicle*) einsteigen; **you can't ~ on, the bus is full** Sie können nicht mehr rein (*ugs.*), der Bus ist voll; B (*make progress*) vorankommen; ~ **on in life/the world** es [im Leben] zu etwas bringen; **you're ~ting on very nicely** Sie machen gute Fortschritte; C (*fare*) **how did you ~ on there?** wie ist es dir dort ergangen?; **he's ~ting on well** es geht ihm gut; **I didn't ~ on too well in my exams** meine Prüfungen sind nicht besonders gut gelaufen (*ugs.*); D (*become late*) vorrücken; **it's ~ting on for five** es geht auf fünf zu; **it's ~ting on for six months since ...:** es sind bald sechs Monate, seit ...; **time is ~ting on** es wird langsam spät; E ▶ **912** (*advance in age*) älter werden; **be ~ting on in years/for seventy** langsam älter werden/auf die Siebzig zugehen; F **there were ~ting on for fifty people** es waren an die fünfzig Leute da; G (*manage*) zurechtkommen; H ⇒ ~ **along** C.
❷ [*stress varies*] *v.t.* A (*climb on*) steigen auf (+ *Akk.*) ‹Fahrrad, Pferd›; (*cause to climb on*) setzen auf (+ *Akk.*); (*enter, board*) einsteigen in (+ *Akk.*) ‹Zug, Bus, Flugzeug›; gehen auf (+ *Akk.*) ‹Schiff›; (*cause to enter or board*) setzen in (+ *Akk.*) ‹Bus, Zug, Flugzeug›; bringen auf (+ *Akk.*) ‹Schiff›; B (*put on*) anziehen ‹Kleider, Schuhe›; aufsetzen ‹Hut, Kessel›; (*load*) [auf]laden auf (+ *Akk.*); ~ **the cover [back] on** den Deckel [wieder] drauftun; (*with some difficulty*) den Deckel [wieder] draufbekommen; C (*coll.*) ~ **something on sb.** (*discover sth. incriminating*) etwas gegen jmdn. in der Hand haben. ⇒ *also* **foot** 1 A; **move** 1 F; **nerve** 1 B

~ **'on to** *v.t.* A ⇒ ~ **on** 2 A; B (*contact*) sich in Verbindung setzen mit; (*by telephone*) anrufen; (*more insistently*) ~ **on to sb.** jmdm. auf die Pelle rücken (*ugs.*); C (*trace, find*) ausfindig machen; ~ **on to sb.'s trail/scent** jmdm. auf die Spur kommen/jmds. Fährte aufnehmen; D (*realize*) ~ **on to sth.** hinter etw. (*Akk.*) kommen; ~ **on to the fact that ...:** dahinter kommen, dass ...; E (*move or pass to*) übergehen zu; (*unintentionally in conversation*) kommen auf (+ *Akk.*); **we don't ~ on to anatomy until next year** zur Anatomie kommen wir erst im nächsten Jahr

~ **'on with** *v.t.* A weitermachen mit; **let sb. ~ on with it** (*coll.*) jmdn. [allein weiter]machen lassen; **enough to be ~ting on with** genug für den Anfang *od.* fürs Erste; B = ~ **along with** ⇒ ~ **along** A, C

~ **'out** ❶ *v.i.* A (*go away*) (*walk out*) rausgehen (**of** aus); (*drive out*) rausfahren (**of** aus); (*alight*) aussteigen (**of** aus); (*climb out*) rausklettern (**of** aus); ~ **out from under** (*fig. coll.*) noch einmal davonkommen; ~ **out [of my room]!** raus [aus meinem Zimmer]!; **we'd better ~ out, and quick!** wir verschwinden hier besser, und zwar schnell!; **you need to ~ out a bit more** du müsstest hier öfter mal raus; **she likes to ~ out for a breath of fresh air** sie geht gern mal vor die Tür, um frische Luft zu schnappen; B (*leak*) austreten (**of** aus); (*escape from cage, jail*) ausbrechen, entkommen (**of** aus); (*fig.*) ‹Geheimnis:› herauskommen; ‹Nachrichten:› durchsickern; C ~ **out [of it]!** (*coll.*) ach, geh *od.* komm!; ach, erzähl mir doch nichts! (*ugs.*); D (*Cricket*) ausgeschlagen werden.
❷ *v.t.* A (*cause to leave*) rausbringen (**of** aus); (*send out*) rausschicken (**of** aus); (*throw out*) rauswerfen (**of** aus); ~ **all the passengers out** alle Passagiere aussteigen lassen; ~ **a nail out/out of the wall** einen Nagel herauskriegen/aus der Wand kriegen (*ugs.*); ~ **a stain out/out of sth.** einen Fleck wegbekommen/aus etw. herausbekommen; B (*bring or take out*) herausholen (**of** aus); herausziehen ‹Korken›; (*drive out*) herausfahren (**of** aus); **you only ~ out what you put in** (*fig.*) man kriegt nur raus, was man reingesteckt hat (*ugs.*); C (*withdraw*) abheben ‹Geld› (**of** von); D (*publish*) herausbringen; E (*speak, utter*) hervorbringen ‹Entschuldigung, Gruß usw.›; herausbringen ‹Wort›; F (*Cricket*) ausschlagen; G (*work out*) herausbekommen, (*ugs.*) herauskriegen ‹Rechenaufgabe, Summe, Rätsel›. ⇒ *also* ~**-out**

~ **'out of** *v.t.* A (*leave*) verlassen ‹Zimmer, Haus, Stadt, Land›; (*cause to leave*) entfernen aus; (*extract from*) herausziehen aus; (*bring or take out of*) herausholen; (*leak from*) austreten aus; (*withdraw from*) abheben von; ~ **a book out of the library** ein Buch aus der Bibliothek ausleihen; ~ **a lazy person out of bed** einen Faulpelz aus dem Bett kriegen (*ugs.*); ~ **him out of my sight!** schaff ihn

g

mir aus den Augen!; ~ **me out of this mess** hol mich aus diesem Schlamassel heraus! (*ugs.*); ~ **sth. out of one's head** *or* **mind** sich (*Dat.*) etw. aus dem Kopf schlagen; **he can't ~ the idea out of his head** er wird den Gedanken nicht los; ⇒ *also* ~ **out** 1 A, B, C, 2 A, B, C; Ⓑ (*draw out of*) herausbringen (*ugs.*) *od.* herausbekommen ‹Wahrheit, Worte› aus; Ⓒ (*escape*) herauskommen aus; (*avoid*) herumkommen um (*ugs.*); sich drücken vor (+ *Dat.*) (*ugs.*) ‹Arbeit›; **I can't ~ out of it now** jetzt muss ich mich auch daran halten; Ⓓ (*gain from*) herausholen ‹Geld› aus; machen (*ugs.*) *od.* erzielen ‹Gewinn› bei; **I couldn't ~ much out of this book** das Buch hat mir nicht viel gegeben; ~ **a word/the truth/a confession out of sb.** aus jmdm. ein Wort/die Wahrheit/ein Geständnis herausbringen; ~ **the best/most/utmost out of sb./sth.** das Beste/Meiste/Äußerste aus jmdm./etw. herausholen. ⇒ *also* **bed** 1 A; **depth** D; **habit** 1 A; **hand** 1 B; **way** 1 L

~ **outside [of]** *v.t.* (*sl.: eat*) sich reinziehen (*ugs.*)

~ **'over** ❶ *v.i.* Ⓐ (*cross*) ~ **over to the other side** auf die andere Seite gehen; **manage to ~ over to the other side** es schaffen, auf die andere Seite zu kommen; **I need to talk to you. When can you ~ over here?** ich muss dich sprechen — wann kannst du mal vorbeikommen?; Ⓑ (*coll.*) ⇒ ~ **across** 1 B. ❷ *v.t.* Ⓐ (*cross*) gehen über (+ *Akk.*); setzen über (+ *Akk.*) ‹Fluss›; (*climb*) klettern über (+ *Akk.*); (*cause to cross*) [hinüber]bringen über (+ *Akk.*); **we got ourselves safely over the river** wir kamen sicher über den Fluss; **manage to ~ over the road** es schaffen, über die Straße zu kommen; Ⓑ ⇒ ~ **across** 2 B; Ⓒ (*surmount*) überwinden; Ⓓ (*overcome*) überwinden; hinwegkommen über (+ *Akk.*); Ⓔ (*recover from*) überwinden; hinwegkommen über (+ *Akk.*); verwinden (*geh.*) ‹Verlust›; sich erholen von ‹Krankheit›; Ⓕ (*fully believe*) **I can't ~ over his cheek/the fact that ...:** solche Frechheit kann ich nicht begreifen/ich kann gar nicht fassen, dass ...; Ⓖ (*travel over*) zurücklegen ‹Strecke›; Ⓗ (*do, so as not to have still to come*) hinter sich bringen; **you might as well ~ it over and done with** je eher du es tust, desto schneller hast du es hinter dir

~ **'over with** *v.t.* ~ **sth. over with** etw. hinter sich (*Akk.*) bringen

~ **'past** ❶ *v.i.* ⇒ ~ **by** 1 A. ❷ *v.t.* ⇒ ~ **by** 2 A, B

~ **'round** ❶ *v.i.* Ⓐ ⇒ ~ **about**; Ⓑ ~ **round to doing sth.** dazu kommen, etw. zu tun. ❷ *v.t.* Ⓐ **she got round the shops very quickly** sie erledigte ihre Besorgungen sehr schnell; Ⓑ (*avoid*) umgehen ‹Gesetz, Bestimmungen›; Ⓒ ~ **sb. round,** ~ **round sb.** (~ *one's way with*) jmdn. herumkriegen (*ugs.*); (*persuade*) jmdn. überzeugen (**to** von); Ⓓ (*overcome*) lösen ‹Problem usw.›; überwinden ‹Hindernis usw.›; umgehen ‹Schwierigkeit usw.›. ⇒ *also* **table** 1 A; **tongue** C

~ **there** *v.i.* Ⓐ (*reach a place*) dorthin kommen; Ⓑ (*coll.: succeed*) es schaffen; Ⓒ (*understand*) verstehen, was gemeint ist; dahinter kommen (*ugs.*)

~ **through** ❶ /-'-/ *v.i.* Ⓐ (*pass obstacle*) durchkommen; (*make contact by radio or telephone*) durchkommen (*ugs.*); Verbindung bekommen (**to** mit); Ⓑ (*be transmitted*) durchkommen (*ugs.*); durchdringen (**to** bis zu *od.* nach); Ⓒ (*win heat or round*) gewinnen; ~ **through to the finals** in die Endrunde kommen; Ⓓ ~ **through [to sb.]** (*make sb. understand*) sich [jmdm.] verständlich machen; Ⓔ (*pass*) bestehen; durchkommen (*ugs.*); Ⓕ ~ **through on** auskommen mit ‹Gehalt›; Ⓖ (*be approved*) angenommen werden; durchkommen (*ugs.*).
❷ [*stress varies*] *v.t.* Ⓐ (*pass through*) [durch]kommen durch; ~ **sth. through sth.** etw. durch etw. [durch]bekommen *od.* (*ugs.*) [durch]kriegen; Ⓑ (*help to make contact*) ~ **sb. through to** jmdn. verbinden mit; Ⓒ (*bring*) [durch]bringen; übermitteln ‹Nachricht› (**to** *Dat.*); ~ **food/a message through to sb.** jmdm. Nahrungsmittel/eine Nachricht zukommen lassen; Ⓓ (*bring as far as*) ~ **a team through to the finals** eine Mannschaft in die Endrunde bringen; Ⓔ (*communicate*) ~ **sth. through to sb.** jmdm. etw. klarmachen; Ⓕ (*pass*) durchkommen bei (*ugs.*), bestehen ‹Prüfung›; (*help to pass*) durchbringen ‹Prüfling›; Ⓖ (*Parl.: cause to be approved*) durchbringen; Ⓗ (*consume, use up*) verbrauchen; verqualmen (*ugs. abwertend*) ‹Zigaretten›; aufessen ‹Essen›; ablatschen (*salopp*) ‹Schuhe›; abtragen ‹Kleidung›; (*spend*) durchbringen ‹Geld, Vermögen›; Ⓘ (*survive*) durchstehen; überstehen; kommen durch; Ⓙ (*manage to deal with*) fertig werden mit, erledigen ‹Arbeit›; durchkriegen ‹Buch›; **let me ~ through this work first** lass mich erst diese Arbeit fertig machen; ~ **through reading a book/writing a letter** ein Buch auslesen/einen Brief fertig schreiben

~ **'through with** *v.t.* Ⓐ (*finish*) fertig werden mit ‹Arbeit›; erledigen ‹Formalitäten›; auslesen ‹Buch›; Ⓑ (*coll.: finish dealing with sb.*) **wait till I ~ through with him!** warte, bis ich mit ihm fertig bin!

~ **to** *v.t.* Ⓐ (*reach*) kommen zu ‹Gebäude›; erreichen ‹Person, Ort›; **I've got to here** ich bin bis hierher gekommen; **he is ~ting to the age when ...:** er wird bald das Alter erreicht haben, wo ...; **where have you got to in German/in this book?** wie weit bist du gekommen in Deutsch/mit *od.* in dem Buch?; **I haven't got to the end [of the novel] yet** ich habe [den Roman] noch nicht zu Ende gelesen; **where has the child/the book got to?** wo ist das Kind hin/das Buch hingekommen?; Ⓑ (*begin*) ~ **to doing sth.** anfangen, etw. zu tun; Ⓒ ~ **to sb.** (*coll.: annoy*) jmdm. auf die Nerven gehen (*ugs.*); **don't let him ~ to you!** lass dir von ihm nicht auf den Nerven rumtrampeln! (*salopp*)

~ **to'gether** ❶ *v.i.* zusammenkommen; **we must ~ together again sometime** wir müssen uns bald mal wieder sehen; **why not ~ together after work?** wollen wir uns nach Feierabend treffen? ❷ *v.t.* Ⓐ (*collect*) zusammenbringen; ~ **one's things together** seine Sachen zusammenpacken; ~ **one's thoughts together** seine Gedanken sammeln; Ⓑ (*coll.: organize*) ~ **it** *or* **things together** die Dinge auf die Reihe kriegen (*ugs.*); ~ **oneself together** sich am Riemen reißen (*ugs.*). ⇒ *also* ~**-together**

~ **'under** *v.t.* (*shelter*) gehen unter (+ *Akk.*); kriechen unter (+ *Akk.*) ‹Decke, Bett›; ~ **sth. under sth.** etw. unter etw. (*Akk.*) tun; **how did my passport manage to ~ under your books?** wie ist mein Pass nur unter deine Bücher gekommen?

~ **up** ❶ /-'-/ *v.i.* Ⓐ (*rise from bed, chair, floor; leave table*) aufstehen; **please don't ~ up!** bitte bleiben Sie sitzen!; Ⓑ (*climb*) [auf]steigen, aufsitzen (**on** auf + *Dat. od. Akk.*); Ⓒ (*rise, increase in force*) zunehmen; **the sea is ~ting up** die See wird immer wilder; Ⓓ (*Cricket*) ‹Ball:› steil hochfliegen; Ⓔ ~ **up and go** (*coll.*) in Gang kommen. ❷ [*stress varies*] *v.t.* Ⓐ (*call, awaken*) wecken; (*cause to leave bed*) aus dem Bett holen; ~ **oneself up** aufwachen; (*leave bed*) aus dem Bett kommen; Ⓑ (*cause to stand up*) aufhelfen (+ *Dat.*); hochkriegen (*ugs.*); Ⓒ (*cause to mount*) ~ **sb. up on the horse** jmdm. aufs Pferd helfen; Ⓓ (*climb*) hinaufsteigen; **your car will not ~ up that hill** dein Auto kommt den Berg nicht hinauf *od.* schafft den Berg nicht; **water got up my nose** ich habe Wasser in die Nase gekriegt (*ugs.*); Ⓔ (*carry up*) ~ **sb./sth. up [sth.]** jmdn./etw. [etw.] her-/hinaufbringen; (*with some difficulty*) jmdn. etw. [etw.] her-/hinaufbekommen; Ⓕ (*organize*) organisieren; auf die Beine stellen; auf die Beine bringen ‹Personen›; Ⓖ (*arrange appearance of, dress up*) zurechtmachen; herrichten ‹Zimmer›; hübsch aufmachen ‹Buch, Geschenk›. ⇒ *also* **back** 1 A; ~**-up**; ~**-up-and-go**; **steam** 1; **wind**[1] 1 E

~ **'up to** *v.t.* Ⓐ (*reach*) erreichen ‹Leistungsniveau›; (*cause to reach*) bringen auf (+ *Akk.*); Ⓑ (*indulge in*) aus sein auf (+ *Akk.*); ~ **up to mischief** etwas anstellen; **what have you been ~ting up to?** was hast du getrieben *od.* angestellt?

**get:** ~**-'at-able** *adj.* zugänglich; ~**away** *n.* Flucht, *die; attrib.* Flucht‹plan, -wagen›; **make one's ~away** entkommen; ~**-out** *n.* Ⓐ (*coll.: evasion*) Ausweg, *der;* Ⓑ **as** *or* **like [all]** ~**-out** (*coll.*) wie nur irgendetwas; ~**-rich-'quick** *adj.* ~**-rich-quick manual/methods** Handbuch/Methoden, wie man schnell reich wird

**gettable** /'getəbl/ *adj.* erhältlich

**get:** ~**-together** *n.* (*coll.*) Zusammenkunft, *die;* (*informal social gathering*) gemütliches Beisammensein; **have a ~-together** sich treffen; zusammenkommen; ~**-up** *n.* (*coll.*) Aufmachung, *die;* **buy a new ~-up** sich neu einkleiden; ~**-up-and-'go** *n.* (*coll.*) Elan, *der;* Schwung, *der*

**geyser** *n.* Ⓐ /'gi:zə(r), 'geɪzə(r)/ (*hot spring*) Geysir, *der;* Ⓑ /'gi:zə(r)/ (*Brit.: water heater*) Durchlauferhitzer, *der*

**Ghana** /'gɑ:nə/ *pr. n.* Ghana (*das*)

**Ghanaian** /gɑ:'neɪən/ ▶ **1340** ❶ *adj.* ghanaisch; **sb. is ~:** jmd. ist Ghanaer/Ghanaerin. ❷ *n.* Ghanaer, *der*/Ghanaerin, *die*

**ghastly** /'gɑ:stlɪ/ *adj.* Ⓐ grauenvoll; grässlich; entsetzlich ‹Verletzungen›; schrecklich ‹Geschichte, Fehler, Irrtum›; Ⓑ (*coll.: objectionable, unpleasant*) scheußlich (*ugs.*); grässlich (*ugs.*); **I feel ~:** ich fühle mich scheußlich; Ⓒ (*pale*) leichenblass; leichenhaft ‹Blässe›; gespenstisch ‹Weiß›; Ⓓ (*forced*) verzerrt ‹Grinsen, Grimasse›

**Ghent** /gent/ *pr. n.* ▶ **1626** Gent (*das*)

**gherkin** /'gɜ:kɪn/ *n.* Essiggurke, *die*

**ghetto** /'getəʊ/ *n., pl.* ~**s** Getto, *das*

**ghetto blaster** /'getəʊblɑ:stə(r)/ *n.* (*coll.*) [großer, tragbarer] Radiorekorder

**ghost** /gəʊst/ ❶ *n.* Ⓐ Geist, *der;* Gespenst, *das;* Ⓑ **give up the ~:** den *od.* seinen Geist aufgeben (*veralt., scherzh.*); (*fig.: give up hope*) die Hoffnung aufgeben; Ⓒ (*shadowy outline*) Schatten, *der;* (*trace*) Spur, *die;* **the ~ of a smile** der Anflug eines Lächelns; **not have the** *or* **a ~ of a chance/an idea** nicht die geringste Chance/Ahnung haben; Ⓓ (*Telev.*) Geisterbild, *das.* ❷ *v.t.* ~ **sb.'s speech** *etc.* für jmdn. eine Rede *usw.* [als Ghostwriter] schreiben. ❸ *v.i.* ~ **[for sb.]** [für jmdn.] als Ghostwriter arbeiten

**ghosting** /'gəʊstɪŋ/ *n., no pl.* (*Telev.*) ein Geisterbild

**'ghostlike** *adj.* gespenstisch

**ghostly** /'gəʊstlɪ/ *adj.* gespenstisch; geisterhaft; **a ~ presence** die Anwesenheit eines Geistes

**ghost:** ~ **story** *n.* Gespenstergeschichte, *die;* ~ **town** *n.* Geisterstadt, *die;* ~ **train** *n.* Geisterbahn, *die;* ~ **writer** *n.* Ghostwriter, *der*

**ghoul** /gu:l/ *n.* *Mensch mit einem Hang zum Makabren*

**ghoulish** /'gu:lɪʃ/ *adj.* teuflisch ‹Freude›; schaurig ‹Gelächter›; makaber ‹Geschichte›

**GHQ** *abbr.* **General Headquarters** HQ; H.-Qu.

**GI** /'dʒi:aɪ, dʒi:'aɪ/ ❶ *adj.* GI-‹Uniform, Haarschnitt›; **GI bride** Amibraut, *die* (*ugs.*); **GI Joe** Amisoldat, *der* (*ugs.*). ❷ *n.* GI, *der*

**giant** /'dʒaɪənt/ ❶ *n.* Ⓐ (*legendary being*) Riese, *der;* (*Greek Mythol.*) Gigant, *der;* Ⓑ (*person*) Riese, *der;* (*animal, plant*) besonders großes Exemplar; **a ~ of a man/plant** ein Riese von einem Mann/eine riesengroße Pflanze; Ⓒ (*person of extraordinary ability*) Größe, *die;* **he was one of the ~s of his time** er war einer der Großen seiner Zeit; Ⓓ (*sth. with power*) Koloss, *der;* **a ~ among rivers** ein gigantischer Strom; Ⓔ (*Astron.*) Riese[nstern], *der.*
❷ *attrib. adj.* riesig; Riesen-(*ugs.*); Riesen‹tier, -pflanze›

**giantess** /'dʒaɪəntɪs/ *n.* Riesin, *die*

**giant:** ~**-killer** *n.* Riesenbezwinger, *der;* ~ **'panda** *n.* Bambusbär, *der;* Riesenpanda, *der;* ~ **'slalom** *n.* Riesenslalom, *der*

**Gib.** /dʒɪb/ *pr. n.* (*coll.*) Gibraltar (*das*)

**gibber** /'dʒɪbə(r)/ *v.i.* plappern; ‹Affe:› schnattern; **I just stood there like a ~ing idiot** ich stand da wie ein Idiot

**gibberish** /'dʒɪbərɪʃ/ *n.* Ⓐ (*unintelligible chatter*) Kauderwelsch, *das;* Ⓑ (*nonsense*)

Geschwafel, *das* (*ugs.*); **talk ~:** schwafeln (*ugs.*)

**gibbet** /ˈdʒɪbɪt/ *n.* (*Hist.*) Galgen, *der*

**gibbon** /ˈɡɪbən/ *n.* (*Zool.*) Gibbon, *der*

**gibe** /dʒaɪb/ ❶ *n.* Spöttelei, *die* (*ugs.*); Stichelei, *die* (*ugs.*); **make ~s at sb.** jmdn. verspotten; gegen jmdn. sticheln (*ugs.*). ❷ *v.i.* **~ at sb./sth.** über jmdn./etw. spötteln; sich über jmdn./etw. lustig machen

**giblets** /ˈdʒɪblɪts/ *n. pl.* [Geflügel]klein, *das*

**Gibraltar** /dʒɪˈbrɔːltə(r)/ *pr. n.* ▶ 1626 Gibraltar (*das*); **the Rock/Straits of ~:** der Felsen/die Straße von Gibraltar

**giddiness** /ˈɡɪdɪnɪs/ *n., no pl.* Schwindel, *der;* **a feeling of ~:** ein Schwindelgefühl; **fits of ~:** Schwindelanfälle *Pl.*

**giddy** /ˈɡɪdɪ/ *adj.* [A] (*dizzy*) schwind[e]lig; **I feel ~, I have a ~ feeling** mir ist schwindlig; mir schwindelt; [B] (*causing vertigo*) Schwindel erregend ‹Höhe, Abgrund›; atemberaubend ‹Geschwindigkeit›; [C] (*fig.: frivolous*) ausgelassen; verrückt (*ugs.*); [D] **my ~ aunt!** (*fig. coll.*) ach, du dicker Vater! (*ugs.*); ach, du dickes Ei! (*ugs.*); ⇒ *also* **goat** A

**gift** /ɡɪft/ *n.* [A] (*present*) Geschenk, *das;* Gabe, *die* (*geh.*); (*to an organization*) Schenkung, *die;* **make sb. a ~ of sth., make a ~ of sth. to sb.** jmdm. etw. schenken *od.* zum Geschenk machen; **it was given to me as a ~:** ich habe es geschenkt bekommen; **a ~ box/pack** eine Geschenkpackung; **I wouldn't [even] have it as a ~:** das würde ich nicht mal geschenkt nehmen; [B] (*money given to charity*) Spende, *die;* [C] (*talent etc.*) Begabung, *die;* **a person of many ~s** ein vielseitig begabter Mensch; **have a ~ for languages/mathematics** sprachbegabt/mathematisch begabt sein; ⇒ *also* **gab** 1; **tongue** C; [D] (*easy task etc.*) **be a ~:** geschenkt sein (*ugs.*); [E] (*right to give*) **sth. is in the ~ of sb.** jmd. hat das Recht, etw. zu vergeben; etw. kann von jmdm. vergeben werden; [F] (*Law*) Schenkung, *die*

**gifted** /ˈɡɪftɪd/ *adj.* begabt (**in, at** für); **highly ~:** hoch begabt; begnadet ‹Künstler›; **be ~ in** *or* **at languages** sprachbegabt sein

**gift: ~ horse** *n.* **never** *or* **don't look a ~ horse in the mouth** (*prov.*) einem geschenkten Gaul schaut man nicht ins Maul (*Spr.*); **~ shop** *n.* Geschenkboutique, *die;* Geschenkladen, *der;* **~ tax** *n.* (*Amer.*) Schenkungssteuer, *die;* **~ token, ~ voucher** *ns.* Geschenkgutschein, *der;* **~-wrap** *v.t.* als Geschenk einpacken; in Geschenkpapier einpacken

**gig**[1] /ɡɪɡ/ *n.* (*boat, vehicle*) Gig, *das*

**gig**[2] *n.* (*coll.: performance*) Gig, *der*

**giga-** /ˈɡɪɡə/ *pref.* giga-/Giga-; **~byte** Gigabyte, *das*

**gigantic** /dʒaɪˈɡæntɪk/ *adj.* gigantisch; riesig; enorm, gewaltig ‹Verbesserung, Appetit, Portion›; **a ~ success/effort** ein Riesenerfolg/eine Riesenanstrengung; **grow to a ~ size** riesengroß werden

**giggle** /ˈɡɪɡl/ ❶ *n.* [A] Kichern, *das;* Gekicher, *das;* **have a ~ about sth.** über etw. (*Akk.*) kichern; **with a ~:** kichernd; **[a fit of] the ~s** ein Kicheranfall; **get/have the ~s** kichern müssen; [B] (*coll.*) (*amusing person*) Witzbold, *der;* (*amusing thing, joke*) Spaß, *der;* **it was a bit of a ~:** es war ganz amüsant; **for a ~:** aus Spaß; **we did it for a ~:** wir wollten unseren Spaß haben. ❷ *v.i.* kichern

**gild**[1] /ɡɪld/ *v.t.* vergolden; (*with gold-coloured paint*) mit Goldbronze überziehen; **~ed cage** (*fig.*) goldener Käfig (*fig.*); **~ed youth** Jeunesse dorée, *die* (*veralt.*); **~ the lily** etwas Vollkommenes [unnötigerweise] noch vervollkommnen [wollen]; des Guten zu viel tun

**gild**[2] ⇒ **guild**

**gilding** /ˈɡɪldɪŋ/ *n.* Goldauflage, *die;* (*process*) Vergoldung, *die;* (*paint*) Goldfarbe, *die*

**gill**[1] /ɡɪl/ *n., usu. in pl.* [A] (*of fish etc.*) Kieme, *die;* **green about the ~s** (*fig.*) grün *od.* blass um die Nase[nspitze] (*ugs.*); [B] (*of mushroom etc.*) Lamelle, *die*

**gill**[2] *n.* (*Brit.*) [A] (*ravine*) [bewaldete] Schlucht; [B] (*torrent*) Wildbach, *der*

**gill**[3] /dʒɪl/ *n.* Viertelpint, *das* (*0,142 l*)

**gillie** /ˈɡɪlɪ/ *n.* (*Hunting*) Jagdgehilfe, *der*

**gilt** /ɡɪlt/ ❶ *n.* [A] (*gilding*) Goldauflage, *die;* (*paint*) Goldfarbe, *die;* **take the ~ off the gingerbread** (*fig.*) der Sache den Reiz nehmen; [B] *in pl.* = **~-edged securities** ⇒ **~-edged.** ❷ *adj.* vergoldet

**gilt-edged** *adj.* (*Commerc.*) **~ securities/stocks** mündelsichere Wertpapiere

**gimcrack** /ˈdʒɪmkræk/ *adj.* schäbig

**gimlet** /ˈɡɪmlɪt/ *n.* [Hand]bohrer, *der;* **~ eye** Luchsauge, *das;* (*fig.*) Scharfblick, *der*

**gimme** /ˈɡɪmɪ/ (*coll.*) = **give me**

**gimmick** /ˈɡɪmɪk/ *n.* (*coll.*) Gag, *der;* **a publicity/public relations/promotional ~:** ein Werbegag

**gimmickry** /ˈɡɪmɪkrɪ/ *n.* (*coll.*) Firlefanz, *der* (*ugs.*); Pipifax, *der* (*ugs.*); **advertising ~:** Werbetricks *od.* -gags *Pl.*

**gimmicky** /ˈɡɪmɪkɪ/ *adj.* (*coll.*) vergagt; **~ publicity stunts** verrückte Werbegags

**gin**[1] /dʒɪn/ *n.* (*drink*) Gin, *der;* **~ and tonic** Gin [und] Tonic, *der;* **~ and it** (*Brit. coll.*) Gin und [italienischer] Wermut; **pink ~:** Gin und Angostura

**gin**[2] *n.* (*trap*) Falle, *die;* (*snare*) Schlinge, *die*

**ginger** /ˈdʒɪndʒə(r)/ ❶ *n.* [A] Ingwer, *der;* [B] (*colour*) Rötlichgelb, *das;* **his hair was a bright shade of ~:** er hatte helles rötliches Haar; [C] (*vigour*) Feuer, *das;* Schwung, *der.* ❷ *adj.* [A] (*flavour*) Ingwer‹gebäck, -geschmack›; [B] (*colour*) rötlich gelb; rotblond ‹Bart, Haare›. ❸ *v.t.* **~ up** (*fig.*) in Schwung bringen

**ginger: ~ ˈale** *n.* Gingerale, *das;* **~ ˈbeer** *n.* Ingwerbier, *das;* Gingerbeer, *das;* **~ beer plant** *Mischung aus Hefe und Bakterie zur Gärung von Gingerbeer;* **~bread** ❶ *n.* [A] Pfefferkuchen, *der;* ⇒ *also* **gilt** 1 A; [B] (*Archit. etc.*) überflüssiger [geschmackloser] Schmuck; ❷ *adj.* (*fig.*) überladen; zuckerbäckerhaft ‹[Bau]stil›; **~ group** *n.* (*Brit.*) Initiative, *die;* Aktionsgruppe, *die*

**gingerly** /ˈdʒɪndʒəlɪ/ *adv.* behutsam; [übertrieben] vorsichtig

**ginger: ~ nut** *n.* Pfeffernuss, *die;* **~ snap** *n.* Ingwerkeks, *der;* **~ ˈwine** *n.* Ingwerwein, *der*

**gingery** /ˈdʒɪndʒərɪ/ *adj.* ingwerartig

**gingham** /ˈɡɪŋəm/ *n.* (*Textiles*) Gingan, *der*

**gingivitis** /dʒɪndʒɪˈvaɪtɪs/ *n.* ▶ 1232 (*Med.*) Gingivitis, *die* (*fachspr.*); Zahnfleischentzündung, *die*

**ginormous** /dʒaɪˈnɔːməs/ *adj.* (*Brit. coll.*) elefantös (*ugs. scherzh.*)

**gin: ~-palace** *n.* auffällig aufgemachte Kneipe; **~ ˈrummy** *n.* Rommé mit Zehn

**ginseng** /ˈdʒɪnseŋ/ *n.* (*Bot., Med.*) Ginseng, *der*

**gin ˈsling** *n.* Ginsling, *der*

**gippy tummy** /dʒɪpɪ ˈtʌmɪ/ *n.* (*coll.*) Durchfall, *der;* Durchmarsch, *der* (*salopp*)

**gipsy** ⇒ **gypsy**

**giraffe** /dʒɪˈrɑːf, dʒɪˈræf/ *n.* Giraffe, *die*

**gird** /ɡɜːd/ *v.t.,* **~ed** *or* **girt** /ɡɜːt/ [A] (*encircle*) **~ sb./sb.'s waist with sth.** jmdn./jmds. Taille mit etw. gürten; etw. um jmdn./jmds. Taille als Gürtel legen; [B] (*surround*) umgeben; [C] (*secure*) **~ on one's armour/sword** seine Rüstung anlegen/sich (*Dat.*) sein Schwert umgürten; [D] (*prepare*) **~ oneself for sth.** sich zu etw. rüsten; **be ~ed for sth.** für etw. gewappnet sein

**~ up** *v.t.* gürten; **~ up one's loins** (*literary*) seine Lenden gürten (*veralt.*); sich gürten

**girder** /ˈɡɜːdə(r)/ *n.* [Eisen-/Stahl]träger, *der*

**girdle**[1] /ˈɡɜːdl/ ❶ *n.* [A] (*corset*) Hüfthalter, *der;* Hüftgürtel, *der;* [B] (*belt, cord, etc.*) Gürtel, *der;* (*sash*) Schärpe, *die;* **a ~ of trees/forests** eine Baumkette *od.* ein Gürtel von Bäumen/ein Waldgürtel; [C] (*Anat.*) ‹Schulter-, Becken›gürtel, *der.* ❷ *v.t.* umgeben; ‹Bäume:› umstehen; ‹Fluss, Wasser:› umfließen, umströmen

**girdle**[2] (*Scot.*) ⇒ **griddle**

**girl** /ɡɜːl/ *n.* [A] Mädchen, *das;* (*teenager*) junges Mädchen; ([*young*] *woman*) Frau, *die;* (*daughter*) Mädchen, *das* (*ugs.*); Tochter, *die;* **baby ~:** kleines Mädchen; **~s' school** Mädchenschule, *die;* **a ~'s name** ein Mädchenname; **a little Italian ~:** eine kleine Italienerin; ein kleines italienisches Mädchen; **[my] ~** (*as address*) [mein] Mädchen; **the ~s** (*female friends*) meine/ihre *usw.* Freundinnen; **the Smith ~s** die Mädchen von Smiths; ⇒ *also* **old girl**; [B] (*worker*) Mädchen, *das;* (*secretary*) Sekretärin, *die;* (*maid*) [Haus-/Dienst]mädchen, *das;* **the ~ at the cash desk/switchboard** die Kassiererin/Telefonistin; [C] (*sweetheart*) Mädchen, *das;* Freundin, *die*

**girl: ~ ˈFriday** *n.* ⇒ **Friday** 1; **~friend** *n.* Freundin, *die;* **~ ˈguide** ⇒ **guide** 1 E

**girlhood** /ˈɡɜːlhʊd/ *n.* Kindheit, *die*

**girlie** /ˈɡɜːlɪ/ ❶ *adj.* mit nackten Mädchen *nachgestellt.* ❷ *n.* [kleines] Mädchen

**girlish** /ˈɡɜːlɪʃ/ *adj.* (*coll.*) mädchenhaft; **a ~ voice** eine Mädchenstimme; **~ laughter** Mädchenlachen, *das*

**girl: ~ power** *n.* (*coll.*) Girlpower, *die;* **~ ˈscout** *n.* (*Amer.*) Pfadfinderin, *die*

**giro** /ˈdʒaɪərəʊ/ *n., pl.* **~s** Giro, *das; attrib.* Giro‹bank, -geschäft, -konto, -scheck›; **post office/bank ~:** Postgiro- *od.* (*veralt.*) Postscheck-/Giroverkehr, *der*

**girt** ⇒ **gird**

**girth** /ɡɜːθ/ *n.* [A] (*circumference*) Umfang, *der;* (*at waist*) Taillenumfang, *der;* (*at belly*) Bauchumfang, *der;* (*of ship*) Spantumfang, *der;* **in ~:** im Umfang *usw.;* [B] (*band round horse*) Bauchgurt, *der*

**gismo** /ˈɡɪzməʊ/ *n.* (*coll.*) Ding, *das* (*ugs.*)

**gist** /dʒɪst/ *n.* Wesentliche, *das;* (*of tale, argument, question, etc.*) Kern, *der;* **this is the ~ of what he said** das hat er im Wesentlichen gesagt; **get the ~ of sth.** das Wesentliche einer Sache mitbekommen; **could you give me the ~ of it/what's been going on?** könntest du mir sagen, worum es hier geht?/was los gewesen ist?

**git** /ɡɪt/ *n.* (*Brit. sl. derog.*) Idiot, *der* (*salopp*); **stupid ~:** Blödmann, *der* (*derb*); (*woman*) blöde Kuh (*derb*)

**give** /ɡɪv/ ❶ *v.t.,* **gave** /ɡeɪv/, **given** /ˈɡɪvn/ [A] (*hand over, pass*) geben; (*transfer from one's authority, custody, or responsibility*) überbringen; übergeben (**to** an + *Akk.*); **she gave him her bag to carry** sie gab ihm ihre Tasche zum Tragen; **G~ it to me! I'll do it** Gib her! Ich mache das; **~ me …** (*on telephone*) geben Sie mir …; verbinden Sie mich mit …; [B] (*as gift*) schenken; (*donate*) spenden; geben; (*bequeath*) vermachen; **~ sb. sth., ~ sth. to sb.** jmdm. etw. schenken; **~ sb. sth.** *or* **~ sth. [to] sb. as a present** jmdm. etw. schenken; (*sth. of great value*) jmdm. etw. zum Geschenk machen; **each of the boys was ~n a book** die Jungen bekamen jeder ein Buch [geschenkt]; **the book was ~n me by my son** das Buch hat mir mein Sohn geschenkt; **I was ~n it by my son** mein Sohn hat es mir geschenkt; ich habe es von meinem Sohn [geschenkt] bekommen; **I wouldn't have it if it was ~n [to] me** ich würde es nicht mal geschenkt nehmen; *abs.* **it is more blessed to ~ than to receive** (*Bibl.*) Geben ist seliger denn Nehmen (*Spr.*); **~ alms/to the poor** Almosen/den Armen geben; **~ towards sth.** zu etw. beisteuern; **~ blood** Blut spenden; **~ [a donation] to charity** für wohltätige Zwecke spenden; **'please ~ generously'** „wir bitten um großzügige Spenden"; **~ and take** (*fig.*) Kompromisse eingehen; (*in marriage etc.*) geben und nehmen; [C] (*sell*) verkaufen; geben; (*pay*) zahlen; geben (*ugs.*); (*sacrifice*) geben; opfern; **I'll ~ you the machine for £2** für 2 Pfund gebe ich dir *od.* hast du die Maschine; **what will you ~ me for this watch?** was *od.* wie viel geben Sie mir für diese Uhr?; **I'll ~ you anything you ask for it** ich zahle Ihnen jeden Preis dafür; **~ sb. sth. [in exchange] for sth.** jmdm. etw. für etw. [im Tausch] geben; **I would ~ anything** *or* **my right arm/a lot to be there** ich würde alles/viel darum geben, wenn ich dort sein könnte; [D] (*assign*) aufgeben ‹Hausaufgaben, Strafarbeit usw.›; (*sentence to*) geben ‹10 Jahre Gefängnis usw.›; **~ sb. a translation to**

**do/an essay to write for homework** jmdm. eine Übersetzung/einen Aufsatz aufgeben; **he was ~n ten years** er bekam zehn Jahre; **E** (*grant, award*) geben ‹Erlaubnis, Arbeitsplatz, Interview, Rabatt, Fähigkeit, Kraft›; verleihen ‹Preis, Titel, Orden usw.›; **be ~n sth.** etw. bekommen; **he was ~n the privilege/honour of doing it** ihm wurde das Vorrecht/die Ehre zuteil, es zu tun; **~ me strength to do it** gib mir Kraft, es zu tun; **it is ~n to few/her** es ist wenigen/ihr gegeben *od.* (*geh.*) beschieden; **~ sb. to understand** *or* **believe that ...:** jmdn. glauben lassen, dass ...; **he gave me to understand** *or* **believe that ...** (*unintentionally*) was er sagte, ließ mich glauben, dass ...; **F** (*entrust sb. with*) übertragen (**to** *Dat.*); **~ sb. the power to do sth.** jmdn. ermächtigen, etw. zu tun; **G** (*allow sb. to have*) geben ‹Recht, Zeit, Arbeit›; überlassen ‹seinen Sitzplatz›; lassen ‹Wahl, Zeit›; **be ~n little freedom** wenig Freiheit haben; **~ sb./a horse a rest** jmdm./einem Pferd eine Pause gönnen; **they gave me [the use of] their car for the weekend** sie überließen mir übers Wochenende ihr Auto; **~ it time and it will work out well** gut Ding will Weile haben (*Spr.*); **I will ~ you a day to think it over** ich lasse dir einen Tag Bedenkzeit; **I can ~ you an hour. Then I must go** Ich habe [für Sie] eine Stunde Zeit. Dann muss ich gehen; **~ yourself time to think about it** lass dir Zeit und denk darüber nach; **~ me the good old times** (*fig. coll.*) es geht doch nichts über die guten alten Zeiten; **~ me London any day** *or* **time** *or* **every time** (*fig. coll.*) London ist mir zehnmal lieber; **I['ll] ~ you/him** *etc.* **that** (*fig. coll.: grant*) das gebe ich zu; zugegeben; **you've got to ~ it to him** (*fig. coll.*) das muss man ihm lassen; **~ or take** (*coll.*) mehr oder weniger; **it cost £5, ~ or take a few pence** es hat fünf Pfund gekostet, vielleicht ein paar Pence mehr oder weniger; **~ or take a few errors, this book is ...:** abgesehen von ein paar Fehlern ist dieses Buch ...; **~ oneself to sb.** (*yield sexually*) sich jmdm. hingeben; **~n that** (*because*) da; (*if*) wenn; **~n the right tools** mit dem richtigen Werkzeug; **~n time/the cash, I'll do/buy it** wenn ich Zeit/das nötige Geld habe, mache/kaufe ich es; **H** (*offer to sb.*) geben, reichen ‹Arm, Hand usw.›; **~ sb. one's attention/confidence** jmdm. seine Aufmerksamkeit/sein Vertrauen schenken; **please ~ me your attention** ich bitte um Ihre Aufmerksamkeit; **~ sb. in marriage** jmdn. verheiraten; **my heart is ~n to another** mein Herz gehört einer/einem anderen; **she gave him an infection/a cold** sie hat ihn angesteckt/mit ihrer Erkältung angesteckt; **she gave him four sons** sie hat ihm vier Söhne geschenkt (*geh.*); ⇒ *also* **~ way**; **I** (*cause sb./sth. to have*) geben; verleihen ‹Charme, Reiz, Gewicht, Nachdruck›; bereiten, machen ‹Freude, Mühe, Kummer›; bereiten, verursachen ‹Schmerz›; bieten ‹Abwechslung, Schutz›; leisten ‹Hilfe›; gewähren ‹Unterstützung›; erteilen ‹Absolution›; **~ sb. sth./be ~n sth. to eat** jmdm. etw. zu essen geben/etw. zu essen bekommen; **~ sb. some refreshment** jmdm. eine Erfrischung reichen; **~ sb. pork for dinner** jmdm. Schweinefleisch zum Abendessen geben *od.* reichen; **I was ~n the guest room** man gab mir das Gästezimmer; **~ a clear picture/~ good reception** (*Telev.*) ein gutes Bild/einen guten Empfang haben; **the answer was ~n me in a dream** die Antwort kam mir im Traum; **her words gave me much pain/quite a shock** ihre Worte schmerzten/schockierten mich sehr; **~ hope to sb.** jmdm. Hoffnung machen; **~ sb. the name of Jim** jmdn. Jim nennen; jmdm. den Namen Jim geben; **the village gave its name to the battle** die Schlacht wurde nach dem Dorf benannt; **Latin, which has ~n the English language so many words** das Lateinische, aus dem so viele englische Wörter stammen; **~ sb. something to cry for/to complain about** jmdm. einen Grund zum Weinen/Klagen geben; **~ one's labour [free of charge]** unbezahlt arbeiten; seine Arbeit unentgeltlich machen; **~ sb. what for** (*coll.*) es jmdm. geben (*ugs.*); **J** (*convey in words, tell, communicate*) angeben ‹Namen, Anschrift, Alter, Grund, Zahl›; nennen ‹Grund, Einzelheiten, Losungswort›; geben ‹Rat, Beispiel, Befehl, Anweisung, Antwort›; fällen ‹Urteil, Entscheidung›; sagen ‹Meinung›; erlassen ‹Gesetze›; bekannt geben ‹Nachricht, Ergebnis›; machen ‹Andeutung›; erteilen ‹Verweis, Rüge›; (*present, set forth*) ‹Wörterbuch, Brief:› enthalten; ‹Zeitung:› bringen ‹Bericht›; **~ details of sth.** Einzelheiten einer Sache (*Gen.*) darlegen; **~ sth. a mention** etw. erwähnen; **~ a brief history of sth.** einen kurzen Abriss der Geschichte einer Sache (*Gen.*) geben; **~ sb. the facts** jmdn. mit den Fakten vertraut *od.* bekannt machen; **she gave us the news/the news of her engagement** sie teilte es uns mit/teilte uns ihre Verlobung mit; **~ it as one's opinion that ...:** die Meinung äußern, dass ...; **~ sb. a decision** jmdm. eine Entscheidung mitteilen; **~ sb. the right time** jmdm. die genaue Zeit sagen; **~ him my best wishes** richte ihm meine besten Wünsche aus; **the average wage is ~n as £6,000** der Durchschnittslohn wird mit 6 000 Pfund angegeben; **don't ~ me 'that** (*coll.*) erzähl mir [doch] nichts! (*ugs.*); **don't ~ me that legal jargon** lass mich mit deinem Juristenkauderwelsch in Ruhe!; **~!** (*coll.: disclose what you know*) [nun] red schon!; **~n** (*in formal dating*) ausgefertigt; **K** **~n** (*specified*) gegeben; **L** (*perform, read, sing, etc.*) geben ‹Vorstellung, Konzert›; halten ‹Vortrag, Seminar›; vorlesen ‹Gedicht, Erzählung›; singen ‹Lied›; spielen ‹Schauspiel, Oper, Musikstück›; **~ us a song** sing mal was; **M** (*in speeches*) ausbringen ‹Toast, Trinkspruch›; (*as toast*) **ladies and gentlemen, I ~ you the Queen** meine Damen, meine Herren, auf die Königin *od.* das Wohl der Königin; (*as speaker*) **I ~ you the Lord Mayor** das Wort hat der Oberbürgermeister; **N** (*produce*) geben ‹Licht, Milch›; tragen ‹Früchte›; ergeben ‹Zahlen, Resultat›; erbringen ‹Ernte›; **~ your answer to the third decimal place** berechnen Sie das Ergebnis auf die dritte Stelle hinter dem Komma; **~ a high yield** sehr ertragreich sein; reichen Ertrag bringen; **O** (*cause to develop*) machen; **sth. ~s me a headache** von etw. bekomme ich Kopfschmerzen; **running ~s me an appetite** Laufen macht mich hungrig; **he did this to ~ himself courage** er tat das, um sich (*Dat.*) Mut zu machen; **P** (*make sb. undergo*) geben; versetzen ‹Schlag, Stoß›; verabreichen (*geh.*), geben ‹Arznei›; **~ sb. a hammering** (*Sport*) jmdm. eine schwere Schlappe beibringen; **~ sb. a [friendly] look** jmdm. einen [freundlichen] Blick zuwerfen; **he gave her hand a squeeze** er drückte ihr die Hand; **~ it to sb.** (*thrash or scold him*) es jmdm. geben (*ugs.*); **~ as good as one gets** (*coll.*) es jmdm. mit gleicher Münze heimzahlen; **Q** (*execute, make, show*) geben ‹Zeichen, Stoß, Tritt›; machen ‹Satz, Ruck›; ausstoßen ‹Schrei, Seufzer, Pfiff›; **~ a [little] smile** [schwach] lächeln; **the flame gave a final flicker** die Flamme flackerte noch einmal auf; **~ sth./sb. a look** sich (*Dat.*) etw./jmdn. ansehen; **R** (*devote, dedicate*) widmen; **be ~n to sth./doing sth.** zu etw. neigen/etw. gern tun; **~ [it] all one's got** (*coll.*) sein Möglichstes tun; **S** (*be host at*) geben ‹Party, Ball, Empfang, Essen usw.›; **T** (*predict time remaining as*) **~ sb./sth. two months/a year** jmdm./einer Sache zwei Monate/ein Jahr geben; **U** **~ birth, ~ chase,** *etc. see the nouns.*

**2** *v.i.*, **gave, given** **A** (*yield, bend*) nachgeben (*auch fig.*); ‹Knie:› weich werden; ‹Bett:› federn; (*break down*) zusammenbrechen; ‹Eisdecke, Boden:› einbrechen; ‹Brücke:› einstürzen; (*fig.*) nachlassen; **something's got to ~:** irgendwo muss man zurückstecken; **B** (*lead*) **~ on to the street/garden/into a room** ‹Tür usw.:› auf die Straße hinaus-/in den Garten/ein Zimmer führen; **C** **what ~s [with you]?** (*coll.*) was ist los [bei dir]?; **D** **~ of sth.** etw. opfern; **~ of oneself** sich [auf]opfern.

**3** *n.* **A** Nachgiebigkeit, *die;* (*elasticity*) Elastizität, *die;* **have [no] ~:** [nicht] nachgeben; **B** **~ and take** (*exchange of ideas*) Gedankenaustausch, *der;* (*compromise*) Kompromiss, *der;* Entgegenkommen, *das;* (*exchange of benefits or mutual concessions*) Geben und Nehmen, *das;* **with a bit of ~ and take** mit etwas Kompromissbereitschaft

**~ a'way** *v.t.* **A** (*without charge, as gift*) verschenken; (*fig.: lose by negligence*) verschenken ‹Punkt, Tor usw.›; vergeben ‹Chance, Tor, Elfmeter›; **B** (*in marriage*) dem Bräutigam zuführen; **C** (*distribute*) verteilen, vergeben ‹Preise›; überreichen ‹Zeugnisse usw.›; **D** (*fig.: betray*) verraten. ⇒ *also* **game**[1] 1 B; **~-away**

**~ 'back** *v.t.* (*lit. or fig.*) zurückgeben; wiedergeben

**~ 'forth** ⇒ **forth** C

**~ in** **1** /'--/ *v.t.* abgeben; **~ sb.'s name in for sth.** jmdn. zu etw. anmelden. **2** /-'-/ *v.i.* nachgeben (**to** *Dat.*); (*in guessing game*) aufgeben; **~ in to temptation/blackmail/a superior force** der Versuchung (*Dat.*) erliegen/auf Erpressung (*Akk.*) eingehen/sich der Übermacht (*Dat.*) ergeben; **~ in to persuasion** sich überzeugen lassen

**~ 'off** *v.t.* ausströmen ‹Rauch, Geruch›; aussenden ‹Strahlen›

**~ out** **1** /'--/ *v.t.* **A** (*distribute*) verteilen ‹Prospekte, Flugblätter, Karten, Preise›; austeilen ‹Stifte, Hefte, Papier usw.›; vergeben ‹Arbeit›; **B** (*declare*) bekannt geben ‹Nachricht›; (*pretend*) vorgeben; **~ oneself out to be ...:** sich als ... ausgeben. **2** /-'-/ *v.i.* ‹Vorräte:› ausgehen; ‹Maschine:› versagen; ‹Kraft:› nachlassen; **my patience/voice gave out** ich war mit meiner Geduld am Ende/mir versagte die Stimme

**~ 'over** *v.t.* **A** **be ~n over to sth.** für etw. beansprucht werden; **the rest of the day was ~n over to pleasure** der Rest des Tages war dem Vergnügen gewidmet; **B** (*abandon*) **~ sth./sb. over to sb.** etw. jmdm. überlassen/jmdn. jmdm. ausliefern; **~ oneself over to sb./sth.** sich jmdm./einer Sache ergeben *od.* hingeben; jmdm./einer Sache verfallen; **C** (*coll.: stop*) **~ over [doing sth.]** aufhören[, etw. zu tun]

**~ 'up** **1** *v.i.* aufgeben. **2** *v.t.* **A** (*abandon, renounce*) aufgeben; ablegen ‹Gewohnheit›; abschaffen ‹Auto, Fernsehgerät, Putzfrau›; widmen ‹Zeit›; (*relinquish, stop using*) verzichten auf (+ *Akk.*) ‹Territorium, Kinder, Süßigkeiten›; **~ sth. up/~ up doing sth.** (*abandon habit*) sich (*Dat.*) etw. abgewöhnen/sich abgewöhnen, etw. zu tun; **~ sb./sth. up as a bad job** (*coll.*) jmdn./etw. abschreiben (*ugs.*); **~ oneself up to sth.** sich einer Sache (*Dat.*) hingeben; **B** **~ sb. up** (*as not coming*) jmdn. nicht mehr erwarten; mit jmdm. nicht mehr rechnen; (*as beyond help*) jmdn. aufgeben; **~ up for lost/dead** verloren geben/für tot halten; **C** (*hand over to police etc.*) übergeben (**to** *Dat.*); ausliefern ‹Spion usw.›; **~ oneself up [to sb.]** sich [jmdm.] stellen

**~ 'way** *v.i.* **A** (*yield, lit. or fig.*) nachgeben; (*collapse*) ‹Brücke, Balkon:› einstürzen; **his legs gave way under him** er knickte [in den Knien] ein; **~ way to sth.** einer Sache (*Dat.*) nachgeben; **~ way to tears** seinen Tränen freien Lauf lassen; **~ way to anger** seinem Ärger Luft machen; **~ way to persuasion** sich überzeugen lassen; **~ way to fear** der Angst erliegen; **his health gave way under this stress** seine Gesundheit hielt dieser Belastung nicht stand; **B** (*in traffic*) **~ way [to traffic from the right]** [dem Rechtsverkehr] die Vorfahrt lassen; **'Give Way'** „Vorfahrt beachten"; **C** (*be succeeded by*) **~ way to sth.** einer Sache (*Dat.*) weichen; von etw. abgelöst werden; **winter ~s way to spring** auf den Winter folgt der Frühling

**'giveaway** *n.* (*coll.*) **A** (*what betrays*) **the tremble in her voice was the ~:** mit ihrer zitternden Stimme hat sie sich verraten; **it was a dead ~:** es verriet alles; **B** *attrib.* (*Commerc.*) **~ prices** Schleuderpreise *Pl.*

**given** ⇒ **give** 1, 2

**'given name** *n.* (*Amer.*) Vorname, *der*

**giver** /'gɪvə(r)/ *n.* Geber, *der*/Geberin, *die;* (*donor*) Spender, *der*/Spenderin, *die*

**give-'way sign** *n.* (*Brit.*) Vorfahrtsschild, *das*

**gizmo** ⇒ **gismo**

**gizzard** /'gɪzəd/ *n.* (*of bird*) Muskelmagen, *der;* (*of insect, fish, etc.*) Kaumagen, *der;* **stick**

**in sb.'s ~** (*fig.*) jmdm. gegen den Strich gehen (*ugs.*)

**Gk.** *abbr.* **Greek** griech./Griech.

**glacé** /'glæseɪ/ *adj.* Ⓐ glasiert ‹Früchte›; (*candied*) kandiert; Ⓑ **~ leather** Glacéleder, *das;* **~ kid gloves** Glacéhandschuhe *Pl.*

**glacial** /'gleɪsɪəl, 'gleɪʃl/ *adj.* Ⓐ (*icy*) eisig; (*fig.*) eiskalt; Ⓑ (*Geol.*) Gletscher-; **~ epoch** *or* **period** Eiszeit, *die;* Glazialzeit, *die* (*fachspr.*)

**glaciation** /gleɪsɪ'eɪʃn, glæsɪ'eɪʃn/ *n.* (*Geol.*) Vergletscherung, *die*

**glacier** /'glæsɪə(r)/ *n.* Gletscher, *der*

**glad** /glæd/ *adj.* Ⓐ *pred.* froh; **be ~ about sth.** sich über etw. (*Akk.*) freuen; **be ~ that ...:** sich freuen, dass ...; (*be relieved*) froh sein [darüber], dass ...; **[I'm] ~ to meet you** es freut mich *od.* ich freue mich, Sie kennen zu lernen; **be ~ to hear sth.** sich freuen, etw. zu hören; (*relieved*) froh sein, etw. zu hören; **I am always ~ to see her** ich freue mich jedes Mal, wenn ich sie sehe; **Don't mention it. I was ~ to be of assistance** Keine Ursache. Das habe ich doch gern [für Sie] getan; **I'm ~ to know that ...:** zu meiner Freude erfahre ich, dass ...; **he's ~ to be alive** er ist froh, dass er lebt; **..., you'll be ~ to know/hear ...**, das freut Sie sicherlich; **I'd be ~ to [help you]** aber gern [helfe ich Ihnen]; **we shall be ~ to come/give further information** wir werden gern kommen/wir geben Ihnen gerne weitere Informationen; **be ~ of sth.** über etw. (*Akk.*) froh sein; für etw. dankbar sein; **Take your gloves. You'll be ~ of them** Nimm deine Handschuhe mit. Du wirst sie gebrauchen können; **a sight which makes one ~ to be alive** ein Anblick, der einem Freude am Leben gibt; **I'd be ~ if you'd do some work** (*iron.*) ich hätte nichts dagegen, wenn du dich jetzt etwas nützlich machst (*iron.*); Ⓑ (*giving joy*) froh ‹Botschaft›; freudig ‹Nachricht, Ereignis, Tag usw.›; (*marked by joy*) fröhlich; (*bright, beautiful*) herrlich ‹Morgen›

**gladden** /'glædn/ *v.t.* erfreuen

**glade** /gleɪd/ *n.* Lichtung, *die*

**glad 'eye** *n.* **give sb. the ~** (*coll.*) jmdm. schöne Augen machen (*ugs.*)

**glad 'hand** *n.* **give sb. the ~** (*coll.*) jmdm. die Hand schütteln

**gladiator** /'glædɪeɪtə(r)/ *n.* (*Roman Ant.*) Gladiator, *der*

**gladiolus** /glædɪ'əʊləs/ *n.*, *pl.* **gladioli** /glædɪ'əʊlaɪ/ *or* **~es** (*Bot.*) Gladiole, *die*

**gladly** /'glædlɪ/ *adv.* Ⓐ (*willingly*) gern; Ⓑ (*with joy*) freudig

**gladness** /'glædnɪs/ *n.*, *no pl.* Freude, *die;* (*of voice etc.*) Fröhlichkeit, *die*

**'glad rags** *n. pl.* (*coll.*) Festkleidung, *die*

**Gladstone bag** /glædstən 'bæg/ *n.* zweiteiliger Reisehandkoffer

**glamor** (*Amer.*) ⇒ **glamour**

**glamorize** (**glamorise**) /'glæməraɪz/ *v.t.* (*add glamour to*) [mehr] Glanz verleihen (+ *Dat.*); (*idealize*) verherrlichen (**into** zu); glorifizieren

**glamorous** /'glæmərəs/ *adj.* glanzvoll; glamourös ‹Filmstar, Lebenswandel usw.›; schillernd ‹Name, Persönlichkeit›; mondän ‹Kleidung›; **a ~ job** ein Traumberuf

**glamorously** /'glæmərəslɪ/ *adv.* mondän ‹gekleidet sein›; glanzvoll ‹darstellen›

**glamour** /'glæmə(r)/ *n.* Glanz, *der;* (*of person*) Ausstrahlung, *die*

**glamour: ~ boy** *n.* Schönling, *der;* **~ girl** *n.* Glamourgirl, *das*

**glamourize** (*Brit.*) ⇒ **glamorize**

**'glamour puss** *n.* (*coll.*) Glitzermieze, *die*

**glance** /glɑːns/ ❶ *n.* Ⓐ (*quick look*) Blick, *der;* **cast** *or* **take** *or* **have a [quick] ~ at sth./sb.** einen [kurzen] Blick auf etw./jmdn. werfen; **cast** *etc.* **a quick ~ at the newspaper/letter** die Zeitung durchblättern/den Brief überfliegen; **cast** *etc.* **a hasty ~ round the room** sich hastig im Zimmer umsehen; **give sb. a [knowing/quick** *etc.***] ~:** jmdm. einen [wissenden/kurzen *usw.*] Blick zuwerfen; **not give sb./sth. so much as a ~:** jmdn./eine Sache keines Blickes würdigen; **at a ~:** auf einen Blick; **at first/a casual ~:** auf den ersten Blick/wenn man flüchtig hinsieht; Ⓑ (*Cricket*) Streifschlag, *der.* ❷ *v.i.* Ⓐ blicken; schauen; **~ at sb./sth.** jmdn./etw. anblicken; **~ at one's watch** auf seine Uhr blicken; **she ~d at herself in the mirror** sie warf einen Blick in den Spiegel; **~ over/across at sb. [nervously** *etc.***]** jmdm. einen [nervösen *usw.*] Blick zuwerfen; **~ down/up [at sth.]** [auf etw. (*Akk.*)] hinunter-/[zu etw.] aufblicken; **~ over** *or* **through the newspaper** *etc.* die Zeitung *usw.* durchblättern; **~ at the newspaper** *etc.* einen Blick in die Zeitung *usw.* werfen; **~ round [the room]** sich [im Zimmer] umsehen; **~ around/from one thing to another** ‹Augen, Blick:› umherwandern/von einem Gegenstand zum anderen wandern; Ⓑ (*allude briefly*) **~ at sth.** etw. nur kurz streifen *od.* ansprechen; Ⓒ **~ [off sth.]** abprallen [an etw. (*Dat.*)]; ‹Messer, Schwert:› abgleiten [an etw. (*Dat.*)]; **strike sb. a glancing blow** jmdn. nur streifen

**gland**[1] /glænd/ *n.* Drüse, *die*

**gland**[2] *n.* (*Mech.*) Dichtung, *die*

**glandular** /'glændjʊlə(r)/ *adj.* Drüsen-; **~ swelling** geschwollene Drüse/Drüsen

**glandular 'fever** *n.* ▶ 1232 Drüsenfieber, *das*

**glans** /glænz/ *n.* **~ [penis]** (*Anat.*) Eichel, *die*

**glare** /gleə(r)/ ❶ *n.* Ⓐ (*dazzle*) grelles Licht; **shine with a ~:** grell scheinen; **the ~ of the sun** die grelle Sonne; das grelle Sonnenlicht; **amidst the ~/in the full ~ of publicity** (*fig.*) im Rampenlicht der Öffentlichkeit; Ⓑ (*hostile look*) feindseliger Blick; **with a ~:** feindselig; Ⓒ (*gaudiness*) Grellheit, *die.* ❷ *v.i.* Ⓐ (*glower*) [finster] starren; **~ at sb./sth.** jmdn./etw. anstarren; Ⓑ ‹Licht:› grell scheinen; (*shine by reflection*) ‹Strand, Straße:› flimmern; **~ down** ‹Sonne:› herunterbrennen. ❸ *v.t.* **~ contempt/defiance/hate** *etc.* **at sb.** jmdn. verächtlich/herausfordernd/hasserfüllt *usw.* anstarren

**glaring** /'gleərɪŋ/ *adj.* (*dazzling*) grell [strahlend/scheinend *usw.*]; gleißend hell ‹Licht›; (*fig.: conspicuous*) schreiend; eklatant; grob ‹Fehler›; krass ‹Gegensatz›

**glaringly** /'gleərɪŋlɪ/ *adv.* Ⓐ grell; **~ bright** gleißend hell; Ⓑ (*fig.*) **be ~ obvious** überdeutlich sein

**glasnost** /'glæsnɒst/ *n.* Glasnost, *die*

**glass** /glɑːs/ ❶ *n.* Ⓐ *no pl.* (*substance*) Glas, *das;* **pieces of/broken ~:** Glasscherben *Pl.;* (*smaller*) Glassplitter *Pl.;* **a pane/sheet of ~:** eine Glasscheibe/Glasplatte; Ⓑ (*drinking ~*) Glas, *das;* **a ~ of milk** ein Glas Milch; **a friendly ~:** ein Gläschen unter Freunden; **he's fond of his ~:** er trinkt gern ein Gläschen; **wine by the ~:** offener Wein; **raise one's ~ [to sb.]** (*fig.*) [auf jmdn.] das Glas erheben; Ⓒ (*of spectacles, watch*) Glas, *das;* (*pane, covering picture*) [Glas]scheibe, *die;* Ⓓ *in pl.* (*spectacles*) **[a pair of] ~es** eine Brille; **she wears thick ~es** sie trägt eine Brille mit dicken Gläsern; **driving/reading ~es** Fahr-/Lesebrille, *die;* Ⓔ (*binoculars*) Fernglas, *das;* **~es** *pl.* ein Fernglas; Ⓕ (*barometer*) Barometer, *das;* Ⓖ ⇒ **looking-glass**. ⇒ *also* **dark glasses**; **eyeglass**; **field glasses**; **ground glass**; **hourglass**; **magnifying glass**; **opera glasses**; **plate glass**; **water glass**. ❷ *attrib. adj.* Glas-; **people who live in ~ houses should not throw stones** (*prov.*) wer im Glashaus sitzt, soll nicht mit Steinen werfen (*Spr.*). ❸ *v.t., usu. in p. p.* verglasen; **~ed in** verglast

**glass: ~-blower** *n.* ▶ 1261 Glasbläser, *der*/Glasbläserin, *die;* **~-blowing** *n.* Glasblasen, *das;* **~ 'case** *n.* Vitrine, *die;* Glaskasten, *der;* **~ 'ceiling** *n.* (*fig.*) unsichtbare Barriere; **~cloth** *n.* Gläsertuch, *das;* **~ 'door** *n.* Glastür, *die;* **~ 'fibre** *n.* Glasfaser, *die*

**glassful** /'glɑːsfʊl/ *n.* Glas, *das* (**of** von); **a ~ of milk** ein Glas Milch

**glass: ~house** *n.* Ⓐ (*~works*) Glashütte, *die;* Ⓑ (*Brit.: greenhouse*) Gewächshaus, *das;* Glashaus, *das;* Ⓒ (*Brit. sl.: military prison*) Bunker, *der* (*Soldatenspr. salopp*); **~-making** *n.* Glasherstellung, *die;* **~-paper** *n.* Glaspapier, *das;* **~ware** *n.* Glas, *das;* **~ wool** *n.* Glaswolle, *die;* **~works** *n. sing.* Glashütte, *die*

**glassy** /'glɑːsɪ/ *adj.* gläsern; (*fig.*) glasig ‹Blick›; spiegelglatt ‹Wasseroberfläche›

**'glassy-eyed** *adj.* glasig; ‹Person› mit glasigem Blick; **begin to look ~:** einen glasigen Blick bekommen

**Glaswegian** /glæz'wiːdʒn/ ❶ *adj.* Glasgower. ❷ *n.* Glasgower, *der*/Glasgowerin, *die*

**glaucoma** /glɔː'kəʊmə/ *n.* ▶ 1232 (*Med.*) Glaukom, *das* (*fachspr.*); grüner Star

**glaze** /gleɪz/ ❶ *n.* (*on food or pottery*) Glasur, *die;* (*of paint*) Lasur, *die;* (*on paper, fabric*) Appretur, *die.* ❷ *v.t.* Ⓐ (*cover with ~*) glasieren ‹Esswaren, Töpferwaren›; satinieren ‹Papier, Leder, Kunststoff, Tuch›; lasieren ‹Farbe, bemalte Fläche›; **~d tile** Kachel, *die;* Ⓑ (*fit with glass*) **~ [in]** verglasen ‹Fenster, Haus usw.›; hinter Glas setzen ‹Bild›. ❸ *v.i.* **~ [over]** ‹Augen:› glasig werden

**glazed** /gleɪzd/ *adj.* glasig ‹Blick›

**glazier** /'gleɪzɪə(r), 'gleɪʒə(r)/ *n.* ▶ 1261 Glaser, *der*

**glazing** /'gleɪzɪŋ/ *n.* (*pane*) [Glas]scheibe, *die;* (*layer*) Glasur, *die;* ⇒ *also* **double glazing**

**gleam** /gliːm/ ❶ *n.* Ⓐ Schein, *der;* (*fainter, transient, or more subdued*) Schimmer, *der;* **~ of light** Lichtschein, *der;* Ⓑ (*fig.: faint trace*) Anflug, *der* (**of** von); **~ of hope/truth** Hoffnungsschimmer, *der*/Funke Wahrheit; **there was a ~ of anticipation in his eyes** seine Augen leuchteten erwartungsvoll. ❷ *v.i.* ‹Sonne, Licht:› scheinen; ‹Fußboden, Fahrzeug, Stiefel:› glänzen; ‹Zähne:› blitzen; ‹Augen:› leuchten

**gleaming** /'gliːmɪŋ/ ❶ *adj.* glänzend ‹Wasser, Metall, Fahrzeug›; schimmernd ‹Licht›; leuchtend ‹Augen›. ❷ *adv.* **~ white** leuchtend *od.* strahlend weiß; blendend *od.* blitzend weiß ‹Zähne›

**glean** /gliːn/ ❶ *v.t.* Ⓐ zusammentragen ‹Angaben, Informationen, Nachrichten usw.›; herausfinden ‹Inhalt eines Briefes, Gesprächs usw.›; **~ sth. from sth.** einer Sache (*Dat.*) etw. entnehmen; Ⓑ (*Agric.*) nachlesen ‹Getreide, Feld›. ❷ *v.i.* Ähren lesen

**gleaner** /'gliːnə(r)/ *n.* Ährenleser, *der*/Ährenleserin, *die*

**gleanings** /'gliːnɪŋz/ *n. pl.* Ⓐ (*of news*) zusammengeklaubte Informationen; (*of research, study*) Ausbeute, *die;* Ⓑ (*of corn etc.*) Nachlese, *die*

**glee** /gliː/ *n.* Ⓐ Freude, *die;* (*gloating joy*) Schadenfreude, *die;* Häme, *die;* **do sth. with** *or* **in ~:** etw. voll [Schaden]freude tun; Ⓑ (*Mus.*) Glee, *der*

**'glee club** *n.* Gesangverein, *der*

**gleeful** /'gliːfl/ *adj.* freudig; vergnügt; (*gloatingly joyful*) schadenfroh; hämisch; **be ~:** sich [hämisch] freuen

**gleefully** /'gliːfəlɪ/ *adv.* freudig; vor Freude ‹lachen usw.›; (*gloatingly*) schadenfroh; hämisch

**glen** /glen/ *n.* [schmales] Tal

**glib** /glɪb/ *adj.* (*derog.*) aalglatt ‹Person›; (*impromptu, offhand*) leicht dahingesagt, unbedacht ‹Antwort›; (*unreflecting*) vorschnell ‹Schluss, Verallgemeinerung›; (*voluble*) gewandt, geschickt ‹Redner, Politiker, Verkäufer›; (*facile in the use of words*) zungenfertig ‹Person›; flink ‹Zunge›; flinkzüngig ‹Antwort›; **be ~ in finding excuses** schnell Entschuldigungen bei der Hand haben

**glide** /glaɪd/ ❶ *v.i.* Ⓐ gleiten; (*through the air*) schweben; (*slip, steal, creep*) schleichen; ‹Gespenst:› huschen; Ⓑ (*Aeronaut.*) ‹Segelflugzeug:› gleiten, schweben; ‹Flugzeug:› im Gleitflug fliegen; ‹Person:› segelfliegen; **~ down** im Gleitflug niedergehen. ❷ *n.* Ⓐ (*Dancing*) Schleifschritt, *der;* Ⓑ (*Mus.*) Portamento, *das* (*fachspr.*); Ⓒ (*Phonet.*) Gleitlaut, *der*

**'glide path** *n.* (*Aeronaut.*) Gleitflugbahn, *die*

**glider** /'glaɪdə(r)/ *n.* Segelflugzeug, *das;* **~ [pilot]** Segelflieger, *der*/-fliegerin, *die*

**gliding** /'glaɪdɪŋ/ *n.* (*Sport*) Segelfliegen, *das; attrib.* Segelflug-

**glimmer** /'glɪmə(r)/ ❶ *n.* (*of light etc.*) [schwacher] Schein; Glimmer, *der* (*selten*); Schimmer, *der* (**of** von) (*auch fig.*); (*of fire, candle*) Glimmen, *das;* **~ of light** Lichtschimmer, *der;* **~ of hope** Hoffnungsschimmer, *der.* ❷ *v.i.* glimmen; ‹Satin usw.:› schimmern

**glimmering** /'glɪmərɪŋ/ *n.* (*lit. or fig.*) Schimmer, *der* (**of** von)

**glimpse** /glɪmps/ ❶ *n.* [kurzer] Blick; **catch** *or* **have** *or* **get a ~ of sb./sth.** jmdn./etw. [kurz] zu sehen *od.* zu Gesicht bekommen; (*fig.*) einen Eindruck von jmdm./Einblick in etw. (*Akk.*) bekommen; **it gives us a ~ of what life must have been like then** es gibt uns einen Einblick in das damalige Leben. ❷ *v.t.* flüchtig sehen; (*fig.*) einen Einblick bekommen in (+ *Akk.*); einen Eindruck gewinnen von

**glint** /glɪnt/ ❶ *n.* Schimmer, *der;* (*reflected flash*) Glitzern, *das;* (*of eyes*) Funkeln, *das;* (*of knife, dagger*) Blitzen, *das.* ❷ *v.i.* blinken; glitzern

**glissando** /glɪ'sændəʊ/ *n., pl.* **glissandi** /glɪ'sændi:/ *or* **~s** (*Mus.*) Glissando, *das*

**glisten** /'glɪsn/ *v.i.* glitzern; ⇨ *also* **glitter** 1 A

**glitch** /glɪtʃ/ *n.* (*coll.*) Panne, *die*

**glitter** /'glɪtə(r)/ ❶ *v.i.* Ⓐ glitzern; ‹Augen, Juwelen, Sterne:› funkeln; **the sky ~s with stars, stars ~ in the sky** am Himmel funkeln Sterne; **all that ~s** *or* **glistens is not gold** (*prov.*) es ist nicht alles Gold, was glänzt (*Spr.*); Ⓑ *esp. in pres. p.* (*fig.*) glänzen; **~ing prizes** verlockende *od.* attraktive Preise. ❷ *n.* Ⓐ Glitzern, *das;* (*of diamonds*) Funkeln, *das;* Ⓑ (*fig.: ~ing attractiveness*) verlockende Aussicht (**of** auf + *Akk.*); Ⓒ (*tinsel etc.*) Flitterwerk, *das;* Glitzerwerk, *das*

**glitterati** /glɪtə'rɑ:tɪ/ *n. pl.* Schickeria, *die* (*Jargon*)

**glitz** /glɪts/ *n.* Glanz, *der*

**glitzy** /'glɪtsɪ/ *adj.* glanzvoll

**gloaming** /'gləʊmɪŋ/ *n., no pl.* **the ~:** die Abenddämmerung

**gloat** /gləʊt/ *v.i.* **~ over sth.** (*look at with selfish delight*) sich an etw. (*Dat.*) weiden *od.* ergötzen; (*derive sadistic pleasure from*) sich hämisch über etw. (*Akk.*) freuen

**gloatingly** /'gləʊtɪŋlɪ/ *adv.* (*with delight*) selbstgefällig; genüsslich; (*with sadistic pleasure*) hämisch

**global** /'gləʊbl/ *adj.* Ⓐ (*worldwide*) global; weltweit; weltumspannend ‹Kommunikationssystem›; **~ warming** globaler Temperaturanstieg; **~ peace/warfare** Weltfrieden/-krieg, *der;* **~ strategy** Globalstrategie, *die;* **the ~ village** das Weltdorf; Ⓑ (*comprehensive*) Gesamt-; umfassend ‹Berichterstattung›; **take a ~ view** die Dinge global betrachten

**globalization** /gləʊbəlaɪ'zeɪʃn/*n.* Globalisierung, *die*

**globalize** /'gləʊbəlaɪz/ *v.t.* globalisieren

**globally** /'gləʊbəlɪ/ *adv.* Ⓐ (*on a worldwide basis*) global; weltweit; Ⓑ (*comprehensively*) umfassend

**globe** /gləʊb/ *n.* Ⓐ (*sphere*) Kugel, *die;* Ⓑ (*sphere with map*) Globus, *der;* Ⓒ (*world*) **the ~:** der Globus; der Erdball; Ⓓ (*spherical object*) Kugel, *die*

**globe:** **~ 'artichoke** ⇨ **artichoke**; **~fish** *n.* Kugelfisch, *der;* **~flower** *n.* Trollblume, *die;* **~trotter** *n.* Globetrotter, *der;* Weltenbummler, *der;* **~trotting** *n.* Globetrotten, *das;* Weltreisen, *das*

**globular** /'glɒbjʊlə(r)/ *adj.* kugelförmig

**globule** /'glɒbju:l/ *n.* Kügelchen, *das;* (*of liquid*) Tröpfchen, *das*

**globulin** /'glɒbjʊlɪn/ *n.* (*Biochem.*) Globulin, *das*

**glockenspiel** /'glɒkənspi:l, 'glɒkənʃpi:l/ *n.* (*Mus.*) Glockenspiel, *das*

**gloom** /glu:m/ *n.* Ⓐ (*darkness*) Dunkel, *das* (*geh.*); Ⓑ (*despondency*) düstere Stimmung; **cast a ~ over sth.** einen Schatten auf etw. (*Akk.*) werfen (*fig.*)

**gloomily** /'glu:mɪlɪ/ *adv.* finster; düster

**gloomy** /'glu:mɪ/ *adj.* Ⓐ (*dark*) düster; finster; dämmrig ‹Tag, Nachmittag usw.›; Ⓑ (*depressing*) düster, finster [stimmend]; bedrückend; (*depressed*) trübsinnig ‹Person›; bedrückt ‹Gesicht›; **he always tends to see the ~ side of things** er sieht immer gleich schwarz; **have a ~ outlook on life** dem Leben erwartungslos *od.* pessimistisch gegenüberstehen; **feel ~ about the future** der Zukunft pessimistisch entgegensehen; **be in a ~ mood** düsterer Stimmung *od.* niedergeschlagen sein; **look ~:** niedergeschlagen *od.* bedrückt aussehen; ein bedrücktes Gesicht machen

**glorification** /glɔ:rɪfɪ'keɪʃn/ *n.* Ⓐ (*praise*) Verherrlichung, *die;* Glorifizierung, *die;* Ⓑ (*worship*) Verehrung, *die;* Anbetung, *die;* Ⓒ (*exaltation*) Verehrung, *die*

**glorify** /'glɔ:rɪfaɪ/ *v.t.* Ⓐ (*extol*) verherrlichen; glorifizieren; (*misrepresent thus*) **glorified** besser... (*ugs.*); **he's no more than a glorified messenger boy** er ist nichts weiter als *od.* doch nur ein besserer Botenjunge; Ⓑ (*worship*) verehren; anbeten; Ⓒ (*exalt*) verehren; ehren ‹Helden, Andenken›

**glorious** /'glɔ:rɪəs/ *adj.* Ⓐ (*illustrious*) ruhmreich ‹Held, Sieg, Geschichte›; rühmlich ‹Tat, Rolle›; verehrungswürdig ‹Heilige›; Ⓑ (*honourable*) ehrenhaft ‹Sache, Angelegenheit›; ehrenvoll, rühmlich ‹Tod, Kampf, Sieg, Tat›; glorreich, glanzvoll ‹Ende einer Karriere, Errungenschaft›; Ⓒ (*delightful*) wunderschön; herrlich; (*iron.*) schön; **it was ~ fun** es war ein prächtiger *od.* köstlicher Spaß

**gloriously** /'glɔ:rɪəslɪ/ *adv.* Ⓐ (*honourably*) rühmlich; (*illustriously*) glanzvoll; **die ~:** in Ehren sterben; Ⓑ (*splendidly*) wunderschön; herrlich

**glory** /'glɔ:rɪ/ ❶ *n.* Ⓐ (*splendour*) Schönheit, *die;* (*majesty*) Herrlichkeit, *die;* **the Empire at the height of its ~:** das Imperium auf dem Höhepunkt seiner Macht; **a lily in all its ~:** eine Lilie in ihrer vollen Pracht; **in all one's ~** (*iron.*) in all seiner Pracht und Herrlichkeit (*iron.*); Ⓑ (*honour*) Ehre, *die;* (*credit*) Verdienst, *das;* (*fame*) Ruhm, *der;* **they did all the work and he got all the ~:** sie haben die ganze Arbeit getan, und ihm wird es als Verdienst angerechnet; **cover oneself with ~:** sich mit Ruhm bedecken (*geh.*); sich mit Ruhm bekleckern (*ugs., iron.*); Ⓒ (*worshipful praise*) Ehre, *die;* Ruhm, *der;* **~ [be] to God in the highest** Ehre sei Gott in der Höhe; **[built] to the ~ of God** [erbaut] zur Ehre/zum Ruhme Gottes; **~ be!** (*dated coll.*) *expr. surprise* ach du lieber Himmel! (*ugs.*); *expr. annoyance* Himmel noch mal! (*ugs.*); *expr. delight* himmlisch!; Ⓓ (*source of distinction*) Größe, *die;* (*deed*) Ruhmestat, *die;* (*achievement*) Glanzleistung, *die;* **be the ~ of a nation** der Stolz *od.* die Zierde eines Volkes sein; ⇨ *also* **Old Glory**; Ⓔ (*heavenly bliss*) ewige Seligkeit; **Christ in ~:** Christus in seiner Herrlichkeit; **go/send to ~** (*arch. coll.*) abfahren (*veralt.*)/ins Jenseits befördern (*salopp*). ❷ *v.i.* **~ in sth./doing sth.** (*be pleased by*) etw. genießen/es genießen, etw. zu tun; (*be proud of*) sich einer Sache (*Gen.*) rühmen/sich rühmen, etw. zu tun; **~ in the name/title of ...:** den stolzen Namen/Titel ... besitzen *od.* führen

**'glory hole** *n.* (*coll.*) Rumpelkammer, *die*

**gloss**[1] /glɒs/ ❶ *n.* Ⓐ (*sheen*) Glanz, *der;* **~ paint** Lackfarbe, *die;* **~ finish** Glanz, *der;* **paper/photo with a ~ finish** Glanzpapier, *das*/Glanzabzug, *der;* **give sth. a high ~:** einer Sache (*Dat.*) Hochglanz verleihen; Ⓑ (*fig.*) Anstrich, *der.* ❷ *v.t.* polieren; auf Hochglanz bringen

**~ over** *v.t.* bemänteln; beschönigen ‹Fehler›; (*conceal*) unter den Teppich kehren (*ugs.*)

**gloss**[2] ❶ *n.* Ⓐ (*comment*) [Wort]erklärung, *die;* (*Ling.*) Glosse, *die* (*fachspr.*); Ⓑ (*misrepresentation of another's words*) [bewusst] falsche Auslegung; Ⓒ (*glossary*) Glossar, *das;* (*translation*) Interlinearübersetzung, *die;* (*continuous explanation*) Kommentar, *der.* ❷ *v.t.* glossieren

**glossary** /'glɒsərɪ/ *n.* Glossar, *das*

**glossy** /'glɒsɪ/ ❶ *adj.* Ⓐ glänzend; (*printed on ~ paper*) Hochglanz-; auf Glanzpapier gedruckt; **~ paper, paper with a ~ finish** Glanzpapier, *das;* **~ [photographic] print** Glanzabzug, *der;* **~ magazine** Hochglanzzeitschrift, *die;* Ⓑ (*fig.*) glanzvoll. ❷ *n.* (*coll.*) Ⓐ (*magazine*) auf [Hoch]glanzpapier gedruckte Zeitschrift; Hochglanzzeitschrift, *die;* Ⓑ (*photograph*) Glanzabzug, *der*

**glottal** /'glɒtl/ *adj.* (*Phonet.*) glottal; Stimmritzen‹laut, -verschluss usw.›

**glottal 'stop** *n.* (*Phonet.*) Glottisschlag, *der;* Knacklaut, *der*

**glottis** /'glɒtɪs/ *n.* (*Anat.*) Glottis, *die*

**glove** /glʌv/ *n.* Ⓐ Handschuh, *der;* **sth. fits sb. like a ~:** etw. passt jmdm. wie angegossen (*ugs.*); (*fig.*) etw. trifft auf jmdn. haargenau zu; **throw down/take up the ~** (*fig.*) den Fehdehandschuh werfen/aufnehmen (*geh.*); Ⓑ ⇨ **boxing glove**; **argue sth. with the ~s off** sich in allem Ernst *od.* offen und ehrlich über etw. (*Akk.*) auseinander setzen. ⇨ *also* **hand** 1 A

**glove:** **~ box** *n.* Ⓐ ⇨ **~ compartment**; Ⓑ (*for toxic material etc.*) Handschuhkasten, *der;* **~ compartment** *n.* Handschuhfach, *das*

**gloved** /glʌvd/ *adj.* behandschuht

**'glove puppet** *n.* Handpuppe, *die*

**glow** /gləʊ/ ❶ *v.i.* Ⓐ glühen; ‹Lampe, Leuchtfarbe:› schimmern, leuchten; Ⓑ (*fig.*) (*with warmth or pride*) ‹Gesicht, Wangen:› glühen (**with** vor + *Dat.*); (*with health or vigour*) strotzen (**with** vor + *Dat.*); (*with pleasure or excitement*) strahlen (**with** vor + *Dat.*); (*with rage or fervour*) glühen (**with** vor + *Dat.*); Ⓒ (*be suffused with warm colour*) [warm] leuchten; **~ with the tints of autumn** in allen Herbstfarben leuchten. ❷ *n.* Ⓐ Glühen, *das;* (*of candle, lamp*) Schein, *der;* (*of embers, lava, sunset*) Glut, *die;* Ⓑ (*fig.*) Glühen, *das;* **feel a ~ of pride** vor Stolz glühen; **his cheeks had a healthy ~:** seine Wangen hatten eine blühende Farbe; **~ of youth/health** blühende Jugend/Gesundheit; **feel a ~ of happiness/passion** ein warmes Glücksgefühl/glühende Leidenschaft verspüren

**glower** /'glaʊə(r)/ *v.i.* finster dreinblicken; **~ at sb.** jmdn. finster anstarren

**glowing** /'gləʊɪŋ/ *adj.* glühend (*auch fig.*); [warm] leuchtend ‹Herbstfarben›; (*fig.: enthusiastic*) begeistert ‹Bericht, Beschreibung›; überschwänglich ‹Lob›; **be in ~ health** sich blühender Gesundheit (*Gen.*) erfreuen; **describe sth. in ~ colours/terms** (*fig.*) etw. in glühenden *od.* leuchtenden Farben/glühenden Worten beschreiben; **~ promises** glänzende Versprechungen

**glow:** **~-lamp** *n.* (*Electr.*) Glühlampe, *die;* **~-worm** *n.* Glühwürmchen, *das*

**gloxinia** /glɒk'sɪnɪə/ *n.* (*Bot.*) Gloxinie, *die*

**glucose** /'glu:kəʊs, 'glu:kəʊz/ *n.* Glucose, *die;* **~ [powder]** (*Med.*) Traubenzucker, *der*

**glue** /glu:/ ❶ *n.* Klebstoff, *der;* Leim, *der;* Kleber, *der* (*ugs.*); **like ~** (*fig.*) wie festgeklebt; **cling like ~ to sth./sb.** (*fig.*) an etw./jmdm. kleben (*ugs.*). ❷ *v.t.* Ⓐ kleben; leimen; **~ sth. together/on** etw. zusammen-/ankleben; **~ sth. to sth.** etw. an etw. (*Dat.*) an- *od.* festkleben; **as though ~d to the spot** wie angewurzelt; Ⓑ (*fig.*) **be ~d to sth./sb.** an etw./jmdm. kleben (*ugs.*); **their eyes** *or* **they were ~d to the TV screen** sie starrten auf den Bildschirm

**glue:** **~ pot** *n.* Leimtopf, *der;* **~-sniffing** *n.* Schnüffeln, *das* (*ugs.*); Sniefen, *das* (*ugs.*)

**glug** /glʌg/ *v.i.*, **-gg-** gluckern; glucksen

**glum** /glʌm/ *adj.*, **glumly** /'glʌmlɪ/ *adv.* verdrießlich; missgelaunt

**glut** /glʌt/ ❶ *n.* (*Commerc.*) Überangebot, *das* (**of** an, von + *Dat.*); **a ~ of apples/talent** eine Apfelschwemme/eine Menge Talente. ❷ *v.t.*, **-tt-:** Ⓐ (*Commerc.*) überschwemmen; Ⓑ (*gorge*) **~ oneself** sich voll stopfen (*ugs.*) (**with, on** mit); **be ~ted with sth.** (*fig.*) einer Sache (*Gen.*) überdrüssig sein

**glutamate** /'glu:təmeɪt/ *n.* (*Chem.*) Glutamat, *das;* **monosodium ~:** [Mono]natriumglutamat, *das*

**gluten** /'glu:tən/ *n.* Gluten, *das;* Kleber, *der* (*fachspr.*); **~ bread** Glutenbrot, *das*

**glutinous** /'glu:tɪnəs/ *adj.* klebrig

**glutton** /'glʌtən/ *n.* **A** Vielfraß, *der* (*ugs.*); **a ~ for books/punishment** (*iron.*)/**work** (*fig.*) eine Leseratte (*ugs.*)/ein Masochist (*fig.*)/ein Arbeitstier (*fig.*); **B** (*Zool.*) Vielfraß, *der*

**gluttonous** /'glʌtənəs/ *adj.* gefräßig

**gluttony** /'glʌtənɪ/ *n.* Gefräßigkeit, *die*

**glycerine** /'glɪsəri:n/ (*Amer.:* **glycerin** /'glɪsərɪn/) *n.* Glyzerin, *das*

**glycogen** /'glaɪkədʒən/ *n.* (*Med., Biol.*) Glykogen, *das*

**glycol** /'glaɪkɒl/ *n.* (*Chem.*) Glykol, *das*

**GM** *abbr.* **genetically modified**

**gm.** *abbr.* ▶ 1683 **gram[s]** g

**G-man** /'dʒi:mæn/ *n., pl.* **G-men** /'dʒi:men/ (*Amer. coll.*) G-Man, *der*

**GMO** *abbr.* **genetically modified organism** GVO

**GMT** *abbr.* **Greenwich mean time** GMT; WEZ

**gnarled** /nɑ:ld/, **gnarly** /'nɑ:lɪ/ *adjs.* knorrig; knotig ‹Finger, Hand›

**gnash** /næʃ/ *v.t.* **~ one's teeth [in anger]** [vor Zorn] mit den Zähnen knirschen; **~ing of teeth** Zähneknirschen, *das*

**gnat** /næt/ *n.* [Stech]mücke, *die;* ⇒ *also* **strain¹** 3 B

**gnaw** /nɔ:/ **1** *v.i.* **A** **~ [away] at sth.** an etw. (*Dat.*) nagen; **~ through a rope/sack** ein Seil/einen Sack durchnagen; **B** (*fig.*) **~ [away] at sth./sb.'s savings** an etw. (*Dat.*) nagen/an jmds. Ersparnissen zehren. **2** *v.t.* **A** nagen an (+ *Dat.*); abnagen ‹Knochen›; kauen an *od.* auf (*Dat.*) ‹Fingernägeln›; **~ a hole in sth.** ein Loch in etw. (*Akk.*) nagen; **B** (*fig.*) nagen an (+ *Dat.*) ‹Gewissen›; zehren an ‹Herzen›

**gnawing** /'nɔ:ɪŋ/ *adj.* nagend ‹Hunger, Schmerz, Zweifel, Kummer usw.›; quälend ‹Zahnschmerzen, Angst›

**gneiss** /gnaɪs, naɪs/ *n.* (*Geol.*) Gneis, *der*

**gnome** /nəʊm/ *n.* **A** Gnom, *der;* (*in garden*) Gartenzwerg, *der;* **B** (*fig. coll.*) **the ~s of Zurich** die Zürcher Gnome; die Schweizer Bankiers

**gnomic** /'nəʊmɪk/ *adj.* gnomisch

**gnostic** /'nɒstɪk/ **1** *adj.* **A** (*relating to or having knowledge*) kognitiv; (*Relig.*) erleuchtet; **B** **G~** (*Relig. Hist.*) gnostisch. **2** *n.* **G~** (*Relig. Hist.*) Gnostiker, *der*

**GNP** *abbr.* **gross national product** BSP

**gnu** /nu:, nju:/ *n.* (*Zool.*) Gnu, *das*

**go¹** /gəʊ/ **1** *v.i., pres.* **he goes** /gəʊz/, *p. t.* **went** /went/, *pres. p.* **going** /'gəʊɪŋ/, *p. p.* **gone** /gɒn, gɔ:n/ **A** gehen; ‹Fahrzeug:› fahren; ‹Flugzeug:› fliegen; ‹Vierfüßer:› laufen; ‹Reptil:› kriechen; (*on horseback etc.*) reiten; (*on skis, roller skates*) laufen; (*in wheelchair, pram, lift*) fahren; **go by bicycle/car/bus/train** *or* **rail/boat** *or* **sea** *or* **ship** mit dem [Fahr]rad/Auto/Bus/Zug/Schiff fahren; **go by plane** *or* **air** fliegen; **go by Lufthansa/Concorde** mit der Lufthansa/der Concorde fliegen; **go on foot** zu Fuß gehen; laufen (*ugs.*); **as one goes [along]** (*fig.*) nach und nach; **do sth. as one goes [along]** (*lit.*) etw. beim Gehen *od.* unterwegs tun; **go on a journey** eine Reise machen; verreisen; **go first-class/at 50 m.p.h.** erster Klasse reisen *od.* fahren/80 Stundenkilometer fahren; **go with sb.** mit jmdm. gehen; jmdn. begleiten; ‹Hund:› jmdm. folgen; **have far to go** weit zu gehen *od.* zu fahren haben; es weit haben; **the doll/dog goes everywhere with her** sie hat immer ihre Puppe/ihren Hund dabei; **who goes there?** (*sentry's challenge*) wer da?; **there you go** (*coll., giving sth.*) bitte!; da! (*ugs.*); **B** (*proceed as regards purpose, activity, destination, or route*) ‹Bus, Zug, Lift, Schiff:› fahren; (*use means of transportation*) fahren; (*fly*) fliegen; (*proceed on outward journey*) weg-, abfahren; (*travel regularly*) ‹Verkehrsmittel:› verkehren (**from ... to** zwischen + *Dat.* ... und); **know where one is going** (*fig.*) wissen, was man will; **his hand went to his pocket** er griff nach seiner Tasche; **go to the toilet/cinema/moon/a museum/a funeral** auf die Toilette/ins Kino gehen/zum Mond fliegen/ins Museum/zu einer Beerdigung gehen; **go to a dance** tanzen gehen; **go [along] to the doctor['s]** *etc.* zum Arzt *usw.* gehen; **go [out] to China** nach China gehen; **go [over] to America** nach Amerika [hinüber]fliegen/-fahren; **go [off] to London** nach London [ab]fahren/[ab]fliegen; **go [over** *or* **across] to the mainland** zum Festland [hinüber]fahren/-fliegen; **last year we went to Italy** letztes Jahr waren wir in Italien; **go this/that way** hier/da entlanggehen/-fahren; **go out of one's way** einen Umweg machen; (*fig.*) keine Mühe scheuen; **go towards sth./sb.** auf etw./jmdn. zugehen; **don't go on the grass** geh nicht auf den Rasen; **go by sth./sb.** ‹Festzug usw.:› an etw./jmdm. vorbeiziehen; ‹Bus usw.:› an etw./jmdm. vorbeifahren; **go in/out** hinein-/hinausgehen; **go in and out [of sth.]** [in etw. (*Dat.*)] ein- und ausgehen; **go into sth.** in etw. (*Akk.*) [hinein]gehen; **I'd never go on motorways** ich würde niemals [auf der] Autobahn fahren; **go out for some fresh air** frische Luft schöpfen gehen; **go out to the postbox** zum Briefkasten gehen; **go [out] for a walk** einen Spaziergang machen; spazieren gehen; **go bathing** baden gehen; **go cycling** Rad fahren; **go looking for sb.** jmdn. suchen gehen; **go chasing after sth./sb.** hinter etw./jmdm. herrennen (*ugs.*); **go to do sth.** gehen, um etw. zu tun; (*while standing still*) etw. tun wollen; **go to live in Berlin** nach Berlin ziehen; **go to sea** in See stechen; (*become sailor*) zur See gehen (*ugs.*); **go to see sb.** jmdn. aufsuchen; **I went to water the garden** ich ging den Garten sprengen; **go and do sth.** [gehen und] etw. tun; **you ought to go and find a flat** du solltest dir eine Wohnung suchen; **I'll go and get my coat** ich hole jetzt meinen Mantel; **I'll just go and put my shoes on** ich ziehe mir nur eben Schuhe an; **go and see whether ...:** nachsehen [gehen], ob ...; **go on a pilgrimage** *etc.* eine Pilgerfahrt *usw.* machen; **go on TV/the radio** im Fernsehen/Radio auftreten; **I'll go!** ich geh schon!; (*answer phone*) ich geh ran *od.* nehme ab; (*answer door*) ich mache auf; **'you go** (*to the phone*) geh du mal ran!; **C** (*start*) losgehen; (*in vehicle*) losfahren; **let's go!** (*coll.*) fangen wir an!; **here goes!** (*coll.*) dann mal los!; **whose turn is it to go?** (*in game*) wer ist an der Reihe?; **go first** (*in game*) anfangen; **from the word go** (*fig. coll.*) [schon] von Anfang an; **D** (*pass, circulate, be transmitted*) gehen; **a shiver went up** *or* **down my spine** ein Schauer lief mir über den Rücken *od.* den Rücken hinunter; **go to** (*be given to*) ‹Preis, Sieg, Gelder, Job:› gehen an (+ *Akk.*); ‹Titel, Krone, Besitz:› übergehen auf (+ *Akk.*); ‹Ehre, Verdienst:› zuteil werden (*Dat.*); **go towards** (*be of benefit to*) zugute kommen (+ *Dat.*); **go according to** (*be determined by*) sich richten nach; ⇒ *also* **head** 1 A; **E** (*make specific motion, do something specific*) **go round** ‹Rad:› sich drehen; **there he** *etc.* **goes again** (*coll.*) da, schon wieder!; **here we go again** (*coll.*) jetzt geht das wieder los!; **F** (*act, work, function effectively*) gehen; ‹Mechanismus, Maschine:› laufen; **get the car to go** das Auto ankriegen (*ugs.*) *od.* starten; **at midnight we were still going** um Mitternacht waren wir immer noch dabei *od.* im Gange; **go by electricity** mit Strom betrieben werden; **the clock doesn't go** die Uhr geht nicht; **go to it!** (*coll.*) an die Arbeit!; **keep going** (*in movement*) weitergehen/-fahren; (*in activity*) weitermachen; (*not fail*) sich aufrecht halten; **the car still keeps going** das Auto läuft noch immer; **keep oneself going** durchhalten; **keep sb. going** (*enable to continue*) jmdn. aufrecht halten; **that'll keep me going** das reicht mir; damit komme ich aus; **keep sth. going** etw. in Gang halten; **make sth. go, get/set sth. going** etw. in Gang bringen; **set sb. going** (*iron.*) jmdn. aufs Thema bringen (*ugs.*); jmdn. in Fahrt bringen (*ugs.*); **G** **go to** (*attend*): **go to work** zur Arbeit gehen; **go to church/kindergarten/school** in die Kirche/den Kindergarten/die Schule gehen; **go to Eton/Oxford** Eton besuchen/in Oxford studieren; **go to a comprehensive school** eine Gesamtschule besuchen; auf eine Gesamtschule gehen; **go as a witch** *etc.* als Hexe *usw.* gehen; **what should I go in?** was soll ich anziehen?; **H** (*have recourse*) **go to the police** zur Polizei gehen; **go to the originals** auf die Quellen zurückgreifen; **go to the relevant authority/UN** sich an die zuständige Behörde/UN wenden; **go on hunger strike** in den Hungerstreik treten; **go into the army** zur Armee gehen; **where do we go from here?** (*fig.*) und was nun? (*ugs.*); **I** (*depart*) gehen; ‹Bus, Zug:› [ab]fahren; ‹Post:› rausgehen (*ugs.*); (*resign*) zurücktreten; (*abdicate*) abdanken; **go away** weggehen; (*move away*) wegziehen; **he/the bus has gone** er/der Bus ist schon weg (*ugs.*); **I must go** ich muss gehen; **I must be going now** ich muss allmählich gehen; **time to go!** wir müssen/ihr müsst *usw.* gehen!; **'gone away'** (*on envelope*) „verzogen"; **Oh no! There goes my quiet weekend** Oh nein, jetzt ist mein geruhsames Wochenende dahin!; **to go** (*Amer.*) ‹Speisen, Getränke› zum Mitnehmen; **my headache has gone** mein Kopfweh ist weg; **J** (*euphem.: die*) sterben; **be dead and gone** tot sein; **after I go** wenn ich einmal nicht mehr bin; **K** (*fail*) ‹Gedächtnis, Kräfte:› nachlassen; (*cease to function*) kaputtgehen; ‹Maschine, Computer usw.:› ausfallen; ‹Sicherung:› durchbrennen; (*break*) brechen; ‹Seil usw.:› reißen; (*collapse*) einstürzen; ‹Mast:› umstürzen; (*fray badly*) ausfransen; **the jacket has gone at the elbows** die Jacke ist an den Ellbogen durchgescheuert *od.* abgewetzt; **his memory is going** sein Gedächtnis lässt nach; **L** (*disappear*) weggehen; ‹Mantel, Hut, Fleck:› verschwinden; ‹Zahn:› ausfallen; ‹Kultur:› vergehen; ‹Geruch, Rauch:› sich verziehen; ‹Geld, Zeit:› draufgehen (*ugs.*) **(in, on** für); (*be relinquished*) aufgegeben werden; ‹Absatz usw.:› gestrichen werden; ‹Unterrichtsfach:› entfallen; ‹Tradition:› abgeschafft werden; (*be dismissed*) ‹Arbeitskräfte:› entlassen werden; (*Cricket*) (*be out*) aus sein; **be gone from sight** außer Sicht geraten sein; **my coat/the stain has gone** mein Mantel/der Fleck ist weg; **where has my hat gone?** wo ist mein Hut [geblieben]?; **I don't know where my money goes** ich weiß nicht, wo das Geld bleibt; **that aid to developing countries goes on the growing of food** diese Entwicklungshilfe wird für den Anbau von Nahrungsmitteln verwendet; **this paragraph will have to go** dieser Absatz muss gestrichen werden; **all his money goes on women** er gibt sein ganzes Geld für Frauen aus; **all hope has gone** alle Hoffnung ist dahin; **M** (*elapse*) ‹Zeit:› vergehen; ‹Interview usw.:› vorüber-, vorbeigehen; **that has all gone by** das ist jetzt alles vorbei; **in days gone by** in längst vergangenen Zeiten; **N** **to go** (*still remaining*) **have sth. [still] to go** [noch] etw. übrig haben; **he has two years to go before he can retire** an der Rente fehlen ihm noch zwei Jahre; **there's hours to go** es dauert noch Stunden; **one week** *etc.* **to go to ...:** noch eine Woche *usw.* bis ...; **there's only another mile to go** [es ist] nur noch eine Meile; **still have a mile to go** noch eine Meile vor sich (*Dat.*) haben; **one down, two to go** einer ist bereits erledigt, bleiben noch zwei übrig (*salopp*); **O** (*be sold*) weggehen (*ugs.*); verkauft werden; **it went for £1** es ging für 1 Pfund weg; **I shan't let it go for less** für weniger gebe ich es nicht her; **go to sb.** an jmdn. gehen; **going! going! gone!** Zum Ersten! zum Zweiten! zum Dritten!; **P** (*run*) ‹Grenze, Straße usw.:› verlaufen, gehen; (*afford access, lead*) gehen; führen; (*extend*) reichen; (*fig.*) gehen; **go high[er]** ‹Preis:› [noch weiter] steigen, [noch weiter] in die Höhe gehen; **the line goes across the page/to the corner/upwards** der Strich geht quer über die Seite/bis in die Ecke/verläuft nach oben; **my holiday goes from ... to ...:** ich habe Urlaub von ... bis ...; **as** *or* **so far as he/it goes** so weit; **sth.**

g

**is correct as** *or* **so far as it goes** etw. ist so weit in Ordnung; **go a long way** ‹Geld, Vorräte:› lange reichen; **he will go a long way** (*fig.*) er wird es weit bringen; **go some/a long way to[wards] achieving sth.** ein kleines/ganzes Stück weiterhelfen *od.* einiges/eine Menge dazu beitragen, etw. zu erreichen; **ten pounds in those days went a long way** damals waren zehn Pfund noch etwas wert; **a little of his company goes a long way** (*coll. derog.*) wenn man nur kurze Zeit mit ihm verbracht hat, reicht das erst mal für eine Weile *od.* (*salopp*) ist man erst mal für eine Weile bedient; **Q** (*fig.: advance*) **we'll go halfway to meet the cost** wir kommen ihnen *usw.* bei den Kosten halbwegs entgegen; **I'll go as high as £100** (*at auction*) ich gehe *od.* biete bis zu 100 Pfund [mit]; ⇒ *also* **bother** 3 B; **expense** 1 A; **trouble** A; **way** 1 E; **R** (*turn out, progress*) ‹Ereignis, Projekt, Interview, Abend:› verlaufen; **go for/against sb./sth.** ‹Wahl, Kampf:› zu jmds./einer Sache Gunsten/Ungunsten ausgehen; ‹Entscheidung, Urteil:› zu jmds./einer Sache Gunsten/Ungunsten ausfallen; ‹Rechtsfall:› zu jmds./einer Sache Gunsten/Ungunsten entschieden werden; **how did your holiday/party go?** wie war Ihr Urlaub/Ihre Party?; **how is the book going?** was macht [denn] das Buch?; **how are the rehearsals going?** was machen die Proben?; wie läuft es mit den Proben?; **go according to plan** nach Plan gehen; planmäßig verlaufen; **things have been going well/badly/smoothly** *etc.* **of late** in der letzten Zeit läuft alles gut/schief/glatt *usw.*; **the way things are going, ...:** so wie es aussieht *od.* so wie die Dinge liegen, ...; **how are things going?, how is it going?**, (*coll. joc.*) **how goes it?** wie stehts *od.* (*ugs.*) läufts?; **S** (*be, have form or nature, be in temporary state*) sein; ‹Sprichwort, Gedicht, Titel:› lauten; **this is how things go, that's the way it goes** so ist es nun mal; **go against sth.** mit etw. nicht übereinstimmen; **go against one's principles** gegen seine Prinzipien gehen; **go against logic** der Logik widersprechen; gegen alle Logik sein; **go armed/naked** bewaffnet sein/nackt herumlaufen; **go in rags** in Lumpen *od.* zerlumpt gehen; **go hungry** hungern; hungrig bleiben; **go without food/water** es ohne Essen/Wasser aushalten; **go in fear of one's life** in beständiger Angst um sein Leben leben; **may the blessings of God go with you** möge der Segen des Herrn dich begleiten; der Segen des Herrn sei mit dir; **how does the tune/song/wording go [now]?** wie geht die Melodie/das Lied/lauten die Worte [denn nun]?; **the argument goes like this** das Argument ist folgendes; **now the tale/rumour/theory goes that ...:** es wird erzählt/es geht das Gerücht/es wird die Theorie vertreten, dass ...; **go to the tune of ...:** der Melodie von ... folgen; **this noun/verb goes like ...:** dieses Substantiv/Verb geht genauso wie ...; **as things/canteens/actors** *etc.* **go** verglichen mit anderen Dingen/Kantinen/Schauspielern *usw.*; **as things go, it's not expensive** das ist verhältnismäßig billig; **go by** *or* **under the name of ...:** unter dem Namen ... bekannt sein; **T** (*become*) werden; **the tyre has gone flat** der Reifen ist platt; **the phone has gone dead** die Leitung ist tot; **go on the blink** kaputtgehen (*ugs.*); **go all freaky/Indian** *etc.* völlig ausflippen (*ugs.*)/ganz auf indisch *usw.* machen; **go serious/arty on sb.** jmdm. auf die ernste Tour/Künstlertour kommen (*ugs.*); **go nuclear/metric** (*coll.*) zur Atommacht werden/das metrische System einführen; **the constituency/York went Tory** der Wahlkreis/York ging an die Tories; **U** (*have usual place*) kommen; (*belong*) gehören; **where does the box go?** wo kommt *od.* gehört die Kiste hin?; **where do you want this chair to go?** wo soll *od.* kommt der Stuhl hin?; **that chair will go nicely in the corner** dieser Stuhl macht sich gut in der *od.* passt gut in die Ecke; **this goes under a different heading** das gehört unter eine andere Überschrift; **each drink goes** *or* **all drinks go on the bill** alle Getränke kommen *od.* gehen auf die Rechnung; **the cheque is to go in[to] my account** der Scheck geht auf mein Konto; **V** (*fit*) passen; **go in[to] sth.** in etw. (*Akk.*) gehen *od.* [hinein]passen; **it won't go [in]** es geht nicht rein (*ugs.*); **go through sth.** durch etw. [hindurch]gehen *od.* [hindurch]passen; **six into twelve goes twice** sechs geht zweimal in zwölf; **five goes into forty exactly** vierzig durch fünf geht auf; **W** (*harmonize, match*) passen (**with** zu); **the two colours don't go** die beiden Farben passen nicht zusammen *od.* beißen sich; **X** (*serve, contribute*) dienen; **the qualities that go to make a leader** die Eigenschaften, die einen Führer ausmachen; **the sounds that go to make up a language** die Laute, aus denen eine Sprache besteht; **this fact goes to prove that ...** folgende Tatsache belegt, dass ...; **it just goes to show that ...:** daran zeigt sich, dass ...; **Y** (*make sound of specified kind*) machen; (*emit sound*) ‹Turmuhr, Gong:› schlagen; ‹Glocke:› läuten; **There goes the bell. School is over** Es klingelt. Die Schule ist aus; **the fire alarm went at 3 a. m.** der Feueralarm ging um 3 Uhr morgens los; **a police car with its siren going** ein Polizeiwagen mit eingeschalteter Sirene; **Z** *as intensifier* (*coll.*) **don't go making** *or* **go and make him angry** verärgere ihn bloß nicht; **he might go and hang himself** nachher hängt er sich womöglich auf; **don't go and make a fool of yourself** mach dich doch nicht lächerlich; **don't go looking for trouble** such keinen Streit; **don't go thinking ...:** glaube doch ja nicht, dass ....; **I gave him a £10 note and, of course, he had to go and lose it** (*iron.*) ich gab ihm einen 10-Pfund-Schein, und er musste ihn natürlich prompt verlieren; **now you've been and gone and done it** (*coll.*) du hast ja was Schönes angerichtet! (*ugs. iron.*); **go tell him I'm ready** (*coll./Amer.*) geh und sag ihm, dass ich fertig bin; **she said to her dog 'Go fetch it'** sie sagte zu ihrem Hund: „Los, hols!"; **let's go get ourselves a drink** (*coll./Amer.*) holen wir uns was zu trinken; **AA** (*coll.: be acceptable or permitted*) erlaubt sein; gehen (*ugs.*); **everything/anything goes** es ist alles erlaubt; **it/that goes without saying** es/das ist doch selbstverständlich; es/das versteht sich von selbst; **what he** *etc.* **says, goes** was er *usw.* sagt, gilt; wenn er *usw.* etwas sagt, dann gilt es auch; ⇒ *also* **let**[1] 1 A; **BB** (*coll. euphem.: defecate or urinate*) auf die Toilette gehen; **really have to go** wirklich müssen (*ugs.*); **I want to go somewhere** ich muss mal wohin *od.* verschwinden (*ugs.*); **CC** **go astray, go into action, go blackberrying, go to the country,** *etc. see the noun, adverb, etc.* ⇒ *also* **going**; **gone**.

**2** *v.t., forms as* 1 **A** (*Cards*) spielen; **B** (*coll.*) **go it** es toll treiben; (*work hard*) rangehen; **he has been going it a bit too hard** er hat es etwas zu weit getrieben; **go it!** los!; weiter!; **100 m.p.h.? That's really going it!** 160 km/h? Das ist wirklich ein tolles Tempo; ⇒ *also* **alone** 1.

**3** *n., pl.* **goes** /gəʊz/ (*coll.*) **A** (*attempt, try*) Versuch, *der;* (*chance*) Gelegenheit, *die;* **have a go** es versuchen *od.* probieren; **have a go at doing sth.** versuchen, etw. zu tun; **have a go at sth.** sich an etw. (*Dat.*) versuchen; **someone has had a go at this lock** jmd. hat sich an dem Schloss zu schaffen gemacht; **he's had several goes at the driving test** er hat schon mehrere Anläufe genommen, den Führerschein zu bekommen; **have a good go with the vacuum cleaner** gründlich saugen; **let me have/can I have a go?** lass mich [auch ein]mal/kann ich [auch ein]mal? (*ugs.*); **it's my go** ich bin an der Reihe *od.* dran; **I've had my go already** ich hab[e] schon (*ugs.*); ich war schon dran (*ugs.*); **it's your turn to have a go** du bist jetzt dran (*ugs.*); **now 'you have a go** jetzt mach du mal; **you missed one go** du hast einmal ausgesetzt; du bist einmal übersprungen worden; **in two/three goes** bei zwei/drei Versuchen; **at one go** auf einmal; **at the first go** auf Anhieb; **give sth. a go** etw. mal versuchen (*ugs.*); **B** **have a go at sb.** (*scold*) sich (*Dat.*) jmdn. vornehmen *od.* vorknöpfen (*ugs.*); (*attack*) über jmdn. herfallen; **have a go at a policeman** sich mit einem Polizisten anlegen (*ugs.*); **C** (*period of activity*) **in one go** auf einmal; **he downed his beer in one go** er trank sein Bier in einem Zug aus; **the dentist said he'd fill the teeth in two goes** der Zahnarzt meinte, dass er die Füllungen in zwei Sitzungen machen würde; **D** (*energy*) Schwung, *der;* **be full of go** voller Schwung *od.* Elan sein; **have plenty of** *or* **a lot of go** einen enormen Schwung *od.* Elan haben; **E** (*vigorous activity*) **it's all go** es ist alles eine einzige Hetzerei (*ugs.*); **it's all go at work** es ist ganz schön was los bei der Arbeit; wir müssen ganz schön ran bei der Arbeit; **be on the go** auf Trab sein (*ugs.*); **keep sb. on the go** jmdn. auf Trab halten (*ugs.*); **have two jobs** *etc.* **on the go** zwei Jobs *usw.* gleichzeitig haben; **F** (*success*) Erfolg, *der;* **make a go of sth.** (*turn sth. into a success*) mit etw. Erfolg haben; eine Sache zum Erfolg führen; (*not let sth. be a failure*) das Beste aus etw. machen; **it's no go** da ist nichts zu machen; **it's a go** (*dated coll.*) [es ist] abgemacht; ⇒ *also* **no-go**; **G** **be all the go** der letzte Schrei sein (*ugs.*); groß in Mode sein; **H** **that was a near go** das war knapp; das wäre beinahe schief gegangen; **I** (*dated coll.: incident*) Geschichte, *die;* **a rum go** eine komische Geschichte.

**4** *adj.* (*coll.*) **all systems go** alles in Ordnung; alles klar

**go about** **1** /--'-/ *v.i.* **A** (*move from place to place*) herumgehen; (*by vehicle*) herumfahren; **go about in groups** in Gruppen herumziehen; **go about in leather gear/dressed like a tramp** in Lederkleidung/wie ein Landstreicher herumlaufen; **go about doing sth.** (*be in the habit of*) etw. immer tun; **B** (*circulate*) ‹Gerücht, Geschichte, Grippe:› umgehen; **C** (*Naut.*) wenden. **2** /'---/ *v.t.* **A** (*set about*) erledigen ‹Arbeit›; angehen ‹Problem›; **how does one go about it?** wie geht man da vor?; wie stellt man das am besten an?; **go about it [in] the right way** es richtig angehen; **go about it tactfully** *etc.* taktvoll *usw.* vorgehen; **B** (*busy oneself with*) nachgehen (+ *Dat.*) ‹Arbeit usw.›

**'go after** *v.t.* (*hunt*) jagen; zu stellen versuchen; (*fig.*) anstreben; sich bemühen um ‹Job›; **decide what you want and go after it** werd dir darüber klar, was du willst, und dann versuche, es auch zu bekommen

**'go against** *v.t.* zuwiderhandeln (+ *Dat.*); handeln gegen ‹Prinzip, Gesetz›; **go against sb.** sich jmdm. in den Weg stellen *od.* widersetzen; ⇒ *also* **go**[1] 1 R, S

**go a'head** *v.i.* **A** (*in advance*) vorausgehen (**of** *Dat.*); (*Sport*) an die Spitze gehen; die Führung übernehmen; **the runner went ahead of the others** der Läufer zog an den anderen vorbei; **You go ahead. I'll meet you there** Geh mal schon vor. Wir treffen uns dann dort; **B** (*proceed*) weitermachen; (*make progress*) ‹Arbeit:› fortschreiten, vorangehen; **go ahead with a plan** einen Plan durchführen; **go ahead and do it** es einfach machen; **go ahead!** nur zu!; **May I explain it to you? — OK. Go ahead** Darf ich es Ihnen erklären? — Ja, schießen Sie nur los (*ugs.*). ⇒ *also* **go-ahead**

**go a'long** **1** *v.i.* dahingehen/-fahren; (*attend*) hingehen. **2** *v.t.* entlanggehen/-fahren

**go a'long with** *v.t.* **A** **go along with sth.** (*share sb.'s opinion*) einer Sache (*Dat.*) zustimmen; (*agree to*) sich einer Sache (*Dat.*) anschließen; **B** **go along with you!** (*coll.*) ach, geh *od.* komm (*ugs.*); ach, erzähl mir doch nichts! (*ugs.*)

**go a'round** ⇒ **go about** 1 A, B; **go round**

**'go at** *v.t.* **go at sb.** (*attack*) über jmdn. herfallen; auf jmdn. losgehen; **go at sth./it** (*work at*) sich hinter etw. (*Akk.*) klemmen/sich dahinter klemmen (*ugs.*); sich an etw. (*Akk.*) machen/sich dranmachen

**go a'way** *v.i.* weggehen; (*on holiday or business*) wegfahren; verreisen; **what did the bride wear to go away in?** was trug die Braut, als sie auf Hochzeitsreise ging?; **the problem won't go away** das Problem kann man nicht einfach ignorieren; ⇒ *also* **go¹** 1 I; **going-away**

**go 'back** *v.i.* **A** (*return*) zurückgehen/-fahren; (*restart*) ‹Schule, Fabrik:› wieder anfangen; (*fig.*) zurückgehen; **I wouldn't want to go back to that place** dorthin wollte ich auf keinen Fall wieder zurück; **go back to a subject** auf ein Thema zurückkommen; **go back to the beginning** noch mal von vorne anfangen; **there'll be/there's no going back** da gibt es kein Zurück mehr; **B** (*be returned*) zurückgegeben werden; ‹Waren:› zurückgehen (**to** an + *Akk.*); **C** (*be put back*) ‹Uhren:› zurückgestellt werden

**go 'back on** *v.t.* nicht [ein]halten ‹Versprechen, Wort›

**go before** ❶ /--'-/ *v.i.* (*live before*) früher leben; (*happen before*) vorher *od.* früher geschehen. ❷ /'---/ *v.t.* **A** (*live before*) **go before sb.** vor jmds. Zeit (*Dat.*) leben; **B** (*appear before*) **go before sth./sb.** ‹Person:› vor etw./jmdm. erscheinen; ‹Sache:› vor etw./jmdn. kommen

**'go by** *v.t.* **go by sth.** sich nach etw. richten; (*adhere to*) sich an etw. (*Akk.*) halten; **if the report is anything to go by** wenn man nach dem Bericht gehen kann; **go by appearances** nach dem Äußeren gehen *od.* urteilen; ⇒ *also* **go¹** 1 B, M; **go-by**

**go 'down** *v.i.* **A** hinuntergehen/-fahren; ‹Taucher:› [hinunter]tauchen; (*set*) ‹Sonne:› untergehen; (*sink*) ‹Schiff:› sinken, untergehen; (*drown*) ‹Person:› untergehen, ertrinken; (*fall to ground*) ‹Flugzeug usw.:› abstürzen; **go down to the bottom of the garden/to the doctor/to the beach** zum hinteren Ende des Gartens gehen/zum Arzt gehen/an den Strand gehen; **B** (*be digested*) verdaut werden; (*be swallowed*) hinuntergeschluckt werden; **go down the wrong way** in die falsche Kehle geraten; **sugar helps the medicine go down** mit Zucker kriegt man die Arznei besser hinunter (*ugs.*); **C** (*become less*) sinken; ‹Umsatz, Schwellung:› zurückgehen; ‹Vorräte usw.:› abnehmen; ‹Währung:› fallen; (*become lower*) fallen; (*subside*) ‹Wind usw.:› nachlassen; **go down in sb.'s estimation/in the world** in jmds. Achtung (*Dat.*) sinken/sich verschlechtern; **D** **go down well/all right** *etc.* **[with sb.]** [mit jmdm.] gut *usw.* klarkommen (*ugs.*); ‹Film, Schauspieler, Vorschlag:› [bei jmdm.] gut *usw.* ankommen (*ugs.*); **that didn't go down [at all] well with his wife** das hat ihm seine Frau nicht abgenommen; **E** (*be defeated*) unterliegen; **go down to sb.** gegen jmdn. verlieren; **F** (*be recorded in writing*) niedergeschrieben werden; schriftlich vermerkt werden; **G** (*Bridge*) den Kontrakt nicht erfüllen; (*Cards*) [seine Karten] aufdecken; **H** (*Brit. Univ.*) abgehen; (*at end of term*) in die Semesterferien gehen; **I** ‹Maschine, Computer usw.:› ausfallen

**go 'down with** *v.t.* bekommen ‹Krankheit›; ⇒ *also* **go down d**

**'go for** *v.t.* **A** (*go to fetch*) **go for sb./sth.** jmdn./etw. holen; **B** (*apply to*) **go for sb./sth.** für jmdn./etw. gelten; **that goes for me too** das gilt auch für mich; ich auch; **what goes for me goes for you too** was für mich gilt, gilt auch für dich; **C** (*attack*) **go for sb. [with a knife** *etc.***]** [mit einem Messer *usw.*] auf jmdn. losgehen; **D** (*pass for*) **go for sth.** als etw. durchgehen; **E** (*like*) **go for sb./sth.** jmdn./etw. gut finden; **I could go for 'him** der könnte mir gefallen; **F** (*count for*) **go for nothing/little** nichts/wenig gelten *od.* zählen; **G** (*aim at*) es abgesehen haben auf (+ *Akk.*). ⇒ *also* **go¹** 1 O, R; **going** 2 F

**go 'forth** ⇒ **forth** C

**go 'forward** *v.i.* weitergehen/-fahren; (*fig.*) voranschreiten; ‹Uhren:› vorgestellt werden

**go 'forward with** *v.t.* weiter durchführen; weiter verfolgen ‹Plan usw.›

**go 'in** *v.i.* **A** (*go indoors*) hineingehen; reingehen (*ugs.*); **B** (*be covered by cloud*) verschwinden; weggehen (*ugs.*); **C** (*be learnt*) [in den Kopf] reingehen (*ugs.*); **it just won't go in** es will einfach nicht in den Kopf; **D** (*Cricket*) zum Schlagen drankommen; **E** **go in and win!** Bangemachen gilt nicht! (*fam.*); nur Mut! ⇒ *also* **go¹** 1 B, V

**go 'in for** *v.t.* **go in for sth.** (*choose as career*) etw. [er]lernen wollen; (*enter*) an etw. (*Dat.*) teilnehmen; (*indulge in, like*) für etw. zu haben sein; (*have as one's hobby, pastime, etc.*) sich auf etw. (*Akk.*) verlegen; **so you'd like to go in for teaching** du willst also Lehrer/Lehrerin werden; **I don't really go in for jogging** ich habe nicht viel übrig fürs Joggen; **go in for wearing loud colours** gern knallige Farben tragen

**'go into** *v.t.* **A** (*join*) eintreten in (+ *Akk.*) ‹Orden, Geschäft usw.›; gehen in (+ *Akk.*) ‹Industrie, Politik›; gehen zu ‹Film, Fernsehen, Armee›; beitreten (+ *Dat.*) ‹Bündnis›; **go into law/the church** Jurist/Geistlicher werden; **go into nursing** Krankenschwester/-pfleger werden; **go into publishing** ins Verlagswesen gehen; **go into general practice** (*Med.*) sich als allgemeiner Mediziner niederlassen; **B** (*go and live in*) gehen in (+ *Akk.*) ‹Krankenhaus, Heim usw.›; ziehen in (+ *Akk.*) ‹Wohnung, Heim›; **go into digs/lodgings** sich (*Dat.*) eine Bude (*ugs.*)/ein Zimmer nehmen; **C** (*consider*) eingehen auf (*Akk.*); (*investigate, examine*) sich befassen mit; (*explain*) darlegen; **D** (*crash into*) [hinein]fahren in (+ *Akk.*); fahren gegen ‹Baum usw.›; **E** (*pass into specified state*) verfallen in (+ *Akk.*); **go into hysterics/a fit** hysterisch werden/einen Anfall bekommen; **go [off] into laughter** *etc.* in Lachen *usw.* ausbrechen; **the book is going into paperback/its fifth edition** das Buch erscheint als Paperback/in der fünften Auflage; **F** ([*begin to*] *wear*) tragen. ⇒ *also* **go¹** 1 B, V

**go 'in with** *v.t.* **go in with sb.** [mit jmdm.] mitmachen

**go off** ❶ /-'-/ *v.i.* **A** (*Theatre*) abgehen; **B** **go off with sb./sth.** sich mit jmdm./etw. auf- und davonmachen (*ugs.*); **his wife has gone off with the milkman** seine Frau ist mit dem Milchmann durchgebrannt (*ugs.*); **C** ‹Alarm, Schusswaffe, Klingel:› losgehen; ‹Wecker:› klingeln; ‹Bombe:› hochgehen; **D** (*turn bad*) schlecht werden; (*turn sour*) sauer werden; (*fig.*) sich verschlechtern; **E** ‹Strom, Gas, Wasser:› ausfallen; **F** **go off [to sleep]** einschlafen; **G** (*be sent*) abgehen (**to** an + *Akk.*); **H** **go off well** *etc.* gut *usw.* verlaufen. ⇒ *also* **go¹** 1 B.
❷ /'--, -'-/ *v.t.* **A** (*begin to dislike*) **go off sth.** von etw. abkommen; **go off sb.** jmdn. nicht mehr mögen; **go off beer/the cinema** sich (*Dat.*) nichts mehr aus Bier/Kino machen; **B** **go off the gold standard** vom Goldstandard abgehen; **C** **go off into** ⇒ **go into f**

**go on** ❶ /-'-/ *v.i.* **A** weitergehen/-fahren; (*by vehicle*) die Reise/Fahrt *usw.* fortsetzen; (*go ahead*) vorausgehen; (*drive ahead*) vorausfahren; **B** (*continue*) weitergehen; ‹Kämpfe:› anhalten; ‹Verhandlungen, Arbeiten:› [an]dauern; (*continue to act*) weitermachen; (*continue to live*) weiterleben; **I can't go on** ich kann nicht mehr; ich weiß nicht mehr weiter; **go on for weeks** *etc.* Wochen *usw.* dauern; **this has been going on for months** das geht schon seit Monaten so; **the case went on for years** der Prozess hat sich jahrelang hingezogen; **go on to say** *etc.* fortfahren und sagen *usw.*; **'moreover', he went on, ...:** „außerdem", fuhr er fort, ...; **go on and on** dauern und dauern; kein Ende nehmen wollen; sich endlos hinziehen; **go on [and on]** (*coll.*) (*chatter*) reden und reden; **she does go on so** sie redet unaufhörlich; **go on about sb./sth.** stundenlang von jmdm./etw. erzählen; (*complain*) sich ständig über jmdn./etw. beklagen; **go on at sb.** (*coll.*) auf jmdm. herumhacken (*ugs.*); **C** (*elapse*) ‹Zeit:› vergehen; **as time/the years went on** im Laufe der Zeit/Jahre; **D** (*happen*) passieren; vor sich gehen; **there's more going on in the big cities** in den großen Städten ist mehr los; **the things that go on there** die Dinge, die da vor sich gehen; **what's going on?, what goes on?** was geht vor?; was ist los?; **E** **be going on [for] ...** (*be nearly*) fast ... sein; **he is going on [for] ninety** er geht auf die Neunzig zu; **he is seven going on [for] eight** er ist fast acht; **it is going on [for] ten o'clock** es geht auf 10 Uhr zu; **F** (*behave*) sich benehmen; sich aufführen; **G** ‹Kleidung:› passen; **my dress wouldn't go on** ich kriegte mein Kleid nicht an (*ugs.*); ich kam nicht in mein Kleid rein (*ugs.*); **this hat won't go on** diesen Hut kriege ich nicht auf (*ugs.*); **H** (*Theatre*) auftreten; (*Cricket*) mit dem Werfen beginnen; **I** ⇒ **go forward**; **J** (*be lit*) ‹Licht:› angehen; (*be supplied*) ‹Strom, Wasser:› kommen; **go on again** ‹Strom, Gas, Wasser:› wiederkommen; **K** **go on!** (*proceed*) los, mach schon! (*ugs.*); (*resume*) fahren Sie fort!; (*coll.: stop talking nonsense*) ach, geh *od.* komm (*ugs.*); ach, erzähl mir doch nichts! (*ugs.*); ⇒ *also* **goings-on**.
❷ /'--/ *v.t.* **A** (*ride on*) fahren mit; **go on the roundabout/swings/Big Dipper** Karussell/Schiffschaukel/Achterbahn fahren; **B** (*continue*) **go on working/talking** *etc.* weiterarbeiten/weiterreden *usw.*; **go on trying** es weiter[hin] versuchen; **C** (*coll.: be guided by*) sich stützen auf (+ *Akk.*); **there's little evidence to go on** es gibt wenig Beweismaterial, auf das man sich stützen kann; **D** (*begin to receive*) bekommen, erhalten ‹Arbeitslosengeld, Sozialfürsorge›; ⇒ *also* **dole** 1; **E** ⇒ **go on to b**; **F** (*start to take*) nehmen ‹Medikament, Drogen›; **go on a diet** eine Abmagerungs- *od.* Schlankheitskur machen; **G** (*coll.: like*) ⇒ **much** 2. ⇒ *also* **go¹** 1 L; **stage** 1 B

**go 'on for** ⇒ **go on** 1 E

**go 'on to** *v.t.* **A** (*proceed to*) übergehen zu; **he went on to become ...:** er wurde schließlich ...; **B** (*change working arrangements to*) übergehen zu ‹Kurzarbeit, Überstunden›

**go 'on with** *v.t.* **A** **go on with sth.** mit etw. weitermachen; **something/enough to go on with** *or* **be going on with** etwas/genug für den Anfang *od.* fürs Erste; **here's something to be going on with** hiermit kann man schon [ein]mal anfangen; **here's £10 to be going on with** hier sind erst [ein]mal 10 Pfund [für den Anfang] (*ugs.*); **here's a cup of tea to be going on with** hier hast du erst einmal eine Tasse Tee; **B** ⇒ **go along with b**

**go 'out** *v.i.* **A** (*from home*) ausgehen; **go out to work/go out charring/for a meal** arbeiten/putzen/essen gehen; **go out and about** unterwegs sein; auf den Beinen sein; **out you go!** hinaus *od.* (*ugs.*) raus mit dir!; **go out with sb.** (*regularly*) mit jmdm. gehen (*ugs.*); **B** **go out [on strike]** in den Ausstand treten; **C** (*be extinguished*) ‹Feuer, Licht, Zigarre usw.:› ausgehen; **go out like a light** (*fig. coll.: fall asleep*) sofort weg sein (*ugs.*) *od.* einschlafen; **D** (*ebb*) ‹Ebbe, Wasser:› ablaufen, zurückgehen; **the tide has gone out** es ist Ebbe; **E** (*Polit.*) [aus der Regierung] ausscheiden; ‹Regierung:› abgelöst werden; **F** (*be issued*) verteilt werden; (*Radio, Telev.: be transmitted*) übertragen werden; ausgestrahlt werden; **G** (*euphem.: die*) [hinüber]gehen (*verhüll.*); **he went out peacefully in his sleep** er ist sanft entschlafen (*geh.*); **H** (*end*) ‹Monat, Jahr:› zu Ende gehen; **I** (*of fashion*) unmodern werden; ‹Brauch:› aussterben; **J** (*Sport: be defeated*) unterliegen (**to** *Dat.*). ⇒ *also* **go¹** 1 B; **business** B; **walk** 3 A

**go 'out to** *v.t.* ‹Sympathie:› sein mit; **my heart/sympathy goes out to them** ich fühle mit ihnen mit. ⇒ *also* **go out j**

**go over** ❶ /-'--/ *v.i.* **A** **he went over to the fireplace/man in the corner** er ging zum Kamin/zu dem Mann in der Ecke hinüber; **we're going over to our friends** wir fahren zu unseren Freunden; **I'm just going over to the shop** ich gehe kurz ins Geschäft hinüber; **B** (*be received*) ‹Rede, Ankündigung, Plan:› ankommen (**with** bei); **C** (*Radio, Telev.*) **go over to sb./sth./Belfast** zu jmdm./in etw. (*Akk.*)/nach Belfast umschalten. ⇒ *also* **go¹** 1 B; **go over to**.
❷ /'---/ *v.t.* **A** (*re-examine, think over, rehearse*) durchgehen; **go over sth./the facts in one's head** *or* **mind** etw. im Geiste durchgehen/die Fakten überdenken; **B** (*clean*) sauber machen; (*inspect and repair*) durchsehen ‹Maschine, Auto usw.›; **go over the house with the Hoover/duster** durchsaugen/mit dem Staubtuch durchs Haus gehen; **C** (*survey*) begutachten; sich (*Dat.*)

ansehen; Ⓓ **go over sth. with a pen** etw. mit dem Stift nachziehen. ⇒ *also* **going-over**

**go 'over to** *v.t.* Ⓐ hinübergehen zu; übertreten zu ‹Glauben, Partei›; überwechseln zu ‹Revolutionären›; ‹Verräter:› überlaufen zu ‹Feind›; überlaufen in (+ *Akk.*) ‹Lager des Feindes›; Ⓑ (*change to*) übergehen zu. ⇒ *also* **go¹** 1 B, H; **go over** 1

**go round** ❶ /'-'-/ *v.i.* Ⓐ (*call*) **go round and** *or* **to see sb.** jmdn. besuchen; bei jmdm. vorbeigehen (*ugs.*); **go round to sb.'s house** (*call at*) jmdn. aufsuchen; Ⓑ (*look round*) sich umschauen; Ⓒ (*suffice*) reichen; langen (*ugs.*); **enough coffee to go round** genug Kaffee für alle; Ⓓ (*spin*) sich drehen; **my head is going round** mir dreht sich alles; Ⓔ (*circulate*) **the word went round that ...:** es ging die Parole um, dass ...; Ⓕ (*Golf*) **go round in 70** eine 70er Runde spielen.
❷ /'--/ *v.t.* Ⓐ (*inspect*) besichtigen; Ⓑ (*encompass*) ‹Gürtel:› herumreichen um ‹Taille›; **the trousers won't go round my waist** die Hose passt mir nicht in der Taille *od.* um die Taille herum; Ⓒ **have enough food to go round [so many people]** [für so viele Leute] genügend zu essen haben

**go through** ❶ /'-'-/ *v.i.* ‹Ernennung, Gesetzesvorlage:› durchkommen; ‹Geschäft:› [erfolgreich] abgeschlossen werden; ‹Antrag, Bewerbung:› durchgehen; **go through to the final** in die Endrunde kommen; **as soon as his divorce has gone through** sobald seine Scheidung durch ist.
❷ /'--/ *v.t.* Ⓐ (*execute, undergo*) erledigen ‹Formalität, Anforderung›; abwickeln ‹Geschäft›; absolvieren ‹Kurs, Lehre›; durchziehen (*ugs.*) ‹Programm›; **go through a marriage ceremony/divorce proceedings** sich trauen lassen/die Scheidung durchmachen; Ⓑ (*rehearse*) durchgehen; Ⓒ (*examine*) durchsehen ‹Post, Unterlagen›; (*search*) durchsuchen ‹Taschen›; Ⓓ (*endure*) durchmachen ‹schwere Zeiten›; durchstehen ‹Belastung›; (*suffer*) erleiden ‹Schmerzen›; Ⓔ (*use up*) verbrauchen; durchbringen ‹Erbschaft›; aufbrauchen ‹Vorräte›; Ⓕ (*be published in*) erleben ‹Auflagen›. ⇒ *also* **go¹** 1 V

**go 'through with** *v.t.* zu Ende führen; ausführen ‹Hinrichtung›; **she realized that she would have to go through with it** sie sah ein, dass sie jetzt nicht mehr zurückkonnte; **she told him that she couldn't go through with the wedding** sie sagte ihm, dass aus der Hochzeit nichts würde

**go to'gether** *v.i.* Ⓐ (*coincide*) zusammengehen; Ⓑ (*match*) zusammenpassen; Ⓒ (*date regularly*) miteinander gehen (*ugs.*)

**go 'under** *v.i.* (*sink below surface*) untergehen; (*fig.: fail*) ‹Geschäftsmann:› scheitern; ‹Unternehmen:› eingehen; **go under under to sth.** einer Sache (*Dat.*) zum Opfer fallen

**go 'up** *v.i.* Ⓐ hinaufgehen/-fahren; ‹Ballon:› aufsteigen; ‹Flugzeug, Flieger:› fliegen; (*Theatre*) ‹Vorhang:› aufgehen, hochgehen; ‹Lichter:› angehen; Ⓑ (*increase*) ‹Bevölkerung, Zahl:› wachsen; ‹Preis, Wert, Zahl, Niveau:› steigen; **everything is going up these days** heutzutage wird alles teurer; Ⓒ (*be constructed*) ‹Gebäude, Barrikade:› errichtet werden; Ⓓ (*be destroyed*) in die Luft fliegen (*ugs.*); hochgehen (*ugs.*); ⇒ *also* **flame** 1 A; **smoke** 1 A; Ⓔ (*Brit. Univ.*) sein Studium aufnehmen; **go up to Oxford** sein Studium in Oxford aufnehmen; (*at beginning of term*) nach den Semesterferien nach Oxford zurückkehren; Ⓕ **go up to sb.** (*approach for talk*) auf jmdn. zugehen; Ⓖ **go up in the world** [gesellschaftlich] aufsteigen

**'go with** *v.t.* Ⓐ (*be concomitant with*) einhergehen mit; Ⓑ (*be included with*) gehören zu; Ⓒ (*date regularly*) gehen mit (*ugs.*). ⇒ *also* **go¹** 1 A, W

**go without** ❶ /'---/ *v.t.* verzichten auf (+ *Akk.*); **have to go without sth.** ohne etw. auskommen müssen. ❷ /--'-/ *v.i.* (*receive nothing*) **if you won't eat that dinner, you'll have to go without** wenn du das Essen nicht isst, musst du eben ohne auskommen

**go²** *n.* (*game*) Go, *das*

**goad** /gəʊd/ ❶ *v.t.* Ⓐ **~ sb. into sth./doing sth.** jmdn. zu etw. anstacheln/dazu anstacheln, etw. zu tun; **~ sb. into a fury** jmdn. in Wut bringen; Ⓑ antreiben ‹Vieh usw.›. ❷ *n.* Stachelstock, *der;* (*fig.*) Stachel, *der;* (*stimulus*) Ansporn, *der*
**~ 'on** *v.t.* **~ sb. on** jmdn. anstiften

**'go-ahead** ❶ *adj.* (*enterprising*) unternehmungslustig; (*progressive*) fortschrittlich; **~ spirit** Unternehmungsgeist, *der.* ❷ *n.* grünes Licht (*fig.*); **give sb./sth. the ~:** jmdm./einer Sache grünes Licht geben

**goal** /gəʊl/ *n.* Ⓐ (*aim*) Ziel, *das;* **what do you have as your ~?** welches Ziel hast du dir gesetzt?; **attain** *or* **reach** *or* **accomplish one's ~:** sein Ziel erreichen; Ⓑ (*Assoc. Footb., Hockey*) Tor, *das;* (*Rugby*) Mal, *das;* **keep ~:** das Tor hüten; **[play] in ~:** im Tor [stehen]; **score/kick a ~:** einen Treffer erzielen; **win by two ~s to one** zwei zu eins gewinnen; Ⓒ (*of race*) Ziellinie, *die;* Ziel, *das*

**goal: ~ area** *n.* Torraum, *der;* **~ average** *n.* **on ~ average** nach Toren; **~ difference** *n.* Tordifferenz, *die*

**goalie** /'gəʊlɪ/ *n.* (*coll.*) Tormann, *der;* Schlussmann, *der* (*ugs.*)

**goal: ~keeper** *n.* ▶ **1261** Torwart, *der;* **~ kick** *n.* (*Assoc. Footb.*) Abstoß, *der;* (*Rugby*) Tritt nach dem Mal

**goalless** /'gəʊllɪs/ *adj.* torlos; **end in a ~ draw** torlos [unentschieden] enden

**goal: ~-line** *n.* (*Assoc. Footb., Hockey*) Torlinie, *die;* (*Rugby*) Mallinie, *die;* **~minder** *n.* (*Amer.*) Torwart, *der;* **~mouth** *n.* Raum unmittelbar vor dem Tor; **~post** *n.* Torpfosten, *der;* **move the ~posts** (*fig. coll.*) sich nicht an die Spielregeln halten; **~-tender** *n.* (*Amer.*) Torwart, *der*

**go-as-you-'please** *adj.* ungezwungen

**goat** /gəʊt/ *n.* Ⓐ Ziege, *die;* **act** *or* **play the [giddy] ~:** den Clown spielen; herumalbern; **get sb.'s ~** (*coll.*) jmdn. aufregen (*ugs.*); Ⓑ (*Astrol.*) **the G~:** der Steinbock; ⇒ *also* **archer** B; Ⓒ (*coll.: fool*) Idiot, *der* (*ugs. abwertend*); Esel, *der* (*ugs.*); Ⓓ (*coll.: licentious man*) **old ~:** alter [geiler] Bock (*salopp*); Ⓔ (*Amer.: scape~*) Sündenbock, *der* (*ugs.*)

**goatee** /gəʊ'ti:/ *n.* **~ [beard]** Kinnbart, *der;* Spitzbart, *der*

**'goatherd** *n.* Ziegenhirt[e], *der*

**goatish** /'gəʊtɪʃ/ *adj.* (*fig.*) geil

**goat: ~skin** *n.* Ziegenleder, *das;* (*bottle*) Ziegenlederflasche, *die;* **~'s milk** *n.* Ziegenmilch, *die;* **~sucker** ⇒ **nightjar**

**gob¹** /gɒb/ *n.* (*sl.*) Gosche, *die* (*landsch. derb*); Schnauze, *die* (*derb abwertend*); Maul, *das* (*derb abwertend*); **shut your ~!** halts Maul! (*derb*); halt die Schnauze! (*derb*)

**gob²** *v.i.* (*sl.: spit*) rotzen (*derb*)

**gobble¹** /'gɒbl/ ❶ *v.t.* **~ [down** *or* **up]** hinunterschlingen. ❷ *v.i.* schlingen
**~ up** *v.t.* (*fig. coll.*) verschlingen; ‹Land, Imperium:› sich (*Dat.*) einverleiben ‹kleineres Land usw.›

**gobble²** *v.i.* (*make sound*) kollern

**gobbledegook, gobbledygook** /'gɒbldɪgu:k, 'gɒbldɪgʊk/ *n.* Kauderwelsch, *das*

**'go-between** *n.* Vermittler, *der*/Vermittlerin, *die;* (*in love affair*) Postillon d'Amour, *der*

**Gobi** /'gəʊbɪ/ *pr. n.* **the ~ [Desert]** die [Wüste] Gobi

**goblet** /'gɒblɪt/ *n.* Kelchglas, *das*

**goblin** /'gɒblɪn/ *n.* Kobold, *der*

**gobsmacked** /'gɒbsmækt/ *adj* (*Brit. coll.*) geplättet (*salopp*); baff (*salopp*)

**'gobstopper** *n.* (*Brit.*) Riesenlutscher, *der;* Maulstopfer, *der* (*ugs.*)

**goby** /'gəʊbɪ/ *n.* (*Zool.*) Grundel, *die*

**'go-by** *n.* **give the ~ to sb., give sb. the ~:** jmdn. schneiden

**'go-cart** *n.* Ⓐ (*handcart*) Handwagen, *der;* Ⓑ (*for child*) Sport[kinder]wagen, *der*

**god** /gɒd/ *n.* Ⓐ Gott, *der;* **the drink of the ~s** der Göttertrank; **be** *or* **lie in the lap** *or* **on the knees of the ~s** im Schoß der Götter liegen; **a feast [fit] for the ~s** ein göttliches Mahl; **a gift from the ~s** ein Geschenk des Himmels; **a sight [fit] for the ~s** eine Augenweide; (*with grandeur*) ein majestätischer Anblick; (*iron.*) ein Bild für die Götter (*ugs. scherzh.*); **ye ~s [and little fishes]!** mein Gott!; Ⓑ **G~** *no pl.* (*Theol.*) Gott; **Almighty G~:** der allmächtige Gott; **G~ the Father, Son, and Holy Ghost** Gott Vater, Sohn und Heiliger Geist; **G~ moves in a mysterious way** (*prov.*) die Wege des Herrn sind unerforschlich; **G~ helps those who help themselves** (*prov.*) hilf dir selbst, so hilft dir Gott (*Spr.*); **G~ knows** (*as G~ is witness*) weiß Gott (*ugs.*); **G~ knows, I tried** ich habe es, weiß Gott, versucht; **G~ [only] knows** (*coll.: nobody knows*) weiß der Himmel (*ugs.*); **G~ willing, if it is G~'s will** so Gott will; **an act of G~:** höhere Gewalt; **before G~:** bei Gott; **play G~:** sich zum Gott aufwerfen; **under G~:** auf Erden (*geh.*); **G~'s gift** ein Geschenk Gottes; ein Gottesgeschenk; **she thinks she's G~'s gift to men** sie denkt, sie ist der Traum aller Männer; **G~'s truth** [nichts als] die reine Wahrheit (*geh.*); **be with G~:** bei Gott sein (*bibl.*); **G~'s [own] country** Paradies auf Erden; **G~'s earth** Gottes [weite] Erde; **G~!/good G~!/my G~!/oh G~!/G~ in Heaven!** [ach] Gott!/großer *od.* allmächtiger *od.* guter Gott!/mein Gott!/o Gott!/[guter] Gott im Himmel!; **dear G~!** lieber Gott!; **for G~'s sake!** um Himmels *od.* Gottes willen!; **I hope to G~ that ...:** ich hoffe bei Gott, dass ...; **G~ be with you** Gott mit euch; **G~, he's so stupid!** [mein] Gott, ist er dumm!; **by G~:** bei Gott; **thank G~!** Gott sei Dank!; **G~ damn it!** zum Teufel noch mal! (*ugs.*); **G~ damn you/him** *etc.* Gott verfluche dich/ihn *usw.*; **G~ help you/him** *etc.* möge Gott dir/ihm *usw.* helfen; Gott steh dir/ihm *usw.* bei; **G~ grant ...:** Gott gebe ...; **please G~!** so es Gott gefällt; **as G~ is my witness/judge** Gott ist mein Zeuge; ⇒ *also* **bless** A; **forbid** B; **help** 1 E; **man** 1 A, B; **name** 1 D; Ⓒ (*fig.*) Gott, *der;* Götze, *der* (*geh., abwertend*); ⇒ *also* **tin ~**; Ⓓ (*Theatre*) **the ~s** der Olymp (*ugs. scherzh.*)

**'God-awful** *adj.* (*sl.*) fürchterlich

**god: ~child** *n.* Patenkind, *das;* **~dam, ~damn, ~damned** ❶ *adj.* gottverdammt (*derb*); **[it is] none of your ~dam business** das geht dich einen Dreck an (*salopp*); ❷ *adv.* gottverdammt (*derb*); **you're ~dam right!** du hast, verdammt noch mal, Recht! (*derb*); **~-daughter** *n.* Patentochter, *die*

**goddess** /'gɒdɪs/ *n.* Göttin, *die*

**'godfather** *n.* Ⓐ Pate, *der;* Patenonkel, *der;* **my ~s!** [ach] du meine *od.* liebe Güte!; Ⓑ (*fig.*) Boss, *der* (*ugs.*); (*of Mafia etc.*) Pate, *der*

**'God-fearing** *adj.* gottesfürchtig

**'godforsaken** *adj.* gottverlassen

**'God-given** *adj.* gottgegeben

**godhead** /'gɒdhed/ *n.* Göttlichkeit, *die;* **the G~:** die Gottheit; Gott, *der*

**godless** /'gɒdlɪs/ *adj.* gottlos

**godlike** /'gɒdlaɪk/ *adj.* göttlich; göttergleich (*geh.*)

**godliness** /'gɒdlɪnɪs/ *n., no pl.* Gottgefälligkeit, *die*

**godly** /'gɒdlɪ/ *adj.* gottgefällig; gottergeben

**god: ~mother** *n.* Patin, *die;* Patentante, *die;* **~parent** *n.* (*male*) Pate, *der;* (*female*) Patin, *die;* **~parents** Paten *Pl.;* **~send** *n.* Gottesgabe, *die;* **be a ~send to sb.** für jmdn. ein Geschenk des Himmels sein; **~son** *n.* Patensohn, *der*

**God'speed** *n.* (*dated*) **wish** *or* **bid sb. ~:** jmdm. eine glückliche Reise wünschen

**godwit** /'gɒdwɪt/ *n.* (*Ornith.*) Pfuhlschnepfe, *die*

**goer** /'gəʊə(r)/ *n.* Ⓐ (*horse*) Geher, *der;* **be a good ~:** gut gehen; Ⓑ (*active person*) Energiebündel, *das* (*ugs.*); Ⓒ *in comb.* -gänger, *der;* -besucher, *der;* ⇒ *also* **churchgoer, filmgoer,** *etc.*

**goes** ⇒ **go¹** 1, 2

**Goethian (Goethean)** /'gɜ:tɪən/ *adj.* goethisch; goethesch

**'go-getter** *n.* Draufgänger, *der*

**'go-getting** *adj.* draufgängerisch; Ellbogen gebrauchend

**goggle** /'gɒgl/ ❶ *n. in pl.* **[a pair of] ~s** eine Schutzbrille. ❷ *adj.* **~ eyes** Glupschaugen

*Pl.* (*nordd.*); Froschaugen *Pl.* (*ugs.*). ❸ *v.i.* glotzen (*ugs.*); **~ at sb./sth.** jmdn./etw. anglotzen (*ugs.*)

**goggle: ~-box** *n.* (*Brit. coll.*) Glotze, *die* (*salopp*); Glotzkiste, *die* (*salopp*); **~-eyed** *adj.* glotzäugig (*ugs.*)

**'go-go** *adj.* (*coll.*) Go-go-; **~ dancer** *or* **girl** Go-Go-Girl, *das*

**going** /'gəʊɪŋ/ ❶ *n.* Ⓐ *vbl. n. of* **go¹** 1; Ⓑ (*progress*) Vorankommen, *das;* (*Horseracing, Hunting, etc.*) Geläuf, *das;* **150 miles in two hours, that is good ~:** 150 Meilen in zwei Stunden, das ist wirklich gut; **the ~ was slow/heavy** man kam nur langsam/schwer voran; **the journey was slow ~:** die Reise zog sich [in die Länge]; **interviewing her is heavy ~:** ein Gespräch mit ihr ist ganz schön mühsam *od.* ein schwieriges Geschäft; **this book is heavy ~:** dieses Buch liest sich schwer; **while the ~ is good** solange noch Zeit dazu ist *od.* es noch geht.
❷ *adj.* Ⓐ *pres. p. of* **go¹** 1, 2; Ⓑ (*available*) erhältlich; **there is sth. ~:** es gibt etw.; **take any job ~:** jede Arbeit annehmen, die es nur gibt; **this cabbage was the best one ~:** das war der beste Kohl, den man bekommen konnte; Ⓒ **be ~ to do sth.** etw. tun [werden/wollen]; **he's ~ to be a ballet dancer when he grows up** wenn er groß ist, wird er Balletttänzer; **I was ~ to say** ich wollte sagen; **I was not ~** (*did not intend*) **to do sth.** ich hatte nicht die Absicht, etw. zu tun; **it's ~ to snow** es wird schneien; Ⓓ (*current*) [derzeit/damals/dann] geltend; **the ~ rate of exchange** der augenblickliche Wechselkurs; Ⓔ **a ~ concern** eine gesunde Firma; Ⓕ **have a lot/nothing** *etc.* **~ for one** (*coll.*) viel/nichts *usw.* haben, was für einen spricht; Ⓖ **to be ~ on with** ⇒ **go on with**; **set/keep sth. ~, keep sb. ~** ⇒ **go¹** 1 F; **get ~** ⇒ **get** 1 O, 2 B; **be ~ on fifteen** *etc.* ⇒ **go on** 1 E; **~ strong** ⇒ **strong** 2; **~ great guns** ⇒ **gun** 1 A

**going: ~-a'way** *attrib. adj.* ‹Ausstattung, Kleid› für die Hochzeitsreise; **~-over** *n.* Ⓐ (*coll.: overhaul*) (*of list etc.*) Durchsicht, *die;* (*of engine etc.*) Überholung, *die;* Überprüfung, *die;* **give sth. a [good etc.] ~-over** eine Sache [gründlich *usw.*] durchgehen *od.* durchsehen; **give the room a ~-over with the Hoover/duster** das Zimmer durchsaugen/im Zimmer Staub wischen; Ⓑ (*coll.: thrashing*) **give sb. a [good] ~-over** jmdn. [ordentlich] verprügeln (*ugs.*); Ⓒ (*Amer. coll.: scolding*) **give sb. a [good] ~-over** sich (*Dat.*) jmdn. [einmal ordentlich] vorknöpfen (*ugs.*)

**goings-on** /gəʊɪŋz'ɒn/ *n. pl.* Ereignisse *Pl.;* Vorgänge; **there have been some strange ~:** es sind seltsame Dinge passiert; **be disgusted by sb.'s ~:** empört über jmds. Treiben *od.* Geschichten (*Akk.*) sein

**goitre** (*Brit.; Amer.:* **goiter**) /'gɔɪtə(r)/ *n.* (*Med.*) Kropf, *der*

**'go-kart** *n.* Gokart, *der*

**gold** /gəʊld/ ❶ *n.* Ⓐ *no pl., no indef. art.* Gold, *das;* **the price of ~:** der Goldpreis; **be worth one's weight in ~:** nicht mit Gold aufzuwiegen sein; **a heart of ~:** ein goldenes Herz; **she is pure ~:** sie ist Gold wert; Ⓑ *no pl., no indef. art.* (*wealth*) Geld, *das;* (*coins*) Goldmünzen *Pl.;* **a crock** *or* **pot of ~ at the end of the rainbow** ein Krug/Topf voll Gold am Ende des Regenbogens (*ein unerfüllbarer Wunsch*); Ⓒ (*colour*) Gold, *das;* **the ~ of her hair** ihr goldenes Haar; Ⓓ (*medal*) Gold, *das;* **win six Olympic ~s** sechsmal olympisches Gold gewinnen; Ⓔ (*Archery*) Gold, *das.* ⇒ *also* **glitter** 1 A; **good** 1 F.
❷ *attrib. adj.* golden; Gold‹münze, -stück, -kette, -krone usw.›

**gold: ~ 'brick** *n.* Ⓐ (*coll.: fraud*) Schwindel, *der;* **sell sb. a ~ brick** jmdn. übers Ohr hauen (*ugs.*); jmdm. etwas andrehen (*ugs.*); Ⓑ (*Amer. coll.: shirker*) Drückeberger, *der* (*ugs. abwertend*); **~-coloured** *adj.* goldfarben; **~crest** *n.* (*Ornith.*) Wintergoldhähnchen, *das;* **~-digger** *n.* Goldgräber, *der;* **she's a ~-digger** (*fig. coll.*) sie ist nur auf das Geld der Männer aus; **~ 'disc** *n.* Goldene Schallplatte; **~ dust** *n.* Ⓐ Goldstaub, *der;* **be like ~ dust** eine Rarität sein; Ⓑ (*Bot.*) Felsensteinkraut, *das*

**golden** /'gəʊldn/ *adj.* Ⓐ golden; **~ brown/yellow** goldbraun/goldgelb; Ⓑ (*fig.*) golden; einmalig ‹Gelegenheit›

**golden: ~ age** *n.* goldenes Zeitalter; **~ boy** *n.* Goldjunge, *der;* **~ 'calf** *n.* Goldenes Kalb; **~ 'disc** ⇒ **gold disc**; **~ 'eagle** *n.* Steinadler, *der;* **G~ 'Fleece** *n.* (*Greek Mythol.*) Goldenes Vlies; **G~ 'Gate** *pr. n.* (*Geog.*) Goldenes Tor; **the ~ Gate Bridge** die Golden-Gate-Brücke; **~ girl** *n.* Goldmädchen, *das;* **~-haired** *adj.* mit goldenem Haar *nachgestellt* (*dichter.*); **~ 'hamster** *n.* Goldhamster, *der;* **~ 'handshake** *n.* Abfindung[ssumme], *die;* **~ hel'lo** *n.* ≈ Handgeld, *das;* **~ 'jubilee** *n.* goldenes Jubiläum; **~ 'mean** *n.* goldene Mitte; **~ re'triever** *n.* Golden Retriever, *der;* **~ rod** *n.* (*Bot.*) Goldrute, *die;* **~ 'rule** *n.* goldene Regel; **~ 'syrup** *n.* (*Brit.*) Sirup, *der;* **~ 'wedding** *n.* goldene Hochzeit

**gold: ~ fever** *n.* Goldrausch, *der;* **~field** *n.* Goldfeld, *das;* **~finch** *n.* Stieglitz, *der;* Distelfink, *der;* **~fish** *n.* Goldfisch, *der;* **~fish bowl** *n.* Goldfischglas, *das;* **like being in a ~fish bowl** (*fig.*) wie auf dem Präsentierteller; **~ 'foil** *n.* Goldfolie, *die*

**goldilocks** /'gəʊldɪlɒks/ *n.* Blondkopf, *der*

**gold: ~ 'leaf** *n.* Blattgold, *das;* **~ 'medal** *n.* Goldmedaille, *die;* **~ 'medallist** *n.* Goldmedaillengewinner, *der*/-gewinnerin, *die;* **~ mine** *n.* Goldmine, *die;* (*fig.*) Goldgrube, *die;* **~ 'plate** *n., no pl., no indef. art.* Ⓐ vergoldete Ware; (*coating*) Goldauflage, *die;* **be ~ plate** vergoldet sein; Ⓑ (*vessels, tableware*) Goldgeschirr, *das;* **~-plate** *v.t.* vergolden; **~ reserve** *n.* Goldreserve, *die;* **~ rush** *n.* **the ~ rush to Alaska** der Strom von Goldgräbern nach Alaska; **~smith** *n.* ▶ **1261** Goldschmied, *der*/-schmiedin, *die;* **~ standard** *n.* Goldstandard, *der;* ⇒ *also* **go off** 2 B; **~ 'thread** *n.* Goldfaden, *der*

**golf** /gɒlf/ ❶ *n., no pl.* Golf, *das; attrib.* Golf‹platz, -schlag usw.›. ❷ *v.i.* Golf spielen; **his ~ing friends** seine Golffreunde

**golf: ~ bag** *n.* Golftasche, *die;* **~ ball** *n.* Ⓐ Golfball, *der;* Ⓑ (*in typewriter*) Kugelkopf, *der;* **~ club** *n.* Ⓐ (*implement*) Golfschläger, *der;* Ⓑ (*association*) Golfklub, *der;* **~ course** *n.* Golfplatz, *der*

**golfer** /'gɒlfə(r)/ *n.* Golfer, *der*/Golferin, *die;* Golfspieler, *der*/Golfspielerin, *die*

**golf links** *n. pl.* Golfplatz, *der*

**Goliath** /gə'laɪəθ/ *n.* (*lit. or fig.*) Goliath, *der*

**golliwog** /'gɒlɪwɒg/ *n.* Negerpuppe, *die;* **have hair like a ~:** wie ein Struwwelpeter aussehen

**golly¹** /'gɒlɪ/ ⇒ **golliwog**

**golly²** *int.* meine Güte!; **by ~:** Menschenskind!

**golosh** (*Brit.*) ⇒ **galosh**

**gonad** /'gəʊnæd/ *n.* (*Anat., Zool.*) Gonade, *die*

**gondola** /'gɒndələ/ *n.* Ⓐ (*boat*) Gondel, *die;* Ⓑ (*Amer. Railw.*) **~ [car]** offener Güterwagen; offener Flachwagen; Ⓒ (*of ski lift, airship*) Gondel, *die;* Ⓓ (*in shop*) Gondel, *die;* Verkaufsregal, *das*

**gondolier** /gɒndə'lɪə(r)/ *n.* ▶ **1261** Gondoliere, *der*

**gone** /gɒn/ ❶ *p. p. of* **go¹** 1, 2.
❷ *pred. adj.* Ⓐ (*away*) weg; **it's time you were ~:** es ist *od.* wird Zeit, dass du gehst; **he has been ~ ten minutes** er ist seit zehn Minuten fort *od.* weg; **he will be ~ a year** er wird ein Jahr lang weg sein; **no, it's ~ again** (*fig.: forgotten*) es ist mir schon wieder entfallen; Ⓑ ▶ **1012** (*of time: after*) nach; **not be back until ~ ten o'clock** erst nach zehn Uhr zurückkommen; **it's ~ ten o'clock** es ist zehn Uhr vorbei; **at ~ midnight** nach Mitternacht; Ⓒ (*used up*) **be all ~:** alle sein (*ugs.*); Ⓓ (*coll.: pregnant*) **be six** *etc.* **months ~:** im sechsten *usw.* Monat sein; Ⓔ **be ~ on sb./sth.** (*coll.*) ganz weg von jmdm./etw. sein (*ugs.*). ⇒ *also* **far** 1 D; **forget** 1 A; **go¹** 1 K

**goner** /'gɒnə(r)/ *n.* (*coll.*) **he is a ~:** er hat die längste Zeit gelebt (*ugs.*); **the ship is a ~:** das Schiff macht es nicht mehr lange *od.* wird bald seinen Geist aufgeben (*ugs.*)

**gong** /gɒŋ/ *n.* Ⓐ Gong, *der;* Ⓑ (*Brit coll.: medal*) Orden, *der; in pl.* Blech, *das* (*ugs.*); Lametta, *das* (*ugs.*)

**gonna** /'gɒnə/ (*coll./Amer.*) = **going to;** ⇒ **going** 2 C

**gonorrhoea** (*Amer.:* **gonorrhea**) /gɒnə'rɪə/ *n.* ▶ **1232** (*Med.*) Gonorrhö, *die* (*fachspr.*); Tripper, *der*

**goo** /gu:/ *n.* (*coll.*) Schmiere, *die* (*ugs.*); (*fig.*) Gefühlsduselei, *die* (*ugs. abwertend*); (*in film etc.*) Schmalz, *der* (*ugs. abwertend*)

**good** /gʊd/ ❶ *adj.*, **better** /'betə(r)/, **best** /best/ Ⓐ (*satisfactory*) gut; (*reliable*) gut; zuverlässig; (*sufficient*) gut; ausreichend ‹Vorrat›; ausgiebig ‹Mahl›; (*competent*) gut; geeignet; **his ~ eye/leg** sein gesundes Auge/Bein; **in ~ health** bei guter Gesundheit; **come in a ~ third** einen guten dritten Platz belegen; **come ~** (*coll.*) groß rauskommen (*ugs.*); **Late again! It's just not ~ enough** (*coll.*) Schon wieder zu spät. So geht es einfach nicht!; **your excuse is not ~ enough** diese Entschuldigung reicht nicht; **in ~ time** frühzeitig; **all in ~ time** alles zu seiner Zeit; **take ~ care of sb.** gut für jmdn. sorgen; **be ~ at sth.** in etw. (*Dat.*) gut sein; **be ~ at doing sth.** etw. gut können; **speak ~ English** gut[es] Englisch sprechen; **be ~ with people** *etc.* mit Menschen *usw.* gut *od.* leicht zurechtkommen; **the ~ ship 'Victory'** die gute alte „Victory"; Ⓑ (*favourable, advantageous*) gut; günstig ‹Gelegenheit, Augenblick, Angebot›; **a ~ chance of succeeding** gute Erfolgschancen; **too ~ to be true** zu schön, um wahr zu sein; **in the ~ sense** im positiven Sinn; **I've heard so many ~ things about you** ich habe schon so viel Gutes von Ihnen gehört; **the ~ thing about it is that ...:** das Gute daran ist, dass ...; **be on to a ~ thing** was Gutes aufgetan haben (*ugs.*); **be too much of a ~ thing** zu viel des Guten sein; **you can have too much of a ~ thing** man kann es auch übertreiben; **be ~ for sb./sth.** gut für jmdn./etw. sein; **apples are ~ for you** Äpfel sind gesund; **eat more than is ~ for one** mehr essen, als einem gut tut; **know what is ~ for one** wissen, was sich gehört; **it's a ~ thing you told him** nur gut, dass du es ihm gesagt hast; **make a ~ death** *or* **end** einen schönen Tod haben; **the water isn't ~ to drink** das Wasser kann man nicht trinken; Ⓒ (*prosperous*) gut; **~ times** eine schöne Zeit; **have it ~:** es gut haben; Ⓓ (*enjoyable*) schön ‹Leben, Urlaub, Wochenende›; **the ~ things** alles, was gut und schön ist; **the ~ things in life** Annehmlichkeiten; **the ~ old days** die gute alte Zeit; **the ~ life** das angenehme[, sorglose] Leben; **have a ~ time!** viel Spaß *od.* Vergnügen!; **did you have a ~ time in Spain?** war es schön in Spanien?; **be after a ~ time** auf sein Vergnügen aus sein; **have a ~ journey!** gute Reise!; **it's ~ to be alive** es ist eine Lust zu leben; **it's ~ to be home again** es ist schön, wieder zu Hause zu sein; **ox liver is not very ~ to eat** Rinderleber ist nicht gut zum Verzehr geeignet; **Did you have a ~ day at the office?** Wie war es heute im Büro?; Ⓔ (*cheerful*) gut; angenehm ‹Patient›; **~ humour** *or* **spirits** *or* **mood** gute Laune; **feel ~:** sich wohl fühlen; **I'm not feeling too ~** (*coll.*) mir geht es nicht sehr gut; Ⓕ (*well-behaved*) gut; brav; **be ~!, be a ~ girl/boy!** sei brav *od.* lieb!; **[as] ~ as gold** ganz artig *od.* brav; Ⓖ (*virtuous*) rechtschaffen; (*kind*) nett; gut ‹Absicht, Wünsche, Benehmen, Tat›; **the ~ guy** der Gute; **be ~ to sb.** gut zu jmdm. sein; **would you be so ~ as to** *or* **~ enough to do that?** wären Sie so freundlich *od.* nett, das zu tun?; **how ~ of you!** wie nett von Ihnen!; **that/it is ~ of you** das/es ist nett *od.* lieb von dir; **he has a very ~ nature** er ist sehr gutmütig; **~ works** gute Taten *od.* Werke; ⇒ *also* **turn** 1 L; Ⓗ (*commendable*) gut; **~ for 'you** *etc.* (*coll.*), **~ 'on you** *etc.* (*esp. Austral. and NZ coll.*) bravo!; **~ old Jim** *etc.* (*coll.*) der gute alte Jim *usw.* (*ugs.*); **~ man!** (*coll.*) mein lieber Mann!; alle Achtung!; **my ~ man/friend** (*coll.*) mein lieber Herr/Freund (*ugs.; auch iron.*); **the ~ man/woman** (*dated*) der werte Herr/die werte Dame (*geh.*); **your ~**

g

**man/lady** Ihr lieber Mann/Ihre liebe Frau; Ihr werter Gatte/Ihre werte Gattin; **~ men and true** rechtschaffene Leute; **that's a ~ one** (*coll.*) der ist gut! (*ugs.*); (*iron.*) das ist'n Ding! (*ugs.*); ⇒ *also* **fellow** 1 A; **I** (*attractive*) schön; gut ‹Figur, Haltung›; gepflegt ‹Erscheinung, Äußeres›; wohlgeformt ‹Nase, Beine›; **look ~** gut aussehen; **~ looks** gutes Aussehen; **have ~ looks** gut aussehen; **J** (*thorough*) gut; **take a ~ look round** sich gründlich umsehen; **give sb. a ~ beating/scolding** jmdn. tüchtig verprügeln/ausschimpfen; **give sth. a ~ polish** etw. ordentlich polieren; **have a ~ weep/rest/sleep** sich richtig ausweinen/ausruhen/[sich] richtig ausschlafen (*ugs.*); **K** (*considerable*) [recht] ansehnlich ‹Menschenmenge›; ganz schön, ziemlich (*ugs.*) ‹Stück Wegs, Entfernung, Zeitraum, Strecke›; gut, anständig ‹Preis, Erlös›; hoch ‹Alter›; **a ~ bit better** (*coll.*) ein ganzes Stück besser; **a ~ dose of ...:** eine gute Dosis ...; (*fig.*) eine gehörige Portion ...; **take a ~ long time** ziemlich *od.* recht lange dauern; seine Zeit brauchen; **have a ~ long sleep** [sich] richtig ausschlafen; **live to a ~ old age** ein recht hohes Alter erreichen; **a ~ four hours** *etc.* volle *od.* ganze vier Stunden *usw.*; gut vier Stunden *usw.*; **a ~ half pound** ein gutes halbes Pfund; **he is a ~ seventy** (*coll.*) er ist gute siebzig (*ugs.*); **L** (*sound, valid*) gut ‹Grund, Rat, Gedanke›; berechtigt ‹Anspruch›; (*Commerc.*) solide ‹Kunde›; sicher ‹Anleihe, Kredit›; gedeckt ‹Scheck›; **good sense** Vernünftigkeit, *die;* **have the ~ sense to do sth.** so vernünftig sein, etw. zu tun; **be ~ for a year** es ein Jahr machen; ‹Gerät usw.:› ein Jahr halten; ‹Ticket:› ein Jahr gelten; **~ for five journeys** gültig für fünf Fahrten; **I'm ~ for another hour's walk** ich kann noch eine Stunde weiterlaufen; **he's ~ for £5,000** er wird bestimmt 5 000 Pfund geben (*ugs.*); **how much is he ~ for?** wie viel wird er wohl geben? (*ugs.*); **the draft is ~ for ...:** der Wechsel ist auf ... (*Akk.*) ausgestellt; **M** ▶ **1191** *in greeting* gut; **~ afternoon/day** guten Tag!; **~ evening/morning** *or* (*Brit. arch.*) **morrow** guten Abend/Morgen!; **~ night** gute Nacht!; **a ~-night kiss** ein Gutenachtkuss; **N** *in exclamation* gut; **very ~, sir** sehr wohl!; **~ God/Lord** *etc. see the nouns;* **O** (*best*) gut ‹Geschirr, Anzug›; **P** (*serious*) ernst ‹Musik›; schön ‹Künste›; **Q** (*orthodox*) gut ‹Christ, Moslem›; **R** (*correct, fitting*) gut; (*appropriate*) angebracht; ratsam; **S** (*socially prestigious*) gut; **be of a ~/very ~ family** aus guter Familie/bestem Hause stammen; **T as ~ as** so gut wie; ⇒ *also* **give** 1 P; **U make ~** (*succeed*) erfolgreich sein; (*effect*) in die Tat umsetzen; ausführen ‹Plan›; erfüllen ‹Versprechen›; (*compensate for*) wieder gutmachen ‹Fehler›; (*indemnify*) ersetzen ‹Schaden, Ausgaben›; (*prove*) belegen ‹Behauptung, Anschuldigung›; **the film made ~ at the box office** der Film war ein Kassenerfolg; **they soon made ~ in Australia** sie brachten es bald zu was in Australien (*ugs.*). ⇒ *also* **best** 1; **better** 1; **egg**[1]; **form** 1 F, H; **luck** A; **temper** 1 A.

**2** *adv.* **A** (*coll.*) *as intensifier* **~ and ...** richtig ...; **~ and angry** (*Amer.*) richtig böse; **hit sb. ~ and proper** jmdn. ordentlich verprügeln; **it was raining ~ and hard** es hat [so] richtig gegossen; **they quizzed him ~ and proper** sie haben ihn ordentlich in die Mangel genommen (*ugs.*); **B** (*Amer. coll.: well*) gut; **get along ~** gut zurechtkommen; **he's doing pretty ~ these days** es geht ihm in letzter Zeit sehr gut. ⇒ *also* **best** 2; **better** 2.

**3** *n.* **A** (*use*) Nutzen, *der;* **be some ~ to sb./sth.** jmdm./einer Sache nützen; **he'll never be any ~** aus dem wird nichts Gutes werden; **is this book any ~?** taugt dieses Buch etwas?; **you're a lot of ~, I must say!** (*iron.*) du bist mir vielleicht einer! (*ugs.*); **be no ~ to sb./sth.** für jmdn./etw. nicht zu gebrauchen sein; **not be any ~ for work** nicht zur Arbeit taugen *od.* geeignet sein; **it is no/not much ~ doing sth.** es hat keinen/kaum einen Sinn, etw. zu tun; **what's the ~ of ...?, what ~ is ...?** was nützt ...?; **what's the ~ of knowing Latin?** was nützt einem Latein?; wozu ist Latein gut?; ⇒ *also* **no-~**; **B** (*benefit*) **for your/his** *etc.* **own ~** zu deinem/seinem *usw.* Besten *od.* eigenen Vorteil; **for the ~ of mankind/the country** zum Wohl[e] der Menschheit/des Landes; **for ~ or ill** ⇒ **ill** 2 A; **do no/little ~:** nichts/wenig helfen *od.* nützen; **do sb./sth. ~** jmdm./einer Sache nützen; ‹Ruhe, Erholung:› jmdm./einer Sache gut tun; ‹Arznei:› jmdm./einer Sache helfen; **I'll tell him, but what ~ will that do?** ich sag es ihm, aber was nützt *od.* hilft das schon?; **do sb. a lot/a world of ~** jmdm. sehr gut tun; **just sitting there won't do you any ~** einfach dasitzen hilft dir auch nicht weiter; **you aren't doing yourself any ~** du tust dir keinen Gefallen; **much ~ may it do you** (*iron.*) [na, dann] viel Vergnügen; **look what ~** *or* **a lot of ~** *or* **much ~ it did him** (*iron.*) [und] was hat es ihm genützt?; und das hat er nun davon gehabt (*iron.*); **to the ~** (*for the best*) zum Guten; (*in profit*) plus; **this development was all to the ~** diese Entwicklung war nur von Vorteil; **the delay was partly to the ~** die Verspätung hatte auch ihr Gutes; **end up [a game** *etc.*] **£10 to the ~** [bei einem Spiel *usw.*] 10 Pfund gutmachen; **come home £10 to the ~** mit 10 Pfund plus nach Hause kommen; **be 4 points/wins to the ~** 4 Punkte/Siege voraus *od.* im Vorteil sein; **finish the work with two days to the ~** zwei Tage früher mit der Arbeit fertig sein; **come to no ~** kein gutes Ende nehmen; **C** (*goodness*) Gute, *das;* **the highest ~** (*Philos.*) das Höchste Gut; **there's ~ and bad in everyone** in jedem steckt Gutes und Böses; **the difference between ~ and bad** *or* **evil** der Unterschied zwischen Gut und Böse; **D** (*kind acts*) Gute, *das;* **be up to** *or* **after no ~** nichts Gutes im Sinn haben *od.* im Schilde führen; **do ~** Gutes tun; **E for ~ [and all]** (*finally*) ein für alle Mal; (*permanently*) für immer [und ewig]; endgültig; **F** *constr. as pl.* (*virtuous people*) **the ~** die Guten; **G** *in pl.* (*wares etc.*) Waren *Pl.*; (*belongings*) Habe, *die;* (*Brit. Railw.*) Fracht, *die; attrib.* Fracht‹büro, -tarif, -schiff, -flugzeug, -zettel usw.›; Güter‹abfertigung, -bahnhof, -produktion, -verkehr, -wagen, -zug usw.›; **~s and chattels** Sachen *Pl.*; **canned/manufactured ~s** Konserven/Fertigwaren *Pl.*; **stolen ~s** gestohlene Waren; Diebesgut, *das;* **by ~s** per Bahnfracht; als Frachtgut; **H** *in pl.* **the ~s** (*coll.: what is wanted*) das Gewünschte; das Verlangte; **deliver the ~s** (*fig.*) halten, was man verspricht; **sb. is the ~s** jmd. ist der Richtige; **he's got the ~s** er ist der richtige Mann

**good: ~'bye** (*Amer.:* **~'by**) /gʊd'baɪ/ ▶ **1191** **1** *int.* auf Wiedersehen!; (*on telephone*) auf Wiederhören!; **2** *n., pl.* **~'byes** (*Amer.:* **~'bys**) (*farewell remark or gesture*) Lebewohl, *das* (*geh.*); (*parting*) Abschied, *der;* **say ~bye to sb.** jmdm. Auf Wiedersehen sagen; **say ~bye, say one's ~byes** sich verabschieden; **nod/wave ~bye** zum Abschied nicken/winken; **kiss sb. ~bye** jmdm. einen Abschiedskuss geben; **say ~bye to sth.** Abschied nehmen von etw.; **say ~bye to sth., kiss sth. ~bye** (*fig.: accept its loss*) etw. abschreiben (*ugs.*); **~ 'fellowship** *n.* Kameradschaftlichkeit, *die;* **~-for-nothing** (*derog.*) **1** *adj.* nichtsnutzig; **2** *n.* Taugenichts, *der;* **G~ 'Friday** ⇒ **Friday** 1; **~-hearted** /'gʊdhɑ:tɪd/ *adj.* gutherzig; gut gemeint ‹Bemühungen›; **~-humoured** /gʊd'hju:məd/ *adj.*, **~-humouredly** /gʊd'hju:mədlɪ/ *adv.* gutmütig

**goodies** /'gʊdɪz/ *n. pl.* (*coll.*) (*food*) Naschereien *Pl.*; (*sweets*) Süßigkeiten *Pl.*; (*attractive things*) Attraktionen *Pl.*; tolle Sachen

**goodish** /'gʊdɪʃ/ *adj.* **A** (*quite good*) ganz gut; recht gut; **B** (*considerable*) ganz schön

**good: ~-looker** *n.* flotte Erscheinung (*ugs.*); **be a ~-looker** gut aussehen; **~-'looking** *adj.* gut aussehend

**goodly** /'gʊdlɪ/ *adj.* stattlich; ansehnlich

**good: ~-'natured** *adj.* gutwillig; gutmütig; **~-naturedly** /gʊd'neɪtʃədlɪ/ *adv.* gutmütig; **~-'neighbour** *attrib. adj.* gutnachbarlich; **a ~-neighbour policy** eine Politik der guten Nachbarschaft

**goodness** /'gʊdnɪs/ **1** *n., no pl.* **A** (*virtue*) Güte, *die;* **have the ~ to do sth.** die Güte haben, etw. zu tun (*geh., auch iron.*); **B** (*of food*) Nährgehalt, *der;* Güte, *die;* (*of soil*) Fruchtbarkeit, *die;* Güte, *die.* **2** *int.* **[my] ~** *expr. surprise* meine Güte! (*ugs.*); **[oh] my ~** *expr. shock* lieber Himmel!; **~ gracious** *or* **me!** [ach] du lieber Himmel *od.* liebe Güte! (*ugs.*); **for ~' sake** um Himmels willen; **~ [only] knows** weiß der Himmel (*ugs.*); **I hope to ~ that ...:** gebe Gott, dass ...; **I wish to ~ I'd never met him** wenn ich ihn doch bloß nie kennen gelernt hätte!; **surely to ~ you don't mean that** das ist doch wohl nicht dein Ernst?; **thank ~:** Gott sei Dank

**good: ~-o, ~-oh** *int.* (*coll.*) toll! prima!

**goods** ⇒ **good** 3 G, H

**good: ~-sized** ⇒ **-sized**; **~s station** *n.* (*Brit. Railw.*) Güterbahnhof, *der;* **~s train** *n.* (*Brit. Railw.*) Güterzug, *der;* **~s vehicle** *n.* Nutzfahrzeug, *das;* **~s yard** *n.* (*Brit. Railw.*) Güterbahnhof, *der;* **~-'tempered** *adj.* ausgeglichen; gutmütig; verträglich ‹Person›; **~-time** *adj.* **a ~-time girl** ein leichtes Mädchen (*abwertend*); **~ 'will** *n.* gute Absicht; **~'will** *n.* **A** (*friendly feeling*) guter Wille; *attrib.* Goodwill‹botschaft, -reise usw.›; **men of ~will** Menschen, die guten Willens sind; **B** (*willingness*) Bereitwilligkeit, *die;* **with ~will** bereitwillig; **C** (*Commerc.*) Goodwill, *der*

**goody**[1] /'gʊdɪ/ *n.* (*coll.: hero*) Gute, *der/die;* ⇒ *also* **goodies**

**goody**[2] *int.* (*coll.*) toll; prima; **~, ~ gumdrops!** juhu!; juchhe!

**goody: ~-~ 1** *n.* Tugendbold, *der* (*iron.*); **2** *adj.* [scheinheilig] tugendhaft; musterhaft (*iron.*); **~-'two-shoes** *n.* Tugendlamm, *das* (*iron.*)

**gooey** /'gu:ɪ/ *adj.*, **gooier** /'gu:ɪə(r)/, **gooiest** /'gu:ɪɪst/ (*coll.*) klebrig; (*fig.*) rührselig; schnulzig (*ugs. abwertend*)

**goof** /gu:f/ (*coll.*) **1** *n.* **A** (*fool*) Döskopp, *der* (*salopp*); Doofi, *der* (*ugs.*); **B** (*gaffe*) Schnitzer, *der* (*ugs.*); Patzer, *der* (*ugs.*). **2** *v.i.* Mist machen *od.* bauen (*salopp*). **3** *v.t.* vermasseln (*salopp*); Murks machen bei (*salopp*)

**~ about, ~ around** *v.i.* (*coll.*) herumpfuschen (*ugs. abwertend*); (*spend time idly*) herumhängen (*salopp*); herumtrödeln

**goofy** /'gu:fɪ/ *adj.* (*coll.*) **A** dämlich (*ugs.*); bescheuert (*salopp*); **B** vorstehend ‹Zähne›

**googly** /'gu:glɪ/ *n.* (*Cricket*) (*zur Täuschung des Schlagmanns*) gedrehter Ball

**gook** /gu:k, gʊk/ *n.* (*Amer. sl. derog.*) Schlitzauge, *das* (*salopp abwertend*)

**goon** /gu:n/ *n.* (*coll.*) **A** (*hatchet man*) Schläger, *der* (*abwertend*); **B** (*fool*) Blödmann, *der* (*salopp*)

**goosander** /gu:'sændə(r)/ *n.* (*Ornith.*) Gänsesäger, *der*

**goose** /gu:s/ *n., pl.* **geese** /gi:s/ **A** Gans, *die;* **all mothers think their geese are swans** jede Mutter glaubt, ihre Kinder seien etwas Besonderes; **kill the ~ that lays the golden eggs** (*fig.*) das Huhn, das goldene Eier legt, schlachten; **roast ~:** Gänsebraten, *der;* ⇒ *also* **boo** 1; **cook** 2 A; **B** (*simpleton*) Gans, *die* (*ugs.*)

**gooseberry** /'gʊzbərɪ/ *n.* **A** (*berry, shrub*) Stachelbeere, *die;* **B play ~:** das fünfte Rad am Wagen sein (*ugs.*)

**'gooseberry bush** *n.* Stachelbeerstrauch, *der;* **we found you under a ~** (*fig.*) dich hat uns der Klapperstorch gebracht (*Kinderspr.*)

**goose: ~ bumps** *n. pl.* (*Amer.*) Gänsehaut, *die;* **~ egg** *n.* Gänseei, *das;* **~flesh** *n., no pl.* Gänsehaut, *die;* **~foot** *n., pl.* **~foots** (*Bot.*) Gänsefuß, *der;* **~grass** *n.* Klebkraut, *das;* **~neck** *n.* Schwanenhals, *der* (*fig.*); **~ pimples** *n. pl.* **have ~ pimples** eine Gänsehaut haben; **~ step 1** *n.* Stechschritt, *der;* **2** *v.i.* im Stechschritt marschieren

**gopher** /'gəʊfə(r)/ *n.* **A** (*Zool.*) Taschenratte, *die;* (*squirrel*) Ziesel, *der;* **B** (*Computing*) Gopher, *der*

**gorblimey** /gɔ:'blaɪmɪ/ *int.* (*Brit. sl.*) Mensch! (*salopp*)

**Gordian knot** /gɔːdɪən 'nɒt/ *n.* gordischer Knoten; **cut the ~:** den gordischen Knoten durchhauen

**gore**[1] /gɔː(r)/ *v.t.* [mit den Hörnern] aufspießen *od.* durchbohren; **be ~d to death by a bull** von den Hörnern eines Stieres durchbohrt [und tödlich verletzt] werden

**gore**[2] *n.* (*blood*) Blut, *das*

**gore**[3] *n.* Keil, *der;* (*of skirt*) [Rock]bahn, *die*

**gorge** /gɔːdʒ/ **1** *n.* **A** Schlucht, *die;* Klamm, *die;* **B** **sb.'s ~ rises at sth.** (*fig.*) jmdm. wird schlecht *od.* übel von *od.* bei etw.; **C** (*rhet.: throat*) (*of person*) Kehle, *die;* (*of animal*) Schlund, *der.* **2** *v.i.* sich voll stopfen (**on** mit) (*ugs.*); ‹Tier:› sich voll fressen (**on** mit). **3** *v.t.* **A** (*satiate*) voll stopfen (*ugs.*); **~ oneself with** *or* **on sth.** sich mit etw. voll stopfen (*ugs.*); **B** (*fill full*) anfüllen (**with** mit)

**gorgeous** /'gɔːdʒəs/ *adj.* **A** (*magnificent*) prächtig; hinreißend ‹Frau, Mann, Lächeln›; (*richly coloured*) farbenprächtig; **the ~ colours of sth.** die Farbenpracht einer Sache; **B** (*coll.: splendid*) sagenhaft (*ugs.*)

**gorgeously** /'gɔːdʒəslɪ/ *adv.* **A** prächtig; hinreißend ‹lächeln›; **B** (*coll.: splendidly*) sagenhaft

**gorgon** /'gɔːgən/ *n.* **A** (*Greek Mythol.*) Gorgo, *die;* **B** (*person*) Drachen, *der* (*ugs. abwertend*)

**gorilla** /gə'rɪlə/ *n.* Gorilla, *der*

**gormandize (gormandise)** /'gɔːməndaɪz/ *v.i.* prassen; schlemmen

**gormless** /'gɔːmlɪs/ *adj.* (*Brit. coll.*) dämlich (*ugs.*)

**gorse** /gɔːs/ *n.* Stechginster, *der*

**gory** /'gɔːrɪ/ *adj.* **A** blutbefleckt ‹Hände›; blutbeschmiert ‹Waffe›; blutig ‹Schlacht›; **B** (*fig.: sensational*) blutrünstig

**gosh** /gɒʃ/ *int.* (*coll.*) Gott

**goshawk** /'gɒshɔːk/ *n.* (*Ornith.*) [Hühner]habicht, *der*

**gosling** /'gɒzlɪŋ/ *n.* Gänseküken, *das;* Gössel, *das* (*nordd.*)

**'go-slow** *n.* (*Brit.*) Bummelstreik, *der*

**gospel** /'gɒspl/ *n.* **A** (*Relig.*) Evangelium, *das;* (*reading*) Lesung, *die;* **B** (*fig.*) Evangelium, *das;* **take sth. for** *or* **as ~:** etw. für bare Münze nehmen; **preach the ~ of non-violence** Gewaltlosigkeit predigen

**gospel: ~ 'oath** *n.* Eid auf die Bibel; **~ singer** *n.* Gospelsänger, *der*/-sängerin, *die;* **~ 'truth** *n.* absolute *od.* reine Wahrheit

**gossamer** /'gɒsəmə(r)/ *n.* **A** Altweibersommer, *der;* **like ~:** wie Spinnfäden; **B** (*fig.*) Spinnfäden *Pl.* (*fig.*); *attrib.* hauchdünn ‹Flügel›

**gossip** /'gɒsɪp/ **1** *n.* **A** (*person*) Klatschbase, *die* (*ugs. abwertend*); **B** (*talk*) Schwatz, *der;* (*malicious*) Klatsch, *der* (*ugs. abwertend*); **the latest ~ is that ...:** seit neustem wird geklatscht, dass ... **2** *v.i.* schwatzen; (*maliciously*) klatschen (*ugs. abwertend*)

**gossip: ~ column** *n.* Klatschspalte, *die* (*ugs. abwertend*); **~ columnist** *n.* ▶ **1261** Klatschspaltenkolumnist, *der*/-kolumnistin, *die* (*abwertend*)

**gossiper** /'gɒsɪpə(r)/ ⇒ **gossip 1 A**

**'gossipmonger** *n.* (*derog.*) Klatschmaul, *das* (*ugs. abwertend*)

**gossipy** /'gɒsɪpɪ/ *adj.* geschwätzig (*abwertend*); (*conversational*) plaudernd ‹Ton, Stil›; im Plauderton geschrieben ‹Buch, Brief›

**got** ⇒ **get**

**Goth** /gɒθ/ *n.* Gote, *der*

**Gothic** /'gɒθɪk/ **1** *adj.* **A** gotisch; **B** (*Lit.*) *für den Schauerroman charakteristisch;* **~ novel** Schauerroman, *der;* **C** (*Printing*) gotisch. **2** *n.* **A** (*Ling.*) Gotisch[e], *das;* **B** (*Archit.*) Gotik, *die;* **C** (*type, script*) Gotisch, *das*

**Gothic Re'vival** *n.* (*Archit.*) Neugotik, *die*

**gotta** /'gɒtə/ (*coll.*) = **got to, got a; I['ve] ~ go** ich muss gehen; **I['ve] ~ present for you** ich habe da ein Geschenk für dich

**gotten** ⇒ **get**

**gouache** /guː'ɑːʃ/ *n.* (*Art*) Gouache, *die*

**gouge** /gaʊdʒ/ **1** *v.t.* **A** aushöhlen; ausmeißeln; **~ a channel** ‹Fluss:› eine Rinne auswaschen; **B** (*Amer.: overcharge*) betrügen. **2** *n.* **A** Hohleisen, *das;* Hohlmeißel, *der;* **B** (*Amer.: overcharging*) Betrug, *der*

**~ out** *v.t.* ausschneiden; ausstechen; **~ sb.'s eye out** jmdm. ein Auge ausstechen

**goulash** /'guːlæʃ/ *n.* (*Gastr.*) Gulasch, *das od. der*

**gourd** /gʊəd/ *n.* **A** (*fruit, plant*) [Flaschen]kürbis, *der;* **B** (*bottle, bowl*) Kürbisflasche, *die;* Kalebasse, *die*

**gourmand** /'gʊəmənd/ *n.* (*glutton*) Gourmand, *der*

**gourmet** /'gʊəmeɪ/ *n.* Gourmet, *der; attrib.* **~ meal/restaurant** Feinschmeckergericht, *das*/-lokal, *das*

**gout** /gaʊt/ *n.* ▶ **1232** (*Med.*) Gicht, *die*

**gouty** /'gaʊtɪ/ *adj.* (*Med.*) gichtkrank; gichtig

**Gov.** *abbr.* **A** **Government** Reg.; Rg.; **B** **Governor** Gouv.

**govern** /'gʌvn/ **1** *v.t.* **A** (*rule*) regieren ‹Land, Volk›; (*administer*) verwalten ‹Provinz, Kolonie›; **B** (*dictate*) bestimmen; **be ~ed by sth.** sich von etw. leiten lassen; **self-interest ~s all his actions** Eigennutz beherrscht all sein Tun; **C** (*regulate proceedings of*) leiten ‹Geschäft, Unternehmen›; ‹Vorschriften:› regeln; **D** (*be in command of*) den Befehl haben über (+ *Akk.*) ‹Festung, Stadt›; **E** (*restrain*) zügeln ‹Temperament, Leidenschaften›; **F** (*constitute a law or principle for*) ‹Prinzipien:› die Grundlage bilden für; **the laws which ~ the animal kingdom** die Gesetze, denen das Tierreich unterworfen ist; **G** (*Ling.*) verlangen; regieren ‹Kasus›.
**2** *v.i.* regieren

**governable** /'gʌvənəbl/ *adj.* regierbar

**governance** /'gʌvənəns/ *n.* Regieren, *das;* (*office, function*) Regierungsgewalt, *die;* (*control*) Herrschaft, *die*

**governess** /'gʌvənɪs/ *n.* ▶ **1261** Gouvernante, *die* (*veraltet*); Hauslehrerin, *die*

**governing** /'gʌvənɪŋ/ *adj.* **A** (*ruling*) regierend; **B** (*guiding*) dominierend ‹Einfluss›; geltend ‹Vorschriften›; **sb.'s ~ principle** das Prinzip, von dem jmd. sich leiten lässt; **~ body** leitendes Gremium

**government** /'gʌvnmənt/ *n.* **A** Regierung, *die;* **form a G~:** die Regierung bilden; **B** (*system, form*) Regierungsform, *die;* **C** (*an administration or ministry*) **[central] ~:** Zentralregierung, *die; attrib.* Regierungs-; **~ money** Staatsgelder *Pl.;* **~ securities** *or* **stocks** Staatspapiere *od.* -anleihen *Pl.;* **~-controlled establishment** staatlich kontrollierte Einrichtung; ⇒ *also* **body 1 D**

**governmental** /gʌvn'mentl/ *adj.* Regierungs-

**government: ~ department** *n.* Regierungsstelle, *die;* **~-funded** *adj.* staatlich finanziert; **~ official** *n.* Regierungsbeamte, *der*/Regierungsbeamtin, *die;* **~ 'surplus** *n.* Waren aus Regierungsbeständen; *attrib.* **~ surplus radio** Radio aus Regierungsbeständen

**governor** /'gʌvənə(r)/ *n.* ▶ **1261** **A** (*ruler*) Herrscher, *der;* **B** (*of province, town, etc.*) Gouverneur, *der;* Statthalter, *der* (*hist.*); **C** (*of State of US*) Gouverneur, *der;* **D** (*of institution*) Direktor, *der*/Direktorin, *die;* **[board of] ~s** Vorstand, *der;* (*of school*) Schulleitung, *die;* (*of bank, company*) Direktorium, *das;* Direktion, *die;* **E** (*of prison*) Gefängnisdirektor, *der*/-direktorin, *die;* **F** (*commandant*) Kommandant, *der;* Gouverneur, *der;* **G** (*coll.*) (*employer*) Boss, *der* (*ugs.*); (*father*) Alte, *der* (*salopp*); **hey, ~!** (*as voc.: mister*) hallo, Chef! (*salopp*); **H** (*Mech.*) Regler, *der*

**Governor-'General** *n.* Generalgouverneur, *der*

**governorship** /'gʌvənəʃɪp/ *n.* Gouverneursamt, *das*

**Govt.** *abbr.* **Government** Reg.; Rg.

**gown** /gaʊn/ *n.* **A** [elegantes] Kleid; **bridal/baptismal ~:** Braut-/Taufkleid, *das;* **B** (*official or uniform robe*) Talar, *der;* Robe, *die;* **town and ~:** Bürger und Studenten; **C** (*surgeon's overall*) [Operations]kittel, *der*

**GP** *abbr.* **A** **general practitioner;** **B** **Grand Prix**

**GPO** *abbr.* **A** (*Hist.*) **General Post Office** Post, *die;* **B** (*Amer.*) **Government Printing Office** Staatsdruckerei, *die*

**gr.** *abbr.* **A** **grain[s]** Gran, *der* (*veralt.*); **B** **gram[s]** g; **C** **gross** bto.

**grab** /græb/ **1** *v.t.*, **-bb-:** **A** greifen nach; (*seize*) packen; (*capture, arrest*) schnappen (*ugs.*); **~ sth. away from sb.** jmdm. etw. entreißen; **~ sb. by the arm** *etc.* jmdn. am Arm *usw.* packen; **should we ~ some food** *or* **a bite to eat?** (*coll.*) sollen wir schnell etwas essen?; **could you ~ a table while I ...** (*coll.*) versuch du, einen Tisch zu ergattern, während ich ... (*ugs.*); **I managed to ~ her before she got on the bus** (*stop her*) ich konnte sie gerade noch aufhalten, bevor sie in den Bus stieg; **~ the chance** die Gelegenheit ergreifen; **I would ~ an offer like that** ein solches Angebot würde ich mir nicht entgehen lassen; **~ hold of sb./sth.** sich (*Dat.*) jmdn./etw. schnappen (*ugs.*); **B** (*coll.: impress*) **how does that ~ you?** wie findest du das?; **this doesn't [really] ~ me** das lässt mich [im Grunde] kalt.
**2** *v.i.*, **-bb-** **A** **~ at sth.** nach etw. greifen; **don't ~ like that!** grapsch nicht so! (*ugs.*); **B** (*act jerkily*) ‹Bremse:› ruckartig greifen.
**3** *n.* **A** **make a ~ at** *or* **for sb./sth.** nach jmdm./etw. greifen *od.* (*ugs.*) grapschen; **be up for ~s** (*coll.*) zu erwerben sein; ‹Posten:› frei sein; **B** (*coll.: robbery*) Raubüberfall, *der;* (*burglary*) Bruch, *der* (*ugs.*); **C** (*Mech.*) Greifer, *der.* ⇒ *also* **smash-and-grab [raid]**

**grab: ~ bag** *n.* (*Amer.*) Grabbelsack, *der* (*ugs.*); **~ handle** *n.* Haltegriff, *der;* **~ rail** *n.* Haltestange, *die*

**grace** /greɪs/ **1** *n.* **A** (*charm*) Anmut, *die* (*geh.*); Grazie, *die;* **B** (*attractive feature*) Charme, *der;* **airs and ~s** vornehmes Getue (*ugs. abwertend*); affektiertes Benehmen; **C** (*accomplishment*) **social ~s** Umgangsformen *Pl.;* **D** (*decency*) Anstand, *der;* **have the ~ to do sth.** so anständig sein und etw. tun; **he didn't even have the ~ to apologize** er brachte es nicht einmal fertig, sich zu entschuldigen; (*civility*) **with [a] good/bad ~:** bereitwillig/widerwillig; **he accepted my criticism with good/bad ~:** er trug meine Kritik mit Fassung/nahm meine Kritik mit Verärgerung hin; **E** (*favour*) Wohlwollen, *das;* Gunst, *die;* (*Theol.*) Gnade, *die;* **be in sb.'s good ~s** in jmds. Gunst stehen; bei jmdm. gut angeschrieben sein (*ugs.*); **~ and favour house/residence** *etc. von der Regierung od. Krone zur Verfügung gestelltes Haus/gestellte Residenz usw.;* **act of ~:** Gnadenakt, *der;* **there, but for the ~ of God, go I** es hätte leicht auch mich erwischen können; **by the ~ of God Queen of ...:** von Gottes Gnaden Königin von ...; **state of ~** (*Theol.*) Stand der Gnade; **he fell from ~:** er fiel in Ungnade; **in the year of ~ 1892** (*literary*) im Jahr des Herrn 1892; **F** (*favour shown by granting delay*) Frist, *die;* (*Commerc.*) Zahlungsfrist, *die;* **give sb. a day's ~:** jmdm. einen Tag Aufschub gewähren; **we will grant you two weeks' ~:** wir lassen Ihnen zwei Wochen Zeit; **G** (*prayers*) Tischgebet, *das;* **say ~:** das Tischgebet sprechen; **H** ▶ **1617** *in address* **Your G~:** Euer Gnaden; **I** (*Mus.*) ⇒ **~-note**; **J** (*Greek Mythol.*) **the Graces** die Grazien. ⇒ *also* **saving ~.**
**2** *v.t.* **A** (*adorn*) zieren (*geh.*); schmücken; **B** (*honour*) auszeichnen; ehren; **~ a première by** *or* **with one's presence** eine Premiere mit seiner Anwesenheit beehren (*geh.*)

**graceful** /'greɪsfl/ *adj.* elegant; graziös ‹Bewegung, Eleganz›; geschmeidig ‹Katze, Pferd›

**gracefully** /'greɪsfəlɪ/ *adv.* elegant; graziös ‹tanzen, sich bewegen›; **grow old ~:** mit Würde alt werden

**gracefulness** /'greɪsflnɪs/ *n., no pl.* Eleganz, *die;* (*of movement, form, style*) Grazie, *die*

g

**graceless** /ˈgreɪslɪs/ *adj.* (*lacking sense of decency*) taktlos; (*lacking charm and elegance*) ungehobelt, schroff ‹Benehmen, Person›

**ˈgrace note** *n.* (*Mus.*) Verzierung, *die;* Manier, *die* (*fachspr.*)

**gracious** /ˈgreɪʃəs/ ❶ *adj.* Ⓐ liebenswürdig; freundlich; (*iron./joc.*) gütig; **~ living** kultivierter Lebensstil; **our ~ Queen** unsere gnädige Königin; Ⓑ (*merciful*) gnädig. ❷ *int.* **~!, good[ness] ~!, [goodness] ~ me!** [ach] du meine *od.* liebe Güte!

**graciously** /ˈgreɪʃəslɪ/ *adv.* liebenswürdig; freundlich; (*with condescension*) gnädig

**gradation** /grəˈdeɪʃn/ *n.* Ⓐ *usu. in pl.* (*stage*) **~s of madness/an illness** Stufen *od.* Grade des Wahnsinns/einer Krankheit; Ⓑ (*degree in rank, merit, intensity, etc.*) Stufung, *die;* **~s of colour** Farbskala, *die;* **~ on a thermometer** Gradeinteilung, *die*

**grade** /greɪd/ ❶ *n.* Ⓐ Rang, *der;* (*Mil.*) Dienstgrad, *der;* (*salary ~*) Gehaltsstufe, *die;* (*in things: degree of quality, size, or value*) [Handels-, Güte]klasse, *die;* (*of textiles*) Qualität, *die;* (*position, level*) Stufe, *die;* (*intensity of illness*) Grad, *der;* **what ~ is your job?** in welcher Gehaltsklasse sind Sie?; **a high ~ of intelligence** ein hohes Maß an Intelligenz; Ⓑ (*Amer. Sch.: class*) Klasse, *die;* Ⓒ (*Sch., Univ.: mark*) Note, *die;* Zensur, *die;* **attain ~ B or a higher ~:** eine Zwei oder eine bessere Note erreichen; Ⓓ (*Amer.: gradient*) (*ascent*) Steigung, *die;* (*descent*) Neigung, *die;* **at ~:** auf gleicher Höhe; ebenerdig ‹Wohnung usw.›; Ⓔ **on the up/down ~** (*lit.*) ansteigend/abfallend; (*fig.*) auf dem auf-/absteigenden Ast; **make the ~:** es schaffen.
❷ *v.t.* Ⓐ einstufen ‹Arbeit nach Gehalt, Schüler nach Fähigkeiten, Leistungen›; [nach Größe/Qualität] sortieren ‹Eier, Kartoffeln›; Ⓑ (*mark*) benoten; zensieren.
❸ *v.i.* (*pass gradually*) übergehen (**into** in + *Akk.*)

**ˈgrade crossing** *n.* (*Amer.*) Kreuzung, *die;* (*of railroad tracks and road*) schienengleicher Bahnübergang

**grader** /ˈgreɪdə(r)/ *n.* (*Amer. Sch.*) **a ninth/tenth-~:** ein Schüler der 9./10. Klasse; ein Neunt-/Zehntklässler (*südd., schweiz.*)

**ˈgrade school** *n.* (*Amer.*) Grundschule, *die*

**gradient** /ˈgreɪdɪənt/ *n.* Ⓐ (*amount of slope*) (*ascent*) Steigung, *die;* (*descent*) Gefälle, *das;* (*inclined part of road*) Neigung, *die;* **a ~ of 1 in 10** eine Steigung/ein Gefälle von 10%; Ⓑ ([*rate of*] *rise or fall of temperature etc.*) Gradient, *der* (*bes. Math.*); (*ascent*) Anstieg, *der;* (*descent*) Abfall, *der*

**gradual** /ˈgrædʒʊəl/ *adj.* allmählich; sanft ‹Steigung, Gefälle usw.›

**gradually** /ˈgrædʒʊəlɪ/ *adv.* allmählich; sanft ‹ansteigen, abfallen›

**graduate** ❶ /ˈgrædʒʊət/ *n.* Ⓐ Graduierte, *der/die;* (*who has left university*) Akademiker, *der*/Akademikerin, *die;* **university ~:** Hochschulabsolvent, *der*/-absolventin, *die;* **he is an Oxford ~:** er hat seinen Universitätsabschluss in Oxford gemacht; Ⓑ (*Amer. Sch.*) Schulabgänger, *der*/-abgängerin, *die.*
❷ /ˈgrædʒʊeɪt/ *v.i.* Ⓐ einen akademischen Grad/Titel erwerben; **he ~d from Oxford University** er schloss sein Studium an der Universität von Oxford ab; Ⓑ (*Amer. Sch.*) die [Schul]abschlussprüfung bestehen (**from** an + *Dat.*); Ⓒ (*move up*) **he's ~d from comics to detective stories** er hat sich vom Comicleser zum Krimileser entwickelt; Ⓓ (*pass by degrees*) **~ into** allmählich übergehen in (+ *Akk.*).
❸ /ˈgrædʒʊeɪt/ *v.t.* Ⓐ (*mark out*) mit Gradeinteilung versehen; graduieren (*bes. Technik*) ‹Thermometer›; (*arrange in gradations*) gradweise abstufen; Ⓑ (*Amer. Univ.*) graduieren; (*Amer. Sch.*) aus der Schule entlassen

**graduated** /ˈgrædʒʊeɪtɪd/ *adj.* (*marked with lines*) mit einer Skala versehen; (*arranged in grades*) abgestuft; **~ markings** unterteilte Markierung

**graduate school** /ˈgrædʒʊət skuːl/ *n.* (*Amer.*) *Hochschulabteilung für Fortgeschrittenenstudium*

**graduation** /grædʒʊˈeɪʃn/ *n.* Ⓐ (*Univ.*) Graduierung, *die;* Ⓑ (*Amer. Sch.*) Entlassung, *die;* Ⓒ *attrib.* Abschluss-; Ⓓ (*mark on a scale*) Graduation, *die* (*bes. Technik*)

**graffiti** /grəˈfiːtiː/ *n. sing. or pl.* Graffiti *Pl.; attrib.* **~ artist** Graffitikünstler, *der*/-künstlerin, *die*

**graft¹** /grɑːft/ ❶ *n.* Ⓐ (*Bot.*) (*shoot, scion*) Edelreis, *das;* Pfropfreis, *das;* (*process*) Pfropfung, *die;* (*place*) Pfropfstelle, *die;* Ⓑ (*Med.*) Transplantat, *das;* Ⓒ (*Brit. coll.: work*) Plackerei, *die* (*ugs.*). ❷ *v.t.* Ⓐ (*Bot.*) pfropfen; Ⓑ (*fig.*) **~ sth. on to sth.** etw. einer Sache (*Dat.*) aufpfropfen; Ⓒ (*Med.*) transplantieren (*fachspr.*); verpflanzen. ❸ *v.i.* Ⓐ (*Bot.*) pfropfen; Ⓑ (*Brit. coll.: work*) schuften (*ugs.*)

**graft²** (*coll.*) ❶ *n.* (*dishonesty*) Gaunerei, *die;* (*profit*) Fischzug, *der.* ❷ *v.i.* mit kleinen Gaunereien Geld machen

**grafter** /ˈgrɑːftə(r)/ *n.* (*Brit. coll.*) Ⓐ (*dishonest person*) Gauner, *der;* Ⓑ (*worker*) Wühler, *der* (*ugs.*); Arbeitstier, *das* (*ugs.*)

**Grail** /greɪl/ *n.* **[Holy] ~:** [Heiliger] Gral

**grain** /greɪn/ ❶ *n.* Ⓐ Korn, *das;* (*collect.:* [*species of*] *corn*) Getreide, *das;* Korn, *das;* Ⓑ (*particle*) Korn, *das;* Ⓒ (*unit of weight*) Gran, *das* (*veralt.*); (*fig.: small amount*) **a ~ of truth** ein Gran *od.* Körnchen Wahrheit; **not a ~ of love/sense** kein Fünkchen Liebe/Funke [von] Verstand; Ⓓ (*texture*) Korn, *das* (*fachspr.*); Griff, *der;* (*of fibre in wood*) Maserung, *die;* (*in paper*) Faser, *die;* Faserverlauf, *der;* (*in leather*) Narbung, *die;* **go against the ~ [for sb.]** (*fig.*) jmdm. gegen den Strich gehen (*ugs.*).
❷ *v.t.* körnen ‹Papier›; masern ‹Holz›; narben ‹Leder›

**grained** /greɪnd/ *adj.* gekörnt ‹Papier›; genarbt ‹Leder›; maserig, gemasert ‹Holz›

**ˈgrain elevator** *n.* Getreideheber, *der*

**grainy** /ˈgreɪnɪ/ *adj.* körnig; gemasert ‹Holz›; genarbt ‹Leder›

**gram** /græm/ *n.* ▶ 1683 | Gramm, *das*

**grammar** /ˈgræmə(r)/ *n.* Ⓐ (*also book*) Grammatik, *die;* **sth. is [bad] ~:** etw. ist grammat[ikal]isch [nicht] richtig *od.* korrekt; Ⓑ (*Brit. coll.*) ⇨ **grammar school a**

**ˈgrammar book** *n.* Grammatik, *die;* Sprachlehre, *die*

**grammarian** /grəˈmeərɪən/ *n.* Grammatiker, *der*/Grammatikerin, *die*

**ˈgrammar school** *n.* Ⓐ (*Brit.*) ≈ Gymnasium, *das;* Ⓑ (*Amer.*) ≈ Realschule, *die*

**grammatical** /grəˈmætɪkl/ *adj.* Ⓐ grammat[ikal]isch richtig *od.* korrekt; Ⓑ (*of grammar*) grammatisch

**grammatically** /grəˈmætɪkəlɪ/ *adv.* grammat[ikal]isch ‹richtig, falsch›; **speak English ~:** grammatisch richtiges *od.* korrektes Englisch sprechen

**gramme** ⇨ **gram**

**gramophone** /ˈgræməfəʊn/ *n.* Plattenspieler, *der*

**ˈgramophone record** *n.* Schallplatte, *die*

**gran** /græn/ *n.* (*coll./child lang.*) Oma, *die* (*Kinderspr./ugs.*)

**granary** /ˈgrænərɪ/ *n.* Ⓐ Getreidesilo, *der od. das;* Kornspeicher, *der;* Ⓑ **~ [loaf]** Vollkornbrot, *das* (*mit in die Kruste eingebackenen Getreidekörnern*)

**ˈgranary bread** *n.* Ganzkornbrot, *das*

**grand** /grænd/ ❶ *adj.* Ⓐ (*in official titles: chief*) Groß‹meister, -herzog usw.›; ⇨ *also* **cross 1 G; lodge 1 C;** Ⓑ (*most or very important*) groß; **~ finale** großes Finale; ⇨ *also* **slam²;** Ⓒ (*final*) **~ total** Gesamtsumme, *die;* Ⓓ (*main*) Haupt‹eingang, -raum, -halle usw.›; Ⓔ (*great*) groß ‹Armee, Leidenschaft usw.›; Ⓕ (*splendid*) grandios; (*impressive*) eindrucksvoll ‹Erscheinung, Figur, Person›; (*conducted with solemnity, splendour, etc.*) glanzvoll; **live in ~ style** auf großem Fuß leben; Ⓖ (*distinguished*) vornehm; **put on a ~ air** die Nase hoch tragen (*ugs. abwertend*); Ⓗ (*dignified, lofty*) erhaben; groß ‹Versprechungen, Pläne, Worte›; (*noble, admirable*) ehrwürdig; Ⓘ (*coll.: excellent*) großartig.
❷ *n.* Ⓐ (*piano*) Flügel, *der;* Ⓑ *pl. same* (*coll.: thousand pounds or* (*Amer.*) *dollars*) Riese, *der* (*salopp*)

**grandad** /ˈgrændæd/ *n.* (*coll./child lang.*) Großpapa, *der* (*fam.*); Opa, *der* (*Kinderspr./ugs.*)

**grand: ~aunt** *n.* Großtante, *die;* **~child** *n.* Enkel, *der*/Enkelin, *die;* Enkelkind, *das;* **~dad[dy]** /ˈgrændæd(ɪ)/ *n.* (*coll./child lang.*) *see* **grandad; ~daughter** *n.* Enkelin, *die;* Enkeltochter, *die;* **~ ˈduchess** *n.* Großherzogin, *die;* **~ ˈduchy** *n.* Großherzogtum, *das;* **~ ˈduke** *n.* Großherzog, *der*

**grandee** /grænˈdiː/ *n.* Grande, *der*

**grandeur** /ˈgrændʒə(r), ˈgrændjə(r)/ *n.* Ⓐ Erhabenheit, *die;* Ⓑ (*splendour of living, surroundings, etc.*) Großartigkeit, *die;* Glanz, *der;* **live a life of ~:** in Glanz und Herrlichkeit leben; Ⓒ (*nobility of character*) Größe, *die;* Erhabenheit, *die;* Ⓓ (*power, rank*) Größe, *die;* Macht, *die*

**ˈgrandfather** *n.* Großvater, *der;* **~ clock** Standuhr, *die*

**grandiloquence** /grænˈdɪləkwəns/ *n., no pl.* Großsprecherei, *die* (*abwertend*); (*of style*) Pathos, *das*

**grandiloquent** /grænˈdɪləkwənt/ *adj.* großtönend (*geh. abwertend*); hochtrabend (*abwertend*) ‹Stil, Worte, Rede›

**grandiose** /ˈgrændɪəʊs/ *adj.* Ⓐ (*impressive*) grandios; Ⓑ (*pompous*) bombastisch (*abwertend*); großtönend (*geh. abwertend*) ‹Worte, Art›

**grand ˈjury** *n.* (*Hist./Amer.*) Großes Geschworenengericht

**grandly** /ˈgrændlɪ/ *adv.* großartig; aufwendig ‹sich kleiden›; in großem Stil ‹leben›

**grand: ~ma[ma]** *n.* (*coll./child lang.*) Großmama, *die* (*fam.*); Oma, *die* (*Kinderspr./ugs.*); **~ ˈmaster** *n.* Großmeister, *der;* **~mother** *n.* Großmutter, *die;* ⇨ *also* **egg¹; G~ ˈNational** *n.* (*Brit. Horseracing*) Grand National, *das;* **~nephew** *n.* Großneffe, *der*

**grandness** /ˈgrændnɪs/ *n., no pl.* Großartigkeit, *die;* (*pomp*) Pracht[fülle], *die*

**grand: ~niece** *n.* Großnichte, *die;* **~ old man** *n.* Grand Old Man, *der; älteste bedeutende männliche Persönlichkeit in einem bestimmten Bereich;* **G~ Old Party** *n.* (*Amer.*) Republikanische Partei; **~ ˈopera** *n.* große Oper; **~pa[pa]** *n.* (*coll./child lang.*) Großpapa, *der* (*fam.*); Opa, *der* (*Kinderspr./ugs.*); **~parent** *n.* (*male*) Großvater, *der;* (*female*) Großmutter, *die;* **~parents** Großeltern *Pl.;* **~ piˈano** *n.* [Konzert]flügel, *der;* **G~ Prix** /grɑ̃ ˈpriː/ *n.* Grand Prix, *der;* **~sire** *n.* (*arch.*) (*~father*) Großvater, *der;* (*ancestor*) Ahne, *der* (*geh.*); **~son** *n.* Enkel, *der;* Enkelsohn, *der;* **~stand** *n.* [Haupt]tribüne, *die;* **~stand finish** packendes Finish; **~stand view** guter Überblick (**of** über + *Akk.*); **~stand play** (*Amer.*) Effekthascherei, *die;* **~ ˈtour** *n.* Ⓐ (*Hist.*) Bildungsreise, *die;* Kavalierstour, *die;* Ⓑ (*fig.*) große Fahrt *od.* Reise (*scherzh.*); **make the ~ tour of** auf große Fahrt *od.* Reise gehen zu (*scherzh.*); **~uncle** *n.* Großonkel, *der*

**grange** /greɪndʒ/ *n.* Gutshof, *der;* Landsitz, *der*

**granite** /ˈgrænɪt/ *n.* Ⓐ Granit, *der;* Ⓑ (*fig.: unyieldingness*) Unnachgiebigkeit, *die*

**granny (grannie)** /ˈgrænɪ/ *n.* Ⓐ (*coll./child lang.*) Großmama, *die* (*fam.*); Oma, *die* (*Kinderspr./ugs.*); Ⓑ ⇨ **granny knot**

**granny: ~ flat** *n.* Einliegerwohnung, *die;* **~ knot** *n.* Altweiberknoten, *der* (*Seemannsspr.*)

**grant** /grɑːnt/ ❶ *v.t.* Ⓐ (*consent to fulfil*) erfüllen ‹Wunsch›; erhören ‹Gebet, Flehen›; stattgeben (+ *Dat.*) ‹Gesuch›; gewähren ‹Gunst›; **~ sb. his wish** jmdm. seinen Wunsch erfüllen; Ⓑ (*concede, give*) gewähren; gestatten ‹Blick›; geben ‹Zeit›; bewilligen ‹Geldmittel›; verleihen ‹akademischen Grad, Auszeichnung›; zugestehen ‹Recht›; erteilen ‹Erlaubnis›; (*transfer legally*) übertragen (**to** auf + *Akk.*); Ⓒ (*in argument*) zugeben; einräumen (*geh.*); **~ed that ...:** zugegeben, dass ...; **~ing this to be true** *or* **that this is true** nehmen wir einmal an, dass das stimmt; **take sb./sth. [too much] for ~ed** sich (*Dat.*) jmds. [allzu] sicher sein/etw. für [allzu] selbstverständlich halten; **he's a good fellow, [that] I ~ you** er ist ein guter Kumpel *od.* Kerl, das gebe ich zu; **I beg your pardon — G~ed** Entschuldigen Sie! — Bitte; **nobody likes to be taken for ~ed** keiner mag es, wenn man sich nicht um ihn bemüht.

**2** *n.* **A** (*sum of money*) Zuschuss, *der;* (*financial aid* [*to student*]) [Studien]beihilfe, *die;* (*scholarship*) Stipendium, *das;* **B** (*conceding, allowing*) (*of request, respite*) Gewährung, *die;* (*of pension, holiday*) Bewilligung, *die;* (*of award, degree*) Verleihung, *die;* (*of permission*) Erteilung, *die*

**'grant-aided school** *n.* (*Brit.*) subventionierte Schule

**grant-in-'aid** *n., pl.* **grants-in-aid** (*Educ.*) [staatlicher Schul]zuschuss

**granular** /'grænjʊlə(r)/ *adj.* körnig; granulös (*Med.*)

**granulate** /'grænjʊleɪt/ *v.t.* granulieren (*bes. Technik*); **~d sugar** [Zucker]raffinade, *die;* Kristallzucker, *der*

**granule** /'grænju:l/ *n.* Körnchen, *das*

**grape** /greɪp/ *n.* Weintraube, *die;* Weinbeere, *die;* **a bunch of ~s** eine Traube; **the juice of the ~** (*literary*) der Saft der Rebe[n] (*dichter.*); **[it's] sour ~s** (*fig.*) die Trauben hängen zu hoch

**grape: ~fruit** *n., pl. same* Grapefruit, *die;* **~ harvest** *n.* Weinlese, *die;* **~ 'hyacinth** *n.* Traubenhyazinthe, *die;* **~ juice** *n.* Traubensaft, *der;* **~-shot** *n., pl. same* (*Mil. Hist.*) Kartätsche, *die;* **~vine** *n.* **A** Wein, *der;* **B** (*fig.*) **the ~vine** die Flüsterpropaganda; **I heard [it] on the ~vine that they were getting married** es wird geflüstert, dass sie heiraten wollen

**graph** /græf, grɑ:f/ **1** *n.* grafische Darstellung; Graph, *der* (*Math.*). **2** *v.t.* grafisch darstellen

**graphic** /'græfɪk/ **1** *adj.* **A** grafisch; **~ art** Grafik, *die;* **~ artist** Grafiker, *der*/Grafikerin, *die;* **B** (*clear, vivid*) plastisch; anschaulich; **in ~ detail** in allen Einzelheiten. **2** *n.* **A** (*product*) Grafik, *die;* **B** *in pl.* ⇒ **graphics**

**graphical** /'græfɪkl/ ⇒ **graphic 1**

**graphically** /'græfɪkəlɪ/ *adv.* **A** (*clearly, vividly*) plastisch; anschaulich; **B** (*by use of graphic methods*) grafisch

**graphic 'arts** *n. pl.* Grafik, *die*

**graphics** /'græfɪks/ *n.* (*design and decoration*) grafische Gestaltung; (*use of diagrams*) grafische Darstellung; **computer ~:** Computergraphik, *die*

**graphite** /'græfaɪt/ *n.* Graphit, *der*

**graphologist** /grə'fɒlədʒɪst/ *n.* ▶ **1261** Graphologe, *der*/Graphologin, *die*

**graphology** /grə'fɒlədʒɪ/ *n.* Graphologie, *die*

**'graph paper** *n.* Diagrammpapier, *das*

**grapnel** /'græpnəl/ *n.* Draggen, *der* (*bes. Seew.*); Dreghaken, *der;* (*to seize ship*) Enterhaken, *der*

**grapple** /'græpl/ **1** *v.i.* (*in fighting*) handgemein werden; **they ~d together** (*Wrestling*) sie rangen miteinander; **~ with** (*fig.*) sich auseinander setzen *od.* (*ugs.*) herumschlagen mit; **~ with death** mit dem Tode ringen. **2** *v.t.* **A** (*seize, fasten*) [mit Enterhaken] festhaken ‹Schiff›; (*drag*) [mit Dreghaken] absuchen ‹Fluss›; **B** (*grip with hands*) packen

**grappling** /'græplɪŋ/: **~-hook, ~-iron** ⇒ **grapnel**

**grasp** /grɑ:sp/ **1** *v.i.* **~ at** (*lit. or fig.*) ergreifen; sich stürzen auf (+ *Akk.*) ‹Angebot›; ⇒ *also* **straw B**.

**2** *v.t.* **A** (*clutch at, seize*) ergreifen (*auch fig.*); **manage to ~:** zu fassen bekommen; **B** (*hold firmly*) festhalten; **~ sb. in one's arms** jmdn. [fest] in den Armen halten; **~ the nettle** (*fig.*) das Problem beherzt anpacken; **C** (*understand*) verstehen; erfassen ‹Bedeutung›.

**3** *n.* **A** (*firm hold*) Griff, *der;* **twist from sb.'s ~:** sich jmds. Griff (*Dat.*) entwinden; **he had my hand in a firm ~:** er hielt meine Hand mit festem Griff; **tighten/loosen one's ~:** fester zupacken/den Griff lockern; **sth. is within/beyond sb.'s ~:** etwas ist in/außer jmds. Reichweite (*Dat.*); **success was almost within/was completely beyond his ~** (*fig.*) der Erfolg war zum Greifen nah/in unerreichbarer Ferne; **B** (*mental hold*) **have a good ~ of sth.** etw. gut beherrschen; **his ~ of this subject is remarkable** er beherrscht das Thema außergewöhnlich gut; **sth. is beyond/within sb.'s ~:** etw. überfordert jmds. [intellektuelle] Fähigkeiten/kann von jmdm. verstanden werden

**graspable** /'grɑ:spəbl/ *adj.* (*fig.*) verständlich

**grasping** /'grɑ:spɪŋ/ *adj.* (*greedy*) habgierig

**grass** /grɑ:s/ **1** *n.* **A** Gras, *das;* **be as green as ~** (*fig.*) noch feucht hinter den Ohren sein (*ugs.*); **not let the ~ grow under one's feet** (*fig. coll.*) die Sache nicht auf die lange Bank schieben (*ugs.*); **the ~ is always greener on the other side [of the hill** *or* **fence]** (*prov.*) die Kirschen aus Nachbars Garten schmecken immer viel besser; **B** *no pl.* (*lawn*) Rasen, *der;* **C** *no pl.* (*grazing, pasture*) Weide, *die;* (*pastureland*) Weideland, *das;* **be out at ~:** auf der Weide sein; **put** *or* **turn out to ~:** auf die Weide treiben *od.* führen; (*fig.*) in den Ruhestand versetzen; nicht mehr zur Arbeit einsetzen ‹Pferd›; **D** (*sl.: marijuana*) Grass, *das* (*ugs.*); **E** (*Brit. sl.: police informer*) Spitzel, *der.*

**2** *v.t.* **A** (*cover with turf*) mit Rasen bedecken; **B** (*Brit. sl.: betray*) verpfeifen (*ugs.*).

**3** *v.i.* (*Brit. sl.: inform police*) singen (*salopp*); **~ on sb.** jmdn. verpfeifen (*ugs.*)

**grass: ~box** *n.* Grasfangkorb, *der;* **~ 'court** *n.* Rasenplatz, *der;* Grasplatz, *der;* **~-green** *adj.* grasgrün; **~hopper** *n.* Grashüpfer, *der;* ⇒ *also* **knee-high**; **~land** *n.* Grasland, *das;* (*for grazing*) Weideland, *das;* **~-root[s]** *attrib. adj.* (*Polit.*) Basis-; **~ roots** *n. pl.* (*fig.*) (*source*) Wurzeln *Pl.;* (*Polit.*) Basis, *die;* **~ seed** *n.* Grassamen, *der;* **~ 'skirt** *n.* Baströckchen, *das;* **~ snake** *n.* **A** (*Brit.: ringed snake*) Ringelnatter, *die;* **B** (*Amer.: green snake*) Grasnatter, *die;* **~ widow** *n.* Strohwitwe, *die* (*ugs. scherzh.*); **~ widower** *n.* Strohwitwer, *der* (*ugs. scherzh.*)

**grassy** /'grɑ:sɪ/ *adj.* mit Gras bewachsen

**grate**[1] /greɪt/ *n.* Rost, *der;* (*fireplace*) Kamin, *der*

**grate**[2] **1** *v.t.* **A** (*reduce to particles*) reiben; (*less finely*) raspeln; **B** (*grind*) **~ one's teeth in anger/in one's sleep** vor Wut/im Schlaf mit den Zähnen knirschen; **C** (*utter in harsh tone*) [durch die Zähne] knirschen. **2** *v.i.* **A** (*rub*) knirschen; **the door ~s [up]on its hinges** die Tür knirscht in den Angeln; **B** (*have irritating effect*) **~ [up]on sb./sb.'s nerves** jmdm. auf die Nerven gehen; **C** (*sound harshly*) knirschen; **her shrill voice ~d [up]on our ears** ihre schrille Stimme gellte uns in den Ohren

**grateful** /'greɪtfl/ *adj.* **A** dankbar (**to** *Dat.*); **a ~ word of thanks** ein herzliches Wort des Dankes; **B** (*pleasant, agreeable*) wohltuend

**gratefully** /'greɪtfəlɪ/ *adv.* dankbar; **thank sb. ~:** jmdm. aufrichtig danken

**grater** /'greɪtə(r)/ *n.* Reibe, *die;* (*less fine*) Raspel, *die*

**gratification** /grætɪfɪ'keɪʃn/ *n.* **A** (*pleasure*) Genugtuung, *die;* **the ~ of doing sth.** die Genugtuung, etw. zu tun; **B** (*satisfaction*) ⇒ **gratify B**: Befriedigung, *die;* Erfüllung, *die;* Stillung, *die*

**gratify** /'grætɪfaɪ/ *v.t.* **A** (*please*) freuen; **be gratified by** *or* **with** *or* **at sth.** über etw. (*Akk.*) erfreut sein; **I was gratified** *or* **it gratified me to hear that ...:** mit Genugtuung erfuhr ich, dass ...; **B** (*satisfy*) befriedigen ‹Neugier, Bedürfnis, Eitelkeit›; erfüllen ‹Wunsch›; stillen ‹Sehnsucht, Verlangen›

**gratifying** /'grætɪfaɪɪŋ/ *adj.* erfreulich

**gratin** /'grætæ̃/ *n.* (*Cookery*) Gratin, *das;* **cauliflower au ~** /əʊ 'grætæ̃/ gratinierter Blumenkohl

**grating** /'greɪtɪŋ/ *n.* (*framework*) Gitter, *das*

**gratis** /'greɪtɪs, 'grætɪs, 'grɑ:tɪs/ **1** *adv.* gratis, kostenlos ‹bekommen, abgeben›; umsonst, unentgeltlich ‹tun›. **2** *adj.* gratis *nicht attr.;* Gratis‹mahlzeit, -vorstellung usw.›

**gratitude** /'grætɪtju:d/ *n., no pl.* Dankbarkeit, *die* (**to** gegenüber); **show one's ~ to sb.** sich jmdm. gegenüber dankbar zeigen

**gratuitous** /grə'tju:ɪtəs/ *adj.* **A** (*uncalled-for, motiveless*) grundlos; unnötig; (*without logical reason*) unbegründet; **B** (*got or given free*) unentgeltlich ‹Dienstleistung›

**gratuitously** /grə'tju:ɪtəslɪ/ *adv.* **A** (*without motive or reason*) ohne Grund; **B** (*free of cost*) unentgeltlich

**gratuity** /grə'tju:ɪtɪ/ *n.* **A** (*formal: tip*) Trinkgeld, *das;* **B** (*Brit.: bounty*) Sonderzuwendung, *die*

**graunch** /grɔ:nʃ/ **1** *v.t.* **~ the gears** knirschend schalten. **2** *v.i.* (*make grinding sound*) knirschen

**grave**[1] /greɪv/ *n.* Grab, *das;* **the house was as quiet** *or* **silent** *or* **still as the ~:** im Haus herrschte Grabesstille; **dig one's own ~** (*fig.*) sich (*Dat.*) selbst sein Grab graben (*fig.*); **he would turn in his ~** (*fig.*) er würde sich im Grabe herumdrehen; **sb. is walking on** *or* **over my/his** *etc.* **~** (*fig.*) es überläuft mich/ihn *usw.* eiskalt; **carry a scar** *etc.* **to one's ~:** eine Narbe *usw.* bis an sein Lebensende tragen; **a message from beyond the ~:** eine Botschaft aus dem Jenseits; **take a secret to the ~:** ein Geheimnis mit ins Grab nehmen; ⇒ *also* **cradle 1 A**; **foot 1 A**

**grave**[2] *adj.* **A** (*important, dignified, solemn*) ernst; **B** (*formidable, serious*) schwer, gravierend ‹Fehler, Irrtum, Verfehlung›; ernst ‹Situation, Lage, Schwierigkeit›; groß ‹Gefahr, Risiko, Verantwortung›; schlimm ‹Nachricht, Zeichen›

**grave**[3] /grɑ:v, greɪv/ *adj.* (*Ling.*) **~ accent** Accent grave, *der;* Gravis, *der*

**gravedigger** /'greɪvdɪgə(r)/ *n.* ▶ **1261** Totengräber, *der*

**gravel** /'grævl/ **1** *n.* **A** (*small stones*) Kies, *der; attrib.* **~ path/pit** Kiesweg, *der*/-grube, *die;* **B** (*Geol., Mining*) Geröll, *das;* **C** (*Med.*) **[bladder/kidney] ~:** Harn-/Nierengrieß, *der.* **2** *v.t.,* (*Brit.*) **-ll-** kiesen

**gravelly** /'grævəlɪ/ *adj.* **A** kieshaltig ‹Boden›; **B** rau, heiser ‹Stimme›

**gravely** /'greɪvlɪ/ *adv.* **A** (*in grave manner*) ernst; **B** (*seriously*) ernstlich; **be ~ mistaken** sich schwer irren (*ugs.*)

**graven image** /greɪvn 'ɪmɪdʒ/ *n.* Götzenbild, *das*

**grave** /greɪv/: **~side** *n.* **at the ~side** am Grab; **~stone** *n.* Grabstein, *der;* **~yard** *n.* Friedhof, *der;* **be a ~yard of reputations** manch einen guten Ruf zerstört haben

**graving dock** /'greɪvɪŋ dɒk/ ⇒ **dry dock**

**gravitas** /'grævɪtɑ:s/ *n.* (*literary*) Gravität, *die* (*veralt.*)

**gravitate** /'grævɪteɪt/ *v.i.* gravitieren (*Phys., Astron., geh.*); **young people ~ to[wards] the cities** junge Leute zieht es in die Städte

**gravitation** /grævɪ'teɪʃn/ *n.* Gravitation, *die;* Schwerkraft, *die;* (*fig.*) Streben, *das*

**gravitational** /grævɪ'teɪʃənl/ *adj.* Gravitations‹feld, -energie usw.›; **~ pull** Anziehungskraft, *die;* **~ force** Schwerkraft, *die*

**gravity** /'grævɪtɪ/ *n.* **A** (*solemnity*) Feierlichkeit, *die;* **B** (*importance*) (*of mistake, offence*) Schwere, *die;* (*of situation*) Ernst, *der;* **C** (*seriousness, staidness*) Ernst, *der;* **the ~ of his manner** seine Ernsthaftigkeit; **keep** *or* **preserve one's ~:** ernst bleiben; **D** (*Phys., Astron.*) Gravitation, *die;* Schwerkraft, *die;* **the law/force of ~:** das Gravitationsgesetz/die Schwerkraft; **centre of ~** (*lit. or fig.*) Schwerpunkt, *der;* **specific ~** (*Phys.*) spezifisches Gewicht; Wichte, *die* (*fachspr.*)

**'gravity feed** *n.* Schwerkraftzufuhr, *die* (*Technik*)

**gravy** /'greɪvɪ/ *n.* **A** (*juices*) Bratensaft, *der;* **B** (*dressing*) [Braten]soße, *die;* **C** (*coll.: money*) Nebenverdienst, *der;* (*tip*) Trinkgeld, *das*

**gravy: ~ boat** *n.* Sauciere, *die;* Soßenschüssel, *die;* **~ train** *n.* **ride/board the ~ train** (*coll.*) leichtes Geld machen (*ugs.*)

**gray** *etc.* (*Amer.*) ⇒ **grey** *etc.*

**grayling** /'greɪlɪŋ/ *n., pl. same* (*Zool.*) Äsche, *die*

g

**graze**[1] /greɪz/ **1** *v.i.* **A** grasen; weiden; **B** (*snack*) zwischendurch dies und jenes naschen; **I had been grazing all day** ich hatte den ganzen Tag herumgenascht (*ugs.*); **~ on sth.** etw. essen *od.* naschen. **2** *v.t.* **A** (*feed*) weiden ‹Schafe, Rinder›; **B** (*feed on*) abweiden ‹Feld, Wiese›

**graze**[2] **1** *n.* Schürfwunde, *die.* **2** *v.t.* **A** (*touch lightly*) streifen; **B** (*scrape*) abschürfen ‹Haut›; zerkratzen ‹Oberfläche›; **~ one's knee/elbow** sich (*Dat.*) das Knie/den Ellbogen aufschürfen. **3** *v.i.* **~ against/by** *or* **past the wall** an der Mauer entlang-/vorbeischrammen

**grazier** /'greɪzɪə(r), 'greɪʒə(r)/ *n.* **A** Viehzüchter, *der;* **B** (*Austral.: sheep farmer*) Schafzüchter, *der*

**grazing** /'greɪzɪŋ/ **1** *n.* (*feeding*) Weiden, *das;* (*land*) Weide, *die;* Weideland, *das.* **2** *adj.* weidend; **~ land** Weideland, *das;* **~ rights** Weiderecht, *das*

**grease** **1** [gri:s] *n.* Fett, *das;* (*lubricant*) Schmierfett, *das.* **2** [gri:z, gri:s] *v.t.* einfetten; einreiben ‹Haut, Rücken usw.›; (*lubricate*) schmieren; **like ~d lightning** (*coll.*) wie ein geölter Blitz (*ugs.*); **~ sb.'s palm** (*fig.*) jmdn. schmieren (*salopp abwertend*); **~ the wheels** (*fig.*) der Sache (*Dat.*) nachhelfen

**grease:** **~ gun** *n.* Fettpresse, *die* (*Technik*); **~ monkey** *n.* (*coll.*) Schmiermaxe, *der* (*ugs.*); **~paint** *n.* [Fett]schminke, *die;* **~proof** *adj.* fettdicht; **~proof paper** Pergament- *od.* Butterbrotpapier, *das*

**greasy** /'gri:zɪ, 'gri:sɪ/ *adj.* **A** fettig; fett ‹Essen›; speckig ‹Kleidung›; (*lubricated*) geschmiert; (*slippery, dirty with lubricant*) schmierig; **B** (*fig.: unctuous*) schmierig (*abwertend*)

**great** /greɪt/ **1** *adj.* **A** (*large*) groß; **~ big** (*coll.*) riesengroß (*ugs.*); **~ thick** (*coll.*) mordsdick (*ugs.*); **give sb. a ~ big hug** (*coll.*) jmdn. mit großer Herzlichkeit umarmen; **a ~ many** sehr viele; **a ~ amount of patience** eine Menge Geduld (*ugs.*); ⇨ *also* **deal**[2]; **B** (*beyond the ordinary*) groß; sehr gut ‹Freund›; sehr schwer ‹Krise›; **a ~ [old] age** ein hohes Alter; **take ~ care of/a ~ interest in** sich sehr kümmern um/interessieren für; **C** (*important*) groß ‹Tag, Ereignis, Attraktion, Hilfe›; (*powerful, influential, of remarkable ability*) groß ‹Person, Komponist, Schriftsteller›; (*impressive*) großartig; **the ~ thing is** die Hauptsache ist; *in titles or names* **Peter the G~:** Peter der Große; *in excl.* **G~ Scott!** großer Gott!; (*having much skill*) **be ~ at sth.** in etw. (*Dat.*) ganz groß sein (*ugs.*); (*having much knowledge*) **be ~ on modern music** in zeitgenössischer Musik sehr beschlagen sein (*ugs.*); **be a ~ one for sth.** etw. sehr gern tun; ⇨ *also* **spirit** 1 H; **D** (*coll.: splendid*) großartig; **E** (*in relationship*) Groß‹onkel, -tante, -neffe, -nichte›; Ur‹großmutter, -großvater, -enkel, -enkelin›; **~-~-** Urgroß‹onkel, -tante, -neffe, -nichte›; Urur‹großmutter, -großvater, -enkel, -enkelin›.
**2** *n.* **A** (*person*) Größe, *die;* **literary/football ~s** literarische Größen/Fußballgrößen; *as pl.* **the ~:** die Großen [der Geschichte/Literatur *usw.*]; **the ~est** (*coll.*) der/die Größte/die Größten (*ugs.*); **B** **G~s** (*Brit. Univ.*) klassische Philologie

**Great:** **~ 'Bear** *n.* (*Astron.*) Großer Bär; **~ 'Britain** *pr. n.* Großbritannien (*das*); **g~coat** *n.* [Winter]mantel, *der;* **~ 'Dane** *n.* Deutsche Dogge

**Greater:** **~ 'London** *pr. n.* Groß-London; **~ London 'Council** *n.* (*Hist.*) Stadtrat von Groß-London

**great:** **~-hearted** *adj.* hochherzig; großmütig; **~ 'house** *n.* Gutshaus, *das;* Herrenhaus, *das;* **the ~ houses of England** englische Schlösser und Adelssitze; **G~ 'Lakes** *pr. n. pl.* Große Seen *Pl.*

**greatly** /'greɪtlɪ/ *adv.* sehr; höchst ‹verärgert›; stark ‹beeinflusst, beunruhigt›; weit ‹überlegen›; bedeutend ‹verbessert›; **sth. is ~ to be feared** etw. muss ernstlich befürchtet werden; **it doesn't ~ matter** es ist nicht so wichtig

**greatness** /'greɪtnɪs/ *n., no pl.* Größe, *die;* (*extent, degree*) Ausmaß, *das;* **~ of heart/mind/soul** Hochherzigkeit, *die*/Großmut, *die*/Seelengröße, *die*

**Great:** **~ 'Power** *n.* Großmacht, *die;* **~ Salt 'Lake** *pr. n.* Großer Salzsee; **g~ tit** *n.* (*Ornith.*) Kohlmeise, *die;* **g~ 'toe** *n.* großer Zeh; **~ 'War** *n.* Erster Weltkrieg

**grebe** /gri:b/ *n.* (*Ornith.*) Lappentaucher, *der*

**Grecian** /'gri:ʃn/ **1** *adj.* griechisch. **2** *n.* Grieche, *der*/Griechin, *die*

**Greece** /gri:s/ *pr. n.* Griechenland (*das*)

**greed** /gri:d/ *n.* Gier, *die* (**for** nach); (*gluttony*) Gefräßigkeit, *die* (*abwertend*); (*of animal*) Fressgier, *die;* **~ for money/power** Geld-/Machtgier, *die*

**greedily** /'gri:dɪlɪ/ *adv.* gierig

**greediness** /'gri:dɪnɪs/ *n., no pl.* Gier, *die*

**greedy** /'gri:dɪ/ *adj.* gierig; (*gluttonous*) gefräßig (*abwertend*); (*eager*) begierig; **be ~ for sth.** nach etw. gieren; **~ for money/power/success** geldgierig/machthungrig/erfolgshungrig; **be ~ to do/get sth.** etw. unbedingt tun/bekommen wollen

**'greedy-guts** *n. sing.* (*coll.*) Vielfraß, *der* (*ugs.*)

**Greek** /gri:k/ ▶ 1275, ▶ 1340 **1** *adj.* griechisch; **sb. is ~:** jmd. ist Grieche/Griechin; ⇨ *also* **calends**; **English** 1. **2** *n.* **A** (*person*) Grieche, *der*/Griechin, *die;* **B** (*language*) Griechisch, *das;* **modern ~:** Neugriechisch, *das;* **it's all ~ to me** (*fig.*) das sind mir *od.* für mich böhmische Dörfer; ⇨ *also* **English** 2 A

**Greek:** **~ 'Church** ⇨ **~ Orthodox Church**; **~ 'god** *n.* (*fig.*) Adonis, *der;* **~ Orthodox 'Church** *n.* griechisch-orthodoxe Kirche

**green** /gri:n/ **1** *adj.* **A** grün; **have ~ fingers** *or* **a ~ thumb** (*fig.*) eine grüne Hand haben (*ugs.*); **~ vegetables** Grüngemüse, *das;* **B** (*Polit.*) **G~:** grün; **he/she is ~:** er ist ein Grüner/sie ist eine Grüne; **the Greens** die Grünen; **C** (*environmentally safe*) ökologisch; **D** (*unripe, young, tender*) grün ‹Obst, Apfel, Banane, Zweig›; **E** (*not dried, seasoned, smoked, or tanned*) grün ‹Holz, Speck, Heringe›; nicht gegerbt ‹Fell›; **F** (*pale*) **his face turned ~ at the sight of the blood** beim Anblick des Blutes wurde er ganz grün im Gesicht; **be/turn ~ with envy/jealousy** vor Neid/Eifersucht grün sein/werden; **G** (*immature, naïve*) unreif; (*gullible*) naiv; einfältig; (*inexperienced*) grün.
**2** *n.* **A** (*colour*) Grün, *das;* **B** (*piece of land*) Grünfläche, *die;* **village ~:** Dorfanger, *der;* **C** *in pl.* (**~** *vegetables*) Grüngemüse, *das;* **D** (*verdure, vegetation*) Grün, *das;* **E** (*Snooker*) grüne Kugel; **F** (**~** *clothes*) **dressed in ~:** grün gekleidet; **G** (*traffic light*) Grün, *das;* **the traffic light is at ~:** die Ampel steht auf Grün.

**green:** **~back** *n.* (*Amer.*) [Geld]schein, *der;* **~ 'belt** *n.* Grüngürtel, *der;* **~ 'card** *n.* (*Insurance*) grüne Karte (*Verkehrsw.*)

**greenery** /'gri:nərɪ/ *n., no pl.* Grün, *das*

**green:** **~-eyed** *adj.* grünäugig; (*fig.*) neidisch; **be ~-eyed** grüne Augen haben; **~-'field site** *n.* Bauplatz im Grünen; **~finch** *n.* Grünfink, *der;* **~fly** *n.* (*Brit.*) grüne Blattlaus; **~gage** *n.* Reineclaude, *die;* **~grocer** *n.* ▶ 1261 (*Brit.*) Obst- und Gemüsehändler, *der*/-händlerin, *die;* ⇨ *also* **baker**; **~grocery** *n.* (*Brit.*) **A** Obst- und Gemüsehandlung, *die;* **B** *in sing. or pl.* (*goods*) Obst und Gemüse; **~horn** *n.* Greenhorn, *das;* **~house** *n.* Gewächshaus, *das;* **~house effect** Treibhauseffekt, *der;* **~house gas** Treibhausgas, *das*

**greenish** /'gri:nɪʃ/ *adj.* grünlich

**'greenkeeper** *n.* (*Golf*) Golfwart, *der*

**Greenland** /'gri:nlənd/ *pr. n.* Grönland (*das*)

**Greenlander** /'gri:nləndə(r)/ *n.* ▶ 1340 Grönländer, *der*/Grönländerin, *die*

**green 'light** *n.* **A** grünes Licht; (*as signal*) Grün, *das;* **it's a ~:** die Ampel ist grün; **B** (*fig. coll.*) **give sb./get the ~:** jmdm. grünes Licht geben/grünes Licht erhalten

**greenness** /'gri:nnɪs/ *n., no pl.* **A** (*of colour*) Grün, *das;* grüne Farbe; **B** (*of sth. covered with herbage*) Grün, *das;* **C** (*unripeness*) grüner Zustand; **D** (*fig.: youth, immaturity*) Unreife, *die;* (*inexperience*) Unerfahrenheit, *die;* (*gullibility*) Naivität, *die;* Einfalt, *die*

**green:** **G~ 'Paper** *n.* (*Brit.*) *öffentliches Diskussionspapier über die Regierungspolitik;* **G~ Party** *n.* (*Polit.*) die Grünen; **~ 'pepper** ⇨ **pepper** 1 B; **~ revo'lution** *n.* grüne Revolution; **~-room** *n.* (*Theatre*) Konversationszimmer, *das;* **~sward** *n.* (*literary*) Grünfläche, *die*

**Greenwich** /'grɪnɪdʒ, 'grenɪdʒ, 'grɪnɪtʃ, 'grenɪtʃ/ *n.* **~ [mean] time** Greenwicher Zeit; [mittlere] Greenwich-Zeit

**'greenwood** *n.* [grüner] Wald

**greet** /gri:t/ *v.t.* **A** begrüßen; (*in passing*) grüßen; (*receive*) empfangen; **~ sb. with sth.** jmdn. mit etw. begrüßen/grüßen/empfangen; **B** (*meet*) empfangen; **~ sb.'s eyes/ears** sich jmds. Augen (*Dat.*) darbieten/an jmds. Ohr (*Akk.*) dringen

**greeting** /'gri:tɪŋ/ *n.* ▶ 1191 Begrüßung, *die;* (*in passing*) Gruß, *der;* (*words*) Grußformel, *die;* (*reception*) Empfang, *der;* **please give my ~s to your parents** grüßen Sie bitte Ihre Eltern von mir; **my husband also sends his ~s** mein Mann lässt auch grüßen

**greeting:** **~[s] card** *n.* Grußkarte, *die;* (*for anniversary, birthday*) Glückwunschkarte, *die;* **~[s] telegram** *n.* Glückwunschtelegramm, *das*

**gregarious** /grɪ'geərɪəs/ *adj.* **A** (*Zool.*) gesellig; Herden‹tier, -trieb›; **B** (*fond of company*) gesellig

**gregariousness** /grɪ'geərɪəsnɪs/ *n., no pl.* **A** (*Zool.*) Herdenleben, *das;* **B** (*of person*) Geselligkeit, *die*

**Gregorian** /grɪ'gɔ:rɪən/ *adj.* gregorianisch; **~ calendar/chant** gregorianischer Kalender/Gesang

**Gregory** /'gregərɪ/ *pr. n.* (*Hist., as name of pope*) Gregor

**gremlin** /'gremlɪn/ *n.* (*coll. joc.*) ≈ Kobold, *der*

**grenade** /grɪ'neɪd/ *n.* Granate, *die;* ⇨ *also* **hand grenade**

**Grenadier Guards** /grenədɪə(r) 'gɑ:dz/ *n. pl.* (*Brit.*) Grenadiergarde, *die*

**grew** ⇨ **grow**

**grey** /greɪ/ **1** *adj.* **A** (*lit. or fig.*) grau; **he** *or* **his hair went** *or* **turned ~:** er wurde grau *od.* ergraute; **grow ~ in sb.'s service** (*fig.*) in jmds. Diensten ergrauen; **~ area** (*fig.*) Grauzone, *die;* **B** (*anonymous*) gesichtslos ‹Person›. **2** *n.* **A** Grau, *das;* **B** (**~** *clothes*) **dressed in ~:** grau gekleidet; **C** (*horse*) Grauschimmel, *der*

**grey:** **~beard** *n.* Graubart, *der* (*ugs.*); **~ cells** *n. pl.* graue Substanz (*Anat.*); **~ e'conomy** *n.* graue Wirtschaft; **~ 'eminence** ⇨ **éminence grise**; **G~ Friar** *n.* Franziskaner, *der;* **~ goose** *n.* Graugans, *die;* **~-haired, ~-headed** *adjs.* grauhaarig; **~-hen** *n.* Birkhenne, *die*

**'greyhound** *n.* Windhund, *der*

**'greyhound racing** *n.* Windhundrennen, *das*

**greyish** /'greɪɪʃ/ *adj.* gräulich

**greylag** /'greɪlæg/ *n.* **~ [goose]** Graugans, *die*

**grey:** **~ matter** *n.* graue Substanz (*Anat.*); (*fig.: intelligence*) graue Zellen; **~ 'squirrel** *n.* Grauhörnchen, *das*

**grid** /grɪd/ *n.* **A** (*grating*) Rost, *der;* **B** (*of lines*) Gitter[netz], *das;* **C** (*for supply*) [Versorgungs]netz, *das;* **D** ⇨ **gridiron** A; **E** (*Motor racing*) Startmarkierung, *die;* **F** (*of town streets*) rechtwinkliges Straßennetz; **~ pattern** rechtwinkliges Straßensystem; **G** (*Electronics*) Gitter, *das*

**griddle** /'grɪdl/ *n.* [*beheizbare*] *runde Eisenplatte zum Backen;* **~ cake** Crêpe, *die*

**grid:** **~iron** *n.* **A** (*Cookery*) Bratrost, *der;* **B** (*Amer.: football field*) Footballfeld, *das;* **~lock** *n.* Verkehrsinfarkt, *der;* (*fig.*) völliger Stillstand; **save the city centre from the threat of ~lock** das Stadtzentrum vor dem Verkehrsinfarkt bewahren; **~locked** /'grɪdlɒkt/ *adj.* total verstopft ‹Straße, Stadt›; (*fig.*) festgefahren; **the traffic is ~locked** der Verkehr ist völlig zusammengebrochen; **~ reference** *n.* Positionsangabe, *die*

# Greetings ····> Letter-writing

■ **ON A POSTCARD**

***Greetings*** or ***Best wishes from Freiburg***
= Schöne *or* Herzliche Grüße aus Freiburg

***Having a wonderful time***
= Es gefällt uns hier ausgezeichnet

***Wish you were here!***
≈ Das hättest Du alles sehen sollen!

***See you soon***
= Bis bald

***All best wishes, Steve and Cathy***
= Herzlichst *or* Herzliche Grüße *or* Es grüßen recht herzlich Steve und Cathy

■ **FOR A BIRTHDAY**

***Many happy returns [of the day], Happy birthday***
= Herzlichen Glückwunsch zum Geburtstag

***All good*** or ***best wishes for your birthday***
= Alles Gute zum Geburtstag

■ **FOR CHRISTMAS AND THE NEW YEAR**

***Happy Christmas!***
= Frohe Weihnachten!

***[Best wishes for] a Merry*** or ***Happy Christmas and a Prosperous New Year***
= Frohe Weihnachten *or* Fröhliche Weihnachten *or* Ein gesegnetes Weihnachtsfest und viel Glück im neuen Jahr

***Happy New Year!***
= Glückliches neues Jahr!; (*when drinking*) Prost *or* Prosit Neujahr!

■ **FOR EASTER**

***[Best wishes for a] Happy Easter***
= Frohe Ostern, Ein fröhliches Osterfest

■ **FOR A WEDDING**

***Every good wish to the happy couple*** or ***to the bride and groom on their wedding day and in the years to come***
= Dem glücklichen Paar alles Schöne am Hochzeitstag und viel Glück in der Zukunft

■ **FOR AN EXAM**

***Every success in your [forthcoming] exams***
= Viel Erfolg bei deiner *or* der bevorstehenden Prüfung

***All good wishes for your A levels/GCSEs***
≈ Alles Gute zum Abitur

■ **FOR A HOUSE MOVE**

***Every happiness in your new home***
= Viel Glück im neuen Heim

■ **FOR AN ILLNESS**

***Get well soon!***
= Gute Besserung!

***Best wishes for a speedy recovery***
= Die besten Wünsche zur baldigen Genesung

## Spoken greetings

Equivalents can only be approximate in some cases, and in others do not really exist.

■ **MEETING SOMEONE**

***Hello*** or ***Hallo*** or ***Hullo [there]!, Hi!***
= Hallo! (*more colloquial*); Guten Tag! (*more formal*); Grüß Gott! (*South German*)

***Good morning!***
= Guten Morgen!

***Good afternoon!***
= *no equivalent; say* Guten Tag!

***Good evening!***
= Guten Abend!

***How are you?***
= Wie geht es Ihnen? (*formal*); Wie gehts? (*more colloquial*)

***How do you do?***
≈ (*when being introduced*) Freut mich!; Angenehm! (*dated*)

■ **SAYING GOODBYE**

***Goodbye!***
= Auf Wiedersehen!

***'Bye now!***
= Wiedersehen!; Tschüs! (*more colloquial*)

***Look after yourself!, Take care!***
= Machs gut!

g

**grief** /gri:f/ *n.* Ⓐ Kummer, *der* (**over, at** über + *Akk.*, um); (*at loss of sb.*) Trauer, *die* (**for** um); **she felt [real] ~:** es bekümmerte sie sehr; **be a [great] ~ to sb.** jmdm. [großen *od.* viel] Kummer machen; **come to ~** (*fail*) scheitern; **the car came to ~:** das Auto wurde beschädigt (*ugs. scherzh.*); Ⓑ **good** *or* **great ~!** guter *od.* großer Gott!

'**grief-stricken** *adj.* untröstlich (**at** über + *Akk.*); **say sth. in a ~ voice** etw. mit vor Kummer erstickter Stimme sagen; **the ~ look on his face** sein gramvolles Gesicht

**grievance** /'gri:vəns/ *n.* (*complaint*) Beschwerde, *die;* Klage, *die;* (*resentment, grudge*) Groll, *der;* **air one's ~s** seine Beschwerden vorbringen/seinem Groll Luft machen; **I have no ~s against him personally** ich habe nichts gegen ihn persönlich

'**grievance procedure** *n.* Schlichtungsverfahren, *das*

**grieve** /gri:v/ ❶ *v.t.* betrüben; bekümmern. ❷ *v.i.* trauern (**for** um) ; **my heart ~s** *or* **I ~ for you** (*sympathize*) ich trauere mit dir; **~ over sb./sth.** jmdm./einer Sache nachtrauern

**grievous** /'gri:vəs/ *adj.* Ⓐ (*causing grief*) schmerzlich; Ⓑ (*flagrant, heinous*) schwer; **~ wrong[s]** schreiendes Unrecht; Ⓒ (*severe*) schwer ‹Verwundung, Krankheit›; groß ‹Schmerz›; Ⓓ (*bringing serious trouble*) folgenschwer ‹Irrtum, Dummheit›; schwer ‹Autounfall›; **~ bodily harm** (*Law*) schwere Körperverletzung

**grievously** /'gri:vəslɪ/ *adv.* Ⓐ (*seriously*) schwer ‹verletzt, benachteiligt›; Ⓑ (*strongly, exceedingly*) stark, ernstlich ‹beunruhigt›

**griffin** /'grɪfɪn/ *n.* Greif, *der*

**grill**[1] /grɪl/ ❶ *v.t.* Ⓐ (*cook*) grillen; Ⓑ (*fig.: question*) in die Mangel nehmen (*ugs.*). ❷ *v.i.* grillen; **be ~ing in the hot sun** (*fig.*) sich von *od.* in der heißen Sonne braten lassen (*ugs.*). ❸ *n.* Ⓐ (*Gastr.*) Grillgericht, *das;* **mixed ~:** Mixed Grill, *der;* gemischte Grillplatte; Ⓑ (*restaurant*) Grillrestaurant, *das;* Ⓒ (*on cooker*) Grill, *der;* Ⓓ ⇒ **gridiron** A

**grille (grill**[2]**)** *n.* Ⓐ (*grating*) Gitter, *das;* Ⓑ (*Motor Veh.*) [Kühler]grill, *der*

'**grill room** ⇒ **grill**[1] 3 B

**grim** /grɪm/ *adj.* (*stern*) streng; grimmig ‹Lächeln, Gesicht, Blick, Schweigen, Humor›; Furcht erregend ‹Krieger›; (*unrelenting, merciless, severe*) erbittert ‹Widerstand, Kampf, Schlacht›; grimmig ‹Entschlossenheit, Winter›; eisern ‹Vorsatz›; (*sinister, ghastly*) grauenvoll ‹Aufgabe, Anblick, Nachricht›; grausig ‹Wetter, Zeiten›; trostlos ‹Wetter, Winter, Tag, Landschaft, Aussichten›; (*mirthless*) grimmig ‹Humor, Spaß›; **hold** *or* **hang** *or* **cling on [to sth.] like ~ death** sich mit aller Kraft [an etw. (*Dat.*)] festklammern; ⇒ *also* **reaper** B

**grimace** /grɪ'meɪs/ ❶ *n.* Grimasse, *die;* **make a ~:** eine Grimasse machen *od.* schneiden. ❷ *v.i.* Grimassen machen *od.* schneiden; **~ with pain/disgust** vor Schmerz/Ekel das Gesicht verziehen

**grime** /graɪm/ *n.* Schmutz, *der;* (*soot*) Ruß, *der*

**grimly** /'grɪmlɪ/ *adv.* grimmig; eisern ‹entschlossen sein, sich festhalten›; verbissen, erbittert ‹kämpfen›

**Grimm's Law** /'grɪmz lɔ:/ *n.* (*Ling.*) germanische *od.* erste Lautverschiebung

**grimy** /'graɪmɪ/ *adj.* schmutzig; schwarz (*ugs.*); **buildings ~ with soot** rußgeschwärzte Gebäude

**grin** /grɪn/ ❶ *n.* Grinsen, *das.* ❷ *v.i.*, **-nn-** grinsen; **~ at sb.** jmdn. angrinsen; **~ and bear it** gute Miene zum bösen Spiel machen; ⇒ *also* **Cheshire cat**. ❸ *v.t.*, **-nn-: ~ approval/satisfaction** *etc.* beifällig/zufrieden *usw.* grinsen

**grind** /graɪnd/ ❶ *v.t.*, **ground** /graʊnd/ Ⓐ (*reduce to small particles*) **~ [up]** zermahlen; pulverisieren ‹Metall›; mahlen ‹Kaffee, Pfeffer, Getreide›; **~ sth. to dust/[a] powder/into flour** *etc.* etw. zu Staub/[einem] Pulver/zu Mehl *usw.* zermahlen; Ⓑ (*sharpen*) schleifen ‹Schere, Messer›; schärfen ‹Klinge›; (*smooth, shape*) schleifen ‹Linse, Edelstein›; **~ sth. to a sharp edge** etw. scharf schleifen; ⇒ *also* **axe** 1 A; Ⓒ (*rub harshly*) zerquetschen; **~ a cigarette end into the ground** einen Zigarettenstummel austreten; **~ facts into pupils** Schülern Fakten einhämmern; **~ dirt**

**into sth.** Schmutz in etw. (*Akk.*) treten; **~ one's teeth** mit den Zähnen knirschen; **D** (*produce by grinding*) mahlen ‹Mehl›; **E** (*turn, cause to work*) drehen ‹Leier›; **~ the coffee mill** den Kaffee mahlen; **~ a barrel organ** eine Drehorgel spielen; **F** (*fig.: oppress, harass*) auspressen (*fig.*); **~ the faces of the poor** (*literary*) die Armen [grausam] ausbeuten; **~ing poverty/tyranny** erdrückende Armut/Tyrannei.

❷ *v.i.*, **ground** **A** (*toil*) hart arbeiten; (*study*) büffeln (*ugs.*); **B** (*rub gratingly*) knirschen (**on** auf + *Dat.*); **bring sth. ~ing to a halt** etw. lahm legen; **~ to a halt, come to a ~ing halt** ‹Fahrzeug:› quietschend zum Stehen kommen; (*fig.*) ‹Verkehr:› zum Erliegen kommen; ‹Maschine:› stehen bleiben; ‹Projekt:› sich festfahren.

❸ *n.* Plackerei, *die* (*ugs.*); **the daily ~** (*coll.*) der alltägliche Trott

**~ a'way** ❶ *v.t.* abschleifen. ❷ *v.i.* (*fig.*) hart arbeiten (**at** an + *Dat.*); (*study*) büffeln (*ugs.*) (**at** *Akk.*)

**~ 'down** *v.t.* **A** zermahlen; pulverisieren ‹Metall›; mahlen ‹Kaffee›; **B** (*fig.: oppress*) ‹Tyrann, Regierung:› unterdrücken; ‹Armut, Verantwortung:› erdrücken; **C** (*sharpen*) abschleifen

**~ 'in** *v.t.* **A** (*Mech.*) einschleifen ‹Ventil›; **B** **~ the dirt in** den Schmutz ein- *od.* festtreten; **~ in facts** (*fig. coll.*) Fakten einhämmern

**~ 'on** *v.i.* sich mühsam voranarbeiten

**~ 'out** *v.t.* (*fig.*) sich (*Dat.*) abquälen ‹Verse, Melodie, Aufsatz›

**grinder** /ˈgraɪndə(r)/ *n.* **A** Schleifmaschine, *die;* (*pulverizing machine*) Mühle, *die;* **B** *in comb.* (*person*) ‹Messer-, Scheren›schleifer, *der;* **C** (*tooth*) Mahlzahn, *der;* **D** (*millstone*) Läufer, *der.* ⇒ *also* **organ-grinder**

**'grindstone** *n.* Schleifstein, *der;* **hold** *or* **keep one's/sb.'s nose to the ~** (*fig.*) sich dahinter klemmen (*ugs.*)/dafür sorgen, dass jmd. sich dahinter klemmt (*ugs.*); **get back to the ~:** sich wieder an die Arbeit machen

**gringo** /ˈgrɪŋgəʊ/ *n., pl.* **~s** (*often derog.*) Gringo, *der* (*abwertend*)

**grip** /grɪp/ ❶ *n.* **A** (*firm hold*) Halt, *der;* (*fig.: power*) Umklammerung, *die;* **hold sth. with a firm ~:** etw. mit festem Griff halten; **have a ~ on sth.** etw. festhalten; **loosen one's ~:** loslassen; **take a ~:** festhalten (**on** *Akk.*); **get** *or* **take a ~ on oneself** (*fig.*) sich zusammenreißen (*ugs.*); **gain a ~:** einen Halt finden; ‹Reifen:› greifen; **have/get a ~ on sth.** (*fig.*) etw. im Griff haben/in den Griff bekommen; **winter tightened its ~:** der Winter wurde noch strenger; **come** *or* **get to ~s with sth./sb.** (*fig.*) mit etw. fertig werden/sich (*Dat.*) jmdn. vorknöpfen *od.* vornehmen (*ugs.*); **be in the ~ of** (*fig.*) beherrscht werden von ‹Angst, Leidenschaft, Furcht›; heimgesucht werden von ‹Naturkatastrophe, Armut, Krieg›; **lose one's ~** (*fig.*) nachlassen; **lose one's ~ on reality** (*fig.*) den Bezug zur Realität verlieren; **the Prime Minister is losing his ~** (*fig.*) der Premierminister hat die Situation nicht mehr richtig im Griff; **B** (*strength or way of ~ping*) Griff, *der;* **shorten/lengthen one's ~:** den Schläger *o. Ä.* kürzer/länger fassen; **C** (*holding-device*) Klammer, *die;* (*part which is held*) Griff, *der;* (*of oar*) Holm, *der;* **D** ⇒ **hairgrip**; **E** (*bag*) Reisetasche, *die.*

❷ *v.t.*, **-pp-** greifen nach; ‹Reifen:› greifen; (*fig.*) ergreifen; fesseln ‹Publikum, Aufmerksamkeit›; **~ sb.'s collar/hand** *or* **sb. by the collar/hand** jmdn. am Kragen packen/sich an jmds. Hand (*Akk.*) klammern; **~ sb.'s imagination** (*fig.*) jmdn. fesseln.

❸ *v.i.*, **-pp-** ‹Räder, Bremsen usw.:› greifen; **~ at** greifen nach

**gripe** /graɪp/ ❶ *n.* **A** (*coll.: complaint*) Meckern, *das* (*ugs. abwertend*); **one more ~ about my driving ...:** noch ein Wort über meinen Fahrstil ...; **his favourite ~ is ...:** am liebsten schimpft er über (+ *Akk.*) ...; **have a good ~ about sth./at sb.** sich über etw. (*Akk.*) ausschimpfen/jmdn. tüchtig ausschimpfen; **B** *in pl.* (*colic*) **get/have the ~s** Bauchschmerzen *od.* (*ugs.*) Bauchweh bekommen/haben. ❷ *v.i.* (*coll.*) meckern (*ugs. abwertend*) (**about** über + *Akk.*)

**gripping** /ˈgrɪpɪŋ/ *adj.* (*fig.*) packend

**grisly** /ˈgrɪzlɪ/ *adj.* grausig

**Grisons** /ˈgriːzɔ̃/ *pr. n.* Graubünden (*das*)

**grist** /grɪst/ *n.* **A** Mahlgut, *das;* (*Brewing*) Malzschrot, *der od. das;* **B** (*fig.*) **it's all ~ to the/sb.'s mill** man kann aus allem etwas machen/jmd. versteht es, aus allem etwas zu machen

**gristle** /ˈgrɪsl/ *n.* Knorpel, *der*

**gristly** /ˈgrɪslɪ/ *adj.* knorp[e]lig

**grit** /grɪt/ ❶ *n.* **A** Sand, *der;* **B** ⇒ **gritstone**; **C** (*coll.: courage, endurance*) Schneid, *der* (*ugs.*). ❷ *v.t.*, **-tt-** **A** streuen ‹vereiste Straßen›; **B** **~ one's teeth** die Zähne zusammenbeißen (*ugs.*)

**grits** /grɪts/ *n. pl.* **A** (*oats*) geschälte Haferkörner; **B** (*oatmeal*) Haferschrot, *der od. das*

**'gritstone** *n.* (*Geol.*) Grit, *der* (*fachspr.*); Sandstein, *der*

**gritty** /ˈgrɪtɪ/ *adj.* **A** (*containing grit*) sandig ‹Weg, Boden, Butterbrot›; (*full of hard particles*) grobkörnig ‹Struktur, Sand›; **B** (*fig.: courageous*) **be ~:** Schneid haben

**grizzle** /ˈgrɪzl/ *v.i.* (*Brit. coll.*) quengeln (*ugs.*)

**grizzled** /ˈgrɪzld/ *adj.* grau ‹Haar, Bart›; grauhaarig ‹Person›; (*partly grey*) grau meliert ‹Haar›

**grizzly** /ˈgrɪzlɪ/ *n.* **~ [bear]** Grislybär, *der*

**groan** /grəʊn/ ❶ *n.* (*of person*) Stöhnen, *das;* (*of thing*) Ächzen, *das* (*fig.*); **give a ~ of pain** vor Schmerz stöhnen; **a ~ rose from the crowd** die Menge stöhnte auf. ❷ *v.i.* **A** ‹Person:› [auf]stöhnen (**at** bei); ‹Tisch, Planken:› ächzen (*fig.*); **~ inwardly** innerlich aufstöhnen; **a ~ing board** (*literary*) ein reich gedeckter Tisch; **B** (*fig.: be oppressed*) stöhnen. ❸ *v.t.* stöhnen

**groats** /grəʊts/ *n. pl.* (*hulled*) geschälte [Hafer]körner; (*hulled and crushed*) [Hafer]grütze, *die*

**grocer** /ˈgrəʊsə(r)/ *n.* Lebensmittelhändler, *der*/-händlerin, *die;* ⇒ *also* **baker**

**grocery** /ˈgrəʊsərɪ/ *n.* **A** *in pl.* (*goods*) Lebensmittel *Pl.;* **B** **~ [store]** Lebensmittelgeschäft, *das;* **C** (*trade*) Lebensmittelhandel, *der*

**grog** /grɒg/ *n.* Grog, *der;* (*Austral. and NZ coll.*) (*beer*) Bier, *das;* (*spirits*) Schnaps, *der* (*ugs.*)

**groggily** /ˈgrɒgɪlɪ/ *adv.* benommen ‹sprechen, gehen›; auf unsicheren *od.* (*ugs.*) auf wackeligen Beinen ‹gehen›

**groggy** /ˈgrɒgɪ/ *adj.* wackelig auf den Beinen (*ugs.*) *präd.;* groggy (*ugs.*) *präd.*

**groin** /grɔɪn/ *n.* **A** ▶ **966** (*Anat.*) Leistengegend, *die;* (*euphem.: genitals*) Weichteile *Pl.* (*verhüll.*); **B** (*Archit.*) Grat, *der* (*fachspr.*)

**grommet** ⇒ **grummet**

**groom** /gruːm, grʊm/ ❶ *n.* **A** (*stable boy*) Stallbursche, *der;* Stallknecht, *der* (*veralt.*); (*stable girl*) Stallgehilfin, *die;* **B** (*bride~*) Bräutigam, *der;* **C** (*Brit.: officer of Royal Household*) *Bediensteter des britischen Hofes.* ❷ *v.t.* **A** striegeln ‹Pferd›; (*smarten*) pflegen ‹Kleidung›; **~ oneself** sich zurechtmachen; **well/badly ~ed** gepflegt/ungepflegt; **B** (*fig.: prepare*) **~ sb. for/as sth.** jmdn. für/als etw. aufbauen; **~ sb. for a career** jmdn. auf *od.* für eine Laufbahn vorbereiten

**groove** /gruːv/ ❶ *n.* **A** (*channel*) Nut, *die* (*bes. Technik*); (*of gramophone record*) Rille, *die;* **B** (*fig.: routine*) **get into a ~** ‹Arbeit:› routinemäßig ablaufen; ‹Person:› zum Gewohnheitsmenschen werden; **be stuck in a ~:** aus dem Trott nicht mehr herauskommen; **C** **be in the ~** (*dated coll.*) gut drauf sein (*salopp*); (*perform excellently*) groß in Form sein (*ugs.*); (*be appreciative*) ‹Publikum:› begeistert mitgehen.
❷ *v.t.* nuten

**groovy** /ˈgruːvɪ/ *adj.* (*coll.*) (*excellent, very good*) klasse (*ugs.*); **be ~** (*Jazz*) in Form sein (*ugs.*); gut drauf sein (*salopp*)

**grope** /grəʊp/ ❶ *v.i.* tasten (**for** nach); **~ for the right word/truth** nach dem richtigen Wort/der Wahrheit suchen; **~ after sth.** (*fig.*) etw. herauszufinden versuchen. ❷ *v.t.* **A** **~ one's way [along]** sich [entlang]tasten; (*fig.*) [sich durch]lavieren (*ugs. abwertend*); **B** (*coll.: caress*) **~ sb.** jmdn. betatschen (*ugs. abwertend*)

**grosgrain** /ˈgrəʊgreɪn/ *n.* (*Textiles*) grob gerippter Stoff; Grosgrain, *der* (*fachspr.*)

**gros point** /ˈgrəʊ pwæ̃/ *n.* **A** (*embroidery*) Kreuzstichstickerei, *die;* **B** (*stitch*) Kreuzstich, *der*

**gross**[1] /grəʊs/ ❶ *adj.* **A** (*flagrant*) grob ‹Fahrlässigkeit, Fehler, Irrtum›; übel ‹Laster, Beleidigung›; schwer ‹Verbrechen, Beleidigung›; schreiend ‹Ungerechtigkeit›; **B** (*obese*) fett (*abwertend*); (*luxuriant*) üppig, dicht ‹Vegetation›; **C** (*coarse, rude*) ordinär (*abwertend*); (*coll.: disgusting*) **that's really ~!** das ist wirklich ekelhaft!; **D** (*total*) Brutto-; Gesamt‹umsatz, -absatz›; **earn £15,000 ~:** 15 000 Pfund brutto verdienen; **~ national product** Bruttosozialprodukt, *das;* **E** (*dull, not delicate*) grob ‹Person, Geschmack›; **F** (*coarse*) deftig ‹Mahlzeit, Essen›.

❷ *v.t.* **A** (*yield*) [insgesamt] einbringen ‹Geld›; **B** **~ up** einbeziehen; **~ed up** Brutto‹dividende, -rendite›

**gross**[2] *n., pl. same* Gros, *das;* **by the ~:** en gros

**grossly** /ˈgrəʊslɪ/ *adv.* **A** (*flagrantly*) äußerst; grob ‹übertreiben›; schwer ‹beleidigen›; **B** (*coarsely, rudely*) ordinär ‹sich benehmen, sprechen›; ohne Manieren ‹essen›

**grotesque** /grəʊˈtesk/ ❶ *adj.* grotesk. ❷ *n.* **A** (*decoration*) Groteske, *die;* **B** (*Printing*) Grotesk, *die*

**grotesquely** /grəʊˈtesklɪ/ *adv.* grotesk

**grotto** /ˈgrɒtəʊ/ *n., pl.* **~es** *or* **~s** Grotte, *die*

**grotty** /ˈgrɒtɪ/ *adj.* (*Brit. coll.*) mies (*ugs.*); (*dirty*) dreckig (*ugs.*); **the bathroom looks ~:** das Bad ist total versifft (*salopp*)

**grouch** /graʊtʃ/ (*coll.*) ❶ *v.i.* schimpfen; mosern (*ugs.*). ❷ *n.* **A** (*person*) Miesepeter, *der* (*ugs. abwertend*); **B** (*cause*) Ärger, *der;* **have a ~ against sb.** auf jmdn. sauer sein (*salopp*)

**grouchy** /ˈgraʊtʃɪ/ *adj.* (*coll.*) griesgrämig

**ground**[1] /graʊnd/ ❶ *n.* **A** Boden, *der;* **work above/below ~:** über/unter der Erde arbeiten; **1,000 feet above the ~:** 1 000 Fuß über dem Erdboden; **deep under the ~:** tief unter der Erde; **uneven, hilly ~:** unebenes, hügeliges Gelände; **on high ~:** in höheren Lagen; **cover much ~** (*distance*) eine weite Strecke zurücklegen; **B** (*fig.*) **be above/below ~:** am Leben *od.* unter den Lebenden sein/unter der Erde sein *od.* liegen; **cut the ~ from under sb.'s feet** jmdm. den Wind aus den Segeln nehmen (*ugs.*); **be** *or* **suit sb. down to the ~** (*coll.*) genau das Richtige für jmdn. sein; **Friday suits me down to the ~:** Freitag passt mir prima (*ugs.*); **that's Billy down to the ~** (*coll.*) das ist typisch Billy (*ugs.*); **fall to the ~:** zunichte werden; **be dashed to the ~:** [mit einem Schlag] zunichte werden; **from the ~ up** (*coll.*) (*thoroughly*) von der Pike auf (*ugs.*) ‹lernen›; (*entirely anew*) ganz von vorne ‹anfangen›; **get off the ~** (*coll.*) konkrete Gestalt annehmen; **get sth. off the ~** (*coll.*) etw. in die Tat umsetzen; **hit the ~ running** (*coll.*) voll durchstarten (*ugs.*); **go to ~** ‹Fuchs usw.:› im Bau verschwinden; ‹Person:› untertauchen; **run to ~:** aufstöbern; **run sb./oneself into the ~** (*coll.*) jmdn./sich kaputtmachen (*ugs.*); **run a car into the ~** (*coll.*) ein Auto so lange fahren, bis es schrottreif ist; **on the ~** (*in practice*) an Ort und Stelle; **be/not be on firm** *or* **solid ~:** sich auf sicherem/schwankendem Boden bewegen; **thin/thick on the ~:** dünn/dicht gesät; **break fresh** *or* **new ~:** Neuland betreten; **cover much** *or* **a lot of ~:** weit vorankommen; **cover the ~** ‹Student:› den Stoff erarbeiten; ‹Buch:› eine umfassende Darstellung geben; **cover the same ~** ‹Vorträge, Buch:› denselben Stoff behandeln; **gain** *or* **make ~:** Boden gewinnen (**on** gegenüber); (*become established*) Fuß fassen; **give** *or* **lose ~:** an Boden verlieren; **hold** *or* **keep** *or* **stand one's ~:** nicht nachgeben; **shift one's ~:** umschwenken; ⇒ *also* **foot** 1 A; **C** (*special area*) Gelände, *das;* **[sports] ~:** Sportplatz, *der;* **[cricket] ~:** Cricketfeld, *das;* ⇒ *also* **common ground**; **forbidden** 2; **D** *in pl.* (*attached to house*) Anlage,

die; Ⓔ (*Brit.: floor*) Boden, *der;* Ⓕ (*motive, reason*) Grund, *der;* **on the ~[s] of, on ~s of** aufgrund (+ *Gen.*); (*giving as one's reason*) unter Berufung auf (+ *Akk.*); **on the ~s that ...:** unter Berufung auf die Tatsache, dass ...; **on health/religious** *etc.* **~s** aus gesundheitlichen/religiösen *usw.* Gründen; **on what ~s do you suspect him?** mit welcher Begründung verdächtigen Sie ihn?; **the ~s for divorce are ...:** als Scheidungsgrund gilt ...; **there are no ~s for this assumption** es besteht kein Grund zu dieser Annahme; **have/give [no] ~s for sth.** [k]einen Grund für etw. haben/[keine] Gründe für etw. angeben; **have no ~s for sth./to do sth.** keinen Grund für etw. haben/keinen Grund haben, etw. zu tun; **have no ~s for complaint** keinen Grund zur Klage haben; **have good ~s for doing sth.** allen Grund haben, etw. zu tun; Ⓖ (*in embroidery, painting, etc.*) Grund, *der;* **on a white ~:** auf weißem Grund; Ⓗ *in pl.* (*sediment*) **~s** Satz, *der;* (*of coffee*) Kaffeesatz, *der;* Ⓘ (*Electr.*) Erde, *die;* **~ed plug** (*Amer.*) Schukostecker, *der;* Ⓙ (*bottom of sea*) Grund, *der;* **touch ~** (*fig.*) wieder Grund unter den Füßen haben.
❷ *v.t.* Ⓐ (*cause to run ashore*) auf Grund setzen; **be ~ed** auf Grund gelaufen sein; Ⓑ (*base, establish*) gründen (**on** auf + *Akk.*); **be ~ed on** gründen auf (+ *Dat.*); **well ~ed** wohl begründet; Ⓒ (*instruct*) **~ sb. [in the essentials]** jmdn. in die Anfangsgründe einführen; **be well/not well ~ed in a subject** über gute/keine guten Grundkenntnisse auf einem Gebiet verfügen; Ⓓ (*Mil.*) niederlegen; Ⓔ (*Aeronaut.*) am Boden festhalten; (*prevent from flying*) nicht fliegen lassen ‹Piloten›; **be ~ed by bad weather/owing to a defect** *etc.* wegen schlechten Wetters/eines Defekts *usw.* nicht starten können; Ⓕ (*Electr.*) erden; Ⓖ (*esp. Amer.: confine to home*) **be ~ed** Stubenarrest *od.* Hausarrest haben.
❸ *v.i.* (*run ashore*) ‹Schiff:› auf Grund laufen

**ground²** ❶ ⇒ **grind** 1, 2. ❷ *adj.* gemahlen ‹Kaffee, Getreide›; pulverisiert ‹Holz, Gummi›; **~ meat** (*Amer.*) Hackfleisch, *das;* **~ coffee** Kaffeepulver, *das;* **fine-/coarse-/medium-~ coffee** fein/grob/mittelfein gemahlener Kaffee

**ground: ~bait** *n.* Grundköder, *der;* **~ bass** /ˈgraʊnd beɪs/ *n.* (*Mus.*) Basso ostinato, *der;* Ground, *der;* **~ control** *n.* (*Aeronaut.*) Ⓐ (*personnel, equipment, etc.*) Flugsicherungskontrolldienst, *der;* Ⓑ (*directing*) **~ control approach** GCA-Verfahren, *das;* **~ crew** *n.* (*Aeronaut.*) Bodenpersonal, *das;* **~ effect** *n.* Bodeneffekt, *der* (*Technik*); **~ 'floor** ⇒ **floor** 1 B; **~ forces** *n. pl.* Bodentruppen *Pl.;* **~ frost** *n.* Bodenfrost, *der;* **~ 'glass** *n.* Mattglas, *das*

**grounding** /ˈgraʊndɪŋ/ *n.* Ⓐ Grundkenntnisse *Pl.;* Grundwissen, *das;* Ⓑ (*Aeronaut.*) **the ~ of the plane was ordered** dem Flugzeug wurde Startverbot erteilt

**ground: ~ ivy** *n.* Gundelrebe, *die;* **~keeper** (*Amer.*) ⇒ **groundsman**

**groundless** /ˈgraʊndlɪs/ *adj.* unbegründet; **these reports/rumours/statements are ~:** diese Berichte/Gerüchte/Aussagen entbehren jeder Grundlage

**ground: ~ level** *n.* **above/below ~ level** oberhalb/unterhalb der ebenen Erde; **on** *or* **at ~ level** ebenerdig; ‹Wohnung, Fenster› zu ebener Erde; **~nut** *n.* (*Brit.*) Erdnuss, *die;* **~ plan** *n.* Grundriss, *der;* (*fig.*) Grundstruktur, *die;* **~ rent** *n.* Grundrente, *die;* **~ 'rice** *n.* Reismehl, *das;* **~ rule** *n.* Ⓐ (*Sport*) Platzregel, *die;* Ⓑ (*basic principle*) Grundregel, *die*

**groundsel** /ˈgraʊnsl/ *n.* (*Bot.*) Greiskraut, *das*

**ground: ~sheet** *n.* Bodenplane, *die;* **~sman** /ˈgraʊndzmən/ *n., pl.* **~smen** /ˈgraʊndzmən/ (*Sport*) Platzwart, *der;* **~ speed** *n.* (*Aeronaut.*) Grundgeschwindigkeit, *die;* **~ squirrel** *n.* Erdhörnchen, *das;* **~ staff** *n.* (*Aeronaut.*) Bodenpersonal, *das;* **~ station** *n.* (*Astronaut., Communications*) Bodenstation, *die;* **~swell** *n.* schwere Dünung; **the ~swell of public opinion** (*fig.*) der wachsende Druck der öffentlichen Meinung; **~ traffic** *n.* Bodenverkehr, *der;* **~ water** *n.* Grundwasser, *das;* **~work** *n.* Vorarbeiten *Pl.;* (*fig.*) Grundlage, *die;* **do the ~work for sth.** die Vorarbeiten für etw. machen; **~ 'zero** *n.* [Boden]nullpunkt, *der*

**group** /gru:p/ ❶ *n.* Ⓐ Gruppe, *die; attrib.* Gruppen‹verhalten, -dynamik, -bewusstsein›; **~ of houses/trees/islands** Häuser-/Baum-/Inselgruppe, *die;* **the Germanic ~ of languages** die germanische Sprachfamilie; Ⓑ (*Commerc.*) [Unternehmens]gruppe, *die;* Ⓒ (*Polit.*) Gruppe, *die;* (*Parl.*) Fraktion, *die;* Ⓓ ⇒ **pop group**; Ⓔ (*Math., Chem.*) Gruppe, *die.* ❷ *v.t.* gruppieren; **~ books according to their subjects** Bücher nach ihrer Thematik ordnen; **~ flowers together** Blumen zusammenstellen; **you can't ~ all criminals together** man kann nicht alle Verbrecher in einen Topf werfen (*ugs.*); **be ~ed into classes** Klassen zugeordnet werden

**group: ~ captain** *n.* (*Air Force*) Oberst der Luftwaffe; **~ discussion** *n.* Gruppendiskussion, *die*

**groupie** /ˈgru:pɪ/ *n.* (*coll.*) Groupie, *das*

**grouping** /ˈgru:pɪŋ/ *n.* (*placing in groups*) Gruppierung, *die;* (*classification*) Klassifizierung, *die;* **blood ~:** Bestimmung der Blutgruppe; ([*belonging to a*] *blood group*) Blutgruppe[nzugehörigkeit], *die*

**group: ~ practice** *n.* Gemeinschaftspraxis, *die;* **~ sex** *n.* Gruppensex, *der;* **~ therapy** *n.* Gruppentherapie, *die*

**grouse¹** /graʊs/ *n.* Ⓐ *pl. same* Raufußhuhn, *das;* **[red] ~** (*Brit.*) Schottisches Moorschneehuhn; Ⓑ *no pl.* (*as food*) Waldhuhn, *das;* schottisches Moorhuhn

**grouse²** (*coll.*) ❶ *v.i.* meckern (*ugs.*), mosern (*ugs.*) (**about** über + *Akk.*). ❷ *n.* Meckerei, *die* (*ugs.*); Moserei, *die* (*ugs.*); **my only ~ is that ...:** mir stinkt nur, dass ... (*salopp*)

**grouser** /ˈgraʊsə(r)/ *n.* (*coll.*) Meckerer, *der;* Meckerfritze, *der*/-liese, *die* (*ugs.*)

**ˈgrouse-shooting** *n.* Jagd auf Moorhühner

**grout** /graʊt/ ❶ *n.* Mörtelschlamm, *der.* ❷ *v.t.* verstreichen ‹Fugen, Löcher›; [aus]fugen ‹Mauer, Fliesen›

**grove** /grəʊv/ *n.* Wäldchen, *das;* Hain, *der* (*dichter. veralt.*)

**grovel** /ˈgrɒvl/ *v.i.,* (*Brit.*) **-ll-** Ⓐ (*lie prone*) auf dem Bauch liegen; (*go down on one's knees*) sich auf die Knie werfen; **be ~ling on the floor** auf dem Fußboden kriechen; Ⓑ (*fig.: be subservient*) katzbuckeln (*abwertend*); (*in apology*) zu Kreuze kriechen (*abwertend*) (**before** vor + *Dat.*)

**grovelling** (*Amer.:* **groveling**) /ˈgrɒvəlɪŋ/ *adj.* kriechend; (*fig.*) kriecherisch (*abwertend*)

**grow** /grəʊ/ ❶ *v.i.,* **grew** /gru:/, **grown** /grəʊn/ Ⓐ (*sprout*) ‹Pflanze:› wachsen; **leaves are beginning to ~ on the trees** an den Bäumen bilden sich allmählich Blätter; Ⓑ (*in size etc.*) wachsen; **haven't you ~n!** du bist aber gewachsen *od.* groß geworden!; **~ing lad** Junge, der noch im Wachsen ist *od.* noch wächst; **it just ~ed** (*coll.*) es hat sich einfach so entwickelt; Ⓒ (*develop, expand*) wachsen; (*increase numerically*) ‹Bevölkerung:› zunehmen, wachsen; **~ out of** *or* **from sth.** sich aus etw. entwickeln; (*from sth. abstract*) aus etw. erwachsen; von etw. herrühren; ‹Situation, Krieg usw.:› die Folge von etw. sein; ‹Plan:› aus etw. erwachsen; **~ in** zunehmen *od.* gewinnen an (+ *Dat.*) ‹Größe, Bedeutung, Autorität, Ansehen, Weisheit›; gewinnen an (+ *Dat.*) ‹Popularität, Format›; Ⓓ (*become*) werden; **~ used to sth./sb.** sich an etw./jmdn. gewöhnen; **~ like sb.** jmdm. ähnlich werden; **~ apart** (*fig.*) sich auseinander leben; **~ away from sb.** (*fig.*) sich jmdm. entfremden; **~ to be sth.** allmählich etw. werden; **he grew to be a man** er wuchs zum Manne heran (*geh.*); **~ to love/hate** *etc.* **sb./sth.** jmdn./etw. lieben/hassen *usw.* lernen; **~ to like sb./sth.** nach und nach Gefallen an jmdm./etw. finden; **~ old [gracefully]** [mit Würde] alt werden. ⇒ *also* **growing**; **grown** 2.
❷ *v.t.,* **grew, grown** Ⓐ (*cultivate*) (*on a small scale*) ziehen; (*on a large scale*) anpflanzen; züchten ‹Blumen›; (*produce*) züchten ‹Kristalle›; Ⓑ **~ one's hair [to a great length]** sich (*Dat.*) die Haare [sehr lang] wachsen lassen; **~ a beard** sich (*Dat.*) einen Bart wachsen lassen; **the lizard will ~ a new tail** der Eidechse wächst ein neuer Schwanz

**~ into** *v.t.* Ⓐ (*become*) werden zu; Ⓑ (*become big enough for*) hineinwachsen in (+ *Akk.*) ‹Kleidungsstück›

**~ on** *v.t.* **it ~s on you** man findet mit der Zeit Geschmack *od.* Gefallen daran; **he grew on us** wir haben ihn schätzen gelernt

**~ 'out of** *v.t.* Ⓐ (*become too big for*) herauswachsen aus ‹Kleidungsstück›; Ⓑ (*lose in the course of time*) ablegen ‹Angewohnheit›; entwachsen (+ *Dat.*) ‹Kindereien›; überwinden ‹Zustand›; ⇒ *also* **~** 1 C

**~ 'up** *v.i.* Ⓐ (*spend early years*) aufwachsen; (*become adult*) erwachsen werden; **she grew up to be a gifted pianist** sie wuchs zu einer begabten Pianistin heran; **what do you want to be** *or* **do when you ~ up?** was willst du denn mal werden, wenn du groß bist?; Ⓑ (*fig.: behave more maturely*) erwachsen werden; **~ up!** werde endlich erwachsen!; Ⓒ (*develop*) ‹Freundschaft, Feindschaft, Streit:› sich entwickeln; ‹Legende:› entstehen, sich bilden; ‹Tradition, Brauch:› sich herausbilden

**~ 'up into** *v.t.* werden *od.* sich entwickeln zu

**grower** /ˈgrəʊə(r)/ *n.* Ⓐ *usu. in comb.* (*person*) Produzent, *der*/Produzentin, *die;* **fruit/apple/vegetable ~:** Obst-/Apfel-/Gemüsebauer, *der;* **coffee/tobacco ~:** Kaffee-/Tabakpflanzer, *der;* Ⓑ (*plant*) **be a slow/free ~:** langsam/schnell wachsen; eine langsam/schnell wachsende Pflanze sein

**growing** /ˈgrəʊɪŋ/ ❶ *adj.* wachsend; sich verdichtend ‹Anzeichen›; immer umfangreicher werdend ‹Sachgebiet›; sich immer mehr verbreitend ‹Praktik›. ❷ *n.* Anbau, *der; attrib.* **~ season** Vegetationsperiode, *die;* **good/bad ~ weather** dem Pflanzenwachstum förderliches/abträgliches Wetter

**ˈgrowing pains** *n. pl.* Wachstumsschmerzen *Pl.;* (*fig.*) Anfangsschwierigkeiten *Pl.*

**growl** /graʊl/ ❶ *n.* (*of dog, lion*) Knurren, *das;* (*of bear*) Brummen, *das;* **a ~ of disapproval** ein missbilligendes Knurren. ❷ *v.i.* Ⓐ ‹Hund, Löwe:› knurren; ‹Bär:› [böse] brummen; **~ at sb.** jmdn. anknurren/anbrummen; Ⓑ (*murmur angrily*) knurren. ❸ *v.t.* **~ [out]** knurren

**grown** /grəʊn/ ❶ ⇒ **grow.** ❷ *adj.* erwachsen; **fully ~:** ausgewachsen

**ˈgrown-up** ❶ *n.* Erwachsene, *der/die.* ❷ *adj.* erwachsen; **~ books/clothes** Bücher/Kleider für Erwachsene; **act in a ~ way** sich wie ein Erwachsener verhalten

**growth** /grəʊθ/ *n.* Ⓐ (*of industry, economy, population*) Wachstum, *das* (**of, in** *Gen.*); (*of interest, illiteracy*) Zunahme, *die* (**of, in** *Gen.*); *attrib.* Wachstums‹hormon, -rate›; Ⓑ (*growing of organisms, crystals*) Wachstum, *das;* (*cultivation*) Anbau, *der;* Ⓒ (*amount grown*) Wachstum, *das;* Ⓓ (*thing grown*) Vegetation, *die;* Pflanzenwuchs, *der;* (*in classification of vineyards*) Lage, *die;* **a thick ~ of weeds** dicht wucherndes Unkraut; **cut away the old ~:** die alten Triebe ab- *od.* wegschneiden; **a four days' ~ [of beard]** ein vier Tage alter Bart; Ⓔ (*Med.*) Geschwulst, *die;* Gewächs, *das*

**growth: ~ area** *n.* Wachstumsbereich, *der;* **~ industry** *n.* Wachstumsindustrie, *die;* **~ rate** *n.* Wachstumsrate, *die;* **~ ring** *n.* Wachstumsring, *der;* **~ stock** *n.* Wachstumsaktien *Pl.*

**groyne** /grɔɪn/ *n.* Buhne, *die*

**grub** /grʌb/ ❶ *n.* Ⓐ Larve, *die;* (*maggot*) Made, *die;* (*ugs.*) Wurm, *der;* (*caterpillar*) Raupe, *die;* (*larva of cockchafer etc.*) Engerling, *der;* Ⓑ (*coll.: food*) Futterage, *die* (*ugs.*); Fressen, *das* (*salopp*); (*victuals*) Fressalien *Pl.* (*ugs.*); **~['s] up!** ran an die Futterkrippe! (*ugs.*); **lovely ~!** ein Spitzenfraß! (*salopp*); **pub ~** (*Brit.*) Kneipenessen, *das* (*ugs.*).
❷ *v.i.,* **-bb-** Ⓐ (*dig*) wühlen, buddeln (*ugs.*) (**for** nach); Ⓑ (*search*) (*in bag, cupboard, etc.*) wühlen, kramen (**for** nach); **~ about**

g

[herum]wühlen; [herum]kramen; ~ **about for sth.** nach etw. wühlen *od.* kramen.
❸ *v.t.*, **-bb-** [A] (*dig*) umgraben ‹Land, Boden›; ‹Tier:› aufwühlen; (*remove roots or stumps from*) roden ‹Land›; (*extract by digging*) ausgraben; (*uproot*) [aus]roden ‹Buschwerk, Baum›; [B] (*fig.*) **barely ~bing a subsistence** gerade eben in der Lage zu existieren

~ **'out** *v.t.* roden ‹Land›; [aus]roden ‹Wurzelstock›; (*fig.*) zutage fördern

~ **'up** *v.t.* ausgraben; [aus]jäten ‹Unkraut›; [aus]roden ‹Wurzelstock›

**grubby** /'grʌbɪ/ *adj.* (*dirty*) schmudd[e]lig (*ugs. abwertend*); (*slovenly*) schlampig (*ugs. abwertend*)

**'grub screw** *n.* (*Mech. Engin.*) Gewindestift, *der*

**grudge** /grʌdʒ/ ❶ *v.t.* ~ **sb. sth.** jmdm. etw. missgönnen *od.* nicht gönnen; **I don't ~ him his success** ich gönne ihm seinen Erfolg; ~ **every penny that is taken in tax** der Steuer jeden Pfennig missgönnen; ~ **doing sth.** (*be unwilling to do sth.*) nicht bereit sein, etw. zu tun; (*do sth. reluctantly*) etw. ungern tun; **I ~ paying £20 for this** es geht mir gegen den Strich, dafür 20 Pfund zu zahlen (*ugs.*). ❷ *n.* Groll, *der*; **have** *or* **hold a ~ against sb.** einen Groll *od.* (*ugs.*) Hass auf jmdn. haben; jmdm. grollen; **I owe him a ~:** den habe ich gefressen (*ugs.*); ⇒ *also* **bear²** 1 H

**grudging** /'grʌdʒɪŋ/ *adj.* widerwillig ‹Lob, Bewunderung, Unterstützung›; widerwillig gewährt ‹Zuschuss›; **be ~ in one's approval** nur widerwillig zustimmen

**grudgingly** /'grʌdʒɪŋlɪ/ *adv.* widerwillig

**gruel** /'gru:əl/ *n.* [Hafer]schleim, *der;* Schleimsuppe, *die*

**gruelling** (*Amer.:* **grueling**) /'gru:əlɪŋ/ ❶ *adj.* aufreibend; zermürbend; [äußerst] strapaziös ‹Reise, Marsch›; mörderisch (*ugs.*) ‹Tempo, Rennen›. ❷ *n.* (*Brit.*) **the boxer got a ~:** der Boxer bezog tüchtig Prügel (*ugs.*); **take a ~ from sth.** durch etw. sehr leiden

**gruesome** /'gru:səm/ *adj.*, **gruesomely** /'gru:səmlɪ/ *adv.* grausig; schaurig

**gruff** /grʌf/ *adj.* barsch; schroff; ruppig, bärbeißig ‹Benehmen, Wesen›; (*low-pitched, hoarse*) rau ‹Stimme, Lachen›

**grumble** /'grʌmbl/ ❶ *v.i.* [A] murren; ~ **at sb. about** *or* **over sth.** sich bei jmdm. über etw. (*Akk.*) *od.* wegen etw. beklagen; **put up with sth. without grumbling** etw. ohne Murren ertragen; [B] (*rumble*) ‹[Geschütz]donner:› grollen. ❷ *n.* [A] (*act*) Murren, *das;* (*complaint*) Klage, *die;* **without a ~:** ohne Murren; **she's always full of ~s** sie hat immer etwas zu murren; **my chief ~ is that ...:** vor allem missfällt mir, dass ...; am meisten stört mich, dass ...; [B] (*rumble of thunder, cannon*) Grollen, *das*

**grumbler** /'grʌmblə(r)/ *n.* Querulant, *der*/Querulantin, *die*

**grumbling a'ppendix** *n.* (*Med.*) Blinddarmreizung, *die*

**grummet** /'grʌmɪt/ *n.* [A] (*Naut.*) Grummet, *das;* Grummetstropp, *der;* [B] (*washer*) Durchführung, *die;* [C] (*in cap*) Versteifungsring, *der*

**grumpily** /'grʌmpɪlɪ/ *adv.* unleidlich; grantig (*ugs.*)

**grumpiness** /'grʌmpɪnɪs/ *n.*, *no pl.* Unleidlichkeit, *die;* Grantigkeit, *die* (*ugs.*)

**grumpy** /'grʌmpɪ/ *adj.* unleidlich; grantig (*ugs.*)

**grunge** /grʌndʒ/ *n.*, *no. pl.* [A] (*Amer. coll.: grime*) Dreck, *der* (*ugs.*); Siff, *der* (*salopp*); [B] (*music*) Grunge, *der;* [C] (*fashion*) Grunge[look], *der*/-[stil], *der*

**grunt** /grʌnt/ ❶ *n.* Grunzen, *das;* **give a ~:** grunzen. ❷ *v.i.* grunzen; **he only ~ed in answer** er gab nur ein Grunzen zur Antwort. ❸ *v.t.* ~ **[out]** grunzen

**gruyère** /'gru:jeə(r)/ *n.* Gruyère[käse], *der;* Greyerzer [Käse], *der*

**gryphon** /'grɪfn/ ⇒ **griffin**

**GSOH** *abbr.* (*in advertisements*) **good sense of humour** Humor, *der;* **outgoing, friendly, ~:** kontaktfreudig, freundlich, humorvoll

**'G-string** *n.* [A] (*Mus.*) G-Saite, *die;* [B] (*garment*) (*of showgirl*) ≈ Cachesexe, *das;* G-String, *die od. der;* (*of tribesman*) Lendenschurz, *der*

**'G-suit** *n.* (*Aeronaut.*) Anti-g-Anzug, *der*

**Gt.** *abbr.* **Great** Gr.

**guano** /'gwɑ:nəʊ/ *n.*, *pl.* **~s** Guano, *der*

**guarantee** /gærən'ti:/ ❶ *v.t.* [A] garantieren; garantieren für, bürgen für ‹Echtheit usw.›; ~ **sth. to sb.** jmdm. etw. zusichern; [B] (*by formal agreement*) garantieren für; [eine] Garantie geben auf (+ *Akk.*); ~ **sth. for a year** auf etw. (*Akk.*) ein Jahr Garantie geben; **is the clock ~d?** hat die Uhr Garantie?; gibt es auf die Uhr Garantie?; **the clock is ~d for a year** die Uhr hat ein Jahr Garantie; ~ **sb. regular employment** jmdm. eine Beschäftigungsgarantie geben; **~d wage** Garantielohn, *der;* **~d genuine** *etc.* garantiert echt *usw.;* [C] (*Law: take responsibility for*) bürgen für ‹Darlehen, Schuld usw.›; [D] (*in popular use*) (*promise*) garantieren (*ugs.*); (*ensure*) bürgen für ‹Qualität›; garantieren ‹Erfolg›; **be ~d to do sth.** etw. garantiert tun; **there's no ~ing he'll get a work permit** es ist gar nicht gesagt, dass er eine Arbeitserlaubnis kriegt.
❷ *n.* [A] (*Commerc. etc.*) Garantie, *die;* (*document*) Garantieschein, *der;* (*Law*) Bürgschaft, *die;* **there's a year's ~ on this radio, this radio has** *or* **carries a year's ~:** auf dieses Radio gibt es *od.* dieses Radio hat ein Jahr Garantie; **is it still under ~?** ist noch Garantie darauf?; **come under** *or* **be covered by the ~:** unter die Garantie fallen; [B] (*guarantor*) Garant, *der;* (*Law*) Bürge, *der*/Bürgin, *die;* [C] (*in popular use: promise*) Garantie, *die* (*ugs.*); **give sb. a ~ that ...:** jmdm. garantieren, dass ...; **you have my ~:** das garantiere ich dir; **be a ~ of sth.** (*ensure*) eine Garantie für etw. sein

**guarantor** /'gærəntə(r), gærən'tɔ:(r)/ *n.* Bürge, *der*/Bürgin, *die;* **be** *or* **stand ~ for sb., be sb.'s ~:** eine Bürgschaft für jmdn. übernehmen; für jmdn. bürgen

**guaranty** /'gærəntɪ/ *n.* [A] (*undertaking*) Garantie, *die;* (*to pay another's debt*) Bürgschaft, *die;* [B] (*basis of security*) Garantie, *die;* Gewähr, *die*

**guard** /gɑ:d/ ❶ *n.* ▶ 1261 [A] (*Mil.: ~sman*) Wachtposten, *der;* [B] *no pl.* (*Mil.: group of soldiers*) Wache, *die;* Wachmannschaft, *die;* ~ **of honour** Ehrenwache, *die;* Ehrengarde, *die;* **change ~:** Wachablösung machen; **relieve ~:** die Wache ablösen; **mount ~:** Wache beziehen; ⇒ *also* **old guard**; [C] **Guards** (*Brit. Mil.: household troops*) Garderegiment, *das;* Garde, *die;* ⇒ *also* **Foot Guards**; **Horse Guards**; **Life Guards**; [D] (*watch; also Mil.*) Wache, *die;* **be on ~:** Wache haben; **keep** *or* **stand ~:** Wache halten *od.* stehen; **keep** *or* **mount** *or* **stand ~ over sth./sb.** etw./jmdn. bewachen; **be on [one's] ~ [against sb./sth.]** (*lit. or fig.*) [vor jmdm./etw.] auf der Hut sein; sich [vor jmdm./etw.] hüten; **be off [one's] ~** (*fig.*) nicht auf der Hut sein; **be caught** *or* **taken off [one's] ~ [by sth.]** (*fig.*) [von etw.] überrascht werden; **put sb. on [his/her] ~:** jmdn. misstrauisch machen; **put** *or* **throw sb. off [his/her] ~:** jmdn. überrumpeln (*ugs.*); **under ~:** unter Bewachung; **be [kept/held] under ~:** bewacht werden; unter Bewachung stehen; **keep** *or* **hold/put under ~:** bewachen/unter Bewachung stellen; **put a ~ on sb./sth.** jmdn./etw. bewachen lassen; [E] (*Brit. Railw.*) [Zug]schaffner, *der*/-schaffnerin, *die;* [F] (*Amer.: prison warder*) [Gefängnis]wärter, *der*/-wärterin, *die;* [G] (*safety device*) Schutz, *der;* Schutzvorrichtung, *die;* (*worn on body*) Schutz, *der;* Schützer, *der;* (*crossbar on sword*) Parierstange, *die;* (*of rapier*) Stichblatt, *das;* (*Fencing: of weapon*) Glocke, *die;* [H] (*posture*) (*Boxing, Fencing*) Deckung, *die;* (*Cricket*) Abwehrhaltung, *die;* **on ~!** (*Fencing*) en garde!; **take ~:** in Verteidigungsstellung gehen; **drop** *or* **lower one's ~:** die Deckung fallen lassen; (*fig.*) seine Reserve aufgeben; **have one's ~ down** (*fig.*) sich ungezwungen verhalten *od.* bewegen. ⇒ *also* **security guard**.
❷ *v.t.* [A] (*watch over*) bewachen; (*keep safe*) hüten ‹Geheimnis, Schatz, Juwelen›; schützen ‹Leben›; beschützen ‹Blinden, Schwächeren, Prominenten›; ~ **sb./oneself against sth.** jmdn. vor etw. (*Dat.*) beschützen/sich vor etw. (*Dat.*) schützen; [B] (*keep in check*) hüten, im Zaum halten ‹Zunge›; mäßigen ‹Worte›

~ **against** *v.t.* sich hüten vor (+ *Dat.*); verhüten ‹Unfall›; vorbeugen (+ *Dat.*) ‹Krankheit, Gefahr, Irrtum›; ~ **against doing sth.** sich [davor] hüten, etw. zu tun

**guard:** ~ **dog** *n.* Wachhund, *der;* ~ **duty** *n.* Wachdienst, *der;* **be on** *or* **do ~ duty** Wachdienst haben

**guarded** /'gɑ:dɪd/ *adj.*, **guardedly** /'gɑ:dɪdlɪ/ *adv.* zurückhaltend; vorsichtig

**'guardhouse** *n.* (*Mil.*) Wache, *die;* Wach[t]haus, *das*

**guardian** /'gɑ:dɪən/ *n.* [A] Hüter, *der;* Wächter, *der;* [B] (*Law*) Vormund, *der;* **place sb. under the care of a ~:** jmdm. einen Vormund geben

**guardian 'angel** *n.* Schutzengel, *der*

**guardianship** /'gɑ:dɪənʃɪp/ *n.* [A] *no pl.* Schutz, *der;* [B] (*Law*) Vormundschaft, *die;* **have [legal] ~ of sb.** jmds. Vormund sein

**guard:** ~ **rail** *n.* Geländer, *das;* (*Railw.*) Radlenker, *der;* **~room** *n.* (*Mil.*) Wachstube, *die;* Wachlokal, *das*

**guardsman** /'gɑ:dzmən/ *n.*, *pl.* **guardsmen** /'gɑ:dzmən/ ▶ 1261 (*belonging to guard*) Wachtposten, *der;* (*belonging to Guards*) Gardist, *der;* Gardesoldat, *der*

**'guard's van** *n.* (*Brit. Railw.*) Gepäckwagen (*mit Dienstabteil*)

**Guatemala** /gwætɪ'mɑ:lə/ *pr. n.* Guatemala (*das*)

**Guatemalan** /gwætɪ'mɑ:lən/ ▶ 1340 ❶ *adj.* guatemaltekisch; **sb. is ~:** jmd. ist Guatemalteke/Guatemaltekin. ❷ *n.* Guatemalteke, *der*/Guatemaltekin, *die*

**guava** /'gwɑ:və/ *n.* [A] (*fruit*) Guave, *die;* Guajave, *die;* [B] (*tree*) Guajavabaum, *der*

**gubbins** /'gʌbɪnz/ *n.* (*Brit.*) [A] *no pl.* (*trash*) Schund, *der* (*ugs. abwertend*); Ramsch, *der* (*ugs. abwertend*); (*personal effects*) Kram, *der* (*ugs.*); Krempel, *der* (*ugs.*); (*gadgetry*) Zeug, *das;* [B] (*coll.: fool*) Simpel, *der* (*ugs.*)

**gubernatorial** /gju:bənə'tɔ:rɪəl/ *adj.* (*Amer.*) Gouverneurs-

**gudgeon** /'gʌdʒn/ *n.* (*Zool.*) Gründling, *der*

**'gudgeon pin** *n.* (*Mech. Engin.*) Kolbenbolzen, *der*

**guelder rose** /'geldə rəʊz/ *n.* (*Bot.*) Schneeball, *der*

**guerilla** ⇒ **guerrilla**

**Guernsey** /'gɜ:nzɪ/ *n.* [A] *pr. n.* Guernsey (*das*); [B] (*animal*) Guernseyrind, *das*

**guerrilla** /gə'rɪlə/ *n.* Guerillakämpfer, *der*/-kämpferin, *die;* (*in Latin America*) Guerillero, *der*/Guerillera, *die; attrib.* Guerilla-

**guess** /ges/ ❶ *v.t.* [A] (*estimate*) schätzen; (*surmise correctly*) erraten; raten ‹Rätsel›; **I ~ her [age] to be ten** ich schätze sie auf zehn; **can you ~ his weight?** schätz mal, wie viel er wiegt; ~ **who's here!** rate mal, wer da ist!; ~ **what!** (*coll.*) stell dir vor!; **he ~ed from their manner that ...:** er entnahm aus ihrem Verhalten, dass ...; **you'd never ~ that ...:** man würde nie vermuten, dass ...; **I ~ed as much** das habe ich mir schon gedacht; [B] (*esp. Amer.: suppose*) **I ~:** ich glaube; ich schätze (*ugs.*); **I ~ I ought to apologize** ich sollte mich wohl entschuldigen; **I ~ we'll have to** wir müssen wohl; **I ~ so/not** ich glaube schon *od.* ja/nicht *od.* kaum.
❷ *v.i.* (*estimate*) schätzen; (*make assumption*) vermuten; (*surmise correctly*) es erraten; ~ **at sth.** etw. schätzen; (*surmise*) über etw. (*Akk.*) Vermutungen anstellen; **I'm just ~ing** das ist nur eine Schätzung/eine Vermutung; **you've ~ed right/wrong** deine Vermutung ist richtig/falsch; **Do you know what he said? — No, but I can ~:** Weißt du, was er gesagt hat? — Nein, aber ich kann es mir denken; **well, ~!** na, rate mal!; **keep sb. ~ing** (*coll.*) jmdn. im Unklaren *od.* Ungewissen lassen; **how did you ~?** wie hast du

das nur erraten?; **you'll never ~!** darauf kommst du nie!
❸ *n.* Schätzung, *die;* **at a ~:** schätzungsweise; **what's your ~?** was schätzen Sie?; **make** *or* **have a ~:** schätzen; **have a ~!** rate *od.* schätz mal!; **my ~ is [that] ...:** ich schätze, dass ...; **miss one's ~** (*Amer.*) sich verschätzen; **I'll give you three ~es** (*coll.*) dreimal darfst du raten (*ugs.*); **have another ~ coming** (*coll.*) sich verrechnet haben (*ugs.*); ⇒ *also* **anybody** B

**guessing game** /ˈgesɪŋgeɪm/ *n.* Ratespiel, *das*

**guesstimate** /ˈgestɪmət/ *n.* (*coll.*) grobe Schätzung

**ˈguesswork** *n., no pl., no indef. art.* **be ~:** eine Vermutung sein; **rely largely on ~:** [weitgehend] auf Vermutungen angewiesen sein; **How did you know? — Oh, it was only [by] ~:** Woher wusstest du das? — Ach, ich habe nur geraten

**guest** /gest/ *n.* Gast, *der; attrib.* Gast‹auftritt, -spiel, -vortrag, -redner›; Gäste‹handtuch›; **be my ~** (*fig. coll.*) tun Sie sich/tu dir keinen Zwang an; **as [the] ~ of** als Gast (+ *Gen.*); **~ of honour** Ehrengast, *der*

**guest: ~ house** *n.* Pension, *die;* **~ list** *n.* Gästeliste, *die* (**at** *Gen.*); **~ night** *n.* Gästeabend, *der;* **~ room** *n.* Gästezimmer, *das;* **~ worker** *n.* Gastarbeiter, *der*/-arbeiterin, *die*

**guff** /gʌf/ *n.* (*coll.*) Mumpitz, *der* (*ugs.*)

**guffaw** /gʌˈfɔː, ˈgʌfɔː/ ❶ *n.* brüllendes Gelächter; **give a [great] ~:** in brüllendes Gelächter ausbrechen. ❷ *v.i.* brüllend lachen

**guidance** /ˈgaɪdəns/ *n., no pl., no indef. art.* Ⓐ (*leadership, direction*) Führung, *die;* (*by teacher, tutor, etc.*) [An]leitung, *die;* **pray for God's ~:** Gott bitten, einem den rechten Weg zu weisen; Ⓑ (*advice*) Rat, *der;* **turn to sb. for ~:** jmdn. um Rat fragen *od.* bitten; **give sb. ~ on sth.** jmdn. in etw. (*Dat.*) beraten; **financial/vocational ~:** Finanz-/Berufsberatung, *die*

**guide** /gaɪd/ ❶ *n.* Ⓐ Führer, *der*/Führerin, *die;* (*Tourism*) [Fremden]führer, *der*/-führerin, *die;* (*professional mountain climber*) [Berg]führer, *der*/-führerin, *die;* Ⓑ (*fig.: mentor*) Lehrer, *der*/Lehrerin, *die;* **God is my ~:** Gott leitet mich; Ⓒ (*directing principle*) Richtschnur, *die;* **always let your conscience be your ~:** lass dich stets von deinem Gewissen leiten; Ⓓ (*indicator*) **be a [good/bad] ~ to sth.** ein [guter/schlechter] Anhaltspunkt für etw. sein; **be no/little ~ to sth.** keine/nur begrenzte Rückschlüsse auf etw. (*Akk.*) zulassen; Ⓔ (*Brit.: member of girls' organization*) **[Girl] G~:** Pfadfinderin, *die;* **the G~s** (*organization*) die Pfadfinderinnen; **King's/Queen's G~** (*im Britischen Commonwealth*) *Pfadfinderin der höchsten Rangstufe;* Ⓕ (*handbook*) Handbuch, *das;* **a ~ to healthier living** ein Ratgeber für ein gesünderes Leben; Ⓖ (*book for tourists*) [Reise]führer, *der;* (*on entertainment, with dates*) Veranstaltungskalender, *der;* **a ~ to York/the cathedral/the museum** ein Führer für *od.* durch York/für die Kathedrale/ein Museumsführer; Ⓗ (*Mech. Engin.*) Führung, *die.*
❷ *v.t.* Ⓐ führen ‹Personen, Pflug, Maschinenteil usw.›; Ⓑ (*fig.*) bestimmen ‹Handeln, Urteil›; anleiten ‹Schüler, Lehrling›; **be ~d by sth./sb.** sich von etw./jmdm. leiten lassen; **guiding star** (*fig.*) Leitstern, *der* (*geh.*); **guiding hand** (*fig.*) leitende Hand; Ⓒ (*conduct affairs of*) führen, lenken ‹Land, Staat›; lenken ‹Angelegenheit›; führen ‹Finanzen›

**ˈguidebook** ⇒ **guide** 1 G

**guided missile** /gaɪdɪd ˈmɪsaɪl/ *n.* Lenkflugkörper, *der*

**ˈguide dog** *n.* **~ [for the blind]** Blinden[führ]hund, *der*

**guided tour** /gaɪdɪd ˈtʊə(r)/ *n.* Führung, *die* (**of** durch)

**guide: ~line** *n.* (*fig.*) Richtlinie, *die;* (*model*) Vorlage, *die;* **~post** *n.* Wegweiser, *der*

**Guider** /ˈgaɪdə(r)/ *n.* (*Brit.*) Pfadfinderführerin, *die*

**guild** /gɪld/ *n.* Ⓐ Verein, *der;* Vereinigung, *die;* Ⓑ (*Hist.*) (*of merchants*) Gilde, *die;* (*of artisans*) Zunft, *die*

**ˈguildhall** *n.* Ⓐ (*town hall*) Rathaus, *das;* **[the] Guildhall** (*Brit.*) die Guildhall (*in London*); Ⓑ (*Hist.*) (*for merchants*) Gildehaus, *das;* (*for artisans*) Zunfthaus, *das*

**guile** /gaɪl/ *n., no pl.* Arglist, *die* (*geh.*); Hinterlist, *die;* (*wiliness*) List, *die;* **be without ~:** ohne Arg *od.* Falsch sein (*geh.*)

**guileful** /ˈgaɪlfl/ *adj.* arglistig (*geh.*); hinterlistig; (*wily*) listig

**guileless** /gaɪllɪs/ *adj.* arglos

**guillemot** /ˈgɪlɪmət/ *n.* (*Ornith.*) (*Uria*) Lumme, *die;* (*Cepphus*) Teiste, *die*

**guillotine** /ˈgɪlətiːn/ ❶ *n.* Ⓐ Guillotine, *die;* Fallbeil, *das;* Ⓑ (*for paper*) Papierschneidemaschine, *die;* (*for metal*) Schlagschere, *die;* Ⓒ (*Brit. Parl.*) Begrenzung der Beratungszeit (*im Gesetzgebungsverfahren*). ❷ *v.t.* Ⓐ (*behead*) guillotinieren; mit der Guillotine *od.* dem Fallbeil hinrichten; Ⓑ (*cut*) schneiden

**guilt** /gɪlt/ *n., no pl.* Ⓐ Schuld, *die* (**of, for** an + *Dat.*); **bear the ~ of** *or* **for sth.** die Schuld für etw. auf sich (*Akk.*) tragen; Ⓑ (*awareness of being in the wrong*) Schuldbewusstsein, *das;* (*guilty feeling*) Schuldgefühle *Pl.*; **feel [full of] ~:** [starke] Schuldgefühle haben; **~ was written all over his face** sein schlechtes Gewissen stand ihm im Gesicht geschrieben; **~ complex** (*Psych.*) Schuldkomplex, *der;* **~-feelings** Schuldgefühle

**guiltily** /ˈgɪltɪlɪ/ *adv.* schuldbewusst

**guiltless** /ˈgɪltlɪs/ *adj.* unschuldig (**of** an + *Dat.*)

**guilty** /ˈgɪltɪ/ *adj.* Ⓐ schuldig; **the ~ person** der/die Schuldige; **be ~ of murder** des Mordes schuldig sein; **find sb. ~/not ~ [of sth.]** jmdn. [an etw. (*Dat.*)] schuldig sprechen/[von etw.] freisprechen; **the jury found him not ~ of murder** die Geschworenen entschieden, dass er des Mordes nicht schuldig war; **~ thoughts** böse Gedanken; **[return** *or* **find a verdict of] ~/not ~:** [auf] „schuldig"/„nicht schuldig" [erkennen]; **feel ~ about sth./having done sth.** ein schlechtes Gewissen haben wegen etw./, weil man etw. getan hat; **everyone is/we're all ~ of that** (*coll.*) das tut jeder/das tun wir alle; **I've often been ~ of that myself** (*coll.*) das habe ich auch schon oft gemacht; **be ~ of bad taste** eine Geschmacklosigkeit begangen haben; Ⓑ (*prompted by guilt*) schuldbewusst ‹Miene, Blick, Verhalten›; schlecht ‹Gewissen›

**guinea** /ˈgɪnɪ/ *n.* (*Hist.*) Guinee, *die*

**Guinea** /ˈgɪnɪ/ *pr. n.* Guinea (*das*)

**guinea: ~fowl, ~ hen** *ns.* Perlhuhn, *das*

**Guinean** /ˈgɪnɪən/ ❶ *adj.* guineisch. ❷ *n.* Guineer, *der*/Guineerin, *die*

**ˈguinea pig** *n.* Ⓐ (*animal*) Meerschweinchen, *das;* Ⓑ (*fig.: subject of experiment*) (*person*) Versuchsperson, *die;* Versuchskaninchen, *das* (*ugs. abwertend*); (*thing*) Versuchsobjekt, *das;* **act as ~:** Versuchskaninchen spielen

**guise** /gaɪz/ *n.* Ⓐ (*semblance*) Gestalt, *die;* **in** *or* **under the ~ of** in Gestalt (+ *Gen.*); Ⓑ (*pretence*) Vorwand, *der;* Ⓒ (*external appearance*) Äußere, *das*

**guitar** /gɪˈtɑː(r)/ *n.* Gitarre, *die; attrib.* Gitarren‹musik, -spieler, -konzert›; **electric ~:** elektrische Gitarre; Elektrogitarre, *die*

**guitarist** /gɪˈtɑːrɪst/ *n.* ▶ **1261** Gitarrist, *der*/Gitarristin, *die*

**Gujarati** /guːdʒəˈrɑːtɪ/ ▶ **1275** ❶ *adj.* gudscharatisch. ❷ *n.* Ⓐ (*person*) Gudscharate, *der*/Gudscharatin, *die;* Ⓑ (*language*) Gudscharati, *das*

**gulch** /gʌltʃ/ *n.* (*Amer.*) Schlucht, *die;* Klamm, *die*

**gules** /gjuːlz/ (*esp. Her.*) ❶ *n.* Rot, *das.* ❷ *adj.* rot

**gulf** /gʌlf/ *n.* Ⓐ (*portion of sea*) Golf, *der;* Meerbusen, *der;* **the [Arabian** *or* **Persian] G~:** der Persische Golf; **the G~ of Bothnia/Mexico** der Bottnische Meerbusen/der Golf von Mexiko; Ⓑ (*wide difference, impassable gap*) Kluft, *die;* **there is a great ~ between them** es besteht eine tiefe Kluft zwischen ihnen; Ⓒ (*chasm*) Abgrund, *der*

**Gulf: ~ States** *pr. n. pl.* Golfstaaten *Pl.*; **~ Stream** *pr. n.* Golfstrom, *der*

**gull** /gʌl/ *n.* Möwe, *die*

**gullet** /ˈgʌlɪt/ *n.* Ⓐ (*food passage*) Speiseröhre, *die;* Ⓑ (*throat*) Kehle, *die;* Gurgel, *die*

**gullible** /ˈgʌlɪbl/ *adj.* leichtgläubig; (*trusting*) gutgläubig

**ˈgull-wing** *adj.* **~ door** Flügeltür, *die*

**gully** /ˈgʌlɪ/ *n.* Ⓐ (*artificial channel*) Abzugskanal, *der;* Abzugsrinne, *die;* Ⓑ (*drain*) Gully, *der;* Ⓒ (*water-worn ravine*) [Erosions]rinne, *die;* Runse, *die* (*Geol.*); Ⓓ (*Cricket*) *Position/Feldspieler seitlich hinter dem Schlagmann*

**ˈgully hole** ⇒ **gully** B

**gulp** /gʌlp/ ❶ *v.t.* hinunterschlingen; hinuntergießen ‹Getränk›. ❷ *v.i.* (*swallow with difficulty*) würgen; (*choke, swallow on account of shock*) schlucken; **~ for air** nach Luft ringen *od.* schnappen. ❸ *n.* Ⓐ (*act of ~ing, effort to swallow*) Schlucken, *das;* **swallow in** *or* **at one ~:** mit einem Schluck herunterstürzen ‹Getränk›; in einem Bissen herunterschlingen ‹Speise›; Ⓑ (*large mouthful*) (*of drink*) kräftiger Schluck; (*of food*) großer Bissen; Ⓒ (*act of swallowing due to shock*) **give a ~:** schlucken

**~ ˈback** *v.t.* hinunterschlucken ‹Tränen›; unterdrücken ‹Schluchzer›

**~ ˈdown** *v.t.* hinunterschlingen; hinuntergießen ‹Getränk›

**gum**[1] /gʌm/ *n., usu. in pl.* ▶ **966** (*Anat.*) **~[s]** Zahnfleisch, *das*

**gum**[2] ❶ *n.* Ⓐ (*viscous secretion*) Gummi, *das;* (*glue*) Klebstoff, *der;* Ⓑ (*sweet*) Gummibonbon, *der od. das;* Ⓒ (*Amer.*) ⇒ **chewing gum;** Ⓓ (*tree*) ⇒ **gum tree.** ❷ *v.t.,* **-mm-** Ⓐ (*smear with ~*) mit Klebstoff bestreichen; gummieren ‹Briefmarken, Etiketten usw.›; Ⓑ (*fasten with ~*) kleben

**~ ˈup** *v.t.* aufkleben; **~ up the works** (*fig. coll.*) alles vermasseln (*salopp*)

**gum: ~ ˈarabic** ⇒ **Arabic** 1; **~boil** *n.* ▶ **1232** Zahnfleischabszess, *der;* **~boot** *n.* Gummistiefel, *der*

**gummy** /ˈgʌmɪ/ *adj.* Ⓐ (*sticky*) klebrig; Ⓑ (*covered with gum*) mit Klebstoff verschmiert

**gumption** /ˈgʌmpʃn/ *n., no pl., no indef. art.* (*coll.*) Ⓐ (*resourcefulness*) Grips, *der* (*ugs.*); (*enterprising spirit*) Unternehmungsgeist, *der;* **she had the ~ to open the door** sie war clever genug, die Tür zu öffnen; Ⓑ (*practical sense*) praktische Veranlagung; **have a lot of ~:** sehr praktisch veranlagt sein

**gum: ~shield** *n.* Mundschutz, *der;* **~ tree** *n.* Gummiharz liefernder Baum; (*eucalyptus*) [Australischer] Gummibaum; **be up a ~ tree** (*fig.*) in der Klemme sitzen (*ugs.*)

**gun** /gʌn/ ❶ *n.* Ⓐ Schusswaffe, *die;* (*piece of artillery*) Geschütz, *das;* (*rifle*) Gewehr, *das;* (*pistol*) Pistole, *die;* (*revolver*) Revolver, *der;* **big ~** (*coll.: important person*) hohes *od.* großes Tier (*ugs.*); **be going great ~s** laufen wie geschmiert (*ugs.*); ‹Person:› toll in Schwung sein (*ugs.*); **son of a ~** (*coll.*) Hund, *der* (*salopp*); (*joc.*) alter Hund (*salopp*); **stick to one's ~s** auf seinem Posten bleiben; (*fig.*) auf seinem Standpunkt beharren; **give it the ~!** (*coll.*) drück auf die Tube! (*ugs.*); **~s or butter** (*fig.*) Macht oder Wohlleben; Ⓑ (*starting pistol*) Startpistole, *die;* **wait for the ~:** auf den Startschuss warten; **beat** *or* **jump the ~:** einen Fehlstart verursachen; (*fig.*) vorpreschen; (*by saying sth.*) vorzeitig etwas bekannt werden lassen; Ⓒ (*member of shooting party*) Schütze, *der.*
❷ *v.t.,* **-nn-:** Ⓐ (*Amer. coll.*) erschießen; umlegen (*salopp*); Ⓑ (*coll.*) **~ the engine** den Motor hochdrehen

**~ ˈdown** *v.t.* niederschießen

**~ for** *v.t.* Ⓐ (*seek with ~*) Jagd machen auf (+ *Akk.*); Ⓑ (*fig.*) auf dem Kieker haben (*ugs.*)

**gun:** ~ **battle** *n.* Schießerei, *die;* ~**boat** *n.* Kanonenboot, *das;* ~**boat diplomacy** Kanonenbootpolitik, *die;* ~ **carriage** *n.* [fahrbare] Geschützlafette; ~ **control** *n.* Bestimmungen *Pl.* über den Besitz und den Gebrauch von Schusswaffen; ~ **control law** Waffengesetz, *das;* ~ **control legislation** Waffengesetze *Pl.;* ~**cotton** *n.* Schießbaumwolle, *die;* ~ **crew** *n.* Geschützbedienung, *die;* ~ **dog** *n.* Jagdhund, *der;* ~**fight** *n.* (*Amer. coll.*) Schießerei, *die;* ~**fighter** *n.* Revolverheld, *der;* ~**fire** *n.* Geschützfeuer, *das;* (*of small arms*) Schießerei, *die*

**gunge** /gʌndʒ/ (*Brit. coll.*) ❶ *n.* Schmiere, *die.* ❷ *v.t.* ~ **up** verschmieren; **be/get** ~**d up** schmierig werden

**gung-ho** /gʌŋ'həʊ/ *adj.* wild entschlossen; **be very** ~ **for sth.** ein leidenschaftlicher Verfechter einer Sache (*Gen.*) sein

**gungy** /'gʌndʒɪ/ *adj.* (*Brit. coll.*) schmierig

**gunk** /gʌŋk/ *n.* (*coll.*) Schmiere, *die*

**gun:** ~ **laws** *pl.* Waffengesetze *Pl.;* ~**man** /'gʌnmən/ *n., pl.* ~**men** /'gʌnmən/ [mit einer Schusswaffe] bewaffneter Mann; ~**metal** *n.* Geschützbronze, *die;* (*colour*) Metallgrau, *das;* ~ **moll** *n.* (*Amer. coll.*) Ⓐ (*armed woman criminal*) Revolverbraut, *die* (*salopp*); Ⓑ ⇒ **moll**

**gunnel** /'gʌnl/ ⇒ **gunwale**

**gunner** /'gʌnə(r)/ *n.* Artillerist, *der;* (*private soldier*) Kanonier, *der*

**gunnery** /'gʌnərɪ/ *n., no pl.* Geschützwesen, *das*

**gunny** /'gʌnɪ/ *n.* Rupfen, *der;* ~ **cloth** Rupfenleinwand, *die;* ~**-sack** Rupfensack, *der*

**gun:** ~**play** *n., no pl., no indef. art.* Schießereien *Pl.;* (*single fight*) Schießerei, *die;* ~ **point** ⇒ **point** 1 B; ~**powder** *n.* Schießpulver, *das;* **Gunpowder Plot** (*Hist.*) Pulververschwörung, *die;* ~**room** *n.* Ⓐ (*in house*) Waffenkammer, *die;* Ⓑ (*in warship*) Kadettenmesse, *die;* ~**-runner** *n.* Waffenschmuggler, *der*/-schmugglerin, *die;* ~**-running** *n.* Waffenschmuggel, *der;* ~**ship** *n.* Kampfhubschrauber, *der;* ~**shot** *n.* Ⓐ (*shot*) Schuss, *der;* ~**shot wound** Schusswunde, *die;* Ⓑ **within/out of** ~**shot** in/außer Schussweite; ~**slinger** ⇒ **gunman;** ~**smith** *n.* ▶ 1261 Büchsenmacher, *der*

**gunwale** /'gʌnl/ *n.* (*Naut.*) Schandeck, *das;* Schandeckel, *der;* (*of rowing boat*) Dollbord, *der*

**guppy** /'gʌpɪ/ *n.* (*Zool.*) Guppy, *der*

**gurgle** /'gɜːgl/ ❶ *n.* Gluckern, *das;* (*of brook*) Plätschern, *das;* (*of baby*) Lallen, *das;* (*with delight*) Glucksen, *das.* ❷ *v.i.* gluckern; ‹Bach:› plätschern; ‹Baby:› lallen/glucksen. ❸ *v.t.* glucksen

**Gurkha** /'gɜːkə, 'gʊəkə/ *n.* Gurkha, *der*

**guru** /'gʊruː/ *n.* Ⓐ Guru, *der;* Ⓑ (*mentor*) Mentor, *der*

**gush** /gʌʃ/ ❶ *n.* Ⓐ (*sudden stream*) Schwall, *der;* Ⓑ (*effusiveness*) Überschwänglichkeit, *die;* Ⓒ (*sentimental affectation*) Schmalz, *der* (*abwertend*). ❷ *v.i.* Ⓐ strömen; schießen; (*fig.: speak or act effusively*) überschwänglich sein; ~ **out** herausströmen; herausschießen; **water** ~**ed down through the ceiling** das Wasser floss in Strömen durch die Decke; Ⓑ (*fig.: speak or act with sentimental affectation*) schwärmen. ❸ *v.t.* Ⓐ **sth.** ~**es water/oil/blood** Wasser/Öl/Blut schießt aus etw. hervor; Ⓑ **'...' she** ~**ed** „...", sagte sie begeistert

**gusher** /'gʌʃə(r)/ *n.* Ⓐ (*oil well*) [natürlich sprudelnde] Ölquelle; Ⓑ (*person*) exaltierter Mensch

**gushing** /'gʌʃɪŋ/ *adj.* Ⓐ reißend ‹Strom›; strömend ‹Regen›; Ⓑ (*effusive*) exaltiert

**gusset** /'gʌsɪt/ *n.* (*strengthening*) Verstärkung, *die;* (*enlarging*) Einsatz, *der;* (*triangular*) Zwickel, *der;* Keil, *der*

**gust** /gʌst/ ❶ *n.* ~ **[of wind]** Windstoß, *der;* Bö[e], *die.* ❷ *v.i.* böig wehen

**gusto** /'gʌstəʊ/ *n., no pl.* (*enjoyment*) Genuss, *der;* (*vitality*) Schwung, *der*

**gusty** /'gʌstɪ/ *adj.* böig; ~ **rain** Regenböen *Pl.*

**gut** /gʌt/ ❶ *n.* Ⓐ (*material*) Darm, *der;* (*for fishingline*) Seidenwurmdarm, *der;* (*Med.: for stitches*) Katgut, *das;* Ⓑ *in pl.* (*bowels*) Eingeweide *Pl.;* Gedärme *Pl.;* **hate sb.'s** ~**s** (*coll.*) jmdn. auf den Tod nicht ausstehen können; **sweat** *or* **work one's** ~**s out** (*coll.*) sich dumm und dämlich schuften (*ugs.*); Ⓒ *in pl.* (*fig.: substantial contents*) Innereien *Pl.* (*scherzh.*); (*of problem, matter*) Kern, *der;* **sth. has no** ~**s in it** etw. ist ohne Saft und Kraft; etw. ist fad[e]; Ⓓ *in pl.* (*coll.: pluck*) Schneid, *der* (*ugs.*); Mumm, *der* (*ugs.*); Ⓔ (*intestine*) Darm, *der;* **large/small** ~: Dick-/Dünndarm, *der;* **bust a** ~ (*coll.*) sich totarbeiten (*ugs.*); Ⓕ (*narrow water passage*) (*of sea*) Meerenge, *die;* Sund, *der;* (*of river*) Fluss-, Stromenge, *die.*
❷ *v.t.*, **-tt-:** Ⓐ (*take out* ~*s of*) ausnehmen; Ⓑ (*remove or destroy fittings in*) ausräumen; **the fire** ~**ted the house** bei dem Feuer ist das Haus ausgebrannt; **it was** ~**ted [by the fire]** es brannte aus; Ⓒ (*extract essence of*) ≈ exzerpieren ‹Buch›.
❸ *attrib. adj.* Ⓐ (*fundamental*) grundlegend ‹Problem›; Ⓑ (*instinctive*) gefühlsmäßig ‹Reaktion›; ~ **feeling** instinktives Gefühl; **have a** ~ **feeling that ...** es im Gefühl *od.* (*salopp*) Urin haben, dass...; **rely on one's** ~ **feelings** sich auf seine Gefühle *od.* (*ugs.*) seinen Bauch verlassen

**gutless** /'gʌtlɪs/ *adj.* feige; **be** ~: keinen Mumm haben (*ugs.*)

**gutsy** /'gʌtsɪ/ *adj.* (*coll.: courageous*) mutig

**gutta-percha** /gʌtə'pɜːtʃə, gʌtə'pɜːkə/ *n.* Guttapercha, *die od. das*

**gutter** /'gʌtə(r)/ ❶ *n.* Ⓐ (*below edge of roof*) Dach- *od.* Regenrinne, *die;* (*at side of street*) Rinnstein, *der;* Gosse, *die;* (*open conduit*) Rinne, *die;* **the** ~ (*fig.*) die Gosse; Ⓑ (*track worn by water*) Rinne, *die.* ❷ *v.i.* ‹Kerze:› tropfen; ‹Flamme:› [immer schwächer] flackern

**guttering** /'gʌtərɪŋ/ *n.* (*on roof*) Dachrinnen *Pl.;* (*in floor*) Rinnen *Pl.*

**gutter:** ~ **press** *n.* Sensationspresse, *die* (*abwertend*); ~**snipe** *n.* Gassenjunge, *der* (*abwertend*)

**guttural** /'gʌtərl/ ❶ *adj.* Ⓐ (*from the throat*) guttural; kehlig; Ⓑ (*of the throat*) Kehl-; (*of the larynx*) Kehlkopf-; Ⓒ (*Phonet.*) Kehl-; guttural (*Sprachw. veralt.*). ❷ *n.* (*Phonet.*) Gaumensegellaut, *der;* Guttural[laut], *der* (*Sprachw. veralt.*)

**guv**, /gʌv/, **guv'nor** /'gʌvnə(r)/ (*Brit. coll.*) ⇒ **governor** G

**guy**[1] /gaɪ/ *n.* (*rope, wire*) Halteseil, *das;* (*for hoisted things*) Lenkseil, *das*

**guy**[2] ❶ *n.* Ⓐ (*coll.: man*) Typ, *der* (*ugs.*); Ⓑ *in pl.* (*Amer.: everyone*) **[listen,] you** ~**s!** [hört mal,] Kinder! (*ugs.*); Ⓒ (*Brit.: effigy*) Guy-Fawkes-Puppe, *die;* **Guy Fawkes Day** *Festtag (5. November) zum Gedenken an die Pulververschwörung.* ❷ *v.t.* (*ridicule*) sich lustig machen über (+ *Akk.*)

**Guyana** /gaɪ'ænə/ *pr. n.* Gu[a]yana (*das*)

**Guyanese** /gaɪə'niːz/ ▶ 1340 ❶ *adj.* gu[a]yanisch. ❷ *n.* Gu[a]yaner, *der*/Gu[a]yanerin, *die*

**guy:** ~**-rope** *n.* Zelt[spann]leine, *die;* ~**-wire** *n.* Spanndraht, *der;* Drahtseilabspannung, *die*

**guzzle** /'gʌzl/ ❶ *v.t.* (*eat*) hinunterschlingen; (*drink*) hinuntergießen; (*eat or drink up*) wegputzen (*ugs.*). ❷ *v.i.* schlingen

**gybe** /dʒaɪb/ (*Naut.*) ❶ *v.i.* Ⓐ (*swing across*) übergehen; Ⓑ (*change course*) halsen; (*accidentally*) eine Patenthalse machen. ❷ *n.* (*change of course*) Halse, *die;* (*accidental*) Patenthalse, *die;* (*swing of boom*) Schwenken, *das;* ~**-oh!** rund achtern!

**gym** /dʒɪm/ *n.* (*coll.*) Ⓐ (*gymnasium*) Turnhalle, *die;* (*fitness studio*) Fitnessstudio, *das;* Ⓑ *no pl., no indef. art.* (*gymnastics*) Turnen, *das;* ~ **teacher** Turnlehrer, *der*/Turnlehrerin, *die*

**gymkhana** /dʒɪm'kɑːnə/ *n.* Ⓐ (*meeting*) Gymkhana, *das;* Ⓑ (*display*) Sportfest, *das*

**gymnasium** *n.* Ⓐ /dʒɪm'neɪzɪəm/ *pl.* ~**s** *or* **gymnasia** /dʒɪm'neɪzɪə/ Turnhalle, *die;* Ⓑ /dʒɪm'neɪzɪəm, gɪm'nɑːzɪʊm/ *pl.* ~**s** (*German school*) Gymnasium, *das*

**gymnast** /'dʒɪmnæst/ *n.* Turner, *der*/Turnerin, *die*

**gymnastic** /dʒɪm'næstɪk/ *adj.* turnerisch ‹Können›; ~ **exercise** gymnastische Übung; (*esp. with apparatus*) Turnübung, *die;* ~ **equipment** Turngeräte *Pl.;* (*portable*) gymnastische Geräte

**gymnastics** /dʒɪm'næstɪks/ *n., no pl.* Ⓐ (*exercise*) Gymnastik, *die;* (*esp. with apparatus*) Turnen, *das; attrib.* Gymnastik-/Turn‹stunde, -lehrer›; Ⓑ (*fig.*) **mental** ~: Gehirnakrobatik, *die* (*ugs. scherzh.*); **verbal** ~: Wortakrobatik, *die* (*ugs. scherzh.*)

**gym:** ~ **shoe** *n.* Turnschuh, *der;* ~**slip**, ~ **tunic** *ns.* Trägerrock, *der* (*für die Schule*)

**gynaecological** /gaɪnɪkə'lɒdʒɪkl/ *adj.* (*Med.*) gynäkologisch

**gynaecologist** /gaɪnɪ'kɒlədʒɪst/ *n.* ▶ 1261 (*Med.*) Gynäkologe, *der*/Gynäkologin, *die;* Frauenarzt, *der*/Frauenärztin, *die*

**gynaecology** /gaɪnɪ'kɒlədʒɪ/ *n.* (*Med.*) Gynäkologie, *die;* Frauenheilkunde, *die*

**gynecological** *etc.* (*Amer.*) ⇒ **gynaec-**

**gyp** /dʒɪp/ *n.* **give sb.** ~ (*coll.*) (*scold sb.*) jmdn. zusammenstauchen (*ugs.*); (*pain sb.*) jmdm. sehr zu schaffen machen (*ugs.*)

**gypsophila** /dʒɪp'sɒfɪlə/ *n.* (*Bot.*) Gipskraut, *das*

**gypsum** /'dʒɪpsəm/ *n.* Gips, *der*

**gypsy, Gypsy** /'dʒɪpsɪ/ *n.* Zigeuner, *der*/Zigeunerin, *die;* **family of gypsies** Zigeunerfamilie, *die*

**gypsy:** ~ **moth** *n.* (*Zool.*) Schwammspinner, *der;* ~ **rose** *n.* (*Bot.*) Krätz[en]kraut, *das*

**gyrate** /dʒaɪə'reɪt/ *v.i.* sich drehen; kreiseln

**gyration** /dʒaɪə'reɪʃn/ *n.* Drehung, *die;* kreiselnde Bewegung

**gyratory** /'dʒaɪərətərɪ/ *adj.* kreiselnd

**gyrfalcon** /'dʒɜːfɔːlkn, 'dʒɜːfɒlkn/ *n.* (*Ornith.*) Gerfalke, *der*

**gyro** /'dʒaɪərəʊ/ *n., pl.* ~**s** (*coll.*) ⇒ **gyroscope**

**'gyrocompass** *n.* Kreiselkompass, *der*

**gyroscope** /'dʒaɪərəskəʊp/ *n.* (*Phys., Naut., Aeronaut.*) Kreisel, *der;* (*for scientific purposes*) Gyroskop, *das*

**gyroscopic** /dʒaɪərə'skɒpɪk/ *adj.* Kreisel-

**gyro-'stabilizer** *n.* Schiffskreisel, *der*

# Hh

**H¹, h** /eɪtʃ/ *n., pl.* **Hs** *or* **H's** /'eɪtʃɪz/ (*letter*) H, h, *das;* ⇒ *also* **drop** 3 G

**H²** *abbr.* (*on pencil*) **hard** H

**h.** *abbr.* Ⓐ **hecto-** h; Ⓑ **hour[s]** Std[n].; **at 17⁰⁰h** um 17.00 h

**ha** /hɑ:/ ❶ *int. expr. surprise, triumph* ha; *expr. hesitation* hm. ❷ *v.i.* ⇒ **hum** 1 A. ❸ *n., pl.* **ha's** ⇒ **hum** 3 B

**ha.** *abbr.* **hectare[s]** ha

**habeas corpus** /heɪbɪəs 'kɔ:pəs/ *n., no pl.* (*Law*) Anordnung eines Haftprüfungstermins; **Habeas Corpus Act** Habeaskorpusakte, *die*

**haberdasher** /'hæbədæʃə(r)/ *n.* ▶ **1261** Ⓐ (*Brit.*) Kurzwarenhändler, *der*/-händlerin, *die;* Ⓑ (*Amer.*) (*dealer in men's accessories*) Inhaber eines Geschäfts für Herrenartikel; (*dealer in menswear*) Herrenausstatter, *der;* Ⓒ **~'s** ⇒ **haberdashery** B

**haberdashery** /'hæbədæʃərɪ/ *n.* Ⓐ (*goods*) (*Brit.*) Kurzwaren *Pl.;* (*Amer.: men's accessories*) Herrenartikel; (*Amer.: menswear*) Herrenmoden; Ⓑ (*shop*) (*Brit.*) Kurzwarengeschäft, *das;* Kurzwarenhandlung, *die;* (*Amer.*) Geschäft für Herrenartikel/Herrenmodengeschäft, *das;* Ⓒ (*department*) (*Brit.*) Kurzwarenabteilung, *die;* (*Amer.*) Abteilung für Herrenartikel/Herrenmodenabteilung, *die*

**habit** /'hæbɪt/ ❶ *n.* Ⓐ (*set practice*) Gewohnheit, *die;* **good/bad ~:** gute/schlechte [An]gewohnheit; **the ~ of smoking** das [gewohnheitsmäßige] Rauchen; **have a** *or* **the ~ of doing sth.** die Angewohnheit haben, etw. zu tun; **the sun has a ~ of disappearing at the weekend** (*iron.*) zum Wochenende verzieht sich die Sonne regelmäßig; **make a [regular] ~ of doing sth.** sich (*Dat.*) angewöhnen, etw. [regelmäßig] zu tun; **you shouldn't make a ~ of it** du solltest es nicht zur Gewohnheit werden lassen; **let sth. become** *or* (*coll.*) **get to be a ~:** etw. zur Gewohnheit werden *od.* (*ugs.*) einreißen lassen; **out of ~, from [force of] ~:** aus Gewohnheit; **old ~s die hard** der Mensch ist ein Gewohnheitstier (*ugs.*); **be in the ~ of doing sth.** die Gewohnheit haben, etw. zu tun; **not be in the ~ of doing sth.** es nicht gewohnt sein, etw. zu tun; **I'm not in the ~ of accepting lifts from strangers** ich pflege mich nicht von Fremden im Auto mitnehmen zu lassen; **get** *or* **fall into a** *or* **the ~ of doing sth.** [es] sich (*Dat.*) angewöhnen, etw. zu tun; **get into** *or* **form** *or* **acquire good ~s** gute Angewohnheiten annehmen; **get** *or* **fall into** *or* (*coll.*) **pick up bad ~s** schlechte [An]gewohnheiten annehmen; **get out of** *or* **give up** *or* **stop a/the ~:** sich (*Dat.*) etwas/das abgewöhnen; eine/die Angewohnheit ablegen; **get out of the ~ of doing sth.** [es] sich (*Dat.*) abgewöhnen, etw. zu tun; Ⓑ (*coll.*) (*addiction*) Süchtigkeit, *die;* [Drogen]abhängigkeit, *die;* (*craving*) Sucht, *die;* **have got the ~:** süchtig sein; User sein (*Drogenjargon*); Ⓒ (*dress*) Habit, *der od. das;* (*woman's riding dress*) Reitkostüm, *das;* (*arch.: clothing*) Gewand, *das;* Ⓓ (*Psych.*) Habit, *das od. der;* Ⓔ (*Biol., Chem.*) Habitus, *der.*
❷ *v.t.* (*formal: clothe*) kleiden

**habitable** /'hæbɪtəbl/ *adj.* bewohnbar

**habitat** /'hæbɪtæt/ *n.* Ⓐ (*of animals, plants*) Habitat, *das* (*Zool., Bot.*); Lebensraum, *der;* Standort, *der* (*Bot.*); (*of humans*) Lebensraum, *der;* Ⓑ ⇒ **habitation** B

**habitation** /hæbɪ'teɪʃn/ *n.* Ⓐ (*inhabiting*) [Be]wohnen, *das;* **fit/unfit** *or* **not fit for human ~:** bewohnbar/unbewohnbar; Ⓑ (*place*) Wohnstätte, *die* (*geh.*)

**habit-forming** /'hæbɪtfɔ:mɪŋ/ *adj.* Abhängigkeit erzeugend; **be ~:** Abhängigkeit erzeugen; abhängig machen; (*fig.*) leicht zur Gewohnheit werden [können]

**habitual** /hə'bɪtjʊəl/ *adj.* Ⓐ (*customary*) gewohnt; üblich; Ⓑ (*continual, recurring*) ständig; **that's a ~ problem of hers** das ist immer wieder ihr Problem; Ⓒ (*given to habit*) gewohnheitsmäßig; Gewohnheits‹trinker›; notorisch (*abwertend*), gewohnheitsmäßig ‹Lügner›

**habitually** /hə'bɪtjʊəlɪ/ *adv.* Ⓐ (*regularly, recurrently*) regelmäßig; Ⓑ (*incessantly*) ständig

**habituate** /hə'bɪtjʊeɪt/ *v.t.* **~ sb./oneself to sth./sb.** jmdn./sich an etw./jmdn. gewöhnen; **~ sb./oneself to doing sth.** jmdn./sich daran gewöhnen, etw. zu tun; **become [too] ~d to sth.** sich [zu sehr] an etw. (*Akk.*) gewöhnen

**habitué** /hə'bɪtjʊeɪ/ *n.* Habitué, *der* (*veralt.*); regelmäßiger Besucher; (*of hotel, casino, etc.*) Stammgast, *der*

**Habsburg** /'hæpsbɜ:g/ *pr. n.* Ⓐ (*place*) Habsburg (*das*); Ⓑ (*family name*) Habsburger, *der;* **the ~ family** die Habsburger *Pl.;* **the ~ emperors** die habsburgischen Kaiser; die Habsburgerkaiser

**hack¹** /hæk/ ❶ *v.t.* Ⓐ (*cut*) hacken ‹Holz›; **~ sb./sth. to bits** *or* **pieces** jmdn. zerstückeln/etw. in Stücke hacken; **~ to bits** *or* **pieces** (*fig.*) zerpflücken; kaputtmachen ‹Ruf›; verreißen ‹Artikel›; **~ sth. out of sth.** etw. aus etw. heraushacken; **~ one's way [through/along/out of sth.]** sich (*Dat.*) einen Weg [durch etw./etw. entlang/aus etw. heraus] [frei]schlagen; Ⓑ (*Footb.*) **~ sb.'s shin** jmdm. *od.* jmdn. vors *od.* gegen das Schienbein treten; Ⓒ (*Computing*) eindringen in (+ *Akk.*) ‹Computersystem›.
❷ *v.i.* Ⓐ (*deal blows*) **~ at** herumhacken auf (+ *Dat.*); **~ through the undergrowth** sich (*Dat.*) einen Weg durchs Unterholz schlagen; Ⓑ **~ing cough** trockener Husten; Reizhusten, *der;* Ⓒ (*Computing*) **~ into sth.** in etw. (*Akk.*) eindringen

**~ a'bout** *v.t.* verpfuschen (*ugs.*); (*fig.*) zurechtstutzen

**~ a'way** ❶ *v.i.* **~ away at sth.** auf etw. (*Akk.*) einhacken; (*fig.*) etw. aushöhlen. ❷ *v.t.* weghacken

**~ 'off** *v.t.* abhacken; abschlagen

**~ 'out** *v.t.* heraushauen (**from** aus); (*fig.: work out*) zustande bringen

**hack²** ❶ *n.* Ⓐ (*drudge*) ≈ Gelegenheitsarbeiter, *der;* Mietling, *der* (*veralt. abwertend*); (*uninspired worker*) Arbeitstier, *das;* (*writer*) Schreiberling, *der* (*abwertend*); **newspaper ~:** Zeitungsschreiber, *der;* **publisher's ~:** Lohnschreiber, *der;* Auftragsschreiber, *der;* Ⓑ (*hired horse*) Mietpferd, *das;* Ⓒ (*horse for ordinary riding*) Reitpferd, *das;* Ⓓ ⇒ **jade¹** 1 A; Ⓔ (*Amer.*) (*taxi*) Taxi, *das;* (*taxi driver*) Taxifahrer, *der.* ❷ *adj.* Ⓐ **~ writer** Lohnschreiber, *der;* Ⓑ (*mediocre*) Nullachtfünfzehn- (*ugs. abwertend*)

**hacker** /'hækə(r)/ *n.* (*Computing*) Hacker, *der*

**hacking**/'hækɪŋ/: **~ coat, ~ jacket** *ns.* Reitjackett, *das;* (*sports jacket*) Sportjacke, *die*

**hackle** /'hækl/ *n.* Ⓐ (*long feather/feathers*) Schmuckfeder, *die*/Schmuckfedern; (*neck plumage*) Kragen, *der;* Kragenfedern; **a cock's ~s are up** ein Hahn sträubt die Federn *od.* stellt die Federn auf; Ⓑ *in pl.* (*animal's hair*) Nacken[- und Rücken]haare *Pl.;* **a dog's ~s are up** einem Hund sträubt sich das Fell; **sb.'s ~s rise/are up** (*fig.*) jmd. gerät/ist in Harnisch; **get sb.'s ~s up, make sb.'s ~s rise** (*fig.*) jmdn. wütend machen; **that kind of thing always gets his ~s up** bei so was sieht er immer rot (*ugs.*); so etwas bringt ihn immer in Harnisch; Ⓒ (*comb*) Hechel, *die* (*Landw.*)

**hackney** /'hæknɪ/ *n.* [gewöhnliches] Pferd; Gaul, *der* (*ugs.*)

**hackney:** **~ 'cab, ~ 'carriage** *ns.* Droschke, *die* (*veralt.*); Taxe, *die;* **~ 'coach** *n.* (*Hist.*) [Pferde]droschke, *die*

**hackneyed** /'hæknɪd/ *adj.* abgegriffen; abgedroschen (*ugs.*)

**'hacksaw** *n.* [Metall]bügelsäge, *die*

**had** ⇒ **have** 1, 2

**haddie** /'hædɪ/ (*Scot.*) ⇒ **haddock**

**haddock** /'hædək/ *n., pl. same* Schellfisch, *der;* **smoked ~:** Haddock, *der*

**Hades** /'heɪdi:z/ *n., no pl.* Ⓐ (*Greek Mythol.*) Hades, *der;* **to/in ~:** in den/im Hades; Ⓑ (*coll. euphem.*) ⇒ **hell** A

**hadji** /'hædʒɪ/ *n.* Hadschi, *der*

**hadn't** /'hædnt/ (*coll.*) = **had not;** ⇒ **have** 1, 2

**Hadrian's Wall** /heɪdrɪənz 'wɔ:l/ *n.* (*Hist.*) Hadrianswall, *der*

**haematology** /hi:mə'tɒlədʒɪ/ *n.* (*Med.*) Hämatologie, *die*

**haemoglobin** /hi:mə'gləʊbɪn/ *n.* (*Anat., Zool.*) Hämoglobin, *das*

**haemophilia** /hi:mə'fɪlɪə/ *n.* ▶ **1232** (*Med.*) Hämophilie, *die* (*fachspr.*); Bluterkrankheit, *die*

**haemophiliac** /hi:mə'fɪlɪæk/ *n.* (*Med.*) Bluter, *der*/Bluterin, *die*

**haemorrhage** /'hemərɪdʒ/ (*Med.*) ❶ *n.* Hämorrhagie, *die* (*fachspr.*); Blutung, *die.* ❷ *v.i.* starke Blutungen haben

**haemorrhoid** /'hemərɔɪd/ *n., usu. in pl.* (*Med.*) Hämorrhoide, *die*

**haft** /hɑ:ft/ *n.* Griff, *der;* Heft, *das* (*geh.*)

**hag** /hæg/ *n.* Ⓐ (*old woman*) [alte] Hexe; Ⓑ (*witch*) Hexe, *die;* Ⓒ ⇒ **hagfish**

**'hagfish** *n.* Inger, *der;* Schleimaal, *der*

**haggard** /'hægəd/ *adj.* (*worn*) ausgezehrt; (*with worry*) abgehärmt; (*tired*) abgespannt

**haggis** /'hægɪs/ *n.* (*Gastr.*) Haggis, *der; gefüllter Schafsmagen*

**haggle** /'hægl/ ❶ *v.i.* sich zanken (**over, about** wegen); (*over price*) feilschen (*abwertend*) (**over, about** um). ❷ *n.* Gezänk, *das* (*abwertend*); (*over price*) Gefeilsche, *das* (*abwertend*)

**hagiography** /hægɪ'ɒgrəfɪ/ *n.* Hagiographie, *die*

**'hag-ridden** *adj.* **be ~ by sth.** von etw. geplagt *od.* gequält werden; **look ~:** niedergedrückt aussehen

**Hague** /heɪg/ *pr. n.* ▶ **1626** **The ~:** Den Haag (*das*); der Haag (*geh.*); **The ~ Conventions** die Haager Konventionen

**ha ha** /hɑ: 'hɑ:/ *int.* haha!

**ha-ha** /'hɑ:hɑ:/ *n.* Umfassungsgraben, *der;* Aha, *das* (*Bauw.*)

**haiku** /'haɪku:/ *n., pl. same* (*Lit.*) Haiku, *das*

**hail¹** /heɪl/ ❶ *n.* Ⓐ *no pl., no indef. art.* (*Meteorol.*) Hagel, *der;* Ⓑ (*fig.: shower*) Hagel, *der;* (*of curses, insults, questions, praise*) Schwall, *der;* Flut, *die;* **a ~ of bullets/missiles/stones/arrows** ein Kugel-/Geschoss-/Stein-/Pfeilhagel *od.* -regen. ❷ *v.i.* Ⓐ *impers.* (*Meteorol.*) **it ~s** *or* **is ~ing** es hagelt; Ⓑ (*fig.: descend*) **~ down** niederprasseln (**on** auf + *Akk.*); **~ down on sb.** ‹Beschimpfungen, Vorwürfe usw.:› auf jmdn. einprasseln. ❸ *v.t.* niederhageln *od.* niederprasseln lassen

**hail²** ❶ *v.t.* **A** (*call out to*) anrufen, (*fachspr.*) anpreien ‹Schiff›; (*signal to*) heranwinken, anhalten ‹Taxi›; **within/not within ~ing distance** in/außer Rufweite; **B** (*salute*) grüßen; (*receive, welcome*) begrüßen; empfangen; **C** (*acclaim*) zujubeln (+ *Dat.*); bejubeln (**as** als); **~ sb. king** jmdm. als König zujubeln. ❷ *v.i.* **A** rufen; **B where does the ship ~ from?** woher kommt das Schiff?; **where do you ~ from?** woher kommst du?; wo bist du her? (*ugs.*). ❸ *n.* **A** (*salutation*) Gruß, *der;* (*shout of acclamation*) Jubelruf, *der;* **B** (*call*) [Zu]ruf, *der;* **within/out of ~:** in/außer Rufweite. ❹ *int.* (*arch.*) sei gegrüßt (*geh.*); **~ Macbeth/to thee, O Caesar** Heil Macbeth/dir, o Cäsar; **H~ Mary** ⇒ **ave Maria**; **~-fellow-well-met** kumpelhaft; **be ~-fellow-well-met with sb.** jmdn. kumpelhaft behandeln; **say ~ and farewell to sb.** jmdn. begrüßen und von ihm [zugleich] Abschied nehmen; ⇒ *also* **all** 1 A

**hail: ~stone** *n.* (*Meteorol.*) Hagelkorn, *das;* **~storm** *n.* (*Meteorol.*) heftiger Hagelfall; Hagelschauer, *der*

**hair** /heə(r)/ *n.* **A** (*one strand*) Haar, *das;* **a dog's ~:** ein Hundehaar; **without turning a ~** (*fig.*) ohne eine Miene zu verziehen; **not harm a ~ of sb.'s head** (*fig.*) jmdm. kein Haar krümmen; ⇒ *also* **dog** 1 A; **hang** 2 A; **short** 1 A; **split** 3 B; **B** ▶966 *collect., no pl.* (*many strands, mass*) Haar, *das;* Haare *Pl.; attrib.* Haar-; (*horse~*) Rosshaar-; **the cat has a lovely coat of black ~:** die Katze hat ein wunderschönes schwarzes Fell; **do one's/sb.'s ~:** sich/jmdm. das Haar machen (*ugs.*); **do one's own ~:** sich (*Dat.*) das Haar selbst machen (*ugs.*); **have** *or* **get one's ~ done** sich (*Dat.*) das Haar *od.* die Haare machen lassen (*ugs.*); **where did you get your ~ done?** bei welchem Friseur warst du?; **pull sb.'s ~:** jmdn. an den Haaren ziehen; **he's losing his ~:** ihm gehen die Haare aus; **he has still not lost his ~:** er hat seine Haare noch [alle]; **keep your ~ on!** (*coll.*), **don't lose your ~!** (*coll.*) geh [mal] nicht gleich an die Decke! (*ugs.*); **let one's ~ down** sein Haar aufmachen *od.* lösen; (*fig. coll.*) [ganz] locker sein (*ugs.*); sich [ganz] locker geben (*ugs.*); (*give free expression to one's feelings etc.*) aus sich herausgehen; (*have a good time*) auf den Putz hauen (*ugs.*); die Sau rauslassen (*salopp*); **sb.'s ~ stands on end** (*fig.*) jmdm. stehen die Haare zu Berge (*ugs.*); **get in sb.'s ~** (*fig. coll.*) jmdm. auf die Nerven *od.* den Wecker gehen *od.* fallen (*ugs.*); **get out of my ~!** (*coll.*) lass mich in Ruhe! (*ugs.*); **keep out of sb.'s ~** (*coll.*) jmdn. in Ruhe lassen; ⇒ *also* **curl** 1 A, 2 A; **tear¹** 2 B; **C** (*Bot.*) Haar, *das;* **D** (*thin filament*) Faden, *der;* **E** (*minute amount*) **a ~:** eine Idee; **by a ~:** knapp ‹gewinnen›; **to a ~:** haargenau; (*in every detail*) haarklein

**hair: ~breadth** ❶ *n.* winzige Kleinigkeit; **by [no more than] a ~breadth** [nur] um Haaresbreite ‹verfehlen›; nur knapp ‹gewinnen›; **the firm was within a ~breadth of bankruptcy** die Firma wäre um ein Haar (*ugs.*) bankrott gegangen; ❷ *adj.* minimal; hauchdünn (*ugs.*) ‹Chance›; **that was a ~breadth escape** das war äußerst *od.* (*ugs.*) verdammt knapp; **~brush** *n.* Haarbürste, *die;* **~ conditioner** *n.* Pflegespülung *die;* **~ cream** *n.* Haarcreme, *die;* Pomade, *die;* **~ curler** *n.* Lockenwickler, *der;* **~cut** *n.* **A** (*act*) Haareschneiden, *das;* **go for/need a ~cut** zum Friseur gehen/müssen; **give sb. a ~cut** jmdm. die Haare schneiden; **get/have a ~cut** sich (*Dat.*) die Haare schneiden lassen; **B** (*style*) Haarschnitt, *der;* **~do** *n.* (*coll.*) **A get a ~do** sich (*Dat.*) das Haar machen lassen (*ugs.*); **give sb. a ~do** jmdm. das Haar machen (*ugs.*); **B** (*style*) Frisur, *die;* **~dresser** *n.* ▶1261 **A** (*Brit.*) Friseur, *der*/Friseuse, *die;* **men's ~dresser** Herrenfriseur, *der*/-friseuse, *die;* **ladies' ~dresser** Damenfriseur, *der*/-friseuse, *die;* **go to the ~dresser['s]** zum Friseur gehen; **B** (*Amer.: for women*) Damenfriseur, *der*/-friseuse, *die;* **~dresser's** Damen[frisier]salon, *der;* **go to the ~dresser['s]** zum Friseur gehen; **~dressing** *n.* der Friseurberuf; *attrib.* **~dressing salon** Friseursalon, *der;* **~drier** *n.* Haartrockner, *der;* Fön ⓌⓏ, *der;* (*with a hood*) Trockenhaube, *die;* **~ dye** *n.* Haarfärbemittel, *das;* **use ~ dye** sich (*Dat.*) das Haar färben

**-haired** /heəd/ *adj. in comb.* ▶966 **black-/dark-/frizzy-~:** schwarz-/dunkel-/kraushaarig; **greasy-~:** mit fettigem Haar *nachgestellt*

**hair: ~ follicle** *n.* Haarbalg, *der;* **~grip** *n.* (*Brit.*) Haarklammer, *die;* **~ lacquer** ⇒ **~spray**

**hairless** /ˈheəlɪs/ *adj.* unbehaart ‹Körper[teil], Pflanze, Blatt›; kahlköpfig ‹Person›; kahl ‹Kopf›

**hair: ~line** *n.* **A** (*edge of hair*) Haaransatz, *der;* **his ~line is receding, he has a receding ~line** er bekommt eine Stirnglatze; **B** (*narrow line*) haarfeine Linie; haarfeiner Strich; **C** (*crack*) haarfeiner Riss; **~line crack** (*esp. Metallurgy, Mech. Engin.*) Haarriss, *der;* **~line fracture** (*Med.*) Fissur, *die;* **D** (*in writing or printing*) Haarstrich, *der;* **~net** *n.* Haarnetz, *das;* **~piece** *n.* Haarteil, *das;* **~pin** *n.* Haarnadel, *die;* **~pin 'bend** *n.* Haarnadelkurve, *die;* **~-raising** /ˈheəreɪzɪŋ/ *adj.* Furcht erregend; (*very bad*) haarsträubend; mörderisch ‹Rennstrecke; Abstieg vom Berg usw.›; **~-restorer** *n.* Haarwuchsmittel, *das;* **~'s breadth** ⇒ **~breadth**; **~ 'shirt** *n.* härenes Hemd (*geh.*); Härenhemd, *das* (*veralt.*); (*worn as a penance*) Büßerhemd, *das;* **~slide** *n.* (*Brit.*) Haarspange, *die;* **~-space** *n.* (*Printing*) Haarspatium, *das;* **~-splitting** (*derog.*) ❶ *adj.* haarspalterisch (*abwertend*); ❷ *n.* Haarspalterei, *die* (*abwertend*); **~spray** *n.* Haarspray, *das;* **~spring** *n.* (*Horol.*) Unruhfeder, *die;* **~style** *n.* Frisur, *die;* **~stylist** *n.* ▶1261 Friseur, *der*/Friseuse, *die;* Hair-Stylist, *der*/-Stylistin, *die;* **~-trigger** *n.* (*Arms*) Stecher, *der*

**hairy** /ˈheərɪ/ *adj.* **A** (*having hair*) behaart; flauschig ‹Schal, Pullover, Teppich›; **you're beginning to get a ~ chest** du bekommst Haare auf der Brust; **a very ~ dog** ein Hund mit einem dichten Fell; (*having very long hair*) ein sehr langhaariger Hund; **be all ~:** voller Haare sein; **B** (*made of hair*) aus Haar (*nachgestellt*); hären (*geh.*) ‹Gewand›; **C** (*coll.: difficult, dangerous*) haarig; **D** (*coll.: unpleasant, frightening*) eklig (*ugs.*); **E** (*coll.: crude, clumsy*) unmöglich (*ugs.*)

**Haiti** /hɑːˈiːtɪ, ˈheɪtɪ/ *pr. n.* Haiti (*das*)

**Haitian** /hɑːˈiːʃn, ˈheɪʃn/ ▶1340 ❶ *adj.* haitianisch; **sb. is ~:** jmd. ist Haitianer/Haitianerin. ❷ *n.* Haitianer, *der*/Haitianerin, *die*

**hajji** ⇒ **hadji**

**hake** /heɪk/ *n., pl. same* (*Zool.*) Seehecht, *der*

**halal** /hɑːˈlɑːl/ (*Islam*) ❶ *v.t.* nach muslimischem Ritus schlachten. ❷ *n.* Fleisch von einem nach muslimischem Ritus geschlachteten Tier. ❸ *adj.* ‹Fleisch› von einem nach muslimischem Ritus geschlachteten Tier

**halberd** /ˈhælbəd/, **halbert** /ˈhælbət/ *ns.* (*Arms Hist.*) Hellebarde, *die*

**ˈhalcyon days** /ˈhælsɪən deɪz/ *n. pl.* (*happy days*) glückliche Tage *Pl.;* glückliche Zeiten *Pl.*

**hale¹** /heɪl/ *adj.* kräftig ‹Körper, Konstitution›; rege ‹Geist›; **~ and hearty** gesund und munter

**hale²** *v.t.* (*literary*) **~ sb. to prison** jmdn. ins Gefängnis werfen (*geh.*); **~ sb. before the magistrate** jmdn. vor den Friedensrichter *od.* das Schiedsgericht zerren

**half** /hɑːf/ ❶ *n., pl.* **halves** /hɑːvz/ **A** ▶912, ▶1012, ▶1352 (*part*) Hälfte, *die;* **~ [of sth.]** die Hälfte [von etw.]; **~ of Europe** halb Europa; **I've only ~ left** ich habe nur noch die Hälfte; **~ [of] that** die Hälfte [davon]; **I don't believe ~ of it!** ich glaube nicht die Hälfte davon; **cut sth. in ~** *or* **into [two] halves** etw. in zwei Hälften schneiden; **divide sth. in ~** *or* **into halves** etw. halbieren; **one/two and a ~ hours, one hour/two hours and a ~:** anderthalb *od.* eineinhalb/zweieinhalb Stunden; **she is three and a ~:** sie ist dreieinhalb; **that was a performance/game/job and a ~** (*fig. coll.*) das war vielleicht eine Vorstellung/ein Spiel/eine Arbeit (*ugs.*); **an idiot/a joker/a fool/a woman and a ~** (*fig. coll.*) ein Oberidiot/-witzbold/-trottel (*ugs.*)/eine Superfrau (*ugs.*); **not/never do anything/things by halves** keine halben Sachen machen; **you don't do things by halves, do you?** (*iron.*) du meinst wohl, wenn schon, denn schon?; **be too cheeky/big by ~:** entschieden zu frech/groß sein; **be too clever by ~** (*iron.*) oberschlau (*ugs. iron.*) *od.* superklug (*ugs. iron.*) sein; **go halves** *or* **go ~ and ~ [with sb.] in** *or* (*coll.*) **on sth.** sich (*Dat.*) etw. [mit jmdm.] teilen; bei etw. halbe-halbe [mit jmdm.] machen (*ugs.*); **how the other ~ lives** wie andere Leute leben; **that's only** *or* **just** *or* **not the ~ of it** das ist noch nicht alles; **you don't know the ~ of it** [ja,] wenn es nur das wäre!; **my other ~** (*coll.*) meine bessere Hälfte (*ugs.*); ⇒ *also* **better** 1; **B** (*coll.:* **~** *pint*) kleines Glas; (*of beer*) kleines Bier; Kleine, *das* (*ugs.*); **a ~ of bitter/lager/cider** ein kleines Bitter/ein kleines Lager/ein kleiner Apfelwein; **C** (*Brit. Hist. coll.:* **~** *a new penny*) Halbe, *der* (*ugs.*); **D** (*child's ticket*) Fahrkarte zum halben Preis; halbe Fahrkarte; **one and a ~ to Oxford** eineinhalbmal nach Oxford; **two halves to Oxford** zwei halbe [Fahrkarten] nach Oxford; **E** (*Brit. Sch.: term*) Halbjahr, *das;* **F** (*Footb. etc.*) (*period*) Halbzeit, *die;* (*of pitch*) [Spielfeld]hälfte, *die;* (*coll.:* **~***-back*) Läufer, *der*/Läuferin, *die;* **G** (*Golf*) halbiertes Loch; **the outward/inward ~:** die Löcher 1-9/10-18.

❷ *adj.* **A** (*equal to a ~*) halb; **~ the house/books/staff/time** die Hälfte des Hauses/der Bücher/des Personals/der Zeit; **~ the world** die halbe Welt; **he is drunk ~ the time** (*very often*) er ist fast immer betrunken; **she knits ~ the time/the day** (*a lot of, a good deal of*) sie strickt die ganze Zeit/den halben Tag; **~ an hour** eine halbe Stunde; **be only ~ the man/woman one used to be** (*fig.*) längst nicht mehr der/die alte sein; **B** (*forming a ~*) **they each have a ~ share in the boat** das Boot gehört jedem [von ihnen] zur Hälfte; **be given a ~ day's holiday** einen halben Tag freibekommen; **C** (*Bookbinding*) Halb‹leder, -leinen›; ⇒ *also* **battle** 1 C; **ear¹** A; **eye** 1 A; **mind** 1 B.

❸ *adv.* **A** (*to the extent of ~*) zur Hälfte; halb ‹öffnen, schließen, aufessen, fertig, voll, geöffnet›; (*almost*) fast ‹fallen, ersticken, tot sein›; **our journey was now ~ done** die Hälfte der Reise lag hinter uns; **~ as much/many/big/heavy** halb so viel/viele/groß/schwer; **~ run [and] ~ walk** teils laufen, teils gehen; **~ cough and ~ sneeze** halb husten, halb niesen; **we had only ~ entered the room when ...:** wir waren noch nicht ganz eingetreten, als ...; **I ~ wished/hoped that ...:** ich wünschte mir/hoffte fast, dass ...; **only ~ hear what ...:** nur zum Teil hören, was ...; **~ listen for/to** mit halbem Ohr horchen auf (+ *Akk.*)/zuhören (+ *Dat.*); **I ~ laughed** (*almost*) ich hätte fast [los]gelacht; **I felt ~ dead** (*fig.*) ich war halbtot; **be only ~ ready** *or* **done** (*Cookery*) erst halb gar sein; **~ cook sth.** etw. halb gar werden lassen; **be ~ happy, ~ worried about sth.** teils glücklich, teils besorgt über etw. (*Akk.*) sein; **leave the food ~ eaten** die Hälfte von dem Essen übrig lassen; **go ~ crazy/wild** halb verrückt (*ugs.*) werden; **not ~ cooked yet** noch lange nicht gar; **not ~ finished yet** noch lange nicht fertig; **not ~ long/strong enough** bei weitem nicht lang/stark genug; **not ~** (*coll.*) (*most certainly*) und ob!; (*extremely*) irrsinnig (*ugs.*); **not ~ bad** (*coll.*) toll (*ugs.*); **not ~ a bad fellow/meal** (*coll.*) ein toller Typ/ein tolles Essen (*ugs.*); **not ~ he wouldn't!** (*coll.*) und ob er das wäre/tun würde!; **it wasn't ~ a problem** (*coll.*) es war ein großes *od.* (*ugs.*) wahnsinniges Problem; **she can't ~ be stubborn** (*coll.*) sie ist wahnsinnig (*ugs.*) dickköpfig; **there won't ~ be trouble** (*coll.*) es wird einen Riesenkrach geben; ⇒ *also* **again** A; **B** ▶1012 (*by the amount of a ~-hour*) halb; **at ~ past the hour** um halb; **from eight o'clock till ~ past** von acht bis halb neun; **~ past** *or* (*coll.*) **~ one/two/three** *etc.* halb zwei/drei/vier *usw.;* **~ past twelve** halb eins; **~ past midday/midnight** halb eins mittags/nachts

**half-** *in comb.* ▶ 1012| halb ‹gar, verbrannt, betrunken, voll, leer›; **~cold** fast kalt; **~starved** halb verhungert; **a ~dozen** ein halbes Dutzend; **~pound bag/~litre glass** Halbpfundtüte, *die*/-literglas, *das;* **a ~mile** eine halbe Meile; **~year** Halbjahr, *das;* halbes Jahr

**half: ~-and-'~** ❶ *n.* **Does it contain a or b? — H~-and-~:** Enthält es a oder b? — Halb und halb; **it is all silver, not ~-and-~:** es ist reines Silber, nicht halb Silber und halb etwas anderes; **settle for ~-and-~:** sich für eine Kombination aus beidem entscheiden; ❷ *adj.* [A] *(equal)* **take a ~-and-~ share in the duties** sich mit jmdm. die Pflichten teilen; **~-and-~ mixture of a and b** Mischung, die je zur Hälfte aus a und b besteht; [B] *(indecisive)* halb ‹Maßnahme›; ❸ *adv.* zu gleichen Teilen; **they divide their earnings/share the duties ~-and-~:** sie teilen ihre Einkünfte/die Pflichten gleichmäßig untereinander auf; **~-arse[d]** /'hɑːfɑːs(t)/ *adj.* (*sl.*) bescheuert (*salopp*); beknackt (*salopp*); **do a ~-arse[d] job** Murks machen (*ugs.*); pfuschen (*ugs.*); **~-back** *n.* (*Footb., Hockey*) Läufer, *der*/Läuferin, *die;* **~-baked** /hɑːf'beɪkt/ *adj.* [A] (*Cookery*) nicht richtig durchgebacken; [B] (*fig.*) (*not thorough[ly planned]*) unausgegoren (*abwertend*), unausgereift ‹Plan, Aufsatz›; (*not earnest, lacking in strength of purpose*) lasch ‹Haltung, Person›; [C] (*~-witted*) nicht ganz gar *od.* dicht (*ugs.*); **~-binding** *n.* (*Bookbinding*) Halblederereinband, *der;* Halbfranzeinband, *der;* **~-blood** ⇒ **~-breed** A; **~-'blue** *n.* (*Brit. Univ.*) **get a** *or* **one's ~-blue** die Universität bei weniger wichtigen Sportwettkämpfen oder als Reservespieler vertreten; **~-'board** *n.* Halbpension, *die;* **~-board accommodation** [Unterkunft mit] Halbpension; **~-boot** *n.* Halbstiefel, *der;* **~-breed** *n.* [A] Mischling, *der;* Halbblut, *das;* [B] ⇒ **cross-breed** 1; **~-brother** *n.* Halbbruder, *der;* **be ~-brother to sb.** jmds. Halbbruder sein; **~-caste** ❶ *n.* Mischling, *der;* Halbblut, *das;* ❷ *adj.* Mischlings-; **~ 'cock** ⇒ **cock**[1] 1 E; **~-cocked** /hɑːf'kɒkt/ *adj., adv.* (*Amer.*) = **at ~ cock** ⇒ **cock**[1] 1 E; **~-conscious** *adj.* [nur] halb bewusst ‹Wunsch, Wahrnehmung usw.›; **be only ~-conscious** ‹Person:› nicht bei vollem Bewusstsein sein; **~-'crown** *n.* (*Brit. Hist.*) Halfcrown, *die;* **~-day** *n.* halber Tag; *attrib.* halbtägig ‹Kurs, Test›; **take a ~-day's holiday** einen halben Tag Urlaub nehmen; **it's ~-day closing today** heute ist nur halbtägig geöffnet; **~-'hardy** *adj.* (*Hort.*) [bedingt] winterhart; **~-hearted** /hɑːf'hɑːtɪd/ *adj.*, **~-heartedly** /hɑːf'hɑːtɪdlɪ/ *adv.* halbherzig; **~ hitch** ⇒ **hitch** 3 B; **~ 'holiday** *n.* halber freier Tag; **I'll take a ~ holiday on Wednesday** ich werde [am] Mittwoch einen halben Tag Urlaub nehmen; **there will be a ~ holiday in May** im Mai gibt es einen halben Tag frei; **~-hose** ⇒ **hose** 1 B; **~-'hour** *n.* ▶ 1012| halbe Stunde; **at the ~-hour** um halb; **the clock chimes at the ~-hour** die Uhr schlägt jeweils um halb; **~-'hourly** ▶ 1012| ❶ *adj.* halbstündlich; halbstündlich verkehrend ‹Bus usw.›; **the bus service is ~-hourly** der Bus verkehrt halbstündlich; ❷ *adv.* jede halbe Stunde; halbstündlich; **~-hunter** ⇒ **hunter** E; **~-'inch** ❶ *n.* halber Inch; halber Zoll; *attrib.* /'--/ halbzollig; Halbzoll‹bohrer, -schraube›; ❷ *v.t.* (*Brit. sl.*) klauen (*ugs.*); klemmen (*salopp*); **~-landing** *n.* Treppenabsatz, *der;* Zwischenpodest, *das* (*Bauw.*); **~-life** *n.* (*Phys.*) Halbwertszeit, *die;* **~-light** *n.* Halblicht, *das;* **~ 'mast** *n.* **be [flown] at ~ mast** ‹Flagge:› auf halbmast gehisst sein *od.* stehen; **raise/lower to ~ mast** auf halbmast hissen/setzen ‹Flagge›; **~ measure** *n.* [A] **a ~ measure of whisky** ein halber Whisky; [B] *in pl.* halbe Maßnahme; Halbheit, *die* (*abwertend*); **there are no ~ measures with him** er macht keine halben Sachen (*ugs.*); bei ihm gibt es keine Halbheiten; **~ 'moon** *n.* [A] Halbmond, *der;* [B] (*Anat.*) Möndchen, *das;* **the ~ moons of his nails** seine Nagelmöndchen; **~ 'nelson** *n.* (*Wrestling*) Halbnelson, *der;* **get/have got a ~ nelson on sb./sth.** (*fig.*) jmdn./etw. unter Kontrolle bringen/haben; ‹Erpresser usw.:› jmdn./etw. in die Hand kriegen/in der Hand haben; **~ note** (*Amer. Mus.*) ⇒ **minim** A; **~ 'pay** *n.* Ruhegehalt, *das;* Pension, *die;* **be on ~ pay** Ruhegehalt *od.* Pension beziehen; **~penny** /'heɪpnɪ/, *pl. usu.* **~pennies** /'heɪpnɪz/ *for separate coins,* **~pence** /'heɪpəns/ *for sum of money* (*Brit. Hist.*) (*coin*) Halfpenny, *der;* (*sum*) halber Penny; **~pennyworth** /'heɪpəθ/ *n.* (*Brit.*) [A] (*Hist.: amount*) **a ~pennyworth of ...:** für einen halben Penny ...; [B] (*fig.: small amount*) **not a** *or* **one ~pennyworth of** nicht für fünf Pfennig (*ugs.*) ‹Verstand›; nicht das kleinste bisschen ‹Ruhe, Gastfreundschaft, Entgegenkommen usw.›; **~-'pint** *n.* [A] (*quantity*) halbes Pint; [B] (*coll.: small or insignificant person*) halbe Portion (*ugs. spött.*); **~-'price** ❶ *n.* halber Preis; **all articles are at ~-price** alle Artikel gibt es zum halben Preis; **bring sth. down** *or* **reduce sth. to ~-price** etw. um die Hälfte heruntersetzen *od.* reduzieren; ❷ *adj.* zum halben Preis *nachgestellt;* **~-price air fares** um die Hälfte herabgesetzte Flugpreise; ❸ *adv.* zum halben Preis; **~-seas-over** /hɑːfsiːz'əʊvə(r)/ *adj.* (*coll.*) angesäuselt (*ugs.*); **~-shell** *n.* Austernschale, *die:* **lobster on the ~-shell** (*Gastr.*) auf einer Austernschale servierter Hummer; **~-sister** *n.* Halbschwester, *die;* **be ~-sister to sb.** jmds. Halbschwester sein; **~-size** ❶ *n.* Zwischengröße, *die;* halbe Größe; **a ~-size larger** eine halbe Nummer größer; ❷ *adj.* halb ‹Portion›; klein ‹Blumentopf, Spaten›; **~-'staff** (*Amer.*) ⇒ **~-mast**; **~ step** (*Amer. Mus.*) ⇒ **semitone**; **~-'term** *n.* (*Brit.*) [A] **it is nearly ~-term** das Trimester ist fast zur Hälfte vorüber; **by/at/towards ~-term** bis zur/in der/gegen die Mitte des Trimesters; [B] (*holiday*) **~-term [holiday/break]** Ferien in der Mitte des Trimesters; **before ~-term** in der ersten Trimesterhälfte; **~-timbered** /hɑːf'tɪmbəd/ *adj.* Fachwerk‹haus, -bauweise›; **be ~-timbered** ein Fachwerkbau sein; **~-'time** ❶ *n.* [A] (*Sport*) Halbzeit, *die; attrib.* /'--/ Halbzeit‹pfiff, -stand›; **blow the whistle for ~-time** die erste Halbzeit abpfeifen; **by/to ~-time** bis zur Halbzeit; **at ~-time** bei *od.* bis zur Halbzeit; (*during interval*) in der Halbzeitpause; [B] (*Industry*) Kurzarbeit, *die* (*mit um 50 Prozent gekürzter Arbeitszeit*); **~-time working** Kurzarbeit, *die;* **several cotton mills were put on ~-time** in mehreren Baumwollspinnereien wurde Kurzarbeit eingeführt; **1,150 workers were put on ~-time** *or* **had to go on ~-time schedules** 1150 Arbeiter mussten kurzarbeiten; ❷ *adv.* (*Industry*) kurz‹arbeiten›; **~-title** *n.* (*Printing*) [A] Schmutztitel, *der;* Vortitel, *der;* [B] (*section title*) Zwischentitel, *der;* **~-tone** *n.* [A] (*Printing etc.*) Rasterbild, *das;* [B] (*Amer. Mus.*) ⇒ **semitone**; **~-track** *n.* [A] (*system*) Halbkettenantrieb, *der;* [B] (*vehicle*) Halbkettenfahrzeug, *das;* **~-truth** *n.* Halbwahrheit, *die;* **you've only told us a ~-truth** du hast uns nur die halbe Wahrheit gesagt; **~-'volley** ⇒ **volley** 1 C; **~'way** ❶ *adj.* halb ‹Maßnahme›; **~way point** Mitte, *die;* **we're well over the ~way mark** wir haben gut die Hälfte geschafft; **~way house** Gasthaus auf halbem Weg; (*fig.: compromise*) Kompromiss, *der;* Mittelweg, *der;* **~way line** (*Footb.*) Mittellinie, *die;* ❷ *adv.* die Hälfte des Weges ‹begleiten, fahren›; **not ~way satisfactory** nicht einmal halbwegs zufrieden stellend; **by midday they had climbed ~way up the mountain** bis zum Mittag hatten sie den halben Aufstieg hinter sich; ⇒ *also* **go**[1] 1 Q; **meet**[1] 1 B; **~wit** *n.* Schwachkopf, *der;* (*scatterbrain*) Schussel, *der;* **~-witted** /hɑːf'wɪtɪd/ *adj.* dumm; (*mentally deficient*) debil; schwachsinnig; **~-witted person** Schwachkopf, *der;* **~-'yearly** ❶ *adj.* halbjährlich; **at ~-yearly intervals** in halbjährigen Abständen; halbjährlich; ❷ *adv.* halbjährlich; jedes halbe Jahr

**halibut** /'hælɪbət/ *n., pl. same* (*Zool.*) Heilbutt, *der*

**halide** /'heɪlaɪd, 'hælaɪd/ *n.* (*Chem.*) Halogenid, *das;* Halid, *das*

**halitosis** /hælɪ'təʊsɪs/ *n., pl.* **halitoses** /hælɪ'təʊsiːz/ (*Med.*) Halitose, *die* (*fachspr.*); schlechter Atem

**hall** /hɔːl/ *n.* [A] (*large [public] room*) Saal, *der;* (*public building*) Halle, *die;* (*for receptions, banquets*) Festsaal, *der;* (*in medieval house: principal living room*) Wohnsaal, *der;* **school/church ~:** Aula, *die*/Gemeindehaus, *das;* ⇒ *also* **servants' hall**; [B] (*mansion*) Herrenhaus, *das;* Herrensitz, *der;* [C] (*Univ.*) (*residential building*) **~ [of residence]** Studentenwohnheim, *das;* (*Hist.: college*) Kolleg, *das;* **live in ~:** im [Studenten]wohnheim wohnen; [D] (*Univ.: dining room*) Speisesaal, *der;* Mensa, *die;* **in ~:** im Speisesaal; in der Mensa; [E] *no art.* (*dinner taken in ~*) Abendessen in der Mensa; [F] ⇒ **guildhall** B; [G] *in pl.* (*music ~s*) Varietee, *das;* **be on the ~s** im Varietee auftreten; **do a turn on the ~s** mit einer Nummer im Varietee auftreten; [H] (*entrance passage*) Diele, *die;* Flur, *der;* [I] (*Amer.: corridor*) Korridor, *der;* Flur, *der*

**hallal** ⇒ **halal**

**halliard** ⇒ **halyard**

**'hallmark** ❶ *n.* [Feingehalts]stempel, *der;* Repunze, *die;* (*fig.: distinctive mark*) Kennzeichen, *das;* **be the ~ of quality/perfection** (*fig.*) für Qualität/Vollkommenheit bürgen *od.* stehen. ❷ *v.t.* stempeln; repunzieren

**hallo** /hə'ləʊ/ ❶ *int.* [A] (*to call attention*) hallo!; [B] (*Brit.*) ⇒ **hello.** ❷ *n., pl.* **~s** Hallo, *das;* Halloruf, *der;* **give a ~:** Hallo rufen. ❸ *v.i.* Hallo rufen; **~ to sb.** jmdn. anrufen

**hall of 'fame** *n.* Ruhmeshalle, *die*

**halloo** /hə'luː/ ❶ *int.* [A] ⇒ ⇒(*Hunting*) horrido!; [B] ⇒ **hallo** 1 A. ❷ *n.* [A] (*Hunting*) Horrido, *das;* [B] ⇒ **hallo** 2. ❸ *v.i.* (*Hunting*) Horrido rufen. ❹ *v.t.* (*Hunting*) anfeuern ‹Jagdhund›

**hallow** /'hæləʊ/ ❶ *n.* **All H~s, H~mas** = **All Saints' Day** ⇒ **all** 1 B. ❷ *v.t.* [A] (*sanctify*) heiligen; **~ed** geheiligt (*auch fig.*); heilig ‹Boden›; [B] (*honour*) als heilig verehren; **~ed be Thy Name** (*in Lord's Prayer*) geheiligt werde dein Name

**Hallowe'en** /hæləʊ'iːn/ *n.* Halloween, *das;* *Abend vor Allerheiligen;* **on** *or* **at ~:** [an] Halloween

**hall: ~ 'porter** *n.* (*Brit.*) [Hotel]portier, *der;* **~ stand** *n.* [Flur]garderobe, *die*

**hallucinant** /hə'luːsɪnənt/ ❶ *adj.* ⇒ **hallucinogenic.** ❷ *n.* ⇒ **hallucinogen**

**hallucinate** /hə'luːsɪneɪt/ *v.i.* halluzinieren (*Med., Psych.*); Halluzinationen haben

**hallucination** /həluːsɪ'neɪʃn/ *n.* (*act*) Halluzinieren, *das;* (*instance, imagined object*) Halluzination, *die;* Sinnestäuschung, *die*

**hallucinatory** /hə'luːsɪneɪtərɪ/ *adj.* [A] (*producing hallucinations*) ⇒ **hallucinogenic**; [B] (*associated with hallucinations*) halluzinatorisch (*Med., Psych.*); [C] (*unreal*) imaginär (*geh.*); **be purely ~:** reine Einbildung sein

**hallucinogen** /hə'luːsɪnədʒen/ *n.* (*Med.*) Halluzinogen, *das*

**hallucinogenic** /həluːsɪnə'dʒenɪk/ *adj.* (*Med.*) halluzinogen

**'hallway** *n.* [A] ⇒ **hall** H; [B] (*corridor*) Flur, *der;* Korridor, *der;* Gang, *der* (*bes. südd., österr., schweiz.*)

**halm** ⇒ **haulm**

**halo** /'heɪləʊ/ *n., pl.* **~es** [A] (*Meteorol.*) Halo, *der* (*fachspr.*); Hof, *der;* **there was a ~ round** *or* **a ~ surrounded the moon** der Mond hatte einen Hof *od.* (*fachspr.*) Halo; [B] (*circle*) Ring, *der;* (*of light*) Lichthof, *der;* [C] (*around head*) Heiligen-, Glorienschein, *der;* [D] (*fig.: aura*) Nimbus, *der;* **put a romantic ~ about sth.** etw. mit einer romantischen Gloriole umgeben

**halogen** /'hælədʒən/ *n.* (*Chem.*) Halogen, *das* (*fachspr.*); Salzbildner, *der;* **~ lamp** Halogenlampe, *die*

**halt**[1] /hɒlt, hɔːlt/ ❶ *n.* [A] (*temporary stoppage*) Pause, *die;* (*on march or journey*) Rast, *die;* Pause, *die;* (*esp. Mil. also*) Halt, *der;* **make a ~:** Rast/eine Pause machen/Halt machen; **call a ~:** eine Pause machen lassen/Halt machen lassen; **let's call a ~:** machen wir eine Pause!; [B] (*interruption*) Unterbrechung, *die;* **come to a ~** = **come to**

h

a standstill ⇒ standstill; ⇒ *also* call 2 F; come 1 H; grind 2 B; C (*Brit. Railw.*) Haltepunkt, *der.* 2 *v.i.* A (*stop*) ‹Fußgänger, Tier:› stehen bleiben; ‹Fahrer:› anhalten; (*for a rest*) eine Pause machen; (*esp. Mil.*) Halt machen; (*to collect one's thoughts etc.*) innehalten; ~, who goes there? (*Mil.*) halt, wer da?; B (*end*) eingestellt werden. 3 *v.t.* A (*cause to stop*) anhalten; Halt machen lassen ‹Marschkolonne usw.›; he could not be ~ed (*fig.*) er war nicht aufzuhalten *od.* (*ugs.*) zu bremsen; B (*cause to end*) stoppen ‹Inflation, Diskussion›; beenden ‹Herrschaft›; einstellen ‹Projekt›

**halt**[2] *v.i.* (*not progress smoothly*) ‹Argument:› schwach sein; ‹Verse, Übersetzung:› holprig sein; ~ing schleppend ‹Stimme, Redeweise, Fortschritt›; holprig ‹Verse›; zögernd ‹Antwort›; schwach ‹Argument›; in a ~ing way *or* manner schleppend ‹sprechen›

**halter** /ˈhɒltə(r), ˈhɔːltə(r)/ *n.* A (*for horse*) Halfter, *das;* (*for cattle*) [rope] ~: Strick, *der;* B (*for hanging*) Strick, *der;* Strang, *der;* you'll find a ~ round your neck if ...: du findest dich am Galgen wieder, wenn ...; the ~ (*arch./literary: hanging*) Strang, *der* (*geh.*); C (*Dressmaking*) (*strap*) Nackenträger, *der;* Nackenband, *das;* (*top with a* ~) Oberteil *od.* Top mit Nackenträger; ~ dress/bodice/top/bra Kleid/Mieder/Oberteil *od.* Top/Büstenhalter mit Nackenträger; ~ neck Nackenband, *das*

**halting** ⇒ halt[2]

**haltingly** /ˈhɒltɪŋlɪ, ˈhɔːltɪŋlɪ/ *adv.* schleppend ‹vorankommen›; (*with uncertain steps*) mit unsicheren Schritten ‹gehen›; (*hesitantly*) zögernd; come ~ to the point nur auf Umwegen zur Sache kommen

**halve** /hɑːv/ *v.t.* A (*divide*) halbieren; B (*share*) [ehrlich] teilen; they ~d the cake [between them] sie haben sich (*Dat.*) den Kuchen ehrlich geteilt; C (*reduce*) halbieren; auf *od.* um die Hälfte verringern; 'sale — all prices ~d!' „Ausverkauf — alles zum halben Preis!"; ~ the amount of beer one drinks/number of nights one goes out nur noch halb so viel Bier trinken/halb so oft abends ausgehen; D (*Golf*) mit der gleichen Anzahl von Schlägen erreichen ‹Loch› (with wie); durchspielen ‹Runde›; beenden ‹Spiel›; the hole was ~d in 5 beide Spieler erreichten das Loch mit fünf Schlägen; be ~d ‹Spiel:› unentschieden enden

**halves** *pl. of* half

**halyard** /ˈhæljəd/ *n.* (*Naut.*) Fall, *das;* (*for flag*) Flagg[en]leine, *die*

**ham** /hæm/ 1 *n.* A ([*meat from*] *thigh of pig*) Schinken, *der;* B *usu. in pl.* (*back of thigh*) Hinterseite des Oberschenkels; squat *or* sit on one's ~s in der Hocke sitzen; C (*coll.*) (*amateur*) Amateur, *der;* (*poor actor*) Schmierenkomödiant, *der* (*abwertend*); radio ~: Funkamateur, *der;* D *no pl., no art.* (*coll.: inexpert acting*) Schmierentheater, *das* (*abwertend*). 2 *adj.* (*coll.*) überzogen; a very ~ performance ein ziemliches Schmierentheater (*abwertend*). 3 *v.i.*, -mm- (*coll.*) überziehen. 4 *v.t.*, -mm- (*coll.*) überzogen spielen

~ 'up *v.t.* (*coll.*) überzogen spielen ‹Stück›; ~ it up überziehen

**hamadryad** /hæməˈdraɪæd/ *n.* A (*Greek and Roman Mythol.*) Hamadryade, *die;* B (*Zool.: cobra*) Königskobra, *die;* C (*Zool.: baboon*) Mantelpavian, *der*

**Hamburg** /ˈhæmbɜːg/ ▶ 1626 1 *pr. n.* Hamburg (*das*). 2 *attrib. adj.* Hamburger

**hamburger** /ˈhæmbɜːgə(r)/ *n.* A (*beef cake*) Hacksteak, *das;* (*filled roll*) Hamburger, *der;* B H~ (*person*) Hamburger, *der*/Hamburgerin, *die*

**Hamelin** /ˈhæməlɪn/ *pr. n.* Hameln (*das*)

**ham:** ~-fisted /hæmˈfɪstɪd/, ~-handed /hæmˈhændɪd/ *adjs.* (*coll.*) tollpatschig (*ugs.*) ‹Mensch, Art›; dilettantisch ‹Bearbeitung, Vorgehensweise›; plump (*abwertend*) ‹Vorstellung, Humor›; ~-fisted *or* ~-handed actions Tollpatschigkeiten

**Hamitic** /həˈmɪtɪk/ *adj.* (*Ling.*) hamitisch

**hamlet** /ˈhæmlɪt/ *n.* Weiler, *der*

**hammer** /ˈhæmə(r)/ 1 *n.* A (*tool; also Anat.*) Hammer, *der;* the H~ and Sickle Hammer und Sichel; go *or* be at sth. ~ and tongs sich bei etw. schwer ins Zeug legen (*ugs.*); go *or* be at it ~ and tongs (*quarrel*) sich streiten, dass die Fetzen fliegen; B (*of gun*) Hahn, *der;* C (*auctioneer's mallet*) Hammer, *der;* come under the ~: unter den Hammer kommen; D (*Athletics*) [Wurf]hammer, *der;* [throwing] the ~ (*event*) das Hammerwerfen. 2 *v.t.* A (*strike with* ~) hämmern; (*fig.*) hämmern auf (*Akk.*) ‹Tasten, Tisch›; einhämmern auf (*Akk.*) ‹Gegner, Opfer›; ~ a nail into sth. einen Nagel in etw. (*Akk.*) hämmern *od.* schlagen; ~ sth. into sb.['s head] (*fig.*) jmdm. etw. einhämmern; ~ home einschlagen ‹Nagel, Bolzen usw.›; He must not do that. We'll ~ it home Er darf das nicht tun. Wir werden es ihm einbläuen; B (*coll.: inflict heavy defeat on*) abservieren (*ugs.*) ‹Gegner›; vernichtend schlagen ‹Feind›; ausstechen ‹Konkurrenten›; C (*St. Exch.*) für zahlungsunfähig erklären. 3 *v.i.* A (*give blows*) hämmern; klopfen; ~ at sth. an etw. (*Dat.*) [herum]hämmern; ~ at *or* on the door an *od.* gegen die Tür hämmern; B (*fig. coll.: travel fast*) düsen (*ugs.*); kacheln (*salopp*)

~ a'way *v.i.* hämmern; ~ away at herumhämmern *od.* (*ugs.*) -kloppen auf (+ *Dat.*); (*fig.: work hard at*) sich hineinknien in (+ *Akk.*) (*ugs.*) ‹Tätigkeit›; [herum]bosseln an (+ *Dat.*) (*ugs.*) ‹Aufsatz›

~ 'down *v.t.* festhämmern, -klopfen

~ 'out *v.t.* A (*make smooth*) ausklopfen ‹Delle, Beule›; ausbeulen ‹Kotflügel usw.›; glatt klopfen ‹Blech usw.›; B (*fig.: devise*) ausarbeiten ‹Plan, Methode, Vereinbarung›; kommen zu ‹Entscheidung, Entschluss›

**hammock** /ˈhæmək/ *n.* Hängematte, *die*

**hammy** /ˈhæmɪ/ *adj.* A (*resembling ham*) schinkenartig; Schinken‹geschmack, -geruch›; have a ~ taste nach Schinken schmecken; B (*coll.: of ham actors*) theatralisch (*abwertend*) ‹Nummer, Rolle, Aufführung, Darstellung›

**hamper**[1] /ˈhæmpə(r)/ *n.* A (*basket*) [Deckel]korb, *der;* B (*consignment of food*) Präsentkorb, *der;* Christmas ~: Weihnachtsgeschenkkorb, *der*

**hamper**[2] *v.t.* behindern; hemmen ‹Entwicklung, Wachstum usw.›; ~ sb. in his progress, ~ sb.'s progress ‹Hindernis:› jmdn. aufhalten; ~ sb. in his movements jmdn. behindern *od.* in seiner Bewegungsfreiheit beeinträchtigen

**hamster** /ˈhæmstə(r)/ *n.* Hamster, *der;* ⇒ *also* golden hamster

**'hamstring** 1 *n.* (*Anat.*) A (*in man, ape*) Kniesehne, *die;* B (*in quadruped*) Achillessehne, *die.* 2 *v.t.*, hamstrung *or* ~ed A (*cripple*) die Kniesehnen/Achillessehnen durchtrennen (+ *Dat.*); B (*fig.: destroy efficiency of*) lähmen

**hand** /hænd/ 1 *n.* A ▶ 966 (*Anat., Zool.*) Hand, *die;* eat from *or* out of sb.'s ~ (*lit. or fig.*) jmdm. aus der Hand fressen; I need an extra/a strong pair of ~s ich brauche noch jmdn., der/eine kräftige Person, die mir hilft; get one's ~s dirty, dirty *or* soil one's ~s (*lit. or fig.*) sich (*Dat.*) die Hände schmutzig machen; give sb. one's ~ (*reach, shake*) jmdm. die Hand geben *od.* reichen; give *or* lend [sb.] a ~ [with *or* in sth.] [jmdm.] [bei etw.] helfen; not/never do a ~'s turn keine/niemals eine Hand rühren (*ugs.*); keinen/niemals einen Finger krumm machen (*ugs.*); pass *or* go through sb.'s ~s (*fig.*) durch jmds. Hand *od.* Hände gehen; pass through many/several ~s durch viele/etliche Hände gehen; many ~s make light work (*prov.*) viele Hände machen der Arbeit bald ein Ende (*Spr.*); ~ in ~: Hand in Hand; go ~ in ~ [with sth.] (*fig.*) [mit etw.] Hand in Hand gehen; the problem/project/matter in ~: das vorliegende Problem/Projekt/die vorliegende Angelegenheit; ⇒ *also* d; hold hands Händchen halten (*ugs. scherzh.*); sich bei den Händen halten; hold sb.'s ~: jmds. Hand halten; jmdm. die Hand halten; (*fig.: give sb. close guidance*) jmdn. bei der Hand nehmen; (*fig.: give sb. moral support or backing*) jmdn. moralisch unterstützen; jmdm. das Händchen halten (*iron.*); take one's child's/big brother's ~ ‹Erwachsener:› sein Kind an die Hand nehmen/‹Kind:› sich von seinem großen Bruder an die Hand nehmen lassen; ~s off! Hände *od.* Finger weg!; ~s off my wife/Chile! Hände weg von meiner Frau/Chile!; take/keep one's ~s off sb./sth. jmdn./etw. loslassen/nicht anfassen; take your ~s off me this instant! nimm sofort die Finger weg!; keep one's ~s off sth. (*fig.*) die Finger von etw. lassen (*ugs.*); show of ~s Handzeichen, *das;* ~s up [all those in favour] (*as sign of assent*) wer dafür ist, hebt die Hand!; ~s up! (*as sign of surrender*) Hände hoch!; ~s down (*fig.*) (*easily*) mit links (*ugs.*); (*without a doubt, by a large margin*) ganz klar (*ugs.*); eindeutig (*ugs.*); be good with one's ~s [handwerklich] geschickt sein; change *or* (*coll.*) swap ~s die Hand wechseln; die andere Hand nehmen; ⇒ *also* c; turn one's ~ to sth. sich einer Sache (*Dat.*) zuwenden; put *or* set one's ~ to sich machen an (+ *Akk.*) ‹Arbeit, Aufgabe›; ⇒ *also* l; put *or* set one's ~ to doing sth. sich daran machen, etw. zu tun; have sth. at ~: etw. zur Hand haben; have sb. at ~: jmdn. bei sich haben; be at ~ (*be nearby*) in der Nähe sein; (*be about to happen*) unmittelbar bevorstehen; out of ~ (*without delay*) unverzüglich; (*summarily*) kurzerhand; ⇒ *also* b; be to hand (*be readily available, within reach*) zur Hand sein; (*be received*) ‹Brief, Notiz, Anweisung:› vorliegen; come to ~ (*turn up*) sich finden; (*be received*) ‹Brief, Mitteilung:› eingehen; she uses whatever comes to ~: sie nimmt, was gerade da ist; fight ~ to ~: Mann gegen Mann kämpfen; go/pass from ~ to ~: von Hand zu Hand gehen; ~ over ~ *or* fist Zug um Zug ‹hinaufklettern, einziehen›; ~ over fist (*fig.*) (*with steady progress*) laufend; (*with rapid progress*) rapide; live from ~ to mouth von der Hand in den Mund leben; be ~ in glove [with] unter einer Decke stecken [mit]; bind sb. ~ and foot jmdn. an Händen und Füßen fesseln; wait on *or* serve sb. ~ and foot (*fig.*) jmdn. vorn und hinten bedienen (*ugs.*); on [one's] ~s and knees auf Händen und Knien; crawl on [one's] ~s and knees auf allen vieren kriechen (*ugs.*); get down on one's ~s and knees auf die Knie gehen; his ~s are tied (*fig.*) ihm sind die Hände gebunden; have one's ~s full die Hände voll haben; (*fig.: be fully occupied*) alle Hände voll zu tun haben (*ugs.*); ~ on *or* over heart (*fig.*) Hand aufs Herz; get one's ~s on sb./sth. jmdn. erwischen *od.* (*ugs.*) in die Finger kriegen/etw. auftreiben; lay *or* put one's ~ on sth. etw. finden; lay [one's] ~s on sth. sich einer Sache bemächtigen; everything *or* anything *or* all they could lay [their] ~s on alles, wessen sie habhaft werden konnten; lay ~s on sb. jmdm. etw. tun; Hand an jmdn. legen (*geh.*); (*violate*) sich an jmdm. vergreifen; by ~ (*manually*) mit der *od.* von Hand; (*in ~writing*) handschriftlich; (*by messenger*) durch Boten; be made by ~: Handarbeit sein; bring up by ~: mit der Flasche aufziehen; I could do that with one ~ tied behind my back das mache ich doch mit links (*ugs.*); ⇒ *also* banana A; clean 1 B; finger 1 A; hand-to-hand; hand-to-mouth; join 1 A; shake 2 A; sit 1 B; wash 1 A; B (*fig.: authority*) with a strict/firm/iron ~: mit fester/starker Hand/eiserner Faust ‹regieren›; with a heavy ~: mit eiserner Strenge; he needs a father's ~: er braucht die väterliche Hand; hold one's ~: abwarten; hold one's ~ and not do sth. davon Abstand nehmen, etw. zu tun; keep in ~: unter Kontrolle behalten ‹Schüler, Demonstranten› (⇒ *also* d); get out of ~: außer Kontrolle geraten; give sb. a free ~: jmdm. freie Hand lassen; have a free ~ to do sth. freie Hand haben, etw. zu tun; ⇒ *also* a; ⇒ *also* free hand; take 1 A; upper 1 A; C *in pl.* (*custody*) in sb.'s ~s, in the ~s of sb. (*in sb.'s possession*) in jmds. Besitz; (*in sb.'s care*) in jmds. Obhut; I am in your ~s die Entscheidungen überlasse ich Ihnen; put oneself in sb.'s ~s sich jmdm. anvertrauen; be in the ~s of the police ‹Verdächtiger:› sich in Polizeigewahrsam befinden; may I leave

**the matter in your ~s?** darf ich die Angelegenheit Ihnen überlassen?; **the matter/the decision is now out of my ~s** ich bin für die Angelegenheit/die Entscheidung nicht mehr zuständig; **take sth. out of sb.'s ~s** (*withdraw sth. from sb.*) jmdm. etw. entziehen *od.* aus der Hand nehmen; (*relieve sb. of sth.*) jmdm. etw. abnehmen; **fall into sb.'s ~s** ‹Person, Geld:› jmdm. in die Hände fallen; ‹Verantwortung:› jmdm. zufallen; **be in good/bad ~s** in guten/schlechten Händen sein; **have [got] sth./sb. on one's ~s** sich um etw./jmdn. kümmern müssen; **he's got such a lot/enough on his ~s at the moment** er hat augenblicklich so viel/genug um die Ohren (*ugs.*); **suddenly we had a riot on our ~s** plötzlich sahen wir uns mit Ausschreitungen konfrontiert; **have time on one's ~s** [viel] Zeit haben; (*too much*) mit seiner Zeit nichts anzufangen wissen; **they are off our ~s at last** endlich sind wir sie los (*ugs.*); **have [got] sth./sb. off one's ~s** etw./jmdn. los sein (*ugs.*); **take sb./sth. off sb.'s ~s** jmdm. jmdn./etw. abnehmen; **change ~s** den Besitzer wechseln; ⇒ *also* **a**; (D) (*disposal*) **have sth. in ~:** etw. zur Verfügung haben; (*not used up*) etw. [übrig] haben; **keep in ~:** in Reserve halten ‹Geld› (⇒ *also* **b**); **have on ~:** dahaben; **be on ~:** da sein; (E) (*share*) **have a ~ in sth.** bei etw. seine Hände im Spiel haben; **take a ~ [in sth.]** sich [an etw. (*Dat.*)] beteiligen; **take a ~ [at bridge]** [Bridge] mitspielen; ⇒ *also* **bear²** 1 K; (F) (*agency*) Wirken, *das* (*geh.*); **the ~ of a thief/artist/craftsman has been at work here** hier war ein Dieb/Künstler/Handwerker am Werk; **the ~ of God** die Hand Gottes; **these two paintings are by the same ~:** diese beiden Gemälde stammen von derselben Hand; **suffer/suffer injustice at the ~s of sb.** unter jmdm./jmds. Ungerechtigkeit zu leiden haben; **die by one's own ~[s]** (*literary*) Hand an sich (*Akk.*) legen (*geh.*); (G) (*pledge of marriage*) **ask for** *or* **seek sb.'s ~ [in marriage]** um jmds. Hand bitten *od.* (*geh.*) anhalten; um jmdn. anhalten (*geh.*); **ask sb. for his daughter's ~:** jmdn. um die Hand seiner Tochter bitten; bei jmdm. um die Hand seiner Tochter anhalten (*geh.*); **win sb.'s ~:** jmdn. zur Frau *od.* jmds. Hand gewinnen; (H) (*worker*) Arbeitskraft, *die;* Arbeiter, *der;* (*Naut.: seaman*) Hand, *die* (*fachspr.*); Matrose, *der;* **the ship sank with all ~s** das Schiff sank mit der gesamten Mannschaft; (I) (*person having ability*) **be a good/poor/rotten ~ at [playing] tennis** ein guter/schwacher/miserabler Tennisspieler sein; **I'm no ~ at painting** ich kann nicht malen; ⇒ *also* **old** 1 B; (J) (*source*) Quelle, *die;* **at first/second/third ~:** aus erster/zweiter/dritter Hand; ⇒ *also* **first-hand**; **second-hand**; (K) (*skill*) Geschick, *das;* (*characteristic style*) Handschrift, *die;* **get one's ~ in** wieder in Übung kommen *od.* (*ugs.*) reinkommen; **get one's ~ in at sth.** etw. lernen; **keep one's ~ in [at singing/dancing]** [im Singen/Tanzen] in der Übung bleiben *od.* nicht aus der Übung kommen; ⇒ *also* **try** 2 B; (L) (*style of ~writing*) Handschrift, *die;* Hand, *die* (*veralt.*); (*signature*) Unterschrift, *die;* **witness the ~ of J. C.** laut eigener Unterschrift — J. C.; **set one's ~ to sth.** seine Unterschrift unter etw. (*Akk.*) setzen; ⇒ *also* **a**; (M) (*of clock or watch*) Zeiger, *der;* (N) (*side*) Seite, *die;* **on the right/left ~:** rechts/links; rechter/linker Hand; **on sb.'s right/left ~:** rechts/links von jmdm.; zu jmds. Rechten/Linken; **on either ~:** zu *od.* auf beiden Seiten; **on every ~, on all ~s** von allen Seiten ‹umringt sein›; ringsum ‹etw. sehen›; von überallher ‹eintreffen›; **on the one ~ ..., [but] on the other [~] ...:** einerseits ..., andererseits ...; auf der einen Seite ..., auf der anderen Seite ...; **[but] on the other ~:** aber andererseits *od.* auf der anderen Seite; ⇒ *also* **left-hand**; **right-hand**; (O) (*measurement*) Handbreit, *die;* (P) (*Cards*) Karte, *die;* (*player*) Mitspieler, *der*/-spielerin, *die;* (*period of play*) Runde, *die;* **have a good/bad ~:** ein gutes/schlechtes Blatt haben; eine gute/schlechte Karte haben; **play a good ~:** gut spielen; ⇒ *also* **force¹** 2 B; **play** 2 A; **show** 2 A; (Q) (*coll.: applause*) Beifall, *der;* Applaus, *der;* **give him a big ~, let's have a big ~ for him** viel Applaus *od.* Beifall für ihn!

❷ *v.t.* (A) (*deliver*) geben; (Überbringer:) übergeben ‹Sendung, Lieferung›; **~ sth. from one to another** etw. von einem zum anderen weitergeben *od.* -reichen; **~ sth. [a]round [to sb.]** (*offer for distribution*) [jmdm.] etw. anbieten; **~ sth. [a]round** (*pass round, circulate*) etw. herumgeben *od.* -reichen; (*among group*) etw. herumgehen lassen; **you've got to ~ it to them/her** *etc.* (*fig. coll.*) das muss man ihnen/ihr *usw.* lassen; (B) (*help*) helfen; **~ sb. out of/into/over sth.** jmdm. aus etw./in etw. (*Akk.*)/über etw. (*Akk.*) helfen

**~ 'back** *v.t.* (*return*) zurückgeben

**~ 'down** *v.t.* (A) (*pass on*) überliefern ‹Geschichte, Information, Tradition›; weitergeben ‹Gegenstand› (**to** an + *Akk.*); [weiter]vererben ‹Erbstück› (**to** an + *Akk.*); **that ring has been ~ed down from your great-great-grandmother** der Ring ist ein Erbstück von deiner Ururgroßmutter; (B) (*Law*) verhängen ‹Strafe› (**to** über + *Akk.*); fällen ‹Entscheidung›; verkünden ‹Urteil›; **~ down a fine to sb.** jmdn. mit einer Geldstrafe belegen; (C) (*give to person below*) hinunter-/herunterreichen

**~ 'in** *v.t.* abgeben ‹Klausur, Arbeit, Aufsatz› (**to, at** bei); einreichen ‹Petition, Bewerbung› (**to, at** bei)

**~ 'on** *v.t.* weitergeben ‹Rundschreiben, Nachricht, Erfahrungen, Information› (**to** an + *Akk.*); **at 65 he ~ed the business on to his son** mit 65 hat er das Geschäft seinem Sohn übergeben

**~ 'out** *v.t.* aus-, verteilen (**to** an + *Akk.*, **among** unter + *Dat.*); geben ‹Ratschläge, Tipps, Winke› (**to** an + *Akk.*); verteilen ‹Komplimente, Lob› (**to** an + *Akk.*); ⇒ *also* **handout**

**~ 'over** ❶ *v.t.* (A) (*deliver*) übergeben (**to** *Dat.*); freilassen ‹Geisel›; **~ over your guns/money!** Waffen/Geld her!; gebt eure Waffen/euer Geld her!; **he ~ed the housekeeping money over to his wife** er händigte seiner Frau das Haushaltsgeld aus; (B) (*transfer*) übergeben *od.* -reichen (**to** *Dat.*); (*pass*) herüber- *od.* rübergeben *od.* -reichen (**to** *Dat.*); (*allow to have*) abgeben. ❷ *v.i.* (*to next speaker/one's successor*) das Wort/die Arbeit übergeben (**to** an + *Akk.*)

**~ 'up** *v.t.* heraufreichen (**to** *Dat.*)

**hand-** *in comb.* (A) (*operated by hand, held in the hand*) Hand‹hammer, -hebel, -gepäck, -werkzeug, -mixer›; (B) (*done by hand*) hand‹gestickt›; mit der Hand *od.* von Hand ‹glasiert, verziert, gebacken›

**hand: ~bag** *n.* Handtasche, *die;* **~ baggage** *n.* Handgepäck, *das;* **~bell** *n.* Handglocke, *die;* (*musical instrument*) Glocke, *die;* **~bill** *n.* Handzettel, *der;* **~book** *n.* Handbuch, *das;* (*guidebook*) Führer, *der;* **~brake** *n.* Handbremse, *die*

**h & c** *abbr.* **hot and cold running water** fl. h. u. k. W.

**hand: ~cart** *n.* Handwagen, *der;* **~clap** *n.* (A) (*single clap*) In-die-Hände-Klatschen, *das;* **give three ~claps** dreimal in die Hände klatschen; (B) (*applause*) [Hände]klatschen, *das;* ⇒ *also* **slow handclap**; **~clasp** *n.* Händedruck, *der;* **~craft** ❶ *n.* ⇒ **handicraft** A; ❷ *v.t.* in Handarbeit herstellen; **~cream** *n.* Handcreme, *die;* **~cuff** ❶ *n., usu. in pl.* Handschelle, *die;* ❷ *v.t.* in Handschellen (*Akk.*) legen ‹Hände›; **~cuff sb.** jmdm. Handschellen anlegen

**handed-'down** *adj.* abgelegt ‹Kleidungsstück›; (*to posterity*) überliefert

**hand-'finished** *adj.* ⇒ **finish** 1 F: mit der Hand *od.* von Hand geglättet/appretiert/glasiert/poliert/lackiert *usw.*

**handful** /'hændfʊl/ *n.* (A) (*quantity, or fig.: small number*) Handvoll, *die;* **a few ~s of nuts** ein paar Hand voll *od.* ein paar Hände voll Nüsse; **they picked them up by the ~:** sie sammelten ganze Hände voll davon auf; **come out in ~s** *or* **by the ~** ‹Haar:› büschelweise ausgehen; (B) (*fig. coll.: troublesome person[s] or thing[s]*) **these children are/this dog is a real ~:** die Kinder halten/der Hund hält einen ständig auf Trab (*ugs.*); **it's quite a ~ looking after the children** mit der Versorgung der Kinder hat man alle Hände voll zu tun; **that car is quite a ~ to steer** das Auto zu lenken ist Schwerarbeit (*ugs.*)

**hand: ~ grenade** *n.* (*Mil.*) Handgranate, *die;* **~gun** *n.* (*Arms*) Faustfeuerwaffe, *die;* **~-held** *adj.* **~-held camera** Handkamera, *die;* **~hold** *n.* Halt, *der;* **provide ~holds/a ~hold for sb.** jmdm. Halt bieten; **use sth. as a ~hold** sich an etw. (*Dat.*) festhalten

**handicap** /'hændɪkæp/ ❶ *n.* (A) (*Sport*) (*advantage*) Handikap, *das* (*fachspr.*); Vorgabe, *die;* (*disadvantage*) **carry a ~** ‹Jockey:› ein Ergänzungsgewicht mitführen; ‹Pferd:› ein Ergänzungsgewicht tragen; (B) (*race, competition*) Handikaprennen, *das;* Ausgleichsrennen, *das;* (C) (*fig.: hindrance*) Handikap, *das;* **have a mental/physical ~:** geistig behindert/körperbehindert sein; **be a ~/more of a ~ than a help** hinderlich/eher hinderlich als eine Hilfe sein; **don't let the child become a ~ to you** lass dich durch das Kind nicht zu sehr einschränken.

❷ *v.t.*, **-pp-** (A) (*Sport: impose a ~ on*) ein Handikap festlegen für; (B) (*fig.: put at a disadvantage*) benachteiligen; handikapen (*ugs.*); (*fig.: obstruct*) ein Hemmnis darstellen für

**handicapped** /'hændɪkæpt/ ❶ *adj.* behindert; **mentally/physically ~:** geistig behindert/körperbehindert. ❷ *n. pl.* **the [mentally/physically] ~:** die [geistig/körperlich] Behinderten; **a home for the ~:** ein Heim für Behinderte; ein Behindertenheim

**handicapper** /'hændɪkæpə(r)/ *n.* (*Sport*) (*person*) Handikapper, *der*/Handikapperin, *die;* Ausgleicher, *der*/Ausgleicherin, *die*

**handicraft** /'hændɪkrɑːft/ *n.* (A) (*craft*) [Kunst]handwerk, *das;* (*knitting, weaving, needlework*) Handarbeit, *die;* (B) *no pl.* (*manual skill*) Handfertigkeit, *die*

**handily** /'hændɪlɪ/ *adv.* praktisch; günstig ‹gelegen›; deutlich ‹gewinnen, schlagen›

**handiness** /'hændɪnɪs/ *n., no pl.* (A) (*convenience*) Vorteil, *der;* (*nearness*) günstige Lage; (B) (*adroitness*) Geschicklichkeit, *die*

**handiwork** /'hændɪwɜːk/ *n., no pl., no indef. art.* (A) (*working*) handwerkliche Arbeit; **he enjoys ~:** er arbeitet gern handwerklich; **a nice piece of ~!** (*fig.*) gute Arbeit!; (B) (*piece of work*) [Hand]arbeit, *die;* **this painting is the ~ of a master** dieses Bild ist das Werk eines Meisters *od.* ein Meisterwerk; **this ring/newly decorated kitchen is all my own ~:** diesen Ring habe ich selbst gemacht *od.* (*geh.*) gearbeitet/diese Küche habe ich selbst renoviert; (C) (*derog.: bad piece of work*) Werk, *das* (*ugs.*); **whose ~ is this?** wer hat das [denn] verbrochen? (*ugs.*)

**handkerchief** /'hæŋkətʃɪf, 'hæŋkətʃiːf/ *n., pl.* **~s** *or* **handkerchieves** /'hæŋkətʃiːvz/ Taschentuch, *das*

**handle** /'hændl/ ❶ *n.* (A) (*part held*) [Hand]griff, *der;* (*of bag etc.*) [Trag]griff, *der;* (*of knife, chisel*) Heft, *das;* Griff, *der;* (*of axe, brush, comb, broom, saucepan*) Stiel, *der;* (*of handbag*) Bügel, *der;* (*of door*) Klinke, *die;* (*of bucket, watering can, cup, jug*) Henkel, *der;* (*of pump*) Schwengel, *der;* **fly off the ~** (*fig. coll.*) an die Decke gehen (*ugs.*); ausflippen (*salopp*); (B) (*coll.: title*) Titel, *der;* **have a ~ to one's name** einen Titel haben; (C) (*fact used against one*) Handhabe, *die;* (D) (*feel*) Griff, *der;* **have a natural/give a warm ~:** sich natürlich/warm anfühlen.

❷ *v.t.* (A) (*touch, feel*) anfassen; **'Fragile! H~ with care!'** „Vorsicht! Zerbrechlich!"; **mind how you ~ those glasses** geh bitte vorsichtig mit den Gläsern um; (B) (*deal with*) umgehen mit ‹Person, Tier, Situation›; führen ‹Verhandlung›; erledigen ‹Korrespondenz, Telefonat usw.›; (*cope with*) fertig werden *od.* zurechtkommen mit ‹Person, Tier, Situation›; **train sb. to ~ dogs** jmdn. zum Hundeführer ausbilden; (C) (*control*) handhaben ‹Fahrzeug, Flugzeug›; (D) (*treat*) behandeln ‹Person›; (E) (*process, transport*) umschlagen ‹Fracht›; **Heathrow ~s x passengers per year** in Heathrow werden pro Jahr x Passagiere abgefertigt; **the railway ~s x tons of coal a**

h

**week** die Bahn befördert wöchentlich x Tonnen Kohle; **F** (*discuss*) behandeln ‹Thema, Ansicht, Frage›; **G** (*deal in*) handeln mit.
❸ *v.i.* ‹Gerät:› sich handhaben lassen; ‹Fahrzeug, Boot:› sich fahren; ‹Flugzeug:› sich fliegen

**handlebar** /'hændlbɑ:(r)/ *n.* Lenkstange, *die;* Lenker, *der; attrib.* ~ **moustache** Schnauzbart, *der*

'**handlebar tape** *n.* Lenkerband, *das*

**handler** /'hændlə(r)/ *n.* **A** ▶ **1261** (*of police dog*) Hundeführer, *der/*-führerin, *die;* **B** (*dealer*) **be a ~ of sth.** mit etw. handeln; **a ~ of stolen goods** ein Hehler

**handling** /'hændlɪŋ/ *n., no pl.* **A** (*management*) Handhabung, *die;* (*of troops, workforce, bargaining, discussion*) Führung, *die;* (*of situation, class, crowd*) Umgang, *der* (**of** mit); **B** (*use*) Handhabung, *die;* (*Motor Veh.*) Fahrverhalten, *das;* Handling, *das;* **what's your car's ~ like?** wie fährt sich dein Auto?; **C** (*treatment*) Behandlung, *die;* **the child needs firm/considerate ~:** das Kind braucht eine feste Hand/muss rücksichtsvoll behandelt werden; **come in for some rough ~** ‹Sache:› schlecht behandelt werden; ‹Person:› ganz schön etwas abbekommen (*ugs.*); **D** (*processing*) Beförderung, *die;* (*of passengers*) Abfertigung, *die*

'**handling charge** *n.* (*Commerc.*) Bearbeitungsgebühr, *die*

**hand:** ~**list** *n.* Aufstellung, *die;* Liste, *die;* ~ **lotion** *n.* Handlotion, *die;* ~ **luggage** *n.* Handgepäck, *das;* ~**made** *adj.* handgearbeitet; in Handarbeit hergestellt; handgeschöpft ‹Papier›; ~**maid**, ~**maiden** *ns.* **A** (*arch.: female attendant*) Kammerfrau, *die;* [Kammer]zofe, *die;* **B** (*fig.: subordinate*) Dienerin, *die;* ~**-me-down** ❶ *n.* **A** (*garment handed down*) abgelegtes *od.* getragenes *od.* gebrauchtes Kleidungsstück (**from** *Gen.*); **I got the hat/ring as a ~-me-down from my aunt** den Hut/Ring habe ich von meiner Tante übernommen *od.* (*scherzh.*) geerbt; **B** (*ready-made garment*) [billiges] Kleidungsstück von der Stange; ❷ *adj.* gebraucht; alt; ~**out** *n.* **A** (*alms*) Almosen, *das;* Gabe, *die;* **B** (*information*) Handout, *das;* (*press release*) Presseerklärung, *die;* ~**over** *n.* Übergabe, *die;* ~**-painted** *adj.* handbemalt ‹Gegenstand›; handgemalt ‹Muster, Bild›; ~**-'picked** *adj.* sorgfältig ausgewählt; handverlesen (*ugs. scherzh.*); ~**rail** *n.* Geländer, *das;* Handlauf, *der* (*Bauw.*); (*on ship*) Handläufer, *der;* ~**set** *n.* (*Teleph.*) Handapparat, *der*

'**hands-free kit** *n.* Freisprechanlage, *die*

'**handshake** *n.* Händedruck, *der;* Handschlag, *der;* ⇒ *also* **golden handshake**

**hands-'off** *adj.* **have a ~-off approach** sich heraushalten (**to** aus); **be a ~ manager** seinen Mitarbeitern freie Hand lassen

**handsome** /'hænsəm/ *adj.,* ~**r** /'hænsəmə(r)/, ~**st** /'hænsəmɪst/ **A** (*good-looking*) gut aussehend ‹Mann, Frau›; schön, edel ‹Tier, Möbel, Vase usw.›; ~ **is as ~ does** (*prov.*) man soll nicht nach dem Äußeren urteilen; **B** (*generous*) großzügig ‹Geschenk, Belohnung, Mitgift›; nobel ‹Behandlung, Verhalten, Empfang›; (*considerable*) stattlich, ansehnlich ‹Vermögen, Summe, Preis›; stolz ‹Preis, Summe›

**handsomely** /'hænsəmlɪ/ *adv.* großzügig; mit großem Vorsprung ‹gewinnen›

**hand:** ~**s-'on** *adj.* praktisch; ~**spring** *n.* Handstandüberschlag, *der;* ~**stand** *n.* Handstand, *der;* ~**-to-~** *adj.* ~**-to-~ combat** ein Kampf Mann gegen Mann; ~**-to-mouth** *adj.* **A** (*meagre*) kärglich, kümmerlich ‹Leben, Dasein›; **eke out/lead a ~-to-mouth life/existence** von der Hand in den Mund leben; **B** (*precarious*) Gelegenheits‹arbeit›; **operate on a ~-to-mouth basis** von der Hand in den Mund leben (*fig.*); ~ **towel** *n.* [Hände]handtuch, *das;* ~**work** *n., no pl.* Handarbeit, *die;* ~**writing** *n.* [Hand]schrift, *die;* **his style of ~writing** seine [Hand]schrift; ~**'written** *adj.* handgeschrieben; handschriftlich

**handy** /'hændɪ/ *adj.* **A** (*ready to hand*) griffbereit; greifbar; **keep/have sth. ~:** etw. griffbereit *od.* greifbar haben; **there is a ~ socket just by my bed** ich habe direkt am Bett eine Steckdose; **the house is very ~ for the market/town centre** *etc.* von dem Haus aus ist man sehr schnell auf dem Markt/in der Stadt *usw.;* **B** (*useful*) praktisch; nützlich; **come in ~:** sich als nützlich erweisen; **that'll come in ~!** das kann ich gebrauchen!; **C** (*adroit*) geschickt; **be ~ about the house** handwerklich geschickt sein; **be [quite/very] ~ with sth.** [ganz gut/sehr gut] mit etw. umgehen können; **he is too ~ with his gun/fists** er greift zu schnell zum Gewehr/ihm sitzen die Fäuste allzu locker

'**handyman** *n.* Handwerker, *der;* **[home] ~:** Heimwerker, *der;* **be a ~:** handwerklich geschickt sein

**hang** /hæŋ/ ❶ *v.t.,* **hung** /hʌŋ/ (⇒ *also* **f**): **A** (*support from above*) hängen; aufhängen ‹Gardinen›; ~ **sth. from sth.** etw. an etw. (*Dat.*) aufhängen; ~ **sth. on sb.** (*fig. coll.*) jmdm. etw. anhängen (*ugs. abwertend*); **B** (*place on wall*) aufhängen ‹Bild, Gemälde, Zeichnung›; ~ **a picture from a nail** ein Bild an *od.* mit einem Nagel aufhängen; **C** (*paste up*) ankleben ‹Tapete›; ~ **[the] wallpaper** tapezieren; **D** (*install*) aufhängen ‹Glocke›; einhängen ‹Tür, Tor›; **E** (*Cookery*) abhängen lassen ‹Fleisch, Wild›; **be well hung** gut abgehangen sein; **F** *p.t., p.p.* **hanged** (*execute*) hängen, (*ugs.*) aufhängen (**for** wegen); ~ **oneself** sich erhängen *od.* (*ugs.*) aufhängen; **be ~ed, drawn, and quartered** (*Hist.*) gehängt werden(, die Eingeweide herausgenommen bekommen) und gevierteilt werden; **I'll be** *or* **I am ~ed if ...** (*fig.*) der Henker soll mich holen, wenn ...; **[well,] I'm ~ed!** beim *od.* zum Henker! (*derb*); **I'm ~ed if I will** (*said as a retort*) den Teufel werd' ich (*salopp*); ~ **it!** zum Henker! (*derb*); ~ **the expense!** die Kosten interessieren mich nicht; **G** (*let droop*) ~ **one's head in** *or* **for shame** beschämt den Kopf senken; **H** (*decorate*) schmücken

❷ *v.i.,* **hung** **A** (*be supported from above*) hängen; ‹Kleid usw.› fallen; ~ **from the ceiling** an der Decke hängen; von der Decke [herab]hängen; ~ **by a rope** an einem Strick hängen; ~ **in folds** ‹Haut, Segel, Markise, Zelt:› Falten werfen; ~ **loose** lose sein; ~ **tough** (*coll.*) hart bleiben; ~ **in there!** (*coll.*) halte durch!; ~ **by a hair** (*fig.*) an einem seidenen Faden hängen; **he had the threat of prison ~ing over his head** ihm drohte eine Gefängnisstrafe; **time ~s heavily** *or* **heavy** die Zeit wird einem lang; **time ~s heavily** *or* **heavy on sb.** die Zeit wird jmdm. lang; ⇒ *also* **balance** 1 C; **lip** A; **thereby**; **thread** 1 B; **B** (*be executed*) hängen; **let sth. go ~** (*coll.*) etw. schleifen lassen (*ugs.*); **let things go ~:** alles schleifen lassen (*ugs.*); **let sb. go ~:** jmdn. abschreiben (*ugs.*); **C** (*droop*) **the dog's ears and tail hung [down]** der Hund ließ die Ohren und den Schwanz hängen; **his head hung** er hielt den Kopf gesenkt; **with his head ~ing** mit gesenktem Kopf.

❸ *n., no pl.* **A** (*how sth. hangs*) Sitz, *der;* **the ~ of those clothes is perfect** die Kleider sitzen perfekt; **get the ~ of** (*fig. coll.*) (*get the knack of, understand*) klarkommen mit (*ugs.*) ‹Gerät, Arbeit›; (*see the meaning of*) kapieren (*ugs.*) ‹Sprache, Argument›; **you'll soon get the ~ of it/doing it** du wirst den Bogen bald raushaben (*ugs.*)/wirst bald raushaben, wie man es macht; **B** **I don't give** *or* **care a ~ about that/him** (*coll.*) das/er kümmert mich nicht die Bohne (*ugs.*)

~ **about** (*Brit.*), ~ **around** ❶ /--'-/ *v.i.* **A** (*loiter about*) herumlungern (*salopp*); **we ~ about** *or* **around there all evening** wir hängen da den ganzen Abend rum (*ugs.*); **B** (*coll.: wait*) warten; **keep sb. ~ing about** *or* **around** jmdn. warten lassen; **don't ~ about, get a move on!** trödel nicht, beeile dich!; ~ **about!** (*coll.*) wart mal!; Sekunde mal! (*ugs.*). ❷ /'---/ *v.t.* herumlungern an/in/*usw.* (+ *Dat.*) (*salopp*); ~ **about the exit** am Ausgang herumlungern

~ **'back** *v.i.* **A** (*be reluctant*) sich zieren; **don't ~ back!** na komm schon!; **B** (*keep rearward position*) zurückbleiben

~ **on** ❶ /-'-/ *v.i.* **A** (*hold fast*) sich festhalten; ~ **on to** (*lit.: grasp*) sich festhalten an (+ *Dat.*) ‹Gegenstand›; (*fig. coll.: retain*) behalten ‹Eigentum, Stellung›; **B** (*stand firm, survive*) durchhalten; **C** (*coll.: wait*) warten; ~ **on [a minute]!** Moment *od.* (*ugs.*) Sekunde mal!; **D** (*coll.: not ring off*) dranbleiben (*ugs.*). ❷ /'--/ *v.t.* ~ **on sth.** (*fig.*) von etw. abhängen; ~ **on sb.'s words** jmdm. gespannt zuhören

~ **'out** ❶ *v.t.* **A** (*suspend*) aufhängen ‹Wäsche›; **B** (*cause to protrude*) heraushängen lassen ‹Zunge, Tentakel›. ❷ *v.i.* **A** (*protrude*) heraushängen; **the dog's tongue hung out** dem Hund hing die Zunge heraus; **let it all ~ out** (*fig. coll.*) die Sau rauslassen (*ugs.*); **just let it all ~ out!** mach einfach das, wozu du lustig bist! (*ugs.*); **B** (*coll.*) (*reside*) wohnen; seine Bude haben (*ugs.*); (*be often present*) sich herumtreiben (*ugs.*); rumhängen (*ugs.*)

~ **to'gether** *v.i.* **A** (*be coherent*) ‹Handlung:› stimmig sein; ‹Teile eines Ganzen:› sich zusammenfügen; ‹Aussagen:› zusammenstimmen; **B** (*be or remain associated*) zusammenhalten

~ **'up** ❶ *v.t.* **A** (*suspend*) aufhängen; ~ **up sth. on a hook** etw. an einen Haken hängen *od.* an einem Haken aufhängen; **B** (*fig.: put aside*) an den Nagel hängen (*ugs.*); **C** (*postpone*) aufschieben, vertagen ‹Entscheidung›; (*indefinitely*) auf die lange Bank schieben; **D** (*cause delay to*) aufhalten ‹Person›; **the negotiations were hung up for a week** die Verhandlungen kamen für eine Woche zum Stillstand; **E** (*coll.: cause inhibition to*) **be hung up about sth.** ein gestörtes Verhältnis zu etw. haben. ⇒ *also* ~**-up**. ❷ *v.i.* (*Teleph.*) einhängen; auflegen; ~ **up on sb.** einfach einhängen *od.* auflegen

**hangar** /'hæŋə(r), 'hæŋgə(r)/ *n.* Hangar, *der;* Flugzeughalle, *die*

'**hangdog** *adj.* zerknirscht

**hanger** /'hæŋə(r)/ *n.* **A** (*for clothes*) Bügel, *der;* **B** (*loop on clothes etc.*) Aufhänger, *der*

**hanger-'on** *n.* **there are many hangers-on in every political party** in jeder politischen Partei gibt es viele, denen es nur um den persönlichen Vorteil geht; **the rock group with its usual [crowd of] hangers-on** die Rockgruppe mit ihrem üblichen Anhang

**hang:** ~**-glider** *n.* Hängegleiter, *der;* Drachen, *der;* ~**-glider pilot** Drachenflieger, *der/*-fliegerin, *die;* ~**-gliding** *n.* Drachenfliegen, *das*

**hanging** /'hæŋɪŋ/ ❶ *n.* **A** ⇒ **hang** 1: [Auf]hängen, *das;* Ankleben, *das;* Einhängen, *das;* Abhängen, *das;* **B** (*execution*) Hinrichtung [durch den Strang]; ~ **is too good for sb.** der Strang wäre noch eine zu milde Strafe [für jmdn.]; **this is a ~ matter** *or* **crime** darauf steht der Tod durch Erhängen; **it's/that's not a** *or* **no ~ matter** (*fig.*) das ist doch kein Beinbruch! (*ugs.*); **C** *in pl.* (*drapery*) Behang, *der.* ❷ *adj.* ~ **basket/staircase/balcony** Hängekorb, *der*/freitragende Treppe/vorstehender Balkon

**hanging:** ~ **'gardens** *n. pl.* hängende Gärten; ~ **judge** *n.* Richter, *der schnell mit der Todesstrafe bei der Hand ist;* ~ **'paragraph** *n.* (*Printing*) *Absatz mit ausgerückter erster Zeile;* ~ **'valley** *n.* (*Geog.*) Hängetal, *das;* ~ **'wardrobe** *n.* Kleiderschrank, *der*

**hang:** ~**man** /'hæŋmən/ *n., pl.* ~**men** /'hæŋmən/ Henker, *der;* ~**over** *n.* **A** (*after-effects*) Kater, *der* (*ugs.*); **B** (*remainder*) Relikt, *das;* ~**-up** *n.* (*coll.*) **A** (*difficulty*) Problem, *das;* **we have no ~-ups about morals** die Moral ist bei uns kein Thema; **B** (*inhibition*) Macke, *die* (*ugs.*); **have a ~-up about sth.** ein gestörtes Verhältnis zu etw. haben; **C** (*fixation*) Komplex, *der* (**about** wegen); **he has a ~-up about his mother** er hat einen Mutterkomplex

**hank** /hæŋk/ *n.* Strang, *der*

**hanker** /'hæŋkə(r)/ *v.i.* ~ **after** *or* **for** ein [heftiges] Verlangen haben nach ‹Person, etwas Neuem, Zigarette›; sich (*Dat.*) sehnlichst wünschen ‹Gelegenheit›

**hankering** /'hæŋkərɪŋ/ *n.* (*craving*) Verlangen, *das* (**after, for** nach); (*longing*) Sehnsucht, *die* (**after, for** nach)

**hanky** /'hæŋkɪ/ *n.* (*coll.*) Taschentuch, *das*

**hanky-panky** /hæŋkɪ'pæŋkɪ/ *n.*, *no pl.*, *no indef. art.* (*coll.*) Ⓐ (*underhand dealing*) Mauschelei, *die* (*abwertend*); **there's been some ~/there was some ~ going on** es ist gemauschelt worden (*ugs. abwertend*); Ⓑ (*love affair*) Techtelmechtel, *das;* **be involved in some ~ with sb.** ein Techtelmechtel mit jmdm. haben; Ⓒ (*illicit sexual activity*) Knutscherei, *die* (*ugs.*); Gefummel, *das* (*ugs. abwertend*); **there was some ~ going on** es wurde geknutscht *od.* gefummelt (*ugs.*)

**Hanover** /'hænəʊvə(r)/ *pr. n.* ▶ 1626 Hannover (*das*); **the House of ~** (*Hist.*) das Haus Hannover

**Hanoverian** /hænə'vɪərɪən/ ▶ 1626 ❶ *n.* (*Hist.*) Hannoveraner, *der*/Hannoveranerin, *die;* **be a ~:** aus dem Haus Hannover sein. ❷ *adj.* hannoversch

**Hansard** /'hænsɑ:d/ *n.* Hansard, *der: die britischen Parlamentsberichte*

**Hanse** /'hæns/ *n.* (*Hist.*) Hanse, *die*

**Hanseatic** /hænsɪ'ætɪk/ *adj.* (*Hist.*) hansisch; **~ town** Hansestadt, *die;* **the ~ League** der Hansebund

**hansom [cab]** /'hænsəm (kæb)/ *n.* (*Hist.*) Hansom, *der*

**Hants** *abbr.* **Hampshire**

**haphazard** /hæp'hæzəd/ ❶ *adj.* willkürlich ‹Auswahl›; unbedacht ‹Bemerkung›; **arranged in a ~ fashion** willkürlich *od.* wahllos angeordnet; **the whole thing was rather ~:** das Ganze geschah ziemlich planlos. ❷ *adv.* (*at random*) willkürlich; wahllos

**haphazardly** /hæp'hæzədlɪ/ *adv.* willkürlich; wahllos; **~ planned** planlos

**hapless** /'hæplɪs/ *adj.* unglückselig

**ha'p'orth** /'heɪpəθ/ ⇒ **halfpennyworth**

**happen** /'hæpn/ *v.i.* Ⓐ (*occur*) geschehen; ‹Vorhergesagtes:› eintreffen; **these things [do] ~:** das kommt vor; **it was the only thing that 'could ~:** es konnte [gar] nicht anders kommen; **what's ~ing?** was ist los?; **what's ~ing this evening?** was ist für heute Abend geplant?; **I can't** *or* **don't see 'that ~ing** das kann ich mir nicht vorstellen; **it all ~ed like this ...:** das war so ...; **nothing ever ~s here** hier ist nichts los; **don't let it ~ again!** dass mir das nicht wieder vorkommt!; **that's what ~s!** das kommt davon!; **~ to sb.** jmdm. passieren; **what has ~ed to him/her arm?** was ist mit ihm/ihrem Arm?; **what can have ~ed to him?** was mag mit ihm los sein?; **it all ~ed so quickly that ...:** es ging alles so schnell, dass ...; **it's all ~ing** (*coll.*) es ist was los (*ugs.*); **it's all ~ing for him** (*coll.*) es läuft gut bei ihm (*ugs.*); Ⓑ (*chance*) **~ to do sth./be sb.** zufällig etw. tun/jmd. sein; **it so ~s** *or* **as it ~s I have ...:** zufällig habe ich *od.* ich habe zufällig ...; **how does it ~ that ...?** wie kommt es, dass ...?; **do you ~ to know him?** kennen Sie ihn zufällig?

**~ 'by** *v.i.* zufällig vorbeikommen

**~ [up]on** *v.t.* zufällig treffen ‹Person›; zufällig finden ‹Arbeit, Gegenstand›

**happening** /'hæpnɪŋ/ *n.* Ⓐ *usu. in pl.* (*event*) Ereignis, *das;* **a regrettable ~:** ein bedauerlicher Vorfall; **such ~s cannot be tolerated** solche Vorfälle können nicht toleriert werden; Ⓑ (*improvised performance*) Happening, *das*

**happenstance** /'hæpnstæns, 'hæpnstɑ:ns/ *n.* (*Amer.*) Zufall, *der*

**happily** /'hæpɪlɪ/ *adv.* Ⓐ glücklich ‹lächeln›; fröhlich, vergnügt ‹spielen, lachen›; gut ‹zurechtkommen›; **they lived ~ ever after[wards]** (*at end of fairy tale*) sie lebten fortan glücklich und zufrieden[, und wenn sie nicht gestorben sind, dann leben sie noch heute]; Ⓑ (*gladly*) mit Vergnügen; Ⓒ (*aptly*) gut; treffend, passend ‹ausdrücken, formulieren›; Ⓓ (*fortunately*) glücklicherweise; zum Glück; **it ended ~:** es ging gut aus

**happiness** /'hæpɪnɪs/ *n.*, *no pl.* ▶ 1191 ⇒ **happy** A: Glück, *das;* Heiterkeit, *die;* Zufriedenheit, *die;* **I wish you every ~:** [ich wünsche Ihnen] alles Gute

**happy** /'hæpɪ/ *adj.* Ⓐ ▶ 1191 (*joyful*) glücklich; heiter ‹Bild, Veranlagung, Ton›; (*contented*) zufrieden; (*causing joy*) erfreulich ‹Gedanke, Erinnerung, Szene›; froh ‹Ereignis›; glücklich ‹Zeiten›; **I'm not ~ with her work** ich bin mit ihrer Arbeit nicht zufrieden; **not be ~ about sth./doing sth.** nicht froh über etw. (*Akk.*) sein/etw. nicht gern tun; **are you ~?** (*not needing help*) kommen Sie allein zurecht?; **~ birthday!** herzlichen Glückwunsch zum Geburtstag!; **~ anniversary!** herzlichen Glückwunsch! (*zum Jahrestag*); **~ Christmas!** frohe Weihnachten!; **~ New Year!** ein glückliches neues Jahr!; **~ days/landings!** (*dated coll.*) viel Glück!; **~ event** (*euphem.: birth*) freudiges Ereignis (*verhüll.*); **[strike] a ~ medium** den goldenen Mittelweg [wählen]; **~ release** (*death*) Erlösung, *die;* ⇒ *also* **day** A; **lark[1]**; **return** 3 A; **sandboy**; Ⓑ (*glad*) **be ~ to do sth.** etw. gern *od.* mit Vergnügen tun; **[I'm] ~ to meet you** [es] freut mich, Sie kennen zu lernen; **I'm ~ for you** das freut mich für dich; **make sb. ~:** jmdn. zufrieden stellen; **yes, I'd be ~ to** (*as reply to request*) ja, gern *od.* mit Vergnügen; **I'd be only too ~ to do that** ich würde das nur zu gern tun; Ⓒ (*lucky*) glücklich; **by a ~ chance/accident/coincidence** durch einen glücklichen Zufall; Ⓓ (*apt*) glücklich ‹Einfall›; gut ‹Wahl, Methode›; Ⓔ *in comb.* (*quick to use sth.*) **bomb-~:** mit Bomben schnell bei der Hand *nur präd.;* **gun-~:** schießwütig (*ugs.*); ⇒ *also* **slap-happy; trigger-happy**

**happy: ~ 'ending** *n.* Happy End, *das;* **~ 'families** *n. sing.* (*Cards*) Quartett, *das;* **~-go-'lucky** *adj.* sorglos; unbekümmert; **~ hour** *n. Zeitspanne am frühen Abend, in der die Getränke in einer Bar o. Ä. billiger verkauft werden;* **~ 'hunting ground[s]** *n.* [*pl.*] Ⓐ (*N. Amer. Ind. Mythol.*) **the ~ hunting grounds** die ewigen Jagdgründe; Ⓑ (*fig.*) Eldorado, *das*

**hara-kiri** /hærə'kɪrɪ/ *n.* Harakiri, *das*

**harangue** /hə'ræŋ/ ❶ *n.* Tirade, *die* (*abwertend*). ❷ *v.t.* eine Ansprache halten an (+ *Akk.*); **stop haranguing me about how ...:** hör auf, mir ständig zu predigen (*ugs.*), wie ...

**harass** /'hærəs/ *v.t.* schikanieren; **constantly ~ the enemy** den Feind nicht zur Ruhe kommen lassen; **~ sb. with complaints** jmdn. mit [ständigen] Beschwerden belästigen; **~ sb. into doing sth.** jmdm. so sehr zusetzen, dass er etw. tut

**harassed** /'hærəst/ *adj.* geplagt (**with** von); gequält ‹Blick, Ausdruck›

**harassment** /'hærəsmənt/ *n.* Schikanierung, *die;* **constant ~ of/by the enemy** ständiger Kleinkrieg mit dem Feind; **sexual ~:** [sexuelle] Belästigung

**harbinger** /'hɑ:bɪndʒə(r)/ *n.* Vorbote, *der*/Vorbotin, *die*

**harbour** (*Brit.; Amer.:* **harbor**) /'hɑ:bə(r)/ ❶ *n.* Ⓐ (*for ships*) Hafen, *der;* **in ~:** im Hafen; Ⓑ (*shelter*) Unterschlupf, *der.* ❷ *v.t.* beherbergen; Unterschlupf gewähren (+ *Dat.*) ‹Verbrecher, Flüchtling›; (*fig.*) hegen (*geh.*) ‹Hoffnung, Groll, Verdacht›

**'harbour master** *n.* Hafenmeister, *der*

**hard** /hɑ:d/ ❶ *adj.* Ⓐ hart; fest ‹Gelee, Eiscreme, Preis›; stark, heftig ‹Regen›; hart, streng ‹Frost›; gesichert ‹Beweis, Zahlen, Daten, Informationen›; **~ water area** Gebiet mit hartem Wasser; **drive a ~ bargain** hart verhandeln; **a drop of the ~ stuff** (*coll.*) etw. Hochprozentiges; **the ~ fact is that ...:** es ist einfach eine Tatsache, dass ...; **~ facts** nackte *od.* unumstößliche Tatsachen; ⇒ *also* **cheese** C; **iron** 1 A; **liquor** A; **nail** 1 B; **nut** A; Ⓑ (*difficult*) schwer; schwierig; **this is ~ to believe** das ist kaum zu glauben; es fällt schwer, das zu glauben; **it is ~ to do sth.** es ist schwer, etw. zu tun; **he's ~ to get on with** mit ihm ist schwer auszukommen; **this is a [very] ~ thing [for me] to say** es fällt mir [sehr] schwer, das zu sagen; **make it ~ for sb. [to do sth.]** es jmdm. schwer machen[, etw. zu tun]; **make sth. ~ for sb.** jmdm. etw. schwer machen; **[choose to] go about/do sth. the ~ way** es sich (*Dat.*) bei etw. unnötig schwer machen; **learn sth. the ~ way** etw. durch schlechte Erfahrungen lernen; **be [a] ~ [person] to please/prove wrong/catch out** schwer zufrieden zu stellen/zu widerlegen/zu überführen sein; **be ~ to convince [of sth.]** schwer [von etw.] zu überzeugen sein; **be ~ to understand** schwer zu verstehen sein; **have a ~ row to hoe** (*fig. dated*) es nicht leicht haben; **be ~ of hearing** schwerhörig sein; **be ~ going** ‹Buch:› sich schwer lesen; ‹Arbeit:› anstrengend sein; **play ~ to get** (*coll.*) so tun, als sei man nicht interessiert; **have a ~ time doing sth.** Schwierigkeiten haben, etw. zu tun; **give sb. a ~ time** jmdm. das Leben schwer machen; **it's a ~ life** (*joc.*) das Leben ist schwer; Ⓒ (*involving suffering*) hart, anstrengend, beschwerlich ‹Marsch›; **it is [a bit] ~ on him** es ist [schon] schlimm für ihn; **~ luck** Pech; ⇒ *also* **line[1]** 1 A; Ⓓ (*strenuous*) hart; beschwerlich ‹Reise›; konzentriert ‹Gespräch, Diskussion›; leidenschaftlich ‹Spieler›; **be a ~ drinker** viel trinken; **this is really ~ work!** (*coll.*) das ist wirklich nicht leicht; **go in [too much] for ~ drinking/gambling** zu viel trinken/spielen; **be a ~ worker/campaigner** sehr viel arbeiten/sich im Wahlkampf voll einsetzen; **try one's ~est to do sth.** sich nach Kräften bemühen, etw. zu tun; **I worked my very ~est** ich arbeitete, so hart ich konnte; Ⓔ (*vigorous*) heftig ‹Angriff, Schlag›; kräftig ‹Schlag, Stoß, Tritt, Klaps›; (*severe*) streng ‹Winter›; (*strong*) hart, hochprozentig ‹alkoholisches Getränk›; Ⓕ (*unfeeling*) hart; streng ‹Kritiker›; **be ~ [up]on sb.** streng mit jmdm. sein; **take a ~ line [with sb. on sth.]** [in Bezug auf etw. (*Akk.*)] eine harte Linie [gegenüber jmdm.] vertreten; ⇒ *also* **nail** 1 B; Ⓖ (*harsh*) hart; **be ~ on sb./sth.** jmdn./etw. strapazieren; Ⓗ (*Phonet.*) hart.

❷ *adv.* Ⓐ (*strenuously*) hart ‹arbeiten, trainieren›; schnell ‹laufen›; fleißig ‹lernen, studieren, üben›; genau ‹überlegen, beobachten, ansehen›; scharf ‹nachdenken›; gut ‹aufpassen, zuhören, sich festhalten›; fest ‹kleben›; **he drinks ~:** er ist ein starker Trinker; **concentrate ~/~er** sich sehr/mehr konzentrieren; **try ~:** sich sehr bemühen; **work ~ and play ~:** intensiv arbeiten und leben; **be ~ at work on sth.** an etw. (*Dat.*) intensiv *od.* konzentriert arbeiten; **go ~ at it** sich richtig hineinknien (*ugs.*); **be ~ 'at it** schwer arbeiten; **we found him already ~ 'at it** wir fanden ihn schon mitten in der Arbeit; **it's freezing ~ outside** es friert Stein und Bein draußen (*ugs.*); Ⓑ (*vigorously*) heftig; herzhaft ‹küssen›; laut ‹rufen›; fest ‹schlagen, drücken, klopfen›; Ⓒ (*severely, drastically*) hart; streng ‹zensieren›; **come down ~ on sb.** jmdn. zusammenstauchen (*ugs.*); **cut back** *or* **down ~ on sth.** etw. drastisch einschränken; **he took the news very ~:** die Nachricht traf ihn hart *od.* sehr; **be ~ up** knapp bei Kasse sein (*ugs.*); **be ~ up for sth.** um etw. verlegen sein; Ⓓ (*with difficulty*) **it goes ~ with sb.** jmd. bekommt Schwierigkeiten; **be ~ put to it [to do sth.]** große Schwierigkeiten haben[, etw. zu tun]; Ⓔ hart ‹kochen›; fest ‹gefrieren [lassen]›; **bake ~:** abbacken; **set ~:** fest werden; Ⓕ (*close*) **darkness/trouble is ~ at hand** es wird gleich dunkel/gibt gleich Ärger; **follow ~ upon sth.** unmittelbar auf etw. (*Akk.*) folgen; **~ by** in nächster Nähe; **~ by sth.** nahe an etw. (*Dat.*); ⇒ *also* **heel[1]** 1 A; **trail** 1 B; Ⓖ (*Naut.*) hart; **~ a-port!** hart backbord!

**hard: ~ and 'fast** ⇒ **fast[2]** 1 A; **~back** (*Printing*) ❶ *n.* gebundene Ausgabe; Hardcoverausgabe, *die; attrib.* Hardcover‹verlag, -verkäufe›; **in ~back** gebunden; mit festem Einband; ❷ *adj.* gebunden; Hardcover-; **~backed** /'hɑ:dbækt/ *adj.* ⇒ **~back** 2; **~bitten** *adj.* hartgesotten; abgebrüht (*ugs.*) ‹Veteran, Journalist, Karrieremacher›; **~board** *n.* Hartfaserplatte, *die; attrib.* Hartfaser‹trennwand, -unterlage›; **~-boiled** *adj.* Ⓐ (*boiled solid*) hart gekocht; Ⓑ (*fig.*) (*shrewd*) ausgekocht (*ugs.*); (*realistic, unsentimental*) realistisch; (*tough*) hartgesotten; **~ 'case** *n.* (*intractable person*) ausgebuffter Typ (*ugs.*); (*criminal*) Gangster, *der;* **~ 'cash** *n.* Ⓐ

h

(*coins*) Hartgeld, *das;* Ⓑ (*actual money*) Bargeld, *das;* **in ~ cash** in bar ‹bezahlen›; **~ 'coal** *n.* Anthrazit, *der;* ≈ Steinkohle, *die;* **~ 'copy** *n.* (*Computing*) Hardcopy, *die;* Papierausdruck, *der;* **~ core** *n.* Ⓐ /-'-/ (*nucleus*) harter Kern; (*of a problem*) Kern, *der;* Ⓑ /'--/ (*Brit.: material*) Packlage, *die* (*Bauw.*); **~-core** *attrib. adj.* hart ‹Pornographie›; zum harten Kern gehörend ‹Terrorist›; **~ 'court** *n.* (*Tennis*) Hartplatz, *der;* **~ 'cover** *n.* Hardcovereinband, *der; attrib.* Hardcover‹ausgabe›; **in ~ covers** als Hardcover ‹herauskommen›; **~ 'currency** *n.* (*Econ.*) harte Währung; *attrib.* ‹Markt, Land› mit harter Währung; **~-currency shop** Geschäft, in dem nur harte Währungen angenommen werden; **~ 'disk** ⇒ **disk**; **~-drinking** *attrib. adj.* ‹Mann/Frau,› der/die viel [Alkohol] trinkt; **~ drive** *n.* (*Computing*) Festplattenlaufwerk, *das;* **~ drug** *n.* harte Droge; **~-earned** *adj.* schwer verdient

**harden** /'hɑːdn/ ❶ *v.t.* Ⓐ (*make hard*) härten; Ⓑ (*fig.: reinforce*) bestärken (**in** in + *Dat.*); **~ sb.'s attitude/conviction** jmdn. in seiner Haltung/Überzeugung bestärken; Ⓒ (*make robust*) abhärten (**to** gegen); Ⓓ (*make tough*) unempfindlich machen (**to** gegen); **~ sb./oneself to sth.** jmdn./sich gegenüber etw. hart machen; **~ sb. to killing** jmdn. an das Töten gewöhnen; **he ~ed his heart against her** er verhärtete sich gegen sie. ❷ *v.i.* Ⓐ (*become hard*) hart werden; härten; Ⓑ (*become confirmed*) sich verhärten; Ⓒ ‹Preis:› sich festigen; Ⓓ (*become severe*) ‹Gesicht:› einen harten Ausdruck annehmen; ‹Gesichtsausdruck:› hart werden; **his face ~ed into anger** sein Gesicht verhärtete sich zornig

**~ 'off** *v.t.* widerstandsfähig machen ‹Pflanze›

**hardened** /'hɑːdnd/ *adj.* Ⓐ verhärtet ‹Arterie›; Ⓑ (*grown tough*) abgehärtet, unempfindlich (**to, against** gegen); hartgesotten ‹Verbrecher, Sünder, Krieger›; **be ~ to sth.** gegen etw. unempfindlich sein; **become** *or* **get ~ to sth.** gegen etw. unempfindlich werden; **a ~ drinker** jemand, der viel verträgt; Ⓒ (*seasoned*) eingefleischt

**hardener** /'hɑːdnə(r)/ *n.* Härter, *der*

**hardening** /'hɑːdnɪŋ/ *n.* Ⓐ (*of steel*) Härten, *das;* (*of arteries*) Verhärtung, *die;* Ⓑ (*making callous*) Verhärtung, *die*

**hard: ~-featured** *adj.* ‹Person› mit harten Gesichtszügen; hart ‹Gesicht›; **~ 'feelings** *n. pl.* (*coll.*) **no ~ feelings** schon gut; **make sure there are no ~ feelings** dafür sorgen, dass er/sie/*usw.* nicht mehr böse ist; **with no ~ feelings on either side** ohne dass es einer dem anderen nachtrug; **~-fought** *adj.* heftig ‹Kampf›; hart ‹Spiel, Wettbewerb›; **~ 'hat** *n.* Ⓐ (*Brit.: bowler hat*) Bowler, *der;* Ⓑ (*protective headgear*) Schutzhelm, *der;* **~-headed** *adj.* sachlich; nüchtern; **be ~-headed about what one wants** genau wissen, was man will; **~-hearted** /hɑːd'hɑːtɪd/ *adj.* hartherzig (**towards** gegenüber); **~-'hitting** *adj.* schlagkräftig; (*fig.*) aggressiv ‹Rede, Politik, Kritik›

**hardiness** /'hɑːdɪnɪs/ *n., no pl.* Widerstandsfähigkeit, *die*

**hard: ~ 'labour** *n.* Zwangsarbeit, *die;* **~ 'landing** *n.* (*Astronaut.*) harte Landung; **~line** *adj.* kompromisslos; **~'liner** *n.* Befürworter einer harten Linie (**on** gegenüber); **~-'luck story** *n.* Leidensgeschichte, *die*

**hardly** /'hɑːdlɪ/ *adv.* kaum; **he can ~ have arrived yet** er kann kaum jetzt schon angekommen sein; **~ anyone** *or* **anybody/anything** kaum jemand/etwas; fast niemand/nichts; **~ any wine/beds** kaum Wein/Betten; fast kein Wein/keine Betten; **~ ever** so gut wie nie; **~ at all** fast überhaupt nicht

**hard 'money** *n.* (*Amer.*) Hartgeld, *das*

**hardness** /'hɑːdnɪs/ *n., no pl.* Härte, *die;* (*of blow*) Heftigkeit, *die;* (*of person*) Strenge, *die;* **~ of hearing** Schwerhörigkeit, *die*

**hard: ~ 'news** *n. sing.* gesicherte Fakten; **~-nose[d]** /'hɑːdnəʊz(d)/ *adj.* (*coll.*) abgebrüht; **~-on** *n.* (*sl.*) Ständer, *der* (*ugs.*); **~ 'palate** *n.* (*Anat.*) harter Gaumen; **~ 'pressed** *adj.* hart bedrängt; **be ~ pressed** große Schwierigkeiten haben; **~ 'rock** *n.* (*Mus.*) Hardrock, *der;* **~-scrabble** (*Amer.*) ❶ *n.* karger Boden; ❷ *adj.* ertragsarm ‹Bauernhof›; karg ‹Boden, Feld, Acker›; **~ sell** *n.* aggressive Verkaufsmethoden; *attrib.* aggressiv ‹Werbung, [Verkaufs]methode›

**hardship** /'hɑːdʃɪp/ *n.* Ⓐ *no pl., no indef. art.* Not, *die;* Elend, *das;* **life of ~:** entbehrungsreiches *od.* hartes Leben; Ⓑ (*instance*) Notlage, *die;* **~s** Not, *die;* Entbehrungen; **if it's not too much of a ~ for you** wenn es nicht zu viel verlangt ist; Ⓒ (*sth. causing suffering*) Unannehmlichkeit, *die*

**hard: ~ 'shoulder** *n.* Standspur, *die;* **~ 'standing** *n., no pl., no indef. art.* befestigter Abstellplatz; **~ 'tack** *n.* Schiffszwieback, *der;* **it'll be ~ tack from now on** (*fig.*) von jetzt an gibt es nur noch trocken Brot (*fig.*); **~ top** *n.* Hardtop, *das;* **~ware** *n., no pl., no indef. art.* Ⓐ (*goods*) Eisenwaren *Pl.;* (*for domestic use also*) Haushaltswaren *Pl.; attrib.* Eisen-/Haushaltswaren‹geschäft›; Ⓑ (*coll.: weapons*) Schießeisen (*ugs.*); **military ~ware** Waffen *Pl.;* Ⓒ (*Computing*) Hardware, *die;* **~-wearing** *adj.* strapazierfähig; **~ 'wheat** *n.* Hartweizen, *der;* **~-wired** *adj.* (*Computing*) festverdrahtet; **~-won** *adj.* schwer errungen *od.* erkämpft ‹Sieg›; mühsam gewonnen ‹Schlacht›; schwer erarbeitet ‹Reichtum›; **~wood** *n.* Hartholz, *das; attrib.* Hartholz‹möbel, -fußboden, -baum›; **~ 'words** *n. pl.* Ⓐ (*difficult to understand*) schwierige Wörter; Ⓑ (*angry*) harte Worte; **~-working** *adj.* fleißig ‹Person›

**hardy** /'hɑːdɪ/ *adj.* Ⓐ (*robust*) abgehärtet; zäh, robust ‹Rasse›; Ⓑ (*Hort.*) winterhart; Ⓒ (*bold*) unerschrocken

**hardy: ~ 'annual** *n.* Ⓐ (*Hort.*) winterharte einjährige Pflanze; Ⓑ (*fig. joc.*) nicht totzukriegendes Thema (*scherzh.*); **~ per'ennial** *n.* Ⓐ (*Hort.*) winterharte mehrjährige Pflanze; Ⓑ (*fig. joc.*) Dauerbrenner, *der* (*ugs.*)

**hare** /heə(r)/ ❶ *n.* Hase, *der;* **run like a ~:** wie ein geölter Blitz laufen (*ugs.*); **[as] mad as a March ~** (*fig.*) völlig verrückt (*ugs.*); **run with the ~ and hunt with the hounds** (*fig.*) auf beiden Schultern *od.* Achseln Wasser tragen (*veralt.*). ❷ *v.i.* sausen (*ugs.*); **go haring about** herumsausen (*ugs.*)

**hare: ~ and 'hounds** *n. sing.* Schnitzeljagd, *die;* **~bell** *n.* (*Bot.*) Ⓐ (*Scottish bluebell*) Rundblättrige Glockenblume; Ⓑ (*English bluebell*) Hasenglöckchen, *das;* **~-brained** *adj.* unüberlegt; **~'lip** *n.* Hasenscharte, *die*

**harem** /'hɑːriːm, hɑː'riːm/ *n.* Harem, *der*

**haricot** /'hærɪkəʊ/ *n.* Ⓐ (*Cookery*) Ragout, *das;* **~ of veal** Kalbsragout, *das;* Ⓑ ⇒ **haricot bean**

**haricot bean** *n.* Gartenbohne, *die;* (*pod also*) grüne Bohne; (*seed also*) weiße Bohne

**hark** /hɑːk/ *v.i.* Ⓐ (*arch.: listen*) **~ [to sb.]** hören [auf jmdn.]; **~!** horch!/horcht!; Ⓑ (*coll.*) **just ~ at him!** hör ihn dir/hört ihn euch nur an!

**~ 'back** *v.i.* **~ back to** (*come back to*) zurückkommen auf (+ *Akk.*); zurückgreifen auf (+ *Akk.*) ‹Tradition›; wieder anfangen von ‹alten Zeiten›; (*go back to*) ‹Idee, Brauch:› zurückgehen auf (+ *Akk.*)

**Harlequin** /'hɑːlɪkwɪn/ *n.* Harlekin, *der*

**harlot** /'hɑːlət/ (*arch./derog.*) *n.* Metze, *die* (*veralt.*)

**harlotry** /'hɑːlətrɪ/ *n.* (*arch./derog.*) Prostitution, *die*

**harm** /hɑːm/ ❶ *n.* Schaden, *der;* **do ~:** Schaden anrichten; **do ~ to sb., do sb. ~:** jmdm. schaden; (*injure*) jmdn. verletzen; **the blow didn't do him any ~:** der Schlag war harmlos; **the dog won't do you any ~:** der Hund tut dir nichts; **it will do you no** *or* **won't do you any ~** (*iron.*) es würde dir nichts schaden; **do ~ to sth.** einer Sache (*Dat.*) schaden; **sb./sth. comes to no ~:** jmdm./einer Sache passiert nichts; **there is no ~ done** nichts ist passiert; **there's no ~ in doing sth., it will do no ~ to do sth.** (*could be of benefit*) es kann nicht schaden, etw. zu tun; **there's no ~ in asking** Fragen kostet nichts; **it will do more ~ than good** es wird mehr schaden als nützen; **where's** *or* **what's the ~ in it?** was ist denn schon dabei?; **see no ~ in it/sth./doing sth.** nichts dabei/bei etw. finden/dabei finden, etw. zu tun; **let's hope no ~ will come of it** wir wollen hoffen, dass es sich nicht negativ auswirkt; **stay here, out of ~'s way** bleib hier, wo dir nichts passieren kann; **keep out of ~'s way** der Gefahr fernbleiben; an einem sicheren Ort aufbewahren ‹Medikamente›; von der Gefahr fern halten ‹Person›; **get sb. out of ~'s way** jmdn. in Sicherheit bringen; ⇒ *also* **intend** A; **mean**[3] A. ❷ *v.t.* etwas [zuleide] tun (+ *Dat.*); schaden (+ *Dat.*) ‹Beziehungen, Land, Karriere, Ruf›

**harmful** /'hɑːmfl/ *adj.* schädlich (**to** für); schlecht ‹Angewohnheit›

**harmfulness** /'hɑːmflnɪs/ *n., no pl.* Schädlichkeit, *die*

**harmless** /'hɑːmlɪs/ *adj.* harmlos; **make** *or* **render ~:** unschädlich machen; entschärfen ‹Bombe›

**harmlessly** /'hɑːmlɪslɪ/ *adv.* ohne Schaden anzurichten

**harmlessness** /'hɑːmlɪsnɪs/ *n., no pl.* Harmlosigkeit, *die*

**harmonic** /hɑː'mɒnɪk/ ❶ *adj.* (*also Mus., Math.*) harmonisch. ❷ *n.* Ⓐ (*Mus.*) Oberton, *der;* Ⓑ (*component frequency*) Harmonische, *die* (*Physik*); **upper ~s** harmonische Oberschwingungen (*Physik*)

**harmonica** /hɑː'mɒnɪkə/ *n.* (*Mus.*) Mundharmonika, *die*

**harmonious** /hɑː'məʊnɪəs/ *adj.*, **harmoniously** /hɑː'məʊnɪəslɪ/ *adv.* harmonisch

**harmonise** ⇒ **harmonize**

**harmonium** /hɑː'məʊnɪəm/ *n.* (*Mus.*) Harmonium, *das*

**harmonize** /'hɑːmənaɪz/ ❶ *v.t.* Ⓐ (*bring into harmony*) aufeinander abstimmen; **~ sth. with sth.** etw. mit etw. in Einklang bringen *od.* auf etw. (*Akk.*) abstimmen; Ⓑ (*Mus.*) harmonisieren. ❷ *v.i.* (*be in harmony*) harmonieren (**with** mit); ‹Interessen, Ansichten, Wort und Tat:› miteinander im *od.* in Einklang stehen; **~ well together** ‹Farben, Klänge:› gut harmonieren

**harmony** /'hɑːmənɪ/ *n.* Ⓐ Harmonie, *die;* **live in perfect ~:** völlig harmonisch *od.* in vollkommener Harmonie zusammenleben; **peace and ~:** Friede und Eintracht; **be in ~** ⇒ **harmonize** 2; **be in harmony with sth.** mit etw. im *od.* in Einklang stehen; **be out of ~ with sth.** mit etw. nicht im *od.* in Einklang stehen; Ⓑ (*Mus.*) Harmonie, *die;* (*theory of ~*) Harmonielehre, *die;* **sing in ~:** mehrstimmig singen; ⇒ *also* **sphere** C

**harness** /'hɑːnɪs/ ❶ *n.* Ⓐ Geschirr, *das;* Ⓑ (*on parachute*) Gurtzeug, *das;* (*for toddler, dog*) Laufgeschirr, *das;* (*for window cleaner, steeplejack, etc.*) Sicherheitsgürtel, *der;* **in ~** (*fig.*) (*in the daily routine*) in der Tretmühle (*ugs. abwertend*); (*together*) gemeinsam; **die in ~:** in den Sielen sterben; **out of ~** (*fig.*) außer Dienst; ⇒ *also* **double harness.** ❷ *v.t.* Ⓐ (*put ~ on*) anschirren; **~ a horse to a cart** ein Pferd vor einen Wagen spannen; Ⓑ (*fig.*) nutzen

**'harness racing** Trabrennen, *das*

**harp** /hɑːp/ ❶ *n.* Harfe, *die.* ❷ *v.i.* **~ on [about] sth.** [immer wieder] von etw. reden; (*critically*) auf etw. (*Dat.*) herumreiten (*salopp*); (*complainingly*) über etw. (*Akk.*) lamentieren (*ugs.*); **don't ~ on about it!** hör auf damit!

**harpist** /'hɑːpɪst/ *ns.* Harfenist, *der*/Harfenistin, *die;* Harfenspieler, *der*/-spielerin, *die*

**harpoon** /hɑː'puːn/ ❶ *n.* Harpune, *die.* ❷ *v.t.* harpunieren

**harpoon-'gun** *n.* Harpunengeschütz, *das*

**'harp seal** *n.* (*Zool.*) Sattelrobbe, *die*

**harpsichord** /'hɑːpsɪkɔːd/ *n.* (*Mus.*) Cembalo, *das*

**harpy** /'hɑːpɪ/ *n.* Ⓐ (*grasping person*) Hyäne, *die* (*ugs. abwertend*); Ⓑ (*Greek and Roman Mythol.*) Harpyie, *die*

**harridan** /'hærɪdən/ *n.* Schreckschraube, *die* (*ugs. abwertend*)

**harrier** /'hærɪə(r)/ *n.* Ⓐ (*Ornith.*) Weihe, *die;* Ⓑ (*Hunting*) Harrier, *der* (*Hund für die Hasenjagd*); Ⓒ (*Sport*) Querfeldeinläufer, *der*/-läuferin, *die*

**Harris tweed** /hærɪs 'twi:d/ *n.* Harristweed, *der; attrib.* Harristweed‹jackett›

**harrow** /'hærəʊ/ ❶ *n.* Egge, *die.* ❷ *v.t.* Ⓐ eggen; Ⓑ (*distress*) quälen

**harrowing** /'hærəʊɪŋ/ *adj.* entsetzlich; (*horrific*) grauenhaft ‹Anblick, Geschichte›

**harry** /'hærɪ/ *v.t.* Ⓐ ~ **[continuously]** wiederholt angreifen; Ⓑ (*harass*) bedrängen; **be harried by telephone calls** von Anrufern belästigt *od.* behelligt werden

**harsh** /hɑ:ʃ/ *adj.* Ⓐ rau ‹Gewebe, Oberfläche, Gegend, Land, Klima›; schrill ‹Ton, Stimme›; grell ‹Licht, Farbe, Ton›; schroff, stark ‹Kontrast›; scharf ‹Geschmack›; stechend, streng ‹Geruch›; hart ‹Bedingungen, Leben›; Ⓑ (*excessively severe*) [sehr] hart; [äußerst] streng ‹Richter, Disziplin›; rücksichtslos ‹Tyrann, Herrscher, Verhalten, Politik›; **back to ~ reality** zurück zur grauen Wirklichkeit; **don't be ~ on him** sei nicht zu streng mit ihm

**harshly** /'hɑ:ʃlɪ/ *adv.* Ⓐ (*disagreeably*) grell ‹klingen›; in schroffem Ton ‹reden›; Ⓑ (*extremely severely*) [sehr] hart

**harshness** /'hɑ:ʃnɪs/ *n., no pl.* Ⓐ ⇒ **harsh** A: Rauheit, *die;* schriller Klang; Grelle, *die;* Schroffheit, *die;* Schärfe, *die;* (*of life conditions*) Härte, *die;* Ⓑ ⇒ **harsh** B: Härte, *die;* Strenge, *die;* Rücksichtslosigkeit, *die*

**hart** /hɑ:t/ *n.* Hirsch, *der*

**harum-scarum** /heərəm'skeərəm/ (*coll.*) ❶ *adj.* unbesonnen. ❷ *n.* Wildfang, *der*

**harvest** /'hɑ:vɪst/ ❶ *n.* Ⓐ Ernte, *die;* **timber ~:** Holzschlag, *der;* **find/reap a [rich] ~** (*fig.*) einen [tollen] Fang machen; Ⓑ (*time*) Ernte[zeit], *die.* ❷ *v.t.* ernten; schlagen ‹Holz›; lesen ‹Weintrauben›; fangen ‹Fisch›; (*fig.*) gewinnen ‹Energie›; ansammeln ‹Vermögen›; **~ the crops** die Ernte einbringen; **~ the fruits of one's labours** (*fig.*) die Früchte seiner Arbeit ernten

**harvester** /'hɑ:vɪstə(r)/ *n.* Ⓐ (*machine*) Erntemaschine, *die;* ⇒ *also* **combine** 3 B; Ⓑ (*person*) Erntearbeiter, *der*/-arbeiterin, *die*

**harvest:** ~ **'festival** *n.* Erntedankfest, *das;* ~ **'home** *n.* Erntefest, *das;* **~man** /'hɑ:vɪstmən/ *n., pl.* **-men** /'hɑ:vɪstmən/ (*Zool.*) Weberknecht, *der;* ~ **'moon** *n. Vollmond zur Zeit der Herbst-Tagundnachtgleiche;* ~ **mouse** *n.* Zwergmaus, *die*

**has** ⇒ **have** 1, 2

**has-been** /'hæzbi:n/ *n.* (*coll.*) **be [a bit of] a ~:** seine besten Jahre hinter sich haben; **a seedy ~ of an actor** ein abgetakelter Schauspieler

**hash¹** /hæʃ/ ❶ *n.* (*Cookery*) Haschee, *das;* (*fig.*) Aufguss, *der* (*abwertend*); **make a ~ of sth.** (*coll.*) etw. verpfuschen *od.* verpatzen (*ugs.*); **settle sb.'s ~** (*coll.*) jmdn. zur Vernunft bringen; (*by forceful methods*) jmdn. unschädlich machen; **I'll settle his ~:** dem werd ichs zeigen (*ugs.*). ❷ *v.t.* haschieren; (*fig. coll.*) verpfuschen (*ugs.*); verpatzen (*ugs.*); **~ and rehash sth.** etw. x-mal durchkauen (*ugs.*)

~ **'up** *v.t.* zerkleinern; (*fig. coll.*) verpfuschen (*ugs.*); verpatzen (*ugs.*)

**hash²** *n.* (*coll.: drug*) Hasch, *das* (*ugs.*)

**'hash browns** *n. pl.: Bratkartoffeln mit Zwiebeln;* ≈ Rösti mit Zwiebeln

**hashish** /'hæʃɪʃ/ *n.* Haschisch, *das od. der*

**Hasidic** /hə'sɪdɪk/ *adj.* chassidisch

**hasn't** /'hæznt/ = **has not;** ⇒ **have** 1, 2

**hasp** /hɑ:sp/ *n.* Haspe, *die;* (*fastener snapping into a lock*) [Schnapp]schloss, *das;* (*fastener for book or cape*) Schließe, *die*

**hassle** /'hæsl/ (*coll.*) ❶ *n.* **~[s]** Krach, *der* (*ugs.*); (*trouble, problem*) Ärger, *der;* **get involved in ~s with sb.** mit jmdm. Ärger kriegen (*ugs.*); **no end of ~[s]** nichts als Ärger; **it's a real ~:** das ist ein echtes Problem; **it's too much [of a]/such a ~:** das macht zu viel/so viel Umstände. ❷ *v.t.* schikanieren; **don't ~ me** nerv mich nicht (*ugs.*)

**hassock** /'hæsək/ *n.* Ⓐ (*cushion*) Kniekissen, *das;* Ⓑ (*tuft of grass*) Grasbüschel, *das*

**haste** /heɪst/ *n., no pl.* Eile, *die;* (*rush*) Hast, *die;* **in his ~:** in seiner Hast; **no need for ~:** kein Grund zur Eile; **more ~, less speed** (*prov.*) eile mit Weile (*Spr.*); **do sth. in ~:** etw. eilig tun; **yours in ~** (*at end of letter*) in Eile, Dein/Deine; **make ~:** sich beeilen

**hasten** /'heɪsn/ ❶ *v.t.* (*cause to hurry*) drängen; (*accelerate*) beschleunigen. ❷ *v.i.* eilen; (*precipitately*) hasten (*geh.*); **~ away** davoneilen; **~ to do sth.** sich beeilen, etw. zu tun; **I ~ to add/say** ich muss *od.* möchte gleich hinzufügen/sagen

**hastily** /'heɪstɪlɪ/ *adv.* (*hurriedly*) eilig; (*precipitately*) hastig; (*rashly*) übereilt; (*quick-temperedly*) heftig; hitzig; **judge sb. too ~:** jmdn. vorschnell beurteilen

**hasty** /'heɪstɪ/ *adj.* (*hurried*) eilig; flüchtig ‹Skizze, Blick›; (*precipitate*) hastig; (*rash*) übereilt; (*quick-tempered*) heftig; hitzig; **beat a ~ retreat** sich schnellstens zurückziehen *od.* (*ugs.*) aus dem Staub machen; (*fig.*) schnell einen Rückzieher machen; **he's a man of ~ temper/disposition** er hat eine recht hitzige Art

**hasty 'pudding** *n.* (*Brit.*) Mehlbrei, *der;* (*Amer.*) Maismehlbrei, *der*

**hat** /hæt/ *n.* Ⓐ Hut, *der;* **[sailor's/woollen/knitted] ~:** [Matrosen-/Woll-/Strick]mütze, *die;* **without a ~:** ohne Hut/Mütze; **raise** *or* (*dated*) **doff one's ~ to sb.** vor jmdm. den Hut ziehen; **take off one's ~, take one's ~ off** seinen *od.* den Hut abnehmen; **take one's ~ off** *or* **take off one's ~ to sb./sth.** (*lit. or fig.*) vor jmdm./etw. den Hut ziehen; **~s off to him!** Hut ab vor ihm!; Ⓑ (*fig.*) **bad ~** (*Brit. coll.*) übler Kunde (*ugs.*); **at the drop of a ~:** auf der Stelle; **sb. will/would eat his ~ if ...:** jmd. frisst einen Besen/will einen Besen fressen, wenn ... (*salopp*); **somewhere** *or* **a place to hang [up] one's ~:** ein Ort, an dem man zu Hause ist; **throw one's ~ in the ring** seine Kandidatur anmelden; **my ~!** *expr. surprise* ist es/[denn] das die Möglichkeit! (*ugs.*); *expr. disbelief* dass ich nicht lache!; **be old ~** (*coll.*) ein alter Hut sein (*ugs.*); **become old ~** (*coll.*) aus der Mode kommen; **they pulled his name out of a ~:** er wurde ganz zufällig ausgewählt; **produce sth. out of a ~:** etw. aus dem Ärmel schütteln; **pass** *or* **send round the ~** *or* **the ~ round** (*coll.*) den Hut herumgehen lassen; **with ~ in hand** demütig; **talk through one's ~** (*coll.*) dummes Zeug reden (*ugs.*); **keep sth. under one's ~:** etw. für sich behalten; **[when he is] wearing his ... ~:** in seiner Rolle als ...; **switch ~s** die Rollen vertauschen; **wear two ~s** zwei Interessen gleichzeitig vertreten

**hat:** **~band** *n.* Hutband, *das;* **~box** *n.* Hutschachtel, *die*

**hatch¹** /hætʃ/ *n.* Ⓐ (*opening*) Luke, *die;* **under ~es** unter Deck; **down the ~!** (*fig. coll.*) runter damit! (*ugs.*); Ⓑ (*serving ~*) Durchreiche, *die.* ⇒ *also* **escape-hatch**

**hatch²** ❶ *v.t.* (*lit. or fig.*) ausbrüten. ❷ *v.i.* [aus]schlüpfen; ⇒ *also* **chicken** 1 A. ❸ *n.* Ⓐ (*act of ~ing*) Schlüpfen, *das;* Ⓑ (*brood ~ed*) Brut, *die*

~ **'out** ❶ *v.i.* ausschlüpfen; **the eggs have ~ed out** die Eier sind ausgebrütet. ❷ *v.t.* ausbrüten

~ **'up** *v.t.* ausbrüten (*fig.*); aushecken (*ugs.*)

**hatch³** *v.t.* (*Art*) schraffieren

**'hatchback** *n.* Ⓐ (*door*) Heckklappe, *die;* **a ~ model** ein Modell mit Heckklappe; Ⓑ (*vehicle*) Schräghecklimousine, *die*

**hatchery** /'hætʃərɪ/ *n.* (*for birds*) Brutplatz, *der;* (*for fish*) Laichplatz, *der*

**hatchet** /'hætʃɪt/ *n.* Beil, *das;* **bury the ~** (*fig.*) das Kriegsbeil begraben

**hatchet:** ~ **face** *n.* scharf geschnittenes Gesicht; **~-faced** *adj.* mit scharfen Gesichtszügen *nachgestellt;* ~ **job** *n.* **do a ~ job on sb./sth.** jmdn./etw. in der Luft zerreißen (*salopp*); ~ **man** Ⓐ (*professional killer*) Killer, *der;* **be a real ~ man** (*fig.*) kein Pardon kennen; Ⓑ (*henchman*) Erfüllungsgehilfe, *der* (*fig. abwertend*)

**hatchling** /'hætʃlɪŋ/ *n.* Junge, *das*

**hatchment** /'hætʃmənt/ *n.* (*Her.*) Totenschild, *der od. das*

**hate** /heɪt/ ❶ *n.* Ⓐ Hass, *der;* **~ for sb.** Hass auf *od.* gegen jmdn.; Ⓑ (*coll.: object of dislike*) **be sb.'s ~:** jmdm. verhasst sein; **my pet ~ at the moment is ...:** ... hasse ich zurzeit am meisten.

❷ *v.t.* hassen; **I ~ having to get up at seven** ich hasse es, um sieben Uhr aufstehen zu müssen; **I ~ to say this** (*coll.*) ich sage das nicht gern; **I ~ [having] to trouble you** (*coll.*) tut mir Leid, dass ich Sie damit behelligen muss; **I ~ to think what would have happened if .../I ~ the thought of having to leave this job** (*coll.*) ich darf gar nicht daran denken, was geschehen wäre, wenn .../wie es wäre, wenn ich die Stelle aufgeben müsste

**hateful** /'heɪtfl/ *adj.* abscheulich; verabscheuenswürdig (*geh.*); **that would be a ~ thing to do** das [zu tun] wäre abscheulich

**'hate mail** *n.* hasserfüllte Briefe *Pl.*

**hatful** /'hætfʊl/ *n.* Ⓐ **a ~ of eggs** ein Hut voll[er] Eier; Ⓑ (*fig.: considerable number/amount*) **a ~ of** eine ganze Menge (*ugs.*)

**hatless** /'hætlɪs/ *adj.* ohne Hut *nachgestellt*

**hat:** ~ **peg** *n.* Huthaken, *der;* **~pin** *n.* Hutnadel, *die*

**hatred** /'heɪtrɪd/ *n.* Hass, *der;* **feel ~ for** *or* **of sb./sth.** Hass auf *od.* gegen jmdn./etw. empfinden

**'hatstand** *n.* Hutständer, *der*

**hatter** /'hætə(r)/ *n.* Hutmacher, *der;* **[as] mad as a ~** (*fig.*) völlig verrückt (*ugs.*)

**'hat trick** *n.* Hattrick, *der;* **make** *or* **score a ~:** einen Hattrick erzielen; **be on a ~:** vor einem Hattrick stehen

**haughtily** /'hɔ:tɪlɪ/ *adv.* hochmütig

**haughtiness** /'hɔ:tɪnɪs/ *n., no pl.* Hochmut, *der*

**haughty** /'hɔ:tɪ/ *adj.* hochmütig

**haul** /hɔ:l/ ❶ *v.t.* Ⓐ (*pull*) ziehen; schleppen; (*Fishing*) einholen ‹Netze›; **~ sth. up the wall** etw. die Mauer hochziehen; **~ the boat up on the beach** das Boot auf den Strand ziehen; **be ~ed before the court** (*fig. coll.*) vor Gericht gestellt werden; **~ down** einholen ‹Flagge, Segel›; ⇒ *also* **coal** B; Ⓑ (*transport*) transportieren; befördern; Ⓒ (*Naut.*) (*mit geändertem Kurs*) steuern; **~ the ship into the wind** anluven. ❷ *v.i.* ziehen; **~ [up]on** *or* **at sth.** an etw. (*Dat.*) [kräftig] ziehen. ❸ *n.* Ⓐ Ziehen, *das;* Schleppen, *das;* (*Fishing*) Einholen, *das;* Ⓑ (*catch*) Fang, *der;* (*fig.*) Beute, *die;* Ⓒ (*distance*) Strecke, *die;* ⇒ *also* **long haul**; **short haul**

**haulage** /'hɔ:lɪdʒ/ *n., no pl.* Ⓐ (*hauling*) Transport, *der;* Ⓑ (*charges*) Transportkosten *Pl.*

**hauler** /'hɔ:lə(r)/ (*Amer.*), **haulier** /'hɔ:lɪə(r)/ (*Brit.*) *n.* (*person*) Spediteur, *der;* (*firm*) Spedition[sfirma], *die*

**haulm** /hɔ:m, hɑ:m/ *n.* Ⓐ *no pl., no indef. art.* (*Agric.*) Kraut, *das;* Ⓑ (*stem*) (*of grass, straw*) Halm, *der;* (*of leaf, fruit*) Stiel, *der*

**haunch** /hɔ:nʃ/ *n.* Ⓐ **sit on one's/its ~es** auf seinem Hinterteil sitzen; Ⓑ (*Gastr.*) Keule, *die;* Ⓒ (*Archit.*) [Bogen]schenkel, *der*

**haunt** /hɔ:nt/ ❶ *v.t.* Ⓐ **~ a house/castle** in einem Haus/Schloss spuken *od.* umgehen; **the old farmhouse is ~ed by ghosts** in dem alten Bauernhaus spuken Geister; Ⓑ (*fig.: trouble*) ‹Erinnerung, Gedanke:› plagen, verfolgen; Ⓒ (*frequent*) häufig besuchen ‹Ort, Lokal›. ❷ *n.* **a favourite ~ of artists** ein beliebter Treffpunkt für Künstler; **these are my old ~s** hier habe ich mich früher immer herumgetrieben (*ugs.*)

**haunted** /'hɔ:ntɪd/ *adj.* Ⓐ **a ~ house** ein Haus, in dem es spukt; **a ~ castle** ein Spukschloss; Ⓑ (*fig.: troubled*) gehetzt ‹Blick, Eindruck›

**haunting** /'hɔ:ntɪŋ/ *adj.* sehnsüchtig ‹Klänge, Musik›; lastend ‹Erinnerung›; drückend ‹Schuld›

**Hausa** /'haʊsə/ *n., pl. same* Ⓐ (*person*) Haus[s]a, *der*/Haus[s]afrau, *die;* Ⓑ (*language*) Hausa, *das*

**hausfrau** /'haʊsfraʊ/ *n.* [biedere] Hausfrau

**haute couture** /əʊt ku:'tjʊə(r)/ *n., no pl.* Haute Couture, *die*

h

**haute école** /əʊt eɪˈkɒl/ *n.*, *no pl.* [die] hohe Schule

**hauteur** /əʊˈtɜː(r)/ *n.*, *no pl.* Stolz, *der*

**Havana** /həˈvænə/ *n.* ❶ Ⓐ (*cigar*) Havanna, *die;* Ⓑ *pr. n.* ▶ 1626 Havanna (*das*)

**have** ❶ /hæv/ *v.t.*, *pres.* **he has** /hæz/, *p.t.* & *p.p.* **had** /hæd/ Ⓐ (*possess*) haben; **I ~ it!** ich habs[!]; **and what ~ you** (*coll.*) und so weiter; **I ~ something to say [to you]** ich habe Ihnen etwas zu sagen; **~ nothing to do/wear/say** nichts zu tun/anzuziehen/zu sagen haben; **they ~ some French** sie können etwas Französisch; **I still ~ some work to do** ich muss noch etwas arbeiten; **you ~ some explaining to do** du schuldest mir eine Erklärung; **you ~ five minutes [in which] to do it** Sie haben fünf Minuten [Zeit], um es zu tun; Ⓑ (*obtain*) bekommen; **there was no money/help to be had** es war kein Geld/keine Hilfe zu bekommen *od.* (*ugs.*) aufzutreiben; **we shall ~ snow** es wird schneien; **let's not ~ any ...:** lass uns ... vermeiden; **come on, let's ~ it!** (*coll.*) rück schon raus damit! (*ugs.*); Ⓒ (*take*) nehmen; **~ a cigarette** nehmen Sie eine Zigarette; ⇒ *also* E; Ⓓ (*keep*) behalten; haben; **you can ~ that pencil** Sie können den Bleistift behalten *od.* haben; Ⓔ (*eat, drink, etc.*) **~ breakfast/dinner/lunch** frühstücken/zu Abend/zu Mittag essen; **~ a cup of tea** eine Tasse Tee trinken; **~ a cigarette** eine Zigarette rauchen; ⇒ *also* C; Ⓕ (*experience*) haben ‹Spaß, Vergnügen›; Ⓖ (*suffer*) haben ‹Krankheit, Schmerz, Enttäuschung, Abenteuer›; erleiden ‹Schock›; (*feel*) haben ‹Gefühl, Idee›; (*show*) haben ‹Güte, Freundlichkeit, Frechheit›; **let him/them ~ it** (*coll.*) gibs ihm/ihnen (*ugs.*); Ⓗ (*engage in*) **~ a game of football** Fußball spielen; **~ a try** es [einmal] versuchen; **~ it [with sb.]** (*sl.: copulate*) es [mit jmdm.] machen (*salopp*); Ⓘ (*accept*) **I won't ~ it** das lasse ich mir nicht bieten; **I won't ~ him in the house** er kommt mir nicht ins Haus; **I won't ~ you behaving like that** so kannst du dich nicht benehmen; Ⓙ (*give birth to*) **~ a baby/children** ein Baby/Kinder bekommen; **~ pups** *etc.* Junge bekommen; Ⓚ (*sl.: copulate with*) **he had her on the sofa** er machte es mit ihr auf dem Sofa (*salopp*); Ⓛ (*coll.: beat*) **you ~ me there** da bringen Sie mich aber in Verlegenheit; Ⓜ (*coll.: swindle*) **I was had** ich bin [he]reingelegt worden (*ugs.*); **ever been had!** da bist du ganz schön reingefallen (*ugs.*); Ⓝ (*know*) **I ~ it on good authority that ...:** ich weiß es aus zuverlässiger Quelle, dass ...; **she 'will ~ it that ...:** sie besteht darauf, dass ...; **she won't ~ it that ...:** sie will nichts davon hören, dass ...; **rumour/legend/tradition has it that they escaped** einem Gerücht/der Legende/der Überlieferung zufolge sind sie entkommen; **as Goethe has it** wie Goethe sagt; Ⓞ (*as guest*) **~ sb. to stay** jmdn. zu Besuch haben; **thanks for having me** danke für die Einladung; Ⓟ (*summon*) **he had me into his office** er hat mich in sein Büro beordert; Ⓠ (*in coll. phrases*) **you've had it now** jetzt ist es aus (*ugs.*); **if you want another drink, you've had it** falls du noch was trinken willst, da geht nichts mehr (*ugs.*); **this car/dress has had it** dieser Wagen/dieses Kleid hat ausgedient. ❷ /həv, əv, *stressed* hæv/ *v. aux.*, **he has** /həz, əz, *stressed* hæz/, **had** /həd, əd, *stressed* hæd/ Ⓐ *forming past tenses* **I've** *or* **I ~/I had read** ich habe/hatte gelesen; **I've** *or* **I ~/I had gone** ich bin/war gegangen; **having seen him** (*because*) weil ich ihn gesehen habe/hatte; (*after*) wenn ich ihn gesehen habe/nachdem ich ihn gesehen hatte; **if I had known ...:** wenn ich gewusst hätte ...; Ⓑ (*cause to be*) **~ sth. made/repaired** etw. machen/reparieren lassen; **~ the painters in** die Maler haben; **~ sb. do sth.** jmdn. etw. tun lassen; **~ a tooth extracted** sich (*Dat.*) einen Zahn ziehen lassen; **~ oneself tattooed** sich tätowieren lassen; Ⓒ **she had her purse stolen** man hat ihr das Portemonnaie gestohlen; Ⓓ *expr. obligation* **~ to** müssen; **you don't ~ to** du brauchst *od.* musst nicht; **I only ~ to do the washing-up** ich muss nur noch den Abwasch machen; **I ~ only to see him to feel annoyed** ich brauche ihn nur zu sehen, und ich ärgere mich; **he 'has to be guilty** er ist fraglos schuldig. ❸ /hæv/ *n. in pl.* **the ~s and the ~-nots** die Besitzenden und die Besitzlosen

**~ a'way** ⇒ **~ off b**

**~ 'off** *v.t.* Ⓐ abmachen; Ⓑ **~ it off [with sb.]** (*sl.*) es [mit jmdm.] treiben (*salopp*)

**~ 'on** *v.t.* Ⓐ **~ the light on** das Licht anhaben; Ⓑ (*wear*) **~ a dress/hat on** ein Kleid/einen Hut tragen; ein Kleid anhaben/einen Hut aufhaben (*ugs.*); Ⓒ (*Brit. coll.: deceive*) **~ sb. on** jmdn. auf den Arm nehmen (*ugs.*)

**~ 'out** *v.t.* Ⓐ entfernen; **~ a tooth/one's tonsils out** sich (*Dat.*) einen Zahn ziehen lassen/sich (*Dat.*) die Mandeln herausnehmen lassen; Ⓑ (*discuss and settle*) **~ sth. out** sich über etw. (*Akk.*) offen [mit jmdm.] aussprechen; **~ it out with sb.** mit jmdm. offen sprechen

**~ 'up** *v.t.* Ⓐ aufgehängt haben ‹Vorhang, Bild›; Ⓑ (*coll.: bring to court*) **~ sb. up** jmdn. rankriegen (*ugs.*)

**haven** /ˈheɪvn/ *n.* Ⓐ (*mooring*) geschützte Anlegestelle, *die;* (*fig.*) Zufluchtsort, *der;* **a ~ of peace** eine Insel des Friedens; Ⓑ (*arch.: harbour*) Port, *der* (*veralt.*)

**have-not** /ˈhævnɒt/ ⇒ **have** 3

**haven't** /ˈhævnt/ = **have not;** ⇒ **have** 1, 2

**haver** /ˈheɪvə(r)/ *v.i.* Ⓐ (*talk foolishly*) **~ [on] about sth.** über etw. (*Akk.*) schwafeln (*ugs.*); Ⓑ (*vacillate*) zögern

**haversack** /ˈhævəsæk/ *n.* Brotbeutel, *der*

**havoc** /ˈhævək/ *n.*, *no pl.* Ⓐ (*devastation*) Verwüstungen *Pl.*; **cause** *or* **create** *or* **wreak ~:** Verwüstungen anrichten; **play ~ with** ruinieren ‹Gesundheit, Frisur usw.›; Ⓑ (*confusion*) Chaos, *das;* **play ~ with sth.** etw. völlig durcheinander bringen

**haw¹** /hɔː/ *n.* (*Bot.*) Ⓐ (*tree*) (*white*) Weißdorn, *der;* (*red*) Rotdorn, *der;* Ⓑ (*fruit*) Weißdorn-/Rotdornfrucht, *die*

**haw²** ⇒ **hum** 1 A, 3 B

**Hawaii** /həˈwaɪiː/ *pr. n.* Hawaii (*das*)

**Hawaiian** /həˈwaɪən/ ▶ 1275, ▶ 1340 ❶ *adj.* hawaiisch. ❷ *n.* Ⓐ (*person*) Hawaiianer, *der*/Hawaiianerin, *die;* Ⓑ (*language*) Hawaiisch, *das*

**'hawfinch** *n.* [Kirsch]kernbeißer, *der*

**haw-haw** /ˈhɔːhɔː/ ❶ *int.* (*laughter*) haha. ❷ *n.* **let out a loud ~:** laut auflachen

**hawk¹** /hɔːk/ ❶ *n.* (*Ornith., Polit.*) Falke, *der;* **watch sb. like a ~:** jmdn. mit Argusaugen beobachten; **have eyes like a ~:** Augen wie ein Luchs *od.* Adleraugen haben. ❷ *v.i.* mit dem Falken jagen; beizen (*Jägerspr.*)

**hawk²** *v.t.* (*peddle*) **~ sth.** (*at door*) mit etw. hausieren [gehen]; (*in street*) etw. [auf der Straße] verkaufen; **~ sth. around** (*fig.*) mit etw. hausieren [gehen]

**hawk³** ❶ *v.t.* **~ [up] phlegm** Schleim auswerfen. ❷ *v.i.* Schleim hochziehen [im Hals]

**hawker** /ˈhɔːkə(r)/ *n.* Hausierer, *der*/Hausiererin, *die;* (*in street*) fliegender Händler

**'hawk-eyed** *adj.* adleräugig; **be ~:** Falkenaugen *od.* Adleraugen haben

**hawkish** /ˈhɔːkɪʃ/ *adj.* raubvogelartig ‹Aussehen›; (*Polit.*) militant

**'hawklike** *adj.* falkenartig

**hawk: ~moth** *n.* (*Zool.*) Schwärmer, *der;* **~-nosed** *adj.* hakennasig; **be ~-nosed** eine Hakennase *od.* Habichtsnase haben; **~weed** *n.* (*Bot.*) Habichtskraut, *das*

**hawser** /ˈhɔːzə(r)/ *n.* (*Naut.*) Trosse, *die*

**hawthorn** /ˈhɔːθɔːn/ *n.* (*Bot.*) (*white*) Weißdorn, *der;* (*red*) Rotdorn, *der*

**hay** /heɪ/ *n.*, *no pl.* Heu, *das;* **make ~:** Heu machen; **make ~ while the sun shines** (*prov.*) die Zeit nutzen; ⇒ *also* **hit** 1 I

**hay: ~cock** *n.* Heuhaufen, *der;* **~ fever** *n.*, *no pl.* ▶ 1232 Heuschnupfen, *der;* **~field** *n.* Heuwiese, *die;* **~maker** *n.* Ⓐ Heumacher, *der;* Ⓑ (*coll.: blow*) weit ausholender Schlag; Heumacher, *der* (*Boxen Jargon*); **~making** *n.*, *no pl.* Heuernte, *die;* **~rick** ⇒ **~stack;** **~seed** *n.* Ⓐ Heublumen *Pl.*; Ⓑ (*Amer. derog.: yokel*) Bauerntölpel, *der;* **~stack** *n.* Heuschober, *der* (*südd.*); Heudieme, *die* (*nordd.*); ⇒ *also* **needle** 1

**haywire** /ˈheɪwaɪə(r)/ *adj.* (*coll.*) **go ~** ‹Instrument:› verrückt spielen (*ugs.*); ‹Plan:› über den Haufen geworfen werden (*ugs.*); ‹Person:› durchdrehen (*ugs.*)

**hazard** /ˈhæzəd/ ❶ *n.* Ⓐ (*danger*) Gefahr, *die;* (*on road*) Gefahrenstelle, *die;* **occupational ~:** Berufsrisiko, *das;* ⇒ *also* **fire hazard;** Ⓑ (*chance*) Schicksal, *das;* Ⓒ (*Golf*) Hindernis, *das.* ❷ *v.t.* Ⓐ (*endanger*) in Gefahr bringen; Ⓑ (*venture*) riskieren; **~ a guess** mit Raten probieren

**'hazard lights** *ns. pl.* (*Motor Veh.*) Warnblinkanlage, *die*

**hazardous** /ˈhæzədəs/ *adj.* (*dangerous*) gefährlich; (*risky*) riskant

**hazardously** /ˈhæzədəslɪ/ *adv.* (*dangerously*) gefährlich; (*riskily*) riskant

**hazard 'warning lights** ⇒ **hazard lights**

**haze** /heɪz/ ❶ *n.* Dunst[schleier], *der;* (*fig.*) Nebel, *der.* ❷ *v.t.* vernebeln

**hazel** /ˈheɪzl/ ❶ *n.* Ⓐ (*Bot.*) Haselnussstrauch, *der;* (*wood*) Haselholz, *das* (*veralt.*); Ⓑ (*colour*) Haselnussbraun, *das.* ❷ *adj.* haselnussbraun

**'hazelnut** *n.* Haselnuss, *die*

**hazily** /ˈheɪzɪlɪ/ *adv.* (*lit. or fig.*) verschwommen; unscharf; vage ‹verstehen›; unklar ‹sich vorstellen›

**haziness** /ˈheɪzɪnɪs/ *n.*, *no pl.* Dunst, *der;* (*fig.*) Vagheit, *die*

**hazy** /ˈheɪzɪ/ *adj.* dunstig, diesig ‹Wetter, Tag[eszeit]›; verschwommen, unscharf ‹Konturen›; (*fig.*) vage; **I have a ~ recollection that ...:** ich erinnere mich dunkel, dass ...

**H-bomb** /ˈeɪtʃbɒm/ *n.* H-Bombe, *die*

**HDTV** *abbr.* **high-definition television** HDTV

**he¹** /hɪ, *stressed* hiː/ ❶ *pron.* er; *referring to personified things or animals which correspond to German feminines/neuters* sie/es; **it was he** (*formal*) er war es; **he who** wer; (*Games*) **be 'he'** dran sein; ⇒ *also* **him; himself; his.** ❷ *n.*, *pl.* **hes** /hiːz/ Er, *der* (*ugs.*)

**he²** /hiː/ *int.* haha!

**he-** /hiː/ *pref.* männlich; **he-goat** [Ziegen]bock, *der*

**HE** *abbr.* Ⓐ **high explosive;** Ⓑ **His Eminence;** Ⓒ **His/Her Excellency**

**head** /hed/ ❶ *n.* Ⓐ ▶ 966 Kopf, *der;* Haupt, *das* (*geh.*); **count ~s** die Anzahl feststellen; **mind your ~!** Vorsicht, dein Kopf!; (*on sign*) Vorsicht — geringe Durchgangshöhe!; **turn sb.'s ~** (*fig.*) jmdm. den Kopf verdrehen; **laugh/scream one's ~ off** wie verrückt lachen/schreien; **from ~ to foot** von Kopf bis Fuß; **get one's ~ down** (*coll.*) sich aufs Ohr hauen (*ugs.*); **keep one's ~ down** (*lit. or fig.*) in Deckung bleiben; **stand on one's ~:** [einen] Kopfstand machen; **I could do that [standing] on my ~** (*fig. coll.*) das kann *od.* mache ich mit links (*ugs.*); **he has a price on his ~:** auf seinen Kopf ist eine Belohnung *od.* ein Preis ausgesetzt; **have a [bad] ~** (*fig. coll.: headache*) einen Brummschädel haben (*ugs.*); **the crowned ~s of Europe** die gekrönten Häupter Europas; **taller by a ~, a ~ taller** einen Kopf größer; **win by a ~/short ~:** mit einer Kopflänge/Nasenlänge gewinnen; **be** *or* **stand ~ and shoulders above sb.** (*fig.*) jmdm. haushoch überlegen sein; **give a horse its ~:** einem Pferd die Zügel schießen lassen; **give sb.** *or* **let sb. have his/her ~** (*fig.*) jmdm. freie Hand lassen; **go to sb.'s ~:** jmdm. in den *od.* zu Kopf steigen; **have a [good] ~ for heights** schwindelfrei sein; **~ first** mit dem Kopf zuerst/voran; (*fig.*) kopfüber; **not know whether one is [standing] on one's ~ or one's heels** nicht wissen, wo einem der Kopf steht; **~ over heels** kopfüber; **~ over heels in love** bis über beide Ohren verliebt (*ugs.*); **I can hold up my ~ [again]** ich brauche mich nicht [mehr] zu schämen; **keep one's ~:** einen klaren Kopf behalten; **keep one's ~ above water** (*fig.*) sich über Wasser halten; **put our/your/their ~s together [on sth.]** sich [wegen etw.] zusammensetzen; **lose one's ~:** enthauptet werden; (*fig.*) den Kopf verlieren; **~ to tail** in einer Reihe dicht hintereinander;

(~ *beside tail*) nebeneinander in umgekehrter Richtung; **be unable to make ~ or tail of sth./sb.** aus etw./jmdm. nicht klug werden; **be off one's ~** (*coll.*) übergeschnappt sein (*ugs.*); **off the top of one's ~** (*coll.*) aus dem Stegreif; (*as estimate*) über den Daumen gepeilt; **on your** *etc.* **[own] ~ be it** das hast du *usw.* selbst zu verantworten; **promote sb. over sb.'s ~:** jmdn. jmdm. bei der Beförderung vorziehen; **go over sb.'s ~:** jmdn. übergehen; ⇒ *also* **ear¹** A; **hole** 1 A; **raise** 1 A; Ⓑ (*mind*) Kopf, *der;* **in one's ~:** im Kopf; **enter sb.'s ~:** jmdm. in den Sinn kommen; **two ~s are better than one** (*prov.*) zwei Köpfe sind besser als einer; **it went right out of my ~:** ich habe das völlig vergessen; **take it into one's ~ [to do sth.]** auf die Idee kommen[, etw. zu tun]; **put sth. into sb.'s ~:** jmdn. auf etw. (*Akk.*) bringen; **it went above** *or* **over my ~** (*fig.*) das war zu hoch für mich (*ugs.*); **talk over sb.'s ~:** sich zu kompliziert für jmdn. ausdrücken; **I've got a good/bad ~ for figures** ich kann gut rechnen/rechnen kann ich überhaupt nicht; **use your ~:** gebrauch deinen Verstand; **not quite right in the ~** (*coll.*) nicht ganz richtig [im Kopf] (*ugs.*); **get sth. into one's ~:** etw. begreifen; **get this into your ~!** schreib dir das hinter die Ohren! (*ugs.*); **have got it into one's ~ that ...:** fest [davon] überzeugt sein, dass ...; **the first thing that comes into sb.'s ~:** das Erste, was jmdm. einfällt; **you ought to have your ~ examined** (*joc.*) ich glaube, du musst mal deinen Kopf untersuchen lassen (*ugs. scherzh.*); **the ~ rules the heart** der Verstand kontrolliert die Gefühle; Ⓒ (*person*) **a** *or* **per ~:** pro Kopf; Ⓓ *pl. same* (*in counting*) Stück [Vieh], *das;* Ⓔ *in pl.* (*on coin*) **~s or tails?** Kopf oder Zahl?; **~s [it is]** Kopf; **~s I go, tails I stay** bei Kopf gehe ich, bei Zahl bleibe ich; **~s I win, tails you lose** es läuft auf dasselbe hinaus; Ⓕ (*working end etc.; also Mus.*) Kopf, *der;* (*of axe*) Blatt, *das;* (*of spear*) Spitze, *die;* (*of cylinder*) Zylinderkopf, *der;* **drilling/cutting ~:** Bohr-/Schneidkopf, *der;* **playback/erasing ~:** Wiedergabe-/Löschkopf, *der;* Ⓖ (*of plant*) Kopf, *der;* (*of grain*) Ähre, *die;* **~ of lettuce** Salatkopf, *der;* Ⓗ (*on beer*) Blume, *die;* Ⓘ (*highest part*) Kopf, *der;* (*of stairs*) oberes Ende; (*of list, column*) oberste Reihe; (*of mast*) Topp, *der;* Ⓙ (*upper or more important end*) Kopf, *der;* (*of table*) Kopf, *der;* Kopfende, *das;* (*of lake, valley*) oberes Ende; (*of river*) Quelle, *die;* (*of bed*) Kopfende, *das;* Ⓚ (*of boil etc.*) Spitze, *die;* (*fig.: crisis*) **come to a ~:** sich zuspitzen; **bring matters to a ~:** die Sache auf die Spitze treiben; (*force a decision*) die Entscheidung herbeiführen; Ⓛ (*leader*) Leiter, *der*/Leiterin, *die;* (*of church, family*) Oberhaupt, *das;* **~ of government** Regierungschef, *der*/-chefin, *die;* **~ of state** Staatsoberhaupt, *das;* Ⓜ ⇒ **~master**; **~mistress**; Ⓝ (*leadership*) Spitze, *die;* **he is at the ~ of his profession** er hat eine Spitzenstellung in seinem Beruf; Ⓞ (*of ship*) Bug, *der;* Ⓟ ⇒ **~land**; Ⓠ (*body of water*) gestautes Wasser; Oberwasser, *das;* (*height of liquid*) Höhe, *die;* (*pressure*) Druck, *der;* **under a full ~ of steam** mit Volldampf; Ⓡ (*title*) Überschrift, *die;* (*fig.: category*) Rubrik, *die.*

❷ *attrib. adj.* (*senior*) **~ boy/girl** ≈ Schulsprecher, *der*/-sprecherin, *die* (*vom Lehrkörper eingesetzt*); **~ waiter** Oberkellner, *der;* **~ clerk** Bürovorsteher, *der;* (*main*) **~ office** Hauptverwaltung, *die;* (*Commerc.*) Hauptbüro, *das;* (*Banking, Insurance*) Hauptgeschäftsstelle, *die.*

❸ *v.t.* Ⓐ (*provide with heading*) überschreiben; betiteln; **~ed notepaper** Briefpapier mit Kopf; Ⓑ (*stand at top of*) anführen ‹Liste›; (*lead*) leiten; führen ‹Bewegung›; Ⓒ (*precede*) anführen; Ⓓ (*direct*) **~ sth. towards sth.** etw. auf etw. zusteuern; **we were ~ed towards Plymouth** wir fuhren mit Kurs auf Plymouth; Ⓔ (*Football*) köpfen; Ⓕ (*overtake and stop*) **~ sb./sth. [off]** jmdn./etw. abdrängen; Ⓖ (*surpass*) überholen.

❹ *v.i.* steuern; **~ for London** ‹Flugzeug, Schiff:› Kurs auf London nehmen; ‹Auto:› in Richtung London fahren; **~ towards** *or* **for sb./the buffet** auf jmdn./das Büfett zusteuern; **where are you ~ing?** wo gehst du hin?; **you're ~ing in the wrong direction** (*fig.*) du bist auf dem Holzweg; **you're ~ing for trouble** du wirst Ärger bekommen

**~ 'up** *v.t.* (*Amer.*) leiten

**head: ~ache** *n.* ▸**1232** Kopfschmerzen *Pl.;* (*fig. coll.*) Problem, *das;* **~achy** *adj.* (*coll.*) drückend ‹Wetter›; **feel ~achy** einen Druck im Kopf haben; **~band** *n.* Stirnband, *das;* **~board** *n.* (*of bed*) Kopfende, *das;* **~butt** ❶ *n.* Kopfstoß, *der;* ❷ *v.t.* einen Kopfstoß geben (+ *Dat.*); **~ case** *n.* (*coll.*) Hirni, *der* (*ugs.*); **be some sort of ~ case** sie nicht alle haben (*ugs.*); **~ count** *n.* Ⓐ **take a ~ count** abzählen; die Anzahl feststellen; Ⓑ (*number of people*) Kopfzahl, *die;* **~ covering** *n.* Kopfbedeckung, *die;* **~dress** *n.* Kopfschmuck, *der*

**-headed** /'hedɪd/ *adj. in comb.* -köpfig

**header** /'hedə(r)/ *n.* Ⓐ (*Footb.*) Kopfball, *der;* Ⓑ (*dive*) Kopfsprung, *der;* Ⓒ (*Building*) Binder, *der*

**head: ~gear** *n., no pl.* Ⓐ Kopfbedeckung, *die;* (*hats*) Kopfbedeckungen *Pl.;* **protective ~gear** Kopfschutz, *der;* Ⓑ (*Mining*) Fördergerüst, *das;* **~hunter** *n.* (*lit. or fig.*) Kopfjäger, *der*

**heading** /'hedɪŋ/ *n.* Ⓐ (*title*) Überschrift, *die;* (*in encyclopaedia*) Stichwort, *das;* (*fig.: category*) Rubrik, *die;* **come under the ~ [of] X** unter die Rubrik X fallen; **let's discuss these problems under separate ~s** diese Probleme sollten gesondert behandelt werden; Ⓑ (*direction*) Kurs, *der*

**head: ~lamp** *n.* Scheinwerfer, *der;* **~land** /'hedlənd, 'hedlænd/ *n.* Ⓐ (*Geog.*) Landspitze, *die;* Ⓑ (*Agric.*) Vorgewende, *das*

**headless** /'hedlɪs/ *adj.* ohne Kopf; **run around like a ~ chicken** herumrennen wie ein aufgescheuchtes Huhn/wie aufgescheuchte Hühner

**head: ~light** *n.* Scheinwerfer, *der;* **~line** *n.* Schlagzeile, *die;* **be ~line news, make [the] ~lines,** (*coll.*) **hit the ~lines** Schlagzeilen machen; **the [news] ~lines** (*Radio, Telev.*) die Kurznachrichten; (*within news programme*) der [Nachrichten]überblick; ⇒ *also* **running head[line]**; **~liner** *n.* (*Amer.*) Star (*der ständig in den Schlagzeilen ist*); **~lock** *n.* (*Wrestling*) Schwitzkasten, *der*

**'headlong** ❶ *adv.* Ⓐ (*head first*) **fall/plunge ~ into sth.** kopfüber in etw. fallen/springen; Ⓑ (*uncontrollably*) blindlings; **rush ~ into sth.** (*fig.*) etw. überstürzen. ❷ *adj.* Ⓐ (*head first*) **~ dive** Kopfsprung, *der;* Ⓑ (*impetuous*) überstürzt ‹Flucht, Entscheidung›

**head: ~man** *n.* Häuptling, *der;* **~'master** *n.* ▸**1261**, ▸**1617** Schulleiter, *der;* (*in secondary school*) Direktor, *der;* (*in primary school*) Rektor, *der;* **~'mistress** *n.* ▸**1261**, ▸**1617** ⇒ **~master**: Schulleiterin, *die;* Direktorin, *die;* Rektorin, *die;* **~-on** ❶ /'-'-/ *adj.* frontal; offen ‹Konfrontation, Konflikt›; **a ~-on collision** *or* **crash** ein Frontalzusammenstoß; ❷ /-'-/ *adv.* frontal; **meet sth./sb. ~-on** (*fig.: resolutely*) einer Sache/jmdm. entschieden entgegentreten; **~phones** *n. pl.* Kopfhörer, *der;* **~'quarters** *n. sing. or pl.* Hauptquartier, *das;* (*of firm*) Zentrale, *die;* **police ~quarters** Polizeidirektion, *die;* **~rest** *n.* Kopfstütze, *die;* **~room** *n., no pl.* [lichte] Höhe, *die;* (*in car*) Kopffreiheit, *die;* **low ~room** geringe Durchfahrtshöhe; **~scarf** *n.* Kopftuch, *das;* **~set** *n.* Kopfhörer, *der*

**headship** /'hedʃɪp/ *n.* Posten des Schulleiters/der Schulleiterin

**head: ~shrinker** *n.* Ⓐ Kopfjäger, *der;* Ⓑ (*coll.: psychiatrist*) Seelenklempner, *der* (*salopp*); **~square** *n.* [viereckiges] Kopftuch; **~ 'start** *n.* **a ~ start [over sb.]** eine Vorgabe [gegenüber jmdm.]; **~stock** *n.* Spindelstock, *der;* **~stone** *n.* Ⓐ (*gravestone*) Grabstein, *der;* Ⓑ (*of building*) Grundstein, *der;* (*fig.*) Grundpfeiler, *der;* **~strong** *adj.* eigensinnig; störrisch ‹Pferd, Esel›; **~ tax** *n.* (*Amer.*) Kopfsteuer, *die;* **~ 'teacher** *n.* ⇒ **headmaster**; **headmistress**; **~ voice** *n.* Kopfstimme, *die;* **~water** *n., usu. in pl.* Quellfluss, *der;* **~way** *n., no pl.* (*progress*) **make ~way** Fortschritte machen; **~ wind** *n.* Gegenwind, *der;* **~word** *n.* Ⓐ Stichwort, *das;* Ⓑ (*Ling.*) Nukleus, *der;* **~work** *n., no pl.* Kopfarbeit, *die*

**heady** /'hedɪ/ *adj.* Ⓐ vorschnell; unbesonnen; Ⓑ (*intoxicating*) berauschend

**heal¹** /hi:l/ ❶ *v.t.* Ⓐ (*lit. or fig.*) heilen; **time ~s all** (*fig.*) die Zeit heilt [alle] Wunden; Ⓑ (*arch.*) ⇒ **cure** 2 A. ❷ *v.i.* **~ [up]** [ver]heilen

**heal²** ⇒ **hele**

**healer** /'hi:lə(r)/ *n.* (*person*) Heilkundige, *der*/*die;* **time is a great ~:** die Zeit heilt alle Wunden

**healing** /'hi:lɪŋ/ ❶ *n.* Heilung, *die;* **powers of ~:** Heilkräfte. ❷ *attrib. adj.* **~ effect** Heilwirkung, *die;* **~ influence** heilsamer Einfluss; **~ ointment** Heilsalbe, *die*

**health** /helθ/ *n.* Ⓐ *no pl.* (*state*) Gesundheitszustand, *der;* (*healthiness*) Gesundheit, *die;* **in good/very good ~:** bei guter/bester Gesundheit; **sb. suffers from poor** *or* **bad ~:** jmdm. geht es gesundheitlich schlecht; **be restored to ~:** wieder hergestellt sein; **be in poor ~:** in schlechtem gesundheitlichen Zustand sein; **[not] be in the best of ~:** [nicht] bei bester Gesundheit sein; **in my state of ~:** in meinem Gesundheitszustand; **I'm not doing it for [the good of] my ~:** ich mache das nicht meiner Gesundheit zuliebe *od.* (*fig.*) nicht zum Vergnügen; **at least you have your ~:** du bist wenigstens gesund; Ⓑ (*toast*) **drink sb.'s ~** *or* **a ~ to sb.** auf jmds. Gesundheit trinken; **good** *or* **your ~!** auf deine Gesundheit!; zum Wohl!; pros[i]t!

**health: ~ authority** *n.* Gesundheitsbehörde, *die;* **~ care** *n.* Gesundheitsfürsorge, *die; attrib.* **~-care worker** im Gesundheitswesen Beschäftigte, *der*/*die;* **inadequate ~ care** unzureichende medizinische Versorgung; **~ centre** *n.* medizinisches Versorgungszentrum; Poliklinik, *die;* **~ certificate** *n.* Gesundheitszeugnis, *das;* **~ check** *n.* Gesundheitsuntersuchung, *die;* **~ education** *n.* Gesundheitslehre, *die;* **~ farm** *n.* Gesundheitsfarm, *die* (*ugs.*); **~ food** *n.* Reformhauskost, *die; attrib.* **~ food shop** Reformhaus, *das;* **~-giving** *adj.* gesund; **~ hazard** *n.* Gesundheitsrisiko, *das*

**healthily** /'helθɪlɪ/ *adv.* gesund

**healthiness** /'helθɪnɪs/ *n., no pl.* (*lit. or fig.*) Gesundheit, *die*

**health: ~ insurance** *n.* Krankenversicherung, *die;* **~ 'physics** *n.* Strahlenhygiene, *die;* **~ resort** *n.* Kurort, *der;* **~ salts** *n. pl.* leichtes Magenmittel; **H~ Secretary** *n.* (*Brit.*) Gesundheitsminister, *der*/-ministerin, *die;* **~ service** *n.* Gesundheitsdienst, *der;* **~ visitor** *n.* ▸**1261** Krankenschwester/-pfleger im Sozialdienst; **~ warning** *n.* Warnhinweis, *der; Hinweis auf die Gesundheitsgefährdung*

**healthy** /'helθɪ/ *adj.* Ⓐ gesund; (*fig.*) **the engine sounds ~:** der Motor hat einen gesunden Klang; **a ~ attitude towards sex** ein gesundes *od.* natürliches Verhältnis zum Sex; Ⓑ (*salutary*) gut ‹Zeichen›; **~ living** ein gesundes Leben; (*safe*) **stay at a ~ distance** in sicherer Entfernung bleiben

**heap** /hi:p/ ❶ *n.* Ⓐ (*pile*) Haufen, *der;* **a ~ of clothes** ein Kleiderhaufen; **at the bottom/top of the ~** (*fig.*) bei den Verlierern/Gewinnern; **lying in a ~/in ~s** auf einem/in Haufen liegen; **he was lying in a ~ on the ground** er lag zusammengesackt am Boden; Ⓑ (*fig. coll.: quantity*) **a [whole] ~ of** eine [ganze] Menge; **~s of** jede Menge (*ugs.*); Ⓒ (*fig. coll. derog.: vehicle*) Klapperkiste, *die* (*ugs.*). ❷ *v.t.* (*pile*) aufhäufen; **a ~ed spoonful of sugar** ein gehäufter Löffel Zucker; **~ sth. up** etw. aufhäufen; **~ sth. with sth.** etw. mit etw. [hoch] beladen; **~ sth. on sb.** (*fig.*) jmdn. mit etw. überhäufen

**hear** /hɪə(r)/ ❶ *v.t.,* **heard** /hɜ:d/ Ⓐ hören; **they ~d the car drive away** sie hörten den Wagen abfahren; **did you ~ him leaving** *or* **leave?** hast du ihn weggehen gehört *od.* hören?; **I have ~d it said that ...:** ich

habe sagen hören, dass ...; **I can hardly ~ myself think/speak** ich kann keinen klaren Gedanken fassen/kann mein eigenes Wort nicht verstehen; **let's ~ it!** nun sags schon!; **from what one ~s** wie man hört; **what's this I ~?** was muss ich da hören?; **you haven't ~d the last of this matter** das letzte Wort in dieser Sache ist noch nicht gesprochen; ⇒ *also* **end** 1 G; **last**[1] 3 A; **B** (*understand*) verstehen; **C** (*Law*) [an]hören; verhandeln ‹Fall›; **D** (*answer*) **our prayers have been ~d** unsere Gebete sind erhört worden.
❷ *v.i.*, **heard: ~ about sb./sth.** von jmdm./etw. [etwas] hören; **I've ~d all a'bout you** ich habe schon viel von Ihnen gehört; **~ from sb.** von jmdm. hören; **have you ~d from Tokyo/Smith yet?** haben Sie schon Nachricht aus Tokio/von Smith?; **I never ~d of such a thing!** hat man so was schon gehört!; **he was never ~d of again** von ihm hat man nie wieder [etwas] gehört; **he wouldn't ~ of it** er wollte davon nichts hören.
❸ *int.* **H~! H~!** bravo!; richtig!
**~ 'out** *v.t.* ausreden lassen

**heard** ⇒ **hear** 1, 2

**hearer** /'hɪərə(r)/ *n.* Hörer, *der*/Hörerin, *die*

**hearing** /'hɪərɪŋ/ *n.* **A** *no pl., no art.* (*faculty*) Gehör, *das;* **have good ~:** gut hören können; **be hard of ~:** schwerhörig sein; **B** *no pl.* (*distance*) **within/out of ~:** in/außer Hörweite; **C** *no pl.* **a fair ~:** eine faire Chance zu sprechen; **get a ~:** sich (*Dat.*) Gehör verschaffen können; **D** (*Law etc.*) Hearing, *das*

**'hearing aid** *n.* Hörgerät, *das*

**hearken** /'hɑːkn/ *v.i.* (*arch./literary*) **~ to sb./sth.** jmdm./einer Sache lauschen

**hearsay** /'hɪəseɪ/ *n., no pl., no indef. art.* Gerücht, *das;* Klatsch, *der* (*abwertend*); **~ evidence** (*Law*) Beweis vom Hörensagen

**hearse** /hɜːs/ *n.* Leichenwagen, *der*

**heart** /hɑːt/ *n.* **A** ▶ 966 (*Anat.; also ~-shaped object*) Herz, *das;* **he has a weak ~** (*Med.*) er hat ein schwaches Herz; **know/learn sth. by ~:** etw. auswendig wissen/lernen; **B** (*seat of feeling*) **at ~:** im Grunde seines/ihres Herzens; **sb. has sth. at ~, sth. is near** *or* **close to sb.'s ~:** jmdm. liegt etw. am Herzen; **a matter near** *or* **close to sb.'s ~:** ein Herzensanliegen; **go to sb.'s ~:** jmdm. ans Herz gehen; **in one's ~ [of ~s]** im tiefsten Herzen; **from the** *or* **one's ~:** von Herzen; **from the bottom of one's ~:** aus tiefstem Herzen; **with all one's ~ [and soul]** von ganzem Herzen; **put one's ~ and soul into sth.** etw. mit Leib und Seele tun; **put one's ~ into sth.** mit ganzem Herzen bei einer Sache sein; **cry one's ~ out** sich (*Dat.*) die Augen ausweinen *od.* aus dem Kopf weinen; **eat one's ~ out** sich vor Gram/Sehnsucht/Trauer *usw.* verzehren; **eat your ~ out!** da kannst du grün vor Neid werden!; **set one's ~ on sth./on doing sth.** sein Herz an etw. (*Akk.*) hängen/daran hängen, etw. zu tun; **to one's ~'s content** nach Herzenslust; **take sth. to ~:** sich (*Dat.*) etw. zu Herzen nehmen; (*accept*) beherzigen ‹Rat›; **take sb. to one's ~:** jmdn. in sein *od.* ins Herz schließen; **my ~ goes out to them** ich verspüre großes Mitleid mit ihnen; **my ~ bleeds for him** ich habe tiefstes Mitgefühl mit ihm; (*iron.*) mir blutet das Herz; **it does my ~ good** es erfreut mein Herz; **somebody after my own ~:** jemand ganz nach meinem Herzen; **have a ~ to ~ talk** offen und ehrlich miteinander sprechen; **her ~ is in the right place** sie hat das Herz auf dem rechten Fleck; **lose one's ~ to sb./sth.** sein Herz an jmdn./etw. verlieren; **give one's ~:** sein Herz schenken; **be sick at ~:** verzweifelt sein; **with a light/heavy ~:** leichten/schweren Herzens; **his ~ is not in it** er ist nicht mit dem Herzen dabei; **all the ~ could desire** alles, was das Herz begehrt; **bless his/her ~:** das liebe Kind!; **wear one's ~ [up]on one's sleeve** das Herz auf der Zunge tragen; **find it in one's ~ to do sth.** es übers Herz bringen, etw. zu tun; **have a ~!** hab' Erbarmen!; **not have the ~ to do sth.** nicht das Herz haben, etw. zu tun; **C** (*seat of courage*) **take ~:** Mut schöpfen (**from** bei); **put new ~ into sb.** jmdn. neuen Mut geben; **in good ~:** voll Zuversicht; **lose ~:** den Mut verlieren; **his ~ stood still** ihm stand das Herz still; **my ~ was in my boots** ich war am Boden zerstört (*ugs.*); **my ~ sank** mein Mut sank; **D** (*Cards*) Herz, *das;* ⇒ *also* **club** 1 D; **E** (*centre*) (*of cabbage*) Strunk, *der;* (*of lettuce*) Herz, *das;* (*of tree*) Kernholz, *das;* **the ~ of the matter** der wahre Kern der Sache; **go to the ~ of a problem** zum Kern eines Problems kommen; **in the ~ of the forest/England** mitten im Wald/im Herzen Englands. ⇒ *also* **break**[1] 1 H, 2 A; **change** 1 A; **dear** 1 A; **desire** 1 C; **gold** 1 A; **stone** 1 A

**heart: ~ache** *n.* [seelische] Qual; **~ attack** *n.* ▶ 1232 Herzanfall, *der;* (*fatal*) Herzschlag, *der;* **~beat** *n.* Herzschlag, *der;* **~['s]-blood** *n.* (*fig.*) Herzblut, *das* (*geh.*); **~break** *n.* Herzeleid, *das* (*geh.*); tiefer Kummer; **~breaking** *adj.* herzzerreißend; **~broken** *adj.* **she was ~broken** ihr Herz war gebrochen; **~burn** *n., no pl.* **A** Groll, *der;* **B** ▶ 1232 (*Med.*) Sodbrennen, *das;* **~ disease** *n., no pl.* ▶ 1232 Herzkrankheiten *Pl.;* **die of/from ~ disease** einem Herzleiden erliegen

**hearten** /'hɑːtn/ *v.t.* ermutigen

**heartening** /'hɑːtənɪŋ/ *adj.* ermutigend; **~ news** erfreuliche Nachrichten

**heart: ~ failure** *n.* ▶ 1232 Herzversagen, *das;* **~felt** *adj.* tief empfunden ‹Beileid›; aufrichtig ‹Dankbarkeit›; **a ~felt wish** ein Herzenswunsch

**hearth** /hɑːθ/ *n.* **A** [*gekachelter o. ä.*] *Platz vor dem Kamin;* **~ and home** (*fig.*) der heimische Herd; **B** (*in furnace*) Ofenraum, *der;* (*smith's ~*) Esse, *die*

**hearthrug** *n.* Kaminvorleger, *der*

**heartily** /'hɑːtɪlɪ/ *adv.* von Herzen; **eat ~:** tüchtig essen; **be ~ sick of sth.** etw. herzlich leid sein

**'heartland** *n.* Landesinnere, *das*

**heartless** /'hɑːtlɪs/ *adj.*, **heartlessly** /'hɑːtlɪslɪ/ *adv.* herzlos; unbarmherzig

**heartlessness** /'hɑːtlɪsnɪs/ *n., no pl.* Unbarmherzigkeit, *die*

**heart: ~-'lung machine** *n.* (*Med.*) Herz-Lungen-Maschine, *die;* **~ rate** *n.* Herzfrequenz, *die;* **an abnormally rapid ~ rate** ein abnorm schneller Herzschlag; **~-rending** *adj.* herzzerreißend; **~-searching** *n.* Gewissenserforschung, *die;* **~'s-ease** *n.* (*Bot.*) Veilchen, *das;* (*Viola tricolor*) Stiefmütterchen, *das;* **~-shaped** *adj.* herzförmig; **~sick** *adj.* verzweifelt; **~strings** *n. pl.* **touch sb.'s ~strings** jmdm. zu Herzen gehen; **~-throb** *n.* (*person*) Idol, *das;* **~-to-~** *n.* **have a ~-to-~:** offen und ehrlich miteinander sprechen; **~ transplant** *n.* (*operation*) Herztransplantation, *die* (*fachspr.*); Herzverpflanzung, *die;* (*transplanted heart*) Herztransplantat, *das* (*fachspr.*); **receive a ~ transplant from sb.** jmds. Herz eingepflanzt *od.* implantiert bekommen; **~ trouble** *n.* ▶ 1232 Probleme mit dem Herzen; **~-warming** *adj.* herzerfreuend; **~wood** *n.* (*Bot.*) Kernholz, *das*

**hearty** /'hɑːtɪ/ ❶ *adj.* **A** (*wholehearted*) ungeteilt ‹Unterstützung, Zustimmung›; (*enthusiastic, unrestrained*) herzlich; begeistert ‹Gesang›; **a ~ eater** ein guter Esser; **B** (*large*) herzhaft ‹Mahlzeit›; gesund ‹Appetit›; **C** (*vigorous*) herzhaft ‹Ruck, Tritt›; ⇒ *also* **hale**[1]. ❷ *n.* (*Naut.*) **come on, my hearties!** auf gehts, Jungs!

**heat** /hiːt/ ❶ *n.* **A** (*hotness*) Hitze, *die;* (*temperature*) Temperatur, *die;* (*temperature setting*) Temperaturstufe, *die;* (*fig.: sensation*) Brennen, *das;* **remove sth. from/return sth. to the ~:** etw. vom Feuer nehmen/wieder erhitzen; **B** (*Phys.*) Wärme, *die;* **latent ~:** Umwandlungswärme, *die;* **specific ~:** spezifische Wärme; **C** (*fig.*) (*anger*) Erregung, *die;* **generate a lot of ~/more ~ than light** die Gemüter erregen/mehr Erregung als Erleuchtung erzeugen; **take the ~ out of a situation** eine Situation entschärfen; **in the ~ of the moment** in der Hitze des Gefechts; (*coll.: pressure*) **the ~ is on** die Sache ist heiß (*ugs.*); **put the ~ on** Druck machen; **put the ~ on sb.** jmdn. unter Druck setzen; **the ~ is off** die Lage hat sich entspannt; **D** (*Zool.*) Brunst, *die;* **come into** *or* **on/be in** *or* **on ~:** brünstig werden/sein; ‹Stute:› rossig werden/sein; ‹Hündin:› läufig werden/sein; ‹Katze:› rollig werden/sein; **E** (*Sport*) Vorlauf, *der;* ⇒ *also* **dead heat.**
❷ *v.t.* heizen ‹Raum›; erhitzen ‹Substanz, Lösung›; vorheizen ‹Backofen›.
❸ *v.i.* warm werden
**~ 'up** *v.t.* heiß machen ‹Essen, Wasser›

**heated** /'hiːtɪd/ *adj.* erhitzt; (*fig.: angry*) hitzig; **a ~ exchange** ein heftiger Schlagabtausch (*fig.*)

**heatedly** /'hiːtɪdlɪ/ *adv.* hitzig

**heater** /'hiːtə(r)/ *n.* **A** Ofen, *der;* (*for water*) Boiler, *der;* **B** (*dated coll.: firearm*) Kanone, *die* (*salopp*)

**'heat exchanger** *n.* Wärmetauscher, *der*

**heath** /hiːθ/ *n.* **A** Heide, *die;* **B** (*Bot.*) (*Calluna*) Heidekraut, *das;* (*Erica*) Erika, *die;* Glockenheide, *die*

**'heat haze** *n.* Hitzeschleier, *der;* **sth. shimmers in the ~** etw. flimmert in der Hitze; **through 'the shimmering ~:** durch die flimmernde Hitze

**heathen** /'hiːðn/ ❶ *adj.* heidnisch. ❷ *n.* Heide, *der*/Heidin, *die;* (*fig. derog.*) gottloser Mensch

**heather** /'heðə(r)/ *n.* **A** (*plant*) Heidekraut, *das;* **B** (*colour*) Erikarot, *das*

**heating** /'hiːtɪŋ/ *n., no pl.* Heizung, *die*

**heat: ~proof** *adj.* feuerfest; **~ pump** *n.* Wärmepumpe, *die;* **~ rash** *n.* (*Med.*) Hitzebläschen *Pl.;* **~-resistant** *adj.* hitzebeständig; **~ shield** *n.* (*Astronaut.*) Hitzeschild, *der;* **~stroke** *n.* Hitzschlag, *der;* **~ treatment** *n.* (*Metall., Med.*) Wärmebehandlung, *die;* **~wave** *n.* Hitzewelle, *die*

**heave** /hiːv/ ❶ *v.t.* **A** (*lift*) heben; wuchten (*ugs.*); **B** *p.t. & p.p.* **hove** /həʊv/ (*coll.: throw*) werfen; schmeißen (*ugs.*); (*Naut.: cast, haul up*) hieven; **C** (*utter*) **~ a sigh [of relief]** [erleichtert] aufseufzen. ❷ *v.i.* **A** (*pitch*) [auf und nieder] schwanken; ‹Schiff:› stampfen (*Seemannsspr.*); (*rise*) sich heben; **B** (*pull*) ziehen; **~ ho!** hau ruck!; holt auf (*Seemannsspr.*); **C** (*pant*) keuchen; **D** (*retch*) sich übergeben; **E** *p.t. & p.p.* **hove** (*move*) **~ in sight** in Sicht kommen; **~ to** (*Naut.*) beidrehen. ❸ *n.* **A** (*pull*) Zug, *der;* **B** (*throw*) Schwung, *der*

**heaven** /'hevn/ *n.* **A** Himmel, *der;* **in ~:** im Himmel; **go** *or* **ascend to ~:** in den Himmel kommen; **~ on earth** (*fig.*) der Himmel auf Erden; **be sent from ~** (*fig.*) ein Geschenk des Himmels sein; **it was ~ [to her]** (*fig.*) es war der Himmel auf Erden [für sie]; **seventh ~** (*fig.*) der siebte Himmel; **move ~ and earth** (*fig.*) Himmel und Erde in Bewegung setzen; **B** *in pl.*, (*poet.*) *in sing.* (*sky*) Firmament, *das;* Himmelszelt, *das* (*dichter.*); **in the ~s** am Himmel; **the ~s opened** es prasselte los; **C** (*God, Providence*) **by H~!** bei Gott; **[good] H~s!** gütiger Himmel!; **H~s above!** du lieber Himmel!; **H~ [only] knows** weiß der Himmel; **H~ help us** der Himmel steh uns bei; **for H~'s sake** um Gottes *od.* Himmels willen; **thank H~[s]** Gott sei Dank; **I hope to H~ that ...:** ich hoffe zu Gott, dass ...; ⇒ *also* **forbid** B; **name** 1 D

**heavenly** /'hevnlɪ/ *adj.* **A** (*also coll.: delightful*) himmlisch; **B** **~ body** Himmelskörper, *der;* **C** (*of heaven*) himmlisch; **the H~ City** das Himmelreich

**'heaven-sent** *adj.* **a ~ opportunity** eine Gelegenheit, die wie gerufen kommt/kam

**heavenward[s]** /'hevnwəd(z)/ *adv.* himmelwärts

**heavily** /'hevɪlɪ/ *adj.* **A** (*with great weight, severely, with difficulty*) schwer ‹beladen, bestraft, atmen›; **~ guarded** streng bewacht; **B** (*to a great extent*) stark; schwer ‹bewaffnet›; tief ‹schlafen›; dicht ‹bevölkert›; **smoke/drink ~:** ein starker Raucher/Trinker sein; **eat too ~:** zu schwer essen; **gamble ~:** ein [leidenschaftlicher] Spieler sein; **rely ~ on sb./sth.** von jmdm./etw. [vollkommen] abhängig sein; **C** (*with great force*) **it rained/**

snowed **~:** es regnete/schneite stark; **fall ~:** hart fallen; **~ underlined** dick unterstrichen; **weigh ~ [up]on sb.** (*fig.*) schwer auf jmdm. lasten; **~ built** kräftig gebaut

**heaviness** /'hevɪnɪs/ *n.*, *no pl.* **A** (*weight*) Gewicht, *das;* **B** (*great extent*) Ausmaß, *das;* (*severity*) Härte, *die;* **C** (*clinging quality*) Schwere, *die;* **D** (*tiredness*) Schwerfälligkeit, *die*

**heavy** /'hevɪ/ ❶ *adj.* **A** ▶1683 (*in weight*) schwer; dick ‹Mantel›; fest ‹Schuh›; **~ traffic** Schwerlastverkehr, *der;* (*dense*) hohes Verkehrsaufkommen; **~ work** Schwerarbeit, *die;* **a ~ crop** (*fig.*) eine [sehr] reiche Ernte; **a ~ silence** eine atemlose Stille; **B** (*severe*) schwer ‹Schaden, Verlust, Strafe, Kampf›; hoch ‹Steuern, Schulden, Anforderungen›; massiv ‹Druck, Unterstützung›; **~ responsibilities** schwere Verantwortung; **C** (*excessive*) unmäßig ‹Trinken, Essen, Rauchen›; ausgiebig ‹Necking, Petting›; **be ~ on the sugar/petrol** (*coll.*) viel Zucker nehmen/viel Benzin verbrauchen; **a ~ smoker/drinker** ein starker Raucher/Trinker; **a ~ gambler** ein [leidenschaftlicher] Spieler; **be a ~ sleeper** sehr fest schlafen; **D** (*violent*) schwer ‹Schlag, Sturm, Regen, Sturz, Seegang›; hart ‹Aufprall›; **~ weather** ungünstiges Wetter; **make ~ weather of sth.** (*fig.*) die Dinge unnötig komplizieren; **E** (*clinging*) schwer ‹Boden›; ⇨ *also* **going** 1 B; **F** (*hard to digest*) schwer ‹Mahlzeit›; **G** (*overcast*) bedeckt ‹Himmel›; **H** (*in sound*) **~ footsteps** schwere Schritte; **I** (*clumsy*) plump; (*intellectually slow*) schwerfällig; **~ with sleep** schlaftrunken; **our eyes were ~ with sleep** wir konnten [vor Müdigkeit] kaum noch die Augen offen halten; **J** (*tedious*) schwerfällig; (*serious*) seriös ‹Zeitung›; ernst ‹Musik, Theaterrolle›; (*stern*) streng; gestreng (*veralt.*) ‹Vater, Ehemann›; **lie ~ on sb.'s stomach/conscience** jmdm. schwer im Magen liegen/auf der Seele liegen; **time lies ~ on my hands** mir wird die Zeit lang; ⇨ *also* **hand** 1 B; **K** (*Phys.*) **~ hydrogen/water** schwerer Wasserstoff/schweres Wasser.
❷ *n.* (*coll.*) **A** (*newspaper*) seriöse Zeitung; **B** (*coll.: thug*) Schlägertyp, *der* (*ugs.*)

**heavy: ~-duty** *adj.* strapazierfähig ‹Kleidung, Material›; schwer ‹Werkzeug, Maschine›; **~-'footed** *adj.* schwerfällig; **~ 'goods vehicle** *n.* Schwerlastwagen, *der;* **~-'handed** *adj.* (*clumsy*) ungeschickt ‹Person›; umständlich ‹Stil›; (*oppressive*) unbarmherzig ‹Tyrannei, Diktatur›; **~-'hearted** *adj.* traurig; **~ 'industry** *n.* Schwerindustrie, *die;* **~ 'metal** *n.* **A** Schwermetall, *das;* **B** (*Mus.*) Heavy-Metal, *das;* **a ~-metal band** eine Heavy-Metal-Band; **~ 'type** *n.* (*Printing*) fette Schrift; **~weight** *n.* (*Boxing etc.*) Schwergewicht, *das;* (*person also*) Schwergewichtler, *der;* (*fig.*) Größe, *die*

**Hebraic** /hi:'breɪɪk/ *adj.* hebräisch

**Hebrew** /'hi:bru:/ ▶1275 ❶ *adj.* hebräisch; ⇨ *also* **English** 1. ❷ *n.* **A** (*Israelite*) Hebräer, *der*/Hebräerin, *die;* **B** *no pl.* (*language*) Hebräisch, *das;* **a ~ scholar** ein Hebraist; ⇨ *also* **English** 2 A

**Hebrides** /'hebrɪdi:z/ *pr. n. pl.* Hebriden *Pl.;* **Inner/Outer ~:** Innere/Äußere Hebriden

**heck** /hek/ (*coll. euphem.*) ⇨ **hell** B

**heckle** /'hekl/ *v.t.* **~ sb./a speech** jmdn./eine Rede durch Zwischenrufe unterbrechen

**heckler** /'heklə(r)/ *n.* Zwischenrufer, *der*

**hectare** /'hektɑ:(r), 'hekteə(r)/ *n.* ▶928 Hektar, *das od. der*

**hectic** /'hektɪk/ *adj.* hektisch

**hecto-** /'hektə/ *pref.* hekto-/Hekto-

**hector** /'hektə(r)/ ❶ *v.t.* einschüchtern. ❷ *v.i.* bramarbasieren (*geh.*)

**hectoring** /'hektərɪŋ/ *adj.* überheblich

**he'd** /hɪd, *stressed* hi:d/ **A** = **he had; B** = **he would**

**hedge** /hedʒ/ ❶ *n.* (*of bushes, trees, etc.*) Hecke, *die;* (*fig.: barrier*) Mauer, *die;* (*fig.: means of protection*) Schutzwall, *der;* (*against financial loss*) Absicherung, *die.* ❷ *v.t.* **A** (*surround with ~*) mit einer Hecke umgeben; **~ sb. [in or round]** (*fig.*) jmdn. in seiner Handlungsfreiheit einschränken; **B** (*protect*) **~ one's bets** mit verteiltem Risiko wetten; (*fig.*) nicht alles auf eine Karte setzen. ❸ *v.i.* (*avoid commitment*) sich nicht festlegen; **stop hedging and give me a straight answer** weich nicht dauernd aus, und gib mir eine klare Antwort

**'hedge clippers** *n. pl.* Heckenschere, *die*

**hedgehog** /'hedʒhɒg/ *n.* Igel, *der*

**'hedge-hop** *v.i.* im Tiefflug fliegen

**hedge: ~row** *n.* Hecke, *die* [als Feldbegrenzung]; **~ sparrow** *n.* Heckenbraunelle, *die*

**hedonism** /'hi:dənɪzm/ *n.*, *no pl.* Hedonismus, *der*

**hedonist** /'hi:dənɪst/ *n.* Hedonist, *der*/Hedonistin, *die*

**hedonistic** /hi:də'nɪstɪk/ *adj.* hedonistisch

**heebie-jeebies** /hi:bɪ'dʒi:bɪz/ *n. pl.* (*coll.*) **give sb. the ~:** jmdn. kribblig machen (*ugs.*)

**heed** /hi:d/ ❶ *v.t.* beachten; beherzigen ‹Rat, Lektion›; **~ the danger/risk** sich (*Dat.*) der Gefahr/des Risikos bewusst sein. ❷ *n.*, *no art.*, *no pl.* **give** *or* **pay ~ to, take ~ of** Beachtung schenken (+ *Dat.*); **give** *or* **pay no ~ to, take no ~ of** nicht beachten

**heedful** /'hi:dfl/ *adj.* achtsam; **be ~ of sth.** etw. beachten; **be ~ of the danger/necessity** sich (*Dat.*) der Gefahr/Notwendigkeit (*Gen.*) bewusst sein; **be ~ of sb.'s warning** jmds. Warnung beherzigen

**heedless** /'hi:dlɪs/ *adj.* unachtsam; **be ~ of sth.** auf etw. (*Akk.*) nicht achten; **be ~ of the danger/risks** die Gefahr/Risiken nicht beachten

**hee-haw** /'hɪ:hɔ:/ ❶ *int.* iah. ❷ *n.* Iah, *das.* ❸ *v.i.* iahen; (*fig.*) wiehern

**heel**[1] /hi:l/ ❶ *n.* **A** ▶966 Ferse, *die;* **~ of the hand** Handballen, *der;* **Achilles' ~** (*fig.*) Achillesferse, *die;* **bring a dog to ~:** einen Hund bei Fuß rufen; **bring sb. to ~** (*fig.*) jmdn. auf Vordermann bringen (*ugs.*); **come to ~:** bei Fuß gehen; (*fig.*) parieren (*ugs.*); **[to] ~!** bei Fuß!; **at ~:** bei Fuß; **be on sb.'s ~s** (*fig.*) jmdm. auf den Fersen sein (*ugs.*); **[hard** *or* **close] on** *or* **at the ~s of sb./sth.** [dicht] hinter jmdm./etw.; (*in time or quality*) gleich nach jmdm./etw.; **show a clean pair of ~s** (*fig.*) sich aus dem Staub machen (*ugs.*); **show sb. a clean pair of ~s** (*fig.*) jmdn. abhängen (*ugs.*); **take to one's ~s** (*fig.*) Fersengeld geben (*ugs.*); **cool one's ~s** (*fig. coll.*) lange warten [müssen]; **kick one's ~s** (*fig. coll.*) rumhängen (*ugs.*); **be under the ~ of sb.** (*fig.*) unter jmds. Herrschaft sein; ⇨ *also* **dig in** 2 B; **B** (*of shoe*) Absatz, *der;* (*of stocking*) Ferse, *die;* **down at ~:** abgetreten; (*fig.*) heruntergekommen (*ugs.*); **turn on one's ~:** auf dem Absatz kehrtmachen; ⇨ *also* **high heel; C** (*of violin bow*) Frosch, *der;* (*of golf club*) Ferse, *die;* (*of ski*) hinteres Ende; (*of loaf*) Endstück, *das;* **D** (*coll.: person*) Schuft, *der* (*abwertend*).
❷ *v.t.* **A** **~ a shoe** einen Schuh mit einem [neuen] Absatz versehen; **B** (*Golf*) mit der Ferse schlagen; **C** (*Rugby*) mit dem Absatz spielen

**heel**[2] (*Naut.*) ❶ *v.i.* krängen. ❷ *v.t.* zum Krängen bringen. ❸ *n.* Krängung, *die*

**heel**[3] ⇨ **hele**

**heel: ~ bar** *n.* Absatzschnelldienst, *der;* **~ bone** *n.* (*Anat.*) Fersenbein, *das*

**heelless** /'hi:llɪs/ *adj.* ‹Schuhe› ohne Absatz

**heft** /heft/ ❶ *v.t.* anheben (*und dabei das Gewicht feststellen*). ❷ *n.* (*Amer.*) Gewicht, *das*

**heftily** /'heftɪlɪ/ *adv.* kräftig; (*fig.*) stark

**hefty** /'heftɪ/ *adj.* kräftig; (*heavy*) schwer; (*fig.: large*) hoch ‹Rechnung, Summe, Strafe, Anteil›; deutlich ‹Mehrheit›; stark ‹Erhöhung›

**Hegelian** /he'gi:lɪən, her'gi:lɪən/ (*Philos.*) ❶ *adj.* hegelianisch. ❷ *n.* Hegelianer, *der*/Hegelianerin, *die*

**hegemony** /hɪ'gemənɪ, hɪ'dʒemənɪ/ *n.* Hegemonie, *die*

**hegira** /'hedʒɪrə/ *n.* Hedschra, *die;* (*fig. literary*) Exodus, *der*

**heh** /heɪ/ *int.* he

**he-he** /hi:'hi:/ *int.* haha

**heifer** /'hefə(r)/ *n.* Färse, *die*

**heigh-ho** /heɪ'həʊ/ *int.* ach ja

**height** /haɪt/ *n.* **A** ▶1210 Höhe, *die;* (*of person, animal, building*) Größe, *die;* **lose ~** (*Aeron.*) an Höhe verlieren; **be three metres in ~:** drei Meter hoch sein; **at a ~ of three metres** in einer Höhe von drei Metern; **be six feet in ~** ‹Person:› 1,80 m groß sein; **what is your ~?** wie groß sind Sie?; **B** *usu. in pl.* (*high place*) **the ~s** die Anhöhe; **be afraid of ~s** nicht schwindelfrei sein; **~ of land** (*Amer. Geog.*) Wasserscheide, *die;* **C** (*fig.: highest point*) Höhepunkt, *der;* **at the ~ of one's fame** auf dem Gipfel seines Ruhms; **the ~ of luxury** das Nonplusultra an Luxus; **the ~ of folly** der Gipfel der Dummheit; **at the ~ of summer** im Hochsommer; ⇨ *also* **fashion** 1 B

**heighten** /'haɪtn/ ❶ *v.t.* aufstocken; (*fig.: intensify*) verstärken. ❷ *v.i.* (*fig.*) sich verstärken

**heinous** /'heɪnəs/ *adj.* schändlich; ruchlos (*geh.*, *veralt.*)

**heir** /eə(r)/ *n.* (*lit. or fig.*) Erbe, *der*/Erbin, *die;* **the ~ to the throne** der Thronerbe/die Thronerbin; ⇨ *also* **apparent** A; **presumptive**

**heiress** /'eərɪs/ *n.* Erbin, *die* (*bes. eines Vermögens*); ⇨ *also* **heir**

**heirloom** /'eəlu:m/ *n.* **A** Erbstück, *das;* (*fig.*) Erbe, *das;* **B** (*Law*) *von einem Erbe nicht abtrennbarer Teil*

**heist** /haɪst/ (*Amer. coll.*) ❶ *n.* Raubüberfall, *der.* ❷ *v.t.* (*steal*) rauben; (*rob*) ausrauben

**hejira** ⇨ **hegira**

**held** ⇨ **hold**[2] 1, 2

**hele** /hi:l/ *v.t.* (*Hort.*) **~ sth. [in]** etw. einpflanzen

**Helen** /'helən/ *pr. n.* **~ of Troy** [die schöne] Helena

**heli-** /'helɪ/ *in comb.* Heli-

**helical** /'helɪkl/ *adj.* spiralförmig; spiralig; **~ gear** Schrägstirnrad, *das;* **~ spring** Schraubenfeder, *die*

**helices** *pl. of* **helix**

**helicopter** /'helɪkɒptə(r)/ *n.* Hubschrauber, *der*

**Heligoland** /'helɪgəlænd/ *pr. n.* Helgoland (*das*)

**helio-** /'hi:lɪə/ *in comb.* helio-/Helio-

**'heliograph** ❶ *n.* Heliograph, *der.* ❷ *v.t.* mit dem Heliographen übermitteln

**heliotrope** /'hi:lɪətrəʊp, 'helɪətrəʊp/ ❶ *n.* **A** (*Bot.*, *Min.*) Heliotrop, *das;* **B** (*colour*) Bläulichviolett, *das;* Heliotrop, *das.* ❷ *adj.* bläulich violett; heliotrop

**heliport** /'helɪpɔ:t/ *n.* Heliport, *der*

**helium** /'hi:lɪəm/ *n.* Helium, *das*

**helix** /'hi:lɪks/ *n.*, *pl.* **helices** /'hi:lɪsi:z/ **A** Spirale, *die;* **B** (*Archit.*) Volute, *die;* **C** (*Anat.*) Helix, *die*

**hell** /hel/ *n.* **A** Hölle, *die;* **suffer the torments of ~:** Höllenqualen erleiden; **make sb.'s life [a] ~, make life ~ for sb.** jmdm. das Leben zur Hölle machen; **all ~ was let loose** (*fig.*) es war die Hölle los; **~ on earth** (*fig.*) die Hölle auf Erden; **B** (*coll.: in imprecations and phrases*) **[oh] ~!** verdammter Mist! (*ugs.*); **what the ~!** ach, zum Teufel! (*ugs.*); **to** *or* **the ~ with it!** ich habs satt (*ugs.*); **who the ~ are you?** wer, zum Teufel, sind Sie? (*ugs.*); **~'s bells!** (*coll.*) Mensch, Scheiße! (*salopp*); **get the ~ 'out of here!, go to ~!** scher dich zum Teufel! (*ugs.*); **play [merry] ~ with sth.** etw. [ganz schön] ins Schleudern bringen (*ugs.*); **there'll be ~ to pay if you get caught** wenn sie dich erwischen, ist der Teufel los (*ugs.*); **as tired/angry as ~:** unheimlich müde/wütend; **a** *or* **one ~ of a** *or* **a helluva [good] party** eine unheimlich gute Party (*ugs.*); **a ~ of a** *or* **a helluva noise** ein Höllenlärm (*salopp*); **like sb./sth. a ~ of a lot** jmdn./etw. wahnsinnig gern mögen (*ugs.*); **a ~ of a lot of money** wahnsinnig viel Geld (*ugs.*); **he thinks he's a ~ of a fellow** er denkt, er ist ein Teufelskerl (*ugs.*); **that was**

h

# Height and depth

1 inch = 25,4 mm
1 foot = 30,48 cm

## Height

■ **PEOPLE**

***How tall is she?, What height is she?***
= Wie groß ist sie?

***She's five foot six***
= Sie ist ein Meter achtundsechzig (1,68 m) groß

***He's smaller*** or ***less tall than his brother***
= Er ist kleiner als sein Bruder

***A is the same height*** or ***as tall as B***
= A ist [genau]so groß wie B

***They are the same height***
= Sie sind gleich groß

***an athlete six feet tall***
≈ ein 1,80 Meter großer Athlet

■ **THINGS**

***How high is it?, What height is it?***
= Wie hoch ist es?

***It's about thirty feet high*** or ***in height***
= Es ist ungefähr neun Meter hoch

***A is lower/higher than B***
= A ist niedriger/höher als B

***A is the same height*** or ***as high as B***
= A ist [genau]so hoch wie B

***The towers are the same height***
= Die Türme sind gleich hoch

***The aircraft was flying at a height*** or ***an altitude of 10,000 feet***
≈ Die Maschine flog in einer Höhe von 3 000 Metern

***The treeline is at a height of about 6,500 feet***
≈ Die Baumgrenze liegt bei etwa 2 000 Meter Höhe *or* bei etwa 2 000 Metern

***waves ten feet high***
≈ drei Meter hohe Wellen

***a mountain of over 20,000 feet*** or ***over 20,000 feet in height***
≈ ein Berg von über 6 000 Metern *or* von über 6 000 Meter Höhe

## Depth

***How deep*** or ***What depth is the river?***
= Wie tief ist *or* Welche Tiefe hat der Fluss?

***It's ten feet deep***
≈ Er ist drei Meter tief *or* hat eine Tiefe von drei Metern

***The treasure is at a depth of fifty feet*** or ***is fifty feet down***
≈ Der Schatz liegt in einer Tiefe von fünfzehn Metern *or* fünfzehn Meter tief

***A is the same depth as B***
= A hat die gleiche Tiefe wie B

***A and B are the same depth***
= A und B sind gleich tief

***A is shallower than B***
= A ist flacher *or* seichter als B

***a hole ten feet deep***
≈ ein drei Meter tiefes Loch

**a ~ of a thing to do** das war ungeheuerlich (*abwertend*)/(*praising*) grandios; **work/run like ~:** wie der Teufel arbeiten/rennen (*ugs.*); **like ~!** nie im Leben! (*ugs.*); **it hurt like ~:** es tat höllisch weh (*ugs.*); **beat** *or* **knock [the] ~ out of sb.** jmdn. grün und blau schlagen (*ugs.*); **give sb. ~:** jmdm. die Hölle heiß machen (*ugs.*); ‹Schmerzen usw.:› jmdn. verrückt machen (*ugs.*); **get ~:** großen Ärger kriegen (*ugs.*); **come ~ or high water** [völlig] egal, was passieren sollte (*ugs.*); **do sth. [just] for the ~ of it** etw. [nur so] aus Jux und Tollerei tun (*ugs.*); **~ for leather** wie der Teufel (*ugs.*); **I'll see you in ~ first** ich denke nicht im Traum daran!; ⇒ *also* **hope** 1; **raise** 1 G

**he'll** /hɪl, *stressed* hi:l/ = **he will**

**hell: ~bender** *n.* (*Amer. Zool.*) Schlammteufel, *der;* **~-'bent** *adj.* **be ~-bent on doing sth.** (*coll.*) wild entschlossen sein, etw. zu tun (*ugs.*); **~cat** *n.* (*derog.*) Wildkatze, *die*

**hellebore** /'helɪbɔ:(r)/ *n.* (*Bot.*) Nieswurz, *die*

**Hellenic** /he'li:nɪk/ *adj.* hellenisch

**Hellenist** /'helɪnɪst/ *n.* Hellenist, *der*/Hellenistin, *die*

**Hellenistic** /helɪ'nɪstɪk/ *adj.* hellenistisch

**'hellfire** *n.* Höllenfeuer, *das*

**'hellhound** *n.* Höllenhund, *der;* (*fig.*) Teufel, *der*

**hellish** /'helɪʃ/ ❶ *adj.* höllisch ‹Qual, Schmerz›; scheußlich ‹Arbeit, Zeit›. ❷ *adv.* (*coll.*) verdammt (*ugs.*)

**hellishly** /'helɪʃlɪ/ *adv.* höllisch; scheußlich; (*coll. as intensive*) verdammt (*ugs.*)

**hello** /hə'ləʊ, he'ləʊ/ ▶ **1191** ❶ *int.* (*greeting*) hallo!; (*surprise*) holla! ❷ *n.* Hallo, *das*

**hell's 'angel** *n.* Rocker, *der*

**helluva** /'heləvə/ = **hell of a;** ⇒ **hell** B

**helm¹** /helm/ *n.* (*Naut.*) Ruder, *das;* **be at the ~** (*lit. or fig.*) am Ruder sein; **take the ~** (*lit. or fig.*) das Ruder übernehmen

**helm²** *n.* (*arch.: helmet*) Helm, *der*

**helmet** /'helmɪt/ *n.* Helm, *der*

**helmeted** /'helmɪtɪd/ *adj.* behelmt

**helmsman** /'helmzmən/ *n., pl.* **helmsmen** /'helmzmən/ (*Naut.*) Rudergänger, *der*

**helot** /'helət/ *n.* Helot, *der*

**help** /help/ ❶ *v.t.* Ⓐ **~ sb. [to do sth.]** jmdm. helfen[, etw. zu tun]; **~ [sb.] with sth.** [jmdm.] bei etw. helfen; **~ oneself** sich (*Dat.*) selbst helfen; **can I ~ you?** was kann ich für Sie tun?; (*in shop also*) was möchten Sie bitte?; **~ sb. over a difficulty** jmdm. über eine Schwierigkeit hinweghelfen; **~ sb. on/off with his coat** jmdm. in den/aus dem Mantel helfen; **every little ~s** auch der kleinste Beitrag hilft weiter; **it would ~ [matters], if ...:** es wäre von Nutzen, wenn ...; **how does that ~?** was sollte *od.* könnte das nützen?; Ⓑ (*serve*) **~ oneself** sich (*Dat.*) nehmen; sich bedienen; **~ oneself to sth.** sich (*Dat.*) etw. nehmen; (*coll.: steal*) etw. mitgehen lassen (*ugs.*); **~ sb. to some soup** jmdm. etwas Suppe geben; Ⓒ (*avoid*) **if I/you can ~ it** wenn es irgend zu vermeiden ist; **not if I can ~ it** nicht wenn ich es verhindern kann; **it can't be ~ed** es lässt sich nicht ändern; (*remedy*) **I can't ~ it** ich kann nichts dafür (*ugs.*); Ⓓ (*refrain from*) **I can't ~ it** *or* **myself** ich kann mir nicht helfen; **I can't ~ thinking** *or* **can't ~ but think that ...:** ich kann mir nicht helfen, ich glaube, ...; **I couldn't ~ hearing what you said** ich konnte nicht umhin zu hören, was Sie sagten; **I can't ~ laughing** ich muss einfach lachen; Ⓔ (*in oath*) **so ~ me [God]** so wahr mir Gott helfe.
❷ *n.* Ⓐ Hilfe, *die;* **can I be of ~?** kann ich Ihnen behilflich sein?; **a cry for ~:** ein Hilferuf; **give sb. some ~:** jmdm. helfen (**with** bei); **be of [some]/no/much ~ to sb.** jmdm. eine gewisse/keine/eine große Hilfe sein; **with the ~ of sth./sb.** mit Hilfe einer Sache/mit jmds. Hilfe; mit Hilfe von etw./jmdm.; **walk without the ~ of a stick** ohne Stock gehen; **that's no ~:** das hilft nicht; **there's no ~ for it** daran lässt sich nichts ändern; **be a great ~ to sb.** jmdm. eine große Hilfe sein; Ⓑ (*employee*) Aushilfskraft, *die;* **home ~** (*Brit.*) Haushaltshilfe, *die*

**~ 'out** ❶ *v.i.* aushelfen. ❷ *v.t.* **~ sb. out** jmdm. helfen

**'help desk** *n.* Help Desk, *das* (*fachspr.*); *Auskunftsstelle für Computerbenutzer*

**helper** /'helpə(r)/ *n.* Helfer, *der*/Helferin, *die;* (*paid assistant*) Aushilfskraft, *die*

**helpful** /'helpfl/ *adj.* (*willing*) hilfsbereit; (*useful*) hilfreich; nützlich

**helpfully** /'helpfəlɪ/ *adv.* hilfsbereit

**helpfulness** /'helpflnɪs/ *n., no pl.* (*willingness*) Hilfsbereitschaft, *die;* (*usefulness*) Nützlichkeit, *die*

**helping** /'helpɪŋ/ ❶ *adj.* **lend [sb.] a ~ hand [with sth.]** (*fig.*) [jmdm.] [bei etw.] helfen; **need a ~ hand** jmdn. brauchen, der einem hilft; **be ready with a ~ hand** bereit sein zu helfen. ❷ *n.* Portion, *die*

**helpless** /'helplɪs/ *adj.* hilflos; (*powerless*) machtlos

**helplessly** /'helplɪslɪ/ *adv.* hilflos

**helplessness** /'helplɪsnɪs/ *n., no pl.* Hilflosigkeit, *die;* (*powerlessness*) Machtlosigkeit, *die*

**'helpline** *n.* Hotline, *die;* **a ~ for parents** ein telefonischer Beratungsdienst für Eltern; **the AIDS ~:** das AIDS-Telefon

**helpmate** /'helpmeɪt/, **helpmeet** /'helpmi:t/ *n.* Gefährte, *der*/Gefährtin, *die* (*geh.*)

**helter-skelter** /'heltəskeltə(r)/ ❶ *adv.* in wildem Durcheinander. ❷ *adj.* unkontrolliert. ❸ *n.* Ⓐ wildes Durcheinander; Ⓑ (*in funfair*) [spiralförmige] Rutschbahn

**helve** /helv/ *n.* Stiel, *der*

**hem¹** /hem/ ❶ *n.* Saum, *der.* ❷ *v.t.*, **-mm-:** Ⓐ säumen; Ⓑ (*surround*) **~ sb./sth. in** *or* **about** jmdn./etw. einschließen; **feel ~med in** (*fig.*) sich eingeengt fühlen

**hem²** /hem, həm, hm/ ❶ *int.* hm! ❷ *n.* (*sound*) Räuspern, *das;* **give a loud ~:** sich laut räuspern. ❸ *v.i.*, **-mm-** sich räuspern; **~ and haw** (*coll.*) herumdrucksen (*ugs.*)

**he-man** /ˈhi:mæn/ *n.* **a real ~:** ein richtiger Mann

**hematology** (*Amer.*) ⇒ **haematology**

**hemi-** /ˈhemɪ/ *pref.* hemi-/Hemi-

**hemiplegia** /hemɪˈpli:dʒɪə/ *n.* (*Med.*) Halbseitenlähmung, *die;* Hemiplegie, *die* (*fachspr.*)

**hemiplegic** /hemɪˈpli:dʒɪk/ *adj.* (*Med.*) halbseitig gelähmt

**ˈhemisphere** *n.* [A] Halbkugel, *die;* Hemisphäre, *die;* **the Southern ~** (*Geog., Astron.*) die südliche Halbkugel; [B] (*Anat.*) Hemisphäre, *die*

**hemiˈspherical** *adj.* halbkugelig; halbkugelförmig

**ˈhemline** *n.* Saum, *der;* **~s are up/down** die Röcke sind kurz/lang; **Yves St. Laurent's new ~:** die neue Rocklänge bei Yves St. Laurent

**hemlock** /ˈhemlɒk/ *n.* Schierling, *der*

**hemlock** [**ˈfir, ˈspruce**] *ns.* (*Amer. Bot.*) Hemlocktanne, *die*

**hemo-** (*Amer.*) ⇒ **haemo-**

**hemp** /hemp/ *n.* [A] (*Bot., Textiles*) Hanf, *der;* [B] (*drug*) Haschisch, *das od. der*

**ˈhem-stitch** ❶ *n.* Hohlsaum, *der.* ❷ *v.t.* mit Hohlsaum versehen

**hen** /hen/ *n.* [A] (*Ornith.*) Huhn, *das;* Henne, *die* (*bes. im Gegensatz zu „Hahn"*); [B] (*Zool.*) (*lobster, crab*) weiblicher Hummer/Krebs; (*salmon*) Lachsweibchen, *das*

**ˈhenbane** *n., no pl.* (*Bot., Med.*) Bilsenkraut, *das*

**hence** /hens/ *adv.* [A] (*therefore*) daher; [B] (*from this time*) **a week/ten years ~:** in einer Woche/zehn Jahren; [C] (*arch./poet.: from here*) [**from**] **~:** von hinnen (*veralt.*)

**henceˈforth, henceˈforward** *advs.* von nun an; fürderhin (*veralt.*)

**henchman** /ˈhentʃmən/ *n., pl.* **henchmen** /ˈhentʃmən/ (*derog.*) Handlanger, *der*

**ˈhen-coop** *n.* Hühnerstall, *der*

**hendeca-** /henˈdekə/ *in comb.* elf-/Elf-

**ˈhen house** *n.* Hühnerhaus, *das;* Hühnerstall, *der*

**henna** /ˈhenə/ *n.* (*dye*) Henna, *das*

**hen: ~-party** *n.* (*coll.*) [Damen]kränzchen, *das;* **~pecked** /ˈhenpekt/ *adj.* **a ~pecked husband** ein Pantoffelheld (*ugs.*); **be ~pecked** unter dem Pantoffel stehen (*ugs.*); **~-run** *n.* [Hühner]auslauf, *der*

**Henry** /ˈhenrɪ/ *pr. n.* (*Hist., as name of ruler etc.*) Heinrich (*der*)

**hep** *adj.* (*dated coll.*) [über alles Moderne] informiert; **be ~ to sth.** über etw. (*Akk.*) auf dem Laufenden sein

**hepatic** /hɪˈpætɪk/ *adj.* (*Anat., Med.*) Leber-

**hepatitis** /hepəˈtaɪtɪs/ *n.* ▶ 1232 (*Med.*) Leberentzündung, *die;* Hepatitis, *die* (*fachspr.*)

**heptagon** /ˈheptəgən/ *n.* (*Geom.*) Siebeneck, *das;* Heptagon, *das* (*fachspr.*)

**heptagonal** /hepˈtægənl/ *adj.* (*Geom.*) siebeneckig; heptagonal (*fachspr.*)

**her¹** /hə(r), *stressed* hɜ:(r)/ *pron.* sie; *as indirect object* ihr; *reflexively* sich; *referring to personified things or animals which correspond to German masculines/neuters* ihn/es; *as indirect object* ihm; **it was ~:** sie wars; **~ and me** (*coll.*) sie und ich; **if I were ~** (*coll.*) wenn ich sie wäre

**her²** *poss. pron. attrib.* ihr; *referring to personified things or animals which correspond to German masculines/neuters* sein; **she opened ~ eyes/mouth** sie öffnete die Augen/den Mund; **~ father and mother** ihr Vater und ihre Mutter; **she has problems of ~ own** sie hat ihre eigenen Probleme; **she has a room of ~ own** sie hat ein eigenes Zimmer; **he complained about ~ being late** er beklagte sich darüber, dass sie zu spät kam; er beklagte sich über ihr Zuspätkommen

**herald** /ˈherəld/ ❶ *n.* [A] Herold, *der;* [B] (*messenger*) Bote, *der;* (*fig.: forerunner*) Vorbote, *der;* [C] (*Brit.: official of Heralds' College*) *Beamter des Heroldamtes.* ❷ *v.t.* (*lit. or fig.*) ankündigen

**heraldic** /heˈrældɪk/ *adj.* heraldisch; **~ animal** Wappentier, *das*

**heraldry** /ˈherəldrɪ/ *n., no pl.* [A] Wappenkunde, *die;* Heraldik, *die;* [B] (*armorial bearings*) Wappenschmuck, *der*

**herb** /hɜ:b/ *n.* [A] Kraut, *das;* (*Cookery*) Gewürzkraut, *das;* [B] (*Med.*) [Heil]kraut, *das*

**herbaceous** /hɜ:ˈbeɪʃəs/ *adj.* (*Bot.*) krautartig ‹Pflanze›; krautig ‹Stiel›; **~ border** Staudenrabatte, *die*

**herbage** /ˈhɜ:bɪdʒ/ *n., no pl.* (*Agric.*) (*herbs*) Weide, *die;* (*succulent parts*) Kraut, *das*

**herbal** /ˈhɜ:bl/ ❶ *attrib. adj.* Kräuter‹tee, -arznei›; ‹Behandlung› mit Heilkräutern. ❷ *n.* Pflanzenbuch, *das*

**herbalist** /ˈhɜ:bəlɪst/ *n.* [A] ▶ 1261 Kräuterhändler, *der*/Kräuterhändlerin, *die* [für Heilkräuter]; [B] (*Hist.*) Herbalist, *der*

**herbarium** /hɜ:ˈbeərɪəm/ *n., pl.* **herbaria** /hɜ:ˈbeərɪə/ Herbarium, *das*

**ˈherb garden** *n.* Kräutergarten, *der*

**herbicide** /ˈhɜ:bɪsaɪd/ *n.* Unkrautvertilgungsmittel, *das;* Herbizid, *das*

**herbivore** /ˈhɜ:bɪvɔ:(r)/ *n.* (*Zool.*) Pflanzenfresser, *der;* Herbivore, *der* (*fachspr.*)

**herbivorous** /hɜ:ˈbɪvərəs/ *adj.* Pflanzen fressend; herbivor (*fachspr.*)

**ˈherb tea** *n.* Kräuteraufguss, *der*

**herby** /ˈhɜ:bɪ/ *adj.* **a ~ taste/smell** ein Geschmack/Geruch nach Kräutern

**Herculean** /hɜ:kjʊˈli:ən, hɜ:ˈkju:lɪən/ *adj.* übermenschlich ‹Anstrengung›; bärenstark ‹Person›; herkulisch (*geh.*), ungeheuer ‹Kraft›; **~ labour** Herkulesarbeit, *die*

**Hercules** /ˈhɜ:kjʊli:z/ *pr. n.* Herakles, *der;* Herkules, *der* (*auch fig.*); **the labours of ~:** die zwölf Arbeiten des Herakles

**herd** /hɜ:d/ ❶ *n.* [A] Herde, *die;* (*of wild animals*) Rudel, *das;* **a ~ of sheep/elephants** eine Herde Schafe/Elefanten; eine Schaf-/Elefantenherde; **ride ~ on sb.** (*Amer.*) jmdn. im Auge behalten; [B] (*fig.*) Masse, *die;* **the common ~** (*derog.*) die breite Masse; **the ~ instinct** der Herdentrieb; **follow the ~** (*fig.*) der Herde folgen; mit der Herde laufen. ❷ *v.t.* [A] (*lit. or fig.*) treiben; **~** [**people**] **together** (*fig.*) [Menschen] zusammenpferchen; [B] (*tend*) hüten. ❸ *v.i.* sich zu einer Herde zusammenschließen; (*fig.*) sich drängen

**ˈherdsman** /ˈhɜ:dzmən/ *n., pl.* **herdsmen** /ˈhɜ:dzmən/ ▶ 1261 Hirt[e], *der*

**here** /hɪə(r)/ ❶ *adv.* [A] (*in or at this place*) hier; **Schmidt ~** (*on telephone*) Schmidt; **spring is ~:** der Frühling ist da; **stay ~:** hier bleiben; **down/in/up ~:** hier unten/drin/oben; **~ below** (*fig. literary*) hienieden (*geh.*); auf dieser Erde; **~ goes!** (*coll.*) dann mal los! (*ugs.*); **~'s to you!** auf dein Wohl!; **~, there, and everywhere** überall; **that's neither ~ nor there** (*coll.*) das ist völlig nebensächlich; **~ today and gone tomorrow** (*of traveller*) heute hier, morgen dort; (*of money*) wie gewonnen, so zerronnen; **~ you are** (*giving sth.*) hier; **~ we are** (*on arrival*) da sind *od.* wären wir; **~ we go again** (*coll.*) jetzt geht das wieder los! (*ugs.*); [B] (*to this place*) hierher; **in**[**to**] **~:** hierherein; **come/bring ~:** herkommen/-bringen; hierher kommen/bringen; **put sth. ~:** etw. hierhin *od.* hierher tun; **~ comes the bus** hier *od.* da kommt der Bus.
❷ *n.* **leave ~:** von hier abreisen; **near ~:** hier in der Nähe; **up to ~, as far as ~:** bis hierhin; **he is up to ~ in problems** die Probleme sind ihm über den Kopf gewachsen; **from ~ on** von nun an; **where do we go from ~?** (*fig.*) was machen wir jetzt?
❸ *int.* (*attracting attention*) he; (*at roll-call*) hier

**here: ~aˈbout**[**s**] *adv.* hier [in dieser Gegend]; **~ˈafter** *adv.* (*formal*) im Folgenden; (*in the future*) fürderhin (*veralt.*); (*literary: in the next world*) dereinst (*geh.*); **the life ~after** das Leben im Jenseits; **~ˈat** *adv.* (*arch.*) daraufhin; **~ˈby** *adv.* (*formal*) hiermit

**hereditary** /hɪˈredɪtərɪ/ *adj.* [A] erblich ‹Titel, Amt›; ererbt ‹Reichtum›; **~ monarchy/right** Erbmonarchie, *die*/Erbrecht, *das;* [B] (*Biol.*) angeboren ‹Instinkt, Verhaltensweise›; **~ disease** Erbkrankheit, *die;* [C] (*of a family*) **~ feud/enemy** Erbfehde, *die*/-feind, *der*

**heredity** /hɪˈredɪtɪ/ *n.* (*Biol.*) [A] (*transmission of qualities*) Vererbung, *die;* [B] (*genetic constitution*) Erbgut, *das*

**here: ~ˈin** *adv.* (*formal*) hierin; **~inˈafter** *adv.* (*formal*) im Folgenden; **~ˈof** *adv.* (*formal*) davon

**heresy** /ˈherɪsɪ/ *n.* Ketzerei, *die;* Häresie, *die* (*geh.*)

**heretic** /ˈherɪtɪk/ *n.* Ketzer, *der*/Ketzerin, *die;* Häretiker, *der*/Häretikerin, *die* (*geh.*)

**heretical** /hɪˈretɪkl/ *adj.* ketzerisch; häretisch (*geh.*)

**here: ~ˈto** /hɪəˈtʊ, hɪəˈtu:/ *adv.* (*formal*) darauf/hierauf; **~toˈfore** *adv.* (*formal*) (*up to now*) bisher; (*up until that time*) bis dahin; **~ˈunder** *adv.* (*formal*) im Folgenden; **~uˈpon** *adv.* hierauf; **~ˈwith** *adv.* [A] (*with this*) in der Anlage; **we enclose ~with your cheque** wir legen Ihren Scheck diesem Schreiben bei; [B] ⇒ **~by**

**heritage** /ˈherɪtɪdʒ/ *n.* (*lit. or fig.*) Erbe, *das*

**hermaphrodite** /hɜ:ˈmæfrədaɪt/ ❶ *n.* Zwitter, *der* (*auch fig.*); Hermaphrodit, *der.* ❷ *adj.* zwittrig; hermaphroditisch

**hermeneutics** /hɜ:mɪˈnju:tɪks/ *n., no pl.* Hermeneutik, *die*

**hermetic** /hɜ:ˈmetɪk/ *adj.* (*airtight*) luftdicht; (*fig.*) hermetisch (*geh.*)

**hermetically** /hɜ:ˈmetɪkəlɪ/ *adv.* hermetisch

**hermit** /ˈhɜ:mɪt/ *n.* [A] Einsiedler, *der*/Einsiedlerin, *die;* [B] (*Relig.*) Eremit, *der*

**hermitage** /ˈhɜ:mɪtɪdʒ/ *n.* Einsiedelei, *die*

**ˈhermit crab** *n.* Einsiedlerkrebs, *der*

**hernia** /ˈhɜ:nɪə/ *n., pl.* **~s** *or* **~e** /ˈhɜ:nɪi:/ (*Med.*) Bruch, *der;* Hernie, *die* (*Med.*)

**hero** /ˈhɪərəʊ/ *n., pl.* **~es** Held, *der;* (*demigod*) Heros, *der;* **~ of the hour** Held des Tages

**heroic** /hɪˈrəʊɪk/ *adj.* [A] heldenhaft; heroisch (*geh.*); [B] (*Lit.*) **~ epic/legend** Heldenepos, *das*/-legende, *die;* **~ couplet** Heroic Couplet, *das;* **~ verse** heroischer Vers; [C] (*high-flown*) erhaben; (*very large*) gewaltig

**heroically** /hɪˈrəʊɪkəlɪ/ *adv.* heldenhaft

**heroics** /hɪˈrəʊɪks/ *n. pl.* [A] (*language*) Theatralische, *das;* (*foolhardiness*) Draufgängertum, *das;* [B] (*Lit.*) heroischer Vers

**heroin** /ˈherəʊɪn/ *n., no pl.* Heroin, *das*

**heroine** /ˈherəʊɪn/ *n.* Heldin, *die;* Heroin, *die* (*geh.*); Heroine, *die* (*Theater*)

**heroism** /ˈherəʊɪzm/ *n., no pl.* Heldentum, *das*

**heron** /ˈhern/ *n.* Reiher, *der*

**hero: ~-worship** ❶ *n.* Heldenverehrung, *die;* ❷ *v.t.* vergöttern; **~-worshipper** *n.* Heldenverehrer, *der*/-verehrerin, *die*

**herpes** /ˈhɜ:pi:z/ *n.* ▶ 1232 (*Med.*) Herpes, *der*

**herring** /ˈherɪŋ/ *n.* Hering, *der*

**herring: ~bone** ❶ *n.* [A] (*Textiles*) (*stitch*) Fischgrätenstich, *der;* (*cloth*) Fischgrat, *der;* [B] (*Archit.*) Fischgrätenverband, *der;* ❷ *adj.* **~bone pattern** (*Textiles*) Fischgrätenmuster, *das;* **~ gull** *n.* Silbermöwe, *die;* **~ pond** *n.* (*joc.*) Atlantik, *der*

**hers** /hɜ:z/ *poss. pron. pred.* ihrer/ihre/ihres; der/die/das ihre *od.* ihrige (*geh.*); **the book is ~:** das Buch gehört ihr; **that car is ~:** das ist ihr Wagen; der Wagen gehört ihr; **some friends of ~:** ein paar Freunde von ihr; **a book of ~:** ein Buch von ihr; eins ihrer Bücher; **those children of ~:** ihre Gören (*ugs.*); **~ is a difficult job** sie hat einen schwierigen Job (*ugs.*)

**herself** /hɜ:ˈself/ *pron.* [A] *emphat.* selbst; **she ~ said so** sie selbst hat das gesagt; **she saw it ~:** sie hat es selbst gesehen; **she wanted to be ~:** sie wollte sie selbst sein; **she was just being ~:** sie gab sich einfach so, wie sie ist; **she is** [**quite**] **~ again** sie ist wieder ganz die Alte; (*after an illness*) sie ist wieder

h

auf der Höhe (*ugs.*); **all right in ~:** im Wesentlichen gesund; **she's not quite ~:** sie ist nicht ganz in Ordnung; **[all] by ~** (*on her own, by her own efforts*) [ganz] allein[e]; **B** *refl.* sich; allein[e] ‹tun, wählen›; **she wants to see for ~** sie will [es] selbst sehen; **she wants it for ~:** sie will es für sich [selbst]; **she won't believe anything that she hasn't seen for ~:** sie glaubt nichts, was sie nicht selbst gesehen hat; **younger than/ as heavy as ~:** jünger als/so schwer wie sie selbst; **... she thought to ~:** ... dachte sie sich [im Stillen]; ... dachte sie bei sich

**hertz** /hɜ:ts/ *n.*, *pl. same* (*Phys.*) Hertz, *das*

**he's** /hɪz, *stressed* hi:z/ **A** = **he is; B** = **he has**

**hesitance** /ˈhezɪtəns/, **hesitancy** /ˈhezɪtənsɪ/ *n.*, *no pl.* Unschlüssigkeit, *die*

**hesitant** /ˈhezɪtənt/ *adj.* zögernd ‹Politik, Reaktion›; stockend ‹Rede›; unsicher ‹Person, Stimme›; **be ~ to do sth.** *or* **about doing sth.** Bedenken haben, etw. zu tun

**hesitantly** /ˈhezɪtəntlɪ/ *adv.* zögernd ‹handeln, reagieren›; stockend ‹sprechen›

**hesitate** /ˈhezɪteɪt/ *v.i.* **A** (*show uncertainty*) zögern; **he who ~s is lost** (*prov.*) man muss die Gelegenheit beim Schopfe fassen; **B** (*falter*) ins Stocken geraten; **C** (*show reluctance*) **~ to do sth.** Bedenken haben, etw. zu tun

**hesitation** /hezɪˈteɪʃn/ *n.* **A** *no pl.* (*indecision*) Unentschlossenheit, *die;* **without the slightest ~:** ohne im Geringsten zu zögern; **have no ~ in doing sth.** nicht zögern, etw. zu tun; **B** (*instance of faltering*) Unsicherheit, *die;* **C** *no pl.* (*reluctance*) Bedenken *Pl.*

**Hesse** /ˈhesə/ *pr. n.* Hessen (*das*)

**hessian** *n.* Sackleinen, *das;* Hessian, *das* (*fachspr.*)

**Hessian** /ˈhesɪən/ ❶ *adj.* hessisch. ❷ *n.* Hesse, *der*/Hessin, *die*

**het** /het/ *adj.* (*coll.*) **~ up** aufgeregt; **get ~ up over sth.** sich über etw. (*Akk.*) aufregen

**hetero** /ˈhetərəʊ/ *n.* (*coll.*) ❶ *n.* Hetero *der*/ *die;* **be a ~:** hetero sein. ❷ *adj.* heterosexuell; *attrib. also* Hetero-

**hetero-** /ˈhetərə/ *in comb.* hetero-/Hetero-

**heterodox** /ˈhetərədɒks/ *adj.* heterodox

**heterodoxy** /ˈhetərədɒksɪ/ *n.* Heterodoxie, *die*

**heterogeneity** /hetərədʒɪˈni:ɪtɪ/ *n.* Ungleichartigkeit, *die;* Heterogenität, *die*

**heterogeneous** /hetərəˈdʒi:nɪəs, hetərəˈdʒenɪəs/ *adj.* ungleichartig; heterogen

**heterosexual** ❶ *adj.* heterosexuell. ❷ *n.* Heterosexuelle, *der/die*

**heterosexuality** /hetərəʊseksjʊˈælətɪ/ *n.*, *no pl.* Heterosexualität, *die*

**heuristic** /hjʊəˈrɪstɪk/ ❶ *adj.* heuristisch. ❷ *n.* (*procedure*) heuristische Methode

**hew** /hju:/ ❶ *v.t.*, *p. p.* **~n** /hju:n/ *or* **~ed** /hju:d/ **A** (*cut*) hacken ‹Holz›; fällen ‹Baum›; losschlagen ‹Kohle, Gestein›; **~ away** *or* **off** abschlagen; **B** (*shape*) hauen ‹Stufen›; behauen ‹Holz, Stein›. ❷ *v.i.*, *p. p.* **~n** *or* **~ed A** zuschlagen; **~ at sth.** auf etw. (*Akk.*) einschlagen; **B** (*Amer.: conform*) **~ to sth.** sich an etw. (*Akk.*) halten

**hex** /heks/ (*Amer.*) ❶ *v.t.* (*lit. or fig.*) verhexen. ❷ *n.* **A put a ~ on sb./sth.** jmdn./ etw. verhexen; **B** (*witch, lit. or fig.*) Hexe, *die*

**hexagon** /ˈheksəgən/ *n.* (*Geom.*) Sechseck, *das;* Hexagon, *das* (*fachspr.*)

**hexagonal** /hekˈsægənl/ *adj.* (*Geom.*) sechseckig; hexagonal (*fachspr.*)

**hexameter** /hekˈsæmɪtə(r)/ *n.* (*Pros.*) Hexameter, *der*

**hey** /heɪ/ *int.* he!; **~ presto!** simsalabim!

**heyday** /ˈheɪdeɪ/ *n.*, *no pl.* Blütezeit, *die*

**hf.** *abbr.* **half**

**HF** *abbr.* **high frequency** HF

**HGV** *abbr.* (*Brit.*) **heavy goods vehicle**

**HH** *abbr.* ▶**1617** **A Her/His Highness** I. H./S. H.; **B His Holiness**

**hi** /haɪ/ *int.* ▶**1191** hallo (*ugs.*)

**hiatus** /haɪˈeɪtəs/ *n.* **A** (*gap*) Bruch, *der;* (*interruption*) Unterbrechung, *die;* **B** (*Ling.*) Hiatus, *der*

**hibernate** /ˈhaɪbəneɪt/ *v.i.* Winterschlaf halten

**hibernation** /haɪbəˈneɪʃn/ *n.* Winterschlaf, *der;* **go into/come out of ~:** sich zum Winterschlaf zurückziehen/aus dem Winterschlaf erwachen

**Hibernian** /haɪˈbɜ:nɪən/ ❶ *adj.* irisch. ❷ *n.* Ire, *der*/Irin, *die*

**hibiscus** /hɪˈbɪskəs/ *n.* (*Bot.*) Hibiskus, *der*

**hic** /hɪk/ *int.* hick (*ugs.*)

**hiccup** /ˈhɪkəp/ ❶ *n.* **A** Schluckauf, *der;* **have/get [the] ~s** [den] Schluckauf haben/ bekommen; **give a ~:** schlucksen (*ugs.*); hick machen (*ugs.*); hicksen (*landsch.*); **an attack of [the] ~s** ein Schluckaufanfall; **B** (*fig.: stoppage*) Störung, *die;* **without any ~s** reibungslos. ❷ *v.i.* schlucksen (*ugs.*); hicksen (*landsch.*); hick machen (*ugs.*); (*many times*) den Schluckauf haben

**hick** /hɪk/ *n.* (*Amer. coll.*) **[country] ~:** Provinzler, *der* (*ugs. abwertend*); Hinterwäldler, *der* (*spött.*); **~ town** Provinzstadt, *die;* Provinznest, *das* (*ugs. abwertend*)

**hickey** /ˈhɪkɪ/ *n.* (*Amer.*) Dings, *das* (*ugs.*)

**hickory** /ˈhɪkərɪ/ *n.* **A** (*tree*) Hickory[baum], *der;* **B** (*wood*) Hickory[holz], *das*

**hid** ⇨ **hide**[1] 1, 2

**hidden** ⇨ **hide**[1] 1, 2

**hidden reˈserve** *n.* (*Econ.*) stille Reserve *od.* Rücklage

**hide**[1] /haɪd/ ❶ *v.t.*, **hid** /hɪd/, **hidden** /ˈhɪdn/ **A** (*put or keep out of sight*) verstecken ‹Gegenstand, Person usw.› (**from** vor + *Dat.*); **~ one's head [in embarrassment/ shame]** (*fig.*) sich [vor Verlegenheit/Scham (*Dat.*)] verstecken; **~ one's face in one's hands** sein Gesicht in den Händen bergen; ⇨ *also* **bushel**; **B** (*keep secret*) verbergen ‹Gefühle, Sinn, Freude usw.› (**from** vor + *Dat.*); verheimlichen ‹Tatsache, Absicht, Grund usw.› (**from** *Dat.*); **have nothing to ~:** nichts zu verbergen haben; **the future is hidden from us** die Zukunft ist uns verborgen; **C** (*obscure*) verdecken; **~ sth. [from view]** etw. verstecken; (*by covering*) etw. verdecken; ‹Nebel, Rauch usw.:› etw. einhüllen.

❷ *v.i.*, **hid, hidden** sich verstecken *od.* verbergen (**from** vor + *Dat.*); **where is he hiding?** wo hält er sich versteckt *od.* verborgen? ❸ *n.* (*Brit.*) Versteck, *das;* (*hunter's ~*) Ansitz, *der* (*Jägerspr.*)

**~ aˈway** *v.i.* sich verstecken *od.* verbergen; ⇨ *also* **hideaway**

**~ ˈout, ~ ˈup** *v.i.* sich versteckt *od.* verborgen halten; ⇨ *also* **hideout**

**hide**[2] *n.* (*animal's skin*) Haut, *die;* (*of furry animal*) Fell, *das;* (*dressed*) Leder, *das;* (*joc.: human skin*) Haut, *die;* Fell, *das;* **tan sb.'s ~:** jmdm. das Fell gerben *od.* versohlen (*salopp*); **save one's own ~:** die eigene Haut retten (*ugs.*); **when I returned I could find neither ~ nor hair of them** als ich zurückkam, waren sie spurlos verschwunden

**hide: ~-and-ˈseek** (*Amer.:* **~-and-go-ˈseek**) *n.* Versteckspiel, *das;* **play ~-and-seek** Verstecken spielen; **~away** ⇨ **~out;** **~bound** *adj.* engstirnig, borniert (*abwertend*) ‹Person, Ansicht›

**hideous** /ˈhɪdɪəs/ *adj.* **A** (*extremely ugly, offensive to the ear*) scheußlich; (*repulsive, horrific*) entsetzlich; grauenhaft; **B** (*coll.: unpleasant*) furchtbar (*ugs.*), schrecklich (*ugs.*)

**hideously** /ˈhɪdɪəslɪ/ *adv.* **A** entsetzlich, grauenhaft ‹verstümmelt, entstellt, schreien›; **B** (*coll.: unpleasantly*) furchtbar (*ugs.*), schrecklich (*ugs.*) ‹langweilig, teuer, kalt, laut usw.›

**ˈhideout** *n.* Versteck, *das;* (*of bandits, partisans, etc.*) Versteck, *das;* Unterschlupf, *der;* (*retreat*) Refugium, *das*

**hidey-hole** ⇨ **hidy-hole**

**hiding**[1] /ˈhaɪdɪŋ/ *n.* **go into ~:** sich verstecken; (*to avoid police, public attention*) untertauchen; **be/stay in ~:** sich versteckt halten/sich weiterhin versteckt halten; (*to avoid police, public attention*) untergetaucht sein/ bleiben; **come out of ~:** aus seinem Versteck kommen; (*no longer avoid police, public attention*) wieder auftauchen

**hiding**[2] *n.* (*coll.: beating*) Tracht Prügel; (*fig.*) Schlappe, *die;* **give sb. a [good] ~:** jmdm. eine [ordentliche] Tracht Prügel verpassen; (*fig.*) jmdm. eine [klare] Abfuhr erteilen; **get/ be given/take a real ~ [from sb.]** [von jmdm.] gehörige Prügel beziehen *od.* einstecken müssen; (*fig.*) sich (*Dat.*) [von jmdm.] eine klare Abfuhr holen; **be on a ~ to nothing** eine undankbare Rolle haben

**ˈhiding place** *n.* Versteck, *das*

**hidy-hole** /ˈhaɪdɪhəʊl/ *n.* (*coll.*) Versteck, *das*

**hierarchic** /haɪəˈrɑ:kɪk/, **hierarchical** /haɪəˈrɑ:kɪkl/ *adj.* hierarchisch

**hierarchy** /ˈhaɪərɑ:kɪ/ *n.* Hierarchie, *die*

**hieroglyph** /ˈhaɪərəglɪf/ *n.* **A** Hieroglyphe, *die;* **B** *in pl.* (*joc.: scrawl*) Hieroglyphen (*scherzh.*)

**hieroglyphic** /haɪərəˈglɪfɪk/ ❶ *adj.* **A** (*composed of hieroglyphs*) hieroglyphisch; **B** (*symbolical*) geheimnisvoll ‹Zeichen›. ❷ *n. in pl.* (*also joc.*) Hieroglyphen

**hi-fi** /ˈhaɪfaɪ/ (*coll.*) ❶ *adj.* Hi-Fi-. ❷ *n.* **A** (*equipment*) Hi-Fi-Anlage, *die;* **B** (*use of ~*) Hi-Fi, *das; attrib.* Hi-Fi-‹Fan usw.›

**higgledy-piggledy** /hɪgldɪˈpɪgldɪ/ ❶ *adv.* wie Kraut und Rüben (*ugs.*). ❷ *adj.* wirr, kunterbunt ‹Ansammlung usw.›

**high** /haɪ/ ❶ *adj.* **A** ▶**1210** (*reaching far up*) hoch ‹Berg, Gebäude, Mauer›; **a wall eight feet** *or* **foot ~:** eine acht Fuß hohe Mauer; **I've known him since he was only so ~** (*coll.*) ich kannte ihn schon, als er [noch] so [klein] war; **B** (*above normal level*) hoch ‹Stiefel›; **a dress with a ~ neckline** ein hochgeschlossenes Kleid; **the river/water is ~:** der Fluss/das Wasser steht hoch; **~ and dry** ‹Boot:› auf dem Trockenen; hoch und trocken (*Seemannsspr.*); **be left ~ and dry** (*fig.*) auf dem Trock[e]nen sitzen (*ugs.*); (*be stuck without transport*) festsitzen (*ugs.*); **C** (*far above ground or sea level*) hoch ‹Gipfel, Punkt›; groß ‹Höhe›; Hoch‹ebene, -moor›; **be ~** ‹Ort:› hoch liegen; ‹Sonne, Mond:› hoch stehen; **D** (*to or from far above the ground*) hoch ‹Aufstieg, Sprung›; **~ diving** Turmspringen, *das;* **a ~ dive** ein Sprung vom Turm; ⇨ *also* **bar**[1] 1 B; **E** (*of exalted rank*) hoch ‹Beamter, Amt, Gericht›; **the Most H~** (*Bibl.*) der Allerhöchste; **~ and low** Arm und Reich (*veralt.*); **a ~er court** eine höhere Instanz; **~er mammals/plants** höhere Säugetiere/ Pflanzen; **~ and mighty** (*coll.: high-handed*) selbstherrlich; (*coll.: self-important*) wichtigtuerisch; (*coll.: superior*) hochnäsig (*ugs.*); (*arch.: exalted*) hoch ‹Adlige›; groß ‹Häuptling›; **aim for ~er things** (*fig.*) nach Höherem streben; **be born** *or* **destined for ~er things** zu Höherem geboren *od.* bestimmt sein; **in ~ places** an höherer Stelle; höheren Orts; **people in ~ places** Leute in hohen Positionen; **those in ~ places** die Oberen; **F** (*great in degree*) hoch; groß ‹Gefallen, Bedeutung›; stark ‹Wind›; **be ~ in iodine** einen hohen Jodgehalt aufweisen; **be held in ~ regard/esteem** hohes Ansehen/hohe Wertschätzung genießen; hoch angesehen/geschätzt sein; **~ blood pressure** Bluthochdruck, *der;* **~ vacuum** Hochvakuum, *das;* **her ~est aspiration** ihr größter Wunsch; **get a nice ~ polish on the car** das Auto auf Hochglanz polieren; **a/his** *etc.* **~ colour** ein/sein *usw.* rotes Gesicht; **have a ~ opinion of sb./sth.** eine hohe Meinung von jmdm./etw. haben (*geh.*); viel von jmdm./etw. halten; **G** (*extreme in opinion*) extrem; **H** (*noble, virtuous*) hoch ‹Ideal, Ziel, Prinzip, Berufung›; edel ‹Charakter›; **of ~ birth** von hoher Geburt (*geh.*); **~ art/comedy** hohe Kunst/ Komödie; **I** (*Geog.*) **~ latitudes** hohe Breiten; **J** (*of time, season*) **it is ~ time you left** es ist *od.* wird höchste Zeit, dass du gehst; **~ noon** Mittag; **it was ~ noon** es war genau Mittag; **~ summer** Hochsommer, *der;* **K** (*fully developed*) hoch; Hoch‹mittelalter, -renaissance usw.›; **L** (*long since passed*) fern ‹Vergangenheit›; **M** (*luxurious, extravagant*) üppig ‹Leben›; **N** (*enjoyable*) **have a ~ [old] time** sich bestens amüsieren; **have a ~ [old] time doing sth.** Spaß damit haben, etw. zu tun; **O** (*coll.*) (*under the influence*) (*of* *a drug*) high *nicht attr.* (*ugs.*) (**on** von); angeturnt (*ugs.*) (**on** von); (*on cannabis*) bekifft (*ugs.*); (*on alcohol*) blau (*ugs.*) (**on** von); **get ~ on** sich anturnen mit (*ugs.*) ‹Haschisch, Ecstasy usw.›; sich besaufen mit (*salopp*) ‹Whisky, Bier usw.›; P (*in pitch*) hoch ‹Ton, Stimme, Lage, Klang usw.›; Q (*slightly decomposed*) angegangen (*landsch.*) ‹Fleisch›; ‹Wild› mit Hautgout; R (*Cards*) hoch; **ace is ~:** Ass ist hoch; **I'm queen** *etc.* **~:** Dame *usw.* ist das Höchste, was ich habe; S (*Ling.*) ⇒ **close** 1 N. ⇒ *also* **horse** 1 A.

**2** *adv.* A (*in or to a ~ position*) hoch; **~ on our list of priorities** weit oben auf unserer Prioritätenliste; **~er up the valley** weiter oben im Tal; **we climbed ~er up the cliff** wir kletterten das Kliff ein Stück höher hinauf; **search** *or* **hunt** *or* **look ~ and low** überall suchen; **search** *or* **hunt** *or* **look ~ and low for sb./sth.** jmdn./etw. suchen wie eine Stecknadel; ⇒ *also* **aim** 2 A; B (*to a ~ level*) hoch; **prices have gone too ~:** die Preise sind zu stark gestiegen; **I'll go as ~ as two thousand pounds** ich gehe bis zweitausend Pfund; C (*at or to a ~ pitch*) hoch ‹singen›; D **play ~** (*Cards*) etwas Hohes spielen; (*Gambling*) mit hohen Einsätzen spielen.

**3** *n.* A (*~est level/figure*) Höchststand, *der;* ⇒ *also* **all-time;** B ▶ **1603** (*Meteorol.*) Hoch, *das;* C (*Amer. coll.: ~ school*) Oberschule, *die;* **in junior ~:** in der Unterstufe [der Oberschule]; D (*coll.: drug-induced euphoria*) Rausch[zustand], *der;* **give sb. a ~** ‹Droge:› jmdn. high machen (*ugs.*); E (*~ position*) **on ~:** hoch oben *od.* (*geh., südd., österr.*) droben; (*in heaven*) im Himmel; **from on ~:** von hoch oben; (*from heaven*) vom Himmel; (*fig.: from a ~ authority*) von oben; **a judgement from on ~:** eine Strafe des Himmels

**high: ~ 'altar** *n.* (*Eccl.*) Hochaltar, *der;* **~-altitude** *adj.* Höhen-; **~ball** *n.* (*Amer.*) A (*drink*) Highball, *der;* B (*Railw.: signal*) Freie-Fahrt-Signal, *das;* **~ 'beam** *n.* Fernlicht, *das;* **I was on ~ beam most of the time** ich fuhr die meiste Zeit mit Fernlicht; **~binder** *n.* (*Amer.*) A (*thug*) Schläger, *der;* B (*assassin*) [chinesischer] Killer; C (*swindler*) Schwindler, *der;* Ganove, *der* (*ugs.*); **~-born** *adj.* hochgeboren (*veralt.*); **~boy** *n.* (*Amer.*) (*hochbeinige*) hohe Kommode; Highboy, *der* (*fachspr.*); **~brow 1** *n.* Intellektuelle, *der/die;* **2** *adj.* intellektuell ‹Person, Gerede usw.›; hochgestochen (*abwertend*) ‹Person, Gerede, Musik, Literatur usw.›; hochgeistig ‹Interessen, Beschäftigung, Gerede›; **~ chair** *n.* (*for baby*) Hochstuhl, *der;* **H~ 'Church** *n.* High Church, *die;* Hochkirche, *die; attrib.* hochkirchlich; **~-class** *adj.* hochwertig ‹Erzeugnis›; erstklassig ‹Unterkunft, Konditor usw.›; **~ com'mand** *n.* (*Mil.*) Oberkommando, *das;* **H~ Com'mission** *n.* Hohe Kommission; **H~ Com'missioner** *n.* Hoher Kommissar; **H~ 'Court [of Justice]** *n.* (*Brit. Law*) *oberster Gerichtshof für Zivil- und Strafsachen;* **~ day** *n.* **on ~ days and holidays** zu besonderen Anlässen; **~-definition 'television** *n.* hoch auflösendes Fernsehen; **~ 'diving** *n.* Turmspringen, *das*

**higher** /'haɪə(r)/**: ~ edu'cation** *n., no pl., no art.* Hochschul[aus]bildung, *die;* **he works in ~ education** er ist im Hochschulbereich tätig; **more funds are needed for ~ education** das Hochschulwesen braucht mehr Mittel; **~ mathe'matics** *n.* höhere Mathematik

**high: ~ ex'plosive** ⇒ **explosive** 2; **~-falutin** /haɪfə'lu:tɪn/, **~-faluting** /haɪfə'lu:tɪŋ/ *adj.* (*coll. derog.*) hochtrabend ‹Gerede, Stil, Sprache usw.›; aufgeblasen (*ugs. abwertend*) ‹Person›; **~ 'fashion** ⇒ **haute couture;** **~ fi'delity** *n.* High Fidelity, *die;* **reproduce sth. in ~ fidelity** etw. in Hi-Fi-Qualität wiedergeben; **~ fi'nance** *n.* Hochfinanz, *die;* **~-'flier** ⇒ **~-flyer;** **~-flown** *adj.* geschwollen (*abwertend*) ‹Stil, Ausdrucksweise›; hochfliegend ‹Ideen, Pläne›; **~-'flyer** *n.* A (*ambitious person*) Ehrgeizling, *der* (*ugs., abwertend*); **be a ~-flyer** große Rosinen im Kopf haben (*ugs.*); hoch hinaus wollen; B (*successful person*) Senkrechtstarter, *der;* (*person with great potential*) Hochbegabte, *der/die;* **~-'flying** *adj.* hoch fliegend; (*fig.: ambitious*) hochfliegend ‹Pläne, Ideen›; erfolgreich ‹Person›; **~ 'frequency** *n.* hohe Frequenz; (*radio frequency*) Hochfrequenz, *die;* **~-frequency** *adj.* hochfrequent ‹Welle, Schwingung, Strahlung, Strom, Ton, Signal›; Hochfrequenz‹welle, -schwingung, -signal, -gerät, -sender usw.›; ‹Sendung› ≈ auf Kurzwelle; ‹Verluste› im Hochfrequenzbereich; **~ 'German** ⇒ **German** 2 B; **~-grade** *adj.* hochwertig; **~-grade ore** hochhaltiges Erz; Reicherz, *das;* **~-grade steel** Edelstahl, *der;* **~-handed** /haɪ'hændɪd/ *adj.* selbstherrlich; **~ 'hat** *n.* A (*tall hat*) Zylinder, *der;* B (*fig.: snobbish person*) dünkelhafter Mensch; **~ 'heel** *n.* A hoher Absatz; B *in pl.* (*shoes*) hochhackige Schuhe; **~-heeled** /haɪ'hi:ld/ *adj.* ‹Schuhe› mit hohen Absätzen; **~ 'holiday** *n.* (*Relig.*) *einer der beiden höchsten jüdischen Feiertage;* höchster Feiertag; **~-income** *adj.* einkommensstark; **~-income earners** Bezieher hoher Einkommen; **~-income area/country** Gebiet/Land mit hohem Pro-Kopf-Einkommen; **~-income investment** Investition mit hoher Rendite; **~ 'jinks** /'haɪ dʒɪŋks/ *n. pl.* [übermütige] Ausgelassenheit; **~ jump** *n., no pl.* A (*Sport*) Hochsprung, *der;* B (*fig.: reprimand, punishment*) **he is for the ~ jump, it's the ~ jump for him** er kann sich auf was gefasst machen (*ugs.*); **~ jumper** *n.* (*Sport*) Hochspringer, *der*/-springerin, *die;* **~-'key** *adj.* (*Photog.*) High-key-‹Bild, Aufnahme usw.› (*fachspr.*); **~ 'kick** *n.* hoher Beinwurf; **~land** /'haɪlənd/ **1** *n., usu. in pl.* Hochland, *das;* **the H~lands** (*in Scotland*) die Highlands; **2** *adj.* hochländisch; **H~land 'cattle** *n. pl.* schottische Hochlandrinder; **H~land 'dress** *n., no pl.* [schottische] Hochlandtracht; **~lander** /'haɪ ləndə(r)/ *n.* Hochländer, *der*/-länderin, *die;* **H~lander** schottischer Hochländer/schottische Hochländerin; **~-level** *adj.* ‹Verhandlungen usw.› auf hoher Ebene; **~-level talks** Spitzengespräche; **~-level computer language** problemorientierte Programmiersprache; **~ life** *n., no pl.* A (*life of upper class*) das Leben der Oberschicht; B (*luxurious living*) **the ~ life** das Leben auf großem Fuße; **~light 1** *n.* A (*outstanding moment*) Höhepunkt, *der;* **the ~light of the week's events** das herausragende Ereignis der Woche; B (*bright area*) Licht, *das;* C (*in hair*) *usu. pl.* Strähnchen, *das;* **2** *v.t.*, **~ed** ein Schlaglicht werfen auf (+ *Akk.*) ‹Probleme usw.›; markieren ‹Text, Wort etc.› **~lighter** *n.* Textmarker, *der*

**highly** /'haɪlɪ/ *adv.* A (*to a high degree*) sehr; äußerst; hoch‹interessant, -gebildet, -modern, -aktuell›; hoch‹begabt, -bezahlt, angesehen›; leicht ‹entzündlich›; stark ‹gewürzt›; **feel ~ honoured** sich hoch geehrt fühlen; **I can ~ recommend the restaurant** ich kann dieses Restaurant sehr empfehlen; ⇒ *also* **polish** 1 B; B (*favourably*) **think ~ of sb./sth., regard sb./sth. ~:** eine hohe Meinung von jmdm./etw. haben; **speak/write ~ of sb./sth.** jmdn./etw. sehr loben

**'highly strung** *adj.* übererregbar

**high: ~ 'mass** ⇒ **mass**[1]; **~-minded** /haɪ'maɪndɪd/ *adj.* hochgesinnt ‹Person›; hoch, (*geh.*) hehr ‹Prinzipien, Dienstauffassung usw.›; **~-necked** *adj.* hochgeschlossen ‹Kleidungsstück›

**Highness** /'haɪnɪs/ *n.* ▶ **1617** Hoheit, *die;* **His/Her/Your [Royal] ~:** Seine/Ihre/Eure [Königliche] Hoheit

**high: ~-octane** *adj.* hochoktanig; **~performance** *adj.* Hochleistungs-; **~-pitched** *adj.* A hoch ‹Ton, Stimme›; B (*Archit.*) steil ‹Dach›; C (*lofty*) anspruchsvoll; hochgeistig ‹Unterhaltung›; **be too ~-pitched intellectually for sb.** jmdm. *od.* für jmdn. zu hoch sein (*ugs.*); **~ point** *n.* Höhepunkt, *der;* Gipfelpunkt, *der;* **~-powered** /'haɪpaʊəd/ *adj.* A (*powerful*) stark ‹Fahrzeug, Motor, Glühbirne usw.›; B (*forceful*) dynamisch ‹Geschäftsmann, Manager usw.›; C (*authoritative*) mit umfangreichen Vollmachten ausgestattet; (*intellectually excellent*) [äußerst] fähig; hochkarätig (*ugs.*) ‹Examen›; **~ 'pressure** *n.* A (*Meteorol.*) Hochdruck, *der;* **an area of ~ pressure** ein Hochdruckgebiet; B (*Mech. Engin.*) Überdruck, *der;* C (*fig.: high degree of activity*) Hochdruck, *der;* **work at ~ pressure** mit Hochdruck arbeiten (*ugs.*); **~-pressure** *adj.* Hochdruck-; (*fig.: persuasive*) aggressiv ‹Verkaufsmethoden›; aufdringlich ‹Vertreter›; **~-priced** /haɪ'praɪst/ *adj.* teuer; **~ 'priest** *n.* Hohepriester, *der;* **~ 'profile** ⇒ **profile** 1 G; **~-ranking** *adj.* hochrangig; von hohem Rang *nachgestellt;* hoch ‹Beamter, Offizier›; **~ re'lief** ⇒ **relief**[2] A; **~-rise** *adj.* Hochhaus-; **~-rise building** Hochhaus, *das;* **~-rise [block of] flats/office block** Wohn-/Bürohochhaus, *das;* **~-risk** *attrib. adj.* risikoreich; Risiko‹gruppe, -sportart›; hochgradig gefährdet ‹Person›; **take a ~-risk gamble** viel aufs Spiel setzen; viel riskieren; **a ~-risk investment** eine Geldanlage mit hohem Risiko; **~ road** *n.* Hauptstraße, *die;* **the ~ road to ruin** der sichere Weg zum Ruin; **a ~ road to happiness** ein sicherer Weg zum Glück; **~ school** *n.* ≈ Oberschule, *die;* **~ 'seas** *n. pl.* **the ~ seas** die hohe See; **~ season** *n.* Hochsaison, *die;* **~ sign** *n.* (*Amer. coll.*) **give sb. the ~ sign** jmdm. signalisieren, dass die Luft rein ist; **~-sounding** *adj.* hochtönend; hochtrabend (*abwertend*); **~-speed** *adj.* A schnell [fahrend]; **~-speed train** Hochgeschwindigkeitszug, *der;* **~-speed steel** Schnell[arbeits]stahl, *der;* B (*Photog.*) ⇒ **fast**[2] 1 H; **~-spirited** ⇒ **spirited** B; **~ 'spirits** ⇒ **spirit** 1 H; **~ spot** *n.* (*coll.*) Höhepunkt, *der;* **~ street** *n.* Hauptstraße, *die;* **~ street shop/office** Geschäft/Büro in der Hauptstraße; **~ street banks** Großbanken; **~-'strung** ⇒ **highly strung;** **~ 'table** *n.* A (*at public dinner*) erhöhte Speisetafel; B (*table for college fellows*) Dozententisch, *der;* **~tail [it]** *v.i.* & *t.* (*Amer. coll.*) abhauen (*salopp*); verduften (*ugs.*); sich aus dem Staub machen (*ugs.*); **~ 'tea** ⇒ **tea** B; **~-tech** *adj.* (*coll.*) Hightech-; **~ 'tech** (*coll.*), **~ tech'nology** *ns.* Spitzentechnologie, *die;* Hochtechnologie, *die;* **~-technology** *adj.* hoch technisiert; Hightech-; **~ 'tension** ≈ **~ voltage** ⇒ **voltage;** **~-'tension** ⇒ **~-voltage;** **~ 'tide** ⇒ **tide** 1 A; **~ 'treason** ⇒ **treason** A; **~-up** *n.* (*coll.*) hohes Tier (*ugs.*); **~ 'voltage** ⇒ **voltage;** **~-'voltage** *adj.* (*Electr.*) Hochspannungs-; **~ 'water** *n.* Hochwasser, *das;* **~ 'water mark** *n.* A (*level reached by tide*) Hochwassermarke, *die;* B (*maximum value*) höchster Stand; Höchststand, *der;* (*highest point of excellence*) Höhepunkt, *der;* **~way** *n.* A (*public road*) öffentliche Straße; (*public path*) öffentlicher Weg; **H~ways Department** Straßenbauamt, *das;* **the King's/Queen's ~way** (*Brit.*) *eine öffentliche Straße;* B (*main route*) Verkehrsweg, *der;* **the spinal cord is the ~way for all nervous impulses** das Rückenmark ist die Bahn, die alle Nervenimpulse nehmen; C (*fig.: course of action*) **the ~way to ruin** der sichere Weg zum Ruin; **H~way 'Code** *n.* (*Brit.*) Straßenverkehrsordnung, *die;* **~wayman** /'haɪweɪmən/ *n., pl.* **~waymen** /'haɪweɪmən/ (*Hist.*) Straßenräuber, *der;* Wegelagerer, *der;* **~ 'wire** *n.* [Hoch]seil, *das*

**hijack** /'haɪdʒæk/ **1** *v.t.* A (*seize*) in seine Gewalt bringen; **they ~ed an aircraft to Cuba** sie haben ein Flugzeug nach Kuba entführt; **he ~ed the lorry to London** er zwang den Fahrer des LKWs, nach London zu fahren; B (*coll.: steal*) sich (*Dat.*) unter den Nagel reißen (*ugs.*). **2** *n.* (*of aircraft*) Entführung, *die* (**of** *Gen.*); (*of vehicle*) Überfall, *der* (**of** auf + *Akk.*)

**hijacker** /'haɪdʒækə(r)/ *n.* Entführer, *der;* (*of aircraft*) Hijacker, *der;* Flugzeugentführer, *der;* **be seized by ~s** entführt werden

**hike** /haɪk/ **1** *n.* A (*long walk*) Wanderung, *die;* **go on a ~:** eine Wanderung machen; wandern gehen; **be on a ~:** auf einer Wanderung sein; eine Wanderung machen; B (*esp. Amer.: increase*) Anstieg, *der;* Erhöhung, *die* (**in** *Gen.*). **2** *v.i.* A wandern; eine Wanderung machen; B (*walk vigorously*) wandern; marschieren. **3** *v.t.* A (*hoist*) hieven (*ugs.*); B (*esp. Amer.: raise*) erhöhen, anheben ‹Preise usw.› (**to** auf + *Akk.*)

h

~ **'up** *v.i.* ‹Kleidungsstück:› hochrutschen (*ugs.*), sich hochschieben

**hiker** /'haɪkə(r)/ *n.* Wanderer, *der*/Wanderin, *die*

**hilarious** /hɪ'leərɪəs/ *adj.* **A** (*extremely funny*) urkomisch; rasend komisch (*ugs.*); **B** (*boisterously merry*) ausgelassen ‹Party, Stimmung›

**hilariously** /hɪ'leərɪəslɪ/ *adv.* **be ~ funny** rasend komisch sein (*ugs.*); zum Schreien sein (*ugs.*)

**hilarity** /hɪ'lærɪtɪ/ *n.*, *no pl.* **A** (*gaiety*) Fröhlichkeit, *die;* **B** (*merriment*) übermütige Ausgelassenheit; (*loud laughter*) Heiterkeit, *die*

**Hilary term** /hɪlərɪ 'tɜ:m/ *n.* (*Brit. Univ.*) Frühjahrstrimester, *das*

**hill** /hɪl/ *n.* **A** Hügel, *der;* (*higher*) Berg, *der;* **walk in the ~s** in den Bergen wandern; **built on a ~:** am Hang gebaut; **be over the ~** (*fig. coll.*) auf dem absteigenden Ast sein (*ugs.*); (*past the crisis*) über den Berg sein (*ugs.*); **[as] old as the ~s** (*fig.*) uralt; ‹Person› [so] alt wie Methusalem; ⇒ *also* **up** 2 A; **up~**; **B** (*heap*) Hügel, *der;* (*ant~, dung~, mole~*) Haufen, *der;* **C** (*sloping road*) Steigung, *die;* **park on a ~:** am Berg parken

**hill: ~billy** *n.* (*Amer.*) **A** Hinterwäldler, *der*/Hinterwäldlerin, *die* (*spött.*); Landpomeranze, *die* (*ugs. abwertend, auch scherzh.*); (*of the SE US*) Hillbilly, *der;* **B** (*Mus.*) Hillbilly, *der;* **~ climb** *n.* (*Motor Racing*) Bergrennen, *das;* **~ fort** *n.* Bergfestung, *die;* (*Archaeol.*) Hillfort, *das;* **~man** *n.* Bergbewohner, *der*

**hillock** /'hɪlək/ *n.* [kleiner] Hügel

**hill: ~side** *n.* Hang, *der;* **~ start** *n.* (*Motor Veh.*) Anfahren am Berg, *das;* **do a ~ start** am Berg anfahren; **~top** *n.* [Berg]gipfel, *der*

**hilly** /'hɪlɪ/ *adj.* hüg[e]lig; (*higher*) bergig

**hilt** /hɪlt/ *n.* Griff, *der;* Heft, *das* (*geh.*, *fachspr.*); **[up] to the ~** (*fig.*) voll und ganz ‹unterstützen usw.›; schlagend, stichhaltig ‹beweisen›

**him** /ɪm, *stressed* hɪm/ *pron.* ihn; *as indirect object* ihm; *reflexively* sich; *referring to personified things or animals which correspond to German feminines/neuters* sie/es; *as indirect object* ihr/ihm; **it was ~:** er wars; ⇒ *also* **her**[1]

**Himalayan** /hɪmə'leɪən/ *adj.* Himalaja-

**Himalayas** /hɪmə'leɪəz/ *pr. n. pl.* Himalaja, *der*

**himself** /hɪm'self/ *pron.* **A** *emphat.* selbst; **B** *refl.* sich. ⇒ *also* **herself**

**hind**[1] /haɪnd/ *n.* Hirschkuh, *die*

**hind**[2] *adj.* hinter...; **~ legs** Hinterbeine; **get up on one's ~ legs** (*fig. joc.*) sich hinstellen; ⇒ *also* **donkey**

**hinder** /'hɪndə(r)/ **1** *v.t.* (*impede*) behindern; (*delay*) verzögern ‹Vollendung einer Arbeit, Vorgang›; aufhalten ‹Person›; **~ sb. in his work** jmdn. bei der Arbeit behindern; **~ sb. from doing sth.** jmdn. daran hindern, etw. zu tun. **2** *v.i.* **will it help or ~?** bedeutet es eine Erleichterung oder eine Erschwernis?

**Hindi** /'hɪndi:/ **▸1275** **1** *adj.* Hindi-; ⇒ *also* **English** 1. **2** *n.* Hindi, *das;* ⇒ *also* **English** 2 A

**hind: ~most** *adj.* (*furthest behind*) hinterst...; ⇒ *also* **devil** 1 C; **~quarters** *n. pl.* Hinterteil, *das;* (*of large quadruped*) Hinterteil, *das;* Hinterhand, *die* (*fachspr.*)

**hindrance** /'hɪndrəns/ *n.* **A** (*action*) Behinderung, *die;* ⇒ *also* **let**[2] A; **B** (*obstacle*) Hindernis, *das* (**to** für); **he is more of a ~ than a help** er stört mehr, als dass er hilft; **be a ~ to navigation** ein Hindernis für die Schifffahrt sein *od.* darstellen

**'hindsight** *n.* **in ~, with [the benefit of] ~:** im Nachhinein

**Hindu** /'hɪndu:, hɪn'du:/ **▸1340** **1** *n.* Hindu, *der.* **2** *adj.* hinduistisch; Hindu‹gott, -tempel›

**Hinduism** /'hɪndu:ɪzm/ *n.*, *no pl.* Hinduismus, *der*

**Hindustani** /hɪndə'stɑ:ni:/ **▸1275** **1** *adj.* **A** hindustanisch; **B** (*Ling.*) Hindustani-; hindustanisch; ⇒ *also* **English** 1. **2** *n.* Hindustani, *das;* ⇒ *also* **English** 2 A

**hinge** /hɪndʒ/ **1** *n.* **A** Scharnier, *das;* (*continuous*) Klavierband, *das;* **off its ~s** ‹Tür› aus den Angeln gehoben; **B** (*Zool.: of bivalve*) Schloss, *das;* **C** (*Philat.*) **[stamp] ~:** Klebefalz, *der.* **2** *v.t.* mit Scharnieren/einem Scharnier versehen; **~ sth. to sth.** etw. mit Scharnieren/einem Scharnier an etw. (*Dat.*) befestigen. **3** *v.i.* **A** (*hang and turn*) **~ [up]on sth.** mit Scharnieren/einem Scharnier an etw. (*Dat.*) befestigt sein; **B** (*fig.: depend*) abhängen (**[up]on** von); hängen (*ugs.*) (**[up]on** an + *Dat.*)

**hinged** /hɪndʒd/ *adj.* mit Scharnieren/einem Scharnier versehen; **~ lid** Klappdeckel, *der*

**hinny** /'hɪnɪ/ *n.* (*Zool.*) Maulesel, *der*

**hint** /hɪnt/ **1** *n.* **A** (*suggestion*) Wink, *der;* Hinweis, *der;* **give a ~ that ...:** andeuten, dass ...; **give no ~ that ...:** nicht einmal andeutungsweise zu erkennen geben, dass ...; **is that a ~?** ist das ein Wink mit dem Zaunpfahl? (*scherzh.*); **~, ~!** (*joc.*) wenn ich mal mit dem Zaunpfahl winken darf (*scherzh.*); ⇒ *also* **broad** 1 B; **drop** 3 D; **take** 1 V; **B** (*slight trace*) Spur, *die* (**of** von); **the ~/no ~ of a smile** der Anflug/nicht die Spur eines Lächelns; **there was a ~ of sadness in his smile** in seinem Lächeln zeigte sich ein Anflug von Traurigkeit; **a ~ of aniseed** ein Hauch von Anis; **C** (*practical information*) Tipp, *der* (**on** für); **car repair ~s** Tips für die Autoreparatur.

**2** *v.t.* andeuten; **nothing has yet been ~ed about it** darüber hat man noch nichts herausgelassen (*ugs.*).

**3** *v.i.* **~ at** andeuten

**hinterland** /'hɪntəlænd/ *n.* Hinterland, *das;* (*area surrounding city*) Umland, *das*

**hip**[1] /hɪp/ *n.* **A** **▸966** Hüfte, *die;* **with one's hands on one's ~s** die Arme in die Hüften gestemmt; **shoot from the ~** (*lit. or fig.*) aus der Hüfte schießen; **B** *in sing. or pl.* (*~ measurement*) Hüftumfang, *der;* Hüftweite, *die;* (*of man, boy*) Gesäßumfang, *der;* Gesäßweite, *die;* **have thirty-seven-inch ~s** *or* **a thirty-seven-inch ~:** eine Hüftweite/Gesäßweite von vierundneunzig Zentimetern haben; **how large are your ~s?** welche Hüftweite/Gesäßweite hast du?; **C** (*Archit.*) Grat, *der*

**hip**[2] *n.* (*Bot.*) Hagebutte, *die*

**hip**[3] *int.* ⇒ **hurrah** 1

**hip**[4] *adj.* ⇒ **hep**

**hip: ~ bath** *n.* Sitzbad, *das;* **~ bone** *n.* (*Anat.*) Hüftbein, *das;* Hüftknochen, *der;* **~ flask** *n.* Taschenflasche, *die;* Flachmann, *der* (*ugs. scherzh.*); **~ joint** *n.* (*Anat.*) Hüftgelenk, *das;* **~-length** *adj.* hüftlang ‹Kleidungsstück›; **~ measurement** *n.* Hüftumfang, *der;* Hüftweite, *die;* (*of man, boy*) Gesäßumfang, *der;* Gesäßweite, *die*

**hippie** /'hɪpɪ/ *n.* (*coll.*) Hippie, *der*

**hippo** /'hɪpəʊ/ *n.*, *pl.* **~s** (*coll.*) ⇒ **hippopotamus**

**hip 'pocket** *n.* Gesäßtasche, *die*

**Hippocratic oath** /hɪpəkrætɪk 'əʊθ/ *n.* (*Med.*) Eid des Hippokrates

**hippopotamus** /hɪpə'pɒtəməs/ *n.*, *pl.* **~es** *or* **hippopotami** /hɪpə'pɒtəmaɪ/ (*Zool.*) Nilpferd, *das;* Flusspferd, *das*

**hippy** /'hɪpɪ/ ⇒ **hippie**

**hip: ~ roof** *n.* (*Archit.*) Walmdach, *das;* **~ size** ⇒ **~ measurement**

**hipster** /'hɪpstə(r)/ **1** *adj.* auf der Hüfte sitzend ‹Hose›. **2** *in pl.* Hüfthose, *die*

**hire** /haɪə(r)/ **1** *n.* **A** (*action*) Mieten, *das;* (*of servant*) Einstellen, *das;* **conditions of ~:** Mietbedingungen; **B** (*condition*) **be on ~ [to sb.]** [an jmdn.] vermietet sein; **for** *or* **on ~:** zu vermieten; **'for ~'** „frei"; **there are boats for** *or* **on ~:** man kann Boote mieten; **C** (*amount*) Leihgebühr, *die;* **D** (*arch.: wages*) Lohn, *der;* **the labourer is worthy of his ~** (*prov.*) jede Arbeit ist ihres Lohnes wert (*Spr.*). **2** *v.t.* **A** (*employ*) anwerben; engagieren ‹Anwalt, Berater usw.›; **~d assassin** gedungener Mörder; **B** (*obtain use of*) mieten; **~ sth. from sb.** etw. bei jmdm. mieten; **C** (*grant use of*) vermieten; **~ sth. to sb.** etw. jmdm. *od.* an jmdn. vermieten

**~ 'out** *v.t.* vermieten

**'hire car** *n.* Mietwagen, *der;* Leihwagen, *der*

**hired** /haɪəd/: **~ car** ⇒ **hire car**; **~ girl** *n.* (*Amer.*) Hausmädchen, *das;* (*on farm*) Magd, *die* (*veralt.*); **~ man** *n.* (*Amer.*) Gehilfe, *der;* (*on farm*) Knecht, *der* (*veralt.*)

**hireling** /'haɪəlɪŋ/ *n.* Söldling, *der* (*abwertend*); Mietling, *der* (*abwertend*)

**hire 'purchase** *n.*, *no pl.*, *no art.* (*Brit.*) Ratenkauf, *der;* Teilzahlungskauf, *der;* *attrib.* Raten-; Teilzahlungs-; **pay for/buy sth. on ~:** etw. in Raten bezahlen/auf Raten *od.* Teilzahlung kaufen

**hirer** /'haɪərə(r)/ *n.* Mieter, *der*/Mieterin, *die;* (*who grants use*) Vermieter, *der*/Vermieterin, *die*

**hirsute** /'hɜ:sju:t/ *adj.* behaart; (*unkempt*) zottelig; struppig

**hirsuteness** /'hɜ:sju:tnɪs/ *n.*, *no pl.* starke Behaarung; (*unkempt appearance*) Struppigkeit, *die*

**his** /ɪz, *stressed* hɪz/ *poss. pron.* **A** *attrib.* sein; *referring to personified things or animals which correspond to German feminines/neuters* ihr/sein; ⇒ *also* **her**[2]; **B** *pred.* (*the one[s] belonging to him*) seiner/seine/sein[e]s; der/die/das seine *od.* seinige (*geh.*); **towels labelled '~' and 'hers'** mit „Er" und „Sie" gekennzeichnete Handtücher; ⇒ *also* **hers**

**Hispanic** /hɪ'spænɪk/ **1** *adj.* lateinamerikanisch; **~ studies** Hispanistik, *die;* **~ Americans** Hispanoamerikaner. **2** *n.* Lateinamerikaner, *der*/-amerikanerin, *die;* Hispanoamerikaner, *der*/-amerikanerin, *die*

**Hispanicist** /hɪ'spænɪsɪst/, **Hispanist** /'hɪspənɪst/ *n.* Hispanist, *der*/Hispanistin, *die*

**hiss** /hɪs/ **1** *n.* (*of goose, snake, escaping steam, crowd, audience*) Zischen, *das;* (*of cat, locomotive*) Fauchen, *das.* **2** *v.i.* ‹Gans, Schlange, Dampf, Publikum, Menge:› zischen; ‹Katze, Lokomotive:› fauchen. **3** *v.t.* **A** (*express disapproval of*) auszischen ‹Redner, Schauspieler›; **B** (*utter with a hiss*) zischen

**histamine** /'hɪstəmɪn, 'hɪstəmi:n/ *n.* (*Physiol.*) Histamin, *das*

**histogram** /'hɪstəgræm/ *n.* (*Statistics*) Histogramm, *das*

**histology** /hɪ'stɒlədʒɪ/ *n.* (*Biol.*) Histologie, *die*

**historian** /hɪ'stɔ:rɪən/ *n.* **A** **▸1261** (*writer of history*) Geschichtsschreiber, *der*/Geschichtsschreiberin, *die;* **B** (*scholar of history*) Historiker, *der*/Historikerin, *die*

**historic** /hɪ'stɒrɪk/ *adj.* **A** (*famous*) historisch; **B** (*Ling.*) historisch ‹Tempus usw.›

**historical** /hɪ'stɒrɪkl/ *adj.* **A** historisch; geschichtlich ‹Belege, Hintergrund›; **~ research** Geschichtsforschung, *die;* **of ~ interest** von historischem *od.* geschichtlichem Interesse; **B** (*belonging to the past*) in früheren Zeiten üblich ‹Methode›; **be ~:** der Geschichte angehören

**historically** /hɪ'stɒrɪkəlɪ/ *adv.* **A** (*with respect to history*) historisch; **B** (*as a matter of history*) in der Geschichte

**history** /'hɪstərɪ/ *n.* **A** (*continuous record*) Geschichte, *die;* **histories** historische Darstellungen; **B** *no pl.*, *no art.* Geschichte, *die;* (*study of past events*) Geschichte, *die;* Geschichtswissenschaft, *die;* **~ relates ...:** die Geschichte erzählt ...; **that's [all] [past] ~:** das ist [alles] [längst] vergangen [und vergessen]; das gehört [alles] [längst] der Vergangenheit an; **~ repeats itself** die Geschichte wiederholt sich; **make [boxing] ~:** Geschichte [im Boxen] machen; **go down in ~:** in die Geschichte eingehen; **and the rest is ~:** und das Weitere ist [ja] bekannt; **C** (*train of events*) Geschichte, *die;* (*of person*) Werdegang, *der;* **have a ~ of asthma/shoplifting** schon lange an Asthma leiden/eine Vorgeschichte als Ladendieb haben; **D** (*eventful past career*) Geschichte, *die;* **he has quite a ~:** er hat eine bewegte Vergangenheit; **E** (*Theatre*) historisches Drama; **Shakespeare's histories** Shakespeares Historien. ⇒ *also* **ancient** 1 A; **case history**; **life history**; **medieval history**; **natural history**

**'history book** *n.* Geschichtsbuch, *das*

**histrionic** /hɪstrɪ'ɒnɪk/ ❶ *adj.* **A** schauspielerisch ‹Talent, Fähigkeiten›; **~ art** Schauspielkunst, *die;* **B** (*stagy*) theatralisch (*abwertend*). ❷ *n. in pl.* **A** (*theatrical art*) Schauspielkunst, *die;* Schauspielerei, *die;* **B** (*melodramatic behaviour*) theatralisches Getue (*abwertend*); **forget the ~s!** lass die Schauspielerei! (*ugs. abwertend*)

**hit** /hɪt/ ❶ *v.t.*, **-tt-**, **hit** **A** (*strike with blow*) schlagen; (*strike with missile*) treffen; ‹Geschoss, Ball usw.:› treffen; **I've been ~!** (*struck by bullet*) ich bin getroffen!; **I could ~ him** (*fig. coll.*) ich könnte ihm eine runterhauen (*ugs.*); **the ball ~ me in the face** der Ball traf mich ins Gesicht; **~ sb. over the head** jmdm. eins überziehen (*ugs.*); **~ one's thumb** sich (*Dat.*) auf den Daumen schlagen; **~ by lightning** vom Blitz getroffen; **~ a man when he's down** (*fig.*) jmdn. treten, der schon am Boden liegt; ⇒ *also* **belt** 1 A; **nail** 1 B; **note** 1 A; **B** (*come forcibly into contact with*) ‹Fahrzeug:› prallen gegen ‹Mauer usw.›; ‹Schiff:› laufen gegen ‹Felsen usw.›; **the aircraft ~ the ground** das Flugzeug schlug auf den Boden auf; **the noise of the hammer ~ting the anvil** das Geräusch des Hammers beim Auftreffen auf den Amboss; **~ the roof** *or* **ceiling** (*fig. coll.: become angry*) an die Decke *od.* in die Luft gehen (*ugs.*); **C** (*cause to come into contact*) [an]stoßen; [an]schlagen; **~ one's head on sth.** mit dem Kopf gegen etw. stoßen; sich (*Dat.*) den Kopf an etw. (*Dat.*) stoßen; **D** (*deliver*) **~ a blow at sb.**, **~ sb. a blow** jmdm. einen Schlag verpassen (*ugs.*); **E** (*fig.: cause to suffer*) **~ badly** *or* **hard** schwer treffen; **I will ~ them very hard** (*take severe measures against*) ich werde mit aller Schärfe gegen sie vorgehen; **F** (*fig.: affect*) treffen; **have been ~ by frost/rain** *etc.* durch Frost/Regen *usw.* gelitten haben; **G** (*fig.: light upon*) finden; stoßen *od.* treffen auf (+ *Akk.*); finden ‹Bodenschätze›; **you've ~ it!** du sagst es!; **H** (*fig.: characterize*) ⇒ **~ off**; **I** (*fig. coll.*) (*encounter*) Bekanntschaft machen mit (+ *Dat.*) (*ugs.*); (*arrive at*) erreichen ‹Höchstform, bestimmten Ort, bestimmte Höhe, bestimmtes Alter usw.›; **I think we've ~ a snag** ich glaube, jetzt gibts Probleme; **~ a pool of water** ‹Auto:› in eine [Wasser]pfütze fahren; **~ an all-time high** ‹Preis:› eine Rekordhöhe erreichen; **the car can ~ 100 miles an hour** das Auto schafft 100 Meilen in der Stunde (*ugs.*); **they ~ all the night spots** sie statteten allen Nachtlokalen einen Besuch ab (*ugs.*); **~ town** ankommen; **~ the trail** (*Amer. coll.*) *or* **the road** sich auf den Weg *od.* (*ugs.*) die Socken machen; **~ the hay** (*coll.*) in die Falle gehen (*ugs.*); sich in die Falle hauen (*ugs.*); **J** (*fig. coll.: indulge in*) zuschlagen bei (+ *Dat.*) (*salopp*); **[begin to] ~ the bottle** das Trinken anfangen; **K** (*Cricket*) erzielen ‹Lauf›; **~ the ball for six** (*Brit.*) sechs Läufe auf einmal erzielen; **~ sb. for six** (*Brit.*) gegen jmdn. sechs Läufe erzielen; (*fig.: defeat*) jmdn. übertrumpfen

❷ *v.i.*, **-tt-**, **hit** **A** (*direct a blow*) schlagen; **~ hard** fest *od.* hart zuschlagen; **~ at sb./sth.** auf jmdn./etw. einschlagen; (*fig.: criticize*) jmdn./etw. kritisieren; **~ at sth. as being extravagant** etw. als extravagant geißeln; **~ and run** ‹Autofahrer:› Fahrer- *od.* Unfallflucht begehen; ‹Angreifer:› einen Blitzüberfall machen; ⇒ *also* **~-and-run**; **B** (*come into forcible contact*) **~ against** *or* **upon sth.** gegen *od.* auf etw. (*Akk.*) stoßen.

❸ *n.* **A** (*blow*) Schlag, *der;* **B** (*sarcastic remark*) Seitenhieb, *der* (**at** gegen); Spitze, *die* (**at** gegen); (*censure, rebuke*) Angriff, *der;* **that's a ~ at me** das geht gegen mich; **C** (*shot or bomb striking target*) Treffer, *der;* **D** (*success*) Erfolg, *der;* Knüller, *der* (*ugs.*); (*success in entertainment*) Schlager, *der;* Hit, *der* (*ugs.*); **make a ~:** gut ankommen; **make** *or* **be a ~ with sb.** bei jmdm. einschlagen *od.* gut ankommen; **I'm sure she'll be** *or* **make a [big] ~:** ich bin sicher, sie wird [ganz] groß herauskommen (*ugs.*); **E** (*stroke of luck*) Glückstreffer, *der;* **F** (*Computing*) (*in search*) Treffer, *der;* (*on Web site*) Hit, *der*

**~ 'back** ❶ *v.t.* zurückschlagen. ❷ *v.i.* zurückschlagen; (*verbally*) kontern; sich wehren; **~ back at sb.** (*fig.*) jmdm. Kontra geben

**~ 'off** *v.t.* **A** (*characterize*) genau treffen; treffend charakterisieren; **B** **~ it off [with each other]** gut miteinander auskommen; **~ it off with sb.** gut mit jmdm. auskommen

**~ on** ⇒ **~ upon**

**~ 'out** *v.i.* **A** (*aim blows*) drauflosschlagen; **B** **~ out at** *or* **against sb./sth.** (*fig.*) jmdn./etw. scharf angreifen *od.* attackieren

**~ upon** *v.t.* stoßen auf (+ *Akk.*); finden ‹richtige Antwort, Methode›; kommen auf (+ *Akk.*) ‹Idee›

**hit: ~-and-'miss** ⇒ **~-or-miss**; **~-and-'run** *adj.* **A** unfallflüchtig ‹Fahrer›; **~-and-run accident** Unfall mit Fahrerflucht; **B** Blitz‹angriff, -überfall›; **~-and-run tactics** Taktik des Blitzüberfalls

**hitch** /hɪtʃ/ ❶ *v.t.* **A** (*move by a jerk*) rücken; **B** (*fasten*) [fest]binden ‹Tier› (**to** an + *Akk.*); binden ‹Seil› (**round** um + *Akk.*); [an]koppeln ‹Anhänger usw.› (**to** an + *Akk.*); spannen ‹Zugtier, -maschine usw.› (**to** vor + *Akk.*); **get ~ed** (*coll.*) heiraten; ⇒ *also* **wagon** A; **C** **~ a lift** *or* **ride** (*coll.*) per Anhalter fahren; trampen; **he was trying to ~ a lift** *or* **ride** er wollte mitgenommen werden.

❷ *v.i.* ⇒ **hitch-hike** 1.

❸ *n.* **A** (*jerk*) Ruck, *der;* **give sth. a ~:** an etw. (*Dat.*) rucken; **B** (*Naut.: knot*) Stek, *der* (*Seemannsspr.*); **half ~:** halber Schlag; ⇒ *also* **clove hitch**; **C** (*stoppage*) Unterbrechung, *die;* **go off without a ~:** glatt *od.* reibungslos über die Bühne gehen; **D** (*impediment*) Problem, *das;* Schwierigkeit, *die;* **have one ~:** einen Haken haben (*ugs.*); **E** ⇒ **hitch-hike** 2

**~ 'up** *v.t.* **A** hochheben ‹Rock›; **~ up one's trousers** seinen Hosenbund hochziehen; **B** (*Amer.: attach*) anspannen

**hitch: ~-hike** ❶ *v.i.* per Anhalter fahren; trampen; ❷ *n.* Tramptour, *die;* **~-hiker** *n.* Anhalter, *der*/Anhalterin, *die;* Tramper, *der*/Tramperin, *die;* **~-hiking** *n.* Trampen, *das*

**hitching post** /'hɪtʃɪŋpəʊst/ *n.* Pfosten, *der* (*zum Anbinden von Zug- und Reittieren*)

**hi-tech** ⇒ **high-tech**

**hither** /'hɪðə(r)/ *adv.* (*literary*) hierher; **~ and thither** *or* **yon** hierhin und dorthin; ⇒ *also* **come-~**

**hitherto** /'hɪðətʊ, hɪðə'tu:/ *adv.* (*literary*) bisher; bislang; (*up to that time*) bis dahin

**hit: ~ list** *n.* **A** (*charts*) ⇒ **~ parade**; **B** (*victims*) Abschussliste, *die* (*fig.*); **~ man** *n.* (*Amer.*) Killer, *der* (*salopp*); **~-or-'miss** *adj.* (*coll.*) (*random*) unsicher, unzuverlässig ‹Methode›; (*careless*) schlampig, schluderig (*ugs. abwertend*) ‹Arbeit›; **it was a very ~-or-miss affair** das ging alles aufs Geratewohl (*ugs.*); **~ parade** *n.* Hitparade, *die;* Schlagerparade, *die;* **~ 'record** *n.* Hit, *der* (*ugs.*)

**Hittite** /'hɪtaɪt/ ▶ **1275**, ▶ **1340** ❶ *n.* **A** Hethiter, *der*/Hethiterin, *die;* **B** (*Ling.*) Hethitisch, *das.* ❷ *adj.* hethitisch

**HIV** *abbr.* (*Med.*) **human immunodeficiency virus** HIV; **~-positive/-negative** HIV-positiv/-negativ; **~-infected** HIV-infiziert

**hive** /haɪv/ ❶ *n.* **A** [Bienen]stock, *der;* (*of straw*) Bienenkorb, *der;* **frame ~:** Bienenkasten, *der;* **B** (*fig.: busy place*) **what a ~ of industry!** der reinste Bienenstock! (*ugs.*); **the office is a [regular] ~ of industry** in dem Büro geht es zu wie in einem Bienenstock. ❷ *v.t.* in einen Stock bringen, einfangen ‹Bienen›

**~ 'off** (*Brit.*) ❶ *v.i.* ‹Firma, Abteilung:› sich abspalten (**from** von). ❷ *v.t.* (*separate and make independent*) verselbstständigen; (*assign*) zuweisen, übertragen ‹Aufgabe usw.› (**to** *Dat.*); **the firm was ~d off from the parent company** die Firma wurde aus der Muttergesellschaft ausgegliedert

**hiya** /'haɪjə/ *int.* (*coll.*) hallo!

**HM** *abbr.* **A** **Her/His Majesty** I. M./S. M.; **B** **Her/His Majesty's**; **C** **headmaster/headmistress** ≈ Dir.

**HMG** *abbr.* (*Brit.*) **Her/His Majesty's Government**

**HMI** *abbr.* (*Brit.*) **Her/His Majesty's Inspector [of Schools]**

**HMS** *abbr.* (*Brit.*) **Her/His Majesty's Ship** H.M.S.

**HMSO** *abbr.* (*Brit.*) **Her/His Majesty's Stationery Office**

**HNC** *abbr.* (*Brit.*) **Higher National Certificate**

**HND** *abbr.* (*Brit.*) **Higher National Diploma**

**ho** /həʊ/ *int.* **A** *expr. surprise* oh; nanu; *expr. admiration* oh; *expr. triumph* ha; *drawing attention* he; heda; *expr. derision* haha; **land ho!** Land in Sicht!; **B** (*Naut.: rallying cry*) **westward ho!** auf nach Westen!

**hoard** /hɔ:d/ ❶ *n.* **A** (*store laid by*) Vorrat, *der;* **make/collect a ~ of sth.** etw. horten; **B** (*fig.: amassed stock*) Sammlung, *die;* **he had accumulated a ~ of grievances** bei ihm hatten sich eine Menge Klagen angehäuft *od.* angestaut; **C** (*Archaeol.*) Hort, *der* (*fachspr.*). ❷ *v.t.* **~ [up]** horten ‹Geld, Brennmaterial, Lebensmittel usw.›; hamstern ‹Lebensmittel›. ❸ *v.i.* horten

**hoarder** /'hɔ:də(r)/ *n.* Hamsterer, *der*/Hamsterin, *die*

**hoarding**[1] /'hɔ:dɪŋ/ *n.* Horten, *das;* Hamstern, *das*

**hoarding**[2] *n.* **A** (*fence*) Bretterzaun, *der;* Bretterwand, *die;* (*round building site*) Bauzaun, *der;* **B** (*Brit.: for advertisements*) Reklamewand, *die;* Plakatwand, *die*

**hoar frost** /'hɔ:frɒst/ *n.* [Rau]reif, *der*

**hoarse** /hɔ:s/ *adj.* **A** (*rough, husky*) heiser ‹Laut›; heiser, rau ‹Stimme›; (*croaking*) krächzend ‹Laut›; (*with emotion*) belegt ‹Stimme›; **B** (*having a dry, husky voice*) heiser; **shout oneself ~:** sich heiser schreien

**hoarsely** /'hɔ:slɪ/ *adv.* (*in a hoarse voice*) heiser ‹sprechen›; mit heiserer Stimme ‹reden, schreien, singen›; (*in an emotional voice*) mit belegter Stimme

**hoarseness** /'hɔ:snɪs/ *n.* Heiserkeit, *die*

**hoary** /'hɔ:rɪ/ *adj.* **A** (*grey*) grau; ergraut (*geh.*); (*white*) [schloh]weiß; **become ~:** grau werden, (*geh.*) ergrauen/weiß werden; **B** (*having grey hair*) grauhaarig; ergraut (*geh.*); (*having white hair*) weißhaarig; **C** (*very old*) altehrwürdig ‹Gebäude›; **~ old joke** uralter Witz

**hoax** /həʊks/ ❶ *v.t.* anführen (*ugs.*); foppen; zum Besten haben *od.* halten; **I'd been ~ed** ich hatte mich anführen (*ugs.*) *od.* foppen lassen; **~ sb. into believing sth.** jmdm. etw. weismachen. ❷ *n.* (*deception*) Schwindel, *der;* (*false report*) Falschmeldung, *die;* Ente, *die* (*ugs.*); (*practical joke*) Streich, *der;* (*false alarm*) blinder Alarm

**hoaxer** /'həʊksə(r)/ *n.* Schwindler, *der*/Schwindlerin, *die*

**hob** /hɒb/ *n.* **A** (*of cooker*) Kochmulde, *die* (*Fachspr.*); [Koch]platte, *die;* Kochstelle, *die;* **B** (*at side of fireplace*) Kamineinsatz, *der;* **C** (*peg*) Zielpflock, *der*

**hobble** /'hɒbl/ ❶ *v.i.* **~ [about]** [herum]humpeln *od.* -hinken. ❷ *v.t.* **A** (*cause to ~*) [beim Gehen] behindern; **B** (*tie together legs of*) an den Füßen fesseln ‹Pferd usw.›; **C** (*tie together*) fesseln ‹Vorderbeine›. ❸ *n.* **A** *no pl.* (*uneven gait*) Humpeln, *das;* Hinken, *das;* **B** (*device for hobbling*) [Fuß]fessel, *die*

**hobby**[1] /'hɒbɪ/ *n.* Hobby, *das;* Steckenpferd, *das;* **do sth. as a ~:** etw. als Hobby tun

**hobby**[2] *n.* (*Ornith.*) Baumfalke, *der*

**'hobby horse** *n.* **A** (*wicker horse*) Pferdemaske, *die;* **B** (*child's toy*) Steckenpferd, *das;* **C** ⇒ **rocking horse**; **D** (*favourite topic*) Lieblingsthema, *das;* **get on to/start on one's ~:** anfangen, sein Steckenpferd zu reiten (*scherzh.*)

**hob: ~goblin** *n.* **A** (*mischievous imp*) Kobold, *der;* Puck, *der;* **B** (*bogy*) Schreckgespenst, *das;* **~nail** *n.* [starker] Schuh- *od.* Stiefelnagel; **~nailed** /'hɒbneɪld/ *adj.* Nagel‹schuh, -stiefel›; **~-nob** *v.i.*, **-bb-: I've seen them ~-nobbing [together] a lot recently** ich habe sie in letzter Zeit viel zusammen gesehen; **he's always ~-nobbing**

h

**with the aristocracy** er verkehrt viel in adeligen Kreisen

**hobo** /'həʊbəʊ/ *n., pl.* **~es** (*Amer.*) Landstreicher, *der*/-streicherin, *die*

**Hobson's choice** /hɒbsnz 'tʃɔɪs/ *n.* **it was [a case of] ~:** es gab eigentlich gar keine Wahl

**hock**[1] /hɒk/ (*joint of quadruped's leg*) Sprunggelenk, *das*

**hock**[2] *n.* (*Brit.: wine*) Rheinwein, *der*

**hock**[3] (*Amer. coll.*) ❶ *v.t.* versetzen. ❷ *n.* **be in ~** (*in pawn*) versetzt sein; (*in prison*) [im Kittchen *od.* Knast] sitzen (*ugs.*); Knast schieben (*salopp*); (*in debt*) in Schulden stecken; **put sth. in ~:** etw. versetzen; **put sb. in ~** (*in debt*) jmdn. in Schulden stürzen; (*in prison*) jmdn. einlochen (*salopp*); **be in ~ to sb.** bei jmdm. in der Kreide stehen (*ugs.*)

**hockey** /'hɒkɪ/ *n.* Ⓐ Hockey, *das;* Ⓑ (*Can.*) ⇒ **ice hockey**

**hockey: ~ player** *n.* Hockeyspieler, *der*/-spielerin, *die;* **~ stick** *n.* Hockeystock, *der;* Hockeyschläger, *der*

**hocus-pocus** /həʊkəs'pəʊkəs/ *n.* (*deception*) Zauberei, *die*

**hod** /hɒd/ *n.* Ⓐ (*Building*) Tragmulde, *die;* Ⓑ (*for coal*) Kohlenschütte, *die*

**hodgepodge** /'hɒdʒpɒdʒ/ ⇒ **hotchpotch**

**hoe** /həʊ/ ❶ *n.* Hacke, *die;* ⇒ *also* **Dutch hoe**. ❷ *v.t.* hacken ‹Beet, Acker›; **~ up** weg- *od.* heraushacken ‹Unkraut›; **~ down** weg- *od.* umhacken ‹Büsche›; **~ in** einhacken; ⇒ *also* **hard** 1 B. ❸ *v.i.* hacken

**'hoedown** *n.* (*Amer.*) Ⓐ (*dance*) Hoedown, *der;* Ⓑ (*party*) Schwof, *der* (*ugs.*)

**hog** /hɒg/ ❶ *n.* Ⓐ (*domesticated pig*) [Mast]schwein, *das;* **go the whole ~** (*coll.*) Nägel mit Köpfen machen (*ugs.*); **go the whole ~ with sb.** so weit wie jmd. gehen; **live high off** *or* **on the ~** (*Amer.*) aus dem Vollen leben; Ⓑ (*Zool.: animal of family Suidae*) Schwein, *das;* Ⓒ (*fig.: person*) Schwein, *das* (*derb*); Sau, *die* (*derb*); Ferkel, *das* (*derb*). ❷ *v.t.*, **-gg-** (*coll.*) sich (*Dat.*) unter den Nagel reißen; **~ the middle of the road** ‹Fahrer:› die ganze Straße für sich beanspruchen; **~ the bathroom** das Badezimmer mit Beschlag belegen

**'hogback** *n.* (*Geog.*) [scharfer, steiler und langer] Grat

**hoggish** /'hɒgɪʃ/ *adj.* verfressen (*salopp abwertend*)

**Hogmanay** /'hɒgməneɪ/ *n.* (*Scot., N. Engl.*) Silvester, *der od. das*

**hog's back** /'hɒgz bæk/ ⇒ **hogback**

**hogshead** /'hɒgzhed/ *n.* Ⓐ (*cask*) [großes] Fass; Oxhoftfass, *das;* Ⓑ (*measure*) Oxhoft, *das*

**hog: ~-tie** *v.t.* (*Amer.*) Ⓐ (*secure*) an Händen und Füßen fesseln ‹Person›; an allen vieren fesseln ‹Tier›; Ⓑ (*fig.: impede*) in ein zu enges Korsett zwängen; **sb. is ~-tied** jmdm. sind Hände und Füße gebunden; **~-wash** *n.* Ⓐ (*coll.: nonsense*) Quatsch, *der* (*salopp*); Ⓑ (*pigswill*) Schweinefutter, *das;* **~weed** *n.* (*Bot.*) Wiesenbärenklau, *der*

**ho-'ho** *int. expr. surprise* ach ne!; *expr. triumph, derision* haha!

**hoick** /hɔɪk/ *v.t.* (*Brit. coll.*) wuchten ‹[schweren] Gegenstand› (**over** über + *Akk.*, **into** in + *Akk.*)

**hoi polloi** /hɔɪ pɒ'lɔɪ/ *n. pl.* (*literary*) **[the] ~:** das [gemeine] Volk; die Masse; der Pöbel (*abwertend*)

**hoist** /hɔɪst/ ❶ *v.t.* Ⓐ (*raise aloft*) hoch-, aufziehen, hissen ‹Flagge usw.›; heißen (*Seemannsspr.*) ‹Flagge usw.›; setzen (*Seemannsspr.*) ‹Signal usw.›; **~ sth. up a mast** etw. an einem Mast hoch-/aufziehen/hissen/heißen/setzen; Ⓑ (*raise by tackle etc.*) hieven ‹Last›; setzen ‹Segel›. ❷ *n.* Ⓐ (*act of hoisting*) [Hoch]hieven, *das;* Ⓑ (*part of flag*) Liek, *das;* Ⓒ (*goods lift*) [Lasten]aufzug, *der.* ❸ *adj.* **be ~ with one's own petard** sich in seiner eigenen Schlinge fangen

**hoity-toity** /hɔɪtɪ'tɔɪtɪ/ *adj.* (*coll.*) hochnäsig (*abwertend*); eingebildet; (*petulant*) pikiert

**hokum** /'həʊkəm/ *n.* (*coll.*) Humbug, *der*

**hold**[1] /həʊld/ *n.* (*of ship*) Laderaum, *der;* (*of aircraft*) Frachtraum, *der*

**hold**[2] ❶ *v.t.*, **held** /held/ Ⓐ (*grasp*) halten; (*carry*) tragen; (*keep fast*) festhalten; **~ sb. by the arm** jmdn. am Arm festhalten; **they held each other tight** sie hielten sich fest umschlungen; **~ one's belly/head** *etc.* sich (*Dat.*) den Bauch/Kopf *usw.* halten; **~ tight!** (*in bus etc.*) festhalten!; ⇒ *also* **baby** 1 A; **clock** 1 A; **hand** 1 A; **nose** 1 A; Ⓑ (*support*) ‹tragendes Teil:› halten, stützen, tragen ‹Decke, Dach usw.›; aufnehmen ‹Gewicht, Kraft›; Ⓒ (*keep in position*) halten; **~ the door open for sb.** jmdm. die Tür aufhalten; **~ sth. in place** etw. halten; **~ sth. over sb.** (*fig.*) jmdm. ständig mit etw. drohen; ⇒ *also* **candle** 1 A; Ⓓ (*grasp to control*) halten ‹Kind, Hund, Zügel›; Ⓔ (*keep in particular attitude*) **~ oneself well/badly/straight** sich gut/schlecht/gerade halten; **~ oneself still** stillhalten; **~ oneself ready** *or* **in readiness** sich bereit *od.* in Bereitschaft halten; **~ oneself ready** *or* **in readiness to do sth.** jederzeit bereit sein, etw. zu tun; **~ one's head high** (*fig.*) (*be confident*) selbstbewusst sein *od.* auftreten; (*be proud*) den Kopf hoch tragen; Ⓕ (*contain*) enthalten; bergen ‹Gefahr, Geheimnis›; (*be able to contain*) fassen ‹Liter, Personen usw.›; **the bag ~s flour** in dem Sack wird Mehl aufbewahrt; **the room ~s ten people** in dem Raum haben 10 Leute Platz; der Raum bietet 10 Leuten Platz; **the box won't ~ these books** diese Bücher gehen nicht in die Kiste; **the disaster may ~ lessons for the future** aus dem Unglück kann man vielleicht Lehren für die Zukunft ziehen; **no one knows what the future will ~:** niemand weiß, was die Zukunft bringt *od.* bringen wird; **~ water** ‹Behälter:› wasserdicht sein; Wasser halten; (*fig.*) ‹Argument, Theorie:› stichhaltig sein, hieb- und stichfest sein; ‹Annahme, Theorie, Alibi:› haltbar sein; Ⓖ (*not be intoxicated by*) **he can/can't ~ his drink** *or* **liquor** er kann etwas/nichts vertragen; Ⓗ (*possess*) besitzen; haben; halten (*Wirtsch.*) ‹Aktien, Anteile›; Ⓘ (*Cards: have in one's hand*) [auf der Hand] haben; Ⓙ (*have gained*) halten ‹Rekord›; haben ‹Diplom, Doktorgrad›; Ⓚ (*keep possession of*) halten ‹Stützpunkt, Stadt, Stellung›; (*Mus.: sustain*) [aus]halten ‹Ton›; **~ one's own** (*fig.*) sich behaupten; **~ one's position** (*fig.*) auf seinem Standpunkt beharren; **~ the line on the price/over one's demands** den Preis [stabil] halten/in seinen Forderungen hart *od.* fest bleiben; ⇒ *also* L; **fort**; **ground**[1] 1 B; Ⓛ (*occupy*) innehaben, (*geh.*) bekleiden ‹Posten, Amt, Stellung›; **~ office** im Amt sein; **~ the line** (*Teleph.*) am Apparat bleiben; ⇒ *also* K; **~ the road** nicht von der Straße abkommen; **~ the road well** ‹Auto:› eine gute Straßenlage haben; Ⓜ (*engross*) fesseln, (*geh.*) gefangen halten ‹Aufmerksamkeit, Publikum›; Ⓝ (*dominate*) **~ the stage** *or* **house** das Publikum *od.* ganze Haus in Bann halten (*geh.*); **~ the floor** das Wort führen; das Gespräch/die Diskussion/Debatte *usw.* beherrschen *od.* bestimmen; ⇒ *also* **field** 1 E; Ⓞ (*keep in specified condition*) halten; **~ the ladder steady** die Leiter festhalten; **~ the audience in suspense** das Publikum fesseln; ⇒ *also* **bay**[4] 1; **ransom** 1; Ⓟ (*detain*) (*in custody*) in Haft halten, festhalten; (*imprison*) festsetzen; inhaftieren; (*arrest*) festnehmen; **be held in a prison** in einem Gefängnis einsitzen; **~ a [connecting] train** einen [Anschluss]zug warten lassen; **there was nothing to ~ me there** da hielt mich nichts mehr; Ⓠ (*oblige to adhere*) **~ sb. to the terms of the contract/to a promise** darauf bestehen, dass jmd. sich an die Vertragsbestimmungen hält/dass jmd. ein Versprechen hält *od.* einlöst; **You can have the car when I go abroad — I'll ~ you to that** Du kannst das Auto haben, wenn ich ins Ausland gehe — Ich werde dich beim Wort nehmen; Ⓡ (*Sport: restrict*) **~ one's opponent [to a draw]** ein Unentschieden [gegen den Gegner] halten *od.* verteidigen; **~ one's opponents to three goals** die Zahl der gegnerischen Tore bei drei halten; Ⓢ (*cause to take place*) stattfinden lassen; abhalten ‹Veranstaltung, Konferenz, Gottesdienst, Sitzung, Prüfung›; veranstalten ‹Festival, Auktion›; austragen ‹Meisterschaften›; führen ‹Unterhaltung, Gespräch, Korrespondenz›; durchführen ‹Untersuchung›; geben ‹Empfang›; halten ‹Vortrag, Rede›; **be held** stattfinden; **~ a conversation with sb.** eine Unterhaltung mit jmdm. führen *od.* haben; sich mit jmdm. unterhalten; ⇒ *also* **court** 1 C; Ⓣ (*restrain*) [fest]halten; **~ sb. from doing sth.** jmdn. davon abhalten, etw. zu tun; **~ one's noise** leise sein; **~ one's fire** [noch] nicht schießen; (*fig.: refrain from criticism*) mit seiner Kritik zurückhalten; **~ your fire!** nicht schießen!; (*fig.*) nun mal sachte! (*ugs.*); **there is/was no ~ing sb.** jmd. ist/war nicht mehr zu halten *od.* (*ugs.*) bremsen; für jmdn. gibt/gab es kein Halten mehr; ⇒ *also* **breath** A; **hand** 1 B; **peace** B; Ⓤ (*coll.: withhold*) zurückhalten; **~ one's payments** mit der Abzahlung säumig sein; **~ it!** [einen] Moment mal!; **~ everything!** stopp! (*ugs.*); ⇒ *also* **horse** 1 A; Ⓥ (*think, believe*) **~ a view** *or* **an opinion** eine Ansicht haben (**on** über + *Akk.*); **~ that ...:** dafürhalten, dass ...; der Ansicht sein, dass ...; **~ sb. to be ...:** jmdn. für ... halten; glauben, dass jmd. ... ist; **~ sb./oneself guilty/blameless** jmdn./sich für schuldig/unschuldig halten (**for** an + *Dat.*); **~ oneself responsible for sth.** sich für etw. verantwortlich fühlen; **~ sb. in high/low regard** *or* **esteem** viel/wenig von jmdm. halten; jmdn. hoch schätzen (*geh.*)/gering schätzen; **~ sth. against sb.** jmdm. etw. vorwerfen; **~ it against sb. that ...:** jmdm. vorwerfen, dass ...; ⇒ *also* **cheap** 1 C; **dear** 1 A; **responsible** A; Ⓦ (*Law: pronounce*) **~ that ...:** entscheiden, dass ...

❷ *v.i.*, **held** Ⓐ (*not give way*) ‹Seil, Nagel, Anker, Schloss, Angeklebtes:› halten; ‹Damm:› [stand]halten; Ⓑ (*remain unchanged*) anhalten; [an]dauern; ‹Wetter:› sich halten, so bleiben; ‹Angebot, Versprechen:› gelten; **his luck held** er hatte auch weiterhin Glück; Ⓒ (*remain steadfast*) **~ to sth.** bei etw. bleiben; an etw. (*Dat.*) festhalten; **~ to** *or* **by one's family** zur Familie stehen *od.* halten; **~ by one's beliefs/convictions** tun, was man für richtig hält; **he still ~s to the view that ...:** er ist nach wie vor der Ansicht, dass ...; ⇒ *also* **aloof** 1; Ⓓ (*be valid*) **~ [good** *or* **true]** gelten; Gültigkeit haben; Ⓔ (*arch.: wait*) einhalten; **~ [hard]!** halt[et] ein! ⇒ *also* **still**[1] 1 A.

❸ *n.* Ⓐ (*grasp*) Griff, *der;* **grab** *or* **seize ~ of sth.** etw. ergreifen; **get** *or* **lay** *or* **take ~ of sth.** etw. fassen *od.* packen; (*manage to gain a grip on sth.*) etw. zu fassen kriegen (*ugs.*) *od.* bekommen; (*in order to carry it*) etw. nehmen; **keep ~ of sth.** etw. festhalten; **keep/lose one's ~:** den Halt nicht verlieren/den Halt verlieren; **lose one's ~ on reality** den Sinn für die Realität verlieren; **take ~** (*fig.*) sich durchsetzen; ‹Krankheit:› fortschreiten; **get ~ of sth.** (*fig.*) etw. bekommen *od.* auftreiben; **if the newspapers get ~ of the story** wenn die Zeitungen Wind von der Sache bekommen (*ugs.*); **get ~ of sb.** (*fig.*) jmdn. erreichen; **get a ~ on oneself** sich fassen; **have a ~ over sb.** jmdn. in der Hand halten; ⇒ *also* **catch** 1 A; Ⓑ (*influence*) Einfluss, *der* (**on, over** *auf* + *Akk.*); **lose one's ~:** seinen Einfluss verlieren; **gain a ~:** zu Einfluss gelangen; Ⓒ (*Sport*) Griff, *der;* **there are no ~s barred** (*fig.*) alles ist erlaubt; Ⓓ (*thing to ~ by*) Griff, *der;* Ⓔ **put on ~:** auf Eis legen ‹Plan, Programm›

**~ 'back** ❶ *v.t.* Ⓐ (*restrain*) zurückhalten; **~ sb. back from doing sth.** jmdn. [daran] hindern, etw. zu tun; Ⓑ (*impede progress of*) hindern; **nothing can ~ him back** er ist nicht mehr aufzuhalten; Ⓒ (*withhold*) zurückhalten; zurückhalten mit ‹Bekanntgabe von Ergebnissen, Veröffentlichung eines Berichts›; **~ sth. back from sb.** jmdm. etw. vorenthalten. ❷ *v.i.* zögern; **~ back from doing sth.** zögern, etw. zu tun

**~ 'down** *v.t.* Ⓐ festhalten; (*repress*) unterdrücken; niederhalten ‹Volk›; (*fig.: keep at low level*) niedrig halten ‹Preise, Löhne usw.›; Ⓑ (*keep*) sich halten in (+ *Dat.*) ‹Stellung, Position›

~ **'forth** ❶ *v.t.* (*offer*) anpreisen. ❷ *v.i.* sich in langen Reden ergehen (*oft abwertend*); ~ **forth about** *or* **on sth.** sich über etw. (*Akk.*) auslassen (*abwertend*)
~ **'in** *v.t.* zügeln ‹Pferd, Temperament›; einziehen ‹Bauch›; ~ **oneself in** (*temper, emotions*) sich beherrschen; an sich (*Akk.*) halten; (*stomach*) den Bauch einziehen
~ **'off** ❶ *v.t.* (*keep at bay*) von sich fernhalten, (*ugs.*) sich (*Dat.*) vom Leib halten ‹Fans, Presse›; in Schach halten ‹gegnerische Stürmer›; abwehren ‹Angriff›; Einhalt gebieten (+ *Dat.*) ‹Inflation, Arbeitslosigkeit›; **he's been ~ing her off for years** er hat sie jahrelang immer wieder abgewiesen; ~ **your dog off!** halten Sie Ihren Hund zurück! ❷ *v.i.* (*restrain oneself*) ‹Käufer usw.:› sich zurückhalten; ‹Feind:› sich ruhig verhalten; (*be delayed*) ‹Regen, Monsun, Winter:› ausbleiben, auf sich (*Akk.*) warten lassen
~ **'on** ❶ *v.t.* (*keep in position*) [fest]halten. ❷ *v.i.* Ⓐ (*grip*) sich festhalten; ~ **on to sb./sth.** sich an jmdm./etw. festhalten; (*fig.: retain*) jmdn./etw. behalten; **the firm should make every effort to ~ on to him** die Firma sollte alles versuchen, ihn zu halten; Ⓑ (*continue*) andauern; weitergehen; Ⓒ (*stand firm*) durchhalten; aushalten; ‹Regierung:› sich halten; Ⓓ (*Teleph.*) am Apparat bleiben; dranbleiben (*ugs.*); Ⓔ (*coll.: wait*) warten; ~ **on!** einen Moment!; **just [you] ~ on now!** (*calm yourself*) nun mal ganz ruhig!; Moment mal!
~ **'out** ❶ *v.t.* Ⓐ (*stretch forth*) ausstrecken ‹Hand, Arm usw.›; ausbreiten ‹Arme›; hinhalten ‹Tasse, Teller›; Ⓑ (*fig.: offer*) in Aussicht stellen (**to** *Dat.*); **he did not ~ out much hope** er hat mir/dir *usw.* nicht viel Hoffnung gemacht. ❷ *v.i.* Ⓐ (*maintain resistance*) sich halten; Ⓑ (*last*) ‹Vorräte:› vorhalten; ‹Motor:› halten; durchhalten (*ugs.*); Ⓒ ~ **out for sth.** etw. herauszuschinden versuchen (*ugs.*); Ⓓ ~ **out [on sb.]** (*coll.: withhold knowledge*) [jmdm.] etwas verschweigen
~ **'over** *v.t.* vertagen (**till** auf + *Akk.*)
~ **to'gether** ❶ *v.t.* zusammenhalten. ❷ *v.i.* (*lit. or fig.*) zusammenhalten
~ **'under** *v.t.* unter Wasser drücken; (*fig.*) unterdrücken ‹Land, Volk, usw.›
~ **'up** ❶ *v.t.* Ⓐ (*raise*) hochhalten; hochheben ‹Person›; [hoch]heben ‹Hand, Kopf›; ~ **sth. up to the light** etw. ins Licht/(*to see through it*) gegen das Licht halten; ~ **up one's head** (*fig.*) seine Selbstachtung nicht verlieren; **he'd never be able to ~ his head up again** er könnte seine Selbstachtung niemals mehr wiedergewinnen; Ⓑ (*fig.: offer as an example*) ~ **sb. up as ...:** jmdn. als ... hinstellen; ~ **sb. up as an example** jmdn. als [leuchtendes] Vorbild hinstellen; ~ **sb./sth. up to ridicule/scorn** jmdn./etw. dem Spott/Hohn preisgeben; Ⓒ (*support*) stützen; tragen ‹Dach usw.›; (*fig.: give support to*) stützen ‹Regime›; ~ **sth. up with sth.** etw. mit etw. abstützen; Ⓓ (*delay*) aufhalten; behindern ‹Verkehr, Versorgung›; verzögern ‹Friedensvertrag›; (*halt*) ins Stocken bringen ‹Produktion›; Ⓔ (*rob*) überfallen [und ausrauben]. ⇒ *also* **~-up**. ❷ *v.i.* Ⓐ (*under scrutiny*) sich als stichhaltig erweisen; Ⓑ ‹Wetter:› schön bleiben, sich halten
~ **with** *v.t.* **~/not ~ with sth.** mit etw. einverstanden sein/etw. ablehnen

**holdall** /'həʊldɔːl/ *n.* Reisetasche, *die*

**holder** /'həʊldə(r)/ *n.* Ⓐ (*of post*) Inhaber, *der*/Inhaberin, *die;* Ⓑ (*of title*) Träger, *der*/Trägerin, *die;* Inhaber, *der*/Inhaberin, *die;* (*Sport*) Titelhalter, -inhaber, *der;* (*share~*) Aktionär, *der;* Aktieninhaber, *der;* **in the Cup Final, the ~s were beaten** im Pokalendspiel wurden die Pokalverteidiger geschlagen; Ⓒ ‹Zigaretten›spitze, *die;* ‹Schirm›ständer, *der;* ‹Papier-, Feder-, Zahnputzglas›halter, *der;* **flowerpot ~:** Übertopf, *der*

**holding** /'həʊldɪŋ/ *n.* Ⓐ (*tenure*) Land-, Grundbesitz, *der;* Ⓑ (*land held*) Gut, *das;* ⇒ *also* **smallholding**; Ⓒ (*property held*) Besitz, *der;* (*stocks or shares*) Anteil, *der*

**holding:** ~ **company** *n.* (*Commerc.*) Holding[gesellschaft], *die;* ~ **operation** *n.* Aktion zur Schadensbegrenzung

**'hold-up** *n.* Ⓐ (*robbery*) [Raub]überfall, *der;* Ⓑ (*stoppage*) Unterbrechung, *die;* (*delay*) Verzögerung, *die;* **run into a traffic ~:** in einen [Verkehrs]stau geraten; **there are ~s on the motorway** auf der Autobahn kommt es zu erheblichen Behinderungen

**hole** /həʊl/ ❶ *n.* Ⓐ Loch, *das;* **make a ~ in sth.** (*fig.*) eine ganze Menge von etw. verschlingen; **be a round/square peg in a square/round ~** (*fig.*) es nicht gut getroffen haben; **be in ~s** voller Löcher sein; **pick ~s in** Löcher machen in (+ *Akk.*) ‹Pullover usw.›; (*fig.: find fault with*) zerpflücken (*ugs.*); auseinander nehmen (*ugs.*); madig machen (*ugs.*) ‹Person›; **be full of ~s** (*fig.*) viele Schwächen haben; ~ **in the heart** Loch in der Herzscheidewand; Septumdefekt, *der* (*fachspr.*); **they need it like a ~ in the head** (*coll.*) das ist das Letzte, was sie gebrauchen können (*ugs.*); Ⓑ (*burrow*) (*of fox, badger, rabbit*) Bau, *der;* (*of mouse*) Loch, *das;* Ⓒ (*coll.*) (*dingy abode*) Loch, *das* (*salopp abwertend*); (*wretched place*) Kaff, *das* (*ugs. abwertend*); Nest, *das* (*ugs. abwertend*); Ⓓ (*coll.: awkward situation*) Klemme, *die* (*ugs.*); Patsche, *die* (*ugs.*); **be in a ~:** in der Klemme sein *od.* Patsche sitzen; Ⓔ (*Golf*) Loch, *das;* (*space between tee and ~*) [Spiel]bahn, *die;* (*point scored*) Loch, *das;* ~ **in one** Hole-in-One, *das;* Ass *das.* ⇒ *also* **burn**[1] 2 A.
❷ *v.t.* Ⓐ Löcher/ein Loch machen in (+ *Akk.*); **be ~d** Löcher/ein Loch haben; Ⓑ (*Naut.: pierce side of*) **be ~d** leckschlagen (*Seemannsspr.*); Ⓒ (*Golf*) ⇒ ~ **out**
~ **'out** *v.t.* (*Golf*) einlochen; *abs.* ~ **out in one** ein Hole-in-One *od.* As spielen
~ **'up** *v.i.* (*Amer. coll.*) sich verkriechen (*ugs.*)

**hole-and-'corner** *adj.* zwielichtig; anrüchig

**'hole-in-the-wall** *adj.* ~ **[cash] machine** Geldautomat, *der*

**holiday** /'hɒlɪdeɪ, 'hɒlɪdɪ/ ❶ *n.* Ⓐ (*day of recreation*) [arbeits]freier Tag; (*day of festivity*) Feiertag, *der;* **the whole country was given a ~:** das ganze Land bekam einen Tag [arbeits]frei; **tomorrow is a ~:** morgen ist frei/Feiertag; ⇒ *also* **bank holiday; national holiday; public holiday;** Ⓑ *in sing. or pl.* (*Brit.: vacation*) Urlaub, *der;* (*Sch.*) [Schul]ferien *Pl.;* **need a ~:** urlaubsreif sein; **have a good ~!** schönen Urlaub!; (*at Christmas etc.*) schöne Feiertage!; **go to Cornwall for one's ~[s]** im Urlaub/in den Ferien nach Cornwall fahren; in Cornwall urlauben (*ugs.*); **take** *or* **have a/one's ~:** Urlaub nehmen *od.* machen/seinen Urlaub nehmen; **on ~, on one's ~s** im *od.* in seinem Urlaub; **be [away] on ~** *or* **on one's ~s** in *od.* im *od.* auf Urlaub sein; **go on [a] ~** *or* **on one's ~s** (*leave work*) in Urlaub gehen; (*go away*) in Urlaub fahren; ⇒ *also* **busman.**
❷ *attrib. adj.* Urlaubs-/Ferien‹stimmung, -pläne›; Freizeit‹kleidung›.
❸ *v.i.* Urlaub/Ferien machen; urlauben (*ugs.*)

**holiday:** ~ **camp** *n.* Feriendorf, *das;* Ferienpark, *der;* ~ **home** *n.* Feriendomizil, *das;* ~ **job** *n.* Ferienjob, *der;* **~maker** *n.* Urlauber, *der*/Urlauberin, *die;* ~ **resort** *n.* Ferienort, *der;* ~ **season** *n.* Urlaubszeit, *die*

**holier-than-thou** /həʊlɪəðən'ðaʊ/ *adj.* (*coll.*) selbstgerecht

**holiness** /'həʊlɪnɪs/ *n.*, *no pl.* ▶ **1617** Heiligkeit, *die;* **His H~:** Seine Heiligkeit

**holism** /'hɒlɪzm, 'həʊlɪzm/ *n.*, *no pl.* (*Philos.*) Holismus, *der*

**holistic** /hɒ'lɪstɪk, həʊ'lɪstɪk/ *adj.* (*Philos.*) holistisch

**Holland** /'hɒlənd/ *pr. n.* Holland (*das*)

**hollandaise** /'hɒləndeɪz/ *n.* (*Gastr.*) ~ **[sauce]** holländische Soße; Sauce hollandaise, *die*

**holler** /'hɒlə(r)/ (*Amer.*) ❶ *v.i.* schreien; brüllen. ❷ *v.t.* schreien

**hollow** /'hɒləʊ/ ❶ *adj.* Ⓐ (*not solid*) hohl; Hohl‹ziegel, -mauer, -zylinder, -kugel›; **have ~ legs** (*joc.*) nicht satt zu kriegen sein (*ugs.*); Ⓑ (*sunken*) eingefallen ‹Wangen, Schläfen›; hohl, tief liegend ‹Augen›; nach innen gewölbt ‹Stück Blech usw.›; **a ~ place in the ground/road** *etc.* eine Vertiefung im Boden/in der Straße *usw.;* Ⓒ (*hungry*) **feel ~:** ein Loch im Bauch haben (*ugs.*); Ⓓ (*echoing*) hohl ‹Ton, Klang›; **speak with a ~ voice** mit Grabesstimme sprechen; Ⓔ (*fig.: empty*) wertlos; eitel (*geh.*) ‹Reichtum›; oberflächlich ‹Person›; Ⓕ (*fig.: cynical*) verlogen; leer ‹Versprechen›; gequält ‹Lachen›.
❷ *n.* [Boden]senke, *die;* [Boden]vertiefung, *die;* (*area below general level*) Niederung, *die;* **hold sth. in the ~ of one's hand** etw. in der hohlen Hand halten.
❸ *adv.* **beat sb. ~** (*coll.*) jmdn. um Längen schlagen (*ugs.*).
❹ *v.t.* ~ **out** aushöhlen; graben ‹Höhle›; bohren, graben ‹Tunnel›

**'hollow-eyed** *adj.* hohläugig

**hollowly** /'hɒləʊlɪ/ *adv.* hohl ‹widerhallen›

**hollowness** /'hɒləʊnɪs/ *n.* *no pl.* Ⓐ Hohlheit, *die;* Ⓑ (*of voice*) Hohlheit, *die;* Ⓒ (*fig.*) (*emptiness*) Hohlheit, *die;* (*falseness*) Verlogenheit, *die*

**'hollowware** *n.*, *no pl.* Geschirr, *das;* Gefäße *Pl.*

**holly** /'hɒlɪ/ *n.* Ⓐ (*tree*) Stechpalme, *die;* Ilex, *der* (*fachspr.*); Ⓑ (*foliage*) Stechpalmenzweige *Pl.*

**'hollyhock** *n.* (*Bot.*) Stockrose, *die*

**holm**[1] /həʊm/ *n.* (*Brit.*) (*islet*) kleine Insel; Holm, *der* (*nordd.*); (*in a river*) Werder, *der*

**holm**[2] *n.* ~ **[oak]** (*Bot.*) Steineiche, *die*

**holocaust** /'hɒləkɔːst/ *n.* (*destruction*) Massenvernichtung, *die;* **the H~:** der Holocaust; die Judenvernichtung; **nuclear ~:** atomarer Holocaust

**Holocene** /'hɒləsiːn/ *n.* (*Geol.*) Holozän, *das*

**hologram** /'hɒləgræm/ *n.* Hologramm, *das*

**holography** /hɒ'lɒgrəfɪ/ *n.*, *no pl.*, *no art.* Holographie, *die*

**hols** /hɒlz/ *n. pl.* (*Brit. coll.*) Ferien *Pl.*

**holster** /'həʊlstə(r)/ *n.* [Pistolen]halfter, *die od. das*

**holy** /'həʊlɪ/ *adj.* heilig; fromm ‹Zweck›; ~ **saints** Heilige; ~ **smoke** *or* **cow!** (*coll.*) heiliger Bimbam (*ugs.*) *od.* (*salopp*) Strohsack!

**holy: H~ 'Bible** *n.* Heilige Schrift; **H~ 'City** *n.* Heilige Stadt; **H~ Com'munion** ⇒ **communion** A; ~ **'cross** *n.* Kreuz Christi, *das;* **the sign of the ~ cross** das Kreuzzeichen; ~ **day** *n.* religiöser Feiertag; **H~ 'Family** *n.* Heilige Familie; **H~ 'Father** ⇒ **father** 1 F; **H~ 'Ghost** ⇒ **H~ Spirit**; **H~ Grail** ⇒ **Grail**; ~ **'Joe** *n.* (*coll. derog.*) Pfaffe, *der* (*abwertend*); **H~ Land** *n.* Ⓐ **the H~ Land** das Heilige Land; Ⓑ (*revered land*) geheiligtes *od.* heiliges Land; ~ **of 'holies** *n.* (*inner chamber, fig.: sacred place*) Allerheiligste, *das;* ~ **'orders** ⇒ **order** 1 H; ~ **place** *n.* Ⓐ Heilige, *das;* Ⓑ *in pl.* (*places of pilgrimage*) heilige Stätten *Pl.;* **H~ Roman 'Empire** ⇒ **Roman Empire**; **H~ 'Sacrament** ⇒ **sacrament** A; **H~ 'Saturday** *n.* Karsamstag, *der;* **H~ 'Scripture** ⇒ **scripture**; **H~ 'See** ⇒ **see**[2]; **H~ 'Spirit** *n.* (*Relig.*) Heiliger Geist; ~ **'terror** ⇒ **terror** C; **H~ 'Trinity** ⇒ **Trinity** A; ~ **'war** *n.* heiliger Krieg; ~ **'water** *n.* (*Eccl.*) Weihwasser, *das;* **H~ Week** *n.* Karwoche, *die*

**homage** /'hɒmɪdʒ/ *n.* (*tribute*) Huldigung, *die* (**to** an + *Akk.*); **pay** *or* **do ~ to sb./sth.** jmdm./einer Sache huldigen

**Homburg** /'hɒmbɜːg/ *n.* ~ **[hat]** Homburg, *der*

**home** /həʊm/ ❶ *n.* Ⓐ (*place of residence*) Heim, *das;* (*flat*) Wohnung, *die;* (*house*) Haus, *das;* (*household*) [Eltern]haus, *das;* **my ~ is in Leeds** ich bin in Leeds zu Hause *od.* wohne in Leeds; **a ~ of one's own** ein eigenes Zuhause; **give sb./an animal a ~:** jmdm./einem Tier ein Zuhause geben; **work/be away from ~:** auswärts arbeiten/nicht zu Hause sein; **leave/have left ~:** aus dem Haus gehen/sein; **have a good ~:** ein gutes Zuhause haben; **live at ~:** im Elternhaus wohnen; **they had no ~/~s [of their own]** sie hatten kein Zuhause; **safety in the ~:** Sicherheit im Haus[halt]; **make one's ~ in the country/abroad** aufs Land ziehen/

h

ins Ausland gehen; **at ~:** zu Hause; (*not abroad*) im Inland; **be at ~ [to sb.]** (*be available to caller*) [für jmdn.] zu sprechen sein *od.* da sein; (*Sport: play on one's own ground*) auf eigenem Platz *od.* zu Hause [gegen jmdn.] spielen; **who/what is X when he's/it's at ~?** (*joc.*) wer/was ist das denn?; **is our next match at ~ or away?** ist unser nächstes Spiel ein Heimspiel oder ein Auswärtsspiel?; **be/feel at ~** (*fig.*) sich wohl fühlen; **make sb. feel at ~:** es jmdm. behaglich machen; **make yourself at ~:** fühl dich wie zu Hause; **he is quite at ~ in French** er ist im Französischen ganz gut zu Hause; ⇒ *also* D; **at-~; there's no place like ~** (*prov.*) es geht [doch] nichts über das eigene Zuhause; **~ from ~:** zweites Zuhause; **B** (*fig.*) **this was something very near ~:** das war etwas, das einen sehr direkt betraf; **to take an example nearer ~, ...:** um ein Beispiel zu nehmen, das uns näher liegt, ...; ⇒ *also* **from** D; **second ~**; **C** (*Amer., Austral., NZ: dwelling house*) Haus, *das;* **D** (*native country*) die Heimat; **at ~:** zu Hause; in der Heimat; ⇒ *also* A; **E** (*place where thing is native*) Heimat, *die;* **F** (*institution*) Heim, *das;* (*coll.: mental home*) Anstalt, *die* (*salopp*); **you ought to be in a ~:** du gehörst in die Klapsmühle; ⇒ *also* **mental ~**; **nursing ~**; **G** *no art.* (*Games: safe place*) das Mal; (*in Ludo etc.*) das Haus; (*finishing point*) das Ziel; **H** (*Sport: home win*) Heimsieg, *der.* ❷ *adj.* **A** (*connected with home*) Haus-; Haushalts‹gerät usw.›; **she enjoyed her ~ life** sie genoss das Zuhausesein; **B** (*done at home*) häuslich; Selbst‹backen, -brauen usw.›; **C** (*in the neighbourhood of home*) nahe gelegen; **D** (*Sport*) Heim‹spiel, -sieg, -mannschaft›; ‹Anhänger, Spieler› der Heimmannschaft; **~ ground** eigener Platz; **E** (*not foreign*) [ein]heimisch; inländisch; ⇒ *also* **trade.**
❸ *adv.* **A** (*to home*) nach Hause; **find one's way ~:** nach Hause finden; **on one's way ~:** auf dem Weg nach Hause *od.* Nachhauseweg; **get ~:** nach Hause kommen; (*to the finishing point*) das Ziel erreichen; **get ~ by inches** um eine Nasenlänge gewinnen; **Pierre is going ~ to France tomorrow** Pierre fährt morgen nach Frankreich zurück; **be going ~** (*fig.: be becoming unserviceable*) den Geist aufgeben (*ugs.*); **he takes ~ £200 a week after tax** er verdient 200 Pfund netto in der Woche; **nothing to write ~ about** (*coll.*) nichts Besonderes *od.* Aufregendes; **B** (*arrived at home*) zu Hause; **the first competitor ~ was Paul** als erster [Teilnehmer] traf Paul am Ziel ein *od.* ging Paul durchs Ziel; **be ~ and dry** (*fig.*) aus dem Schneider sein (*ugs.*); **C** (*Amer.: at home*) zu Hause; **D** (*to the point aimed at*) **go ~** ‹Schlag usw.:› sitzen (*ugs.*); ‹Schuss:› treffen; (*fig.*) ‹Bemerkungen usw.:› ins Schwarze treffen, (*ugs.*) sitzen; **E** (*as far as possible*) **push ~:** [ganz] hineinschieben ‹Schublade›; forcieren ‹Angriff›; ausnutzen ‹Vorteil›; **press ~:** [ganz] hinunterdrücken ‹Hebel›; forcieren ‹Angriff›; [voll] ausnutzen ‹Vorteil›; **drive ~:** [ganz] einschlagen ‹Nagel›; **F come** *or* **get ~ to sb.** (*become fully realized*) jmdm. in vollem Ausmaß bewusst werden; **bring sth. ~ to sb.** jmdm. etw. klarmachen *od.* vor Augen führen; ⇒ *also* **roost** 1.
❹ *v.i.* **A** ‹Vogel usw.:› zurückkehren; **B** (*be guided*) **these missiles ~ [in] on their targets** diese Flugkörper suchen sich (*Dat.*) ihr Ziel; **C ~ in on sth.** (*fig.*) etw. herausgreifen

**home: ~ address** *n.* Privatanschrift, *die;* **~ 'banking** *n.* Homebanking, *das;* **~-based** /'həʊmbeɪst/ *adj.* zu Hause arbeitend; **be ~-based** zu Hause arbeiten; seinen Arbeitsplatz zu Hause haben; **~ bird** *n.* häuslicher Mensch; **~ brew** *n.* selbst gebrautes Bier; **~-brewed** /'həʊmbru:d/ *adj.* selbst gebraut; **~ 'comforts** *n. pl.* häuslicher Komfort; **~coming** *n.* Heimkehr, *die;* **~ com'puter** *n.* Heimcomputer, *der;* **H~ Counties** *n. pl.* (*Brit.*) **the Home Counties** die Home Countys; *die Grafschaften um London;* **~ eco'nomics** *n. sing.* ⇒ **domestic science**; **~ farm** *n.* (*Brit.*) Herrenhof, *der;* **~ 'ground** *n.* **on [one's] ~ ground** auf heimischem Boden; (*fig.*) zu Hause (*ugs.*); **~-grown** *adj.* selbst gezogen ‹Gemüse, Obst›; **H~ 'Guard** *n.* (*Brit. Hist.*) **A** (*army*) Bürgerwehr, *die;* **B** (*person*) Mitglied der Bürgerwehr; **~ 'help** (*Brit.*) ⇒ **help** 2 B; **~land** *n.* **A** (*native land*) Heimat, *die;* Heimatland, *das;* **B** (*in South Africa*) Homeland, *das;* **~ leave** *n.* Heimaturlaub, *der*

**homeless** /'həʊmlɪs/ ❶ *adj.* obdachlos. ❷ *n.* **the ~:** die Obdachlosen

**homelessness** /'həʊmlɪsnɪs/ *n.* Obdachlosigkeit, *die*

**'homelike** *adj.* wohnlich

**'home-loving** *adj.* häuslich

**homely** /'həʊmlɪ/ *adj.* **A** (*unpretentious, simple*) einfach, schlicht ‹Worte, Stil, Sprache usw.›; warmherzig ‹Person›; bescheiden ‹kleines Haus›; **B** (*Amer.: not attractive*) nicht sehr attraktiv; wenig attraktiv

**home: ~-made** *adj.* selbst gemacht; selbst gebacken ‹Brot›; hausgemacht ‹Lebensmittel›; **~maker** *n.* Hausfrau, *die;* (*man*) Hausmann, *der;* **~ 'movie** *n.* Amateurfilm, *der;* **H~ Office** *n.* (*Brit.*) Innenministerium, *das*

**homeopathic** *etc.* (*Amer.*) ⇒ **homoeo-**

**home: ~owner** *n.* Eigenheimbesitzer, *der*/-besitzerin, *die;* **~ page** *n.* (*Computing*) Homepage *die;* **~ 'perm** *n.* selbst gemachte Dauerwelle; **~ 'plate** ⇒ **plate** 1 L; **~ 'port** *n.* Heimathafen, *der*

**Homer** *pr. n.* Homer (*der*)

**Homeric** /hə'merɪk, həʊ'merɪk/ *adj.* homerisch

**home: ~ 'rule** *n.* Autonomie, *die;* Selbstbestimmung, *die;* **~ 'run** *n.* (*Baseball*) Homerun, *der;* **H~ 'Secretary** *n.* (*Brit.*) Innenminister, *der;* **~ 'shopping** *n.* Teleshopping, *das;* **~sick** *adj.* heimwehkrank; **become/be ~sick** Heimweh bekommen/haben; **~sickness** *n., no pl.* Heimweh, *das;* **~spun** *adj.* **A** (*spun [and woven] at ~*) selbst gesponnen [und gewoben]; (*of ~ manufacture*) in Heimarbeit gesponnen; **B** (*unsophisticated*) schlicht; einfach; **~spun philosophy** Lebensweisheiten; **~stead** *n.* **A** (*house with land*) Anwesen, *das;* (*farm*) Gehöft, *das;* **B** (*Austral., NZ: residence*) Herrenhaus, *das;* **C** (*Amer.: area of land*) Parzelle, *die;* ≈ Heimstätte, *die;* **~ 'straight** (*Amer.:* **~ 'stretch**) *n.* (*lit. or fig.*) Zielgerade, *die;* **~ 'town** *n.* Heimatstadt, *die;* Vaterstadt, *die* (*geh.*); (*town of residence*) Wohnort, *der;* **~ 'truth** *n.* unangenehme Wahrheit; **tell** *or* **give sb. a few ~ truths** jmdm. [gehörig] die Meinung sagen; **now you're going to listen to a few ~ truths** jetzt hörst du mir mal zu!

**homeward** /'həʊmwəd/ ❶ *adj.* nach Hause *nachgestellt;* Nachhause‹weg›; (*return*) Rück‹fahrt, -reise, -weg›; ⇒ *also* **bound**³. ❷ *adv.* nach Hause; heimwärts

**homewards** /'həʊmwədz/ ⇒ **homeward** 2

**'homework** *n.* (*Sch.*) Hausaufgabe, *die;* **Latin ~:** Hausaufgaben in Latein; **be given ~:** Hausaufgaben aufbekommen *od.* aufhaben; **give/set sb. too much ~:** jmdm. zu viel [Hausaufgaben] aufgeben; **for ~:** als Hausaufgabe; **do one's ~** (*fig.*) sich mit der Materie vertraut machen; seine Hausaufgaben machen (*scherzh.*)

**homicidal** /hɒmɪ'saɪdl/ *adj.* gemeingefährlich; **~ tendency** Drang zum Töten

**homicide** /'hɒmɪsaɪd/ *n.* **A** (*act*) Tötung, *die;* (*manslaughter*) Totschlag, *der;* **B** (*person*) *jemand, der einen Menschen getötet hat*

**homily** /'hɒmɪlɪ/ *n.* **A** (*sermon*) Homilie, *die* (*Theol.*); **B** (*tedious discourse*) Moralpredigt, *die;* Predigt, *die* (*ugs.*); **give sb. a ~:** jmdm. eine [Moral]predigt halten

**homing** /'həʊmɪŋ/ *attrib. adj.* zielsuchend ‹Flugkörper, Torpedo›; Zielsuch‹einrichtung, -kopf›; **~ instinct/sense** Heimfindevermögen, *das*

**'homing pigeon** *n.* Brieftaube, *die*

**hominid** /'hɒmɪnɪd/ (*Zool.*) ❶ *adj.* zu den Hominiden gehörend. ❷ *n.* Hominide, *der*

**homo** /'həʊməʊ/ (*coll.*) ❶ *adj.* homosexuell; homo *nicht attr.* (*ugs.*). ❷ *n., pl.* **~s** Homo, *der* (*ugs.*)

**homo-** /həʊməʊ, hɒməʊ/ *in comb.* homo-/Homo-

**homoeopathic** /həʊmɪə'pæθɪk, hɒmɪə'pæθɪk/ *adj.* homöopathisch

**homoeopathy** /həʊmɪ'ɒpəθɪ, hɒmɪ'ɒpəθɪ/ *n.* Homöopathie, *die*

**homogeneity** /hɒmədʒɪ'ni:ɪtɪ, həʊmədʒɪ'ni:ɪtɪ/ *n., no pl.* Homogenität, *die*

**homogeneous** /hɒmə'dʒi:nɪəs, həʊmə'dʒi:nɪəs/ *adj.* homogen

**homogenisation, homogenise, homogeniser** ⇒ **homogeniz-**

**homogenization** /həmɒdʒɪnaɪ'zeɪʃn/ *n.* Homogenisierung, *die*

**homogenize** /hə'mɒdʒɪnaɪz/ *v.t.* (*lit. or fig.*) homogenisieren

**homogenizer** /hə'mɒdʒɪnaɪzə(r)/ *n.* Homogenisator, *der*

**'homograph** *n.* (*Ling.*) Homograph, *das*

**homologous** /hə'mɒləgəs/ *adj.* homolog

**homonym** /'hɒmənɪm/ *n.* (*Ling.*) Homonym, *das*

**homonymous** /hə'mɒnɪməs/ *adj.* homonym

**'homophone** *n.* (*Ling.*) Homophon, *das*

**Homo sapiens** /hɒməʊ 'sæpɪenz/ *n., no pl.* Homo sapiens, *der*

**homo'sexual** ❶ *adj.* homosexuell. ❷ *n.* Homosexuelle, *der/die;* **he is a ~:** er ist homosexuell

**homosexu'ality** *n.* Homosexualität, *die*

**homy** /'həʊmɪ/ *adj.* wohnlich; heimelig (*veralt.*) ‹Zimmer, Haus›; vertraut ‹Anblick›

**Hon.** /ɒn/ *abbr.* **A Honorary; B** ▶ **1617** **Honourable**

**honcho** /'hɒntʃəʊ/ *n.* (*Amer. coll.*) Boss, *der* (*ugs.*)

**Honduran** /hɒn'djʊərən/ ▶ **1340** ❶ *adj.* honduranisch; **sb. is ~:** jmd. ist Honduraner/Honduranerin. ❷ *n.* Honduraner, *der*/Honduranerin, *die*

**Honduras** /hɒn'djʊərəs/ *pr. n.* Honduras (*das*)

**hone** /həʊn/ ❶ *n.* Wetzstein, *der.* ❷ *v.t.* wetzen ‹Messer, Klinge usw.›; **~ a razor to a sharp edge** ein Rasiermesser wetzen, bis die Schneide scharf ist

**honest** /'ɒnɪst/ *adj.* **A** (*acting fairly*) ehrlich; **~ broker** ehrlicher Makler; **B** (*sincere*) ehrlich; **the ~ truth** die reine Wahrheit; **to be ~ [with you]** offen *od.* ehrlich gesagt; **C** (*showing righteousness*) redlich; ehrenhaft ‹Absicht, Tat, Plan›; ehrlich ‹Arbeit›; **D** (*blameless*) rechtschaffen; **he made an ~ woman of her** (*joc.*) er heiratete sie; **E** (*got by fair means*) ehrlich erworben ‹Besitz›; ehrlich verdient ‹Geld›; ehrlich erwirtschaftet ‹Gewinn›; **make an ~ living** sein Leben auf ehrliche Weise verdienen; **earn** *or* **turn an ~ penny** sich (*Dat.*) sein Brot ehrlich verdienen; **F** (*unsophisticated*) [gut und] einfach; (*unadulterated*) rein; **~ bread** gutes, einfaches Brot; **G ~ [to God], ~ to goodness!** (*coll.*) ehrlich! (*ugs.*); ⇒ *also* **honest-to-God**

**honestly** /'ɒnɪstlɪ/ *adv.* **A** (*fairly*) ehrlich; redlich ‹handeln›; **B** (*frankly*) ehrlich; offen; **C** (*genuinely, really*) ehrlich (*ugs.*); wirklich; **~!** ehrlich!; (*annoyed*) also wirklich!

**honest: ~-to-God, ~-to-goodness** *adjs.* echt

**honesty** /'ɒnɪstɪ/ *n.* **A** (*truthfulness*) Ehrlichkeit, *die;* Aufrichtigkeit, *die;* **in all ~:** ganz ehrlich; **in all ~, I have to admit ...:** ich muss ehrlicherweise zugeben ...; **B** (*upright conduct*) Redlichkeit, *die;* Anständigkeit, *die;* **~ is the best policy** (*prov.*) ehrlich währt am längsten (*Spr.*); **C** (*Bot.*) Silberblatt, *das*

**honey** /'hʌnɪ/ *n.* **A** Honig, *der;* **B** (*colour*) Honiggelb, *das;* **C** (*fig.: sweetness*) Lieblichkeit, *die;* **D sb. is a [real] ~:** jmd. ist ein Schatz (*ugs.*); **E** (*Amer., Ir.: darling*) Schatz, *der* (*ugs.*)

**honey: ~ bee** *n.* Honigbiene, *die;* **~ blonde** *adj.* honigblond; **~-coloured** *adj.* honigfarben; **~comb** *n.* Bienenwabe, *die;* (*filled with honey*) Honigwabe, *die;* **~combed** /'hʌnɪkəʊmd/ *adj.* (*with cavities*) wabenartig durchsetzt *od.* durchzogen; **~dew** *n.* (*lit. or* *fig.*) Honigtau, *der;* **~dew [melon]** Honigmelone, *die*

**honeyed** /ˈhʌnɪd/ *adj.* honigsüß ‹Worte›

**honey: ~moon** ❶ *n.* Ⓐ Flitterwochen *Pl.;* Honigmond, *der* (*scherzh.*); (*journey*) Hochzeitsreise, *die;* **where did you go for your ~moon?** wohin habt ihr eure Hochzeitsreise gemacht?; **be a ~moon couple** sich auf der Hochzeitsreise befinden; Ⓑ (*fig.: initial period*) anfängliche Begeisterung; **the ~moon period** die Phase der Begeisterung; ❷ *v.i.* seine Flitterwochen verbringen; flittern (*ugs. scherzh.*); **~pot** *n.* Honigtopf, *der;* **~suckle** *n.* (*Bot.*) Geißblatt, *das;* **~-sweet** *adj.* honigsüß

**honk** /hɒŋk/ ❶ *n.* Ⓐ (*of horn*) Hupen, *das;* **I gave him a ~ [on my horn]** ich hupte ihn an; **~s** Hupsignale; Ⓑ (*of goose or seal*) Schrei, *der.* ❷ *v.i.* Ⓐ ‹Fahrzeug, Fahrer:› hupen; Ⓑ ‹Gans, Seehund:› schreien. ❸ *v.t.* **~ one's horn** ⇒ **horn** 1 D

**honky-tonk** /ˈhɒŋkɪtɒŋk/ *n.* (*coll.*) Ⓐ (*nightclub*) Schuppen, *der* (*ugs.*); Ⓑ (*music*) Ragtime, *der*

**honor, honorable, honorably** (*Amer.*) ⇒ **honour** *etc.*

**honorarium** /ɒnəˈreərɪəm/ *n., pl.* **~s** *or* **honoraria** /ɒnəˈreərɪə/ Honorar, *das*

**honorary** /ˈɒnərərɪ/ *adj.* Ⓐ ehrenamtlich; Ehren‹mitglied, -präsident, -doktor, -bürger›; Ⓑ (*conferred as an honour*) Ehren-; **~ degree** ehrenhalber verliehener akademischer Grad; **the position is an ~ one** der Posten ist ehrenamtlich

**honour** /ˈɒnə(r)/ (*Brit.*) ❶ *n.* Ⓐ *no indef. art.* (*reputation*) Ehre, *die;* **win/achieve ~:** zu Ehren kommen; **to his ~, he refused** es ehrt ihn, dass er abgelehnt hat; **do ~ to sb./sth.** jmdm./einer Sache zur Ehre gereichen (*geh.*); jmdm./einer Sache Ehre machen; Ⓑ (*respect*) Hochachtung, *die;* **he was treated with** *or* **shown ~:** ihm wurde große Achtung entgegengebracht; **hold sb./sth. in ~:** jmdn./etw. achten; **do sb. ~, do ~ to sb.** jmdm. Ehre erweisen; (*show appreciation of*) jmdn. würdigen; **do ~ to sth.** etw. würdigen; **in ~ of sb.** jmdm. zu Ehren; **in ~ of sth.** um etw. gebührend zu feiern; Ⓒ (*privilege*) Ehre, *die;* **have the ~ to do** *or* **of doing sth.** die Ehre haben, etw. zu tun; **may I have the ~ [of the next dance]?** darf ich [um den nächsten Tanz] bitten?; **do sb. an ~:** jmdm. eine Ehre erweisen; **you do me too great an ~:** Sie tun mir zu viel Ehre an; **do sb. the ~ of doing sth.** jmdm. die Ehre erweisen, etw. zu tun; Ⓓ *no art.* (*ethical quality*) Ehre, *die;* **he is a man of ~** *or* **with a sense of ~:** er ist ein Ehrenmann *od.* Mann von Ehre; **feel [in] ~ bound to do sth.** sich moralisch verpflichtet fühlen, etw. zu tun; **promise [up]on one's ~:** sein Ehrenwort geben; **be on one's ~:** sein Ehrenwort gegeben haben; **[up]on my ~!** Ehrenwort!; bei meiner Ehre! (*geh.*); **the prisoner was put [up]on his ~ not to escape** der Gefangene musste sich auf Ehrenwort verpflichten, nicht zu fliehen; **~ bright** (*coll.*) großes Ehrenwort! (*ugs.*); **[there is] ~ among thieves** [es gibt so etwas wie] Ganovenehre; Ⓔ (*chastity*) Ehre, *die* (*veralt.*); Ⓕ (*distinction*) Auszeichnung, *die;* (*title*) Ehrentitel, *der;* ⇒ *also* **birthday; new year;** Ⓖ *in pl.* (*recognition*) Auszeichnungen; Ⓗ *in pl.* (*Univ.*) **she gained ~s in her exam, she passed [the exam] with ~s** sie hat das Examen mit Auszeichnung bestanden; Ⓘ *in pl.* **do the ~s** (*coll.*) (*introduce guests*) die Honneurs machen; (*serve guests*) den Gastgeber spielen; Ⓙ (*ceremony*) **funeral** *or* **last ~s** Trauerfeierlichkeiten *Pl.;* **pay the last ~s to sb.** jmdm. die letzte Ehre erweisen (*geh.*); **military ~s** militärische Ehren; Ⓚ *in title* **your H~** (*Brit. Law*) hohes Gericht; Euer Ehren; Ⓛ (*person or thing that brings credit*) **be an ~ to sb./sth.** jmdm./einer Sache Ehre machen; Ⓜ (*Cards*) Honneur, *das;* **~s are even** es gibt keinen Verlierer. ⇒ *also* **affair** F; **code** 1 A; **companion**[1] C; **debt; guard** 1 B; **guest; legion** C; **maid of honour; matron** B; **point** 1 C; **word** 1 C.

❷ *v.t.* Ⓐ ehren; würdigen ‹Verdienste, besondere Eigenschaften›; **be ~ed as an artist** als Künstler Anerkennung finden; **~ your father and your mother** du sollst Vater und Mutter ehren; **be ~ed with a knighthood** in den Ritterstand erhoben werden; **~ sb. with one's presence** (*iron.*) jmdn. mit seiner Gegenwart beehren; Ⓑ (*acknowledge*) beachten ‹Vorschriften›; respektieren ‹Gebräuche, Rechte›; Ⓒ (*fulfil*) sich halten an (+ *Akk.*); (*Commerc.*) honorieren; begleichen ‹Rechnung, Schuld›

**honourable** /ˈɒnərəbl/ *adj.* (*Brit.*) Ⓐ (*worthy of respect*) ehrenwert (*geh.*); ehrbar (*geh.*); Ⓑ (*bringing credit*) achtbar; (*consistent with honour*) ehrenvoll ‹Frieden, Rückzug, Entlassung›; Ⓒ (*ethical*) rechtschaffen; redlich ‹Geschäftsgebaren›; **sb.'s intentions are ~:** jmd. hat ehrliche Absichten; Ⓓ ▶ **1617** *in title* **the H~ ...** ≈ der/die ehrenwerte ...; **the ~ gentleman/lady, the ~ member [for X]** (*Brit. Parl.*) der Herr/die Frau Abgeordnete [für den Wahlkreis X]; ≈ der [verehrte] Herr Kollege/die [verehrte] Frau Kollegin; **the Most H~ ...** (*Brit.*) ≈ der/die höchst ehrenwerte ...; **the Right H~ ...** (*Brit.*) ≈ der/die sehr ehrenwerte ... ⇒ *also* **mention** 1 B

**honourably** /ˈɒnərəblɪ/ *adv.* (*Brit.*) Ⓐ (*with credit*) ehrenvoll; Ⓑ (*ethically*) ehrenhaft ‹handeln›

**honours: ~ degree** *n.* Examen mit Auszeichnung; **~ list** *n.* Ⓐ (*Univ.*) *Liste der Kandidaten, die das Examen mit Auszeichnung bestanden haben;* Ⓑ (*of sovereign*) *Liste der Titel- und Rangverleihungen*

**Hon. Sec.** /ɒn ˈsek/ *abbr.* **Honorary Secretary**

**hooch** /huːtʃ/ *n.* (*Amer. coll.*) [schwarz gebrannter] Schnaps; Fusel, *der* (*ugs. abwertend*)

**hood**[1] /hʊd/ *n.* Ⓐ Kapuze, *die;* Ⓑ (*of vehicle*) (*Brit.: waterproof top*) Verdeck, *das;* (*Amer.: bonnet*) [Motor]haube, *die;* (*of pram*) Verdeck, *das;* **drive with the ~ down** mit offenem Verdeck fahren; Ⓒ (*over hearth*) [Rauch]abzug, *der;* (*over stove*) Abzugshaube, *die*

**hood**[2] /hʊd, huːd/ *n.* (*coll.: gangster*) Gangster, *der*

**hooded** /ˈhʊdɪd/ *adj.* (*wearing hood*) mit einer Kapuze bekleidet; (*with hood attached*) ‹Mantel usw.› mit Kapuze; **a ~ figure** eine Gestalt mit [einer] Kapuze

**hooded ˈcrow** *n.* (*Ornith.*) Nebelkrähe, *die*

**hoodlum** /ˈhuːdləm/ *n.* Ⓐ (*young thug*) Rowdy, *der* (*abwertend*); Ⓑ (*Amer.: gangster*) ⇒ **hood**[2]

**hoodoo** /ˈhuːduː/ *n.* Ⓐ (*bad spell*) Fluch, *der;* **there is a ~ on that house** es liegt ein Fluch über diesem Haus; **put a ~ on sb.** ‹Hexe:› jmdn. verwünschen; Ⓑ (*bringer of bad luck*) **be a ~:** Unglück bringen

**hoodwink** /ˈhʊdwɪŋk/ *v.t.* hinters Licht führen; täuschen

**hooey** /ˈhuːɪ/ (*coll.*) ❶ *n.* Quatsch, *der* (*ugs.*); Blödsinn, *der* (*ugs.*). ❷ *int.* Quatsch [mit Soße]! (*ugs.*)

**hoof** /huːf/ ❶ *n., pl.* **~s** *or* **hooves** /huːvz/ Ⓐ Huf, *der;* (*coll. derog.: human foot*) Pedal, *das* (*ugs. scherzh.*); Ⓑ **buy cattle on the ~** (*for meat*) Lebendvieh kaufen; **on the ~** (*fig.*) auf der Stelle. ⇒ *also* **cloven** 2. ❷ *v.t.* (*coll.*) Ⓐ (*kick*) **he ~ed him out of** *or* **through the door** er gab ihm einen Tritt, dass er durch die Tür flog; **get ~ed out of the army** (*fig.*) aus der Armee fliegen (*ugs.*); Ⓑ (*walk*) **~ it** tippeln (*ugs.*)

**ˈhoofbeat** *n.* Hufschlag, *der*

**hoo-ha** /ˈhuːhɑː/ *n.* (*coll.*) Wirbel, *der;* **make a [lot of** *or* **big] ~ [about sth.]** [viel] Wind [um etw.] machen (*ugs.*)

**hook** /hʊk/ ❶ *n.* Ⓐ Haken, *der;* (*Fishing*) [Angel]haken, *der;* **~ and eye** Haken und Öse; **swallow sth. ~, line, and sinker** (*fig.*) etw. blind glauben; **they fell for it ~, line, and sinker** (*fig.*) sie sind voll und ganz darauf hereingefallen; **get sb. off the ~** (*fig. coll.*) jmdn. herauspauken (*ugs.*); **get oneself off the ~** (*fig. coll.*) den Kopf aus der Schlinge ziehen; **that lets me/him off the ~** (*fig. coll.*) da bin ich/ist er noch einmal davongekommen; **by ~ or by crook** mit allen Mitteln; Ⓑ (*telephone cradle*) Gabel, *die;* **the telephone was off the ~:** das Telefon war ausgehängt; Ⓒ (*Agric.*) (*for cutting grass or grain*) Sense, *die;* (*for cutting and lopping*) Hippe, *die;* Ⓓ (*Boxing*) Haken, *der;* Ⓔ (*Baseball, Bowling, Cricket, Golf*) Hook, *der;* Ⓕ (*Geog., Geol.*) (*in river*) [scharfe] Krümmung; (*sand spit*) spitz zulaufende Sandbank; (*projecting land*) gekrümmte Landzunge; **the H~** (*coll.*) ⇒ **Hook of Holland;** Ⓖ (*Mus.*) [Noten]fähnchen, *das.*

❷ *v.t.* Ⓐ (*grasp*) mit Haken/mit einem Haken greifen; Ⓑ (*fasten*) mit Haken/mit einem Haken befestigen (**to** an + *Dat.*); festhaken ‹Tor› (**to** an + *Akk.*); haken ‹Bein, Finger› (**over** über + *Akk.*, **in** in + *Akk.*); **~ a caravan to a car** einen Wohnwagen an ein Auto hängen; Ⓒ **be ~ed [on sth./sb.]** (*coll.*) (*addicted harmfully*) [von etw./jmdm.] abhängig sein; (*addicted harmlessly*) [auf etw./jmdn.] stehen (*ugs., bes. Jugendspr.*); (*captivated*) [von etw./jmdm.] fasziniert sein; **be ~ed on heroin/drugs** heroin-/drogenabhängig sein; Ⓓ (*catch*) an die Angel bekommen ‹Fisch›; (*fig.*) sich (*Dat.*) angeln; Ⓔ **~ it** (*sl.: leave*) abhauen (*salopp*); Ⓕ (*Boxing*) einen Haken versetzen *od.* geben (+ *Dat.*); Ⓖ (*Rugby*) hakeln; (*Golf*) ‹Rechtshänder:› einen Linksdrall geben (+ *Dat.*), nach links verziehen ‹Ball›; ‹Linkshänder:› einen Rechtsdrall geben (+ *Dat.*), nach rechts verziehen ‹Ball›; (*Cricket*) *mit waagerechtem Schläger in Schulterhöhe hinter sich schlagen* ‹Ball›

**~ ˈon** ❶ *v.t.* anhaken (**to** an + *Akk.*); anhängen ‹Wagen, Anhänger, Schiff› (**to** an + *Akk.*). ❷ *v.i.* angehakt werden (**to** an + *Akk.*)

**~ ˈup** ❶ *v.t.* Ⓐ festhaken (**to** an + *Akk.*); zuhaken ‹Kleid›; Ⓑ (*Radio and Telev. coll.*) zusammenschalten ‹Sender›; ⇒ *also* **hook-up.** ❷ *v.i.* ‹Kleid:› mit Haken geschlossen werden

**hookah** /ˈhʊkə/ *n.* Huka, *die;* [indische] Wasserpfeife

**hooked** /hʊkt/ *adj.* Ⓐ (*hook-shaped*) hakenförmig; **~ nose** Hakennase, *die;* Ⓑ (*having hook[s]*) mit Haken/mit einem Haken versehen. ⇒ *also* **hook** 2 C

**hooker** /ˈhʊkə(r)/ *n.* Ⓐ (*Rugby*) Hakler, *der;* Ⓑ (*Amer. sl.: prostitute*) Nutte, *die* (*salopp*)

**hookey** /ˈhʊkɪ/ *n.* (*Amer. coll.*) **play ~:** [die] Schule schwänzen (*ugs.*)

**hook: ~ ˈnose** *n.* Hakennase, *die;* **~-nosed** /ˈhʊknəʊzd/ *adj.* mit einer Hakennase *nachgestellt;* hakennasig; **be ~-nosed** eine Hakennase haben; **H~ of ˈHolland** *pr. n.* Hoek van Holland (*das*); **~-up** *n.* (*Radio and Telev. coll.*) Zusammenschaltung, *die* (*zu einer Gemeinschaftssendung*); **~worm** *n.* Ⓐ (*worm*) Hakenwurm, *der;* Ⓑ *no art.* (*disease*) die Hakenwurmkrankheit

**hooky** ⇒ **hookey**

**hooligan** /ˈhuːlɪgən/ *n.* Rowdy, *der*

**hooliganism** /ˈhuːlɪgənɪzm/ *n., no pl.* Rowdytum, *das*

**hoop** /huːp/ *n.* Ⓐ (*circular band*) Reifen, *der;* (*of barrel*) Fassreifen, *der;* Fassband, *das;* Ⓑ (*toy*) Reifen, *der;* Ⓒ (*Croquet*) [Krocket]tor, *das;* Ⓓ (*in circus, show, etc.*) Springreifen, *der;* **go** *or* **be put/put sb. through the ~[s]** (*fig.*) durch die Mangel gedreht werden/jmdn. durch die Mangel drehen (*salopp*)

**hoop-la** /ˈhuːplɑː/ *n.* Ringwerfen, *das*

**hoopoe** /ˈhuːpuː/ *n.* (*Ornith.*) Wiedehopf, *der*

**hooray** ⇒ **hurray**

**Hooray ˈHenry** *n.* (*Brit.*) [reicher, extrovertierter] Schickimicki (*ugs.*)

**hoosegow** /ˈhuːsgaʊ/ *n.* (*Amer. coll.*) Knast, *der* (*ugs.*)

**hoot** /huːt/ ❶ *v.i.* Ⓐ (*call out*) johlen; **~ with laughter** in johlendes Gelächter ausbrechen; Ⓑ ‹Eule:› schreien; Ⓒ ‹Fahrzeug, Fahrer:› hupen, tuten; ‹Sirene, Nebelhorn usw.:› heulen, tuten; **~ at sb./sth.** jmdn./etw. anhupen. ❷ *v.t.* Ⓐ (*assail with derision*) ausbuhen (*ugs.*); Ⓑ heulen *od.* tuten lassen ‹Sirene, Nebelhorn›; **~ one's horn** ⇒ **horn** 1 D.

❸ *n.* Ⓐ (*shout*) **~s of derision/scorn** verächtliches Gejohle; **~s of laughter** johlendes Gelächter; Ⓑ (*owl's cry*) Schrei, *der;* Ⓒ (*signal*) (*of vehicle*) Hupen, *das;* (*of siren, foghorn*) Heulen, *das;* Tuten, *das;* **give a ~ of** *or* **on one's horn** ‹Fahrer:› hupen; Ⓓ (*coll.*) **I don't care** *or* **give a ~** *or* **two ~s what you do** es ist mir völlig piepegal *od.* schnuppe (*ugs.*), was du tust; **not matter a ~** *or* **two ~s [to sb.]** [jmdm.] völlig schnuppe sein (*ugs.*); Ⓔ (*coll.: cause of laughter*) **what a ~!** zum Kaputtlachen! (*ugs.*); **be a ~:** zum Schießen sein (*ugs.*)

**hooter** /ˈhuːtə(r)/ *n.* (*Brit.*) Ⓐ (*siren*) Sirene, *die;* Ⓑ (*motor horn*) Hupe, *die;* **sound one's ~:** hupen; Ⓒ (*coll.: nose*) Zinken, *der* (*ugs. scherzh.*)

**hoots** /huːts/ *int.* (*Scot., N. Engl.*) ach was!

**hoover** /ˈhuːvə(r)/ (*Brit.*) ❶ *n.* Ⓐ **H~** ® [Hoover]staubsauger, *der;* Ⓑ (*made by any company*) Staubsauger, *der.* ❷ *v.t.* staubsaugen; saugen ‹Boden, Teppich›; absaugen ‹Möbel›. ❸ *v.i.* [staub]saugen

**hooves** *pl. of* **hoof**

**hop**[1] /hɒp/ *n.* Ⓐ (*Bot.*) (*plant*) Hopfen, *der; in pl.* (*cones*) Hopfendolden; Ⓑ *in pl.* (*Brewing*) Hopfen, *der*

h

**hop**[2] ❶ *v.i.*, **-pp-:** Ⓐ hüpfen; ‹Hase:› hoppeln; **be ~ping mad [about** *or* **over sth.]** (*coll.*) [wegen etw.] fuchsteufelswild sein (*ugs.*); Ⓑ (*fig. coll.*) **~ out of bed** aus dem Bett springen; **~ into the car/on [to] the bus/train/bicycle** sich ins Auto/in den Bus/Zug/aufs Fahrrad schwingen (*ugs.*); **~ into bed with sb.** mit jmdm. ins Bett steigen (*ugs.*); **~ off/out** aussteigen; Ⓒ (*coll.: change location*) **be always ~ping [about] from place to place/country to country** ständig unterwegs sein.
❷ *v.t.*, **-pp-:** Ⓐ (*jump over*) springen über (+ *Akk.*); Ⓑ (*coll.: jump aboard*) aufspringen auf (+ *Akk.*); Ⓒ **~ it** (*Brit. coll.: go away*) sich verziehen (*ugs.*). ⇒ *also* **hedge-hop**.
❸ *n.* Ⓐ (*action*) Hüpfer, *der;* Hopser, *der* (*ugs.*); **~, step, and jump** ⇒ **triple jump**; Ⓑ **be on the ~** (*Brit. coll.: be bustling about*) auf Trab sein (*ugs.*); **keep sb. on the ~** (*Brit. coll.*) jmdn. in Trab halten (*ugs.*); Ⓒ **catch sb. on the ~** (*Brit. coll.*) (*unprepared*) jmdn. überraschen *od.* überrumpeln; (*in the act*) jmdn. auf frischer Tat ertappen; Ⓓ (*coll.: dance*) Schwof, *der* (*ugs.*); Ⓔ (*distance flown*) Flugstrecke, *die;* (*stage of journey*) Teilstrecke, *die;* Etappe, *die;* (*flight*) kurzer Flug; (*trip*) kurze Reise

**hope** /həʊp/ ❶ *n.* Hoffnung, *die;* **~ springs eternal [in the human breast]** (*prov.*) der Mensch hofft, solange er lebt; **give up ~:** die Hoffnung aufgeben; **that is my [dearest] ~:** darauf setze ich meine [ganze] Hoffnung; **hold out ~ [for sb.]** [jmdm.] Hoffnung machen; **I don't hold out much ~ for his recovery** ich habe nicht viel Hoffnung, dass er sich wieder erholt; **beyond** *or* **past ~:** hoffnungslos; **in the ~/in ~[s] of sth./doing sth.** in der Hoffnung auf etw. (*Akk.*)/, etw. zu tun; **live in ~[s] of sth.** in der Hoffnung auf etw. (*Akk.*) leben; **sb.'s ~[s] of sth.** jmds. Hoffnung auf etw. (*Akk.*); **I have some ~[s] of success** *or* **of succeeding** *or* **that I shall succeed** es besteht die Hoffnung, dass ich Erfolg habe; **set** *or* **put** *or* **place one's ~s on** *or* **in sth./sb.** seine Hoffnung auf etw./jmdn. setzen; **raise sb.'s ~s** jmdm. Hoffnung machen; **raise sb.'s ~s too much** *or* **high** jmdm. zu große Hoffnungen machen; **high ~s** große Hoffnungen; **have high ~s of sth./doing sth.** sich (*Dat.*) große Hoffnungen auf etw. (*Akk.*) machen/sich (*Dat.*) große Hoffnungen machen, etw. zu tun; **there is no/some/little ~ that ...:** es besteht keine/einige/wenig Hoffnung, dass ...; **not have a ~ [in hell] [of sth.]** (*coll.*) sich (*Dat.*) keine[rlei] Hoffnung [auf etw. (*Akk.*)] machen können; **there's not a ~ in hell that ...** (*coll.*) es besteht nicht die leiseste Chance, dass ...; **not a ~ [in hell]!** (*coll. iron.*) völlig ausgeschlossen!; **what a ~!** (*coll.*), **some ~[s]!** (*coll. iron.*) schön wärs!; **be hoping against ~ that ...:** trotz allem die Hoffnung nicht aufgeben, dass ...; **be the great new tennis ~:** die große neue Hoffnung im Tennis sein; **hard work is our only ~ for** *or* **of a better way of life** nur wenn wir hart arbeiten, können wir auf ein besseres Leben hoffen; **my ~ is that ...:** ich hoffe, dass ...; ⇒ *also* **alive** A; **forlorn** A.
❷ *v.i.* hoffen (**for** auf + *Akk.*); **I ~ so/not** hoffentlich/hoffentlich nicht; ich hoffe es/ich hoffe nicht; **~ for the best** das Beste hoffen.
❸ *v.t.* **~ to do sth./that sth. may be so** hoffen, etw. zu tun/dass etw. so eintrifft; **I ~ to go to Paris** (*am planning*) ich habe vor, nach Paris zu fahren; **I ~ [that] that is true** hoffentlich stimmt das; **hoping to see you soon** in der Hoffnung, Sie bald zu sehen

ˈ**hope chest** *n.* (*Amer.*) Aussteuertruhe, *die*

**hoped-for** /ˈhəʊptfɔː(r)/ *attrib. adj.* erhofft

**hopeful** /ˈhəʊpfl/ ❶ *adj.* Ⓐ zuversichtlich; **I'm ~/not ~ that ...:** ich hoffe zuversichtlich/bezweifle, dass ...; **feel ~:** zuversichtlich sein; **be** *or* **feel ~ about the future** hoffnungsvoll *od.* zuversichtlich in die Zukunft blicken; **if you think he will help you, you are very ~ indeed** wenn du denkst, dass er dir helfen wird, dann bist du wirklich ein Optimist; **be ~ of sth./of doing sth./that sth. may be so** auf etw. (*Akk.*) hoffen/voller Hoffnung sein, etw. zu tun/dass etw. so eintrifft; Ⓑ (*promising*) viel versprechend; aussichtsreich ‹Kapitalanlage, Kandidat›.
❷ *n.* **[young] ~:** hoffnungsvoller junger Mensch

**hopefully** /ˈhəʊpfəlɪ/ *adv.* Ⓐ (*expectantly*) voller Hoffnung; Ⓑ (*promisingly*) viel versprechend; Ⓒ (*coll.: it is hoped that*) hoffentlich; **~, all our problems should now be over** wir wollen hoffen, dass unsere ganzen (*ugs.*) Probleme jetzt beseitigt sind; **~, it will be available in the autumn** wir hoffen, dass es im Herbst zur Verfügung steht

**hopeless** /ˈhəʊplɪs/ *adj.* Ⓐ hoffnungslos; Ⓑ (*inadequate, incompetent*) miserabel; **be ~,** **be a ~ case** ein hoffnungsloser Fall sein (*ugs.*) (**at** in + *Dat.*); **be ~ at doing sth.** etw. überhaupt nicht können

**hopelessly** /ˈhəʊplɪslɪ/ *adv.* Ⓐ hoffnungslos; **be ~ in love** (*fig.*) rettungslos verliebt sein (*ugs.*); **I'm ~ bad at maths** in Mathematik bin ich ein hoffnungsloser Fall (*ugs. scherzh.*); Ⓑ (*inadequately*) miserabel

**hopelessness** /ˈhəʊplɪsnɪs/ *n., no pl.* Hoffnungslosigkeit, *die*

ˈ**hop garden** *n.* (*Brit. Agric.*) Hopfengarten, *der*

**hopper** /ˈhɒpə(r)/ *n.* (*Mech.*) Trichter, *der*

**hop: ~sack** *n.* Ⓐ (*bag*) Hopfensack, *der;* Ⓑ (*Textiles*) Sackleinen, *das;* Sackleinwand, *die;* **~scotch** *n.* Himmel-und-Hölle-Spiel, *das;* **play ~scotch** „Himmel und Hölle" spielen

**horde** /hɔːd/ *n.* (*huge number*) große Menge; (*derog./of wild animals*) Horde, *die;* **in [their] ~s** in Scharen; **~s of tourists** Scharen von Touristen

**horizon** /həˈraɪzn/ *n.* Ⓐ Horizont, *der;* **on/over the ~:** am Horizont; **the sun dropped below the ~:** die Sonne verschwand hinter dem Horizont; **there is trouble on the ~** (*fig.*) am Horizont tauchen Probleme auf; **there's nothing on the ~** (*fig.*) da ist nichts in Sicht (*ugs.*); ⇒ *also* **artificial horizon**; Ⓑ (*fig.: perceptual limit*) Horizont, *der;* Gesichtskreis, *der;* **broaden one's/sb.'s ~s** seinen/jmds. Horizont erweitern; Ⓒ (*Geol.*) Horizont, *der;* Ⓓ (*Archaeol.*) Kulturschicht, *die;* Ⓔ (*Soil Science*) Bodenhorizont, *der*

**horizontal** /hɒrɪˈzɒntl/ ❶ *adj.* horizontal; waagerecht; ⇒ *also* **bar**[1] 1 B; **integration** D.
❷ *n.* Horizontale, *die;* Waagerechte, *die*

**horizontally** /hɒrɪˈzɒntəlɪ/ *adv.* horizontal; (*flat*) waagerecht; flach ‹liegen›

**hormonal** /hɔːˈməʊnl, ˈhɔːmənl/ *adj.* (*Biol., Pharm.*) hormonal; hormonell; **~ deficiency** Hormonmangel, *der*

**hormone** /ˈhɔːməʊn/ *n.* (*Biol., Pharm.*) Hormon, *das*

**hormone reˈplacement therapy** *n.* (*Med.*) Hormonsubstitutionstherapie, *die*

**horn** /hɔːn/ ❶ *n.* Ⓐ (*of animal or devil*) Horn, *das;* (*of deer*) Geweihstange, *die* (*Jägerspr.*); **~s** Geweih, *das;* **lock ~s [with sb.]** (*fig.*) [mit jmdm.] die Klinge[n] kreuzen (*geh.*); Ⓑ (*substance*) Horn, *das; attrib.* Horn-; Ⓒ (*Mus.*) Horn, *das;* **[French] ~:** [Wald]horn, *das;* ⇒ *also* **English horn**; Ⓓ (*of vehicle*) Hupe, *die;* (*of ship*) [Signal]horn, *das;* (*of factory*) [Fabrik]sirene, *die;* **sound** *or* **blow** *or* **hoot** *or* **honk the** *or* **one's ~ [at sb.]** ‹Fahrer:› [jmdn. an]hupen; Ⓔ (*of snail*) Horn, *das;* (*of insect*) Fühler, *der;* **draw in one's ~s** (*fig.*) sich zurückhalten; (*restrain one's ambition*) zurückstecken; Ⓕ (*vessel*) Horn, *das;* (*to drink from*) Trinkhorn, *das* (*hist.*); (*for gunpowder*) Pulverhorn, *das* (*hist.*); **~ of plenty** Füllhorn, *das;* Ⓖ (*loudspeaker*) [Schall]trichter, *der;* Ⓗ (*of crescent*) Horn, *das;* **the ~s of the moon** die Hörnerspitzen des Mondes; Ⓘ (*Geog.*) (*of land*) Horn, *das* (*veralt.*); **the H~:** das Kap Hoorn; Ⓙ (*coarse: erect penis*) Latte, *die* (*salopp*). ⇒ *also* **bull**[1] 1 A; **dilemma**; **foghorn**; **shoehorn**.
❷ *v.i.* (*coll.*) **~ in [on sth.]** sich [in etw. (*Akk.*)] reinhängen (*salopp*)

**horn: ~beam** *n.* (*Bot.*) Hainbuche, *die;* Hornbaum, *der;* **~bill** *n.* (*Ornith.*) Nashornvogel, *der*

**horned** /hɔːnd/ *adj.* Ⓐ gehörnt; (*with antlers*) Geweih tragend; Ⓑ (*poet.: crescent-shaped*) sichelförmig

**horned: ~ ˈowl** *n.* Ohreule, *die;* **~ ˈtoad** *n.* Texaskrötenechse, *die*

**hornet** /ˈhɔːnɪt/ *n.* Hornisse, *die;* **stir up** *or* **walk into a ~s' nest** (*fig.*) in ein Wespennest stechen *od.* greifen (*ugs.*); **bring a ~s' nest about one's ears** (*fig.*) sich in ein Wespennest setzen (*ugs.*)

**hornless** /ˈhɔːnlɪs/ *adj.* hornlos; (*without antlers*) geweihlos

ˈ**hornpipe** *n.* (*Mus.*) Hornpipe, *die*

ˈ**horn-rimmed** *adj.* **~ spectacles** *or* **glasses** Hornbrille, *die*

**horny** /ˈhɔːnɪ/ *adj.* Ⓐ (*hard*) hornig ‹Fußsohlen, Haut, Hände›; Ⓑ (*made of horn*) aus Horn *nachgestellt;* (*like horn*) hornartig; Ⓒ (*sl.: sexually aroused*) spitz (*ugs.*); geil (*oft abwertend*)

**horology** /həˈrɒlədʒɪ/ *n., no pl.* Ⓐ (*science*) Lehre von der Zeitmessung; Ⓑ (*clockmaking*) Uhrmacherkunst, *die*

**horoscope** /ˈhɒrəskəʊp/ *n.* (*Astrol.*) Horoskop, *das;* **draw up** *or* **cast sb.'s ~:** jmdm. das Horoskop stellen

**horrendous** /həˈrendəs/ *adj.* (*coll.*) schrecklich (*ugs.*); entsetzlich (*ugs.*) ‹Dummheit›; horrend ‹Preis›

**horrendously** /həˈrendəslɪ/ *adv.* (*coll.*) entsetzlich (*ugs.*); horrend ‹teuer›

**horrible** /ˈhɒrɪbl/ *adj.* Ⓐ grauenhaft; grausig ‹Monster, Geschichte›; grauenvoll ‹Verbrechen, Albtraum›; schauerlich ‹Maske›; **I find all insects ~:** mir graust vor jeder Art von Insekten; Ⓑ (*coll.: unpleasant, excessive*) grauenhaft (*ugs.*); horrend ‹Ausgaben, Kosten›; **have a ~ surprise** eine ganz böse Überraschung erleben (*ugs.*); **don't be so ~ to me** sei nicht so garstig zu mir; **I have a ~ feeling that ...:** ich habe das ungute Gefühl, dass ...

**horribly** /ˈhɒrɪblɪ/ *adv.* Ⓐ entsetzlich ‹entstellt›; scheußlich ‹grinsen›; **it was a ~ frightening story** es war eine überaus grausige Geschichte; Ⓑ (*coll.: unpleasantly, excessively*) entsetzlich (*ugs.*); fürchterlich (*ugs.*) ‹aufregen›; horrend ‹teuer›

**horrid** /ˈhɒrɪd/ *adj.* scheußlich; **don't be so ~ to me** (*coll.*) sei nicht so garstig zu mir

**horrific** /həˈrɪfɪk/ *adj.* schrecklich; grausig ‹Geistergeschichte›; (*coll.*) horrend ‹Preis›

**horrify** /ˈhɒrɪfaɪ/ *v.t.* Ⓐ (*excite horror in*) mit Schrecken erfüllen; **it horrifies me to think what ...:** ich denke mit Schrecken daran, was ...; **I was horrified to see my car rolling into the river** voller Entsetzen sah ich, wie mein Auto in den Fluss rollte; Ⓑ (*shock, scandalize*) **be horrified** entsetzt sein (**at, by** über + *Akk.*)

**horrifying** /ˈhɒrɪfaɪɪŋ/ *adj.* grauenhaft; grausig ‹Film›; **it is ~ to think that ...:** der Gedanke, dass ..., ist schrecklich

**horrifyingly** /ˈhɒrɪfaɪɪŋlɪ/ *adv.* erschreckend

**horror** /ˈhɒrə(r)/ ❶ *n.* [A] Entsetzen, *das* (**at** über + *Akk.*); (*repugnance*) Grausen, *das;* **she screamed in ~:** sie schrie voller Entsetzen; **there was [an expression of] ~ on her face** Entsetzen/Grauen stand ihr im Gesicht geschrieben; **have a ~ of sb./sth./doing sth.** einen Horror vor jmdm./etw. haben/einen Horror davor haben, etw. zu tun (*ugs.*); **have a fit of the ~s** weiße Mäuse sehen (*ugs.*); **spiders gave her the ~s** vor Spinnen hatte sie eine panische Angst; **he gives me the ~s** er ist mir unheimlich; [B] (*coll.: dismay*) Entsetzen, *das* (**at** über + *Akk.*); [C] (*horrifying quality*) Grauenhaftigkeit, *die;* (*horrifying thing*) Gräuel, *der;* (*horrifying person*) Scheusal, *das;* **'Six Die in Blaze H~'** „Sechs Tote in flammendem Inferno"; **Chamber of H~s** (*lit. or fig.*) Schreckenskabinett, *das.*
❷ *attrib. adj.* Horror‹comic, -film, -geschichte›.
❸ *int.* **~[s]!** wie schrecklich!; o Graus! (*ugs. scherzh.*); **~ of ~s!** o Schreck, o Graus! (*ugs. scherzh.*)

**horror: ~-stricken, ~-struck** *adjs.* von Entsetzen gepackt; **be ~-stricken** *or* **-struck at sth.** über etw. (*Akk.*) furchtbar entsetzt sein

**hors de combat** /ɔː də ˈkɔ̃bɑː/ *pred. adj.* kampfunfähig; **put** *or* **render sb./sth. ~:** jmdn./etw. außer Gefecht setzen

**hors d'œuvre** /ɔːˈdɜːvr, ɔːˈdɜːv/ *n.* (*Gastr.*) Horsd'œuvre, *das;* ≈ Vorspeise, *die*

**horse** /hɔːs/ ❶ *n.* [A] Pferd, *das;* (*adult male*) Hengst, *der;* **be/get on one's high ~** (*fig.*) auf dem hohen Ross sitzen/sich aufs hohe Ross setzen (*ugs.*); **get [down] off one's high ~** (*fig.*) von seinem hohen Ross herunterkommen *od.* -steigen (*ugs.*); **hold your ~s!** (*fig.*) immer sachte mit den jungen Pferden! (*ugs.*); **he ought to hold his ~s** er sollte erst einmal abwarten; **that's/he is a ~ of a different** *or* **of another colour** (*fig.*) das ist etwas anderes/mit ihm sieht die Sache anders aus; **as strong as a ~:** bärenstark (*ugs.*); **eat/work like a ~:** wie ein Scheunendrescher essen (*salopp*)/wie ein Pferd arbeiten; **I could eat a ~** (*coll.*) ich habe einen Bärenhunger (*ugs.*); **[right** *or* **straight] from the ~'s mouth** (*fig.*) aus erster Hand *od.* Quelle; **change** *or* **swap ~s in midstream** (*fig.*) auf halbem Wege die Richtung ändern; **to ~!** aufgesessen!; **it's [a question** *or* **matter of] ~s for courses** (*fig.*) jeder sollte die Aufgaben übernehmen, für die er am besten geeignet ist; **you can lead** *or* **take a ~ to water, but you can't make it drink** (*prov.*) man kann ein Pferd zur Tränke bringen, aber es nicht zwingen zu trinken; [B] *constr. as pl.* (*Mil.*) Kavallerie, *die;* Reiterei, *die;* **800 ~:** 800 Reiter *od.* Berittene; [C] (*Gymnastics*) **[vaulting] ~:** [Sprung]pferd, *das;* [D] (*framework*) Gestell, *das;* (*for planks or beams*) [Auflager]bock, *der;* **[clothes] ~:** Wäscheständer, *der;* [E] (*coll.: ~power*) PS, *das.* ⇒ *also* **cart** 1; **carthorse; dark ~; flog** A; **gift-~; hobby ~; light ~; lock²** 2 A; **marine** 2 A; **pommel ~; rocking ~; sea ~; Trojan ~; white ~; wild ~; wooden ~.**
❷ *v.i.* **~ about** *or* **around** (*coll.*) herumalbern (*ugs.*)

**horse: ~-and-'buggy** *adj.* (*Amer. fig.*) aus der Zeit der Postkutschen (*fig.*) *nachgestellt;* **~back** ❶ *n.* [A] **on ~back** zu Pferd; **ride on ~back** reiten; [B] *attrib.* (*Amer.*) **~back riding** Reiten, *das;* **go in for** *or* **enjoy ~back rides** gerne reiten; ❷ *adv.* **go ~back** reiten; **~box** *n.* (*trailer*) Pferdeanhänger, *der;* (*Motor Veh.*) Pferdetransporter, *der;* **~ brass** ⇒ **brass** 1 C; **~breaker** *n.* Zureiter, *der;* **~ breeder** ⇒ **breeder; ~ 'chestnut** *n.* (*Bot.*) Rosskastanie, *die;* **~-drawn** *attrib. adj.* pferdebespannt; von Pferden gezogen; **~-drawn vehicle** Pferdewagen, *der;* Pferdefuhrwerk, *das;* **~flesh** *n.* [A] (*meat*) Pferdefleisch, *das;* [B] (*horses*) Pferde; **~fly** *n.* (*Zool.*) Pferdebremse, *die;* **H~ Guards** *n. pl.* (*Brit. Mil.*) (*brigade*) Gardekavallerie, *die;* **~hair** *n.* [A] (*single hair*) Pferdehaar, *das;* [B] *no pl., no indef. art.* (*mass of hairs*) Rosshaar, *das;* [C] (*fabric*) Rosshaar, *das;* **~ latitudes** *n. pl.* (*Geog.*) Rossbreiten *Pl.;* **~ laugh** *n.* laute Lache (*ugs.*); **~man** /ˈhɔːsmən/ *n., pl.* **~men** /ˈhɔːsmən/ [A] ([*skilled*] *rider*) [guter] Reiter; [B] (*Amer.: breeder*) Pferdezüchter, *der*

**horsemanship** /ˈhɔːsmənʃɪp/ *n., no pl.* [**skills of**] **~:** reiterliches Können

**horse: ~ opera** *n.* (*Amer. coll.*) Pferdeoper, *die* (*ugs.*); **~play** *n.* Balgerei, *die;* Alberei, *die;* **~power** *n., pl. same* (*Mech.*) Pferdestärke, *die;* **a 40 ~power car** ein Auto mit 40 PS; **what ~power is your car?** wie viel PS hat dein Auto?; **~ race** *n.* Pferderennen, *das;* **~racing** *n.* Pferderennsport, *der;* **~radish** *n.* Meerrettich, *der;* **~ sense** *n.* (*coll.*) [gesunder Menschen]verstand; **~shoe** *n.* Hufeisen, *das;* (*Archit.*) Hufeisenbogen, *der; attrib.* hufeisenförmig; **~shoe magnet** Hufeisenmagnet, *der;* **~shoe crab** (*Amer. Zool.*) Königskrabbe, *die;* **~ show** *n.* Pferdeschau, *die;* **~tail** *n.* [A] (*Bot.*) Schachtelhalm, *der;* [B] ⇒ **ponytail; ~-trader** *n.* Pferdehändler, *der;* **~-trading** *n.* [A] (*Amer.: dealing in horses*) Pferdehandel, *der;* [B] (*fig.: bargaining*) Kuhhandel, *der* (*ugs. abwertend*); **~whip** ❶ *n.* Reitpeitsche, *die;* ❷ *v.t.* auspeitschen; **~woman** *n.* Reiterin, *die*

**horsy (horsey)** /ˈhɔːsɪ/ *adj.* [A] (*horselike*) pferdeähnlich; **~ face/laugh** Pferdegesicht, *das*/wieherndes Lachen (*ugs.*); [B] (*much concerned with horses*) pferdenärrisch; **~ people** Pferdenarren

**horticultural** /hɔːtɪˈkʌltʃərl/ *adj.* gartenbaulich; Gartenbau‹zeitschrift, -ausstellung›; **~ society** Gesellschaft für Gartenbau; **~ show** Gartenschau, *die*

**horticulture** /ˈhɔːtɪkʌltʃə(r)/ *n.* Gartenbau, *der*

**horticulturist** /hɔːtɪˈkʌltʃərɪst/ *n.* ▶ **1261** Gärtner, *der*/Gärtnerin, *die*

**hosanna** /həʊˈzænə/ (*Bibl.*) ❶ *int.* hosianna. ❷ *n.* Hosianna, *das*

**hose** /həʊz/ ❶ *n.* [A] (*flexible tube*) Schlauch, *der;* **garden ~:** Gartenschlauch, *der;* [B] *constr. as pl.* (*stockings*) Strümpfe; **half-~:** Socken; [C] *constr. as pl.* (*Hist.*) (*tights*) Strumpfhose, *die;* (*breeches*) Kniehose, *die;* ⇒ *also* **doublet** A. ❷ *v.t.* sprengen

**~ 'down** *v.t.* abspritzen

**'hosepipe** ⇒ **hose** 1 A

**hosiery** /ˈhəʊʒərɪ/ *n., no pl.* Strumpfwaren *Pl.*

**hospice** /ˈhɒspɪs/ *n.* [A] (*Brit.*) (*for the destitute*) Heim für Mittellose; (*for the terminally ill*) Sterbeklinik, *die;* [B] (*for travellers or students*) Hospiz, *das*

**hospitable** /ˈhɒspɪtəbl/ *adj.* [A] (*welcoming*) gastfreundlich ‹Person, Wesensart›; gastlich ‹Haus, Hotel, Klima›; freundlich ‹Einladung›; **be ~ to sb.** jmdn. gastfreundlich *od.* gastlich aufnehmen; [B] (*fig.: favourably disposed*) **be ~ [to sth.]** aufgeschlossen [gegenüber etw.] sein

**hospitably** /ˈhɒspɪtəblɪ/ *adv.* (*welcomingly*) gastlich; gastfreundlich

**hospital** /ˈhɒspɪtl/ *n.* Krankenhaus, *das;* **in ~** (*Brit.*), **in the ~** (*Amer.*) im Krankenhaus; **into** *or* **to ~** (*Brit.*), **to the ~** (*Amer.*) ins Krankenhaus ‹gehen, bringen›; **veterinary/dolls' ~:** Tier-/Puppenklinik, *die*

**hospital: ~ bed** *n.* Krankenhausbett, *das;* **~ case** *n.* Fall fürs Krankenhaus

**hospitalisation, hospitalise** ⇒ **hospitaliz-**

**hospitality** /hɒspɪˈtælɪtɪ/ *n., no pl.* (*of person*) Gastfreundschaft, *die;* (*of thing, action, environment*) Freundlichkeit, *die*

**hospitalization** /hɒspɪtəlaɪˈzeɪʃn/ *n.* Einweisung ins Krankenhaus; **long periods of ~:** lange Krankenhausaufenthalte

**hospitalize** /ˈhɒspɪtəlaɪz/ *v.t.* ins Krankenhaus einweisen

**hospital: ~ nurse** *n.* ▶ **1261** Krankenschwester, *die*/Krankenpfleger, *der;* **~ porter** *n.* ▶ **1261** ≈ Krankenpflegehelfer, *der*/-helferin, *die;* **~ ship** *n.* Lazarettschiff, *das*

**host¹** /həʊst/ *n.* [A] (*large number*) Menge, *die;* **in [their] ~s** in Scharen; **a ~ of people/children** eine Menge Leute/eine Schar von Kindern; **he has ~s** *or* **a ~ of things to do/friends** er hat eine Menge zu erledigen/eine Menge Freunde; [B] (*arch.: army*) Heer, *das;* [C] (*Bibl.*) **the Lord [God] of ~s** der Herr der Heerscharen; **the heavenly ~** (*angels*) die himmlischen Heerscharen (*bibl.*)

**host²** ❶ *n.* [A] Gastgeber, *der*/Gastgeberin, *die;* **be** *or* **play ~ to sb.** jmdn. zu Gast haben; **~ country** Gastland, *das;* [B] (*landlord*) [Gast]wirt, *der;* **mine ~** (*arch./joc.*) der Herr Wirt; [C] (*compère*) Moderator, *der;* **your ~ for the show is ...:** durch die Show führt Sie ...; (*for chat show*) Gastgeber ist heute Abend ...; [D] (*Biol.: with parasite*) Wirt, *der;* [E] (*Biol./Med.: recipient*) Empfänger [eines Transplantats]; (*of organ*) [Organ]empfänger, *der.* ❷ *v.t.* [A] (*act as host at*) Gastgeber sein bei; **China is to ~ the Olympic Games** China soll die Olympischen Spiele ausrichten; [B] (*compère*) moderieren; **~ a programme** durch ein Programm führen

**host³** *n.* (*Eccl.: bread*) Hostie, *die*

**hostage** /ˈhɒstɪdʒ/ *n.* Geisel, *die;* **hold/take sb. ~:** jmdn. als Geisel festhalten/nehmen; **a ~ to fortune** etwas, was einem das Schicksal nehmen kann; **give ~s to fortune** *or* **history** *or* **time** sich dem Schicksal in die Hand geben (*geh.*)

**hostel** /ˈhɒstl/ *n.* (*Brit.*) [A] Wohnheim, *das;* [B] ⇒ **youth hostel**

**hostelry** /ˈhɒstlrɪ/ *n.* (*arch./literary*) Herberge, *die* (*veralt.*)

**hostess** /ˈhəʊstɪs/ *n.* [A] Gastgeberin, *die;* **take flowers for the ~:** der Dame des Hauses Blumen mitbringen; [B] (*in nightclub*) Animierdame, *die;* [C] (*euphem.: prostitute*) Hostess, *die* (*verhüll.*); [D] (*in passenger transport*) Hostess, *die;* ⇒ *also* **air hostess;** [E] (*compère*) Moderatorin, *die*

**'hostess gown** *n.* Hausmantel, *der*

**hostile** /ˈhɒstaɪl/ *adj.* [A] feindlich; [B] (*unfriendly*) feindselig (**to[wards]** gegenüber); **give sb. a ~ look** jmdn. feindselig ansehen; **be ~ to** *or* **towards sb.** jmdm. mit Feindseligkeit begegnen; **be ~ to sth.** etw. ablehnen; **a government ~ to change** eine Veränderungen ablehnende Regierung; [C] (*inhospitable*) unwirtlich; feindselig ‹Atmosphäre›; rau ‹Wirklichkeit›

**hostility** /hɒˈstɪlɪtɪ/ *n.* [A] *no pl.* (*enmity*) Feindschaft, *die;* [B] *no pl.* (*antagonism*) Feindseligkeit, *die* (**to[wards]** gegenüber); **feel no ~ towards anybody** niemandem feindlich gesinnt sein; **show ~ to sth.** einer Sache (*Dat.*) feindlich gegenüberstehen; [C] (*state of war, act of warfare*) Feindseligkeit, *die;* **an act of ~:** eine feindselige Handlung

**hot** /hɒt/ ❶ *adj.* [A] heiß; (*cooked*) warm ‹Mahlzeit, Essen›; (*fig.: potentially dangerous, difficult*) heiß (*ugs.*) ‹Thema, Geschichte›; ungemütlich, gefährlich ‹Lage›; **bake in a ~ oven** bei hoher Temperatur backen; **the room is much too ~:** in dem Zimmer ist es viel zu heiß; **~ and cold running water** fließend warm und kalt Wasser; **I've climbed more mountains than you've had ~ dinners** (*coll.*) ich habe schon mehr Berge bestiegen, als du dir vorstellen kannst; **be too ~ to handle** (*fig.*) eine zu heiße Angelegenheit sein (*ugs.*); **things were getting too ~ for him [to handle]** (*fig.*) die Sache wurde ihm zu brenzlig (*ugs.*); **make it** *or* **things [too] ~ for sb.** (*fig.*) jmdm. die Hölle heiß machen (*ugs.*); [B] (*feeling heat*) **I am/feel ~:** mir ist heiß; **I got ~:** mir wurde heiß; **I went ~ and cold all over** es überlief mich heiß und kalt; [C] (*pungent*) scharf ‹Gewürz, Senf usw.›; scharf gewürzt ‹Essen›; [D] (*suggesting heat*) grell, flammend ‹Farbe›; [E] (*passionate, lustful*) glühend ‹Begeisterung›; heiß ‹Küsse, Tränen, Umarmung›; **be ~ for sth.** heiß auf etw. (*Akk.*) sein (*ugs.*); **be ~ on sth./sb.** (*keen*) auf etw./jmdn. wild sein (*ugs.*); auf etw./jmdn. versessen sein; **he's really ~ on her** (*sexually*) er ist richtig scharf auf sie (*ugs.*); **have a ~ temper** ein hitziges Temperament haben; [F] (*agitated, angry*) hitzig; **get ~ over sth.** sich an etw. (*Dat.*) erhitzen; **be**

h

[all] ~ **and bothered** ganz aufgelöst sein; **get [all]** ~ **and bothered** sich [fürchterlich] (*ugs.*)] aufregen; **G** (*intense*) heiß ‹[Wett]kampf, Auseinandersetzung›; **H** (*coll.: good, skilful*) toll (*ugs.*); **be** ~ **at sth.** in etw. (*Dat.*) [ganz] groß sein (*ugs.*); **I'm not too** ~ **at that** darin bin ich nicht besonders umwerfend (*ugs.*); **be** ~ **on sth.** (*interested*) sich in *od.* mit etw. (*Dat.*) gut auskennen; **not so** *or* **too** ~ (*coll.*) nicht gerade berauschend (*ugs.*); **I** (*recent*) (*Hunting*) warm, frisch ‹Fährte›; (*fig.*) noch warm ‹Nachrichten›; **this is really** ~ **[news]** das ist wirklich das Neueste vom Neuen; ~ **off the press[es]** (*Journ., Printing*) frisch aus der Presse; **J** (*close*) **you are getting** ~/**are** ~ (*in children's games*) es wird schon wärmer/[jetzt ist es] heiß; **follow** ~ **on sb.'s heels** jmdm. dicht auf den Fersen folgen (*ugs.*); **be** ~ **on sb.'s track** *or* **trail** jmdm. dicht auf den Fersen sein (*ugs.*); **in** ~ **pursuit** dicht auf den Fersen (*ugs.*); **K** (*Mus.: rhythmical*) heiß; schräg (*ugs.*) ‹Musik›; **he is a really** ~ **saxophonist** er spielt ein heißes Saxophon; **L** (*coll.: in demand*) zugkräftig; **they are the** ~**test items just now** sie sind die augenblicklichen Renner (*ugs.*); **a** ~ **property** (*singer, actress, etc.*) eine ertragreiche Zugnummer; (*company, invention, etc.*) eine ertragreiche Geldanlage; **M** (*coll.: radioactive*) heiß (*Kernphysik*); **N** (*Sport; also fig.*) heiß (*ugs.*) ‹Tipp, Favorit›; **O** (*coll.: illegally obtained*) heiß ‹Ware, Geld›. ⇒ *also* **blow**[1] 1 B; **cake** 1 B; **collar** 1 A; **potato** A; **red-hot**; **white-hot**.

❷ *adv.* heiß.

❸ *n. in pl.* **have the** ~**s for sb.** (*coll.*) richtig scharf auf jmdn. sein (*ugs.*)

~ **'up** (*Brit. coll.*) ❶ *v.t.* **A** (*heat*) warm machen; **B** (*excite*) auf Touren bringen (*ugs.*); **C** (*make more exciting*) in Schwung bringen; (*make more dangerous*) verschärfen; **D** (*intensify*) anheizen (*ugs.*); **E** (*Motor Veh.*) frisieren (*ugs.*). ❷ *v.i.* **A** (*rise in temperature*) heiß werden; **the weather** ~**s up** es wird wärmer; **B** (*become exciting*) in Schwung kommen; (*become dangerous*) sich verschärfen; **C** (*become more intense*) sich verstärken; ‹Wortgefecht:› zunehmend heißer *od.* hitziger werden

**hot:** ~ **'air** *n.* (*coll.: idle talk*) leeres Gerede (*ugs.*); **talk** ~ **air** dummes Gewäsch von sich geben (*ugs. abwertend*); ⇒ *also* **balloon** 1 A; ~**bed** *n.* (*Hort.*) Mistbeet, *das;* Frühbeet, *das;* (*fig.: place favouring growth*) Nährboden, *der* (**of** für); (*of vice, corruption, etc.*) Brutstätte, *die* (**of** für); ~**-blooded** /ˈhɒtblʌdɪd/ *adj.* heißblütig

**hotchpotch** /ˈhɒtʃpɒtʃ/ *n.* (*mixture*) Mischmasch, *der* (*ugs.*) (**of** aus); **a** ~ **of people** eine bunte Mischung von Leuten (*scherzh.*)

**hot:** ~ **cross 'bun** *n.: mit einem Kreuz aus Teig verziertes Rosinenbrötchen, das am Karfreitag gegessen wird;* ~**-'desking** *n.: Mehrfachnutzung von Arbeitsplätzen;* ~ **dog** *n.* (*coll.*) Hotdog, *das od. der; attrib.* ~**-dog stand** ≈ Würstchenbude, *die*

**hotel** /həˈtel, həʊˈtel/ *n.* **A** Hotel, *das;* ⇒ *also* **private hotel**; **B** (*Austral., NZ: public house*) Wirtshaus, *das*

**hotelier** /həˈtelɪə(r)/ *n.* ▶ **1261** Hotelier, *der*

**hot:** ~ **'flush** *n.* (*Med.*) **suffer from** ~ **flushes** unter fliegender Hitze leiden; ~**foot** ❶ *adv.* stehenden Fußes; ❷ *adj.* **in** ~**foot pursuit** dicht auf den Fersen (*ugs.*); ❸ *v.i.* (*Amer. coll.*) ~**foot home** machen, dass man nach Hause kommt (*ugs.*); ❹ *v.t.* ~**foot it** sich hastig davonmachen; ~**head** *n.* Hitzkopf, *der;* ~**-headed** *adj.* hitzköpfig; ~**house** *n.* Treibhaus, *das; attrib.* (*lit. or fig.*) Treibhaus-; ~**line** *n.* Hotline, *die;* (*Polit.*) heißer Draht

**hotly** /ˈhɒtlɪ/ *adv.* heftig; **they were** ~ **pursued by the police** die Polizei war ihnen dicht auf den Fersen (*ugs.*); **his cheeks flushed** ~: er wurde über und über rot

**hot:** ~**-'metal** *adj.* (*Printing*) Bleisatz-; ~ **'money** *n.* (*Finance*) heißes Geld

**hotness** /ˈhɒtnɪs/ *n., no pl.* **A** (*temperature*) Hitze, *die;* **test the** ~: die Wärme prüfen; **B** (*hot sensation*) Hitze, *die;* **C** (*pungency*) Schärfe, *die;* **D** (*ardour*) Feuer, *das;* Glut, *die* (*geh.*)

**hot:** ~**plate** *n.* Kochplatte, *die;* (*for keeping food* ~) Warmhalteplatte, *die;* ~**pot** *n.* (*Gastr.*) **[Lancashire]** ~**pot** *Fleischeintopf mit Kartoffeleinlage;* ~ **rod** *n.* (*Motor Veh.*) hochfrisiertes Auto (*ugs.*); ~ **seat** *n.* (*coll.*) **A** (*electric chair*) elektrischer Stuhl; **B** (*uneasy situation*) Folterbank, *die* (*fig.*); (*involving heavy responsibility*) **be in the** ~ **seat** den Kopf hinhalten müssen (*ugs.*); ~ **shoe** *n.* (*Photog.*) [Blitzlicht]mittenkontakt, *der;* ~**shot** *n.* (*coll.*) Ass, *das* (*ugs.*); ~ **spot** *n.* **A** heiße Gegend; **B a** ~ **spot of political instability** (*fig.*) ein politischer Krisenherd; **C** (*nightclub*) Nachtlokal, *das;* **D** (*difficult situation*) **find oneself** *or* **be in/get into a** ~ **spot** in der Bredouille sein/in die Bredouille kommen *od.* geraten (*ugs.*); ~ **'spring** *n.* heiße Quelle; Thermalquelle, *die;* ~ **'stuff** *n., no pl., no art.* (*coll.*) **sb./sth. is** ~ **stuff** jmd./etw. ist große Klasse (*ugs.*); ~**-tempered** *adj.* heißblütig

**Hottentot** /ˈhɒtntɒt/ *n.* (*person*) Hottentotte, *der*/Hottentottin, *die; attrib.* ‹Gebräuche, Lebensweise› der Hottentotten

**hot:** ~ **'water** *n.* (*fig. coll.*) **be in/get into** ~ **water** in der Bredouille sein/in die Bredouille geraten (*ugs.*); **he got into** ~ **water with the authorities** er bekam Ärger mit den Behörden; ~**-'water bag** (*Amer.*), ~**-'water bottle** *ns.* Wärmflasche, *die*

**hound** /haʊnd/ ❶ *n.* **A** Jagdhund, *der;* **the [pack of]** ~**s** (*Brit. Hunting*) die Meute (*Jägerspr.*); **ride to** ~**s** mit der Meute jagen; **B** (*despicable man*) Lump, *der.* ❷ *v.t.* jagen; (*fig.*) verfolgen; **they were** ~**ed from country to country** sie wurden von einem Land ins andere gejagt

~ **'down** *v.t.* (*lit. or fig.*) zur Strecke bringen

~ **'on** *v.t.* antreiben; ~ **sb. on to do sth.** jmdn. [dazu] antreiben, etw. zu tun

~ **'out** *v.t.* **A** (*hunt out*) aufspüren; **B** (*force to leave*) vertreiben (**of** aus); verjagen (**of** aus)

**hound's-tooth** *n.* (*Textiles*) (*pattern*) Hahnentritt, *der;* (*fabric*) Stoff mit Hahnentrittmuster

**hour** /ˈaʊə(r)/ *n.* ▶ **1012** **A** Stunde, *die;* **half an** ~: eine halbe Stunde; **an** ~ **and a half** anderthalb Stunden; **be paid by the** ~: stundenweise bezahlt werden; **it takes her** ~**s to get ready** sie braucht Stunden, bis sie fertig ist; **I did two** ~**s' work** ich habe zwei Stunden [lang] gearbeitet; **there aren't enough** ~**s in the day** der Tag hat nicht genug Stunden [für all die Dinge, die man erledigen möchte]; **an eight-**~ **day** ein Achtstundentag; **a two-**~ **session** eine zweistündige Sitzung; **the 24-**~ **clock** die Vierundzwanzigstundenuhr; ⇒ *also* **lunch hour**; **B** (*time o'clock*) Zeit, *die;* **the** ~ **grows late** (*literary*) es wird spät; **strike the** ~: die volle Stunde schlagen; **on the** ~: zur vollen Stunde; **every** ~ **on the** ~: jede volle Stunde; **at this late** ~: zu so später Stunde (*geh.*); **at an early/a late** ~: zu früher/später *od.* vorgerückter Stunde (*geh.*); **at all** ~**s** zu jeder [Tages- oder Nacht]zeit; (*late at night*) spät in der Nacht; **till all** ~**s [of the morning/night]** bis zum Morgengrauen/bis in die späte Nacht; **the small** ~**s [of the morning]** die frühen Morgenstunden; **0100/0200/1700/1800** ~**s** (*on 24-*~ *clock*) 1.00/2.00/17.00/18.00 Uhr; **C** *in pl.* **doctor's** ~**s** Sprechstunde, *die;* **post office** ~**s** Schalterstunden der Post; **what** ~**s do you work?, what are your working** ~**s?** wie ist deine Arbeitszeit?; **strike for shorter** ~**s** für eine kürzere Arbeitszeit streiken; **work long** ~**s** einen langen Arbeitstag haben; **during school** ~**s** während der Schulstunden *od.* des Unterrichts; **out of/after** ~**s** (*in office, bank, etc.*) außerhalb der Dienstzeit; (*of doctor*) außerhalb der Sprechstunde; (*in shop*) außerhalb der Geschäftszeit; (*in pub*) außerhalb der Ausschankzeit; (*in school*) außerhalb der Unterrichtszeit; **keep regular/irregular** ~**s** geregelte/keine geregelten Zeiten einhalten; **what sort of** ~**s do you keep?** was hast du für einen Tagesrhythmus?; **be accustomed to late** ~**s** gewöhnlich lange aufbleiben; **D** (*particular time*) Stunde, *die;* **don't desert me in my** ~ **of need** verlass mich nicht in der Stunde der Not; ~ **of glory** Stunde des Ruhmes; **sb.'s finest** ~: jmds. größte Stunde; **one's dying** *or* **final** ~ *or* ~ **of death** jmds. letzte Stunde *od.* Todesstunde; **at an unhappy/a happy** ~: in einer unglücklichen/glücklichen Stunde; **E** (*present*) **the question** *etc.* **of the** ~: das Problem *usw.* der Stunde; **F** (*distance*) Stunde, *die;* **they are two** ~**s from us by train** sie wohnen zwei Bahnstunden von uns entfernt; **he lives an** ~ **from the sea** er wohnt eine Stunde vom Meer entfernt; **G** *in pl.* (*RC Ch.*) (*times*) Gebetsstunden; (*prayers*) Stundengebete; **book of** ~**s** Stundenbuch, *das.* ⇒ *also* **eleventh** 1

**hour:** ~**glass** *n.* Sanduhr, *die;* Stundenglas, *das* (*veralt.*); **a woman with an** ~**glass figure** eine kurvenreiche Frau (*ugs. scherzh.*); ~ **hand** *n.* Stundenzeiger, *der;* kleiner Zeiger

**houri** /ˈhʊərɪ/ *n.* (*Muslim Mythol.*) Huri, *die*

**'hour-long** ❶ *attrib. adj.* einstündig. ❷ *adv.* eine Stunde [lang]

**hourly** /ˈaʊəlɪ/ ❶ *adj.* **A** (*happening every hour*) stündlich; **at** ~ **intervals** jede Stunde; stündlich; **there are** ~ **trains to London** jede *od.* alle Stunde fährt ein Zug nach London; **the bus service is** ~: der Bus verkehrt stündlich; **B** (*reckoned by the hour*) **he is paid an** ~ **rate of £6** er hat einen Stundenlohn von 6 Pfund; **on an** ~ **basis** stundenweise ‹mieten›; **C** (*continual*) ständig; **D** **two-**~: zweistündlich. ❷ *adv.* stündlich; **be paid** ~: stundenweise bezahlt werden

**house** ❶ /haʊs/ *n., pl.* ~**s** /ˈhaʊzɪz/ **A** (*dwelling, occupants*) Haus, *das;* **a collection from** ~ **to** ~: eine Haussammlung; **to/at my** ~: zu mir [nach Hause]/bei mir [zu Hause]; ~ **of cards** (*lit. or fig.*) Kartenhaus, *das;* **H**~ **of God** Gotteshaus, *das;* ~ **and home** Haus und Hof; **keep** ~ **[for sb.]** [jmdm.] den Haushalt führen; **keep open** ~: ein offenes Haus haben *od.* führen; **set up** ~: einen eigenen Hausstand gründen; **put** *or* **set one's** ~ **in order** (*fig.*) seine Angelegenheiten in Ordnung bringen; **[as] safe as** ~**s** absolut sicher; **[get on] like a** ~ **on fire** (*fig.*) prächtig [miteinander auskommen]; **go all [a]round the** ~**s** (*fig.*) überall herumlaufen; (*in discussion*) sich lange im Kreise drehen; **man/lady** *or* **woman of the** ~: Hausherr, *der*/Dame des Hauses; **B** *in comb.* (*for animals*) **lion/reptile/monkey** ~: Löwen-/Reptilien-/Affenhaus, *das;* **C** (*Parl.*) (*building*) Parlamentsgebäude, *das;* (*assembly*) Haus, *das;* **the H**~ (*Brit.*) das Parlament; **H**~ **of Keys** *Unterhaus der Insel Man;* ⇒ *also* **commons** A; **lord** 1 C; **Lower House**; **parliament**; **representative** 1 B; **Upper House**; **D** (*institution*) Haus, *das;* **fashion** ~: Modehaus, *das;* **Broadcasting H**~: das Funkhaus; **Congress H**~: das Gewerkschaftshaus; **E** (*inn etc.*) Wirtshaus, *das;* **keep a good** ~: ein gepflegtes Haus führen; **on the** ~: auf Kosten des Hauses; ~ **of ill fame** *or* **repute** (*arch./joc.*), ~ (*Amer.*) (*brothel*) öffentliches Haus (*verhüll.*); ⇒ *also* **free house**; **tied**; **F** (*Relig.*) (*residence*) Ordenshaus, *das;* (*members*) Ordensgemeinschaft, *die;* Orden, *der;* **a** ~ **of friars** ein Mönchskloster; **she entered a** ~ **of nuns** sie ging in ein Kloster; **G** (*Univ.*) College, *das;* **H** (*Sch.*) *eine von mehreren Schülergruppen innerhalb einer Privatschule;* **I** (*Theatre*) (*building*) Haus, *das;* (*audience*) Publikum, *das;* (*performance*) Vorstellung, *die;* **an empty** ~: ein leeres Haus; **a good/bad** ~: eine gut/schlecht besuchte Vorstellung; **bring the** ~ **down, bring down the** ~: stürmischen Beifall auslösen; (*cause laughter*) Lachstürme entfesseln; ⇒ *also* **full house** a; **J** (*family*) Haus, *das;* Geschlecht, *das;* **the H**~ **of Windsor** das Haus Windsor; **K** (*Astrol.*) Haus, *das.*

❷ /haʊz/ *v.t.* **A** (*provide with home*) ein Heim geben (+ *Dat.*); **be** ~**d in sth.** in etw. (*Dat.*) untergebracht sein; **B** (*receive in* ~) beherbergen; **be** ~**d by sb.** bei jmdm. unterkommen *od.* Unterkunft finden; **C** (*keep, store*) unterbringen; einlagern ‹Waren›; **D** (*fig.: encase*) in sich (*Dat.*) bergen (*geh.*)

**house**/haʊs/: **~ agent** *n.* ▸1261 (*Brit.*) Häusermakler, *der;* **~ arrest** *n.* Hausarrest, *der;* **~boat** *n.* Hausboot, *das;* **~-bound** *adj.* ans Haus gefesselt; **~boy** *n.* Boy, *der;* **~breaker** *n.* (*burglar*) Einbrecher, *der;* **~breaking** *n.*, *no pl.* (*burglary*) Einbruch, *der;* **~coat** *n.* Hausmantel, *der;* Morgenmantel, *der;* **~craft** *n.*, *no pl.*, *no art.* (*Brit.*) Hauswirtschaft, *die;* **~father** *n.* Hausvater, *der;* **~ flag** *n.* (*Naut.*) Hausflagge, *die;* **~fly** *n.* Stubenfliege, *die*

**houseful** /ˈhaʊsfʊl/ *n.* **a ~ of guests** ein Haus voll[er] Gäste; **we've already got a ~:** wir haben das Haus schon voll (*ugs.*)

**house guest** /ˈhaʊs gest/ *n.* Logiergast, *der*

**household** /ˈhaʊshəʊld/ *n.* Ⓐ Haushalt, *der; attrib.* Haushalts-; **~ chores** Hausarbeit, *die;* Ⓑ **the H~** (*Brit.: royal family*) die königliche Hofhaltung

**household ˈcavalry** *n.* (*Brit. Mil.*) berittene königliche Leibgarde

**householder** /ˈhaʊshəʊldə(r)/ *n.* Ⓐ (*homeowner*) Wohnungsinhaber, *der/*-inhaberin, *die;* Ⓑ (*head of household*) Haushaltsvorstand, *der*

**household: ~ ˈgods** *n. pl.* (*Roman Ant.; also fig.*) Hausgötter; **~ ˈmanagement** *n.* Hauswirtschaft, *die;* **~ ˈname** *n.* geläufiger Name; **be a ~ name** ein Begriff sein; **~ ˈtroops** *n. pl.* (*Brit. Mil.*) königliche Leibgarde; **~ ˈword** *n.* geläufiger Ausdruck

**house** /haʊs/: **~-hunter** *n.* Haussuchende, *der/die;* **~-hunting** *n.*, *no indef. art.* Suche nach einem Haus; **go ~-hunting** sich nach einem Haus umsehen; **~ husband** *n.* Hausmann, *der;* **~keep** *v.i.* (*coll.*) den Haushalt führen (**for** *Dat.*); **~keeper** *n.* ▸1261 (*woman managing household affairs*) Haushälterin, *die;* Wirtschafterin, *die;* (*person running own home*) Hausfrau, *die*/Hausmann, *der;* (*person in charge*) Hausmeister, *der/*-meisterin, *die;* **~keeping** *n.* Ⓐ (*management*) Hauswirtschaft, *die;* Haushaltsführung, *die;* **he does most of/helps with the ~keeping** er besorgt fast den ganzen Haushalt/hilft im Haushalt; **~keeping money,** (*coll.*) **~keeping** Haushalts- *od.* Wirtschaftsgeld, *das;* Ⓑ (*fig.: maintenance, record-keeping, etc.*) Wirtschaften, *das;* **~leek** *n.* (*Bot.*) Hauswurz, *die;* **~ lights** *n. pl.* (*Theatre*) Lichter im Zuschauerraum; **~ magazine** *n.* Hauszeitschrift, *die;* **~maid** *n.* ▸1261 Hausgehilfin, *die;* **~maid's ˈknee** *n.* (*Med.*) Dienstmädchenknie, *das;* **~man** /ˈhaʊsmən/ *n.*, *pl.* **~men** /ˈhaʊsmən/ Ⓐ Hausdiener, *der;* Ⓑ (*Brit. Med.*) Medizinalassistent, *der;* **~ martin** ⇒ **martin;** **~master** *n.* (*Sch.*) *für ein „house" zuständiger Lehrer;* **~mistress** *n.* (*Sch.*) *für ein „house" zuständige Lehrerin;* **~mother** *n.* Hausmutter, *die;* **~ painter** *n.* Maler, *der/*Malerin, *die;* Anstreicher, *der/*Anstreicherin, *die;* **~ party** *n.* ≈ Gesellschaft, *die; mehrtägiges Fest in einem Landhaus;* **~ physician** *n.* (*in hospital*) *im Krankenhaus wohnender Arzt;* (*elsewhere*) Hausarzt, *der;* Anstaltsarzt, *der;* **~ plant** *n.* Zimmerpflanze, *die;* **~ prices** *n. pl.* Immobilienpreise; **~-proud** *adj.* **he/she is ~-proud** Ordnung und Sauberkeit [im Haushalt] gehen ihm/ihr über alles; **~room** *n.*, *no pl.*, *no indef. art.* **find ~room for sth.** einen Platz für etw. [in der Wohnung] finden; **I wouldn't give it ~room** das käme mir nicht ins Haus; **~-sit** *v.i.* das Haus hüten; **~-sitter** *n.* House-sitter, *der* (*ugs.*); *Person, die für jemanden das Haus hütet;* **~ ˈstyle** *n.* (*Printing, Publishing*) hauseigener Stil; **~ surgeon** *n.* (*in hospital*) *im Krankenhaus wohnender Chirurg;* (*elsewhere*) Hauschirurg, *der;* Anstaltschirurg, *der;* **~-to-~** ❶ *adj.* **make ~-to-~ enquiries** von Haus zu Haus gehen und fragen; **a ~-to-~ delivery** eine Lieferung von Haus zu Haus; ❷ *adv.* von Haus zu Haus ‹gehen usw.›; **~top** *n.* [Haus]dach, *das;* **cry** *or* **proclaim** *or* **shout sth. from the ~tops** (*fig.*) etw. öffentlich verkünden; **~-train** *v.t.* (*Brit.*) **~-train a cat/child** eine Katze/ein Kleinkind dazu bringen, dass sie/es stubenrein/sauber wird; **~-trained** *adj.* (*Brit.*) stubenrein ‹Hund, Katze›; sauber ‹Kleinkind›; **~-training** *n.* (*of pet*) Stubenreinmachen, *das;* (*of child*) Sauberkeitserziehung, *die;* Sauberkeitsgewöhnung, *die;* **~-warming** /ˈhaʊs wɔːmɪŋ/ *n.* **~-warming [party]** Einzugsfeier, *die;* **~wife** *n.* Hausfrau, *die;* **~wifely** *adj.* hausfraulich; **~work** *n.*, *no pl.* Hausarbeit, *die*

**housey-housey, housie-housie** /haʊsɪ ˈhaʊsɪ/ *n.* Lotto, *das*

**housing** /ˈhaʊzɪŋ/ *n.* Ⓐ *no pl.* (*dwellings collectively*) Wohnungen; (*provision of dwellings*) Wohnungsbeschaffung, *die; attrib.* Wohnungs-; **there was insufficient ~:** es gab zu wenig Wohnungen; **this piece of land has been set aside for ~:** auf diesem Stück Land sollen neue Wohnungen gebaut werden; **~ programme** Wohnungsbauprogramm, *das;* Ⓑ *no pl.* (*shelter*) Unterkunft, *die;* Ⓒ (*Mech. Engin.*) Gehäuse, *das*

**housing: ~ association** *n.* (*Brit.*) Gesellschaft für sozialen Wohnungsbau; **~ benefit** *n.* (*Brit.*) Wohngeld, *das;* **~ estate** *n.* (*Brit.*) Wohnsiedlung, *die*

**hove** ⇒ **heave** 1 B, 2 E

**hovel** /ˈhɒvl/ *n.* [armselige] Hütte; (*joc.*) Bruchbude, *die* (*ugs. abwertend*)

**hover** /ˈhɒvə(r)/ *v.i.* Ⓐ (*hang in air*) schweben; Ⓑ (*linger*) sich herumdrücken (*ugs.*); **~ about** *or* **round sb./sth.** um jmdn./etw. herumschleichen (*ugs.*); Ⓒ (*move to and fro*) herumstrolchen (*ugs. abwertend*); Ⓓ (*waver*) schwanken; **~ between doing this and doing that** schwanken, ob man dieses oder jenes tun soll; **~ between life and death** (*fig.*) zwischen Leben und Tod schweben

**hover: ~craft** *n.*, *pl. same* Hovercraft, *das;* Luftkissenfahrzeug, *das;* **~ mower** *n.* Luftkissenmäher, *der;* **~port** *n.* Anlegestelle [für Hovercrafts]; **~train** *n.* Luftkissenzug, *der;* (*magnetic*) Magnetschwebebahn, *die*

**how** /haʊ/ ❶ ▸1191 *adv.* wie; **learn ~ to ride a bike/swim** *etc.* Rad fahren/schwimmen *usw.* lernen; **this is ~ to do it** so macht man das; **~ do you know that?** woher weißt du das?; **~ to find the answer?** wie soll man die Lösung finden?; **~ should I know?** woher soll ich das wissen?; **~ ˈcould you?** wie konntest du nur?; **here's ~!** (*as toast*) zum Wohl!; **~ is it/does it happen that ...?** wie kommt es, dass ...?; **~'s that?** (**~** *did that happen?*) wie kommt das [denn]?; (*is that as it should be?*) ist es so gut?; (*will you agree to that?*) was hältst du davon?; (*Cricket*) ist der Schlagmann aus?; **~'s that for impudence?** ist das nicht eine Unverschämtheit?; **~ so?** wieso [das]?; **~ can that be?** wie kommt das?; **~ would it be if ...?** wie wäre es, wenn ...?; **~ would this dress be?** wie wäre es mit diesem Kleid?; **~ now?** (*arch.*) wie?; **[I know/see] ~ it is** [ich weiß,] wie das ist; **~ is she/the car?** (*after accident*) wie geht es ihr?/was ist mit dem Auto?; **~ ˈare you?** wie geht es dir?; (*greeting*) guten Morgen/Tag/Abend!; **~ do you ˈdo?** (*formal*) guten Morgen/Tag/Abend!; **~ ˈdo?** (*coll.*) Morgen/Tag/ˈn Abend! (*ugs.*); **~ much?** wie viel?; (*joc.: I did not hear*) wie bitte?; **~ many?** wie viel?; wie viele?; **~ many times?** wie oft?; **~ crazy** *etc.* **can you get?** verrückter *usw.* gehts wohl nicht! (*ugs.*); **~ far** (*to what extent*) inwieweit; **~ marvellous/perfect!** wie herrlich *od.* wunderbar! **~ right/wrong you are!** da hast du völlig Recht/da irrst du dich gewaltig!; **~ naughty of him** das war aber frech von ihm; **and ~!** (*coll.*) und wie! (*ugs.*); **we must earn a living ~ [best] we can** wir müssen uns unseren Lebensunterhalt, so gut es geht, verdienen; **~ about ...?** wie ist es mit ...?; (*in invitation, proposal, suggestion*) wie wäre es mit ...?; **~ about all the overtime I've done?** wie ist das eigentlich mit meinen ganzen Überstunden?; **~ about having a drink?** wie wäre es mit etwas zu trinken?; **~ about getting up?** wie wäre es, wenn du aufstehst/wir aufstehen?; **~ about [giving me] a lift?** wie sieht's aus, kannst du mich mitnehmen? (*ugs.*); **~ about tomorrow?** wie siehts morgen aus? (*ugs.*); **~ about it/that?** na, wie ist das?/was sagst du nun?; (*is that acceptable?*) was hältst du davon?; ⇒ *also* **come** M; **do**[1] 2 F; **ever** E; **go**[1] 1 R, S. ❷ *n.* Wie, *das*

**howbeit** /haʊˈbiːɪt/ *adv.* (*arch./literary*) nichtsdestominder

**howdah** /ˈhaʊdə/ *n.* [*baldachinartig überdachter*] *Sitz auf einem Elefanten*

**how-de-do** /haʊdɪˈduː/, **how-do-you-do** /haʊdjʊˈduː/ *ns.* **[this is] a fine** *or* **pretty how-do-you-do [we have landed in]** das ist ja eine schöne Bescherung (*ugs. iron.*)

**howdy** /ˈhaʊdɪ/ *int.* (*Amer.*) = **how do;** ⇒ **how** 1

**how-d'ye-do** /haʊdjəˈduː/ ⇒ **how-de-do**

**however** /haʊˈevə(r)/ *adv.* Ⓐ wie ... auch; egal, wie (*ugs.*); **it's a long journey ~ you choose to travel, whether by train or by car** es ist eine lange Fahrt, ganz gleich, ob du mit dem Zug oder mit dem Auto fährst; **~ beautiful she is** wie schön sie auch ist; ganz gleich, wie schön sie ist; **I shall never win this race, ~ hard I try** ich werde dieses Rennen nie gewinnen, und wenn ich mich noch so anstrenge *od.* wie sehr ich mich auch anstrenge; Ⓑ (*nevertheless*) jedoch; aber; **I don't like him very much. H~, he has never done me any harm** Ich mag ihn nicht sehr. Er hat mir allerdings noch nie etwas getan; **~, the rain soon stopped, and ...:** es hörte jedoch *od.* aber bald auf zu regnen, und ...; **this, ~, seems not to be true** das scheint jedoch *od.* aber nicht wahr zu sein; Ⓒ (*coll.*) = **how ever** ⇒ **ever** E

**howitzer** /ˈhaʊɪtsə(r)/ *n.* (*Mil.*) Haubitze, *die*

**howl** /haʊl/ ❶ *n.* Ⓐ (*of animal*) Heulen, *das;* (*of distress*) Schrei, *der;* **the repeated ~s of the dog** das wiederholte Heulen des Hundes; **a ~ of pain** *or* **agony** ein Schmerzensschrei; **~s of protest/rage** Protestgeschrei, *das*/wütendes Geschrei; **~s of laughter** brüllendes Gelächter; **~s of delight/merriment** Freudengeheul, *das;* **~s of derision/scorn** verächtliches Gejohle; Ⓑ (*Electr.*) Pfeifgeräusch, *das.* ❷ *v.i.* ‹Tier, Wind:› heulen; (*with distress*) schreien; **~ in** *or* **with pain/hunger** *etc.* vor Schmerz/Hunger *usw.* schreien; **~ with laughter** vor Lachen brüllen. ❸ *v.t.* [hinaus]schreien
**~ ˈdown** *v.t.* niederbrüllen

**howler** /ˈhaʊlə(r)/ *n.* (*coll.: blunder*) Schnitzer, *der* (*ugs.*); **make a ~:** sich (*Dat.*) einen Schnitzer leisten

**howling** /ˈhaʊlɪŋ/ ❶ *n.* Heulen, *das;* (*of distress*) Schreien, *das.* ❷ *adj.* Ⓐ heulend ‹Tier, Wind›; (*crying with distress*) schreiend; (*with laughter*) johlend; **the ~ mob** der johlende Pöbel; **five ~ brats/children** fünf Schreihälse (*ugs.*); **there is a ~ draught in this room** (*coll.*) hier im Zimmer zieht es höllisch (*ugs.*); Ⓑ (*coll.: extreme*) enorm; fürchterlich ‹Katastrophe›; **a ~ mistake** ein Riesenfehler (*ugs.*)

**howsoˈe'er** (*poet.*), **howsoˈever** *adv.* Ⓐ (*arch.*) wie auch immer; Ⓑ (*to whatsoever extent*) wie ... auch immer

**hoy** /hɔɪ/ *int.* he! (*ugs.*)

**HP** *abbr.* Ⓐ /eɪtʃˈpiː/ (*Brit.*) **hire purchase; on HP** auf Teilzahlungsbasis; Ⓑ **horsepower** PS; Ⓒ **high pressure**

**HQ** *abbr.* **headquarters** HQ

**HRH** *abbr.* **Her/His Royal Highness** I./S. Kgl. H.

**hr[s].** *abbr.* **hour[s]** Std[n].; **at 0800 hrs.** um 8.00 Uhr

**HRT** *abbr.* **hormone replacement therapy**

**HT** *abbr.* **high tension**

**HTML** *abbr.* (*Computing*) **hypertext markup language** HTML

**hub** /hʌb/ *n.* Ⓐ (*of wheel*) [Rad]nabe, *die;* Ⓑ (*fig.: central point*) Mittelpunkt, *der;* Zentrum, *das;* **the ~ of the universe** (*fig.*) der Nabel der Welt (*geh.*)

**hubbub** /ˈhʌbʌb/ *n.* Ⓐ (*din*) Lärm, *der;* **a ~ of conversation/voices** ein Stimmengewirr; Ⓑ (*disturbance*) Tumult, *der;* **be in a ~:** sich in Aufruhr befinden

**hubby** /ˈhʌbɪ/ *n.* (*coll.*) Mann, *der;* (*iron./joc.*) der Herr des Hauses

**hub: ~cap** *n.* Radkappe, *die;* **~ dynamo** *n.* Nabendynamo, *der* **~ gear** *n.* Nabenschaltung, *die*

**hubris** /'hju:brɪs/ *n., no pl.* Überheblichkeit, *die;* Hybris, *die (geh.)*

**huckleberry** /'hʌklbərɪ/ *n. (Bot.)* **A** *(Gaylussacia)* Gaylussacie, *die (fachspr.);* ≈ Heidelbeere, *die; attrib.* ≈ Heidelbeer-; **B** *(Vaccinium)* Heidel- *od.* Blaubeere, *die*

**huckster** /'hʌkstə(r)/ *n.* **A** *(pedlar)* Straßenhändler, *der; (from door to door)* Hausierer, *der;* **B** *(mercenary person)* Profitjäger, *der (abwertend);* **C** *(Amer.) (salesman using showmanship)* Werbefachmann, *der; (Radio, Telev.: presenter)* Propagandist, *der*

**huddle** /'hʌdl/ **1** *v.i.* sich drängen; *(curl up, nestle)* sich kuscheln; **~ against each other/together** sich aneinander drängen/sich zusammendrängen; **a few cottages ~d on the hillside** ein paar kleine Häuser kauerten sich an den Hang. **2** *v.t.* **A** *(put on)* **~ one's coat around one** sich in den Mantel hüllen; **B** *(crowd together)* [eng] zusammendrängen; **the sheep were ~d against the fence/together** die Schafe drängten sich gegen den Zaun/aneinander. **3** *v. refl.* **~ oneself against sb./sth.** sich an jmdn./etw. kuscheln; **~ oneself up** sich zusammenkauern. **4** *n.* **A** *(tight group)* dicht gedrängte Menge *od.* Gruppe; **[stand] in a ~:** dicht zusammengedrängt [stehen]; **B** *(coll.: conference)* Besprechung, *die;* **be in a ~/go [off] in[to] a ~:** die Köpfe zusammenstecken *(ugs.)*

**~ 'up** *v.i. (nestle up)* sich zusammenkauern; *(crowd together)* sich [zusammen]drängen; **~ up to sb./sth.** sich an jmdn./etw. kuscheln

**hue**[1] /hju:/ *n.* **A** Farbton, *der;* **his face was of** *or* **had** *or* **looked a very sickly ~:** er hatte eine sehr ungesunde Gesichtsfarbe; **the sky took on a reddish ~:** der Himmel färbte sich rötlich; **B** *(fig.: aspect)* Schattierung, *die;* Couleur, *die*

**hue**[2] *n.* **~ and cry** *(outcry)* lautes Geschrei; *(protest)* Gezeter, *das (abwertend);* **raise a ~ and cry against sb./sth.** ein lautes Geschrei/Gezeter über jmdn./etw. anstimmen

**huff** /hʌf/ **1** *v.i.* **~ and puff** schnaufen und keuchen; *(fig.: speak threateningly and bombastically)* sich aufblasen *(ugs.).* **2** *n.* **be in a ~:** beleidigt *od. (ugs.)* eingeschnappt sein; **get into a ~:** einschnappen *(ugs.);* den Beleidigten/die Beleidigte spielen *(ugs.);* **go off in a ~:** beleidigt *od.* eingeschnappt abziehen *(ugs.)*

**huffy** /'hʌfɪ/ *adj.* **A** *(indignant)* ungehalten *(geh.);* **get ~ [about** *or* **over sth.]** [wegen etw.] beleidigt *od. (ugs.)* eingeschnappt sein; *(become irritated)* [über etw. *(Akk.)*] aufgebracht sein; **B** *(easily offended)* empfindlich; gereizt ‹Stimmung, Laune›

**hug** /hʌg/ **1** *n. (squeeze)* Umarmung, *die; (of animal)* Umklammerung, *die;* **give sb. a ~:** jmdn. umarmen. **2** *v.t.,* **-gg-:** **A** *(squeeze)* umarmen; ‹Tier:› umklammern; **~ sb./sth. to oneself** jmdn./etw. an sich *(Akk.)* drücken *od.* pressen; **~ one's knees** seine Knie umfassen; **the bear ~ged him to death** der Bär drückte ihn zu Tode; **B** *(keep close to)* sich dicht halten an (+ *Dat.*); ‹Schiff, Auto usw.:› dicht entlangfahren an (+ *Dat.*); **C** *(fit tightly around)* eng anliegen an (+ *Dat.*); **a pullover that ~s the figure** ein Pullover, der die Figur betont. **3** *v. refl.,* **-gg-** die Arme um sich schlagen; **we ~ged ourselves for** *or* **on managing to win** *(fig.)* wir beglückwünschten uns dazu, den Sieg errungen zu haben

**huge** /hju:dʒ/ *adj.* riesig; gewaltig ‹Unterschied, Verbesserung, Interesse›; **the problem is ~:** das Problem ist außerordentlich schwierig; **she is not just fat: she is ~:** sie ist nicht einfach dick: sie ist ein Monstrum; **tell ~ lies** wie gedruckt lügen *(ugs.)*

**hugely** /'hju:dʒlɪ/ *adv.* gewaltig; riesig ‹sich freuen, sich amüsieren›; außerordentlich ‹intelligent›; ungeheuer ‹erfolgreich›

**Huguenot** /'hju:gənɒt, 'hju:gənəʊ/ *pr. n.* Hugenotte, *der*/Hugenottin, *die; attrib.* Hugenotten-

**huh** /hʌ/ *int. (Amer.)* pah!

**hula hoop** /'hu:lə hu:p/ *n.* Hula-Hoop-Reifen, *der*

**hulk** /hʌlk/ *n.* **A** *(body of ship)* [Schiffs]rumpf, *der; (as store etc.)* Hulk, *die od. der (Seew.);* **B** *(wreck) (of car, machine, etc.)* Wrack, *das; (of house)* Ruine, *die;* **C** *(unwieldy ship)* dicker Pott *(ugs.);* **D** *(fig.) (big thing)* Klotz, *der; (big person)* Koloss, *der (ugs. scherzh.);* **a ~ of a man** ein Klotz von [einem] Mann *(fig. ugs.)*

**hulking** /'hʌlkɪŋ/ *adj. (coll.) (bulky)* wuchtig; *(clumsy)* klotzig *(abwertend);* **a ~ great person/thing** ein klobiger Mensch/ein klobiges Etwas; **a ~ great brute of a man/dog** ein grobschlächtiger, brutaler Kerl/ein scheußliches Ungetüm von einem Hund

**hull**[1] /hʌl/ *n. (Naut.)* Schiffskörper, *der; (Aeronaut.)* Rumpf, *der;* **be ~ down on the horizon** ‹Schiff:› am Horizont entschwinden/auftauchen

**hull**[2] **1** *n. (Bot.) (pod, husk)* Hülse, *die; (of peas)* Schote, *die; (of barley, oats, etc.)* Spelze, *die.* **2** *v.t.* enthülsen ‹Erbsen, Bohnen, Korn›; entstielen ‹Erdbeeren›

**hullabaloo** /hʌləbə'lu:/ *n.* **A** *(noise)* Radau, *der (ugs.);* Lärm, *der; (of show business life, city)* Trubel, *der;* **B** *(controversy)* Aufruhr, *der;* **make a ~ about sth.** viel Lärm um etw. machen; **I don't see what all the ~ is about** ich verstehe nicht, was das ganze Theater *(ugs.)* eigentlich soll

**hullo** /hə'ləʊ/ ⇒ **hallo; hello**

**hum** /hʌm/ **1** *v.i.,* **-mm-:** **A** summen; ‹Motor, Maschine, Kreisel:› brummen; **~ and ha** *or* **haw** *(coll.)* herumdrucksen *(ugs.);* **the workshop was ~ming with the noise of machinery** die Werkstatt war vom Brummen der Maschinen erfüllt; **B** *(coll.: be in state of activity)* voller Leben *od.* Aktivität sein; **things are ~ming** die Sache ist in Schwung gekommen *od.* läuft *(ugs.);* **make things ~, set things ~ming** die Sache in Schwung bringen *(ugs.);* **C** *(Brit. coll.: smell)* riechen. **2** *v.t.,* **-mm-** summen ‹Melodie, Lied›. **3** *n.* **A** Summen, *das; (of spinning top, machinery, engine)* Brummen, *das;* **B** *(inarticulate sound)* Hm, *das;* **~s and ha's** *or* **haws** verlegenes Geräusper; **C** *(of voices, conversation)* Gemurmel, *das; (of insects and small creatures)* Gesumme, *das; (of traffic)* Brausen, *das;* **D** *(Electronics)* Brummen, *das;* **E** *(Brit. coll.: smell)* Geruch, *der.* **4** *int.* hm

**human** /'hju:mən/ **1** *adj.* menschlich; **~ biology** Humanbiologie, *die;* **result in a terrible loss of ~ life** ‹Katastrophe:› erschreckend viele Menschenleben fordern *(geh.);* **untouched by ~ hand** hygienisch verpackt ‹Lebensmittel›; **the ~ condition** das Menschsein; **the ~ race** die menschliche Rasse; das Menschengeschlecht *(geh.);* **~ sacrifice** Menschenopfer, *das;* **~ dustbin** *(joc.)* Resteesser, *der;* **they formed a ~ chain** sie bildeten eine Kette; *(as demonstration)* sie bildeten eine Menschenkette; **do everything within ~ power** alles Menschenmögliche tun; **that is not ~:** das ist unmenschlich; **I sometimes wonder if he's ~** *(iron.)* manchmal frage ich mich, ob er überhaupt ein Mensch ist; **I'm only ~:** ich bin auch nur ein Mensch; **it's only ~:** es ist menschlich; **~ error** menschliches Versagen; **the ~ element** *or* **factor** das menschliche Element; der menschliche Faktor; **lack the ~ touch** menschliche Wärme vermissen lassen; **be ~!** sei kein Unmensch!; ⇒ *also* **nature** D. **2** *n.* Mensch, *der*

**human: ~ 'being** *n.* Mensch, *der;* **~ 'comedy** *n.* menschliche Komödie *(fig.)*

**humane** /hju:'meɪn/ *adj.* **A** human; **B** *(tending to civilize)* humanistisch

**humane 'killer** *n. Instrument zur schmerzlosen Tötung von Tieren (bes. im Schlachthof)*

**humanely** /hju:'meɪnlɪ/ *adv.* human

**human: ~ engi'neering** *n. (Industry)* Human engineering, *das;* Ergonomie, *die;* **~ 'interest** *n., no pl.* **a story full of/an occupation with a lot of ~ interest** eine Geschichte, in der/ein Beruf, in dem das Menschliche eine große Rolle spielt; **~-interest story** Geschichte aus dem Leben

**humanise** ⇒ **humanize**

**humanism** /'hju:mənɪzm/ *n., no pl.* **A** Humanität, *die;* Menschlichkeit, *die;* **B** *(literary culture; also Philos.)* Humanismus, *der*

**humanist** /'hju:mənɪst/ *n.* Humanist, *der*/Humanistin, *die*

**humanistic** /hju:mə'nɪstɪk/ *adj.* **A** *(Philos.)* humanistisch; **B** *(humanitarian)* humanitär ‹Einstellung, Zwecke›; von Menschlichkeit zeugend ‹Äußerung›; **C** *(of classical study)* humanistisch; *(as opposed to scientific study)* geisteswissenschaftlich

**humanitarian** /hju:mænɪ'teərɪən/ **1** *adj.* humanitär. **2** *n. (philanthropist)* Menschenfreund, *der; (promoter of human welfare)* Humanitarist, *der*/Humanitaristin, *die*

**humanitarianism** /hju:mænɪ'teərɪənɪzm/ *n., no pl.* Humanitarismus, *der*

**humanity** /hju:'mænɪtɪ/ *n.* **A** *no pl.* Menschsein, *das;* **he was a pathetic specimen of ~:** er war ein jämmerliches Exemplar der Gattung Mensch; **B** *no pl., no art. (mankind)* Menschheit, *die; (people collectively)* Menschen; **C** *no pl. (being humane)* Humanität, *die;* Menschlichkeit, *die;* **D** *in pl. (cultural learning)* **[the] humanities** [die] Geisteswissenschaften; *(study of Latin and Greek classics)* [die] Altphilologie; [die] klassische Philologie

**humanize** /'hju:mənaɪz/ *v.t.* **A** *(make human)* vermenschlichen; **B** *(adapt to human use)* den menschlichen Bedürfnissen anpassen; humanisieren ‹Industrie›; **C** *(make humane)* humanisieren ‹Strafvollzug›; zivilisieren ‹Wilde›; geistig bilden ‹Gesellschaft›

**'humankind** *n., no pl., no art.* die Menschheit; **all ~:** die ganze Menschheit

**humanly** /'hju:mənlɪ/ *adv.* menschlich; *(by human means)* mit menschlichen Mitteln; **do everything ~ possible** alles Menschenmögliche tun; **would it be ~ possible to obtain a copy?** wäre es zu viel verlangt, ein Exemplar zu bekommen?

**human: ~ re'lations** *n. pl. (Social Psych., Industry)* Human Relations *Pl.;* **~ re'sources** *n.* **A** *pl.* [Arbeits]kräfte *Pl.;* Personal, *das;* **B** *sing. (department)* Personalabteilung, *die;* **~ 'right** *n.* **~ rights** Menschenrechte *Pl.;* **fundamental ~ right** Grundrecht, *das;* **Court of H~ Rights** Europäischer Gerichtshof für Menschenrechte; *attrib.* **~ rights group** Menschenrechtsorganisation, *die*

**humble** /'hʌmbl/ **1** *adj.* **A** ▶ **924** *(modest)* bescheiden; ergeben ‹Untertan, Diener, Gefolgsmann›; bescheiden ‹Vorschlag, Meinung›; demütig ‹Gebet›; ehrfurchtsvoll ‹Bewunderung›; unterwürfig *(oft abwertend)* ‹Haltung, Knechtschaft›; **when I look up at the vast universe, it makes me feel very ~:** wenn ich das unermessliche Universum betrachte, komme ich mir sehr klein und unbedeutend vor; **may I offer** *or* **please accept my ~ apologies** ich bitte ergebenst um Verzeihung; **eat ~ pie** klein beigeben; ⇒ *also* **servant** C; **B** *(low-ranking)* einfach; niedrig ‹Status, Rang usw.›; **he stems from very ~ stock/origins** er ist von sehr niedriger Geburt *od.* Herkunft; **C** *(unpretentious)* einfach; bescheiden ‹Zuhause, Wohnung, Anfang›; **the meal/gift was a very ~ offering** es war ein sehr einfaches Essen/nur eine bescheidene Gabe. **2** *v.t.* **A** *(abase)* demütigen; **feel ~d** sich *(Dat.)* klein vorkommen; **~ oneself** sich demütigen *od.* erniedrigen; **B** *(remove power of)* entmachten; *(defeat decisively)* [vernichtend] schlagen; **~ oneself** sich [selbst] erniedrigen

**'humble-bee** *n.* Hummel, *die*

**humbly** /'hʌmblɪ/ *adv.* **A** *(with humility)* demütig; ergebenst ‹um Verzeihung bitten›; ergeben ‹dienen›; *(meekly)* unterwürfig; *(in formal address)* höflichst ‹bitten, ersuchen›; **B** *(in low rank)* **~ born** von niedriger Herkunft; **C**

(*unpretentiously*) einfach; bescheiden; spärlich ‹ausgestattet›

**humbug** /'hʌmbʌg/ *n.* Ⓐ *no pl., no art.* (*deception, nonsense*) Humbug, *der* (*ugs. abwertend*); Ⓑ (*fraud*) Schwindel, *der;* Betrug, *der;* Ⓒ (*impostor*) Schwindler, *der*/Schwindlerin, *die* (*abwertend*); Ⓓ (*Brit.: sweet*) [Pfefferminz]bonbon, *der od. das*

**humdinger** /'hʌmdɪŋə(r), hʌm'dɪŋə(r)/ *n.* (*coll.*) **be a ~:** Spitze *od.* große Klasse sein (*ugs.*); **she's a real ~:** sie ist absolute Spitze; **when we have a quarrel, it's a real ~:** wenn wir uns streiten, fliegen die Fetzen (*ugs.*)

**humdrum** /'hʌmdrʌm/ *adj.* Ⓐ alltäglich; eintönig ‹Leben›; langweilig ‹Person›; Ⓑ (*monotonous*) stumpfsinnig; **the ~ routine of life/things** das tägliche Einerlei

**humerus** /'hju:mərəs/ *n., pl.* **humeri** /'hju:məraɪ/ (*Anat., Zool.*) Humerus, *der*

**humid** /'hju:mɪd/ *adj.* feucht; humid (*Geogr.*)

**humidifier** /hju:'mɪdɪfaɪə(r)/ *n.* Luftbefeuchter, *der*

**humidify** /hju:'mɪdɪfaɪ/ *v.t.* befeuchten

**humidity** /hju:'mɪdɪtɪ/ *n.* Ⓐ *no pl.* Feuchtigkeit, *die;* **I don't mind the heat but I cannot stand ~:** die Hitze macht mir nichts aus, aber die [hohe] Luftfeuchtigkeit kann ich nicht vertragen; **the ~ of the atmosphere** die [hohe] Luftfeuchtigkeit; Ⓑ (*degree of moisture*) **~ [of the atmosphere]** Luftfeuchtigkeit, *die* (*Met.*); Luftfeuchte, *die* (*bes. fachspr.*)

**humiliate** /hju:'mɪlɪeɪt/ *v.t.* demütigen; **I was** *or* **felt totally ~d** ich war zutiefst beschämt

**humiliation** /hju:mɪlɪ'eɪʃn/ *n.* Demütigung, *die*

**humility** /hju:'mɪlɪtɪ/ *n.* Demut, *die;* (*of servant*) Ergebenheit, *die;* (*absence of pride or arrogance*) Bescheidenheit, *die*

**humming**/'hʌmɪŋ/**: ~bird** *n.* Kolibri, *der;* **~-top** *n.* Brummkreisel, *der*

**hummock** /'hʌmək/ *n.* Ⓐ (*hillock*) [kleiner] Hügel; Ⓑ (*Amer.: rise*) Waldinsel, *die;* Ⓒ (*in ice field*) Eishügel, *der*

**humor** (*Amer.*) ⇒ **humour**

**humoresque** /hju:mə'resk/ *n.* (*Mus.*) Humoreske, *die*

**humorist** /'hju:mərɪst/ *n.* Ⓐ (*facetious person*) Spaßvogel, *der;* Komiker, *der* (*fig.*); Ⓑ (*talker, writer*) Humorist, *der*/Humoristin, *die*

**humorless** (*Amer.*) ⇒ **humourless**

**humorous** /'hju:mərəs/ *adj.* Ⓐ (*comic*) lustig, komisch ‹Geschichte, Name, Situation›; witzig ‹Bemerkung›; **I fail to see anything ~ in the situation** ich finde die Situation überhaupt nicht komisch *od.* lustig; **the ~ side of the situation** das Komische der Situation; **stop trying to be ~:** hör auf damit, komisch wirken zu wollen!; Ⓑ (*showing sense of humour*) humorvoll ‹Person›; **be/not be in a ~ mood** in heiterer Stimmung sein/nicht zum Lachen aufgelegt sein

**humorously** /'hju:mərəslɪ/ *adv.* Ⓐ (*comically*) komisch; lustig; **his remarks were meant ~, not offensively** seine Bemerkungen sollten belustigen und nicht verletzen; **~ enough, ...:** lustigerweise ...; Ⓑ (*with sense of humour*) humorvoll; **look ~ at the problems of life** den Problemen des Alltags mit Humor begegnen

**humour** /'hju:mə(r)/ (*Brit.*) ❶ *n.* Ⓐ *no pl., no indef. art.* (*faculty, comic quality*) Humor, *der;* (*of situation*) Komische, *das;* **see the ~ of sth.** einer Sache (*Dat.*) die komische Seite abgewinnen; **sense of ~:** Sinn für Humor; **he has no sense of ~:** er hat keinen Humor; Ⓑ *no pl., no indef. art.* (*facetiousness*) Witzigkeit, *die;* **a funeral is no place for ~:** bei einer Beerdigung macht man keine Witze; Ⓒ (*mood*) Laune, *die;* **his ~ is sometimes melancholy** er ist manchmal [in] melancholisch[er Stimmung]; **be in a good/bad ~:** in guter Stimmung sein/schlechte Laune haben; **what sort of ~ are you in?** wie ist deine Stimmung?; **in good ~:** gut gelaunt; **be out of ~:** schlechte Laune haben; **a fit of ill ~:** ein Anfall von schlechter Laune; **have recovered one's good ~:** wieder bei Laune sein; Ⓓ (*disposition*) Temperament, *das;* **be of a pleasant/jovial ~:** eine angenehme/joviale Art haben; Ⓔ (*Hist.: body fluid*) Körpersaft, *der;* Humor, *der* (*Med. veralt.*); **the cardinal ~s** die Hauptsäfte des Körpers; ⇒ *also* **aqueous humour**; **vitreous** B.

❷ *v.t.* (*indulge*) willfahren (*geh.*) (+ *Dat.*); **~ sb.** jmdm. seinen Willen lassen; **~ sb.'s taste** jmds. Geschmack *od.* Vorliebe (*Dat.*) entsprechen; **don't [try to] ~ me!** sei nicht so übertrieben rücksichtsvoll!; **do it just to ~ her/him** tus doch, damit sie ihren/er seinen Willen hat

**humourless** /'hju:məlɪs/ *adj.* (*Brit.*) humorlos; todernst ‹Gesicht›; trocken ‹Buch›

**humous** /'hju:məs/ *adj.* humos (*Bodenk.*)

**hump** /hʌmp/ ❶ *n.* Ⓐ (*human*) Buckel, *der;* Höcker, *der* (*ugs.*); (*of animal*) Höcker, *der;* **he has a ~ on his back** er hat einen Buckel; **live on one's ~** (*fig.*) von seinen Reserven leben; Ⓑ (*mound*) Hügel, *der;* (*Railw.*) Ablaufberg, *der;* Ⓒ (*fig.: critical point*) Wendepunkt, *der;* **be over the ~:** über den Berg sein (*ugs.*); Ⓓ (*Brit. coll.*) **have the ~:** sauer sein (*ugs.*); **get the ~:** [stink]sauer werden (*ugs.*). ❷ *v.t.* (*Brit. coll.*) (*carry*) schleppen; (*hoist*) **~ a sack on to one's shoulders** einen Sack buckeln *od.* auf den Buckel nehmen (*ugs.*)

**hump: ~back** *n.* Ⓐ ⇒ **hunchback**; Ⓑ ⇒ **~back whale**; **~back 'bridge** *n.* gewölbte Brücke; **~backed** /'hʌmpbækt/ *adj.* ⇒ **hunchbacked**; **~back 'whale** *n.* Buckelwal, *der;* **~ 'bridge** ⇒ **~back bridge**

**humph** /hmf/ ❶ *int.* hm. ❷ *n.* Hm, *das;* Grunzen, *das* (*ugs.*)

**humus** /'hju:məs/ *n.* Humus, *der*

**Hun** /hʌn/ *n.* Ⓐ (*Hist.*) Hunne, *der*/Hunnin, *die; attrib.* Hunnen-; Ⓑ (*derog.: German*) Sauerkrautfresser, *der* (*ugs. abwertend*); **the ~** (*collect.*) der Teutone (*abwertend*)

**hunch**[1] /hʌntʃ/ ❶ *v.t.* hochziehen ‹Schultern›; **sit ~ed in a corner** zusammengekauert in einer Ecke sitzen; **he/the cat ~ed his/its back** er/die Katze machte einen Buckel. ❷ *v.i.* (*Amer.*) Ⓐ (*adopt bent posture*) sich krümmen; (*curl up*) sich zusammenrollen; **~ in a chair** gebeugt *od.* mit krummem Rücken auf einem Stuhl sitzen; Ⓑ (*rise in hump*) sich buckelartig erheben; sich nach oben wölben; **his shoulders ~ed** er zog die Schultern hoch

**~ 'up** ❶ *v.t.* hochziehen; **don't sit ~ed up like that** sitz nicht so krumm da!; **~ oneself up** einen Buckel machen. ❷ *v.i.* (*Amer.*) ⇒ **hunch**[1] 2

**hunch**[2] *n.* (*intuitive feeling*) Gefühl, *das;* **I have a ~ that ..., my ~ is that ...:** ich habe das [leise] Gefühl, dass ...; **the detective followed a ~:** der Detektiv folgte einem inneren Gefühl

**hunch: ~back** *n.* Ⓐ (*back*) Buckel, *der;* Ⓑ (*person*) Bucklige, *der/die;* **be a ~back** einen Buckel haben; **the H~back of Notre Dame** der Glöckner von Notre-Dame; **~backed** /'hʌntʃbækt/ *adj.* buck[e]lig; höckerig ‹Kamel›

**hundred** /'hʌndrəd/ ▶ **912**, ▶ **1012**, ▶ **1352** ❶ *adj.* Ⓐ hundert; **a** *or* **one ~:** [ein]hundert; **two/several ~:** zweihundert/mehrere hundert; **a** *or* **one ~ and one** [ein]hundert[und]eins; **a** *or* **one ~ and one people** hundert[und]ein Menschen *od.* Mensch; **the ~ metres race** der Hundertmeterlauf; **the H~ Years War** (*Hist.*) der Hundertjährige Krieg; **eighteen ~ hours** 18.00 Uhr; Ⓑ **a ~ [and one]** (*fig.: innumerable*) hundert (*ugs.*); **I've told you a ~ times** ich habe es dir schon hundertmal gesagt; **never** *or* **not in a ~ years** nie im Leben; **I've got a ~ [and one] things to do** ich habe hunderterlei zu tun (*ugs.*); Ⓒ **a** *or* **one ~ per cent** hundertprozentig; **I'm not a ~ per cent at the moment** (*fig.*) momentan geht es mir nicht sehr gut. ⇒ *also* **eight** 1; **mile** A.

❷ *n.* Ⓐ (*number*) hundert; **a** *or* **one/two ~:** [ein]hundert/zweihundert; **count up to a** *or* **one ~:** bis hundert zählen; **not if I live to be a ~:** nie im Leben; **in** *or* **by ~s** hundertweise; **the seventeen-~s** *etc.* das achtzehnte *usw.* Jahrhundert; **a ~ and one** *etc.* [ein]hundert[und]eins *usw.*; **a** *or* **one/two ~ of the men died** einhundert/zweihundert der Männer starben; **there are five ~ of us** wir sind zu fünfhundert; **it's a ~ to one that ...:** die Chancen stehen hundert zu eins, dass ...; Ⓑ (*symbol, written figure*) Hundert, *die; in adding numbers by columns* Hunderter, *der* (*Math.*); (*set or group of 100*) Hundert, *das;* (*~-pound etc. note*) Hunderter, *der;* Ⓒ (*indefinite amount*) **~s** Hunderte *Pl.;* **tourists flock to Rome by the ~[s]** *or* **in their ~s** die Touristen reisen zu Hunderten nach Rom; **~s of times** hundertmal; Ⓓ (*Brit. Hist.: county division*) Zent, *die;* ⇒ *also* **Chiltern Hundreds**. ⇒ *also* **eight** 2 A

**hundredfold** /'hʌndrədfəʊld/ ❶ *adv.* hundertfach. ❷ *adj.* hundertfach. ❸ *n.* Hundertfache, *das;* **improve a ~** (*fig.*) sich um ein Vielfaches verbessern; **she had repaid his kindness a ~:** sie hatte seine Güte tausendfach vergolten; **by a ~:** um das Hundertfache. ⇒ *also* **eightfold**

**hundreds and 'thousands** *n. pl.* (*sweets*) Liebesperlen *Pl.*

**hundredth** /'hʌndrədθ/ ❶ *adj.* hundertst...; **the one-/two-~ person** der [ein]hundertste/zweihundertste Mensch; **a ~ part** ein Hundertstel; ⇒ *also* **eighth** 1. ❷ *n.* Ⓐ (*fraction*) Hundertstel, *das;* **a ~ of a second** eine Hundertstelsekunde; Ⓑ (*in sequence, rank*) Hunderstte, *der/die/das;* **Old H~** (*Eccl.*) der hunderstte Psalm. ⇒ *also* **eighth** 2

**hundredweight** /'hʌndrədweɪt/ *n., pl. same or* **~s** ▶ **1683** Ⓐ (*Brit.*) **[long] ~:** 50,8 kg; ≈ Zentner, *der;* Ⓑ (*in metric weight*) **[metric] ~:** Zentner, *der;* Ⓒ (*Amer.*) **[short] ~:** 45,36 kg; ≈ Zentner, *der* (*45,36 kg*)

**hung** ⇒ **hang** 1, 2

**Hungarian** /hʌŋ'geərɪən/ ▶ **1275**, ▶ **1340** ❶ *adj.* ungarisch; **sb. is ~:** jmd. ist Ungar/Ungarin; ⇒ *also* **English** 1. ❷ *n.* Ⓐ (*person*) Ungar, *der*/Ungarin, *die;* Ⓑ (*language*) Ungarisch, *das;* ⇒ *also* **English** 2 A

**Hungary** /'hʌŋgərɪ/ *pr. n.* Ungarn (*das*)

**hunger** /'hʌŋgə(r)/ ❶ *n.* (*lit. or fig.*) Hunger, *der;* **pang[s] of ~:** quälender Hunger; **the pangs of ~ were getting stronger** der Hunger plagte mich *usw.* immer mehr; **~ is the best sauce** (*prov.*) Hunger ist der beste Koch (*Spr.*); **die of ~:** verhungern; (*fig.: be very hungry*) vor Hunger sterben (*ugs.*); **~ for sth.** (*lit. or fig.*) Hunger nach etw. (*geh.*); **~ for revenge/knowledge** Rache-/Wissensdurst, *der.* ❷ *v.i.* (*have craving*); **~ after** *or* **for sb./sth.** [heftiges] Verlangen nach jmdm./etw. haben

**hunger: ~ march** *n.* Hungermarsch, *der;* **~ marcher** *n.* Hungermarschierer, *der;* **~ strike** ❶ *n.* Hungerstreik, *der;* **stage a/go on ~ strike** in den Hungerstreik treten; ❷ *v.i.* in den Hungerstreik treten; **be ~ striking** sich im Hungerstreik befinden; **~ striker** *n.* Hungerstreikende, *der/die*

**hung: ~ 'jury** *n. Geschworenengericht, das zu keinem einstimmigen Urteil/keinem Mehrheitsurteil gelangen kann;* **~-'over** *adj.* (*coll.*) verkatert (*ugs.*); **~ 'parliament** *n. Parlament, in dem keine Partei die absolute Mehrheit hat*

**hungrily** /'hʌŋgrɪlɪ/ *adv.* Ⓐ hungrig; **my stomach was rumbling/growling ~:** mir knurrte vor Hunger der Magen; Ⓑ (*fig.: longingly*) sehnsüchtig ‹an etw. denken›; [be]gierig ‹etw. verfolgen›

**hungry** /'hʌŋgrɪ/ *adj.* Ⓐ (*feeling hunger*) hungrig; (*regularly feeling hunger or lacking food*) hungernd; (*showing hunger*) hungrig, gierig ‹Augen, Blick›; **be ~:** Hunger haben; hungrig sein; **we were poor and ~:** wir waren arm und litten Hunger; **[as] ~ as a hunter** *or* **lion** *or* **wolf** hungrig wie ein Löwe *od.* Wolf; **go ~:** hungern; hungrig bleiben; **I don't like fish. — Go ~, then!** Ich mag keinen Fisch. — Dann musst du eben hungern; **~ years** Hungerjahre *Pl.;* Ⓑ (*inducing hunger*) hungrig machend; Ⓒ (*fig.:*

*eager, avaricious*) [hab]gierig ‹Spekulant›; stürmisch ‹Liebhaber›; brennend, glühend ‹Verlangen›; hungrig ‹Ozean, Kriegsmaschine usw.›; **be ~ for sb./sth.** sich nach jmdm. sehnen/nach etw. hungern (*geh.*); **be ~ to do sth.** darauf brennen, etw. zu tun; **~ for success/power/knowledge/love** erfolgs-/macht-/bildungs-/liebeshungrig; **~ to learn** lernbegierig; **be ~ after sth.** nach etw. hungern (*geh.*); **success-/war-/freedom-~:** erfolgshungrig/kriegslustig/freiheitsdurstig; (D) (*barren*) karg

**hunk** /hʌŋk/ *n.* (A) (*large piece*) [großes] Stück; (*clumsy piece*) Brocken, *der;* (*of bread*) Brocken, *der;* Ranken, *der* (*landsch.*); **~s of wood** große Holzscheite; (B) (*coll.: large person*) stattliche Erscheinung; **he is a gorgeous great ~:** er ist ein blendend aussehender, stattlicher Mann; **a great ~ of a weightlifter** ein Koloss (*ugs. scherzh.*) von einem Gewichtheber

**hunky** /ˈhʌŋkɪ/ *adj.* (*coll.*) stattlich

**hunky-dory** /hʌŋkɪˈdɔːrɪ/ *adj.* (*Amer. coll.*) prima (*ugs.*); **everything's ~, it's all ~:** es ist alles in [bester] Ordnung

**hunt** /hʌnt/ ❶ *n.* (A) (*pursuit of game*) Jagd, *die;* **the ~ is up** (*Sport*) die Jagd ist eröffnet; Jagd frei! (*Jägerspr.*); **badger-/deer-~:** Dachs-/Hirschjagd, *die;* (B) (*search*) Suche, *die;* (*strenuous search*) Jagd, *die;* **be on the ~ for sb./sth.** auf der Suche/Jagd nach jmdm./etw. sein; **the ~ is on/up [for sb./sth.]** die Suche/Jagd [nach jmdm./etw.] hat begonnen/die Jagd [nach jmdm./etw.] ist eröffnet; (C) (*body of fox-hunters*) Jagd[gesellschaft], *die;* (*association*) Jagdverband, *der;* **the local ~:** der örtliche Jägerverein; (D) (*district*) Jagd, *die;* Jagdrevier, *das.*

❷ *v.t.* (A) jagen; Jagd machen auf (+ *Akk.*); **he spends his weekends ~ing foxes** am Wochenende geht er auf die Fuchsjagd; (B) (*search for*) Jagd machen auf (+ *Akk.*) ‹Mörder usw.›; fahnden nach ‹vermisster Person›; **~ the thimble/slipper** (*Games*) Fingerhutverstecken, *das*/Pantoffelverstecken, *das;* (C) (*drive, lit. or fig.*) jagen; **he was ~ed from office/out of society** er wurde aus dem Amt gejagt/aus der Gesellschaft ausgestoßen; (D) (*Amer.: shoot*) schießen ‹Wildenten›.

❸ *v.i.* (A) jagen; **go ~ing** jagen; auf die Jagd gehen; **~ after** *or* **for** Jagd machen auf (+ *Akk.*), jagen ‹Tier›; (B) (*seek*) **~ after** *or* **for sb./sth.** nach jmdm./etw. suchen; **he ~ed through his pockets for a coin** er durchsuchte seine Taschen nach einer Münze; **the police are ~ing for him** die Polizei ist auf der Suche nach ihm; (C) (*operate irregularly*) abwechselnd zu schnell und zu langsam laufen; pendeln (*Technik*)

**~ aˈbout, ~ aˈround** *v.i.* **~ about** *or* **around for sb./sth.** [überall] nach jmdm./etw. suchen

**~ ˈdown** *v.t.* (A) (*bring to bay*) hetzen und stellen; **the animal was finally ~ed down** das Tier wurde schließlich zur Strecke gebracht (*Jägerspr.*); (B) (*pursue and overcome*) zur Strecke bringen ‹Person›; abschießen ‹feindliches Flugzeug›; (C) (*fig.: track down*) aufstöbern

**~ ˈout** *v.t.* (A) (*drive from cover*) aufstöbern; (B) (*seek out*) suchen; (C) (*fig.: track down*) ausfindig machen ‹Tatsachen, Antworten›

**~ ˈup** *v.t.* aufspüren

**hunt ˈball** *n. Ball eines Jagdverbandes*

**hunted** /ˈhʌntɪd/ *adj.* (A) (*pursued*) gejagt; **the deer is a much ~ beast** der Hirsch ist ein viel bejagtes *od.* intensiv bejagtes Tier; (B) (*fig.: sought*) gesucht; (C) (*expressing fear*) gejagt, gehetzt ‹Blick, Gesichtsausdruck›

**hunter** /ˈhʌntə(r)/ *n.* (A) Jäger, *der;* **big-game ~:** Großwildjäger, *der;* **whale ~:** Walfänger, *der;* (B) (*fig.: seeker*) **be a ~ after glory/truth** dem Ruhm nachjagen/der Wahrheit nachspüren; **autograph ~:** Autogrammjäger, *der;* **treasure ~:** Schatzsucher, *der;* ⇒ *also* **fortune-hunter**; (C) (*horse*) Jagdpferd, *das;* (D) (*dog*) Jagdhund, *der;* (E) (*watch*) Sprungdeckeluhr, *die;* **half-~** *Sprungdeckeluhr mit teilweise durchsichtigem Deckel*

**hunter-ˈkiller** *n.: zur Jagd auf Schiffe eingesetztes U-Boot*

**hunter's ˈmoon** *n. Vollmond nach dem „harvest moon"*

**hunting** /ˈhʌntɪŋ/ ❶ *n., no pl.* (A) die Jagd (**of** auf + *Akk.*); das Jagen (**of** *Gen.*); **there's good ~** *or* **the ~ is good in this forest** dieser Wald ist ein gutes Jagdgebiet; **~, shooting, [and] fishing,** (*iron.*) **huntin', shootin', and fishin'** Fischen und Jagen; **otter-~:** Otterjagd, *die;* ⇒ *also* **fox-hunting**; (B) (*fig.: searching*) Suche, *die* (**for** nach); **the ~ of a criminal** die Verbrecherjagd; **after months of/much ~:** nach monatelanger/langer Suche; **[I wish you] good ~** (*fig.*) [ich wünsche dir] viel Glück bei der Suche; ⇒ *also* **house-hunting**; **job-hunting**; (C) (*searching through*) (*of house*) Durchsuchen, *das;* (*of area*) Absuchen, *das;* (*in pursuit of game*) Jagen, *das* (**of** in + *Dat.*); (D) (*Amer.: shooting*) Schießen, *das.*

❷ *adj.* jagend

**hunting: ~ box** *n.* (*Brit.*) Jagdhütte, *die;* **~ crop** ⇒ **crop** 1 C; **~ ground** *n.* (*lit. or fig.*) Jagdrevier, *das;* ⇒ *also* **happy hunting ground[s]**; **~ horn** *n.* Jagdhorn, *das;* **~ lodge** *n.* Jagdhaus, *das;* **~ ˈpink** *n.* Rot des Jagdrocks

**ˈhunt saboteur** *n.* Jagdsaboteur, *der*

**huntsman** /ˈhʌntsmən/ *n., pl.* **huntsmen** /ˈhʌntsmən/ (A) (*hunter*) Jäger, *der;* (*riding to hounds*) Jagdreiter, *der;* (B) (*manager of hunt*) Rüdemeister, *der* (*Jagdw. hist.*); (*in foxhunting*) Pikör, *der* (*Jagdw. hist.*)

**huntswoman** /ˈhʌntswʊmən/ *n.* Jägerin, *die;* (*riding to hounds*) Jagdreiterin, *die*

**hurdle** /ˈhɜːdl/ ❶ *n.* (A) (*Athletics*) Hürde, *die;* **~ race, ~s** Hürdenlauf, *der;* (*for horses*) Hürdenrennen, *das;* **the 400 metres ~s** der 400-m-Hürdenlauf; die 400 m Hürden (*Sportjargon*); (B) (*fig.: obstacle*) Hürde, *die;* **fall at the last ~:** an der letzten Hürde scheitern; **get over** *or* **negotiate a ~:** eine Hürde nehmen; (C) (*for fence*) Hürde, *die.* ❷ *v.t.* überspringen ‹Zaun, Hecke usw.›

**hurdler** /ˈhɜːdlə(r)/ *n.* (*Athletics*) Hürdenläufer, *der*/-läuferin, *die*

**hurdy-gurdy** /ˈhɜːdɪgɜːdɪ/ *n.* (A) (*Mus. Hist.*) Drehleier, *die* (*hist.*); (B) (*coll.: barrel organ*) Drehorgel, *die;* Leierkasten, *der* (*ugs.*)

**hurl** /hɜːl/ ❶ *v.t.* (A) (*throw*) werfen; (*violently*) schleudern; (*throw down*) stürzen; **~ sb. [down] into the street** jmdn. auf die Straße hinunterstürzen; **she ~ed herself to her death from a 15th-floor window** sie stürzte sich aus einem Fenster im 15. Stock zu Tode; (B) (*fig.*) **~ insults at sb.** jmdm. Beleidigungen ins Gesicht schleudern; **~ defiant looks/glances at sb.** trotzige Blicke auf jmdn. schleudern; (C) (*drive*) werfen; **be ~ed around the ship/against each other** durch das Schiff geschleudert/gegeneinander geschleudert werden; **~ oneself at** *or* **upon sb.** sich auf jmdn. stürzen; **~ oneself into a new job** (*fig.*) sich in eine neue Arbeit stürzen.

❷ *n.* (*throwing*) Stürzen, *das;* (*violent*) Schleudern, *das*

**hurling** /ˈhɜːlɪŋ/ *n.* (*Sport*) Hurling, *das;* irisches Hockey; *attrib.* Hurling-

**hurly-burly** /ˈhɜːlɪbɜːlɪ/ *n.* Tumult, *der;* **the ~ of city life** der Großstadtrummel (*ugs.*)

**hurrah** /hʊˈrɑː, hʊˈrɑː/, **hurray** /həˈreɪ, hʊˈreɪ/ ❶ *int.* hurra; **~ for sb./sth.!** jmd./etw. lebe hoch!; **~ for the Queen!** ein Hoch der Königin!; **hip, hip, ~!** hipp, hipp, hurra!. ❷ Hurra, *das;* **their joyous ~s** ihre freudigen Hurrarufe. ❸ *v.i.* Hurra rufen

**hurricane** /ˈhʌrɪkən/ *n.* (A) (*tropical cyclone*) Hurrikan, *der;* (*storm, lit. or fig.*) Orkan, *der;* **it's/the wind is blowing a ~ outside** draußen tobt ein Orkan; (B) (*Meteorol.*) Orkan, *der; attrib.* **~ force** Orkanstärke, *die;* **~ force winds** Winde, die Orkanstärke erreichen

**hurricane: ~ lamp** *n.* Sturmlaterne, *die;* **~ season** *n. Jahreszeit, in der Hurrikane am häufigsten auftreten*

**hurried** /ˈhʌrɪd/ *adj.* eilig; überstürzt ‹Abreise›; eilig *od.* hastig geschrieben ‹Brief, Aufsatz›; eilig vollzogen ‹Zeremonie›; in Eile ausgeführt ‹Arbeit›; **our farewells were ~:** wir verabschiedeten uns eilig

**hurriedly** /ˈhʌrɪdlɪ/ *adv.* eilig; überstürzt ‹abreisen›; in Eile ‹ausführen›

**hurry** /ˈhʌrɪ/ ❶ *n.* (A) (*great haste*) Eile, *die;* **what is** *or* **why the [big] ~?** warum die Eile?; **amongst all the ~ at the airport** in der allgemeinen Hetze am Flughafen; **in a ~:** eilig; **be in a [great** *or* **terrible] ~:** es [furchtbar] eilig haben; in [großer] Eile sein; **do sth. in a ~:** etw. in Eile tun; **leave in a ~:** davoneilen; **I have to get there in a ~:** ich muss so schnell wie möglich dort sein; **I need it in a ~:** ich brauche es dringend; **the handle won't come off again in a ~** (*coll.*) der Griff wird so schnell nicht wieder abgehen; **I shall not ask again in a ~** (*coll.*) ich frage so schnell nicht wieder; **be in a/not be in a** *or* **be in no ~ to do sth.** es eilig/nicht eilig haben, etw. zu tun; (B) (*urgent requirement*) **there is a ~ for sth.** etw. ist sehr gefragt; **there is a ~ for us to get out** wir müssen uns beeilen, hinauszukommen; **what's the [big] ~?** wozu die Eile?; **there's no ~:** es eilt nicht; es hat keine Eile; **is there any ~ for this letter [to be sent off]?** ist dieser Brief eilig?

❷ *v.t.* (*transport fast*) schnell bringen; (*urge to go or act faster*) antreiben; (*quicken process of*) beschleunigen; (*consume fast*) hinunterschlingen ‹Essen›; hinunterstürzen ‹Getränk›; **~ sb. out of the house** dafür sorgen, dass jmd. bald aus dem Haus herauskommt; **~ dinner** sich mit dem Abendessen beeilen; **~ a soufflé** ein Soufflé zu schnell zubereiten; **~ one's work** seine Arbeit in zu großer Eile erledigen.

❸ *v.i.* sich beeilen; (*to or from place*) eilen; **~ downstairs/out/in** nach unten/nach draußen/nach drinnen eilen; **she hurried from shop to shop** sie hastete von einem Laden zum andern

**~ aˈlong** ❶ *v.i.* sich beeilen. ❷ *v.t.* zur Eile antreiben; beschleunigen ‹Vorgang›

**~ ˈon** ❶ *v.i.* weitereilen; **the teacher is ~ing on too fast** (*fig.*) der Lehrer geht zu schnell weiter; **I must ~ on** ich muss [rasch] weiter. ❷ *v.t.* antreiben; beschleunigen ‹Vorgang›

**~ through** *v.t.* (A) /--ˈ-/ beschleunigen; (B) /ˈ---/ schnell durcheilen; (*fig.*) möglichst schnell durchziehen (*ugs.*); (*Parl.*) durchpeitschen ‹Gesetz›

**~ ˈup** ❶ *v.i.* sich beeilen. ❷ *v.t.* antreiben; beschleunigen, vorantreiben ‹Vorgang›

**ˈhurry-scurry** ❶ *adv.* in wilder Hast. ❷ *n.* Hektik, *die.* ❸ *v.i.* in wilder Hast laufen

**hurt** /hɜːt/ ❶ *v.t.,* **hurt** (A) ▶ **1232** (*cause pain to*) wehtun (+ *Dat.*); (*injure physically*) verletzen; **~ one's arm/leg/head/back** sich (*Dat.*) am Arm/Bein/Kopf/Rücken wehtun; (*injure*) sich (*Dat.*) den Arm/das Bein/am Kopf/am Rücken verletzen; **you are ~ing me/my arm** du tust mir weh/am Arm weh; **my arm is ~ing me** mein Arm tut [mir] weh; mir tut der Arm weh; **it ~s me to move my arm** es tut [mir] weh, wenn ich den Arm bewege; **it ~s my ears to listen to that noise** dieser Lärm tut meinen Ohren weh; **he wouldn't ~ a fly** (*fig.*) er tut keiner Fliege etwas zuleide; **sth. won't** *or* **wouldn't ~ sb.** etw. tut nicht weh; (*fig.*) etw. würde jmdm. nichts schaden (*ugs.*); **~ oneself** sich (*Dat.*) wehtun; (*injure oneself*) sich verletzen; (B) (*damage, be detrimental to*) schaden (+ *Dat.*); **sth. won't** *or* **wouldn't ~ sth.** etw. würde einer Sache (*Dat.*) nichts schaden; (C) (*distress emotionally*) verletzen, kränken ‹Person›; verletzen ‹Ehrgefühl, Stolz›; **~ sb.'s feelings** jmdn. verletzen; **it ~s me to have to tell you this** es ist mir schmerzlich, Ihnen dies sagen zu müssen; **~ sb.'s sense of honour** jmdn. in seiner Ehre kränken.

❷ *v.i.,* **hurt** (A) ▶ **1232** (*cause pain*) wehtun; schmerzen; (B) (*cause damage, be detrimental*) schaden; **does it ~ to drive the car with the handbrake on?** schadet es dem Auto, wenn man mit angezogener Handbremse fährt?; **I don't think it really ~s** ich glaube nicht, dass es wirklich etwas schadet; **publicity never ~s** Publicity kann nie

schaden (*ugs.*); **sth. won't** *or* **wouldn't ~** (*also iron.*) etw. würde nichts schaden (*ugs.*); **it won't ~ to have another biscuit** noch ein Keks kann doch nichts schaden; **C** (*cause emotional distress*) wehtun; ‹Worte, Beleidigungen:› verletzen; ‹Person:› verletzend sein; **D** (*suffer*) **I ~ all over** es tut mir überall weh; **my leg ~s** mein Bein tut [mir] weh; **does your hand ~?** tut dir die Hand weh?; **I ~ inside** (*emotionally*) es tut mir innerlich weh.
**3** *adj.* gekränkt ‹Tonfall, Miene›.
**4** *n.* **A** (*bodily injury*) Verletzung, *die;* **B** (*detriment*) Schaden, *der;* **C** (*emotional pain*) Schmerz, *der;* (*emotional injury*) Kränkung, *die*

**hurtful** /ˈhɜːtfl/ *adj.* **A** (*physically harmful, detrimental*) schädlich (**to** für); **be ~ to sb./sth.** jmdm./einer Sache schaden; **B** (*fig.: painful*) schmerzlich; **C** (*emotionally wounding*) verletzend; **be ~ [in what one says] about sth.** sich in verletzender Form über etw. äußern; **what a ~ thing to say/do!** wie kann man nur so etwas Verletzendes sagen/tun!

**hurtle** /ˈhɜːtl/ **1** *v.i.* **A** (*move rapidly*) rasen (*ugs.*); **he went hurtling down the street/round the corner** er raste die Straße hinunter/um die Ecke; **the car was hurtling along** das Auto brauste *od.* sauste dahin; **B** (*move with clattering sound*) **the saucepans came hurtling to the floor** die Kochtöpfe fielen mit lautem Klappern auf den Boden.
**2** *v.t.* schleudern

**husband** /ˈhʌzbənd/ **1** *n.* Ehemann, *der;* **my/your/her ~:** mein/dein/ihr Mann; **give my regards to your ~:** grüßen Sie Ihren Mann *od.* (*geh.*) Gatten von mir; **~ and wife** Mann und Frau; **they are a ~-[and-]wife team of interior decorators** die Eheleute arbeiten gemeinsam als Innenarchitekten. **2** *v.t.* regeln ‹Angelegenheiten›; haushalten mit ‹Mitteln›; bewirtschaften ‹Land›

**husbandry** /ˈhʌzbəndrɪ/ *n., no pl.* **A** (*farming*) Landwirtschaft, *die;* (*application of farming technique*) Bewirtschaftung, *die;* **animal/dairy ~:** Viehzucht, *die*/Milchviehhaltung, *die;* **B** (*management*) **bad/good ~:** schlechtes/sparsames Wirtschaften; **bad/good ~ of sth.** verschwenderischer/haushälterischer Umgang mit etw.; **C** (*careful management*) sparsames Wirtschaften

**hush** /hʌʃ/ **1** *n.* **A** (*silence*) Schweigen, *das;* **a sudden ~ fell over them** sie verstummten plötzlich; **can we have a bit of ~ now, please?** (*coll.*) ein bisschen mehr Ruhe jetzt, wenn ich bitten dürfte!; **B** (*stillness*) Stille, *die;* **dead ~:** Totenstille, *die;* **C** (*secrecy*) Geheimhaltung, *die;* **why all the ~?** wozu die ganze Geheimnistuerei? (*ugs.*).
**2** *v.t.* (*silence*) zum Schweigen bringen; zum Verstummen bringen ‹Vogelgesang, Gerüchte›; (*still*) beruhigen; besänftigen; (*quieten*) dämpfen ‹Stimme›; **she tried to ~ her baby to sleep/her baby's crying** sie versuchte, ihr Baby zum Schlafen zu bringen/ihr schreiendes Baby zu beruhigen.
**3** *v.i.* still sein; (*become silent*) verstummen; **~!** still!

**~ 'up** *v.t.* **A** (*make silent*) zum Schweigen bringen; **B** (*keep secret*) **~ sth. up** etw. vertuschen

**hushaby[e]** /ˈhʌʃəbaɪ/ *int.* eiapopeia

**hushed** /hʌʃt/ *adj.* schweigend ‹Publikum›; gedämpft ‹Flüstern, Stimme›; **~ atmosphere** Stille, *die;* **there was a ~ silence** alles schwieg; **with ~ respect/attention** mit respektvollem/gespanntem Schweigen

**hush: ~-~** *adj.* (*coll.*) geheim; **strictly/terribly/very ~-~:** streng geheim; **keep sth. ~-~:** etw. geheim halten; **~ money** *n.* Schweigegeld, *das*

**husk** /hʌsk/ **1** *n.* Schale, *die;* (*of wheat, grain, rice*) Spelze, *die;* (*Amer.: of maize*) Hüllblatt, *das;* Liesche, *die* (*Bot.*); (*fig.: useless remainder*) Hülse, *die.* **2** *v.t.* schälen

**huskily** /ˈhʌskɪlɪ/ *adv.* heiser

**husky¹** /ˈhʌskɪ/ **1** *adj.* **A** (*hoarse*) heiser; **her voice has a natural/an attractive ~ quality** ihre Stimme ist von Natur aus rau/sie hat eine anziehende rauchige Stimme; **B** (*coll.: tough*) bärenstark (*ugs.*). **2** *n.* (*Amer. coll.: strong person*) bärenstarker Typ (*ugs.*)

**husky²** *n.* (*dog*) Eskimohund, *der;* (*Siberian ~*) Husky, *der;* (*sledge dog*) Schlittenhund, *der*

**hussar** /hʊˈzɑː(r)/ *n.* (*Mil.*) Husar, *der*

**hussy** /ˈhʌsɪ, ˈhʌzɪ/ *n. fem.* **A** (*improper woman*) Flittchen, *das* (*ugs. abwertend*); **B** (*pert girl*) Göre, *die* (*nordd.*); Fratz, *der* (*fam.*)

**hustings** /ˈhʌstɪŋz/ *n. pl.* **A** *constr. as sing. or pl.* (*proceedings*) Wahlveranstaltungen; **B** (*Hist.: platform*) *Rednerbühne für die Kandidaten einer Wahl;* **C** (*fig.*) **he gave a good speech from the ~:** er hielt eine gute Wahlrede

**hustle** /ˈhʌsl/ **1** *v.t.* **A** drängen (**into** zu); **B** (*jostle*) anrempeln (*salopp*); schubsen (*ugs.*); (*thrust*) [hastig] drängen; **the guide ~d the tourists along/from one church to another** der Führer scheuchte die Touristen voran/von einer Kirche zur anderen (*ugs.*); **~ a Budget through the Senate** ein Budget im Senat durchpeitschen (*ugs.*); **C** (*coll.: exert pressure on*) bedrängen; **~ sb. to do sth.** jmdn. dazu bringen wollen, etw. zu tun.
**2** *v.i.* **A** (*push roughly*) **~ against sb./sth.** jmdn. anrempeln/gegen etw. stoßen; **~ through the crowds** sich durch die Menge drängeln; **B** (*hurry*) hasten; **~ about the house** durchs Haus wirbeln; **we'll have to ~:** wir müssen uns beeilen; **~ and bustle about** geschäftig hin und her eilen *od.* sausen; **C** (*coll.: strive for business*) **~ for sth.** etw. zu kriegen versuchen (*ugs.*); **D** (*sl.: solicit*) **~ [on the street]** auf den Strich gehen (*salopp*); **he ~s for her** er besorgt ihr die Freier (*ugs.*).
**3** *n.* **A** (*jostling*) Gedränge, *das;* **B** (*hurry*) Hetze, *die;* **~ and bustle** Geschäftigkeit, *die;* (*in street*) geschäftiges Treiben

**hustler** /ˈhʌslə(r)/ *n.* (*sl.: prostitute*) Strichmädchen, *das*/Strichjunge, *der* (*salopp*)

**hut** /hʌt/ *n.* Hütte, *die;* (*Mil.*) Baracke, *die*

**hutch** /hʌtʃ/ *n.* **A** (*for rabbit*) Stall, *der;* (*for guinea pig*) Käfig, *der;* **B** (*derog.: hut, small house*) Hütte, *die*

**hyacinth** /ˈhaɪəsɪnθ/ *n.* **A** (*Bot.*) Hyazinthe, *die;* **wild** *or* **wood ~:** Hasenglöckchen, *das;* ⇒ *also* **grape hyacinth**; **B** (*colour*) **~ [blue]** Hyazinthblau, *das*

**hybrid** /ˈhaɪbrɪd/ **1** *n.* **A** (*Biol.*) Hybride, *die od. der* (**between** aus); Kreuzung, *die;* **B** (*Ethnol.*) Mischling, *der;* **C** (*fig.: mixture*) Mischung, *die;* **D** (*Ling.*) hybride Bildung.
**2** *adj.* **A** (*Biol.*) hybrid ‹Züchtung›; **this is a ~ rose** diese Rose ist eine Hybride; **a ~ species/animal/plant** eine Hybridzüchtung; ein[e] Hybride; **B** (*Ethnol.*) mischerbig; **C** (*fig.: mixed*) gemischt; Misch‹kultur, -sprache›; **D** (*Ling.*) hybrid

**hybridize (hybridise)** /ˈhaɪbrɪdaɪz/ *v.t.* **A** (*Biol.*) hybridisieren (*fachspr.*); kreuzen; **B** (*Ling.*) **~ words** hybride Wörter bilden

**hydra** /ˈhaɪdrə/ *n.* **A** (*Greek Mythol.*) Hydra, *die;* **B** (*Zool.: polyp*) Süßwasserpolyp, *der;* Hydra, *die*

**hydrangea** /haɪˈdreɪndʒə/ *n.* (*Bot.*) Hortensie, *die;* Hydrangea, *die* (*fachspr.*)

**hydrant** /ˈhaɪdrənt/ *n.* Hydrant, *der*

**hydrate** /ˈhaɪdreɪt/ *n.* (*Chem.*) Hydrat, *das*

**hydration** /haɪˈdreɪʃn/ *n.* **A** (*addition of fluid*) Flüssigkeitszufuhr, *die;* **B** (*Chem.*) Hydra[ta]tion, *die*

**hydraulic** /haɪˈdrɔːlɪk/ *adj.* (*Mech. Engin.*) hydraulisch; **~ engineer** Wasserbauingenieur, *der;* **~ engineering** Wasserbau, *der*

**hydraulic: ~ 'brake** *n.* (*Mech. Engin.*) hydraulische Bremse; **~ 'fluid** *n.* (*Mech. Engin.*) hydraulische Flüssigkeit; (*in brake system*) Bremsflüssigkeit, *die;* **~ 'ram** *n.* (*Mech. Engin.*) **A** (*pump*) hydraulischer Widder; **B** (*piston*) Hydraulikkolben, *der*

**hydride** /ˈhaɪdraɪd/ *n.* (*Chem.*) Hydrid, *das*

**hydrocarbon** /haɪdrəˈkɑːbən/ *n.* (*Chem.*) Kohlenwasserstoff, *der*

**hydrochloric acid** /haɪdrəklɔːrɪk ˈæsɪd/ *n.* (*Chem.*) Salzsäure, *die*

**hydrodynamics** /haɪdrədaɪˈnæmɪks/ *n., no pl.* (*Phys.*) Hydrodynamik, *die*

**hydroelectric** /haɪdrəʊɪˈlektrɪk/ *adj.* (*Electr.*) hydroelektrisch; **~ power plant** *or* **station** Wasserkraftwerk, *das*

**hydrofoil** /ˈhaɪdrəfɔɪl/ *n.* (*Naut.*) **A** (*structure*) Tragfläche, *die;* Tragflügel, *der;* **B** (*vessel*) Tragflächenboot, *das;* Tragflügelboot, *das*

**hydrogen** /ˈhaɪdrədʒən/ *n.* Wasserstoff, *der;* Hydrogen[ium], *das* (*fachspr.*); **a ~-filled balloon** ein mit Wasserstoff gefüllter Ballon; ⇒ *also* **peroxide** 1 B

**'hydrogen bomb** *n.* Wasserstoffbombe, *die*

**hydrological** /haɪdrəˈlɒdʒɪkl/ *adj.* hydrologisch

**hydrology** /haɪˈdrɒlədʒɪ/ *n., no pl.* Hydrologie, *die*

**hydrolyse** /ˈhaɪdrəlaɪz/ *v.t.* (*Chem.*) hydrolysieren

**hydrolysis** /haɪˈdrɒlɪsɪs/ *n., pl.* **hydrolyses** /haɪˈdrɒlɪsiːz/ (*Chem.*) Hydrolyse, *die*

**hydrolyze** (*Amer.*) ⇒ **hydrolyse**

**hydrometer** /haɪˈdrɒmɪtə(r)/ *n.* Hydrometer, *das*

**hydrophobia** /haɪdrəˈfəʊbɪə/ *n.* ▶ 1232 **A** (*Med.*) (*rabies*) Tollwut, *die;* (*symptom*) Hydrophobie, *die* (*Med.*); **B** (*Psych.*) Hydrophobie, *die* (*fachspr.*); krankhafte Wasserscheu

**hydrophobic** /haɪdrəˈfəʊbɪk/ *adj.* **A** (*Med.*) tollwutkrank, tollwutinfiziert ‹Tier, Person›; tollwütig ‹Tier›; **be ~:** Tollwut haben; **B** (*water-resistant*) hydrophob (*Chemie, Technik*)

**hydroplane** /ˈhaɪdrəpleɪn/ *n.* **A** (*Naut.: fin-like device*) Gleitfläche, *die;* (*of submarine*) Tiefenruder, *das;* **B** (*motor boat*) Gleitboot, *das*

**hydroponics** /haɪdrəˈpɒnɪks/ *n., no pl.* (*Hort.*) Hydroponik, *die* (*fachspr.*); Hydrokultur, *die*

**hydrosphere** /ˈhaɪdrəsfɪə(r)/ *n.* (*Geog.*) Hydrosphäre, *die*

**hydrostatic** /haɪdrəˈstætɪk/ *adj.* (*Phys.*) hydrostatisch

**hydrostatics** /haɪdrəˈstætɪks/ *n., no pl.* (*Phys.*) Hydrostatik, *die*

**hydrous** /ˈhaɪdrəs/ *adj.* (*Chem., Min.*) wasserhaltig ‹Salz, Substanz›

**hydroxide** /haɪˈdrɒksaɪd/ *n.* (*Chem.*) Hydroxid, *das*

**hydrozoan** /haɪdrəˈzəʊən/ (*Zool.*) **1** *adj.* zu den Hydrozoen gehörend; **~ polyp** Hydroidpolyp, *der.* **2** *n.* Hydrozoon, *das*

**hyena** /haɪˈiːnə/ *n.* **A** (*Zool.*) Hyäne, *die;* **laughing** *or* **spotted ~:** Tüpfel- *od.* Fleckenhyäne, *die;* **laugh like a ~:** wie eine Hyäne kreischen; ≈ wiehernd lachen; **B** (*fig.: person*) Hyäne, *die* (*ugs. abwertend*); **C** (*Austral. Zool.*) Beutelwolf, *der*

**hygiene** /ˈhaɪdʒiːn/ *n., no pl.* **A** Hygiene, *die;* **conditions of bad ~:** schlechte hygienische Verhältnisse; **domestic ~:** häusliche Hygiene; **feminine ~:** Monatshygiene, *die;* **B** *no art.* (*science*) Hygiene, *die* (*Med.*); **dental ~:** Zahnhygiene, *die*

**hygienic** /haɪˈdʒiːnɪk/ *adj.* hygienisch; **not ~:** unhygienisch

**hygienically** /haɪˈdʒiːnɪkəlɪ/ *adv.* hygienisch

**hygienist** /haɪˈdʒiːnɪst/ *n.* ▶ 1261 Hygieniker, *der*/Hygienikerin, *die;* **dental ~:** Zahnhygieniker, *der*/-hygienikerin, *die*

**hygrometer** /haɪˈgrɒmɪtə(r)/ *n.* (*Meteorol.*) Hygrometer, *das*

**hymen** /ˈhaɪmen/ *n.* (*Anat.*) Hymen, *das od. der* (*fachspr.*); Jungfernhäutchen, *das*

**hymn** /hɪm/ **1** *n.* **A** (*Relig.*) Hymne, *die;* Loblied, *das;* (*sung in service*) Kirchenlied, *das;* **Easter ~, ~ for Easter** Osterlied, *das;* **B** (*song of praise, lit. or fig.*) Hymne, *die;* **a ~ to nature** eine Hymne an die Natur; **a ~ to Venus/England/the new age** eine Hymne auf Venus/England/das neue Zeitalter. **2** *v.t.* (*praise with songs*) besingen (*geh.*); lobpreisen (*dichter.*) ‹Gott, Werke Gottes›; (*fig.: praise*) preisen (*geh.*)

**hymnal** /ˈhɪmnl/, **hymnary** /ˈhɪmnərɪ/ *ns.* Gesangbuch, *das;* Hymnar[ium], *das*

h

**'hymn book** *n.* Gesangbuch, *das*

**hyoid** /'haɪɔɪd/ (*Anat.*) *adj.* & *n.* ~ **[bone]** Zungenbein, *das*

**hype** /haɪp/ (*coll.*) ❶ *n.* Ⓐ (*deception*) Schwindel, *der* (*ugs.*); Ⓑ (*misleading publicity*) Reklameschwindel, *der* (*ugs.*); **media** ~: Medienrummel, *der.* ❷ *v.t.* Ⓐ (*cheat*) reinlegen (*ugs.*); ~ **sb. into sth./doing sth.** jmdn. [durch Tricks] zu etw. bringen/ jmdn. [durch Tricks] dazu bringen, etw. zu tun; Ⓑ ~ **[up]** (*publicize excessively*) groß herausbringen

~ **up** *v.t.* (*coll.*) hochputschen (*ugs.*); **feel ~d up** überdreht sein (*ugs.*)

**hyper** /'haɪpə(r)/ *adj.* (*coll.*) aufgedreht (*ugs.*); überdreht (*ugs.*); **there's no need to get so** ~: kein Grund zur Panik! (*ugs.*)

**hyperactive** /haɪpə'ræktɪv/ *adj.* überaktiv

**hyperbola** /haɪ'pɜ:bələ/ *n., pl.* ~**s** *or* ~**e** /haɪ'pɜ:bəli:/ (*Geom.*) Hyperbel, *die*

**hyperbole** /haɪ'pɜ:bəlɪ/ *n.* (*Rhet.*) Hyperbel, *die*

**hyperbolic** /haɪpə'bɒlɪk/ *adj.* Ⓐ (*Geom.*) hyperbolisch; Ⓑ ⇒ **hyperbolical** A

**hyperbolical** /haɪpə'bɒlɪkl/ *adj.* Ⓐ (*Rhet.*) hyperbolisch ‹Stil, Wendung usw.›; Ⓑ ⇒ **hyperbolic** A

**hyper:** ~**critical** /haɪpə'krɪtɪkl/ *adj.* hyperkritisch; übertrieben kritisch; ~**link** *n.* (*Computing*) Hyperlink, *der*

**hypermarket** /'haɪpəmɑ:kɪt/ *n.* Verbrauchermarkt, *der*

**hypersensitive** /haɪpə'sensɪtɪv/ *adj.* hypersensibel; überempfindlich; **be ~ to sth.** überempfindlich auf etw. (*Akk.*) reagieren

**hypersensitivity** /haɪpəsensɪ'tɪvɪtɪ/ *n., no pl.* Überempfindlichkeit, *die*

**hypertension** /haɪpə'tenʃn/ *n.* (*Med.*) Hypertonie, *die* (*fachspr.*); Bluthochdruck, *der*

**hypertensive** /haɪpə'tensɪv/ *adj.* (*Med.*) hypertonisch

**hypertext** *n., no pl.* (*Computing*) Hypertext, *der;* ~ **link** Hyperlink, *der*

**hypertrophied** /haɪ'pɜ:trəfɪd/ *adj.* hypertroph ‹Organ›; (*fig.: excessive*) hypertroph[isch] (*geh.*); hypertrophiert (*geh.*)

**hyper'ventilate** *v.i.* hyperventilieren (*Med.*)

**hypha** /'haɪfə/ *n., pl* ~**e** /'haɪfi:/ (*Bot.*) Hyphe, *die* (*fachspr.*); Pilzfaden, *der*

**hyphen** /'haɪfn/ ❶ *n.* Ⓐ Bindestrich, *der;* Ⓑ (*connecting separate syllables*) Trennungsstrich, *der;* Divis, *das* (*fachspr.*). ❷ *v.t.* mit Bindestrich schreiben

**hyphenate** /'haɪfəneɪt/ ⇒ **hyphen** 2

**hyphenation** /haɪfə'neɪʃn/ *n., no pl.* Kopplung, *die*

**hypnosis** /hɪp'nəʊsɪs/ *n., pl.* **hypnoses** /hɪp'nəʊsi:z/ Hypnose, *die;* (*act, process*) Hypnotisierung, *die;* **under** ~: in Hypnose (*Dat.*)

**hypnotic** /hɪp'nɒtɪk/ ❶ *adj.* hypnotisch; (*producing hypnotism*) hypnotisch; hypnotisierend ‹Wirkung, Blick›; **have a ~ effect on sb.** hypnotisierend *od.* einschläfernd auf jmdn. wirken. ❷ *n.* Schlafmittel, *das;* (*Med. also*) Hypnotikum, *das* (*fachspr.*)

**hypnotism** /'hɪpnətɪzm/ *n.* Hypnotik, *die;* (*act*) Hypnotisieren, *das*

**hypnotist** /'hɪpnətɪst/ *n.* Hypnotiseur, *der*/ Hypnotiseuse, *die*

**hypnotize** /'hɪpnətaɪz/ *v.t.* (*lit. or fig.*) hypnotisieren; (*fig.: fascinate*) faszinieren

**hypo** /'haɪpəʊ/ *n.* (*Photog.*) Fixiernatron, *das;* Fixiersalz, *das*

**hypocaust** /'haɪpəkɔ:st/ *n.* (*Roman Ant.*) Hypokaustum, *das*

**hypochondria** /haɪpə'kɒndrɪə/ *n.* Hypochondrie, *die*

**hypochondriac** /haɪpə'kɒndrɪæk/ ❶ *adj.* hypochondrisch. ❷ *n.* Hypochonder, *der*

**hypocrisy** /hɪ'pɒkrɪsɪ/ *n.* Ⓐ Heuchelei, *die;* Hypokrisie, *die* (*geh.*); Ⓑ (*simulation of virtue*) Scheinheiligkeit, *die*

**hypocrite** /'hɪpəkrɪt/ *n.* Ⓐ Heuchler, *der*/ Heuchlerin, *die;* Hypokrit, *der* (*geh. veralt.*); Ⓑ (*person feigning virtue*) Scheinheilige, *der/die*

**hypocritical** /hɪpə'krɪtɪkl/ *adj.* Ⓐ heuchlerisch; Ⓑ (*feigning virtue*) scheinheilig; hypokritisch (*geh. veralt.*)

**hypodermic** /haɪpə'dɜ:mɪk/ (*Med.*) ❶ *adj.* subkutan ‹Injektion›; subkutan verabreicht ‹Medikament›; ~ **syringe** Injektionsspritze, *die.* ❷ *n.* Ⓐ (*injection*) subkutane Injektion; Ⓑ (*syringe*) Injektionsspritze, *die*

**hypotension** /haɪpəʊ'tenʃn/ *n.* (*Med.*) Hypotonie, *die* (*fachspr.*); zu niedriger Blutdruck

**hypotensive** /haɪpəʊ'tensɪv/ *adj.* (*Med.*) hypotonisch; (*tending to lower the blood pressure*) blutdrucksenkend ‹Medikament›

**hypotenuse** /haɪ'pɒtənju:z/ *n.* (*Geom.*) Hypotenuse, *die;* **square on the** ~: Hypotenusenquadrat, *das*

**hypothermia** /haɪpə'θɜ:mɪə/ *n.* (*Med.*) Hypothermie, *die* (*fachspr.*); Unterkühlung, *die*

**hypothesis** /haɪ'pɒθɪsɪs/ *n., pl.* **hypotheses** /haɪ'pɒθɪsi:z/ Hypothese, *die;* (*unproved assumption also*) Annahme, *die*

**hypothesize** (**hypothesise**) /haɪ'pɒθɪsaɪz/ ❶ *v.i.* eine Hypothese aufstellen; mutmaßen; spekulieren. ❷ *v.t.* annehmen

**hypothetical** /haɪpə'θetɪkl/ *adj.* hypothetisch; angenommen; **it will remain** ~: darüber wird man nur mutmaßen *od.* spekulieren können

**hypothetically** /haɪpə'θetɪkəlɪ/ *adv.* hypothetisch

**hyrax** /'haɪəræks/ *n.* (*Zool.*) Klippschliefer, *der*

**hyssop** /'hɪsəp/ *n.* (*Bot.*) Ysop, *der*

**hysterectomy** /hɪstə'rektəmɪ/ *n.* (*Med.*) Hysterektomie, *die* (*fachspr.*); operative Entfernung der Gebärmutter

**hysteria** /hɪ'stɪərɪə/ *n.* Hysterie, *die*

**hysterical** /hɪ'sterɪkl/ *adj.* hysterisch

**hysterically** /hɪ'sterɪkəlɪ/ *adv.* hysterisch; ~ **funny** urkomisch

**hysterics** /hɪ'sterɪks/ *n. pl.* (*laughter*) hysterischer Lachanfall; (*crying*) hysterischer Weinkrampf; **have** ~: hysterisch lachen/ weinen

**Hz** *abbr.* **hertz** Hz

# I i

**I**[1], **i** /aɪ/ *n., pl.* **Is** *or* **I's** A (*letter*) I, i, *das;* ⇒ *also* **dot** 2 B; B (*Roman numeral*) I

**I**[2] ❶ *pron.* ich; **it was I** (*formal*) ich war es; **it was I who locked the door** (*formal*) ich war es, der die Tür abgeschlossen hat; ich habe die Tür abgeschlossen; ⇒ *also* **me**[1]; **mine**[2]; **my**; **myself**. ❷ *n., no pl.* **the I** (*Philos.*) das Ich

**I.** *abbr.* A **Island[s]** I.; B **Isle[s]** I.

**iamb** /ˈaɪæm/ ⇒ **iambus**

**iambic** /aɪˈæmbɪk/ (*Pros.*) ❶ *adj.* jambisch; **~ pentameter** fünffüßiger Jambus. ❷ *n. in pl.* Jamben

**iambus** /aɪˈæmbəs/ *n., pl.* **~es** *or* **iambi** /aɪˈæmbaɪ/ (*Pros.*) Jambus, *der*

**IATA** /ɪˈɑːtə, aɪˈɑːtə/ *abbr.* **International Air Transport Association** IATA, *die*

**IBA** *abbr.* (*Brit.*) **Independent Broadcasting Authority** *Kontrollgremium für den privaten Rundfunk und das Privatfernsehen*

**Iberia** /aɪˈbɪərɪə/ *pr. n.* (*Hist., Geog.*) Iberische Halbinsel

**Iberian** /aɪˈbɪərɪən/ ❶ *adj.* iberisch. ❷ *n.* (*inhabitant of* [*ancient*] *Iberia*) Iberer, *der*/Ibererin, *die*

**Iberian Peˈninsula** *pr. n.* (*Geog.*) Iberische Halbinsel

**ibex** /ˈaɪbeks/ *n.* (*Zool.*) Steinbock, *der*

**ibid.** *abbr.* **ibidem** ib.; ibd.; ibid.

**ibidem** /ˈɪbɪdem, ɪˈbaɪdəm/ *adv.* ibidem; ebenda; ebendort

**ibis** /ˈaɪbɪs/ *n.* (*Ornith.*) Ibis, *der*

**i/c** *abbr.* A **in charge;** B **in command**

**ICBM** *abbr.* **intercontinental ballistic missile**

**ice** /aɪs/ ❶ *n.* A *no pl.* Eis, *das;* **become ~:** [zu Eis] gefrieren; **feel/be like ~** (*be very cold*) eiskalt sein; **there was ~ over the pond** eine Eisschicht bedeckte den Teich; **fall through the ~:** auf dem Eis einbrechen; **be on ~** (*coll.*) (*be held in reserve*) ‹Plan:› auf Eis (*Dat.*) liegen (*ugs.*); **put on ~** (*coll.*) auf Eis (*Akk.*) legen (*ugs.*); **be on thin ~** (*fig.*) sich auf dünnes Eis begeben haben; **break the ~** (*fig.: make a beginning*) den Anfang machen; (*break through reserve*) das Eis brechen; ⇒ *also* **cut** 1 B; **skate**[2] 2; B (*confection*) [Speise]eis, *das;* Eiscreme, *die;* **an ~/two ~s** ein/zwei Eis; C *no pl., no indef. art.* (*Amer. coll.: diamonds*) Diamanten.
❷ *v.t.* A (*freeze*) einfrieren, tiefkühlen ‹Lebensmittel›; ⇒ *also* **lolly** A; B (*cool with ~*) [mit Eis] kühlen; **~d coffee/tea** Eiskaffee, *der*/Tee mit Eis; **be ~d** eisgekühlt sein; C glasieren ‹Kuchen›

**~ ˈover** *v.i.* ‹Gewässer:› zufrieren; ‹Straße, Flugzeug:› vereisen

**~ ˈup** *v.i.* A (*freeze*) ‹Wasserleitung:› einfrieren; B ⇒ **~ over**

**ice: ~ age** *n.* Eiszeit, *die;* **~ axe** *n.* Pickel, *der*

**iceberg** /ˈaɪsbɜːg/ *n.* Eisberg, *der;* **the tip of the ~** (*fig.*) die Spitze des Eisbergs

**ice: ~ blue** ❶ /ˈ-ˈ-/ *n.* Eisblau, *das;* ❷ /ˈ--/ *adj.* eisblau; **~-bound** *adj.* eingefroren ‹Schiff›; durch Vereisung abgeschnitten ‹Hafen, Küste›; **~box** *n.* (*Amer.*) Kühlschrank, *der;* **~-breaker** *n.* (*Naut.*) Eisbrecher, *der;* **~ bucket** *n.* Eisbehälter, *der;* **~ cap** *n.* Eisdecke, -schicht, *die;* (*polar*) Eiskappe, *die;* **~-cold** *adj.* eiskalt; **~ ˈcream** *n.* Eis, *das;* Eiscreme, *die;* **one ~ cream/two/too many ~ creams** ein/zwei/zu viel Eis; **~ ˈcream parlour** *n.* Eisdiele, *die;* Eiscafé, *das;* **~ cube** *n.* Eiswürfel, *der;* **~ floe** ⇒ **floe**; **~ hockey** *n.* Eishockey, *das*

**Iceland** /ˈaɪslənd/ *pr. n.* Island (*das*)

**Icelander** /ˈaɪsləndə(r)/ *n.* ▶ **1340** Isländer, *der*/Isländerin, *die*

**Icelandic** /aɪsˈlændɪk/ ▶ **1275**, ▶ **1340** ❶ *adj.* isländisch; ⇒ *also* **English** 1. ❷ *n.* Isländisch, *das;* ⇒ *also* **English** 2 A

**ice: ~ ˈlolly** ⇒ **lolly** A; **~ machine** *n.* Gefrierapparat, *der;* **~ pack** *n.* A (*to relieve pain*) Eispackung, *die;* B (*to keep food cool*) Kälteakku *od.* Kühlakku, *der* (*ugs.*); C (*sea ~*) [Pack]eisdecke, *die;* **~ rink** *n.* Schlittschuh-, Eisbahn, *die;* **~ skate** *n.* Schlittschuh, *der;* **~-skate** *v.i.* Schlittschuh laufen; Eis laufen; **~ skater** *n.* Schlittschuhläufer, *der;* **~ skating** *n.* Schlittschuhlaufen, *das;* **~ water** *n.* Eiswasser, *das*

**ichthyologist** /ɪkθɪˈɒlədʒɪst/ *n.* Ichthyologe, *der*/Ichthyologin, *die;* Fischkundler, *der*/-kundlerin, *die*

**ichthyology** /ɪkθɪˈɒlədʒɪ/ *n.* Ichthyologie, *die;* Fischkunde, *die*

**icicle** /ˈaɪsɪkl/ *n.* Eiszapfen, *der*

**icily** /ˈaɪsɪlɪ/ *adv.* eisig; (*fig.*) kalt ‹ablehnend, lächelnd›; eisig, frostig ‹empfangen, begrüßen, anblicken›; **~ cold** eiskalt

**iciness** /ˈaɪsɪnɪs/ *n., no pl.* Eis[es]kälte, *die;* (*of road*) Eisglätte, *die*

**icing** /ˈaɪsɪŋ/ *n.* A *no pl.* Vereisen, *das;* (*cooling*) Kühlen, *das;* (*of cake*) Überziehen mit Zuckerguss; B (*Cookery: sugar coating*) Zuckerguss, *der;* Zuckerglasur, *die;* **[the] ~ on the cake** (*fig.*) das Tüpfelchen auf dem i

**ˈicing sugar** *n.* (*Brit.*) Puderzucker, *der*

**icon** /ˈaɪkən, ˈaɪkɒn/ *n.* A (*statue*) Standbild, *das;* B (*Orthodox Ch.*) Ikone, *die;* C (*Computing*) Icon, *das;* D (*representative symbol*) Kultsymbol, *das;* (*Person*) Ikone, *die*

**iconoclast** /aɪˈkɒnəklæst/ *n.* (*lit. or fig.*) Bilderstürmer, *der*

**iconoclastic** /aɪkɒnəˈklæstɪk/ *adj.* (*lit. or fig.*) bilderstürmerisch

**icterus** /ˈɪktərəs/ *n.* (*Med.*) Ikterus, *der* (*fachspr.*); Gelbsucht, *die*

**icy** /ˈaɪsɪ/ *adj.* A vereist ‹Berge, Landschaft, Straße, See›; eisreich ‹Region, Land›; **in ~ conditions** bei Eis; B (*very cold*) eiskalt; eisig; (*fig.*) frostig ‹Benehmen, Ton›

**id** /ɪd/ *n.* (*Psych.*) Es, *das*

**I'd** /aɪd/ A = **I had;** B = **I would**

**ID** /aɪˈdiː/ *n.* **ID card/disc/plate** *etc.* ⇒ **identification** C; **have you [got] some** *or* **any ID?** können Sie sich ausweisen?

**idea** /aɪˈdɪə/ *n.* A (*conception*) Idee, *die;* Gedanke, *der;* **arrive at an ~:** auf eine Idee *od.* einen Gedanken kommen; **get one's** *or* **the ~ from sth.** sich durch etw. anregen *od.* inspirieren lassen; **the ~ of going abroad** der Gedanke *od.* die Vorstellung, ins Ausland zu fahren; **have a good ~ of sth.** über etw. (*Akk.*) Bescheid wissen; **give/get some ~ of sth.** einen Überblick über etw. (*Akk.*) geben/einen Eindruck von etw. bekommen; **get the ~ [of sth.]** verstehen, worum es [bei etw.] geht; **be getting the ~ quickly** schnell [damit] zurechtkommen; **sb.'s ~ of sth.** (*coll.*) jmds. Vorstellung von etw.; **not my ~ of ...** (*coll.*) nicht, was ich mir unter ... (*Dat.*) vorstelle; **he has no ~** (*coll.*) er hat keine Ahnung (*ugs.*); B (*mental picture*) Vorstellung, *die;* **what gave you ˈthat ~?** wie bist du darauf gekommen?; **get the ~ that ...:** den Eindruck bekommen, dass ...; **I don't want her to get the ~ that ...:** ich will nicht, dass sie glaubt *od.* den Eindruck bekommt, dass ...; **he's got the ~ that ...:** er bildet sich (*Dat.*) ein, dass ...; **get** *or* **have ~s** (*coll.*) (*be rebellious*) auf dumme Gedanken kommen (*ugs.*); (*be ambitious*) sich (*Dat.*) Hoffnungen machen; **put ~s into sb.'s head** jmdn. auf dumme Gedanken bringen; C (*vague notion*) Ahnung, *die;* Vorstellung, *die;* **have you any ~ [of] how ...?** weißt du ungefähr, wie ...?; **have no ~ [of] where ...:** keine Ahnung haben, wo ...; **you can have no ~ [of] how ...:** du kannst dir gar nicht vorstellen, wie ...; **not have the remotest** *or* **slightest** *or* **faintest** *or* (*coll.*) **foggiest ~:** nicht die entfernteste *od.* mindeste *od.* leiseste Ahnung haben; keinen blassen Schimmer haben (*ugs.*); **I suddenly had the ~ that ...:** mir kam plötzlich der Gedanke, dass ...; **I've an ~ that ...:** ich habe so eine Ahnung, dass ...; **the ~ of his having committed a murder** die Vorstellung, dass er einen Mord begangen hat *od.* er könne einen Mord begangen haben; **the [very] ~!, what an ~!** (*coll.*) unvorstellbar!; allein die Vorstellung!; D (*way of thinking*) Vorstellung, *die;* E (*plan*) Idee, *die;* **man of ~s** kluger Kopf; einfallsreicher Mensch; **have you any ~s for the future?** hast du [irgendwelche] Zukunftspläne?; **be full of good/new ~s** viele gute/neue Ideen haben; voller guter/neuer Ideen sein; **good ~!** [das ist eine] gute Idee!; **ˈthat's an ~** (*coll.*) das ist eine gute Idee; **that gives me an ~:** das hat mich auf eine Idee gebracht; **the ~ was that ...:** der Plan war, dass ...; **have big ~s** große Rosinen im Kopf haben; **what's the big ~?** (*iron.*) was soll das?; was soll der Blödsinn? (*ugs.*); F (*archetype*) Leitgedanke, *der;* (*Platonic Philos.*) Idee, *die*

**ideal** /aɪˈdɪəl/ ❶ *adj.* A ideal; vollendet ‹Genuss, Ehemann, Gastgeber, Rittertum›; vollkommen ‹Glück, Welt›; B (*embodying an idea, existing only in idea*) ideell; gedacht; C (*visionary*) idealistisch. ❷ *n.* A (*perfect type*) Ideal, *das;* Idealvorstellung, *die;* B (*standard for imitation*) Vorbild, *das*

**ideal ˈgas** *n.* (*Phys.*) ideales Gas

**idealise** ⇒ **idealize**

**idealism** /aɪˈdɪəlɪzm/ *n., no pl.* A Idealismus, *der;* B (*representation of things in idealized form*) Idealisierung, *die*

**idealist** /aɪˈdɪəlɪst/ *n.* Idealist, *der*/Idealistin, *die*

**idealistic** /aɪdɪəˈlɪstɪk/ *adj.* idealistisch; **~ young people** junge Idealisten *Pl.*

**idealize** /aɪˈdɪəlaɪz/ *v.t.* A (*exalt*) idealisieren; verklären; B (*represent in ideal form*) idealisieren; idealisierend darstellen

**ideally** /aɪˈdɪəlɪ/ *adv.* ideal; **~, the work should be finished in two weeks** im Idealfalle *od.* idealerweise sollte die Arbeit in zwei Wochen abgeschlossen sein

**idée fixe** /iːdeɪ ˈfiːks/ *n., pl.* **idées fixes** /iːdeɪ ˈfiːks/ fixe Idee; Idée fixe, *die* (*geh.*)

**identical** /aɪˈdentɪkl/ *adj.* A (*same*) identisch; **the ~ species** dieselbe Art; **he is the ~ convict who ...:** er ist genau der Sträfling, der ...; B (*agreeing in every detail*) identisch; sich (*Dat.*) gleichend; **be ~:** sich (*Dat.*) völlig gleichen; **~ twins** eineiige Zwillinge

**identically** /aɪˈdentɪkəlɪ/ *adv.* völlig, genau ‹gleich, übereinstimmend›; völlig gleich, völlig einheitlich ‹bauen usw.›

**identifiable** /aɪˈdentɪfaɪəbl/ *adj.* erkennbar (**by** an + *Dat.*); nachweisbar ‹Stoff, Substanz›; bestimmbar ‹Pflanzen-, Tierart›; diagnostizierbar ‹Krankheit›

**identification** /aɪdentɪfɪˈkeɪʃn/ *n.* A (*treating as identical*) Gleichsetzung, *die;* B (*association*) Identifikation, *die;* Identifizierung, *die;* [C] (*determination of identity*) (*of person*) Identifizierung, *die;* Wiedererkennen, *das;* (*of plants or animals*) Bestimmung, *die;* **means of ~:** Ausweispapiere *Pl.;* **have you any means of ~?** können Sie sich ausweisen?; **~ card** [Personal]ausweis, *der;* **~ disc** Erkennungsmarke, *die;* **~ plate** Kennzeichenschild, *das;* **~ badge** Ausweisplakette, *die;* Legitimationsabzeichen, *das*

**identifi'cation parade** *n.* (*Brit.*) Gegenüberstellung [zur Identifizierung], *die*

**identify** /aɪ'dentɪfaɪ/ **1** *v.t.* [A] (*treat as identical*) gleichsetzen (**with** mit); [B] (*associate*) identifizieren (**with** mit); **Guy Fawkes will always be identified with the Gunpowder Plot** bei Guy Fawkes wird jeder sofort an die Pulververschwörung denken; [C] (*recognize*) identifizieren; bestimmen ‹Pflanze, Tier›; [D] (*establish*) ermitteln. **2** *v.i.* **~ with sb.** sich mit jmdm. identifizieren

**Identikit** ® /aɪ'dentɪkɪt/ *n.* Phantombild, *das*

**identity** /aɪ'dentɪtɪ/ *n.* [A] (*sameness*) Übereinstimmung, *die;* [B] (*individuality, being specified person*) Identität, *die;* **proof of ~:** Identitätsnachweis, *der;* **[case of] mistaken ~:** [Personen]verwechslung, *die;* [C] (*Math.*) Identität, *die;* identische Gleichung; [D] **~ card/disc/plate** *etc.* ⇒ **identification** C

**identity: ~ crisis** *n.* Identitätskrise, *die;* **~ parade** ⇒ **identification parade**

**ideogram** /'ɪdɪəgræm/, **ideograph** /'ɪdɪəgrɑːf/ *ns.* Ideogramm, *das;* Begriffszeichen, *das*

**ideological** /aɪdɪə'lɒdʒɪkl, ɪdɪə'lɒdʒɪkl/ *adj.*, **ideologically** /aɪdɪə'lɒdʒɪkəlɪ, ɪdɪə'lɒdʒɪkəlɪ/ *adv.* ideologisch; weltanschaulich

**ideologue** /'aɪdɪəlɒg, 'ɪdɪəlɒg/ *n.* Ideologe, *der*/Ideologin, *die*

**ideology** /aɪdɪ'ɒlədʒɪ, ɪdɪ'ɒlədʒɪ/ *n.* Ideologie, *die;* Weltanschauung, *die*

**ides** /aɪdz/ *n. pl.* Iden *Pl.;* **the ~ of March** die Iden des März

**idiocy** /'ɪdɪəsɪ/ *n.* [A] (*foolishness*) Dummheit, *die;* Idiotie, *die* (*abwertend*); [B] *no pl.* (*Med.*) Idiotie, *die;* hochgradiger Schwachsinn

**idiolect** /'ɪdɪəlekt/ *n.* (*Ling.*) Idiolekt, *der*

**idiom** /'ɪdɪəm/ *n.* [A] (*set phrase*) [Rede]wendung, *die;* idiomatischer Ausdruck; [B] (*expression peculiar to a group*) Ausdrucksweise, *die;* (*expression peculiar to a person*) Stil, *der;* Diktion, *die* (*geh.*); **the legal ~:** die Juristensprache; [C] (*national language*) Idiom, *das;* [National]sprache, *die;* [D] (*style of artistic expression*) Ausdrucksform, *die;* **the New Orleans ~:** der New-Orleans-Stil

**idiomatic** /ɪdɪə'mætɪk/ *adj.*, **idiomatically** /ɪdɪə'mætɪkəlɪ/ *adv.* idiomatisch

**idiosyncrasy** /ɪdɪə'sɪŋkrəsɪ/ *n.* [A] (*mental constitution*) [geistige] Einstellung; [B] (*view, behaviour*) Eigentümlichkeit, *die;* Eigenheit, *die*

**idiosyncratic** /ɪdɪəsɪŋ'krætɪk/ *adj.*, **idiosyncratically** /ɪdɪəsɪŋ'krætɪkəlɪ/ *adv.* eigenwillig

**idiot** /'ɪdɪət/ *n.* [A] (*coll.: fool*) Idiot, *der* (*ugs.*); Trottel, *der* (*ugs.*); [B] (*Med.*) Schwachsinnige, *der/die;* Idiot, *der*/Idiotin, *die* (*veralt.*)

**idiotic** /ɪdɪ'ɒtɪk/ *adj.* idiotisch (*ugs. abwertend*); schwachsinnig (*abwertend*); **what an ~ thing to do/say** was für ein Schwachsinn

**idiotically** /ɪdɪ'ɒtɪkəlɪ/ *adv.* idiotisch (*ugs.*); schwachsinnig

**idle** /'aɪdl/ **1** *adj.* [A] (*lazy*) faul; träge; [B] (*not in use*) außer Betrieb *nachgestellt;* **be** *or* **stand ~** ‹Maschinen, Fabrik:› stillstehen; ⇒ *also* **lie²** 2 B; [C] (*having no special purpose*) bloß ‹Neugier›; nutzlos, leer ‹Geschwätz›; [D] (*groundless*) unbegründet ‹Annahme, Mutmaßung›; bloß, rein ‹Spekulation, Angeberei, Gerücht, Behauptung›; **no ~ jest** kein Scherz; **no ~ boast** *or* **jest** (*iron.*) kein leeres Versprechen; [E] (*ineffective*) sinnlos, (*geh.*) müßig ‹Diskussion, Streit›; fruchtlos, vergeblich ‹Versuch›; leer ‹Versprechen›; [F] (*unoccupied*) frei ‹Zeit, Stunden, Tag›; **Satan** *or* **the devil finds** *or* **makes work for ~ hands [to do]** (*prov.*) Müßiggang ist aller Laster Anfang (*Spr.*). [G] (*unemployed*) arbeitslos; **be made ~** ‹Arbeiter:› arbeitslos werden. **be ~ for an hour** eine Stunde lang untätig sein *od.* nichts tun. **2** *v.i.* [A] faulenzen; [B] ‹Motor:› leer laufen, im Leerlauf laufen

**~ a'way** *v.t.* vertun ‹Zeit, Leben, Chancen›

**idleness** /'aɪdlnɪs/ *n., no pl.* (*being unoccupied*) Untätigkeit, *die;* (*avoidance of work*) Müßiggang, *der* (*geh.*)

**idler** /'aɪdlə(r)/ *n.* Faulenzer, *der*/Faulenzerin, *die;* Faulpelz, *der* (*fam.*)

**idly** /'aɪdlɪ/ *adv.* [A] (*carelessly*) leichtsinnig; gedankenlos; [B] (*inactively*) untätig; **stand ~ by while ...** (*fig.*) untätig zusehen, wie ...; [C] (*indolently*) faul; **spend one's time ~:** seine Zeit mit Faulenzen verbringen

**idol** /'aɪdl/ *n.* [A] (*false god*) Götze, *der;* (*image of deity*) Götzenbild, *das;* [B] (*person venerated*) Idol, *das;* (*thing venerated*) Götze, *der*

**idolater** /aɪ'dɒlətə(r)/ *n.* [A] (*worshipper of idols*) Götzendiener, *der;* [B] (*devoted admirer*) Verehrer, *der*/Verehrerin, *die*

**idolatrous** /aɪ'dɒlətrəs/ *adj.* götzendienerisch ‹Religion, Person›; abgöttisch, götzenhaft ‹Verehrung›

**idolatry** /aɪ'dɒlətrɪ/ *n.* [A] (*worship of false gods*) Götzenverehrung, *die;* [B] (*veneration of person or thing*) Vergötterung, *die*

**idolize** (**idolise**) /'aɪdəlaɪz/ *v.t.* [A] (*make an idol of*) anbeten; verehren; [B] (*fig.: venerate*) vergöttern; zum Idol erheben

**idyll** (**idyl**) /'ɪdɪl/ *n.* [A] (*description of scene*) Idylle, *die;* **prose ~** Idylle in Prosa; [B] (*episode*) Idyll, *das*

**idyllic** /aɪ'dɪlɪk, ɪ'dɪlɪk/ *adj.* idyllisch

**i.e.** /aɪ'iː/ *abbr.* **that is** d. h.; i. e.

**if** /ɪf/ **1** *conj.* [A] wenn; **if anyone should ask ...:** falls jemand fragt, ...; wenn jemand fragen sollte, ...; **if you were a bird ...:** wenn du ein Vogel wärest; **if you would lend me some money ...:** wenn du mir Geld leihen würdest, ...; **if I knew what to do ...:** wenn ich wüsste, was ich tun soll ...; **if I were you** an deiner Stelle; **if and when ...:** im Falle, dass ...; unter der Voraussetzung, dass ...; **write down the items you wish to buy, if any** schreib auf, welche Artikel du kaufen willst, wenn *od.* falls du etwas möchtest; **better, if anything** vielleicht etwas besser; **tell me what I can do to help, if anything** falls ich irgendwie helfen kann, sag es mir; **if so/not** wenn ja/nein *od.* nicht; **if then/that/at all** wenn überhaupt; **if only for today** wenn auch nur für heute; **if only because/to ...:** schon allein, weil/um ... zu ...; **as if** als ob; **he nodded, as if to say ...:** er nickte, als ob er sagen wollte *od.* wie um zu sagen ...; **as if you didn't know!** als ob du es nicht gewusst hättest!; **it isn't** *or* **it's not as if we were** *or* (*coll.*) **we're rich** es ist nicht etwa so, dass wir reich wären; [B] (*whenever*) [immer] wenn; [C] (*whether*) ob; [D] *in excl. of wish* **if I only knew, if only I knew!** wenn ich das nur wüsste!; das wüsste ich gern!; **if only he arrives in time!** wenn er nur rechtzeitig ankommt!; **if only you could** *or* **if you could only have seen it!** wenn du es nur hättest sehen können!; [E] *expr. surprise etc.* **if it isn't Ronnie!** das ist doch Ronnie!; **and if he didn't try to knock me down!** und er hat doch tatsächlich versucht, mich niederzuschlagen!; [F] *in polite request* **if you will wait a moment** wenn Sie einen Augenblick warten wollen; **if you wouldn't mind holding the door open** wenn Sie so freundlich wären und die Tür aufhielten; wenn Sie freundlicherweise die Tür aufhielten; [G] (*though*) und wenn; auch *od.* selbst wenn; **if I'm mistaken, you're mistaken too** wenn ich mich auch irre, du irrst dich genauso; **even if he did say that, ...:** selbst wenn er das gesagt hat, ...; [H] (*despite being*) wenn auch; **likeable, if somewhat rough** liebenswürdig, wenn auch etwas derb.

**2** *n.* Wenn, *das;* Einschränkung, *die;* **ifs and buts** Wenn und Aber, *das*

**iffish** /'ɪfɪʃ/, **iffy** /'ɪfɪ/ *adjs.* (*coll.*) ungewiss; zweifelhaft

**igloo** /'ɪgluː/ *n.* Iglu, *der od. das*

**igneous** /'ɪgnɪəs/ *adj.* **~ rock** (*Geol.*) Extrusivgestein, *das;* Eruptivgestein, *das*

**ignite** /ɪg'naɪt/ **1** *v.t.* [A] anzünden; entzünden (*geh.*); [B] (*Chem.: heat*) [bis zur Verbrennung] erhitzen. **2** *v.i.* sich entzünden

**ignition** /ɪg'nɪʃn/ *n.* [A] (*igniting*) Zünden, *das;* Entzünden, *das* (*geh.*); (*being ignited*) Entzündung, *die;* **we have ~:** wir haben gezündet; [B] (*Motor Veh.*) Zündung, *die*

**ignition: ~ key** *n.* (*Motor Veh.*) Zündschlüssel, *der;* **~ system** *n.* (*Motor Veh.*) Zündanlage, *die*

**ignoble** /ɪg'nəʊbl/ *adj.* niedrig ‹Geburt, Herkunft›; niederträchtig ‹Person›; schändlich ‹Tat›

**ignominious** /ɪgnə'mɪnɪəs/ *adj.* [A] verwerflich (*geh.*) ‹Tat, Idee, Praktik›; schändlich, verworfen ‹Person›; [B] (*humiliating*) schändlich; schmachvoll (*geh.*)

**ignominiously** /ɪgnə'mɪnɪəslɪ/ *adv.* (*in a humiliating manner*) auf entehrende *od.* erniedrigende Weise; schmachvoll (*geh.*)

**ignominy** /'ɪgnəmɪnɪ/ *n.* Schande, *die*

**ignoramus** /ɪgnə'reɪməs/ *n.* Ignorant, *der;* Nichtswisser, *der*

**ignorance** /'ɪgnərəns/ *n., no pl.* Ignoranz, *die* (*abwertend*); Unwissenheit, *die;* **keep sb. in ~ of sth.** jmdn. in Unkenntnis über etw. (*Akk.*) lassen; **~ is bliss** das ist das Glück der Unwissenden; was ich nicht weiß, macht mich nicht heiß (*Spr.*); **his ~ of physics** seine mangelnden Kenntnisse in Physik

**ignorant** /'ɪgnərənt/ *adj.* [A] (*lacking knowledge*) unwissend; ungebildet; [B] (*behaving in uncouth manner*) unkultiviert (*abwertend*); [C] (*uninformed*) **be ~ of sth.** über etw. (*Akk.*) nicht informiert sein; von etw. keine Ahnung haben; **remain ~ of sth.** über etw. (*Akk.*) nie etwas erfahren; **be ~ in** *or* **of mathematics** mangelnde Kenntnisse in Mathematik haben *od.* (*geh.*) aufweisen

**ignorantly** /'ɪgnərəntlɪ/ *adv.* unwissend; in Unwissenheit; **behave ~:** sich ungehobelt benehmen

**ignore** /ɪg'nɔː(r)/ *v.t.* ignorieren; nicht beachten; nicht befolgen ‹Befehl, Rat›; übergehen, überhören ‹Frage, Bemerkung›; **he ~d me in the street** er ist [auf der Straße] einfach an mir vorbeigegangen; **I shall ~ that remark!** ich habe das nicht gehört!

**iguana** /ɪ'gwɑːnə/ *n.* (*Zool.*) Leguan, *der*

**ikon** ⇒ **icon**

**Iliad** /'ɪlɪæd/ *n.* Ilias, *die*

**ilk** /ɪlk/ *n.* [A] (*coll.*) **Bill and [others of] his ~:** Bill und seinesgleichen; **... and that ~:** ... und dergleichen; **he's another of the same ~:** er gehört auch zu *od.* ist auch von derselben Sorte; **people of that ~:** solche Leute; [B] **of that ~** (*Scot.*) aus dem Clan/Ort gleichen Namens

**ill** /ɪl/ **1** *adj.*, **worse** /wɜːs/, **worst** /wɜːst/ [A] ▶ 1232 (*sick*) krank; **be ~ with flu** an Grippe (*Dat.*) erkrankt sein; [die] Grippe haben; **be ~ with worry** vor Sorgen [ganz] krank sein; sich vor Sorgen verzehren (*geh.*); [B] (*morally bad*) schlecht, zweifelhaft ‹Ruf, Ansehen›; ⇒ *also* **fame**; [C] (*hostile*) schlimm, böse ‹Gerücht›; schlecht, übel ‹Laune, Stimmung›; [D] (*harmful*) **~ effects** schädliche Wirkungen; **do an ~ turn to sb.** jmdm. Schaden zufügen; [E] (*unfavourable*) ungünstig ‹Zeitpunkt›; widrig ‹Schicksal, Umstand›; **~ fate** *or* **fortune** *or* **luck** Pech, *das;* **it's an ~ wind that blows nobody [any] good** (*prov.*) des einen Leid, des andern Freud' (*Spr.*); **as ~ luck would have it** wie es das Unglück wollte; [F] (*improper*) schlecht ‹Benehmen, Manieren›.

**2** *n.* [A] (*evil*) Übel, *das;* **for good or ~:** komme, was will; **through good and ~:** im Glück wie im Unglück; [B] (*harm*) Schlechte, *das;* Unglück, *das;* **wish sb. ~:** jmdm. nichts Gutes *od.* nur das Schlechteste wünschen; **speak ~ of sb./sth.** Schlechtes über jmdn. *od.* von jmdm./von etw. sagen; **let's not speak ~ of the dead** die Toten soll man ruhen lassen; [C] *in pl.* (*misfortunes*) Missstände *Pl.;* **the ~s that flesh is heir to** die Leiden, mit denen die Menschheit geschlagen ist.

**3** *adv.*, **worse, worst** [A] (*badly*) schlecht, unschicklich ‹sich benehmen›; [B] (*unfavourably*) ungünstig ‹gelegen›; **it goes ~**

**with sb.** es geht jmdm. schlecht; **C** (*imperfectly*) schlecht, unzureichend ‹versorgt, ausgestattet›; **he can ~ afford it** er kann es sich (*Dat.*) kaum leisten; **it ~ becomes sb. to do sth.** es ist nicht jmds. Sache *od.* steht jmdm. nicht zu, etw. zu tun; **~ at ease** verlegen

**I'll** /aɪl/ **A** = **I shall**; **B** = **I will**

**ill: ~-advised** *adj.* unklug; schlecht beraten ‹Kunde›; **be ~-advised** ‹Person:› schlecht beraten sein; **~-ad'visedly** *adv.* in unüberlegter Weise; unüberlegt, unklug ‹handeln›; **~-assorted** *adj.* schlecht zusammenpassend; nicht harmonierend, unverträglich ‹Ehepaar usw.›; bunt zusammengewürfelt ‹Sammlung›; **~-behaved** /ˈɪlbɪheɪvd/ *adj.* ⇒ **behave** 1 A; **~-bred** *adj.* schlecht erzogen ‹Kind, Jugendlicher›; unkultiviert (*abwertend*) ‹Leute, Kerl usw.›; **~-conceived** /ˈɪlkənsiːvd/ *adj.* schlecht durchdacht; **~-defined** /ˈɪldɪfaɪnd/ *adj.* ungenau definiert, unklar ‹Verfahren, Vorgehen›; verschwommen [formuliert] ‹Gesetz, Verordnung›; nicht klar *od.* fest umrissen ‹Aufgabenbereich›; **~-disposed** /ˈɪldɪspəʊzd/ *adj.* ⇒ **disposed**

**illegal** /ɪˈliːgl/ *adj.* ungesetzlich; illegal; (*Games, Sport: contrary to rules*) regelwidrig; unerlaubt; **it is ~ to drive a car without a licence** es ist verboten, ohne Führerschein Auto zu fahren

**illegality** /ɪlɪˈgælɪtɪ/ *n.* **A** *no pl.* Ungesetzlichkeit, *die;* **be unaware of the ~ of sth.** nicht wissen, dass etw. verboten ist; **B** (*illegal act*) Gesetzesübertretung, *die*

**illegally** /ɪˈliːgəlɪ/ *adv.* illegal; **bring sth. into the country ~:** etw. illegal *od.* auf illegalem Wege einführen

**illegibility** /ɪledʒɪˈbɪlɪtɪ/ *n., no pl.* Unleserlichkeit, *die*

**illegible** /ɪˈledʒɪbl/ *adj.*, **illegibly** /ɪˈledʒɪblɪ/ *adv.* unleserlich

**illegitimacy** /ɪlɪˈdʒɪtɪməsɪ/ *n., no pl.* ⇒ **illegitimate**: **A** Unehelichkeit, *die;* Illegitimität, *die;* **B** Unrechtmäßigkeit, *die;* **C** Unzulässigkeit, *die*

**illegitimate** /ɪlɪˈdʒɪtɪmət/ *adj.* **A** (*not from wedlock*) unehelich; illegitim; **B** (*not authorized by law*) unrechtmäßig ‹Machtergreifung, Geschäft›; mit dem Gesetz unvereinbar ‹Maßnahme, Vorgehen, Beweggrund›; **C** (*wrongly inferred*) unzulässig

**illegitimately** /ɪlɪˈdʒɪtɪmətlɪ/ *adv.* ⇒ **illegitimate**: **A** unehelich; **B** zu Unrecht; **C** auf unzulässige Weise

**ill: ~-'fated** *adj.* unglückselig; verhängnisvoll ‹Entscheidung, Stunde, Tag›; **~-'favoured** *adj.* (*unattractive*) unansehnlich ‹Person›; **~ 'feeling** *n.* Verstimmung, *die;* **cause ~ feeling** böses Blut machen *od.* schaffen; **no ~ feeling[s]?** sind Sie jetzt verstimmt *od.* (*fam.*) böse?; **no ~ feeling[s]** das macht [doch] nichts; ich nehme es nicht übel; **~-founded** /ˈɪlfaʊndɪd/ *adj.* haltlos ‹Theorie, Gerücht›; **be ~-founded** völlig haltlos sein; jeder Grundlage entbehren; **~-gotten** *adj.* unrechtmäßig erworben; **~ 'health** *n.* schwache Gesundheit; **~ humour** *n.* schlechte Laune; Gereiztheit, *die;* **~-humoured** /ɪlˈhjuːməd/ *adj.* schlecht gelaunt

**illicit** /ɪˈlɪsɪt/ *adj.* verboten ‹Glücksspiel›; unerlaubt ‹[Geschlechts]verkehr, Beziehung›; Schwarz‹handel, -verkauf, -arbeit, -brennerei›; **~ traffic in drugs** illegaler Drogenhandel

**illicitly** /ɪˈlɪsɪtlɪ/ *adv.* illegal ‹Handel treiben, Schnaps brennen›

**'ill-informed** *adj.* schlecht informiert; auf Unkenntnis beruhend ‹Bemerkung, Schätzung, Urteil›

**illiteracy** /ɪˈlɪtərəsɪ/ *n., no pl.* Analphabetentum, *das;* Analphabetismus, *der*

**illiterate** /ɪˈlɪtərət/ **1** *adj.* **A** des Lesens und Schreibens unkundig; analphabetisch ‹Bevölkerung›; **he is ~:** er ist Analphabet; **B** (*showing lack of learning*) primitiv (*abwertend*); **musically ~:** auf musikalischem Gebiet *od.* musikalisch völlig unbedarft; **he is politically ~:** er ist ein politischer Analphabet. **2** *n.* Analphabet, *der*/Analphabetin, *die*

**ill: ~-judged** /ɪlˈdʒʌdʒd/ *adj.* unklug; (*rash*) unüberlegt; leichtfertig; **~-mannered** /ɪlˈmænəd/ *adj.* rüpelhaft (*abwertend*); ungezogen ‹Kind›; **an ~-mannered fellow** ein Rüpel; **~-matched** *adj.* schlecht zusammenpassend; **~-natured** /ɪlˈneɪtʃəd/ *adj.*, **~-naturedly** /ɪlˈneɪtʃədlɪ/ *adv.* übellaunig

**illness** /ˈɪlnɪs/ *n.* ▶ **1232** **A** (*a disease*) Krankheit, *die;* Erkrankung, *die;* **children's ~:** Kinderkrankheit, *die;* **B** *no pl.* Krankheit, *die;* **because of ~:** wegen [einer] Krankheit

**illogical** /ɪˈlɒdʒɪkl/ *adj.* unlogisch; unbegründet ‹Ärger, Verstimmung›

**illogicality** /ɪlɒdʒɪˈkælɪtɪ/ *n.* **A** *no pl.* Unlogik, *die;* **B** (*illogical thing*) Ungereimtheit, *die;* logischer Fehler

**illogically** /ɪˈlɒdʒɪkəlɪ/ *adv.* auf unlogische Weise; ohne jede Logik

**ill: ~-omened** /ɪlˈəʊmənd/ *adj.* unheilvoll; **~-starred** /ˈɪlstɑːd/ *adj.* unglücklich ‹Liebesverhältnis›; unheilvoll, verhängnisvoll ‹Tag, Jahr, Zufall›; **the trip was ~-starred** die Reise stand unter einem Unstern *od.* ungünstigen Stern; **~ 'temper** ⇒ **ill humour**; **~-tempered** /ɪlˈtempəd/ ⇒ **ill-humoured**; **~-timed** /ɪlˈtaɪmd/ *adj.* [zeitlich] ungelegen; ungünstig; unpassend, unbesonnen ‹Bemerkung›; **~-'treat** *v.t.* misshandeln ‹Lebewesen›; nicht schonend behandeln, schlecht umgehen mit ‹Gegenstand›; **~-'treatment** *n., no pl.* (*of living thing*) Misshandlung, *die;* (*of object*) wenig pflegliche Behandlung; **suffer/receive ~-treatment** misshandelt/wenig schonend *od.* pfleglich behandelt werden

**illuminate** /ɪˈljuːmɪneɪt, ɪˈluːmɪneɪt/ *v.t.* **A** (*light up*) ‹Lampe usw.:› beleuchten; ‹Mond, Sonne:› erleuchten; **B** (*give enlightenment to*) erleuchten; **C** (*help to explain*) erhellen; [näher] beleuchten; **~ a period of history** Licht in eine Geschichtsepoche bringen; **D** (*decorate with lights*) festlich beleuchten; illuminieren; **~d advertisements** Leuchtreklamen; **E** (*decorate with colours*) ausmalen, (*fachspr.*) illuminieren ‹Handschriften usw.›; **~d initial letters** verzierte *od.* ausgemalte Initialen

**illuminating** /ɪˈljuːmɪneɪtɪŋ, ɪˈluːmɪneɪtɪŋ/ *adj.* aufschlussreich

**illumination** /ɪljuːmɪˈneɪʃn, ɪluːmɪˈneɪʃn/ *n.* **A** (*lighting*) Beleuchtung, *die;* **B** (*enlightenment*) Erleuchtung, *die;* **C** (*decorative lights*) *often in pl.* **~[s]** Festbeleuchtung, *die;* Illumination, *die;* **D** (*of manuscript*) Buchmalerei, *die;* Illumination, *die* (*fachspr.*)

**illumine** /ɪˈljuːmɪn, ɪˈluːmɪn/ *v.t.* (*literary*) **A** (*light up*) erhellen; illuminieren (*geh.*); **B** (*enlighten*) erleuchten; Erleuchtung bringen (+ *Dat.*); illuminieren (*geh.*)

**ill-use** **1** /ɪlˈjuːz/ *v.t.* ⇒ **ill-treat**. **2** /ɪlˈjuːs/ *n.* ⇒ **ill-treatment**

**illusion** /ɪˈljuːʒn, ɪˈluːʒn/ *n.* **A** (*false sense-perception*) [Sinnes]täuschung, *die;* Illusion, *die;* **have the ~ of seeing sth.** sich (*Dat.*) einbilden, etw. zu sehen; etw. zu sehen glauben; **the ointment produces an ~ of warmth** die Salbe ruft die Empfindung *od.* Illusion von Wärme hervor; **B** (*deception*) Wunschbild, *das;* Illusion, *die;* (*misapprehension*) falsche Vorstellung; Illusion, *die;* **be under an ~:** sich Illusionen (*Dat.*) hingeben; sich (*Dat.*) Illusionen machen; **be under the ~ that ...:** sich (*Dat.*) einbilden, dass ...; **have no ~s about sb./sth.** sich (*Dat.*) über jmdn./etw. keine Illusionen machen *od.* nichts vormachen

**illusionist** /ɪˈljuːʒənɪst, ɪˈluːʒənɪst/ ⇒ **conjurer**

**illusory** /ɪˈljuːsərɪ, ɪˈluːsərɪ/ *adj.* **A** (*deceptive*) illusorisch; trügerisch; **B** (*of the nature of an illusion*) imaginär (*geh.*) ‹Gestalt›; Wahn‹bild, -idee, -vorstellung›; irrig ‹Lehre, Ansicht, Annahme›

**illustrate** /ˈɪləstreɪt/ *v.t.* **A** (*serve as example of*) veranschaulichen; illustrieren; **B** (*elucidate by pictures*) [bildlich] darstellen ‹Vorgang, Ablauf›; illustrieren ‹Buch, Erklärung›; **C** (*explain*) verdeutlichen; erläutern; (*make clear by examples*) anschaulicher machen; illustrieren; **D** (*ornament*) illustrieren; bebildern

**illustration** /ɪləˈstreɪʃn/ *n.* **A** (*example*) Beispiel, *das* (**of** für); (*drawing*) Abbildung, *die;* bildliche Darstellung; **B** (*picture*) Abbildung, *die;* Illustration, *die;* **C** *no pl.* (*with example*) Illustration, *die;* Erläuterung, *die;* (*with picture*) Illustration, *die;* Illustrierung, *die;* **by way of ~:** zur Illustration *od.* Verdeutlichung

**illustrative** /ˈɪləstrətɪv/ *adj.* erläuternd; illustrativ; **be ~ of sth.** beispielhaft *od.* typisch für etw. sein; **~ material** Beispielmaterial, *das*

**illustrator** /ˈɪləstreɪtə(r)/ *n.* ▶ **1261** Illustrator, *der*/Illustratorin, *die*

**illustrious** /ɪˈlʌstrɪəs/ *adj.* berühmt ‹Person› (**for** wegen); ruhmreich ‹Tat, Herrschaft›

**ill 'will** *n.* Böswilligkeit, *die*

**I'm** /aɪm/ = **I am**

**image** /ˈɪmɪdʒ/ *n.* **A** Bildnis, *das* (*geh.*); (*statue*) Standbild, *das;* Statue, *die;* **B** (*Optics, Math.*) Bild, *das;* **C** (*semblance*) Bild, *das;* (*counterpart*) Ebenbild, *das* (*geh.*); (*archetype*) Verkörperung, *die;* **God created man in his own ~** (*Bibl.*) Gott schuf den Menschen nach seinem Bilde; **she is the [very] ~ of her mother** sie ist das [getreue] Ebenbild ihrer Mutter; **D** (*Lit.: simile, metaphor*) Bild, *das;* Metapher, *die* (*fachspr.*); **E** (*mental representation*) Bild, *das;* (*conception*) Vorstellung, *die;* **F** (*perceived character*) Image, *das;* **improve one's ~:** sein Image aufbessern; **public ~:** Image [in der Öffentlichkeit], *das*

**'image-conscious** *adj.* imagebewusst

**imagery** /ˈɪmɪdʒərɪ, ˈɪmɪdʒrɪ/ *n., no pl.* **A** (*images*) Bilder *Pl.;* bildliche Darstellungen *Pl.;* (*statues*) Statuen *Pl.;* Standbilder *Pl.;* **B** (*mental images*) Vorstellungen *Pl.;* **C** (*Lit.: figurative illustration*) Metaphorik, *die*

**imaginable** /ɪˈmædʒɪnəbl/ *adj.* erdenklich; **the biggest lie ~:** die unverschämteste Lüge, die man sich (*Dat.*) vorstellen kann

**imaginary** /ɪˈmædʒɪnərɪ/ *adj.* **A** imaginär (*geh.*); konstruiert ‹Bildnis›; eingebildet ‹Krankheit›; **B** (*Math.*) imaginär

**imagination** /ɪmædʒɪˈneɪʃn/ *n.* **A** *no pl., no art.* Fantasie, *die;* **do/see sth. in one's ~:** sich (*Dat.*) vorstellen, etw. zu tun/etw. vor seinem geistigen Auge sehen; **use your ~!** hab doch ein bisschen Fantasie! (*ugs.*); entwickel doch mal etwas Fantasie!; **B** *no pl., no art.* (*fancy*) Einbildung, *die;* **catch sb.'s ~:** jmdn. begeistern; **it's just your ~:** das bildest du dir nur ein; **it's all in your ~:** das bildest du dir alles [nur] ein

**imaginative** /ɪˈmædʒɪnətɪv/ *adj.* **A** imaginativ (*geh.*); **~ faculties** Vorstellungsvermögen, *das;* **B** (*given to using imagination*) fantasievoll; **be too ~:** zu viel Fantasie haben; **C** (*showing imagination*) einfallsreich

**imaginatively** /ɪˈmædʒɪnətɪvlɪ/ *adv.* **A** einfallsreich; **B** (*using imagination*) fantasievoll

**imagine** /ɪˈmædʒɪn/ *v.t.* **A** (*picture to oneself*) sich (*Dat.*) vorstellen; **can you ~?** stell dir vor!; **it cannot be ~d** es ist unvorstellbar; **~ things** sich (*Dat.*) Dinge einbilden[, die gar nicht stimmen]; **..., or am I imagining things?** ..., oder bilde ich mir das bloß ein?; **B** (*think*) sich (*Dat.*) vorstellen; **~ sb./sth. to be/do ...:** denken *od.* sich (*Dat.*) vorstellen, dass jmd./etw. ... ist/tut; **~ sth. to be easy/difficult** *etc.* sich (*Dat.*) etw. leicht/schwer *usw.* vorstellen; **~ oneself to be sth.** sich (*Dat.*) einbilden, etw. zu sein; **do not ~ that ...:** bilden Sie sich (*Dat.*) bloß nicht ein, dass ...; **C** (*guess*) sich (*Dat.*) vorstellen; **as you can ~, as may be ~d** wie du dir denken *od.* vorstellen kannst/wie man sich denken *od.* vorstellen kann; **D** (*suppose*) glauben; **E** (*get the impression*) **~ [that ...]:** sich (*Dat.*) einbilden[, dass ...]

**imago** /ɪˈmeɪgəʊ/ *n., pl.* **imagines** /ɪˈmeɪdʒɪniːz/ *or* **~s** *or* (*Amer.*) **~es** (*Biol., Psych.*) Imago, *die*

**imam** /ɪˈmɑːm/ *n.* (*Muslim Rel.*) Imam, *der*

**imbalance** /ɪmˈbæləns/ *n.* Unausgeglichenheit, *die*

**imbecile** /ˈɪmbɪsiːl, ˈɪmbɪsaɪl/ **1** *adj.* **A** (*stupid*) schwachsinnig (*ugs. abwertend*); **B** (*Med.*) imbezil[l]. **2** *n.* **A** (*stupid person*)

# Illnesses, aches and pains

## Injuries

***Where does it hurt?***
= Wo haben Sie Schmerzen?; (*to child*) Wo tut es weh?

***My right arm is hurting***
= Der rechte Arm tut mir weh, Mir tut der rechte Arm weh

***She has hurt her foot***
= (*e.g. twisted it*) Sie hat sich am Fuß wehgetan; (*wounded it, e.g. cut it or stuck something into it*) Sie hat sich am Fuß verletzt

***I have sprained my ankle***
= Ich habe mir den Fuß verstaucht

***He has broken his leg***
= Er hat sich das Bein gebrochen

***She has a fractured skull/pelvis***
= Sie hat einen Schädelbruch/Beckenbruch

***You've burnt your hand***
= Du hast dir die Hand verbrannt

Note the number of expressions where the English possessive with a part of the body is translated by a definite article and a personal pronoun in the dative.

 The body

## Aches and pains

***I've got toothache/a headache/a stomach ache***
= Ich habe Zahnschmerzen/Kopfschmerzen/Magenschmerzen *or* (*coll.*) Zahnweh/Kopfweh/Magenweh

***She has a pain in her knee***
= Sie hat Schmerzen im Knie

***something to relieve the pain***
= etwas gegen die Schmerzen

***a stab of pain***
= ein stechender Schmerz

***A gnawing pain went right through him***
= Ein bohrender Schmerz durchfuhr ihn

Note that **Schmerz** referring to physical pain is mostly used in the plural for continuing or repeated pain, and in the singular only when a single occurrence is meant.

## Being ill

***I feel ill***
= Ich fühle mich krank; (*esp. sick*) Mir ist übel *or* schlecht

***He is ill with flu, He has [got] flu***
= Er ist an Grippe erkrankt, Er hat [die] Grippe

***He is seriously/terminally ill***
= Er ist schwer krank/unheilbar krank

***She has caught*** or ***gone down with a cold***
= Sie hat sich erkältet *or* sich (*Dat.*) eine Erkältung zugezogen

***You'll catch pneumonia***
= Du holst dir eine Lungenentzündung

***They suffer from asthma/bronchitis***
= Sie leiden an Asthma/Bronchitis

***a bout of malaria***
= ein Malariaanfall

***an asthma attack***
= ein Asthmaanfall

## Illnesses and conditions

More permanent illnesses are usually translated as **-leiden**:

***He has a heart condition/a stomach complaint***
= Er hat ein Herzleiden/ein Magenleiden

But:

***a skin complaint***
= eine Hautkrankheit

Indicating often general and less well defined pain or discomfort, the German **-beschwerden** (plural) corresponds approximately to the English "trouble" (also translated by **-probleme**):

***heart/stomach trouble***
= Herzbeschwerden *or* Herzprobleme/Magenbeschwerden *or* Magenprobleme

***She suffers from back trouble***
= Sie hat Rückenprobleme, Sie hats mit dem Rücken (*coll.*)

In some cases, the noun describing the person is used rather than the word for the illness:

***He has epilepsy***
= Er ist Epileptiker

German forms many words for people with certain illnesses by adding **-kranke(r)**:

***people with Aids, Aids sufferers***
= Aidskranke

***a cancer patient*** or ***victim***
= ein Krebskranker/eine Krebskranke

## Treatment

***She is having*** or ***receiving treatment [from a specialist]***
= Sie ist [bei einem Facharzt] in Behandlung

***He is being treated for cancer/a stomach ulcer***
= Er wird wegen Krebs/eines Magengeschwürs behandelt

In this last example **auf** + accusative can also be used, but this gives the phrase the sense "given the treatment for", i.e. the condition has not necessarily been diagnosed (or not correctly):

***They treated him for a stomach ulcer, but it turned out that he had cancer***
= Sie haben ihn auf ein Magengeschwür behandelt, aber es stellte sich heraus, dass er Krebs hatte

***What can I take for hay fever?***
= Was kann ich gegen Heuschnupfen nehmen?

***To be taken three times a day***
= Dreimal täglich einzunehmen

***Shake the bottle***
= Vor Gebrauch schütteln

***There is no cure for Aids***
= Es gibt kein Mittel gegen Aids, Aids ist nicht heilbar

***I had four operations***
= Ich bin viermal operiert worden

***Have you been vaccinated against cholera?***
= Sind Sie gegen Cholera geimpft [worden]?

***She gave me an injection***
= Sie gab mir eine Spritze

## Recovery

***He is getting better*** or ***is on the mend*** or ***is on the road to recovery***
= Er ist auf dem Wege der Besserung

***She is much better***
= Es geht ihr *or* Sie fühlt sich viel besser

***I am completely cured/fully recovered***
= Ich bin völlig geheilt/habe mich vollständig erholt

Idiot, *der* (*ugs.*); Schwachkopf, *der;* B (*Med.*) Imbezil[l]e, *der/die*

**imbibe** /ɪm'baɪb/ *v.t.* A (*drink*) trinken; B (*fig.: assimilate*) in sich (*Akk.*) aufsaugen

**imbroglio** /ɪm'brəʊljəʊ/ *n., pl.* **~s** A **a financial ~:** ein finanzielles Chaos; ein Finanzchaos; B (*dramatic situation*) Verwicklungen *Pl.;* (*political situation*) Wirrwarr, *das*

**imbue** /ɪm'bju:/ *v.t.* A (*tinge*) färben; B (*permeate*) durchdringen; **~d with sth.** von etw. durchdrungen

**IMF** *abbr.* **International Monetary Fund** IWF, *der*

**imitate** /'ɪmɪteɪt/ *v.t.* A (*mimic*) nachahmen; nachmachen (*ugs.*); **~ sb.** (*follow example of*) es jmdm. gleichtun; B (*produce sth. like*) kopieren; C (*be like*) imitieren

**imitation** /ɪmɪ'teɪʃn/ ❶ *n.* A (*imitating*) Nachahmung, *die;* **Tim's ~ of his brother** die Art und Weise, wie Tim seinen Bruder nachahmt/nachahmte; **a style developed in ~ of classical models** ein nach klassischen Vorbildern entwickelter Stil; **do ~s of sb.** jmdn. imitieren *od.* nachahmen; **he sings, tells jokes, and does ~s** er singt, erzählt Witze und ahmt andere Leute nach; **~ is the sincerest [form of] flattery** nachgeahmt zu werden ist das größte Kompliment; B (*copy*) Kopie, *die;* Nachbildung, *die;* (*counterfeit*) Imitation, *die.*
❷ *adj.* imitiert; Kunst‹leder, -horn›; **~ marble/ivory/teak/fur** *etc.* Marmor-/Elfenbein-/Teak-/Pelzimitation *usw.*, *die*

**imitative** /'ɪmɪtətɪv, 'ɪmɪteɪtɪv/ *adj.* A uneigenständig; epigonal (*geh.*); **be ~ of sb./sth.** jmdn./etw. nachahmen; **~ arts** bildende Künste; B (*prone to copy*) imitativ (*geh.*)

**imitator** /'ɪmɪteɪtə(r)/ *n.* Nachahmer, *der/*Nachahmerin, *die;* (*one who mimics another*) Imitator, *der*/Imitatorin, *die;* **be an ~ of sb.** jmdn. nachahmen

**immaculate** /ɪ'mækjʊlət/ *adj.* A (*spotless*) makellos ‹Kleidung, Weiß›; B (*faultless*) tadellos

**Immaculate Con'ception** *n.* (*RC Ch.*) Unbefleckte Empfängnis

**immaculately** /ɪ'mækjʊlətlɪ/ *adv.* A (*spotlessly*) makellos; **~ white** blütenweiß; B (*faultlessly*) tadellos

**immanence** /'ɪmənəns/ *n., no pl.* Immanenz, *die*

**immanent** /'ɪmənənt/ *adj.* A immanent; **be ~ in sth.** einer Sache (*Dat.*) innewohnen (*geh.*); B (*Theol.*) allgegenwärtig

**immaterial** /ɪmə'tɪərɪəl/ *adj.* A (*unimportant*) unerheblich; **it's quite ~ to me** das ist für mich vollkommen uninteressant; B (*not consisting of matter*) immateriell (*geh.*); körperlos ‹Wesen›

**immature** /ɪmə'tjʊə(r)/ *adj.* A noch nicht voll entwickelt ‹Lebewesen›; noch nicht voll ausgereift ‹Begabung, Talent›; noch etwas unausgegoren ‹Kunststil›; unreif ‹Persönlichkeit, Einstellung›; B (*Biol.: unripe*) unreif; noch nicht voll entwickelt ‹Organ›

**immaturity** /ɪmə'tjʊərɪtɪ/ *n.* A *no pl.* Unreife, *die;* B *no pl.* (*Biol.: unripeness*) Unreife, *die;* **in ~:** vor der Reife

**immeasurable** /ɪ'meʒərəbl/ *adj.* unermesslich; unmessbar ‹Entfernung›

**immeasurably** /ɪ'meʒərəblɪ/ *adv.* A unmessbar; unendlich ‹lang›; B (*immensely*) ungeheuer

**immediate** /ɪ'mi:djət/ *adj.* A unmittelbar; (*nearest*) nächst... ‹Nachbar[schaft], Umgebung, Zukunft›; engst... ‹Familie›; unmittelbar ‹Kontakt›; **your ~ action must be to ...:** als Erstes müssen Sie ...; **~ inference** direkter Schluss; **his ~ plan is to ...:** zunächst einmal will er ...; B (*occurring at once*) prompt; unverzüglich ‹Handeln, Maßnahmen›; umgehend ‹Antwort›

**immediately** /ɪ'mi:djətlɪ/ ❶ *adv.* A unmittelbar; direkt; B (*without delay*) sofort.
❷ *conj.* sobald

**immemorial** /ɪmɪ'mɔ:rɪəl/ *adj.* undenklich; **from time ~:** seit undenklichen Zeiten

**immense** /ɪ'mens/ *adj.* A ungeheuer; immens; B (*coll.: great*) enorm

**immensely** /ɪ'menslɪ/ *adv.* A ungeheuer; B (*coll.: very much*) unheimlich (*ugs.*)

**immensity** /ɪ'mensɪtɪ/ *n., no pl.* (*great size*) Ungeheuerlichkeit, *die*

**immerse** /ɪ'mɜ:s/ *v.t.* A (*dip*) [ein]tauchen; **he ~d his head in cold water** er tauchte den Kopf in kaltes Wasser; B (*cause to be under water*) versenken; (*Eccl.*) untertauchen; **~d in water** unter Wasser; C **be ~d in thought/one's work** (*fig.: involved deeply*) in Gedanken versunken/in seine Arbeit vertieft sein

**immersion** /ɪ'mɜ:ʃn/ *n.* A Eintauchen, *das;* B (*Relig.*) Untertauchen, *das;* C (*fig.*) (*in work*) Vertiefung, *die;* (*in thought*) Versunkenheit, *die* (*geh.*)

**im'mersion heater** *n.* Heißwasserbereiter, *der;* (*small, portable*) Tauchsieder, *der*

**immigrant** /'ɪmɪgrənt/ ❶ *n.* Einwanderer, *der*/Einwanderin, *die;* Immigrant, *der*/Immigrantin, *die.* ❷ *adj.* Einwanderer-; **~ population** Einwanderer *Pl.;* **~ workers** ausländische Arbeitnehmer

**immigrate** /'ɪmɪgreɪt/ *v.i.* einwandern, immigrieren (**into** nach, **from** aus)

**immigration** /ɪmɪ'greɪʃn/ *n.* Einwanderung *die*, Immigration, *die* (**into** nach, **from** aus); *attrib.* Einwanderungs‹kontrolle, -beschränkung, -gesetz›; **go through ~:** durch die Passkontrolle gehen; *attrib.* **~ officer** Beamte/Beamtin der Einwanderungsbehörde; **~ authorities** Einwanderungsbehörden *Pl.;* **~ Service** Einwanderungsbehörde, *die*

**imminence** /'ɪmɪnəns/ *n., no pl.* Bevorstehen, *das*

**imminent** /'ɪmɪnənt/ *adj.* unmittelbar bevorstehend; drohend ‹Gefahr›; **be ~:** unmittelbar bevorstehen/drohen

**imminently** /'ɪmɪnəntlɪ/ *adv.* unmittelbar; **the President's arrival is expected ~:** die Ankunft des Präsidenten wird jeden Moment erwartet

**immiscible** /ɪ'mɪsɪbl/ *adj.* nicht mischbar

**immobile** /ɪ'məʊbaɪl/ *adj.* A (*immovable*) unbeweglich; (*Mil.*) immobil; B (*motionless*) bewegungslos

**immobilisation, immobilise** ⇨ **immobiliz-**

**immobility** /ɪmə'bɪlɪtɪ/ *n., no pl.* A (*immovableness*) Unbeweglichkeit, *die;* (*of army*) Immobilität, *die;* B (*motionlessness*) Bewegungslosigkeit, *die*

**immobilization** /ɪməʊbɪlaɪ'zeɪʃn/ *n.* A (*fixing immovably*) Verankerung, *die;* B (*Med.: restricting in movement*) Ruhigstellung, *die*

**immobilize** /ɪ'məʊbɪlaɪz/ *v.t.* A (*fix immovably*) verankern; (*fig.*) lähmen; B (*restrict movement of*) feststellen ‹Tür usw.›; ruhig stellen ‹Tier, Körperteil, Patienten›; C gegen Wegfahren sichern ‹Fahrzeug›

**immobilizer** /ɪ'məʊbɪlaɪzə(r)/ *n.* (*Motor Veh.*) Wegfahrsperre, *die*

**immoderate** /ɪ'mɒdərət/ *adj.* A (*excessive*) unmäßig ‹Rauchen, Trinken›; überhöht ‹Geschwindigkeit, Preis›; übermäßig ‹Lärm›; B (*extreme*) extrem ‹Ansichten, Politiker›; maßlos ‹Lebensstil›

**immoderately** /ɪ'mɒdərətlɪ/ *adv.* A (*excessively*) übermäßig ‹hoch›; unmäßig ‹essen, trinken usw.›; übertrieben ‹schnell, laut›; B (*to an extreme degree*) extrem

**immodest** /ɪ'mɒdɪst/ *adj.* A (*impudent*) unbescheiden; B (*improper*) unanständig

**immodestly** /ɪ'mɒdɪstlɪ/ *adv.* A (*impudently*) unbescheidenerweise; B (*improperly*) unanständig

**immodesty** /ɪ'mɒdɪstɪ/ *n., no pl.* A (*impudence*) Unbescheidenheit, *die;* B (*impropriety*) Unanständigkeit, *die;* **the ~ of her short skirt** ihr unanständig kurzer Rock

**immolate** /'ɪməleɪt/ *v.t.* (*literary*) A (*kill*) opfern (**to** *Dat.*); B (*fig.: sacrifice*) zum Opfer bringen, aufopfern (*geh.*) (**to** *Dat.*)

**immolation** /ɪmə'leɪʃn/ *n.* (*literary*) A Opferung, *die;* B (*fig.*) Aufopferung, *die*

**immoral** /ɪ'mɒrəl/ *adj.* A (*not conforming to morality*) unmoralisch; unsittlich; sittenwidrig (*Rechtsspr.*); B (*morally evil*) pervers; (*unchaste*) sittenlos; C (*dissolute*) zügellos

**immoral 'earnings** *n. pl.* (*Law*) Einkünfte aus gewerbsmäßiger Unzucht

**immorality** /ɪmə'rælɪtɪ/ *n.* A *no pl.* Unsittlichkeit, *die;* Unmoral, *die;* Sittenwidrigkeit, *die* (*Rechtsspr.*); B *no pl.* (*wickedness*) Verdorbenheit, *die;* (*unchastity*) Sittenlosigkeit, *die;* C *no pl.* (*dissoluteness*) Zügellosigkeit, *die;* D (*morally evil or unchaste act*) Unsittlichkeit, *die;* E (*dissolute act*) Ausschweifung, *die*

**immorally** /ɪ'mɒrəlɪ/ *adv.* A (*without regard for morality*) unmoralisch; unsittlich; B (*wickedly*) unmoralisch; (*unchastely*) sittenlos; C (*dissolutely*) ausschweifend; zügellos

**immortal** /ɪ'mɔ:tl/ ❶ *adj.* A (*living for ever*) unsterblich; B (*divine*) ewig; **~ life, the life ~:** das ewige Leben; C (*incorruptible*) unvergänglich; D (*famous for all time*) unsterblich, unvergänglich ‹Kunstwerk›. ❷ *n.* A Unsterbliche, *der/die;* B *in pl.* (*Greek and Roman Mythol.*) Unsterbliche; Götter

**immortality** /ɪmɔ:'tælɪtɪ/ *n., no pl.* ⇨ **immortal** 1 A, C, D: Unsterblichkeit, *die;* Unvergänglichkeit, *die*

**immortalize** /ɪ'mɔ:təlaɪz/ *v.t.* unsterblich machen

**immortally** /ɪ'mɔ:təlɪ/ *adv.* A (*eternally*) ewig[lich]; B (*perpetually*) [immer und] ewig

**immovable** /ɪ'mu:vəbl/ *adj.* A unbeweglich; **be ~:** sich nicht bewegen lassen; B (*motionless*) bewegungslos; C (*not subject to change*) unveränderbar; ⇨ *also* **feast** 1 A; D (*steadfast*) unerschütterlich; unverrückbar ‹Entschluss›; E (*emotionless*) unbewegt; F (*Law*) unbeweglich

**immovably** /ɪ'mu:vəblɪ/ *adv.* A fest; **be ~ stuck** feststecken; B (*in a motionless manner*) bewegungslos; C (*unchangeably*) unveränderbar; D (*steadfastly*) unerschütterlich; **be ~ resolved** fest entschlossen sein; E (*in an emotionless manner*) unbewegt

**immune** /ɪ'mju:n/ *adj.* A (*exempt*) sicher (**from** vor + *Dat.*); geschützt (**from, against** vor + *Dat.*); gefeit (*geh.*) (**from, against** gegen); **~ from criminal liability** nicht strafmündig; **make oneself ~ from criticism** sich gegen Kritik abschirmen; B (*insusceptible*) unempfindlich (**to** gegen); (*to hints, suggestions, etc.*) unempfänglich (**to** für); immun (**to** gegen); C (*Med.*) (*resistant to disease*) immun (**to** gegen); (*relating to immunity*) Immun‹defekt, -körper, -schwäche, -serum›; **~ system** Immunsystem, *das*

**immunisation, immunise** ⇨ **immuniz-**

**immunity** /ɪ'mju:nɪtɪ/ *n.* A (*freedom*) **~ from criminal liability** Strafunmündigkeit, *die;* **~ from prosecution** Schutz vor Strafverfolgung; **give sb. ~ from punishment** ‹Person:› jmdn. von der Bestrafung ausnehmen; ‹Umstand:› jmdn. vor Strafe schützen; ⇨ *also* **diplomatic immunity;** B ⇨ **immune** B: Unempfindlichkeit, *die* (**to** gegen); Unempfänglichkeit, *die* (**to** für); Immunität, *die* (**to** gegen); C (*Law*) Immunität, *die* (**from** vor + *Dat.*); D (*Med.: capacity to resist disease*) Immunität, *die;* **have ~ to infection** gegen Infektion immun sein

**immunization** /ɪmjʊnaɪ'zeɪʃn/ *n.* (*Med.*) Immunisierung, *die*

**immunize** /'ɪmjʊnaɪz/ *v.t.* (*Med.*) immunisieren

**immunodeficiency** /ɪ'mju:nəʊdɪfɪʃənsɪ/ *n.* (*Med.*) Immunschwäche, *die*

**immunodeficient** /ɪ'mju:nəʊdɪfɪʃənt/ *adj.* (*Med.*) immunschwach

**immunology** /ɪmjʊ'nɒlədʒɪ/ *n.* (*Med.*) Immunologie, *die*

**immure** /ɪ'mjʊə(r)/ (*literary*) ❶ *v.t.* einkerkern (*geh.*). ❷ *v. refl.* **~ oneself** sich abkapseln

**immutability** /ɪmju:tə'bɪlɪtɪ/ *n., no pl.* Unveränderlichkeit, *die*

**immutable** /ɪ'mju:təbl/ *adj.* unveränderlich

**imp** /ɪmp/ *n.* A Kobold, *der;* B (*fig.: mischievous child*) Racker, *der* (*fam.*)

**impact** ❶ /'ɪmpækt/ *n.* A Aufprall, *der* (**on, against** auf + *Akk.*); (*of shell or bomb*) Einschlag, *der;* (*collision*) Zusammenprall, *der;* **B** (*fig.: effect*) Wirkung, *die;* **the ~ of plastics on modern life** die Auswirkung von Kunststoffen auf das moderne Leben; **have an ~ on sb./sth.** Auswirkungen auf jmdn./etw. haben; **make an ~ on sb./sth.** Eindruck auf jmdn./etw. machen. **2** /ɪmˈpækt/ *v.t.* pressen

**impacted** /ɪmˈpæktɪd/ *adj.* **A** (*Dent.*) impaktiert ‹Zahn›; **B** (*Med.*) **~ fracture** Knocheneinkeilung, *die*

**ˈimpact strength** *n.* (*Metallurgy*) Stoßfestigkeit, *die*

**impair** /ɪmˈpeə(r)/ *v.t.* **A** (*damage*) beeinträchtigen; schaden (+ *Dat.*) ‹Gesundheit›; **B** (*weaken*) beeinträchtigen; **~ed vision** Sehschwäche, *die;* **~ed hearing** Schwerhörigkeit, *die*

**impairment** /ɪmˈpeəmənt/ *n.* Beeinträchtigung, *die;* **~ of memory** Gedächtnisschwäche, *die*

**impale** /ɪmˈpeɪl/ *v.t.* **A** aufspießen; (*Hist.*) pfählen; **B** (*Her.*) spalten ‹Wappen›

**impalpable** /ɪmˈpælpəbl/ *adj.* **A** (*imperceptible to touch*) nicht fühlbar; **B** (*not easily grasped by the mind*) unfassbar

**impart** /ɪmˈpɑːt/ *v.t.* **A** (*give*) [ab]geben (**to** an + *Akk.*); vermachen (**to** *Dat.*); **B** (*communicate*) kundtun (*geh.*) (**to** *Dat.*); vermitteln ‹Kenntnisse› (**to** *Dat.*)

**impartial** /ɪmˈpɑːʃl/ *adj.* unparteiisch; gerecht ‹Entscheidung, Behandlung, Urteil›

**impartiality** /ɪmpɑːʃɪˈælɪtɪ/ *n.*, *no pl.* Unparteilichkeit, *die*

**impartially** /ɪmˈpɑːʃəlɪ/ *adv.* unparteiisch

**impassable** /ɪmˈpɑːsəbl/ *adj.* unpassierbar (**to** für); (*to vehicles*) unbefahrbar (**to** für)

**impasse** /ˈæmpɑːs/ *n.* (*lit. or fig.*) Sackgasse, *die;* **the negotiations have reached an ~:** die Verhandlungen sind in eine Sackgasse geraten

**impassioned** /ɪmˈpæʃnd/ *adj.* leidenschaftlich

**impassive** /ɪmˈpæsɪv/ *adj.* **A** ausdruckslos; **B** (*incapable of feeling emotion*) leidenschaftslos

**impassively** /ɪmˈpæsɪvlɪ/ *adv.* ⇒ **impassive**: **A** ausdruckslos; **B** leidenschaftslos

**impatience** /ɪmˈpeɪʃəns/ *n.*, *no pl.* **A** Ungeduld, *die* (**at** über + *Akk.*); **B** (*intolerance*) Unduldsamkeit, *die* (**of** gegen); **C** (*eager desire*) [ungeduldige] Erwartung (**for** *Gen.*)

**impatient** /ɪmˈpeɪʃənt/ *adj.* **A** ungeduldig; **~ at sth./with sb.** ungeduldig über etw. (*Akk.*)/mit jmdm.; **B** (*intolerant*) unduldsam (**of** gegen); **be ~ of sth.** etw. nicht ertragen können; **C** (*eagerly desirous*) **be ~ for sth.** etw. kaum erwarten können; **be ~ to do sth.** unbedingt etw. tun wollen

**impatiently** /ɪmˈpeɪʃəntlɪ/ *adv.* **A** ungeduldig; **B** (*intolerantly*) unduldsam; **C** (*with eager desire*) begierig

**impeach** /ɪmˈpiːtʃ/ *v.t.* **A** (*call in question*) infrage stellen; **B** **~ sb. with sth.** jmdn. einer Sache (*Gen.*) beschuldigen; **C** (*find fault with*) anzweifeln; in Zweifel ziehen; **D** (*Law*) anklagen (**of** *Gen.*, wegen)

**impeachment** /ɪmˈpiːtʃmənt/ *n.* **A** (*calling in question*) Infragestellung, *die;* **B** (*finding of fault*) Anzweif[e]lung, *die;* **C** (*Law*) Impeachment, *das*

**impeccable** /ɪmˈpekəbl/ *adj.* makellos; tadellos ‹Manieren›

**impeccably** /ɪmˈpekəblɪ/ *adv.* tadellos; makellos ‹rein›

**impecunious** /ɪmpɪˈkjuːnɪəs/ *adj.* mittellos

**impedance** /ɪmˈpiːdəns/ *n.* (*Electr.*) Impedanz, *die*

**impede** /ɪmˈpiːd/ *v.t.* behindern

**impediment** /ɪmˈpedɪmənt/ *n.* **A** Hindernis, *das* (**to** für); **B** (*speech defect*) Sprachfehler, *der*

**impedimenta** /ɪmpedɪˈmentə/ *n. pl.* (*also Mil.*) Gepäck, *das*

**impel** /ɪmˈpel/ *v.t.*, **-ll-:** **A** (*drive by moral action*) treiben; **feel ~led to do sth.** sich genötigt *od.* gezwungen fühlen, etw. zu tun; **~ sb. to greater efforts** jmdn. zu größeren Bemühungen anspornen; **B** (*drive forward*) treiben; antreiben ‹Turbine usw.›

**impend** /ɪmˈpend/ *v.i.* **A** (*be about to happen*) bevorstehen; ‹Gefahr:› drohen

**impenetrable** /ɪmˈpenɪtrəbl/ *adj.* **A** undurchdringlich (**by, to** für); unbezwingbar, uneinnehmbar ‹Festung›; **B** (*inscrutable*) unergründlich

**impenetrably** /ɪmˈpenɪtrəblɪ/ *adv.* **A** undurchdringlich; **B** (*inscrutably*) unergründlich; **C** hoffnungslos ‹dumm›

**impenitent** /ɪmˈpenɪtənt/ *adj.* reu[e]los; **be quite ~:** keine Spur von Reue zeigen

**impenitently** /ɪmˈpenɪtəntlɪ/ *adv.* reu[e]los

**imperative** /ɪmˈperətɪv/ **1** *adj.* **A** (*commanding*) gebieterisch (*geh.*) ‹Stimme, Geste›; **B** (*urgent*) dringend erforderlich; **C** (*obligatory*) zwingend ‹Verpflichtung›; **D** (*Ling.*) imperativisch; **~ mood** Imperativ, *der.* **2** *n.* **A** (*command*) Befehl, *der;* **B** (*Ling.*) Imperativ, *der;* Befehlsform, *die*

**imperceptible** /ɪmpəˈseptɪbl/ *adj.* **A** nicht wahrnehmbar (**to** für); unsichtbar ‹Schranke (fig.)›; **be ~ to sb./the senses** von jmdm./den Sinnen nicht wahrgenommen werden können; **B** (*very slight or gradual*) unmerklich; (*subtle*) kaum zu erkennen *nicht attr.;* kaum zu erkennend *nicht präd.;* minimal ‹Unterschied›

**imperceptibly** /ɪmpəˈseptɪblɪ/ *adv.* **A** unmerklich; kaum wahrnehmbar ‹sich bewegen›; **B** (*very gradually*) unmerklich; (*very slightly*) geringfügig

**imperfect** /ɪmˈpɜːfɪkt/ **1** *adj.* **A** (*not fully formed*) unfertig; (*incomplete*) unvollständig; **drainage in this region is ~:** die Entwässerung in dieser Gegend ist mangelhaft; **slightly ~ stockings/pottery** *etc.* Strümpfe/Keramik *usw.* mit kleinen Fehlern; **B** (*faulty*) mangelhaft; **human beings are ~:** der Mensch ist unvollkommen; **C** (*Ling.*) Imperfekt-; **the ~ tense** das Imperfekt. **2** *n.* (*Ling.*) Imperfekt, *das*

**imperfection** /ɪmpəˈfekʃn/ *n.* **A** *no pl.* (*incompleteness*) Unvollständigkeit, *die;* **B** *no pl.* (*faultiness*) Mangelhaftigkeit, *die;* (*of human beings*) Unvollkommenheit, *die;* **C** (*fault*) Mangel, *der*

**imperfectly** /ɪmˈpɜːfɪktlɪ/ *adv.* **A** (*incompletely*) unvollständig; **B** (*faultily*) fehlerhaft; mangelhaft

**imperial** /ɪmˈpɪərɪəl/ *adj.* **A** kaiserlich; imperial (*geh.*); Reichs‹adler, -insignien›; **I~ Rome** das Rom der Kaiserzeit; das kaiserliche Rom; **B** (*Brit. Hist.*) des Britischen Weltreiches *nachgestellt;* **C** (*of an emperor*) Kaiser-; **the I~ Court** der Kaiserhof; der kaiserliche Hof; **Her I~ Majesty** Ihre Kaiserliche Hoheit; **D** (*majestic*) majestätisch; (*haughty*) hochmütig; erhaben (*iron.*); **E** (*magnificent*) fürstlich; glanzvoll ‹Stadt›; **F** (*fixed by statute*) britisch ‹Maße, Gewichte›; ⇒ *also* **gallon**

**imperialism** /ɪmˈpɪərɪəlɪzm/ *n.*, *no pl.* (*derog.*) Imperialismus, *der;* **US/Soviet ~:** der US-/Sowjetimperialismus

**imperialist** /ɪmˈpɪərɪəlɪst/ *n.* (*derog.*) Imperialist, *der*/Imperialistin, *die;* **~ countries** imperialistische Länder

**imperialistic** /ɪmpɪərɪəˈlɪstɪk/ *adj.* (*derog.*) imperialistisch

**imperil** /ɪmˈperl/ *v.t.*, (*Brit.*) **-ll-** gefährden

**imperious** /ɪmˈpɪərɪəs/ *adj.* **A** (*overbearing*) herrisch; **B** (*urgent*) zwingend; mächtig ‹Triebe usw.›

**imperiously** /ɪmˈpɪərɪəslɪ/ *adv.* **A** (*overbearingly*) herrisch; **B** (*urgently*) zwingend

**imperishable** /ɪmˈperɪʃəbl/ *adj.* **A** (*immortal*) unvergänglich; **B** (*not decaying*) alterungsbeständig ‹Material›; unverderblich ‹Lebensmittel›

**imperishably** /ɪmˈperɪʃəblɪ/ *adv.* unvergänglich

**impermanence** /ɪmˈpɜːmənəns/ *n.*, *no pl.* Vergänglichkeit, *die*

**impermanent** /ɪmˈpɜːmənənt/ *adj.* vorübergehend; vergänglich ‹Leben›

**impermeable** /ɪmˈpɜːmɪəbl/ *adj.* undurchlässig; impermeabel (*fachspr.*)

**impermissible** /ɪmpəˈmɪsɪbl/ *adj.* unzulässig

**impersonal** /ɪmˈpɜːsənl/ *adj.* **A** (*having no personality*) **an ~ thing** etwas [rein] Dingliches; **B** (*not connected with any particular person*) unpersönlich ‹Art, Zimmer usw.›

**impersonality** /ɪmpɜːsəˈnælɪtɪ/ *n.*, *no pl.* Unpersönlichkeit, *die*

**impersonal: ~ ˈpronoun** ⇒ **pronoun**; **~ ˈverb** *n.* (*Ling.*) unpersönliches Verb; Impersonale, *das* (*fachspr.*)

**impersonate** /ɪmˈpɜːsəneɪt/ *v.t.* (*pretend to be*) (*for entertainment*) imitieren; nachahmen; (*for purpose of fraud*) sich ausgeben als

**impersonation** /ɪmpɜːsəˈneɪʃn/ *n.* **A** (*personification*) Verkörperung, *die;* **B** (*imitation*) Imitation, *die;* Nachahmung, *die;* **he does ~s** er ist Imitator; **his ~ of Tony Blair** seine Tony-Blair-Imitation; **do an ~ of sb.** jmdn. imitieren *od.* nachahmen; **~ of sb.** (*for purpose of fraud*) Auftreten als jmd.

**impersonator** /ɪmˈpɜːsəneɪtə(r)/ *n.* (*entertainer*) Imitator, *der*/Imitatorin, *die;* (*sb. with fraudulent intent*) Betrüger, *der*/Betrügerin, *die;* **an ~ posing as a policeman** jemand, der sich als Polizist ausgibt; ⇒ *also* **female 1 A**

**impertinence** /ɪmˈpɜːtɪnəns/ *n.* Unverschämtheit, *die;* Impertinenz, *die* (*geh.*)

**impertinent** /ɪmˈpɜːtɪnənt/ *adj.* unverschämt; impertinent (*geh.*)

**impertinently** /ɪmˈpɜːtɪnəntlɪ/ *adv.* unverschämterweise; **behave ~:** sich unverschämt benehmen

**imperturbability** /ɪmpətɜːbəˈbɪlɪtɪ/ *n.*, *no pl.* Gelassenheit, *die*

**imperturbable** /ɪmpəˈtɜːbəbl/ *adj.* gelassen; **be completely ~:** durch nichts zu erschüttern sein; die Ruhe weghaben (*ugs.*)

**imperturbably** /ɪmpəˈtɜːbəblɪ/ *adv.* gelassen; **..., he said ~:** ..., sagte er in aller Ruhe

**impervious** /ɪmˈpɜːvɪəs/ *adj.* **A** undurchlässig; **~ to water/bullets/rain** wasserdicht/kugelsicher/regendicht; **B** (*fig.: impenetrable*) unergründlich; **C** **be ~ to sth.** (*fig.*) unempfänglich für etw. sein; **be ~ to argument** Argumenten unzugänglich sein

**impetigo** /ɪmpɪˈtaɪgəʊ/ *n.* ▶ **1232** (*Med.*) Impetigo, *die* (*fachspr.*); Eiterflechte, *die*

**impetuosity** /ɪmpetjʊˈɒsɪtɪ/ *n.* **A** *no pl.* (*quality*) Impulsivität, *die;* **B** (*act, impulse*) Ausbruch, *der*

**impetuous** /ɪmˈpetjʊəs/ *adj.* impulsiv ‹Person›; unüberlegt ‹Handlung, Entscheidung›; (*vehement*) stürmisch; ungestüm ‹Person, Angriff›

**impetuousness** /ɪmˈpetjʊəsnɪs/ ⇒ **impetuosity A**

**impetus** /ˈɪmpɪtəs/ *n.* **A** Kraft, *die;* (*of impact*) Wucht, *die;* **B** (*fig.: impulse*) Motivation, *die;* **give an ~ to sth.** einer Sache (*Dat.*) Impulse geben; **give sth. new** *or* **fresh ~:** einer Sache (*Dat.*) neuen Auftrieb geben; **the ~ behind the development of nuclear power** die treibende Kraft bei der Entwicklung der Kernkraft

**impiety** /ɪmˈpaɪətɪ/ *n.* **A** *no pl.* (*ungodliness*) Gottlosigkeit, *die;* **B** *no pl.* (*lack of dutifulness*) Respektlosigkeit, *die;* **C** (*act*) Pietätlosigkeit, *die*

**impinge** /ɪmˈpɪndʒ/ *v.i.* **A** (*make impact*) **~ [up]on sth.** auf etw. (*Akk.*) auftreffen; **B** (*encroach*) **~ [up]on sth.** auf etw. (*Akk.*) Einfluss nehmen

**impious** /ˈɪmpɪəs/ *adj.* **A** (*wicked*) gottlos; **B** (*lacking in respect*) respektlos

**impish** /ˈɪmpɪʃ/ *adj.* lausbübisch; diebisch ‹Freude›; verschmitzt ‹Grinsen, Blick›

**impishly** /ˈɪmpɪʃlɪ/ *adv.* lausbübisch; diebisch ‹sich freuen›; verschmitzt ‹grinsen›

**implacable** /ɪmˈplækəbl/ *adj.* unversöhnlich; erbittert ‹Gegner›; erbarmungslos ‹Verfolgung›; unerbittlich ‹Schicksal›

**implacably** /ɪmˈplækəblɪ/ *adv.* unerbittlich; unaufhaltsam ‹voranschreiten›

**implant** **1** /ɪmˈplɑːnt/ *v.t.* **A** (*Med.*) implantieren (*fachspr.*), einpflanzen (**in** *Dat.*); **~ sb./sth. with sth.** jmdm./einer Sache etw. einpflanzen; **B** (*Physiol.*) **be ~ed** sich einnisten; **C** (*fig.: instil*) einpflanzen (**in**

*Dat.*); **D** (*plant*) [ein]pflanzen. **2** /'ɪmplɑ:nt/ *n.* (*Med.*) Implantat, *das*

**implantation** /ɪmplɑ:n'teɪʃn/ *n.* **A** (*Med.*) Implantation, *die* (*fachspr.*); Einpflanzung, *die;* **B** (*fig.: instilling*) Einpflanzung, *die*

**implausibility** /ɪmplɔ:zɪ'bɪlɪtɪ/ *n., no pl.* Unglaubwürdigkeit, *die*

**implausible** /ɪm'plɔ:zɪbl/ *adj.*, **implausibly** /ɪm'plɔ:zɪblɪ/ *adv.* unglaubwürdig

**implement 1** /'ɪmplɪmənt/ *n.* Gerät, *das.* **2** /'ɪmplɪment/ *v.t.* **A** (*fulfil, complete*) erfüllen ‹Versprechen, Vertrag›; einhalten ‹Termin usw.›; vollziehen ‹Erlass usw.›; **B** (*put into effect*) [in die Tat] umsetzen ‹Politik, Plan usw.›

**implementation** /ɪmplɪmen'teɪʃn/ *n.* ⇒ **implement** 2: Erfüllung, *die;* Einhaltung, *die;* Vollzug, *der;* Umsetzung [in die Tat], *die*

**implicate** /'ɪmplɪkeɪt/ *v.t.* **A** (*show to be involved*) belasten ‹Verdächtigen usw.›; **be ~d in a scandal** in einen Skandal verwickelt sein; **B** (*affect*) **be ~d in sth.** von etw. betroffen sein

**implication** /ɪmplɪ'keɪʃn/ *n.* **A** *no pl.* (*implying*) Implikation, *die* (*geh.*); **by ~:** implizit; implizite (*geh.*); **B** *no pl.* (*being involved*) Verwicklung, *die* (**in** in + *Akk.*); **C** *no pl.* (*being affected*) Betroffenheit, *die* (**in** von); **D** (*thing implied*) Implikation, *die*

**implicit** /ɪm'plɪsɪt/ *adj.* **A** (*implied*) implizit (*geh.*); unausgesprochen ‹Drohung, Zweifel›; **B** (*virtually contained*) **be ~ in sth.** in etw. (*Dat.*) enthalten sein; **C** (*resting on authority*) unbedingt; blind ‹Vertrauen›

**implicitly** /ɪm'plɪsɪtlɪ/ *adv.* **A** (*by implication*) implizit (*geh.*); **B** (*unquestioningly*) blind ‹vertrauen, gehorchen usw.›

**implode** /ɪm'pləʊd/ **1** *v.i.* implodieren. **2** *v.t.* implodieren lassen; **be ~d** implodieren

**implore** /ɪm'plɔ:(r)/ *v.t.* **A** (*beg for*) erflehen (*geh.*); flehen um; **'please', she ~d** „bitte", flehte sie; **B** (*entreat*) anflehen (**for** um); **~ sb. to do/not to do sth.** jmdn. anflehen *od.* inständig bitten, etw. zu tun/nicht zu tun

**imploring** /ɪm'plɔ:rɪŋ/ *adj.* flehend

**imploringly** /ɪm'plɔ:rɪŋlɪ/ *adv.* flehentlich (*geh.*)

**imply** /ɪm'plaɪ/ *v.t.* **A** (*involve the existence of*) implizieren (*geh.*); (*by inference*) schließen lassen auf (+ *Akk.*); **be implied in sth.** in etw. (*Dat.*) enthalten sein; **silence sometimes implies consent** Schweigen bedeutet manchmal Zustimmung; **B** (*express indirectly*) hindeuten auf (+ *Akk.*); (*insinuate*) unterstellen; **are you ~ing that ...?** willst du damit etwa sagen, dass ...?

**impolite** /ɪmpə'laɪt/ *adj.*, **~r** /ɪmpə'laɪtə(r)/, **~st** /ɪmpə'laɪtɪst/ unhöflich; ungezogen ‹Kind›

**impolitely** /ɪmpə'laɪtlɪ/ *adv.* unhöflich

**impoliteness** /ɪmpə'laɪtnɪs/ *n., no pl.* Unhöflichkeit, *die;* (*of child*) Ungezogenheit, *die*

**impolitic** /ɪm'pɒlɪtɪk/ *adj.* (*inexpedient*) unklug; unratsam

**imponderable** /ɪm'pɒndərəbl/ **1** *adj.* unwägbar; imponderabel (*geh. veralt.*). **2** *n.* Unwägbarkeit, *die;* **~s** Unwägbarkeiten; Imponderabilien (*geh.*)

**import 1** /ɪm'pɔ:t/ *v.t.* **A** importieren, einführen ‹Waren› (**from** aus, **into** nach); importieren ‹Kulturgüter›; **~ing country** Einfuhrland, *das;* **oil-~ing countries** [Erd]öl importierende Länder; **B** (*signify*) bedeuten. **2** /'ɪmpɔ:t/ *n.* **A** (*process, amount imported*) Import, *der;* Einfuhr, *die;* **~s of beef/sugar** Zucker-/Rindfleischimporte *od.* -einfuhren; **ban on the ~ of sth.** Einfuhrverbot für etw.; **B** (*article imported*) Importgut, *das;* **C** (*meaning*) Bedeutung, *die;* Sinn, *der;* **the ~ of his speech was that ...:** was aus seiner Rede hervorging, war, dass ...; **D** (*importance*) Bedeutung, *die;* **an event of great ~:** ein sehr bedeutungsvolles Ereignis

**importance** /ɪm'pɔ:təns/ *n., no pl.* **A** Bedeutung, *die;* Wichtigkeit, *die;* **be of great ~ to sb./sth.** für jmdn./etw. äußerst wichtig sein; **B** (*significance*) Bedeutung, *die;* (*of decision*) Tragweite, *die;* **increase in ~:** an Bedeutung zunehmen; **be of/without ~:** wichtig/unwichtig sein; **C** (*personal consequence*) Bedeutung, *die;* Gewicht, *das;* **a man of considerable ~:** ein sehr wichtiger Mann; **speak with an air of ~:** mit gewichtiger Miene sprechen; **full of one's own ~:** von seiner eigenen Wichtigkeit überzeugt

**important** /ɪm'pɔ:tənt/ *adj.* **A** bedeutend; (*in a particular matter*) wichtig (**to** für); **the most ~ thing is ...:** die Hauptsache ist ...; **B** (*momentous*) wichtig ‹Entscheidung›; bedeutsam ‹Tag›; **C** (*having high rank*) wichtig ‹Persönlichkeit›; **very ~ person** wichtige Persönlichkeit; VIP; **D** (*considerable*) beträchtlich; erheblich; **E** (*pompous*) wichtigtuerisch; gewichtig (*iron.*)

**importantly** /ɪm'pɔ:təntlɪ/ *adv.* **A** **bear ~ [up]on sth.** auf etw. bedeutsame Auswirkungen haben; **more/most ~** *as sentence-modifier* was noch wichtiger/am wichtigsten ist; **B** (*pompously*) wichtigtuerisch

**importation** /ɪmpɔ:'teɪʃn/ ⇒ **import** 2 A

**'import duty** *n.* Einfuhrzoll, *der*

**importer** /ɪm'pɔ:tə(r)/ *n.* Importeur, *der;* **be an ~ of cotton** Baumwollimporteur sein; ‹Land:› Baumwolle importieren

**'import permit** *n.* Einfuhrerlaubnis, *die*

**importunate** /ɪm'pɔ:tjʊnət/ *adj.* zudringlich

**importunately** /ɪm'pɔ:tʃʊnətlɪ/ *adv.* zudringlich; nachdrücklich ‹beharren auf, instruieren›

**importune** /ɪmpɔ:'tju:n/ **1** *v.t.* **A** behelligen; **she ~d her neighbours and relatives for money** sie belästigte ihre Nachbarn und Verwandten mit Bitten um Geld; **B** (*solicit for immoral purpose*) belästigen. **2** *v.i.* sich aufdrängen; lästig fallen

**importunity** /ɪmpɔ:'tju:nɪtɪ/ *n.* Aufdringlichkeit, *die*

**impose** /ɪm'pəʊz/ **1** *v.t.* **A** auferlegen (*geh.*) ‹Bürde, Verpflichtung› (**[up]on** *Dat.*); erheben ‹Steuer, Zoll› (**on** auf + *Akk.*); verhängen ‹Kriegsrecht›; anordnen ‹Rationierung›; verhängen ‹Sanktionen› (**on** gegen); **~ a ban on sth.** etw. mit einem Verbot belegen; **~ a tax on sth.** etw. mit einer Steuer belegen; **~ a nervous strain on sb.** jmdn. nervlich belasten; **B** (*compel compliance with*) **~ sth. [up]on sb.** jmdm. etw. aufdrängen; **~ one's company [up]on sb.** sich jmdm. aufdrängen; **~ restraints [up]on sb.** jmdm. Grenzen setzen; **C** (*Printing*) ausschießen ‹Seiten›. **2** *v.i.* **A** (*exert influence*) imponieren; Eindruck machen; **B** (*take advantage*) **I would** *or* **do not want** *or* **wish to ~:** ich will nicht aufdringlich sein. **3** *v. refl.* **~ oneself on sb.** sich jmdm. aufdrängen

**~ on** *v.t.* **A** (*take advantage of*) ausnutzen ‹Gutmütigkeit, Toleranz usw.›; **~ on sb. for help** jmdn. mit der Bitte um Hilfe belästigen; **B** (*force oneself on*) **~ on sb.** sich jmdm. aufdrängen

**~ upon** ⇒ **~ on**

**imposing** /ɪm'pəʊzɪŋ/ *adj.* imposant

**imposition** /ɪmpə'zɪʃn/ *n.* **A** *no pl.* (*action*) Auferlegung, *die;* (*of tax*) Erhebung, *die;* **B** *no pl.* (*enforcement*) Durchsetzung, *die;* **C** *no pl.* (*Printing*) Ausschießen, *das;* **D** (*tax*) Abgabe, *die;* Steuer, *die;* **E** (*piece of advantage-taking*) Ausnützung, *die;* **I am weary of the ~s of my relatives** ich bin es leid, mich von meinen Verwandten ausnützen zu lassen; **I hope it's not too much of an ~:** ich hoffe, es macht nicht zu viele Umstände; **F** (*Brit. Sch.: work set as punishment*) Strafarbeit, *die*

**impossibility** /ɪmpɒsɪ'bɪlɪtɪ/ *n.* **A** *no pl.* Unmöglichkeit, *die;* **the ~ of a man's flying** die Tatsache, dass der Mensch nicht fliegen kann *od.* dass es dem Menschen nicht möglich ist zu fliegen; **B** **go after impossibilities** das Unerreichbare wollen; **that's an absolute ~:** das ist völlig unmöglich *od.* ausgeschlossen *od.* ein Ding der Unmöglichkeit (*ugs.*)

**impossible** /ɪm'pɒsɪbl/ **1** *adj.* **A** unmöglich; **it is ~ for me to do it** es ist mir nicht möglich, es zu tun; **B** (*not easy*) schwer; (*not easily believable*) unmöglich (*ugs.*); **his car is becoming ~ to start** sein Auto lässt sich kaum noch starten; **C** (*coll.: intolerable*) unmöglich (*ugs.*). **2** *n.* **the ~:** das Unmögliche; Unmögliches; **achieve the ~:** das Unmögliche erreichen

**impossibly** /ɪm'pɒsɪblɪ/ *adv.* **A** unmöglich; **the stone was ~ heavy to lift** der Stein war so schwer, dass man ihn unmöglich anheben konnte; **B** (*to an inconvenient degree*) unheimlich (*ugs.*) ‹schwierig, teuer usw.›; **C** (*coll.: intolerably*) unmöglich (*ugs.*); **he is ~ idealistic** er ist unmöglich mit seinem Idealismus (*ugs.*)

**impost** /'ɪmpəʊst/ *n.* **A** (*tax*) Abgabe, *die;* **B** (*Archit.*) Kämpfer[stein], *der*

**impostor** /ɪm'pɒstə(r)/ *n.* Hochstapler, *der*/-staplerin, *die;* (*swindler*) Betrüger, *der*/Betrügerin, *die*

**imposture** /ɪm'pɒstʃə(r)/ *n.* **A** *no pl.* (*practice of deception*) Hochstapelei, *die;* (*swindling*) Betrügerei, *die;* **B** (*act of deception*) Betrug, *der;* Schwindel, *der;* **C** (*fake*) Fälschung, *die*

**impotence** /'ɪmpətəns/, **impotency** /'ɪmpətənsɪ/ *n., no pl.* **A** (*powerlessness*) Machtlosigkeit, *die;* **B** (*helplessness*) Hilflosigkeit, *die;* **C** (*lack of sexual power; in popular use: sterility*) Impotenz, *die*

**impotent** /'ɪmpətənt/ *adj.* **A** (*powerless*) machtlos; kraftlos ‹Argument›; **be ~ to do sth.** nicht in der Lage sein, etw. zu tun; **B** (*helpless*) hilflos; **C** (*lacking in sexual power; in popular use: sterile*) impotent

**impotently** /'ɪmpətəntlɪ/ *adv.* **A** (*powerlessly*) machtlos; **B** (*helplessly*) hilflos

**impound** /ɪm'paʊnd/ *v.t.* **A** (*shut up*) einpferchen ‹Vieh›; einsperren ‹streunende Hunde usw.›; (*fig.: confine*) einsperren ‹Person›; **B** (*take possession of*) beschlagnahmen; requirieren (*Milit.*)

**impoverish** /ɪm'pɒvərɪʃ/ *v.t.* **A** verarmen lassen; **be/become ~ed** verarmt sein/verarmen; **B** (*exhaust*) auslaugen ‹Boden›

**impoverishment** /ɪm'pɒvərɪʃmənt/ *n., no pl.* **A** (*making poor*) Verarmung, *die;* (*being poor*) Armut, *die;* **B** (*exhaustion*) (*process*) Auslaugung, *die;* (*state*) Ausgelaugtheit, *die*

**impracticability** /ɪmpræktɪkə'bɪlɪtɪ/ *n.* **A** *no pl.* (*of plan*) Undurchführbarkeit, *die;* (*of prediction*) Unmöglichkeit, *die;* **B** (*thing*) **be an ~:** undurchführbar sein; **it's an ~:** es lässt sich nicht durchführen

**impracticable** /ɪm'præktɪkəbl/ *adj.* undurchführbar; impraktikabel (*geh.*)

**impractical** /ɪm'præktɪkl/ **A** ⇒ **unpractical**; **B** ⇒ **impracticable**

**impracticality** /ɪmpræktɪ'kælɪtɪ/ ⇒ **impracticability**

**imprecation** /ɪmprɪ'keɪʃn/ *n.* Verwünschung, *die*

**imprecise** /ɪmprɪ'saɪs/ *adj.*, **imprecisely** /ɪmprɪ'saɪslɪ/ *adv.* ungenau; unpräzise (*geh.*)

**imprecision** /ɪmprɪ'sɪʒn/ *n.* Ungenauigkeit, *die*

**impregnability** /ɪmpregnə'bɪlɪtɪ/ *n., no pl.* Uneinnehmbarkeit, *die;* (*of strongroom etc.*) Einbruch[s]sicherheit, *die;* (*fig.*) Unanfechtbarkeit, *die*

**impregnable** /ɪm'pregnəbl/ *adj.* uneinnehmbar ‹Festung, Bollwerk›; einbruch[s]sicher ‹Tresorraum usw.›; (*fig.*) unanfechtbar ‹Ruf, Tugend, Stellung›

**impregnate** /'ɪmpregneɪt, ɪm'pregneɪt/ *v.t.* **A** imprägnieren; **B** (*make pregnant*) schwängern; (*Biol.: fertilize*) befruchten; **Mary was ~d by the Holy Ghost** Maria empfing vom Heiligen Geist

**impregnation** /ɪmpreg'neɪʃn/ *n., no pl.* **A** Imprägnierung, *die;* **B** (*making pregnant*) Schwängerung, *die;* (*Biol.: fertilization*) Befruchtung, *die*

**impresario** /ɪmprɪ'sɑ:rɪəʊ/ *n., pl.* **~s** Intendant, *der*/Intendantin, *die;* Impresario, *der* (*veralt.*)

**impress 1** /ɪm'pres/ *v.t.* **A** (*apply*) drücken; **~ a pattern** *etc.* **on/in sth.** ein Muster *usw.* auf etw. (*Akk.*) aufdrücken *od.* aufprägen/in etw. (*Akk.*) eindrücken *od.* einprägen; **B** (*arouse strong feeling in*) beeindrucken; Eindruck machen auf (+ *Akk.*); *abs.* Eindruck machen (**with** mit); **be ~ed by** *or* **with sth.** von etw. beeindruckt sein; **C** (*affect favourably*) beeindrucken; *abs.* Eindruck machen; **D** (*mark*) stempeln ‹Dokument›; **~ a**

i

**child with the right attitude** (*fig.*) einem Kind die richtige Einstellung vermitteln; **E** (*affect*) ~ **sb. favourably/unfavourably** auf jmdn. einen günstigen/ungünstigen Eindruck machen.
**2** /ˈɪmpres/ *n.* **A** Druck, *der;* **B** (*mark*) Abdruck, *der;* **bear the ~ of sth.** (*fig.*) den Stempel *od.* (*geh.*) das Gepräge von etw. tragen
~ **[up]on** *v.t.* einprägen, einschärfen (+ *Dat.*); **they have had ~ed [up]on them the danger of doing that** ihnen ist eingeschärft worden, wie gefährlich es sei, das zu tun; ~ **sth. [up]on sb.'s memory** jmdm. etw. einprägen *od.* einschärfen

**impression** /ɪmˈpreʃn/ *n.* **A** (*impressing*) Druck, *der;* **B** (*mark*) Abdruck, *der;* **C** (*print*) Druck, *der;* **take an ~ of sth.** einen Abzug von etw. machen; (*of painting, engraving, etc.*) Druck, *der;* **D** (*Printing*) (*quantity of copies*) Auflage, *die;* (*unaltered reprint*) Nachdruck, *der;* **E** (*effect on persons*) Eindruck, *der* (**of** von); (*effect on inanimate things*) Wirkung, *die;* **make an ~ on sb.** Eindruck auf jmdn. machen; **make a good/bad/strong** *etc.* ~ **on sb.** einen guten/schlechten/starken *usw.* Eindruck auf jmdn. machen; bei jmdm. einen guten/schlechten/starken *usw.* Eindruck hinterlassen; **he had made quite an ~ on the weed-choked flower bed** nachdem er sich des im Unkraut erstickenden Blumenbeets angenommen hatte, war es kaum noch wieder zu erkennen; **first ~/~s** erster Eindruck/erste Eindrücke; **F** (*impersonation*) **do an ~ of sb.** jmdn. imitieren; **do ~s** andere Leute imitieren; **G** (*notion*) Eindruck, *der;* **it's my ~ that ...:** ich habe den Eindruck, dass ...; **what's your ~ of him?** welchen Eindruck hast du von ihm *od.* macht er auf dich?; **form an ~ of sb.** sich (*Dat.*) ein Bild von jmdm. machen; **it's only an ~:** es ist nur eine Vermutung; **give [sb.] the ~ that .../of being bored** [bei jmdm.] den Eindruck erwecken, als ob .../als ob man sich langweile; **be under the ~ that ...:** der Auffassung *od.* Überzeugung sein, dass ...; (*less certain*) den Eindruck haben, dass ...

**impressionable** /ɪmˈpreʃənəbl/ *adj.* beeinflussbar; **have an ~ mind, be ~:** sich leicht beeinflussen lassen; **children who are at the ~ age** Kinder in dem Alter, in dem sie noch formbar sind

**impressionism** /ɪmˈpreʃənɪzm/ *n., no pl.* Impressionismus, *der*

**impressionist** /ɪmˈpreʃənɪst/ *n.* Impressionist, *der*/Impressionistin, *die; attrib.* impressionistisch ‹Kunst usw.›

**impressionistic** /ɪmpreʃəˈnɪstɪk/ *adj.* impressionistisch

**impressive** /ɪmˈpresɪv/ *adj.* beeindruckend; imponierend; **be ~ on account of** *or* **~ for sth.** durch etw. beeindrucken

**impressively** /ɪmˈpresɪvlɪ/ *adv.* beeindruckend; imponierend

**imprimatur** /ɪmprɪˈmɑːtə(r), ɪmpraɪˈmeɪtə(r)/ *n.* **A** (*RC Ch.*) Imprimatur, *das;* **B** (*fig.: sanction*) **put the ~ of approval on sth.** etw. gutheißen *od.* billigen; **bear the ~ of sb./an institution** jmds. Plazet/das Plazet einer Institution haben (*geh.*)

**imprint** **1** /ˈɪmprɪnt/ *n.* **A** Abdruck, *der;* **publisher's/printer's ~:** Impressum, *das;* **B** (*fig.*) Stempel, *der;* **leave one's ~ on sb./sth.** jmdm./einer Sache seinen Stempel aufdrücken; **the ~ of suffering upon sb.'s face** die Spuren des Leidens in jmds. Gesicht. **2** /ɪmˈprɪnt/ *v.t.* **A** (*stamp*) aufdrucken; aufdrücken ‹Poststempel›; (*on metal*) aufprägen; **B** (*fix indelibly*) **sth. is ~ed in** *or* **on sb.'s memory** etw. hat sich jmdm. [unauslöschlich] eingeprägt; **C** (*Ethol.*) ~ **on** *or* **to** prägen auf (+ *Akk.*)

**imprison** /ɪmˈprɪzn/ *v.t.* **A** in Haft nehmen; **be ~ed** sich in Haft befinden; eine Freiheitsstrafe verbüßen; **be ~ed for three months** (*be sentenced to three months in prison*) eine dreimonatige Freiheitsstrafe erhalten; **B** (*fig.: confine*) einsperren; (*hold*) festhalten

**imprisonment** /ɪmˈprɪznmənt/ *n.* **A** Haft, *die;* **a long term** *or* **period of ~:** eine langjährige Haft- *od.* Freiheitsstrafe; **serve a sentence of ~:** eine Gefängnisstrafe verbüßen; **B** (*fig.: being confined*) Gefangenschaft, *die;* ~ **by sb./sth.** Gefangensein durch jmdn./etw.

**improbability** /ɪmprɒbəˈbɪlɪtɪ/ *n.* Unwahrscheinlichkeit, *die*

**improbable** /ɪmˈprɒbəbl/ *adj.* **A** (*not likely*) unwahrscheinlich; **B** (*incongruous*) unmöglich (*ugs.*); **he is an ~ person to be in charge of a large company** es ist eigentlich erstaunlich, dass er der Chef einer großen Firma ist

**impromptu** /ɪmˈprɒmptjuː/ **1** *adj.* improvisiert; **an ~ speech** eine Stegreifrede; **an ~ visit** ein Überraschungsbesuch; ein unangekündigter Besuch. **2** *adv.* aus dem Stegreif. **3** *n.* **A** Improvisation, *die;* **B** (*Mus.*) Impromptu, *das*

**improper** /ɪmˈprɒpə(r)/ *adj.* **A** (*wrong*) unrichtig; ungeeignet ‹Werkzeug›; **B** (*unseemly*) ungehörig; unpassend; (*indecent*) unanständig; **C** (*not in accordance with rules of conduct*) unangebracht; unzulässig ‹Gebühren›; **D** ~ **fraction** (*Math.*) unechter Bruch

**improperly** /ɪmˈprɒpəlɪ/ *adv.* **A** (*wrongly*) unrichtig; **use sth. ~:** etw. unsachgemäß gebrauchen; **B** (*in unseemly fashion*) unpassend; (*indecently*) unanständig; **C** (*in contravention of rules of conduct*) unzulässigerweise; **use sth. ~:** etw. missbrauchen

**impropriety** /ɪmprəˈpraɪətɪ/ *n.* **A** *no pl.* Unrichtigkeit, *die;* (*unfitness*) Ungeeignetheit, *die;* **say/state** *etc.* **without ~ that ...:** mit Recht sagen/behaupten *usw.*, dass ...; **B** *no pl.* (*unseemliness*) Unpassende, *das;* (*indecency*) Unanständigkeit, *die;* **the ~ of sb.'s clothing** jmds. unpassende/unschickliche Kleidung; **C** *no pl.* (*lack of accordance with rules of conduct*) Unrechtmäßigkeit, *die;* Unredlichkeit, *die;* **see no ~ in doing sth.** nichts Unrechtmäßiges *od.* Unredliches darin sehen, etw. zu tun; **D** (*instance of improper conduct*) Unanständigkeit, *die;* **moral ~:** moralisches Fehlverhalten

**improvable** /ɪmˈpruːvəbl/ *adj.* verbesserungsfähig

**improve** /ɪmˈpruːv/ **1** *v.i.* sich verbessern; besser werden; ‹Person, Wetter:› sich bessern; (*become more attractive*) sich zu seinem Vorteil verändern; **he was ill, but he's improving now** er war krank, aber es geht ihm jetzt schon besser; **things are improving** es sieht schon besser aus. **2** *v.t.* verbessern; erhöhen, steigern ‹Produktion›; ausbessern ‹Haus usw.›; verschönern ‹öffentliche Anlage usw.›; **~d health** ein besserer Gesundheitszustand; ~ **one's mind** sich [weiter]bilden; ~ **one's situation** sich verbessern. **3** *v. refl.* ~ **oneself** sich weiterbilden
~ **[up]on** *v.t.* überbieten ‹Rekord, Angebot›; verbessern ‹Leistung›

**improvement** /ɪmˈpruːvmənt/ *n.* **A** *no pl.* Verbesserung, *die;* Besserung, *die;* (*in trading*) Steigerung, *die;* **there is need for ~ in your handwriting** deine Handschrift müsste besser werden; **an ~ on** *or* **over sth.** eine Verbesserung gegenüber etw.; **B** (*addition*) Verbesserung, *die;* **make ~s to sth.** Verbesserungen an etw. (*Dat.*) vornehmen

**improvidence** /ɪmˈprɒvɪdəns/ *n., no pl.* **A** Sorglosigkeit, *die;* **B** (*heedlessness*) Leichtsinn, *der;* **C** (*thriftlessness*) Verschwendungssucht, *die*

**improvident** /ɪmˈprɒvɪdənt/ *adj.* **A** sorglos; leichtsinnig; **he is ~:** er ist ein unbekümmerter Mensch; ~ **action** unbedachtes Handeln; **B** (*heedless*) leichtsinnig; **C** (*thriftless*) verschwenderisch

**improvidently** /ɪmˈprɒvɪdəntlɪ/ *adv.* **A** leichtsinnigerweise; **B** (*thriftlessly*) verschwenderisch

**improvisation** /ɪmprəvaɪˈzeɪʃn, ɪmprɒvɪˈzeɪʃn/ *n.* **A** *no pl.* Improvisieren, *das;* (*composing while performing*) Improvisation, *die;* **his talent for ~:** sein Improvisationstalent; (*in speaking*) sein Talent für Stegreifreden; **B** (*thing*) Improvisation, *die;* **the speech was an ~:** die Rede war improvisiert *od.* aus dem Stegreif vorgetragen; **the bench was only an ~:** die Bank war nur ein Provisorium

**improvise** /ˈɪmprəvaɪz/ *v.t.* improvisieren; aus dem Stegreif vortragen ‹Rede›

**imprudence** /ɪmˈpruːdəns/ *n.* **A** *no pl.* Unüberlegtheit, *die;* **with great ~:** sehr unüberlegt; **B** (*rash act*) Unbesonnenheit, *die*

**imprudent** /ɪmˈpruːdənt/ *adj.* unklug; (*showing rashness*) unbesonnen

**imprudently** /ɪmˈpruːdəntlɪ/ *adv.* unbesonnenerweise; bedenklich ‹nah, schnell›

**impudence** /ˈɪmpjʊdəns/ *n.* **A** Unverschämtheit, *die;* **B** (*brazenness*) Dreistigkeit, *die*

**impudent** /ˈɪmpjʊdənt/ *adj.*, **impudently** /ˈɪmpjʊdəntlɪ/ *adv.* unverschämt; (*brazen*) dreist

**impugn** /ɪmˈpjuːn/ *v.t.* in Zweifel ziehen; anfechten ‹Anspruch›

**impulse** /ˈɪmpʌls/ *n.* **A** (*act of impelling*) Stoß, *der;* Impuls, *der;* (*fig.: motivation*) Impuls, *der;* **give an ~ to sth.** einer Sache (*Dat.*) neue Impulse geben; **B** (*mental incitement*) Impuls, *der;* **be seized with an irresistible ~ to do sth.** von einem unwiderstehlichen Drang ergriffen werden, etw. zu tun; **C** (*tendency to act without reflection*) Impulsivität, *die;* **from pure ~:** rein impulsiv; **be ruled/guided by ~:** impulsiv sein; **be a creature of ~:** ein impulsives Wesen haben; **act/do sth. on [an] ~:** impulsiv handeln/etw. tun; **D** (*impetus*) Stoßkraft, *die;* **E** (*Biol., Electr., Phys.*) Impuls, *der*

**ˈimpulse buying** *n.* Spontankäufe *Pl.*

**impulsion** /ɪmˈpʌlʃn/ *n.* **A** (*impelling push*) Stoß, *der;* **B** (*mental impulse*) Antrieb, *der;* **C** (*impetus*) Impuls, *der;* **give an ~ to sth.** einer Sache (*Dat.*) neue Impulse geben

**impulsive** /ɪmˈpʌlsɪv/ *adj.* **A** impulsiv; **B** (*driving*) vorwärts treibend; ~ **force** Antriebskraft, *die;* **C** (*Phys.*) stoßartig

**impulsively** /ɪmˈpʌlsɪvlɪ/ *adv.* impulsiv

**impulsiveness** /ɪmˈpʌlsɪvnɪs/ *n., no pl.* Impulsivität, *die*

**impunity** /ɪmˈpjuːnɪtɪ/ *n., no pl.* Straffreiheit, *die;* **be able to do sth. with ~:** etw. gefahrlos tun können; (*without being punished*) etw. ungestraft tun können

**impure** /ɪmˈpjʊə(r)/ *adj.* **A** (*dirty*) unsauber; schmutzig ‹Wasser›; **B** (*unchaste*) unrein; unanständig ‹Person, Sprache›; schmutzig ‹Gedanke›; **C** (*mixed with extraneous substance*) unrein; (*fig.: of mixed nature*) unrein; uneinheitlich ‹Stilform›

**impurity** /ɪmˈpjʊərɪtɪ/ *n.* **A** *no pl.* (*being dirty*) Unsauberkeit, *die;* (*of water*) Verschmutzung, *die;* **B** *no pl.* (*not being chaste*) Unreinheit, *die;* **moral ~:** moralische Verfehlung; **C** *no pl.* (*being mixed with extraneous substance*) Unreinheit, *die;* **D** *in pl.* (*dirt*) Schmutz, *der;* **E** (*foreign matter*) Fremdkörper, *der;* Fremdstoff, *der*

**imputation** /ɪmpjʊˈteɪʃn/ *n.* **A** *no pl.* Zuschreibung, *die;* (*accusing*) Bezichtigung, *die;* [ungerechtfertigte] Beschuldigung; Imputation, *die* (*veralt.*); **B** (*charge*) Anschuldigung, *die;* Beschuldigung, *die*

**impute** /ɪmˈpjuːt/ *v.t.* ~ **sth. to sb./sth.** jmdm./einer Sache etw. zuschreiben; ~ **bad intentions to sb.** jmdm. schlechte Absichten unterstellen

**in** /ɪn/ **1** *prep.* **A** (*position; also fig.*) in (+ *Dat.*); **I looked into all the boxes, but there was nothing in them** ich sah in alle Kisten hinein, aber es war nichts darin; **in the 'Mauretania'** auf der „Mauretania"; **in the fields** auf den Feldern; **a ride in a motor car** eine Autofahrt; **shot/wounded in the leg** ins Bein geschossen/am Bein verwundet; **in this heat** bei dieser Hitze; **the highest mountain in the world** der höchste Berg der Welt; ⇒ *also* **bed** 1 A; **clover; country** B; **dark** 2 A; **prison** B; **rage** 1 A; **sky** 1; **sleep** 1 B; **street** A; **tear**[2]; **B** (*wearing as dress*) in (+ *Dat.*); (*wearing as headgear*) mit; **in brown shoes** mit braunen Schuhen; **a**

lady in black eine Dame in Schwarz; a group of youths in leather jackets eine Gruppe Jugendlicher in od. mit Lederjacken; ⇒ also shirtsleeve 1; C (with respect to) two feet in diameter mit einem Durchmesser von zwei Fuß; young in years jung an Jahren; a change in attitude eine Änderung der Einstellung; ⇒ also herself A; itself A; D (as a proportionate part of) eight dogs in ten acht von zehn Hunden; pay 33 pence in the pound as interest 33 Prozent Zinsen zahlen; ⇒ also gradient A; E (as a member of) in (+ Dat.); be in the Scouts bei den Pfadfindern sein; be employed in the Civil Service als Beamter/Beamtin beschäftigt sein; F (as content of) there are three feet in a yard ein Yard hat drei Fuß; is there anything in the notion of ...? ist an der Vorstellung ... etwas dran?; what is there in this deal for me? was springt für mich bei dem Geschäft heraus? (ugs.); there is nothing of the hero in him er hat nichts von einem Helden an sich (Dat.); there is nothing/not much or little in it (difference) da ist kein/kein großer Unterschied [zwischen ihnen]; there is something in what you say an dem, was Sie sagen, ist etwas dran (ugs.); G (as a kind of) in (+ Dat.); the latest thing in fashion/in luxury der letzte Modeschrei/der neueste Luxus; H expr. identity in (+ Dat.); have a faithful friend in sb. an jmdm. einen treuen Freund haben; we have lost a first-rate teacher in Jim wir haben mit Jim einen erstklassigen Lehrer verloren; I (concerned with) in (+ Dat.); what line of business are you in? in welcher Branche sind Sie?; he's in politics er ist Politiker; she's in insurance sie ist in der Versicherungsbranche tätig; J be [not] in it (as competitor) [nicht] dabei od. im Rennen sein; K (Mus.) in; in [the key of] D flat in Des; L (Ling.) (ending with) [endend] auf (+ Akk.); (beginning with) beginnend mit; M (with arrangement of) in (+ Dat.); sell eggs in half-dozens Eier im halben Dutzend verkaufen; ⇒ also order 1 A; N (with the means of; having as material, colour) a message in code eine verschlüsselte Nachricht; in writing schriftlich; in this way auf diese Weise; so; in a few words mit wenigen Worten; bind in leather in Leder binden; a dress in velvet ein Kleid aus Samt; this sofa is also available in leather/blue dieses Sofa gibt es auch in Leder/Blau; write sth. in red etw. in Rot schreiben; write in red mit Rot schreiben; pay in pounds/dollars in Pfund/Dollars bezahlen; draw in crayon/ink etc. mit Kreide/Tinte usw. zeichnen; be cast in brass etc. aus Messing usw. gegossen sein; ⇒ also English 2 A; O ▶ 1055 (while, during) in crossing the river beim Überqueren des Flusses; in fog/rain etc. bei Nebel/Regen usw.; in the 20th century im 20. Jahrhundert; in the eighties/nineties in den Achtzigern/Neunzigern; 4 o'clock in the morning/afternoon 4 Uhr morgens/abends; in 1990 [im Jahre] 1990; P (after a period of) in (+ Dat.); in three minutes/years in drei Minuten/Jahren; Q (within the ability of) have it in one [to do sth.] fähig sein[, etw. zu tun]; I didn't know you had it in you das hätte ich dir nicht zugetraut; he has in him the makings of a good soldier er hat das Zeug zu einem guten Soldaten; be in human nature in der menschlichen Natur liegen; there is no malice in him er hat nichts Bösartiges an sich (Dat.); R (into) in (+ Akk.); get the whole of sth. in a photo etwas ganz auf ein Foto kriegen (ugs.) od. bekommen; S in that insofern als; ⇒ also far 1 D; T in doing this (by so doing) indem jmd. das tut/tat; dadurch; hierdurch.

❷ adv. A (inside) hinein‹gehen usw.›; (towards speaker) herein‹kommen usw.›; when the animal is in, shut the cage door wenn das Tier drin ist, mach die Käfigtür zu; is everyone in? sind alle drin? (ugs.); in with you! rein mit dir! (ugs.); 'In' „Einfahrt"/„Eingang"; the children have been in and out all day die Kinder sind den ganzen Tag raus- und reingerannt (ugs.); B (at home, work, etc.) be in da sein; find sb. in jmdn. antreffen; ask sb. in jmdn. hereinbitten; he's been in and out all day er war den ganzen Tag über mal da und mal nicht da; C (included) darin; drin (ugs.); cost £50 all in 50 Pfund kosten, alles inbegriffen; the word is not in das Wort ist nicht aufgeführt; your article is not in dein Artikel steht nicht drin (ugs.); D (inward) innen; E (in fashion) in (ugs.); in Mode; F (elected) be in gewählt sein; the Tories are in die Tories sind am Ruder; the Tories are in by three votes die Tories haben die Wahl mit einer Mehrheit von drei Stimmen gewonnen; G (Cricket) our team is in unsere Mannschaft ist am Schlag; H (Brit.: burning) be in ‹Feuer:› an sein, brennen; keep the fire in das Feuer brennen lassen; I (having arrived) be in ‹Zug, Schiff, Ware, Bewerbung:› da sein; ‹Ernte:› eingebracht sein; the coach is not due in for another hour der Bus wird nicht vor einer Stunde da sein; J (present) be in at the start/climax beim Start/Höhepunkt dabei sein; K sb. is in for sth. (about to undergo sth.) jmdm. steht etw. bevor; (in competition for sth.) jmd. nimmt im Wettbewerb um etw. teil; (taking part in sth.) jmd. nimmt an etw. (Dat.) teil; we're in for it now! (coll.) jetzt blüht uns was! (ugs.); have it in for sb. es auf jmdn. abgesehen haben (ugs.); L (coll.: as participant, accomplice, observer, etc.) be in on the secret/discussion in das Geheimnis eingeweiht sein/bei der Diskussion dabei sein; be in on the action dabei sein; be [well] in with sb. mit jmdm. [gut] auskommen; be in with the right/wrong people mit den richtigen/falschen Leuten verkehren; M (Sport) be in ‹Ball:› drin sein. ⇒ also all 3; eye 1 A; far 1 D; luck B; penny C; tide 1 A.

❸ attrib. adj. (fashionable) Mode-; the in crowd die Clique, die gerade in ist (ugs.); in joke Insiderwitz, der.

❹ n. know the ins and outs of a matter sich in einer Sache genau auskennen; I don't know the ins and outs of the argument ich weiß nicht [genau], worum es bei diesem Streit geht

**in.** abbr. ▶ 1210, ▶ 1284 inch[es]

**inability** /ɪnəˈbɪlɪtɪ/ n., no pl. A (being unable) Unfähigkeit, die; B (lack of power) Unvermögen, das

**in absentia** /ɪn æbˈsentɪə, ɪn æbˈsenʃɪə/ adv. in absentia (bes. Rechtsw.)

**inaccessibility** /ɪnəksesɪˈbɪlɪtɪ/ n., no pl. A (unreachableness) Unzugänglichkeit, die; B (unapproachableness) Unnahbarkeit, die

**inaccessible** /ɪnəkˈsesɪbl/ adj. A (that cannot be reached) unzugänglich; B (unapproachable) unnahbar; unzugänglich

**inaccuracy** /ɪnˈækjʊrəsɪ/ n. A (incorrectness) Unrichtigkeit, die; an example of ~ in the use of ...: ein Beispiel für den unrichtigen Gebrauch von ...; B (imprecision) Ungenauigkeit, die

**inaccurate** /ɪnˈækjʊrət/ adj. A (incorrect) unrichtig; B (imprecise) ungenau

**inaccurately** /ɪnˈækjʊrətlɪ/ adv. A (incorrectly) falsch; B (imprecisely) ungenau

**inaction** /ɪnˈækʃn/ n., no pl., no indef. art. A Untätigkeit, die; B (sluggishness) Trägheit, die

**inactive** /ɪnˈæktɪv/ adj. A untätig; B (sluggish) träge

**inactivity** /ɪnækˈtɪvɪtɪ/ n., no pl. A Untätigkeit, die; B (sluggishness) Trägheit, die

**inadequacy** /ɪnˈædɪkwəsɪ/ n. A Unzulänglichkeit, die; B (incompetence) mangelnde Eignung

**inadequate** /ɪnˈædɪkwət/ adj. A unzulänglich; his response was ~ [to the situation] seine Antwort war [der Situation] nicht angemessen; the resources are ~ to his needs die Mittel reichen für seine Bedürfnisse nicht aus; B (incompetent) ungeeignet; feel ~: sich überfordert fühlen

**inadequately** /ɪnˈædɪkwətlɪ/ adv. A unzulänglich; B (incompetently) mangelhaft

**inadmissibility** /ɪnədmɪsɪˈbɪlɪtɪ/ n., no pl. Unzulässigkeit, die

**inadmissible** /ɪnədˈmɪsɪbl/ adj. unzulässig

**inadvertent** /ɪnədˈvɜːtənt/ adj. ungewollt; versehentlich

**inadvertently** /ɪnədˈvɜːtəntlɪ/ adv. versehentlich

**inadvisability** /ɪnədvaɪzəˈbɪlɪtɪ/ n., no pl. (inappropriateness) Unangebrachtheit, die; (foolishness) Unvernünftigkeit, die; see the ~ of sth. sehen, dass etw. nicht ratsam ist

**inadvisable** /ɪnədˈvaɪzəbl/ adj. nicht ratsam; unratsam

**inalienable** /ɪnˈeɪlɪənəbl/ adj. unveräußerlich ‹Recht›

**inane** /ɪˈneɪn/ adj., **inanely** /ɪˈneɪnlɪ/ adv. dümmlich

**inanimate** /ɪnˈænɪmət/ adj. unbelebt

**inanity** /ɪˈnænɪtɪ/ n. Dümmlichkeit, die

**inapplicability** /ɪnæplɪkəˈbɪlɪtɪ/ n., no pl. Nichtanwendbarkeit, die

**inapplicable** /ɪnˈæplɪkəbl, ɪnəˈplɪkəbl/ adj. nicht anwendbar (to auf + Akk.); delete if ~: Unzutreffendes [bitte] streichen

**inappropriate** /ɪnəˈprəʊprɪət/ adj. unpassend; be ~ for sth. für etw. nicht geeignet sein; be ~ to the occasion dem Anlass nicht angemessen sein; this translation is ~: diese Übersetzung ist nicht angemessen

**inappropriately** /ɪnəˈprəʊprɪətlɪ/ adv. unpassend

**inapt** /ɪnˈæpt/ adj., **inaptly** /ɪnˈæptlɪ/ adv. unpassend

**inarticulate** /ɪnɑːˈtɪkjʊlət/ adj. A she's rather/very ~: sie kann sich ziemlich schlecht/sehr schlecht ausdrücken; a clever but ~ mathematician ein kluger Mathematiker, der sich aber nur schlecht ausdrücken kann; B (indistinct) unverständlich; inartikuliert (geh.) C (dumb) unfähig zu sprechen

**inarticulately** /ɪnɑːˈtɪkjʊlətlɪ/ adv. inartikuliert (geh.); unverständlich ‹murmeln›

**inartistic** /ɪnɑːˈtɪstɪk/ adj. unkünstlerisch ‹Person›

**inasmuch** /ɪnəzˈmʌtʃ/ adv. ~ as A insofern als; B (because) da

**inattention** /ɪnəˈtenʃn/ n., no pl. Unaufmerksamkeit, die (to gegenüber); ~ to detail Ungenauigkeit im Detail

**inattentive** /ɪnəˈtentɪv/ adj. unaufmerksam (to gegenüber)

**inattentiveness** /ɪnəˈtentɪvnɪs/ n., no pl. Unaufmerksamkeit, die

**inaudible** /ɪnˈɔːdɪbl/ adj., **inaudibly** /ɪnˈɔːdɪblɪ/ adv. unhörbar

**inaugural** /ɪˈnɔːgjʊrl/ adj. A (first in series) Eröffnungs-; B (given at inauguration) ~ lecture or address Antrittsrede, die; (of professor) Antrittsvorlesung, die

**inaugurate** /ɪˈnɔːgjʊreɪt/ v.t. A (admit to office) in sein Amt einführen; inaugurieren (geh.); B (begin) einführen; aufnehmen ‹Frachtverkehr usw.›; in Angriff nehmen ‹Projekt›; C (officially open) seiner Bestimmung übergeben; (with ceremony) einweihen

**inauguration** /ɪnɔːgjʊˈreɪʃn/ n. A (admission to office) Amtseinführung, die; Inauguration, die (geh.); B (beginning) Einführung, die; (of service) Aufnahme, die; (of project) Inangriffnahme, die; C (official opening) Übergabe, die; (with ceremony) Einweihung, die

**inauspicious** /ɪnɔːˈspɪʃəs/ adj. A (ominous) Unheil verkündend; unheilvoll; we made an ~ start to the project schon der Beginn des Projekts verhieß nichts Gutes; B (unlucky) unglücklich

**'inboard** (Naut., Aeronaut., Motor Veh.) ❶ adv. binnenbords. ❷ adj. Innen[bord]-

**'inborn** adj. angeboren (in Dat.)

**'in-box** n. (Computing) Inbox, die; Posteingang, der

**in'bred** adj. A angeboren; B (impaired by inbreeding) they are/have become ~: bei ihnen herrscht Inzucht

**in'breeding** n. Inzucht, die

**'inbuilt** adj. jmdm./einer Sache eigen

**Inc.** abbr. (Amer.) Incorporated e. G.

**Inca** /ˈɪŋkə/ ❶ n. Inka, der/die. ❷ adj. der Inkas nachgestellt

**incalculable** /ɪn'kælkjʊləbl/ *adj.* Ⓐ (*very great*) unermesslich; Ⓑ (*unpredictable*) unabsehbar; unberechenbar ‹Person, Temperament›

**in camera** ⇒ **camera** B

**incandescent** /ɪnkæn'desənt/ *adj.* glühend; **~ lamp** Glühlampe, *die*

**incantation** /ɪnkæn'teɪʃn/ *n.* Ⓐ (*words*) Zauberspruch, *der;* Ⓑ (*spell*) Beschwörung, *die*

**incapability** /ɪnkeɪpə'bɪlɪtɪ/ *n., no pl.* Unvermögen, *das;* Unfähigkeit, *die*

**incapable** /ɪn'keɪpəbl/ *adj.* Ⓐ (*lacking ability*) **be ~ of doing sth.** außerstande sein, etw. zu tun; **be ~ of sth.** zu etw. unfähig sein; **she is ~ of such an act** sie ist zu einer solchen Tat nicht fähig; Ⓑ **be ~ of** (*not allow*) nicht zulassen ‹Beweis, Messung usw.›; **sb. is ~ of any improvement** jmd. ist zu keiner Besserung fähig; **a statement that is ~ of proof** eine Feststellung, die nicht beweisbar ist; Ⓒ (*incompetent*) unfähig; **he was drunk to the point of being completely ~:** er war so betrunken, dass er zu nichts mehr fähig war

**incapacitate** /ɪnkə'pæsɪteɪt/ *v.t.* Ⓐ (*render unfit*) unfähig machen; **~ sb. for** *or* **from doing sth.** es jmdm. unmöglich machen, etw. zu tun; **physically ~d/~d by illness** körperlich/durch Krankheit behindert; Ⓑ (*disqualify*) ausschließen (**for** von)

**incapacity** /ɪnkə'pæsɪtɪ/ *n., no pl.* Unfähigkeit, *die* (**for** zu); **civil ~** (*Law*) Geschäftsunfähigkeit, *die*

**incarcerate** /ɪn'kɑːsəreɪt/ *v.t.* einkerkern (*geh.*)

**incarceration** /ɪnkɑːsə'reɪʃn/ *n.* Einkerkerung, *die* (*geh.*)

**incarnate** /ɪn'kɑːnət/ *adj.* Ⓐ **be the devil ~:** der leibhaftige Satan *od.* der Teufel in Person sein; **the Word I~** (*Theol.*) das Fleisch gewordene Wort; Ⓑ (*in perfect form*) **be beauty/wisdom** *etc.* **~:** die personifizierte Schönheit/Weisheit *usw.* sein

**incarnation** /ɪnkɑː'neɪʃn/ *n.* Inkarnation, *die*

**incautious** /ɪn'kɔːʃəs/ *adj.*, **incautiously** /ɪn'kɔːʃəslɪ/ *adv.* unbedacht

**incendiary** /ɪn'sendɪərɪ/ ❶ *adj.* Ⓐ **~ attack** Brandstiftung, *die;* **~ device** Brandsatz, *der;* **~ bomb** ⇒ **2** B; Ⓑ (*fig.*) aufwieglerisch; Hetz-. ❷ *n.* Ⓐ (*person*) Brandstifter, *der*/-stifterin, *die;* (*fig.*) Aufwiegler, *der*/Aufwieglerin, *die;* Ⓑ (*bomb*) Brandbombe, *die*

**incense[1]** /'ɪnsens/ *n.* Weihrauch, *der*

**incense[2]** /ɪn'sens/ *v.t.* erzürnen; erbosen; **be ~d at** *or* **by sth./with sb.** über etw./jmdn. erbost *od.* erzürnt sein

**incentive** /ɪn'sentɪv/ *n.* Ⓐ (*motivation*) Anreiz, *der;* **~ to achievement** Leistungsanreiz, *der; attrib.* **~ payment system** System des finanziellen Anreizes; Ⓑ (*payment*) finanzieller Anreiz

**inception** /ɪn'sepʃn/ *n.* Einführung, *die;* **from** *or* **since/at its ~:** von Beginn an/zu Beginn

**incessant** /ɪn'sesənt/ *adj.*, **incessantly** /ɪn'sesəntlɪ/ *adv.* unablässig; unaufhörlich

**incest** /'ɪnsest/ *n.* Inzest, *der;* Blutschande, *die*

**incestuous** /ɪn'sestjʊəs/ *adj.* (*lit. or fig.*) inzestuös

**inch** /ɪnʃ/ ❶ *n.* Ⓐ ▶928, ▶1210, ▶1284 Inch, *der;* Zoll, *der* (*veralt.*); **a 2½-~ map** eine Landkarte im Maßstab 1 Meile : 2½ Inches; **he could hardly see an ~ in front of him** er konnte kaum die Hand vor Augen sehen; **miss sth./sb. by ~es** etw./jmdn. um Haaresbreite verfehlen; Ⓑ (*small amount*) **~ by ~:** ≈ Zentimeter um Zentimeter; **by ~es** ≈ zentimeterweise; **escape death by an ~:** dem Tod mit knapper Not entrinnen; **she came within an ~ of winning** sie hätte um ein Haar gewonnen; **give him an ~ and he will take a mile** wenn man ihm den kleinen Finger reicht, nimmt er gleich die ganze Hand; **not give** *or* **yield an ~:** keinen Fingerbreit nachgeben; keinen Zoll weichen (*geh.*); **he is every ~ a soldier** er ist Zoll für Zoll ein Soldat (*geh.*); **he was flogged within an ~ of his life** er wurde fast zu Tode geprügelt; Ⓒ *in pl.* (*stature*) Körpergröße, *die.*
❷ *v.t.* ≈ zentimeterweise bewegen; **~ one's way forward** sich Zoll für Zoll vorwärts bewegen.
❸ *v.i.* ≈ sich zentimeterweise bewegen; **~ along/forward** sich ganz langsam entlangbewegen/vorwärts bewegen

**inchoate** /'ɪnkəʊət/ *adj.* Ⓐ (*just begun*) beginnend; Ⓑ (*undeveloped*) unausgereift

**incidence** /'ɪnsɪdəns/ *n.* Ⓐ (*occurrence*) Auftreten, *das;* Vorkommen, *das;* Ⓑ (*manner or range of occurrence*) Häufigkeit, *die;* **~ of crime/accidents** Verbrechens-/Unfallrate, *die;* Ⓒ (*Phys.*) Einfall, *der;* **angle of ~:** Einfall[s]winkel, *der;* Inzidenzwinkel, *der* (*fachspr.*)

**incident** /'ɪnsɪdənt/ ❶ *n.* Ⓐ (*notable event*) Vorfall, *der;* (*minor occurrence*) Begebenheit, *die;* Vorkommnis, *das;* **the evening passed without ~:** der Abend verging ohne besondere Vorkommnisse; Ⓑ (*clash*) Zwischenfall, *der;* **frontier ~:** Grenzzwischenfall, *der;* Ⓒ (*in play, novel, etc.*) Episode, *die.* ❷ *adj.* Ⓐ (*attaching*) **~ to** verbunden mit; Ⓑ (*falling*) einfallend ‹Licht, Strahl›

**incidental** /ɪnsɪ'dentl/ ❶ *adj.* Ⓐ (*casual*) beiläufig ‹Art, Bemerkung›; Neben‹ausgaben, -einnahmen, -gewinn›; Ⓑ (*attaching*) **~ to** verbunden mit. ❷ *n., in pl.* Nebensächlichkeiten; (*expenses*) Nebenausgaben

**incidentally** /ɪnsɪ'dentəlɪ/ *adv.* Ⓐ (*by the way*) nebenbei [bemerkt]; Ⓑ (*by chance*) zufällig; Ⓒ (*as not essential*) am Rande

**inci'dental music** *n.* Begleitmusik, *die*

**'incident room** *n.* [*temporäres*] *lokales Einsatzzentrum der Polizei*

**incinerate** /ɪn'sɪnəreɪt/ *v.t.* verbrennen

**incinerator** /ɪn'sɪnəreɪtə(r)/ *n.* Verbrennungsofen, *der;* (*in garden*) Abfallverbrenner, *der*

**incipient** /ɪn'sɪpɪənt/ *adj.* anfänglich; einsetzend ‹Schmerzen›; aufkommend ‹Zweifel, Angst›

**incise** /ɪn'saɪz/ *v.t.* einschneiden

**incision** /ɪn'sɪʒn/ *n.* Ⓐ (*cutting*) Einschneiden, *das;* Ⓑ (*cut*) Einschnitt, *der;* **abdominal ~:** Bauchschnitt, *der*

**incisive** /ɪn'saɪsɪv/ *adj.* schneidend ‹Ton›; scharf ‹Verstand›; scharfsinnig ‹Genie, Kritik, Methode, Frage, Bemerkung, Argument›; präzise ‹Sprache, Stil›

**incisively** /ɪn'saɪsɪvlɪ/ *adv.* scharfsinnig; präzise ‹sich ausdrücken›

**incisor** /ɪn'saɪzə(r)/ *n.* (*Anat., Zool.*) Schneidezahn, *der*

**incitation** /ɪnsɪ'teɪʃn/ ⇒ **incitement** A

**incite** /ɪn'saɪt/ *v.t.* anstiften; aufstacheln, aufwiegeln ‹Massen, Volk›

**incitement** /ɪn'saɪtmənt/ *n.* Ⓐ (*act*) Anstiftung, *die;* (*of masses, crowd*) Aufstachelung, *die;* Aufwiegelung, *die;* Ⓑ (*encouragement*) Antrieb, *der*

**incivility** /ɪnsɪ'vɪlɪtɪ/ *n.* Unhöflichkeit, *die;* **it is gross ~ to refuse** es ist eine grobe Unhöflichkeit abzulehnen

**incl.** *abbr.* **including** inkl.; einschl.

**inclement** /ɪn'klemənt/ *adj.* unfreundlich ‹Wetter›

**inclination** /ɪnklɪ'neɪʃn/ *n.* Ⓐ (*slope*) [Ab]hang, *der;* (*of roof*) Neigung, *die;* Ⓑ (*preference, desire*) Neigung, *die;* **have a strong ~ to[wards]** *or* **for sth.** eine ausgeprägte Neigung für etw. haben; **my ~ is to let the matter rest** ich neige dazu, die Sache auf sich beruhen zu lassen; **by ~ he tended to be a recluse** er hatte eine Neigung zum Einsiedlertum; **have neither the time nor the ~ to pursue the matter** weder die Zeit noch die Lust haben, die Sache zu verfolgen; **my immediate ~ was to throw him out** mein erster Gedanke war, ihn hinauszuwerfen; **show no ~ to go to bed** keine Anstalten machen, ins Bett zu gehen; Ⓒ (*liking*) **~ for sb.** Zuneigung für jmdn.; Ⓓ (*bow, nod*) Neigung, *die*

**incline** ❶ /ɪn'klaɪn/ *v.t.* Ⓐ (*bend*) neigen; Ⓑ (*dispose*) veranlassen; **all her instincts ~d her to stay** alles in ihr drängte sie zu bleiben. ❷ *v.i.* Ⓐ (*be disposed*) neigen (**to[wards]** zu); **~ to believe that ...:** geneigt sein zu glauben, dass ...; **~ to suppose that ...:** zu der Annahme neigen, dass ...; Ⓑ (*lean*) sich neigen. ❸ /'ɪnklaɪn/ *n.* Steigung, *die*

**inclined** /ɪn'klaɪnd/ *adj.* Ⓐ (*disposed*) geneigt; **be mathematically ~:** sich für Mathematik interessieren; **he is not very much ~ to believe me** er zeigt wenig Neigung, mir zu glauben; **they are ~ to be slow** sie neigen zur Langsamkeit; **if you feel [so] ~:** wenn Sie Lust dazu haben; **if you are that way ~:** wenn das Ihren Neigungen entspricht; **he is that way ~:** er neigt dazu; **be ~ to believe that ...:** geneigt sein zu glauben, dass ...; **the door is ~ to bang** die Tür schlägt leicht zu; Ⓑ (*sloping*) abfallend

**inclined 'plane** *n.* (*Phys.*) schiefe Ebene

**inclose** ⇒ **enclose**

**include** /ɪn'kluːd/ *v.t.* einschließen; (*contain*) enthalten; **his team ~s a number of people who ...:** zu seiner Mannschaft gehören einige, die ...; **..., [the] children ~d ...,** [die] Kinder eingeschlossen; **does that ~ 'me?** gilt das auch für mich?; **the list ~d several prominent politicians** die Liste enthielt mehrere prominente Politiker; **your name is not ~d in the list** dein Name steht nicht auf der Liste; **have you ~d the full amount?** haben Sie den vollen Betrag einbezogen?; **~ sth. in an essay** *etc.* etw. in einen Aufsatz *usw.* aufnehmen; **~d in the price** im Preis inbegriffen; **postage ~d** einschließlich Porto

**~ 'out** *v.t.* (*coll. joc.*) auslassen; **[you can] ~ me out** ohne mich!

**including** /ɪn'kluːdɪŋ/ *prep.* einschließlich; **I make that ten ~ the captain** mit dem Kapitän sind das nach meiner Rechnung zehn; **up to and ~ the last financial year** bis einschließlich des letzten Geschäftsjahres; **~ VAT** inklusive Mehrwertsteuer; **the lights cost me £10, ~ the batteries** die Lampen kosteten mich, einschließlich Batterien, 10 Pfund

**inclusion** /ɪn'kluːʒn/ *n.* Aufnahme, *die*

**inclusive** /ɪn'kluːsɪv/ *adj.* Ⓐ inklusive (*bes. Kaufmannsspr.*); einschließlich; **be ~ of sth.** etw. einschließen; **the rent is not ~ of gas and electricity charges** in der Miete sind Gas und Strom nicht enthalten; **from 2 to 6 January ~:** vom 2. bis einschließlich 6. Januar; **pages 7 to 26 ~:** Seite 7 bis 26 einschließlich; Ⓑ (*including everything*) Pauschal-; Inklusiv-; **~ terms** Pauschalpreis, *der;* **cost £50 ~:** 50 Pfund kosten, alles inbegriffen

**incognito** /ɪnkɒg'niːtəʊ/ ❶ *adj., adv.* inkognito. ❷ *n.* Inkognito, *das*

**incoherent** /ɪnkəʊ'hɪərənt/ *adj.* zusammenhanglos; **~ person/talk** sich ohne Zusammenhang ausdrückende Person/zusammenhangloses Gerede

**incoherently** /ɪnkəʊ'hɪərəntlɪ/ *adv.* zusammenhanglos

**incombustible** /ɪnkəm'bʌstɪbl/ *adj.* unbrennbar

**income** /'ɪnkəm/ *n.* Einkommen, *das;* **~s** (*receipts*) Einkünfte *Pl.;* **live within/beyond one's ~:** entsprechend seinen Verhältnissen/über seine Verhältnisse leben

**income: ~ bracket, ~ group** *ns.* Einkommensklasse, *die;* **~s policy** *n.* Einkommenspolitik, *die;* **~ sup'port** *n.* (*Brit.*) zusätzliche Hilfe zum Lebensunterhalt; **~ tax** *n.* Einkommensteuer, *die;* (*on wages, salary*) Lohnsteuer, *die; attrib.* **~ tax return** Einkommensteuererklärung, *die*/Lohnsteuererklärung, *die*

**'incoming** *adj.* Ⓐ (*arriving*) ankommend; einlaufend ‹Zug, Schiff›; landend ‹Flugzeug›; einfahrend ‹Zug›; eingehend ‹Telefongespräch, Auftrag›; **the ~ post** *or* **mail** der Posteingang (*Bürow.*); **the ~ tide** die Flut; Ⓑ (*succeeding*) neu ‹Vorsitzender, Präsident, Mieter, Regierung›

**incomings** /'ɪnkʌmɪŋz/ *n. pl.* (*revenue, income*) Einnahmen *Pl.;* Einkünfte *Pl.*

**incommensurable** /ɪnkə'menʃərəbl/ *adj.* inkommensurabel

**incommensurate** /ɪnkəˈmenʃərət/ *adj.* (*not comparable*) **be ~ with** *or* **to sth.** einer Sache (*Gen.*) unangemessen sein

**incommode** /ɪnkəˈməʊd/ *v.t.* (*formal*) **A** (*annoy*) belästigen; inkommodieren (*geh. veralt.*); **B** (*inconvenience*) behindern

**incommunicado** /ɪnkəmju:nɪˈkɑ:dəʊ/ *pred. adj.* von der Außenwelt abgeschnitten; **hold sb. ~:** jmdn. ohne Verbindung zur Außenwelt halten

**incomparable** /ɪnˈkɒmpərəbl/ *adj.*, **incomparably** /ɪnˈkɒmpərəblɪ/ *adv.* unvergleichlich

**incompatibility** /ɪnkəmpætɪˈbɪlɪtɪ/ *n.*, *no pl.* **A** (*inability to harmonize*) Unverträglichkeit, *die;* **divorce on grounds of ~:** Scheidung wegen unüberwindlicher Abneigung; **B** (*unsuitability for use together*) Nichtübereinstimmung, *die;* (*of medicines*) Unverträglichkeit, *die;* **C** (*inconsistency*) Unvereinbarkeit, *die*

**incompatible** /ɪnkəmˈpætɪbl/ *adj.* **A** (*unable to harmonize*) unverträglich; **they were ~ and they separated** sie passten nicht zueinander und trennten sich; **B** (*unsuitable for use together*) unvereinbar; inkompatibel (*Technik*); unverträglich ‹Medikamente›; **C** (*inconsistent*) unvereinbar

**incompetence** /ɪnˈkɒmpɪtəns/, **incompetency** /ɪnˈkɒmpɪtənsɪ/ *n.* Unfähigkeit, *die;* Unvermögen, *das*

**incompetent** /ɪnˈkɒmpɪtənt/ ❶ *adj.* unfähig; unzulänglich ‹Arbeit›; **he was ~ at his job** in seinem Beruf war er völlig unfähig. ❷ *n.* Unfähige, *der/die*

**incompetently** /ɪnˈkɒmpɪtəntlɪ/ *adv.* stümperhaft

**incomplete** /ɪnkəmˈpli:t/ *adj.*, **incompletely** /ɪnkəmˈpli:tlɪ/ *adv.* unvollständig

**incompleteness** /ɪnkəmˈpli:tnɪs/ *n.*, *no pl.* Unvollständigkeit, *die*

**incomprehensible** /ɪnkɒmprɪˈhensɪbl/ *adj.* unbegreiflich; unverständlich ‹Sprache, Rede, Theorie, Argument›

**incomprehension** /ɪnkɒmprɪˈhenʃn/ *n.*, *no pl.* Verständnislosigkeit, *die* (**of** gegenüber)

**inconceivable** /ɪnkənˈsi:vəbl/ *adj.*, **inconceivably** /ɪnkənˈsi:vəblɪ/ *adv.* unvorstellbar

**inconclusive** /ɪnkənˈklu:sɪv/ *adj.* ergebnislos; nicht schlüssig ‹Beweis, Argument›; **the result was ~:** das Ergebnis gab keinen Aufschluss

**inconclusively** /ɪnkənˈklu:sɪvlɪ/ *adv.* ergebnislos; nicht schlüssig ‹argumentieren›

**incongruity** /ɪnkɒŋˈgru:ɪtɪ/ *n.* **A** *no pl.* (*quality*) Deplatziertheit, *die;* **without ~:** ohne deplatziert zu wirken; **B** (*instance*) Absurdität, *die*

**incongruous** /ɪnˈkɒŋgrʊəs/ *adj.* **A** (*inappropriate*) unpassend; **B** (*inharmonious*) unvereinbar; nicht zusammenpassend ‹Farben, Kleidungsstücke›

**incongruously** /ɪnˈkɒŋgrʊəslɪ/ *adv.* (*inappropriately*) unpassend; *as sentence-modifier* unpassenderweise

**incongruousness** /ɪnˈkɒŋgrʊəsnɪs/ ⇒ **incongruity A**

**inconsequent** /ɪnˈkɒnsɪkwənt/ *adj.* **A** (*irrelevant*) sprunghaft ‹Abweichung, Eingebung›; zusammenhanglos ‹Bemerkung›; **B** (*illogical*) unlogisch; **C** (*disconnected*) unzusammenhängend

**inconsequential** /ɪnkɒnsɪˈkwenʃl/ *adj.* **A** (*unimportant*) belanglos; **B** ⇒ **inconsequent A**

**inconsiderable** /ɪnkənˈsɪdərəbl/ *adj.* unbeträchtlich; unerheblich; **the costs were not ~:** die Kosten waren nicht unerheblich

**inconsiderate** /ɪnkənˈsɪdərət/ *adj.* **A** (*unkind*) rücksichtslos; **B** (*rash*) unbedacht; unüberlegt

**inconsiderately** /ɪnkənˈsɪdərətlɪ/ *adv.* (*unkindly*) rücksichtslos; *as sentence-modifier* rücksichtsloserweise

**inconsistency** /ɪnkənˈsɪstənsɪ/ *n.* **A** (*incompatibility, self-contradiction*) Widersprüchlichkeit, *die* (**with** zu); **B** (*illogicality*) Inkonsequenz, *die;* **C** (*irregularity*) Unbeständigkeit, *die;* Inkonsistenz, *die* (*geh.*)

**inconsistent** /ɪnkənˈsɪstənt/ *adj.* **A** (*incompatible, self-contradictory*) widersprüchlich; **be ~ with sth.** zu etw. im Widerspruch stehen; **results ~ with the others** Ergebnisse, die nicht zu den anderen passen; **B** (*illogical*) inkonsequent; **C** (*irregular*) unbeständig; inkonsistent (*geh.*)

**inconsistently** /ɪnkənˈsɪstəntlɪ/ *adv.* **A** (*in a self-contradictory manner*) widersprüchlich; **B** (*illogically*) inkonsequent; **C** (*irregularly*) unbeständig; inkonsistent (*geh.*)

**inconsolable** /ɪnkənˈsəʊləbl/ *adj.* untröstlich

**inconspicuous** /ɪnkənˈspɪkjʊəs/ *adj.* unauffällig; **make oneself ~:** sich so verhalten, dass man nicht auffällt

**inconspicuously** /ɪnkənˈspɪkjʊəslɪ/ *adv.* unauffällig

**inconstancy** /ɪnˈkɒnstənsɪ/ *n.*, *no pl.* ⇒ **inconstant**: Unstetigkeit, *die;* Wankelmut, *der* (*geh.*); Ungleichmäßigkeit, *die*

**inconstant** /ɪnˈkɒnstənt/ *adj.* **A** (*fickle*) unstet; wankelmütig (*geh.*); **B** (*irregular*) ungleichmäßig

**incontestable** /ɪnkənˈtestəbl/ *adj.* unbestreitbar; unwiderlegbar ‹Beweis›

**incontinence** /ɪnˈkɒntɪnəns/ *n.* (*Med.*) Inkontinenz, *die*

**incontinent** /ɪnˈkɒntɪnənt/ *adj.* (*Med.*) inkontinent; **be ~:** an Inkontinenz leiden

**incontrovertible** /ɪnkɒntrəˈvɜ:tɪbl/ *adj.* unbestreitbar; unwiderlegbar ‹Beweis›

**incontrovertibly** /ɪnkɒntrəˈvɜ:tɪblɪ/ *adv.* unbestreitbar; unwiderlegbar ‹beweisen›

**inconvenience** /ɪnkənˈvi:nɪəns/ ❶ *n.* **A** *no pl.* (*discomfort, disadvantage*) Unannehmlichkeiten (**to** für); **put sb. to a lot of ~:** jmdm. große Unannehmlichkeiten bereiten; **go to a great deal of ~:** große Unannehmlichkeiten auf sich (*Akk.*) nehmen; **B** (*instance*) **if it's no ~:** wenn es keine Umstände macht; **it is rather an ~ to have to wait** es ist ziemlich unangenehm, warten zu müssen. ❷ *v.t.* Unannehmlichkeiten bereiten (+ *Dat.*); (*disturb*) stören; **don't ~ yourself just for me** *or* **on my account** mach [dir] meinetwegen nur keine Umstände!

**inconvenient** /ɪnkənˈvi:nɪənt/ *adj.* unbequem; ungünstig ‹Lage, Standort›; unpraktisch ‹Design, Konstruktion, Schnitt›; **a very ~ time** eine sehr ungünstige Zeit; **come at an ~ time** zu ungelegener Zeit kommen; **if it is not ~ [to you]** wenn es Ihnen recht ist

**inconveniently** /ɪnkənˈvi:nɪəntlɪ/ *adv.* ungünstig ‹gelegen›; unbequem ‹klein›

**incorporate** /ɪnˈkɔ:pəreɪt/ *v.t.* **A** (*make a legal corporation*) vereinigen; **~ a company** eine Gesellschaft gründen; **be ~d as a company** zu einer Gesellschaft zusammengeschlossen sein; **B** (*include*) aufnehmen (**in[to], with** in + *Akk.*); **your suggestion will be ~d in the plan** dein Vorschlag wird in den Plan eingehen; **the new plan ~s many of your suggestions** in dem neuen Plan sind viele deiner Vorschläge enthalten; **C** (*unite*) verbinden (**into** zu); **~ one's ideas in an essay** seine Gedanken in einem Essay zusammenfassen

**incorporated** /ɪnˈkɔ:pəreɪtɪd/ *adj.* eingetragen ‹[Handels]gesellschaft›

**incorporation** /ɪnkɔ:pəˈreɪʃn/ *n.* **A** (*formation*) Gründung, *die;* **B** (*inclusion*) Eingliederung, *die;* (*of material, chemical*) Aufnahme, *die;* **C** (*union*) Verbindung, *die* (**into** zu)

**incorporeal** /ɪnkɔ:ˈpɔ:rɪəl/ *adj.* (*not composed of matter; also Law*) unkörperlich; geisterhaft ‹Erscheinung, Wesen›

**incorrect** /ɪnkəˈrekt/ *adj.* **A** unrichtig; inkorrekt; **be ~:** nicht stimmen; **it is ~ to say that ...:** es stimmt nicht, dass ...; **you are ~ in believing that ...:** du irrst, wenn du glaubst, dass ...; **B** (*improper*) inkorrekt; unschicklich

**incorrectly** /ɪnkəˈrektlɪ/ *adv.* **A** unrichtigerweise; falsch ‹beantworten, aussprechen›; **B** (*improperly*) inkorrekt; unschicklich

**incorrectness** /ɪnkəˈrektnɪs/ *n.*, *no pl.* **A** Unrichtigkeit, *die;* Inkorrektheit, *die;* **B** (*impropriety*) Inkorrektheit, *die;* Unschicklichkeit, *die*

**incorrigible** /ɪnˈkɒrɪdʒɪbl/ *adj.*, **incorrigibly** /ɪnˈkɒrɪdʒɪblɪ/ *adv.* unverbesserlich

**incorruptible** /ɪnkəˈrʌptɪbl/ *adj.* **A** (*upright*) unbestechlich; **B** (*not subject to decay*) unzerstörbar

**increase** ❶ /ɪnˈkri:s/ *v.i.* zunehmen; ‹Schmerzen:› stärker werden; ‹Lärm:› größer werden; ‹Verkäufe, Preise, Nachfrage:› steigen; **~ in skill** größere Fertigkeit gewinnen; **~ in weight/size/price** schwerer/größer/teurer werden; **~ in maturity/value/popularity** an Reife/Wert/Popularität (*Dat.*) gewinnen.
❷ *v.t.* **A** (*make greater*) erhöhen; vermehren ‹Besitz›; **wages are ~d** die Löhne steigen; **B** (*intensify*) verstärken; **~ one's efforts/commitment** sich mehr anstrengen/engagieren.
❸ /ˈɪnkri:s/ *n.* **A** (*becoming greater*) Zunahme, *die* (**in** *Gen.*); (*in measurable amount*) Anstieg, *der* (**in** *Gen.*); (*deliberately caused*) Steigerung, *die* (**in** *Gen.*); **~ in weight/size** Gewichtszunahme, *die*/Vergrößerung, *die;* **~ in popularity** Popularitätsgewinn, *der;* **be on the ~:** [ständig] zunehmen; **B** (*by reproduction*) Zunahme, *die;* Zuwachs, *der;* **C** (*amount*) Erhöhung, *die;* (*of growth*) Zuwachs, *der*

**increasing** /ɪnˈkri:sɪŋ/ *adj.* steigend; wachsend; **an ~ number of people** mehr und mehr Menschen

**increasingly** /ɪnˈkri:sɪŋlɪ/ *adv.* in zunehmendem Maße; **become ~ apparent** immer deutlicher werden; **I am ~ of the opinion that ...:** ich bin immer mehr der Meinung, dass ...; **~, the husband looks after the children** immer häufiger kümmert sich der Mann um die Kinder

**incredibility** /ɪnkredɪˈbɪlɪtɪ/ *n.*, *no pl.* Unglaublichkeit, *die*

**incredible** /ɪnˈkredɪbl/ *adj.* **A** (*beyond belief*) unglaublich; **B** (*coll.*) (*remarkable*) unglaublich (*ugs.*); (*wonderful*) toll (*ugs.*)

**incredibly** /ɪnˈkredɪblɪ/ *adv.* **A** unglaublich; **B** (*coll.: remarkably*) unglaublich (*ugs.*); unwahrscheinlich (*ugs.*); **C** *as sentence-modifier* es ist/war kaum zu glauben, aber ...

**incredulity** /ɪnkrɪˈdju:lɪtɪ/ *n.*, *no pl.* Ungläubigkeit, *die*

**incredulous** /ɪnˈkredjʊləs/ *adj.* ungläubig; **be ~ of sth.** einer Sache (*Dat.*) keinen Glauben schenken

**incredulously** /ɪnˈkredjʊləslɪ/ *adv.* ungläubig

**increment** /ˈɪnkrɪmənt/ *n.* Erhöhung, *die;* (*amount of growth*) Zuwachs, *der*

**incriminate** /ɪnˈkrɪmɪneɪt/ *v.t.* belasten; **incriminating evidence** belastendes Material

**incriminatory** /ɪnˈkrɪmɪnətərɪ/ *adj.* belastend

**incrustation** /ɪnkrʌsˈteɪʃn/ *n.* **A** (*encrusting*) Überkrustung, *die;* **B** (*deposit*) Inkrustation, *die* (*Geol.*); Verkrustung, *die*

**incubate** /ˈɪnkjʊbeɪt/ ❶ *v.t.* bebrüten; (*to hatching; also fig.*) ausbrüten. ❷ *v.i.* **A** ‹Henne:› brüten; **B** (*be developed*) ‹Kulturen:› bebrütet werden

**incubation** /ɪnkjʊˈbeɪʃn/ *n.* **A** Inkubation, *die* (*Biol.*); Bebrütung, *die;* (*fig.*) Ausbrüten, *das;* **B** (*Med.*) Inkubation, *die;* **~ period** Inkubationszeit, *die*

**incubator** /ˈɪnkjʊbeɪtə(r)/ *n.* Inkubator, *der* (*Biol.*, *Med.*); (*for babies also*) Brutkasten, *der;* (*for eggs*) Brutapparat, *der*

**incubus** /ˈɪŋkjʊbəs/ *n.*, *pl.* **~es** *or* **incubi** /ˈɪnkjʊbaɪ/ **A** Albdruck, *der;* **B** (*spirit*) Inkubus, *der*

**inculcate** /ˈɪnkʌlkeɪt/ *v.t.* **~ sth. in[to] sb.**, **~ sb. with sth.** jmdm. etw. einpflanzen

**inculpate** /ˈɪnkʌlpeɪt/ *v.t.* **A** (*accuse*) **~ sb. [for a crime]** jmdn. [eines Verbrechens] beschuldigen; **B** (*involve*) **~ sb. [in sth.]** jmdn. der Mittäterschaft (*Gen.*) [bei etw.] beschuldigen

i

**inculpation** /ɪnkʌlˈpeɪʃn/ *n.* Beschuldigung, *die*

**incumbency** /ɪnˈkʌmbənsɪ/ *n.* Amt, *das*

**incumbent** /ɪnˈkʌmbənt/ ❶ *n.* Ⓐ (*Eccl.*) **the ~ of the parish** der Inhaber der Pfarrstelle; Ⓑ (*office-holder*) Amtsinhaber, *der.* ❷ *adj.* (*imposed*) **the duty ~ on me** die mir obliegende Pflicht; **it is ~ on sb. to do it** es ist jmds. Pflicht *od.* obliegt jmdm., es zu tun; **I feel it ~ on me** ich sehe es als meine Pflicht an

**incur** /ɪnˈkɜː(r)/ *v.t.*, **-rr-** sich (*Dat.*) zuziehen ‹Unwillen, Ärger›; **~ a loss** einen Verlust erleiden; **~ debts/expenses/risks** Schulden machen/Ausgaben haben/Risiken eingehen; **they had ~red fines** sie waren mit Geldstrafen belegt worden

**incurable** /ɪnˈkjʊərəbl/ ❶ *adj.* Ⓐ (*Med.*) unheilbar; Ⓑ (*fig.*) unheilbar (*ugs.*); unstillbar ‹Sehnsucht, Verlangen›; unüberwindbar ‹Scheu, Zurückhaltung›. ❷ *n.* unheilbar Kranker/Kranke

**incurably** /ɪnˈkjʊərəblɪ/ *adv.* unheilbar ‹krank›

**incurious** /ɪnˈkjʊərɪəs/ *adj.* uninteressiert

**incursion** /ɪnˈkɜːʃn/ *n.* (*invasion*) Eindringen, *das;* (*by sudden attack*) Einfall, *der*

**indebted** /ɪnˈdetɪd/ *pred. adj.* Ⓐ **be/feel deeply ~ to sb.** tief in jmds. Schuld (*Dat.*) stehen (*geh.*); **he was ~ to the book/a friend for this information** er verdankte dem Buch/einem Freund diese Information; **be [much] ~ to sb. for sth.** jmdm. für etw. [sehr] verbunden sein (*geh.*) *od.* zu Dank verpflichtet sein; Ⓑ (*owing money*) **be ~ to the bank for a large sum** bei der Bank mit einer hohen Summe verschuldet sein; **be [heavily] ~ to a friend** bei einem Freund [große] Schulden haben

**indebtedness** /ɪnˈdetɪdnɪs/ *n.* Ⓐ (*something owed*) Dankesschuld, *die* (*geh.*) (**to** bei); Ⓑ (*condition of owing money*) Verschuldung, *die*

**indecency** /ɪnˈdiːsənsɪ/ *n.* Unanständigkeit, *die*

**indecent** /ɪnˈdiːsənt/ *adj.* Ⓐ (*immodest, obscene*) unanständig; ⇒ *also* **exposure** A; Ⓑ (*unseemly*) ungehörig; **with ~ haste** mit unziemlicher Hast (*geh.*)

**indecent asˈsault** *n.* (*Law*) Notzucht, *die* (*Rechtsw.*)

**indecently** /ɪnˈdiːsəntlɪ/ *adv.* unanständig

**indecipherable** /ɪndɪˈsaɪfərəbl/ *adj.* unentzifferbar

**indecision** /ɪndɪˈsɪʒn/ *n., no pl.* Unentschlossenheit, *die*

**indecisive** /ɪndɪˈsaɪsɪv/ *adj.* Ⓐ (*not conclusive*) ergebnislos ‹Streit, Diskussion›; nichts entscheidend ‹Krieg, Schlacht›; nichts sagend ‹Ergebnis, Beobachtung›; Ⓑ (*hesitating*) unentschlossen; **be ~ about one's plans** keine festen Pläne haben; **~ about which line of action to choose** unschlüssig, wie man vorgehen soll

**indecisively** /ɪndɪˈsaɪsɪvlɪ/ *adv.* Ⓐ (*inconclusively*) ohne Entscheidung; Ⓑ (*hesitatingly*) unentschlossen

**indecisiveness** /ɪndɪˈsaɪsɪvnɪs/ *n., no pl.* Ⓐ Ergebnislosigkeit, *die;* Unentschlossenheit, *die;* Ⓑ (*hesitation*) **~ over a crucial issue** Unentschlossenheit in einer äußerst wichtigen Sache

**indeclinable** /ɪndɪˈklaɪnəbl/ *adj.* (*Ling.*) indeklinabel

**indecorous** /ɪnˈdekərəs/ *adj.* (*improper*) ungehörig; (*in bad taste*) unschicklich

**indeed** /ɪnˈdiːd/ *adv.* Ⓐ (*in truth*) in der Tat; tatsächlich; **~ that is correct** das stimmt tatsächlich *od.* in der Tat; Ⓑ *emphat.* **thank you very much ~:** haben Sie vielen herzlichen Dank; **it was very kind of you ~:** es war wirklich sehr freundlich von Ihnen; **I shall be very glad ~ when ...:** ich bin wirklich sehr froh, wenn ...; **~ it is** in der Tat; allerdings; **yes ~, it certainly is/I certainly did** *etc.* ja, das kann man wohl sagen; **no, ~:** nein, ganz bestimmt nicht; Ⓒ (*in fact*) ja sogar; **~, he can ...:** ja, er kann sogar ...; **if ~ such a thing is possible** wenn so etwas überhaupt möglich ist; **I feel, ~ I know, she will come** ich habe das Gefühl, [ja] ich weiß sogar, dass sie kommen wird; Ⓓ (*admittedly*) zugegebenermaßen; zwar; Ⓔ *interrog.* **~?** wirklich?; ist das wahr?; Ⓕ *expr. irony, surprise, interest, etc.* **He expects to win — Does he ~!** Er glaubt, dass er gewinnt — Tatsächlich?; **I want a fortnight off work — [Do you] ~!** Ich möchte 14 Tage freihaben — Ach wirklich?; **smoked salmon, ~!** soso *od.* sieh mal einer an, geräucherter Lachs [also]!; Ⓖ *echoing question* **Who is this Mr Smith? — Who is he, ~!** (*you may well ask*) Wer ist denn dieser Mr. Smith? — Ja, wer ist er eigentlich?

**indefatigable** /ɪndɪˈfætɪgəbl/ *adj.* unermüdlich

**indefensible** /ɪndɪˈfensɪbl/ *adj.* Ⓐ (*insecure*) unhaltbar; Ⓑ (*untenable*) unvertretbar; unhaltbar; Ⓒ (*intolerable*) unverzeihlich

**indefinable** /ɪndɪˈfaɪnəbl/ *adj.* undefinierbar; **have a certain ~ something** etwas Gewisses haben

**indefinite** /ɪnˈdefɪnɪt/ *adj.* Ⓐ (*vague*) unbestimmt; **she was rather ~ about it** sie äußerte sich ziemlich vage darüber; Ⓑ (*unlimited*) unbegrenzt; **~ leave** Urlaub auf unbestimmte Zeit; Ⓒ (*Ling.*) unbestimmt; indefinit (*fachspr.*); infinit (*fachspr.*) ‹Verbform›; ⇒ *also* **article** 1 C; **pronoun**

**indefinitely** /ɪnˈdefɪnɪtlɪ/ *adv.* Ⓐ (*vaguely*) unbestimmt; Ⓑ (*unlimitedly*) unbegrenzt; **it can't go on ~:** es kann nicht endlos so weitergehen; **postponed ~:** auf unbestimmte Zeit verschoben; **it would be easy to prolong the list ~:** die Liste ließe sich beliebig verlängern

**indelible** /ɪnˈdelɪbl/ *adj.* unauslöschlich (*auch fig.*); nicht zu entfernend ‹Fleck›; **~ ink** Wäschetinte, *die;* **~ pencil** Kopierstift, *der;* Tintenstift, *der*

**indelibly** /ɪnˈdelɪblɪ/ *adv.* unauslöschlich

**indelicacy** /ɪnˈdelɪkəsɪ/ *n.* ⇒ **indelicate**: Ungehörigkeit, *die;* Geschmacklosigkeit, *die;* Mangel an Feingefühl

**indelicate** /ɪnˈdelɪkət/ *adj.* (*coarse*) ungehörig; (*almost indecent*) geschmacklos; (*slightly tactless*) nicht sehr feinfühlig

**indelicately** /ɪnˈdelɪkətlɪ/ *adv.* ⇒ **indelicate**: ungehörig; geschmacklos; wenig feinfühlend

**indemnification** /ɪndemnɪfɪˈkeɪʃn/ *n.* Entschädigung, *die*

**indemnify** /ɪnˈdemnɪfaɪ/ *v.t.* Ⓐ (*protect*) **~ sb. against sth.** jmdn. gegen etw. absichern; Ⓑ (*compensate*) entschädigen

**indemnity** /ɪnˈdemnɪtɪ/ *n.* Ⓐ (*security*) Absicherung, *die;* Ⓑ (*compensation*) Entschädigung, *die*

**inˈdemnity policy** *n.* Haftpflichtversicherung, *die*

**indent**[1] ❶ /ˈɪndent/ *n.* Ⓐ (*incision*) Einschnitt, *der;* Ⓑ (*Brit.: requisition*) Requisition, *die;* Ⓒ ⇒ **indentures**. ❷ /ɪnˈdent/ *v.t.* Ⓐ (*make notches in*) einkerben; Ⓑ (*form recesses in*) einschneiden in (+ *Akk.*); **an ~ed coastline** eine Küste mit tiefen Einschnitten; Ⓒ (*from margin*) einrücken; Ⓓ (*Brit.: order*) requirieren. ❸ *v.i.* (*Brit.: make requisition*) **~ [on sb.] for sth.** etw. [bei jmdm.] requirieren

**indent**[2] /ɪnˈdent/ *v.t.* (*imprint*) eindrücken

**indentation** /ɪndenˈteɪʃn/ *n.* Ⓐ (*indenting, notch*) Einkerbung, *die;* Ⓑ (*recess*) Einschnitt, *der*

**indentures** /ɪnˈdentʃəz/ *n. pl.* Ausbildungsvertrag, *der*

**independence** /ɪndɪˈpendəns/ *n.* Unabhängigkeit, *die;* **declaration of ~:** Unabhängigkeitserklärung, *die;* **~ of mind/spirit** geistige Selbstständigkeit

**Indeˈpendence Day** *n.* (*Amer.*) Unabhängigkeitstag, *der*

**independent** /ɪndɪˈpendənt/ ❶ *adj.* Ⓐ unabhängig; **~ income/means** eigenes Einkommen; Ⓑ (*not wanting obligations*) selbstständig. ❷ *n.* (*Polit.*) Unabhängige, *der/die*

**independently** /ɪndɪˈpendəntlɪ/ *adv.* unabhängig (**of** von); **they work ~:** sie arbeiten unabhängig voneinander

**indeˈpendent school** *n.* (*Brit.*) Schule in nichtstaatlicher Trägerschaft

**ˈin-depth** ⇒ **depth** C

**indescribable** /ɪndɪˈskraɪbəbl/ *adj.*, **indescribably** /ɪndɪˈskraɪbəblɪ/ *adv.* unbeschreiblich

**indestructible** /ɪndɪˈstrʌktɪbl/ *adj.* unzerstörbar; unerschütterlich ‹Glaube›

**indeterminable** /ɪndɪˈtɜːmɪnəbl/ *adj.* unbestimmbar

**indeterminacy** /ɪndɪˈtɜːmɪnəsɪ/ *n., no pl.* Unbestimmtheit, *die*

**indeterminate** /ɪndɪˈtɜːmɪnət/ *adj.* Ⓐ (*not fixed, vague*) unbestimmt ‹Form, Menge›; unklar ‹Konzept, Bedeutung›; Ⓑ (*left undecided*) ergebnislos; offen ‹Rechtsfrage›; Ⓒ (*Math.*) unbestimmt

**index** /ˈɪndeks/ ❶ *n.* Ⓐ (*list*) Index, *der;* Register, *das;* **~ of sources** Quellenverzeichnis, *das;* ⇒ *also* **card index**; Ⓑ *pl.* **indices** /ˈɪndɪsiːz/ (*Phys.*) **refractive ~:** Brechzahl, *die;* Brechungsindex, *der;* Ⓒ *pl.* **indices** (*Math.*) Index, *der;* (*exponent*) Exponent, *der;* Ⓓ (*pointer on scale*) Zeiger, *der;* Ⓔ (*Econ.*) Index, *der;* Ⓕ *pl.* **indices** (*indication*) [An]zeichen, *das;* Ⓖ **the I~** (*Hist.*) der Index; **put on the I~:** auf den Index setzen. ❷ *v.t.* Ⓐ (*furnish with ~*) mit einem Register *od.* Index versehen; Ⓑ (*enter in ~*) ins Register aufnehmen; Ⓒ (*Econ.*) indexieren; **~ pensions** Renten dynamisieren

**indexation** /ɪndekˈseɪʃn/ *n.* (*Econ.*) Indexierung, *die*

**ˈindex card** *n.* Karteikarte, *die*

**indexer** /ˈɪndeksə(r)/ *n.* Verfasser eines Registers/von Registern

**index: ~ finger** *n.* Zeigefinger, *der;* Index, *der* (*Anat.*); **~ gears** *pl.* Indexschaltung, *die;* **~-linked** *adj.* (*Econ.*) indexiert; dynamisch ‹Rente›; **~-linking** *n.* (*Econ.*) Indexierung, *die;* **~-linking of pensions** ≈ Rentenanpassung, *die;* **~ number** *n.* Indexzahl, *die* (*bes. Statistik*)

**India** /ˈɪndɪə/ *pr. n.* Indien (*das*); **~ ink** (*Amer.*) ⇒ **Indian ink**

**Indian** /ˈɪndɪən/ ▶ 1340 ❶ *adj.* Ⓐ indisch; Ⓑ **[American] ~:** indianisch. ⇒ *also* **file**[3] 1 A; **Red Indian**; **West Indian** 1. ❷ *n.* Ⓐ Inder, *der*/Inderin, *die;* Ⓑ **[American] ~:** Indianer, *der*/Indianerin, *die*

**Indian: ~ ˈclub** *n.* Keule, *die;* **~ ˈcorn** *n.* Mais, *der;* **~ ˈink** *n.* (*Brit.*) Tusche, *die;* **~ ˈOcean** *pr. n.* Indischer Ozean; **~ ˈrope-trick** *n.* indischer Seiltrick; **~ ˈsummer** *n.* Altweibersommer, *der;* Nachsommer, *der* (*auch fig.*)

**ˈIndia rubber** ⇒ **rubber**[1] A, B

**indicate** /ˈɪndɪkeɪt/ ❶ *v.t.* Ⓐ (*be a sign of*) erkennen lassen; **this ~s something about his attitude** dies gibt Aufschlüsse über seine Haltung; Ⓑ (*state briefly*) andeuten; **~ the rough outlines of a project** ein Projekt kurz umreißen *od.* in groben Umrissen darstellen; **they ~d that they might take action** sie gaben zu verstehen, dass sie Schritte unternehmen könnten; Ⓒ (*mark, point out*) anzeigen; Ⓓ (*suggest, make evident*) zum Ausdruck bringen (**to** gegenüber); Ⓔ (*Med.*) **be ~d** indiziert sein. ❷ *v.i.* blinken (*bes. Verkehrsw.*)

**indication** /ɪndɪˈkeɪʃn/ *n.* Ⓐ (*sign, guide*) [An]zeichen, *das* (**of** *Gen.*, für); **he gave no ~ that he understood** nichts wies darauf hin, dass er verstand; **there is every/no ~ that ...:** alles/nichts weist darauf hin, dass ...; **give a clear ~ of one's intentions** seine Absichten klar zum Ausdruck bringen; **first ~s are that ...:** die ersten Anzeichen deuten darauf hin, dass ...; **that is some ~ of his feelings/the seriousness of the situation** das lässt seine Gefühle erkennen/das deutet darauf hin, wie ernst die Lage ist; **give me a rough ~ of when you will arrive** sagen Sie mir ungefähr, wann Sie kommen; Ⓑ (*Med.*) Indikation, *die*

**indicative** /ɪnˈdɪkətɪv/ ❶ *adj.* Ⓐ (*suggestive*) **be ~ of sth./that ...:** auf etw. (*Akk.*) schließen lassen/darauf schließen lassen, dass ...; Ⓑ (*Ling.*) indikativisch; **~ mood** Indikativ, *der.* ❷ *n.* (*Ling.*) Indikativ, *der*

**indicator** /ˈɪndɪkeɪtə(r)/ *n.* Ⓐ *(instrument)* Anzeiger, *der;* Ⓑ *(board)* Anzeigetafel, *die;* Ⓒ *(on vehicle)* Blinker, *der;* Ⓓ *(fig.: pointer)* Indikator, *der (bes. Wirtsch.);* Ⓔ *(Chem.)* Indikator, *der*

**indices** *pl. of* **index** 1 B, C, F

**indict** /ɪnˈdaɪt/ *v.t.* anklagen (**for, on a charge of** *Gen.*)

**indictable** /ɪnˈdaɪtəbl/ *adj.* strafrechtlich verfolgbar ‹Person›; strafbar ‹Handlung›

**indictment** /ɪnˈdaɪtmənt/ *n.* Ⓐ *(Law)* Anklageerhebung, *die;* **~ for** *or* **on a charge of murder** Mordanklage, *die;* **bring an ~ against sb.** Anklage gegen jmdn. erheben; **[bill of] ~:** Anklageschrift, *die;* Ⓑ *(fig.: accusation)* **~ of sth.** Anklage gegen etw. *(geh.)*

**indie** /ˈɪndɪ/ *(coll.)* ❶ *adj.* Indie‹Gruppe, Szene, Charts usw.›. ❷ *n. (record company)* Indie-Label, *das; (band)* Indie-Band, *die*

**Indies** /ˈɪndɪz/ *pr. n. pl.* Ⓐ **the ~** *(arch.)* Indien; der indische Subkontinent; Ⓑ **East ~:** Malaiischer Archipel; Ostindischer Archipel *(veralt.);* **West ~:** Westindische Inseln

**indifference** /ɪnˈdɪfərəns/ *n., no pl.* Ⓐ *(unconcern)* Gleichgültigkeit, *die* (**to[wards]** gegenüber); Ⓑ *(neutrality)* Indifferenz, *die;* Ⓒ *(unimportance)* **a matter of ~:** eine Belanglosigkeit; **this is a matter of complete ~ to** *or* **for him** das ist für ihn völlig belanglos

**indifferent** /ɪnˈdɪfərənt/ *adj.* Ⓐ *(without concern or interest)* gleichgültig; unbeteiligt ‹Beobachter›; **be ~ to[wards] sb./sth.** sich für jmdn./etw. nicht interessieren; Ⓑ *(not good)* mittelmäßig; *(fairly bad)* mäßig; *(neither good nor bad)* durchschnittlich; **very ~:** schlecht

**indifferently** /ɪnˈdɪfərəntlɪ/ *adv.* Ⓐ *(unconcernedly)* gleichgültig; Ⓑ *(badly)* mäßig

**indigence** /ˈɪndɪdʒəns/ *n., no pl.* Armut, *die*

**indigenous** /ɪnˈdɪdʒɪnəs/ *adj.* einheimisch; eingeboren ‹Bevölkerung›; **a species ~ to India** eine in Indien heimische *od.* beheimatete Art; **~ inhabitant** Ureinwohner, *der*

**indigent** /ˈɪndɪdʒənt/ *adj.* arm

**indigestible** /ɪndɪˈdʒestɪbl/ *adj. (lit. or fig.)* unverdaulich

**indigestion** /ɪndɪˈdʒestʃn/ *n., no pl., no indef. art.* Magenverstimmung, *die; (chronic)* Verdauungsstörungen *Pl.*

**indignant** /ɪnˈdɪgnənt/ *adj.* entrüstet (**at, over, about** über + *Akk.*); indigniert ‹Blick, Geste›; **grow ~:** sich entrüsten; **it makes me ~:** es regt mich auf; **he was ~ with his wife** er ärgerte sich über seine Frau; **it's no use getting ~:** es hat keinen Zweck, sich aufzuregen

**indignantly** /ɪnˈdɪgnəntlɪ/ *adv.* entrüstet; indigniert

**indignation** /ɪndɪgˈneɪʃn/ *n., no pl.* Entrüstung, *die* (**about, at, against, over** über + *Akk.*); **feel great ~ at sb.** sehr entrüstet über jmdn. sein

**indignity** /ɪnˈdɪgnɪtɪ/ *n.* Ⓐ *no pl., no art. (humiliation)* Demütigung, *die;* **be treated with great ~:** äußerst demütigend behandelt werden; Ⓑ *no pl. (lack of dignity)* **the ~ of my position** das Demütigende [an] meiner Situation; **oh, the ~ of it!** o Schmach und Schande!; **the ~ of having to do sth.** die Demütigung, etw. tun zu müssen

**indigo** /ˈɪndɪgəʊ/ ❶ *n., pl.* **~s** Ⓐ *(dye)* Indigo, *der od. das;* Ⓑ *(plant)* Indigopflanze, *die;* Ⓒ *(colour)* **~ [blue]** Indigoblau, *das.* ❷ *adj.* **~ [blue]** indigoblau

**indirect** /ɪndɪˈrekt, ɪndaɪˈrekt/ *adj.* indirekt; *(long-winded)* umständlich; **follow an ~ route** nicht den direkten Weg nehmen; **that's the more ~ way** das ist der weniger direkte *od.* geradlinige Weg; **that road is rather ~:** diese Straße ist ein ziemlicher Umweg; **by ~ means** auf Umwegen *(fig.)*

**indirectly** /ɪndɪˈrektlɪ, ɪndaɪˈrektlɪ/ *adv.* indirekt; auf Umwegen ‹hören, herausfinden›

**indirect: ~ ˈobject** *n. (Ling.)* indirektes Objekt; *(in German)* Dativobjekt, *das;* **~ ˈquestion** *n. (Ling.)* indirekte Frage; **~ ˈspeech** *n. (Ling.)* indirekte Rede

**indiscernible** /ɪndɪˈsɜːnɪbl/ *adj.* unmerklich; **the sound was virtually ~:** das Geräusch war kaum wahrnehmbar

**indiscipline** /ɪnˈdɪsɪplɪn/ *n., no pl., no indef. art.* Disziplinlosigkeit, *die*

**indiscreet** /ɪndɪˈskriːt/ *adj.* indiskret; taktlos ‹Benehmen›; **she was ~ to do that** es war indiskret von ihr, das zu tun

**indiscreetly** /ɪndɪˈskriːtlɪ/ *adv.* indiskret; taktlos ‹sich benehmen›

**indiscretion** /ɪndɪˈskreʃn/ *n.* Ⓐ *(conduct)* Indiskretion, *die; (tactlessness)* Taktlosigkeit, *die;* Ⓑ *(imprudence)* Unbedachtheit, *die;* Ⓒ *(action)* Unbedachtsamkeit, *die; (love affair)* Affäre, *die;* Ⓓ *(revelation of official secret etc.)* Indiskretion, *die*

**indiscriminate** /ɪndɪˈskrɪmɪnət/ *adj.* Ⓐ *(undiscriminating)* unkritisch; **hand out ~ condemnations** unterschiedslos alles verurteilen; Ⓑ *(unrestrained, promiscuous)* wahllos; willkürlich ‹Anwendung›; unüberlegt ‹Ausgaben›

**indiscriminately** /ɪndɪˈskrɪmɪnətlɪ/ *adv.* ⇒ **indiscriminate**: unkritisch; wahllos; willkürlich; unüberlegt

**indispensability** /ɪndɪspensəˈbɪlɪtɪ/ *n., no pl.* Unentbehrlichkeit, *die* (**to** für)

**indispensable** /ɪndɪˈspensəbl/ *adj.* unentbehrlich (**to** für); unabdingbar ‹Voraussetzung›; **make oneself ~:** sich unentbehrlich machen

**indispose** /ɪndɪˈspəʊz/ *v.t. (make averse)* einnehmen (**towards** gegen)

**indisposed** /ɪndɪˈspəʊzd/ *adj.* Ⓐ *(unwell)* unpässlich; indisponiert ‹Sänger, Schauspieler›; Ⓑ *(disinclined)* **be ~ to do sth.** abgeneigt sein, etw. zu tun; **she was ~ to be polite** sie war nicht geneigt, höflich zu sein

**indisposition** /ɪndɪspəˈzɪʃn/ *n.* Ⓐ *(ill health)* Unpässlichkeit, *die; (of singer, actor)* Indisposition, *die;* Ⓑ *(disinclination)* **an ~ to do sth.** eine Abneigung dagegen, etw. zu tun

**indisputable** /ɪndɪˈspjuːtəbl/ *adj.*, **indisputably** /ɪndɪˈspjuːtəblɪ/ *adv.* unbestreitbar

**indissoluble** /ɪndɪˈsɒljʊbl/ *adj.*, **indissolubly** /ɪndɪˈsɒljʊblɪ/ *adv.* unauflöslich

**indistinct** /ɪndɪˈstɪŋkt/ *adj.* undeutlich; *(blurred)* verschwommen; **grow ~ in the twilight** in der Dämmerung verschwimmen

**indistinctly** /ɪndɪˈstɪŋktlɪ/ *adv.* undeutlich ‹sprechen›; verschwommen ‹sich erinnern›

**indistinguishable** /ɪndɪˈstɪŋgwɪʃəbl/ *adj.* Ⓐ *(not distinguishable)* nicht unterscheidbar; **the twins are ~:** die Zwillinge sind nicht voneinander zu unterscheiden; Ⓑ *(imperceptible)* nicht erkennbar; nicht wahrnehmbar ‹Geräusch›

**individual** /ɪndɪˈvɪdjʊəl/ ❶ *adj.* Ⓐ *(single)* einzeln; Ⓑ *(special, personal)* besonder... ‹Vorteil, Merkmal›; **give ~ attention to one's pupils** seine Schüler individuell betreuen; **~ case** Einzelfall, *der;* Ⓒ *(intended for one)* für eine [einzelne] Person bestimmt; **~ portions** Einzelportionen; **~ pie** Pastete für eine [einzelne] Person; Ⓓ *(distinctive)* eigentümlich; individuell; **be ~ in one's view** individuelle *od.* eigene Ansichten vertreten; Ⓔ *(characteristic)* eigen; individuell.
❷ *n.* Ⓐ *(one member)* Einzelne, *der/die; (animal)* Einzeltier, *das;* einzelnes Tier; **~s** Einzelne; Ⓑ *(one being)* Individuum, *das;* Einzelne, *der/die;* **the rights of ~s** die Rechte des Individuums *od.* des Einzelnen; Ⓒ *(coll.: person)* Individuum, *das (abwertend);* **who is that ~?** wer ist dieses Individuum?

**individualise** ⇒ **individualize**

**individualist** /ɪndɪˈvɪdjʊəlɪst/ *n.* Individualist, *der*/Individualistin, *die*

**individualistic** /ɪndɪvɪdjʊəˈlɪstɪk/ *adj.* individualistisch

**individuality** /ɪndɪvɪdjʊˈælɪtɪ/ *n., no pl.* Ⓐ *(character)* eigene Persönlichkeit; Individualität, *die;* Ⓑ *(separate existence)* individuelle Existenz

**individualize** /ɪndɪˈvɪdjʊəlaɪz/ *v.t.* **~ sth.** einer Sache *(Dat.)* einen eigenen Charakter geben

**individually** /ɪndɪˈvɪdjʊəlɪ/ *adv.* Ⓐ *(singly)* einzeln; Ⓑ *(distinctively)* individuell; Ⓒ *(personally)* persönlich

**indivisibility** /ɪndɪvɪzɪˈbɪlɪtɪ/ *n., no pl.* Unteilbarkeit, *die*

**indivisible** /ɪndɪˈvɪzɪbl/ *adj.* Ⓐ *(not divisible)* unteilbar; Ⓑ *(not distributable)* nicht aufteilbar

**indivisibly** /ɪndɪˈvɪzɪblɪ/ *adv.* unteilbar

**Indo-** /ɪndəʊ/ *in comb.* Indo-

**Indo-ˈChina** *pr. n.* Indochina *(das)*

**indoctrinate** /ɪnˈdɒktrɪneɪt/ *v.t.* indoktrinieren *(abwertend)*

**indoctrination** /ɪndɒktrɪˈneɪʃn/ *n.* Indoktrination, *die (abwertend)*

**Indo: ~-Euroˈpean, ~-Gerˈmanic** ❶ *adjs.* indoeuropäisch; indogermanisch. ❷ *ns. (Ling.)* Indogermanisch, *das*

**indolence** /ˈɪndələns/ *n., no pl.* Trägheit, *die;* Indolenz, *die (geh.)*

**indolent** /ˈɪndələnt/ *adj.*, **indolently** /ˈɪndələntlɪ/ *adv.* träge; indolent *(geh.)*

**indomitable** /ɪnˈdɒmɪtəbl/ *adj.* unbeugsam; unbezähmbar ‹Begeisterung›

**Indonesia** /ɪndəˈniːzɪə/ *pr. n.* Indonesien *(das)*

**Indonesian** /ɪndəˈniːzɪən/ ▶1275, ▶1340 ❶ *adj.* indonesisch; **sb. is ~:** jmd. ist Indonesier/Indonesierin; ⇒ *also* **English** 1. ❷ *n.* Ⓐ *(person)* Indonesier, *der*/Indonesierin, *die;* Ⓑ *(language)* Indonesisch, *das;* ⇒ *also* **English** 2 A

**ˈindoor** *adj.* **~ shoes** Schuhe für zu Hause; **~ swimming pool/sports/tennis** Hallenbad, *das*/-sport, *der*/-tennis, *das;* **~ plants** Zimmerpflanzen; **~ games** Spiele im Haus; *(Sport)* Hallenspiele; **~ aerial** Innenantenne, *die; (in room)* Zimmerantenne, *die;* **I don't enjoy ~ work** ich arbeite nicht gern drinnen *od.* im Haus/Büro *usw.;* **he's not one for [the] ~ life** er ist lieber draußen als drinnen

**indoors** /ɪnˈdɔːz/ *adv.* drinnen; im Haus; **come/go ~:** nach drinnen *od.* ins Haus kommen/gehen

**indorse** ⇒ **endorse**

**indubitable** /ɪnˈdjuːbɪtəbl/ *adj.* unzweifelhaft

**indubitably** /ɪnˈdjuːbɪtəblɪ/ *adv.* zweifellos; zweifelsohne

**induce** /ɪnˈdjuːs/ *v.t.* Ⓐ *(persuade)* **~ sb. to do sth.** jmdn. dazu bringen, etw. zu tun; Ⓑ *(bring about)* hervorrufen; verursachen, führen zu ‹Krankheit›; Ⓒ *(Med.)* einleiten ‹Wehen, Geburt›; herbeiführen ‹Schlaf›; Ⓓ *(Electr., Phys., Philos.)* induzieren

**inducement** /ɪnˈdjuːsmənt/ *n. (incentive)* Anreiz, *der;* **as an added ~:** als besonderer Anreiz *od.* Ansporn; **no ~ would persuade her to give up her home** kein noch so verlockendes Angebot könnte sie dazu bewegen, ihr Zuhause aufzugeben

**induct** /ɪnˈdʌkt/ *v.t.* Ⓐ einführen (**to** in + *Akk.*); Ⓑ *(Amer. Mil.)* einziehen; einberufen

**inductance** /ɪnˈdʌktəns/ *n. (Electr.)* Induktanz, *die*

**inductee** /ɪndʌkˈtiː/ *n. (Amer. Mil.)* Einberufene, *der/die*

**induction** /ɪnˈdʌkʃn/ *n.* Ⓐ *(formal introduction)* Amtseinführung, *die;* Ⓑ *(initiation)* Einführung, *die* (**into** in + *Akk.*); **~ course** Einführungskurs[us], *der;* Ⓒ *(Med.)* Einleitung, *die; (of sleep)* Herbeiführen, *das;* Ⓓ *(Electr., Phys., Math., Philos.)* Induktion, *die;* Ⓔ *(Amer. Mil.)* Einberufung, *die*

**induction: ~ coil** *n. (Electr.)* Induktionsspule, *die;* **~ heating** *n.* Induktionsheizung, *die*

**inductive** /ɪnˈdʌktɪv/ *adj.*, **inductively** /ɪnˈdʌktɪvlɪ/ *adv. (Electr., Phys., Math., Logic)* induktiv

**indue** ⇒ **endue**

**indulge** /ɪnˈdʌldʒ/ ❶ *v.t.* Ⓐ *(yield to)* nachgeben (+ *Dat.*) ‹Wunsch, Verlangen, Verlockung›; frönen *(geh.)* (+ *Dat.*) ‹Leidenschaft, Neigung›; Ⓑ *(please)* verwöhnen; **~ sb. in sth.** jmdm. in etw. *(Dat.)* nachgeben; **~ oneself in** schwelgen in *(geh.)* (+ *Dat.*); sich gütlich tun an (+ *Dat.*) ‹Speisen, Leckereien›. ❷ *v.i.* Ⓐ *(allow oneself pleasure)* **~ in** frönen *(geh.)* (+ *Dat.*) ‹Leidenschaft, Neigung›; sich gütlich tun an (+ *Dat.*)

‹Speisen, Leckereien›; **B** (*coll.: take alcoholic drink*) sich (*Dat.*) einen genehmigen (*ugs.*); **I'd better not ~:** ich halte mich besser zurück

**indulgence** /ɪn'dʌldʒəns/ *n.* **A** Nachsicht, *die;* (*humouring*) Nachgiebigkeit, *die* (**with** gegenüber); **B sb.'s ~ in sth.** jmds. Hang zu etw.; **constant ~ in bad habits** ständiges Nachgeben gegenüber schlechten Gewohnheiten; **C** (*thing indulged in*) Luxus, *der;* **D** (*privilege*) Vorrecht, *das;* **E** (*Relig.: remission*) Ablass, *der*

**indulgent** /ɪn'dʌldʒənt/ *adj.* nachsichtig (**with, to[wards]** gegenüber); **she's so ~ with that dog of hers** sie verhätschelt ihren Hund so sehr

**indulgently** /ɪn'dʌldʒəntlɪ/ *adv.* nachsichtig

**industrial** /ɪn'dʌstrɪəl/ *adj.* **A** industriell; betrieblich ‹Ausbildung, Forschung›; Arbeits‹unfall, -medizin, -psychologie›; **B** (*intended for industry*) Industrie‹alkohol, -diamant usw.›; **C** (*characterized by industry*) industrialisiert; **the ~ nations** die Industrienationen. ⇒ *also* **archaeology; estate B**

**industrial: ~ 'action** *n.* Arbeitskampfmaßnahmen *Pl.;* **take ~ action** in den Ausstand treten; **~ di'sease** *n.* Berufskrankheit, *die;* **~ di'spute** *n.* Arbeitskonflikt, *der;* **~ 'espionage** *n.* Industriespionage, *die;* **~ estate** *n.* Industriegebiet, *das;* **~ exhibition** *n.* Industrieausstellung, *die;* **~ 'injury** *n.* Arbeitsverletzung, *die*

**industrialisation, industrialise** ⇒ **industrializ-**

**industrialist** /ɪn'dʌstrɪəlɪst/ *n.* Industrielle, *der/die*

**industrialization** /ɪndʌstrɪəlaɪ'zeɪʃn/ *n.* Industrialisierung, *die*

**industrialize** /ɪn'dʌstrɪəlaɪz/ *v.i. & t.* industrialisieren

**industrially** /ɪn'dʌstrɪəlɪ/ *adv.* industriell

**industrial: ~ park** *n.* Industriegebiet, *das;* **~ plant** *n.* Industrieanlage, *die;* **~ re'lations** *n. pl.* Industrialrelations *Pl.* (*Wirtsch.*); *Beziehungen zwischen Arbeitgebern und Gewerkschaften;* **I~ Revo'lution** *n.* (*Hist.*) industrielle Revolution; **~ town** *n.* Industriestadt, *die;* **~ tribunal** *n.* Arbeitsgericht, *das;* **~ un'rest** *n.* Unruhe in der Arbeitnehmerschaft; **~ 'waste** *n.* Industriemüll, *der;* **~ wastes** Industrieabfälle *Pl.*

**industrious** /ɪn'dʌstrɪəs/ *adj.* fleißig; (*busy*) emsig

**industriously** /ɪn'dʌstrɪəslɪ/ *adv.* fleißig; (*busily*) emsig

**industry** /'ɪndəstrɪ/ *n.* **A** Industrie, *die;* **several industries** mehrere Industriezweige; **steel/coal ~:** Stahl-/Kohleindustrie, *die;* **the nation's ~:** die Industrie des Landes; **incentives to ~:** Maßnahmen zur Förderung des industriellen Wachstums; **the leaders of ~:** die Industriebosse (*ugs.*); die Industriemanager; **~ is thriving** die Industrie blüht; **his experience of ~:** seine Erfahrungen auf dem industriellen Sektor; **the Shakespeare/abortion ~** (*coll.*) die Vermarktung Shakespeares/das Geschäft mit der Abtreibung; **B** ⇒ **industrious**: Fleiß, *der;* Emsigkeit, *die*

**inebriated** /ɪ'ni:brɪeɪtɪd/ *adj.* **A** (*drunk*) betrunken; **B** (*fig.*) berauscht (**with** von); trunken (*geh.*) (**with** von, vor + *Dat.*)

**inedible** /ɪn'edɪbl/ *adj.* ungenießbar

**ineducable** /ɪn'edjʊkəbl/ *adj.* lernunfähig

**ineffable** /ɪn'efəbl/ *adj.* unbeschreiblich

**ineffective** /ɪnɪ'fektɪv/ *adj.* **A** unwirksam; ineffektiv; fruchtlos ‹Anstrengung, Versuch›; ineffizient ‹Produktionsmethoden›; wirkungslos ‹Argument›; **B** (*inefficient*) untauglich; **C** (*lacking artistic effect*) reizlos

**ineffectively** /ɪnɪ'fektɪvlɪ/ *adv.* unwirksam; ineffektiv

**ineffectiveness** /ɪnɪ'fektɪvnɪs/ *n., no pl.* ⇒ **ineffective**: Unwirksamkeit, *die;* Ineffizienz, *die;* Fruchtlosigkeit, *die;* Wirkungslosigkeit, *die;* Untauglichkeit, *die;* Reizlosigkeit, *die*

**ineffectual** /ɪnɪ'fektjʊəl/ *adj.* unwirksam; ineffektiv; fruchtlos ‹Versuch, Bemühung›; ineffizient ‹Methode, Person›

**ineffectually** /ɪnɪ'fektjʊəlɪ/ *adv.* vergebens; ohne Aussagekraft ‹schreiben›

**inefficacious** /ɪnefɪ'keɪʃəs/ *adj.* unwirksam; wirkungslos

**inefficacy** /ɪn'efɪkəsɪ/ *n., no pl.* (*of measures*) Unwirksamkeit, *die;* Wirkungslosigkeit, *die*

**inefficiency** /ɪnɪ'fɪʃənsɪ/ *n.* Ineffizienz, *die;* (*incapability*) Unfähigkeit, *die*

**inefficient** /ɪnɪ'fɪʃənt/ *adj.* ineffizient; (*incapable*) unfähig; **the worker/machine is ~:** der Arbeiter/die Maschine leistet nicht genug

**inefficiently** /ɪnɪ'fɪʃəntlɪ/ *adv.* ineffizient; **do one's job too ~:** zu wenig leisten

**inelastic** /ɪnɪ'læstɪk, ɪnɪ'lɑ:stɪk/ *adj.* **A** (*not elastic*) unelastisch; **B** (*unadaptable*) nicht flexibel

**inelegance** /ɪn'elɪgəns/ *n., no pl.* **A** (*of dress*) Mangel an Eleganz; (*of gestures, movements, gait*) Schwerfälligkeit, *die;* **B** (*lack of refinement, polish*) Ungeschliffenheit, *die* (*abwertend*)

**inelegant** /ɪn'elɪgənt/ *adj.* **A** unelegant; schwerfällig ‹Bewegung, Gang›; **B** (*unrefined, unpolished*) ungeschliffen (*abwertend*)

**inelegantly** /ɪn'elɪgəntlɪ/ *adv.* **A** unelegant; schwerfällig ‹sich bewegen›; **B** (*without refinement or polish*) ungeschliffen (*abwertend*)

**ineligible** /ɪn'elɪdʒɪbl/ *adj.* ungeeignet; **be ~ for** nicht infrage kommen für ‹Beförderung, Position, Mannschaft›; nicht berechtigt sein zu ‹Leistungen des Staats usw.›; **be ~ for a pension** nicht pensionsberechtigt sein

**ineluctable** /ɪnɪ'lʌktəbl/ *adj.* (*literary*) (*remorseless*) unbarmherzig; (*not to be opposed*) unausweichlich; unentrinnbar (*geh.*) ‹Schicksal›

**inept** /ɪ'nept/ *adj.* **A** (*unskilful, clumsy*) unbeholfen; **B** (*inappropriate*) unangemessen, unpassend ‹Vergleich›; unpassend, unangebracht ‹Bemerkung, Eingreifen›; **C** (*foolish*) albern

**ineptitude** /ɪ'neptɪtju:d/ *n., no pl.* **A** (*unskilfulness, clumsiness*) Unbeholfenheit, *die;* **B** (*inappropriateness*) (*of comparison*) Unangemessenheit, *die;* (*of remark, intervention*) Unangebrachtheit, *die;* **C** (*foolishness*) Albernheit, *die*

**ineptly** /ɪ'neptlɪ/ *adv.* **A** (*unskilfully, clumsily*) unbeholfen; **B** (*inappropriately*) **intervene ~:** in unangebrachter Weise eingreifen; **C** (*foolishly*) albern

**ineptness** ⇒ **ineptitude**

**inequable** /ɪn'ekwəbl/ *adj.* **A** (*not uniform*) ungleichmäßig; **B** (*not fair*) ungleich

**inequality** /ɪnɪ'kwɒlɪtɪ/ *n.* **A** (*lack of equality*) Ungleichheit, *die;* **great inequalities between rich and poor** große Ungleichheit zwischen arm und reich; **educational ~:** Ungleichheit der Bildungschancen; **the inequalities in income** die ungleiche Einkommensverteilung; **B** (*variableness*) Veränderlichkeit, *die;* (*in time*) Unbeständigkeit, *die;* **C** (*irregularity*) Unebenheit, *die;* **D** (*Math.*) Ungleichheit, *die;* (*expression*) Ungleichung, *die*

**inequitable** /ɪn'ekwɪtəbl/ *adj.*, **inequitably** /ɪn'ekwɪtəblɪ/ *adv.* ungerecht

**inequity** /ɪn'ekwɪtɪ/ *n.* Ungerechtigkeit, *die*

**ineradicable** /ɪnɪ'rædɪkəbl/ *adj.* unausrottbar ‹Vorurteil, Aberglaube›

**inert** /ɪ'nɜ:t/ *adj.* **A** reglos; (*sluggish*) träge; (*passive*) untätig; **B** (*Chem.: neutral*) inert

**inert 'gas** *n.* (*Chem.*) Edelgas, *das*

**inertia** /ɪ'nɜ:ʃə, ɪ'nɜ:ʃjə/ *n.* (*also Phys.*) Trägheit, *die;* ⇒ *also* **moment C**

**inertial** /ɪ'nɜ:ʃl/ *adj.* **A** Trägheits-; **B** (*performed automatically*) Automatik-

**inertia: ~ reel** *n.* Aufrollautomatik, *die;* **~ reel seat belt** Automatikgurt, *der;* **~ selling** *n.* unverlangte Warenzusendung

**inertly** /ɪ'nɜ:tlɪ/ *adv.* reglos; (*sluggishly*) träge; (*passively*) untätig

**inescapable** /ɪnɪ'skeɪpəbl/ *adj.* unausweichlich ‹Schlussfolgerung, Logik›; **the facts were ~:** man konnte sich den Tatsachen nicht entziehen

**inessential** /ɪnɪ'senʃl/ **1** *adj.* (*not necessary*) unwesentlich; (*dispensable*) entbehrlich. **2** *n.* Nebensächlichkeit, *die*

**inestimable** /ɪn'estɪməbl/ *adj.* unschätzbar

**inevitability** /ɪnevɪtə'bɪlɪtɪ/ *n., no pl.* Unvermeidlichkeit, *die;* (*of fate, event*) Unabwendbarkeit, *die*

**inevitable** /ɪn'evɪtəbl/ *adj.* unvermeidlich; unabwendbar ‹Ereignis, Krieg, Schicksal›; zwangsläufig ‹Ergebnis, Folge›; **bow to the ~:** sich in das Unvermeidliche fügen

**inevitably** /ɪn'evɪtəblɪ/ *adv.* zwangsläufig

**inexact** /ɪnɪg'zækt/ *adj.* ungenau

**inexactitude** /ɪnɪg'zæktɪtju:d/ ⇒ **inexactness**

**inexactly** /ɪnɪg'zæktlɪ/ *adv.* ungenau

**inexactness** /ɪnɪg'zæktnɪs/ *n.* Ungenauigkeit, *die*

**inexcusable** /ɪnɪk'skju:zəbl/ *adj.*, **inexcusably** /ɪnɪk'skju:zəblɪ/ *adv.* unverzeihlich; unentschuldbar

**inexhaustible** /ɪnɪg'zɔ:stɪbl/ *adj.* unerschöpflich ‹Reserven, Quelle, Energie›; unverwüstlich ‹Person›

**inexorable** /ɪn'eksərəbl/ *adj.*, **inexorably** /ɪn'eksərəblɪ/ *adv.* unerbittlich

**inexpediency** /ɪnɪk'spi:dɪənsɪ/ *n., no pl.* Unklugheit, *die;* (*of plan, measure*) Ungeeignetheit, *die*

**inexpedient** /ɪnɪk'spi:dɪənt/ *adj.* unklug ‹Entscheidung, Politik›; ungeeignet ‹Plan, Maßnahme›; **she thought it somewhat ~ to reveal the names** es erschien ihr wenig ratsam, die Namen preiszugeben

**inexpensive** /ɪnɪk'spensɪv/ *adj.* preisgünstig; **the car is ~ to run** der Wagen ist sparsam im Verbrauch

**inexpensively** /ɪnɪk'spensɪvlɪ/ *adv.* günstig ‹kaufen›; unaufwendig ‹leben›; ohne viel Geld ‹einrichten›

**inexperience** /ɪnɪk'spɪərɪəns/ *n.* Unerfahrenheit, *die;* Mangel an Erfahrung; **his ~ with this machine** seine mangelnde Vertrautheit mit dieser Maschine

**inexperienced** /ɪnɪk'spɪərɪənst/ *adj.* unerfahren; **~ at doing sth.** wenig damit vertraut, etw. zu tun; **~ in sth.** wenig vertraut mit etw.

**inexpert** /ɪn'ekspɜ:t/ *adj.* unerfahren; (*unskilled*) ungeschickt; unsachgemäß ‹Behandlung›

**inexpertly** /ɪn'ekspɜ:tlɪ/ *adv.* ungeschickt; unsachgemäß ‹behandeln›

**inexplicable** /ɪnek'splɪkəbl/ *adj.* unerklärlich

**inexplicably** /ɪnek'splɪkəblɪ/ *adv.* unerklärlich ‹hoch, langsam›; *as sentence-modifier* unerklärlicherweise

**inexpressible** /ɪnɪk'spresɪbl/ *adj.*, **inexpressibly** /ɪnɪk'spresɪblɪ/ *adv.* unbeschreiblich

**inextinguishable** /ɪnɪk'stɪŋgwɪʃəbl/ *adj.* nicht löschbar ‹Feuer, Flamme›; unauslöschlich ‹Liebe, Hoffnung, Sehnsucht, Verlangen›

**in extremis** /ɪn ek'stri:mɪs/ *adv.* **A** (*in great difficulties*) in äußerster Not; **B** (*at point of death*) in extremis (*Med.*); **be ~:** im Sterben liegen

**inextricable** /ɪn'ekstrɪkəbl/ *adj.* **A** (*that cannot be unravelled*) unentwirrbar; **B** unüberschaubar ‹Durcheinander›

**inextricably** /ɪn'ekstrɪkəblɪ/ *adv.* **become ~ entangled** sich vollkommen verheddern (*ugs.*); **[be] ~ linked** untrennbar verbunden [sein]

**INF** *abbr.* **intermediate-range nuclear force** Mittelstrecken-Nuklearkräfte *Pl.*

**infallibility** /ɪnfælɪ'bɪlɪtɪ/ *n., no pl.* Unfehlbarkeit, *die;* **Papal I~:** päpstliche Unfehlbarkeit; Infallibilität, *die* (*kath. Kirche*)

**infallible** /ɪn'fælɪbl/ *adj.*, **infallibly** /ɪn'fælɪblɪ/ *adv.* unfehlbar

**infamous** /'ɪnfəməs/ *adj.* **A** berüchtigt; **of ~ repute** verrufen; **B** (*wicked*) infam; niederträchtig

**infamy** /'ɪnfəmɪ/ *n.* **A** Verrufenheit, *die;* **B** (*wickedness*) Infamie, *die;* Niederträchtigkeit, *die*

**infancy** /ˈɪnfənsɪ/ *n.* Ⓐ frühe Kindheit; Ⓑ (*fig.: early state*) Frühzeit, *die;* **be in its ~:** noch in den Anfängen *od.* Kinderschuhen stecken; Ⓒ (*Law*) Minderjährigkeit, *die*

**infant** /ˈɪnfənt/ ❶ *n.* Ⓐ kleines Kind; **teach ~s** ≈ Vorschulklassen unterrichten; Ⓑ (*Law*) Minderjährige, *der/die.* ❷ *adj.* Ⓐ kindlich; Ⓑ (*fig.: not developed*) in den Anfängen steckend

**infanta** /ɪnˈfæntə/ *n.* (*Hist.*) Infantin, *die*

**infanticide** /ɪnˈfæntɪsaɪd/ *n.* Kindesmord, *der;* (*custom*) Kindestötung, *die*

**infantile** /ˈɪnfəntaɪl/ *adj.* Ⓐ (*relating to infancy*) kindlich; Ⓑ (*childish*) kindisch (*abwertend*); infantil (*abwertend*)

**infant: ~ morˈtality** *n.* Säuglingssterblichkeit, *die;* **~ ˈprodigy** *n.* Wunderkind, *das*

**infantry** /ˈɪnfəntrɪ/ *n. constr. as sing. or pl.* Infanterie, *die*

**infantryman** /ˈɪnfəntrɪmən/ *n., pl.* **infantrymen** /ˈɪnfəntrɪmən/ Infanterist, *der*

**ˈinfant school** *n.* (*Brit.*) ≈ Vorschule, *die; Grundschule für die ersten beiden Jahrgänge*

**infarction** /ɪnˈfɑːkʃn/ *n.* (*Med.*) Infarkt, *der*

**infatuated** /ɪnˈfætjʊeɪtɪd/ *adj.* betört (*geh.*); verzaubert; **be ~ with sb./oneself** in jmdn./sich selbst vernarrt sein

**infatuation** /ɪnfætjʊˈeɪʃn/ *n.* Vernarrtheit, *die* (**with** in + *Akk.*)

**infect** /ɪnˈfekt/ *v.t.* Ⓐ (*contaminate*) verseuchen; Ⓑ (*affect with disease*) infizieren (*Med.*); **~ sb. with sth.** jmdn. mit etw. infizieren *od.* anstecken; **the wound became ~ed** die Wunde entzündete sich; **be ~ed with sth.** (*fig.*) von etw. infiziert sein; Ⓒ (*imbue*) anstecken

**infection** /ɪnˈfekʃn/ *n.* ▶ **1232** Infektion, *die;* **throat/ear/eye ~:** Hals-/Ohren-/Augenentzündung, *die*

**infectious** /ɪnˈfekʃəs/ *adj.* Ⓐ ▶ **1232** infektiös (*Med.*), ansteckend ‹Krankheit›; **be ~** ‹Person:› eine ansteckende Krankheit haben; ansteckend sein (*ugs.*); Ⓑ (*fig.*) ansteckend ‹Heiterkeit, Begeisterung, Lachen›

**infectiously** /ɪnˈfekʃəslɪ/ *adv.* ansteckend ‹lachen usw.›

**infectiousness** /ɪnˈfekʃəsnɪs/ *n., no pl.* Ⓐ Infektiosität, *die* (*Med.*); Ansteckungsfähigkeit, *die;* Ⓑ (*fig.*) **the ~ of her enthusiasm** ihre ansteckend wirkende *od.* mitreißende Begeisterung

**infelicitous** /ɪnfɪˈlɪsɪtəs/ *adj.,* **infelicitously** /ɪnfɪˈlɪsɪtəslɪ/ *adv.* unangebracht

**infelicity** /ɪnfɪˈlɪsɪtɪ/ *n.* Unangebrachtheit, *die;* **infelicities of style** stilistische Ungeschicklichkeiten

**infer** /ɪnˈfɜː(r)/ *v.t.,* **-rr-** schließen (**from** aus); erschließen ‹Voraussetzung›; gewinnen ‹Kenntnisse›; ziehen ‹Schlussfolgerung›

**inference** /ˈɪnfərəns/ *n.* [Schluss]folgerung, *die;* **make ~s** [Schluss]folgerungen ableiten *od.* ziehen; **by ~:** schlussfolgernd

**inferential** /ɪnfəˈrenʃl/ *adj.* Ⓐ auf [Schluss]folgerungen beruhend; schlussfolgernd; Ⓑ (*deduced by inference*) gefolgert

**inferior** /ɪnˈfɪərɪə(r)/ ❶ *adj.* Ⓐ (*of lower quality*) minderwertig ‹Ware›; minder... ‹Qualität›; gering ‹Kenntnis›; unter..., nieder... ‹Klasse, Kaste›; unterlegen ‹Gegner›; **~ to sth.** schlechter als etw.; **feel ~:** Minderwertigkeitsgefühle haben; **feel ~ to sb.** sich jmdm. gegenüber unterlegen fühlen; Ⓑ (*having lower rank*) untergeordnet (**to** *Dat.*); Ⓒ (*Printing*) tiefgestellt ‹Buchstabe, Zahl›. ❷ *n.* Untergebene, *der/die;* **his social ~s** die gesellschaftlich unter ihm Stehenden

**inferiority** /ɪnfɪərɪˈɒrɪtɪ/ *n., no pl.* Unterlegenheit, *die* (**to** gegenüber); (*of goods*) schlechtere Qualität

**inferiˈority complex** *n.* (*Psych.*) Minderwertigkeitskomplex, *der*

**infernal** /ɪnˈfɜːnl/ *adj.* Ⓐ (*of hell*) höllisch; ‹Regionen, Geister, Götter› der Unterwelt; Ⓑ (*hellish*) teuflisch; Ⓒ (*coll.: detestable*) verdammt (*salopp*)

**infernally** /ɪnˈfɜːnəlɪ/ *adv.* (*coll.*) verdammt; **he is too ~ clever for me** er ist, verdammt noch mal, zu clever für mich (*ugs.*)

**inferno** /ɪnˈfɜːnəʊ/ *n., pl.* **~s** Inferno, *das;* **a blazing ~:** ein flammendes Inferno; **the ~ of the blazing house** das Flammenmeer des brennenden Hauses

**infertile** /ɪnˈfɜːtaɪl/ *adj.* unfruchtbar

**infertility** /ɪnfɜːˈtɪlɪtɪ/ *n., no pl.* Unfruchtbarkeit, *die*

**infest** /ɪnˈfest/ *v.t.* ‹Ungeziefer, Schädlinge:› befallen; ‹Unkraut:› überwuchern; (*fig.*) heimsuchen; **~ed with** befallen/überwuchert/heimgesucht von

**infestation** /ɪnfesˈteɪʃn/ *n.* **~ of rats/insects** Ratten-/Insektenplage, *die*

**infidel** /ˈɪnfɪdəl/ *n.* (*Relig. Hist.*) Ungläubige, *der/die*

**infidelity** /ɪnfɪˈdelɪtɪ/ *n.* Untreue, *die* (**to** gegenüber); **infidelities** (*to lover, wife, husband*) Seitensprünge

**ˈinfighting** *n.* Ⓐ (*in organization*) interne Machtkämpfe; Ⓑ (*Boxing*) Nahkampf, *der*

**infiltrate** /ˈɪnfɪltreɪt/ ❶ *v.t.* Ⓐ (*penetrate into*) infiltrieren ‹feindliche Reihen›; unterwandern ‹Partei, Organisation›; Ⓑ (*cause to enter*) einschleusen ‹Agenten›; Ⓒ (*esp. Biol., Med.: pass into, permeate*) infiltrieren. ❷ *v.i.* Ⓐ (*penetrate*) einsickern (*fig.*); **~ into** unterwandern ‹Partei, Organisation›; infiltrieren ‹feindliche Reihen›; Ⓑ ‹Flüssigkeit:› eindringen

**infiltration** /ɪnfɪlˈtreɪʃn/ *n.* Ⓐ (*penetration*) (*of enemy lines*) Infiltration, *die;* (*of party, organization*) Unterwanderung, *die* (**into** *Gen.*); Ⓑ (*of spies, agents*) Einschleusung, *die;* Ⓒ (*of liquid*) Einsickern, *das*

**infiltrator** /ˈɪnfɪltreɪtə(r)/ *n.* Eindringling, *der;* (*of party, organization*) Unterwanderer, *der*

**infinite** /ˈɪnfɪnɪt/ *adj.* Ⓐ (*endless*) unendlich; **I don't have an ~ amount of time/money** ich habe nicht unbegrenzt Zeit/keine unbegrenzten Mittel; Ⓑ (*very great*) ungeheuer; unendlich groß; Ⓒ (*very many*) endlos; **his problems seemed to be ~:** seine Probleme schienen kein Ende zu nehmen; Ⓓ (*Math.*) unendlich

**infinitely** /ˈɪnfɪnɪtlɪ/ *adv.* Ⓐ (*endlessly*) unendlich ‹mitfühlend, dumm usw.›; endlos ‹sich erstrecken, teilbar›; Ⓑ (*vastly*) unendlich; unendlich viel ‹weiser, stärker, besser›

**infinitesimal** /ɪnfɪnɪˈtesɪml/ *adj.* Ⓐ (*Math.*) infinitesimal; ⇒ *also* **calculus** A; Ⓑ (*very small*) äußerst gering; winzig ‹Menge›; **be of ~ value** so gut wie wertlos sein

**infinitive** /ɪnˈfɪnɪtɪv/ (*Ling.*) ❶ *n.* Infinitiv, *der.* ❷ *adj.* Infinitiv-

**infinity** /ɪnˈfɪnɪtɪ/ *n.* Ⓐ (*boundlessness, boundless extent*) Unendlichkeit, *die;* Ⓑ (*indefinite amount*) **an ~ of [stars** *etc.*] unendlich viele [Sterne *usw.*]; Ⓒ (*Geom.: infinite distance*) **at ~:** im Unendlichen ‹sich schneiden›; **focus on ~** (*Photog.*) auf unendlich stellen; Ⓓ (*Math.: infinite quantity*) unendliche Menge

**infirm** /ɪnˈfɜːm/ *adj.* Ⓐ (*weak*) gebrechlich; Ⓑ (*irresolute*) schwach; **~ of purpose** (*literary*) willensschwach

**infirmary** /ɪnˈfɜːmərɪ/ *n.* Ⓐ (*hospital*) Krankenhaus, *das;* Ⓑ (*sick-quarters*) Krankenstation, *die;* (*room*) Krankenzimmer, *das*

**infirmity** /ɪnˈfɜːmɪtɪ/ *n.* Ⓐ *no pl.* (*feebleness*) Gebrechlichkeit, *die;* Ⓑ (*malady*) Gebrechen, *das* (*geh.*); Ⓒ (*weakness of character*) Schwäche, *die*

**in flagrante [delicto]** /ɪn flæˈgræntɪ (dɪˈlɪktəʊ)/ *adv.* in flagranti

**inflame** /ɪnˈfleɪm/ *v.t.* Ⓐ (*excite*) entflammen (*geh.*); **~d with patriotic fever** in patriotischem Fieber entbrannt; Ⓑ (*aggravate*) schüren ‹Feindschaft, Hass›; Ⓒ (*Med.*) **become/be ~d** ‹Auge, Wunde:› sich entzünden/entzündet sein; Ⓓ (*make hot*) erhitzen; **his face was ~d with anger/passion** sein Gesicht glühte vor Zorn/Leidenschaft

**inflammability** /ɪnflæməˈbɪlɪtɪ/ *n., no pl.* Feuergefährlichkeit, *die;* Entflammbarkeit, *die* (*Chemie*)

**inflammable** /ɪnˈflæməbl/ *adj.* Ⓐ (*easily set on fire*) feuergefährlich; leicht entzündlich *od.* entflammbar; **'highly ~'** „feuergefährlich"; Ⓑ explosiv ‹Situation›

**inflammation** /ɪnfləˈmeɪʃn/ *n.* Ⓐ (*Med.*) Entzündung, *die;* Inflammation, *die* (*fachspr.*); Ⓑ (*fig.: of feeling etc.*) Entfachung, *die* (*geh.*)

**inflammatory** /ɪnˈflæmətərɪ/ *adj.* Ⓐ aufrührerisch; **an ~ speech** eine Hetzrede (*abwertend*); Ⓑ (*Med.*) entzündlich

**inflatable** /ɪnˈfleɪtəbl/ ❶ *adj.* aufblasbar; **~ dinghy** Schlauchboot, *das.* ❷ *n.* Ⓐ (*boat*) Schlauchboot, *das;* Ⓑ (*to jump around on*) Luftkissen, *das*

**inflate** /ɪnˈfleɪt/ *v.t.* Ⓐ (*distend*) aufblasen; (*with pump*) aufpumpen; Ⓑ (*Econ.*) in die Höhe treiben ‹Preise, Kosten›; inflationieren ‹Währung›; **~ the economy** Inflationspolitik betreiben; Ⓒ (*fig.: puff up*) **be ~d with pride** von Stolz geschwellt sein

**inflated** /ɪnˈfleɪtɪd/ *adj.* (*lit or fig.*) aufgeblasen; geschwollen ‹Stil›; **have an ~ opinion of oneself** aufgeblasen sein (*ugs. abwertend*); **have an ~ ego** ein übertriebenes Selbstbewusstsein haben

**inflation** /ɪnˈfleɪʃn/ *n.* Ⓐ Aufblasen, *das;* (*with pump*) Aufpumpen, *das;* Ⓑ (*Econ.*) Inflation, *die*

**inflationary** /ɪnˈfleɪʃənərɪ/ *adj.* (*Econ.*) inflationär; **~ policies** Inflationspolitik, *die*

**inˈflation-proofed** *adj.* mit Inflationsausgleich *nachgestellt*

**inflect** /ɪnˈflekt/ *v.t.* Ⓐ (*Ling.*) flektieren; beugen; Ⓑ (*change pitch*) modulieren ‹Stimme›

**inflection** ⇒ **inflexion**

**inflectional** ⇒ **inflexional**

**inflective** /ɪnˈflektɪv/ ⇒ **inflexional**

**inflexibility** /ɪnfleksɪˈbɪlɪtɪ/ *n., no pl.* Ⓐ (*stiffness*) Unbiegsamkeit, *die;* Ⓑ (*obstinacy*) [geistige] Unbeweglichkeit; (*lack of versatility*) mangelnde Flexibilität

**inflexible** /ɪnˈfleksɪbl/ *adj.* Ⓐ (*stiff*) unbiegsam; Ⓑ (*obstinate*) [geistig] unbeweglich ‹Person›; wenig flexibel ‹Einstellung, Meinung›

**inflexion** /ɪnˈflekʃn/ *n.* (*Brit.*) Ⓐ (*in voice*) Tonfall, *der;* **a rising ~:** ein Heben der Stimme; Ⓑ (*bending*) Biegung, *die;* Ⓒ (*Ling.*) (*form*) Flexionsform, *die;* (*suffix*) Flexionsendung, *die*

**inflexional** /ɪnˈflekʃənl/ *adj.* (*Brit. Ling.*) flektierend ‹Sprache›; **~ ending** Flexionsendung, *die*

**inflict** /ɪnˈflɪkt/ *v.t.* zufügen ‹Leid, Schmerzen›, beibringen ‹Wunde›, versetzen ‹Schlag› (**on** *Dat.*); **~ punishment [on sb.]** eine Strafe [über jmdn.] verhängen; [jmdm.] eine Strafe auferlegen (*geh.*); **~ oneself** *or* **one's company on sb.** sich jmdm. aufdrängen

**infliction** /ɪnˈflɪkʃn/ *n.:* ⇒ **inflict**: Zufügen, *das;* Beibringen, *das;* Versetzen, *das;* Verhängung, *die*

**ˈin-flight** *adj.* Bord‹verpflegung, -programm›

**inflorescence** /ɪnfləˈresəns/ *n.* (*Bot.*) Blütenstand, *der*

**ˈinflow** *n.* Zustrom, *der*

**influence** /ˈɪnflʊəns/ ❶ *n.* (*also thing, person*) Einfluss, *der;* **exercise ~:** Einfluss ausüben (**over** auf + *Akk.*); **owe sth. to ~:** etw. seinen guten Beziehungen verdanken; **have ~ with/over sb.** Einfluss bei jmdm./auf jmdn. haben; **use one's ~ to do sth.** seinen Einfluss nutzen, um etw. zu tun; **you have to have ~ to get a job** man muss Beziehungen haben, um eine Stelle zu bekommen; **a person of ~:** eine einflussreiche Persönlichkeit; **be a good/bad/major ~ [on sb.]** einen guten/schlechten/bedeutenden Einfluss [auf jmdn.] ausüben; **under the ~ of alcohol** unter Alkoholeinfluss; **be under the ~** (*coll.*) betrunken sein; **steal a car while under the ~** (*coll.*) in betrunkenem Zustand ein Auto stehlen. ❷ *v.t.* beeinflussen; **be too easily ~d** sich zu leicht beeinflussen lassen

**influential** /ɪnflʊˈenʃl/ *adj.* einflussreich ‹Person›; **be ~ in sb.'s decision/on sb.'s career** jmdn. in seiner Entscheidung beeinflussen/jmds. Karriere beeinflussen; **have been ~ in the successful outcome of sth.** den erfolgreichen Ausgang einer Sache (*Gen.*) beeinflusst haben

**influenza** /ɪnflʊ'enzə/ *n.* ▶ 1232| Grippe, *die;* ⇒ *also* **gastric influenza**
**influx** /'ɪnflʌks/ *n.* Zustrom, *der*
**info** /'ɪnfəʊ/ *n., no pl. (coll.)* Infos *Pl. (ugs.)*
**inform** /ɪn'fɔ:m/ ❶ *v.t.* Ⓐ informieren **(of, about** über + *Akk.*); **I am pleased to ~ you that ...:** ich freue mich, Ihnen mitteilen zu können, dass ...; **keep sb./oneself ~ed** jmdn./sich auf dem Laufenden halten; **he is not very well ~ed** er ist nicht besonders gut informiert; **why wasn't I ~ed?** warum wurde ich nicht [darüber] informiert?; Ⓑ (*animate, inspire*) durchdringen; Ⓒ (*give character or essence to*) prägen. ❷ *v.i.* **~ against** *or* **on sb.** jmdn. anzeigen *od.* (*abwertend*) denunzieren **(to** bei)
**informal** /ɪn'fɔ:ml/ *adj.* Ⓐ (*without formality*) zwanglos; ungezwungen ‹Ton, Sprache›; leger ‹Kleidungsstück›; **'dress: ~'** „keine festliche Garderobe"; Ⓑ (*unofficial*) informell ‹Gespräch, Treffen›
**informality** /ɪnfɔ:'mælɪtɪ/ *n. no pl.* Zwanglosigkeit, *die;* Ungezwungenheit, *die*
**informally** /ɪn'fɔ:məlɪ/ *adv.* Ⓐ (*casually*) zwanglos; leger ‹gekleidet›; Ⓑ (*unofficially*) informell; **talks are proceeding ~:** die Gespräche laufen auf informeller Ebene
**informant** /ɪn'fɔ:mənt/ *n.* Informant, *der*/Informantin, *die;* Gewährsmann, *der*
**informatics** /ɪnfə'mætɪks/ *n. sing. (Brit.)* Informatik, *die*
**information** /ɪnfə'meɪʃn/ *n., no pl.* Ⓐ *no indef. art.* Informationen; **give ~ on sth.** Auskunft über etw. (*Akk.*) erteilen; **piece** *or* **bit of ~:** Information, *die;* **some/any ~:** einige/irgendwelche Informationen; **source of ~:** Informationsquelle, *die;* **where can we get hold of some ~?** wo können wir uns informieren?; wo können wir Auskunft bekommen?; **have ~ about sth.** über etw. (*Akk.*) informiert sein; **have no ~ on sb.** nichts über jmdn. wissen; **we have ~ that ...:** uns (*Dat.*) liegen Informationen [darüber] vor, dass ...; **for your ~:** zu Ihrer Information; (*iron.*) damit du Bescheid weißt!; Ⓑ (*Law*) Anklage, *die*
**information: ~ bureau, ~ centre** *ns.* Auskunftsbüro, *das;* **~ desk** *n.* Informationsschalter, *der;* **~ explosion** *n.* Informationsflut, *die;* **~ highway** *n.* (*Computing*) Datenautobahn, *die;* **~ office** ⇒ **~ bureau**; **~ pack** *n.* Informationspaket, *das;* (*folder etc.*) Informationsmappe, *die;* (*for journalists*) Pressemappe, *die;* **~ retrieval** *n.* (*Computing*) Retrieval, *das;* **~ retrieval system** Retrievalsystem, *das;* **~ science** *n.* Informatik, *die;* **~ scientist** *n.* Informatiker, *der*/Informatikerin, *die;* **~ superhighway** *n.* (*Computing*) Datenautobahn, *die;* Datensuperhighway, *der;* **~ system** *n.* Informationssystem, *das;* **management ~ system** Managementinformationssystem, *das;* **~ technology** *n.* Informationstechnologie, *die;* Informationstechnik, *die;* **~ theory** *n.* Informationstheorie, *die*
**informative** /ɪn'fɔ:mətɪv/ *adj.* informativ; **not very ~:** nicht sehr aufschlussreich ‹Dokument, Schriftstück›; **he was not very ~ about his qualifications** er war nicht sehr mitteilsam, was seine Qualifikationen anbelangte
**informed** /ɪn'fɔ:md/ *adj.* Ⓐ informiert; fundiert ‹Schätzung›; **very ~:** sehr gut informiert; ⇒ *also* **ill-informed**; **well-informed**; Ⓑ (*educated*) kultiviert; **~ opinion suggests that ...:** Kundige meinen, dass ...
**informer** /ɪn'fɔ:mə(r)/ *n.* Denunziant, *der*/Denunziantin, *die* (*abwertend*); Informant, *der*/Informantin, *die;* **police ~:** Polizeispitzel, *der* (*abwertend*)
**infraction** /ɪn'frækʃn/ *n.* Übertretung, *die;* Regelverstoß, *der* (*Sport*)
**infra dig.** /ɪnfrə'dɪg/ *pred. adj. (coll.)* unter meiner/seiner *usw.* Würde
**infra-red** /ɪnfrə'red/ *adj.* Ⓐ infrarot; Ⓑ (*using ~ radiation*) Infrarot-
**infrastructure** /'ɪnfrəstrʌktʃə(r)/ *n.* Infrastruktur, *die*
**infrequency** /ɪn'fri:kwənsɪ/ *n., no pl.* Seltenheit, *die*
**infrequent** /ɪn'fri:kwənt/ *adj.* Ⓐ (*uncommon*) selten; Ⓑ (*sparse*) vereinzelt
**infrequently** /ɪn'fri:kwəntlɪ/ *adv.* selten
**infringe** /ɪn'frɪndʒ/ ❶ *v.t.* verstoßen gegen. ❷ *v.i.* **~ [up]on** verstoßen gegen ‹Recht, Gesetz usw.›; unbefugt betreten ‹Privatgelände usw.›; **~ upon sb.'s privacy** jmds. Privatsphäre verletzen
**infringement** /ɪn'frɪndʒmənt/ *n.* Ⓐ (*violation*) Verstoß, *der* (**of** gegen); **~ of the contract** Vertragsverletzung, *die;* Vertragsbruch, *der;* Ⓑ (*encroachment*) Übergriff, *der* (**on** auf + *Akk.*); (*on privacy*) Eingriff, *der* (**on** in + *Akk.*)
**infuriate** /ɪn'fjʊərɪeɪt/ *v.t.* wütend machen; **be ~d** wütend sein (**by** über + *Akk.*)
**infuriating** /ɪn'fjʊərɪeɪtɪŋ/ *adj.* **she is an ~ person** sie kann einen zur Raserei bringen; **it is ~ when/that ...:** es ist wahnsinnig ärgerlich, wenn/dass ... (*ugs.*); **he has some ~ habits** er hat einige Angewohnheiten, die einen rasend machen können; **~ calmness/slowness** aufreizende Gelassenheit/Langsamkeit
**infuriatingly** /ɪn'fjʊərɪeɪtɪŋlɪ/ *adv.* aufreizend ‹gleichgültig, langsam›
**infuse** /ɪn'fju:z/ ❶ *v.t.* Ⓐ (*instil*) **~ sth. into sb., ~ sb. with sth.** jmdm. etw. einflößen *od.* (*geh.*) eingeben; **~ new life into an ancient institution** eine altehrwürdige Institution mit neuem Leben erfüllen; **~ vitality into** mit Vitalität erfüllen; **be ~d with new hope** neue Hoffnung schöpfen; Ⓑ (*steep*) aufgießen ‹Tee usw.›. ❷ *v.i.* ‹Tee usw.:› ziehen; **let the tea [stand to] ~:** den Tee ziehen lassen
**infusion** /ɪn'fju:ʒn/ *n.* Ⓐ (*Med.*) Infusion, *die;* **an ~ of new blood into the organization is essential** (*fig.*) die Organisation braucht dringend frisches Blut; Ⓑ (*imparting*) Einflößen, *das;* Ⓒ (*steeping*) Aufgießen, *das;* Ⓓ (*liquid*) Aufguss, *der*
**ingenious** /ɪn'dʒi:nɪəs/ *adj.* Ⓐ (*resourceful*) einfallsreich; (*skilful*) geschickt; Ⓑ (*cleverly constructed*) genial ‹Methode, Idee›; raffiniert ‹Spielzeug, Werkzeug, Maschine›
**ingeniously** /ɪn'dʒi:nɪəslɪ/ *adv.* genial; raffiniert ‹konstruiert›
**ingénue** /'æ̃ʒeɪnju:/ *n.* unschuldiges junges Mädchen; (*Theatre*) Naive, *die*
**ingenuity** /ɪndʒɪ'nju:ɪtɪ/ *n., no pl.* Ⓐ (*resourcefulness*) Einfallsreichtum, *der;* (*skill*) Geschicklichkeit, *die;* Ⓑ (*cleverness of construction*) Genialität, *die;* **a plan of some ~:** ein recht raffinierter Plan
**ingenuous** /ɪn'dʒenjʊəs/ *adj.* Ⓐ (*frank*) freimütig; Ⓑ (*innocent*) naiv; unschuldig ‹Augen, Lächeln›
**ingenuously** /ɪn'dʒenjʊəslɪ/ *adv.* freimütig
**ingest** /ɪn'dʒest/ *v.t.* aufnehmen
**ingestion** /ɪn'dʒestʃn/ *n.* Aufnahme, *die;* **~ of food** Nahrungsaufnahme, *die*
**inglenook** /'ɪŋglnʊk/ *n.* Kaminecke, *die*
**inglorious** /ɪn'glɔ:rɪəs/ *adj.* unrühmlich; schmählich (*geh.*) ‹Niederlage›
**ingot** /'ɪŋgət/ *n.* Ingot, *der* (*Metall.*)
**ingrained** /'ɪngreɪnd, ɪn'greɪnd/ *adj.* Ⓐ (*embedded*) **the stain was deeply ~ in the fibres** der Fleck war tief in die Fasern eingedrungen; **hands ~ with dirt** stark verschmutzte Hände; Ⓑ (*fig.*) tief eingewurzelt ‹Vorurteil usw.›; Ⓒ (*thorough*) eingefleischt ‹Skeptiker usw.›
**ingrate** /'ɪngreɪt, ɪn'greɪt/ *n.* (*arch.*) Undankbare, *der/die;* **be an ~:** undankbar sein
**ingratiate** /ɪn'greɪʃɪeɪt/ *v. refl.* **~ oneself with sb.** sich bei jmdm. einschmeicheln
**ingratiating** /ɪn'greɪʃɪeɪtɪŋ/ *adj.* schmeichlerisch
**ingratitude** /ɪn'grætɪtju:d/ *n., no pl.* Undankbarkeit, *die* (**to[wards]** gegenüber)
**ingredient** /ɪn'gri:dɪənt/ *n.* Zutat, *die;* Ingredienz, *die;* **the ~s of a successful marriage** (*fig.*) die Voraussetzungen für eine gute Ehe; **all the ~s of success** (*fig.*) alles, was man zum Erfolg braucht
**'in-group** *n.* Ingroup, *die* (*Soziol.*); Eigengruppe, *die* (*Soziol.*)
**ingrowing** /'ɪngrəʊɪŋ/ *adj.* eingewachsen ‹Zehennagel usw.›
**inhabit** /ɪn'hæbɪt/ *v.t.* bewohnen; **the region was ~ed by penguins/the Celts** in der Gegend lebten Pinguine/die Kelten; **a region ~ed by a rich flora** eine Gegend mit einer reichen Flora
**inhabitable** /ɪn'hæbɪtəbl/ *adj.* bewohnbar
**inhabitant** /ɪn'hæbɪtənt/ *n.* Bewohner, *der*/Bewohnerin, *die;* (*of village etc. also*) Einwohner, *der*/Einwohnerin, *die;* **that district has few ~s** in diesem Bezirk leben nur wenige Menschen
**inhalant** /ɪn'heɪlənt/ *n.* (*Med.*) Inhalationsmittel, *das*
**inhalation** /ɪnhə'leɪʃn/ *n.* (*Med.*) Inhalation, *die*
**inhale** /ɪn'heɪl/ ❶ *v.t.* (*breathe in*) einatmen; (*take into the lungs*) inhalieren (*ugs.*) ‹Zigarettenrauch usw.›; (*Med.*) inhalieren. ❷ *v.i.* einatmen; (*Med.*) inhalieren; ‹Raucher:› inhalieren (*ugs.*), über die Lunge rauchen
**inhaler** /ɪn'heɪlə(r)/ *n.* (*Med.*) Inhalationsapparat, *der*
**inharmonious** /ɪnhɑ:'məʊnɪəs/ *adj.* Ⓐ disharmonisch; misstönend; Ⓑ (*fig.*) unharmonisch
**inharmoniously** /ɪnhɑ:'məʊnɪəslɪ/ *adv.* Ⓐ disharmonisch; Ⓑ (*fig.*) unharmonisch
**inhere** /ɪn'hɪə(r)/ *v.i.* **~ in sth.** einer Sache (*Dat.*) innewohnen (*geh.*); einer Sache (*Dat.*) inhärieren (*Philos.*)
**inherent** /ɪn'hɪərənt, ɪn'herənt/ *adj.* (*belonging by nature*) innewohnend (*geh.*); natürlich ‹Anmut, Eleganz›; inhärent (*Philos.*); **our ~ indolence** die uns (*Dat.*) innewohnende Trägheit
**inherently** /ɪn'hɪərəntlɪ, ɪn'herəntlɪ/ *adv.* von Natur aus
**inherit** /ɪn'herɪt/ *v.t.* erben
**inheritable** /ɪn'herɪtəbl/ *adj.* erblich; **~ disease** Erbkrankheit, *die*
**inheritance** /ɪn'herɪtəns/ *n.* Ⓐ (*what is inherited*) Erbe, *das;* **come into one's ~:** sein Erbe antreten; Ⓑ *no pl.* (*inheriting*) Erbschaft, *die*
**in'heritance tax** *n.* Erbschaftssteuer, *die*
**inhibit** /ɪn'hɪbɪt/ *v.t.* hemmen; **~ sb. from doing sth.** jmdn. daran hindern, etw. zu tun
**inhibited** /ɪn'hɪbɪtɪd/ *adj.* gehemmt
**inhibition** /ɪnhɪ'bɪʃn/ *n.* Ⓐ Unterdrückung, *die;* Ⓑ (*Psych.*) Hemmung, *die;* Ⓒ (*coll.: emotional resistance*) Hemmung, *die;* **without ~:** hemmungslos; **have no ~s about doing sth.** keine Hemmungen haben, etw. zu tun
**inhomogeneity** /ɪnhɒmədʒɪ'ni:ɪtɪ, ɪnhəʊmədʒɪ'ni:ɪtɪ/ *n.* Ⓐ *no pl.* (*lack of homogeneity*) Inhomogenität, *die;* Ⓑ (*irregularity*) Unregelmäßigkeit, *die*
**inhomogeneous** /ɪnhɒmə'dʒi:nɪəs, ɪnhəʊmə'dʒi:nɪəs/ *adj.* inhomogen
**inhospitable** /ɪnhɒs'pɪtəbl/ *adj.* Ⓐ ungastlich ‹Person, Verhalten›; Ⓑ unwirtlich ‹Gegend, Klima›
**'in-house** *adj.* hausintern
**inhuman** /ɪn'hju:mən/ *adj.* Ⓐ (*brutal*) unmenschlich ‹Tyrann, Grausamkeit, Strenge›; inhuman ‹Arbeitgeber, Verhalten›; Ⓑ (*not human*) nicht menschlich
**inhumane** /ɪnhju:'meɪn/ *adj.* unmenschlich; inhuman (*geh.*); menschenunwürdig ‹Zustände, Behandlung›
**inhumanity** /ɪnhju:'mænɪtɪ/ *n.* ⇒ **inhumane**: Unmenschlichkeit, *die;* Inhumanität, *die* (*geh.*); Menschenunwürdigkeit, *die;* **man's ~ to man** die Unmenschlichkeit unter den Menschen
**inimical** /ɪ'nɪmɪkl/ *adj.* Ⓐ (*hostile*) feindselig ‹Blick, Beziehungen›; feindlich [gesinnt] ‹Macht›; **be ~ to sb.** jmdm. feindlich gesinnt sein; jmdm. Feind sein (*geh.*); Ⓑ (*harmful*) abträglich (**to** *Dat.*) (*geh.*); nachteilig (**to** für); schädlich (**to** für)
**inimitable** /ɪ'nɪmɪtəbl/ *adj.* unnachahmlich ‹Gabe, Fähigkeit›; einzigartig ‹Persönlichkeit›
**iniquitous** /ɪ'nɪkwɪtəs/ *adj.* Ⓐ (*wicked*) schändlich; Ⓑ (*unjust*) ungerecht ‹Urteil›; ungeheuer hoch ‹Preis›

**iniquity** /ɪ'nɪkwɪtɪ/ *n.* Ⓐ (*wickedness*) Schändlichkeit, *die;* (*sin*) Missetat, *die;* Ⓑ (*injustice*) Ungerechtigkeit, *die*

**initial** /ɪ'nɪʃl/ ❶ *adj.* anfänglich; zu Anfang auftretend ‹Symptome›; Anfangs‹stadium, -schwierigkeiten›; ~ **costs** *or* **expenses** Startkosten. ❷ *n. esp. in pl.* Initiale, *die;* **what do the ~s s.a.e. stand for?** wofür steht *od.* was bedeutet die Abkürzung s.a.e.? ❸ *v.t.*, (*Brit.*) **-ll-** abzeichnen ‹Scheck, Quittung, Beleg›; paraphieren ‹Vertrag, Abkommen usw.›

**initial 'letter** *n.* Anfangsbuchstabe, *der*

**initially** /ɪ'nɪʃəlɪ/ *adv.* anfangs; am *od.* zu Anfang

**initiate** ❶ /ɪ'nɪʃɪeɪt/ *v.t.* Ⓐ (*admit*) [feierlich] aufnehmen; initiieren (*Soziol.*, *Völkerk.*); (*introduce*) einführen (**into** in + *Akk.*); ~ **sb. into sth.** (*into club, group, etc.*) jmdn. in etw. (*Akk.*) aufnehmen; (*into knowledge, mystery, etc.*) jmdn. in etw. (*Akk.*) einweihen; Ⓑ (*begin*) initiieren (*geh.*); in die Wege leiten ‹Vorhaben›; einleiten ‹Verhandlungen, Reformen›; eröffnen ‹Diskussion, Verhandlung, Feierlichkeiten, Feindseligkeiten›; anstrengen ‹Prozess, Klage›. ❷ /ɪ'nɪʃɪət/ *n.* Eingeweihte, *der/die*

**initiation** /ɪnɪʃɪ'eɪʃn/ *n.* Ⓐ (*beginning*) Initiierung, *die* (*geh.*); (*of hostilities, discussion, negotiation, festivities*) Eröffnung, *die;* (*of reforms, negotiations*) Einleitung, *die;* Ⓑ (*admission*) Aufnahme, *die* (**into** in + *Akk.*); (*into knowledge, mystery, etc.*) Einweihung, *die;* Initiation, *die* (*Soziol.*, *Völkerk.*); (*introduction*) Einführung, *die* (**into** in + *Akk.*); ~ **ceremony** Aufnahmezeremonie, *die;* Initiationsritus, *der* (*Soziol.*, *Völkerk.*)

**initiative** /ɪ'nɪʃətɪv, ɪ'nɪʃɪətɪv/ *n.* Ⓐ (*power*) **the ~ is ours/lies with them** die Initiative liegt bei uns/ihnen; **have the ~** (*Mil.*) den Kampf bestimmen; Ⓑ *no pl., no indef. art.* (*ability*) Initiative, *die;* **lack ~:** keine Initiative haben *od.* besitzen; Ⓒ (*first step*) Initiative, *die;* **take the ~:** die Initiative ergreifen; den ersten Schritt tun; **on one's own ~:** aus eigener Initiative; Ⓓ (*citizen's right to initiate legislation*) Gesetzesinitiative, *die*

**initiator** /ɪ'nɪʃɪeɪtə(r)/ *n.* Initiator, *der*/Initiatorin, *die*

**inject** /ɪn'dʒekt/ *v.t.* Ⓐ [ein]spritzen; injizieren (*Med.*); Ⓑ (*put fluid into*) ~ **a vein with sth.** etw. in eine Vene spritzen *od.* (*Med.*) injizieren; ~ **a mould with plastic** Plastik in eine Form spritzen; Ⓒ (*administer sth. to*) ~ **sb. with sth.** jmdm. etw. spritzen *od.* (*Med.*) injizieren; ~ **sb. against smallpox** jmdn. gegen Pocken impfen; Ⓓ (*fig.*) pumpen ‹Geld›; ~ **new life/vigour into sth.** einer Sache (*Dat.*) neues Leben geben/neue Kraft verleihen

**injection** /ɪn'dʒekʃn/ *n.* ▶ **1232** Ⓐ (*injecting*) Einspritzung, *die;* Injektion, *die* (*Med.*); **give sb. an ~:** jmdm. eine Spritze *od.* Injektion geben; Ⓑ (*liquid injected*) Injektion, *die;* Injektionslösung, *die;* Ⓒ (*fig.*) ~ **of money/capital, financial ~:** Geldzuschuss, *der;* Finanzspritze, *die* (*ugs.*); ⇒ *also* **fuel injection**

**in'jection moulding** *n.* Spritzguss, *der*

**injudicious** /ɪndʒu:'dɪʃəs/ *adj.* unklug; ungünstig ‹Moment›

**Injun** /'ɪndʒən/ *n.* (*coll.*) Indianer, *der*/Indianerin, *die*

**injunction** /ɪn'dʒʌŋkʃn/ *n.* Ⓐ (*order*) Verfügung, *die;* Ⓑ (*Law*) [richterliche] Verfügung; **a court ~:** eine richterliche Verfügung

**injure** /'ɪndʒə(r)/ *v.t.* Ⓐ (*hurt*) verletzen; (*fig.*) verletzen ‹Stolz, Gefühle›; kränken ‹Person›; **his leg was ~d** er wurde/(*state*) war am Bein verletzt; **six people were badly ~d** es gab sechs Schwerverletzte; Ⓑ (*impair*) schaden (+ *Dat.*); schädigen ‹Gesundheit›; beeinträchtigen ‹Beziehungen›; Ⓒ (*do harm to*) schädigen ‹Ruf, Ansehen›

**injured** /'ɪndʒəd/ *adj.* Ⓐ (*hurt, lit. or fig.*) verletzt; verwundet ‹Soldat›; **because of his ~ hand** wegen seiner Handverletzung; **the ~:** die Verletzten/Verwundeten; Ⓑ (*wronged*) geschädigt; hintergangen, betrogen ‹Ehemann›; **the ~ party** (*Law*) der/die Geschädigte; Ⓒ (*offended*) gekränkt ‹Stimme, Blick›; verletzt, beleidigt ‹Person›; **with an ~ air** mit gekränkter Miene; **speak in an ~ voice** mit gekränkter Stimme sprechen

**injurious** /ɪn'dʒʊərɪəs/ *adj.* Ⓐ (*wrongful*) ungerecht ‹Behandlung›; Ⓑ (*hurtful*) schädlich; **be ~ to sb./sth.** jmdm./einer Sache schaden; **smoking is ~ to health** Rauchen schadet der Gesundheit

**injury** /'ɪndʒərɪ/ *n.* Ⓐ (*harm*) Verletzung, *die* (**to** *Gen.*); **risk ~ to life and limb** Leben und Gesundheit aufs Spiel setzen; Ⓑ (*instance of harm*) Verletzung, *die* (**to** *Gen.*); (*fig.*) Kränkung, *die* (**to** *Gen.*); **add insult to ~:** das Ganze noch schlimmer machen; **do sb./oneself an ~:** jmdm./sich wehtun; **I'll do him an ~ if he doesn't shut up!** (*coll.*) ich tu ihm jetzt [gleich] was, wenn er nicht ruhig ist!; Ⓒ (*wrongful action*) Verletzung, *die* (*to Gen.*)

**'injury time** *n.* (*Brit. Footb.*) Nachspielzeit, *die;* **be into/play ~:** nachspielen

**injustice** /ɪn'dʒʌstɪs/ *n.* Ⓐ (*unfairness*) Ungerechtigkeit, *die;* **fight against ~:** gegen die Ungerechtigkeit *od.* das Unrecht kämpfen; **protest at the ~ of a statement** gegen eine ungerechte Behauptung protestieren; Ⓑ (*wrong act*) Ungerechtigkeit, *die;* **do sb. an ~:** jmdm. unrecht tun

**ink** /ɪŋk/ ❶ *n.* Ⓐ Tinte, *die;* (*for stamp pad*) Farbe, *die;* (*for drawing*) Tusche, *die;* **my ballpoint has run out of ~:** meine [Kugelschreiber]mine ist leer; Ⓑ (*in printing*) Druckfarbe, *die;* (*in duplicating, newsprint*) Druckerschwärze, *die;* Ⓒ (*Zool.*) Tinte, *die.* ❷ *v.t.* Ⓐ ~ **in** mit Tinte/Tusche nachziehen ‹Bleistiftstrich usw.›; mit Tusche ausmalen ‹Teil eines Bildes›; ~ **over** mit Tusche übermalen ‹Papier, Blatt›; Ⓑ (*apply ink to*) einfärben ‹Druckform›; mit Farbe schwärzen ‹Stempel›

**'ink bottle** *n.* Tintenfass, *das*

**'ink-jet printer** *n.* Tintenstrahldrucker, *der*

**inkling** /'ɪŋklɪŋ/ *n.* Ahnung, *die;* **I haven't an ~:** ich habe nicht die leiseste Ahnung *od.* (*ugs.*) keinen blassen Schimmer; **have an ~ of sth.** etw. ahnen; **get an ~ of sth.** etw. merken; Wind von etw. bekommen (*ugs.*)

**ink: ~-pad** *n.* Stempelkissen, *das;* **~well** *n.* [eingelassenes] Tintenfass

**inky** /'ɪŋkɪ/ *adj.* Ⓐ (*covered with ink*) tintenbeschmiert; tintig; **I have ~ fingers** meine Finger sind voller Tinte; Ⓑ (*black*) tintenschwarz; tintig

**inlaid** ⇒ **inlay** 1

**inland** ❶ /'ɪnlənd, 'ɪnlænd/ *adj.* Ⓐ (*placed ~*) Binnen-; binnenländisch; ~ **town** Stadt im Landesinneren; **an ~ state** ein Binnenstaat; Ⓑ (*carried on ~*) inländisch; Binnen‹handel, -verkehr›; Inlands‹brief, -paket, -gebühren›. ❷ /ɪn'lænd/ *adv.* landeinwärts; im Landesinneren ‹leben›

**inland: ~ navi'gation** *n.* Binnenschifffahrt, *die;* ~ **'revenue** *n.* Steuereinnahmen *Pl.;* **I~ 'Revenue** *n.* (*Brit.*) ≈ Finanzamt, *das;* ~ **'sea** *n.* Binnenmeer, *das*

**'in-law** *n., usu. in pl.* (*coll.*) angeheirateter Verwandter/angeheiratete Verwandte; **~s** (*parents-in-law*) Schwiegereltern

**inlay** ❶ /-'-/ *v.t.*, **inlaid** Ⓐ (*embed*) einlassen; Ⓑ (*ornament*) einlegen. ❷ /'--/ *n.* Ⓐ (*work*) Einlegearbeit, *die;* Intarsie, *die;* Ⓑ (*material*) **~s** Intarsien *Pl.* (**of** aus); Ⓒ (*Dent.*) Inlay, *das*

**inlet** /'ɪnlet, 'ɪnlɪt/ *n.* Ⓐ [schmale] Bucht; Ⓑ (*piece inserted*) eingelegtes Stück; Einsatz, *der;* Ⓒ (*way of entry*) Einlassöffnung, *die;* ~ **pipe** Zuleitungsrohr, *das;* Zuleitung, *die;* ~ **valve** Einlassventil, *das*

**in-liners** /ɪn'laɪnəz/, **'in-line skates** *ns. pl.* Inliner, *Pl.;* Inlineskates, *Pl.*

**'inmate** *n.* (*of hospital, prison, etc.*) Insasse, *der*/Insassin, *die;* (*of house*) Bewohner, *der*/Bewohnerin, *die*

**in memoriam** /ɪn mɪ'mɔ:rɪæm/ *n.* Gedenkinschrift, *die*

**inmost** /'ɪnməʊst, 'ɪnmɒst/ *adj.* Ⓐ (*deepest*) tiefst...; Ⓑ (*fig.: most inward*) innerst... ‹Gefühle, Wesen›

**inn** /ɪn/ *n.* Ⓐ (*hotel*) Herberge, *die* (*veralt.*); Gasthof, *der;* **no room at the ~** (*fig.*) alles ausgebucht (*scherzh.*); Ⓑ (*pub*) Wirtshaus, *das;* Gastwirtschaft, *die;* **'The Swan Inn'** „Wirtshaus zum Schwan"

**innards** /'ɪnədz/ *n. pl.* (*coll.*) Eingeweide *Pl.;* (*in animals for slaughter*) Innereien *Pl.*

**innate** /ɪ'neɪt, 'ɪneɪt/ *adj.* Ⓐ (*inborn*) angeboren; natürlich ‹Schönheit, Fähigkeit›; **be ~ in sb.** jmdm. angeboren sein; **we all have an ~ desire for happiness** das Streben nach Glück ist uns allen angeboren; Ⓑ (*Philos.*) angeboren ‹Ideen›

**inner** /'ɪnə(r)/ *adj.* Ⓐ inner...; Innen‹hof, -tür, -fläche, -seite usw.›; ~ **ear** (*Anat.*) Innenohr, *das;* Ⓑ (*fig.*) inner... ‹Gefühl, Wesen, Zweifel, Ängste›; verborgen ‹Bedeutung›; ~ **life** Seelenleben, *das;* ~ **circle of friends** engster Freundeskreis; ⇒ *also* **bar**[1] 1 I

**inner: ~ 'city** *n.* Innenstadt, *die;* City, *die;* ~ **city areas** Innenbezirke; Innenstadtgebiete; ~ **man** *n.* (*soul, mind*) Innere, *das;* **the needs of the ~ man** die inneren Bedürfnisse

**innermost** /'ɪnəməʊst/ *adj.* innerst...; **one's ~ thoughts** seine geheimsten Gedanken; **in the ~ depths of the forest** im tiefsten Wald

**inner: ~-spring** (*Amer.*) ⇒ **interior-sprung**; ~ **tube** *n.* Schlauch, *der*

**'inner woman** ⇒ **inner man**

**inning** /'ɪnɪŋ/ *n.* (*Amer. Baseball*) Inning, *das*

**innings** /'ɪnɪŋz/ *n., pl. same or* (*coll.*) **~es** Ⓐ (*Cricket*) Durchgang, *der;* Innings, *das* (*fachspr.*); Ⓑ (*period of office*) Amtszeit, *die;* (*dominance of political party*) Legislaturperiode, *die;* Ⓒ (*period of life etc.*) **a good ~:** eine gute Gelegenheit; **he had a good/long ~:** er hatte ein langes, ausgefülltes Leben

**'innkeeper** *n.* [Gast]wirt, *der*/-wirtin, *die*

**innocence** /'ɪnəsəns/ *n., no pl.* Ⓐ Unschuld, *die;* **a presumption of ~:** eine Unschuldsvermutung; **lose one's ~:** die Unschuld verlieren; Ⓑ (*freedom from cunning*) Naivität, *die;* Ⓒ (*lack of knowledge*) Unkenntnis, *die;* **in all ~:** in aller Unschuld; **in all ~ of the fact that ...:** ohne die leiseste Ahnung davon zu haben, dass ...

**innocent** /'ɪnəsənt/ ❶ *adj.* Ⓐ unschuldig (**of** an + *Dat.*); **be ~ of the charge/accusation** unschuldig sein; **the ~ party** der/die Unschuldige; **he is not as ~ as he appears** er ist nicht der Unschuldsengel, der er scheint (*ugs.*); Ⓑ (*simple*) einfältig; naiv ‹Wortwahl›; Ⓒ (*harmless*) harmlos; Ⓓ (*naïve*) unschuldig; **he is ~ about the ways of the world** er ist völlig unerfahren; Ⓔ (*pretending to be guileless*) arglos, unschuldig ‹Blick, Erscheinung›; **adopt an ~ air** eine Unschuldsmiene aufsetzen. ❷ *n.* (*innocent person*) Unschuldige, *der/die;* **he was such an ~ when he went to London** er war noch so unschuldig *od.* unverdorben, als er nach London ging

**innocently** /'ɪnəsəntlɪ/ *adv.* unschuldig ‹blicken›; in aller Unschuld ‹etw. sagen, tun›

**innocuous** /ɪ'nɒkjʊəs/ *adj.* (*not injurious*) unschädlich ‹Tier, Mittel›; (*inoffensive*) harmlos

**innocuously** /ɪ'nɒkjʊəslɪ/ *adv.* harmlos

**Inn of 'Court** *n., pl.* **Inns of Court** (*Brit.*) (*society*) *englischer Anwaltsverband;* (*building*) *Gebäude dieses Verbandes*

**innovate** /'ɪnəveɪt/ *v.i.* Ⓐ (*bring in novelties*) Innovationen vornehmen; innovieren (*fachspr.*); Ⓑ (*make changes*) Änderungen vornehmen

**innovation** /ɪnə'veɪʃn/ *n.* Ⓐ (*introduction of something new*) Innovation, *die* (*geh.*, *fachspr.*); (*thing introduced*) Neuerung, *die;* Ⓑ (*change*) [Ver]änderung, *die;* Neuerung, *die;* Innovation, *die* (*geh.*, *fachspr.*)

**innovative** /'ɪnəvətɪv/ *adj.* innovativ

**innovator** /'ɪnəveɪtə(r)/ *n.* Neuerer, *der*/Neuerin, *die*

**'inn sign** *n.* Gasthausschild, *das*

**innuendo** /ɪnju:'endəʊ/ *n., pl.* **~es** *or* **~s** versteckte Andeutung; Anspielung, *die;* Innuendo, *das* (*geh.*); **make ~es about sb.** über jmdn. Andeutungen fallen lassen *od.* machen

**innumerable** /ɪ'nju:mərəbl/ *adj.* unzählig; zahllos; (*uncountable*) unzählbar

**innumeracy** /ɪ'nju:mərəsɪ/ *n., no pl.* (*Brit.*) Nicht-rechnen-Können, *das*

**innumerate** /ɪ'nju:mərət/ *adj.* (*Brit.*) **be ~:** nicht rechnen können; des Rechnens unkundig sein (*geh.*)

**inoculate** /ɪ'nɒkjʊleɪt/ *v.t.* **(A)** (*treat by injection*) impfen (**against, for** gegen); **(B)** (*implant*) einimpfen (**into** in + *Akk.*); **~ sb. with a virus** jmdm. einen Virus einimpfen

**inoculation** /ɪnɒkjʊ'leɪʃn/ *n.* Impfung, *die*, Inokulation, *die* (*Med.*) (**against, for** gegen); **give sb. an ~:** jmdn. impfen

**inoffensive** /ɪnə'fensɪv/ *adj.* **(A)** (*unoffending*) harmlos; gutartig ‹Tier›; **(B)** (*not objectionable*) harmlos ‹Bemerkung›; unaufdringlich ‹Geruch, Art, Person›; **be ~ to the eye** dem Auge nicht wehtun

**inoffensively** /ɪnə'fensɪvlɪ/ *adv.* harmlos

**inoperable** /ɪn'ɒpərəbl/ *adj.* **(A)** (*Surg.*) inoperabel (*fachspr.*); nicht operierbar; **(B)** (*fig.*) undurchführbar ‹Politik›

**inoperative** /ɪn'ɒpərətɪv/ *adj.* ungültig; außer Kraft *nicht attr.*; **render sth. ~:** etw. außer Betrieb setzen

**inopportune** /ɪn'ɒpətju:n/ *adj.* inopportun (*geh.*); unpassend, unangebracht ‹Bemerkung›; ungelegen, unpassend ‹Augenblick, Besuch›; **it was very ~ that …:** es kam sehr ungelegen, dass …

**inopportunely** /ɪn'ɒpətju:nlɪ/ *adv.* zur Unzeit ‹kommen›; unpassenderweise, im unpassenden Moment ‹vorbringen, äußern›

**inordinate** /ɪ'nɔ:dɪnət/ *adj.* (*immoderate*) unmäßig; ungeheuer ‹[Menschen]menge›; überzogen, übertrieben ‹Forderung›; **an ~ amount of work/money** ungeheuer viel Arbeit/eine Unmenge Geld

**inordinately** /ɪ'nɔ:dɪnətlɪ/ *adv.* unmäßig; ungeheuer ‹groß, hoch, weit usw.›; **he is ~ fond of …:** seine Zuneigung zu … ist übertrieben

**inorganic** /ɪnɔ:'gænɪk/ *adj.* **(A)** (*Chem.*) anorganisch; **(B)** (*fig.*) unorganisch (*geh.*)

**inorganic 'chemist** *n.* Anorganiker, *der*/Anorganikerin, *die*

**'inpatient** *n.* stationär behandelter Patient/behandelte Patientin; **be an ~:** stationär behandelt werden

**'input** ❶ *n.* **(A)** (*esp. Computing: what is put in*) Input, *der od. das;* (*of capital*) Investition, *die;* (*of manpower*) [Arbeits]aufwand, *der;* (*of electricity*) Energiezufuhr, *die;* **(B)** (*esp. Computing: place where information etc. enters system*) Eingang, *der.* ❷ *v.t.*, **-tt-**, **~** *or* **~ted** (*esp. Computing*) eingeben ‹Daten, Programm›; zuführen ‹Strom, Energie›; **~ data to the computer** Daten in den Computer eingeben

**input: ~ circuit** *n.* Eingangsstromkreis, *der;* Primärstromkreis, *der;* **~ data** *n. pl.* Eingabedaten *Pl.;* Rechnerdaten *Pl.*

**inquest** /'ɪnkwest, 'ɪŋkwest/ *n.* **(A)** (*legal inquiry*) gerichtliche Untersuchung; **(B)** (*inquiry by coroner's court*) **~ [into the causes of death]** gerichtliche Untersuchung der Todesursache; **(C)** (*coll.: discussion*) ⇒ **post-mortem** 3 B; **(D)** (*inquisition*) Untersuchung, *die* (**into** *Gen.*)

**inquietude** /ɪn'kwaɪɪtju:d, ɪŋ'kwaɪɪtju:d/ *n., no pl.* Unruhe, *die*

**inquire** /ɪn'kwaɪə(r), ɪŋ'kwaɪə(r)/ ❶ *v.i.* **(A)** (*make search*) Untersuchungen anstellen (**into** über + *Akk.*); **~ into a matter** eine Angelegenheit untersuchen *od.* prüfen; **(B)** (*seek information*) sich erkundigen (**about, after** nach, **of** bei); **(C)** (*ask*) fragen (**for** nach). ❷ *v.t.* sich erkundigen nach, fragen nach ‹Weg, Namen›; **~ how/whether** *etc.* **…:** fragen *od.* sich erkundigen, wie/ob *usw.* …

**inquirer** /ɪn'kwaɪərə(r), ɪŋ'kwaɪərə(r)/ *n.* (*for the way, a name, etc.*) Fragende, *der/die;* (*into a matter*) Untersuchende, *der/die;* Nachforschende, *der/die*

**inquiring** /ɪn'kwaɪərɪŋ, ɪŋ'kwaɪərɪŋ/ *adj.* fragend; forschend ‹Geist›

**inquiry** /ɪn'kwaɪərɪ, ɪŋ'kwaɪərɪ/ *n.* **(A)** (*asking*) Anfrage, *die;* **on ~:** auf Anfrage; **give sb. a look of ~:** jmdn. fragend ansehen; **(B)** (*question*) Erkundigung, *die* (**into** über + *Akk.*); **make inquiries** Erkundigungen einziehen; Nachforschungen anstellen; **(C)** (*investigation*) Untersuchung, *die;* (*research*) Forschung, *die;* **hold an ~:** eine Untersuchung durchführen (**into** *Gen.*); **court of ~** (*Mil.*) Untersuchungskommission, *die*

**inquiry: ~ agent** *n.* (*Brit.*) Privatdetektiv, *der;* **~ desk, ~ office** *ns.* Auskunft, *die*

**inquisition** /ɪnkwɪ'zɪʃn, ɪŋkwɪ'zɪʃn/ *n.* **(A)** (*search*) Nachforschung, *die* (**into** über + *Akk.*); **(B)** (*judicial inquiry*) gerichtliche Untersuchung; (*fig. coll.*) Verhör, *das;* **(C)** **I~** (*Hist.*) Inquisition, *die*

**inquisitive** /ɪn'kwɪzɪtɪv, ɪŋ'kwɪzɪtɪv/ *adj.* **(A)** (*unduly inquiring*) neugierig; **(B)** (*inquiring*) wissbegierig; **be ~ about sth.** alles über etw. (*Akk.*) wissen wollen; **give sb. an ~ look** jmdn. forschend ansehen

**inquisitively** /ɪn'kwɪzɪtɪvlɪ, ɪŋ'kwɪzɪtɪvlɪ/ *adv.* ⇒ **inquisitive** A, B: neugierig; wissbegierig

**inquisitiveness** /ɪn'kwɪzɪtɪvnɪs, ɪŋ'kwɪzɪtɪvnɪs/ *n., no pl.* ⇒ **inquisitive** A, B: Neugier[de], *die;* Wissbegier[de], *die*

**inquorate** /ɪn'kwɔ:reɪt, ɪŋ'kwɔ:reɪt/ *adj.* nicht beschlussfähig

**'inroad** *n.* **(A)** (*intrusion*) Eingriff, *der* (**on, into** in + *Akk.*); **make ~s into the market** in den Markt eindringen; **make ~s into sb.'s savings** jmds. Ersparnisse angreifen; **(B)** (*hostile incursion*) Einfall, *der* (**into** in + *Akk.*); Überfall, *der* (**[up]on** auf + *Akk.*); **make ~s on a country** in ein Land einfallen

**'inrush** *n.* Zustrom, *der;* (*of water*) Einbruch, *der;* **an ~ of air/water** ein Luftzug/Wassereinbruch

**insane** /ɪn'seɪn/ *adj.* **(A)** (*not of sound mind*) geisteskrank; **(B)** (*extremely foolish*) wahnsinnig (*ugs.*); irrsinnig (*ugs.*)

**insanely** /ɪn'seɪnlɪ/ *adv.* **(A)** (*in a mad manner*) wahnsinnig (*ugs.*) ‹eifersüchtig›; irr[e] ‹reden›; **(B)** (*very foolishly*) verrückt ‹sich benehmen›

**insanitary** /ɪn'sænɪtərɪ/ *adj.* unhygienisch

**insanity** /ɪn'sænɪtɪ/ *n.* **(A)** Geisteskrankheit, *die;* Wahnsinn, *der;* **(B)** (*extreme folly*) Irrsinn, *der;* Wahnsinn, *der* (*ugs.*); (*instance*) Verrücktheit, *die*

**insatiable** /ɪn'seɪʃəbl/ *adj.* unersättlich; unstillbar ‹Verlangen, Neugierde›; **he has an ~ thirst for knowledge** er ist unersättlich in seinem Wissensdurst

**inscribe** /ɪn'skraɪb/ *v.t.* **(A)** (*write*) schreiben; (*on ring etc.*) eingravieren; (*on stone, rock*) einmeißeln; **~ sth. on sth.** etw. auf etw. (*Akk.*) schreiben/in etw. (*Akk.*) eingravieren/einmeißeln; **(B)** (*enter*) eintragen ‹Namen› (**on** in + *Akk.*); **~ one's name in the Visitors' Book** sich in das Gästebuch eintragen; **(C)** (*mark*) mit einer Inschrift versehen ‹Denkmal, Grabstein›; **~ a tombstone/locket with a name** einen Namen in einen Grabstein einmeißeln/ein Medaillon eingravieren; **(D)** (*with informal dedication*) **~ sth. to sb.** jmdm. etw. widmen

**inscription** /ɪn'skrɪpʃn/ *n.* **(A)** (*words inscribed*) Inschrift, *die;* (*on coin*) Aufschrift, *die;* **(B)** (*informal dedication*) Widmung, *die*

**inscrutability** /ɪnskru:tə'bɪlɪtɪ/ *n., no pl.* Unergründlichkeit, *die;* (*of facial expression*) Undurchdringlichkeit, *die*

**inscrutable** /ɪn'skru:təbl/ *adj.* **(A)** (*mysterious*) unergründlich; geheimnisvoll ‹Lächeln›; undurchdringlich ‹Miene›; **he remained ~:** seine Miene *od.* sein Gesichtsausdruck blieb undurchdringlich; **(B)** (*incomprehensible*) unerforschlich (*geh.*)

**inscrutably** /ɪn'skru:təblɪ/ *adv.* unergründlich; geheimnisvoll ‹lächeln›

**insect** /'ɪnsekt/ *n.* Insekt, *das;* Kerbtier, *das*

**insect: ~ bite** *n.* Insektenstich, *der;* **~-borne** *adj.* durch Insekten übertragen ‹Krankheit›; **~ control** *n.* Insektenbekämpfung, *die*

**insecticide** /ɪn'sektɪsaɪd/ *n.* Insektizid, *das*

**insectivore** /ɪn'sektɪvɔ:(r)/ *n.* (*Zool.*) Insektenfresser, *der*

**insect: ~ powder** *n.* Insektenpulver, *das;* **~-proof** *adj.* insektensicher; **~ repellent** *n.* Insektenschutzmittel, *das*

**insecure** /ɪnsɪ'kjʊə(r)/ *adj.* **(A)** (*unsafe*) unsicher; **(B)** (*not firm, liable to give way*) nicht sicher; nicht fest ‹Knoten›; unstabil, instabil ‹Regal›; **(C)** (*Psych.*) unsicher; **feel ~:** sich nicht sicher fühlen

**insecurely** /ɪnsɪ'kjʊəlɪ/ *adv.* nicht sicher ‹befestigt›; nicht fest ‹verschlossen›

**insecurity** /ɪnsɪ'kjʊərɪtɪ/ *n., no pl.* (*also Psych.*) Unsicherheit, *die;* **the ~ of his job** sein unsicherer Arbeitsplatz

**inseminate** /ɪn'semɪneɪt/ *v.t.* inseminieren (*Med., Zool., Landw.*); befruchten ‹Frau›; besamen ‹Vieh›

**insemination** /ɪnsemɪ'neɪʃn/ *n.* Insemination, *die* (*Med., Zool., Landw.*); (*of woman*) Befruchtung, *die;* (*of animal*) Besamung, *die;* ⇒ *also* **artificial insemination**

**insensibility** /ɪnsensɪ'bɪlɪtɪ/ *n., no pl.* **(A)** (*lack of emotional feeling, indifference*) Gefühllosigkeit, *die* (**to** gegenüber); **(B)** (*unconsciousness*) Bewusstlosigkeit, *die;* **(C)** (*lack of physical feeling*) Unempfindlichkeit, *die* (**to** gegen); **~ to pain** Schmerzunempfindlichkeit, *die*

**insensible** /ɪn'sensɪbl/ *adj.* **(A)** (*imperceptible*) unmerklich; nicht wahrnehmbar; **(B)** (*unconscious*) bewusstlos; **they drank themselves ~:** sie betranken sich bis zur Bewusstlosigkeit; **(C)** (*unaware*) **be ~ of** *or* **to sth.** sich (*Dat.*) einer Sache (*Gen.*) nicht bewusst sein; **(D)** (*deprived of sensation*) unempfindlich (**to** gegen); **be ~ to the cold/to pain** keine Kälte/keinen Schmerz empfinden; **(E)** (*emotionless*) gefühllos ‹Person, Art›; unempfindlich (**to** für)

**insensitive** /ɪn'sensɪtɪv/ *adj.* **(A)** (*lacking feeling*) gefühllos ‹Person, Art›; **be ~ to the needs of others** kein Gefühl für die Bedürfnisse anderer haben; **(B)** (*unappreciative*) unempfänglich (**to** für); **(C)** (*not physically sensitive*) unempfindlich (**to** gegen); **~ to light/heat** licht-/hitzeunempfindlich

**insensitively** /ɪn'sensɪtɪvlɪ/ *adv.* gefühllos, ohne Gefühl ‹reagieren, sprechen›

**insensitiveness** /ɪn'sensɪtɪvnɪs/, **insensitivity** /ɪnsensɪ'tɪvɪtɪ/ *ns., no pl.* **(A)** (*lack of feeling*) Gefühllosigkeit, *die* (**to** gegenüber); **(B)** (*unappreciativeness*) Unempfindlichkeit, *die* (**to** für); **(C)** (*lack of physical sensitiveness*) Unempfindlichkeit, *die* (**to** gegen); **~** *or* **insensitivity to heat** Hitzeunempfindlichkeit, *die*

**inseparable** /ɪn'sepərəbl/ *adj.* **(A)** untrennbar; (*fig.*) unzertrennlich ‹Freunde, Zwillinge usw.›; **sth. is ~ from sth.** etw. ist mit etw. untrennbar verbunden; **he is ~ from his teddy bear** der Junge und sein Teddybär sind unzertrennlich; **(B)** (*Ling.*) untrennbar

**inseparably** /ɪn'sepərəblɪ/ *adv.* untrennbar

**insert** ❶ /ɪn'sɜ:t/ *v.t.* **(A)** einlegen ‹Film›; einwerfen ‹Münze›; einsetzen ‹Herzschrittmacher›; einstechen ‹Nadel›; **~ a piece of paper into the typewriter** ein Blatt Papier in die Schreibmaschine einspannen; **~ sth. in/between sth.** etw. in/zwischen etw. (*Akk.*) stecken/legen *usw.*; **~ the key [into the lock]** den Schlüssel ins Schloss stecken; **~ a page into a book** ein Blatt in ein Buch einlegen; **(B)** (*introduce into*) einfügen ‹Wort, Satz usw.› (**in** in + *Akk.*); **~ an advertisement in 'The Times'** eine Anzeige in die „Times" setzen; in der „Times" inserieren; **(C)** (*Computing*) einfügen; **~ key** Einfügetaste, *die.*
❷ /'ɪnsɜ:t/ *n.* (*in magazine*) Beilage, *die;* (*in garment*) Einsatz, *der;* (*in book*) Einlage, *die;* (*printed in newspaper*) Inserat, *das*

**insertion** /ɪn'sɜ:ʃn/ *n.* **(A)** (*inserting*) ⇒ **insert** 1 A: Einlegen, *das;* Einwerfen, *das;* Einsetzen, *das;* Einstechen, *das;* **(B)** (*thing inserted*) (*words, sentences in a text*) Einfügung, *die;* Beifügung, *die;* (*in newspaper*) Inserat, *das;* **(C)** (*each appearance of an advertisement*) Insertion, *die*

**in-service 'training** *n.* Fort- *od.* Weiterbildung [für Berufstätige]

**inset** ❶ /'--/ *n.* (*small map*) Nebenkarte, *die;* (*small photograph, diagram*) Nebenbild, *das.* ❷ /-'-/ *v.t.*, **-tt-**, ~ *or* **~ted** einfügen ‹Karte, Seite› (**in** in + *Akk.*)

**inshore** ❶ /'--/ *adj.* Küsten‹fischerei, -gewässer, -schifffahrt›; ~ **currents** sich auf die Küste zu bewegende Strömungen. ❷ /-'-/ *adv.* auf die Küste zu ‹treiben›; in Küstennähe ‹sein, fischen›; **close ~:** dicht an der Küste ‹sein, liegen›; dicht an die Küste ‹heranfahren›

**inside** ❶ /-'-, '--/ *n.* Ⓐ (*internal side*) Innenseite, *die;* **on the ~:** innen; **to/from the ~:** nach/von innen; **overtake sb. on the ~** (*in driving*) jmdn. auf der falschen Seite überholen; **on the ~ of the door** innen an der Tür; **lock the door from the ~:** die Tür von innen abschließen; Ⓑ (*inner part*) Innere, *das;* **the ~ of the cupboard needs a good clean-out** der Schrank muss innen richtig sauber gemacht werden; Ⓒ *in sing. or pl.* (*coll.: stomach and bowels*) Eingeweide *Pl.;* Innere, *das;* **have a pain in one's ~[s]** Bauch- *od.* Leibschmerzen haben; Ⓓ (*position affording ~ information*) **he knows Parliament from the ~:** er kennt das Parlament von innen; **be on the ~:** eingeweiht *od.* ein Insider sein; Ⓔ **the wind blew her umbrella ~ out** der Wind hat ihren Regenschirm umgestülpt; **wear one's sweater ~ out** seinen Pullover verkehrt *od.* falsch herum anhaben; **know sth. ~ out** etw. in- und auswendig kennen; **turn a jacket ~ out** eine Jacke nach links wenden; **turn sth. ~ out** (*fig.*) etw. auf den Kopf stellen (*ugs.*). ❷ /'--/ *adj.* (*of, on, nearer the ~*) inner...; Innen‹wand, -einrichtung, -ansicht, -reparatur, -durchmesser›; (*fig.*) intern; **be on an ~ page** im Inneren [der Zeitung] stehen; **give the ~ story of sth.** etw. von innen beleuchten (*fig.*); **~ information** interne Informationen; **the burglary was an ~ job** (*coll.*) der Einbruch war das Werk von Leuten, die sich auskannten; **~ pocket** Innentasche, *die;* **~ lane** Innenspur, *die;* **~ track** (*Racing*) Innenbahn, *die.* ❸ /-'-/ *adv.* Ⓐ (*on or in the ~*) innen; (*to the ~*) nach innen hinein/herein; (*indoors*) drinnen; **come ~:** hereinkommen; **take a look ~:** hineinsehen; (*in search of sth.*) innen nachsehen; **go ~:** [ins Haus] hineingehen; **see ~ for further details** weitere Informationen finden Sie in diesem Brief/in dieser Broschüre; Ⓑ (*sl.: in prison*) **be ~:** sitzen (*ugs.*); **put sb. ~:** jmdn. einlochen (*salopp*); Ⓒ **~ of** ⇒ **4**. ❹ /-'-/ *prep.* Ⓐ (*on inner side of*) [innen] in (+ *Dat.*); (*with direction*) in (+ *Akk.*) hinein; **sit/get ~ the house** im Haus sitzen/ins Haus hineinkommen; **what's ~ that package?** was ist in diesem Paket?; **leave your shoes just ~ the door** lass deine Schuhe gerade [innen] an der Tür stehen; Ⓑ (*in less than*) **~ an hour** innerhalb [von] einer Stunde; in weniger als einer Stunde

**inside: ~ edge** *n.* (*Skating, Cricket*) Innenkante, *die;* **~ 'forward** *n.* (*Footb., Hockey*) Halbstürmer, *der;* Innenstürmer, *der;* Inside, *der* (*schweiz. Fußball*); **~ 'left** *n.* (*Footb., Hockey*) Halblinke, *der/die;* **~-leg** *adj.* **~-leg measurement** Schrittlänge, *die*

**insider** /ɪn'saɪdə(r)/ *n.* Ⓐ (*within a society*) Mitglied, *das;* Zugehörige, *der/die;* Ⓑ (*person privy to secret*) Eingeweihte, *der/die;* Insider, *der;* **~ dealing** *or* **trading** (*Stock Exch.*) Insiderhandel, *der*

**inside 'right** *n.* (*Footb., Hockey*) Halbrechte, *der/die*

**insidious** /ɪn'sɪdɪəs/ *adj.* heimtückisch; **an ~ disease** eine heimtückische *od.* (*fachspr.*) insidiöse Krankheit

**insidiously** /ɪn'sɪdɪəslɪ/ *adv.* auf heimtückische Weise

**insidiousness** /ɪn'sɪdɪəsnɪs/ *n., no pl.* Heimtücke, *die*

**'insight** *n.* Ⓐ (*penetration, discernment*) Verständnis, *das;* **be lacking in ~:** einen Mangel an Verständnis zeigen; **~ into human nature** Menschenkenntnis, *die;* Ⓑ (*instance*) Einblick, *der* (**into** in + *Akk.*); **be** *or* **give an ~ into sth.** einen Einblick in etw. (*Akk.*) geben; **gain an ~ into sth.** [einen] Einblick in etw. (*Akk.*) gewinnen *od.* bekommen

**insignia** /ɪn'sɪɡnɪə/ *n., pl. same* Insigne, *das*

**insignificance** /ɪnsɪɡ'nɪfɪkəns/ *n., no pl.* Ⓐ (*unimportance*) Bedeutungslosigkeit, *die;* Unwichtigkeit, *die;* Ⓑ (*contemptibility*) Unscheinbarkeit, *die;* Ⓒ (*meaninglessness*) Belanglosigkeit, *die*

**insignificant** /ɪnsɪɡ'nɪfɪkənt/ *adj.* Ⓐ (*unimportant*) unbedeutend; geringfügig ‹Summe›; unbedeutend, geringfügig ‹Unterschied›; unscheinbar ‹Äußeres›; Ⓑ (*contemptible*) unscheinbar ‹Person›; Ⓒ (*meaningless*) belanglos ‹Bemerkung›

**insincere** /ɪnsɪn'sɪə(r)/ *adj.* unaufrichtig; falsch ‹Lächeln›

**insincerely** /ɪnsɪn'sɪəlɪ/ *adv.* unaufrichtig; falsch ‹lächeln›

**insincerity** /ɪnsɪn'serɪtɪ/ *n.* Unaufrichtigkeit, *die;* (*of smile, person*) Falschheit, *die*

**insinuate** /ɪn'sɪnjʊeɪt/ *v.t.* Ⓐ (*introduce*) [auf geschickte Art] einflößen ‹Propaganda›; insinuieren (*veralt.*); **~ doubts into sb.'s mind** jmdm. geschickt Zweifel einpflanzen; Ⓑ (*convey*) andeuten (**to sb.** jmdm. gegenüber); unterstellen; insinuieren (*geh.*); **how dare you ~ that ...?** wie können Sie es wagen, zu behaupten, dass ...?; **insinuating remarks** Andeutungen; Unterstellungen; Ⓒ **~ oneself into sb.'s favour** sich bei jmdm. einschmeicheln

**insinuation** /ɪnsɪnjʊ'eɪʃn/ *n.* Anspielung, *die* (**about** auf + *Akk.*); versteckte Andeutung; **by ~:** andeutungsweise

**insipid** /ɪn'sɪpɪd/ *adj.* Ⓐ (*tasteless*) fad[e] ‹Essen›; schal ‹Getränk›; Ⓑ (*lacking liveliness*) fad[e] (*ugs.*), geistlos ‹Person›; schal, fad[e] (*ugs.*) ‹Witz, Spaß›; geistlos ‹Gespräch›; langweilig ‹Farbe, Musik›

**insist** /ɪn'sɪst/ ❶ *v.i.* bestehen ([**up**]**on** auf + *Dat.*); **~ on doing sth./on sb.'s doing sth.** darauf bestehen, etw. zu tun/dass jmd. etw. tut; **if you ~:** wenn du darauf bestehst; **he 'will ~ on ringing us late at night** er ruft uns beharrlich spätabends an; **she ~s on her innocence** sie behauptet beharrlich, unschuldig zu sein. ❷ *v.t.* Ⓐ **~ that ...:** darauf bestehen, dass ...; Ⓑ (*maintain positively*) **they keep ~ing that ...:** sie beharren *od.* bestehen beharrlich darauf, dass ...; **he ~ed that he was right** er bestand darauf, dass er Recht habe

**insistence** /ɪn'sɪstəns/, **insistency** /ɪn'sɪstənsɪ/ *n., no pl.* Bestehen, *das* (**on** auf + *Dat.*); **I only came here at your ~:** ich kam nur auf dein Drängen hierher

**insistent** /ɪn'sɪstənt/ *adj.* Ⓐ beharrlich, hartnäckig ‹Person›; aufdringlich ‹Musik›; nachdrücklich ‹Forderung›; **be most ~ that .../about sth.** hartnäckig darauf bestehen, dass .../auf etw. (*Dat.*) bestehen; Ⓑ ([*annoyingly*] *persistent*) penetrant (*abwertend*)

**insistently** /ɪn'sɪstəntlɪ/ *adv.* Ⓐ mit Nachdruck ‹betonen, fordern›; Ⓑ (*persistently*) penetrant (*abwertend*)

**in situ** /ɪn 'sɪtju:/ *adv.* in situ; in natürlicher Lage (*Med.*); in originaler Lage (*Archäol.*)

**insobriety** /ɪnsə'braɪətɪ/ *n., no pl.* Trunkenheit, *die*

**insofar** /ɪnsəʊ'fɑ:(r)/ *adv.* = **in so far;** ⇒ **far 1 D**

**insole** /'ɪnsəʊl/ *n.* Ⓐ Einlegesohle, *die;* Ⓑ (*part of shoe or boot*) Brandsohle, *die*

**insolence** /'ɪnsələns/ *n., no pl.* Unverschämtheit, *die;* Frechheit, *die;* Insolenz, *die* (*geh.*)

**insolent** /'ɪnsələnt/ *adj.*, **insolently** /'ɪnsələntlɪ/ *adv.* Ⓐ (*contemptuous*[*ly*]) anmaßend; überheblich; Ⓑ (*insulting*[*ly*]) unverschämt; frech; insolent (*geh.*)

**insolubility** /ɪnsɒljʊ'bɪlɪtɪ/ *n., no pl.* ⇒ **insoluble**: Unlösbarkeit, *die;* Unlöslichkeit, *die*

**insoluble** /ɪn'sɒljʊbl/ *adj.* Ⓐ unlösbar ‹Problem, Rätsel usw.›; Ⓑ unlöslich ‹Substanz›; insolubel (*Chem.*) ‹Verbindung›

**insolvency** /ɪn'sɒlvənsɪ/ *n.* Insolvenz, *die* (*bes. Wirtsch.*); Zahlungsunfähigkeit, *die*

**insolvent** /ɪn'sɒlvənt/ ❶ *adj.* (*unable to pay debts*) insolvent (*bes. Wirtsch.*); zahlungsunfähig. ❷ *n.* zahlungsunfähiger Schuldner

**insomnia** /ɪn'sɒmnɪə/ *n.* Schlaflosigkeit, *die;* Insomnie, *die* (*Med.*)

**insomniac** /ɪn'sɒmnɪæk/ *n.* an Schlaflosigkeit Leidender/Leidende; **be an ~:** an Schlaflosigkeit leiden

**insomuch** /ɪnsəʊ'mʌtʃ/ *adv.* Ⓐ (*to such an extent*) **~ that** so sehr *od.* dermaßen, dass; Ⓑ (*inasmuch*) insofern (**as** als)

**insouciance** /ɪn'su:sɪəns, æ̃'su:sjɑ̃s/ *n., no pl.* Unbekümmertheit, *die;* Sorglosigkeit, *die*

**insouciant** /ɪn'su:sɪənt, æ̃'su:sjɑ̃/ *adj.* unbekümmert; sorglos

**inspect** /ɪn'spekt/ *v.t.* Ⓐ (*view closely*) prüfend betrachten; **let me ~ your hands** lass mich mal deine Hände sehen; zeig mal deine Hände vor; **~ a cat for fleas** eine Katze auf Flöhe untersuchen; Ⓑ (*examine officially*) überprüfen; inspizieren, kontrollieren ‹Räumlichkeiten›; abschreiten ‹Ehrenformation›

**inspection** /ɪn'spekʃn/ *n.* Überprüfung, *die;* (*of premises*) Kontrolle, *die;* Inspektion, *die;* **tour of ~:** Inspektionsrunde, *die;* (*on foot also*) Inspektionsgang, *der* (**of** durch); **present/show/submit sth. for ~:** etw. zur Prüfung vorlegen; **hold out your hands for ~:** zeigt eure Hände vor; **on [closer] ~:** bei näherer Betrachtung *od.* Prüfung

**in'spection copy** *n.* Ansichtsexemplar, *das;* (*for teachers*) Lehrerprüfstück, *das*

**inspector** /ɪn'spektə(r)/ *n.* Ⓐ (*official*) (*on bus, train etc.*) Kontrolleur, *der*/Kontrolleurin, *die;* **~ [of schools]** Schulrat, *der*/-rätin, *die;* **health ~** *Beamter/Beamtin in der Gesundheitsfürsorge;* Ⓑ (*Brit.: police officer*) ≈ Polizeiinspektor, *der*

**inspector: ~ 'general** *n.* Oberinspektor, *der;* **~ of 'taxes** *n.* (*Brit.*) Finanzbeamte, *der*/Finanzbeamtin, *die*

**inspiration** /ɪnspə'reɪʃn/ *n.* Ⓐ Inspiration, *die* (*geh.*); **get one's ~ from sth.** sich von etw. inspirieren lassen; **I have just had an ~:** ich hatte gerade eine [plötzliche] Eingebung; mir ist gerade eine Erleuchtung gekommen (*oft iron.*); **sth. is an ~ to sb.** etw. inspiriert jmdn.; Ⓑ (*drawing in of breath*) Inspiration, *die* (*Med.*); Einatmung, *die*

**inspire** /ɪn'spaɪə(r)/ *v.t.* Ⓐ (*instil thought or feeling into*) inspirieren (*geh.*); **in an ~d moment** (*coll.*) in einem Augenblick der Erleuchtung; Ⓑ (*breathe in*) einatmen ‹Luft›; Ⓒ (*animate*) inspirieren; anregen; (*encourage*) anspornen; **~ sb. with hope/confidence/respect** jmdn. mit Hoffnung/Vertrauen/Respekt erfüllen; **~d playing** beseeltes Spiel; **~d idea** genialer Gedanke; **~d guess** intuitiv richtige Vermutung; Ⓓ (*instil*) einflößen ‹Mut, Angst, Respekt› (**in** *Dat.*); [er]wecken ‹Vertrauen, Gedanke, Hoffnung› (**in** in + *Dat.*); hervorrufen ‹Hass, Abneigung› (**in** bei); (*incite*) anstiften; anzetteln (*abwertend*) ‹Unruhen usw.›; **what ~d this piece of music?** woher kamen die Anregungen zu diesem Musikstück?

**inspiring** /ɪn'spaɪərɪŋ/ *adj.* inspirierend (*geh.*); **his speech was not particularly ~:** seine Rede riss einen nicht gerade vom Stuhl (*ugs.*)

**inst.** *abbr.* (*Commerc.*) **instant** d. M.

**instability** /ɪnstə'bɪlɪtɪ/ *n.* (*mental, physical*) Labilität, *die;* (*inconstancy*) Instabilität, *die*

**install** /ɪn'stɔ:l/ *v.t.* Ⓐ (*establish*) **~ oneself** sich installieren; (*in a chair etc.*) sich niederlassen; sich pflanzen (*ugs.*); (*in a house etc.*) sich einrichten; **when we're ~ed in our new house** wenn wir in unserem neuen Haus eingerichtet sind; Ⓑ (*set up for use*) installieren ‹Heizung, Leitung, Software›; anschließen ‹Telefon›; einbauen ‹Badezimmer›; aufstellen, anschließen ‹Herd›; Ⓒ (*place ceremonially*) installieren (*geh.*); **~ sb. in an office/a post** jmdn. in ein Amt einführen *od.* einsetzen

**installation** /ɪnstə'leɪʃn/ *n.* Ⓐ (*installing*) (*in an office or post*) Amtseinsetzung, *die;* Amtseinführung, *die;* Installation, *die* (*schweiz., sonst veralt.*); (*setting up for use*) Installation, *die;* (*of bathroom etc.*) Einbau, *der;* (*of telephone, cooker*) Anschluss, *der;* **~ charges** Installationskosten; Ⓑ (*apparatus etc. installed*) Anlage, *die;* **kitchen ~:** Kücheneinrichtung, *die*

i

**instalment** (*Amer.*: **installment**) /ɪn'stɔ:lmənt/ *n.* Ⓐ (*part payment*) Rate, *die;* **pay by** *or* **in ~s** in Raten *od.* ratenweise zahlen; **monthly ~:** Monatsrate, *die;* Ⓑ (*of serial, novel*) Fortsetzung, *die;* (*of film, radio programme*) Folge, *die;* Ⓒ **installment plan** (*Amer.*) Ratenzahlung, *die;* Teilzahlung, *die;* **buy on an installment plan** auf Raten kaufen

**instance** /'ɪnstəns/ ❶ *n.* Ⓐ (*example*) Beispiel, *das* (**of** für); **as an ~ of ...:** als [ein] Beispiel für ...; **for ~:** zum Beispiel; Ⓑ (*particular case*) **in your/this ~:** in deinem/diesem Fall[e]; **in many ~s** in vielen Fällen; **isolated ~s** Einzelfälle; Ⓒ **at the ~ of ...:** auf Ersuchen *od.* Betreiben (+ *Gen.*); **at his ~:** auf seine Veranlassung [hin]; auf sein Betreiben; **court of first ~** (*Law*) erste Instanz; Ⓓ **in the first ~:** zuerst *od.* zunächst einmal; (*at the very beginning*) gleich zu Anfang; **it will be for six months in the first ~:** es ist zunächst auf sechs Monate befristet. ❷ *v.t.* Ⓐ (*cite as an ~*) anführen; Ⓑ *usu. in pass.* (*exemplify*) exemplifizieren

**instant** /'ɪnstənt/ ❶ *adj.* Ⓐ (*occurring immediately*) unmittelbar; sofortig ‹Wirkung, Linderung, Ergebnis›; **these new showers give you ~ hot water** mit diesen neuen Duschen hat man sofort heißes Wasser; Ⓑ **~ coffee/tea** Instant- *od.* Pulverkaffee/Instanttee, *der;* **~ potatoes** fertiger Kartoffelbrei; **~ cake mix** fertige Backmischung; **~ meal** Fertiggericht, *das;* Ⓒ (*fig.: hurriedly produced*) eilig angefertigt/geschrieben *usw.;* Ⓓ (*Commerc.*) dieses Monats.
❷ *n.* Augenblick, *der;* **at that very ~:** genau in dem Augenblick; **come here this ~:** komm sofort *od.* auf der Stelle her; **we were just this ~ talking about you** wir haben gerade eben von dir gesprochen; **the ~ he walked in at the door ...:** in dem Augenblick, als er hereintrat, ...; **in an ~:** augenblicklich; sofort; **not [for] an ~:** keinen Augenblick

**instantaneous** /ɪnstən'teɪnɪəs/ *adj.* unmittelbar; **his reaction was ~:** er reagierte sofort; **death was ~:** der Tod trat sofort *od.* unmittelbar ein

**instantaneously** /ɪnstən'teɪnɪəslɪ/ *adv.* sofort; unverzüglich

**instantly** /'ɪnstəntlɪ/ *adv.* sofort; **he is ~ likeable** er ist einem sofort sympathisch

**instant 'replay** *n.* (*Sport*) [sofortige] Wiederholung

**instead** /ɪn'sted/ *adv.* stattdessen; **~ of doing sth.** [an]statt etw. zu tun; **~ of sth.** anstelle einer Sache (*Gen.*); **I will go ~ of you** ich gehe an deiner Stelle; **Friday ~ of Saturday** Freitag anstelle von *od.* [an]statt Sonnabend

**'instep** *n.* Ⓐ (*of foot*) Spann, *der;* Fußrücken, *der;* Ⓑ (*of shoe*) Blatt, *das*

**instigate** /'ɪnstɪgeɪt/ *v.t.* Ⓐ (*urge on*) anstiften (**to** zu); **~ sb. to do sth.** jmdn. dazu anstiften, etw. zu tun; Ⓑ (*bring about*) initiieren (*geh.*) ‹Reformen, Projekt usw.›; anzetteln (*abwertend*) ‹Streik usw.›

**instigation** /ɪnstɪ'geɪʃn/ *n.* Ⓐ (*urging*) Anstiftung, *die;* **at sb.'s ~:** auf jmds. Betreiben (*Akk.*); Ⓑ (*bringing about*) Anzettelung, *die* (*abwertend*); (*of reforms etc.*) Initiierung, *die* (*geh.*)

**instigator** /'ɪnstɪgeɪtə(r)/ *n.* Ⓐ (*of bank raid etc.*) Anstifter, *der*/Anstifterin, *die;* Ⓑ (*of riot, strike*) Anzettler, *der*/Anzettlerin, *die* (*abwertend*); (*of reforms*) Initiator, *der*/Initiatorin, *die* (*geh.*)

**instil** (*Amer.*: **instill**) /ɪn'stɪl/ *v.t.*, **-ll-** Ⓐ (*introduce gradually*) einflößen (**in** *Dat.*); einimpfen (**in** *Dat.*); beibringen ‹gutes Benehmen, Wissen› (**in** *Dat.*); Ⓑ (*put in by drops*) einträufeln (**into** in + *Akk.*)

**instinct** /'ɪnstɪnkt/ *n.* Ⓐ Instinkt, *der;* **~ for survival, survival ~:** Überlebenstrieb, *der;* ⇨ *also* **herd** 1 B; Ⓑ (*intuition*) Instinkt, *der;* instinktives Gefühl (**for** für); (*unconscious skill*) natürliche Begabung (**for** für); Sinn, *der* (**for** für); **~ warns them when danger is near** der Instinkt warnt sie bei drohender Gefahr; **have an ~ for business** Geschäftssinn *od.* -instinkt haben; Ⓒ (*innate impulse*) angeborener *od.* natürlicher *od.* instinktiver Drang

**instinctive** /ɪn'stɪnktɪv/ *adj.*, **instinctively** /ɪn'stɪnktɪvlɪ/ *adv.* instinktiv

**institute** /'ɪnstɪtju:t/ ❶ *n.* Institut, *das;* ⇨ *also* **Women's Institute**. ❷ *v.t.* einführen ‹Reform, Brauch, Beschränkung›; einleiten ‹Suche, Verfahren, Untersuchung›; gründen ‹Gesellschaft›; anstrengen ‹Prozess, Klage›; schaffen ‹Posten›; einrichten ‹Ausstellung›; **his wife ~d divorce proceedings against him** seine Ehefrau reichte die Scheidung [gegen ihn] ein

**institution** /ɪnstɪ'tju:ʃn/ *n.* Ⓐ (*instituting*) Einführung, *die;* Ⓑ (*law, custom*) Institution, *die;* Ⓒ (*coll.: familiar object*) Institution, *die;* **become an ~:** zur Institution werden; **he's one of the ~s of the place** er gehört dort/hier schon zum Inventar (*scherzh.*); Ⓓ (*institute*) Heim, *das;* Anstalt, *die;* **charitable/educational ~:** Wohltätigkeitseinrichtung/Erziehungsanstalt, *die*

**institutional** /ɪnstɪ'tju:ʃənl/ *adj.* Ⓐ (*of, like, organized through institutions*) institutionell (*geh.*); Ⓑ (*suggestive of typical charitable institutions*) Heim-; Anstalts-; **~ care/catering** Heim-/Anstaltsfürsorge, *die*/Heim-/Anstaltsverpflegung, *die;* Ⓒ (*Amer.*) **~ advertising** Prestigewerbung, *die;* institutionelle Werbung (*fachspr.*)

**instruct** /ɪn'strʌkt/ *v.t.* Ⓐ (*teach*) unterrichten ‹Klasse, Fach›; Ⓑ (*direct, command*) anweisen; die Anweisung erteilen (+ *Dat.*); instruieren; **we were ~ed to do it in this way** wir hatten Weisung (*Amtsspr.*) *od.* Anweisung, es so zu machen; Ⓒ (*inform*) unterrichten; in Kenntnis setzen; instruieren (*geh.*); Ⓓ (*Law: appoint*) beauftragen ‹Anwalt›

**instruction** /ɪn'strʌkʃn/ *n.* Ⓐ (*teaching*) Unterricht, *der;* **a course of ~:** ein Lehrgang; **give ~ in judo** Judounterricht erteilen; **'Driver under ~'** ≈ „Fahrschule“; Ⓑ *esp. in pl.* (*direction, order*) Anweisung, *die;* Instruktion, *die;* **~ manual/~s for use** Gebrauchsanleitung, *die;* (*for machine etc.*) Betriebsanleitung, *die;* **they had precise ~s as to where to go** sie hatten genaue Anweisung, wo sie hinzugehen hatten; **under ~s from** *or* **on the ~s of the committee** auf Anweisung *od.* Anordnung des Komitees; **be under strict ~s to do sth.** strenge Anweisung haben, etw. zu tun; Ⓒ (*Computing*) Befehl, *der*

**instructional** /ɪn'strʌkʃənl/ *adj.* Schulungs-; lehrreich ‹Erfahrung›; **an ~ film** ein Lehrfilm

**instructive** /ɪn'strʌktɪv/ *adj.* aufschlussreich; instruktiv; lehrreich ‹Erfahrung, Buch›

**instructively** /ɪn'strʌktɪvlɪ/ *adv.* aufschlussreich; instruktiv; **an ~ written book** ein lehrreiches Buch

**instructor** /ɪn'strʌktə(r)/ *n.* ▶ **1261** Ⓐ Lehrer, *der*/Lehrerin, *die;* (*Mil.*) Ausbilder, *der;* **riding ~:** Reitlehrer, *der*/-lehrerin, *die;* Ⓑ (*Amer. Univ.*) Dozent, *der*/Dozentin, *die*

**instrument** /'ɪnstrʊmənt/ *n.* Ⓐ (*tool, implement*) Instrument, *das;* **~s of torture** Folterwerkzeuge *od.* -instrumente; Ⓑ (*measuring device*) Instrument, *das;* **~ failure** Versagen der Instrumente; Ⓒ (*Mus.*) Instrument, *das;* Ⓓ (*person*) Werkzeug, *das;* Instrument, *das* (*geh.*); Ⓔ (*means, cause*) Mittel, *das;* Ⓕ (*Law*) Urkunde, *die;* **~ of abdication** Abdankungsurkunde, *die*

**instrumental** /ɪnstrʊ'mentl/ *adj.* Ⓐ (*serving as instrument or means*) dienlich (**to** *Dat.*); förderlich (**to** *Dat.*); **he was ~ in finding me a post** er hat mir zu einer Stelle verholfen; Ⓑ (*Mus.*) instrumental; Instrumental‹musik, -version, -nummer›; Ⓒ (*Ling.*) instrumental

**instrumentalist** /ɪnstrʊ'mentəlɪst/ *n.* Instrumentalist, *der*/Instrumentalistin, *die*

**instrumentation** /ɪnstrʊmen'teɪʃn/ *n.* Ⓐ (*Mus.*) Instrumentation, *die;* Ⓑ (*provision*) Instrumentierung, *die;* (*use*) Anwendung von Instrumenten

**instrument: ~ board**, **~ panel** *ns.* Instrumentenbrett, *das;* Paneel, *das*

**insubordinate** /ɪnsə'bɔ:dɪnət/ *adj.* aufsässig; widersetzlich; (*Mil.*) ungehorsam; **~ behaviour** Widersetzlichkeit, *die;* (*Mil.*) Ungehorsam, *der*

**insubordination** /ɪnsəbɔ:dɪ'neɪʃn/ *n., no pl.* Aufsässigkeit, *die;* Widersetzlichkeit, *die;* (*Mil.*) Gehorsamsverweigerung, *die*

**insubstantial** /ɪnsəb'stænʃl/ *adj.* Ⓐ (*lacking solidity*) wenig substanziell (*geh.*); gegenstandslos ‹Anschuldigung›; dürftig ‹Essen, Kleidung›; gering[fügig] ‹Menge, Betrag›; Ⓑ (*not real*) unwirklich; gegenstandslos ‹Hoffnung, Angst›

**insufferable** /ɪn'sʌfərəbl/ *adj.* Ⓐ (*unbearably arrogant*) unausstehlich; Ⓑ (*intolerable*) unerträglich

**insufferably** /ɪn'sʌfərəblɪ/ *adv.* unerträglich

**insufficiency** /ɪnsə'fɪʃənsɪ/ *n.* Ⓐ Unzulänglichkeit, *die;* (*of money, provisions, information*) Mangel, *der* (**of** an + *Dat.*); (*inability, incompetence*) Unfähigkeit, *die;* mangelnde Eignung; **an ~ of money** Geldknappheit, *die;* Ⓑ (*Med.*) Insuffizienz, *die;* **cardiac/renal ~:** Herz-/Niereninsuffizienz, *die*

**insufficient** /ɪnsə'fɪʃənt/ *adj.* nicht genügend ‹Arbeit, Gründe, Geld›; unzulänglich ‹Beweise›; unzureichend ‹Versorgung, Beleuchtung›; **we have ~ membership** wir haben nicht genügend *od.* zu wenig Mitglieder; **give sb. ~ notice** jmdm. nicht rechtzeitig Bescheid geben

**insufficiently** /ɪnsə'fɪʃəntlɪ/ *adv.* ungenügend; unzulänglich; unzureichend ‹versorgen›

**insular** /'ɪnsjʊlə(r)/ *adj.* Ⓐ (*of an island*) Insel-; insular (*fachspr.*); **an ~ people** *or* **race** ein Inselvolk; Ⓑ (*fig.: narrow-minded*) provinziell (*abwertend*)

**insularity** /ɪnsjʊ'lærɪtɪ/ *n.* Provinzialität, *die* (*abwertend*)

**insulate** /'ɪnsjʊleɪt/ *v.t.* Ⓐ (*isolate*) isolieren (**against, from** gegen); **~ floors against noise** Fußböden schallisolieren *od.* gegen Schall isolieren; Ⓑ (*detach from surrounding*) isolieren (**from** von)

**insulating**/'ɪnsjʊleɪtɪŋ/: **~ material** *n.* Isoliermaterial, *das;* **~ tape** *n.* Isolierband, *das*

**insulation** /ɪnsjʊ'leɪʃn/ *n.* Isolierung, *die;* **put ~ in the loft** den Dachboden isolieren

**insulator** /'ɪnsjʊleɪtə(r)/ *n.* Isolator, *der*

**insulin** /'ɪnsjʊlɪn/ *n.* (*Med.*) Insulin, *das*

**'insulin shock** *n.* (*Med.*) Insulinschock, *der*

**insult** ❶ /'ɪnsʌlt/ *n.* Beleidigung, *die* (**to** *Gen.*); **fling an ~ in sb.'s face** jmdm. eine Beleidigung an den Kopf werfen (*ugs.*); ⇨ *also* **injury** B. ❷ /ɪn'sʌlt/ *v.t.* beleidigen

**insulting** /ɪn'sʌltɪŋ/ *adj.* beleidigend

**insuperable** /ɪn'su:pərəbl, ɪn'sju:pərəbl/ *adj.*, **insuperably** /ɪn'su:pərəblɪ, ɪn'sju:pərəblɪ/ *adv.* unüberwindlich

**insupportable** /ɪnsə'pɔ:təbl/ *adj.* Ⓐ (*unendurable*) unerträglich; Ⓑ (*unjustifiable*) nicht zu rechtfertigen *präd.;* nicht zu rechtfertigend *nicht präd.*

**insurance** /ɪn'ʃʊərəns/ *n.* Ⓐ (*insuring*) Versicherung, *die;* (*fig.*) Sicherheit, *die;* Gewähr, *die;* **take out ~ against/on sth.** eine Versicherung gegen etw. abschließen/etw. versichern lassen; **travel ~:** Reisegepäck- und -unfallversicherung, *die;* **~ against fire/theft/accident** Feuer-/Diebstahl-/Unfallversicherung, *die;* Ⓑ (*sum received*) Versicherungssumme, *die;* (*sum paid*) Versicherungsbetrag, *der;* **I got £50 ~ when my bike was stolen** ich bekam 50 Pfund von der Versicherung, als mein Fahrrad gestohlen wurde; **I've been paying ~ for the last 15 years** ich zahle jetzt schon 15 Jahre in die Versicherung ein; **claim the ~:** den Versicherungsanspruch geltend machen

**insurance: ~ agent** *n.* ▶ **1261** Versicherungsvertreter, *der*/-vertreterin, *die;* Versicherungsagent, *der*/-agentin, *die;* **~ broker** *n.* ▶ **1261** Versicherungsmakler, *der;* **~ claim** *n.* Versicherungsanspruch, *der;* **make an ~ claim** eine Versicherung in Anspruch nehmen; **~ company** *n.* Versicherungsgesellschaft, *die;* **~ policy** *n.* Versicherungspolice, *die;* (*fig.*) Sicherheit, *die;* Gewähr, *die;* **take out an ~ policy** eine Versicherung abschließen; **~ stamp** *n.* (*Brit.*) Versicherungsmarke, *die*

**insure** /ɪnˈʃʊə(r)/ *v.t.* **A** (*secure payment to*) versichern ‹Person› (**against** gegen); ~ **[oneself] against sth.** sich gegen etw. versichern; **the ~d** der/die Versicherte; der Versicherungsnehmer/die Versicherungsnehmerin (*fachspr.*); **B** (*secure payment for*) ‹Versicherungsgesellschaft:› versichern; ‹Versicherungsnehmer:› versichern lassen ‹Gepäck, Gemälde usw.›; ~ **one's life** eine Lebensversicherung abschließen; **C** (*Amer.*) ⇒ **ensure**

**insurer** /ɪnˈʃʊərə(r)/ *n.* Versicherer, *der;* Versicherungsgeber, *der* (*fachspr.*)

**insurgent** /ɪnˈsɜːdʒənt/ ❶ *attrib. adj.* aufständisch. ❷ *n.* Aufständische, *der/die*

**insurmountable** /ɪnsəˈmaʊntəbl/ *adj.* unüberwindlich

**insurrection** /ɪnsəˈrekʃn/ *n.* (*uprising*) Aufstand, *der*

**intact** /ɪnˈtækt/ *adj.* **A** (*entire*) unbeschädigt; unversehrt; intakt ‹Uhr, Maschine usw.›; **keep one's capital ~:** sein Kapital unangetastet lassen; **B** (*unimpaired*) unversehrt; **keep one's reputation ~:** sich (*Dat.*) einen guten Ruf bewahren; **C** (*untouched*) unberührt; unangetastet; **the package was returned to me ~:** das Paket wurde ungeöffnet an mich zurückgesandt

**intaglio** /ɪnˈtælɪəʊ, ɪnˈtɑːlɪəʊ/ *n., pl.* **~s** **A** (*engraved design*) eingeschnittene Figur; **B** (*carving in hard material*) Steinschneidekunst, *die;* Glyptik, *die;* **in ~:** in negativer Gravierung; **C** (*printing process*) Tiefdruck, *der;* **D** (*gem with incised design*) Intaglio, *das*

ˈ**intake** *n.* **A** (*action*) Aufnahme, *die;* ~ **of breath** Atemholen, *das;* **B** (*where water enters channel or pipe*) Einströmungsöffnung, *die;* (*where air or fuel enters engine*) Ansaugöffnung, *die;* (*airway into mine*) Einziehschacht, *der;* **C** (*persons or things taken in*) Neuzugänge; (*amount taken in*) aufgenommene Menge; (*number of persons taken in*) Zahl der aufgenommenen Personen; ~ **of alcohol** Alkoholkonsum, *der;* ~ **of calories** Kalorienzufuhr, *die;* aufgenommene Kalorienmenge; ~ **of students** Zahl der Studienanfänger

**intangible** /ɪnˈtændʒɪbl/ *adj.* **A** (*that cannot be touched*) nicht greifbar; **feel an ~ presence in the room** spüren, dass etwas Unwirkliches anwesend ist; **B** (*that cannot be grasped mentally*) unbestimmbar; unbestimmt ‹Gefühl›; vage ‹Vorstellung›; ~ **assets** (*Econ.*) immaterielle Anlagewerte

**integer** /ˈɪntɪdʒə(r)/ *n.* (*Math.*) ganze Zahl

**integral** /ˈɪntɪgrl/ ❶ *adj.* **A** (*of a whole*) wesentlich, integral ‹Bestandteil›; **B** (*whole, complete*) vollständig; vollkommen; **C** (*forming a whole*) ein Ganzes bildend; integrierend; **an ~ group** eine aus verschiedenen integrierenden Teilen zusammengesetzte Gruppe; **D** (*Math.*) (*of or denoted by an integer*) ganzzahlig; (*involving only integers*) Integral-; ⇒ *also* **calculus A**. ❷ *n.* (*Math.*) Integral, *das*

**integrate** /ˈɪntɪgreɪt/ ❶ *v.t.* **A** (*combine into a whole*) integrieren; **an ~d Europe** ein vereintes Europa; **an ~d personality** eine in sich (*Dat.*) ausgewogene Persönlichkeit; **B** (*into society*) integrieren; ~ **sb. into a society** jmdn. in eine Gesellschaft integrieren *od.* eingliedern; **C** (*open to all racial groups*) ~ **a school/college** eine Schule/ein College für alle Rassen zugänglich machen; **an ~d school** eine Schule ohne Rassentrennung; **D** (*Math.*) integrieren.
❷ *v.i.* integrieren; ‹Schulen:› auch für Farbige zugänglich werden

**integrated** ˈ**circuit** *n.* (*Electronics*) integrierter Schaltkreis

**integration** /ɪntɪˈgreɪʃn/ *n.* **A** (*integrating; also Math.*) Integration, *die;* **B** (*ending of segregation*) Integration, *die* (**into** in + *Akk.*); **the ~ of the schools** die Aufhebung der Rassentrennung an den Schulen; **racial ~:** Rassenintegration, *die;* **C** (*Psych.*) Integration, *die;* **D** (*Commerc.*) **horizontal ~:** horizontale Integration; **vertical ~:** Vertikalkonzentration, *die*

**integrationist** /ɪntɪˈgreɪʃənɪst/ *n.* Integrationist, *der*/Integrationistin, *die*

**integrity** /ɪnˈtegrɪtɪ/ *n.* **A** (*uprightness, honesty*) Redlichkeit, *die;* (*of business, venture*) Seriosität, *die;* (*of style*) Echtheit, *die;* Unverfälschtheit, *die;* **intellectual ~:** intellektuelle Redlichkeit *od.* Integrität; **business ~:** honoriges Geschäftsgebaren; **a writer of ~:** ein redlicher Autor; **B** (*wholeness*) (*of country, empire*) Einheit, *die;* (*of person*) Ganzheit, *die;* (*of fossil etc.*) Unversehrtheit, *die;* **territorial ~:** territoriale Integrität; **C** (*soundness*) Intaktheit, *die*

**integument** /ɪnˈtegjʊmənt/ *n.* (*Biol.*) Integument, *das*

**intellect** /ˈɪntəlekt/ *n.* **A** (*faculty*) Verstand, *der;* Intellekt, *der;* **~ distinguishes man from the animals** das Denkvermögen unterscheidet den Menschen vom Tier; **B** (*understanding*) Intelligenz, *die;* **powers of ~:** Verstandeskräfte; intellektuelle Fähigkeiten; **C** (*person*) großer Geist

**intellectual** /ɪntəˈlektjʊəl/ ❶ *adj.* **A** (*of intellect*) intellektuell; geistig ‹Klima, Interessen, Waffe, Arbeit›; abstrakt ‹Mitgefühl, Sympathie›; **~ powers** intellektuelle Fähigkeiten; **B** (*possessing good understanding or intelligence*) geistig anspruchsvoll ‹Person, Publikum›. ❷ *n.* Intellektuelle, *der/die*

**intellectually** /ɪntəˈlektjʊəlɪ/ *adv.* intellektuell; geistig; **it's ~ stimulating** es regt den Geist an

**intelligence** /ɪnˈtelɪdʒəns/ *n.* **A** (*quickness of understanding*) Intelligenz, *die;* **have the ~ to do sth.** so intelligent sein, etw. zu tun; **have ~:** intelligent sein; **B** (*intellect, understanding*) Intelligenz, *die;* **a man of no mean ~:** ein sehr intelligenter Mann; **C** (*being*) Geist, *der;* (*spirit*) Geistwesen, *das;* **D** (*information*) Informationen *Pl.;* (*news*) Nachrichten *Pl.;* Meldungen *Pl.;* **a source of ~:** eine Informationsquelle; **E** ([*persons employed in*] *collecting information*) Nachrichtendienst, *der;* **military ~:** militärischer Geheimdienst; **be in ~:** dem Nachrichtendienst angehören

**intelligence: ~ department** *n.* Nachrichtendienst, *der;* **~ officer** *n.* Nachrichtenoffizier, *der;* **~ quotient** *n.* Intelligenzquotient, *der;* **~ service** *n.* Nachrichtendienst, *der;* **~ test** *n.* Intelligenztest, *der*

**intelligent** /ɪnˈtelɪdʒənt/ *adj.* intelligent; intelligent geschrieben, geistreich ‹Buch›; (*clever also*) klug; gescheit; **is there ~ life on other planets?** gibt es intelligente *od.* vernunftbegabte Lebewesen auf anderen Planeten?

**intelligently** /ɪnˈtelɪdʒəntlɪ/ *adv.* intelligent

**intelligentsia** /ɪntelɪˈdʒentsɪə/ *n.* Intelligenzija, *die* (*geh.*); Intelligenz, *die*

**intelligibility** /ɪntelɪdʒɪˈbɪlɪtɪ/ *n., no pl.* Verständlichkeit, *die*

**intelligible** /ɪnˈtelɪdʒɪbl/ *adj.* verständlich (**to** für); intelligibel (*Philos.*); **is their language ~ to you?** verstehst du ihre Sprache?

**intelligibly** /ɪnˈtelɪdʒɪblɪ/ *adv.* deutlich

**intemperance** /ɪnˈtempərəns/ *n.* Maßlosigkeit, *die;* Unmäßigkeit, *die;* (*addiction to drinking*) Trunksucht, *die*

**intemperate** /ɪnˈtempərət/ *adj.* **A** (*immoderate*) maßlos; überzogen, übertrieben ‹Verhalten, Bemerkung›; unmäßig, maßlos ‹Verlangen, Appetit, Konsum›; übermäßig ‹Eifer›; ausschweifend ‹Leben›; **his ~ conduct** seine Maßlosigkeit; **B** (*addicted to drinking*) trunksüchtig

**intemperately** /ɪnˈtempərətlɪ/ *adv.* unmäßig

**intend** /ɪnˈtend/ *v.t.* **A** (*have as one's purpose*) beabsichtigen; **~ doing sth.** *or* **to do sth.** beabsichtigen, etw. zu tun; **did you ~ that [to happen]?** hattest du das beabsichtigt?; **we ~ed no harm** wir haben nichts Böses damit bezweckt; (*we didn't mean to cause offence*) wir haben es nicht böse gemeint; **it isn't really what we ~ed** es ist eigentlich nicht das, was wir wollten; **longer than was ~ed** länger als geplant *od.* beabsichtigt; **B** (*design, mean*) **we ~ed it as a stopgap** das sollte eine Notlösung sein; **we ~ him to go** wir wollen, dass er geht; er soll gehen; **this dish is ~ed to be cooked slowly** dieses Gericht sollte langsam gekocht werden; **it was ~ed as a joke** das sollte ein Witz sein; **what do you ~ by that remark?** was willst du mit dieser Bemerkung sagen?; **what does the author ~ here?** was will der Autor hier sagen? ⇒ *also* **intended**

**intended** /ɪnˈtendɪd/ ❶ *adj.* beabsichtigt ‹Wirkung›; erklärt ‹Ziel›; absichtlich ‹Beleidigung›; **be ~ for sb./sth.** für jmdn./etw. bestimmt *od.* gedacht sein; **~ for adults/beginners** für Erwachsene/Anfänger; **~ for drinking** zum Trinken [gedacht]. ❷ *n.* (*coll.*) Zukünftige, *der/die* (*ugs.*)

**intense** /ɪnˈtens/ *adj.*, **~r** /ɪnˈtensə(r)/, **~st** /ɪnˈtensɪst/ **A** intensiv; groß ‹Hitze, Belastung›; stark, ‹Schmerzen›; kräftig, intensiv ‹Farbe›; äußerst groß ‹Aufregung›; ungeheuer ‹Kälte, Helligkeit›; **the day before the play opens is a period of ~ activity** am Tag vor der Premiere herrscht große Geschäftigkeit; **B** (*eager, ardent*) eifrig, lebhaft ‹Diskussion›; stark, ausgeprägt ‹Interesse›; brennend, glühend ‹Verlangen›; äußerst groß ‹Empörung, Aufregung, Betrübnis›; tief ‹Gefühl›; rasend ‹Hass, Eifersucht›; **C** (*with strong emotion*) stark gefühlsbetont ‹Person, Brief›; (*earnest*) ernst

**intensely** /ɪnˈtenslɪ/ *adv.* äußerst ‹schwierig, verärgert, enttäuscht, kalt›; ernsthaft, intensiv ‹studieren›; intensiv ‹fühlen›

**intensification** /ɪntensɪfɪˈkeɪʃn/ *n.* Intensivierung, *die*

**intensifier** /ɪnˈtensɪfaɪə(r)/ *n.* (*Ling.*) intensivierendes Wort

**intensify** /ɪnˈtensɪfaɪ/ ❶ *v.t.* intensivieren. ❷ *v.i.* zunehmen; ‹Hitze, Schmerzen:› stärker werden; ‹Kampf:› sich verschärfen

**intensity** /ɪnˈtensɪtɪ/ *n.* **A** Intensität, *die;* (*of feeling also*) Heftigkeit, *die;* **the heat had lost some of its ~:** die Hitze hatte etwas abgenommen *od.* nachgelassen; **B** (*measurable amount*) Intensität, *die*

**intensive** /ɪnˈtensɪv/ ❶ *adj.* **A** (*vigorous, thorough*) intensiv; Intensiv‹kurs›; **B** (*Ling.*) verstärkend; intensivierend; **C** (*concentrated, directed to a single point or area*) intensiv; heftig ‹Beschuss›; gezielt ‹Entwicklung›; **D** (*Econ.*) intensiv ‹Landwirtschaft›; **E** *in comb.* **capital-~/labour-~:** kapital-/arbeitsintensiv. ❷ *n.* ⇒ **intensifier**

**intensive** ˈ**care** *n.* Intensivpflege, *die* (*Med.*); **be in ~:** auf der Intensivstation sein; **~ unit** Intensivstation, *die*

**intensively** /ɪnˈtensɪvlɪ/ *adv.* intensiv

**intent** /ɪnˈtent/ ❶ *n.* Absicht, *die;* **by ~:** beabsichtigt; **with good/malicious ~:** in guter/schlechter Absicht; **with ~ to do sth.** (*Law*) in der Absicht *od.* mit dem Vorsatz, etw. zu tun; **do sth. with ~:** etw. vorsätzlich tun; **to all ~s and purposes** im Grunde; praktisch; ⇒ *also* **loiter**. ❷ *adj.* **A** (*resolved*) erpicht, versessen (**[up]on** auf + *Akk.*); **be ~ on achieving sth.** etw. unbedingt erreichen wollen; **be ~ upon revenge** auf Rache sinnen; **B** (*attentively occupied*) eifrig beschäftigt (**on** mit); **be ~ on one's work** auf seine Arbeit konzentriert sein; in seine Arbeit vertieft sein; **C** (*earnest, eager*) aufmerksam; konzentriert; forschend ‹Blick›

**intention** /ɪnˈtenʃn/ *n.* **A** Absicht, *die;* Intention, *die;* **have no ~/every ~ of doing sth.** nicht die Absicht haben/die feste Absicht haben, etw. zu tun; **it was my ~ to visit him** ich hatte die Absicht *od.* beabsichtigte, ihn zu besuchen; **with the best of ~s** in der besten Absicht; **the road to hell is paved with good ~s** (*prov.*) der Weg zur Hölle ist mit guten Vorsätzen gepflastert (*Spr.*); **what is the author's ~ here?** was will der Autor hier sagen?; **B** *in pl.* (*coll.: in respect of marriage*) [Heirats]absichten

**intentional** /ɪnˈtenʃənl/ *adj.* absichtlich; vorsätzlich (*bes. Rechtsspr.*); **it wasn't ~:** es war keine Absicht

**intentionally** /ɪnˈtenʃənəlɪ/ *adv.* absichtlich; mit Absicht

**intently** /ɪnˈtentlɪ/ *adv.* aufmerksam ‹zuhören, lesen, beobachten›

**inter** /ɪnˈtɜː(r)/ *v.t.*, **-rr-** (*literary*) bestatten (*geh.*) ‹Leichnam›

**interact** /ɪntər'ækt/ *v.i.* Ⓐ ‹Ideen:› sich gegenseitig beeinflussen; ‹Chemikalien usw.:› aufeinander einwirken, miteinander reagieren; Ⓑ (*Sociol., Psych.*) interagieren

**interaction** /ɪntər'ækʃn/ *n.* Ⓐ gegenseitige Beeinflussung; (*Chem., Phys.*) Wechselwirkung, *die;* Reaktion, *die;* Ⓑ (*Sociol., Psych.*) Interaktion, *die*

**interactive** /ɪntər'æktɪv/ *adj.* Ⓐ (*Chem.*) miteinander reagierend; Ⓑ (*Sociol., Psych., Computing*) interaktiv; **~ television** interaktives Fernsehen

**inter alia** /ɪntər'eɪlɪə/ *adv.* unter anderem

**interbreed** /ɪntə'bri:d/ ❶ *v.t.*, **interbred** /ɪntə'bred/ bastardieren (*fachspr.*); kreuzen ‹Pflanzen, Tiere›. ❷ *v.i.*, **interbred** bastardisieren (*fachspr.*); sich kreuzen

**intercede** /ɪntə'si:d/ *v.i.* sich einsetzen (**with** bei; **for, on behalf of** für)

**intercept** /ɪntə'sept/ *v.t.* Ⓐ (*seize*) abfangen; **~ the enemy** dem Feind den Weg abschneiden; Ⓑ (*check, stop*) abwehren ‹Schlag, Angriff›; Ⓒ (*listen in to*) abhören ‹Gespräch, Funkspruch›

**interception** /ɪntə'sepʃn/ *n.* ⇒ **intercept**: Abfangen, *das;* Abwehr, *die;* Abhören, *das*

**interceptor** /ɪntə'septə(r)/ *n.* (*Air Force*) Abfangjäger, *der*

**intercession** /ɪntə'seʃn/ *n.* (*mediation*) Vermittlung, *die,* (*entreaty*) Fürsprache, *die* (**for, on behalf of** für)

**interchange** ❶ /'ɪntətʃeɪndʒ/ *n.* Ⓐ (*reciprocal exchange*) Austausch, *der;* Ⓑ (*road junction*) [Autobahn]kreuz, *das.* ❷ /ɪntə'tʃeɪndʒ/ *v.t.* Ⓐ (*exchange with each other*) austauschen; wechseln ‹Briefe, Blicke, Worte, Grüße›; Ⓑ (*put each in the other's place*) [miteinander] vertauschen; **they can be ~d** sie sind austauschbar; Ⓒ (*alternate*) wechseln; [aus]wechseln ‹Kulissen usw.›

**interchangeable** /ɪntə'tʃeɪndʒəbl/ *adj.* austauschbar; synonym ‹Wörter, Ausdrücke›

**inter-city** /ɪntə'sɪtɪ/ *adj.* Intercity-; **~ train** Intercity[zug], *der*

**intercom** /'ɪntəkɒm/ *n.* (*coll.*) Gegensprechanlage, *die;* (*Aeronaut.*) Eigenverständigungsanlage, *die*

**intercommunicate** /ɪntəkə'mju:nɪkeɪt/ *v.i.* Ⓐ ‹Räume:› miteinander verbunden sein; Ⓑ ‹Personen, Organisationen:› Kontakt haben zueinander

**interconnect** /ɪntəkə'nekt/ ❶ *v.t.* miteinander verbinden; zusammenschalten ‹Stromkreise, Verstärker, Lautsprecher›; **~ed facts/results** zusammenhängende Tatsachen/Ergebnisse; **the events are ~ed** es besteht ein Zusammenhang zwischen den Ereignissen. ❷ *v.i.* miteinander in Zusammenhang stehen; **~ing rooms** miteinander verbundene Zimmer

**interconnection** /ɪntəkə'nekʃn/ *n.* (*of parts, components*) Zusammenwirken, *das;* (*of circuits*) Zusammenschalten, *das;* (*of facts, events, ideas*) Zusammenhang, *der*

**intercontinental** /ɪntəkɒntɪ'nentl/ *adj.* interkontinental; Interkontinental‹rakete, -flug, -reise›

**intercourse** /'ɪntəkɔ:s/ *n., no pl.* Ⓐ (*social communication*) Umgang, *der;* **social ~:** gesellschaftlicher Verkehr; **human ~:** menschliche Kontakte; die Beziehungen der Menschen; Ⓑ (*sexual ~*) [Geschlechts]verkehr, *der*

**interdenominational** /ɪntədɪnɒmɪ'neɪʃənl/ *adj.* interkonfessionell

**interdepartmental** /ɪntədi:pɑ:t'mentl/ *adj.* ‹Konferenz, Zusammenarbeit, Streit› zwischen den Abteilungen/Fachbereichen

**interdependence** /ɪntədɪ'pendəns/ *n.* gegenseitige Abhängigkeit; Interdependenz, *die*

**interdependent** /ɪntədɪ'pendənt/ *adj.* voneinander abhängig; interdependent

**interdict** /'ɪntədɪkt/ *n.* Ⓐ (*authoritative prohibition*) Verbot, *das;* Ⓑ (*RC Ch.*) Interdikt, *das*

**interdisciplinary** /ɪntədɪsɪ'plɪnərɪ/ *adj.* fachübergreifend; interdisziplinär

**interest** /'ɪntrəst, 'ɪntrɪst/ ❶ *n.* Ⓐ (*concern, curiosity*) Interesse, *das;* Anliegen, *das;* **take** *or* **have an ~ in sb./sth.** sich für jmdn./etw. interessieren; **show/develop a [lively] ~ in sb./sth.** [lebhaftes] Interesse an jmdm./etw. zeigen/entwickeln; **take** *or* **have/show no further ~ in sb./sth.** das Interesse an jmdm./etw. verloren haben/kein Interesse mehr an jmdm./etw. zeigen; **[just] for** *or* **out of ~:** [nur] interessehalber; **with ~:** interessiert (⇒ *also* **e**); **lose ~ in sb./sth.** das Interesse an jmdm./etw. verlieren; **~ in life/food** Lust am Leben/Essen; Ⓑ (*quality of sth.*) Interesse, *das;* Bedeutung, *die;* **this has no great ~ for me** das ist nicht sehr wichtig für mich; **be of ~:** interessant *od.* von Interesse sein (**to** für); **this is of no ~ to me** das ist belanglos für mich; Ⓒ (*advantage, profit*) Interesse, *das;* **act in one's own/sb.'s ~[s]** im eigenen/in jmds. Interesse handeln; **it is in your ~ to go** es liegt in deinem Interesse zu gehen; **in the ~[s] of humanity** zum Wohle der Menschheit; Ⓓ (*thing in which one is concerned*) Angelegenheit, *die;* Belange *Pl.;* **have a wide range of ~s** viele Interessen haben; Ⓔ (*Finance*) Zinsen *Pl.;* **rate of ~, ~ rate** Zinssatz, *der;* **~ on one's capital** Zinsen auf sein Kapital; **~ on a mortgage** Hypothekenzinsen *Pl.;* **at ~:** gegen *od.* auf Zinsen; **at 6% ~:** zu 6% Zinsen; **with ~** (*fig.: with increased force etc.*) überreichlich; doppelt und dreifach (*ugs.*) (⇒ *also* **a**); **give back** *or* **return blows with ~** (*fig.*) Schläge mit doppelter Härte zurückgeben; Ⓕ (*financial stake*) Beteiligung, *die;* Anteil, *der;* **have [financial] ~s all over the world** an Firmen *od.* Unternehmungen in der ganzen Welt finanziell beteiligt sein; **American ~s in the Caribbean** amerikanische Interessen in der Karibik; **declare an ~:** seine Interessen darlegen; Ⓖ (*legal concern*) [Rechts]anspruch, *der;* Ⓗ (*party having common ~*) Interessengruppe, *die;* **banking ~s** Bankkreise *Pl.;* die Banken; **business ~s** die Großindustrie. ⇒ *also* **compound ~; simple ~; vested**.
❷ *v.t.* interessieren (**in** für); **be ~ed in sb./sth.** sich für jmdn./etw. interessieren; **~ oneself in ...:** sich für ... interessieren; **sb. is ~ed by sb./sth.** jmd./etw. erregt jmds. Interesse; ⇒ *also* **interested**

**interested** /'ɪntrəstɪd, 'ɪntrɪstɪd/ *adj.* Ⓐ (*taking or showing interest*) interessiert; **be ~ in music/football/sb.** sich für Musik/Fußball/jmdn. interessieren; **I shall be ~ to hear about your trip** ich bin gespannt darauf, von deiner Reise zu hören; **I should be ~ to know why ...:** es würde mich interessieren, warum ...; **be ~ in doing sth.** sich dafür interessieren, etw. zu tun; **he is ~ in buying a car** er würde gern ein Auto kaufen; **not ~ in his work** nicht an seiner Arbeit interessiert; **the ~ parties** die beteiligten Parteien; **he looked ~:** er zeigte sich interessiert; Ⓑ (*not impartial*) voreingenommen; eigennützig ‹Beweggründe›; befangen ‹Zeuge›

**interest: ~-free** *adj., adv.* unverzinslich ‹Schuldverschreibung›; zinsfrei ‹Darlehen›; **~ group** *n.* Interessengruppe, *die*

**interesting** /'ɪntrəstɪŋ, 'ɪntrɪstɪŋ/ *adj.* interessant

**interestingly** /'ɪntrəstɪŋlɪ, 'ɪntrɪstɪŋlɪ/ *adv.* interessant; **~ [enough], ...:** interessanterweise ...

**'interest rate** *n.* Zinssatz, *der;* Zinsfuß, *der*

**interface** /'ɪntəfeɪs/ *n.* Ⓐ (*surface*) Grenzfläche, *die;* Ⓑ (*place where interaction occurs*) Nahtstelle, *die;* Schnittstelle, *die;* (*fig.*) Verbindung, *die;* Kontakt, *der;* Ⓒ (*Computing*) Schnittstelle, *die*

**interfacing** /'ɪntəfeɪsɪŋ/ *n.* (*Dressm.*) Einlage, *die*

**interfere** /ɪntə'fɪə(r)/ *v.i.* Ⓐ (*meddle*) sich einmischen (**in** in + *Akk.*); **~ with sth.** sich an etw. (*Dat.*) zu schaffen machen; Ⓑ (*come into opposition*) in Konflikt geraten (**with** mit); **~ with sth.** etw. beeinträchtigen; **~ with sb.'s plans** jmds. Pläne durchkreuzen; Ⓒ (*Radio, Telev.*) stören (**with** *Akk.*); Ⓓ **~ with sb.** (*sexually*) jmdn. sexuell missbrauchen; Ⓔ (*Phys.*) interferieren

**interference** /ɪntə'fɪərəns/ *n.* Ⓐ (*interfering*) Einmischung, *die;* Ⓑ (*Radio, Telev.*) Störung, *die;* **~ suppressor** Siebkreis, *der;* Entstörgerät, *das;* Ⓒ (*sexual*) Notzucht, *die* (*veralt.*); Missbrauch, *der;* Ⓓ (*Phys.*) Interferenz, *die*

**interfering** /ɪntə'fɪərɪŋ/ *attrib. adj.* sich einmischend; **she is an ~ old busybody** sie mischt sich in alles und jedes ein

**intergovernmental** /ɪntəgʌvn'mentl/ *adj.* zwischenstaatlich; **~ agreement/conference** Regierungsabkommen, *das*/-konferenz, *die;* **~ discussions** Gespräche auf Regierungsebene; **~ cooperation** internationale Zusammenarbeit

**interim** /'ɪntərɪm/ ❶ *n.* **in the ~:** in der Zwischenzeit. ❷ *adj.* Ⓐ (*intervening*) dazwischenliegend; **the ~ period** die Zwischenzeit; Ⓑ (*temporary, provisional*) vorläufig ‹Vereinbarung, Bericht, Anordnung, Zustand, Maßnahme›; Zwischen‹lösung, -abkommen, -kredit, -finanzierung, -zinsen›; Übergangs‹regierung, -regelung, -hilfe›

**interim 'dividend** *n.* (*Finance*) Abschlagsdividende, *die*

**interior** /ɪn'tɪərɪə(r)/ ❶ *adj.* Ⓐ inner...; Innen‹fläche, -einrichtung, -wand›; Ⓑ (*inland*) im Landesinneren befindlich; Ⓒ (*internal, domestic*) Inlands-; Binnen‹markt, -handel›; Ⓓ (*Cinemat.*) **~ shots/photography** Innenaufnahmen *Pl.* ❷ *n.* Ⓐ (*inland region*) [Landes]innere, *das;* Ⓑ (*~ part*) Innere, *das;* **redecorate the ~ of the shop** den Laden innen renovieren; Ⓒ (*[picture of] inside of building, room, etc.*) Innere, *das;* (*picture*) Interieur, *das;* Ⓓ (*Cinemat.*) Innenaufnahme, *die;* (*Theatre*) Szene eines Innenraumes; Ⓔ (*home affairs*) **Department of the I~** (*US, Canada*), **Ministry of the I~** (*France, Germany, etc.*) Innenministerium, *das;* Ministerium des Innern

**interior: ~ deco'ration** *n.* Raumgestaltung, *die;* **~ 'decorator** *n.* Raumgestalter, *der*/-gestalterin, *die;* **~ de'sign** *n.* Innenarchitektur, *die;* **~ de'signer** *n.* Innenarchitekt, *der*/-architektin, *die;* **~-sprung** *adj.* (*Brit.*) **~-sprung mattress** Federkernmatratze, *die*

**interject** /ɪntə'dʒekt/ *v.t.* Ⓐ (*interpose*) einwerfen ‹Behauptung, Bemerkung, Frage›; **~ remarks** Einwürfe *od.* Zwischenbemerkungen machen; **..., he ~ed ...,** rief er dazwischen; Ⓑ (*remark parenthetically*) einflechten; nebenbei bemerken

**interjection** /ɪntə'dʒekʃn/ *n.* Ⓐ (*exclamation*) Ausruf, *der;* (*Ling.*) Interjektion, *die;* Ⓑ (*interposed remark*) Einwurf, *der;* Zwischenbemerkung, *die*

**interlace** /ɪntə'leɪs/ *v.t.* Ⓐ (*bind together*) zusammenfügen; Ⓑ (*interweave*) [miteinander] verflechten; (*fig.*) [miteinander] verbinden; **cloth ~d with gold threads** mit Goldfäden durchwirktes Tuch; Ⓒ (*mingle*) [miteinander] kombinieren ‹zwei Muster›; spicken ‹Rede, Schreiben› (**with** mit)

**interlard** /ɪntə'lɑ:d/ *v.t.* spicken (**with** mit); **be heavily ~ed with quotations** von Zitaten strotzen

**interleave** /ɪntə'li:v/ *v.t.* (*Printing*) durchschießen (**with** mit); (*fig.*) abwechseln (**with** mit)

**inter-library loan** /ɪntəlaɪbrərɪ 'ləʊn/ *n.* Fernleihe, *die;* **get a book on ~:** ein Buch über die Fernleihe bekommen

**interlink** /ɪntə'lɪŋk/ *v.t.* miteinander verbinden

**interlock** /ɪntə'lɒk/ ❶ *v.i.* sich ineinander haken; ‹Teile eines Puzzles:› sich zusammenfügen. ❷ *v.t.* Ⓐ (*lock together*) zusammenfügen; verflechten ‹Fasern›; Ⓑ (*connect*) (*Railw.*) verriegeln; (*Cinemat.*) synchronisieren

**interloper** /'ɪntələʊpə(r)/ *n.* Eindringling, *der*

**interlude** /'ɪntəlu:d, 'ɪntəlju:d/ *n.* Ⓐ (*Theatre: break*) Pause, *die;* Ⓑ (*occurring in break*) Zwischenspiel, *das;* Intermezzo, *das;* **musical ~:** musikalisches Zwischenspiel; Ⓒ (*intervening time*) kurze Phase *od.* Periode; **a few brief ~s of sleep** wenige kurze Schlafpausen; Ⓓ (*event interposed*) Intermezzo, *das*

**intermarriage** /ɪntə'mærɪdʒ/ *n.* Ⓐ (*between groups*) Mischehen *Pl.;* Ⓑ (*within groups*)

Heirat untereinander; (*between related persons*) Verwandtenehe, *die*

**intermarry** /ɪntə'mærɪ/ *v.i.* Ⓐ (*between groups*) Mischehen schließen; Ⓑ (*within groups*) untereinander heiraten; (*between related persons*) Verwandtenehen schließen

**intermediary** /ɪntə'mi:dɪərɪ/ *n.* Vermittler, *der*/Vermittlerin, *die*

**intermediate** /ɪntə'mi:djət/ ❶ *adj.* Ⓐ Zwischen-; **~ level/point between ...:** Niveau/Punkt zwischen ...; Ⓑ (*Educ.*) Mittel‹stufe, -schule›; **~ education** ≈ Realschulausbildung, *die;* mittlere Reife; **~ French** Französisch für fortgeschrittene Anfänger. ❷ *n.* Ⓐ fortgeschrittener Anfänger; Ⓑ (*Chem.*) Zwischenprodukt, *das*

**intermediate-range [ballistic] 'missile** *n.* Mittelstreckenrakete, *die*

**interment** /ɪn'tɜ:mənt/ *n.* Bestattung, *die* (*geh.*); Beisetzung, *die* (*geh.*)

**intermesh** /ɪntə'meʃ/ *v.i.* ‹Zahnräder:› ineinander greifen; ‹Fäden, Garne:› sich ineinander fügen

**intermezzo** /ɪntə'metsəʊ/ *n., pl.* **intermezzi** /ɪntə'metsi:/ *or* **~s** Intermezzo, *das*

**interminable** /ɪn'tɜ:mɪnəbl/ *adj.*, **interminably** /ɪn'tɜ:mɪnəblɪ/ *adv.* (*lit. or fig.*) endlos

**intermingle** /ɪntə'mɪŋgl/ ❶ *v.i.* sich vermischen; ‹Personen:› miteinander in Kontakt treten. ❷ *v.t.* vermischen

**intermission** /ɪntə'mɪʃn/ *n.* Ⓐ (*pause*) Unterbrechung, *die;* Ⓑ (*period of inactivity*) Pause, *die;* Ⓒ (*Amer.: interval in performance*) Pause, *die*

**intermittent** /ɪntə'mɪtənt/ *adj.* in Abständen auftretend ‹Signal, Fehler, Geräusch›; **be ~:** in Abständen auftreten; **there was ~ rain all day** es hat den ganzen Tag mit kurzen Unterbrechungen geregnet; **~ fever** Wechselfieber, *das;* intermittierendes Fieber (*fachspr.*)

**intermittently** /ɪntə'mɪtəntlɪ/ *adv.* in Abständen

**intern** ❶ /ɪn'tɜ:n/ *v.t.* gefangen halten; internieren ‹Kriegsgefangenen usw.›. ❷ /'ɪntɜ:n/ *n.* (*Amer.*) Ⓐ (*Med.*) Medizinalassistent, *der*/-assistentin, *die;* Ⓑ (*teacher*) Lehramtskandidat, *der*/-kandidatin, *die*

**internal** /ɪn'tɜ:nl/ *adj.* Ⓐ inner...; Innen‹winkel, -durchmesser, -fläche, -druck, -gewinde, -abmessungen›; Ⓑ (*Physiol.*) inner... ‹Blutung, Sekretion, Verletzung›; **~ temperature** Innentemperatur, *die;* Ⓒ (*intrinsic*) inner... ‹Logik, Stimmigkeit›; Ⓓ (*within country*) inner... ‹Angelegenheiten, Frieden, Probleme›; Binnen‹handel, -markt›; innenpolitisch ‹Angelegenheiten, Streitigkeiten, Probleme›; (*within organization*) [betriebs-/partei]intern ‹Auseinandersetzung, Post, Praxis, Verfahren[sweise]›; inner[betrieblich/-kirchlich/-gewerkschaftlich *usw.*] ‹Streitigkeiten›; **~ telephone** Haustelefon, *das;* Ⓔ (*Med.*) innerlich ‹Anwendung›; Ⓕ (*of the mind*) inner... ‹Monolog, Bewegung, Regung, Widerstände, Groll›; Ⓖ (*Univ.*) ordentlich ‹Student›; **~ examination** *an der Universität, an der man immatrikuliert ist, abgelegte Prüfung*

**internal: ~ 'clock** *n.* innere Uhr; **~-com'bustion engine** *n.* Verbrennungsmotor, *der;* **~ 'evidence** *n.* impliziter Beweis

**internalize (internalise)** /ɪn'tɜ:nəlaɪz/ *v.t.* (*Psych.*) verinnerlichen; internalisieren (*fachspr.*)

**internally** /ɪn'tɜ:nəlɪ/ *adv.* innerlich; (*within organization*) [partei-/betriebs]intern; **not to be taken ~:** nicht zum Einnehmen; nur zur äußerlichen Anwendung; **bleed ~:** innere Blutungen haben; **~ inconsistent** in sich (*Dat.*) unstimmig

**internal: ~ 'medicine** *n.* innere Medizin; **~ 'revenue** *n.* (*Amer.*) Steuereinnahmen *Pl.;* **I~ 'Revenue Service** *n.* (*Amer.*) ≈ Finanzamt, *das;* **~ 'rhyme** *n.* (*Pros.*) Binnenreim, *der*

**international** /ɪntə'næʃənl/ ❶ *adj.* international; **it was a very ~ gathering** das Treffen hatte ausgesprochen internationalen Charakter; **~ travel** Auslandsreisen *Pl.;* **~ team** (*Sport*) Nationalmannschaft, *die.* ❷ *n.* Ⓐ (*Sport: contest*) Länderkampf, *der;* (*in team sports*) Länderspiel, *das;* Ⓑ (*Sport: participant*) Internationale, *der/die;* (*in team sports*) Nationalspieler, *der*/-spielerin, *die;* Ⓒ **I~** (*Polit.*) Internationale, *die*

**international: ~ call** *n.* (*Teleph.*) Auslandsgespräch, *das;* **~ 'code** *n.* (*Naut.*) internationales Signalbuch; **I~ Court of 'Justice** *n.* Internationaler Gerichtshof; **~ date line** ⇒ **date line**; **~ 'driving licence** *or* **permit** *n.* internationaler Führerschein

**internationalism** /ɪntə'næʃənəlɪzm/ *n.* Internationalismus, *der*

**internationalize (internationalise)** /ɪntə'næʃənəlaɪz/ *v.t.* internationalisieren

**international 'law** *n.* Völkerrecht, *das*

**internationally** /ɪntə'næʃənəlɪ/ *adv.* international

**international: I~ 'Monetary Fund** *n.* Internationaler Währungsfonds; **~ re'ply coupon** ⇒ **reply coupon**; **~ system of 'units** *n.* (*Phys.*) Internationales Einheitensystem

**internecine** /ɪntə'ni:saɪn/ *adj.* (*mutually destructive*) [für beide Seiten] vernichtend; (*bloody*) Vernichtungs‹krieg, -feldzug›; (*internal*) intern ‹Streitigkeiten, Zwist›

**internee** /ɪntɜ:'ni:/ *n.* Internierte, *der/die*

**Internet** /'ɪntənet/ *n.* **the ~** das Internet; **on the ~:** im Internet; **~ connection** Internetanschluss, *der*

**Internet 'service provider** *n.* (*Computing*) Internetprovider, *der*

**internist** /ɪn'tɜ:nɪst/ *n.* Ⓐ (*specialist*) Facharzt/-ärztin für innere Krankheiten; Internist, *der*/Internistin, *die;* Ⓑ (*Amer.: general practitioner*) praktischer Arzt/praktische Ärztin

**internment** /ɪn'tɜ:nmənt/ *n.* Internierung, *die;* **~ camp** Internierungslager, *das*

**interpersonal** /ɪntə'pɜ:sənl/ *adj.* interpersonal; interpersonell

**interplanetary** /ɪntə'plænɪtərɪ/ *adj.* (*Astron.*, *Astronaut.*) interplanetar[isch] ‹Rakete, Raum, Raumfahrt›

**interplay** /'ɪntəpleɪ/ *n.* Ⓐ (*interaction*) Wechselwirkung, *die;* Ⓑ (*reciprocal action*) Zusammenspiel, *das*

**Interpol** /'ɪntəpɒl/ *n.* Interpol, *die*

**interpolate** /ɪn'tɜ:pəleɪt/ *v.t.* Ⓐ (*interpose orally*) einwerfen ‹Satz, Bemerkung›; (*in programme*) einschieben ‹Warnung usw.›; Ⓑ (*introduce by insertion*) einfügen ‹Worte›; Ⓒ (*Math.*) interpolieren

**interpolation** /ɪntɜ:pə'leɪʃn/ *n.* Ⓐ Einfügung, *die;* **his ~ of that remark** sein Einwurf; Ⓑ (*Math.*) Interpolation, *die*

**interpose** /ɪntə'pəʊz/ ❶ *v.t.* Ⓐ (*insert*) dazwischenlegen; **~ sth. between sb./sth. and sb./sth.** etw. zwischen jmdn./etw. und jmdn./etw. bringen; Ⓑ (*say as interruption*) einwerfen ‹Frage, Bemerkung›; Ⓒ (*exercise, advance*) **~ one's veto** sein Veto einlegen; von seinem Veto[recht] Gebrauch machen; **~ one's authority** seinen Einfluss geltend machen; **~ an objection** einen Einwand vorbringen; Einspruch einlegen (*Rechtsw.*). ❷ *v.i.* Ⓐ (*intervene*) **~ on sb.'s side** *or* **behalf** sich für jmdn. einsetzen; **~ in sth.** in etw. (*Akk.*) [vermittelnd] eingreifen; Ⓑ (*make an interruption*) [kurz] unterbrechen

**interpret** /ɪn'tɜ:prɪt/ ❶ *v.t.* Ⓐ interpretieren; deuten ‹Traum, Zeichen›; auslegen ‹Heilige Schrift›; Ⓑ (*between languages*) dolmetschen; Ⓒ (*decipher*) entziffern ‹Schrift, Inschrift›. ❷ *v.i.* dolmetschen

**interpretation** /ɪntɜ:prɪ'teɪʃn/ *n.* Ⓐ Interpretation, *die;* (*of dream, symptoms*) Deutung, *die;* (*of biblical passage*) Auslegung, *die;* Ⓑ (*deciphering*) Entzifferung, *die*

**interpretative** /ɪn'tɜ:prɪtətɪv/ *adj.* erläuternd ‹Artikel, Aufsatz›; interpretativ ‹Kraft, Talent›; interpretierend ‹Künstler›

**interpreter** /ɪn'tɜ:prɪtə(r)/ *n.* Ⓐ (*between languages*) Dolmetscher, *der*/Dolmetscherin, *die;* Ⓑ (*of dreams, hieroglyphics*) Deuter, *der;* Ⓒ (*performer on stage etc.*) Interpret, *der*/Interpretin, *die*

**interpretive** /ɪn'tɜ:prɪtɪv/ ⇒ **interpretative**

**interregnum** /ɪntə'regnəm/ *n., pl.* **~s** *or* **interregna** /ɪntə'regnə/ Ⓐ (*period*) Zwischenregierung, *die;* Interregnum, *das* (*Politik*); Ⓑ (*interval*) Unterbrechung, *die*

**interrelated** /ɪntərɪ'leɪtɪd/ *adj.* zusammenhängend ‹Tatsachen, Ereignisse, Themen›; verwandt ‹Sprachen, Fachgebiete›; **be ~:** zusammenhängen/verwandt sein

**interrelation** /ɪntərɪ'leɪʃn/ *n.* Wechselbeziehung, *die;* (*between events*) Zusammenhang, *der*

**interrogate** /ɪn'terəgeɪt/ *v.t.* vernehmen ‹Zeugen, Angeklagten›; verhören ‹Angeklagten, Verdächtigen, Spion, Gefangenen›; ausfragen ‹Freund, Kind, Schüler usw.›

**interrogation** /ɪnterə'geɪʃn/ *n.* (*interrogating*) Verhör, *das; attrib.* Verhör-; **under ~:** beim Verhör; **be under ~:** verhört werden

**interrogative** /ɪntə'rɒgətɪv/ *adj.* Ⓐ (*having question form*) Frage-; fragend ‹Tonfall›; Ⓑ (*inquiring*) fragend ‹Ton, Blick›; Ⓒ (*Ling.*) Interrogativ‹pronomen, -adverb, -form›

**interrogator** /ɪn'terəgeɪtə(r)/ *n.* Vernehmer, *der*

**interrupt** /ɪntə'rʌpt/ ❶ *v.t.* unterbrechen; **~ sb.'s sleep** jmds. Schlaf stören; **don't ~ me when I'm busy** stör mich nicht, wenn ich zu tun habe; **~ sb.'s view** jmdm. die Sicht versperren. ❷ *v.i.* unterbrechen; stören; **stop ~ing!** unterbrich *od.* stör nicht dauernd!

**interruption** /ɪntə'rʌpʃn/ *n.* (*of work etc.*) Unterbrechung, *die;* Störung, *die;* (*of peace, sleep*) Störung, *die;* (*of services*) [zeitweiliger] Ausfall; **without ~:** ohne Unterbrechung; ununterbrochen

**intersect** /ɪntə'sekt/ ❶ *v.t.* Ⓐ ‹Kanäle, Schluchten, [Quarz]adern:› durchziehen ‹Land, Boden›; **streets ~ing each other** einander kreuzende Straßen; Ⓑ (*Geom.*) schneiden; **~ each other** sich schneiden. ❷ *v.i.* Ⓐ ‹Straßen:› sich kreuzen; Ⓑ (*Geom.*) sich schneiden

**intersection** /ɪntə'sekʃn/ *n.* Ⓐ (*intersecting; road etc. junction*) Kreuzung, *die;* Ⓑ (*Geom.*) **[point of] ~:** Schnittpunkt, *der;* Ⓒ (*Logic, Math.*) Schnittmenge, *die*

**intersperse** /ɪntə'spɜ:s/ *v.t.* Ⓐ (*scatter*) [hier und da] einfügen; Ⓑ **be ~d with** durchsetzt sein mit; ‹Erzählung, Arbeit, Routine:› unterbrochen werden durch ‹Pausen, Ruhe, Aufregungen›

**interstate** /'ɪntəsteɪt/ *adj.* (*Amer.*) zwischen den [Bundes]staaten *nachgestellt;* zwischenstaatlich; **~ highway** Fernstraße (*die durch mehrere Bundesstaaten führt*)

**interstellar** /ɪntə'stelə(r)/ *adj.* interstellar ‹Materie, Staub, Raum›; **~ travel** [Welt-]raumfahrt, *die*

**interstice** /ɪn'tɜ:stɪs/ *n.* (*intervening space*) Zwischenraum, *der;* (*of net*) Masche, *die;* (*between panels etc.*) Fuge, *die*

**intertwine** /ɪntə'twaɪn/ ❶ *v.t.* flechten (**in** in + *Akk.*); **he ~d his fingers with hers** er schlang *od.* flocht seine Finger zwischen ihre *od.* die ihren (*geh.*). ❷ *v.i.* sich [ineinander] verschlingen

**interval** /'ɪntəvl/ *n.* Ⓐ (*intervening space*) Zwischenraum, *der;* (*intervening time*) [Zeit]abstand, *der;* **at ~s** in Abständen; **at 20-minute ~s** in Abständen von 20 Minuten; **at frequent** *or* **short/wide ~s** in kurzen/weiten Abständen; **at ~s along the road/river** hier und da an der Straße/am Flussufer; **after an ~ of three years** nach [Ablauf von] drei Jahren; Ⓑ (*break; also Brit. Theatre etc.*) Pause, *die;* **an ~ of silence** eine Schweige- *od.* Gedenkminute; **an ~ in the shooting** eine Unterbrechung der Schießereien; **sunny** *or* **bright ~s** (*Meteorol.*) Aufheiterungen *Pl.;* **~ music** Pausenmusik, *die;* Ⓒ (*period*) Pause, *die;* **~s of sanity** lichte Momente; Ⓓ (*Mus.*) Intervall, *das;* **perfect ~:** reines Intervall

**'interval signal** *n.* (*Broadcasting*) Pausenzeichen, *das*

**intervene** /ɪntə'vi:n/ *v.i.* Ⓐ [vermittelnd] eingreifen (**in** in + *Akk.*); (*come between persons*) vermitteln (**between** zwischen + *Dat.*); **if nothing ~s** wenn nichts dazwischenkommt; **if fate had not ~d** wenn das Schicksal nicht eingegriffen hätte; Ⓑ (*occur*) **the years that ~d, the intervening years** die dazwischenliegenden Jahre; Ⓒ (*Law*) **~**

i

**in** eintreten in (+ *Akk.*) ‹Vertrag usw.›; beitreten (+ *Dat.*) ‹Verfahren›

**intervention** /ɪntəˈvenʃn/ *n.* Eingreifen, *das;* Intervention, *die* (*bes. Politik*); **surgical ~:** chirurgischer Eingriff; **at my ~:** auf mein Eingreifen/meine Intervention [hin]; **I~ Board** ≈ Interventionsstelle, *die*

**interventionist** /ɪntəˈvenʃənɪst/ ❶ *n.* Interventionist, *der.* ❷ *adj.* interventionistisch

**interview** /ˈɪntəvjuː/ ❶ *n.* [A] (*for job etc.*) Vorstellungsgespräch, *das;* [B] (*Journ., Radio, Telev.*) Interview, *das;* [C] (*discussion*) Gespräch, *das;* Unterredung, *die.* ❷ *v.t.* ein Vorstellungsgespräch/Vorstellungsgespräch[e] führen mit ‹Stellen-, Studienbewerber›; interviewen ‹Politiker, Filmstar, Konsumenten usw.›; vernehmen ‹Zeugen›

**interviewee** /ɪntəvjuːˈiː/ *n.* (*for opinion poll*) Befragte, *der/die;* (*candidate, applicant*) [Stellen-, Studien]bewerber, *der/*-bewerberin, *die;* (*politician, celebrity, etc.*) Interviewpartner, *der/*-partnerin, *die;* Interviewte, *der/die*

**interviewer** /ˈɪntəvjuːə(r)/ *n.* (*reporter, pollster, etc.*) Interviewer, *der*/Interviewerin, *die;* (*for job etc.*) Leiter/Leiterin des Vorstellungsgesprächs

**inter-war** /ˈɪntəwɔː(r)/ *attrib. adj.* ‹Zeit, Jahre› zwischen den [Welt]kriegen

**interweave** /ɪntəˈwiːv/ *v.t.,* **interwove** /ɪntəˈwəʊv/, **interwoven** /ɪntəˈwəʊvn/ [miteinander] verweben ‹Fäden, Wolle, Seide usw.›; [miteinander] verflechten ‹Zweige, Bänder›; **our lives are interwoven** unsere Lebenswege sind miteinander verschlungen

**intestacy** /ɪnˈtestəsɪ/ *n.* Sterben ohne Hinterlassung eines Testaments

**intestate** /ɪnˈtestət/ *adj.* Intestat‹erbe, -erbfolge, -nachlass›; **die ~:** ohne Hinterlassung eines Testaments sterben

**intestinal** /ɪnˈtestɪnl/ *adj.* (*Med.*) Darm-; intestinal (*fachspr.*)

**intestine** /ɪnˈtestɪn/ *n.* **▶966** *in sing. or pl.* (*Anat.*) Darm, *der;* Gedärme *Pl.;* **large/small ~:** Dick-/Dünndarm, *der*

**intimacy** /ˈɪntɪməsɪ/ *n.* [A] (*state*) Vertrautheit, *die;* (*close personal relationship*) enges [Freundschafts]verhältnis; [B] (*euphem.: sexual intercourse*) Intimität, *die;* **~ took place** es kam zu Intimitäten; [C] *in pl.* (*caresses*) Intimitäten; Vertraulichkeiten

**intimate** ❶ /ˈɪntɪmət/ *adj.* [A] (*close, closely acquainted*) eng ‹Freund, Freundschaft, Beziehung, Verhältnis›; vertraulich ‹Ton›; **be on ~ terms with sb.** zu jmdm. ein enges *od.* vertrautes Verhältnis haben; [B] (*euphem.: having sexual intercourse*) intim ‹Beziehungen›; **be/become ~ with sb.** mit jmdm. intim sein/werden; [C] (*from close familiarity*) **~ knowledge of sth.** genaue *od.* intime Kenntnis einer Sache; **~ acquaintance with sth.** enge Vertrautheit mit etw.; [D] (*closely personal*) persönlich ‹Problem›; privat ‹Angelegenheit, Gefühl, Dinge›; geheim ‹Gedanken›; (*euphem.*) Intim‹bereich, -spray›; [E] innig ‹Verbindung, Verschmelzung, Zusammenhang›; [F] intim ‹Tagebuch, Brief, Darstellung, Raum, Theater, Restaurant, Musik, Feier, Treffen›; **the party was a small, ~ affair** die Feier fand im intimsten Kreis statt.
❷ *n.* (*close friend*) Vertraute, *der/die.*
❸ /ˈɪntɪmeɪt/ *v.t.* [A] **~ sth. [to sb.]/[to sb.] that ...** (*make known*) [jmdm.] etw. mitteilen/[jmdm.] mitteilen, dass ...; (*show clearly*) [jmdm.] etw. deutlich machen *od.* zu verstehen geben/[jmdm.] zu verstehen geben, dass ...; [B] (*imply*) andeuten

**intimately** /ˈɪntɪmətlɪ/ *adv.* genau[estens] ‹kennen›; bestens ‹vertraut›; gründlich ‹vermischen›; eng ‹verbinden›; **he is ~ involved in the planning of the project** er ist an der Planung des Projekts maßgeblich beteiligt; **we know each other, but not ~:** wir kennen uns, aber nicht näher

**intimation** /ɪntɪˈmeɪʃn/ *n.* [A] Mitteilung, *die;* (*of sb.'s death etc.*) Anzeige, *die;* **give an ~:** eine Mitteilung machen; [B] (*hint*) Andeutung, *die;* (*of trouble, anger, pain*) Anzeichen, *das;* **give ~s** Andeutungen machen

**intimidate** /ɪnˈtɪmɪdeɪt/ *v.t.* einschüchtern; **~ sb. into doing sth.** jmdn. einschüchtern *od.* unter Druck setzen, damit er etw. tut; **use intimidating behaviour** zum Mittel der Einschüchterung greifen

**intimidation** /ɪntɪmɪˈdeɪʃn/ *n.* Einschüchterung, *die*

**into** /*before vowel* ˈɪntʊ, *before consonant* ˈɪntə/ *prep.* [A] *expr. motion or direction* in (+ *Akk.*); (*against*) gegen; **I went out ~ the street** ich ging auf die Straße hinaus; **they disappeared ~ the night** sie verschwanden in die Nacht hinein; **you don't have to go ~ London** (*coll.*) du brauchst nicht nach London rein (*ugs.*); **he was [straight] ~ the biscuit tin** er machte sich über die Keksdose her; **baptized ~ the Catholic Church** katholisch getauft; **they were soon ~ their clothes and on deck** sie waren in kurzer Zeit angekleidet auf Deck; **4 [divided] ~ 20 = 5** 20 [geteilt] durch 4 = 5; **until well ~ this century** bis weit in unser Jahrhundert hinein; **it was 15 minutes ~ the second half before ...:** erst in der 15. Minute der zweiten Halbzeit ...; [B] *expr. change, result* **translate sth. ~ English** etw. ins Englische übersetzen; **the book is ~ its third edition** das Buch liegt schon in dritter Auflage vor; **poke the fire ~ a blaze** das Feuer [durch Schüren] zum Auflodern bringen; [C] (*coll.*) **be ~ sth./sb.** (*interested in*) auf etw./jmdn. stehen (*ugs.*); auf etw./jmdn. abfahren (*salopp*); **be ~ sth.** (*knowledgeable about*) mit etw. vertraut sein; **he's heavily ~ meditation** er ist völlig auf Meditation abgefahren (*salopp*)

**intolerable** /ɪnˈtɒlərəbl/ *adj.* unerträglich; **it's ~:** es ist nicht auszuhalten; **an ~ place to live in** ein Ort, an dem das Leben unerträglich ist

**intolerably** /ɪnˈtɒlərəblɪ/ *adv.* unerträglich

**intolerance** /ɪnˈtɒlərəns/ *n., no pl.* Intoleranz, *die;* Unduldsamkeit, *die* (**of** gegenüber); (*Med.*) [Über]empfindlichkeit, *die* (**to, of** gegen)

**intolerant** /ɪnˈtɒlərənt/ *adj.* intolerant, unduldsam (**of** gegenüber)

**intonation** /ɪntəˈneɪʃn/ *n.* (*modulation*) Intonation, *die* (*Sprachw.*); Sprachmelodie, *die;* **speak with a Russian ~:** in russischem Tonfall sprechen

**intone** /ɪnˈtəʊn/ *v.t.* intonieren

**intoxicant** /ɪnˈtɒksɪkənt/ ❶ *n.* Rauschmittel, *das.* ❷ *adj.* berauschend

**intoxicate** /ɪnˈtɒksɪkeɪt/ *v.t.* [A] (*make drunk*) betrunken machen; **be/become ~d** betrunken sein/werden; [B] (*excite*) berauschen; **be ~d by/with sth.** durch/von etw. berauscht sein

**intoxicating** /ɪnˈtɒksɪkeɪtɪŋ/ *adj.* berauschend ‹Wirkung, Schönheit›; mitreißend ‹Worte, Rhythmus›; **~ liquors** alkoholische Getränke

**intoxication** /ɪntɒksɪˈkeɪʃn/ *n.* [A] Rausch, *der;* **in a state of ~:** in betrunkenem Zustand; im Rausch; [B] (*excitement*) Hochgefühl, *das;* Euphorie, *die* (*geh.*)

**intra-** /ɪntrə/ *pref.* inner-; (*mit Fremdwörtern meist*) intra-

**intractable** /ɪnˈtræktəbl/ *adj.* widerspenstig ‹Verhalten, Kind, Tier›; aufrührerisch ‹[Menschen]menge, -masse›; unbeugsam ‹Wille›; hartnäckig ‹Krankheit, Schmerzen, Problem›

**intraˈmural** *adj.* (*Univ.*) innerhalb der Universität; inneruniversitär

**intraˈmuscular** *adj.* (*Med.*) intramuskulär

**ˈIntranet** *n.* Intranet, *das*

**intransigence** /ɪnˈtrænsɪdʒəns, ɪnˈtrænzɪdʒəns/ *n., no pl.* ⇒ **intransigent**: Kompromisslosigkeit, *die;* Unnachgiebigkeit, *die;* Intransigenz, *die* (*geh.*); Unerschütterlichkeit, *die*

**intransigent** /ɪnˈtrænsɪdʒənt, ɪnˈtrænzɪdʒənt/ ❶ *adj.* kompromisslos, unnachgiebig, (*geh.*) intransigent ‹Haltung, Einstellung›; unerschütterlich ‹Wille, Grundsätze, Glaube›. ❷ *n.* (*in politics*) Radikale, *der/die*

**intransitive** /ɪnˈtrænsɪtɪv, ɪnˈtrɑːnsɪtɪv/ *adj.,* **intransitively** /ɪnˈtrænsɪtɪvlɪ, ɪnˈtrɑːnsɪtɪvlɪ/ *adv.* (*Ling.*) intransitiv

**intra-uterine** /ɪntrəˈjuːtəraɪn/ *adj.* (*Med.*) intrauterin; **~ [contraceptive] device** Intrauterinpessar, *das*

**intraˈvenous** *adj.* (*Med.*) intravenös

**ˈin-tray** *n.* Ablage für Eingänge

**intrepid** /ɪnˈtrepɪd/ *adj.,* **intrepidly** /ɪnˈtrepɪdlɪ/ *adv.* unerschrocken

**intricacy** /ˈɪntrɪkəsɪ/ *n.* [A] *no pl.* (*quality*) Kompliziertheit, *die;* **increase the ~ of sth.** etw. [noch] komplizierter machen; [B] *in pl.* (*things*) Feinheiten *Pl.*

**intricate** /ˈɪntrɪkət/ *adj.* verschlungen ‹Pfad, Windung›; kompliziert ‹System, Muster, Fabel, Werkstück, Maschinenteil, Aufgabe›; (*obscure*) schwer verständlich

**intricately** /ˈɪntrɪkətlɪ/ *adv.* kompliziert; **an ~ designed pattern** ein kompliziertes Muster

**intrigue** /ɪnˈtriːg/ ❶ *v.t.* faszinieren; **I'm ~d to find out what ...:** ich bin gespannt darauf, zu erfahren, was ... ❷ *v.i.* **~ against sb.** gegen jmdn. intrigieren; **~ with sb.** mit jmdm. Ränke schmieden *od.* Intrigen spinnen. ❸ /ɪnˈtriːg, ˈɪntriːg/ *n.* Intrige, *die;* **~s** Machenschaften *Pl.* (*abwertend*)

**intriguer** /ɪnˈtriːgə(r)/ *n.* Intrigant, *der*/Intrigantin, *die*

**intriguing** /ɪnˈtriːgɪŋ/ *adj.,* **intriguingly** /ɪnˈtriːgɪŋlɪ/ *adv.* faszinierend

**intrinsic** /ɪnˈtrɪnsɪk, ɪnˈtrɪnzɪk/ *adj.* (*inherent*) innewohnend; inner... ‹Verdorbenheit, Aufbau, Logik›; immanent (*geh.*); (*essential*) wesentlich, (*Philos.*) essenziell ‹Eigenschaft, Bestandteil, Mangel›; **be ~ in *or* to a thing** wesentliches Merkmal einer Sache sein; **~ value** innerer Wert; (*of sth. concrete*) Eigenwert, *der*

**intrinsically** /ɪnˈtrɪnsɪkəlɪ, ɪnˈtrɪnzɪkəlɪ/ *adv.* im Wesentlichen; (*Philos.*) essenziell

**intro** /ˈɪntrəʊ/ *n., pl.* **~s** (*coll.*) (*presentation*) Vorstellung, *die;* (*Mus.*) Einleitung, *die;* Intro, *das* (*fachspr.*)

**introduce** /ɪntrəˈdjuːs/ *v.t.* [A] (*bring in*) [erstmals] einführen ‹Ware, Tier, Pflanze› (**into** in + *Akk.*, **from ... into** von ... nach); einleiten ‹Maßnahmen›; einflechten ‹Episoden in Roman›; einschleppen ‹Krankheit›; **~ irrelevancies into the discussion** Unwesentliches in die Diskussion bringen; [B] einführen ‹Katheter, Schlauch› (**into** in + *Akk.*); stecken ‹Schlüssel, Draht, Rohr, Schlauch› (**into** in + *Akk.*); **~ sth. into the flame** etw. der Flamme aussetzen; [C] (*bring into use*) einführen ‹Neuerung, Verfahren, Brauch, Mode, Kalender, Nomenklatur›; aufbringen ‹Gerücht, Schlagwort, Mode›; [D] (*make known*) vorstellen; einführen ‹Vortragenden›; **~ oneself/sb. [to sb.]** sich/jmdn. [jmdm.] vorstellen; **I ~d them to each other** ich machte sie miteinander bekannt *od.* stellte sie einander vor; **I don't think we've been ~d** ich glaube, wir kennen uns noch nicht; **~ sb. to a hobby/to drugs** jmdn. in ein Hobby einführen/mit Drogen bekannt machen; [E] (*usher in, begin, precede*) einleiten ‹Buch, Thema, Musikstück, Epoche›; [F] (*present*) ankündigen ‹Programm, Darsteller›; [G] (*Parl.*) einbringen ‹Antrag, Entwurf, Gesetz›; einleiten ‹Reform›

**introduction** /ɪntrəˈdʌkʃn/ *n.* [A] (*of methods, measures, process, machinery*) Einführen, *das;* Einführung, *die;* (*of rules*) Aufstellung, *die;* (*of fashion*) Aufbringen, *das;* [B] (*of tube, catheter*) Einführen, *das;* [C] **an ~ to London nightlife** eine Einführung ins Londoner Nachtleben; **~ to heroin** erste Bekanntschaft mit Heroin; [D] (*formal presentation*) Vorstellung, *die;* (*into society*) Einführung, *die;* (*of reform*) Einleiten, *das;* (*of parliamentary bill*) Einbringen, *das;* **X needs no ~ from me** ich brauche X nicht vorzustellen; **do the ~s** die Anwesenden miteinander bekannt machen; **letter of ~:** Empfehlungsschreiben, *das;* [E] (*preliminary matter*) Einleitung, *die;* Introduktion, die (*Musik*); [F] (*introductory treatise*) Einführung, *die* (**to** in + *Akk.*); Leitfaden, *der* (**to** *Gen.*); [G] (*thing introduced*) Eingeführte, *das;* (*exotic plant or animal*) Eingebürgerte, *der/die/das;* **mechanized sowing was a later ~:** [die] maschinelle Aussaat wurde [erst] später eingeführt

**introˈduction agency** *n.* Partnervermittlung[sagentur], *die;* **join an ~:** sich bei einer Partnervermittlung registrieren lassen

**introductory** /ɪntrəˈdʌktərɪ/ *adj.* einleitend; Einführungs‹kurs, -vortrag›; Einleitungs‹kapitel, -rede›

**introspection** /ɪntrəˈspekʃn/ *n.* Selbstbeobachtung, *die;* Introspektion, *die* (*geh., Psych.*)

**introspective** /ɪntrəˈspektɪv/ *adj.* in sich (*Akk.*) gerichtet; verinnerlicht; introspektiv (*geh., Psych.*)

**introvert** /ˈɪntrəvɜːt/ ❶ *n.* Introvertierte, *der/die;* introvertierter Mensch; **be an ~:** introvertiert sein. ❷ *adj.* introvertiert; **have ~ tendencies** zur Introvertiertheit neigen

**introverted** /ɪntrəˈvɜːtɪd/ *adj.* introvertiert

**intrude** /ɪnˈtruːd/ ❶ *v.i.* stören; **~ [up]on sb.'s grief/leisure time/privacy** jmdn. in seiner Trauer stören/ jmds. Freizeit beanspruchen/in jmds. Privatsphäre (*Akk.*) eindringen; **~ [up]on sb.'s time** jmds. Zeit in Anspruch nehmen; **~ in[to] sb.'s affairs/conversation** sich in jmds. Angelegenheiten/Unterhaltung (*Akk.*) einmischen. ❷ *v.t.* aufdrängen (**into,** **[up]on** *Dat.*); **the idea** *or* **thought ~d itself into my mind** der Gedanke drängte sich mir auf; **~ oneself** *or* **one's presence upon sb.** sich jmdm. aufdrängen

**intruder** /ɪnˈtruːdə(r)/ *n.* Eindringling, *der;* (*Mil.*) Intruder, *der*

**in'truder alarm** *n.* Einbruchmeldeanlage, *die*

**intrusion** /ɪnˈtruːʒn/ *n.* Ⓐ (*intruding*) Störung, *die;* **an ~/numerous ~s upon** *or* **into sb.'s privacy** ein/wiederholtes Eindringen in jmds. Privatsphäre (*Akk.*); **~ on sb.'s leisure time** Inanspruchnahme von jmds. Freizeit; Ⓑ (*into building, country, etc.*) [gewaltsames] Eindringen; (*Mil.*) Einmarsch, *der* (**into** in + *Akk.*); Ⓒ (*forcing oneself in*) Einmischung, *die* (**upon** in + *Akk.*); Ⓓ (*Geol.*) Intrusion, *die*

**intrusive** /ɪnˈtruːsɪv/ *adj.* Ⓐ aufdringlich ‹Person›; aggressiv ‹Bemerkung, Kultur, Journalismus›; Ⓑ (*Phonet.*) intrusiv; Ⓒ (*Geol.*) **~ rock** Intrusivgestein, *das*

**intuition** /ɪntjuːˈɪʃn/ *n.* Intuition, *die;* **know sth. by ~:** etw. intuitiv wissen; **have an ~ that ...:** eine Eingebung haben *od.* intuitiv spüren, dass ...

**intuitive** /ɪnˈtjuːɪtɪv/ *adj.* intuitiv; gefühlsmäßig ‹Ablehnung, Beurteilung›; instinktiv ‹Annahme, Gefühl›

**intuitively** /ɪnˈtjuːɪtɪvlɪ/ *adv.* intuitiv; gefühlsmäßig

**inundate** /ˈɪnəndeɪt/ *v.t.* überschwemmen; ‹Meer:› überfluten; (*fig.*) (*with inquiries, letters, complaints, goods, information*) überschwemmen; (*with work, praise, advice*) überhäufen; **~d with tourists** von Touristen überlaufen; **we've been ~d with letters** eine Flut von Zuschriften ist bei uns eingegangen

**inundation** /ɪnənˈdeɪʃn/ *n.* Überschwemmung, *die;* (*by the sea*) Überflutung, *die;* (*fig.*) Flut, *die*

**inure** /ɪˈnjʊə(r)/ *v.t.* gewöhnen (**to** an + *Akk.*); (*toughen*) abhärten (**to** gegen); **become ~d to/~ oneself to sth.** sich an etw. (*Akk.*) gewöhnen

**in vacuo** /ɪn ˈvækjʊəʊ/ *adv.* (*fig.*) im luftleeren Raum; (*lit.*) in einem Vakuum

**invade** /ɪnˈveɪd/ *v.t.* Ⓐ einfallen in (+ *Akk.*) ‹Gebiet, Staat›; **Poland was ~d by the Germans** die Deutschen marschierten in Polen (*Akk.*) ein; Ⓑ (*swarm into*) ‹Touristen, Kinder:› überschwemmen ‹Land, Strand, Schwimmbad›; Ⓒ (*fig.*) ‹unangenehmes Gefühl, Krankheit, Schwäche:› befallen ‹Personen, Gewebe, Körper›; ‹Krankheit, Seuche, Unwetter:› heimsuchen ‹Person, Stadt, Gebiet›; ‹Glücksgefühl, Geruch:› durchströmen ‹Person, Raum›; ‹Thema, Vorstellung:› Eingang finden in (+ *Akk.*) ‹Literatur, Sprache›; Ⓓ (*encroach upon*) verletzen ‹Rechte›; stören ‹Ruhe, Frieden›; eindringen in (+ *Akk.*) ‹Haus, Bereich, Privatsphäre›

**invader** /ɪnˈveɪdə(r)/ *n.* (*hostile*) Angreifer, *der;* Invasor, *der* (*bes. Milit.*); (*intruder*) Eindringling, *der* (**of** in + *Akk.*)

**invalid[1]** ❶ /ˈɪnvəlɪd/ *n.* (*Brit.*) Kranke, *der/die;* (*disabled person*) Körperbehinderte, *der/die;* (*from war injuries*) Kriegsinvalide *der/*-invalidin, *die.* ❷ *adj.* (*Brit.*) körperbehindert; (*from war injuries*) kriegsbeschädigt; kriegsinvalide. ❸ /ˈɪnvəliːd, ɪnvəˈliːd/ *v.t.* **~ home** *or* **out** als dienstuntauglich entlassen; **~ out of the army** wegen Dienstuntauglichkeit aus der Armee entlassen

**invalid[2]** /ɪnˈvælɪd/ *adj.* nicht schlüssig ‹Argument, Behauptung, Folgerung, Theorie›; nicht zulässig ‹Annahme›; ungerechtfertigt ‹Forderung, Vorwurf›; nichtig ‹Entschuldigung›; ungültig ‹Fahrkarte, Garantie, Vertrag, Testament, Ehe›

**invalidate** /ɪnˈvælɪdeɪt/ *v.t.* aufheben; widerlegen ‹Theorie, These, Behauptung›

**invalid/'ɪnvəlɪd/: ~ carriage** *n.* Kranken[fahr]stuhl, *der;* **~ chair** *n.* Rollstuhl, *der;* **~ diet** *n.* Krankenkost, *die*

**invalidity** /ɪnvəˈlɪdɪtɪ/ *n., no pl.* ⇒ **invalid[2]**: mangelnde Schlüssigkeit; Unzulässigkeit, *die;* Ungerechtigkeit, *die;* Nichtigkeit, *die;* Ungültigkeit, *die*

**invalidly** /ɪnˈvælɪdlɪ/ *adv.* nicht ordnungsgemäß

**invaluable** /ɪnˈvæljʊəbl/ *adj.* unbezahlbar; unersetzlich ‹Mitarbeiter, Person›; unschätzbar ‹Dienst, Verdienst, Hilfe, Bedeutung›; außerordentlich wichtig ‹Rolle, Funktion›; außerordentlich wertvoll ‹Rat[schlag]›; **be ~ to sb.** für jmdn. von unschätzbarem Wert sein

**invariable** /ɪnˈveərɪəbl/ *adj.* Ⓐ (*fixed*) unveränderlich ‹Wert, Einheit›; Ⓑ (*always the same*) [stets] gleich bleibend ‹Druck, Temperatur, Höflichkeit, gute Laune›; ständig ‹Pech›

**invariably** /ɪnˈveərɪəblɪ/ *adv.* immer; ausnahmslos ‹falsch, richtig›; **it's ~ wet when I am on holiday** wenn ich Urlaub habe, regnet es garantiert

**invasion** /ɪnˈveɪʒn/ *n.* Ⓐ (*of troops, virus, locusts*) Invasion, *die;* (*of weeds etc.*) massenweise Ausbreitung; (*intrusion*) [überfallartiges] Eindringen (**of** in + *Akk.*); **the ~ of Belgium by German troops** der Einmarsch deutscher Truppen in Belgien; **the Viking ~ of Britain** der Einfall der Wikinger in Britannien; Ⓑ (*encroachment*) ⇒ **invade** D: Verletzung, *die;* Störung, *die;* Eindringen, *das*

**invective** /ɪnˈvektɪv/ *n.* Ⓐ (*abusive language*) Beschimpfungen *Pl.;* Ⓑ (*violent attack in words*) Schmähung, *die;* Invektive, *die* (*geh.*)

**inveigh** /ɪnˈveɪ/ *v.i.* **~ against sb./sth.** über jmdn./etw. schimpfen *od.* sich empören; **~ against fate/the elements** gegen das Schicksal/die Elemente aufbegehren

**inveigle** /ɪnˈviːgl, ɪnˈveɪgl/ *v.t.* Ⓐ (*entice*) **~ sb. into sth./doing sth.** jmdn. zu etw. verleiten/dazu verleiten, etw. zu tun; **~ sb. into the house** jmdn. ins Haus locken; Ⓑ (*cajole*) **~ sb. into doing sth.** jmdn. überreden *od.* (*ugs.*) beschwatzen, etw. zu tun

**invent** /ɪnˈvent/ *v.t.* Ⓐ (*create*) erfinden ‹Maschine, Verfahren, Spiel›; ersinnen ‹Melodie›; entwickeln ‹Schrift›; Ⓑ (*concoct*) erfinden; sich (*Dat.*) ausdenken

**invention** /ɪnˈvenʃn/ *n.* Ⓐ (*thing invented, inventing*) Erfindung, *die;* (*concept*) Idee, *die;* **it's a device of my own ~:** das habe ich mir selbst ausgedacht; **a story of his own ~:** eine von ihm [selbst] erfundene Geschichte; Ⓑ (*inventiveness*) Erfindungsgabe, *die;* [schöpferische] Fantasie; Ⓒ (*fictitious story*) Erfindung, *die;* Lüge, *die*

**inventive** /ɪnˈventɪv/ *adj.* Ⓐ schöpferisch ‹Person, Kraft, Geist, Begabung›; fantasievoll ‹Künstler, Kind›; Ⓑ (*produced with originality*) originell; einfallsreich

**inventiveness** /ɪnˈventɪvnɪs/ *n., no pl.* Erfindungsgabe, *die;* Kreativität, *die*

**inventor** /ɪnˈventə(r)/ *n.* Erfinder, *der/*Erfinderin, *die*

**inventory** /ˈɪnvəntərɪ/ ❶ *n.* Ⓐ (*list*) Bestandsliste, *die;* **make** *or* **take an ~ of sth.** von etw. ein Inventar aufstellen; Inventur machen; Ⓑ (*stock*) Lagerbestand, *der;* Ⓒ (*Amer.: trader's stock*) Warenbestand, *der.* ❷ *v.t.* Ⓐ (*make ~ of*) eine Bestandsliste *od.* ein Inventar aufstellen von; Ⓑ (*enter in ~*) inventarisieren

**inverse** /ɪnˈvɜːs, ˈɪnvɜːs/ ❶ *adj.* umgekehrt ‹Reihenfolge›. ❷ *n.* (*opposite*) Gegenteil, *das;* (*inversion*) Umkehrung, *die*

**inversely** /ɪnˈvɜːslɪ, ˈɪnvɜːslɪ/ *adv.* umgekehrt

**inverse: ~ pro'portion** *n.* umgekehrtes Verhältnis; **be in ~ proportion to sth.** im umgekehrten Verhältnis zu etw. stehen; **~ 'ratio** *n.* umgekehrtes Verhältnis; **~ 'square law** *n.* (*Phys.*) [quadratisches] Abstandsgesetz

**inversion** /ɪnˈvɜːʃn/ *n.* Ⓐ (*turning upside down*) Umdrehen, *das;* Ⓑ (*reversal of role, relation*) Umkehrung, *die;* Ⓒ (*Ling., Meteorol., Mus.*) Inversion, *die*

**invert** /ɪnˈvɜːt/ *v.t.* Ⓐ (*turn upside down*) umstülpen; **~ sth. over sth.** etw. über etw. (*Akk.*) stülpen; Ⓑ umkehren ‹Wortstellung›; vertauschen ‹Wörter, Filmrollen usw.›; Ⓒ (*Mus.*) umkehren

**invertebrate** /ɪnˈvɜːtɪbrət, ɪnˈvɜːtɪbreɪt/ (*Zool.*) ❶ *adj.* wirbellos. ❷ *n.* wirbelloses Tier; Evertebrat, *der* (*fachspr.*)

**inverted: ~ 'commas** *n. pl.* (*Brit.*) Anführungszeichen *Pl.;* Gänsefüßchen *Pl.* (*ugs.*); **in ~ commas** (*also iron.*) in Anführungszeichen; **~ 'pleat** *n.* Kellerfalte, *die;* **~ 'snob** *n.* Edelproletarier, *der* (*salopp*); **~ 'snobbery** *n.* Edelproletariertum, *das* (*salopp*)

**invest** /ɪnˈvest/ ❶ *v.t.* Ⓐ (*Finance*) anlegen (**in** in + *Dat.*); investieren (**in** in + *Dat. od. Akk.*); **~ time and effort in sth.** Zeit und Mühe in etw. (*Akk.*) investieren; Ⓑ **~ sb. with** (*cause to have*) jmdm. übertragen ‹Aufgabe, Amt, Leitung›; jmdm. verleihen ‹Orden, Titel, Amt, Rechte, Kraft›; jmdn. ausstatten mit ‹Geldmitteln, Vollmacht, Insignien›; Ⓒ **~ sth. with sth.** einer Sache (*Dat.*) etw. verleihen; **be ~ed with [an air of] mystery** den Anschein des Geheimnisvollen haben; Ⓓ (*Mil.*) belagern. ❷ *v.i.* investieren (**in** in + *Akk.*, **with** bei); **~ in sth.** (*coll.: buy*) sich (*Dat.*) etw. zulegen (*ugs.*)

**investigate** /ɪnˈvestɪgeɪt/ ❶ *v.t.* untersuchen; überprüfen; prüfen ‹Rechtsfrage, Material, Methode›; ermitteln ‹Produktionskosten›; **~ a case** einen Fall untersuchen; in einem Fall ermitteln; **~ a crime** ein Verbrechen untersuchen; wegen eines Verbrechens ermitteln. ❷ *v.i.* nachforschen; ‹Kripo, Staatsanwaltschaft:› ermitteln; **~ into sth.** etw. untersuchen

**investigation** /ɪnvestɪˈgeɪʃn/ *n.* ⇒ **investigate**: Untersuchung, *die;* Überprüfung, *die;* Prüfung, *die;* Ermittlung, *die;* **sth. is under ~:** etw. wird überprüft; **sb. is under ~:** gegen jmdn. wird ermittelt; **a scientific ~:** eine wissenschaftliche Untersuchung

**investigative** /ɪnˈvestɪgətɪv/ *adj.* detektivisch; **~ journalism** Enthüllungsjournalismus, *der*

**investigator** /ɪnˈvestɪgeɪtə(r)/ *n.* Ermittler, *der/*Ermittlerin, *die;* (*government official*) Untersuchungsbeamte, *der/*-beamtin, *die;* **[private] ~:** [Privat]detektiv, *der/*-detektivin, *die*

**investigatory** /ɪnˈvestɪgeɪtərɪ/ *adj.* **~ proceedings/tests/studies** Untersuchungen *Pl.*

**investiture** /ɪnˈvestɪtʃə(r)/ *n.* Investitur, *die;* **~ with the Order of the Garter** Verleihung des Hosenbandordens

**investment** /ɪnˈvestmənt/ *n.* Ⓐ (*of money*) Investition, *die* (*auch fig.*); Anlage, *die;* (*fig.*) Einsatz, *der;* Aufwand, *der; attrib.* Investitions-; Anlage-; **~ of capital** Kapitalanlage, *die;* **make an ~ [of £1,000 in sth.]** [1000 Pfund in etw. (*Akk.*)] investieren; **~ advice** Anlageberatung, *die;* **~ income** Kapitaleinkommen, *das;* **~ capital** Anlagekapital, *das;* **~ trust** Investmenttrust, *der;* Investmentgesellschaft, *die;* Ⓑ (*money invested*) angelegtes Geld; **his large ~ in the company** seine hohe Beteiligung an dem Unternehmen; Ⓒ (*property*) Kapitalanlage, *die;* **be a good ~** (*fig.*) sich bezahlt machen; eine gute Investition sein; Ⓓ ⇒ **investiture**; Ⓔ (*Mil.*) (*siege*) Belagerung, *die;* (*blockade*) Blockade, *die*

**investor** /ɪnˈvestə(r)/ *n.* Investor, *der/*Investorin, *die;* [Kapital]anleger, *der/*-anlegerin, *die;* **~s in that company** Anteilseigner dieser Firma; **small ~s** Kleinanleger

**inveterate** /ɪnˈvetərət/ *adj.* Ⓐ (*deep-rooted*) unüberwindbar ‹Vorurteil, Misstrauen›; unversöhnlich ‹Hass›; unverbesserlich ‹Faulheit usw.›; Ⓑ (*habitual*) eingefleischt ‹Trinker, Raucher, Individualist, Spieler›; unverbesserlich ‹Lügner›

**invidious** /ɪnˈvɪdɪəs/ *adj.* undankbar ‹Aufgabe›; unpassend, unfair ‹Vergleich, Bemerkung›

**invidiously** /ɪnˈvɪdɪəslɪ/ *adv.* ⇒ **invidious**: auf eine undankbare/unpassende *od.* unfaire Art; *as sentence-modifier* unfairerweise

**invigilate** /ɪnˈvɪdʒɪleɪt/ *v.i.* (*Brit.: in examination*) Aufsicht führen

**invigilation** /ɪnvɪdʒɪˈleɪʃn/ *n.* (*Brit.*) Aufsichtführung, *die*

**invigilator** /ɪnˈvɪdʒɪleɪtə(r)/ *n.* (*Brit.*) Aufsichtsperson, *die;* Aufsichtführende, *der/die;* **there were no ~s** es gab keine Aufsicht

**invigorate** /ɪnˈvɪgəreɪt/ *v.t.* Ⓐ (*make vigorous*) stärken; (*physically*) kräftigen; Ⓑ (*animate*) beleben; anregen ‹Fantasie›

**invigorating** /ɪnˈvɪgəreɪtɪŋ/ *adj.* kräftigend ‹Getränk, Mahlzeit, Klima›; stärkend ‹Schlaf, Mittel›; belebend ‹Brise, Dusche, Rasierwasser›; (*fig.*) anregend ‹Idee, Erfahrung›

**invincibility** /ɪnvɪnsɪˈbɪlɪtɪ/ *n., no pl.* Unbesiegbarkeit, *die*

**invincible** /ɪnˈvɪnsɪbl/ *adj.* unbesiegbar; unerschütterlich ‹Entschlossenheit, Mut, Überzeugung, Stolz›; unüberwindlich ‹Schwierigkeiten, Unwissenheit, Skepsis›

**inviolable** /ɪnˈvaɪələbl/ *adj.* Ⓐ (*not to be violated*) unantastbar; **maintain ~ secrecy** unverbrüchliches Stillschweigen bewahren; Ⓑ (*to be kept sacred*) unantastbar; sakrosankt (*geh.*)

**inviolate** /ɪnˈvaɪələt/ *adj.* Ⓐ (*not violated*) unversehrt; ungestört ‹Friede, Ruhe›; nicht verletzt ‹Abkommen›; Ⓑ (*unbroken*) ungetrübt ‹Freundschaft›; unerschüttert ‹Glaube›; Ⓒ (*unprofaned*) unangetastet

**invisibility** /ɪnvɪzɪˈbɪlɪtɪ/ *n.* Unsichtbarkeit, *die*

**invisible** /ɪnˈvɪzɪbl/ *adj.* (*also Econ.*) unsichtbar; (*hidden because of fog etc.; too small*) nicht sichtbar; **almost ~:** kaum zu sehen; **~ mending** Kunststopfen, *das;* **~ earnings** (*Commerc.*) unsichtbare Einkünfte

**invisibly** /ɪnˈvɪzɪblɪ/ *adv.* [für das Auge] nicht sichtbar; **~ repaired** *or* **mended** so repariert, dass man nichts [davon] sieht; kunstgestopft ‹Gewebe›

**invitation** /ɪnvɪˈteɪʃn/ *n.* (*lit. or fig.*) Einladung, *die;* **at sb.'s ~:** auf jmds. Einladung (*Akk.*); **admission by ~ only** Einlass nur mit Einladung; **an [open] ~ to thieves** eine Aufforderung zum Diebstahl

**invite** ❶ /ɪnˈvaɪt/ *v.t.* Ⓐ (*request to come*) einladen; **~ oneself** (*iron.*) sich selbst einladen; **before an ~d audience** vor geladenen Gästen; **~ sb. in/over/round** jmdn. hereinbitten/herüberbitten/[zu sich] einladen (**for, to** zu); Ⓑ (*request to do sth.*) auffordern; **she ~d him to accompany her** sie forderte ihn auf *od.* lud ihn ein, sie zu begleiten; **they ~d him to ascend the throne** sie boten ihm an, den Thron zu besteigen; sie trugen ihm den Thron an (*geh.*); Ⓒ (*ask for*) erbitten; bitten um; Ⓓ (*bring on*) herausfordern ‹Kritik, Verhängnis, Spott, Verachtung, Protest›; **you're inviting ridicule** du machst dich lächerlich *od.* zum Gespött; Ⓔ (*attract*) einladen; **~ interest in sth.** Interesse an etw. (*Dat.*) wecken.

❷ /ˈɪnvaɪt/ *n.* (*coll.*) Einladung, *die*

**invitee** /ɪnvaɪˈtiː/ *n.* geladener Gast

**inviting** /ɪnˈvaɪtɪŋ/ *adj.* einladend; verlockend ‹Gedanke, Vorstellung, Aussicht›; freundlich ‹Klima›; ansprechend ‹Anblick, Schriftbild›; **make sth. ~ to sb.** etw. für jmdn. attraktiv machen

**invitingly** /ɪnˈvaɪtɪŋlɪ/ *adv.* einladend

**in-vitro fertiliˈzation** /ɪnˈviːtrəʊ fɜːtɪlaɪˈzeɪʃn/ *n.* künstliche Befruchtung [im Reagenzglas]; In-vitro-Fertilisation, *die* (*fachspr.*)

**invocation** /ɪnvəˈkeɪʃn/ *n.* Anrufung, *die;* Invokation, *die* (*geh.*)

**invoice** /ˈɪnvɔɪs/ ❶ *n.* (*bill*) Rechnung, *die;* (*list*) Lieferschein, *der.* ❷ *v.t.* Ⓐ (*make ~ for*) eine Rechnung ausstellen für; (*enter in ~*) in Rechnung stellen ‹Waren›; Ⓑ (*send to*) **~ sb.** jmdm. eine Rechnung schicken; **~ sb. for sth.** jmdm. etw. in Rechnung stellen; **be ~d for sth.** für etw. eine Rechnung erhalten

**invoke** /ɪnˈvəʊk/ *v.t.* Ⓐ (*call on*) anrufen; Ⓑ (*appeal to*) sich berufen auf (+ *Akk.*); **~ an example/sth. as an example** ein Beispiel/etw. als Beispiel anführen; **~ sth. to justify/explain sth.** etw. bemühen, um etw. zu rechtfertigen/erklären; Ⓒ (*summon*) beschwören; Ⓓ (*ask earnestly for*) erbitten; bitten um

**involucre** /ˈɪnvəluːkə(r)/ *n.* (*Bot.*) Hülle, *die*

**involuntarily** /ɪnˈvɒləntərɪlɪ/ *adv.*, **involuntary** /ɪnˈvɒləntərɪ/ *adj.* unwillkürlich

**involve** /ɪnˈvɒlv/ *v.t.* Ⓐ (*implicate*) verwickeln; **~ sb. in a charge** jmdn. zum Mitangeklagten machen; Ⓑ (*draw in as a participant*) **~ sb. in a game/fight** jmdn. an einem Spiel beteiligen/in eine Schlägerei [mit] hineinziehen; **become** *or* **get ~d in a fight** in eine Schlägerei verwickelt *od.* hineingezogen werden; **be ~d in a project** (*employed*) an einem Projekt mitarbeiten; **get ~d with sb.** sich mit jmdm. einlassen; (*sexually, emotionally*) eine Beziehung mit jmdm. anfangen; **sth. is ~d** (*concerned*) etw. kommt mit ins Spiel; **no other vehicle was ~ in the accident** kein anderes Fahrzeug war an dem Unfall beteiligt; Ⓒ (*include*) enthalten; (*contain implicitly*) beinhalten; **this event ~s us all** dieses Ereignis betrifft uns alle *od.* geht uns alle an; Ⓓ (*be necessarily accompanied by*) mit sich bringen; (*require as accompaniment*) erfordern; (*cause, mean*) bedeuten

**involved** /ɪnˈvɒlvd/ *adj.* verwickelt; (*complicated*) kompliziert; (*complex*) komplex

**involvement** /ɪnˈvɒlvmənt/ *n.* Ⓐ **my ~ in this affair began only recently** ich habe mit dieser Angelegenheit erst seit kurzem zu tun; **his ~ in the company** seine Beteiligung an der Firma; **I don't know the extent of his ~ in this affair** ich weiß nicht, inwieweit er mit dieser Sache zu tun hat; Ⓑ (*implication*) **~ in a conflict** Einmischung in einen Konflikt; **his increasing ~ in public life** die Rolle, die er in zunehmendem Maße im öffentlichen Leben spielt; **have an ~ with sb.** (*sexually*) eine Affäre mit jmdm. haben; **you may not take on any other ~:** Sie dürfen sich nicht anderweitig engagieren

**invulnerable** /ɪnˈvʌlnərəbl/ *adj.* unverwundbar ‹Lebewesen, Waffensystem›; (*impregnable*) uneinnehmbar ‹Festung, Stadt usw.›; (*fig.*) unantastbar ‹Würde, Stellung›; **be ~ to sth.** gegen etw. gefeit sein (*geh.*)

**inward** /ˈɪnwəd/ ❶ *adj.* Ⓐ (*situated within*) inner...; Ⓑ (*mental, spiritual*) inner... ‹Impuls, Regung, Friede, Kampf›; innerlich (*geh.*) ‹Leben›; **his ~ thoughts** seine innersten *od.* geheimsten Gedanken; Ⓒ (*directed inside*) nach innen gehend; nach innen gerichtet; **'goods ~'** „Eingänge"; **~ slope** Innenneigung, *die;* Neigung nach innen. ❷ *adv.* einwärts ‹gerichtet, gebogen›; **open ~:** nach innen öffnen; **an ~-looking person** (*fig.*) ein in sich (*Akk.*) gekehrter Mensch

**inwardly** /ˈɪnwədlɪ/ *adv.* im Inneren; innerlich

**inwards** /ˈɪnwədz/ ⇒ **inward** 2

**iodide** /ˈaɪədaɪd/ *n.* (*Chem.*) Jodid, *das*

**iodine** /ˈaɪədiːn, ˈaɪədɪn/ *n.* Jod, *das*

**IOM** *abbr.* **Isle of Man**

**ion** /ˈaɪən/ *n.* (*Phys., Chem.*) Ion, *das*

**ion exˈchange** *n.* Ionenaustausch, *der*

**ionic** /aɪˈɒnɪk/ *adj.* (*Phys., Chem.*) Ionen-; in Ionenform vorliegend ‹Grundstoff›; ionisch ‹Bindung, Verbindung usw.›

**ionisation, ionise** ⇒ **ioniz-**

**ionization** /aɪənaɪˈzeɪʃn/ *n.* Ionisation, *die*

**ionize** /ˈaɪənaɪz/ *v.t.* ionisieren

**ionosphere** /aɪˈɒnəsfɪə(r)/ *n.* Ionosphäre, *die*

**iota** /aɪˈəʊtə/ *n.* Ⓐ (*smallest amount*) Jota, *das* (*geh.*); **not an** *or* **one ~:** nicht ein Jota (*geh.*); kein Jota (*geh.*); **there's not an ~ of truth in that** daran ist nicht e̲i̲n Fünkchen Wahrheit; Ⓑ (*Greek letter*) Jota, *das*

**IOU** /aɪəʊˈjuː/ *n.* Schuldschein, *der*

**IOW** *abbr.* **Isle of Wight**

**IPA** *abbr.* **International Phonetic Alphabet/Association** IPA

**i.p.s.** *abbr.* **inches per second** inch/s

**ipso facto** /ɪpsəʊ ˈfæktəʊ/ *adv.* Ⓐ (*by that very fact*) eo ipso (*geh.*); eben dadurch; Ⓑ (*thereby*) aufgrund dessen; Ⓒ (*by the very nature of the case*) eo ipso; naturgemäß

**IQ** *abbr.* **intelligence quotient** IQ, *der;* **IQ-test** IQ-Test, *der*

**IRA** *abbr.* **Irish Republican Army** IRA, *die*

**Iran** /ɪˈrɑːn/ *pr. n.* Iran, *der*

**Iranian** /ɪˈreɪnɪən/ ▶ **1275**, ▶ **1340** ❶ *adj.* iranisch; **sb. is ~:** jmd. ist Iraner/Iranerin. ❷ *n.* Ⓐ (*person*) Iraner, *der*/Iranerin, *die;* Ⓑ (*Ling.*) Iranisch, *das;* **speak ~:** eine iranische Sprache sprechen

**Iraq** /ɪˈrɑːk/ *pr. n.* Irak, *der*

**Iraqi** /ɪˈrɑːkɪ/ ▶ **1275**, ▶ **1340** ❶ *adj.* irakisch; **sb. is ~:** jmd. ist Iraker/Irakerin. ❷ *n.* Ⓐ (*person*) Iraker, *der*/Irakerin, *die;* Ⓑ (*dialect*) Irakisch, *das*

**irascible** /ɪˈræsɪbl/ *adj.* (*hot-tempered*) aufbrausend; (*irritable*) reizbar

**irate** /aɪˈreɪt/ *adj.* wütend ‹Person, Tier, Menge›; erbost (*geh.*) ‹Person›

**irately** /aɪˈreɪtlɪ/ *adv.* wütend

**ire** /aɪə(r)/ *n.* (*rhet./poet.*) Zorn, *der*

**Ireland** /ˈaɪələnd/ *pr. n.* **[Republic of] ~:** Irland (*das*)

**iridescence** /ɪrɪˈdesəns/ *n.* Schillern, *das;* Irisieren, *das*

**iridescent** /ɪrɪˈdesənt/ *adj.* regenbogenfarben; (*changing colour with position*) schillernd; irisierend

**iridium** /ɪˈrɪdɪəm/ *n.* (*Chem.*) Iridium, *das*

**iris** /ˈaɪərɪs/ *n.* Ⓐ (*Anat.*) Iris, *die;* Regenbogenhaut, *die;* Ⓑ (*Bot.*) Iris, *die;* Schwertlilie, *die;* Ⓒ (*Optics*) Irisblende, *die*

**Irish** /ˈaɪərɪʃ/ ▶ **1275**, ▶ **1340** ❶ *adj.* Ⓐ irisch; **sb. is ~:** jmd. ist Ire/Irin; **~ joke** Irenwitz, *der;* ⇒ *also* **English** 1; Ⓑ (*coll.: contradictory*) komisch. ❷ *n.* Ⓐ (*language*) Irisch, *das;* ⇒ *also* **English** 2 A; Ⓑ *constr. as pl.* **the ~:** die Iren

**Irish:** **~ ˈbull** *n.* Widerspruch in sich; Paradox, *das* (*geh.*); **~ ˈcoffee** *n.* Irishcoffee, *der;* **~ ˈGaelic** *n.* Irisch-Gälisch, *das;* **~man** /ˈaɪərɪʃmən/ *n., pl.* **~men** /ˈaɪərɪʃmən/ Ire, *der;* **~ Reˈpublic** *pr. n.* Irische Republik; **~ ˈSea** *pr. n.* Irische See; **~ ˈstew** *n.* Irishstew, *das;* **~ ˈwhisk[e]y** *n.* irischer Whisk[e]y; **~woman** *n.* Irin, *die*

**irk** /ɜːk/ *v.t.* ärgern

**irksome** /ˈɜːksəm/ *adj.* lästig

**iron** /ˈaɪən/ ❶ *n.* Ⓐ (*metal*) Eisen, *das;* **~ tablets** Eisentabletten; **man of ~** (*fig.*) stahlharter Mann; **with a grip of ~:** mit eisernem Griff; **as hard as ~:** eisenhart; **will of ~:** eiserner Wille; **strike while the ~ is hot** (*prov.*) das Eisen schmieden, solange es heiß ist (*Spr.*); ⇒ *also* **pyrites, rod c;** Ⓑ (*tool*) Eisen, *das;* **have several ~s in the fire** mehrere Eisen im Feuer haben (*ugs.*); **have too many ~s in the fire** sich verzetteln; sich (*Dat.*) zu viel auf einmal vornehmen; Ⓒ (*Golf*) Eisen, *das;* Eisenschläger, *der;* Ⓓ (*for smoothing*) Bügeleisen, *das;* Ⓔ *usu. in pl.* (*fetter*) Eisen, *das;* **put sb. in ~s** jmdn. in Eisen legen (*dichter., veralt.*).

❷ *attrib. adj.* Ⓐ (*of iron*) eisern; Eisen‹platte usw.›; Ⓑ (*very robust*) eisern ‹Konstitution›; stählern ‹Muskeln›; Ⓒ (*unyielding*) eisern; ehern (*geh.*) ‹Stoizismus›; **~ rule/his ~ rule** ein/sein eisernes Regiment.

❸ *v.t.* bügeln.

❹ *v.i.* Ⓐ ‹Kleidungsstück:› sich bügeln lassen; Ⓑ ‹Person:› bügeln

**~ ˈon** *v.t.* aufbügeln; ⇒ *also* **iron-on**

**~ ˈout** *v.t.* herausbügeln ‹Falten›; (*flatten*) glätten ‹Papier›; (*fig.*) beseitigen ‹Kurve, Unregelmäßigkeit›; aus dem Weg räumen ‹Schwierigkeit, Problem›; ausgleichen ‹Interessengegensatz›

**Iron:** **~ Age** *n.* Eisenzeit, *die;* **i~clad** ❶ *adj.* Ⓐ (*clad in iron*) eisenbewehrt; gepanzert ‹Schiff›; Ⓑ (*fig.*) (*rigorous*) eisern; unverbrüchlich ‹Eid›; unnachsichtig ‹Kontrolle›; **there are no ~clad rules in this matter**

dafür gibt es keine starren Regeln; ❷ *n.* (*Navy Hist.*) Panzerschiff, *das;* ~ **'Cross** *n.* Eisernes Kreuz; ~ **'Curtain** *n.* (*fig.*) Eiserner Vorhang; **i~-grey** ❶ *adj.* eisengrau; grau ‹Herbsttag›; ❷ *n.* Eisengrau, *das*

**ironic** /aɪˈrɒnɪk/, **ironical** /aɪˈrɒnɪkl/ *adj.* ironisch; **it is ~ that ...:** es ist paradox, dass ...

**ironically** /aɪˈrɒnɪkəlɪ/ *adv.* ironisch; *as sentence-modifier* ironischerweise

**ironing** /ˈaɪənɪŋ/ *n.* Bügeln, *das;* (*things [to be] ironed*) Bügelwäsche, *die;* **do the ~:** bügeln

**'ironing board** *n.* Bügelbrett, *das*

**iron 'lung** *n.* eiserne Lunge

**ironmonger** /ˈaɪənmʌŋgə(r)/ *n.* ▶ **1261** (*Brit.*) Eisenwarenhändler, *der*/-händlerin, *die;* ⇒ *also* **baker**

**ironmongery** /ˈaɪənmʌŋgərɪ/ *n.* (*Brit.*) **A** (*hardware*) Eisenwaren *Pl.;* **B** (*coll.: firearms*) Schießeisen (*ugs.*)

**iron:** **~-on** *adj.* aufbügelbar; zum Aufbügeln *nachgestellt;* **~ ore** *n.* Eisenerz, *das;* **~ 'ration** *n.* eiserne Ration; **~ware** *n., no pl.* Eisenwaren *Pl.;* (*household utensils*) Haushaltswaren *Pl.;* **~work** *n., no pl.* Eisenarbeit, *die;* (*part*) Eisenwerk, *das;* (*articles*) Eisenwaren *Pl.;* **~works** *n. sing., pl. same* Eisenhüttenwerk, *das;* Eisenhütte, *die*

**irony** /ˈaɪrənɪ/ *n.* Ironie, *die;* **one of life's [little] ironies** eine Ironie des Schicksals; **the ~ was that ...:** die Ironie lag darin, dass ...; das Ironische war, dass ...; ⇒ *also* **tragic B**

**irradiate** /ɪˈreɪdɪeɪt/ *v.t.* **A** (*shine upon*) bescheinen; **B** (*light up*) erstrahlen lassen; zum Leuchten bringen; **C** (*Phys., Med., Gastr.*) bestrahlen

**irradiation** /ɪreɪdɪˈeɪʃn/ *n.* **A** (*illumination*) Leuchten, *das;* **B** (*fig.*) Erleuchtung, *die;* **C** (*Phys., Med.*) Bestrahlung, *die;* **D** **[food] ~:** [Lebensmittel]bestrahlung, *die*

**irrational** /ɪˈræʃənl/ *adj.* **A** (*unreasonable*) irrational (*geh.*); vernunftwidrig; **B** (*incapable of reasoning*) nicht vernunftbegabt; **C** (*Math.*) irrational ‹Zahl›

**irrationality** /ɪræʃəˈnælɪtɪ/ *n.* Irrationalität, *die* (*geh.*); (*of situation*) Absurdität, *die*

**irrationally** /ɪˈræʃənəlɪ/ *adv.* irrationalerweise (*geh.*); ohne vernünftigen Grund

**irreconcilable** /ɪˈrekənsaɪləbl/ *adj.* **A** (*implacably hostile*) unversöhnlich; unüberwindlich ‹Abneigung›; **B** (*incompatible*) unvereinbar; unversöhnlich ‹Gegensätze›; **theory and practice are completely ~:** Theorie und Praxis widersprechen sich total

**irrecoverable** /ɪrɪˈkʌvərəbl/ *adj.* unwiederbringlich verloren; endgültig ‹Verlust›; nicht eintreibbar ‹Schuld›; **the situation was ~:** die Situation war nicht mehr zu retten

**irredeemable** /ɪrɪˈdiːməbl/ *adj.* nicht wieder gutzumachend ‹Fehler›; **be ~:** nicht wieder gutzumachen sein; **the mistake is not yet ~:** noch kann der Fehler wieder gutgemacht werden

**irreducible** /ɪrɪˈdjuːsɪbl/ *adj.* nicht [mehr *od.* weiter] reduzierbar; Mindest‹menge›

**irrefutable** /ɪˈrefjʊtəbl, ɪrɪˈfjuːtəbl/ *adj.* unwiderlegbar

**irregular** /ɪˈregjʊlə(r)/ ❶ *adj.* **A** (*not conforming*) unkorrekt ‹Verhalten, Handlung usw.›; **this is most ~!** das ist eigentlich nicht erlaubt!; **B** (*uneven in duration, order, etc.*) unregelmäßig; ⇒ *also* **hour C**; **C** (*abnormal*) sonderbar; eigenartig; **D** (*not symmetrical*) unregelmäßig; uneben ‹Oberfläche, Gelände›; **E** (*disorderly*) ungeregelt ‹Leben[sweise]›; (*lawless*) zwielichtig; **F** (*Mil.*) irregulär ‹Truppen›; **G** (*Ling., Bot.*) unregelmäßig. ❷ *n. in pl.* (*Mil.*) Irreguläre *Pl.*

**irregularity** /ɪregjʊˈlærɪtɪ/ *n.* **A** (*of behaviour, action*) Unkorrektheit, *die;* (*instance also*) Unregelmäßigkeit, *die;* **B** (*unevenness in duration, order, etc.*) Unregelmäßigkeit, *die;* **C** (*abnormality*) Sonderbarkeit, *die;* Eigenartigkeit, *die;* **D** (*disorderliness*) Ungeregeltheit, *die;* (*lawlessness*) Zwielichtigkeit, *die;* **E** (*lack of symmetry*) Unregelmäßigkeit, *die;* (*of surface*) Unebenheit, *die*

**irregularly** /ɪˈregjʊləlɪ/ *adv.* **A** (*not in conformity*) unkorrekt; (*lawlessly*) unzulässigerweise; **B** (*unevenly*) unregelmäßig

**irrelevance** /ɪˈrelɪvəns/, **irrelevancy** /ɪˈrelɪvənsɪ/ *n.* (*being irrelevant*) Belanglosigkeit, *die;* Irrelevanz, *die* (*geh.*); (*irrelevant detail, information, etc.*) Belanglosigkeit, *die*

**irrelevant** /ɪˈrelɪvənt/ *adj.* belanglos; irrelevant (*geh.*); **be ~ to a subject** für ein Thema ohne Belang *od.* (*geh.*) irrelevant sein

**irreligious** /ɪrɪˈlɪdʒəs/ *adj.* irreligiös (*geh.*), ungläubig ‹Person›; gottlos ‹Verhaltensweise, Idee, Person›

**irremediable** /ɪrɪˈmiːdɪəbl/ *adj.* nicht wieder gutzumachend *nicht präd.* ‹Tat, Verlust, Schaden, Fehler, Irrtum›; nicht wettzumachend *nicht präd.* ‹Verschlechterung›; nicht zu behebend *nicht präd.* ‹Mangel›; nicht zu verbessernd *nicht präd.* ‹Situation›; **be ~:** nicht wieder gutzumachen/wettzumachen/zu beheben/zu verbessern sein

**irreparable** /ɪˈrepərəbl/ *adj.* nicht wieder gutzumachend *nicht präd.;* irreparabel (*geh., Med.*)

**irreparably** /ɪˈrepərəblɪ/ *adv.* irreparabel (*geh.*); **be ~ damaged** einen nicht behebbaren *od.* (*geh.*) irreparablen Schaden haben

**irreplaceable** /ɪrɪˈpleɪsəbl/ *adj.* **A** (*not replaceable*) nicht ersetzbar; nicht nachlieferbar ‹Waren›; **B** (*of which the loss cannot be made good*) unersetzlich

**irrepressible** /ɪrɪˈpresɪbl/ *adj.* nicht zu unterdrückend *nicht präd.;* unbezähmbar ‹Neugier, Verlangen›; unerschütterlich ‹Optimismus›; unbändig ‹Freude, Entzücken›; unbezwingbar ‹Neigung›; sonnig ‹Gemüt›; **he/she is ~:** er/sie ist nicht unterzukriegen (*ugs.*); **an ~ chatterbox** eine unentwegte Quasselstrippe (*ugs.*)

**irreproachable** /ɪrɪˈprəʊtʃəbl/ *adj.* untadelig ‹Charakter, Lebenswandel, Benehmen›; unanfechtbar ‹Ehrlichkeit›; tadellos ‹Kleidung, Manieren›; makellos ‹Vergangenheit [eines Menschen]›

**irresistible** /ɪrɪˈzɪstɪbl/ *adj.* unwiderstehlich; bestechend ‹Argument›

**irresistibly** /ɪrɪˈzɪstɪblɪ/ *adv.* unwiderstehlich; unaufhaltsam ‹näher kommen›

**irresolute** /ɪˈrezəluːt, ɪˈrezəljuːt/ *adj.* **A** (*undecided*) unentschlossen; unschlüssig; **B** (*lacking in resoluteness*) unentschlossen

**irresolutely** /ɪˈrezəluːtlɪ, ɪˈrezəljuːtlɪ/ *adv.* unentschlossen; unschlüssig

**irresoluteness** /ɪˈrezəluːtnɪs, ɪˈrezəljuːtnɪs/, **irresolution** /ɪrezəˈluːʃn, ɪrezəˈljuːʃn/ *ns., no pl.* **A** (*being undecided*) Unentschlossenheit, *die;* Unschlüssigkeit, *die;* **B** (*lack of resoluteness*) Unentschlossenheit, *die;* Entschlusslosigkeit, *die*

**irrespective** /ɪrɪˈspektɪv/ *adj.* **~ of** ungeachtet (+ *Gen.*); (*independent of*) unabhängig von; **~ of what ...:** unabhängig davon, was ...; **~ of the consequences** ungeachtet der *od.* ohne Rücksicht auf die Folgen

**irresponsibility** /ɪrɪspɒnsɪˈbɪlɪtɪ/ *n., no pl.* ⇒ **irresponsible**: Verantwortungslosigkeit, *die;* Unverantwortlichkeit, *die;* **it is sheer ~ to ...:** es ist einfach unverantwortlich, zu ...

**irresponsible** /ɪrɪˈspɒnsɪbl/ *adj.* verantwortungslos ‹Person›; unverantwortlich ‹Benehmen›; (*mentally inadequate to bear responsibility*) der Verantwortung nicht gewachsen; **[financially] ~:** zahlungsunwillig

**irresponsibly** /ɪrɪˈspɒnsɪblɪ/ *adv.* verantwortungslos; unverantwortlich; in verantwortungsloser Weise

**irretrievable** /ɪrɪˈtriːvəbl/ *adj.* nicht mehr wiederzubekommen *nicht attr.;* nicht mehr korrigierbar ‹Fehler›; (*irreversible*) endgültig ‹Ruin, Verfall, Verlust›; unheilbar ‹Zerrüttung einer Ehe›; ausweglos ‹Situation›

**irretrievably** /ɪrɪˈtriːvəblɪ/ *adv.* unwiederbringlich ‹verloren›; (*for ever*) endgültig; für alle Zeiten; **the marriage has ~ broken down** die Ehe ist unheilbar zerrüttet

**irreverence** /ɪˈrevərəns/ *n.* ⇒ **irreverent**: Respektlosigkeit, *die;* Pietätlosigkeit, *die* (*geh.*); **an [act of] ~:** eine Respektlosigkeit/Pietätlosigkeit (*geh.*)

**irreverent** /ɪˈrevərənt/ *adj.*, **irreverently** /ɪˈrevərəntlɪ/ *adv.* respektlos; (*towards religious values or the dead*) pietätlos (*geh.*)

**irreversible** /ɪrɪˈvɜːsɪbl/ *adj.* **A** (*unalterable*) unabänderlich, unumstößlich ‹Entscheidung, Entschluss, Tatsache›; unwiderruflich ‹Entschluss, Entscheidung, Anordnung, Befehl usw.›; **B** (*not reversible*) irreversibel (*geh.*) ‹Vorgang›; (*inexorable*) unaufhaltsam ‹Entwicklung, Verfall›; **~ damage** nicht wieder gutzumachender *od.* (*geh.*) irreparabler Schaden

**irrevocable** /ɪˈrevəkəbl/ *adj.* **A** (*unalterable, final*) unwiderruflich ‹Gelübde, Entscheidung, Entschluss, Befehl›; unabänderlich ‹Entschluss›; **B** (*gone beyond recall*) unwiederbringlich ‹Vergangenheit, Augenblick›

**irrevocably** /ɪˈrevəkəblɪ/ *adv.* unwiederbringlich, unwiderruflich ‹verloren, vorüber›

**irrigate** /ˈɪrɪgeɪt/ *v.t.* **A** bewässern; **B** (*Med.*) [aus]spülen

**irrigation** /ɪrɪˈgeɪʃn/ *n.* **A** Bewässerung, *die;* **overhead ~:** Beregnung, *die;* **B** (*Med.*) Spülung, *die;* Irrigation, *die* (*fachspr.*)

**irritability** /ɪrɪtəˈbɪlɪtɪ/ *n.* ⇒ **irritable A**: Reizbarkeit, *die;* Gereiztheit, *die*

**irritable** /ˈɪrɪtəbl/ *adj.* **A** (*quick to anger*) reizbar; (*temporarily*) gereizt; **B** (*of organ*) empfindlich; **~ to the touch** empfindlich gegen Berührung; **C** (*Biol.*) reizbar

**irritably** /ˈɪrɪtəblɪ/ *adv.* gereizt

**irritant** /ˈɪrɪtənt/ ❶ *adj.* Reiz-; **be ~:** reizen. ❷ *n.* Reizstoff, *der;* **the spicy food proved to be an ~ to his stomach** sein Magen vertrug das scharf gewürzte Essen nicht; **be an ~ to sb./sb.'s nerves** (*fig.*) jmdm. auf die Nerven gehen (*ugs.*)

**irritate** /ˈɪrɪteɪt/ *v.t.* **A** ärgern; **get ~d** ärgerlich werden; **be ~d** sich ärgern; ungehalten sein (*geh.*); **be ~d by** *or* **feel ~d at sth.** sich über etw. (*Akk.*) ärgern; **be ~d with sb.** sich über jmdn. aufregen *od.* ärgern; **be ~d that ...:** verärgert *od.* (*geh.*) ungehalten [darüber] sein, dass ...; **she was ~d to hear this** sie war ärgerlich *od.* (*geh.*) ungehalten, als sie dies hörte; **B** (*Med., Biol.*) reizen

**irritating** /ˈɪrɪteɪtɪŋ/ *adj.* lästig; **I find him ~:** er geht mir auf die Nerven (*ugs.*)

**irritatingly** /ˈɪrɪteɪtɪŋlɪ/ *adv.* ärgerlich; *as sentence-modifier* ärgerlicherweise; **the tap was dripping ~:** der Wasserhahn tropfte nervtötend

**irritation** /ɪrɪˈteɪʃn/ *n.* **A** Ärger, *der;* **[source** *or* **cause of] ~:** Ärgernis, *das;* **B** (*Med., Biol.*) Reizung, *die*

**is** ⇒ **be**

**Is.** *abbr.* **Island[s]; Isle[s]** I[n].

**Isaac** /ˈaɪzək/ *pr. n.* (*Bibl.*) Isaak (*der*)

**Isaiah** /aɪˈzaɪə/ *pr. n.* (*Bibl.*) Jesaja (*der*)

**ISBN** *abbr.* **international standard book number** ISBN

**isinglass** /ˈaɪzɪŋglɑːs/ *n.* Hausenblase, *die;* Fischleim, *der*

**Islam** /ˈɪzlɑːm, ˈɪzlæm, ɪzˈlɑːm/ *n.* Islam, *der*

**Islamic** /ɪzˈlæmɪk/ *adj.* islamisch

**island** /ˈaɪlənd/ *n.* (*lit. or fig.*) Insel, *die;* ⇒ *also* **traffic island**

**islander** /ˈaɪləndə(r)/ *n.* Inselbewohner, *der*/-bewohnerin, *die;* Insulaner, *der*/Insulanerin, *die*

**island:** **~-hop** *v.i.* **go ~ping** eine Inselhoppingtour machen; **~-hopping** *n.; no pl.* Inselhopping, *das; attrib.* **an ~-hopping holiday** eine Urlaubsreise von Insel zu Insel

**isle** /aɪl/ *n.* Insel, *die;* Eiland, *das* (*dichter.*)

**Isle of Man** /aɪl əv ˈmæn/ *pr. n.* Insel Man, *die*

**Isle of Wight** /aɪl əv ˈwaɪt/ *pr. n.* Insel Wight, *die*

**islet** /ˈaɪlɪt/ *n.* **A** (*little island*) kleine Insel; kleines Eiland (*dichter.*); **B** (*isolated spot*) Insel, *die;* **C** (*Anat.*) Insel, *die*

**ism** /ɪzm/ *n.* (*derog.*) Ismus, *der* (*abwertend*)

**isn't** /ˈɪznt/ (*coll.*) = **is not;** ⇒ **be**

**ISO** *abbr.* **International Organization for Standardization** ISO, *die*

**isobar** /ˈaɪsəbɑː(r)/ *n.* (*Meteorol., Phys.*) Isobare, *die*

# It

The tendency when translating *it* into German is to put **es** whatever it refers to. This is of course correct if *it* refers back to a neuter noun (**Brot, Messer, Auto** etc.). Remember the dative form is **ihm**.

***Where's the knife? It's on the table***
= Wo ist das Messer? Es liegt auf dem Tisch

***The car is stuck. Can you give it a shove?***
= Das Auto sitzt fest. Kannst du ihm einen Schubs geben?

The translation is also **es** where *it* stands for an idea which may be expressed in a whole sentence or clause (which is the case with actions, statements and impersonal subjects):

***Who did it/said it?***
= Wer hat es getan/gesagt?

***It was very kind of you***
= Es war sehr nett von Ihnen

***It's true that I can't stand him***
= Es stimmt, ich kann ihn nicht leiden

There are also impersonal verbs and constructions which always have *it* as the subject:

***It's snowing/raining***
= Es schneit/regnet

***It was ten o'clock***
= Es war zehn Uhr

But if *it* refers back to a noun which is masculine in German, it must be translated by **er** (or **ihn** if *it* is accusative and **ihm** in the dative):

***The winter was over; it had been cold***
= Der Winter war vorüber; er war kalt gewesen

***That's my pencil — give it to me***
= Das ist mein Bleistift — gib ihn mir

***There's the river; the road follows it***
= Dort ist der Fluss; die Straße folgt ihm

Similarly, if the noun referred to is feminine *it* must be translated by **sie** (or **ihr** in the dative):

***The flower is wilting — it needs water/you must water it***
= Die Blume ist welk — sie braucht Wasser/du musst sie begießen

***He found a track and followed it***
= Er fand eine Spur und folgte ihr

There are some exceptions to this requirement for agreement, in particular when the noun referred to follows *it's* or *it was*:

***It's a good film***
= Es ist ein guter Film

***It was a lovely evening***
= Es war ein schöner Abend

In other cases, an expression with **es** may be seen as a set phrase which does not need to reflect the gender of the noun referred to. In the example with the pencil above, *give it to me* could also be translated by 'gibs her'.

## After prepositions

Combinations such as *with it*, *from it*, *to it* etc. are translated by the prepositions with the prefix **da-** (**damit, davon, dazu** etc.). Prepositions beginning with a vowel insert an **r** (**daran, darauf, darunter, darüber** etc., in which the **a** is elided in colloquial speech to give **dran, drauf, drunter, drüber** etc.). This makes it possible to distinguish between a person and a thing in examples such as:

***It suits him***
= Es passt zu ihm

and:

***It goes well with it***
= Es passt dazu

Other examples:

***I can't do anything with it***
= Ich kann nichts damit anfangen

***Don't lean on it!***
= Lehn dich nicht daran!

***Put something under it/on top of it***
= Leg etwas darunter *or* drunter/darauf *or* drauf

Sometimes the separable verb prefixes with **hin-** are sufficient:

***It won't fit into it***
= Es passt nicht hinein

***Add sugar to it***
= Geben Sie Zucker hinzu

**isolate** /'aɪsəleɪt/ *v.t.* isolieren; (*Electr.*) vom Stromkreis trennen; **~ sb. from sb.** jmdn. von jmdm. trennen; **he felt completely ~d** er kam sich (*Dat.*) völlig verloren vor

**isolated** /'aɪsəleɪtɪd/ *adj.* [A] (*single*) einzeln; (*occasional*) vereinzelt; (*unique*) einmalig; **~ instances/cases** Einzelfälle; [B] (*solitary*) einsam; (*remote*) abgelegen (**from** von); (*cut off*) abgeschnitten (**from** von)

**isolation** /aɪsə'leɪʃn/ *n.* [A] (*act*) Isolierung, *die;* Absonderung, *die;* [B] (*state*) Isoliertheit, *die;* Isolation, *die;* Abgeschnittenheit, *die;* (*remoteness*) Abgeschiedenheit, *die;* **examine/look at/treat sth. in ~:** etw. isoliert *od.* gesondert betrachten; *attrib.* **~ hospital** Infektionskrankenhaus, *das;* **~ ward** Isolierstation, *die;* Infektionsabteilung, *die*

**isolationism** /aɪsə'leɪʃənɪzm/ *n.* (*Polit.*) Isolationismus, *der*

**isolationist** /aɪsə'leɪʃənɪst/ *n.* (*Polit.*) Isolationist, *der*/Isolationistin, *die*

**isomer** /'aɪsəmɜ:(r)/ *n.* (*Chem.*) Isomer[e], *das*

**isometric** /aɪsə'metrɪk/ *adj.* (*Geom., Physiol.*) isometrisch

**isometrics** /aɪsə'metrɪks/ *n., no pl.* isometrisches Muskeltraining; Isometrik, *die*

**isomorph** /'aɪsəmɔ:f/ *n.* Isomorphe, *die*

**isomorphic** /aɪsə'mɔ:fɪk/ *adj.* isomorph

**isomorphism** /aɪsə'mɔ:fɪzm/ *n.* Isomorphie, *die;* (*of crystals*) Isomorphismus, *der*

**isosceles** /aɪ'sɒsəli:z/ *adj.* (*Geom.*) gleichschenklig

**isotherm** /'aɪsəθɜ:m/ *n.* (*Meteorol., Phys.*) Isotherme, *die*

**isothermal** /aɪsə'θɜ:ml/ *adj.* (*Meteorol., Phys.*) isotherm

**isotope** /'aɪsətəʊp/ *n.* Isotop, *das*

**isotropic** /aɪsə'trɒpɪk/ *adj.* (*Phys.*) isotrop

**ISP** *abbr.* **Internet service provider** ISP

**Israel** /'ɪzreɪl/ *pr. n.* Israel (*das*)

**Israeli** /ɪz'reɪlɪ/ **▶1340** ❶ *adj.* israelisch. ❷ *n.* Israeli, *der/die*

**Israelite** /'ɪzrɪəlaɪt/ *n.* Israelit, *der*/Israelitin, *die*

**issue** /'ɪʃu:, 'ɪsju:/ ❶ *n.* [A] (*point in question*) Frage, *die;* **the ~ of the day** das Thema des Tages; **contemporary ~s** aktuelle Fragen *od.* Themen; **make an ~ of sth.** etw. aufbauschen; **the real ~s in today's world** die Kernprobleme der heutigen Zeit; **become an ~:** zum Problem werden; **evade** *or* **dodge** *or* **duck the ~:** ausweichen; **~ of fact** (*Law*) Tatsachenfrage, *die;* **the point at ~:** der strittige Punkt; worum es geht; **what is at ~ here?** worum geht es hier eigentlich?; **that's not at ~:** das steht nicht zur Debatte; darum geht es nicht; **be at ~ over sth.** wegen etw. miteinander im Streit liegen; wegen etw. Meinungsverschiedenheiten haben; **join** *or* **take ~ with sb. over sth.** sich mit jmdm. auf eine Diskussion über etw. (*Akk.*) einlassen; [B] (*giving out*) Ausgabe, *die;* (*of document*) Ausstellung, *die;* (*of shares*) Emission, *die;* **date of ~:** Ausgabedatum, *das;* Ausgabetag, *der;* (*of document*) Ausstellungsdatum, *das;* (*of stamps*) Ausgabetag, *der;* [C] (*of magazine, journal, etc.*) Ausgabe, *die;* [D] (*total number of copies*) Auflage, *die;* [E] (*quantity of coins*) Emissionszahl, *die;* (*quantity of stamps*) Auflage, *die;* [F] (*result, outcome*) Ergebnis, *das;* Ausgang, *der;* **decide the ~:** den Ausschlag geben; **force the ~:** eine Entscheidung erzwingen; [G] (*termination*) Ende, *das;* [H] (*Law: progeny*) Nachkommen (*Pl.;*) [I] (*outgoing, outflow*) Austritt, *der.*
❷ *v.t.* [A] (*give out*) ausgeben; ausstellen ‹Pass, Visum, Zeugnis, Haft-, Durchsuchungsbefehl›; erteilen ‹Lizenz, Befehl›; **~ sb. with sth.** etw. an jmdn. austeilen; [B] (*publish*) herausgeben ‹Publikation›; herausbringen ‹Publikation, Münze, Briefmarke›; emittieren ‹Wertpapiere›; geben ‹Warnung›; [C] (*supply*) ausgeben (**to** an + *Akk.*); **~ sb. with sth.** jmdn. mit etw. ausstatten; **be ~d with sth.** etw. erhalten.
❸ *v.i.* [A] (*go or come out*) ‹Personen:› herausströmen (**from** aus); ‹Gas, Flüssigkeit:› austreten (**from** aus); ‹Rauch:› heraus-, hervorquellen (**from** aus); ‹Ton, Geräusch:› hervor-, herausdringen (**from** aus); [B] (*be derived*) entspringen (**from** *Dat.*); [C] (*result*) sich ergeben (**from** aus)

**isthmus** /'ɪsməs, 'ɪsθməs/ *n.* (*Geog.*) Landenge, *die;* Isthmus, *der*

**IT** *abbr.* **information technology**

**it**[1] /ɪt/ *pron.* **▶1256** [A] (*the thing, animal, young child previously mentioned*) er/sie/es; *as direct obj.* ihn/sie/es; *as indirect obj.* ihm/ihr/ihm; **behind/under it** dahinter/darunter; **the book was not in the cupboard but behind it** das Buch war nicht im Schrank, sondern dahinter; **the animal turned and snarled at the huntsman behind it** das Tier drehte sich um und knurrte den Jäger hinter sich (*Dat.*) an; **the cathedral and the buildings around it** der Dom und die umliegenden Gebäude; [B] (*the person in question*) **who is it?** wer ist da?; **it was**

**the children** es waren die Kinder; **is it you, father?** bist du es, Vater?; **Are you the one responsible for all this mess? — No, it's him** Sind Sie für dieses Durcheinander verantwortlich? — Nein, er; **C** *subj. of impers. v.* es; **it is snowing/warm** es schneit/ist warm; **it is winter/midnight/ten o'clock** es ist Winter/Mitternacht/zehn Uhr; **it is ten miles to Oxford** es sind zehn Meilen bis Oxford; **it says in the Bible that ...:** in der Bibel heißt es, dass ...; in der Bibel steht, dass ...; **had it not been a Sunday ...:** wenn nicht Sonntag gewesen wäre ...; **if it hadn't been for you ...:** wenn du nicht gewesen wärst, ...; **D** *anticipating subj. or obj.* es; **it is typical of her to do that** es ist typisch für sie, so etwas zu tun; **it is absurd talking** *or* **to talk like that** es ist absurd, so zu reden; **it is a difficult time, winter** es ist eine schwierige Zeit, der Winter; **it is not often that we see them** wir sehen sie nicht oft; **it was for our sake that he did it** um unseretwillen hat er es getan; **it is to him that you must apply** an ihn musst du dich wenden; **E** *as antecedent to relative* es; **it was us who saw him** wir waren es, die ihn gesehen haben; wi̲r haben ihn gesehen; **it was a large sum of money that he found** was er fand, war ein großer Geldbetrag; **F** *as indef. obj.* es; **I can't cope with it any more** ich halte das nicht mehr länger aus; **have a hard time of it** eine schwere Zeit haben; **what is it?** was ist los?; was ist denn?; **G** (*exactly what is needed*) **That's it! That's exactly what I've been looking for** Das ist es! Genau das habe ich gesucht; **a gift that is really 'it** das ideale Geschenk (*ugs.*); **he thinks he's really 'it** er denkt, er ist der Größte (*ugs.*); **H** (*the extreme limit of achievement*) **this is really 'it** das ist wirklich [einsame *od.* absolute] Spitze (*ugs.*); **I** (*coll.: sexual appeal*) das gewisse Etwas (*ugs.*); **J** **that's 'it** (*coll.*) (*that's the problem*) das ist es [eben]; (*that's the end*) jetzt ist Schluss; (*my patience is at an end*) jetzt reichts [mir]; (*that's true*) genau (*ugs.*); **when you've done your stint, that's 'it!** wenn du deinen Anteil geleistet hast, dann fertig *od.* dann wars das; **this is 'it** (*coll.*) (*the time for action*) es ist so weit; (*the real problem*) das ist es [eben]; **K** (*in children's games*) **you're 'it!** du bist! (*ugs.*). ⇨ *also* **its**; **itself**

**it²** *n.* (*Brit. coll.*) [italienischer] Wermut

**Italian** /ɪ'tæljən/ ▶ 1275, ▶ 1340 **1** *adj.* italienisch; **sb. is ~:** jmd. ist Italiener/Italienerin; ⇨ *also* **English** 1. **2** *n.* **A** (*person*) Italiener, *der*/Italienerin, *die;* **B** (*language*) Italienisch, *das;* ⇨ *also* **English** 2 A

**Italianate** /ɪ'tæljənət, ɪ'tæljəneɪt/ *adj.* italienisch beeinflusst

**italic** /ɪ'tælɪk/ **1** *adj.* kursiv. **2** *n. in pl.* Kursivschrift, *die;* **in ~s** kursiv; **my ~s** Hervorhebung von mir

**italicize** (**italicise**) /ɪ'tælɪsaɪz/ *v.t.* kursiv setzen

**italic: ~ 'script** *n.* Kursive, *die;* **~ 'type** *n.* (*Printing*) Kursivschrift, *die*

**Italy** /'ɪtəlɪ/ *pr. n.* Italien (*das*)

**itch** /ɪtʃ/ **1** *n.* **A** Juckreiz, *der;* Jucken, *das;* **I have an ~:** es juckt mich; ich habe einen Juckreiz; **when you get an ~:** wenn es [dich] juckt; **B** (*disease*) Krätze, *die;* **C** (*restless desire*) Drang, *der;* **I have an ~ to do it** es juckt (*ugs.*) *od.* reizt mich, es zu tun; **an ~ for money/success** ein Verlangen nach Geld/Erfolg.
**2** *v.i.* **A** einen Juckreiz haben; **I'm ~ing** es juckt mich; **woollen jumpers make me ~:** Wollpullover jucken mich; **this heat makes me ~ all over** bei der Hitze juckt es mich überall; **it ~es** es juckt; **my back ~es** mein Rücken juckt; es juckt mich am Rücken; ⇨ *also* **finger** 1 A; **B** (*feel a desire*) **~ or be ~ing to do sth.** darauf brennen, etw. zu tun; **~ for sth.** sich nach etw. sehnen; **he is ~ing for a fight** er ist nur darauf aus, sich zu prügeln

**itching powder** /'ɪtʃɪŋpaʊdə(r)/ *n.* Juckpulver, *das*

**itchy** /'ɪtʃɪ/ *adj.* kratzig ‹Socken, Laken›; **be ~** ‹Körperteil:› jucken; **I feel ~:** es juckt mich; **I've got ~ feet** (*fig. coll.*) mich hält es hier nicht länger; (*by temperament*) mich hält es nirgends lange

**it'd** /'ɪtəd/ (*coll.*) **A** = **it had;** **B** = **it would**

**item** /'aɪtəm/ *n.* **A** Ding, *das;* Sache, *die;* (*in shop, catalogue*) Artikel, *der;* (*in variety show, radio, TV*) Nummer, *die;* **~ of clothing/furniture** Kleidungs-/Möbelstück, *das;* **~ of equipment** Ausrüstungsgegenstand, *der;* **B** **~ [of news]** Nachricht, *die;* **C** (*in account or bill*) Posten, *der;* (*in list, programme, agenda*) Punkt, *der*

**itemize** (**itemise**) /'aɪtəmaɪz/ *v.t.* einzeln aufführen; spezifizieren ‹Rechnung›; **~ the stock** den Bestand auflisten

**iterative** /'ɪtərətɪv/ *adj.*, **iteratively** /'ɪtərətɪvlɪ/ *adv.* (*Ling.*) iterativ

**itinerant** /ɪ'tɪnərənt, aɪ'tɪnərənt/ **1** *adj.* reisend; umherziehend; Wander‹prediger, -arbeiter›; fahrend ‹Sänger›. **2** *n.* Landfahrer, *der*/Landfahrerin, *die*

**itinerary** /aɪ'tɪnərərɪ, ɪ'tɪnərərɪ/ *n.* **A** (*route*) [Reise]route, *die;* [Reise]weg, *der;* **B** (*record of travel*) Reisebericht, *der;* Reisebeschreibung, *die;* **C** (*guidebook*) Reiseführer, *der*

**it'll** /ɪtl/ (*coll.*) = **it will**

**its** /ɪts/ *poss. pron. attrib.* sein/ihr/sein; ⇨ *also* **her²**

**it's** /ɪts/ **A** = **it is;** **B** = **it has**

**itself** /ɪt'self/ *pron.* **A** *emphat.* selbst; **by ~** (*automatically*) von selbst; (*alone*) allein; (*taken in isolation*) für sich; **in ~:** für sich genommen; **which ~ is reason enough** was allein schon Grund genug ist; **he is generosity ~:** er ist die Großzügigkeit in Person; **B** *refl.* sich; **the rocket destroys ~:** die Rakete zerstört sich selbst; **the machine switches ~ off** die Maschine schaltet sich [von] selbst aus. ⇨ *also* **herself**

**itsy-bitsy** /ɪtsɪ'bɪtsɪ/, **itty-bitty** /ɪtɪ'bɪtɪ/ *adjs.* (*coll.*) klitzeklein (*ugs.*); **~ little** klitzeklitzeklein (*ugs.*)

**ITV** *abbr.* (*Brit.*) **Independent Television** *kommerzielles britisches Fernsehprogramm*

**IUD** *abbr.* **intrauterine device**

**Ivan** /'aɪvn/ *pr. n.* (*Hist., as name of ruler etc.*) Iwan (*der*); **~ the Terrible** Iwan der Schreckliche

**I've** /aɪv/ = **I have**

**IVF** *abbr.* **in-vitro fertilization**

**ivory** /'aɪvərɪ/ *n.* **A** (*substance*) Elfenbein, *das; attrib.* elfenbeinern; Elfenbein-; **B** (*object*) Elfenbeinschnitzerei, *die;* **C** (*colour*) Elfenbein, *das; attrib.* elfenbeinfarbig; **D** **tickle the ivories** (*coll.*) ein bisschen auf dem Klavier spielen

**ivory: I~ 'Coast** *pr. n.* Elfenbeinküste, *die;* **~ 'tower** *n.* Elfenbeinturm, *der*

**ivy** /'aɪvɪ/ *n.* Efeu, *der;* ⇨ *also* **ground ivy**

**'ivy-clad** *adj.* efeubewachsen

**'Ivy League** *n.* (*Amer.*) *Eliteuniversitäten im Osten der USA*

# J j

**J, j** /dʒeɪ/ *n., pl.* **Js** *or* **J's** J, j, *das*

**J.** *abbr.* [A] (*Cards*) **jack** B; [B] (*Phys.*) **joule[s]** J

**jab** /dʒæb/ ❶ *v.t.,* **-bb-** [A] (*poke roughly*) stoßen; **he ~bed my arm with his finger** er pikste mir mit dem Finger in den Arm; **he ~bed his elbow into my side** er stieß mir den Ellbogen in die Seite; [B] (*stab*) stechen; **he ~bed the needle into my leg** er stach mir mit der Nadel ins Bein; [C] (*thrust abruptly*) stoßen. ❷ *v.i.,* **-bb-:** **~ at sb. [with sth.]** auf jmdn. [mit etw.] einhauen; (*stab at*) auf jmdn. [mit etw.] einstechen. ❸ *n.* [A] (*abrupt blow*) Schlag, *der;* (*with stick, elbow*) Stoß, *der;* (*with needle*) Stich, *der;* (*Boxing*) Jab, *der;* **give sb. a ~:** jmdm. einen Schlag/Stoß/Stich versetzen; [B] (*Brit. coll.: hypodermic injection*) Spritze, *die;* **give sb./oneself a ~:** jmdm./sich eine Spritze verpassen (*ugs.*); **have you had your cholera ~s yet?** bist du schon gegen Cholera geimpft worden?

**jabber** /ˈdʒæbə(r)/ ❶ *v.i.* plappern (*ugs.*); **~ at sb.** auf jmdn. einreden. ❷ *v.t.* brabbeln (*ugs.*). ❸ *n.* [A] (*fast*) Geplapper, *das* (*ugs.*); [B] (*unclear*) Gebrabbel, *das* (*ugs. abwertend*); Kauderwelsch, *das*

**jabot** /ˈʒæbəʊ/ *n.* Jabot, *das*

**jack** /dʒæk/ ❶ *n.* [A] (*Cards*) Bube, *der;* **~ of hearts** Herzbube, *der;* [B] (*for lifting vehicle wheel*) Wagenheber, *der;* [C] **J~** (*man*) Hans; **every man ~ [of them]** (*coll.*) alle miteinander; allesamt; **on one's J~ [Jones]** (*Brit. sl.*) ganz allein; **all work and no play makes J~ a dull boy** (*prov.*) zu viel Arbeit ist ungesund; **I'm all right, J~** (*fig. coll.*) was kümmern *od.* interessieren mich die anderen?; [D] ⇒ **Jack tar**; [E] (*for turning spit*) Bratenwender, *der;* [F] (*on clock*) Glockenschläger, *der;* [G] (*Teleph. etc.*) Buchse, *die;* Klinke, *die* (*Postw.*); (*wall socket*) Steckdose, *die;* [H] (*Bowls*) Malkugel, *die;* [I] (*Zool.*) Männchen, *das;* [J] (*ship's flag*) Gösch, *die* (*Seemannsspr.*). ⇒ *also* **Union Jack**.
❷ *v.t.* [A] **~ in** *or* **up** (*Brit. coll.: abandon*) [auf]stecken (*ugs.*); [B] **~ up** (*lift*) aufbocken ‹Fahrzeug›; (*fig. coll.: increase*) was draufsatteln auf (+ *Akk.*) (*ugs.*)

**jackal** /ˈdʒækl/ *n.* (*Zool.*) Schakal, *der*

**jackanapes** /ˈdʒækəneɪps/ *n.* (*arch.: impertinent fellow*) Laffe, *der* (*veralt. abwertend*)

**jackass** /ˈdʒækæs/ *n.* [A] (*male ass*) Eselhengst, *der;* [B] (*stupid person*) Esel, *der* (*ugs.*); [C] **laughing ~** (*Austral. Ornith.*) Lachender Hans

**jack:** **~boot** *n.* [A] [Stulpen]stiefel, *der;* [B] (*fig.*) **be under the ~boot** brutalen *od.* rücksichtslosen Methoden ausgeliefert sein; **~daw** /ˈdʒækdɔː/ *n.* (*Ornith.*) Dohle, *die*

**jacket** /ˈdʒækɪt/ *n.* [A] Jacke, *die;* (*of suit*) Jackett, *das;* **sports ~:** Sakko, *der;* **a new ~ and trousers** ein neues Jackett und Hosen; eine neue Kombination; **~ pocket** Jackentasche, *die*/Jacketttasche, *die;* [B] (*round a boiler etc.*) Mantel, *der;* [C] (*of book*) Schutzumschlag, *der;* [D] (*of a potato*) Schale, *die;* **~ potatoes** in der Schale gebackene Kartoffeln; [E] (*Amer.*) ⇒ **sleeve** B

**jack:** **J~ 'Frost** *n.* Väterchen Frost (*scherzh.*); **~-in-the-box** *n.* Schachtelteufel, *der;* Kastenteufel, *der;* **~-knife** ❶ *n.* [A] (*large clasp knife*) Klappmesser, *das;* [B] (*dive*) Hechtsprung, *der;* [C] (*Motor Veh.*) Querstellen des Anhängers; ❷ *v.i.* **the lorry ~-knifed** der Anhänger des Lastwagens stellte sich quer; **~ of 'all trades** *n.* Hansdampf [in allen Gassen]; **he is a ~ of all trades and master of none** er versteht von allem ein bisschen was, aber von nichts sehr viel; **~pot** *n.* Jackpot, *der;* **hit the ~pot** (*fig.*) das große Los ziehen; **J~ Robinson** /dʒæk ˈrɒbɪnsn/ *n.* **before you can/could say J~ Robinson** im Nu (*ugs.*); in null Komma nichts (*ugs.*); **J~ Russell** /dʒæk ˈrʌsl/ *n. eine Terrierart;* **J~ 'tar** *n.* Teerjacke, *die* (*scherzh.*)

**Jacob** /ˈdʒeɪkəb/ *pr. n.* (*Bibl.*) Jakob (*der*); **~'s ladder** (*Bot.*) Jakobsleiter, *die;* Sperrkraut, *das*

**Jacobean** /dʒækəˈbiːən/ *adj.* (*Hist.*) [aus] der Zeit Jakobs I. *nachgestellt*

**Jacobite** /ˈdʒækəbaɪt/ *n.* (*Hist.*) Jakobit, *der*

**Jacquard [loom]** /ˈdʒækɑːd (luːm)/ *n.* Jacquardwebstuhl, *der*

**jacuzzi,** (*Amer.:* ®) /dʒəˈkuːzɪ/ *n.* ≈ Whirlpool, *der*

**jade**[1] /dʒeɪd/ ❶ *n.* (*derog.*) [A] (*horse*) alter Klepper (*abwertend*); Schindmähre, *die* (*abwertend*); [B] (*woman*) Weib, *das;* Weibsbild, *das* (*abwertend*). ❷ *v.t., esp. in p.p.* (*tire*) ermüden; abstumpfen ‹Geschmacksnerven›; **look ~d** abgespannt *od.* erschöpft aussehen

**jade**[2] *n.* [A] (*stone*) Jade, *der od. die;* (*carvings*) Jade[arbeiten], *die;* [B] (*colour*) Jadegrün, *das*

**Jaffa** /ˈdʒæfə/, **Jaffa orange** /dʒæfə ˈɒrɪndʒ/ *n.* Jaffaapfelsine, *die*

**jag**[1] *n.* Zacke, *die;* Spitze, *die*

**jag**[2] *n.* (*sl.: drinking bout*) Besäufnis, *das* (*salopp*); Sauferei, *die* (*derb abwertend*); **go on a ~:** saufen (*derb*); **be on a ~:** am Saufen sein (*derb*)

**Jag** /dʒæg/ *n.* (*Brit. coll.: car*) Jaguar, *der*

**jagged** /ˈdʒægɪd/ *adj.* [A] (*irregularly cut*) gezackt; ausgefranst ‹Loch/Riss in Kleidungsstücken›; ‹Wunde› mit [unregelmäßig] gezackten *od.* zerfetzten Rändern; [B] (*deeply indented*) zerklüftet ‹Küste›

**jaguar** /ˈdʒægjʊə(r)/ *n.* (*Zool.*) Jaguar, *der*

**jail** /dʒeɪl/ ❶ *n.* (*place*) Gefängnis, *das;* (*confinement*) Haft, *die;* **in ~:** im Gefängnis; **be sent to ~:** ins Gefängnis kommen; eingesperrt werden; **go to ~:** ins Gefängnis gehen. ❷ *v.t.* ins Gefängnis bringen; einsperren

**jail:** **~bird** *n.* Knastbruder, *der* (*ugs.*); **~break** *n.* Gefängnisausbruch, *der*

**jailer, jailor** /ˈdʒeɪlə(r)/ *n.* Gefängniswärter, *der*/Gefängniswärterin, *die*

**jalopy** /dʒəˈlɒpɪ/ *n.* (*coll.*) Klapperkiste, *die* (*ugs.*)

**jam**[1] /dʒæm/ ❶ *v.t.,* **-mm-** [A] (*squeeze and fix between two surfaces*) einklemmen; **~ sth. into sth.** etw. in etw. (*Akk.*) zwängen; **the key had become ~med in the lock** der Schlüssel hatte sich im Schloss verklemmt; [B] (*make immovable*) blockieren; (*fig.*) lähmen; lahm legen; **I seem to ~ the car door every time I lock it** die Autotür verklemmt sich anscheinend jedes Mal, wenn ich sie abschließe; [C] (*squeeze together in compact mass*) stopfen (**into** in + *Akk.*); **~ together** zusammenpferchen ‹Personen›; [D] (*thrust into confined space*) stopfen (**into** in + *Akk.*); stecken ‹Schlüssel, Münze› (**into** in + *Akk.*); [E] (*block by crowding*) blockieren; versperren, blockieren ‹Eingang›; verstopfen, blockieren ‹Rohr›; **the switchboard was ~med with calls** sämtliche Leitungen waren durch Anrufe blockiert; [F] (*Radio*) stören.
❷ *v.i.,* **-mm-** [A] (*become tightly wedged*) sich verklemmen; [B] (*become unworkable*) ‹Maschine:› klemmen.
❸ *n.* [A] (*crush, stoppage*) Blockierung, *die;* Klemmen, *das;* [B] (*crowded mass*) Stau, *der;* [C] (*coll.: dilemma*) Klemme, *die* (*ugs.*); Patsche, *die* (*ugs.*); **be in a ~:** in der Klemme stecken; in der Patsche sitzen; **get into a ~:** in die Klemme geraten; [D] ⇒ **jam session**. ⇒ *also* **logjam; traffic jam**

**~ 'in** *v.t.* hineinzwängen; **we were ~med in** wir waren eingepfercht

**~ 'on** *v.t.* **~ the brakes [full] on** [voll] auf die Bremse steigen (*ugs.*); eine Vollbremsung machen

**~ 'up** *v.t.* verstopfen ‹Straße usw.›; lahm legen ‹System›; verklemmen ‹Mechanismus›

**jam**[2] *n.* [A] Marmelade, *die;* Konfitüre, *die* (*bes. Kaufmannsspr.*); **make ~:** Marmelade einmachen; **[promises of] ~ tomorrow** (*fig.*) schöne Zukunftsverheißungen; **sb. wants ~ on it** (*fig. coll.*) jmdm. genügt etw. noch nicht; [B] (*Brit. coll.: sth. easy*) kinderleichte Sache (*fam.*); Kinderspiel, *das;* ⇒ *also* **money** A

**Jamaica** /dʒəˈmeɪkə/ *pr. n.* Jamaika (*das*)

**Jamaican** /dʒəˈmeɪkən/ ▶**1340** ❶ *adj.* jamaik[an]isch; **sb. is ~:** jmd. ist Jamaikaner/Jamaikanerin. ❷ *n.* Jamaikaner, *der*/Jamaikanerin, *die*

**jamb** /dʒæm/ *n.* (*of doorway, window*) Pfosten, *der*

**jamboree** /dʒæmbəˈriː/ *n.* [A] fröhliches Beisammensein; Fete, *die* (*ugs. scherzh.*); (*carousal*) Zechgelage, *das* (*veralt.*); [B] (*large rally of Scouts*) Jamboree, *das*

**James** /dʒeɪmz/ *pr. n.* (*Hist., as name of ruler etc.*) Jakob (*der*)

**'jam jar** *n.* Marmeladenglas, *das*

**jammy** /ˈdʒæmɪ/ *adj.* [A] (*sticky with jam*) von Marmelade klebrig; marmeladeverklebt; [B] (*Brit. coll.*) (*easy*) kinderleicht (*fam.*); (*lucky*) **that was ~:** das war Schwein (*ugs.*); **~ beggar** Glückspilz, *der* (*ugs.*)

**jam:** **~-packed** *adj.* (*coll.*) knallvoll (*ugs.*), proppenvoll (*ugs.*) (**with** von); **~ session** *n.* (*Jazz coll.*) Jamsession, *die;* **~ 'tart** *n.* Marmeladentörtchen, *das*

**Jan.** *abbr.* **January** Jan.

**jane** /dʒeɪn/ *n.* (*sl.*) Mieze, *die* (*salopp*); ⇒ *also* **plain** 1 D

**jangle** /ˈdʒæŋgl/ ❶ *v.i.* klimpern; ‹Klingel:› bimmeln. ❷ *v.t.* [A] (*sound*) rasseln mit; bimmeln mit ‹Glocke›; klimpern mit ‹[Klein]geld›; [B] (*irritate*) **~ sb.'s nerves** jmdn. nerven (*salopp*); jmdm. auf die Nerven gehen. ❸ *n.* Geklapper, *das;* (*of bell*) Schrillen, *das*

**janitor** /ˈdʒænɪtə(r)/ *n.* [A] (*doorkeeper*) Portier, *der;* [B] (*caretaker*) Hausmeister, *der*

**January** /ˈdʒænjʊərɪ/ *n.* ▶**1055** Januar, *der;* ⇒ *also* **August**

**Jap** /dʒæp/ *n.* (*coll., often derog.*) Japs, *der* (*ugs., oft abwertend*)

**japan** ❶ *n.* Japanlack, *der.* ❷ *v.t.,* **-nn-** mit Japanlack überziehen; **a ~ned table** ein Lacktisch

**Japan** /dʒəˈpæn/ *n.* Japan (*das*)

**Japanese** /dʒæpəˈniːz/ ▶**1275**, ▶**1340** ❶ *adj.* japanisch; **sb. is ~:** jmd. ist Japaner/Japanerin; ⇒ *also* **English** 1. ❷ *n., pl. same* [A] (*person*) Japaner, *der*/Japanerin, *die;* [B] (*language*) Japanisch, *das;* ⇒ *also* **English** 2 A

**Japanese:** **~ [flowering] 'cherry** *n.* Japanische Kirsche; **~ 'quince** *n.* Japanische Quitte; **~ 'silk** *n.* Japanseide, *die*

**jape** /dʒeɪp/ ❶ *v.i.* spotten (**with** über + *Akk.*); **~ at** verspotten. ❷ *n.* Scherz, *der;* Spaß, *der;* (*practical joke*) Streich, *der*

**japonica** /dʒəˈpɒnɪkə/ *n.* (*Bot.*) Japanische Quitte

**jar¹** /dʒɑ:(r)/ ❶ *n.* [A] (*harsh or grating sound*) Quietschen, *das;* [B] (*jolt*) Stoß, *der;* (*thrill of nerves, shock*) Schlag, *der;* **stop with a ~:** mit einem Ruck halten; [C] (*lack of harmony*) Misston, *der.* ❷ *v.i.*, **-rr-** [A] (*sound discordantly*) quietschen; (*rattle*) ‹Fenster:› scheppern (*ugs.*); **~ on** *or* **against sth.** über etw. (*Akk.*) knirschen; **a ~ring sound** ein Geräusch, das einem durch und durch geht [B] (*have discordant or painful effect*) **~ [up]on sb./sb.'s nerves** jmdm. auf die Nerven gehen; **~ on the ears** durch Mark und Bein gehen (*ugs. scherzh.*); **these two colours ~:** diese beiden Farben beißen sich (*ugs.*); [C] (*fig.: be out of harmony*) **~ with sth.** sich mit etw. nicht vertragen. ❸ *v.t.*, **-rr-** [A] (*cause to vibrate*) erschüttern; [B] (*send shock through*) **~ sb.'s nerves** jmdm. auf die Nerven gehen; **~ one's elbow** sich (*Dat.*) den Ellbogen anschlagen

**jar²** *n.* [A] (*vessel*) Topf, *der;* (*of glass*) Glas, *das;* **~ of jam** *etc.* Topf/Glas Marmelade *usw.;* [B] (*Brit. coll.: glass of beer*) Bierchen, *das* (*fam.*)

**jar³** *n.* (*arch./coll.*) **on the ~** (*ajar*) angelehnt

**jardinière** /ʒɑ:dɪ'njeə(r)/ *n.* Jardiniere, *die;* **à la ~:** nach Gärtnerinart

**jarful** /'dʒɑ:fʊl/ *n.* Topf, *der;* (*contents of glass jar*) Glas, *das;* **a ~ of jam** ein Topf/Glas Marmelade; **a ~ of pebbles** ein Topf/Glas voll Kieselsteine

**jargon** /'dʒɑ:gən/ *n.* [A] (*speech familiar only to a particular group*) Jargon, *der;* [B] (*unintelligible words*) Gebrabbel, *das* (*ugs. abwertend*)

**Jas.** *abbr.* **James**

**jasmin[e]** /'dʒæsmɪn, 'dʒæzmɪn/ *n.* Jasmin, *der;* **common** *or* **white ~:** echter Jasmin; Kletterjasmin, *der;* **red ~:** rot blühende Plumeria; **winter ~:** Winterjasmin, *der*

**jasper** /'dʒæspə(r)/ *n.* (*Min.*) Jaspis, *der*

**jaundice** /'dʒɔ:ndɪs/ ❶ *n.* ▶ 1232 (*Med.*) Gelbsucht, *die.* ❷ *v.t.* [A] ▶ 1232 (*Med.*) **be [badly] ~d** eine [schwere] Gelbsucht haben; [B] *usu. in p.p.* (*fig.: affect with bitterness*) verbittern; **~d** verbittert; (*cynical*) zynisch; **~ sb. against sth./towards sb.** jmdn. gegen etw./jmdn. einnehmen; **with [a] ~d eye** (*enviously*) neidvoll; mit Neid; **have a very ~d view of life** dem Leben voller Verbitterung gegenüberstehen

**jaunt** /dʒɔ:nt/ ❶ *n.* Ausflug, *der;* **be off on/go for a ~:** einen Ausflug machen. ❷ *v.i.* **~ [about]** herumziehen; **are you ~ing off again on some new trip?** geht es mal wieder auf Tour?

**jauntily** /'dʒɔ:ntɪlɪ/ *adv.* unbeschwert

**jaunty** /'dʒɔ:ntɪ/ *adj.* unbeschwert; keck ‹Hut›; **with a ~ gait** beschwingten Schrittes; **he wore his hat at a ~ angle** er hatte sich (*Dat.*) den Hut keck aufs Ohr gesetzt

**Java** /'dʒɑ:və/ *pr. n.* Java (*das*)

**javelin** /'dʒævəlɪn, 'dʒævlɪn/ *n.* [A] Speer, *der;* **throwing the ~** (*Sport*) Speerwerfen, *das;* [B] (*Sport: event*) Speerwerfen, *das*

**jaw** /dʒɔ:/ ❶ *n.* [A] ▶ 966 (*Anat.*) Kiefer, *der;* **his ~ dropped** er ließ die Kinnlade herunterfallen; **upper/lower ~:** Ober-/Unterkiefer, *der;* **set one's ~:** ein entschlossenes Gesicht machen; [B] *in pl.* (*of valley, channel*) Schlund, *der;* [C] (*of machine*) [Klemm]backe, *die;* [D] *in pl.* (*large dangerous mouth*) Rachen, *der;* (*fig.: of fate, death, etc.*) Klauen; **snatch sb. from the ~s of death** jmdn. vor dem sicheren Tod retten; **snatch victory from the ~s of defeat** kurz vor der drohenden Niederlage doch noch den Sieg erringen. ❷ *v.i.* (*coll.*) quatschen (*ugs.*); **~ at sb.** jmdn. voll quatschen (*ugs.*)

**jaw: ~bone** *n.* ▶ 966 Kieferknochen, *der;* **~-breaker** *n.* (*coll.*) Zungenbrecher, *der*

**jay** /dʒeɪ/ *n.* (*Ornith.*) [A] (*Garrulus glandarius*) Eichelhäher, *der;* [B] (*Garrulinae*) Häher, *der*

**jay: ~-walk** *v.i.* als Fußgänger im Straßenverkehr unachtsam sein; **~walker** *n.* im Straßenverkehr unachtsamer Fußgänger

**jazz** /dʒæz/ ❶ *n.* [A] Jazz, *der; attrib.* Jazz‹musik, -musiker›; [B] (*coll.: nonsense*) Quatsch, *der* (*ugs. abwertend*); Gewäsch, *das* (*ugs. abwertend*); **and all that ~** (*coll.*) und der ganze Kram (*ugs.*). ❷ *v.t.* **~ up** aufpeppen (*ugs.*); aufmotzen (*ugs.*)

**jazz: ~ band** *n.* Jazzband, *die;* **~ 'rock** *n.* Jazzrock, *der*

**jazzy** /'dʒæzɪ/ *adj.* poppig; **a ~ sports car** ein aufgemotzter Sportwagen (*ugs.*)

**JCR** *abbr.* (*Brit. Univ.*) **Junior Common Room; Junior Combination Room**

**jealous** /'dʒeləs/ *adj.* [A] (*feeling resentment*) eifersüchtig (**of** auf + *Akk.*); [B] (*possessive*) eifersüchtig ‹Liebe›; **be ~ of sth.** eifersüchtig über etw. (*Akk.*) wachen; **be ~ for sth.** peinlich auf etw. (*Akk.*) bedacht sein; **he kept a ~ eye on her** er wachte eifersüchtig über sie

**jealously** /'dʒeləslɪ/ *adv.* eifersüchtig

**jealousy** /'dʒeləsɪ/ *n.* Eifersucht, *die;* **little jealousies** [kleine] Eifersüchteleien

**jean** /dʒi:n/ *n.* [A] (*cloth*) Baumwolldrell, *der;* [B] *in pl.* (*trousers*) Jeans *Pl.;* Jeans, *die;* **a pair of ~s** ein Paar Jeans; eine Jeans; ⇒ *also* **blue jeans**

**Jeep** ® /dʒi:p/ *n.* Jeep ⓌⓏ, *der*

**jeer** /dʒɪə(r)/ ❶ *v.i.* höhnen (*geh.*); **~ at sb.** jmdn. verhöhnen; **~ing** höhnisch johlend ‹Menge, Mob›. ❷ *v.t.* verhöhnen; **the crowd ~ed every tackle he made** die Menge johlte höhnisch bei jedem Tackling, das er machte. ❸ *n.* höhnisches Johlen; (*remark*) höhnische Bemerkung; **~s** höhnisches Gejohle/höhnische Bemerkungen

**jehad** ⇒ **jihad**

**Jehovah** /dʒɪ'həʊvə/ *n.* (*Relig.*) Jehova (*der*)

**Jehovah's 'Witness** *n.* (*Relig.*) Zeuge Jehovas

**jejune** /dʒɪ'dʒu:n/ *adj.* [A] (*intellectually unsatisfying*) unergiebig; unzulänglich ‹Erklärung, Begründung, Leistung›; [B] (*puerile*) läppisch (*abwertend*); infantil (*abwertend*)

**jejunum** /dʒɪ'dʒu:nəm/ *n.* (*Anat.*) Leerdarm, *der*

**jell** /dʒel/ *v.i.* [A] (*set as jelly*) fest werden; gelieren; [B] (*fig.: take definite form*) Gestalt annehmen; **not ~ as a group** als Gruppe nicht zusammenpassen

**Jell-O** ®, **jello** /'dʒeləʊ/ *n.* (*esp. Amer.*) Götterspeise, *die*

**jelly** /'dʒelɪ/ ❶ *n.* [A] Gelee, *das;* (*dessert*) Götterspeise, *die;* [B] (*substance of similar consistency*) gallertartige Masse; **her legs felt like ~:** ihr schlotterten die Knie; sie hatte Pudding in den Knien (*ugs.*); [C] (*coll.: gelignite*) Plastiksprengstoff, *der.* ❷ *v.t.* [A] zu einer gallertartigen Masse erstarren lassen; Gelee machen aus ‹Obst›; [B] **jellied eels** Aal in Aspik. ❸ *v.i.* (*become ~*) gelieren

**jelly: ~ baby** *n.* ≈ Gummibärchen, *das;* **~ bean** *n.* [bohnenförmiges] Geleebonbon; **~fish** *n.* Qualle, *die;* **~-like** *adj.* gallertartig; gallertig ‹Konsistenz›

**jemmy** /'dʒemɪ/ *n.* (*Brit.*) Brecheisen, *das*

**jeopardize** (**jeopardise**) /'dʒepədaɪz/ *v.t.* gefährden

**jeopardy** /'dʒepədɪ/ *n., no pl.* Gefahr, *die;* **put** *or* **place sth./sb. in ~:** etw. aufs Spiel setzen/jmdn. in Gefahr bringen; etw./jmdn. gefährden; **in ~:** in Gefahr; gefährdet; **her life is in ~:** sie schwebt in Lebensgefahr

**jerbil** ⇒ **gerbil**

**jerboa** /dʒɜ:'bəʊə/ *n.* (*Zool.*) Springmaus, *die*

**Jeremiah** /dʒerɪ'maɪə/ *n.* [A] (*Bibl.*) Jeremia[s] (*der*); [B] (*fig.*) Schwarzseher, *der*

**Jericho** /'dʒerɪkəʊ/ *pr. n.* ▶ 1626 (*Geog.*) Jericho (*das*)

**jerk** /dʒɜ:k/ ❶ *n.* [A] (*sharp sudden pull*) Ruck, *der;* ruckartige Bewegung; **with a series of ~s** ruckartig; ruckend; **with a ~ of his thumb, he indicated the direction in which …:** mit einer kurzen Daumenbewegung zeigte er die Richtung, in die …; **give sth. a ~:** einer Sache (*Dat.*) einen Ruck geben; an etw. (*Dat.*) rucken; [B] (*involuntary movement*) Zuckung, *die;* Zucken, *das;* [C] (*coll.: person*) Null, *die* (*ugs.*); Blödmann, *der* (*ugs.*). ❷ *v.t.* [A] reißen an (+ *Dat.*) ‹Seil usw.›; **~ sth. away/back** *etc.* etw. weg-/zurückreißen *usw.;* **~ sth. off/out of sth.** *etc.* etw. von etw. [herunter]reißen/aus etw. [heraus]reißen *usw.;* **he ~ed his thumb in the direction of the town** er zeigte mit einer kurzen Bewegung seines Daumens in Richtung Stadt; **a noise ~ed him out of his reverie** ein Geräusch riss ihn aus seinen Träumereien; [B] (*Weightlifting*) stoßen. ❸ *v.i.* ruckeln; (*move in a spasmodic manner*) zucken; **the lever ~ed out of his hand** der Hebel sprang ihm aus der Hand; **his head ~ed back** sein Kopf zuckte zurück

**~ 'off** (*coarse*) ❶ *v.t.* **~ sb. off** jmdm. einen abwichsen (*vulg.*). ❷ *v.i.* wichsen (*derb*)

**jerkily** /'dʒɜ:kɪlɪ/ *adv.* ruckartig; eckig ‹gehen, sich verbeugen›

**jerkin** /'dʒɜ:kɪn/ *n.* ≈ Wams, *das;* (*modern*) Weste, *die*

**jerky** /'dʒɜ:kɪ/ *adj.* [A] abgehackt, holprig ‹Art zu schreiben/sprechen›; holprig ‹Busfahrt›; holpernd ‹Fahrzeug›; ruckartig ‹Bewegung›; [B] (*spasmodic*) zuckend; **the ~ movements of a puppet** die eckigen Bewegungen einer Marionette

**Jerome** /dʒə'rəʊm/ *pr. n.* **St ~:** der heilige Hieronymus

**jerrican** ⇒ **jerry-can**

**Jerry** /'dʒerɪ/ *n.* (*Brit. dated coll.*) [A] (*soldier*) Deutsche, *der;* [B] *no pl.* (*Germans collectively*) der Deutsche

**jerry: ~-builder** *n.* Baupfuscher, *der* (*ugs. abwertend*); **~-building** *n.* Pfusch am Bau (*ugs. abwertend*); **~-built** *adj.* unsolide gebaut; **~can** *n.* Kanister, *der*

**jersey** /'dʒɜ:zɪ/ *n.* [A] Pullover, *der;* (*Sport*) Trikot, *das;* Jersey, *das;* [B] (*vest*) Unterhemd, *das;* [C] (*fabric*) Jersey, *der;* [D] **J~** (*cow*) Jerseyrind, *das;* [E] **J~** *pr. n.* (*island*) Jersey (*das*)

**Jerusalem** /dʒə'ru:sələm/ *pr. n.* ▶ 1626 Jerusalem (*das*)

**Jerusalem 'artichoke** *n.* Topinambur, *der*

**jest** /dʒest/ ❶ *n.* [A] (*joke*) Scherz, *der;* Witz, *der;* **make ~s** scherzen; Witze machen; [B] *no pl.* (*fun*) Spaß, *der;* **in ~:** im Scherz. ❷ *v.i.* scherzen; Witze machen

**jester** /'dʒestə(r)/ *n.* Spaßmacher, *der;* (*at court*) Hofnarr, *der;* (*fool*) Hanswurst, *der*

**Jesu** /'dʒi:zju:/ *pr. n. voc.* Jesu

**Jesuit** /'dʒezjʊɪt/ *n.* Jesuit, *der*

**Jesuitical** /dʒezjʊ'ɪtɪkl/ *adj.* jesuitisch

**Jesus** /'dʒi:zəs/ ❶ *pr. n.* Jesus (*der*); **Society of ~:** Jesuitenorden, *der.* ❷ *int.* (*sl.*) **~ [Christ]!** Herrgott noch mal! (*ugs.*)

**jet¹** /dʒet/ ❶ *n.* [A] (*stream*) Strahl, *der;* **~ of flame/steam/water** Feuer-/Dampf-/Wasserstrahl, *der;* [B] (*spout, nozzle*) Düse, *die;* [C] (*aircraft*) Düsenflugzeug, *das;* Jet, *der;* (*engine*) Düsentriebwerk, *das.* ❷ *v.i.*, **-tt-** [A] (*spurt out*) ‹Wasser:› herausschießen (**from** aus); ‹Gas, Dampf:› ausströmen (**from** aus); [B] (*coll.: travel by ~ plane*) jetten (*ugs.*); **~ in/out** *or* **off** [per Jet] einfliegen/abfliegen

**jet²** *n.* (*Min.*) Jett, *der od. das;* Gagat, *der*

**jet: ~-black** *adj.* pechschwarz; kohlrabenschwarz; **~ engine** *n.* Düsen- *od.* Strahltriebwerk, *das;* **~ fighter** *n.* Düsenjäger, *der;* **~foil** *n.* [Jetfoil-]Tragflügelboot, *das;* **~ lag** *n.* Jetlag, *der;* **~-lagged** *adj.* **sb. is ~-lagged** jmdm. macht der Jetlag zu schaffen; **~ plane** *n.* Düsenflugzeug, *das;* **~-propelled** *adj.* düsen- *od.* strahlgetrieben; mit Düsen- *od.* Strahlantrieb *nachgestellt;* **~ pro'pulsion** *n.* Düsen- *od.* Strahlantrieb, *der*

**jetsam** /'dʒetsəm/ *n.* sinkendes Seewurfgut (*Seew.*); (*on seashore*) Strandgut, *das;* ⇒ *also* **flotsam**

**jet: ~ set** *n.* Jetset, *der;* **~-setter** *n.* Jetsetter, *der*/-setterin, *die;* **~ ski** *n.* Jetski, *der;* **~-ski** *v.i.* Jetski fahren **~ stream** *n.* [A] (*Meteorol.*) Jetstream, *der;* Strahlstrom, *der;* [B] (*of jet engine*) Düsenstrahl, *der*

**jettison** /'dʒetɪsən/ *v.t.* [A] (*from ship*) über Bord werfen; (*from aircraft*) abwerfen ‹Ballast, Bombe›; (*discard*) wegwerfen; (*Astronaut.*) (*separate*) abtrennen; (*blast off*) absprengen; [B] (*fig.: abandon*) aufgeben; über Bord werfen ‹Plan›

**jetty** /ˈdʒetɪ/ *n.* Ⓐ (*protecting harbour or coast*) [Hafen]mole, *die;* Ⓑ (*landing pier*) Landungsbrücke, *die;* Anleger, *der* (*Seemannsspr.*); (*smaller*) [Landungs]steg, *der*

**Jew** /dʒuː/ *n.* Jude, *der*/Jüdin, *die;* ⇒ *also* **wandering Jew**

ˈ**Jew-baiting** *n.* Judenhetze, *die;* Judenverfolgung, *die*

**jewel** /ˈdʒuːəl/ ➊ *n.* Ⓐ (*ornament*) [kostbares] Schmuckstück; **~s** *collect.* Schmuck, *der;* Juwelen *Pl.;* Ⓑ (*precious stone*) Juwel, *das od. der;* [wertvoller] Edelstein; (*of watch*) Stein, *der;* Ⓒ (*fig.*) (*person*) Goldstück, *das;* Juwel, *das;* (*thing*) Kleinod, *das.* ➋ *v.t.*, (*Brit.*) **-ll-;** *esp. in p.p.* Ⓐ (*adorn with jewels*) mit Juwelen besetzen; **~led hand** juwelengeschmückte Hand; Ⓑ (*fit with jewels*) mit Steinen versehen

**jewel: ~ box**, **~ case** *ns.* Schmuckkasten, *der*

**jeweller** (*Amer.:* **jeweler**) /ˈdʒuːələ(r)/ *n.* ▶ 1261 Juwelier, *der;* **~'s rouge** Polierrot, *das;* ⇒ *also* **baker**

**jewellery** (*Brit.*), **jewelry** /ˈdʒuːəlrɪ/ *n.* Schmuck, *der;* **~ box** Schmuckkasten, *der*

**Jewess** /ˈdʒuːɪs/ *n.* Jüdin, *die*

**Jewish** /ˈdʒuːɪʃ/ *adj.* jüdisch; **he/she is ~:** er ist Jude/sie ist Jüdin

**Jewry** /ˈdʒʊərɪ/ *n.* Judentum, *das;* Judenheit, *die*

**Jew's ˈharp** *n.* (*Mus.*) Maultrommel, *die*

**jib¹** /dʒɪb/ *n.* Ⓐ (*Naut.*) (*on sailing ship*) Stagsegel, *das* (*Seew.*); (*on sailing yacht or dinghy*) Fock, *die* (*Seew.*); **I don't like the cut of his ~** (*fig.*) mir gefällt sein Gesicht *od.* (*ugs.*) seine Nase nicht; Ⓑ (*of crane*) Ausleger, *der*

**jib²** *v.i.*, **-bb-** Ⓐ (*refuse to go on*) ‹Pferd usw.:› bocken; (*because of fright*) scheuen; Ⓑ (*fig.*) sich sträuben; streiken (*ugs.*); **~ at sth./at doing sth.** sich gegen etw. sträuben/sich dagegen sträuben, etw. zu tun; **he ~bed at the idea** er wollte nichts davon wissen

**jibe¹** /dʒaɪb/ *v.i.* (*Amer.*) (*fit*) sich decken; (*match*) zusammenpassen

**jibe²** ⇒ **gibe; gybe**

**jiff** /dʒɪf/, **jiffy** /ˈdʒɪfɪ/ *n.* (*coll.*) Augenblick, *der;* Moment, *der;* **in a ~:** sofort; gleich; **half a ~:** ein Momentchen!

ˈ**Jiffy bag** ® *n.* gefütterte Versandtasche

**jig** /dʒɪg/ ➊ *n.* Ⓐ (*dance, music*) Jig, *die;* (*movement of suite*) Gigue, *die;* **dance** *or* **do a ~:** einen Freudentanz vollführen; Ⓑ (*appliance*) Einspannvorrichtung, *die.* ➋ *v.i.*, **-gg-** (*dance a ~/gigue*) eine Jig/eine Gigue tanzen; (*fig.*) herumhüpfen; **~ up and down** herumhüpfen

**jigger** /ˈdʒɪgə(r)/ *n. Messbecher für alkoholische Getränke*

**jiggered** /ˈdʒɪgəd/ *adj.* (*coll.*) **I'll be ~:** gibts denn so was! (*ugs.*); **I'll be ~ if …:** der Teufel soll mich holen, wenn … (*salopp*)

**jiggery-pokery** /dʒɪgərɪˈpəʊkərɪ/ *n.* (*Brit. coll.*) Ⓐ (*underhand scheming*) Schmu, *der* (*ugs.*); **there is some [sort of] ~ going on** hier ist was faul; **he's up to some [sort of] ~:** er hat 'n krummes Ding vor (*ugs.*); Ⓑ (*nonsense*) Stuss, *der* (*ugs. abwertend*)

**jiggle** /ˈdʒɪgl/ ➊ *v.t.* rütteln an, wackeln an (+ *Dat.*). ➋ *v.i.* rütteln; wackeln

ˈ**jigsaw** *n.* Ⓐ Dekupiersäge, *die;* (*electric*) Stichsäge, *die;* Ⓑ **~ [puzzle]** Puzzle, *das*

**jihad** /dʒɪˈhæd, dʒɪˈhɑːd/ *n.* (*war*) Dschihad, *der*

**jilt** /dʒɪlt/ *v.t.* sitzen lassen (*ugs.*)

**Jim Crow** /dʒɪm ˈkrəʊ/ *n.* (*Amer. derog.*) Ⓐ (*a Black*) Nigger, *der* (*abwertend*); Ⓑ *no pl.* (*racial segregation*) Rassentrennung, *die;* (*racial discrimination*) Rassendiskriminierung, *die*

**jim-jams** /ˈdʒɪmdʒæmz/ *n. pl.* (*coll.: fit of depression*) Muffe, *die* (*ugs.*); **she got [an attack of] the ~:** ihr ging die Muffe

**jimmy** /ˈdʒɪmɪ/ (*Amer.*) ⇒ **jemmy**

**jimson [weed]** /ˈdʒɪmsən (wiːd)/ *n.* (*Amer. Bot.*) Stechapfel, *der*

**jingle** /ˈdʒɪŋgl/ ➊ *n.* Ⓐ Klingeln, *das;* Bimmeln, *das* (*ugs.*); (*of cutlery, chains, spurs*) Klirren, *das;* (*of coins, keys*) Geklimper, *das;* Ⓑ (*repetition*) Aneinanderreihen lautähnlicher Wörter; (*trivial verse*) Wortgeklingel, *das* (*abwertend*); (*Commerc.*) Werbespruch, *der;* Jingle, *der* (*Werbespr.*); Ⓒ (*thing designed to ~*) Schelle, *die.* ➋ *v.i.* Ⓐ ‹Metallgegenstände:› klimpern; ‹Kasse, Schelle:› klingeln; ‹Glöckchen:› bimmeln; Ⓑ (*be full of alliterations, rhymes, etc.*) ‹Text:› sich reimen und stabreimen. ➌ *v.t.* klingeln mit, (*ugs.*) bimmeln mit ‹Glöckchen›; klimpern mit ‹Münzen, Schlüsseln, Armreifen›

ˈ**jingle-jangle** *n.* Geklimper, *das* (*abwertend*)

**jingo** /ˈdʒɪŋgəʊ/ *n.*, *pl.* **~es** Ⓐ Chauvinist, *der* (*abwertend*); Hurrapatriot, *der* (*ugs. abwertend*); Ⓑ **by ~!** beim Zeus!; bei Gott!

**jingoism** /ˈdʒɪŋgəʊɪzm/ *n.*, *no pl.* Chauvinismus, *der* (*abwertend*); Hurrapatriotismus, *der* (*ugs. abwertend*)

**jingoist** /ˈdʒɪŋgəʊɪst/ ⇒ **jingo** A

**jink** ⇒ **high jinks**

**jinx** /dʒɪŋks/ ➊ *n.* (*coll.*) Fluch, *der;* **there seemed to be a ~ on him** er schien vom Pech verfolgt zu sein; **break the ~:** den Bann brechen. ➋ *v.t.* verhexen

**jitterbug** /ˈdʒɪtəbʌg/ ➊ *n.* Ⓐ Nervenbündel, *das* (*ugs.*); Ⓑ (*dance*) Jitterbug, *der.* ➋ *v.i.* Jitterbug tanzen

**jitters** /ˈdʒɪtəz/ *n. pl.* (*coll.*) großes Zittern; Bammel, *der* (*salopp*); **an attack** *or* **a case of the ~:** ein Bammel (*salopp*); **give sb. the ~:** jmdm. Schiss machen (*salopp*)

**jittery** /ˈdʒɪtərɪ/ *adj.* (*nervous*) nervös; (*frightened*) verängstigt

**jive** /dʒaɪv/ ➊ *n.* Jive, *der.* ➋ *v.i.* Jive tanzen

**Jnr.** *abbr.* **Junior** jr.; jun.

**Joan of Arc** /dʒəʊn əv ˈɑːk/ *pr. n.* die Jungfrau von Orleans

**job** /dʒɒb/ ➊ *n.* Ⓐ (*piece of work*) **~ [of work]** Arbeit, *die;* **we have five ~s to do today** wir haben heute fünf Dinge zu erledigen; (*orders to be fulfilled*) wir haben heute fünf Aufträge zu erledigen; **I have a little ~ for you** ich habe eine kleine Aufgabe *od.* einen kleinen Auftrag für dich; **do a ~ for sb.** für jmdn. etw. erledigen; **try to do sb.'s ~ for him** (*fig. coll.*) jmdm. ins Handwerk pfuschen (*ugs.*); **it is sb.'s ~ to do sth.** es ist jmds. Arbeit, etw. zu tun; **you've got a really tough ~ on your hands!** da hast du aber eine Heidenarbeit *od.* ein schönes Stück Arbeit!; **you're doing an excellent ~:** Sie machen das ausgezeichnet; **nose ~** (*coll.*) Nasenoperation, *die;* Ⓑ ▶ 1261 (*position of employment*) Stelle, *die;* Anstellung, *die;* Job, *der* (*ugs.*); **he is, after all, only doing his ~!** er tut schließlich nur seine Pflicht; **he knows his ~:** er versteht sein Handwerk *od.* versteht etwas von der Sache; **~ vacancies** offene Stellen; (*in newspaper*) „Stellenangebote"; **have ~ security** einen sicheren Arbeitsplatz haben; **~ situation** Arbeitsmarktsituation, *die;* **it's as much as my ~'s worth** es würde mich meinen Job kosten; **it's not my ~** (*fig.*) es ist nicht meine Sache *od.* Aufgabe; **the man for the ~:** der richtige Mann; **~s for the boys** (*coll.*) ≈ wer gute Beziehungen hat, kriegt einen Job (*ugs.*); **it is a case** *or* **matter of ~s for the boys** alle Posten *od.* (*ugs.*) Jobs werden unter der Hand vergeben; **just the ~** (*fig. coll.*) genau das Richtige; die Sache (*ugs.*); **on the ~:** bei der Arbeit; **out of a ~:** arbeitslos; ohne Stellung; Ⓒ (*coll.: crime*) [krummes] Ding (*ugs.*); **do a [bank] ~:** ein Ding [in einer Bank] drehen (*ugs.*); **this was a professional ~:** hier war ein Profi/hier waren Profis am Werk; Ⓓ (*result of work*) Ergebnis, *das;* **make a [good] ~ of sth.** bei etw. gute Arbeit leisten; **make a thorough ~ of it** ganze Arbeit machen; **be a good** *etc.* **~:** gut *usw.* sein; **this respray/rebuilt car is a superb ~!** diese Neulackierung/dieses restaurierte Auto ist großartig geworden!; Ⓔ (*coll.: difficult task*) [schönes] Stück Arbeit; **I had a [hard** *or* **tough] ~ convincing** *or* **to convince him** es war gar nicht so einfach für mich *od.* ich hatte [einige] Mühe, ihn zu überzeugen; Ⓕ (*state of affairs*) **a bad ~:** eine schlimme *od.* üble Sache; **it's a bad ~: the company is virtually bankrupt** es sieht schlecht aus: die Firma ist praktisch pleite; **give sb./sth. up as a bad ~** ⇒ **give up** 2 A; **a good ~:** ein Glück; **we've finished, and a good ~ too!** wir sind fertig, zum Glück; **what** *or* **it's a good ~ he doesn't know about it!** nur gut, dass er nichts davon weiß!
➋ *v.i.*, **-bb-** Ⓐ (*do jobs*) Gelegenheitsarbeiten verrichten; jobben (*ugs.*); Ⓑ (*deal in stocks*) als Börsenhändler arbeiten; Ⓒ (*turn position of trust to private advantage*) sein Amt [zum eigenen Vorteil] missbrauchen; Ⓓ (*buy and sell as middleman*) als Vermittler Geschäfte machen; (*Amer.: trade in wholesale lots*) als Zwischenhändler tätig sein.
➌ *v.t.*, **-bb-** im Zwischenhandel verkaufen; makeln ‹Häuser, Grundstücke›

**Job** /dʒəʊb/ *pr. n.* Hiob (*der*); **he would try the patience of ~:** bei ihm braucht man eine Engelsgeduld; **~'s ˈcomforter** schlechter Trostspender

**jobber** /ˈdʒɒbə(r)/ *n.* Ⓐ (*Amer.: wholesaler*) Zwischenhändler, *der;* Ⓑ (*stock~*) Börsen- *od.* Effektenhändler, *der;* Jobber, *der*

**jobbery** /ˈdʒɒbərɪ/ *n.* Schiebung, *die*

**jobbing** /ˈdʒɒbɪŋ/ *adj.* Gelegenheits-; **~ gardener** Gelegenheits- *od.* Aushilfsgärtner, *der;* **~ printer** Akzidenzdrucker, *der*

**job: ~centre** *n.* (*Brit.*) Arbeitsvermittlungsstelle, *die;* **~ creation** *n.* Schaffung von Arbeitsplätzen; **~ description** *n.* Arbeitsplatzbeschreibung, *die;* Tätigkeitsbeschreibung, *die;* **~ evaluation** *n.* Arbeitsbewertung, *die;* **~-hunt** *v.i.* **go/be ~-hunting** auf Arbeits- *od.* Stellensuche gehen/sein; **~-hunter** *n.* Stellen- *od.* Arbeitssuchende, *der/die;* **~-hunting** *n.* Arbeitssuche, *die;* Stellensuche, *die*

**jobless** /ˈdʒɒblɪs/ *adj.* beschäftigungslos; arbeitslos

**job: ~ ˈlot** *n.* Partieware, *die* (*Kaufmannsspr.*); (*fig.*) Sammelsurium, *das* (*abwertend*); **~ satisfaction** ⇒ **satisfaction** B; **~ security** *n.* Arbeitsplatzsicherheit, *die;* **there is no ~ security in this industry** in dieser Branche gibt es keine sicheren Arbeitsplätze; **~-share** ➊ *n.* geteilter Arbeitsplatz; **look for a ~-share:** eine Jobsharing-Stelle suchen; ➋ *v.t.* aufteilen ‹Arbeitsplatz›; ➌ *v.i.* sich (*Dat.*) einen Arbeitsplatz teilen (**with** mit); **~-sharing** *n.* Jobsharing, *das;* Arbeitsplatzteilung, *die;* **~sheet** *n.* Arbeitsbericht, *der*

**jobsworth** /ˈdʒɒbzwɜːθ/ *n.* (*Brit. coll.*) Beamtenseele, *die* (*abwertend*); sturer Bürokratentyp

**jock** (*coll.*) ⇒ **jockey**

**Jock** /dʒɒk/ *n.* (*Brit. coll., often derog.*) Schotte, *der*

**jockey** /ˈdʒɒkɪ/ ➊ *n.* ▶ 1261 Jockei, *der;* Jockey, *der.* ➋ *v.i.* rangeln (**for** um); **~ for position** (*lit. or fig.*) alles daransetzen, eine möglichst gute Position zu erringen; **all the ~ing behind the scenes** das ganze Gerangel hinter den Kulissen. ➌ *v.t.* **~ sb. into/out of doing sth.** jmdn. dazu bringen, etw. zu tun/nicht mehr zu tun

**jockey: ~ cap** *n.* Jockeymütze, *die;* **J~ Club** *n.* (*Brit.*) *oberste Behörde des Galoppsports in England;* **~ shorts** *n. pl.* (*Amer.*) Unterhose, *die;* Unterhosen *Pl.*

**jockstrap** /ˈdʒɒkstræp/ *n.* [Sport]suspensorium, *das*

**jocose** /dʒəˈkəʊs/ *adj.* Ⓐ (*playful, fond of joking*) launig ‹Stimmung, Bemerkung, Wesensart›; **~ person** Spaßvogel, *der;* Ⓑ (*waggish*) schalkhaft

**jocular** /ˈdʒɒkjʊlə(r)/ *adj.* lustig, witzig ‹Bemerkung, Antwort›; spaßig, scherzhaft ‹Person›; **his ~ conversation bored her** seine Witze langweilten sie

**jocularly** /ˈdʒɒkjʊləlɪ/ *adv.* scherzhaft

**jocund** /ˈdʒɒkənd/ *adj.* (*literary*) fröhlich

**jodhpurs** /ˈdʒɒdpəz/ *n. pl.* Reithose, *die;* Jodhpur[hose], *die*

**Joe** /dʒəʊ/ *n.* **~ [Q.] Public** (*coll.*) Otto Normalverbraucher (*der*) (*ugs.*)

**joey** /ˈdʒəʊɪ/ *n.* (*Austral.*) junges Känguru

**jog** /dʒɒg/ ➊ *v.t.*, **-gg-:** Ⓐ (*shake with push or jerk*) rütteln; schütteln; **the horse ~ged its**

# Jobs

***What's your job?, What do you do [for a living]?***
= Was machen Sie beruflich?, Was sind Sie von Beruf?

***I work in a bank/in a bookshop***
= Ich arbeite bei einer Bank/in einer Buchhandlung

***He is in insurance/in the city***
= Er ist in der Versicherungsbranche/in der City tätig

***I am with a small company*** or ***firm/a large combine*** or ***group/a multinational***
= Ich bin bei einem kleinen Unternehmen/einem großen Konzern/einem Multi

***She owns/runs a small business***
= Sie hat/führt einen kleinen Betrieb

***My husband works for*** or ***is employed by the same firm***
= Mein Mann ist bei derselben Firma angestellt

***She works full time/part time***
= Sie arbeitet ganztags *or* hat eine Ganztagsbeschäftigung/ist als Teilzeitkraft angestellt *or* hat eine Teilzeitbeschäftigung

***I work freelance/am self-employed***
= Ich arbeite freiberuflich/bin selbstständig

There is no article in German when giving someone's specific trade or profession. Also there are feminine forms for all nouns denoting professions, usually with the **-in** ending:

***He's a baker***
= Er ist Bäcker

***She's a teacher***
= Sie ist Lehrerin

***George wants to be a systems analyst***
= George will Systemanalytiker werden

***Jane works as a journalist***
= Jane ist als Journalistin tätig

However if an adjective is included, then there is an indefinite article as in English:

***She is a good teacher***
= Sie ist eine gute Lehrerin

## Looking for a job

***I'm looking for a job as a childminder***
= Ich suche eine Stellung als Tagesmutter

***I didn't find anything suitable in the situations vacant***
= Ich habe in den Stellenangeboten nichts Geeignetes gefunden

***I want to apply for this job***
= Ich will mich um diese Stellung bewerben

***A CV should be sent with the application***
= Der Bewerbung ist ein Lebenslauf beizufügen

***Could you come for an interview on March 24th?***
= Könnten Sie bitte am 24. März zu einem Vorstellungsgespräch kommen?

***What is the earliest you could start work?***
= Wann könnten Sie frühestens anfangen?



**rider up and down** das Pferd schüttelte seinen Reiter durch; **B** (*nudge*) [an]stoßen; **~ sb.'s elbow** jmdn. [am Ellbogen] anstoßen; **C** (*stimulate*) **~ sb.'s memory** jmds. Gedächtnis (*Dat.*) auf die Sprünge helfen. **2** *v.i.*, **-gg-: A** (*move up and down*) auf und ab hüpfen; **~ around/about** herumhüpfen; **his holster was ~ging against his hip** sein Halfter schlug ihm im Rhythmus gegen die Hüfte; **B** (*move at ~trot*) ‹Pferd:› [dahin]trotten; **C** (*run at slow pace*) [in mäßigem Tempo] laufen; traben (*Sport*); (*for physical exercise*) joggen; [einen] Dauerlauf machen; laufen; **~ along** *or* **on** (*fig.*) ‹Geschäft, Projekt:› laufen, seinen Gang gehen; ‹Person:› vor sich hin wursteln (*ugs.*). **3** *n.* **A** (*shake, nudge*) Stoß, *der;* Schubs, *der* (*ugs.*); **B** (*slow walk or trot*) (*of horse*) Trott, *der;* (*of person for physical exercise*) Dauerlauf, *der;* **go for a ~:** joggen gehen; **he went off at a ~:** er trabte davon

**jogger** /ˈdʒɒɡə(r)/ *n.* Jogger, *der*/Joggerin, *die*

**jogging** /ˈdʒɒɡɪŋ/ *n.* Jogging, *das;* Joggen, *das*

**joggle** /ˈdʒɒɡl/ **1** *v.t.* schütteln; wackeln an (+ *Dat.*) ‹Tisch›. **2** *v.i.* wackeln (**to and fro** hin und her); wippen (**up and down** auf und ab); (*in the air*) taumeln. **3** *n.* (*slight shake*) Holpern, *das*

**ˈjogtrot** *n.* (*lit. or fig.*) Trott, *der*

**john** *n.* (*Amer. sl.: lavatory*) Lokus, *der* (*salopp*)

**John** /dʒɒn/ *pr. n.* (*Hist., as name of ruler etc.*) Johann (*der*); ⇒ *also* **Baptist** B

**John: ~ ˈBull** *n.* John Bull (*der*); **a real ~ Bull** ein typischer Engländer; **~ ˈCitizen** *n.* Otto Normalverbraucher (*der*); **~ ˈDoe** *n.* **A** (*Law*) ≈ Meier (*der*); ≈ die Partei A; *fiktiver Name einer Prozesspartei;* **B** (*Amer.: average man*) Otto Normalverbraucher (*der*)

**johnny** /ˈdʒɒnɪ/ *n.* (*Brit. coll.: chap*) Heini, *der* (*ugs.*)

**Johnny-come-ˈlately** *n.* (*coll.*) Neuankömmling, *der*

**joie de vivre** /ʒwɑː də ˈviːvr/ *n.* Lebensfreude, *die;* Lebenslust, *die*

**join** /dʒɔɪn/ **1** *v.t.* **A** (*put together, connect*) verbinden (**to** mit); **~ two things [together]** zwei Dinge miteinander verbinden; zwei Dinge zusammenfügen; **~ hands** sich (*Dat.*) die Hände reichen; **~ hands [with sb.]** (*fig.*) ‹Nation, Partei usw.:› sich [mit jmdm.] vereinen; **~ sb. [with** *or* **to sb.] in marriage/in holy matrimony** jmdn. [mit jmdm.] ehelich verbinden/durch das heilige Band der Ehe vereinen (*geh.*); ⇒ *also* **force**[1] 1 D; **B** (*come into company of*) sich gesellen zu; sich zugesellen (+ *Dat.*); (*meet*) treffen; (*come with*) mitkommen mit; sich anschließen (+ *Dat.*); **you go on ahead — I'll ~ you in a minute** geh nur schon voraus — ich komme gleich nach; **may I ~ you [at the table]?** kann ich mich zu euch [an den Tisch] setzen?; **do ~ us for lunch** iss doch mit uns zu Mittag; **would you like to ~ me in a drink?** hast du Lust, ein Glas mit mir zu trinken?; **if you can't beat them, ~ them** wenn man mit dem Gegner nicht fertig wird, läuft man eben zu ihm über; **C** (*become member of*) eintreten in (+ *Akk.*) ‹Armee, Firma, Orden, Verein, Partei›; beitreten (+ *Dat.*) ‹Verein, Partei, Orden›; **I thought of ~ing the Army/the Scouts** ich dachte daran, zur Armee/zu den Pfadfindern zu gehen; **D** (*take one's place in*) sich einreihen in (+ *Akk.*) ‹Umzug, Demonstrationszug›; **~ one's ship** an Bord seines Schiffs gehen; **~ one's regiment** sich bei seinem Regiment einfinden; **E** ‹Fluss, Straße:› münden in (+ *Akk.*). ⇒ *also* **battle** 1 A. **2** *v.i.* **A** (*come together*) ‹Flüsse:› sich vereinigen, zusammenfließen; ‹Straßen:› sich vereinigen, zusammenlaufen; ‹Grundstücke:› aneinander grenzen, aneinander stoßen; ‹gebrochener Knochen:› zusammenwachsen; ‹Einzelteile:› zusammenpassen; **B** (*take part*) **~ with sb.** sich jmdm. anschließen; **my wife ~s with me in wishing you ...:** auch meine Frau wünscht Ihnen ...; **C** (*become member*) Mitglied werden; (*become employee*) in die Firma eintreten. **3** *n.* Verbindung, *die;* (*line*) Nahtstelle, *die*

**~ in 1** /-ˈ-/ *v.i.* mitmachen (**with** bei); (*in conversation*) sich beteiligen (**with** an + *Dat.*); (*in singing*) einstimmen; mitsingen; **they all ~ed in together** sie machten/sangen alle mit. **2** /ˈ--/ *v.t.* mitmachen bei ‹Spiel, Spaß›; sich beteiligen an (+ *Dat.*) ‹Spiel, Festlichkeiten, Gespräch›; mitsingen ‹Refrain›; sich einreihen in (+ *Akk.*), sich anschließen (+ *Dat.*) ‹Demonstrations-, Umzug›

**~ ˈon** *v.i.* befestigt werden (**to** an + *Dat.*); ‹Grundstück:› [an]grenzen (**to** an + *Akk.*)

**~ ˈup 1** *v.i.* **A** (*Mil.*) einrücken; Soldat werden; **B** ‹Straßen:› zusammenlaufen; ‹Nebenstraße:› [ein]münden (**with** in + *Akk.*); ‹Straße:› zusammenlaufen (**with** mit). **2** *v.t.* miteinander verbinden

**joiner** /ˈdʒɔɪnə(r)/ *n.* ▶ **1261** Tischler, *der*/Tischlerin, *die*

**joinery** /ˈdʒɔɪnərɪ/ *n., no pl.* **A** *no art.* (*craft*) Tischlerei, *die;* Tischlerhandwerk, *das;* **B** *no indef. art.* (*products*) Tischlerarbeiten

**joint** /dʒɔɪnt/ **1** *n.* **A** (*place of joining*) Verbindung, *die;* (*line*) Nahtstelle, *die;* (*Building*) Fuge, *die;* **B** ▶ **966** (*Anat.*) Gelenk, *das;* **be out of ~** ‹Körperteil:› ausgerenkt sein; (*fig.: be out of order*) ‹Zeit, Welt:› aus den Fugen sein; ⇒ *also* **nose** 1 A; **C** (*Bot.*) Knoten, *der;* **D** (*Mech. Engin. etc.*) Gelenk, *das;* **E** (*part of carcass*) **a ~ [of meat]** ein Stück Fleisch; (*for roasting, roast*) ein Braten; **a roast ~:** ein Braten; **a ~ of roast beef** ein Rinderbraten; **chicken ~s** Hähnchenteile *Pl.;* **carve/cut sth. into ~s** etw. tranchieren/zerlegen; **F** (*coll.*) (*place*) Laden, *der* (*ugs.*); (*pub*) Kaschemme, *die* (*abwertend*); (*dwelling*) Bude, *die* (*ugs.*); **jazz ~:** Jazzschuppen, *der* (*ugs.*); **G** (*sl.: marijuana cigarette*) Joint, *der;* **H** (*Amer. sl.: prison*) Knast, *der* (*ugs.*). **2** *adj.* **A** (*of two or more*) gemeinsam ‹Anstrengung, Bericht, Besitz, Projekt, Ansicht, Konto›; **~ venture** Gemeinschaftsunternehmen, *das;* Jointventure, *das* (*Wirtsch.*); ⇒ *also* **several** 1 B; **B** Mit‹autor, -erbe, -besitzer›. **3** *v.t.* **A** (*connect*) verbinden; **B** (*Building*) [aus-, ver-]fugen ‹Wand, Decke, Belag›; **C** (*divide*) zerlegen ‹Tier›

**jointed** /ˈdʒɔɪntɪd/ *adj.* Glieder‹puppe, -tier›; knotig ‹Stamm›

**jointly** /ˈdʒɔɪntlɪ/ *adv.* gemeinsam; **he is ~ responsible** er ist mitverantwortlich

**joint: ~ ˈstock** *n.* (*Econ.*) Gesellschafts- *od.* Aktienkapital, *das;* **~ stock bank/company** Aktienbank, *die*/Aktiengesellschaft, *die;* **~ ˈventure** *n.* (*Commerc.*) Jointventure, *das*

**joist** /dʒɔɪst/ *n.* (*Building*) Deckenbalken, *der;* (*steel*) [Decken]träger, *der*

**joke** /dʒəʊk/ **1** *n.* **A** Witz, *der;* Scherz, *der;* **sb.'s little ~** (*iron.*) jmds. Scherzchen; **make a ~:** einen Scherz machen; **do sth. for a ~:** etw. spaßeshalber *od.* zum Spaß tun; **tell a ~:** einen Witz erzählen; **have a ~ with sb.** mit jmdm. scherzen *od.* spaßen; **play a ~ on sb.** jmdm. einen Streich spielen; **he can/can't take a ~:** er versteht Spaß/keinen Spaß; **the ~ was on him** er

war der Narr; **a ~ is a ~:** das ist gar nicht so komisch; **this is getting beyond/is** *or* **goes beyond a ~:** da hört der Spaß auf/das ist kein Spaß mehr; **this is no ~:** das ist nicht zum Lachen; **B** (*ridiculous thing or circumstance*) Witz, *der* (*ugs.*); (*ridiculous person*) Witzfigur, *die;* **he/it is a standing ~:** alle Welt lacht nur noch über ihn/darüber; **treat sth. as a ~:** etw. nicht weiter ernst nehmen.
**2** *v.i.* scherzen, Witze machen (**about** über + *Akk.*); **I was only joking** ich habe nur Spaß gemacht (*ugs.*); **joking apart** Scherz *od.* Spaß beiseite!; **you are/must be** *or* (*coll.*) **have [got] to be joking!** das soll wohl ein Witz sein!; mach keine Witze!

**joker** /ˈdʒəʊkə(r)/ *n.* **A** (*person fond of making jokes*) Spaßvogel, *der;* Witzbold, *der* (*ugs.*); **B** (*coll.: person*) Vogel, *der* (*salopp*); **C** (*Cards*) Joker, *der;* **~ in the pack** (*fig.*) Unsicherheitsfaktor, *der;* **D** (*Amer.: clause*) versteckte Klausel; **E** (*unexpected factor*) Pferdefuß, *der;* Haken, *der* (*ugs.*)

**jokey** /ˈdʒəʊkɪ/ *adj.* witzig; spaßig

**jokingly** /ˈdʒəʊkɪŋlɪ/ *adv.* im Scherz; **..., he said ~:** ..., scherzte er

**joky** ⇒ **jokey**

**jollification** /dʒɒlɪfɪˈkeɪʃn/ *n.* (*coll.*) Vergnügen, *das*

**jollity** /ˈdʒɒlɪtɪ/ *n.* Fröhlichkeit, *die;* Lustigkeit, *die;* (*merrymaking, festivity*) Festlichkeit, *die*

**jolly** /ˈdʒɒlɪ/ **1** *adj.* **A** (*cheerful*) fröhlich; knallig ‹Farbe›; (*multicoloured*) bunt; **B** (*euphem.: drunk*) angeheitert; **C** (*festive*) lustig; **D** (*coll.: delightful*) klasse (*ugs.*); prima (*ugs.*). **2** *adv.* (*Brit. coll.*) ganz schön (*ugs.*); sehr ‹nett›; **~ good** wirklich gut; **~ good!** ausgezeichnet! **I should ~ well think so!** das möchte ich auch meinen!; **we ~ well 'are coming!** und ob wir kommen! **3** *v.t.* (*coll.*) aufmuntern; **~ sb. into doing sth.** jmdn. dazu überreden, etw. zu tun
**~ a'long** *v.t.* bei Laune halten
**~ 'up** *v.t.* aufmuntern

**'jolly boat** *n.* Jolle, *die*

**Jolly 'Roger** *n.* Piratenflagge, *die;* Totenkopfflagge, *die*

**jolt** /dʒəʊlt/ **1** *v.t.* **A** (*shake*) ‹Fahrzeug:› durchrütteln, durchschütteln; **~ sb./sth. out of/on to sth.** jmdn./etw. aus etw./auf etw. (*Akk.*) schleudern *od.* werfen; **B** (*shock*) aufschrecken; **~ sb. into action** jmdn. auf Trab bringen (*ugs.*); **~ sb. into doing sth.** jmdn. so aufschrecken, dass er etw. tut. **2** *v.i.* ‹Fahrzeug:› holpern, rütteln, rumpeln (*ugs.*). **3** *n.* **A** (*jerk*) Stoß, *der;* Ruck, *der;* **B** (*fig.*) (*shock*) Schock, *der;* Schreck, *der;* (*surprise*) Überraschung, *die;* **give sb. a ~:** jmdm. einen Schock versetzen *od.* einen Schreck[en] einjagen/jmdn. überraschen

**Jonah** /ˈdʒəʊnə/ *n.* **A** Unglücksvogel, *der;* **B** (*Bibl.*) Jonas (*der*)

**Joneses** /ˈdʒəʊnzɪz/ ⇒ **keep up** 1 A

**jonquil** /ˈdʒɒŋkwɪl/ *n.* (*Bot.*) Jonquille, *die*

**Jordan** /ˈdʒɔːdn/ *pr. n.* **A** ▶ **1480** (*river*) Jordan, *der;* **B** (*country*) Jordanien (*das*)

**Jordanian** /dʒɔːˈdeɪnɪən/ ▶ **1340** **1** *adj.* jordanisch; **sb. is ~:** jmd. ist Jordanier/Jordanierin. **2** *n.* Jordanier, *der*/Jordanierin, *die*

**josh** /dʒɒʃ/ (*coll.*) **1** *v.t.* aufziehen. **2** *v.i.* scherzen

**joss stick** /ˈdʒɒs stɪk/ *n.* Räucherstäbchen, *das*

**jostle** /ˈdʒɒsl/ **1** *v.i.* **A** (*knock*) **~ [against each other]** aneinander stoßen; **B** (*struggle*) [sich] streiten (**for** um, **with** mit); **~ with each other** [miteinander *od.* sich] streiten. **2** *v.t.* **A** stoßen; **~ sb.'s arm** jmdn. [am Arm] anstoßen; **~ sb. aside/off the pavement** jmdn. zur Seite/vom Bürgersteig stoßen; **the defender ~d the forward off the ball** der Verteidiger trennte den Stürmer mit einem Rempler vom Ball; **B** (*Racing*) behindern

**jot** /dʒɒt/ **1** *n.* **[not] a ~:** [k]ein bisschen; (*of truth, sympathy also*) [k]ein Fünkchen; **not one ~ or tittle** (*coll.*) nicht das kleinste bisschen. **2** *v.t.*, **-tt-** [rasch] aufschreiben *od.* notieren; **~ sth. on a piece of paper** etw. rasch auf einen Zettel schreiben
**~ 'down** *v.t.* [rasch] aufschreiben *od.* notieren; **~ down notes** [sich (*Dat.*)] rasch Notizen machen

**jotter** /ˈdʒɒtə(r)/ *n.* (*pad*) Notizblock, *der;* (*notebook*) Notizbuch, *das*

**jotting** /ˈdʒɒtɪŋ/ *n.*, *usu. pl.* Notiz, *die*

**joule** /dʒuːl/ *n.* (*Phys.*) Joule, *das*

**journal** /ˈdʒɜːnl/ *n.* **A** (*newspaper*) Zeitung, *die;* (*periodical*) Zeitschrift, *die;* **weekly ~:** Wochenzeitung, *die;* **B** (*Bookk.*) Journal, *das;* Tagebuch, *das;* **C** (*daily record of events*) Tagebuch, *das;* **D** (*Naut.*) **[captain's/ship's] ~:** Schiffstagebuch, *das;* Journal, *das* (*veralt.*); **E** (*part of shaft or axle*) Zapfen, *der*

**'journal bearing** *n.* (*Mech. Engin.*) Zapfenlager, *das*

**journalese** /dʒɜːnəˈliːz/ *n.* (*derog.*) [schlechter] Zeitungsstil

**journalism** /ˈdʒɜːnəlɪzm/ *n.* Journalismus, *der*

**journalist** /ˈdʒɜːnəlɪst/ *n.* ▶ **1261** Journalist, *der*/Journalistin, *die*

**journalistic** /dʒɜːnəˈlɪstɪk/ *adj.* journalistisch ‹Stil›; **~ circles** Journalistenkreise

**journey** /ˈdʒɜːnɪ/ **1** *n.* **A** Reise, *die;* (*distance*) Weg, *der;* **go on a ~:** verreisen; eine Reise machen; **a ~ by car/train/ship** eine Auto-/Bahn-/Schiffsreise; eine Reise mit dem Auto/der Bahn/dem Schiff; **go on a train/car ~:** eine Reise mit dem Zug *od.* Zugreise/eine Reise mit dem Auto *od.* Autoreise machen; **~'s end** die Endstation (*fig.*); **a three-hour ~:** eine Fahrt von drei Stunden; eine dreistündige Fahrt; (*on foot*) ein dreistündiger Weg; **London is three hours' ~ from here** man fährt drei Stunden von hier nach London; **a fruitless ~:** ein vergeblicher Gang; **B** (*fig.*) Weg, *der;* **~ through life** Lebensreise, *die* (*geh.*); **a ~ into history** ein Ausflug in die Geschichte; **C** (*of vehicle*) Fahrt, *die;* **~ time** Fahrzeit, *die.*
**2** *v.i.* (*formal/literary*) fahren; ziehen

**journeyman** /ˈdʒɜːnɪmən/ *n.*, *pl.* **journeymen** /ˈdʒɜːnɪmən/ Geselle, *der;* **a ~ butcher** ein Fleischergeselle

**joust** /dʒaʊst/ **1** *n.* Tjost, *die.* **2** *v.i.* tjostieren

**Jove** /dʒəʊv/ *n.* **A** (*Mythol.*) Jupiter (*der*); **B by ~!** (*dated coll.*) *expr. surprise* potztausend! (*veralt.*); *expr. approval* Hut ab! (*ugs.*); alle Achtung!

**jovial** /ˈdʒəʊvɪəl/ *adj.* (*hearty*) herzlich, freundlich ‹Gruß›; (*merry*) fröhlich ‹Ausdruck, Person›; launig ‹Bemerkung›; (*convivial*) lustig ‹Versammlung, Gesellschaft›

**jovially** /ˈdʒəʊvɪəlɪ/ *adv.* fröhlich ‹zustimmen, rufen›; herzlich, freundlich ‹begrüßen›

**jowl** /dʒaʊl/ *n.* (*jaw*) Unterkiefer, *der;* (*lower part of face*) Kinnbacken *Pl.;* (*double chin*) Doppelkinn, *das;* (*flabby cheek*) Hängebacke, *die;* (*of cattle*) Wamme, *die;* (*of bird*) Kehllappen, *der;* ⇒ *also* **cheek** 1 A

**joy** /dʒɔɪ/ *n.* **A** Freude, *die;* **wish sb. ~:** jmdm. viel Spaß *od.* Vergnügen wünschen; **I wish you ~ of it** (*also iron.*) ich wünsche dir viel Vergnügen damit; **sing for/weep with ~:** vor Freude (*Dat.*) singen/weinen; **we heard with ~ that ...:** wir haben zu unserer Freude erfahren, dass ...; **the ~s of hunting** das Vergnügen des Jagens; **be full of the ~s of spring** (*fig. coll.*) vor Freude ganz aus dem Häuschen sein (*ugs.*); **that is the ~ of the Highlands** das ist der Reiz *od.* das Reizvolle an den Highlands; **it was a ~ to look at** es war eine Augenweide; ⇒ *also* **jump** 2 C; **B** *no pl.*, *no art.* (*coll.: success, satisfaction*) Erfolg, *der;* **he didn't get much ~ out of it** es hat ihm nicht viel gebracht; **any ~?** Erfolg gehabt?; was erreicht? (*ugs.*)

**joyful** /ˈdʒɔɪfl/ *adj.* froh [gestimmt] ‹Person›; froh ‹Gesicht›; freudig ‹Blick, Ereignis, Umarmung, Gesang, Beifall›; freudig, froh ‹Nachricht, Kunde›; erfreulich ‹Nachricht, Ergebnis, Anblick›; Freuden‹tag, -schrei›; **she was ~ [at his return]** sie freute sich [über seine Rückkehr]

**joyfully** /ˈdʒɔɪfəlɪ/ *adv.* freudig

**joyless** /ˈdʒɔɪlɪs/ *adj.* traurig ‹Ausdruck, Nachricht, Ergebnis, Anlass›; freudlos ‹Zeit, Leben›; verdrossen ‹Person›

**joyous** /ˈdʒɔɪəs/ *adj.* freudig ‹Anlass, Ereignis›; froh ‹Lachen, Herz›; Freuden‹tag, -schrei›

**joy:** **~ride** *n.* (*coll.*) Spritztour [im gestohlenen Auto]; **~rider** *n.* Autodieb (*der den Wagen nur für eine Spritztour gestohlen hat*); **~stick** *n.* **A** (*Aeronaut. coll.*) Knüppel, *der;* **B** (*on computer etc.*) Hebel, *der;* Joystick, *der* (*DV*)

**JP** *abbr.* ▶ **1261** **Justice of the Peace**

**Jr.** *abbr.* **Junior** jun.; jr.

**jt.** *abbr.* **joint;** ⇒ **joint** 2

**jubilant** /ˈdʒuːbɪlənt/ *adj.* jubelnd; (*exultingly glad*) freudestrahlend ‹Miene›; (*triumphant*) triumphierend ‹Miene›; **be ~** ‹Person:› frohlocken

**jubilation** /dʒuːbɪˈleɪʃn/ *n.* Jubel, *der*

**jubilee** /ˈdʒuːbɪliː/ *n.* (*anniversary*) Jubiläum, *das;* ⇒ *also* **diamond jubilee; golden jubilee; silver jubilee**

**Judaism** /ˈdʒuːdeɪɪzm/ *n.*, *no pl.*, *no art.* Judentum, *das;* Judaismus, *der*

**Judas** /ˈdʒuːdəs/ *n.* (*traitor*) Judas, *der*

**'Judas tree** *n.* (*Bot.*) Judasbaum, *der*

**judder** /ˈdʒʌdə(r)/ **1** *v.i.* rattern. **2** *n.* Rattern, *das;* **give a ~:** rattern; **with a ~:** ratternd

**judge** /dʒʌdʒ/ **1** *n.* **A** ▶ **1261**, ▶ **1617** Richter, *der*/Richterin, *die;* **[the Book of] Judges** (*Bibl.*) das Buch der Richter; **~ and jury** das Gericht; **be ~ and jury** (*fig.*) sich zum alleinigen Richter aufwerfen; ⇒ *also* **sober** A; **B** (*in contest*) Juror, *der*/Jurorin, *die;* Preisrichter, *der*/-richterin, *die;* (*Sport*) Kampfrichter, *der*/-richterin, *die;* Schiedsrichter, *der*/-richterin, *die;* (*in cycle racing*) Zielrichter, *der*/-richterin, *die;* (*in dispute*) Schiedsrichter, *der*/-richterin, *die;* **C** (*fig.: connoisseur, critic*) Kenner, *der*/Kennerin, *die;* **~ of character/poetry** Menschen-/Lyrikkenner, *der;* **be a good ~ of sth.** etw. gut beurteilen können; **if I'm any ~/any ~ of sth.** soweit ich das/etw. beurteilen kann; **D** (*person who decides question*) Schiedsrichter, *der;* **be the ~ of sth.** über etw. (*Akk.*) entscheiden *od.* befinden.
**2** *v.t.* **A** (*pronounce sentence on*) richten (*geh.*); **~ sb.** (*Law*) jmds. Fall entscheiden; in jmds. Fall das Urteil fällen; **B** (*try*) verhandeln ‹Fall›; **C** (*act as adjudicator of*) Juror/Jurorin *od.* Preisrichter/-richterin sein bei; (*Sport*) Kampfrichter/-richterin *od.* Schiedsrichter/-richterin sein bei; **D** (*form opinion about*) urteilen *od.* ein Urteil fällen über (+ *Akk.*); beurteilen; **~ a book to be worth reading** ein Buch für lesenswert erachten *od.* befinden; **~ sth. [to be] necessary** etw. für *od.* als notwendig erachten; **be good at judging distances** gut Entfernungen schätzen können; **~d by modern standards** nach heutigen Maßstäben; **E** (*decide*) entscheiden ‹Angelegenheit, Frage›; **F** (*conclude*) **I ~d that the meat was done** ich war der Meinung, dass das Fleisch gar war; **I can't ~ whether it's any good** ich kann nicht beurteilen, ob er/sie/es etwas taugt.
**3** *v.i.* **A** (*form a ~ment*) urteilen; **to ~ by its size, ...:** der Größe nach zu urteilen, ...; **judging** *or* **to ~ by the look on his face ...:** nach dem Gesicht zu schließen, das er macht/machte, ...; **judging from what you say, ...:** nach dem, was du sagst, ...; **as far as I can ~, ...:** soweit ich es beurteilen kann, ...; **as near as I could ~, ...:** nach meiner Schätzung ...; **B** (*act as ~*) ⇒ **1** A, B: Richter/Richterin sein; Kampfrichter/-richterin sein; Schiedsrichter/-richterin sein

**judgement, judgment** /ˈdʒʌdʒmənt/ *n.* **A** Urteil, *das;* **the J~ of Paris** (*Greek Mythol.*) das Urteil des Paris; **~ was given in favour of/against sb.** das Urteil fiel zu jmds. Gunsten/Ungunsten aus; **pass [a] ~** ein Urteil abgeben (**on** über + *Akk.*); **give one's ~** ein Urteil fällen; **in** *or* **according to my ~** meines Erachtens; **in the ~ of most people** nach Meinung der meisten Leute; **form a ~** sich (*Dat.*) ein Urteil *od.* eine Meinung bilden; **against one's better ~** entgegen seiner besseren Einsicht; ⇒ *also* **sit** 1 B; **Solomon**; **B** (*critical faculty*) Urteilsfähigkeit, die; Urteilsvermögen, das; **error of ~** Fehlurteil, das; Fehleinschätzung, die; **a man of ~** ein urteilsfähiger Mann; **critical ~** Kritikfähigkeit, die; **I leave it to your ~** ich stelle das in Ihr Ermessen; **use your own ~** verfahren Sie nach Ihrem Gutdünken; **C** (*trial by God*) Gericht, das; **day of ~, J~ Day** Tag des Jüngsten Gerichts; (*fig.*) Stunde der Wahrheit; **the last ~** das Jüngste od. Letzte Gericht; **D** (*misfortune*) **it's a ~ on you for ...** (*joc.*) das ist die Strafe dafür, dass du ...

**judicature** /'dʒu:dɪkətʃə(r)/ n. (*Law*) Judikatur, die (*fachspr.*); Rechtsprechung, die; **Supreme Court of J~** (*Brit.*) Oberster Gerichtshof

**judicial** /dʒu:'dɪʃl/ adj. **A** gerichtlich; richterlich ‹Gewalt›; Recht sprechend ‹Versammlung›; **~ error** Justizirrtum, der; **~ murder** Justizmord, der; **take** or **bring ~ proceedings against sb.** gegen jmdn. gerichtlich vorgehen; **B** (*of a judge*) richterlich; **in his ~ capacity** in seiner Eigenschaft als Richter; **C** (*expressing judgement*) kritisch; **D** (*impartial*) unvoreingenommen

**judiciary** /dʒu:'dɪʃərɪ/ n. (*Law*) Richterschaft, die

**judicious** /dʒu:'dɪʃəs/ adj. **A** (*discerning*) klar blickend; **B** (*sensible*) besonnen

**judiciously** /dʒu:'dɪʃəslɪ/ adv. mit Bedacht

**judo** /'dʒu:dəʊ/ n., pl. **~s** Judo, das

**jug** /dʒʌg/ **1** n. **A** Krug, der; (*with lid, water ~*) Kanne, die; (*small milk ~*) Kännchen, das; **a ~ of water** ein Krug/eine Kanne Wasser; **B** (*sl.: prison*) Loch, das (*salopp*); **put/be in ~:** ins Loch stecken/im Loch sitzen. **2** v.t., **-gg-** (*Cookery*) schmoren; **~ged hare** Hasenpfeffer, der

**jugful** /'dʒʌgfʊl/ n. ⇒ **jug** 1 A: Krug, der; Kanne, die; Kännchen, das; **a ~ of ...:** ein Krug/eine Kanne/ein Kännchen [voll] ...

**juggernaut** /'dʒʌgənɔ:t/ n. **A** (*institution, notion*) Moloch, der (*geh.*); **B** (*large object*) Ungetüm, das; **~ [lorry]** (*Brit.*) schwerer Brummer (*ugs.*)

**juggins** /'dʒʌgɪnz/ n. (*Brit. coll. dated*) Dämel, der (*salopp*); Dämlack, der (*salopp*)

**juggle** /'dʒʌgl/ **1** v.i. **A** jonglieren; (*perform conjuring tricks*) zaubern; **B ~ with** (*misrepresent*) jonglieren mit ‹Fakten, Zahlen›. **2** v.t. (*lit., or fig.: manipulate*) jonglieren [mit]

**juggler** /'dʒʌglə(r)/ n. **A** Jongleur, der/Jongleuse, die; **B** (*conjurer*) Zauber[künstl]er, der/Zauber[künstler]in, die; **C** (*trickster*) Betrüger, der/Betrügerin, die

**Jugoslav** etc. ⇒ **Yugoslav** etc.

**jugular** /'dʒʌgjʊlə(r)/ (*Anat.*) **1** adj. jugular (*fachspr.*); **~ vein** Jugularvene, die (*fachspr.*); Drosselvene, die. **2** n. Jugularvene, die (*fachspr.*); Drosselvene, die; **go for the ~** (*fig.*) versuchen, den Lebensnerv zu treffen

**juice** /dʒu:s/ n. **A** Saft, der; ⇒ also **stew** 3 A; **B** (*sl.*) (*electricity*) Saft, der (*salopp*); (*petrol*) Sprit, der (*ugs.*)

**juicy** /'dʒu:sɪ/ adj. **A** saftig; **B** (*coll.*) (*racy*) saftig (*ugs.*) ‹Anekdote, Witz, Geschichte, Skandal›; (*suggestive*) schlüpfrig; (*profitable*) fett (*ugs.*) ‹Vertrag, Geschäft usw.›

**ju-jitsu** /dʒu:'dʒɪtsu:/ n. Jiu-Jitsu, das

**jukebox** /'dʒu:kbɒks/ n. Jukebox, die; Musikbox, die

**Jul.** abbr. **July** Jul.

**julep** /'dʒu:lep/ n. Julep, das od. der

**Julian** /'dʒu:lɪən/ adj. **~ calendar** julianischer Kalender

**July** /dʒʊ'laɪ/ n. ▶ **1055** Juli, der; ⇒ also **August**

**jumble** /'dʒʌmbl/ **1** v.t. **~ up** or **together** or **about** durcheinander bringen; durcheinander werfen; **~ sth. up with sth.** etw. mit etw. durcheinander bringen od. -werfen; **they've got my clothes ~d up with yours** sie haben meine und deine Sachen durcheinander gebracht. **2** n. **A** Wirrwarr, der; Gewirr, das; (*muddle*) Durcheinander, das; **the cupboard was in a complete ~:** im Schrank herrschte ein heilloses Durcheinander; **a ~ of clothes, books, and toys** ein kunterbuntes Durcheinander von Kleidungsstücken, Büchern und Spielsachen; **B** no pl., no indef. art. (*Brit.: articles for ~ sale*) alte od. gebrauchte Sachen

**'jumble sale** n. (*Brit.*) Trödelmarkt, der; (*for charity*) Wohltätigkeitsbasar, der

**jumbo** /'dʒʌmbəʊ/ **1** n., pl. **~s** **A** (*very large specimen*) riesiges Exemplar; **B** (*jet*) Jumbo, der. **2** adj. **~[-sized]** riesig; Riesen- (*ugs.*)

**jumbo 'jet** n. Jumbojet, der

**jump** /dʒʌmp/ **1** n. **A** Sprung, der; **be on the ~** (*fig. coll.*) in Bewegung od. in Aktion sein; **keep sb. on the ~** (*fig. coll.*) jmdn. auf Trab halten (*ugs.*); **take a running ~ [at oneself]** (*fig. coll.*) verschwinden; **get the ~ on sb.** (*coll.*) sich (*Dat.*) einen Vorsprung vor jmdm. verschaffen; **always be one ~ ahead of sb.** jmdm. immer um eine Nasenlänge voraus sein (*ugs.*); **B** (*sudden movement*) **give a ~:** zusammenzucken od. -fahren; **have got the ~s** (*coll.*) ganz zapp[e]lig od. (*landsch.*) fick[e]rig sein; **give sb. the ~s** (*coll.*) jmdn. ganz zapp[e]lig od. (*landsch.*) fick[e]rig machen; **C** (*sudden transition*) Sprung, der; sprunghafter Wechsel; (*gap*) Lücke, die; **D** (*abrupt rise*) sprunghafter Anstieg; **~ in value/temperature** plötzliche Wertsteigerung/plötzlicher Temperaturanstieg; **there has been a considerable ~ in prices** die Preise sind beträchtlich in die Höhe geschnellt; **E** (*Sport: obstacle*) (*in steeplechase*) Sprung, der; (*in athletics*) Hindernis, das; **set of ~s** Sprungkombination, die; **F** (*Parachuting*) Absprung, der. ⇒ also **broad jump**; **high jump**; **long jump**.

**2** v.i. **A** springen; ‹Fallschirmspringer:› abspringen; **~ to one's feet/from one's seat** aufspringen/vom Sitz aufspringen; **~ down sb.'s throat** (*fig. coll.*) jmdn. anblaffen (*salopp*); **~ in the lake** or **off a cliff** (*fig. coll.*) sich zum Teufel scheren (*ugs.*); **~ on sb.** or (*Amer.*) **all over sb.** (*fig. coll.*) jmdn. zur Minna machen (*salopp*); ⇒ also **skin** 1 A; **B** (*fig.: come over-hastily*) voreilig gelangen (**to** zu) ‹Annahme, Lösung›; **~ to the conclusion that ...:** den voreiligen Schluss ziehen, dass ...; **~ to conclusions** voreilige Schlüsse ziehen; **C** (*make sudden movement*) springen; (*start*) zusammenzucken; **~ for joy** einen Freudensprung/Freudensprünge machen; (*fig.*) vor Freude ganz aus dem Häuschen sein; wahre Freudentänze vollführen; **~ up and down with excitement** aufgeregt herumspringen od. -hüpfen; **her heart ~ed** ihr Herz machte einen Sprung; **D** (*rise suddenly*) ‹Kosten, Preise usw.› sprunghaft steigen, in die Höhe schnellen; **E** (*rise in status, prominence*) plötzlich aufsteigen; **F ~ to it** (*coll.*) zupacken; **~ to it!** (*coll.*) mach/macht schon!

**3** v.t. **A** springen über (+ *Akk.*); überspringen ‹Mauer, Zaun usw.›; **B** springen lassen ‹Pferd›; **~ one's horse over a fence** mit dem Pferd über einen Zaun setzen; **C** (*move to point beyond*) überspringen; **D** (*not stop at*) überfahren ‹rote Ampel›; **~ the lights** bei Rot [durch]fahren; **E ~ the rails** or **track** ‹Zug:› entgleisen; **F ~ ship** ‹Seemann:› [unter Bruch des Heuervertrages vorzeitig] den Dienst quittieren; **G ~ the starting signal by half a second** eine halbe Sekunde vor dem Startsignal starten; **~ the [bus] queue** (*Brit.*) sich [an der Bushaltestelle] vordrängeln; **H** (*skip over*) überspringen ‹Seite, Kapitel usw.›; **I** (*attack*) herfallen über (+ *Akk.*). ⇒ also **bail1**[1] A; **gun** 1 B

**~ a'bout, ~ a'round** v.i. herumspringen (*ugs.*)

**~ at** v.t. **A** anspringen; (*fig.: rebuke*) anfahren; **B** (*fig.: seize, accept eagerly*) sofort [beim Schopf] ergreifen ‹Gelegenheit›; sofort zugreifen od. (*ugs.*) zuschlagen bei ‹Angebot›; sofort aufgreifen od. (*ugs.*) anspringen auf ‹Vorschlag›

**~ 'in** v.i. reinspringen (*ugs.*)

**~ 'off** **1** v.i. **A** abspringen; **he ~ed off from his horse/bicycle** er sprang vom Pferd/Rad; **B** (*Showjumping*) am Stechen teilnehmen; ⇒ also **jump-off**. **2** v.t. **~ off sth.** von etw. springen

**~ on** **1** /'-'-/ v.i. aufspringen; **~ on to a bus/train** in einen Bus/Zug springen; **~ on to one's bicycle/horse** sich aufs Fahrrad/Pferd schwingen. **2** /'--/ v.t. **~ on a bus/train** in einen Bus/Zug springen; **~ on one's bicycle** sich aufs Fahrrad schwingen

**~ 'out** v.i. hinaus-/herausspringen; **~ out of** springen aus

**~ 'up** v.i. aufspringen (**from** von); **the dog ~ed up at him** der Hund sprang an ihm hoch; **~ up on to sth.** auf etw. (*Akk.*) springen; ⇒ also **~** 2 C

**jumped-up** /'dʒʌmptʌp/ adj. (*coll.*) emporgekommen

**jumper** /'dʒʌmpə(r)/ n. **A** (*Brit.: pullover*) Pullover, der; Pulli, der (*ugs.*); **B** (*loose jacket*) Jumper, der; Buseruntje, die (*Seemannsspr.*); **C** (*Sport*) Springer, der/Springerin, die; **D** (*Amer.: pinafore dress*) Trägerkleid, das

**jumping**/'dʒʌmpɪŋ/: **~ bean** n. Springbohne, die; **~ jack** n. **A** Hampelmann, der; **B** (*firework*) Knallfrosch, der; **~-'off place** n. Ausgangsbasis, die

**jump: ~ jet** n. (*Aeronaut.*) Senkrechtstarter, der; **~ leads** n. pl. (*Brit. Motor Veh.*) Starthilfekabel, das; **~-off** n. (*Showjumping*) Stechen, das; **~ seat** n. (*Amer. Motor Veh.*) Klappsitz, der; **~-start** **1** v.t. **A ~-start a car** einem Auto Starthilfe geben; **B** (*fig.*) [wieder] in Gang bringen; [wieder] ankurbeln ‹Wirtschaft, Industrie›; **2** n. Start durch Starthilfe; (*fig.*) neuer Impuls od. Auftrieb; **the car needs a ~-start** das Auto braucht Starthilfe; **the economy received a ~-start** die Wirtschaft erfuhr [einen] neuen Aufschwung; **~suit** n. Overall, der

**jumpy** /'dʒʌmpɪ/ adj. nervös; aufgeregt

**Jun.** abbr. **A June** Jun.; **B Junior** jun.

**junction** /'dʒʌŋkʃn/ n. **A** Verbindungspunkt, der; Verbindungsstelle, die; (*of rivers*) Zusammenfluss, der; (*of railway lines, roads*) ≈ Einmündung, die; (*of motorway*) Anschlussstelle, die; (*crossroads*) Kreuzung, die; **the ~ of two roads** ≈ eine Straßeneinmündung; **B** (*Electr.*) [Leitungs]verbindung, die; (*Electronics*) Übergang, der

**'junction box** n. (*Electr.*) Verteilerkasten, der

**juncture** /'dʒʌŋktʃə(r)/ n. **at this ~:** unter diesen Umständen; (*at this point of time*) zu diesem Zeitpunkt

**June** /dʒu:n/ n. ▶ **1055** Juni, der; ⇒ also **August**

**jungle** /'dʒʌŋgl/ n. Dschungel, der (*auch fig.*); Urwald, der; **tropical ~:** tropischer Urwald; **~ life** das Leben im Dschungel; **the law of the ~:** das Gesetz des Dschungels; **concrete ~:** Betondschungel, der (*ugs.*)

**junior** /'dʒu:nɪə(r)/ **1** adj. **A** ▶ **912** (*below a certain age*) jünger; **~ team** Juniorenmannschaft, die; **~ member** ≈ Mitglied der Jugendabteilung; **be ~ to sb.** jünger sein als jmd.; **B** (*of lower rank*) rangniedriger ‹Person›; niedriger ‹Rang›; einfach ‹Angestellter›; **be ~ to sb.** eine niedrigere Stellung haben als jmd.; **be ~ to sb. by two years** zwei Jahre kürzer im Dienst sein als jmd.; **C** *appended to name* (*the younger*) **Mr Smith J~:** Mr. Smith junior; **D** (*Brit. Sch.*) Grundschul‹klasse›; Grund‹schule›; **E** (*Brit. Univ.*) **~ combination** or **common room** Gemeinschaftsraum für Studenten; **F** (*Amer. Sch., Univ.*) **~ year** vorletztes Jahr vor der Abschlussprüfung.

**2** n. **A** ▶ **912** (*younger person*) Jüngere, der/die; (*person of lower rank*) Untergebene, der/die; (*in an office*) jmd., der in einem Büro die niedrigste Stellung hat; **be sb.'s ~ [by six years]** or **[six years] sb.'s ~:** [sechs Jahre] jünger sein als jmd.; **B** (*Brit. Sch.*) (*at primary school*) Grundschüler, der/-schülerin, die; (*at secondary school*) Unterstufenschüler, der/-schülerin, die; **C** (*Amer.*) (*Univ.*) Student/Studentin im vorletzten Studienjahr; (*Sch.*) Schüler/Schülerin im vorletzten Schuljahr; **D** *no art.* (*Amer. coll.: son in the family*) der Junge; der Junior (*scherzh.*); **come on, ~:** komm, Junior (*scherzh.*) od. Junge!

**junior: ~ 'minister** n. (*Brit.*) ≈ Ministerialdirektor, der/-direktorin, die; **~ 'partner** n. Juniorpartner, der/-partnerin, die

J

**juniper** /ˈdʒuːnɪpə(r)/ *n.* (*Bot.*) Wacholder, *der;* **oil of ~:** Wacholderöl, *das*

**junk**[1] /dʒʌŋk/ ❶ *n.* Ⓐ (*discarded material*) Trödel, *der* (*ugs.*); Gerümpel, *das;* (*trash*) Plunder, *der* (*ugs.*); Ramsch, *der* (*ugs.*); Ⓑ (*Naut.*) (*cables or ropes*) [altes] Tauwerk; Junk, *der* (*fachspr.*); (*cable or rope*) [alter] Tampen (*fachspr.*); Ⓒ (*sl.: drug, esp. heroin*) Junk, *der* (*Drogenjargon*). ❷ *v.t.* wegwerfen; ausmisten (*ugs.*); (*fig.*) aufgeben

**junk**[2] *n.* (*ship*) Dschunke, *die*

ˈ**junk bonds** *n. pl.* Junk bonds *Pl.* (*Wirtsch.*)

**junket** /ˈdʒʌŋkɪt/ ❶ *n.* Ⓐ (*dessert of set milk*) Dickmilchdessert, *das;* Ⓑ (*dated: feast*) [Fest]schmaus, *der* (*veralt.*); Festmahl, *das* (*geh.*); Ⓒ (*Amer.*) (*pleasure outing*) Vergnügungsfahrt, *die;* (*official's tour*) Vergnügungsreise auf Kosten des Steuerzahlers. ❷ *v.i.* Ⓐ (*dated: feast, banquet*) schlemmen; Ⓑ (*esp. Amer.: tour*) eine Vergnügungsreise/Vergnügungsreisen machen

**junketing** /ˈdʒʌŋkɪtɪŋ/ *n.* Ⓐ (*dated*) Schlemmerei, *die;* Ⓑ (*esp. Amer.: by official*[*s*]) Vergnügungsreisen auf Kosten des Steuerzahlers

**junk: ~ food** *n.* minderwertige Kost; **~ heap** *n.* Ⓐ ⇒ **scrap heap**; Ⓑ (*sl.: old car etc.*) Schrotthaufen, *der* (*ugs.*)

**junkie** /ˈdʒʌŋkɪ/ *n.* (*sl.*) Junkie, *der* (*Drogenjargon*)

**junk: ~ mail** *n.* Postwurfsendungen *Pl.;* Reklame, *die;* **~ shop** *n.* Trödelladen, *der* (*ugs.*); **~yard** ⇒ **scrapyard**

**junta** /ˈdʒʌntə/ *n.* Junta, *die;* **military ~:** Militärjunta, *die*

**Jupiter** /ˈdʒuːpɪtə(r)/ *pr. n.* Ⓐ (*Astron.*) Jupiter, *der;* Ⓑ (*Roman Mythol.*) Jupiter (*der*)

**Jura** /ˈdʒʊərə/ *pr. n.* Jura, *der*

**Jurassic** /dʒʊəˈræsɪk/ (*Geol.*) ❶ *adj.* jurassisch; Jura-. ❷ *n.* Jura, *der*

**juridical** /dʒʊəˈrɪdɪkl/ *adj.* Ⓐ (*of judicial proceedings*) gerichtlich; Ⓑ (*of law*) juristisch

**jurisdiction** /dʒʊərɪsˈdɪkʃn/ *n.* (*authority*) Jurisdiktion, *die;* Gerichtsbarkeit, *die;* (*authority of a sovereign power*) Hoheit, *die;* (*extent*) Zuständigkeit, *die;* (*territory*) Zuständigkeitsbereich, *der;* **fall** *or* **come under** *or* **within the ~ of sth./sb.** in die Zuständigkeit *od.* den Zuständigkeitsbereich von etw./jmdm. fallen; **have ~ over sb./in a matter** für jmdn./in einer Angelegenheit zuständig sein

**jurisprudence** /dʒʊərɪsˈpruːdəns/ *n., no pl.* Rechtswissenschaft, *die;* Jurisprudenz, *die*

**jurist** /ˈdʒʊərɪst/ *n.* ▶ **1261** Ⓐ Rechtswissenschaftler, *der*/-wissenschaftlerin, *die;* Jurist, *der*/Juristin, *die;* Ⓑ (*Amer.: lawyer*) [Rechts]anwalt, *der*/-anwältin, *die*

**juror** /ˈdʒʊərə(r)/ *n.* Geschworene, *der/die;* (*in Germany, in some Austrian courts*) Schöffe, *der*/Schöffin, *die*

**jury** /ˈdʒʊərɪ/ *n.* Ⓐ (*in court*) **the ~:** die Geschworenen; (*in Germany, in some Austrian courts*) die Schöffen; **sit on the ~:** auf der Geschworenen-/Schöffenbank sitzen; **do ~ service** das Amt eines Geschworenen/Schöffen ausüben; **a ~ consists of ...:** eine Geschworenen-/Schöffenbank besteht aus ...; **trial by ~:** Schwurgerichtsverfahren, *das;* **the ~ of public opinion** (*fig.*) die Instanz der öffentlichen Meinung; ⇒ *also* **grand jury**; **judge** 1 A; Ⓑ (*in competition*) Jury, *die;* Preisgericht, *das;* (*Sport*) Schiedsgericht, *das;* Kampfgericht, *das*

**jury: ~ box** *n.* Geschworenenbank, *die;* (*in Germany, in some Austrian courts*) Schöffenbank, *die;* **~man** /ˈdʒʊərɪmən/ *n., pl.* **~men** /ˈdʒʊərɪmən/ Geschworene, *der;* (*in Germany, in some Austrian courts*) Schöffe, *der;* **~woman** *n.* Geschworene, *die;* (*in Germany, in some Austrian courts*) Schöffin, *die*

**just** /dʒʌst/ ❶ *adj.* Ⓐ (*morally right, deserved*) gerecht; anständig, korrekt ‹Verhalten, Benehmen›; ⇒ *also* **desert**[1] A; Ⓑ (*legally right*) rechtmäßig; Ⓒ (*well-grounded*) berechtigt ‹Angst, Zorn, Groll›; gerechtfertigt ‹Verhalten›; begründet ‹Verdacht, Ansicht›; Ⓓ (*right in amount*) recht, richtig ‹Proportion, Maß, Verhältnis›.

❷ *adv.* Ⓐ (*exactly*) genau; **~ then/enough** gerade da/genug; **~ as** (*exactly as, in the same way as*) genauso wie; (*when*) gerade, als; **~ as you like** *or* **please** ganz wie Sie wünschen/du magst; **~ as good/tidy** *etc.* genauso gut/ordentlich *usw.;* **come ~ as you are** komm so, wie du bist; **~ as fast as I can** so schnell wie ich nur kann; **~ about** (*coll.*) so ziemlich (*ugs.*); **it'll ~ about be enough** (*coll.*) es wird in etwa reichen; **I've had ~ about enough of you** (*coll.*) ich hab langsam genug von dir; **that is ~ ˈit** das ist es ja gerade; genau das ist es ja; **that's ~ like him** das ist typisch er *od.* für ihn; **~ ˈso** (*in an orderly manner*) ordentlich; *expr. agreement* ganz recht; **be ~ ˈso** (*be exactly arranged*) tadellos in Ordnung sein; **~ what ...?** was genau ...?; **I wonder ~ how good he is** ich frage mich, wie gut er eigentlich wirklich ist; Ⓑ (*barely*) gerade [eben]; (*with very little time to spare*) gerade [eben] noch; (*no more than*) nur; **~ under £10** nicht ganz zehn Pfund; **we had only ~ enough time for a cup of tea** wir hatten gerade [genug] Zeit, eine Tasse Tee zu trinken; **it's ~ possible** das ist gerade noch möglich; **there will be enough, but only ~:** es wird reichen, aber [nur] gerade eben *od.* [nur] gerade so; **it's ~ on/before/after 8 a.m.** es ist fast 8 Uhr/es ist kurz vor/nach 8 Uhr; **it's ~ after/before the traffic lights** es ist direkt hinter/vor der Verkehrsampel; Ⓒ (*exactly or nearly now or then, in immediate past*) gerade [eben]; [so]eben; (*at this moment*) gerade; **I have ~ seen him** (*Brit.*), **I ~ saw him** (*Amer.*) ich habe ihn gerade [eben] *od.* eben gesehen; **~ now** (*at this moment*) [im Moment] gerade; (*a little time ago*) gerade eben; **not ~ now** im Moment nicht; Ⓓ (*coll.*) (*simply*) einfach; (*only*) nur; *esp. with imperatives* mal [eben]; **it ~ so happens that ...:** es ist ganz zufällig, dass ...; **it is ~ that I don't like them** ich mag sie einfach nicht; **I've come here ~ to see you** ich bin nur gekommen, um dich zu besuchen; **~ [you] wait till I catch you!** warte nur *od.* na warte, wenn ich dich erwische!; **~ anybody** irgendjemand; **~ another car** ein ganz gewöhnliches Auto; **~ look at that!** guck dir das mal an!; **could you ~ turn round?** kannst du dich mal [eben] umdrehen?; **~ come here a moment** komm [doch] mal einen Moment her; **~ a moment, please** einen Moment mal; **~ like that** einfach so; ohne weiteres; **~ in case** für alle Fälle; **~ in case it rains** falls es regnet; Ⓔ (*coll.: positively*) einfach; echt (*ugs.*); **that's ~ ridiculous/fantastic** das ist einfach lächerlich/fantastisch; Ⓕ (*quite*) **not ~ yet** noch nicht ganz; **it is ~ as well that ...:** [es ist] nur gut *od.* es ist doch gut, dass ...; **you might ~ as well ...:** du könntest genauso gut ...; Ⓖ (*coll.: really, indeed*) wirklich; echt (*ugs.*); **You wouldn't dare do that! — Oh, wouldn't I ~?** Das würdest du nicht wagen! — Und ob!; **That's lovely. — Isn't it ~?** Das ist schön. — Ja, und wie; **~ the same** (*nevertheless*) trotzdem; **that's ~ too bad** das ist Pech.

❸ *n. pl.* **the ~:** die Gerechten; ⇒ *also* **sleep** 3 A

**justice** /ˈdʒʌstɪs/ *n.* Ⓐ Gerechtigkeit, *die;* **administer ~:** Recht sprechen; **poetic[al] ~:** ausgleichende Gerechtigkeit; **treat sb. with ~:** jmdn. gerecht behandeln; **do ~ to sth.** einer Sache (*Dat.*) gerecht werden; (*to food or drink*) einer Sache (*Dat.*) gebührend zusprechen; **~ was done in the end** der Gerechtigkeit wurde schließlich Genüge getan; **do oneself ~:** sich richtig zur Geltung bringen; **in ~ to sb.** um jmdm. gerecht zu werden; **with ~:** mit Recht; **in all ~:** um gerecht zu sein; ⇒ *also* **rough justice**; Ⓑ (*judicial proceedings*) **bring sb. to [a court of] ~:** jmdn. vor Gericht bringen *od.* stellen; **let ~ take its course, not interfere with the course of ~:** der Gerechtigkeit ihren Lauf lassen; **Department of J~** (*Amer.*) Justizministerium, *das;* Ⓒ ▶ **1261** (*magistrate*) Schiedsrichter, *der*/-richterin, *die;* Schiedsmann, *der*/-männin, *die;* (*Brit.: judge of Supreme Court*) *Richter/Richterin des Obersten Gerichtshofs;* **Mr/Mrs J~ Smith** (*Brit.*) Richter/Richterin Smith; **J~ of the Peace** Friedensrichter, *der*/-richterin, *die;* ⇒ *also* **chief** 2 A

**justifiable** /dʒʌstɪˈfaɪəbl/ *adj.* berechtigt; gerechtfertigt ‹Maßnahme, Handlung›; **it is ~ to state that ...:** man kann mit Recht behaupten, dass ...

**justifiably** /dʒʌstɪˈfaɪəblɪ/ *adv.* zu Recht; berechtigterweise (*Papierdt.*); **and ~ so** und das zu Recht

**justification** /dʒʌstɪfɪˈkeɪʃn/ *n.* Ⓐ Rechtfertigung, *die;* (*condition of being justified*) Berechtigung, *die;* **with some ~:** mit einigem Recht; **in sb.'s ~:** zu jmds. Rechtfertigung; Ⓑ (*Printing*) Randausgleich, *der*

**justify** /ˈdʒʌstɪfaɪ/ *v.t.* Ⓐ (*show justice of, vindicate*) rechtfertigen; (*demonstrate correctness of*) belegen, beweisen ‹Behauptung, Argument, Darstellung›; (*offer adequate grounds for*) begründen ‹Verhalten, Vorstellung, Behauptung›; **~ oneself/sth. to sb.** sich/etw. jmdm. gegenüber *od.* vor jmdm. rechtfertigen; **the end justifies the means** der Zweck heiligt die Mittel; **be justified in doing sth.** etw. zu Recht tun; **this cannot be justified** das ist nicht zu rechtfertigen; Ⓑ (*Printing*) ausschließen

**just-in-ˈtime** *adj.* just-in-time-‹Produktion, Lieferung usw.›

**justly** /ˈdʒʌstlɪ/ *adv.* (*with justice, fairly*) gerecht; (*rightly*) mit *od.* zu Recht

**jut** /dʒʌt/ *v.i.*, **-tt-: ~ [out]** [her]vorragen; herausragen; **his chin ~s out rather a lot** er hat ein ziemlich stark vorspringendes Kinn

**jute** *n.* Jute, *die*

**Jute** /dʒuːt/ *n.* (*Ethnol., Hist.*) Jüte, *der*/Jütin, *die*

**Jutland** /ˈdʒʌtlənd/ *pr. n.* Jütland (*das*)

**juvenile** /ˈdʒuːvənaɪl/ ❶ *adj.* Ⓐ (*young, characteristic of youth*) jugendlich, (*geh.*) juvenil ‹Geschmack, Einstellung›; Jugend‹literatur, -mode›; **~ crime** Jugendkriminalität, *die;* Ⓑ (*immature*) kindisch (*abwertend*); infantil (*abwertend*). ❷ *n.* Jugendliche, *der/die; attrib.* **~ lead** (*Theatre*) jugendlicher Held

**juvenile: ~ court** *n.* (*Law*) Jugendgericht, *das;* **~ deˈlinquency** *n.* Jugendkriminalität, *die;* **~ deˈlinquent, ~ offender** *ns.* jugendlicher Straftäter/jugendliche Straftäterin

**juxtapose** /dʒʌkstəˈpəʊz/ *v.t.* nebeneinander stellen (**with, to** und)

**juxtaposition** /dʒʌkstəpəˈzɪʃn/ *n.* (*action*) Nebeneinanderstellung, *die;* (*condition*) Nebeneinander, *das;* **be in ~:** nebeneinander gestellt sein

# Kk

**K**[1], **k**[1] /keɪ/ *n., pl.* **Ks** *or* **K's** K, k, *das*

**K**[2] *abbr.* **A King['s]** kgl.; **B** *(Phys.)* **kelvin[s]** K; **C** *(Computing)* **kilobyte** K; **D** *(Chess)* **king** K; **E** *(£1,000)* Tsd. £; **earn 35K a year** 35 000 im Jahr verdienen

**k**[2] *abbr.* **kilo-** k-

**Kaffir** /ˈkæfə(r)/ **1** *n.* **A** *(Ethnol.)* Kaffer, *der*/Kaffernfrau, *die;* **B** *(derog.: South African Black)* Kaffer, *der*/Kaffernweib, *das (abwertend).* **2** *adj.* Kaffern-

**Kafkaesque** /kæfkəˈesk/ *adj.* kafkaesk *(geh.)*

**kale** /keɪl/ *n. (Bot.)* **[curly/Scotch] ~:** Grünkohl, *der;* Krauskohl, *der;* ⇒ *also* **seakale**

**kaleidoscope** /kəˈlaɪdəskəʊp/ *n. (lit. or fig.)* Kaleidoskop, *das*

**kaleidoscopic** /kəlaɪdəˈskɒpɪk/ *adj. (lit. or fig.)* kaleidoskopisch

**kamikaze** /kæmɪˈkɑːzɪ/ *n. (Hist.)* **A** *(pilot)* Kamikaze[flieger], *der;* **B** *(aircraft)* Kamikazeflugzeug, *das*

**Kampuchea** /kæmpʊˈtʃiːə/ *pr. n.* Kamputschea *(das)*

**kangaroo** /kæŋgəˈruː/ *n.* Känguru, *das*

**kangaˈroo court** *n.* Femegericht, *das;* Feme, *die*

**Kantian** /ˈkæntɪən/ *(of Kant)* Kantisch; *(of Kantianism)* kant[ian]isch

**kaolin** /ˈkeɪəlɪn/ *n.* Kaolin, *das od. (fachspr.) der*

**kaput** /kæˈpʊt/ *pred. adj. (coll.)* kaputt *(ugs.)*

**karaoke** /kærɪˈəʊkɪ/ *n., no pl., no indef. art.* Karaoke, *das; attrib.* Karaoke-; **~ machine** Karaokegerät, *das*

**karate** /kəˈrɑːtɪ/ *n., no pl., no indef. art.* Karate, *das*

**kaˈrate chop** *n.* Karateschlag, *der;* Handkantenschlag, *der*

**karma** /ˈkɑːmə/ *n. (Buddhism, Hinduism)* Karma[n], *das*

**karst** /kɑːst/ *n. (Geog.)* Karst, *der*

**kart** /kɑːt/ ⇒ **go-kart**

**Kashmir** /kæʃˈmɪə(r)/ *pr. n.* Kaschmir *(das)*

**Katherine** /ˈkæθrɪn/ *pr. n. (Hist., as name of ruler etc.)* Katharina *(die)*

**kayak** /ˈkaɪæk/ *n.* Kajak, *der*

**kc** *abbr.* **kilocycle[s]** kHz

**KC** *abbr. (Brit.)* **King's Counsel**

**kc/s** *abbr.* **kilocycles per second** kHz

**kebab** /kɪˈbæb/ *n. (Cookery)* Kebab, *der*

**kedgeree** /ˈkedʒəriː, kedʒəˈriː/ *n. (Gastr.)* Kedgeree, *das; indisches Reisgericht mit Hülsenfrüchten, Zwiebeln, Eiern; (European dish) Reisgericht mit Fisch und Eiern*

**keel** /kiːl/ **1** *n. (Naut.)* Kiel, *der;* **lay down a ~:** ein Schiff auf Kiel legen; ⇒ *also* **even**[1] 1 B. **2** *v.i.* **~ over** **A** *(overturn)* umstürzen; ‹Schiff:› kentern; **B** *(fall)* ‹Person:› umkippen; **he ~ed over on to the bed** er fiel aufs Bett. **3** *v.t.* **~ over** *(Naut.)* zum Kentern bringen; kieloben legen *(Seemannsspr.); (on one side)* kielholen *(Seemannsspr.)*

**ˈkeelhaul** *v.t.* kielholen *(Seemannsspr.); (fig.)* zusammenstauchen *(ugs.)*

**keen**[1] /kiːn/ *adj.* **A** *(sharp)* scharf ‹Messer, Klinge, Schneide›; *(fig.)* scharf ‹Hohn, Spott›; beißend ‹Sarkasmus›; **B** *(piercingly cold)* scharf, schneidend ‹Wind, Kälte›; *(penetrating, strong)* grell ‹Licht›; durchdringend, stechend ‹Geruch›; **C** *(eager)* begeistert, leidenschaftlich ‹Fußballfan, Amateurfotograf, Sportler›; ausgeprägt, lebhaft ‹Interesse›; heftig ‹Konkurrenz, Verlangen›; **be ~ to do sth.** darauf erpicht sein, etw. zu tun; **he's really ~ to win** er will unbedingt gewinnen; **be ~ on doing sth.** etw. gern[e] tun; **although he's inexperienced, he's really ~:** obwohl er unerfahren ist, ist er doch wirklich sehr interessiert; **she was not particularly ~ to see the play** sie war nicht besonders scharf darauf, das Stück zu sehen *(ugs.)*; **be [as] ~ as mustard** mit Feuereifer dabei sein; **not be ~ on sth.** nicht gerade begeistert von etw. sein; **I'm not too** *or* **not very** *or* **not madly ~ on it** ich bin nicht so wild darauf *(ugs.)*; **my father's very ~ on my going to college** mein Vater will unbedingt, dass ich aufs College gehe; **be ~ on sb.** scharf auf jmdn. sein *(ugs.)*; **D** *(highly sensitive)* scharf ‹Augen›; fein ‹Sinne›; ausgeprägt ‹Sinn für etw.›; **E** *(intellectually sharp)* scharf ‹Verstand, Intellekt›; clever ‹Geschäftsmann›; scharfsinnig, geistreich ‹Bemerkung, Frage usw.›; rasch ‹Auffassungsgabe›; **~ wit** Scharfsinn, *der;* **F** *(acute)* heftig, stark ‹Schmerzen, Qualen›; **G** *(Brit.: exceptionally low)* niedrig, günstig ‹Preis›; günstig ‹Angebot›; **H** *(coll.: excellent)* [einfach] klasse *(ugs.)*

**keen**[2] **1** *n.* Totenklage, *die.* **2** *v.i.* die Totenklage halten *od.* singen **(over** für)

**keenly** /ˈkiːnlɪ/ *adv.* **A** *(sharply)* scharf ‹geschliffen›; **B** *(coldly)* scharf; **C** *(eagerly)* eifrig ‹arbeiten›; brennend ‹interessiert sein›; **look forward ~ to sth.** auf etw. *(Akk.)* sehr gespannt sein; **D** *(piercingly)* scharf ‹ansehen›; **E** *(acutely)* **be ~ aware of sth.** sich *(Dat.)* einer Sache *(Gen.)* voll bewusst sein; **feel sth. ~:** etw. deutlich fühlen

**keenness** /ˈkiːnnɪs/ *n., no pl.* **A** *(sharpness, coldness, acuteness of sense)* Schärfe, *die;* **B** *(eagerness)* Eifer, *der;* **C** *(of intellect)* Schärfe, *die;* **the ~ of his wit** seine Scharfsinnigkeit; **D** *(of pain etc.)* Heftigkeit, *die*

**keep** /kiːp/ **1** *v.t.,* **kept** /kept/ **A** *(observe)* halten ‹Versprechen, Schwur usw.›; einhalten ‹Verabredung, Vereinbarung, Vertrag, Sonntagsruhe, Zeitplan›; begehen, feiern ‹Fest›; halten, einhalten ‹Sabbat, Fasten›; ⇒ *also* **hour** C; **B** *(guard)* behüten, beschützen ‹Person›; hüten ‹Herde, Schafe›; schützen ‹Stadt, Festung›; verwahren ‹Wertgegenstände›; **may God ~ you!** Gott beschütze dich!; **~ sb. [safe] from sth.** jmdn. vor etw. *(Dat.)* bewahren; **~ sb. safe** jmdn. beschützen; **~ sth. locked away** etw. unter Verschluss halten *od.* aufbewahren; **C** *(have charge of)* aufbewahren; verwahren; **D** *(retain possession of)* behalten; *(not lose or destroy)* aufheben ‹Quittung, Rechnung›; **I'll give you that book to ~:** ich schenke dir das Buch; **~ one's position** seine Stellung behaupten *od.* halten; **you can ~ it** *(coll.: I do not want it)* das kannst du behalten *od.* dir an den Hut stecken *(ugs.)*; **Another talk on architecture? You can ~ it** Noch ein Vortrag über Architektur? Nein danke, kein Bedarf *(ugs.)*; **E** *(maintain)* unterhalten, instand halten ‹Gebäude, Straße usw.›; pflegen ‹Garten›; **neatly kept** gut gepflegt; **F** *(carry on, manage)* unterhalten, führen, betreiben ‹Geschäft, Lokal, Bauernhof›; **G** halten ‹Schweine, Bienen, Hund, Katze usw›; sich *(Dat.)* halten ‹Diener, Auto›; **H** führen ‹Tagebuch, Liste usw.›; **~ an account of expenditure** über seine Ausgaben Buch führen; **~ the books** die Bücher führen; **I** *(provide for sustenance of)* versorgen, unterhalten ‹Familie›; **~ sb./oneself in cigarettes** *etc.* jmdn./sich mit Zigaretten *usw.* versorgen; **~ sb. in luxury** jmdm. ein Leben in Luxus bieten; **~ sb. in the style to which he is accustomed** jmdm. den gewohnten Lebensstil bieten; **she has to ~ herself on £20 a week** sie muss mit 20 Pfund pro Woche auskommen; **J** sich *(Dat.)* halten ‹Geliebte, Mätresse usw.›; sich *(Dat.)* als Geliebte halten ‹Frau›; sich *(Dat.)* als Liebhaber halten ‹Mann›; **she is a kept woman** sie lässt sich von einem Mann aushalten; **K** *(have on sale)* führen ‹Ware›; **~ a stock of sth.** etw. [am Lager] haben; **we always ~ a bit of cheese** wir haben immer ein bisschen Käse da; **L** *(maintain in quality, state, or position)* halten ‹Rhythmus›; **~ one's hands in one's pockets** die Hände in den Taschen behalten; **~ sth. in one's head** etw. [im Kopf] behalten; sich *(Dat.)* etw. merken; **~ sth. in a cool place** etw. an einem kühlen Ort aufbewahren; **a cold kept her in bed** eine Erkältung zwang sie, im Bett zu bleiben; **~ sb. to his word/promise** jmdn. beim Wort nehmen; **~ sb. waiting** jmdn. warten lassen; **~ the water boiling** das Wasser am Kochen halten; **~ the office running smoothly** dafür sorgen, dass im Büro weiterhin alles reibungslos [ab]läuft; **~ sb. alive** jmdn. am Leben halten; **~ the traffic moving** den Verkehr in Fluss halten; **~ a plant watered** eine Pflanze feucht halten; **~ sth. shut/tidy** etw. geschlossen/in Ordnung halten; **~ the engine running** den Motor laufen lassen; **~ sth. under [the] water** etw. unter Wasser halten; **M** *(maintain as quality)* **~ silence** schweigen; **~ its shape** seine Form nicht verlieren; **~ one's beauty** sich *(Dat.)* seine Schönheit bewahren; **N** *(detain)* festhalten; **there was no longer anything to ~ him there** es hielt ihn dort nichts mehr; **what kept you [so long]?** wo bleibst du denn [so lange]?; **don't let me ~ you, I mustn't ~ you** lass dich [von mir] nicht aufhalten; **~ sb. in prison** jmdn. in Haft halten; **~ sb. in hospital a few days longer** jmdn. noch ein paar Tage länger im Krankenhaus behalten; **~ sb. indoors** jmdn. nicht aus dem Haus lassen; **the teacher kept Peter behind after the lesson** der Lehrer rief Peter nach der Stunde zu sich; **~ sb. from doing sth.** jmdn. davon abhalten *od.* daran hindern, etw. zu tun; **~ sth. from doing sth.** verhindern, dass etw. etw. tut; **to ~ myself from falling** um nicht zu fallen; **I couldn't ~ myself from laughing** [ich konnte mir nicht helfen,] ich musste einfach lachen; **we must ~ them from seeing each other** wir müssen verhindern, dass sie sich sehen; **O** *(reserve)* aufheben; aufsparen; **I asked him to ~ a seat for me** ich bat ihn, mir einen Platz freizuhalten; **~ it for oneself** es für sich behalten; **~ sth. for later** *etc.* sich *(Dat.)* etw. für später *usw.* aufheben *od.* aufsparen; **let's ~ the business talk for later** verschieben wir das Geschäftliche erst mal auf später; **P** *(conceal)* **~ sth. to oneself** etw. für sich behalten; **~ sth. a mystery** ein Geheimnis aus etw. machen; **~ sth. from sb.** jmdm. etw. verheimlichen; **he kept the news from them** er verschwieg ihnen die Neuigkeit; **Q** *(continue to follow)* folgen (+ *Dat.*) ‹Straße, Weg›; **~ a straight path** immer geradeaus gehen.

**2** *v.i.,* **kept** **A** *(remain in specified place, condition)* bleiben; **~ together** zusammenbleiben; **~ warm/clean** sich warm/sauber halten; **how are you ~ing?** *(coll.)* wie gehts [dir] denn so? *(ugs.)*; **are you ~ing well?** gehts dir gut?; ⇒ *also* **calm** 2 A; **cool** 1 B; **fit**[2] 1 E; **silent** A; **B** *(continue in course, direction, or action)* **~ [to the] left/[to the] right/straight ahead** *or* **straight on** sich links/rechts halten/immer geradeaus fahren/gehen *usw.;* **~ on until you get to the traffic lights** geh/fahr *usw.* weiter bis zur Ampel; **'~ left'** *(traffic sign)* „links vorbeifahren"; *(sign to pedestrians)* „links gehen"; **traffic in Britain ~s [to the] left** in Großbritannien herrscht Linksverkehr *od.* fährt man links; **the lorry kept to the middle of the road** der Lastwagen fuhr die ganze Zeit auf der Straßenmitte; **~ behind me** halte dich *od.* bleib hinter mir; **~ doing sth.** (*not stop*) etw. weiter tun; (*repeatedly*) etw. immer wieder tun; (*constantly*) etw. dauernd *od.* immer tun; **~ talking/working** *etc.* **until ...:** weiterreden/-arbeiten *usw.*, bis ...; ⇒ *also* **smile** 2; **C** (*remain good*) ‹Lebensmittel:› sich halten; (*fig.*) ‹Geheimnis:› gewahrt bleiben; **that story can ~:** diese Geschichte kann warten *od.* eilt nicht; **your report will have to ~ until the next meeting** mit Ihrem Bericht müssen wir bis zum nächsten Treffen warten; **what I have to say won't ~:** was ich zu sagen habe, ist eilig *od.* eilt; **will your news ~ till tomorrow?** haben ihre Neuigkeiten Zeit bis morgen?. ⇒ *also* **go**[1] 1 F; **touch** 3 H. ❸ *n.* **A** (*maintenance*) Unterhalt, *der;* **I get £100 a month and my ~:** ich bekomme 100 Pfund monatlich und Logis; **you don't earn your ~:** du bist nichts als ein unnützer Esser; **sth. doesn't earn its ~:** etw. zahlt sich nicht aus (*ugs.*); **B for ~s** (*coll.*) auf Dauer; (*to be retained*) zum Behalten; **you can have it** *or* **it's yours for ~s** du kannst es behalten; **C** (*Hist.: tower*) Bergfried, *der*

**~ 'after** *v.t.* verfolgen; jagen; (*fig.: chivvy*) antreiben

**~ at** *v.t.* **A** (*work persistently*) weitermachen mit; **~ 'at it!** nicht nachlassen!; **B** (*cause to work at*) **~ sb. at sth.** jmdn. dazu anhalten, dass er etw. weitermacht; **C** /'-'-/ (*nag*) nicht in Ruhe lassen; [ständig] zusetzen (+ *Dat.*); **don't ~ at me all the time!** lass mich endlich einmal in Ruhe!; **they kept at him for the money he owed** sie lagen ihm ständig wegen des Geldes, das er ihnen schuldete, in den Ohren (*ugs.*)

**~ a'way** ❶ *v.i.* wegbleiben (*ugs.*) (**from** von); sich fern halten (**from** von); **I just can't ~ away** es zieht mich immer wieder hin. ❷ *v.t.* fern halten (**from** von); **~ them away from each other!** halte sie auseinander!; **~ him away from me!** halte ihn mir vom Hals! (*ugs.*); **what kept you away?** warum bist du nicht gekommen?

**~ 'back** ❶ *v.i.* zurückbleiben; **~ back from sth.** sich von etw. fern halten; von etw. wegbleiben (*ugs.*); **~ back!** bleib, wo du bist!; **~ back and wait your turn** halte dich zurück und warte, bis du an der Reihe bist. ❷ *v.t.* **A** (*restrain*) zurückhalten ‹Menschenmenge, Tränen›; **~ sb. back from sb./sth.** jmdn. von jmdm./etw. fern halten; **B** (*withhold*) verschweigen ‹Informationen, Tatsachen› (**from** *Dat.*); einbehalten ‹Geld, Zinsen, Zahlung›; **don't try to ~ any secrets back** versuch nicht, etwas zu verheimlichen

**~ 'down** ❶ *v.i.* unten bleiben; (*Mil.: lie low in skirmishing*) in Deckung bleiben; ‹Wind:› nicht stärker werden; **~ down!** bleib unten!; duck dich! ❷ *v.t.* **A** (*oppress, suppress*) unterdrücken ‹Volk, Person, Tränen›; bändigen ‹Hund›; niederhalten ‹rebellische Person›; **you can't ~ a good man down** (*prov.*) er/sie *usw.* lässt/lassen sich nicht unterkriegen (*ugs.*); **B** (*prevent increase of*) niedrig halten ‹Steuern, Preise, Zinssatz, Ausgaben, usw.›; eindämmen ‹Epidemie›; **~ one's weight down** nicht zunehmen; **~ the weeds down** dafür sorgen, dass das Unkraut nicht überhand nimmt; **~ down insects** Insekten bekämpfen; **C** (*not raise*) unten lassen ‹Kopf›; **~ that noise/your voice down** sei/rede nicht so laut; **could you ~ the volume down on your radio?** könntest du dein Radio leiser stellen?; **D** (*not vomit*) bei sich behalten ‹Essen›

**~ from** *v.t.* **~ from doing sth.** etw. nicht tun; (*avoid doing*) es vermeiden, etw. zu tun; **I couldn't ~ from smiling** ich musste einfach lächeln *od.* konnte ein Lächeln nicht unterdrücken; **it is impossible to ~ from getting wet** es ist nicht zu vermeiden, dass man nass wird

**~ 'in** ❶ *v.i.* **A** (*remain indoors*) drinnen bleiben; im Haus bleiben; **B** (*remain in favour*) **~ in with sb.** sich mit jmdm. gut stellen; sich (*Dat.*) jmdn. warm halten (*ugs.*). ❷ *v.t.* **A** (*confine*) unterdrücken ‹Gefühle›; verbergen ‹Überraschung›; einziehen ‹Bauch›; **B** (*keep burning*) am Brennen halten ‹Feuer›; (*not extinguish*) anlassen ‹Feuer›; **C** (*Sch.*) nachsitzen lassen ‹Schüler›; **be kept in [after school]** nachsitzen müssen. ⇒ *also* **hand** 1 K

**~ 'off** ❶ *v.i.* ‹Person:› wegbleiben; ‹Regen, Sturm usw.:› ausbleiben; **let's hope the snow ~s off** hoffen wir, dass es nicht anfängt zu schneien *od.* keinen Schnee gibt; **'~ off'** (*on building site etc.*) „Betreten verboten". ❷ *v.t.* **A** fern halten ‹Person, Tier›; abhalten ‹Sonne›; **~ sb./sth. off sth.** jmdn./etw. von etw. fern halten/abhalten; **~ your dog off our lawn** lassen Sie Ihren Hund nicht auf unseren Rasen; **B** (*not go on*) nicht betreten; nicht begehen/befahren ‹Weg, Straße usw.›; **~ off the flower beds** nicht in die Blumenbeete treten; **'~ off the grass'** „Betreten des Rasens verboten"; **C** (*not touch*) **~ off my whisky!** Hände *od.* Finger weg von meinem Whisky!; **D** (*not eat or drink*) **~ off chocolates/brandy** keine Schokolade essen/keinen Weinbrand trinken; **~ off cigarettes** keine Zigaretten rauchen; **~ off the drink** keinen Alkohol *od.* (*ugs.*) nichts trinken; **if you don't ~ off drugs ...:** wenn du die Finger nicht von den Drogen lässt, ... (*ugs.*); wenn du Drogen nimmst, ...; **E** (*not mention*) **~ off a subject** ein Thema vermeiden; **do ~ off religion when the vicar comes to tea** sprich nicht über Religion, wenn der Pfarrer zum Tee kommt

**~ 'on** ❶ *v.i.* **A** (*continue, persist*) weitermachen (**with** *Akk.*); **~ on doing sth.** etw. [immer] weiter tun; (*repeatedly*) etw. immer wieder tun; (*constantly*) etw. dauernd *od.* immer tun; **I ~ on telling you this** das sage ich dir ja immer; **~ on driving down this road until ...:** fahr diese Straße immer weiter [entlang], bis ...; **I hope you'll ~ on coming to visit us** ich hoffe, du wirst uns auch weiterhin besuchen kommen; **B** (*Brit.: talk tiresomely*) **he does ~ on** er redet von nichts anderem; **~ on about sth.** immer wieder von etw. anfangen; **~ on at sb. about sth.** jmdm. mit etw. ständig in den Ohren liegen (*ugs.*). ❷ *v.t.* **A** weiterbeschäftigen, behalten ‹Angestellten›; behalten ‹Wohnung, Auto›; verlängern ‹Ausstellung, Film›; anlassen, laufen lassen ‹Radio, Fernseher›; **the film was kept on for another three months/till Easter** der Film blieb drei weitere Monate/bis Ostern im Programm; **B** anbehalten, anlassen ‹Kleid, Mantel›; aufbehalten ‹Hut›; ⇒ *also* **hair** B

**~ 'out** ❶ *v.i.* draußen bleiben; **'~ out'** „Zutritt verboten". ❷ *v.t.* **A** (*not let enter*) nicht hereinlassen ‹Person, Tier›; **B** abhalten ‹Kälte›; abweisen ‹Nässe›; **central heating helps ~ out the cold** eine Zentralheizung sorgt dafür, dass es nie zu kalt wird

**~ 'out of** *v.t.* **A** (*stay outside*) **~ out of a room/an area/a country** ein Zimmer/eine Gegend nicht betreten/nicht in ein Land reisen; **B** (*avoid*) **~ out of danger** Gefahren meiden; sich nicht in Gefahr begeben; **~ out of the rain/sun** *etc.* nicht in den Regen/die Sonne *usw.* gehen; **~ out of a quarrel** sich aus einem Streit heraushalten; **~ out of sb.'s way** jmdm. aus dem Weg gehen; **~ out of the way of those boys!** halt dich von diesen Jungen fern!; **~ out of trouble** zurechtkommen; **C** (*not let enter*) nicht hereinlassen in (+ *Akk.*); **D** (*cause to avoid*) **~ him/the dog out of my way** halte mir ihn/den Hund vom Leibe (*salopp*); **~ sb. out of danger** jmdn. vor Gefahr bewahren; **~ the plants out of the sun** die Pflanzen vor Sonne schützen; **I want to ~ him out of it** ich möchte ihn da heraushalten; **he wanted his name to be kept out of the papers** er wollte, dass sein Name in den Zeitungen nicht erwähnt wird

**~ to** *v.t.* **A** (*not leave*) bleiben auf (+ *Dat.*) ‹Straße, Weg›; **~ to the left!** halte dich links!; bleib links!; **B** (*follow, observe*) sich halten an (+ *Akk.*) ‹Regeln, Muster, Gesetz, Diät usw.›; einhalten ‹Zeitplan›; halten ‹Versprechen›; **~ to one's word** Wort halten; **C** (*remain in*) **~ to one's bed** im Bett bleiben; **D ~ [oneself] to oneself** für sich bleiben; **they ~ themselves to themselves** sie bleiben unter sich; **he ~s to himself [most of the time]** er bleibt [meist] für sich allein. ⇒ *also* **~** 1 L, 2 B

**~ 'under** *v.t.* **A** (*hold in subjection*) unterdrücken; **B** (*maintain in state of unconsciousness etc.*) unter Narkose halten

**~ 'up** ❶ *v.i.* **A** (*proceed equally*) **~ up with sb./sth.** mit jmdm./etw. Schritt halten; **he can't ~ up with the rest** er kommt mit den anderen nicht mit; **~ up with the Joneses** mit den andern gleichziehen; **B** (*maintain contact*) **~ up with sb.** mit jmdm. Kontakt halten; **~ up with sth.** sich über etw. (*Akk.*) auf dem Laufenden halten; **~ up with fashions/the times** (*follow*) mit der Mode/Zeit gehen; **C** ‹Regen, Wetter:› anhalten. ❷ *v.t.* **A** (*prevent from falling*) festhalten ‹Leiter, Zelt usw.›; **wear a belt to ~ one's trousers up** einen Gürtel tragen, damit die Hosen nicht rutschen; **B** (*prevent from sinking*) aufrechterhalten ‹Produktion, Standard usw.›; auf gleichem Niveau halten ‹Preise, Löhne usw.›; **C** (*maintain*) aufrechterhalten ‹Bräuche, Traditionen, Freundschaft, Lebensstil, Tempo, jmds. Moral›; (*provide means for the maintenance of*) unterhalten ‹Anwesen›; (**~** *in repair*) instand *od.* (*ugs.*) in Schuss halten ‹Haus›; (**~** *in proper condition*) in Ordnung *od.* (*ugs.*) in Schuss halten ‹Garten›; **D** (*continue*) fortsetzen ‹Angriff, Belagerung›; weiterhin zahlen ‹Raten›; **such old customs are no longer kept up** solche alten Bräuche werden nicht mehr gepflegt; **~ one's courage/spirits up** den Mut nicht sinken lassen; **~ one's strength up** sich bei Kräften halten; **~ it up** weitermachen; **~ it up!** weiter so!; **he'll never be able to ~ it up** er wird es nicht durchhalten [können]; **I'm trying to ~ up my French** ich versuche, mit meinem Französisch nicht aus der Übung zu kommen; **~ up one's chess/painting** weiterhin Schach spielen/malen; **they kept up a correspondence for many years** sie haben jahrelang [miteinander] im Briefwechsel gestanden; ⇒ *also* **appearance** B; **chin**; **end** 1 A; **E** (*prevent from going to bed*) am Schlafengehen hindern; **are we ~ing you up?** halten wir dich vom Schlafengehen ab?; **they kept me up all night** sie haben mich die ganze Nacht nicht schlafen lassen; **they were kept up by their baby crying** wegen ihres schreienden Babys kamen sie nicht zum Schlafen

**keeper** /'ki:pə(r)/ *n.* **A** ▶ **1261** ⇒ **gamekeeper**; **B** ▶ **1261** ⇒ **goalkeeper**; **wicketkeeper**; **C** ▶ **1261** (*custodian*) Wärter, *der*/Wärterin, *die;* (*zoo~*) Tierwärter, *der*/-wärterin, *die;* **~ of the keys** Schlüsselverwahrer, *der* (*veralt.*); **am I my brother's ~?** (*Bibl.*) soll ich meines Bruders Hüter sein? (*bibl.*); **D** (*fruit that keeps*) **these apples are good ~s** diese Äpfel halten sich gut

**keep-'fit** *n.* Fitnesstraining, *das*

**keep-'fit class** *n.* Fitnessgruppe, *die;* **go to ~es** zu Fitnessübungen gehen

**keeping** /'ki:pɪŋ/ *n., no pl.* **A** *no art.* **be in ~ with sth.** einer Sache (*Dat.*) entsprechen; (*be suited to sth.*) zu etw. passen; **be out of ~ with sth.** einer Sache (*Dat.*) nicht entsprechen; **the dress she wore was rather out of ~:** das Kleid, das sie anhatte, war ziemlich unpassend; **B** (*custody*) **give sth. into sb.'s ~:** jmdm. etw. zur Aufbewahrung [über]geben; **the keys are in his ~:** er bewahrt die Schlüssel auf; **take sth. into one's ~:** etw. in Gewahrsam nehmen; **leave sb. in sb.'s ~:** jmdn. jmds. Obhut anvertrauen; **C the apples will improve with ~:** die Äpfel werden besser, wenn man sie eine Zeit lang liegen lässt

**'keepsake** *n.* Andenken, *das;* **take it as** *or* **for a ~ [to remind you] of me** nimm es als *od.* zum Andenken an mich

**keg** /keg/ *n.* **A** (*barrel*) [kleines] Fass; Fässchen, *das;* **B** *attrib.* **~ beer** *aus luftdichten Metallbehältern gezapftes, mit Kohlensäure versetztes Bier;* ≈ Fassbier, *das*

**kelp** /kelp/ *n.* [See]tang, *der*

**kelvin** /'kelvɪn/ *n.* (*Phys.*) Kelvin, *das*

**'Kelvin scale** *n.* (*Phys.*) Kelvinskala, *die*

**ken**[1] /ken/ *n.* **this is beyond** *or* **outside my ~:** das geht über meinen Horizont; das ist zu hoch für mich (*ugs.*); (*beyond range of knowledge*) das übersteigt mein Wissen

**ken**[2] *v.t.*, **~ned** *or* **kent** /kent/, **~ned** (*Scot.*) ⇒ **know** 1

**kennel** /ˈkenl/ *n.* Ⓐ Hundehütte, *die;* Ⓑ *in pl.* [**boarding**] **~s** Hundepension, *die;* [**breeding**] **~s** Zwinger, *der*

**Kentish** /ˈkentɪʃ/ *adj.* kentisch

**Kenya** /ˈkenjə, ˈkiːnjə/ *pr. n.* Kenia (*das*)

**Kenyan** /ˈkenjən, ˈkiːnjən/ ▶ 1340 ❶ *adj.* kenianisch; **sb. is ~:** jmd. ist Kenianer/Kenianerin. ❷ *n.* Kenianer, *der*/Kenianerin, *die*

**kepi** /ˈkepɪ, ˈkeɪpɪ/ *n.* Käppi, *das*

**kept** ⇒ **keep** 1, 2

**kerb** /kɜːb/ *n.* (*Brit.*) Bordstein, *der*

**kerb: ~-crawling** *n.* (*Brit.*) (*langsames*) *Fahren auf dem Autostrich zur Kontaktaufnahme mit einer Prostituierten;* **~ drill** *n.* (*Brit.*) richtiges [Verhalten beim] Überqueren der Fahrbahn; **~stone** *n.* (*Brit.*) Bordstein, *der;* **~ weight** *n.* (*Brit.*) [Fahrzeug]leergewicht, *das*

**kerchief** /ˈkɜːtʃɪf, ˈkɜːtʃiːf/ *n.* (*worn on the head*) Kopftuch, *das;* (*worn around the neck*) [Hals]tuch, *das*

**kerfuffle** /kəˈfʌfl/ *n.* (*Brit. coll.*) Wirbel, *der;* Affenzeck, *der* (*ugs. abwertend*)

**kernel** /ˈkɜːnl/ *n.* (*lit. or fig.*) Kern, *der;* **a ~ of truth** ein Körnchen Wahrheit

**kerosene**, **kerosine** /ˈkerəsiːn/ *n.* (*Amer., Austral., NZ/as tech. term*) Paraffin[öl], *das;* (*for jet engines*) Kerosin, *das;* (*for lamps etc.*) Petroleum, *das;* **~ lamp** Petroleumlampe, *die*

**kestrel** /ˈkestrəl/ *n.* (*Ornith.*) Turmfalke, *der*

**ketch** /ketʃ/ *n.* (*Naut.*) Ketsch, *die*

**ketchup** /ˈketʃʌp/ *n.* Ketchup, *der od. das*

**ketone** /ˈkiːtəʊn/ *n.* (*Chem.*) Keton, *das*

**kettle** /ˈketl/ *n.* [Wasser]kessel, *der;* **a pretty** *or* **fine ~ of fish** (*iron.*) eine schöne Bescherung (*ugs. iron.*); **a different** *or* **another ~ of fish** eine ganz andere Sache

**kettle: ~drum** *n.* (*Mus.*) [Kessel]pauke, *die;* **~-drummer** *n.* (*Mus.*) Paukist, *der*/Paukistin, *die*

**kettleful** /ˈketlfʊl/ *n.* Kessel, *der;* **a ~ of water** ein Kessel [voll] Wasser

**key**[1] /kiː/ ❶ *n.* Ⓐ (*lit. or fig.*) Schlüssel, *der;* **the ~ to success** der Schlüssel zum Erfolg; **the ~ to the mystery** des Rätsels Lösung; der Schlüssel zum Geheimnis; Ⓑ (*place*) Schlüsselstellung, *die* (*Milit.*); Ⓒ (*set of answers*) [Lösungs]schlüssel, *der;* (*to map etc.*) Zeichenerklärung, *die;* (*to cipher*) Schlüssel, *der;* Ⓓ (*translation*) [wörtliche] Übersetzung; Ⓔ (*on piano, typewriter, etc.*) Taste, *die;* (*on wind instrument*) Klappe, *die;* Ⓕ (*Electr.*) Taste, *die;* Ⓖ (*Mus.*) Tonart, *die;* (*fig.: of speech or writing*) Ton, *der;* Tonart, *die;* **sing/play in/off ~:** richtig/falsch singen/spielen; Ⓗ (*Bot.*) Flügelfrucht, *die;* Ⓘ (*for grasping screws etc.*) [Schrauben]schlüssel, *der;* (*for winding a clock etc.*) Schlüssel, *der.* ⇒ *also* **house** 1 C.
❷ *attrib. adj.* entscheidend; Schlüssel‹frage, -position, -rolle, -figur, -industrie›.
❸ *v.t.* (*Computing*) **~ [in]** eintasten

**~ up** *v.t.* Ⓐ (*stimulate*) **key sb. up to sth./to a state of excitement** jmdn. zu etw. hinreißen/in einen Zustand der Erregung versetzen; **the crowd was keyed up for the match** die Menge war auf das Spiel eingestimmt; Ⓑ (*make extremely tense*) **be all keyed up** ganz aufgeregt sein; **he was all keyed up for the great event** er fieberte dem großen Ereignis entgegen

**key**[2] *n.* (*Geog.*) [Korallen]insel, *die*

**key: ~bar** *n.* Typenhebel, *der;* **~board** ❶ *n.* (*of piano etc.*) Klaviatur, *die;* (*of typewriter, computer, etc.*) Tastatur, *die;* **~board instrument** Tasteninstrument, *das;* **~board operator** Taster, *der*/Tasterin, *die;* ❷ *v.t.* tasten; **~boarder**, *n.* ▶ 1261 Taster, *der*/Tasterin, *die;* **~boarding** *n., no pl.* Tasten, *das;* **~boarding error** Tastfehler, *der;* **~hole** *n.* Schlüsselloch, *das;* **~hole surgery** *n.* Schlüssellochchirurgie, *die;* Knopflochchirurgie, *die*

**ˈkeying** *n., no pl.* ⇒ **keyboarding**

**key: ~note** *n.* Ⓐ (*Mus.*) Grundton, *der;* Ⓑ (*fig.*) Grundgedanke, *der;* [Grund]tenor, *der;* *attrib.* **~note speech** programmatische Rede; **~pad** *n.* Tastenfeld, *das;* **~punch operator** *n.* Locher, *der*/Locherin, *die;* **~ring** *n.* Schlüsselring, *der;* **~ signature** *n.* (*Mus.*) Tonartvorzeichnung, *die;* **~stone** *n.* (*Archit.*) Schlussstein, *der;* (*fig.*) Grundpfeiler, *der;* **~stroke** *n.* (*Computing*) Anschlag, *der;* **~word** *n.* Ⓐ (*key to cipher*) Schlüsselwort, *das;* Ⓑ (*significant word in indexing*) Stichwort, *das;* Schlüsselwort, *das* (*bes. DV*)

**kg.** *abbr.* ▶ 1683 **kilogram[s]** kg

**KG** *abbr.* (*Brit.*) **Knight [of the Order] of the Garter**

**khaki** /ˈkɑːkɪ/ ❶ *adj.* khakifarben; **~ colour/cloth** Khaki, *das*/Khaki, *der.* ❷ *n.* (*cloth*) Khaki, *der;* **~-coloured** khakifarben

**kHz** *abbr.* **kilohertz** kHz

**kibbutz** /kɪˈbʊts/ *n., pl.* **kibbutzim** /kɪbʊtˈsiːm/ Kibbuz, *der*

**kibitzer** /ˈkɪbɪtsə(r), kɪˈbɪtsə(r)/ *n.* (*coll.*) Kiebitz, *der* (*ugs.*); (*meddlesome person*) wichtigtuerischer Besserwisser

**kibosh** /ˈkaɪbɒʃ/ *n.* (*coll.*) **put the ~ on sth.** etw. vermasseln (*salopp*); **that's put the ~ on his hopes, hasn't it?** damit sind seine Hoffnungen wohl im Eimer, was? (*salopp*)

**kick** /kɪk/ ❶ *n.* Ⓐ [Fuß]tritt, *der;* (*Footb.*) Schuss, *der;* **give sb. a ~:** jmdm. einen Tritt geben *od.* versetzen; **give a ~ at sth., give sth. a ~:** gegen etw. treten; **give sb. a ~ in the pants** (*fig. coll.*) jmdm. Feuer unterm Hintern machen (*salopp*); **a ~ in the teeth** (*fig.*) ein Schlag ins Gesicht; **give sb. a ~ in the teeth** (*fig. coll.*) jmdn. vor den Kopf stoßen; Ⓑ (*Sport: burst of speed*) Spurt, *der;* Ⓒ (*coll.: sharp effect, thrill*) Kitzel, *der;* (*of wine*) Feuer, *das;* **give sb. a ~:** jmdm. Spaß machen; **this beer has plenty of ~ in it** dieses Bier hat es in sich (*Dat.*); **he gets a ~ out of it** er hat Spaß daran; es macht ihm Spaß; **do sth. for ~s** etw. zum Spaß tun; Ⓓ (*coll.: temporary interest*) Fimmel, *der* (*ugs. abwertend*); Tick, *der* (*ugs.*); **be on a** *or* **the fitness ~:** auf einem *od.* dem Fitnesstrip sein (*ugs.*); Ⓔ (*recoil of gun*) Rückstoß, *der.*
❷ *v.i.* Ⓐ treten; ‹Pferd:› ausschlagen; ‹Baby:› strampeln; ‹Tänzer:› das Bein hochwerfen; **~ at sth.** gegen etw. treten; **you have to ~ with your legs when doing the crawl** beim Kraulen musst du mit den Beinen schlagen; **~ing and screaming** (*fig.*) in heftigem *od.* wildem Protest; Ⓑ (*show opposition*) sich zur Wehr setzen (**at, against** gegen). ⇒ *also* **alive** D; **prick** 3 E; **trace**[2].
❸ *v.t.* Ⓐ einen Tritt geben (+ *Dat.*) ‹Person, Hund›; treten gegen ‹Gegenstand›; kicken (*ugs.*), schlagen, schießen ‹Ball›; **~ the door open/shut** die Tür auf-/zutreten; **he ~ed the ball straight at me** er kickte den Ball genau in meine Richtung; **~ sb. in the teeth** (*fig. coll.*) jmdn. vor den Kopf stoßen; **~ sb. upstairs** (*fig. coll.*) *jmdm. eine nach außen bessere Position geben, aber seinen Einflussbereich einschränken;* ≈ jmdn. fortloben; **I could ~ myself!** (*coll.*) ich könnte mir *od.* mich in den Hintern beißen (*salopp*); Ⓑ (*coll.: abandon*) ablegen ‹schlechte Angewohnheit›; aufgeben ‹Rauchen›; **~ the habit** es aufstecken (*ugs.*). ⇒ *also* **bucket1** A; **heel**[1] 1 A

**~ aˈbout**, **~ aˈround** ❶ *v.t.* Ⓐ [in der Gegend] herumkicken (*ugs.*); Ⓑ (*treat badly*) herumstoßen; schikanieren; Ⓒ (*coll.: discuss unsystematically*) bekakeln (*ugs.*); bequatschen (*salopp*). ❷ *v.i.* Ⓐ (*coll.: wander about*) rumziehen (*ugs.*); Ⓑ **be ~ing about** *or* **around** (*coll.: be present, alive*) rumhängen (*ugs.*); **old Thompson is still ~ing around** (*is still alive*) der alte Thompson machts immer noch (*ugs.*); Ⓒ **be ~ing about** *or* **around** (*coll.: lie scattered*) rumliegen (*ugs.*); rumfliegen (*salopp*); **is there a sandwich ~ing around?** gibts hier irgendwo 'n Sandwich? (*ugs.*)

**~ ˈback** ❶ *v.i.* Ⓐ (**~** *in retaliation*) zurücktreten; (*fig.*) zurückschlagen; Ⓑ (*recoil*) ‹Gewehr:› zurückschlagen. ❷ *v.t.* Ⓐ zurückschlagen ‹Ball›; mit dem Fuß zurückschlagen ‹Bettdecke›; Ⓑ (**~** *in retaliation*) wieder treten. ⇒ *also* **kickback**

**~ ˈin** *v.t.* (*break, damage*) eintreten

**~ ˈoff** ❶ *v.t.* von sich schleudern ‹Kleidungsstück, Schuhe›. ❷ *v.i.* (*Footb.*) anstoßen; ‹Spiel:› beginnen; (*fig. coll.: start*) anfangen; ⇒ *also* **kick-off**

**~ ˈout** *v.t.* (*force to leave*) hinauswerfen; rausschmeißen (*ugs.*); **get ~ed out** rausfliegen (*ugs.*); **get ~ed out of one's job** [aus der Stellung] fliegen (*ugs.*)

**~ ˈup** *v.t.* Ⓐ (*raise by ~ing*) [mit den Füßen] aufwirbeln ‹Sand, Staub›; ‹Autoreifen:› hochschleudern ‹Steine›; mit dem Fuß umschlagen ‹Teppich›; Ⓑ (*coll.: create*) **~ up a fuss/row** Krach schlagen/anfangen (*ugs.*); **~ up a stink** Rabatz machen (*ugs.*)

**kick: ~back** *n.* (*coll.: bribe*) Prozente (*fig. ugs.*); **~-down** *n.* (*Motor Veh.*) Kickdown, *der;* **~-off** *n.* Ⓐ (*Footb.*) Anstoß, *der;* (*fig.: start*) Beginn, *der;* **for a ~-off** (*coll.*) zunächst einmal; Ⓑ (*inaugural event*) Eröffnung, *die;* **~-start** ❶ *n.* Ⓐ Kickstarter, *der;* Ⓑ (*fig.*) [neuer] Auftrieb; ❷ *v.t.* Ⓐ [mit dem Kickstarter] starten; Ⓑ (*fig.*) ankurbeln ‹Industrie, Wirtschaft›; vorantreiben, forcieren ‹Friedensprozess, Entwicklung›; **~-start sb.'s career** jmds. Karriere einen [neuen] Schub geben; **~-starter** *n.* (*Motor Veh.*) Kickstarter, *der;* **~-turn** *n.* (*Skiing*) Spitzkehre, *die*

**kid** /kɪd/ ❶ *n.* Ⓐ (*young goat*) Kitz, *das;* Zickel, *das;* Ⓑ (*leather*) Ziegenleder, *das;* *attrib.* Ziegenleder-; Ⓒ (*coll.: child*) Kind, *das;* (*Amer. coll.: young person*) Jugendliche, *der/die;* Kid, *das* (*ugs.*); **these ~s are driving me mad today** diese Bälger machen mich heute verrückt (*ugs.*); **you're still only a ~:** du bist noch zu jung [dazu]; **OK, ~s, let's go** (*Amer.*) also gut, Leute, gehen wir (*ugs.*); **college ~** (*Amer.*) Student, *der*/Studentin, *die;* **what a great ~ she is!** (*Amer.*) sie ist wirklich schwer in Ordnung (*ugs.*); **it's ~[s'] stuff** (*coll.: easy*) das ist ein Kinderspiel; **I'm too old for that ~s' stuff** ich bin zu alt für diese Kindereien; **~ brother/sister** (*coll.*) kleiner Bruder/kleine Schwester; Brüderchen, *das*/Schwesterchen, *das.*
❷ *v.t.*, **-dd-** (*coll.*) (*hoax*) anführen (*ugs.*); auf den Arm nehmen (*ugs.*); (*deceive*) was vormachen (+ *Dat.*) (*ugs.*); (*tease*) aufziehen (*ugs.*); **I ~ you 'not** ehrlich!; **~ oneself** sich (*Dat.*) was vormachen (*ugs.*).
❸ *v.i.*, **-dd-** (*coll.*) **be ~ding** Spaß machen (*ugs.*); **you've got to be ~ding!** das ist doch nicht dein Ernst!; **no ~ding** [ganz] im Ernst *od.* ohne Scherz

**kiddie** /ˈkɪdɪ/ (*coll.*) Kindchen, *das;* **all right ~s, off to bed with you** okay, Kinder, ab ins Bett (*ugs.*); **I wish I had some ~s of my own** ich wünschte, ich hätte selbst kleine Kinder

**kid ˈglove** *n.* Glacéhandschuh, *der;* **handle** *or* **treat sb. with ~s** (*fig.*) jmdn. mit Samt- *od.* Glacéhandschuhen anfassen (*ugs.*)

**kid-ˈglove** *adj.* sanft; behutsam; **give sb. the ~ treatment** jmdn. mit Samt- *od.* Glacéhandschuhen anfassen (*ugs.*)

**kidnap** /ˈkɪdnæp/ *v.t.*, (*Brit.*) **-pp-** entführen ‹Person›; stehlen ‹Tier›; (*to obtain ransom*) kidnappen; entführen

**kidnapper** /ˈkɪdnæpə(r)/ *n.* Entführer, *der*/Entführerin, *die;* Kidnapper, *der*/Kidnapperin, *die*

**kidney** /ˈkɪdnɪ/ *n.* Ⓐ ▶ 966 (*Anat., Gastr.*) Niere, *die;* **steak and ~ pie/pudding** ⇒ **steak;** Ⓑ (*fig.: temperament*) [Menschen]schlag, *der;* **of the same/right** *etc.* **~:** vom gleichen/richtigen *usw.* Schlag

**kidney: ~ bean** *n.* Gartenbohne, *die;* (*scarlet runner bean*) Feuerbohne, *die;* **red ~ bean** Kidneybohne, *die;* **~ dish** *n.* Nierenschale, *die;* **~ failure** *n.* ▶ 1232 Nierenversagen, *das;* **~ machine** *n.* künstliche Niere; Dialysegerät, *das;* **~-shaped** *adj.* nierenförmig; **~ table** *n.* Nierentisch, *der;* **~-vetch** *n.* Gemeiner Wundklee; gelber Klee

**Kiel Canal** /kiːl kəˈnæl/ *pr. n.* Nord-Ostsee-Kanal, *der*

**Kilkenny cat** /kɪlkenɪ ˈkæt/ *n.* **fight like ~s** wie zwei Wildkatzen kämpfen; (*fig.*) sich bis zum letzten Blutstropfen bekämpfen

**kill** /kɪl/ ❶ *v.t.* A töten; (*deliberately*) umbringen; ‹Rauchen usw.:› tödliche Folgen haben für; sterben lassen ‹Romanfigur usw.›; **be ∼ed in action/war** im Kampf/Krieg fallen; **shoot to ∼:** gezielt schießen; **too much drink can ∼ you** zu viel Alkohol kann tödlich sein; **∼ or cure sb./sth.** jmdn./etw. entweder umbringen oder wieder auf die Beine bringen; **be ∼ed in a car crash** bei einem Autounfall umkommen *od.* ums Leben kommen; **grief/the shock almost ∼ed her** sie wäre vor Gram/Schreck fast gestorben; **it won't ∼ you** (*iron.*) es wird dich [schon] nicht *od.* nicht gleich umbringen; **that last stretch [nearly] ∼ed me!** das letzte Stück hat mich fast umgebracht; **∼ oneself** sich umbringen; **I'm ∼ing myself with this work** ich arbeite mich [dabei] zu Tode; **∼ oneself laughing** (*fig.*) sich totlachen; B (*coll.: cause severe pain to*) **it is ∼ing me** das bringt mich noch um; **my feet are ∼ing me** meine Füße tun wahnsinnig weh (*ugs.*); C abtöten ‹Krankheitserreger, Schmerz, Ungeziefer, Hefe›; erfolgreich bekämpfen ‹Krankheit›; absterben lassen ‹Bäume, Pflanzen›; totschlagen ‹Geschmack, Farbe›; verderben ‹Witz›; (*put an end to*) [ab]töten ‹Gefühl›; zerstören ‹Glauben›; **∼ sb.'s ambition** jmdn. resignieren lassen; jmds. Ehrgeiz erkalten lassen (*geh.*); D **∼ time** sich (*Dat.*) die Zeit vertreiben; die Zeit totschlagen (*abwertend*); **I've got such a lot of time to ∼ at the moment** ich habe zur Zeit so viel Leerlauf; **∼ an hour** sich (*Dat.*) eine Stunde lang die Zeit vertreiben; E (*obtain meat from*) schlachten ‹Tier›; **∼ meat** schlachten; F (*overwhelm*) überwältigen; **dress to ∼:** sich herausputzen; G (*switch off*) ausschalten; (*extinguish*) ausdrücken, (*ugs.*) töten ‹Zigarette›; H (*coll.*) (*eat*) verdrücken (*ugs.*); (*drink*) leer machen ‹Flasche›; I (*Footb.*) stoppen ‹Ball›; (*Tennis*) unretournierbar schlagen ‹Ball›; J (*defeat, veto*) zu Fall bringen; abschmettern (*ugs.*). ⇒ *also* **bird** A.
❷ *n.* A (*∼ing of game*) Abschuss, *der;* (*prey*) Beute, *die;* **the tiger has made a ∼/is on the ∼:** der Tiger hat eine Beute geschlagen/ist auf der Jagd; **move in for the ∼** ‹Raubtier:› die Beute anschleichen, zum Sprung auf die Beute ansetzen; (*fig.*) zum entscheidenden Schlag ausholen; **be in at the ∼ = be in at the death** ⇒ **death** A; B (*Hunting: amount*) Strecke, *die* (*Jägerspr.*); C (*destruction*) (*of aircraft*) Abschuss, *der;* (*of ship*) Versenkung, *die*

**∼ 'off** *v.t.* vernichten ‹Feinde, Konkurrenz›; ausrotten ‹Tierart›; abschlachten ‹Vieh›; sterben lassen ‹Romanfigur usw.›; vertilgen ‹Ungeziefer, Unkraut›; scheitern lassen ‹Projekt›; ‹Frost:› eingehen lassen ‹Pflanze›

**killer** /'kɪlə(r)/ *n.* Mörder, *der*/Mörderin, *die;* (*murderous ruffian*) Killer, *der* (*salopp*); **be a ∼** ‹Krankheit:› tödlich sein; *attrib.* **the ∼ instinct** der Instinkt zum Töten; der Killerinstinkt (*Sportjargon*); ⇒ *also* **humane killer**

**'killer whale** *n.* Mörderwal, *der*

**killing** /'kɪlɪŋ/ ❶ *n.* A Töten, *das;* Tötung, *die;* **the ∼ of the three children** der Mord an den drei Kindern; B (*instance*) Mord[fall], *der;* C (*fig. coll.: great success*) Coup, *der* (*ugs.*); **make a ∼** (*make a great profit*) einen [Mords]reibach machen (*ugs.*). ❷ *adj.* A tödlich; B (*coll.: exhausting*) mörderisch (*ugs.*); C (*coll.: attractive, amusing etc.*) umwerfend

**killingly** /'kɪlɪŋlɪ/ *adv.* **∼ funny** zum Totlachen [komisch] (*ugs.*)

**'killjoy** *n.* Spielverderber, *der*/-verderberin, *die*

**kiln** /kɪln/ *n.* (*for burning/drying*) [Brenn-/Trocken]ofen, *der;* (*hop-∼*) Darre, *die*

**'kiln-dry** *v.t.* [im Ofen] brennen ‹Keramik›; darren ‹Hopfen, Getreide usw.›

**kilo** /'ki:ləʊ/ *n., pl.* **∼s** ▶ **1683** Kilo, *das*

**kilo-** /'kɪlə/ *pref.* kilo-/Kilo-

**'kilobyte** *n.* (*Computing*) Kilobyte, *das*

**'kilocycle** *n.* (*frequency unit*) Kilohertz, *das*

**'kilogram, 'kilogramme** *n.* ▶ **1683** Kilogramm, *das*

**'kilohertz** *n.* (*Phys.*) Kilohertz, *das*

**kilometre** (*Brit.; Amer.:* **kilometer**) /'kɪləmi:tə(r) (*Brit.*), kɪ'lɒmɪtə(r)/ *n.* ▶ **1552** Kilometer, *der*

**'kilowatt** *n.* (*Electr., Phys.*) Kilowatt, *das*

**'kilowatt-hour** *n.* (*Electr., Phys.*) Kilowattstunde, *die*

**kilt** /kɪlt/ *n.* A (*Scot.*) Kilt, *der;* B (*women's garment*) Schottenrock, *der;* Kiltrock, *der*

**kilted** /'kɪltɪd/ *adj.* kiltbekleidet; kilttragend; **be ∼:** einen Kilt tragen

**kilter** /'kɪltə(r)/ *n.* (*Amer.*) **be out of ∼** (*out of order*) nicht in Ordnung sein; (*out of alignment*) schief sein

**kimono** /kɪ'məʊnəʊ/ *n., pl.* **∼s** Kimono, *der*

**kin** /kɪn/ ❶ *n.* (*ancestral stock*) Geschlecht, *das;* (*relatives*) Verwandte; (*relation*) Verwandte, *der/die;* ⇒ *also* **kith; next** 3 C. ❷ *pred. adj.* verwandt (**to** mit)

**kind**[1] /kaɪnd/ *n.* A (*class, sort*) Art, *die;* **several ∼s of apples** mehrere Sorten Äpfel; **all ∼s of things/excuses** alles Mögliche/alle möglichen Ausreden; **all ∼s of people enjoy that programme** das Programm gefällt den verschiedensten Leuten; **no ... of any ∼:** keinerlei ...; **good of its ∼:** auf seine Art ganz gut; **books of every ∼:** Bücher aller Art; **be [of] the same ∼:** von derselben Sorte *od.* Art sein; **I know [you and] your ∼:** deine Sorte kenne ich; **people/things of this ∼:** diese Art Leute/solche Dinge; **she's not the ∼ [of person] to talk scandal** es ist nicht ihre Art, zu tratschen; **something/nothing of the ∼:** so etwas Ähnliches/nichts dergleichen; **you'll do nothing of the ∼!** das kommt gar nicht in Frage!; **two of a ∼:** zwei Gleiche; **they differ** *or* **are different in ∼:** sie unterscheiden sich wesentlich; **I suppose it was art of a ∼** (*derog.*) das sollte wohl Kunst sein; **Was there any entertainment? — Well, of a ∼** (*derog.*) Gab es irgendwelche Unterhaltung? — Na ja, es sollte wohl so was sein; **what ∼ is it?** was für einer/eine/eins ist es?; **what ∼ of [a] tree is this?** was für ein Baum ist das?; **what ∼ of people are they?** was für Leute sind sie?; **what ∼ of thing are you going to wear?** was ziehst du an?; **what ∼ of [a] fool do you take me for?** für wie dumm hältst du mich?; **what ∼ of [a] person do you think I am?** für wen hältst du mich?; **the ∼ of person we need** der Typ, den wir brauchen; **this is exactly the ∼ of house we're looking for** genau so ein Haus suchen wir; **they are the ∼ of people who ...:** sie gehören zu der Sorte von Leuten, die ...; das sind solche Leute, die ...; **this ∼ of food/atmosphere** diese Art *od.* solches Essen/solch *od.* so eine Stimmung; **these ∼ of people/things** (*coll.*) solche Leute/Sachen; B (*implying vagueness*) **a ∼ of ...:** [so] eine Art ...; **∼ of interesting/cute** *etc.* (*coll.*) irgendwie interessant/niedlich *usw.* (*ugs.*); C (*race*) **the human ∼:** die Menschheit; das Menschengeschlecht; **one's own ∼:** seinesgleichen; D **in ∼** (*not in money*) in Sachwerten; **pay in ∼:** in Naturalien zahlen/bezahlen; **benefits in ∼:** Sachbezüge *Pl.;* **pay back** *or* **repay sth. in ∼** (*fig.*) etw. mit *od.* in gleicher Münze zurückzahlen

**kind**[2] *adj.* (*of gentle nature*) liebenswürdig; (*showing friendliness*) freundlich; (*affectionate*) lieb; **if the weather is ∼:** bei schönem Wetter; **have a ∼ heart** gutherzig sein; **would you be so ∼ as to** *or* **∼ enough to do that?** wären Sie so freundlich *od.* nett, das zu tun?; **be ∼ to animals/children** gut zu Tieren/Kindern sein; **oh, you 'are ∼!, that 'is ∼ of you** sehr nett *od.* liebenswürdig von Ihnen; **how ∼ !** wie nett [von ihm/ihr/Ihnen *usw.*]!

**kinda** /'kaɪndə/ (*coll.*) = **kind of; I ∼ like that** ich mag das irgendwie *od.* (*ugs.*) irgendwo; **that ∼ thing** so was (*ugs.*)

**kindergarten** /'kɪndəgɑ:tn/ *n.* Kindergarten, *der;* (*forming part of a school*) ≈ Vorklasse, *die*

**kind-hearted** /kaɪnd'hɑ:tɪd/ *adj.* gutherzig; liebenswürdig ‹Geste, Handlung›

**kindle** /'kɪndl/ ❶ *v.t.* A (*light*) anzünden, (*geh.*) entzünden ‹Holz, Feuer›; entfachen (*geh.*) ‹Flamme›; (*fig.: inflame*) entzünden, entfachen (*geh.*) ‹Zorn, Leidenschaft›; wecken ‹Interesse, Gefühl›; B (*make bright*) erglühen lassen (*geh.*). ❷ *v.i.* A (*catch fire*) sich entzünden; (*fig.: become animated*) aufleben; (*fig.: flare up*) aufflammen; entbrennen (*geh.*); B (*become bright*) ‹Augen:› aufflammen (*geh.*) (**with** vor + *Dat.*); ‹Licht:› aufscheinen (*geh.*); (*start to glow*) erglühen (*geh.*)

**kindliness** /'kaɪndlɪnɪs/ *n., no pl.* Freundlichkeit, *die;* (*gentleness of nature*) Liebenswürdigkeit, *die*

**kindling** /'kɪndlɪŋ/ *n., no pl., no indef. art.* (*for lighting fire*) Anmachholz, *das*

**kindly** /'kaɪndlɪ/ ❶ *adv.* A freundlich; nett; **..., she said ∼:** ..., sagte sie freundlich; B *in polite request etc.* freundlicherweise; C **take sth. ∼:** etw. gern annehmen; **take ∼ to sth./sb.** sich mit etw./jmdm. schnell anfreunden; **he didn't take at all ∼ to the suggestion** er konnte sich mit dem Vorschlag gar nicht recht anfreunden; **I wouldn't take ∼ to anything like that** für dergleichen könnte ich mich kaum erwärmen; D **thank sb. ∼:** jmdm. herzlich danken; **thank you ∼:** herzlichen Dank.
❷ *adj.* A freundlich; nett; liebenswürdig; (*good-natured, kind-hearted*) gütig; wohlwollend; gut ‹Herz, Tat›; B (*pleasant*) angenehm ‹Wetter, Klima›; (*favourable*) günstig; gut

**kindness** /'kaɪndnɪs/ *n.* A *no pl.* (*kind nature*) Freundlichkeit, *die;* Liebenswürdigkeit, *die;* **do sth. out of ∼:** etw. aus Gefälligkeit tun; **out of the ∼ of one's heart** aus reiner Freundlichkeit; B (*kind act*) Gefälligkeit, *die;* **do sb. a ∼:** jmdm. eine Gefälligkeit erweisen *od.* einen Gefallen tun

**kindred** /'kɪndrɪd/ ❶ *n., no pl.* A (*blood relationship*) Blutsverwandtschaft, *die;* B (*one's relatives*) Verwandtschaft, *die;* Verwandte.
❷ *adj.* A (*related by blood*) blutsverwandt; B (*fig.*) (*connected*) verwandt; (*similar*) ähnlich

**kindred 'spirit** *n.* Gleichgesinnte, *der/die;* verwandte Seele (*geh.*)

**kinetic** /kɪ'netɪk, kaɪ'netɪk/ *adj.* kinetisch

**king** /kɪŋ/ *n.* A ▶ **1617** König, *der;* **live like a ∼:** leben wie ein Fürst; **a feast fit for a ∼:** ein königliches Mahl; **[the First/Second Book of] K∼s** (*Bibl.*) [das erste/zweite Buch der] Könige; **K∼ of ∼s** (*God*) König aller Könige; **K∼ of the Castle** *ein Kinderspiel, bei dem man versucht, den Gegner von einem Hügel zu verdrängen;* **be the ∼ of the castle** (*fig.*) das Sagen haben; **∼ of beasts/birds** König der Tiere/Vögel; B (*great merchant, player, etc.*) König, *der;* **oil ∼:** Ölkönig, *der;* Ölmagnat, *der;* C (*Chess, Cards*) König, *der;* (*Draughts*) Dame, *die;* **∼'s bishop/knight/pawn/rook** Königsläufer/-springer/-bauer/-turm, *der;* **∼ of hearts** Herzkönig, *der.* ⇒ *also* **bench** H; **colour** 1 J; **counsel** 1 C; **English** 2 A; **evidence** 1 B; **guide** 1 E; **highway** A; **messenger** B; **ransom** 1; **save** 1 C; **scout**[1] 1 A; **shilling**

**king: ∼ 'cobra** *n.* Königskobra, *die;* **∼ crab** *n.* A Königskrabbe, *die;* B (*Amer.: edible spider crab*) Steinkrabbe, *die;* **∼cup** *n.* (*Bot.*) A (*buttercup*) Hahnenfuß, der; B (*Brit.: marsh marigold*) Sumpfdotterblume, *die*

**kingdom** /'kɪŋdəm/ *n.* A Königreich, *das;* **the ∼ of Naples** das Königreich Neapel; ⇒ *also* **United Kingdom**; B (*reign of God, sphere of reign*) Reich, *das;* **the ∼ of God** das Reich Gottes; **thy ∼ come** dein Reich komme; **the ∼ of heaven** das Himmelreich; **wait till ∼ come** (*coll.*) bis in alle Ewigkeit warten (*ugs.*); **blast sb. to ∼ come** (*coll.*) jmdn. umnieten (*salopp*); C (*domain*) Welt, *die;* **the ∼ of thought** das Reich der Gedanken; D (*province of nature*) Reich, *das;* **animal/vegetable/mineral ∼:** Tier-/Pflanzen-/Mineralreich, *das;* **∼ of nature** Naturreich, *das*

**king: ∼fisher** *n.* (*Ornith.*) Eisvogel, *der;* **K∼ 'James['s] Bible** *or* **Version = Authorized Version;** ⇒ **authorize** B

**kingly** /ˈkɪŋlɪ/ *adj.* königlich

**king: ~maker** *n.* Königsmacher, *der;* **~ ˈpenguin** *n.* Königspinguin, *der;* **~pin** *n.* (*lit., or fig.: essential person or thing*) Hauptstütze, *die;* (*most prominent person or organization*) Nummer eins; **he's the ~pin in the team** mit ihm steht und fällt die Mannschaft

**kingship** /ˈkɪŋʃɪp/ *n.* Ⓐ *no pl., no art.* (*office of king*) Königsamt, *das;* Ⓑ (*rule of king*) Königtum, *das*

**ˈking-size[d]** *adj.* extragroß; Kingsize-‹Zigaretten›

**kink** /kɪŋk/ ❶ *n.* Ⓐ (*in pipe, wire, etc.*) Knick, *der;* (*in rope*) Kink, *der* (*Seemannsspr.*); (*in hair, wool*) Welle, *die;* Ⓑ (*fig.: mental peculiarity*) Tick, *der* (*ugs.*); Spleen, *der.* ❷ *v.i.* Knicke kriegen; ‹Haar:› sich wellen. ❸ *v.t.* knicken; Knicke machen in (+ *Akk.*); einen Kink machen in (+ *Akk.*) (*Seemannsspr.*)

**kinkajou** /ˈkɪŋkədʒuː/ *n.* (*Zool.*) Kinkaju, *der;* Wickelbär, *der*

**kinky** /ˈkɪŋkɪ/ *adj.* Ⓐ geknickt; wellig ‹Haar›; Ⓑ (*coll.: bizarre, perverted*) spleenig; (*sexually*) abartig

**kinsfolk** /ˈkɪnzfəʊk/ *n. pl.* Verwandtschaft, *die;* Verwandte

**kinship** /ˈkɪnʃɪp/ *n.* Ⓐ (*blood relationship*) Blutsverwandtschaft, *die;* Ⓑ (*similarity*) Ähnlichkeit, *die;* (*spiritual*) Verwandtschaft, *die*

**kinsman** /ˈkɪnzmən/ *n., pl.* **kinsmen** /ˈkɪnzmən/ Verwandte, *der*

**kinswoman** /ˈkɪnzwʊmn/ *n.* Verwandte, *die*

**kiosk** /ˈkiːɒsk/ *n.* Ⓐ (*outdoor structure*) Kiosk, *der;* (*Brit.: indoor structure*) [Verkaufs]stand, *der;* Ⓑ (*public telephone booth*) [Telefon]zelle, *die*

**kip** /kɪp/ (*Brit. coll.*) ❶ *n.* Ⓐ (*sleep*) Schlaf, *der;* **have a** *or* **get some ~:** eine Runde pennen (*salopp*); Ⓑ (*bed*) Falle, *die* (*salopp*). ❷ *v.i.,* **-pp-** pennen (*salopp*); **~ down** sich hinhauen (*salopp*)

**kipper** /ˈkɪpə(r)/ ❶ *n.* Kipper, *der;* ≈ Bückling, *der.* ❷ *v.t.* räuchern ‹Fisch›; **~ed** Räucher‹fisch, -lachs, -hering›

**kirk** /kɜːk/ *n.* (*Brit.*) Ⓐ (*Scot., N. Engl.: church*) Kirche, *die;* Ⓑ **the K~ [of Scotland]** die Kirche von Schottland

**kirsch[wasser]** /ˈkɪəʃ(vɑsə(r))/ *n.* Kirsch, *der;* Kirschwasser, *das*

**kiss** /kɪs/ ❶ *n.* Kuss, *der;* **the ~ of death** (*apparently friendly act causing ruin*) ein Danaergeschenk; (*act putting an end to sth.*) der Todesstoß; **give sb./** (*fig.*) **sth. the ~ of life** (*Brit.*) jmdn. von Mund zu Mund beatmen/versuchen, etw. wieder zu beleben; **by administering the ~ of life** durch Mund-zu-Mund-Beatmung; **the ~ of peace** der Friedenskuss; ⇨ *also* **blow¹** 2 B.
❷ *v.t.* küssen; **~ sb. good night/goodbye** jmdm. einen Gutenacht-/Abschiedskuss geben; **it hurts, mummy — ~ it better** (*child lang.*) es tut weh, Mami — puste mal; **~ sb.'s hand** jmdm. einen Handkuss geben.
❸ *v.i.* sich küssen; **~ and make up** sich mit einem Kuss versöhnen

**~ aˈway** *v.t.* wegküssen; **~ away sb.'s tears** jmdm. die Tränen wegküssen

**kissable** /ˈkɪsəbl/ *adj.* **~ lips/mouth** Kussmund, *der*

**kisser** /ˈkɪsə(r)/ *n.* (*sl.: mouth, face*) Fresse, *die* (*derb*); Schnauze, *die* (*derb*)

**kissing** /ˈkɪsɪŋ/ ❶ *adj.* Kuss-. ❷ *n.* Küsserei, *die* (*ugs.*); Geküsse, *das* (*oft abwertend*)

**kissogram** /ˈkɪsəgræm/ *n. Glückwunsch o. Ä., der mit Küssen überbracht wird*

**ˈkiss-proof** *adj.* kussecht

**kit** /kɪt/ ❶ *n.* Ⓐ (*personal equipment*) Sachen; **have you got all your ~ together?** hast du deine Siebensachen beisammen? (*ugs.*); Ⓑ (*Brit.: set of items*) Set, *das;* **construction/self-assembly ~:** Bausatz, *der;* **repair ~:** Reparatursatz, *der;* Reparaturset, *das;* ⇨ *also* **tool kit**; Ⓒ (*Brit.: clothing etc.*) **sports ~:** Sportzeug, *das;* Sportsachen *Pl.;* **riding/skiing/shooting ~:** Reit-/Ski-/Jagdausrüstung, *die;* Ⓓ (*Brit. Mil.*) Ausrüstung, *die;* (*pack*) [Feld]gepäck, *das;* (*uniform*) Montur, *die.*
❷ *v.t.,* **-tt-** (*Brit.*) **~ out** *or* **up** (*equip*) ausrüsten; (*give clothes or uniforms to*) einkleiden

**ˈkitbag** *n.* (*knapsack*) Knappsack, *der* (*veralt.*); Tornister, *der;* (*travelling bag*) Reisetasche, *die*

**kitchen** /ˈkɪtʃɪn/ *n.* Küche, *die; attrib.* Küchen-; ⇨ *also* **soup kitchen**

**kitchenette** /kɪtʃɪˈnet/ *n.* kleine Küche; Kitchenette, *die;* (*alcove*) Kochnische, *die*

**kitchen: ~ ˈgarden** *n.* Küchengarten, *der;* Nutzgarten, *der;* **~ maid** *n.* Küchenmädchen, *das;* Küchenhilfe, *die;* **~ paper** *n.* Küchenkrepp, *der;* Küchentücher *Pl.;* **~ police** *n. pl.* (*Amer. Mil.*) Küchendienst, *der;* **~ roll** *n.* Küchenrolle, *die;* (*kitchen paper*) Küchenkrepp, *der;* **~ ˈsink** *n.* [Küchen]ausguss, *der;* Spüle, *die;* **everything but the ~ sink** (*fig.*) der halbe Hausrat; *attrib.* (*Brit.*) ≈ neonaturalistisch ‹Drama, Kunst usw.›; **~ unit** *n.* Küchenelement, *das;* **~ units** Küchenmöbel; **~ utensil** *n.* Küchengerät, *das;* **~ware** *n., no pl.* Küchengeräte *Pl.*

**kite** /kaɪt/ *n.* Ⓐ (*toy*) Drachen, *der;* Ⓑ (*Ornith.*) habichtartiger Greifvogel; (*species*) Roter Milan; Gabelweihe, *die;* Ⓒ (*Brit. coll. dated: aeroplane*) Vogel, *der;* Kiste, *die* (*salopp*). ⇨ *also* **fly²** 2 B

**kith** /kɪθ/ *n.* **~ and kin** Freunde und Verwandte

**kitsch** /kɪtʃ/ *n.* Kitsch, *der;* **it's a piece of ~:** es ist Kitsch

**kitschy** /ˈkɪtʃɪ/ *adj.* kitschig

**kitten** /ˈkɪtn/ *n.* Ⓐ [Katzen]junge, *das;* Kätzchen, *das;* **the cat has had ~s** die Katze hat Junge bekommen; **as weak as a ~:** schwach und matt; **be as nervous as a ~:** furchtbar ängstlich sein; (*be easily startled*) vor dem eigenen Schatten erschrecken; Ⓑ (*coll.*) **have ~s** (*be upset*) Zustände kriegen (*ugs.*); **be having ~s** (*be nervous*) am Rotieren sein (*ugs.*)

**kittenish** /ˈkɪtənɪʃ/ *adj.* verspielt; kokett ‹junges Mädchen›

**kittiwake** /ˈkɪtɪweɪk/ *n.* (*Ornith.*) Dreizehenmöwe, *die*

**kitty¹** /ˈkɪtɪ/ *n.* (*kitten*) Kätzchen, *das;* (*child lang.*) Miez[e], *die* (*fam.*); Miezekätzchen, *das* (*fam.*); **~, ~, ~!** Miez, Miez, Miez!

**kitty²** *n.* Ⓐ (*Cards*) [Spiel]kasse, *die;* Ⓑ (*joint fund*) Kasse, *die;* **raid the ~:** die Kasse plündern (*scherzh.*)

**kiwi** /ˈkiːwiː/ *n.* Ⓐ (*Ornith.*) Kiwi, *der;* Ⓑ **K~** (*coll.: New Zealander*) Neuseeländer, *der*/Neuseeländerin, *die*

**kiwi: ~ berry, ~ fruit** *ns.* Kiwi[frucht], *die*

**klaxon** ® /ˈklæksn/ *n.* Horn, *das*

**Kleenex** ® /ˈkliːneks/ *n.* Papier[taschen]tuch, *das*

**kleptomania** /kleptəˈmeɪnɪə/ *n., no pl.* (*Psych.*) Kleptomanie, *die*

**kleptomaniac** /kleptəˈmeɪnɪæk/ *n.* Kleptomane, *der*/Kleptomanin, *die*

**km.** *abbr.* **kilometre[s]** km

**knack** /næk/ *n.* Ⓐ (*faculty*) Talent, *das;* **have a ~ for** *or* **of doing sth.** das Talent haben, etw. zu tun; **get the ~ [of doing sth.]** den Bogen rauskriegen[, wie man etw. macht] (*ugs.*); **there's a [real] ~ in doing sth.** es gehört schon [einiges] Geschick dazu, etw. zu tun; **have lost the ~:** es nicht mehr zustande bringen *od.* (*ugs.*) hinkriegen; Ⓑ (*habit*) **have a ~ of doing sth.** es [mit seltenem Talent] verstehen, etw. zu tun (*iron.*)

**knacker** /ˈnækə(r)/ *n.* (*Brit.*) (*horse slaughterer*) Abdecker, *der;* **~'s yard** Abdeckerei, *die*

**knackered** /ˈnækəd/ *adj.* (*Brit. coll.*) geschlaucht (*ugs.*)

**knapsack** /ˈnæpsæk/ *n.* Rucksack, *der;* (*Mil.*) Tornister, *der*

**knave** /neɪv/ *n.* Ⓐ (*rogue*) Schurke, *der;* Ⓑ (*Cards*) ⇨ **jack** 1 A

**knavery** /ˈneɪvərɪ/ *n.* Schurkerei, *die*

**knavish** /ˈneɪvɪʃ/ *adj.* schurkisch

**knead** /niːd/ *v.t.* Ⓐ kneten; **~ sth. with sth.** etw. mit etw. verkneten; **~ together** miteinander verkneten; Ⓑ (*manipulate*) kneten ‹Muskeln›

**knee** /niː/ *n.* Ⓐ ▶ **966** Knie, *das;* **the ~s of his trousers were torn** seine Hose war an den Knien zerrissen; **bend** *or* **bow the ~:** das Knie beugen (**to** vor + *Dat.*); (*fig.: behave humbly*) sich beugen (**to** *Dat.*); **on one's ~s/on bended ~[s]** auf Knien; **be on one's ~s** knien; (*fig.: be defeated*) in die Knie gezwungen sein (*geh.*); **bring** *or* **force sb. to his ~s** (*fig.*) jmdn. in die Knie zwingen (*geh.*); **go down on one's ~s [to** *or* **before sb.]** [vor jmdm.] auf die Knie sinken (*geh.*); Ⓑ (*of animal*) Kniegelenk, *das;* Ⓒ (*thigh*) **hold a child** *etc.* **on one's ~:** ein Kind *usw.* auf den Knien *od.* auf dem Schoß haben; **put a child** *etc.* **over one's ~:** ein Kind *usw.* übers Knie legen (*ugs.*)

**knee: ~ breeches** *n. pl.* Kniebundhose, *die;* **~cap** *n.* Ⓐ (*Anat.*) Kniescheibe, *die;* Ⓑ (*protective covering*) Knieschoner, *der;* **~capping** *n.* Knieschuss, *der;* **~-deep** *adj.* Ⓐ knietief; Ⓑ (*fig.: deeply involved*) **be ~-deep in sth.** bis über den Hals in etw. (*Dat.*) stecken (*ugs.*); **~-high** *adj.* kniehoch; **be ~-high to a grasshopper** (*coll.*) ein Dreikäsehoch sein (*ugs. scherzh.*); **~-jerk** *n.* Kniesehnenreflex, *der; attrib.* **~-jerk reaction** (*fig.*) automatische Reaktion; **~ joint** *n.* Kniegelenk, *das*

**kneel** /niːl/ *v.i.,* **knelt** /nelt/ *or* (*esp. Amer.*) **~ed** knien; **~ down** niederknien; **~ [down] to do sth.** niederknien *od.* sich [hin]knien, um etw. zu tun; **~ to sb.** vor jmdm. [nieder]knien

**ˈknee-length** *adj.* knielang

**kneeler** /ˈniːlə(r)/ ⇨ **hassock** A

**knees-up** /ˈniːzʌp/ *n.* (*coll.*) Schwof, *der* (*ugs.*)

**knell** /nel/ *n.* Glockengeläut, *das;* (*at funeral*) Totengeläut, *das;* **ring** *or* **sound the ~ of sth.** (*fig.*) das Ende einer Sache (*Gen.*) einläuten

**knelt** ⇨ **kneel**

**knew** ⇨ **know** 1

**knickerbockers** /ˈnɪkəbɒkəz/ *n. pl.* Knickerbocker *Pl.*

**knickers** /ˈnɪkəz/ ❶ *n. pl.* Ⓐ (*Brit.: undergarment*) [Damen]schlüpfer, *der;* **get one's ~ in a twist** (*Brit. fig. coll.*) sich aufregen; Ⓑ (*Amer.*) ⇨ **knickerbockers.** ❷ *int.* (*Brit. coll.*) was solls (*ugs.*)

**knick-knack** /ˈnɪknæk/ *n.* Ⓐ (*dainty thing*) **~s** Schnickschnack, *der* (*ugs.*); Ⓑ (*ornament*) Nippfigur, *die*

**knife** /naɪf/ ❶ *n., pl.* **knives** /naɪvz/ Messer, *das;* **put a ~ into sb.** jmdm. ein Messer zwischen die Rippen jagen; **like a ~ through butter** mühelos; **have got one's ~ into sb.** (*fig.*) einen Hass auf jmdn. haben (*ugs.*); **you could [have] cut the atmosphere** (*fig.*)/**air with a ~** (*coll.*) die Atmosphäre war zum Zerreißen gespannt/die Luft war zum Schneiden; **before you can say ~** (*coll.*) ehe man sichs versieht; **turn** *or* **twist the ~ [in the wound]** (*fig.*) Salz in die Wunde streuen; **the knives are out [for sb.]** (*fig.*) das Messer wird [für jmdn.] gewetzt; ⇨ *also* **fork** 1 A.
❷ *v.t.* (*stab*) einstechen auf (+ *Akk.*); (*kill*) erstechen; **~ sb. in the chest** jmdm. ein/das Messer in die Brust stoßen

**knife: ~-edge** *n.* Schneide, *die;* **be [balanced] on a ~-edge** (*fig.*) auf des Messers Schneide stehen; **~ grinder** *n.* Messerschleifer, *der;* **~ pleat** *n.* (*Dressm.*) Plisseefalte, *die;* **~point** ⇨ **point** 1 B; **~ sharpener** *n.* Messerschärfer, *der;* (*steel*) Wetzstahl, *der;* **~-throwing** *n., no pl., no indef. art.* Messerwerfen, *das*

**knifing** /ˈnaɪfɪŋ/ *n.* **there were three ~s on one day** an einem Tag wurden drei Menschen niedergestochen

**knight** /naɪt/ ❶ *n.* Ⓐ *Träger des Titels „Sir“;* Ⓑ (*Hist.*) Ritter, *der;* **~ in shining armour** (*fig.*) Märchenprinz, *der;* Ⓒ

(*Chess*) Springer, *der;* **D** ~ **of the road** (*lorry driver*) Kapitän der Landstraße (*ugs.*). ⇒ *also* **bachelor** C; **Templar**. ❷ *v.t.* adeln; zum Ritter schlagen (*hist.*); in den Ritterstand erheben (*hist.*)

**knight:** ~ **'errant** *n.* (*lit. or fig.*) fahrender Ritter; (*fig.*) Don Quichotte, *der;* ~**-'errantry** /naɪt'erəntrɪ/ *n.*, *no pl.* ≈ höfisches Rittertum; (*fig.: quixotic behaviour*) Donquichotterie, *die*

**knighthood** /'naɪthʊd/ *n.* **A** (*rank*) Ritterwürde, *die;* **receive one's** ~: geadelt werden; in den Ritterstand erhoben werden (*hist.*); **B** (*Hist.: vocation*) Rittertum, *das;* **C** (*Hist.: body of knights*) Ritterschaft, *die*

**knightly** /'naɪtlɪ/ *adj.* ritterlich

**knit** /nɪt/ ❶ *v.t.*, **-tt-**, **knitted** *or* (*esp. fig.*) **knit** **A** stricken ‹Kleidungsstück usw.›; **B** ~ **a stitch** eine [rechte] Masche stricken; ~ **2, purl 2** zwei rechts, zwei links [stricken]; **C** ~ **one's brow** die Stirn runzeln; **D** (*make compact*) zusammenfügen (**into** zu); **closely** *or* **tightly** ~ (*fig.*) festgefügt; hieb- und stichfest ‹Argument›; ⇒ *also* **well-knit**. ❷ *v.i.* sich verbinden; ‹Teile:› zusammenhalten; ‹Knochenbruch:› verheilen; ‹Knochen:› zusammenwachsen. ❸ *n.* (*garment*) Strickware, *die;* **this pattern is for a heavy** ~: dieses Muster eignet sich für Grobgestricktes

~ **to'gether** ❶ *v.t.* zusammenhalten ‹Familie, Gemeinschaft›. ❷ *v.i.* ‹Knochen:› zusammenwachsen; ‹Knochenbruch:› zusammenheilen

**knitter** /'nɪtə(r)/ *n.* Stricker, *der*/Strickerin, *die*

**knitting** /'nɪtɪŋ/ *n.*, *no pl.*, *no indef. art.* Stricken, *das;* (*work in process of being knitted*) Strickarbeit, *die;* **do one's/some** ~: stricken; **carry on with one's** ~: weiterstricken

**knitting:** ~ **machine** *n.* Strickmaschine, *die;* ~ **needle** *n.* Stricknadel, *die;* ~ **pattern** *n.* Strickmuster, *das*

**'knitwear** *n.*, *no pl.*, *no indef. art.* Strickwaren *Pl.*

**knives** *pl. of* **knife** 1

**knob** /nɒb/ *n.* **A** (*protuberance*) Verdickung, *die;* (*on club, tree trunk, etc.*) Knoten, *der;* **B** (*on door, walking stick, etc.*) Knauf, *der;* (*control on radio etc.*) Knopf, *der;* **the same to you with [brass]** ~**s on!** (*coll.*) danke gleichfalls! (*iron.*); **C** (*of butter, sugar*) Klümpchen, *das;* (*of coal*) Brocken, *der*

**knobbly** /'nɒblɪ/ *adj.* knotig ‹Finger, Stock›; knorrig ‹Baum›; ~ **knees competition** Knubbelkniewettbewerb, *der*

**knock** /nɒk/ ❶ *v.t.* **A** (*strike*) (*lightly*) klopfen gegen *od.* an (+ *Akk.*); (*forcefully*) schlagen gegen *od.* an (+ *Akk.*); ⇒ *also* **wood** B; **B** (*make by striking*) schlagen; ~ **two rooms/houses into one** zwei Zimmer/Häuser zu einem umbauen; ~ **a hole in sth.** ein Loch in etw. (*Akk.*) schlagen; **C** (*drive by striking*) schlagen; ~ **sb.'s brains out** jmdm. den Schädel einschlagen; **I'll** ~ **those ideas out of your head** (*fig.*) diese Flausen werde ich dir austreiben (*ugs.*); ~ **the handle off a cup** von einer Tasse den Henkel abschlagen; **I'd like to** ~ **their heads together** (*lit.*) ich könnte ihre Köpfe gegeneinander schlagen; (*fig.: reprove them*) ich möchte ihnen mal gehörig die Leviten lesen; ~ **sb. into the middle of next week** (*coll.*) jmdm. ein Ding verpassen, dass ihm Hören und Sehen vergeht (*ugs.*); ~ **for six** = **hit for six** ⇒ **hit** 1 K; ⇒ *also* **bottom** 1 A; **cock**[1] 2 C; **spot** 1 D; **D** ~ **sb. cold** jmdn. bewusstlos schlagen; (*fig.*) jmdn. am Boden zerstören; ~ **sb. on the head** jmdm. eins über *od.* auf den Schädel geben; ~ **sth. on the head** (*fig.: put an end to*) einer Sache (*Dat.*) ein Ende setzen; **E** (*coll.: criticize*) herziehen über (+ *Akk.*) (*ugs.*); **don't** ~ **it** halt dich zurück; **F** (*Brit. coll.: astonish*) umhauen (*salopp*).
❷ *v.i.* **A** (*strike*) (*lightly*) klopfen; (*forcefully*) schlagen; ⇒ *also* **wood** B; **B** (*seek admittance*) klopfen (**at** an + *Akk.*); **C** (*Mech. Engin.*) klappern; **D** (*Motor Veh.*) klopfen.
❸ *n.* **A** (*rap*) Klopfen, *das;* **there was a** ~ **on** *or* **at the door** es klopfte an der Tür; **give sb. a** ~: bei jmdm. klopfen; **B** (*blow*) Schlag, *der;* (*gentler*) Stoß, *der;* **have had a** ~: einen Schlag/Stoß abbekommen haben; **he got a bad** ~ **when he fell** er schlug beim Fallen hart auf; ~ **for** ~ **agreement** (*Insurance*) gegenseitige Regressverzichtserklärung; **C** (*fig.: blow of misfortune*) [Schicksals]schlag, *der;* **take a [bad** *or* **hard]** ~: einen [schweren *od.* harten] Schlag erleiden; **D** (*Mech. Engin.*) Klappern, *das;* **make a** ~: klappern; **E** (*Motor Veh.: high-pitched explosive sound*) Klopfen, *das*

~ **a'bout** ❶ *v.t.* **A** schlagen; verprügeln; **be** ~**ed about** Schläge *od.* Prügel einstecken müssen; **the building has been** ~**ed about** das Haus ist ziemlich ramponiert worden; **B** ~ **about the world** in der Welt herumkommen. ❷ *v.i.* herumhängen (*ugs.*); ‹Gegenstand:› herumfliegen (*ugs.*); **he's** ~**ed about a bit** er hat sich in der Welt umgetan; ~ **about with sb.** sich mit jmdm. herumtreiben (*ugs.*). ⇒ *also* **knockabout**

~ **against** *v.t.* stoßen gegen; ~ **against each other** gegeneinander stoßen; gegeneinander prallen

~ **a'round** ⇒ ~ **about**

~ **'back** *v.t.* (*coll.*) **A** (*eat quickly*) verputzen (*ugs.*); (*drink quickly*) hinunterkippen (*ugs.*); **B** (*cost*) ~ **sb. back a thousand** jmdn. um einen Tausender ärmer machen; **C** (*disconcert*) einen Schlag versetzen (+ *Dat.*)

~ **'down** *v.t.* **A** (*strike to the ground*) niederreißen, umstürzen ‹Zaun, Hindernis›; (*with fist or weapon*) niederschlagen; (*with car etc.*) umfahren; **B** (*demolish*) abreißen; abbrechen; **C** (*fig.: defeat*) bezwingen; **D** (*sell by auction*) zuschlagen; ~ **sth. down to sb.** jmdm. etw. zuschlagen; **E** (*coll.: lower*) heruntersetzen (*ugs.*) ‹Preis›; herunterdrücken (*ugs.*) ‹Kosten›; **F** (*Amer. coll.: steal*) mitgehen lassen (*ugs.*); klauen (*salopp*). ⇒ *also* **feather** 1 A; **knock-down**

~ **'off** ❶ *v.t.* **A** (*leave off*) aufhören mit; ~ **off painting** zu malen *od.* mit dem Malen aufhören; ~ **off work** Feierabend machen; ~ **it off!** (*coll.*) hör auf [damit]!; **B** (*coll.*) (*produce rapidly*) aus dem Ärmel schütteln (*ugs.*); (*dispatch rapidly*) schnell erledigen; **C** (*deduct*) ~ **five pounds off the price** es fünf Pfund billiger machen; **how much will you** ~ **off for me?** wie viel billiger kriege ich es denn?; **D** (*coll.*) (*steal*) mitgehen lassen (*ugs.*); klauen (*salopp*); (*rob*) ausräumen ‹Bank, Laden, Kasse›; **E** (*sl.: copulate with*) bumsen (*salopp*); **F** (*sl.: kill*) umlegen (*salopp*). ❷ *v.i.* Feierabend machen; ~ **off for an hour/for lunch** eine Stunde aussetzen/Mittag machen

~ **'on** *v.t.* (*Rugby*) ~ **on a pass** bei der Annahme eines Passes ein Vorfallen verursachen; ⇒ *also* **knock-on** 1

~ **'out** *v.t.* **A** (*make unconscious*) bewusstlos umfallen lassen; **he collided with a lamp post and** ~**ed himself out** er stieß mit einem Laternenpfahl zusammen und fiel bewusstlos um; **B** (*Boxing*) k.o. schlagen; kampfunfähig schlagen; **C** (*fig.: defeat*) **be** ~**ed out [of the Cup]** [aus dem Pokal] ausscheiden *od.* (*ugs.*) rausfliegen; **they** ~**ed us out of the Cup** sie warfen uns aus dem Pokal; **D** (*make useless*) außer Funktion setzen; **E** (*coll.: astonish*) umhauen (*salopp*); **be [completely** *or* **totally]** ~**ed out** [völlig] fertig sein (*ugs.*); **F** (*coll.: exhaust*) kaputtmachen (*ugs.*); **G** (*coll.: produce rapidly*) aus dem Ärmel schütteln; **H** (*empty*) ausklopfen ‹Pfeife›; ~ **the ashes out** die Asche herausklopfen. ⇒ *also* **knockout**

~ **'over** *v.t.* umstoßen; ‹Fahrer, Fahrzeug:› umfahren ‹Person›

~ **to'gether** ❶ *v.t.* zusammenzimmern (*ugs.*) ‹Hütte, Tisch, Bühne›; ⇒ *also* **knock** 1 C. ❷ *v.i.* **my knees were** ~**ing together** mir schlotterten die Knie

~ **'up** ❶ *v.t.* **A** (*make hastily*) zusammenzimmern (*ugs.*) ‹Hütte, Schrank›; [her]zaubern ‹Mahlzeit, Imbiss›; grob skizzieren ‹Plan›; **B** (*score*) erzielen; **C** (*Brit.: awaken*) durch Klopfen wecken; (*unexpectedly*) herausklopfen; **D** (*exhaust*) fertig machen (*ugs.*); **be** ~**ed up** fertig *od.* groggy sein (*ugs.*); **E** (*sl.: make pregnant*) dick machen (*derb*). ❷ *v.i.* (*Sport*) sich warm spielen; ⇒ *also* **knock-up**

**knock:** ~**about** *adj.* **A** (*boisterous*) Klamauk‹film, -stück, -szene›; burlesk ‹Komödie, Komik›; wild ‹Spiel›; **B** (*for rough use*) strapazierfähig; ~**-down** *adj.* **A** (*low*) ~**-down cost/prices** minimale Kosten/Schleuderpreise; **B** (*minimum*) Mindest‹preis, -gebot›; **C** (*easily disassembled*) zerlegbar ‹Möbelstück, Boot›; **D** niederschmetternd ‹Schlag, Hieb›; (*fig.: conclusive*) hieb- und stichfest, schlagend ‹Argument›

**knocker** /'nɒkə(r)/ *n.* **A** (*on door*) [Tür]klopfer, *der;* **B** *in pl.* (*coarse: breasts*) **[pair of]** ~**s** Vorbau, *der* (*salopp scherzh.*); Titten (*derb*); **C** (*coll.: critic*) Beckmesser, *der*

**knocking-'off time** *n.* (*coll.*) Feierabend, *der*

**'knocking shop** *n.* (*Brit. sl.*) Puff, *der od. das* (*salopp*)

**knock:** ~**-kneed** /'nɒkni:d/ *adj.* x-beinig ‹Person usw.›; kuhhessig ‹Pferd›; ~ **'knees** *n. pl.* X-Beine *Pl.;* ~**-on** ❶ *n.* (*Rugby*) Vorfallen, *das;* ❷ *attrib. adj.* ~**-on effect** mittelbare Auswirkung; ~**out** ❶ *n.* **A** (*blow*) Knockout[-Schlag], *der;* K.-o.[-Schlag], *der;* (*to armed forces*) vernichtender Schlag; **B** (*competition*) Ausscheidungs[wett]kampf, *der;* **C** (*coll.: outstanding person or thing*) **sb./sth. is a [real]** ~**out** jmd./etw. ist eine Wucht (*salopp*); ❷ *adj.* **A** (*that stuns*) betäubend; (*that incapacitates*) vernichtend; ~**out blow** K.-o.-Schlag, *der;* ~**out drops** K.-o.-Tropfen (*ugs.*); **B** Ausscheidungs‹spiel, -[wett]kampf, -runde›; ~**-up** *n.* (*Sport*) Warmspielen, *das;* **have a** ~**-up** sich warm spielen

**knoll** /nəʊl/ *n.* Anhöhe, *die*

**knot** /nɒt/ ❶ *n.* **A** Knoten, *der;* **the wool has got into a [complete]** ~: die Wolle hat sich völlig verheddert; **tie sb. [up] in** ~**s** (*fig. coll.*) jmdn. in Widersprüche verwickeln; **B** (*ornament*) Schleife, *die;* (*cockade*) Kokarde, *die;* (*epaulette*) Schulterstück, *das;* **C** (*problem*) Verwicklung, *die;* Haken, *der* (*ugs.*); **D** (*cluster*) Pulk, *der;* **E** (*in wood*) Ast, *der;* **F** (*speed unit*) Knoten, *der;* **make** *or* **log ten** ~**s** zehn Knoten machen *od.* fahren; **at a rate of** ~**s** (*coll.*) mit einem Affenzahn (*salopp*); **G** (*Naut.: unit of length*) Knotenlänge, *die;* **H** (*in popular use: nautical mile*) Seemeile, *die;* **I** (*bond*) Bund, *der;* **tie the** ~ (*marry*) den Bund der Ehe eingehen (*geh.*); den Bund fürs Leben schließen (*geh.*); **J** (*lump*) Knoten, *der;* Verdickung, *die.*
❷ *v.t.*, **-tt-:** **A** (*tie*) knoten ‹Seil, Faden usw.›; knoten ‹Schnürsenkel›; knoten, binden ‹Krawatte›; ~ **threads together** Fäden verknoten; ~ **clothes into a bundle** Kleider zu einem Bündel zusammenknoten; ~ **a rope** Knoten in ein Seil machen; **B** (*entangle*) verfilzen; **C** **get** ~**ted!** (*coll.*) rutsch mir den Buckel runter! (*ugs.*); **D** ⇒ **knit** 1 C; **E** (*unite closely*) verknüpfen (**into** zu)

**knot:** ~ **garden** *n.* Boskettgarten, *der;* ~**hole** *n.* Astloch, *das*

**knotty** /'nɒtɪ/ *adj.* **A** (*full of knots*) ‹Seil, Peitsche› mit Knoten; knotig ‹Tisch, Gewebe, Finger›; ineinander gewachsen ‹Gestrüpp, Kriechpflanzen, Ausläufer›; knorrig, astig ‹Holz, Baumstamm›; **B** (*fig.: puzzling*) verwickelt

**know** /nəʊ/ ❶ *v.t.*, **knew** /nju:/, ~**n** /nəʊn/ **A** (*recognize*) erkennen (**by** an + *Dat.*, **for** als + *Akk.*); **B** (*be able to distinguish*) ~ **sth. from sth.** etw. von etw. unterscheiden können; ~ **right from wrong**, ~ **the difference between right and wrong** den Unterschied zwischen Gut und Böse kennen; **he wouldn't** ~ **the difference** er wüsste den Unterschied nicht; ⇒ *also* **Adam**; **C** (*be aware of*) wissen; kennen ‹Person›; **I** ~ **who she is** ich weiß, wer sie ist; **I** ~ **for a fact that ...:** ich weiß ganz bestimmt, dass ...; **it is** ~**n that ...:** man weiß, dass ...; es ist bekannt, dass ...; **they knew they could never become rich** sie wussten [nur zu gut], dass sie niemals reich werden konnten; ~ **sb./sth. to be ...:** wissen, dass jmd./etw. ... ist; **I** ~ **him to be an honest man** ich weiß, dass er ein ehrlicher Mensch ist; **that's/that might be worth**

**~ing** das ist gut/wäre wichtig zu wissen; **it's worth ~ing whether ...:** es ist wichtig zu wissen, ob ...; **he doesn't want to ~:** er will nichts davon wissen *od.* hören; **not if I ~ it** nicht mit mir; **I 'knew it** ich habs ja geahnt; **'I ~ what** ich weiß was (*ugs.*); **you ~** (*coll.*) (*as reminder*) weißt du [noch]; (*as conversational filler*) **they think we might be, you ~, glamorous or something** sie meinen, wir wären vielleicht, na ja, superschick oder so (*ugs.*); **I went to see the doctor, you ~:** ich war beim Arzt, weißt du; **you ~ something** *or* **what?** weißt du was?; **you never ~:** man kann nie wissen (*ugs.*); **sb. has [never] been ~n to do sth.** jmd. hat bekanntlich [noch nie] etw. getan; **for all** *or* (*arch.*) **aught I ~ they may be looking for us** ich könnte mir gut denken, dass sie uns suchen; **and I don't ~ what [all]** (*coll.*) und ich weiß nicht, was noch alles (*ugs.*); **and he ~s it** und er weiß das auch; **don't I ~ it!** (*coll.*) das weiß ich nur zu gut; **I don't ~ that ...** (*coll.: don't believe*) ich glaube nicht, dass ...; **before sb. ~s where he is** ehe jmd. sichs versieht; **what do you ~ [about that]?** (*coll.: that is surprising*) was sagst du dazu?; **sb. is not to ~** (*is not to be told*) jmd. soll nichts wissen (**about, of** von); (*has no way of learning*) jmd. kann nicht wissen; **I was not to ~ until years later** ich sollte erst Jahre später davon erfahren; **not ~ what hit one** (*fig.*) gar nicht begreifen, was geschehen ist; **that's all 'you ~ [about it]** das glaubst du vielleicht; **I'll have you ~ that ...:** ich möchte Sie darauf hinweisen, dass ...; **if you 'must ~:** wenn du es unbedingt wissen willst; **~ different** *or* **otherwise** es besser wissen; **~ what's what** wissen, wie es in der Welt zugeht; **how should I ~?** woher soll ich das wissen?; **I might have ~n** das hätte ich mir denken können; **do you ~, ...:** stell dir [mal] vor, ...; ⇨ *also* **best** 2; **better** 2 D; **god** B; **heaven** C; **let**[1] 1 B; **lord** 1 B; **thing** C; **who** A; **you** A; **D** (*have understanding of*) können ‹ABC, Einmaleins, Deutsch usw.›; beherrschen ‹Grundlagen, Regeln, Grammatik›; sich auskennen mit ‹Gerät, Verfahren, Gesetz›; **they ~ their Latin well** sie haben gute Kenntnisse in Latein; **do you ~ any German?** können Sie etwas Deutsch?; **~ 'how** wissen, wie das geht; **~ how to mend fuses** wissen, wie man Sicherungen repariert; **~ how to drive a car** Auto fahren können; **~ how to write vividly** [es] verstehen, lebendig zu schreiben; **he doesn't ~ much about computers** er hat nicht viel Ahnung von Computern; **do all one ~s [how]** sein Bestes geben; ⇨ *also* **onion**; **rope** 1 C; **stuff** 1 E; **E** (*be acquainted with*) kennen; **we have ~n each other for years** wir kennen uns [schon] seit Jahren; **surely you ~ me better than that** du müsstest mich eigentlich besser kennen; **you don't really ~ him** du kennst ihn nicht gut genug; **you ~ what he/it is** (*is like*) du kennst ihn ja/du weißt ja, wie es ist; **you ~ what it is to be an adolescent** du weißt ja, wie man als Jugendlicher ist; ⇨ *also* **get** 2 C; **sight** 1 A; **F** (*have experience of*) erleben; erfahren; **he ~s no fear, he doesn't ~ what it is to be afraid** er kennt keine Furcht; **~ what it is to be hungry** wissen, was es heißt, Hunger zu haben.

**2** *n.* (*coll.*) **be in the ~:** Bescheid wissen; **those in the ~:** die Eingeweihten

**~ about** *v.t.* wissen über (+ *Akk.*); **oh, I didn't ~ about it/that** oh, das habe ich nicht gewusst; **did you ~ about your son's behaviour?** haben Sie gehört, wie sich Ihr Sohn benommen hat?; **not much is ~n about some of the tribes** über einige Stämme weiß man fast nichts; **I didn't ~ anything about any committee meeting** ich habe nichts von irgendeiner Ausschusssitzung gewusst; **I don't ~ about 'that** na, ich weiß nicht [so recht]; **I don't ~ about beautiful, but it certainly is old** schön — na, ich weiß nicht, auf jeden Fall ist es alt

**~ of** *v.t.* wissen von ‹Plänen, Vorhaben›; kennen, wissen ‹Lokal, Geschäft›; **~ of sb.** von jmdm. gehört haben; **~ of sb. who ...:** jmdn. wissen, der ...; **not that I ~ of** nicht, dass ich wüsste

**knowable** /ˈnəʊəbl/ *adj.* [mit dem Verstand] erkennbar

**know: ~-all** *n.* (*derog.*) Neunmalkluge, *der/die* (*spöttisch*); **~-how** *n.*, *no pl.*, *no indef. art.* praktisches Wissen; (*technical expertise*) Know-how, *das*

**knowing** /ˈnəʊɪŋ/ **1** *adj.* **A** (*shrewd*) verschmitzt ‹Blick, Lachen, Lächeln›; ‹Person› mit wachem Verstand; (*indicating possession of inside information*) viel sagend, wissend ‹Blick, Lächeln›; beredt (*iron.*) ‹Schweigen›; **B** (*derog.: cunning*) verschlagen (*abwertend*). **2** *n.* **there is no ~:** niemand weiß; es lässt sich nicht vorhersagen

**knowingly** /ˈnəʊɪŋlɪ/ *adv.* **A** (*intentionally*) wissentlich ‹lügen, verletzen›; bewusst ‹planen›; **B** (*in a shrewd manner*) verschmitzt ‹lachen, blicken›; (*indicating possession of inside information*) viel sagend ‹lächeln, anblicken, zwinkern, nicken›; **C** (*derog.: cunningly*) verschlagen (*abwertend*)

**'know-it-all** ⇨ **know-all**

**knowledge** /ˈnɒlɪdʒ/ *n.*, *no pl.* **A** (*familiarity*) Kenntnisse (**of** in + *Dat.*); **a ~ of this field** Kenntnisse auf diesem Gebiet; **a little ~ is a dangerous thing** (*prov.*) Halbwissen ist gefährlich; **gain ~ of sb./sth.** Kenntnisse über jmdn./etw. gewinnen; **~ of human nature** Menschenkenntnis, *die;* ⇨ *also* **carnal knowledge**; **B** (*awareness*) Wissen, *das;* **have no ~ of sth.** nichts von etw. wissen; keine Kenntnis von etw. haben (*geh.*); **she had no ~ of it** sie wusste nichts davon; sie war völlig ahnungslos; **the ~ that it was really important** die Gewissheit, dass es wirklich wichtig war; **sth. came to my ~:** etw. ist mir zu Ohren gekommen; **[not] to my** *etc.* **~:** meines *usw.* Wissens [nicht]; **to my certain ~:** wie ich mit Bestimmtheit weiß; **without sb.'s ~:** ohne jmds. Wissen; **C** (*understanding*) **[a] ~ of languages/French** Sprach-/Französischkenntnisse *Pl.;* **sb. with [a] ~ of computers** jmd., der sich mit Computern auskennt; **D** *no art.* (*what is known*) Wissen, *das;* **in the present state of ~:** beim derzeitigen Wissensstand; **branch of ~:** Wissenszweig, *der*

**knowledgeable** /ˈnɒlɪdʒəbl/ *adj.* sachkundig; **be ~ about** *or* **on sth.** viel über etw. (*Akk.*) wissen

**known** /nəʊn/ **1** ⇨ **know. 2** *adj.* bekannt; (*generally recognized*) anerkannt

**knuckle** /ˈnʌkl/ *n.* **A** ▶ **966** (*Anat.*) [Finger]knöchel, *der;* **B** (*joint of meat*) (*pork*) Eisbein, *das;* (*veal or pork*) Hachse, *die;* Haxe, *die* (*südd.*); **C near the ~** (*coll.*) hart an der Grenze [des guten Geschmacks]. ⇨ *also* **rap**[1] 1 A, 2 A

**~ 'down** *v.i.* (*apply oneself*) **~ down to sth.** sich hinter etw. (*Akk.*) klemmen (*ugs.*)

**~ 'under** *v.i.* klein beigeben (**to** gegenüber)

**knuckle: ~ bone** *n.* **A** (*Anat.*) Fingerknochen, *der;* **B** (*Zool.*) Knochen [mit Gelenkkopf]; **~duster** *n.* Schlagring, *der*

**knurled** /nɜːld/ *adj.* geriffelt; kordiert (*Technik*)

**KO** *abbr.* **A kick-off; B knockout** K. o.; **C knocked out** k. o.

**koala** /kəʊˈɑːlə/ *n.* **~ [bear]** (*Zool.*) Koala, *der;* Beutelbär, *der*

**KO'd** /keɪˈəʊd/ ⇨ **KO** C

**kohlrabi** /kəʊlˈrɑːbɪ/ *n.* Kohlrabi, *der*

**kook** /kuːk/ (*Amer. coll.*) **1** *n.* Spinner, *der*/Spinnerin, *die* (*ugs. abwertend*). **2** *adj.* ⇨ **kooky**

**kookaburra** /ˈkʊkəbʌrə/ *n.* (*Austral. Ornith.*) Lachender Hans

**kooky** /ˈkuːkɪ/ *adj.* (*Amer. coll.*) überkandidelt (*ugs.*); idiotisch (*ugs. abwertend*) ‹Leben›

**Koran** /kɔːˈrɑːn, kəˈrɑːn/ *n.* (*Muslim Relig.*) Koran, *der*

**Korea** /kəˈrɪə/ *pr. n.* Korea (*das*)

**Korean** /kəˈriːən/ ▶ **1275**, ▶ **1340** **1** *adj.* koreanisch; **sb. is ~:** jmd. ist Koreaner/Koreanerin; ⇨ *also* **English** 1. **2** *n.* **A** (*person*) Koreaner, *der*/Koreanerin, *die;* **B** (*language*) Koreanisch, *das;* ⇨ *also* **English** 2 A

**kosher** /ˈkəʊʃə(r), ˈkɒʃə(r)/ **1** *adj.* (*lit. or fig.*) koscher. **2** *n.*, *no pl.*, *no art.* (*food*) Koschere, *das;* **eat ~:** koscher essen

**kowtow** /kaʊˈtaʊ/ (**kotow** /kəʊˈtaʊ/) *v.i.* **~ [to sb./sth.]** [vor jmdm./etw.] [s]einen Kotau machen

**k.p.h.** *abbr.* ▶ **1552** **kilometres per hour** km/h

**kraal** /krɑːl/ *n.* Kral, *der*

**Kraut** /kraʊt/ *n.* & *adj.* (*sl. derog.*) *angelsächsische abwertende Bez. für „Deutscher“ und „deutsch“*

**Kremlin** /ˈkremlɪn/ *n.* **the ~:** der Kreml

**Kremlinology** /kremlɪˈnɒlədʒɪ/ *n.*, *no pl.*, *no indef. art.* Sowjetforschung, *die;* Kremlastrologie, *die* (*ugs.*)

**krill** /krɪl/ *n.*, *no pl.*, *no indef. art.* (*Zool.*) Krill, *der*

**kris** /kriːs/ *n.* Kris, *der*

**krugerrand** /ˈkruːgərɑːnt/ *n.* Krügerrand, *der*

**krypton** /ˈkrɪptɒn/ *n.* (*Chem.*) Krypton, *das*

**Kt.** *abbr.* **knight**

**kudos** /ˈkjuːdɒs/ *n.*, *no pl.*, *no indef. art.* Prestige, *das*

**kümmel** /ˈkʊml/ *n.* Kümmellikör, *der*

**kung fu** /kʊŋˈfuː, kʌŋˈfuː/ *n.* Kung-Fu, *das*

**Kurd** /kɜːd/ *n.* Kurde, *der*/Kurdin, *die*

**Kurdish** /ˈkɜːdɪʃ/ ▶ **1275** **1** *adj.* kurdisch. **2** *n.* Kurdisch, *das*

**Kurdistan** /kɜːdɪˈstɑːn/ *pr. n.* Kurdistan (*das*)

**Kuwait** /kʊˈweɪt/ *pr. n.* Kuwait (*das*)

**Kuwaiti** /kʊˈweɪtɪ/ ▶ **1340** **1** *adj.* kuwaitisch; **sb. is ~:** jmd. ist Kuwaiti. **2** *n.* Kuwaiti, *der/die*

**kW** *abbr.* **kilowatt[s]** kW

**kWh** *abbr.* **kilowatt-hour[s]** kWh

# Ll

**L, l** /el/ *n., pl.* **Ls** *or* **L's** A *(letter)* L, l, *das;* B *(Roman numeral)* L

**L.** *abbr.* A **Lake;** B **Liberal** Lib.; C **lire** L.

**£** *abbr.* **pound[s]** £; **cost £5** 5 £ *od.* Pfund kosten

**l.** *abbr.* A ▶ 1671 **litre[s]** l; B **left** l.; C **line** Z.

**LA** *abbr.* **Los Angeles** L. A.

**la** ⇒ **lah**

**lab** /læb/ *n. (coll.)* Labor, *das*

**Lab.** *abbr.* **Labour**

**label** /ˈleɪbl/ ❶ *n.* A *(slip)* Schildchen, *das; (on goods, bottles, jars, in clothes)* Etikett, *das; (tied/stuck to an object)* Anhänger/Aufkleber, *der;* B *(on record)* Label, *das; (record company)* Plattenfirma, *die;* **record on a new ~:** die Plattenfirma *od. (Fachjargon)* das Label gewechselt haben; C *(fig.: classifying phrase)* Etikett, *das;* **hang the ~ ... on sb.** jmdn. als ... etikettieren; **acquire/be given the ~ of ...:** als ... etikettiert werden. ❷ *v.t., (Brit.)* **-ll-:** A *(attach ~ to)* etikettieren; *(attach price tag to)* auszeichnen ‹Waren›; *(write on)* beschriften; *(attach stamp or sticker to)* mit einem Aufkleber versehen; *(tie ~ to)* mit einem Anhänger versehen; B *(fig.: classify)* **~ sb./sth. [as] sth.** jmdn./etw. als etw. etikettieren; **he doesn't like being ~led** er lässt sich nicht gern etikettieren

**labial** /ˈleɪbɪəl/ ❶ *adj.* Lippen-; *(Anat., Zool., Phonet.)* labial; **~ consonant** ⇒ 2. ❷ *n. (Phonet.)* Labial, *der;* Lippenlaut, *der*

**labia majora/minora** /leɪbɪə məˈdʒɔːrə/ mɪˈnɔːrə/ *n. pl. (Anat.)* äußere *od.* große/innere *od.* kleine Schamlippen

**labor** *(Amer.)* ⇒ **labour**

**laboratory** /ləˈbɒrətərɪ/ *n. (lit. or fig.)* Labor[atorium], *das;* **~ animal** Versuchstier, *das;* ⇒ *also* **language laboratory**

**labored, laborer** *(Amer.)* ⇒ **labour-**

**laborious** /ləˈbɔːrɪəs/ *adj.* A mühsam; mühevoll ‹Forschung, Aufgabe usw.›; B *(not fluent)* schwerfällig, umständlich ‹Stil›; schleppend ‹Rede›

**laboriously** /ləˈbɔːrɪəslɪ/ *adv.* A *(with difficulty)* mühevoll; **~ slow** mühsam und schleppend; B *(not fluently)* schwerfällig; schleppend ‹vorangehen›

**laborite** *(Amer.)* ⇒ **labourite**

**ˈlabor union** *(Amer.)* ⇒ **trade union**

**labour** /ˈleɪbə(r)/ *(Brit.)* ❶ *n.* A *(task)* Arbeit, *die;* **sth. is/they did it as a ~ of love** etw. geschieht/sie taten es aus Liebe zur Sache; **~ of Hercules** Herkulesarbeit, *die;* B *(exertion)* Mühe, *die;* **~ in vain, lost ~:** vergebliche *od.* verlorene Mühe; ⇒ *also* **hard labour;** C *(work)* Arbeit, *die;* **cost of ~:** Arbeitskosten *Pl.;* **withdraw one's ~:** die Arbeit niederlegen; D *(body of workers)* Arbeiterschaft, *die;* **immigrant ~:** eingewanderte Arbeitskräfte; E **L~** *(Polit.)* die Labour Party; F *(childbirth)* Wehen *Pl.;* **be in ~:** in den Wehen liegen; **go into ~:** die Wehen bekommen. ⇒ *also* **intensive** 1 E.
❷ *v.i.* A *(work hard)* hart arbeiten (**at, on** an + *Dat.*); *(slave away)* sich abmühen (**at, over** mit); B *(strive)* sich einsetzen (**for** für); **~ to do sth.** sich bemühen, etw. zu tun; C *(be troubled)* leiden; sich quälen; **~ under sth.** sich mit etw. quälen; **~ under a delusion** sich einer Täuschung *(Dat.)* hingeben; D *(Naut.: pitch)* ‹Schiff:› stampfen *(Seemannsspr.);* E *(advance with difficulty)* sich quälen *od.* kämpfen; *(run too slowly)* ‹Motor:› untertourig laufen; **~ up the stairs** sich die Treppe hinaufquälen.
❸ *v.t. (elaborate needlessly)* auswalzen *(ugs.);* **~ the point** sich lange darüber verbreiten; **there's no need to ~ the point** du brauchst dich nicht lange darüber zu verbreiten

**labour: ~ camp** *n.* Arbeitslager, *das;* **L~ Day** *n.* Tag der Arbeit *(in Amerika: erster Montag im September)*

**laboured** /ˈleɪbəd/ *adj. (Brit.)* mühsam; schwerfällig ‹Stil›; mühsam zusammengetragen ‹Argumente›; **his breathing was ~:** er atmete schwer

**labourer** /ˈleɪbərə(r)/ *n.* ▶ 1261 *(Brit.)* Arbeiter, *der*/Arbeiterin, *die; (assisting skilled worker)* Hilfsarbeiter, *der*/-arbeiterin, *die;* **bricklayer's ~:** Maurergehilfe, *der;* **builder's ~:** Bau[hilfs]arbeiter, *der*

**labour: L~ Exchange** *(Hist./coll.)* ⇒ **employment exchange; ~ force** *n.* Arbeitskräfte *Pl.;* **a considerable ~ force** eine beträchtliche Anzahl von Arbeitskräften

**labourite** /ˈleɪbəraɪt/ *n. (Brit. Polit.)* Anhänger/Anhängerin der Labour Party; *(member)* Mitglied der Labour Party

**labour: ~ market** *n.* Arbeitsmarkt, *der;* **~ pains** *n. pl.* Wehenschmerzen; **L~ Party** *n. (Polit.)* Labour Party, *die;* **~ relations** *n. pl.* Beziehungen zwischen Arbeitgebern und Arbeitnehmern; *(within one company)* Betriebsklima, *das;* **~-saving** *adj.* arbeit[s]sparend ‹Methode, Vorrichtung›

**Labrador** /ˈlæbrədɔː(r)/ *n.* **~ [dog** *or* **retriever]** Labrador[hund], *der*

**laburnum** /ləˈbɜːnəm/ *n. (Bot.)* Goldregen, *der*

**labyrinth** /ˈlæbərɪnθ/ *n.* Labyrinth, *das*

**labyrinthine** /læbəˈrɪnθaɪn/ *adj.* A labyrinthisch; labyrinthartig; B *(complex)* verschachtelt

**lac¹** /læk/ *n.* Stocklack, *der;* **~ insect** Lackschildlaus, *die*

**lac²** ⇒ **lakh**

**lace** /leɪs/ ❶ *n.* A *(for shoe)* Schuhband, *das (bes. südd.);* Schnürsenkel, *der (bes. nordd.);* B *(fabric)* Spitze, *die; attrib.* Spitzen-; C *(braid)* **gold/silver ~:** Gold-/Silberlitze, *die.* ❷ *v.t.* A *(fasten)* **~ [up]** [zu]schnüren; B *(interlace)* durchwirken *(geh.);* C *(pass through)* [durch]ziehen; D **~ sth. with alcohol** einen Schuss Alkohol in etw. *(Akk.)* geben; **~d with brandy** mit einem Schuss Weinbrand; **~ sb.'s drink** einen Schuss Alkohol/eine Droge in jmds. Getränk *(Akk.)* geben

**lacerate** /ˈlæsəreɪt/ *v.t.* A *(tear)* aufreißen; **her arm was badly ~d** sie hatte tiefe Wunden am Arm; B *(fig.: afflict)* verletzen

**laceration** /læsəˈreɪʃn/ *n.* A *no pl.* Verletzung, *die (durch Aufreißen);* B *(wound)* Risswunde, *die; (from glass)* Schnittwunde, *die*

**lace: ~-up** ❶ *attrib. adj.* zum Schnüren *nachgestellt;* **~-up boot** Schnürstiefel, *der;* ❷ *n.* Schnürschuh/-stiefel, *der;* **~wing** *n. (Zool.)* Netzflügler, *der*

**lachrymal** /ˈlækrɪml/ *adj. (Anat.)* Tränen-

**lachrymose** /ˈlækrɪməʊs/ *adj.* weinerlich; tränenselig, rührselig ‹Geschichte, Theaterstück, Abschied›

**lacing** /ˈleɪsɪŋ/ *n.* A Schnur, *die; (on shoes)* Schuhband, *das (bes. südd.);* Schnürsenkel, *der (bes. nordd.); (of corset)* Schnüre *Pl.;* B *(quantity of spirits)* Schuss, *der;* **coffee with a ~ of whisky** Kaffee mit einem Schuss Whisky

**lack** /læk/ ❶ *n.* Mangel, *der* (**of** an + *Dat.*); **his ~ of enemies makes his task easier** dass er keine Feinde hat, macht seine Aufgabe leichter; **her ~ of aggression makes her easy to live with** da ihr jegliche Aggressivität abgeht, kann man gut mit ihr zusammenleben; **~ of self-consciousness** Unbefangenheit, *die;* **~ of obedience** mangelnder Gehorsam; **~ of work** Arbeitsmangel, *der;* **there is no ~ of it [for them]** es fehlt [ihnen] nicht daran; **he has no ~ of confidence** an Vertrauen mangelt *od.* fehlt es ihm nicht; **for ~ of sth.** aus Mangel an etw. *(Dat.);* **for ~ of time** aus Zeitmangel.
❷ *v.t.* **sb./sth. ~s sth.** jmdm./einer Sache fehlt es an etw. *(Dat.);* **sb. ~s the creativity/ability to do sth.** jmdm. fehlt die Kreativität/Fähigkeit, etw. zu tun; **what he ~s is ...:** woran es ihm fehlt, ist ...; **his life ~ed something** seinem Leben fehlte etwas; **~ content** inhaltsarm sein.
❸ *v.i.* **sb. ~s for sth.** *(formal)* jmdm. fehlt es an etw. *(Dat.);* **I ~ for nothing** mir fehlt es an nichts; ⇒ *also* **lacking**

**lackadaisical** /lækəˈdeɪzɪkl/ *adj. (unenthusiastic)* gleichgültig; desinteressiert; *(listless)* lustlos

**lackadaisically** /lækəˈdeɪzɪkəlɪ/ *adv.* ⇒ **lackadaisical**: gleichgültig; desinteressiert; lustlos

**lackey** /ˈlækɪ/ *n.* A *(footman)* Lakai, *der;* B *(servant)* Diener, *der;* C *(toady)* Speichellecker, *der (abwertend);* D *(derog.: political follower)* Lakai, *der (fig.: abwertend)*

**lacking** /ˈlækɪŋ/ *adj.* A **be ~** ‹Geld, Ressourcen usw.:› fehlen; **he was found to be ~** *(incapable)* es erwies sich, dass er den Ansprüchen nicht genügte; **he is ~ in stamina/confidence** ihm fehlt es an Stehvermögen *(Dat.)*/er hat nicht genug Selbstvertrauen; B *(coll.: deficient in intellect)* **be ~:** [geistig] unterbelichtet sein *(salopp)*

**ˈlacklustre** *adj.* trüb; glanzlos ‹Augen›; matt ‹Lächeln›; langweilig ‹Aufführung, Party›

**laconic** /ləˈkɒnɪk/ *adj.* A *(concise)* lakonisch; B wortkarg ‹Person, Naturell›

**laconically** /ləˈkɒnɪkəlɪ/ *adv.* lakonisch

**lacquer** /ˈlækə(r)/ ❶ *n.* Lack, *der.* ❷ *v.t.* lackieren; **~ed wood** Lackholz, *das*

**lacrosse** /ləˈkrɒs/ *n. (Sport)* Lacrosse, *das*

**lactation** /lækˈteɪʃn/ *n. (Physiol.)* Laktation, *die*

**lactic acid** /læktɪk ˈæsɪd/ *n. (Chem.)* Milchsäure, *die*

**lactose** /ˈlæktəʊs/ *n. (Chem.)* Laktose, *die;* Milchzucker, *der*

**lacuna** /ləˈkjuːnə/ *n., pl.* **~e** /ləˈkjuːniː/ *or* **~s** Lücke, *die; (in text)* Lakune, *die (Sprachw.);* Textlücke, *die*

**lacy** /ˈleɪsɪ/ *adj.* Spitzen-; *(of metalwork)* spitzenartig; Filigran-

**lad** /læd/ *n.* A *(boy)* Junge, *der;* **young ~:** kleiner Junge; **when I was a ~:** als ich noch ein Junge war; **these are my ~s** das sind meine Jungen *od. (ugs.)* Jungs; B *(man)* Typ, *der;* **the ~s** die Jungs *(ugs.);* **he always goes out for a drink with the ~s** er geht immer mit seinen Kumpels einen trinken *(ugs.);* **my ~:** mein Junge *(ugs.);* C **be a bit of** *or* **quite a ~** *(coll.) (spirited)* kein Kind von Traurigkeit sein *(ugs.); (one for the ladies)* es mit den Mädchen/Frauen haben *(ugs.);* D ⇒ **stable lad**

**ladder** /ˈlædə(r)/ ❶ *n.* A *(lit. or fig.)* Leiter, *die; (fig.: means of advancement)* Aufstiegsmöglichkeit, *die;* **the ~ to political power** der Weg zu politischer Macht; **have a foot on the ~:** die erste Sprosse auf der Leiter des Erfolgs erklommen haben *(geh.);* ⇒ *also* **rung¹** A; **snake** 1 A; **stepladder; top¹** 1 A; B *(Brit.: in tights etc.)* Laufmasche, *die.* ❷ *v.i.*

*(Brit.)* Laufmaschen/eine Laufmasche bekommen. ❸ *v.t.* *(Brit.)* Laufmaschen/eine Laufmasche machen in (+ *Akk.*)

**'ladder-proof** *adj.* *(Brit. Textiles)* maschenfest; laufmaschensicher

**laddie** /'lædɪ/ *n.* Jungchen, *das* *(fam.)*; Bubi, *der* *(bes. südd.)*

**lade** /leɪd/ *v.t., p. p.* **~n** /'leɪdn/ *(Naut.)* **A** *(load with cargo)* laden; **B** *(load on to ship)* verladen

**laden** /'leɪdn/ **A** *(loaded)* beladen (**with** mit); **the air was ~ with moisture** die Luft war schwer von Feuchtigkeit; **trees ~ with blossom** Bäume, schwer von Blüten; **B** *(burdened)* bedrückt; lastend ‹Stille›; bedrückend ‹Schweigen›; **~ with grief/guilt** gramerfüllt/schuldbeladen *(geh.)*

**la-di-da** /lɑːdɪ'dɑː/ *adj.* affektiert; **~ manners** Vornehmtuerei, *die* *(abwertend)*

**ladies'**/'leɪdɪz/**:~ man** *n.* Frauenheld, *der;* **~ night** *n.* Damenabend, *der;* **~ room** *n.* Damentoilette, *die*

**ladified** ⇨ **ladyfied**

**lading** /'leɪdɪŋ/ *n.* **A** *(loading)* Laden, *das;* ⇨ *also* **bill**³ 1 H; **B** *(freight)* Ladung, *die*

**ladle** /'leɪdl/ ❶ *n.* **A** *(utensil)* Schöpfkelle, *die;* Schöpflöffel, *der;* **B** *(Metallurgy)* Pfanne, *die.* ❷ *v.t.* schöpfen

**~ 'out** *v.t.* *(lit. or fig.)* austeilen

**lady** /'leɪdɪ/ *n.* **A** Dame, *die;* *(English, American, etc. also)* Lady, *die;* **~-in-waiting** *(Brit.)* Hofdame, *die;* **ladies' hairdresser** Damenfriseur, *der;* **B** *in pl., constr. as sing.* **the Ladies[']** *(Brit.)* die Damentoilette; **'Ladies'** „Damen"; **C** *as form of address in sing.* *(poet.)* Herrin *(veralt.)*; *in pl.* meine Damen; **Ladies and Gentlemen!** meine Damen und Herren!; **my dear** *or* **good ~:** meine Gnädigste; **D** ▶ **1617** *(Brit.)* *as title* **L~:** Lady; **my ~:** Mylady; **E** *(ruling woman)* Herrin, *die;* **~ of the house** Dame des Hauses; **our sovereign ~[, Queen Elizabeth]** *(Brit.)* unsere gnädige Herrin[, Königin Elisabeth]; **Our L~** *(Relig.)* Unsere Liebe Frau; **find the ~ = three-card trick; F** *(object of a man's devotion)* Angebetete, *die;* *(~-love)* Herzenskönigin, *die* *(dichter.)*; Liebste, *die* *(veralt.)*; **your/his** *etc.* **~:** die Dame deines/seines *usw.* Herzens; **G** *(titled married woman)* Gemahlin, *die* *(geh.)*; **H my/your ~ wife** meine Frau/Ihre Gattin *od.* *(geh.)* Frau Gemahlin; **your good ~:** die Frau Gemahlin *(geh.)*; **I** *attrib.* *(female)* **~ clerk** Angestellte, *die;* **~ doctor** Ärztin, *die;* **~ friend** Freundin, *die;* **~ dog** Hundedame, *die* *(scherzh.)*. ⇨ *also* **easy** 1 C; **first** 2 A; **mayoress**; **old lady**; **painted lady**; **young lady**

**lady: ~bird** *(Amer.)* **~bug** *ns.* *(Zool.)*, Marienkäfer, *der;* **L~ chapel** *n.* *(Eccl.)* Marienkapelle, *die;* **L~ Day** *n., no art.* Mariä Verkündigung; **~ fern** *n.* *(Bot.)* Waldfrauenfarn, *der*

**ladyfied** /'leɪdɪfaɪd/ *adj.* [aufgesetzt] damenhaft; **be ~:** sich [allzu] damenhaft geben

**lady: ~killer** *n.* *(coll.)* Herzensbrecher, *der;* Ladykiller, *der* *(scherzh.)*; **~like** *adj.* **A** damenhaft; **be ~like** sich wie eine Dame benehmen; **B** *(effeminate)* feminin *(abwertend)*; **~-love** *n.* Liebste, *die* *(veralt.)*; **L~'s 'bedstraw** ⇨ **bedstraw**

**ladyship** /'leɪdɪʃɪp/ *n.* ▶ **1617** **her/your ~/their ~s** Ihre/Eure Ladyschaft/Ihre Ladyschaften

**lady: ~'s maid** *n.* [Kammer]zofe, *die;* **~'s man** ⇨ **ladies' man**; **~-smock** ⇨ **cuckoo flower**; **~'s 'slipper** *n.* *(Bot.)* Frauenschuh, *der*

**lag**¹ /læg/ ❶ *v.i.*, **-gg-** *(lit. or fig.)* zurückbleiben; ⇨ *also* **behind** 1 B, 2 C. ❷ *n.* **A** *(delay)* Verzögerung, *die;* *(falling behind)* Zurückbleiben, *das;* **there was a ~ before ...:** es verging einige Zeit, bevor ...; **B** *(Phys.: retardation)* Verzögerung, *die* (**behind** gegenüber); *(amount of retardation)* Verzögerungszeit, *die.* ⇨ *also* **jet lag**; **time lag**

**lag**² *n.* *(Brit. coll.: convict)* Knastbruder, *der* *(ugs.)*; Knacki, *der* *(ugs.)*; **old ~:** alter Knastbruder *(ugs.)*

**lag**³ *v.t.*, **-gg-** *(insulate)* isolieren

**lager** /'lɑːgə(r)/ *n.* Lagerbier, *das;* **a small ~:** ≈ ein kleines Helles

**'lager lout** *n.* Bier trinkender Rüpel

**laggard** /'lægəd/ ❶ *n.* Nachzügler, *der;* *(with work)* Bummelant, *der* *(ugs. abwertend)*. ❷ *adj.* langsam

**lagging**¹ *n.* **no ~!** nicht zurückbleiben!

**lagging**² *n.* *(insulation)* Isolierung, *die*

**lagoon** /lə'guːn/ *n.* **A** Lagune, *die;* **B** *(Amer., Austral., NZ: small lake)* kleiner [abflussloser] See; **C** *(in sewage-works)* Klärteich, *der*

**lah** /lɑː/ *n.* *(Mus.)* la

**laid** ⇨ **lay**² 1, 2

**'laid-back** *adj.* *(coll.)* gelassen

**lain** ⇨ **lie**² 2

**lair** /leər/ *n.* *(of wild animal)* Unterschlupf, *der;* Lager, *das* *(Jägerspr.)*; *(fig.: hiding place)* *(of pirates, bandits)* Schlupfwinkel, *der;* *(of children etc.)* Versteck, *das*

**laird** /leəd/ *n.* *(Scot.)* Gutsbesitzer, *der*

**laisser-faire, laissez-faire** /leɪseɪ'feə(r)/ *n., no pl., no indef. art.* Laisser-faire, *das;* *attrib.* Laisser-faire‹-Kapitalismus, -Einstellung›

**laity** /'leɪɪtɪ/ *n. pl.* Laien; **many of the ~:** viele aus dem Laienstand

**lake**¹ /leɪk/ *n.* See, *der;* **the Great L~s** die Großen Seen

**lake**² *n.* *(pigment from cochineal)* Koschenillerot, *das;* Karmin, *das*

**lake: L~ Constance** /leɪk 'kɒnstəns/ *pr. n.* der Bodensee; **L~ District** *pr. ns.* *(Brit.)* Lake District, *der* *(Seenlandschaft im Nordwesten Englands)*; **~dwelling** *n.* Pfahlbau, *der;* **L~land** /'leɪklənd/ ⇨ **L~ District**; **L~ Lucerne** ⇨ **Lucerne**; **L~ Lugano** /leɪk luː'gɑːnəʊ/ *pr. n.* der Luganer See; **~side** *n.* Seeufer, *das;* **by the ~side** am See[ufer]; **a ~side hotel/promenade** ein Hotel am See/eine Seeuferpromenade; **L~ Su'perior** *pr. n.* der Obere See

**lakh** /læk/ *n.* *(Ind.)* Lakh, *der;* **a ~ of rupees** [ein]hunderttausend Rupien

**lam** /læm/ *(coll.)* ❶ *v.i.*, **-mm-: ~ into sb.** auf jmdn. eindreschen *(ugs.)*; *(verbally)* jmdn. zur Schnecke machen *(ugs.)*. ❷ *v.t.*, **-mm-** dreschen *(salopp)* ‹Ball›; verdreschen *(salopp)* ‹Person›

**lama** /'lɑːmə/ *n.* Lama, *der*

**lamasery** /'lɑːməserɪ/ *n.* Lamakloster, *das*

**lamb** /læm/ ❶ *n.* **A** Lamm, *das;* **as gentle/meek as a ~:** sanft wie ein Lamm; **one may** *or* **might as well be hanged** *or* **hung for a sheep as [for] a ~** *(fig.)* darauf kommt es jetzt auch nicht mehr an; **like a ~ [to the slaughter]** wie ein Lamm [zur Schlachtbank *(geh.)*]; **B** *no pl.* *(flesh)* Lamm[fleisch], *das;* **C** *(mild person)* Lamm, *das;* *(dear person)* Schatz, *der* *(ugs.)*; *(pitiable person)* armes Geschöpf; **the L~ [of God]** *(Bibl.)* das Lamm Gottes. ❷ *v.i.* lammen; **~ing season** Lammzeit, *die*

**lambaste** /læm'beɪst/ (**lambast** /læm'bæst/) *v.t.* *(coll.: thrash, lit. or fig.)* fertig machen *(ugs.)*

**lamb: ~ 'chop** *n.* Lammkotelett, *das;* **~ 'cutlet** *n.* Kammkotelett vom Lamm

**Lambda probe** /'læmdə prəʊb/ *n.* *(Motor Veh.)* Lambdasonde, *die*

**lambkin** /'læmkɪn/ *n.* **A** *(animal)* Lämmchen, *das;* **B** *(person)* Schäfchen, *das* *(fam.)*

**lamb: ~like** *adj.* sanftmütig ‹Wesen, Aussehen›; **~'s fry** *n., no pl., no indef. art.* Gekröse vom Lamm; **~skin** *n.* *(with wool on)* Lammfell, *das;* *(as leather)* Schafleder, *das;* **~'s 'lettuce** *n., no pl., no indef. art.* *(Bot.)* Feldsalat, *der;* **~'s-tails** *n. pl.* *(Brit. Bot.)* Haselkätzchen; **~swool** *n.* Lambswool, *die* *(Textilw.)*

**lame** /leɪm/ ❶ *adj.* **A** *(disabled)* lahm; **go ~:** lahm werden; **be ~ in one's right leg** ein lahmes rechtes Bein haben; **the horse was ~ in one leg** das Pferd lahmte auf einem Bein; **B** *(fig.: unconvincing)* lahm *(ugs. abwertend)*; **C** *(fig.: halting)* holprig ‹Vers, Versmaß›. ❷ *v.t.* lahm reiten ‹Pferd usw.›; *(fig.: hinder)* lähmen ‹Person, Fähigkeiten, Kraft›

**lamé** /'lɑːmeɪ/ *(Textiles)* ❶ *n.* Lamé, *der.* ❷ *adj.* lamé; Lamé-

**lame: ~brain** *n.* *(Amer.)* Schwachkopf, *der* *(abwertend)*; **~ dog** ⇨ **dog** 1 A; **~ 'duck** *n.* **A** *(incapable person)* Versager, *der*/Versagerin, *die;* **B** *(firm)* zahlungsunfähige Firma; **the ~ ducks of industry** die bankrotten Industrieunternehmen; **C** *(Amer.: official about to retire)* *Politiker, der nicht wieder gewählt worden ist*

**lamella** /lə'melə/ *n., pl.* **~e** /lə'meliː/ Lamelle, *die*

**lamely** /'leɪmlɪ/ *adv.* **A** hinkend; **the horse walks ~:** das Pferd geht lahm; **B** *(fig.: unconvincingly)* lahm *(ugs. abwertend)*; **she ~ mumbled an excuse** sie murmelte eine lahme Entschuldigung

**lameness** /'leɪmnɪs/ *n., no pl.* *(lit.; also fig.: unconvincingness)* Lahmheit, *die*

**lament** /lə'ment/ ❶ *n.* **A** *(expression of grief)* Klage, *die* (**for** um); **his great ~ is ...:** sein großer Kummer ist ...; **B** *(dirge)* Klagegesang, *der.* ❷ *v.t.* klagen über (+ *Akk.*) *(geh.)*; klagen um *(geh.)* ‹Freund, Heimat, Glück›; **~ that ...:** beklagen, dass ... ❸ *v.i.* klagen *(geh.)*; **~ over** *or* **for sth.** etw. beklagen *(geh.)*; etw. beweinen; **~ over** *or* **for sb.** jmdn. beweinen; um jmdn. weinen

**lamentable** /'læməntəbl/ *adj.* beklagenswert; kläglich ‹Versuch, Leistung›

**lamentably** /'læməntəblɪ/ *adv.* beklagenswert; kläglich ‹scheitern›; **be ~ ignorant of sth.** beklagenswert wenig über etw. *(Akk.)* wissen

**lamentation** /læmən'teɪʃn/ *n.* **A** *no pl., no art.* *(lamenting)* Wehklagen, *das* *(geh.)*; **B** *(lament)* [Weh]klage, *die* *(geh.)*; **C L~s [of Jeremiah]** *(Bibl.)* Klagelieder [Jeremiä]

**lamented** /lə'mentɪd/ *adj.* betrauert; **the late ~ President** der verschiedene Präsident

**laminate** ❶ /'læmɪneɪt/ *v.t.* **A** *(construct)* lamellieren *(Technik)*; **B** *(make into thin plates)* laminieren *(Metall.)*; **C** *(split)* in [flache] Platten spalten; **D** *(overlay)* beschichten; laminieren *(Technik)*. ❷ *v.i.* sich [in flache Platten] spalten. ❸ /'læmɪnət/ *n.* Schicht[press]stoff, *der* *(Technik)*; Laminat, *das* *(Technik)*; **fibreglass ~:** Glasfaserschichtstoff, *der* *(Technik)*

**laminated** /'læmɪneɪtɪd/ *adj.* lamelliert *(Technik)*; **~ glass** Verbundglas, *das;* **~ fibreglass** Glasfasergewebe, *das*

**lamination** /læmɪ'neɪʃn/ *n.* **A** *(process)* Laminierung, *die* *(Technik)*; **B** *(layer of material)* Schicht, *die*

**lammergeyer** /'læməgaɪə(r)/ *n.* *(Ornith.)* Lämmergeier, *der;* Bartgeier, *der*

**lamp** /læmp/ *n.* Lampe, *die;* *(in street)* [Straßen]laterne, *die;* [Straßen]lampe, *die;* *(of vehicle)* Licht, *das;* *(car headlamp)* Scheinwerfer, *der;* *(fig.: source of hope etc.)* Licht, *das;* ⇨ *also* **fluorescent lamp**; **neon lamp**; **spirit lamp**; **sunlamp**

**lamp: ~black** *n.* Lampenruß, *der;* **~holder** *n.* [Glühlampen]fassung, *die;* **~light** *n.* Lampenlicht, *das;* **~lighter** *n.* Laternenanzünder, *der*

**lampoon** /læm'puːn/ ❶ *n.* Spottschrift, *die;* Pasquill, *das* *(geh.)*. ❷ *v.t.* verhöhnen; verspotten

**'lamp post** *n.* Laternenpfahl, *der;* *(taller)* Lichtmast, *der*

**lamprey** /'læmprɪ/ *n.* *(Zool.)* Neunauge, *das*

**lamp: ~shade** *n.* Lampenschirm, *der;* **~ standard** *n.* Lichtmast, *der*

**Lancastrian** /læŋ'kæstrɪən/ ❶ *adj.* **A** *(of Lancashire)* Lancashire-; ‹Abstammung› aus Lancashire; **B** *(Hist.)* zum Hause Lancaster gehörig; des Hauses Lancaster *nachgestellt.* ❷ *n.* **A** *(native of Lancashire)* **be a ~:** aus Lancashire stammen; **B** *(Hist.)* Mitglied/Anhänger des Hauses Lancaster; **the ~s** die Partei der Lancaster

**lance** /lɑːns/ ❶ *n.* **A** *(weapon)* Lanze, *die;* **B** *(Fishing)* Stoßharpune, *die;* **C** *(pipe)* Sprührohr, *das;* *(for burning a hole)* **[oxygen] ~:** [Sauerstoff]lanze, *die;* **D** *(Mil.)* ⇨ **lancer** A. ❷ *v.t.* **A** *(Med.)* mit der Lanzette öffnen; **B** *(pierce with ~)* mit der Lanze durchbohren

**lance: ~ bombar'dier** *n.* ▶ 1617 (*Mil.*) Obergefreiter der Artillerie; **~ 'corporal** *n.* ▶ 1617 (*Mil.*) Obergefreite, der

**lancer** /'lɑːnsə(r)/ *n.* **A** (*Mil. Hist.*) Lanzenreiter, *der;* **B** *in pl.* (*dance*) Lancier, *der*

**lancet** /'lɑːnsɪt/ *n.* **A** (*Med.*) Lanzette, *die;* **B** (*Archit.*) **~ [arch/light** *or* **window]** Lanzettbogen, *der*/Lanzettfenster, *das*

**land** /lænd/ ❶ *n.* **A** *no pl., no indef. art.* (*solid part of the earth*) Land, *das;* **by ~:** auf dem Landweg; **by ~ or by sea** zu Lande oder zu Wasser ‹reisen›; auf dem Landweg oder auf dem Seeweg ‹schicken, transportieren›; **on ~:** zu Lande; (*not in air*) auf dem Boden; (*not in or on water*) an Land; **~ travel** das Reisen zu Lande; **B** *no indef. art.* (*expanse of country*) Land, *das;* **see/find out how the ~ lies** (*fig.*) herausfinden, wie die Dinge liegen; **how does the ~ lie?** (*fig.*) wie ist die Lage?; ⇒ *also* **lay²** 3 B; **lie²** 1 A; **C** *no pl., no indef. art.* (*ground for farming or building*) Land, *das;* **work the ~:** das Land bebauen; **back to the ~:** zurück aufs Land; **live off the ~:** sich von dem ernähren, was das Land hergibt; **D** (*country*) Land, *das;* **the greatest in the ~:** der/die Größte im ganzen Land; **out of the ~ of Egypt** (*Bibl.*) aus Ägyptenland (*bibl.*); **~ of hope and glory** Land der Hoffnung und des Ruhms; ⇒ *also* **living** 1 E; **promised land**; **E** *no indef. art.* (*landed property*) Land, *das;* **have** *or* **own ~:** Grundbesitz haben; **~s** (*estates*) Ländereien *Pl.*

❷ *v.t.* **A** (*set ashore*) [an]landen ‹Truppen, Passagiere, Waren, Fang›; **B** (*Aeronaut.*) landen ‹[Wasser]flugzeug›; **they were ~ed at an airstrip** ihr Flugzeug landete auf einer Piste; **C** (*bring into a situation*) **~ oneself in trouble** sich in Schwierigkeiten bringen; sich (*Dat.*) Ärger einhandeln (*ugs.*); **this will ~ him in bankruptcy** das wird ihn [noch] bankrott machen; **his recklessness ~ed him in danger** durch seinen Leichtsinn hat er sich in Gefahr gebracht; **~ sb. in [the thick of] it** jmdn. [ganz schön] reinreiten (*salopp*); **D** (*deal*) landen ‹Schlag›; **~ a blow on sb., ~ sb. one** jmdm. einen Schlag versetzen *od.* (*ugs.*) verpassen; **~ sb. one right in the eye** jmdm. eins aufs Auge geben (*ugs.*); **E** (*burden*) **~ sb. with sth., ~ sth. on sb.** jmdm. etw. aufhalsen (*ugs.*); **be ~ed with sb./sth.** jmdn. auf dem Hals haben (*ugs.*)/etw. aufgehalst bekommen (*ugs.*); **this ~ed me with a huge problem** dies stellte mich vor ein ungeheures Problem; **F ~ a fish** einen Fisch an Land ziehen; **G** (*fig.: obtain in face of competition*) an Land ziehen (*ugs.*).

❸ *v.i.* **A** ‹Boot usw.:› anlegen, landen; ‹Passagier:› aussteigen (**from** aus); **we ~ed at Dieppe** wir gingen in Dieppe an Land; **B** (*Aeronaut.*) landen; (*on water*) [auf dem Wasser] aufsetzen; wassern; **be about to ~:** zur Landung angesetzt haben; gerade landen; **C** (*alight*) landen; ‹Ball:› aufkommen; **~ on one's feet** auf den Füßen landen; (*fig.*) [wieder] auf die Füße fallen; **D** (*find oneself in a situation*) landen (*ugs.*) (**at, in** in + *Dat.*); **~ in the middle of a dispute** [mitten] in eine Auseinandersetzung hineingeraten

**~ 'back** *v.i.* wieder landen (*ugs.*)

**~ on** *v.t.* **~ on sb.** (*impose oneself*) jmdn. heimsuchen (*fig.*)

**~ 'up** *v.i.* landen (*ugs.*)

**'land agent** *n.* ▶ 1261 **A** (*Brit.: steward*) Liegenschaftsverwalter, *der*/-verwalterin, *die;* **B** (*selling land*) Grundstücksmakler, *der*/-maklerin, *die*

**landau** /'lændɔː/ *n.* Landauer, *der*

**land: ~ breeze** *n.* Landwind, *der;* **~ crab** *n.* (*Zool.*) Landkrabbe, *die*

**landed** /'lændɪd/ *adj.* **A** (*having land*) **~ gentry/aristocracy** Landadel, *der;* **the ~ interest** die Großgrundbesitzer; **B** (*consisting of land*) Land‹besitz, -gut›

**lander** /'lændə(r)/ *n.* (*Astronaut.*) Landefahrzeug, *das;* Landefähre, *die*

**land: ~fall** *n.* (*Naut.*) Landfall, *der;* **~fill** *n.* **A** (*material*) Müll, *der;* Schutt, *der* (*zur Geländeauffüllung*); **B** (*process*) Geländeauffüllung, *die;* **~fill site** (*mit Erde wieder aufgefüllte*) Müllgrube; **~ force** *n.* **~ force[s** *pl.*] Landstreitkräfte *Pl.;* **~ girl** *n.* (*Brit.*) Landarbeiterin, *die;* Landwirtschaftsgehilfin, *die*

**landing** /'lændɪŋ/ *n.* **A** (*of ship*) Landung, *die;* **on ~** (*disembarkation*) beim Verlassen des Schiffs; **B** (*of aircraft*) Landung, *die;* **emergency ~:** Notlandung, *die;* ⇒ *also* **hard landing; soft landing; C** (*place for disembarkation*) Anlegestelle, *die;* **D** (*between flights of stairs*) Treppenabsatz, *der;* (*passage*) Treppenflur, *der*

**landing: ~ card** *n.* Landekarte, *die;* **~ craft** *n.* (*Navy*) Landungsboot, *das;* **~ flap** *n.* Landeklappe, *die;* **~ gear** *n.* Fahrwerk, *das;* **~ net** *n.* Kescher, *der;* **~ place** ⇒ **landing** C; **~ stage** *n.* Landungssteg, *der;* Landungsbrücke, *die;* (*floating*) Anlegeponton, *der;* **~ strip** ⇒ **airstrip**

**land: ~lady** *n.* **A** (*of rented property*) Vermieterin, *die;* (*of flat also*) Hauswirtin, *die;* (*of room also*) Zimmerwirtin, *die;* **B** (*of public house*) [Gast]wirtin, *die;* **C** (*of lodgings etc.*) [Pensions]wirtin, *die;* **~line** *n.* Landkabel, *das;* **~locked** *adj.* vom Land eingeschlossen ‹Bucht, Hafen›; ‹Staat› ohne Zugang zum Meer; **~lord** *n.* **A** (*of rented property*) Vermieter, *der;* [Haus]wirt, *der;* **B** (*of public house*) [Gast]wirt, *der;* **C** (*of lodgings etc.*) [Pensions]wirt, *der;* **~lubber** /'lændlʌbə(r)/ *n.* (*Naut.*) Landratte, *die* (*ugs.*); **~mark** *n.* **A** (*boundary mark*) Grenzzeichen, *das;* (*stone*) Grenzstein, *der;* **B** (*conspicuous object*) Orientierungspunkt, *der;* (*Naut.*) Landmarke, *die;* **C** (*fig.: significant event*) Markstein, *der;* **stand as a ~mark** einen Meilenstein bedeuten; **~ mass** *n.* (*Geog.*) Landmasse, *die;* **~mine** *n.* (*Mil.*) **A** (*on ground*) Landmine, *die;* **B** (*parachute mine*) Fallschirmmine, *die;* **~owner** *n.* **[large** *or* **big] ~owner** [Groß]grundbesitzer, *der*/-besitzerin, *die*

**landscape** /'lændskeɪp, 'lænskeɪp/ ❶ *n.* **A** Landschaft, *die;* **B** (*picture*) Landschaftsbild, *das;* Landschaft, *die.* ❷ *v.t.* landschaftsgärtnerisch gestalten ‹Garten, Park›

**landscape: ~ architect** *n.* ▶ 1261 Landschaftsarchitekt, *der*/-architektin, *die;* **~ architecture** *n.* Landschaftsgestaltung, *die;* **~ gardener** *n.* ▶ 1261 Landschaftsgärtner, *der*/-gärtnerin, *die;* **~ gardening** *n.* Landschaftsgärtnerei, *die;* **~ painter** *n.* Landschaftsmaler, *der*/-malerin, *die*

**land: ~slide** *n.* **A** Erdrutsch, *der;* **B** (*fig.: majority*) Erdrutsch[wahl]sieg, *der; attrib.* **a ~slide victory** ein Erdrutsch[wahl]sieg; **~slip** ⇒ **~slide** A; **~ tax** *n.* (*Admin.*) Grundsteuer, *die*

**landward** /'lændwəd/ ❶ *adj.* **~ side** Landseite, *die;* **~ view** Blick zur Landseite hin. ❷ *adv.* land[ein]wärts. ❸ *n.* **to [the] ~:** zur Landseite hin

**landwards** /'lændwədz/ ⇒ **landward** 2

**'land wind** *n.* Landwind, *der*

**lane** /leɪn/ *n.* **A** (*in the country*) Landsträßchen, *das;* (*unmetalled*) [Hecken]weg, *der;* **it's a long ~ that has no turning** (*prov.*) alles muss einmal ein Ende haben; **B** (*in town*) Gasse, *die;* **lovers' ~:** Seufzerallee, *die* (*scherzh.*); **C** (*part of road*) [Fahr]spur, *die;* **slow/inside ~** (*in Britain*) linke Spur; (*on the continent*) rechte Spur; **outside ~:** Überholspur, *die;* **'get in ~'** „bitte einordnen"; ⇒ *also* **fast lane; D aircraft ~:** Flugroute, *die;* **shipping ~:** Schifffahrtsweg, *der;* **ocean ~:** Schifffahrtsstraße, *die;* **E** (*for race*) Bahn, *die*

**-lane[d]** /leɪn(d)/ *adj. in comb.* -spurig

**language** /'læŋgwɪdʒ/ *n.* ▶ 1275 **A** Sprache, *die;* **speak the same ~** (*fig.*) die gleiche Sprache sprechen; ⇒ *also* **artificial language; dead language; foreign language; sign language; B** *no pl., no art.* (*words, wording*) Sprache, *die;* **[style of] ~:** [Sprach]stil, *der;* **use of ~:** Sprachgebrauch, *der;* **C** (*style*) Ausdrucksweise, *die;* Sprache, *die;* **use uncompromising ~:** eine unmissverständliche Sprache sprechen; **mind your ~:** drück dich gefälligst anständig aus; **~ of the gutter** Gossensprache, *die;* ⇒ *also* **bad** 1 D; **strong language; D** (*professional vocabulary*) [Fach]sprache, *die;* **the ~ of diplomacy** die Sprache der Diplomatie; **medical ~:** medizinische Fachsprache; **E** (*Computing*) Sprache, *die;* **computer ~s** Computersprachen; **F** *no pl., no art.* (*faculty of speech*) Sprachfähigkeit, *die*

**language: ~ course** *n.* Sprachkurs[us], *der;* **~ laboratory** *n.* Sprachlabor, *das;* **~ teacher** *n.* Sprachlehrer, *der*/-lehrerin, *die*

**languid** /'læŋgwɪd/ *adj.* **A** (*indisposed to exertion, sluggish*) träge; **B** (*inert*) matt; **C** (*apathetic*) lahm

**languidly** /'læŋgwɪdlɪ/ *adv.* **A** (*without vigour, sluggishly*) träge; **B** (*inertly*) matt; **C** (*apathetically*) lustlos

**languish** /'læŋgwɪʃ/ *v.i.* **A** (*lose vitality*) ermatten (*geh.*); ‹Pflanzen:› kümmern; **B** (*live wretchedly*) **~ under sth.** unter etw. (*Dat.*) schmachten (*geh.*); **~ in prison** im Gefängnis schmachten (*geh.*); **C** (*pine*) dahinvegetieren; **~ for sth.** nach etw. schmachten (*geh.*); **~ for sb.** sich nach jmdm. verzehren (*geh.*)

**languor** /læŋgə(r)/ *n.* ⇒ **languorous**: Mattigkeit, *die;* Trägheit, *die;* Verträumtheit, *die*

**languorous** /'læŋgərəs/ *adj.* **A** (*faint*) matt; **B** (*inert*) träge; **C** (*dreamy*) verträumt

**lank** /læŋk/ *adj.* **A** (*tall*) hager; **B** (*thin*) abgemagert; **C** (*limp*) glatt herabhängend ‹Haar›

**lanky** /'læŋkɪ/ *adj.* schlaksig (*ugs.*); [dürr und] lang ‹Arm, Bein›

**lanolin** /'lænəlɪn/ *n.* Lanolin, *das*

**lantern** /'læntən/ *n.* Laterne, *die;* ⇒ *also* **Chinese lantern; magic lantern**

**lantern: ~-jawed** /'læntəndʒɔːd/ *adj.* mit lang geschnittenem Gesicht; **~ slide** *n.* *bemalte Glasplatte oder Dia für die Laterna magica*

**lanyard** /'lænjəd/ *n.* **A** (*Naut.*) Bändsel, *das;* (*in tackle*) Taljenreep, *das;* **B** (*loop of cord*) Kordel, *die;* **C** (*to fire gun*) Abzugsleine, *die*

**Laos** /'laʊs, 'lɑːɒs/ *pr. n.* Laos (*das*)

**Laotian** /laʊʃn/ ▶ 1340 ❶ *adj.* laotisch; **sb. is ~:** jmd. ist Laote/Laotin. ❷ *n.* **A** (*person*) Laote, *der*/Laotin, *die;* **B** (*language*) laotische Sprache

**lap¹** /læp/ *n.* **A** (*part of body*) Schoß, *der;* **live in the ~ of luxury** (*fig.*) im Überfluss leben; **fall** *or* **drop** *or* **be dropped into sb.'s ~** (*fig.*) jmdm. in den Schoß fallen; **end up on** *or* **in sb.'s ~** (*fig.*) bei jmdm. landen (*ugs.*); bei jmdm. abgeladen werden (*fig.*); ⇒ *also* **god** A; **B** (*flap*) [Rock]schoß, *der*

**lap²** ❶ *n.* **A** (*Sport*) Runde, *die;* **on the last ~** (*fig. coll.*) auf der Zielgeraden (*fig.*); **~ of honour** Ehrenrunde, *die;* **B** (*amount of overlap*) Überlappung, *die* (**of** um); (*overlapping part*) überlappender Teil. ❷ *v.t.*, **-pp-: A** (*Sport*) überrunden; **B** (*cause to overlap*) überlappen; **C** (*wrap*) wickeln (**[a]round** um); **D** (*swathe*) umwickeln (**in** mit); wickeln ‹Baby› (**in** in + *Akk.*). ❸ *v.i.*, **-pp-: ~ over sth.** etw. überlappen

**lap³** ❶ *v.i.*, **-pp-: A** (*drink*) schlapppen; schlecken; **B** ‹See, Wasser, Wellen:› plätschern. ❷ *v.t.*, **-pp-: A** (*drink*) **~ [up]** [auf]schlappen; [auf]schlecken; **B** ⇒ **~ up** B; **C** ⇒ **~ up** C; **D** ‹See, Wasser, Wellen:› plätschern an (+ *Akk.*)

**~ 'up** *v.t.* **A** (*drink*) ⇒ **~** 2 A; **B** (*consume greedily*) hinunterschütten; **C** (*fig.: receive eagerly*) schlucken (*ugs.*); begierig aufnehmen ‹Lob›; sich stürzen auf (+ *Akk.*) ‹Sensation›

**laparoscopy** /læpə'rɒskəpɪ/ *n.* (*Med.*) Laparoskopie, *die*

**lap: ~ belt** *n.* Beckengurt, *der;* **~dog** *n.* Schoßhund, *der;* Schoßhündchen, *das*

**lapel** /lə'pel/ *n.* Revers, *das od.* (*österr.*) *der*

**lapidary** /'læpɪdərɪ/ *adj.* **A** (*of gems*) **~ art** (*cutting gems*) Steinschneidekunst, *die;* (*polishing gems*) Kunst des Steinschleifens; **B** (*engraved*) in Stein gehauen; **C** (*dignified and concise*) lapidar

**lapis [lazuli]** /'læpɪs ('læzjʊlɪ), 'leɪpɪs ('læzjʊlaɪ)/ *n., no pl., no indef. art.* **A** (*gem*) Lapislazuli, *der;* Lasurstein, *der;* **B** (*pigment, colour*) Ultramarin, *das;* Lasurblau, *das*

## Languages

With the major European languages, the noun has the same form as the nationality adjective but with a capital, much as in English. All languages are neuter.

***German is difficult to learn***
= Deutsch ist schwer zu lernen

***She writes faultless/cultivated English***
= Sie schreibt ein fehlerloses *or* perfektes Englisch/ein gepflegtes Englisch

***He speaks Spanish without an accent***
= Er spricht akzentfrei Spanisch

***My daughter speaks fluent Russian***
= Meine Tochter spricht fließend Russisch

in with a language is usually **auf:**

***Say it in German***
= Sagen Sie es auf Deutsch

But **in** is also used, especially where there is an adjective:

***a speech in fluent French***
= eine Rede in fließendem Französisch

***The brochure is in English and German***
= Der Prospekt ist in Englisch und Deutsch

Furthermore when the features of a language are being discussed, **im** with the nominalized form of the adjective should be used:

***In English there are fewer endings than in German***
= Im Englischen gibt es weniger Endungen als im Deutschen

The adjective as a noun is also used in relation to translations:

***a translation from German into English***
= eine Übersetzung aus dem Deutschen ins Englische

There are however cases where the adverb is used, which is written with a small letter. This happens because the word or phrase in question answers the question *how*:

***The speech was given in English***
= Die Rede wurde englisch *or* auf Englisch gehalten

***They spoke German*** (*i.e. on this occasion, answering the question 'how did they speak?'*)
= Sie sprachen deutsch

***They speak German*** (*i.e. can speak it, answering the question 'what do they speak?'*)
= Sie sprechen Deutsch

**'lap joint** *n.* Überlappung, *die;* Überlappungsverbindung, *die*

**Lapland** /'læplænd/ *pr. n.* Lappland (*das*)

**Laplander** /'læplændə(r)/ *n.* ▶1340 Lappländer, *der*/Lappländerin, *die*

**Lapp** /læp/ ▶1275, ▶1340 ❶ *n.* Ⓐ (*person*) Lappe, *der*/Lappin, *die;* Ⓑ (*language*) lappische Sprache. ❷ *adj.* Ⓐ lappisch; lappländisch; Ⓑ (*of language*) lappisch

**Lappish** /'læpɪʃ/ ⇒ **Lapp** 2

**lapse** /læps/ ❶ *n.* Ⓐ (*interval*) **a/the ~ of ...:** eine/die Zeitspanne von ...; **a ~ in the conversation** eine Gesprächspause; Ⓑ (*mistake*) Fehler, *der;* Lapsus, *der* (*geh.*); **~ of memory** Gedächtnislücke, *die;* Ⓒ (*deviation*) Verstoß, *der* (**from** gegen); **momentary ~ of concentration** momentane Konzentrationsschwäche; **a ~ from his high standard** eine Abweichung von seinem hohen Standard; **~ from good taste** Geschmacksverirrung, *die;* Ⓓ (*Law: termination of right*) (*of patent*) Erlöschen, *das;* (*of legacy*) Heimfall, *der.*
❷ *v.i.* Ⓐ (*fail*) versagen; **~ from sth.** etw. vermissen lassen; Ⓑ (*sink*) **~ into** verfallen in (+ *Akk.*); fallen in (+ *Akk.*) ‹Schlaf, Koma›; verfallen (+ *Dat.*) ‹Sucht, Ketzerei›; Ⓒ (*become void*) ‹Vertrag, Versicherungspolice usw.:› ungültig werden; ‹Plan, Projekt:› hinfällig werden; ‹Anspruch:› verfallen; Ⓓ **~ to sb.** (*Law*) auf jmdn. übergehen; an jmdn. fallen

**lapsed** /læpst/ *adj.* Ⓐ (*disused*) in Vergessenheit geraten; Ⓑ (*having defected*) abgefallen ‹Christ, Katholik usw.›; Ⓒ abgelaufen, ungültig ‹Pass, Führerschein, Versicherungspolice›; frei geworden ‹Lehen›

**lap: ~top** ❶ *adj.* tragbar, Laptop‹gerät, -PC›; ❷ *n.* Laptop, *der;* tragbarer PC; **~ weld** (*Metalw.*) *n.* Überlapp[schweiß]naht, *die;* **~-weld** (*Metalw.*) *v.t.* überlappt schweißen; **~wing** *n.* (*Ornith.*) Kiebitz, *der*

**larboard** /'lɑ:bəd/ ⇒ **port**[1] 1 C, 2

**larcenous** /'lɑ:sənəs/ *adj.* diebisch

**larceny** /'lɑ:sənɪ/ *n.* (*Law*) Diebstahl, *der*

**larch** /lɑ:tʃ/ *n.* Lärche, *die*

**lard** /lɑ:d/ ❶ *n.* Schweineschmalz, *das;* Schweinefett, *das.* ❷ *v.t.* Ⓐ (*Cookery*) spicken; Ⓑ (*fig.: garnish*) spicken (*ugs.*)

**larder** /'lɑ:də(r)/ *n.* (*room*) Speisekammer, *die;* (*cupboard*) Speiseschrank, *der*

**lardy** /'lɑ:dɪ/ *adj.* fett

**'lardy cake** *n.* ≈ Rosinenbrot, *das*

**large** /lɑ:dʒ/ ❶ *adj.* Ⓐ groß; **a ~ lady** eine stattliche Dame; **~ importer/user** Großimporteur, *der*/Großverbraucher, *der;* ⇒ *also* **intestine**; **life** D; Ⓑ (*comprehensive, broad*) umfassend; **taking the ~ view** im großen Ganzen gesehen. ❷ *n.* Ⓐ **at ~** (*at liberty*) frei; (*not in prison etc.*) auf freiem Fuß; in Freiheit; (*at full length*) ausführlich; (*as a body*) insgesamt; (*Amer. Polit.: representing whole State*) für den ganzen Staat ‹gewählt›; **society at ~:** die Gesellschaft in ihrer Gesamtheit; **students/teachers/doctors at ~:** die [gesamte] Studenten-/Lehrer-/Ärzteschaft; **ambassador at ~** (*Amer.*) Sonderbotschafter, *der*/-botschafterin, *die;* Ⓑ **in [the] ~:** im Großen. ❸ *adv.* ⇒ **bulk** 2; **by**[1] 2 D; **loom**[2]; **write** 2 D

**'large-hearted** *adj.* großherzig (*geh.*)

**largely** /'lɑ:dʒlɪ/ *adv.* weitgehend

**largeness** /'lɑ:dʒnɪs/ *n., no pl.* Größe, *die;* (*of person*) Stattlichkeit, *die*

**larger-than-'life** *attrib. adj.* überlebensgroß

**large: ~-scale** *attrib. adj.* groß angelegt; groß ‹Erfolg, Misserfolg›; ‹Katastrophe› großen Ausmaßes; ‹Modell› in großem Maßstab; **~-scale manufacture** Massenproduktion, *die;* **~-size** ⇒ **-size**

**largess[e]** /lɑ:'ʒes/ *n., no pl.* Ⓐ (*gifts*) Geschenke *Pl.;* **government ~:** staatliche Geschenke; Ⓑ (*bestowal*) [großzügige] Unterstützung *od.* Förderung

**largish** /'lɑ:dʒɪʃ/ *adj.* ziemlich groß; recht stattlich ‹Person›

**largo** /'lɑ:gəʊ/ (*Mus.*) ❶ *adv.* & *adj.* largo. ❷ *n., pl.* **~s** Largo, *das*

**lariat** /'lærɪət/ *n.* Ⓐ (*lasso*) (*lateinamerikanisches*) Lasso; Ⓑ (*tethering-rope*) Seil zum Anpflocken

**lark**[1] /lɑ:k/ *n.* (*Ornith.*) Lerche, *die;* **be up with the ~:** beim *od.* mit dem ersten Hahnenschrei aufstehen; **gay** *or* **happy as a ~:** lustig und vergnügt

**lark**[2] (*coll.*) ❶ *n.* Ⓐ (*frolic*) Jux, *der* (*ugs.*); **they were only having a ~:** sie haben sich (*Dat.*) nur einen Jux gemacht (*ugs.*); **be a real ~:** eine Mordsgaudi sein (*ugs.*); **it'll be a bit of a ~:** es wird bestimmt lustig; **do sth. for a ~:** etw. aus Jux machen (*ugs.*); **what a ~!** das ist/war spitze (*ugs.*); Ⓑ (*Brit.*) (*form of activity*) Blödsinn, *der* (*ugs.*); (*affair*) Geschichte, *die* (*ugs.*); **blow** *or* (*sl.*) **sod** *or* (*coarse*) **bugger this for a ~:** zum Teufel!; verdammte Scheiße (*derb*). ❷ *v.i.* **~ [about** *or* **around]** herumalbern (*ugs.*)

**'larkspur** *n.* (*Bot.*) Rittersporn, *der*

**larva** /'lɑ:və/ *n., pl.* **~e** /'lɑ:vi:/ Larve, *die*

**larval** /'lɑ:vl/ *adj.* Larven-; larval (*fachspr.*); **a ~ fly/frog** eine Fliegen-/Froschlarve

**laryngeal** /lə'rɪndʒɪəl/ ❶ *adj.* Ⓐ (*Anat.*) Kehlkopf-; laryngeal (*fachspr.*); Ⓑ (*Ling.*) Kehl[kopf]-; laryngal (*fachspr.*). ❷ *n.* (*Ling.*) Kehl[kopf]laut, *der;* Laryngal, *der* (*fachspr.*)

**laryngitis** /lærɪn'dʒaɪtɪs/ *n.* ▶1232 (*Med.*) Kehlkopfentzündung, *die;* Laryngitis, *die* (*fachspr.*)

**larynx** /'lærɪŋks/ *n., pl.* **larynges** /lə'rɪndʒi:z/ ▶966 (*Anat.*) Kehlkopf, *der;* Larynx, *der* (*fachspr.*)

**lasagne** /lə'sænjə, lə'sɑ:njə/ *n.* (*Gastr.*) Lasagne *Pl.*

**lascivious** /lə'sɪvɪəs/ *adj.* Ⓐ (*lustful*) lüstern (*geh.*); Ⓑ (*inciting to lust*) lasziv

**lasciviously** /lə'sɪvɪəslɪ/ *adv.* ⇒ **lascivious:** lüstern (*geh.*); lasziv

**lasciviousness** /lə'sɪvɪəsnɪs/ *n., no pl.* ⇒ **lascivious**: Lüsternheit, *die* (*geh.*); Laszivität, *die*

**laser** /'leɪzə(r)/ *n.* Laser, *der*

**laser: ~ beam** *n.* Laserstrahl, *der;* **~disc** *n.* Laserplatte, *die;* **~-guided** *adj.* lasergesteuert; **~ pointer** *n.* Laserpointer, *der;* **~ printer** *n.* Laserdrucker, *der*

**lash** /læʃ/ ❶ *n.* Ⓐ (*stroke*) [Peitschen]hieb, *der;* Ⓑ (*part of whip*) *biegsamer Teil der Peitsche;* (*whipcord*) Peitschenschnur, *die;* (*as punishment*) **the ~:** die Peitsche; Ⓒ (*on eyelid*) Wimper, *die.* ❷ *v.i.* Ⓐ (*make violent movement*) schlagen; ‹Peitsche, Schlange:› zuschlagen; Ⓑ (*strike*) ‹Welle, Regen:› peitschen (**against** gegen, **on** auf + *Akk.*); ‹Person:› [mit der Peitsche] schlagen (**at** nach). ❸ *v.t.* Ⓐ (*fasten*) festbinden (**to** an + *Dat.*); (*Naut.*) festzurren (*bes. Seemannsspr.*); laschen (*Seemannsspr.*); **~ together** zusammenbinden; Ⓑ (*flog*) mit der Peitsche schlagen; (*as punishment*) auspeitschen; **~ oneself** sich geißeln; Ⓒ (*rebuke*) abkanzeln; geißeln ‹Missstand, Laster, Fehler›; (*satirize*) verhöhnen; Ⓓ (*move violently*) schlagen mit; Ⓔ (*beat upon*) peitschen; **the rain ~ed the windows/roof** der Regen peitschte gegen die Fenster/auf das Dach; Ⓕ (*drive*) **~ sb. into sth.** jmdn. zu etw. anstacheln

**~ a'bout** *v.i.* wild um sich schlagen

**~ 'down** ❶ *v.t.* festbinden; (*Naut.*) festzurren (*bes. Seemannsspr.*). ❷ *v.i.* ‹Regen:› niederprasseln

**~ 'into** *v.t.* **~ into sb.** über jmdn. herfallen

**~ 'out** *v.i.* Ⓐ (*hit out*) um sich schlagen; ‹Pferd:› ausschlagen; **~ out at sb.** nach jmdm. schlagen; (*fig.*) über jmdn. herziehen (*ugs.*); Ⓑ **~ out on sth.** (*coll.*) (*spend freely*) sich (*Dat.*) etw. leisten *od.* gönnen; (*pay a lot*) viel Geld für etw. ausgeben

**lashing** /ˈlæʃɪŋ/ *n.* **A** ⇒ **lash** 2: Schlagen, *das usw.;* **B** *(cord)* Zurring, *der (Seemannsspr.);* **C** *in pl. (large amounts)* **~s of sth.** Unmengen von etw.

**ˈlash-up** **1** *adj.* behelfsmäßig; **~ procedures** provisorische Maßnahmen. **2** *n. (improvised structure)* Notbehelf, *der*

**lass** /læs/ *n.* **A** *(Scot./N. Engl./poet.: girl)* Mädchen, *das;* Maid, *die (dichter.);* **B** *(sweetheart)* Liebste, *die (veralt.);* Mädchen, *das (ugs.)*

**lassie** /ˈlæsɪ/ *n. (Scot., N. Engl.)* Mädchen, *das; (sweetheart)* Schätzchen, *das (ugs.)*

**lassitude** /ˈlæsɪtju:d/ *n.* Mattigkeit, *die*

**lasso** /ləˈsu:, ˈlæsəʊ/ **1** *n., pl.* **~s** *or* **~es** Lasso, *das.* **2** *v.t.* mit dem Lasso fangen

**last**[1] /lɑ:st/ **1** *adj.* ▶ **1055**, ▶ **1056** letzt...; **be ~ to arrive** als Letzter/Letzte ankommen; **for the [very] ~ time** zum [aller]letzten Mal; **who was ~?** wer war Letzter?; **the ~ two/three** *etc.* die letzten beiden/drei *usw.;* **he came ~ in the race** er war Letzter bei dem Rennen; **second ~, ~ but one** vorletzt...; **~ but not least** last, not least; nicht zuletzt; **~ evening/night was windy** gestern Abend/gestern *od.* heute Nacht war es windig; **~ week/month/year was cold** letzte Woche/letzten Monat/letztes Jahr war es kalt; **~ month was a memorable one** der letzte Monat war bedeutungsvoll; **~ evening/week we were out** gestern Abend/letzte Woche waren wir aus; **I thought my ~ hour had come** ich dachte, mein letztes Stündlein hätte geschlagen; **sb.'s ~ crust** *(fig.)* jmds. letztes Stück Brot *(fig.);* **I was down to my ~ crust** *(fig.)* ich war völlig abgebrannt *(ugs.);* **I should be the ˈ~ person to do such a thing** ich wäre der Letzte, der so etwas täte; **the ˈ~ thing** das Letzte; **that would be the ˈ~ thing to do in this situation** das wäre das Letzte, was man in dieser Situation tun würde; ⇒ *also* **ditch** 1; **honour** 1 J; **judgment** C; **leg** 1 A; **quarter** 1 J; **resort** 1 A; **respect** 1 E; **straw** B.
**2** *adv.* **A** [ganz] zuletzt; als Letzter/Letzte ‹sprechen, ankommen›; **come ~ with sb.** *(fig.)* für jmdn. an letzter Stelle rangieren; **B** *(on ~ previous occasion)* das letzte Mal; zuletzt; **when did you ~ see him** *or* **see him ~?** wann hast du ihn zuletzt *od.* das letzte Mal gesehen?
**3** *n.* **A** *(mention, sight)* **I shall never hear the ~ of it** das werde ich ständig zu hören bekommen; **you haven't heard the ~ of this matter** das letzte Wort in dieser Sache ist noch nicht gesprochen; **I hope we shall soon see the ~ of him** wir werden ihn hoffentlich bald zum letzten Mal gesehen haben; **that's the ~ we'll see of that old car** jetzt sehen wir dieses alte Auto wohl zum letzten Mal; **that was the ~ we ever saw of him** das war das letzte Mal, dass wir ihn gesehen haben; **B** *(person or thing)* letzt...; **these ~:** Letztere; **be the ~ to arrive** als Letzter/Letzte ankommen; **which ~:** welch letzt...; **I'm always the ~ to be told** ich bin immer der Letzte, der etwas erfährt; **she was the ~ to know about it** sie erfuhr es als Letzte; **the ~ shall be first** *(Bibl.)* die Letzten werden die Ersten sein; **C** *(day, moment[s])* **towards** *or* **at the ~ he was serene** *(just before his death)* am Ende war er gelassen; **to** *or* **till the ~:** bis zuletzt; **D** **look one's ~ on** einen letzten Blick werfen auf (+ *Akk.);* ⇒ *also* **breathe** 2 A; **E** **at [long] ~:** endlich; schließlich [doch noch]

**last**[2] *v.i.* **A** *(continue)* andauern; ‹Wetter, Ärger:› anhalten; **~ all night** die ganze Nacht dauern; **~ till** dauern bis; **~ from ... to ...:** von ... bis ... dauern; **built to ~:** dauerhaft gebaut; **a book that will ~:** ein Buch, das bleibt; **he will not ~ very much longer** *(live)* er hat nicht mehr lange zu leben; *(in job)* ihm wird bald gekündigt werden; **make one's money ~:** mit seinem Geld haushalten; **it can't/won't ~:** das geht nicht mehr lange so; **it's too good to ~:** es ist zu schön, um von Dauer zu sein; **~ sb.'s time** halten, solange jmd. es braucht; **B** *(manage to continue)* es aushalten; **C** *(suffice)* reichen; **while stocks ~:** solange Vorrat reicht; **this knife will ~ [me] a lifetime** dies Messer hält mein ganzes Leben; **memories to ~ a lifetime** Erinnerungen für das ganze Leben

**~ ˈout** **1** *v.t. (complete task)* durchhalten; *(survive)* überstehen; **~ out the winter/journey** ‹Vorräte usw.:› den Winter über/für die Reise ausreichen; **he would probably not ~ out the afternoon** er würde wahrscheinlich den Nachmittag nicht überleben. **2** *v.i.* durchhalten; ‹Vorräte usw:› ausreichen

**last**[3] *n. (for shoemaker)* Leisten, *der;* **the cobbler should stick to his ~** *(prov.)* Schuster, bleib bei deinem Leisten

**Last:** **~ ˈDay** *n. (Relig.)* **the ~ Day** der Jüngste Tag; **l~-ditch** *adj.* **l~-ditch attempt** letzter verzweifelter Versuch

**lasting** /ˈlɑ:stɪŋ/ *adj.* **A** *(permanent)* bleibend; dauerhaft ‹Beziehung›; nachhaltig ‹Eindruck, Wirkung, Bedeutung›; nicht nachlassend ‹Interesse›; **be of no ~ benefit to sb.** sich für jmdn. auf die Dauer nicht auszahlen; **B** *(durable)* haltbar; **[made] in a ~ material** aus haltbarem Material

**lastly** /ˈlɑ:stlɪ/ *adv.* schließlich

**last:** **~-mentioned** *attrib. adj.* letztgenannt; **~ ˈminute** *n.* **at the ~ minute** in letzter Minute; **up to the ~ minute** bis zum letzten Augenblick; **~-minute** *attrib. adj.* in letzter Minute vorgebracht ‹Plan, Aufruf, Ergänzung, Gesuch, Bewerbung›; ‹Sinneswandel› in letzter Minute; **make a ~-minute dash to the airport** in letzter Minute zum Flughafen rasen; **in the ~-minute rush** kurz vor Toresschluss; **~ name** *n.* Zuname, *der;* Nachname, *der;* **~-named** *attrib. adj.* zuletzt genannt; **~ ˈrites** *n. pl.,* **~ ˈsacrament** *n. (Relig.)* Letzte Ölung; **~ ˈsleep** *n., no pl. (literary)* ewiger Schlaf *(geh.);* **L~ ˈSupper** *n., no pl. (Relig.)* **the L~ Supper** das Abendmahl; **~ ˈthing** *adv. (coll.)* als Letztes; **~ ˈtrump** *n. (Relig.)* letzte Posaune; **~ ˈwill** *n.* **~ will [and testament]** letzter Wille; **~ ˈword** *n., no pl., no indef. art.* **A** letztes Wort; **be the ~ word** *(fig.)* nicht zu überbieten sein (in an + *Dat.);* das Letzte sein (**in** an + *Dat.);* **sth. is the ~ word on sth.** mit etw. ist das letzte Wort über etw. *(Akk.)* gesprochen; **B** *(latest fashion)* **the ~ word** das Allerneueste; der letzte Schrei *(ugs.);* **~ ˈwords** *n. pl.* **her/his ~ words** ihre/seine letzten Worte; **[there's] famous ~ words [for you]** *(joc. iron.)* das wollen wir erst mal sehen

**lat.** *abbr.* **latitude** Br.

**latch** /lætʃ/ **1** *n.* **A** *(bar)* Riegel, *der;* **B** *(spring-lock)* Schnappschloss, *das;* **C** **on the ~** *(held by bar)* nur mit einem Riegel verschlossen; *(with lock not in use)* nur eingeklinkt. **2** *v.t.* zuschnappen lassen. **3** *v.i.* zuschnappen

**~ ˈon** *v.i. (coll.)* **A** *(attach oneself)* sich [ungefragt] anschließen; **B** *(understand)* es mitkriegen *(ugs.)*

**~ ˈon to** *v.t. (coll.)* **A** *(attach oneself to)* **~ on to sb.** sich an jmdn. hängen *(ugs.);* **B** *(understand)* kapieren *(ugs.);* **C** *(be enthusiastic about)* abfahren auf (+ *Akk.) (salopp)*

**ˈlatchkey** *n.* Hausschlüssel, *der;* **~ child** *(fig.)* Schlüsselkind, *das*

**late** /leɪt/ **1** *adj.* ▶ **912** **A** spät; *(after proper time)* verspätet; **am I ~?** komme ich zu spät?; **I am rather ~:** ich bin ziemlich spät dran *(ugs.) od.* habe mich ziemlich verspätet; **be ~ for the train** den Zug verpassen; **the train is [ten minutes] ~:** der Zug hat [zehn Minuten] Verspätung; **spring is ~ this year** dieses Jahr haben wir einen späten Frühling; **be [very] ~ for dinner** mit [großer] Verspätung zum Essen kommen; **what makes you so ~ today?** warum kommst du heute so spät?; **~ riser** Spätaufsteher, *der/* -aufsteherin, *die;* **~ entry** verspätete Anmeldung; **~ shift** Spätschicht, *die;* **in the ~ evening** spät am Abend; spätabends; **it is ~:** es ist [schon] spät; **have a ~ dinner** [erst] spät zu Abend essen; **~ summer** Spätsommer, *der;* **~ spring holidays** Ferien im späten Frühjahr; **in ~ July** Ende Juli; **~ Gothic/Victorian** spätgotisch/-viktorianisch; **~ seventeenth-century paintings** Gemälde aus dem späten siebzehnten Jahrhundert; ⇒ *also* **hour** B; **B** *(deceased)* verstorben; ⇒ *also* **lamented**; **C** *(former)* ehemalig; vormalig; **D** *(recent)* letzt...; **in ~ times** in letzter Zeit; **of ~ years** in den letzten Jahren; **E** *(backward in flowering, ripening, etc.)* spät ‹Sorte, Nelken›; **be ~** ‹Blumen:› spät blühen. ⇒ *also* **later**; **latest**.
**2** *adv.* **A** *(after proper time)* verspätet; **[too] ~:** zu spät; **they got home very ~:** sie kamen [erst] sehr spät nach Hause; **better ~ than never** lieber spät als gar nicht; **B** *(far on in time)* spät; **not until quite ~ this year** dieses Jahr erst recht spät; **~ in August** Ende August; **~ last century** [gegen] Ende des letzten Jahrhunderts; **~ in life** erst spät im Leben; erst im fortgeschrittenen Alter; **C** *(at or till a ~ hour)* spät; **be up/sit up ~:** bis spät in die Nacht *od.* lange aufbleiben; **work ~ at the office** [abends] lange im Büro arbeiten; **wait up ~ for sb./sth.** jmds./einer Sache wegen lange aufbleiben; **D** *(formerly)* **~ of ...:** ehemals wohnhaft in ...; ehemaliger Mitarbeiter ‹einer Firma›; **E** *(at ~ stage)* **traces remained as ~ as the seventeenth century** Überreste blieben noch bis ins siebzehnte Jahrhundert erhalten; **she was seen as ~ as yesterday** sie wurde gestern noch gesehen; **[a bit** *or* **somewhat** *or* **rather] ~ in the day** *(fig. coll.)* reichlich spät; **too ~ in the day** *(lit. or fig.)* zu spät.
**3** *n.* **of ~:** in letzter Zeit

**late:** **~ bird** *n. (fig. coll.)* Nachtmensch, *der;* Nachteule, *die (ugs. scherzh.);* **~comer** *n.* Zuspätkommende, *der/die*

**lateen** /ləˈti:n/ *adj. (Naut.)* **A** **~ sail** Lateinersegel, *das;* **B** *(rigged with a ~ sail)* Lateinersegel-; mit Lateinersegel *nachgestellt*

**lately** /ˈleɪtlɪ/ *adv.* in letzter Zeit; **only ~:** erst vor kurzem; **till ~:** bis vor kurzem

**lateness** /ˈleɪtnɪs/ *n., no pl.* **A** *(being after due time)* Verspätung, *die;* **B** *(being far on in time)* **the ~ of the performance** der späte Beginn der Vorstellung; **the ~ of the hour** die späte *od.* vorgerückte Stunde

**ˈlate-night** *attrib. adj.* Spät‹programm, -vorstellung›

**latent** /ˈleɪtənt/ *adj.* **A** latent [vorhanden]; **B** *(Med.)* latent. ⇒ *also* **heat** 1 B

**latent ˈimage** *n. (Photog.)* latentes Bild

**later** /ˈleɪtə(r)/ **1** *adv.* später; **~ on** später; **it must be ready no ~ than next week** es muss bis spätestens nächste Woche fertig sein; **~ [on] the same day** im weiteren Verlauf des Tages; später am Tag; **see you ~:** bis nachher; bis später; ⇒ *also* **soon** B. **2** *adj.* später; *(more recent)* neuer; jünger; **at a ~ date/time** zu einem späteren Zeitpunkt; später; **be ~, be of ~ date** neueren *od.* jüngeren Datums sein

**lateral** /ˈlætərəl/ *adj.* **A** seitlich (**to** von); Seiten‹flügel, -ansicht›; **~ thinking** Querdenken, *das;* **B** *(Anat.)* lateral; **C** *(Bot.)* seitenständig; **~ shoot** Seitentrieb, *der*

**laterally** /ˈlætərəlɪ/ *adv.* seitlich

**latest** /ˈleɪtɪst/ *adj.* **A** *(modern)* neu[e]st...; **the very ~ thing** das Allerneu[e]ste; **the ~ in fashion** der letzte Schrei *(ugs.);* die neu[e]ste Mode; **B** *(most recent)* letzt...; **have you heard the ~?** wissen Sie schon das Neu[e]ste?; **what's the ~?** was gibts Neues?; **C** **at [the] ~/the very ~:** spätestens/allerspätestens

**latex** /ˈleɪteks/ *n., pl.* **~es** *or* **latices** /ˈleɪtɪsi:z/ Latex, *der*

**lath** /lɑ:θ/ *n., pl.* **~s** /lɑ:θs, lɑ:ðz/ Latte, *die;* **~s** *(arrangement)* Lattung, *die;* **~ and plaster** Putzträger und Putz

**lathe** /leɪð/ *n.* Drehbank, *die;* Drehmaschine, *die (Technik)*

**lather** /ˈlɑ:ðə(r), ˈlæðə(r)/ **1** *n.* **A** *(froth)* [Seifen]schaum, *der;* **B** *(sweat)* Schweiß, *der;* Schaum, *der (veralt.);* **get [oneself] into a ~ [about sth.]** *(fig.)* sich [über etw. *(Akk.)*] aufregen. **2** *v.t.* **A** *(cover with froth)* einschäumen; einseifen; **B** *(coll.: thrash)* verprügeln

**Latin** /'lætɪn/ ❶ *adj.* Ⓐ lateinisch; ⇒ *also* **English** 1; Ⓑ (*of ancient Romans*) römisch; Ⓒ (*of RC Ch.*) lateinisch; Ⓓ (*of Southern Europeans*) romanisch; südländisch ‹Temperament, Charme›. ❷ *n.* ▶ 1275 Latein, *das;* **medieval ~:** Mittellatein, *das;* **modern ~:** Neulatein, *das;* **thieves' ~:** Gaunersprache, *die;* ⇒ *also* **English** 2 A

**Latin: ~ A'merica** *pr. n.* Lateinamerika (*das*); **~ A'merican** ❶ *adj.* lateinamerikanisch; ❷ *n.* Lateinamerikaner, *der*/Lateinamerikanerin, *die*

**Latinate** /'lætɪneɪt/ *adj.* (*derived from Latin*) aus dem Lateinischen stammend

**'Latin Church** *n.* lateinische Kirche

**Latinism** /'lætɪnɪzm/ *n.* Latinismus, *der*

**Latinist** /'lætɪnɪst/ *n.* Latinist, *der*/Latinistin, *die*

**Latinize** /'lætɪnaɪz/ *v.t.* latinisieren

**Latino** /lə'ti:nəʊ/ *n., pl.* **~s** (*Amer.*) Lateinamerikaner/-amerikanerin [in den USA]

**Latin: ~ Quarter** *n.* Quartier Latin, *das;* **~ rite** *n.* (*Eccl.*) lateinischer Ritus

**latish** /'leɪtɪʃ/ *adj. & adv.* ziemlich spät

**latitude** /'lætɪtju:d/ *n.* Ⓐ (*freedom*) Freiheit, *die;* (*for differences*) Spielraum, *der;* Ⓑ (*Geog.*) [geographische] Breite; (*of a place*) Breite, *die;* **~s** (*regions*) Breiten *Pl.;* **~ 40° N.** 40° nördlicher Breite; Ⓒ (*Astron.*) Breite, *die*

**latrine** /lə'tri:n/ *n.* Latrine, *die*

**latter** /'lætə(r)/ *attrib. adj.* Ⓐ letzter...; **the ~ ...:** der/die/das letztere; *pl.* die letzteren ...; (*as noun*) der/die/das Letztere; *pl.* die Letzteren; Ⓑ (*later*) letzt...; **the ~ half of the century** die zweite Hälfte des Jahrhunderts; **the ~ part of the year** die zweite Jahreshälfte; **the ~ end** das Ende

**latter: ~ 'day** *n.* Jüngster Tag; **~-day** *adj.* modern; **L~-day 'Saints** *n. pl.* Heilige der Letzten Tage

**latterly** /'lætəlɪ/ *adv.* Ⓐ (*later*) später; gegen Ende; Ⓑ (*lately*) in letzter Zeit

**lattice** /'lætɪs/ *n.* (*also fig., Phys.*) Gitter, *das*

**lattice: ~ frame, ~ girder** *ns.* Gitterträger, *der;* **~work** *n., no pl.* Gitterwerk, *das*

**Latvia** /'lætvɪə/ *pr. n.* Lettland (*das*)

**Latvian** /'lætvɪən/ ▶ 1275, ▶ 1340 ❶ *adj.* lettisch; **sb. is ~:** jmd. ist Lette/Lettin; ⇒ *also* **English** 1. ❷ *n.* Ⓐ (*person*) Lette, *der*/Lettin, *die;* Ⓑ (*language*) Lettisch, *das;* ⇒ *also* **English** 2 A

**laud** /lɔ:d/ *v.t.* (*literary*) preisen (*geh.*); rühmen; **much-~ed** viel gepriesen

**laudable** /'lɔ:dəbl/ *adj.* lobenswert

**laudably** /'lɔ:dəblɪ/ *adv.* lobenswert; löblich

**laudanum** /'lɔ:dnəm, 'lɒdnəm/ *n.* (*Pharm.*) Laudanum, *das*

•**laugh** /lɑ:f/ ❶ *n.* Ⓐ Lachen, *das;* (*loud and continuous*) Gelächter, *das;* **have a [good] ~ about sth.** [herzlich] über etw. (*Akk.*) lachen; **give a loud ~:** laut auflachen; **this line in the play always gets/raises a ~:** diese Zeile im Stück bringt immer einen Lacher; **join in the ~:** mitlachen; **have the last ~:** derjenige sein, der zuletzt lacht (*fig.*); **have** *or* **get the ~ of** *or* **on sb.** jmdn. auslachen können; **the ~ is on me** ich stehe dumm da (*ugs.*); **he is always good for a ~:** bei ihm gibt es immer etwas zu lachen; **it should be good for a ~:** dabei gibt es sicher etwas zu lachen; **sb./sth. is a ~ a minute** bei jmdm./etw. muss man alle Augenblicke lachen; **that sounds like a ~ a minute** (*iron.*) da wird man sicher viel zu lachen haben; **for ~s** zum *od.* aus Spaß; **play Mephisto for ~s** (*Theatre coll.*) aus Mephisto eine komische Figur machen; **for a ~:** [so] zum Spaß; **anything for a ~:** ich bin für alles *od.* für jeden Spaß zu haben (*ugs.*); Ⓑ (*type of ~*) Lachen, *das;* Art zu lachen; Ⓒ (*coll.: comical thing*) **it would be a ~ if ...:** es wäre ja zum [Tot]lachen, wenn ... (*ugs.*); **that's a** *or* **what a ~!** das ist ja zum [Tot]lachen! (*ugs.*); (*iron.*) das ist zum Lachen (*ugs.*); dass ich nicht lache!; **he's a [good] ~:** er ist urkomisch. ❷ *v.i.* lachen; **~ out loud** laut auflachen; **I thought I'd die ~ing** ich hätte mich beinahe totgelacht (*ugs.*); **I ~ed till I cried** ich habe Tränen gelacht; **be ~ing all over one's face** über das ganze Gesicht lachen; **~ at sb./sth.** (*in amusement*) über jmdn./etw. lachen; (*jeer*) jmdn. auslachen/etw. verlachen; über jmdn./etw. lachen; **~ in sb.'s face** jmdm. ins Gesicht lachen; **~ in** *or* **up one's sleeve** sich (*Dat.*) ins Fäustchen lachen; **he'll ~ on the other side of his face when ...:** ihm wird das Lachen [noch] vergehen, wenn ...; **he who ~s last ~s longest** (*prov.*) wer zuletzt lacht, lacht am besten (*Spr.*); **don't make me ~** (*coll. iron.*) dass ich nicht lache!; **~ and the world ~s with you, weep and you weep alone** (*prov.*) Freunde in der Not gehn hundert *od.* tausend auf ein Lot (*Spr.*); ⇒ *also* **laughing**. ❸ *v.t.* lachen; **he was ~ed out of town/off the stage** mit Hohnlachen wurde er aus der Stadt/von der Bühne gejagt; **~ oneself sick** *or* **silly** sich krank- *od.* schieflachen (*ugs.*)

**~ 'off** *v.t.* mit einem Lachen abtun

**laughable** /'lɑ:fəbl/ *adj.* lachhaft (*abwertend*); lächerlich

**laughing** /'lɑ:fɪŋ/ ❶ *n.* **be no ~ matter** nicht zum Lachen sein. ❷ *adj.* (*coll.: fortunate*) **be ~ [all over one's face]** fein raus sein (*ugs.*); ⇒ *also* **hyena** A; **jackass** C

**'laughing gas** *n.* Lachgas, *das*

**laughingly** /'lɑ:fɪŋlɪ/ *adv.* lachend; **what is ~ called ...** (*iron.*) was sich ... nennt (*spött.*)

**'laughing stock** *n.* **make sb. a ~, make a ~ of sb.** jmdn. zum Gespött machen; **he became the ~ of the whole neighbourhood** er wurde zum Gespött der ganzen Nachbarschaft

**laughter** /'lɑ:ftə(r)/ *n.* Lachen, *das;* (*loud and continuous*) Gelächter, *das;* **~ is the best medicine** (*prov.*) Lachen ist die beste Medizin

**'laughter lines** *n. pl.* Lachfältchen

**launch**[1] /lɔ:nʃ/ ❶ *v.t.* Ⓐ zu Wasser lassen, aussetzen ‹Rettungsboot, Segelboot›; vom Stapel lassen ‹neues Schiff›; (*propel*) werfen, abschießen ‹Harpune›; schleudern ‹Speer›; abschießen ‹Torpedo›; **~ a rocket into space** eine Rakete ins All schießen; Ⓑ (*fig.*) lancieren (*bes. Wirtsch.*); auf den Markt bringen ‹Produkt›; vorstellen ‹Buch, Schallplatte, Sänger›; auf die Bühne bringen ‹Theaterstück›; gründen ‹Firma›; **~ an attack** einen Angriff durchführen. ❷ *v.i.* **~ into a song** ein Lied anstimmen; **~ into a long speech/a stream of insults** eine lange Rede/eine Flut von Beschimpfungen vom Stapel lassen *od.* loslassen (*ugs.*). ❸ *n.* Ⓐ (*of spacecraft*) Start, *der;* (*of rocket*) Abschuss, *der;* (*of new ship*) Stapellauf, *der;* (*of boat*) Aussetzen, *das;* Ⓑ (*of product*) Lancieren, *das;* (*of book, record, singer*) Vorstellung, *die;* (*of play*) Premiere, *die;* (*of firm*) Gründung, *die*

**~ 'out** *v.i.* (*fig.*) **~ out into films/a new career/on one's own** sich beim Film versuchen/beruflich etwas ganz Neues anfangen/sich selbstständig machen; **we can really ~ out now** jetzt können wir aus dem Vollen schöpfen *od.* brauchen wir nicht zu sparen; **~ out at sb.** jmdn. anfahren

**launch**[2] *n.* (*boat*) Barkasse, *die*

**launcher** /'lɔ:nʃə(r)/ *n.* Ⓐ (*rocket*) Trägerrakete, *die;* Ⓑ (*structure*) Startrampe, *die*

**launching: ~ pad** *n.* [Raketen]abschussrampe, *die;* **~ site** *n.* [Raketen]abschussbasis, *die*

**'launch pad** ⇒ **launching pad**

**launder** /'lɔ:ndə(r)/ *v.t.* Ⓐ waschen und bügeln; **I have sent the sheets away to be ~ed** ich habe die Bettlaken zum Waschen weggegeben; Ⓑ (*fig.*) waschen ‹Geld›

**launderette** /lɔ:ndə'ret/, **laundrette** /lɔ:n'dret/, (*Amer.*) **laundromat** /'lɔ:ndrəmæt/ *ns.* Waschsalon, *der*

**laundry** /'lɔ:ndrɪ/ *n.* Ⓐ (*place*) Wäscherei, *die;* Ⓑ (*clothes etc.*) Wäsche, *die;* **do the ~:** Wäsche waschen

**laundry: ~ bag** *n.* Wäschebeutel, *der;* **~ basket** *n.* Wäschekorb, *der;* **~man** *n.* ▶ 1261 Wäschemann, *der*

**laureate** /'lɔ:rɪət, 'lɒrɪət/ *n.* Laureat, *der;* **[Poet] L~:** Hofdichter, *der;* Poeta laureatus, *der;* **Nobel ~:** Nobelpreisträger, *der*

**laurel** /'lɒrl/ *n.* Ⓐ (*emblem of victory*) Lorbeer[kranz], *der;* **win one's ~[s]** (*fig.*) Lorbeeren ernten; **have to look to one's ~s** (*fig.*) sich nicht auf seinen Lorbeeren ausruhen dürfen; **rest on one's ~s** (*fig.*) sich auf seinen Lorbeeren ausruhen (*ugs.*); Ⓑ (*Bot.*) **[cherry] ~:** Kirschlorbeer, *der;* Lorbeerkirsche, *die;* **mountain ~:** Lorbeerrose, *die;* ⇒ *also* **spurge laurel**

**lav** /læv/ *n.* (*coll.*) Klo, *das* (*ugs.*)

**lava** /'lɑ:və/ *n.* Lava, *die*

**lavage** /'lævɪdʒ/ *n.* (*Med.*) Spülung, *die*

**lavatory** /'lævətərɪ/ *n.* Toilette, *die;* ⇒ *also* **toilet** A

**lavatory: ~ attendant** *n.* ▶ 1261 Toilettenmann, *der*/Toilettenfrau, *die;* **~ humour** *n.* Fäkalhumor, *der;* **~ paper** ⇒ **toilet paper**; **~ seat** ⇒ **toilet seat**

**lavender** /'lævɪndə(r)/ ❶ *n.* Ⓐ (*Bot.*) Lavendel, *der;* Ⓑ (*colour*) Lavendel[blau], *das.* ❷ *adj.* lavendel[blau]

**'lavender water** *n.* Lavendel[wasser], *das*

**lavish** /'lævɪʃ/ ❶ *adj.* (*generous*) großzügig; überschwänglich ‹Lob, Liebe›; verschwenderisch ‹Ausgaben›; (*abundant*) üppig; **be ~ of** *or* **with sth.** nicht mit etw. geizen; **be too ~ with sth.** mit etw. übertreiben. ❷ *v.t.* **~ sth. on sb.** jmdn. mit etw. überhäufen *od.* überschütten; **~ too much time and money on a project** zu viel Zeit und Geld an ein Projekt verschwenden; **~ care on sth.** seine ganze Mühe auf etw. (*Akk.*) verwenden

**lavishly** /'lævɪʃlɪ/ *adv.* großzügig; überschwänglich ‹loben, lieben›; verschwenderisch ‹Geld ausgeben›; herrschaftlich ‹eingerichtet›

**law** /lɔ:/ *n.* Ⓐ *no pl.* (*body of established rules*) Gesetz, *das;* Recht, *das;* **the ~ forbids/allows sth. to be done** nach dem Gesetz ist es verboten/erlaubt, etw. zu tun; **the ~ is an ass** das Gesetz ist absurd; **according to/under British** *etc.* **~:** nach britischem *usw.* Recht; **break the ~:** gegen das Gesetz verstoßen; **be against the ~:** gegen das Gesetz sein; **the ~ is the ~:** Gesetz ist Gesetz; **be well versed in the ~:** gesetzeskundig *od.* rechtskundig sein; sich gut mit den Gesetzen auskennen; **history of ~:** Rechtsgeschichte, *die;* **laid down by [the] ~:** gesetzlich festgelegt; **under the** *or* **by** *or* **in ~:** nach dem Gesetz; **be/become ~:** vorgeschrieben sein/werden; **one ~ for the rich and another for the poor** zweierlei Recht für Reiche und Arme; **his word is ~** (*fig.*) sein Wort ist Gesetz; **lay down the ~ [about politics]** (*fig.*) [in Sachen Politik] den Ton angeben; **lay down the ~ to sb.** (*fig.*) jmdm. Vorschriften machen; **point** *or* **issue of ~:** Rechtsfrage, *die* (*Rechtsw.*); **~ enforcement** Durchführung der Gesetze/des Gesetzes; Ⓑ *no pl., no indef. art.* (*control through ~*) Gesetz, *das;* **~ and order** Ruhe und Ordnung; **be above the ~:** über dem Gesetz stehen; **outside the ~:** außerhalb der Legalität; Ⓒ (*statute*) Gesetz, *das;* **what are the ~s on drinking and driving?** wie sind die gesetzlichen Bestimmungen bei Trunkenheit am Steuer?; **there ought to be a ~ against it/people like you** so etwas sollte/Leute wie du sollten verboten werden; **be a ~ unto itself** seinen eigenen Gesetzen folgen; **be a ~ unto oneself** machen, was man will; **necessity knows** *or* **has no ~[s]** (*prov.*) Not kennt kein Gebot (*Spr.*); Ⓓ *no pl., no indef. art.* (*litigation*) Rechtswesen, *das;* Gerichtswesen, *das;* **go to ~ [over sth.]** [wegen etw.] vor Gericht gehen; [wegen etw.] den Rechtsweg beschreiten; **have the ~ on sb.** (*coll.*) jmdm. die Polizei auf den Hals schicken (*ugs.*) jmdn. vor den Kadi schleppen (*ugs.*); **take the ~ into one's own hands** sich (*Dat.*) selbst Recht verschaffen; Ⓔ *no pl., no indef. art.* (*profession*) **practise ~:** Jurist/Juristin sein; **go into [the] ~:** die juristische Laufbahn einschlagen; Jurist/Juristin werden; Ⓕ *no pl., no art.* (*Univ.: jurisprudence*) Jura *o. Art.;* Rechtswissenschaft, *die;* *attrib.* Rechts-; **Faculty of L~:** juristische

Fakultät; ~ **school** (*Amer.*) juristische Fakultät; ~ **student** Jurastudent, *der*/-studentin, *die;* **G** *no indef. art.* (*branch of* ~) **commercial** ~: Handelsrecht, *das;* ~ **of contract** Vertragsrecht, *das;* ~ **of nations** Völkerrecht, *das;* **bachelor/doctor of** ~**s** Bakkalaureus/Doktor der Rechte; **H** (*Sci., Philos., etc.*) Gesetz, *das;* (*regularity in nature*) Gesetzmäßigkeit, *die;* ~ **of nature, natural** ~ (*lit., or fig. iron.*) Naturgesetz, *das;* ~ **of supply and demand** Gesetz von Angebot und Nachfrage; ~ **of gravity** *or* **gravitation** Gravitationsgesetz, *das;* **I** (*rule of game, etiquette, or art*) Regel, *die;* ~**s of tennis/chess** Tennis-/Schachregeln; **J** (*Relig.*) Gebot, *das;* Gesetz, *das;* **Divine/God's** ~: göttliche Gebote/Gebote Gottes; **K** (*enforcing agent*) **the** ~: die Rechtsordnung; (*coll.: police, policeman*) Polente, *die* (*salopp*); **be in trouble with the** ~: mit dem Gesetz in Konflikt geraten; **I'll set the** ~ **on you!** ich hole die Polizei!; **the long arm of the** ~ (*rhet./iron.*) der Arm des Gesetzes; **officer of the** ~: Vertreter des Gesetzes

**law:** ~**-abiding** *adj.* gesetzestreu; ~ **agent** (*Scot.*) ⇒ **solicitor** A; ~**breaker** *n.* Gesetzesbrecher, *der*/-brecherin, *die;* Rechtsbrecher, *der*/-brecherin, *die;* ~**court** *n.* Gerichtsgebäude, *das;* (*room*) Gerichtssaal, *der;* **L~ Courts** *n. pl.* (*Brit.*) *Gebäudekomplex von Gerichtshöfen;* ~ **firm** *n.* (*Amer.*) Anwaltskanzlei, *die*

**lawful** /ˈlɔːfl/ *adj.* rechtmäßig, legitim ‹Besitzer, Erbe›; legitim, ehelich ‹Tochter, Sohn, Nachkomme›; legal, gesetzmäßig ‹Vorgehen, Maßnahme›; **by** ~ **means** mit legitimen Mitteln; ⇒ *also* **wife**

**lawfully** /ˈlɔːfəlɪ/ *adv.* legal; auf legalem Weg[e] ‹erwerben›

ˈ**lawgiver** *n.* Gesetzgeber, *der*

**lawless** /ˈlɔːlɪs/ *adj.* **A** gesetzlos; **B** (*unbridled*) zügellos

**law: L~ Lord** *n.* (*Brit.*) *Mitglied des obersten brit. Berufungsgerichts;* Law Lord, *der;* ~**maker** *n.* Gesetzgeber, *der;* ~**man** *n.* (*Amer.*) Vertreter des Gesetzes

**lawn** /lɔːn/ *n.* (*grass*) Rasen, *der;* ~**s** Rasenflächen; **area of** ~: Rasenfläche, *die*

**lawn:** ~**mower** *n.* Rasenmäher, *der;* ~ **seed** *n.* Grassamen, *der;* ~ **sprinkler** *n.* Rasensprenger, *der;* ~ ˈ**tennis** *n.* Rasentennis, *das*

**law:** ~ **officer** *n.* **A** Justizbeamte, *der*/Justizbeamtin, *die;* **B** (*Brit.: member of Government*) Kronanwalt, *der*/Kronanwältin, *die;* ~**suit** *n.* Prozess, *der*

**lawyer** /ˈlɔːjə(r), ˈlɔɪə(r)/ *n.* ▶ **1261** **A** (*solicitor etc.*) Rechtsanwalt, *der*/Rechtsanwältin, *die;* **B** (*expert in law*) Jurist, *der*/Juristin, *die*

**lax** /læks/ *adj.* lax; **be** ~ **about hygiene/paying the rent** *etc.* es mit der Hygiene/der Zahlung der Miete *usw.* nicht sehr genau nehmen; **the guards are** ~ **about whom they allow to enter** die Wachen nehmen es nicht sehr genau damit, wen sie hineinlassen

**laxative** /ˈlæksətɪv/ (*Med.*) **1** *adj.* abführend; stuhlgangfördernd. **2** *n.* Abführmittel, *das;* Laxativ[um] *das* (*fachspr.*)

**laxity** /ˈlæksɪtɪ/, **laxness** /ˈlæksnɪs/ *ns.* Laxheit, *die;* **moral** ~: laxe Moral

**lay**[1] /leɪ/ *adj.* **A** (*Relig.*) laikal; Laien‹bruder, -schwester, -predigt›; ⇒ *also* **vicar**; **B** (*inexpert*) laienhaft; **in** ~ **opinion** nach Ansicht des Laien; **to the** ~ **mind** für den Nichtfachmann *od.* Laien

**lay**[2] **1** *v.t.*, **laid** /leɪd/ **A** (*deposit, put*) legen, verlegen ‹Teppichboden, Rohr, Gleis, Steine, Kabel, Leitung›; legen ‹Parkett, Fliesen, Fundament›; anlegen ‹Straße, Gehsteig›; ~ **to rest** (*euphem.: bury*) zur letzten Ruhe betten (*geh. verhüll.*); ~ **eyes on sb.** jmdn. sehen *od.* erblicken; ⇒ *also* **hand** 1 A; **B** (*fig.*) **feel oneself laid under an obligation** sich verpflichtet fühlen; ~ **one's case before sb.** jmdm. seinen Fall vortragen; ~ **one's plans/ideas before sb.** jmdm. seine Pläne/Vorstellungen unterbreiten; **the facts are laid before us** die Fakten liegen vor uns; ~ **sth. before the Commons** *or* **on the table** (*Brit. Parl.*) etw. dem Unterhaus vorlegen; ~ **damages at £900** (*Law*) 900 Pfund Schadensersatz fordern; **C** (*impose*) auferlegen ‹Verantwortung, Verpflichtung, Geldbuße, Steuern› (**on** *Dat.*); verhängen ‹Strafe› (**on** über + *Akk.*); ~ **a penalty/a tax on sth.** etw. mit einer Strafe/einer Steuer belegen; ~ **a burden of responsibility on sb.'s shoulders** jmdm. Verantwortung aufbürden; **that** ~**s an obligation on me to do it** das verpflichtet mich, es zu tun; ~ **weight on sth.** Gewicht auf etw. (*Akk.*) legen; **D** (*wager*) **I'll** ~ **you five to one that …:** ich wette mit dir fünf zu eins, dass …; **I'll** ~ **you £10 that he'll come** ich wette mit dir um 10 Pfund, dass er kommt; ~ **a wager on sth.** eine Wette auf etw. (*Akk.*) abschließen; auf etw. (*Akk.*) wetten; **E** (*prepare*) ~ **the table/cloth** den Tisch decken/die Tischdecke auflegen; ~ **three places for lunch** drei Gedecke zum Mittagessen auflegen; ~ **[for] breakfast,** ~ **the breakfast things** den Frühstückstisch decken; ⇒ *also* **fire** 1 D; **F** (*Biol.*) legen ‹Ei›; **G** (*apply*) auftragen ‹Farbe usw.› (**on to, over** auf + *Akk.*); (*cover*) ~ **a floor with lino** *etc.* einen Boden mit Linoleum *usw.* auslegen; **H** (*devise*) schmieden, ersinnen ‹Plan›; **I** (*bring into a state*) ~ **idle** stilllegen ‹Fabrik›; ~ **land under water** Land überfluten; **J** (*cause to subside*) glätten ‹See›; binden ‹Staub›; beruhigen ‹Sturm›; (*fig.*) zerstreuen ‹Bedenken, Befürchtungen›; bannen ‹Geist, Gespenst›; **K** (*bring down*) ~ **one on sb.** (*coll.: hit sb.*) jmdm. eine reinschlagen (*salopp*); **the crops were laid [flat] by the rain** der Regen hat das Getreide zu Boden gedrückt; **L** (*sl.: copulate with*) ~ **a woman** eine Frau vernaschen *od.* aufs Kreuz legen (*salopp*); **M** (*make by twisting*) drehen ‹Seil›.

**2** *v.i.*, **laid A** (*Naut.*) liegen; ~ **at anchor** vor Anker liegen; **B** (*used erroneously for 'lie'*) liegen; ~ **down** sich hinlegen.

**3** *n.* **A** (*sl.: sexual partner*) **she's a good/an easy** ~: sie ist gut im Bett/steigt mit jedem ins Bett (*ugs.*); **B** (*way sth. lies*) Lage, *die;* **the** ~ **of the land** (*Amer.*) ≈ **the lie of the land** ⇒ **lie**[2] 1 A

~ **a'bout** *v.t.* (*coll.*) ~ **about sb.** auf jmdn. einschlagen; (*scold*) jmdn. ausschimpfen; ~ **about one** um sich schlagen; ⇒ *also* **layabout**

~ **a'side** *v.t.* beiseite *od.* zur Seite legen, weglegen ‹angefangene Arbeit›; (*fig.*) beilegen ‹Streit, Differenzen›; beiseite *od.* auf die Seite legen ‹Geld›; ablegen ‹Gewohnheiten, Untugenden›

~ ˈ**back** *v.t.* zurückstellen ‹Autositz, Behandlungsstuhl›; ⇒ *also* **laid-back**

~ ˈ**by** *v.t.* beiseite *od.* auf die Seite legen; **have some money laid by** etwas [Geld] auf der hohen Kante haben (*ugs.*)

~ ˈ**down** *v.t.* **A** hinlegen; ~ **sth. down on the table** etw. auf den Tisch legen; **B** (*give up*) niederlegen ‹Amt, Waffen›; ablegen ‹Amtskette›; (*deposit*) hinterlegen ‹Geld›; (*wager*) wetten ‹Betrag›; ~ **down one's arms** sich ergeben; die Waffen strecken (*geh.*); ~ **down one's life for sth./sb.** sein Leben für etw./jmdn. [hin]geben; **C** (*build*) bauen; auf Kiel legen ‹Schiff›; **D** (*formulate*) festlegen ‹Regeln, Richtlinien, Bedingungen›; aufstellen ‹Grundsätze, Regeln, Norm›; festsetzen ‹Preis›; (*in a contract, constitution*) verankern; niederlegen; **E** ~ **the land/field down to pasture** das Land/Feld in Weideland umwandeln; **F** (*store*) einlagern ‹Wein›

~ ˈ**in** *v.t.* einlagern; sich eindecken mit

~ **into** *v.t.* (*coll.*) ~ **into sb.** auf jmdn. losgehen; über jmdn. herfallen; (*fig.*) jmdn. zusammenstauchen (*ugs.*)

~ ˈ**off 1** *v.t.* **A** (*from work*) vorübergehend entlassen; **be laid off [from one's job]** Feierschichten einlegen müssen; **B** (*coll.*) (*stop*) ~ **off shouting!** hör auf zu schreien!; ~ **off it!** lass das!; hör auf damit!; (*stop attacking, lit. or fig.*) ~ **off him!** lass ihn in Ruhe! **2** *v.i.* (*coll.: stop*) aufhören. ⇒ *also* **lay-off**

~ ˈ**on** *v.t.* **A** (*provide*) sorgen für ‹Getränke, Erfrischungen, Unterhaltung›; bereitstellen ‹Auto, Transportmittel›; organisieren ‹Theaterbesuch, Stadtrundfahrt›; anschließen ‹Gas, Wasser, Strom›; **B** (*apply*) auftragen ‹Farbe usw.›; ~ **it on** (*fig.: exaggerate*) dick auftragen (*ugs.*); ⇒ *also* **thick** 1 A; **trowel** A; **C** (*impose*) erheben ‹Steuer, Gebühr›; verhängen ‹Strafe›; **D** ~**ing on of hands** (*Eccl.*) Handauflegung, *die*

~ ˈ**out 1** *v.t.* **A** (*spread out*) ausbreiten; (*ready for use*) zurechtlegen; **the books were laid out on the table** die Bücher waren *od.* lagen auf dem Tisch ausgebreitet; ~ **out sth. for sb. to see** etw. vor jmdm. ausbreiten; **B** (*for burial*) aufbahren; **C** (*arrange*) anlegen ‹Garten, Park, Wege›; das Layout machen für ‹Buch›; ⇒ *also* **layout**; **D** (*coll.: knock unconscious*) ~ **sb. out** jmdn. außer Gefecht setzen; **E** (*spend*) ausgeben; investieren (*ugs.*). **2** *v. refl.* ~ **oneself out to do sth.** sich anstrengen *od.* (*ugs.*) sich mächtig ins Zeug legen, etw. zu tun

~ ˈ**up** *v.t.* **A** (*store*) lagern; **you're** ~**ing up trouble/problems for yourself [later on]** (*fig.*) du handelst dir [für später] nur Ärger/Schwierigkeiten ein; **B** (*put out of service*) [vorübergehend] aus dem Verkehr ziehen ‹Fahrzeug›; (*through illness*) außer Gefecht setzen; **I was laid up in bed for a week** ich musste eine Woche das Bett hüten

**lay**[3] *n.* **A** (*of medieval minstrel*) Leich, *der* (*Literaturw.*); **B** (*narrative poem, song*) Ballade, *die*

**lay**[4] ⇒ **lie**[2] 2

**lay:** ~**about** *n.* (*Brit.*) Gammler, *der* (*ugs. abwertend*); Nichtstuer, *der* (*abwertend*); ~**-by** *n.*, *pl.* ~**s** (*Brit.*) Parkbucht, *die;* Haltebucht, *die;* ~ **clerk** *n.* Kantoreisänger, *der*

**layer** /ˈleɪə(r)/ *n.* **A** Schicht, *die;* **wear several** ~**s of clothing** mehrere Kleidungsstücke übereinander tragen; **several** ~**s of paper** mehrere Lagen Papier; ~ **of dust** Staubschicht, *die;* **B** (*Hort.*) Ableger, *der;* **C** (*poultry*) Leg[e]henne, *die;* **this hen is a poor** ~: dieses Huhn legt schlecht

ˈ**layer cake** *n.* Schichttorte, *die*

**layered** /ˈleɪəd/ *adj.* stufig ‹Haarschnitt›; **three-~ cake** dreischichtige Torte; ~ **skirt** Stufenrock, *der;* ~ **clouds** Schichtwolken *Pl.*

**layette** /leɪˈet/ *n.* **[baby's]** ~: Babyausstattung, *die*

**lay:** ~ **figure** *n.* **A** (*Art*) Gliederpuppe, *die;* **B** (*in dramatic work*) Phantom, *das;* ~**man** /ˈleɪmən/ *n.*, *pl.* ~**men** /ˈleɪmən/ Laie, *der;* ~**-off** *n.* **A** (*temporary dismissal*) vorübergehende Entlassung; **the** ~**-offs lasted longer than expected** es mussten länger als erwartet Feierschichten gefahren werden; **B** (*Sport; coll.: break from work*) Pause, *die;* **take a** ~**-off** [eine] Pause machen; ~**out** *n.* (*of house, office*) Raumaufteilung, *die;* (*of garden, park*) Gestaltung, *die;* Anlage, *die;* (*of book, magazine, poster, advertisement*) Gestaltung, *die;* Layout, *das;* (*of letter*) äußere Form; ~ **reader** *n. Laie, der Teile des Gottesdienstes halten darf;* ≈ Lektor, *der* (*ev. Kirche*); ≈ Diakon, *der* (*kath. Kirche*); ~**shaft** *n.* (*Mech. Engin.*) Vorgelegewelle, *die* (*Technik*)

**laze** /leɪz/ **1** *v.i.* faulenzen; ~ **around** *or* **about** herumfaulenzen (*ugs.*); **spend the whole day lazing in bed** den ganzen Tag faul im Bett liegen. **2** *v.t.* ~ **the day/one's life away** den ganzen Tag/sein ganzes Leben vertrödeln *od.* verbummeln (*ugs. abwertend*)

**lazily** /ˈleɪzɪlɪ/ *adv.* faul; (*sluggishly*) träge

**laziness** /ˈleɪzɪnɪs/ *n.*, *no pl.* Faulheit, *die;* (*sluggishness*) Trägheit, *die*

**lazy** /ˈleɪzɪ/ *adj.* faul; träge ‹Rhythmus, Musik, Geste, Sprechweise›; träge fließend ‹Fluss›; **physically** ~: träge; **mentally** ~: geistig träge; denkfaul; **have a** ~ **day on the beach** einen Tag am Strand faulenzen; **be in a** ~ **mood** sich träge fühlen; **be** ~ **about writing [letters]** schreibfaul sein

**lazy:** ~**bones** *n. sing.* Faulpelz, *der;* ~ ˈ**eye** *n. Auge mit Sehschwäche, das [beim Schielen] weniger belastet wird und deshalb in der Sehkraft weiter nachlässt*

**lb.** *abbr.* ▶ **1683** **pound[s]** ≈ Pfd.

**l.b.w.** /elbiːˈdʌbljʊ/ *abbr.* (*Cricket*) **leg before wicket**

**LCD** *abbr.* **liquid crystal display** LCD

**L/Cpl.** *abbr.* **Lance-Corporal** OG

**L-driver** /ˈeldraɪvə(r)/ (*Brit.*) ⇒ **learner driver**

**LEA** *abbr.* **Local Education Authority** ≈ Schulamt, *das*

**lea** /li:/ *n.* (*poet.*) Wiese, *die*

**leach** /li:tʃ/ ❶ *v.t.* (*make percolate*) durchsickern lassen; (*subject to percolation*) auslaugen; (*remove by percolation*) extrahieren; auslaugen. ❷ *v.i.* (*percolate through*) durchsickern; (*be removed by percolation*) ausgelaugt werden

**lead**[1] /led/ ❶ *n.* Ⓐ (*metal*) Blei, *das;* **white ~:** Bleiweiß, *das;* **[as] heavy as ~:** schwer wie Blei; bleischwer; **go down like a ~ balloon** mit Pauken und Trompeten durchfallen (*ugs.*); ‹Rede, Vorschlag usw.:› überhaupt nicht ankommen; ⇒ *also* **blacklead**; **red lead**; Ⓑ (*in pencil*) [Bleistift]mine, *die;* Ⓒ (*bullets*) Blei, *das* (*veralt.*); **I'll fill** *or* **pump you full of ~:** ich pumpe dich mit Blei voll; Ⓓ (*Naut.*) Lot, *das;* Senkblei, *das;* **cast** *or* **heave the ~:** das Lot [aus]werfen; **swing the ~** (*fig. Brit. coll.*) sich drücken; Ⓔ *in pl.* (*of window*) Bleifassung, *die;* Ⓕ (*Printing*) Reglette, *die.*
❷ *attrib. adj.* Blei-.
❸ *v.t.* Ⓐ in Blei fassen ‹Fenster›; **~ed** bleigefasst; Ⓑ **~ed petrol** bleihaltiges Benzin

**lead**[2] /li:d/ ❶ *v.t.*, **led** /led/ Ⓐ führen; **~ sb. a miserable life** *or* **existence** jmdm. das Leben zur Qual machen; **~ sb. through the procedures** (*fig.*) jmdn. mit dem Verfahren vertraut machen; **~ sb. to do sth.** (*fig.*) jmdn. dazu bringen, etw. zu tun; **~ sb. by the hand** jmdn. an der Hand führen; **~ sb. by the nose** (*fig.*) jmdn. nach seiner Pfeife tanzen lassen; **let oneself be led by the nose** (*fig.*) sich an der Nase herumführen lassen; **~ sb. into trouble/difficulties** (*fig.*) jmdm. Ärger einbringen/jmdn. in Schwierigkeiten bringen; **this is ~ing us nowhere** (*fig.*) das führt zu nichts; ⇒ *also* **astray** 1; **dance** 3 A; **garden** 1 A; **way** 1 B; Ⓑ (*fig.: influence, induce*) **~ sb. to do sth.** jmdn. veranlassen, etw. zu tun; **be easily led** sich leicht beeinflussen lassen; **~ sb. into bad habits** jmdn. zu schlechten Gewohnheiten verleiten; **children are easier led than driven** bei Kindern erreicht man im Guten mehr als im Bösen; **that ~s me to believe that ...:** das lässt mich glauben, dass ...; **I was led to the conclusion that ...:** ich gelangte zu dem Schluss, dass ...; **this ~s me to the conclusion that ...:** daraus schließe ich, dass ...; **Is it true that she was married before? — So I am led to believe** Stimmt es, dass sie schon einmal verheiratet war? — Soweit ich weiß, ja; **he led me to suppose/believe that ...:** er gab mir Grund zu der Annahme/er machte mich glauben, dass ...; Ⓒ führen ‹Leben›; **~ a life of misery/a wretched existence** ein erbärmliches Dasein führen/eine kümmerliche Existenz fristen; Ⓓ (*be first in*) anführen; **~ the world in electrical engineering** auf dem Gebiet der Elektrotechnik in der ganzen Welt führend sein; **Smith led Jones by several yards/seconds** (*Sport*) Smith hatte mehrere Yards/Sekunden Vorsprung vor Jones; ⇒ *also* **field** 1 L; Ⓔ (*direct, be head of*) anführen ‹Bewegung, Abordnung›; leiten ‹Diskussion, Veranstaltung, Ensemble›; ‹Dirigent:› leiten ‹Orchester, Chor›; ‹Konzertmeister:› führen ‹Orchester›; **~ a party** Vorsitzender/Vorsitzende einer Partei sein; **~ the government** an der Spitze der Regierung stehen; Regierungschef/-chefin sein; **Napoleon led his army into Italy/to a great victory** Napoleon führte seine Armee nach Italien/zu einem großen Sieg; Ⓕ (*cause to pass*) **~ water through sth.** Wasser durch etw. [hindurch]leiten; **~ a rope through a pulley** ein Seil über die Rolle[n] eines Flaschenzugs führen; Ⓖ (*Cards*) ausspielen; **~ a spade** Pik ausspielen.
❷ *v.i.*, **led** Ⓐ ‹Straße usw., Tür:› führen; **~ to the town/to the sea/out of the town** zur Stadt/ans Meer/aus der Stadt führen; **~ to confusion** Verwirrung stiften; **one thing led to another** es kam eins zum anderen; **what will it all ~ to?** wo soll das alles [noch] hinführen?; Ⓑ (*be first*) führen; (*go in front*) vorangehen; (*fig.: be leader*) an der Spitze stehen; **~ by 3 metres** mit 3 Metern in Führung liegen; 3 Meter Vorsprung haben; **~ in the race** das Rennen anführen; **it's Smith ~ing from Jones and Brown** Smith führt vor Jones und Brown; Ⓒ (*Journ.*) **a good story to ~ with** eine gute Titelgeschichte; **~ with the latest spy scandal** die jüngste Spionageaffäre groß herausbringen; Ⓓ (*Cards*) ausspielen; **~ with a spade** Pik ausspielen.
❸ *n.* Ⓐ (*precedent*) Beispiel, *das;* (*clue*) Anhaltspunkt, *der;* **follow sb.'s ~, take one's ~ from sb.** jmds. Beispiel (*Dat.*) folgen; **give sb. a ~** (*precedent*) jmdm. mit gutem Beispiel vorangehen; (*clue*) jmdm. einen Anhaltspunkt geben; Ⓑ (*first place*) Führung, *die;* **be in the ~:** in Führung liegen; an der Spitze liegen; **move** *or* **go into the ~:** sich an die Spitze setzen; in Führung gehen; **keep one's ~:** sich an der Spitze *od.* seine Führungsposition behaupten; **we mustn't lose our ~:** wir dürfen unsere Führungsposition nicht verlieren; **hold the ~ in export sales** mit seinen Exportgeschäften die Spitze halten; **take the ~ from sb.** jmdm. den Rang ablaufen; (*in race*) sich vor jmdm. an die Spitze setzen; vor jmdm. in Führung gehen; Ⓒ (*amount*) Vorsprung, *der;* **have a ~ of two metres/minutes over sb.** einen Vorsprung von zwei Metern/Minuten vor jmdm. haben; Ⓓ (*on dog etc.*) Leine, *die;* **on a ~:** an der Leine; **let a dog off the** *or* **its ~:** einen Hund von der Leine losmachen; **put a dog on the ~:** einen Hund anleinen; Ⓔ (*Electr.*) Kabel, *das;* Leitung, *die;* Ⓕ (*Theatre*) Hauptrolle, *die;* (*player*) Hauptdarsteller, *der*/-darstellerin, *die;* Ⓖ (*Cards*) **whose ~ is it?** wer spielt aus?; **the ~ was the jack of clubs** Kreuzbube war gespielt.
❹ *adj.* Lead‹gitarre, -gitarrist usw.›

**~ a'way** *v.t.* abführen ‹Gefangenen, Verbrecher›

**~ 'off** ❶ *v.t.* Ⓐ (*take away*) abführen; Ⓑ (*begin*) beginnen. ❷ *v.i.* beginnen

**~ 'on** ❶ *v.t.* Ⓐ (*entice*) **~ sb. on** jmdn. reizen; **he's ~ing you on** er versucht, dich zu reizen; Ⓑ (*deceive*) auf den Leim führen (*ugs.*); **she's just ~ing him on** sie hält ihn nur zum Narren; Ⓒ (*take further*) **that ~s me on to my next point** das bringt mich zu meinem nächsten Punkt; **~ sb. on to do sth.** jmdn. darauf bringen, etw. zu tun. ❷ *v.i.* Ⓐ *imper.* (*go first*) **~ on!** geh vor!; Ⓑ **~ing on from what you have just said, ...:** um fortzuführen, was Sie eben sagten, ...; **~ on to the next topic** *etc.* zum nächsten Thema *usw.* führen; **~ on to better things** jmdn. weiterbringen

**~ 'up to** *v.t.* [schließlich] führen zu; (*aim at*) hinauswollen auf (+ *Akk.*); **~ up to a very funny punch line** in einer köstlichen Pointe gipfeln; **just as I was ~ing up to the main point of my speech** gerade als ich zum Hauptpunkt meiner Rede kommen wollte

**leaden** /'ledn/ *adj.* Ⓐ bleiern; Ⓑ (*fig.*) (*heavy*) bleiern ‹Schlaf, Augenlider, Glieder›; schleppend ‹Tempo›; bang ‹Herz›; (*oppressive*) drückend ‹Atmosphäre›; lähmend ‹Einfluss›; starr ‹Regeln, Haltung›

**leader** /'li:də(r)/ *n.* Ⓐ Führer, *der*/Führerin, *die;* (*of political party*) Vorsitzende, *der/die;* (*of gang, hooligans, rebels*) Anführer, *der*/Anführerin, *die;* (*of expedition, project, troupe*) Leiter, *der*/Leiterin, *die;* (*of deputation*) Sprecher, *der*/Sprecherin, *die;* (*of tribe*) [Stammes]häuptling, *der;* Stammesführer, *der;* **the Egyptian/Labour ~:** der ägyptische Präsident/der Vorsitzende der Labour Party; **union/the Labour ~s** Gewerkschaftsvorsitzende/die Führenden der Labour Party; **L~ of the House of Commons/Lords** (*Brit. Polit.*) Führer des Unterhauses/Oberhauses; **have the qualities of a ~:** Führungsqualitäten haben; ⇒ *also* **follow-my-leader**; Ⓑ (*one who is first*) **this scientist is a ~ in his field** dieser Wissenschaftler ist eine führende Kapazität auf seinem Gebiet; **be the ~ in a race** in einem Rennen in Führung liegen; **catch up with the ~s** (*in race*) sich an die Spitze des Feldes vorarbeiten; **be no longer amongst the ~s of world tennis** nicht mehr zur internationalen Spitze[nklasse] im Tennis gehören; Ⓒ (*Brit. Journ.*) Leitartikel, *der;* Ⓓ (*tab on film or tape*) Startband, *das;* Ⓔ (*Mus.*) (*leading performer*) Leader, *der*/Leaderin, *die;* (*Brit.: principal first violinist*) Konzertmeister, *der*/-meisterin, *die;* (*Amer.: conductor*) Dirigent, *der*/Dirigentin, *die;* Ⓕ (*Hort.*) Haupttrieb, *der*

**leaderless** /'li:dəlɪs/ *adj.* führerlos

**leadership** /'li:dəʃɪp/ *n.* Ⓐ Führung, *die;* (*capacity to lead*) Führungseigenschaften *Pl.;* **under the ~ of** unter [der] Führung von; Ⓑ (*leaders*) Führung[sspitze], *die;* **~ of the party** Parteivorsitz, *der*

**'leader writer** *n.* Leitartikelschreiber, *der*/-schreiberin, *die;* Leitartikler, *der*/-artiklerin, *die* (*Pressejargon*)

**lead-free** /'ledfri:/ *adj.* bleifrei

**lead-in** /'li:dɪn/ *n.* Einleitung, *die* (**to** *Gen.*); **as a ~ to the film/programme** zur Einleitung des Films/Programms

**leading** /'li:dɪŋ/ *adj.* führend; (*in first position*) ‹Läufer, Pferd, Auto› an der Spitze; **~ role** Hauptrolle, *die;* (*fig.*) führende Rolle

**leading: ~ 'article** *n.* (*Brit. Journ.*) Leitartikel, *der;* **~ 'counsel** *n.* (*Brit. Law*) Kronanwalt, *der*/-anwältin, *die;* (*of the defence*) Hauptverteidiger, *der*/-verteidigerin, *die;* **~ 'edge** *n.* (*foremost edge*) Vorderkante, *die;* (*of sail*) Vorliek, *das;* **~ 'lady** *n.* Hauptdarstellerin, *die;* **his ~ lady** seine Partnerin (*als Hauptdarstellerin*); **~ 'light** *n.* herausragende Persönlichkeit; (*expert*) führende Kapazität; **~ 'man** *n.* Hauptdarsteller, *der;* **her ~ man** ihr Partner (*als Hauptdarsteller*); **~ 'question** *n.* Suggestivfrage, *die;* **~ rein** *n.* Leitzügel, *der*

**lead: ~ pencil** /led 'pensl/ *n.* Bleistift, *der;* **~ poisoning** /'ledpɔɪzənɪŋ/ *n.* Bleivergiftung, *die;* **~ screw** /'li:d skru:/ *n.* Leitspindel, *die* (*Technik*); **~ shot** /led 'ʃɒt/ *n.* Ⓐ *no pl.* (*Angling*) Bleikugeln *Pl.;* Ⓑ *no pl.* (*for shotgun*) Schrot, *der od. das;* Ⓒ (*single projectile*) Blei- *od.* Schrotkugel, *die;* **~ singer** /li:d 'sɪŋə(r)/ *n.* Leadsänger *der*/-sängerin, *die;* **~ story** /'li:d stɔ:rɪ/ *n.* (*Journ.*) Titelgeschichte, *die;* **~ time** /'li:d taɪm/ *n.* (*Econ.*) Entwicklungszeit, *die;* **~-up** /'li:dʌp/ *n.* Vorfeld, *das* (*fig.*); **in/during the ~-up to the election/revolution** im Vorfeld der Wahlen/der Revolution

**leaf** /li:f/ ❶ *n.*, *pl.* **leaves** /li:vz/ Ⓐ Blatt, *das;* **the falling leaves** die fallenden Blätter; das fallende Laub; **shake like a ~:** zittern wie Espenlaub; **be in ~:** grün sein; **come into ~:** grün werden; ausschlagen; Ⓑ (*of paper*) Blatt, *das;* **a ~ of paper** ein Blatt Papier; **turn over a new ~** (*fig.*) einen neuen Anfang machen; sich ändern; ⇒ *also* **book** 1 A; Ⓒ (*of door*) Flügel, *der;* (*of table*) (*hinged/sliding flap*) Platte, *die;* (*for inserting*) Einlegebrett, *das.* ❷ *v.i.* **~ through sth.** etw. durchblättern; in etw. (*Dat.*) blättern

**leaf: ~ green** ❶ /'--/ *adj.* laubgrün; ❷ /-'-/ *n.* Laubgrün, *das;* **~ insect** *n.* Wandelndes Blatt

**leafless** /'li:flɪs/ *adj.* blattlos, kahl ‹Baum›

**leaflet** /'li:flɪt/ ❶ *n.* Ⓐ [Hand]zettel, *der;* (*with manufacturer's instructions*) Gebrauchsanweisung, *die;* Bedienungsanleitung, *die;* (*advertising*) Reklamezettel, *der;* (*political*) Flugblatt, *das;* Ⓑ (*Bot.*) Blättchen, *das.* ❷ *v.t.* [Hand]zettel verteilen an (+ *Akk.*)

**leaf: ~ mould** *n.* Laubkompost, *der;* **~ spring** *n.* (*Mech. Engin.*) Blattfeder, *die* (*Technik*); **~-stalk** *n.* Blattstiel, *der*

**leafy** /'li:fɪ/ *adj.* belaubt; **~ vegetable** Blattgemüse, *das;* **a ~ country lane** eine baumbestandene Landstraße

**league**[1] /li:g/ *n.* Ⓐ (*agreement*) Bündnis, *das;* Bund, *der;* (*in history*) Liga, *die;* **enter into** *or* **form a ~:** ein Bündnis eingehen *od.* schließen; einen Bund schließen; **be in ~ with sb.** mit jmdm. im Bunde sein *od.* stehen; **those two are in ~ [together]** die beiden stecken unter einer Decke (*ugs.*); Ⓑ (*Sport*) Liga, *die;* **the ~ championship** die Ligameisterschaft; **I am not in his ~, he is out of my ~** (*fig.*) ich komme nicht an ihn heran; mit ihm kann ich mich nicht messen; **be in the big ~** (*fig.*) es geschafft haben; ⇒ *also* **Rugby League**

**league**[2] *n.* (*arch.: distance*) ≈ drei Meilen; **travel many a ~:** viele Meilen reisen

**league: ~ 'football** *n.* Ligafußball, *der;* **~ game** *n.* Ligaspiel, *das;* **~ 'leaders** *n. pl.* (*Sport*) Tabellenführer, *der;* **~ match** *n.* Ligaspiel, *das;* **L~ of 'Nations** *n.* (*Hist.*) Völkerbund, *der;* **~ table** *n.* Tabelle, *die* (*Sport*); **be at the top/bottom of the ~ table** an der Tabellenspitze/am Tabellenende sein (*fig.*); an der Spitze rangieren/das Schlusslicht bilden (*ugs.*) (**of** unter + *Dat.*)

**leak** /liːk/ ❶ *n.* Ⓐ (*hole*) Leck, *das;* (*in roof, ceiling, tent*) undichte Stelle; **there's a ~ in the tank** der Tank ist leck; der Tank hat ein Leck; **spring a ~** ‹Schiff:› leckschlagen (*Seemannsspr.*); ‹Gas-, Flüssigkeitsbehälter:› ein Leck bekommen; **stop the ~:** das Leck abdichten *od.* stopfen; Ⓑ (*escaping fluid/gas*) durch ein Leck austretende Flüssigkeit/austretendes Gas; **I can smell a gas ~:** hier riecht es nach Gas; Ⓒ (*instance*) **a gas/oil ~, a ~ of gas/oil** ein Austreten von Gas/Öl; **there has been a gas/oil ~:** es ist Gas/Öl ausgetreten; Ⓓ (*fig.: of information*) undichte Stelle; **government ~s** undichte Stellen in der Regierung; **there has been a ~ to the press/from reliable sources** der Presse sind Informationen zugespielt worden/aus verlässlichen Quellen sind Informationen durchgesickert; **who was responsible for the ~?** wer war dafür verantwortlich, dass Informationen durchgesickert sind?; Ⓔ (*Electr.*) Elektrizitätsverlust, *der;* (*path or point*) Fehlerstelle, *die;* Ⓕ **have a/go for a ~** (*sl.*) pinkeln/pinkeln gehen (*salopp*).
❷ *v.t.* Ⓐ austreten lassen; **the pipe is ~ing water/gas** aus dem lecken Rohr tritt Wasser/Gas aus; Ⓑ (*fig.: disclose*) durchsickern lassen; **~ sth. to sb.** jmdm. etw. zuspielen; **details of the plan have been ~ed** man hat Einzelheiten des Plans durchsickern lassen.
❸ *v.i.* Ⓐ (*escape*) austreten (**from** aus); (*enter*) eindringen (**in** in + *Akk.*); Ⓑ ‹Fass, Tank, Schiff:› lecken; ‹Rohr, Leitung, Dach:› undicht sein; ‹Gefäß, Füller:› auslaufen; **the roof ~s** es regnet durch das Dach; Ⓒ (*fig.*) **~ [out]** durchsickern

**leakage** /'liːkɪdʒ/ *n.* Ⓐ Auslaufen, *das;* (*of fluid, gas*) Ausströmen, *das;* (*fig.: of information*) Durchsickern, *das;* Ⓑ (*substance, amount*) **the ~ is increasing** das Leck wird größer; **mop up the ~:** das ausgelaufene Wasser *usw.* aufwischen; **~ to the Press** (*fig.*) Indiskretionen der Presse gegenüber

**leaky** /'liːkɪ/ *adj.* undicht; leck ‹Schiff, Boot, Tank›

**lean**[1] /liːn/ ❶ *adj.* Ⓐ mager; hager ‹Person, Gesicht›; **we had a ~ time [of it] during the War** es ging uns sehr schlecht während des Krieges; Ⓑ (*Commerc.*) schlank. ❷ *n.* (*meat*) Magere, *das*

**lean**[2] ❶ *v.i.*, **~ed** /liːnd, lent/ *or* (*Brit.*) **~t** /lent/ Ⓐ sich beugen; **~ against the door** sich gegen die Tür lehnen; **~ out of the window** sich aus dem Fenster lehnen *od.* beugen; **~ down/forward** sich herab-/vorbeugen; **~ backwards** sich zurückbeugen; sich nach hinten beugen; **~ back in one's chair** sich im Sessel zurücklehnen; Ⓑ (*support oneself*) **~ against/on sth.** sich gegen/an etw. (*Akk.*) lehnen; **~ on sth.** (*from above*) sich auf etw. (*Akk.*) lehnen; **~ on sb.'s arm** sich auf jmds. Arm (*Akk.*) stützen; Ⓒ (*be supported*) lehnen (**against** an + *Dat.*); Ⓓ (*fig.: rely*) **~ [up]on sb.** auf jmdn. bauen; **I ~ on my friends for moral support** ich baue auf den Beistand meiner Freunde; Ⓔ (*stand obliquely*) sich neigen; **the Leaning Tower of Pisa** der Schiefe Turm von Pisa; Ⓕ (*fig.: tend*) **~ to[wards] sth.** zu etw. neigen; **he ~s to the left politically** er tendiert politisch nach links.
❷ *v.t.*, **~ed** *or* (*Brit.*) **~t** lehnen (**against** gegen *od.* an + *Akk.*).
❸ *n.* Neigung, *die;* **have a definite ~ to the right** deutlich nach rechts geneigt sein; eine deutliche Neigung nach rechts aufweisen; **be on the ~:** schief sein; **have a ~ of 15°** einen Neigungswinkel von 15° haben

**~ on** *v.t.* (*fig. coll.*) unter Druck setzen; **he just needs ~ing on a little** man muss ihm nur ein bisschen gut zureden (*iron.*); ⇒ *also* **~**[2] 1 B, D

**~ over** ❶ /'---/ *v.t.* sich neigen über (+ *Akk.*). ❷ /-'--/ *v.i.* ‹Person:› sich hinüberbeugen; (*forwards*) sich vorbeugen; ‹Gegenstand:› sich neigen; **he ~ed over backwards/sideways** er beugte sich nach hinten/zur Seite; ⇒ *also* **backwards** A

**lean-burn 'engine** *n.* (*Motor Veh.*) Mager[mix]motor, *der*

**leaning** /'liːnɪŋ/ *n.* Hang, *der;* Neigung, *die;* **have Marxist/homosexual ~s** zum Marxismus tendieren/homosexuelle Neigungen haben

**leanness** /'liːnnɪs/ *n.*, *no pl.* Hagerkeit, *die;* (*of times*) Dürftigkeit, *die*

**leant** ⇒ **lean**[2]

**lean-to** /'liːntuː/ *n.*, *pl.* **~s** Anbau, *der*

**leap** /liːp/ ❶ *v.i.*, **~ed** /liːpt, lept/ *or* **~t** /lept/ Ⓐ springen; ‹Herz:› hüpfen; **~ to one's feet** aufspringen; **~ out of/up from one's chair** aus seinem Sessel/von seinem Stuhl aufspringen; **~ down off the table** vom Tisch herunterspringen; **~ back in shock** vor Entsetzen zurückspringen; **~ up and down in excitement** aufgeregt herumspringen; **~ around** *or* **about** herumspringen; Ⓑ (*fig.*) **~ to conclusions** voreilige Schlüsse ziehen; **~ to sb.'s defence** jmdm. beispringen (*geh.*); **~ at the chance** *or* **opportunity** die Gelegenheit beim Schopf packen; **~ to stardom/into prominence** mit einem Schlag zum Star/berühmt werden; **~ at an offer** sofort zugreifen; **~ to the eye** ins Auge *od.* in die Augen springen. ⇒ *also* **look** 1 A.
❷ *v.t.*, **~ed** *or* **~t** Ⓐ (*jump over*) überspringen; springen *od.* setzen über (+ *Akk.*); Ⓑ (*cause to ~*) springen lassen.
❸ *n.* Sprung, *der;* **take a [great] ~ at the fence** [mit einem großen Satz] am Zaun hochspringen; (*successfully*) einen [großen] Satz über den Zaun machen; **with** *or* **in one ~:** mit einem Satz; **by ~s and bounds** (*fig.*) mit Riesenschritten ‹vorangehen›; sprunghaft ‹zunehmen›; ⇒ *also* **dark** 2 C

**'leapfrog** ❶ *n.* Bockspringen, *das.* ❷ *v.i.*, **-gg-** Bockspringen machen; **~ over sb.** einen Bocksprung über jmdn. machen. ❸ *v.t.*, **-gg-** (*fig.*) überspringen

**leapt** ⇒ **leap**

**'leap year** *n.* Schaltjahr, *das*

**learn** /lɜːn/ ❶ *v.t.*, **~t** /lɜːnt/ *or* **~ed** /lɜːnd, lɜːnt/ Ⓐ lernen; (*with emphasis on completeness of result*) erlernen; **~ sth. by** *or* **from experience** etw. durch [die] *od.* aus der Erfahrung lernen; **~ sth. from** *or* **of sb./from a book/an example** etw. von jmdm./aus einem Buch/am Beispiel lernen; **~ one's craft from** *or* **through hard study** seine beruflichen Fähigkeiten durch fleißiges Lernen erwerben; **have you never ~ed any manners/sense?** hat man dir keine Manieren beigebracht/wo hast du nur deinen Verstand?; **I am ~ing [how] to play tennis** ich lerne Tennis spielen; **Can you swim? — No, I never ~ed how [to]** Kannst du schwimmen? — Nein, ich habe es nie gelernt; ⇒ *also* **lesson** C; **rope** 1 E; Ⓑ (*find out*) erfahren; lernen; (*by oral information*) hören; (*by observation*) erkennen; merken; (*by thought*) erkennen; (*be informed of*) erfahren; **I ~ed from the newspaper that ...:** ich habe in der Zeitung gelesen *od.* aus der Zeitung erfahren, dass ...; **I ~ed from his manner what sort of person he was** seine Art verriet mir, was für ein Mensch er war; Ⓒ (*arch./joc./uneducated: teach*) lernen (+ *Dat.*) (*mundartl., ugs.* [*standardsprachlich nicht korrekt*]); **that'll ~ you!** das wird dir 'ne Lehre sein!; **I'll ~ you!** (*threat*) ich werd dir helfen! (*ugs.*).
❷ *v.i.*, **~t** *or* **~ed** Ⓐ lernen; **be slow to ~:** langsam lernen; **you'll soon ~:** du wirst es bald lernen; **will you never ~?** du lernst es wohl nie!; **~ from the experience/mistakes of others** aus den Erfahrungen/Fehlern anderer lernen; **some people never ~:** mancher lernts nie; **~ by one's mistakes** aus seinen Fehlern lernen; **I had to ~ by my mistakes** ich konnte nur aus meinen eigenen Fehlern lernen; **~ about sth.** etwas über etw. (*Akk.*) lernen; **you're never too old** *or* **it's never too late to ~:** man kann immer noch [etwas] dazulernen; zum Lernen ist es nie zu spät; Ⓑ (*get to know*) erfahren (**of** von); **I have ~t about what you get up to** ich habe erfahren, was du so treibst

**~ 'up** *v.t.* Ⓐ **~ up some law** sich (*Dat.*) einige juristische Kenntnisse aneignen; einiges über das Rechtswesen lernen; Ⓑ (*refresh knowledge of*) **~ up one's history** seine Geschichtskenntnisse auffrischen

**learned** /'lɜːnɪd/ *adj.* Ⓐ gelehrt; **very ~ in ancient history** in Alter Geschichte sehr bewandert; Ⓑ (*associated with ~ persons*) wissenschaftlich ‹Gesellschaft, Zeitschrift›; akademisch ‹Stil›; ⇒ *also* **profession** A; Ⓒ (*Brit. Law: in address or reference*) verehrt; geschätzt; **my ~ colleague** *etc.* mein verehrter Herr Kollege/meine verehrte Frau Kollegin *usw.;* ⇒ *also* **friend** D

**learnedly** /'lɜːnɪdlɪ/ *adv.* gelehrt

**learner** /'lɜːnə(r)/ *n.* Lernende, *der/die;* (*beginner*) Anfänger, *der*/Anfängerin, *die;* **be a slow/quick ~:** langsam/schnell lernen; **the car is driven by a ~:** ein Fahrschüler steuert den Wagen; **I'm only a ~ still** ich lerne noch

**learner 'driver** *n.* (*Brit.*) Fahrschüler/-schülerin (*der/die unter Aufsicht fährt*)

**learning** /'lɜːnɪŋ/ *n.* (*scholarship*) Wissen, *das;* (*of person*) Gelehrsamkeit, *die;* **the new ~:** der Humanismus

**learning: ~ difficulties** *n. pl.* Lernschwierigkeiten *Pl.;* **~ disability** *n.* Lernbehinderung, *die*

**learnt** ⇒ **learn**

**lease** /liːs/ ❶ *n.* (*of land, business premises*) Pachtvertrag, *der;* (*of house, flat, office*) Mietvertrag, *der;* **be on [a] ~:** gepachtet/gemietet sein; **have sth. on a 99-year** *etc.* **~:** etw. auf 99 Jahre *usw.* gepachtet/gemietet haben; **take a ~ on** pachten ‹Grundstück, Geschäft›; mieten ‹Haus, Wohnung, Büro›; **enjoy a new ~ of** *or* (*Amer.*) **on life** neuen Auftrieb bekommen; **give sb./sth. a new ~ of life** jmdm. Auftrieb geben/etw. wieder in Schuss bringen (*ugs.*). ❷ *v.t.* Ⓐ (*grant ~ on*) verpachten ‹Grundstück, Geschäft, Rechte›; vermieten ‹Haus, Wohnung, Büro›; Ⓑ (*take ~ on*) pachten ‹Grundstück, Geschäft, Rechte›; mieten ‹Haus, Wohnung, Büro›; leasen ‹Auto›

**lease: ~back** *n.* Verpachtung an den Verkäufer; **~hold** ⇒ **lease** 2: ❶ *n.* **have the ~hold of** *or* **on sth.** etw. gepachtet *od.* in Pacht/gemietet haben; ❷ *adj.* gepachtet/gemietet; ❸ *adv.* **own a property ~hold** einen Besitz in Pacht/gemietet haben; **~holder** *n.* ⇒ **lease** 2: Pächter, *der*/Pächterin, *die;* Mieter, *der*/Mieterin, *die*

**leash** /liːʃ/ *n.* Ⓐ ⇒ **lead**[2] 3 D; Ⓑ **be straining at the ~ to do sth.** (*fig.*) darauf brennen, etw. zu tun; **he was straining at the ~:** er war voller Ungeduld

**least** /liːst/ ❶ *adj.* Ⓐ (*smallest*) kleinst...; (*in quantity*) wenigst...; (*in status*) geringst...; **be ~ in size** am kleinsten sein; **every ~ indication** jedes noch so geringe Anzeichen; **I haven't the ~ idea** ich habe nicht die geringste Ahnung; **not the ~ bit hungry** kein bisschen hungrig; **that's the ~ of our problems** das ist unser geringstes Problem; ⇒ *also* **common denominator**; **common multiple**; **last**[1] 1; **resistance** A; Ⓑ (*Bot., Ornith., Zool.*) Zwerg-. ❷ *n.* Geringste, *das;* **the ~ I can do** das Mindeste, was ich tun kann; **the ~ he could do would be to apologize** er könnte sich wenigstens entschuldigen; **pay the ~:** den niedrigsten Preis zahlen; **to say the ~ [of it]** gelinde gesagt; **~ said, soonest mended** (*prov.*) vieles Reden macht die Sache nur schlimmer; **at ~:** mindestens; (*if nothing more; anyway*) wenigstens; **at the [very] ~:** [aller]mindestens; **not [in] the ~:** nicht im Geringsten. ❸ *adv.* am wenigsten; **not ~ because ...:** nicht zuletzt deshalb, weil ...; **~ of all** am allerwenigsten; **the ~ likely answer** die unwahrscheinlichste Lösung

**leastways** /ˈliːstweɪz/, **leastwise** /ˈliːstwaɪz/ *adv.* (*dial.*) wenigstens

**leather** /ˈleðə(r)/ **1** *n.* **A** Leder, *das;* (*things made of* ~) Lederwaren *Pl.;* **these shoes are genuine ~:** diese Schuhe sind echt Leder *od.* aus echtem Leder; ⇒ *also* **chamois** B; **hell** B; **patent leather**; **B** (*used for polishing*) Leder, *das;* Lederlappen, *der;* **C** (*strap*) Lederriemen, *der;* (*for stirrup*) Steigriemen, *der.* **2** *adj.* ledern; Leder‹jacke, -mantel, -handschuh›. **3** *v.t.* **A** (*polish*) [ab]ledern; **B** (*thrash, whip*) **~ sb.** jmdm. das Leder gerben

**ˈleatherjacket** *n.* (*Brit. Zool.*) Schnakenlarve, *die*

**leathery** /ˈleðərɪ/ *adj.* ledern

**leave¹** /liːv/ *n., no pl.* **A** (*permission*) Erlaubnis, *die;* (*official approval*) Genehmigung, *die;* **grant** *or* **give sb. ~ to do sth.** jmdm. gestatten, etw. zu tun; **beg ~ to do sth.** um Erlaubnis bitten, etw. tun zu dürfen; **be absent without ~:** sich unerlaubt entfernt haben; **get ~ from sb. to do sth.** von jmdm. die Erlaubnis bekommen, etw. zu tun; **by ~ of sb.** mit jmds. Genehmigung; **by your ~** (*formal*) mit Ihrer Erlaubnis; (*iron.*) mit Ihrer gütigen Erlaubnis (*iron.*); **without so much as a by your ~** (*coll.*) ohne auch nur zu fragen; **take ~ to do sth.** sich (*Dat.*) erlauben, etw. zu tun; **B** (*from duty or work*) Urlaub, *der;* **~ [of absence]** Beurlaubung, *die;* Urlaub, *der* (*auch Mil.*); **a fortnight's ~:** vierzehn Tage Urlaub; **book one's ~:** seinen Urlaub anmelden; **when do you intend to go on ~?** wann nehmen Sie Ihren *od.* gehen Sie in Urlaub?; **I've got ~ [of absence] for a couple of days** ich bin für einige Tage beurlaubt; **be on ~:** Urlaub haben; in Urlaub sein; **C take one's ~** (*say farewell*) sich verabschieden; Abschied nehmen (*geh.*); **take [one's] ~ of sb.** sich von jmdm. verabschieden; von jmdm. Abschied nehmen (*geh.*); **have you taken ~ of your senses?** bist du noch bei Sinnen?; **he must have taken ~ of his senses** er muss von Sinnen sein. ⇒ *also* **French leave**; **sick leave**

**leave²** *v.t.,* **left** /left/ **A** (*make or let remain, lit. or fig.*) hinterlassen; **may I ~ my dog/son with you?** kann ich meinen Hund/Sohn bei dir lassen?; **he left a message with me for Mary** er hat bei mir eine Nachricht für Mary hinterlassen; **~ sb. to do sth.** es jmdm. überlassen, etw. zu tun; **I am always left to make the decisions** ich muss immer alles entscheiden; **if he likes the work, ~ him to get on with it** wenn ihm die Arbeit Spaß macht, überlässt du ihn am besten sich (*Dat.*) selbst; **~ be** (*coll.*) sich raushalten (*ugs.*); **6 from 10 ~s 4** 10 weniger 6 ist 4; (*in will*) **~ sb. sth., ~ sth. to sb.** jmdm. etw. hinterlassen; ⇒ *also* **desire** 2 C; **B** (*by mistake*) vergessen; **I left my gloves in your car/my umbrella at the butcher's** ich habe meine Handschuhe in deinem Auto liegen lassen *od.* vergessen/meinen Schirm beim Fleischer stehen lassen *od.* vergessen; **C be left with** nicht loswerden ‹Gefühl, Verdacht›; übrig behalten ‹Geld›; zurückbleiben mit ‹Schulden, Kind›; **I was left with the job/task of clearing up** es blieb mir überlassen, aufzuräumen; **D** (*refrain from doing, using, etc., let remain undisturbed*) stehen lassen ‹Abwasch, Essen›; sich (*Dat.*) entgehen lassen ‹Gelegenheit›; (*spare*) verschonen; **E** (*let remain in given state*) lassen; **~ the door open/the light on** die Tür offen lassen/das Licht anlassen; **~ the curtains drawn/the water running** die Vorhänge zugezogen lassen/das Wasser laufen lassen; **~ the book lying on the table** das Buch auf dem Tisch liegen lassen; **~ sb. in the dark** (*fig.*) jmdn. im Dunkeln lassen; **~ sb. unharmed** jmdn. nichts zuleide tun; **~ one's clothes around** *or* **about/all over the room** seine Kleider überall/im ganzen Zimmer herumliegen lassen; **this ~s me free to do sth.** das erlaubt mir, etw. zu tun; **~ sb. alone** (*allow to be alone*) jmdn. allein lassen; (*stop bothering*) jmdn. in Ruhe lassen; **~ sth. alone** etw. in Ruhe lassen; **~ sb. be** jmdn. in Ruhe *od.* Frieden lassen; **~ him** *etc.* **ˈbe** lass ihn *usw.* [in Ruhe]; **~ go [of] sth.** (*coll.*), **~ hold of sth.** etw. loslassen; **~ it at that** (*coll.*) es dabei bewenden lassen; **how shall we ~ it?** wie verbleiben wir?; **we left it that he'd phone me tomorrow** wir sind so verblieben, dass er mich morgen anruft; ⇒ *also* **well²** 2 B; **F** (*station for a purpose*) postieren; **G** (*refer, entrust*) **~ sth. to sb./sth.** etw. jmdm./einer Sache überlassen; **I ~ the matter entirely in your hands** ich lege diese Angelegenheit ganz in Ihre Hand/Hände; **I ~ the decision to** *or* **with you** ich überlasse dir die Entscheidung; **sit back and ~ the worrying to me** lass mich nur machen; **~ it to me** lass mich nur machen; **~ sb. to himself** *or* **to his own devices** *or* **resources** *or* **to it** jmdn. sich (*Dat.*) selbst überlassen; **H** (*go away from*) verlassen; **~ home at 6 a.m.** um 6 Uhr früh von zu Hause weggehen/-fahren; **the plane ~s Bonn at 6 p.m.** das Flugzeug fliegt um 18 Uhr von Bonn ab; **~ Bonn at 6 p.m.** (*by car, in train*) um 18 Uhr von Bonn abfahren; (*by plane*) um 18 Uhr in Bonn abfliegen; **please may I ~ the room?** (*to go to toilet*) darf ich bitte mal austreten? (*ugs.*); **~ the road** (*crash*) von der Fahrbahn abkommen; **~ the rails** *or* **tracks** entgleisen; **the train ~s the station** der Zug rollt aus dem Bahnhof; **let's ~ here** lass uns hier weggehen; **I left her at the bus stop** (*parted from*) an der Bushaltestelle haben wir uns getrennt; (*set down*) ich habe sie an der Bushaltestelle abgesetzt; **I left her much happier/I left her in tears** als ich ging, war sie schon wieder viel zuversichtlicher/weinte sie; **~ the table** vom Tisch aufstehen; *abs.* **the train ~s at 8.30 a.m.** der Zug fährt *od.* geht um 8.30 Uhr; **~ for Paris** nach Paris fahren/fliegen; **it is time to ~:** wir müssen gehen *od.* aufbrechen; **we're just leaving** wir wollen gerade weggehen; **~ on the 8 a.m. train/flight** mit dem Achtuhrzug fahren/der Achtuhrmaschine fliegen; **I** (*quit permanently*) verlassen; **~ school** die Schule verlassen; (*prematurely*) von der Schule abgehen; **~ work** aufhören zu arbeiten; **~ this world for the next** diese Welt verlassen (*geh. verhüll.*); **all my children have left home now** meine Kinder sind jetzt alle aus dem Haus; *abs.* **I am leaving at Easter** ich gehe zu Ostern; **J** (*desert*) verlassen; **~ sb. for another man/woman** jmdn. wegen eines anderen Mannes/einer anderen Frau verlassen; **~ a house to rot** ein Haus dem Verfall überlassen; **she was left at the altar** der Bräutigam erschien nicht zur Trauung; **~ one's studies halfway through the course** das Studium mittendrin abbrechen; **he was left for dead** man ließ ihn zurück, weil man ihn für tot hielt; ⇒ *also* **mercy** 1 B; **post¹** 1 C; **K** (*pass*) **branch off, leaving the farm on one's right** den Bauernhof rechts liegen lassen und abbiegen

**~ aˈside** *v.t.* beiseite lassen

**~ beˈhind** *v.t.* **A** zurücklassen; **B** (*by mistake*) ⇒ **leave** B

**~ ˈoff** *v.t.* **A** (*cease to wear*) auslassen (*ugs.*); nicht anziehen; **in summer we can ~ off our coats** im Sommer brauchen wir keine Mäntel [anzuziehen]; **B** (*discontinue*) aufhören mit; *abs.* aufhören; **~ off smoking** mit dem Rauchen aufhören; aufhören zu rauchen; **~ off the habit of smoking** sich (*Dat.*) das Rauchen abgewöhnen; **has it left off raining?** hat es aufgehört zu regnen?

**~ ˈout** *v.t.* auslassen

**~ ˈover** *v.t.* **A** (*Brit.: not deal with till later*) zurückstellen; **B be left over** übrig [geblieben] sein; ⇒ *also* **leftover**; **leftovers**

**-leaved** /liːvd/ *adj. in comb.* -blätt[e]rig

**leaven** /ˈlevn/ **1** *n.* **A** Treibmittel, *das;* (*fermenting dough*) Sauerteig, *der;* **B** (*fig.*) (*transforming influence*) Sauerteig, *der* (*geh. veralt.*). **2** *v.t.* **A** mit Treibmittel/Sauerteig ansetzen ‹Teig›; **B** (*fig.: transform*) durchsetzen

**leaves** *pl. of* **leaf**

**ˈleave-taking** *n.* Abschied, *der; attrib.* Abschieds-

**leaving** /ˈliːvɪŋ/ **1** *n. in pl.* Überbleibsel, *das* (*ugs.*); Rest, *der.* **2** *attrib. adj.* Abschieds‹party, -geschenk›; **~ certificate** Abschlusszertifikat, *das;* (*from school*) Abgangszeugnis, *das*

**Lebanese** /lebəˈniːz/ ▶ **1340** **1** *adj.* libanesisch; **sb. is ~:** jmd. ist Libanese/Libanesin. **2** *n., pl. same* Libanese, *der*/Libanesin, *die*

**Lebanon** /ˈlebənən/ *pr. n.* **[the] ~:** [der] Libanon; ⇒ *also* **cedar** A

**lecher** /ˈletʃə(r)/ *n.* Wüstling, *der* (*abwertend*)

**lecherous** /ˈletʃərəs/ *adj.*, **lecherously** /ˈletʃərəslɪ/ *adv.* lüstern (*geh.*); geil (*abwertend*)

**lechery** /ˈletʃərɪ/ *n.* Wollust, *die* (*geh.*)

**lecithin** /ˈlesɪθɪn/ *n.* (*Chem.*) Lezithin, *das*

**lectern** /ˈlektɜːn/ *n.* **A** (*in church*) (*for Bible etc.*) Lektionar[ium], *das;* (*for singers*) Notenpult, *das;* **B** (*Amer.: for lecturer etc.*) Katheder, *das od. der;* Pult, *das*

**lector** /ˈlektə(r)/ *n.* Lektor, *der*/Lektorin, *die*

**lecture** /ˈlektʃə(r)/ **1** *n.* **A** Vortrag, *der;* (*Univ.*) Vorlesung, *die;* **give [sb.] a ~ on sth.** [vor jmdm.] einen Vortrag/eine Vorlesung über etw. (*Akk.*) halten; **B** (*reprimand*) Strafpredigt, *die* (*ugs.*); **give** *or* **read sb. a ~:** jmdm. eine Strafpredigt halten (*ugs.*); jmdm. die Leviten lesen (*ugs.*). **2** *v.i.* **~ [to sb.] [on sth.]** [vor jmdm.] einen Vortrag/(*Univ.*) eine Vorlesung [über etw. (*Akk.*)] halten; (*give ~s*) [vor jmdm.] Vorträge/(*Univ.*) Vorlesungen [über etw. (*Akk.*)] halten. **3** *v.t.* (*scold*) **~ sb.** jmdm. eine Strafpredigt halten (*ugs.*); **he ~d me about** *or* **for** *or* **over being lazy** er hielt mir eine Strafpredigt wegen meiner Faulheit; **stop lecturing me all the time!** mach mir nicht dauernd Vorhaltungen!

**lecture: ~ hall** *n.* Hörsaal, *der;* **~ notes** *n. pl.* Manuskript, *das*

**lecturer** /ˈlektʃərə(r)/ *n.* ▶ **1261** **A** Vortragende, *der/die;* **B** (*Univ.*) Lehrbeauftragte, *der/die;* **senior ~:** Dozent, *der*/Dozentin, *die;* **be a ~ in French** Dozent/Dozentin für Französisch sein

**ˈlecture room** *n.* Vortragsraum, *der;* (*Univ.*) Vorlesungsraum, *der*

**lectureship** /ˈlektʃəʃɪp/ *n.* Dozentur, *die*

**lecture: ~ theatre** *n.* Hörsaal, *der;* **~ tour** *n.* Vortragsreise, *die;* **a ~ tour of America** eine Vortragsreise durch Amerika

**led** ⇒ **lead²** 1, 2

**LED** *abbr.* **light-emitting diode** LED

**ledge** /ledʒ/ *n.* **A** (*of window*) Sims, *der od. das;* **B** (*of rock*) [schmaler] Vorsprung; Band, *das* (*Bergsteigen*)

**ledger** /ˈledʒə(r)/ **1** *n.* (*Commerc.*) Hauptbuch, *das.* **2** *adj.* (*Mus.*) **~ line** Hilfslinie, *die*

**lee** /liː/ *n.* **A** (*shelter*) Schutz, *der;* **in/under the ~ of** im Schutz (+ *Gen.*); **B ~ [side]** (*Naut.*) Leeseite, *die*

**ˈleeboard** *n.* Seitenschwert, *das* (*Seew.*)

**leech** /liːtʃ/ *n.* **A** [Blut]egel, *der;* **stick like a ~** (*fig.*) jmdm. nicht von der Pelle gehen (*ugs.*); **B** (*fig.: sponger*) Blutsauger, *der* (*abwertend*)

**leek** /liːk/ *n.* Porree, *der;* Lauch, *der;* (*as Welsh emblem*) Lauch, *der;* **I like ~s** ich mag Porree *od.* Lauch; **three ~s** drei Stangen Porree/Lauch

**leek ˈsoup** *n.* Lauch[creme]suppe, *die*

**leer** /lɪə(r)/ **1** *n.* **[suggestive/sneering] ~:** anzüglicher/spöttischer Blick; **give sb. a ~ of desire** jmdn. begehrlich ansehen. **2** *v.i.* [anzüglich/spöttisch/begehrlich] blicken; **he just ~ed in reply** ein anzüglicher/spöttischer/begehrlicher [Seiten]blick war seine ganze Antwort; **~ at sb.** jmdm. einen anzüglichen/spöttischen/begehrlichen [Seiten]blick zuwerfen

**leery** /ˈlɪərɪ/ *adj.* (*coll.*) misstrauisch (**of** gegenüber)

**lees** /liːz/ *n. pl.* Bodensatz, *der*

**leeward** /ˈliːwəd, (*Naut.*) ˈluːəd/ (*esp. Naut.*) **1** *adj.* **to/on the ~ side of the ship** nach/in Lee; **to/on the ~ side of the mountain** in den/im Windschatten des Berges; in das Lee/im Lee (*Geogr.*); **L~ Islands** *pr. n. pl.* die Inseln unter dem Winde. **2** *adv.* leewärts;

nach Lee. ❸ *n.* Leeseite, *die;* **to ~:** leewärts; nach Lee

**ˈleeway** *n.* [A] (*Naut.*) Leeweg, *der;* Abdrift, *die;* [B] (*fig.*) Spielraum, *der;* **allow** *or* **give sb. ~:** jmdm. Spielraum lassen; **make up ~:** den Zeitverlust aufholen; **have a great deal of ~ to make up** einiges aufzuholen haben

**left¹** ⇒ **leave²**

**left²** /left/ ❶ *adj.* [A] ▶1679 (*opposite of right*) link...; **on the ~ side** auf der linken Seite; links; **~ field** (*Baseball*) linkes Außenfeld; **have two ~ feet** (*fig.*) zwei linke Füße haben (*ugs.*); ⇒ *also* **turn** 1 C; [B] **L~** (*Polit.*) link...; **her views are very L~:** sie hat sehr linke Ansichten. ❷ *adv.* nach links; **~ of the road** links von der Straße; ⇒ *also* **right** 4 B. ❸ *n.* [A] (**~-*hand side***) linke Seite; **move to the ~:** nach links rücken; **crowds lined the street to ~ and right** eine Menschenmenge säumte links und rechts die Straße; **on** *or* **to the ~ [of sb./sth.]** links [von jmdm./ etw.]; **on** *or* **to my ~, to the ~ of me** links von mir; zu meiner Linken; [B] (*Polit.*) **the L~:** die Linke; (*radicals*) die Linken; **be on the L~ of the Party** dem linken Flügel der Partei angehören; [C] (*Theatre*) **[stage] ~:** rechte Bühnenseite; [D] (*Boxing*) Linke, *die;* [E] (*in marching*) **~, right, ~, right, ~, ...** (*Mil.*) links, zwo, drei, vier, links, ...

**left: ~ ˈback** *n.* (*Footb.*) linker Verteidiger/ linke Verteidigerin; **~ ˈbank** *n.* linkes Ufer; (*in Paris*) Rive Gauche; **~-ˈfooted** *adj.* mit dem linken Fuß geschickter; linksfüßig ‹Fußballspieler›; **~ ˈhand** *n.* [A] linke Hand; Linke, *die;* [B] (*left side*) **on** *or* **at sb.'s ~ hand** zu jmds. Linken; links von jmdm.; **on sb.'s ~ hand** (*not close*) linker Hand; links; **~-hand** *adj.* link...; linksgängig, linksdrehend ‹Schraube›; **~-hand bend** Linkskurve, *die;* **on your ~-hand side you see ...:** links *od.* zur Linken sehen Sie ...; **drive on the ~-hand side** links *od.* auf der linken Seite fahren; ⇒ *also* **drive** 1 I; **~-handed** /leftˈhændɪd/ ❶ *adj.* [A] linkshändig; ‹Werkzeug› für Linkshänder; ‹Schlag› mit der Linken; **be ~-handed** Linkshänder/Linkshänderin sein; [B] (*turning to left*) links angeschlagen ‹Tür›; Links‹gewinde, -drehung›; linksgängig, linksdrehend ‹Schraube›; [C] (*fig.: ambiguous*) zweifelhaft ‹Kompliment, Gefallen›; [D] (*fig.: clumsy*) ungeschickt; unbeholfen; ❷ *adv.* linkshändig; mit der linken Hand; **~-handedness** /leftˈhændɪdnɪs/ *n.* Linkshändigkeit, *die;* **~-hander** /leftˈhændə(r)/ *n.* [A] (*person*) Linkshänder, *der*/-händerin, *die;* [B] (*blow*) Schlag mit der Linken; (*Boxing*) Linke, *die*

**leftie** ⇒ **lefty**

**leftish** /ˈleftɪʃ/ *adj.* (*Polit.*) nach links tendierend; **be ~, have ~ opinions/views** links angehaucht sein; nach links tendieren

**leftism** /ˈleftɪzm/ *n., no pl.* (*Polit.*) linksorientierte Haltung; (*movement*) linke [politische] Strömungen

**leftist** /ˈleftɪst/ (*Polit.*) ❶ *adj.* linksorientiert. ❷ *n.* Linke, *der/die*

**left: ~ ˈluggage [office]** *n.* (*Brit. Railw.*) Gepäckaufbewahrung, *die;* **~-over** *attrib. adj.* übrig geblieben; **~overs** *n. pl.* Reste; (*fig.*) Relikte; Überbleibsel (*ugs.*)

**leftward** /ˈleftwəd/ ❶ *adv.* [nach] links ‹abbiegen›; nach links ‹blicken, sich wenden›; **lie ~ of sth.** links von etw. liegen. ❷ *adj.* linker Hand *nachgestellt*

**leftwards** /ˈleftwədz/ ⇒ **leftward** 1

**left: ~ ˈwing** *n.* linker Flügel; **~-wing** *adj.* [A] (*Sport*) Linksaußen‹spieler, -position›; [B] (*Polit.*) link...; linksgerichtet; Links‹intellektueller, -extremist, -radikalismus›; **~-ˈwinger** *n.* [A] (*Sport*) Linksaußen, *der;* [B] (*Polit.*) Linke, *der/die;* **extreme ~-winger** Linksaußen, *der/die* (*Jargon*); Linksradikale, *der/die*

**lefty** /ˈleftɪ/ *n.* (*coll.*) [A] (*Polit.*) Linke, *der/ die;* Rote, *der/die* (*ugs., oft abwertend*); [B] ⇒ **left-hander** A

**leg** /leg/ ❶ *n.* [A] ▶966 Bein, *das;* **upper/ lower ~:** Ober-/Unterschenkel, *der;* **artificial ~:** Beinprothese, *die;* **wooden ~:** Holzbein, *das;* **as fast as my ~s would carry me** so schnell mich die Füße trugen; **give sb. a ~ up on to a horse/into the saddle/ over the gate** jmdm. auf ein Pferd/in den Sattel/über das Gatter helfen; **give sb. a ~ up in his career** (*fig.*) jmds. Karriere fördern; **be on one's last ~s** sich kaum noch auf den Beinen halten können; (*be about to die*) mit einem Fuß *od.* Bein im Grabe stehen; **the car is on its last ~s** das Auto macht es nicht mehr lange (*ugs.*); **the firm is on its last ~s** die Firma liegt in den letzten Zügen; **on one's ~s** auf den Beinen; **pull sb.'s ~** (*fig.*) jmdn. auf den Arm nehmen (*ugs.*); **pull the other ~, it's got bells on** (*coll.*) das kannst du einem andern erzählen; **be all ~s** staksig sein; **shake a ~** (*fig. coll.*) das Tanzbein schwingen (*ugs. scherzh.*); **show a ~!** (*coll.*) aus den Federn! (*ugs.*); **not have a ~ to stand on** (*fig.*) nichts in der Hand haben (*fig.*); **stretch one's ~s** sich (*Dat.*) die Beine vertreten; **get one's ~ over** (*sl.*) einen wegstecken (*ugs.*); [B] (*of table, chair, etc.*) Bein, *das;* (*of machine*) Stütze, *die;* [C] (*of garment*) Bein, *das;* (*of boot*) Schaft, *der;* **trouser ~s** Hosenbeine; [D] (*Gastr.*) Keule, *die;* Schlegel, *der* (*südd., österr.*); **~ of lamb/veal** Lamm-/Kalbskeule, *die;* [E] (*of journey*) Etappe, *die;* Teilstrecke, *die;* [F] (*of forked object*) Schenkel, *der;* [G] (*Sport coll.*) Durchgang, *der;* (*of relay race*) Teilstrecke, *die;* [H] (*Cricket*) *Spielfeldhälfte rechts bzw., bei linkshändigem Schlagmann, links vom Werfer;* [I] (*Geom.*) Schenkel, *der;* [J] (*straight run*) (*Naut.*) Schlag, *der;* (*Aeronaut.*) Etappe, *die.*
❷ *adj.* (*Cricket*) ‹Seite, Torstab› rechts vom Werfer, (*if batsman is left-handed*) links vom Werfer.
❸ *v.t.*, **-gg-: ~ it** die Beine in die Hand *od.* unter die Arme nehmen (*ugs.*)

**legacy** /ˈlegəsɪ/ *n.* Vermächtnis, *das* (*Rechtsspr.*); Erbschaft, *die;* (*fig.*) Erbe, *das;* **leave sb. sth. as a ~** (*lit. or fig.*) jmdm. etw. hinterlassen; **leave sb. a ~ of £30,000** jmdm. 30 000 Pfund vermachen *od.* hinterlassen

**legal** /ˈli:gl/ *adj.* [A] (*concerning the law*) juristisch; Rechts‹beratung, -berater, -streit, -experte, -angelegenheit, -schutz›; gesetzlich ‹Vertreter›; rechtlich ‹Gründe, Stellung›; (*of the law*) Gerichts‹kosten›; **in ~ matters/affairs** in Rechtsfragen/-angelegenheiten; **seek ~ advice** sich juristisch beraten lassen; **he is a member of the ~ profession** er ist Jurist; **a ~ friend of mine** ein Freund von mir, der Jurist ist; [B] (*required by law*) gesetzlich vorgeschrieben ‹Mindestalter, Zeitraum›; gesetzlich ‹Verpflichtung›; gesetzlich verankert ‹Recht›; **I know my ~ rights** ich kenne meine Rechte; [C] (*lawful*) legal; rechtsgültig ‹Vertrag, Testament›; gesetzlich zulässig ‹Grenze, Höchstwert›; **it is ~/not ~ to do sth.** es ist rechtlich zulässig/gesetzlich verboten, etw. zu tun; **it is not ~ for children to marry** nach dem Gesetz dürfen Kinder nicht heiraten; **make sth. ~:** etw. legalisieren. ⇒ *also* **proceeding** C; **separation** A; **tender³** 3 B

**legal: ~ ˈaction** *n.* Gerichtsverfahren, *das;* Prozess, *der;* **take ~ action against sb.** gerichtlich gegen jmdn. vorgehen; eine Klage gegen jmdn. anstrengen; **take/have recourse to ~ action** den Rechtsweg beschreiten *od.* einschlagen; **~ ˈaid** *n.* ≈ Prozesskostenhilfe, *die;* **~ ˈfiction** *n.* juristische Fiktion (*Rechtsw.*); **~ ˈholiday** (*Amer.*) ⇒ **bank holiday b**

**legalistic** /li:gəˈlɪstɪk/ *adj.* legalistisch (*geh.*); stur legalistisch (*abwertend*)

**legality** /lɪˈgælɪtɪ/ *n.* Legalität, *die;* Rechtmäßigkeit, *die*

**legalization** /li:gəlaɪˈzeɪʃn/ *n.* (*lit. or fig.*) Legalisierung, *die*

**legalize** /ˈli:gəlaɪz/ *v.t.* (*lit. or fig.*) legalisieren

**legally** /ˈli:gəlɪ/ *adv.* rechtlich ‹zulässig, verpflichtet, begründet, unhaltbar, möglich›; gesetzlich ‹verankert, verpflichtet›; vor dem Gesetz ‹verantwortlich›; legal ‹durchführen, abwickeln, erwerben›; **~ and morally** aus rechtlicher und moralischer Sicht; **~ speaking** rechtlich gesehen; vom rechtlichen Standpunkt aus; **~ valid/ binding** rechtsgültig/-verbindlich; **be ~ entitled to sth.** einen Rechtsanspruch auf etw. (*Akk.*) haben

**legate** /ˈlegət/ *n.* (*RC Ch.*) Legat, *der*

**legatee** /legəˈti:/ *n.* Legatar, *der*/Legatarin, *die* (*Rechtsw.*); Vermächtnisnehmer, *der*/ -nehmerin, *die* (*Rechtsw.*)

**legation** /lɪˈgeɪʃn/ *n.* (*Diplom.*) Gesandtschaft, *die;* (*residence also*) Gesandtschaftsgebäude, *das*

**legato** /lɪˈgɑ:təʊ/ (*Mus.*) ❶ *adj.* Legato-. ❷ *adv.* legato. ❸ *n., pl.* **~s** Legato, *das*

**legend** /ˈledʒənd/ *n.* [A] (*myth*) Sage, *die;* (*of life of saint etc.; unfounded belief*) Legende, *die;* **read sb. tales from** *or* **out of Greek ~:** jmdm. aus den griechischen Sagen vorlesen; **~ has it that ...:** es geht die Sage, dass ...; **become a ~ in one's own lifetime** (*fig.*) schon zu Lebzeiten zur Legende werden; **turn sb. into a ~** (*fig.*) jmdn. zur Legende machen; [B] (*inscription*) Inschrift, *die;* (*Num.*) Randinschrift, *die;* [C] (*Printing*) (*caption*) Bildunterschrift, *die;* (*on map*) Legende, *die*

**legendary** /ˈledʒəndərɪ/ *adj.* [A] legendenhaft; (*described in legend*) legendär; sagenhaft; [B] (*coll.: famous*) sagenhaft (*ugs.*); legendär; **become ~:** zur Legende werden

**legerdemain** /ledʒədəˈmeɪn/ *n.* Taschenspielerei, *die;* **diplomatic ~** (*fig.*) diplomatische Kunstgriffe

**leger line** /ˈledʒə laɪn/ *n.* (*Mus.*) Hilfslinie, *die*

**-legged** /legd, legɪd/ *adj. in comb.* ▶966 -beinig; **two-~:** zweibeinig

**leggings** /ˈlegɪŋz/ *n. pl.* Leggings *Pl.;* (*of child*) Gamaschenhose, *die;* (*of baby*) Strampelhose, *die*

**leggy** /ˈlegɪ/ *adj.* langbeinig; hochbeinig; ‹Junge, Fohlen, Welpe› mit [staksigen] langen Beinen

**legibility** /ledʒɪˈbɪlɪtɪ/ *n., no pl.* Leserlichkeit, *die*

**legible** /ˈledʒɪbl/ *adj.* leserlich; **easily/ scarcely ~:** leicht/kaum lesbar

**legibly** /ˈledʒɪblɪ/ *adv.* leserlich

**legion** /ˈli:dʒn/ *n.* [A] (*Roman Ant.*) Legion, *die;* [B] **[Royal] British L~** *Veteranenvereinigung der britischen Streitkräfte;* **American L~** *Veteranenvereinigung der amerikanischen Streitkräfte;* [C] **L~ of Honour** Ehrenlegion, *die;* [D] (*vast number*) Legion, *die;* **they are ~** (*rhet.*) sie sind Legion (*geh.*). ⇒ *also* **foreign legion**

**legionary** /ˈli:dʒənərɪ/ *n.* [A] (*Mil.*) Legionär, *der;* [B] (*of Legion of Honour*) Ritter der Ehrenlegion

**legionnaire** /li:dʒəˈneə(r)/ *n.* Legionär, *der;* (*of British or American Legion*) ≈ Veteran, *der*

**legionˈnaires' disease** *n., no pl., no art.* (*Med.*) Legionärskrankheit, *die*

**legislate** /ˈledʒɪsleɪt/ *v.i.* Gesetze verabschieden; **it is the job of Parliament to ~:** dem Parlament obliegt die Gesetzgebung *od.* (*fachspr.*) Legislatur; **~ for/against sth.** Gesetze zum Schutz von/gegen etw. einbringen; **you cannot ~ for everything** (*fig.*) man kann nicht für alles Vorschriften erlassen

**legislation** /ledʒɪsˈleɪʃn/ *n.* [A] (*laws*) Gesetze *Pl.;* **in German ~:** in den deutschen Gesetzen; **rent-control ~ was extended for another year** die Gesetze zur Mietkontrolle blieben ein weiteres Jahr in Kraft; [B] (*legislating*) Gesetzgebung, *die;* Legislatur, *die* (*fachspr.*)

**legislative** /ˈledʒɪslətɪv/ *adj.* gesetzgebend; legislativ (*fachspr.*); (*created by legislature*) gesetzgeberisch

**legislative: ~ asˈsembly** *n.* gesetzgebende Versammlung; **~ ˈcouncil** *n.* [gesetzgebender] Rat

**legislator** /ˈledʒɪsleɪtə(r)/ *n.* Mitglied der Legislative; (*lawgiver*) Gesetzgeber, *der*

**legislature** /ˈledʒɪsleɪtʃə(r)/ *n.* Legislative, *die*

**legit** /lɪˈdʒɪt/ (*coll.*) ⇒ **legitimate** 1 A

**legitimacy** /lɪˈdʒɪtɪməsɪ/ *n.*, *no pl.* **A** Rechtmäßigkeit, *die;* Legitimität, *die;* **B** (*of child*) Ehelichkeit, *die*

**legitimate** **1** /lɪˈdʒɪtɪmət/ *adj.* **A** (*lawful*) legitim; rechtmäßig ‹Besitzer, Regierung›; legal ‹Vorgehen, Weg, Geschäft, Gewinn›; **I've turned ~:** ich bin jetzt ein gesetzestreuer Bürger; **B** (*valid*) berechtigt; stichhaltig; legitim (*geh.*) ‹Argument›; ausreichend ‹Entschuldigung›; triftig ‹Grund›; **C** (*from wedlock*) ehelich, legitim ‹Kind›; leiblich ‹Vater›. **2** /lɪˈdʒɪtɪmeɪt/ *v.t.* **A** legitimieren; **B** (*justify*) rechtfertigen

**legitimately** /lɪˈdʒɪtɪmətlɪ/ *adv.* **A** (*lawfully*) legal; **be ~ entitled to sth.** einen legitimen Anspruch auf etw. (*Akk.*) haben; **B** (*justifiably*) zu Recht; **C** (*in wedlock*) ehelich, legitim ‹geboren›

**legitimatize (legitimatise)** /lɪˈdʒɪtɪmətaɪz/, **legitimize (legitimise)** /lɪˈdʒɪtɪmaɪz/ *v.t.* legitimieren; [durch Heirat] ehelich machen ‹Kind›

**legless** /ˈleglɪs/ *adj.* **A** (*without legs*) ohne Beine *nachgestellt;* **B** (*coll.: drunk*) sternhagelvoll (*salopp*)

**leg: ~man** *n.* (*Journ.*) Reporter, *der;* **~-of-mutton** *adj.* **~-of-mutton sleeve** Keulenärmel, *der;* Gigot, *das* (*Mode*); **~-pull** *n.* (*coll.*) Jux, *der* (*ugs.*); **~-pulling** *n.*, *no pl.*, *no indef. art.* Aufziehen, *das;* **~room** *n.*, *no pl.*, *no indef. art.* Beinfreiheit, *die;* **~-show** *n.* Revue, *die*

**leguminous** /lɪˈgjuːmɪnəs/ *adj.* (*Bot.*) **~ plant** Hülsenfrucht, *die;* Leguminose, *die* (*fachspr.*)

**leg: ~ warmer** *n.* Überstrumpf, *der;* Legwarmer, *der;* **~work** *n.*, *no pl.*, *no indef. art.* Lauferei, *die* (*ugs.*); (*running errands*) Botengänge *Pl.;* **do a lot of ~work** viel herumlaufen

**leisure** /ˈleʒə(r)/ *n.* Freizeit, *die;* (*for relaxation*) Muße, *die;* *attrib.* Freizeit‹kleidung, -beschäftigung, -zentrum, -industrie›; **a life/day of ~:** ein Leben/Tag der Muße (*geh.*); **I haven't a moment's ~:** ich habe keine freie Minute; **have [the] ~ to do sth./for sth.** [die] Zeit haben, etw. zu tun/Zeit für etw. haben; **lady/gentleman of ~:** Müßiggängerin, *die*/Müßiggänger, *der;* **she has become a lady of ~:** sie verbringt jetzt ihr Leben im Müßiggang; **do sth. at ~:** etw. in Ruhe tun; **do sth. at one's ~:** sich (*Dat.*) Zeit mit etw. lassen; **~ time** *or* **hours** Freizeit, *die*

**leisured** /ˈleʒəd/ *adj.* müßig (*geh.*); **the ~ classes** das Müßiggängertum

**leisurely** /ˈleʒəlɪ/ **1** *adj.* gemächlich; **walk in a ~ manner** gemächlich gehen; **work at a more ~ rate** langsamer *od.* geruhsamer arbeiten; **they made a ~ start** sie ließen es gemächlich angehen. **2** *adv.* langsam; ohne Hast

**'leisurewear** *n.*, *no pl.*, *no indef. art.* Freizeitkleidung, *die*

**leitmotiv (leitmotif)** /ˈlaɪtməʊtiːf/ *n.* (*Mus. etc.; also fig.*) Leitmotiv, *das*

**lemma** /ˈlemə/ *n.*, *pl.* **~ta** /ˈlemətə/ *or* **~s** (*Math., Logic, etc.*) Lemma, *das*

**lemming** /ˈlemɪŋ/ *n.* (*Zool.; also fig.*) Lemming, *der;* **rush like ~s** rennen wie die Lemminge

**lemon** /ˈlemən/ **1** *n.* **A** (*fruit*) Zitrone, *die;* **B** (*tree*) Zitronenbaum, *der;* **C** (*colour*) Zitronengelb, *das;* **D** (*coll.: fool*) Trottel, *der* (*ugs. abwertend*); **E** (*dud*) Reinfall, *der.* **2** *adj.* **A** (*in colour*) zitronengelb; zitronenfarben; **B** (*in taste*) Zitronen‹geschmack, -tee›. ⇒ *also* **verbena**

**lemonade** /leməˈneɪd/ *n.* [Zitronen]limonade, *die*

**lemon: ~ balm** *n.* (*Bot.*) Zitronenmelisse, *die;* **~ 'cheese, ~ 'curd** *ns.* Zitronencreme, *die;* **~ juice** *n.* Zitronensaft, *der;* **~ meringue 'pie** *n.* Zitronenbaisertorte, *die;* **~ 'sole** *n.* Seezunge, *die;* **~ 'squash** *n.* (*Brit.*) Zitronensaftgetränk, *das;* (*concentrated*) Zitronensaftkonzentrat, *das;* **~ squeezer** *n.* Zitronenpresse, *die;* **~ tree** ⇒ **lemon** 1 B; **~ yellow** *adj.* zitronengelb

**lemur** /ˈliːmə/ *n.* (*Zool.*) Lemure, *der*

**lend** /lend/ **1** *v.t.*, **lent** /lent/ **A** leihen; **~ sth. to sb.** jmdm. etw. leihen; **B** (*give, impart*) geben; zur Verfügung stellen ‹Dienste›; verleihen ‹Würde, Glaubwürdigkeit, Zauber›; **~ one's support to sth.** etw. unterstützen; **~ one's name/authority to sth.** seinen Namen/guten Namen für etw. hergeben; ⇒ *also* **credence** A; **ear**[1] A; **hand** 1 A. **2** *v. refl.*, **lent: ~ oneself to sth.** sich für etw. zur Verfügung stellen; (*degradingly*) sich für etw. hergeben; **the book ~s itself/does not ~ itself to use as a learning aid** das Buch eignet sich/eignet sich nicht als Lehrmittel; **the system ~s itself to manipulation** das System bietet sich zur Manipulation an. **3** *n.* (*coll.*) **give me a ~ of your bicycle** leih mir mal dein Fahrrad

**lender** /ˈlendə(r)/ *n.* Verleiher, *der*/Verleiherin, *die*

**lending** /ˈlendɪŋ/ **1** *n.* **~ charge** Leihgebühr, *die.* **2** *adj.* **~ library** (*esp. Brit.*) Leihbücherei, *die.* ⇒ *also* **public lending right**

**length** /leŋθ, leŋkθ/ *n.* **A** ▶ 1284 (*also Horseracing, Rowing, Swimming, Phonet., Pros., Tennis, Fashion*) Länge, *die;* **the river was navigable for most of its ~:** der Fluss war fast in seiner ganzen Länge schiffbar; **a road four miles in ~:** eine vier Meilen lange Straße; **be six feet** *etc.* **in ~:** sechs Fuß *usw.* lang sein; **the room is twice the ~ of yours** das Zimmer ist doppelt so lang wie deins; **travel the ~ and breadth of the British Isles** überall auf den Britischen Inseln herumreisen; **walk the ~ of the street** die ganze Straße entlanglaufen; **a list the ~ of my arm** (*fig.*) eine ellenlange Liste; **win by a ~:** mit einer Länge siegen; **B** (*of time*) Länge, *die;* **a short ~ of time** kurze Zeit; **in that ~ of time** in dieser Zeit; **for some ~ of time** für einige Zeit; **I shouldn't care to live here for any ~ of time** auf die Dauer möchte ich hier nicht wohnen; **spend a ridiculous ~ of time in the bath** unmöglich viel Zeit im Badezimmer verbringen; **the play was three hours in ~:** das Stück dauerte drei Stunden; **depend on ~ of service with the company** von der Dauer der Betriebszugehörigkeit abhängen; **C at ~** (*for a long time*) lange; (*eventually*) schließlich; **at [great] ~** (*in great detail*) lang und breit; sehr ausführlich; **at some ~:** ziemlich ausführlich; **write at undue ~:** übertrieben ausführlich schreiben; **D go to any/great** *etc.* **~s** alles nur/alles Erdenkliche tun; **she went to absurd ~s to save money** sie kam auf die seltsamsten Ideen, nur um Geld zu sparen; **carry sth. to dangerous ~s** mit etw. gefährlich weit gehen; **he even went to the ~ of phoning the police** er ging sogar so weit, die Polizei anzurufen; **E** (*piece of material*) Länge, *die;* Stück, *das;* **six-foot ~s of wood** sechs Fuß lange Holzstücke; **F** (*full extent of body*) [Körper]länge, *die.* ⇒ *also* **arm**[1] A; **full length; measure** 1 A, 2 E

**-length** *adj. in comb.* -lang

**lengthen** /ˈleŋθən, ˈleŋkθən/ **1** *v.i.* länger werden. **2** *v.t.* **A** verlängern; länger machen ‹Kleid›; **B** (*Phonet., Pros.*) längen

**lengthily** /ˈleŋθɪlɪ, leŋkθɪlɪ/ *adv.* ausführlich; lange und gründlich ‹planen›

**lengthiness** /ˈleŋθɪnɪs, ˈleŋkθɪnɪs/ *n.*, *no pl.* Überlänge, *die*

**lengthways** /ˈleŋθweɪz, ˈleŋkθweɪz/ *adv.* der Länge nach

**lengthwise** /ˈleŋθwaɪz, ˈleŋkθwaɪz/ **1** *adv.* ⇒ **lengthways. 2** *adj.* längs angeordnet/verlaufend *usw.*

**lengthy** /ˈleŋθɪ, ˈleŋkθɪ/ *adj.* überlang

**leniency** /ˈliːnɪənsɪ/ *n.*, *no pl.* Nachsicht, *die;* Milde, *die;* **show ~:** Milde walten lassen; Nachsicht zeigen

**lenient** /ˈliːnɪənt/ *adj.* **A** (*tolerant*) nachsichtig; milde, nachsichtig ‹Richter›; **take a ~ view of sth.** Verständnis für etw. haben; **B** (*mild*) mild ‹Urteil, Strafe›

**leniently** /ˈliːnɪəntlɪ/ *adv.* nachsichtig; mit Nachsicht

**lens** /lenz/ *n.* **A** (*Optics, Phys., Anat.*) Linse, *die;* (*in spectacles*) Glas, *das;* **B** (*Photog.*) Objektiv, *das;* **C** (*Zool.*) Einzelauge, *das*

**lens: ~ cap** *n.* (*Photog.*) Objektivdeckel, *der;* **~hood** *n.* (*Photog.*) Gegenlichtblende, *die*

**lent** ⇒ **lend** 1, 2

**Lent** /lent/ *n.* Fastenzeit, *die;* **~ term** (*Brit. Univ.*) Frühjahrstrimester, *das*

**Lenten** /ˈlentən/ *attrib. adj.* Fasten-; **~ fare** Fastenspeise, *die*

**lentil** /ˈlentɪl/ *n.* Linse, *die*

**lentil 'soup** *n.* Linsensuppe, *die*

**Leo** /ˈliːəʊ/ *n.*, *pl.* **~s** (*Astrol., Astron.*) der Löwe; der Leo; ⇒ *also* **Aries**

**leopard** /ˈlepəd/ *n.* (*Zool.*) Leopard, *der;* **hunting ~:** Gepard, *der;* **a ~ can't change** *or* **never changes its spots** niemand kann aus seiner Haut heraus (*ugs.*)

**'leopard skin** *n.* Leopardenfell, *das*

**leotard** /ˈliːətɑːd/ *n.* Turnanzug, *der*

**leper** /ˈlepə(r)/ *n.* Leprakranke, *der/die;* Aussätzige, *der/die* (*auch fig.*)

**'leper colony** *n.* Leprakolonie, *die*

**lepidopterist** /lepɪˈdɒptərɪst/ *n.* Lepidopterologe, *der*/Lepidopterologin, *die*

**leprechaun** /ˈleprəkɔːn/ *n.* (*Ir. Mythol.*) Kobold, *der*

**leprosy** /ˈleprəsɪ/ *n.* **A** (*Med.*) Lepra, *die;* **B** (*fig.*) Seuche, *die*

**leprous** /ˈleprəs/ *adj.* (*Med.*) leprös; lepros

**lesbian** /ˈlezbɪən/ **1** *n.* Lesbierin, *die.* **2** *adj.* lesbisch

**lesbianism** /ˈlezbɪənɪzm/ *n.*, *no pl.* lesbische Liebe; Lesbianismus, *der* (*geh.*)

**lèse-majesté** /leɪzˈmæʒesteɪ/, **lese-majesty** /liːzˈmædʒɪstɪ/ *n.* (*Law*) Majestätsbeleidigung, *die* (*auch scherzh.*); (*treason*) Majestätsverbrechen, *das* (*Rechtsw.*)

**lesion** /ˈliːʒn/ *n.* (*Med.*) Läsion, *die* (*fachspr.*); Verletzung, *die;* (*abnormal change*) krankhafte Veränderung

**less** /les/ **1** *adj.* weniger; **of ~ value/importance/account** *or* **note** weniger wertvoll/wichtig/bedeutend; von geringerem Wert/geringerer Wichtigkeit/Bedeutung; **his chances are ~ than mine** seine Chancen sind geringer als meine; **for ~ time** kürzere Zeit; **the pain is getting ~:** der Schmerz lässt nach; **~ talking, please** etwas mehr Ruhe, bitte.

**2** *adv.* weniger; **I like him ~ than I used to** ich mag ihn [heute] weniger als früher; **I think ~/no ~ of him after what he did** ich halte nicht mehr so viel/nicht weniger von ihm, seit er das getan hat; **~ and ~:** immer weniger; **~ and ~ [often]** immer seltener; **~ so** weniger; **the ~ so because ...:** umso weniger, als *od.* weil ...; **even** *or* **still/far** *or* **much ~:** noch/viel weniger; **not ..., even** *or* **still** *or* **far** *or* **much ~ ...:** ..., geschweige denn ...; ⇒ *also* **more** 3 G; **no** 2 A; **none** 2.

**3** *n.*, *no pl.*, *no indef. art.* weniger; **~ and ~:** immer weniger; **the ~ said [about it] the better** je weniger man darüber sagt, umso besser; **this is ~ of a house than a cottage** das ist weniger ein Haus als ein Cottage *od.* Häuschen; **parking is ~ of a problem with a small car** mit einem kleinen Auto ist das Parken weniger problematisch; **in ~ than no time** (*joc.*) in null Komma nichts (*ugs.*); **~ of that!** (*coll.*) Schluss damit!; **[I'll have] ~ of your clever remarks** (*coll.*) deine schlauen Bemerkungen kannst du dir sparen (*ugs.*); **~ of your cheek!** (*coll.*) sei nicht so frech!; ⇒ *also* **little** 3; **more** 2 C.

**4** *prep.* (*deducting*) **ten ~ three is seven** zehn weniger drei ist sieben; **work every weekend ~ two Saturdays** bis auf zwei Sonnabende an jedem Wochenende arbeiten; **~ £2/tax** abzüglich 2 Pfund/Steuer

**-less** /lɪs/ *adj. suf.* (*without*) -los; **error~:** fehlerlos; **parent~:** elternlos; **window~:** fensterlos; **hat~/trouser~:** ohne Hut/Hose

**lessee** /leˈsiː/ *n.* ⇒ **lease** 2: Pächter, *der*/Pächterin, *die;* Mieter, *der*/Mieterin, *die*

**lessen** /ˈlesn/ **1** *v.t.* (*reduce*) verringern; lindern ‹Schmerz›; dämpfen ‹Lärm›; abschwächen

# Length and width

| | | |
|---|---|---|
| | 1 inch (in.) | = 25,4 mm (fünfundzwanzig Komma vier Millimeter) |
| 12 inches | = 1 foot (ft) | = 30,48 cm (dreißig Komma vier acht Zentimeter) |
| 3 feet | = 1 yard (yd) | = 0,914 m (null Komma neun eins vier Meter) |
| 1,760 yards | = 1 mile | = 1,61 km (eins Komma sechs eins Kilometer) |

***What width/length is it?***
= Wie breit/lang ist es?

***The room is 12 feet [wide] by 15 feet [long]***
= Das Zimmer ist zwölf mal fünfzehn Fuß [groß]

***A is the same length/width as B***
= A hat die gleiche Länge/Breite wie B

***They are the same length*** or ***are equal in length***
= Sie haben die gleiche Länge *or* sind gleich lang

***They are not the same width*** or ***are different widths***
= Sie sind nicht gleich breit *or* sind verschieden breit

***a drive 100 metres long*** or ***in length***
= eine 100 Meter lange Einfahrt

***a plank five centimetres wide*** or ***in width***
= ein fünf Zentimeter breites Brett

German usually puts such measurements before the noun, with the adjective agreeing. However especially if the measurement is more complicated it may also come after:

***a car 14 feet 2 inches long***
= ein Auto von 4,32 Meter Länge

Note that the translations for *wide* and *width* are nearly always **breit** and **Breite; weit** and **Weite** may occasionally occur in relation to clothing, but mainly in compounds such as **Hüftweite** (hip measurement) and **Taillenweite** (waist measurement), or referring to loose fit.

Material is sold in German-speaking countries *by the metre* (**meterweise**):

***three metres of material at £3.50 a metre***
= drei Meter Stoff zu 3,50 Pfund das Meter

***a four-metre length of silk***
= ein vier Meter langes Stück Seide

***two ten-foot lengths of rope***
≈ zwei drei Meter lange Stücke Seil

NB There is no translation of the English *of* after a quantity.

l

‹Aufprall›. ❷ *v.i.* (*become less*) sich verringern; ‹Fieber:› sinken, fallen; ‹Schwierigkeiten:› abnehmen; ‹Zorn:› sich legen; ‹Schmerz:› nachlassen

**lesser** /ˈlesə(r)/ *attrib. adj.* geringer...; weniger bedeutend... ‹Schauspieler, Werk›; **~ in rank, of ~ rank** rangniedriger; **be a ~ man than ...:** kein so großer Mensch sein wie ...; ⇒ *also* **evil** 2 B

**lesson** /ˈlesn/ *n.* Ⓐ (*class*) [Unterrichts]stunde, *die;* (*teaching unit in textbook*) Lektion, *die;* **I like her ~s** mir gefällt ihr Unterricht; **give ~s** Privatstunden *od.* -unterricht geben; **give Italian ~s** Italienischunterricht *od.* -stunden geben; **give [sb.] a [riding] ~:** [jmdm.] eine [Reit]stunde geben; **[give] ~s in/on** Unterricht [erteilen] in (+ *Dat.*); **take piano ~s with sb.** bei jmdm. Klavierstunden nehmen; Ⓑ (*thing to be learnt*) Lektion, *die;* **the first ~ to be learnt** das Erste, was man lernen muss; Ⓒ (*fig.: example, warning*) Lektion, *die;* Lehre, *die;* **teach sb. a ~:** jmdm. eine Lektion erteilen; ‹Vorfall usw.:› jmdm. eine Lehre sein; **he needs to be taught a ~:** er braucht einen Denkzettel; **do that again and I'll teach you a ~ you won't forget!** wenn du das noch mal machst, verpasse ich dir einen Denkzettel, den du nicht vergisst!; **be a ~ to sb.** jmdm. eine Lehre sein; **learn one's** *or* **a ~ from sth.** aus etw. eine Lehre ziehen; **I have learnt my ~:** das soll mir eine Lehre sein; **let that be a ~ to you** lass dir das eine Lehre sein!; Ⓓ (*Eccl.*) Lesung, *die;* **read the ~:** die Lesung halten

**lessor** /leˈsɔ:(r)/ *n.* ⇒ **lease** 2: Verpächter, *der*/Verpächterin, *die;* Vermieter, *der*/Vermieterin, *die*

**lest** /lest/ *conj.* (*literary*) damit ... nicht; [auf] dass ... nicht (*geh.*); **he ran away ~ he [should] be seen** er rannte weg, um nicht gesehen zu werden; **I was afraid ~ he [should] come back before I was ready** ich fürchtete, dass er zurückkommen würde, bevor ich fertig war

**let**¹ /let/ ❶ *v.t.*, **-tt-, let** Ⓐ (*allow to*) lassen; **~ sb. do sth.** jmdn. etw. tun lassen; **don't ~ things get you down/worry you** lass dich nicht entmutigen/mach dir keine Sorgen; **don't ~ him upset you** reg dich seinetwegen nicht auf; **I'll come if you will ~ me** ich komme, wenn ich darf; **~ sb./sth. alone** jmdn./etw. in Ruhe lassen; **~ alone** (*far less*) geschweige denn; **~ sb. be** jmdn. in Ruhe *od.* Frieden lassen; **L~ it be. We can't alter things** Lass doch! Wir können die Dinge nicht ändern; **~ go [of] sth./sb.** (*release hold*) etw./jmdn. loslassen; **~ sb. go** (*from captivity*) jmdn. freilassen; **~ go** (*release hold*) loslassen; (*abandon self-restraint*) sich gehen lassen; (*neglect*) herunterkommen lassen ‹Haus›; (**~ pass**) durchgehen lassen ‹Bemerkung›; **~ it go [at that]** es dabei belassen *od.* bewenden lassen; **~ oneself go** (*neglect oneself*) sich vernachlässigen; nicht auf sich achten; (*abandon self-restraint*) sich gehen lassen; **~ loose** loslassen; Ⓑ (*cause to*) **~ sb. know** jmdn. wissen lassen; **~ sb. think that ...:** jmdn. in dem Glauben lassen, dass ...; **I will ~ you know as soon as ...:** ich gebe Ihnen Bescheid, sobald ...; **I have ~ it be known that ...:** ich habe alle wissen lassen, dass ...; Ⓒ (*release*) ablassen ‹Wasser› **(out of, from** aus); lassen ‹Luft› **(out of** aus); **the practice of ~ting blood** der Brauch des Aderlasses; Ⓓ (*Brit.: rent out*) vermieten ‹Haus, Wohnung, Büro›; verpachten ‹Gelände, Grundstück›; **~ a flat to sb. for a year** jmdm. *od.* an jmdn. eine Wohnung für ein Jahr vermieten; **there were plenty of houses to ~:** es gab viele Häuser, die zu vermieten waren; **'to ~'** „zu vermieten"; Ⓔ (*award*) vergeben ‹Arbeit, Rechte usw.›. ⇒ *also* **fly**² 1 G; **rip**¹ 3 B; **see**¹ 1 F, 2 C; **slip** 1 B; **well**² 2 B.

❷ *v. aux.*, **-tt-, let** Ⓐ *in exhortations* lassen; **~ us [just] suppose that ...:** lassen Sie uns einmal annehmen, dass ...; nehmen wir [nur] einmal an, dass ...; **Let's go to the cinema. — Yes, ~'s/No, ~'s not** *or* **don't ~'s** Komm/Kommt, wir gehen ins Kino. — Ja, gut/Nein, lieber nicht; **~'s pretend** tun wir so, als ob; **~'s have a go on your bike** (*coll.*) lass mich mal mit deinem Rad fahren; Ⓑ *in command, challenge, prayer* lassen; **~ them come in** sie sollen hereinkommen; lassen Sie sie herein; **~ there be light** (*Bibl.*) es werde Licht!; **~ the bells be rung** lasst die Glocken erklingen; **~ him go to the devil!** er soll zum Teufel gehen!; **~ it be said that ...:** es muss gesagt werden, dass ...; **never ~ it be thought/said that ...:** keiner soll glauben/sagen, dass ...; **[just] ~ him try!** das soll er [nur] mal wagen!; **~ him get well** (*in prayer*) lass ihn gesund werden; **~ x be equal to 3 a + b**² (*Math.*) x sei 3 a + b²; ⇒ *also* **pray** 1.

❸ *n.* (*Brit.*) **holiday ~s** ≈ Ferienwohnungen; **rent a flat on a short ~:** eine Wohnung für kurze Zeit mieten

**~ 'down** *v.t.* Ⓐ (*lower*) herunter-/hinunterlassen; herunterkurbeln ‹Autofenster›; **~ sb. down gently** (*fig.*) es jmdm. schonend beibringen (*ugs.*); ⇒ *also* **hair** B; Ⓑ (*deflate*) die Luft [heraus]lassen aus; Ⓒ (*Dressm.*) auslassen ‹Saum, Ärmel, Kleid, Hose›; Ⓓ (*disappoint, fail*) im Stich lassen; **~ oneself down** sich unter sein Niveau begeben; **I ~ myself down in the exam** ich habe in der Prüfung enttäuschend abgeschnitten; ⇒ *also* **~-down**

**~ 'in** *v.t.* Ⓐ (*admit*) herein-/hineinlassen; (*fig.*) die Tür öffnen (+ *Dat.*); **~ oneself/sb. in** sich (*Dat.*) [die Tür] aufschließen/jmdm. aufmachen; **my shoes are ~ting in water** meine Schuhe sind undicht; Ⓑ (*Dressm.*) enger machen; einnähen; Ⓒ **~ oneself in for sth.** sich auf etw. (*Akk.*) einlassen; **~ oneself in for a lot of work/trouble** sich (*Dat.*) viel Arbeit aufhalsen (*ugs.*)/Ärger einhandeln; **~ sb. in for sth.** jmdm. etw. einbrocken (*ugs.*); Ⓓ **~ sb. in on a secret/plan** *etc.* jmdn. in ein Geheimnis/einen Plan *usw.* einweihen

**~ into** *v.t.* Ⓐ (*admit into*) lassen in (+ *Akk.*); Ⓑ (*fig.: acquaint with*) **~ sb. into a secret** jmdn. in ein Geheimnis einweihen; Ⓒ (*set into*) **a safe ~ into the wall** ein in die Wand eingelassener Safe

**~ 'off** *v.t.* Ⓐ (*excuse*) laufen lassen (*ugs.*); (*allow to go*) gehen lassen; **~ sb. off lightly/with a fine** jmdn. glimpflich/mit einer Geldstrafe davonkommen lassen; **~ sb. off sth.** jmdm. etw. erlassen; ⇒ *also* **~-off**; Ⓑ (*fire, explode*) abbrennen ‹Feuerwerk›; abfeuern ‹Kanone, Gewehrsalve›; Ⓒ (*allow to escape*) ablassen ‹Dampf, Flüssigkeit›; Ⓓ (*Brit.: rent out*) einzeln vermieten; Ⓔ (*allow to alight*) aussteigen lassen

**~ 'on** (*coll.*) ❶ *v.i.* **~ on about sth. [to sb.]** [jmdm.] etwas verraten; **don't ~ on!** nichts verraten! ❷ *v.t.* Ⓐ **sb. ~ on to me that ...:** man hat mir gesteckt, dass ... (*ugs.*); Ⓑ (*pretend*) **~ on that ...:** so tun, als ob ... (*ugs.*); **she's not as sick as she ~s on** sie ist nicht so krank, wie sie tut (*ugs.*)

**~ 'out** *v.t.* Ⓐ (*open door for*) **~ sb./an animal out** jmdn./ein Tier heraus-/hinauslassen; **Don't get up. I'll ~ myself out** Bleiben Sie sitzen. Ich finde schon allein hinaus; Ⓑ (*allow out*) rauslassen (*ugs.*); gehen lassen; Ⓒ (*emit*) ausstoßen ‹Schrei›; hören lassen ‹Lachen, Seufzer›; **~ out a groan** aufstöhnen; Ⓓ (*reveal*) verraten, ausplaudern ‹Geheimnis›; **~ out that ...:** durchsickern lassen, dass ...; Ⓔ (*Dressm.*) auslassen; Ⓕ (*Brit.: rent out*) ⇒ **let**¹ 1 D; Ⓖ (*from duty*) **On Saturday? That ~s me out**

Samstag? Da falle ich schon mal aus; **that ~s me out of having to go** dann muss ich nicht hin (*ugs.*); ⇒ *also* **~-out**

**~ 'through** *v.t.* durchlassen

**~ 'up** *v.i.* (*coll.*) nachlassen; **don't you ever ~ up?** wirst du überhaupt nicht müde?; ⇒ *also* **~-up**

**let²** *n.* **A without ~ [or hindrance]** (*formal/Law*) ohne jede Behinderung; **B** (*Tennis*) Let, *der*

**'let-down** *n.* Enttäuschung, *die*

**lethal** /li:θl/ *adj.* tödlich; letal (*Med.*); (*fig.*) vernichtend; **that knife looks ~:** das Messer sieht sehr gefährlich aus

**lethargic** /lɪ'θɑ:dʒɪk/ *adj.* **A** träge; (*apathetic*) lethargisch; (*causing lethargy*) träge machend; einschläfernd ‹Atmosphäre, Musik›; **B** (*Med.*) lethargisch

**lethargically** /lɪ'θɑ:dʒɪkəlɪ/ *adv.* träge; (*apathetically*) lethargisch

**lethargy** /'leθədʒɪ/ *n.* **A** Trägheit, *die;* (*apathy*) Lethargie, *die;* **B** (*Med.*) Lethargie, *die*

**let: ~-off** *n.* **have a ~-off** noch einmal davonkommen; **that was a [lucky] ~-off** da habe ich/hast du *usw.* noch einmal Glück gehabt; **~-out** *n.* Ausrede, *die*

**Lett** /let/ *n.* **A** (*person*) Lette, *der*/Lettin, *die;* **B** (*language*) Lettisch, *das*

**letter** /letə(r)/ ❶ *n.* **A** ▶ 1286 (*written communication*) Brief, *der* (**to** an + *Akk.*); (*official communication*) Schreiben, *das;* **a ~ of appointment** eine [briefliche] Anstellungszusage; **by ~:** brieflich; schriftlich; **'~s to the editor'** „Leserbriefe"; ⇒ *also* **credit** 1 E; **B** (*of alphabet*) Buchstabe, *der;* **how many ~s are there in the word?** wie viele Buchstaben hat das Wort?; **learn one's ~s** die Buchstaben lernen; **write in capital/small ~s** mit Groß-/Kleinbuchstaben schreiben; **have ~s after one's name** Ehrentitel/einen Ehrentitel haben; **C** (*fig.*) **to the ~:** buchstabengetreu; aufs Wort; **the ~ of the law** der Buchstabe des Gesetzes; **in ~ and in spirit** in Geist und Buchstabe; **D** *in pl.* (*literature*) Literatur, *die;* **world of ~s** literarische Welt; **man of ~s** Homme de lettres, *der;* Literat, *der;* **Doctor of L~s** Lit[t]erarum Humaniorum Doctor; **E** (*Printing: type fount*) Letter, *die;* Type, *die;* **F** (*Amer. Sport: mark of proficiency*) Leistungsabzeichen, *das.* ❷ *v.t.* **A** (*classify alphabetically*) mit Buchstaben kennzeichnen; **B** (*inscribe on*) beschriften

**letter: ~ bomb** *n.* Briefbombe, *die;* **~ box** *n.* Briefkasten, *der;* (*slit*) Briefschlitz, *der;* **come** *or* **be put through the ~ box** in den Briefkasten gesteckt werden; **~-card** *n.* Kartenbrief, *der*

**lettered** /'letəd/ *adj.* **A** (*well read, educated*) gebildet; **B** (*inscribed*) beschriftet

**letter: ~head, ~-heading** *ns.* Briefpapier mit Briefkopf; (*heading*) Briefkopf, *der*

**lettering** /'letərɪŋ/ *n.* (*letters*) Typographie, *die;* (*on book cover*) Aufschrift, *die;* (*carved*) Inschrift, *die*

**letter: ~ pad** *n.* Briefblock, *der;* **~ paper** *n.* Briefpapier, *das;* **~ post** *n.* (*Brit. Post*) Briefpost, *die* (*veralt.*); **~press** *n.* **A** (*Brit.: text*) Text, *der;* **B** (*Printing*) Hochdruck, *der;* **~s page** *n.* Leserbriefseite, *die;* **~s 'patent** *n. pl.* Patent, *das;* **~-writer** *n.* Briefschreiber, *der*/Briefschreiberin, *die*

**Lettish** /'letɪʃ/ ❶ *adj.* lettisch. ❷ *n.* ⇒ **Lett** B

**lettuce** /'letɪs/ *n.* [Kopf]salat, *der;* [grüner] Salat; **a [head of] ~:** ein Kopf Salat

**'let-up** *n.* (*coll.*) (*in fighting*) Nachlassen, *das;* (*in work*) Pause, *die;* **there was no ~ in the fighting/bombardment** die Kämpfe ließen/der Beschuss ließ nicht nach

**leucocyte** /lu:kəsaɪt/ *n.* (*Anat.*) Leukozyt, *der* (*fachspr.*); weißes Blutkörperchen

**leucotomy** /lu:'kɒtəmɪ/ *n.* (*Med.*) Leukotomie, *die*

**leukaemia** (*Amer.:* **leukemia**) /lu:'ki:mɪə/ *n.* ▶ 1232 (*Med.*) Leukämie, *die*

**Levant** /lɪ'vænt/ *pr. n.* **the ~:** die Levante

**Levantine** /lɪ'væntaɪn, 'levəntaɪn/ ❶ *adj.* levantinisch. ❷ *n.* Levantiner, *der*/Levantinerin, *die*

**levee** /'levɪ/ *n.* (*Amer. Geog.*) Fluss-, Uferdamm, *der*

**level** /'levl/ ❶ *n.* **A** Höhe, *die;* (*storey*) Etage, *die;* (*fig.: steady state*) Niveau, *das;* (*fig.: basis*) Ebene, *die;* **the water rose to the ~ of the doorsteps** das Wasser stieg bis zur Türschwelle; **live on the same ~:** in *od.* auf derselben Etage wohnen; **prices are at a high/low ~:** die Preise sind hoch/niedrig; **be on a ~ [with sb./sth.]** sich auf gleicher *od.* einer Höhe [mit jmdm./etw.] befinden; (*fig.*) auf dem gleichen Niveau sein *od.* der gleichen Stufe stehen [wie jmd./etw.]; **on the ~** (*fig. coll.*) ehrlich; **he's on the ~:** man kann ihm durchaus trauen; **water finds/seeks its ~:** Wasser verteilt sich gleichmäßig; **find one's ~** (*fig.*) seinen Platz finden; **B** (*height*) **at waist/rooftop** *etc.* **~:** in Taillen-/Dachhöhe *usw.;* **C** (*relative amount*) **sugar/alcohol ~:** [Blut]zucker-/Alkoholspiegel, *der;* **noise ~:** Geräuschpegel, *der;* **high ~s of $CO_2$ in the atmosphere** ein hoher $CO_2$-Gehalt in der Atmosphäre; **D** (*social, moral, or intellectual plane*) Niveau, *das;* (*degree of achievement etc.*) Grad, *der* (**of** an + *Dat.*); (*plane of significance*) Ebene, *die;* **the lower ~s** die unteren Schichten; **on a personal/moral ~:** auf persönlicher/moralischer Ebene; **expenditure is running at high ~s** die Aufwendungen bewegen sich auf einem hohen Niveau; **high ~ of intellect** hoher Intelligenzgrad; **pupils of varying ~s of ability** Schüler unterschiedlicher Begabung; **he has reached an advanced ~ in his course** er hat in seinem Kurs ein fortgeschrittenes Niveau erreicht; **talks at the highest ~ [of government]** Gespräche auf höchster [Regierungs]ebene; **E** (*instrument to test horizontal*) Wasserwaage, *die;* **F** (*Surv.: telescope*) Nivellierinstrument, *das;* **G** (*Mining*) Sohle, *die.*

❷ *adj.* **A** waagerecht; flach ‹Land›; eben ‹Boden, Land›; **a ~ spoonful of flour** ein gestrichener Löffel Mehl; **the picture is not ~:** das Bild hängt nicht gerade; **B** (*on a ~*) **be ~ [with sth./sb.]** auf gleicher Höhe [mit etw./jmdm.] sein; (*fig.*) [mit etw./jmdm.] gleichauf liegen; **the two pictures are not ~:** die beiden Bilder hängen nicht gleich hoch; **draw/keep ~ with a rival** mit einem Gegner gleichziehen/auf gleicher Höhe bleiben; **~ race** Kopf-an-Kopf-Rennen, *das;* ⇒ *also* **peg** 2 C; **C** (*fig.: steady, even*) ausgeglichen ‹Leben, Temperament›; ausgewogen ‹Stil›; **keep a ~ head** einen kühlen Kopf bewahren; **D do one's ~ best** (*coll.*) sein Möglichstes tun.

❸ *v.t.*, (*Brit.*) **-ll-** **A** (*make ~* 2 a) ebnen; **B** (*aim*) richten ‹Blick, Gewehr, Rakete› (**at, against** auf + *Akk.*); (*fig.*) richten ‹Kritik usw.› (**at, against** gegen); erheben ‹Anklage, Vorwurf› (**at, against** gegen); **C** (*raze*) dem Erdboden gleichmachen ‹Stadt, Gebäude›; **D** (*knock down*) zu Boden schlagen ‹Person›; **E** (*abolish*) aufheben, nivellieren ‹Unterschiede›; **F** (*Surv.*) nivellieren.

❹ *v.i.*, (*Brit.*) **-ll-** (*coll.*) **I'll ~ with you** ganz im Ernst; ehrlich (*ugs.*); **~ with sb.** mit jmdm. ehrlich sein

**~ 'down** *v.t.* herabsetzen; abbauen ‹Privilegien, Gehälter, Einkommen›

**~ 'off** ❶ *v.t.* glattmachen. ❷ *v.i.* (*Aeronaut.*) die Flughöhe beibehalten

**~ 'out** ❶ *v.t.* einebnen. ❷ *v.i.* **A** ⇒ **~ off** 2; **B** (*fig.*) sich ausgleichen; ‹Preise, Markt:› sich beruhigen

**~ 'up** *v.t.* anheben ‹Niveau, Leistungsstand, Gehalt, Einkommen›

**level 'crossing** *n.* (*Brit. Railw.*) [schienengleicher] Bahnübergang

**leveler** (*Amer.*) ⇒ **leveller**

**level-'headed** *adj.* besonnen; **remain ~:** einen kühlen Kopf bewahren

**leveller** /'levələ(r)/ *n.* Gleichmacher, *der*

**levelling screw** (*Amer.:* **leveling-screw**) /'levəlɪŋskru:/ *n.* Stellschraube, *die*

**lever** /'li:və(r)/ ❶ *n.* **A** Hebel, *der;* (*crowbar*) Brechstange, *die;* (*Mech.*) Hebel[arm], *der;* **B** (*fig.: means of persuasion*) Druckmittel, *das.* ❷ *v.t.* **~ sth. open** etw. aufhebeln; **~ sth. up** etw. hochhebeln

**leverage** /'li:vərɪdʒ/ *n.* **A** Hebelwirkung, *die;* (*action of lever*) Hebelkraft, *die;* (*system of levers*) Hebelwerk, *das;* **I need more ~ to move this cupboard** ich brauche einen günstigeren Ansatzpunkt, um den Schrank bewegen zu können; **B** (*fig.: influence*) **give sb. [a lot of] ~:** jmds. Position [sehr] stärken

**leveraged buyout** /li:vərɪdʒd 'baɪaʊt/ *n.* (*Commerc.*) Leveraged-Buy-out, *das* (*Wirtsch.*)

**leveret** /'levərɪt/ *n.* (*Zool.*) Junghase, *der*

**leviathan** /lɪ'vaɪəθən/ *n.* **A** (*sea monster*) Seeungeheuer, *das;* **B** (*fig.: huge thing*) Riese, *der;* (*ship*) Ozeanriese, *der*

**Levis** ® /'li:vaɪz/ *n. pl.* Levis, *die* Wz

**levitate** /'levɪteɪt/ *v.i. & t.* levitieren

**levitation** /levɪ'teɪʃn/ *n.* Levitation, *die*

**levity** /'levɪtɪ/ *n.* **A** (*frivolity*) Unernst, *der;* **B** (*inconstancy*) Unbeständigkeit, *die;* Wankelmut, *der* (*geh.*); **C** (*undignified behaviour*) Leichtfertigkeit, *die*

**levy** /'levɪ/ ❶ *n.* **A** [Steuer]erhebung, *die;* **B** (*tax*) Steuer, *die;* **make** *or* **impose a ~ on sth.** eine Steuer auf etw. (*Akk.*) erheben; **C** (*Mil.: conscription*) Einberufung, *die;* (*number of conscripts*) Anzahl von Einberufenen; *in pl.* (*conscripts*) Einberufene. ❷ *v.t.* **A** (*exact*) erheben ‹Steuern, Beträge›; (*seize*) beschlagnahmen; einziehen; (*extort*) erpressen ‹Geld›; **~ a fine on sb./a tax on sth.** jmdn. mit einer Geldstrafe/etw. mit einer Steuer belegen; **B** (*Mil.: conscript*) aufstellen ‹Armee, Truppe›; einberufen ‹Soldat›

**lewd** /lju:d/ *adj.* geil (*oft abwertend*), lüstern (*geh.*) ‹Person›; anzüglich ‹Blick, Geste›; schlüpfrig, unanständig ‹Lied, Ausdruck, Witz›

**lewdly** /'lju:dlɪ/ *adv.* lüstern (*geh.*); anzüglich

**lewdness** /'lju:dnɪs/ *n., no pl.* (*of person*) Geilheit, *die* (*oft abwertend*); Lüsternheit, *die* (*geh.*); (*of look, remark*) Anzüglichkeit, *die;* (*of language, joke*) Schlüpfrigkeit, *die*

**lexical** /'leksɪkl/ *adj.* lexikalisch

**lexicographer** /leksɪ'kɒgrəfə(r)/ *n.* ▶ 1261 Lexikograph, *der*/Lexikographin, *die*

**lexicography** /leksɪ'kɒgrəfɪ/ *n., no pl.* Lexikographie, *die*

**lexicon** /'leksɪkən/ *n.* **A** (*dictionary*) Wörterbuch, *das;* Lexikon, *das* (*veralt.*); **B** (*vocabulary*) Wortschatz, *der*

**lexis** /'leksɪs/ *n.* Wortschatz, *der*

**l. h.** *abbr.* **left hand** l.

**liability** /laɪə'bɪlɪtɪ/ *n.* **A** *no pl.* (*legal obligation*) Haftung, *die;* **limited ~** (*Brit.*) beschränkte Haftung; **~ to pay tax[es]** *or* **for taxation** Steuerpflicht, *die;* **~ for military service** Dienstpflicht, *die;* **B** *no pl.* (*proneness*) (*to disease etc.*) Anfälligkeit, *die* (**to** für); **C** (*sth. one is liable for*) Verpflichtung, *die;* **liabilities** (*debts*) Verbindlichkeiten (*Kaufmannsspr.*); **D** (*cause of disadvantage*) Belastung, *die* (**to** für)

**liable** /'laɪəbl/ *pred. adj.* **A** (*legally bound*) **be ~ for sth.** für etw. haftbar sein *od.* haften; **~ for military service** militärdienstpflichtig; **be ~ to pay tax[es]** steuerpflichtig sein; **B** (*prone*) **be ~ to sth.** ‹Sache:› leicht etw. haben; ‹Person:› zu etw. neigen; **be ~ to do sth.** ‹Sache:› leicht etw. tun; ‹Person:› dazu neigen, etw. zu tun; **C** (*likely*) **difficulties are ~ to occur** mit Schwierigkeiten muss man rechnen; **she is ~ to change her mind** es kann durchaus sein, dass sie ihre Meinung ändert; **it is ~ to be cold there** im Allgemeinen ist es dort kalt

**liaise** /lɪ'eɪz/ *v.i.* eine Verbindung herstellen; **~ on a project** bei einem Projekt zusammenarbeiten; **they ~ on a regular basis** sie haben regelmäßig Kontakt

**liaison** /lɪ'eɪzɒn/ *n.* **A** (*cooperation*) Zusammenarbeit, *die;* (*connection*) Verbindung, *die;* **be in ~ with** in Verbindung stehen mit; **B** (*illicit relation*) Verhältnis, *das;* Liaison, *die* (*geh.*); **form** *or* **enter into a ~:** ein Verhältnis anfangen; **C** (*Phonet.*) Liaison, *die*

**li'aison officer** *n.* Verbindungsmann, *der;* (*Mil.*) Verbindungsoffizier, *der*

# Letter-writing

## Addressing the envelope

German addresses look different.
**LINE 1:** the person's basic title (***Mr*** = Herrn*, ***Mrs*** or ***Ms*** = Frau, ***Miss*** = Fräulein), followed by any other title or rank (Professor, Major etc.), except Dr. and Dipl.-Ing. (Diplomingenieur) which precede the name on **LINE 2**.
**LINE 3:** the street, with the house number after it.
**LINE 4** has the place, preceded by the postcode (**die Postleitzahl**). Finally comes the country on **LINE 5**.

| | | |
|---|---|---|
| Herrn* Professor | Frau | Fräulein |
| Manfred Bauer | Dr. Erika Engelsbach | Inge Walz |
| Fritz-Busch-Str. 48 | Ahornweg 6 | bei Wolf |
| D-86163 Augsburg-Hochzoll | A-4924 Waldzell | Hauptstr. 21 |
| Germany | Austria | 48637 Coesfeld |

*There is an **n** after **Herr** in addresses (and only in addresses) because this is an accusative.

The Postleitzahl may be preceded by D for Germany, A for Austria or CH for Switzerland on letters from outside the country. A district of a large town will often be added after the name of the town and joined with a hyphen.

Writing to someone staying with a family or friend, use **bei** plus the surname, e.g. bei Wolf.

Writing to a firm, **Firma** may precede the name, The name of the department or person you want follows the firm's name (**z. H.** = **zu Händen**, 'for the attention of'). **Postfach** = P.O. Box. And in typed or printed business mail there is a blank line before the place.

| | |
|---|---|
| Firma | Müller-Versand KG |
| Willi Müller | Verkaufsabteilung |
| z. H. Herrn Nesseldorn | Postfach 21 08 03 |
| Endenicher Straße 218 | |
| | 20408 Hamburg |
| 53121 Bonn | |

The sender's address should also be given on the back of the envelope, preceded by **Abs.** or **Absender**.

## Layout

There is usually no address at the top, just the name of the place and the date:

Rastatt, [den] 7.4.1997

■ **BEGINNINGS**

***Dear Hans***
= Lieber Hans

***Dear Karen***
= Liebe Karen

***Dear Hilde and Erwin***
= Liebe Hilde, lieber Erwin

***Dear Mr Engel/Mrs Schulz***
= (*personal letter*) Lieber Herr Engel/Liebe Frau Schulz; (*formal business letter*) Sehr geehrter Herr Engel/Sehr geehrte Frau Schulz

***Dear Sir*** or ***Madam*** (*formal*)
= Sehr geehrte Damen und Herren

To someone with a title, omit the name:

***Dear Professor Wolf***
= Sehr geehrter Herr Professor/Sehr geehrte Frau Professor

An exception is the title **Doktor**, where the name is omitted when writing to a doctor of medicine but not when writing to someone who holds the academic title of **Doktor**.

All these greetings can either be followed by a comma, with the first line then starting with a small letter, or by an exclamation mark, with the first line starting with a capital. In the letter itself, **du, dein, ihr, euer** used to be written with a capital, but this is no longer necessary.

■ **... AND ENDINGS**

Informal:

***Yours***
= Herzliche Grüße

***All my/our love***
= Alles Liebe

***With best wishes, Kind regards***
= Mit herzlichen Grüßen

More formal, standard ending:

***Yours sincerely*** or (Amer.) ***truly***
= Mit freundlichen Grüßen

Formal business letter:

***Yours faithfully***
= Mit freundlichen Empfehlungen, Hochachtungsvoll

**liana** /lɪ'ɑ:nə/ *n.* (*Bot.*) Liane, *die*

**liar** /'laɪə(r)/ *n.* Lügner, *der*/Lügnerin, *die*

**Lib** /lɪb/ *abbr.* Ⓐ **Liberal** Lib.; Ⓑ **liberation**

**libation** /laɪ'beɪʃn, lɪ'beɪʃn/ *n.* Libation, *die;* Trankopfer, *das*

**libel** /'laɪbl/ ❶ *n.* Ⓐ (*schriftliche*) Verleumdung; **[public]** ~: [blasphemische, obszöne, aufrührerische od. landesverräterische] Verleumdung; Ⓑ (*misrepresentation that discredits*) diffamierende Entstellung (**on** *Gen.*). ❷ *v.t.*, (*Brit.*) **-ll-** (*schriftlich*) verleumden

**libellous** (*Amer.:* **libelous**) /'laɪbələs/ *adj.* verleumderisch

**liberal** /'lɪbərl/ ❶ *adj.* Ⓐ (*generous, abundant*) großzügig; freigebig, großzügig ‹Person, Wesen›; **a ~ amount of** reichlich; Ⓑ (*generally educative*) allgemein bildend; **~ education** *or* **culture** Allgemeinbildung, *die;* **~ studies** *geisteswissenschaftliches Nebenfach bei naturwissenschaftlicher, technischer oder berufsspezifischer Ausbildung;* Ⓒ (*not strict*) liberal; frei ‹Auslegung›; Ⓓ (*open-minded*) liberal; aufgeschlossen; Ⓔ (*Polit.*) liberal. ❷ *n.* Ⓐ liberal denkender Mensch; Ⓑ **L~** (*Polit.*) Liberale, *der/die*

**liberal 'arts** *n. pl.* Ⓐ (*Hist.*) Artes liberales *Pl.;* die sieben freien Künste; Ⓑ (*Amer.: arts*) Geisteswissenschaften *Pl.*

**liberalism** /'lɪbərəlɪzm/ *n.* Ⓐ Liberalität, *die;* Ⓑ **L~** (*Polit.*) Liberalismus, *der*

**liberality** /lɪbə'rælɪtɪ/ *n., no pl.* Ⓐ (*generosity*) Großzügigkeit, *die* (**to** gegenüber); Freigebigkeit, *die;* Ⓑ (*open-mindedness*) Liberalität, *die;* **~ of mind** liberale Gesinnung

**liberalize** /'lɪbərəlaɪz/ *v.t.* liberalisieren

**liberally** /'lɪbərəlɪ/ *adv.* (*generously*) großzügig; (*abundantly*) reichlich

**liberate** /'lɪbəreɪt/ *v.t.* Ⓐ befreien (**from** aus); Ⓑ (*Chem.*) freisetzen; Ⓒ (*joc. coll.: steal*) mitgehen lassen (*ugs.*)

**liberation** /lɪbə'reɪʃn/ *n.* Ⓐ Befreiung, *die;* **~ theology** Theologie der Befreiung; ⇒ *also* **Women's Liberation**; Ⓑ (*Chem.*) Freisetzung, *die*

**liberator** /'lɪbəreɪtə(r)/ *n.* Befreier, *der*/Befreierin, *die*

**Liberia** /laɪ'bɪərɪə/ *pr. n.* Liberia (*das*)

**Liberian** /laɪ'bɪərɪən/ ▶ **1340** ❶ *adj.* liber[ian]isch. ❷ *n.* Liberi[an]er, *der*/Liberi[an]erin, *die*

**libertine** /'lɪbəti:n/ *n.* Libertin, *der*

**liberty** /'lɪbətɪ/ *n.* Freiheit, *die;* **the Statue of L~:** die Freiheitsstatue; **you are at ~ to come and go as you please** es steht Ihnen frei, zu kommen und zu gehen, wie Sie wollen; **be at ~:** auf freiem Fuß sein; **set sb. at ~:** jmdn. auf freien Fuß setzen; **~ of the subject** Recht als Staatsbürger; **~ of action/movement** Handlungs-/Bewegungsfreiheit, *die;* **take the ~ to do** *or* **of doing sth.** sich (*Dat.*) die Freiheit nehmen, etw. zu tun; **take liberties with sb.** sich (*Dat.*) Freiheiten gegen jmdn. herausnehmen (*ugs.*); **take liberties with sth.** mit etw. allzu frei umgehen; **if you'll pardon the ~:** wenn ich mir die Bemerkung erlauben darf; ⇒ *also* **conscience**

**liberty: L~ Bell** *n.* (*Amer.*) Freiheitsglocke, *die;* **~ boat** *n.* (*Brit. Naut.*) *Boot, mit dem Seeleute zu einem kurzen Landurlaub an Land* *gebracht werden;* ~ **horse** *n.* Freiheitsdressurpferd, *das*

**libidinal** /lɪˈbɪdɪnl/ *adj.* (*Psych.*) libidinös

**libidinous** /lɪˈbɪdɪnəs/ *adj.* triebhaft

**libido** /lɪˈbiːdəʊ/ *n.* (*Psych.*) Libido, *die*

**Libra** /ˈliːbrə, ˈlɪbrə/ *n.* (*Astrol., Astron.*) die Waage; die Libra; ⇒ *also* **Aries**

**Libran** /ˈliːbrən, ˈlɪbrən/ *n.* (*Astrol.*) Waage, *die*

**librarian** /laɪˈbreərɪən/ *n.* ▶**1261** Bibliothekar, *der*/Bibliothekarin, *die*

**librarianship** /laɪˈbreərɪənʃɪp/ *n.* **A** (*subject*) Bibliothekswesen, *das;* Bibliothekskunde, *die;* **B** (*work*) bibliothekarische Tätigkeit

**library** /ˈlaɪbrərɪ/ *n.* **A** Bibliothek, *die;* Bücherei, *die;* **reference** ~: Präsenzbibliothek, *die;* **public** ~: öffentliche Bücherei; **B** (*collection of films, records, etc.*) Sammlung, *die.* ⇒ *also* **lending** 2; **rental library**

**library:** ~ **book** *n.* Buch aus der Bibliothek *od.* Bücherei; ~ **edition** *n.* Ausgabe mit Bibliothekseinband; ~ **school** *n.* Bibliotheksschule, *die;* ~ **science** *n.* Bibliothekswissenschaft, *die;* ~ **ticket** *n.* Lesekarte, *die*

**librettist** /lɪˈbretɪst/ *n.* Librettist, *der*/Librettistin, *die*

**libretto** /lɪˈbretəʊ/ *n., pl.* **libretti** /lɪˈbretiː/ *or* ~**s** Libretto, *das*

**Libya** /ˈlɪbɪə/ *pr. n.* Libyen (*das*)

**Libyan** /ˈlɪbɪən/ ▶**1340** **1** *adj.* libysch; **sb. is** ~: jmd. ist Libyer/Libyerin. **2** *n.* Libyer, *der*/Libyerin, *die*

**lice** *pl. of* **louse** 1 A

**licence** /ˈlaɪsəns/ **1** *n.* **A** (*official permit*) [behördliche] Genehmigung; Lizenz, *die;* Konzession, *die* (*Amtsspr.*); **hunting** ~: Jagdschein, *der;* **gun** ~: Waffenschein, *der;* ~ **to marry** ⇒ **marriage licence**; **B** ([*excessive*] *liberty of action*) [uneingeschränkte] Handlungsfreiheit; **C** (*licentiousness*) Unzüchtigkeit, *die;* Zügellosigkeit, *die;* **D** (*artist's irregularity*) Freiheit, *die;* **poetic** ~: dichterische Freiheit. **2** *v.t.* ⇒ **license** 1

ˈ**licence dodger** *n.* (*car owner*) Schwarzfahrer, *der;* (*TV*) Schwarzseher, *der*

**license** /ˈlaɪsəns/ **1** *v.t.* ermächtigen; ~ **a building for use as a theatre** ein Gebäude zur Nutzung als Theater freigeben; ~**d to sell alcoholic beverages** (*formal*) [für den Ausschank von alkoholischen Getränken] konzessioniert; ~**d to sell tobacco** berechtigt, Tabakwaren zu verkaufen; **the restaurant is** ~**d to sell drinks** das Restaurant hat eine Schankerlaubnis *od.* -konzession; ~**d** ‹Händler, Makler, Buchmacher› mit [einer] Lizenz; ~**d house** Gastwirtschaft, *die;* **licensing hours** (*in public house*) Ausschankzeiten; **licensing laws** Schankgesetze; ≈ Gaststättengesetz, *das;* ~**d premises** Gaststätte mit Schankerlaubnis; **get a car** ~**d,** ~ **a car** ≈ die Kfz-Steuer für ein Auto bezahlen; ~ **a book/play** *etc.* **[for publication]** ein Buch/Stück *usw.* [zur Veröffentlichung] freigeben; ⇒ *also* **victualler**.
**2** *n.* (*Amer.*) ⇒ **licence** 1

**licensee** /laɪsənˈsiː/ *n.* Lizenzinhaber, *der;* Konzessionsinhaber, *der;* (*of bar*) Wirt, *der*/Wirtin, *die*

ˈ**license plate** *n.* (*Amer.*) Nummernschild, *das*

**licentiate** /laɪˈsenʃɪət/ *n.* **A** (*person*) Inhaber eines Diploms; **B** (*certificate*) Diplom, *das*

**licentious** /laɪˈsenʃəs/ *adj.* zügellos, ausschweifend ‹Leben, Person›; unzüchtig ‹Benehmen, Reden›; freizügig ‹Buch, Theaterstück›

**lichen** /ˈlaɪkn, ˈlɪtʃn/ *n.* Flechte, *die*

**lichgate** /ˈlɪtʃgeɪt/ *n.* überdachtes Friedhofstor

**licit** /ˈlɪsɪt/ *adj.* legal

**lick** /lɪk/ **1** *v.t.* **A** lecken; ~ **a stamp** eine Briefmarke anlecken *od.* belecken; ~ **one's chops** (*coll.*) *or* **lips** (*lit. or fig.*) sich (*Dat.*) die Lippen lecken; ~ **sth./sb. into shape** (*fig.*) etw./jmdn. auf Vordermann bringen (*ugs.*); ~ **sb.'s boots** (*fig.*) jmdm. die Stiefel lecken; ~ **sb.'s arse** (*fig. coarse*) jmdm. hinten reinkriechen (*derb*); ~ **one's wounds** (*lit. or fig.*) seine Wunden lecken; **B** (*play gently over*) ‹Flammen, Feuer:› [empor]züngeln an (+ *Dat.*); ‹Wasser, Wellen:› plätschern über (+ *Akk.*); **C** (*coll.: beat*) verdreschen (*ugs.*); (*fig.*) bewältigen, meistern ‹Problem›; (*in contest*) eine Abfuhr erteilen (+ *Dat.*); **this crossword/problem has [got] me** ~**ed** bei diesem Kreuzworträtsel/Problem steck ich fest (*ugs.*).
**2** *n.* **A** (*act*) Lecken, *das;* **have a** ~ **at sth.** an etw. (*Dat.*) lecken; **give a door a** ~ **of paint** eine Tür [oberflächlich] überstreichen; **give the shoes a** ~ **of polish** die Schuhe flüchtig putzen; **give sth./oneself a** ~ **and a promise** (*fig. coll.*) kurz über etw. (*Akk.*) hinhuschen/Katzenwäsche machen (*ugs.*); **B** (*coll.: fast pace*) **at a great** *or* **at full** ~: mit einem Affenzahn (*ugs.*); **at quite a** ~: mit einem ganz schönen Zahn (*ugs.*); **C** ⇒ **salt lick**

~ ˈ**off** *v.t.* ablecken; ~ **the cream off the cake** die Sahne vom Kuchen lecken

~ ˈ**up** *v.t.* auflecken

**lickety-split** /lɪkətɪˈsplɪt/ *adv.* (*coll.*) wie der Blitz (*ugs.*)

**licking** /ˈlɪkɪŋ/ *n.* (*coll.: beating*) Abreibung, *die* (*ugs.*); **give sb. a good** ~: jmdn. kräftig durchbläuen (*ugs.*); **take a** ~: eine Abreibung kriegen (*ugs.*)

ˈ**lickspittle** *n.* Speichellecker, *der* (*abwertend*)

**licorice** ⇒ **liquorice**

**lid** /lɪd/ *n.* **A** Deckel, *der;* **with the** ~ **off** (*fig.*) unter Aufdeckung aller Mängel/Schwächen/Missstände; **take the** ~ **off sth.** (*fig.*) etw. aufdecken; **keep the** ~ **on sth.** (*fig.*) (*keep under control*) etw. unter Kontrolle halten; (*keep secret*) etw. geheim halten *od.* abschirmen; **put the [tin]** ~ **on sth.** (*Brit. coll.*) (*be the final blow*) einer Sache (*Dat.*) die Krone aufsetzen; (*put an end to*) etw. stoppen; **that [really] puts the tin** ~ **on it** das schlägt dem Fass den Boden aus; ⇒ *also* **flip**[1] 3; **B** (*eyelid*) Lid, *das*

**lido** /ˈliːdəʊ/ *n., pl.* ~**s** Freibad, *das*

**lie**[1] /laɪ/ **1** *n.* **A** (*false statement*) Lüge, *die;* **tell** ~**s/a** ~: lügen; **no, I tell a** ~, **...** (*coll.*) nein, nicht dass ich jetzt lüge, ... (*ugs.*); **white** ~: Notlüge, *die;* **tell a white** ~: eine Notlüge gebrauchen; **give sb. the** ~ **[in his throat]** jmdn. der Lüge bezichtigen; **give the** ~ **to sth.** etw. Lügen strafen; **B** (*thing that deceives*) [einzige] Lüge (*fig.*); Schwindel, *der* (*abwertend*); **he lived a** ~: sein Leben war eine einzige Lüge. **2** *v.i.*, **lying** /ˈlaɪɪŋ/ lügen; ~ **to sb.** jmdn. be- *od.* anlügen; ~ **through one's teeth** (*joc.*) das Blaue vom Himmel herunterlügen (*ugs.*). **3** *v.t.*, **lying:** ~ **one's way out of sth.** sich aus etw. herauslügen

**lie**[2] **1** *n.* **A** (*direction, position*) Lage, *die;* **the** ~ **of the land** (*Brit. fig.: state of affairs*) die Lage der Dinge; die Sachlage; **B** (*Golf*) Lage [des Balles].
**2** *v.i.*, **lying** /ˈlaɪɪŋ/, **lay** /leɪ/, **lain** /leɪn/ **A** liegen; (*assume horizontal position*) sich legen; **many obstacles** ~ **in the way of my success** (*fig.*) viele Hindernisse verstellen mir den Weg zum Erfolg; ~ **resting** ruhen; **she lay asleep/resting on the sofa** sie lag auf dem Sofa und schlief/ruhte sich aus; ~ **still/dying** still liegen/im Sterben liegen; ~ **sick** [krank] daniederliegen; ~ **dead/helpless** tot/hilflos [da]liegen; **B** (*be or remain in specified state*) ~ **in prison** im Gefängnis sitzen; ~ **idle** ‹Feld, Garten:› brachliegen; ‹Maschine, Fabrik:› stillstehen; ‹Gegenstand:› [unbenutzt] herumstehen (*ugs.*); **the money is lying idle in the bank** das Geld liegt ungenutzt auf der Bank; **let sth./things** ~: etw./die Dinge ruhen lassen; **how do things** ~? wie liegen die Dinge?; ⇒ *also* **close** 1 K; **doggo**; **fallow**[1] 2; **heavy** 1 J; **low**[1] 2 E; **wait** 3 B; **waste** 4 B; **C** (*be buried*) [begraben] liegen; ⇒ *also* **state** 1 G; **D** (*be situated*) liegen; **Austria** ~**s to the south of Germany** Österreich liegt südlich von Deutschland; **our road** ~**s northwards/along the river** unsere Straße führt nach Norden/verläuft entlang dem Fluss; ⇒ *also* **land** 1 B; **E** (*be spread out to view*) **the valley/plain/desert lay before us** vor uns lag das Tal/die Ebene/die Wüste; **a brilliant career lay before him** (*fig.*) eine glänzende Karriere lag vor ihm; **these suggestions now** ~ **open to discussion** (*fig.*) diese Vorschläge können jetzt diskutiert werden; **F** (*Naut.*) ~ **at anchor/in harbour** vor Anker/im Hafen liegen; **G** (*fig.*) ‹Gegenstand:› liegen; **her interest** ~**s in languages** ihr Interesse liegt auf sprachlichem Gebiet; **I will do everything that** ~**s in my power to help** ich werde alles tun, was in meiner Macht steht, um zu helfen; **I will ... as far as in me** ~**s** (*literary*) was an mir liegt, so will ich ...; **it** ~**s with you** es liegt bei dir; **H** (*Law: be admissible or sustainable*) zulässig sein; **no objection will** ~: Einspruch kann nicht erhoben werden; **I** ~ **with sb.** (*arch.: have sexual intercourse*) jmdm. beiliegen (*geh. veraltet*)

~ **aˈbout**, ~ **aˈround** *v.i.* herumliegen (*ugs.*)

~ ˈ**back** *v.i.* (*recline against sth.*) sich zurücklegen; (*in sitting position*) sich zurücklehnen

~ ˈ**down** *v.i.* sich hinlegen; **take sth. lying down** (*fig.*) etw. ruhig *od.* tatenlos hinnehmen; ⇒ *also* **lie-down**

~ ˈ**in** *v.i.* **A** (*arch.: labour in childbirth*) im Wochenbett liegen (*veralt.*); **B** (*Brit.: stay in bed*) liegen bleiben; ⇒ *also* **lie-in**

~ ˈ**over** *v.i.* ‹Arbeit:› liegen bleiben; ‹Tagesordnungspunkt, Entscheidung:› vertagt werden

~ ˈ**to** *v.i.* (*Naut.*) beidrehen

~ ˈ**up** *v.i.* **A** (*hide*) sich versteckt halten; **B** (*stay in bed*) das Bett hüten

ˈ**lie-abed** *n.* Langschläfer, *der*/-schläferin, *die*

**lied** /liːt/ *n., pl.* ~**er** /ˈliːdə(r)/ Lied, *das;* (*genre*) Kunstlied, *das*

**lie:** ~ **detector** *n.* Lügendetektor, *der;* ~**-down** *n.* **have a** ~**-down** sich hinlegen

**liege** /liːdʒ/ *n.* (*Hist.*) **A** (*lord*) Lehnsherr, *der;* **my** ~ *as form of address* mein gnädiger Herr; **B** *usu. in pl.* (*vassal*) Lehnsmann, *der*

**Liège** /lɪˈeɪʒ/ *pr. n.* Lüttich (*das*)

ˈ**lie-in** *n.* **A** (*Brit.: extra time in bed*) **have a** ~: [sich] ausschlafen; **B** (*protest*) *Demonstration, bei der sich die Protestierenden auf den Boden legen;* Lie-in, *das*

**lien** /ˈliːən/ *n.* (*Law*) Zurückbehaltungsrecht, *das;* Retentionsrecht, *das*

**lieu** /ljuː, luː/ *n.* **in** ~ **of sth.** anstelle einer Sache (*Gen.*); **get money/holidays in** ~: stattdessen Geld/Urlaub bekommen

**Lieut.** *abbr.* **Lieutenant**

**lieutenant** /lefˈtenənt, ləfˈtenənt/ *n.* ▶**1617** **A** (*Army*) Oberleutnant, *der;* (*Navy*) Kapitänleutnant, *der;* **first** ~ (*Amer. Air Force*) Oberleutnant, *der;* **B** (*Amer.: policeman*) ≈ Polizeioberkommissar, *der*

**lieutenant:** ~ ˈ**colonel** *n.* ▶**1617** Oberstleutnant, *der;* ~ **comˈmander** *n.* ▶**1617** Korvettenkapitän, *der;* ~ ˈ**general** *n.* ▶**1617** Generalleutnant, *der;* ~ ˈ**governor** *n.* ▶**1617** Vizegouverneur, *der*

**life** /laɪf/ *n., pl.* **lives** /laɪvz/ **A** Leben, *das;* **sign of** ~: Lebenszeichen, *das;* **essential for** ~: lebensnotwendig; **it is a matter of** ~ **and death** es geht [dabei] um Leben und Tod; (*fig.: it is of vital importance*) es ist äußerst wichtig (**to** für); **come to** ~ ‹Bild, Statue:› lebendig werden; ‹die Natur:› zu neuem Leben erwachen; (*after unconsciousness*) wieder zu sich kommen; **then the match came to** ~: dann kam Leben in das Spiel; **run** *etc.* **for one's** ~: um sein Leben rennen *usw.;* **I cannot for the** ~ **of me** ich kann beim besten Willen nicht; **lay down one's** ~: sein Leben [hin]geben; **lose one's** ~: sein Leben verlieren; **they lost their lives** sie verloren ihr Leben; **many lives were lost** viele Menschen kamen ums Leben; **risk [losing] one's** ~: sein Leben riskieren; **without loss of** ~: ohne Todesopfer; ~ **begins at forty** das Leben beginnt mit 40; ~ **is not worth living** das Leben ist nicht lebenswert; **not on your** ~ (*coll.*) nie im Leben! (*ugs.*); **save one's/sb.'s** ~: sein Leben/jmdm. das Leben retten; **sth. is as much as sb.'s** ~ **is worth** mit etw. setzt jmd. sein Leben aufs Spiel; **take [sb.'s]** ~: jmdn. töten; **take one's [own]** ~: sich (*Dat.*) das Leben nehmen; **take one's** ~ **in one's hands** sein Leben riskieren; **upon my** ~: meiner Treu (*veralt.*); bei Gott; **get a**

~ (*coll.*) was aus seinem Leben machen; ⇒ *also* book 1 A, lease 1; limb A; price 1 A; sell 1 A; staff 1 G; B (*energy, animation*) Leben, *das;* **be the ~ and soul of the party** der Mittelpunkt der Party sein; **full of ~:** energiegeladen ‹Person›; lebendig ‹Stadt, Straße›; **there is still ~ in sth.** in etw. (*Dat.*) steckt noch Leben; **put some ~ into it!** (*coll.*) ein bisschen flotter!; C (*living things and their activity*) Leben, *das;* **is there ~ on Mars?** gibt es Leben auf dem Mars?; **support ~:** organisches Leben tragen; **bird/insect ~:** die Vogelwelt/die Insekten; D (*living form or model*) **draw sb. from ~:** jmdn. nach dem Leben zeichnen; **as large as ~** (*life-size*) lebensgroß; (*in person*) in voller Schönheit (*ugs. scherzh.*); **larger than ~:** überzeichnet; **larger-than-~ faces** überlebensgroße Gesichter; **true to ~:** wahrheitsgetreu; **to the ~:** lebensgetreu; E (*period from birth to death, from specified time to death*) Leben, *das;* **marry early in ~:** früh heiraten; **late in ~:** erst im fortgeschrittenen Alter; **sb.'s ~ and times** jmds. Leben und die Zeit, in der er *usw.* lebte; **for ~:** auf Lebenszeit; lebenslänglich ‹inhaftiert›; **he's doing ~** (*coll.*) er sitzt lebenslänglich (*ugs.*); **get ~** (*coll.*) lebenslänglich kriegen (*ugs.*); **expectation of ~:** Lebenserwartung, *die;* **get the fright/shock of one's ~** (*coll.*) zu Tode erschrecken/den Schock seines Lebens bekommen (*ugs.*); **have the time of one's ~:** sich hervorragend amüsieren; F (*chance, fresh start*) **a cat has nine lives** eine Katze hat neun Leben; **a player has three lives** (*Sport*) ein Spieler hat drei Versuche; G (*form of existence*) Leben, *das;* **he will do anything for a quiet ~:** für ihn ist die Hauptsache, dass er seine Ruhe hat; **nothing in ~:** nichts auf der Welt; **make ~ easy for oneself/sb.** es sich (*Dat.*)/jmdm. leicht machen; **make ~ difficult for oneself/sb.** sich (*Dat.*)/jmdm. das Leben schwer machen; **this is the ~!** *expr. content* so lässt sichs leben!; **what a ~!** *expr. discontent* so ein Hundeleben! (*ugs.*); **that's ~, ~'s like that** so ist das Leben [nun mal]; H (*specific aspect*) ‹Privat-, Wirtschafts-, Dorf›leben, *das;* **military/national ~:** das militärische/öffentliche Leben; **the bustle of street ~:** das pulsierende Leben in den Straßen; **in this ~** (*on earth*) in diesem Leben; **the other** *or* **the future** *or* **the next ~** (*in heaven*) das zukünftige Leben [nach dem Tode]; **eternal** *or* **everlasting ~:** ewiges Leben; ⇒ *also* depart 1 D, 2; simple A; I (*biography*) Lebensbeschreibung, *die;* J (*active part of existence*) das Leben; **daily ~:** das Alltagsleben; **see ~:** etwas von der Welt sehen; ⇒ *also* high life; K (*of battery, lightbulb, etc.*) Lebensdauer, *die*

**life: ~-and-death** *adj.* ‹Kampf› auf Leben und Tod; (*fig.*) überaus wichtig ‹Frage, Brief›; **~ an'nuity** *n.* Leibrente, *die;* **~ assurance** *n.* (*Brit.*) Lebensversicherung, *die;* **~belt** *n.* Rettungsring, *der;* **~blood** *n.* Blut, *das;* Lebenssaft, *der* (*dichter.*); (*fig.*) Lebensnerv, *der;* **~boat** *n.* Rettungsboot, *das;* **~buoy** *n.* (*ring-shaped*) Rettungsring, *der;* **~ cycle** *n.* Lebenszyklus, *der;* **~ expectancy** *n.* Lebenserwartung, *die;* **~ force** *n.* Elan vital, *der;* **~-giving** *adj.* Leben spendend (*geh.*); **~guard** *n.* ▶ 1261 A (*soldiers*) Leibwache, *die;* B (*expert swimmer*) Rettungsschwimmer, *der*/-schwimmerin, *die;* **L~ Guards** *n. pl.* (*Brit.: regiment*) [Leib]garde, *die;* **~ 'history** *n.* A (*of person*) Lebensgeschichte, *die;* B (*of organism*) Entwicklungsgeschichte, *die;* **~ insurance** *n.* Lebensversicherung, *die;* **~ jacket** *n.* Schwimmweste, *die*

**lifeless** /'laɪflɪs/ *adj.* A leblos; unbelebt ‹Gegend, Planet›; B (*lacking animation*) farblos ‹Stimme, Rede, Aufführung›; ‹Stadt› ohne Leben

**life: ~like** *adj.* lebensecht; **~line** *n.* A (*rope*) Rettungsleine, *die;* Manntau, *das;* (*of diver*) Signalleine, *die;* B (*fig.*) [lebenswichtige] Verbindung; (*support*) Rettungsanker, *der;* C (*Palmistry*) Lebenslinie, *die;* **~long** *adj.* lebenslang; **sb.'s ~long friend** (*future*) jmds. Freund fürs Leben; (*past*) jmds. Freund seit der Kindheit; **~ 'member** *n.* Mitglied auf Lebenszeit; **~ 'membership** *n.* lebenslange Mitgliedschaft; Mitgliedschaft auf Lebenszeit; **~ 'peer** *n.* Peer auf Lebenszeit; **~ 'peerage** *n.* nicht erbliche Peerswürde; **~ preserver** *n.* A (**~** *jacket*) Schwimmweste, *die;* (**~***buoy*) Rettungsring, *der;* B (*stick*) Totschläger, *der*

**lifer** /'laɪfə(r)/ *n.* (*coll.*) Lebenslängliche, *der/die* (*ugs.*)

**life: ~ raft** *n.* Rettungsfloß, *das;* **~saver** *n.* A (*Austral., NZ:* **~***guard*) Rettungsschwimmer, *der;* B (*thing that saves*) Lebensretter, *der* (*fig.*); **it's been a ~saver** es war die letzte Rettung; **~-saving** *n.* Rettungsschwimmen, *das; attrib.* Rettungs‹gerät, -technik›; lebensrettend ‹Medikament›; **~ sciences** *n. pl.* Biowissenschaften *Pl.;* **~ sentence** *n.* lebenslängliche Freiheitsstrafe; **get a ~ sentence** lebenslänglich bekommen; **~-size, ~-sized** *adj.* lebensgroß; in Lebensgröße *nachgestellt;* **~span** *n.* Lebenserwartung, *die;* (*Biol.*) Lebensdauer, *die;* **~ story** *n.* Lebensgeschichte, *die;* **~style** ❶ A *n.* Lebensstil, *der;* B (*Commerc.*) Lifestyle, *der;* ❷ *adj.* (*Commerc.*) Lifestyle-; **~ support** *n.* **~ support system** lebenserhaltende Apparate; **~time** *n.* Lebenszeit, *die;* (*Phys.*) Lebensdauer, *die; attrib.* lebenslang; **once in a ~time** einmal im Leben; **during my ~time** während meines Lebens; **the chance of a ~time** eine einmalige Gelegenheit; die Chance meines/deines *usw.* Lebens; **~ vest** *n.* Schwimmweste, *die;* **~ work** *n.* Lebenswerk, *das*

**lift** /lɪft/ ❶ *v.t.* A heben; (*slightly*) anheben; (*fig.*) erheben ‹Seele, Gemüt, Geist›; **have one's face ~ed** sich (*Dat.*) das Gesicht liften lassen; **~ sb.'s spirits** jmds. Stimmung heben; **not ~ a hand to do sth.** keine Hand rühren (*ugs.*); **~ a hand against sb.** die Hand gegen jmdn. heben; ⇒ *also* finger 1 A; B (*coll.: steal*) klauen (*salopp*); C (*coll.: plagiarize*) abkupfern (*salopp*) (**from** aus); D (*dig up*) ernten ‹Kartoffeln›; aus der Erde nehmen ‹Blumenzwiebeln, -knollen›; E (*end*) aufheben ‹Verbot, Beschränkung, Blockade›.

❷ *v.i.* A (*disperse*) sich auflösen; (*fig.*) ‹schlechte Stimmung, Unmut:› verfliegen; B (*rise*) ‹Stimmung:› sich aufhellen; ‹Herz:› höher schlagen.

❸ *n.* A (*free ride in vehicle*) Mitfahrgelegenheit, *die;* **get a ~ [with** *or* **from sb.]** [von jmdm.] mitgenommen werden; **give sb. a ~:** jmdn. mitnehmen; **would you like a ~?** möchtest du mitfahren?; B (*Brit.: machine for vertical movement*) Aufzug, *der;* Fahrstuhl, *der;* C (**~***ing*) Heben, *das;* (*of eyebrow*) Hochziehen, *das;* (*of prices*) Anstieg, *der;* D (*Mil.*) Lufttransport, *der;* E (*emotional boost*) Auftrieb, *der;* **give sb. a ~:** jmdm. Auftrieb geben; ‹Droge:› jmdn. anturnen (*ugs.*); **get a ~ from sth.** durch etw. Aufschwung bekommen; F (*Mech. Engin.*) Hub, *der;* G (*upward pressure of air*) Auftrieb, *der*

**~ 'down** *v.t.* herunterheben

**~ off** *v.t. & i.* abheben; ⇒ *also* lift-off

**~ 'up** ❶ *v.i.* ‹Sitz:› hochklappbar sein. ❷ *v.t.* (*raise*) hochheben; (*turn upwards*) heben ‹Kopf›; **~ up one's hands** die Hände erheben (*geh.*); **~ up your hearts** erhebet die Herzen! (*geh.*); **~ up one's voice** die Stimme erheben

**lift: ~ attendant, ~ boy, ~ man** *ns.* (*Brit.*) Aufzugführer, *der;* **~-off** ❶ *adj.* abhebbar; (*from backing*) abnehmbar; ❷ *n.* (*Aeronaut., Astronaut.*) Abheben, *das;* **soon after ~-off** bald nach dem Abheben; **we have ~-off** wir haben abgehoben

**ligament** /'lɪgəmənt/ *n.* (*Anat.*) Band, *das;* Ligament[um], *das* (*fachspr.*)

**ligature** /'lɪgətʃə(r)/ ❶ *n.* A Bandage, *die;* (*in surgery*) Ligaturfaden, *der;* B (*Med.: tying; Mus., Printing*) Ligatur, *die.* ❷ *v.t.* (*bind*) abbinden

**light**[1] /laɪt/ ❶ *n.* A Licht, *das;* **in a good ~:** bei gutem Licht; ⇒ *also* j; **be in sb.'s light** jmdm. im Licht sein; **get out of my ~:** geh mir aus dem Weg!; **stand in sb.'s ~** (*fig.*) jmdm. im Weg stehen (*fig.*); **at first ~:** bei Tagesanbruch; **while the ~ lasts** solange es [noch] hell ist; noch bei Tageslicht; **~ of day** (*lit. or fig.*) Tageslicht, *das;* **she was the ~ of his life** (*fig.*) sie war die Sonne seines Lebens; B (*electric lamp*) Licht, *das;* (*fitting*) Lampe, *die;* **~s out** (*in school etc.*) Bettruhe *die;* (*Mil.*) Zapfenstreich, *der;* **go out like a ~** (*fig.*) sofort weg sein (*ugs.*); C (*signal to ships*) Leuchtfeuer, *das;* D *in sing. or pl.* (*signal to traffic*) Ampel, *die;* **at the third set of ~s** an der dritten Ampel; ⇒ *also* green light; red light; traffic lights; E (*to ignite*) Feuer, *das;* **have you got a ~?** haben Sie Feuer?; **put a/set ~ to sth.** etw. anzünden; **strike a ~** (*produce spark or flame*) Feuer schlagen; (*with match*) ein Streichholz anzünden; (*Brit. dated. coll. int.*) *expr. surprise* potz Blitz! (*veralt.*); F (*eminent person*) Größe, *die;* **be a literary ~:** eine literarische Berühmtheit sein; **lesser ~s** weniger berühmte *od.* bekannte Personen; ⇒ *also* leading light; G (*look in eyes*) Leuchten, *das;* H (*fig.: mental illumination*) **throw** *or* **shed ~ [up]on sth.** Licht in etw. (*Akk.*) bringen ; **the ~ of nature** *or* **reason** natürliche Verstandeskräfte; **bring sth. to ~:** etw. ans [Tages]licht bringen; **come to ~:** ans [Tages]licht kommen; ⇒ *also* see[1] 1 A; I *in pl.* (*beliefs, abilities, convictions*) **according to one's ~s** nach bestem Wissen [und Gewissen]; J (*aspect*) **in that ~:** aus dieser Sicht; **seen in this ~:** so gesehen; wenn man es so sieht; **in the ~ of** (*taking into consideration*) angesichts (+ *Gen.*); **show sb. in a bad ~:** ein schlechtes Licht auf jmdn. werfen; **put sb. in a good/bad ~:** jmdn. in einem guten/schlechten Licht erscheinen lassen; K (*Crosswords*) Lösung, *die;* L (*Theol.*) Erleuchtung, *die;* Licht, *das;* M (*window*) Fenster, *das;* (*sky~*) Oberlicht, *das;* (*division in mullion*) Teilfenster, *das.*

❷ *adj.* hell; licht (*geh.*); **~-blue/-brown** *etc.* hellblau/-braun *usw.;* ⇒ *also* blue[1] 2 E.

❸ *v.t.*, **lit** /lɪt/ *or* **~ed** A (*ignite*) anzünden; B (*illuminate*) erhellen; **~ sb.'s/one's way** jmdm./sich leuchten.

❹ *v.i.*, **lit** *or* **~ed** ‹Feuer, Zigarette:› brennen, sich anzünden lassen

**~ 'up** ❶ *v.i.* A (*become lit*) erleuchtet werden; B (*become bright*) aufleuchten (**with** vor); (*become flushed*) aufglühen (**with** vor); **his face lit up in a smile** sein Gesicht hellte sich zu einem Lächeln auf; C (*begin to smoke*) sich (*Dat.*) eine anstecken (*ugs.*). ❷ *v.t.* A (*illuminate*) erleuchten; **~ up with floodlights** mit Flutlicht anstrahlen; B (*make bright*) erhellen; C (*ignite*) anzünden ‹Zigarette usw.›; D **lit up** (*coll.: drunk*) blau (*ugs.*); sternhagelvoll (*salopp*)

**light**[2] ❶ *adj.* A leicht; Leicht‹metall, -öl, -benzin›; **[for] ~ relief** [als] kleine Abwechslung; **be a ~ sleeper** einen leichten Schlaf haben; B (*small in amount*) gering; **traffic is ~ on these roads** auf diesen Straßen herrscht nur wenig Verkehr; C (*Printing*) mager ‹Schrift›; D (*not important*) leicht; **sth. is no ~ matter** etw. ist keine leichte Sache; **make ~ of sth.** etw. bagatellisieren; E (*jesting, frivolous*) leichtfertig; F (*nimble*) leicht ‹Schritt, Bewegungen›; gewandt ‹Hände›; **be ~ of foot** leichtfüßig sein; **have ~ fingers** (*steal*) gern lange Finger machen (*ugs.*); G (*easily borne*) leicht ‹Krankheit, Strafe›; gering ‹Steuern›; unbedeutend ‹Missgeschick›; (*Law*) mild ‹Strafe, Urteil›; H **with a ~ heart** (*carefree*) leichten *od.* frohen Herzens; I **feel ~ in the head** (*giddy*) leicht benommen sein.

❷ *adv.* **travel ~:** mit wenig *od.* leichtem Gepäck reisen

**light**[3] *v.i.*, **lit** /lɪt/ *or* **~ed** A (*come by chance*) **~ [up]on sth.** auf etw. (*Akk.*) kommen *od.* stoßen; B (*coll.: attack*) **~ into sb./sth.** über jmdn./etw. herfallen; C (*coll.: depart*) sich auf den Weg machen (**for** nach/zu)

**light: ~ 'aircraft** *n.* Leichtflugzeug, *das;* **~bulb** *n.* Glühbirne, *die;* Glühlampe, *die* (*fachspr.*); **~-coloured** *adj.* hell

**lighted** /'laɪtɪd/ *adj.* brennend ‹Kerze, Zigarette›; angezündet ‹Streichholz›; beleuchtet ‹Zimmer, Pfad, Schild, Vitrine›

**light-emitting 'diode** /'daɪəʊd/ *n.* Leuchtdiode, *die*

l

**lighten**[1] /ˈlaɪtn/ ❶ *v.t.* **A** (*make less heavy*) leichter machen; leichtern ‹Schiff›; **B** (*make less oppressive*) lindern ‹Not›; mildern ‹Zorn, Erregung›; leichter machen ‹Arbeit, Aufgabe›; verringern ‹Arbeitslast›; kurzweilig gestalten ‹Weg, Reise›; erleichtern ‹Gewissen›; **~ sb.'s burden** jmdn. entlasten; **~ sb.'s duties** jmdm. leichtere Aufgaben zuteilen. ❷ *v.i.* (*become less heavy*) leichter werden; (*fig.*) ‹Stimmung:› sich aufheitern

**lighten**[2] ❶ *v.t.* **A** (*make brighter*) aufhellen; heller machen ‹Raum›; **B** (*arch.: illuminate*) erhellen. ❷ *v.i.* **A** (*become brighter*) sich aufhellen; ‹Auge:› aufleuchten; **B** (*emit lightning*) blitzen

**lighter**[1] /ˈlaɪtə(r)/ *n.* (*device*) Feuerzeug, *das;* (*in car*) Zigarettenanzünder, *der*

**lighter**[2] *n.* (*boat*) Leichter, *der*

**lighterman** /ˈlaɪtəmən/ *n., pl.* **lightermen** /ˈlaɪtəmən/ Leichterschiffer, *der*

**light: ~er-than-ˈair** *adj.* **~er-than-air aircraft/dirigible** Luftschiff, *das*/lenkbares Luftschiff; **~-face** ⇒ **light**[2] 1 D; **~-fingered** /ˈlaɪtfɪŋgəd/ *adj.* langfing[e]rig; **~ fitting** *n.* Lampe, *die;* **~-footed** /ˈlaɪtfʊtɪd/ *adj.* leichtfüßig; **~-ˈheaded** *adj.* **A** (*slightly giddy*) leicht benommen; **B** (*frivolous*) leichtfertig; **~-hearted** *adj.* **A** (*gay, humorous*) unbeschwert; heiter; **B** (*optimistic, casual*) unbekümmert; **~-heartedly** /laɪtˈhɑːtɪdlɪ/ *adv.* unbeschwert ‹lachen›; unbekümmert ‹sich verhalten›; **~ ˈheavyweight** *n.* (*Boxing*) Halbschwergewicht, *das;* (*person also*) Halbschwergewichtler, *der;* **~ ˈhorse** *n., constr. as pl.* (*Mil.*) leichte Kavallerie; **~ ˈhorseman** *n.* (*Mil.*) leichter Kavallerist; **~house** *n.* Leuchtturm, *der;* **~house-keeper** *n.* ▶ 1261 Leuchtturmwärter, *der;* **~ ˈindustry** *n.* Leichtindustrie, *die;* **~ ˈinfantry** *n.* (*Mil.*) leichte Infanterie

**lighting** /ˈlaɪtɪŋ/ *n.* **A** (*supply of light*) Beleuchtung, *die;* **B** (*setting alight*) Anzünden, *das*

**lighting-ˈup time** *n.* Zeit zum Einschalten der Beleuchtung; **at ~:** ≈ wenn es dunkel wird

**lightish** /ˈlaɪtɪʃ/ *adj.* **A** (*in colour*) ziemlich hell; hell ‹Farbe, Haare usw.›; **~-blue/-skinned** [eher] hellblau/-häutig; **B** (*in weight*) ziemlich leicht

**lightly** /ˈlaɪtlɪ/ *adv.* **A** (*not heavily*) leicht; **sleep ~:** einen leichten Schlaf haben; **fall ~:** sacht fallen; **touch ~ on a topic** ein Thema kurz streifen; **B** (*in a small degree*) leicht; **C** (*without serious consideration*) leichtfertig; **D** (*cheerfully, deprecatingly*) leichthin; **not treat sth. ~:** etw. nicht auf die leichte Schulter nehmen; **take sth. ~:** etw. nicht [so] ernst nehmen; **E** (*nimbly*) behänd; **F** **get off ~** (*not receive heavy penalty*) glimpflich davonkommen; **let sb. off ~** (*not inflict heavy penalty*) jmdn. mit Nachsicht behandeln

**light: ~ meter** *n.* Lichtmesser, *der;* (*exposure meter*) Belichtungsmesser, *der;* **~-minded** *adj.* gedankenlos; oberflächlich

**lightness**[1] /ˈlaɪtnɪs/ *n., no pl.* **A** (*having little weight, lit. or fig.*) Leichtigkeit, *die;* **the pianist's ~ of touch** der weiche Anschlag des Pianisten; **B** (*of penalty, weather*) Milde, *die;* (*of infection*) Geringfügigkeit, *die;* **C** (*absence of anxiety*) **~ of heart/spirit** Heiterkeit/Unbekümmertheit, *die;* **D** (*lack of concern*) Leichtfertigkeit, *die;* **E** (*agility of movement*) Leichtigkeit, *die*

**lightness**[2] *n.* (*brightness, paleness of colour*) Helligkeit, *die*

**lightning** /ˈlaɪtnɪŋ/ ❶ *n., no pl., no indef. art.* Blitz, *der;* **flash of ~:** Blitz, *der;* **like ~** (*coll.*) wie der Blitz (*ugs.*); **[as] quick as ~** (*coll.*) schnell wie der Blitz (*ugs.*); **like greased ~** (*coll.*) wie ein geölter Blitz (*ugs.*); **~ never strikes twice [in the same place]** (*prov.*) der Blitz schlägt nie[mals] zweimal am selben Platz *od.* Ort ein; ⇒ *also* **ball lightning**; **sheet lightning**; **summer lightning.** ❷ *adj.* Blitz-; **with ~ speed** blitzschnell; **events moved with ~ speed** die Ereignisse überschlugen sich

**lightning: ~ bug** *n.* (*Amer.*) Leuchtkäfer, *der;* Glühwürmchen, *das* (*ugs.*); **~ conductor** *n.* (*lit. or fig.*) Blitzableiter, *der;* **~ rod** *n.* (*Amer.*) Blitzableiter, *der;* **~ strike**[1] *n.* (*~ hitting object*) Blitzschlag, *der;* **~ ˈstrike**[2] *n.* (*Industry*) überraschender [Kurz]streik

**light: ~ ˈopera** ⇒ **opera**[1] C; **~ pen** *n.* Lichtstift, *der;* **~proof** *adj.* lichtundurchlässig; **~ ˈrailway** *n.* Kleinbahn, *die*

**lights** /laɪts/ *n. pl.* (*lungs*) Lunge, *die*

**light: ~ship** *n.* Feuerschiff, *das;* **~ show** *n.* Lightshow, *die*

**light: ~-tight** *adj.* lichtdicht; **~weight** ❶ *adj.* **A** leicht; **B** (*fig.: of little consequence*) unmaßgeblich; **C** (*Boxing etc.*) Leichtgewichts‹boxer, -kampf›; ❷ *n.* **A** (*Boxing etc.*) Leichtgewicht, *das;* (*person also*) Leichtgewichtler, *der;* **B** (*fig.: person of little ability or importance*) Leichtgewicht, *das* (*fig.*); **~ year** *n.* Lichtjahr, *das;* **~ years [removed] from sth.** (*fig.*) meilenweit von etw. entfernt

**ligneous** /ˈlɪgnɪəs/ *adj.* (*Bot.*) holzig; **~ plants** Holzgewächse

**lignite** /ˈlɪgnaɪt/ *n.* Braunkohle, *die*

**like**[1] /laɪk/ ❶ *adj.* **A** (*resembling*) wie; **your dress is ~ mine** dein Kleid ist so ähnlich wie meins; dein Kleid gleicht meinem (*geh.*); **your dress is very ~ mine** dein Kleid ist meinem sehr ähnlich; **in a case ~ that** in so einem Fall; **there was nothing ~ it** es gab nichts Vergleichbares; **who do you think he's ~?** wem sieht er deiner Ansicht nach ähnlich?; **what is sb./sth. ~?** wie ist jmd./etw.?; **what's he ~ to talk to?** wie redet es sich mit ihm?; **what's it ~ to go up in a balloon?** wie ist es, wenn man im Ballon aufsteigt?; **more ~ twelve** eher zwölf; **that's [a bit] more ~ it** (*coll.: better*) das ist schon [etwas] besser; (*coll.: nearer the truth*) das stimmt schon eher; **a man ~ you** ein Mann [so] wie du; **they are nothing ~ each other** sie sind sich (*Dat.*) nicht im Geringsten ähnlich; **nothing ~ as** *or* **so good/bad/many** *etc.* **as ...:** bei weitem nicht so gut/schlecht/viele *usw.* wie ...; **no, nothing ~:** nein, längst *od.* bei weitem nicht; **Have you finished it yet? — Nothing ~:** Bist du schon damit fertig? — Noch längst nicht; ⇒ *also* **feel** 2 C; **look** 1 D; **something** F; **B** (*characteristic of*) typisch für ‹dich, ihn usw.›; **it's just ~ you to be late!** du musst natürlich wieder zu spät kommen!; **it would be [just] ~ her to do that** das sähe ihr [wieder einmal] ähnlich; **just ~ a woman** typisch Frau (*ugs.*); **C** (*similar*) ähnlich; **in ~ manner** auf die gleiche Weise; **be as ~ as two peas in a pod** sich (*Dat.*) gleichen wie ein Ei dem andern; **~ father, ~ son** (*prov.*) der Apfel fällt nicht weit vom Stamm (*Spr.*); **D** (*Math., Phys.*) **~ signs** gleiche Vorzeichen; **~ charges** gleiche Ladungen; **~ quantities** gleiche Größen.
❷ *prep.* (*in the manner of*) wie; **[just] ~ that** [einfach] so; **you do it ~ so** (*coll.*) so musst du das machen; ⇒ *also* **hell** B; **mad** A, F; **shot** 1 D.
❸ *adv.* **A** (*arch./coll.*) **[as] ~ as not, ~ enough** wahrscheinlich; **B** (*coll.: so to speak*) also; irgendwie; **he kind of hit me, ~:** also, der hat mich irgendwie geschlagen (*ugs.*); **all friendly ~:** ganz freundlich und so (*ugs.*).
❹ *conj.* (*coll.*) **A** (*in same or similar manner as*) wie; **he is not shy ~ he used to be** er ist nicht mehr so schüchtern wie früher; **B** (*coll.: for example*) etwa; beispielsweise; **C** (*Amer.: as if*) als ob; **D** **tell it ~ it is** sagen Sie die ganze Wahrheit!
❺ *n.* **A** (*equal*) **his/her ~:** seines-/ihresgleichen; **the ~ of it** so etwas; dergleichen; **I've never known the ~ [of it]** so etwas habe ich noch nie gehört; **~ attracts ~:** gleich und gleich gesellt sich gern; **compare ~ with ~:** Vergleichbares miteinander vergleichen; **the ~s of me/you** (*coll.*) meines-/deinesgleichen; Leute wie ich/du; **if it weren't for the ~s of them ...** (*coll.*) wenn solche wie die nicht wären, ... (*ugs.*); **that's not for the ~s of us** (*coll.*) das ist nichts für unsereinen (*ugs.*); **I know you and your ~** *or* **the ~s of you** (*coll.*) deine Sorte/Leute von deiner Sorte kenne ich (*ugs.*); **B** (*similar things*) **the ~:** so etwas; **and the ~:** und dergleichen; **or the ~:** oder so etwas; oder so (*salopp*)

**like**[2] ❶ *v.t.* (*be fond of, wish for*) mögen; **~ it or not** ob es dir/ihm *usw.* gefällt oder nicht; **~ vegetables** Gemüse mögen; gern Gemüse essen; **~ doing sth.** etw. gern tun; **would you ~ a drink/to borrow the book?** möchtest du etwas trinken/dir das Buch leihen?; **would you ~ me to do it?** möchtest du, dass ich es tue?; **I'd ~ it back soon** ich hätte es gern bald zurück; **I don't ~ this affair** die Sache gefällt mir nicht; **I didn't ~ to disturb you** ich wollte dich nicht stören; **perhaps you would ~ time to consider it** vielleicht brauchst du etwas Bedenkzeit; **I ~ ˈthat!** (*iron.*) so was hab ich gern! (*ugs. iron.*); **I ~ his cheek!** (*iron.*) der hat vielleicht Nerven! (*ugs. iron.*); **how do you ~ it?** wie gefällt es dir?; **how does he ~ living in America?** wie gefällt es ihm in Amerika?; **how would you ~ an ice cream?** was hältst du von einem Eis?; **how would ˈyou ~ it if ...?** wie würdest du es [denn] finden, wenn ...?; **how do you ~ ˈthat?** was sagst du dazu?; **but what happens ˈthen, I should ~ to know** (*iron.*) aber was dann passiert, wüsste ich gern; **I'd ~ to see you try!** (*iron.*) das möchte ich sehen!; **I should ~ to see them do it** ich möchte mal sehen, wie sie das machen wollen; **if you ~** *expr. assent* wenn du willst *od.* möchtest; *expr. limited assent* wenn man so will; **if one ~s that sort of thing** wenn einem so was gefällt (*ugs.*).
❷ *n., in pl.* **~s and dislikes** Vorlieben und Abneigungen; **tell me your ~s and dislikes** sag mir, was du magst und was nicht

**-like** *adj. suf.* -artig; **bird~:** wie ein Vogel *nachgestellt*

**likeable** /ˈlaɪkəbl/ *adj.* nett; sympathisch

**likelihood** /ˈlaɪklɪhʊd/ *n.* Wahrscheinlichkeit, *die;* **what is the ~ of this happening?** wie wahrscheinlich ist es, dass dies geschieht?; **there is little ~ of his seeing this** *or* **that he will see this** es ist kaum anzunehmen, dass er das sieht; **he saw no ~ of the plan being approved** er hielt es für ausgeschlossen, dass der Plan Zustimmung finden könnte; **in all ~:** aller Wahrscheinlichkeit nach

**likely** /ˈlaɪklɪ/ ❶ *adj.* **A** (*probable*) wahrscheinlich; glaubhaft ‹Geschichte›; voraussichtlich ‹Bedarf, Zukunft›; **be the ~ reason/source** wahrscheinlich der Grund/die Ursache sein; **do you think it ~?** hältst du es für wahrscheinlich?; **is it ~ that he'd do that?** ist ihm so etwas zuzutrauen?; ⇒ *also* **story**[1] A; **B** (*to be expected*) wahrscheinlich; **there are ~ to be [traffic] hold-ups** man muss mit [Verkehrs]staus rechnen; **he is ~ to meet the same fate** er könnte leicht das gleiche Schicksal erleiden; **they are [not] ~ to come** sie werden wohl *od.* wahrscheinlich [nicht] kommen; **am I ~ to do something like that?** sehe ich aus, als ob ich so etwas tun würde?; **is it ~ to rain tomorrow?** wird es morgen wohl regnen?; **this is not ~ to happen** es ist unwahrscheinlich, dass das geschieht; das wird wohl kaum geschehen; **he is ~ to be our next president** er wird voraussichtlich unser nächster Präsident sein; **it seems ~ to have been an accident** es dürfte wohl ein Unfall gewesen sein; **the candidate most ~ to succeed** der Kandidat mit den größten Erfolgsaussichten; **C** (*promising, apparently suitable*) geeignet ‹Person, Ort, Methode, Weg›; **we've looked in all the ~ places** wir haben an allen infrage kommenden Stellen gesucht; **this looks a ~ place to find mushrooms** es sieht so aus, als ob man hier Pilze finden könnte; **this restaurant seems a ~-looking place** dieses Restaurant sieht ganz annehmbar aus; **D** (*strong, capable-looking*) fähig; (*showing promise*) viel versprechend ‹Kandidat, Anwärter›; begabt ‹Student usw.›; **we need a couple of ~ lads** wir brauchen ein paar tüchtige Burschen.

❷ *adv.* (*probably*) wahrscheinlich; **very** *or* **more than** *or* **quite** *or* **most ~:** höchstwahrscheinlich; sehr wahrscheinlich; **as ~ as not** höchstwahrscheinlich; **not ~!** (*coll.*) auf keinen Fall!

**'like-minded** *adj.* gleich gesinnt; **~ people** Gleichgesinnte

**liken** /'laɪkn/ *v.t.* **~ sth./sb. to sth./sb.** etw./jmdn. mit etw./jmdm. vergleichen

**likeness** /'laɪknɪs/ *n.* [A] (*resemblance*) Ähnlichkeit, *die* (**to** mit); [B] (*guise*) Aussehen, *das;* Gestalt, *die;* **take on the ~ of a swan** die Gestalt eines Schwanes annehmen; [C] (*portrait*) Bild, *das;* Bildnis, *das* (*geh.*); **take sb.'s ~** (*arch.*) jmdn. porträtieren

**likewise** /'laɪkwaɪz/ *adv.* ebenso; **do ~:** das Gleiche tun; **if we all did ~:** wenn [wir] das alle machen würden; **I'm not going — L~:** Ich gehe nicht hin — Ich auch nicht

**liking** /'laɪkɪŋ/ *n.* Vorliebe, *die;* **they expressed a ~ for her cakes** sie lobten ihre Kuchen; **take a ~ to sb./sth.** an jmdm./etw. Gefallen finden; **sth. is [not] to sb.'s ~:** etw. ist [nicht] nach jmds. Geschmack

**lilac** /'laɪlək/ ❶ *n.* [A] (*Bot.*) Flieder, *der;* [B] (*colour*) Zartlila, *das.* ❷ *adj.* zartlila; fliederfarben

**lilliputian** /lɪlɪ'pju:ʃn/ ❶ *adj.* Liliput-; winzig ‹Format, Figur›. ❷ *n.* Liliputaner, *der*/Liliputanerin, *die*

**Lilo** ® /'laɪləʊ/ *n.* Luftmatratze, *die*

**lilt** /lɪlt/ (*Scot./literary*) ❶ *n.* [A] (*cadence, swing*) schwingender Rhythmus; (*of voice*) singender Tonfall; **speak with a ~:** mit singendem Tonfall sprechen; [B] (*song, tune*) [fröhliche] Weise; Lied[chen], *das.* ❷ *v.t.* trällern ‹Lied, Melodie›

**lilting** /'lɪltɪŋ/ *adj.* heiter, beschwingt ‹Melodie, Walzer, Lied›; singend ‹Tonfall›

**lily** /'lɪlɪ/ *n.* Lilie, *die;* **~ of the valley** Maiglöckchen, *das;* ⇒ *also* **gild**[1]

**lily: ~-livered** /'lɪlɪlɪvəd/ *adj.* (*literary*) feige; **~ pad** *n.* Seerosenblatt, *das;* **~-white** *adj.* lilienweiß; (*Amer.: excluding Blacks*) rein weiß

**limb** /lɪm/ *n.* [A] ▶ 966 (*Anat.*) Glied, *das;* **~s** Glieder; Gliedmaßen; **a danger to life and ~:** eine Gefahr für Leib und Leben; **tear sb. ~ from ~** (*lit. or fig.*) jmdm. alle Glieder einzeln ausreißen; [B] (*of tree*) Ast, *der;* **be out on a ~** (*fig.*) exponiert sein; **go out** *or* **put oneself out on a ~:** sich exponieren; [C] (*of cross, sea*) Arm, *der*

**limber**[1] /'lɪmbə(r)/ (*Mil.*) *n.* Protze, *die*

**limber**[2] ❶ *adj.* [A] (*flexible*) biegsam ‹Zweig›; elastisch ‹Seil, Leder›; [B] (*nimble*) geschmeidig; elastisch. ❷ *v.t. & i.* ⇒ **limber up**

**~ up** ❶ *v.i.* sich einlaufen/einspielen *usw.*; (*loosen up*) die Muskeln lockern; (*fig.*) sich fit machen (*fig.*) (**for** für); sich vorbereiten (**for** auf + *Akk.*). ❷ *v.t.* warm machen; aufwärmen (*Sport*)

**limbless** /'lɪmlɪs/ *adj.* ‹Person, Tier› ohne Gliedmaßen; ‹Baum› ohne Äste

**limbo**[1] /'lɪmbəʊ/ *n., pl.* **~s** [A] (*region*) Vorhölle, *die;* Limbus, *der* (*Rel.*); [B] (*fig.*) Vergessenheit, *die;* **vanish into ~:** spurlos verschwinden; **be in ~** (*be pending*) in der Schwebe sein; (*be abandoned*) abgeschrieben sein; **live in ~:** in einer Art Niemandsland leben

**limbo**[2] *n., pl.* **~s** (*dance*) Limbo, *der*

**lime**[1] /laɪm/ *n.* [A] **[quick]~:** [ungelöschter] Kalk; **slaked ~:** gelöschter Kalk; Löschkalk, *der;* [B] ⇒ **birdlime**

**lime**[2] *n.* [A] (*fruit*) Limone, *die;* [B] (*juice*) Limonensaft, *der;* [C] ⇒ **lime green**

**lime**[3] ⇒ **lime tree**

**lime: ~ green** ❶ *adj.* [leuchtend] hellgrün; ❷ *n.* Hellgrün, *das;* **~ juice** *n.* Limonensaft, *der;* **~kiln** *n.* Kalkofen, *der;* **~light** *n.* [A] (*light*) Kalklicht, *das;* [B] (*fig.: attention*) **be in the ~light** im Rampenlicht [der Öffentlichkeit] stehen

**limerick** /'lɪmərɪk/ *n.* Limerick, *der*

**lime: ~stone** *n.* Kalkstein, *der;* **~ tree** *n.* Linde, *die;* Lindenbaum, *der* (*geh.*); **~wood** *n.* Lindenholz, *das*

**Limey** /'laɪmɪ/ *n.* (*Amer. sl. derog.*) Engländer, *der;* (*esp. soldier*) Tommy, *der; attrib.* englisch

**limit** /'lɪmɪt/ ❶ *n.* [A] *usu. in pl.* (*boundary*) Grenze, *die;* **within [the] city ~s** innerhalb der Stadtgrenzen; [B] (*point or line that may not be passed*) Limit, *das;* (*of ability, love, etc.*) Grenze, *die;* **set** *or* **put a ~ on sth.** etw. begrenzen *od.* beschränken; **be over the ~** ‹Autofahrer:› zu viel Promille haben; ‹Reisender:› Übergepäck haben; **£400 is my upper ~:** 400 Pfund sind für mich das Äußerste; **there is a ~ to what I can spend/do** ich kann nicht unbegrenzt Geld ausgeben/meine Möglichkeiten sind auch nur begrenzt; **there is a ~ to everything** alles hat seine Grenzen; **there is a ~ to my patience** meine Geduld ist begrenzt; **there is no ~ to his impudence, his impudence knows no ~s** seine Unverschämtheit kennt keine Grenzen; **lower/upper ~:** Untergrenze/Höchstgrenze, *die;* **without ~:** unbegrenzt; **within ~s** innerhalb gewisser Grenzen; **'off ~s'** (*esp. Amer.*) „Zutritt [für Soldaten] verboten"; **this bar is off ~s** zu dieser Bar haben Soldaten keinen Zutritt; [C] (*coll.*) **this is the ~!** das ist [doch] die Höhe!; **he/she is the [very] ~:** er/sie ist [einfach] unmöglich (*ugs.*); [D] (*Math.*) Grenzwert, *der.* ❷ *v.t.* begrenzen (**to** auf + *Akk.*); einschränken ‹Freiheit›

**limitation** /lɪmɪ'teɪʃn/ *n.* [A] (*act*) Beschränkung, *die;* (*of freedom*) Einschränkung, *die;* [B] (*condition*) (*of extent*) Begrenzung, *die;* (*of amount*) Beschränkung, *die;* **know one's ~s** seine Grenzen kennen; [C] (*restrictive circumstance*) Beschränkung, *die;* **due to ~s of space** aus Platzmangel *od.* Platzgründen; [D] (*Law*) Verjährung, *die*

**limited** /'lɪmɪtɪd/ *adj.* [A] (*restricted*) begrenzt; **~ company** (*Brit.*) Gesellschaft mit beschränkter Haftung; **~ edition** limitierte Auflage; **~ train** (*Amer.*) ≈ Schnellzug, *der;* [B] (*intellectually narrow*) beschränkt (*abwertend*); **~ outlook/mind** beschränkter Horizont/Verstand

**limitless** /'lɪmɪtlɪs/ *adj.* grenzenlos

**limo** /'lɪməʊ/ *n., pl.* **~s** (*Amer. coll.*) Limousine, *die*

**limousine** /'lɪmʊzi:n/ *n.* Limousine, *die* (*mit Trennscheibe*)

**limp**[1] /lɪmp/ ❶ *v.i.* (*lit. or fig.*) hinken; **the ship managed to ~ into port** das Schiff schaffte es mit Müh und Not *od.* gerade so in den Hafen. ❷ *n.* Hinken, *das;* **walk with a ~:** hinken; **have a slight/pronounced ~:** leicht/stark hinken

**limp**[2] *adj.* [A] (*not stiff, lit. or fig.*) schlaff; welk ‹Blumen›; **I feel ~ at the thought of it** beim bloßen Gedanken daran wird mir schwach (*ugs.*); [B] (*flexible*) flexibel ‹Einband›

**limpet** /'lɪmpɪt/ *n.* (*Zool.*) Napfschnecke, *die*

**'limpet mine** *n.* Haftmine, *die*

**limpid** /'lɪmpɪd/ *adj.* klar

**limply** /'lɪmplɪ/ *adv.* schlaff; (*weakly*) schwach

**limpness** /'lɪmpnɪs/ *n., no pl.* Schlaffheit, *die;* (*weakness*) Schwäche, *die*

**linchpin** /'lɪntʃpɪn/ *n.* [A] (*pin*) Lünse, *die;* Achsnagel, *der;* [B] (*fig.: essential element*) Kernstück, *das;* **he is the ~ of the company** er ist das Herz der Firma; mit ihm steht und fällt die Firma

**linctus** /'lɪŋktəs/ *n.* (*Med.*) Hustensaft, *der*

**linden** /'lɪndən/ *n.* Linde, *die;* Lindenbaum, *der* (*geh.*)

**line**[1] /laɪn/ ❶ *n.* [A] (*string, cord, rope, etc.*) Leine, *die;* **[fishing]~:** [Angel]schnur, *die;* **the ~s** (*Amer.: reins*) die Zügel; **hard ~s** (*coll.*) ein schwerer Schlag; **[that's] hard ~s, old chap!** Schicksal, alter Junge!; [B] (*telephone or telegraph cable*) Leitung, *die;* **our company has 20 ~s** unsere Firma hat 20 Anschlüsse; **get me a ~ to Washington** verbinden Sie mich mit Washington; **bad ~:** schlechte Verbindung; **be on the ~:** am Apparat sein; ⇒ *also* **cross** 2 A; **hold**[2] 1 L; **party line a;** [C] (*long mark; also Math., Phys.*) Linie, *die;* (*less precise or shorter*) Strich, *der;* (*Telev.*) Zeile, *die;* **capture sth. in a few ~s** etw. mit wenigen Strichen einfangen; **the L~:** die Linie (*Seemannsspr.*); der Äquator; **~ of force** (*Phys.*) Kraftlinie, *die;* **~ of life/fortune** (*Palmistry*) Lebenslinie, *die*/Schicksalslinie, *die;* **straight ~:** gerade Linie; (*Geom.*) Gerade, *die;* **walk in a straight ~:** in einer geraden Linie gehen; **~ of sight** *or* **vision** Blickrichtung, *die;* **the ~s of her face** ihre Gesichtszüge/(*wrinkles*) ihre Falten; ⇒ *also* **yellow line;** [D] *in pl.* (*outline of car, ship, etc.*) Linien *Pl.;* [E] (*boundary*) Linie, *die;* (*fig.*) **somewhere on the ~:** irgendwo dazwischen; **lay sth. on the ~ [for sb.]** [jmdm.] etw. rundheraus sagen; **put sth. on the ~:** etw. aufs Spiel setzen; **put oneself on the ~:** ein Risiko eingehen; **your job is on the ~:** deine Stelle steht auf dem Spiel; ⇒ *also* **draw** 1 G; [F] (*row*) Reihe, *die;* (*Amer.: queue*) Schlange, *die;* **~ of trees** Baumreihe, *die;* **arrange the chairs in a straight ~:** die Stühle in einer Reihe aufstellen; **bring sb. into ~:** dafür sorgen, dass jmd. nicht aus der Reihe tanzt (*ugs.*); **come** *or* **fall into ~:** sich in die Reihe stellen; ‹Gruppe:› sich in einer Reihe aufstellen; (*fig.*) nicht mehr aus der Reihe tanzen (*ugs.*); **be in ~ [with sth.]** [mit etw.] in einer Linie liegen; **be in ~ for promotion** Aussicht auf Beförderung haben; **be in/out of ~ with sth.** (*fig.*) mit etw. in/nicht in Einklang stehen; **all along the ~:** auf der ganzen Linie; **somewhere along the ~:** irgendwann einmal; **stand in ~** (*Amer.: queue*) Schlange stehen; ⇒ *also* **toe** 2; [G] (*Naut.*) **~ abreast** Dwarslinie, *die;* **~ ahead** Kiellinie, *die;* **~ [of battle]** [Kampf]linie, *die;* [H] (*row of words on a page*) Zeile, *die;* **~s** (*actor's part*) Text, *der;* **drop me a ~:** schreib mir ein paar Zeilen; **she has only a few ~s** (*Theatre*) sie hat nur ein paar Worte zu sprechen; **he gave the boy 100 ~s** (*Sch.*) er ließ den Jungen 100 Zeilen abschreiben; ⇒ *also* **read** 1 C; [I] (*system of transport*) Linie, *die;* **[shipping] ~:** Schifffahrtslinie, *die;* [J] (*series of persons or things*) Reihe, *die;* (*generations of family*) Linie, *die;* **be third in ~ to the throne** Dritter in der Thronfolge sein; [K] (*direction, course*) Richtung, *die;* **on these ~s** in dieser Richtung; **on the ~s of** nach Art (+ *Gen.*); **on similar ~s** auf ähnliche Art; **be on the right/wrong ~s** in die richtige/falsche Richtung gehen; **along** *or* **on the same ~s** in der gleichen Richtung; **be on the same ~s** die gleiche Richtung verfolgen; **~ of thought/march** Gedankengang, *der*/Marschrichtung, *die;* **what ~ shall we take with her?** wie sollen wir uns ihr gegenüber verhalten?; **take a strong ~ with sb.** jmdm. gegenüber bestimmt *od.* energisch auftreten; **~ of action** Vorgehensweise, *die;* **get a ~ on sb./sth.** (*coll.*) etwas über jmdn./etw. herausfinden; ⇒ *also* **assembly line; hard** 1 F; **hardline; party line b; resistance** A; [L] (*Railw.*) Bahnlinie, *die;* (*track*) Gleis, *das;* **cross the ~:** die Gleise überqueren; **the ~ was blocked** die Strecke war blockiert; **the Waterloo ~, the ~ to Waterloo** die Linie nach Waterloo; **this is the end of the ~ [for you]** (*fig.*) dies ist das Aus [für dich]; [M] (*field of activity*) Branche, *die;* (*academic*) Fachrichtung, *die;* **what's your ~?** in welcher Branche sind Sie?/was ist Ihre Fachrichtung?; **he's in the building ~:** er ist in der Baubranche; **that's not my ~:** das ist nicht mein Gebiet; **be in the ~ of duty/business** zu den Pflichten/zum Geschäft gehören; ⇒ *also* **shoot** 2 D; [N] (*Commerc.: product*) Artikel, *der;* Linie, *die* (*fachspr.*); [O] (*Fashion*) Linie, *die;* [P] (*Mil.: series of defences*) Linie, *die;* **draw the ~s** Stellungen beziehen; **enemy ~s** feindliche Stellungen *od.* Linien; ⇒ *also* **hold**[2] 1 K; [Q] (*wrinkle*) Falte, *die.*

❷ *v.t.* [A] (*mark with lines*) linieren ‹Papier›; **a ~d face** ein faltiges Gesicht; **a face ~d with worry** ein von Sorgen gezeichnetes Gesicht; [B] (*stand at intervals along*) säumen (*geh.*) ‹Straße, Strecke›

**~ 'up** ❶ *v.t.* antreten lassen ‹Gefangene, Soldaten usw.›; [in einer Reihe] aufstellen ‹Gegenstände›; (*fig.*) **I've got a nice little job/a surprise ~d up for you** ich hab da eine nette kleine Beschäftigung/eine Überraschung für dich (*ugs.*); **have you got anything ~d up for**

**this evening?** haben Sie heute Abend schon etwas vor?; ⇒ *also* **~-up.** ❷ *v.i.* ‹Gefangene, Soldaten:› antreten; ‹Läufer:› Aufstellung nehmen; (*queue up*) sich anstellen

**line²** *v.t.* füttern ‹Kleidungsstück›; auskleiden ‹Magen, Nest›; ausschlagen ‹Schublade usw.›; **~ one's pockets** (*fig.*) sich (*Dat.*) die Taschen füllen

**lineage** /ˈlɪnɪɪdʒ/ *n.* Abstammung, *die*

**lineal** /ˈlɪnɪəl/ *adj.* Ⓐ (*in direct line of descent*) geradlinig ‹Abstammung›; direkt ‹Nachkomme, Vorfahr›; Ⓑ (*linear*) linear

**lineament** /ˈlɪnɪəmənt/ *n., usu. in pl.* [Gesichts]zug, *der;* (*distinctive feature*) Grundzug, *der*

**linear** /ˈlɪnɪə(r)/ *adj.* linear; **~ perspective** Linearperspektive, *die;* **~ extent** Längenausdehnung, *die;* **~ measure** Längenmaß, *das*

**linear acˈcelerator** *n.* (*Phys.*) Linearbeschleuniger, *der*

**line: ~backer** *n.* (*Amer. Footb.*) Gedrängehalbspieler, *der;* **~ dance** ❶ *n.* Linedance, *der;* ❷ *v.i.* Linedance tanzen; **~ dancer** *n.* Linedance-Tanzer, *der*/Linedance-Tänzerin, *die;* **~ dancing** *n.* Linedance-Tanzen, *das;* **~ drawing** *n.* Strichzeichnung, *die;* **~ engraving** *n.* Strichätzung, *die;* **~ fishing** *n.* Angeln, *das;* **~man** /ˈlaɪnmən/ *n., pl.* **~men** /ˈlaɪnmən/ ▶ 1261 (*Amer. Footb.*) Stürmer, *der;* **~ manager** *n.* [unmittelbarer] Vorgesetzter; Linienmanager, *der*

**linen** /ˈlɪnɪn/ ❶ *n.* Ⓐ Leinen, *das;* Ⓑ (*shirts, sheets, clothes, etc.*) Wäsche, *die;* **wash one's dirty ~ in public** (*fig.*) seine schmutzige Wäsche vor anderen Leuten waschen. ❷ *adj.* Leinen‹faden, -bluse, -laken›; Lein‹tuch›

**linen: ~ basket** *n.* (*Brit.*) Wäschekorb, *der;* **~ cupboard** *n.* Wäscheschrank, *der*

**line: ~-out** *n.* (*Sport*) Gasse, *die;* **~ printer** *n.* (*Computing*) Zeilendrucker, *der*

**liner¹** /ˈlaɪnə(r)/ *n.* (*removable metal lining*) Auskleidung, *die;* (*in engine*) Laufbuchse, *die;* **carpet ~:** rutschfeste Teppichunterlage; **[bin] ~:** Müllbeutel, *der*

**liner²** *n.* (*ship*) Linienschiff, *das;* (*aircraft*) Linienflugzeug, *das;* **ocean ~:** [Ozean-]Liner, *der*

**linesman** /ˈlaɪnzmən/ *n., pl.* **linesmen** /ˈlaɪnzmən/ ▶ 1261 Ⓐ (*Sport*) Linienrichter, *der;* Ⓑ (*Brit. Railw.*) Streckenarbeiter, *der;* Ⓒ ⇒ **lineman**

**ˈline-up** *n.* Ⓐ Aufstellung, *die;* **~ of cabaret acts** Zusammenstellung von Kabarettauftritten; Ⓑ (*Amer.*) ⇒ **identification parade**

**ling¹** /lɪŋ/ *n.* (*Zool.*) Leng[fisch], *der*

**ling²** *n.* (*Bot.*) Heidekraut, *das*

**linger** /ˈlɪŋgə(r)/ *v.i.* Ⓐ (*remain, wait*) verweilen (*geh.*); bleiben; (*persist*) fortbestehen; ‹Erkältung, Diskussion, Schmerzen:› andauern; ‹Lied:› nachklingen; **her scent still ~ed in the room** ihr Duft hing noch im Raum; Ⓑ (*dwell*) **~ over** *or* **up[on] a subject** *etc.* bei einem Thema *usw.* verweilen; **~ over a meal** lange beim Essen sitzen

**lingerie** /ˈlæ̃ʒəriː/ *n.* **[women's] ~:** Damenunterwäsche, *die*

**lingering** /ˈlɪŋgərɪŋ/ *adj.* anhaltend; verbleibend ‹Zweifel›; langwierig ‹Krankheit›; langsam ‹Tod›; nachklingend ‹Melodie›; **one last ~ look** ein letzter sehnsuchtsvoller Blick; **any ~ hope was abandoned** alle noch vorhandene Hoffnung schwand dahin (*geh.*)

**lingo** /ˈlɪŋgəʊ/ *n., pl.* **~es** Ⓐ (*derog./joc.: language*) Sprache, *die;* Kauderwelsch, *das* (*abwertend*); Ⓑ (*jargon*) Fachjargon, *der*

**lingua franca** /lɪŋgwə ˈfræŋkə/ *n.* Lingua franca, *die* (*geh.*); Verkehrssprache, *die*

**linguist** /ˈlɪŋgwɪst/ *n.* Ⓐ Sprachkundige, *der/die;* **she's a good ~:** sie kann mehrere Sprachen; **I'm no ~:** Sprachen liegen mir nicht; Ⓑ (*philologist*) Linguist, *der*/Linguistin, *die;* Sprachwissenschaftler, *der*/-wissenschaftlerin, *die*

**linguistic** /lɪŋˈgwɪstɪk/ *adj.* (*of ~s*) linguistisch; sprachwissenschaftlich; (*of language*) sprachlich; Sprach-; **~ science** ⇒ **linguistics;** **~ skills** Sprachbegabung, *die;* **~ fluency** Sprachgewandtheit, *die*

**linguistically** /lɪŋˈgwɪstɪkəlɪ/ *adv.* sprachwissenschaftlich; linguistisch

**linguistics** /lɪŋˈgwɪstɪks/ *n., no pl.* Linguistik, *die;* Sprachwissenschaft, *die*

**liniment** /ˈlɪnɪmənt/ *n.* Liniment, *das* (*Med.*); Einreib[e]mittel, *das*

**lining** /ˈlaɪnɪŋ/ *n.* (*of clothes*) Futter, *das;* (*of stomach*) Magenschleimhaut, *die;* (*of objects, containers, machines, etc.*) Auskleidung, *die*

**ˈlining paper** *n.* Schrankpapier, *das*

**link** /lɪŋk/ ❶ *n.* Ⓐ (*of chain*) Glied, *das;* Ⓑ ⇒ **cuff link;** Ⓒ (*connecting part*) Bindeglied, *das;* Verbindung, *die;* **radio ~:** Funkverbindung, *die;* **road/rail ~:** Straßen-/Zugverbindung, *die;* **what is the ~ between these two?** was verbindet diese beiden?; **~ between two countries** Verbindung zwischen zwei Ländern; **sever all ~s with sb.** alle Bindungen zu jmdm. lösen; **have ~s with the Mafia** Verbindungen zur Mafia haben; ⇒ *also* **cut** 1 B; Ⓓ ⇒ **linkman.** ❷ *v.t.* Ⓐ (*connect*) verbinden; **how are these events ~ed?** was haben diese Ereignisse miteinander zu tun?; **~ sb. with sth.** jmdn. mit etw. in Verbindung bringen; **his name has been ~ed with hers** sein Name wurde mit ihrem in Verbindung gebracht; **be ~ed by telephone to Oslo** telefonisch mit Oslo verbunden sein; Ⓑ (*clasp or hook together*) **~ hands** sich bei den Händen halten; **~ arms** sich unterhaken. ❸ *v.i.* **~ together** sich zusammenfügen; **~ with sth.** sich verbinden mit etw.; ‹Firma:› sich zusammenschließen mit etw.

**~ ˈup** ❶ *v.t.* miteinander verbinden; ankoppeln ‹Wagen, Raumschiff usw.› (**to** an + *Akk.*); miteinander in Verbindung bringen ‹Fakten usw.›; **~ up A with B** A mit B verbinden. ❷ *v.i.* **~ up with sb.** sich mit jmdm. zusammentun *od.* zusammenschließen; **~ up with American TV** sich dem amerikanischen Fernsehen anschließen; **the spacecraft ~ed up** die Raumschiffe wurden angekoppelt; **this road ~s up with the M3** diese Straße mündet in die M3 *od.* geht in die M3 über. ⇒ *also* **link-up**

**linkage** /ˈlɪŋkɪdʒ/ *n.* Ⓐ Verbindung, *die;* Ⓑ (*system of links or bars*) Gestänge, *das;* **steering ~:** Lenkgestänge, *das;* Ⓒ (*Chem.*) Verknüpfung, *die;* Verbindung, *die;* Ⓓ (*Genetics*) Kopplung, *die*

**linkman** /ˈlɪŋkmən/ *n., pl.* **linkmen** /ˈlɪŋkmən/ Ⓐ Verbindungsmann, *der;* Ⓑ (*Radio, Telev.*) Moderator, *der*/Moderatorin, *die;* Ⓒ (*Hockey, Footb.*) Mittelfeldspieler, *der*

**links** /lɪŋks/ *sing. or pl.* **[golf] ~:** Golfplatz, *der*

**ˈlink-up** *n.* Verbindung, *die;* (*of spacecraft etc.*) Ankopplung, *die*

**linnet** /ˈlɪnɪt/ *n.* (*Ornith.*) Hänfling, *der*

**lino** /ˈlaɪnəʊ/ *n., pl.* **~s** Linoleum, *das*

**linocut** *n.* Linolschnitt, *der*

**linoleum** /lɪˈnəʊlɪəm/ *n.* Linoleum, *das*

**linseed** /ˈlɪnsiːd/ *n.* Leinsamen, *der*

**linseed: ~ cake** *n.* (*Agric.*) Leinkuchen, *der;* **~ ˈoil** *n.* Leinöl, *das*

**lint** /lɪnt/ *n.* Ⓐ Mull, *der;* Ⓑ (*fluff*) Fussel, *die*

**lintel** /ˈlɪntl/ *n.* (*Archit.*) Sturz, *der*

**lion** /ˈlaɪən/ *n.* Ⓐ Löwe, *der;* **put one's head into the ~'s mouth** (*fig.*) sich in höchste Gefahr begeben; **the ~'s share** der Löwenanteil; Ⓑ (*celebrity*) **literary ~ [of the day]** literarischer Löwe des Tages (*veralt.*); Ⓒ (*Astrol.*) **the L~:** der Löwe; ⇒ *also* **archer** B

**lioness** /ˈlaɪənɪs/ *n.* Löwin, *die*

**lion: ~heart** *n.* Löwenherz, *das* (*dichter. veralt.*); **Richard [the] L~-heart** Richard Löwenherz; **~-hearted** *adj.* wagemutig; löwenherzig (*dichter. veralt.*)

**lionize (lionise)** /ˈlaɪənaɪz/ *v.t.* [als Berühmtheit] feiern

**ˈlion tamer** *n.* ▶ 1261 Löwenbändiger, *der*

**lip** /lɪp/ *n.* Ⓐ ▶ 966 Lippe, *die;* **lower/upper ~:** Unter-/Oberlippe, *die;* **bite one's ~** (*lit. or fig.*) sich (*Dat.*) auf die Lippen beißen; **escape sb.'s ~s** jmds. Lippen (*Dat.*) entschlüpfen; **hang on sb.'s ~s** an jmds. Lippen (*Dat.*) hängen; **lick one's ~s** (*lit. or fig.*) sich (*Dat.*) die Lippen lecken; **not let a word pass one's ~s** kein Wort über seine Lippen kommen lassen; **not a morsel passed his ~s** er rührte nichts an; **keep a stiff upper ~** (*fig.*) Haltung bewahren; ⇒ *also* **button** 2; **seal²** 2 B; **smack²** 2 B; Ⓑ (*of saucer, cup, crater*) [Gieß]rand, *der;* (*of jug*) Schnabel, *der;* Tülle, *die;* Ⓒ (*coll.: impudence*) **give sb. some ~:** jmdm. gegenüber eine dicke Lippe riskieren (*ugs.*); **none of your ~!** keine frechen Bemerkungen!

**liposuction** /ˈlaɪpəʊsʌkʃn, ˈlɪpəʊsʌkʃn/ ❶ *n.* Fettabsaugung, *die;* Liposuktion, *die* (*Med*). ❷ *v.t.* absaugen ‹Fett›

**lipped** /lɪpt/ *adj.* **thick-/thin-~:** dick-/dünnlippig; **~ vessel** Gefäß mit Schnabel *od.* Gießrand

**lippy** /ˈlɪpɪ/ *adj.* (*coll.*) frech; vorlaut

**lip: ~-read** ❶ *v.i.* von den Lippen lesen; ❷ *v.t.* **be able to ~-read what sb. says** jmdm. von den Lippen ablesen können, was er/sie sagt; **~-reading** *n.* Lippenlesen, *das;* **~ service** *n.* **pay** *or* **give ~ service to sth.** ein Lippenbekenntnis zu etw. ablegen; **~stick** *n.* Lippenstift, *der*

**liquefaction** /lɪkwɪˈfækʃn/ *n.* Verflüssigung, *die*

**liquefier** /ˈlɪkwɪfaɪə(r)/ *n.* Verflüssiger, *der*

**liquefy** /ˈlɪkwɪfaɪ/ ❶ *v.t.* verflüssigen. ❷ *v.i.* sich verflüssigen

**liqueur** /lɪˈkjʊə(r)/ *n.* Likör, *der*

**liqueur: ~ ˈbrandy** *n.* *gut gealterter, hochwertiger Brandy;* **~ ˈchocolate** *n.* Likörpraline, *die;* **~ glass** *n.* Likörglas, *das*

**liquid** /ˈlɪkwɪd/ ❶ *adj.* Ⓐ flüssig; glänzend ‹Augen›; hell klingend ‹Töne, Laute›; **~ air** Flüssigluft, *die;* **~ blue** wasserblau; Ⓑ (*Commerc.*) liquid; **~ assets** flüssige Mittel; Ⓒ (*Phonet.*) **~ consonant** Fließlaut, *der;* Liquida, *die* (*fachspr.*). ❷ *n.* Ⓐ Flüssigkeit, *die;* **he can only take ~s** er kann nur Flüssiges zu sich nehmen; Ⓑ (*Phonet.*) Fließlaut, *der;* Liquida, *die* (*fachspr.*)

**liquidate** /ˈlɪkwɪdeɪt/ ❶ *v.t.* Ⓐ (*Commerc.*) liquidieren; tilgen ‹Schuld›; **~d damages** (*Law*) Konventionalstrafe, *die;* Ⓑ (*eliminate, kill*) liquidieren; beseitigen. ❷ *v.i.* (*Commerc.*) liquidieren

**liquidation** /lɪkwɪˈdeɪʃn/ *n.* Ⓐ (*Commerc.*) Liquidation, *die;* (*of debt*) Tilgung, *die;* **go into ~:** in Liquidation gehen; Ⓑ (*eliminating, killing*) Liquidierung, *die;* Beseitigung, *die*

**liquidator** /ˈlɪkwɪdeɪtə(r)/ *n.* (*Commerc.*) Liquidator, *der*

**liquid: ~ ˈcrystal** *n.* Flüssigkristall, *der;* **~ crystal disˈplay** *n.* Flüssigkristallanzeige, *die*

**liquidity** /lɪˈkwɪdɪtɪ/ *n., no pl.* Ⓐ flüssiger Zustand; Ⓑ (*Commerc.*) Liquidität, *die*

**liquidize** /ˈlɪkwɪdaɪz/ *v.t.* auflösen; (*Cookery*) [im Mixer] pürieren

**liquidizer** /ˈlɪkwɪdaɪzə(r)/ *n.* Mixer, *der*

**liquid ˈmeasure** *n.* Flüssigkeitsmaß, *das*

**liquor** /ˈlɪkə(r)/ *n.* Ⓐ (*drink*) Alkohol, *der;* Spirituosen *Pl.;* **be able to carry** *or* **hold one's ~:** etwas vertragen können; **hard** *or* **strong ~:** hochprozentiger Alkohol; scharfe Sachen (*ugs.*); **be the worse for ~:** betrunken sein; Ⓑ (*Industry*) Beize, *die*

**~ ˈup** (*sl.*) *v.t.* besoffen machen (*derb*); **get/be ~ed up** sich (*Dat.*) einen ansaufen/besoffen sein (*derb*)

**liquorice** /ˈlɪkərɪs/ *n.* Ⓐ (*root*) Süßholz, *das;* (*preparation*) Lakritze, *die;* Ⓑ (*plant*) Süßholzstrauch, *der*

**ˈliquor store** *n.* (*Amer.*) Spirituosenladen, *der*

**lira** /ˈlɪərə/ *n., pl.* **lire** /ˈlɪərə, ˈlɪərɪ/ *or* **~s** ▶ 1328 Lira, *die*

**Lisbon** /ˈlɪzbən/ *pr. n.* ▶ 1626 Lissabon (*das*)

**lisle** /laɪl/ *n.* **~ [thread]** Florgarn, *das* (*Textilw.*)

**lisp** /lɪsp/ ❶ *v.i. & t.* lispeln. ❷ *n.* Lispeln, *das;* **speak with a ~:** lispeln; **have a bad ~:** stark lispeln

l

**lissom[e]** /ˈlɪsəm/ *adj.* geschmeidig

**list¹** /lɪst/ ❶ *n.* [A] Liste, *die;* **active ~** (*Mil.*) Liste der Reserve; **publisher's ~:** Verlagsprogramm, *das;* **shopping ~:** Einkaufszettel, *der;* [B] *in pl.* **enter the ~s [against sb./sth.]** (*fig.*) zum Kampf [gegen jmdn./etw.] antreten. ❷ *v.t.* aufführen; auflisten; (*verbally*) aufzählen; **~ed securities/stock** an der Börse zugelassene Wertpapiere/Aktien

**list²** ❶ *n.* [A] (*Naut.: tilt*) Schlagseite, *die;* **have/develop a pronounced ~:** deutlich Schlagseite haben/bekommen; [B] (*of building, fence, etc.*) Neigung, *die;* **develop a ~:** sich neigen. ❷ *v.i.* [A] (*Naut.*) **~ [to port/starboard]** Schlagseite [nach Backbord/Steuerbord] haben; [B] ‹Gebäude, Zaun usw.:› sich neigen

**listed 'building** *n.* (*Brit.*) Gebäude unter Denkmalsschutz

**listen** /ˈlɪsn/ *v.i.* zuhören; **~ to music/the radio** Musik/Radio hören; **just ~ to the noise they are making!** hör dir bloß mal an, was sie für einen Lärm machen!; **~, nitwit** hör zu, du Trottel; **they ~ed to his words** sie hörten ihm zu; **you never ~ to what I say** du hörst mir nie zu; **we stopped and ~ed** wir hielten inne und horchten; **~ [out] for sth./sb.** auf etw. (*Akk.*) horchen/horchen, ob jmd. kommt; **~ to sth./sb.** (*pay heed*) auf etw./jmdn. hören; **he wouldn't ~** (*heed*) er wollte nicht hören; **~ to sb.'s grievances** sich (*Dat.*) jmds. Beschwerden anhören

**~ 'in** *v.i.* [A] (*Radio*) hören (**on, to** *Akk.*); [B] (*tap line*) mithören; [C] (*eavesdrop*) mithören (**on, to** *Akk.*)

**listener** /ˈlɪsnə(r)/ *n.* [A] Zuhörer, *der*/Zuhörerin, *die;* **be a good ~:** ein guter Zuhörer sein; [B] (*Radio*) Hörer, *der*/Hörerin, *die*

**listening post** /ˈlɪsnɪŋpəʊst/ *n.* (*Mil.; also fig.*) Horchposten, *der*

**listing** /ˈlɪstɪŋ/ *n.* Aufführung, *die;* Auflistung, *die;* (*verbal*) Aufzählung, *die*

**listless** /ˈlɪstlɪs/ *adj.*, **listlessly** /ˈlɪstlɪslɪ/ *adv.* lustlos

**listlessness** /ˈlɪstlɪsnɪs/ *n., no pl.* Lustlosigkeit, *die*

**'list price** *n.* Katalogpreis, *der*

**lit** /lɪt/ ⇒ **light¹** 4; **light³**

**litany** /ˈlɪtənɪ/ *n.* (*lit. or fig.*) Litanei, *die;* **the L~** *die Litanei im Book of Common Prayer*

**litchi** /ˈlaɪtʃɪ, ˈlɪtʃɪ/ *n.* Litschi, *die*

**lite, Lite** ® /laɪt/ ❶ *adj.* kalorienreduziert ‹Bier, Käse etc.›. ❷ *n.* Leichtbier, *das*

**liter** (*Amer.*) ⇒ **litre**

**literacy** /ˈlɪtərəsɪ/ *n., no pl.* Lese- und Schreibfertigkeit, *die;* **adult ~ classes** Kurse für Analphabeten; **~ is low** das Analphabetentum ist groß

**literal** /ˈlɪtərl/ ❶ *adj.* [A] wörtlich; **take sth. in a ~ sense** etw. wörtlich nehmen; [B] (*not exaggerated*) buchstäblich; **the ~ truth** die reine Wahrheit; [C] (*coll.: with some exaggeration*) wahr; [D] (*prosaic*) nüchtern; prosaisch; [E] (*in text*) **~ error** Tippfehler, *der;* (*misprint*) Druckfehler, *der.* ❷ *n.* [A] (*error*) Tippfehler, *der;* (*misprint*) Druckfehler, *der;* [B] (*Computing*) Literal, *das*

**literally** /ˈlɪtərəlɪ/ *adv.* [A] wörtlich; **take sth./sb. ~:** etw./was jmd. sagt, wörtlich nehmen; [B] (*actually*) buchstäblich; [C] (*coll.: with some exaggeration*) geradezu

**literal: ~-'minded** *adj.* nüchtern [denkend *nicht präd.*]; **~-mindedness** /lɪtərl ˈmaɪndɪdnɪs/ *n., no pl.* Nüchternheit [des Denkens]

**literary** /ˈlɪtərərɪ/ *adj.* literarisch; (*not colloquial*) gewählt; **be of a ~ turn of mind** sich für Literatur interessieren

**literary: ~ 'agent** *n.* Literaturagent, *der*/-agentin, *die;* **~ 'critic** *n.* Literaturkritiker, *der*/-kritikerin, *die;* **~ ex'ecutor** ⇒ **executor;** **~ gent** *n.* (*coll.*) Literat, *der* (*oft abwertend*); **~ hi'storian** *n.* Literaturhistoriker, *der*/-historikerin, *die;* **~ 'history** *n.* Literaturgeschichte, *die;* **~ 'luncheon** *n.* literarischer Lunch (*mit Schriftstellern und Verlegern*); **~ man** *n.* Schriftsteller, *der;* (*versed in literature*) Literaturkenner, *der*

**literate** /ˈlɪtərət/ ❶ *adj.* (*able to read and write*) des Lesens und Schreibens kundig; (*educated*) gebildet; **not be ~:** nicht lesen und schreiben können. ❷ *n.* Alphabet, *der*

**literature** /ˈlɪtərətʃə(r), ˈlɪtrətʃə(r)/ *n.* [A] Literatur, *die;* [B] (*writings on a subject*) [Fach]literatur, *die* (**on** zu); [C] (*coll.: printed matter*) Literatur, *die;* Informationsmaterial, *das;* **advertising ~:** Werbeschriften *od.* -material

**lithe** /laɪð/ *adj.* geschmeidig

**lithium** /ˈlɪθɪəm/ *n.* (*Chem.*) Lithium, *das*

**litho** /ˈlaɪθəʊ/ (*coll.*) ❶ *n., pl.* **~s** Litho, *das.* ❷ *adj.* Litho-; **~ print/printing** Litho, *das.* ❸ *v.t.* lithographieren

**lithograph** /ˈlɪθəgrɑːf/ ❶ *n.* Lithographie, *die.* ❷ *v.t.* lithographieren

**lithographer** /lɪˈθɒgrəfə(r)/ *n.* Lithograph, *der*/Lithographin, *die*

**lithographic** /lɪθəˈgræfɪk/ *adj.* lithographisch

**lithography** /lɪˈθɒgrəfɪ/ *n.* Lithographie, *die*

**Lithuania** /lɪθjʊˈeɪnɪə/ *pr. n.* Litauen (*das*)

**Lithuanian** /lɪθjʊˈeɪnɪən/ ▶ **1275**, ▶ **1340** ❶ *adj.* litauisch; **sb. is ~:** jmd. ist Litauer/Litauerin; ⇒ *also* **English** 1. ❷ *n.* [A] (*person*) Litauer, *der*/Litauerin, *die;* [B] (*language*) Litauisch, *das;* ⇒ *also* **English** 2 A

**litigant** /ˈlɪtɪgənt/ ❶ *n.* Prozesspartei, *die.* ❷ *adj.* **~ party** Prozesspartei, *die*

**litigate** /ˈlɪtɪgeɪt/ ❶ *v.i.* prozessieren. ❷ *v.t.* vor Gericht verhandeln

**litigation** /lɪtɪˈgeɪʃn/ *n.* Rechtsstreit, *der;* **in ~:** rechtshängig

**litigious** /lɪˈtɪdʒəs/ *adj.* prozesssüchtig; **a ~ person** ein Prozesshansel (*ugs.*)

**litmus** /ˈlɪtməs/ *n.* Lackmus, *das od. der*

**'litmus paper** *n.* Lackmuspapier, *das*

**litotes** /ˈlaɪtətiːz/ *n.* (*Rhet.*) Litotes, *die*

**litre** /ˈliːtə(r)/ *n.* ▶ **1671** (*Brit.*) Liter, *der od. das*

**Litt. D.** /lɪt ˈdiː/ ⇒ **D. Litt.**

**litter** /ˈlɪtə(r)/ ❶ *n.* [A] (*rubbish*) Abfall, *der;* Abfälle; **'do not leave ~'** „bitte keine Abfälle zurücklassen"; **her desk was strewn with a ~ of books** ihr Schreibtisch war mit Büchern übersät; [B] (*vehicle*) Sänfte, *die;* [C] (*stretcher*) Trage, *die;* Tragbahre, *die;* [D] (*bedding for animals*) Streu, *die;* Einstreu, *die* (*Landw.*); [E] (*young*) Wurf, *der.* ❷ *v.t.* verstreuen; **papers were ~ed about the room** im Zimmer lagen überall Zeitungen herum; **~ the room with one's books** seine Bücher im Zimmer verstreuen. ❸ *v.i.* **'do not ~'** „bitte keine Abfälle zurücklassen"

**litter: ~ basket** *n.* Abfallkorb, *der;* **~ bin** *n.* Abfalleimer, *der;* **~bug, ~ lout** *ns.* Schmutzfink, *der* (*ugs.*)

**little** /ˈlɪtl/ ❶ *adj.*, **~r** /ˈlɪtlə(r)/, **~st** /ˈlɪtlɪst/ (*Note: it is more common to use the compar. and superl. forms* **smaller, smallest**) [A] (*small*) klein; **~ town/book/dog** kleine Stadt/kleines Buch/kleiner Hund; (*showing affection or amusement*) Städtchen, *das*/Büchlein, *das*/Hündchen, *das;* **~ toe** kleine Zehe; **the ~ woman** (*coll.: my wife*) mein kleines Frauchen (*ugs.*); **you poor ~ thing!** du armes kleines Ding!; **don't worry your ~ head** zerbrich dir nicht dein Köpfchen!; **I know your ~ ways** ich kenne deine Tricks; **do one's ~ best** sein Bestes tun; **L~ Venice** Klein-Venedig, *das;* **the ~ people** (*fairies*) die Elfen; ⇒ *also* **bear¹** C; **slam²** A; [B] (*young*) klein; **the ~ Joneses** die Jones-Kinder; **~ man/woman** (*child*) Kleiner/Kleine; **the ~ ones** die Kleinen; **my ~ sister** meine kleine Schwester; [C] (*short*) klein ‹Person›; **a ~ way** ein kleines *od.* kurzes Stück; **after a ~ while** nach kurzer Zeit; nach einer kleinen Weile (*veralt.*); [D] (*not much*) wenig; **you have ~ time left** dir bleibt nicht mehr viel Zeit; **there is very ~ tea left** es ist kaum noch Tee *od.* nur noch ganz wenig Tee da; **make a nice ~ profit** (*coll. iron.*) einen hübschen Gewinn machen (*ugs.*); **a ~ ...** (*a small quantity of*) etwas ...; ein wenig *od.* bisschen ...; **speak a ~ German** etwas Deutsch sprechen; **speak only a ~ German** nur wenig Deutsch sprechen; **a ~ goes a long way** ein bisschen reicht lange; (*fig.*) ein bisschen hat eine große Wirkung; **no ~ ...:** nicht wenig ...; [E] (*trivial*) klein; **get annoyed about ~ things** sich über Kleinigkeiten aufregen; **of course, this 'would occur to your mean ~ mind** einem miesen Kleingeist wie dir muss natürlich so etwas einfallen; **~ things please ~ minds** kleine Geister erfreuen sich an kleinen Dingen. ⇒ *also* **Englander; old** 1 E; **Russian** 2 B.

❷ *n.* wenig; **but ~:** nur wenig; **~ or nothing** kaum etwas; so gut wie nichts; **[do] not a ~:** einiges [tun]; **not a ~ angry** *etc.* ziemlich verärgert *usw.;* **there was ~ we could do** wir konnten nur wenig tun; **a ~** (*a small quantity*) etwas; ein wenig *od.* bisschen; (*somewhat*) ein wenig; **too ~ too late** zu wenig [und] zu spät; **think ~ of sb.** gering von jmdm. denken; **after a ~:** nach einer Weile; **a ~ after eight** kurz nach acht; **for a ~:** ein Weilchen; (*a short way*) ein Stückchen; **we see very ~ of one another** wir sehen sehr wenig voneinander; **~ by ~:** nach und nach; **the ~ I know** das wenige, was ich weiß; ⇒ *also* **help** 1 A; **make** 1 M; **what** 6 A.

❸ *adv.*, **less** /les/, **least** /liːst/ [A] (*not at all*) **she ~ thought that ...:** sie dachte nicht im Geringsten daran, dass ...; **he ~ suspected/knew what ...:** er hatte nicht die geringste Ahnung/wusste überhaupt nicht, was ...; [B] (*to only a small extent*) **~ as he liked it** sowenig es ihm auch gefiel; **he writes ~ now** er schreibt nur noch wenig; **~ more/less than ...:** kaum mehr/weniger als ...; **that is ~ less than ...:** das grenzt schon an (+ *Akk.*) ...; **the holiday was ~ less than a disaster** der Urlaub war ein ziemlicher Reinfall (*ugs.*); **his behaviour is ~ less than disgraceful** sein Benehmen ist schon fast skandalös zu nennen

**little: ~ end** *n.* (*Brit. Motor Veh.*) Pleuelauge, *das* (*Technik*); **~ 'finger** *n.* kleiner Finger; **twist sb. round one's ~ finger** jmdn. um den [kleinen] Finger wickeln (*ugs.*); **~-known** *adj.* wenig bekannt

**littleness** /ˈlɪtlnɪs/ *n., no pl.* Kleinheit, *die*

**'little theatre** *n.* Kleinbühne, *die*

**littoral** /ˈlɪtərl/ ❶ *adj.* litoral (*Geogr.*). ❷ *n.* Litoral, *das* (*Geogr.*); Küstengebiet, *das*

**liturgical** /lɪˈtɜːdʒɪkl/ *adj.* liturgisch

**liturgy** /ˈlɪtədʒɪ/ *n.* [A] Liturgie, *die;* [B] (*Book of Common Prayer*) **the ~:** das Book of Common Prayer

**live¹** /laɪv/ ❶ *adj.* [A] *attrib.* (*alive*) lebend; [B] (*Radio, Telev.*) **~ performance** Live-Aufführung, *die;* **~ broadcast** Livesendung, *die;* Direkt- *od.* Originalübertragung, *die;* **we go ~ tomorrow** (*fig.*) morgen machen wir Ernst; [C] (*topical*) aktuell ‹Thema, Frage›; [D] (*Electr.*) Strom führend; [E] (*unexploded*) scharf ‹Munition usw.›; [F] (*glowing*) glühend ‹Kohle›; [G] (*joc.: actual*) **real ~:** richtig; [H] (*Mech. Engin.*) Trieb‹rad, -feder›; Antriebs‹achse, -rad, -welle›.

❷ *adv.* (*Radio, Telev.*) live ‹übertragen usw.›

**live²** /lɪv/ ❶ *v.i.* [A] leben; **~ and let ~:** leben und leben lassen; **~ by sth.** von etw. leben; **will he ~?** wird er am Leben bleiben?; **you'll ~** (*iron.*) du wirsts [schon] überleben (*iron.*); **as long as I ~ I shall never understand why ...:** mein Leben lang werde ich nicht begreifen, warum ...; **~ to see** [mit]erleben; **she will ~ to regret her stupidity** sie wird ihre Dummheit noch bereuen; **you ~ and learn** man lernt nie aus; **~ for sth./sb.** für etw./jmdn. leben; **~ through sth.** etw. durchmachen (*ugs.*); (*survive*) etw. überleben; **~ to a ripe old age/to be a hundred** ein hohes Alter erreichen/hundert Jahre alt werden; **long ~ the queen!** lang lebe die Königin!; **they ~d violently** ihr Leben stand im Zeichen der Gewalt; **~ beyond one's means** über seine Verhältnisse leben; **~ well** (*eat well*) es sich (*Dat.*) gut gehen lassen; ⇒ *also* **hand** 1 A; [B] (*make permanent home*) wohnen; leben; **the room seems ~d in** das Zimmer scheint bewohnt zu sein; **~ together** zusammenleben; **~ with sb.** mit jmdm. zusammenleben; **~**

**with sth.** (*lit. or fig.*) mit etw. leben.
❷ *v.t.* Ⓐ leben; **~ one's own life** sein eigenes Leben leben; **~ an honest life** ein ehrbares Leben führen; **~ it up** das Leben in vollen Zügen genießen; (*have a good time*) einen draufmachen (*ugs.*); Ⓑ (*express*) **~ one's convictions** nach seiner Überzeugung leben; **what others were preaching, he ~d** was andere nur predigten, lebte er vor
**~ 'down** *v.t.* Gras wachsen lassen über (+ *Akk.*); **he will never be able to ~ it down** das wird ihm ewig anhängen
**~ 'in** *v.i.* (*Brit.*) ‹Personal, Koch usw.:› im Haus wohnen; ‹Student, Krankenschwester:› im Wohnheim wohnen
**~ on** ❶ /'--/ *v.t.* leben von; (*fig.*) zehren von ‹Ruf›; leben von ‹Hoffnung›; **~ on air** (*joc.*) von der Luft *od.* (*ugs. scherzh.*) von Luft und Liebe leben; ⇒ *also* **fat** 2. ❷ /-'-/ *v.i.* weiterleben
**~ out** ❶ /-'-/ *v.i.* (*Brit.*) außerhalb wohnen. ❷ /'--/ *v.t.* Ⓐ (*survive*) überleben; überstehen ‹Winter, Woche›; Ⓑ (*complete, spend*) verbringen; **they had ~d out their lives as fishermen** sie waren ihr Leben lang Fischer gewesen
**~ 'up to** *v.t.* gerecht werden (+ *Dat.*); **~ up to one's principles/faith** nach seinen Prinzipien/seinem Glauben leben; **he's a bright lad — I hope he ~s up to his promise** er ist ein aufgeweckter Bursche — ich hoffe, er hält, was er verspricht; **~ up to one's reputation** seinem Ruf Ehre machen; **~ up to one's income** seinen Verhältnissen entsprechend leben

**liveable** /'lɪvəbl/ *adj.* lebenswert, erträglich ‹Leben›

**live birth** /laɪv 'bɜ:θ/ *n.* Lebendgeburt, *die*

**live-in** /'lɪvɪn/ *attrib. adj.* im Haus wohnend ‹Personal›; **~ cook** Hauskoch *der*/Hausköchin, *die;* **~ lover** Geliebter, der/Geliebte, die bei ihr/ihm *usw.* wohnt

**livelihood** /'laɪvlɪhʊd/ *n.* Lebensunterhalt, *der;* **gain a ~ from sth.** sich (*Dat.*) seinen Lebensunterhalt mit etw. verdienen; **her ~ is her painting** sie lebt von der Malerei

**liveliness** /'laɪvlɪnɪs/ *n., no pl.* Lebhaftigkeit, *die*

**livelong** /'lɪvlɒŋ/ *adj.* (*poet./rhet.*) **all the ~ day/night** den lieben langen Tag/die ganze Nacht [hindurch]

**lively** /'laɪvlɪ/ *adj.* Ⓐ lebhaft; lebendig ‹Gegenwart›; rege ‹Handel›; **things start to get ~ at 9 a.m.** um 9 Uhr wird es lebhaft; **have a ~ sense of humour** immer zu Späßen aufgelegt sein; **look ~** (*coll.*) sich ranhalten (*ugs.*); Ⓑ (*vivid*) lebendig, anschaulich ‹Bericht, Schilderung›; Ⓒ (*joc.: exciting, dangerous, difficult*) **things were getting ~:** die Sache wurde gefährlich; **give sb. a ~ time, make things ~ for sb.** jmdm. zu schaffen machen; Ⓓ (*fresh*) lebhaft ‹Farbe›

**liven** ⇒ **~ up** 1

**liven up** /laɪvn 'ʌp/ ❶ *v.t.* Leben bringen in (+ *Akk.*). ❷ *v.i.* ‹Person:› aufleben; **things will ~ up when ...:** es wird Leben in die Bude kommen (*ugs.*), wenn ...

**liver**[1] /'lɪvə(r)/ *n.* ▶ **966** (*Anat., Gastr.*) Leber, *die*

**liver**[2] *n.* **be a fast/clean ~:** ein flottes/solides Leben führen

**'liver-coloured** *adj.* leberbraun

**liveried** /'lɪvərɪd/ *adj.* livriert

**liverish** /'lɪvərɪʃ/ *adj.* Ⓐ (*unwell*) elend; unwohl; Ⓑ (*grumpy*) mürrisch

**Liverpudlian** /lɪvə'pʌdlɪən/ ❶ *adj.* Liverpooler. ❷ *n.* Liverpooler, *der*/Liverpoolerin, *die*

**liver: ~ salts** *n. pl.* (*Brit.*) ≈ Magenmittel, *das;* **~ sausage** *n.* Leberwurst, *die;* **~wort** *n.* Lebermoos, *das;* **~wurst** /'lɪvəwɜ:st/ (*Amer.*) ⇒ **~ sausage**

**livery** /'lɪvərɪ/ *n.* Livree, *die;* **in/out of ~:** livriert/nicht livriert

**livery: ~ company** *n.* (*Brit.*) Londoner *Zunft;* **~ stable** *n.* Mietstall, *der*

**live** /laɪv/: **~stock** *n. pl.* Vieh, *das;* **large number of ~stock** großer Viehbestand; **~ weight** *n.* Lebendgewicht, *das;* **~ 'wire** *n.* (*Electr.*) Strom führender Draht; (*fig.*) Energiebündel, *das* (*ugs.*)

**livid** /'lɪvɪd/ *adj.* Ⓐ (*bluish*) bleigrau; Ⓑ (*Brit. coll.: furious*) fuchtig (*ugs.*)

**living** /'lɪvɪŋ/ ❶ *n.* Ⓐ Leben, *das;* ⇒ *also* **cost of living; standard** 1 B; Ⓑ (*livelihood*) Lebensunterhalt, *der;* **make a ~:** seinen Lebensunterhalt verdienen; **earn one's [own] ~:** sich (*Dat.*) seinen Lebensunterhalt [selbst] verdienen; **make one's ~ out of farming** von der Landwirtschaft leben; **make a good ~:** viel verdienen; **it's a ~** (*joc.*) man kann davon leben; Ⓒ (*Brit. Eccl.*) Pfründe, *die;* Ⓓ (*way of life*) Lebensstil, *der;* **the art of ~:** die Kunst zu leben; **good ~:** üppiges Leben; (*pious*) guter Lebenswandel; **high ~:** hoher Lebensstandard; Ⓔ *in pl.* **the ~:** die Lebenden; **be still/back in the land of the ~:** noch/wieder unter den Lebenden weilen.
❷ *adj.* Ⓐ lebend; **~ things** Lebewesen *Pl.;* **not a ~ soul** keine Menschenseele; **no man ~:** niemand auf der Welt; **it was a ~ death for him** er fühlte sich dort wie lebendig begraben; **within ~ memory** seit Menschengedenken; **be the ~ image of sb.** jmds. Ebenbild sein; **a ~ monument** ein lebendiges Zeugnis (**to** *Gen.*); ⇒ *also* **daylight** C; Ⓑ (*uncut, unquarried*) gewachsen ‹Stein, Fels›; Ⓒ (*still in vernacular use*) lebend ‹Sprache›

**living: ~ room** *n.* Wohnzimmer, *das;* **~ space** *n.* Ⓐ Lebensraum, *der;* Ⓑ (*in dwelling*) Wohnraum, *der;* **~ 'wage** *n.* Lohn, von dem man leben kann; **~ 'will** *n.* Patientenverfügung, *die*

**Livy** /'lɪvɪ/ *pr. n.* Livius (*der*)

**lizard** /'lɪzəd/ *n.* Eidechse, *die*

**ll.** *abbr.* **lines** Zz.

**'ll** /l/ (*coll.*) = **shall;** [1]**will**

**llama** /'lɑ:mə/ *n.* (*Zool., Textiles*) Lama, *das*

**LL.B/LL.D/LL.M** *abbrs.* **Bachelor/Doctor/Master of Laws;** ⇒ *also* **B. Sc.**

**lo** /ləʊ/ *int.* Ⓐ **lo and behold** (*joc.*) sieh[e] da; Ⓑ (*arch.*) siehe/seh[e]t

**loach** /ləʊtʃ/ *n.* (*Zool.*) Schmerle, *die*

**load** /ləʊd/ ❶ *n.* Ⓐ (*burden, weight*) Last, *die;* (*amount carried*) Ladung, *die;* **a ~ of hay** eine Ladung Heu; **barrow~ of apples** Karre voll Äpfel; **a ~ of [old] rubbish** *or* **tripe** (*fig. coll.*) ein einziger Mist (*ugs.*); **talk a ~ of rubbish** eine Menge Blödsinn reden (*ugs.*); **what a ~ of rubbish!** was für ein Quatsch (*ugs.*) *od.* (*ugs. abwertend*) Schmarren!; **get a ~ of this!** (*coll.*) (*listen*) hör einmal gut *od.* genau zu! (*ugs.*); (*look*) guck mal genau hin! (*ugs.*); Ⓑ (*weight*) Last, *die;* (*Electr.*) Belastung, *die;* Ⓒ (*fig.*) Last, *die;* Bürde, *die* (*geh.*); **a heavy ~ of work** eine große Arbeitsbelastung; **take a ~ off sb.'s mind** jmdm. eine Last von der Seele nehmen; **that's a ~ off my mind** damit fällt mir ein Stein vom Herzen; **teaching ~** (*Sch.*) Deputat, *das;* Ⓓ *usu. in pl.* (*coll.: plenty*) **~s of** jede Menge *od.* massenhaft (*ugs.*) ‹Nahrungsmittel usw.›; **have ~s of sense** sehr vernünftig sein.
❷ *v.t.* Ⓐ (*put ~ on*) beladen; **~ sb. with work** (*fig.*) jmdm. Arbeit auftragen *od.* (*ugs. abwertend*) aufhalsen *od.* (*geh.*) aufbürden; Ⓑ (*put as ~*) laden; Ⓒ (*weight with lead*) mit Blei beschweren; **~ed dice** präparierte Würfel; **the dice were ~ed against him** (*fig.*) er hatte schlechte Karten; Ⓓ (*charge*) laden ‹Gewehr›; **~ a camera** einen Film [in einen Fotoapparat] einlegen; Ⓔ (*insert*) einlegen ‹Film, Tonband usw.› (**into** in + *Akk.*); laden ‹Datei, Dokument›; Ⓕ (*strain*) schwer belasten; **a table ~ed with food** ein mit Speisen beladener Tisch; Ⓖ (*overwhelm*) (*with praise, presents, etc.*) überhäufen; (*with abuse*) überschütten.
❸ *v.i.* laden (**with** *Akk.*); Ladung übernehmen
**~ 'up** *v.i.* laden (**with** *Akk.*)

**'load-bearing** *adj.* tragend ‹Wand, Balken, Konstruktion›

**loaded** /'ləʊdɪd/ *adj.* Ⓐ (*coll.: rich*) **be ~:** [schwer] Kohle haben (*salopp*); Ⓑ (*coll.: drunk*) voll (*ugs.*); Ⓒ (*Amer. sl.: drugged*) high (*Jargon verhüll.*); **be ~ [up] on heroin** sich mit Heroin voll gepumpt haben (*ugs.*); Ⓓ **~ for bear** (*Amer. coll.*) für alles gerüstet; Ⓔ **emotionally ~ words** emotional befrachtete Wörter; **a ~ question** eine suggestive Frage. ⇒ *also* **load** 2

**loader** /'ləʊdə(r)/ *n.* Ⓐ (*person who loads gun*) [Gewehr]lader, *der;* Ⓑ (*machine*) Lader, *der;* Ⓒ *in comb.* (*gun etc.*) ‹Vorder-, Hinter›lader, *der*

**'loading bay** *n.* Ladeplatz, *der*

**load: ~ line** *n.* Ladelinie, *die* (*Seew.*); **~-shedding** *n.* (*Electr.*) Stromabschaltung, *die;* **~star** ⇒ **lodestar; ~stone** *n.* Ⓐ (*oxide*) Magnetit, *der;* Ⓑ (*piece*) Magnet[eisen]stein, *der;* Ⓒ (*fig.*) Magnet, *der*

**loaf**[1] /ləʊf/ *n., pl.* **loaves** /ləʊvz/ Ⓐ Brot, *das;* [Brot]laib, *der;* **a ~ of bread** ein Laib Brot; **a brown/white ~:** ein dunkles Brot/Weißbrot; **half a ~ is better than no bread** *or* **none** (*prov.*) wenig ist besser als gar nichts; Ⓑ (*coll.: head*) **use one's ~:** seinen Grips anstrengen (*ugs.*); Ⓒ **~ sugar** Hutzucker, *der*

**loaf**[2] ❶ *v.i.* Ⓐ **~ round town/the house** in der Stadt/zu Hause herumlungern (*ugs.*); Ⓑ (*saunter*) trödeln (*ugs.*). ❷ *v.t.* **~ away** vertrödeln ‹Zeit›

**loafer** /'ləʊfə(r)/ *n.* Ⓐ (*idler*) Faulenzer, *der;* Ⓑ **L~** ® *bequemer [mokassinartiger] Halbschuh*

**loam** /ləʊm/ *n.* Ⓐ (*paste*) Lehm, *der;* Ⓑ (*soil*) Lehmboden, *der*

**loamy** /'ləʊmɪ/ *adj.* lehmig

**loan** /ləʊn/ ❶ *n.* Ⓐ (*thing lent*) Leihgabe, *die;* Ⓑ (*lending*) **let sb. have/give sb. the ~ of sth.** jmdm. etw. leihen; **may I have the ~ of your mower?** könnte ich mir mal Ihren Rasenmäher ausleihen?; **be [out] on ~** ‹Buch, Schallplatte:› ausgeliehen sein; **have sth. on ~ [from sb.]** etw. [von jmdm.] geliehen haben; Ⓒ (*money lent*) Darlehen, *das;* Kredit, *der;* (*public ~*) Anleihe, *die.* ❷ *v.t.* **~ sth. to sb.** jmdm. etw. leihen; etw. an jmdn. verleihen

**loan: ~ collection** *n.* Leihgaben *Pl;* **~ shark** *n.* (*coll.*) Kredithai, *der* (*ugs. abwertend*); **~ translation** *n.* Lehnübersetzung, *die;* **~word** *n.* Lehnwort, *das*

**loath** /ləʊθ/ *pred. adj.* **be ~ to do sth.** etw. ungern tun; **be nothing ~:** nicht abgeneigt sein

**loathe** /ləʊð/ *v.t.* verabscheuen; nicht ausstehen können; **he ~s eggs** er mag Eier überhaupt nicht; **I ~ ironing** ich kann Bügeln nicht ausstehen; **I ~d having to tell her** ich fand es grässlich, ihr das sagen zu müssen

**loathing** /'ləʊðɪŋ/ *n.* Abscheu, *der* (**of, for** vor + *Dat.*); **have a ~ of sth.** Abscheu vor etw. (*Dat.*) haben; etw. verabscheuen

**loathsome** /'ləʊðsəm/ *adj.* abscheulich; widerlich; verhasst ‹Tätigkeit, Pflicht›

**loaves** *pl. of* **loaf**[1]

**lob** /lɒb/ ❶ *v.t.,* **-bb-** in hohem Bogen werfen; (*Tennis*) lobben. ❷ *n.* (*Tennis*) Lob, *der*

**lobby** /'lɒbɪ/ ❶ *n.* Ⓐ (*pressure group*) Lobby, *die;* Interessenvertretung, *die;* Ⓑ (*of hotel*) Eingangshalle, *die;* (*of theatre*) Foyer, *das;* (*anteroom*) (*narrow*) Flur, *der;* (*larger*) Vorraum, *der;* Ⓒ (*esp. Brit. Parl.: hall*) Lobby, *die;* Wandelhalle, *die.* ❷ *v.t.* (*als Lobby*) zu beeinflussen suchen ‹Abgeordnete›. ❸ *v.i.* (*als Lobby*) seinen Einfluss geltend machen; **~ for/against sth.** (*als Lobby*) sich für etw. einsetzen/gegen etw. wenden

**lobbyist** /'lɒbɪɪst/ *n.* Lobbyist, *der*/Lobbyistin, *die*

**lobe** /ləʊb/ *n.* (*ear~*) Ohrläppchen, *das;* (*of liver, lung, brain*) Lappen, *der;* Lobus, *der* (*fachspr.*); (*of leaf*) Ausbuchtung, *die*

**lobed** /ləʊbd/ *adj.* gelappt

**lobelia** /lə'bi:lɪə/ *n.* (*Bot.*) Lobelie, *die*

**lobotomy** /ləʊ'bɒtəmɪ/ ⇒ **leucotomy**

**lobster** /'lɒbstə(r)/ *n.* Hummer, *der*

**'lobster pot** *n.* Hummerkorb, *der*

**local** /'ləʊkl/ ❶ *adj.* Ⓐ lokal (*bes. Zeitungsw.*); Lokal‹teil, -nachrichten, -sender›; Kommunal‹politiker, -wahl, -abgaben›; (*of this area*) hiesig; (*of that area*) dortig; ortsansässig ‹Firma, Familie›; ‹Wein, Produkt, Spezialität› [aus]

l

der Gegend; (*Bot.*) örtlich begrenzt [vorkommend]; lokal [verbreitet]; ~ **knowledge** Ortskenntnis, *die;* **go into your ~ branch** gehen Sie zu Ihrer Filiale; **our ~ hairdresser** der Friseur bei uns in der Nähe/(*in village*) bei uns im Dorf; **she's a ~ girl** sie ist von hier/dort; ~ **resident** Anwohner, *der*/Anwohnerin, *die;* ~ **bus** hiesiger/dortiger Bus; (*serving immediate area*) Nahverkehrsbus, *der;* **your ~ candidate** der Kandidat Ihres Wahlkreises; ~ **opinion** die Meinung der unmittelbar betroffenen Bevölkerung; B (*Med.*) lokal ‹Schmerzen, Entzündung›; örtlich ‹Betäubung›; C (*Post*) innerstädtisch ‹Briefzustellung, Post›.

**2** *n.* A (*inhabitant*) Einheimische, *der/die;* B (*Brit. coll.: pub*) [Stamm]kneipe, *die*

**local:** ~ **anaes'thetic** *n.* Lokalanästhetikum, *das* (*Med.*); **[be treated] under a ~ anaesthetic** unter örtlicher Betäubung *od.* (*Med.*) Lokalanästhesie [behandelt werden]; ~ **au'thority** *n.* (*Brit.*) Kommunalverwaltung, *die; attrib.* kommunal; ~ **call** *n.* (*Teleph.*) Ortsgespräch, *das;* Nahbereichsgespräch, *das* (*Postw.*); ~ **'colour** ⇒ **colour** 1 G; ~ **'Derby** ⇒ **Derby** A

**locale** /ləʊ'kɑːl/ *n.* Ort, *der;* (*of crime etc.*) Schauplatz, *der*

**local 'government** *n.* Kommunalverwaltung, *die;* ~ **elections/officials** Kommunalwahlen/-beamte

**localise** ⇒ **localize**

**locality** /lə'kælɪtɪ/ *n.* A (*position*) (*of thing*) Position [im Raum]; (*of person*) Aufenthaltsort, *der;* (*of mineral*) Vorkommen, *das;* B (*district*) Ort, *der;* Gegend, *die*

**localize** /'ləʊkəlaɪz/ *v.t.* A (*restrict*) eingrenzen (**to** auf + *Akk.*); lokalisieren (*bes. Politik, Med.*); B (*decentralize*) lokalisieren

**locally** /'ləʊkəlɪ/ *adv.* im/am Ort; in der Gegend

**'local time** *n.* Ortszeit, *die;* **[it's] 3 p.m. ~:** [es ist] 15 Uhr Ortszeit

**locate** /lə'keɪt/ *v.t.* A (*position*) platzieren; **be ~d** liegen; gelegen sein; **the factory is to be ~d on the edge of the town** die Fabrik soll am Stadtrand errichtet werden; B (*determine position of*) ausfindig machen; lokalisieren (*fachspr.*); orten (*Flugw., Seew.*)

**location** /lə'keɪʃn/ *n.* A (*position*) Lage, *die;* (*place*) Ort, *der;* (*of ship, aircraft, police car*) Position, *die;* (*of person, building, etc.*) Standort, *der;* **discover the ~ of sth.** etw. ausfindig machen; B (*positioning*) Positionierung, *die;* C (*determination of position of*) Lokalisierung, *die;* **succeed in the ~ of the buried treasure** den vergrabenen Schatz ausfindig machen; D (*Cinemat.*) Drehort, *der;* **be on ~:** bei Außenaufnahmen sein; **shoot on ~:** Außenaufnahmen drehen; E (*S. Afr.*) [Bantu]siedlung, *die*

**loc. cit.** /lɒk 'sɪt/ *abbr.* **in the passage already quoted** loc. cit.; a. a. O.

**loch** /lɒx, lɒk/ *n.* (*Scot.*) See, *der;* (*in Scotland*) Loch, *der;* (*arm of sea*) Meeresarm, *der;* (*in Scotland*) Loch, *der*

**Loch Ness** /lɒx 'nes, lɒk 'nes/ *pr. n.* Loch Ness (*der*); ~ **monster** Ungeheuer von Loch Ness

**lock¹** /lɒk/ *n.* A (*tress of hair*) [Haar]büschel, *das;* [Haar]strähne, *die;* (*ringlet*) Locke, *die;* B *in pl.* (*hair*) Haar, *das;* C (*of wool, cotton, etc.*) Flocke, *die*

**lock²** **1** *n.* A (*of door etc.*) Schloss, *das;* **under ~ and key** unter [strengem] Verschluss; B (*on canal etc.*) Schleuse, *die;* C (*on wheel*) Sperrvorrichtung, *die;* Sperre, *die;* D (*Wrestling*) Fesselgriff, *der;* Klammergriff, *der;* E (*of gun*) Schloss, *das;* **~, stock, and barrel** (*fig.*) mit allem Drum und Dran (*ugs.*); **condemn sth. ~, stock, and barrel** (*fig.*) etw. in Bausch und Bogen verurteilen; F (*Motor Veh.*) Lenkeinschlag, *der;* **full [left/right] ~:** voller Lenk[rad]einschlag [nach links/rechts]; G (*Rugby*) ~ **[forward]** Gedrängespieler in der zweiten Reihe; H ⇒ **airlock** B.

**2** *v.t.* A (*fasten*) zuschließen; abschließen; ~ *or* **shut the stable door after the horse has bolted** (*fig.*) den Brunnen erst zudecken, wenn das Kind hineingefallen ist; B (*shut*) ~ **sb./sth. in sth.** jmdn./etw. in etw. (*Akk.*) [ein]schließen; ~ **sb./sth. out of sth.** jmdn./etw. aus etw. aussperren; C (*Mech. Engin.: engage*) befestigen (**in** in + *Dat.*); D *in p.p.* (*joined*) **the wrestlers were ~ed in combat** die Ringer hielten sich im Fesselgriff; **the lovers were ~ed in an embrace** die Liebenden hielten sich fest umschlungen. ⇒ *also* **horn** 1 A.

**3** *v.i.* ‹Tür, Kasten usw.:› sich ab-/zuschließen lassen

~ **a'way** *v.t.* einschließen; wegschließen; einsperren ‹Person, Tier›; **he ought to be ~ed away** er gehört hinter Schloss und Riegel

~ **'in** *v.t.* einschließen; (*deliberately*) einsperren ‹Person, Tier›

~ **'on to** *v.t.* A ‹Rakete:› erfassen ‹Ziel›; B ‹Teleskop:› sich einstellen auf (+ *Akk.*) ‹Objekt›

~ **'out** *v.t.* A aussperren; ~ **oneself out** sich aussperren; B (*Industry*) aussperren ‹Arbeiter›; ⇒ *also* **lockout**

~ **'up** **1** *v.i.* abschließen. **2** *v.t.* A abschließen ‹Haus, Tür›; B (*imprison*) einsperren; **he ought to be ~ed up** er gehört hinter Schloss und Riegel; C (*store inaccessibly*) binden ‹Kapital›; (*fig.*) unterdrücken ‹Gefühle›; ~ **sth. up in one's heart** (*fig.*) etw. ganz für sich behalten. ⇒ *also* **lock-up**

**locker** /'lɒkə(r)/ *n.* A Schließfach, *das;* B (*Naut.*) Schapp, *das od. der* (*Seemannsspr.*)

**'locker room** *n.* Umkleideraum, *der*

**locket** /'lɒkɪt/ *n.* Medaillon, *das*

**lock:** ~ **gate** *n.* Schleusentor, *das;* **~jaw** *n.* (*Med.*) Kieferklemme, *die;* (*disease*) Wundstarrkrampf, *der;* **~-keeper** *n.* Schleusenwärter, *der;* **~nut** *n.* (*Mech.*) Kontermutter, *die;* **~out** *n.* Aussperrung, *die;* **~smith** *n.* ▶ **1261** Schlosser, *der;* ~ **stitch** **1** *n.* Doppelsteppstich, *der;* **2** *v.t. & i.* steppen; **~-up** **1** *n.* A (*closing time*) Toresschluss, *der;* B (*jail*) Gewahrsam, *das* (*veralt.*); **2** *adj.* A (*Brit.*) **~-up shop/garage** *Laden in einem Gebäude, in dem der Inhaber nicht wohnt/nicht unmittelbar bei der Wohnung gelegene Garage;* B **~-up time** Toresschluss, *der*

**locomotion** /ləʊkə'məʊʃn/ *n.* Fortbewegung, *die;* Lokomotion, *die* (*fachspr.*)

**locomotive** /'ləʊkəməʊtɪv, ləʊkə'məʊtɪv/ **1** *n.* Lokomotive, *die.* **2** *adj.* A (*of locomotion*) lokomotorisch (*fachspr.*); B (*not stationary*) fahrbar ‹Kran›; ~ **engine** Lokomotive, *die*

**locum** /'ləʊkəm/ *n.* (*coll.*), **locum tenens** /ləʊkəm 'tenenz/ *n., pl.* ~ **tenentes** /ləʊkəm te'nentiːz/ [Stell]vertreter, *der*/-vertreterin, *die*

**locus** /'ləʊkəs/ *n., pl.* **loci** /'ləʊsaɪ/ A (*Math.*) geometrischer Ort; B (*Biol.*) Genort, *der*

**locust** /'ləʊkəst/ *n.* A [Wander]heuschrecke, *die;* B (*Amer.: cicada*) Zikade, *die;* C (*Bot.*) ~ **[bean]** Johannisbrot, *das;* ~ **[tree]** (*carob tree*) Johannisbrotbaum, *der;* (*false acacia*) Robinie, *die;* Scheinakazie, *die*

**locution** /lə'kjuːʃn/ *n.* Lokution, *die* (*geh.*); (*style*) Ausdrucksweise, *die;* (*idiom*) Ausdruck, *der;* Redewendung, *die*

**lode** /ləʊd/ *n.* (*Min.*) Erzgang, *der*

**loden** /'ləʊdn/ *n.* (*cloth*) Loden, *der*

**lode:** **~star** *n.* Leitstern, *der;* (*esp.*) Polarstern, *der;* (*fig.*) Leitbild, *das;* **~stone** ⇒ **loadstone**

**lodge** /lɒdʒ/ **1** *n.* A (*servant's cottage*) Pförtner-/Gärtnerhaus, *das;* (*Sport*) [Jagd-/Ski]hütte, *die;* (*hotel*) Hotel, *das;* B (*porter's room*) [Pförtner]loge, *die;* (*at gate of school etc.*) Pedellloge, *die;* C (*Freemasonry*) Loge, *die;* **grand ~:** Großloge, *die;* D (*lair*) Bau, *der;* E (*of trade union*) Ortsgruppe, *die.*

**2** *v.t.* A (*deposit formally*) einlegen ‹Beschwerde, Protest, Berufung usw.›; (*bring forward*) erheben ‹Einspruch, Protest›; einreichen ‹Klage›; ~ **information against sb.** jmdn. anzeigen; B (*house*) unterbringen; (*receive as guest*) beherbergen; bei sich unterbringen; (*establish as resident*) einquartieren; C (*leave*) ~ **sth. with sb./in a bank** *etc.* etw. bei jmdm./in einer Bank *usw.* hinterlegen *od.* deponieren; D ~ **power** *etc.* **in the hands of** *or* **with sb.** jmdm. Macht *od.* Befugnis[se] *usw.* übertragen; E (*put, fix*) stecken; [hinein]stoßen ‹Schwert, Messer usw.›; **be ~d in sth.** in etw. (*Dat.*) stecken; **become ~d in sth.** ‹Kugel, Messer:› stecken bleiben in etw. (*Dat.*); **the idea became ~d in his mind** der Gedanke setzte sich in ihm fest. **3** *v.i.* A (*be paying guest*) [zur Miete] wohnen; B (*enter and remain*) stecken bleiben (**in** in + *Dat.*); hängen bleiben (**on** an + *Dat.*); ~ **in sb.'s memory** jmdm. im Gedächtnis bleiben; C (*reside*) wohnen; (*pass the night*) übernachten; nächtigen (*geh.*)

**lodger** /'lɒdʒə(r)/ *n.* Untermieter, *der*/Untermieterin, *die;* ⇒ *also* **take in d**

**lodging** /'lɒdʒɪŋ/ *n.* A *usu. in pl.* (*rented room*) [möbliertes] Zimmer; B (*accommodation*) Unterkunft, *die;* **board** *or* **food and ~:** Unterkunft und Verpflegung; Kost und Logis

**'lodging house** *n.* Pension, *die*

**loess** /'ləʊes/ *n.* (*Geol.*) Löss, *der*

**loft** /lɒft/ **1** *n.* A (*attic*) [Dach]boden, *der;* (*Amer.: room*) Dachzimmer, *das;* ~ **conversion** Dachausbau, *der;* B (*over stable*) Heuboden, *der;* C (*pigeon house*) Taubenschlag, *der;* D (*gallery in church*) Empore, *die.* **2** *v.t.* (*Sport*) hochspielen ‹Ball›; ~ **a ball over sth.** einen Ball über etw. (*Akk.*) heben

**loftily** /'lɒftɪlɪ/ *adv.* A (*grandiosely*) feierlich ‹schreiben, sprechen›; B (*haughtily*) hochmütig; überheblich

**lofty** /'lɒftɪ/ *adj.* A (*exalted, grandiose*) hoch; hehr (*geh.*); hochfliegend ‹Ideen›; hoch gesteckt ‹Ziele›; (*fig.: elevated*) feierlich ‹Stil›; B (*high*) hoch [aufragend]; hoch ‹Flug, Raum›; C (*haughty*) hochmütig; überheblich

**log¹** /lɒg/ **1** *n.* A (*rough piece of timber*) [geschlagener] Baumstamm; (*part of tree trunk*) Klotz, *der;* (*as cut for firewood*) [Holz]scheit, *das;* **be as easy as falling off a ~:** kinderleicht sein; **sleep like a ~:** schlafen wie ein Klotz; B **~[book]** Tagebuch, *das;* (*Naut.*) Logbuch, *das;* (*Aeronaut.*) Bordbuch, *das;* C (*Naut.: float etc.*) Log, *das.* **2** *v.t.,* **-gg-:** A (*record*) Buch führen über (*Akk.*); (*Naut.*) ins Logbuch eintragen; B (*achieve*) verbuchen

~ **'in** ⇒ ~ **on**

~ **'off** *v.i.* (*Computing*) sich abmelden

~ **'on** *v.i.* (*Computing*) sich anmelden

~ **'out** ⇒ ~ **off**

**log²** *n.* (*Math.*) Logarithmus, *der*

**loganberry** /'ləʊgnberɪ/ *n.* Loganbeere, *die*

**logarithm** /'lɒgərɪðm/ *n.* (*Math.*) Logarithmus, *der*

**logarithmic** /lɒgə'rɪðmɪk/ *adj.* (*Math.*) logarithmisch

**log:** **~book** *n.* A (*Brit.: of car*) Zulassung, *die;* B ⇒ **log¹** 1 B; ~ **'cabin** *n.* Blockhütte, *die;* ~ **'fire** *n.* Holzfeuer, *das*

**loggerheads** /'lɒgəhedz/ *n. pl.* **be at ~ with sb.** mit jmdm. im Clinch liegen; **they were constantly at ~:** sie lagen ständig miteinander im Clinch

**loggia** /'ləʊdʒjə, 'lɒdʒjə/ *n.* Loggia, *die*

**logging** /'lɒgɪŋ/ *n., no pl., no indef. art.* Holzeinschlag, *der* (*Forstw.*)

**logic** /'lɒdʒɪk/ *n.* Logik, *die*

**logical** /'lɒdʒɪkl/ *adj.* A logisch; **she has a ~ mind** sie denkt logisch; B (*clear-thinking*) logisch denkend; klar denkend

**logicality** /lɒdʒɪ'kælɪtɪ/ *n.* Logik, *die*

**logically** /'lɒdʒɪkəlɪ/ *adv.* logisch

**logical 'positivism** *n.* (*Philos.*) logischer Empirismus

**logician** /lə'dʒɪʃn/ *n.* (*Philos.*) Logiker, *der*/Logikerin, *die*

**logistic** /lə'dʒɪstɪk/ *adj.,* **logistically** /lə'dʒɪstɪklɪ/ *adv.* logistisch

**logistics** /lə'dʒɪstɪks/ *n. pl.* Logistik, *die*

**'logjam** *n. Stau von treibendem Holz/Flößholz;* **the talks failed to move** *or* **break the ~** (*fig.*) die Gespräche haben keinen Durchbruch gebracht

**logo** /'lɒgəʊ, 'ləʊgəʊ/ *n., pl.* **~s** Signet, *das;* Logo, *das*

**'log tables** *n. pl.* Logarithmentafeln

**loin** /lɔɪn/ *n.* A *in pl.* (*Anat.*) Lende, *die;* ⇒ *also* **gird up;** B (*meat*) Lende, *die*

**'loincloth** *n.* Lendenschurz, *der*

**loiter** /'lɔɪtə(r)/ *v.i.* trödeln; bummeln; (*linger suspiciously*) herumlungern; **~ with intent** sich mit gesetzwidriger Absicht herumtreiben

**~ a'way** *v.t.* vertrödeln ‹Zeit›

**loiterer** /'lɔɪtərə(r)/ *n.* Herumtreiber, *der;* Herumlungerer, *der* (*salopp*)

**loll** /lɒl/ *v.i.* **A** (*lounge*) sich lümmeln (*ugs. abwertend*); **don't ~!** lümmel dich nicht so!; **B** (*droop*) ‹Zunge:› heraushängen; ‹Kopf:› hängen

**~ a'bout, ~ a'round** *v.i.* sich herumlümmeln (*ugs. abwertend*)

**lollipop** /'lɒlɪpɒp/ *n.* Lutscher, *der*

**lollipop: ~ man/woman** *ns.* ▶ 1261 (*Brit. coll.*) *Mann/Frau in der Funktion eines Schülerlotsen*

**lollop** /'lɒləp/ *v.i.* (*coll.*) (*bob up and down*) ‹Kaninchen usw.:› hoppeln; (*proceed by clumsy bounds*) zotteln (*ugs.*); trotten

**lolly** /'lɒlɪ/ *n.* **A** (*Brit. coll.: lollipop*) Lutscher, *der;* **ice[d] ~:** Eis am Stiel; **B** *no pl., no indef. art.* (*coll.: money*) Kohle, *die* (*salopp*)

**Lombardy** /'lɒmbədɪ/ *pr. n.* Lombardei, *die;* **~ poplar** (*Bot.*) Pyramidenpappel, *die*

**London** /'lʌndən/ ▶ 1626 **1** *pr. n.* London (*das*). **2** *attrib. adj.* Londoner

**Londoner** /'lʌndənə(r)/ *pr. n.* ▶ 1626 Londoner, *der*/Londonerin, *die*

**lone** /ləʊn/ *attrib. adj.* **A** (*poet./rhet.: solitary*) einsam; **B** (*lonesome*) einsam; **C** **~ hand** (*Cards: player*) Einzelspieler, *der*/-spielerin, *die;* **play *or* hold a ~ hand** allein spielen; **play a ~ hand** (*fig.*) einen Alleingang machen

**loneliness** /'ləʊnlɪnɪs/ *n., no pl.* Einsamkeit, *die;* (*remoteness*) Abgeschiedenheit, *die*

**lonely** /'ləʊnlɪ/ *adj.* einsam; (*remote*) abgeschieden; **~ heart** einsames Herz

**lone 'parent** *n.* allein erziehender Elternteil; Alleinerziehende, *der/die;* **she/he is a ~:** sie/er ist allein erziehend

**loner** /'ləʊnə(r)/ *n.* Einzelgänger, *der*/-gängerin, *die*

**lonesome** /'ləʊnsəm/ *adj.* einsam; **by *or* on one's ~:** ganz allein

**lone 'wolf** *n.* (*fig.*) Einzelgänger, *der*/-gängerin, *die*

**long**[1] /lɒŋ/ **1** *adj.*, **~er** /'lɒŋgə(r)/, **~est** /'lɒŋgɪst/ **A** ▶ 1284 lang; weit ‹Reise, Weg›; **be ~ in the tooth** nicht mehr der/die Jüngste sein; **she's getting a bit ~ in the tooth for that** dafür ist sie allmählich vielleicht doch etwas zu alt; **in two days at the ~est** in spätestens zwei Tagen; **it will take two hours at the ~est** es wird höchstens zwei Stunden dauern; **take a ~ view of sth.** etw. auf lange *od.* weite Sicht sehen; **two inches/weeks ~:** zwei Zoll/Wochen lang; ⇒ *also* **law** K; **way** 1 E; **B** (*elongated*) länglich; schmal; **pull *or* make a ~ face** (*fig.*) ein langes Gesicht ziehen *od.* machen (*ugs.*); **C** (*of extended duration*) lang; **~ service** (*esp. Mil.*) langjähriger Dienst; **in the '~ run** auf die Dauer; auf lange Sicht; **in the '~ term** auf lange Sicht; langfristig; **for a '~ time** lange; (*still continuing*) seit langem; **what a ~ time you've been away!** du warst aber lange [Zeit] fort!; **~ time no see!** (*coll.*) lange nicht gesehen! (*ugs.*); **D** (*tediously lengthy*) lang[atmig]; weitschweifig; **E** (*lasting*) lang; langjährig ‹Gewohnheit, Freundschaft›; alt ‹Brauch, Gewohnheit›; **F** klein, gering ‹Chance›; **it would be a ~ chance that …:** es ist ziemlich unwahrscheinlich, dass …; **G** (*seemingly more than stated*) lang ‹Minute, Tag, Jahre usw.›; **H** (*coll.: tall*) lang (*ugs.*) ‹Person›; hoch ‹Fenster›; **I** lang ‹Gedächtnis›; **have a ~ memory for sth.** etw. nicht so schnell vergessen; **J** *qualifying number or measure:* **~ dozen** dreizehn [Stück]; **~ hundred** hundertzwanzig [Stück]; Großhundert, *das* (*veralt.*); **~ hundredweight** englischer Zentner; **~ ton** Longton, *die;* **K** (*consisting of many items*) lang ‹Liste usw.›; hoch ‹Zahl›; **L** (*Phonet., Pros.*) lang; **M** (*Cards*) **~ suit** lange Farbe; **be sb.'s ~ suit** (*fig.*) jmds. Stärke sein; **N** **be ~ on sth.** (*coll.*) ein Ausbund an etw. (*Dat.*) sein (*ugs.*).

**2** *n.* **A** (*long interval*) **take ~:** lange dauern; **for ~:** lange; (*since ~ ago*) seit langem; **before ~:** bald; **it is ~ since …:** es ist lange her, dass …; **B** **the ~ and the short of it is …:** der langen Rede kurzer Sinn ist …

**3** *adv.*, **~er, ~est** **A** lang[e]; **as *or* so ~ as** so lange wie; ⇒ *also* **B**; **the shop hasn't ~ been open** den Laden gibt es noch nicht lange; **you should have finished ~ before now** du hättest schon längst *od.* viel früher fertig sein sollen; **I knew her ~ before I met you** ich kenne sie schon viel länger als dich; **not ~ before that** kurz davor *od.* zuvor; **not ~ before I …:** kurz bevor ich …; **~ since** [schon] seit langem; **all day/night/summer ~:** den ganzen Tag/die ganze Nacht/den ganzen Sommer [über *od.* lang]; **a quiet resort, ~ the gathering place of …:** ein ruhiger Ferienort, lange/(*still continuing*) schon lange Versammlungsort von …; **not be ~ for this world** nicht mehr lange zu leben haben; **I shan't be ~:** ich bin gleich fertig; (*departing*) bis gleich!; **don't be ~!** beeil dich!; **don't be ~ about [doing] it!** lass dir nicht zu viel Zeit damit!; **sb. is ~ [in *or* about doing sth.]** jmd. braucht lange *od.* viel Zeit[, um etw. zu tun]; **the opportunity was not ~ in coming** es dauerte nicht lange, bis sich die Gelegenheit bot; **much ~er** viel länger; **not wait any/much ~er** nicht mehr länger/viel länger warten; **no ~er** nicht mehr; nicht länger ‹warten usw.›; **we no ~er had any hope** wir hatten keine Hoffnung mehr; **play can't go on much ~er** das Spiel muss bald abgebrochen werden; **how much ~er is he going to sleep?** wie lange schläft er denn noch?; ⇒ *also* **ago**; **so**[1] 1 A; **B** **as *or* so ~ as** (*provided that*) solange; wenn

**long**[2] *v.i.* **~ for sb./sth.** sich nach jmdm./etw. sehnen; **~ for the end of sth./for the summer to come** das Ende einer Sache/den Sommer herbeisehnen; **~ for sb. to do sth.** sich (*Dat.*) [sehr] wünschen, dass jmd. etw. tut; **I ~ for you to come home** ich warte sehnsüchtig darauf, dass du nach Hause kommst; **~ to do sth.** sich danach sehnen, etw. zu tun; **he ~ed to ask his mother the meaning of it** es drängte ihn, seine Mutter zu fragen, was das bedeutete; **[much] ~ed-for** [lang] ersehnt

**long.** *abbr.* **longitude** Lg.

**long: ~ ago** **1** *n.* längst vergangene Zeit[en]; **2** *adj.* längst vergangen; **~boat** *n.* Barkasse, *die;* Langboot, *das;* **~bow** *n.* (*Mil.*) Langbogen, *der;* **~-case 'clock** *n.* Standuhr, *die;* **~-dated** *adj.* (*Finance*) langfristig; **~-distance** **1** /'---/ *adj.* Fern‹gespräch, -verkehr usw.›; Langstrecken‹lauf, -läufer, -flug usw.›; **~-distance coach** Reise- *od.* Überlandbus, *der;* **~-distance lorry driver** ▶ 1261 Fern[last-]fahrer, *der;* **2** /-'--/ *adv.* **phone ~-distance** ein Ferngespräch führen; **~ division** ⇒ **division** G; **~-drawn[-out]** *adj.* lang gezogen ‹Schrei, Ton›; langatmig ‹Erklärung, Diskussion›; ausgedehnt ‹Wanderung›; **~ drink** *n.* Longdrink, *der*

**longevity** /lɒn'dʒevɪtɪ/ *n., no pl.* Langlebigkeit, *die*

**long: ~-forgotten** *adj.* längst vergessen; **~-haired** *adj.* langhaarig; Langhaar‹dackel, -katze›; **~hand** *n.* Langschrift, *die;* **~ haul** *n.* Langstreckentransport, *der;* [Güter]ferntransport, *der;* **it's a ~ haul** das ist ein weiter Weg; **~-haul** *adj.* Fern‹verkehr, -lastwagen›; Langstrecken‹[flug]verkehr›; Fernverkehrs‹bus, -verbindung›; **~ hop** *n.* (*Cricket*) *kurz aufgesetzter und dann weit fliegender Ball;* **~horn** *n.* **A** (*cattle*) Longhorn, *das;* **B** (*beetle*) Bockkäfer, *der*

**longing** /'lɒŋɪŋ/ **1** *n.* Verlangen, *das;* Sehnsucht, *die;* (*craving*) Gelüst, *das* (*geh.*); **I had a sudden ~ for a cigarette** ich hatte plötzlich Lust auf eine Zigarette. **2** *adj.* sehnsüchtig

**longingly** /'lɒŋɪŋlɪ/ *adv.* voll Sehnsucht; sehnsüchtig

**longish** /'lɒŋɪʃ/ *adj.* ziemlich lang

**longitude** /'lɒndʒɪtju:d, 'lɒŋgɪtju:d/ *n.* **A** (*Geog.*) [geographische] Länge; (*of a place*) Länge, *die;* **~ 40° E** 40° östlicher Länge; **B** (*Astron.*) Länge, *die*

**longitudinal** /lɒndʒɪ'tju:dɪnl, lɒŋgɪ'tju:dɪnl/ *adj.* **A** Längen‹ausdehnung, -messung›; **B** (*running lengthwise*) längs gerichtet; **~ stripe** Längsstreifen, *der;* **C** **~ wave** (*Phys.*) Longitudinalwelle, *die*

**long: ~ johns** *n. pl.* (*coll.*) lange Unterhosen; **~ jump** *n.* (*Brit. Sport*) Weitsprung, *der;* **~-lasting** *adj.* lang andauernd; anhaltend ‹Niederschläge, Schneefälle usw.›; dauerhaft ‹Beziehung, Freundschaft›; **~-legged** *adj.* langbeinig; **~ 'lens** *n.* (*Photog.*) Fernobjektiv, *das;* **~-life** *adj.* haltbar [gemacht]; **~-life battery** Batterie mit langer Lebensdauer; **~-life milk** H-Milch, *die;* **~-lived** /'lɒŋlɪvd/ *adj.* (*durable*) andauernd; (*having long life*) langlebig; **be ~-lived** sehr alt werden; **a ~-lived family** eine Familie, in der alle sehr alt werden; **~ 'odds** *n. pl.* (*Racing, also fig.*) geringe Gewinnchancen; **~ 'player, ~-playing 'record** *ns.* Langspielplatte, *die;* **~-range** *adj.* **A** (*having a long range*) Langstrecken‹flugzeug, -rakete usw.›; ‹Geschütz› mit großer Reichweite; **B** (*relating to the future*) langfristig; **~-running** *adj.* anhaltend; Langzeit‹versuch›; wochen-/monate-/jahrelang ‹Debatte, Streit usw.›; lange laufend ‹Theaterstück›; **~ ship** *n.* (*Hist.*) Wikingerschiff, *das;* **~shoreman** /'lɒŋʃɔ:mən/ *n., pl.* **~shoremen** /'lɒŋʃɔ:mən/ *n.* Schauermann, *der;* **~ shot** *n.* **A** (*wild guess*) reine Spekulation; **B** (*bet at long odds*) gewagter Versuch; **C** (*Cinemat.*) Fernaufnahme, *die;* **D** **not by a ~ shot** bei weitem nicht; **~ 'sight** *n.* Weitsichtigkeit, *die;* **have ~ sight** weitsichtig sein; **~-sighted** *adj.* weitsichtig; (*fig.*) weitblickend; vorausschauend; **~-sleeved** /'lɒŋsli:vd/ *adj.* langärmelig; **~-standing** *attrib. adj.* seit langem bestehend; langjährig ‹Freundschaft usw.›; alt ‹Schulden, Rechnung, Streit›; **~stop** *n.* (*fig.*) Notnagel, *der;* **~-suffering** *adj.* schwer geprüft; (*meek*) geduldig; **~-term** *adj.* langfristig; **~-time** *adj.* seit langem bestehend; alt ‹Zwist, Freund›; **~ va'cation** *n.* (*Brit.*) Sommer[semester]ferien *Pl.;* (*Law*) Sommerpause, *die;* **~ wave** *n.* (*Radio*) Langwelle, *die;* **~-wave** *adj.* (*Radio*) Langwellen-; **~ways** *adv.* längs; in Längsrichtung; **~-winded** /lɒŋ'wɪndɪd/ *adj.* langatmig; weitschweifig

**loo** /lu:/ *n.* (*Brit. coll.*) Klo, *das* (*ugs. fam.*) **go to/be on the ~:** aufs Klo gehen/auf dem Klo sein

**loofah** /'lu:fə/ *n.* **A** (*sponge*) Luffaschwamm, *der;* **B** (*Bot.*) Luffa, *die*

**look** /lʊk/ **1** *v.i.* **A** sehen; gucken (*ugs.*); schauen (*bes. südd., sonst geh.*); **~ down at one's feet** zu Boden blicken; **don't ~ now, but …:** sieh jetzt nicht hin, aber …; **~ before you leap** (*prov.*) erst wägen, dann wagen (*Spr.*); **~ the other way** (*fig.*) die Augen verschließen; **not know which way to ~:** nicht wissen, wohin man sehen soll; **as quick *or* soon as ~ [at you]** (*coll.: very readily*) ohne zu zögern; ⇒ *also* **eye** 1 A; **B** (*search*) nachsehen; **C** (*face*) zugewandt sein (**to[wards]** *Dat.*); **the windows ~ north** die Fenster liegen *od.* gehen nach Norden; **the room ~s on to the road/into the garden** das Zimmer liegt zur Straße/zum Garten hin *od.* geht zur Straße/zum Garten; **D** (*appear*) aussehen; **~ as if** [so] aussehen, als ob; **~ well/ill** gut *od.* gesund/schlecht *od.* krank aussehen; **~ like** aussehen wie; **it ~s like rain** es sieht nach Regen aus; **he ~s like winning** es sieht so aus, als ob er gewinnt; **make sb. ~ small** jmdn. herabsetzen; jmdn. heruntermachen (*salopp*); ⇒ *also* **alive** D; **black** 1 D; **fool**[1] 1 A; **E** (*seem to be*) **she ~s her age/her 40 years** man sieht ihr ihr Alter/die 40 Jahre an; **you ~ yourself again** es scheint dir wieder gut zu gehen; **you don't ~ yourself** du siehst schlecht aus; **~ the part** (*lit. or fig.*) so aussehen; **she ~ed the part to perfection** sie war für die Rolle wie geschaffen; **F** (*inquire*) **you haven't ~ed deep enough into it** du hast dich nicht eingehend genug damit befasst; **~ [here]!** (*demanding attention*) hören Sie/hör zu; (*protesting*) passen Sie/pass ja *od.*

bloß auf!; ~ **sharp [about sth.]** (*hurry up*) sich [mit etw.] beeilen; ~ **inwards** in sich (*Akk.*) hineinblicken; nach innen blicken; [G] (*take care, make sure*) ~ **that ...:** dafür sorgen *od.* zusehen *od.* darauf achten, dass ...; ~ **to do sth.** (*expect*) erwarten *od.* hoffen, etw. zu tun.
❷ *v.t.* [A] (*ascertain by sight*) nachsehen; *in exclamation of surprise etc.* sich (*Dat.*) ansehen; ~ **what you've done!** sieh [dir mal an], was du getan *od.* angerichtet hast!; ~ **who's here!** sieh mal, wer da *od.* gekommen ist!; [B] (*express by one's* ~*s*) ~ **a question at sb.** jmdn. fragend ansehen; **she** ~**ed her surprise** die Überraschung stand ihr im Gesicht geschrieben; ⇒ *also* **dagger** A.
❸ *n.* [A] Blick, *der;* **get a good** ~ **at sb.** jmdn. gut *od.* genau sehen [können]; **have** *or* **take a** ~ **at sb./sth.** sich (*Dat.*) jmdn./etw. ansehen; einen Blick auf jmdn./etw. werfen; **have a** ~ **at a town** sich (*Dat.*) eine Stadt ansehen; **let sb. have a** ~ **at sth.** jmdn. etw. sehen lassen; **if** ~**s could kill** wenn Blicke töten könnten; [B] *in sing. or pl.* (*person's appearance*) Aussehen, *das;* (*facial expression*) [Gesichts]ausdruck, *der;* **from** *or* **by the** ~**[s] of sb.** von jmds. Aussehen zu schließen; **good** ~**s** gutes Aussehen; **have good** ~**s** gut aussehen; **she's lost her** ~**s** sie hat ihre Schönheit verloren; **have a hungry** ~**:** hungrig aussehen; **have the** ~ **of an artist** wie ein Künstler aussehen; **put on a** ~ **of innocence** eine Unschuldsmiene aufsetzen; **there were angry** ~**s from them** sie guckten *od.* (*geh.*) blickten böse; ⇒ *also* **black** 1 F; [C] (*thing's appearance*) Aussehen, *das;* (*Fashion*) Look, *der;* **have a neglected** ~**:** verwahrlost aussehen; **from** *or* **by the** ~ **of the furniture** *etc.* [so] wie die Möbel *usw.* aussehen; **by the** ~**[s] of it** *or* **things** [so] wie es aussieht; **the house is empty, by the** ~ **of it** das Haus steht allem Anschein nach leer; **I don't like the** ~ **of this** das gefällt mir gar nicht; **the place has a European** ~**:** der Ort wirkt europäisch; **for the** ~ **of the thing** (*coll.*) um den Schein zu wahren

~ **a'bout** ❶ *v.t.* ~ **about a room** sich in einem Zimmer umsehen; ~ **about one** sich umsehen *od.* umschauen. ❷ *v.i.* [A] sich umsehen; ~ **about everywhere** (*search*) überall gucken; [B] (*be watchful*) sich vorsehen; ~ **about for sth.** sich nach etw. umsehen

~ **'after** *v.t.* [A] (*follow with one's eyes*) nachsehen (+ *Dat.*); [B] (*attend to*) sich kümmern um; [C] (*care for*) sorgen für; ~ **after oneself** allein zurechtkommen; für sich selbst sorgen; ~ **'after yourself!** pass auf dich auf!

~ **a'head** *v.i.* [A] nach vorne sehen; [B] (*fig.: plan for future*) an die Zukunft denken; vorausschauen; ~ **ahead five years/to next year** an die Zeit in fünf Jahren/an nächstes Jahr denken

~ **a'round** ⇒ ~ **about**

~ **at** *v.t.* [A] (*regard*) ansehen; ~ **at one's watch** auf seine Uhr sehen; ~ **directly at the light** direkt ins Licht sehen; **don't** ~ **at me like that!** sieh mich nicht so an!; **be pleasing to** ~ **at** [recht] nett aussehen; **be good/not much to** ~ **at** nach etwas/nach nichts *od.* nicht nach viel aussehen (*ugs.*); **to** ~ **at him, you'd think ...:** wenn man ihn so sieht, würde man meinen, ...; [B] (*examine*) sich (*Dat.*) ansehen; [C] (*consider*) betrachten; in Betracht ziehen ‹Angebot›; **that's the proper way to** ~ **at it** so muss man es sehen; **I wouldn't even** ~ **at such an offer** so ein Angebot wäre für mich völlig undiskutabel; **I can't** ~ **at any more caviare** ich kann Kaviar nicht mehr sehen

~ **a'way** *v.i.* weggucken (*ugs.*); wegsehen

~ **'back** *v.i.* [A] (*glance behind*) sich umsehen; sich umblicken (*geh.*); (*fig.: hesitate*) zurückschauen; **he's never** ~**ed back since then** seitdem läuft bei ihm alles bestens; [B] (*cast one's mind back*) ~ **back [up]on** *or* **to sth.** an etw. (*Akk.*) zurückdenken; auf etw. (*Akk.*) zurückblicken

~ **'down [up]on** *v.t.* [A] herunter-/hinuntersehen, (*ugs.*) runtergucken auf (+ *Akk.*); [B] (*fig.: despise*) herabsehen auf (+ *Akk.*)

~ **for** *v.t.* [A] (*expect*) erwarten; [B] (*seek*) suchen nach; auf der Suche sein nach ‹neuen Ideen›; ~ **for trouble** Streit suchen; (*unintentionally*) sich (*Dat.*) Ärger einhandeln

~ **'forward to** *v.t.* sich freuen auf (+ *Akk.*); ~ **forward to doing sth.** sich darauf freuen, etw. zu tun

~ **'in** *v.i.* [A] hin-/hereinsehen; (*visit*) vorbeikommen (**on** bei); vorbei- *od.* hereinschauen (**on** bei) (*bes. südd. ugs.*); ~ **in at the butcher's** beim Fleischer vorbeigehen; **the doctor** ~**ed in frequently** der Arzt kam häufig vorbei; **the nurse** ~**ed in on the patient every hour** die Schwester sah jede Stunde nach dem Patienten; [B] (*coll.: watch television*) fernsehen. ⇒ *also* **look-in**

~ **into** *v.t.* [A] sehen in (+ *Akk.*); [B] (*fig.: investigate*) [eingehend] untersuchen; unter die Lupe nehmen (*ugs.*); prüfen ‹Beschwerde›

~ **on** ❶ /-'-/ *v.i.* zusehen; zugucken (*ugs.*); ⇒ *also* **looker-on.** ❷ /'--/ *v.t.* ~ **on sb. as a hero** *etc.* jmdn. als Held[en] *usw.* betrachten; ~ **on sb. with distrust/suspicion** jmdn. mit Misstrauen/Argwohn betrachten

~ **'out** ❶ *v.i.* [A] hinaus-/heraussehen (**of** aus); rausgucken (*ugs.*); [B] (*take care*) aufpassen; [C] (*have view*) ~ **out on sth.** ‹Zimmer, Wohnung usw.:› zu etw. gehen (*ugs.*); zu etw. hin liegen; **the house** ~**s out over the river** von dem Haus hat man einen Blick auf den Fluss; **a room** ~**ing out on the green** ein Zimmer mit Blick auf die Wiese. ❷ *v.t.* (*Brit.: select*) [her]aussuchen. ⇒ *also* **lookout**

~ **'out for** *v.t.* (*be prepared for*) aufpassen *od.* achten auf (+ *Akk.*); sich in Acht nehmen vor (+ *Dat.*) ‹gefährliche Person, Sturm›; (*keep watching for*) Ausschau halten nach ‹Arbeit, Gelegenheit, Partner, Sammelobjekt usw.›

~ **'out of** *v.t.* sehen *od.* (*ugs.*) gucken aus

~ **'over** *v.t.* [A] sehen über (+ *Akk.*) ‹Mauer usw.›; überblicken ‹Tal usw.›; [B] (*survey*) inspizieren, sich (*Dat.*) ansehen ‹Haus, Anwesen›; [C] (*scrutinize*) mustern ‹Person›; durchsehen ‹Text›

~ **'round** *v.i.* sich umsehen; sich umgucken (*ugs.*); ~ **round in search of sth.** nach etw. Ausschau halten

~ **through** *v.t.* [A] ~ **through sth.** durch etw. [hindurch]sehen; [B] (*inspect*) durchsehen ‹Papiere›; prüfen ‹Antrag, Vorschlag, Aussage›; [C] (*glance through*) sich (*Dat.*) ansehen ‹Buch, Notizen›; [D] (*fig.: ignore deliberately*) ~ **straight 'through sb.** durch jmdn. hindurchsehen; jmdn. einfach übersehen; [E] (*penetrate*) durchschauen ‹Person, Verhaltensweise›

~ **to** *v.t.* [A] (*rely on, count upon*) ~ **to sb./sth. for sth.** etw. von jmdm./etw. erwarten; ~ **to sb./sth. to do sth.** von jmdm./etw. erwarten, dass er/es etw. tut; **we** ~ **to him for help/to help us** wir zählen auf seine *od.* rechnen mit seiner Hilfe/zählen darauf *od.* rechnen damit, dass er uns hilft; [B] (*be careful about*) sorgen für; (*keep watch upon*) aufpassen auf (+ *Akk.*); ~ **to it that ...:** zusehen *od.* dafür sorgen, dass ...; ~ **to your manners!** benimm dich! (*ugs.*); ⇒ *also* **laurel** A; [C] (*consider*) ~ **to sth.** etw. beachten; einer Sache (*Dat.*) Beachtung schenken; ~ **more to quality than to quantity** mehr auf Qualität als auf Quantität achten; [D] (*take care of*) sich kümmern um ‹Wunde, Kind usw.›

~ **towards** *v.t.* [A] sehen *od.* (*ugs.*) gucken nach/zu; [B] (*face*) **the balcony/room** ~**s towards the sea** der Balkon/das Zimmer liegt zum Meer hin; [C] (*consider*) ~ **towards the future** an die Zukunft denken; [D] (*hope for and expect*) sich (*Dat.*) erhoffen; [E] (*aim at*) abzielen auf (+ *Akk.*)

~ **'up** ❶ *v.i.* [A] aufblicken; ~ **up into the sky** in den Himmel [hinauf]blicken; [B] (*improve*) besser werden; ‹Aktien, Chancen:› steigen; **things are** ~**ing up** es geht bergauf; **business is** ~**ing up again** das Geschäft läuft wieder besser. ❷ *v.t.* [A] (*search for*) nachschlagen ‹Wort›; heraussuchen ‹Telefonnummer, Zugverbindung usw.›; [B] (*coll.: visit*) ~ **sb. up** bei jmdm. reingucken (*ugs.*); bei jmdm. vorbeischauen (*bes. südd. ugs.*); [C] ~ **sb. up and down** jmdn. von Kopf bis Fuß mustern

~ **upon** ⇒ ~ **on** 2

~ **'up to** *v.t.* ~ **up to sb.** (*lit. or fig.*) zu jmdm. aufschauen *od.* aufsehen

**'lookalike** *n.* Doppelgänger, *der*/-gängerin, *die;* **be** ~**s** wie Zwillinge aussehen

**looker** /'lʊkə(r)/ *n.* (*coll.: attractive woman*) gut aussehende Frau; **she's a** ~**:** sie sieht gut aus; ⇒ *also* **good-looker**

**looker-'on** *n.* Zuschauer, *der*/Zuschauerin, *die*

**'look-in** *n.* [A] (*visit*) kurzer Besuch; [B] (*opportunity*) Chance, *die;* **we didn't get a** ~**:** wir hatten überhaupt keine Chance

**-looking** /lʊkɪŋ/ *adj. in comb.* aussehend; **dirty-**~**:** schmutzig wirkend; **European-/oriental-**~**:** europäisch/orientalisch aussehend; ⇒ *also* **good-looking**

**'looking glass** *n.* Spiegel, *der*

**'lookout** *n., pl.* ~**s** [A] (*keeping watch*) (*Naut.*) Ausschauhalten, *das;* (*guard*) Wache, *die;* **keep a** ~ *or* **be on the** ~ **[for sth./sb.]** (*wanted*) [nach etw./jmdm.] Ausschau halten; (*not wanted*) [auf etw./jmdn.] aufpassen; [B] (*observation post*) Ausguck, *der;* Beobachtungsstand, *der;* (*crow's nest*) Krähennest, *das* (*Seemannsspr.*); Mastkorb, *der* (*Seemannsspr.*); (*belvedere*) Aussichtsturm, *der;* [C] (*person*) Wache, *die;* (*Mil.*) Wach[t]posten, *der;* Beobachtungsposten, *der;* (*scout, scouts*) Wachtposten, *der;* [D] (*view*) Ausblick, *der;* (*esp. Brit. fig.: prospect*) Aussichten; **that's a bad** ~**:** das sind schlechte Aussichten; **it's a poor/bleak** *etc.* ~ **for sb./sth.** es sieht schlecht/düster *usw.* aus für jmdn./etw.; [E] (*concern*) Sache, *die;* Problem, *das;* **that's his [own]** ~**:** das ist [allein] sein Problem *od.* seine Sache

**loom**[1] /lu:m/ *n.* (*Weaving*) Webstuhl, *der*

**loom**[2] *v.i.* auftauchen; (*as impending occurrence*) sich [bedrohlich] abzeichnen; ~ **large** [bedrohlich] auftauchen; (*fig.*) eine große Rolle spielen

~ **a'head** *v.i.* [A] auftauchen (**of** vor + *Dat.*); [B] ‹Prüfung:› unausweichlich bevorstehen (**of** *Dat.*); ‹Hindernis, Schwierigkeit, Problem:› sich [bedrohlich] abzeichnen (**of** für)

~ **'up** *v.i.* ~ **up [in front of sb.]** [unmittelbar] [vor jmdm.] auftauchen

**loon** /lu:n/ *n.* [A] (*crazy person*) Idiot, *der* (*ugs. abwertend*); [B] (*Ornith.*) [See]taucher, *der*

**loony** /'lu:nɪ/ (*coll.*) ❶ *n.* Verrückte, *der/die* (*ugs.*). ❷ *adj.* verrückt (*ugs.*); irr; **the** ~ **Left/Right** die hundertfünfzigprozentigen Linken/Rechten

**'loony bin** *n.* (*sl.*) Klapsmühle, *die* (*salopp*)

**loop** /lu:p/ ❶ *n.* [A] Schleife, *die;* [B] (*cord*) Schlaufe, *die;* [C] (*for lifting or fastening*) Schlaufe, *die;* (*eye*) Öse, *die;* ~ **aerial** *or* (*Amer.*) **antenna** Rahmenantenne, *die;* [D] (*contraceptive coil*) Spirale, *die.* ❷ *v.t.* [A] (*form into a loop*) zu einer Schlaufe/Öse formen; [B] (*enclose*) umschlingen; [C] (*fasten*) ~ **up/together** *etc.* mit einer Schlaufe hoch-/zusammenbinden *usw.;* [D] (*Aeronaut.*) ~ **the** ~**:** einen Looping fliegen; loopen (*fachspr.*)

**'loophole** *n.* [A] (*in wall*) Maueröffnung, *die;* (*for shooting through*) Schießscharte, *die;* [B] (*fig.*) Lücke, *die;* ~ **in the law** Gesetzeslücke, *die;* Lücke im Gesetz; **tax** ~**:** Lücke im Steuergesetz

**loopy** /'lu:pɪ/ *adj.* (*coll.*) verrückt (*ugs.*)

**loose** /lu:s/ ❶ *adj.* [A] (*unrestrained*) frei laufend ‹Tier›; (*escaped*) ausgebrochen; (*bolted*) durchgegangen ‹Pferd›; **he finally got one hand** ~**:** er bekam schließlich eine Hand frei; **run** *or* **be** ~**:** los sein; **set** *or* **turn** ~**:** freilassen; **cut the boat/dog** ~**:** das Boot/den Hund losschneiden; **cut** ~ **from sb.** (*fig.*) sich von jmdm. lösen; **cut** ~ (*coll.: behave wildly*) verrückt spielen (*ugs.*); ⇒ *also* **cast** 1 A; **fast**[2] 1 A; **let**[1] 1 A; [B] (*not firm*) locker ‹Zahn, Schraube, Mutter, Knopf, Messerklinge›; **come/get/work** ~ ‹Schraube, Mutter, Knoten, Knopf usw.:› sich lockern; ⇒ *also* **screw** 1 A; [C] (*not fixed*) lose ‹Knopf, Buchseite, Brett, Stein›; **the pages have come** ~**:** die Seiten haben sich gelöst; [D] (*not bound together*) lose; offen ‹Haar›; [E] (*slack*) locker; schlaff ‹Haut, Gewebe usw.›; beweglich ‹Glieder›; ~ **tongue** loses

Mundwerk (*salopp*); ~ **bowels** [Neigung zu] Durchfall; ~ **build** *or* **frame** schlaksige Gestalt; **F** (*not dense*) locker ‹Boden, Gewebe usw.›; **G** (*hanging free*) lose; **be at a ~ end** *or* (*Amer.*) **at ~ ends** (*fig.*) beschäftigungslos sein; (*not knowing what to do with oneself*) nichts zu tun haben; nichts anzufangen wissen; **tie up the ~ ends** *or* **threads** (*fig.*) die letzten Kleinigkeiten erledigen; **H** (*inexact*) ungenau; schief ‹Vergleich›; frei ‹Stil›; unsauber ‹Denken›; unklar, verwaschen ‹Aussage›; **I** (*morally lax*) lose ‹Mundwerk, Person›; liederlich ‹Leben[swandel], Person›; locker ‹Moral, Lebenswandel, Mundwerk›; **a ~ woman** ein leichtes Mädchen; **J** *in comb.* lose; locker; **~-flowing hair** locker fallendes Haar.

**2** *v.t.* **A** loslassen ‹Hund usw.›; **B** (*untie*) lösen; aufmachen (*ugs.*); **C** **~ [off]** abschießen ‹Pfeil›; abfeuern ‹Feuerwaffe, Salve›; abgeben ‹Schuss, Salve›; **D** (*relax*) lockern; **~ [one's] hold** loslassen; **E** (*detach from moorings*) losmachen ‹Schiff›; loswerfen (*Seemannsspr.*) ‹Tau›.

**3** *n.* **A** **be on the ~**: frei herumlaufen; **B** (*Rugby*) **in the ~**: beim offenen Kombinationsspiel

**loose:** ~ **box** ⇒ **box²** 1 G; ~ **'change** ⇒ **change** 1 D; ~ **'cover** *n.* (*Brit.*) Überzug, *der;* Schoner, *der;* **~-fitting** *adj.* bequem geschnitten; **~-knit** *adj.* lose zusammenhängend ‹Organisation, Gemeinschaft usw.›; **~-leaf** *attrib. adj.* Loseblatt-; **~-leaf file** Ringbuch, *das;* **~-limbed** /'lu:slɪmd/ *adj.* gelenkig; geschmeidig; (*gawky*) schlaksig; **~-lipped** /'lu:slɪpt/ *adj.* geschwätzig; **~-living** *adj.* mit lockerem *od.* liederlichem Lebenswandel *nachgestellt*

**loosely** /'lu:slɪ/ *adv.* **A** (*not tightly*) locker; lose; **B** (*not strictly*) locker ‹gruppieren›; lose ‹zusammenhängen›; frei ‹übersetzen›; ~ **speaking** grob gesagt; **use a word ~**: ein Wort in einem weiteren Sinne gebrauchen

**loosen** /'lu:sn/ **1** *v.t.* **A** (*make less tight etc.*) lockern ; **B** (*Med.*) lösen ‹Husten›; **~ the/sb.'s bowels** abführend wirken; **C** (*fig.: relax*) lockern ‹Bestimmungen, Reglement usw.›; **~ sb.'s tongue** (*fig.*) jmds. Zunge lösen. **2** *v.i.* (*become looser*) sich lockern

**~ up 1** /'---/ *v.t.* lockern ‹Glieder, Muskeln›. **2** /--'-/ *v.i.* sich auflockern; (*relax*) auftauen

**looseness** /'lu:snɪs/ *n., no pl.* **A** Lockerheit, *die;* **B** (*Med.*) **~ of the bowels** [Neigung zu] Durchfall

**loot** /lu:t/ **1** *v.t.* **A** (*plunder*) plündern; **B** (*carry off*) rauben. **2** *n.* **A** (*in war*) [Kriegs]beute, *die;* **B** (*gain, esp. illicit*) Beute, *die;* **C** (*coll.: money*) Zaster, *der* (*salopp*); Knete, *die* (*salopp*)

**looter** /'lu:tə(r)/ *n.* Plünderer, *der*

**lop** /lɒp/ *v.t.*, **-pp-** **A** stutzen, beschneiden ‹Baum, Hecke›; **B** **~ sth. [off** *or* **away]** etw. abhauen *od.* abhacken

**lope** /ləʊp/ *v.i.* ‹Hase, Kaninchen:› springen; ‹Wolf, Fuchs:› laufen; ‹Person:› beschwingten Schrittes gehen

**lop-eared** /'lɒpɪəd/ *adj.* schlappohrig (*ugs.*); hängeohrig

**lopsided** /lɒp'saɪdɪd/ *adj.* schief; (*fig.*) einseitig

**loquacious** /lə'kweɪʃəs/ *adj.* redselig; schwatzhaft (*abwertend*)

**loquacity** /lə'kwæsɪtɪ/ *n., no pl.* Redseligkeit, *die;* Geschwätzigkeit, *die* (*abwertend*)

**lord** /lɔ:d/ **1** *n.* **A** (*master*) Herr, *der;* **the ~s of creation** (*fig.: mankind*) die Krone der Schöpfung; **~ and master** (*joc.*) Herr und Gebieter *od.* Meister (*scherzh.*); **B** **L~** (*Relig.*) Herr, *der;* **L~ God [Almighty]** unser Herr[, der allmächtige Gott]; **the L~ [God]** [Gott] der Herr; **Our/the L~** (*Christ*) unser Herr Jesus/der Herr; **in the year of Our L~ ...:** im Jahre des Herrn ...; **the L~'s Prayer** das Vaterunser; **the 'L~'s Day** der Tag des Herrn; **the L~'s Supper** das [heilige] Abendmahl; **L~ only knows** (*coll.*) weiß der Himmel (*ugs.*); **C** ▶ **1617** (*Brit.: nobleman, or as title*) Lord, *der;* **live like a ~** (*fig.*) fürstlich leben; **treat sb. like a ~**: jmdn. fürstlich bewirten; **the L~s** (*Brit.*) die Lords; das Oberhaus; **the House of L~s** (*Brit.*) das Oberhaus; ⇒ *also* **drunk** 1; **D** ▶ **1617** **My L~** (*Brit.*) *form of address* (*to earl, viscount*) Graf; (*to baron*) Baron; (*to bishop*) Exzellenz; (*to ~ mayor, ~ provost*) Herr Oberbürgermeister; (*to judge*) /mlʌd/ Herr Richter; **E** (*Brit.: feudal superior*) Lord, *der;* Lehnsherr, *der.*

**2** *int.* (*coll.*) Gott!; **oh/good L~!** du lieber Himmel *od.* Gott!; großer Gott!; **L~ bless my soul/me/us** *etc.* allmächtiger Gott!

**3** *v.t.* **~ it** (*rule*) das Zepter *od.* Regiment führen; (*put on airs*) sich groß aufspielen; **~ it over sb.** bei jmdm. den großen Herrn/die große Dame spielen

**Lord:** ~ **'Advocate** *n.* (*Scot. Law*) Kronanwalt, *der;* ~ **'Bishop** *n.* (*Brit.*) Lordbischof, *der;* ~ **'Chamberlain** *n.* (*Brit.*) Haushofmeister, *der;* ~ **'Chancellor** *n.* (*Brit.*) Lord-[groß]kanzler, *der;* ~ **Chief 'Justice** ⇒ **chief** 2 A; ~ **Lieu'tenant** *n.* (*Brit.*) Lord Lieutenant, *der; Vertreter der Krone in einer Grafschaft*

**lordly** /'lɔ:dlɪ/ *adj.* **A** (*grand*) herrschaftlich; edel ‹Gegenstand›; herrschaftlich ‹Gebäude›; stattlich ‹Vermögen›; **B** (*haughty*) anmaßend; hochmütig

**Lord:** ~ **'Mayor** ⇒ **mayor**; ~ **President of the 'Council** *n.* (*Brit.*) Lordpräsident, *der;* ~ **Privy 'Seal** *n.* (*Brit.*) Lordsiegelverwalter, *der;* ~ **'Provost** *n.* (*Scot.*) ≈ Oberbürgermeister, *der*

**lordship** /'lɔ:dʃɪp/ *n.* **A** ▶ **1617** (*title, estate*) Lordschaft, *die;* **his/your ~/their/your ~s** seine/Eure Lordschaft/ihre/Eure Lordschaften; **B** (*dominion*) Herrschaft, *die* (**of, over** über + *Akk.*)

**lore** /lɔ:(r)/ *n.* Wissen, *das;* Kunde, *die;* (*body of traditions*) Überlieferung, *die;* (*of a people, an area*) Folklore, *die;* **animal/bird/plant ~**: Tier-/Vogel-/Pflanzenkunde, *die*

**lorgnette** /lɔ:'njet/ *n. in sing. or pl.* Lorgnette, *die*

**Lorraine** /lɒ'reɪn/ *pr. n.* Lothringen (*das*)

**lorry** /'lɒrɪ/ *n.* (*Brit.*) Lastwagen, *der;* Lkw, *der;* Laster, *der* (*ugs.*); **it fell off the back of a ~** (*joc.*) das ist mir/ihm *usw.* zugelaufen (*ugs. scherzh.*)

**'lorry driver** *n.* ▶ **1261** (*Brit.*) Lastwagenfahrer, *der;* Lkw-Fahrer, *der*

**lose** /lu:z/ **1** *v.t.*, **lost** /lɒst/ **A** verlieren; kommen um, verlieren ‹Leben, Habe›; **sb. has something/nothing to ~ [by doing sth.]** es kann jmdm. schaden/nicht schaden[, wenn er etw. tut]; ⇒ *also* **face** 1 A; **grip** 1 A; **ground¹** 1 B; **hold** 3 A, B; **sight** 1 B; **temper** 1 A; **B** (*fail to maintain*) verlieren; (*become slow by*) ‹Uhr:› nachgehen ‹zwei Minuten täglich usw.›; **C** (*become unable to find*) verlieren; **~ one's way** sich verlaufen/verfahren; **be lost/~ oneself in sth.** (*fig.*) ganz in etw. (*Dat.*) aufgehen; **D** (*waste*) vertun ‹Zeit›; (*miss*) versäumen, verpassen ‹Zeitpunkt, Gelegenheit, Ereignis›; ⇒ *also* **time** 1 B; **E** (*fail to obtain*) nicht bekommen ‹Preis, Vertrag usw.›; (*fail to hear*) nicht mitbekommen ‹Teil einer Rede usw.›; (*fail to catch*) verpassen, versäumen ‹Zug, Bus›; **the motion was lost** der Antrag kam nicht durch *od.* scheiterte; **F** (*forfeit*) verlieren, (*geh.*) verwirken ‹Recht›; **G** (*be defeated in*) verlieren ‹Kampf, Spiel, Wette, Prozess usw.›; ⇒ *also* **fight** 2 C; **toss** 3 A; **H** (*cause loss of*) **~ sb. sth.** jmdn. um etw. bringen; **you['ve] lost me** (*fig.*) ich komme nicht mehr mit; **I** (*get rid of*) abschütteln ‹Verfolger›; loswerden ‹Erkältung›; **~ weight** abnehmen. ⇒ *also* **lost**.

**2** *v.i.*, **lost** **A** (*suffer loss*) einen Verlust erleiden; (*in business*) Verlust machen (**on** bei); (*in match, contest*) verlieren; **heads you win, tails you ~**: bei Kopf hast du gewonnen, bei Zahl verloren; **~ in freshness** an Frische verlieren; **the story didn't ~ in the telling** die Geschichte wurde beim Weitererzählen eher noch aufgebauscht; **his poetry ~s in translation** seine Gedichte verlieren durch die Übersetzung; **you can't ~** (*coll.*) du kannst nur profitieren *od.* gewinnen; **B** (*become slow*) ‹Uhr:› nachgehen

**~ 'out** *v.i.* verdrängt werden (**to** von)

**loser** /'lu:zə(r)/ *n.* Verlierer, *der*/Verliererin, *die;* (*failure*) Versager, *der*/Versagerin, *die;* **we'd be the ~s by it** wir wären dabei die Dummen (*ugs.*)

**loss** /lɒs/ *n.* **A** (*process*) Verlust, *der* (**of** Gen.); **B** *in sing. or pl.* (*what is lost*) Verlust, *der;* **sell at a ~**: mit Verlust verkaufen; ⇒ *also* **cut** 1 K; **C** (*state*) Verlust, *der;* **be a great/no ~ to sb.** für jmdn. ein großer *od.* schwerer/kein Verlust sein; **D** **be at a ~**: nicht [mehr] weiterwissen; **be at a ~ what to do** nicht wissen, was zu tun ist; **be at a ~ [how] to do sth.** nicht wissen, wie man etwas machen soll; **be at a ~ to understand sth.** etw. nicht verstehen können; **be at a ~ for words/an answer** um Worte/eine Antwort verlegen sein. ⇒ *also* **dead loss**; **life** A; **profit** 1 A

**loss:** ~ **adjuster** *n.* (*Finance*) Schaden[s]regulierer, *der*/Schaden[s]reguliererin, *die;* **~-leader** *n.* (*Commerc.*) [unter dem Selbstkostenpreis angebotener] Lockartikel; **~-making** *adj.* mit Verlust arbeitend

**lost** /lɒst/ *adj.* **A** (*perished*) verloren; ausgestorben ‹Kunst[fertigkeit]›; **B** (*astray*) verloren; vermisst ‹Person›; **get ~**: sich verlaufen *od.* verirren/verfahren; **get ~!** (*coll.*) verdufte! (*salopp*); **he can get ~!** (*coll.*) er soll verduften! (*salopp*); **I'm ~** (*fig.*) ich verstehe gar nichts mehr; **feel ~ without sb./sth.** (*fig.*) sich (*Dat.*) ohne jmdn./etw. hilflos vorkommen; **~ generation** verlorene Generation; Lostgeneration, *die* (*Literaturw.*); **C** (*wasted*) vertan ‹Zeit, Gelegenheit›; verschwendet ‹Zeit, Mühe›; verpasst, versäumt ‹Gelegenheit›; **D** (*not won*) verloren; aussichtslos ‹Sache›; ⇒ *also* **all** 2 D; **cause** 1 D; **E** **~ in admiration** überwältigt; **be ~ to sb.** für jmdn. verloren sein; **be ~ [up]on sb.** (*unrecognized by*) bei jmdm. keine Anerkennung finden; von jmdm. nicht gewürdigt werden; **sarcasm was ~ on him** mit Sarkasmus konnte er nichts anfangen; **be ~ to all sense of duty** jedes Pflichtgefühl vermissen lassen. ⇒ *also* **lose**; **property** A

**lot** /lɒt/ *n.* **A** (*method of choosing*) Los, *das;* **by ~**: durch das Los; **B** (*destiny*) Los, *das;* **fall to the ~ of sb.** jmdm. bestimmt sein; **C** (*item to be auctioned*) Posten, *der;* **bad ~** (*fig.: disreputable person*) üble Person; **D** (*set of persons*) Haufen, *der;* **the ~**: [sie] alle; **'our/'your/'their ~** (*coll.*) wir/ihr/die; **not an honest man among the '~ [of them]** kein einziger anständiger Kerl in dem ganzen Haufen; **I'm bored with the '~ of you** *or* **with 'you ~**: ihr langweilt mich alle; **E** (*set of things*) Menge, *die;* **we received a new ~ of hats** wir haben eine neue Sendung Hüte erhalten; **divide sth. into five ~s** etw. in fünf Stapel/Haufen *usw.* teilen; **the ~** (*whole set*) alle/alles; **that's the ~** (*coll.*) das ist alles; das wärs (*ugs.*); **'that little ~** (*coll. iron.*) diese Kleinigkeit; **F** (*coll.: large number or quantity*) **~s** *or* **a ~ of money** *etc.* viel *od.* eine Menge Geld *usw.;* **~s of books/coins** eine Menge Bücher/Münzen; **he has a ~ to learn** er muss noch viel lernen; **I have a ~ to be thankful for** ich muss für vieles dankbar sein; **have ~s to do** viel zu tun haben; **we have ~s of time** wir haben viel *od.* (*ugs.*) massenweise Zeit; **sing** *etc.* **a ~**: viel singen *usw.;* **~s** *or* **a ~ better** viel besser; **not a ~ better** nicht viel besser; **like sth. a ~**: etw. sehr mögen; **Did you like it? — Not a ~**: Hat es dir gefallen? — Nicht sehr; **G** (*for choosing*) Los, *das;* **draw/cast/throw ~s [for sth.]** das Los [über etw. (*Akk.*)] entscheiden lassen; [um etw.] losen; **cast/throw in one's ~ with sb.** sich mit jmdm. zusammentun; **draw ~s to determine sth.** etw. durch das Los entscheiden ; **H** (*plot of land*) Gelände, *das;* Platz, *der;* (*measured piece of land*) Parzelle, *die;* **building ~** (*Amer.*) Bauplatz, *der*

**lotion** /'ləʊʃn/ *n.* Lotion, *die*

**lottery** /'lɒtərɪ/ *n.* Lotterie, *die;* (*fig.*) Glücksspiel, *das*

**'lottery ticket** *n.* Lottozahl, *die*

**lotto** /'lɒtəʊ/ *n., no pl.* Lotto, *das*

**lotus** /'ləʊtəs/ *n.* (*Nymphaea*) Seerose, *die;* (*Nelumbo*) Lotusblume, *die*

**'lotus position** *n.* Lotussitz, *der*

**loud** /laʊd/ ❶ *adj.* [A] laut; schreiend ‹Reklame›; lautstark ‹Protest, Kritik›; **he was ~ in his praise/criticism of the government** er lobte die Regierung in höchsten Tönen/er äußerte scharfe Kritik an der Regierung; ⇒ *also* **pedal** 1 A; [B] *(conspicuous)* aufdringlich; laut, aufdringlich ‹Farbe, Muster usw.›; grell, schreiend ‹Farbe›. ❷ *adv.* laut; **laugh out ~:** laut auflachen; **laugh ~ and long** in lautes, anhaltendes Gelächter ausbrechen; **say sth. out ~:** etw. aussprechen; *(fig.)* etw. laut verkünden

**loud hailer** /laʊd 'heɪlə(r)/ *n.* Megaphon, *das;* Flüstertüte, *die (ugs. scherzh.)*

**loudly** /'laʊdlɪ/ *adv.* [A] *(in a loud voice, clamorously)* laut; **he insisted ~ on his rights** er bestand entschieden auf seinen Rechten; [B] *(flashily)* aufdringlich

**loud: ~mouth** *n.* Großmaul, *das;* **~-mouthed** /'laʊdmaʊðd/ *adj.* großmäulig *(ugs. abwertend);* großsprecherisch *(abwertend)*

**loudness** /'laʊdnɪs/ *n., no pl.* Lautstärke, *die;* *(flashiness)* Aufdringlichkeit, *die*

**loud'speaker** *n.* Lautsprecher, *der*

**lough** /lɒx, lɒk/ *n. (Ir.)* See, der

**lounge** /laʊndʒ/ ❶ *v.i.* ~ **[about** *or* **around]** [faul] herumliegen/-sitzen/-stehen; [faul] herumhängen *(ugs.);* *(in chair etc.)* sich lümmeln *(ugs.).* ❷ *n.* [A] *(public room)* Lounge, *die;* *(in hotel)* Lounge, *die;* [Hotel]halle, *die;* *(at station)* Wartesaal, *der;* *(in theatre)* Foyer, *das;* *(at airport)* Lounge, *die;* Wartehalle, *die;* [B] *(sitting room)* Wohnzimmer, *das;* [C] *(Brit.: bar)* ~ **[bar]** ⇒ **saloon bar**

**'lounge lizard** *n. (coll.)* Salonlöwe, *der*

**lounger** /'laʊndʒə(r)/ *n.* [A] Nichtstuer, *der;* [B] *(sunbed)* Liege, *die*

**'lounge suit** *n. (Brit.)* Straßenanzug, *der*

**lour** /'laʊə(r)/ *v.i.* missmutig [drein]blicken; ein finsteres Gesicht machen; *(fig.)* ‹Wolken, Gewitter:› sich [bedrohlich] zusammenziehen; ‹Himmel:› sich [bedrohlich] verfinstern

**louse** /laʊs/ ❶ *n.* [A] *pl.* **lice** /laɪs/ Laus, *die;* [B] *pl.* **~s** *(sl.: person)* Ratte, *die (derb).* ❷ *v.t.* ~ **up** *(coll.)* vermasseln *(salopp)*

**lousy** /'laʊzɪ/ *adj.* [A] *(infested)* verlaust; **be ~ with money** *(coll.)* im Geld schwimmen *(ugs.);* lausig viel Geld haben *(ugs.);* **places ~ with foreigners** von Ausländern wimmelnde Orte; [B] *(coll.)* *(disgusting)* ekelhaft; widerlich; *(very poor)* lausig *(ugs.);* mies *(ugs.);* **feel ~:** sich mies *(ugs.) od.* miserabel fühlen; **men are ~ at housework** Männer stellen sich bei der Hausarbeit miserabel an

**lout** /laʊt/ *n.* Rüpel, *der;* Flegel, *der;* *(bumpkin)* Tollpatsch, *der (ugs.);* Tölpel, *der*

**loutish** /'laʊtɪʃ/ *adj.* rüpelhaft; flegelhaft

**louver, louvre** /'lu:və(r)/ *n.* [A] *(roof turret)* Laterne, *die (Bauw.);* [B] *(slat)* Jalousiebrettchen, *das;* ~ **door** Jalousietür, *die;* ~ **window** Jalousiefenster, *das;* [C] *in pl.* *(blind)* Jalousie, *die;* *(for cooling engine etc.)* Lüftungslamellen

**lovable** /'lʌvəbl/ *adj.* liebenswert

**love** /lʌv/ ❶ *n.* [A] *(affection, sexual ~)* Liebe, *die* **(for** zu); **~ is blind** *(prov.)* die Liebe ist blind; **~'s young dream** junges Liebesglück; **in ~ [with]** verliebt [in (+ *Akk.*)]; **fall in ~ [with]** sich verlieben [in (+ *Akk.*)]; **be/fall out of ~ with sb.** jmdn. nicht mehr lieben; **be/fall out of ~ with sth.** einer Sache *(Gen.)* überdrüssig sein/etw. nicht mehr mögen; **make ~ to sb.** *(court)* um jmdn. werben; jmdm. den Hof machen *(veralt., noch scherzh.);* *(have sex)* mit jmdm. schlafen; jmdn. lieben; **they made ~:** sie schliefen miteinander; sie liebten sich; **for ~:** aus Liebe; *(free)* unentgeltlich; umsonst; *(for pleasure)* aus Spaß an der Freude *(ugs.);* nur zum Vergnügen *od.* Spaß; **not for ~ or money** um nichts in der Welt; **[Happy Christmas,] ~ from Beth** [fröhliche Weihnachten und] herzliche Grüße von Beth; **give my ~ to her** grüß sie von mir; **send one's ~ to sb.** jmdn. grüßen lassen; **Peter sends [you] his ~:** Peter lässt [dich] grüßen; **there is no ~ lost between them** sie sind sich *(Dat.)* nicht grün *(ugs.);* **sb.'s life and ~s** jmds. Lebens- und Liebesgeschichte; see also **fair**[2] 1 A; [B] *(devotion)* Liebe, *die* **(of, for, to[wards]** zu); **~ of life/eating/learning** Freude am Leben/Essen/Lernen; **for [the] ~ of sb.** jmdm. zu Liebe; um jmds. willen; **for the ~ of God** um Gottes willen; ⇒ *also* **Mike**; [C] *(sweetheart)* Geliebte, *der/die;* Liebste, *der/die (veraltet);* **[my] ~** *(coll.: form of address)* [mein] Liebling *od.* Schatz; *(to sb. less close)* mein Lieber/meine Liebe; **sth. is sb.'s first ~:** etw. ist jmds. größte Leidenschaft; **can I help you, ~?** *(in shop)* was darfs denn sein?; [D] *(Tennis)* **fifteen/thirty ~:** fünfzehn/dreißig null; **win the set six games to ~:** den Satz mit sechs zu null Spielen gewinnen; **~ all** null beide; **~ game/victory** *etc.* Zu-null-Spiel, *das/*-Sieg, *der usw.* ❷ *v.t.* [A] lieben; **our/their ~d ones** unsere/ihre Lieben; [B] *(like)* **I'd ~ a cigarette** ich hätte sehr gerne eine Zigarette; **~ to do** *or* **doing sth.** etw. [leidenschaftlich] gern tun. ❸ *v.i.* lieben

**love: ~ affair** *n.* [Liebes]verhältnis, *das;* Liebschaft, *die;* **~bird** *n. (Ornith.)* Unzertrennliche, *der;* *(fig.)* Turteltaube, *die (ugs. scherzh.);* **~ child** *n. (euphem.)* Kind der Liebe *(geh. verhüll.);* uneheliches Kind; **~-'hate** *adj.* von Hassliebe geprägt; **~-hate relationship** Hassliebe, *die;* **~-in-a-'mist** *n. (Bot.)* Jungfer im Grünen; Gretel im Busch; **~ knot** ⇒ **true-love knot**

**loveless** /'lʌvlɪs/ *adj.* [A] *(unloving)* lieblos; hart; [B] *(unloved)* ohne Liebe *nachgestellt*

**love: ~ letter** *n.* Liebesbrief, *der;* **~-lies-'bleeding** *n. (Bot.)* Fuchsschwanz, *der;* **~ life** *n.* Liebesleben, *das*

**loveliness** /'lʌvlɪnɪs/ *n., no pl.* Schönheit, *die*

**lovelorn** /'lʌvlɔ:n/ *adj.* liebeskrank *(geh.)*

**lovely** /'lʌvlɪ/ ❶ *adj.* [A] [wunder]schön; herrlich ‹Tag, Essen›; [B] *(lovable)* liebenswert; [C] *(coll.: delightful)* toll *(ugs.);* wunderbar; **~ and warm/cool** *etc. (coll.)* schön warm/kühl *usw.* ❷ *n.* Schönheit, *die;* Schöne, *die*

**love: ~making** *n.* [A] *(courtship)* Liebeswerben, *das (geh.);* [B] *(sexual intercourse)* körperliche Liebe; **~ match** *n.* Liebesheirat, *die;* **~ nest** *n.* Liebesnest, *das;* **~ potion** *n.* Liebestrank, *der*

**lover** /'lʌvə(r)/ *n.* [A] Liebhaber, *der;* Geliebte, *der;* *(woman)* Geliebte, *die;* **be ~s** ein Liebespaar sein; **~'s knot** ⇒ **true-love knot**; [B] *(person devoted to sth.)* Liebhaber, *der/*Liebhaberin, *die;* Freund, *der/*Freundin, *die;* **~ of the arts** Kunstliebhaber, *der/*-liebhaberin, *die;* Kunstfreund, *der/*-freundin, *die;* **dog ~:** Hundefreund, *der/*-freundin, *die*

**love: ~sick** *adj.* an Liebeskummer leidend; liebeskrank *(geh.);* **be ~sick** Liebeskummer haben; liebeskrank sein *(geh.);* **~ song** *n.* Liebeslied, *das;* **~ story** *n.* Liebesgeschichte, *die;* **~ token** *n.* Liebespfand, *das*

**lovey** /'lʌvɪ/ *n. (coll.)* *usu. as form of address* Liebling, *der;* Schatz, *der*

**lovey-dovey** /lʌvɪ'dʌvɪ/ *adj.* **be ~:** den Verliebten/die Verliebte spielen *(ugs.);* **be ~ with sb.** jmdn. umschmeicheln

**loving** /'lʌvɪŋ/ *adj.* [A] *(affectionate)* liebend; [B] *(expressing love)* liebevoll; **your ~ father** *(in letter)* dein dich liebender Vater; in Liebe dein Vater

**loving: ~ cup** *n.* Pokal, *der;* **~ 'kindness** *n.* Güte, *die*

**lovingly** /'lʌvɪŋlɪ/ *adv.* liebevoll; *(painstakingly)* mit viel Liebe

**low**[1] /ləʊ/ ❶ *adj.* [A] ▶ **1210** *(not reaching far up)* niedrig; niedrig, flach ‹Absätze, Stirn›; flach ‹Relief›; gering ‹Körpergröße›; [B] *(below normal level)* niedrig; tief ‹Flug›; flach ‹Welle›; tief ausgeschnitten ‹Kleid›; tief ‹Ausschnitt›; [C] *(not elevated)* tief liegend ‹Wiese, Grund, Land›; tief hängend ‹Wolke›; tief stehend ‹Gestirne›; tief ‹Verbeugung›; **the river/water is ~:** der Fluss/das Wasser ist niedrig; **the sun/moon is ~:** die Sonne/der Mond steht tief; [D] *(of humble rank)* nieder…; niedrig; ⇒ *also* **high** 1 E; [E] *(inferior)* niedrig; gering ‹Intelligenz, Bildung›; gewöhnlich ‹Geschmack›; *(vulgar)* gewöhnlich; [F] *(not fair)* gemein; [G] *(Cards)* niedrig; [H] ▶ **1603** *(small in degree)* niedrig; gering ‹Sichtweite, Wert›; leicht ‹Fieber›; **be ~ in iodine** einen geringen Jodgehalt aufweisen; **have a ~ opinion of sb./sth.** von jmdm./etw. keine hohe Meinung haben; **temperatures will be in the ~ forties** die Temperaturen werden knapp über 40° [Fahrenheit] liegen; ⇒ *also* **common denominator**; [I] *(in pitch)* tief ‹Ton, Stimme, Lage, Klang›; *(in loudness)* leise ‹Ton, Stimme›; [J] *(Ling.)* ⇒ **open** 1 M; [K] *(weak)* schwach; **~ vitality** Kraftlosigkeit, *die;* **he is very ~** *(physically)* er ist sehr geschwächt; *(emotionally)* er ist sehr niedergeschlagen; **in a ~ state of mind** niedergeschlagen; in gedrückter Stimmung; [L] *(nearly gone)* fast verbraucht *od.* aufgebraucht; **run ~:** allmählich ausgehen *od.* zu Ende gehen; **we are ~/getting ~ on petrol** wir haben nur noch wenig/bald kein Benzin mehr; **the bottle is getting ~:** die Flasche geht allmählich zu Ende *od.* ist bald leer; [M] *(Geog.)* **~ latitudes** niedere Breiten. ⇒ *also* **lower**[2] 1.

❷ *adv.* [A] *(in or to a ~ position)* tief; niedrig, tief ‹hängen›; **that comes ~ on my list of priorities** das hat für mich keine hohe Priorität; ⇒ *also* **high** 2 A; [B] *(to a ~ level)* **prices have gone too ~:** die Preise sind zu weit gefallen; **if the temperature drops any ~er** wenn die Temperatur weiter sinkt; [C] *(not loudly)* leise; [D] *(at ~ pitch)* tief; [E] **lay sb. ~** *(prostrate)* jmdn. niederstrecken *(geh.);* *(confine to sickbed)* jmdn. aufs Krankenlager werfen *(geh.);* **lie ~:** am Boden liegen; *(hide)* untertauchen. ⇒ *also* **bring** A; **lower**[2] 2.

❸ *n.* [A] ▶ **1603** *(Meteorol.)* Tief, *das;* [B] **hit** *or* **reach a new/an all-time ~:** einen neuen/absoluten Tiefststand erreichen

**low**[2] *v.i.* ‹Kuh:› muhen

**low: ~-alcohol** *adj.* alkoholarm ‹Getränk›; **~brow** ❶ *n.* Nichtintellektuelle, *der/die;* ❷ *adj.* schlicht ‹Person›; [geistig] anspruchslos ‹Buch, Programm›; **~-budget** *adj.* Lowbudget-, Billig‹film, -produktion usw.›; **~-calorie** *adj.* kalorienarm ‹Kost, Getränk›; **Low 'Church** *n.* Low Church, *die;* **~-class** *adj. (Brit.)* *(of low quality)* drittklassig; *(of low social class)* Unterschicht[s]-; **~ 'comedy** *n.* Schwank, *der;* Posse, *die;* **~-cost** *adj.* preiswert; **Low Countries** *pr. n. pl. (Hist.)* Niederlande *Pl.;* **~-cut** *adj.* [tief] ausgeschnitten ‹Kleid›; **~-cut neck** tiefer Ausschnitt; **~-cut shoes** Halbschuhe; **~-down** ❶ *adj.* *(mean)* mies *(ugs.);* ❷ *n. (coll.)* **give [sb.]/get the ~-down on sb./sth.** [jmdm.] sagen/rauskriegen, was es mit jmdm./etw. [wirklich] auf sich hat; **~-energy house** *n.* Niedrigenergiehaus, *das*

**lower**[1] /'ləʊə(r)/ ❶ *v.t.* [A] *(let down)* herab-/hinablassen; zu Wasser lassen ‹Boot›; einholen ‹Flagge, Segel›; **~ oneself into** hinuntersteigen in (+ *Akk.*) ‹Kanalschacht, Keller›; **~ oneself into a chair** sich in einen Sessel sinken lassen; *abs.* **~ [away]** *(Naut.)* (~ *boat)* das Boot aussetzen *od.* zu Wasser lassen; (~ *sail)* das Segel einholen; [B] *(reduce in height)* senken ‹Blick›; niederschlagen ‹Augen›; niedriger machen ‹Wand›; absenken ‹Zimmerdecke›; tiefer hängen ‹Bild›; auslassen ‹Saum›; ⇒ *also* **sight** 1 H; [C] *(lessen)* senken ‹Preis, Miete, Zins usw.›; [D] *(degrade)* herabsetzen; verderben ‹Geschmack›; **~ oneself** sich erniedrigen; **~ oneself to do sth.** sich so weit erniedrigen, etw. zu tun; [E] *(weaken)* schwächen; dämpfen ‹Licht, Stimme, Lärm›; **~ one's voice** leiser sprechen; die Stimme senken *(geh.).* ❷ *v.i.* [A] *(weaken)* ‹Stimme:› leiser werden; ‹Licht:› dunkler werden; [B] *(sink)* sinken; ‹Wasservorrat:› weniger werden, abnehmen

**lower**[2] ❶ *compar. adj.* [A] unter… ‹Nil, Themse usw., Atmosphäre›; Unter‹jura, -devon usw., -arm, -lippe usw.›; Nieder‹rhein, -kalifornien›; ⇒ *also* **jaw** 1 A; [B] *(in rank)* unter…; **~ mammals/plants** niedere Säugetiere/Pflanzen; **the ~ orders/classes** die Unterschichten/die unteren Klassen; **~ middle class** untere Mittelschicht. ❷ *compar. adv.* tiefer ‹sinken, hängen usw.›

**lower**[3] /'laʊə(r)/ ⇒ **lour**

**lower: ~ case** ❶ *n.* Kleinbuchstaben *Pl.;* **in ~ case** in Kleinbuchstaben; ❷ *adj.* klein

‹Buchstabe›; **L~ 'Chamber** *n.* (*Parl.*) Unterhaus, *das;* **~ court** *n.* unteres *od.* untergeordnetes Gericht; **~ 'deck** *n.* [A] (*of ship*) Unterdeck, *das;* (*of bus*) unteres Deck; [B] (*Brit.: seamen*) Mannschaft, *die;* **L~ House** *n.* (*Parl.*) Unterhaus, *das;* **~most** *adj.* unterst...; **be ~most** zuunterst liegen; **~ 'regions** *n. pl.* (*Mythol.*) Unterwelt, *die;* **L~ 'Saxon** *adj.* niedersächsisch; **L~ 'Saxony** *pr. n.* Niedersachsen (*das*); **~ 'sixth** *n.* (*Brit.*) ≈ Unterprima, *die;* **~ 'world** *n.* [A] (*the earth*) Erde, *die;* [B] (*hell*) Unterwelt, *die*

**low: ~-fat** *adj.* fettarm; **~-flying** *adj.* tief fliegend; **~-flying aircraft** Tiefflieger, *der;* **~ 'frequency** *n.* Niederfrequenz, *die;* **~-frequency** *adj.* niederfrequent; **Low 'German** ⇒ **German** 2 B; **~-grade** *adj.* minderwertig; leicht ‹Infektion›; **~-grade steel** Stahl minderer Güte; **~-heeled** *adj.* flach ‹Schuh›; ‹Schuhe› mit flachen Absätzen; **~-income** *adj.* einkommensschwach; **~-income families** Familien mit niedrigem Einkommen; **a ~-income country** ein Land mit niedrigem Nationaleinkommen; **~-key** *adj.* zurückhaltend; unaufdringlich ‹Beleuchtung, Unterhaltung›; unauffällig ‹Einsatz›; **~land** /'ləʊlənd/ ❶ *n.* Tiefland, *das;* **the Lowlands of Scotland** die Lowlands; das schottische Tiefland; ❷ *adj.* tiefländisch; Tiefland‹rasse, -farm›; **~lander** /'ləʊləndə(r)/ *n.* Tieflandbewohner, *der*/-bewohnerin, *die;* (*Scot.*) Bewohner/Bewohnerin der Lowlands; **~lights** *n. pl.* (*in hair*) dunkel getönte Strähnen

**lowly** /'ləʊlɪ/ *adj.* [A] (*modest*) bescheiden; [B] (*not highly evolved*) nieder...

**low: ~-lying** *adj.* tief liegend; **~-necked** *adj.* [tief] ausgeschnitten; **~-nicotine** *adj.* nikotinarm; **~-paid** *adj.* niedrig bezahlt; **~-paid families** Familien mit geringem Einkommen; **~-'pitched** *adj.* [A] tief ‹Stimme›; [B] (*Archit.*) wenig geneigt ‹Dach›; **~ point** *n.* Tiefpunkt, *der;* **~-powered** /'ləʊpaʊəd/ *adj.* schwach ‹Motor, Glühbirne›; **~ 'pressure** Tiefdruck, *der;* **an area of ~ pressure** ein Tiefdruckgebiet; **~-priced** /ləʊ'praɪst/ *adj.* preisgünstig; **~ 'profile** ⇒ **profile** 1 G; **~ re'lief** ⇒ **relief**² A; **~-rise** *adj.* ‹Gebäude› mit wenigen Stockwerken; **~ season** *n.* Nebensaison, *die;* **~-'spirited** *adj.* niedergeschlagen; **~-tech** *adj.* Lowtech‹system, -ausrüstung etc.›; **~ 'tension** = **~ voltage** ⇒ **voltage**; **~-tension** ⇒ **~-voltage**; **~ 'tide** ⇒ **tide** 1 A; **~ 'voltage** ⇒ **voltage**; **~-voltage** *adj.* (*Electr.*) Niederspannungs-; **~-wage** *attrib. adj.* schlecht bezahlt; Niedriglohn‹land›; **~ 'water** *n.* Niedrigwasser, *das;* (*fig.*) Tiefpunkt, *der;* **~-'water mark** *n.* Niedrigwassermarke, *die*

**loyal** /'lɔɪəl/ *adj.* (*to person*) treu; (*to government etc.*) treu [ergeben]; loyal

**loyalist** /'lɔɪəlɪst/ ❶ *n.* Loyalist, *der*/Loyalistin, *die.* ❷ *adj.* loyalistisch

**loyally** /'lɔɪəlɪ/ *adv.* treu; loyal

**loyalty** /'lɔɪəltɪ/ *n.* Treue, *die;* Loyalität, *die;* **brand ~:** Markentreue, *die*

**'loyalty card** *n.* Treuekarte, *die* (*für Kunden*)

**lozenge** /'lɒzɪndʒ/ *n.* [A] (*tablet*) Pastille, *die;* [B] (*diamond shape*) Raute, *die;* Rhombus, *der*

**LP** *abbr.* **long-playing record** LP, *die*

**'L-plate** *n.* (*Brit.*) 'L'-Schild, *das;* ≈ „Fahrschule"-Schild, *das*

**LSD** *abbr.* **lysergic acid diethylamide** LSD, *das*

**LSE** *abbr.* **London School of Economics**

**Lt.** *abbr.* **Lieutenant**

**Ltd.** *abbr.* **Limited** GmbH; **... Company ~** ...gesellschaft mbH

**lubricant** /'lu:brɪkənt/ ❶ *n.* Schmiermittel, *das.* ❷ *adj.* Schmier-

**lubricate** /'lu:brɪkeɪt/ *v.t.* schmieren; einfetten ‹Haut›

**lubrication** /lu:brɪ'keɪʃn/ *n.* Schmierung, *die; attrib.* Schmier‹system, -vorrichtung›

**lucerne** *n.* (*Brit. Bot.*) [Blaue] Luzerne

**Lucerne** /lu:'sɜ:n/ *pr. n.* ▶ 1626 | Luzern (*das*); **Lake ~:** der Vierwaldstätter See

**lucid** /'lu:sɪd/ *adj.* klar; [leicht] verständlich; einleuchtend ‹Argumentation›; **~ interval** (*period of sanity*) lichter Augenblick *od.* Moment

**lucidity** /lu:'sɪdɪtɪ/ *n., no pl.* Klarheit, *die*

**lucidly** /'lu:sɪdlɪ/ *adv.* klar [und verständlich] ‹formulieren usw.›

**luck** /lʌk/ *n.* [A] (*good or ill fortune*) Schicksal, *das;* **as ~ would have it** wie das Schicksal es wollte; **good ~:** Glück, *das;* **bad ~:** Pech, *das;* **bring [sb.] good/bad ~:** [jmdm.] Glück/Pech bringen; **better ~ next time** mehr Glück beim nächsten Mal; **good ~ [to you]!** viel Glück!; alles Gute!; viel Erfolg!; **good ~ to him, I say** ich wünsche ihm viel Glück; (*iron.*) na, dann viel Glück!; **it's the ~ of the game** Glück/Pech gehabt!; **just my ~:** typisch für mich; **try one's ~:** sein Glück versuchen; **you never know your ~:** vielleicht hast du ja Glück; ⇒ *also* **down**³ 1 MM; **draw** 3 A; **hard** 1 C; **push** 1 C; **worse** 1; [B] (*good fortune*) Glück, *das;* **with [any] ~:** mit ein bisschen *od.* etwas Glück; **~ was with us all the way** wir hatten die ganze Zeit Glück; **I was in ~'s way** das war wirklich Glück; **wear sth. for ~:** etw. als Glücksbringer tragen; **do sth. for ~:** etw. tun, damit es einem Glück bringen soll; **have the ~ to do sth.** das Glück haben, etw. zu tun; **be in/out of ~:** Glück/kein Glück haben; **sb.'s ~ is in/out** jmd. hat Glück/kein Glück; **no such ~:** schön wärs; ⇒ *also* **stroke**¹ 1 C

**luckily** /'lʌkɪlɪ/ *adv.* glücklicherweise; **~ for her** zu ihrem Glück

**luckless** /'lʌklɪs/ *adj.* glücklos; (*unlucky, unfortunate*) unglücklich

**lucky** /'lʌkɪ/ *adj.* [A] (*favoured by chance*) glücklich; **be ~ [in love/at games]** Glück [in der Liebe/im Spiel] haben; **be ~ to be alive** von Glück sagen können, dass man noch am Leben ist; **be ~ enough to be rescued** das [große] Glück haben, gerettet zu werden; **I should be so ~:** schön wärs; **get ~:** Glück haben; **Could you lend me £100? — 'You'll be ~!:** Könntest du mir 100 Pfund leihen? — So siehst du aus!; **it was ~ [for you/him** *etc.*] **the car stopped in time** dein/sein *usw.* Glück, dass das Auto rechtzeitig gehalten hat; **be a ~ dog** ein Glückspilz sein (*ugs.*); [B] (*favouring sb. by chance*) glücklich ‹Umstand, Zufall, Zusammentreffen usw.›; ⇒ *also* **escape** 1 A; [C] (*bringing good luck*) Glücks‹zahl, -tag usw.›; **~ charm** Glücksbringer, *der;* **be born under a ~ star** ein Glückskind sein; **you can thank your ~ stars** du kannst von Glück sagen

**lucky: ~ bag,** (*Brit.*) **~ 'dip** *ns.* Glückstopf, *der;* (*fig.*) Glücksspiel, *das*

**lucrative** /'lu:krətɪv/ *adj.* einträglich; lukrativ

**lucre** /'lu:kə(r)/ *n.* (*derog.*) Profit, *der;* ⇒ *also* **filthy** 1 B

**Luddite** /'lʌdaɪt/ *n.* [A] Maschinenstürmer, *der;* [B] (*Hist.*) Luddit, *der*

**ludicrous** /'lu:dɪkrəs/ *adj.* lächerlich ‹Anblick, Lohn, Argument, Vorschlag, Idee›; lachhaft ‹Angebot, Ausrede›; **a ~ speed/price** (*low*) eine lächerliche Geschwindigkeit/ein lächerlicher Preis; (*high*) eine haarsträubende Geschwindigkeit/ein haarsträubender Preis

**ludicrously** /'lu:dɪkrəslɪ/ *adv.* lächerlich ‹wenig, billig, langsam, klein›; haarsträubend ‹schnell, teuer›

**ludo** /'lu:dəʊ/ *n., no pl., no art.* Mensch-ärgere-dich-nicht[-Spiel], *das*

**luff** /lʌf/ (*Naut.*) ❶ *v.t.* [A] (*bring nearer wind*) luven ‹Schiff›; [B] (*turn*) **~ the helm** anluven; [C] (*Yacht racing*) durch Luven den Wind nehmen (+ *Dat.*). ❷ *v.i.* anluven. ❸ *n.* Vorliek, *das*

**lug**¹ /lʌg/ ❶ *v.t.,* **-gg-** [A] (*drag*) schleppen; [B] (*force*) **~ sb. along** jmdn. mit herumschleppen (*ugs.*). ❷ *v.i.,* **-gg-** ziehen, zerren (**at** an + *Dat.*)

**lug**² ⇒ **lugworm**

**lug**³ *n.* [A] (*projection*) Henkel, *der;* [B] (*coll./joc.: ear*) Löffel, *der* (*ugs.*)

**luge** /lu:ʒ/ *n.* [Rodel]schlitten, *der*

**luggage** /'lʌgɪdʒ/ *n.* Gepäck, *das*

**luggage: ~ carrier** *n.* Gepäckträger, *der;* **~ locker** *n.* [Gepäck]schließfach, *das;* **~ rack** *n.* Gepäckablage, *die;* **~ trolley** *n.* Kofferkuli, *der;* **~ van** *n.* Gepäckwagen, *der*

**lugger** /'lʌgə(r)/ *n.* (*Naut.*) Logger, *der*

**'lughole** *n.* (*coll.: ear*) Löffel, *der* (*ugs.*)

**lugubrious** /lu:'gu:brɪəs, lʊ'gu:brɪəs/ *adj.* (*mournful*) kummervoll; traurig; (*dismal*) düster; trübselig

**lugubriously** /lu:'gu:brɪəslɪ, lʊ'gu:brɪəslɪ/ *adv.* (*mournfully*) kummervoll; traurig; (*dismally*) düster

**'lugworm** *n.* Köderwurm, *der*

**Luke** /lu:k/ *pr. n.* **St ~:** der hl. Lukas

**lukewarm** /'lu:kwɔ:m, lu:k'wɔ:m/ *adj.* [A] lauwarm; [B] (*fig.*) lau[warm]; halbherzig

**lull** /lʌl/ ❶ *v.t.* [A] (*soothe*) lullen; **~ a child to sleep** ein Kind in den Schlaf lullen; [B] (*fig.*) einlullen; einschläfern ‹Misstrauen›; **~ sb. into a false sense of security** jmdn. in einer trügerischen Sicherheit wiegen. ❷ *n.* Pause, *die;* **the ~ before the storm** (*fig.*) die Ruhe vor dem Sturm; **a ~ in the storm** ein vorübergehendes *od.* kurzes Nachlassen des Sturms

**lullaby** /'lʌləbaɪ/ *n.* Schlaflied, *das;* Wiegenlied, *das*

**lulu** /'lu:lu:/ *n.* (*coll.*) (*thing*) Hammer, *der* (*salopp*); (*person*) bombige Type (*ugs.*)

**lumbago** /lʌm'beɪgəʊ/ *n., pl.* **~s** (*Med.*) Hexenschuss, *der;* Lumbago, *die* (*fachspr.*)

**lumbar** /'lʌmbə(r)/ *adj.* (*Anat.*) Lenden-; lumbal (*fachspr.*); **~ puncture** (*Med.*) Lumbalpunktion, *die*

**lumber**¹ /'lʌmbə(r)/ *v.i.* ‹Person:› schwerfällig gehen; ‹Fahrzeug:› rumpeln

**lumber**² ❶ *n.* [A] (*furniture*) Gerümpel, *das;* [B] (*useless material*) Kram, *der* (*ugs. abwertend*); Krempel, *der* (*ugs. abwertend*); [C] (*Amer.: timber*) [Bau]holz, *das.* ❷ *v.t.* (*fill up, encumber*) voll stopfen (*ugs.*); voll stellen ‹Zimmer›; überladen ‹Stil, Buch›; **~ sb. with sth./sb.** jmdm. etw./jmdn. aufhalsen (*ugs.*); **get ~ed with sth./sb.** etw./jmdn. aufgehalst kriegen (*ugs.*); **~ oneself with too many things** (*lit. or fig.*) sich (*Dat.*) zu viel Krempel (*ugs.*) anschaffen

**lumbering** /'lʌmbərɪŋ/ *adj.* schwerfällig; (*graceless in appearance*) plump

**lumber: ~jack** *n.* ▶ 1261 | (*Amer.*) Holzfäller, *der;* **~jacket** *n.* Lumberjack, *der;* **~man** ⇒ **~jack**; **~ room** *n.* Abstellkammer, *die;* Rumpelkammer, *die* (*ugs.*)

**luminary** /'lu:mɪnərɪ/ *n.* (*person*) Koryphäe, *die*

**luminescence** /lu:mɪ'nesəns/ *n.* Leuchten, *das;* (*Phys.*) Lumineszenz, *die*

**luminescent** /lu:mɪ'nesənt/ *adj.* leuchtend; (*Phys.*) lumineszierend

**luminosity** /lu:mɪ'nɒsɪtɪ/ *n.* (*also Astron.*) Helligkeit, *die*

**luminous** /'lu:mɪnəs/ *adj.* [A] (*bright*) hell ‹Feuer, Licht usw.›; [hell] leuchtend; Leucht‹anzeige, -zeiger usw.›; **~ paint** Leuchtfarbe, *die;* [B] (*of light*) Leucht‹kraft, -stärke usw.›; [C] (*fig.*) brilant; (*enlightening*) erhellend

**lummee** /'lʌmɪ/ *int.* (*Brit. dated. coll.*) großer Gott

**lummox** /'lʌməks/ *n.* (*Amer. coll.*) Tölpel, *der;* Tollpatsch, *der* (*ugs.*)

**lump**¹ /lʌmp/ ❶ *n.* [A] (*shapeless mass*) Klumpen, *der;* (*of sugar, butter, etc.*); Stück, *das;* (*of wood*) Klotz, *der;* (*of dough*) Kloß, *der;* (*of bread*) Brocken, *der;* **a ~ of sugar/dough/bread** ein Stück Zucker/ein Teigkloß/ein Brocken Brot; **a ~ of wood/clay** ein Holzklotz/ein Klumpen Lehm *od.* Lehmklumpen; **have/get a ~ in one's throat** (*fig.*) einen Kloß im Hals haben (*ugs.*); [B] (*swelling*) Beule, *die;* (*caused by cancer*) Knoten, *der;* [C] (*coll.: heap*) Haufen, *der;* [D] (*thickset person*) Klotz, *der* (*ugs.*); **a great ~ of a woman** ein Koloss von Frau; [E] **the ~** (*Brit.: workers*) die Schwarzarbeiter im Baugewerbe; [F] **[taken] in the ~** im Ganzen [gesehen]; **get payment in a ~** die gesamte Summe auf einmal erhalten.

❷ *v.t.* (*mass together*) zusammentun; **~ sth. with sth.** etw. und etw. zusammentun; **~ sb./sth. with the rest** jmdn./etw. mit dem Rest in einen Topf werfen (*ugs.*); **~ the**

**archaeology books under History** die Archäologiebücher mit zur Geschichte stellen
**~ to'gether** *v.t.* zusammenfassen
**lump²** *v.t.* (*coll.*) sich abfinden mit; **he can [like it or] ~ it** er muss sich [wohl oder übel] damit abfinden; **if you don't like it you can ~ it** du musst dich wohl oder übel damit abfinden
**lumpenproletariat** /ˈlʌmpənprəʊləteərɪət/ *n.* (*derog.*) Lumpenproletariat, *das*
**lumpish** /ˈlʌmpɪʃ/ *adj.* (*derog.*) **A** (*clumsy*) plump; (*in movement, speech, action*) schwerfällig; **B** (*dull*) dumpf; stumpf
**lump:** **~ payment** *n.* einmalige Zahlung [einer größeren Summe]; **~sucker** *n.* (*Zool.*) Scheibenbauch, *der;* Lumpfisch, *der;* (*Cyclopterus lumpus*) Seehase, *der;* **~ 'sugar** *n.* Würfelzucker, *der;* **~ 'sum** *n.* (*covering several items*) Pauschalsumme, *die;* (*paid at once*) einmalige Pauschale
**lumpy** /ˈlʌmpɪ/ *adj.* klumpig ‹Brei, Lehm›; ‹Kissen, Matratze› mit klumpiger Füllung
**lunacy** /ˈluːnəsɪ/ *n.* **A** (*insanity*) Wahnsinn, *der;* (*Law*) geistige Unzurechnungsfähigkeit; **B** (*mad folly*) Wahnsinn, *der* (*ugs.*); Irrsinn, *der*
**lunar** /ˈluːnə(r)/ *adj.* Mond-; lunar (*fachspr.*)
**lunar:** **~ e'clipse** *n.* (*Astron.*) Mondfinsternis, *die;* **~ 'module** *n.* Mond[lande]fähre, *die*
**lunatic** /ˈluːnətɪk/ **1** *adj.* **A** (*mad*) wahnsinnig; irre (*veralt.*); ⇒ *also* **fringe** 1 C; **B** (*foolish*) wahnwitzig; Wahnsinns- (*ugs.*); idiotisch (*ugs. abwertend*). **2** *n.* Wahnsinnige, *der/die;* Irre, *der/die;* **be a ~:** wahnsinnig *od.* (*veralt.*) irre sein
**'lunatic asylum** *n.* (*Hist.*) Irrenanstalt, *die* (*veralt., ugs. abwertend*)
**lunch** /lʌnʃ/ **1** *n.* Mittagessen, *das;* **have** *or* **eat** *or* (*formal*) **take [one's] ~:** zu Mittag essen; das Mittagessen einnehmen (*geh.*); **get an hour for ~:** eine Stunde Mittag[spause] haben; **have sth. for ~:** etw. zu Mittag essen; **be at** *or* **eating** *or* **having [one's] ~:** gerade beim Mittagessen sein; zu Tisch sein; **there's no such thing as a free ~** (*fig.*) es wird einem nichts geschenkt. **2** *v.i.* zu Mittag essen
**lunch:** **~ box** *n.* Lunchbox, *die;* **~ break** ⇒ **~ hour**
**luncheon** /ˈlʌnʃn/ *n.* (*formal*) **A** (*midday meal*) Mittagessen, *das;* **B** (*Amer.: light meal*) Imbiss, *der*
**luncheon:** **~ meat** *n.* Frühstücksfleisch, *das;* **~ voucher** *n.* (*Brit.*) Essenmarke, *die;* Essensbon, *der*
**lunch:** **~ hour** *n.* Mittagspause, *die;* **~room** *n.* Imbissraum, *der;* **~time** *n.* Mittagszeit, *die;* **at ~time** mittags
**lung** /lʌŋ/ *n.* ▶ 966 Lunge, *die;* (*right or left*) Lungenflügel, *der;* **have good/weak ~s** eine gute *od.* kräftige/schwache Lunge haben; **the ~s of a city** (*fig.*) die grünen Lungen einer Stadt
**'lung cancer** *n.* ▶ 1232 (*Med.*) Lungenkrebs, *der*
**lunge** /lʌndʒ/ **1** *n.* **A** (*Sport*) Ausfall, *der;* **B** (*sudden forward movement*) Sprung nach vorn; **make a ~ at sb.** sich auf jmdn. stürzen. **2** *v.i.* **A** (*Sport*) einen Ausfall machen (**at** gegen); **B** **~ at sb. with a knife** jmdn. mit einem Messer angreifen
**~ 'out** *v.i.* einen Ausfall machen (**at** gegen); **~ out at sb.** (*make sudden forward movement*) sich auf jmdn. stürzen
**lung:** **~fish** *n.* Lungenfisch, *der;* **~ power** *n.* Stimmkraft, *die*
**lupin, lupine¹** /ˈluːpɪn/ *n.* [Edel]lupine, *die*
**lupine²** /ˈluːpaɪn, ˈljuːpaɪn/ *adj.* Wolfs-; wölfisch; **have ~ features/a ~ appearance** ein Wolfsgesicht haben/wie ein Wolf aussehen
**lupus** /ˈluːpəs/ *n.* (*Med.*) Zehrflechte, *die;* Lupus, *der* (*fachspr.*)
**lurch¹** /lɜːtʃ/ *n.* **leave sb. in the ~:** jmdn. im Stich lassen; jmdn. hängen lassen (*ugs.*)
**lurch²** **1** *n.* Rucken, *das;* (*of ship*) Schlingern, *das;* **give a ~:** rucken; ‹Schiff:› schlingern. **2** *v.i.* rucken; ‹Betrunkener:› torkeln; ‹Schiff:› schlingern
**lurcher** /ˈlɜːtʃə(r)/ *n.* (*Brit.*) *Kreuzung zwischen Collie und Windhund* [*besonders als Spürhund eines Wilderers*]; ≈ Spürhund, *der*
**lure** /ljʊə(r), lʊə(r)/ **1** *v.t.* locken; **~ away from/out of/into sth.** von etw. fortlocken/aus etw. [heraus]locken/in etw. (*Akk.*) [hinein]locken; **~ sb. away from his duty** jmdn. [durch Lockungen] von seinen Pflichten abbringen. **2** *n.* **A** (*Falconry*) Federspiel, *das;* **B** (*Hunting*) Lockvogel, *der;* (*fig.: thing*) Lockmittel, *das;* **C** **the ~ of the sea** der Ruf *od.* die Lockung des Meeres (*geh.*)
**lurid** /ˈljʊərɪd, ˈlʊərɪd/ *adj.* **A** (*ghastly*) gespenstisch; (*highly coloured*) grell ‹Licht, Schein, Himmel›; **B** (*fig.*) (*horrifying*) grässlich, schaurig ‹Einzelheiten, Beispiele›; (*sensational*) reißerisch (*abwertend*); (*showy, gaudy*) reißerisch [aufgemacht] (*abwertend*) ‹Umschlag, Bild›
**luridly** /ˈljʊərɪdlɪ, ˈlʊərɪdlɪ/ *adv.* **A** (*glaringly*) grell; **B** (*fig.*) (*horrifyingly*) grässlich; schaurig; (*showily, gaudily*) reißerisch
**lurk** /lɜːk/ *v.i.* **A** lauern; ‹Raubtier:› auf Lauer liegen; **~ about a place** an einem Ort herumschleichen; **B** (*fig.*) **~ in sb.'s** *or* **at the back of sb.'s mind** ‹Zweifel, Verdacht, Furcht:› an jmdm. nagen
**lurking** /ˈlɜːkɪŋ/ *attrib. adj.* heimlich ‹Zweifel, Verdacht, Angst, Mitgefühl›
**luscious** /ˈlʌʃəs/ *adj.* **A** (*sweet in taste or smell*) köstlich [süß]; saftig [süß] ‹Obst›; **B** (*excessively sweet*) aufdringlich süß ‹Parfüm›; **C** (*appealing to senses*) üppig ‹Figur, Kurven›; knackig (*ugs.*) ‹Mädchen›; voll ‹Lippen›; satt ‹Farbe›
**lush** /lʌʃ/ *adj.* saftig ‹Wiese›; grün ‹Tal›; üppig ‹Vegetation›; (*fig.*) luxuriös, (*ugs.*) feudal ‹Atmosphäre, Räumlichkeiten›
**lust** /lʌst/ **1** *n.* **A** (*sexual drive*) Sinnenlust, *die;* sinnliche Begierde; **B** (*passionate desire*) Gier, *die* (**for** nach); **~ for power/glory/of battle** Machtgier, *die*/Ruhmsucht, *die*/Kampf[es]lust, *die;* **C** (*Bibl., Theol.*) Fleischeslust, *die* (*geh.*); **~s of the flesh** fleischliche Gelüste (*geh.*). **2** *v.i.* **~ after** [lustvoll] begehren (*geh.*); **he ~s after ...:** es gelüstet ihn nach ... (*geh.*); **~ for glory** ruhmbegierig (*geh.*) *od.* ruhmsüchtig sein
**luster** (*Amer.*) ⇒ **lustre**
**lustful** /ˈlʌstfl/ *adj.* lüstern (*geh.*)
**lustily** /ˈlʌstɪlɪ/ *adv.* kräftig; forsch ‹sich bewegen, etw. angehen›; herzhaft ‹lachen, gähnen›; aus voller Kehle ‹rufen, singen›; **he tucked ~ into his dinner** er langte kräftig *od.* tüchtig *od.* herzhaft zu
**lustre** /ˈlʌstə(r)/ *n.* (*Brit.*) **A** Schimmer, *der;* [schimmernder] Glanz; **shine with a ~:** einen schimmernden Glanz haben; **B** (*fig.: splendour*) Glanz, *der;* **add ~ to** *or* **shed ~ on sth.** einer Sache (*Dat.*) Glanz verleihen; **lack ~** ‹Augen:› glanzlos sein; ‹Lächeln:› matt sein; **C** (*glaze*) Glasurglanz, *der;* Lüster, *der* (*fachspr.*)
**lustreless** /ˈlʌstəlɪs/ *adj.* glanzlos; stumpf
**'lustreware** *n.* Lüsterkeramik, *die*
**lustrous** /ˈlʌstrəs/ *adj.* schimmernd; (*fig.*) glanzvoll; erhaben (*geh.*) ‹Geist›
**lusty** /ˈlʌstɪ/ *adj.* **A** (*healthy*) gesund; frisch ‹Gesichtsfarbe›; (*strong, powerful*) kräftig; **B** (*vigorous*) herzhaft ‹Applaus, Tritt›; tüchtig, zupackend ‹Arbeiter›; **a ~ girl from the country** ein strammes Landmädchen
**lutanist** /ˈluːtənɪst, ˈljuːtənɪst/ *n.* ▶ 1261 (*Mus.*) Lautenist, *der*/Lautenistin, *die*
**lute** /luːt, ljuːt/ *n.* (*Mus.*) Laute, *die*
**lutenist** ⇒ **lutanist**
**Lutheran** /ˈluːθərən, ˈljuːθərən/ **1** *adj.* lutherisch. **2** *n.* Lutheraner, *der*/Lutheranerin, *die*
**luvvy** (**luvvie**) /ˈlʌvɪ/ *n.* (*coll. derog.*) Luvvy, *der/die* (*affektierter Schickeriatyp, der seinesgleichen mit 'love' anredet*)
**Luxembourg** *etc.* ⇒ **Luxemburg** *etc.*
**Luxemburg** /ˈlʌksəmbɜːg/ *pr. n.* ▶ 1626 Luxemburg (*das*)
**Luxemburger** /ˈlʌksəmbɜːgə(r)/ *n.* ▶ 1340 Luxemburger, *der*/Luxemburgerin, *die*
**Luxemburgian** /ˈlʌksəmbɜːgɪən/ **1** *adj.* luxemburgisch. **2** *n.* Luxemburgisch, *das;* Letzeburgesch, *das* (*fachspr.*)
**luxuriance** /lʌgˈzjʊərɪəns, lʌkˈsjʊərɪəns/ *n., no pl.* (*superabundance*) Üppigkeit, *die;* (*of hair*) Fülle, *die*
**luxuriant** /lʌgˈzjʊərɪənt, lʌkˈsjʊərɪənt/ *adj.* **A** (*growing profusely, exuberant*) üppig ‹Vegetation, Farbenpracht, Blattwerk›; voll ‹Haar›; ertragreich ‹Ernte›; **B** (*richly ornamented*) reich ausgeschmückt
**luxuriantly** /lʌgˈzjʊərɪəntlɪ, lʌkˈsjʊərɪəntlɪ/ *adv.* üppig
**luxuriate** /lʌgˈzjʊərɪeɪt, lʌkˈsjʊərɪeɪt/ *v.i.* **~ in** sich aalen in (+ *Dat.*) ‹Sonne, Bett usw.›; **~ in the bath** sich genüsslich in der Badewanne rekeln (*ugs.*)
**luxurious** /lʌgˈzjʊərɪəs, lʌkˈsjʊərɪəs/ *adj.* luxuriös; Luxus-; (*self-indulgent*) verwöhnt; luxuriös, verschwenderisch ‹Lebensstil›
**luxuriously** /lʌgˈzjʊərɪəslɪ, lʌkˈsjʊərɪəslɪ/ *adv.* luxuriös; mit allem Luxus; feudal (*ugs.*) ‹wohnen, essen›
**luxury** /ˈlʌkʃərɪ/ **1** *n.* **A** Luxus, *der;* **live** *or* **lead a life of ~:** ein Leben im Luxus führen; ⇒ *also* **lap¹** A; **B** (*article*) Luxusgegenstand, *der;* **luxuries** Luxus, *der;* **C** (*sth. one enjoys*) Luxus, *der.* **2** *attrib. adj.* Luxus-
**LV** *abbr.* (*Brit.*) **luncheon voucher**
**LW** *abbr.* (*Radio*) **long wave** LW
**lychee** /ˈlaɪtʃɪ, ˈlɪtʃɪ/ *n.* Litschi, *die*
**lychgate** ⇒ **lichgate**
**lye** /laɪ/ *n.* Lauge, *die*
**lying** /ˈlaɪɪŋ/ **1** *adj.* **A** (*given to falsehood*) verlogen; **~ scoundrel** Lügenbold, *der;* **B** (*false, untrue*) lügnerisch; lügenhaft; erlogen ‹Geschichte›; falsch, verlogen ‹Sentimentalität›. **2** *n.* Lügen, *das;* **that would be ~:** das wäre gelogen. ⇒ *also* **lie¹** 2, 3
**lymph** /lɪmf/ *n.* **A** (*Physiol.*) Lymphe, *die* (*fachspr.*); Gewebsflüssigkeit, *die;* **B** (*Med.: exudation from sore*) Blutwasser, *das*
**lymphatic** /lɪmˈfætɪk/ **1** *adj.* (*Physiol., Anat.*) Lymph-; lymphatisch. **2** *n.* (*Anat.*) Lymphgefäß, *das*
**lymph:** **~ gland, ~ node** *ns.* (*Anat.*) Lymphknoten, *der*
**lymphocyte** /ˈlɪmfəsaɪt/ *n.* (*Anat.*) Lymphozyt, *der*
**lynch** /lɪnʃ/ *v.t.* lynchen
**'lynch law** *n.* Lynchjustiz, *die*
**lynx** /lɪŋks/ *n.* (*Zool.*) Luchs, *der*
**'lynx-eyed** *adj.* (*fig.*) luchsäugig; mit Luchsaugen *nachgestellt;* **be ~:** Luchsaugen haben
**Lyons** /ˈliːɔ̃, ˈlaɪənz/ *pr. n.* ▶ 1626 Lyon (*das*)
**lyre** /ˈlaɪə(r)/ *n.* (*Mus.*) Lyra, *die;* Leier, *die*
**'lyrebird** *n.* (*Ornith.*) Leierschwanz, *der*
**lyric** /ˈlɪrɪk/ **1** *adj.* lyrisch; **~ poet** Lyriker, *der*/Lyrikerin, *die;* **~ poetry** Lyrik, *die.* **2** *n.* **A** (*poem*) lyrisches Gedicht; **B** *in pl.* (*verses*) lyrische Passagen; (*of song*) Text, *der*
**lyrical** /ˈlɪrɪkl/ *adj.* **A** ⇒ **lyric** 1; **B** (*like lyric poetry*) lyrisch; **C** (*coll.: enthusiastic*) gefühlvoll; **become** *or* **grow** *or* **wax ~ about** *or* **over sth.** über etw. (*Akk.*) ins Schwärmen geraten
**lyrically** /ˈlɪrɪkəlɪ/ *adv.* lyrisch
**lyricism** /ˈlɪrɪsɪzm/ *n.* **A** (*lyric character, a lyrical expression*) Lyrismus, *der;* **B** (*high-flown sentiments*) Gefühlsbetontheit, *die;* Gefühlsseligkeit, *die;* Schwärmerei, *die*
**lyricist** /ˈlɪrɪsɪst/ *n.* ▶ 1261 Texter, *der*/Texterin, *die*

# Mm

**M, m** /em/ *n., pl.* **Ms** *or* **M's** A *(letter)* M, m, *das;* B *(Roman numeral)* M

**M.** *abbr.* A **Master/Member of/Monsieur** M.; B **mega-** M; C *(Brit.)* **motorway** A

**m.** *abbr.* A **male** männl.; B **masculine** m.; C **married** verh.; D ▶1284 **metre[s]** m; E ▶1671 **milli-** m; F **million[s]** Mill.; G ▶1012 **minute[s]** Min.; H **mile[s]** M

**m'** /mə/ *poss. pron.* mein

**MA** *abbr.* **Master of Arts** M. A.; ⇒ *also* **B.Sc.**

**ma** /mɑ:/ *n. (coll.)* Mama, *die;* Mutti, *die (fam.)*

**ma'am** /mɑ:m, mæm/ *n.* gnädige Frau; *(in addressing Queen)* Majestät

**Mac** /mæk/ *n. (coll.)* A *(Scotsman)* Schotte, *der; (in address)* Mac; B *(Amer.: fellow)* Kumpel, *der (ugs.)*; **hi, ~!** Tag, Kumpel!

**mac** ⇒ **mack**

**macabre** /mə'kɑ:br/ *adj.* makaber

**macaque** /mə'kæk/ *n. (Zool.)* Makak, *der*

**macaroni** /mækə'rəʊnɪ/ *n.* Makkaroni *Pl.;* **~ and cheese** *(Amer.)* ⇒ **macaroni cheese**

**macaroni 'cheese** *n. (Brit.)* Käsemakkaroni *Pl.*

**macaroon** /mækə'ru:n/ *n.* Makrone, *die*

**macaw** /mə'kɔ:/ *n. (Ornith.)* Ara, *der;* Langschwanzpapagei, *der*

**mace**[1] /meɪs/ *n.* A *(Hist.: weapon)* Keule, *die;* B *(staff of office)* Amtsstab, *der*

**mace**[2] *n. (Bot., Cookery)* Mazis, *der;* Mazisblüte, *die;* Muskatblüte, *die*

**'mace-bearer** *n.* Träger/Trägerin des Amtsstabes

**macédoine** /'mæsɪdwɑ:n/ *n. (Cookery)* Macedoine, *das*

**Macedonia** /mæsɪ'dəʊnɪə/ *pr. n.* Makedonien *(das)*

**macerate** /'mæsəreɪt/ *v.t.* aufweichen ‹Papier›

**Mach** /mæk, mɑ:k/ *n. (Phys., Aeronaut.)* **~ [number]** Machzahl, *die;* machsche Zahl; **~ one/two** *etc.* Geschwindigkeit von 1/2 *usw.* Mach

**machete** /mə'tʃetɪ, mə'tʃeɪtɪ/ *n.* Machete, *die;* Buschmesser, *das*

**machiavellian** /mækɪə'velɪən/ *adj.* machiavellistisch

**machination** /mækɪ'neɪʃn, mæʃɪ'neɪʃn/ *n.* Machenschaft, *die (abwertend)*

**machine** /mə'ʃi:n/ **1** *n.* A Maschine, *die;* **be made by ~:** maschinell hergestellt werden; B *(bicycle)* [Fahr]rad, *das; (motorcycle)* Maschine, *die (ugs.)*; C *(computer)* Computer, *der;* D *(fig.: person)* Roboter, *der;* Maschine, *die;* E *(system of organization)* Apparat, *der;* **party/propaganda ~:** Partei-/Propagandaapparat, *der.* **2** *v.t. (make with ~)* maschinell herstellen; *(operate on with ~)* maschinell bearbeiten ‹Werkstück›; *(sew)* mit *od.* auf der Maschine nähen

**machine: ~ age** *n.* Maschinenzeitalter, *das;* **~ code** *n. (Computing)* Maschinensprache, *die;* **~ gun** *n.* Maschinengewehr, *das;* **~ language** ⇒ **~ code**; **~-made** *adj.* maschinell hergestellt; **~-minder** *n.* Maschinenwärter, *der;* **~ operator** *n.* [Maschinen]bediener, *der*/-bedienerin, *die;* **~ pistol** *n.* Maschinenpistole, *die;* **~-readable** *adj. (Computing)* maschinenlesbar; **~ room** *n.* Maschinenraum, *der*

**machinery** /mə'ʃi:nərɪ/ *n.* A *(machines)* Maschinen *Pl.;* B *(mechanism)* Mechanismus, *der;* C *(organized system)* Maschinerie, *die;* D *(Lit.)* Kunstmittel *Pl.*

**machine: ~ tool** *n.* Werkzeugmaschine, *die;* **~ trans'lation** *n.* maschinelle Übersetzung; **~-wash** *v.t.* in der Waschmaschine waschen; **~-washable** *adj.* waschmaschinenfest

**machinist** /mə'ʃi:nɪst/ *n.* ▶1261 *(who makes machinery)* Maschinenbauer, *der; (who controls machinery)* Maschinist, *der*/Maschinistin, *die;* **[sewing] ~:** [Maschinen]näherin, *die*/-näher, *der*

**machismo** /mə'tʃɪzməʊ, mə'kɪzməʊ/ *n., no pl.* Machismo, *der;* Männlichkeitswahn, *der*

**macho** /'mætʃəʊ/ **1** *n., pl.* **~s** Macho, *der.* **2** *adj.* Macho-; **he is really ~:** er ist wirklich ein Macho

**mack** /mæk/ *n. (Brit. coll.)* Regenmantel, *der;* Kleppermantel ⓦ, *der (ugs. veralt.)*

**mackerel** /'mækərl/ *n., pl. same or* **~s** *(Zool.)* Makrele, *die*

**mackerel 'sky** *n. (Meteorol.)* Zirrokumulusbewölkung, *die;* Schäfchenwolken *Pl.*

**mackintosh** /'mækɪntɒʃ/ *n.* Regenmantel, *der*

**macramé** /mə'krɑ:mɪ/ *n.* Makramee, *das*

**macro** /'mækrəʊ/ *n. (Computing)* Makro, *das*

**macro-** /'mækrəʊ/ *in comb.* makro-/Makro-

**macrobiotic** /mækrəʊbaɪ'ɒtɪk/ *adj.* makrobiotisch

**macro: ~economic** *adj.* makroökonomisch; **~economics** *n.* Makroökonomie, *die*

**macron** /'mækrɒn/ *n.* übergesetzter waagerechter Strich *(zur Kennzeichnung langer Vokale)*

**macroscopic** /mækrəʊ'skɒpɪk/ *adj.* makroskopisch

**mad** /mæd/ *adj.* A *(insane)* geisteskrank; irr ‹Blick, Ausdruck›; **you must be ~!** du bist wohl verrückt! *(ugs.)*; **are you ~?** bist du völlig verrückt geworden? *(ugs.)*; **like a ~ thing** *(coll.)* wie ein Verrückter/eine Verrückte *(ugs.)*; B *(frenzied)* wahnsinnig; verrückt *(ugs.)*; **it's one ~ rush** *(coll.)* es ist eine einzige Hetze; **make a ~ dash for sth.** sich auf etw. *(Akk.)* stürzen; **drive sb. ~:** jmdn. um den Verstand bringen *od. (ugs.)* verrückt machen; **this noise is enough to drive anyone ~!** dieser Lärm ist ja zum Verrücktwerden! *(ugs.)*; **~ with joy/fear** außer sich vor Freude/Angst; C *(foolish)* verrückt *(ugs.)*; **that was a ~ thing to do** das war eine Dummheit *od. (ugs.)* verrückt; **a ~ hope** eine wahnwitzige Hoffnung; D *(very enthusiastic)* **be/go ~ about** *or* **on sb./sth.** auf jmdn./etw. wild sein/werden *(ugs.)*; **be ~ keen on sth.** *(coll.)* auf etw. *(Akk.)* ganz scharf *od.* wild sein *(ugs.)*; **be ~ keen to do sth.** *(coll.)* ganz scharf *od.* wild darauf sein, etw. zu tun; E *(coll.: annoyed)* **~ [with** *or* **at sb.]** sauer [auf jmdn.] *(ugs.)*; **be ~ about/at missing the train** wütend sein, weil man den Zug verpasst hat; F *(with rabies)* toll; **~ dog** *(fig.)* Verrückte, *der/die (ugs.)*; **[run** *etc.***] like ~** *(coll.)* wie wild *od.* wie ein Wilder/eine Wilde *(ugs.)* [laufen *usw.*]; G *(frivolous)* ausgelassen, *(ugs.)* verrückt ‹Stimmung›

**Madagascan** /mædə'gæskən/ **1** *adj.* madagassisch. **2** *n.* Madagasse, *der*/Madagassin, *die*

**Madagascar** /mædə'gæskə(r)/ *pr. n.* Madagaskar *(das)*

**madam** /'mædəm/ *n.* A ▶1286, ▶1617 *(formal address)* gnädige Frau; **M~ Chairman** Frau Vorsitzende; **Dear M~** *(in letter)* Sehr verehrte gnädige Frau; B *(euphem.: woman brothel-keeper)* Bordellwirtin, *die;* Puffmutter, *die (salopp)*; C *(derog.: conceited, pert young woman)* Kratzbürste, *die (ugs. scherzh.)*

**Madame** /mə'dɑ:m, 'mædəm/ *n., pl.* **Mesdames** /meɪ'dæm, meɪ'dɑ:m/ A *(title)* Madame, *die;* **[the] Mesdames A and B** Madame A und Madame B; B *(formal address)* gnädige Frau; meine Dame

**'madcap** **1** *adj.* unbesonnen. **2** *n.* Heißsporn, *der*

**mad 'cow disease** *n. (coll.)* Rinderwahnsinn, *der*

**madden** /'mædn/ *v.t.* A *(make mad)* wahnsinnig machen *(ugs.)*; um den Verstand bringen; **~ed with grief/loneliness** wahnsinnig vor Kummer/Einsamkeit; B *(irritate)* [ver]ärgern; **be ~ed by sth.** sich über etw. *(Akk.)* [maßlos] aufregen; **it ~s me to think that ...:** es fuchst mich *(ugs.)*, wenn ich daran denke, dass ...

**maddening** /'mædənɪŋ/ *adj.* A *(irritating, tending to infuriate)* [äußerst] ärgerlich; B *(tending to craze)* unerträglich

**maddeningly** /'mædənɪŋlɪ/ *adv.* ⇒ **maddening** A, B: [äußerst] ärgerlich; unerträglich

**madder** /'mædə(r)/ *n.* A *(Bot.)* Krapp, *der;* Färberröte, *die;* B *(dye)* Krappfarbstoff, *der;* C *(Chem.)* synthetisches Alizarin

**made** ⇒ **make** 1, 2

**Madeira** /mə'dɪərə/ **1** *n.* Madeira[wein], *der.* **2** *pr. n.* Madeira *(das)*

**Ma'deira cake** *n.* Madeirakuchen, *der*

**madeleine** /'mædleɪn/ *n. Butterkeks in Form einer Muschel*

**made-to-'measure** *attrib. adj.* Maß-; **a ~ suit** ein Maßanzug *od.* maßgeschneiderter Anzug; ⇒ *also* **measure** 1 A

**'made-up** *attrib. adj.* erfunden ‹Geschichte›

**'madhouse** *n.* Irrenanstalt, *die;* Irrenhaus, *das; (fig.)* Tollhaus, *das*

**Madison Avenue** /mædɪsən 'ævənju:/ *n.* die amerikanische Werbeindustrie

**madly** /'mædlɪ/ *adv.* A wie ein Verrückter/eine Verrückte *(ugs.)*; B *(coll.: passionately, extremely)* wahnsinnig *(ugs.)*

**madman** /'mædmən/ *n., pl.* **madmen** /'mædmən/ Wahnsinnige, *der;* Irre, *der*

**madness** /'mædnɪs/ *n., no pl.* Wahnsinn, *der;* ⇒ *also* **method** B

**madonna** /mə'dɒnə/ *n. (Art, Relig.)* Madonna, *die*

**madrigal** /'mædrɪgl/ *n. (Lit., Mus.)* Madrigal, *das*

**'madwoman** *n.* Wahnsinnige, *die;* Irre, *die*

**maelstrom** /'meɪlstrəm/ *n. (lit. or fig.)* Mahlstrom, *der;* Strudel, *der;* Sog, *der*

**maestro** /'maɪstrəʊ/ *n., pl.* **maestri** /'maɪstri:/ *or* **~s** *(Mus.)* Maestro, *der; (fig.: great performer)* Meister, *der*

**Mae West** /meɪ 'west/ *n.* aufblasbare Schwimmweste

**MAFF** *abbr. (Brit.)* **Ministry of Agriculture, Fisheries, and Food** Landwirtschaftsministerium, *das*

**Mafia** /'mæfɪə/ *n.* A *(secret criminal organization)* Mafia, *die;* B **m~** *(organization exerting influence)* Mafia, *die*

**mag** /mæg/ *n. (coll.: magazine)* Zeitschrift, *die;* **porno ~:** Pornoheft, *das*

**magazine** /mægə'zi:n/ *n.* A *(periodical)* Zeitschrift, *die; (news ~, fashion ~, etc.)* Magazin, *das;* B *(Mil.: store) (for arms)* Waffenkammer, *die; (for ammunition)* Munitionsdepot, *das; (for provisions)* Proviantlager, *das; (for explosives)* Sprengstofflager, *das;* C *(Arms, Photog.)* Magazin, *das*

**magenta** /mə'dʒentə/ **1** *n.* A *(dye)* Fuchsin, *das;* Rosanilin, *das;* B *(colour)* Magenta, *das;* Purpur, *das.* **2** *adj.* purpurrot

m

**maggot** /ˈmægət/ *n.* Made, *die*

**maggoty** /ˈmægətɪ/ *adj.* madig

**Magi** /ˈmeɪdʒaɪ/ *n. pl.* **the [three] ~:** die drei Weisen aus dem Morgenland; die Heiligen Drei Könige

**magic** /ˈmædʒɪk/ ❶ *n.* [A] (*witchcraft, lit. or fig.*) Magie, *die;* **do ~:** zaubern; **as if by ~:** wie durch Zauberei; **black/white ~:** schwarze/weiße Magie; **work like ~:** wie ein Wunder wirken; **like ~** (*rapidly*) blitzartig; [B] (*conjuring tricks*) Zauberei, *die;* **make sth. appear/disappear by ~:** etw. herbei-/wegzaubern; [C] (*fig.: charm, enchantment*) Zauber, *der.*
❷ *adj.* [A] (*of ~*) magisch ‹Eigenschaft, Kraft›; (*resembling ~*) zauberhaft; (*used in ~*) Zauber‹spruch, -trank, -wort, -bann›; **cast a ~ spell on sb.** jmdn. verzaubern; [B] (*fig.: producing surprising results*) wunderbar.
❸ *v.t.*, **-ck-** zaubern; **~ sth./sb. away** ‹Zauberspruch:› etw./jmdn. verschwinden lassen; ‹Person:› etw./jmdn. wegzaubern

**magical** /ˈmædʒɪkl/ *adj.* (*of magic*) magisch; (*resembling magic*) zauberhaft; **the effect was ~:** das wirkte [wahre] Wunder

**magically** /ˈmædʒɪkəlɪ/ *adv.* auf wunderbare Weise ‹schützen, verwandeln, befördern›; zauberhaft ‹beleuchten›

**magic: ~ ˈcarpet** *n.* fliegender Teppich; **~ ˈeye** *n.* [A] (*Electr.: control device*) Photozelle, *die;* [B] (*Radio*) magisches Auge

**magician** /məˈdʒɪʃn/ *n.* (*lit. or fig.*) Magier, *der*/Magierin, *die;* (*conjurer*) Zauberer, *der*/Zauberin, *die;* **I'm not a ~:** ich kann doch nicht zaubern *od.* hexen (*ugs.*)

**magic: ~ ˈlantern** *n.* (*Optics*) Laterna Magica, *die;* **~ ˈsquare** *n.* (*Math.*) magisches Quadrat; **~ ˈwand** *n.* Zauberstab, *der*

**magisterial** /mædʒɪˈstɪərɪəl/ *adj.* [A] (*invested with authority*) gebieterisch (*geh.*); [B] (*dictatorial*) diktatorisch (*abwertend*); herrisch; [C] (*authoritative*) maßgebend

**magistracy** /ˈmædʒɪstrəsɪ/ *n.*, *no pl.* (*position*) Amt des Friedensrichters

**magistrate** /ˈmædʒɪstreɪt/ *n.* ▶ 1261 Friedensrichter, *der*/Friedensrichterin, *die;* **~s' court** ≈ Schiedsgericht, *das*

**magma** /ˈmægmə/ *n.*, *pl.* **~ta** /ˈmægmətə/ *or* **~s** (*Geol.*) Magma, *das*

**Magna Carta, Magna Charta** /mægnə ˈkɑːtə/ *n.* (*Hist.; also fig.*) Magna Charta, *die*

**magnanimity** /mægnəˈnɪmɪtɪ/ *n.*, *no pl.* Großmut, *die;* **with ~:** großmütig

**magnanimous** /mægˈnænɪməs/ *adj.*, **magnanimously** /mægˈnænɪməslɪ/ *adv.* großmütig (**towards** gegen)

**magnate** /ˈmægneɪt/ *n.* Magnat, *der*/Magnatin, *die;* **cotton/steel ~:** Baumwoll-/Stahlmagnat, *der*

**magnesia** /mægˈniːʃə/ *n.* Magnesiaweiß, *das;* ⇒ *also* **milk** 1

**magnesium** /mægˈniːzɪəm/ *n.* (*Chem.*) Magnesium, *das*

**magnet** /ˈmægnɪt/ *n.* (*lit. or fig.*) Magnet, *der*

**magnetic** /mægˈnetɪk/ *adj.* (*lit. or fig.*) magnetisch; (*fig.: very attractive*) sehr anziehend, unwiderstehlich ‹Person›; **~ power** (*fig.*) magnetische Anziehungskraft

**magnetic: ~ atˈtraction** *n.* (*Phys.*) magnetische Anziehungskraft; **~ ˈcompass** *n.* Magnetkompass, *der;* **~ ˈdisc** ⇒ **disc** C; **~ ˈfield** *n.* (*Phys.*) Magnetfeld, *das;* **~ ˈmine** *n.* Magnetmine, *die;* **~ ˈneedle** *n.* Magnetnadel, *die;* **~ ˈnorth** *n.* magnetisch Nord, *das;* **~ ˈpole** *n.* (*Phys.*) Magnetpol, *der;* (*Geog.*) magnetischer Pol; **~ ˈstorm** *n.* (*Phys.*) erdmagnetischer Sturm; **~ ˈtape** *n.* Magnetband, *das*

**magnetise** ⇒ **magnetize**

**magnetism** /ˈmægnɪtɪzm/ *n.* [A] (*Phys.*) (*science*) Magnetik, *die;* (*force, lit. or fig.*) Magnetismus, *der;* **terrestrial ~:** Erdmagnetismus, *der;* [B] (*fig.: personal charm and attraction*) Attraktivität, *die;* Anziehungskraft, *die;* Attraktion, *die*

**magnetize** /ˈmægnɪtaɪz/ *v.t.* [A] (*Phys.*) magnetisieren; [B] (*fig.: attract*) in seinen Bann schlagen *od.* ziehen (*geh.*); **be ~d by sth.** von etw. ganz gebannt sein

**magneto** /mægˈniːtəʊ/ *n.*, *pl.* **~s** Magnetzünder, *der*

**magnification** /mægnɪfɪˈkeɪʃn/ *n.* Vergrößerung, *die;* **under high/low ~/at x ~s** in starker/geringer/x-facher Vergrößerung

**magnificence** /mægˈnɪfɪsəns/ *n.*, *no pl.* (*lavish display*) Pracht, *die;* Üppigkeit, *die;* (*splendour*) Prunk, *der;* Pracht, *die;* (*grandeur*) Stattlichkeit, *die;* Großartigkeit, *die;* (*beauty*) Herrlichkeit, *die*

**magnificent** /mægˈnɪfɪsənt/ *adj.* [A] (*stately, sumptuously constructed or adorned*) prächtig; prachtvoll; (*sumptuous*) prunkvoll; grandios, großartig ‹Pracht, Herrlichkeit, Anblick›; (*beautiful*) herrlich ‹Garten, Umgebung, Kleidung, Vorhang, Kunstwerk, Wetter, Gestalt›; (*lavish*) üppig ‹Freigebigkeit, Mahl›; [B] (*coll.: fine, excellent*) fabelhaft (*ugs.*)

**magnificently** /mægˈnɪfɪsəntlɪ/ *adv.* [A] (*with great stateliness and grandeur*) prächtig; prachtvoll; (*sumptuously*) prunkvoll ‹einrichten, schmücken›; (*with lavishness*) üppig ‹zubereitet›; [B] (*coll.: in fine manner*) fabelhaft (*ugs.*)

**magnifier** /ˈmægnɪfaɪə(r)/ *n.* (*Optics*) Lupe, *die*

**magnify** /ˈmægnɪfaɪ/ *v.t.* [A] vergrößern; [B] (*exaggerate*) aufbauschen; übertrieben darstellen ‹Gefahren›

**ˈmagnifying glass** *n.* Lupe, *die;* Vergrößerungsglas, *das*

**magnitude** /ˈmægnɪtjuːd/ *n.* [A] (*largeness, vastness*) Ausmaß, *das;* (*of explosion, earthquake*) Stärke, *die;* [B] (*size*) Größe, *die;* **problems of this ~:** Probleme dieser Größenordnung; **order of ~:** Größenordnung, *die;* [C] (*importance*) Wichtigkeit, *die;* (*of person*) Bedeutung, *die;* **sth. of the first ~:** etw. von höchster Wichtigkeit; **a writer of the first ~:** ein sehr bedeutender Schriftsteller; [D] (*Astron.*) Helligkeit, *die*

**magnolia** /mægˈnəʊlɪə/ *n.* (*Bot.*) Magnolie, *die*

**magnum** /ˈmægnəm/ *n.* (*bottle*) Magnum, *die;* (*measure*) 1,5 l; **two ~s** drei Liter

**magnum ˈopus** ⇒ **opus** B

**magpie** /ˈmægpaɪ/ *n.* (*Ornith.*) Elster, *die;* **chatter like a ~:** unaufhörlich schnattern (*ugs.*); **be like a ~** (*fig.*) alles Mögliche sammeln [wie eine Elster]

**Magyar** /ˈmægjɑː(r)/ ▶ 1275, ▶ 1340 ❶ *adj.* madjarisch. ❷ *n.* [A] (*person*) Madjar, *der*/Madjarin, *die;* [B] (*language*) Madjarisch, *das*

**maharaja[h]** /mɑːhəˈrɑːdʒə/ *n.* (*Ind. Hist.*) Maharadscha, *der*

**mah-jong[g]** /mɑːˈdʒɒŋ/ *n.* Mah-Jongg, *das*

**mahogany** /məˈhɒgənɪ/ *n.* [A] (*wood*) Mahagoni[holz], *das; attrib.* Mahagoni-; [B] (*tree*) Mahagonibaum, *der;* [C] (*colour*) Mahagonibraun, *das*

**maid** /meɪd/ *n.* [A] (*servant*) Dienstmädchen, *das;* Dienstmagd, *die* (*veralt.*); **~ of ˈall work** (*servant*) Hausangestellte, *die;* Hausmädchen, *das;* (*fig.: person doing many jobs*) Mädchen für alles (*ugs.*); [B] (*arch.: unmarried woman*) unverheiratete Frau; Jungfer, *die* (*veralt., oft abwertend*); [C] (*arch./poet.*) (*girl*) Maid, *die* (*dichter. veralt.*); (*young unmarried woman, virgin*) Jungfrau, *die;* [D] (*rhet.: young woman*) Maid, *die* (*dichter. veralt.*); **the M~ [of Orleans]** die Jungfrau von Orleans. ⇒ *also* **old maid**

**maiden** /ˈmeɪdn/ ❶ *n.* [A] ⇒ **maid** C; **the answer to a ~'s prayer** genau das Richtige; (*attractive man*) der Traum aller Frauen; [B] ⇒ **maiden over.** ❷ *adj.* [A] (*unmarried*) unverheiratet; (*befitting a maid*) jungfräulich ‹Unschuld, Schönheit, Anmut›; mädchenhaft ‹Bescheidenheit, Erröten›; [B] (*first*) **~ voyage/speech** Jungfernfahrt/-rede, *die;* [C] (*unmated*) nicht gedeckt, nicht begattet ‹Tier›; [D] (*that has never won*) sieglos; **~ horse** Maiden, *das;* **~ race** Maidenrennen, *das*

**maiden: ~hair** *n.* (*Bot.*) Frauenhaarfarn, *der;* **~hair tree** Gingko[baum], *der;* Fächerbaum, *der;* **~head** *n.* [A] (*virginity*) Jungfräulichkeit, *die;* [B] (*hymen*) Jungfernhäutchen, *das;* **~ name** *n.* Mädchenname, *der;* **~ ˈover** *n.* (*Cricket*) Serie von sechs Würfen ohne erzielten Lauf

**maid: ~ of ˈhonour** *n.*, *pl.* **~s of honour** [A] (*attendant of queen or princess*) Hofod. Ehrendame, *die;* [B] (*Amer.: chief bridesmaid*) Brautjungfer, *die;* **~servant** *n.* (*arch.*) Hausangestellte, *die;* Hausmädchen, *das*

**mail**[1] /meɪl/ ❶ *n.* [A] ⇒ **post**[2] 1; [B] (*vehicle carrying ~*) Postbeförderungsmittel, *das;* (*train*) Postzug, *der.* ❷ *v.t.* ⇒ **post**[2] 2 A

**mail**[2] *n.* [A] (*armour*) Panzer, *der;* Rüstung, *die;* (*chain ~*) Kettenpanzer, *der;* **coat of ~:** Panzer- *od.* Kettenhemd, *das;* [B] (*Zool.*) Panzer, *der*

**mail: ~bag** *n.* (*postman's bag*) Zustelltasche, *die;* (*sack for transporting ~*) Postsack, *der;* **my ~bag is full of such requests** (*fig.*) ich habe jede Menge Anfragen dieser Art bekommen; **~boat** *n.* Postschiff *od.* -boot, *das;* Postdampfer, *der;* **~ bomb** *n.* (*Amer.*) Briefbombe, *die;* **~box** *n.* (*Amer.*) Briefkasten, *der;* (*slot*) Briefschlitz, *der;* **~ coach** *n.* [A] (*Hist.*) Postkutsche, *die;* [B] (*Railw.*) Post- *od.* Paketwagen, *der*

**mailed** /meɪld/ *adj.* [A] (*armed with mail*) gepanzert; [B] **~ fist** ([*threat of*] *armed force*) gepanzerte Faust

**mailing** /ˈmeɪlɪŋ/: **~ address** *n.* Postanschrift, *die;* **~ list** *n.* Adressenliste, *die*

**mail: ~man** *n.* ▶ 1261 (*Amer.*) Briefträger, *der;* Postbote, *der* (*ugs.*); **~ order** *n.* postalische Bestellung; Mailorder, *die* (*Werbespr., Kaufmannsspr.*); **by ~ order** durch Bestellung *od.* Mailorder; **~ order catalogue** *n.* Versandhauskatalog, *der;* **~ order firm, ~ order house** *ns.* Versandhaus, *das;* **~ room** *n.* Poststelle, *die;* **~shot** *n.* Versand von Werbeschriften; **~ train** *n.* Postzug, *der;* **~ van** *n.* (*Railw.*) Post- *od.* Paketwagen, *der*

**maim** /meɪm/ *v.t.* (*mutilate*) verstümmeln; (*cripple*) zum Krüppel machen; **~ sb. for life** jmdn. zeitlebens zum Krüppel machen

**main** /meɪn/ ❶ *n.* [A] (*channel, pipe*) Hauptleitung, *die;* **sewage ~:** Kanalisation, *die;* **~s [system]** öffentliches Versorgungsnetz; (*of electricity*) Stromnetz, *das;* **turn the gas/water off at the ~[s]** den Haupthahn [für das Gas/Wasser] abstellen; **turn the electricity off at the ~s** [den Strom] am Hauptschalter abschalten; **~s-operated** für Netzbetrieb *nachgestellt;* **the radio works on battery and on ~s** das Radio funktioniert mit Batterie- und Netzstrom; [B] **in the ~:** im Allgemeinen; im Großen und Ganzen.
❷ *attrib. adj.* Haupt-; **the ~ body of troops** das Gros der Truppen; **the ~ doubt/principle** der entscheidende Zweifel/oberste Grundsatz; **~ office** Zentrale, *die;* **~ theme** Hauptthema, *das;* **the ~ points of the news** die wichtigsten Meldungen; **the ~ thing is that ...:** die Hauptsache *od.* das Wichtigste ist, dass ...; **by ~ force** gewaltsam; **have an eye to the ~ chance** auf den eigenen Vorteil bedacht sein; **he married her with an eye to the ~ chance** er war auf seinen eigenen Vorteil bedacht, als er sie heiratete

**main: ~ beam** *n.* (*Motor Veh.*) **on ~ beam** aufgeblendet; **~ brace** *n.* (*Naut.*) Großbrasse, *die;* **splice the ~ brace** (*Hist.*) eine Extraration Rum austeilen; **~ ˈclause** *n.* (*Ling.*) Hauptsatz, *der;* **~ course** *n.* Hauptgang, *der;* Hauptgericht, *das;* **~frame** *n.* (*Computing*) Großrechner, *der;* **~land** /ˈmeɪnlənd/ *n.* Festland, *das;* **~ ˈline** *n.* [A] (*principal line of a railway*) Hauptstrecke, *die; attrib.* **~-line station/train** Fernbahnhof/-zug, *der;* **~-line train service** Fernverkehr, *der;* [B] (*Amer.: chief road or street*) Hauptstraße, *die;* **~line** (*sl.*) ❶ *v.i.* an der Spritze hängen (*ugs.*); ❷ *v.t.* spritzen (*ugs.*) ‹Heroin›

**mainly** /ˈmeɪnlɪ/ *adv.* hauptsächlich; in erster Linie; (*for the most part*) vorwiegend

**main: ~mast** *n.* (*Naut.*) Großmast, *der;* **~ ˈroad** Hauptstraße, *die;* **~sail** /ˈmeɪnseɪl, ˈmeɪnsl/ *n.* (*Naut.*) Großsegel, *das;* **~spring** *n.* Hauptfeder, *die;* (*of clock, watch, etc.; also fig.*) Triebfeder, *die;* **~stay** *n.* (*Naut.*) Großstag, *das;* (*fig.*) [wichtigste] Stütze; **~ ˈstem**

*n.* (*Amer. coll.*) (*street*) Hauptstraße, *die;* (*Railw.*) Hauptstrecke, *die;* **~stream** *n.* **A** (*principal current*) Hauptstrom, *der;* (*fig.*) Hauptrichtung, *die;* **the ~stream of fashion** der vorherrschende Trend in der Mode; **be in the ~stream** der Hauptrichtung angehören; **B** (*Jazz*) Mainstream, *der;* **~ 'street** *n.* /(*Amer.*) '--/ Hauptstraße, *die;* **M~ Street** *n., no pl., no art.* (*Amer. fig.*) Kleinbürgertum, *das*

**maintain** /meɪn'teɪn/ *v.t.* **A** (*keep up*) aufrechterhalten; bewahren ‹Anschein, Haltung, Einstellung, Frieden, Fassung›; unterhalten ‹Beziehungen, Briefwechsel›; [beibe]halten ‹Preise, Geschwindigkeit, Standard, Temperatur›; wahren ‹Rechte, Ruf›; **in order to ~ security** aus Sicherheitsgründen; **B** (*provide for*) **~ sb.** für jmds. Unterhalt aufkommen; **C** (*preserve*) instand halten; warten ‹Maschine, Gerät›; unterhalten ‹Straße›; **the car is too expensive to ~:** der Wagen ist in der Unterhaltung *od.* im Unterhalt zu teuer; **D** (*give aid to*) unterstützen ‹Partei, Wohlfahrtsorganisation, Sache›; **E** (*assert as true*) vertreten ‹Meinung, Lehre›; beteuern ‹Unschuld›; **~ that ...:** behaupten, dass ...

**main'tained school** *n.* (*Brit.*) staatliche Schule

**maintenance** /'meɪntənəns/ *n.* **A** ⇒ **maintain** A: Aufrechterhaltung, *die;* Bewahrung, *die;* Unterhaltung, *die;* [Beibe]halten, *das;* Wahrung, *die;* **B** (*furnishing with means of subsistence*) Unterhaltung, *die;* **C** (*assertion as true*) Vertretung, *die;* (*of innocence*) Beteuerung, *die;* **D** (*Law: money paid to support sb.*) Unterhalt, *der;* ⇒ *also* **separate maintenance**; **E** (*preservation*) Instandhaltung, *die;* (*of machinery*) Wartung, *die;* **~ instructions** (*for car*) Wartungs- und Pflegeanleitung, *die;* **F** (*aiding*) Unterstützung, *die*

**maintenance: ~-'free** *adj.* wartungsfrei; **~ manual** *n.* Wartungsbuch, *das;* **~ order** *n.* Unterhaltsurteil, *das;* **~ worker** *n.* Wartungsmonteur, *der*

**main 'verb** *n.* Hauptverb, *das*

**maison[n]ette** /meɪzə'net/ *n.* [zweistöckige] Wohnung; Maison[n]ette, *die*

**maize** /meɪz/ *n.* Mais, *der;* **~ cob** Maiskolben, *der;* **grain of ~:** Maiskorn, *das;* **field of ~:** Maisfeld, *das*

**Maj.** *abbr.* **Major[-]** Maj.

**majestic** /mə'dʒestɪk/ *adj.* majestätisch; hoheitsvoll (*geh.*); erhaben ‹Erscheinung, Schlichtheit, Schönheit›; gemessen ‹Auftreten, Schritt›; getragen ‹Musik›; (*stately*) stattlich; (*possessing grandeur*) grandios

**majestically** /mə'dʒestɪkəlɪ/ *adv.* majestätisch; gemessen[en Schritts] ‹gehen›

**majesty** /'mædʒɪstɪ/ *n.* ▶ **1617** **A** Majestät, *die* (*geh.*); (*of verse, music*) Erhabenheit, *die;* (*of appearance*) Stattlichkeit, *die;* (*of person, bearing*) Würde, *die;* **B** (*sovereign power*) Hoheit, *die;* Majestät, *die;* **C** **Your/His/Her M~:** Eure/Seine/Ihre Majestät

**major** /'meɪdʒə(r)/ **1** *adj.* **A** *attrib.* (*greater of two*) größer...; **~ part** Großteil, *der;* **B** *attrib.* (*important*) bedeutend...; (*serious*) schwer ‹Unfall, Krankheit, Unglück, Unruhen›; größer... ‹Krieg, Angriff, Durchbruch›; **not a ~ poet** kein bedeutender Dichter; kein Dichter von Bedeutung; **of ~ interest/importance** von größerem Interesse/von größerer Bedeutung; **~ road** (*important*) Hauptverkehrsstraße, *die;* (*having priority*) Vorfahrtsstraße, *die;* **C** *attrib.* (*Med.*) schwer, größer... ‹Operation›; **D** (*Brit. Sch.*) **Jones ~:** der ältere Jones; Jones Nr. 1 (*ugs.*); **E** (*Mus.*) Dur-; **~ key/scale/chord** Durtonart, *die*/Durtonleiter, *die*/Durakkord, *der;* **C ~:** C-Dur; **in a ~ key** in Dur; **~ third** *etc.* große Terz *usw.* **2** *n.* **A** ▶ **1617** (*Mil.*) (*officer above captain*) Major, *der;* (*officer in charge of section of band instruments*) Leiter der Trommler/Trompeter *usw.* einer Regimentskapelle; ⇒ *also* **sergeant major**; **B** (*Amer. Univ.*) Hauptfach, *das;* **with ~ in maths** mit Mathematik als Hauptfach; **be an economics ~:** Wirtschaftswissenschaft als Hauptfach studieren. **3** *v.i.* (*Amer. Univ.*) **~ in sth.** etw. als Hauptfach studieren

**major 'axis** *n.* (*Geom.*) große Achse; Hauptachse, *die*

**Majorca** /mə'jɔ:kə/ *pr. n.* Mallorca (*das*)

**major-domo** /meɪdʒə'dəʊməʊ/ *n., pl.* **~s** (*butler, house steward*) Haushofmeister, *der*

**majorette** /meɪdʒə'ret/ ⇒ **drum majorette**

**major-'general** *n.* ▶ **1617** (*Mil.*) Generalmajor, *der*

**majority** /mə'dʒɒrɪtɪ/ *n.* **A** (*greater number or part*) Mehrheit, *die;* **the great ~:** die überwiegende Mehrheit; der größte Teil; **the ~ of people think ...:** die meisten Menschen denken ...; **be in the ~:** in der Mehrheit *od.* Überzahl sein; überwiegen; **B** (*in vote*) [Stimmen]mehrheit, *die;* Majorität, *die;* (*party with greater/greatest number of votes*) Mehrheitspartei, *die;* **two-thirds ~:** Zweidrittelmehrheit, *die;* **be elected by a narrow** *or* **small ~/a ~ of 3,000** mit knapper Mehrheit/einer Mehrheit von 3000 Stimmen gewählt werden; **C** (*full age*) Volljährigkeit, *die;* **attain** *or* **reach one's ~:** volljährig werden; **the age of ~:** das Volljährigkeitsalter

**majority: ~ de'cision** *n.* Mehrheitsentscheid, *der;* **~ 'holding** *n.* (*Finance*) Mehrheitsanteile *Pl.;* **~ 'rule** *n.* Mehrheitsregierung, *die;* **~ 'verdict** *n.* Mehrheitsentscheid, *der;* **return a ~ verdict** mehrheitlich zu einem Urteil kommen

**major: ~ 'league** *n.* (*Amer.*) Oberliga, *die;* **~ 'planet** *n.* Riesenplanet, *der;* **~ 'prophet** *n.* (*Bibl.*) Großer Prophet; **~ 'suit** *n.* (*Bridge*) hohe Farbe

**make** /meɪk/ **1** *v.t.*, **made** /meɪd/ **A** (*construct*) machen, anfertigen (**of** aus); bauen ‹Damm, Straße, Flugzeug, Geige›; anlegen ‹See, Teich, Weg usw.›; zimmern ‹Tisch, Regal›; basteln ‹Spielzeug, Vogelhäuschen, Dekoration usw.›; nähen ‹Kleider›; durchbrechen ‹Türöffnung›; (*manufacture*) herstellen; (*create*) [er]schaffen ‹Welt›; (*prepare*) zubereiten ‹Mahlzeit›; machen ‹Frühstück, Grog›; machen, kochen ‹Kaffee, Tee, Marmelade›; backen ‹Brot, Kuchen›; (*compose, write*) schreiben, verfassen ‹Buch, Gedicht, Lied, Bericht›; machen ‹Eintrag, Zeichen, Kopie, Zusammenfassung, Testament›; anfertigen ‹Entwurf›; aufsetzen ‹Bewerbung, Schreiben, Urkunde›; **~ a film** einen Film drehen; **as tough/clever/stupid as they ~ them** (*coll.*) zäh/schlau/dumm wie sonst was (*ugs.*); **~ a dress out of the material, ~ the material into a dress** aus dem Stoff ein Kleid machen; **~ wine from grapes/a frame with timber** aus Trauben Wein/Holz einen Rahmen machen; **~ milk into butter** aus Milch Butter machen; **~ a sofa into a bed** aus einem Sofa ein Bett machen; **a table made of wood/of the finest wood** ein Holztisch/ein Tisch aus feinstem Holz; **made in Germany** in Deutschland hergestellt; **be German-made** deutsche Ware sein; **show what one is made of** zeigen, was in einem steckt (*ugs.*); **see what sb. is made of** sehen, was in jmdm. steckt (*ugs.*); **be [simply] 'made of money** (*coll.*) ein [wahrer] Krösus sein (*ugs.*); im Geld [nur so] schwimmen (*ugs.*); **be 'made for sth./sb.** (*fig.: ideally suited*) wie geschaffen für etw./jmdn. sein; **'made for one another** wie für einander geschaffen; **that's the way he's made** so ist er nun einmal; **be 'made for doing sth.** (*fig.*) dazu geschaffen sein, etw. zu tun; **be made [so as] to ...:** so beschaffen sein, dass ...; **a made dish** ein aus mehreren Zutaten bereitetes Gericht; **made road** befestigte *od.* gepflasterte Straße; **~ a bed** (*for sleeping*) ein Bett bauen (*ugs.*); **~ the bed** (*arrange after sleeping*) das Bett machen; **have it made** (*coll.*) ausgesorgt haben (*ugs.*); **she has it made** (*is sure of success*) ihr ist der Erfolg sicher; ⇒ *also* **best** 3 E; **hash**[1] 1; **hay**; **head** 1 E; **light**[2] 1 F; **meal**[1]; **measure** 1 A; **most** 2 C; **nothing** 1 A; **order** 1 E; **B** (*combine into*) sich verbinden zu; bilden; **blue and yellow ~ green** aus Blau und Gelb wird Grün; **~ it a foursome** eine Vierergruppe bilden; **C** (*cause to exist*) machen ‹Ärger, Schwierigkeiten, Lärm, Aufhebens›; **~ enemies** sich (*Dat.*) Feinde machen *od.* schaffen; **~ time for sb./sth.** sich (*Dat.*) für jmdn./etw. Zeit nehmen; **~ time for doing** *or* **to do sth.** sich (*Dat.*) die Zeit dazu nehmen, etw. zu tun; ⇒ *also* **bone** 1 A, D; **book** 1 G; **conversation**; **friend** A; **fun** 1; **game**[1] 1 D; **mark**[1] 1 A, B; **name** 1 E; **peace** B; **point** 1 G; **room** 1 B; **sport** 1 D; **stir**[1] 3 A; **D** (*result in, amount to*) machen ‹Unterschied, Summe›; ergeben ‹Resultat›; **it ~s a difference** es ist ein *od.* (*ugs.*) macht einen Unterschied; **two and two ~ four** zwei und zwei ist *od.* macht *od.* sind vier; **twelve inches ~ a foot** zwölf Inches sind ein Fuß; **these two gloves don't ~ a pair** diese beiden Handschuhe ergeben kein Paar *od.* gehören nicht zusammen; **that would ~ a nice Christmas present** das wäre ein schönes Weihnachtsgeschenk; **~ an unusual sight** ein ungewöhnlicher Anblick sein; **they ~ a handsome pair** sie geben ein hübsches Paar ab; sie sind ein hübsches Paar; **qualities that ~ a man** Eigenschaften, die einen Mann ausmachen; ⇒ *also* **change** 1 A, C, D; **swallow**[2]; **E** (*establish, enact*) bilden ‹Gegensatz›; treffen ‹Unterscheidung, Übereinkommen›; ziehen ‹Vergleich, Parallele›; erlassen ‹Gesetz, Haftbefehl›; aufstellen ‹Regeln, Behauptung›; stellen ‹Forderung›; geben ‹Bericht›; schließen ‹Vertrag›; vornehmen ‹Zahlung›; machen ‹Geschäft, Vorschlag, Geständnis›; erheben ‹Anschuldigung, Protest, Beschwerde›; **F** (*cause to be or become*) **~ angry/happy/known** *etc.* wütend/glücklich/bekannt *usw.* machen; **~ sb. captain/one's wife** jmdn. zum Kapitän/(*veralt.*) zu seiner Frau machen; **~ a good husband of sb.** aus jmdm. einen guten Ehemann machen; **~ a star of sb.** aus jmdm. einen Star machen; **~ a friend of sb.** sich mit jmdm. anfreunden; **~ something of oneself/sth.** etwas aus sich/etw. machen; **~ oneself heard/respected** sich (*Dat.*) Gehör/Respekt verschaffen; **~ oneself understood** sich verständlich machen; **~ oneself/sb. feared** bewirken, dass man/jmd. gefürchtet ist; **~ a weekend of it** ein Wochenende daraus machen; es zu einem Wochenende verlängern; **he was made director/the heir** er wurde Direktor/zum Erben; **shall we ~ it Tuesday then?** sagen wir also Dienstag?; **that ~s it one pound exactly** das macht genau ein Pfund; **~ it a round dozen** ein rundes Dutzend daraus machen; das Dutzend voll machen; **~ it a shorter journey by doing sth.** die Reise abkürzen, indem man etw. tut; ⇒ *also* **example** B; **exhibition** C; **fool**[1] 1 A; **habit** 1 A; **night** A; **practice**[1] A, D; **scarce** 1 B; **G** **~ sb. do sth.** (*cause*) jmdn. dazu bringen, etw. zu tun; (*compel*) jmdn. zwingen, etw. zu tun; **he made her cry** seinetwegen musste sie weinen; er brachte sie zum Heulen (*ugs.*); **~ sb. repeat the sentence** jmdn. den Satz wiederholen lassen; **be made to do sth.** etw. tun müssen; **you can't ~ me** du kannst mich nicht zwingen; **~ oneself do sth.** sich überwinden, etw. zu tun; **what ~s you think that?** wie kommst du darauf?; **~ sth. do sth.** es fertig bringen, dass etw. etw. tut; **H** (*form, be counted as*) **this ~s the tenth time you've failed** das ist nun [schon] das zehnte Mal, dass du versagt hast; du hast nun schon zum zehnten Mal versagt; **will you ~ one of the party?** wirst du dabei *od.* (*ugs.*) mit von der Partie sein?; **I** (*serve for*) abgeben; **this story ~s good reading** diese Geschichte ist guter Lesestoff; **J** (*become by development or training*) **the site would ~ a good playground** der Platz würde einen guten Spielplatz abgeben *od.* würde sich gut als Spielplatz eignen; **he will ~ a good officer/husband** aus ihm wird noch ein guter Offizier/Ehemann; **~ a reliable partner** ein verlässlicher Partner sein; **K** (*gain, acquire, procure*) machen ‹Vermögen, Profit, Verlust›; machen (*ugs.*) ‹Geld›; verdienen ‹Lebensunterhalt›; sich (*Dat.*) erwerben ‹Ruf›; (*obtain as result*) kommen zu *od.* auf, herausbekommen ‹Ergebnis, Endsumme›; (*Cricket: score*) erzielen; (*Cards: win*) machen ‹Stich›; erfüllen ‹Kontrakt›; **how much did you ~?** wie viel hast du verdient?; **that ~s one pound exactly** das macht genau ein Pfund; **that ~s a hundred you've scored** damit hast du insgesamt 100 Punkte; **L** (*execute by physical movement*) machen ‹Geste, Bewegung, Verbeugung, Knicks, Satz›; schlagen ‹Purzelbaum›;

m

(*perform as action*) machen ‹Reise, Besuch, Ausnahme, Fehler, Angebot, Entdeckung, Witz, Bemerkung›; begehen ‹Irrtum›; vornehmen ‹Änderung, Stornierung›; vorbringen ‹Beschwerde›; tätigen, machen ‹Einkäufe›; geben ‹Versprechen, Kommentar›; halten ‹Rede›; ziehen ‹Vergleich›; durchführen, machen ‹Experiment, Analyse, Inspektion›; (*wage*) führen ‹Krieg›; (*accomplish*) schaffen ‹Strecke pro Zeiteinheit›; **~ a good breakfast** *etc.* (*dated: eat*) gut frühstücken *usw.*; ⇒ *also* **back** 1 A; **bow**[2] 3; **face** 1 A; **love** 1 A; **shift** 3 D; **M** **~ much of sth.** etw. betonen; **~ little of sth.** (*play down*) etw. herunterspielen; **they could ~ little of his letter** (*understand*) sie konnten mit seinem Brief nicht viel anfangen; **I couldn't ~ much of the book** (*understand*) ich konnte mit dem Buch nicht viel anfangen; das Buch sagte mir nicht viel; **I don't know what to ~ of him/it** ich werde aus ihm/daraus nicht schlau *od.* klug; **what do you ~ of him?** was hältst du von ihm?; wie schätzt du ihn ein?; **N** (*arrive at*) erreichen ‹Bestimmungsort›; (*achieve place in*) kommen in (+ *Akk.*) ‹Hitparade›; aufsteigen in (+ *Akk.*) ‹1. Liga usw.›; (*coll.: catch*) [noch] kriegen (*ugs.*) ‹Zug usw.›; (*coll.: seduce*) ins Bett kriegen (*ugs.*); **~ it** (*succeed in arriving*) es schaffen; **~ it in business** es geschäftlich zu etwas bringen; **~ it through the winter/night** über den Winter/durch die Nacht kommen; **I can't ~ it tomorrow** (*coll.*) morgen passt es mir nicht; **~ it with sb.** (*coll.: seduce*) es mit jmdm. machen (*ugs.*); mit jmdm. ins Bett steigen (*ugs.*); **O** (*frame in mind*) **~ a judgement/an estimate of sth.** sich (*Dat.*) ein Urteil über etw. (*Akk.*) bilden/etw. [ab- *od.* ein]schätzen; **P** (*secure advancement of*) machen (*ugs.*) ‹Popstar usw.›; zum Erfolg verhelfen (+ *Dat.*); **a made man** ein gemachter Mann; **sth. ~s or breaks** *or* **mars sb.** etw. entscheidet über jmds. Glück oder Verderben (*Akk.*); **~ sb.'s day** jmdm. einen glücklichen Tag bescheren; **Q** (*consider to be*) **What do you ~ the time? — I ~ it five past eight** Wie spät hast du es *od.* ist es bei dir? — Auf meiner Uhr ist es fünf nach acht; **he made the answer/total £10** er bekam 10 Pfund als Antwort heraus/kam zu einer Gesamtsumme von 10 Pfund; **R** (*Electr.*) herstellen ‹Kontakt›; schließen ‹Stromkreis›; **S** (*Naut.*) (*discern*) sichten ‹Land, Hafen usw.›; **~ sail** Segel setzen; (*start on voyage*) lossegeln; **T** **~ do** vorlieb nehmen; **~ do and mend** mit den vorhandenen Sachen vorlieb nehmen und sie ausbessern; **~ do with/without sth.** mit/ohne etw. auskommen.

❷ *v.i.*, **made** **A** (*proceed*) **~ toward sth./sb.** auf etw./jmdn. zusteuern; **B** (*act as if with intention*) **~ to do sth.** Anstalten machen, etw. zu tun; **~ as if** *or* **as though to do sth.** so tun, als wolle man etw. tun; **C** (*profit*) **~ on a deal** bei einem Geschäft Gewinn machen. ⇒ *also* **bold** B; **certain** B; **free** 1 C; **good** 1 U; **merry** A; **sure** 1 E.

❸ *n.* **A** (*kind of structure*) Ausführung, *die;* (*of clothes*) Machart, *die;* **B** (*type of manufacture*) Fabrikat, *das;* (*brand*) Marke, *die;* **~ of car** Automarke, *die;* **a camera of Japanese ~:** eine Kamera japanischer Herstellung *od.* Fabrikation; **C** **on the ~** (*coll.: intent on gain*) hinter dem Geld her (*abwertend*)

**~ a'way with** ⇒ **~ off with**

**~ for** *v.t.* **A** (*move towards*) zusteuern auf (+ *Akk.*); zuhalten auf (+ *Akk.*); (*rush towards*) losgehen auf (+ *Akk.*); zustürzen auf (+ *Akk.*); **~ for home** heimwärts steuern; **B** (*be conducive to*) führen zu, herbeiführen ‹gute Beziehungen, Erfolg, Zuversicht›

**~ 'off** *v.i.* sich davonmachen

**~ 'off with** *v.t.* **~ off with sb./sth.** sich mit jmdm./etw. [auf und] davonmachen

**~ 'out** ❶ *v.t.* **A** (*write*) ausstellen ‹Scheck, Dokument, Rechnung›; aufstellen ‹Liste›; ausfertigen (*Amtsspr.*) ‹Schreiben, Antrag›; **B** (*claim, assert*) behaupten; **the novel wasn't as good as the review had made it out to be** *or* **made out** der Roman war nicht so gut, wie in der Rezension behauptet wurde; **~ out a case for/against sth.** für/gegen etw. argumentieren; **you've made out a convincing case** deine Argumente sind überzeugend; **you ~ me out to be a liar** du stellst mich als Lügner hin; **how do you ~ that out?** wie kommst du darauf?; **C** (*understand*) verstehen; **~ out what sb. wants/whether sb. wants help or not** herausbekommen, was jmd. will/ob jmd. Hilfe möchte oder nicht; **D** (*manage to see or hear*) ausmachen; (*manage to read*) entziffern; **E** (*pretend, assert falsely*) vorgeben.

❷ *v.i.* (*coll.*) (*progress*) zurechtkommen (**at** bei); **how are you making out with your girlfriend?** wie läuft es denn so mit deiner Freundin? (*ugs.*)

**~ 'over** *v.t.* **A** (*transfer*) übereignen, überschreiben ‹Geld, Geschäft, Eigentum› (**to** *Dat.*); **B** (*change, convert*) umändern, umarbeiten ‹Kleidung›; umbauen ‹Haus› (**into** zu); umgestalten ‹Garten, Zimmer›

**~ 'up** ❶ *v.t.* **A** (*replace*) ausgleichen ‹Fehlmenge, Verluste›; **~ up lost ground/time** Boden gut- *od.* wettmachen (*ugs.*)/den Zeitverlust aufholen; **B** (*complete*) komplett machen; **C** (*prepare, arrange*) zubereiten ‹Arznei usw.›; zusammenstellen ‹Picknickkorb usw.›; zurechtmachen ‹Bett›; (*prepare by mixing*) vermischen (**into** zu); (*process material*) verarbeiten (**into** zu); **~ up into bundles** bündeln; **D** (*apply cosmetics to*) schminken; **~ up one's face/eyes** sich schminken/sich (*Dat.*) die Augen schminken; ⇒ *also* **make-up** A; **E** (*assemble, compile*) zusammenstellen; aufstellen ‹Liste usw.›; bilden ‹ein Ganzes›; **F** (*Printing*) umbrechen; ⇒ *also* **make-up** D; **G** (*invent*) erfinden; sich (*Dat.*) ausdenken; **you're just making it up!** das hast du dir doch nur ausgedacht!; **H** (*reconcile*) beilegen ‹Streit, Meinungsverschiedenheit›; **~ up the quarrel** *or* **~ it up with sb.** sich wieder mit jmdm. vertragen; sich mit jmdm. aus- *od.* versöhnen; **they've made it up [again]** sie vertragen sich wieder *od.* haben sich ausgesöhnt; ⇒ *also* **mind** 1 B; **I** (*form, constitute*) bilden; **~ up a man's character** den Charakter eines Menschen ausmachen; **be made up of ...:** bestehen aus ...; ⇒ *also* **make-up** B, C; **J** **~ up the fire** [Holz *usw.* aufs Feuer] nachlegen.

❷ *v.i.* **A** (*apply cosmetics etc.*) sich schminken; ⇒ *also* **make-up** A; **B** (*be reconciled*) sich wieder vertragen

**~ 'up for** *v.t.* **A** (*outweigh, compensate*) wettmachen; **B** (*make amends for*) wieder gutmachen; **C** **~ up for lost time** Versäumtes nachholen *od.* (*ugs.*) wettmachen

**~ 'up to** *v.t.* **A** (*raise to, increase to*) bringen auf (+ *Akk.*); **B** (*coll.: act flirtatiously towards*) sich heranmachen an (+ *Akk.*) (*ugs.*); **C** (*coll.: give compensation to*) **~ it/this up to sb.** jmdn. dafür entschädigen

**~ with** *v.t.* (*Amer. coll.: supply, produce*) **~ with the drinks!** [los,] her mit den Getränken!; **start making with the ideas!** lass dir mal was einfallen!

**'make-believe** ❶ *n.* **it's only ~:** das ist bloß Fantasie; **a world of ~:** eine Scheinwelt. ❷ *adj.* nicht echt; **a ~ world/story** eine Scheinwelt/Fantasiegeschichte

**make-or-'break** *attrib. adj.* alles entscheidend

**maker** /ˈmeɪkə(r)/ *n.* **A** (*manufacturer*) Hersteller, *der;* **~ of laws/rules/regulations** *jmd., der Gesetze macht/Regeln aufstellt/Verordnungen erlässt;* **B** **M~** (*God*) Schöpfer, *der;* **meet one's M~:** vor seinen Schöpfer treten (*verhüll.*)

**-maker** *n. in comb.* -macher, *der*/-macherin, *die;* (*by machine*) -hersteller, *der*/-herstellerin, *die*

**make: ~shift** ❶ *adj.* behelfsmäßig; **a ~shift shelter/bridge** eine Behelfsunterkunft/-brücke; ❷ *n.* Notbehelf, *der;* **~-up** *n.* **A** (*Cosmetics*) Make-up, *das;* (*Theatre*) Maske, *die;* **put on one's ~-up** Make-up auflegen; sich schminken; (*Theatre*) Maske machen; *attrib.* **~-up bag** Kosmetiktasche, *die;* **wear heavy ~-up/one's stage ~-up** stark geschminkt/in Maske sein; **B** (*composition*) Zusammensetzung, *die;* **C** (*character, temperament*) Veranlagung, *die;* **physical ~-up** Konstitution, *die;* **national ~-up** Nationalcharakter, *der;* **honesty is/is not part of his ~-up** er ist seinem Wesen nach aufrichtig/Aufrichtigkeit liegt nicht in seinem Wesen; **D** (*Printing: arrangement of type*) Umbruch, *der;* **~weight** *n.* Gewichtszugabe, *die;* (*fig.: insignificant thing or person*) Lückenbüßer, *der;* (*unimportant point*) *unbedeutender Punkt zur Unterstützung eines Arguments;* **use X as [a] ~weight to Y** Y durch X schwerer machen; (*fig.*) Y durch X mehr Gewicht verleihen

**making** /ˈmeɪkɪŋ/ *n.* **A** (*production*) Herstellung, *die;* **the ~ of the English working class** die Entstehung der englischen Arbeiterklasse; **in the ~:** im Entstehen; im Werden; **a minister in the ~:** ein angehender Minister; **be the ~ of victory/sb.'s career/sb.'s future** zum Sieg/zu jmds. Karriere führen/jmds. Zukunft sichern; **B** *in pl.* (*profit*) Gewinn, *der* (**from** aus); (*earnings*) Verdienst, *der* (**on** für); **C** *in pl.* (*qualities*) Anlagen; Voraussetzungen; **have all the ~s of sth.** alle Voraussetzungen für etw. haben; **have the ~s of a leader** über Führerqualitäten verfügen; das Zeug zum Führer haben (*ugs.*); **D** (*Amer., Austral.*) **the ~s for cigarettes** Zigarettenpapier und Tabak

**malachite** /ˈmæləkaɪt/ *n.* (*Min.*) Malachit, *der; attrib.* aus Malachit *nachgestellt*

**maladjusted** /mæləˈdʒʌstɪd/ *adj.* (*Psych., Sociol.*) **[psychologically/socially] ~:** verhaltensgestört

**maladjustment** /mæləˈdʒʌstmənt/ *n.* (*Psych., Sociol.*) **[psychological/social] ~:** Verhaltensgestörtheit, *die*

**maladministration** /mælədmɪnɪˈstreɪʃn/ *n.* Misswirtschaft, *die*

**maladroit** /mæləˈdrɔɪt, ˈmælədrɔɪt/ *adj.* ungeschickt; taktlos ‹Bemerkung›

**malady** /ˈmælədɪ/ *n.* Leiden, *das;* (*fig.: of society, epoch*) Übel, *das*

**Malaga** /ˈmæləgə/ *n.* (*wine*) Malaga, *der*

**Malagasy** /mæləˈgæsɪ/ ▶ **1275**, ▶ **1340** ❶ *adj.* madagassisch. ❷ *n.* (*person*) Madagasse, *der*/Madagassin, *die;* (*language*) Malagassi, *das;* Madagassisch, *das*

**malaise** /məˈleɪz/ *n.* (*bodily discomfort*) Unwohlsein, *das;* (*feeling of uneasiness*) Unbehagen, *das;* Malaise, *die* (*geh.*)

**malapropism** /ˈmæləprɒpɪzm/ *n.* Malapropismus, *der* (*Literaturw.*); *irrtümlicher Gebrauch eines [schwierigen] Wortes anstelle eines ähnlich klingenden*

**malaria** /məˈleərɪə/ *n.* ▶ **1232** Malaria, *die*

**malarkey** /məˈlɑːkɪ/ *n., no pl., no indef. art.* (*coll.*) Blabla, *das* (*salopp*); **a load of ~:** reinstes Geschwafel (*ugs.*)

**Malawi** /məˈlɑːwɪ/ *pr. n.* Malawi (*das*)

**Malawian** /məˈlɑːwɪən/ ▶ **1340** ❶ *adj.* malawisch. ❷ Malawier, *der*/Malawierin, *die*

**Malay** /məˈleɪ/ ▶ **1275**, ▶ **1340** ❶ *adj.* malaiisch; **sb. is ~:** jmd. ist Malaie/Malaiin; ⇒ *also* **English** 1. ❷ *n.* **A** (*person*) Malaie, *der*/Malaiin, *die;* **B** (*language*) Malaiisch, *das;* ⇒ *also* **English** 2 A

**Malaya** /məˈleɪə/ *pr. n.* Malaya (*das*)

**Malayan** /məˈleɪən/ ⇒ **Malay** 1, 2 A

**Malaysia** /məˈleɪzɪə/ *pr. n.* Malaysia (*das*)

**Malaysian** /məˈleɪzɪən/ ▶ **1340** ❶ *adj.* malaysisch. ❷ *n.* Malaysier, *der*/Malaysierin, *die*

**malcontent** /ˈmælkəntent/ ❶ *adj.* unzufrieden; malkontent (*landsch., sonst veralt.*). ❷ *n.* Nörgler, *der*/Nörglerin, *die* (*abwertend*)

**Maldives** /ˈmɔːldiːvz/ *pr. n. pl.* Malediven *Pl.*

**male** /meɪl/ ❶ *adj.* **A** männlich; Männer‹stimme, -chor, -verein›; **~ child/dog/cat/doctor/nurse/student** Junge/Rüde/Kater/Arzt/Krankenpfleger/Student, *der;* **~ prostitute** *Mann, der der Prostitution nachgeht;* Strichjunge, *der* (*salopp*); Stricher, *der* (*salopp*); **~ animal/bird/fish/insect** Männchen, *das;* **~ ward** Männerstation, *die;* **B** **~ screw** Schraube, *die;* **~ thread** Außengewinde, *das.* ⇒ *also* **chauvinism**; **chauvinist**; **menopause** A. ❷ *n.* (*person*) Mann, *der;* (*foetus, child*) Junge, *der;* (*animal*) Männchen, *das*

**malediction** /mælɪˈdɪkʃn/ *n.* Fluch, *der;* Verwünschung, *die*

**'male-dominated** *adj.* von Männern dominiert; **a ~ field** eine Männerdomäne

**malefactor** /ˈmælɪfæktə(r)/ *n.* Übeltäter, *der*

**maleficent** /məˈlefɪsənt/ *adj.* böse ‹Geist, Macht›

**male voice ˈchoir** *n.* Männerchor, *der*

**malevolence** /məˈlevələns/ *n., no pl.* ⇒ **malevolent**: Bosheit, *die;* Übelwollen, *das;* Böswilligkeit, *die;* Boshaftigkeit, *die;* **feel ~ towards sb.** Missgunst gegenüber jmdm. empfinden

**malevolent** /məˈlevələnt/ *adj.* böse ‹Macht, Tat›; übel wollend ‹Gott›; boshaft, hämisch ‹Gelächter›; böswillig ‹Lüge›; boshaft ‹Person›

**malevolently** /məˈlevələntlɪ/ *adv.* boshaft ‹anstarren›; böswillig ‹verhindern, durchkreuzen›; in böser Absicht ‹überreden›; hämisch ‹lachen›

**malformation** /mælfɔːˈmeɪʃn/ *n.* (*Med.*) Missbildung, *die*

**malformed** /mælˈfɔːmd/ *adj.* (*Med.*) missgebildet

**malfunction** /mælˈfʌŋkʃn/ **1** *n.* Störung, *die;* (*Med.*) Dysfunktion, *die* (*fachspr.*); Funktionsstörung, *die.* **2** *v.i.* ‹Mechanismus, System, Gerät:› nicht richtig funktionieren; ‹Prozess, Vorgang:› nicht richtig ablaufen; **the nervous system/liver ~s** die Funktion des Nervensystems/der Leber ist gestört

**Mali** /ˈmɑːlɪ/ *pr. n.* Mali (*das*)

**Malian** /ˈmɑːlɪən/ ▶1340 **1** *adj.* malisch. **2** *n.* Malier, *der*/Malierin, *die*

**malice** /ˈmælɪs/ *n.* **A** (*active ill will*) Bosheit, *die;* Böswilligkeit, *die;* (*desire to tease*) Schalkhaftigkeit, *die* (*geh.*); **bear ~ to** *or* **towards** *or* **against sb.** jmdm. übel wollen; **B** (*Law*) böse Absicht; Dolus, *der* (*fachspr.*); böser Vorsatz; ⇒ *also* **aforethought**

**malicious** /məˈlɪʃəs/ *adj.* **A** böse ‹Klatsch, Tat, Person, Wort›; böswillig ‹Gerücht, Lüge, Verleumdung›; boshaft ‹Person›; hämisch ‹Vergnügen, Freude›; **B** (*Law*) böswillig ‹Sachbeschädigung, Verleumdung›

**maliciously** /məˈlɪʃəslɪ/ *adv.* **A** mit [böser] Absicht; böse ‹lächeln›; **B** (*Law*) böswillig

**malign** /məˈlaɪn/ **1** *v.t.* (*slander*) verleumden; (*speak ill of*) schlecht machen; **~ sb.'s character** jmdm. Übles nachsagen; ‹Klatsch, Verleumdung:› jmdn. in Verruf bringen. **2** *adj.* **A** (*injurious*) böse ‹Macht, Geist›; schlecht, unheilvoll ‹Eigenschaft, Einfluss›; **B** (*Med.: malignant*) maligne (*fachspr.*), bösartig ‹Krankheit›; schwer ‹Verletzung›; **C** (*malevolent*) böse ‹Absicht›; niederträchtig ‹Motiv›

**malignancy** /məˈlɪgnənsɪ/ *n.* (*Med.*) Bösartigkeit, *die;* Malignität, *die* (*fachspr.*)

**malignant** /məˈlɪgnənt/ *adj.* **A** (*Med.*) maligne (*fachspr.*), bösartig ‹Krankheit, Geschwür›; **~ cancer** Karzinom, *das* (*fachspr.*); Krebs, *der;* **B** (*harmful*) böse ‹Macht›; ungünstig ‹Einfluss›; **C** (*feeling or showing ill will*) böse ‹Geist, Zunge, Klatsch›; bösartig, boshaft ‹Verleumdung›

**malinger** /məˈlɪŋgə(r)/ *v.i.* simulieren

**malingerer** /məˈlɪŋgərə(r)/ *n.* Simulant, *der*/Simulantin, *die*

**mall** /mæl, mɔːl/ *n.* **A** (*promenade*) Promenade, *die;* **B** (*Amer.: shopping precinct*) Einkaufszentrum, *das;* Einkaufsstraße, *die*

**mallard** /ˈmælɑːd/ *n.* (*Ornith.*) Stockente, *die*

**malleable** /ˈmælɪəbl/ *adj.* formbar ‹Material, Person›

**mallet** /ˈmælɪt/ *n.* **A** (*hammer*) Holzhammer, *der;* Schlegel, *der;* (*of stonemason*) Klöpfel, *der;* (*of carpenter*) Klopfholz, *das;* **B** (*Croquet*) Hammer, *der;* (*Polo*) Schläger, *der*

**mallow** /ˈmæləʊ/ *n.* (*Bot.*) Malve, *die*

**malnutrition** /mælnjuːˈtrɪʃn/ *n.* Unterernährung, *die*

**malodorous** /mælˈəʊdərəs/ *adj.* übel riechend

**malpractice** /mælˈpræktɪs/ *n.* **A** (*wrongdoing*) Übeltat, *die* (*geh.*); **B** (*Law, Med.: improper treatment of patient*) Kunstfehler, *der;* **C** (*Law: wrongdoing by official etc.*) Amtsvergehen, *das*

**malt** /mɔːlt, mɒlt/ **1** *n.* **A** ⇒Malz, *das;* **B** (*coll.: malt whisky*) Malzwhisky, *der.* **2** *v.t.* mälzen ‹Gerste›

**Malta** /ˈmɔːltə, ˈmɒltə/ *pr. n.* Malta (*das*)

**malted** /ˈmɔːltɪd, ˈmɒltɪd/ *attrib. adj.* Malz-

**Maltese** /mɔːlˈtiːz, mɒlˈtiːz/ ▶1275, ▶1340 **1** *adj.* maltesisch; **sb. is ~:** jmd. ist Malteser/Malteserin. **2** *n., pl. same* **A** (*person*) Malteser, *der*/Malteserin, *die;* **B** (*language*) Maltesisch (*das*)

**Maltese: ~ ˈcat** *n. blaugraue, kurzhaarige Hauskatze;* **~ ˈcross** *n.* Malteserkreuz, *das*

**malt: ~ ˈextract** *n.* Malzextrakt, *der;* **~house** *n.* Mälzerei, *die;* **~ ˈliquor** *n.* Bier, *das*

**maltreat** /mælˈtriːt/ *v.t.* misshandeln

**maltreatment** /mælˈtriːtmənt/ *n.* Misshandlung, *die*

**malt ˈwhisky** *n.* Malzwhisky, *der*

**mam** /mæm/ *n.* (*Brit. coll./child lang.*) Mama, *die* (*fam.*); Mami, *die* (*fam.*)

**mama** ⇒ **mamma**

**mamba** /ˈmæmbə/ *n.* (*Zool.*) Mamba, *die*

**mamma** /məˈmɑː/ *n.* (*coll./child lang.*) Mama, *die* (*fam.*); Mami, *die* (*fam.*); **~'s boy** (*coll.*) Muttersöhnchen, *das* (*ugs.*)

**mammal** /ˈmæml/ *n.* (*Zool.*) Säugetier, *das;* Säuger, *der*

**mammalian** /məˈmeɪlɪən/ (*Zool.*) **1** *adj.* Säugetier-; eines Säugetiers *nachgestellt.* **2** *n.* Säugetier, *das;* Säuger, *der*

**mammary** /ˈmæmərɪ/ *adj.* (*Anat., Zool.*) Brust-; **~ gland** Brustdrüse, *die*

**mammography** /mæˈmɒgrəfɪ/ *n., no pl.* (*Med.*) Mammographie, *die*

**Mammon** /ˈmæmən/ *n.* **A** (*wealth regarded as idol*) Mammon, *der;* **ye cannot serve God and ~** (*Bibl.*) ihr könnt nicht Gott dienen und dem Mammon; **B** (*the rich*) die Reichen

**mammoth** /ˈmæməθ/ **1** *n.* (*Zool., Palaeont.*) Mammut, *das.* **2** *adj.* Mammut-; riesig ‹Menge›; gigantisch ‹Vorhaben›

**mammy** /ˈmæmɪ/ *n.* **A** (*child lang.: mother*) Mama, *die* (*fam.*); Mami, *die* (*fam.*); **B** (*Amer.: black nurse*) schwarze Kinderfrau

**man** /mæn/ **1** *n., pl.* **men** /men/ **A** *no art., no pl.* (*human being, person*) Mensch, *der;* (*the human race*) der Mensch; **as a ~:** als Mensch; **God was made ~:** Gott ward Mensch (*bibl.*); **~ is a political animal** der Mensch ist ein politisches Wesen; **everything a ~ needs** alles, was der Mensch braucht; **what can a ~ do?** was kann man tun?; **every ~ for himself** rette sich, wer kann; **as one ~:** wie ein Mann; (*unanimously*) geschlossen; **any ~ who ...:** wer ...; jeder, der ...; **no ~:** niemand; **always get one's ~:** den Täter immer finden; **[all] to a ~:** allesamt; **to the last ~:** bis zum letzten Mann; **they were killed to a ~:** sie wurden bis auf den letzten Mann getötet; **the ~ in** *or* (*Amer.*) **on the street** der Mann auf der Straße; **the rights of ~:** die Menschenrechte; **Heidelberg M~:** der Homo heidelbergensis; der Heidelbergmensch; **Java/Peking M~:** der Java-/Pekingmensch; **B** (*adult male, individual male*) Mann, *der;* **every ~, woman, and child** ausnahmslos jeder *od.* alle; **the right ~:** der richtige Mann; der Richtige; **the [very] ~ for sth.** der richtige Mann *od.* der Richtige; **he is your ~:** er ist der richtige Mann *od.* der Richtige für dich; **you have arrested the wrong ~:** Sie haben den Falschen verhaftet; **a ~'s life** ein Leben für Männer; **a ~'s ~:** ein Mann, der sich nur in männlicher Gesellschaft wohl fühlt; **make a ~ out of sb.** (*fig.*) einen Mann aus jmdm. machen; **be only half a ~:** nur ein halber Mann sein; **like a ~:** wie ein Mann; **that's just like a ~:** typisch Mann!; **a ~ of property/great strength** ein vermögender/sehr kräftiger Mann; **that ~ Oakfield** dieser Oakfield; **play the ~:** ein Mann sein; **men's clothing/outfitter** Herrenkleidung, *die*/Herrenausstatter, *der;* **be ~ enough to ...:** Manns genug sein, um zu ...; **a ˈman's voice** eine männliche Stimme; **'the deodorant for men'** „das Herrendeodorant"; **I have lived here, ~ and boy** ich habe hier von frühester Jugend an gewohnt; **sth. sorts out** *or* **separates the men from the boys** (*coll.*) an etw. (*Dat.*) zeigt sich, wer ein ganzer Kerl ist und wer nicht; **~ of God** Gottesmann, *der* (*geh.*); **the ~ in the moon** der Mann im Mond; **he's a local ~:** er ist von hier; **a whisky ~:** ein Whiskytrinker; **he's [not] a drinking ~:** er trinkt [nicht]; **be one's own ~:** wissen, was man will; **you've come to the right ~:** bei mir sind Sie richtig; **men's toilet** Herrentoilette, *die;* **'Men'** „Herren"; **my [good] ~:** mein Guter; **fight ~ to ~:** Mann gegen Mann kämpfen; **~ friend** Freund, *der;* **C** (*husband*) Mann, *der;* **be ~ and wife** verheiratet sein; **D** (*work~*) Mann, *der;* **E** *usu. in pl.* (*soldier, sailor, etc.*) Mann, *der;* **F** (*Chess*) Figur, *die;* (*Draughts*) Stein, *der;* **G** (*coll.: as int. of surprise or impatience, as mode of address*) Mensch! (*salopp*); **nonsense, ~!** Unsinn!; **hurry up, ~!** Mensch, beeil dich!; **H** (*type of ~*) Mann, *der;* Typ, *der;* **a ~ of the people/world/of action** ein Mann des Volkes/von Welt/der Tat; **he is not a** *or* **the ~ to do something like that** er ist nicht der Mann *od.* Typ, der so etwas tut; **he is not a ~ I could trust** ihm könnte ich nicht trauen; **be an Oxford ~:** aus Oxford kommen; (*Univ.*) in Oxford studiert haben; **I** (*~servant*) Diener, *der.* ⇒ *also* **action** A; **alive** A; **best man**; **Clapham**; **handyman**; **honour** 1 D; **house** 1 A; **inner man**; **jack** 1 C; **letter** 1 D; **little** 1 B; **moment** A; **old man**; **outer** B; **part** 1 I; **substance** B; **town** A; **word** 1 B; **world** A.
**2** *v.t.*, **-nn-** bemannen ‹Schiff, Spill›; besetzen ‹Büro, Stelle, Posten, Pumpe, Kontrollpunkt›; bedienen ‹Telefon, Geschütz›; ‹Soldaten:› Stellung beziehen in (+ *Dat.*) ‹Festung›; mit Personal besetzen ‹Fabrik, Werk›; **be ~ned by a crew of 50** ‹Schiff:› eine Besatzung von 50 Mann haben

**manacle** /ˈmænəkl/ **1** *n., usu. in pl.* [Hand]fessel, *die;* Kette, *die.* **2** *v.t.* Handfesseln anlegen (+ *Dat.*)

**manage** /ˈmænɪdʒ/ **1** *v.t.* **A** (*handle, wield*) handhaben ‹Werkzeug, Segel, Boot›; bedienen ‹Schaltbrett›; **the tool is too heavy for him to ~:** er kommt mit dem schweren Gerät nicht zurecht; **B** (*conduct, organize*) durchführen ‹Operation, Unternehmen›; erledigen ‹Angelegenheit›; verwalten ‹Geld, Grundstück›; leiten ‹Geschäft, Büro, Schule, Krankenhaus›; führen ‹Haushalt›; **C** (*Sport etc.: be manager of*) managen, betreuen ‹Team, Mannschaft›; **D** (*cope with*) schaffen; **I could/couldn't ~ another apple** (*coll.*) ich könnte noch einen Apfel schaffen/noch einen Apfel schaffe ich nicht; **I can/can't ~ this suitcase** den Koffer kann ich [alleine] tragen/ich werde mit diesem Koffer nicht fertig; **we can ~ another person in the car** einer hat noch Platz im Wagen; **he can't ~ the stairs** er kommt die Treppe nicht rauf/runter; **E** (*gain one's ends with*) für sich gewinnen ‹Person›; **F** (*succeed in achieving*) zustande bringen ‹Lächeln›; **G** (*contrive*) **~ to do sth.** (*also iron.*) es fertig bringen, etw. zu tun; **he ~d to do it** es gelang ihm, es zu tun; **I don't know how you ~d it** ich weiß nicht, wie du das bewerkstelligt hast; **I'll ~ it somehow** ich werde es schon irgendwie hinkriegen (*ugs.*); **I ~d to get a word in** ich kam endlich zu Wort; **can you ~ to be there at 10 a.m.?** (*coll.*) kannst du um 10 Uhr dort sein?; **how could you ~ to eat all that?** (*coll.*) wie hast du es [bloß] geschafft, das alles zu essen?; **can you ~ 7 [o'clock]?** passt dir 7 Uhr?; **H** (*be in charge of*) hüten ‹Herde›; **I** (*control*) bändigen ‹Person, Tier, Haar›.
**2** *v.i.* zurechtkommen; **~ without sth.** ohne etw. auskommen; **~ on** zurecht- *od.* auskommen mit ‹Geld, Einkommen›; **~ by oneself** allein zurechtkommen; **I can ~:** es geht; **can you ~?** gehts?; geht es?

**manageable** /ˈmænɪdʒəbl/ *adj.* leicht frisierbar ‹Haar›; fügsam ‹Person, Tier›; regierbar ‹Land, Staat›; überschaubar ‹Größe, Menge›; zu bewältigend ‹Portion›; lenkbar ‹Firma›

**management** /ˈmænɪdʒmənt/ *n.* **A** Durchführung, *die;* (*of a business*) Leitung, *die;* Management, *das;* (*of money*) Verwaltung, *die;* **~ studies** Betriebsführung und -organisation (*als Teilgebiet der Betriebswirtschaftslehre*); **it**

m

**was bad ~ to ...:** es war ein Fehler der Geschäftsleitung, zu ...; B (*managers*) Leitung, *die;* Management, *das;* (*of theatre etc.*) Direktion, *die;* **the ~:** die Geschäftsleitung; **'under new ~'** „unter neuer Leitung"; C (*Med.*) Behandlung, *die*

**management: ~ 'buyout** *n.* Management-Buy-out, *das;* **~ consultancy** *n.* Unternehmensberatung, *die;* **~ consultant** *n.* ▶ 1261 Unternehmensberater, *der/*-beraterin, *die*

**manager** /'mænɪdʒə(r)/ *n.* ▶ 1261 (*of branch of shop or bank*) Filialleiter, *der/*-leiterin, *die;* Geschäftsstellenleiter, *der/*-leiterin, *die;* (*of football team*) [Chef]trainer, *der/*-trainerin, *die;* (*of tennis player, boxer, pop group*) Manager, *der/*Managerin, *die;* (*of restaurant, shop, hotel*) Geschäftsführer, *der/*-führerin, *die;* (*of estate, grounds*) Verwalter, *der/*Verwalterin, *die;* (*of department; sales or publicity ~*) Leiter, *der/*Leiterin, *die;* (*of theatre*) Direktor, *der/*Direktorin, *die*

**manageress** /'mænɪdʒəres, mænɪdʒə'res/ *n.* (*of restaurant, shop, hotel*) Geschäftsführerin, *die;* ⇒ *also* **manager**

**managerial** /mænə'dʒɪərɪəl/ *adj.* führend, leitend ‹Stellung›; geschäftlich ‹Aspekt, Seite›; ‹Pflicht, Fähigkeiten› als Führungskraft; **~ skills** Führungsqualitäten; **the ~ class** die Führungsschicht

**managing** /'mænɪdʒɪŋ/ *attrib. adj.* geschäftsführend; leitend; **~ director** Geschäftsführer, *der*

**Manchuria** /mæn'tʃʊərɪə/ *pr. n.* die Mandschurei

**Mancunian** /mæŋ'kju:nɪən/ ❶ *adj.* Manchesterer. ❷ *n.* Manchesterer, *der/*Manchesterin, *die*

**mandala** /'mændələ/ *n.* (*Hinduism, Buddhism, Psych.*) Mandala, *das*

**mandarin[1]** /'mændərɪn/ *n.* **~ [orange]** Mandarine, *die*

**mandarin[2]** *n.* A (*Hist.: Chinese official*) Mandarin, *der;* B ▶ 1275 **M~** (*language*) Hochchinesisch, *das;* C (*party leader*) Parteiboss, *der* (*ugs.*); [Partei]bonze, *der* (*abwertend*); D (*bureaucrat*) Bürokrat, *der/*Bürokratin, *die* (*abwertend*); Apparatschik, *der* (*abwertend*)

**mandarin: ~ 'collar** *n.* Mandarinkragen, *der;* **~ 'duck** *n.* Mandarinente, *die*

**mandarine** /'mændəri:n/ ⇒ **mandarin[1]**

**mandarin 'sleeve** *n.* Bouffonärmel, *der*

**mandate** ❶ /'mændeɪt/ *n.* A (*judicial or legal command*) Verfügung, *die;* B (*commission to act for another*) Mandat, *das;* C (*Polit.*) Mandat, *das;* **electoral ~:** Wählerauftrag, *der.* ❷ /mæn'deɪt/ *v.t.* **~ a territory to a country** ein Gebiet der Verwaltung eines Landes unterstellen

**mandatory** /'mændətərɪ/ *adj.* obligatorisch; **be ~:** Pflicht od. obligatorisch sein; **it is ~ for sb. to do sth.** jmd. muss etw. tun

**'man-day** *n.* (*Work Study*) Manntag, *der;* Arbeitstag pro Mann

**mandible** /'mændɪbl/ *n.* (*Zool.*) A (*of mammal, fish*) Unterkiefer, *der;* B (*of bird*) Schnabel, *der;* **lower ~:** Unterschnabel, *der;* C (*of insect*) Zange, *die;* Kiefer, *der*

**mandolin, mandoline** /mændə'lɪn/ *n.* (*Mus.*) Mandoline, *die*

**mandrake** /'mændreɪk/ *n.* (*Bot.*) Mandragore, *die;* Alraunwurzel, *die*

**mandrel** /'mændrəl/ *n.* (*Mech. Engin.*) A (*shaft in lathe*) Drehspindel, *die;* B (*rod*) Horn, *das*

**mandrill** /'mændrɪl/ *n.* (*Zool.*) Mandrill, *der*

**mane** /meɪn/ *n.* (*lit. or fig.*) Mähne, *die*

**man: ~eater** *n.* (*tiger*) Menschen fressender Tiger; (*shark*) Menschenhai, *der;* (*cannibal*) Kannibale, *der/*Kannibalin, *die;* (*fig.: woman*) Frau, die Männer aussaugt; **~-eating** *adj.* Menschen fressend ‹Löwe, Tiger›; **a ~-eating shark** ein Menschenhai

**maneuver, maneuverable** (*Amer.*) ⇒ **manœuvr-**

**man 'Friday** ⇒ **Friday** 1

**manful** /'mænfl/ *adj.* mannhaft

**manfully** /'mænfəlɪ/ *adv.* mannhaft; wie ein Mann

**manganese** /'mæŋgəni:z, mæŋgə'ni:z/ *n.* A (*Min.*) Braunstein, *der;* Manganoxid, *das* (*fachspr.*); B (*Chem.*) Mangan, *das*

**mange** /meɪndʒ/ *n.* (*Vet. Med.*) Räude, *die*

**mangel[-wurzel]** /'mæŋgl(wɜ:zl)/ *n.* (*Agric.*) Runkelrübe, *die*

**manger** /'meɪndʒə(r)/ *n.* Futtertrog, *der;* (*Bibl.*) Krippe, *die;* ⇒ *also* **dog** 1 A

**mangetout** /mɑ̃ʒ'tu:/ *n.* Zuckererbse, *die*

**mangle[1]** /'mæŋgl/ ❶ *n.* Mangel, *die.* ❷ *v.t.* mangeln ‹Wäsche›

**mangle[2]** *v.t.* verstümmeln, [übel] zurichten ‹Person›; demolieren ‹Sache›; verstümmeln, entstellen ‹Zitat, Musikstück›

**mango** /'mæŋgəʊ/ *n., pl.* **~es** *or* **~s** A (*tree*) Mangobaum, *der;* B (*fruit*) Mango[frucht], *die*

**mangrove** /'mæŋgrəʊv/ *n.* (*Bot.*) Mangrovebaum, *der*

**mangy** /'meɪndʒɪ/ *adj.* A (*Vet. Med.*) räudig; B (*squalid, shabby*) verwahrlost, schäbig ‹Äußeres, Kleidung›; abgenutzt, schäbig ‹Teppich, Decke, Stuhl›

**man: ~handle** *v.t.* A (*move by human effort*) von Hand bewegen ‹Gegenstand›; B (*handle roughly*) grob behandeln ‹Person›; **~hater** *n.* (*misanthrope*) Menschenhasser, *der/*-hasserin, *die;* (*hater of male sex*) Männerfeind, *der/*-feindin, *die;* **~hole** *n.* Mannloch, *das;* (*in tank*) Einstiegsluke, *die;* (*to cables under pavement*) Kabelschacht, *der*

**manhood** /'mænhʊd/ *n., no pl.* A (*state*) Mannesalter, *das;* B (*courage*) Männlichkeit, *die;* C (*men of a country*) Männer *Pl.*

**man: ~-hour** *n.* (*Work Study*) Arbeitsstunde, *die;* **~hunt** *n.* Menschenjagd, *die;* (*for criminal*) Verbrecherjagd, *die*

**mania** /'meɪnɪə/ *n.* A (*madness*) Wahnsinn, *der;* B (*enthusiasm*) Manie, *die;* **~ for detective novels** Leidenschaft für Krimis; **have a ~ for doing sth.** etw. wie besessen *od.* leidenschaftlich gern tun; **there was a ~ at that time for wearing earrings** damals waren die Leute ganz verrückt auf Ohrringen

**-mania** *n. in comb.* (*Psych.*) -manie, *die*

**maniac** /'meɪnɪæk/ ❶ *adj.* wahnsinnig; krankhaft, (*geh.*) manisch ‹Fantasie, Verlangen›. ❷ *n.* A (*Psych.*) Besessene, *der/die;* (*madman/-woman*) Wahnsinnige, *der/die;* B (*person with passion for sth.*) Fanatiker, *der/*Fanatikerin, *die;* **a nation of tennis ~s** ein Volk von Tennisfanatikern

**maniacal** /mə'naɪəkl/ *adj.* wahnsinnig

**manic** /'mænɪk/ *adj.* (*Psych.*) manisch

**manic-de'pressive** (*Psych.*) ❶ *adj.* manisch-depressiv. ❷ *n.* manisch-depressiver Mensch; **be a ~:** manisch-depressiv sein

**manicure** /'mænɪkjʊə(r)/ ❶ *n.* Maniküre, *die;* **give sb. a ~:** jmdn. maniküren. ❷ *v.t.* maniküren

**manicurist** /'mænɪkjʊərɪst/ *n.* ▶ 1261 Maniküre, *die*

**manifest** /'mænɪfest/ ❶ *adj.* offenkundig; offenbar ‹Missverständnis›; sichtbar ‹Erfolg, Fortschritt›; sichtlich ‹Freude›. ❷ *v.t.* A (*show, display*) zeigen, bekunden (*geh.*) ‹Interesse, Missfallen, Begeisterung, Zuneigung›; B (*reveal*) offenbaren (*meist geh.*); **~ itself** ‹Geist:› erscheinen; ‹Natur, Wahrheit:› sich offenbaren; ‹Symptom, Krankheit:› manifest werden. ❸ *n.* A (*cargo list*) Frachtgutliste, *die;* Ladeverzeichnis, *das;* **ship's ~:** [Schiffs]manifest, *das;* B (*list*) (*of passengers in aircraft*) Passagierliste, *die;* (*of trucks etc. in goods train*) Fahrzeugliste, *die*

**manifestation** /mænɪfe'steɪʃn/ *n.* (*of ill will, favour, disapproval*) Ausdruck, *der;* Bekundung, *die* (*geh.*); Bezeugung, *die;* (*appearance*) Erscheinung, *die; in pl.* Erscheinungsformen; (*visible expression, sign*) [An]zeichen, *das* (**of** von)

**manifestly** /'mænɪfestlɪ/ *adv.* offenkundig; **it is ~ unjust that ...:** es ist ganz offensichtlich ungerecht, dass ...

**manifesto** /mænɪ'festəʊ/ *n., pl.* **~s** Manifest, *das*

**manifold** /'mænɪfəʊld/ ❶ *adj.* (*literary*) mannigfaltig (*geh.*); vielfältig; vielseitig ‹Erzählperspektive, Gehalt, Verwendung›. ❷ (*Mech. Engin.*) Verteilerrohr, *das;* **[inlet] ~:** [Ansaug]krümmer, *der;* **[exhaust] ~:** [Auspuff]krümmer, *der*

**manikin** /'mænɪkɪn/ *n.* A (*dwarf*) Zwerg, *der;* B (*Art*) Gliederpuppe, *die;* C (*Med.*) anatomisches Modell

**Manila** /mə'nɪlə/ *n.* A (*cigar*) Manilazigarre, *die;* B (*fibre*) **~ [hemp]** ⇒ **hemp** A; C (*paper*) **~ [paper]** Manilapapier, *das;* **~ [envelope]** Briefumschlag aus Manilapapier; brauner Briefumschlag

**manioc** /'mænɪɒk/ *n.* A (*plant*) Maniok, *der;* B (*flour*) Mandioka, *die*

**manipulate** /mə'nɪpjʊleɪt/ *v.t.* A (*also Med.*) manipulieren; **~ sb. into doing sth.** jmdn. dahin gehend manipulieren, dass er etw. tut; B (*handle*) handhaben

**manipulation** /mənɪpjʊ'leɪʃn/ *n.* A (*also Med.*) Manipulation, *die;* B (*handling*) Handhabung, *die*

**manipulative** /mə'nɪpjʊlətɪv/ *adj.* manipulativ

**mankind** /mæn'kaɪnd/ *n.* Menschheit, *die*

**'manlike** *adj.* A (*like a male, mannish*) männlich; B (*like a human*) menschenähnlich

**manly** /'mænlɪ/ *adj.* männlich; (*brave*) mannhaft (*geh.*)

**'man-made** *adj.* künstlich ‹See, Blumen, Schlucht›; vom Menschen geschaffen ‹Gesetze›; (*synthetic*) Kunst‹faser, -stoff›

**manna** /'mænə/ *n.* (*Bibl.*) Manna, *das;* **be ~ [from heaven]** (*fig.*) ein wahrer Segen sein

**manned** /mænd/ *adj.* bemannt ‹Raumschiff usw.›

**mannequin** /'mænɪkɪn/ *n.* A (*person*) Mannequin, *das;* B (*dummy*) Schaufensterpuppe, *die*

**manner** /'mænə(r)/ *n.* A (*way, fashion*) Art, *die;* Weise, *die;* (*more emphatic*) Art und Weise, *die;* **in this ~:** auf diese Art und Weise; **he did it in a very unorthodox ~:** er machte es auf [eine ganz] unorthodoxe Art; **he acted in such a ~ as to offend her** er benahm sich so, dass sie beleidigt war; **in the French ~:** auf französische Art; **celebrate in the grand ~:** in großem Stil feiern; **[as] to the ~ born** (*coll.*) wie dafür geschaffen; **in a ~ of speaking** mehr oder weniger; **adverb of ~** (*Ling.*) Umstandsbestimmung der Art und Weise; B *no pl.* (*bearing*) Art, *die;* (*towards others*) Auftreten, *das;* C *in pl.* (*social behaviour*) Manieren *Pl.;* Benehmen, *das;* **teach sb. some ~s** jmdm. Manieren beibringen; **forget one's ~s** seine guten Manieren zu Hause lassen; **where are your ~s?** wo hast du deine Manieren gelassen?; **that's good ~s** das gehört sich so; **that's bad ~s** das gehört sich nicht; das macht man nicht; **mind** *or* **watch your ~s!** benimm dich!; **~s maketh man** (*prov.*) es kommt vor allem auf gutes Benehmen an; ⇒ *also* **mend** 1 B; D *in pl.* (*modes of life*) Sitten *Pl.;* E (*artistic style*) Stil, *der;* **~s** Stilrichtungen; F (*type*) **all ~ of** ⇒ **all** 1 B; **no ~ of** keinerlei; **what ~ of man is he?** (*arch.*) was für ein Mensch ist er?; ⇒ *also* **means** C

**mannered** /'mænəd/ *adj.* A (*showing mannerism*) manieriert; B *in comb.* **... -~:** mit ... Manieren *nachgestellt;* **be well-~/bad-~:** gute/schlechte Manieren haben; **he's a mild-~ man** er hat ein sanftes Wesen

**mannerism** /'mænərɪzm/ *n.* A (*addiction to a manner*) Manieriertheit, *die;* B (*trick of style*) Manierismus, *der;* C (*in behaviour*) Eigenart, *die;* D *no pl., no art.* (*Art*) Manierismus, *der*

**manning** /'mænɪŋ/ *n.* (*of ship, aircraft*) Bemannung, *die;* (*of factory, industry, etc.*) Personalausstattung, *die*

**mannish** /'mænɪʃ/ *adj.* männlich; männlich, maskulin ‹Kleidung›; **a ~ woman** ein Mannweib (*abwertend*)

**manœuvrable** /mə'nu:vrəbl/ *adj.* (*Brit.*) manövrierfähig ‹Schiff, Flugzeug, Auto›; **be easily ~:** leicht zu manövrieren *od.* zu lenken sein

**manœuvre** /mə'nu:və(r)/ (*Brit.*) ❶ *n.* A (*Mil., Navy*) Manöver, *das;* **be/go on ~s** im Manöver sein/ins Manöver ziehen *od.* rücken; B (*deceptive movement, scheme; also of*

*vehicle, aircraft*) Manöver, *das;* **room for ~** (*fig.*) Spielraum, *der.*
❷ *v.t.* Ⓐ (*Mil., Navy*) führen; dirigieren; Ⓑ (*bring by ~s*) manövrieren; bugsieren ‹Sperriges›; **~ sb./oneself/sth. into a good position** (*fig.*) jmdn./sich/etw. in eine gute Position manövrieren; Ⓒ (*manipulate*) beeinflussen; **~ sb. into doing sth.** jmdn. dazu bringen, etw. zu tun; **~ sb. away from sth.** jmdn. von etw. abbringen.
❸ *v.i.* Ⓐ (*Mil., Navy*) [ein] Manöver durchführen; Ⓑ (*move, scheme*) manövrieren; **room to ~:** Platz zum Manövrieren; (*fig.*) Spielraum, *der;* **~ for power** auf Machtgewinn hinarbeiten

**man-of-'war** *n., pl.* **men-of-war** Kriegsschiff, *das;* ⇒ *also* **Portuguese man-of-war**

**manor** /'mænə(r)/ *n.* Ⓐ (*land*) [Land]gut, *das;* **lord/lady of the ~:** Gutsherr, *der*/ Gutsherrin, *die;* Ⓑ (*house*) Herrenhaus, das; Ⓒ (*Brit. coll.: police area*) Revier, *das*

**'manor house** ⇒ **manor** B

**manorial** /mə'nɔ:rɪəl/ *adj.* Guts‹hof, -besitz›; gutsherrschaftlich ‹System, Rechte›

**'manpower** *n.* Ⓐ (*available power*) Arbeitspotenzial, *das;* (*workers*) Arbeitskräfte *Pl.; attrib.* Personal‹mangel, -planung›; Ⓑ (*Mil.*) Stärke, *die*

**'man-powered** *adj.* **~ flight** Flug mit [menschlicher] Muskelkraft

**manqué** /'mɑ̃keɪ/ *adj. postpos.* verhindert ‹Poet, Künstler, Intellektueller usw.›

**mansard** /'mænsɑ:d/ *n.* **~ [roof]** (*Archit.*) Mansard[en]dach, *das*

**manse** /mæns/ *n.* Pfarrhaus, *das*

**'manservant** *n., pl.* **'menservants** Diener, *der*

**mansion** /'mænʃn/ *n.* Villa, *die;* (*of lord of the manor*) Herrenhaus, *das*

**man: ~-size, ~-sized** *adj.* (*suitable for a man*) ‹Mahlzeit, Steak› für einen [ganzen] Mann; (*large*) groß; **~slaughter** *n.* (*Law*) Totschlag, *der*

**manta** /'mæntə/ *n.* (*Zool.*) Teufelsrochen, *der;* Manta, *der*

**mantel** /'mæntl/ ⇒ **mantelpiece**

**mantel: ~piece** *n.* Ⓐ (*above fireplace*) Kaminsims, *der od. das;* Ⓑ (*around fireplace*) Kamineinfassung, *die;* **~shelf** ⇒ **~piece** A

**mantis** /'mæntɪs/ *n., pl. same* (*Zool.*) Fang[heu]schrecke, *die;* **praying ~:** Gottesanbeterin, *die*

**mantle** /'mæntl/ ❶ *n.* Ⓐ (*cloak*) Umhang, *der;* (*fig.*) Mantel, *der;* **~ of snow** Schneedecke, *die;* Ⓑ (*Geol.*) Mantel, *der.* ❷ *v.t.* (*literary: cover*) bedecken

**'man-to-man** *adj.* von Mann zu Mann *nachgestellt*

**mantra** /'mæntrə/ *n.* (*Relig.*) Mantra, *das*

**'mantrap** *n.* Fußangel, *die*

**manual** /'mænjʊəl/ ❶ *adj.* Ⓐ manuell; **~ work/labour** manuelle Tätigkeit *od.* Handarbeit/körperliche Arbeit *od.* Schwerarbeit; **~ worker/labourer** Handarbeiter/Schwerarbeiter, *der;* Ⓑ (*not automatic*) handbetrieben; ‹Bedienung, Kontrolle, Schaltung› von Hand; **~ steering/signals** Handsteuerung, *die*/ -zeichen. ❷ *n.* Ⓐ (*handbook*) Handbuch, *das;* Ⓑ (*Mus.*) Manual, *das*

**manually** /'mænjʊəlɪ/ *adv.* manuell; von Hand; mit der Hand; **a ~ operated machine** eine handbetriebene Maschine

**manufacture** /mænjʊ'fæktʃə(r)/ ❶ *n.* Herstellung, *die;* **cost/country of ~:** Herstellungskosten, *Pl.*/-land, *das;* **articles of home/foreign/British ~:** inländische/ausländische/britische Erzeugnisse. ❷ *v.t.* Ⓐ (*Commerc.*) herstellen; **~ iron into steel/ cloth into garments** Eisen zu Stahl verarbeiten/aus Stoff Kleidungsstücke herstellen; **~d goods** Fertigprodukte *Pl.;* **manufacturing costs/firm/fault** Herstellungskosten *Pl.* /Herstellerfirma, *die*/Produktionsfehler, *der;* **manufacturing town** Industriestadt, *die;* Ⓑ (*invent*) erfinden ‹Geschichte, Ausrede usw.›

**manufacturer** /mænjʊ'fæktʃərə(r)/ *n.* Hersteller, *der;* **'~'s recommended [retail] price'** „unverbindliche Preisempfehlung"

**manure** /mə'njʊə(r)/ ❶ *n.* (*dung*) Dung, *der;* (*fertilizer*) Dünger, *der.* ❷ *v.t.* düngen

**manuscript** /'mænjʊskrɪpt/ ❶ *n.* Ⓐ Handschrift, *die;* Ⓑ (*not yet printed*) Manuskript, *das;* **the novel is still in ~:** der Roman liegt [erst] im *od.* als Manuskript vor. ❷ *adj.* handschriftlich

**'man-week** *n.* (*Work Study*) Mannwoche, *die*

**Manx** /mæŋks/ ▶ **1275** ❶ *adj.* der Insel Man *nachgestellt.* ❷ *n.* (*Ling.*) Manx, *das*

**Manx: ~ 'cat** *n.* Man[x]katze, *die;* **~man** /'mæŋksmən/ *n., pl.* **~men** /'mæŋksmən/ Bewohner der Insel Man; Manx, *der*

**many** /'menɪ/ ❶ *adj.* Ⓐ viele; *pred.* zahlreich; **how ~ people/books?** wie viele *od.* wie viel Leute/Bücher?; **as ~ as** so viele wie; **there were as ~ as 50 of them** es waren mindestens *od.* bestimmt 50; **three accidents in as ~ days** drei Unfälle in ebenso vielen *od.* ebenso viel Tagen; **~'s the tale/the time** so manche Geschichte/so manches Mal; **too ~ people/books** zu viele *od.* zu viel Leute/Bücher; **there were too ~ of them** es waren zu viele *od.* zu viel; **two [copies] too ~:** zwei [Exemplare] zu viel; **one is too ~/ there is one too ~:** einer/eine/eins ist zu viel; **he/she is one too ~ here** er/sie ist hier überflüssig; **he's had one too ~** (*is drunk*) er hat einen *od.* ein Glas zu viel getrunken; Ⓑ **~ a man** so mancher; manch einer; **~ a time** so manches Mal.
❷ *n.* viele [Leute]; **there weren't ~ of them there** es waren nicht viele da; **~ of us** viele von uns; **a good/great ~ [of them/of the books]** eine Menge/eine ganze Reihe [von ihnen/der Bücher]; **there were a good ~ there** eine Menge war *od.* waren da

**'many-coloured** *adj.* vielfarbig

**'man-year** *n.* (*Work Study*) Mannjahr, *das*

**'many-sided** *adj.* (*Geom.; also fig.*) vielseitig

**Mao** /maʊ/ *adj.* ‹Jacke, Schirmmütze› im Mao-Look; Mao-‹Jacke, Mütze›

**Maoism** /'maʊɪzm/ *n., no pl.* Maoismus, *der*

**Maoist** /'maʊɪst/ *n.* Maoist, *der; attrib.* maoistisch

**Maori** /'maʊrɪ/ ▶ **1275**, ▶ **1340** ❶ *n.* Ⓐ (*person*) Maori, *der;* Ⓑ (*language*) Maori, *das.* ❷ *adj.* maorisch

**map** /mæp/ ❶ *n.* Ⓐ [Land]karte, *die;* (*street plan*) Stadtplan, *der;* Ⓑ (*fig. coll.*) **off the ~:** abgelegen; **we're a bit off the ~ up here** wir leben hier ein bisschen hinter dem Mond (*ugs.*); **wipe off the ~:** ausradieren; **[put sth./sb.] on the ~:** [etw./jmdn.] populär [machen]. ❷ *v.t.*, **-pp-** (*make ~ of*) kartographieren; (*make survey of*) vermessen

**~ 'out** *v.t.* im Einzelnen festlegen

**maple** /'meɪpl/ *n.* Ahorn, *der*

**maple: ~ leaf** *n.* Ahornblatt, *das;* **~ sugar** *n.* Ahornzucker, *der;* **~ syrup** *n.* Ahornsirup, *der*

**map: ~-maker** *n.* ▶ **1261** Kartograph, *der*/ Kartographin, *die;* **~-reader** *n.* Kartenleser, *der*/-leserin, *die;* **~-reading** *n., no pl.* Kartenlesen, *das*

**mar** /mɑ:(r)/ *v.t.*, **-rr-** Ⓐ (*spoil, disfigure*) verderben; entstellen ‹Aussehen›; stören ‹Veranstaltung›; **the book was ~red by a number of small mistakes** die Qualität des Buches wurde durch eine Reihe kleiner Fehler beeinträchtigt; Ⓑ (*ruin*) ⇒ **make** 1 P

**Mar.** *abbr.* **March** Mrz.

**marabou** /'mærəbu:/ *n.* (*Ornith.*) Ⓐ (*African*) Marabu, *der;* Ⓑ ⇒ **adjutant** B

**maraschino** /mærə'ski:nəʊ/ *n., pl.* **~s** Maraschino, *der;* **~ cherry** Maraschinokirsche, *die*

**marathon** /'mærəθən/ *n.* Ⓐ (*race*) Marathon[lauf], *der; attrib.* Marathon‹läufer›; Ⓑ (*fig.*) Marathon, *das; attrib.* Marathon‹rede, -spiel, -sitzung›; **a chess ~:** ein Schachmarathon

**maraud** /mə'rɔ:d/ ❶ *v.i.* plündern; marodieren (*Soldatenspr.*). ❷ *v.t.* plündern

**marauder** /mə'rɔ:də(r)/ *n.* Plünderer, *der;* Marodeur, *der* (*Soldatenspr.*); (*animal*) Räuber, *der*

**marble** /'mɑ:bl/ *n.* Ⓐ (*stone*) Marmor, *der* (*auch fig.*); *attrib.* Marmor-; aus Marmor *nachgestellt;* marmorn (*dichter., fig.*); Ⓑ *in pl.* (*statues*) Marmorskulpturen; **the Elgin M~s** die Elgin Marbles (*Kunstwiss.*); Ⓒ (*toy*) Murmel, *die;* **[game of] ~s** Murmelspiel, *das;* **play ~s** murmeln; [mit] Murmeln spielen; Ⓓ *in pl.* **not have all** *or* **have lost one's ~s** (*coll.*) nicht alle Tassen im Schrank haben (*ugs.*)

**marbled** /'mɑ:bld/ *adj.* Ⓐ marmoriert ‹Papier, Seife usw.›; Ⓑ (*streaked*) durchwachsen ‹Fleisch›

**march**[1] ❶ *n.* Ⓐ (*Mil., Mus.; hike*) Marsch, *der;* (*gait*) Marschschritt, *der;* Marschtritt, *der;* **on the ~:** auf dem Marsch; (*fig.*) unterwegs; **~ past** Vorbeimarsch, *der;* Defilee, *das;* **a day's/three days' ~:** ein Tagesmarsch/drei Tagesmärsche; **an hour's ~ away** eine Marschstunde *od.* eine Stunde Marsch entfernt; ⇒ *also* **forced march; line**[1] 1 K; **steal** 1 C; Ⓑ (*in protest*) **[protest] ~:** Protestmarsch, *der;* Ⓒ (*progress of time, events, etc.*) Gang, *der;* **the onward ~ of science** der Vormarsch der Wissenschaft.
❷ *v.i.* (*also Mil.*) marschieren; (*fig.*) fortschreiten; **~ away** abmarschieren; **forward/quick ~!** vorwärts/im Eilschritt marsch!; **~ing song** Marschlied, *das;* **~ing order** (*Brit.*) Marschordnung, *die;* **~ing orders** Marschbefehl, *der;* **give sb. his/her ~ing orders** (*fig. coll.*) jmdm. den Laufpass geben (*ugs.*).
❸ *v.t.* (*Mil.*) marschieren lassen

**~ 'off** ❶ *v.i.* losmarschieren. ❷ *v.t.* ‹Polizei usw.:› abführen

**~ on** *v.t.* (*Mil.*) marschieren gegen ‹Feind›; marschieren auf (+ *Akk.*) ‹Stadt›

**march**[2] *n.* (*Hist.: frontier*) Mark, *die;* **the Welsh ~es** das Grenzland zwischen Wales und England

**March** /mɑ:tʃ/ *n.* ▶ **1055** März, *der;* ⇒ *also* **August; hare** 1 A

**marcher** /'mɑ:tʃə(r)/ *n.* **[protest] ~:** Demonstrant, *der*/Demonstrantin, *die;* **~s on a demonstration** Teilnehmer an einem Demonstrationszug

**marchioness** /mɑ:ʃə'nes/ *n.* Marquise, *die*

**Mardi Gras** /mɑ:di: 'grɑ:/ *n.* Ⓐ (*Shrove Tuesday*) Fastnachtsdienstag, *der;* Ⓑ (*carnival*) Karneval, *der*

**mare** /meə(r)/ *n.* Stute, *die*

**Margaret** /'mɑ:grɪt/ *pr. n.* (*Hist., as name of ruler etc.*) Margarete (*die*)

**margarine** /mɑ:dʒə'ri:n, mɑ:gə'ri:n/, (*coll.*) **marge** /mɑ:dʒ/ *ns.* Margarine, *die*

**margin** /'mɑ:dʒɪn/ *n.* Ⓐ (*of page*) Rand, *der;* **notes [written] in the ~:** Randbemerkungen; Anmerkungen am Rand; **~ release** Randlöser, *der;* Randfreigabe, *die;* Ⓑ (*extra amount*) Spielraum, *der;* **profit ~:** Gewinnspanne, *die;* **win by a narrow/wide ~:** knapp/mit großem Vorsprung gewinnen; **~ of error** Spielraum für mögliche Fehler; **allow for a considerable ~ of error** eine beachtliche Fehlerzahl mit einkalkulieren; Ⓒ (*edge*) Rand, *der;* Saum, *der* (*geh.*); **[be] on the ~ of sth.** (*fig.*) am Rande einer Sache (*Gen.*) [sein]

**marginal** /'mɑ:dʒɪml/ *adj.* Ⓐ (*barely adequate, slight*) geringfügig; unwesentlich; **of ~ importance/use** von geringer Bedeutung/geringem Nutzen; Ⓑ (*close to limit*) marginal; (*of profitability*) kaum rentabel; Ⓒ knapp ‹Wahlergebnis›; **~ seat/constituency** (*Brit. Polit.*) wackeliger (*ugs.*) *od.* nur mit knapper Mehrheit gehaltener Parlamentssitz/Wahlkreis; Ⓓ **~ cost** Grenzkosten *Pl.;* Ⓔ (*of or written in margin*) an den Rand geschrieben; **~ notes/references** Randbemerkungen/-verweise; Ⓕ (*of or at the edge*) Rand‹gebiet, -bereich, -besitzung, -bepflanzung usw.›

**marginalia** /mɑ:dʒɪ'neɪlɪə/ *n. pl.* Marginalien *Pl.*

**marginally** /'mɑ:dʒɪnəlɪ/ *adv.* geringfügig; unwesentlich; **only ~ profitable** kaum rentabel

**marguerite** /mɑ:gə'ri:t/ *n.* (*Bot.*) Margerite, *die*

**marigold** /'mærɪgəʊld/ *n.* (*Calendula*) Studentenblume, *die;* Ringelblume, *die;* (*Tagetes*)

m

Studentenblume, *die;* ⇒ *also* **corn marigold; marsh marigold**

**marijuana (marihuana)** /mærɪ'hwɑ:nə/ *n.* Marihuana, *das; attrib.* Marihuana‹zigarette, -raucher, -süchtiger›

**marimba** /mə'rɪmbə/ *n.* (*Mus.*) **A** (*native xylophone*) Marimba, *die;* **B** (*modern instrument*) Marimbaphon, *das*

**marina** /mə'ri:nə/ *n.* Marina, *die;* Jachthafen, *der*

**marinade** /mærɪ'neɪd/ ❶ *n.* **A** (*spiced mixture*) Marinade, *die;* **B** (*marinaded meat*) **a ~ of beef/pork** mariniertes Rind-/Schweinefleisch; **a ~ of fish** marinierter Fisch; eine Marinade. ❷ *v.t.* marinieren

**marinate** /'mærɪneɪt/ ⇒ **marinade** 2

**marine** /mə'ri:n/ ❶ *adj.* **A** (*of the sea*) Meeres-; **~ life** Meeresflora und -fauna; **B** (*of shipping*) See‹versicherung, -recht, -schifffahrt›; **~ engineering** Schiffsmaschinenbau, *der;* **~ engineer** ▶ **1261** Schiffbauingenieur, *der;* **C** (*for use at sea*) Schiffs‹ausrüstung, -chronometer, -kessel, -turbine usw.›. ❷ *n.* **A** (*person*) Marineinfanterist, *der;* **the M~s** die Marineinfanterie; die Marinetruppen; **tell that/it to the [horse] ~s** (*coll.*) das kannst du deiner Großmutter erzählen (*ugs.*); ⇒ *also* **Royal Marine; B** (*shipping*) **merchant** *or* **mercantile ~:** Handelsmarine, *die*

**mariner** /'mærɪnə(r)/ *n.* Seemann, *der;* **master ~:** Kapitän eines Handelsschiffes; ⇒ *also* **compass** 1 B

**marionette** /mærɪə'net/ *n.* Marionette, *die*

**marital** /'mærɪtl/ *adj.* ehelich ‹Rechte, Pflichten, Harmonie›; Ehe‹beratung, -glück, -krach, -krise, -probleme›; **~ status** Familienstand, *der*

**maritime** /'mærɪtaɪm/ *adj.* **A** (*found near the sea*) Küsten‹bewohner, -gebiet, -stadt, -provinz›; **~ climate** Meeresklima, *das;* **B** (*connected with the sea*) See‹recht, -versicherung, -volk, -wesen›

**marjoram** /'mɑ:dʒərəm/ *n.* (*Bot., Cookery*) Majoran, *der*

**mark**[1] ❶ *n.* **A** (*trace*) Spur, *die;* (*of finger, foot also*) Abdruck, *der;* (*stain etc.*) Fleck, *der;* (*scratch*) Kratzer, *der;* **dirty ~:** Schmutzfleck, *der;* **make/leave a ~ on sth.** auf etw. (*Dat. od. Akk.*) einen Fleck/einen Kratzer machen/auf etw. (*Dat.*) einen Fleck/eine Spur/einen Kratzer hinterlassen; **leave one's/its ~ on sth.** (*fig.*) einer Sache (*Dat.*) seinen Stempel aufdrücken; **leave its ~ on sb.** Spuren bei jmdm. hinterlassen; **make one's/its ~** (*fig.*) sich (*Dat.*) einen Namen machen (⇒ *also* **b**); **of ~** *postpos.* von Bedeutung *nachgestellt;* ⇒ *also* **birthmark; B** (*affixed sign, indication, symbol*) Zeichen, *das;* (*in trade names*) Typ, *der* (*Technik*); (*made by illiterate*) Kreuz, *das;* **distinguishing ~:** Kennzeichen, *das;* **M~ 2 version/model** Version/Modell 2; **make one's ~:** ein Kreuz *od.* drei Kreuze machen (⇒ *also* **a**); **bear the ~ of sth.** (*lit. or fig.*) den Stempel von etw. tragen; **have all the ~s of sth.** alle Anzeichen von etw. haben; **be a ~ of good taste/breeding** ein Zeichen guten Geschmacks/guter Erziehung sein; **sth. is the ~ of a good writer** an etw. (*Dat.*) erkennt man einen guten Schriftsteller; **C** (*Sch.: grade*) Zensur, *die;* Note, *die;* (*Sch., Sport: unit of numerical award*) Punkt, *der;* **get good/bad/35 ~s in** *or* **for a subject** gute/schlechte Noten *od.* Zensuren/35 Punkte in einem Fach bekommen; **there are no ~s for guessing that ...** (*fig. coll.*) es ist ja wohl nicht schwer zu erraten, dass ...; ⇒ *also* **black mark; full marks; pass mark; D** (*line etc. to indicate position*) Markierung, *die;* (*Naut.*) Marke, *die* (*an der Lotleine*); **be up to/below** *or* **not up to the ~** (*fig.*) den Anforderungen entsprechen/nicht entsprechen; **his work hasn't really been up to the ~ lately** seine Arbeit war in letzter Zeit wirklich nicht sonderlich; **[not] feel up to the ~:** [nicht] auf der Höhe sein; **E** (*level*) Marke, *die;* **reach the 15%/25 million/£300 ~:** die 15%-Marke/25-Millionen-Marke/300-Pfund-Marke erreichen; **around the 300 ~:** ungefähr 300; **F** (*Sport: starting position*) Startlinie, *die;* **on your ~s! [get set! go!]** auf die Plätze! [Fertig! Los!]; **get off the ~ quickly** (*fig.*) einen guten Start haben; **be quick/slow off the ~:** einen guten/schlechten Start haben; (*fig.*) fix (*ugs.*)/langsam sein; **he is usually the quickest/first off the ~:** er ist gewöhnlich der Schnellste/Erste; **G** (*Rugby*) (*spot*) Marke, *die;* (*fair catch*) Freifang, *der;* '**~!**' „Marke!"; **H** (*target, desired object*) Ziel, *das;* (*coll.: intended victim*) Opfer, *das;* **hit/miss the ~** (*fig.*) ins Schwarze treffen/danebenschießen (*ugs.*) *od.* -treffen; **be wide of the ~** (*lit. or fig.*) danebentreffen; **his calculations were wide of the ~:** mit seinen Berechnungen hat er völlig danebengetroffen; **my guess was off the ~:** mit meiner Schätzung lag ich daneben (*ugs.*); **be close to the ~** (*fig.*) der Sache nahe kommen; ⇒ *also* **overshoot; overstep.**

❷ *v.t.* **A** (*stain, dirty*) Flecke[n] machen auf (+ *Dat.*); schmutzig machen; (*scratch*) zerkratzen; **be ~ed for life** bleibende Narben zurückbehalten; (*fig.*) fürs Leben gezeichnet sein; **B** (*put distinguishing ~ on, signal*) kennzeichnen, markieren (**with** mit); **the bottle was ~ed 'poison'** die Flasche trug die Aufschrift „Gift"; **~ sb.'s name on sth.** etw. mit jmds. Namen kennzeichnen; **~ an item with its price** eine Ware auszeichnen *od.* mit einem Preisschild versehen; **~ a route on a map** eine Route auf *od.* in einer *od.* in eine Landkarte einzeichnen; **ceremonies to ~ the tenth anniversary** Feierlichkeiten aus Anlass des 10. Jahrestages; **C** (*Sch.*) (*correct*) korrigieren; (*grade*) benoten; zensieren; **~ an answer wrong** eine Antwort als falsch bewerten; **D ~ time** (*Mil.; also fig.*) auf der Stelle treten; **E** (*characterize*) kennzeichnen; charakterisieren; **be ~ed by sth.** durch etw. gekennzeichnet *od.* charakterisiert sein; **his style is ~ed by a great variety of metaphors** sein Stil zeichnet sich durch eine reiche Metaphorik aus; **F** (*heed*) hören auf (+ *Akk.*) ‹Person, Wort›; **~ carefully how it is done** pass genau auf, wie es gemacht wird; **[you] ~ my words** höre auf mich; eins kann ich dir sagen; (*as a warning*) lass dir das gesagt sein; **~ you, it may not be true** vielleicht stimmt es ja doch gar nicht; **G** (*manifest*) bekunden ‹Missfallen, Zustimmung usw.›; **H** (*record*) notieren, aufschreiben ‹Spielstand›; **~ a pupil absent** einen Schüler als fehlend eintragen; **I** (*Brit. Sport: keep close to*) markieren (*fachspr.*), decken ‹Gegenspieler›; **J** (*choose as victim*) ⇒ **mark down a; K** (*arch./literary: notice*) bemerken ‹Vorfall, Vorgang›

**~ 'down** *v.t.* **A** (*choose as victim, lit. or fig.*) [sich (*Dat.*)] auswählen; aussersehen (*geh.*); **B** [im Preis] herabsetzen ‹Ware›; herabsetzen ‹Preis›; ⇒ *also* **mark-down**

**~ 'off** *v.t.* abgrenzen (**from** von, gegen)

**~ 'out** *v.t.* **A** (*trace out boundaries of*) markieren ‹Spielfeld›; **~ out a tennis court** auf einen Tennisplatz die Spielfeldlinien markieren; **B** (*plan*) festlegen ‹Strategie, Vorgehen›; **C** (*destine*) vorsehen; ‹Schicksal:› bestimmen, aussersehen

**~ 'up** *v.t.* [im Preis] heraufsetzen ‹Ware›; heraufsetzen ‹Preis›; ⇒ *also* **mark-up**

**mark**[2] *n.* ▶ **1328** (*monetary unit*) Mark, *die*

**Mark** /mɑ:k/ *pr. n.* **St ~:** der hl. Markus

**'mark-down** *n.* (*Econ.*) Preissenkung, *die;* **there has been a ~:** der Preis ist/die Preise sind gesenkt worden

**marked** /mɑ:kt/ *adj.* **A** (*noticeable*) deutlich ‹Gegensatz, Unterschied, [Ver]besserung, Veränderung›; ausgeprägt ‹Akzent, Sprachfehler, Kennzeichen, Merkmal, Fähigkeit, Neigung›; **B** (*given distinctive mark*) gezinkt ‹Spielkarte›; **C be a ~ man** auf der schwarzen Liste stehen (*ugs.*)

**markedly** /'mɑ:kɪdlɪ/ *adv.* eindeutig; deutlich

**marker** /'mɑ:kə(r)/ *n.* **A** (*to mark place*) Markierung, *die;* **B** ⇒ **bookmark; C** (*of examination etc.*) Korrektor, *der*/Korrektorin, *die;* **be a fair/severe ~:** gerecht/streng [korrigieren und] benoten; **D** (*Aeronaut.: flare*) Marker, *der* (*fachspr.*); Sichtzeichen, *das*

**'marker pen** *n.* Markierstift, *der*

**market** /'mɑ:kɪt/ ❶ *n.* **A** Markt, *der; attrib.* Markt‹händler, -stand›; **at the ~:** auf dem Markt; **go to ~:** auf den Markt gehen; **take sth. to ~:** etw. auf den Markt bringen; **there is a ~ every Friday** freitags *od.* jeden Freitag ist Markt; **B** (*demand*) Markt, *der;* **find a [ready] ~:** [guten] Absatz finden; **price oneself/one's goods out of the ~:** sich/seine Waren durch Überteuerung konkurrenzunfähig machen; **C** (*area of demand*) Absatzmarkt, *der;* (*persons*) Abnehmer *Pl.;* **D** (*conditions for buying and selling, trade*) Markt, *der;* **the corn/coffee** *etc.* **~:** der Getreide-/Kaffeemarkt *usw.;* **be in the ~ for sth.** an etw. (*Dat.*) interessiert sein; **be on/come into** *or* **on to the ~** ‹Haus:› zum Verkauf stehen/kommen; ‹neue Produkte:› auf dem Markt sein/auf den Markt kommen; **put on the ~:** zum Verkauf anbieten ‹Haus›; **bring on to the ~:** auf den Markt bringen ‹neues Produkt›; **make a ~** (*St. Exch.*) [künstlich] Nachfrage erzeugen; **the M~** (*Brit. Polit.*) der Gemeinsame Markt; ⇒ *also* **buyer c; Common Market; corner** 2 B; **play** 3 I; **seller** A.

❷ *v.t.* vermarkten

**marketable** /'mɑ:kɪtəbl/ *adj.* **A** (*suitable for the market*) marktfähig; **B** (*wanted by purchasers*) marktgängig; **~ securities** börsengängige Effekten

**market: ~ day** *n.* Markttag, *der;* **~ e'conomy** *n.* Marktwirtschaft, *die;* **~ 'forces** *n. pl.* Kräfte des freien Marktes; **~ 'garden** *n.* (*Brit.*) Gartenbaubetrieb, *der;* **~ 'gardener** *n.* ▶ **1261** (*Brit.*) Gemüseanbauer, *der*/-anbauerin, *die;* **~ 'gardening** *n.* (*Brit.*) Gemüseanbau, *der*

**marketing** /'mɑ:kɪtɪŋ/ *n.* (*Econ.*) Marketing, *das; attrib.* Marketing-; **~ research** Marketingresearch, *das*

**market: ~ 'leader** *n.* (*company, brand*) Marktführer, *der;* (*product*) meistverkauftes Produkt; **the company is the ~ leader in its field** die Firma ist marktführend auf ihrem Gebiet; **~-maker** *n.* (*St. Exch.*) *die Preise bestimmender Wertpapierhändler;* **~ place** *n.* Marktplatz, *der;* (*fig.*) Markt, *der;* **~ 'price** *n.* Marktpreis, *der;* **~ 'research** *n.* Marktforschung, *die;* **~ 'square** *n.* Marktplatz, *der;* **~ town** *n.* Marktort, *der;* **~ 'value** *n.* Marktwert, *der*

**marking** /'mɑ:kɪŋ/ *n.* **A** (*identification symbol*) Markierung, *die;* Kennzeichen, *das;* **B** (*on animal*) Zeichnung, *die;* **C** (*Sch.*) (*correcting*) Korrektur, *die;* (*grading*) Benotung, *die;* Zensieren, *das;* **I've got some ~ to do** ich muss noch korrigieren

**'marking ink** *n.* Wäschetinte, *die*

**marksman** /'mɑ:ksmən/ *n., pl.* **marksmen** /'mɑ:ksmən/ Scharfschütze, *der*

**marksmanship** /'mɑ:ksmənʃɪp/ *n., no pl.* Treffsicherheit, *die*

**'mark-up** *n.* (*Econ.*) **A** (*price increase*) Preiserhöhung, *die;* **B** (*amount added*) Handelsspanne, *die* (*Kaufmannsspr.*)

**marl** /mɑ:l/ *n.* Mergel, *der*

**marmalade** /'mɑ:məleɪd/ *n.* **[orange] ~:** Orangenmarmelade, *die;* **tangerine/lime ~:** Mandarinen-/Limonenmarmelade, *die*

**marmalade 'cat** *n.* orangefarbene Katze

**marmoset** /'mɑ:məzet/ *n.* (*Zool.*) Marmosette, *die*

**marmot** /'mɑ:mət/ *n.* (*Zool.*) Murmeltier, *das*

**maroon**[1] /mə'ru:n/ ❶ *adj.* kastanienbraun. ❷ *n.* Kastanienbraun, *das*

**maroon**[2] *v.t.* **A** (*Naut.: put ashore*) aussetzen; **B** ‹Flut, Hochwasser:› von der Außenwelt abschneiden; **she was ~ed at home without transport** ohne Transportmittel saß sie zu Hause fest

**marque** /mɑ:k/ *n.* Marke, *die;* (*of cars also*) Fabrikat, *das*

**marquee** /mɑ:'ki:/ *n.* **A** (*large tent*) großes Zelt; (*for public entertainment*) Festzelt, *das;* **B** (*Amer.: canopy*) Vordach, *das*

**marquess** ⇒ **marquis**

**marquetry** /'mɑ:kɪtrɪ/ *n.* Marketerie, *die* (*Kunstwiss.*); Einlegearbeit, *die;* Intarsie, *die; attrib.* Intarsien‹arbeit, -schrank›

**marquis** /'mɑ:kwɪs/ *n.* Marquis, *der*

**marriage** /'mærɪdʒ/ *n.* **A** Ehe, *die* (**to** mit); **state of ~:** Ehestand, *der;* **proposal** *or* **offer of ~:** Heiratsantrag, *der;* **his son by**

a former ~: sein Sohn aus einer früheren Ehe; **related by ~:** verschwägert; **uncle/cousin by ~:** angeheirateter Onkel/Cousin; **take sb. in ~:** jmdn. zum Mann/zur Frau nehmen; ⇒ *also* **convenience** A; **give** 1 H; **B** (*wedding*) Hochzeit, *die;* (*act of marrying*) Heirat, *die;* (*ceremony*) Trauung, *die;* **~ ceremony** Trauzeremonie, *die;* Eheschließung, *die;* **church ~:** kirchliche Trauung; ⇒ *also* **civil marriage**; **C** (*fig.*) Verbindung, *die*

**marriageable** /ˈmærɪdʒəbl/ *adj.* heiratsfähig; **of ~ age** im heiratsfähigen Alter

**marriage: ~ broker** *n.* Heiratsvermittler, *der*/-vermittlerin, *die;* **~ bureau** *n.* Eheanbahnungs- *od.* Ehevermittlungsinstitut, *das;* **~ certificate** *n.* Trauschein, *der;* (*record of civil marriage also*) Heiratsurkunde, *die;* **~ 'guidance** *n.* Eheberatung, *die;* **~ licence** *n.* Heirats- *od.* Eheerlaubnis, *die;* **~ lines** *n. pl.* (*Brit.*) ⇒ **~ certificate**; **~ market** *n.* Heiratsmarkt, *der;* **~ settlement** *n.* (*Law*) Ehevertrag, *der;* **~ stakes** *n. pl.* (*joc.*) Heiratsmarkt, *der;* **~ vows** *n. pl.* Ehegelöbnis, *das* (*geh.*)

**married** /ˈmærɪd/ ❶ *adj.* **A** verheiratet; **~ couple** Ehepaar, *das;* **B** (*marital*) ehelich ‹Leben, Liebe›; Ehe‹leben, -name, -stand›; **~ quarters** Verheiratetenquartiere. ❷ *n.* Verheiratete, *der/die;* **young/newly ~s** Jungverheiratete

**marron glacé** /mærɒn ˈglɑːseɪ/ *n.* kandierte Kastanie

**marrow** /ˈmærəʊ/ *n.* **A** **[vegetable] ~:** Speisekürbis, *der;* **B** (*Anat.*) [Knochen]mark, *das;* **spinal ~:** Rückenmark, *das;* **to the ~** (*fig.*) durch und durch; **be chilled to the ~** (*fig.*) völlig durchgefroren sein

**marrow: ~bone** *n.* Markknochen, *der;* **~fat** *n.* Markerbse, *die;* **~ squash** (*Amer.*) ⇒ **marrow** A

**marry** /ˈmærɪ/ ❶ *v.t.* **A** (*take in marriage*) heiraten; **~ money** Geld *od.* (*ugs.*) reich heiraten; (*for financial gain only*) jmds. Geld heiraten; **B** (*join in marriage*) trauen; **they were** *or* **got married last summer** sie haben letzten Sommer geheiratet; **C** (*give in marriage*) verheiraten ‹Kind› (**to** mit); **D** (*fig.: unite intimately*) verquicken; eng miteinander verbinden; **~ sth. with** *or* **to sth.** etw. mit etw. verquicken *od.* eng verbinden. ❷ *v.i.* heiraten; **~ for money** wegen des Geldes heiraten; **~ in haste, repent at leisure** (*prov.*) Heirat in Eile bereut man in Weile (*Spr.*); **~ into a [rich] family** in eine [reiche] Familie einheiraten

**~ 'off** *v.t.* verheiraten ‹Tochter› (**to** mit)

**marrying** /ˈmærɪɪŋ/ *adj.* **he's not the ~ sort** *or* **kind** *or* **type** er ist nicht der Typ [von Mann], der heiratet

**Mars** /mɑːz/ *pr. n.* **A** (*Astron.*) Mars, *der;* **B** (*Roman Mythol.*) Mars (*der*)

**Marsala** /mɑːˈsɑːlə/ *n.* Marsala[wein], *der*

**Marseillaise** /mɑːsəˈleɪz, mɑːseɪˈjeɪz/ *n.* Marseillaise, *die*

**Marseilles** /mɑːˈseɪlz, mɑːˈseɪ/ *pr. n.* ▶ **1626** Marseille (*das*)

**marsh** /mɑːʃ/ *n.* Sumpf, *der; attrib.* (*Bot., Zool.*) Sumpf‹klee, -kresse, -[kratz]distel, -krokodil, -hirsch›

**marshal** /ˈmɑːʃl/ ❶ *n.* **A** (*officer of state*) [Hof]marschall, *der;* **B** (*officer in army*) Marschall, *der;* ⇒ *also* **Field Marshal**; **C** (*Sport*) Ordner, *der;* **D** (*Amer.*) (*head of police department*) Polizeipräsident, *der;* (*head of fire department*) Branddirektor, *der.* ⇒ *also* **provost marshal.** ❷ *v.t.*, (*Brit.*) **-ll-** **A** (*arrange in order*) aufstellen ‹Truppen›; sich (*Dat.*) zurechtlegen ‹Argumente›; ordnen ‹Fakten›; **the teacher ~led the children on to the coach** der Lehrer führte die Kinder zu ihren Plätzen im Bus; **B** (*Her.*) vereinigen, verbinden ‹Wappen›

**'marshalling yard** /ˈmɑːʃəlɪŋ jɑːd/ *n.* (*Railw.*) Rangierbahnhof, *der*

**marsh: ~ gas** *n.* (*Chem.*) Sumpfgas, *das;* **~ 'harrier** *n.* (*Ornith.*) Rohrweihe, *die;* **~land** *n.* Sumpfland, *das;* **~ mallow** *n.* **A** (*Bot.*) Eibisch, *der;* **B** (*confection*) Marshmallow, *das;* süßer Speck; **~'mallow** *n.* (*sweet*) ≈ Mohrenkopf, *der;* **~ 'marigold** *n.* Sumpfdotterblume, *die;* **~ tit** *n.* (*Ornith.*) Nonnenmeise, *die*

**marshy** /ˈmɑːʃɪ/ *adj.* sumpfig; Sumpf‹boden, -gebiet, -land›

**marsupial** /mɑːˈsjuːpɪəl, mɑːˈsuːpɪəl/ (*Zool.*) ❶ *adj.* Beutel‹tier, -frosch, -mulle›. ❷ *n.* Beuteltier, *das*

**mart** /mɑːt/ *n.* **A** (*market place*) Markt, *der;* **B** (*auction-room*) Auktionsraum, *der;* **sale ~:** Verkaufsraum, *der*

**marten** /ˈmɑːtɪn/ *n.* (*Zool.*) Marder, *der;* **stone ~:** Steinmarder, *der;* ⇒ *also* **pine marten**

**martial** /ˈmɑːʃl/ *adj.* kriegerisch; ⇒ *also* **court martial**

**martial: ~ 'arts** *n. pl.* (*Sport*) Kampfsportarten; **~ 'law** *n.* Kriegsrecht, *das;* **state of ~ law** Kriegszustand, *der*

**martin** /ˈmɑːtɪn/ *n.* (*Ornith.*) **[house] ~:** Mehlschwalbe, *die*

**martinet** /mɑːtɪˈnet/ *n.* Zuchtmeister, *der* (*veralt., noch scherzh.*)

**Martini** ® /mɑːˈtiːnɪ/ *n.* Martini, *der;* **dry ~:** Martini dry, *der*

**martyr** /ˈmɑːtə(r)/ ❶ *n.* (*Relig.; also fig.*) Märtyrer, *der*/Märtyrerin, *die;* **die a ~'s death** den Märtyrertod erleiden *od.* sterben; **a ~ to** *or* **in the cause of sth.** Märtyrer/Märtyrerin einer Sache (*Gen.*); **be a ~ to rheumatism** entsetzlich unter Rheumatismus leiden; **make a ~ of oneself** den Märtyrer/die Märtyrerin spielen; **make sb. a ~, make a ~ of sb.** jmdn. zum Märtyrer/zur Märtyrerin machen. ❷ *v.t.* **A** den Märtyrertod sterben lassen; **be ~ed** den Märtyrertod sterben; **B** (*fig.: torment*) martern (*geh.*); **a ~ed expression** eine Duldermiene

**martyrdom** /ˈmɑːtədəm/ *n.* Martyrium, *das;* **suffer ~:** ein Martyrium durchleiden

**marvel** /ˈmɑːvl/ ❶ *n.* Wunder, *das;* **work ~s** Wunder wirken; **it's a ~ to me how ...:** es ist mir schleierhaft, wie ...; **it will be a ~ if ...:** es wäre ein Wunder, wenn ...; **be a ~ of patience/neatness** eine sagenhafte Geduld haben/sagenhaft ordentlich sein (*ugs.*). ❷ *v.i.*, (*Brit.*) **-ll-** (*literary*) **A** (*be surprised*) **~ at sth.** über etw. (*Akk.*) staunen; etw. bestaunen; **~ that ...:** erstaunt sein, dass ...; **B** (*wonder*) sich wundern; sich fragen; **~ how/why** *etc.* sich fragen *od.* (*bes. schweiz.*) sich wundern, wie/warum *usw.*

**marvellous** /ˈmɑːvələs/ *adj.*, **marvellously** /ˈmɑːvələslɪ/ *adv.* wunderbar

**marvelous, marvelously** (*Amer.*) ⇒ **marvell-**

**Marxian** /ˈmɑːksɪən/ ⇒ **Marxist**

**Marxism** /ˈmɑːksɪzm/ *n.* Marxismus, *der*

**Marxist** /ˈmɑːksɪst/ ❶ *n.* Marxist, *der*/Marxistin, *die.* ❷ *adj.* marxistisch

**Mary** /ˈmeərɪ/ *pr. n.* (*Hist., as name of ruler, saint, etc.*) Maria (*die*); ⇒ *also* **Bloody Mary**

**marzipan** /ˈmɑːzɪpæn/ *n.* Marzipan, *das*

**mascara** /mæˈskɑːrə/ *n.* Mascara, *das*

**mascot** /ˈmæskɒt/ *n.* Maskottchen, *das*

**masculine** /ˈmæskjʊlɪn/ ❶ *adj.* **A** (*of men*) männlich; **B** (*manly, manlike*) maskulin; **C** (*Ling.*) männlich; maskulin (*fachspr.*). ❷ *n.* (*Ling.*) Maskulinum, *das*

**masculine 'rhyme** *n.* (*Pros.*) männlicher *od.* stumpfer Reim

**masculinity** /mæskjʊˈlɪnɪtɪ/ *n.*, *no pl.* Männlichkeit, *die*

**maser** /ˈmeɪzə(r)/ *n.* (*Phys.*) Maser, *der*

**mash** /mæʃ/ ❶ *n.* **A** (*Brewing*) Maische, *die;* **B** (*as fodder*) Mischfutter, *das;* **C** (*pulp*) Brei, *der;* **D** (*Brit. coll.: ~ed potatoes*) Kartoffelbrei, *der.* ❷ *v.t.* zerdrücken, zerquetschen, stampfen ‹Kartoffeln›; zerdrücken, zerquetschen ‹Gemüse, Obst›; **~ed potatoes** Kartoffelbrei, *der*

**mask** /mɑːsk/ ❶ *n.* (*also fig., Phot.*) Maske, *die* ; (*worn by surgeon*) Gesichtsmaske, *die;* Mundschutz, *der;* **throw off the ~** (*fig.: abandon pretence*) die Maske fallen lassen. ❷ *v.t.* **A** (*cover with mask*) maskieren; **B** (*Mil.*) tarnen; **C** (*fig.: disguise, conceal*) maskieren; ‹Wolken, Bäume:› verdecken; überdecken ‹Geschmack›; **D** (*cover for protection*) abdecken

**masked 'ball** *n.* Maskenball, *der*

**'masking tape** *n.* Abklebeband, *das*

**masochism** /ˈmæsəkɪzm/ *n.* Masochismus, *der*

**masochist** /ˈmæsəkɪst/ *n.* Masochist, *der*/Masochistin, *die*

**masochistic** /mæsəˈkɪstɪk/ *adj.* masochistisch

**mason** /ˈmeɪsn/ *n.* **A** (*builder*) ▶ **1261** Baumeister, *der;* Steinmetz, *der;* **B** **M~** (*Free~*) [Frei]maurer, *der*

**Masonic** /məˈsɒnɪk/ *adj.* [frei]maurerisch; **~ lodge** [Frei]maurerloge, *die*

**masonry** /ˈmeɪsnrɪ/ *n.* **A** (*stonework*) Mauerwerk, *das;* (*work of a mason*) Steinmetzarbeit, *die;* **B** **M~** (*Free~*) [Frei]maurertum, *das*

**masque** /mɑːsk/ *n.* Maskenspiel, *das*

**masquerade** /mæskəˈreɪd, mɑːskəˈreɪd/ ❶ *n.* (*lit. or fig.*) Maskerade, *die.* ❷ *v.i.* **~ as sb./sth.** sich als jmd./etw. ausgeben; vorgeben, jmd./etw. zu sein

**mass**[1] /mæs/ *n.* (*Eccl., Mus.*) Messe, *die; attrib.* Mess‹buch, -gewand›; **say/hear ~:** die Messe lesen/hören; **go to** *or* **attend ~:** zur Messe gehen; **high ~:** Hochamt, *das;* **low ~:** stille Messe; ⇒ *also* **black mass**

**mass**[2] ❶ *n.* **A** (*solid body of matter*) Brocken, *der;* (*of dough, rubber*) Klumpen, *der;* **a ~ of rock/stone** ein Felsbrocken/Steinblock; **B** (*dense aggregation of objects*) Masse, *die;* **a tangled ~ of threads** ein wirres Knäuel von Fäden; **a ~ of curls** eine Fülle von Locken; **a confused ~ of ideas** ein Wust von Ideen; **C** (*large number or amount of*) **a ~ of ...:** eine Unmenge von ...; **a ~ of people** eine große Menschenmenge; **~es of ...:** massenhaft ... (*ugs.*); eine Masse ... (*ugs.*); **D** (*unbroken expanse*) **a ~ of blossom/colour/red** ein Blütenmeer/Farbenmeer/Meer von Rot; **be a ~ of bruises/mistakes/inhibitions** (*coll.*) voll blauer Flecken sein/von Fehlern nur so wimmeln/nur aus Hemmungen bestehen; **E** (*main portion*) Masse, *die;* **the [great] ~ of people/voters** die breite Masse des Volkes/der Wähler; **the ~es** die breite Masse; die Massen; **in the ~:** als Ganzes; **F** (*Phys.*) Masse, *die;* **centre of ~:** Massenmittelpunkt, *der;* **G** (*bulk*) massige Form; **the huge ~ of the pyramid** die riesige Größe der Pyramide; **H** *attrib.* (*for many people*) Massen-.
❷ *v.t.* **A** anhäufen; **~ed bands** mehrere gleichzeitig spielende Kapellen; **B** (*Mil.*) massieren, zusammenziehen ‹Truppen›.
❸ *v.i.* sich ansammeln; ‹Truppen:› sich massieren, sich zusammenziehen; ‹Wolken:› sich zusammenziehen

**massacre** /ˈmæsəkə(r)/ ❶ *n.* **A** (*slaughter*) Massaker, *das;* **make a ~ of ...:** ein Massaker anrichten unter (+ *Dat.*) ...; **B** (*coll.: defeat*) völlige Zerstörung. ❷ *v.t.* **A** (*slaughter*) massakrieren; **B** (*coll.: defeat heavily*) massakrieren (*ugs., meist scherzh.*)

**massage** /ˈmæsɑːʒ/ ❶ *n.* Massage, *die;* **give sb./sb.'s back a ~:** jmdn./jmds. Rücken massieren; **~ parlour** (*often euphem.*) Massagesalon, *der.* ❷ *v.t.* massieren

**mass communi'cations** *n. pl.* Massenkommunikation, *die*

**masseur** /mæˈsɜː(r)/ *n.* ▶ **1261** Masseur, *der*

**masseuse** /mæˈsɜːz/ *n.* ▶ **1261** *fem.* Masseurin, *die;* Masseuse, *die* (*oft verhüll.*)

**mass: ~ 'grave** *n.* Massengrab, *das;* **~ hy'steria** *n.* Massenhysterie, *die*

**massif** /mæˈsiːf/ *n.* (*Geog.*) Massiv, *das*

**massive** /ˈmæsɪv/ *adj.* (*lit. or fig.*) massiv; wuchtig ‹Statur, Stirn›; kräftig ‹Augenbrauen, Gesicht›; gewaltig ‹Ausmaße, Aufgabe›; enorm ‹Schulden, Vermögen›; **be [conceived] on a ~ scale** groß angelegt sein; **receive aid on a ~ scale** massive Unterstützung erhalten

**massively** /ˈmæsɪvlɪ/ *adv.* (*lit. or fig.*) massiv

**mass: ~ market** *n.* Massenmarkt, *der;* **~-market** *attrib. adj.* für den Massenmarkt nachgestellt; **~ 'media** *n. pl.* Massenmedien *Pl.;* **~ 'meeting** *n.* Massenversammlung, die; (*Pol.*) Massenkundgebung, *die;* (*Industry*) Belegschaftsversammlung, *die;* ~ '**murder** *n.* Massenmord, *der;* ~ '**murderer** *n.* Massenmörder, *der;* ~**-pro'duced** *adj.* serienmäßig produziert *od.* hergestellt; Massen‹artikel›; ~**-pro'ducer** *n.* Massenproduzent, *der;* ~ **pro'duction** *n.* Massenproduktion, *die*

**mast¹** /mɑːst/ *n.* (*for sail, flag, aerial, etc.*) Mast, *der;* **work** *or* **serve** *or* **sail before the** ~: als Matrose dienen; [**mooring**] ~: Ankermast, *der;* ⇒ *also* **colour** 1 J; **half mast**

**mast²** *n.* (*for fodder*) Mast, *die*

**mastectomy** /mæ'stektəmɪ/ *n.* (*Med.*) Mastektomie, *die* (*fachspr.*); Brustamputation, *die*

**-masted** /mɑːstɪd/ *adj. in comb.* (*Naut.*) -mastig; **two-**~: zweimastig

**master** /'mɑːstə(r)/ ❶ *n.* Ⓐ Herr, *der;* **be** ~ **of sth./oneself** Herr über etw. (*Akk.*)/sich selbst sein; **be** ~ **of the situation/[the]** ~ **of one's fate** Herr der Lage/seines Schicksals sein; **be one's own** ~: sein eigener Herr sein; **make oneself** ~ **of sth.** sich zum Herrn über etw. (*Akk.*) machen; Ⓑ (*of animal, slave*) Halter, *der;* (*of dog*) Herrchen, *das;* (*Hunting*) Master, *der;* (*of ship*) Kapitän, *der;* (*of college*) Rektor, *der;* (*of livery company, masonic lodge*) Meister, *der;* ~ **of the house** Hausherr, *der;* **be** ~ **in one's own house** Herr im eigenen Hause sein; ~**'s certificate** *or* **ticket** (*Naut.*) Kapitänspatent, *das;* ⇒ *also* **mariner**; Ⓒ ▶ **1261** (*Sch.: teacher*) Lehrer, *der;* **French** ~: Französischlehrer, *der;* Ⓓ **find** *or* **meet [in sb.] one's** ~: [in jmdm.] seinen Meister finden; Ⓔ (*employer*) Herr, *der;* Ⓕ *in titles* ‹Hofkapell-, Schatz-, Ritt-, Waffen- usw.›meister, *der;* **M**~ **of Ceremonies** Zeremonienmeister, *der;* (*for variety programme etc.*) Conférencier, *der;* **M**~ **of the Rolls** (*Brit. Law*) Präsident des Berufungsgerichts; Ⓖ (*original of document, film, etc.*) Original, *das;* Ⓗ (*expert, great artist*) Meister, *der* (**at** in + *Dat.*); **be a** ~ **of sth.** etw. meisterhaft beherrschen; ⇒ *also* **grand master**; **old master**; **past master**; Ⓘ (*skilled workman*) ~ **craftsman/carpenter** Handwerks-/Tischlermeister, *der;* Ⓙ (*Univ.: postgraduate degree*) ≈ Magister, *der;* ~ **of Arts/Science** ≈ Magister Artium/rerum naturalium; **he got his** ~**'s degree in 1971** ≈ er hat 1971 den *od.* seinen Magister gemacht; Ⓚ (*boy's title*) ≈ junger Herr (*veralt.*); **M**~ **Theo/Richard** *etc.* Master Theo/Richard *usw.*
❷ *adj.* Ⓐ (*commanding*) **the** ~ **race** die Herrenrasse; ~ **card** Leitkarte, *die* (*DV*); Ⓑ (*principal*) Haupt‹strategie, -liste›; ~ **bedroom** großes Schlafzimmer; ≈ Elternschlafzimmer, *das;* ~ **tape/copy** Originalband, *das*/Original, *das;* ~ **plan** Gesamtplan, *der.*
❸ *v.t.* Ⓐ (*learn*) erlernen; **have** ~**ed a language/subject/instrument** eine Sprache/ein Fach/ein Instrument beherrschen; Ⓑ (*overcome*) meistern ‹Probleme usw.›; besiegen ‹Feind›; beherrschen ‹Natur›; zügeln ‹Emotionen, Gefühle›

**-master** *n. in comb.* (*Naut.*) -master, *der;* **two-**~: Zweimaster, *der*

'**master class** *n.* (*Mus. etc.*) Meisterklasse, *die*

**masterful** /'mɑːstəfl/ *adj.* Ⓐ (*imperious*) herrisch ‹Haltung, Ton, Person›; Ⓑ (*masterly*) meisterhaft ‹Beherrschung, Fähigkeit›

**masterfully** /'mɑːstəfəlɪ/ *adv.* ⇒ **masterful**: herrisch; meisterhaft

**master:** ~ **hand** *n.* (*person*) Meister, *der* (**at** im + *Dat.*); ~ **key** *n.* General- *od.* Hauptschlüssel, *der;* (*fig.*) Schlüssel, *der*

**masterly** /'mɑːstəlɪ/ *adj.* meisterhaft

**master:** ~**mind** ❶ *n.* führender Kopf; ❷ *v.t.* ~**mind the plot/conspiracy** *etc.* der Kopf des Komplotts/der Verschwörung *usw.* sein; ~**piece** *n.* (*work of art*) Meisterwerk, *das;* (*production showing masterly skill*) Meisterstück, *das;* **a** ~**piece of tact/irony** ein Meisterstück an Takt/Ironie *od.* des Taktes/der Ironie; ~**singer** *n.* (*Hist.*) Meistersinger, *der;* ~ **stroke** *n.* Geniestreich, *der;* **be a** ~ **stroke** genial sein; ~ **switch** *n.* Hauptschalter, *der;* ~**work** ⇒ ~**piece**

**mastery** /'mɑːstərɪ/ *n.* Ⓐ (*skill*) Meisterschaft, *die;* Ⓑ (*knowledge*) Beherrschung, *die* (**of** *Gen.*); Ⓒ (*upper hand*) Oberhand, *die;* **gain** ~ **over sb.** die Oberhand über jmdn. gewinnen; Ⓓ (*control*) Herrschaft, *die* (**of** über + *Akk.*)

'**masthead** *n.* Ⓐ (*Naut.*) [Mast]topp, *der;* Ⓑ (*Journ.*) Impressum, *das;* (*title*) Titel, *der*

**mastic** /'mæstɪk/ *n.* Ⓐ (*gum, resin, asphalt*) Mastix, *der;* Ⓑ (*cement*) Mastik, *der*

**masticate** /'mæstɪkeɪt/ *v.t.* zerkauen

**mastication** /mæstɪ'keɪʃn/ *n.* Zerkauen, *das*

**mastiff** /'mæstɪf/ *n.* (*Zool.*) Mastiff, *der*

**mastitis** /mæs'taɪtɪs/ *n.* ▶ **1232** (*Med.*) Mastitis, *die*

**mastodon** /'mæstədɒn/ *n.* (*Zool., Palaeont.*) Mastodon, *das*

**mastoid** /'mæstɔɪd/ *n.* (*Anat.*) Mastoid, *das*

**masturbate** /'mæstəbeɪt/ *v.i. & t.* masturbieren

**masturbation** /mæstə'beɪʃn/ *n.* Masturbation, *die*

**mat¹** /mæt/ ❶ *n.* Ⓐ (*on floor, Sport*) Matte, *die;* **pull the** ~ **from under sb.'s feet** (*fig.*) jmdm. den Boden unter den Füßen wegziehen; **be on the** ~ (*coll.: be in trouble*) zusammengestaucht werden (*ugs.*); Ⓑ (*to protect table etc.*) Untersetzer, *der;* (*as decorative support*) Deckchen, *das;* Ⓒ (*tangled mess*) (*of hair*) Wust, *der* (*ugs.*); (*of weeds, foliage*) Gewirr, *das.* ❷ *v.t.,* **-tt-** Ⓐ (*furnish with mats*) mit Matten belegen ‹Boden›; mit Matten auslegen ‹Zimmer›; Ⓑ *usu. in p.p.* (*entangle*) verflechten ‹Äste, Unkraut›; verfilzen ‹Haar›; ~**ted** verflochten; verfilzt. ❸ *v.i.,* **-tt-** ‹Äste, Unkraut usw.:› sich [ineinander] verflechten; ‹Haare, Wolle:› verfilzen

**mat²** ⇒ **matt**

**matador** /'mætədɔː(r)/ *n.* Matador, *der*

**match¹** /mætʃ/ ❶ *n.* Ⓐ (*equal*) Ebenbürtige, *der/die;* **be a/no** ~ **for sb.** es mit jmdm. aufnehmen/nicht aufnehmen [können]; sich mit jmdm. messen/nicht messen können; **she is more than a** ~ **for him** sie ist ihm mehr als gewachsen; **find** *or* **meet one's** ~: einen ebenbürtigen Gegner finden; (*be defeated*) seinen Meister finden; Ⓑ (*sb./sth. similar or appropriate*) **be a [good** *etc.*] ~ **for sth.** [gut *usw.*] zu etw. passen; **the colours are a poor** ~: die Farben passen schlecht zueinander *od.* zusammen; **find a** ~ **for this paint** genau die gleiche Farbe finden; Ⓒ (*Sport*) Spiel, *das;* (*Football, Tennis, etc. also*) Match, *das;* (*Boxing*) Kampf, *der;* (*Athletics*) Wettkampf, *der;* Ⓓ (*marriage*) Heirat, *die;* (*marriage partner*) Partie, *die;* **make a** ~: sich verheiraten; **make a good** ~: eine gute Partie machen.
❷ *v.t.* Ⓐ (*equal*) ~ **sb. at chess/in shooting/in argument/in originality** es mit jmdm. im Schach/Schießen/Argumentieren/an Originalität (*Dat.*) aufnehmen [können]; **can you** ~ **that for impudence?** das ist eine Unverschämtheit ohnegleichen!; ~ **that if you can!** das mach [mir] erst mal einer nach!; Ⓑ (*pit*) ~ **sb. with** *or* **against sb.** jmdn. jmdm. gegenüberstellen; **be** ~**ed against sb.** gegen jmdn. antreten; ~ **one's skill/strength against sb.** sein Können/seine Kräfte mit jmdm. messen; Ⓒ **be well** ~**ed** ‹Mann u. Frau:› gut zusammenpassen; ‹Spieler, Mannschaften:› sich (*Dat.*) ebenbürtig sein; **they are a well** ~**ed couple/pair** die beiden passen gut zusammen; Ⓓ (*harmonize with*) passen zu; **a handbag and** ~**ing shoes** eine Handtasche und [dazu] passende Schuhe; ~ **each other exactly** genau zueinander passen; **form a** ~**ing pair** [als Paar] gut zueinander passen; Ⓔ (*find matching material etc. for*) ~ **sth. with sth.** etw. auf etw. abstimmen; ~ **people with jobs** geeignete Personen für die Stellen finden.
❸ *v.i.* (*correspond*) zusammenpassen; **with a scarf** *etc.* **to** ~: mit [dazu] passendem Schal *usw.*
~ **'up** ❶ *v.i.* Ⓐ (*correspond*) zusammenpassen; Ⓑ (*be equal*) ~ **up to sth.** einer Sache (*Dat.*) entsprechen; ~ **up to the situation** der Situation gewachsen sein. ❷ *v.t.* aufeinander abstimmen ‹Farben usw.›; passend zusammenfügen ‹Teile, Hälften›; ~ **up one colour with another** eine Farbe auf eine andere abstimmen

**match²** *n.* (*for lighting*) Streichholz, *das;* Zündholz, *das* (*südd., österr.*)

**match:** ~**box** *n.* Streichholzschachtel, *die;* ~**-fit** *adj.* (*Sport*) spielfähig

**matchless** /'mætʃlɪs/ *adj.* unvergleichlich; beispiellos

**match:** ~**maker** *n.* Ehestifter, *der*/Ehestifterin, *die;* ~**making** *n.* Ehestiftung, *die;* ~ **point** *n.* (*Tennis etc.*) Matchball, *der;* ~**stick** *n.* Ⓐ Streichholz, *das;* Zündholz, *das* (*südd., österr.*); Ⓑ ~**stick man** ⇒ **stick figure**; ~**wood** *n.* **make** ~**wood of sth., smash sth. to** ~**wood** Kleinholz aus etw. machen; **the storm had made** ~**wood of the boat** der Sturm hatte das Boot zertrümmert

**mate¹** /meɪt/ ❶ *n.* Ⓐ Kumpel, *der* (*ugs.*); (*friend also*) Kamerad, *der*/Kameradin, *die;* (*workmate also*) [Arbeits]kollege, *der*/-kollegin, *die;* Ⓑ (*coll.: as form of address*) Kumpel, *der* (*ugs.*); **look** *or* **listen,** ~, ...: jetzt hör [mir] mal gut zu, Freundchen, ...; Ⓒ (*Naut.: officer on merchant ship*) ≈ Kapitänleutnant, *der;* **chief** *or* **first/second** ~: Erster/Zweiter Offizier; Ⓓ (*workman's assistant*) Gehilfe, *der;* Ⓔ (*spouse*) Lebensgefährte, *der*/-gefährtin, *die* (*geh.*); Ⓕ (*Zool.*) (*male*) Männchen, *das;* (*female*) Weibchen, *das.*
❷ *v.i.* Ⓐ (*for breeding*) sich paaren; Ⓑ (*Mech.: fit well*) ~ **with sth.** [genau] auf/in etw. (*Akk.*) passen.
❸ *v.t.* paaren ‹Tiere›; ~ **a mare and** *or* **with a stallion** eine Stute von einem Hengst decken lassen

**mate²** (*Chess*) ⇒ **checkmate** 1, 3

**material** /mə'tɪərɪəl/ ❶ *adj.* Ⓐ (*physical, tangible, bodily*) materiell; Ⓑ (*not spiritual*) materiell (*oft abwertend*) ‹Mensch, Einstellung, Lebensführung›; Ⓒ (*relevant, important*) wesentlich; **be not** ~ **to sth.** für etw. nicht relevant sein.
❷ *n.* Ⓐ (*matter from which thing is made*) Material, *das;* **cost of** ~**s** Materialkosten *Pl.;* ⇒ *also* **raw material**; Ⓑ *in sing. or pl.* (*elements*) Material, *das;* (*for novel, sermon also*) Stoff, *der;* Ⓒ (*cloth*) Stoff, *der;* Ⓓ *in pl.* **building/writing** ~**s** Bau-/Schreibmaterial, *das;* **cleaning** ~**s** Reinigungsmaterial, *das;* **reading** ~: Lesestoff, *der;* Ⓔ **be leadership/university/officer** *etc.* ~: das Zeug für einen Führungsposten/zum Hochschulstudium/zum Offizier *usw.* haben

**materialise** ⇒ **materialize**

**materialism** /mə'tɪərɪəlɪzm/ *n., no pl.* Materialismus, *der*

**materialist** /mə'tɪərɪəlɪst/ *n.* Materialist, *der*/Materialistin, *die; attrib.* materialistisch ‹Philosophie›

**materialistic** /mətɪərɪə'lɪstɪk/ *adj.* materialistisch

**materialize** /mə'tɪərɪəlaɪz/ *v.i.* Ⓐ ‹Hoffnung:› sich erfüllen; ‹Plan, Idee:› sich verwirklichen; ‹Treffen, Versammlung:› zustande kommen; **he promised help/money, but it never** ~**d** aus seiner versprochenen Hilfe/seinem versprochenen Geld wurde nichts; **this idea will never** ~: aus dieser Idee wird nie etwas; **problems kept materializing** dauernd traten Probleme auf; Ⓑ (*come into view, appear*) [plötzlich] auftauchen; (*coll.*) ‹Person:› sich blicken lassen (*ugs.*), kommen

**materially** /mə'tɪərɪəlɪ/ *adv.* Ⓐ (*considerably*) wesentlich; Ⓑ (*in respect of material interests*) materiell

**matériel** /mətɪərɪ'el/ *n.* Ausrüstung, *die*

**maternal** /mə'tɜːnl/ *adj.* Ⓐ (*motherly*) mütterlich ‹Liebe, Sorge, Typ›; Mutter‹instinkt›; Ⓑ (*related*) ‹Großeltern, Onkel, Tante› mütterlicherseits

**maternity** /mə'tɜːnɪtɪ/ *n.* (*motherhood*) Mutterschaft, *die*

**maternity:** ~ **allowance** *n.* Mutterschaftshilfe, *die;* ~ **benefit** *n.* Mutterschaftsgeld, *das;* ~ **dress** *n.* Umstandskleid, *das;* ~ **home,** ~ **hospital** *ns.* Entbindungsheim, *das;* ~ **leave** *n.* Mutterschaftsurlaub, *der;*

~ **nurse** *n.* Hebamme, *die;* ~ **pay** *n.* Mutterschaftsgeld, *das;* ~ **unit,** ~**ward** *ns.* Entbindungsstation, *die;* ~ **wear** *n.* Umstandskleidung, *die*

**matey** /ˈmeɪtɪ/ (*Brit. coll.*) ❶ *adj.*, **matier** /ˈmeɪtɪə(r)/, **matiest** /ˈmeɪtɪɪst/ kameradschaftlich ‹Typ, Atmosphäre›; **be/get ~ with sb.** mit jmdm. vertraulich sein/werden. ❷ *n.* Kumpel, *der* (*ugs.*); **watch it, ~!** pass bloß auf, Freundchen!

**math** /mæθ/ (*Amer. coll.*) ⇒ **maths**

**mathematical** /mæθɪˈmætɪkl/ *adj.* **A** mathematisch; **B** (*precise*) mathematisch ‹Genauigkeit, Exaktheit, Bestimmtheit›; mathematisch genau ‹Beweis›

**mathematically** /mæθɪˈmætɪkəlɪ/ *adv.* mathematisch; **prove sth. ~:** etw. mathematisch genau beweisen

**mathematician** /mæθɪməˈtɪʃn/ *n.* ▶ 1261 Mathematiker, *der*/Mathematikerin, *die*

**mathematics** /mæθɪˈmætɪks/ *n., no pl.* **A** (*subject*) Mathematik, *die;* **pure/applied ~:** reine/angewandte Mathematik; **B** *constr. as pl.* (*application*) **the ~ of this problem are complicated** diese Aufgabe ist mathematisch kompliziert; **your ~ are good** du bist gut in Mathematik

**maths** /mæθs/ *n.* (*Brit. coll.*) Mathe, *die* (*Schülerspr.*)

**matinée** (*Amer.:* **matinee**) /ˈmætɪneɪ/ *n.* Matinee, *die;* Frühvorstellung, *die;* (*in the afternoon*) Nachmittagsvorstellung, *die*

**mating**/ˈmeɪtɪŋ/: ~ **call,** ~ **cry** *ns.* Paarungsruf, *der;* ~ **season** *n.* Paarungszeit, *die*

**matins** /ˈmætɪnz/ *n., constr. as sing. or pl.* **A** (*RC Ch.*) Matutin, *die;* **B** (*Anglican Ch.*) Früh- *od.* Morgenandacht, *die*

**matriarchal** /meɪtrɪˈɑːkl/ *adj.* matriarchalisch

**matriarchy** /ˈmeɪtrɪɑːkɪ/ *n.* Matriarchat, *das*

**matrices** *pl. of* **matrix**

**matricide** /ˈmætrɪsaɪd/ *n.* **A** (*murder*) Muttermord, *der;* **B** (*murderer*) Muttermörder, *der*/-mörderin, *die*

**matriculate** /məˈtrɪkjʊleɪt/ (*Univ.*) ❶ *v.t.* immatrikulieren (**in** an + *Dat.*). ❷ *v.i.* sich immatrikulieren

**matriculation** /mətrɪkjʊˈleɪʃn/ *n.* (*Univ.*) Immatrikulation, *die*

**matrimonial** /mætrɪˈməʊnɪəl/ *adj.* Ehe-

**matrimony** /ˈmætrɪmənɪ/ *n.* **A** (*rite of marriage*) Eheschließung, *die;* **sacrament of ~:** Ehesakrament, *das;* **B** (*married state*) Ehestand, *der;* **enter into [holy] ~:** in den [heiligen] Stand der Ehe treten (*geh.*)

**matrix** /ˈmeɪtrɪks, ˈmætrɪks/ *n., pl.* **matrices** /ˈmeɪtrɪsiːz, ˈmætrɪsiːz/ *or* ~**es** **A** (*Geol., Math.*) Matrix, *die;* **B** (*mould*) Matrize, *die*

**matron** /ˈmeɪtrən/ *n.* **A** ▶ 1261 (*in school*) ≈ Hausmutter, *die;* (*in hospital*) Oberin, *die;* Oberschwester, *die;* **B** (*arch./literary: married woman*) Matrone, *die;* ~ **of honour** (*verheiratete*) Brautführerin

**matronly** /ˈmeɪtrənlɪ/ *adj.* matronenhaft (*meist abwertend*)

**matt** /mæt/ *adj.* matt; **have a ~ finish** ‹Fotografie:› auf mattem Papier abgezogen sein

**matter** /ˈmætə(r)/ ❶ *n.* **A** (*affair*) Angelegenheit, *die;* ~**s** die Dinge; **business ~s** geschäftliche Angelegenheiten *od.* Dinge; **money ~s** Geldangelegenheiten *od.* -fragen; ~**s of state** Staatsangelegenheiten; **raise an important ~:** einen wichtigen Punkt ansprechen; **police investigation into the ~:** polizeiliche Ermittlung in dieser Sache; **it's only a minor** *or* **it's no great ~:** es ist nicht wichtig; **that's another** *or* **a different ~ altogether** *or* **quite another ~:** das ist etwas ganz anderes; **it will only make ~s worse** das macht die Sache nur schlimmer; **and to make ~s worse ...:** und was die Sache noch schlimmer macht/machte, ...; **B** (*cause, occasion*) **a/no ~ for** *or* **of ...:** ein/kein Grund *od.* Anlass zu ...; **it's a ~ of complete indifference to me** es ist mir völlig gleichgültig; **C** (*topic*) Thema, *das;* Gegenstand, *der;* ~ **on the agenda** Punkt der Tagesordnung; **it's a ~ for the committee [to decide]** das muss der [zuständige] Ausschuss entscheiden; **D a ~ of ...** (*something that amounts to*) eine Frage (+ *Gen.*) ...; eine Sache von ...; **it's a ~ of taste/habit** das ist Geschmacks-/Gewohnheitssache; **it's a ~ of common knowledge** es ist allgemein bekannt; **it's a ~ of policy with us** das ist für uns eine Grundsatzfrage; **a ~ of how fast I can type** eine Frage, wie schnell ich tippen kann; **[only] a ~ of time** [nur noch] eine Frage der Zeit; **it's a ~ of repairing the switch** der Schalter muss repariert werden; **it's just a ~ of working harder** man muss sich ganz einfach [bei der Arbeit] mehr anstrengen; **it's a ~ of a couple of hours** es wird ein paar Stunden dauern; das ist eine Sache von ein paar Stunden; **in a ~ of minutes** in wenigen Minuten; **it's only a ~ of seconds** das ist eine Sache von Sekunden; **a [plain] ~ of fact** eine [schlichte] Tatsache; **That's odd! As a ~ of fact, I was just thinking the same** Das ist komisch! Ich habe nämlich gerade dasselbe gedacht; **Do you know him? — Yes, as a ~ of fact, I do/I know him quite well** Kennst du ihn? — Ja, und ob [ich ihn kenne]/und sogar recht gut; **no, as a ~ of fact, you're wrong** nein, da irrst du dich aber; ~ **of fact** (*Law*) Tatfrage, *die;* ~ **of law** Rechtsfrage, *die;* ⇒ *also* **course** 1 B; **form** 1 H; **E what's the ~?** was ist [los]?; **is something the ~?** stimmt irgendetwas nicht?; ist [irgend]was (*ugs.*)?; **there's nothing the ~:** gar nichts ist los; **there must be something the ~:** irgendetwas stimmt da nicht; **What's the ~ with you? — There's nothing the ~ with me** Was hast du *od.* ist [los] mit dir? — Gar nichts [ist los mit mir]; **there's nothing the ~ with him really, he's just pretending** es fehlt ihm eigentlich gar nichts, er tut nur so; **F for that ~:** eigentlich; **... and for that ~ so am/do I ...** und ich eigentlich auch; **G no ~!** [das] macht nichts!; **no ~ how/who/what/why** *etc.* ganz gleich *od.* egal (*ugs.*), wie/wer/was/warum *usw.;* **no ~ how hard he tried** sosehr er sich auch bemühte; **H in the ~ of sth.** was etw. (*Akk.*) anbelangt; **in the ~ of A versus B** (*Law*) in Sachen A gegen B; **I** (*material, as opposed to mind, spirit, etc.*) Materie, *die;* **[in]organic/solid/vegetable ~:** [an]organische/feste/pflanzliche Stoffe; **the triumph of mind over ~:** der Sieg des Geistes über die Materie; **J** (*Physiol.*) Substanz, *die;* (*pus*) Eiter, *der;* **faecal ~:** Fäzes *Pl.;* ⇒ *also* **grey matter**; **K** *no pl., no indef. art.* (*written or printed material*) **reading ~:** Lesestoff, *der;* **advertising ~:** Reklame, *die;* **L** (*material for thought etc.*) Material, *das;* **M** (*content*) Inhalt, *der.*
❷ *v.i.* etwas ausmachen; **what does it ~?** was macht das schon?; was machts? (*ugs.*); **what ~s is that ...:** worum es geht, ist ...; **not ~ a damn** vollkommen egal sein; **[it] doesn't ~:** [das] macht nichts (*ugs.*); **it ~s a great deal** es macht eine ganze Menge aus; **it doesn't ~ how/when** *etc.* es ist einerlei, wie/wann *usw.;* **does it ~ to you if ...?** macht es dir etwas aus, wenn ...?; **it doesn't ~ at all to me** es ist mir völlig einerlei; **some things ~ rather more than others** manche Dinge sind eben wichtiger als andere; **that's all that ~s** das ist die Hauptsache; **the things which ~ in life** [das,] worauf es im Leben ankommt; **she knows the people who really ~:** sie kennt die Leute, die wirklich etwas gelten

**ˈmatter-of-fact** *adj.* sachlich; nüchtern

**matter-of-ˈfactly** /mætərəvˈfæktlɪ/ *adv.* sachlich; nüchtern

**Matthew** /ˈmæθjuː/ *pr. n.* **St ~:** der hl. Matthäus *od.* (*ökumen.*) Mattäus

**matting** /ˈmætɪŋ/ *n.* (*fabric*) **coconut/straw/reed ~:** Kokos-/Stroh-/Schilf- *od.* Rohrgeflecht, *das;* (*as floor covering*) Kokos-/Stroh-/Schilfmatten *Pl.;* **a piece of ~:** ein Stück Matte

**mattock** /ˈmætək/ *n.* (*Agric.*) Breithacke, *die*

**mattress** /ˈmætrɪs/ *n.* Matratze, *die;* ⇒ *also* **spring mattress**

**maturation** /mætjʊˈreɪʃn/ *n.* **A** (*maturing*) Reifung, *die;* **B** (*of fruit*) [Heran]reifen, *das*

**mature** /məˈtjʊə(r)/ ❶ *adj.*, ~**r** /məˈtjʊərə(r)/, ~**st** /məˈtjʊərɪst/ **A** reif; ausgereift ‹Plan, Methode, Stil, Käse, Portwein, Sherry›; durchgegoren ‹Wein›; ausgewachsen ‹Pflanze, Tier›; voll entwickelt ‹Zellen›; ~ **student** Spätstudierende, *der/die;* **a man of ~ years** ein Mann im reiferen Alter *od.* in reiferen Jahren; **B** (*Finance*) fällig ‹Rechnung, Schuldschein usw.›. ❷ *v.t.* reifen lassen ‹Frucht, Wein, Käse›; reifer machen ‹Personen›; ausreifen lassen ‹Plan›; **port is ~d in oak casks** Portwein reift in Eichenfässern. ❸ *v.i.* **A** ‹Frucht, Wein, Käse usw.:› reifen; **B** ‹Person:› reifen, reifer werden; **C** ‹Rechnung, Police usw.:› fällig werden

**maturity** /məˈtjʊərɪtɪ/ *n.* **A** Reife, *die;* **reach ~, come to ~** ‹Person:› erwachsen werden; ‹Tier:› ausgewachsen sein; **B** (*Finance*) Fälligkeit, *die;* **come to ~:** fällig werden

**maty** ⇒ **matey**

**maudlin** /ˈmɔːdlɪn/ *adj.* gefühlsselig

**maul** /mɔːl/ ❶ *v.t.* **A** ‹Tiger, Löwe, Bär usw.:› Pranken-/Tatzenhiebe versetzen (+ *Dat.*); (*fig.*) malträtieren; verreißen ‹Theaterstück, Buch›; ‹Boxer:› losgehen auf (+ *Akk.*) ‹Gegner›; **he was ~ed by a lion** er wurde von einem Löwen angefallen; **B** (*fondle roughly*) betatschen (*ugs.*). ❷ *n.* **A** (*brawl*) Schlägerei, *die;* **B** (*Rugby*) **[loose] ~:** offenes Gedränge

**Maundy** /ˈmɔːndɪ/ *n.* (*Brit.*) *Verteilung von Almosen am Gründonnerstag*

**Maundy:** ~ **money** *n.* (*Brit.*) *englische silberne Sondermünzen, die am Gründonnerstag als Almosen verteilt werden;* Maundy money, *das;* ~ **ˈThursday** *n.* Gründonnerstag, *der*

**Mauritania** /mɒrɪˈteɪnɪə/ *pr. n.* Mauretanien (*das*)

**Mauritian** /məˈrɪʃn/ ▶ 1340 ❶ *adj.* mauritisch; **sb. is ~:** jmd. ist Mauritier/Mauritierin. ❷ *n.* Mauritier, *der*/Mauritierin, *die*

**Mauritius** /məˈrɪʃəs/ *pr. n.* Mauritius (*das*)

**mausoleum** /mɔːsəˈliːəm/ *n.* Mausoleum, *das*

**mauve** /məʊv/ *adj.* mauve

**maverick** /ˈmævərɪk/ ❶ *n.* Einzelgänger, *der*/Einzelgängerin, *die;* (*Amer.: politician*) Alleingänger, *der.* ❷ *adj.* einzelgängerisch

**maw** /mɔː/ *n.* **A** (*stomach*) Magen, *der;* (*of ruminant*) Labmagen, *der;* **B** (*jaws*) Rachen, *der*

**mawkish** /ˈmɔːkɪʃ/ *adj.* (*sentimental*) rührselig

**max.** *abbr.* **maximum** (*adj.*) max., (*n.*) Max.

**maxi** /ˈmæksɪ/ *n.* (*coll.*) (*dress*) Maxi, *das* (*ugs.*); (*skirt*) Maxi, *der* (*ugs.*)

**maxi-** *in comb.* Maxi‹kleid, -mantel, -rock›

**maxim** /ˈmæksɪm/ *n.* Maxime, *die*

**maximal** /ˈmæksɪml/ *adj.*, **maximally** /ˈmæksɪməlɪ/ *adv.* maximal

**maximisation, maximise** ⇒ **maximiz-**

**maximization** /mæksɪmaɪˈzeɪʃn/ *n.* Maximierung, *die;* ~ **of profit** Profitmaximierung, *die*

**maximize** /ˈmæksɪmaɪz/ *v.t.* maximieren

**maximum** /ˈmæksɪməm/ ❶ *n., pl.* **maxima** /ˈmæksɪmə/ Maximum, *das;* **a ~ of happiness** ein Maximum *od.* Höchstmaß an Glück; **production is at a ~:** die Produktion befindet sich auf einem Höchststand. ❷ *adj.* ▶ 1603 maximal; Maximal-; ~ **security prison** Hochsicherheitsgefängnis, *das;* ~ **temperatures today around 20°** Höchsttemperaturen heute um 20°

**ˈmaximum-security** *attrib. adj.* Hochsicherheits‹[gefängnis]trakt›

**May** /meɪ/ *n.* **A** ▶ 1055 (*month*) Mai, *der;* ⇒ *also* **August; queen** A; **B** **may** (*hawthorn*) Weißdorn, *der*

**may** *v. aux., only in pres.* **may,** *neg.* (*coll.*) **mayn't** /meɪnt/, *past* **might** /maɪt/, *neg.* (*coll.*) **mightn't** /ˈmaɪtnt/ ▶ 1312 **A** *expr. possibility* können; **it ~ be true** das kann stimmen; **it ~ or ~ not be true** vielleicht stimmts, vielleicht auch nicht; **I ~ be wrong** vielleicht irre ich mich; **they ~ be related** es kann sein, dass sie verwandt sind; vielleicht sind sie verwandt; **it ~ not be possible** das wird vielleicht nicht möglich

m

## May/might

### Possibility

Where *may* simply means *can*, **können** is used in German:

***These flowers may be grown in any soil***
= Diese Blumen kann man in jeder Erde pflanzen

But where *may* in English is used to express degrees of possibility and uncertainty, there are a number of possible translations in German:

***She may come*** (*it's possible*)
= Es kann sein *or* Es ist möglich, dass sie kommt

***She may come* (and on the other hand she may not)**
= Vielleicht kommt sie (und vielleicht auch nicht)

***She may*** or ***might come*** (*a more distant possibility*)
= Sie könnte kommen

***She may* (well) *come*** (= *there's a good possibility*)
= Es kann schon sein *or* Es ist schon möglich, dass sie kommt

***She may yet come***
= Sie kann immerhin noch kommen; Es ist immerhin möglich, dass sie noch kommt

With *may have*, the perfect tense is applied to the verb governed and not to the translation of *may*:

***I may have seen him***
= Es kann sein *or* Es ist möglich, dass ich ihn gesehen habe

***The train may have been late***
= Vielleicht hat der Zug Verspätung gehabt

***I might have said it* (but I don't remember)**
= Es könnte sein, dass ich es gesagt habe (aber ich weiß es nicht mehr)

***She might have come if she had known***
= Sie wäre vielleicht gekommen, wenn sie es gewusst hätte

However, where *might* is **könnte**, *might have* is **hätte ... können**:

***It might have been worse*** (= *could have been*)
= Es hätte schlimmer sein können

***You might have told me***
= Du hättest es mir doch sagen können

### Permission

This can always be translated by **dürfen**:

***May I have the next dance?***
= Darf ich [um den nächsten Tanz] bitten?

***You may not smoke***
= Sie dürfen nicht rauchen

***Dear Bertie* (if I may)**
= Lieber Bertie (wenn ich dich so nennen darf)

sein; **he ~ have missed his train** vielleicht hat er seinen Zug verpasst; **he ~ have finished already** vielleicht ist er schon fertig; **it ~** *or* **might be true, though I doubt it** das kann schon *od.* könnte stimmen, obwohl ich es bezweifle; **it ~** *or* **might rain** es könnte regnen; **he might come round later** vielleicht kommt er später noch vorbei; **they might decide to stay** womöglich beschließen sie zu bleiben; **he might have been right** vielleicht hat er [ja] Recht gehabt; er könnte Recht gehabt haben; **he might have agreed if ...:** vielleicht hätte er zugestimmt, wenn ...; **it's not so bad as it might have been** es hätte schlimmer kommen können; **that ~ well be** das ist durchaus möglich; das kann durchaus sein; **it ~** *or* **might well be true** das kann *od.* könnte durchaus stimmen; **it ~** *or* **might well turn out to be quite easy** es ist durchaus möglich, dass es sich als recht einfach herausstellt; **you ~ well say so** das kann man wohl sagen; **as well he ~/might** wozu er [auch] allen Grund hat/hatte; **we ~** *or* **might as well go** wir könnten eigentlich ebenso gut [auch] gehen; (*we are not achieving anything here*) dann können wir ja gehen; **that is as '~ be** das kann *od.* mag schon sein; **be that as it ~:** wie dem auch sei; Ⓑ *expr. permission* dürfen; **you ~ go now** du kannst *od.* darfst jetzt gehen; **~ I ask why ...?** darf ich fragen, warum ...?; **if I ~ say so ...:** wenn ich das sagen darf, ...; **~** *or* **might I be permitted to ...?** (*formal*) gestatten Sie, dass ...?; **we ~ safely assert that ...:** wir dürfen wohl behaupten, dass ...; **~** *or* **might I ask** (*iron.*) ..., wenn ich [mal] fragen darf?; Ⓒ *expr. wish* mögen; **~ you be happy together!** ich hoffe, ihr werdet glücklich miteinander!; **~ the best man win!** auf dass der Beste gewinnt!; **~ God bless you** Gott segne dich; Ⓓ *expr. request* **you might help me with this** du könntest mir dabei helfen; **you might offer to help instead of ...:** du solltest lieber helfen, statt ...; **you might at least try [it]** du könntest es wenigstens versuchen; **you might have asked permission** du hättest um Erlaubnis fragen können; Ⓔ *used concessively* **he ~ be slow but he's accurate** mag *od.* kann sein, dass er langsam ist, aber dafür ist er auch genau; Ⓕ *in clauses* **so that I ~/might do sth.** damit ich etw. tun kann; **I hope he ~ succeed** ich hoffe, es gelingt ihm; **I wish it might happen** ich wünschte, es würde geschehen; **you never know what ~ happen** man weiß nie, was passieren kann; **come what ~, whatever ~ happen** geschehe was will; was auch geschieht; **whatever you ~ say ...:** ganz gleich, was du sagst ...; Ⓖ **who ~ you be?** wer bist du denn *od.* bist denn du?; **how old might she be?** wie alt mag sie *od.* wird sie wohl sein?

**maybe** /'meɪbi:, 'meɪbɪ/ *adv.* vielleicht

**'Mayday** *n.* (*distress signal*) Mayday; **~ signal/call** Maydaysignal, *das*

**'May Day** *n.* der Erste Mai; **~ celebrations/demonstrations** Maifeiern/-demonstrationen; **the ~ holiday** der Maifeiertag

**'mayfly** *n.* (*Zool.*) Eintagsfliege, *die*

**mayhem** /'meɪhem/ *n.* Ⓐ (*confusion, chaos*) Chaos, *das;* **there was ~:** es gab ein Chaos; **cause** *or* **create ~:** ein Chaos verursachen *od.* hervorrufen; Ⓑ (*Brit. Hist./Amer.*) schwere Körperverletzung

**mayn't** /meɪnt/ (*coll.*) = **may not;** ⇒ **may**

**mayonnaise** /meɪə'neɪz/ *n.* Mayonnaise, *die;* **egg/fish ~:** Ei/Fisch in Mayonnaise

**mayor** /meə(r)/ *n.* ▶ 1261, ▶ 1617 Bürgermeister, *der;* **Lord M~** (*Brit.*) Lord Mayor, *der;* ≈ Oberbürgermeister, *der;* **Lord Mayor's Show** (*Brit.*) *Festzug des Lord Mayor durch die City von London*

**mayoral** /'meərl/ *adj.* des Bürgermeisters *nachgestellt*

**mayoralty** /'meərltɪ/ *n.* (*office*) Amt des Bürgermeisters; (*period of office*) Amtszeit eines Bürgermeisters

**mayoress** /'meərɪs/ *n.* ▶ 1261, ▶ 1617 (*woman mayor*) Bürgermeisterin, *die;* (*mayor's wife*) [Ehe]frau des Bürgermeisters; **Lady M~** (*Brit.*) Oberbürgermeisterin, *die*/[Ehe]frau des Oberbürgermeisters

**'maypole** *n.* Maibaum, *der*

**'May queen** *n.* Maikönigin, *die*

**maze** /meɪz/ *n.* (*lit. or fig.*) Labyrinth, *das*

**mazurka** /mə'zɜ:kə/ *n.* (*Mus.*) Mazurka, *die*

**MB** *abbr.* Ⓐ (*Computing*) **megabyte** MB; Ⓑ **Bachelor of Medicine** ≈ zweites medizinisches Staatsexamen; ⇒ *also* **B. Sc.**

**MBA** *abbr.* **Master of Business Administration** *Diplom in Betriebswirtschaft;* ⇒ *also* **B. Sc.**

**MBE** *abbr.* (*Brit.*) **Member [of the Order] of the British Empire** Träger des Ordens des British Empire 5. Klasse

**Mbyte** *abbr.* **megabyte** Mbyte; MByte

**MC** *abbr.* Ⓐ **Master of Ceremonies;** Ⓑ (*Brit.*) **Military Cross** *militärisches Verdienstkreuz*

**MCC** /emsɪ:'sɪ:/ *n. britischer Kricketverband*

**McCoy** /mə'kɔɪ/ **the real ~** (*coll.*) der/die/das Echte; (*not a fake or replica*) das Original

**MCP** *abbr.* (*coll.*) **male chauvinist pig**

**MD** *abbr.* Ⓐ **Doctor of Medicine** Dr. med.; ⇒ *also* **B. Sc.**; Ⓑ **Managing Director** Ltd. Dir.

**me**[1] /mɪ, *stressed* mi:/ *pron.* mich; *as indirect object* mir; **bigger than/as big as me** größer als/so groß wie ich; **silly me** ich Dussel! (*salopp*); **why me?** warum ich/mich/mir?; **who, me?** wer, ich?; **not me** ich/mich/mir nicht; **it's me** ich bins; **it isn't me** das bin ich nicht; **yes, me** ja, ich/mich/mir; **the real me** mein wahres Ich

**me**[2] /mi:/ *n.* (*Mus.*) mi

**ME** *abbr.* (*Med.*) **myalgic encephalomyelitis**

**mead**[1] /mi:d/ *n.* (*drink*) Met, *der*

**mead**[2] *n.* (*poet./arch.: meadow*) Aue, *die*

**meadow** /'medəʊ/ *n.* Wiese, *die;* **in the ~:** auf der Wiese

**meadow: ~ grass** *n.* [Wiesen]rispengras, *das;* **~ pipit** *n.* (*Ornith.*) Wiesenpieper, *der;* **~ 'saffron** *n.* (*Bot.*) Herbstzeitlose, *die;* **~sweet** *n.* (*Bot.*) (*Brit.*) Mädesüß, *das;* (*Amer.*) Weidenblättriger Spierstrauch

**meager, meagerly, meagerness** (*Amer.*) ⇒ **meagre** *etc.*

**meagre** /'mi:gə(r)/ *adj.* Ⓐ spärlich; dürftig (*auch fig.*); mager ‹Boden›; **a ~ attendance** eine geringe Teilnehmerzahl; Ⓑ mager ‹Gesicht, Mensch›; hager ‹Gestalt›

**meagrely** /'mi:gəlɪ/ *adv.* spärlich; dürftig ‹leben, sich ernähren, behandeln›

**meagreness** /'mi:gənɪs/ *n., no pl.* Spärlichkeit, *die;* Dürftigkeit, *die*

**meal**[1] /mi:l/ *n.* Mahlzeit, *die;* **stay for a ~:** zum Essen bleiben; **go out for a ~:** essen gehen; **have a [hot/cold/light] ~:** [warm/kalt/etwas Leichtes] essen; **enjoy your ~:** guten Appetit!; **did you enjoy your ~?** hat es Ihnen geschmeckt?; **~s on wheels** (*Brit.*) Essen auf Rädern; **make a ~ of sth.** etw. verzehren *od.* essen; (*fig.*) eine große Sache aus etw. machen

**meal²** *n.* Ⓐ (*ground grain*) Schrot[mehl], *das;* Ⓑ (*Scot.: oatmeal*) Hafermehl, *das;* Ⓒ (*Amer.: maize flour*) Maismehl, *das*

**mealies** /ˈmiːlɪz/ *n. pl.* (*S. Afr.*) Ⓐ (*maize*) Mais, *der;* Ⓑ (*corn cob*) Maiskolben, *der*

**meal: ~ ticket** *n.* Essenmarke, *die;* (*fig. coll.*) melkende Kuh (*ugs.*); **~time** *n.* Essenszeit, *die;* **at ~times** während des Essens; bei Tisch; **my usual ~time is ...:** ich esse gewöhnlich um ...

**mealy** /ˈmiːlɪ/ *adj.* mehlig ‹Kartoffeln, Äpfel›

**mealy-mouthed** /ˈmiːlɪmaʊðd/ *adj.* (*derog.*) unaufrichtig

**mean¹** /miːn/ *n.* Ⓐ Mittelweg, *der;* Mitte, *die;* **a happy ~:** der goldene Mittelweg; ⇒ *also* **golden mean**; Ⓑ (*Math.*) Mittelwert, *der*

**mean²** *adj.* Ⓐ (*niggardly*) schäbig (*abwertend*); **you ~ old thing!** du alter Geizhals! (*abwertend*); Ⓑ (*ignoble*) schäbig (*abwertend*), gemein ‹Person, Verhalten, Gesinnung›; (*malicious*) hinterhältig ‹Blick›; Ⓒ (*unimpressive*) schäbig (*abwertend*) ‹Haus, Wohngegend›; armselig ‹Verhältnisse›; **be no ~ athlete/feat** kein schlechter Sportler/keine schlechte Leistung sein; Ⓓ (*coll.: ashamed*) **feel ~ [about sth.]** sich [wegen etw.] schäbig vorkommen; **he made me feel ~:** ich kam mir ihm gegenüber richtig schäbig vor; Ⓔ (*inferior*) minder... ‹Qualität›; **this is clear to the ~est intelligence** das ist selbst dem Dümmsten klar; Ⓕ (*Amer.: vicious*) bösartig, heimtückisch ‹Person, Tier›; Ⓖ (*Amer. coll.: unwell*) **feel ~:** sich mies fühlen (*ugs.*); Ⓗ (*coll.: skilful*) spitze (*ugs.*); klasse (*ugs.*); **blow a ~ trumpet** spitze *od.* klasse Trompete spielen

**mean³** *v.t.*, **meant** /ment/ Ⓐ (*have as one's purpose*) beabsichtigen; **~ well** es gut meinen; **~ sb. well, ~ well by** *or* **to** *or* **towards sb.** es gut mit jmdm. meinen; **I ~t no harm** ich habs nicht böse gemeint; **I ~t him no harm** ich wollte ihm nichts Böses; **what do you ~ by [saying] that?** was willst du damit sagen?; **what do you ~ by entering without first knocking?** was fällt dir ein, einfach, ohne anzuklopfen, hereinzukommen? **I ~t it** *or* **it was ~t as a joke** das sollte ein Scherz sein; **~ to do sth.** etw. tun wollen; **I ~ to do it** ich bin fest dazu entschlossen; **I ~ to be obeyed** ich verlange, dass man mir gehorcht; **if he ~s to come ...:** wenn er [schon] unbedingt kommen will, ...; **I ~t to write, but forgot** ich hatte [fest] vor zu schreiben, aber habe es [dann] vergessen; **I only ~t to be helpful** ich wollte [doch] nur helfen; **I didn't ~ to be rude** ich wollte nicht unhöflich sein; **I never ~t to imply that** das habe ich niemals sagen wollen; **do you ~ to say that ...?** willst du damit sagen, dass ...?; ⇒ *also* **business** F; Ⓑ (*design, destine*) **these plates are ~t to be used** diese Teller sind zum Gebrauch bestimmt *od.* sind da, um benutzt zu werden; **what's this gadget ~t to be?** welche Funktion hat dieses Gerät?; **I ~t it to be a surprise/as a surprise for him** es sollte eine Überraschung für ihn sein; ich wollte ihn damit überraschen; **you were never ~t for a diplomat** du bist eben nicht der geborene Diplomat; **they are ~t for each other** sie sind füreinander bestimmt; **I am ~t for greater things than this** ich bin zu Höherem bestimmt; **is this ~t for me?** soll das für mich sein?; **I ~t you to read the letter** ich wollte, dass du den Brief liest; **be ~t to do sth.** etw. tun sollen; **you are ~t to arrive on time** es wird erwartet, dass Sie pünktlich eintreffen *od.* sind; **you weren't ~t to say that** das hättest du nicht sagen sollen; **I am ~t to be giving a lecture** ich soll einen Vortrag halten; **are we ~t to go this way?** (*permitted*) dürfen wir hier langgehen?; **the Russians are ~t to be good at chess** die Russen sollen gut im Schach sein; Ⓒ (*intend to convey, refer to*) meinen; **I ~ [to say], ...:** ich meine ...; **if you know** *or* **see what I ~:** du verstehst, was ich meine?; **what do you ~ by that?** was hast du damit gemeint?; **what I ~ is, will you marry me?** ich meine, willst du mich heiraten?; **I really ~ it, I ~ what I say** ich meine das ernst; es ist mir Ernst damit; **I didn't ~ it literally** ich habe das nicht wörtlich gemeint; Ⓓ (*signify, entail, matter*) bedeuten; **the name ~s/the instructions ~ nothing to me** der Name sagt mir nichts/ich kann mit der Anleitung nichts anfangen; **this ~s serious problems for him** das wird ihn in ernste Schwierigkeiten bringen

**meander** /mɪˈændə(r)/ ❶ *v.i.* Ⓐ ‹Fluss:› sich schlängeln *od.* winden; mäandern (*Geogr.*); Ⓑ ‹Person:› schlendern. ❷ *n. in pl.* Windungen; (*of river also*) Mäander (*Geogr.*)

**meanderings** /mɪˈændərɪŋz/ *n. pl.* Windungen; (*of stream also*) Mäander (*Geogr.*)

**meanie** /ˈmiːnɪ/ *n.* (*coll.*) Geizhals, *der* (*abwertend*); Geizkragen, *der* (*ugs. abwertend*)

**meaning** /ˈmiːnɪŋ/ ❶ *n.* Bedeutung, *die;* (*of text etc., life*) Sinn, *der;* **this sentence has no ~:** dieser Satz ergibt keinen Sinn; **if you get my ~:** du verstehst, was ich meine?; **I don't get your ~:** ich verstehe dich nicht; ich weiß nicht, was du meinst; **I mistook his ~:** ich habe ihn missverstanden; **what's the ~ of this?** was hat [denn] das zu bedeuten?; **you don't know the ~ of suffering/of the word** du weißt ja gar nicht, was Leiden bedeutet *od.* ist/was das bedeutet; **with ~:** bedeutungsvoll.
❷ *adj.* bedeutungsvoll

**meaningful** /ˈmiːnɪŋfl/ *adj.* sinntragend ‹Wort, Einheit›; (*fig.*) bedeutungsvoll ‹Blick, Ergebnis, Folgerung›; sinnvoll ‹Leben, Aufgabe, Arbeit, Gespräch›

**meaningless** /ˈmiːnɪŋlɪs/ *adj.* ‹Wort, Satz, Gespräch› ohne Sinn; (*fig.*) sinnlos ‹Aktivität, Leben, Leiden, Opfer, Verhalten›

**meanly** /ˈmiːnlɪ/ *adv.* schäbig (*abwertend*) gemein ‹sich verhalten, jmdn. behandeln›; armselig, dürftig ‹bekleidet, ausgestattet, ausgerüstet›; **live ~:** in armseligen Verhältnissen leben

**meanness** /ˈmiːnnɪs/ *n., no pl.* Ⓐ (*stinginess*) Schäbigkeit, *die* (*abwertend*); Ⓑ (*baseness*) Schäbigkeit, *die* (*abwertend*); Gemeinheit, *die;* Ⓒ (*shabbiness*) ⇒ **mean²** C: Schäbigkeit, *die;* Armseligkeit, *die*

**means** /miːnz/ *n. pl.* Ⓐ *usu. constr. as sing.* (*way, method*) Möglichkeit, *die;* [Art und] Weise; **by this ~:** hierdurch; auf diese Weise; **by what ~?** wie? auf welche Weise?; **by some ~ or other** auf die eine oder andere Weise; irgendwie; **a ~ to an end** ein Mittel zum Zweck; **do the ends justify the ~?** heiligt der Zweck die Mittel?; **we have no ~ of doing this** wir haben keine Möglichkeit, dies zu tun; **he used poetry as a ~ of expressing his ideas** er benutzte Dichtung als Mittel, um seine Gedanken auszudrücken; **an easy ~ of escape** eine bequeme Fluchtmöglichkeit; **~ of transport** Transportmittel, *das;* **a ~ of communicating with sb.** eine Möglichkeit *od.* ein Weg, sich mit jmdm. zu verständigen; **how this happened we have no ~ of telling/knowing** wie es passierte *od.* (*geh.*) geschah, können wir nicht sagen/wissen; ⇒ *also* **way** 1 C; Ⓑ (*resources*) Mittel *Pl.;* **live within/beyond one's ~:** seinen Verhältnissen entsprechend/über seine Verhältnisse leben; **he/she is a man/woman of ~:** er/sie ist vermögend; Ⓒ **Will you help me? — By all ~:** Hilfst du mir? — Selbstverständlich!; **May I go now? — By all ~:** Darf ich jetzt gehen? — Ja, gern *od.* sicher; **do so by all ~, but ...:** tu das ruhig, aber ...; **by no [manner of] ~, not by any [manner of] ~:** ganz und gar nicht; keineswegs; **by ~ of** durch; mit [Hilfe von]

**~ test** ❶ *n.* Überprüfung der Bedürftigkeit. ❷ *v.t.* jmds. Bedürftigkeit überprüfen; **means test tested benefits** nach Bedürftigkeit gestaffelte Unterstützungszahlungen

**meant** ⇒ **mean³**

**mean: ~time** ❶ *n.* **in the ~time** in der Zwischenzeit; inzwischen. ❷ *adv.* inzwischen. **~while** *adv.* inzwischen

**meany** ⇒ **meanie**

**measles** /ˈmiːzlz/ *n., constr. as pl. or sing.* ▶ 1232 Masern *Pl.;* ⇒ *also* **German measles**

**measly** /ˈmiːzlɪ/ *adj.* (*coll. derog.*) pop[e]lig (*ugs. abwertend*); **a ~ little portion** eine mickrige Portion (*ugs. abwertend*)

**measurable** /ˈmeʒərəbl/ *adj.* messbar ‹Anzahl, Menge, Größe›; (*fig.*) merklich ‹Besserung, Veränderung, Fortschritte›; **bring sb. within ~ distance of bankruptcy** jmdn. an den Rand des Bankrotts bringen

**measurably** /ˈmeʒərəblɪ/ *adv.* merklich ‹besser, größer›

**measure** /ˈmeʒə(r)/ ❶ *n.* Ⓐ ▶ 928, ▶ 1683 Maß, *das;* **~ of length** Längenmaß, *das;* **weights and ~s** Maße und Gewichte; **for good ~:** sicherheitshalber; (*as an extra*) zusätzlich; **give short/full ~** (*in public house*) zu wenig/vorschriftsmäßig ausschenken; (*in shop*) zu wenig/vorschriftsmäßig abwiegen; **made to ~** *pred.* (*Brit., lit. or fig.*) maßgeschneidert; Ⓑ (*degree*) Menge, *die;* **in some ~:** in gewisser Hinsicht; **in large/full ~:** in hohem/vollem Maße; **a ~ of freedom/responsibility** ein gewisses Maß an Freiheit/Verantwortung (*Dat.*); Ⓒ (*instrument or utensil for measuring*) Maß, *das;* (*for quantity also*) Messglas, *das;* Messbecher, *der;* (*for size also*) Messstab, *der;* Maßstab, *der* (*selten*); (*fig.*) Maßstab, *der;* **be a/the ~ of sth.** Maßstab für etw. sein; **it gave us some ~ of the problems** das gab uns eine Vorstellung *od.* einen Begriff von den Problemen; **beyond [all] ~:** grenzenlos; über die *od.* alle Maßen *adv.*; Ⓓ (*Pros.*) Versmaß, *das;* Metrum, *das;* Ⓔ (*Mus.: time, bar*) Takt, *der;* Ⓕ (*step, law*) Maßnahme, *die;* (*Law: bill*) Gesetzesvorlage, *die;* **take ~s to stop/ensure sth.** Maßnahmen ergreifen *od.* treffen, um etw. zu unterbinden/sicherzustellen; ⇒ *also* **half measure b**; Ⓖ (*Geol.*) ⇒ **coal measures**.
❷ *v.t.* Ⓐ messen ‹Größe, Menge usw.›; ausmessen ‹Raum›; **~ sb. for a suit** [bei] jmdm. Maß *od.* die Maße für einen Anzug nehmen; Ⓑ (*fig.: estimate*) abschätzen; **~ sb. by one's own standards** jmdn. an seinen eigenen Maßstäben messen; Ⓒ (*mark off*) **~ sth. [off]** etw. abmessen; Ⓓ (*fig.: put in competition*) messen (*geh.*); **~ oneself against sb.** sich mit jmdm. messen (*geh.*); Ⓔ **~ one's length** (*fig.*) der Länge nach hinfallen.
❸ *v.i.* Ⓐ (*have a given size*) messen; Ⓑ (*take measurement[s]*) Maß nehmen

**~ 'out** *v.t.* abmessen

**~ 'up to** *v.t.* entsprechen (+ *Dat.*) ‹Maßstäben, Erwartungen›; gewachsen sein (+ *Dat.*) ‹Anforderungen›

**measured** /ˈmeʒəd/ *adj.* rhythmisch, gleichmäßig ‹Geräusch, Bewegung›; gemessen ‹Schritt, Worte, Ausdrucksweise›; **speak in ~ terms** sich gemessen ausdrücken

**measureless** /ˈmeʒəlɪs/ *adj.* unermesslich

**measurement** /ˈmeʒəmənt/ *n.* ▶ 928 Ⓐ (*act, result*) Messung, *die;* Ⓑ *in pl.* (*dimensions*) Maße *Pl.;* **take sb.'s ~s** [bei] jmdm. Maß *od.* die Maße nehmen

**measuring** /ˈmeʒərɪŋ/**: ~ jug** *n.* Messbecher, *der;* **~ tape** *n.* Bandmaß, *das*

**meat** /miːt/ *n.* Ⓐ Fleisch, *das;* Ⓑ (*arch.: food*) Essen, *das;* (*for animals*) Futter, *das;* **~ and drink** Speis und Trank (*geh.*); **one man's ~ is another man's poison** (*prov.*) was dem einen sein Uhl, ist dem andern sin Nachtigall (*Spr.*); **be ~ and drink to sb.** (*fig.*) genau das sein, was jmd. braucht; Ⓒ (*fig.: chief part, essence*) Substanz, *die*

**meat: ~ axe** *n.* Fleischbeil, *das;* Spalter, *der* (*fachspr.*); **~ball** *n.* Fleischkloß, *der;* Fleischklößchen, *das;* **~-fly** *n.* Fleischfliege, *die;* **~ grinder** (*Amer.*) ⇒ **mincer**

**meatless** /ˈmiːtlɪs/ *adj.* fleischlos

**meat: ~ loaf** *n.* Hackbraten, *der;* **~ 'pie** *n.* Fleischpastete, *die;* **~ safe** *n.* (*Brit.*) Fliegenschrank, *der*

**meaty** /ˈmiːtɪ/ *adj.* Ⓐ (*full of meat*) fleischig; ‹Gulasch usw.› mit reichlich Fleisch; **have a ~ taste** nach Fleisch schmecken; Ⓑ (*fig.: full of substance*) gehaltvoll

**Mecca** /ˈmekə/ *n.* ▶ 1626 Mekka, *das;* **the ~ of golfers** das Mekka für Golfer

**mechanic** /mɪˈkænɪk/ *n.* ▶ 1261 Mechaniker, *der*

m

**mechanical** /mɪˈkænɪkl/ *adj.* (*lit. or fig.*) mechanisch; **produced by ~ means** maschinell produziert; maschinell erzeugt ‹Strom›; **~ contrivance** Mechanismus, *der*

**mechanical: ~ engiˈneer** *n.* Maschinenbauer, *der*/-bauerin, *die;* (*graduate*) Maschinenbauingenieur, *der*/-ingenieurin, *die;* **~ engiˈneering** *n.* Maschinenbau, *der*

**mechanically** /mɪˈkænɪkəlɪ/ *adv.* (*lit. or fig.*) mechanisch; **~ inclined/minded** technisch interessiert/veranlagt

**mechanical ˈpencil** *n.* (*Amer.*) Drehbleistift, *der*

**mechanics** /mɪˈkænɪks/ *n., no pl.* **A** Mechanik, *die;* **B** *constr. as pl.* (*means of construction or operation*) Mechanismus, *der;* (*of writing, painting, etc.*) Technik, *die;* **understand the ~ of sth.** wissen, wie etw. funktioniert

**mechanisation, mechanise** ⇒ **mechaniz-**

**mechanism** /ˈmekənɪzm/ *n.* Mechanismus, *der*

**mechanization** /mekənaɪˈzeɪʃn/ *n.* Mechanisierung, *die*

**mechanize** /ˈmekənaɪz/ *v.t.* **A** mechanisieren; **B** (*Mil.*) motorisieren

**Med** /med/ *pr. n.* (*coll.*) **the ~:** das Mittelmeer

**medal** /ˈmedl/ *n.* Medaille, *die;* (*decoration*) Orden, *der;* **~ for bravery/pole-vaulting** Tapferkeitsmedaille, *die*/Medaille im Stabhochsprung; **the reverse of the ~** (*fig.*) die Kehrseite der Medaille

**medalist** (*Amer.*) ⇒ **medallist**

**medallion** /mɪˈdæljən/ *n.* **A** (*large medal*) [große] Medaille; **B** (*thing shaped like medal*) Medaillon, *das*

**medallist** /ˈmedəlɪst/ *n.* Medaillengewinner, *der*/-gewinnerin, *die* (*Sport*); **be a ~:** eine Medaille gewonnen haben

**meddle** /ˈmedl/ *v.i.* **~ with sth.** sich (*Dat.*) an etw. (*Dat.*) zu schaffen machen; **~ in sth.** sich in etw. (*Akk.*) einmischen; **don't ~:** Finger weg! (*ugs.*); (*stop interfering*) misch dich nicht ein!; **she's always meddling** sie muss sich immer in alles einmischen

**meddler** /ˈmedlə(r)/ *n.* **he's [such] a ~** (*with things*) er muss immer alles in die Finger nehmen *od.* (*ugs.*) an allem herumspielen; (*in things*) er muss sich immer in alles einmischen

**meddlesome** /ˈmedlsəm/ *adj.* **she is so ~** *or* **such a ~ person** (*interferes with things*) sie muss sich (*Dat.*) immer an was zu schaffen machen; (*interferes in things*) sie muss sich in alles einmischen

**Mede** /mi:d/ *n.* **law of the ~s and Persians** (*fig.*) unumstößliches Gesetz

**media** /ˈmi:dɪə/ ⇒ **mass media; medium** 1 A

**mediaeval** ⇒ **medieval**

**medial** /ˈmi:dɪəl/ *adj.* mittler...; ‹Buchstabe, Zeichen› mitten im Wort

**median** /ˈmi:dɪən/ **1** *adj.* mittler...; median (*Anat.*). **2** *n.* (*Statistics*) Median[wert], *der;* Zentralwert, *der*

**median strip** /mi:dɪən ˈstrɪp/*n.* (*Amer.*) Mittelstreifen, *der*

**ˈmedia studies** *n. sing.* Medienwissenschaft, *die;* (*school subject*) Medienkunde, *die*

**mediate** /ˈmi:dɪeɪt/ **1** *v.i.* vermitteln. **2** *v.t.* **A** (*settle*) vermitteln in (+ *Dat.*); **B** (*bring about*) vermitteln

**mediation** /mi:dɪˈeɪʃn/ *n.* Vermittlung, *die*

**mediator** /ˈmi:dɪeɪtə(r)/ *n.* Vermittler, *der*/Vermittlerin, *die*

**medic** /ˈmedɪk/ ⇒ **medico**

**Medicaid** /ˈmedɪkeɪd/ *n.* (*Amer.*) [*bundes*]*staatliches Programm, das Unterstützungsbedürftigen Beihilfe zur Deckung von Arzt- und Heilmittelkosten gewährt*

**medical** /ˈmedɪkl/ **1** *adj.* medizinisch; ärztlich ‹Behandlung›; **~ ward** ≈ medizinische *od.* innere Abteilung. **2** *n.* (*coll.*) ⇒ **medical examination**

**medical: ~ attendant** *n.* Leibarzt, *der*/-ärztin, *die;* **~ certificate** *n.* Attest, *das;* **~ examiˈnation** *n.* ärztliche Untersuchung; **~ ˈhistory** *n.* **A** Geschichte der Medizin; **make ~ history** auf dem Gebiet der Medizin Geschichte machen; **B** (*of person*) Krankengeschichte, *die;* **~ insurance** *n.* Krankenversicherung, *die;* **have ~ insurance** krankenversichert sein

**medically** /ˈmedɪkəlɪ/ *adv.* medizinisch

**medical: ~ officer** *n.* (*Brit.*) **A** Amtsarzt, *der*/-ärztin, *die;* **B** (*Mil.*) Sanitätsoffizier, *der;* **~ pracˈtitioner** *n.* ▶ **1261** praktischer Arzt/praktische Ärztin; Arzt/Ärztin für Allgemeinmedizin; **~ report** *n.*. medizinisches Gutachten; **~ school** *n.* medizinische Hochschule; (*faculty*) medizinische Fakultät; **~ student** *n.* Medizinstudent, *der*/-studentin, *die*

**medicament** /mɪˈdɪkəmənt, ˈmedɪkəmənt/ *n.* Medikament, *das*

**Medicare** /ˈmedɪkeə(r)/ *n.* (*Amer.*) [*bundes*]*staatliches Krankenversicherungssystem für Personen über 65 Jahre*

**medicated** /ˈmedɪkeɪtɪd/ *adj.* **~ shampoo/soap** medizinisches Haarwaschmittel/medizinische Seife; **~ gauze** imprägnierter Mull

**medication** /medɪˈkeɪʃn/ *n.* **A** (*treatment*) Behandlung, *die;* Medikation, *die* (*Med.*); **B** (*medicament*) Medikament, *das*

**medicinal** /mɪˈdɪsɪnl/ *adj.* medizinisch; Arznei‹mittel, -kohle›; **~ qualities** Heilkräfte

**medicinally** /mɪˈdɪsɪnəlɪ/ *adv.* medizinisch; **use sth. ~:** etw. zu medizinischen Zwecken *od.* Heilzwecken verwenden

**medicine** /ˈmedsən, ˈmedɪsɪn/ *n.* (*science*) Medizin, *die;* (*preparation*) Medikament, *das;* Medizin, *die* (*veralt.*); **give sb. some** *or* **a little** *or* **a dose** *or* **a taste of his/her own ~** (*fig.*) es jmdm. mit gleicher Münze heimzahlen; **they got a taste of their own ~** (*fig.*) man zahlte es ihnen mit gleicher Münze heim; **take one's ~** (*fig.*) die bittere Pille schlucken (*ugs.*); (*bear the consequences*) die Suppe auslöffeln (*ugs.*)

**medicine: ~ ball** *n.* Medizinball, *der;* **~ chest** *n.* Medikamentenschränkchen, *das;* (*in home*) Hausapotheke, *die;* **~ man** *n.* Medizinmann, *der*

**medico** /ˈmedɪkəʊ/ *n., pl.* **~s** (*coll.*) **A** (*doctor*) Doktor, *der* (*ugs.*); **B** (*student*) Medizinér, *der*/Medizinerin, *die* (*ugs.*)

**medieval** /medɪˈi:vl/ *adj.* (*lit. or fig.*) mittelalterlich; **the ~ period** das Mittelalter; **~ studies** Mediävistik, *die;* **in ~ times** im Mittelalter; **~ Latin** ⇒ **Latin** 2

**medieval ˈhistory** *n.* Geschichte des Mittelalters; (*as subject*) mittelalterliche Geschichte

**medievalist** /medɪˈi:vəlɪst/ *n.* Mediävist, *der*/Mediävistin, *die*

**mediocre** /mi:dɪˈəʊkə(r)/ *adj.* mittelmäßig

**mediocrity** /mi:dɪˈɒkrɪtɪ/ *n.* **A** *no pl.* Mittelmäßigkeit, *die;* **B** (*person*) mittelmäßiger Mensch; **he is a ~/they are mediocrities** er ist/sie sind [ausgesprochenes] Mittelmaß

**meditate** /ˈmedɪteɪt/ **1** *v.t.* (*consider*) denken an (+ *Akk.*); erwägen; (*design*) planen; **~ revenge** auf Rache (*Akk.*) sinnen (*geh.*). **2** *v.i.* nachdenken, (*esp. Relig.*) meditieren ([**up**]**on** über + *Akk.*)

**meditation** /medɪˈteɪʃn/ *n.* **A** (*act of meditating*) Nachdenken, *das;* **B** (*Relig.*) Meditation, *die*

**meditative** /ˈmedɪtətɪv/ *adj.*, **meditatively** /ˈmedɪtətɪvlɪ/ *adv.* nachdenklich; (*esp. Relig.*) meditativ

**Mediterranean** /medɪtəˈreɪnɪən/ **1** *pr. n.* **the ~:** das Mittelmeer. **2** *adj.* mediterran (*Geogr.*); südländisch; **~ coast/countries** Mittelmeerküste, *die*/Mittelmeerländer

**Mediterranean: ~ ˈclimate** *n.* (*Geog.*) mediterranes Klima; **~ ˈSea** *pr. n.* Mittelmeer, *das*

**medium** /ˈmi:dɪəm/ **1** *n., pl.* **media** /ˈmi:dɪə/ *or* **~s** **A** (*substance*) Medium, *das;* (*fig.: environment*) Umgebung, *die;* **B** (*intermediate agency*) Mittel, *das;* **by** *or* **through the ~ of** durch; **C** *pl.* **~s** (*Spiritualism*) Medium, *das;* **D** (*means of communication or artistic expression*) Medium, *das;* **E** *in pl.* (*means of mass communication*) Medien *Pl.;* **F** (*middle degree*) Mittelweg, *der;* ⇒ *also* **happy** A; **G** (*liquid*) Bindemittel, *das.* **2** *adj.* mittler...; medium *nur präd.*, halb durchgebraten ‹Steak›; ⇒ *also* **-size**

**medium: ~-dry** *adj.* halbtrocken ‹Wein, Sherry›; **~-size[d]** *adj.* mittelgroß; **~-sweet** *adj.* mittelsüß ‹Wein, Sherry›; **~ term** ⇒ **term** 1 D; **~ wave** *n.* (*Radio*) Mittelwelle, *die*

**medlar** /ˈmedlə(r)/ *n.* (*Bot.*) Mispel, *die*

**medley** /ˈmedlɪ/ *n.* **A** (*forming a whole*) buntes Gemisch; (*collection of items*) Sammelsurium, *das* (*abwertend*); (*of colours*) Kunterbunt, *das;* **his mind was confused with a ~ of thoughts** die verschiedensten Gedanken schossen durch seinen verwirrten Kopf; **B** (*Mus.*) Potpourri, *das;* Medley, *das;* **C** ⇒ **medley relay**

**medley ˈrelay** *n.* (*Athletics*) Schwellstaffel, *die;* (*Swimming*) Lagenstaffel, *die*

**medulla** /mɪˈdʌlə/ *n.* (*Anat.*) **A** Medulla, *die* (*fachspr.*); ‹Knochen-, Rücken-, Haar›mark, *das;* **B** (*of brain*) ⇒ **medulla oblongata**

**medulla oblongata** /mɪdʌlə ɒblɒŋˈgɑ:tə/ *n.* (*Anat.*) verlängertes Rückenmark; Medulla oblongata, *die* (*fachspr.*)

**meek** /mi:k/ *adj.* **A** (*humble*) sanftmütig; **B** (*tamely submissive*) zu nachgiebig; **be [far] too ~:** sich (*Dat.*) [viel] zu viel gefallen lassen; **[as] ~ as a lamb** fromm wie ein Lamm

**meekly** /ˈmi:klɪ/ *adv.* **A** (*humbly*) demütig; **B** (*submissively*) widerstandslos

**meekness** /ˈmi:knɪs/ *n., no pl.* **A** (*humbleness*) Sanftmütigkeit, *die;* **B** (*submissiveness*) [zu große] Nachgiebigkeit

**meerschaum** /ˈmɪəʃəm/ *n.* **A** (*Min.*) Meerschaum, *der;* **B** (*pipe*) Meerschaumpfeife, *die*

**meet[1]** /mi:t/ **1** *v.t.*, **met** /met/ **A** (*come face to face with or into the company of*) treffen; **I have to ~ my boss at 11 a.m.** ich muss um 11 Uhr zum Chef (*ugs.*) *od.* habe um 11 Uhr einen Termin beim Chef; **arrange to ~ sb.** sich mit jmdm. verabreden; **B** (*go to place of arrival of*) treffen; (*collect*) abholen; **I'll ~ your train** ich hole dich vom Zug ab; **~ sb. halfway** (*fig.*) jmdm. [auf halbem Wege] entgegenkommen; **~ trouble halfway** sich (*Dat.*) unnötig Sorgen machen; **C** (*make the acquaintance of*) kennen lernen; **I'd like you to ~ my wife** ich möchte Sie gern meiner Frau vorstellen *od.* mit meiner Frau bekannt machen; **I have never met her** ich kenne sie nicht persönlich; **pleased to ~ you** [sehr] angenehm; sehr erfreut; **Maimie, ~ Charlene. Charlene, ~ Maimie** (*Amer.*) Maimie, [dies ist] Charlene. Charlene, [dies ist] Maimie; **D** (*reach point of contact with*) treffen auf (+ *Akk.*); **~ the eye/sb.'s eye[s]** sich den/jmds. Blicken darbieten; **~ the ear/sb.'s ears** das/jmds. Ohr treffen; **she met his eye[s], her eyes met his** (*fig.*) sie sah ihn an, er sah sie an; **he could not ~ his father's eyes** er konnte seinem Vater nicht in die Augen sehen; **there's more to** *or* **in it/him** *etc.* **than ~s the eye** da ist *od.* steckt mehr dahinter, als man zuerst denkt/in ihm *usw.* steckt mehr, als man auf den ersten Blick denkt; **E** (*oppose*) treffen auf (+ *Akk.*) ‹Feind, Herausforderer usw.›; (*grapple with*) begegnen (+ *Dat.*); **F** (*experience*) stoßen auf (+ *Akk.*) ‹Widerstand, Problem›; ernten ‹Gelächter, Drohungen›; **~ [one's] death** *or* **one's end/disaster/one's fate** den Tod finden (*geh.*)/von einer Katastrophe/seinem Schicksal ereilt werden (*geh.*); **~ one's fate bravely** sich seinem Schicksal tapfer stellen; **G** (*satisfy*) entsprechen (+ *Dat.*) ‹Forderung, Wunsch, Bedürfnis, Erfordernis›; einhalten ‹Termin, Zeitplan›; Rechnung tragen (+ *Dat.*) ‹Einwand, Kritik›; **~ the case** angemessen sein; **H** (*pay*) decken ‹Kosten, Auslagen›; bezahlen ‹Rechnung›; **~ one's obligations** seinen Verpflichtungen nachkommen.
**2** *v.i.*, **met** **A** (*come face to face*) (*by chance*) sich (*Dat.*) begegnen; (*by arrangement*) sich treffen; **goodbye, until we ~ again** auf Wiedersehen bis zum nächsten Mal; **we've met before** wir kennen uns bereits; **B** (*assemble*) ‹Komitee, Ausschuss usw.:› tagen; **~ together** sich versammeln; **C** (*be in opposition*) aufeinander treffen; **D** (*come together*)

‹Bahnlinien, Straßen usw.:› aufeinander treffen; ‹Flüsse:› zusammenfließen; **their eyes/lips met** ihre Blicke/Lippen begegneten sich; **the tables don't quite ~:** die Tische stehen nicht ganz dicht aneinander; ⇒ *also* **end** 1 H, N; Ⓔ *(be united)* **~ in sb.** in jmdm. zusammentreffen; sich in jmdm. vereinen *(geh.)*. ❸ *n. (Hunting)* Treffen, *das*

**~ 'up** *v.i.* sich treffen; **~ up with sb.** *(coll.)* jmdn. [zufällig] treffen

**~ with** *v.t.* Ⓐ *(encounter)* begegnen (+ *Dat.*); Ⓑ *(experience)* haben ‹Erfolg, Unfall›; finden ‹Zustimmung, Verständnis, Tod›; stoßen auf (+ *Akk.*) ‹Widerstand›; **be met with sth.** etw. hervorrufen; **all her attempts met with failure** alle ihre Bemühungen endeten in einem Misserfolg; Ⓒ *(Amer.)* ⇒ **~** 1 A

**meet**[2] *adj. (arch.)* **it is ~ to do sth.** es ziemt sich *(geh. veralt.)*, etw. zu tun

**meeting** /'mi:tɪŋ/ *n.* Ⓐ Begegnung, *die (auch fig.)*; *(by arrangement)* Treffen, *das*; *(of rivers)* Zusammenfluss, *der*; **~ of minds** Verständigung, *die;* Annäherung der Standpunkte; Ⓑ *(assembly) (of shareholders, club members, etc.; also Relig.)* Versammlung, *die; (of committee, Cabinet, council, etc.)* Sitzung, *die; (social gathering)* Treffen, *das;* **call a ~ of the committee** den Ausschuss einberufen; Ⓒ *(persons assembled)* Versammlung, *die;* Ⓓ *(Sport)* Treffen, *das; (Racing)* Rennen, *das*

**meeting: ~ place** *n.* Treffpunkt, *der;* **~ point** *n. (of lines, roads)* Schnittpunkt, *der; (of rivers)* Zusammenfluss, *der;* **at the ~ point of the roads** wo die Straßen zusammentreffen

**mega** /'megə/ *(coll.)* ❶ *adj.* Ⓐ *(enormous)* Mega- *(Jugendspr.)*; Ⓑ *(excellent)* geil *(Jugendspr.)*. ❷ *adv.* äußerst; **be ~ rich** superod. megareich *(Jugendspr.)* sein; **be ~ talented** höchst talentiert sein

**mega-** /'megə/ *pref.* mega-/Mega-

**'megabyte** *n. (Computing)* Megabyte, *das*

**'megacycle** *n.* Megahertz, *das*

**'megadeath** *n.* Megatote *Pl.;* **one ~:** 1 Million Tote

**'megahertz** *n. (Phys.)* Megahertz, *das*

**megalithic** /megə'lɪθɪk/ *adj. (Archaeol.)* megalithisch

**megalomania** /megələ'meɪnɪə/ *n.* Größenwahn, *der;* Megalomanie, *die (Psych.)*

**megalomaniac** /megələ'meɪnɪæk/ ❶ *n.* Größenwahnsinnige, *der/die;* Megalomane, *der/ die (Psych.)*; **he's a ~:** er ist größenwahnsinnig. ❷ *adj.* größenwahnsinnig; megaloman[isch] *(Psych.)*

**'megaphone** *n.* Megaphon, *das*

**'megastar** *n.* Megastar, *der (ugs.)*

**'megaton[ne]** *n.* Megatonne, *die*

**'megawatt** *n. (Electr.)* Megawatt, *das*

**meiosis** /maɪ'əʊsɪs/ *n., pl.* **meioses** /maɪ'əʊsi:z/ *(Biol.)* Meiose, *die*

**Meissen** /'maɪsn/ *pr. n.* **~ [porcelain]** ⇒ **porcelain** A

**melancholia** /melən'kəʊlɪə/ *n. (Med.)* Melancholie, *die*

**melancholic** /melən'kɒlɪk/ *adj.* melancholisch; schwermütig

**melancholy** /'melənkəlɪ/ ❶ *n.* Melancholie, *die; (pensive sadness)* Schwermut, *die.* ❷ *adj.* Ⓐ *(gloomy, expressing sadness)* melancholisch; schwermütig; Ⓑ *(saddening)* deprimierend

**Melanesia** /melə'ni:ʃə/ *pr. n.* Melanesien *(das)*

**Melanesian** /melə'ni:ʃən/ ▶1275, ▶1340 ❶ *adj.* melanesisch. ❷ *n.* Ⓐ *(person)* Melanesier, *der*/Melanesierin, *die;* Ⓑ *(language)* Melanesisch, *das*

**melanin** /'melənɪn/ *n.* Melanin, *das*

**Melba** /'melbə/ ⇒ **peach Melba**

**Melba 'toast** *n. dünner, knuspriger Toast*

**meld** /meld/ *(Amer.)* ❶ *v.t.* verschmelzen **(into** zu). ❷ *v.i.* [miteinander] verschmelzen

**mêlée** *(Amer.:* **melee)** /'meleɪ/ *n.* Ⓐ *(scuffle)* Handgemenge, *das;* Ⓑ *(muddle)* Durcheinander, *das; (of things or people moving to and fro)* Gewühl, *das*

**mellifluous** /me'lɪflʊəs/ *adj.* einschmeichelnd ‹Stimme, Melodie›

**mellow** /'meləʊ/ ❶ *adj.* Ⓐ *(softened by age or experience)* abgeklärt; Ⓑ *(ripe, well-matured)* reif; ausgereift ‹Wein›; Ⓒ *(genial)* freundlich; *(slightly drunk)* angeheitert; **~ in mood** heiter gestimmt; aufgeräumt; Ⓓ *(full and soft)* weich ‹Stimme, Ton, Licht, Farben›. ❷ *v.t.* reifer machen ‹Person›; [aus]reifen lassen ‹Wein›. ❸ *v.i.* ‹Person, Obst, Wein:› reifen; ‹Licht, Farbe:› weicher werden

**melodic** /mɪ'lɒdɪk/ *adj.* melodisch; **~ minor** melodisches Moll

**melodious** /mɪ'ləʊdɪəs/ *adj.*, **melodiously** /mɪ'ləʊdɪəslɪ/ *adv.* melodisch

**melodrama** /'melədrɑ:mə/ *n. (lit. or fig.)* Melodrama, *das*

**melodramatic** /melədrə'mætɪk/ *adj.*, **melodramatically** /melədrə'mætɪkəlɪ/ *adv. (lit. or fig.)* melodramatisch

**melody** /'melədɪ/ *n.* Ⓐ *(pleasing sound)* Gesang, *der;* Ⓑ *(tune)* Melodie, *die;* Ⓒ *no pl. (musical quality)* Melodik, *die;* Ⓓ *(Mus.: part in harmonized music)* Melodiestimme, *die*

**melon** /'melən/ *n.* Melone, *die*

**melt** /melt/ ❶ *v.i.* Ⓐ schmelzen; *(dissolve)* sich auflösen; **~ in one's** *or* **the mouth** auf der Zunge zergehen; ⇒ *also* **butter** 1; Ⓑ *(fig.: be softened)* dahinschmelzen *(geh.)* **(at** bei); sich erweichen lassen **(at** durch); **her heart ~ed with pity** ihr Herz schmolz vor Mitleid; **~ into tears** in Tränen zerfließen. ❷ *v.t.* Ⓐ schmelzen ‹Schnee, Eis, Metall›; *(Cookery)* zerlassen ‹Butter›; Ⓑ *(fig.: make tender)* erweichen ‹Person, Herz›; **he was ~ed by her entreaties** er ließ sich durch ihre Bitten erweichen

**~ a'way** *v.i.* ‹Schnee, Eis:› [weg]schmelzen; *(fig.: dwindle away)* ‹Nebel, Dunst, Menschenmenge:› sich auflösen; ‹Verdacht, Mehrheit, Furcht:› dahinschwinden *(geh.)*; ‹Geld:› dahinschmelzen

**~ 'down** ❶ *v.i.* schmelzen. ❷ *v.t.* einschmelzen ‹Metall, Glas›. ⇒ *also* **meltdown**

**~ into** *v.t.* übergehen in (+ *Akk.*)

**'meltdown** *n.* Schmelzen, *das*

**melting**/'meltɪŋ/**: ~ point** *n.* Schmelzpunkt, *der;* **~ pot** *n. (fig.)* Schmelztiegel, *der;* **be in the ~ pot** in rascher Veränderung begriffen sein

**member** /'membə(r)/ *n.* Ⓐ Mitglied, *das; attrib.* Mitglieds‹staat, -land›; **be a ~ of the club** Mitglied des Vereins sein; Vereinsmitglied sein; **~ of the expedition** Expeditionsteilnehmer, *der*/-teilnehmerin, *die;* **be a ~ of an expedition** an einer Expedition teilnehmen; **~ of a/the family** Familienangehörige, *der/die;* Ⓑ ▶1617 **M~ [of Parliament]** *(Brit. Polit.)* Abgeordnete [des Unterhauses], *der/die;* **M~ of Congress** *(Amer. Polit.)* Kongressabgeordnete, *der/die;* Ⓒ *(limb)* Gliedmaße, *die;* Glied, *das; (organ of the body)* [Körper]organ, *das*

**membership** /'membəʃɪp/ *n.* Ⓐ *(being a member)* Mitgliedschaft, *die* **(of** in + *Dat.*); *attrib.* Mitglieds‹karte, -ausweis, -beitrag›; Mitglieder‹liste, -verzeichnis›; **he was elected to ~ of the Society** er wurde zum Mitglied der Gesellschaft gewählt; Ⓑ *(number of members)* Mitgliederzahl, *die;* **the club has a ~ of a few hundred** der Verein hat einige hundert Mitglieder; Ⓒ *(body of members)* Mitglieder *Pl.*

**membrane** /'membreɪn/ *n. (Biol.)* Membran, *die*

**membranous** /'membrənəs/ *adj. (Biol.)* membranös; **~ bag** Hautsack, *der*

**memento** /mɪ'mentəʊ/ *n., pl.* **~es** *or* **~s** Andenken, *das* **(of** an + *Akk.*)

**memo** /'meməʊ/ *n., pl.* **~s** *(coll.)* ⇒ **memorandum** A, B

**memoir** /'memwɑ:(r)/ *n.* Ⓐ *in pl. (autobiography)* Memoiren *Pl.;* Ⓑ *(biography)* Biografie, *die*

**memorabilia** /memərə'bɪlɪə/ *n. pl.* Erinnerungsstücke *Pl.;* Memorabilien *Pl. (veralt.)*

**memorable** /'memərəbl/ *adj.* denkwürdig ‹Ereignis, Gelegenheit, Tag›; unvergesslich ‹Film, Buch, Aufführung›; **not a very ~ play** kein sehr beeindruckendes Stück

**memorably** /'memərəblɪ/ *adv.* nachhaltig ‹beeindrucken›; auf unvergessliche Weise ‹spielen›

**memorandum** /memə'rændəm/ *n., pl.* **memoranda** /memə'rændə/ *or* **~s** Ⓐ *(note)* Notiz, *die;* **make a ~ of sth.** sich *(Dat.)* etw. notieren; Ⓑ *(letter)* Mitteilung, *die;* Ⓒ *(Diplom.)* Memorandum, *das;* Ⓓ *(Law)* rechtskräftiges Dokument

**memorial** /mɪ'mɔ:rɪəl/ ❶ *adj.* Gedenk‹stein, -gottesdienst, -ausstellung›. ❷ *n.* Ⓐ *(monument)* Denkmal, *das* **(to** für); *(ceremony)* Gedenkzeremonie, *die;* Ⓑ *(statement of facts)* Denkschrift, *die* **(to** an + *Akk.*); Ⓒ *(Diplom.)* Memorandum, *das*

**Me'morial Day** *n. (Amer.) Trauertag zum Gedenken an die Gefallenen;* ≈ Volkstrauertag, *der*

**memorize (memorise)** /'meməraɪz/ *v.t.* sich *(Dat.)* merken *od.* einprägen; *(learn by heart)* auswendig lernen

**memory** /'memərɪ/ *n.* Ⓐ *(faculty or capacity, recovery of knowledge)* Gedächtnis, *das;* **have a good/poor ~ for faces** ein gutes/schlechtes Personengedächtnis haben; **commit sth. to ~** ⇒ **memorize**; Ⓑ *(recollection, person or thing remembered, act of remembering)* Erinnerung, *die* **(of** an + *Akk.*); **have a vague ~ of sth.** sich nur ungenau *od.* vage an etw. *(Akk.)* erinnern; **to the best of my ~:** soweit ich mich erinnere *od.* erinnern kann; **if my ~ is right** wenn ich mich recht erinnere; **search one's ~:** versuchen, sich zu erinnern; **it slipped** *or* **escaped my ~:** es ist mir entfallen; **from ~:** aus dem Gedächtnis *od.* Kopf; **speaking from ~, ...:** soweit *od.* soviel ich mich erinnere, ...; **in ~ of** zur Erinnerung an (+ *Akk.*); *attrib.* **a trip down ~ lane** eine Reise in die Vergangenheit; Ⓒ *(remembered time)* **a time within the ~ of men still living** eine Zeit, an die sich heute lebende Menschen noch erinnern können; **it is beyond the ~ of anyone alive today** es lebt niemand mehr, der sich daran erinnern könnte; ⇒ *also* **living** 2 A; Ⓓ *(posthumous repute)* Andenken, *das* **(of** an + *Akk.*); **of happy** *or* **blessed ~:** seligen Angedenkens *(veralt.)*; Ⓔ *(Computing)* Speicher, *der*

**'memory bank** *n.* Speicherbank, *die*

**men** *pl. of* **man**

**menace** /'menɪs/ ❶ *v.t.* bedrohen ‹Person›; **~ sb. with sth.** jmdm. mit etw. drohen. ❷ *v.i.* drohen. ❸ *n.* Ⓐ Plage, *die;* **an absolute** *or* **a public ~** *(fig. coll.) (dangerous person)* eine öffentliche Gefahr; *(obnoxious person)* ein [richtiges] Ekel *(ugs.)*; *(child)* ein kleiner Teufel; Ⓑ *(literary: threat)* Drohung, *die;* **a sense of ~:** ein Gefühl der Bedrohung; ⇒ *also* **demand** 2 A

**menacing** /'menɪsɪŋ/ *adj.* drohend

**ménage** /meɪ'nɑ:ʒ/ *n.* Haushalt, *der;* **~ à trois** /meɪnɑ:ʒ ɑ: 'trwɑ:/ Menage à trois, *die;* ≈ Dreiecksverhältnis, *das*

**menagerie** /mɪ'nædʒərɪ/ *n.* Tierschau, *die;* Menagerie, *die (veralt.)*; *(fig. iron.: collection of persons)* Gesellschaft, *die*

**mend** /mend/ ❶ *v.t.* Ⓐ *(repair)* reparieren; ausbessern, flicken ‹Kleidung, Fischernetz›; kleben, kitten ‹Glas, Porzellan, Sprung›; beheben ‹Schaden›; beseitigen ‹Riss›; Ⓑ *(improve)* **~ one's manners** sich *(Dat.)* bessere Umgangsformen angewöhnen; **~ one's ways** sich bessern; **~ matters** die Sache bereinigen; **it is never too late to ~** *(prov.)* zum Bessermachen/Verbessern ist es nie zu spät; ⇒ *also* **fence** 1 A; **least** 2.
❷ *v.i.* gesund werden; genesen *(geh.)*; *(knit together)* ‹Knochen, Bein, Finger usw:› heilen; **has his leg ~ed yet?** ist sein Bein schon verheilt?
❸ *n. (in glass, china, etc.)* Kleb[e]stelle, *die; (in cloth)* ausgebesserte Stelle; *(repair)* Ausbesserung, *die;* **be on the ~** ‹Person:› auf dem Wege der Besserung sein; ‹Verhältnisse, Lage:› sich bessern

**mendacious** /men'deɪʃəs/ *adj.* unwahr ‹Bericht, Behauptung, Darstellung›; verlogen *(abwertend)* ‹Person, Rede, Buch›

**mendacity** /men'dæsɪtɪ/ *n.* Ⓐ *no pl. (untruthfulness)* ⇒ **mendacious**: Unwahrheit,

m

*die;* Verlogenheit, *die* (*abwertend*); [B] (*a lie*) Lüge, *die*

**Mendelian** /men'di:lɪən/ *adj.* (*Biol.*) mendelsch

**mender** /'mendə(r)/ *n.* Ausbesserer, *der*/Ausbesserin, *die;* (*of clocks, watches, machines*) Reparateur, *der;* **take one's watch/shoes to the ~'s** seine Uhr zum Uhrmacher *od.* zur Reparatur/seine Schuhe zum Schuster *od.* zur Reparatur bringen

**mendicant** /'mendɪkənt/ ❶ *adj.* bettelnd; **~ friar** Bettelmönch, *der.* ❷ *n.* [A] (*beggar*) Bettler, *der*/Bettlerin, *die;* [B] (*friar*) Bettelmönch, *der*

**menfolk** /'menfəʊk/ *n. pl.* Männer

**menial** /'mi:nɪəl/ ❶ *adj.* niedrig; untergeordnet ‹Aufgabe›. ❷ *n.* (*derog.*) Domestik, *der* (*veralt. abwertend*)

**meningitis** /menɪn'dʒaɪtɪs/ *n.* ▶ 1232 (*Med.*) Meningitis, *die* (*fachspr.*); Hirnhautentzündung, *die*

**menopausal** /'menəpɔ:zl/ *adj.* (*Physiol.*) klimakterisch; menopausal

**menopause** /'menəpɔ:z/ *n.* [A] (*period of life*) Wechseljahre *Pl.;* Klimakterium, *das* (*fachspr.*); **male ~:** Wechseljahre des Mannes; [B] (*Physiol.*) Menopause, *die*

**menstrual** /'menstrʊəl/ *adj.* (*Physiol.*) menstrual (*fachspr.*); Menstruations-

**menstruate** /'menstrʊeɪt/ *v.i.* (*Physiol.*) menstruieren

**menstruation** /menstrʊ'eɪʃn/ *n.* (*Physiol.*) Menstruation, *die*

**menswear** /'menzweə(r)/ *n., no pl.* Herrenbekleidung, *die; attrib.* Herrenbekleidungs-; für Herrenbekleidung *od.* -moden *nachgestellt*

**mental** /'mentl/ *adj.* [A] (*of the mind*) geistig; seelisch ‹Belastung, Labilität›; Geistes‹zustand, -verfassung, -störung›; **the previous ~ history of the patient** die Vorgeschichte der seelischen Erkrankungen des Patienten; [B] (*done by the mind*) geistig; gedanklich; **make a quick ~ calculation** es im Kopf schnell überschlagen; **~ process** Denkprozess, -vorgang, *der;* **make a ~ note of sth.** sich (*Dat.*) etw. merken; **make a ~ note to do sth.** versuchen, daran zu denken, etw. zu tun; [C] (*Brit. coll.: mad*) verrückt (*salopp*); bekloppt (*salopp*)

**mental: ~ age** *n.* geistiger Entwicklungsstand; Intelligenzalter, *das* (*Psych.*); **~ a'rithmetic** *n.* Kopfrechnen, *das;* **~ asylum** ⇒ **~ hospital; ~ 'block** ⇒ **block** 1 L; **~ case** (*coll.*) Verrückte, *der/die* (*salopp*); (*mental patient*) Geisteskranke, *der/die;* **~ 'cruelty** *n., no pl.* seelische Grausamkeit; **~ de'fective** *n.* Schwachsinnige, *der/die;* **~ de'ficiency** *n.* Geistesschwäche, *die;* **~ 'health** *n.* seelische Gesundheit; **~ health services** psychiatrische Versorgung; **~ home** *n.* Nervenklinik, *die;* **~ hospital** *n.* psychiatrische Klinik; Nervenklinik, *die;* **~ 'illness** *n.* Geisteskrankheit, *die*

**mentality** /men'tælɪtɪ/ *n.* [A] (*outlook*) Mentalität, *die;* [B] (*mental capacity*) geistige Fähigkeit

**mentally** /'mentəlɪ/ *adv.* [A] geistig; geistes‹gestört, -krank›; **~ deficient** *or* **defective** schwachsinnig; [B] (*inwardly*) innerlich *od.* im Geiste ‹fluchen, sich Vorwürfe machen›; im Kopf ‹rechnen›

**mental: ~ patient** *n.* Geisteskranke, *der/die;* **~ reser'vation** *n.* geheimer Vorbehalt

**menthol** /'menθɒl/ *n.* Menthol, *das*

**mention** /'menʃn/ ❶ *n.* [A] Erwähnung, *die;* **there is a brief/no ~ of sth.** etw. wird kurz/nicht erwähnt; **the earliest ~ of this is in ...:** das wird zum ersten Mal in ... (*Dat.*) erwähnt; **get a ~:** erwähnt werden; **make [no] ~ of sth.** etw. [nicht] erwähnen; [B] (*commendation*) Belobigung, *die;* **honourable ~:** ehrenvolle Erwähnung.
❷ *v.t.* [A] erwähnen (**to** gegenüber); **~ as the reason for sth.** als Grund für etw. nennen; **now that you [come to] ~ it** jetzt, wo Sie es sagen; **not to ~ ...:** ganz zu schweigen von ...; **not to ~ the fact that ...:** ganz abgesehen davon, dass ...; **Thank you very much. — Don't ~ it** Vielen Dank. — Keine Ursache; [B] (*commend*) **be ~ed** lobend erwähnt werden. ⇒ *also* **dispatch** 2 A

**mentor** /'mentɔ:(r)/ *n.* Mentor, *der*/Mentorin, *die*

**menu** /'menju:/ *n.* [A] [Speise]karte, *die;* **ensure a varied ~:** für einen abwechslungsreichen Speiseplan sorgen; **a ~ at 40 marks** ein Menü zu 40 Mark; [B] (*fig.: diet*) Nahrung, *die;* [C] (*fig.: programme*) Angebot, *das;* [D] (*Computing, Telev.*) Menü, *das*

**'menu bar** *n.* (*Computing*) Menüleiste, *die*

**MEP** *abbr.* **Member of the European Parliament** MdEP

**Mephistopheles** /mefɪ'stɒfɪli:z/ *n.* [A] *pr. n.* Mephisto[pheles] (*der*); [B] *n.* (*fiendish person*) Mephisto, *der*

**mercantile** /'mɜ:kəntaɪl/ *adj.* [A] (*commercial*) Handels-; **the ~ system** der Merkantilismus; das Merkantilsystem; [B] (*trading*) Handel treibend (*nicht präd.*) ‹Nation›; **~ marine** ⇒ **merchant navy**

**Mercator** /mɜ:'keɪtə(r)/ *n.* **~'s projection** (*Geog.*) Mercatorprojektion, *die;* Zylinderprojektion, *die*

**mercenary** /'mɜ:sɪnərɪ/ ❶ *adj.* [A] ⇒ gewinnsüchtig; [B] (*hired*) Söldner-. ❷ *n.* Söldner, *der*

**merchandise** /'mɜ:tʃəndaɪz/ ❶ *n., no pl., no indef. art.* [Handels]ware, *die.* ❷ *v.t.* auf den Markt bringen

**merchant** /'mɜ:tʃənt/ *n.* [A] (*trader*) Kaufmann, *der;* **corn/timber ~:** Getreide-/Holzhändler, *der*/-händlerin, *die;* ⇒ *also* **coal merchant; scrap merchant; wine merchant;** [B] (*Amer., Scot.: retailer*) Einzelhändler, *der*/-händlerin, *die;* [C] (*coll.: person engaged in specified activity*) **rip-off ~:** Halsabschneider, *der* (*ugs. abwertend*); **gloom ~:** Schwarzseher, *der*/-seherin, *die;* ⇒ *also* **speed merchant**

**merchant: ~ 'bank** *n.* Handelsbank, *die;* **~ 'banker** *n.* ▶ 1261 Leiter einer Handelsbank; ≈ Bankier, *der;* **~ 'fleet** ⇒ **~ navy; ~man** /'mɜ:tʃəntmən/ *n., pl.* **~men** /'mɜ:tʃəntmən/ ⇒ **~ ship; ~ ma'rine** (*Amer.*), **~ 'navy** (*Brit.*) *ns.* Handelsmarine, *die;* **~ 'prince** *n.* Großkaufmann, *der;* Handelsherr, *der* (*veralt.*); **~ 'seaman** *n.* Matrose bei der Handelsmarine; **~ service** ⇒ **~ navy; ~ ship** *n.* Handelsschiff, *das*

**merciful** /'mɜ:sɪfl/ *adj.* gnädig; **his death must have come as a ~ release from his sufferings** der Tod muss für ihn eine Erlösung gewesen sein; **~ Heavens!** gütiger *od.* barmherziger Himmel!; **God is ~ to sinners** Gott ist den Sündern gnädig

**mercifully** /'mɜ:sɪfəlɪ/ *adv.* gnädig; *as sentence-modifier* (*fortunately*) glücklicherweise

**merciless** /'mɜ:sɪlɪs/ *adj.*, **mercilessly** /'mɜ:sɪlɪslɪ/ *adv.* gnadenlos; unbarmherzig

**mercurial** /mɜ:'kjʊərɪəl/ *adj.* (*quick-witted*) quecksilbrig; (*changeable*) wechselhaft

**mercury** /'mɜ:kjʊrɪ/ *n.* [A] Quecksilber, *das;* **the ~ is rising/falling** das Barometer steigt/fällt; [B] *pr. n.* **M~** (*Roman Mythol.*) Merkur (*der*); [C] *pr. n.* **M~** (*Astron.*) Merkur, *der;* [D] (*Bot.*) Bingelkraut, *das*

**mercy** /'mɜ:sɪ/ ❶ *n.* [A] *no pl., no indef. art.* (*compassion; also Theol.*) Erbarmen, *das* (**on** mit); **show sb. [no] ~:** mit jmdm. [kein] Erbarmen haben; **beg for ~:** um Gnade bitten *od.* flehen; **act of ~:** Gnadenakt, *der;* **God's great ~:** Gottes große Barmherzigkeit; **be at the ~ of sb./sth.** jmdm./einer Sache [auf Gedeih und Verderb] ausgeliefert sein; **the ship was at the ~ of the waves** das Schiff war den Wellen preisgegeben; **have ~!** Gnade!; **Lord have ~ [up]on us** (*Relig.*) Herr, erbarme dich [unser]; **~ [me]!, ~ [up]on us!** gütiger Himmel!; [B] (*instance*) glückliche Fügung; **one** *or* **we must be thankful** *or* **grateful for small mercies** (*coll.*) man darf [ja] nicht zu viel verlangen; **leave sb. to the [tender] mercies of sb.** (*iron.*) jmdn. jmds. [liebevoller] Fürsorge überlassen; **it is a ~:** es ist ein Glück *od.* Segen; **what a ~ it is that ...:** welch ein Glück *od.* Segen, dass ...
❷ *attrib. adj.* Hilfs-, Rettungs‹einsatz, -flug›; **~ killing** aktive Sterbehilfe; **~ killings** Fälle aktiver Sterbehilfe

**mere**[1] /mɪə(r)/ *adj.* bloß; rein ‹Tautologie, Versehen›; **he is a ~ child** er ist nur ein Kind; **it's a ~ copy** es ist bloß eine Kopie; **~ courage is not enough** Mut allein genügt nicht; **the ~st hint/trace of sth.** die kleinste Andeutung/Spur von etw.; **~ words won't help** Worte allein tun es nicht

**mere**[2] *n.* (*arch./literary*) See, *der*

**merely** /'mɪəlɪ/ *adv.* bloß; lediglich; **not ~ ...:** nicht bloß ...

**meretricious** /merɪ'trɪʃəs/ *adj.* trügerisch ‹Argument, Methode›

**merge** /mɜ:dʒ/ ❶ *v.t.* [A] (*combine*) zusammenschließen ‹Firmen, Unternehmen› (**into** zu); zusammenlegen ‹Anteile, Abteilungen›; **~ one firm/department with another** eine Firma mit einer anderen zusammenschließen/eine Abteilung mit einer anderen zusammenlegen; [B] (*blend gradually*) verschmelzen (**with** mit); **his library should not be ~d with another collection** seine Bibliothek sollte nicht einer anderen Sammlung einverleibt werden.
❷ *v.i.* [A] (*combine*) ‹Firma, Unternehmen:› sich zusammenschließen, fusionieren (**with** mit); ‹Abteilung:› zusammengelegt werden (**with** mit); [B] (*blend gradually*) ‹Straße:› zusammenlaufen (**with** mit); **~ with sth.** ‹Kontur, Muster:› verschmelzen mit etw.; ‹Unterhaltung:› untergehen in etw. (*Dat.*); **~ into sth.** ‹Farbe usw.:› in etw. (*Akk.*) übergehen

**merger** /'mɜ:dʒə(r)/ *n.* (*of departments, parties*) Zusammenschluss, *der;* Vereinigung, *die;* (*of companies*) Fusion, *die*

**meridian** /mə'rɪdɪən/ *n.* (*Astron., Geog.*) Meridian, *der;* ⇒ *also* **prime meridian**

**meringue** /mə'ræŋ/ *n.* Meringe, *die;* Baiser, *das*

**merino** /mə'ri:nəʊ/ *n., pl.* **~s** [A] **~ [sheep]** Merinoschaf, *das;* Merino, *der;* [B] (*material*) Merino, *der;* [C] (*yarn*) Merinogarn, *das*

**merit** /'merɪt/ ❶ *n.* [A] *no pl.* (*worth*) Verdienst, *das;* **a man of great ~:** ein Mann von hohen Verdiensten (*geh.*); ein sehr verdienter Mann; **promotion is by ~:** Beförderung richtet sich nach Leistung; **there is no ~ in doing that** es ist nicht [sehr] sinnvoll, das zu tun; **be without ~** ‹Buch, Film:› kein Niveau haben; [B] (*good feature*) Vorzug, *der;* **on his/its ~s** nach seinen Vorzügen; [C] *in pl.* (*rights and wrongs*) Für und Wider, *das;* [D] (*Theol.*) Verdienst, *der;* [E] **Order of M~** (*Brit.*) Order of Merit, *der; britischer Verdienstorden.*
❷ *v.t.* verdienen; **sb. ~s reward/punishment** jmd. hat eine Belohnung/Strafe verdient

**'merit award, 'merit increase** *ns.* Leistungszulage, *die*

**meritocracy** /merɪ'tɒkrəsɪ/ *n.* Meritokratie, *die;* Verdienstadel, *der* (*veralt.*)

**meritorious** /merɪ'tɔ:rɪəs/ *adj.* verdienstvoll ‹Tat, Verhalten, Person›; verdient ‹Person›

**'merit system** *n.* (*Amer.*) Leistungsprinzip im öffentlichen Dienst

**mermaid** /'mɜ:meɪd/ *n.* Nixe, *die*

**merrie England** ⇒ **merry England**

**merrily** /'merɪlɪ/ *adv.* munter

**merriment** /'merɪmənt/ *n., no pl.* Fröhlichkeit, *die;* **fall into fits of helpless ~:** sich vor Lachen nicht mehr halten können

**merry** /'merɪ/ *adj.* [A] ▶ 1191 (*full of laughter or gaiety*) fröhlich; **the M~ Widow/Wives of Windsor** die lustige Witwe/die lustigen Weiber von Windsor; **a ~ time was had by all** alle haben sich prächtig amüsiert; **make ~:** sich amüsieren; **make ~ over sb./sth.** sich über jmdn./etw. lustig machen; **the more the merrier** je mehr, desto besser; **~ Christmas!** frohe *od.* fröhliche Weihnachten!; [B] (*coll.: tipsy*) beschwipst (*ugs.*)

**merry: ~ 'England** *pr. n.* das gute alte England; **~-go-round** *n.* Karussell, *das;* **~ 'hell** ⇒ **hell** B; **~making** *n.* [A] *no pl., no indef. art.* Feiern, *das;* **the sound of ~making** fröhlicher Festlärm; [B] (*occasion*) Fest, *das;* **~ 'men** *n. pl.* Getreue; Kumpane (*ugs.*)

**mesa** /'meɪsə/ *n.* (*Amer. Geog.*) Tafelberg, *der*

**Mesdames** *pl. of* **Madame; Mrs**

**mesh** /meʃ/ ❶ *n.* Ⓐ Masche, *die;* Ⓑ (*netting; also fig.: network*) Geflecht, *das;* **wire ~ [fence]** Maschendraht[zaun], *der;* Ⓒ *in pl.* (*fig.: snare*) Maschen; Ⓓ (*fabric*) Netzgewebe, *das; attrib.* Netz‹strumpf, -hemd, -vorhang›; Ⓔ **be in ~** ‹Zahnräder:› ineinander greifen, im Eingriff stehen (*Technik*). ❷ *v.i.* Ⓐ (*Mech. Engin.*) ‹Zahnräder:› ineinander greifen; **~ with** eingreifen in (*Akk.*); Ⓑ (*fig.: be harmonious*) harmonisieren (**with** mit)

**mesmerism** /'mezmərɪzm/ *n., no pl.* Ⓐ Mesmerismus, *der;* Ⓑ (*dated: influence*) hypnotische Kraft; **powers of ~:** hypnotische Fähigkeiten

**mesmerize** /'mezməraɪz/ *v.t.* faszinieren; erstarren lassen ‹Tier›

**Mesopotamia** /mesəpə'teɪmɪə/ *pr. n.* Mesopotamien (*das*); Zweistromland, *das*

**Mesozoic** /mesəʊ'zəʊɪk/ (*Geol.*) ❶ *adj.* mesozoisch. ❷ *n.* Mesozoikum, *das*

**mess** /mes/ ❶ *n.* Ⓐ (*dirty/untidy state*) **[be] a ~** *or* **in a ~:** schmutzig/unaufgeräumt [sein]; **[be] a complete** *or* **in an awful ~:** in einem fürchterlichen Zustand [sein]; **what a ~!** was für ein Dreck (*ugs.*)/Durcheinander; **look a ~:** schlimm aussehen; **your hair is a ~:** dein Haar ist ganz durcheinander; **don't make too much ~:** mach nicht zu viel Schmutz/Durcheinander; Ⓑ (*sth. out of place*) **leave a lot of ~ behind one** (*dirt*) viel Schmutz hinterlassen; (*untidiness*) eine große Unordnung hinterlassen; **I'm not tidying up your ~:** ich mache deinen Schmutz/räume deinen Kram nicht weg (*ugs.*); **make a ~ with sth.** mit etw. Schmutz machen; Ⓒ (*excreta*) **dog's/cat's ~es** Hunde-/Katzenkot, *der;* **make/leave a ~ on the carpet** auf den Teppich machen (*ugs.*); Ⓓ (*bad state*) **be [in] a ~:** sich in einem schlimmen Zustand befinden; ‹Person:› schlimm dran sein; **get into a ~:** in Schwierigkeiten geraten; **clear up the ~:** die Dinge wieder in Ordnung bringen; **what a ~!** (*troubled situation*) das ist ja eine schöne Bescherung!; (*unpleasant sight*) das sieht ja schlimm aus!; **make a ~ of** verpfuschen (*ugs.*) ‹Arbeit, Leben, Bericht, Vertrag›; ruinieren ‹Wirtschaft›; durcheinander bringen ‹Pläne›; **make a ~ of things** alles verpfuschen (*ugs.*); Ⓔ (*food*) **give sth. away for a ~ of pottage** (*fig. arch.*) etw. für ein Linsengericht hergeben (*geh.*); Ⓕ (*derog.: disagreeable concoction*) Mischmasch, *der* (*ugs.*); Ⓖ (*eating place*) Kantine, *die;* (*for officers*) Kasino, *das;* (*on ship*) Messe, *die;* **officers' ~:** Offizierskasino, *das*/Offiziersmesse, *die.* ❷ *v.i.* (*Mil., Navy*) essen. ❸ *v.t.* ⇒ **~ up**

**~ a'bout, ~ a'round** ❶ *v.i.* Ⓐ (*potter*) herumwerken; (*fool about*) herumalbern; **~ about with cars** an Autos herumbasteln (*ugs.*); Ⓑ (*interfere*) **~ about** *or* **around with** sich einmischen in (+ *Akk.*) ‹Angelegenheit›; herumspielen an (+ *Dat.*) ‹Mechanismus, Stromkabel usw.›. ❷ *v.t.* **~ sb. about** *or* **around** mit jmdm. nach Belieben umspringen (*abwertend*); **he's been ~ed about** *or* **around by the doctors** die Ärzte haben ihn in der Mangel gehabt (*ugs.*)

**~ 'up** *v.t.* Ⓐ (*make dirty*) schmutzig machen; (*make untidy*) in Unordnung bringen; Ⓑ (*bungle*) verpfuschen; Ⓒ (*interfere with*) durcheinander bringen ‹Plan›. ⇒ *also* **~-up**

**message** /'mesɪdʒ/ *n.* Ⓐ (*communication*) Mitteilung, *die;* Nachricht, *die;* **send/take/leave a ~:** eine Nachricht übermitteln/entgegennehmen/hinterlassen; **give sb. a ~:** jmdm. etwas ausrichten; **did you give him my ~?** haben Sie ihm meine Nachricht übermittelt?; **can I take a ~?** kann *od.* soll ich etw. ausrichten?; **send sb. a ~ by sb.** (*orally*) jmdm. etwas durch jmdn. ausrichten lassen; (*in writing*) jmdm. durch jmdn. eine Nachricht zukommen lassen; Ⓑ (*teaching*) Aussage, *die;* (*Relig.*) Botschaft, *die;* **get the ~** (*fig. coll.*) verstehen; es schnallen (*salopp*)

**messenger** /'mesɪndʒə(r)/ *n.* Ⓐ Bote, *der*/Botin, *die;* Ⓑ **King's/Queen's M~:** königlicher Kurier

**'messenger boy** *n.* ▶ 1261 Botenjunge, *der*

**Messiah** /mɪ'saɪə/ *n.* (*lit. or fig.*) Messias, *der*

**Messianic** /mesɪ'ænɪk/ *adj.* messianisch

**messily** /'mesɪlɪ/ *adv.* nachlässig; unordentlich ‹arbeiten›; **eat/drink ~:** sich beim Essen/Trinken bekleckern

**mess: ~ jacket** *n.* (*Mil., Navy*) Messjackett, *das;* **~mate** *n.* (*Mil., Navy*) Kamerad, *der;* **he was a ~mate of mine** er und ich waren Kameraden [in der Armee/Marine]

**Messrs** /'mesəz/ *n. pl.* Ⓐ (*in name of firm*) ≈ Fa.; Ⓑ *pl. of* **Mr;** (*in list of names*) **~ A, B, and C** die Herren A, B und C

**'mess-up** *n.* Durcheinander, *das;* **there has been a ~ with your order** bei deiner Bestellung ist etwas durcheinander geraten

**messy** /'mesɪ/ *adj.* Ⓐ (*dirty*) schmutzig; (*untidy*) unordentlich; **be a ~ workman** unordentlich arbeiten; **be a ~ eater** sich beim Essen bekleckern; Ⓑ (*awkward*) vertrackt (*ugs.*)

**met**[1] ⇒ **meet**[1] 1, 2

**met**[2] /met/ (*coll.*) ❶ *adj.* ⇒ **meteorological.** ❷ *n.* **the Met** Ⓐ (*Brit.*) **The Metropolitan Police** ⇒ **metropolitan** 1 A; Ⓑ (*Amer.: Metropolitan Opera*) die Met

**metabolic** /metə'bɒlɪk/ *adj.* (*Physiol.*) metabolisch (*fachspr.*); Stoffwechsel‹krankheit, -typ›

**metabolism** /mɪ'tæbəlɪzm/ *n.* (*Physiol.*) Metabolismus, *der* (*fachspr.*); Stoffwechsel, *der;* **basal ~:** Grundumsatz, *der*

**metabolize** /mɪ'tæbəlaɪz/ *v.t.* (*Physiol.*) umsetzen

**metal** /'metl/ ❶ *n.* Ⓐ Metall, *das;* ⇒ *also* **gunmetal; white metal;** Ⓑ *in pl.* (*Brit.: rails*) Schienen; Gleise; **leave the ~s** entgleisen. ❷ *adj.* Metall-; **be ~:** aus Metall sein. ❸ *v.t.,* (*Brit.*) **-ll-** (*Brit.: surface*) schottern ‹Straße›

**'metal detector** *n.* Metallsuchgerät, *das*

**metalize** (*Amer.*) ⇒ **metallize**

**metallic** /mɪ'tælɪk/ *adj.* Ⓐ (*of metal*) metallisch ‹Element, Substanz›; Metall‹salz, -oxid›; **~ currency** Hart- *od.* Metallgeld, *das;* Ⓑ (*like metal*) metallisch ‹Härte, Glanz, Farbe, Geräusch, Stimme›; metallisch glänzend ‹Glasur, Anstrich›; **have a ~ taste** nach Metall schmecken

**metallize (metallise)** /'metəlaɪz/ *v.t.* metallisieren

**metallurgic** /metə'lɜːdʒɪk/, **metallurgical** /metə'lɜːdʒɪkl/ *adj.* metallurgisch

**metallurgist** /mɪ'tælədʒɪst, 'metəlɜːdʒɪst/ *n.* ▶ 1261 Metallurg, *der*/Metallurgin, *die*

**metallurgy** /mɪ'tælədʒɪ, 'metəlɜːdʒɪ/ *n., no pl.* Metallurgie, *die*

**metal: ~ polish** *n.* Metallputzmittel, *das;* **~work** *n., no pl.* Ⓐ (*activity*) Metallbearbeitung, *die;* Ⓑ (*metal products*) Metallarbeiten *Pl.;* **a piece of ~work** eine Metallarbeit; **~worker** *n.* Metallarbeiter, *der*/-arbeiterin, *die*

**metamorphic** /metə'mɔːfɪk/ *adj.* (*Geol.*) metamorph ‹Gestein›

**metamorphose** /metə'mɔːfəʊz/ ❶ *v.t.* verwandeln (**into** in + *Akk.*). ❷ *v.i.* sich verwandeln (**into** in + *Akk.*)

**metamorphosis** /metə'mɔːfəsɪs, metəmɔː'fəʊsɪs/ *n., pl.* **metamorphoses** /metə'mɔːfəsiːz, metəmɔː'fəʊsiːz/ Ⓐ (*change of form or character*) Metamorphose, *die* (**into** in + *Akk.*); **undergo a [gradual] ~:** sich [allmählich] verändern; Ⓑ (*Zool.*) Metamorphose, *die*

**metaphor** /'metəfə(r)/ *n.* Ⓐ *no pl., no art.* (*stylistic device*) **[the use of] ~:** der Gebrauch von Metaphern; Ⓑ (*instance*) Metapher, *die;* **mixed ~:** Bildbruch, *der;* Katachrese, *die* (*Literaturw.*)

**metaphoric** /metə'fɒrɪk/, **metaphorical** /metə'fɒrɪkl/ *adj.* metaphorisch

**metaphorically** /metə'fɒrɪkəlɪ/ *adv.* metaphorisch; **be ~ true** metaphorisch betrachtet zutreffen; **~ speaking** bildlich gesprochen

**metaphysical** /metə'fɪzɪkl/ *adj.* Ⓐ (*Philos.*) metaphysisch; **~ language/terminology** Sprache/Terminologie der Metaphysik; Ⓑ (*in popular use: abstract*) theoretisch

**metaphysics** /metə'fɪzɪks/ *n., no pl.* Ⓐ (*Philos.*) Metaphysik, *die;* Ⓑ (*in popular use: abstract talk or theory*) abstrakte Theorie

**metastasis** /me'tæstəsɪs/ *n., pl.* **metastases** /me'tæstəsiːz/ (*Med.*) Metastasierung, *die*

**mete** /miːt/ *v.t.* (*literary*) **~ out** zuteil werden lassen (*geh.*) ‹Belohnung› (**to** *Dat.*); auferlegen ‹Strafe› (**to** *Dat.*); **~ out justice** Recht sprechen

**meteor** /'miːtɪə(r)/ *n.* (*Astron.*) Meteor, *der;* **~ shower** Meteorschauer, *der*

**meteoric** /miːtɪ'ɒrɪk/ *adj.* Ⓐ (*Astron.*) Meteor‹schweif, -tätigkeit›; meteorisch; Ⓑ (*fig.*) kometenhaft; meteorhaft

**meteorite** /'miːtɪəraɪt/ *n.* (*Astron.*) Meteorit, *der*

**meteorological** /miːtɪərə'lɒdʒɪkl/ *adj.* meteorologisch ‹Instrument›; Wetter‹ballon, -bericht›; **M~ Office** (*Brit.*) Meteorologisches Amt; Wetteramt, *das*

**meteorologist** /miːtɪə'rɒlədʒɪst/ *n.* ▶ 1261 Meteorologe, *der*/Meteorologin, *die*

**meteorology** /miːtɪə'rɒlədʒɪ/ *n.* Ⓐ *no pl.* Meteorologie, *die;* Ⓑ (*weather of region*) meteorologische Bedingungen

**meter**[1] /'miːtə(r)/ ❶ *n.* Ⓐ (*measuring device*) Zähler, *der;* (*for coins*) Münzzähler, *der;* **humidity ~:** Hygrometer, *das;* ⇒ *also* **electricity meter; gas meter; water meter;** Ⓑ (*parking ~*) Parkuhr, *die;* **feed the ~** (*coll.*) Geld [in die Parkuhr] nachwerfen; Ⓒ ⇒ **taximeter.** ❷ *v.t.* [mit einem Zähler] messen ‹[Wasser-, Gas-, Strom]verbrauch›

**meter**[2] (*Amer.*) ⇒ **metre**[1]

**meter**[3] (*Amer.*) ⇒ **metre**[2]

**'meter maid** *n.* (*coll.*) Politesse, *die*

**methadone** /'meθədəʊn/ *n.* Methadon, *das*

**methane** /'miːθeɪn, 'meθeɪn/ *n.* (*Chem.*) Methan, *das*

**methinks** /mɪ'θɪŋks/ *v.i. impers., p. t.* **methought** /mɪ'θɔːt/ (*arch.*) mich dünkt *od.* deucht (*geh. veralt.*)

**method** /'meθəd/ *n.* Ⓐ (*procedure*) Methode, *die;* **~ of proceeding** *or* **procedure** Vorgehensweise, *die;* **brew by the traditional ~:** nach traditionellem Verfahren brauen; **police ~s** die Arbeitsweise der Polizei; Ⓑ *no pl., no art.* (*arrangement of ideas, orderliness*) System, *das;* Systematik, *die;* **there was a lack of** *or* **was no ~ in the book** das Buch war unmethodisch *od.* unsystematisch aufgebaut; **a man of ~:** ein systematisch denkender Mensch; **use ~:** methodisch *od.* systematisch vorgehen; **there's ~ in his madness** (*fig. joc.*) der Wahnsinn hat Methode; Ⓒ (*scheme of classification*) System, *das*

**methodic** /mɪ'θɒdɪk/ *adj.* (*Amer.*) Ⓐ ⇒ **methodical;** Ⓑ (*relating to methodology*) methodologisch

**methodical** /mɪ'θɒdɪkl/ *adj.* methodisch; systematisch; **in a ~ way** methodisch; systematisch; **be ~:** methodisch *od.* systematisch vorgehen

**methodically** /mɪ'θɒdɪkəlɪ/ *adv.* mit Methode; systematisch

**Methodism** /'meθədɪzm/ *n., no pl.* (*Relig.*) Methodismus, *der*

**Methodist** /'meθədɪst/ *n.* (*Relig.*) Methodist, *der*/Methodistin, *die; attrib.* Methodisten‹kapelle, -gottesdienst, -pfarrer›

**methodology** /meθə'dɒlədʒɪ/ *n.* Ⓐ *no pl., no art.* (*science of method*) Methodik, *die;* Methodologie, *die;* Ⓑ (*methods used*) Methodik, *die*

**methought** ⇒ **methinks**

**meths** /meθs/ *n., no pl., no indef. art.* (*Brit. coll.*) [Brenn]spiritus, *der*

**'meths drinker** *n.* (*Brit. coll.*) ≈ Fuseltrinker, *der*/-trinkerin, *die*

**Methuselah** /mɪ'θjuːzələ/ *n.* Ⓐ *pr. n.* (*Bibl.*) Methusalem (*der*); Ⓑ **[old] ~:** Methusalem, *der* (*ugs.*)

**methyl** /'meθɪl, 'miːθaɪl/ *n.* (*Chem.*) Methyl, *das*

**methyl 'alcohol** *n.* (*Chem.*) Methylalkohol, *der;* Methanol, *das*

m

**methylated spirit[s]** /meθɪleɪtɪd 'spɪrɪt(s)/ *n.* [*pl.*] Brennspiritus, *der;* vergällter *od.* denaturierter Alkohol (*fachspr.*)

**meticulous** /mɪ'tɪkjʊləs/ *adj.* (*scrupulous*) sorgfältig; (*overscrupulous*) übergenau; pedantisch (*abwertend*); **be ~ about sth.** es peinlich genau mit etw. nehmen; **be a ~ person** es sehr genau nehmen

**meticulously** /mɪ'tɪkjʊləslɪ/ *adv.* Ⓐ (*scrupulously*) sorgfältig; (*overscrupulously*) übergenau; pedantisch (*abwertend*); **~ clean** peinlich sauber; Ⓑ (*coll.: carefully*) sehr sorgfältig; haargenau (*ugs.*) ‹abbilden, wiedergeben›

**métier** /'metjeɪ/ *n.* Ⓐ (*calling*) Metier, *das;* Ⓑ (*forte*) Stärke, *die*

**metonymy** /mɪ'tɒnɪmɪ/ *n.* (*Rhet.*) Metonymie, *die*

**metre**[1] /'mi:tə/ *n.* (*Brit.*) Ⓐ (*poetic rhythm*) Metrum, *das* (*Verslehre*); Versmaß, *das;* **written in an iambic ~:** in Jamben geschrieben; Ⓑ (*Pros.: metrical group*) Metrum, *das*

**metre**[2] *n.* ▶ 1079, ▶ 1284 (*Brit.: unit*) Meter, *der od. das;* **sell cloth by the ~:** Stoff meterweise verkaufen; ⇨ *also* **cubic** B; **square** 2 B

**metric** /'metrɪk/ *adj.* metrisch; **~ system** metrisches System; **go ~:** das metrische System einführen; ⇨ *also* **hundredweight**; **ton** A

**metrical** /'metrɪkl/ *adj.*, **metrically** /'metrɪkəlɪ/ *adv.* metrisch

**metricate** /'metrɪkeɪt/ *v.t. & i.* auf das metrische System umstellen

**metrication** /metrɪ'keɪʃn/ *n.* Umstellung auf das metrische System

**metro** /'metrəʊ/ *n., pl.* **~s** U-Bahn, *die;* **the Paris M~** die [Pariser] Metro

**metronome** /'metrənəʊm/ *n.* (*Mus.*) Metronom, *das*

**metropolis** /mɪ'trɒpəlɪs/ *n.* (*capital*) Hauptstadt, *die;* (*chief city*) Metropole, *die;* **the ~** (*Brit.*) London (*das*)

**metropolitan** /metrə'pɒlɪtən/ ❶ *adj.* Ⓐ (*of a metropolis*) **[the] ~ hotels/cinemas** die Hotels/Kinos der Metropole; **~ New York/Tokyo** der Großraum New York/Tokio; **~ London** Großlondon (*das*); **the M~ Police** die Londoner Polizei; **~ borough/district** (*Brit. Admin.*) Gemeinde/Bezirk im Großraum einer Großstadt; **~ county** (*Brit. Admin.*) *eines von sechs Ballungsgebieten außerhalb Großlondons;* Ⓑ (*not colonial*) mutterländisch; **~ France** das Mutterland Frankreich.
❷ *n.* ⇨ **metropolitan bishop**

**metropolitan 'bishop** *n.* (*Gk. Orthodox Ch., RC Ch.*) Metropolit, *der;* (*Anglican Ch.*) Erzbischof, *der*

**mettle** /'metl/ *n.* Ⓐ (*quality of temperament*) Wesensart, *die;* **show one's ~:** zeigen, aus welchem Holz man [geschnitzt] ist; Ⓑ (*spirit*) Mut, *der;* **a man of ~:** ein mutiger Mann; **be on one's ~:** zeigen müssen, was man kann; **put sb./sth. on his/its ~:** jmdn./etw. fordern; Ⓒ (*animal's vigour*) Feuer, *das*

**Meuse** /mɜ:z/ *pr. n.* (*Geog.*) Maas (*die*)

**mew** /mju:/ ❶ *v.i.* ‹Katze:› miauen; ‹Möwe:› kreischen. ❷ *n.* (*of cat*) Miauen, *das;* (*of seagull*) Kreischen, *das*

**mews** /mju:z/ *n., pl. same* (*Brit.*) Stallungen *Pl.;* (*converted into dwellings/garages*) *zu* [*eleganten*] *Wohnhäusern/Garagen umgebaute ehemalige Stallungen* [*in ruhigen Seitenstraßen*]

**Mexican** /'meksɪkən/ ▶ 1340 ❶ *adj.* mexikanisch; **sb. is ~:** jmd. ist Mexikaner/Mexikanerin; **~ wave** La-Ola[-Welle], *die;* ⇨ *also* **English** 1. ❷ *n.* Mexikaner, *der*/Mexikanerin, *die*

**Mexico** /'meksɪkəʊ/ *pr. n.* ▶ 1626 Mexiko (*das*); **~ City** Mexiko [City] (*das*)

**mezzanine** /'metsəni:n, 'mezəni:n/ *n.* Ⓐ (*Archit.*) Mezzanin, *das* (*fachspr.*); Halbgeschoss, *das;* Ⓑ (*Amer. Theatre*) erster Rang

**mezzo** /'metsəʊ/: **~-soprano** *n.* Mezzosopranistin, *die;* **~tint** *n.* (*Art*) Mezzotinto, *das;* (*method*) Mezzotinto, *das;* Schabkunst, *die*

**mg.** *abbr.* ▶ 1683 **milligram[s]** mg

**MHz** *abbr.* **megahertz** MHz

**mi** /mi:/ ⇨ **me**[2]

**mi.** *abbr.* (*Amer.*) **mile[s]** M

**MI** *n.* (*Brit. Hist./coll.*) **MI5** *die britische Spionageabwehr;* **MI6** *der britische Nachrichtendienst*

**miaow** /mɪ'aʊ/ ❶ *v.i.* miauen. ❷ *n.* Miauen, *das*

**miasma** /mɪ'æzmə, maɪ'æzmə/ *n., pl.* **~ta** /mɪ'æzmətə, maɪ'æzmətə/ *or* **~s** Miasma, *das;* Gestank, *der*

**mica** /'maɪkə/ *n.* (*Min.*) Glimmer, *der*

**mice** *pl. of* **mouse**

**Michaelmas** /'mɪklməs/ *n.* Michaeli[s] (*das*); Michaelistag, *der*

**Michaelmas: ~ 'daisy** *n.* (*Bot.*) Herbstaster, *die;* **~ term** *n.* (*Brit. Univ.*) Herbsttrimester, *das*

**mickey** /'mɪkɪ/ *n.* (*Brit. coll.*) **take the ~ [out of sb./sth.]** jmdn./etw. durch den Kakao ziehen (*ugs.*)

**Mickey 'Mouse** *attrib. adj.* (*derog.*) lächerlich; **croquet is a bit of a ~ sport** Krocket ist doch gar kein richtiger Sport; **this is a ~ job** diese Arbeit ist ein Witz

**mickle** /'mɪkl/ (*arch./Scot.*) ❶ groß. ❷ *n.* **many a ~ makes a muckle** (*prov.*) Kleinvieh macht auch Mist (*ugs.*)

**micky** ⇨ **mickey**

**micro** /'maɪkrəʊ/ *n., pl.* **~s** ⇨ **microcomputer**

**micro-** /maɪkrəʊ/ *in comb.* mikro-/Mikro-

**microbe** /'maɪkrəʊb/ *n.* (*Biol.*) Mikrobe, *die*

**micro: ~bi'ology** *n.* Mikrobiologie, *die;* **~brewery** *n.* Mikrobrauerei, *die;* **M~card** ® *n.* Mikrokarte, *die;* **~chip** *n.* (*Electronics*) [Mikro]chip, *der;* **~computer** *n.* (*Computing*) Mikrocomputer, *der;* **~con'troller** *n.* (*Electronics*) Mikrocontroller, *der;* **~dot** *n.* Mikrat, *das;* **~economic** *adj.* mikroökonomisch; **~economics** *n.* Mikroökonomie, *die;* **~elec'tronics** *n.* Mikroelektronik, *die;* **~fibre** *n.* Mikrofaser, *die;* **~fiche** *n., pl. same or* **~s** Mikrofiche, *das od. der;* **~film** ❶ *n.* Mikrofilm, *der;* ❷ *v.t.* auf Mikrofilm (*Akk.*) aufnehmen; **~light ['aircraft]** *n.* (*Aeronaut.*) Ultraleichtflugzeug, *das*

**micrometer** /maɪ'krɒmɪtə(r)/ *n.* (*Mech. Engin.*) [Fein]messschraube, *die*

**micron** /'maɪkrɒn/ *n.* Mikrometer, *der od. das*

**Micronesia** /maɪkrə'ni:ʃə/ *pr. n.* Mikronesien (*das*)

**micro-'organism** *n.* Mikroorganismus, *der;* Kleinstlebewesen, *das*

**microphone** /'maɪkrəfəʊn/ *n.* Mikrofon, *das*

**micro: ~'photograph** *n.* Mikrokopie, *die;* **~'processor** *n.* (*Computing*) Mikroprozessor, *der*

**microscope** /'maɪkrəskəʊp/ *n.* Mikroskop, *das;* **examine sth. through** *or* **under a ~:** etw. unter dem Mikroskop untersuchen; **put** *or* **have sth. under the ~** (*fig.*) etw. unter die Lupe nehmen (*ugs.*); **be under the ~** (*fig.*) unter die Lupe genommen werden (*ugs.*); auf den Zahn gefühlt werden (*ugs.*)

**microscopic** /maɪkrə'skɒpɪk/ *adj.* Ⓐ mikroskopisch; sehr stark vergrößernd ‹Linse›; Ⓑ (*fig.: very small*) winzig ‹Portion, Auto›; mikroskopisch klein ‹Tier, Portion›

**microscopy** /maɪ'krɒskəpɪ/ *n., no pl., no art.* Mikroskopie, *die;* **by ~:** mikroskopisch; unter dem Mikroskop

**micro: ~surgery** *n., no pl., no art.* (*Med.*) Mikrochirurgie, *die;* **~wave** *n.* Mikrowelle, *die;* **~wave ['oven]** *n.* Mikrowellenherd, *der*

**mid-** /mɪd/ *in comb.* ▶ 912 Ⓐ **in ~air/-stream** in der Luft/Strommitte; **~air collision** Zusammenstoß in der Luft; **in ~flight/-sentence** mitten im Flug/Satz; **in ~course** mittendrin; **[in] ~afternoon** [mitten] am Nachmittag; Ⓑ *forming compound adj. used attrib.* **~afternoon siesta** Nachmittagsschläfchen, *das;* **~morning break** ≈ Frühstückspause, *die;* große Pause (*Schulw.*); **a ~season game** ein Spiel in der Mitte der Saison; **~term exams** Prüfungen in der Mitte des Trimesters; **~term elections** (*Amer.*) Kongress- und Kommunalwahlen in der Mitte der Amtszeit des Präsidenten; Ⓒ *with months, decades, persons' ages* **~July** Mitte Juli; **the ~60s** die Mitte der Sechzigerjahre; **a man in the** *or* **his ~fifties** ein Mittfünfziger; **be in one's ~thirties** Mitte dreißig sein

**Midas touch** /'maɪdəs tʌtʃ/ *n.* **he has the ~:** was er anfasst, wird zu Gold (*fig.*)

**midday** /'mɪddeɪ, mɪd'deɪ/ *n.* ▶ 1012 Ⓐ (*noon*) zwölf Uhr; **round about ~:** um die Mittagszeit; Ⓑ (*middle of day*) Mittag, *der; attrib.* Mittags-

**midden** /'mɪdn/ *n.* Ⓐ (*dunghill*) Misthaufen, *der;* Ⓑ (*refuse heap*) Abfallhaufen, *der*

**middle** /'mɪdl/ ❶ *attrib. adj.* Ⓐ mittler...; **the ~ one** der/die/das mittlere; **~ space** Zwischenraum, *der;* **the ~ years of the 19th century** die Jahre in der Mitte des 19. Jahrhunderts; **man/house of ~ height/size** mittelgroßer Mann/-großes Haus; Ⓑ (*equidistant from extremities*) **~ point** Mittelpunkt, *der;* Ⓒ (*Ling.*) Mittel‹latein, -hochdeutsch›; ⇨ *also* **English** 2 A.
❷ *n.* Ⓐ ▶ 1055 Mitte, *die;* (*central part*) Mittelteil, *der;* **in the ~ of the room/the table** in der Mitte des Zimmers/des Tisches; (*emphatic*) mitten im Zimmer/auf dem Tisch; **right in the ~ of Manchester** genau im Zentrum von Manchester; **in the ~ of the forest** mitten im Wald; **the boat sank in the ~ of the Atlantic** das Schiff sank mitten im Atlantik; **grasp the ~ of sth.** etw. in der Mitte festhalten; **fold sth. down the ~:** etw. in der Mitte falten; **in the ~ of the day** mittags; **in the ~ of the morning/afternoon** mitten am Vor-/Nachmittag; **in the ~ of the night/week** mitten in der Nacht/Woche; **happen in the ~ of next week/month** Mitte nächster Woche/nächsten Monats geschehen; **the ~ of the day** die Mitte des Tages; **be in the ~ of doing sth.** (*fig.*) gerade mitten dabei sein, etw. zu tun; **in the ~ of the operation/washing her hair** (*fig.*) mitten in der Operation/im Haarewaschen; ⇨ *also* **knock** 1 C; **nowhere** 2; Ⓑ (*waist*) Taille, *die*

**middle: ~ 'age** *n.* mittleres [Lebens]alter; **a man in ~ age** ein Mann mittleren Alters; **complaints of ~ age** Beschwerden von Menschen mittleren Alters; **~-aged** /'mɪdleɪdʒd/ *adj.* mittleren Alters *nachgestellt;* **acquire a ~-aged spread** [in den mittleren Jahren] Speck ansetzen; **M~ 'Ages** *n. pl.* **the M~ Ages** das Mittelalter; **~brow** (*coll.*) ❶ *adj.* für den [geistigen] Normalverbraucher *nachgestellt* (*ugs.*); ❷ *n.* [geistiger] Normalverbraucher (*ugs.*); **~ 'C** *n.* (*Mus.*) das eingestrichene C; **~ 'class** *n.* Mittelstand, *der;* Mittelschicht, *die;* **~-class** *adj.* bürgerlich ‹Vorort, Einstellung, Moral, Werte›; ‹Moral, Werte› des Mittelstandes; **~-class people** Mittelständler; **~ 'common room** *n.* (*Brit. Univ.*) Gemeinschaftsraum für graduierte Studenten; **~ 'course** *n.* Mittelweg, *der;* **~ 'distance** ⇨ **distance** 1 D; **~-distance runner** Mittelstreckenläufer, *der*/-läuferin, *die;* **~ 'ear** *n.* (*Anat.*) Mittelohr, *das;* **M~ 'East** *pr. n.* **the M~ East** der Nahe [und Mittlere] Osten; **M~ 'Eastern** *adj.* nahöstlich; des Nahen Ostens *nachgestellt;* ‹Person› aus dem Nahen Osten; **~ 'England** *n.* die konservative englische Mittelklasse *od.* -schicht; **~ finger** *n.* Mittelfinger, *der;* **~ 'life** *n., no pl.* mittleres Lebensalter; **~man** *n.* (*Commerc.*) Zwischenhändler, *der*/-händlerin, *die;* (*fig.*) Vermittler, *der*/Vermittlerin, *die;* **~ 'management** *n.* mittleres Management; **~ 'manager** *n.* **be a ~ manager** im mittleren Management arbeiten; **~ name** *n.* Ⓐ zweiter Vorname; Ⓑ (*fig.: characteristic quality*) **carefulness is my ~ name** ich bin die Vorsicht in Person; **modesty is not his ~ name** Bescheidenheit ist nicht seine Stärke; **~-of-the-'road** *adj.* gemäßigt; moderat; **~-of-the-road politician/politics** Politiker/Politik der Mitte; **~ school** *n.* (*Brit.*) Ⓐ (*State school*) *Schule für 9- bis 13-Jährige;* Ⓑ (*third and fourth forms*) *dritte und vierte Klasse einer höheren Schule;* **~-size[d]** *adj.*

mittelgroß; ~ **'way** *n.* [A] ⇒ ~ **course**; [B] (*Buddhism*) **the** ~ **way** der mittlere Weg; **~weight** *n.* (*Boxing etc.*) Mittelgewicht, *das;* (*person also*) Mittelgewichtler, *der;* **M~ 'West** *pr. n.* (*Amer.*) **the M~ West** der Mittlere Westen; **M~ 'Western** *adj.* (*Amer.*) des Mittleren Westens *nachgestellt*

**middling** /'mɪdlɪŋ/ ❶ *adj.* [A] (*second-rate*) mittelmäßig; [B] (*moderately good*) **[fair to]** ~: ganz ordentlich (*ugs.*); [ganz] passabel; [C] (*coll.: in fairly good health*) mittelprächtig (*ugs. scherzh.*); **How are you? — Oh,** ~: Wie geht es dir? — Ach, so einigermaßen; [D] (*Commerc.*) mittler... ‹Qualität, Ware›. ❷ *adv.* recht; (*only moderately*) ganz

**middlingly** /'mɪdlɪŋlɪ/ *adv.* [A] ganz ordentlich *od.* passabel; [B] (*only moderately well*) mäßig

**'Mideast** (*Amer.*) ⇒ **Middle East**

**Mid'eastern** (*Amer.*) ⇒ **Middle Eastern**

**'midfield** *n.* (*Footb.*) Mittelfeld, *das;* **play in** ~: im Mittelfeld spielen; *attrib.* ~ **player** Mittelfeldspieler, *der*

**midge** /mɪdʒ/ *n.* [A] (*in popular use*) Stechmücke, *die;* [B] (*Zool.*) Zuckmücke, *die*

**midget** /'mɪdʒɪt/ ❶ *n.* [A] (*person*) Liliputaner, *der*/Liliputanerin, *die;* Zwerg, *der*/Zwergin, *die;* [B] (*thing*) Zwerg, *der* (*fig.*); (*animal*) Zwergform, *die.* ❷ *adj.* winzig; (*in design*) Mini‹flugzeug, -U-Boot›

**midi** /'mɪdɪ/ *n.* Midi[rock], *der;* (*dress*) Midikleid, *das;* **~-length coat** Midimantel, *der*

**midland** /'mɪdlənd/ ❶ *n.* Binnenland, *das;* **the M~s** (*Brit.*) Mittelengland. ❷ *adj.* im Landesinnern *nachgestellt;* **M~[s]** (*Brit.*) in den Midlands *nachgestellt;* ‹Dialekt› der Midlands

**midlander** /'mɪdləndə(r)/ *n.* Bewohner/Bewohnerin des Binnenlandes; **M~** (*Brit.*) Bewohner/Bewohnerin der Midlands

**midlife crisis** /mɪdlaɪf 'kraɪsɪs/ *n.* Midlifecrisis, *die*

**'midline** *n.* Mittellinie, *die*

**'midnight** *n.* ▶1012 Mitternacht, *die; attrib.* Mitternachts‹stunde, -messe, -zug›; mitternächtlich ‹Festgelage, Feiern›

**midnight:** ~ **'oil** ⇒ **oil** 1 A; ~ **'sun** *n.* Mitternachtssonne, *die*

**mid-'off** *n.* (*Cricket*) Feldspieler links vom Werfer (*bei rechtshändigem Schlagmann*)

**mid-'on** *n.* (*Cricket*) Feldspieler rechts vom Werfer (*bei rechtshändigem Schlagmann*)

**'midpoint** *n.* Mitte, *die*

**'midrib** *n.* (*Bot.*) [mittlere] Blattrippe

**midriff** /'mɪdrɪf/ *n.* [A] **the bulge below his** ~: die Wölbung seiner Taillengegend; **with bare** ~: nabelfrei; **he landed a blow on his opponent's** ~: er traf seinen Gegner unterhalb des Brustkorbs; [B] (*diaphragm*) Zwerchfell, *das;* [C] (*Amer.: garment exposing* ~) die Taille freilassender Zweiteiler

**midshipman** /'mɪdʃɪpmən/ *n., pl.* **midshipmen** /'mɪdʃɪpmən/ (*Navy*) [A] (*Brit.*) Midshipman, *der; unterster Seeoffiziersrang;* [B] (*Amer.*) Midshipman, *der;* Seeoffiziersanwärter, *der*

**midst** /mɪdst/ *n.* **in the** ~ **of sth.** mitten in einer Sache; **be in the** ~ **of doing sth.** gerade mitten dabei sein, etw. zu tun; **in our/their/your** ~: in unserer/ihrer/eurer Mitte

**midsummer** /'mɪdsʌmə(r), mɪd'sʌmə(r)/ *n.* die [Zeit der] Sommersonnenwende; der Mittsommer; **[on] M~['s] Day** [am] Johannistag; ~ **madness** [heller] Wahnsinn (*ugs.*)

**'midtown** *n.* (*Amer.*) *am Rande des Zentrums gelegener Stadtbezirk; attrib.* am Rande des Zentrums *nachgestellt*

**midway** /'mɪdweɪ, mɪd'weɪ/ *adv.* auf halbem Weg[e] ‹sich treffen, sich befinden›; ~ **through sth.** (*fig.*) mitten in etw. (*Dat.*)

**midweek** /'mɪdwi:k, mɪd'wi:k/ *n.* **in** ~: in der Wochenmitte; ~ **flights** Flüge in der Wochenmitte

**'Midwest** (*Amer.*) ⇒ **Middle West**

**Mid'western** (*Amer.*) ⇒ **Middle Western**

**midwife** /'mɪdwaɪf/ *n., pl.* **midwives** /'mɪdwaɪvz/ ▶1261 Hebamme, *die*

**midwifery** /'mɪdwɪfrɪ, mɪd'wɪfərɪ/ *n., no pl., no art.* Geburtshilfe, *die*

**mid'winter** *n.* die [Zeit der] Wintersonnenwende; der Mittwinter

**mien** /mi:n/ *n.* (*literary*) (*look*) Miene, *die;* (*bearing*) Gebaren, *das*

**miff** /mɪf/ (*coll.*) ❶ *n.* [A] (*huff*) **get into a** ~: sich auf den Schlips getreten fühlen **(about** wegen) (*ugs.*); **be in a** ~: beleidigt *od.* eingeschnappt sein (*ugs.*); [B] (*quarrel*) Knies, *der* (*ugs.*); **have a** ~ **with sb.** mit jmdm. Ärger *od.* (*ugs.*) Knies haben. ❷ *v.t.* verärgern; **be ~ed** beleidigt *od.* (*ugs.*) eingeschnappt sein

**might**[1] /maɪt/ ⇒ **may**

**might**[2] *n.* [A] (*force*) Gewalt, *die;* (*inner strength*) Macht, *die;* **with all one's** ~: mit aller Kraft; **with** ~ **and main** mit aller Macht; [B] (*power*) Macht, *die;* ~ **is right** Macht geht vor Recht

**might-have-been** /'maɪtəvbi:n/ *n.* [A] nicht verwirklichte Möglichkeit; **the ~s** das, was hätte sein können; [B] (*person*) *jemand, der es zu etwas hätte bringen können;* **he is a** ~: er hat seine Chancen verpasst

**mightily** /'maɪtɪlɪ/ *adv.* [A] mit aller Kraft; [B] (*coll.: very*) überaus; **be** ~ **amused** sich köstlich amüsieren

**mightn't** /'maɪtnt/ (*coll.*) = **might not;** ⇒ **may**

**mighty** /'maɪtɪ/ ❶ *adj.* [A] (*powerful*) mächtig; gewaltig ‹Krieger, Anstrengung›; [B] (*massive*) gewaltig; [C] (*coll.: great*) riesig; stark ‹Trinker›. ⇒ *also* **high** 1 E. ❷ *adv.* (*coll.*) verdammt (*ugs.*)

**mignonette** /mɪnjə'net/ *n.* [A] (*plant*) Reseda, *die;* (*Reseda odorata*) Gartenresede, *die;* [B] (*colour*) Resedagrün, *das*

**migraine** /'mi:greɪn, 'maɪgreɪn/ *n.* ▶1232 (*Med.*) Migräne, *die*

**migrant** /'maɪgrənt/ ❶ *adj.* [A] ~ **tribe** Nomadenstamm, *der;* ~ **worker** Wanderarbeiter, *der*/-arbeiterin, *die;* (*in EEC*) Gastarbeiter, *der*/-arbeiterin, *die;* [B] (*coming and going with the seasons*) ~ **bird/fish** Zugvogel, *der*/Wanderfisch, *der;* ~ **herds** wandernde Herden. ❷ *n.* [A] Auswanderer, *der*/Auswanderin, *die;* (*worker*) Wanderarbeiter, *der*/-arbeiterin, *die;* [B] (*bird*) Zugvogel, *der;* (*fish*) Wanderfisch, *der*

**migrate** /maɪ'greɪt/ *v.i.* [A] (*from rural area to town*) abwandern; (*to another country*) auswandern; (*to another town*) übersiedeln **(to** nach); (*to another place of work*) überwechseln; [B] (*with the seasons*) ‹Vogel:› fortziehen; ‹Fisch:› wandern; ~ **to the south/sea** nach Süden ziehen/zum Meer wandern

**migration** /maɪ'greɪʃn/ *n.* [A] ⇒ **migrate** A: Abwandern, *das;* Auswandern, *das;* Übersiedeln, *das;* Überwechseln, *das;* **a great** ~: eine große Auswanderungswelle; [B] (*with the seasons*) (*of birds*) Fortziehen, *das;* (*of fish*) Wandern, *das;* (*instance*) (*of birds*) Zug, *der;* (*of fish*) Wanderung, *die*

**migratory** /'maɪgrətərɪ, maɪ'greɪtərɪ/ *adj.* [A] ~ **tribe** Nomadenstamm, *der;* **these workers are** ~: dies sind Wanderarbeiter/(*in EEC*) Gastarbeiter; [B] (*moving according to seasons*) ~ **bird/fish** Zugvogel, *der*/Wanderfisch, *der*

**mike** *n.* (*coll.*) Mikro, *das*

**Mike** /maɪk/ *pr. n.* **for the love of** ~ (*coll.*) um Himmels willen

**milady** /mɪ'leɪdɪ/ *n.* [A] Lady, *die;* [B] (*form of address*) Mylady; gnädige Frau

**Milan** /mɪ'læn/ *pr. n.* ▶1626 Mailand (*das*)

**Milanese** /mɪlə'ni:z/ ❶ *n.* Mailänder, *der*/Mailänderin, *die.* ❷ *adj.* mailändisch; Mailänder

**milch** /mɪltʃ/ *attrib. adj.* ~ **cow** Milchkuh, *die*

**mild** /maɪld/ ❶ *adj.* [A] (*gentle*) sanft ‹Person›; [B] (*not severe*) mild ‹Urteil, Bestrafung, Kritik›; leicht ‹Erkrankung, Gefühlsregung›; gemäßigt ‹Ausdrucksweise, Sprache, Satire›; (*moderate*) leicht ‹Ermutigung, Aufregung›; [C] (*moderately warm*) mild ‹Wetter, Winter›; [D] (*having gentle effect*) mild, leicht ‹Arzneimittel, Stimulans›; [E] (*not strong in taste*) mild; leicht ‹Bier›; [F] (*feeble*) zahm (*ugs.*) ‹Versuch, Spiel›. ⇒ *also* **draw** 1 C. ❷ *n. schwach gehopfte englische Biersorte;* ~ **and bitter** (*Brit.*) *Mischgetränk aus schwach und stark gehopftem Bier*

**mildew** /'mɪldju:/ ❶ *n.* [A] (*on paper, cloth, wood*) Schimmel, *der;* **be spotted with** ~: Stockflecke haben; [B] (*on plant*) Mehltau, *der.* ❷ *v.t.* **be/become ~ed** schimm[e]lig sein/verschimmeln; ‹Pflanze:› von Mehltau befallen sein/werden

**mildewy** /'mɪldju:ɪ/ *adj.* schimm[e]lig ‹Papier, Stoff, Holz›; von Mehltau befallen ‹Pflanze›; muffig, mod[e]rig ‹Atmosphäre, Luft›; (*spotted with mildew*) stock[fleck]ig

**mildly** /'maɪldlɪ/ *adv.* [A] (*gently*) mild[e]; [B] (*slightly*) ein bisschen *od.* wenig ‹enttäuscht, bestürzt, ermutigend, begeistert›; [C] **to put it** ~: gelinde gesagt; **and that's putting it** ~: und das ist noch gelinde ausgedrückt

**mild 'steel** *n.* weicher *od.* kohlenstoffarmer Stahl

**mile** /maɪl/ *n.* [A] ▶928, ▶1079, ▶1552 Meile, *die;* ~ **after** *or* **upon** ~ *or* **~s and ~s of sand/beaches** meilenweit Sand/Strände; **~s per hour** Meilen pro Stunde; **not a hundred** *or* **thousand** *or* **million ~s from** (*joc.*) nicht allzu weit von; **someone not a hundred** *etc.* **~s from here** (*joc.*) einer ganz hier in der Nähe; **go the extra** ~ (*fig.*) [noch] einen Schritt weiter gehen; ⇒ *also* **square** 2 B; [B] **geographical** *or* **nautical** *or* **sea** ~ ⇒ **nautical mile;** [C] (*fig. coll.: great amount*) **win/miss by a** ~: haushoch gewinnen/meilenweit verfehlen; **~s better/too big** tausendmal besser/viel zu groß; **beat sb. by ~s** jmdn. haushoch schlagen; **be ~s ahead of sb.** jmdm. weit voraus sein; **be ~s out [in one's answers]** [mit seinen Antworten] völlig danebenliegen (*ugs.*); **run a** ~ (*fig.*) das Weite suchen; **you can see it a** ~ **off** (*fig.*) das sieht doch ein Blinder [mit dem Krückstock] (*ugs.*); **sb. is ~s away** (*in thought*) jmd. ist mit seinen Gedanken ganz woanders; ⇒ *also* **stand out b; stick out** 2 B; [D] (*race*) Meilenlauf, *der;* **run the** ~ **in under four minutes** die Meile in weniger als vier Minuten laufen

**mileage** /'maɪlɪdʒ/ *n.* [A] (*number of miles*) [Anzahl der] Meilen; **state the exact** ~ **travelled** die gefahrenen Meilen genau angeben; **a low** ~ (*on milometer*) ein niedriger Meilenstand; [B] (*number of miles per gallon*) [Benzin]verbrauch, *der;* **what** ~ **do you get with your car?** wie viel verbraucht dein Auto?; [C] (*fig.: benefit*) Nutzen, *der;* **get** ~ **out of sth.** Nutzen aus etw. ziehen; **there is no** ~ **in the idea** dieser Vorschlag rentiert sich nicht; [D] (*expenses*) ≈ Kilometergeld, *das*

**mile:** **~post** *n.* [A] Meilenpfosten, *der;* [B] (*Sport*) Meilenmarkierung, *die;* **by/at the ~post** eine Meile vor dem Ziel; **~stone** *n.* (*lit. or fig.*) Meilenstein, *der*

**milieu** /mɪ'ljɜ:, 'mi:ljɜ:/ *n., pl.* **~x** /mɪ'ljɜ:z, 'mi:ljɜ:z/ *or* **~s** Milieu, *das*

**militancy** /'mɪlɪtənsɪ/ *n., no pl.* Kampfbereitschaft, *die;* Militanz, *die*

**militant** /'mɪlɪtənt/ ❶ *adj.* [A] (*aggressively active*) kämpferisch; militant; (*less aggressive*) aktiv; [B] (*engaged in warfare*) Krieg führend. ❷ *n.* Militante, *der/die*

**militaria** /mɪlɪ'teərɪə/ *n. pl.* Militaria *Pl.*

**militarism** /'mɪlɪtərɪzəm/ *n.* Militarismus, *der*

**militarize (militarise)** /'mɪlɪtəraɪz/ *v.t.* militarisieren; (*equip*) militärisch ausrüsten

**military** /'mɪlɪtərɪ/ ❶ *adj.* militärisch; Militär‹regierung, -akademie, -uniform, -parade›; ~ **man** Soldat, *der;* ~ **service** Militärdienst, *der;* Wehrdienst, *der.* ❷ *n., constr. as sing. or pl.* **the** ~: das Militär

**military:** ~ **'band** *n.* Militärkapelle, *die;* ~ **po'lice** *n.* Militärpolizei, *die*

**militate** /'mɪlɪteɪt/ *v.i.* ~ **against/in favour of sth.** [deutlich] gegen/für etw. sprechen; (*have effect*) sich zuungunsten/zugunsten einer Sache (*Gen.*) auswirken

**militia** /mɪ'lɪʃə/ *n.* Miliz, *die;* Bürgerwehr, *die* (*hist.*)

**militiaman** /mɪ'lɪʃəmən/ *n., pl.* **militiamen** /mɪ'lɪʃəmən/ Milizionär, *der*

**milk** /mɪlk/ ❶ *n.* Milch, *die;* **it's no use crying over spilt ~** (*prov.*) [was] passiert ist[, ist] passiert; **be [like] ~ and water** bieder und harmlos sein; **~-and-water** (*fig.*) nichts sagend ‹Rede, Predigt, Meinung, Buch›; halbherzig ‹Politik›; **a land of** *or* **flowing with ~ and honey** (*fig.*) ein Land, darin Milch und Honig fließt (*bibl. fig.*); **the ~ of human kindness** die Milch der frommen Denkart (*dichter.*); **M~ of Magnesia,** (P) Magnesiamilch, *die;* ⇒ *also* **condense** 1 A; **dried**; **powder** 2 B.
❷ *v.t.* (*draw ~ from*) melken; (*fig.: get money out of*) melken (*salopp*); **be ~ed dry by sb.** von jmdm. ausgenommen werden (*ugs.*)

**milk:** ~ **bar** *n.* Milchbar, *die;* ~ **bottle** *n.* Milchflasche, *die;* ~ **'chocolate** *n.* Milchschokolade, *die;* ~ **churn** *n.* Milchkanne, *die;* ~ **float** *n.* (*Brit.*) Milchwagen, *der*

**milking** /ˈmɪlkɪŋ/ *n.* Melken, *das*

**milking:** ~ **machine** *n.* Melkmaschine, *die;* ~ **stool** *n.* Melkschemel, *der*

**milk:** ~ **jug** *n.* Milchkrug, *der;* (*with tea, coffee, etc.*) Milchkännchen, *das;* ~ **loaf** *n.* Milchbrot, *das;* **~maid** *n.* ▶1261 Melkerin, *die;* **~man** /ˈmɪlkmən/ *n., pl.* **~men** /ˈmɪlkmən/ ▶1261 Milchmann, *der;* ~ **powder** *n.* Milchpulver, *das;* ~ **'pudding** *n.* Milchpudding, *der;* ~ **run** *n.* (*fig.*) [übliche] Tour; ~ **shake** *n.* Milkshake, *der;* Milchshake, *der;* **~sop** *n.* Weichling, *der;* ~ **tooth** *n.* Milchzahn, *der;* ~ **train** *n.* Milkzug, *der;* **take the ~ train into London** (*fig.*) den ersten Zug nach London nehmen; **~-white** *adj.* milchweiß

**milky** /ˈmɪlkɪ/ *adj.* milchig; ~ **coffee** Milchkaffee, *der*

**Milky 'Way** *n.* Milchstraße, *die*

**mill** /mɪl/ ❶ *n.* Ⓐ Mühle, *die;* **he really went** *or* **was put through the ~** (*fig.*) er wurde ganz schön in die Mangel genommen (*ugs.*); Ⓑ (*factory*) Fabrik, *die;* (*machine*) Maschine, *die;* ~ **town** ≈ Textilstadt, *die.* ❷ *v.t.* Ⓐ mahlen ‹Getreide›; Ⓑ fräsen ‹Metallgegenstand›; rändeln ‹Münze›. ❸ *v.i.* ‹Vieh:› im Kreis laufen; **crowds of customers were ~ing in the corridors** die Kunden schoben sich in Scharen durch die Gänge

~ **a'bout** (*Brit.*), **mill a'round** *v.i.* durcheinander laufen; **a mass of people ~ing about** *or* **around in the square** eine Menschenmenge, die sich hin und her über den Platz schiebt/schob

**milled** /mɪld/ *adj.* gemahlen ‹Korn›; gerändelt ‹Münze›

**millennium** /mɪˈlenɪəm/ *n., pl.* **~s** *or* **millennia** /mɪˈlenɪə/ Ⓐ Jahrtausend, *das;* Millennium, *das;* Ⓑ (*Relig.*) Tausendjähriges Reich; Millennium, *das* (*fachspr.*)

**mil'lennium bug** *n.* (*Computing*) Jahrtausendvirus, *der od. das*

**millepede** /ˈmɪlɪpiːd/ *n.* (*Zool.*) Ⓐ (*myriapod*) Tausendfüß[l]er, *der;* Ⓑ (*crustacean*) Assel, *die*

**miller** /ˈmɪlə(r)/ *n.* ▶1261 Müller, *der*

**millet** /ˈmɪlɪt/ *n.* (*Bot.*) Hirse, *die*

**milli-** /ˈmɪlɪ/ *pref.* milli-/Milli-

**milliard** /ˈmɪljəd/ *n.* (*Brit.*) Milliarde, *die*

**'millibar** *n.* (*Meteorol.*) Millibar, *das*

**'milligram** *n.* ▶1683 Milligramm, *das*

**'millilitre** (*Brit.; Amer.:* **milliliter**) *n.* ▶1671 Milliliter, *der od. das*

**'millimetre** (*Brit.; Amer.:* **millimeter**) *n.* ▶1210, ▶1284 Millimeter, *der*

**milliner** /ˈmɪlɪnə(r)/ *n.* ▶1261 Putzmacher, *der*/-macherin, *die;* Modist, *der*/Modistin, *die*

**millinery** /ˈmɪlɪnərɪ/ *n.* Ⓐ *no pl.* (*articles*) Hüte *Pl.;* Ⓑ *no pl.* (*business*) Hutmacherei, *die;* Ⓒ (*shop*) Hutgeschäft, *das*

**million** /ˈmɪljən/ ▶1352 ❶ *adj.* Ⓐ **a** *or* **one ~:** eine Million; **two/several ~:** zwei/mehrere Millionen; **a** *or* **one ~ and one** eine Million ein; **half a ~:** eine halbe Million; Ⓑ **a ~ [and one]** (*fig.: innumerable*) tausend; **a ~ books/customers** eine Unmenge Bücher/Kunden; **never in a ~ years** nie im Leben (*ugs.*); **I've got a ~ [and one] things to do** ich habe tausend Sachen zu erledigen; ⇒ *also* **dollar**; **mile** A. ❷ *n.* Ⓐ Million, *die;* **a** *or* **one/two ~:** eine Million/zwei Millionen; **a ~-to-one chance** eine Chance von einer Million zu eins; **in** *or* **by ~s** millionenweise; **a ~ and one** *etc.* eine Million einer/eine/eins; **the starving ~s** die Millionen [von] Hungerleidenden; **make a ~:** eine Million machen; Ⓑ (*indefinite amount*) **there were ~s of people** eine Unmenge Leute waren da; **thanks a ~:** tausend Dank; **~s of times** tausendmal; x-mal (*ugs.*); **he is a man/she is one in a ~:** so jemanden wie ihn/sie findet man nicht noch einmal; **the ~[s]** die breite Masse

**millionaire** /mɪljəˈneə(r)/ *n.* (*lit. or fig.*) Millionär, *der*/Millionärin, *die*

**millionth** /ˈmɪljənθ/ ❶ *adj.* ▶1352 millionst...; **a ~ part** ein Millionstel. ❷ *n.* (*fraction*) Millionstel, *das;* **a ~ of a second** eine Millionstelsekunde

**millipede** ⇒ **millepede**

**mill:** ~ **owner** *n.* Textilfabrikant, *der;* **~pond** *n.* Mühlteich, *der;* **the sea was like a ~pond** die See war ruhig wie ein Teich; ~ **race** *n.* Mühlbach, *der;* **~stone** *n.* Mühlstein, *der;* **be a ~stone round sb.'s neck** (*fig.*) jmdm. ein Klotz am Bein sein (*ugs.*); ~ **wheel** *n.* Mühlrad, *das*

**milometer** /maɪˈlɒmɪtə(r)/ *n.* Meilenzähler, *der*

**mime** /maɪm/ ❶ *n.* Ⓐ (*performance*) Pantomime, *die;* Ⓑ *no pl., no art.* (*art*) Pantomimik, *die;* Pantomime, *die* (*ugs.*); Ⓒ (*performer*) Pantomime, *der*/Pantomimin, *die.* ❷ *v.i.* pantomimisch agieren. ❸ *v.t.* pantomimisch darstellen

**mimeograph** /ˈmɪmɪəgrɑːf/ ❶ *n.* (*machine*) Mimeograph, *der.* ❷ *v.t.* [auf einen Mimeographen] herstellen ‹Kopien›/vervielfältigen ‹Vorlage›

**mimic** /ˈmɪmɪk/ ❶ *n.* Imitator, *der;* **that child is such a ~!** das Kind macht/plappert alles nach!. ❷ *v.t.,* **-ck-** Ⓐ nachahmen; imitieren; (*ridicule by imitating*) parodieren; Ⓑ (*resemble closely*) aussehen wie

**mimicry** /ˈmɪmɪkrɪ/ *n.* Ⓐ *no pl.* Nachahmen, *das;* Nachäffen, *das* (*abwertend*); Ⓑ (*instance of imitation*) (*of person*) Parodie, *die;* Ⓒ (*Zool.*) Mimikry, *die*

**mimosa** /mɪˈməʊzə/ *n.* Mimose, *die*

**min.** *abbr.* Ⓐ **minute[s]** Min; Ⓑ **minimum** (*adj.*) mind., (*n.*) Min.

**Min.** *abbr.* **Minister/Ministry** Min.

**mina** /ˈmaɪnə/ *n.* (*Ornith.*) Maina, *der;* (*talking species*) Beo, *der*

**minaret** /ˈmɪnəret/ *n.* Minarett, *das*

**mince** /mɪns/ ❶ *n.* Hackfleisch, *das;* Gehackte, *das.* ❷ *v.t.* in kleine Stücke schneiden; (*chop*) klein hacken; ~ **beef in a machine** Rindfleisch durch den [Fleisch]wolf drehen; **~d meat** Hackfleisch, *das;* **not ~ matters** die Dinge beim Namen nennen; **there is no point in mincing matters** es hat keinen Sinn, etwas zu beschönigen; **she doesn't ~ her words** sie spricht ganz offen und unverblümt. ❸ *v.i.* trippeln

**mince:** **~meat** *n.* Ⓐ Hackfleisch, *das;* Gehackte, *das;* **make ~meat of sb.** (*fig.*) Hackfleisch aus jmdm. machen (*ugs.*); **make ~meat of sb.'s arguments** (*fig.*) jmds. Argumente zerpflücken; Ⓑ (*sweet*) *süße Pastetenfüllung aus Obst, Rosinen, Gewürzen, Nierenfett usw.;* ~ **'pie** *n. mit süßem „mincemeat" gefüllte Pastete*

**mincer** /ˈmɪnsə(r)/ *n.* Fleischwolf, *der*

**mind** /maɪnd/ ❶ *n.* Ⓐ (*remembrance*) **bear** *or* **keep sth. in ~:** an etw. (*Akk.*) denken; etw. nicht vergessen; **have [it] in ~ to do sth.** vorhaben, etw. zu tun; etw. zu tun gedenken (*geh.*); **we have in ~ a new project** uns (*Dat.*) schwebt ein neues Projekt vor; **bring sth. to ~:** etw. in Erinnerung rufen; **call sth. to ~:** sich (*Dat.*) an etw. erinnern; **many things came to ~:** vielerlei kam mir/ihm *usw.* in den Sinn; **sth. comes into sb.'s ~:** jmdm. fällt etw. ein; **it went out of my ~:** ich habe es vergessen; es ist mir entfallen; **put sb. in ~ of sb./sth.** jmdn. an jmdn./etw. erinnern; **put sth./sb. out of one's ~:** etw./jmdn. aus seinem Gedächtnis streichen; ⇒ *also* **sight** 1 F; **time** 1 B; Ⓑ (*opinion*) **in** *or* **to my ~:** meiner Meinung *od.* Ansicht nach; **be of a** *or* **of one** *or* **of the same ~, be in one ~:** einer Meinung sein; **be in two ~s about sth.** [sich (*Dat.*)] unschlüssig über etw. (*Akk.*) sein; **change one's ~:** seine Meinung ändern; **have a ~ of one's own** seinen eigenen Kopf haben; **I have a good ~/a** *or* **half a ~ to do that** ich hätte große Lust/nicht übel Lust, das zu tun; **he doesn't know his own ~:** er weiß nicht, was er will; **make up one's ~, make one's ~ up** sich entscheiden; **make up one's ~ to do sth.** sich entschließen, etw. zu tun; **I've finally made up my ~:** ich bin zu einem Entschluss gekommen; **if your ~ is made up** wenn Sie einen Entschluss gefasst haben; **he made up my ~ for me** er nahm mir die Entscheidung ab; (*made my decision easy*) er machte mir die Entscheidung leicht; **tell sb. one's ~ frankly** freimütig jmdm. seine Meinung sagen; **give sb. a piece of one's ~:** jmdm. gründlich die Meinung sagen; **read sb.'s ~:** jmds. Gedanken lesen; ⇒ *also* **speak** 2 B; Ⓒ (*direction of thoughts*) **his ~ is on other things** er ist mit den Gedanken woanders; **give** *or* **put** *or* **set** *or* **turn one's ~ to** sich konzentrieren auf (+ *Akk.*) ‹Arbeit, Aufgabe, Angelegenheit›; **I have had sb./sth. on my ~:** jmd./etw. hat mich beschäftigt; (*remembered*) ich habe an jmdn./etw. gedacht; (*worried*) ich habe mir Sorgen wegen jmdm./etw. gemacht; **she has a lot of things on her ~:** sie hat viele Sorgen; **sth. preys** *or* **weighs on sb.'s ~:** etw. macht jmdm. zu schaffen *od.* lässt jmdn. nicht los; **take sb.'s ~ off sth.** jmdn. von etw. ablenken; **keep one's ~ on sth.** sich auf etw. (*Akk.*) konzentrieren; **close one's ~ to sth.** sich einer Sache (*Dat.*) verschließen (*geh.*); **have a closed ~:** sich entschieden haben; **set one's ~ on sth./on doing sth.** sich (*Dat.*) etw. in den Kopf setzen/sich (*Dat.*) in den Kopf setzen, etw. zu tun; ⇒ *also* **absence** C; **open** 1 G; **presence** E; Ⓓ (*way of thinking and feeling*) Denkweise, *die;* **frame of ~:** [seelische] Verfassung; **state of ~:** [Geistes]zustand, *der;* **be in a frame of ~ to do sth.** in der Verfassung sein, etw. zu tun; **be in a calm frame of ~:** ruhig sein; **her state of ~ was confused** sie konnte nicht mehr klar denken; **have a logical ~:** logisch denken; **he has the ~ of a child** er hat ein kindliches Gemüt; **the secrets of the human ~:** die Geheimnisse des menschlichen Geistes; **the Victorian/Classical** *etc.* **~:** die Denkweise des viktorianischen Zeitalters/der Klassik *usw.;* Ⓔ (*seat of consciousness, thought, volition*) Geist, *der;* **a triumph/the power of ~ over matter** ein Triumph/die Macht des Geistes über die Materie; **it was a case of ~ over matter** der Geist hat über die Materie triumphiert; **it's all in the ~:** es ist alles nur Einstellung; **in one's ~:** im Stillen; **in my ~'s eye** vor meinem geistigen Auge; im Geiste; **nothing could be further from my ~ than ...:** nichts läge mir ferner, als ...; **no such thought ever entered his ~:** so etwas kam ihm nie in den Sinn; **his ~ was filled with gloomy forebodings** er war von düsteren Vorahnungen erfüllt; Ⓕ (*intellectual powers*) Verstand, *der;* Intellekt, *der;* **have a very fine** *or* **good ~:** einen klaren *od.* scharfen Verstand haben; **[not] have a good ~:** [nicht] intelligent sein; **great ~s think alike** (*joc.*) große Geister denken [eben] gleich; Ⓖ (*normal mental faculties*) Verstand, *der;* **lose** *or* **go out of one's ~:** den Verstand verlieren; **be out of one's ~:** verrückt sein; den Verstand verloren haben; **in one's right ~:** im Vollbesitz seiner geistigen Kräfte; bei klarem Verstand; Ⓗ (*person*) Geist, *der;* **a fine ~:** ein großer Geist *od.* (*ugs.*) kluger Kopf.
❷ *v.t.* Ⓐ (*heed*) **don't ~ what he says** gib nichts auf sein Gerede *od.* (*geh.*) seine Worte; **~ what I say** glaub mir; **let's do it, and never ~ the expense** machen wir es doch, egal, was es kostet; Ⓑ (*concern oneself about*) **he ~s a lot what people think of him** es ist für ihn sehr wichtig, was die Leute von

ihm denken; **I can't afford a bicycle, never ~ a car** ich kann mir kein Fahrrad leisten, geschweige denn ein Auto; **never ~ him/that** (*don't be anxious*) er/das kann dir doch egal sein (*ugs.*); **never ~ him — what about me/my predicament?** er interessiert mich nicht — was ist mit mir/mit meinem Dilemma?; **never ~ how/where ...:** es tut nichts zur Sache, wie/wo ...; **never ~ your mistake** lass dir über diesen Fehler *od.* wegen dieses Fehlers keine grauen Haare wachsen (*ugs.*); **don't ~ me** nimm keine Rücksicht auf mich; (*don't let my presence disturb you*) lass dich [durch mich] nicht stören; (*iron.*) nimm bloß keine Rücksicht auf mich; **~ the doors!** Vorsicht an den Türen!; **~ your back[s]!** (*coll.*) Bahn frei! (*ugs.*); **~ one's P's and Q's** sich anständig benehmen; (*follow the correct procedure*) sich nichts zuschulden kommen lassen; Ⓒ (*apply oneself to*) sich kümmern um; ⇒ *also* **business** C; Ⓓ *usu. neg. or interrog.* (*object to*) **did he ~ being woken up?** hat es ihm was ausgemacht, aufgeweckt zu werden?; **would you ~ opening the door?** würdest du bitte die Tür öffnen?; **do you ~ my asking you a personal question?** darf ich Sie etwas Persönliches fragen?; **do you ~ my smoking?** stört es Sie *od.* haben Sie etwas dagegen, wenn ich rauche?; **I don't ~ what he says** es ist mir gleichgültig *od.* egal, was er sagt; **I don't ~ him** ich habe nichts gegen ihn; **I wouldn't ~ a new car/a walk** ich hätte nichts gegen ein neues Auto/einen Spaziergang; **Have a cup of tea. — I don't ~ if I do** Eine Tasse Tee? — Ach ja, warum nicht?; **do you ~ not helping yourself to all the sweets?** (*iron.*) wie wärs, wenn du ein paar von den Süßigkeiten übrig ließest?; Ⓔ (*remember and take care*) **~ you don't go too near the cliff edge!** pass auf, dass du nicht zu nah an den Felsenrand gehst!; **~ [that] you wash your hands before lunch!** denk daran *od.* vergiss nicht, vor dem Essen die Hände zu waschen!; **~ you don't leave anything behind** denk daran, nichts liegen lassen!; **~ how you go!** pass auf! sei vorsichtig!; (*as general farewell*) machs gut! (*ugs.*); **~ you get this work done** sieh zu, dass du mit dieser Arbeit fertig wirst!; Ⓕ (*have charge of*) aufpassen auf (+ *Akk.*); hüten ‹Schafe›; **~ the shop** *or* (*Amer.*) **the store** (*fig.*) sich um den Laden kümmern (*ugs.*); Ⓖ (*Amer.: be obedient to*) gehorchen (+ *Dat.*) ‹Person›; befolgen ‹Befehl›; **~ what they tell you** tu, was sie sagen!.
❸ *v.i.* Ⓐ **~!** Vorsicht!; Achtung!; Ⓑ *usu. in imper.* (*take note*) **follow the signposts, ~, or ...:** denk daran und halte dich an die Wegweiser, sonst...; **I didn't know that, ~, or ...:** das habe ich allerdings nicht gewusst, sonst ...; wohlgemerkt, das habe ich nicht gewusst, sonst ...; **~ you, I could see he was good** dass er gut war, war mir durchaus klar; Ⓒ (*care*) **do you '~?** (*iron.*) ich muss doch sehr bitten!; **turn it on; nobody will ~:** mach es an — es wird keinen stören *od.* keiner wird etwas dagegen haben; **he doesn't ~ about your using the car** er hat nichts dagegen, wenn Sie den Wagen benutzen; **do you ~?** (*may I?*) hätten Sie etwas dagegen?; (*please do not*) darf ich bitten! (*iron.*); **if you don't ~:** wenn es Ihnen recht ist; (*iron.*) wenn ich bitten darf!; Ⓓ (*give heed*) **never [you] ~** (*it's not important*) macht nichts; ist nicht schlimm; **never ~: I can do it** schon gut — das kann ich machen; **never you ~** (*do not be inquisitive*) das braucht dich nicht zu interessieren; **Never ~ about that now! This work is more important** Lass das jetzt mal [sein/liegen]! Dies hier ist wichtiger; **never ~ about him — what happened to her?** er interessiert mich nicht — was ist ihr passiert?

**~ 'out** *v.i.* **I told them to ~ out** ich sagte ihnen, sie sollten aufpassen; **~ out for sth.** auf etw. (*Akk.*) aufpassen; **~ out!** Vorsicht!

**mind: ~-bending,** (*coll.*) **~-blowing** *adjs.* bewusstseinsverändernd; **the concert was ~-blowing** das Konzert war wahnsinnig (*ugs.*); **~-boggling** /'maɪndbɒglɪŋ/ *adj.* (*coll.*) wahnsinnig (*ugs.*)

**minded** /'maɪndɪd/ *adj.* Ⓐ (*disposed*) **be ~ to do sth.** bereit *od.* (*geh.*) geneigt sein, etw. zu tun; **he could do it if he were so ~:** er könnte es tun, wenn ihm der Sinn danach stünde; Ⓑ **mechanically ~:** technisch veranlagt; **he is not in the least politically ~:** er ist vollkommen unpolitisch; **romantically ~:** romantisch veranlagt; **religious-~:** religiös; **be Establishment-~:** sich nach dem Establishment richten

**minder** /'maɪndə(r)/ *n.* Ⓐ (*for child*) **we need a ~ for the child** wir brauchen jemanden, der auf das Kind aufpasst *od.* das Kind betreut; Ⓑ (*for machine*) Maschinenwart, *der;* Ⓒ (*sl.: protector of criminal*) Gorilla, *der* (*salopp*)

**mindful** /'maɪndfl/ *adj.* **be ~ of sth.** (*take into account*) etw. bedenken *od.* berücksichtigen; (*give attention to*) an etw. (*Akk.*) denken

**mindless** /'maɪndlɪs/ *adj.* geistlos, (*ugs.*) hirnlos ‹Person›; sinnlos ‹Handlung, Gewalt›

**'mind: ~-reader** ⇒ **thought-reader**; **~set** *n.* Denkart, *die*

**mine**[1] /maɪn/ ❶ *n.* Ⓐ (*for coal*) Bergwerk, *das;* (*for metal, diamonds, etc.*) Bergwerk, *das;* Mine, *die;* **go** *or* **work down the ~:** unter Tage arbeiten; Ⓑ (*fig.: abundant source*) unerschöpfliche Quelle; **he is a ~ of useful facts/of information** von ihm kann man eine Menge Nützliches/eine Menge erfahren; Ⓒ (*explosive device*) Mine, *die.*
❷ *v.t.* Ⓐ graben ‹Loch, unterirdischen Gang›; Ⓑ schürfen ‹Gold›; abbauen, fördern ‹Erz, Kohle, Schiefer›; Ⓒ (*dig into for ore etc.*) **~ an area** in einem Gebiet Bergbau betreiben; **~ an area for ore** *etc.* in einem Gebiet Erz *usw.* abbauen *od.* fördern; Ⓓ (*Mil.: lay ~s in*) verminen.
❸ *v.i.* (*dig the earth*) Bergbau betreiben; **~ for** ⇒ **2** B

**mine**[2] *poss. pron.* Ⓐ *pred.* meiner/meine/mein[e]s; der/die/das Meinige (*geh.*); **you do your best and I'll do ~:** du tust dein Bestes und ich auch; **look at that dog of ~!** sieh dir bloß mal meinen Hund an! (*ugs.*); **those big feet of ~:** meine großen Quanten (*ugs.*); **when will you be ~?** wann wirst du die Meine/der Meine sein? (*veralt.*); **vengeance is ~:** die Rache ist mein (*geh., veralt.*); ⇒ *also* **hers**; Ⓑ *attrib.* (*arch./poet.*) mein

**mine: ~-detector** *n.* Minensuchgerät, *das;* **~field** *n.* (*lit. or fig.*) Minenfeld, *das;* **~layer** *n.* Minenleger, *der*

**miner** /'maɪnə(r)/ *n.* ▶ 1261 Bergmann, *der;* Kumpel, *der* (*Bergmannsspr.*)

**mineral** /'mɪnərl/ ❶ *adj.* mineralisch; Mineral‹salz, -quelle›; **~ wealth** Mineralienreichtum, *der;* Reichtum an Bodenschätzen; ⇒ *also* **kingdom** D. ❷ *n.* Ⓐ (*~ substance*) Mineral, *das;* **a country rich in ~s** ein an Bodenschätzen reiches Land; Ⓑ *esp. in pl.* (*Brit.: soft drink*) Erfrischungsgetränk, *das*

**mineralize** /'mɪnərəlaɪz/ *v.t. & i.* mineralisieren

**mineralogist** /mɪnə'rælədʒɪst/ *n.* Mineraloge, *der*/Mineralogin, *die*

**mineralogy** /mɪnə'rælədʒɪ/ *n.* Mineralogie, *die*

**mineral: ~ oil** *n.* Mineralöl, *das;* **~ water** *n.* Mineralwasser, *das*

**'mineshaft** *n.* [Gruben]schacht, *der*

**minestrone** /mɪnɪ'strəʊnɪ/ *n.* (*Gastr.*) Minestrone, *die*

**mine: ~sweeper** *n.* Minensuchboot, *das;* **~worker** *n.* ▶ 1261 Bergmann, *der;* Kumpel, *der* (*Bergmannsspr.*)

**mingle** /'mɪŋgl/ ❶ *v.t.* [ver]mischen. ❷ *v.i.* sich [ver]mischen (**with** mit); **~ with** *or* **among the crowds** sich unters Volk mischen; **he ~s with millionaires** er hat Umgang mit Millionären

**mingy** /'mɪndʒɪ/ *adj.* (*Brit. coll.*) mick[e]rig (*ugs.*) ‹Gegenstand›; knick[e]rig (*ugs.*) ‹Person›; lumpig (*ugs.*) ‹Betrag›

**mini** /'mɪnɪ/ *n.* (*coll.*) Ⓐ (*car*) **M~, (P)** Mini, *der;* Ⓑ (*skirt*) Mini, *der* (*ugs.*)

**mini-** /'mɪnɪ/ *in comb.* Mini-; Klein‹bus, -wagen, -taxi›

**miniature** /'mɪnɪtʃə(r)/ ❶ *n.* Ⓐ (*picture*) Miniatur, *die;* Ⓑ *no pl., no art.* (*branch of painting*) Miniaturmalerei, *die;* **a portrait in ~:** ein Miniaturportrait; Ⓒ (*small version*) Miniaturausgabe, *die;* **in ~:** im Kleinformat. ❷ *adj.* Ⓐ (*small-scale*) Miniatur-; Ⓑ (*smaller than normal*) Mini- (*ugs.*); Kleinst-; **~ poodle** Zwergpudel, *der;* **~ golf** Minigolf, *das;* **~ camera** Kleinstbildkamera, *die;* **~ railway** Miniaturbahn, *die*

**miniaturise** ⇒ **miniaturize**

**miniaturist** /'mɪnɪtʃərɪst/ *n.* Miniaturmaler, *der*/-malerin, *die*

**miniaturize** /'mɪnɪtʃəraɪz/ *v.t.* verkleinern

**mini: ~bus** *n.* Kleinbus, *der;* **~cab** *n.* Kleintaxi, *das;* Minicar, *das;* **~computer** *n.* Minicomputer, *der*

**minim** /'mɪnɪm/ *n.* Ⓐ (*Brit. Mus.*) halbe Note; Ⓑ (*fluid measure*) Minim, *das* (*ca. 0,06 cm³*)

**minimal** /'mɪnɪml/ *adj.* minimal

**minimally** /'mɪnɪməlɪ/ *adv.* minimal

**minimisation, minimise** ⇒ **minimiz-**

**minimization** /mɪnɪmaɪ'zeɪʃn/ *n.* Ⓐ Minimierung, *die;* Ⓑ (*understating*) Verharmlosung, *die*

**minimize** /'mɪnɪmaɪz/ *v.t.* Ⓐ (*reduce*) minimieren; auf ein Mindestmaß reduzieren; Ⓑ (*understate*) bagatellisieren; verharmlosen ‹Gefahr›; herunterspielen ‹Bedeutung›

**minimum** /'mɪnɪməm/ ❶ *n., pl.* **minima** /'mɪnɪmə/ Minimum, *das* (**of** an + *Dat.*); **reduce to a ~:** auf ein Minimum reduzieren; **keep sth. to a ~:** etw. so gering/niedrig wie möglich halten; **a ~ of £5** mindestens 5 Pfund; **at the ~:** mindestens. ❷ *attrib. adj.* ▶ 1603 Mindest-; **~ temperatures tonight around** 5° nächtliche Tiefsttemperaturen um 5°

**minimum: ~ 'lending rate** *n.* (*Finance*) *Mindestausleihsatz [der Bank von England];* ≈ Mindestdiskontsatz, *der;* **~ 'wage** *n.* Mindestlohn, *der*

**minimum 'wage** *n.* Mindestlohn, *der*

**mining** /'maɪnɪŋ/ *n.* Bergbau, *der; attrib.* Bergbau-; **~ area** *or* **district** Bergbaugebiet, *das;* Revier, *das*

**mining: ~ engineer** *n.* ▶ 1261 Berg[bau]ingenieur, *der;* **~ engineering** *n.* Bergbautechnik, *die;* **~ industry** *n.* Montanindustrie, *die;* Bergbau, *der;* **~ town** *n.* Bergbaustadt, *die;* **~ village** *n.* Bergbaudorf, *das*

**minion** /'mɪnjən/ *n.* (*derog.*) Ⓐ (*servile agent*) Ergebene, *der/die;* Lakai, *der* (*abwertend*); Ⓑ (*favourite of king etc.*) Günstling, *der* (*abwertend*); Protegé, *der*

**'mini roundabout** *n.* (*Brit.*) *sehr kleiner, oft nur aufs Pflaster aufgezeichneter Kreisverkehr*

**'miniskirt** *n.* Minirock, *der*

**minister** /'mɪnɪstə(r)/ ❶ *n.* ▶ 1261 Ⓐ ▶ 1617 (*Polit.*) Minister, *der*/Ministerin, *die;* **M~ of the Crown** (*Brit.*) Kabinettsminister, *der*/-ministerin, *die;* **M~ of State** (*Brit.*) ≈ Staatssekretär, *der*/-sekretärin, *die;* ⇒ *also* **portfolio** B; **prime minister**; Ⓑ (*diplomat*) Gesandte, *der*/Gesandtin, *die;* Ⓒ (*Eccl.*) **~ [of religion]** Geistliche, *der/die;* Pfarrer, *der*/Pfarrerin, *die.* ❷ *v.i.* **~ to sb.** sich um jmdn. kümmern; **~ to sb.'s wants/needs** jmds. Wünsche/Bedürfnisse befriedigen; **~ing angel** barmherziger Engel

**ministerial** /mɪnɪ'stɪərɪəl/ *adj.* Ⓐ (*Eccl.*) geistlich; **~ candidate** Kandidat [für das Pfarramt]; Ⓑ (*Polit.*) Minister-; ministeriell

**ministration** /mɪnɪ'streɪʃn/ *n.* Ⓐ (*giving aid*) Hilfe[leistung], *die;* Fürsorge, *die;* **under the ~s of sb.** durch jmds. Fürsorge *od.* Pflege; Ⓑ (*Relig.*) Seelsorge, *die;* seelsorgerischer Dienst (**to** an + *Dat.*)

**ministry** /'mɪnɪstrɪ/ *n.* Ⓐ (*Government department or building*) Ministerium, *das;* **~ official** Ministerialbeamte, *der*/-beamtin, *die;* Ⓑ (*Polit.: body of ministers*) Kabinett, *das;* Regierung, *die;* Ⓒ (*Eccl.: body of ministers*) Geistlichkeit, *die;* Ⓓ (*profession of clergyman*) geistliches Amt; **go into** *or* **enter the ~:** Geistlicher werden; Ⓔ (*Relig.*) (*office as minister*) geistliches Amt; (*period of*

m

*tenure)* Amtszeit als Geistlicher; **perform a ~ among the poor** die Armen seelsorgerisch betreuen; **F** *(Polit.: period of office)* Amtszeit [als Minister]

**mink** /mɪŋk/ *n.* Nerz, *der; attrib.* **~ coat** Nerzmantel, *der*

**minnow** /ˈmɪnəʊ/ *n.* *(Zool.)* Elritze, *die; (fig.)* kleiner Fisch

**minor** /ˈmaɪnə(r)/ **1** *adj.* **A** *(lesser)* kleiner...; leicht ‹Operation, Verletzung, Anfall›; Neben‹figur, -rolle›; **~ piece** *(Chess)* Leichtfigur, *die;* **B** *(comparatively unimportant)* weniger bedeutend; geringer ‹Bedeutung›; **~ matter** Nebensächlichkeit, *die;* **~ road** kleine Straße; **C** *(Brit. Sch.)* **Jones ~:** der jüngere Jones; Jones No. 2 *(ugs.)*; **D** *(Mus.)* Moll-; **~ key/scale/chord** Molltonart, *die*/Molltonleiter, *die*/Mollakkord, *der;* **A ~:** a-Moll; **in a ~ key** in Moll; **~ third** *etc.* kleine Terz *usw.* **2** *n.* **A** *(person)* Minderjährige, *der/die;* **be a ~:** minderjährig sein; **B** *(Amer. Univ.)* Nebenfach, *das.* **3** *v.i.* *(Amer.)* **~ in sth.** etw. als Nebenfach haben

**minor 'axis** *n.* *(Geom.)* kleine Achse

**minority** /maɪˈnɒrɪtɪ, mɪˈnɒrɪtɪ/ *n.* **A** Minderheit, *die;* Minorität, *die;* **be in a ~ of one** allein dastehen; **in the ~:** in der Minderheit; **B** *attrib.* Minderheits‹regierung, -bericht›; **~ group** Minderheit, *die;* Minorität, *die;* **~ rights** Minderheitenrechte

**minority 'rule** *n.* Herrschaft einer/der Minderheit; **white ~:** die Herrschaft der weißen Minderheit

**minor: ~ league** *(Amer.)* *n.* untere Liga; *attrib.* Unterliga-; **~ planet** ⇒ **planet**; **~ suit** *n.* *(Bridge)* niedrige Farbe

**minster** /ˈmɪnstə(r)/ *n.* Münster, *das;* **York M~:** die Kathedrale von York

**minstrel** /ˈmɪnstrl/ *n.* **A** *(medieval singer or musician)* Spielmann, *der;* fahrender Sänger; **~s' gallery** Musikantengalerie, *die;* **B** *(Hist.: entertainer)* Minstrel, *der* *(hist.)*

**mint¹** /mɪnt/ **1** *n.* **A** *(place)* Münzanstalt, *die;* Münze, *die;* **Royal M~** *(Brit.)* Königlich-Britische Münzanstalt; **B** *(sum of money)* **a ~ [of money]** eine schöne Stange *od.* ein Haufen Geld *(ugs.)*; **have a ~ [of money]** Geld wie Heu haben *(ugs.)*; im Geld schwimmen *(ugs.)*; **C** *(fig.: source)* Prägestätte, *die.* **2** *adj.* funkelnagelneu *(ugs.)*; vorzüglich ‹Münze› *(fachspr.)*; ungestempelt ‹Briefmarke›; **in ~ condition** *or* **state** ‹Auto, Bild usw.› in tadellosem Zustand. **3** *v.t.* *(lit. or fig.)* prägen

**mint²** *n.* **A** *(plant)* Minze, *die;* **B** *(peppermint)* Pfefferminz, *das; attrib.* Pfefferminz-

**mint 'sauce** *n.* Minzsoße, *die*

**minty** /ˈmɪntɪ/ *adj.* Pfefferminz‹aroma, -geschmack›; **be/taste ~:** nach Pfefferminz schmecken

**minuet** /mɪnjʊˈet/ *n.* *(Mus.)* Menuett, *das*

**minus** /ˈmaɪnəs/ **1** *prep.* **A** *(with the subtraction of)* minus; weniger; *(without)* ohne; abzüglich(+ *Gen.*);; **B** *(below zero)* minus; **a temperature of ~ 20 degrees** [eine Temperatur von] 20 Grad Kälte *od.* minus 20 Grad; **C** *(coll.: lacking)* ohne. **2** *adj.* **A** *(Math.)* negativ ‹Wert, Menge, Größe›; Minus‹zeichen, -betrag›; **B** *(Electr.)* **~ pole/terminal** Minuspol, *der.* **3** *n.* **A** *(Math.)* *(symbol)* Minus[zeichen], *das;* *(negative quantity)* negative Größe; **B** *(disadvantage)* Minus, *das;* Nachteil, *der*

**minuscule** /ˈmɪnəskju:l/ **1** *adj.* winzig. **2** *n.* *(lower-case letter)* Minuskel, *die* *(Druckw.)*; Kleinbuchstabe, *der*

**minute¹** /ˈmɪnɪt/ **1** *n.* **A** ▶ 1012 Minute, *die;* *(moment)* Moment, *der;* Augenblick, *der;* **I expect him [at] any ~ [now]** ich erwarte ihn jeden Augenblick; **for a ~:** eine Minute/einen Moment [lang]; **I'm not for a ~ saying you're wrong** ich will keinesfalls sagen, dass du Unrecht hast; **in a ~** *(very soon)* gleich; **half a ~!** einen Augenblick!; **have not a ~ to spare** keine [Minute] Zeit haben; **have you got a ~?** hast du mal eine Minute *od.* einen Augenblick Zeit?; **can you just give me a ~'s peace?** kannst du mich mal eine Minute *od.* einen Augenblick in Frieden lassen?; **come back this ~!** komm sofort *od.* auf der Stelle zurück!; **at that very ~:** genau in diesem Augenblick; **at the ~** *(coll.)* momentan; im Moment; **to the ~:** auf die Minute; **up to the ~:** hochaktuell; **the ~ [that] I left** in dem Augenblick, als ich wegging; **the ~ he gets home, he's out in the garden** kaum ist er zu Hause, geht er in den Garten; **just a ~!, wait a ~!** *(coll.)* einen Augenblick!; *(objecting)* Augenblick mal! *(ugs.)*; **would you mind waiting a ~?** würden Sie sich einen Moment gedulden?; **live ten ~s from town** zehn Minuten von der Stadt entfernt wohnen; **be five ~s' walk [away]** fünf Minuten zu Fuß entfernt sein; ⇒ *also* **last minute**; **B** *(of angle)* Minute, *die;* **C** *(draft)* Entwurf, *der;* *(note)* Notiz, *die;* Vermerk, *der;* **D** *in pl.* *(brief summary)* Protokoll, *das;* **keep** *or* **take** *or* **record the ~s** das Protokoll führen; **E** *(official memorandum)* Memorandum, *das.* **2** *v.t.* **A** *(record)* protokollieren ‹Vernehmung, Aussage›; zu Protokoll nehmen ‹Bemerkung›; **B** *(send note to)* **~ sb. [about sth.]** jmdn. schriftlich [von etw.] unterrichten

**minute²** /maɪˈnju:t/ *adj.*, **~r** /maɪˈnju:tə(r)/, **~st** /maɪˈnju:tɪst/ **A** *(tiny)* winzig; **not the ~st interest** nicht das geringste Interesse; **B** *(petty)* [völlig] unbedeutend; **C** *(precise)* minutiös; exakt; **with ~ care** mit peinlicher Sorgfalt

**minute hand** /ˈmɪnɪthænd/ *n.* Minutenzeiger, *der;* großer Zeiger

**minutely** /maɪˈnju:tlɪ/ *adv.* *(with precision)* genauestens; sorgfältigst; **~ planned** bis ins kleinste Detail geplant; **a ~ detailed analysis** eine Untersuchung bis ins kleinste Detail

**minuteman** /ˈmɪnɪtmæn/ *n.* *(Amer. Hist.)* *auf Abruf bereitstehender Freiwilliger im amerikanischen Unabhängigskeitskrieg;* Minuteman, *der* *(fachspr.)*

**minute steak** /ˈmɪnɪt steɪk/ *n.* Minutensteak, *das*

**minutiae** /maɪˈnju:ʃɪi:, mɪˈnju:ʃɪi:/ *n. pl.* Details

**minx** /mɪŋks/ *n.* kleines Biest *(ugs.)*

**miracle** /ˈmɪrəkl/ *n.* Wunder, *das;* **perform** *or* **work ~s** Wunder tun *od.* vollbringen; ‹Mittel, Behandlung usw.:› Wunder wirken; **be nothing short of a ~:** an ein Wunder *od.* ans Wunderbare grenzen; **the age of ~s is not past** es geschehen noch Zeichen und Wunder; **economic ~:** Wirtschaftswunder, *das;* **we'll do our best but we can't promise ~s!** wir tun unser Bestes, aber wir können nicht hexen *od.* zaubern; **be a ~ of ingenuity** ein Wunder an Genialität sein

**'miracle play** *n.* *(Hist.)* Mirakel[spiel], *das*

**miraculous** /mɪˈrækjʊləs/ *adj.* **A** wunderbar; wundersam *(geh.)*; *(supernatural)* übernatürlich ‹Ereignisse›; *(having ~ power)* wunderkräftig; **B** *(surprising)* erstaunlich; unglaublich

**miraculously** /mɪˈrækjʊləslɪ/ *adv.* **A** auf wunderbare *od.* *(geh.)* wundersame Weise; **~, he escaped injury** wie durch ein Wunder blieb er unverletzt; **B** *(surprisingly)* erstaunlicherweise

**mirage** /ˈmɪrɑ:ʒ, mɪˈrɑ:ʒ/ *n.* **A** *(optical illusion)* Fata Morgana, *die;* Luftspiegelung, *die;* **B** *(illusory thing)* Illusion, *die;* Trugbild, *das*

**mire** /maɪə(r)/ *n.* Morast, *der;* **be** *or* **stick** *or* **find oneself in the ~** *(fig.)* im Dreck *od.* in der Klemme stecken *od.* sitzen *(ugs.)*; **drag sb.'s name through the ~** *(fig.)* jmds. Namen in den Schmutz *od.* *(ugs.)* Dreck ziehen

**mirror** /ˈmɪrə(r)/ **1** *n.* *(lit. or fig.)* Spiegel, *der;* **hold the ~ up to sb./sth.** *(fig.)* jmdm./einer Sache den Spiegel vorhalten; **it's all done with ~s** *(coll.)* das Ganze ist nur ein Trick. **2** *v.t.* *(lit. or fig.)* [wider]spiegeln; **be ~ed in sth.** sich in etw. *(Dat.)* [wider]spiegeln

**mirror: ~ 'image** *n.* Spiegelbild, *das;* **~ writing** *n.* Spiegelschrift, *die*

**mirth** /mɜ:θ/ *n.* *(literary)* Frohsinn, *der;* Fröhlichkeit, *die;* *(laughter)* Heiterkeit, *die*

**mirthful** /ˈmɜ:θfl/ *adj.* *(literary)* heiter, fröhlich ‹Lachen›

**misadventure** /mɪsədˈventʃə(r)/ *n.* **A** *(piece of bad luck)* Missgeschick, *das;* **I had a ~:** mir ist ein Missgeschick passiert; **B** *(Law)* **death by ~:** Tod durch Unfall

**misalliance** /mɪsəˈlaɪəns/ *n.* Mesalliance, *die* *(geh.)*; Missheirat, *die*

**misanthrope** /ˈmɪzənθrəʊp/, **misanthropist** /mɪˈzænθrəpɪst/ *ns.* Misanthrop, *der* *(geh.)*; Menschenfeind, *der*

**misanthropic** /mɪzənˈθrɒpɪk/ *adj.* misanthropisch *(geh.)*; menschenfeindlich

**misanthropy** /mɪˈzænθrəpɪ/ *n.* Menschenfeindlichkeit, *die*

**misapprehend** /mɪsæprɪˈhend/ *v.t.* missverstehen

**misapprehension** /mɪsæprɪˈhenʃn/ *n.* Missverständnis, *das;* **be under a ~:** einem Irrtum unterliegen; **have a lot of ~s about sth.** völlig falsche Vorstellungen von etw. haben

**misappropriate** /mɪsəˈprəʊprɪeɪt/ *v.t.* unterschlagen, *(Rechtsspr.)* veruntreuen ‹Geld usw.›; stehlen ‹Idee›

**misappropriation** /mɪsəprəʊprɪˈeɪʃn/ *n.* *(of money)* Unterschlagung, *die;* Veruntreuung, *die* *(Rechtsspr.)*

**misbegotten** /mɪsbɪˈgɒtn/ *adj.* **A** *(badly conceived)* schlecht konzipiert ‹Plan, Vorhaben, Projekt›; **B** *(dated: illigitimate)* unehelich ‹Kind›

**misbehave** /mɪsbɪˈheɪv/ **1** *v.i.* sich schlecht benehmen. **2** *v. refl.* **~ oneself** sich schlecht benehmen; sich danebenbenehmen *(ugs.)*; **he and his girlfriend have been misbehaving themselves** *(euphem.)* er und seine Freundin haben sich miteinander eingelassen

**misbehaviour** *(Amer.:* **misbehavior)** /mɪsbɪˈheɪvɪə(r)/ *n.* schlechtes Benehmen *od.* Betragen

**miscalculate** /mɪsˈkælkjʊleɪt/ **1** *v.t.* falsch berechnen ‹Menge›; *(misjudge)* falsch einschätzen ‹Folgen, Auswirkungen, Stärke›; **~ the distance/the budget** sich bei der Entfernung/beim Budget verkalkulieren *od.* verschätzen. **2** *v.i.* sich verrechnen

**miscalculation** /mɪskælkjʊˈleɪʃn/ *n.* *(arithmetical error)* Rechenfehler, *der;* *(misjudgement)* Fehleinschätzung, *die;* **make a ~ about sth.** *(misjudge sth.)* etw. falsch einschätzen

**miscarriage** /mɪsˈkærɪdʒ/ *n.* **A** *(Med.)* Fehlgeburt, *die;* **B** *(of plans, projects, etc.)* Fehlschlagen, *das;* Misslingen, *das;* **~ of justice** Justizirrtum, *der*

**miscarry** /mɪsˈkærɪ/ *v.i.* **A** *(Med.)* eine Fehlgeburt haben; **B** ‹Plan, Vorhaben usw.:› fehlschlagen; **C** *(not reach destination)* ‹Brief usw.:› fehlgeleitet werden

**miscast** /mɪsˈkɑ:st/ *v.t.*, **miscast** falsch *od.* schlecht besetzen ‹Rolle, Film, Theaterstück›; fehlbesetzen ‹Rolle›

**miscellaneous** /mɪsəˈleɪnɪəs/ *adj.* **A** *(mixed)* [kunter]bunt ‹[Menschen]menge, Sammlung›; **B** *with pl. n.* *(of various kinds)* verschieden; verschiedenerlei

**miscellany** /mɪˈselənɪ/ *n.* **A** *(mixture)* [bunte] Sammlung; [buntes] Gemisch; **B** *(book)* Sammelband, *der*

**mischance** /mɪsˈtʃɑ:ns/ *n.* **A** *(piece of bad luck)* unglücklicher Zufall; **by a** *or* **some ~:** durch einen unglücklichen Zufall; **B** *no pl., no art.* *(bad luck)* Pech, *das*

**mischief** /ˈmɪstʃɪf/ *n.* **A** Unsinn, *der;* Unfug, *der;* *(pranks)* [dumme] Streiche *Pl.;* *(playful malice)* Schalk, *der;* **mean ~:** etwas im Schilde führen; **be up to ~ again** wieder etwas im Schilde führen; **be** *or* **get up to [some] ~:** etwas anstellen; **keep out of ~:** keine Dummheiten *od.* keinen Unfug machen; **keep sb. out of ~:** jmdn. vor Dummheiten bewahren; **what ~ have you been up to now?** was hast du denn jetzt schon wieder angestellt?; **sb.'s eyes are full of ~:** jmdm. sieht *od.* schaut der Schalk aus den Augen; **B** *(harm)* Schaden, *der;* **do sb./oneself a ~** *(coll.)* jmdm./sich etwas antun;

**make** *or* **stir up ~:** Ärger machen; **C** (*person*) Schlawiner, *der* (*ugs.*); (*child also*) Racker, *der*

'**mischief-maker** *n.* Böswillige, *der/die*

**mischievous** /'mɪstʃɪvəs/ *adj.* **A** spitzbübisch, schelmisch ‹Blick, Gesichtsausdruck, Lächeln›; schalkhaft (*geh.*); **~ trick** Schabernack, *der;* [dummer] Streich; **B** (*malicious*) boshaft ‹Person›; böse ‹Absicht›; **C** (*harmful*) schädlich ‹Effekt›; bösartig ‹Gerücht›; böse ‹Zeitungsartikel›

**mischievously** /'mɪstʃɪvəslɪ/ *adv.* **A** spitzbübisch; schalkhaft (*geh.*); **behave ~:** Schabernack treiben; Unfug anstellen; **B** (*maliciously*) aus [reiner] Bosheit

**miscible** /'mɪsɪbl/ *adj.* mischbar

**misconceive** /mɪskən'si:v/ **1** *v.i.* **~ of sth.** eine falsche Vorstellung von etw. haben; etw. verkennen. **2** *v.t.* **be ~d** ‹Projekt, Vorschlag, Aktion:› schlecht konzipiert sein

**misconception** /mɪskən'sepʃn/ *n.* falsche Vorstellung (**about** von); **be [labouring] under a ~ about sth.** sich (*Dat.*) eine falsche Vorstellung von etw. machen; etw. verkennen; **it is a ~ to think that ...:** es ist ein Irrtum, anzunehmen, dass ...

**misconduct 1** /mɪs'kɒndʌkt/ *n.*, *no pl.* **A** (*improper conduct*) unkorrektes Verhalten; (*Sport*) unsportliches *od.* unfaires Verhalten; **he was accused of gross ~:** er wurde grober Verfehlungen bezichtigt; **professional ~:** standeswidriges Verhalten; **B** (*bad management*) schlechte Verwaltung; **~ of the war** schlechte Kriegsführung. **2** /mɪskən'dʌkt/ *v. refl.* sich unkorrekt verhalten

**misconstrue** /mɪskən'stru:/ *v.t.* missdeuten; missverstehen; **~ sb.'s meaning** jmdn. missverstehen; **~ sth. as sth.** etw. irrtümlicherweise für etw. halten

**miscount** /mɪs'kaʊnt/ **1** *n.* falsche Zählung; (*of votes*) falsche Auszählung; **there had been a ~:** bei der Zählung hatte es einen Fehler gegeben. **2** *v.i.* sich verzählen; (*when counting votes*) falsch [aus]zählen; (*when calculating*) sich verrechnen. **3** *v.t.* falsch zählen; falsch ausrechnen ‹Zahl›

**misdeal** /mɪs'di:l/ (*Cards*) **1** *v.i.*, *forms as* **deal**[1] 1 sich vergeben; falsch geben. **2** *v.t.*, *forms as* **deal**[1] 2 vergeben, falsch geben ‹Karten›

**misdeed** /mɪs'di:d/ *n.* **A** (*evil deed*) Missetat, *die* (*geh. veralt.*); **B** (*crime*) Verbrechen, *das;* Untat, *die*

**misdemeanour** (*Amer.:* **misdemeanor**) /mɪsdɪ'mi:nə(r)/ *n.* **A** (*misdeed*) Missetat, *die* (*veralt., scherzh.*); **B** (*Law*) Vergehen, *das;* Übertretung, *die*

**misdirect** /mɪsdɪ'rekt, mɪsdaɪ'rekt/ *v.t.* **A** (*direct wrongly*) falsch adressieren ‹Brief›; vergeuden, falsch einsetzen ‹Energien›; in die falsche Richtung schicken ‹nach dem Weg Fragenden›; **B** (*Law*) falsch informieren; falsch belehren ‹Geschworene›

**miser** /'maɪzə(r)/ *n.* Geizhals, *der;* Geizkragen, *der* (*ugs.*)

**miserable** /'mɪzərəbl/ *adj.* **A** (*unhappy*) unglücklich; erbärmlich, elend ‹Leben[sbedingungen]›; **make sb.'s life ~:** jmdm. das Leben schwer machen; **feel ~:** sich elend fühlen; **B** (*causing wretchedness*) trostlos; trist ‹Wetter, Urlaub›; elend, armselig ‹Wohnviertel, Slums›; öde ‹Beschäftigung›; [sehr] unglücklich ‹Ehe›; **C** (*contemptible, mean*) armselig; **a ~ five pounds** klägliche *od.* (*ugs. abwertend*) miese fünf Pfund

**miserably** /'mɪzərəblɪ/ *adv.* **A** (*uncomfortably, unhappily*) unglücklich; elend, jämmerlich ‹leben, zugrunde gehen›; elend ‹kalt, nass›; **~ poor** bettelarm; **B** (*meanly*) spärlich ‹beleuchtet, möbliert›; miserabel, (*ugs.*) mies ‹bezahlt›; **C** (*to a deplorable extent*) kläglich, jämmerlich ‹versagen›; völlig, total ‹verpfuscht, unzureichend›

**miserliness** /'maɪzəlmɪs/ *n.*, *no pl.* Geiz, *der*

**miserly** /'maɪzəlɪ/ *adj.* geizig; armselig ‹Portion, Essen›; **~ creature** Geizhals, *der;* Geizkragen, *der* (*ugs.*)

**misery** /'mɪzərɪ/ *n.* **A** (*wretched state*) Elend, *das;* **make sb.'s life a ~:** jmdm. das Leben zur Qual *od.* zur Hölle machen; **live in ~, live a life of ~:** ein erbärmliches *od.* jämmerliches Leben führen; **put an animal out of its ~:** ein Tier von seinen Qualen erlösen; **put sb. out of his ~** (*fig.*) jmdn. nicht länger auf die Folter spannen; **B** (*thing*) **the ~ of it was that ...:** das Unglück dabei war, dass ...; **miseries** Elend, *das;* Nöte; **C** (*coll.: discontented person*) **~[ guts]** Miesepeter, *der* (*ugs. abwertend*)

**misfire** /mɪs'faɪə(r)/ **1** *v.i.* **A** ‹Motor:› eine Fehlzündung/Fehlzündungen haben; ‹Kanone, Gewehr:› versagen, nicht losgehen; **B** ‹Plan, Versuch:› fehlschlagen; ‹Streich, Witz:› danebengehen. **2** *n.* **A** (*of engine*) Fehlzündung, *die;* (*of gun*) Versager, *der;* **B** (*of plan, attempt*) Fehlschlag, *der;* **C** (*sth. that fails*) Schlag ins Wasser; (*book, play*) Flop, *der*

**misfit** /'mɪsfɪt/ *n.* (*person*) Außenseiter, *der/* Außenseiterin, *die*

**misfortune** /mɪs'fɔ:tʃən, mɪs'fɔ:tʃu:n/ *n.* **A** *no pl., no art.* (*bad luck*) Missgeschick, *das;* **suffer ~:** [viel] Unglück haben; **companions in ~:** Leidensgenossen; **B** (*stroke of fate*) Schicksalsschlag, *der;* (*unlucky incident*) Missgeschick, *das;* **bear one's ~s bravely** sein Schicksal tapfer tragen; **it was his ~** *or* **he had the ~ to ...:** er hatte das Pech, zu ...; **~s rarely come singly** ein Unglück kommt selten allein

**misgiving** /mɪs'gɪvɪŋ/ *n.* Bedenken *Pl.;* Zweifel, *der;* **have some ~s about sth.** wegen einer Sache Bedenken haben

**misgovern** /mɪs'gʌvn/ *v.t.* schlecht regieren

**misgovernment** /mɪs'gʌvnmənt/ *n.*, *no pl.* politische Misswirtschaft

**misguided** /mɪs'gaɪdɪd/ *adj.* töricht ‹Mensch›; unangebracht ‹Eifer, Freundlichkeit›; unsinnig ‹Bemühung, Maßnahme›

**misguidedly** /mɪs'gaɪdɪdlɪ/ *adv.* (*in error*) irrigerweise; (*ill-advisedly*) törichterweise

**mishandle** /mɪs'hændl/ *v.t.* **A** (*deal with incorrectly*) falsch behandeln ‹Angelegenheit›; schlecht verwalten ‹Finanzen›; **B** (*handle roughly*) misshandeln

**mishap** /'mɪshæp, mɪs'hæp/ *n.* Missgeschick, *das;* **sb. suffers** *or* **meets with a ~:** jmdm. passiert ein Missgeschick; **without further ~:** ohne weitere Zwischenfälle

**mishear** /mɪs'hɪə(r)/, **misheard** /mɪs'hɜ:d/ **1** *v.i.* sich verhören. **2** *v.t.* falsch verstehen

**mishit 1** /'mɪshɪt/ *n.* Fehlschlag, *der;* **have** *or* **make a ~:** [den Ball] verschlagen. **2** /mɪs'hɪt/ *v.t.*, *forms as* **hit** 1 verschlagen ‹Ball›

**mishmash** /'mɪʃmæʃ/ *n.* Mischmasch, *der* (*ugs.*) (**of** aus)

**misinform** /mɪsɪn'fɔ:m/ *v.t.* falsch informieren *od.* unterrichten

**misinformation** /mɪsɪnfə'meɪʃn/ *n.*, *no pl.*, *no indef. art.* Fehlinformationen *Pl.;* (*on radio, in newspaper*) Falschmeldungen *Pl.*

**misinterpret** /mɪsɪn'tɜ:prɪt/ *v.t.* **A** (*interpret wrongly*) fehlinterpretieren, falsch auslegen ‹Text, Inschrift, Buch›; ‹Übersetzung:› falsch wiedergeben ‹Sinn›; **B** (*make wrong inference from*) falsch deuten; missdeuten; **he ~ed her letter as meaning that ...:** er las fälschlicherweise aus ihrem Brief heraus, dass ...

**misinterpretation** /mɪsɪntɜ:prɪ'teɪʃn/ *n.* Fehlinterpretation, *die;* **be open to ~:** leicht falsch ausgelegt werden können

**misjudge** /mɪs'dʒʌdʒ/ **1** *v.t.* falsch einschätzen; falsch beurteilen ‹Person›; **~ the height/distance/length of time** sich in der Höhe/Entfernung/Zeit verschätzen. **2** *v.i.* sich verschätzen

**misjudgement**, **misjudgment** /mɪs'dʒʌdʒmənt/ *n.* Fehleinschätzung, *die;* (*of person*) falsche Beurteilung; (*of distance, length, etc.*) falsche Einschätzung

**mislay** /mɪs'leɪ/ *v.t.*, **mislaid** /mɪs'leɪd/ verlegen

**mislead** /mɪs'li:d/ *v.t.*, **misled** /mɪs'led/ irreführen; täuschen; **~ sb. about sth.** jmdm. ein falsches Bild von etw. vermitteln

**misleading** /mɪs'li:dɪŋ/ *adj.* irreführend

**mismanage** /mɪs'mænɪdʒ/ *v.t.* herunterwirtschaften ‹Firma, Land›; schlecht führen ‹Haushalt›; schlecht handhaben *od.* abwickeln ‹Angelegenheit, Projekt, Sache›; schlecht abwickeln ‹Geschäft›

**mismanagement** /mɪs'mænɪdʒmənt/ *n.* Misswirtschaft, *die;* (*of finances*) schlechte Verwaltung; (*of matters or affairs*) schlechte Handhabung *od.* Abwicklung

**mismatch 1** /mɪs'mætʃ/ *v.t.* **~ parts of sth.** Teile von etw. nicht richtig zusammenfügen; **~ colours/fabrics/patterns** Farben/Gewebe/Muster miteinander kombinieren, die nicht zusammenpassen; **a badly ~ed couple** ein Paar, das absolut nicht zusammenpasst. **2** /'mɪsmætʃ/ *n.* Nichtübereinstimmung, *die;* (*Boxing*) ungleicher Kampf; **their marriage was a ~:** sie passten als Eheleute nicht zusammen

**misnomer** /mɪs'nəʊmə(r)/ *n.* **A** (*use of wrong name*) falsche Bezeichnung *od.* Benennung; **this seems like a slight ~** (*iron.*) das ist wohl etwas danebengegriffen; **B** (*wrong name*) unzutreffende Bezeichnung

**misogynist** /mɪ'sɒdʒɪnɪst/ *n.* Frauenhasser, *der;* Misogyn, *der* (*geh.*)

**misogyny** /mɪ'sɒdʒɪnɪ/ *n.* Frauenhass, *der;* Misogynie, *die* (*geh.*)

**misplace** /mɪs'pleɪs/ *v.t.* **A** (*put in wrong place*) an die falsche Stelle *od.* den falschen Platz stellen/legen/setzen *usw.*; **B** (*bestow on wrong object*) **~ one's affection/confidence** seine Zuneigung/sein Vertrauen dem Falschen/der Falschen schenken; **have a ~d reliance on sb./sth.** so töricht sein, fest auf jmdn./etw. zu vertrauen; **C be ~d** (*inappropriate*) unangebracht *od.* fehl am Platz sein

**misplay** /mɪs'pleɪ/ *v.t.* verschießen ‹Elfmeter, Eckball usw.›; schlecht spielen, verschlagen ‹Ball, Return›; **~ one's stroke** den Ball verschlagen

**misprint 1** /'mɪsprɪnt/ *n.* Druckfehler, *der.* **2** /mɪs'prɪnt/ *v.t.* verdrucken

**mispronounce** /mɪsprə'naʊns/ *v.t.* falsch aussprechen

**mispronunciation** /mɪsprənʌnsɪ'eɪʃn/ *n.* falsche Aussprache; (*mistake*) Aussprachefehler, *der*

**misquotation** /mɪskwəʊ'teɪʃn/ *n.* falsches Zitat; **he is given to ~:** er zitiert oft falsch

**misquote** /mɪs'kwəʊt/ *v.t.* falsch zitieren; **he was ~d as saying that ...:** man unterstellte ihm, gesagt zu haben, dass ...

**misread** /mɪs'ri:d/ *v.t.*, **misread** /mɪs'red/ (*read wrongly*) falsch *od.* nicht richtig lesen ‹Text, Wort, Schrift›; (*interpret wrongly*) falsch verstehen ‹Anweisungen›; missdeuten ‹Text, Absichten›; **~ an 'a' as a 'b'** ein „a" als „b" lesen

**misremember** /mɪsrɪ'membə(r)/ *v.t.* **~ sth.** etw. nicht richtig in Erinnerung haben

**misrepresent** /mɪsreprɪ'zent/ *v.t.* falsch darstellen; verdrehen ‹Tatsachen›; **~ sb.'s character** ein falsches Bild von jmds. Charakter geben

**misrepresentation** /mɪsreprɪzen'teɪʃn/ *n.* falsche Darstellung; (*of facts*) Verdrehung, *die*

**miss 1** *n.* **A** (*failure to hit or attain*) Fehlschlag, *der;* (*shot*) Fehlschuss, *der;* (*throw*) Fehlwurf, *der;* **be a ~:** danebengehen (*ugs.*); **a ~ is as good as a mile** (*prov.*) fast getroffen ist auch daneben; **B give sb./sth. a ~:** sich (*Dat.*) jmdn./etw. schenken; **we'll give the pub a ~ tonight** wir werden heute Abend mal nicht in die Kneipe gehen; ⇒ *also* **near** 3 C.

**2** *v.t.* **A** (*fail to hit, lit. or fig.*) verfehlen; **~ed!** nicht getroffen!; **the car just ~ed the tree** das Auto wäre um ein Haar gegen den Baum geprallt; **we just ~ed having an accident** wir hätten um ein Haar einen Unfall gehabt; **B** (*fail to get*) nicht bekommen; (*fail to find or meet*) verpassen; **they ~ed each other** sie verpassten *od.* verfehlten sich; **~ a catch** einen Ball nicht fangen; **~ the goal** am Tor vorbeischießen; danebenschießen; **he just ~ed being first** er wäre um ein Haar Erster geworden; **C** (*let slip*) verpassen; versäumen; **~ an opportunity** sich (*Dat.*) eine Gelegenheit entgehen lassen; **you don't know what you're ~ing** du weißt ja gar

m

nicht, was dir entgeht; **it is too good to ~ or is not to be ~ed** das darf man sich (*Dat.*) [einfach] nicht entgehen lassen; **an experience he would not have ~ed** eine Erfahrung, die er nicht hätte missen wollen; **D** (*fail to catch*) versäumen, verpassen ‹Bus, Zug, Flugzeug›; **~ the boat** *or* **bus** (*fig.*) den Anschluss verpassen (*fig.*); **E** (*fail to take part in*) versäumen; **~ school** in der Schule fehlen; **F** (*fail to see*) übersehen; (*fail to hear or understand*) nicht mitbekommen; **you can't ~ it** es ist nicht zu übersehen; **he doesn't ~ much** ihm entgeht so schnell nichts; **G** (*feel the absence of*) vermissen; **she ~es him** er fehlt ihr; **H** (*fail to keep or perform*) versäumen ‹Verabredung, Vorstellung›; **she ~ed her pill** sie hat vergessen, ihre Pille zu nehmen.

❸ *v.i.* **A** (*not hit sth.*) nicht treffen; (*not catch sth.*) danebengreifen; **B** ‹Ball, Schuss usw.:› danebengehen; **C** ‹Motor:› aussetzen

**~ 'out** ❶ *v.t.* weglassen; **his name was ~ed out from the list** sein Name fehlte auf der Liste. ❷ *v.i.* **~ out on sth.** (*coll.*) sich (*Dat.*) etw. entgehen lassen; **he can't afford to ~ out** er kann es sich nicht leisten, sich das entgehen zu lassen

**Miss** /mɪs/ *n.* ▶ **1617** **A** ▶ **1286** (*title of unmarried woman*) **~ Brown** Frau Brown; Fräulein Brown (*veralt.*); (*girl*) Fräulein Brown; **the ~es Smith[s]** die Damen/Fräulein Smith; **B** (*title of beauty queen*) **~ France** Miss Frankreich; **~ World Contest** Miss-Universum-Wahl, *die;* **C** (*as form of address to teacher etc.*) Frau Schmidt *usw.;* (*from servant*) gnädiges Fräulein; **D** **m~** (*derog. or playful: girl*) **the young ~es** die jungen Dinger (*ugs.*); **she is a saucy [little] ~:** sie ist ein freches [junges] Ding (*ugs.*)

**missal** /'mɪsl/ *n.* **A** (*RC Ch.*) Missal[e], *das;* **B** (*book of prayers*) [illuminiertes] Gebetbuch

**missel [thrush]** /'mɪsl(θrʌʃ)/ *n.* (*Ornith.*) Misteldrossel, *die*

**misshapen** /mɪs'ʃeɪpn/ *adj.* missgebildet, missgestaltet ‹Körper[teil]›; verwachsen ‹Baum, Pflanze›; verbogen ‹Münze›

**missile** /'mɪsaɪl/ *n.* **A** (*thrown*) [Wurf]geschoss, *das;* **B** (*self-propelled*) Missile, *das;* Flugkörper, *der;* **intercontinental ballistic ~:** [ballistische] Interkontinentalrakete

**missile: ~ base** *n.* [Raketen]abschussbasis, *die;* **~launcher** *n.* [Raketen]abschussrampe, *die*

**missilery** /'mɪslrɪ/ *n., no pl.* **A** (*missiles*) Geschosse *Pl.;* (*modern*) Raketen *Pl.;* **B** (*science*) Raketentechnik, *die*

**'missile site** ⇨ **missile base**

**missing** /'mɪsɪŋ/ *adj.* vermisst; fehlend ‹Seite, Kapitel, Teil, Hinweis, Indiz›; **be ~** ‹Kapitel, Wort, Seite:› fehlen; ‹Brille, Bleistift usw.:› verschwunden sein; ‹Mensch:› vermisst werden; (*not be present*) nicht da sein; fehlen; **she went ~ two hours ago** sie wird seit zwei Stunden vermisst; **the jacket has two buttons ~:** an der Jacke fehlen zwei Knöpfe; **I am ~ £10** mir fehlen 10 Pfund; **the dead, wounded, and ~:** die Toten, Verwundeten und Vermissten; **~ person** Vermisste *der/die;* **~ link** (*Biol.*) Missing Link, *das*

**mission** /'mɪʃn/ *n.* **A** (*task*) Mission, *die;* Auftrag, *der;* **B** (*journey*) Mission, *die;* **go/come on a ~ to do sth.** mit dem Auftrag reisen/kommen, etw. zu tun; **C** (*planned operation*) Einsatz, *der;* (*order*) Befehl, *der;* **space ~:** Weltraumflug, *der;* **D** (*vocation*) Mission, *die;* **~ in life** Lebensaufgabe, *die;* **have a ~ to do sth.** dazu berufen sein, etw. zu tun; **E** (*persons*) Mission, *die;* **F** (*Relig.*) Mission, *die;* (*missionary post*) Mission[sstation], *die;* (*religious body*) Mission[sgesellschaft], *die;* **foreign/home ~** (*campaign*) äußere/innere Mission

**missionary** /'mɪʃənərɪ/ ❶ *adj.* missionarisch; Missions‹station, -arbeit, -schrift›; **~ box** Opferbüchse [für die Mission]. ❷ *n.* ▶ **1261** Missionar, *der*/Missionarin, *die*

**'mission statement** *n.* Unternehmensleitbild, *das*

**missis** /'mɪsɪz, 'mɪsɪs/ *n.* **A** (*uneducated/joc.: wife*) **the** *or* **my/his/your ~:** die *od.* meine/seine/deine Alte (*salopp*); meine/seine/deine bessere Hälfte (*ugs. scherzh.*); **B** (*coll.: as form of address*) **well, ~. ...:** na, die Dame, ... (*ugs.*)

**missive** /'mɪsɪv/ *n.* (*formal/joc.*) Missiv, *das* (*veralt.*); Schreiben, *das*

**misspell** /mɪs'spel/ *v.t., forms as* **spell**[1] falsch schreiben

**misspelling** /mɪs'spelɪŋ/ *n.* falsch geschriebenes Wort

**misspend** /mɪs'spend/ *v.t., forms as* **spend** verschwenden; vergeuden; **his was a misspent youth** er hat seine Jugend vertan

**misstate** /mɪs'steɪt/ *v.t.* falsch darstellen

**misstatement** /mɪs'steɪtmənt/ *n.* falsche Darstellung

**missus** /'mɪsɪz/ ⇨ **missis**

**mist** /mɪst/ ❶ *n.* **A** (*fog*) Nebel, *der;* (*haze*) Dunst, *der;* (*on windscreen etc.*) Beschlag, *der;* ⇨ *also* **Scotch mist**; **B** **in the ~s of time** *or* **antiquity** (*fig.*) im Dunkel *od.* (*geh.*) Nebel der Vergangenheit; **C** (*of spray, vapour, etc.*) Wolke, *die;* **D** (*blurring of sight*) Schleier, *der.* ❷ *v.t.* beschlagen lassen ‹Glas›; ‹Tränen:› verschleiern ‹Blick›

**~ 'over** ❶ *v.i.* ‹Glas usw.:› [sich] beschlagen; **his eyes ~ed over** Tränen verschleierten seinen Blick. ❷ *v.t.* beschlagen lassen

**~ 'up** *v.i.* ‹Glas, Brille:› [sich] beschlagen

**mistakable** /mɪ'steɪkəbl/ *adj.* verwechselbar (**for** mit)

**mistake** /mɪ'steɪk/ ❶ *n.* Fehler, *der;* (*misunderstanding*) Missverständnis, *das;* **make a ~:** einen Fehler machen; (*in thinking*) sich irren; **there was a ~ about sth.** man hat sich in etw. (*Dat.*) geirrt; **there's some ~!** da liegt ein Irrtum *od.* Fehler vor!; **we all make ~s** jeder macht mal einen Fehler; (*in thinking*) jeder kann sich mal irren; **the ~ is mine** der Fehler liegt bei mir; **it is a ~ to assume that ...:** es ist ein Irrtum anzunehmen, dass ...; **by ~:** versehentlich; aus Versehen; **... and no ~:** ..., aber wirklich; **I was properly scared and no ~:** ich habe einen ganz schönen Schrecken gekriegt, kann ich dir sagen; **make no ~ about it, ...:** täusch dich nicht, ...

❷ *v.t., forms as* **take** 1 **A** (*misunderstand meaning of*) falsch verstehen; missverstehen; **~ sth./sb. as meaning that ...:** etw./jmdn. [fälschlicherweise] so verstehen, dass ...; **B** (*wrongly take one for another*) **~ x for y** x mit y verwechseln; x [fälschlich] für y halten; **there is no mistaking what ought to be done** es steht außer Frage *od.* ist ganz klar, was getan werden muss; **there is no mistaking him** man kann ihn gar nicht verwechseln; **~ sb.'s identity** jmdn. [mit jmd. anderem] verwechseln; **C** (*choose wrongly*) verfehlen ‹Beruf, Weg›

**mistaken** /mɪ'steɪkn/ *adj.* **be ~:** sich täuschen; **you're ~ in believing that** wenn du das glaubst, täuschst du dich; **~ kindness/zeal** unangebrachte Freundlichkeit/unangebrachter Eifer; **or** *or* **unless I'm very much ~:** wenn mich nicht alles täuscht; **a case of ~ identity** eine Verwechslung

**mistakenly** /mɪ'steɪknlɪ/ *adv.* irrtümlicherweise

**mister** /'mɪstə(r)/ *n.* **A** (*coll./joc.*) **hey, ~:** he, Meister *od.* Chef (*ugs.*); **B** (*person without title*) **a mere ~:** ein gewöhnlicher Bürger

**mistime** /mɪs'taɪm/ *v.t.* einen ungünstigen Zeitpunkt wählen für; schlecht timen (*bes. Sport*)

**mistletoe** /'mɪsltəʊ/ *n.* Mistel, *die;* (*sprig*) Mistelzweig, *der*

**mistook** ⇨ **mistake** 2

**mistral** /mɪs'trɑ:l/ *n.* (*Meteorol.*) Mistral, *der*

**mistranslate** /mɪstræns'leɪt/ *v.t.* falsch übersetzen

**mistranslation** /mɪstræns'leɪʃn/ *n.* falsche Übersetzung; (*error*) Übersetzungsfehler, *der*

**mistreat** /mɪs'tri:t/ *v.t.* schlecht behandeln; (*violently*) misshandeln; **~ one's tools** nachlässig mit seinem Werkzeug umgehen

**mistreatment** /mɪs'tri:tmənt/ *n.* schlechte Behandlung; (*violent*) Misshandlung, *die*

**mistress** /'mɪstrɪs/ *n.* **A** (*of a household*) Hausherrin, *die;* **the ~ of the house** *or* **family** die Frau des Hauses; **B** (*person in control, employer*) Herrin, *die;* **she is ~ of the situation** sie ist Herr der Lage; **she is her own ~:** sie ist ihr eigener Herr; **the dog's ~:** das Frauchen [des Hundes]; **C** (*Brit. Sch.: teacher*) Lehrerin, *die;* **'French ~:** Französischlehrerin, *die;* **D** (*man's illicit lover*) Geliebte, *die;* Mätresse, *die* (*veralt. abwertend*); **E** (*expert*) Expertin, *die;* Meisterin, *die;* **F** (*of college*) Rektorin, *die*

**mistrial** /mɪs'traɪəl/ *n.* (*Law*) **A** (*invalid trial*) fehlerhaft geführter Prozess; **on the grounds that there had been a ~:** wegen Verfahrensfehlern in der Prozessführung; **B** (*Amer.: inconclusive trial*) ergebnisloser Prozess

**mistrust** /mɪs'trʌst/ ❶ *v.t.* misstrauen (+ *Dat.*); **~ oneself** sich (*Dat.*) selbst misstrauen. ❷ *n., no pl.* Misstrauen, *das* (**of** gegenüber + *Dat.*); **[show] ~ towards sb.** Misstrauen gegen jmdn. [hegen]

**mistrustful** /mɪs'trʌstfl/ *adj.* misstrauisch; **be ~ of sb./sth.** jmdm./einer Sache gegenüber misstrauisch sein

**misty** /'mɪstɪ/ *adj.* **A** verschleiert ‹Augen, Blick›; neb[e]lig, dunstig ‹Tag, Morgen›; in Nebel *od.* Dunst gehüllt ‹Berg, Hügel›; nebelverhangen (*geh.*), dunstig ‹Tal›; **~ blue** rauchiges Blau; **B** (*indistinct in form*) unklar; verschwommen

**'misty-eyed** *adj.* mit verschleiertem Blick *nachgestellt;* **be ~:** einen [tränen]verschleierten Blick haben

**misunderstand** /mɪsʌndə'stænd/ *v.t., forms as* **understand** missverstehen; falsch verstehen; **~ the word x as meaning y** das Wort x im Sinne von y verstehen; **don't ~ me** versteh mich nicht falsch

**misunderstanding** /mɪsʌndə'stændɪŋ/ *n.* Missverständnis, *das;* **there has been a ~:** da lag ein Missverständnis vor; **I don't want there to be any ~ about it** ich möchte nicht, dass deswegen ein Missverständnis aufkommt

**misunderstood** /mɪsʌndə'stʊd/ *adj.* unverstanden; verkannt ‹Künstler, Genie›; **be ~:** kein Verständnis finden

**misuse** ❶ /mɪs'ju:z/ *v.t.* missbrauchen; zweckentfremden ‹Werkzeug, Gelder›; falsch bedienen ‹Maschine›; nichts Rechtes machen aus ‹Gelegenheit, Talent›; vergeuden, verschwenden ‹Reserven, Zeit›. ❷ /mɪs'ju:s/ *n.* Missbrauch, *der;* (*of funds*) Zweckentfremdung, *die;* (*of resources, time*) Vergeudung, *die;* Verschwendung, *die;* **a ~ of language** eine unangemessene *od.* unangebrachte Ausdrucksweise

**mite** /maɪt/ *n.* **A** (*Zool.*) Milbe, *die;* **B** (*contribution*) Scherflein, *das;* **give one's ~ to sth.** sein Scherflein zu etw. beitragen; **the widow's ~:** das Scherflein der armen Witwe; **C** (*small object*) Dingelchen, *das;* kleines Ding; (*small child*) Würmchen, *das* (*fam.*); **poor little ~:** armes Kleines; **D** (*coll.: somewhat*) **a ~ too strong/outspoken** ein bisschen *od.* etwas zu stark/geraderaus

**miter, mitered** (*Amer.*) ⇨ **mitre, mitred**

**mitigate** /'mɪtɪgeɪt/ *v.t.* **A** (*alleviate*) lindern; **B** (*make less severe*) mildern; **mitigating circumstances** mildernde Umstände; **C** (*appease*) besänftigen ‹Zorn, Wut›

**mitigation** /mɪtɪ'geɪʃn/ *n.* ⇨ **mitigate**: Linderung, *die;* Milderung, *die;* Besänftigung, *die;* **it must be said, in ~ of his faults, that ...:** es muss zu seiner Verteidigung *od.* Entlastung gesagt werden, dass ...; **~ of punishment** Strafmilderung, *die*

**mitre** /'maɪtə(r)/ *n.* (*Brit.*) **A** (*Eccl.*) Mitra, *die;* **B** (*joint*) Gehrung, *die* (*bes. Technik*)

**mitred** /'maɪtəd/ *adj.* **A** (*Brit. Eccl.*) eine Mitra tragend; **B** **~ joint** (*Carpentry*) Gehrungsverbindung, *die*

**mitten** /'mɪtn/ *n.* Fausthandschuh, *der;* Fäustling, *der;* (*not covering fingers*) fingerloser Handschuh

**Mitty** /ˈmɪtɪ/ *n., pl.* **~s: [Walter] ~ [figure]** *Mensch, der sich gern Tagträumen von eigenen Großtaten hingibt*

**mix** /mɪks/ ❶ *v.t.* Ⓐ (*combine*) [ver]mischen; vermengen; verrühren ‹Zutaten›; verbinden ‹Harmonien, Komponenten, Stilrichtungen›; **~ one's drinks** alles durcheinander trinken; **~ an egg into the batter** ein Ei in den Teig rühren; Ⓑ (*prepare by mixing*) mischen, mixen ‹Cocktail›; anrühren, ansetzen ‹Lösung, Teig›; zubereiten ‹Medikament›; Ⓒ **~ it [with sb.]** (*coll.*) sich [mit jmdm.] prügeln.
❷ *v.i.* Ⓐ (*become ~ed*) sich vermischen; Ⓑ (*be sociable, participate*) Umgang mit anderen [Menschen] haben; **~ well** kontaktfreudig *od.* gesellig sein; **you should ~ with other people** du solltest unter Leute gehen; **I don't ~ with that sort of people/in those circles** ich verkehre nicht mit solchen Leuten/in diesen Kreisen; Ⓒ (*be compatible*) zusammenpassen; sich [miteinander] vertragen; ‹Ideen:› sich verbinden lassen.
❸ *n.* Ⓐ (*coll.: mixture*) Mischung, *die* (**of** aus); Ⓑ (*proportion*) [Mischungs]verhältnis, *das;* Ⓒ (*ready ingredients*) [gebrauchsfertige] Mischung; **[cake] ~:** Backmischung, *die;* Ⓓ (*Radio, Cinemat., TV*) **~[es]** Mischung, *die*

**~ ˈin** ❶ *v.i.* Ⓐ (*be compatible*) zu jmdm./etw. passen; Ⓑ (*start fighting*) aufeinander losgehen. ❷ *v.t.* einrühren

**~ ˈup** *v.t.* Ⓐ vermischen; verrühren ‹Zutaten›; Ⓑ (*make a muddle of*) durcheinander bringen; (*confuse one with another*) verwechseln; ⇒ *also* **mix-up**; Ⓒ *in pass.* (*involve*) **be/get ~ed up in sth.** in etw. (*Akk.*) verwickelt sein/werden; **get ~ed up with a gang** sich mit einer Gang einlassen

**mixed** /mɪkst/ *adj.* Ⓐ (*diverse*) unterschiedlich ‹Reaktionen, Kritiken›; **a ~ assortment** eine [bunte] Mischung (**of** von); **~ feelings** gemischte Gefühle; **get ~ reviews** sehr unterschiedliche Kritiken bekommen; Ⓑ (*containing people from various backgrounds etc.*) gemischt ‹Gesellschaft›; **a ~ bunch** ein bunt gemischter Haufen; Ⓒ (*for both sexes*) gemischt

**mixed: ~ ˈbag** *n.* bunte Mischung; **a very ~ bag of people** eine bunt gemischte Gruppe [von Leuten]; **~ ˈblessing** *n.* **be a ~ blessing** nicht nur Vorteile haben; **children are a ~ blessing** Kinder sind kein reiner Segen; **~ ˈcompany** *n.* **in ~ company** in Gesellschaft von Damen [und Kindern]; **~ ˈdoubles** ⇒ **double** 3 J; **~ ˈfarming** *n.* Kombination von Ackerbau und Viehzucht; **~ ˈgrill** *n.* Mixed grill, *der* (*Gastr.*); gemischte Grillplatte; **~ ˈmarriage** *n.* Mischehe, *die;* **~ ˈmetaphor** ⇒ **metaphor** B; **~ ˈup** *adj.* (*fig. coll.*) verwirrt, konfus ‹Person›; **be/feel very ~ up** völlig durcheinander sein; **[crazy] ~ up kids** Jugendliche ohne [jeden] inneren Halt

**mixer** /ˈmɪksə(r)/ *n.* Ⓐ (*for foods*) Mixer, *der;* (*for concrete*) Mischmaschine, *die;* Ⓑ (*merging pictures*) (*apparatus*) Mischpult, *das;* (*person*) Bildmischer, *der;* Ⓒ (*combining sounds*) (*apparatus*) Mischpult, *das;* Tonmischer, *der;* (*person*) Tonmischer, *der;* Ⓓ (*drink*) Getränk zum Mischen; Ⓔ (*in society*) **be a good ~:** mit den unterschiedlichsten Leuten gut zurechtkommen

**mixture** /ˈmɪkstʃə(r)/ *n.* Ⓐ (*mixing, being mixed*) Mischen, *das;* (*of harmonies*) Verbinden, *das;* Ⓑ (*result*) Mischung, *die* (**of** aus); **~ of gases** Gasgemisch, *das;* **he is such a ~** (*fig.*) er ist so unausgeglichen; Ⓒ (*medicinal preparation*) Mixtur, *die;* **the ~ as before** (*fig.*) die altbekannte Mischung; Ⓓ (*Motor Veh.: gas or vaporized petrol*) Gemisch, *das;* Ⓔ (*ready ingredients*) ⇒ **mix** 3 C; Ⓕ **[mechanical] ~** (*act*) Vermengen, *das;* (*product*) Gemenge, *das*

**ˈmix-up** *n.* Durcheinander, *das;* (*misunderstanding*) Missverständnis, *das;* **there has been some sort of ~:** da ist irgendetwas schief gelaufen (*ugs.*); **there's been a ~ about who should be invited** es gab einige Verwirrung darüber, wer eingeladen werden sollte

**mizen** /ˈmɪzn/ *n.* (*Naut.*) Besan, *der*

**mizen: ~mast** *n.* (*Naut.*) Besanmast, *der;* **~sail** *n.* (*Naut.*) Besansegel, *das*

**mizzen** ⇒ **mizen**

**Mk.** *abbr.* ⇒ **mark[1] b**

**ml.** *abbr.* Ⓐ ▶**1671** **millilitre[s]** ml; Ⓑ **mile[s]** M

**MLR** *abbr.* **minimum lending rate**

**mm.** *abbr.* ▶**1210**, ▶**1284** **millimetre[s]** mm

**mnemonic** /nɪˈmɒnɪk/ *n.* Gedächtnishilfe, *die;* Eselsbrücke, *die* (*ugs.*)

**mo** /məʊ/ *n., pl.* **~s** /məʊz/ (*coll.*) Moment, *der;* **half a ~, wait a ~** Momentchen!

**mo.** *abbr.* (*Amer.*) **month** Mo.

**moa** /ˈməʊə/ *n.* (*Ornith.*) Moa, *der*

**moan** /məʊn/ ❶ *n.* Ⓐ Stöhnen, *das;* (*fig.: of wind*) Heulen, *das;* Ⓑ (*complaint*) **have a ~** (*complain at length*) jammern; (*have a grievance*) eine Beschwerde haben. ❷ *v.i.* Ⓐ stöhnen (**with** vor + *Dat.*); (*fig.*) ‹Wind:› heulen; Ⓑ (*complain*) jammern (**about** über + *Akk.*); **what is he ~ing [and groaning] about now?** was hat er denn jetzt wieder zu jammern?; **~ at sb.** jmdm. etwas vorjammern. ❸ *v.t.* stöhnen

**moat** /məʊt/ ❶ *n.* [Wasser]graben, *der;* **[castle] ~:** Burggraben, *der.* ❷ *v.t.* mit einem Wassergraben umgeben

**mob** /mɒb/ ❶ *n.* Ⓐ (*rabble*) Mob, *der* (*abwertend*); Pöbel, *der* (*abwertend*); **a ~ gathered outside the police station** eine aufgebrachte Menge versammelte sich vor der Polizeiwache; Ⓑ (*coll.: associated group*) **~ [of criminals]** Bande, *die* (*abwertend*); **Peter and his ~:** Peter und seine ganze Blase (*salopp*); **~ law/rule** Gesetz/Herrschaft der Straße; Ⓒ (*derog.: populace*) **the ~:** die [breite] Masse. ❷ *v.t.*, **-bb-:** Ⓐ (*crowd round*) belagern (*ugs.*) ‹Schauspieler, Star›; stürmen ‹Kino›; Ⓑ (*attack*) herfallen über (+ *Akk.*); sich stürzen auf (+ *Akk.*); **he was ~bed** sie fielen über ihn her

**mobile** /ˈməʊbaɪl/ ❶ *adj.* Ⓐ (*able to move easily*) beweglich; (*on wheels*) fahrbar; Ⓑ lebhaft ‹Gesicht[szüge]›; Ⓒ (*Mil.*) mobil; Ⓓ (*accommodated in vehicle*) mobil; fahrbar; **~ library** Fahrbücherei, *die;* **~ canteen** Kantine auf Rädern; Ⓔ (*in social status*) mobil (*bes. Soziol.*); **upwardly ~:** sozial aufsteigend; **be upwardly ~:** sozial aufsteigen; **downwardly ~:** im sozialen Abstieg begriffen; **be downwardly ~:** sich im sozialen Abstieg befinden. ❷ *n.* Ⓐ (*decorative structure*) Mobile, *das;* Ⓑ (**~ phone**) Handy, *das*

**mobile: ~ ˈhome** *n.* transportable Wohneinheit; (*caravan*) Wohnwagen, *der;* **~ ˈphone** *n.* Mobiltelefon, *das*

**mobilisation, mobilise** ⇒ **mobiliz-**

**mobility** /məˈbɪlɪtɪ/ *n.* Ⓐ (*ability to move*) (*of person*) Beweglichkeit, *die;* (*on wheels*) Fahrbarkeit, *die;* Ⓑ (*in social status*) Mobilität, *die* (*bes. Soziol.*)

**moˈbility allowance** *n.* (*Brit.*) *staatliche Geldleistung, die Gehbehinderten gewährt werden kann*

**mobilization** /məʊbɪlaɪˈzeɪʃn/ *n.* Ⓐ (*act of mobilizing*) Mobilisierung, *die;* Ⓑ (*Mil.*) Mobilmachung, *die*

**mobilize** /ˈməʊbɪlaɪz/ *v.t.* Ⓐ (*render movable or effective*) mobilisieren; Ⓑ (*Mil.*) mobil machen; *abs.* **make preparations to ~:** die Mobilmachung vorbereiten

**mobster** /ˈmɒbstə(r)/ *n.* (*coll.*) Gangster, *der*

**moccasin** /ˈmɒkəsɪn/ *n.* Mokassin, *der*

**mocha** /ˈmɒkə/ *n.* Mokka, *der*

**mock** /mɒk/ ❶ *v.t.* Ⓐ (*subject to ridicule*) sich lustig machen über (+ *Akk.*); verspotten; **he was ~ed** man machte sich über ihn lustig; Ⓑ (*ridicule by imitation*) **~ sb./sth.** jmdn./etw. nachmachen[, um sich über ihn/darüber lustig zu machen]. ❷ *v.i.* **~ at sb./sth.** sich über jmdn./etw. mokieren *od.* lustig machen. ❸ *attrib. adj.* gespielt ‹Feierlichkeit, Bescheidenheit, Ernst›; Schein‹kampf, -angriff, -ehe›; **~ Tudor style** Pseudotudorstil, *der;* **~ examination** simulierte Prüfung; ⇒ *also* **orange** 1 B. ❹ *n.* (*thing deserving scorn*) **make [a] ~ of sb./sth.** sich über jmdn./etw. lustig machen

**mocker** /ˈmɒkə(r)/ *n.* Ⓐ Spötter, *der*/Spötterin, *die;* Ⓑ **put the ~s on sb./sth.** (*coll.*) jmdm. alles vermasseln/etw. vermasseln (*salopp*)

**mockery** /ˈmɒkərɪ/ *n.* Ⓐ (*inadequate form*) **be a ~ of justice/the truth** der Gerechtigkeit/Wahrheit (*Dat.*) hohnsprechen (*geh.*); **he received only the ~ of a trial** sein Verfahren war eine einzige Farce; Ⓑ (*futile action*) **it would be a ~ to ...** (*be absurd*) es wäre grotesk *od.* absurd, zu ...; (*be impudent*) es wäre geschmacklos *od.* unverschämt, zu ...; Ⓒ *no pl., no indef. art.* (*derision*) Spott, *der;* Ⓓ (*person or thing derided*) Gespött, *das;* **make a ~ of sth.** etw. zur Farce machen

**mock-heˈroic** *adj.* komisch-heroisch (*Literaturw.*); **~ poem** komisches Heldengedicht *od.* Epos

**mocking** /ˈmɒkɪŋ/ ❶ *adj.* spöttisch. ❷ *n.* Spott, *der*

**ˈmockingbird** *n.* Spottdrossel, *die*

**ˈmock turtle soup** *n.* Mockturtlesuppe, *die*

**ˈmock-up** *n.* Modell [in Originalgröße]; (*of book etc.*) Layout, *das*

**Mod** /mɒd/ *n.* (*Brit.*) *sich modisch kleidender [Motorroller fahrender] Jugendlicher in den Sechzigerjahren;* Mod, *der*

**MOD** *abbr.* (*Brit.*) **Ministry of Defence** Verteidigungsministerium, *das*

**modal** /ˈməʊdl/ *adj.* Ⓐ (*of mode, form*) formal; Ⓑ (*Ling.*) modal; **~ auxiliary** *or* **verb** Modalverb, *das;* Ⓒ (*Mus.*) modal

**modality** /məˈdælɪtɪ/ *n.* **the modalities are** *or* **the ~ is as follows** die Modalitäten sind wie folgt

**mod cons** /mɒd ˈkɒnz/ *n. pl.* (*Brit. coll.*) [moderner] Komfort; **have all ~:** mit allem Komfort *od.* (*ugs.*) allen Schikanen ausgestattet sein

**mode** /məʊd/ *n.* Ⓐ (*way in which thing is done*) Art [und Weise], *die;* (*method of procedure*) Methode, *die;* (*Computing*) Betriebsart, *die;* **~ of behaviour** *or* **conduct/life** Verhaltens-/Lebensweise, *die;* **~ of transport** Transportmittel, *das;* Ⓑ (*fashion*) Mode, *die;* **the ~ for short skirts** die Mode der kurzen Röcke; **~s and fashions** Moden und Modetrends; Ⓒ (*Mus.*) Tonart, *die;* Ⓓ (*Statistics*) Modus, *der* (*fachspr.*); statistischer Mittelwert

**model** /ˈmɒdl/ ❶ *n.* Ⓐ Modell, *das;* **a sports ~:** ein Sportmodell; ⇒ *also* **working model**; Ⓑ (*perfect example*) Muster, *das* (**of** an + *Dat.*); (*to be imitated*) Vorbild, *das;* **be a ~ of industry** ein Muster an Fleiß (*Dat.*) sein; **on the ~ of sth.** nach dem Vorbild einer Sache (*Gen.*); **make sth. on the ~ of sth.** etw. einer Sache (*Dat.*) nachbilden; **take sb. as a ~:** [sich (*Dat.*)] jmdn. zum Vorbild nehmen; Ⓒ (*person employed to pose*) Modell, *das;* (*Fashion*) Model, *das;* Mannequin, *das;* (*male*) Dressman, *der;* **photographer's ~:** Fotomodell, *das;* **be a painter's ~:** einem Maler Modell stehen/sitzen.
❷ *adj.* Ⓐ (*exemplary*) vorbildlich; mustergültig; Muster- (*oft iron.*); **~ child** Musterkind, *das;* (*boy*) Musterknabe, *der* (*iron.*); Ⓑ (*miniature*) Modell‹stadt, -eisenbahn, -flugzeug›.
❸ *v.t.*, (*Brit.*) **-ll-:** Ⓐ (*shape figure of*) modellieren; formen; **~ sth. in clay** etw. in Ton modellieren; **delicately ~led features** (*fig.*) fein geschnittene Gesichtszüge; Ⓑ (*form in imitation of sth.*) **~ sth. after** *or* **[up]on sth.** etw. einer Sache (*Dat.*) nachbilden; **we ~led our system on the European one** wir haben unser System nach europäischem Vorbild aufgebaut; **~ oneself on sb.** sich (*Dat.*) jmdn. zum Vorbild nehmen; Ⓒ (*Fashion*) vorführen ‹Kleid, Entwurf usw.›.
❹ *v.i.*, (*Brit.*) **-ll-:** Ⓐ (*Fashion*) als Mannequin *od.* Model arbeiten; ‹Mann:› als Dressman arbeiten; (*Photog.*) als [Foto]modell arbeiten; (*Art*) Modell stehen/sitzen; Ⓑ **~ in clay** *etc.* in Ton *usw.* modellieren

**modelling** (*Amer.:* **modeling**) /ˈmɒdəlɪŋ/ *n.* Ⓐ *no art.* (*posing*) **do ~** (*Fashion*) als

Mannequin *od.* Model arbeiten; ‹Mann:› als Dressman arbeiten; (*Photog.*, *Art*) als Modell arbeiten; **do [some] ~ for sb.** (*Fashion*) jmds. Kreationen vorführen; (*Photog.*, *Art*) jmdm. Modell stehen/sitzen; **B** *no indef. art.* (*sculpturing*) Modellieren, *das;* **~ clay** Modellierton, *der*

**modem** /'məʊdem/ *n.* (*Communications*) Modem, *der*

**moderate** **1** /'mɒdərət/ *adj.* **A** (*avoiding extremes*) gemäßigt ‹Partei, Ansichten›; mäßig, maßvoll ‹Person, bes. Trinker, Esser; Forderungen›; mäßig ‹Begeisterung, Interesse›; **be ~ in one's demands** maßvolle Forderungen erheben *od.* stellen; **B** (*fairly large or good*) mittler... ‹Größe, Menge, Wert›; nicht allzu groß ‹Entfernung, Wert›; **[only] ~:** mäßig ‹Qualität, Ernte›; **a ~ amount of coal** eine gewisse Menge Kohle; **the water was of only ~ depth** das Wasser war nicht besonders *od.* nur mäßig tief; **C** (*reasonable*) angemessen, vernünftig ‹Preis, Summe›; **D** mäßig ‹Wind›.
**2** /'mɒdərət/*n.* Gemäßigte, *der/die;* **be a ~ in politics** gemäßigte politische Ansichten vertreten.
**3** /'mɒdəreɪt/ *v.t.* mäßigen ‹Begierde, Ungeduld, Gefühl›; lindern ‹Schmerzen, Sorgen›; dämpfen ‹Eifer›; zügeln ‹Begeisterung›; senken ‹Stimme›; mildern ‹negativen Effekt›; **~ one's demands** seine Forderungen einschränken *od.* abschwächen.
**4** /'mɒdəreɪt/*v.i.* nachlassen; ‹Forderungen:› gemäßigter *od.* maßvoller werden

**moderately** /'mɒdərətlɪ/ *adv.* einigermaßen; mäßig ‹begeistert, groß, begabt; rauchen›; **there was only a ~ large audience** es waren nicht übermäßig viele Zuschauer da; **be only ~ enthusiastic/concerned about sth.** sich nicht allzu sehr *od.* übermäßig für etw. begeistern/sich keine allzu großen Sorgen um etw. machen

**moderation** /mɒdə'reɪʃn/ *n.* **A** (*moderating*) Mäßigung, *die;* (*of wind, fever*) Nachlassen, *das;* **B** *no pl.* (*moderateness*) Mäßigkeit, *die;* (*of demands etc.*) Angemessenheit, *die;* Vernünftigkeit, *die;* **~ in all things** alles mit Maßen; **in ~:** mit *od.* in Maßen

**moderator** /'mɒdəreɪtə(r)/ *n.* **A** (*arbitrator*) Schlichter, *der;* (*mediator*) Vermittler, *der*/Vermittlerin, *die;* **B** (*presiding officer*) Vorsitzende, *der/die;* **C** (*Eccl.*) Moderator, *der*

**modern** /'mɒdn/ **1** *adj.* **A** (*of the present*) modern; heutig ‹Zeit[alter], Welt, Mensch›; **~ jazz** Modern Jazz, *der;* **in ~ times** in der heutigen Zeit; **~ English** modernes Englisch; **~ history** neuere Geschichte; **~ languages** neuere Sprachen; (*subject of study*) Neuphilologie, *die;* **~ maths** die neue Mathematik; ⇒ *also* **Latin** 2; **B** (*in current fashion*) modern; neumodisch (*oft abwertend*); **the ~ fashion is to wear a hat** es ist [jetzt] Mode, einen Hut zu tragen. **2** *n. usu. in pl.* moderner Mensch; (*Art*) Modernist, *der*/Modernistin, *die;* (*person alive at present*) Zeitgenosse, *der*/-genossin, *die*

**'modern-day** *attrib. adj.* von heute *nachgestellt;* heutig

**modernisation**, **modernise** ⇒ **moderniz-**

**modernism** /'mɒdənɪzm/ *n.* Modernismus, *der*

**modernist** /'mɒdənɪst/ *n.* Modernist, *der*/Modernistin, *die*

**modernistic** /mɒdə'nɪstɪk/ *adj.* modernistisch

**modernity** /mə'dɜ:nɪtɪ/ *n.* Modernität, *die*

**modernization** /mɒdənaɪ'zeɪʃn/ *n.* **A** (*modernizing*) Modernisierung, *die;* **B** (*version*) modernisierte Fassung

**modernize** /'mɒdənaɪz/ **1** *v.t.* modernisieren. **2** *v.i.* sich der modernen Zeit anpassen

**modest** /'mɒdɪst/ *adj.* **A** (*not conceited*) bescheiden; (*shy*) bescheiden; zurückhaltend; **be ~ about one's achievements** nicht mit seinen Leistungen prahlen; **B** (*not excessive*) bescheiden (*auch iron.*); genügsam, anspruchslos ‹Mensch›; vorsichtig ‹Schätzung›; **C** (*unpretentious in appearance, amount, etc.*) bescheiden; einfach, unauffällig ‹Haus, Kleidung›; **have a ~ lifestyle** bescheiden *od.* einfach leben; **~ in appearance** unauffällig; **D** (*decorous, chaste*) anständig ‹Charakter›; anständig, (*veralt.*) sittsam ‹Mensch, Benehmen›; schicklich ‹Benehmen, Ausdrucksweise›; dezent, unauffällig ‹Kleidung›

**modestly** /'mɒdɪstlɪ/ *adv.* **A** (*not conceitedly*) bescheiden; **B** (*decently*) dezent, unauffällig ‹sich kleiden›; schicklich, sittsam (*veralt.*) ‹sich benehmen›

**modesty** /'mɒdɪstɪ/ *n., no pl.* **A** (*freedom from conceit*) Bescheidenheit, *die;* **in all ~:** bei aller Bescheidenheit; **the [sheer] ~ of the man!** (*iron.*) die Bescheidenheit in Person!; **B** **the ~ of their demands** ihre maßvollen Forderungen; **C** (*regard for propriety*) ⇒ **modest** D: Anständigkeit, *die;* Sittsamkeit, *die* (*veralt.*); Schicklichkeit, *die;* Unauffälligkeit, *die;* Dezentheit, *die*

**modicum** /'mɒdɪkəm/ *n.* Minimum, *das;* **a ~ of luck/truth** ein Quäntchen Glück/ein Körnchen Wahrheit

**modification** /mɒdɪfɪ'keɪʃn/ *n.* [Ab]änderung, *die;* Modifizierung, *die;* **without any sort of ~:** ohne jede Änderung

**modifier** /'mɒdɪfaɪə(r)/ *n.* (*esp. Ling., Biol.*) Modifikator, *der*

**modify** /'mɒdɪfaɪ/ *v.t.* **A** (*make changes in*) [ab-, ver]ändern; modifizieren; **B** (*tone down*) mäßigen; mildern ‹Klima›; **~ one's position** in seiner Haltung gemäßigter werden; **you'd better ~ your tone** mäßigen Sie sich mal in Ihrem Ton!; **C** (*Ling.*) (*qualify sense of*) näher bestimmen ‹Verb, Adjektiv usw.›; (*change by umlaut*) umlauten ‹Vokal›

**modish** /'məʊdɪʃ/ *adj.* modisch

**modular** /'mɒdjʊlə(r)/ *adj.* **A** (*employing module[s]*) aus Elementen [zusammengesetzt]; (*in construction*) aus Baueinheiten *od.* -elementen [zusammengesetzt]; **~ system** Baukastensystem, *das;* **~ construction/design** Konstruktion/Entwurf nach dem Baukastensystem; **~ unit** [Bau-, Konstruktions]element, *das;* **B** (*Educ.*) **~ course** *aus vielen verschiedenen, beliebig kombinierten Unterrichtseinheiten bestehender Kurs*

**modulate** /'mɒdjʊleɪt/ **1** *v.t.* **A** (*regulate*) abstimmen (**to** auf + *Akk.*); anpassen (**to** *Dat.*, an + *Akk.*); **B** (*adjust pitch*) modulieren ‹Stimme, Sprache, Ton›; **C** (*Radio*) modulieren ‹Welle, Sender›. **2** *v.i.* modulieren; **~ from one key to another** von einer Tonart in die andere übergehen

**modulation** /mɒdjʊ'leɪʃn/ *n.* Modulation, *die*

**modulator** /'mɒdjʊleɪtə(r)/ *n.* (*Electronics*) Modulator, *der*

**module** /'mɒdju:l/ *n.* **A** (*in construction or system*) Bauelement, *das;* (*Electronics*) Modul, *das;* **B** (*Educ.*) Unterrichtseinheit, *die;* **C** (*Astronaut.*) **command ~:** Kommandoeinheit *od.* -kapsel, *die;* ⇒ *also* **lunar module**

**modulus** /'mɒdjʊləs/ *n., pl.* **moduli** /'mɒdjʊlaɪ/ (*Math., Phys.*) Modul, *der*

**modus operandi** /məʊdəs ɒpə'rændi:/ *n.* Modus operandi, *der* (*geh.*)

**modus vivendi** /məʊdəs vɪ'vendɪ:/ *n.* Modus vivendi, *der* (*geh.*)

**mog** /mɒg/, **moggie** /'mɒgɪ/ *ns.* (*Brit. coll.*) Katze, *die;* Katzenvieh, *das* (*abwertend*)

**Mogul** /'məʊgl, məʊ'gʌl/ **1** *n.* **A** (*Hist.: Mongolian*) Mongole, *der*/Mongolin, *die;* **the Great** *or* **Grand ~:** der Großmogul; **B** **m~** (*coll.: important person*) Mogul, *der* (*fig.*). **2** *adj.* (*Hist.*) mongolisch; **the ~ empire** das Reich der Moguln

**mohair** /'məʊheə(r)/ *n.* Mohair, *der;* (*yarn*) Mohair- *od.* Angorawolle, *die*

**Mohammedan** /mə'hæmɪdən/ ⇒ **Muhammadan**

**moist** /mɔɪst/ *adj.* feucht (**with** von)

**moisten** /'mɔɪsn/ *v.t.* anfeuchten; feucht machen; **~ one's lips** sich (*Dat.*) die Lippen [mit der Zunge] befeuchten

**moisture** /'mɔɪstʃə(r)/ *n.* Feuchtigkeit, *die;* **~ in the air** Luftfeuchtigkeit, *die;* **film of ~:** Feuchtigkeitsfilm, *der*

**moisturise**, **moisturiser**, **moisturising** ⇒ **moisturiz-**

**moisturize** /'mɔɪstjʊraɪz, 'mɔɪstʃəraɪz/ *v.t.* befeuchten; **~ the skin** der Haut (*Dat.*) Feuchtigkeit zuführen; ‹Creme:› der Haut (*Dat.*) Feuchtigkeit verleihen

**moisturizer** /'mɔɪstjʊraɪzə(r), 'mɔɪstʃəraɪzə(r)/, **'moisturizing cream** *ns.* Feuchtigkeitscreme, *die*

**moke** /məʊk/ *n.* (*Brit. coll.*) Esel, *der*

**molar** /'məʊlə(r)/ **1** *n.* Backenzahn, *der;* Molar[zahn], *der* (*Anat.*); Mahlzahn, *der* (*bes. Zool.*). **2** *adj.* **~ tooth** ⇒ **1**

**molasses** /mə'læsɪz/ *n.* **A** (*syrup drained from raw sugar*) Melasse, *die;* **B** (*Amer.: treacle*) Sirup, *der*

**mold** (*Amer.*) ⇒ **mould**[1, 2, 3]

**Moldavia** /mɒl'deɪvɪə/ *pr. n.* Moldau, *die*

**molder**, **molding**, **moldy** (*Amer.*) ⇒ **mould-**

**mole**[1] /məʊl/ *n.* (*on skin*) Leberfleck, *der;* Pigmentfleck, *der* (*Med.*); (*prominent*) Muttermal, *das*

**mole**[2] *n.* **A** (*animal*) Maulwurf, *der;* **B** (*coll.: spy*) Maulwurf, *der* (*ugs.*)

**mole**[3] *n.* **A** (*breakwater*) Mole, *die;* **B** (*artificial harbour*) [künstlicher] Hafen

**mole**[4] *n.* (*Chem.*) Mol, *das*

**molecular** /mɒ'lekjʊlə(r)/ *adj.* (*Phys., Chem.*) molekular; **~ weight/biology** Molekulargewicht, *das*/-biologie, *die*

**molecule** /'mɒlɪkju:l, 'məʊlɪkju:l/ *n.* **A** (*Phys., Chem.*) Molekül, *das;* **B** (*small particle*) winziges Teilchen

**'molehill** *n.* Maulwurfshügel, *der;* **make a mountain out of a ~** (*fig.*) aus einer Mücke einen Elefanten machen (*ugs.*)

**molest** /mə'lest/ *v.t.* **A** belästigen; (*to rob*) überfallen; **B** (*sexually*) [unsittlich] belästigen

**molestation** /məʊlɪ'steɪʃn, mɒlɪ'steɪʃn/ *n.* **A** Belästigung, *die;* (*to rob*) Überfallen, *das;* **B** (*sexual*) [unsittliche] Belästigung

**moll** /mɒl/ *n.* (*coll.*) Gangsterbraut, *die*

**mollify** /'mɒlɪfaɪ/ *v.t.* besänftigen; beschwichtigen; **be finally mollified** sich schließlich beruhigen

**mollusc**, (*Amer.*) **mollusk** /'mɒləsk/ *n.* (*Zool.*) Molluske, *die* (*fachspr.*); Weichtier, *das*

**mollycoddle** /'mɒlɪkɒdl/ **1** *v.t.* [ver]hätscheln (*oft abwertend*); verzärteln (*abwertend*). **2** *n.* Weichling, *der* (*abwertend*)

**molt** (*Amer.*) ⇒ **moult**

**molten** /'məʊltn/ *adj.* geschmolzen; flüssig ‹Lava›

**molybdenum** /mə'lɪbdɪnəm/ *n.* (*Chem.*) Molybdän, *das*

**mom** /mɒm/ (*Amer. coll.*) ⇒ **mum**[2]

**moment** /'məʊmənt/ *n.* **A** Moment, *der;* Augenblick, *der;* **barely a ~ had elapsed ...:** es war kaum eine Minute vergangen ...; **help came not a ~ too soon** die Hilfe hätte keinen Moment später kommen dürfen; **for a ~ or two** für einen kurzen Augenblick; **for a few ~s** für ein paar Augenblicke; ein paar Augenblicke lang; **there was never a dull ~:** man langweilte sich keinen Augenblick lang; **at this ~ in time** in diesem Moment *od.* Augenblick; **after a ~'s hesitation** nach kurzem Zögern; **at any ~,** (*coll.*) **any ~:** jeden Augenblick *od.* Moment; **on the spur of the ~:** ganz spontan; **it was over in just a few ~s** es dauerte nur wenige Augenblicke *od.* war im Nu geschehen; **it is the ~ [for sth.]** es ist der richtige Zeitpunkt [für etw.]; **this is the ~!** dies ist der geeignete Augenblick!; **a few ~s of peace** ein paar Minuten der Ruhe; ein paar ruhige Minuten; **the film had its ~s** der Film hatte einige starke Stellen; **he has his ~s** manchmal ist er gar nicht so übel (*ugs.*); **at odd ~s** gelegentlich[, wenn ein wenig Zeit ist]; **a ~ to remember** ein denkwürdiger Augenblick; **at the precise ~ she came in ...:** genau in dem Augenblick *od.* gerade, als sie hereintrat, ...; **the ~ I get home** gleich *od.* sofort, wenn ich nach Hause komme; **one** *or* **half a** *or* **just a** *or* **wait a ~!** einen Moment *od.* Augenblick!; Moment[chen] *od.* Augenblick mal!; **in a ~** (*instantly*) im Nu (*ugs.*); (*very soon*) sofort; gleich; **for a ~:** einen Moment [lang]; für einen Moment; **not for a ~:** keinen Moment [lang]; **[at] the [very] ~ it happened** in dem *od.* im selben Augenblick, als es passierte; **the ~ of truth** die Stunde der Wahrheit; **at the ~:** im Augenblick; momentan; **for the ~:** im *od.* für den Augenblick; vorläufig; **I shan't be a ~** (*I'll be back very soon*) ich bin sofort zurück; (*I have very nearly finished*) ich bin sofort so weit; **have you got a ~?** hast du mal einen Augenblick Zeit?; **be the man of the ~:** der Mann des Tages sein; **come here this ~!** komm sofort *od.* auf der Stelle her!; **just this ~:** soeben; gerade *od.* eben [erst]; **from ~ to ~:** alle Augenblicke; **B** (*formal: importance*) **of ~:** von Bedeutung; **of little** *or* **small/no ~:** von geringer/ohne Bedeutung; **C** (*Phys.*) Moment, *das;* **~ of inertia** Trägheitsmoment, *das*

**momentarily** /'məʊməntərɪlɪ/ *adv.* **A** (*for a moment*) einen Augenblick lang; (*for a while*) vorübergehend; **B** (*Amer.*) (*at any moment*) jeden Augenblick *od.* Moment; (*in a few minutes*) in wenigen Minuten

**momentary** /'məʊməntərɪ/ *adj.* **A** (*lasting only a moment*) kurz; **a ~ forgetfulness/aberration** ein Augenblick geistiger Abwesenheit/der Verwirrung; **B** (*transitory*) vorübergehend

**momentous** /mə'mentəs/ *adj.* (*important*) bedeutsam; bedeutungsvoll; (*of consequence*) folgenschwer; von großer Tragweite *nachgestellt;* **of ~ importance** von entscheidender Bedeutung

**momentum** /mə'mentəm/ *n., pl.* **momenta** /mə'mentə/ **A** (*impetus*) Schwung, *der;* **lose ~:** Schwung *od.* Fahrt verlieren; (*fig.*) [an] Schwung *od.* Fahrt verlieren; **gain** *or* **gather ~:** schneller werden; (*fig.*) in Schwung kommen; ‹Idee:› an Boden gewinnen; **B** (*Mech.*) Impuls, *der;* ⇒ *also* **angular** C; **conservation** B

**mommy** /'mɒmɪ/ (*Amer. coll.*) ⇒ **mummy²**

**Mon.** *abbr.* ▶ **1056** **Monday** Mo.

**Monaco** /'mɒnəkəʊ/ *pr. n.* Monaco (*das*)

**monarch** /'mɒnək/ *n.* (*king, emperor, etc.*) Monarch, *der*/Monarchin, *die;* (*supreme ruler*) [Allein]herrscher, *der*/-herrscherin, *die*

**monarchic** /mə'nɑːkɪk/, **monarchical** /mə'nɑːkɪkl/ *adj.* **A** (*of government*) monarchisch; **B** (*of monarchy*) monarchistisch

**monarchism** /'mɒnəkɪzm/ *n.* (*monarchical government*) Monarchie, *die;* (*attachment to monarchy*) Monarchismus, *der*

**monarchist** /'mɒnəkɪst/ *n.* Monarchist, *der*/Monarchistin, *die*

**monarchy** /'mɒnəkɪ/ *n.* Monarchie, *die;* ⇒ *also* **constitutional** 1 B

**monastery** /'mɒnəstrɪ/ *n.* [Mönchs]kloster, *das*

**monastic** /mə'næstɪk/ *adj.* **A** (*of or like monks*) mönchisch; **B** (*of monasteries*) klösterlich; Kloster‹gebäude, -architektur›

**monasticism** /mə'næstɪsɪzm/ *n.* Mönch[s]tum, *das*

**Monday** /'mʌndeɪ, 'mʌndɪ/ ▶ **1056** ❶ *n.* Montag, *der.* ❷ *adv.* (*coll.*) **she comes ~s** sie kommt montags. ⇒ *also* **Friday**

**monetarism** /'mʌnɪtərɪzm/ *n.* (*Econ.*) Monetarismus, *der*

**monetarist** /'mʌnɪtərɪst/ *n.* (*Econ.*) Monetarist, *der*/Monetaristin, *die*

**monetary** /'mʌnɪtərɪ/ *adj.* **A** (*of the currency in use*) monetär; Währungs‹politik, -system›; **~ union** Währungsunion, *die;* **B** (*of money*) finanziell; **~ gift** Geldgeschenk, *das*

**money** /'mʌnɪ/ *n.* ▶ **1328** **A** *no pl.* Geld, *das;* **your ~ or your life!** Geld oder Leben!; **be in the ~** (*coll.*) (*be winning ~ prizes*) am Scheffeln sein (*ugs.*); (*have plenty of ~*) im Geld schwimmen (*ugs.*); **there is ~ in sth.** mit etw. kann man [viel] Geld verdienen; **~ for jam** *or* **old rope** (*Brit. fig. coll.*) leicht *od.* schnell verdientes Geld; **make ~** ‹Person:› [viel] Geld verdienen, (*ugs.*) [das große] Geld machen; ‹Geschäft:› etwas einbringen, sich rentieren; **earn good ~:** gut verdienen; **come into ~:** zu Geld kommen; **~ talks** das Geld machts (*ugs.*); **~ makes the world go round** Geld regiert die Welt; **put ~ into sth.** Geld in etw. (*Akk.*) investieren *od.* (*ugs.*) hineinstecken; **have ~ to burn** (*fig. coll.*) Geld wie Heu haben (*ugs.*); **[not] be made of ~** (*fig. coll.*) [k]ein Goldesel *od.* Krösus sein; **spend ~ like water** mit dem Geld nur so um sich werfen (*ugs.*); **good ~** (*earned/spent*) gutes/teueres Geld; **this would only be to throw** *or* **pour good ~ after bad** das wäre nur rausgeschmissenes *od.* rausgeworfenes Geld (*ugs.*); **for 'my ~:** wenn man mich fragt; **he/she is the one for my ~:** ich tippe auf ihn/sie; **put one's ~ on sth.** auf etw. (*Akk.*) wetten *od.* setzen; (*fig.*) [seine Hoffnung] auf etw. (*Akk.*) setzen; **the best that ~ can buy** das Beste, was es für Geld gibt; **~ can't buy happiness!** Geld allein macht nicht glücklich!; **~ supply** Geldmenge, *die;* **B** *pl.* **~s** *or* **monies** /'mʌnɪz/ (*sum of money*) Geld, *das;* [Geld]betrag, *der;* **the rent ~:** [das Geld für] die Miete; **C** (*rich person[s]*) **that's not where the real ~ lives** da ist nicht das große Geld zu Hause. ⇒ *also* **account** 3 A; **big** 1 A; **conscience money**; **cost** 2 A; **love** 1 A; **run** 1 A

**money: ~-back** *attrib. adj.* **~-back guarantee** Geld-zurück-Garantie, *die;* **~ bag** *n.* Geldsack, *der;* **~ bags** *n. sing.* (*coll.: person*) Geldsack, *der* (*ugs. abwertend*); **~ belt** *n.* Geldgürtel, *der;* **~ box** *n.* Sparbüchse, *die;* (*for collection*) Sammelbüchse, *die;* **~ changer** *n.* ▶ **1261** Geldwechsler, *der*

**moneyed** /'mʌnɪd/ *adj.* (*rich*) vermögend; begütert; **the ~ classes** die besitzenden Klassen

**money: ~-grubber** *n.* Raffzahn, *der* (*ugs.*); **~-grubbing** ❶ *adj.* geldgierig (*abwertend*); ❷ *n.* Geldgier, *die* (*abwertend*); **~lender** *n.* ▶ **1261** Geldverleiher, *der;* **~maker** *n.* **be a ~maker** ‹Projekt, Produkt, Film:› Geld bringen; **~making** ❶ *adj.* Gewinn bringend, einträglich ‹Geschäft, Beschäftigung›; ❷ *n., no pl.* Geldverdienen, *das;* **~ market** *n.* Geldmarkt, *der;* **~ order** *n.* Zahlungsanweisung, *die;* (*issued by Post Office*) Postanweisung, *die;* **~-spinner** *n.* (*Brit.*) Verkaufsschlager, *der;* (*business*) Goldgrube, *die* (*ugs.*); **he turned that idea into a ~-spinner** er hat diese Idee versilbert (*ugs.*); **~'s worth** *n.* **get** *or* **have one's ~'s worth** etwas für sein Geld bekommen

**Mongol** /'mɒŋgl/ ❶ *n.* **A** Mongole, *der*/Mongolin, *die;* (*Anthrop.*) Mongolide, *der/die;* **B** **m~** (*Med.*) Mongoloide, *der/die;* **she is a m~** sie ist mongoloid. ❷ *adj.* **A** mongolisch; (*Anthrop.*) mongolid; **B** **m~** (*Med.*) mongoloid

**Mongolia** /mɒŋ'gəʊlɪə/ *pr. n.* Mongolei, *die*

**Mongolian** /mɒŋ'gəʊlɪən/ ❶ *adj.* **A** ▶ **1340** mongolisch; **B** (*Anthrop.*) mongolid (*fachspr.*); mongolisch. ❷ *n.* **A** ▶ **1340** (*person*) Mongole, *der*/Mongolin, *die;* **B** (*Anthrop.*) Mongolide, *der/die;* **C** (*language*) Mongolisch, *das;* das Mongolische

**mongolism** /'mɒŋgəlɪzm/ *n.* (*Med.*) Mongolismus, *der*

**mongoose** /'mɒŋguːs/ *n.* (*Zool.*) Indischer Mungo

**mongrel** /'mʌŋgrəl, 'mɒŋgrəl/ ❶ *n.* **A** (*Bot., Zool.*) Bastard, *der* (*fachspr.*); Hybride, *der* (*fachspr.*); Kreuzung, *die;* (*often derog.: dog*) Promenadenmischung, *die* (*scherzh., auch abwertend*); **B** (*derog.: person*) Mischling, *der;* Bastard, *der* (*derb abwertend*). ❷ *adj.* (*of mixed origin*) hybrid (*fachspr.*) ‹Pflanze, Tier›; **~ animal/plant** [tierischer/pflanzlicher] Hybride *od.* Bastard (*fachspr.*); [Tier-/Pflanzen]kreuzung, *die*

**moni[c]ker** /'mɒnɪkə(r)/ *n.* (*coll.*) Name, *der;* (*nickname*) Spitzname, *der*

**monitor** /'mɒnɪtə(r)/ ❶ *n.* **A** (*Sch.*) Aufsichtsschüler, *der*/-schülerin, *die;* **pencil/milk/lunch ~:** Bleistift-/Milch-/Essen[s]wart, *der;* **school ~:** Präfekt, *der;* **B** (*Zool.*) **~ [lizard]** Waran, *der;* **C** (*listener*) Mithörer, *der*/Mithörerin, *die;* **D** (*Mech. Engin., Phys., Med., Telev.*) Monitor, *der.* ❷ *v.t.* **A** (*maintain surveillance over*) kontrollieren ‹Strahlungsintensität›; beobachten ‹Wetter, Flugzeug, Gewohnheit, Bewegung›; abhören ‹Sendung, Telefongespräch›; **B** (*regulate*) kontrollieren ‹Radio-, Fernsehempfang›; überwachen ‹Verteilung, Ein-/Ausfuhr›

**monk** /mʌŋk/ *n.* Mönch, *der;* **order of ~s** Mönchsorden, *der;* ⇒ *also* **White Monk**

**monkey** /'mʌŋkɪ/ ❶ *n.* **A** Affe, *der;* **the three wise ~s** (*Mythol.*) die „Drei Affen"; **make a ~ of sb.** (*coll.*) jmdn. zum Gespött machen; **get one's ~ up** (*Brit. coll.*) auf die Palme gehen (*ugs.*); **sb.'s ~ is up** (*Brit. coll.*) jmd. ist auf der Palme; **I'll be a ~'s uncle!** (*coll.*) ich denk, mich laust der Affe (*ugs.*); **B** (*in playful abuse*) Schlingel, *der* (*scherzh.*); **cheeky ~:** Frechdachs, *der* (*fam.*); **C** (*coll.: £500, $500*) halber Riese (*salopp*). ❷ *v.i.* **~ about** *or* **around [with]** (*coll.*) herumalbern [mit] (*ugs.*) ‹Person›; (*interfere*) herumspielen [mit *od.* an (+ *Dat.*)] ‹Gegenstand›

**monkey: ~ business** *n.* (*coll.*) (*mischief*) Schabernack, *der;* (*unlawful or unfair activities*) krumme Touren *Pl.* (*ugs.*); **~ jacket** *n.* (*Naut., Fashion*) Monkijacke, *die;* Affenjäckchen, *das* (*Soldatenspr. scherzh.*); **~ nut** *n.* (*Bot.*) Erdnuss, *die;* **~ puzzle** *n.* (*Bot.*) Chilefichte, *die;* Araukarie, *die* (*fachspr.*); **~ tricks** *n. pl.* (*Brit. coll.*) **be up to one's ~ tricks** etwas aushecken; **no ~ tricks!** mach keinen Quatsch (*ugs.*); **~ wrench** *n.* Rollgabelschlüssel, *der* (*fachspr.*); Universalschraubenschlüssel, *der*

**monkish** /'mʌŋkɪʃ/ *adj.* **A** mönchisch; Mönchs‹kleidung›; Kloster‹leben, -bibliothek›; **B** (*derog.: sanctimonious*) pfäffisch (*abwertend*); **C** (*modest*) anspruchslos; **D** (*derog.: unsociable*) ungesellig

**monkshood** /'mʌŋkshʊd/ *n.* (*Bot.*) Blauer Eisenhut

**mono** /'mɒnəʊ/ *adj.* Mono‹platte[nspieler], -wiedergabe›

**monochrome** /'mɒnəkrəʊm/ ❶ *n.* **A** (*picture*) monochromes (*fachspr.*) *od.* einfarbiges Bild; **B** (*representation*) monochrome (*fachspr.*) *od.* einfarbige Darstellung; **in ~:** monochrom (*fachspr.*); einfarbig; Schwarzweiß- (*Ferns.*). ❷ *adj.* monochrom (*fachspr.*); einfarbig; Schwarzweiß- (*Ferns.*)

**monocle** /'mɒnəkl/ *n.* Monokel, *das;* Einglas, *das* (*veralt.*)

**monocotyledon** /mɒnəkɒtɪ'liːdn/ *n.* (*Bot.*) Monokotyle[done], *die* (*fachspr.*); einkeimblättrige Pflanze

**monocycle** /'mɒnəsaɪkl/ *n.* Einrad, *das*

**monogamous** /mə'nɒgəməs/ *adj.* monogam

**monogamy** /mə'nɒgəmɪ/ *n.* Monogamie, *die;* Einehe, *die*

**monogram** /'mɒnəgræm/ *n.* Monogramm, *das*

**monogrammed** /'mɒnəgræmd/ *adj.* monogrammiert; ‹Taschentuch usw.:› mit Monogramm

**monograph** /'mɒnəgrɑːf/ *n.* Monographie, *die;* Einzeldarstellung, *die*

**monohull** /'mɒnəhʌl/ *n.* (*Naut.*) Einrumpfschiff, *das;* Einkörperschiff, *das*

**monolingual** /mɒnə'lɪŋgwəl/ *adj.* einsprachig

**monolith** /'mɒnəlɪθ/ *n.* (*Prehist., Building; lit. or fig.*) Monolith, *der*

**monolithic** /mɒnə'lɪθɪk/ *adj.* (*Prehist., Building; lit. or fig.*) monolithisch; Monolith‹denkmal, -säule, -charakter, -beton›

**monologue** (*Amer.:* **monolog**) /'mɒnəlɒg/ *n.* (*lit. or fig.*) Monolog, *der*

**monomania** /mɒnə'meɪnɪə/ *n.* **A** (*Med., Psych.*) Monomanie, *die;* **B** (*fig.*) übertriebene Begeisterung (**for** für); Leidenschaft, *die* (**for** für)

**monophonic** /mɒnə'fɒnɪk/ *adj.* monophon

**monoplane** /'mɒnəpleɪn/ *n.* (*Aeronaut.*) Eindecker, *der*

**monopolisation**, **monopolise** ⇒ **monopoliz-**

**monopolistic** /mənɒpə'lɪstɪk/ *adj.* (*Econ.*) monopolistisch ‹Wettbewerb usw.›

**monopolization** /mənɒpəlaɪ'zeɪʃn/ *n.* (*Econ.*) Monopolisierung, *die*

**monopolize** /mə'nɒpəlaɪz/ *v.t.* (*Econ.*) monopolisieren; (*fig.*) mit Beschlag belegen; **~ the conversation** den/die anderen nicht zu Wort kommen lassen

m

# Money

## German money

***90 pfennigs***
= 90 Pf, 0,90 DM = neunzig Pfennig

***one mark***
= 1 DM = eine Mark

***1 mark 90 [pfennigs]***
= 1,90 DM = eine Mark neunzig, eine Mark und neunzig Pfennig

***50 marks***
= 50 DM = fünfzig Mark

***1,000 marks***
= 1 000 DM = [ein]tausend Mark

***100 pfennigs make one mark***
= 100 Pfennig sind eine Mark

***a 20 mark note***
= ein Zwanzigmarkschein *or* 20-Mark-Schein

***a five mark piece***
= ein Fünfmarkstück *or* 5-Mark-Stück

***a 50 pfennig coin***
= ein Fünfzigpfennigstück *or* 50-Pfennig-Stück

Although **DM** stands for "Deutsche Mark", this term is only occasionally used in full to denote the currency, and is not used when quoting amounts; however **D-Mark** will often be heard as a more specific alternative for the basic **Mark**. The abbreviation **DM** may also precede the number when prices are given in catalogues or advertisements, or is omitted altogether.

Note that there is a comma before the number of pfennigs, also that as with all denominations (not only marks and pfennigs) the plural form is the same as the singular when an amount is being quoted (and on most other occasions), although the form **Pfennige** will sometimes be heard.

## Austrian and Swiss money

The Austrian unit of currency is the schilling (**Schilling**, abbreviation S, öS, or ATS), and the Swiss unit the Swiss franc (**Schweizer Franken**, abbreviation sfr or sFr). The abbreviations precede the number when prices are given in catalogues or advertisements, or are omitted, while in a text "Schilling" is usually written in full.

The Swiss franc is worth slightly more than the German mark, but there are about 7 Austrian schillings to one mark. In each case there are smaller denominations, with 100 centimes (**Rappen** in Swiss German) to the Swiss franc and 100 **Groschen** to the Austrian schilling. Not surprisingly one does not often see amounts in groschen, although some firms still quote prices such as "99,90".

***Price including VAT 250 schillings***
= Preis inkl. MWS S *or* öS 250,—
= Preis inklusive Mehrwertsteuer 250 Schilling

***Special offer 18 Swiss francs 90 centimes***
= Sonderangebot sfr *or* sFr 18,90

## British money

***one penny = 1p***
= ein Penny

***five pence = 5p***
= fünf Pence

***one pound fifty [pence] = £1.50***
= ein Pfund fünfzig [Pence]

***eight pounds thirty-four pence = £8.34***
= acht Pfund vierunddreißig Pence

***one thousand two hundred and fifty pounds or twelve hundred and fifty pounds = £1 250***
= [ein]tausendzweihundertfünfzig Pfund *or* zwölfhundertfünfzig Pfund

***a five-pound note***
= ein Fünfpfundschein

***a pound coin***
= ein Pfundstück

***a 50 pence piece***
= ein Fünfzigpencestück

## American money

| | | |
|---|---|---|
| ***one cent*** | = 1c | = ein Cent |
| ***five cents*** | = 5c | = fünf Cent |
| ***one dollar*** | = \$1 *or* \$1.00 | = ein Dollar |
| ***one dollar fifty*** | = \$1.50 | = ein Dollar fünfzig [Cent] |

***a ten dollar bill***
= ein Zehndollarschein

***a dollar bill***
= ein Dollarschein

***a dollar coin***
= ein Dollarstück

***a dime, a ten cent piece***
= ein Zehncentstück

***a quarter, a twenty-five cent piece***
= ein Vierteldollarstück

## Other money phrases

***What or How much does it cost?***
= Was *or* Wie viel kostet das?

***It costs just under/just over £950***
= Es kostet knapp 950/etwas über 950 Pfund

***The potatoes are 30p a pound***
= Die Kartoffeln kosten 30 Pence das Pfund

***\$100 in cash***
= 100 Dollar in bar

***Can I pay by cheque/by credit card?***
= Kann ich mit Scheck/mit Kreditkarte zahlen?

***a cheque for £50***
= ein Scheck über 50 Pfund

***a dollar/sterling traveller's cheque*** or (Amer.) ***traveler's check***
= ein Reisescheck in Dollar/Pfund [Sterling]

***Can you change or give me change for a 20 mark note?***
= Können Sie mir einen 20-Mark-Schein wechseln *or* auf einen 20-Mark-Schein herausgeben?

***I want to change marks into dollars***
= Ich will Mark in Dollar wechseln

***Our pounds are hardly worth anything***
= Unsere Pfunde sind kaum etwas wert

Notice again that the plural form of the various currencies is the same as the singular. The one exception is the use of the plural form with an ending in examples such as the last one (here "Pfunde" – one can also talk of "Schillinge" and "Franken", but marks are always **Mark**).

**monopoly** /məˈnɒpəlɪ/ *n.* Ⓐ (*Econ.*) Monopol, *das* (**of** auf + *Akk.*, für); Ⓑ (*exclusive possession*) alleiniger Besitz; **have a ~ on sth.** ein Monopol auf etw. (*Akk.*) haben; **you can't have a ~ on the car** du kannst das Auto nicht ständig mit Beschlag belegen; Ⓒ (*thing monopolized*) Monopol, *das;* Ⓓ **M~, (P)** (*game*) Monopoly Ⓦⓩ, *das*

**monorail** /ˈmɒnəreɪl/ *n.* Ⓐ (*single rail*) Einschienengleis, *das;* Ⓑ (*vehicle*) Einschienenbahn, *die;* Ⓒ (*overhead*) Schwebebahn, *die*

**monosyllabic** /mɒnəsɪˈlæbɪk/ *adj.* Ⓐ einsilbig ‹Antwort, Person›; aus einsilbigen Wörtern bestehend ‹Rede, Dichtung, Schrift, Sprache›; Ⓑ (*Ling.*) monosyllabisch

**monosyllable** /ˈmɒnəsɪləbl/ *n.* Ⓐ einsilbiges Wort; **speak** *or* **talk/answer in ~s** einsilbig reden/antworten; Ⓑ (*Ling.*) Einsilber, *der*

**monotheism** /ˈmɒnəθiːɪzm/ *n.* (*Relig.*) **[doctrine of/belief in] ~:** Monotheismus, *der*

**monotheistic** /mɒnəθiːˈɪstɪk/ *adj.* (*Relig.*) monotheistisch

**monotone** /ˈmɒnətəʊn/ ❶ *n.* Ⓐ gleich bleibender Ton; Ⓑ (*uniformity*) (*general*) Einerlei, *das;* (*of colour*) Einfarbigkeit, *die;*

(*of style*) eintöniger *od.* monotoner Stil; **grey ~:** graues Einerlei; **engravings in ~:** einfarbige Stiche. ❷ *adj.* A (*monotonous*) eintönig, monoton ‹Geräusch, Sprache, Akzent, Rezitation›; B (*in one colour*) einfarbig

**monotonous** /mə'nɒtənəs/ *adj.* eintönig, monoton ‹Laut, Leben, Landschaft usw.›

**monotonously** /mə'nɒtənəslɪ/ *adv.* eintönig

**monotonousness** /mə'nɒtənəsnɪs/, **monotony** /mə'nɒtənɪ/ *ns.* Eintönigkeit, *die;* Monotonie, *die*

**monoxide** /mə'nɒksaɪd/ *n.* (*Chem.*) Monoxid, *das;* Monoxid, *das* (*fachspr.*)

**Monseigneur** /mɔ̃se'njɜ:(r)/ *n., pl.* **Messeigneurs** /mese'njɜ:(r)/ Monseigneur, *der*

**Monsignor** /mɒn'si:njɔ:(r)/ *n., pl.* **~i** /mɒnsi:'njɔ:ri:/ (*Eccl.*) Monsignore, *der*

**monsoon** /mɒn'su:n/ *n.* (*Geog.*) A (*wind*) **summer** *or* **wet/dry ~:** Sommer-/Wintermonsun, *der;* B (*season*) Regenzeit, *die*

**monster** /'mɒnstə(r)/ ❶ *n.* A (*imaginary or huge creature*) Ungeheuer, *das;* Monster, *das;* (*huge thing*) Ungetüm, *das;* Monstrum, *das;* **a ~ of a fish/car** ein Ungeheuer/Ungetüm von einem Fisch/Auto; **that's a real ~!, what a ~!** (*in surprise or admiration*) das ist ja ungeheuer!; B (*inhuman person*) Unmensch, *der;* (*iron.: naughty child*) Monster, *das* (*scherzh.*). ❷ *adj.* riesig; monströs; Mammut‹sitzung, -veranstaltung›

**monstrance** /'mɒnstrəns/ *n.* (*RC Ch.*) Monstranz, *die*

**monstrosity** /mɒn'strɒsɪtɪ/ *n.* A (*physical deformity*) Missbildung, *die;* (*deviation from the norm, unnatural thing*) Abnormität, *die;* Widernatürlichkeit, *die;* B (*outrageous thing*) Ungeheuerlichkeit, *die;* (*hideous building etc.*) Ungetüm, *das;* C (*imaginary or huge creature*) Ungeheuer, *das;* Monster, *das*

**monstrous** /'mɒnstrəs/ *adj.* A (*huge*) monströs (*geh.*); ungeheuer ‹Lärm, Jubel, Menge›; riesig ‹Lkw, Kuchen, Buch›; unnatürlich groß ‹Gemüse, Person, Baum, Pflanze›; B (*outrageous*) ungeheuerlich (*abwertend*) ‹Vorschlag, Vorstellung, Glaube, Einstellung, Wahl, Entscheidung›; C (*atrocious*) scheußlich; monströs (*meist abwertend*); D (*misshapen*) missgestaltet

**monstrously** /'mɒnstrəslɪ/ *adv.* A (*hugely*) schrecklich (*ugs.*), furchtbar (*ugs.*) ‹hoch, beschäftigt, kurz, dick›; B (*outrageously*) unmöglich (*ugs. meist abwertend*) ‹sich benehmen›

**mons Veneris** /mɒnz 'venərɪs/ *n.* (*Anat.*) Venushügel, *der* (*fachspr.*); weiblicher Schamberg

**montage** /mɒn'tɑ:ʒ/ *n.* (*Photog., Art, Radio, Film*) Montage, *die;* (*Mus.*) Collage, *die;* **work in ~:** Montagen herstellen

**month** /mʌnθ/ *n.* ▶ 1055 A Monat, *der;* **last day of the ~:** Monatsletzte, *der;* Ultimo, *der* (*Kaufmannsspr.*); **on the last day of the ~:** ultimo; am Monatsletzten; **the ~ of January** der [Monat] Januar; **come every ~:** jeden Monat kommen; **for a ~/several ~s** einen Monat [lang]/mehrere Monate [lang] *od.* monatelang; **for ~s [on end]** monatelang; **I haven't seen him for ~s** ich habe ihn seit Monaten nicht mehr gesehen; **~s ago** vor Monaten; **every six ~s** alle sechs Monate; halbjährlich; **once every** *or* **a ~:** einmal monatlich *od.* im Monat; **in a ~['s time]** in einem Monat; **in two ~s[' time]** in zwei Monaten; **in alternate ~s** alle zwei Monate; **take a ~'s holiday** [sich (*Dat.*)] einen Monat Urlaub nehmen; **£10 a** *or* **per ~:** zehn Pfund im Monat; **from ~ to ~:** Monat um *od.* für Monat; **she is in the third/last ~ of her pregnancy** sie ist im dritten/neunten Monat schwanger; **a ~ from today** heute in einem Monat; **a three-~ period** ein Zeitraum von drei Monaten; **a six-~[s]-old baby/strike** ein sechs Monate altes *od.* sechsmonatiges Baby/ein bereits sechsmonatiger Streik; ⇒ *also* **calendar** A; **next** 1 B; **Sunday** 1 A; **this** 1 E; B (*period of 28 days*) vier Wochen; 28 Tage

**'month-long** *attrib. adj.* einmonatig

**monthly** /'mʌnθlɪ/ ❶ *adj.* A (*of or relating to a month*) monatlich; Monats‹umsatz, -einkommen, -gehalt›; **three-~:** dreimonatlich; vierteljährlich; B (*lasting a month*) einmonatig ‹Abstand›; Monats‹zyklus, -karte›; **three-~ season ticket** Dreimonats- *od.* Vierteljahreskarte, *die;* C (*happening every month*) monatlich; (*happening once a month*) [ein]monatlich; **a woman's ~ period** die Periode *od.* Monatsblutung einer Frau. ❷ *adv.* [ein]monatlich; einmal im Monat. ❸ *n.* (*publication*) monatlich erscheinende Zeitschrift; Monatsschrift, *die*

**monument** /'mɒnjʊmənt/ *n.* A Denkmal, *das;* ⇒ *also* **ancient** 1 B; B (*on grave*) Grabmal, *das* (*geh.*); C **the M~** *in der Londoner Innenstadt stehende Säule zur Erinnerung an den großen Brand von 1666*

**monumental** /mɒnjʊ'mentl/ *adj.* A (*of a monument*) Denkmals‹architekt, -inschrift›; B (*massive*) gewaltig ‹Auffahrt, Skulptur›; monumental ‹Plastik, Gemälde, Gebäude›; C (*extremely great*) kolossal (*ugs.*)

**monumentally** /mɒnjʊ'mentəlɪ/ *adv.* enorm ‹stur, schlau, kreativ›; **~ boring/stupid** sterbenslangweilig/strohdumm

**monumental 'mason** *n.* Steinmetz, *der*

**moo** /mu:/ ❶ *n.* Muhen, *das;* **give** *or* **utter a loud ~:** laut muhen. ❷ *v.i.* muhen

**mooch** /mu:tʃ/ (*coll.*) ❶ *v.i.* **~ about** *or* **around/along** herumschleichen (*ugs.*)/zockeln (*ugs.*). ❷ *v.t.* (*Amer.*) A (*steal*) mopsen (*fam.*); B (*beg*) schnorren (*ugs.*)

**'moo-cow** *n.* (*child lang.*) Muhkuh, *die* (*Kinderspr.*)

**mood**[1] /mu:d/ *n.* A (*state of mind*) Stimmung, *die;* **there was a [general] ~ of optimism** es herrschte allgemeiner Optimismus; **be in a very good/good/bad ~:** [bei] bester/guter/schlechter Laune sein; **be in a cheerful ~:** froh gelaunt *od.* fröhlich gestimmt sein; **be in a militant ~:** in Kampfstimmung sein; **be in a serious/pensive ~:** ernst/nachdenklich gestimmt sein; **be in no ~ for joking/dancing** nicht zum Scherzen/Tanzen aufgelegt sein;; **I'm not in the ~:** ich hab keine Lust dazu; B (*fit of melancholy or bad temper*) Verstimmung, *die;* schlechte Laune; **have one's ~s** [seine] Launen haben

**mood**[2] *n.* (*Ling.*) Modus, *der* (*fachspr.*); Aussageweise, *die;* **the subjunctive ~:** der Konjunktiv (*fachspr.*); die Möglichkeitsform

**moodily** /'mu:dɪlɪ/ *adv.* übel gelaunt; missgestimmt; (*in a sullen manner*) missmutig; verdrossen

**'mood music** *n.* stimmungsvolle Musik

**moody** /'mu:dɪ/ *adj.* A (*sullen*) missmutig; verdrossen; (*gloomy*) niedergeschlagen; B (*subject to moods*) launenhaft

**moon** /mu:n/ ❶ *n.* A Mond, *der;* **light of the ~:** Mondlicht, *das;* Mondschein, *der;* **the ~ is full/waning/waxing** es ist Vollmond/abnehmender/zunehmender Mond; **there is no ~ tonight** heute Nacht ist der Mond nicht zu sehen; **be over the ~** (*fig. coll.*) im siebten Himmel sein (*ugs.*); **offer sb. the ~** (*fig.*) jmdm. ein Vermögen bieten; **promise sb. the ~** (*fig.*) jmdm. das Blaue vom Himmel versprechen (*ugs.*); **ask for the ~:** Unmögliches verlangen; ⇒ *also* **blue moon**; **cry** 3 A; **full moon**; **half moon**; **man** 1 B; **new moon**; **shoot** 2 D; B (*poet.: month*) Mond, *der* (*dichter. veralt.*); C **that was many ~s ago** das liegt schon lange zurück. ❷ *v.i.* (*coll.*) **~ about** *or* **around [the house]** trübselig [im Haus] herumschleichen (*ugs.*)

**~ over** *v.t.* in Gedanken an ... (*Akk.*) verloren *od.* versunken *od.* vertieft sein

**moon: ~beam** *n.* Mondstrahl, *der;* **~beams** Mondschein, *der;* Mondlicht, *das;* **~face** *n.* Mondgesicht, *das*

**Moonie** /'mu:nɪ/ *n.* (*coll.*) Anhänger der Mun-Sekte

**moon: ~ landing** *n.* Mondlandung, *die;* **~less** *adj.* mondlos ‹Nacht, Himmel›; **~light** ❶ *n.* Mondlicht, *das;* Mondschein, *der;* ❷ *attrib. adj.* mondhell (*geh.*) ‹Nacht›; **do a ~light [flit]** (*Brit. coll.*) bei Nacht und Nebel wegziehen, ohne die Schulden zu bezahlen; ❸ *v.i.* (*coll.*) nebenberuflich abends arbeiten; (*hold two jobs at once*) zwei Jobs gleichzeitig haben; **~lit** *adj.* mondbeschienen (*geh.*); **~shine** *n.* A (*visionary ideas*) Unsinn, *der;* B (*liquor*) schwarz gebrannter Alkohol; **~shine whisky** schwarz gebrannter Whiskey; **~shot** *n.* (*Astronaut.*) Mondflug, *der;* **~stone** *n.* (*Min.*) Mondstein, *der;* Adular, *der* (*fachspr.*)

**moor**[1] *n.* A (*Geog.*) [Hoch]moor, *das;* B (*for shooting*) *im Moor gelegenes Wildhegegebiet*

**moor**[2] ❶ *v.t.* festmachen; vertäuen. ❷ *v.i.* festmachen

**Moor** /mʊə(r), mɔ:(r)/ *n.* Maure, *der*/Maurin, *die*

**'moorhen** *n.* (*Ornith.*) [Grünfüßiges] Teichhuhn

**mooring** /'mʊərɪŋ, 'mɔ:rɪŋ/ *n.* A *usu. in pl.* (*means of attachment*) Vertäuung, *die;* B *usu. in pl.* (*place*) Anlegestelle, *die;* **set sail from one's ~:** ablegen; C (*action of making fast*) Vertäuung, *die*

**mooring: ~ line** *n.* Festmacher, *der;* **~-mast** ⇒ **mast**[1]; **~ post** *n.* Pfahl, *der;* ≈ Duckdalben, *der;* **~ rope** *n.* Festmachetrosse, *die*

**Moorish** /'mʊərɪʃ, 'mɔ:rɪʃ/ *adj.* maurisch

**moorland** /'mʊələnd, 'mɔ:lənd/ *n.* (*Geog.*) Moorland, *das*

**moose** /mu:s/ *n., pl. same* (*Zool.*) Amerikanischer Elch

**moot** /mu:t/ ❶ *adj.* umstritten; offen ‹Frage›; strittig ‹Punkt›. ❷ *v.t.* (*broach, suggest*) zur Sprache bringen ‹Maßnahme, Plan›; anschneiden ‹Thema›; erörtern ‹Frage, Punkt›

**mop** /mɒp/ ❶ *n.* A Mopp, *der;* (*for washing up*) ≈ Spülbürste, *die;* (*Naut.*) Dweil, *der;* **Mrs M~[p]** (*Brit.*) [die/unsere] Parkettkosmetikerin (*ugs. scherzh.*); B **~ [of hair]** Wuschelkopf, *der.* ❷ *v.t.*, **-pp-** A (*clean with mop*) moppen ‹Fußboden›; B (*wipe*) abwischen ‹Träne, Schweiß, Stirn›; C **~ the floor with sb.** (*fig. coll.*) jmdn. fertig machen (*ugs.*)

**~ 'up** *v.t.* A (*wipe up*) aufwischen ‹Flüssigkeit›; **here's some bread to ~ up the gravy** hier ist etwas Brot, um die Soße vom Teller zu wischen; B (*Brit. coll.*) (*drink greedily*) wegschlabbern (*ugs.*) ‹Getränk›; (*eat greedily*) reinstopfen (*ugs.*) ‹Essen›; C (*Mil.*) ausheben ‹Widerstandsnest›; aufreiben ‹versprengte Truppen›; säubern ‹Gebiet›

**'mopboard** *n.* (*Amer.*) Fußleiste, *die*

**mope** /məʊp/ *v.i.* Trübsal blasen (*ugs.*); **~ about** *or* **around** trübselig herumschleichen (*ugs.*)

**moped** /'məʊped/ *n.* Moped, *das*

**'mophead** *n.* A (*at end of mop*) Mopp, *der;* B (*of hair; person*) Wuschelkopf, *der* (*ugs.*)

**Mopp** ⇒ **mop** 1 A

**moppet** /'mɒpɪt/ *n.* A (*endearing: baby, little girl*) Fratz, *der* (*fam.*); B (*coll.: child*) Matz, *der* (*fam.*)

**moquette** /mɒ'ket/ *n.* (*Textiles*) Mokett, *der* (*fachspr.*); Möbelplüsch aus Wolle

**moraine** /mə'reɪn/ *n.* (*Geol.*) Moräne, *die*

**moral** /'mɒrl/ ❶ *adj.* A (*of right and wrong*) moralisch ‹Gefühl, Bewusstsein›; sittlich ‹Wert›; Moral‹begriff, -prinzip, -vorstellung›; B (*dealing with regulation of conduct*) moralisch ‹Erzählung, Rede›; Lehr‹gedicht, -stück›; C (*concerned with rules of morality*) Moral‹philosoph[ie], -psychologie›; D (*virtuous*) moralisch, sittlich, (*veralt.*) tugendhaft ‹Leben, Person›; E (*founded on ~ law*) moralisch, sittlich ‹Verpflichtung, Pflicht›; **be under a ~ obligation** eine moralische *od.* sittliche Pflicht haben; F (*not physical*) moralisch ‹Stärke, Zusammenbruch›.
❷ *n.* A (*lesson*) Moral, *die;* **draw the ~ from sth.** die Lehre aus etw. ziehen; B *in pl.* (*habits*) Moral, *die;* Moralvorstellungen *Pl.;* C (*maxim*) Moral, *die;* Lehre, *die;* **point a ~:** einen moralischen Grundsatz aufstellen

**moral: ~ 'certainty** *n.* **it is a ~ certainty [that ...]** es ist so gut wie sicher[, dass ...]; **~ 'courage** *n.* Rückgrat, *das;* Zivilcourage, *die;* **~ 'cowardice** *n.* Mangel an Rückgrat *od.* Zivilcourage

m

**morale** /mə'rɑ:l/ Moral, *die;* **high/low ~:** gute/schlechte Moral

**mo'rale-booster** *n.* **be a** *or* **work** *or* **act as a ~ for sb.** jds. Moral heben *od.* stärken

**moralise** ⇒ **moralize**

**moralist** /'mɒrəlɪst/ *n.* **A** (*one who practises morality*) moralischer *od.* sittlicher Mensch; **B** (*philosopher*) Moralist, *der*/Moralistin, *die;* Moralphilosoph, *der*/Moralphilosophin, *die*

**moralistic** /mɒrə'lɪstɪk/ *adj.* moralistisch

**morality** /mə'rælɪtɪ/ *n.* **A** (*conduct*) Moral, *die;* Sittlichkeit, *die;* Moralität, *die* (*geh.*); **B** (*moral science*) Moralphilosophie, *die;* Ethik, *die;* Sittenlehre, *die;* **C** *in pl.* (*moral principles*) Moralgesetze *Pl.;* Moralprinzipien *Pl.;* **D** (*particular system*) Ethik, *die;* **E** (*conformity to moral principles*) Sittlichkeit, *die;* Moralität, *die* (*geh.*); **F** (*Hist., Lit.*) **~ [play]** Moralität, *die*

**moralize** /'mɒrəlaɪz/ *v.i.* moralisieren (*geh.*); moralische Betrachtungen anstellen (**[up]on** über + *Akk.*); **do stop moralizing!** hör auf mit deinen Moralpredigten!

**moral 'law** *n.* Moralgesetz, *das*

**morally** /'mɒrəlɪ/ *adv.* **A** (*as regards right and wrong*) moralisch ‹verantwortlich›; **B** (*virtuously*) moralisch einwandfrei, integer ‹sich benehmen›; **C** (*virtually*) praktisch, so gut wie ‹sicher›; **D** (*not physically*) moralisch; psychisch

**moral: ~ 'majority** *n. vermutete Mehrheit, die für strengere öffentliche Moral eintritt;* **~ phi'losophy** *n.* Moralphilosophie, *die;* **~ 'pressure** *n.* moralischer Druck; **~ 'sense** *n.* moralisches *od.* sittliches Bewusstsein; **~ sup'port** *n.* moralische Unterstützung; **~ the'ology** *n.* Moraltheologie, *die;* **~ 'victory** *n.* moralischer Sieg

**morass** /mə'ræs/ *n.* **A** (*bog*) Morast, *der;* **B** (*fig.: entanglement*) Wirrnis, *die* (*geh.*); Labyrinth, *das;* **a ~ of confusion** heillose Verwirrung

**moratorium** /mɒrə'tɔ:rɪəm/ *n., pl.* **~s** *or* **moratoria** /mɒrə'tɔ:rɪə/ **A** vorläufige Einstellung (**on** *Gen.*); [vorläufiger] Stopp (**on** für); **declare a ~ on sth.** etw. vorläufig einstellen *od.* stoppen; **B** (*authorized delay*) Moratorium, *das*

**Moravia** /mə'reɪvɪə/ *pr. n.* Mähren (*das*)

**morbid** /'mɔ:bɪd/ *adj.* **A** (*unwholesome, having such feelings*) krankhaft; makaber, (*geh.*) morbid ‹Freude, Faszination, Fantasie, Neigung›; **B** (*coll.: melancholy*) trübselig; **make sb. feel ~:** jmdn. trübselig machen; **C** (*Med.*) pathologisch (*fachspr.*) ‹Anatomie›; krankhaft ‹Zustand, Veränderung›; krank ‹Körper›; pathogen (*fachspr.*) ‹Substanz›

**morbidity** /mɔ:'bɪdɪtɪ/ *n., no pl.* **A** Krankhaftigkeit, *die;* **B** (*Med.*) (*diseased state*) Krankheit, *die;* (*rate of sickness*) Morbidität, *die* (*fachspr.*)

**morbidly** /'mɔ:bɪdlɪ/ *adv.* **A** (*Med.*) krankhaft; **B** (*coll.: in melancholy way*) trübselig

**mordant** /'mɔ:dənt/ *adj.* bissig ‹Bemerkung, Rede›; beißend ‹Humor›; sarkastisch ‹Person›

**more** /mɔ:(r)/ ❶ *adj.* **A** (*additional*) mehr; **would you like any** *or* **some/a few ~?** (*apples, books, etc.*) möchten Sie noch welche/ein paar?; **would you like any** *or* **some ~ apples?** möchten Sie noch Äpfel?; **would you like any** *or* **some/a little ~?** (*tea, paper, etc.*) möchten Sie noch etwas/ein wenig?; **would you like any** *or* **some ~ tea/paper?** möchten Sie noch Tee/Papier?; **I haven't any ~ [apples/tea]** ich habe keine [Äpfel]/keinen [Tee] mehr; **~ and ~:** immer mehr; **offer ~ coffee** noch Kaffee anbieten; **for a few dollars ~:** für ein paar Dollar mehr; **[just] one ~ thing before I go** [nur] noch eins, bevor ich gehe; **one ~ word and ...:** noch ein Wort und ...; **many ~ things** noch viel mehr [Dinge]; **two/twenty ~ things** noch zwei/zwanzig Dinge; **some ~ things** noch einige Dinge; noch einiges; **B** (*greater in degree*) größer; **~'s the pity** leider!; **the ~ fool 'you** du bist vielleicht ein Dummkopf.

❷ *n., no pl., no indef. art.* **A** (*greater amount or number or thing*) mehr; **he is ~ of a poet than a musician** er ist mehr Dichter als Musiker; **~ and ~:** mehr und mehr; immer mehr; **six or ~:** mindestens sechs; **I hope to see ~ of you** hoffentlich sehen wir uns öfter; **the ~ the merrier** ⇒ **merry** A; **B** (*additional number or amount or thing*) mehr; **what is ~ ...:** außerdem ...; **do no ~ than do sth.** nur etw. tun; **~ means worse** ein Mehr an Zahl heißt ein Weniger an Qualität; **water is no ~ than thawed ice** Wasser ist nichts weiter *od.* anderes als aufgetautes Eis; **and ~:** mindestens *vorangestellt;* oder mehr; **there's plenty ~ where that came from** es ist noch viel mehr da; man braucht keineswegs zu geizen; **there's no need to do/say [any] ~:** da braucht nichts weiter getan/gesagt zu werden; ⇒ *also* **say** 1 A; **C** **~ than** (*coll.: exceedingly*) über‹satt, -glücklich, -froh›; hoch‹erfreut, -willkommen›; sehr ‹aufgeregt›; tief‹traurig›; **at least you enjoyed yourself, which is ~ than I did** im Gegensatz zu mir *od.* anders als ich hast du dich wenigstens noch amüsiert; **which is ~ than you** *or* **one can say of X** und das kann man nicht von X behaupten; **neither ~ nor less [than ridiculous** *etc.*] [lächerlich *usw.*,] nicht mehr und nicht weniger.

❸ *adv.* **A** mehr ‹mögen, interessieren, gefallen, sich wünschen›; *forming compar.* **a ~ interesting book** ein interessanteres Buch; **this book is ~ interesting** dieses Buch ist interessanter; **~ often** häufiger; **~ than a little tiresome** ziemlich langweilig; **~ than anything [else]** vor allem; **~ than sb. can say** mehr als jmd. sagen kann; **B** (*nearer, rather*) eher; **~ ... than ...:** eher ... als ...; **~ dead than alive** mehr tot als lebendig; **C** **you couldn't be ~** (*are extremely*) **mistaken** *or* **wrong** du irrst dich gewaltig; **I couldn't be ~** (*am extremely*) **sorry** es tut mir schrecklich leid; **D** (*again*) wieder; **never ~:** nie wieder *od.* mehr; **not any ~:** nicht mehr; **once ~:** noch einmal; **a couple of times ~:** noch ein paarmal; **E** **~ and ~ ...:** mehr und mehr *od.* immer mehr ...; *with adj. or adv.* immer ... (+ *Komp.*); **become ~ and ~ absurd** immer absurder werden; **F** **~ or less** (*fairly*) mehr oder weniger; (*approximately*) annähernd; **G** **~ so** noch mehr; **Is she equally attractive? — Rather ~ so, if anything** Ist sie genauso attraktiv? — Ja, wenn nicht noch attraktiver; **the ~ so because ...:** umso mehr, als *od.* weil ...; **H** **not any ~ [than]** nicht mehr [als]. ⇒ *also* **like**[1] 1 A; **little** 3 B; **no**[1] 2 A; **the** 2; **what** 6 A

**moreish** /'mɔ:rɪʃ/ *adj.* (*coll.*) lecker; **this cake is rather ~:** dieser Kuchen schmeckt nach mehr

**morel** /mə'rel/ *n.* (*Bot.: edible fungus*) [Speise]morchel, *die*

**morello** /mə'reləʊ/ *n., pl.* **~s** (*Bot.*) Schattenmorelle, *die*

**moreover** /mɔ:'rəʊvə(r)/ *adv.* und außerdem; zudem (*geh.*)

**mores** /'mɔ:ri:z, 'mɔ:reɪz/ *n. pl.* Sitten *Pl.;* **sexual ~:** Sexualethik *od.* -moral, *die*

**morganatic** /mɔ:gə'nætɪk/ *adj.* morganatisch; **~ marriage** morganatische Ehe; Ehe zur linken Hand (*hist.*)

**morgue** /mɔ:g/ *n.* **A** ⇒ **mortuary**; **B** (*Journ.*) Archiv, *das*

**moribund** /'mɒrɪbʌnd/ *adj.* (*lit. or fig.*) moribund (*Med.*); dem Tode geweiht (*geh.*); im Sterben liegend ‹Person›; im Aussterben begriffen ‹Spezies›; dem Untergang geweiht ‹Nation, Volk, Brauch›

**Mormon** /'mɔ:mən/ ❶ *n.* Mormone, *der*/Mormonin, *die;* **Book of ~:** Buch Mormon. ❷ *adj.* mormonisch

**morn** /mɔ:n/ *n.* **A** (*poet.: morning*) Morgen, *der;* **from ~ to** *or* **till night** von früh bis spät; **B** (*poet.: dawn*) Morgengrauen, *das*

**mornay** /'mɔ:neɪ/ *n.* (*Gastr.*) Sauce Mornay, *die* (*eine Käsesoße*)

**morning** /'mɔ:nɪŋ/ *n.* **A** ▶ **1012**, ▶ **1056** Morgen, *der;* (*as opposed to afternoon*) Vormittag, *der;* **this ~:** heute Morgen *od.* früh; **tomorrow ~:** morgen früh; **during the ~:** am Morgen/Vormittag; **[early] in the ~:** am [frühen] Morgen; (*regularly*) [früh] morgens; **at one** *etc.* **in the ~ = at one a.m.** *etc.* ⇒ **a.m.** 1; **begin next morning:** am anderen Morgen beginnen; **on Wednesday ~s/~:** Mittwoch morgens/[am] Mittwochmorgen *od.* Mittwoch früh; **one ~:** eines Morgens; **the other ~:** neulich morgens *od.* früh; **~, noon, and night** Tag und Nacht; **~ came** es wurde Morgen; **~s, of a ~:** morgens; ⇒ *also* **good** 1 M; **B** **in the ~** (*coll.: next ~*) morgen früh; **see you in the ~!** bis morgen früh!; **C** (*spent in a particular way*) **a ~ of shopping** ein mit Einkaufen verbrachter Morgen; **D** ▶ **1191** (*coll. greeting*) **~, all!** Morgen, zusammen!; **E** (*fig.*) Anfang, *der;* Beginn, *der;* **F** *attrib.* morgendlich; Morgen‹kaffee, -spaziergang›

**morning: ~ 'after** *n.* (*coll.: hangover*) **~-'after [feeling]** Katzenjammer, *der;* Kater, *der;* **~-'after pill** *n.* Pille [für den Morgen] danach; **~ coat** *n.* Cut[away], *der;* **~ dress** *n.* Stresemann, *der;* **~ 'glory** *n.* (*Bot.*) Winde, *die;* **~ 'paper** *n.* Morgenzeitung, *die;* **~ 'prayer** *n.* Morgenandacht, *die;* **~ 'service** *n.* (*Eccl.*) Morgenandacht, *die;* (*RC Ch.*) Frühmesse, *die;* **~ sickness** *n.* morgendliche Übelkeit; **~ 'star** *n.* Morgenstern, *der*

**Moroccan** /mə'rɒkən/ ▶ **1340** ❶ *adj.* marokkanisch; **sb. is ~:** jmd. ist Marokkaner/Marokkanerin. ❷ *n.* Marokkaner, *der*/Marokkanerin, *die*

**morocco** *n., pl.* **~s** Maroquin, *der*

**Morocco** /mə'rɒkəʊ/ *pr. n.* Marokko (*das*)

**moron** /'mɔ:rɒn/ *n.* **A** (*coll.*) Trottel, *der* (*ugs. abwertend*); Schwachkopf, *der* (*ugs.*); **B** (*mental defective*) Geistesschwache, *der/die;* Schwachsinnige, *der/die*

**moronic** /mə'rɒnɪk/ *adj.* geistesschwach; schwachsinnig; debil (*fachspr.*)

**morose** /mə'rəʊs/ *adj.,* **morosely** /mə'rəʊslɪ/ *adv.* verdrießlich

**morpheme** /'mɔ:fi:m/ *n.* (*Ling.*) Morphem, *das*

**morphia** /'mɔ:fɪə/, **morphine** /'mɔ:fi:n/ *ns.* Morphin, *das* (*fachspr.*); Morphium, *das;* **be a ~ addict** morphiumsüchtig sein

**morphing** /'mɔ:fɪŋ/ *n., no pl.* (*Cinemat., Computing*) Morphing, *das*

**morphological** /mɔ:fə'lɒdʒɪkl/ *adj.* (*Biol., Ling.*) morphologisch

**morphology** /mɔ:'fɒlədʒɪ/ *n.* **A** (*Biol.*) Morphologie, *die;* Gestaltlehre, *die;* **B** (*Ling.*) Morphologie, *die* (*fachspr.*); Formen- und Wortbildungslehre, *die*

**morris** /'mɒrɪs/: **~ dance** *n.* Moriskentanz, *der;* **~ dancer** *n.* Moriskentänzer, *der;* **~ dancing** *n.* Moriskentanzen, *das*

**morrow** /'mɒrəʊ/ *n.* (*literary*) **the ~** (*the next day*) der folgende *od.* kommende Tag; **on the ~:** tags drauf; am nächsten Tag. ⇒ *also* **good** 1 M

**Morse** /mɔ:s/ *n.* ▶ **1275** Morseschrift, *die;* Morsezeichen *Pl.;* **can you use ~?** können Sie morsen?

**Morse 'code** *n.* Morseschrift, *die;* Morsealphabet, *das*

**morsel** /'mɔ:sl/ *n.* **A** (*of food*) Bissen, *der;* Happen, *der;* **B** (*fragment*) Stückchen, *das;* Bröckchen, *das;* (*fig.*) Quäntchen, *das*

**mortal** /'mɔ:tl/ ❶ *adj.* **A** (*that must die*) sterblich; **B** (*fatal, fought to the death, intense*) tödlich (**to** für); **~ combat** ein Kampf auf Leben und Tod; **give ~ offence to sb.** jmdn. tödlich beleidigen; **~ sin** Todsünde, *die;* **C** (*implacable*) tödlich; erbittert; **~ enemy** Todfeind, *der;* **D** (*coll.: whatsoever*) **every ~ thing** alles Menschenmögliche; **E** (*accompanying death*) Todes‹strudel, -kampf, -angst›; **F** (*human, earthly*) vergänglich; irdisch ‹Dasein›; menschlich ‹Verlangen, Geist›. ❷ *n.* Sterbliche, *der/die;* **be a mere ~:** auch nur ein Mensch sein

**mortality** /mɔ:'tælɪtɪ/ *n.* **A** Sterblichkeit, *die;* **B** (*loss of life*) [Dahin]sterben, *das;* **C** (*number of deaths*) Sterblichkeit, *die;* Todesfälle *Pl.;* Mortalität, *die* (*Med.*); **D** **~ [rate]** Sterblichkeitsrate, *die;* Sterbeziffer, *die;* Mortalität, *die* (*Med.*)

**mortally** /ˈmɔːtəlɪ/ *adv.* **A** ~ **wounded** tödlich verletzt; **B** (*intensely*) ~ **offended** zutiefst *od.* tödlich beleidigt

**mortar** /ˈmɔːtə(r)/ *n.* **A** (*substance*) Mörtel, *der;* **B** (*vessel*) Mörser, *der;* **C** (*cannon*) Minenwerfer, *der;* Mörser, *der*

ˈ**mortarboard** *n.* (*Univ.*) *bei bestimmten Anlässen zum Talar getragene viereckige Kopfbedeckung der Studenten und Lehrer an britischen und amerikanischen Universitäten;* ≈ Barett, *das*

**mortgage** /ˈmɔːɡɪdʒ/ **1** *n.* **A** Hypothek, *die;* **B** (*deed*) Pfandverschreibung, *die;* Hypothekenbrief, *der;* **C** *attrib.* Hypotheken‹schuld, -zinssatz, -darlehen, -geld›; ~ **repayment** Hypothekenzahlung, *die.* **2** *v.t.* **A** mit einer Hypothek *od.* hypothekarisch belasten; **B** (*pledge*) verpfänden

**mortgagee** /mɔːɡɪˈdʒiː/ *n.* Hypothekar, *der;* Hypothekengläubiger, *der*

**mortgager** /ˈmɔːɡɪdʒə(r)/, **mortgagor** /mɔːɡɪˈdʒɔː(r)/ *n.* Hypothekenschuldner, *der*

**mortice** ⇒ **mortise**

**mortician** /mɔːˈtɪʃn/ *n.* ▶ **1261** (*Amer.*) Leichenbestatter, *der*/-bestatterin, *die*

**mortification** /mɔːtɪfɪˈkeɪʃn/ *n.* (*humiliation*) Beschämung, *die;* Kränkung, *die;* **feel great** ~ **at sth.** etw. als eine große Schmach empfinden; tief beschämt über etw. (*Akk.*) sein

**mortify** /ˈmɔːtɪfaɪ/ *v.t.* **A** (*humiliate*) beschämen; kränken; **he felt mortified** er empfand es als beschämend; **B** (*subdue desires of*) ~ **the flesh/oneself** sich kasteien

**mortise** /ˈmɔːtɪs/ *n.* **A** (*Woodw.*) Zapfenloch, *das;* ~ **and tenon [joint]** Zapfenverbindung, *die;* Verzapfung, *die;* **B** *attrib.* ~ **lock** Steckschloss, *das*

**mortuary** /ˈmɔːtjʊərɪ/ *n.* Leichenschauhaus, *das*

**mosaic** /məʊˈzeɪɪk/ *n.* (*lit. or fig.*) Mosaik, *das; attrib.* Mosaik‹fußboden, -arbeit, -stein usw.›

**Moscow** /ˈmɒskəʊ/ ▶ **1626** **1** *pr. n.* Moskau (*das*). **2** *attrib. adj.* Moskauer

**moselle** *n.* (*wine*) Mosel[wein], *der*

**Moselle** /məʊˈzel/ *pr. n.* ▶ **1480** Mosel, *die*

**Moses** /ˈməʊzɪz/ *pr. n.* (*Bibl.*) Moses (*der*); Mose (*der*) (*ökum.*)

**Moslem** /ˈmɒzləm/ ⇒ **Muslim**

**mosque** /mɒsk/ *n.* Moschee, *die*

**mosquito** /mɒsˈkiːtəʊ/ *n., pl.* ~**es** Stechmücke, *die;* (*in tropics*) Moskito, *der;* ~ **bite** Mücken-/Moskitostich, *der*

**mos**ˈ**quito net** *n.* Moskitonetz, *das*

**moss** /mɒs/ *n.* **A** Moos, *das;* **B** (*Scot., N. Engl.: bog*) Moor, *das;* Sumpf, *der*

**moss:** ~**-covered** *adj.* bemoost; moosbedeckt; ~**-green** *adj.* moosgrün

**mossy** /ˈmɒsɪ/ *adj.* moosig; bemoost; moosbewachsen

**most** /məʊst/ **1** *adj.* (*in greatest number, the majority of*) die meisten; (*in greatest amount*) meist...; größt... ‹Fähigkeit, Macht, Bedarf, Geduld, Lärm›; **make the** ~ **mistakes/noise** die meisten Fehler/den meisten *od.* größten Lärm machen; ~ **people** die meisten Leute; die Mehrheit [der Leute]; **he has the** ~ **need of it** er braucht es am nötigsten; **for the** ~ **part** größtenteils; zum größten Teil.
**2** *n.* **A** (*greatest amount*) das meiste; **offer [the]** ~ **for it** das meiste *od.* am meisten dafür bieten; **pay the** ~**:** am meisten bezahlen; **want sth. the** ~**:** sich (*Dat.*) etw. am meisten wünschen; **the** ~ **one can say** das Beste, was man sagen kann; **B** (*the greater part*) ~ **of the girls** die meisten Mädchen; ~ **of his friends** die meisten seiner Freunde; ~ **of the poem** der größte Teil des Gedichts; ~ **of the time** die meiste Zeit; (*on* ~ *occasions*) meistens; **lead for** ~ **of the race** während des größten Teils des Rennens führen; **be more enterprising than** ~**:** unternehmungslustiger als die meisten anderen sein; ~ **of what he said** das meiste von dem, was er sagte; **C** **make the** ~ **of sth., get the** ~ **out of sth.** etw. voll ausschöpfen; (*employ to the best advantage*) etw. voll ausnützen; (*represent at its best*) das Beste aus etw. machen; **D** **at [the]** ~**:** höchstens; **at the very** ~**:** allerhöchstens.
**3** *adv.* **A** (*more than anything else*) am meisten ‹mögen, interessieren, gefallen, sich wünschen, verlangt›; ~ **of all** am allermeisten; **B** *forming superl.* **the** ~ **interesting book** das interessanteste Buch; **this book is the** ~ **interesting** dieses Buch ist das interessanteste; ~ **probably** höchstwahrscheinlich; ~ **often** am häufigsten; **C** (*exceedingly*) überaus; äußerst; ~ **decidedly** ganz entschieden; ausgesprochen; ~ **certainly** ohne jeden Zweifel; **D** (*Amer. coll.: almost*) fast

**mostly** /ˈməʊstlɪ/ *adv.* (*most of the time*) meistens; (*mainly*) größtenteils; hauptsächlich

**MOT** /eməʊˈtiː/ ⇒ **MOT test**

**mote** /məʊt/ *n.* **the** ~ **in sb.'s eye** (*fig. dated*) die Schwächen anderer

**motel** /məʊˈtel/ *n.* Motel, *das*

**motet** /məʊˈtet/ *n.* (*Mus.*) Motette, *die*

**moth** /mɒθ/ *n.* Nachtfalter, *der;* (*in clothes*) Motte, *die;* **[the]** ~ (*collect.*) die [Kleider]motten *Pl.*

**moth:** ~**ball** **1** *n.* Mottenkugel, *die;* **in** ~**balls** (*fig.: stored*) eingemottet ‹Kleidung›; (*Mil.*) eingelagert, eingemottet ‹Schiffe, Waffen›; beiseite geschoben ‹Plan, Projekt›; **put sth. in** ~**balls** etw. einmotten; **2** *v.t.* einmotten ‹Kleider, alte Sachen, Vorschlag›; einlagern, einmotten ‹militärisches Gerät›; beiseite schieben ‹Plan, Projekt›; ~**-eaten** *adj.* von Motten zerfressen; vermottet; (*fig.: antiquated*) verstaubt ‹Idee, Politik›; altmodisch ‹Person, System›

**mother** /ˈmʌðə(r)/ **1** *n.* **A** Mutter, *die;* **she is a** *or* **the** ~ **of six [children]** sie ist Mutter von sechs Kindern; **like** ~ **used to make** ‹Essen› wie bei Muttern (*ugs.*); **every** ~**'s son [of you]** jeder Einzelne [von euch]; ~ **animal** Muttertier, *das;* ~ **hen** Glucke, *die;* ⇒ *also* **expectant** B; **B** (*Relig.*) **M**~ **Superior** Äbtissin, *die;* **C** (*fig.: source*) Ursprung, *der;* Wurzel, *die;* **necessity is the** ~ **of invention** (*prov.*) Not macht erfinderisch (*Spr.*). **2** *v.t.* **A** großziehen ‹Familie›; hervorbringen ‹Idee, Gerücht›; **B** (*over-protect*) bemuttern

**mother:** **M**~ **Church** *n.* **A** /ˈ---/ Mutterkirche, *die;* **B** /--ˈ-/ (*authority*) Mutter Kirche *o. Art.;* die Kirche; ~ **country** *n.* Mutterland, *das;* ~**craft** *n., no pl.* Kinderpflege, *die;* ~ ˈ**earth** *n.* Mutter Erde; ~ **fixation** *n.* (*Psych.*) Mutterbindung, *die;* **M**~ ˈ**Goose rhyme** *n.* (*Amer.*) Kinderreim, *der*

**motherhood** /ˈmʌðəhʊd/ *n., no pl.* Mutterschaft, *die*

**Mothering Sunday** /ˈmʌðərɪŋ sʌndɪ/ (*Brit. Eccl.*) ⇒ **Mother's Day**

**mother:** ~**-in-law** *n., pl.* ~**s-in-law** Schwiegermutter, *die;* ~**-in-law's** ˈ**tongue** *n.* (*Bot.*) Bajonettpflanze, *die;* Frauenzunge, *die;* ~**land** *n.* Vaterland, *das;* Heimatland, *das*

**motherless** /ˈmʌðəlɪs/ *adj.* mutterlos; **the child was left** ~**:** das Kind verlor seine Mutter

**motherly** /ˈmʌðəlɪ/ *adj.* mütterlich; ~ **love** Mutterliebe, *die*

**mother:** **M**~ **of** ˈ**God** *n.* Mutter Gottes, *die;* Muttergottes, *die;* ~**-of-**ˈ**pearl** *n.* Perlmutt, *das;* ~**'s boy** *or* **darling** *n.* (*coll. derog.*) Muttersöhnchen, *das* (*ugs.*); **M**~**'s Day** *n.* Muttertag, *der;* ~**s'** ˈ**meeting** *n.* (*Brit.*) Müttertreffen [der Pfarrgemeinde], *das;* (*fig.*) aufgeregte Debatte; ~ ˈ**tongue** *n.* Muttersprache, *die;* ~ **wit** *n.* Mutterwitz, *der*

**moth:** ~ **hole** *n.* Mottenloch, *das;* ~**proof** **1** *adj.* mottenfest; **2** *v.t.* mottenfest machen

**motif** /məʊˈtiːf/ *n.* **A** Motiv, *das;* **B** (*on goods*) Markenzeichen, *das;* **the BMW** ~**:** das BMW-Zeichen; **C** (*Mus.*) [Leit]motiv, *das;* **D** (*on clothing*) Applikation, *die* (*fachspr.*); Aufnäher, *der*

**motion** /ˈməʊʃn/ **1** *n.* **A** (*movement*) Bewegung, *die;* Gang, *der;* **be in** ~**:** in Bewegung sein; sich bewegen; ‹Maschine:› laufen; ‹Fahrzeug:› fahren; **set** *or* **put sth. in** ~ (*lit. or fig.*) etw. in Bewegung *od.* Gang setzen; ⇒ *also* **perpetual motion; slow motion**; **B** (*gesture*) Bewegung, *die;* Wink, *der;* **make a** ~ **to sb. to do sth.** jmdm. ein Zeichen geben, etw. zu tun; **a** ~ **of the hand** ein Zeichen mit der Hand; eine Handbewegung; **C** (*formal proposal; also Law*) Antrag, *der;* **put forward** *or* **propose a** ~**:** einen Antrag stellen; **D** (*of bowels*) Stuhlgang, *der;* **have** *or* **make a** ~**:** Stuhlgang haben; **E** *in sing. or pl.* (*faeces*) Stuhl, *der;* **F** (*manner of moving*) [Körper]haltung, *die;* **G** (*change of posture*) Bewegung, *die;* **make a** ~ **to leave** Anstalten machen wegzugehen; **H** **go through the** ~**s of doing sth.** (*simulate*) so tun, als ob man etw. täte; (*do superficially*) etw. pro forma tun; **go through the** ~**s** (*simulate*) nur so tun; (*do superficially*) es nur pro forma tun.
**2** *v.t.* ~ **sb. to do sth.** jmdm. bedeuten (*geh.*) *od.* winken, etw. zu tun; ~ **sb. to[wards]/away from sth.** jmdm. bedeuten (*geh.*), zu etw. [hin]zugehen/von etw. wegzugehen; ~ **sb. aside/to a seat** jmdn. zur Seite winken/jmdm. bedeuten (*geh.*), Platz zu nehmen.
**3** *v.i.* winken; ~ **to sb. to come in** jmdn. hereinwinken; ~ **to** *or* **for sb. to do sth.** jmdm. bedeuten (*geh.*), etw. zu tun

**motionless** /ˈməʊʃnlɪs/ *adj.* reg[ungs]los; bewegungslos; unbewegt ‹See, Teich›; **be/stay** *or* **remain** ~**:** sich nicht bewegen

ˈ**motion picture** *n.* (*esp. Amer.*) Film, *der; attrib.* Film-

**motivate** /ˈməʊtɪveɪt/ *v.t.* **A** (*be motive of, stimulate*) motivieren; **B** (*cause to act*) ~ **sb. to do sth.** jmdn. veranlassen, etw. zu tun

**motivation** /məʊtɪˈveɪʃn/ *n.* **A** (*process*) Motivierung, *die;* **give/receive** ~**:** motivieren/motiviert werden; **B** (*incentive*) Motivation, *die* (**for** zu); Anreiz, *der;* **C** (*condition*) Motiviertheit, *die;* Motivation, *die;* **have good/poor** *or* **little** ~**:** sehr/wenig motiviert sein

**motive** /ˈməʊtɪv/ **1** *n.* **A** Motiv, *das;* Beweggrund, *der;* **the** ~ **for the crime** das Tatmotiv; **do sth. from** ~**s of kindness** etw. aus Freundlichkeit tun; **B** ⇒ **motif** A, C. **2** *adj.* (*moving to action*) treibend ‹Geist, Kraft›; (*productive of motion*) Antriebs-

**motiveless** /ˈməʊtɪvlɪs/ *adj.* unmotiviert

ˈ**motive power** *n.* Antriebskraft, *die*

**mot juste** /məʊ ˈʒuːst/ *n., pl.* **mots justes** /məʊ ˈʒuːst/ treffender *od.* passender Ausdruck

**motley** /ˈmɒtlɪ/ **1** *adj.* **A** [bunt] gescheckt; (*multicoloured*) [kunter]bunt; **B** (*varied*) bunt gemischt; bunt ‹Auswahl›; ⇒ *also* **crew** 1 B. **2** *n.* (*Hist.: jester's dress*) Narrenkostüm, *das;* Narrenkleid, *das*

**motocross** /ˈməʊtəʊkrɒs/ *n., no pl., no art.* Motocross, *das*

**motor** /ˈməʊtə(r)/ **1** *n.* **A** (*machine*) Motor, *der;* **B** (*Brit.:* ~ *car*) Auto, *das.* **2** *adj.* **A** (*driven by engine or* ~) Motor‹schlitten, -mäher, -jacht usw.›; **B** (*of* ~ *vehicles*) Kraftfahrzeug‹ersatzteile, -mechaniker, -verkehr, -motor›. **3** *v.t.* (*Brit.*) fahren. **4** *v.i.* (*Brit.*) [mit dem Auto] fahren

**Motorail** /ˈməʊtəreɪl/ *n.* (*Brit.*) Autoreisezug, *der*

**motor:** ~**bike** (*coll.*) ⇒ **motorcycle**; ~ **boat** *n.* Motorboot, *das*

**motorcade** /ˈməʊtəkeɪd/ *n.* Fahrzeug- *od.* Wagenkolonne, *die*

**motor:** ~ **car** *n.* (*Brit.*) Kraftfahrzeug, *das;* Automobil, *das* (*geh.*); ~ **caravan** *n.* (*Brit.*) Caravan, *der;* Wohnmobil, *das;* ~ **cycle** *n.* Motorrad, *das;* Kraftrad, *das* (*Amtsspr.*); *attrib.* ~**cycle combination** (*Brit.*) Motorrad mit Beiwagen; ~**cyclist** *n.* Motorradfahrer, *der*/-fahrerin, *die;* ~ **home** *n.* Reisemobil, *das;* ~ **industry** *n.* Kraftfahrzeugindustrie, *die*

**motoring** /ˈməʊtərɪŋ/ *n.* (*Brit.*) Autofahren, *das;* ~ **correspondent** Motorjournalist, *der;* /-journalistin, *die;* **school of** ~**:** Fahrschule, *die;* ~ **offence** Verstoß gegen die [Straßen]verkehrsordnung; ~ **organisation** Automobilklub, *der*

**motorise** ⇒ **motorize**

**motorist** /ˈməʊtərɪst/ *n.* Autofahrer, *der*/-fahrerin, *die*

**motorize** /ˈməʊtəraɪz/ *v.t.* motorisieren

**motor:** ~**man** *n.* Wagenführer, *der;* ~ **nerve** *n.* (*Anat.*) motorischer Nerv; ~ **racing** *n.* Autorennsport, *der;* ~ **scooter** ⇒ **scooter** B; ~ **show** *n.* Auto[mobil]ausstellung, *die;*

m

~ **trade** *n.* Kraftfahrzeughandel, *der;* ~ **vehicle** *n.* Kraftfahrzeug, *das;* ~**way** *n.* (*Brit.*) Autobahn, *die*

**motte** /mɒt/ *n.* Motte, *die* (*fachspr.*); Erdhügelburg, *die*

**MO'T test** *n.* (*Brit.*) ≈ TÜV, *der*

**mottle** /'mɒtl/ *v.t.* sprenkeln

**mottled** /'mɒtld/ *adj.* gesprenkelt

**motto** /'mɒtəʊ/ *n., pl.* ~**es** Ⓐ Motto, *das;* **my ~ is 'live and let live'** meine Devise ist „leben und leben lassen"; Ⓑ (*in cracker*) Spruch, *der;* Ⓒ (*Mus.*) Leitmotiv, *das*

**moufflon** /'mu:flən/ *n.* (*Zool.*) Mufflon, *der*

**mould**[1] /məʊld/ *n.* Ⓐ (*earth*) Erde, *die;* Ⓑ (*upper soil*) [Mutter]boden, *der*

**mould**[2] ❶ *n.* Ⓐ (*hollow*) Form, *die;* (*Metallurgy*) Kokille, *die;* (*Plastics*) Pressform, *die;* (*Papermaking*) Schöpfform, *die;* **break the ~ of sth.** (*fig.*) neue Wege in etw. (*Dat.*) gehen; Ⓑ (*Cookery: hollow utensil*) [Kuchen-/Back-/Pudding]form, *die;* Ⓒ (*fig.*) Wesensart, *die;* **be cast in heroic/pedantic** *etc.* ~: von heldischer/pedantischer *usw.* Wesensart sein. ❷ *v.t.* formen (**out of, from** aus); ~ **sth. into a certain shape** etw. in bestimmter Weise formen; ~ **sb. into a fine character/person** einen feinen Menschen aus jmdm. machen

**mould**[3] *n.* (*Bot.*) Schimmel, *der;* (*in Roquefort, Stilton, etc. cheese*) Edelschimmelpilz, *der;* **grow [a]/get ~:** schimmlig werden

**moulder** /'məʊldə(r)/ *v.i.* ~ **[away]** (*lit. or fig.*) [ver]modern

**moulding** /'məʊldɪŋ/ *n.* Ⓐ (*process of forming, lit. or fig.*) Formen, *das;* Ⓑ (*object*) Formteil, *das* (**of, in** aus); Formling, *der* (*fachspr.*); (*Archit.*) Zierleiste, *die;* Ⓒ (*wooden strip*) Leiste, *die*

**mouldy** /'məʊldɪ/ *adj.* (*overgrown with mould*) schimmlig ‹Lebensmittel›; verschimmelnd, [ver]modernd ‹Buch, Vorhang, Teppich›; **a ~ smell** ein Modergeruch; **become** *or* **grow** *or* **get** *or* **go ~:** verschimmeln; schimmlig werden

**moult** /məʊlt/ ❶ *v.t.* Ⓐ (*Ornith.*) verlieren ‹Federn, Gefieder›; Ⓑ (*Zool.*) verlieren ‹Haar›; abstreifen ‹Haut›; abwerfen ‹Horn, Geweih›. ❷ *v.i.* ‹Vogel:› sich mausern; ‹Hund, Katze:› sich haaren; ‹Schlange, Krebs usw.:› sich häuten. ❸ *n.* (*of bird*) Mauser, *die;* (*of snake, crab, etc.*) Häutung, *die*

**mound** /maʊnd/ *n.* Ⓐ (*of earth*) Hügel, *der;* (*of stones*) Steinhaufen, *der;* **defensive ~:** Verteidigungshügel, *der;* **burial** *or* **sepulchral** *or* **grave ~:** Grabhügel, *der;* Ⓑ (*hillock*) Anhöhe, *die;* Ⓒ (*heap*) Haufen, *der;* Ⓓ (*Baseball*) [erhöhtes] Wurfmal

**mount** /maʊnt/ ❶ *n.* Ⓐ (*mountain, hill*) Berg, *der;* **M~ Vesuvius/Everest** der Vesuv/der Mount Everest; ⇒ *also* **sermon** A; Ⓑ (*animal*) Reittier, *das;* (*horse*) Pferd, *das;* Ⓒ (*of picture, photograph*) Passepartout, *das;* (*backing*) Unterlage, *die;* Ⓓ (*for gem*) Fassung, *die;* Ⓔ (*Philat.*) [Klebe]falz, *der.*

❷ *v.t.* Ⓐ (*ascend*) hinaufsteigen ‹Treppe, Leiter, Stufe›; steigen auf (+ *Akk.*) ‹Plattform, Berg, Kanzel›; besteigen ‹Thron›; Ⓑ (*get on*) steigen auf (*Akk.*) ‹Reittier, Fahrzeug›; *abs.* aufsitzen; ~ **the pavement** auf den Bürgersteig fahren; Ⓒ (*place on support*) montieren (**on** auf + *Akk.*); Ⓓ (*prepare*) aufstellen ‹Maschine, Apparat›; präparieren ‹Exemplar, Haut, Skelett›; (*fasten*) in ein Album einkleben ‹Briefmarke›; (*for microscope*) fixieren; (*raise into position*) in Stellung bringen ‹Kanone, Geschütz, Mörser›; Ⓔ (*Art*) aufziehen ‹Bild usw.›; [ein]fassen ‹Edelstein usw.›; Ⓕ (*put on stage*) inszenieren ‹Stück, Show, Oper›; organisieren ‹Festspiele, Ausstellung›; Ⓖ (*carry out*) durchführen ‹Angriff, Operation usw.›; ⇒ *also* **guard** 1 B, D; Ⓗ (*for copulation*) bespringen ‹Tier›; besteigen (*salopp*) ‹Frau›.

❸ *v.i.* Ⓐ (*move up, rise in rank*) aufsteigen; Ⓑ ~ **[up]** (*fig.: increase*) steigen (**to** auf + *Akk.*); ‹Unruhe, Besorgnis, Unwillen:› wachsen; **it all ~s up** es summiert sich

**mountain** /'maʊntɪn/ *n.* Ⓐ (*lit. or fig.*) Berg, *der;* **in the ~s** im Gebirge; **~s high** (*fig.*) berg[e]hoch; **~s of books** (*fig.*) Berge von Büchern; **butter/grain** *etc.* ~ (*fig.*) Butter-/Getreideberg *usw., der;* **move ~s** (*fig.*) Berge versetzen; Himmel und Hölle in Bewegung setzen; ⇒ *also* **molehill**; Ⓑ *attrib.* Gebirgs-; ~ **lake** Bergsee, *der*

**mountain:** ~ **'ash** *n.* (*Bot.*) Eberesche, *die;* ~ **bike** *n.* Mountainbike, *das;* ~ **chain** *n.* (*Geog.*) Gebirgskette, *die*

**mountaineer** /maʊntɪ'nɪə(r)/ *n.* ▶ 1261 Bergsteiger, *der*/Bergsteigerin, *die*

**mountaineering** /maʊntɪ'nɪərɪŋ/ *n.* Bergsteigen, *das;* ~ **expedition/party** Bergpartie, *die*/Seilschaft, *die; attrib.* ~ **experience** bergsteigerische Erfahrung; ~ **equipment/club** Bergsteigerausrüstung, *die*/-verein, *der*

**mountain 'goat** *n.* Schneeziege, *die*

**mountainous** /'maʊntɪnəs/ *adj.* Ⓐ (*characterized by mountains*) gebirgig; Ⓑ (*huge*) riesig ‹Gegenstand, Welle›; riesenhaft ‹Person›; groß ‹Leistung›

**mountain:** ~ **'railway** *n.* [Schienen]bergbahn, *die;* ~ **'range** *n.* Gebirgszug, *der;* ~ **'road** *n.* Gebirgsstraße, *die;* ~ **sickness** *n.* Höhenkrankheit, *die;* ~**side** *n.* [Berg]hang, *der;* ~ **top** *n.* Berggipfel, *der*

**mountebank** /'maʊntɪbæŋk/ *n.* Ⓐ (*derog.: quack*) Quacksalber, *der* (*abwertend*); Ⓑ (*derog.: charlatan*) Scharlatan, *der* (*abwertend*)

**mounted** /'maʊntɪd/ *adj.* Ⓐ (*on animal*) beritten; Ⓑ (*on support*) montiert ‹Gerät›; aufgezogen ‹Stich›; (*for display*) präpariert ‹Tier›

**Mountie** /'maʊntɪ/ *n.* (*coll.*) Mountie, *der; berittener kanadischer Polizist*

**mounting** /'maʊntɪŋ/ *n.* Ⓐ (*of performance*) Inszenierung, *die;* (*of programme*) Durchführung, *die;* Ⓑ (*support*) (*Art: of drawing*) Passepartout, *das;* (*backing*) Unterlage, *die;* (*of engine, axle, etc.*) Aufhängung, *die* (*Technik*)

**Mount of 'Olives** *pr. n.* Ölberg, *der*

**mourn** /mɔ:n/ ❶ *v.i.* Ⓐ (*feel sorrow or regret*) trauern; ~ **for** *or* **over** trauern um ‹Toten›; nachtrauern (+ *Dat.*) ‹Jugend, Augenlicht, Haustier›; betrauern ‹Verlust, Missgeschick›; Ⓑ (*observe conventions of ~ing*) trauern; Trauer tragen. ❷ *v.t.* betrauern; nachtrauern ‹etw. Verlorenem›

**mourner** /'mɔ:nə(r)/ *n.* Ⓐ (*one who mourns*) Trauernde, *der/die;* Trauergast, *der;* Ⓑ (*person hired to attend funeral*) (*man*) Klagemann, *der;* (*woman*) Klageweib, *das*

**mournful** /'mɔ:nfl/ *adj.* traurig, bitter ‹Träne›; klagend ‹Stimme, Ton, Schrei, Geheul›; trauervoll (*geh.*) ‹Person›

**mournfully** /'mɔ:nfəlɪ/ *adv.* traurig; klagend ‹sprechen, tönen›

**mourning** /'mɔ:nɪŋ/ *n.* Ⓐ (*clothes*) Trauer[kleidung], *die;* **be [dressed] in** *or* **wear/put on** *or* **go into ~:** Trauer tragen/anlegen; ⇒ *also* **deep mourning**; Ⓑ (*sorrowing, lamentation*) Trauer, *die;* (*period*) Trauer[zeit], *die;* **a national day of ~:** eintägige Staatstrauer

**mouse** /maʊs/ ❶ *n., pl.* **mice** /maɪs/ Ⓐ Maus, *die;* **as quiet as a ~:** ganz leise; mucksmäuschenstill (*fam.*) ‹dasitzen›; (*by nature*) sehr still; ⇒ *also* **cat** A; **church mouse**; Ⓑ (*fig.: timid person*) Angsthase, *der* (*ugs.*); **a man or a ~:** ein Mann oder ein Schwächling; Ⓒ (*Computing*) Maus, *die.* ❷ *v.i.* mausen; **go mousing** auf Mäusejagd gehen

**mouse:** ~ **button** *n.* (*Computing*) Maustaste, *die;* ~ **click** *n.* (*Computing*) Mausklick, *der;* ~**-coloured** *adj.* mausfarben; mausgrau; ~ **hole** *n.* Mauseloch, *das;* ~ **mat** *n.* (*Computing*) Mauspad, *das;* ~ **pointer** *n.* (*Computing*) Mauszeiger, *der*

**mouser** /'maʊsə(r)/ *n.* Mäusefänger, *der*

**'mousetrap** *n.* Ⓐ Mausefalle, *die;* Ⓑ (*joc.: cheese*) billiger *od.* einfacher Käse

**moussaka** /mʊ'sɑ:kə/ *n.* (*Gastr.*) Moussaka, *die*

**mousse** /mu:s/ *n.* Mousse, *die*

**moustache** /mə'stɑ:ʃ/ *n.* Schnurrbart, *der*

**mousy** /'maʊsɪ/ *adj.* Ⓐ (*nondescript*) mattbraun ‹Haar›; Ⓑ (*timid*) scheu ‹Blick, Wesen›

**mouth** ❶ /maʊθ/ *n., pl.* ~**s** /maʊðz/ Ⓐ ▶ 966 (*of person*) Mund, *der;* (*of animal*) Maul, *das;* **his ~ quivered/twitched/moved** seine Lippen zitterten/zuckten/bewegten sich; **hit sb. in the ~:** jmdn. auf den Mund schlagen; **with one's ~ open** mit offenem Mund; **keep one's ~ shut** (*fig. sl.*) die *od.* seine Klappe halten (*salopp*); **put one's money where one's ~ is** (*fig. coll.*) seinen Worten Taten folgen lassen; **shut sb.'s ~** (*fig. sl.*) jmdm. den Mund stopfen (*ugs.*); **with one's ~ full** mit vollem Mund; **my ~ feels dry** ich habe einen trockenen Mund; **out of sb.'s own ~** (*fig.*) aus jmds. eigenem Mund; von jmdm. selbst; **hear sb. say sth. out of his own ~:** hören, wie jmd. etw. selbst sagt; **out of the ~s of babes [and sucklings]!** (*fig.*) Kindermund tut Wahrheit kund (*Spr.*); **put words into sb.'s ~:** jmdm. etwas in den Mund legen; (*misrepresent*) jmdm. das Wort im Munde [her]umdrehen; **have got many ~s to feed** viele hungrige Mäuler zu stopfen haben (*ugs.*); **take the words out of sb.'s ~:** jmdm. das Wort aus dem Mund *od.* von der Zunge nehmen; **go** *or* **be passed** *or* **be spread from ~ to ~:** von Mund zu Mund gehen; Ⓑ (*fig.*) (*entrance to harbour*) [Hafen]einfahrt, *die;* (*of valley, gorge, mine, burrow, tunnel, cave*) Eingang, *der;* (*of well*) Loch, *das;* (*of volcano*) Krater, *der;* (*of bottle, cannon*) Mündung, *die;* (*of pocket, womb, pit*) Öffnung, *die;* Ⓒ ▶ 1480 (*of river*) Mündung, *die.* ⇒ *also* **down**[3] 1 DD; **open** 1 A, 3 A; **shoot off** 1; **water** 3 B; **word** 1 D.

❷ /maʊð/ *v.t.* Ⓐ (*declaim*) schwülstig vortragen ‹Gedicht, Rede, Zitat, Satz›; Ⓑ (*express by silent lip-movement*) mit Lippenbewegungen sagen; ~ **sth. to oneself** etw. unhörbar vor sich (*Akk.*) hin sagen.

❸ /maʊð/ *v.i.* Ⓐ (*grimace*) den Mund verziehen; Ⓑ (*move lips silently*) lautlos die Lippen bewegen; ~ **to oneself** unhörbar vor sich (*Akk.*) hin sprechen

**mouthful** /'maʊθfʊl/ *n.* Ⓐ (*bite*) Mundvoll, *der;* (*of solid food*) Bissen, *der;* (*of drink*) Schluck, *der;* **a ~ of abuse** ein Schwall Schimpfwörter; Ⓑ (*small quantity*) **a ~:** ein Bisschen; Ⓒ (*sth. difficult to say*) Zungenbrecher, *der* (*ugs.*); Ⓓ (*Amer. coll.: sth. important*) etwas Wichtiges

**mouth:** ~ **organ** *n.* Mundharmonika, *die;* ~**piece** *n.* Ⓐ (*Mus., Med.; for cigar[ette], pipe*) Mundstück, *das;* (*of telephone*) Sprechmuschel, *die;* Ⓑ (*speaker for others*) Sprachrohr, *das;* **act as the ~piece** Sprachrohr sein; ~**-to-~ resusci'tation** *n.* Wiederbelebung durch Mund-zu-Mund-Beatmung; ~**wash** *n.* Mundwasser, *das;* ~**-watering** *adj.* appetitlich ‹Essen, Geruch, Anblick›; lecker ‹Essen, Geruch, Geschmack›

**movable** /'mu:vəbl/ *adj.* Ⓐ (*capable of being moved*) beweglich ‹Möbel, Teppich, Regal›; Ⓑ (*Law*) beweglich ‹Vermögen, Güter›; (*Scot. Law*) nicht vererbbar. ⇒ *also* **doh**; **feast** 1 A

**move** /mu:v/ ❶ *n.* Ⓐ (*change of residence*) Umzug, *der;* (*change of job*) **after three years with the same firm it was time for a ~:** nach drei Jahren bei derselben Firma war es Zeit, sich (*Dat.*) eine neue Stelle zu suchen; Ⓑ (*action taken*) Schritt, *der;* (*Footb. etc.*) Spielzug, *der;* Ⓒ (*turn in game*) Zug, *der;* (*fig.*) [Schach]zug, *der;* **make a ~:** ziehen; **it's your ~:** du bist am Zug; Ⓓ **be on the ~** (*moving about*) ‹Person:› unterwegs *od.* (*ugs.*) auf Achse sein; ‹Tier, Tramp:› umherziehen; (*progressing*) ‹Land usw.:› sich weiterentwickeln; ‹Person:› vorankommen; Ⓔ **make a ~** (*initiate action*) etwas tun *od.* unternehmen; (~ *from motionless position*) sich rühren; (*rise from table*) aufstehen; (*coll.: leave, depart*) losziehen (*ugs.*); **make the first ~:** den Anfang machen; **make no ~:** sich nicht rühren; **make no ~ to help sb.** keine Anstalten machen, jmdm. zu helfen; Ⓕ **get a ~ on** (*coll.*) einen Zahn zulegen (*ugs.*); **get a ~ on!** (*coll.*) [mach] Tempo! (*ugs.*).

❷ *v.t.* Ⓐ (*change position of*) bewegen; wegräumen ‹Hindernis, Schutt›; (*transport*) befördern; ~ **the chair over here** rück den Stuhl hier herüber!; ~ **sth. somewhere else** etw. anderswohin tun; ~ **sth. from the spot/its place** etw. von der Stelle/seinem Platz wegnehmen; ~ **sth. to a new position** etw. an einen neuen Platz bringen; ~ **house** umziehen; ~ **the furniture about** umräumen; **who has ~d my papers?** wer war an meinen Papieren?; **please ~ your car** bitte fahren Sie Ihr Auto weg; ~ **the luggage/equipment into the building** das Gepäck/die Ausrüstung ins Gebäude hineinbringen; **not ~ a muscle** sich nicht rühren; ~ **one's/sb.'s bowels** Stuhlgang haben/jmds. Verdauung in Gang bringen; **please ~ your head [to one side]** bitte tun Sie Ihren Kopf zur Seite; **please ~ your legs out of the way** bitte nehmen Sie Ihre Beine aus dem Weg; ~ **it!** (*coll.*) Beeilung! (*ugs.*); ~ **yourself!** (*coll.*) Beeilung! (*ugs.*); ~ **sb. to another department/job** jmdn. in eine andere Abteilung/Position versetzen; **the residents were ~d out of the area** die Bewohner wurden aus dem Gebiet evakuiert; ~ **one's child to a different school** sein Kind in eine andere Schule schicken; **the patient was ~d to a different ward** der Patient wurde in eine andere Abteilung verlegt; ~ **police/troops into an area** Polizeikräfte/Truppen in ein Gebiet schicken; ~ **sb. into new accommodation** jmdn. in eine neue Unterkunft bringen lassen; **B** (*in game*) ziehen; **C** (*put or keep in motion*) bewegen; in Marsch setzen ‹Truppe›; auseinander treiben ‹Demonstranten›; in Bewegung setzen ‹Mechanismus›; **D** (*provoke*) erregen ‹Ärger, Eifersucht, Begierde›; wecken ‹Ehrgeiz, Hass›; hervorrufen ‹Gelächter›; ~ **sb. to laughter** jmdn. zum Lachen bringen; ~ **sb. to anger** jmds. Ärger erregen; **E** (*affect*) bewegen; berühren; ~ **sb. to tears** jmdn. zu Tränen rühren; ~ **sb. to pity/compassion** jmds. Mitleid erregen; **be ~d to pity/compassion** vor Mitleid ergriffen sein; **be ~d by sth.** über etw. (*Akk.*) gerührt sein; **F** (*prompt*) ~ **sb. to do sth.** jmdn. dazu bewegen, etw. zu tun; **he was ~d by this** *or* **this ~d him to do it** das bewog ihn dazu, es zu tun; ~ **sb. to action** jmdn. aktivieren *od.* mobilisieren; **I shall not be ~d** ich bleibe dabei; **sb. is not to be ~d** jmd. lässt sich nicht erschüttern; **G** (*propose*) beantragen ‹Beendigung, Danksagung›; stellen ‹Antrag›; ~ **that sth. should be done** beantragen, dass etw. getan wird; **H** (*make formal application to*) einen Antrag stellen bei ‹Gericht usw.›; **I** (*Commerc.: sell*) absetzen. **3** *v.i.* **A** (*go from place to place*) sich bewegen; (*by car, bus, train*) fahren; (*on foot*) gehen; (*coll.: start, leave*) gehen; ‹Wolken:› ziehen (**across** über + *Akk.*); ~ **with the times** (*fig.*) mit der Zeit gehen; **it's time we got moving** es ist Zeit aufzubrechen; **get moving!** beeil dich!; **start to ~** ‹Fahrzeug:› sich in Bewegung setzen; **nobody ~d** niemand rührte sich von der Stelle; **keep moving!** bewegt euch!; (~ *on*) gehen Sie bitte weiter; **Don't ~. You're not in the way** Bleiben Sie sitzen/stehen. Sie sind nicht im Weg; **he has ~d to another department** er ist jetzt in einer anderen Abteilung; **Don't ~. I'll be back soon** Bleib hier *od.* Geh nicht weg. Ich bin gleich zurück; **in which direction are your thoughts moving?** in welche Richtung gehen Ihre Gedanken?; **B** (*in games*) ziehen; **it's your turn to ~:** du bist am Zug; **White to ~** (*Chess*) Weiß zieht; **C** (*fig.: initiate action*) handeln; aktiv werden; ~ **quickly** *etc.* **to do sth.** schnell *usw.* handeln und etw. tun; **D** (*be socially active*) (*in certain circles, part of society, part of town*) verkehren; (*in certain part of country*) sich aufhalten; **E** (*change residence or accommodation*) umziehen (**to** nach); (*into flat etc.*) einziehen (**into** in + *Akk.*); (*out of town*) wegziehen (**out of** aus); (*out of flat etc.*) ausziehen (**out of** aus); **I want to ~ to London** ich will nach London ziehen; **I hate moving** ich hasse Umzüge; **F** (*change posture or state*) sich bewegen; (*in order to make oneself comfortable etc.*) eine andere Haltung einnehmen; **don't ~ or I'll shoot** keine Bewegung, oder ich schieße; **nobody/nothing ~d** niemand/nichts rührte sich; ~ **aside to make room** zur Seite gehen/rücken, um Platz zu machen; ~ **back/forward in one's seat** sich auf seinem Sitz zurücklehnen/vorbeugen; **have your bowels ~d?** hatten Sie Stuhlgang?; haben Sie abgeführt?; **lie without moving** regungslos daliegen; **G** (*operate*) ‹Maschine:› laufen; ‹Pendel:› schwingen; **H** (*make progress*) vorankommen; **get things moving** vorankommen; **things are moving now** jetzt geht es voran; ~ **towards** näher kommen (+ *Dat.*) ‹Einigung, Höhepunkt, Kompromiss›; ~ **away from** abrücken von ‹Standpunkt›; ~ **in the direction of sth.** sich auf etw. (*Akk.*) zubewegen; **I** (*Commerc.: be sold*) ‹Waren:› Absatz finden, sich absetzen lassen; **J** (*coll.: go fast*) **that car can really ~:** der Wagen ist enorm schnell (*ugs.*); **that's really moving!** das nenn ich Tempo! (*ugs.*)

~ **a'bout** **1** *v.i.* zugange sein; (*travel*) unterwegs sein; **I need more room to ~ about** ich brauche mehr Bewegungsfreiheit *od.* Spielraum. **2** *v.t.* herumräumen ‹Möbel, Bücher›; herumschieben ‹Teile einer Collage›

~ **a'long** **1** *v.i.* **A** gehen/fahren; **B** (*make room*) Platz machen; ~ **along, please!** gehen/fahren Sie bitte weiter!; (*on bus etc.*) bitte weiter [durch]gehen! **2** *v.t.* zum Weitergehen/-fahren auffordern

~ **a'round** ⇒ ~ **about**

~ **'in** **1** *v.i.* **A** einziehen; (*to start work*) ‹Bauarbeiter:› kommen; **B** (*come closer*) ‹Truppen, Polizeikräfte:› anrücken; ‹Kamera:› näher herangehen; ~ **in on** ‹Truppen, Polizeikräfte:› vorrücken gegen; ~ **in on a new market** beginnen, sich auf einem neuen Markt zu etablieren. **2** *v.t.* einrücken lassen ‹Truppen, Polizeikräfte›; hineinbringen ‹Gepäck, Ausrüstung›

~ **'off** *v.i.* sich in Bewegung setzen

~ **'on** **1** *v.i.* weitergehen/-fahren; (*leave job*) sich verändern; ~ **on to another question** (*fig.*) zu einer anderen Frage übergehen. **2** *v.t.* zum Weitergehen/-fahren auffordern

~ **'out** *v.i.* ausziehen (**of** aus); (*in car*) nach rechts/(*im Rechtsverkehr*) links ausbiegen

~ **'over** *v.i.* rücken; ~ **over!** (*said rudely*) Platz da!; **would you mind moving over a little?** würden Sie bitte ein Stück [weiter]rücken?

~ **'up** **1** *v.i.* **A** (*in queue, hierarchy*) aufrücken; ‹Fahrzeug:› vorfahren; (*to new class*) versetzt werden; (*to new school*) wechseln (**to** auf); **she's moving up in the world** sie kommt voran [im Leben]; **B** ⇒ ~ **over**. **2** *v.t.* versetzen ‹Schüler›

**movement** /'mu:vmənt/ *n.* **A** (*change of position or posture, or to and fro*) Bewegung, *die;* (*of people: towards city, country, etc.*) [Ab]wanderung, *die;* (*of clouds*) Zug, *der;* (*of air*) Regung, *die;* (*trend, tendency*) Tendenz, *die,* (*fashion*) Trend, *der* (**towards** zu); **a ~ of the head/arm/leg** eine Kopf-/Arm-/Beinbewegung; **without ~:** bewegungslos; **B** *in pl.* Aktivitäten *Pl.;* **keep track of sb.'s ~s** jmdn. überwachen; **C** (*Mus.*) Satz, *der;* **D** (*concerted action for purpose*) Bewegung, *die;* **E** *in sing. or pl.* (*Mech. esp. in clock, watch*) Räderwerk, *das;* **F** (*Mil.*) Manöver, *das;* (*shifting*) Verlegung, *die;* (*advance*) Vorstoß, *der;* **G** (*mental impulse*) Regung, *die;* **H** (*progressive development*) (*of plot*) Fortgang, *der;* (*of story, poem, etc.*) Handlung, *die;* **I** (*Commerc.: activity*) Geschäft, *das* (**in** mit); Bewegung im Handel (**in** mit); **J** (*rise or fall in price*) Preisbewegung, *die;* **a downward/an upward ~ in shares** *or* **share prices/[the price of] coffee** ein Rückgang/Anstieg der Aktienkurse/des Kaffeepreises; **K** (*of bowels*) ⇒ **motion** 1 D

**mover** /'mu:və(r)/ *n.* **A** (*of proposition*) Antragsteller, *der*/-stellerin, *die;* **B** (*Amer.: of furniture*) Möbelspediteur, *der;* (*employee*) Möbelpacker, *der;* **firm** *or* **company of ~s** Möbelspedition, *die;* **C** **prime ~** (*God*) Schöpfer, *der;* (*source of motive power*) Energiequelle, *die;* (*fig.: of plan etc.*) Urheber, *der*/Urheberin, *die;* **D** **this animal is a slow** *etc.* **~:** die Bewegungen dieses Tieres sind langsam *usw.;* **she is a beautiful ~:** ihre Bewegungen sind anmutig; **be a slow ~** (*think slowly*) langsam schalten (*ugs.*); (*work slowly*) langsam arbeiten; **be a fast ~:** von der schnellen Truppe sein (*ugs.*)

**movie** /'mu:vɪ/ *n.* (*Amer. coll.*) Film, *der; attrib.* Film‹publikum, -projektor, -studio usw.›; **the ~s** (*art form, cinema industry*) der Film; (*cinema*) das Kino; **go to the ~s** ins Kino gehen

**movie:** **~-goer** *n.* (*Amer. coll.*) Kinogänger, *der*/-gängerin, *die;* ~ **house,** ~ **theater** *ns.* (*Amer. coll.*) Kino, *das*

**moving** /'mu:vɪŋ/ *adj.* **A** beweglich; **from a ~ car** ‹sehen, erkennen› von einem fahrenden Auto aus; ‹fallen, werfen, schießen› aus einem fahrenden Auto; **B** (*affecting*) ergreifend; bewegend; rührend

**movingly** /'mu:vɪŋlɪ/ *adv.* in rührender Weise; ergreifend ‹schreiben, sprechen›

**moving:** ~ **'pavement** *n.* (*Brit.*) Rollbürgersteig, *der;* ~ **'picture** *n.* Film, *der;* ~ **'sidewalk** (*Amer.*) ⇒ ~ **pavement;** ~ **'spirit** *n.* treibende Kraft; ~ **'staircase** ⇒ **escalator** A

**mow** /məʊ/ *v.t., p.p.* **~n** /məʊn/ *or* **~ed** /məʊd/ mähen ‹Gras, Getreide, Rasen, Feld usw.›; **newly-~n** frisch gemäht

~ **'down** *v.t.* niedermähen ‹Soldaten›; überfahren ‹Fußgänger›; (*fig.: rout, smash*) zerschlagen ‹Opposition›

**mower** /'məʊə(r)/ *n.* **A** (*lawn~*) Rasenmäher, *der;* **B** (*Agric.*) Mäher, *der*

**'mowing machine** ⇒ **mower** B

**Mozambican** /məʊzəm'bi:kn/ ▶ 1340 **1** *adj.* mosambikanisch, mosambikisch. **2** *n.* Mosambikaner, *der*/Mosambikanerin, *die*

**Mozambique** /məʊzəm'bi:k/ *pr. n.* Mosambik (*das*)

**MP** *abbr.* **A** **Member of Parliament; committee of MPs** Unterhausausschuss, *der;* **B** **military police** MP; **C** **military policeman/policewoman** Militärpolizist, *der*/-polizistin, *die;* **D** **melting point** Schmp.

**m.p.g.** /empi:'dʒi:/ *abbr.* (*Motor Veh.*) **miles per gallon; do/get 34 ~** (*Brit.*) 8,3 l auf 100 km [ver]brauchen

**m.p.h.** /empi:'eɪtʃ/ *abbr.* ▶ 1552 **miles per hour**; **How many ~ are we doing? — We are travelling at/driving at/doing 30 ~** Wie schnell fahren wir? — Wir fahren 50 [km/h]

**MPV** *abbr.* **multi-purpose vehicle**

**Mr** /'mɪstə(r)/ *n., pl.* **Messrs** /'mesəz/ ▶ 1286, ▶ 1617 (*title*) Herr; (*third person also*) Hr.; (*in an address*) Herrn; **Messrs** Hrn.; (*firm*) Fa.; **Mr Right** (*joc.: destined husband*) der Richtige (*ugs.*); **Mr Big** (*coll.*) der Boss (*ugs.*)

**Mrs** /'mɪsɪz/ *n., pl. same or* **Mesdames** /meɪ'dæm, meɪ'dɑ:m/ **A** ▶ 1286, ▶ 1617 (*title*) Frau; (*third person also*) Fr.; **B** (*coll.: wife*) **the** *or* **my/your** *etc.* **~:** meine/deine *usw.* Madam (*ugs. scherzh.*). ⇒ *also* **Grundy**; **mop** 1 A

**Ms** /mɪz/ *n., no pl.* ▶ 1286, ▶ 1617 Frau

**MS** *abbr.* **A** **manuscript** Ms.; **B** ▶ 1232 (*Med.*) **multiple sclerosis** MS

**M.Sc.** /emes'si:/ *abbr.* **Master of Science** ≈ Mag. rer. nat. (*österr.*); ⇒ *also* **B.Sc.**

**MSS** *abbr.* /em'esɪz/ **manuscripts** Mss.

**Mt.** *abbr.* **Mount;** ~ **Etna/Everest/Sinai** (*Geog.*) der Ätna/der Mount Everest/der Berg Sinai

**mth** *abbr.* **month**

**much** /mʌtʃ/ **1** *adj.,* **more** /mɔ:(r)/, **most** /məʊst/ **A** viel; groß ‹Erleichterung, Sorge, Dankbarkeit, Verachtung›; **with ~ love** voller Liebe; **with ~ love from ...** (*familiar ending to letter*) herzlichst, ...; **he never eats ~ breakfast/lunch/supper** er isst nicht viel zum Frühstück/zu Mittag/zum Abendbrot; **too ~:** zu viel *indekl.;* **B** **be a bit ~** (*coll.*) ein bisschen zu viel sein; (*fig.*) ein bisschen zu weit gehen. ⇒ *also* **good** 3 B; **how** 1; **nothing** 1 A; **so** 1 A; **this** 3; **too** A.

**2** *n.;* ⇒ *also* **more** 2; **most** 2; vieles; **we don't see ~ of her any more** wir sehen sie kaum noch; **we haven't ~ to go on yet** bis jetzt haben wir noch nicht viel; **that doesn't come** *or* **amount to ~:** es kommt nicht viel dabei heraus; **he/this beer isn't up to ~** (*coll.*) mit ihm/diesem Bier ist nicht viel los (*ugs.*); **spend ~ of the day/week/month doing sth.** den Großteil des Tages/der Woche/des Monats damit verbringen, etw. zu tun; **they have done ~ to improve the situation** sie haben viel für die Verbesserung der Situation getan; **not be ~ of a cinema-goer** *etc.* (*coll.*) kein großer Kinogänger *usw.* sein (*ugs.*); **not have ~ of a singing voice/head for heights** keine besonders schöne Stimme haben/leicht schwindelig werden; **it isn't ~ of a bicycle/car/house** es ist kein besonders tolles Fahrrad/Auto/Haus (*ugs.*); **not be ~ to look at** nicht sehr ansehnlich sein; **he/the plan/plant didn't come to ~:** aus ihm/dem Plan/der Pflanze ist nichts Richtiges geworden; **it's as ~ as she can do to get up the stairs** sie kommt gerade noch die Treppe hinauf; **I expected/thought as ~:** das habe ich erwartet/mir gedacht; **he stared at me as ~ as to say ...:** er starrte mich an, als ob er sagen wollte: ...; **you are as ~ to blame as he is** du bist ebenso sehr schuld wie er; **she knows as ~ as we do** sie weiß genauso viel wie wir; **we didn't have so ~ as the bus fare home** wir hatten nicht einmal das Geld für den Bus nach Hause; **without so ~ as saying goodbye/a backward glance** ohne auch nur Auf Wiedersehen zu sagen/einen Blick zurückzuwerfen; ⇒ *also* **again** A; **as** 1; **in** A; **make** 1 M; **so** 1 A; **think of** g; **up** 1 V. ❸ *adv.*, **more, most** A *modifying comparatives* viel ‹besser›; **~ more lively/happy/attractive** viel lebhafter/glücklicher/attraktiver; B *modifying superlatives* mit Abstand ‹der/die/das Beste, Schlechteste, Klügste usw.›; C *modifying passive participles and predicative adjectives* sehr; **he is ~ improved** (*in behaviour*) er hat sich sehr gebessert; (*in health*) es geht ihm viel besser; D *modifying verbs* (*greatly*) sehr ‹lieben, mögen, genießen›; (*often*) oft ‹sehen, treffen, besuchen›; (*frequently*) viel; **she loved him too ~:** sie liebte ihn zu sehr; **I don't ~ like him** *or* **like him ~:** ich mag ihn nicht besonders; **not go ~ on sb./sth.** (*coll.*) nicht viel von jmdm./etw. halten; **it doesn't matter ~:** es ist nicht so wichtig; **I don't very ~ want to come** ich habe keine sehr große Lust zu kommen; **I would ~ prefer to stay at home** ich würde viel lieber zu Hause bleiben; **~ to my surprise/annoyance, I found that ...:** zu meiner großen Überraschung/Verärgerung stellte ich fest, dass ...; **it's not so ~ a problem of money as of time** es ist nicht so sehr ein finanzielles als ein zeitliches Problem; E (*approximately*) fast; **[pretty** *or* **very] ~ the same** fast [genau] der-/die-/dasselbe; **the old house was ~ as it had always been** das alte Haus hatte sich kaum verändert; F (*for a large part of time*) viel ‹gärtnern, lesen, spielen›; (*often*) oft; häufig; G **~ as** *or* **though** (*although*) sosehr ... auch; **~ as he disliked the idea** sosehr ihm die Idee auch missfiel; **~ as I should like to go** so gern ich auch gehen würde; H **not ~** (*coll.: certainly not*) nicht die Bohne (*ugs.*); denkste! (*ugs.*). ⇒ *also* **less** 2; **oblige** 1 D; **same** 1

**muchly** /ˈmʌtʃlɪ/ *adv.* (*joc.*) sehr ‹beeindruckt›; **ta** *or* **thanks ~!** tausend Dank! (*ugs.*)

**muchness** /ˈmʌtʃnɪs/ *n.*, *no pl.*, *no def. art.* **be much of a ~** (*coll.*) sich (*Dat.*) so ziemlich gleichen (*ugs.*); **they are much of a ~ when it comes to ...:** wenn es um ... geht, kann der eine es nicht besser als der andere

**muck** /mʌk/ ❶ *n.* A (*farmyard manure*) Mist, *der*; ⇒ *also* **common** 1 E; B (*coll.: anything disgusting*) Dreck, *der* (*ugs.*); (*liquid*) Brühe, *die* (*ugs. abwertend*); **covered in ~:** verdreckt (*ugs.*); C (*coll.: defamatory remarks, nonsense*) Mist, *der* (*ugs.*); Dreck, *der* (*ugs.*); D (*coll.: untidy state*) Schweinerei, *die* (*derb abwertend*); **make a ~ of sth.** (*coll.*) [bei einer Sache] Mist bauen (*ugs.*). ❷ *v.t.* ⇒ **muck up** b

**~ aˈbout, ~ aˈround** (*Brit. coll.*) ❶ *v.i.* A herumalbern (*ugs.*); B (*tinker*) herumfummeln (**with** an + *Dat.*). ❷ *v.t.* A herumstreifen *od.* umherstreifen in (+ *Dat.*) (*ugs.*) ‹Stadt, Straße›; B **~ sb. about** *or* **around** jmdn. verarschen (*derb*); **the bank really ~ed us about** es war ein ewiges Hin und Her mit der Bank (*ugs.*)

**~ ˈin** *v.i.* (*coll.*) mit zugreifen *od.* mit anpacken (**with** bei)

**~ ˈout** *v.t.* ausmisten ‹Stall›; (*fig.*) aufräumen ‹Haus, Garage, Zimmer›

**~ ˈup** *v.t.* A (*Brit. coll.: bungle*) vermurksen, verbocken (*ugs.*); **~ it up** Mist bauen (*ugs.*); B (*make dirty*) voll schmieren, dreckig machen (*ugs.*); einsauen (*derb*); C (*coll.: spoil*) vermasseln (*salopp*). ⇒ *also* **muck-up**

**muckle** /ˈmʌkl/ ⇒ **mickle**

**muck: ~raker** /ˈmʌkreɪkə(r)/ *n.* **he's just a ~raker** er ist nur auf Sensationen aus; **~raking** /ˈmʌkreɪkɪŋ/ ❶ *adj.* skandalträchtig ‹Rede, Brief, Angriff, Politik›; skandalsüchtig (*abwertend*) ‹Person›; Skandal‹artikel, -blatt, -journalismus, -presse› (*abwertend*); ❷ *n.* Skandalhascherei, *die* (*abwertend*); Sensationsmache, *die* (*ugs. abwertend*); **~-up** *n.* (*Brit. coll.*) (*confusing or confused situation*) Kuddelmuddel, *der od. das* (*ugs.*); (*blunder, mess*) Mist, *der* (*ugs.*); **make a ~-up of sth.** etw. vermasseln (*salopp*)

**mucky** /ˈmʌkɪ/ *adj.* dreckig (*ugs.*); (*with manure*) mistig; (*fig.*) schmierig ‹Zeitung, Witz, usw.›

**mucous** /ˈmju:kəs/ *adj.* (*Med., Bot., Zool.*) schleimig; Schleim-; mukös (*fachspr.*)

**mucous ˈmembrane** *n.* Schleimhaut, *die*

**mucus** /ˈmju:kəs/ *n.* (*Med., Bot., Zool.*) Schleim, *der*

**mud** /mʌd/ *n.* A Schlamm, *der*; Morast, *der*; **patch/expanse** *or* **area of ~:** schlammige *od.* morastige Stelle/Fläche; **covered with ~:** schlammbedeckt; **be as clear as ~** (*joc. iron.*) absolut unklar sein; **[here's] ~ in your eye!** (*coll. dated.*) Prösterchen! (*fam.*); B (*hard ground*) Lehm, *der*; *attrib.* Lehm-; lehmig; **~ hut** Lehmhütte, *die*; C (*fig.*) **be dragged through the ~:** in den Schmutz gezogen werden; **his name is ~** (*coll.*) er ist unten durch (*ugs.*) (**with** bei); **fling** *or* **sling** *or* **throw ~ at sb.** (*fig.*) jmdn. mit Dreck (*ugs.*) *od.* Schmutz bewerfen; ⇒ *also* **stick** 1 E; **stick-in-the-mud**

**ˈmudbath** *n.* (*Med.*; *also fig.*) Schlammbad, *das*

**muddle** /ˈmʌdl/ ❶ *n.* Durcheinander, *das*; **the room is in a hopeless ~:** in dem Zimmer herrscht ein heilloses Durcheinander *od.* eine heillose Unordnung; **get sth. in a ~:** etw. in Unordnung bringen; etw. durcheinander bringen; **my mind/brain is in a ~:** ich bin ganz durcheinander; ich kann nicht klar denken; **get/get sb. in[to] a ~:** durcheinander kommen (*ugs.*)/jmdn. durcheinander bringen; **make a ~ of sth.** (*bungle*) etw. verpfuschen. ❷ *v.t.* A **~ [up]** durcheinander bringen; **~ up** (*mix up*) verwechseln (**with** mit); **be ~d up** (*out of order*) durcheinander geraten sein; B (*mismanage*) verderben. ❸ *v.i.* wursteln (*ugs.*) (**with** an + *Dat.*)

**~ aˈlong, ~ ˈon** *v.i.* vor sich (*Akk.*) hin wursteln (*ugs.*) (**with** bei); **~ on towards sth.** planlos auf etw. (*Akk.*) hinarbeiten

**~ ˈthrough** *v.i.* sich durchwursteln (*ugs.*)

**muddled** /ˈmʌdld/ *adj.* A (*confused*) benebelt ‹Person›; konfus ‹Verhalten, Denken›; B (*mixed-up, jumbled*) verworren ‹Situation, Information, Ideen›

**muddle-ˈheaded** *adj.* wirr; **a ~ thinker/person** ein Wirrkopf

**muddy** /ˈmʌdɪ/ ❶ *adj.* A schlammig; **get** *or* **grow** *or* **become ~:** verschlammen; B (*turbid, dull*) trübe ‹Flüssigkeit, Licht, Farbe›; grau ‹Haut›; C (*obscure*) wirr; **a ~ thinker** ein Wirrkopf. ❷ *v.t.* (*cover with mud*) schmutzig machen; (*make turbid*) trüben ‹Flüssigkeit›; **~ the waters** (*fig.*) die Dinge [noch] undurchschaubarer *od.* verworrener machen; für zusätzliche Verwirrung sorgen

**mud: ~flap** *n.* (*Motor Veh.*) Schmutzfänger, *der*; **~flat[s]** *n.* [*pl.*] (*Geog.*) Watt, *das*; **~guard** *n.* Schutzblech, *das*; (*of car*) Kotflügel, *der*; **~pack** *n.* Schlammpackung [für das Gesicht]; Gesichtsmaske aus Schlamm; **~ ˈpie** *n.* Kuchen *aus Sand usw.*; **~ volˈcano** *n.* (*Geog.*) Schlammvulkan, *der*; Salse, *die* (*fachspr.*)

**muesli** /ˈmju:zlɪ/ *n.* Müsli, *das*

**muezzin** /mʊˈezɪn/ *n.* Muezzin, *der*

**muff**[1] /mʌf/ *n.* (*for hands*) Muff, *der*; ⇒ *also* **earmuffs**; **footmuff**

**muff**[2] ❶ *n.* (*person*) Tölpel, *der* (*abwertend*). ❷ *v.t.* A (*bungle*) verderben; verpatzen (*ugs.*); verhauen (*ugs.*) ‹Examen›; **I ~ed everything today** mir ging heute alles daneben (*ugs.*); B (*Theatre*) verpatzen (*ugs.*); **~ a line** einen Patzer machen (*ugs.*)

**muffin** /ˈmʌfɪn/ *n.* Muffin, *der*

**muffle** /ˈmʌfl/ *v.t.* A (*envelop*) **~ [up]** einhüllen; einmumme[l]n (*ugs.*); B (*deaden [sound of]*) dämpfen ‹Geräusch›; [zur Schalldämpfung] umwickeln ‹Fuß, Schuh, Ruder, Trommel, Glocke›; **~ sb.'s cries/screams** ‹Kopfkissen, Wand:› jmds. Schreie dämpfen; ‹Person:› jmdn. am Schreien hindern; C (*suppress sound of*) unterdrücken ‹Fluch, Bemerkung›; hinunterschlucken ‹Fluch›

**muffler** /ˈmʌflə(r)/ *n.* A (*wrap, scarf*) Schal, *der*; B (*deadener of sound*) Dämpfer, *der*; C (*Amer. Motor Veh.: silencer*) Schalldämpfer, *der*; Auspufftopf, *der*

**mufti** /ˈmʌftɪ/ *n.* A (*plain clothes*) Zivil, *das*; **in ~** in Zivil; B (*Muslim priest*) Mufti, *der*

**mug**[1] /mʌg/ ❶ *n.* A (*vessel, contents*) Becher, *der* (*meist mit Henkel*); (*for beer etc.*) Krug, *der*; **a ~ of milk** ein Becher Milch; B (*coll.: face, mouth*) Visage, *die* (*salopp*); Fresse, *die* (*derb*); C (*Brit. coll.: simpleton*) Schwachkopf, *der* (*ugs.*); D (*Brit. coll.: gullible person*) Trottel, *der* (*ugs. abwertend*); Doofi, *der* (*ugs.*); **make a ~ of sb.** jmdn. anschmieren *od.* beschupsen (*salopp*); **that's a ˈmug's game** das ist doch Schwachsinn (*ugs.*); E (*Amer. coll.: hoodlum*) Ganove, *der* (*ugs.*). ❷ *v.t.*, **-gg-** (*rob*) überfallen und berauben

**mug**[2] (*Brit. coll.: study*) *v.t.*, **-gg-: ~ up** büffeln (*ugs.*) ‹Fach, Zitate, Formeln›; durchackern (*ugs.*) ‹Buch, Notizen›

**mugful** /ˈmʌgfʊl/ (*contents*) ⇒ **mug**[1] 1 A

**mugger** /ˈmʌgə(r)/ *n.* Straßenräuber, *der*/Straßenräuberin, *die*

**mugginess** /ˈmʌgɪnɪs/ *n.*, *no pl.* Schwüle, *die*

**mugging** /ˈmʌgɪŋ/ *n.* Straßenraub, *der* (**of** an + *Dat.*)

**muggins** /ˈmʌgɪnz/ *n.*, *pl.* **~es** *or same* (*coll.*) A (*simpleton*) Dummkopf, *der* (*ugs.*); Esel, *der* (*ugs.*); B (*myself, stupidly*) ich Dummkopf (*ugs.*)

**muggy** /ˈmʌgɪ/ *adj.* schwül; drückend ‹Klima, Zeit, Tag, Luft›; **a ~ place** ein Ort mit schwülem Klima

**ˈmug shot** *n.* (*coll.*) A **[police] ~s of criminals** Verbrecherfotos; B (*passport photo etc.*) [Pass]foto, *das*

**mugwort** /ˈmʌgwɜ:t/ *n.* (*Bot.*) Beifuß, *der*

**Muhammadan** /məˈhæmədn/ (*Relig.*) ❶ *n.* Moslem, *der*. ❷ *adj.* moslemisch

**Muhammadanism** /məˈhæmədənɪzm/ *n.*, *no pl.* (*Relig.*) Islam, *der*

**mulatto** /mju:ˈlætəʊ/ *n.*, *pl.* **~s** (*Amer.*: **~es**) Mulatte, *der*/Mulattin, *die*

**mulberry** /ˈmʌlbərɪ/ *n.* A (*fruit*) Maulbeere, *die*; *attrib.* Maulbeer-; B (*tree*) Maulbeerbaum, *der*; *attrib.* Maulbeer-

**mulch** /mʌltʃ/ (*Agric., Hort.*) ❶ *n.* Mulch, *der*. ❷ *v.t.* mulchen

**mulct** /mʌlkt/ *v.t.* A (*Law: fine*) eine Geldstrafe auferlegen (*geh.*) (+ *Dat.*); B (*literary: deprive*) berauben (*geh.*) (**of** *Gen.*)

**mule**[1] /mju:l/ *n.* A (*Zool.*) Maultier, *das*; **have a kick like a ~** (*fig.*) einen umwerfen; ⇒ *also* **obstinate**; **stubborn** A; B (*coll.*) (*stupid person*) Esel, *der* (*ugs.*); (*obstinate person*) Dickkopf, *der* (*ugs.*); C (*Textiles*) Mule-Maschine, *die*

**mule**[2] *n.* (*slipper*) Pantoffel, *der*

**muleteer** /mju:lɪˈtɪə(r)/ *n.* Maultiertreiber, *der*/Maultiertreiberin, *die*

**mulish** /ˈmju:lɪʃ/ *adj.* (*stubborn*) stur; **~ stubbornness/obstinacy** Sturheit, *die*

**mull**[1] /mʌl/ *v.t.* **~ over** nachdenken über (+ *Akk.*); (*in conversation*) diskutieren

**mull**[2] *v.t.* (*prepare*) erhitzen und würzen ‹Wein›; **~ wine** Glühwein zubereiten; **~ed wine** Glühwein, *der*

**mull**[3] *n.* (*Scot.: promontory*) Kap, *das*

**mullah** /ˈmʌlə/ *n.* (*Islam*) Mullah, *der*

**mullet** /ˈmʌlɪt/ *n.*, *pl.* **~s** *or same* (*Zool.*) **red ~:** Gewöhnliche Meerbarbe; **grey ~:** Meeräsche, *die*

**mulligatawny** /mʌlɪgəˈtɔ:nɪ/ *n.* ~ **[soup]** Mulligatawny-Suppe, *die* (*mit Curry scharf gewürzte indische Geflügelsuppe*)

**mullion** /ˈmʌljən/ *n.* A (*Archit.*) Längspfosten, *der;* B *in pl.* (*Gothic Archit.*) Stabwerk, *das*

**mullioned** /ˈmʌljənd/ *adj.* längs unterteilt; ~ **windows** Fenster mit Stabwerk

**multi-** /ˈmʌltɪ/ *pref.* (*several*) mehr-/Mehr-; (*many*) viel-/Viel-; multi-/Multi-, poly-/Poly- (*bes. mit Fremdwörtern*)

**multi:** **~coloured** (*Brit.; Amer.:*) **~colored** *adj.* (*with several colours*) mehrfarbig, (*with many colours*) vielfarbig ‹Gegenstand, Tier, Pflanze›; bunt ‹Stoff, Kleid›; **~'cultural** *adj.* multikulturell

**multifarious** /mʌltɪˈfeərɪəs/ *adj.* A (*having great variety*) vielgestaltig; B (*many and various*) mannigfach; vielfältig

**multi:** **~function button** *n.* Multifunktionstaste, *die;* **~grade** *adj.*, *n.* **~grade [oil]** Mehrbereichsöl, *das;* **~gym** *n.* A (*equipment*) Multifunktionsfitnessgerät, *das;* B (*room*) Fitnessraum, *der;* **~'lateral** *adj.* mehrseitig; (*Polit.*) multilateral

**multilingual** /mʌltɪˈlɪŋgwəl/ *adj.* mehrsprachig

**multi:** **~media** *n. sing.* Multimedia, *das; attrib.* Multimedia-; **~millio'naire** *n.* Multimillionär, *der*/-millionärin, *die*

**multi'national** ❶ *adj.* multinational. ❷ *n.* (*Econ.*) multinationaler Konzern; Multi, *der* (*ugs.*)

**multiple** /ˈmʌltɪpl/ ❶ *adj.* A (*manifold*) mehrfach; ~ **birth** Mehrlingsgeburt, *die;* ~ **crash/pile-up** Massenkarambolage, *die;* B (*many and various*) vielerlei; vielfältig; mannigfach; C (*Bot.*) multipel; ~ **fruit** Sammelfrucht, *die.* ⇒ *also* **sclerosis** A. ❷ *n.* A (*Math.*) Vielfache, *das;* ⇒ *also* **common multiple**; B ⇒ **multiple store**

**multiple:** **~-'choice** *adj.* Multiple-Choice- ‹Verfahren, Test, Frage›; ~ **'store** *n.* (*Brit. Commerc.*) Kettenladen, *der*

**multiplex** /ˈmʌltɪpleks/ ❶ *adj.* Multiplex- ‹kino, -filmtheater etc.›. ❷ *n.* (*Cinema*) Multiplex[-kino], *das*

**multiplication** /mʌltɪplɪˈkeɪʃn/ *n.* (*increase*) Vervielfachung, *die;* (*Math.*) Multiplikation, *die* (*fachspr.*); Malnehmen, *das; attrib.* Multiplikations-; **do/use ~:** multiplizieren (*fachspr.*); malnehmen; ~ **sign** Malzeichen, *das;* ~ **table** Multiplikationstabelle, *die;* **do** *or* **learn/recite** *or* **say/practise one's ~ table[s]** das Einmaleins lernen/aufsagen/üben

**multiplicity** /mʌltɪˈplɪsɪtɪ/ *n.* A (*manifold variety*) Vielfalt, *die* (**of**, **in** an, von + *Dat. Pl.*); ~ **in size/age** Größen-/Altersvielfalt, *die;* ~ **of habits/beliefs/ideas** vielfältige Gewohnheiten/Überzeugungen/Ideen; B (*great number*) Vielzahl, *die* (**of** von, an + *Dat.*)

**multiply**[1] /ˈmʌltɪplaɪ/ ❶ *v.t.* A (*Math., also abs.*) multiplizieren (*fachspr.*), malnehmen (**by** mit); B (*increase*) vervielfachen; **be multiplied** sich vervielfachen; C (*Biol.*) fortpflanzen; züchten. ❷ *v.i.* (*Biol.*) sich vermehren; sich fortpflanzen; **be fruitful and ~** (*Bibl.*) seid fruchtbar und mehret euch (*bibl.*)

**multiply**[2] /ˈmʌltɪplɪ/ *adv.* mehrfach

**'multi-purpose** *adj.* Mehrzweck-

**multi-purpose 'vehicle** *n.* Großraumlimousine, *die*

**multi'racial** *adj.* mehrrassig; gemischtrassig

**'multi-stage** *adj.* mehrstufig; Mehrstufen-

**multi:** **'~-storey** *adj.* mehrstöckig; mehrgeschossig; **~-storey car park/block of flats** Parkhaus/Wohnhochhaus, *das;* **~track** *adj.* mehrspurig; Mehrspur‹aufnahme, -ton, -tonbandgerät›

**multitude** /ˈmʌltɪtju:d/ *n.* A (*crowd*) Menge, *die;* (*great number*) Vielzahl, *die;* **cover a ~ of sins** (*joc.*) ein weites Feld umfassen; (*compensate*) vieles aufwiegen; **a ~ of animals/vehicles/men** eine Vielzahl von Tieren/Fahrzeugen/Männern; B **the [common] ~:** die [breite] Masse (*oft abwertend*); C (*numerousness*) Vielheit, *die*

**multitudinous** /mʌltɪˈtju:dɪnəs/ *adj.* A (*comprising many individuals*) vielköpfig ‹Herde, Versammlung›; B (*very many*) zahlreich

**'multi-volume** *adj.* vielbändig

**mum**[1] /mʌm/ (*coll.*) ❶ *int.* pst; **~'s the word** nicht weitersagen!; (*I won't tell anyone else*) ich sags nicht weiter. ❷ *adj.* leise; ruhig; still; **keep ~:** den Mund halten (*ugs.*); **keep ~ about sth.** etw. nicht weitersagen

**mum**[2] *n.* (*Brit. coll.: mother*) Mama, *die* (*fam.*)

**mumble** /ˈmʌmbl/ ❶ *v.i.* nuscheln (*ugs.*); ~ **[away] about sth.** über etw. (*Akk.*) nuscheln (*ugs.*). ❷ *v.t.* A (*utter indistinctly*) nuscheln (*ugs.*); ~ **one's words/phrases** *etc.* nuscheln (*ugs.*); B (*chew*) mit zahnlosem Mund kauen. ❸ *n.* Nuscheln, *das*

**mumbo-jumbo** /mʌmbəʊˈdʒʌmbəʊ/ *n.*, *pl.* **~s** A (*meaningless ritual*) Brimborium, *das* (*ugs.*); Theater, *das* (*ugs. abwertend*); B (*gibberish*) Kauderwelsch, *das;* C (*object of senseless veneration*) Idol, *das;* Götze, *der*

**mummer** /ˈmʌmə(r)/ *n.* (*Theatre*) Pantomime, *der*/Pantomimin, *die*

**mummery** /ˈmʌmərɪ/ *n.* (*derog.*) Mummenschanz, *der* (*abwertend*)

**mummify** /ˈmʌmɪfaɪ/ *v.t.* A mumifizieren; B (*shrivel*) austrocknen

**mummy**[1] /ˈmʌmɪ/ *n.* Mumie, *die*

**mummy**[2] *n.* (*Brit. coll.: mother*) Mutti, *die* (*fam.*); Mami, *die* (*fam.*); Mama, *die* (*fam.*)

**mumps** /mʌmps/ *n. sing.* ▶ **1232** (*Med.*) Mumps, *der*

**munch** /mʌnʃ/ ❶ *v.t.* ~ **one's food** mampfen (*salopp*); schmatzend kauen. ❷ *v.i.* mampfen (*salopp*); ~ **[away] at sth.** an etw. (*Dat.*) kauen

**mundane** /mʌnˈdeɪn/ *adj.* A (*dull*) banal; profan (*geh.*); stumpfsinnig ‹Entschluss, Routine›; B (*worldly*) weltlich; irdisch

**Munich** /ˈmju:nɪk/ *pr. n.* München (*das*); *attrib.* Münchner

**municipal** /mju:ˈnɪsɪpl/ *adj.* gemeindlich; kommunal; Kommunal‹politik, -verwaltung›; Gemeinde‹rat, -verwaltung, -beschluss›; ~ **district** (*Can., Austral.*) Landgemeinde, *die*

**municipality** /mju:nɪsɪˈpælɪtɪ/ *n.* A (*political unit*) Gemeinde, *die;* B (*governing body*) Gemeindeverwaltung, *die*

**munificence** /mju:ˈnɪfɪsəns/ *n.* (*formal*) Generosität, *die;* Hochherzigkeit, *die* (*geh.*)

**munificent** /mju:ˈnɪfɪsənt/ *adj.*, **munificently** /mju:ˈnɪfɪsəntlɪ/ *adv.* (*formal*) generös (*geh.*)

**munition** /mju:ˈnɪʃn/ *n.*, *usu. in pl.* Kriegsmaterial, *das;* **~[s] factory** Rüstungsbetrieb, *der;* **~[s] worker** Arbeiter in einem Rüstungsbetrieb

**muntjak (muntjac)** /ˈmʌntdʒæk/ *n.* (*Zool.*) Muntjak, *der*

**mural** /ˈmjʊərl/ ❶ *adj.* (*on a wall*) Wand-; an Wänden *nachgestellt.* ❷ *n.* Wandbild, *das;* Wandgemälde, *das;* (*on ceiling*) Deckengemälde, *das*

**murder** /ˈmɜ:də(r)/ ❶ *n.* A (*Law*) Mord, *der* (**of** an + *Dat.*); ~ **investigation** Ermittlungen *Pl.* in dem/einem Mordfall; ~ **hunt** Fahndung nach dem/einem Mörder; **be accused of ~:** des Mordes beschuldigt werden; **be arrested on a charge of ~:** unter Mordverdacht verhaftet werden; ~ **will out** (*prov.: sth. cannot be hidden*) die Wahrheit kommt doch an den Tag; B (*fig.*) **the exam/journey was ~:** die Prüfung/Reise war der glatte *od.* reine Mord (*ugs.*). ⇒ *also* **blue murder**; **get away with c**; **judicial** A.
❷ *v.t.* A (*kill unlawfully*) ermorden; ~ **sb. with a gun/knife** jmdn. erschießen/erstechen; **I could ~ him/a hamburger/a beer** (*fig. coll.*) ich könnte ihn umbringen/einen Hamburger vertragen/ein Bier vertragen (*ugs.*); B (*kill inhumanly*) umbringen; C (*coll.: spoil*) verhunzen (*ugs.*); D (*coll.: defeat*) fertig machen (*ugs.*)

**murderer** /ˈmɜ:dərə(r)/ *n.* Mörder, *der*/Mörderin, *die;* **be accused of being a ~:** des Mordes beschuldigt werden

**murderess** /ˈmɜ:dərɪs/ *n.* Mörderin, *die*

**murderous** /ˈmɜ:dərəs/ *adj.* tödlich; Mord‹absicht, -drohung›; vernichtend ‹Blick›; mörderisch (*ugs.*) ‹Fahrweise, Wetter, Kampf, Bedingung›; ~ **nature/mentality/psychology** Wesen/Mentalität/Psyche eines Mörders

**murk** /mɜ:k/ *n.* Dunkelheit, *die;* Nebelnacht, *die* (*geh.*)

**murky** /ˈmɜ:kɪ/ *adj.* A (*dark*) düster; trüb ‹Tag, Wetter›; B (*dirty*) schmutzig-trüb ‹Wasser›; C (*thick, opaque*) trüb ‹Luft, Atmosphäre›; verhangen ‹Himmel›; tief ‹Dunkelheit›; (*fig.: obscure*) dunkel; undurchsichtig; unergründlich ‹Geheimnis, Tiefen›; ~ **past** dunkle Vergangenheit

**murmur** /ˈmɜ:mə(r)/ ❶ *n.* A (*subdued sound*) Rauschen, *das;* (*of brook also*) Murmeln, *das* (*dichter.*); (*of bee*) Summen, *das;* B (*Med.*) **heart ~:** Herzgeräusch, *das;* Klappengeräusch, *das;* C (*expression of discontent*) Murren, *das;* **raise a few ~s** einige unzufriedene Stimmen laut werden lassen; ~ **of disagreement/impatience** ablehnendes/ungeduldiges Murren; **without a ~:** ohne Murren; ohne zu murren; D (*soft speech*) Murmeln, *das;* ~ **of approval/delight** beifälliges/freudiges Murmeln; **a ~ of voices** ein Gemurmel; **say sth. in a ~:** etw. murmeln.
❷ *v.t.* murmeln; raunen (*geh.*), hauchen ‹Zärtlichkeiten›.
❸ *v.i.* A ‹Person:› murmeln; (*make soft sound*) ‹Brise:› rauschen; B (*complain*) murren (**against**, **at** über + *Akk.*)

**murphy** /ˈmɜ:fɪ/ *n.* (*coll.*) Kartoffel, *die;* Knolle, *die* (*ugs.*)

**muscadel** ⇒ **muscatel**

**muscat** /ˈmʌskət/ *n.* (*grape*) Muskattraube, *die;* (*vine*) Muskatrebe, *die*

**muscatel** /mʌskəˈtel/ *n.* A (*raisin*) Muskadinerosine, *die;* B (*wine*) Muskateller[wein], *der*

**muscle** /ˈmʌsl/ ❶ *n.* A ▶ **966** Muskel, *der;* **not move a ~** (*fig.*) sich nicht rühren; B (*tissue*) Muskeln *Pl.*; **be all ~:** nur aus Muskeln bestehen; C (*muscular power*) [Muskel-, Körper]kraft, *die;* Muskeln *Pl.*; (*fig.: force, power, influence*) Stärke, *die;* **have financial ~:** finanzkräftig *od.* -stark sein; [finanziell] potent sein; **have industrial ~:** eine leistungsfähige Industrie haben. ❷ *v.i.* ~ **'in** (*coll.*) sich hineindrängen (**on** in + *Akk.*); **they're muscling in on our market** sie machen sich auf unserem Markt breit (*ugs.*); **you're muscling in [on my territory** (*fig.*)] du kommst mir ins Gehege

**muscle:** **~-bound** *adj.* A (*with powerful muscles*) muskelbepackt (*ugs.*); B (*with stiff muscles*) **be ~-bound** Muskelkater haben; (*fig.*) verknöchert sein; **become ~-bound** (*fig.*) verknöchern; **~man** *n.* A (*intimidator*) Gorilla, *der* (*ugs.*); B (*sb. with powerful physique*) Muskelmann, *der* (*ugs.*)

**Muscovite** /ˈmʌskəvaɪt/ ❶ *n.* Moskauer, *der*/Moskauerin, *die;* Moskowiter, *der*/Moskowiterin, *die* (*veralt.*). ❷ *adj.* moskauisch, Moskauer ‹Winter, Arbeiter›

**muscular** /ˈmʌskjʊlə(r)/ *adj.* A (*Med.*) Muskel-; muskulär (*fachspr.*); B (*strong*) muskulös. ⇒ *also* **dystrophy**

**muscularity** /mʌskjʊˈlærɪtɪ/ *n.*, *no pl.* Muskulosität, *die*

**muse**[1] /mju:z/ *n.* A **M~** (*Greek and Roman Mythol.*) Muse, *die;* B (*Lit.*) Genius, *der* (*geh.*)

**muse**[2] (*literary*) ❶ *v.i.* (*ponder*) grübeln; [nach]sinnen (*geh.*), sinnieren (**on**, **about**, **over** über + *Akk.*). ❷ *v.t.* sinnieren

**museum** /mju:ˈzi:əm/ *n.* Museum, *das;* **an art ~, a ~ of art** ein Kunstmuseum; **a ~ of modern art** ein Museum für moderne Kunst

**mu'seum piece** *n.* A (*specimen of art*) Museumsstück, *das;* B (*joc. derog.*) (*old-fashioned thing*) Museumsstück, *das* (*ugs. iron.*); (*old-fashioned person*) Fossil, *das*

**mush**[1] /mʌʃ/ *n.* A (*soft pulp*) Mus, *das;* Brei, *der;* **boil into a ~** ‹Kartoffeln:› zu Mus kochen *od.* verkochen; ~ **of mud/snow** Matsch,

m

der; **B** (*weak sentimentality*) Schmalz, *der* (*ugs. abwertend*)

**mush²** /mʊʃ/ *n.* (*sl.: face, mouth*) Schnauze, *die* (*derb*)

**mushroom** /'mʌʃrʊm, 'mʌʃru:m/ **1** *n.* **A** Pilz, *der;* (*edible*) [Speise]pilz, *der;* (*cultivated, esp. Agaricus campestris*) Champignon, *der; attrib.* Pilz-; **grow like ~s** (*fig.*) wie Pilze aus dem Boden schießen; **B** (*fig.*) **~ of smoke** Rauchpilz, *der;* ⇒ *also* **mushroom cloud. 2** *v.i.* **A** (*spring up*) wie Pilze aus dem Boden schießen; (*grow rapidly*) **demand ~ed overnight** die Nachfrage schoss über Nacht in die Höhe; **B** (*expand and flatten*) ‹Aschenwolke, Rauch:› sich pilzförmig ausbreiten

**mushroom: ~ cloud** *n.* Rauchpilz, *der;* (*after nuclear explosion*) Atompilz, *der;* **~-colour** *n.* blasses Gelbbraun; **~-coloured** *adj.* blass gelbbraun

**mushy** /'mʌʃɪ/ *adj.* **A** (*soft*) breiig; matschig ‹Boden›; **B** (*feebly sentimental*) schmalzig (*abwertend*); gefühlsduselig (*ugs. abwertend*) ‹Mensch›; **be full of ~ sentiment** vor Schmalz triefen (*abwertend*)

**music** /'mju:zɪk/ *n.* **A** Musik, *die;* **make ~:** Musik machen; musizieren; **student of ~:** Musikstudent, *der*/-studentin, *die;* **piece of ~:** Musikstück, *das;* Musik, *die;* **set** *or* **put sth. to ~:** etw. vertonen *od.* in Musik setzen; **have a gift for ~:** musikalisch begabt *od.* musikbegabt sein; **be ~ to sb.'s ears** (*fig.*) Musik in jmds. Ohren sein (*ugs.*); ⇒ *also* **face** 2 C; **set** 1 S; **sphere** C; **B** (*of waves, wind, brook*) Rauschen, *das;* (*of birds*) Gesang, *der;* **C** (*score*) Noten *Pl.;* (*as merchandise also*) Musikalien *Pl.;* **sheet of ~:** Notenblatt, *das;* **play from ~:** nach Noten spielen

**musical** /'mju:zɪkl/ **1** *adj.* **A** (*of music*) musikalisch ‹Abend, Begabung›; Musik‹instrument, -verein, -verständnis, -notation, -abend›; **B** (*melodious*) musikalisch ‹Stimme, Klänge›; melodiös, melodisch ‹Stück›; **C** (*fond of or skilled in music*) musikalisch; **D** (*set to music*) musikalisch; Musik‹film, -theater›. **2** *n.* (*Mus., Theatre*) Musical, *das*

**musical: ~ box** *n.* (*Brit.*) Spieldose, *die;* **~ 'chairs** *n. sing.* Reise nach Jerusalem; **~ director** *n.* (*Theatre*) Musikdirektor, *der*/-direktorin, *die;* (*conductor*) Kapellmeister, *der*/-meisterin, *die*

**musically** /'mju:zɪkəlɪ/ *adv.* (*with regard to music*) musikalisch; (*melodiously*) melodisch; melodiös; **~ gifted** musikalisch [begabt]; musikbegabt

**music: ~ box** (*Amer.*) ⇒ **musical box; ~ centre** *n.* Kompaktanlage, *die;* **~ drama** *n.* Musikdrama, *das;* **~ hall** *n.* (*Brit.*) **1** *n.* Varietee, *das;* **2** *attrib. adj.* Varietee-

**musician** /mju:'zɪʃn/ *n.* ▶ **1261** Musiker, *der*/Musikerin, *die;* (*minstrel, street ~ etc.*) Musikant, *der*/Musikantin, *die*

**'music lesson** *n.* Musikstunde, *die*

**musicologist** /mju:zɪ'kɒlədʒɪst/ *n.* ▶ **1261** Musikwissenschaftler, *der*/-wissenschaftlerin, *die;* Musikologe, *der*/Musikologin, *die* (*geh.*)

**musicology** /mju:zɪ'kɒlədʒɪ/ *n.* Musikwissenschaft, *die;* Musikologie, *die* (*geh.*)

**music: ~ paper** *n.* Notenpapier, *das;* **~ rest** *n.* Notenpult, *das;* **~ room** *n.* Musiksaal, *der;* (*for concerts*) Konzertsaal, *der;* **~ stand** *n.* Notenständer, *der;* **~ stool** *n.* Klavierhocker, *der;* Klavierschemel, *der;* **~ teacher** *n.* ▶ **1261** Musiklehrer, *der*/-lehrerin, *die;* **~ video** *n.* Musikvideo, *das*

**musk** /mʌsk/ *n.* **A** (*substance*) Moschus, *der;* **~-scented** mit Moschus parfümiert; **B** (*odour*) Moschusgeruch, *der;* **C** (*Bot.*) Moschusgauklerblume, *die*

**'musk deer** *n.* (*Zool.*) Moschushirsch, *der*

**musket** /'mʌskɪt/ *n.* (*Arms Hist.*) Muskete, *die*

**musketeer** /mʌskɪ'tɪə(r)/ *n.* (*Hist.*) Musketier, *der*

**musketry** /'mʌskɪtrɪ/ *n.* (*Hist.*) (*muskets*) Musketen *Pl.;* (*musketeers*) Musketiere *Pl.*

**musk: ~ melon** *n.* Zuckermelone, *die;* Gartenmelone, *die;* **~ ox** *n.* (*Zool.*) Moschusochse, *der;* **~rat** *n.* **A** (*Zool.*) Bisamratte, *die;* **B** (*fur*) Bisam, *der;* **~ rose** *n.* (*Bot.*) Moschusrose, *die*

**musky** /'mʌskɪ/ *adj.* moschusartig duftend; moschusartig ‹Duft, Geruch, Geschmack›; Moschus‹duft, -parfüm›

**Muslim** /'mʊslɪm, 'mʌzlɪm/ **1** *adj.* muslimisch (*bes. fachspr.*); moslemisch; **be ~** ‹Person:› Muslim/Muslime sein, Moslem/Moslime sein. **2** *n.* Muslim, *der*/Muslime, *die* (*bes. fachspr.*); Moslem, *der*/Moslime, *die*

**muslin** /'mʌzlɪn/ **1** *n.* Musselin, *der.* **2** *adj.* musselinen; Musselin-

**musquash** /'mʌskwɒʃ/ *n.* **A** (*Zool.*) Bisamratte, *die;* **B** (*fur*) Bisam, *der*

**muss** /mʌs/ *v.t.* (*Amer. coll.*) verstrubbeln (*ugs.*) ‹Haar, Frisur›; zerknittern ‹Stoff›

**~ 'up** *v.t.* durcheinander bringen; verstrubbeln (*ugs.*) ‹Haar›; zerknittern ‹Kleidung›

**mussel** /'mʌsl/ *n.* Muschel, *die;* **bed of ~s, ~ bed** Muschelbank, *die*

**must¹** /məst, *stressed* mʌst/, *stressed* **1** *v. aux., only in pres. and past ~, neg.* (*coll.*) **~n't** /'mʌsnt/ **A** (*have to*) müssen; *with negative* dürfen; **you ~ not/never do that** das darfst du nicht/nie tun; **you ~ remember ...:** du darfst nicht vergessen, ...; du musst daran denken, ...; **you ~ stop that noise/listen to me!** hör mit dem Lärm auf/hör mir zu!; **you ~n't do that again!** tu das [ja] nie wieder!; **I ~ get back to the office** ich muss wieder ins Büro; **I ~ go to London** ich muss nach London; **I ~ leave at 6 o'clock** ich muss um 6 Uhr weg *od.* los; **do it if you ~:** wenn es sein muss, tu es eben; tu, was du nicht lassen kannst (*ugs.*); **I will go if I ~:** wenn es sein muss, gehe ich; **~ I?** muss das sein?; **'~ you shout so loudly?** musst du denn so laut schreien?; **I ~ away** (*arch.*) ich muss fort; **I ~ have a new dress** ich brauche ein neues Kleid; **why ~ it always rain on Saturdays?** warum muss es ausgerechnet sonnabends immer regnen?; **I '~ say ...:** ich muss sagen ...; **[that] I'~ say** [das] muss ich schon sagen; **if you '~ know** wenn du es unbedingt wissen willst; **B** (*ought to*) müssen; *with negative* dürfen; **I ~ ask you to leave** ich muss Sie bitten zu gehen; **you ~ think about it** du solltest [unbedingt] darüber nachdenken; **I ~ not sit here drinking coffee** ich sollte *od.* dürfte eigentlich nicht hier sitzen und Kaffee trinken; **C** (*be certain to*) müssen; **you ~ be tired** du musst müde sein; du bist bestimmt müde; **you ~ be crazy** du bist wohl wahnsinnig!; **there ~ be a reason** es muss einen Grund geben; **it ~ be about 3 o'clock** es wird wohl *od.* dürfte *od.* müsste etwa 3 Uhr sein; **I ~ have lost it** ich muss es verloren haben; **it ~ have stopped raining by now** es dürfte *od.* müsste inzwischen aufgehört haben zu regnen; **I think they ~ have left** ich denke, sie sind sicher *od.* bestimmt weggegangen; **20 people ~ have visited me** es haben mich bestimmt 20 Leute besucht; **there ~ have been forty of them** (*forty*) es müssen vierzig gewesen sein; (*probably about forty*) es dürften etwa vierzig gewesen sein; **you ~ have seen it** (*necessarily would have*) du hättest es sehen müssen; *expr. indignation or annoyance* **he ~ come just when ...** er muss/musste natürlich *od.* ausgerechnet kommen, wenn/als ...; **what ~ I do but break my leg?** Was musste natürlich kommen? Ich musste mir das Bein brechen; ⇒ *also* **joke** 2.

**2** *n.* (*coll.*) Muss, *das;* **be a ~ for sb./sth.** ein Muss für jmdn./unerlässlich für etw. sein

**must²** *n.* **A** (*wine*) neuer Wein; **B** (*grape juice*) Most, *der*

**must³** ⇒ **mustiness**

**mustache** ⇒ **moustache**

**mustachio** /mə'stɑ:ʃəʊ/ *n., pl.* **~s** Schnauzbart, *der*

**mustachioed** /mə'stɑ:ʃəʊd/ *adj.* schnauzbärtig

**mustang** /'mʌstæŋ/ *n.* Mustang, *der*

**mustard** /'mʌstəd/ *n.* **A** Senf, *der; attrib.* Senf‹geschmack usw.›; **~ and cress** (*Brit.*) Senfkeimlinge und Kresse; **B** (*colour*) Senffarbe, *die; attrib.* senffarben; **C** (*Amer. coll.: thing that provides zest*) Pep, *der* (*ugs.*); **cut the ~:** es bringen (*ugs.*); **I can't cut the ~:** ich bringe es nicht (*ugs.*)

**mustard: ~-coloured** *adj.* senffarben; **~ gas** *n.* (*Chem., Mil.*) Senfgas, *das;* **~ plaster** *n.* Senfpflaster, *das;* **~ pot** *n.* Senftopf, *der;* **~-yellow** *adj.* senfgelb

**muster** /'mʌstə(r)/ **1** *n.* **A** (*Mil.*) Appell, *der;* **pass ~** (*fig.*) akzeptabel sein; **B** (*assembly*) Zusammenkunft, *die.*

**2** *v.t.* **A** (*summon*) versammeln; (*Mil., Naut.*) [zum Appell] antreten lassen; **B** (*collect*) zusammenbringen; zusammenziehen ‹Streitkräfte, Truppen›; zusammentreiben ‹Vieh›; (*raise*) aufstellen ‹Armee›; ausheben ‹Truppen›; **C** (*fig.: summon up*) zusammennehmen ‹Kraft, Mut, Verstand›; aufbringen ‹Unterstützung›; **~ [the] strength to do sth.** all seine Kräfte zusammennehmen, um etw. zu tun; **he couldn't ~ [the] courage to do it** er brachte nicht den Mut auf, es zu tun.

**3** *v.i.* sich [ver]sammeln; ‹Truppen:› aufmarschieren; (*for parade*) antreten

**~ 'up** *v.t.* aufbringen ‹Unterstützung, Mut, Verständnis›; **~ up all one's courage** seinen ganzen *od.* all seinen Mut zusammennehmen

**mustiness** /'mʌstɪnɪs/ *n., no pl.* **A** (*of smell, taste*) Muffigkeit, *die;* Muff, der (*nordd.*); **B** (*mouldiness*) Stockigkeit, *die*

**mustn't** /'mʌsnt/ (*coll.*) ... **must not**

**musty** /'mʌstɪ/ *adj.* **A** (*smelling or tasting stale*) muffig; **B** (*mouldy*) stockig; **C** (*fig.: stale, antiquated*) verstaubt

**mutable** /'mju:təbl/ *adj.* **A** (*formal: liable to change*) wandelbar (*geh.*); **B** (*Ling., Biol.*) mutabel (*fachspr.*)

**mutant** /'mju:tənt/ (*Biol.*) **1** *adj.* mutiert ‹Gen, Zelle, Stamm›. **2** *n.* Mutante, *die*

**mutate** /mju:'teɪt/ (*Biol.*) **1** *v.t.* zur Mutation anregen; **be ~d** mutieren. **2** *v.i.* mutieren

**mutation** /mju:'teɪʃn/ *n.* **A** (*formal: change*) Wandel, *der;* Wandlung, *die;* **B** (*Biol.*) Mutation, *die; attrib.* Mutations-

**mute** /mju:t/ **1** *adj.* (*dumb, silent; also Ling.*) stumm; (*silent also*) schweigend; (*temporarily bereft of speech also*) sprachlos; **be ~ with rage/amazement/grief/from shock** vor Zorn/Staunen/Kummer/Entsetzen kein Wort hervorbringen *od.* über die Lippen bringen. **2** *n.* **A** (*dumb person*) Stumme, *der/die;* **B** (*Mus.*) Dämpfer, *der.* **3** *v.t.* dämpfen

**muted** /'mju:tɪd/ *adj.* gedämpft; verhalten ‹Kritik, Begeisterung›

**mutely** /'mju:tlɪ/ *adv.* stumm; (*silently also*) schweigend

**mute 'swan** *n.* Höckerschwan, *der*

**mutilate** /'mju:tɪleɪt/ *v.t.* (*deprive of limb; fig.: render imperfect*) verstümmeln; mutilieren (*Med.*); (*cut off*) abtrennen ‹Gliedmaße›

**mutilation** /mju:tɪ'leɪʃn/ *n.* (*deprivation of limb; fig.: rendering imperfect*) Verstümmelung, *die;* Mutilation, *die* (*Med.*)

**mutineer** /mju:tɪ'nɪə(r)/ *n.* Meuterer, *der*

**mutinous** /'mju:tɪnəs/ *adj.* rebellisch ‹Geist, Person›; aufrührerisch ‹Rede, Gedanke›; meuternd ‹Mannschaft eines Schiffs, Truppen›; **~ acts** Akte der Meuterei; **become ~:** meutern

**mutinously** /'mju:tɪnəslɪ/ *adj.* rebellisch, aufrührerisch ‹sich benehmen›

**mutiny** /'mju:tɪnɪ/ **1** *n.* Meuterei, *die.* **2** *v.i.* meutern

**mutt** /mʌt/ *n.* (*coll.*) **A** (*person*) Schafskopf, *der* (*ugs.*); **poor ~:** armer Irrer (*salopp*); **B** (*derog.: dog*) Köter, *der* (*abwertend*)

**mutter** /'mʌtə(r)/ **1** *v.i.* **A** (*speak low*) murmeln; brummeln; **~ [away] to oneself** vor sich (*Akk.*) hin murmeln *od.* brummeln; **B** (*grumble*) murren (**at, about** über + *Akk.*). **2** *v.t.* (*utter*) murmeln ‹Beleidigung, Gebet, Drohung›; **~ sth. under one's breath/to oneself** sich (*Dat.*) etw. in den Bart/etw. vor sich (*Akk.*) hin murmeln. **3** *n.* Gemurmel, *das;* **~ of voices** Gemurmel [von Stimmen]

**muttering** /'mʌtərɪŋ/ *n.* **A** *no pl.* (*low speech*) Gemurmel, *das;* **B** **~[s]** (*complaints*) Gemurre, *das*

**mutton** /'mʌtn/ *n.* Hammelfleisch, *das;* Hammel, *der;* **[a case of] ~ dressed [up] as**

m

lamb (*coll. derog.*) eine Alte, die auf jugendlich macht (*ugs.*); ⇒ *also* **dead** 1 A

**mutton:** ~ **'chop** *n.* Ⓐ Hammelkotelett, *das;* Ⓑ **~-chop [whiskers]** [Bart]koteletten *Pl.;* **~head** *n.* (*coll. derog.*) Schafskopf, *der* (*ugs.*)

**mutual** /'mju:tjʊəl/ *adj.* Ⓐ (*given and received*) gegenseitig; beiderseitig ‹Einvernehmen, Vorteil, Bemühung›; wechselseitig ‹Abhängigkeit›; **look at each other with ~ suspicion** sich argwöhnisch ansehen; **I can't bear you! — The feeling's ~:** Ich kann dich nicht riechen! — Das beruht auf Gegenseitigkeit; **to our ~ satisfaction/benefit** zu unser beider Zufriedenheit/Nutzen; **~ aid programme** Programm zur gegenseitigen Hilfe; **be ~ well-wishers** es gut miteinander meinen; Ⓑ (*coll.: shared*) gemeinsam ‹Interesse, Freund, Abneigung usw.›

**mutual:** ~ **admi'ration society** *n.* (*joc.*) *Kreis von Leuten, die alle eine ungerechtfertigt hohe Meinung voneinander haben;* **~ 'fund** *n.* (*Amer. Econ.*) Investmentgesellschaft, *die;* **~ in'surance company** *n.* Versicherungsverein auf Gegenseitigkeit

**mutuality** /mju:tjʊ'ælɪtɪ/ *n., no pl.* Gegenseitigkeit, *die;* (*of interests*) Gemeinsamkeit, *die*

**mutually** /'mju:tjʊəlɪ/ *adv.* Ⓐ gegenseitig; **be ~ exclusive** einander (*geh.*) *od.* sich [gegenseitig] ausschließen; **~ beneficial/accepted** für beide Seiten vorteilhaft/von beiden Seiten akzeptiert; Ⓑ (*in common*) gemeinsam

**muzak** /'mju:zæk/ *n.* (*often derog.*) Hintergrundmusik, *die;* Berieselungsmusik, *die* (*ugs. abwertend*)

**muzzle** /'mʌzl/ ❶ *n.* Ⓐ (*of dog*) Schnauze, *die;* (*of horse, cattle*) Maul, *das;* Ⓑ (*of gun*) Mündung, *die;* Ⓒ (*put over animal's mouth*) Maulkorb, *der.* ❷ *v.t.* Ⓐ einen Maulkorb umbinden *od.* anlegen (+ *Dat.*) ‹Hund›; Ⓑ (*fig.*) mundtot machen, einen Maulkorb anlegen (*ugs.*) (+ *Dat.*) ‹Presse, Kritiker›; knebeln ‹Presse, Redefreiheit›; unterdrücken ‹Protest›

**muzzle:** **~-loader** *n.* Vorderlader, *der;* **~ velocity** *n.* Mündungsgeschwindigkeit, *die*

**muzzy** /'mʌzɪ/ *adj.* Ⓐ (*mentally hazy, blurred*) verschwommen; verworren ‹Verstand›; **feel ~:** ein dumpfes Gefühl haben; Ⓑ (*from intoxication*) benebelt (**with** von)

**MW** *abbr.* Ⓐ (*Radio*) **medium wave** MW; Ⓑ (*Electr., Phys.*) **megawatt[s]** MW

**my** /maɪ/ *poss. pron. attrib.* Ⓐ (*belonging to me*) mein; Ⓑ *in affectionate, jocular, patronizing, etc. use* mein; **my poor fellow** du Ärmster; ⇒ *also* **man** 1 B; Ⓒ *in excl. of surprise* **my[, my]!, [my] oh my!** [ach du] meine Güte! (*ugs.*); ach du grüne Neune! (*ugs.*). ⇒ *also* **god** B; **her²**; **word** 1 C

**myalgic encephalomyelitis** /maɪæld͡ʒɪk ensefələʊmaɪə'laɪtɪs/ *n.* ▶ **1232** (*Med.*) myalgische Enzephalomyelitis

**mycelium** /maɪ'si:lɪəm/ *n., pl.* **mycelia** /maɪ'si:lɪə/ (*Bot.*) Myzel[ium], *das*

**Mycenaean** /maɪsɪ'ni:ən/ *adj.* (*Archaeol.*) mykenisch

**mycology** /maɪ'kɒləd͡ʒɪ/ *n.* Mykologie, *die*

**myna, mynah** ⇒ **mina**

**myopia** /maɪ'əʊpɪə/ *n.* Kurzsichtigkeit, *die* (*auch fig.*); Myopie, *die* (*fachspr.*)

**myopic** /maɪ'əʊpɪk/ *adj.* kurzsichtig (*auch fig.*); myopisch (*fachspr.*)

**myriad** /'mɪrɪəd/ (*literary*) ❶ *adj.* unzählig; Myriaden von (*geh.*) ‹Insekten, Sternen›. ❷ *n.* (*great number*) Unzahl, *die;* Myriade, *die* (*geh.*); **a ~ of possibilities** Myriaden von Möglichkeiten

**myriapod, myriopod** /'mɪrɪəpɒd/ *n.* (*Zool.*) Myriapode, *der;* Myriopode, *der*

**myrrh** /mɜ:(r)/ *n.* Myrrhe, *die*

**myrtle** /'mɜ:tl/ *n.* (*Bot.*) Ⓐ **common ~:** Myrte, *die;* Ⓑ (*Amer.: periwinkle*) Immergrün, *das*

**myself** /maɪ'self/ *pron.* Ⓐ *emphat.* selbst; **I thought so ~:** das habe ich auch gedacht; **I haven't been there, ~:** ich war nicht selbst da; **[even] though/if I say it ~:** wenn ich es auch selbst sage; **I am quite ~ again** mir geht es wieder gut; **I want to be ~:** ich will ich selbst sein; Ⓑ **you know more than ~:** du weißt mehr als ich [selbst]; **there were the three of them and ~:** da waren die drei und ich [selbst]; Ⓒ *refl.* mich/mir; **I washed ~:** ich wusch mich; **I'm going to get ~ a car** ich werde mir ein Auto zulegen; **I said to ~:** ich sagte mir; **I need to have time to ~:** ich brauche Zeit für mich. ⇒ *also* **herself**

**mysterious** /mɪ'stɪərɪəs/ *adj.* Ⓐ (*curious, strange*) mysteriös; rätselhaft; geheimnisvoll ‹Fremder, Orient›; **~-looking** geheimnisvoll aussehend; **he did it for some ~ reason of his own** er hat es aus irgendeinem unerfindlichen Grunde getan; Ⓑ (*secretive*) geheimnisvoll; **be very ~ about sth.** ein großes Geheimnis aus etw. machen; **why are you being so ~?** warum tust du so geheimnisvoll?

**mysteriously** /mɪ'stɪərɪəslɪ/ *adv.* auf mysteriöse *od.* rätselhafte Weise; sonderbar ‹erfreut usw.›; geheimnisvoll ‹lächeln usw.›

**mystery** /'mɪstərɪ/ *n.* Ⓐ (*hidden, inexplicable matter*) Rätsel, *das;* **it's a ~ to me why ...:** es ist mir schleierhaft (*ugs.*) *od.* ein Rätsel, warum ...; **make a ~ [out] of sth.** ein Geheimnis aus etw. machen; **make no ~ of sth.** kein *od.* keinen Hehl aus etw. machen; **the mysteries of a trade** die Geheimnisse eines Handwerks; **he's a bit of a ~:** er hat etwas Rätselhaftes *od.* Geheimnisvolles; Ⓑ (*secrecy*) Geheimnis, *das;* **wrapped in** *or* **shrouded in** *or* **surrounded by ~:** geheimnisumwittert *od.* -umwoben (*geh.*); **there's no ~ about it** das ist überhaupt kein Geheimnis; **~ man, man of ~:** rätselhafter Mann; Ⓒ (*making a secret of things*) Heimlichtuerei, *die;* Ⓓ (*religious truth*) Mysterium, *das* (*geh.*); Ⓔ ⇒ **mystery play**; **mystery story**

**mystery:** ~ **novel** *n.* ≈ Detektiv- *od.* Kriminalroman, *der;* **~ play** *n.* Mysterienspiel, *das;* **~ story** *n.* (*detective story*) ≈ Detektiv- *od.* Kriminalgeschichte, *die;* (*mysterious story*) rätselhafte Erzählung; **~ tour, ~ trip** *ns.* Fahrt ins Blaue (*ugs.*); **~ writer** Kriminalschriftsteller, *der*/-schriftstellerin, *die;* Krimiautor, *der*/-autorin, *die* (*ugs.*)

**mystic** /'mɪstɪk/ ❶ *adj.* Ⓐ mystisch; Ⓑ (*mysterious*) geheimnisvoll. ❷ *n.* Mystiker, *der*/Mystikerin, *die*

**mystical** /'mɪstɪkl/ *adj.* mystisch

**mysticism** /'mɪstɪsɪzm/ *n.* Mystik, *die;* Mystizismus, *der* (*geh.*)

**mystification** /mɪstɪfɪ'keɪʃn/ *n.* Verwirrung, *die;* **add to sb.'s ~:** jmdn. noch mehr verwirren

**mystify** /'mɪstɪfaɪ/ *v.t.* verwirren; **this mystifies me** das ist mir ein Rätsel *od.* rätselhaft; **the police are completely mystified** die Polizei steht vor einem absoluten Rätsel

**mystique** /mɪ'sti:k/ *n.* geheimnisvoller Nimbus

**myth** /mɪθ/ *n.* Ⓐ Mythos, *der;* Ⓑ (*fictitious thing or idea*) Mythos, *der;* (*untrue tale*) Legende, *die;* (*rumour*) Gerücht, *das*

**mythical** /'mɪθɪkl/ *adj.* Ⓐ (*based on myth*) mythisch; **~ creatures** Sagengestalten; **the ~ land of Atlantis** das sagenhafte Land Atlantis; Ⓑ (*invented*) fiktiv

**mythological** /mɪθə'lɒd͡ʒɪkl/ *adj.* mythologisch

**mythology** /mɪ'θɒləd͡ʒɪ/ *n.* Mythologie, *die*

**myxomatosis** /mɪksəmə'təʊsɪs/ *n., pl.* **myxomatoses** /mɪksəmə'təʊsi:z/ (*Vet. Med.*) Myxomatose, *die*

m

# Nn

**N¹, n** /en/ *n., pl.* **Ns** *or* **N's** Ⓐ *(letter)* N, n, *das;* Ⓑ *(Math.)* n; **nth** /enθ /:/ **to the nth [degree]** in der n-ten Potenz; *(fig.: to the utmost)* in höchster Potenz *(ugs.)*; **for the nth time** zum x-ten Mal *(ugs.)*

**N²** *abbr.* Ⓐ ▶ 1024 **north** N; Ⓑ ▶ 1024 **northern** n.; Ⓒ *(Chess)* **knight** S; Ⓓ **nuclear; N-weapons** A-Waffen; Ⓔ *(Phys.)* **newton** N

**'n, 'n'** /ən/ *conj. (coll.: and)* und

**n.** *abbr.* Ⓐ **note** Anm.; Ⓑ **nano-** n; Ⓒ **neuter** n.

**n/a** *abbr.* Ⓐ **not available** n. bek.; Ⓑ **not applicable** entf.

**NAAFI** /ˈnæfɪ/ *abbr. (Brit.)* **Navy, Army and Air Force Institutes** *Kaufhaus für Angehörige der britischen Truppen*

**nab** /næb/ *v.t.*, **-bb-** *(coll.)* Ⓐ *(arrest)* schnappen *(ugs.)*; Ⓑ *(seize)* sich *(Dat.)* schnappen; **~ him before he goes** sieh zu, dass du ihn noch erwischst, bevor er geht *(ugs.)*; **all the best seats had been ~bed** die besten Plätze waren alle schon weggeschnappt; Ⓒ *(steal)* klauen *(salopp)*; krallen *(salopp)*

**nacelle** /næˈsel/ *n.* Gondel, *die*

**nacre** /ˈneɪkə(r)/ ⇒ **mother-of-pearl**

**nadir** /ˈneɪdɪə(r)/ *n.* Ⓐ *(lowest point)* Tief[st]punkt, *der;* **at the ~:** auf dem Tiefpunkt; **he was at the ~ of despair** er war zutiefst verzweifelt; Ⓑ *(Astron.)* Nadir, *der*

**naff** /næf/ *(coll.)* ❶ *adj.* ätzend *(ugs.)*. ❷ *v.i.* **~ off** abhauen *(ugs.)*

**nag¹** /næg/ ❶ *v.i.*, **-gg-** Ⓐ *(scold)* nörgeln *(abwertend)*; meckern *(ugs. abwertend)*; **~ at sb.** an jmdm. herumnörgeln *od.* -meckern; **~ at sb. to do sth.** jmdm. zusetzen *(ugs.)*, dass er etw. tut; Ⓑ *(cause distress)* **~ at sb.** jmdn. plagen; jmdm. zusetzen *(ugs.) od.* keine Ruhe lassen. ❷ *v.t.*, **-gg-** Ⓐ *(scold)* herumnörgeln an (+ *Dat.*) *(abwertend)*; herummeckern an (+ *Dat.*) *(abwertend)*; **don't ~ me!** lass mich [mit deinem Genörgel *od. (ugs.)* Gemecker] in Ruhe!; **~ sb. about sth./to do sth.** jmdm. wegen etw. zusetzen *(ugs.)*/jmdm. zusetzen *(ugs.)*, dass er etw. tut; Ⓑ *(cause distress)* plagen; keine Ruhe lassen (+ *Dat.*)

**nag²** *n.* Ⓐ *(coll.: horse)* Gaul, *der;* Ⓑ *(old or inferior horse)* Klepper, *der (abwertend)*

**nagging** /ˈnægɪŋ/ ❶ *adj.* Ⓐ *(annoying)* nörglerisch *(abwertend)*; ständig nörgelnd *(abwertend)*; Ⓑ *(persistent)* quälend ‹Durst, Angst, Sorge, Zweifel›; bohrend ‹Schmerz›; **a ~ conscience** [quälende] Gewissensbisse *Pl.* ❷ *n.* Genörgel, *das (abwertend)*; Gemecker, *das (ugs. abwertend)*; **stop your ~:** hör auf zu nörgeln *od.* meckern

**naiad** /ˈnaɪæd/ *n., pl.* **~s** *or* **~es** /ˈnaɪədiːz/ Najade, *die*

**naïf** /nɑːˈiːf/ ❶ *adj.* ⇒ **naïve**. ❷ *n.* Naive, *der/die;* Naivling, *der (ugs. abwertend)*

**nail** /neɪl/ ❶ *n.* Ⓐ ▶ 966 *(on finger, toe)* Nagel, *der;* **cut one's ~s** sich *(Dat.)* die Nägel schneiden; **bite one's ~s** an den Nägeln kauen; *(fig.)* wie auf Kohlen sitzen; Ⓑ *(metal spike)* Nagel, *der;* **be hard as ~s** *(fig.)* steinhart sein; *(fit)* topfit sein; *(unfeeling, insensitive)* knallhart sein *(ugs.)*; **hit the [right] ~ on the head** *(fig.)* den Nagel auf den Kopf treffen *(ugs.)*; **be a ~ in sb.'s/sth.'s coffin, drive a ~ into sb.'s/sth.'s coffin** *(fig.)* ein Nagel zu jmds. Sarg/ein Sargnagel für etw. sein *(ugs.)*; **on the ~** *(fig. coll.)* pünktlich ‹bezahlen, sein Geld kriegen›; Ⓒ *(claw, talon)* Kralle, *die.* ⇒ *also* **tooth** A.

❷ *v.t.* Ⓐ *(fasten)* nageln (**to** an + *Akk.*); **~ planks over sth.** etw. mit Brettern vernageln; **~ two planks together** zwei Bretter zusammennageln; Ⓑ *(fig.: expose)* **~ sth. [to the counter** *or* **barn door]** etw. anprangern; Ⓒ *(fig.: fix)* **be ~ed to the spot/ground** wie angenagelt sein *(ugs.)*; **~ one's eyes/attention on sth.** seine Augen auf etw. *(Akk.)* heften *(geh.)*/seine Aufmerksamkeit auf etw. *(Akk.)* konzentrieren; Ⓓ *(fig.: secure, catch, engage)* an Land ziehen *(ugs.)* ‹Vertrag, Auftrag›; festlegen ‹Strategie›; *(bind)* **~ sb. down to sth.** jmdn. auf etw. *(Akk.)* festnageln Ⓔ *(coll.: arrest)* einkassieren *(salopp)*. ⇒ *also* **colour** 1 J

**~ 'down** *v.t.* Ⓐ festnageln; zunageln ‹Kiste, Fenster›; Ⓑ *(fig.)* *(define)* untermauern ‹Argument›; festlegen ‹Strategie›; *(bind)* **~ sb. down to sth.** jmdn. auf etw. *(Akk.)* festnageln

**~ 'up** *v.t.* Ⓐ *(close)* vernageln; Ⓑ *(affix with ~)* annageln (**against** an + *Akk.*)

**nail: ~-biting** ❶ *n., no pl.* Nägelkauen, *das;* ❷ *adj. (fig.)* bang ‹Minuten, Schweigen, Sorge›; angstvoll ‹Spannung›; spannungsgeladen ‹Spiel, Film›; **~ brush** *n.* Nagelbürste, *die;* **~ clippers** *n. pl.* **[pair of] ~ clippers** Nagelknipser, *der;* **~ enamel** *(Amer.)* ⇒ **~ polish**; **~ file** *n.* Nagelfeile, *die;* **~ polish** *n.* Nagellack, *der;* **~ polish remover** Nagellackentferner, *der;* **~ scissors** *n. pl.* **[pair of] ~ scissors** Nagelschere, *die;* **~ varnish** *(Brit.)* ⇒ **~ polish**

**naïve, naive** /nɑːˈiːv, naɪˈiːv/ *adj.* naiv; einfältig

**naïvely, naively** /nɑːˈiːvlɪ, naɪˈiːvlɪ/ *adv.* naiv; *as sentence-modifier* naiverweise

**naïvety, naivety** /nɑːˈiːvtɪ, naɪˈiːvtɪ/, **(naïveté** /nɑːˈiːveɪ/) *n.* Ⓐ *(state, quality)* Naivität, *die;* Einfalt, *die;* Ⓑ *(action)* Naivität, *die*

**naked** /ˈneɪkɪd/ *adj.* Ⓐ nackt; **as ~ as the day I was born** wie Gott mich geschaffen hat *(scherzh.)*; **go ~:** nackt herumlaufen; **strip sb. ~:** jmdn. nackt ausziehen; **I feel ~ without my make-up on** ohne mein Make-up fühle ich mich nackt; Ⓑ *(unshaded)* nackt ‹Glühbirne›; *(unshielded)* offen ‹Licht, Flamme›; Ⓒ *(defenceless)* wehrlos; Ⓓ *(without covering)* blank ‹Schwert›; bloß ‹Faust›; Ⓔ *(plain)* nackt ‹Tatsache, Wahrheit, Aggression, Gier, Ehrgeiz›

**naked: ~ 'eye** *n.* **visible to** *or* **with the ~ eye** mit bloßem Auge zu erkennen; **~-eye** *adj.* mit bloßem Auge sichtbar

**nakedness** /ˈneɪkɪdnɪs/ *n., no pl.* Nacktheit, *die;* Blöße, *die (geh.)*

**namby-pamby** /næmbɪˈpæmbɪ/ *adj.* seicht *(abwertend)* ‹Literatur usw.›; verzärtelt *(abwertend)* ‹Person›; lax *(oft abwertend)* ‹Handhabung, Normen›

**name** /neɪm/ ❶ *n.* Ⓐ Name, *der;* **what's your ~/the ~ of this place?** wie heißt du/dieser Ort?; **my ~ is Jack** ich heiße Jack; mein Name ist Jack; **call sb. by his ~:** jmdn. bei seinem Namen rufen; **no one of** *or* **by that ~:** niemand mit diesem Namen *od. (geh.)* dieses Namens; **last ~:** Zuname, *der,* Nachname, *der;* **know sb./sth. by** *or* **under another ~:** jmdn./etw. unter einem anderen Namen kennen; **the ~ of Edwards** der Name Edwards; **mention no ~s** keine Namen nennen; **fill in one's ~ and address** Name und Adresse eintragen; **she took her mother's ~:** sie nahm den Mädchennamen ihrer Mutter an; **what ~ shall I say?** wen darf ich melden?; **I can't put a ~ to the plant/his face** ich kann die Pflanze nicht benennen/sein Gesicht mit keinem Namen in Verbindung bringen; **a man of** *or* **by the ~ of Miller** ein Mann namens Miller *od.* mit Namen Miller; **go** *or* **be known by** *or* **under the ~ of ...:** unter dem Namen ... bekannt sein; **by ~:** namentlich ‹erwähnen, aufrufen usw.›; **refer to sb./sth. by ~:** jmdn./etw. namentlich nennen; **know sb. by ~/by ~ only** jmdn. mit Namen/nur dem Namen nach kennen; **she goes by the ~ of Madame Lola** sie ist unter dem Namen Madame Lola bekannt; **that's the ~ of the game** *(coll.)* darum geht es; **with us speed is the ~ of the game** *(coll.)* bei uns heißt die Devise Schnelligkeit; **put one's/sb.'s ~ down for sth.** sich/jmdn. für etw. vormerken lassen; **put one's/sb.'s ~ down on the waiting list** sich auf die Warteliste setzen lassen/jmdn. auf die Warteliste setzen; **take sb.'s ~ off the books** jmdn. ausschließen *od.* von der Mitgliederliste streichen; **without a penny to his ~:** ohne einen Pfennig in der Tasche; **he hasn't a pair of shoes to his ~:** er kann nicht einmal ein Paar Schuhe sein eigen nennen *(ugs.)*; **what's in a ~?** Name ist Schall und Rauch; **... or my ~ is not John Smith** ... so wahr ich John Smith heiße; **if this doesn't work, my ~ is not Peter Brown** *etc.* wenn das nicht funktioniert, will ich Emil heißen *(ugs.)*; **that bullet had my ~ [and number] on it** die Kugel war für mich bestimmt; **have/see one's ~ [up] in lights** ganz groß herauskommen *(ugs.)*; ⇒ *also* **mud** C; Ⓑ *(word denoting object of thought)* Bezeichnung, *die;* Name, *der;* **~s cannot hurt me** Beschimpfungen tun mir nicht weh; Ⓒ **in ~ [only]** [nur] auf dem Papier; **a Christian/town in ~ only** nur dem Namen nach ein Christ/eine Stadt; **in all but ~:** im Grunde genommen; Ⓓ **in the ~ of** im Namen (+ *Gen.*); **in God's ~, in the ~ of God** um Gottes willen; **in Heaven's ~:** um Himmels willen; **in one's own ~:** im eigenen Namen; *(independently)* von sich aus; Ⓔ *(reputation)* Ruf, *der;* **have a ~ for honesty** für seine Ehrlichkeit bekannt sein; **make a ~ for oneself, win oneself a ~:** sich *(Dat.)* einen Namen machen; **make one's/sb.'s ~:** berühmt werden/jmdn. berühmt machen; **this book made his ~:** mit diesem Buch machte er sich einen Namen; **clear one's/sb.'s ~:** seine/jmds. Unschuld beweisen; Ⓕ *(famous person)* Name, *der;* **many great** *or* **big ~s** viele namhafte Persönlichkeiten; viele Größen; **be a big ~:** einen großen Namen haben; Ⓖ *attrib.* **~ brand** Markenartikel, *der;* **~ band** Starband, *die.* ⇒ *also* **assume** C; **bad** 1 A; **call** 2 I; **dog** 1 A; **false** 1 B; **proper name**; **take** 1 Y; **use** 2 A; **what** 5 A.

❷ *v.t.* Ⓐ *(give name to)* einen Namen geben (+ *Dat.*); **~ sb. John** jmdn. John nennen; jmdm. den Namen John geben; **~ a ship 'Mary'** ein Schiff [auf den Namen] „Mary" taufen; **~ sb./sth. after** *or (Amer.)* **for sb.** jmdn./etw. nach jmdm. benennen; **be ~d John** John heißen; **a man ~d Smith** ein Mann namens *od.* mit Namen Smith; **~ sb. John after** *or (Amer.)* **for sb.** jmdn. nach jmdm. John nennen; Ⓑ *(call by right name)* benennen; **~ the capital of Zambia** nenne die Hauptstadt von Sambia; **can you ~ the books of the Bible?** kannst du die Bücher der Bibel aufzählen?; Ⓒ *(nominate)* ernennen; **~ sb. [as] sth.** jmdn. zu etw. ernennen; **~ sb. to an office/a post** jmdn. in ein Amt berufen *od.* einsetzen/auf einen Posten berufen; **~ one's successor/heir** seinen Nachfolger/Erben bestimmen; **he has been ~d as the winner** ihm wurde der Sieg zuerkannt; **be ~d actress of the year** zur Schauspielerin des Jahres gewählt werden; Ⓓ *(mention)* nennen; *(specify)* benennen; **~ sb. as witness** jmdn. als Zeugen benennen; **~ ~s** Namen nennen; **he was ~d as the thief** er wurde als der Dieb genannt;

n

**~ the time and I'll meet you there** sag die Zeit, und dann treffen wir uns dort; **~ the day** (*choose wedding day*) den Tag der Hochzeit festlegen *od.* -setzen; **to ~ but a few** um nur einige zu nennen; **we were given champagne, oysters, you ~ it** (*coll.*) wir kriegten Champagner, Austern, und, und, und; **you ~ it, he's got/done** *etc.* **it** (*coll.*) es gibt nichts, was er nicht hat/noch nicht gemacht hat *usw.*

**name: ~-calling** *n.* Beschimpfungen *Pl.*; **the debate degenerated into mere ~-calling** die Debatte artete in bloße gegenseitige Beschimpfungen aus; **~ day** *n.* Namenstag, *der;* **~-drop** *v.i.* [scheinbar beiläufig] bekannte Namen fallen lassen; **she is always ~-dropping** sie lässt dauernd einfließen, wen sie alles kennt; **~-dropping** *n.* Namedropping, *das; Nennung bedeutender Namen, um Eindruck zu machen*

**nameless** /ˈneɪmlɪs/ *adj.* (A) (*having no name, obscure*) namenlos; **a ~ grave** das Grab eines Unbekannten *od.* Namenlosen; (B) (*not mentioned by name*) **a person who shall remain ~:** eine Person, die ungenannt bleiben soll; (C) (*anonymous*) namenlos; anonym; **a ~ woman** eine namentlich nicht bekannte Frau; eine Unbekannte; (D) (*abominable*) unaussprechlich; unsäglich (*geh.*); (E) (*inexpressible*) unbeschreiblich

**namely** /ˈneɪmlɪ/ *adv.* nämlich

**name: ~ part** *n.* Titelrolle, *die;* **~plate** *n.* Namensschild, *das;* **~sake** *n.* Namensvetter, *der*/-schwester, *die;* **~ tag** *n.* Namensschild, *das;* **~ tape** *n.* Namensschildchen, *das;* ≈ Wäschezeichen, *das*

**Namibia** /nəˈmɪbɪə/ *pr. n.* Namibia (*das*)

**nan** /næn/ *n.* (*child lang./coll.*) Omi, *die* (*Kinderspr.*)

**nancy** /ˈnænsɪ/ (*coll.*) ❶ *n.* **~ [boy]** Tunte, *die* (*salopp*). ❷ *adj.* tuntig (*salopp*)

**nanny** /ˈnænɪ/ *n.* (A) (*Brit.: nursemaid*) Kindermädchen, *das;* (B) (*coll.: granny*) Großmama, *die* (*fam.*); (C) ⇒ **nanny goat**

**nanny: ~ goat** *n.* Ziege, *die;* Geiß, *die* (*südd., österr., schweiz., westmd.*); **~ 'state** *n.* (*derog.*) Versorgungsstaat, *der*

**nanotechnology** /ˈnænəʊteknɒlədʒɪ/ *n.* Nanotechnologie, *die*

**nap¹** /næp/ ❶ *n.* Schläfchen, *das* (*ugs.*); Nickerchen, *das* (*fam.*); **take *or* have a ~:** ein Schläfchen *od.* Nickerchen machen *od.* halten; **have an afternoon ~:** ein [Nach]mittagsschläfchen machen *od.* halten. ❷ *v.i.*, **-pp-** dösen (*ugs.*); **catch sb. ~ping** (*fig.*) jmdn. überrumpeln

**nap²** *n.* (*of cloth*) Flor, *der*

**nap³** *n.* (A) **go ~** (*Cards*) die höchste Zahl von Stichen ansagen; (*fig.: risk everything*) alles auf eine Karte setzen; (B) (*Horseracing etc. coll.: tip*) Tipp auf Sieg

**napalm** /ˈneɪpɑːm/ *n.* Napalm, *das*

**nape** /neɪp/ *n.* **~ [of the neck]** Nacken, *der;* Genick, *das*

**naphtha** /ˈnæfθə/ *n.* Naphtha, *das*

**naphthalene** /ˈnæfθəliːn/ *n.* Naphthalin, *das*

**napkin** /ˈnæpkɪn/ *n.* (A) Serviette, *die;* (B) (*Brit.: nappy*) Windel, *die;* (C) (*waiter's*) Serviertuch, *das.* ⇒ *also* **sanitary napkin**

**'napkin ring** *n.* Serviettenring, *der*

**Naples** /ˈneɪplz/ *pr. n.* ▶ **1626** Neapel (*das*)

**Napoleonic** /nəpəʊlɪˈɒnɪk/ *adj.* napoleonisch; **the ~ Wars** die Napoleonischen Kriege

**nappy** /ˈnæpɪ/ *n.* (*Brit.*) Windel, *die;* **when you were still in nappies** als du noch in den Windeln gelegen hast

**narcissism** /nɑːˈsɪsɪzm/ *n.*, *no pl.* (*Psych.*) Narzissmus, *der*

**narcissistic** /nɑːsɪˈsɪstɪk/ *adj.* (*Psych.*) narzisstisch

**narcissus** /nɑːˈsɪsəs/ *n.*, *pl.* **narcissi** /nɑːˈsɪsaɪ/ *or* **~es** (*Bot.*) Narzisse, *die*

**narcosis** /nɑːˈkəʊsɪs/ *n.*, *pl.* **narcoses** /nɑːˈkəʊsiːz/ Betäubung, *die;* (*Med.: general anaesthesia*) Narkose, *die*

**narcotic** /nɑːˈkɒtɪk/ ❶ *n.* (A) (*drug*) Rauschgift, *das;* Betäubungsmittel, *das* (*Rechtsw.*); **~s squad** Rauschgiftdezernat, *das;* (B) (*active ingredient*) Betäubungsmittel, *das;* Narkotikum, *das* (*Med.*); (*fig.*) Narkotikum, *das;* Droge, *die.* ❷ *adj.* (A) narkotisch; **~ drug** Rauschgift, *das;* Betäubungsmittel, *das* (*Rechtsw.*); (B) (*inducing drowsiness, fig.*) einschläfernd

**nark** /nɑːk/ (*sl.*) ❶ *n.* (A) (*Brit.: informer*) Spitzel, *der* (*abwertend*); (B) (*Brit.: policeman*) Bulle, *der* (*salopp*). ❷ *v.t.* (*annoy*) stinken (+ *Dat.*) (*salopp*); **be ~ed [about sb./at *or* about sth.]** [auf jmdn./über etw. (*Akk.*)] sauer sein (*ugs.*); **that really got me ~ed** das hat mir echt gestunken (*salopp*)

**narrate** /nəˈreɪt/ *v.t.* (A) (*give account of*) erzählen; schildern ‹Ereignisse›; (B) kommentieren ‹Film›; *abs.* erzählen

**narration** /nəˈreɪʃn/ *n.* (A) Erzählen, *das;* Erzählung, *die;* (*of events*) Schilderung, *die;* Schildern, *das;* (B) ⇒ **narrative** 1 A

**narrative** /ˈnærətɪv/ ❶ *n.* (A) (*tale, story*) Geschichte, *die;* Erzählung, *die;* (B) *no pl.* (*kind of composition*) **be written in ~:** in der Erzählform geschrieben sein; **writer of ~:** erzählender Autor; Erzähler, *der.* ❷ *adj.* narrativ (*Sprachw.*); erzählend; erzählerisch ‹Gabe, Talent›; Erzähl‹kunst, -technik›; **~ writer** Erzähler, *der*/Erzählerin, *die*

**narrator** /nəˈreɪtə(r)/ *n.* Erzähler, *der*/Erzählerin, *die;* (*of film*) Kommentator, *der*/Kommentatorin, *die;* **first-/third-person ~:** Ich-/Er-Erzähler, *der*

**narrow** /ˈnærəʊ/ ❶ *adj.* (A) schmal; schmal geschnitten ‹Rock, Hose, Ärmel usw.›; eng ‹Tal, Gasse›; **the road became ~:** die Straße verschmälerte sich; (B) (*limited*) eng; begrenzt, schmal ‹Auswahl›; **in the ~est sense** im engsten Sinne; (C) (*with little margin*) knapp ‹Sieg, Führung, Mehrheit›; **have a ~ escape** mit knapper Not entkommen (**from** *Dat.*); **win by a ~ margin** knapp gewinnen; (D) (*not tolerant*) spießig (*abwertend*); engstirnig (*abwertend*); **have a ~ mind** engstirnig *od.* spießig sein; **a ~ existence** ein Spießerdasein; (E) (*restricted*) eng ‹Grenzen, Toleranzen›; klein, begrenzt ‹Freundeskreis›; beengt ‹Verhältnisse›; schmal ‹Einkommen›; (F) (*precise*) genau; gründlich, eingehend ‹Prüfung, Befragung›.

❷ *n. usu. in pl.* (*of sea*) Meerenge, *die.*

❸ *v.i.* sich verschmälern; ‹Augen, Tal:› sich verengen; (*fig.*) [zusammen]schrumpfen; **the road ~s to one lane** die Straße wird einspurig.

❹ *v.t.* verschmälern; (*fig.*) einengen; enger fassen ‹Definition›; **~ one's eyes** die Augen zusammenkneifen; **~ the field** (*fig.*) eine Vorauswahl treffen

**~ 'down** ❶ *v.t.* einengen, beschränken (**to** auf + *Akk.*). ❷ *v.i.* sich reduzieren (**to** auf + *Akk.*); **the choice ~s down to two possibilities** es bleiben zwei Möglichkeiten [übrig]

**narrow: ~ boat** *n.* (*Brit.*) *besonders schmales Binnenschiff;* **~-gauge** *adj.* schmalspurig; Schmalspur-

**narrowly** /ˈnærəʊlɪ/ *adv.* (A) (*with little width*) schmal; (B) (*only just*) knapp; mit knapper Not ‹entkommen›; **he ~ escaped being run over by a car** er wäre um ein Haar (*ugs.*) überfahren worden; **~ miss winning [the election/race]** [bei der Wahl/in dem Rennen] knapp unterliegen; (C) (*closely*) genau; eng ‹auslegen›

**narrow: ~-'minded** *adj.*, **~-mindedly** /nærəʊˈmaɪndɪdlɪ/ *adv.* engstirnig (*abwertend*); **~-mindedness** /nærəʊˈmaɪndɪdnɪs/ *n.*, *no pl.* Engstirnigkeit, *die* (*abwertend*); **~-'shouldered** *adj.* schmalschultrig; **~ 'squeak** ⇒ **squeak** 1 B

**narwhal** /ˈnɑːwəl/ *n.* (*Zool.*) Narwal, *der*

**nary** /ˈneərɪ/ *adj.* (*coll./dial.*) **~ a ...:** kein einziger/keine einzige/kein einziges ...

**NASA** /ˈnæsə/ *abbr.* (*Amer.*) **National Aeronautics and Space Administration** NASA, *die*

**nasal** /ˈneɪzl/ ❶ *adj.* (A) (*Anat.*) Nasen-; (B) näselnd; **speak in a ~ voice** durch die Nase sprechen; näseln; **have a ~ intonation** näselnd sprechen; näseln; (C) (*Ling.*) nasal; Nasal-. ❷ *n.* (*Ling.*) Nasal[laut], *der*

**nasalize** /ˈneɪzəlaɪz/ *v.t.* (*Ling.*) nasalieren

**nascent** /ˈnæsnt/ *adj.* (A) (*literary: coming into existence*) werdend; im Entstehen begriffen; aufkommend, (*geh.*) aufkeimend ‹Hoffnung, Stolz›; (B) (*Chem.*) naszierend

**nastily** /ˈnɑːstɪlɪ/ *adv.* (A) (*disagreeably, unpleasantly*) scheußlich; (B) (*ill-naturedly*) gemein; gehässig; ärgerlich ‹etwas sagen›; **behave ~:** hässlich sein; (C) (*disgustingly*) eklig; widerlich

**nasturtium** /nəˈstɜːʃəm/ *n.* (A) (*in popular use: garden plant*) Kapuzinerkresse, *die;* (B) (*Bot.: cruciferous plant*) Brunnenkresse, *die*

**nasty** /ˈnɑːstɪ/ ❶ *adj.* (A) (*disagreeable, unpleasant*) scheußlich ‹Geruch, Geschmack, Arznei, Essen, Wetter›; gemein ‹Trick, Verhalten, Äußerung, Mensch›; hässlich ‹Angewohnheit›; **her ~ little ways** ihre kleinen Gemeinheiten; **that was a ~ thing to say/do** das war gemein *od.* eine Gemeinheit; **that's a ~ one** (*awkward question*) das ist vertrackt; (*injury*) das ist übel *od.* sieht böse aus; **a ~ bit *or* piece of work** (*coll.*) (*man*) ein fieser Kerl (*ugs. abwertend*); (*woman*) ein fieses Weibsstück (*ugs. abwertend*); ⇒ *also* **cheap** 1 A; (B) (*ill-natured*) böse; **be ~ to sb.** hässlich zu jmdm. sein; **he has a ~ temper** er ist jähzornig; **cut up *or* turn ~** (*coll.*) eklig werden (*ugs.*); (C) (*serious*) übel; böse ‹Verletzung, Husten usw.›; schlimm ‹Krankheit, Husten, Verletzung, Wende›; **that's a ~-looking wound** die Wunde sieht übel *od.* böse aus; **she had a ~ fall** sie ist übel *od.* böse gefallen; **He had to have his leg amputated — N~!** Sein Bein musste amputiert werden — Das ist schlimm!; (D) (*disgusting*) eklig; widerlich; **don't touch that, it's ~:** pfui, fass das nicht an! (*fam.*); nicht anfassen, das ist bä bä (*Kinderspr.*); (E) (*obscene*) schweinisch (*ugs. abwertend*); **call sb. ~ names** jmdn. mit schweinischen Ausdrücken beschimpfen.

❷ *n.* (A) (*person*) Ekel, *das* (*ugs. abwertend*); Fiesling, *der* (*salopp abwertend*); (B) (*thing*) ekliges Ding; ⇒ *also* **video nasty**

**Nat.** *abbr.* (*Polit.*) **Nationalist**

**natal** /ˈneɪtl/ *adj.* Geburts-

**natch** /nætʃ/ *adv.* (*coll.*) versteht sich (*ugs.*); logisch (*ugs.*)

**nation** /ˈneɪʃn/ *n.* Nation, *die;* (*people*) Volk, *das;* **law of ~s** Völkerrecht, *das;* **throughout the ~:** im ganzen Land. ⇒ *also* **League of Nations; United Nations**

**national** /ˈnæʃənl/ ❶ *adj.* national; National‹flagge, -denkmal, -held, -theater, -tanz, -gericht, -charakter, -kirche, -ökonomie, -einkommen›; Landes‹durchschnitt, -sprache›; Volks‹wirtschaft, -charakter, -held›; Staats‹sicherheit, -religion, -symbol›; überregional ‹Rundfunkstation, Zeitung›; landesweit ‹Streik›; **the rose is the ~ flower of England** die Rose ist das Symbol Englands. ❷ *n.* (A) (*citizen*) Staatsbürger, *der*/-bürgerin, *die;* **foreign ~:** Ausländer, *der*/Ausländerin, *die;* (B) (*fellow countryman*) Landsmann, *der*/-männin, *die;* (C) *usu. in pl.* (*newspaper*) überregionale Zeitung; [großes] überregionales Blatt; (D) (*Brit.: horse race*) **the N~:** das Grand National

**national: ~ 'anthem** *n.* Nationalhymne, *die;* **N~ As'sembly** *n.* Nationalversammlung, *die;* **N~ As'sistance** *n.* (*Brit. dated*) Sozialhilfe, *die;* **be on N~ Assistance** Sozialhilfe beziehen; **~ 'bank** *n.* (*Amer.*) Nationalbank, *die;* **~ call** *n.* (*Brit. Teleph.*) Inlandsgespräch, *das;* **~ con'vention** *n.* (*Amer.*) Nationalkonvent, *der;* ≈ Bundeskongress, *der;* **~ 'costume** *n.* Nationaltracht, *die;* Landestracht, *die;* **N~ Cur'riculum** *n.* (*Brit.*) Nationales Curriculum; **N~ 'Debt** ⇒ **debt; ~ 'dress** ⇒ **~ costume; ~ 'football** *n.* (*Austral.*) australischer Fußball; **N~ 'Front** *n.* (*Brit.*) National Front, *die* (*britische Organisation mit extremen reaktionären Positionen z. B. in Bezug auf die Einwanderungspolitik*); *attrib.* National-Front-‹Mitglied, Slogan usw.›; **~ 'grid** *n.* (*Brit.*) (A) (*Electr.*) nationales Verbundnetz; **~ grid system** nationales Verbundsystem; (B) (*Geog.*) nationales Gitternetz; **N~ 'Guard** *n.* (*Amer.*) Nationalgarde, *die;* **N~ 'Health [Service]** *n.* (*Brit.*) *staatlicher Gesundheitsdienst;* **he had his teeth done on the N~ Health** er hat sich (*Dat.*)

# Nationalities

In English, words such as German, French, Italian etc. are both adjectives referring to the language and the people and nouns meaning a language or a person, and are always written with a capital. In German, the words **deutsch, französisch, italienisch** and so on are also used as both adjectives and nouns, with the differences that only the nouns are written with a capital, and the noun meaning a person is only in a few cases the same as the noun meaning a person (e.g. **ein Deutscher**), and then it has endings while that meaning a language usually does not.

For full details of these ····➤ **Languages**

## Adjectives

Translating adjective plus noun combinations is straightforward (remembering the small letter for the adjective):

***an Italian car***
= ein italienisches Auto

***the French government***
= die französische Regierung

***a German painter***
= ein deutscher Maler/eine deutsche Malerin

When referring to a unique national institution, the name of the country in the genitive is often preferred (just as one can also use of plus the name of the country in English):

***the Indian capital*** = ***the capital of India***
= die Hauptstadt Indiens

When the adjective is predicative, i.e. standing on its own, and refers to a person or persons, the English nationality adjective will always be translated by the noun in German:

***He is Italian***
= Er ist Italiener

***She is Indian***
= Sie ist Inderin

***The tourists are French***
= Die Touristen sind Franzosen

Referring to a thing, German often prefers to avoid having the adjective standing on its own:

***The car is Italian***
= Es ist ein italienisches Auto, *rather than* Das Auto ist italienisch

## Nouns

As in English, the nouns for people of different nationalities vary in form, but in German there are feminine forms in all cases ending in **-in**. A large number of them have the **-er** ending added to the word for the country for the masculine, and **-erin** for the feminine:

***an Englishman/Englishwoman***
= ein Engländer/eine Engländerin

***an Italian***
= ein Italiener/eine Italienerin (*Italy* = Italien)

***an Austrian***
= ein Österreicher/eine Österreicherin (*Austria* = Österreich)

***a Japanese***
= ein Japaner/eine Japanerin

A number of these nouns end in **-e**, and this disappears when the feminine ending is added:

***a Frenchman/Frenchwoman***
= ein Franzose/eine Französin

***a Chinese***
= ein Chinese/eine Chinesin

***a Dane***
= ein Däne/eine Dänin

***a Russian***
= ein Russe/eine Russin

The plural in these cases adds an **-n** (**Franzosen, Chinesen, Dänen, Russen**) to the masculine, and it is this masculine plural form that is used when referring to a group of mixed gender, or the whole nation:

***the French***
= die Franzosen

***the English***
= die Engländer

Last but not least, the noun for a German is the adjective as a noun:

***a German***
= ein Deutscher/eine Deutsche

***the Germans***
= die Deutschen

***He was the only German***
= Er war der einzige Deutsche

***The prize was awarded to a German***
= Der Preis wurde einem Deutschen verliehen

## Phrases

***She is Spanish by birth***
= Sie ist von Geburt Spanierin *or* gebürtige Spanierin

***He is of German extraction***
= Er ist deutscher Abstammung

***I come from the north of England***
= Ich stamme *or* komme aus Nordengland

***He's a Belgian national or citizen***
= Er ist belgischer Staatsbürger

***a naturalized Swiss citizen***
= ein eingebürgerter *or* naturalisierter Schweizer/eine eingebürgerte *or* naturalisierte Schweizerin

seine Zähne auf Kosten des staatlichen Gesundheitsdienstes in Ordnung bringen *od.* (*ugs.*) machen lassen; *attrib.* **National Health doctor/patient/spectacles** ≈ Kassenarzt, *der*/-patient, *der*/-brille, *die;* ~ **'holiday** *n.* Nationalfeiertag, *der;* (*statutory holiday*) gesetzlicher Feiertag; **N~ In'surance** *n.* (*Brit.*) Sozialversicherung, *die*

**nationalisation, nationalise** ⇒ **nationaliz-**

**nationalism** /'næʃənəlɪzm/ *n.* Nationalismus, *der;* (*patriotism*) nationale Gesinnung; **feelings of ~:** nationale Gefühle

**nationalist** /'næʃənəlɪst/ ❶ *n.* Nationalist, *der*/Nationalistin, *die.* ❷ *adj.* nationalistisch

**nationalistic** /næʃənə'lɪstɪk/ *adj.* Ⓐ (*patriotic*) nationalistisch; Ⓑ (*national*) national

**nationality** /næʃə'nælɪtɪ/ *n.* Ⓐ Staatsangehörigkeit, *die;* Nationalität, *die* (*geh.*); **be of** *or* **have British ~:** britischer Nationalität sein (*geh.*); die britische Staatsangehörigkeit haben; **what's his ~?** welche Staatsangehörigkeit hat er?; welcher Nationalität ist er? (*geh.*); Ⓑ (*ethnic group*) Nationalität, *die;* Volksgruppe, *die;* Ⓒ (*of ship, aircraft, company*) Nationalität, *die*

**nationalization** /næʃənəlaɪ'zeɪʃn/ *n.* Ⓐ (*bringing under state control*) Verstaatlichung, *die;* Nationalisierung, *die;* Ⓑ (*making national*) Nationalisierung, *die*

**nationalize** /'næʃənəlaɪz/ *v.t.* Ⓐ (*bring under state control*) verstaatlichen, nationalisieren ‹Betriebe, Industriezweige›; Ⓑ (*make national*) nationalisieren

**nationally** /'næʃənəlɪ/ *adv.* als Nation; (*throughout the nation*) landesweit

**National: n~ 'park** *n.* Nationalpark, *der;* ~ **'Savings** *n. pl.* (*Brit.*) Staatsschuldverschreibungen *Pl.; attrib.* ~ **Savings certificate** Sparkassengutschein, *der;* öffentlicher Sparbrief; **n~ 'service** *n.* (*Brit.*) Wehrdienst, *der;* **do n~ service** seinen Wehrdienst ableisten; ~ **'Socialist** *n.* (*Hist.*) Nationalsozialist, *der*/-sozialistin, *die; attrib.* nationalsozialistisch; ~ **'Trust** *n.* (*Brit.*) *nationale Einrichtung für Naturschutz und Denkmalpflege;* ~ **Vo'cational Qualification** *n.* (*Brit.*) *staatliches Berufsausbildungsprogramm*

**nationhood** /'neɪʃnhud/ *n.* nationale Selbstständigkeit

**nation:** ~ **'state** *n.* Nationalstaat, *der;* **~wide** ❶ /'---/ *adj.* landesweit; national ‹Bedeutung›. ❷ /--'-/ *adv.* landesweit; im ganzen Land

**native** /'neɪtɪv/ ❶ *n.* Ⓐ (*of specified place*) **a ~ of Britain** ein gebürtiger Brite/eine gebürtige Britin; **speak English like a ~:** Englisch wie seine Muttersprache sprechen; Ⓑ (*indigenous person*) Eingeborene, *der/die;* Ⓒ (*local inhabitant*) Einheimische, *der/die;* **the ~s** die Einheimischen; die einheimische Bevölkerung; Ⓓ (*Zool., Bot.*) **be a ~ of a place** in einem Ort beheimatet *od.* heimisch sein; Ⓔ (*S. Afr.: Black*) Schwarze, *der/die.*
❷ *adj.* Ⓐ (*indigenous*) eingeboren; (*local*) einheimisch ‹Pflanze, Tier›; **be a ~ American**

gebürtiger Amerikaner/gebürtige Amerikanerin sein; **the ~ habitat of the zebra** die Heimat des Zebras; **~ inhabitant** Eingeborene/Einheimische, *der/die;* **B** (*of one's birth*) Geburts-, Heimat‹land, -stadt›; Vater‹land, -stadt› (*geh.*); Mutter‹sprache, -sprachler›; heimatlich ‹Wälder›; **one's ~ soil** die Heimaterde; **in his ~ France** in seiner Heimat Frankreich; **~ speaker** Muttersprachler, *der* (*fachspr.*); **he's not a ~ speaker of English** Englisch ist nicht seine Muttersprache; **C** (*innate*) angeboren ‹Qualitäten, Schläue, Humor, Wissen›; **D** (*of the ~s*) Eingeborenen-; **go ~:** die Lebensweise der Eingeborenen annehmen; **E** (*Mining*) gediegen

**native: ~ 'bear** (*Austral., NZ*) ⇒ **koala bear**; **~ 'rock** *n.* anstehendes Gestein; gewachsener Fels

**nativity** /nə'tɪvɪtɪ/ *n.* **A** Geburt, *die;* **the N~ [of Christ]** die Geburt Christi; **B** (*festival*) **the N~ of Christ** das Fest der Geburt Christi; **C** (*picture*) Geburt Christi

**na'tivity play** *n.* Krippenspiel, *das*

**NATO, Nato** /'neɪtəʊ/ *abbr.* **North Atlantic Treaty Organization** NATO, *die*

**natter** /'nætə(r)/ (*Brit. coll.*) **1** *v.i.* quatschen (*ugs.*); quasseln (*ugs.*). **2** *n.* Schwatz, *der* (*fam.*); Schwätzchen, *das* (*fam.*); **have a bit of a ~:** ein bisschen quatschen (*ugs.*); ein Schwätzchen halten (*fam.*)

**natterjack** /'nætədʒæk/ *n.* (*Zool.*) **~ [toad]** Kreuzkröte, *die*

**nattily** /'nætɪlɪ/ *adv.* (*coll.*) schick; flott (*ugs.*)

**natty** /'nætɪ/ *adj.* (*coll.*) **A** (*spruce*) schick, (*ugs.*) flott ‹Kleidungs[stück]›; **be a ~ dresser** immer schick *od.* flott angezogen sein; **B** (*handy*) praktisch ‹Gerät, Werkzeug usw.›

**natural** /'nætʃrəl/ **1** *adj.* **A** (*existing in or by nature*) natürlich; Natur‹zustand, -begabung, -talent, -seide, -schwamm, -faser, -gewalt, -erscheinung›; gediegen ‹Gold, Mineralien›; naturgetreu ‹Wiedergabe, Darstellung›; **the ~ world** die Natur[welt]; **in its ~ state** im ursprünglichen Zustand *od.* Naturzustand; **be a ~ blonde** naturblondes Haar haben; von Natur aus blond sein; **B** (*normal*) natürlich; **it is ~ for dogs to fight** es ist natürlich, dass Hunde kämpfen; **it is ~ for you to think that** es ist klar, dass du das denkst; **die of** *or* **from ~ causes** eines natürlichen Todes sterben; **have a ~ tendency to ...:** naturgemäß dazu neigen, ... zu ...; **C** (*unaffected*) natürlich ‹Art, Lächeln, Stil›; **D** (*destined*) natürlich ‹Feinde›; **be a ~ artist** *etc.* der geborene Künstler *usw.* sein; **E** (*related by nature*) leiblich ‹Eltern, Kind usw.›; natürlich (*Rechtsspr. veralt.*) ‹Kind›; **F** (*instinctive*) Natur‹recht›; auf das Naturrecht gegründet ‹Gerechtigkeit›. **2** *n.* **A** (*person naturally expert or endowed*) Naturtalent, *das;* **she's a ~ for the part** die Rolle ist ihr auf den Leib geschrieben; **he was a ~ for the job** er war der Mann für die Stelle; **B** (*arch.: mentally deficient person*) Schwachsinnige, *der/die;* **C** (*Mus.*) (*symbol*) Auflösungszeichen, *das;* (*note*) Stammton, *der;* (*white key on piano*) weiße Taste; **he played C sharp instead of C ~:** er hat cis statt c gespielt

**natural: ~ 'childbirth** *n.* natürliche Geburt; **~ 'death** *n.* natürlicher Tod; **die a ~ death** eines natürlichen Todes sterben; **let the gossip die a ~ death** warten, bis sich das Gerede von selber legt; **~ 'food** *n.* naturreines Nahrungsmittel; **~ food[s]** Naturkost, *die;* **~ 'gas** ⇒ **gas** 1 A; **~ hi'storian** *n.* Naturkundler, *der/*-kundlerin, *die;* **~ 'history** *n.* **A** (*study*) Naturkunde, *die; attrib.* Naturkunde-; naturkundlich ‹Museum›; **B** (*facts*) Naturgeschichte, *die*

**naturalisation, naturalise** ⇒ **naturaliz-**

**naturalism** /'nætʃrəlɪzm/ *n.* Naturalismus, *der*

**naturalist** /'nætʃrəlɪst/ *n.* **A** Naturforscher, *der/*-forscherin, *die;* **B** (*believer in naturalism*) Naturalist, *der/*Naturalistin, *die*

**naturalistic** /nætʃrə'lɪstɪk/ *adj.* naturalistisch

**naturalization** /nætʃrəlaɪ'zeɪʃn/ *n.* (*admission to citizenship*) Einbürgerung, *die;* Naturalisierung, *die; attrib.* Einbürgerungs-

**naturalize** /'nætʃrəlaɪz/ **1** *v.t.* **A** (*admit to citizenship*) einbürgern; naturalisieren; **B** (*adopt*) übernehmen ‹Fremdwort, Sitte›; **C** (*introduce*) naturalisieren, einbürgern ‹Tiere, Pflanzen›; **this plant has become ~d here** diese Pflanze wurde hier heimisch. **2** *v.i.* eingebürgert werden

**natural: ~ 'language** *n.* natürliche Sprache; **~-language programming** Programmieren in natürlicher Sprache; **~ 'law** *n.* Naturrecht, *das;* (*regularity*) Naturgesetz, *das;* **~ 'life** *n.* Erdenleben, *das* (*meist dichter., geh. od. veralt.*); **~ 'logarithm** *n.* natürlicher Logarithmus

**naturally** /'nætʃrəlɪ/ *adv.* **A** (*by nature*) von Natur aus ‹musikalisch, blass, fleißig usw.›; (*in a true-to-life way*) naturgetreu; (*with ease*) natürlich; (*in a natural manner*) auf natürliche Weise; **a ~ posed photograph** ein natürlich wirkendes Foto; **it comes ~ to her** es fällt ihr leicht; es liegt in ihrer Natur; **leadership comes so ~ to him** die Führungsrolle liegt ihm sehr; **lead ~ to sth.** naturgemäß zu etw. führen; **B** (*of course*) natürlich

**naturalness** /'nætʃrəlnɪs/ *n.* Natürlichkeit, *die*

**natural: ~ note** *n.* (*Mus.*) Stammton, *der;* **~ 'number** *n.* (*Math.*) natürliche Zahl; **~ 'order** *n.* (*Biol.*) natürliche Kategorie; **~ phi'losopher** *n.* Naturphilosoph, *der/*-philosophin, *die;* **~ phi'losophy** *n.* **A** (*physics*) Naturphilosophie, *die;* **B** (**~ science**) die Naturwissenschaften; **~ re'ligion** *n.* natürliche Religion; **~ re'sources** *n. pl.* natürliche Ressourcen; Naturschätze *Pl.;* **~ 'scale** *n.* (*Mus.*) Grundskala, *die;* **~ 'science** *n.* **science, the ~ sciences** die Naturwissenschaften; **~ se'lection** *n.* (*Biol.*) natürliche Auslese

**nature** /'neɪtʃə(r)/ *n.* **A** Natur, *die;* **a gift from N~:** ein Geschenk der Natur; **balance of ~:** Gleichgewicht der Natur; **against** *or* **contrary to ~:** wider die Natur *od.* widernatürlich; **back to ~:** zurück zur Natur; **get back** *or* **return to ~:** zu einer natürlichen Lebensweise zurückkehren; **paint from ~:** nach der Natur malen; **in ~** (*actually existing*) in der Wirklichkeit; (*anywhere*) auf Erden; **one of ~'s gentlemen** ein geborener Gentleman; **one of ~'s innocents** die Unschuld selbst; **in a state of ~** (*undomesticated, uncultivated*) in der Wildform; ⇒ *also* **call** 3 F; **course** 1 A; **law** H; **B** (*essential qualities*) Beschaffenheit, *die;* **in the ~ of things** naturgemäß; **it is in** *or* **by the [very] ~ of the case/of things** es liegt in der Natur der Sache/Dinge; **C** (*kind, sort*) Art, *die;* **things of this ~:** Derartiges; Dinge dieser Art; **or something of that ~:** oder etwas in der Art; **it's in** *or* **of the ~ of a command** es hat Befehlscharakter; **D** (*character*) [Wesens]art, *die;* Wesen, *das;* **have a happy ~:** eine Frohnatur sein; ein glückliches Naturell haben; **be of** *or* **have a placid ~:** eine ruhige Art haben; **have a jealous ~:** eifersüchtig sein; **it is not in her ~ to lie** es ist nicht ihre Art zu lügen; **be proud/friendly** *etc.* **by ~:** ein stolzes/freundliches *usw.* Wesen haben; **[human] ~:** menschliche Natur; **it's only human ~ to ...:** es ist nur menschlich, ... zu ...; ⇒ *also* **better** 1; **second nature**; **E** (*inherent impulses*) Natur, *die;* **commit a sin/crime against ~:** sich wider die Natur versündigen (*geh.*); **F** (*person*) Natur, *die*

**nature: ~ conservation** *n.* Naturschutz, *der;* **~ cure** *n.* Naturheilverfahren, *das*

**-natured** /'neɪtʃəd/ *adj. in comb.* -artig; ⇒ *also* **good-natured**; **ill-natured**

**nature: ~ lover** *n.* Naturfreund, *der/*-freundin, *die;* **~ reserve** *n.* Naturschutzgebiet, *das;* **~ study** *n.* Naturkunde, *die;* **~ trail** *n.* Naturlehrpfad, *der;* **~ worshipper** *n.* Naturanbeter, *der/*-anbeterin, *die*

**naturism** /'neɪtʃərɪzm/ *n.* (*nudism*) Naturismus, *der;* Freikörperkultur, *die*

**naturist** /'neɪtʃərɪst/ *n.* (*nudist*) Naturist, *der/*Naturistin, *die;* FKK-Anhänger, *der/*FKK-Anhängerin, *die*

**naught** /nɔːt/ *n.* (*arch./dial.*) **~ but** nur; **I care ~ for what they say** ich scher mich keinen Deut darum, was sie sagen; **bring to ~:** zunichte machen; **come to ~:** zunichte werden; **it matters ~:** es ist ohne Belang

**naughtily** /'nɔːtɪlɪ/ *adv.* ungezogen, unartig ‹sich benehmen›; frech ‹etw. tun, bemerken›

**naughtiness** /'nɔːtɪnɪs/ *n.* Ungezogenheit, *die;* Unartigkeit, *die*

**naughty** /'nɔːtɪ/ *adj.* **A** (*disobedient*) unartig; ungezogen; **the dog has been ~ on the carpet** (*coll. euphem.*) der Hund hat auf den Teppich gemacht (*ugs.*); **you ~ boy/dog** du böser Junge/Hund; **B** (*indecent*) unanständig; **how ~ of him** das war aber frech *od.* kess von ihm; **~, ~!** du bist ja ein ganz Schlimmer!/eine ganz Schlimme!

**nausea** /'nɔːzɪə, 'nɔːsɪə/ *n.* **A** ▶ 1232 Übelkeit, *die;* **even the idea fills me with ~:** schon beim bloßen Gedanken daran wird mir übel; **B** (*fig.: disgust*) Ekel, *der,* Abscheu, *der* (**with, at** vor + *Dat.*)

**nauseate** /'nɔːzɪeɪt, 'nɔːsɪeɪt/ *v.t.* **A** ▶ 1232 **~ sb.** in jmdm. Übelkeit erregen; **the smell ~d him** bei dem Geruch wurde ihm übel; **B** (*fig.: disgust*) anekeln; anwidern

**nauseating** /'nɔːzɪeɪtɪŋ, 'nɔːsɪeɪtɪŋ/ *adj.* **A** Übelkeit verursachend *od.* erregend; **B** (*fig.: disgusting*) widerlich; Ekel erregend ‹Anblick, Geruch, Essen›; ekelhaft ‹Mensch›

**nauseatingly** /'nɔːzɪeɪtɪŋlɪ, 'nɔːsɪeɪtɪŋlɪ/ *adv.* (*lit. or fig.*) widerlich

**nauseous** /'nɔːzɪəs, 'nɔːsɪəs/ *adj.* **A** ▶ 1232 **sb. is** *or* **feels ~:** jmdm. ist übel; **B** (*fig.: nasty, disgusting*) widerlich

**nautical** /'nɔːtɪkl/ *adj.* nautisch; seemännisch ‹Ausdruck, Können›; **~ map** Seekarte, *die;* **be interested in ~ matters** sich für die Seefahrt interessieren

**nautically** /'nɔːtɪkəlɪ/ *adv.* nautisch

**nautical 'mile** *n.* Seemeile, *die;* nautische Meile

**nautilus** /'nɔːtɪləs/ *n., pl.* **~es** *or* **nautili** /'nɔːtɪlaɪ/ (*Zool.*) Nautilus, *der*

**naval** /'neɪvl/ *adj.* Marine-; Flotten‹parade, -abkommen›; See‹schlacht, -macht, -streitkräfte›; ‹Überlegenheit› zur See; **~ ship** Kriegsschiff, *das*

**naval: ~ a'cademy** *n.* Marineakademie, *die;* **~ 'architect** *n.* ▶ 1261 Schiffsbauingenieur, *der;* **~ base** *n.* Flottenstützpunkt, *der;* **~ officer** *n.* Marineoffizier, *der;* **~ 'stores** *n. pl.* Schiffsvorräte *Pl.;* **~ 'warfare** *n.* Seekrieg, *der;* Krieg zur See

**nave** /neɪv/ *n.* (*Archit.*) [Mittel-, Haupt]schiff, *das*

**navel** /'neɪvl/ *n.* Nabel, *der;* **contemplate one's ~** (*fig.*) Nabelschau halten (*ugs. abwertend*)

**'navel orange** *n.* Navelorange, *die*

**navigable** /'nævɪgəbl/ *adj.* **A** (*suitable for ships*) schiffbar; befahrbar; **B** (*seaworthy*) seetüchtig ‹Schiff, Zustand›; **C** (*steerable*) lenkbar, steuerbar ‹Ballon, Luftschiff›

**navigate** /'nævɪgeɪt/ **1** *v.t.* **A** (*sail on*) beschiffen (*veralt.*), befahren ‹Kanal, Fluss, Gewässer›; **B** (*direct course of*) navigieren ‹Schiff, Flugzeug›; **C** (*fig.*) **~ one's way to the bar** sich (*Dat.*) einen Weg zur Bar bahnen. **2** *v.i.* **A** (*in ship, aircraft*) navigieren; **B** (*assist driver*) den Lotsen spielen (*ugs.*); franzen (*Rallyesport*); **you drive, I'll ~:** du fährst, und ich dirigiere *od.* lotse dich

**navigation** /nævɪ'geɪʃn/ *n.* **A** (*navigating*) Navigation, *die;* Navigieren, *das;* (*sailing on river etc.*) Befahren, *das;* (*assisting driver*) Dirigieren, *das;* Lotsen, *das;* Franzen, *das* (*Rallyesport*); **I'm relying on you to do the ~:** ich verlasse mich darauf, dass du mich richtig dirigierst; **B** (*art, science*) Navigation, *die;* **C** (*voyage*) Fahrt, *die;* Reise, *die*

**navi'gation lights** *n. pl.* (*Naut.*) Lichter; (*Aeronaut.*) Kennlichter

**navigator** /'nævɪgeɪtə(r)/ *n.* **A** (*one skilled in navigation*) Navigator, *der/*Navigatorin, *die;* **his co-driver was acting as ~:** sein

n

Beifahrer dirigierte *od.* lotste ihn; [B] (*sea explorer*) Seefahrer, *der*

**navvy** /'nævɪ/ (*Brit.*) ❶ *n.* (*labourer*) Bau-/Straßenarbeiter, *der.* ❷ *v.i.* Bau-/Straßenarbeiter sein

**navy** /'neɪvɪ/ *n.* [A] [Kriegs]marine, *die;* (*ships also*) [Kriegs]flotte, *die;* [B] ⇒ **navy blue**

**navy:** ~ **'blue** *n.* Marineblau, *das;* **~-blue** *adj.* marineblau; **N~ Department** *n.* (*Amer.*) Marineministerium, *das;* **N~ List** *n.* (*Brit.*) Rangliste der Marine; ~ **yard** *n.* (*Amer.*) Marinewerft, *die*

**nay** /neɪ/ ❶ *adv.* ⇒ (*literary: or rather*) ja [sogar]; [AA] (*arch./dial.: no*) nein. ❷ *n.* [A] (*negative vote*) Neinstimme, *die;* [B] (*arch./dial.: no*) Nein, *das.* ⇒ *also* **yea** 2

**Nazi** /'nɑːtsɪ/ ❶ *n.* [A] (*party member*) Nationalsozialist, *der*/-sozialistin, *die;* Nazi, *der;* [B] (*fig. derog.*) Faschist, *der*/Faschistin, *die* (*abwertend*); Nazi, *der* (*abwertend*). ❷ *adj.* [A] nazistisch; Nazi-; [B] (*fig. derog.*) faschistisch (*abwertend*); Nazi- (*abwertend*)

**Naziism** /'nɑːtsɪɪzm/, **Nazism** /'nɑːtsɪzm/ *n.* Nazismus, *der*

**NB** *abbr.* **nota bene** NB

**NCO** *abbr.* **non-commissioned officer** Uffz.

**NE** *abbr.* ▶1024 [A] /nɔːθ'iːst/ **north-east** NO; [B] /nɔːθ'iːstən/ **north-eastern** nö.

**Neanderthal** /nɪ'ændətɑːl/ *adj.* Neandertaler-; (*fig.*) neandertalerhaft; ~ **man** Neandertaler, *der*

**neap** /niːp/ ⇒ **neap-tide**

**Neapolitan** /niːə'pɒlɪtn/ ❶ *n.* Neapolitaner, *der*/Neapolitanerin, *die.* ❷ *adj.* Neapolitaner; neapolitanisch

**'neap tide** *n.* Nipptide, *die*

**near** /nɪə(r)/ ❶ *adv.* [A] ▶1079, ▶1679 (*at a short distance*) nah[e]; **stand/live [quite] ~:** [ganz] in der Nähe stehen/wohnen; **come** *or* **draw ~/~er** ‹Tag, Zeitpunkt:› nahen/näher rücken; **take the one ~est to you** nimm das am nächsten Liegende; **get ~er together** näher zusammenrücken; **~ at hand** in Reichweite (*Dat.*); ‹Ort› ganz in der Nähe; **be ~ at hand** ‹Ereignis:› nahe bevorstehen; **~ by** in der Nähe; **so ~ and yet so far** so nah und doch so fern; [B] (*closely*) **it is 7.10 or as ~ as makes no difference** *or* **matter** es ist ziemlich genau *od.* fast 7.10 Uhr; **as ~ as I can judge** soweit ich es beurteilen kann; **no, but ~ enough** nein, aber beinah[e] *od.* fast; [C] **~ to** = 2 A, B, C; **he came ~ to being the winner/to tears** er hätte fast *od.* beinah[e] gewonnen/war den Tränen nahe; **we were ~ to being drowned** wir wären fast *od.* beinah[e] ertrunken.
❷ *prep.* [A] ▶1079 (*in space*) (*position*) nahe an/bei (+ *Dat.*); (*motion*) nahe an (+ *Akk.*); (*fig.*) nahe (*geh.*) *nachgestellt* (+ *Dat.*); in der Nähe (+ *Gen.*); **go ~ the water's edge** nahe ans Ufer gehen; **keep ~ me** halte dich *od.* bleib in meiner Nähe; **~ where ...:** in der Nähe *od.* unweit der Stelle (*Gen.*), wo ...; **move it ~er her** rücke es näher zu ihr; **I won't go ~ the police** (*fig.*) ich gehe der Polizei aus dem Weg; **don't stand so ~ the fire** geh nicht so nahe *od.* dicht an das Feuer; **when we got ~er Oxford** als wir in die Nähe von Oxford kamen; **wait till we're ~er home** warte, bis wir nicht mehr so weit von zu Hause weg sind; **don't come ~ me** komm mir nicht zu nahe; **it's ~ here** es ist hier in der Nähe; **the man ~/~est you** der Mann, der bei dir/der dir am nächsten steht; [B] (*in quality*) **nobody comes anywhere ~ him at swimming** im Schwimmen kommt bei weitem keiner an ihn heran; **we're no ~er solving the problem** wir sind der Lösung des Problems nicht näher gekommen; **be very ~ the original** dem Original sehr nahe kommen; **be ~ completion** kurz vor der Vollendung stehen; [C] (*in time*) **it's getting ~ the time when I must leave** der Zeitpunkt, wo ich gehen muss, rückt näher; **ask me again ~er the time** frag mich, wenn der Zeitpunkt etwas näher gerückt ist, noch einmal; **the Monday ~est Christmas** der Montag, der dem Weihnachtstag am nächsten liegt; **it's drawing ~ Christmas** es geht auf Weihnachten zu; **come back ~er 8 o'clock/the appointed time** komm kurz vor 8 Uhr/dem verabredeten Zeitpunkt noch einmal zurück; **~ the end/the beginning of sth.** gegen Ende/zu Anfang einer Sache (*Gen.*); [D] *in comb.* (*close in nature*) Beinahe‹unfall, -zusammenstoß, -katastrophe›; **~-hysterical/-human** fast hysterisch/menschlich; **a state of ~-panic** ein panikähnlicher Zustand; **be in a state of ~-collapse** kurz vor dem Zusammenbruch stehen; **a ~-miracle** fast *od.* beinahe ein Wunder; **~-famine conditions** Zustände schon fast wie bei einer Hungersnot. ⇒ *also* **heart** 1 B; **knuckle** C; **nowhere1** C; **wind**[1] 1 A.
❸ *adj.* [A] (*in space or time*) nahe; **in the ~ future** in nächster Zukunft; **the ~est man** der am nächsten stehende Mann; **the chair is ~er** der Stuhl steht näher; **our ~est neighbours** unsere nächsten Nachbarn; [B] (*closely related*) nahe ‹Verwandte, Freunde›; eng ‹Freund›; **~ and dear** lieb und teuer; *abs.* **my/your** *etc.* **~est and dearest** meine/deine *usw.* Lieben; [C] (*in nature*) fast richtig ‹Vermutung›; groß ‹Ähnlichkeit›; genau ‹Übersetzung›; **£30 or ~/~est offer** 30 Pfund oder nächstbestes Angebot; **this is the ~est equivalent** dies entspricht dem am ehesten; **that's the ~est you'll get to an answer** eine weiter gehende Antwort wirst du nicht bekommen; **~ escape** Entkommen mit knapper Not; **round it up to the ~est penny** runde es auf den nächsthöheren Pfennigbetrag; **be a ~ miss** ‹Schuss, Wurf:› knapp danebengehen; **I had a ~ miss** (*accident*) ich hätte um Haaresbreite einen Unfall gehabt; **that was a ~ miss** (*escape*) das war aber knapp!; [D] **the ~ side** (*Brit.*) (*travelling on the left/right*) die linke/rechte Seite; [E] (*direct*) **4 miles by the ~est road** 4 Meilen auf dem kürzesten Wege.
❹ *v.t.* sich nähern (+ *Dat.*); **the building is ~ing completion** das Gebäude geht seiner Vollendung entgegen *od.* steht kurz vor seiner Vollendung; **he's ~ing his end** sein Ende naht.
❺ *v.i.* ‹Zeitpunkt:› näher rücken, (*geh.*) nahen

**'nearby** *adj.* nahe gelegen

**Near:** ~ **'East** *n.* [A] ⇒ **Middle East**; [B] (*arch.: Turkey and Balkans*) Balkan, *der;* ~ **'Eastern** *adj.* nahöstlich

**nearly** /'nɪəlɪ/ *adv.* [A] ▶912 (*almost*) fast; **it ~ fell over** es wäre fast umgefallen; **be ~ crying** *or* **in tears** den Tränen nahe sein; **it is ~ six o'clock** es ist kurz vor sechs Uhr; **are you ~ ready?** bist du bald fertig?; [B] (*closely*) nah[e] ‹verwandt›; sehr ‹ähneln›; weitgehend ‹sich entsprechen›; [C] (*at all*) **not ~:** nicht annähernd; bei weitem nicht

**nearness** /'nɪənɪs/ *n., no pl.* [A] (*proximity*) Nähe, *die;* **their ~ in age** der geringe Altersunterschied zwischen ihnen; [B] (*similarity*) große Ähnlichkeit

**near:** **~-sighted** *adj.* (*Amer.*) kurzsichtig; ~ **'thing** *n.* **that was a ~ thing/what a ~ thing [that was]!** das war knapp!/war das aber knapp!

**neat** /niːt/ *adj.* [A] (*tidy, clean*) sauber, ordentlich ‹Handschrift, Arbeit›; gepflegt ‹Haar, Person›; **keep one's desk ~:** auf seinem Schreibtisch Ordnung halten; [B] (*undiluted*) pur ‹Getränk›; **she drinks vodka ~:** sie trinkt Wodka pur; [C] (*smart*) gepflegt ‹Erscheinung, Kleidung›; elegant, schick ‹Anzug, Auto, Haus›; [D] (*deft*) geschickt; raffiniert ‹Diebstahl, Trick, Plan, Lösung, Gerät›; **make a ~ job of sth./repairing sth.** etw. sehr geschickt machen/reparieren; [E] (*brief, clear*) prägnant ‹Beschreibung, Antwort, Formulierung›; [F] (*esp. Amer. coll.: excellent*) toll; geil (*Jugendspr. salopp*)

**neath** /niːθ/ *prep.* (*arch./poet.*) unter (+ *Dat.*); nid (+ *Dat.*) (*schweiz. veralt.*)

**neatly** /'niːtlɪ/ *adv.* [A] (*tidily*) ordentlich; [fein] säuberlich; [B] (*smartly*) gepflegt; **~ groomed** äußerst gepflegt; [C] (*deftly*) geschickt; auf raffinierte [Art und] Weise; [D] (*briefly, clearly*) prägnant; **a ~ turned phrase** eine prägnante Formulierung

**neatness** /'niːtnɪs/ *n., no pl.* ⇒ **neat** A, C, D, E: Sauberkeit, *die;* Ordentlichkeit, *die;* Gepflegtheit, *die;* Eleganz, *die;* Geschick, *das;* Geschicktheit, *die;* Raffiniertheit, *die;* Prägnanz, *die*

**nebula** /'nebjʊlə/ *n., pl.* **~e** /'nebjʊliː/ *or* **~s** (*Astron.*) Nebel, *der*

**nebular** /'nebjʊlə(r)/ *adj.* (*Astron.*) Nebel-

**nebulous** /'nebjʊləs/ *adj.* [A] (*hazy*) nebelhaft, (*geh.*) nebulös ‹Vorstellung, Werte›; verschwommen ‹Grenze›; unbestimmt, vage ‹Angst, Hoffnung›; [B] (*cloudlike*) wolkenartig ‹Form›

**necessarily** /nesɪ'serɪlɪ/ *adv.* notwendigerweise; zwangsläufig; **it is not ~ true** es muss nicht [unbedingt] stimmen; **Do we have to do it? — Not ~:** Müssen wir es tun? — Nicht unbedingt

**necessary** /'nesɪsərɪ/ ❶ *adj.* [A] (*indispensable*) nötig; notwendig; unbedingt ‹Erfordernis›; **be ~ to life** lebensnotwendig sein; **patience is ~ for a teacher** ein Lehrer muss Geduld haben; **it is not ~ for you to go** es ist nicht nötig *od.* notwendig, dass du gehst; du brauchst nicht zu *od.* musst nicht gehen; **it may be ~ for him to leave** vielleicht muss er gehen; **they made it ~ for him to attend** ihretwegen musste er hingehen; **do no more than is ~:** nur das Nötigste tun; **do everything ~** (*that must be done*) das Nötige *od.* Notwendige tun; [B] (*inevitable*) zwangsläufig ‹Ergebnis, Folge›; zwingend ‹Schluss›; [C] **a ~ evil** ein notwendiges Übel.
❷ *n.* **the necessaries of life** das Lebensnotwendige; **will he come up with the ~?** (*coll.: money*) wird er die Kohle auftreiben? (*salopp*); **will you do the ~?** kümmerst du dich drum?

**necessitate** /nɪ'sesɪteɪt/ *v.t.* [A] (*make necessary*) erforderlich machen; [B] (*Amer.: force*) zwingen; nötigen; **be ~d to do sth.** gezwungen *od.* genötigt sein, etw. zu tun

**necessitous** /nɪ'sesɪtəs/ *adj.* (*formal*) bedürftig

**necessity** /nɪ'sesɪtɪ/ *n.* [A] (*power of circumstances*) Not, *die;* äußerer Zwang; **bow to ~:** der Not gehorchen (*geh.*); **do sth. out of** *or* **from ~:** etw. notgedrungen *od.* gezwungenermaßen tun; **make a virtue of ~:** aus der Not eine Tugend machen; **of ~:** notwendigerweise; [B] (*necessary thing*) Notwendigkeit, *die;* **the necessities of life** das Lebensnotwendige; **be a ~ of life** lebensnotwendig sein; **be a ~ for sth.** eine notwendige Voraussetzung für etw. sein; [C] (*indispensability, imperative need*) Notwendigkeit, *die;* **there is no ~ for rudeness** es besteht keine Notwendigkeit *od.* es ist nicht notwendig, unhöflich zu sein; **if the ~ arises** wenn es unbedingt nötig ist; **in case of ~:** nötigenfalls; **~ is the mother of invention** (*prov.*) Not macht erfinderisch (*Spr.*); [D] (*want*) Not, *die;* Bedürftigkeit, *die;* **be/live in ~:** Not leiden

**neck** /nek/ ❶ *n.* [A] ▶966 Hals, *der;* **be breathing down sb.'s ~** (*fig.*) (*be close behind sb.*) jmdm. im Nacken sitzen (*ugs.*); (*watch sb. closely*) jmdm. ständig auf die Finger sehen; **get it in the ~** (*coll.*) eins auf den Deckel *od.* das Dach kriegen (*ugs.*); **be** *or* **come down on sb.'s ~** (*coll.*) jmdm. eins auf den Deckel *od.* aufs Dach geben (*ugs.*); **give sb./be a pain in the ~** (*coll.*) jmdm. auf die Nerven *od.* den Wecker gehen (*ugs.*); **have sb. round one's ~** (*coll.*) jmdn. auf dem *od.* am Hals haben (*ugs.*); **you'll bring the police down on our ~s** wir werden deinetwegen die Polizei auf den Hals kriegen (*ugs.*); **break one's/sb.'s ~** (*fig. coll.*) sich/jmdm. den Hals brechen; **risk one's ~:** Kopf und Kragen riskieren; **save one's ~:** seinen Kopf retten; **be up to one's ~ in work** (*coll.*) bis über den Hals in Arbeit stecken (*ugs.*); **be [in it] up to one's ~** (*coll.*) bis über den Hals drinstecken (*ugs.*); **~ and ~:** Kopf an Kopf; **~ or nothing** alles oder nichts; **it's [a matter of] ~ or nothing** es geht um die Wurst (*ugs.*); ⇒ *also* **dead** 1 A; **millstone**; **stick out** 1 A; [B] (*length*) Halslänge, *die;* (*fig.*) Nasenlänge, *die;* **short ~** (*Horseracing*) kurze Halslänge; [C] (*cut of meat*) Hals, *der;* **~ of lamb/mutton** *etc.* Lammfleisch/Hammelfleisch *usw.* vom Hals; [D] (*part of garment*) Kragen, *der;* **that**

**dress has a high ~:** das Kleid ist hochgeschlossen; **E** (*narrow part*) Hals, *der;* **F** (*Geog.: isthmus*) Landenge, *die;* **~ of land** Landzunge, *die;* **G** **~ of the woods** (*coll.*) Breiten *Pl.*
**2** *v.i.* (*coll.*) knutschen (*ugs.*)

**neck: ~band** *n.* Halsbündchen, *das;* **~cloth** *n.* (*Hist.*) Halstuch, *das*

**-necked** /nekt/ *adj. in comb.* **red/long-~:** rot-/langhalsig; **polo-~:** Rollkragen-

**neckerchief** /ˈnekətʃɪf/ *n.* Halstuch, *das*

**necklace** /ˈneklɪs/ *n.* [Hals]kette, *die;* (*with jewels*) Collier, *das*

**neck: ~line** *n.* [Hals]ausschnitt, *der;* **~tie** *n.* Krawatte, *die;* Binder, *der*

**necromancy** /ˈnekrəmænsɪ/ *n.* Nekromantie, *die*

**necrophilia** /nekrəˈfɪlɪə/ *n.* Nekrophilie, *die*

**necrosis** /neˈkrəʊsɪs/ *n., pl.* **necroses** /neˈkrəʊsiːz/ (*Med.*) Nekrose, *die*

**nectar** /ˈnektə(r)/ *n.* **A** (*Bot., Greek and Roman Mythol.*) Nektar, *der;* **B** (*delicious drink*) Göttertrank, *der* (*scherzh.*); (*drink of blended fruit juices*) Nektar, *der* (*fachspr.*)

**nectarine** /ˈnektərɪn, ˈnektəriːn/ *n.* Nektarine, *die*

**nectary** /ˈnektərɪ/ *n.* (*Bot.*) Nektarium, *das* (*fachspr.*); Honigdrüse, *die*

**NEDC** *abbr.* (*Brit. Hist.*) **National Economic Development Council** Rat für Wirtschaftsentwicklung

**neddy** /ˈnedɪ/ *n.* (*child lang.: donkey*) Esel, *der;* Langohr, *das* (*scherzh.*)

**née** (*Amer.:* **nee**) /neɪ/ *adj.* geborene

**need** /niːd/ **1** *n.* **A** *no pl.* Notwendigkeit, *die* **(for, of** *Gen.***)**; (*demand*) Bedarf, *der* **(for, of** an + *Dat.***)**; **as the ~ arises** nach Bedarf; **if ~ arise/be** nötigenfalls; falls nötig; **the ~ for discussion** die Notwendigkeit zu diskutieren; **there's no ~ for that** (*as answer*) [das ist] nicht nötig; **there's no ~ to do sth.** es ist nicht nötig *od.* notwendig, etw. zu tun; **there is no ~ to worry/get angry** es besteht kein Grund zur Sorge/sich zu ärgern; **is there any ~ [for us] to hurry?** müssen wir uns beeilen?; **there was a ~ for caution** Vorsicht war geboten; **be in ~ of sth.** etw. brauchen *od.* nötig haben; **there is no ~ for such behaviour** solch ein Verhalten ist unnötig; **is there any ~ for all this hurry?** ist diese Eile nötig *od.* notwendig?; **there's no ~ for you to apologize** du brauchst dich nicht zu entschuldigen; **feel the ~ to do sth.** sich gezwungen *od.* genötigt sehen, etw. zu tun; **feel the ~ to confide in sb.** das Bedürfnis haben, sich jmdm. anzuvertrauen; **have ~ to do sth.** (*dated*) es nötig haben, etw. zu tun; **be badly in ~ of sth.** etw. dringend nötig haben; etw. nötig brauchen; **be in ~ of a coat of paint** einen Anstrich nötig haben; **be in ~ of repair** reparaturbedürftig sein; **have ~ of sb./sth.** jmdn./etw. brauchen *od.* nötig haben; **your ~ is greater than mine** du hast es nötiger als ich; du brauchst es dringender als ich; **B** *no pl.* (*emergency*) Not, *die;* **in case of ~:** im Notfall; **in times of ~:** in Notzeiten; ⇒ *also* **friend** A; **C** *no pl.* (*destitution*) Not, *die;* Bedürftigkeit, *die;* **be in ~:** Not leiden; **those in ~:** die Notleidenden *od.* Bedürftigen; **D** (*thing*) Bedürfnis, *das;* **my ~s are few** ich brauche nicht viel; **each will receive according to his ~s** jeder bekommt, was er braucht.
**2** *v.t.* **A** (*require*) brauchen; **sth. that urgently ~s doing** etw., was dringend gemacht werden muss; **much ~ed** dringend notwendig; **that's all I ~ed!** (*iron.*) auch das noch!; das hat mir gerade noch gefehlt!; **it ~s a coat of paint** es muss gestrichen werden; **it ~s careful consideration** es muss gut überlegt werden; **~ correction** berichtigt werden müssen; **Education? Who ~s it?** (*coll.*) Bildung? Wozu?; **B** *expr. necessity* müssen; **I ~ to do it** ich muss es tun; **it ~s/doesn't ~ to be done** es muss getan werden/es braucht nicht getan zu werden; **you don't ~ to do that** das brauchst du nicht zu tun; **I don't ~ to be reminded** du brauchst/ihr braucht mich nicht daran zu erinnern; **it ~ed doing** es musste getan werden; **he ~s cheering up** er muss [ein bisschen] aufgeheitert werden; **he doesn't ~ to be told** das braucht man ihm nicht erst zu sagen; **you shouldn't ~ to be told** das solltest *od.* müsstest du eigentlich wissen; **it doesn't ~ me to tell you** das muss ich dir nicht sagen *od.* brauche ich dir nicht zu sagen; **she ~s everything [to be] explained to her** man muss ihr alles erklären; **you ~ only ask** du brauchst nur zu fragen; **don't be away longer than you ~ [be]** bleib nicht länger als nötig weg; **C** *pres.* **he need**, *neg.* **need not** *or* (*coll.*) **needn't** /ˈniːdnt/ *expr. desirability* müssen; *with neg.* brauchen zu; **~ anybody be there?** muss jemand dort sein?; **~ I say more?** muss ich noch mehr sagen?; **~ she have come at all?** hätte sie überhaupt kommen müssen?; **N~ you go? — No, I ~n't** Musst du gehen? — Nein; **I ~ hardly** *or* **hardly ~ say that ...:** ich brauche wohl kaum zu sagen, dass ...; **I don't think that ~ be considered** ich glaube, das braucht nicht berücksichtigt zu werden; **no one ~ know this** das braucht niemand zu wissen; **he ~n't be told** (*let's keep it secret*) das braucht er nicht zu wissen; **we ~n't** *or* **~ not have done it, if ...:** wir hätten es nicht zu tun brauchen, wenn ...; **it ~ not follow that ...:** daraus folgt nicht unbedingt, dass ...; daraus muss nicht [unbedingt] folgen, dass ...; **that ~ not be the case** das muss nicht so sein *od.* der Fall sein

**needful** /ˈniːdfl/ *adj.* (*arch.*) nötig; **it is ~ to do it** es ist vonnöten *od.* (*geh., veralt.*) tut not, dass es getan wird; **everything/the ~:** alles/das Nötige

**needle** /ˈniːdl/ **1** *n.* Nadel, *die;* **it is like looking/searching for a ~ in a haystack** es ist, als wollte man eine Stecknadel in einem Heuhaufen finden; **~ and thread** *or* **cotton** Nadel und Faden; **~'s eye** Nadelöhr, *das;* **give sb. the ~** (*Brit. coll.*) jmdn. ärgern; **get the ~** (*Brit. coll.*) sich ärgern; ⇒ *also* **pin** 1 A. **2** *v.t.* (*coll.*) ärgern; nerven (*ugs.*); **what's needling him?** was fuchst ihn [denn so]? (*ugs.*)

**needle: ~cord** *n.* (*Textiles*) Feinkord, *der;* **~craft** *n.* Nadelarbeit, *die;* **~ game, ~ match** *ns.* (*Brit.*) erbitterter Fight (*Sportjargon*); **~point** *n.* **A** Nadelspitze, *die;* (*fig.*) springender Punkt; **B** (*embroidery*) Stickerei, *die*

**needless** /ˈniːdlɪs/ *adj.* unnötig; (*senseless*) sinnlos; **~ to say** *or* **add, he didn't do it** überflüssig zu sagen, dass er es nicht getan hat

**needlessly** /ˈniːdlɪslɪ/ *adv.* unnötigerweise; (*senselessly*) sinnlos

**needle: ~ valve** *n.* (*Mech. Engin.*) Nadelventil, *das;* **~woman** *n.* (*seamstress*) Näherin, *die;* **be a good/bad ~woman** gut nähen [können]/schlecht nähen *od.* nicht gut nähen können; **~work** *n.* Handarbeit, *die;* Nadelarbeit, *die* (*veralt.*); (*school subject*) Handarbeiten, *das;* Nadelarbeit, *die* (*veralt.*); **do ~work** handarbeiten; **a piece of ~work** eine Handarbeit

**needn't** /ˈniːdnt/ (*coll.*) = **need not;** ⇒ **need** 2 C

**needs** /niːdz/ *adv.* (*dated*) **~ must when the devil drives** (*prov.*) was sein muss, muss sein; **if ~ must** wenn es [unbedingt] sein muss *od.* nötig ist

**needy** /ˈniːdɪ/ *adj.* **A** (*poor*) Not leidend, bedürftig ‹Person, Familie›; **the neediest cases** die schlimmsten Fälle von Bedürftigkeit; **the ~:** die Notleidenden *od.* Bedürftigen; **B** ärmlich, dürftig ‹Verhältnisse›

**ne'er** /neə(r)/ *adv.* (*poet.: never*) nimmer (*geh. veralt.*); nie; **~ a ...:** kein einziger/keine einzige/kein einziges ...

**ne'er-do-well** /ˈneəduwel/ **1** *n.* Tunichtgut, *der.* **2** *adj.* nichtsnutzig (*veralt. abwertend*); **~ fellow** Tunichtgut, *der*

**nefarious** /nɪˈfeərɪəs/ *adj.* ruchlos (*geh.*); frevelhaft (*geh.*)

**negate** /nɪˈgeɪt/ *v.t.* **A** (*formal: be negation of*) widersprechen (+ *Dat.*); **B** (*nullify*) zunichte machen; **C** (*Ling.*) negieren (*fachspr.*); verneinen

**negation** /nɪˈgeɪʃn/ *n.* **A** (*refusal to accept*) Ablehnung, *die;* (*refusal to accept existence of sth.*) Verleugnung, *die;* **B** (*negative statement*) negative Aussage; **be the ~ of sth.** im Widerspruch zu etw. stehen; **C** (*opposite of sth. positive*) Negation, *die;* **D** (*Ling.*) Negation, *die* (*fachspr.*); Verneinung, *die*

**negative** /ˈnegətɪv/ **1** *adj.* **A** (*also Math.*) negativ; **~ vote** Neinstimme, *die;* **B** (*Ling.*) verneint; Negations‹partikel›; **C** (*Electr.*) **~ pole/terminal** Minuspol, *der;* **D** (*Photog.*) negativ; Negativ-. ⇒ *also* **feedback** B. **2** *n.* **A** (*Photog.*) Negativ, *das;* **B** (**~** *statement*) negative Aussage; (*answer*) Nein, *das;* **two ~s make an affirmative** doppelte Verneinung ergibt Bejahung; **be in the ~** ‹Antwort:› negativ *od.* „Nein" sein; ‹Votum:› ablehnend ausfallen; **C** (**~** *quality*) negative Eigenschaft; fehlende Eigenschaft; **D** (*Ling.*) Negation, *die* (*fachspr.*); Verneinung, *die.* **3** *v.t.* **A** (*veto*) ablehnen; **B** (*disprove*) widerlegen

**negative 'equity** *n.* Negativwert, *der*

**negatively** /ˈnegətɪvlɪ/ *adv.* **A** (*in the negative*) negativ; **answer ~:** eine negative Antwort geben; **B** (*unsympathetically*) negativ; ablehnend; **C** (*Electr.*) negativ

**'negative sign** *n.* (*Math.*) negatives Vorzeichen; (*symbol*) Minuszeichen, *das*

**neglect** /nɪˈglekt/ **1** *v.t.* **A** (*disregard, leave uncared for*) vernachlässigen; nicht hören auf (+ *Akk.*) ‹Rat›; versäumen ‹Gelegenheit›; **B** (*leave undone*) unerledigt lassen, liegen lassen ‹Korrespondenz, Arbeit›; **C** (*omit*) versäumen; **she ~ed to write** sie hat es versäumt zu schreiben; **not ~ doing** *or* **to do sth.** es nicht versäumen, etw. zu tun. **2** *n.* **A** (*neglecting, disregard*) Vernachlässigung, *die;* **be in a state of ~** ‹Gebäude:› verwahrlost sein; **years of ~:** jahrelange Vernachlässigung; **suffer from ~:** vernachlässigt werden; **~ of duty** Pflichtvergessenheit, *die;* **B** (*negligence*) Nachlässigkeit, *die;* Fahrlässigkeit, *die*

**neglectful** /nɪˈglektfl/ *adj.* (*careless*) gleichgültig **(of** gegenüber**)**; **be ~ of** sich nicht kümmern um

**négligé, negligee** /ˈneglɪʒeɪ/ *n.* Negligee, *das*

**negligence** /ˈneglɪdʒəns/ *n., no pl.* (*carelessness*) Nachlässigkeit, *die;* (*Law, Insurance, etc.*) Fahrlässigkeit, *die;* ⇒ *also* **contributory** A

**negligent** /ˈneglɪdʒənt/ *adj.* **A** nachlässig; **be ~ about sth.** sich um etw. nicht kümmern; **be ~ of one's duties/sb.** seine Pflichten/jmdn. vernachlässigen; **B** (*offhand*) ungezwungen; zwanglos

**negligently** /ˈneglɪdʒəntlɪ/ *adv.* **A** nachlässig ‹arbeiten›; unvorsichtig ‹fahren›; *as sentence-modifier* nachlässigerweise/unvorsichtigerweise; **B** (*in an offhand manner*) lässig

**negligible** /ˈneglɪdʒɪbl/ *adj.* unerheblich; unbedeutend ‹Fehler›; ⇒ *also* **quantity** E

**negotiable** /nɪˈgəʊʃəbl/ *adj.* **A** (*open to discussion*) verhandlungsfähig ‹Forderung, Bedingungen›; **B** (*that can be got past*) zu bewältigend *nicht präd.;* zu bewältigen *nicht attr.;* passierbar ‹Straße, Fluss›; **C** (*Commerc.*) übertragbar ‹Sicherheit, Scheck usw.›

**negotiate** /nɪˈgəʊʃɪeɪt/ **1** *v.i.* verhandeln **(for, on, about** über + *Akk.***)**; **the negotiating table** der Verhandlungstisch. **2** *v.t.* **A** (*arrange*) aushandeln; **B** (*get past*) bewältigen; überwinden ‹Hindernis›; passieren ‹Straße, Fluss›; nehmen ‹Kurve›; **~ the stairs** die Treppe schaffen (*ugs.*); **C** (*Commerc.*) (*convert into cash*) einlösen ‹Scheck›; (*transfer*) übertragen ‹Wechsel, Papiere usw.›

**negotiation** /nɪgəʊʃɪˈeɪʃn, nɪgəʊsɪˈeɪʃn/ *n.* **A** (*discussion*) Verhandlung, *die* **(for, about** über + *Akk.***)**; **by ~:** durch Verhandeln *od.* Verhandlungen; **enter into ~:** in Verhandlungen (*Akk.*) eintreten; **be in ~ with sb.** mit jmdm. verhandeln; **be a matter of ~:** Verhandlungssache sein; **B** *in pl.* (*talks*) Verhandlungen *Pl.;* **C** ⇒ **negotiate** 2

B: Bewältigung, *die;* Überwindung, *die;* Passieren, *das;* D ⇒ **negotiate** 2 C: Einlösung, *die;* Übertragung, *die*

**negotiator** /nɪˈgəʊʃɪeɪtə(r)/ *n.* Unterhändler, *der*/-händlerin, *die*

**Negress** /ˈni:grɪs/ *n.* Negerin, *die*

**Negro** /ˈni:grəʊ/ ❶ *n., pl.* **~es** Neger, *der.* ❷ *adj.* Neger-; **~ woman** Negerin, *die;* **~ art/music** Kunst/Musik der Neger; ⇒ *also* **spiritual** 2

**Negroid** /ˈni:grɔɪd/ ❶ *adj.* negrid; (*akin to or resembling Negroes*) negroid. ❷ *n.* Negride, *der/die;* (*akin to or resembling Negro*) Negroide, *der/die*

**neigh** /neɪ/ ❶ *v.i.* wiehern. ❷ *n.* Wiehern, *das*

**neighbor** *etc.* (*Amer.*) ⇒ **neighbour** *etc.*

**neighbour** /ˈneɪbə(r)/ ❶ *n.* Nachbar, *der*/Nachbarin, *die;* (*at table*) [Tisch]nachbar, *der*/[Tisch]nachbarin, *die;* (*thing*) der/die/das daneben; (*building/country*) Nachbargebäude/-land, *das;* **we're next-door ~s** wir wohnen Tür an Tür; **my next-door ~s** meine unmittelbaren Nachbarn; meine Nachbarn von nebenan; **we were ~s at dinner** wir haben beim Essen nebeneinander gesessen. ❷ *v.t. & i.* **~ [upon]** grenzen an (+ *Akk.*)

**neighbourhood** /ˈneɪbəhʊd/ *n.* A (*district*) Gegend, *die;* **sb.'s ~:** jmds. Nachbarschaft; **the children from the ~:** die Kinder aus der Nachbarschaft *od.* Umgebung; B (*nearness*) Nähe, *die;* **it was [somewhere] in the ~ of £100** es waren [so] um [die] 100 Pfund; C (*neighbours*) Nachbarschaft, *die;* D *attrib.* an der *od.* um die Ecke *nachgestellt* (*ugs.*); **small ~ shop/store** [kleiner] Laden um die Ecke; **your friendly ~ bobby/milkman** *etc.* (*coll. joc.*) der nette Polizist, der bei uns die Runde macht/der nette Milchmann, der uns täglich die Milch bringt

**ˈneighbourhood watch** *n.* Bürgerwehr, *die*

**neighbouring** /ˈneɪbərɪŋ/ *adj.* benachbart; Nachbar-; angrenzend ‹Felder›

**neighbourliness** /ˈneɪbəlmɪs/ *n., no pl.* gut- *od.* freundnachbarliche Art

**neighbourly** /ˈneɪbəlɪ/ *adj.* A (*characteristic of neighbours*) [gut]nachbarlich; B (*friendly*) freundlich

**neither** /ˈnaɪðə(r), ni:ðə(r)/ ❶ *adj.* keiner/keine/keins der beiden; **in ~ case** in keinem Falle.
❷ *pron.* keiner/keine/keins von *od.* der beiden; **~ of them** keiner von *od.* der beiden; (*none*) keiner von ihnen; **~ of the accusations** keine der [beiden] Beschuldigungen; **Which will you have? — N~:** Welches nehmen Sie? — Keins [von beiden]; **we ~ of us moved** keiner von uns [beiden] hat sich bewegt.
❸ *adv.* (*also not*) auch nicht; **I'm not going — N~ am I** *or* (*coll.*) **Me ~:** Ich gehe nicht — Ich auch nicht; **if you don't go, ~ shall I** wenn du nicht gehst, gehe ich auch nicht; **he didn't go and ~ did I** er ging nicht und ich auch nicht.
❹ *conj.* A (*not either, not on the one hand*) weder; **~ ... nor** weder ... noch; **he ~ knows nor cares** weder weiß er es, noch will er es wissen; **he ~ ate, drank, nor smoked** er aß nicht, noch trank oder rauchte er; ⇒ *also* **here** 1 A; B (*arch.: and also not*) noch

**nelly** /ˈnelɪ/ *n.* **not on your ~** (*Brit. coll.*) nie im Leben (*ugs.*); im Leben nicht (*ugs.*)

**nelson** /ˈnelsn/ *n.* (*Wrestling*) Nelson, *der*

**nem. con.** /nem ˈkɒn/ *abbr.* **nemine contradicente** nem. con.

**nemesis** /ˈnemɪsɪs/ *n., pl.* **nemeses** /ˈnemɪsi:z/ A (*formal: justice*) Nemesis, *die;* ausgleichende Gerechtigkeit; B (*downfall*) gerechte Strafe (**of** für)

**neo-** /ni:əʊ/ *in comb.* neo-/Neo-

**neoˈclassic, neoˈclassical** *adj.* klassizistisch

**neoˈclassicism** *n.* Klassizismus, *der*

**neolithic** /ni:əˈlɪθɪk/ *adj.* (*Archaeol.*) neolithisch (*fachspr.*); jungsteinzeitlich; (*fig.*) vorsintflutlich; **~ period** Neolithikum, *das;* Jungsteinzeit, *die;* **~ man** Neolithiker, *der*

**neologism** /nɪˈɒlədʒɪzm/ *n.* Neubildung, *die;* Neologismus, *der* (*Sprachw.*)

**neon** /ˈni:ɒn/ *n.* (*Chem.*) Neon, *das*

**neon: ~ ˈlamp** *n.* Neonlampe, *die;* **~ ˈlight** *n.* Neonlicht, *das;* (*fitting*) Neonlampe, *die;* **~ ˈsign** *n.* Neonreklame, *die*

**neophyte** /ˈni:əfaɪt/ *n.* A (*Relig.*) Neophyt, *der;* B (*beginner*) Anfänger, *der*

**Nepal** /nɪˈpɔ:l/ *pr. n.* Nepal (*das*)

**Nepalese** /nepəˈli:z/, **Nepali** /nɪˈpɔ:lɪ/ ▶ **1275**, ▶ **1340** ❶ *adj.* nepalesisch. ❷ *n.* A *pl.* **Nepalese, Nepalis** (*person*) Nepalese, *der*/Nepalesin, *die;* B (*language*) Nepali, *das*

**nephew** /ˈnevju:, ˈnefju:/ *n.* Neffe, *der*

**nephritis** /nɪˈfraɪtɪs/ *n.* ▶ **1232** (*Med.*) Nephritis, *die* (*fachspr.*); Nierenentzündung, *die*

**nepotism** /ˈnepətɪzm/ *n.* Nepotismus, *der* (*geh.*); Vetternwirtschaft, *die* (*abwertend*)

**Neptune** /ˈneptju:n/ *pr. n.* A (*Roman Mythol.*) Neptun (*der*); B (*Astron.*) Neptun, *der*

**NERC** *abbr.* (*Brit.*) **Natural Environment Research Council** ≈ Umweltbundesamt

**nerd** /nɜ:d/ *n.* (*coll. derog.*) Depp, *der* (*abwertend*)

**nerve** /nɜ:v/ ❶ *n.* A Nerv, *der;* **~ tissue** Nervengewebe, *das;* B *in pl.* (*fig., of mental state*) **be suffering from ~s** nervös sein; **bundle of ~s** Nervenbündel, *das* (*ugs.*); **have a fit of ~s** durchdrehen (*ugs.*); sehr nervös werden; **get on sb.'s ~s** jmdm. auf die Nerven gehen *od.* fallen (*ugs.*); **~s of steel** Nerven wie Drahtseile (*ugs.*); C **strain every ~** (*fig.*) alle Anstrengungen machen; D (*coolness, boldness*) Kaltblütigkeit, *die;* Mut, *der;* **not have the ~ for sth.** für *od.* zu etw. nicht die Nerven haben; **lose one's ~:** die Nerven verlieren; **a man with an iron ~:** ein Mann mit eisernen Nerven; E (*coll.: audacity*) **of all the ~!** das ist doch die Höhe!; **what [a] ~!** [so eine] Frechheit!; **have the ~ to do sth.** den Nerv haben, etw. zu tun (*ugs.*); **he's got a ~:** der hat Nerven (*ugs.*).
❷ *v.t.* A (*give strength or courage to*) ermutigen; **~ oneself** *or* **one's heart** seinen ganzen Mut zusammennehmen; B (*brace*) **~ oneself** *or* **one's mind** sich wappnen (*geh.*)

**nerve: ~ cell** *n.* Nervenzelle, *die;* **~ centre** *n.* A (*Anat.*) Nervenzentrum, *das;* B (*fig.*) Schaltzentrale, *die;* **~ gas** *n.* Nervengas, *das*

**nerveless** /ˈnɜ:vlɪs/ *adj.* A (*inert*) schwach; kraftlos ‹Arm, Hand›; B (*flabby*) kraftlos ‹Stil›; C (*cool, confident*) nervenstark

**nerve: ~-racking** *adj.* nervenaufreibend; **~-shattering** *adj.* nervenzerrüttend

**nervous** /ˈnɜ:vəs/ *adj.* A (*Anat., Med.*) Nerven-; **[central] ~ system** [Zentral]nervensystem, *das;* **~ breakdown** Nervenzusammenbruch, *der;* B (*having delicate nerves*) nervös; **be a ~ wreck** mit den Nerven völlig am Ende sein; C (*Brit.: timid*) **be ~ of** *or* **about** Angst haben vor (+ *Dat.*); **I'm ~ of offending him** ich habe Angst, ihn zu kränken; **be a ~ person** ängstlich sein

**nervously** /ˈnɜ:vəslɪ/ *adv.* nervös

**nervousness** /ˈnɜ:vəsnɪs/ *n., no pl.* Ängstlichkeit, *die;* (*temporary*) Angst, *die*

**nervure** /ˈnɜ:vjə(r)/ *n.* A (*Zool.*) [Flügel]ader, *die;* B (*Bot.*) [Blatt]ader, *die*

**nervy** /ˈnɜ:vɪ/ *adj.* A (*jerky, nervous*) nervös; unruhig; B (*Amer. coll.*) (*cool, confident*) dreist; (*impudent*) unverschämt

**nest** /nest/ ❶ *n.* A (*of bird, animal, insect*) Nest, *das;* **foul one's own ~** (*fig.*) (*denigrate one's own family*) das eigene *od.* sein eigenes Nest beschmutzen; (*harm one's own interests*) sich (*Dat.*) selbst schaden; ⇒ *also* **feather** 2 A; B (*fig.: retreat, shelter, receptacle*) Nest, *das* (*fig.*); Zufluchtsort, *der;* **leave the ~:** flügge werden; C (*haunt of robbers etc.*) Nest, *das;* Schlupfwinkel, *der;* D (*place fostering vice etc.*) Brutstätte, *die;* E (*brood or swarm in a ~*) Nest, *das;* (*of rabbits*) Satz, *der* (*Jägerspr.*); (*of wasps, hornets, ants*) Schwarm, *der;* F (*group of machine guns*) (*Mil.*) [MG-]Nest, *das;* G (*set*) Satz, *der;* **~ of tables** Satz Tische.
❷ *v.i.* A (*make or have ~*) nisten; B (*take ~s*) Nester entfernen; (*take eggs*) Nester ausnehmen *od.* ausheben; C (*fit together*) **~ [into one another]** ineinander passen.
❸ *v.t.* A (*place as in ~*) einbetten; B (*pack one inside the other*) ineinander setzen ‹Töpfe usw.›; (*fig.*) einbetten

**ˈnest egg** *n.* A Nestei, *das;* B (*fig.*) Notgroschen, *der*

**ˈnesting box** *n.* Nistkasten, *der*

**nestle** /ˈnesl/ ❶ *v.i.* A (*settle oneself*) sich kuscheln; **~ down in a sleeping bag** sich in einen Schlafsack kuscheln; B (*press oneself affectionately*) sich schmiegen (**to, against** an + *Akk.*); **they ~d [up] together** sie schmiegten sich aneinander; C (*lie half hidden*) eingebettet sein. ❷ *v.t.* A (*push affectionately or snugly*) kuscheln, schmiegen (**against** an + *Akk.*); B (*hold as in nest*) **~ a baby in one's arms** ein Baby schützend in den Armen halten

**nestling** /ˈnestlɪŋ/ *n.* Nestling, *der*

**net**[1] /net/ ❶ *n.* (*lit. or fig.*) Netz, *das;* **cast one's ~ wide** (*fig.*) seine Netze weit spannen; **spread one's ~** (*fig.*) seine Netze stellen *od.* spannen; **the Net** (*Computing*) das Netz. ❷ *v.t.,* **-tt-:** A (*cover*) **~ [over]** mit einem Netz überziehen ‹Baum, Busch›; (*catch*) [mit einem Netz] fangen ‹Tier›; einfangen ‹Person›; **~ sb. sth.** (*fig. coll.*) jmdm. etw. einbringen; B (*put in net*) ins Netz schlagen; (*put in goal*) ins Tor schießen; **~ a goal** ein Tor schießen

**net**[2] ❶ *adj.* A (*free from deduction*) netto; Netto‹einkommen, -[verkaufs]preis usw.›; B (*not subject to discount*); **~ price** gebundener Preis; **~ book** preisgebundenes Buch; **N~ ˈBook Agreement** Vereinbarung zur Preisbindung bei Büchern; C ▶ **1683** (*excluding weight of container etc.*) netto; **~ weight** Nettogewicht, *das;* D (*effective, ultimate*) End‹ergebnis, -effekt›. ❷ *v.t.,* **-tt-** (*gain*) netto einnehmen; (*yield*) netto einbringen

**net: ~ball** *n.* Korbball, *der;* **~ cord** *n.* (*Tennis*) A Spannseil, *das;* B (*stroke*) Netzball, *der;* **~ ˈcurtain** *n.* Store, *der* [aus Gittertüll]; Tüllgardine, *die*

**nether** /ˈneðə(r)/ *adj.* (*arch./joc.*) unter...; Unter‹lippe, -kiefer›

**Netherlands** /ˈneðələndz/ ❶ *pr. n. sing. or pl.* Niederlande *Pl.* ❷ *attrib. adj.* niederländisch

**nether ˈregions, nether ˈworld** *ns.* Unterwelt, *die*

**netiquette** /ˈnetɪket/ *n.* (*Computing*) Netiquette, *die;* **breaches of ~:** Verstöße gegen die Netiquette

**net ˈprofit** *n.* Reingewinn, *der*

**nett** ⇒ **net**[2]

**netting** /ˈnetɪŋ/ *n.* A (*making net*) Knüpfen, *das;* B ([*piece of*] *net*) Netz, *das;* (*needlework*) Filet- *od.* Netzarbeit, *die;* **cover with ~:** mit Netzen/mit einem Netz bedecken; **wire ~:** Drahtgeflecht, *das;* Maschendraht, *der*

**nettle** /ˈnetl/ ❶ *n.* Nessel, *die;* ⇒ *also* **grasp** 2 B; **stinging nettle.** ❷ *v.t.* reizen; aufbringen

**ˈnettlerash** *n.* (*Med.*) Nesselsucht, *die;* Nesselausschlag, *der*

**ˈnetwork** ❶ *n.* A (*of intersecting lines, electrical conductors*) Netzwerk, *das;* B (*of railways etc., persons, operations*) Netz, *das;* C (*of broadcasting stations*) [Sender]netz, *das;* (*company*) Sender, *der;* D (*Computing*) Netzwerk, *das.* ❷ *v.t.* (*broadcast*) [im ganzen Sendebereich] ausstrahlen

**ˈnetwork provider** *n.* (*Computing, Teleph.*) Netzanbieter, *der*

**Neuchâtel** /nɜ:ʃæˈtel/ *pr. n.* ▶ **1626** Neuenburg (*das*)

**neural** /ˈnjʊərl/ *adj.* (*Anat.*) neural (*fachspr.*); Nerven-

**neuralgia** /njʊəˈrældʒə/ *n.* ▶ **1232** (*Med.*) Neuralgie, *die* (*fachspr.*); Nervenschmerz, *der*

**neuritis** /njʊəˈraɪtɪs/ *n.* ▶ **1232** (*Med.*) Neuritis, *die* (*fachspr.*); Nervenentzündung, *die*

**neurological** /njʊərəˈlɒdʒɪkl/ *adj.* neurologisch

**neurologist** /njʊəˈrɒlədʒɪst/ *n.* ▶ **1261** Neurologe, *der*/Neurologin, *die;* Nervenarzt, *der*/Nervenärztin, *die*

**neurology** /njʊəˈrɒlədʒɪ/ *n.* Neurologie, *die*

**neuron** /ˈnjʊərɒn/, **neurone** /ˈnjʊərəʊn/ *n.* (*Anat.*) Neuron, *das*

**neurosis** /njʊəˈrəʊsɪs/ *n., pl.* **neuroses** /njʊəˈrəʊsi:z/ Neurose, *die*

**neurosurgeon** /njʊərəʊˈsɜ:dʒn/ *n.* ▶ 1261 Neurochirurg, *der*/-chirurgin, *die*

**neurosurgery** /njʊərəʊˈsɜ:dʒərɪ/ *n.* Neurochirurgie, *die*

**neurotic** /njʊəˈrɒtɪk/ ❶ *adj.* Ⓐ (*suffering from neurosis*) nervenkrank; Ⓑ (*of neurosis*) neurotisch; ~ **affection** *or* **ailment** Nervenkrankheit, *die;* Ⓒ (*coll.: unduly anxious*) neurotisch; **don't get ~ about it** lass es nicht zu einer Neurose werden. ❷ *n.* Neurotiker, *der*/Neurotikerin, *die*

**neurotically** /njʊəˈrɒtɪkəlɪ/ *adv.* neurotisch

**neuter** /ˈnju:tə(r)/ ❶ *adj.* Ⓐ (*Ling.*) sächlich; neutral (*fachspr.*); Ⓑ (*Bot.: asexual*) weder männlich noch weiblich; ungeschlechtlich ‹Blüte›; Ⓒ (*Zool.: sterile*) unfruchtbar. ❷ *n.* Ⓐ (*Ling.*) Neutrum, *das;* Ⓑ (*Zool.*) (*insect*) unfruchtbares Insekt; (*ant, bee*) Arbeiterin, *die;* Ⓒ (*castrated animal*) kastriertes Tier. ❸ *v.t.* kastrieren

**neutral** /ˈnju:trl/ ❶ *adj.* neutral; ~ **gear** Leerlauf, *der;* ⇒ *also* **equilibrium**. ❷ *n.* Ⓐ Neutrale, *der/die;* **be ~s/a ~:** neutral sein; Ⓑ (~ *gear*) Leerlauf, *der;* **in ~:** im Leerlauf

**neutralise** ⇒ **neutralize**

**neutrality** /nju:ˈtrælɪtɪ/ *n.* Neutralität, *die*

**neutralize** /ˈnju:trəlaɪz/ *v.t.* Ⓐ (*Chem.*) neutralisieren; Ⓑ (*counteract*) neutralisieren; entkräften ‹Argument›

**neutrally** /ˈnju:trəlɪ/ *adv.* neutral

**neutrino** /nju:ˈtri:nəʊ/ *n., pl.* **~s** (*Phys.*) Neutrino, *das*

**neutron** /ˈnju:trɒn/ *n.* (*Phys.*) Neutron, *das*

**neutron: ~ bomb** *n.* Neutronenbombe, *die;* **~ star** *n.* Neutronenstern, *der*

**never** /ˈnevə(r)/ *adv.* Ⓐ (*at no time*) nie; **I ~ thought I would see her again** ich hätte nie gedacht, dass ich sie wiedersehen würde; **the rain seemed as if it would ~ stop** der Regen schien gar nicht mehr aufhören zu wollen; **will the rain ~ stop?** hört denn der Regen überhaupt nicht mehr auf?; **he has ~ been abroad** er war [noch] nie im Ausland; **he ~ so much as apologized** er hat sich nicht einmal entschuldigt; **I ~ slept a wink all night** ich habe die ganze Nacht kein Auge zugetan; **~ is a long time** man soll niemals nie sagen; **~, ~:** nie, nie; niemals; (*more emphatic*) nie im Leben; **~ so** [auch] noch so; **be it ~ so great** wenn es auch noch so groß ist; mag es auch noch so groß sein; **~-to-be-forgotten** unvergesslich; **~-satisfied** unersättlich; **~-ending** endlos; **~-failing** unfehlbar; unerschöpflich ‹Quelle›; Ⓑ (*not … at any time, not … at all*) nie; **he was ~ one to do sth.** es war nicht seine Art, etw. zu tun; **he is ~ likely to succeed** er wird es nie schaffen; **I ~ remember her winning** ich kann mich nicht erinnern, dass sie je gewonnen hätte; **~ a** (*not one*) kein Einziger/keine Einzige/kein Einziges; Ⓒ (*coll.*) *expr. surprise* **you ~ believed that, did you?** du hast das doch wohl nicht geglaubt?; **He ate the whole turkey. — N~!** Er hat den ganzen Truthahn aufgegessen. — Nein! (*ugs.*); **well, I ~ [did]!** [na *od.* nein *od.* also] so was!

**never: ~ˈmore** *adv.* nie wieder; **~-ˈ~** *n.* (*Brit. coll.*) Abzahlungskauf, *der;* **on the ~-~ [system]** auf Stottern (*ugs.*); auf Raten; **~theˈless** *adv.* trotzdem; nichtsdestoweniger

**new** /nju:/ ❶ *adj.* Ⓐ (*not existing before*) neu; **ˈ~ boy/girl** (*lit. or fig.*) Neuling, *der;* **a ~ baby** ein neugeborenes Kind; ein Neugeborenes; Ⓑ (*unfamiliar*) neu; **flying was an experience ~ to him** Fliegen war für ihn eine neue Erfahrung; **that's a ~ one on me** (*coll.*) das ist mir neu; (*of joke etc.*) den habe ich noch nicht gehört; (*of style etc.*) das habe ich noch nicht gesehen; **visit ~ places** unbekannte Orte besuchen; **so what else is ~?** (*iron.*) sonst was Neues? (*ugs.*); **that is not** *or* **nothing ~ to me** das ist mir nichts Neues; Ⓒ (*renewed, additional, changed*) neu; (*in place names*) Neu-; **the ~ mathematics** die neue Mathematik; **the ~ poor** die erst vor kurzem Verarmten; **the ~ rich** die Neureichen (*abwertend*); **the ~ woman** die moderne Frau; die Frau von heute; **be like a ~ man/woman** wie neugeboren sein; ⇒ *also* **birth** A; **broom** A; **deal**[1] 3 A; **leaf** 1 B; Ⓓ (*of recent origin, growth, or manufacture*) neu; frisch ‹Brot, Gemüse›; neu ‹Kartoffeln›; neu, jung ‹Wein›; neu, lebend ‹Sprache›; **as good as ~:** so gut wie neu; **as ~:** neuwertig.
❷ *adv.* Ⓐ (*recently*) vor kurzem; frisch ‹gebacken, gewaschen, geschnitten›; gerade erst ‹erblüht›; Ⓑ (*afresh*) neu

**ˈNew Age** *n.* Newage, *das; attrib.* Newage-

**ˈnewborn** *adj.* Ⓐ (*recently born*) neugeboren; Ⓑ (*regenerated*) neu gewonnen ‹Mut, Kraft usw.›; neu ‹Person›

**ˈnewcomer** *n.* Newcomer, *der;* (*new arrival also*) Neuankömmling, *der;* (*one having no experience also*) Neuling, *der* (**to** in + *Dat.*); (*thing also*) Neuheit, *die* (**to** für)

**New Delhi** /nju: ˈdelɪ/ *pr. n.* ▶ 1626 Neu-Delhi (*das*)

**newel** /ˈnju:əl/ *n.* Ⓐ (*pillar*) Spindel, *die;* Ⓑ **~ [post]** (*supporting stair handrail*) [Treppen]pfosten, *der*

**New ˈEngland** ❶ *n.* Neuengland (*das*). ❷ *attrib. adj.* aus Neuengland; ‹Stadt usw.› in Neuengland

**New Englander** /nju: ˈɪŋgləndə(r)/ *n.* Neuengländer, *der*/Neuengländerin, die

**new: ~fangled** /nju:ˈfæŋgld/ *adj.* (*derog.*) neumodisch (*abwertend*); **~-found** *adj.* neu; (*recently discovered*) neu [entdeckt]

**Newfoundland** /nju:ˈfaʊndlənd/ ❶ *n.* Ⓐ *pr. n.* Neufundland (*das*); Ⓑ (*dog*) Neufundländer, *der.* ❷ *adj.* neufundländisch; **~ dog** Neufundländer, *der*

**Newfoundlander** /nju:ˈfaʊndləndə(r)/ *n.* Neufundländer, *der*/Neufundländerin, *die*

**New ˈGuinea** *pr. n.* Neuguinea (*das*)

**newish** /ˈnju:ɪʃ/ *adj.* ziemlich neu

**new: ~-laid** *adj.* frisch [gelegt]; **New ˈLeft** *n.* neue Linke; **~ ˈlook** *n.* (*coll.*) neuer Stil; **~-look** *adj.* neu

**newly** /ˈnju:lɪ/ *adv.* Ⓐ (*recently*) neu; **~ married** seit kurzem verheiratet; Ⓑ (*in new way*) neu

**ˈnewly-wed** *n.* Jungverheiratete, *der/die*

**new: New ˈMan** *n.* der neue Mann; **~ ˈmoon** *n.* Neumond, *der;* **~-mown** *adj.* frisch gemäht

**news** /nju:z/ *n., no pl.* Ⓐ (*new information*) Nachricht, *die;* **items** *or* **pieces** *or* **bits of ~:** Neuigkeiten; **be in the** *or* **make ~:** Schlagzeilen machen; **that's ~ to me** (*coll.*) das ist mir neu; **what's the latest ~?** was gibt es Neues?; **have you heard the/this ~?** hast du schon gehört/das schon gehört?; weißt du schon das Neueste? (*ugs.*); **have you had any ~ of your brother?** hast du etwas von deinem Bruder gehört?; hast du Nachricht von deinem Bruder?; **I have ~ for you** (*also iron.*) ich habe eine Neuigkeit für dich; **bad/good ~:** schlechte/gute Nachrichten; **sb./sth. is good ~** (*coll.*) jmd./etw. ist wirklich toll (*ugs.*); **he/she/that firm is bad ~** (*coll.*) er/sie/diese Firma ist mit Vorsicht zu genießen (*ugs.*); **no ~ is good ~** (*prov.*) keine Nachricht, gute Nachricht; Ⓑ (*Radio, Telev.*) Nachrichten *Pl.;* **the 10 o'clock ~:** die 10-Uhr-Nachrichten; **listen to/watch the ~:** [die] Nachrichten hören/sehen; **I heard it on the ~:** ich habe es in den Nachrichten gehört; **here is the ~** (*Radio*) Sie hören Nachrichten; (*Telev.*) ≈ ich begrüße Sie zu den Nachrichten; **summary of the ~:** Nachrichtenüberblick, *der*

**news: ~ agency** *n.* Nachrichtenagentur, *die;* **~agent** *n.* ▶ 1261 Zeitungshändler, *der*/-händlerin, *die;* **~boy** *n.* Zeitungsjunge, *der;* **~ bulletin** *n.* Nachrichten *Pl.;* **~cast** *n.* Nachrichtensendung, *die;* **~caster** *n.* ▶ 1261 Nachrichtensprecher, *der*/-sprecherin, *die;* **~ conference** *n.* Pressekonferenz, *die;* **~dealer** *n.* (*Amer.*) Zeitungshändler, *der*/-händlerin, *die;* **~ desk** *n.* Nachrichtenredaktion, *die;* **this is Joe Smith at the ~ desk** (*Radio*) hier ist Joe Smith mit den Nachrichten; **~flash** *n.* Kurzmeldung, *die;* **~girl** *n.* (*delivering*) Zeitungsausträgerin, *die;* (*selling*) Zeitungsverkäuferin, *die;* **~group** *n.* (*Computing*) Newsgroup, *die;* **~hawk** ⇒ **~hound**; **~ ˈheadline** *n.* Schlagzeile, *die;* **~hound** *n.* (*Amer.*) Zeitungsmann, *der* (*ugs.*); Journalist, *der;* **~letter** *n.* Rundschreiben, *das;* **~man** *n.* Reporter, *der;* **~paper** *n.* Ⓐ Zeitung, *die; attrib.* **~paper boy/girl** Zeitungsausträger, *der*/-austrägerin, *die;* Ⓑ (*material*) Zeitungspapier, *das;* **~paperman** *n.* ▶ 1261 Zeitungsmann, *der* (*ugs.*); Journalist, *der;* **~print** *n.* Zeitungspapier, *das;* (*ink*) Druckerschwärze, *die;* **~reader** *n.* ▶ 1261 Nachrichtensprecher, *der*/-sprecherin, *die;* **~reel** *n.* Wochenschau, *die;* **~room** *n.* Nachrichtenredaktion, *die;* **~-sheet** *n.* Informationsblatt, *das;* **~stand** *n.* Zeitungskiosk, *der;* Zeitungsstand, *der;* **~ summary** *n.* Kurznachrichten *Pl.*

**new ˈstar** *n.* (*Astron.*) Nova, *die*

**news: ~ vendor** *n.* Zeitungsverkäufer, *der*/-verkäuferin, *die;* **~worthy** *adj.* [für die Medien] interessant ‹Person, Ereignis›; berichtenswert ‹Ereignis›

**newsy** /ˈnju:zɪ/ *adj.* (*coll.*) Ⓐ (*full of news*) voller Neuigkeiten *nachgestellt;* Ⓑ (*newsworthy*) interessant

**newt** /nju:t/ *n.* [Wasser]molch, *der;* ⇒ *also* **pissed** A

**New ˈTestament** ⇒ **testament** A

**newton** /ˈnju:tn/ *n.* (*Phys.*) Newton, *das*

**new: ~ town** *n.: mit Unterstützung der Regierung völlig neu entstandene Ansiedlung;* **~ ˈworld** ⇒ **world** A; **~ ˈyear** *n.* ▶ 1191 Neujahr, *das;* **over the New Year** über Neujahr; **the Jewish New Year** das jüdische Neujahrsfest; **a Happy New Year** ein glückliches *od.* gutes neues Jahr; **New Year honours** (*Brit.*) Titel- und Ordensverleihungen am Neujahrstag; **bring in the New Year** Silvester feiern; ⇒ *also* **resolution** B; **New ˈYear's** (*Amer.*), **New Year's ˈDay** *ns.* Neujahrstag, *der;* **New Year's ˈEve** *n.* Silvester, *der od. das;* Neujahrsabend, *der*

**New Yorker** /nju: ˈjɔ:kə(r)/ *n.* New Yorker, *der*/New Yorkerin, *die*

**New Zealand** /nju: ˈzi:lənd/ ❶ *pr. n.* Neuseeland (*das*). ❷ *attrib. adj.* neuseeländisch

**New Zealander** /nju: ˈzi:ləndə(r)/ *n.* Neuseeländer, *der*/Neuseeländerin, *die*

**next** /nekst/ ❶ *adj.* Ⓐ (*nearest*) nächst...; **[the] ~ thing to sth.** fast *od.* beinahe etw.; **the seat ~ to me** der Platz neben mir; **the ~ room** das Nebenzimmer; **~ friend** (*Law*) ≈ Beistand, *der;* **the ~ but one** der/die/das Übernächste; **be the one ~ to the door** der/die neben der Tür sein; **~ to** (*fig.: almost*) fast; nahezu; **get ~ to sb.** (*Amer. coll.: friendly*) sich an jmdn. ranmachen (*ugs.*); Ⓑ ▶ 1055 (*in order*) nächst...; **within the ~ few days** in den nächsten Tagen; **~ week/month/year** nächste Woche/nächsten Monat/nächstes Jahr; **on the first of ~ month** am nächsten Ersten; **~ year's results** die Ergebnisse des nächsten Jahres; **during the ~ year** während der nächsten zwölf Monate; **we'll come ~ May** wir kommen im Mai nächsten Jahres; **the ~ largest/larger** der/die/das Nächstkleinere/Nächstgrößere; **[the] ~ time** das nächste Mal; **the ~ best** der/die/das Nächstbeste; **taking one year** *etc.* **with the ~:** im Ganzen gesehen; **am I ~?** komme ich jetzt dran?; **he's as able as the ˈ~ man** er kann es wie jeder andere auch; ⇒ *also* **door** A; **world** A.
❷ *adv.* (*in the next place*) als Nächstes; (*on the next occasion*) das nächste Mal; **when I ~ see him** wenn ich ihn das nächste Mal sehe; **whose name comes ~?** wessen Name kommt als Nächstes *od.* Nächster?; **it is my turn ~:** ich komme als Nächster dran; **what ˈwill they think of ~?** was fällt denen als Nächstes ein?; **sit/stand ~ to sb.** neben jmdm. sitzen/stehen; **place sth. ~ to sb./sth.** etw. neben jmdn./etw. stellen; **come ~ to last** (*in race*) Zweitletzter/Zweitletzte

werden; **come ~ to bottom** (*in exam*) der/die Zweitschlechteste sein; ❸ *n.* Ⓐ (*letter, issue, etc.*) nächster Brief/nächste Ausgabe *usw.*; Ⓑ (*period of time*) **from one day to the ~:** von einem Tag zum andern; **the week after ~:** [die] übernächste Woche; Ⓒ (*person*) **~ of kin** nächster/nächste Angehörige; **~ please!** der Nächste, bitte!

**'next-door** *adj.* gleich nebenan *nachgestellt;* ⇒ *also* **neighbour** 1

**nexus** /'neksəs/ *n.* Nexus, *der* (*fachspr.*)

**NHS** *abbr.* (*Brit.*) **National Health Service**; *attrib.* **~ Trust** NHS-Trust, *der*

**NI** *abbr.* (*Brit.*) **National Insurance**

**Niagara Falls** /naɪægərə 'fɔ:lz/ *pr. n. pl.* Niagarafälle

**nib** /nɪb/ *n.* Feder, *die;* (*tip*) Spitze, *die*

**nibble** /'nɪbl/ ❶ *v.t.* knabbern; **~ off** abknabbern. ❷ *v.i.* knabbern (**at, on** an + *Dat.*); **the cheese had been ~d at** der Käse war angeknabbert worden; **they are nibbling at the idea** (*fig.*) sie beginnen, sich langsam für die Idee zu interessieren. ❸ *n.* Ⓐ (*lit. or fig.*) Anbeißen, *das;* **he didn't get a single ~:** bei ihm biss nicht einer an; Ⓑ *in pl.* (*coll.: things to eat*) etwas zum Knabbern

**nibs** /nɪbz/ *n.* (*coll./joc.*) **his ~:** der hohe Herr (*scherzh.*)

**Nicaragua** /nɪkə'rægjʊə/ *pr. n.* Nicaragua (*das*)

**Nicaraguan** /nɪkə'rægjʊən/ ▶**1340** ❶ *adj.* nicaraguanisch; **sb. is ~:** jmd. ist Nicaraguaner/Nicaraguanerin. ❷ *n.* Nicaraguaner, *der*/Nicaraguanerin, *die*

**nice** /naɪs/ *adj.* Ⓐ (*pleasing*) nett; angenehm ‹Stimme›; schön ‹Wetter›; (*iron.: disgraceful, difficult*) schön; sauber (*iron.*); **the hotel is ~ enough** das Hotel ist nicht schlecht *od.* ganz ordentlich; **she has a ~ smile** sie lächelt so nett; **a ~ friend you are!** (*iron.*) du bist mir [ja] ein schöner Freund!; **you're a ~ one, I must say** (*iron.*) du bist mir vielleicht einer; **be in a ~ mess** (*iron.*) in einem schönen Schlamassel sitzen (*ugs.*); **[do a piece of] ~ work** saubere *od.* gute Arbeit [leisten]; **~ to meet you** freut mich, Sie kennen zu lernen; **~ [and] warm/fast/high** schön warm/schnell/hoch; **a ~ long holiday** schöne lange Ferien; **~-looking** hübsch; gut aussehend, hübsch ‹Person›; **not very ~** (*unpleasant*) nicht sehr nett; nicht sehr schön ‹Wetter›; **he is not very ~ to his sister** er ist nicht gerade nett zu seiner Schwester; **~ one!** (*coll.*) nicht schlecht!; **~ one, Cyril!** (*Brit. coll.*) so ein Schlaumeier!; **~ work if you can get it** (*iron.*) das ließe ich mir auch gefallen!; Ⓑ (*fastidious*) anspruchsvoll; (*punctilious*) genau; Ⓒ (*requiring precision*) fein, genau ‹Unterscheidung›; Ⓓ (*subtle*) fein ‹Bedeutungsunterschied›

**Nice** /ni:s/ *pr. n.* Nizza (*das*)

**nicely** /'naɪslɪ/ *adv.* Ⓐ (*well*) nett; gut ‹arbeiten, sich benehmen, platziert sein›; **a ~ behaved child** ein wohlerzogenes Kind; Ⓑ (*all right*) gut; **he's got a new job and is doing very ~:** er hat eine neue Arbeit und kommt prima (*ugs.*) *od.* sehr gut damit zurecht; **the patient is doing ~:** der Patient macht gute Fortschritte; **that will do ~:** das reicht völlig; ⇒ *also* **thank**

**nicety** /'naɪsɪtɪ/ *n.* Ⓐ *no pl.* (*punctiliousness*) [peinliche] Genauigkeit; Ⓑ *no pl.* (*precision, accuracy*) Feinheit, *die;* Genauigkeit, *die;* **to a ~:** perfekt ‹arrangieren›; sehr genau ‹schätzen›; Ⓒ *no pl.* (*intricate or subtle quality*) Feinheit, *die;* **make a point of great ~:** höchst subtil argumentieren; Ⓓ *in pl.* (*minute distinctions*) Feinheiten

**niche** /nɪtʃ, ni:ʃ/ *n.* Ⓐ (*in wall*) Nische, *die;* Ⓑ (*fig.: suitable place*) Platz, *der;* **there he soon carved out a ~ for himself** dort fand er bald den richtigen Platz für sich

**Nicholas** /'nɪkələs/ *pr. n.* (*Hist., as name of ruler etc.*) Nikolaus (*der*)

**nick** ❶ *n.* Ⓐ (*notch*) Kerbe, *die;* Ⓑ (*sl.: prison*) Kittchen, *das* (*ugs.*); Knast, *der* (*salopp*); Ⓒ (*Brit. sl.: police station*) Wache, *die;* Revier, *das;* Ⓓ **in good/poor ~** (*coll.*) gut/nicht gut in Schuss (*ugs.*); Ⓔ **in the ~ of time** gerade noch rechtzeitig. ❷ *v.t.* Ⓐ (*make ~ in*) einkerben ‹Holz›; **~ one's chin** sich am Kinn schneiden; Ⓑ (*Brit. coll.*) (*catch*) schnappen (*ugs.*); (*arrest*) einlochen (*salopp*); Ⓒ (*Brit. coll.: steal*) klauen (*salopp*); mitgehen lassen (*ugs.*)

**Nick** /nɪk/ *n.* **Old ~:** der Teufel; der Leibhaftige (*verhüll.*)

**nickel** /'nɪkl/ *n.* Ⓐ (*metal*) Nickel, *das;* Ⓑ (*US coin*) Fünfcentstück, *das*

**nickel-'plate** *v.t.* vernickeln

**nicker** /'nɪkə(r)/ *n., pl. same* (*Brit. coll.*) Pfund, *das;* **it's a hundred ~:** ≈ es sind dreihundert Eier (*salopp*)

**nickname** /'nɪkneɪm/ ❶ *n.* Ⓐ (*name added or substituted*) Spitzname, *der;* Ⓑ (*abbreviation*) Spitzname, *der;* (*affectionate*) Koseform, *die.* ❷ *v.t.* einen Spitznamen geben (+ *Dat.*); **~ sb. ...:** jmdm. den Spitznamen ... geben; jmdn. ... taufen

**nicotine** /'nɪkəti:n/ *n.* Nikotin, *das*

**'nicotine patch** *n.* Nikotinpflaster, *das*

**niece** /ni:s/ *n.* Nichte, *die*

**nifty** /'nɪftɪ/ *adj.* (*coll.*) Ⓐ (*smart, excellent*) klasse (*ugs.*); flott ‹Kleidung›; Ⓑ (*clever*) geschickt; clever ‹Plan, Idee›

**Niger**[1] /'naɪdʒə(r)/ *pr. n.* ▶**1480** (*river*) Niger, *der*

**Niger**[2] /ni:'ʒeə(r)/ *pr. n.* (*country*) Niger (*das od. der*)

**Nigeria** /naɪ'dʒɪərɪə/ *pr. n.* Nigeria (*das*)

**Nigerian** /naɪ'dʒɪərɪən/ ▶**1340** ❶ *adj.* nigerianisch; **sb. is ~:** jmd. ist Nigerianer/Nigerianerin. ❷ *n.* Nigerianer, *der*/Nigerianerin, *die*

**niggardly** /'nɪgədlɪ/ *adj.* Ⓐ (*miserly*) knaus[e]rig (*ugs. abwertend*); Ⓑ (*given in small amounts*) armselig, kümmerlich (*abwertend*) ‹Portion›

**nigger** /'nɪgə(r)/ *n.* (*derog.: Negro, dark-skinned person*) Nigger, *der* (*abwertend*); **there's a ~ in the woodpile** *or* (*Amer.*) **in the fence** (*fig.*) es gibt einen Haken bei *od.* an der Sache; **who's the ~ in the woodpile?** (*fig.*) wer schießt hier quer?

**niggle** /'nɪgl/ ❶ *v.i.* Ⓐ (*spend time on petty details*) **~ over** [endlos] herumtüfteln an (+ *Dat.*) ‹Vertrag, Klausel›; **~ over every small point** sich mit jeder winzigen Einzelheit aufhalten; Ⓑ (*find fault pettily*) [herum]nörgeln (*ugs. abwertend*) (**at** an + *Dat.*). ❷ *v.t.* herumnörgeln an (+ *Dat.*); **be ~d** verärgert sein

**niggling** /'nɪglɪŋ/ *adj.* Ⓐ (*petty*) belanglos; Ⓑ (*trivial*) nichts sagend; oberflächlich ‹Kritik›; krittelig ‹Rezension, Rezensent›; Ⓒ (*nagging*) nagend ‹Zweifel›; quälend ‹Gefühl›

**niggly** /'nɪglɪ/ *adj.* Ⓐ (*irritable*) gereizt; Ⓑ ⇒ **niggling** A

**nigh** /naɪ/ (*arch./literary/dial.*) ❶ *adv.* nahe; **come** *or* **draw ~:** näher kommen; ‹Tag, Zeitpunkt:› nahen; **it's ~ on impossible** es ist nahezu unmöglich; ⇒ *also* **wellnigh.** ❷ *prep.* nahe (*geh.*) *nachgestellt* (+ *Dat.*)

**night** /naɪt/ *n.* ▶**1012**, ▶**1056** Ⓐ Nacht, *die;* (*evening*) Abend, *der;* **~ after ~:** Nacht für Nacht/Abend für Abend; **the following ~:** die Nacht/der Abend darauf; **the previous ~:** die vorausgegangene Nacht/der vorausgegangene Abend; **one ~ he came** eines Nachts/Abends kam er; **two ~s ago** vorgestern Nacht/Abend; **the other ~:** neulich abends/nachts; **far into the ~:** bis spät *od.* tief in die Nacht; **on Sunday ~:** Sonntagnacht/[am] Sonntagabend; **on Sunday ~s** sonntagabends; **on the ~ of Friday the 13th** am Freitag, dem 13., nachts/abends; **[on] the ~ after/before** die Nacht danach/davor; **[on] the ~ after/before sth.** die Nacht nach/vor etw. (*Dat.*); **for the ~:** über Nacht; **late at ~:** spätabends; **a ~ raid** ein nächtlicher Überfall; ein Nachtangriff (*Milit.*); **a ~'s rest will make you feel better** wenn du eine Nacht richtig geschlafen hast, wirst du dich wieder besser fühlen; **take all ~** (*fig.*) den ganzen Abend brauchen; **at ~** (*in the evening, at ~fall*) abends; (*during the ~*) nachts; bei Nacht; **make a ~ of it** die Nacht durchfeiern; durchmachen (*ugs.*); **~ and day** Tag und Nacht; **as ~ follows day** so sicher wie das Amen in der Kirche; **a ~ off** eine Nacht/ein Abend frei; **~ out** (*of servant*) freier Abend; **it is her ~ out** sie hat ihren freien Abend; **have a ~ out** (*festive evening*) [abends] ausgehen; **she works one ~ a week** sie arbeitet einen Abend/eine Nacht in der Woche; **spend the ~ with sb.** bei jmdm. übernachten; (*implying sexual intimacy*) die Nacht mit jmdm. verbringen; **stay the ~** *or* **over ~:** über Nacht bleiben; **work ~s** nachts arbeiten; (*be on ~shift*) ‹Krankenschwester:› Nachtdienst haben; ‹Schichtarbeiter:› Nachtschicht haben; ⇒ *also* **good** 1 M; **last**[1] 1; Ⓑ (*darkness, lit. or fig.*) Nacht, *die;* **black as ~:** schwarz wie die Nacht; **it went as dark as ~:** es wurde stockdunkel; Ⓒ (*~fall*) Einbruch der Dunkelheit; **wait for ~:** darauf warten, dass es Nacht wird; **when ~ comes** wenn es dunkel wird; Ⓓ (*~'s sleep*) **have a good/bad ~:** gut/schlecht schlafen; **have a sleepless ~:** eine schlaflose Nacht haben; Ⓔ (*evening of performance etc.*) Abend, *der;* **opening ~:** Premiere, *die;* ⇒ *also* **first night; ladies' night;** Ⓕ *attrib.* Nacht-/Abend-

**night: ~ bell** *n.* (*Brit.*) Nachtglocke, *die;* **~bird** *n.* (*person*) Nachteule, *die* (*ugs. scherzh.*); **~ blindness** *n.* Nachtblindheit, *die;* **~cap** *n.* Ⓐ Nachtmütze, *die;* (*woman's*) Nachthaube, *die;* Ⓑ (*drink*) Schlaftrunk, *der;* **~clothes** *n. pl.* Nachtwäsche, *die;* **in one's ~clothes** im Nachthemd/Schlafanzug; **~club** *n.* Nachtklub, *der;* Nachtlokal, *das;* **~dress** *n.* Nachthemd, *das;* **~ duty** *n.* Nachtdienst, *der;* **be on ~ duty** Nachtdienst haben; **~fall** *n., no art.* Einbruch der Dunkelheit; **at/after ~fall** bei/nach Einbruch der Dunkelheit; **~ fighter** *n.* (*Air Force*) Nachtjäger, *der;* **~ flying** *n.* Nachtfliegen, *das;* **~gown** ⇒ **~dress**

**nightie** /'naɪtɪ/ *n.* (*coll.*) Nachthemd, *das*

**nightingale** /'naɪtɪŋgeɪl/ *n.* Nachtigall, *die*

**night: ~jar** *n.* (*Ornith.*) Ziegenmelker, *der;* **~life** *n.* Nachtleben, *das;* **~ light** *n.* Nachtlicht, *das;* **~-long** ❶ *adj.* sich über die ganze Nacht hinziehend; **keep a ~-long vigil** die ganze Nacht wachen; ❷ *adv.* die ganze Nacht [lang *od.* über]

**nightly** /'naɪtlɪ/ ❶ *adj.* (*happening, done, etc. in the night/evening*) nächtlich/abendlich; (*happening every night/evening*) allnächtlich/allabendlich. ❷ *adv.* (*every night*) jede Nacht; (*every evening*) jeden Abend; **twice ~** (*Theatre etc.*) zweimal pro Abend

**night: ~mare** *n.* (*lit. or fig.*) Albtraum, *der;* **~marish** /'naɪtmeərɪʃ/ *adj.* albtraumhaft; **~-'~** *int.* (*coll.*) [gute] Nacht; **~ nurse** *n.* Nachtschwester, *die;* **~ owl** *n.* Ⓐ (*Ornith.*) Eule, *die;* Nachteule, *die* (*veralt.*); Ⓑ (*coll.: person*) Nachteule, *die* (*ugs. scherzh.*); Nachtschwärmer, *der* (*scherzh.*); **~ porter** *n.* Nachtportier, *der;* **~robe** (*Amer.*) ⇒ **nightdress; ~ safe** *n.* Nachttresor, *der;* **~-scented 'stock** *n.* (*Bot.*) Abendlevkoje, *die;* **~ school** *n.* Abendschule, *die;* **~shade** *n.* (*Bot.*) Nachtschatten, *der;* **black ~shade** Schwarzer Nachtschatten; **woody ~shade** Bittersüß, *das;* Bittersüßer Nachtschatten; ⇒ *also* **deadly; ~ shelter** *n.* Nachtasyl, *das;* **~ shift** *n.* Nachtschicht, *die;* **be on ~ shift** Nachtschicht haben *od.* machen; **~shirt** *n.* [Herren]nachthemd, *das;* **~ 'sky** *n.* Nachthimmel, *der;* **~ spot** (*coll.*) ⇒ **~club; ~stick** *n.* (*Amer.*) Schlagstock, *der;* **~ 'storage heater** *n.* Nachtspeicherofen, *der;* **~time** *n., no indef. art.* Nacht, *die;* **at ~-time** nachts; **wait until ~-time** warten, bis es Nacht *od.* dunkel wird; **in the ~-time** während der Nacht; nachts; **~ 'watch** *n.* Nachtwache, *die;* **in the ~ watches** während der Nacht; **~'watchman** *n.* Ⓐ ▶**1261** Nachtwächter, *der;* Ⓑ (*Cricket*) *Auswechselspieler, der am Ende eines Tages eingesetzt wird, damit ein besserer Spieler geschont wird;* **~wear** *n. sing.:* ⇒ **nightclothes**

**nig-nog** /'nɪgnɒg/ *n.* (*Brit. derog.*) Nigger, *der* (*abwertend*)

**nihilism** /'naɪɪlɪzm, 'nɪhɪlɪzm/ *n.* Nihilismus, *der*

**nihilist** /'naɪlɪst, 'nɪhɪlɪst/ *n.* Nihilist, *der*

**nihilistic** /naɪ'lɪstɪk, nɪhɪ'lɪstɪk/ *adj.* nihilistisch

**nil** /nɪl/ *n.* Ⓐ nichts; **his chances were ~:** seine Chancen waren gleich null; **our investment has shown a ~ return** unsere Investition hat keinen Gewinn gebracht; Ⓑ (*Sport*) null; **win one ~** *or* **by one goal to ~:** eins zu null gewinnen

**Nile** /naɪl/ *pr. n.* ▶ 1480 Nil, *der*

**nimble** /'nɪmbl/ *adj.* Ⓐ (*quick in movement*) flink; behände; Ⓑ (*quick in mind*) beweglich ‹Geist›; lebhaft ‹Fantasie›; **his mind remained ~:** er blieb geistig beweglich; Ⓒ (*dextrous*) geschickt

**nimbly** /'nɪmblɪ/ *adv.* flink ‹arbeiten, sich bewegen›

**nimbus** /'nɪmbəs/ *n., pl.* **nimbi** /'nɪmbaɪ/ *or* **~es** Ⓐ (*halo*) Nimbus, *der* (*bild. Kunst*); Heiligenschein, *der;* Ⓑ (*Meteorol.*) Nimbostratus, *der*

**nincompoop** /'nɪŋkəmpu:p/ *n.* Trottel, *der* (*ugs. abwertend*)

**nine** /naɪn/ ▶ 912, ▶ 1012, ▶ 1352 ❶ *adj.* neun; **~-tenths of the time/inhabitants** (*fig.*) fast die ganze Zeit/fast *od.* so gut wie alle Einwohner; **~ times out of ten** (*fig.: nearly always*) in den weitaus meisten Fällen; **a ~ days' wonder** nur eine Eintagsfliege (*ugs.*); ⇒ *also* **eight** 1. ❷ *n.* Ⓐ (*number, symbol*) Neun, *die;* **work from ~ to five** die übliche Arbeitszeit [von 9 bis 17 Uhr] haben; **the ~-to-five world** die Welt des geregelten Achtstundentags; **~-to-five mentality** Angestelltenmentalität, *die* (*abwertend*); Ⓑ (*Amer.: baseball team*) Mannschaft, *die;* „Neun", *die;* Ⓒ **the N~** (*literary: the Muses*) die neun Musen; Ⓓ **dressed [up] to the ~s** sehr festlich gekleidet; **~-~-~, 999** (*Brit.: emergency number*) ≈ eins, eins, null. ⇒ *also* **eight** 2 A, C, D

**ninefold** /'naɪnfəʊld/ *adj., adv.* neunfach; ⇒ *also* **eightfold**

**'ninepins** *n.* (*Brit.*) Ⓐ (*game*) Kegeln, *das;* **play ~:** kegeln; Ⓑ *constr. as pl.* (*pins*) Kegel; **go down like ~** (*fig.*) reihenweise umfallen (*ugs.*)

**nineteen** /naɪn'ti:n/ ▶ 912, ▶ 1012, ▶ 1352 ❶ *adj.* neunzehn; ⇒ *also* **eight** 1. ❷ *n.* Ⓐ Neunzehn, *die;* ⇒ *also* **eight** 2 A; **eighteen** 2; Ⓑ **talk ~ to the dozen** (*Brit.*) wie ein Wasserfall reden (*ugs.*)

**nineteenth** /naɪn'ti:nθ/ ▶ 1055 ❶ *adj.* ▶ 1352 neunzehnt...; **~ hole** (*joc.: golf club's bar*) neunzehntes Loch (*fig. scherzh.*); ⇒ *also* **eighth** 1. ❷ *n.* (*fraction*) Neunzehntel, *das;* ⇒ *also* **eighth** 2

**ninetieth** /'naɪntɪɪθ/ ❶ *adj.* ▶ 1352 neunzigst...; ⇒ *also* **eighth** 1. ❷ *n.* (*fraction*) Neunzigstel, *das;* ⇒ *also* **eighth** 2

**ninety** /'naɪntɪ/ ▶ 912, ▶ 1352 ❶ *adj.* neunzig; **one-and-~** (*arch.*) ⇒ **ninety-one** 1; ⇒ *also* **eight** 1. ❷ *n.* Neunzig, *die;* **one-and-~** (*arch.*) ⇒ **~-one** 2. ⇒ *also* **eight** 2 A; **eighty** 2

**ninety: ~-'first** *etc. adj.* ▶ 1352 einundneunzigst... *usw.;* ⇒ *also* **eighth** 1; **~-'one** *etc.* ❶ *adj.* einundneunzig *usw.;* **~-nine times out of a hundred** (*fig.: nearly always*) so gut wie immer; ⇒ *also* **eight** 1; ❷ *n.* ▶ 1352 Einundneunzig *usw., die;* ⇒ *also* **eight** 2 A

**ninny** /'nɪnɪ/ *n.* Dummkopf, *der* (*ugs.*); Dussel, *der* (*ugs.*)

**ninth** /naɪnθ/ ❶ *adj.* ▶ 1352 neunt...; ⇒ *also* **eighth** 1. ❷ *n.* Ⓐ (*in sequence, rank*) Neunte, *der/die/das;* (*fraction*) Neuntel, *das;* Ⓑ (*Mus.*) None, *die;* Ⓒ ▶ 1055 (*day*) **the ~ of May** der neunte Mai; **the ~ [of the month]** der Neunte [des Monats]. ⇒ *also* **eighth** 2

**niobium** /naɪ'əʊbɪəm/ *n.* (*Chem.*) Niobium, *das*

**nip**[1] ❶ *v.t.*, **-pp-** Ⓐ (*pinch, squeeze, bite*) zwicken; **~ sb.'s toe/sb. on the leg** jmdn. *od.* jmdm. in den Zeh/jmdn. am Bein zwicken; Ⓑ **~ off** abzwicken; (*with scissors*) abknipsen. ⇒ *also* **bud** 1. ❷ *v.i.*, **-pp-** (*Brit. coll.: step etc. quickly*) **~ in** hinein-/hereinflitzen (*ugs.*); **~ out** hinaus-/herausflitzen (*ugs.*); **~ up** hochflitzen (*ugs.*); **~ out to get a paper** kurz rausgehen, um eine Zeitung zu holen (*ugs.*); **~ across to Mrs Jones and ...:** spring mal zu Frau Jones rüber und ... ❸ *n.* Ⓐ (*pinch, squeeze*) Kniff, *der;* (*bite*) Biss, *der;* **give sb.'s cheek a ~,** **give sb. a ~ on the cheek** jmdn. in die Wange zwicken; Ⓑ (*coldness of air*) Kälte, *die;* **there's a ~ in the air** es ist frisch

**nip**[2] *n.* (*of spirits etc.*) Schlückchen, *das;* **have a ~ of wine** ein Schlückchen Wein nehmen

**Nip** /nɪp/ *n.* (*sl. derog.*) Japs, *der* (*ugs., oft abwertend*)

**nip and 'tuck** *n.* (*Amer.*) **it was ~:** es war ganz knapp

**nipper** /'nɪpə(r)/ *n.* Ⓐ (*Brit. coll.: child*) Gör, *das* (*nordd.*); Balg, *das* (*ugs.*); Ⓑ *in pl.* (*pincers*) Beißzange, *die;* Kneifzange, *die;* Ⓒ (*claw*) Schere, *die;* Zange, *die*

**nipple** /'nɪpl/ *n.* Ⓐ (*on breast*) Brustwarze, *die;* Ⓑ (*of feeding bottle*) Sauger, *der;* Ⓒ **[grease] ~:** [Schmier]nippel, *der*

**Nippon** /'nɪpɒn/ *pr. n.* Nippon (*das*)

**nippy** /'nɪpɪ/ *adj.* (*coll.*) Ⓐ (*nimble*) flink; spritzig ‹Auto›; Ⓑ (*cold*) frisch; kühl

**nirvana** /nə:'vɑ:nə, nɪə'vɑ:nə/ *n.* Nirwana, *das*

**nisi** /'naɪsaɪ/ *adj.* (*Law*) vorläufig; mit Vorbehalt; ⇒ *also* **decree** 1 B

**Nissen hut** /'nɪsn hʌt/ *n.* Nissenhütte, *die*

**nit** /nɪt/ *n.* Ⓐ (*egg*) Nisse, *die;* Ⓑ (*coll.: stupid person*) Dussel, *der* (*ugs.*); Blödmann, *der* (*salopp*)

**niter** (*Amer.*) ⇒ **nitre**

**'nit: ~-pick** *v.i.* kritteln (*abwertend*); **~-picking** (*coll.*) ❶ *n.* Kritteleien *Pl.* (*abwertend*); ❷ *adj.* kleinlich (*abwertend*)

**nitrate** /'naɪtreɪt/ *n.* Ⓐ (*salt*) Nitrat, *das;* Ⓑ (*fertilizer*) Nitratdünger, *der*

**nitre** /'naɪtə(r)/ *n.* (*Brit.*) Salpeter, *der*

**nitric** /'naɪtrɪk/ *adj.* (*Chem.: of or containing nitrogen*) stickstoffhaltig; Stickstoff-

**nitric: ~ 'acid** *n.* (*Chem.*) Salpetersäure, *die;* **~ 'oxide** *n.* (*Chem.*) Stickoxid, *das*

**nitride** /'naɪtraɪd/ *n.* (*Chem.*) Nitrid, *das*

**nitrite** /'naɪtraɪt/ *n.* (*Chem.*) Nitrit, *das*

**nitrogen** /'naɪtrədʒən/ *n.* Stickstoff, *der*

**nitrogen: ~ cycle** *n.* (*Bot.*) Stickstoffkreislauf, *der;* **~ fixation** *n.* (*Bot.*) Bindung des freien Stickstoffs

**nitrogenous** /naɪ'trɒdʒɪnəs/ *adj.* stickstoffhaltig

**nitroglycerine** /naɪtrəʊ'glɪsəri:n/ *n.* Nitroglyzerin, *das*

**nitrous**/'naɪtrəs/: **~ 'acid** *n.* (*Chem.*) salpet[e]rige Säure; **~ 'oxide** *n.* (*Chem.*) Distickstoff[mon]oxid, *das*

**nitty-gritty** /nɪtɪ'grɪtɪ/ *n.* (*coll.*) **the ~ [of the matter]** der Kern [der Sache]; **the ~ of the situation** das, worum es eigentlich geht; **get down to the ~:** zur Sache kommen

**nitwit** /'nɪtwɪt/ *n.* (*coll.*) Trottel, *der* (*ugs.*)

**nitwitted** /'nɪtwɪtɪd/ *adj.* dämlich (*ugs.*)

**nix** /nɪks/ *n.* (*coll.*) Ⓐ (*nothing*) nix (*ugs.*); Ⓑ ⇒ **no** 2 B

**NNE** /nɔ:θnɔ:θ'i:st/ *abbr.* ▶ 1024 **north-north-east** NNO

**NNW** /nɔ:θnɔ:θ'west/ *abbr.* ▶ 1024 **north-north-west** NNW

**no** /nəʊ/ ❶ *adj.* Ⓐ (*not any*) kein; Ⓑ (*not a*) kein; (*quite other than*) alles andere als; **she is no beauty** sie ist keine Schönheit *od.* nicht gerade eine Schönheit; **you are no friend** du bist kein [wahrer] Freund; **friend or no friend** Freund oder nicht; Freund hin oder her; ⇒ *also* **go**[1] 3 F; Ⓒ (*hardly any*) **it's no distance from our house to the shopping centre** von unserem Haus ist es nicht weit bis zum Einkaufszentrum; ⇒ *also* **time** B. ❷ *adv.* Ⓐ (*by no amount*) nicht; **we went no further than the Post Office** wir gingen nicht weiter als bis zum Postamt; **no fewer than** nicht weniger als; **no less [than]** nicht weniger [als]; **it is no different from before** es hat sich nichts geändert; **it was no less a person than Gladstone** *or* **Gladstone, no less** es war kein Geringerer als Gladstone; **I ask no more of you other than ...:** ich verlange nicht mehr von dir als ...; **no more wine?** keinen Wein mehr?; **no more war!** nie wieder Krieg!; **he is no more upper-class than I am** er ist auch nicht mehr *od.* nichts Besseres (*ugs.*) als ich; **I'm not entirely innocent in this matter — No more am I** Ich bin nicht ganz unschuldig in dieser Sache — Und ich [bins] ebenso wenig; **I saw no more of him** ich habe ihn nicht mehr gesehen; **he is no more** (*is dead*) er ist nicht mehr (*geh.*); Ⓑ (*equivalent to negative sentence*) nein; **say/answer 'no'** Nein sagen/mit Nein antworten; **I won't take 'no' for an answer** ein Nein lasse ich nicht gelten; **I won't say 'no'** da kann ich nicht Nein sagen; Ⓒ (*not*) nicht; **like it or no** ob es mir *usw.* [nun] passt/passte oder nicht; **whether or no anyone else helps** [egal] ob sonst jemand hilft oder nicht; Ⓓ **no can do** (*coll.*) geht nicht (*ugs.*). ❸ *n., pl.* **noes** /nəʊz/ Nein, *das;* (*vote*) Neinstimme, *die;* **the ayes and noes** die Stimmen für und wider; **the noes have it** die Mehrheit ist dagegen

**No.** *abbr.* Ⓐ **number** Nr.; Ⓑ ▶ 1024 (*Amer.*) **North** N

**'no-account** *adj.* unbedeutend

**Noah's ark** /nəʊəz 'ɑ:k/ Ⓐ (*Bibl.*) die Arche Noah; Ⓑ (*toy*) Arche Noah (*als Spielzeug*)

**nob**[1] /nɒb/ *n.* (*coll.: head*) Rübe, *die* (*salopp*)

**nob**[2] *n.* (*Brit. coll.: wealthy or upper-class person*) **the ~s** die besseren Leute

**no-'ball** (*Cricket*) ❶ *n.* Fehlball, *der.* ❷ *v.t.* **~ sb.** jmds. Wurf für ungültig erklären

**nobble** /'nɒbl/ *v.t.* (*Brit. coll.*) Ⓐ (*tamper with*) (*durch Spritzen o. Ä.*) langsam machen ‹Rennpferd›; Ⓑ (*get the favour of*) (*durch Bestechung o. Ä.*) auf seine Seite ziehen ‹Person›; Ⓒ (*take dishonestly*) klauen (*salopp*) ‹Geld, Schmuck›; Ⓓ (*catch*) schnappen (*ugs.*) ‹Dieb›

**nobbut** /'nɒbət/ *adv.* (*dial.*) bloß (*ugs.*); nur; **it's ~ Thursday** es ist erst Donnerstag

**Nobel prize** /nəʊbel 'praɪz/ *n.* Nobelpreis, *der*

**nobility** /nə'bɪlɪtɪ/ *n.* Ⓐ *no pl.* (*character*) hohe Gesinnung; Adel, *der;* **a true ~ of character** ein wahrhaft nobler Charakter; **~ of soul** Seelenadel, *der* (*geh.*); Ⓑ (*class*) Adel, *der;* **many of the ~:** viele Adlige; **be born into the ~:** von adliger Geburt sein (*geh.*)

**noble** /'nəʊbl/ ❶ *adj.* Ⓐ (*by rank, title, or birth*) ad[e]lig; **be of ~ birth** von adliger *od.* edler Geburt sein (*geh.*); adlig sein; **the ~ Lord/Earl** der edle Lord/Graf (*geh.*); Ⓑ (*of lofty character*) edel ‹Gedanken, Gefühle›; **~ ideals** hohe Ideale; Ⓒ (*showing greatness of character*) edel; hochherzig (*geh.*); **make ~ efforts** sich in hochherziger Weise bemühen (*geh.*); Ⓓ (*splendid*) edel (*geh.*); vortrefflich. ❷ *n.* Adlige, *der/die;* Edelmann, *der/*Edelfrau, *die* (*hist.*); **the ~s** die Adligen; die Edelleute (*hist.*)

**noble: ~man** /'nəʊblmən/ *n., pl.* **~men** /'nəʊblmən/ Adlige, *der;* Edelmann, *der* (*hist.*); **~ 'metal** *n.* (*Chem.*) Edelmetall, *das;* **~-'minded** *adj.* edel gesinnt; edel ‹Tat›; **~ 'savage** *n.* edler Wilder (*Literaturw.*)

**noblesse** /nə'bles/ *n., no pl.* Noblesse, *die* (*veralt.*); Adel, *der;* **~ oblige** /nəʊbles əʊ 'bli:ʒ/ noblesse oblige (*geh., oft scherzh.*); Adel verpflichtet

**'noblewoman** *n.* Adlige, *die;* Edelfrau, *die* (*hist.*); (*unmarried*) Edelfräulein, *das* (*hist.*)

**nobly** /'nəʊblɪ/ *adv.* Ⓐ (*with noble spirit*) edel [gesinnt]; Ⓑ (*generously*) edelmütig (*geh.*); Ⓒ (*splendidly*) edel (*geh.*)

**nobody** /'nəʊbədɪ/ *n. & pron.* niemand; keiner; (*person of no importance*) Niemand, *der;* ⇒ *also* **business** C; **fool**[1] 1 A

**no-'claim[s] bonus** *n.* (*Insurance*) Schadenfreiheitsrabatt, *der*

**nocturnal** /nɒk'tɜ:nl/ *adj.* nächtlich; nachtaktiv ‹Tier›; **~ animal/bird** Nachttier, *das/* -vogel, *der*

**nocturne** /'nɒktɜ:n/ *n.* Ⓐ (*Mus.*) Nocturne, *das od. die;* Ⓑ (*Art*) Nachtstück, *das*

**nod** /nɒd/ ❶ *v.i.*, **-dd-** Ⓐ (*as signal*) nicken; **~ to sb.** jmdm. zunicken; **have a ~ding acquaintance with sth.** nur über geringe Kenntnisse in etw. (*Dat.*) verfügen; **he's only**

n

**a ~ding acquaintance** ich kenne ihn nur flüchtig; **he ~ded to him to take charge** er gab ihm durch ein Nicken zu verstehen, dass er das Kommando übernehmen solle; ⇒ *also* **goodbye** 2; **B** (*in drowsiness*) **she sat ~ding by the fire** sie war neben dem Kamin eingenickt (*ugs.*); **her head started to ~:** sie begann einzunicken (*ugs.*); **C** (*make a mistake*) patzen (*ugs.*); einen Fehler machen; **D** (*move up and down*) nicken (*fig. dichter.*).

**2** *v.t.*, **-dd- A** (*incline*) **~ one's head [in greeting]** [zum Gruß] mit dem Kopf nicken; **B** (*signify by nod*) **~ approval** *or* **agreement** zustimmend nicken; **~ sb. a welcome, ~ a welcome to sb.** jmdm. zum Gruß *od.* zur Begrüßung zunicken.

**3** *n.* **A** (*nodding*) [Kopf]nicken, *das;* **a ~ is as good as a wink [to a blind man** *or* **horse]** (*fig.*) es bedarf/bedurfte keiner weiteren Worte; **land of N~:** Land der Träume (*geh.*); **on the ~** (*coll.*) (*on credit*) auf Pump (*salopp*); (*with merely formal assent*) ohne große Diskussion; **B** (*Amer.: sign of approval*) **get the ~ from sb.** von jmdm. grünes Licht bekommen; **give sth. the ~:** grünes Licht für etw. geben

**~ 'off** *v.i.* einnicken (*ugs.*)

**noddle** /ˈnɒdl/ *n.* (*coll.: head*) Birne, *die* (*salopp*)

**noddy** /ˈnɒdɪ/ *n.* Dummkopf, *der*

**node** /nəʊd/ *n.* **A** (*Bot., Astron.*) Knoten, *der;* **B** (*Phys.*) Schwingungsknoten, *der;* **C** (*Math.*) Knoten[punkt], *der*

**nodule** /ˈnɒdju:l/ *n.* **A** Klümpchen, *das;* **B** (*Bot.*) Knötchen, *das*

**Noel** /nəʊˈel/ *n.* (*esp. in carols*) Weihnachten, *das od. Pl.;* Weihnacht, *die* (*geh.*)

**'no 'entry** (*for people*) „Zutritt verboten"; (*for vehicles*) „Einfahrt verboten"; **a ~ sign** ein Schild mit der Aufschrift „Zutritt/Einfahrt verboten"

**'no-fault insurance** *n.* (*Amer.*) ≈ Vollkaskoversicherung

**no-'fly zone** *n.* Flugverbotszone, *die*

**noggin** /ˈnɒgɪn/ *n.* **A** (*mug*) Becher, *der;* (*drink*) Schlückchen, *das;* **B** (*Amer. coll.: head*) Birne, *die* (*salopp*)

**no-'go** *adj.* Sperr‹gebiet, -zone›

**'no-good** *adj.* (*coll.*) nichtsnutzig (*abwertend*)

**no-hoper** /nəʊˈhəʊpə(r)/ *n.* absoluter Außenseiter; **be a ~:** keine Chance haben; **a team of ~s** eine völlig chancenlose Mannschaft

**nohow** /ˈnəʊhaʊ/ *adv.* (*Amer. coll.*) in keiner Weise

**noise** /nɔɪz/ **1** *n.* **A** (*loud outcry*) Lärm, *der;* Krach, *der;* **don't make so much ~/such a loud ~:** sei nicht so laut/mach nicht solchen Lärm *od.* Krach; **make a ~ about sth.** (*fig.: complain*) wegen etw. Krach machen *od.* schlagen (*ugs.*); **make a ~** (*fig.: be much talked about*) von sich reden machen; Aufsehen erregen; ⇒ *also* **hold²** 1 T; **B** (*any sound*) Geräusch, *das;* (*loud, harsh, unwanted*) Lärm, *der;* **~s off** Geräuschkulisse, *die;* **C** (*Communications: irregular fluctuations of signal*) Geräusch, *das;* (*hissing*) Rauschen, *das;* **D** *in pl.* (*conventional remarks or sounds*) **make friendly** *etc.* **~s [at sb.]** [jmdm. gegenüber] freundliche *usw.* Bemerkungen von sich geben; **make ~s about doing sth.** davon reden, etw. tun zu wollen.

**2** *v.t.* (*dated/formal*) **~ sth. abroad** *or* **about** etw. verbreiten

**'noise abatement** *n.* Lärmbekämpfung, *die*

**noise: ~less** /ˈnɔɪzlɪs/ *adj.*, **noiselessly** /ˈnɔɪzlɪslɪ/ *adv.* **A** (*silent[ly]*) lautlos; **B** (*making no avoidable noise*) geräuschlos; **~ level** *n.* Geräuschpegel, *der;* (*of unpleasant noise*) Lärmpegel, *der*

**'noise pollution** *n.* Lärmbelästigung, *die*

**noisily** /ˈnɔɪzɪlɪ/ *adv.* laut; lärmend ‹spielen›; geräuschvoll ‹stolpern, schlürfen›

**noisome** /ˈnɔɪsəm/ *adj.* (*literary*) **A** (*harmful, noxious*) gefährlich; übel (*geh.*) ‹Umgebung›; **B** (*evil-smelling*) übel riechend; **C** (*objectionable, offensive*) unangenehm

**noisy** /ˈnɔɪzɪ/ *adj.* laut; lärmend, laut ‹Menschenmasse, Kinder›; lautstark ‹Diskussion, Begrüßung›; geräuschvoll ‹Aufbruch, Ankunft›

**nomad** /ˈnəʊmæd/ **1** *n.* **A** Nomade, *der;* **B** (*wanderer*) jmd., der ein Nomadendasein führt. **2** *adj.* **A** nomadisch; **B** (*wandering*) **~ existence** Nomadendasein, *das*

**nomadic** /nəʊˈmædɪk/ *adj.* nomadisch; **~ tribe** Nomadenstamm, *der*

**'no man's land** *n.* Niemandsland, *das*

**nom de plume** /nɒm də ˈplu:m/ *n., pl.* **noms de plume** /nɒm də ˈplu:m/ Schriftstellername, *der;* Pseudonym, *das*

**nomenclature** /nəˈmenklətʃə(r), ˈnəʊmənkleɪtʃə(r)/ *n.* **A** (*system of names*) Vokabular, *das;* **B** (*terminology, systematic naming, catalogue*) Nomenklatur, *die*

**nominal** /ˈnɒmɪnl/ *adj.* **A** (*in name only*) nominell; **B** (*virtually nothing*) äußerst gering; äußerst niedrig ‹Preis, Miete›; **C** (*Ling.*) nominal; Nominal‹phrase, -präfix›

**nominalism** /ˈnɒmɪnəlɪzm/ *n.* (*Philos.*) Nominalismus, *der*

**nominally** /ˈnɒmɪnəlɪ/ *adv.* namentlich

**nominal 'value** *n.* (*Econ.*) Nennwert, *der*

**nominate** /ˈnɒmɪneɪt/ *v.t.* **A** (*call by name of*) nennen; **B** (*propose for election*) nominieren; **C** (*appoint to office*) ernennen

**nomination** /nɒmɪˈneɪʃn/ *n.* **A** (*appointment to office*) Ernennung, *die;* **B** (*proposal for election*) Nominierung, *die*

**nominative** /ˈnɒmɪnətɪv/ (*Ling.*) **1** *adj.* Nominativ-; nominativisch; **~ case** Nominativ, *der.* **2** *n.* Nominativ, *der;* ⇒ *also* **absolute** C

**nominee** /nɒmɪˈni:/ *n.* **A** (*candidate*) Kandidat, *der*/Kandidatin, *die;* **B** (*representative*) Stellvertreter, *der*/-vertreterin, *die*

**non-** /nɒn/ *pref.* nicht-

**non-ac'ceptance** *n.* (*Commerc.*) Annahmeverweigerung, *die*

**nonagenarian** /nəʊnədʒɪˈneərɪən/ **1** *adj.* neunzigjährig; (*more than 90 years old*) in den Neunzigern *nachgestellt.* **2** *n.* Neunziger, *der*/Neunzigerin, *die*

**non-ag'gression** *n.* Gewaltverzicht, *der;* **~ pact** *or* **treaty** Nichtangriffspakt, *der*

**non-alco'holic** *adj.* alkoholfrei

**non-a'ligned** *adj.* blockfrei

**non-a'lignment** *n., no pl.* Blockfreiheit, *die*

**non-bel'ligerent 1** *adj.* nicht Krieg führend. **2** *n.* nicht Krieg führendes Land

**nonce** /nɒns/ *n.* **for the ~:** einstweilen

**'nonce word** *n.* Ad-hoc-Bildung, *die*

**nonchalance** /ˈnɒnʃələns/ *n.* Nonchalance, *die* (*geh.*); Unbekümmertheit, *die;* (*lack of interest*) Desinteresse, *das;* Gleichgültigkeit, *die*

**nonchalant** /ˈnɒnʃələnt/ *adj.*, **nonchalantly** /ˈnɒnʃələntlɪ/ *adv.* nonchalant (*geh.*); unbekümmert; (*without interest*) desinteressiert; gleichgültig

**non-'combatant 1** *n.* Nichtkämpfende, *der/die.* **2** *adj.* nicht am Kampf beteiligt

**non-com'missioned** *adj.* ohne Patent *nachgestellt;* **~ officer** Unteroffizier, *der*

**non-com'mittal** *adj.* unverbindlich

**non compos [mentis]** /nɒn ˈkɒmpɒs (ˈmentɪs)/ *pred. adj.* nicht im Vollbesitz seiner/ihrer *usw.* geistigen Kräfte

**non-con'ducting** *adj.* (*Phys.*) nicht leitend

**non-con'ductor** *n.* (*Phys.*) Nichtleiter, *der*

**noncon'formism** *n.* Nonkonformismus, *der*

**noncon'formist** *n.* Nonkonformist, *der*/Nonkonformistin, *die*

**noncon'formity** *n.* **A** Nonkonformismus, *der;* **B** (*lack of correspondence or agreement*) Nonkonformität, *die*

**non-con'tributory** *adj.* beitragsfrei

**non-cooper'ation** *n.* Verweigerung der Kooperation

**non-denomi'national** *adj.* konfessionslos

**nondescript** /ˈnɒndɪskrɪpt/ *adj.* unscheinbar; undefinierbar ‹Farbe›

**'non-drip** *adj.* nicht tropfend ‹Farbe›

**non-'driver** *n.* Nicht[auto]fahrer, *der*

**none** /nʌn/ **1** *pron.* kein...; **I want ~ of your cheek!** sei nicht so frech!; **~ of them** keiner/keine/keines von ihnen; **~ of this money is mine** von diesem Geld gehört mir nichts; **~ of these houses** kein[e]s dieser Häuser; **~ but they/he** keiner *od.* niemand außer ihnen/ihm; nur sie/er; **~ other than ...:** kein anderer/keine andere als ...; **Is there any bread left? — No, ~ at all** Ist noch Brot da? — Nein, gar keins mehr; **it is ~ of my concern** das geht mich nichts an; **his understanding is ~ of the clearest** seine Auffassungsgabe ist nicht gerade die beste.

**2** *adv.* keineswegs; **I'm ~ the wiser now** jetzt bin ich um nichts klüger; **~ the less** nichtsdestoweniger; ⇒ *also* **too** A

**non'entity** *n.* (*non-existent thing, person or thing of no importance*) Nichts, *das*

**nonesuch** ⇒ **nonsuch**

**'non-event** *n.* Reinfall, *der* (*ugs.*); Enttäuschung, *die*

**non-ex'istence** *n., no pl.* Nichtvorhandensein, *das*

**non-ex'istent** /nɒnɪgˈzɪstənt/ *adj.* nicht vorhanden

**non-'ferrous** *adj.* Nichteisen-

**non-'fiction** *n.* **~ [literature]** Sachliteratur, *die;* **~ novel** Tatsachenroman, *der*

**non-'flammable** *adj.* nicht entzündbar

**non-inter'ference, non-inter'vention** *ns., no pl.* Nichteinmischung, *die*

**non-'iron** *adj.* bügelfrei

**non-'member** *n.* Nichtmitglied, *das*

**non-'metal** *n.* (*Chem.*) Nichtmetall, *das*

**non-me'tallic** *adj.* (*Chem.*) nichtmetallisch

**non-'net** *adj.* nicht preisgebunden

**non-'nuclear** *adj.* Nichtnuklear-; **~ club** Gruppe der Nichtnuklearstaaten; **~ weapons** konventionelle Waffen

**'no-no** *n., pl.* **~es** (*coll.*) **be a ~:** nicht infrage kommen (*ugs.*); **that's a ~:** das kannste vergessen (*ugs.*)

**no-'nonsense** ⇒ **nonsense** 1 C

**nonpareil** /nɒnpəˈreɪl/ *n.* (*person*) jemand, der nicht seinesgleichen hat; Ausnahmeerscheinung, *die;* (*thing*) Nonplusultra, *das*

**non-'party** *adj.* **A** (*not attached to a party*) parteilos; **B** (*not related to a party*) überparteilich; **C** (*nonpartisan*) unparteiisch

**non-'payment** *n.* Nichtzahlung, *die*

**non-'playing** *adj.* nicht mitspielend; zuschauend; **~ captain** Mannschaftsführer, *der*

**nonplus** /nɒnˈplʌs/ *v.t.*, **-ss-** verblüffen; **he was ~sed by sth.** etw. verblüffte ihn

**non-'profit[-making]** *adj.* nicht auf Gewinn ausgerichtet

**non-prolife'ration** *n., no pl.* Nichtverbreitung von Atomwaffen; Nonproliferation, *die* (*Politik*); **~ treaty** Atom[waffen]sperrvertrag, *der*

**non-'resident 1** *adj.* (*residing elsewhere*) nicht im Haus wohnend; (*outside a country*) nicht ansässig; **a ~ landlord** ein Vermieter, der nicht im [selben] Haus wohnt. **2** *n.* nicht im Haus Wohnende, *der/die;* (*outside a country*) Nichtansässige, *der/die;* **the bar is open to ~s** die Bar ist auch für Gäste geöffnet, die nicht im Hotel wohnen

**non-re'turnable** *adj.* Einweg‹behälter, -flasche, -[ver]packung›; nicht rückzahlbar ‹Anzahlung›

**nonsense** /ˈnɒnsəns/ **1** *n.* **A** *no pl., no art.* (*meaningless words, ideas, or behaviour*) Unsinn, *der;* **make ~ of sth.** etw. ad absurdum führen; **piece of ~:** Firlefanz, *der* (*ugs. abwertend*); **talk ~:** Unsinn reden; **it's all a lot of ~:** das ist alles Unsinn; **B** (*instance*) Unsinn, *der;* **~s** Unsinn; **make a ~ of** verpfuschen (*ugs.*); ‹Ereignis:› unsinnig *od.* widersinnig machen; ad absurdum führen ‹Idee, Ideal›; **C** (*sth. one disapproves of*) Unsinn, *der;* (*trifles*) Firlefanz, *der* (*ugs. abwertend*); **what's all this ~ about ...?** was soll das [dumme] Gerede über (+ *Akk.*) ...?; **let's have no more ~, stop your ~:** Schluss mit dem Unsinn; **stand no ~:** keinen Unfug dulden; **no-~:** nüchtern; **come along now, and no ~:** kommt jetzt, und mach keinen Unsinn.

**2** *int.* Unsinn!

n

**'nonsense verses** *n. pl.* (*Lit.*) Nonsensdichtung, *die*

**nonsensical** /nɒn'sensɪkl/ *adj.* unsinnig

**nonsensically** /nɒn'sensɪkəlɪ/ *adv.* unsinnigerweise; ohne Sinn und Verstand ‹handeln›

**non sequitur** /nɒn 'sekwɪtə(r)/ *n.* unlogische Folgerung

**non-'skid** *adj.* rutschfest

**non-'slip** *adj.* rutschfest

**non-'smoker** *n.* Ⓐ (*person*) Nichtraucher, *der*/Nichtraucherin, *die;* Ⓑ (*train compartment*) Nichtraucherabteil, *das*

**non-'starter** *n.* Ⓐ (*Sport*) Nichtstartende, *der/die;* Ⓑ (*fig. coll.*) Reinfall, *der* (*ugs.*); (*person*) Blindgänger, *der* (*fig. salopp*)

**non-'stick** *adj.* **~ frying pan** *etc.* Bratpfanne *usw.* mit Antihaftbeschichtung

**non-stop** ❶ /'--/ *adj.* durchgehend ‹Zug, Busverbindung›; Nonstop‹flug, -revue›. ❷ /-'-/ *adv.* ohne Unterbrechung ‹tanzen, reden, reisen, senden›; nonstop, im Nonstop ‹fliegen, tanzen, fahren›

**nonsuch** /'nʌnsʌtʃ/ *n.* Ⓐ Ausnahmeerscheinung, *die;* Ⓑ (*plant*) Hopfenklee, *der*

**'non-toxic** *adj.* ungiftig; nichttoxisch (*fachspr.*)

**non-U** /nɒn'ju:/ *adj.* (*coll.*) nicht vornehm

**non-'union** *adj.* nicht organisiert; (*made by ~ members*) von Nichtorganisierten hergestellt ‹Fabrikat›

**non-'violence** *n., no pl.* Gewaltlosigkeit, *die*

**non-'violent** *adj.* gewaltlos

**non-'white** ❶ *adj.* farbig. ❷ *n.* Farbige, *der/die*

**noodle**[1] /'nu:dl/ *n.* (*pasta*) Nudel, *die*

**noodle**[2] *n.* (*dated coll.: simpleton*) Dummkopf, *der* (*ugs.*); **gape like a ~:** dumm gucken (*ugs.*)

**nook** /nʊk/ *n.* Winkel, *der;* Ecke, *die;* **in every ~ and cranny** in allen Ecken und Winkeln

**nooky** /'nʊkɪ/ *n.* (*sl.*) Aufhupfer, *der* (*ugs.*)

**noon** /nu:n/ *n.* ▶ 1012 Mittag, *der;* zwölf Uhr [mittags]; **at/before ~:** um/vor zwölf [Uhr mittags]

**'noonday** *n.* Mittag, *der; attrib.* Mittags‹sonne, -hitze›; **at ~:** mittags

**'no one** ❶ *pron.* Ⓐ **~ of them** keiner/keine/keines von ihnen; Ⓑ ⇒ **nobody**. ❷ *adj.* **~ person could do that** einer allein könnte das nicht tun

**'noontide** (*dated/rhet.*), **'noontime** (*Amer.*) *ns.* Mittagszeit, *die;* **at ~:** zur Mittagszeit

**noose** /nu:s/ ❶ *n.* Schlinge, *die;* **put one's head in a ~** (*fig.*) den Kopf in die Schlinge stecken. ❷ *v.t.* [mit einer Schlinge] fangen

**nope** /nəʊp/ *adv.* (*Amer. coll.*) nee (*ugs.*)

**'no place** *adv.* (*Amer.*) ⇒ **nowhere** 1

**nor** /nə(r), *stressed* nɔ:(r)/ *conj.* noch; **neither ... ~ ..., not ... ~ ...:** weder ... noch ...; **he can't do it, ~ can I, ~ can you** er kann es nicht, ich auch nicht und du auch nicht; **~ will I deny that ...:** [und] ich will auch nicht bestreiten, dass ...

**Nordic** /'nɔ:dɪk/ ❶ *adj.* nordisch. ❷ *n.* nordischer Typus; Nordide, *der/die* (*Ethnol.*)

**norm** /nɔ:m/ *n.* Norm, *die;* **IQ above the ~:** überdurchschnittlicher IQ; **rise above the ~:** über den Normalwert steigen; **behavioural ~:** Verhaltensnorm *od.* -regel, *die*

**normal** /'nɔ:ml/ ❶ *adj.* Ⓐ normal; **be back to ~ working hours** wieder normal arbeiten; **recover one's ~ self** sein seelisches Gleichgewicht wieder finden; Ⓑ (*Geom.*) senkrecht (**to** auf + *Dat.*, zu). ❷ *n.* Ⓐ (*normal value*) Normalwert, *der;* Ⓑ (*usual state*) normaler Stand; **everything is back to** *or* **has returned to ~:** es hat sich wieder alles normalisiert; **his temperature is above ~:** er hat erhöhte Temperatur; Ⓒ (*Geom.*) Normale, *die*

**normalcy** /'nɔ:mlsɪ/ *n., no pl.* (*normality*) Normalität, *die*

**normalise** ⇒ **normalize**

**normality** /nɔ:'mælɪtɪ/ *n., no pl.* Normalität, *die;* **return to ~ after Christmas** nach Weihnachten wieder zum gewohnten Alltag zurückkehren

**normalize** /'nɔ:məlaɪz/ ❶ *v.t.* normalisieren. ❷ *v.i.* sich normalisieren

**normally** /'nɔ:məlɪ/ *adv.* Ⓐ (*in normal way*) normal; Ⓑ (*ordinarily*) normalerweise

**Norman** /'nɔ:mn/ ❶ *n.* Ⓐ Normanne, *der*/Normannin, *die;* Ⓑ (*king*) normannischer König; Ⓒ (*Ling.*) Normannisch, *das;* Ⓓ (*Archit.*) normannischer Baustil. ❷ *adj.* normannisch; ⇒ *also* **conquest** A

**Normandy** /'nɔ:məndɪ/ *pr. n.* Normandie, *die*

**Norman: ~ 'French** *n.* (*Ling.*) Normannisch, *das;* **~ style** *n.* (*Archit.*) normannischer Baustil

**normative** /'nɔ:mətɪv/ *adj.* normativ (*geh.*)

**Norse** /nɔ:s/ ❶ *n.* (*Ling.*) Ⓐ (*Scandinavian language group*) nordische Sprachen; Ⓑ **[Old] ~:** Altnordisch, *das.* ❷ *adj.* nordisch

**Norseman** /'nɔ:smən/ *n., pl.* **Norsemen** /'nɔ:smən/ (*Hist.*) Wikinger, *der*

**north** /nɔ:θ/ ▶ 1024 ❶ *n.* Ⓐ Norden, *der;* **the ~:** Nord (*Met., Seew.*); **in/to[wards]/from the ~:** im/nach *od.* (*geh.*) gen/von Norden; **to the ~ of** nordwestlich von; nördlich (+ *Gen.*); **magnetic ~:** magnetischer Nordpol; Ⓑ *usu.* **N~** (*part lying to the ~*) Norden, *der;* **from the N~:** aus dem Norden; **the N~** (*Brit.: of England*) Nordengland (*das*); der Norden; (*the Arctic*) die Arktis; der Nordpol; (*Amer.: the Northern states*) die Nordstaaten; der Norden; Ⓒ (*Cards*) Nord. ❷ *adj.* nördlich; Nord‹wind, -küste, -grenze, -tor›. ❸ *adv.* nordwärts; nach Norden; **~ of** nördlich von; nördlich (+ *Gen.*); **~ and south** nach Norden und Süden ‹verlaufen, sich erstrecken›; ⇒ *also* **by**[1] 1 D

**north: N~ 'Africa** *pr. n.* Nordafrika (*das*); **N~ A'merica** *pr. n.* Nordamerika (*das*); **N~ A'merican** ❶ *adj.* nordamerikanisch; ❷ *n.* Nordamerikaner, *der*/-amerikanerin, *die;* **N~ At'lantic** *pr. n.* Nordatlantik, *der;* **North Atlantic Treaty Organization** Nordatlantikpakt, *der;* **~bound** *adj.* ▶ 1024 ‹Zug, Verkehr usw.› in Richtung Norden; **~ country** *n.* (*Brit.*) Nordengland (*das*); Norden, *der;* **~-country** *adj.* (*Brit.*) nordenglisch; **~-'countryman** *n.* (*Brit.*) Nordengländer, *der;* **~-'east** ▶ 1024 ❶ *n.* Nordosten, *der;* **in/to[wards]/from the ~-east** im/nach *od.* (*geh.*) gen/von Nordosten; **to the ~-east of** nordöstlich von; nordöstlich (+ *Gen.*); ❷ *adj.* nordöstlich; Nordost‹wind, -küste›; **~-east passage** Nordostpassage, *die;* ❸ *adv.* nordostwärts; nach Nordosten; **~-east of** nordöstlich von; nordöstlich (+ *Gen.*); ⇒ *also* **by**[1] 1 D; **~-'easter** Nordostwind, *der;* **~-'easterly** ▶ 1024 ❶ *adj.* nordöstlich; ❷ *adv.* (*position*) im Nordosten; (*direction*) nach Nordosten; **~-'eastern** *adj.* ▶ 1024 nordöstlich

**northerly** /'nɔ:ðəlɪ/ ▶ 1024 ❶ *adj.* Ⓐ (*in position or direction*) nördlich; **in a ~ direction** nach Norden; Ⓑ (*from the north*) ‹Wind› aus nördlichen Richtungen; **the wind was ~:** der Wind kam aus nördlichen Richtungen. ❷ *adv.* Ⓐ (*in position*) nördlich; (*in direction*) nordwärts; Ⓑ (*from the north*) aus *od.* von Nord[en]. ❸ *n.* Nord[wind], *der*

**northern** /'nɔ:ðən/ *adj.* ▶ 1024 nördlich; Nord‹grenze, -hälfte, -seite, -fenster, -wind›

**northerner** /'nɔ:ðənə(r)/ *n.* (*male*) Nordengländer/-deutsche *usw., der;* (*female*) Nordengländerin/-deutsche *usw., die;* (*Amer.*) Nordstaatler, *der*/-staatlerin, *die;* **he's a ~:** er kommt aus dem Norden

**Northern: ~ 'Europe** *pr. n.* Nordeuropa (*das*); **~ Euro'pean** ❶ *adj.* nordeuropäisch; ❷ *n.* Nordeuropäer, *der*/Nordeuropäerin, *die;* **~ 'Ireland** *pr. n.* Nordirland (*das*); **n~ 'lights** *n. pl.* Nordlicht, *das*

**northernmost** /'nɔ:ðənməʊst/ *adj.* ▶ 1024 nördlichst...

**North: ~ 'German** ❶ *adj.* norddeutsch; ❷ *n.* Norddeutsche, *der/die;* **~ 'Germany** *pr. n.* Norddeutschland (*das*); **~ Ko'rea** *pr. n.* Nordkorea (*das*); **~ Ko'rean** ❶ *adj.* nordkoreanisch; ❷ *n.* Nordkoreaner, *der*/-koreanerin, *die;* **'~land** *n.* (*poet.*) Nordland, *das* (*selten*); **n~ 'light** *n.* Licht von Norden; **~man** /'nɔ:θmən/ *n., pl.* **Northmen** /'nɔ:θmən/ ⇒ **Norseman**; **n~-~-'east** ▶ 1024 ❶ *n.* Nordnordosten, *der;* ❷ *adj.* nordnordöstlich; ❸ *adv.* nordnordostwärts; **n~-~-'west** ▶ 1024 ❶ *n.* Nordnordwesten, *der;* ❷ *adj.* nordnordwestlich; ❸ *adv.* nordnordwestwärts; **~ of 'England** *pr. n.* Nordengland (*das*); *attrib.* nordenglisch; **~ 'Pole** *pr. n.* Nordpol, *der;* **~ Rhine West'phalia** *pr. n.* Nordrhein-Westfalen (*das*); **n~ 'Sea** *pr. n.* Nordsee, *die;* **North Sea gas/oil** Nordseegas/-öl, *das;* **~ 'star** *n.* Nordstern, *der*

**northward** /'nɔ:θwəd/ ▶ 1024 ❶ *adj.* nach Norden gerichtet; (*situated towards the north*) nördlich; **in a ~ direction** nach Norden; [in] Richtung Norden. ❷ *adv.* nordwärts; **they are ~ bound** sie fahren nach *od.* [in] Richtung Norden. ❸ *n.* Norden, *der*

**northwards** /'nɔ:θwədz/ ▶ 1024 ⇒ **northward** 2

**north: ~-'west** ▶ 1024 ❶ *n.* Nordwesten, *der;* **in/to[wards]/from the ~-west** im/nach *od.* (*geh.*) gen/von Nordwesten; **to the ~-west of** nordwestlich von; nordwestlich (+ *Gen.*); ❷ *adj.* nordwestlich; Nordwest‹wind, -küste›; **~-west passage** Nordwestpassage, *die;* ❸ *adv.* nordwestwärts; nach Nordwesten; **~-west of** nordwestlich von; nordwestlich (+ *Gen.*); ⇒ *also* **by**[1] 1 D; **~-wester** /nɔ:θ'westə(r)/ *n.* Nordwestwind, *der;* **~-'westerly** ▶ 1024 ❶ *adj.* nordwestlich; ❷ *adv.* (*position*) im Nordwesten; (*direction*) nach Nordwesten; **~-'western** *adj.* ▶ 1024 nordwestlich

**Norway** /'nɔ:weɪ/ *pr. n.* Norwegen (*das*)

**Norwegian** /nɔ:'wi:dʒn/ ▶ 1275, ▶ 1340 ❶ *adj.* norwegisch ⇒ *also* **English** 1. ❷ *n.* Ⓐ (*person*) Norweger, *der*/Norwegerin, *die;* Ⓑ (*language*) Norwegisch, *das;* ⇒ *also* **English** 2 A

**Nos.** *abbr.* **numbers** Nrn.

**nose** /nəʊz/ ❶ *n.* Ⓐ ▶ 966 Nase, *die;* **have one's ~ [stuck] in a book** (*coll.*) die Nase in ein Buch stecken (*ugs.*); **it's as plain as the ~ on your face** (*coll.*) das sieht doch ein Blinder [mit dem Krückstock] (*ugs.*); **[win] by a ~:** mit einer Nasenlänge [gewinnen]; **follow one's ~** (*fig.*) (*be guided by instinct*) seinem Instinkt folgen; (*go forward*) der Nase nachgehen; **then just follow your ~:** dann einfach immer der Nase nach (*ugs.*); **get up sb.'s ~** (*coll.: annoy sb.*) jmdm. auf den Wecker gehen *od.* fallen (*salopp*); **hold one's ~:** sich (*Dat.*) die Nase zuhalten; **keep one's ~ clean** (*fig. coll.*) eine saubere Weste behalten (*ugs.*); **keep your ~ clean!** bleib sauber! (*ugs.*); **on the ~** (*Amer. coll.: on time*) pünktlich auf die Minute; **hit it** *or* **be right on the ~** (*Amer. coll.*) den Nagel auf den Kopf treffen (*ugs.*); **parson's** *or* **pope's ~** (*Gastr.*) Bürzel, *der;* **pay through the ~:** tief in die Tasche greifen müssen (*ugs.*); **poke** *or* **thrust** *etc.* **one's ~ into sth.** (*fig.*) seine Nase in etw. (*Akk.*) stecken (*fig. ugs.*); **put sb.'s ~ out of joint** (*fig. coll.*) jmdn. vor den Kopf stoßen (*ugs.*); **rub sb.'s ~ in it** (*fig.*) es jmdm. ständig unter die Nase reiben (*ugs.*); **see no further than one's ~** (*fig.*) nicht weiter sehen, als seine Nase reicht (*ugs.*); **speak through one's ~:** näseln; durch die Nase sprechen; **turn up one's ~ at sth.** (*fig. coll.*) die Nase über etw. (*Akk.*) rümpfen; **under sb.'s ~** (*fig. coll.*) vor jmds. Augen (*Dat.*); **keep one's ~ out of sth.** (*fig. coll.*) sich aus etw. [he]raushalten; **keep your ~ out of this!** halt [du] dich da raus!; **go** *or* **walk about with one's ~ in the air** die Nase hoch tragen; ⇒ *also* **blow**[1] 2 G; **grindstone**; **lead**[2] 1 A; **spite** 2; **thumb** 2 C; Ⓑ (*sense of smell*) Nase, *die;* **have a good ~ for sth.** eine gute Nase für etw. haben; Ⓒ (*of ship, aircraft*) Nase, *die;* (*of torpedo*) Schnauze, *die* (*ugs.*); Ⓓ (*of wine*) Blume, *die.*
❷ *v.t.* Ⓐ (*detect, smell out*) **~ [out]** aufspüren; Ⓑ **~ one's way** sich (*Dat.*) vorsichtig seinen Weg bahnen.
❸ *v.i.* sich vorsichtig bewegen; **~ out of sth.** sich vorsichtig aus etw. hinausbewegen
**~ a'bout, ~ a'round** *v.i.* (*coll.*) herumschnüffeln (*ugs.*)

**nose: ~bag** *n.* Futterbeutel, *der;* **~band** *n.* Nasenriemen, *der;* **~bleed** *n.* Nasenbluten, *das;* **~ cone** *n.* [Rumpf]spitze, *die;* **~dive**

n

❶ *n.* (A) Sturzflug, *der;* (B) (*fig.*) Einbruch, *der;* **take a ~dive** einen Einbruch erleben; ❷ *v.i.* im Sturzflug hinuntergehen; ‹Schiff:› mit dem Bug wegtauchen; **~ flute** *n.* Nasenflöte, *die;* **~gay** *n.* [duftendes] Blumensträußchen; **~ring** *n.* Nasenring, *der;* **~ wheel** *n.* (*Aeronaut.*) Bugrad, *das*

**nosey** ⇒ **nosy**

**nosh** /nɒʃ/ (*esp. Brit. coll.*) ❶ *v.t. & i.* (*eat*) futtern (*ugs.*); (*between meals*) naschen. ❷ *n.* (*snack*) Imbiss, *der;* (*food*) Futter, *das* (*salopp*)

**no-'show** *n.* (*for a flight*) No-show, *der* (*fachspr.*); **be a ~ at a dinner/at an event/on a flight /in a hotel** bei einem Abendessen/einer Veranstaltung nicht erscheinen/eine Flug-/Hotelreservierung nicht in Anspruch nehmen

**'nosh-up** *n.* (*Brit. coll.*) Essen, *das;* (*good meal*) Festessen, *das;* **have a ~:** spachteln (*ugs.*)

**no 'side** *n.* (*Rugby*) Spielende, *das*

**nostalgia** /nɒ'stældʒə/ *n.* Nostalgie, *die;* **~ for sth.** Sehnsucht nach etw.

**nostalgic** /nɒ'stældʒɪk/ *adj.* nostalgisch

**nostril** /'nɒstrɪl/ *n.* ▶ 966 Nasenloch, *das;* (*of horse*) Nüster, *die*

**nostrum** /'nɒstrəm/ *n.* (A) (*medicine*) Mittelchen, *das;* **his pet ~ is** er schwört auf (+ *Akk.*); (B) (*pet scheme*) Patentrezept, *das*

**nosy** /'nəʊzɪ/ *adj.* (*coll.*) neugierig

**Nosy 'Parker** *n.* Schnüffler, *der*/Schnüfflerin, *die* (*ugs. abwertend*)

**not** /nɒt/ *adv.* (A) nicht; **he is ~ a doctor** er ist kein Arzt; **isn't she pretty?** ist sie nicht hübsch?; **I do ~ feel like doing it** ich habe keine Lust, es zu tun; (B) *in ellipt. phrs.* nicht; **I hope ~:** hoffentlich nicht; **~ so** keineswegs; **~ at all** überhaupt nicht; (*in polite reply to thanks*) keine Ursache; gern geschehen; **~ that [I know of]** nicht, dass [ich wüsste]; (C) *in emphat. phrs.* **~ … but …** nicht …, sondern …; **it was ~ a small town but a big one** es war keine kleine Stadt, sondern eine große; **lazy he is ~:** faul ist er keineswegs; **~ I/they** *etc.* ich/sie *usw.* [bestimmt] nicht; **~ a moment/grey hair** nicht ein *od.* kein einziger Augenblick/einziges graues Haar; **~ a thing** gar nichts; **come ~ a day too soon** keinen Tag zu früh kommen; **~ a few/everybody** nicht wenige/jeder; **~ a small sacrifice** kein kleines Opfer; **~ once or** *or* **nor twice, but …:** nicht nur ein- oder zweimal, sondern …; **feel ~ so** *or* **too well** sich nicht besonders gut fühlen

**notability** /nəʊtə'bɪlɪtɪ/ *n.* (A) *no pl.* (*being notable*) Ansehen, *das;* **a painter of [some] ~:** ein [ziemlich] angesehener Maler; (B) (*person*) ⇒ **notable** 2

**notable** /'nəʊtəbl/ ❶ *adj.* bemerkenswert; bedeutend, angesehen ‹Person›; **be ~ for sth.** für etw. bekannt sein. ❷ *n.* bekannte Persönlichkeit; Notabilität, *die* (*geh.*)

**notably** /'nəʊtəblɪ/ *adv.* besonders

**notarial** /nəʊ'teərɪəl/ *adj.* (*Law*) (A) (*of a notary*) Notariats-; (B) (*prepared by a notary*) notariell ‹Urkunde›

**notary** /'nəʊtərɪ/ *n.* ▶ 1261 **~ [public]** Notar, *der*/Notarin, *die*

**notation** /nəʊ'teɪʃn/ *n.* (A) (*Math., Mus., Chem.*) Notation, *die* (*fachspr.*); Notierung, *die;* (B) (*Amer.: annotation*) Anmerkung, *die.* ⇒ *also* **scale**³ 1 F

**notch** /nɒtʃ/ ❶ *n.* Kerbe, *die;* (*in damaged blade*) Scharte, *die;* (*in belt*) Loch, *das;* **be a ~ above the others** (*fig.*) eine Klasse besser als die anderen sein; **tighten one's belt another ~** (*lit. or fig.*) seinen Gürtel ein Loch enger schnallen. ❷ *v.t.* (A) (*make ~es in*) kerben; (B) (*score by ~es*) mit Kerben notieren; (*fig.: score, achieve*) erreichen; erzielen ‹Tor, Eckstoß›; erringen ‹Sieg›

**~ 'up** *v.t.* erreichen; aufstellen ‹Rekord›; erringen ‹Sieg›

**notched** /nɒtʃt/ *adj.* kerbig; gekerbt ‹Blattrand›

**note** /nəʊt/ ❶ *n.* (A) (*Mus.*) (*sign*) Note, *die;* (*key of piano*) Taste, *die;* (*single sound*) Ton, *der;* (*bird's song*) Gesang, *der;* **strike a false ~:** unangebracht sein; **strike the right ~** ‹Sprecher, Redner, Brief:› den richtigen Ton treffen; **hit the wrong ~:** einen falschen Ton anschlagen; (B) (*tone of expression*) [Unter]ton, *der;* **~ of discord** Missklang, *der;* **~ of caution/anger** warnender/ärgerlicher [Unter]ton; **sound a ~ of caution** eine Warnung aussprechen; **on a ~ of optimism, on an optimistic ~:** in optimistischem Ton; **his voice had a peevish ~:** seine Stimme klang gereizt; **a festive ~, a ~ of festivity** eine festliche Note; (C) (*jotting*) Notiz, *die;* **take** *or* **make ~s** sich (*Dat.*) Notizen machen; **take** *or* **make a ~ of sth.** sich (*Dat.*) etw. notieren; **speak without ~s** frei sprechen; (D) (*annotation, footnote*) Anmerkung, *die;* **author's ~:** Anmerkung des Verfassers; (E) (*short letter*) [kurzer] Brief; **write a ~:** ein paar Zeilen schreiben; (F) (*Diplom.*) Note, *die;* (G) ▶ 1328 (*Finance*) **~ [of hand]** Schuldschein, *der;* **£10 ~:** Zehn-Pfund-Schein, *der;* (H) *no pl.*, *no art.* (*importance*) Bedeutung, *die;* **person/sth. of ~:** bedeutende Persönlichkeit/etw. Bedeutendes; **nothing of ~:** nichts von Bedeutung; **be of ~:** bedeutend sein; (I) *no pl.*, *no art.* (*attention*) Beachtung, *die;* **worthy of ~:** beachtenswert; **take ~ of sth.** (*heed*) einer Sache (*Dat.*) Beachtung schenken; (*notice*) etw. zur Kenntnis nehmen.

❷ *v.t.* (A) (*register*) beobachten; (B) (*pay attention to*) beachten; (C) (*notice*) bemerken; (D) (*set down*) **~ [down]** [sich (*Dat.*)] notieren

**note: ~book** *n.* (A) Notizbuch, *das;* (*for lecture notes*) Kollegheft, *das;* (B) **~book [computer]** Notebook, *das;* **~case** *n.* Brieftasche, *die*

**noted** /'nəʊtɪd/ *adj.* (A) (*famous*) bekannt, berühmt (**for** für, wegen); (B) (*significant*) beachtlich

**notelet** /'nəʊtlɪt/ *n.* Grußkarte, *die*

**note: ~pad** *n.* Notizblock, *der;* **~paper** *n.* Briefpapier, *das;* **~-row** *n.* (*Mus.*) Tonreihe, *die;* **~worthy** *adj.* bemerkenswert

**nothing** /'nʌθɪŋ/ ❶ *n.* (A) nichts; **~ interesting** nichts Interessantes; **~ much** nichts Besonderes; **~ more than** nur; **~ more, ~ less** nicht mehr, nicht weniger; **I should like ~ more than sth./to do sth.** ich würde etw. nur zu gern haben/tun; **next to ~:** so gut wie nichts; **~ less than the best treatment** die bestmögliche Behandlung; **~ less than a miracle is needed to save …:** nur ein Wunder kann … retten; **it's ~ less than suicidal to do this** es ist reiner *od.* glatter Selbstmord, dies zu tun; **there's ~ so good as …:** es gibt nichts Besseres als …; **be ~ [when] compared to sth.** nichts sein im Vergleich zu etw.; **~ else than, ~ [else] but** nur; **do ~ [else] but grumble** nur murren; **there was ~ [else] for it but to do sth.** es blieb nichts anderes übrig, als etw. zu tun; **he is ~ if not active** wenn er eins ist, dann [ist er] aktiv; **be ~ if not conscientious/brutal** überaus gewissenhaft/brutal sein; **there is ~ in it** (*in race etc.*) es ist noch nichts entschieden; (*it is untrue*) es ist nichts daran wahr; **there's ~ 'of him** (*he is very thin*) an ihm ist nichts dran; **there is ~ 'to it** es ist kinderleicht (*fam.*); **he/she is ~ to me** er/sie interessiert mich nicht; **your problems are ~ compared to his** deine Probleme sind nichts im Vergleich zu seinen; **~ ventured ~ gained, ~ venture ~ win** (*prov.*) wer nicht wagt, der nicht gewinnt (*Spr.*); **£300 is ~ to him** 300 Pfund sind ein Klacks für ihn (*ugs.*); **have [got]** *or* **be ~ to do with sb./sth.** (*not concern*) nichts zu tun haben mit jmdm./etw.; **have ~ to do with sb./sth.** (*avoid*) jmdm./einer Sache aus dem Weg gehen; **[not] for ~:** [nicht] umsonst; **count** *or* **go for ~** (*be unappreciated*) ‹Person:› nicht zählen; (*be profitless*) ‹Arbeit, Bemühung:› umsonst *od.* vergebens sein; **have [got] ~ on sb./sth.** (*be not better than; iron.: be inferior to*) nicht mit jmdm./etw. zu vergleichen sein; nichts sein im Vergleich zu jmdm./etw.; **have [got] ~ on sb.** (*know ~ bad about*) nichts gegen jmdn. in der Hand haben; **have ~ on** (*be naked*) nichts anhaben; (*have no engagements*) nichts vorhaben; **make ~ of sth.** (*make light of*) keine große Sache aus etw. machen; (*not understand*) mit etw. nichts anfangen [können]; **it means ~ to me** (*is not understood*) ich werde nicht klug daraus; (*is not loved*) es bedeutet mir nichts; **no ~** (*coll.*) kein gar nichts (*ugs.*); **to say ~ of** ganz zu schweigen von; (B) (*zero*) **multiply by ~:** mit null multiplizieren; **register ~** ‹Thermometer:› null Grad anzeigen; (C) (*trifling event*) Nichtigkeit, *die;* (*trifling person*) Nichts, *das;* Niemand, *der;* **soft** *or* **sweet ~s** Zärtlichkeiten *Pl.* ⇒ *also* **do**¹ 1 B, 2 J; **like**¹ 1 A; **short** 1 D; **stop** 1 C, 2 B; **think of g.**

❷ *adv.* keineswegs; **~ near so bad as …:** nicht annähernd so schlecht wie …

**nothingness** /'nʌθɪŋnɪs/ *n.*, *no pl.* Nichts, *das*

**notice** /'nəʊtɪs/ ❶ *n.* (A) Anschlag, *der;* Aushang, *der;* (*in newspaper*) Anzeige, *die;* **no-smoking ~:** Rauchverbotsschild, *das;* (B) (*warning*) **~ of a forthcoming strike** Meldungen über einen bevorstehenden Streik; **give [sb.] [three days'] ~ of one's arrival** [jmdm.] seine Ankunft [drei Tage vorher] mitteilen; **have [no] ~ [of sth.]** [von etw.] [keine] Kenntnis haben; **at short/a moment's/ten minutes' ~:** kurzfristig/von einem Augenblick zum andern/innerhalb von zehn Minuten; (C) (*formal notification*) Ankündigung, *die;* **give ~ of appeal** Berufung einlegen; **until further ~:** bis auf weiteres; **~ is given of sth.** etw. wird angekündigt; ⇒ *also* **quit** 2 B; (D) (*ending an agreement*) Kündigung, *die;* **give sb. a week's/month's ~:** jmdm. mit einer Frist von einer Woche/einem Monat kündigen; **hand in one's ~** *or* **give ~** (*Brit.*), **give one's ~** (*Amer.*) kündigen; (E) (*attention*) Beachtung, *die;* **attract ~:** Beachtung finden; **bring sb./sth. to sb.'s ~:** jmdn. auf jmdn./etw. aufmerksam machen; **worthy of ~:** beachtenswert; **it has come to my ~ that …:** ich habe bemerkt *od.* mir ist aufgefallen, dass …; **not take much ~ of sb./sth.** jmdm./einer Sache keine große Beachtung schenken; **take no ~ of sb./sth.** (*not observe*) jmdn./etw. nicht bemerken; (*disregard*) keine Notiz von jmdm./etw. nehmen; **take no ~:** sich nicht darum kümmern; **take ~ of** wahrnehmen; hören auf ‹Rat›; zur Kenntnis nehmen ‹Leistung›; (F) (*review*) Besprechung, *die;* Rezension, *die.*

❷ *v.t.* (A) (*perceive, take notice of*) bemerken; **~ the details [on this painting]** beachten Sie die Einzelheiten [auf diesem Gemälde]; **he likes to get himself ~d** er drängt sich gern in den Vordergrund; *abs.* **I pretended not to ~:** ich tat so, als ob ich es nicht bemerkte; **but not so you'd ~** (*coll.*) aber es fällt/fiel nicht auf; (B) (*remark upon*) erwähnen; (C) (*acknowledge*) Notiz nehmen von

**noticeable** /'nəʊtɪsəbl/ *adj.* (A) (*perceptible*) wahrnehmbar ‹Fleck, Schaden, Geruch›; merklich ‹Verbesserung›; spürbar ‹Mangel›; (B) (*worthy of notice*) bemerkenswert

**noticeably** /'nəʊtɪsəblɪ/ *adv.* sichtlich ‹größer, kleiner›; merklich ‹verändern›; spürbar ‹kälter›

**'noticeboard** *n.* (*Brit.*) Anschlagbrett, *das;* schwarzes Brett

**notifiable** /'nəʊtɪfaɪəbl/ *adj.* meldepflichtig ‹Krankheit›

**notification** /nəʊtɪfɪ'keɪʃn/ *n.* Mitteilung, *die* (**of sb.** an jmdn.; **of sth.** über etw. [*Akk.*]); (*of disease*) Meldung, *die* (**of** über + *Akk.*)

**notify** /'nəʊtɪfaɪ/ *v.t.* (A) (*make known*) ankündigen; (B) (*inform*) benachrichtigen (**of** über + *Akk.*)

**notion** /'nəʊʃn/ *n.* (A) Vorstellung, *die;* **not have the faintest/least ~ of how/what** *etc.* nicht die blasseste/geringste Ahnung haben, wie/was *usw.*; **he has no ~ of time** er hat kein Verhältnis zur Zeit; (B) (*intention*) **have no ~ of doing sth.** nicht beabsichtigen *od.* vorhaben, etw. zu tun; (C) (*knack, inkling*) **have no ~ of sth.** keine Ahnung von etw. haben; (D) *in pl.* (*Amer.: haberdashery*) Kurzwaren *Pl.*

n

**notional** /ˈnəʊʃənl/ *adj.* Ⓐ (*imaginary*) imaginär; Ⓑ (*theoretical*) theoretisch ‹Ansatz, Wissen, Gewinn›; (*token*) symbolisch; (*hypothetical*) angenommen; Ⓒ (*vague, abstract*) abstrakt

**notionally** /ˈnəʊʃənəlɪ/ *adv.* theoretisch

**notoriety** /nəʊtəˈraɪətɪ/ *n., no pl.* traurige Berühmtheit

**notorious** /nəˈtɔːrɪəs/ *adj.* bekannt; (*infamous*) berüchtigt; notorisch ‹Lügner›; niederträchtig ‹List›; **be** *or* **have become ~ for sth.** wegen *od.* für etw. bekannt/berüchtigt sein

**notoriously** /nəˈtɔːrɪəslɪ/ *adv.* notorisch

**no 'trump** *n.* (*Bridge*) Sans atout, *das*

**notwithstanding** /nɒtwɪθˈstændɪŋ, nɒt wɪðˈstændɪŋ/ ❶ *prep.* ungeachtet. ❷ *adv.* dennoch; dessen ungeachtet. ❸ *conj.* **~ that ...** ungeachtet dessen, dass ...

**nougat** /ˈnuːgɑː/ *n.* Nougat, *das od. der*

**nought** /nɔːt/ *n.* Ⓐ ▶1352 (*zero*) Null, *die;* **~s and crosses** (*Brit.*) *Spiel, bei dem innerhalb eines Feldes von Kästchen Dreierreihen von Kreisen bzw. Kreuzen zu erzielen sind;* Ⓑ (*poet./arch.: nothing*) ⇒ **naught**

**noun** /naʊn/ *n.* (*Ling.*) Substantiv, *das;* Hauptwort, *das;* Nomen, *das* (*fachspr.*)

**nourish** /ˈnʌrɪʃ/ *v.t.* Ⓐ ernähren (**on** mit); (*fig.*) nähren (*geh.*); Ⓑ (*in one's heart*) hegen, nähren (*geh.*) ‹Gefühl, Hoffnung›

**nourishing** /ˈnʌrɪʃɪŋ/ *adj.* nahrhaft

**nourishment** /ˈnʌrɪʃmənt/ *n.* (*food*) Nahrung, *die;* (*fig.*) Förderung, *die*

**nous** /naʊs/ *n.* (*coll.*) Grips, *der* (*ugs.*); **use a bit of ~:** seinen Grips ein bisschen anstrengen

**nouveau riche** /nuːvəʊ ˈriːʃ/ ❶ *n., pl.* **nouveaux riches** /nuːvəʊ ˈriːʃ/ Neureiche, *der/die.* ❷ *adj.* neureich

**Nov.** *abbr.* **November** Nov.

**nova** /ˈnəʊvə/ *n., pl.* **~e** /ˈnəʊviː/ *or* **~s** (*Astron.*) Nova, *die*

**Nova Scotia** /nəʊvə ˈskəʊʃə/ *pr. n.* Neuschottland (*das*)

**novel** /ˈnɒvl/ ❶ *n.* Roman, *der.* ❷ *adj.* neuartig

**novelette** /nɒvəˈlet/ *n.* Novelette, *die* (*Literaturw.*); (*Brit. derog.*) Groschenroman, *der*

**novelist** /ˈnɒvəlɪst/ *n.* ▶1261 Romanautor, *der/*-autorin, *die*

**novella** /nəˈvelə/ *n.* Novelle, *die*

**novelty** /ˈnɒvltɪ/ *n.* Ⓐ **be a/no ~:** etwas/nichts Neues sein; Ⓑ (*newness*) Neuheit, *die;* Neuartigkeit, *die;* **the ~ will wear off** der Reiz des Neuen wird nachlassen; **have a certain ~ value** den Reiz des Neuen haben; Ⓒ (*gadget*) Überraschung, *die;* **jokes and novelties** Scherzartikel

**November** /nəˈvembə(r)/ *n.* ▶1055 November, *der;* ⇒ *also* **August**

**novice** /ˈnɒvɪs/ *n.* Ⓐ (*Relig.*) Novize, *der/*Novizin, *die;* Ⓑ (*new convert*) Neubekehrte, *der/die;* Ⓒ (*beginner*) Anfänger, *der/*Anfängerin, *die*

**noviciate, novitiate** /nəˈvɪʃɪət/ *n.* Ⓐ (*Relig.: period, quarters*) Noviziat, *das;* (*fig.: period or state of initiation*) Lehrzeit, *die;* Lehre, *die;* Ⓑ ⇒ **novice** A, C

**now** /naʊ/ ❶ *adv.* Ⓐ jetzt; (*nowadays*) heutzutage; (*immediately*) [jetzt] sofort; (*this time*) jetzt [schon wieder]; **it's ten years ago ~ that** *or* **since he died** es ist schon zehn Jahre her, seit er gestorben ist; **just ~** (*very recently*) gerade eben; (*at this particular time*) gerade jetzt; **I can't see you just ~:** ich habe im Augenblick leider keine Zeit für Sie; **~ for a cup of tea** jetzt eine Tasse Tee; **[every] ~ and then** *or* **again** hin und wieder; **~ sunshine, ~ showers** bald Sonne, bald Regen; **[it's] ~ or never!** jetzt oder nie!; Ⓑ (*not referring to time*) **well ~:** also; **come ~:** na, komm (*ugs.*); **~, ~:** na, na; **~, what happened is this ...:** also, passiert ist Folgendes: ...; **~ just listen to me** jetzt hör mir mal gut zu; **~ then** na (*ugs.*); **quickly ~!** nun aber schnell; **goodbye ~:** also dann, auf Wiedersehen; **He thinks he can stay here for nothing. — Does he, ~!** Er glaubt, er könnte hier umsonst bleiben. — Da hat er sich aber geirrt! ❷ *conj.* **~ [that] ...** jetzt, wo *od.* da ... ❸ *n.* **the here and ~:** das Hier und Jetzt; **~ is the time to do sth.** es ist jetzt an der Zeit, etw. zu tun; **before ~:** früher; **up to** *or* **until ~:** bis jetzt; **never before ~:** noch nie; **by ~:** inzwischen; **a week from ~:** [heute] in einer Woche; **you've got from ~ till Friday to do it** du hast bis Freitag Zeit, es zu tun; **between ~ and Friday** bis Freitag; **from ~ on** von jetzt an; **as of ~:** jetzt; **that's all for ~:** das ist im Augenblick alles; **put it aside for ~:** leg es einstweilen zur Seite; **bye** *etc.* **for ~!** (*coll.*) bis bald!

**nowadays** /ˈnaʊədeɪz/ *adv.* heutzutage

**nowhere** /ˈnəʊweə(r)/ ❶ *adv.* Ⓐ (*in no place*) nirgends; nirgendwo; Ⓑ (*to no place*) nirgendwohin; Ⓒ **~ near** (*not even nearly*) nicht annähernd; **be ~ near prepared** völlig unzureichend vorbereitet sein. ❷ *pron.* **as if from ~:** wie aus dem Nichts; **live in the middle of ~** (*coll.*) am Ende der Welt *od.* (*ugs.*) jwd wohnen; **the train stopped in the middle of ~:** der Zug hielt mitten in der Wildnis (*ugs.*); **start from ~:** bei Null anfangen; **come from ~:** wie aus dem Nichts auftauchen; **come [in]/be ~** (*in race etc.*) unter „ferner liefen" rangieren (*ugs.*); **get ~** (*make no progress*) nicht vorankommen; (*have no success*) nichts erreichen; **get sb. ~:** [jmdm.] nichts nützen

**no-'win** *attrib. adj.* Verlierer-

**nowt** /naʊt/ *n.* (*Brit. dial. or coll.*) nix (*ugs.*)

**noxious** /ˈnɒkʃəs/ *adj.* giftig

**nozzle** /ˈnɒzl/ *n.* Düse, *die;* (*of gun*) Mündung, *die;* (*of petrol pump*) Zapfhahn, *der*

**nr.** *abbr.* **near**

**NSPCC** *abbr.* (*Brit.*) **National Society for the Prevention of Cruelty to Children** ≈ Kinderschutzbund, *der*

**NT** *abbr.* **New Testament** N.T.

**nth** /enθ/ ⇒ **N**[1], n B

**nuance** /ˈnjuːɑ̃s/ ❶ *n.* Nuance, *die;* (*Mus.*) Nuancierung, *die;* **~s of meaning** Bedeutungsnuancen; **~ of colour** Farbnuance, *die;* Farbschattierung, *die.* ❷ *v.t.* nuancieren (*geh.*)

**nub** /nʌb/ *n.* Ⓐ (*small lump*) Stückchen, *das;* (*stub*) Stummel, *der;* Ⓑ (*fig.*) Kernpunkt, *der*

**nubile** /ˈnjuːbaɪl/ *adj.* Ⓐ (*marriageable*) heiratsfähig; Ⓑ (*sexy*) sexy (*ugs.*); anziehend

**nuclear** /ˈnjuːklɪə(r)/ *adj.* Ⓐ Kern-; Ⓑ (*using ~ energy or weapons*) Atom-; Kern‹explosion, -technik›; atomar ‹Antrieb, Gefechtskopf, Bedrohung, Gegenschlag, Wettrüsten›; nuklear ‹Abschreckungspotenzial, Sprengkörper, Streitkräfte›; atomgetrieben ‹Unterseeboot, Schiff›

**nuclear: ~ 'bomb** *n.* Atombombe, *die;* **~ capa'bility** *n.* nukleares Potenzial; **a missile with ~ capability** eine nuklearfähige Rakete; **have ~ capability** nuklearfähig sein; **~ de'terrent** *n.* atomare *od.* nukleare Abschreckung; **~ dis'armament** *n.* atomare *od.* nukleare Abrüstung; **~ 'energy** *n., no pl.* Atom- *od.* Kernenergie, *die;* **~ 'family** *n.* (*Sociol.*) Kernfamilie, *die;* **~ 'fission** *n.* Kernspaltung, *die;* **~-free** *adj.* atomwaffenfrei ‹Zone›; **~ 'fuel** *n.* Kernbrennstoff, *der;* **~ 'fusion** *n.* Kernfusion, *die;* **~ 'physics** *n.* Kernphysik, *die;* **~ 'power** *n.* Ⓐ Atom- *od.* Kernkraft, *die;* Ⓑ (*country*) Atom- *od.* Nuklearmacht, *die;* **~-'powered** *adj.* atomgetrieben; **~ 'power station** *n.* Atom- *od.* Kernkraftwerk, *das;* **~ re'actor** ⇒ **reactor** A; **~ 'testing** *n.* Atomversuche *Pl.;* **~ 'warfare** *n., no pl.* Atomkrieg, *der;* **~ 'waste** *n.* Atommüll, *der;* **~ 'winter** *n.* nuklearer Winter

**nuclei** *pl. of* **nucleus**

**nucleic acid** /njuːkliːɪk ˈæsɪd/ *n.* (*Biochem.*) Nukleinsäure, *die*

**nucleus** /ˈnjuːklɪəs/ *n., pl.* **nuclei** /ˈnjuːklɪaɪ/ Kern, *der;* (*of collection*) Grundstock, *der*

**nude** /njuːd/ ❶ *adj.* nackt; **~ figure/revue** Akt, *der/*Nacktrevue, *die.* ❷ *n.* Ⓐ (*Art*) (*figure*) Akt, *der;* (*painting*) Aktgemälde, *das;* Ⓑ **in the ~:** nackt; Ⓒ (*person*) Nackte, *der/die*

**nudge** /nʌdʒ/ ❶ *v.t.* Ⓐ (*push gently*) anstoßen; **~ aside** zur Seite schieben; **~ sth.** (*fig.*) einer Sache (*Dat.*) einen Schubs geben (*ugs.*); Ⓑ (*touch*) stoßen an (+ *Akk.*) ‹Mauer›. ❷ *n.* Stoß, *der;* Puff, *der;* **give sb. a ~:** jmdn. anstoßen

**nudism** /ˈnjuːdɪzm/ *n.* Nudismus, *der;* Freikörperkultur, *die*

**nudist** /ˈnjuːdɪst/ *n.* Nudist, *der/*Nudistin, *die;* FKK-Anhänger, *der/*-Anhängerin, *die; attrib.* Nudisten-

**nudity** /ˈnjuːdɪtɪ/ *n.* Nacktheit, *die*

**nugatory** /ˈnjuːgətərɪ/ *adj.* (*literary*) belanglos

**nugget** /ˈnʌgɪt/ *n.* Ⓐ (*Mining*) Klumpen, *der;* (*of gold*) Goldklumpen, *der;* Nugget, *das;* Ⓑ (*fig.*) **~s of wisdom** goldene Weisheiten; **~s of information** wertvolle Informationen

**nuisance** /ˈnjuːsəns/ *n.* Ⓐ Ärgernis, *das;* Plage, *die;* **what a ~!** so etwas Dummes!; **be a bit of a ~:** eine ziemliche Plage sein; **make a ~ of oneself** lästig werden; Ⓑ (*Law*) Belästigung, *die*

**nuke** /njuːk/ (*Amer. coll.*) ❶ *n.* (*bomb*) Atombombe, *die.* ❷ *v.t.* Atombomben/eine Atombombe werfen auf (+ *Akk.*)

**null** /nʌl/ *adj.* (*Law*) **declare sth. ~ [and void]** etw. für null und nichtig erklären

**nullify** /ˈnʌlɪfaɪ/ *v.t.* Ⓐ (*cancel*) für null und nichtig *od.* rechtsungültig erklären ‹Vertrag, Testament›; Ⓑ (*neutralize*) zunichte machen; entkräften ‹Beweis›

**nullity** /ˈnʌlɪtɪ/ *n.* (*Law*) Ungültigkeit, *die*

**numb** /nʌm/ ❶ *adj.* (*without sensation*) gefühllos, taub (**with** vor + *Dat.*); (*fig.*) (*without emotion*) benommen; (*unable to move*) starr; gelähmt; **go ~ with horror** vor Entsetzen (*Dat.*) erstarren. ❷ *v.t.* Ⓐ ‹Kälte, Schock:› gefühllos machen; ‹Narkosemittel:› betäuben; Ⓑ (*fig.*) **her emotions were ~ed** sie war betäubt *od.* benommen; **be ~ed by horror/with fear** vor Entsetzen/Angst (*Dat.*) erstarren

**number** /ˈnʌmbə(r)/ ❶ *n.* ▶1352 Ⓐ (*in series*) Nummer, *die;* **~ 3 West Street** West Street [Nr.] 3; **my ~ came up** (*fig.*) ich war dran (*ugs.*) *od.* an der Reihe; **the ~ of sb.'s car** jmds. Autonummer; **you've got the wrong ~** (*Teleph.*) Sie sind falsch verbunden; **dial a wrong ~:** sich verwählen (*ugs.*); **what page ~ is it?** welche Seite ist es?; **~ one** (*oneself*) man selbst; *attrib.* Nummer eins *nachgestellt;* erstklassig ‹Darstellung›; Spitzen‹position, -platz›; **take care of** *or* **look after ~ one** an sich (*Akk.*) selbst denken; **be sb.'s ~ one priority** bei jmdm. an erster Stelle stehen; **~ two** (*in organisation*) zweiter Mann; (*of sb. else*) rechte Hand; **N~ Ten [Downing Street]** (*Brit.*) *Amtssitz des britischen Premierministers/der britischen Premierministerin;* **paint by ~s** nach einer Vorlage [mit nummerierten Farbfeldern] malen; **have [got] sb.'s ~** (*fig. coll.*) jmdn. durchschaut haben; **sb.'s ~ is up** (*coll.*) jmds. Stunde hat geschlagen; Ⓑ (*esp. Math.: numeral*) Zahl, *die;* **memory for ~s** Zahlengedächtnis, *das;* Ⓒ (*sum, total, quantity*) [An]zahl, *die;* **a ~ of people/things** einige Leute/Dinge; **a ~ of times/on a ~ of occasions** mehrfach *od.* -mals; **a small ~:** eine geringe [An]zahl; **large ~s** eine große [An]zahl; **in [large** *or* **great] ~s** in großer Zahl; **in a small ~ of cases** in einigen wenigen Fällen; **a and b in equal ~s** a und b in gleicher Anzahl; **a fair ~:** eine ganze Anzahl *od.* Reihe; **any ~:** beliebig viele; **on any ~ of occasions** oft[mals]; **without** *or* **beyond ~:** ohne Zahl (*geh.*); **times without ~:** unzählige Male; **in ~[s]** zahlenmäßig ‹überlegen sein, überwiegen›; **ten in ~:** zehn an der Zahl; **be few in ~:** gering an Zahl sein; Ⓓ (*person, song, turn, edition*) Nummer, *die;* **final/May ~:** Schluss-/Mainummer, *die;* Ⓔ (*coll.*) (*outfit*) Kluft, *die;* (*girl*) Mieze, *die* (*salopp*); (*job*) Job, *der* (*ugs.*); **it's not a bad little ~** (*job*) da kann man eine ruhige Kugel schieben (*ugs.*); Ⓕ (*Bibl.*) **[the Book of] Numbers** das vierte Buch Mose; Ⓖ (*company*) [Personen]kreis, *der;* Gruppe, *die;* **he was [one] of our ~:** er war einer von uns; Ⓗ *in pl.* (*arithmetic*) Rechnen, *das;* Ⓘ (*Ling.*)

# Numbers

## Cardinal numbers = Kardinalzahlen

**0 (*nought, zero*)** = null
**1 (*one*)** = eins, ein...[1]
**2 (*two*)** = zwei
**3 (*three*)** = drei
**4 (*four*)** = vier
**5 (*five*)** = fünf
**6 (*six*)** = sechs
**7 (*seven*)** = sieben
**8 (*eight*)** = acht
**9 (*nine*)** = neun
**10 (*ten*)** = zehn
**11 (*eleven*)** = elf
**12 (*twelve*)** = zwölf
**13 (*thirteen*)** = dreizehn
**14 (*fourteen*)** = vierzehn
**15 (*fifteen*)** = fünfzehn
**16 (*sixteen*)** = sechzehn
**17 (*seventeen*)** = siebzehn
**18 (*eighteen*)** = achtzehn
**19 (*nineteen*)** = neunzehn
**20 (*twenty*)** = zwanzig
**21 (*twenty-one*)** = einundzwanzig
**22 (*twenty-two*)** = zweiundzwanzig
**30 (*thirty*)** = dreißig
**40 (*forty*)** = vierzig
**50 (*fifty*)** = fünfzig
**60 (*sixty*)** = sechzig
**70 (*seventy*)** = siebzig
**80 (*eighty*)** = achtzig
**90 (*ninety*)** = neunzig
**100 (*a* or *one hundred*)** = [ein]hundert
**101 (*a* or *one hundred and one*)** = [ein]hundert[und]ein[s][2]
**555 (*five hundred and fifty-five*)** = fünfhundert[und]fünfundfünfzig
**1,000 (*a* or *one thousand*)** = [ein]tausend[3]
**1,001 (*a* or *one thousand and one*)** = [ein]tausend[und]ein[s][2]
**1,200 (*one thousand two hundred* or *twelve hundred*)** = [ein]tausendzweihundert *or* zwölfhundert[4]
**100,000 (*a* or *one hundred thousand*)** = [ein]hunderttausend
**1,000,000 (*a* or *one million*)** = eine Million
**3,536,000 (*three million five hundred and thirty-six thousand*)** = drei Millionen fünfhundertsechsunddreißigtausend
**1,000,000,000 (*a* or *one billion, a* or *one thousand million*)** = eine Milliarde
**1,000,000,000,000 (*a* or *one trillion, a* or *one million million*)** = eine Billion

[1] The form **eins** is used when the number appears on its own, e.g. when counting (eins, zwei, drei), calculating, giving times or scores (***a quarter to one*** = Viertel vor eins, ***to win one-nil*** = eins zu null gewinnen) or quoting decimals (***0 point one*** = null Komma eins, ***one point five*** = eins Komma fünf).

Where the number comes before a noun, it is declined like an indefinite article.

***I would like one large knob and two small ones***
= Ich möchte einen großen Knopf und zwei kleine

***You mustn't use one new battery and three old ones***
= Man darf nicht eine neue Batterie und drei alte verwenden

For other uses see the entry for *one*.

In larger numbers ending in **eins** it is not usually declined before a noun

***201 days***
= zweihundert[und]eins Tage

But note

***A Thousand and one Nights***
= Tausendundeine Nacht

[2] The bracketed **und** is usually included in numbers from 101 to 109, but omitted from 110 (hundertzehn) onwards except when counting. The bracketed **ein** may be included for emphasis. For the use of the final **s** see the note on **eins** above.

[3] Where English style usually has a comma for thousands, Continental European usage has a space:

1,000 = 1 000; 5,500 = 5 500; 123,467 = 123 467; 6,327,456 = 6 327 456

[4] Note that in dates the **hundert** should not be omitted:

***1895 = eighteen ninety-five***
= achtzehnhundertfünfundneunzig

## Fractions = Brüche

| | | | |
|---|---|---|---|
| 1/2 | ein halb | 1 1/2 | ein[und]einhalb |
| 1/4 | ein viertel | 2 3/4 | zwei[und]dreiviertel |
| 1/3 | ein drittel | 5 2/3 | fünf[und]zweidrittel |
| 1/8 | ein achtel | 8 7/8 | acht[und]siebenachtel |

Fractions are formed in German by adding **-tel** to the number, except where the number ends in **t, d** or **g**. In these cases an **s** is inserted before the **-tel**:

ein hundertstel  ein tausendstel  ein zwanzigstel

The fractions are written as above with a small letter in a calculation or with units of measure, but when combined with other nouns they are written with a capital:

***two thirds of the distance***
= zwei Drittel des Weges

***one eighth of the amount***
= ein Achtel des Betrages

but:

***an eighth of a litre***
= ein achtel Liter, ein Achtelliter

Note that with measures, "of a" is not translated and the fraction is often written with the unit to form one word. Also with plural fractions the unit of measure is in the plural:

***five eighths of a mile***
= fünf achtel Meilen

***six hundredths of a second***
= sechs hundertstel Sekunden, sechs Hundertstelsekunden

►

**NUMBERS** CONTINUED

## Ordinal numbers = Ordinalzahlen

**1st (*first*)** = 1. (erst...)[5]
**2nd (*second*)** = 2. (zweit...)
**3rd (*third*)** = 3. (dritt...)
**4th (*fourth*)** = 4. (viert...)
**5th (*fifth*)** = 5. (fünft...)
**6th (*sixth*)** = 6. (sechst...)
**7th (*seventh*)** = 7. (sieb[en]t...)
**8th (*eighth*)** = 8. (acht...)
**9th (*ninth*)** = 9. (neunt...)
**10th (*tenth*)** = 10. (zehnt...)
**11th (*eleventh*)** = 11. (elft...)
**12th (*twelfth*)** = 12. (zwölft...)
**13th (*thirteenth*)** = 13. (dreizehnt...)
**14th (*fourteenth*)** = 14. (vierzehnt...)
**15th (*fifteenth*)** = 15. (fünfzehnt...)
**16th (*sixteenth*)** = 16. (sechzehnt...)
**17th (*seventeenth*)** = 17. (siebzehnt...)
**18th (*eighteenth*)** = 18. (achtzehnt...)
**19th (*nineteenth*)** = 19. (neunzehnt...)
**20th (*twentieth*)** = 20. (zwanzigst...)
**21st (*twenty-first*)** = 21. (einundzwanzigst...)
**22nd (*twenty-second*)** = 22. (zweiundzwanzigst...)
**30th (*thirtieth*)** = 30. (dreißigst...)
**40th (*fortieth*)** = 40. (vierzigst...)
**50th (*fiftieth*)** = 50. (fünfzigst...)
**60th (*sixtieth*)** = 60. (sechzigst...)
**70th (*seventieth*)** = 70. (siebzigst...)
**80th (*eightieth*)** = 80. (achtzigst...)
**90th (*ninetieth*)** = 90. (neunzigst...)
**100th ([*one*] *hundredth*)** = 100. ([ein]hundertst...)
**101st ([*one*] *hundred and first*)** = 101. ([ein]hundert[und]erst...)
**555th (*five hundred and fifty-fifth*)** = 555. (fünfhundert[und]fünfundfünfzigst...)
**1,000th ([*one*] *thousandth*)** = 1 000. ([ein]tausendst...)
**1,001st (*one thousand and first*)** = 1 001. ([ein]tausend[und]erst...)
**1,200th (*one thousand two hundredth* or *twelve hundredth*)** = 1 200. ([ein]tausendzweihundertst... *or* zwölfhundertst...)
**100,000th ([*one*] *hundred thousandth*)** = 100 000. ([ein]hunderttausendst...)
**1,000,000th ([*one*] *millionth*)** = 1 000 000. (millionst...)
**3,536,000th (*three million five hundred and thirty-six thousandth*)** = 3 536 000.
(drei Millionen fünfhundertsechsunddreißigtausendst...)
**1,000,000,000th ([*one*] *billionth*, [*one*] *thousand millionth*)** = 1 000 000 000. (milliardst...)
**1,000,000,000,000th ([*one*] *trillionth*, [*one*] *million millionth*)** = 1 000 000 000 000. (billionst...)

[5] Ordinal numbers are declined like adjectives:

***the first time***
= das erste Mal

***her ninetieth birthday***
= ihr neunzigster Geburtstag

***at the tenth attempt***
= beim zehnten Versuch

***the end of his fifth symphony***
= der Schluss seiner fünften Symphonie

For the use of ordinals in dates ••••➤ **Dates**

For order in races, note the following phrases:

***He came (in) first***
= Er kam als Erster ins Ziel

***She finished third***
= Sie ging als Dritte durchs Ziel *or* belegte den dritten Platz

***I was sixth***
= Ich wurde Sechster/Sechste

## Decimal numbers = Dezimalzahlen

| | |
|---|---|
| 0.1 | = 0,1 (null Komma eins) |
| 0.015 | = 0,015 (null Komma null eins fünf) |
| 1.43 | = 1,43 (eins Komma vier drei) |
| 11.70 | = 11,70 (elf Komma sieben null) |
| 12.333 recurring | = 12,$\bar{3}$ (zwölf Komma Periode drei) |

## Calculations

7 + 3 = 10 (sieben plus drei ist [gleich] zehn)
10 – 3 = 7 (zehn minus drei ist [gleich] sieben)
10 x 3 = 30 (zehn mal *or* multipliziert mit drei ist [gleich] dreißig)
30 ÷ 3 = 10 (dreißig [dividiert *or* geteilt] durch drei ist [gleich] zehn)

## Powers = Potenzen

$3^2$ = ***three squared*** = drei [im *or* zum] Quadrat, drei hoch zwei
$3^3$ = ***three cubed*** = drei hoch drei
$3^{10}$ = ***three to the power of ten*** = drei hoch zehn
$\sqrt{25}$ = ***the square root of twenty-five***
= die [Quadrat]wurzel aus fünfundzwanzig

••••➤ **Age** **Area** **the Clock** **Distance** **Height and Depth** **Length and Width** **Money** **Temperature** **Volume** **Weight**

n

Numerus, *der* (*fachspr.*). ⇨ *also* **eight** 2 A; **opposite number**; **round number**.
❷ *v.t.* Ⓐ (*assign* ~ *to*) beziffern; nummerieren; Ⓑ (*amount to, comprise*) zählen; **the nominations ~ed ten in all** es wurden insgesamt zehn Kandidaten nominiert; **a town ~ing x inhabitants** eine Stadt mit x Einwohnern; Ⓒ (*include, regard as*) zählen, rechnen (**among, with** zu); Ⓓ **be ~ed** (*be limited*) begrenzt sein; **sb.'s days** *or* **years are ~ed** jmds. Tage sind gezählt; Ⓔ (*count*) zählen
~ **'off** *v.i.* abzählen

**numbering** /ˈnʌmbərɪŋ/ *n.* Nummerierung, *die*

**numberless** /ˈnʌmbəlɪs/ *adj.* unzählig; zahllos

ˈ**number plate** *n.* Nummernschild, *das*

**numbly** /ˈnʌmlɪ/ *adv.* wie betäubt

**numbness** /ˈnʌmnɪs/ *n., no pl.* (*caused by cold*) Gefühllosigkeit, *die;* Taubheit, *die;* (*caused by anaesthetic, sleeping pill*) Betäubung, *die;* (*fig.: stupor*) Benommenheit, *die*

**numbskull** ⇨ **numskull**

**numeracy** /ˈnjuːmərəsɪ/ *n.* rechnerische Fähigkeiten

**numeral** /ˈnjuːmərl/ *n.* Ziffer, *die;* (*word*) Zahlwort, *das;* **cardinal ~:** Kardinal- *od.* Grundzahl, *die*

**numerate** /ˈnjuːmərət/ *adj.* rechenkundig; **be ~:** rechnen können

**numerator** /ˈnjuːməreɪtə(r)/ *n.* (*Math.*) Zähler, *der*

**numerical** /njuːˈmerɪkl/ *adj.* Zahlen‹wert, -folge›; numerisch ‹Reihenfolge, Stärke, Überlegenheit›; zahlenmäßig ‹Überlegenheit›; rechnerisch ‹Fähigkeiten›

**numerically** /njuːˈmerɪkəlɪ/ *adv.* numerisch; **~ speaking, ...:** numerisch *od.* zahlenmäßig ...

**numerous** /ˈnjuːmərəs/ *adj.* zahlreich

**numismatics** /njuːmɪzˈmætɪks/ *n., no pl.* Numismatik, *die;* Münzkunde, *die*

**numismatist** /njuːˈmɪzmətɪst/ *n.* ▶ **1261** Numismatiker, *der*/Numismatikerin, *die*

**numskull** /ˈnʌmskʌl/ *n.* Hohlkopf, *der* (*abwertend*)

**nun** /nʌn/ *n.* Nonne, *die*

**nuncio** /ˈnʌnʃɪəʊ/ *n., pl.* **~s** (*RC Ch.*) Nuntius, *der*

**nunnery** /ˈnʌnərɪ/ *n.* [Nonnen]kloster, *das*

**nuptial** /ˈnʌpʃl/ ❶ *adj.* ehelich; **~ vow/feast/day** Eheversprechen, *das*/Hochzeitsfest, *das*/Hochzeitstag, *der.* ❷ *n. in pl.* (*literary/joc.*) Hochzeit, *die*

**nurd** ⇨ **nerd**

**nurse** /nɜːs/ ❶ *n.* ▶ **1261** Krankenschwester, *die;* **thank you, ~:** danke, Schwester; **hospital ~:** Krankenhausschwester, *die;* **[male] ~:** Krankenpfleger, *der;* **~s' home/uniform** Schwesternwohnheim, *das*/-tracht, *die.* ❷ *v.t.* Ⓐ (*act as* ~ *to*) pflegen ‹Kranke›; **take up nursing the handicapped/sick** in der Behinderten-/Krankenpflege tätig werden; **~ sb. through an illness** jmdn. während seiner Krankheit pflegen; **~ sb. back to health** jmdn. gesund pflegen; Ⓑ (*act as ~maid to*) betreuen ‹Kind›; (*fig.: foster, tend*) hegen (*geh.*) ‹Projekt›; fördern ‹Begabung›; Ⓒ (*try to cure*) versorgen; auskurieren ‹Erkältung›; Ⓓ (*suckle*) die Brust geben (+ *Dat.*), stillen ‹Säugling›; Ⓔ (*manage carefully*) hegen, pflegen ‹Pflanze›; Ⓕ (*cradle*) vorsichtig halten; wiegen ‹Baby›; Ⓖ (*keep burning*) hüten ‹Feuer›; Ⓗ (*treat carefully*) **~ gently/carefully** behutsam *od.* schonend umgehen mit; Ⓘ (*fig.: harbour*) hegen (*geh.*) ‹Gefühl, Plan, Groll›.
❸ *v.i.* Ⓐ (*act as wet* ~) stillen; Ⓑ (*be a sick* ~) Krankenschwester/-pfleger sein. ⇨ *also* **wet nurse**

ˈ**nursemaid** *n.* (*lit. or fig.*) Kindermädchen, *das*

**nursery** /ˈnɜːsərɪ/ *n.* Ⓐ (*room for children*) Kinderzimmer, *das;* Ⓑ (*crèche*) Kindertagesstätte, *die;* Ⓒ ⇨ **nursery school**; Ⓓ (*Agric.*) (*for plants*) Gärtnerei, *die;* (*for trees*) Baumschule, *die;* (*fig.: training ground*) Schule, *die*

**nursery: ~man** /ˈnɜːsərɪmən/ *n., pl.* **~men** /ˈnɜːsərɪmən/ Gärtner, *der;* **~ nurse** *n.* Kindermädchen, *das;* Kinderpflegerin, *die;* **~ rhyme** *n.* Kinderreim, *der;* **~ school** *n.* Kindergarten, *der;* **~-school teacher** *n.* ▶ **1261** (*female*) Kindergärtnerin, *die;* Erzieherin, *die;* (*male*) Erzieher, *der;* **~ slopes** *n. pl.* (*Skiing*) Idiotenhügel, *der* (*ugs. scherzh.*)

**nursing** /ˈnɜːsɪŋ/ *n., no pl., no art.* ▶ **1261** (*profession*) Krankenpflege, *die; attrib.* Pflege‹personal, -beruf›

**nursing: ~ auxiliary** *n.* ▶ **1261** (*female*) Schwesternhelferin, *die;* (*male*) Hilfspfleger, *der;* **~ home** *n.* (*Brit.*) (*for the aged, infirm*) Pflegeheim, *das;* (*for convalescents*) Genesungsheim, *das;* (*maternity hospital*) Entbindungsheim, *das;* ~ ˈ**mother** *n.* stillende Mutter

**nurture** /ˈnɜːtʃə(r)/ ❶ *n.* Ⓐ *no pl.* (*bringing up*) Erziehung, *die;* Ⓑ (*nourishment, lit. or fig.*) Nahrung, *die.* ❷ *v.t.* Ⓐ (*rear*) aufziehen; Ⓑ (*fig.: foster*) nähren (*geh.*); Ⓒ (*train*) erziehen; schulen, bilden ‹Geist›

**nut** /nʌt/ *n.* Ⓐ Nuss, *die;* **she can't sing/spell for ~s** (*Brit. coll.*) sie kann nicht für fünf Pfennig (*ugs.*) singen/schreiben; **be a hard** *or* **tough ~ [to crack]** (*fig.*) eine harte Nuss sein (*ugs.*); ‹Person:› schwierig sein; **~s to you** (*coll.*) du kannst/ihr könnt mir den Buckel runterrutschen (*ugs.*); Ⓑ (*Mech. Engin.*) [Schrauben]mutter, *die;* **~s and bolts** (*fig.*) praktische Grundlagen; Ⓒ (*coll.: head*) Kürbis, *der* (*salopp*); **go/be off one's ~:** verrückt (*ugs.*) werden/sein; **do one's ~:** durchdrehen (*ugs.*); Ⓓ (*crazy person*) Verrückte, *der/die* (*ugs.*); **be a bit of a ~:** ein bisschen spinnen (*ugs.*); Ⓔ *in pl.* (*coarse: testicles*) Eier (*derb*). ⇨ *also* **nuts**

**nut: ~-brown** *adj.* nussbraun; ~ ˈ**butter** *n.* [Erd]nussbutter, *die;* **~case** *n.* (*coll.*) Verrückte, *der/die* (*ugs.*); **~crackers** *n. pl.* Nussknacker, *der;* **~ cutlet** *n.* Nussschnitzel, *das;* **~hatch** *n.* (*Ornith.*) Kleiber, *der;* **~house** *n.* (*sl.*) Klapsmühle, *die* (*salopp*); **~ meat** *n.* (*Amer.*) Nusskern, *der*

**nutmeg** /ˈnʌtmeg/ *n.* Muskatnuss, *die;* Muskat, *der*

**nutrient** /ˈnjuːtrɪənt/ ❶ *adj.* Ⓐ (*serving as nourishment*) nahrhaft; Ⓑ (*providing nourishment*) Ernährungs-; Nähr‹lösung, -salze›. ❷ *n.* Nährstoff, *der*

**nutriment** /ˈnjuːtrɪmənt/ *n.* (*lit. or fig.*) Nahrung, *die*

**nutrition** /njuːˈtrɪʃn/ *n.* Ⓐ (*nourishment, diet*) Ernährung, *die;* Ⓑ (*food, lit. or fig.*) Nahrung, *die*

**nutritional** /njuːˈtrɪʃənl/ *adj.* nahrhaft; **~ value** Nährwert, *der;* **~ deficiency/deficiencies** Nährstoffmangel, *der*

**nutritionist** /njuːˈtrɪʃənɪst/ *n.* Ernährungswissenschaftler, *der*/-wissenschaftlerin, *die*

**nutritious** /njuːˈtrɪʃəs/ *adj.* nahrhaft

**nutritive** /ˈnjuːtrɪtɪv/ *adj.* nahrhaft; **~ value/function** Nährwert, *der*/Ernährungsfunktion, *die*

ˈ**nut roast** *n.* Nussbraten, *der*

**nuts** /nʌts/ *pred. adj.* (*coll.*) verrückt (*ugs.*); **be ~ about** *or* **on sb./sth.** nach jmdm./etw. verrückt sein (*ugs.*)

ˈ**nutshell** *n.* Ⓐ Nussschale, *die;* Ⓑ (*fig.*) **in a ~:** in aller Kürze; **to put it** *or* **the matter** *or* **the whole thing in a ~:** kurz gesagt

**nutter** /ˈnʌtə(r)/ *n.* (*coll.*) Verrückte, *der/die* (*ugs.*); **be a ~:** verrückt sein (*ugs.*)

ˈ**nut tree** *n.* Haselnussstrauch, *der;* (*walnut*) Nussbaum, *der*

**nutty** /ˈnʌtɪ/ *adj.* Ⓐ (*tasting like nuts*) nussig; Ⓑ (*abounding in nuts*) voller Nüsse *nachgestellt;* Ⓒ (*coll.: crazy*) verrückt (*ugs.*); **be ~ about** *or* **on sb./sth.** (*coll.*) nach jmdm./etw. verrückt sein (*ugs.*); ⇨ *also* **fruit cake**

**nuzzle** /ˈnʌzl/ ❶ *v.i.* Ⓐ (*with nose*) **~ in** *or* **into sth.** die Schnauze in etw. (*Akk.*) drücken; **~ against sth.** die Schnauze gegen etw. drücken; Ⓑ (*nestle*) sich kuscheln (**[up] to, at, against** an + *Akk.*). ❷ *v.t.* schmiegen ‹Gesicht, Kopf, Schulter›

**NVQ** *abbr.* (*Brit.*) **National Vocational Qualification**

**NW** *abbr.* ▶ **1024** Ⓐ /nɔːθˈwest/ **north-west** NW; Ⓑ /nɔːθˈwestən/ **north-western** nw.

**NY** *abbr.* New York

**nylon** /ˈnaɪlɒn/ *n.* Ⓐ *no pl.* (*Textiles*) Nylon, *das; attrib.* Nylon-; Ⓑ *in pl.* (*stockings*) Nylonstrümpfe; Nylons (*ugs.*)

**nymph** /nɪmf/ *n.* (*Mythol., Zool.*) Nymphe, *die*

**nymphet** /ˈnɪmfet, nɪmˈfet/ *n.* Nymphchen, *das*

**nympho** /ˈnɪmfəʊ/ *n., pl.* **~s** (*coll.*) Nymphomanin, *die*

**nymphomania** /nɪmfəˈmeɪnɪə/ *n.* Nymphomanie, *die;* Mannstollheit, *die* (*veralt.*)

**nymphomaniac** /nɪmfəˈmeɪnɪæk/ ❶ *n.* Nymphomanin, *die.* ❷ *adj.* nymphoman; mannstoll (*veralt.*)

**NZ** *abbr.* **New Zealand**

n

# O o

**O[1], o** /əʊ/ *n., pl.* **Os** *or* **O's** [A] (*letter*) O, o, *das;* [B] (*zero*) Null, *die*

**O[2]** *int.* (*arch./poet./rhet.*) o; **O God** *etc.* o Herr *usw.;* ⇒ *also* **that** 6 C

**o'** /ə/ *prep.* (*esp. arch./poet./dial.*) [A] = **of** von; **man-o'-war** Kriegsschiff, *das;* **cup o' tea** (*coll.*) Tasse Tee; ⇒ *also* **o'clock**; [B] = **on: o' nights/Sundays** nachts/sonntags

**oaf** /əʊf/ *n., pl.* **~s** *or* **oaves** /əʊvz/ [A] (*stupid person*) Dummkopf, *der* (*ugs.*); **great ~:** Riesenrindvieh, *das* (*ugs.*); [B] (*awkward lout*) Stoffel, *der* (*ugs.*); **you clumsy ~!** du Trampeltier! (*ugs.*)

**oafish** /'əʊfɪʃ/ *adj.* stoffelig (*ugs.*)

**oak** /əʊk/ *n.* Eiche, *die; attrib.* Eichen‹wald, -möbel, -kiste, -blatt›

**'oak apple** *n.* (*Bot.*) Gallapfel, *der*

**oaken** /'əʊkn/ *attrib. adj.* eichen

**'oak tree** *n.* Eiche, *die*

**OAP** *abbr.* (*Brit.*) **old-age pensioner** Rentner, *der*/Rentnerin, *die;* **~ [social] club** Seniorenklub, *der*

**oar** /ɔ:(r)/ *n.* [A] Ruder, *das;* Riemen, *der* (*Sport, Seemannsspr.*); **put in one's ~, put one's ~ in** (*fig. coll.*) seinen Senf dazugeben (*ugs.*); sich einmischen; **rest on one's ~s, lie** *or* (*Amer.*) **lay on one's ~s** die Riemen hochnehmen; (*fig.: relax one's efforts*) sich ausruhen; [B] (*rower*) Ruderer, *der*/Ruderin, *die*

**-oared** /ɔ:d/ *adj. in comb.* mit … Riemen *nachgestellt;* -ruderig

**oarsman** /'ɔ:zmən/ *n., pl.* **oarsmen** /'ɔ:zmən/ Ruderer, *der*

**oarsmanship** /'ɔ:zmənʃɪp/ *n., no pl.* ruderisches Können

**oarswoman** /'ɔ:zwʊmn/ *n.* Ruderin, *die*

**oasis** /əʊ'eɪsɪs/ *n., pl.* **oases** /əʊ'eɪsi:z/ (*lit. or fig.*) Oase, *die*

**oast** /əʊst/ *n.* (*Agric., Brewing*) Darre, *die*

**'oast house** *n.* (*Agric., Brewing*) Hopfendarre, *die*

**oat** /əʊt/ *n.* [A] **~s** Hafer, *der;* **be off one's ~s** (*fig.*) keinen Appetit haben; **rolled ~s** Haferflocken *Pl.;* [B] (*plant*) Haferpflanze, *die;* **field of ~s** Haferfeld, *das;* **wild ~:** Flug- *od.* Windhafer, *der;* **sow one's wild ~s** (*fig.*) sich (*Dat.*) die Hörner abstoßen (*ugs.*)

**'oatcake** *n.* [flacher] Haferkuchen

**oath** /əʊθ/ *n., pl.* **~s** /əʊðz/ [A] Eid, *der;* Schwur, *der;* **be bound by ~:** durch einen Eid *od.* Schwur gebunden sein; **take** *or* **swear an ~ [on sth.] that …:** einen Eid [auf etw. (*Akk.*)] schwören, dass …; [B] (*Law*) **swear** *or* **take the ~:** vereidigt werden; **on** *or* **under ~:** unter Eid; **be on** *or* **under ~ to do sth.** geschworen haben, etw. zu tun; **put sb. on** *or* **under ~:** jmdn. vereidigen *od.* unter Eid nehmen; **[I swear] on my ~ I am telling the truth** ich schwöre, dass ich die Wahrheit sage; **~ of office** Amts- *od.* Diensteid, *der;* **~ of allegiance/supremacy** Treu-/Suprematseid, *der;* [C] (*expletive*) Fluch, *der*

**'oatmeal** *n.* [A] Hafermehl, *das;* [B] (*colour*) Graubeige, *das*

**OAU** *abbr.* (*Polit.*) **Organization of African Unity** OAE

**oaves** *pl. of* **oaf**

**obbligato** /ɒblɪ'gɑ:təʊ/ (*Mus.*) ❶ *adj.* obligat. ❷ *n., pl.* **~s** Obligato, *das*

**obduracy** /'ɒbdjʊrəsɪ/ *n., no pl.* (*hard-heartedness*) Unerbittlichkeit, *die;* (*stubbornness*) Verstocktheit, *die*

**obdurate** /ɒb'djʊərət/ *adj.* (*hardened*) unerbittlich ‹Brutalität›; verstockt ‹Herz, Sünder›; (*stubborn*) verstockt; hartnäckig ‹Weigerung, Ablehnung›

**OBE** *abbr.* (*Brit.*) **Officer [of the Order] of the British Empire**

**obedience** /ə'bi:dɪəns/ *n.* Gehorsam, *der;* **show ~:** gehorsam sein; **in ~ to** gemäß

**obedient** /ə'bi:dɪənt/ *adj.* gehorsam; (*submissive*) fügsam; **teach a dog to be ~:** einem Hund Gehorsam beibringen; **be ~ to sb./sth.** jmdm./einer Sache gehorchen; ⇒ *also* **servant** C

**obediently** /ə'bi:dɪəntlɪ/ *adv.* gehorsam; (*submissively*) fügsam

**obeisance** /əʊ'beɪsəns/ *n.* [A] (*gesture*) Verbeugung, *die;* Verneigung, *die* (*geh.*); (*prostration*) Fußfall, *der;* [B] *no pl.* (*homage*) Ehrerbietung, *die* (*geh.*); Reverenz, *die* (*geh.*); **do** *or* **make** *or* **pay ~ to sb.** jmdm. seine Reverenz bezeigen *od.* erweisen (*geh.*)

**obelisk** /'ɒbəlɪsk, 'ɒbɪlɪsk/ *n.* [A] (*pillar*) Obelisk, *der;* [B] (*Printing*) Kreuzchen, *das;* **double ~:** Doppelkreuzchen, *das*

**obese** /əʊ'bi:s/ *adj.* fett (*abwertend*); fettleibig (*bes. Med.*)

**obesity** /əʊ'bi:sɪtɪ/ *n., no pl.* Fettheit, *die* (*abwertend*); Fettleibigkeit, *die* (*bes. Med.*); Obesität, *die* (*Med.*)

**obey** /əʊ'beɪ/ ❶ *v.t.* gehorchen (+ *Dat.*); ‹Kind, Hund:› folgen (+ *Dat.*), gehorchen (+ *Dat.*); sich halten an (+ *Akk.*) ‹Vorschrift, Regel›; befolgen ‹Befehl›; folgen (+ *Dat.*) ‹Aufforderung›; nachkommen (*geh.*) (+ *Dat.*), Folge leisten (+ *Dat.*) ‹Vorladung›. ❷ *v.i.* gehorchen; ‹Kind, Hund:› folgen, gehorchen; **refuse to ~:** den Gehorsam verweigern

**obfuscate** /'ɒbfəskeɪt/ *v.t.* (*literary*) (*obscure*) vernebeln; (*confuse*) verwirren

**obituary** /ə'bɪtjʊərɪ/ ❶ *n.* Nachruf, *der* (**to, of** auf + *Akk.*); (*notice of death*) Todesanzeige, *die.* ❷ *adj.* **~ notice/memoir** Todesanzeige, *die*/Nachruf, *der;* **the ~ page/column** die Todesanzeigen

**object** ❶ /'ɒbdʒɪkt/ *n.* [A] (*thing*) Gegenstand, *der;* (*Philos.*) Objekt, *das;* **he was no longer the ~ of her affections** ihre Zuneigung gehörte ihm nicht mehr; [B] (*purpose*) Ziel, *das;* **~ in life** Lebensziel, *das od.* -zweck, *der;* **with this ~ in mind** *or* **view** mit diesem Ziel [vor Augen]; **with the ~ of doing sth.** in der Absicht, etw. zu tun; **make it one's ~ [in life]** es sich (*Dat.*) zum Ziel setzen; es zu seinem Lebensziel machen; ⇒ *also* **defeat** 1 B; **exercise** 1 B; [C] (*obstacle, hindrance*) **money/time** *etc.* **is no ~:** Geld/Zeit *usw.* spielt keine Rolle; [D] (*Ling.*) Objekt, *das;* ⇒ *also* **direct object**; **indirect object**.

❷ /əb'dʒekt/ *v.i.* [A] (*state objection*) Einwände/einen Einwand erheben (**to** gegen); (*protest*) protestieren (**to** gegen); **I ~, your Honour** (*Law*) Einspruch, Herr Vorsitzender!; [B] (*have objection or dislike*) etwas dagegen haben; **~ to sb./sth.** etwas gegen jmdn./etw. haben; **if you don't ~:** wenn Sie nichts dagegen haben; **I ~ to your smoking** es stört mich, dass du rauchst; **~ to sb.'s doing sth.** etw. dagegen haben, dass jmd. etw. tut; **I strongly ~ to this tone** ich verbitte mir diesen Ton; **I ~ to being blamed for this error** ich verwahre mich dagegen, für diesen Fehler verantwortlich gemacht zu werden.

❸ *v.t.* einwenden

**objectify** /əb'dʒektɪfaɪ/ *v.t.* objektivieren

**objection** /əb'dʒekʃn/ *n.* [A] Einwand, *der;* Einspruch, *der* (*Amtsspr., Rechtsw.*); **raise** *or* **make an ~ [to sth.]** einen Einwand *od.* (*Rechtsw.*) Einspruch [gegen etw.] erheben; **make no ~ to sth.** nichts gegen etw. einzuwenden haben; [B] (*feeling of opposition or dislike*) Abneigung, *die;* **have an/no ~ to sb./sth.** etw./nichts gegen jmdn./etw. haben; **have an/no ~:** etwas/nichts dagegen haben; **have no ~ to sb.'s doing sth.** nichts dagegen haben, dass jmd. etw. tut

**objectionable** /əb'dʒekʃənəbl/ *adj.* unangenehm ‹Anblick, Geruch›; anstößig ‹Bemerkung, Wort, Benehmen›; unausstehlich ‹Kind›

**objectionably** /əb'dʒekʃənəblɪ/ *adv.* unerträglich ‹überheblich, aufdringlich›; anstößig ‹sich benehmen›

**objective** /əb'dʒektɪv/ ❶ *adj.* [A] (*unbiased*) objektiv; sachlich; [B] (*esp. Philos.: real*) objektiv. ❷ *n.* (*goal*) Ziel, *das;* **establish one's ~:** sich (*Dat.*) ein Ziel setzen

**objective: ~ case** *n.* (*Ling.*) **be in the ~ case** Objekt sein; **~ 'genitive** *n.* (*Ling.*) Genitivus obiectivus, *der*

**objectively** /əb'dʒektɪvlɪ/ *adv.* [A] objektiv; [B] (*Ling.*) als Objekt ‹gebrauchen›

**objectiveness** /əb'dʒektɪvnɪs/, **objectivity** /ɒbdʒek'tɪvɪtɪ/ *ns., no pl.* Objektivität, *die;* **maintain objectivity** objektiv bleiben

**'object lesson** *n.* (*warning*) Denkzettel, *der;* (*very clear example*) Musterbeispiel, *das* (**in, on** für); **it was an ~ to him** es war ihm eine Lehre; **an ~ in** *or* **on how to do sth.** ein Musterbeispiel dafür, wie man etw. macht

**objector** /əb'dʒektə(r)/ *n.* Gegner, *der*/Gegnerin, *die* (**to** *Gen.*); ⇒ *also* **conscientious**

**objet d'art** /ɒbʒeɪ 'dɑ:(r)/ *n., pl.* **objets d'art** /ɒbʒeɪ 'dɑ:(r)/ Kunstgegenstand, *der*

**obligate** /'ɒblɪgeɪt/ *v.t., usu. in p.p.* verpflichten

**obligation** /ɒblɪ'geɪʃn/ *n.* [A] Verpflichtung, *die;* (*constraint*) Zwang, *der;* **be under** *or* **have an/no ~ to do sth.** verpflichtet/nicht verpflichtet sein, etw. zu tun; **have an/no ~ to[wards] sb.** jmdm. gegenüber eine/keine Verpflichtung haben; **there's no ~ to buy** es besteht kein Kaufzwang; **without ~:** unverbindlich; [B] (*indebtedness*) Dankesschuld, *die* (*geh.*); **put** *or* **place sb. under an ~:** jmdm. eine Dankespflicht auferlegen; **be under an ~ to sb.** in jmds. Schuld stehen (*geh.*); jmdm. verpflichtet sein; **be under no ~ to sb.** jmdm. nicht verpflichtet sein

**obligatory** /ə'blɪgətərɪ/ *adj.* obligatorisch; **make sth. ~ for sb.** etw. für jmdn. vorschreiben; **it has become ~ to do sth.** es ist zur Pflicht geworden, etw. zu tun

**oblige** /ə'blaɪdʒ/ ❶ *v.t.* [A] (*be binding on*) **~ sb. to do sth.** jmdm. vorschreiben, etw. zu tun; **one is ~d by law to do sth.** etw. ist gesetzlich vorgeschrieben; [B] (*constrain, compel*) zwingen; nötigen; **be ~d to do sth.** gezwungen *od.* genötigt sein, etw. zu tun; **you are not ~d to answer these questions** Sie sind nicht verpflichtet, diese Fragen zu beantworten; **feel ~d to do sth.** sich verpflichtet fühlen, etw. zu tun; [C] (*be kind to*) **~ sb. by doing sth.** jmdm. den Gefallen tun und etw. tun; **would you please ~ me by doing it?** würden Sie bitte so gut sein und es tun?; **~ sb. with sth.** (*help out*) jmdm. mit etw. aushelfen; **could you ~ me with a lift?** könnten Sie mich freundlicherweise mitnehmen?; [D] **~d** (*bound by gratitude*) **be much/greatly ~d to sb. [for sth.]** jmdm. [für etw.] sehr verbunden sein; **much ~d** besten Dank!

❷ *v.i.* **be always ready to ~:** immer sehr gefällig sein; **anything to ~** (*as answer*) stets zu Diensten; **~ with a song** *etc.* ein Lied *usw.* zum Besten geben

**obliging** /ə'blaɪdʒɪŋ/ *adj.* entgegenkommend

**obligingly** /ə'blaɪdʒɪŋlɪ/ *adv.* entgegenkommenderweise

**oblique** /ə'bli:k/ ❶ *adj.* **A** (*slanting*) schief ‹Gerade, Winkel›; **B** (*fig.: indirect*) indirekt ‹Bemerkung, Hinweis, Frage›; versteckt ‹Hinweis›. ❷ *n.* Schrägstrich, *der*

**obliquely** /ə'bli:klɪ/ *adv.* **A** (*in a slanting direction*) schräg ‹einfallen, abzweigen›; **B** (*fig.: indirectly*) indirekt ‹sich beziehen, antworten›

**obliterate** /ə'blɪtəreɪt/ *v.t.* **A** auslöschen; (*cancel*) entwerten ‹Briefmarke›; **B** (*fig.*) verschleiern ‹Wahrheit›; auslöschen ‹Erinnerung›; zerstreuen ‹Bedenken›; vernichtend schlagen ‹Gegner›

**obliteration** /əblɪtə'reɪʃn/ *n.* ⇒ **obliterate**: Auslöschung, *die;* Verschleierung, *die;* Zerstreuung, *die*

**oblivion** /ə'blɪvɪən/ *n., no pl.* **A** (*being forgotten*) Vergessenheit, *die;* **sink** *or* **fall into ~:** in Vergessenheit geraten; **rescued from ~:** der Vergessenheit (*Dat.*) entrissen; **B** (*forgetting*) Vergessen, *das*

**oblivious** /ə'blɪvɪəs/ *adj.* **be ~ to** *or* **of sth.** (*be unconscious of*) sich (*Dat.*) einer Sache (*Gen.*) nicht bewusst sein; (*not notice*) etw. nicht bemerken *od.* wahrnehmen

**oblong** /'ɒblɒŋ/ ❶ *adj.* rechteckig. ❷ *n.* Rechteck, *das*

**obloquy** /'ɒbləkwɪ/ *n.* (*literary*) **A** (*abuse*) Beschimpfungen *Pl.;* **B** (*disgrace*) Schande, *die*

**obnoxious** /əb'nɒkʃəs/ *adj.*, **obnoxiously** /əb'nɒkʃəslɪ/ *adv.* widerlich (*abwertend*)

**oboe** /'əʊbəʊ/ *n.* (*Mus.*) Oboe, *die*

**oboist** /'əʊbəʊɪst/ *n.* ▶ **1261** (*Mus.*) Oboist, *der*/Oboistin, *die*

**obscene** /əb'si:n/ *adj.* obszön; (*coll.: offensive*) widerlich (*abwertend*); unanständig ‹Profit›

**obscenely** /əb'si:nlɪ/ *adv.* obszön; (*coll.: offensively*) widerlich (*abwertend*); unanständig ‹reich›

**obscenity** /əb'senɪtɪ/ *n.* Obszönität, *die;* (*coll.: offensive nature*) Widerlichkeit, *die* (*abwertend*)

**obscurantism** /ɒbskjʊə'ræntɪzm/ *n.* Obskurantismus, *der*

**obscurantist** /ɒbskjʊə'ræntɪst/ ❶ *n.* Obskurant, *der*/Obskurantin, *die* (*geh.*). ❷ *adj.* **~ doctrine/argument** Obskurantentum, *das* (*geh.*)

**obscure** /əb'skjʊə(r)/ ❶ *adj.* **A** (*unexplained*) dunkel; **for some ~ reason** aus irgendeinem unerfindlichen (*geh.*) *od.* verborgenen Grund; **B** (*hard to understand*) schwer verständlich ‹Argument, Dichtung, Autor, Stil›; unklar ‹Hinweis, Textstelle›; **C** (*unknown*) unbekannt ‹Herkunft, Schriftsteller›; (*undistinguished*) unbedeutend; **D** (*indistinct, vague*) undeutlich ‹Spur, Gemurmel›; vage ‹Anhaltspunkt›; **E** (*remote*) abgelegen, entlegen ‹Ort›; **F** (*dark, dim*) dunkel. ❷ *v.t.* **A** (*make indistinct*) verdunkeln; (*block*) versperren ‹Aussicht›; (*conceal*) ‹Nebel:› verhüllen; **B** (*fig.: make unintelligible*) unverständlich machen; **be ~d** unverständlich werden; **C** (*fig.: outshine*) in den Schatten stellen

**obscurely** /əb'skjʊəlɪ/ *adv.* **A** (*indirectly*) vage; **B** (*in obscurity*) im Verborgenen

**obscurity** /əb'skjʊərɪtɪ/ *n.* **A** *no pl.* (*being unknown or inconspicuous*) Unbekanntheit, *die;* **rise out of ~:** bekannt werden; **sink into ~:** in Vergessenheit geraten; **in ~:** unbeachtet, unauffällig ‹leben›; **B** *no pl.* (*being not clearly known or understood*) **be lost in [the mists of] ~:** im Dunkeln liegen; **C** (*unintelligibleness, unintelligible thing*) Unverständlichkeit, *die;* **D** *no pl.* (*darkness*) Dunkelheit, *die*

**obsequies** /'ɒbsɪkwɪz/ *n. pl.* (*funeral rites*) Beisetzungsfeierlichkeiten (*geh.*)

**obsequious** /əb'si:kwɪəs/ *adj.*, **obsequiously** /əb'si:kwɪəslɪ/ *adv.* unterwürfig (*abwertend*)

**observable** /əb'zɜ:vəbl/ *adj.* erkennbar; spürbar ‹Mangel, Zunahme, Übergewicht›

**observance** /əb'zɜ:vəns/ *n.* **A** *no pl.* (*observing, keeping*) Einhaltung, *die;* Befolgung, *die;* (*of prescribed times*) Einhaltung, *die;* **B** (*esp. Relig.: practice, rite*) Regel, *die;* **C** (*rule*) Ordensregel, *die*

**observant** /əb'zɜ:vənt/ *adj.* **A** aufmerksam; **be ~ of sth.** ein Auge für etw. haben; **how very ~ of you!** sehr scharf beobachtet!; **B** (*mindful, regardful*) **be ~ of** beachten, sich halten an (+ *Akk.*) ‹Gesetz, Regel›

**observation** /ɒbzə'veɪʃn/ *n.* **A** *no pl.* Beobachtung, *die;* **escape ~:** unbeobachtet bleiben; **powers of ~:** Beobachtungsgabe, *die;* **stay in hospital for ~:** zur Beobachtung im Krankenhaus bleiben; **be [kept] under ~:** beobachtet werden; (*by police, detectives*) observiert *od.* überwacht werden; **B** (*remark*) Bemerkung, *die* (**on** über + *Akk.*); **make an ~ on sth.** sich zu etw. äußern

**observational** /ɒbzə'veɪʃənl/ *adj.* Beobachtungs‹gabe, -methode›

**observation: ~ car** *n.* (*Railw.*) Aussichtswagen, *der;* **~ post** *n.* (*Mil.*) Beobachtungsposten, *der*

**observatory** /əb'zɜ:vətərɪ/ *n.* Observatorium, *das;* (*Astron. also*) Sternwarte, *die;* (*Meteorol. also*) Wetterstation, *die*

**observe** /əb'zɜ:v/ *v.t.* **A** (*watch*) beobachten; ‹Polizei, Detektiv:› observieren, überwachen; *abs.* aufpassen; (*perceive*) bemerken; **B** (*abide by, keep*) einhalten; feiern ‹Weihnachten, Jahrestag›; einlegen ‹Schweigeminute›; halten ‹Gelübde›; nachkommen (*geh.*) (+ *Dat.*) ‹Bitte›; **C** (*say*) bemerken

**observer** /əb'zɜ:və(r)/ *n.* Beobachter, *der*/Beobachterin, *die*

**obsess** /əb'ses/ *v.t.* **~ sb.** von jmdm. Besitz ergreifen (*fig.*); **be/become ~ed with** *or* **by sb./sth.** von jmdm./etw. besessen sein/werden; **don't let yourself become ~ed by her** versuch in deiner Beziehung zu ihr einen kühlen Kopf zu behalten

**obsession** /əb'seʃn/ *n.* **A** (*persistent idea*) Zwangsvorstellung, *die;* **be/become an ~ with sb.** für jmdn. zur Sucht geworden sein/werden; **have an ~ with sb.** von jmdm. besessen sein; **have an ~ with sex** sexbesessen sein; **have an ~ with cleanliness/guns** einen Sauberkeits-/Waffenfimmel haben; **have an ~ with detail** ein Kleinkrämer sein; **B** *no pl.* (*Psych.: condition*) Obsession, *die* (*fachspr.*); Besessenheit, *die;* **develop an ~ about washing** einen Waschzwang entwickeln

**obsessional** /əb'seʃənl/ *adj.* zwanghaft; obsessiv (*Psych.*)

**obsessive** /əb'sesɪv/ *adj.* zwanghaft; obsessiv (*Psych.*); **be ~ about sth.** von etw. besessen sein; **be an ~ eater/gambler** unter Esszwang leiden/dem Spiel verfallen sein

**obsessively** /əb'sesɪvlɪ/ *adv.* zwanghaft

**obsolescence** /ɒbsə'lesəns/ *n., no pl.* Veralten, *das;* **fall into ~:** veralten; **built-in** *or* **planned ~:** geplanter Verschleiß

**obsolescent** /ɒbsə'lesənt/ *adj.* veraltend; **become/have become** *or* **be ~:** allmählich veralten/nahezu veraltet sein

**obsolete** /'ɒbsəli:t/ *adj.* veraltet; obsolet (*geh.*); **become/have become ~:** veralten/veraltet sein

**obstacle** /'ɒbstəkl/ *n.* Hindernis, *das* (**to** für); **put ~s in sb.'s path** (*fig.*) jmdm. Hindernisse *od.* Steine in den Weg legen; **give rise to ~s** Schwierigkeiten verursachen

**obstacle: ~ course** *n.* Hindernisparcours, *der;* **~ race** *n.* Hindernisrennen, *das*

**obstetric** /ɒb'stetrɪk/, **obstetrical** /ɒb'stetrɪkl/ *adj.* (*Med.*) Geburts‹schock, -kanal›; **~ ward** Entbindungsstation, *die*

**obstetrician** /ɒbstə'trɪʃn/ *n.* ▶ **1261** (*Med.*) Geburtshelfer, *der*/-helferin, *die*

**obstetrics** /ɒb'stetrɪks/ *n., no pl.* (*Med.*) Obstetrik, *die* (*fachspr.*); Geburtshilfe, *die*

**obstinacy** /'ɒbstɪnəsɪ/ *n., no pl.* ⇒ **obstinate**: Starrsinn, *der;* Hartnäckigkeit, *die;* Sturheit, *die* (*ugs.*)

**obstinate** /'ɒbstɪnət/ *adj.* starrsinnig; (*adhering to particular course of action*) hartnäckig; stur (*ugs.*); **an ~ cold** eine hartnäckige Erkältung; **be as ~ as a mule** ein sturer Bock sein (*ugs. abwertend*)

**obstinately** /'ɒbstɪnətlɪ/ *adv.* ⇒ **obstinate**: starrsinnig; hartnäckig; stur (*ugs.*)

**obstreperous** /əb'strepərəs/ *adj.* **A** randalierend; **be/become ~:** randalieren/zu randalieren beginnen; **B** (*protesting*) widerspenstig; **stop being so ~!** mach nicht so ein Geschrei! (*ugs.*)

**obstruct** /əb'strʌkt/ *v.t.* **A** (*block*) versperren; blockieren; (*Med.*) verstopfen; behindern ‹Verkehr›; versperren ‹Sicht›; **~ sb.'s view** jmdm. die Sicht versperren; **B** (*fig.: impede; also Sport*) behindern; **C** (*Parl.*) obstruieren

**obstruction** /əb'strʌkʃn/ *n.* **A** *no pl.* (*blocking*) Blockierung, *die;* (*Med.*) Verstopfung, *die;* Obstruktion, *die* (*Med.*); (*of progress; also Sport*) Behinderung, *die;* (*to success*) Hindernis, *das* (**to** für); **B** (*Parl.*) Obstruktion, *die;* **C** (*obstacle*) Hindernis, *das;* Hemmnis, *das*

**obstructionism** /əb'strʌkʃənɪzm/ *n., no pl.* (*Polit.*) **[policy of] ~:** Obstruktionspolitik, *die*

**obstructionist** /əb'strʌkʃənɪst/ *n.* (*Polit.*) Obstruktionspolitiker, *der*/-politikerin, *die*

**obstructive** /əb'strʌktɪv/ *adj.* hinderlich; obstruktiv ‹Politik, Taktik›; **be ~** ‹Person:› sich quer legen (*ugs.*)

**obtain** /əb'teɪn/ ❶ *v.t.* bekommen ‹Ware, Information, Hilfe›; erreichen, erzielen ‹Resultat, Wirkung›; erwerben, erlangen ‹akademischen Grad›; **~ a divorce** geschieden werden. ❷ *v.i.* Geltung haben; ‹Ansicht, Brauch:› herrschen, verbreitet sein; ‹Regelung:› in Kraft sein

**obtainable** /əb'teɪnəbl/ *adj.* erhältlich ‹Ware, Eintrittskarte›; erzielbar ‹Wirkung›

**obtrude** /əb'tru:d/ ❶ *v.t.* **~ one's beliefs/opinions on sb.** jmdm. seine Überzeugung/Meinung aufdrängen; **~ oneself [up]on sb./into sth.** sich jmdm. aufdrängen/sich in etw. (*Akk.*) hineindrängen. ❷ *v.i.* sich aufdrängen (**upon** *Dat.*); **~ upon sb.'s grief** jmdn. in seinem Kummer stören

**obtrusive** /əb'tru:sɪv/ *adj.* aufdringlich; (*conspicuous*) auffällig

**obtrusively** /əb'tru:sɪvlɪ/ *adv.* in aufdringlicher Weise

**obtrusiveness** /əb'tru:sɪvnɪs/ *n., no pl.* Aufdringlichkeit, *die;* (*conspicuousness*) Auffälligkeit, *die*

**obtuse** /əb'tju:s/ *adj.* **A** (*blunt; also Geom.*) stumpf ‹Winkel, Messer›; **B** (*stupid*) einfältig; **he's being deliberately ~:** er stellt sich dumm

**obtusely** /əb'tju:slɪ/ *adv.* einfältig

**obverse** /'ɒbvɜ:s/ *n.* **A** (*of coin or medal*) Vorderseite, *die;* Avers, *der* (*Münzk.*); **B** (*front*) Schauseite, *die;* **C** (*fig.: counterpart*) Gegenstück, *das* (**of** zu)

**obviate** /'ɒbvɪeɪt/ *v.t.* begegnen (+ *Dat.*) ‹Gefahr, Risiko, Einwand›; **~ the necessity of sth.** etw. unnötig machen

**obvious** /'ɒbvɪəs/ *adj.* offenkundig; eindeutig ‹Sieger›; (*easily seen*) augenfällig; sichtlich ‹Empfindung, innerer Zustand›; plump ‹Trick, Mittel›; **she was the ~ choice** es lag nahe, dass die Wahl auf sie fiel; **the answer is ~:** die Antwort liegt auf der Hand; **the ~ thing to do is …:** das Naheliegende ist …; **it's not ~ what we should do next** es ist nicht ersichtlich, was wir als Nächstes tun sollten; **with the ~ exception of …:** natürlich mit Ausnahme von …; **be ~ [to sb.] that …:** [jmdm.] klar sein, dass …; **that's stating the ~:** das ist nichts Neues

**obviously** /'ɒbvɪəslɪ/ *adv.* offenkundig; sichtlich ‹enttäuschen, überraschen usw.›; **~, we can't expect any help** es ist klar, dass wir keine Hilfe erwarten können

**ocarina** /ɒkə'ri:nə/ *n.* (*Mus.*) Okarina, *die*

**Occam's razor** /ɒkəmz 'reɪzə(r)/ *n.* (*Philos.*) Ökonomieprinzip, *das;* Ockham's Razor, *der*

**occasion** /ə'keɪʒn/ ❶ *n.* **A** (*opportunity*) Gelegenheit, *die;* **rise to the ~:** sich der Situation gewachsen zeigen; **B** (*reason*) Grund, *der* (**for** zu); (*cause*) Anlass, *der;* **should the ~ arise** falls sich die Gelegenheit ergibt;

**there is no ~ for alarm** es besteht kein Grund zur Sorge; **be [an] ~ for celebration** ein Grund zum Feiern sein; **have ~ to do sth.** [eine] Gelegenheit haben, etw. zu tun; **I had ~ to be in Rome** ich hatte in Rom zu tun; **C** *(point in time)* Gelegenheit, *die;* **on several ~s** bei mehreren Gelegenheiten; **on that ~:** bei der Gelegenheit; damals; **[up]on ~[s]** gelegentlich; **D** *(special occurrence)* Anlass, *der;* **on state ~s** bei offiziellen Anlässen; **it was quite an ~:** es war ein Ereignis; **on the ~ of** anlässlich (+ *Gen.*). ❷ *v.t.* verursachen; erregen, Anlass geben zu ‹Besorgnis›; geben ‹Denkanstoß, Anregung›; **~ sb. to do sth.** jmdn. veranlassen, etw. zu tun

**occasional** /ə'keɪʒənl/ *adj.* **A** *(happening irregularly)* gelegentlich; vereinzelt ‹Regenschauer›; **take an** *or* **the ~ break** gelegentlich eine Pause machen; **B** *(specially written)* Gelegenheits‹musik, -dichtung›

**occasionally** /ə'keɪʒənəlɪ/ *adv.* gelegentlich; **[only] very ~:** gelegentlich einmal

**oc'casional table** *n.* Beistelltisch, *der*

**Occident** /'ɒksɪdənt/ *n. (poet./rhet.)* **the ~** *(the west, European civilization)* der Okzident; das Abendland

**occidental** /ɒksɪ'dentl/ ❶ *adj.* ⇒abendländisch; **AA** *(Polit.)* westlich. ❷ **O~** *n.* Abendländer, *der*/Abendländerin, *die*

**occlude** /ə'klu:d/ *v.t.* **A** *(Med.)* verschließen; **B** *(Chem.)* okkludieren ‹Gas›; **C** *(Meteorol.)* **~d front** Okklusion, *die*

**occlusion** /ə'klu:ʒn/ *n.* **A** *(Med.)* Okklusion, *die (fachspr.)*; Verschluss, *der;* **B** *(Chem., Meteorol., Dent.)* Okklusion, *die*

**occult** /ɒ'kʌlt, ə'kʌlt/ *adj.* **A** *(mystical)* okkult ‹Kunst, Wissenschaft›; **the ~:** das Okkulte; **B** *(mysterious)* unergründlich, dunkel ‹Rätsel, Geheimnis›; **C** *(secret)* verborgen

**occultism** /ɒ'kʌltɪzm, ə'kʌltɪzm/ *n.* Okkultismus, *der*

**occultist** /ɒ'kʌltɪst, ə'kʌltɪst/ *n.* Okkultist, *der*/Okkultistin, *die*

**occupancy** /'ɒkjʊpənsɪ/ *n. (residence in a place)* Bewohnung, *die; (moving into property)* Einzug, *der*

**occupant** /'ɒkjʊpənt/ *n.* **A** *(resident)* Bewohner, *der*/Bewohnerin, *die; (of post)* Inhaber, *der*/Inhaberin, *die; (of car, bus, etc.)* Insasse, *der*/Insassin, *die; (of room)* [Zimmer]bewohner, *der*/-bewohnerin, *die;* **B** *(Law)* Besitzer, *der*/Besitzerin, *die*

**occupation** /ɒkjʊ'peɪʃn/ *n.* **A** *(of property) (tenure)* Besitz, *der; (occupancy)* Bewohnung, *die;* **take over the ~ of** in Besitz nehmen; einziehen in (+ *Akk.*) ‹Haus, Wohnung, Zimmer›; **the owners of the house are [still]/the new tenants are already in ~:** die Hausbesitzer sind noch nicht ausgezogen/die neuen Mieter sind schon eingezogen; **B** *(Mil.)* Okkupation, *die;* Besetzung, *die; (period)* Besatzungszeit, *die;* **army of ~:** Besatzungsarmee, *die;* **C** *(activity)* Beschäftigung, *die; (pastime)* Zeitvertreib, *der;* **D** *(profession)* Beruf, *der;* **his ~ is civil engineering** er ist Bauingenieur [von Beruf]; **what's her ~?** was ist sie von Beruf?

**occupational** /ɒkjʊ'peɪʃənl/ *adj.* Berufs‹beratung, -risiko›; betrieblich ‹Altersversorgung›

**occupational: ~ di'sease** *n. (also joc.)* Berufskrankheit, *die;* **~ 'therapist** *n.* **▶ 1261** Beschäftigungstherapeut, *der*/-therapeutin, *die;* **~ 'therapy** *n.* Beschäftigungstherapie, *die*

**occupier** /'ɒkjʊpaɪə(r)/ *n. (Brit.)* Besitzer, *der*/Besitzerin, *die; (tenant)* Bewohner, *der*/Bewohnerin, *die*

**occupy** /'ɒkjʊpaɪ/ *v.t.* **A** *(Mil.; Polit. as demonstration)* besetzen; **the terrorists are ~ing the building** die Terroristen halten das Gebäude besetzt; **B** *(reside in, be a tenant of)* bewohnen; **~ a flat on a one-year lease** eine Wohnung für ein Jahr gemietet haben; **C** *(take up, fill)* einnehmen; liegen in (+ *Dat.*) ‹Bett›; besetzen ‹Sitzplatz, Tisch›; belegen ‹Zimmer›; in Anspruch nehmen ‹Zeit, Aufmerksamkeit›; **how did you ~ your time?** wie hast du die Zeit verbracht?; **the hotel occupies an attractive site** das Hotel ist schön gelegen; **~ a special place in sb.'s affections** einen besonderen Platz in jmds. Herzen haben; **D** *(hold)* innehaben ‹Stellung, Amt›; **E** *(busy, employ)* beschäftigen; **~ oneself [with doing sth.]** sich [mit etw.] beschäftigen; **be occupied with** *or* **in doing sth.** damit beschäftigt sein, etw. zu tun; **keep sb.['s mind] occupied** jmdn. [geistig] beschäftigen

**occur** /ə'kɜ:(r)/ *v.i.*, **-rr-** **A** *(be met with)* vorkommen; ‹Gelegenheit, Schwierigkeit, Problem:› sich ergeben; ‹Gelegenheit:› sich bieten; ‹Krankheit, Problem, Schwierigkeit:› auftreten; **if the case should ~ that ...:** sollte der Fall eintreten, dass ...; **B** *(happen)* ‹Veränderung:› eintreten; ‹Unfall, Vorfall, Zwischenfall:› sich ereignen; ‹Olympiade:› stattfinden; ‹Todesfall:› auftreten; **how did your injuries ~?** wie kam es zu deinen Verletzungen?; **this must not ~ again** das darf nicht wieder vorkommen; **C ~ to sb.** *(be thought of)* jmdm. einfallen *od.* in den Sinn kommen; ‹Idee:› jmdm. kommen; **it ~red to me that she was looking rather pale** mir fiel auf, dass sie ziemlich blass aussah; **it never ~red to me** auf den Gedanken *od.* darauf bin ich nie gekommen

**occurrence** /ə'kʌrəns/ *n.* **A** *(incident)* Ereignis, *das;* Begebenheit, *die;* **B** *(occurring)* Vorkommen, *das; (of disease)* Vorkommen, *das;* Auftreten, *das;* **be of frequent ~:** häufig vorkommen

**ocean** /'əʊʃn/ *n.* **A** Ozean, *der;* Meer, *das; attrib.* Meeres‹strömung, -boden›; **B** *in pl. (fig. coll.)* **~s of time** massenhaft Zeit *(ugs.)*; **he's got ~s of money** er hat Geld wie Heu *(ugs.)*; **weep ~s of tears** Ströme von Tränen vergießen

**'ocean-going** *adj.* Übersee‹handel, -dampfer, -schiff›

**Oceania** /əʊʃɪ'ɑ:nɪə, əʊsɪ'ɑ:nɪə/ *pr. n.* Ozeanien *(das)*

**oceanic** /əʊʃɪ'ænɪk, əʊsɪ'ænɪk/ *adj.* ozeanisch; Meeres‹tier, -klima, -tiefe, -strömung›; See‹vogel, -klima›; *(fig.)* gewaltig

**oceanography** /əʊʃə'nɒgrəfɪ/ *n.* Ozeanographie, *die;* Meereskunde, *die*

**ocelot** /'ɒsɪlɒt/ *n. (Zool.)* Ozelot, *der*

**och** /ɒx/ *int. (Scot., Ir.)* ach

**ochre** *(Amer.:* **ocher)** /'əʊkə(r)/ *n.* Ocker, *der od. das*

**ocker** /'ɒkə(r)/ *n. (Austral. coll.) ungehobelter, rüpelhafter Australier*

**o'clock** /ə'klɒk/ *adv.* **A ▶ 1012** **it is two/six ~:** es ist zwei/sechs Uhr; **at two/six ~:** um zwei/sechs Uhr; **six ~** *attrib.* Sechs-Uhr-‹Zug, Maschine, Nachrichten›; **B** *indicating direction or position* **see a plane at 3/6/9/12 ~:** ein Flugzeug rechts/genau unter sich *(Dat.)*/links/genau über sich *(Dat.)* sehen; *(horizontally)* ein Flugzeug rechts/genau hinter sich *(Dat.)*/links/genau vor sich *(Dat.)* sehen

**Oct.** *abbr.* **October** Okt.

**octagon** /'ɒktəgən/ *n. (Geom.)* Achteck, *das;* Oktogon, *das (fachspr.)*

**octagonal** /ɒk'tægənl/ *adj. (Geom.)* achteckig; oktogonal *(fachspr.)*

**octahedron** /ɒktə'hi:drən/ *n., pl.* **~s** *or* **octahedra** /ɒktə'hi:drə/ *(Geom.)* Oktaeder, *das (fachspr.)*; Achtflächner, *der*

**octane** /'ɒkteɪn/ *n.* Oktan, *das*

**octave** /'ɒktɪv/ *n. (Mus.)* Oktave, *die*

**octavo** /ɒk'tɑ:vəʊ/ *n., pl.* **~s** **A** *(book)* Oktavband, *der; (page)* Oktavseite, *die;* **B** *(size)* Oktav[format], *das*

**octet, octette** /ɒk'tet/ *n. (Mus.)* Oktett, *das;* **string ~** Streichoktett, *das*

**October** /ɒk'təʊbə(r)/ *n.* **▶ 1055** Oktober, *der;* **the ~ Revolution** *(Hist.)* die Oktoberrevolution; ⇒ *also* **August**

**octogenarian** /ɒktədʒɪ'neərɪən/ ❶ *adj.* achtzigjährig; *(more than 80 years old)* in den Achtzigern *nachgestellt.* ❷ *n.* Achtziger, *der*/Achtzigerin, *die*

**octopus** /'ɒktəpəs/ *n. (lit. or fig.)* Tintenfisch, *der;* Krake, *der;* Octopus, *der (Zool.)*

**ocular** /'ɒkjʊlə(r)/ *adj.* Augen‹maß, -krankheit, -täuschung›

**oculist** /'ɒkjʊlɪst/ *n.* **▶ 1261** Augenarzt, *der*/Augenärztin, *die*

**OD** *abbr. (esp. Amer. coll.)* ❶ **overdose 1.** ❷ **OD's, OD'd, ODing: overdose 3**

**odd** /ɒd/ *adj.* **A** *(surplus, spare)* übrig ‹Stück›; überzählig ‹Spieler›; restlich, übrig ‹Silbergeld›; **B** *(additional)* **£25 and a few ~ pence** 25 Pfund und ein paar Pence; **1,000 and ~ pounds** etwas über 1 000 Pfund; **C** *(occasional, random)* gelegentlich; **use the occasional ~ moment to do sth.** etw. tun, wenn sich die Gelegenheit ergibt; **I like the ~ whisky** gelegentlich trinke ich gern einen Whisky; **the ~ bit of translating** gelegentliche kleine Übersetzungen; **~ job/~-job man** Gelegenheitsarbeit, *die*/-arbeiter, *der;* **do ~ jobs** Gelegenheitsarbeiten verrichten; *(about the house)* anfallende Arbeiten erledigen; **D** *(one of pair or group)* einzeln; **~ socks/gloves** *etc.* nicht zusammengehörende Socken/Handschuhe *usw.;* **~ numbers/volumes** Einzelnummern/Einzelbände; **E** *(uneven)* ungerade ‹Zahl, Seite, Hausnummer›; **F** *(plus something)* **she must be forty ~:** sie muss etwas über vierzig sein; **sixty thousand ~:** etwas über sechzigtausend; **twelve pounds ~:** etwas mehr als zwölf Pfund; **G** *(extraordinary)* merkwürdig; *(strange, eccentric)* seltsam

**odd: ~ball, ~ 'fish** *ns. (coll.)* komischer Kauz *(ugs.)*

**oddity** /'ɒdɪtɪ/ *n.* **A** *(strangeness, peculiar trait)* Eigentümlichkeit, *die;* **B** *(odd person)* Sonderling, *der;* **C** *(fantastic object, strange event)* Kuriosität, *die*

**oddly** /'ɒdlɪ/ *adv.* seltsam; merkwürdig; **~ enough** seltsamer- *od.* merkwürdigerweise

**odd 'man** *n.* **be the ~:** die entscheidende Stimme haben; **~ out** Außenseiter, *der*/Außenseiterin, *die;* **be the ~ out** *(extra person)* überzählig sein; *(thing)* zu etw. nicht passen; **find the ~ out** das finden, was überzählig ist/nicht passt

**oddment** /'ɒdmənt/ *n.* **A** *(left over)* [Über]rest, *der; (in sales)* Reststück, *das;* **B** *in pl. (odds and ends)* Kleinigkeiten; **~s of furniture** einzelne Möbelstücke

**oddness** /'ɒdnɪs/ *n., no pl.* Merkwürdigkeit, *die; (strangeness)* Seltsamkeit, *die*

**odd: ~numbered** *adj.* ungerade; **~ one** ⇒ **odd man**

**odds** /ɒdz/ *n. pl.* **A** *(Betting)* Odds *pl.;* **the ~ were on Black Bess** Black Bess hatte die besten Chancen; **lay** *or* **give/take ~ of six to one in favour of/against sb./a horse** eine 6 : 1-Wette auf/gegen jmdn./ein Pferd anbieten/annehmen; **I'll lay ~ that ...** *(fig.)* ich wette, dass ...; **take ~ on sth.** auf etw. *(Akk.)* wetten; **over the ~** *(fig.)* zu viel; **pay over the ~ for sth.** einen überhöhten Preis für etw. bezahlen; **be/go over the ~** *(more than is reasonable)* zu weit gehen; ⇒ *also* **long odds; short odds; B** *(chances for or against)* Möglichkeit, *die; (chance for)* Aussicht, *die;* Chance, *die;* **[the] ~ are that she did it** wahrscheinlich hat sie es getan; **the ~ are against/in favour of sb./sth.** jmds. Aussichten *od.* Chancen/die Aussichten *od.* Chancen für etw. sind gering/gut; **the ~ are against/in favour of sth. happening** es besteht kaum/durchaus die Möglichkeit, dass etw. geschieht; **struggle against considerable/impossible ~:** mit ziemlich geringen Chancen/völlig chancenlos kämpfen; **by all ~:** bei weitem; **C** *(balance of advantage)* **against [all] the ~:** allen Widrigkeiten zum Trotz; **D** *(difference)* Unterschied, *der;* **make no/little ~ [whether ...]** es ist völlig/ziemlich gleichgültig[, ob ...]; **what's the ~?** was macht das schon?; **E** *(variance)* **be at ~ [with sb./sth.]** sich nicht [mit jmdm./etw.] vertragen; **be at ~ with sb. over sth.** mit jmdm. in etw. *(Dat.)* uneinig sein; **F ~ and ends,** *(coll.)* **~ and bobs** Kleinigkeiten; *(of food)* Reste; **~ and sods** *(coll.) (things)* Krempel, *der (ugs. abwertend)*; *(persons)* Figuren *(salopp)*

**'odds-on** ❶ *adj.* gut ‹Chance, Aussicht›; hoch, klar ‹Favorit›; **be ~ [favourite] to win/for sth.** klarer *od.* hoher Favorit/Favorit für etw. sein. ❷ *adv.* wahrscheinlich; **it's ~ that he is alive** die Chancen stehen gut, dass er am Leben ist

**ode** /əʊd/ *n.* Ode, *die* (**to** an + *Akk.*)

**odious** /ˈəʊdɪəs/ *adj.*, **odiously** /ˈəʊdɪəslɪ/ *adv.* widerwärtig

**odium** /ˈəʊdɪəm/ *n.* (*hatred*) Hass, *der;* **be held in ~ by sb.** bei jmdm. verhasst sein

**odometer** /əˈdɒmɪtə(r)/ *n.* Hodometer, *das;* Wegmesser, *der*

**odor** *etc.* (*Amer.*) ⇨ **odour** *etc.*

**odoriferous** /əʊdəˈrɪfərəs/ *adj.* wohlriechend (*geh.*); duftend

**odorous** /ˈəʊdərəs/ *adj.* A (*fragrant*) wohlriechend (*geh.*); duftend; B (*malodorous*) übel riechend; übel ‹Geruch›

**odour** /ˈəʊdə(r)/ *n.* A (*smell*) Geruch, *der;* (*fragrance*) Duft, *der;* **~ of cats** Katzengeruch, *der;* ⇨ *also* **body odour**; B (*fig.*) Note, *die;* **be in/fall** *or* **get into good/bad ~ with sb.** bei jmdm. in gutem/schlechtem Geruch stehen/in guten/schlechten Geruch kommen

**odourless** /ˈəʊdəlɪs/ *adj.* geruchlos

**Odysseus** /əˈdɪsjuːs/ *pr. n.* Odysseus (*der*)

**odyssey** /ˈɒdɪsɪ/ *n.* abenteuerliche Reise; Odyssee, *die* (*geh.*); **the O~** (*Myth.*) die Odyssee

**OECD** *abbr.* **Organization for Economic Cooperation and Development** OECD, *die*

**oedema** /ɪˈdiːmə/ *n.* (*Med.*) Ödem, *das;* Gewebewassersucht, *die*

**Oedipus complex** /ˈiːdɪpəs kɒmpleks/ *n.* (*Psych.*) Ödipuskomplex, *der*

**o'er** /ɔː(r)/ (*poet.*) ⇨ **over** 1, 2

**oesophagus** /iːˈsɒfəgəs/ *n.*, *pl.* **oesophagi** /iːˈsɒfədʒaɪ/ *or* **~es** (*Anat.*) Ösophagus, *der* (*fachspr.*)

**oestrogen** /ˈiːstrədʒən/ *n.* (*Biochem.*) Östrogen, *das*

**œuvre** /ɜːvr/ *n.* Œuvre, *das* (*geh.*); Werk, *das*

**of** /əv, *stressed* ɒv/ *prep.* A *indicating belonging, connection, possession* **articles of clothing** Kleidungsstücke; **be a thing of the past** der Vergangenheit (*Dat.*) angehören; **topic of conversation** Gesprächsthema, *das;* **the brother of her father** der Bruder ihres Vaters; **a friend of mine/the vicar's** ein Freund von mir/des Pfarrers; **that dog of yours** Ihr Hund da; **it's no business of theirs** es geht sie nichts an; **where's that pencil of mine?** wo ist mein Bleistift?; B *indicating starting point* von; **within a mile of the centre** nicht weiter als eine Meile vom Zentrum entfernt; **for upwards of 10 years** seit mehr als 10 Jahren; C *indicating origin, cause, agency* **have a taste of garlic** nach Knoblauch schmecken; **it was clever of you to do that** es war klug von dir, das zu tun; **the approval of sb.** jmds. Zustimmung; **be of a good family** aus guter Familie sein; **the works of Shakespeare** Shakespeares Werke; **R. T. Smith, of Oxford** R. T. Smith, Oxford; **Lord Morrison of Lambeth** Lord Morrison von Lambeth; D *indicating material, substance* aus; **a dress of cotton** ein Kleid aus Baumwolle; **be made of ...:** aus ... [hergestellt] sein; E *indicating closer definition, identity, or contents* **a pound of apples** ein Pfund Äpfel; **a glass of wine** ein Glas Wein; **a painting of the queen** ein Gemälde der Königin; **the city of Chicago** die Stadt Chicago; **the Republic of Ireland** die Republik Irland; **Professor of Chemistry** Professor der Chemie; **the Gospel of St Mark** das Markusevangelium; das Evangelium des Markus; **family of eight** achtköpfige Familie; **increase of 10%** Zuwachs/Erhöhung von zehn Prozent; **battle of Hastings** Schlacht von *od.* bei Hastings; **University of Oxford** Universität [von] Oxford; **President of the Philippines** Präsident[in] der Philippinen; **the Queen of Spades** die Pikdame; **the love of God** die Liebe Gottes; **the fifth of January** der fünfte Januar; **your letter of 2 January** Ihr Brief vom 2. Januar; **that fool of a personnel manager** dieser Idiot von Personalleiter; **a fool of a woman** eine törichte Frau; **the worst liar of any man I know** der gemeinste Lügner, den ich kenne; **be of value/interest to** von Nutzen/von Interesse *od.* interessant sein für; **the whole of ...:** der/die/das ganze ...; **tales of adventure** Abenteuergeschichten; F *indicating concern, reference, respect* **do not speak of such things** sprich nicht von solchen Dingen; **inform sb. of sth.** jmdn. über etw. (*Akk.*) informieren; **well, what of it?** (*asked as reply*) na und?; G *indicating objective relation* **love of virtue** Tugendliebe, *die;* **his love of his father** seine Liebe zu seinem Vater; H *indicating description, quality, condition* **a frown of disapproval** ein missbilligendes Stirnrunzeln; **person of extreme views** Mensch mit extremen Ansichten; **work of authority** maßgebendes Werk; **a boy of 14 years** ein vierzehnjähriger *od.* ein 14 Jahre alter Junge; **a city of wide boulevards** eine Stadt mit breiten Alleen; I *indicating partition, classification, inclusion, selection* von; **of these, three ...:** drei von ihnen ...; (*inanimate*) drei davon; **the five of us** wir fünf; **the five of us went there** wir sind zu fünft hingegangen; **some/five of us** einige/fünf von uns; **there are five of us waiting to see the doctor** wir sind fünf, die auf den Doktor warten; **the most dangerous of enemies** ein sehr gefährlicher Feind; **be too much of a gentleman to do sth.** zu sehr Gentleman sein, um etw. zu tun; **he of all men** (*most unsuitably*) ausgerechnet er; (*especially*) gerade er; **of all the impudence!** das ist doch die Höhe!; **here of all places** ausgerechnet hier; **on this night of nights** in solch einer herrlichen Nacht; **of an evening** (*coll.*) abends; des Abends; **of an evening in June** an einem Juniabend; J (*Amer.: before the hour of*) **a quarter of two** Viertel vor zwei; K (*arch.: by*) von; **beloved of all** von allen geliebt

**off** /ɒf/ 1 *adv.* A (*away, at or to a distance*) **be a few miles ~:** wenige Meilen entfernt sein; **the lake is not far ~:** der See ist nicht weit [weg *od.* entfernt]; **Christmas is not far ~:** es ist nicht mehr lang bis Weihnachten; **some way ~:** in einiger Entfernung; **where are you ~ to?** wohin gehst du?; **I must be ~:** ich muss fort *od.* weg *od.* los; **I'm ~ now** ich gehe jetzt; **~ with you!** geh/geht!; los jetzt!; **~ with his head!** schlagt ihm den Kopf ab!; **~ we go!** (*we are starting*) los *od.* ab gehts!; (*let us start*) gehen/fahren wir!; **they're ~!** sie sind gestartet!; ⇨ *also* **make off**; **put off**; **straight off**; B (*not on or attached or supported*) **get the lid ~:** den Deckel abbekommen; C (*not in good condition*) mitgenommen; **the meat** *etc.* **is ~:** das Fleisch *usw.* ist schlecht [geworden]; **be a bit ~** (*Brit. fig.*) ein starkes Stück sein (*ugs.*); D **be ~** (*switched or turned ~*) ‹Wasser, Gas, Strom:› abgestellt sein; **the light/radio** *etc.* **is ~:** das Licht/Radio *usw.* ist aus; **put the light ~:** das Licht ausmachen; **leave the bathroom tap ~:** den Hahn im Badezimmer zulassen; **is the gas tap ~?** ist der Gashahn zu?; **neither the water nor the electricity was ~:** weder Wasser noch Strom waren abgestellt; E **be ~** (*cancelled*) abgesagt sein; ‹Verlobung:› [auf]gelöst sein; **the strike is ~:** der Streik ist abgeblasen (*ugs.*); **is Sunday's picnic ~?** fällt das Picknick am Sonntag aus?; **~ and on** immer mal wieder (*ugs.*); F (*not at work*) frei; **on my day ~:** an meinem freien Tag; **take/get/have a week** *etc.* **~:** eine Woche *usw.* Urlaub nehmen/bekommen/haben; **be given a day ~ from school** einen Tag schulfrei haben; **be ~ sick** wegen Krankheit fehlen; G (*no longer available*) **soup** *etc.* **is ~:** es gibt keine Suppe *usw.* mehr; H (*entirely, to the end*) **drink ~:** austrinken; I (*situated as regards money etc.*) **he is badly** *etc.* **~:** er ist schlecht *usw.* gestellt; ihm geht es [finanziell] schlecht *usw.*; **we'd be better ~ without him** ohne ihn wären wir besser dran; **there are many people worse ~ than you** vielen geht es schlechter als dir; **he left her comfortably ~:** er hinterließ ihr genug, um gut zu leben; **how are you ~ for food?** wie viel Essbares hast du noch?; **be badly ~ for sth.** mit etw. knapp sein; ⇨ *also* **well off**; J (*Theatre*) **take place ~:** hinter der Bühne stattfinden; ⇨ *also* **noise** 1 B.
2 *prep.* A (*from*) von; **take a little ~ the price** ein bisschen vom Preis nachlassen; **cut a couple of slices ~ the loaf** einige Scheiben Brot abschneiden; **be a few inches ~ the finish** ein paar Zentimeter vom Ziel entfernt sein; **be ~ school/work** in der Schule/am Arbeitsplatz fehlen; B (*diverging from*) **get ~ the subject, talk ~ the point** [vom Thema] abschweifen; **be ~ the point** nicht zur Sache gehören; C (*designed not to cover*) **~-the-shoulder** schulterfrei ‹Kleid›; **an ~-the-face hat** ein Hut, der das Gesicht nicht verdeckt; D (*having lost interest in*) **be ~ sth.** etw. leid sein *od.* haben (*ugs.*); **be ~ one's food** keinen Appetit haben; **be quite ~ sth.** von etw. vollkommen abgekommen sein; E (*no longer obliged to use*) **be ~ drugs** vom Rauschgift losgekommen sein; clean sein (*ugs.*); **be ~ one's diet** seine Diät abgesetzt haben; **be ~ the tablets** ohne Tabletten auskommen; F (*leading from, not far from*) **just ~ the square** ganz in der Nähe des Platzes; **a street ~ the main road** eine Straße, die von der Hauptstraße abgeht; **take a turning ~ the main road** von der Hauptstraße abbiegen; G (*to seaward of*) vor (+ *Dat.*); H (*Golf*) **play ~ three** mit Vorgabe drei spielen. ⇨ *also* **offside**.
3 *adj.* A **the ~ side** (*Brit.*) (*when travelling on the left/right*) die rechte/linke Seite; B (*Cricket*) ‹Seite, Torstab:› links vom Werfer, (*if batsman is left-handed*) rechts vom Werfer; **~ drive** Treibschlag nach rechts; (*by left-handed batsman*) Treibschlag nach links; **~ side** ⇨ **4** A.
4 *n.* A (*Cricket*) *Spielfeldhälfte rechts vom rechtshändigen bzw. links vom linkshändigen Schlagmann;* B (*start of race*) Start, *der*

**offal** /ˈɒfl/ *n.*, *no pl.* A (*parts of animal's carcass*) Innereien *Pl.;* B (*carrion*) Aas, *das;* C (*refuse*) Abfall, *der;* D (*fig.: dregs, scum*) Abschaum, *der*

**off: ~beat** 1 *n.* (*Mus.*) unbetonter Taktteil; Off-Beat, *der* (*fachspr.*); 2 *adj.* A (*Mus.*) Off-Beat-; B (*fig.: eccentric*) unkonventionell ‹Mensch, Lebensweise›; außergewöhnlich ‹Vorlesung, Kursus›; **~-'centre** 1 *adj.* nicht zentriert; 2 *adv.* nicht [genau] in der Mitte; **~ chance** ⇨ **chance** 1 C; **~ 'colour** *adj.* A (*not in good health*) unwohl; **be** *or* **feel ~ colour** sich unwohl *od.* schlecht fühlen; B (*Amer.: somewhat indecent*) schlüpfrig; **~cut** *n.* Rest, *der;* **~ day** *n.* schlechter Tag; **~-duty** *attrib. adj.* Freizeit-; dienstfrei ‹Zeit›; ‹Polizist usw.,› der dienstfrei hat

**offence** /əˈfens/ *n.* (*Brit.*) A (*hurting of sb.'s feelings*) Kränkung, *die;* **I meant** *or* **intended no ~:** ich wollte Sie/ihn *usw.* nicht kränken; **your behaviour caused [great] ~:** Ihr Benehmen war [sehr] kränkend *od.* verletzend; B (*annoyance*) **give ~:** Missfallen erregen; **take ~:** beleidigt *od.* verärgert sein; **don't take ~, but ...:** nimm es mir nicht übel, aber ...; **no ~** (*coll.*) nichts für ungut; **no ~ to you, but ...** (*coll.*) nichts gegen dich, aber ... (*ugs.*); C (*transgression*) Verstoß, *der;* (*crime*) Delikt, *das;* Straftat, *die;* **an ~ against good taste** eine Beleidigung des guten Geschmacks; **criminal/petty ~:** strafbare Handlung/geringfügiges Vergehen; D (*attacking*) Angriff, *der*

**offend** /əˈfend/ 1 *v.i.* verstoßen (**against** gegen). 2 *v.t.* **~ sb.** bei jmdm. Anstoß erregen; (*hurt feelings of*) jmdn. kränken; **she was ~ed with him** sie war ihm böse; **~ the eye** das Auge beleidigen; **her delicacy was ~ed** ihr Zartgefühl war verletzt; *abs.* **a refusal often ~s** eine Ablehnung wird oft als Kränkung empfunden

**offender** /əˈfendə(r)/ *n.* (*against law*) Straffällige, *der/die;* Täter, *der*/Täterin, *die;* (*against rule*) Zuwiderhandelnde, *der/die;* ⇨ *also* **first offender**

**offending** /əˈfendɪŋ/ *attrib. adj.* A (*that outrages*) anstößig; Anstoß erregend; **he removed the ~ object** er beseitigte den Stein des Anstoßes; B (*that transgresses*) zuwiderhandelnd; **there are penalties for ~ persons** Zuwiderhandlungen werden bestraft

**offense** (*Amer.*) ⇒ **offence**

**offensive** /əˈfensɪv/ ❶ *adj.* **A** (*aggressive*) offensiv; Angriffs‹waffe, -krieg›; **B** (*giving offence, insulting*) ungehörig; (*indecent*) anstößig; **~ language** Beschimpfungen *Pl.*; **C** (*repulsive*) widerlich; **be ~ to sb.** jmdm. zuwider sein; auf jmdn. abstoßend wirken. ❷ *n.* **A** (*attitude of assailant*) offensive Haltung; **take the** *or* **go on the ~:** in die *od.* zur Offensive übergehen; **be on the ~:** aggressiv sein; **B** (*attack*) Offensive, *die;* Angriff, *der;* **C** (*fig.: forceful action*) Offensive, *die*

**offensively** /əˈfensɪvlɪ/ *adv.* **A** (*aggressively*) offensiv; **B** (*insultingly*) auf beleidigende Weise; (*indecently*) unverschämt; **C** (*repulsively*) widerlich; abstoßend

**offer** /ˈɒfə(r)/ ❶ *v.t.* **A** anbieten; vorbringen ‹Entschuldigung›; bieten ‹Chance›; aussprechen ‹Beileid›; sagen ‹Meinung›; unterbreiten, machen ‹Vorschläge›; bieten, spenden ‹Schatten›; **have something to ~:** etwas zu bieten haben; **the job ~s good prospects** der Arbeitsplatz hat Zukunft; **B** (*present to deity etc.*) **~ [up]** opfern; **~ up a sacrifice** ein Opfer darbringen (*geh.*); **~ prayers for the dead** für die Toten beten; **C** (*have for sale*) anbieten; **D** (*show readiness for*) **~ resistance** Widerstand leisten; **~ violence** gewalttätig werden; **~ peace** für den Frieden eintreten; **~ to do sth.** anbieten, etw. zu tun; **~ to help** seine Hilfe anbieten; **E** (*present to sight or notice*) bieten
❷ *v.i.* ‹Gelegenheit, Chance:› sich bieten.
❸ *n.* **A** Angebot, *das;* (*in auction*) Gebot, *das;* **all ~s of help** alle Hilfeangebote; **[have/be] on ~:** im Angebot [haben/sein]; **B** (*marriage proposal*) Antrag, *der*

**offering** /ˈɒfərɪŋ/ *n.* **A** *no pl.* (*act*) Anbieten, *das;* (*to deity*) Opfern, *das;* **B** (*thing*) Angebot, *das;* (*to a deity*) Opfer, *das;* **the latest ~ from the publishers** (*joc.*) was die Verleger als Neuestes anbieten

**offertory** /ˈɒfətərɪ/ *n.* (*Eccl.*) **A** (*part of Mass*) Offertorium, *das;* **B** (*collection of money*) Kollekte, *die*

**off: ~ˈhand** ❶ *adv.* **A** (*without preparation*) auf Anhieb, aus der Hand (*ugs.*) ‹sagen, wissen›; spontan ‹beschließen, entscheiden›; **B** (*casually*) leichthin; ❷ *adj.* **A** (*without preparation*) impulsiv; spontan; **B** (*casual*) beiläufig; **be ~hand with sb.** zu jmdm. kurz angebunden sein; **he was very ~hand about the whole business** er war, was die ganze Geschichte betrifft, sehr kurz angebunden; **~handed** /ɒfˈhændɪd/ ⇒ **~hand** 2 B

**office** /ˈɒfɪs/ *n.* **A** Büro, *das;* **goods ~:** Güterabfertigung, *die;* **B** (*branch of organization*) Zweigstelle, *die;* Geschäftsstelle, *die;* **C** (*position with duties*) Amt, *das;* **be in/out of ~:** im/nicht mehr im Amt sein; ‹Partei:› an der/nicht mehr an der Regierung sein; **resign ~:** sein Amt niederlegen; **hold ~:** amtieren; **D** (*government department*) **Home O~** (*Brit.*) ≈ Innenministerium, *das;* **the Passport O~:** das Passamt; **E** **the usual ~s** (*Brit.: of house*) ≈ Küche, Bad, WC *usw.*; **F** (*Eccl.*) (*service*) Gottesdienst, *der;* (*mass*) Messe, *die* (*kath. Kirche*); **O~ for Baptism** Taufbekenntnis *od.* -versprechen, *das;* **O~ for the Dead** Trauergottesdienst, *der;* Totenmesse, *die* (*kath. Kirche*); **G** **the Holy O~** (*RC Ch.*) das Heilige Officium; **H** (*kindness*) **[good]** **~s** Hilfe, *die;* Unterstützung, *die;* **use one's good ~s to help sb.** jmdm. mit Rat und Tat zur Seite stehen; **I** (*Amer.: consulting-room*) Büro, *das;* (*of lawyer*) Kanzlei, *die;* Büro, *das;* (*of physician*) Sprechzimmer, *das*

**office: ~-bearer** *n.* Amtsinhaber, *der*/-inhaberin, *die;* **~ block** *n.* Bürogebäude, *das;* **~ boy** *n.* Bürogehilfe, *der;* **~ girl** *n.* Bürogehilfin, *die;* **~ hours** *n. pl.* Dienststunden *Pl.*; Dienstzeit, *die;* **after ~ hours** nach Dienstschluss; **~ job** *n.* Bürotätigkeit, *die;* Bürojob, *der* (*ugs.*); **~ ˈjunior** *n.* Bürogehilfe, *der*/-gehilfin, *die*

**officer** /ˈɒfɪsə(r)/ *n.* **A** (*Army etc.*) Offizier, *der;* **~ of the day** Offizier vom Dienst; **B** (*holder of office*) Beamte, *der*/Beamtin, *die;* **~ of arms** (*Her.*) Mitglied des Heroldskollegiums; **C** (*of club etc.*) Funktionär, *der*/Funktionärin, *die;* **D** ▶ **1617** (*constable*) Polizeibeamte, *der*/-beamtin, *die;* **yes, ~:** jawohl, Herr Wachtmeister/Frau Wachtmeisterin; **E** ▶ **1261** (*bailiff*) **[sheriff's] ~:** Vollstreckungsbeamte, *der*/-beamtin, *die;* **F** (*member of honorary Order*) **O~ of the Order of the British Empire** Träger des britischen Verdienstordens; **O~ of the Legion of Honour** Ritter der Ehrenlegion

**office: ~ technology** *n.* Bürotechnik, *die;* **~ worker** *n.* ▶ **1261** Büroangestellte, *der*/*die*

**official** /əˈfɪʃl/ ❶ *adj.* **A** Amts‹pflicht, -robe, -person›; **B** (*derived from authority, formal*) offiziell; amtlich ‹Verlautbarung›; regulär ‹Streik›; **he is here on ~ business** er ist dienstlich hier; **~ secret** Staatsgeheimnis, *das;* **O~ Secrets Act** (*Brit.*) Gesetz über Landesverrat und Gefährdung der äußeren Sicherheit; **is it ~ yet?** (*coll.*) ist das schon amtlich? ❷ *n.* Beamte, *der*/Beamtin, *die;* (*party, union, or sports ~*) Funktionär, *der*/Funktionärin, *die*

**officialdom** /əˈfɪʃldəm/ *n.*, *no pl.*, *no art.* Beamtentum, *das;* Bürokratie, *die*

**officialese** /əfɪʃəˈliːz/ *n.*, *no pl.* (*derog.*) Behördensprache, *die;* (*German*) Amtsdeutsch, *das*

**officially** /əˈfɪʃəlɪ/ *adv.* offiziell

**officiate** /əˈfɪʃɪeɪt/ *v.i.* **A** **~ as ...:** fungieren als ...; **she ~d as hostess** sie übernahm die Rolle der Gastgeberin; **B** (*perform religious ceremony*) **~ at the service** den Gottesdienst abhalten; **~ at a wedding** eine Trauung vornehmen

**officious** /əˈfɪʃəs/ *adj.*, **officiously** /əˈfɪʃəslɪ/ *adv.* übereifrig

**officiousness** /əˈfɪʃəsnɪs/ *n.*, *no pl.* Übereifer, *der*

**offing** /ˈɒfɪŋ/ *n.* **be in the ~** (*fig.*) bevorstehen; ‹Gewitter:› aufziehen

**off: ~-ˈkey** ❶ *adj.* verstimmt; (*fig.: incongruous*) falsch; ❷ *adv.* falsch ‹singen, spielen›; **~-licence** *n.* (*Brit.*) **A** (*premises*) ≈ Wein- und Spirituosenladen, *der;* **B** (*licence*) Konzession für den Verkauf alkoholischer Getränke über die Straße; **~-line** (*Computing*) ❶ /ˈ--/ *adj.* Offline‹gerät, -betrieb›; ❷ /-ˈ-/ *adv.* offline; **~load** *v.t.* abladen; **~load sth. on to sb.** (*fig.: get rid of*) etw. bei jmdm. loswerden; **~-peak** *attrib. adj.* **during ~-peak hours** außerhalb der Spitzenlastzeiten; (*of traffic*) außerhalb der Stoßzeiten; **at ~-peak times** (*Telev.*) außerhalb der Haupteinschaltzeit; **~-peak power** *or* **electricity** Nachtstrom, *der;* **~-peak storage heating** Nachtspeicherheizung, *die;* **~print** *n.* Sonderdruck, *der;* **~-putting** /ˈɒfpʊtɪŋ/ *adj.* (*Brit.*) abstoßend ‹Gesicht, Äußeres, Weg›; abschreckend ‹Umfang›; deprimierend ‹Anblick›; **~-ramp** *n.* (*Amer.*) Abfahrt, *die;* **~-road** *attrib. adj.* Gelände-, Offroad‹fahrzeug, -fahrrad, -wagen, -fahrt, -einsatz›; **~-road driving** Fahren im Gelände; **~ season** *n.* Nebensaison, *die;* **~set** ❶ *n.* **A** (*compensation*) Ausgleich, *der;* **act as an ~set to sth., be an ~set for sth.** etw. ausgleichen *od.* aufwiegen; **B** (*Printing: unwanted transfer of ink*) Schmutzen, *das;* Abliegen, *das;* **C** **~set [process]** (*Printing*) Offsetdruck, *der;* **D** (*Archit.*) Vorsprung, *der;* ❷ /ˈ--, -ˈ-/ *v.t.*, *forms as* **set** **A** (*counterbalance*) ausgleichen; **B** (*place out of line*) versetzen; **C** (*Printing*) im Offsetverfahren drucken; **~shoot** *n.* **A** (*of plant*) Spross, *der;* (*of mountain range*) Ausläufer, *der;* **B** (*fig.: descendant*) Spross, *der* (*geh.*); Nachkomme, *der;* **C** (*derivative*) Ableger, *der* (*fig.*); (*of religion, philosophy, etc.*) Nebenströmung, *die;* **~shore** *adj.* **A** (*situated at sea*) küstennah; offshore (*Energiewirtsch.*); **~shore island** küstennahe Insel; **B** (*made or registered abroad*) Auslands-; **~shore order** Offshoreauftrag, *der;* **C** (*blowing seawards*) ablandig (*Seemannsspr.*); **~ˈside** *adj.* (*Sport*) Abseits-; **be ~side** abseits *od.* im Abseits sein; **~side trap** Abseitsfalle, *die;* **~spring** *n.*, *pl. same* (*progeny*) (*human*) Nachkommenschaft, *die;* (*of animal*) Junge; **~-ˈstage** ❶ *adj.* in den Kulissen *nachgestellt;* ❷ *adv.* in den Kulissen; **go ~-stage** abgehen; **~-street** *adj.* außerhalb des Straßenbereiches *nachgestellt;* **~-street parking** Stellplatz, *der;* (*for several cars*) Stellplätze; **~-the-peg** *attrib. adj.* Konfektions-; von der Stange *nachgestellt;* **~-the-shoulder** *attrib. adj.* schulterfrei ‹Kleid, T-Shirt›; **~-the-wall** *attrib. adj.* (*esp. Amer. coll.*) ausgeflippt (*ugs.*); **~ time** *n.* ruhige Zeit; **~-ˈwhite** *adj.* gebrochen weiß; (*yellowish*) vergilbt; **~ year** *n.* (*Amer.*) Wahljahr, in dem kein Präsident gewählt wird

**oft** /ɒft/ *adv.* (*arch./literary*) oft; **the ~-told tales** die immer wieder erzählten Geschichten; **~-repeated/-recurring** häufig wiederholt/wiederkehrend; **many a time and ~:** oft genug

**often** /ˈɒfn, ˈɒftn/ *adv.* oft; **more ~:** häufiger; **do sth. as ~ as not** etw. genauso oft tun wie man es nicht tut; **more ~ than not** meistens; **every so ~:** gelegentlich; hin und wieder; **once too ~:** einmal zu viel

**ogee** /ˈəʊdʒiː, əʊˈdʒiː/ ❶ *n.* Karnies, *das* (*Archit.*); (*line*) S-Kurve, *die.* ❷ *adj.* S-förmig; **~ arch** (*Archit.*) Eselsrücken, *der*

**ogle** /ˈəʊgl/ ❶ *v.i.* gaffen (*ugs. abwertend*); **~ at sb.** jmdn. angaffen (*ugs. abwertend*). ❷ *v.t.* **~ sb.** jmdn. angaffen (*ugs. abwertend*)

**ogre** /ˈəʊgə(r)/ *n.* **A** (*giant*) Oger, *der;* [menschenfressender] Riese; **B** (*terrifying person*) Ungeheuer, *das;* (*terrifying thing*) Schreckbild, *das*

**oh**[1] /əʊ/ *int.* oh; *expr. pain* au; **ˈoh no [you don't]!** auf keinen Fall!; **oh ˈno!** oh nein!; oje!; **oh ˈwell** na ja (*ugs.*); tja (*ugs.*); **ˈoh yes** oh ja; **oh ˈyes?** ach ja?; **oh, ˈhim/ˈthat!** ach, der/das!; ⇒ *also* **boy** 2

**oh**[2] *n.* (*zero*) Null, *die*

**ohm** /əʊm/ *n.* (*Electr.*) Ohm, *das;* **Ohm's law** das ohmsche Gesetz

**OHMS** *abbr.* **on Her/His Majesty's service** ⇒ **service** 1 M

**oho** /əʊˈhəʊ/ *int.* he

**ˈoh-so-** *pref.* (*coll. derog.*) ach so ‹schlau, schick›

**oil** /ɔɪl/ ❶ *n.* **A** Öl, *das;* **burn the midnight ~** (*fig.*) bis spät in die Nacht arbeiten; **strike ~** (*lit.*) auf Öl stoßen; (*fig.*) das große Los ziehen; ⇒ *also* **mineral oil**; **pour** 1 A; **B** *in pl.* (*paints*) Ölfarben; **paint in ~s** in Öl malen; **C** (*coll.: picture*) Ölbild, *das.* ❷ *v.t.* **A** (*apply ~ to*) ölen; **~ the wheels** (*fig.*) den Karren schmieren; **B** (*supply with ~*) [mit Öl] betanken ‹Schiff usw.›; **C** (*impregnate with ~*) mit Öl behandeln; **~ed silk** Ölseide, *die;* **D** **well ~ed** (*fig. coll.: drunk*) abgefüllt

**oil: ~-burner** *n.* **A** (*steamship/locomotive*) Dampfschiff/Lokomotive mit Ölfeuerung; **B** (*device*) Ölbrenner, *der;* **~-burning** *adj.* ölbetrieben; ölgeheizt ‹Ofen›; ölgefeuert ‹Lokomotive, Schiff›; Ölfeuerungs‹anlage, -kessel›; Öl‹ofen, -heizung, -lampe›; **~cake** *n.*, *no pl.* (*Agric.*) Ölkuchen, *der;* **~can** *n.* Ölkanne, *die;* **~ change** *n.* (*Motor Veh.*) Ölwechsel, *der;* **~cloth** *n.* **A** *no pl.* (*waterproofed fabric*) Öltuch, *das;* **B** (*covering for tables or shelves*) Wachstuch, *das;* Öltuch, *das;* (*covering for floor*) ≈ Linoleum, *das;* **~ colour** *n.*, *usu. in pl.* Ölfarbe, *die;* **[painted] in ~ colours** in Öl [gemalt]; **~ drum** *n.* Ölfass, *das;* **~field** *n.* Ölfeld, *das;* **~-fired** *adj.* ölgefeuert; ölbetrieben ‹Zentralheizung›; **~ gauge** *n.* (*Mech. Engin.*) Ölstandsanzeiger, *der;* **~ heater** *n.* Ölofen, *der;* **~ industry** *n.* Mineralölindustrie, *die;* **~ lamp** *n.* Öllampe, *die;* Petroleumlampe, *die;* **~ level** *n.* Ölstand, *der;* **~man** *n.* **A** (*seller of ~*) Ölhändler, *der*/-händlerin, *die;* **B** (*industrialist*) Unternehmer in der Ölbranche; (*worker*) Ölarbeiter, *der;* **~ paint** ⇒ **~ colour**; **~ painting** *n.* **A** (*activity*) Ölmalerei, *die;* **B** (*picture*) Ölgemälde, *das;* **he/she is no ~ painting** (*coll.*) er/sie ist keine [strahlende] Schönheit; **~-producing** *attrib. adj.* Öl‹pflanze, -saat, -schiefer, -sand, -schicht›; [Erd]öl fördernd ‹Land›; **~ rag** *n.* Öllappen, *der;* **~ refinery** *n.* [Erd]ölraffinerie, *die;* **~-rich** *adj.* ‹Land, Gebiet› mit großem [Erd]ölvorkommen; ölhaltig ‹Schiefer, Sand usw.›; **~ rig** ⇒ **rig**[1] 1 B; **~ shale** *n.* (*Geol.*) Ölschiefer, *der;* **~skin** *n.* **A** (*material*) Öltuch, *das;* *attrib.* aus Öltuch *nachgestellt;*

~**skin jacket** Öljacke, *die;* **B** (*garment*) **put on ~skins/an ~skin** Ölzeug anziehen; **~ slick** ⇒ **slick** 2; **~-soluble** *adj.* öllöslich; **~ stove** *n.* Ölofen, *der;* **~ tanker** *n.* Öltanker, *der;* **~ well** *n.* Ölquelle, *die*

**oily** /'ɔɪlɪ/ *adj.* **A** ölig ‹Oberfläche, Hände, Lappen, Flüssigkeit, Geschmack›; Öl‹lache, -fleck›; ölverschmiert ‹Gesicht, Hände›; verölt ‹Motor›; (*containing oil*) viel Öl enthaltend ‹Soße›; fettig ‹Haut, Haar›; **the food is very ~:** das Essen schwimmt in Öl (*ugs.*); **B** (*fig.: unctuous, fawning*) schmierig (*abwertend*) ‹Kerl, Art›; ölig ‹Lächeln, Stimme›

**ointment** /'ɔɪntmənt/ *n.* Salbe, *die;* ⇒ *also* **fly**[1] A

**OK** /əʊ'keɪ/ (*coll.*) **1** *adj.* in Ordnung; okay (*ugs.*); **[it's] OK by me** mir ist es recht. **2** *adv.* gut; **be doing OK** seine Sache gut machen. **3** *int.* okay (*ugs.*); **OK?** [ist das] klar?; okay?. **4** *n.* Zustimmung, *die;* Okay, *das* (*ugs.*). **5** *v.t.* (*approve*) zustimmen (+ *Dat.*); sein Okay geben (+ *Dat.*) (*ugs.*); **be OK'd by sb.** von jmdm. das Okay bekommen (*ugs.*)

**okay** /əʊ'keɪ/ ⇒ **OK**

**okey-doke** /əʊkɪ'dəʊk/ (*coll.*), **okey-dokey** /əʊkɪ'dəʊkɪ/ (*coll.*) ⇒ **OK** 3

**old** /əʊld/ **1** *adj.* **A** ▶ 912 alt; **[not] be ~ enough to do sth.** [noch nicht] alt genug sein, um etw. zu tun; **he is ~ enough to know better** aus diesem Alter ist er heraus; **he/she is ~ enough to be your father/mother** er/sie könnte dein Vater/deine Mutter sein; **be/get too ~ for doing sth.** *or* **to do sth.** zu alt sein/langsam zu alt sein, um etw. zu tun; **be ~ beyond one's years** seinem Alter voraus sein; **if I live to be that ~:** wenn ich je so alt werde; **grow ~ [gracefully]** [mit Würde] alt werden; **that dress/that new hairstyle makes you look ~:** dieses Kleid/diese neue Frisur macht dich alt; **make/get/be/seem ~ before one's time** frühzeitig altern lassen/altern/gealtert sein/gealtert wirken; **be [more than] 30 years ~:** [über] 30 Jahre alt sein; **at ten years ~:** im Alter von 10 Jahren; mit 10 Jahren; ⇒ *also* **buffer**[2]; **fogy; fool**[1] 1 A; **shoulder** 1 B; **B** (*experienced*) **be an ~ hand** *or* (*Brit.*) **stager** ein alter Hase sein (*ugs.*); **an ~ offender** ein mehrfach Vorbestrafter; ⇒ *also* **campaigner** B; **contemptible; lag**[2]; **retainer** A; **salt** 1 D; **C** (*long in use, matured with keeping, long familiar*) alt; **~ iron** Alteisen, *das;* **be still working for one's** *or* **the same ~ firm** noch immer in seiner alten *od.* derselben Firma arbeiten; **you see the same ~ people/faces wherever you go** man sieht immer dieselben Leute/Gesichter, wohin man auch geht; **keep quarrelling over the same ~ thing** immer wieder über dasselbe leidige Thema streiten; **O~ Pals Act** (*Brit. joc.*) ≈ Vitamin B (*ugs. scherzh.*); **the ~ firm** (*fig. coll.*) das altbewährte Team; **of the ~ school** (*fig.*) der alten Schule; **that's an '~ one!** (*joke*) der ist [doch] alt!; (*excuse*) das kennen wir schon!; **[as] ~ as the hills** uralt; **that joke is [as] ~ as the hills** dieser Witz hat so einen Bart (*ugs.*); **be as ~ as time** seit Urzeiten bestehen; ⇒ *also* **brigade** A; **score** 1 F; **story**[1] A; **world** D; **D** *in playful or friendly mention* alt (*ugs.*); **you lucky ~ so-and-so!** du bist vielleicht ein alter Glückspilz!; **I saw ~ George today** ich habe heute unsern Freund George getroffen; **I pulled out the ~ cigarette lighter** ich holte mein Feuerzeug raus; **~ chap/fellow/son** alter Junge (*fam.*); **~ bean/stick/thing** (*coll.*) altes Haus (*ugs. scherzh.*); **[such] a dear ~ thing** [so] ein lieber Mensch; **O~ Bill** (*Brit. coll.*) (*police force*) die Polente (*salopp*); (*policeman*) Polyp, *der* (*salopp*); **O~ Harry** *or* **Nick** der Teufel; der Leibhaftige (*verhüll.*); **good/dear ~ Harry/London** (*coll.*) der gute alte Harry/das gute alte London; **that car needs a good ~ clean** *or* **wash** (*coll.*) das Auto muss einmal ordentlich gewaschen werden; **have a fine** *or* **good ~ time** (*coll.*) sich köstlich amüsieren; **a fair ~ wind** (*coll.*) ein ganz schöner Wind; **poor ~ Jim/my poor ~ arm** armer Jim/mein armer Arm (*ugs.*); **there was little ~ me, not knowing what to do** (*Amer.*) da war ich nun und wusste nicht, was ich tun sollte; **your silly** *or* **stupid ~ camera** deine blöde (*ugs.*) Kamera; **you silly ~ thing** du dummer Kerl/(*woman*) dummes Ding (*ugs.*); **a load of ~ rubbish** (*coll.*) nichts als blanker Unsinn; **any ~ thing** (*coll.*) irgendwas (*ugs.*); irgendetwas; **any ~ how** (*coll.*) irgendwie; **he just pulls his hat on any ~ how** er setzt sich den Hut auf, wies grad kommt (*ugs.*); **any ~ place** *or* **where** (*coll.*) irgendwo; **any ~ place will do for me** mir ist alles *od.* jeder Ort recht; **any ~ time** (*coll.*) jederzeit; **any ~ piece of paper** (*coll.*) irgendein Blatt Papier; ⇒ *also* **high** 1 N; **E** (*belonging to past times*) alt; **in the ~ days** früher; ⇒ *also* **bad** 1 A; **good** 1 D, H; **F** (*former*) alt ‹Wohnung, Firma, Arbeit, Name›; **at 'my ~ school** in meiner Schule; **~ school tie** *Krawatte mit den Farben der Public School;* (*fig.*) *Begünstigung von Absolventen der Public Schools;* ≈ Vitamin B (*ugs. scherzh.*); **the ~ year** das alte Jahr; ⇒ *also* **flame** 1 C; **G** (*Ling.*) alt‹englisch, -lateinisch›. **2** *n.* **A** **the ~** *constr. as pl.* (*old people*) alte Menschen; *constr. as sing.* (*old things*) Altes; das Alte; **young and ~, ~ and young** Jung und Alt; Alt und Jung; **B** **the customs/knights of ~:** die Sitten/Ritter früherer Zeiten; die alten Sitten/Ritter; **in [the] days of ~:** in [den] alten Zeiten; **of ~** (*formerly*) einst; (*since the old days*) seit jeher; **I know him of ~:** ich kenne ihn von früher; **as of ~:** wie eh und je; wie seit jeher; **from of ~:** von alters her (*geh.*)

**old:** **~ 'age** *n., no pl.* [fortgeschrittenes] Alter; **it must be the effect of ~ age** das muss das Alter bewirken; **die of ~ age** an Altersschwäche sterben; **in ~ age** im [fortgeschrittenen] Alter; **in my** *etc.* **~ age** auf meine *usw.* alten Tage; **you've become quite sensible in your ~ age** (*joc.*) du bist ja doch noch ein ganz vernünftiger Mensch geworden; **live to a ripe ~ age/to the ripe ~ age of ...** (*coll.*) ein hohes Alter/das hohe Alter von ... erreichen; **~-age** *attrib. adj.* Alters‹rente, -ruhegeld, -versicherung›; **~-age pensioner** Rentner, *der*/Rentnerin, *die;* **Old 'Bailey** ⇒ **bailey**; **~ boy** *n.* **A** ehemaliger Schüler; Ehemalige, *der;* **old boys' reunion** Ehemaligentreffen, *das;* **B** (*coll.: elderly man or male animal*) alter Knabe (*ugs.*); **C** *as voc.* alter Junge *od.* Knabe (*ugs.*); Alter (*ugs.*); **~ boy network** *n. Filzokratie* (*ugs.*) *der Absolventen britischer Eliteschulen und -universitäten;* **~ 'clothes** *n. pl.* (*worn, shabby clothes*) alte Kleidung *od.* (*ugs.*) Klamotten; (*discarded clothes*) getragene Kleidung *od.* Kleider; Altkleider *Pl.;* **~ 'country** *n.* **the ~ country** das Heimatland; die Heimat; **~ 'dear** *n.* (*woman*) ältere Frau; (*iron.*) Alte, *die* (*ugs.*)

**olden** /'əʊldn/ *adj.* (*literary*) alt; **in [the] ~ days** *or* **times** in alten Zeiten; **people** *etc.* **of ~ times** Menschen *usw.* früherer Zeiten

**Old 'English** **1** *n.* (*Ling.*) ⇒ **English** 2 A. **2** *adj.* altenglisch; **~ marmalade** englische Marmelade nach altem Rezept; ⇒ *also* **sheepdog**

**old-es'tablished** *adj.* alt ‹Tradition, Brauch›; alteingesessen ‹Firma, Geschäft, Familie›

**olde-worlde** /əʊldɪ'wɜ:ldɪ/ *adj.* (*coll. joc.*) altertümlich

**old:** **~-fashioned** /əʊld'fæʃnd/ **1** *adj.* altmodisch; ‹Weihnachtsfest› nach altem Brauch; **an ~-fashioned look** ein missbilligender Blick; **2** *n.* (*Amer.*) Old Fashioned, *der;* **~ 'folk's home** ⇒ **old people's home**; **Old 'French** (*Ling.*) **1** *n.* Altfranzösisch, *das;* **2** *adj.* altfranzösisch; **~ 'girl** *n.* **A** ehemalige Schülerin; Ehemalige, *die;* **B** (*coll.: elderly woman or female animal*) altes Mädchen (*ugs.*); alte Dame; **C** **the/one's ~ girl** (*coll.*) (*mother*) die/seine Alte (*ugs.*); (*car*) die/seine alte Kutsche (*ugs.*); **D** *as voc.* altes Mädchen; **Old 'Glory** *n., no pl., no art.* (*Amer.*) das Sternenbanner; **~ 'gold** **1** *n.* Altgold, *das;* **2** *adj.* altgolden; **~ guard** *n.* alte Garde; **a man** *or* **one of the ~ guard** einer von der alten Garde; **~ 'hat** *pred. adj.* ⇒ **hat** B; **Old High 'German** (*Ling.*) **1** *n.* Althochdeutsch, *das;* **2** *adj.* althochdeutsch; **Old 'Hundredth** ⇒ **hundredth** 2 B

**oldie** /'əʊldɪ/ *n.* (*coll.*) (*person*) Oldie, *der* (*ugs.*); Oldtimer, *der* (*scherzh.*); (*song, record, etc.*) Oldie, *der* (*ugs.*); (*film*) alter Streifen (*ugs.*); (*joke*) olle *od.* alte Kamelle (*ugs.*); **golden ~:** guter Oldie

**oldish** /'əʊldɪʃ/ *adj.* älter

**old:** **~ 'lady** *n.* **A** alte *od.* ältere Dame; **quite an ~ lady** eine recht alte Dame; **B** **the/one's ~ lady** (*coll.*) ⇒ **~ girl** C; **the Old Lady of Threadneedle Street** (*Brit.*) die Bank von England; **~-line** *adj.* (*Amer.*) (*established, experienced*) alterfahren ‹Personen›; alteingeführt ‹Unternehmen, Institution›; (*conservative*) konservativ; (*traditional*) ‹Diplomat› alter Schule; **~ 'maid** *n.* **A** (*elderly spinster*) alte Jungfer (*abwertend*); **B** (*fig.: precise, fussy, prim person*) altjüngferliche Person; **~-maidish** /əʊld'meɪdɪʃ/ *adj.* altjüngferlich; **~ 'man** *n.* **A** (*aged man*) alter Mann; **B** (*coll.: superior*) **the ~ man** der Alte (*ugs.*); **C** (*coll.: father, husband*) **the/one's ~ man** der Alte/sein Alter (*ugs.*); **D** *as voc.* alter Junge *od.* Knabe (*ugs. oft scherzh.*); Alter (*ugs.*); **~ man's 'beard** *n.* (*Bot.*) Waldrebe, *die;* **~ 'master** *n.* (*Art*) alter Meister; **~ 'people's home** *n.* Altenheim, *das;* Altersheim, *das;* **Old Pre'tender** ⇒ **pretender**; **~ 'soldier** *n.* alt[gedient]er Soldat; (*fig.*) alter Hase (*ugs.*); **come the ~ soldier over sb.** (*fig.*) sich jmdm. gegenüber als der Erfahrenere aufspielen; **~ soldiers never die** ein alter Soldat ist nicht so leicht unterzukriegen (*ugs.*)

**oldster** /'əʊldstə(r)/ *n.* alter Mensch; **the/we ~s** die/wir Alten

**old:** **~-style** *attrib. adj.* alten Stils *nachgestellt;* alt ‹Geldschein, Münze›; **Old 'Testament** ⇒ **testament** A; **~-time** *adj.* früherer Zeiten *nachgestellt;* von anno dazumal *nachgestellt;* **~-time dancing** alte Tänze; **~-'timer** *n.* **A** (*person with long experience*) alter Hase (*ugs.*); Oldtimer, *der* (*scherzh.*); **B** (*Amer.*) (*old person*) Alte, *der/die;* (*old or antique thing*) Oldtimer, *der;* **~ 'wives' tale** *n.* Ammenmärchen, *das;* Altweibermärchen, *das;* **~ 'woman** *n.* **A** alte Frau; (*fig.: fussy or timid person*) altes Weib (*abwertend*); **B** (*coll.: mother, wife*) **the/one's ~ woman** ⇒ **old girl** C; **~-'womanish** *adj.* altweiberhaft; **~-world** *adj.* (*belonging to old times, quaint*) altertümlich; altväterisch ‹Höflichkeit, Benehmen›

**oleaginous** /əʊlɪ'ædʒɪnəs/ *adj.* **A** (*oily, greasy*) ölig; **B** (*producing oil*) ölhaltig

**oleander** /əʊlɪ'ændə(r)/ *n.* (*Bot.*) Oleander, *der*

**O level** /'əʊ levl/ *n.* (*Brit. Sch. Hist.*) *Abschluss der Mittelstufe* (*auch in der Erwachsenenbildung als Qualifikation*); **he has five ~s** er hat die 'O'-Level-Prüfung in fünf Fächern bestanden

**olfactory** /ɒl'fæktərɪ/ *adj.* olfaktorisch (*geh.*); Geruchs‹nerv, -sinn›

**oligarchic[al]** /ɒlɪ'gɑ:kɪk(l)/ *adj.* (*Polit.*) oligarchisch

**oligarchy** /'ɒlɪgɑ:kɪ/ *n.* (*Polit.*) Oligarchie, *die*

**olive** /'ɒlɪv/ **1** *n.* **A** (*tree*) Ölbaum, *der;* Olivenbaum, *der;* **B** (*fruit*) Olive, *die;* **C** (*emblem of peace*) Ölzweig, *der;* **D** **~[ wood]** Olivenholz, *das;* **E** (*Cookery*) **[beef] ~:** [Rinds]roulade, *die;* **F** (*colour*) Olivgrün, *das.* **2** *adj.* **A** olivgrün; **B** (*in complexion*) oliv[farben]; olivbraun

**olive:** **~ branch** *n.* (*fig.*) Friedensangebot, *das;* **offer the ~ branch** ein Versöhnungs- *od.* Friedensangebot machen; **~ 'drab** *n.* Olivgrau, *das;* **~-green** **1** /'--'-/ *adj.* olivgrün; **2** /--'-/ *n.* Olivgrün, *das;* **~ 'oil** *n.* Olivenöl, *das*

**Olympiad** /ə'lɪmpɪæd/ *n.* Olympiade, *die*

**Olympian** /ə'lɪmpɪən/ **1** *adj.* **A** (*Greek Mythol.*) olympisch; **the ~ gods** die Götter des Olymp; **B** (*superior*) olympisch (*geh.*); **C** ⇒ **Olympic**. **2** *n.* **A** (*Greek Mythol.*) Olympier, *der*/Olympierin, *die;* **B** (*competitor in modern Olympics*) olympischer

O

[Wett]kämpfer/olympische [Wett]kämpferin; Olympionike, *der*/Olympionikin, *die*

**Olympic** /əˈlɪmpɪk/ *adj.* olympisch; ~ **Games** Olympische Spiele; ~ **champion** Olympiasieger, *der*/-siegerin, *die*

**Olympics** /əˈlɪmpɪks/ *n. pl.* Olympiade, *die;* **Winter** ~: Winterolympiade, *die*

**Olympus** /əˈlɪmpəs/ (*Greek Ant.*) Olymp, *der*

**OM** *abbr.* (*Brit.*) **Order of Merit**

**ombudsman** /ˈɒmbʊdzmən/ *n., pl.* **ombudsmen** /ˈɒmbʊdzmən/ Ombudsmann, *der*

**omega** /ˈəʊmɪgə/ *n.* (*letter*) Omega, *das;* ⇒ *also* **alpha** A

**omelette (omelet)** /ˈɒmlɪt/ *n.* (*Gastr.*) Omelett, *das;* **one cannot make an ~ without breaking eggs** wo gehobelt wird, [da] fallen Späne (*Spr.*)

**omen** /ˈəʊmən/ *n.* Omen, *das;* Vorzeichen, *das*

**ominous** /ˈɒmɪnəs/ *adj.* (*of evil omen*) ominös; (*worrying*) beunruhigend; **seem ~:** Schlimmes ahnen lassen

**ominously** /ˈɒmɪnəslɪ/ *adv.* bedrohlich; beunruhigend ‹still›

**omissible** /əˈmɪsɪbl/ *adj.* weglassbar; **that is ~:** das kann man weglassen

**omission** /əˈmɪʃn/ *n.* **A** Auslassung, *die;* **B** (*non-performance*) Unterlassung, *die;* **sins of ~ and commission** Unterlassungs- und Begehungssünden

**omit** /əˈmɪt/ *v.t.,* **-tt-** **A** (*leave out*) weglassen; **B** (*not perform*) versäumen; **~ to do sth.** es versäumen, etw. zu tun

**omnibus** /ˈɒmnɪbəs/ **1** *n.* **A** (*arch.*) ⇒ **bus** 1 A; **Clapham**; **B** (*book*) Sammelband, *der.* **2** *adj.* Sammel‹band, -ausgabe›

**omnidirectional** /ɒmnɪdɪˈrekʃənl, ɒmnɪdaɪˈrekʃənl/ *adj.* allseitig empfindlich ‹Mikrofon›; allseitig abstrahlend ‹Lautsprecher›; **~ aerial** Rundstrahler, *der*

**omnipotence** /ɒmˈnɪpətəns/ *n., no pl.* Allmacht, *die* (*geh.*); Omnipotenz, *die* (*geh.*)

**omnipotent** /ɒmˈnɪpətənt/ *adj.* allmächtig; omnipotent (*geh.*); **be made ~:** unbeschränkte Machtbefugnisse erhalten

**omniscience** /ɒmˈnɪsɪəns, ɒmˈnɪʃjəns/ *n., no pl.* Allwissenheit, *die*

**omniscient** /ɒmˈnɪsɪənt, ɒmˈnɪʃjənt/ *adj.* allwissend

**omnivorous** /ɒmˈnɪvərəs/ *adj.* **A** omnivor (*Zool.*); **~ animal** Allesfresser, *der;* **B** (*fig.*) unstillbar ‹Appetit, Neugier, Wissbegier›

**on** /ɒn/ **1** *prep.* **A** (*position*) auf (+ *Dat.*); (*direction*) auf (+ *Akk.*); (*attached to*) an (+ *Dat./Akk.*); **put sth. on the table** etw. auf den Tisch legen *od.* stellen; **be on the table** auf dem Tisch sein; **put/keep a dog on a lead** den Hund an die Leine nehmen/an der Leine halten; **write sth. on the wall** etw. an die Wand schreiben; **be hanging on the wall** an der Wand hängen; **have sth. on one** etw. bei sich (*Dat.*) haben; **on the mountain [side]** am Berghang; **on the bus/train** im Bus/Zug; (*by bus/train*) mit dem Bus/Zug; **on the shore** am Ufer; **be on the board/committee** im Vorstand/Ausschuss sein; **be on the team** (*Amer.*)/**staff** zum Team/zur Belegschaft gehören; **on Oxford 56767** unter der Nummer Oxford 56767; **B** (*with basis, motive, etc. of*) **on the evidence** aufgrund des Beweismaterials; **borrow money on one's house** eine Grundschuld auf sein Haus aufnehmen; **on the assumption/hypothesis that ...:** angenommen, ...; **C** (*close to*) an ‹einer Straße›; (*in the direction of*) auf ‹eine Stadt› zu; **D** (*coll.: in a position to get*) **the player is on a hat-trick** der Spieler steht vor einem Hattrick; **E** ▶ **1055**, ▶ **1056** *in expressions of time* an ‹einem Abend, Tag usw.›; **on Sundays** sonntags; **it's just on nine** es ist gerade 9; **on [his] arrival** bei seiner Ankunft; **on entering the room ...:** beim Betreten des Zimmers ...; **on time** *or* **schedule** pünktlich; **F** *expr. state etc.* **be on heroin** heroinabhängig sein; **be on beer** (*coll.*) Bier trinken; **Armstrong on trumpet** Armstrong, Trompete; **the drinks are on me** (*coll.*) die Getränke gehen auf mich; **the fire went out on me** (*coll.*) mir ist das Feuer ausgegangen; **there is a lot of money on that horse** auf das Pferd ist viel gesetzt worden; **be on £20,000 a year** 20 000 Pfund im Jahr kriegen *od.* haben; **G** (*added to*) **failure on failure** Fehlschlag auf Fehlschlag; **trouble on trouble** nichts als Ärger; **loss on loss** anhaltende Verluste; **H** (*concerning, about*) über (+ *Akk.*).

**2** *adv.* **A** **with/without a hat/coat on** mit/ohne Hut/Mantel; **have a hat on** einen Hut aufhaben; **your hat is on crooked** dein Hut sitzt schief; **boil sth. with/without the lid on** etw. in geschlossenem/offenem Topf kochen; **the potatoes are on** die Kartoffeln sind aufgesetzt; **B** (*in some direction*) **face on** mit dem Gesicht voran; **on and on** immer weiter; **speak/wait/work** *etc.* **on** (*in time*) weiterreden/-warten/-arbeiten *usw.;* **wait on until ...:** so lange warten, bis ...; **C** (*switched or turned on*) **the light/radio** *etc.* **is on** das Licht/Radio *usw.* ist an; **put the light on** das Licht anmachen; **leave the bathroom tap on** das Wasser im Badezimmer laufen lassen; **is there a gas tap on?** ist ein Gashahn aufgedreht?; **neither the water nor the electricity was on** es gab weder Wasser noch Strom; **D** (*arranged*) **the strike is still on** der Streik wird [weiterhin] fortgesetzt; **is Sunday's picnic on?** findet das Picknick am Sonntag statt?; **I have nothing of importance on** ich habe nichts Wichtiges vor; **E** *ellipt.* (= **go on** *etc.*) weiter; **on with the show!** weitermachen!; **F** (*being performed*) **what's on at the cinema?** was gibt es *od.* läuft im Kino?; **his play is currently on in London** sein Stück wird zurzeit in London aufgeführt *od.* gespielt; **the race is on** (*fig.*) das Wettrennen hat begonnen; **G** **be on** (*on the stage*) auftreten; (*on the playing field*) spielen; **H** (*on duty*) **come/be on** seinen Dienst antreten/Dienst haben; **I** **sth. is on** (*feasible*)/**not on** etw. ist möglich/ausgeschlossen; **are you on?** (*coll.: will you agree?*) machst du mit?; **you're on!** (*coll.: I agree*) abgemacht!; (*making bet*) die Wette gilt!; **be on about sb./sth.** (*coll.*) [dauernd] über jmdn./etw. sprechen; es von jmdm./etw. haben (*ugs.*); **what is he on about?** was will er [sagen]?; **be on at/keep on and on at sb.** (*coll.*) jmdm. in den Ohren/dauernd in den Ohren liegen (*ugs.*); **on to, onto** auf (+ *Akk.*); **be on to sb.** (*be aware of sb.'s intentions etc.*) jmdn. *od.* jmds. Absichten durchschauen; (*nag sb., suspect sb.*) jmdn. auf dem Kieker haben (*ugs.*); **be on to sb. to do sth.** jmdn. bearbeiten, etw. zu tun; **be on to sth.** (*have discovered sth.*) etw. ausfindig gemacht haben; (*realize importance of sth.*) etw. [klar] erkennen; **the police/researchers are on to something** die Polizei hat/die Forscher haben eine heiße Spur; **on and off** = **off and on** ⇒ **off** 1 C. ⇒ *also* **right** 4 D.

**3** *adj.* (*Cricket*) rechts vom Werfer; (*if batsman is left-handed*) links vom Werfer; **on drive** Treibschlag nach links; (*by lefthanded batsman*) Treibschlag nach rechts; **on side** ⇒ **4**.

**4** *n.* (*Cricket*) *Spielfeldhälfte links vom rechtshändigen bzw. rechts vom linkshändigen Schlagmann*

**once** /wʌns/ **1** *adv.* **A** einmal; **~ a week/month** einmal die Woche/im Monat; **~ or twice** ein paarmal; einige Mal; **~ again** *or* **more** noch einmal; **~ [and] for all** ein für alle Mal; **[every] ~ in a while** *or* (*Brit.*) **way** von Zeit zu Zeit; hin und wieder; **for ~ in a way** (*Brit.*) [wenigstens] dieses eine Mal; ausnahmsweise einmal; **~ an X always an X** X bleibt X; **~ seen never forgotten** jmd./etw. ist unvergesslich; ⇒ *also* **for** 1 O; **B** (*multiplied by one*) ein mal; **C** (*even for one or the first time*) je[mals]; **never/not ~:** nicht ein einziges Mal; **D** (*formerly*) früher einmal; einst (*geh.*); **~ upon a time there lived a king** es war einmal ein König; **E** **at ~** (*immediately*) sofort; sogleich; (*at the same time*) gleichzeitig; **all at ~** (*all together*) alle auf einmal; (*without warning*) mit einem Mal; **they were all shouting at ~:** sie schrien alle durcheinander.

**2** *conj.* wenn; (*with past tense*) als; **~ past the fence we are safe** wenn wir [nur] den Zaun hinter uns bringen, sind wir in Sicherheit; **will you get it, ~ he finds out how valuable it is?** wirst du es auch bekommen, wenn er [einmal] herausfindet, wie wertvoll es ist?

**3** *n.* **[just** *or* **only] this ~, for [this/that] ~:** [nur] dieses eine Mal; **~ was enough for her** sie hatte nach dem ersten Mal schon genug

**'once-over** *n.* **give sb./sth. a/the ~:** jmdn./etw. kurz in Augenschein nehmen; **sth. needs a ~ every month** etw. muss einmal im Monat kurz überprüft/(*cleaning*) gereinigt werden

**oncology** /ɒŋˈkɒlədʒɪ/ *n., no pl., no art.* (*Med.*) Onkologie, *die*

**'oncoming** *adj.* [heran]nahend ‹Person›; entgegenkommend ‹Fahrzeug, Verkehr›; aufkommend ‹Sturm›; **'caution: ~ vehicles'** „Vorsicht! Gegenverkehr"

**one** /wʌn/ ▶ **912**, ▶ **1012**, ▶ **1352** **1** *adj.* **A** *attrib.* ein; **~ thing I must say/admit** ein[e]s muss ich sagen/zugeben; **~ man, ~ vote** ≈ gleiches Wahlrecht für alle; **~ or two** (*fig.: a few*) ein paar; **~ more ...:** noch ein ...; **~ more time** noch einmal; **Act O~** (*Theatre*) erster Akt; **from day ~:** vom ersten Tag an; **it's ~ [o'clock]** es ist eins *od.* ein Uhr; ⇒ *also* **eight** 1; **half** 1 A, 3 A; **many** 1 A; **quarter** 1 A; **B** *attrib.* (*single, only*) einzig; **the ~ thing** das Einzige; **any ~:** irgendein; **in any ~ day/year** an einem Tag/in einem Jahr; **at any ~ time** zu jeder Zeit; **no ~:** kein; **not ~ [little] bit** überhaupt nicht; **not** *or* **never for ~ [single] moment** *or* **minute** nicht einen Augenblick *od.* eine Minute [lang]; ⇒ *also* **only** 1, 2 A; **thing** A, C, F, G; **C** (*identical, same*) ein; **the writer and his principal character are ~:** der Autor und sein Protagonist sind identisch; **~ and the same person/thing** ein und dieselbe Person/Sache; **it's ~ and the same thing** das ist ein und dasselbe; **at ~ and the same time** gleichzeitig; ⇒ *also* **all** 2 A; **D** *pred.* (*united, unified*) **be ~:** eine Einheit bilden; **we are ~:** wir sind uns einig; **be ~ as a family/nation** eine einige Familie/Nation sein; **become ~:** sich vereinigen; **be made ~** (*married*) getraut werden; ⇒ *also* **with**; **E** *attrib.* (*a particular but undefined*) **at ~ time** einmal; einst (*geh.*); **~ morning/evening/night** eines Morgens/Abends/Nachts; **~ day** (*on day specified*) einmal; (*at unspecified future date*) eines Tages; **~ day soon** bald einmal; **~ day next week** irgendwann nächste Woche; **~ Sunday/weekend/afternoon** an einem Sonntag/Wochenende/Nachmittag; **F** *attrib. contrasted with 'other'/'another'* ein; **for ~ thing** zum einen; **~ book** *etc.* **after another** *or* **the other** ein Buch *usw.* nach dem anderen; **deal with ~ thing after the other** eins nach dem andern machen; **what with ~ thing and another** wie das so ist *od.* geht, wenn viel zusammenkommt; **neither ~ thing nor the other** weder das eine noch das andere; **for ~ reason or another** aus irgendeinem Grund; **at ~ time or another** irgendwann einmal; zu irgendeinem Zeitpunkt; ⇒ *also* **hand** 1 N; **way** 1 C, J; **G** *qualifying implied n.* ein...; (*Brit.: one-pound coin or note*) Pfundnote, *die;* (*Amer.: one-dollar bill*) Dollarnote, *die;* **three to ~, three-~** (*Sport*) drei zu eins; **~-nil** (*Sport*) eins zu null; **in ~** (*coll.: at first attempt*) auf Anhieb; **got it in ~!** (*coll.*) [du hast es] erraten!; ⇒ *also* **every** A; **hole** 1 E.

**2** *n.* **A** eins; **~, two, three ...!** eins, zwei, drei ...!; **B** (*number, symbol*) Eins, *die;* **a Roman/arabic ~:** eine römische/arabische Eins; ⇒ *also* **eight** 2 A; **C** (*unit*) **in ~s** einzeln; **in** *or* **by ~s and twos** (*fig.*) kleckerweise (*ugs.*); **two for the price of ~:** zwei zum Preis von einem; ⇒ *also* **number** 1 A; **ten** 2 C.

**3** *pron.* **A** **~ of ...:** ein... (+ *Gen.*); **~ of the boys/books** einer der Jungen/eins der Bücher; **~ of them/us** *etc.* einer von ihnen/uns *usw.;* **any ~ of them** jeder/jede/jedes von ihnen; **every ~ of them** jeder/jede/jedes [Einzelne] von ihnen; **not ~ of them** keiner/keine/keines von ihnen; ⇒ *also* **thing**

O

G; Ⓑ *replacing n. implied or mentioned* ein...; **red ~s and yellow ~s, big ~s and little ~s** rote und gelbe, große und kleine; **the jacket is an old ~:** die Jacke ist [schon] alt; **the older/younger ~:** der/die/das Ältere/Jüngere; **the problem is ~ of great complexity/is not ~ that will simply go away** das Problem ist sehr komplex/wird sich nicht von selbst lösen; **not that book — the ~ on the table** nicht das Buch — das auf dem Tisch; **who is that man, the ~ in the blue suit?** wer ist dieser Mann, der im blauen Anzug?; **of the three books, this is the ~ which appealed to me most** von den drei Büchern hat mir dieses am besten gefallen; **this is the ~ I like** den/die/das mag ich; **my husband is the tall ~ over there** mein Mann ist der Große da; **you are** *or* **were the ~ who insisted on going to Scotland** du warst der-/diejenige, der/die unbedingt nach Schottland wollte; **this ~:** dieser/diese/dieses [da]; **that ~:** der/die/das [da]; **these ~s** *or* **those ~s?** (*coll.*) die [da] oder die [da]?; **these/those blue** *etc.* **~s** diese/die blauen *usw.*; **which ~?** welcher/welche/welches?; **which ~s?** welche?; **not ~:** keiner/keine/keines; *emphatic* nicht einer/eine/eines; **never a ~:** kein Einziger; **many a ~:** viele; **all but ~:** alle außer einem/einer/einem; **the last house but ~:** das vorletzte Haus; **[all] in ~:** in einem; (*in a person*) in einer Person; **I for ~:** ich für mein[en] Teil; **~ by ~, ~ after another** *or* **the other** einzeln; **love/like/hate ~ another** sich *od.* (*geh.*) einander lieben/mögen/hassen; **be kind to ~ another** nett zueinander sein; ⇒ *also* **all** 2 A; **better** 2 E; **many** 1 A; Ⓒ (*contrasted with 'other'/'another'*) **[the] ~ ... the other** der/die/das eine ... der/die/das andere; Ⓓ (*person or creature of specified kind*) **the little ~:** der/die/das Kleine; **dear** *or* **loved ~:** lieber Mensch; **our dear** *or* **loved ~s** unsere Lieben; **my sweet ~:** mein Liebling *od.* Schatz; **young ~** (*youngster*) Kind, *das;* (*young animal*) Junge, *das;* **the Holy O~, the O~ above** Gott; der Vater im Himmel; **like ~ dead** wie ein Toter; **as ~ enchanted/bewitched** wie verzaubert/verhext; **~ John Smith** ein John Smith; Ⓔ **[not] ~ who does** *or* **to do** *or* **for doing sth.** [nicht] der Typ, der etw. tut; **[not] be ~ for parties** *or* **for going to parties** [k]ein Partytyp sein; **be a great ~ for tennis** ein begeisterter Tennisspieler; **be a great ~ for playing practical jokes** gerne anderen einen Streich spielen; ein großer Witzbold sein; **not be much of a ~ for sth./doing sth.** nicht sehr für etw. sein/etw. nicht gern tun; **you 'are a ~** (*coll.*) du bist [mir] vielleicht einer/eine; Ⓕ (*representing people in general; also coll.: I, we*) man; *as indirect object* einem; *as direct object* einen; **~'s** sein; **lose ~'s job** seinen Arbeitsplatz verlieren; **wash ~'s hands** sich (*Dat.*) die Hände waschen; Ⓖ (*coll.: joke, story*) **a good/naughty ~:** ein guter/unanständiger Witz; **have you heard the ~ about the Irishman who ...?** kennst du den von dem Iren, der ...?; ⇒ *also* **good** 1 H; Ⓗ (*coll.: drink*) **I'll have just a little ~:** ich trinke nur einen Kleinen (*ugs.*); **this ~'s on me/the house** der geht auf mich/auf Kosten des Hauses; **have ~ on me** ich geb dir einen aus; **have ~ too many** einen über den Durst trinken (*ugs.*); ⇒ *also* **quick one**; **road** A; Ⓘ (*coll.: blow*) **give sb. ~ on the head/nose** jmdm. eins über den Kopf/auf die Nase geben (*ugs.*); **he hit me ~ between the eyes** er verpasste mir einen zwischen die Augen (*ugs.*); Ⓙ (*Knitting, Crochet: stitch*) eine Masche; **knit ~, purl ~:** eins rechts, eins links; **make ~:** eine Masche zunehmen

**one: ~-armed** *adj.* einarmig; **~-armed bandit** (*coll.*) einarmiger Bandit (*ugs.*); **~-day** *attrib. adj.* eintägig; [für] einen Tag gültig ‹Karte, Genehmigung›; **~-eyed** *adj.* einäugig; **in the land of the blind the ~-eyed [man] is king** (*prov.*) unter [den] Blinden ist der Einäugige König (*Spr.*); **~-handed** /wʌnhændɪd/ ❶ /'---/ *adj.* einhändig; ❷ /-'--/ *adv.* mit einer Hand; **~-horse** *attrib. adj.* Ⓐ (*drawn by only ~ horse*) einspännig; (*having only ~ horse*) mit nur einem Pferd *nachgestellt;* **it's a ~-horse race** (*fig.*) das Rennen ist schon so gut wie gelaufen; Ⓑ (*fig. coll.: second-rate*) **~-horse firm** *or* **outfit** kleine Klitsche (*ugs.*); **~-horse town** [verschlafenes] Nest (*ugs.*); **~-legged** *adj.* einbeinig; **~-line** *attrib. adj.* einzeilig; **~-'liner** *n.* Einzeiler, *der;* **~-man** *attrib. adj.* Einmann‹boot, -betrieb usw.›; **a ~-man fight/war against sth.** ein einsamer Kampf/Krieg gegen etw.; **~-man band** Einmannkapelle, *die;* (*fig.: firm etc.*) Einmannbetrieb, *der;* **~-man show** (*exhibition*) Einzelausstellung, *die;* (*play etc.*) Einmannstück, *das;* (*fig.: firm etc.*) Einmannbetrieb, *der*

**oneness** /'wʌnnɪs/ *n., no pl.* Ⓐ (*singleness*) **~ of purpose** Zielstrebigkeit, *die;* Ⓑ (*unity, harmony*) Übereinstimmung, *die;* Einklang, *der* (*geh.*)

**one: ~-night 'stand** *n.* (*coll.*) Ⓐ (*single performance*) Einzelauftritt, *der;* Ⓑ (*sexual*) [sexuelles] Abenteuer für eine Nacht; (*partner*) Bettgenosse/-genossin für eine Nacht; **~-off** (*Brit.*) ❶ *n.* (*article*) Einzelstück, *das;* Einzelexemplar, *das;* (*operation*) einmalige Sache; ❷ *adj.* einmalig ‹Zahlung, Angebot, Produktion, Verkauf›; Einzel‹stück, -modell, -anfertigung, -auftritt, -arbeit›; **~-parent family** *n.* Einelternfamilie, *die;* **~-party** *adj.* (*Polit.*) Einparteien‹system, -staat›; **~-piece** *adj.* einteilig; **~'quarter** *attrib. adj.* Viertel-; ‹Anteil› von einem Viertel; ‹Anstieg› um ein Viertel; **~-room[ed]** /'wʌnru:m(d)/ *adj.* Einzimmer‹wohnung, -appartement›; **a ~-room school/shack** eine aus einem [einzigen] Raum bestehende Schule/Hütte

**onerous** /'ɒnərəs, 'əʊnərəs/ *adj.* schwer; **find sth. increasingly ~:** etw. zunehmend als Belastung empfinden

**onerously** /'ɒnərəslɪ, 'əʊnərəslɪ/ *adv.* schwer

**one: ~'self** *pron.* Ⓐ *emphat.* selbst; **as old/rich as ~self** so alt/reich wie man selbst; **older/richer than ~self** älter/reicher als man selbst; **be ~self** man selbst sein; Ⓑ *refl.* sich; ⇒ *also* **herself**; **~-shot** *adj.* (*coll.*) einmalig; Einzel‹auftritt, -anfertigung›; ‹Medikament, Verfahren› zur einmaligen Anwendung; **a ~-shot solution to a problem** eine auf Anhieb wirksame Lösung eines Problems; **~-sided** *adj.* einseitig; **~step** *n.* Onestep, *der;* **~-storey** *adj.* eingeschossig; **~-'third** *attrib. adj.* Drittel-; ‹Anteil› von einem Drittel; ‹Anstieg› um ein Drittel; **~-time** *adj.* Ⓐ (*former*) ehemalig; Ⓑ (*used once only*) einmalig; **~-to-'~** *adj.* **~-to-~ relation/correspondence** hundertprozentige Parallelität; **~-to-~ translation** Wort-für-Wort-Übersetzung, *die;* **~-to-~ teaching** Einzelunterricht, *der;* **~-touch** *adj.* **~-touch dialling** Zielwahl, *die;* Zielwahlverfahren, *das;* **~-touch cooking** Kochen per Knopfdruck; Kochen mit einem einzigen Knopfdruck; **~-track** *adj.* eingleisig; **have a ~-track mind** (*lack flexibility*) eingleisig denken; (*be obsessed by one subject*) [immer] nur eins im Kopf haben; **~-'two** *n.* (*coll.*) (*Boxing*) Einszwei-Schlag, *der;* (*Sport*) Doppelpass, *der;* **~-'up** *pred. adj.* (*coll.*) **be ~-up [on** *or* **over sb.]** (*Sport*) [vor jmdm.] mit einem Punkt/Tor in Führung liegen; (*fig.*) [jmdm.] um eine Nasenlänge voraus sein; **it is ~-up for** *or* **to sb.** jmd. ist im Vorteil; **~-up for** *or* **to you** (*fig.*) eins zu null für dich; **~-upmanship** /wʌn'ʌpmənʃɪp/ *n., no pl., no indef. art.* die Kunst, den anderen immer um eine Nasenlänge voraus zu sein; **~-way** *adj.* Ⓐ in einer Richtung *nachgestellt;* Einbahn‹straße, -verkehr›; Einweg‹spiegel, -scheibe›; **~-way radio** Funkempfänger, *der;* **~-way switch** (*Electr.*) einfacher Schalter; Ⓑ (*single*) einfach ‹Fahrpreis, Fahrkarte, Flug usw.›; Ⓒ (*fig.: ~-sided*) einseitig; **~-woman** *attrib. adj.* Einfrau‹betrieb, -job, -firma›; **a ~-woman fight/war against sth.** ein einsamer Kampf/Krieg gegen etw.; **~-woman show** (*exhibition*) Einzelausstellung [einer Künstlerin]; (*play etc.*) Einfraustück, *das;* (*fig.: firm etc.*) Einfraubetrieb, *der*

**'ongoing** *adj.* aktuell ‹Problem, Aktivitäten, Debatte›; laufend ‹Forschung, Projekt›; andauernd ‹Situation›

**onion** /'ʌnjən/ *n.* Zwiebel, *die;* **know one's ~s** (*fig. coll.*) sein Geschäft verstehen

**onion: ~ dome** *n.* (*Archit.*) Zwiebelkuppel, *die;* **~ skin** *n.* Ⓐ Zwiebelschale, *die;* Ⓑ (*paper*) Florpost, *die;* **~ 'soup** *n.* Zwiebelsuppe, *die*

**oniony** /'ʌnjənɪ/ *adj.* Zwiebel‹geruch, -geschmack›

**online** (*Computing*) ❶ /'--/ *adj.* Online‹computer, -betrieb›. ❷ /-'-/ *adv.* online

**'onlooker** *n.* Zuschauer, *der*/Zuschauerin, *die;* (*at scene of accident*) Schaulustige, *der/die*

**only** /'əʊnlɪ/ ❶ *attrib. adj.* Ⓐ einzig...; **the ~ person** der/die Einzige; **my ~ regret is that ...:** ich bedaure nur, dass ...; **for the first and ~ time** zum ersten und einzigen Mal; **an ~ child** ein Einzelkind; **the ~ one/ones** der/die/das Einzige/die Einzigen; **the ~ thing** das Einzige; **one and ~** (*sole*) einzig...; (*incomparable*) einzigartig; ⇒ *also* **pebble**; **thing** B, C; Ⓑ (*best by far*) **the ~:** der/die/das einzig wahre; **he/she is the ~ one for me** es gibt nur ihn/sie für mich; **the ~ thing** das einzig Wahre.

❷ *adv.* Ⓐ nur; **we had been waiting ~ 5 minutes when ...:** wir hatten erst 5 Minuten gewartet, als ...; **it's ~/~ just 6 o'clock** es ist erst 6 Uhr/gerade erst 6 Uhr vorbei; **the meat is ~ half done** das Fleisch ist erst halb durch; **I ~ wish I had known** wenn ich es doch nur gewusst hätte; **you ~ have** *or* **you have ~ to ask** *etc.* du brauchst nur zu fragen *usw.;* **you may each take one and one ~:** ihr dürft euch jeder einen/eine/eins nehmen, aber [wirklich] nur einen/eine/eins; **you ~ live once** man lebt nur einmal; **you're ~ young once** man ist nur einmal jung; **~ ever** (*coll.: never more than*) lediglich; **~ if** nur [dann] ..., wenn; **~ if the weather is fine** nur bei gutem Wetter; **he ~ just managed it/made it** er hat es gerade so/gerade noch geschafft; **not ~ ... but also** nicht nur ... sondern auch; ⇒ *also* **if** 1 D; Ⓑ (*no longer ago than*) erst; **~ the other day/week** erst neulich *od.* kürzlich; **~ the other evening** erst neulich abends; **~ just** gerade erst; **it is ~ now I realize ...:** erst jetzt wird mir klar ...; Ⓒ (*with no better result than*) **~ to find/discover that ...:** nur, um zu entdecken, dass ...; Ⓓ **~ too ...** *in context of desirable circumstances* [sogar] ausgesprochen ‹froh, begierig, bereitwillig›; *in context of undesirable circumstances* viel zu; **be ~ too aware of sth.** sich (*Dat.*) einer Sache (*Gen.*) voll bewusst sein; **it's ~ too true** es ist nur zu wahr; **~ too well** nur zu gut ‹wissen, kennen, sich erinnern›; gerne ‹mögen›; nur zu genau ‹hören, aufpassen auf›.

❸ *conj.* Ⓐ (*but then*) nur; Ⓑ (*were it not for the fact that*) **~ [that] I am/he is** *etc.* **...:** ich bin/er ist *usw.* nur ...

**only-be'gotten** *adj.* (*Relig.*) **Jesus Christ, the ~ Son of the Father** Jesus Christus, Gottes eingeborener Sohn

**o.n.o.** /əʊ en 'əʊ/ *abbr.* (*Brit.*) **or near offer** ≈ VHB

**'on-off** *adj.* **~ switch** Ein-aus-Schalter, *der*

**onomatopoeia** /ɒnəmætə'pi:ə/ *n.* (*Ling.*) Onomatopöie, *die*

**onomatopoeic** /ɒnəmætə'pi:ɪk/ *adj.* (*Ling.*) onomatopoetisch

**'onrush** *n.* Ansturm, *der*

**on-screen** ❶ *adj.* Ⓐ (*Computing, TV*) Bildschirm-; **~ editing** redaktionelle Bearbeitung am Bildschirm; Ⓑ (*Cinemat.*) Leinwand-; **~ violence** Gewalt im Fernsehen/im Film; **her ~ daughter** ihre Filmtochter. ❷ *adv.* Ⓐ (*Computing, TV*) auf dem Bildschirm; Ⓑ (*Cinemat.*) auf der Leinwand; **appear ~ simultaneously** gleichzeitig im Bild sein; **~ they were lovers** im Film waren sie ein Liebespaar

**'onset** *n.* Ⓐ (*attack*) [Sturm]angriff, *der;* Ⓑ (*beginning*) (*of storm*) Einsetzen, *das;* (*of winter*) Einbruch, *der;* (*of disease*) Ausbruch, *der*

**'onshore** *adj.* auflandig (*Seemannsspr.*)

**on'side** *adj.* (*Footb.*) nicht abseits

**onslaught** /'ɒnslɔ:t/ *n.* [heftige] Attacke (*fig.*)

**on-'stage** ❶ *adj.* auf der Bühne *nachgestellt.* ❷ *adv.* auf die Bühne ‹gehen›; auf der Bühne ‹stehen›

**ˈon-street** *adj.* auf der Straße *nachgestellt*

**ˈon-target** *attrib. adj.* **~ earnings £50,000** Verdienst bei erfolgreicher Tätigkeit 50 000 Pfund

**ˈon-the-job** *attrib. adj.* berufsbegleitend ‹Unterricht, Fortbildungskurs usw.›; **~ experience** Berufserfahrung, *die;* **~ training** Ausbildung am Arbeitsplatz

**on-the-ˈspot** *adj.* vor Ort *nachgestellt*

**onto** ⇒ **on** 2 I

**ontological** /ɒntəˈlɒdʒɪkl/ *adj.* (*Philos.*) ontologisch

**ontology** /ɒnˈtɒlədʒɪ/ *n.* (*Philos.*) Ontologie, *die*

**onus** /ˈəʊnəs/ *n.* Last, *die;* **the ~ [of proof]** die Beweislast; **the ~ is on him to do it** es ist seine Sache, es zu tun

**onward** /ˈɒnwəd/ **1** *adv.* **A** (*in space*) vorwärts; **from X ~:** von X an; **they moved ~ into the forest** sie gingen *od.* zogen weiter in den Wald [hinein]; **B** (*in time*) **from that day ~:** von diesem Tag an; **history from the 12th century ~:** Geschichte vom 12. Jahrhundert an. **2** *adj.* nach vorn *nachgestellt;* **~ movement** Vorwärtsbewegung, *die;* **~ march** Vormarsch, *der*

**onwards** /ˈɒnwədz/ ⇒ **onward** 1

**onyx** /ˈɒnɪks/ *n.* (*Min.*) Onyx, *der;* **~ marble** Onyxmarmor, *der*

**oodles** /ˈuːdlz/ *n. pl., constr. as sing. or pl.* (*coll.*) **~ of** haufenweise (*ugs.*); jede Menge (*ugs.*)

**ooh** /uː/ **1** *n.* Oh, *das;* Ah, *das;* **the ~s [and ahs] of the audience** die Ohs und Ahs der Zuschauer. **2** *int. expr. disapproval or delight* oh; *expr. pain* au

**oojah** /ˈuːdʒɑː/ *n.* (*coll.*) Ding, *das* (*ugs.*)

**oompah** /ˈuːmpɑː/ *n.* Humpta, *das*

**oomph** /ʊmf/ *n.* (*coll.*) **A** (*attractiveness*) Sex-Appeal, *der;* **B** (*energy*) Elan, *der*

**oops** /uːps/ *int.* (*coll.*) *expr. surprise* huch; *expr. apology* oh; oje; *expr. apology for a faux pas* oh

**ooze** /uːz/ **1** *v.i.* **A** (*percolate, exude*) sickern (**from** aus); (*more thickly*) quellen (**from** aus); **the juice ~s out** der Saft trieft heraus; **B** (*become moistened*) triefen (**with** von, vor + *Dat.*). **2** *v.t.* **A ~ [out]** triefen von *od.* vor (+ *Dat.*); **B** (*fig.: radiate*) ausstrahlen ‹Charme, Optimismus›; ausströmen ‹Sarkasmus›. **3** *n.* **A** (*mud*) Schlick, *der;* **B** (*sluggish flow*) Sickern, *das;* (*sluggish stream*) Rinnsal, *das* (**of** von + *Dat.*)

**op** /ɒp/ *n.* (*coll.*) **A** (*Med.*) Operation, *die;* **B** (*Mil., Navy, Air Force*) Einsatz, *der;* **C** (*radio operator*) Funker, *der*/Funkerin, *die;* (*telegraph operator*) Telegrafist, *der*/Telegrafistin, *die*

**op.** /ɒp/ *abbr.* (*Mus.*) **opus** op.

**opacity** /əˈpæsɪtɪ/ *n., no pl.* **A** (*not transmitting light*) Opazität, *die* (*Optik*); Lichtundurchlässigkeit, *die;* **B** (*obscurity*) Undurchsichtigkeit, *die*

**opal** /ˈəʊpl/ *n.* (*Min.*) Opal, *der*

**opalescence** /əʊpəˈlesəns/ *n.* Schillern, *das;* Opaleszenz, *die* (*Optik*)

**opalescent** /əʊpəˈlesənt/ *adj.* schillernd; opalisierend; opaleszierend (*Optik*)

**ˈopal glass** *n.* Opalglas, *das*

**opaque** /əʊˈpeɪk/ *adj.* **A** (*not transmitting light*) lichtundurchlässig; opak (*fachspr.*); **B** (*obscure*) dunkel; unverständlich

**opaqueness** /əʊˈpeɪknɪs/ ⇒ **opacity**

**ˈop art** *n., no pl., no indef. art.* Op-Art, *die*

**op. cit.** /ɒp ˈsɪt/ *abbr.* **in the work already quoted** op. cit.

**OPEC** /ˈəʊpek/ *abbr.* **Organization of Petroleum Exporting Countries** OPEC, *die*

**open** /ˈəʊpn/ **1** *adj.* **A** offen; **with the window ~:** bei geöffnetem Fenster; **~ goal** (*Sport*) leeres Tor; **wear an ~ shirt** sein Hemd offen tragen; **be [wide/half] ~:** [weit/halb] offen stehen; **stand ~:** offen stehen; **swing ~:** aufschwingen; **come ~:** aufgehen; **get sth. ~:** etw. aufbekommen; **hold the door ~ [for sb.]** [jmdm.] die Tür aufhalten; **push/pull/kick the door ~:** die Tür aufstoßen/aufziehen/eintreten; **force sth. ~:** etw. mit Gewalt öffnen; **fling** *or* **throw a door/window [wide] ~:** eine Tür/ein Fenster [weit] aufreißen; **tear** *or* **rip sth. ~:** etw. aufreißen; **with one's mouth ~:** mit offenem Mund; **have one's eyes ~:** die Augen geöffnet haben; **[not] be able to keep one's eyes ~:** [nicht mehr] die Augen offen halten können; **with ~ eyes** (*attentive, surprised*) mit großen Augen; ⇒ *also* **eye**[1] A; **B** (*unconfined*) offen ‹Gelände, Feuer›; frei ‹Feld, Blick›; **~ country** (*with wide views*) weites Land; (*without buildings*) offenes Land; **on the ~ road** auf freier Strecke; **the ~ road lay before me** vor mir lag die freie Landstraße; **the ~ sea** die offene See; **in the ~ air** im Freien; ⇒ *also* **sky** 1 A; **C** (*not blocked or obstructed*) frei; offen, eisfrei ‹Hafen, Fluss, Wasser›; frostfrei ‹Winter, Wetter›; **D** (*ready for business or use*) **be ~** ‹Laden, Museum, Bank usw.:› geöffnet sein; **'~'/'~ on Sundays'/'~ 24 hours'** „geöffnet"/„Sonntags geöffnet"/„24 Stunden geöffnet"; **declare a building/an exhibition ~:** ein Gebäude/eine Ausstellung für eröffnet erklären; **E** (*accessible*) offen; öffentlich ‹Treffen, Rennen›; (*available*) frei ‹Stelle›; freibleibend ‹Angebot›; **it is ~ to you to refuse** es steht dir frei abzulehnen; **lay ~:** offen legen ‹Plan›; **be ~ to the public** für die Öffentlichkeit zugänglich sein; **the competition is ~ to children under 16** [nur] Kinder unter 16 Jahren sind zum Wettbewerb zugelassen; **the job/offer is ~ to men over 25 years of age** die Stelle ist für/das Angebot gilt für Männer über 25 Jahren; **the offer remains** *or* **will be kept ~ until the end of the month** das Angebot bleibt bestehen *od.* gilt noch bis Ende des Monats; **keep a position ~ for sb.** jmdm. eine Stelle freihalten; **keep an account ~:** ein Konto [weiterhin] bestehen lassen; **~ champion** Sieger einer offenen Meisterschaft; **~ cheque** (*Brit.*) Barscheck, *der;* **in ~ court** in öffentlicher Sitzung *od.* Verhandlung; **~ ward** offene Station; ⇒ *also* **house** 1 A; **F be ~ to** (*exposed to*) ausgesetzt sein (+ *Dat.*) ‹Wind, Sturm›; (*receptive to*) offen sein für ‹Ratschlag, andere Meinung, Vorschlag›; **~ to infection** infektionsgefährdet *od.* -anfällig; **be ~ to criticism** kritisierbar sein; **~ to attack by dry rot** anfällig für Trockenfäule; **be ~ to attack from the air** aus der Luft angreifbar sein; **sth. may be ~ to misinterpretation** etw. kann [leicht] falsch ausgelegt werden; **be ~ to sb.'s influence** sich leicht von jmdm. beeinflussen lassen; **I hope to sell it for £1,000, but I am ~ to offers** ich möchte es für 1 000 Pfund verkaufen, aber ich lasse mit mir handeln; **lay sb. wide ~** (*fig.*) jmdn. bloßstellen; **lay oneself [wide] ~ to ridicule/attack/criticism** *etc.* sich der Lächerlichkeit preisgeben/sich Angriffen/der Kritik *usw.* aussetzen; **lay oneself [wide] ~ to blackmail/a charge** sich der Gefahr der Erpressung/einer Anklage aussetzen; **be ~ to question/doubt/argument** fraglich/zweifelhaft/umstritten sein; **I am ~ to correction** ich lasse mich gern korrigieren; **G** (*undecided*) offen; **~ invitation** Einladung, gelegentlich einmal zu Besuch zu kommen; **~ return ticket** nicht termingebundene Rückfahrkarte; **have an ~ mind about** *or* **on sth.** einer Sache gegenüber aufgeschlossen *od.* unvoreingenommen sein; **with an ~ mind** aufgeschlossen; **have/keep an ~ mind on a question** in einer Sache unvoreingenommen sein/bleiben; **be [wide] ~:** [völlig] offen sein; **leave sth. ~:** etw. offen lassen; ⇒ *also* **verdict** A; **H** (*undisguised, manifest*) unverhohlen ‹Bewunderung, Hass, Verachtung›; offen ‹Verachtung, Empörung, Bruch, Widerstand›; offensichtlich ‹Spaltung, Zwiespalt›; **~ war/warfare** offener Krieg/Kampf; ⇒ *also* **secret** 2 A; **I** (*frank, communicative*) offen ‹Wesen, Streit, Abstimmung, Gesicht, Regierungsstil›; (*not secret*) öffentlich ‹Wahl›; **be ~ [about sth./with sb.]** [in Bezug auf etw. (*Akk.*)/gegenüber jmdm.] offen sein; **J** (*not close*) grob ‹Muster, Gewebe, Maserung›; offen ‹Anordnung›; **~ order** (*Mil., Navy*) offene Ordnung; **K** (*expanded, unfolded*) offen, geöffnet ‹Pore, Regenschirm›; aufgeblüht ‹Blume, Knospe›; aufgeschlagen ‹Zeitung, Landkarte, Stadtplan›; **~ book** offenes *od.* aufgeschlagenes Buch; **sb./sth. is an ~ book [to sb.]** (*fig.*) jmd./etw. ist ein aufgeschlagenes *od.* offenes Buch [für jmdn.]; **an ~ hand** eine aufgehaltene Hand; (*fig.*) eine milde *od.* offene Hand; **with an ~ hand, with ~ hands** (*fig.*) mit einer milden *od.* offenen Hand; **with [an] ~ heart** (*frankly*) offenherzig; (*kindly*) herzlich; ⇒ *also* **arm**[1] A; **~-heart**; **L** (*Mus.*) **~ string** leere Saite; **~ pipe** offene Pfeife; **~ note** Naturton, *der;* **M** (*Ling.*) offen ‹Vokal, Silbe›.

**2** *n.* **A the ~:** das offene Land; **in the ~** (*outdoors*) unter freiem Himmel; (*in an open space*) auf offenem Gelände; (*in open water*) auf offener *od.* hoher See; **[out] in the ~** (*fig.*) [öffentlich] bekannt; **come [out] into the ~** (*fig.*) (*become obvious*) herauskommen (*ugs.*); an den Tag kommen; (*speak out*) offen sprechen; **bring sth. [out] into the ~** (*fig.*) etw. an die Öffentlichkeit bringen; **B** (*Sport*) offene Meisterschaft; Open, *das* (*fachspr.*).

**3** *v.t.* **A** öffnen; aufmachen (*ugs.*); **~ sth. with a key** etw. aufschließen; **~ sth. wide** etw. weit aufmachen (*ugs.*) *od.* öffnen; **half ~ sth.** etw. halb aufmachen (*ugs.*) *od.* öffnen; **[not] ~ one's mouth** *or* **lips** (*fig.*) den Mund [nicht] aufmachen *od.* auftun (*ugs.*); **~ one's big mouth [to sb. about sth.]** (*fig.*) [etw. jmdm. aus]plaudern; **~ the** *or* **one's bowels** den Darm entleeren; ⇒ *also* **eye** 1 A; **floodgate**; **B** (*allow access to*) **~ sth. [to sb./sth.]** etw. öffnen [für jmdn./etw.]; (*fig.*) [jmdm./einer Sache] etw. öffnen; **~ a road to traffic** eine Straße für den Verkehr freigeben; **~ sth. to the public** etw. der Öffentlichkeit (*Dat.*) zugänglich machen; ⇒ *also* **door** B; **C** (*establish*) eröffnen ‹Konferenz, Kampagne, Diskussion, Laden›; aufmachen (*ugs.*) ‹Laden›; beginnen ‹Verhandlungen, Krieg, Spiel›; (*declare open*) eröffnen ‹Gebäude usw.›; **~ the scoring** (*Sport*) den ersten Treffer erzielen; (*Cricket*) den ersten Lauf machen; (*Rugby*) die ersten Punkte machen; **~ the betting with a £5 stake** das Spiel mit einem Einsatz von 5 Pfund eröffnen; **~ the bidding** (*in auction*) das erste Gebot abgeben; (*Bridge*) eröffnen; **~ an account** ein Konto eröffnen; **~ fire [on sb./sth.]** das Feuer [auf jmdn./etw.] eröffnen; ⇒ *also* **ball**[2]; **parliament**; **D** (*unfold, spread out*) aufschlagen ‹Zeitung, Landkarte, Stadtplan, Buch›; aufspannen, öffnen ‹Schirm›; öffnen ‹Fallschirm, Poren›; **~ one's hand** die *od.* seine Hand öffnen; **~ one's arms [wide]** die *od.* seine Arme [weit] ausbreiten; **~ one's legs** die *od.* seine Beine spreizen; **E** (*reveal, expose*) **~ a view** *or* **prospect of sth. [to sb.]** [jmdm.] den Blick auf etw. freigeben; **sth. ~s new prospects/horizons/a new world to sb.** (*fig.*) etw. eröffnet jmdm. neue Aussichten/Horizonte/eine neue Welt; **~ one's heart to sb.** (*fig.*) sich jmdm. öffnen; **F** (*make more receptive*) **~ one's mind** aufgeschlossener werden; **~ one's heart** *or* **mind to sb./sth.** sich jmdm./einer Sache öffnen; **~ sb.'s mind to sth.** jmdm. etw. nahe bringen; **G** (*cut*) graben ‹Stollen, Brunnen, Loch, Gang›; bauen ‹Straße durch Berge/Wald›; (*break up*) bearbeiten ‹Boden›; **~ a hole in the wall** ein Loch in die Wand machen.

**4** *v.i.* **A** sich öffnen; aufgehen; ‹Spalt, Kluft:› sich auftun; **'Doors ~ at 7 p.m.'** „Einlass ab 19 Uhr"; **the safe ~s with a special key** der Tresor lässt sich mit einem Spezialschlüssel öffnen; **~ inwards/outwards** nach innen/außen aufgehen; **the door would not ~:** die Tür ging nicht auf *od.* ließ sich nicht öffnen; **his mouth ~ed in a big yawn** sein Mund öffnete sich zu einem ausgiebigen Gähnen; **his eyes ~ed wide** er riss die Augen weit auf; **~ into/on to sth.** zu etw. führen; sich zu etw. hin öffnen; **the kitchen ~s into the living room** die Küche hat eine Tür zum Wohnzimmer; **the road ~s into a square** die Straße öffnet sich zu einem Platz; ⇒ *also* **heaven** B; **B** (*become open to customers*) öffnen; aufmachen (*ugs.*); (*start trading etc.*) eröffnet werden; **the shop does not ~ on Sundays** der Laden ist sonntags geschlossen; **C** (*make a start*) beginnen; ‹Ausstellung:› eröffnet werden; ‹Theaterstück:› Premiere haben; **shares ~ed steady** *or* **firm** (*St. Exch.*) die Aktien eröffneten fest; **~ for the prosecution** (*Law*) das Eröffnungsplädoyer [in der Hauptverhandlung] halten; D (*become visible*) **~ before sb./sb.'s eyes** sich jmdm./jmds. Augen bieten; (*fig.*) sich jmdm. eröffnen

**~ 'out** ❶ *v.t.* A (*unfold*) auseinander falten; B (*enlarge, widen*) erweitern; C (*develop*) erweitern. ❷ *v.i.* A (*unfold*) ‹Landkarte:› sich auseinander falten lassen; ‹Knospe:› sich öffnen; (*fig.*) ‹Person:› auftauen; B (*widen, expand*) **~ out into sth.** sich zu etw. erweitern *od.* verbreitern; C (*be revealed*) **~ out before sb./sb.'s eyes** vor jmdm./jmds. Augen liegen

**~ 'up** ❶ *v.t.* A aufmachen (*ugs.*); öffnen; aufschlagen ‹Buch›; aufspannen, öffnen ‹Schirm›; **~ up a room/house** ein Zimmer/ein Haus öffnen *od.* zugänglich machen; B (*form or make by cutting etc.*) machen ‹Loch, Riss›; **~ up a path through the jungle** einen Weg durch den Urwald schlagen; **the frost has ~ed up big cracks** durch den Frost sind große Risse entstanden; **~ up a lead** *or* **gap of ten metres/points** einen Vorsprung von zehn Metern/Punkten gewinnen; C (*establish, make more accessible*) eröffnen ‹Laden, Filiale›; erschließen ‹neue Märkte usw.›; **~ up a region to trade/tourism** ein Gebiet für den Handel/Tourismus erschließen; **~ up a new world to sb.** jmdm. eine neue Welt erschließen; **~ up new opportunities for sb.** jmdm. neue Möglichkeiten eröffnen; D (*make more lively, accelerate*) aufdrehen (*ugs.*).
❷ *v.i.* A (*open a door*) aufmachen; B ‹Blüte, Knospe:› sich öffnen; C (*be established*) ‹Filiale:› eröffnet werden; ‹Firma:› sich niederlassen; D (*appear, be revealed*) entstehen; ‹Aussichten, Möglichkeiten:› sich eröffnen; **~ up before sb.** ‹Blick, Aussicht:› sich jmdm. bieten; ‹neue Welt:› sich vor jmdm. auftun; E (*talk freely*) gesprächig werden; **~ up to sb.** sich jmdm. anvertrauen; sich jmdm. eröffnen (*geh.*); F (*begin shooting*) das Feuer eröffnen; (*begin sounding*) ertönen; G (*become more lively or active*) ‹Spiel, Handel:› sich beleben; (*accelerate*) aufdrehen (*ugs.*)

**open: ~ 'access library** *n.* Freihandbibliothek, *die;* **~-air** *attrib. adj.* Open-Air-‹Konzert›; Freiluft‹restaurant, -aktivitäten›; Freilicht‹kino, -aufführung›; ‹Ausstellung, Markt, Versammlung› im Freien *od.* unter freiem Himmel; **~-air [swimming] pool** Freibad, *das;* **~-and-'shut case** *n.* (*coll.*) klarer Fall; **~-armed** *adj.* herzlich; **receive** *or* **welcome sb. ~-armed** jmdn. mit offenen Armen aufnehmen *od.* empfangen; **~cast** *adj.* (*Mining*) **~cast mining/coal/method** Tagebau, *der*/Kohle aus dem Tagebau/Methode des Tagebaus; **~ day** *n.* Tag der offenen Tür; **~-'door** *attrib. adj.* **~-door policy** Politik der offenen Tür; **~-ended** /əʊpən'endɪd/ *adj.* [am Ende] offen; (*fig.: with no predetermined limit*) unbefristet ‹Aufenthalt, Vertrag›; uneingeschränkt ‹Verpflichtung›; unbegrenzt ‹Unterstützung, Kredit›; Open-End-‹Diskussion, Debatte›; offen ‹Frage›; unerschöpflich ‹Thema›; **~-ended spanner** Gabelschlüssel, *der*

**opener** /'əʊpənə(r)/ *n.* A Öffner, *der;* B (*opening item or event*) (*of entertainment*) Eröffnungsnummer, *die;* (*of a serial*) erste Folge; (*Sport*) Eröffnungsspiel, *das;* C (*Cricket*) eröffnender Schlagmann; D **for ~s** (*coll.*) zu Beginn; zunächst einmal

**open: ~-eyed** *adj.* A mit offenen Augen *nachgestellt;* **in ~-eyed amazement** mit großen Augen; **gaze/stare ~-eyed at sb./sth.** jmdn./etw. mit großen Augen ansehen/anstarren; **gaze/stare ~-eyed** große Augen machen; B (*watchful, alert*) **do sth. ~eyed** etw. bewusst tun; **~-'field system** *n.* (*Agric.*) alte Dreifelderwirtschaft; **~-'fronted** *adj.* vorne offen; **~-'handed** *adj.* freigebig; **~-'heart** *attrib. adj.* (*Med.*) am offenen Herzen *nachgestellt;* **~-'hearted** *adj.* aufrichtig ‹Person, Mitgefühl›; herzlich ‹Empfang›

**opening** /'əʊpnɪŋ/ ❶ *n.* A Öffnen, *das;* (*becoming open*) Sichöffnen, *das;* (*of crack, gap, etc.*) Entstehen, *das;* (*of exhibition, new centre*) Eröffnen, *das;* (*of road to traffic*) Freigabe, *die* (**to** für); **hours** *or* **times of ~:** Öffnungszeiten; **it's late ~:** heute haben die Läden länger geöffnet; **'late ~ Thursday'** „donnerstags auch abends geöffnet"; B (*establishment, inauguration, ceremony*) Eröffnung, *die;* **~ of Parliament** Parlamentseröffnung, *die;* C (*first performance*) Premiere, *die;* D (*initial part*) Anfang, *der;* (*Chess*) Eröffnung, *die;* E (*gap, aperture*) Öffnung, *die;* F (*opportunity*) Möglichkeit, *die;* (*for goods*) Absatzmöglichkeit, *die;* (*vacancy*) freie *od.* offene Stelle; **wait for an ~:** auf eine günstige Gelegenheit warten; **give sb. an ~:** jmdm. eine Gelegenheit geben; **give sb. an ~ into sth.** ‹Person:› jmdm. den Einstieg in etw. (*Akk.*) ermöglichen; ‹Job:› für jmdn. ein Einstieg in etw. (*Akk.*) sein; G (*facing pages of book etc.*) Seitenpaar, *das.*
❷ *adj.* einleitend; **the ~ lines** (*of play, poem, etc.*) die ersten Zeilen; **~ night** (*Theatre*) Premiere, *die;* **~ speech/address** Eröffnungsrede/-ansprache, *die;* **~ move** (*Chess*) Eröffnung, *die;* (*fig.*) erster Schachzug; **~ bid** (*at auction; also Bridge*) erstes Gebot; **~ batsman** (*Cricket*) eröffnender Schlagmann

**opening: ~ ceremony** *n.* feierliche Eröffnung (**for** *Gen.*); **~ hours** *n. pl.* Öffnungszeiten *Pl.;* **~ time** *n.* A Öffnungszeit, *die;* **wait for ~ time** darauf warten, dass geöffnet wird; B **~ times** ⇒ **~ hours**

**open 'letter** *n.* offener Brief

**openly** /'əʊpnlɪ/ *adv.* A (*publicly*) in der Öffentlichkeit; öffentlich ‹zugeben, verurteilen, abstreiten›; **quite ~:** in aller Öffentlichkeit; B (*frankly*) offen

**open: ~ 'market** *n.* offener *od.* freier Markt; **~-'minded** *adj.* aufgeschlossen (**about** für); **~-mindedness** /əʊpn'maɪndɪdnɪs/ *n., no pl.* Aufgeschlossenheit, *die;* **~-mouthed** /əʊpn'maʊðd/ *adj.* mit offenem Mund; **gape in ~-mouthed amazement** mit offenem Munde staunen; **~-necked** *adj.* ‹Hemd, Bluse› mit offenem Kragen; ausgeschnitten ‹Kleid, Pullover›

**openness** /'əʊpnnɪs/ *n., no pl.* A (*of countryside etc.*) Weite, *die;* B (*susceptibility*) Empfindlichkeit, *die* (**to** gegen); C (*receptiveness*) Empfänglichkeit, *die;* **~ of mind** Aufgeschlossenheit, *die;* D (*manifestness*) Offenheit, *die;* **I was surprised by the ~ of the people's resistance** ich war überrascht, wie offen die Leute Widerstand leisteten; E (*frankness*) Offenheit, *die;* F (*being spread out*) Grobheit, *die;* (*of arrangement*) Offenheit, *die*

**open: ~-plan** *adj.* mit ineinander übergehenden Räumen *nachgestellt;* offen angelegt ‹Haus›; **~-plan office** Großraumbüro, *das;* **~ 'prison** *n.* offene Anstalt; **~ 'sandwich** *n.* belegtes Brot; **~ season** *n.* (*Brit.*) Jagdzeit, *die;* (*for fish*) Fangzeit, *die;* **it is [the] ~ season for** *or* **on sth.** (*fig.*) etw. ist an der Tagesordnung; **~ 'sesame** ⇒ **sesame** C; **~ 'shelf library** (*Amer.*) ⇒ **~ access library;** **~ 'shelves** *n. pl.* **these books are on ~ shelves** diese Bücher sind in der Freihandzone [aufgestellt]; **~ 'shop** *n.* Open Shop, *der;* nicht gewerkschaftspflichtiger Betrieb; **~ so'ciety** *n.* (*Sociol.*) offene Gesellschaft; **~-toe[d]** /əʊpn'təʊ(d)/ *adj.* vorn offen ‹Schuh, Sandale›; **~-top** *attrib. adj.* offen; oben offen ‹Bus›; **O~ Uni'versity** *pr. n.* (*Brit.*) **the O~ University** die Open University (*britische Fernuniversität*); *attrib.* ‹Kurs› an der Fernuniversität; ‹akademischer Grad› der Fernuniversität; **~ 'weave** *n.* (*Textiles*) loses *od.* grobes Gewebe; *attrib.* locker *od.* grob gewebt ‹Stoff, Struktur›; **~work** *n.* durchbrochene Struktur; (*Sewing*) Durchbrucharbeit, *die; attrib.* durchbrochen

**opera**[1] /'ɒpərə/ *n.* A Oper, *die;* B *no pl.* (*branch of art*) **[the] ~:** die Oper; C **light ~:** Operette, *die*

**opera**[2] *pl. of* **opus**

**operable** /'ɒpərəbl/ *adj.* (*Med.*) operabel

**opera: ~ glasses** *n. pl.* Opernglas, *das;* **~ hat** *n.* Chapeau claque, *der;* **~ house** *n.* Opernhaus, *das;* **~ singer** *n.* ▶ 1261 Opernsänger, *der*/-sängerin, *die*

**operate** /'ɒpəreɪt/ ❶ *v.i.* A (*be in action*) in Betrieb sein; ‹Bus, Zug usw.:› verkehren; (*have an effect*) sich auswirken; **the system ~s against our interests/in our favour** das System, wie es derzeit funktioniert, bringt uns Nachteile/Vorteile; **the hospital is operating normally again** im Krankenhaus herrscht wieder normaler Betrieb; B (*function*) arbeiten; **the torch ~s on batteries** die Taschenlampe arbeitet mit Batterien; C (*perform operation*) operieren; arbeiten; **~ on sth.** etw. bearbeiten; **~ [on sb.]** (*Med.*) [jmdn.] operieren; D (*exercise influence*) **~ [up]on sb./sth.** auf jmdn./etw. einwirken; E (*follow course of conduct*) agieren; **the gang ~d by posing as workmen** die Methode der Bande bestand darin, dass sie sich als Arbeiter ausgaben; F (*produce effect*) wirken; G (*Mil.*) operieren.
❷ *v.t.* A (*accomplish*) herbeiführen; B (*cause to work*) bedienen ‹Maschine›; betätigen ‹Hebel, Bremse›; betreiben ‹Unternehmen›; unterhalten ‹Werk, Post, Busverbindung, Telefondienst›

**operatic** /ɒpə'rætɪk/ *adj.* A Opern‹sänger, -musik›; B (*like opera*) opernhaft

**operating: ~ room** *n.* (*Med.*) Operationssaal, *der;* **~ system** *n.* (*Computing*) Betriebssystem. *das;* **~ table** *n.* (*Med.*) Operationstisch, *der;* **~ theatre** *n.* (*Brit. Med.*) Operationssaal, *der*

**operation** /ɒpə'reɪʃn/ *n.* A (*causing to work*) (*of machine*) Bedienung, *die;* (*of factory, mine, etc.*) Betrieb, *der;* (*of bus service, telephone service, etc.*) Unterhaltung, *die;* **ease of ~:** leichte Bedienbarkeit; B (*way sth. works*) Arbeitsweise, *die;* **the engine is noted for its quiet ~** *or* **quietness in ~:** der Motor ist für seinen leisen Lauf bekannt; C (*being operative*) **come into ~** ‹Maschine, Gerät:› zu arbeiten beginnen; ‹Gesetz, Gebühr usw.:› in Kraft treten; **be in ~** ‹Maschine, Gerät usw.:› in Betrieb sein; ‹Service:› zur Verfügung stehen; ‹Gesetz:› in Kraft sein; **be out of ~** ‹Maschine, Gerät usw.:› außer Betrieb sein; ‹Service:› nicht zur Verfügung stehen; D (*active process*) Vorgang, *der;* **drilling ~s** Bohrarbeiten; **~[s] research** ⇒ **operational research;** E (*performance*) Tätigkeit, *die;* **repeat the ~:** das Ganze [noch einmal] wiederholen; F ▶ 1232 (*Med.*) Operation, *die;* **have an ~ [on one's foot]** [am Fuß] operiert werden; **an ~ for appendicitis** eine Blinddarmoperation; G (*Air Force, Mil., Navy*) Einsatz, *der;* Operation, *die;* **night ~s** Nachteinsätze; **~s room** Befehlsstelle, *die;* ⇒ *also* **combined;** H (*financial transaction*) [Geschäfts]tätigkeit, *die;* I (*Math., Computing*) Operation, *die*

**operational** /ɒpə'reɪʃənl/ *adj.* A (*concerned with operations*) Einsatz‹flugzeug, -breite›; Betriebs‹wirtschaftlichkeit, -personal›; (*Mil.*) Einsatz-; B (*esp. Mil.: ready to function*) einsatzbereit

**operational re'search** *n.* (*Brit.*) Unternehmensforschung, *die*

**operative** /'ɒpərətɪv/ ❶ *adj.* A (*in operation*) **the law became ~:** das Gesetz trat in Kraft; **the scheme is fully ~:** das Programm läuft; B (*effective*) wirksam; C (*most relevant*) **the ~ word is 'quietly'** die Betonung liegt auf „leise"; D (*Med.*) operativ. ❷ *n.* [Fach]arbeiter, *der*/-arbeiterin, *die;* **machine ~:** Maschinist, *der*/Maschinistin, *die*

**operator** /'ɒpəreɪtə(r)/ *n.* A ▶ 1261 (*worker*) [Maschinen]bediener, *der*/-bedienerin, *die;* Bedienungskraft, *die;* (*of crane, excavator, etc.*) Führer, *der;* B ▶ 1261 (*Teleph.*) (*at exchange*) Vermittlung, *die;* (*at switchboard*) Telefonist, *der*/Telefonistin, *die;* C (*person engaged in business*) Unternehmer, *der*/Unternehmerin, *die;* (*coll.: shrewd person*) Schlitzohr, *das* (*ugs.*); **a sly ~** (*coll.*) ein gewiefter Bursche (*ugs.*); D (*Math., Computing*) Operator, *der*

**operetta** /ɒpə'retə/ *n.* (*Mus.*) Operette, *die*

**ophthalmic** /ɒf'θælmɪk/ *adj.* Augen‹arterie, -krankheit, -chirurg, -salbe›

**ophthalmic op'tician** *n.* ▶ 1261 (*Brit.*) Augenoptiker, *der*/-optikerin, *die*

O

**ophthalmology** /ɒfθæl'mɒlədʒɪ/ *n.* (*Med.*) Ophthalmologie, *die* (*fachspr.*); Augenheilkunde, *die*

**opiate** /'əʊpɪət/ *n.* Ⓐ (*Med.*) Opiat, *das;* Ⓑ (*fig.*) Betäubungsmittel, *das;* (*causing addiction*) Droge, *die*

**opine** /ə'paɪn/ *v.t.* Ⓐ (*express as one's opinion*) meinen; Ⓑ (*hold as opinion*) denken

**opinion** /ə'pɪnjən/ *n.* Ⓐ (*belief, judgement*) Meinung, *die* (**on** über + *Akk.*, zu); Ansicht, *die* (**on** von, zu, über + *Akk.*); **his [political] ~s** seine [politische] Einstellung; **his ~s on the matter/on religion** seine Meinung dazu/seine Einstellung zur Religion; **in my ~:** meiner Meinung nach; **be of [the] ~ that ...:** der Ansicht sein, dass ...; **be a matter of ~:** Ansichtssache sein; ⇒ *also* **difference** A; Ⓑ *no pl., no art.* (*beliefs etc. of group*) Meinung, *die* (**on** über + *Akk.*); **~ is swinging in his favour** es gibt einen Meinungsumschwung zu seinen Gunsten; **public ~:** die öffentliche Meinung; Ⓒ (*estimate*) **have a high/low ~ of sb.** eine hohe/schlechte Meinung von jmdm. haben; **I formed a better ~ of the place** ich bekam einen besseren Eindruck von dem Ort; **have a great ~ of oneself** sehr von sich überzeugt sein; **have no ~ of sth./sb.** von etw./jmdm. nicht sehr überzeugt sein; Ⓓ (*formal statement of expert*) Gutachten, *das;* **[get *or* secure a] solicitor's/expert's ~:** [ein] Rechts-/Sachverständigengutachten [einholen]; **another *or* a second ~:** die Meinung eines weiteren *od.* zweiten Sachverständigen; Ⓔ (*Law*) (*expression of reasons for decision*) Urteilsbegründung, *die;* (*judgement, decision*) Entscheidung, *die;* Urteil, *das*

**opinionated** /ə'pɪnjəneɪtɪd/ *adj.* Ⓐ (*obstinate*) rechthaberisch; Ⓑ (*self-willed*) eigensinnig

**o'pinion poll** *n.* Meinungsumfrage, *die*

**opium** /'əʊpɪəm/ *n.* Opium, *das*

**opium: ~ den** *n.* Opiumhöhle, *die* (*abwertend*); **~ pipe** *n.* Opiumpfeife, *die*

**opossum** /ə'pɒsəm/ *n.* (*Zool.*) Ⓐ Opossum, *das;* Ⓑ (*Austral., NZ*) ⇒ **possum** C

**oppo** /'ɒpəʊ/ *n., pl.* **~s** (*Brit. coll.*) Kumpel, *der* (*salopp*)

**opponent** /ə'pəʊnənt/ *n.* Gegner, *der*/Gegnerin, *die*

**opportune** /'ɒpətju:n/ *adj.* Ⓐ (*favourable*) günstig; Ⓑ (*well-timed*) zur rechten Zeit *nachgestellt;* **be ~:** zur rechten Zeit kommen

**opportunely** /'ɒpətju:nlɪ/ *adv.* ⇒ **opportune:** günstig; zur rechten Zeit; **be ~ timed** zeitlich günstig liegen

**opportunism** /ɒpə'tju:nɪzm/ *n., no pl.* Opportunismus, *der*

**opportunist** /ɒpə'tju:nɪst/ *n.* Opportunist, *der*/Opportunistin, *die*

**opportunity** /ɒpə'tju:nɪtɪ/ *n.* Gelegenheit, *die;* **have plenty of/little ~ for doing *or* to do sth.** reichlich/wenig Gelegenheit haben, etw. zu tun; **~ knocks for sb.** eine Gelegenheit bietet sich jmdm.; ⇒ *also* **equal opportunity; take** 1 E

**opposable** /ə'pəʊzəbl/ *adj.* (*Anat., Zool.*) opponierbar

**oppose** /ə'pəʊz/ ❶ *v.t.* Ⓐ (*set oneself against*) sich wenden gegen; opponieren gegen; Ⓑ (*place as obstacle*) entgegenstellen (**to** *Dat.*); Ⓒ (*set as contrast*) gegenüberstellen (**to, against** *Dat.*); Ⓓ (*Anat., Zool.*) opponieren. ❷ *v.i.* ‹Opposition:› opponieren; **the opposing team** die gegnerische Mannschaft

**opposed** /ə'pəʊzd/ *adj.* Ⓐ (*contrary, opposite*) gegensätzlich; entgegengesetzt; **X and Y are diametrically ~:** X und Y sind einander diametral entgegengesetzt; **as ~ to** im Gegensatz zu; Ⓑ (*hostile*) **be ~** ‹Personen:› Gegner sein; **be ~ to sth.** gegen etw. sein

**opposite** /'ɒpəzɪt/ ❶ *adj.* Ⓐ (*on other or farther side*) gegenüberliegend ‹Straßenseite, Ufer›; entgegengesetzt ‹Ende›; Ⓑ (*contrary*) entgegengesetzt ‹Weg, Richtung›; Ⓒ (*very different in character*) entgegengesetzt, gegensätzlich ‹Beschreibungen, Aussagen›; **be ~ to sth.** das Gegenteil von etw. sein; **be of an ~ kind from ...:** von einer ganz anderen Art sein als ...; Ⓓ **the ~ sex** das andere Geschlecht. ❷ *n.* Gegenteil, *das* (**of** von); **be the extreme ~ of sth.** das genaue Gegenteil von etw. sein; **be ~s** einen Gegensatz bilden. ❸ *adv.* gegenüber; **sit ~:** auf der gegenüberliegenden Seite sitzen. ❹ *prep.* gegenüber; **~ each other** einander gegenüber; **play ~ sb.** (*Theatre*) neben jmdm. spielen

**opposite 'number** *n.* (*fig.*) Pendant, *das*

**opposition** /ɒpə'zɪʃn/ *n.* Ⓐ *no pl.* (*antagonism*) Opposition, *die;* (*resistance*) Widerstand, *der* (**to** gegen); **in ~ to** entgegen; **offer ~ to sth.** einer Sache (*Dat.*) Widerstand entgegensetzen; **without ~:** ohne Widerstand; Ⓑ (*Brit. Polit.*) **the O~, Her Majesty's O~:** die Opposition; **Leader of the O~:** Oppositionsführer, *der*/-führerin, *die;* **[be] in ~:** in der Opposition [sein]; Ⓒ (*body of opponents or competitors*) Gegner *Pl.;* Ⓓ (*contrast, antithesis*) Gegensatz, *der* (**to** zu); Ⓔ (*placing or being placed opposite*) Platzierung an gegenüberliegenden Stellen; **by the ~ of sth. to sth.** indem man etw. gegenüber einer Sache (*Dat.*) platziert; Ⓕ (*Astron., Astrol.*) **be in ~:** in Opposition stehen (**with** zu); *abs.* in Opposition zur Sonne stehen

**oppress** /ə'pres/ *v.t.* Ⓐ (*govern cruelly*) unterdrücken; Ⓑ (*fig.: weigh down*) ‹Gefühl:› bedrücken; ‹Hitze:› schwer zu schaffen machen (+ *Dat.*)

**oppression** /ə'preʃn/ *n.* Unterdrückung, *die*

**oppressive** /ə'presɪv/ *adj.* Ⓐ (*tyrannical*) repressiv; Ⓑ (*fig.: hard to endure*) bedrückend ‹Ängste, Atmosphäre› (**to** für); Ⓒ (*fig.: hot and close*) drückend ‹Wetter, Klima, Tag›; Ⓓ (*fig.: burdensome*) drückend ‹Steuer›; repressiv ‹Gesetz, Beschränkung›

**oppressively** /ə'presɪvlɪ/ *adv.* Ⓐ (*tyrannically*) mit unterdrückerischen Methoden; repressiv ‹regieren›; Ⓑ (*fig.: so as to weigh down*) drückend ‹heiß›; **weigh ~ on sb.** schwer auf jmdm. lasten

**oppressor** /ə'presə(r)/ *n.* Unterdrücker, *der*

**opprobrious** /ə'prəʊbrɪəs/ *adj.* Ⓐ (*abusive*) verächtlich; Ⓑ (*shameful*) schändlich

**opprobrium** /ə'prəʊbrɪəm/ *n.* Schande, *die*

**opt** /ɒpt/ *v.i.* sich entscheiden (**for** für); **~ to do sth.** sich dafür entscheiden, etw. zu tun; **~ out** (*not join in*) nicht mitmachen; (*cease taking part*) nicht länger mitmachen; **~ out of** nicht/nicht länger mitmachen bei; (*give up membership of*) austreten aus; (*not take up invitation to*) sich entschließen, doch nicht teilzunehmen an (+ *Dat.*)

**optic** /'ɒptɪk/ ❶ *adj.* (*Anat.*) Seh‹nerv, -hügel, -bahn›; (*Med.*) Sehnerven‹entzündung, -atrophie›. ❷ *n.* Ⓐ (*in optical instrument*) optisches Element; Ⓑ (*arch./joc.: eye*) Auge, *das;* Ⓒ *or* **O~** ® (*Brit.: for measuring out spirits*) Portionierer, *der*

**optical** /'ɒptɪkl/ *adj.* optisch ‹Zielvorrichtung, Täuschung, Gerät, Fernrohr›; **~ microscope** Lichtmikroskop, *das;* **~ aid** Sehhilfe, *die*

**optical: ~ 'character reader** *n.* (*Computing*) Klarschriftleser, *der;* **~ 'fibre** *n.* Lichtleitfaser, *die*

**optically** /'ɒptɪkəlɪ/ *adv.* optisch

**optician** /ɒp'tɪʃn/ *n.* ▶ 1261 Ⓐ (*maker or seller of spectacles etc.*) Optiker, *der*/Optikerin, *die;* Ⓑ ⇒ **ophthalmic optician**

**optics** /'ɒptɪks/ *n., no pl.* Optik, *die*

**optima** *pl. of* **optimum**

**optimal** /'ɒptɪml/ ⇒ **optimum** 2

**optimise** ⇒ **optimize**

**optimism** /'ɒptɪmɪzm/ *n., no pl.* Optimismus, *der*

**optimist** /'ɒptɪmɪst/ *n.* Optimist, *der*/Optimistin, *die*

**optimistic** /ɒptɪ'mɪstɪk/ *adj.* optimistisch

**optimistically** /ɒptɪ'mɪstɪkəlɪ/ *adv.* optimistisch; **~ speaking, ...:** mit etwas Optimismus kann man sagen, dass ...

**optimize** /'ɒptɪmaɪz/ *v.t.* Ⓐ (*make optimum*) optimieren; Ⓑ (*make the most of*) das Beste machen aus

**optimum** /'ɒptɪməm/ ❶ *n., pl.* **optima** /'ɒptɪmə/ Ⓐ (*most favourable conditions*) Optimum, *das;* Ⓑ (*best compromise*) goldener Mittelweg. ❷ *adj.* optimal

**option** /'ɒpʃn/ *n.* Ⓐ (*choice*) Wahl, *die;* (*thing that may be chosen*) Wahlmöglichkeit, *die;* (*Brit. Univ., Sch.*) Wahlfach, *das;* **I have no ~ but to do sth.** mir bleibt nichts [anderes] übrig, als etw. zu tun; **keep *or* leave one's ~s open** sich (*Dat.*) alle Möglichkeiten offen halten; ⇒ *also* **soft option;** Ⓑ *no pl.* (*freedom of choice*) Entscheidungsfreiheit, *die;* **she had no ~ about accepting ...:** sie hatte keine andere Wahl, als ... anzunehmen; **that leaves us no ~ [but to ...]** dann bleibt uns keine andere Wahl[, als zu ...]; Ⓒ (*St. Exch.*) Option, *die*

**optional** /'ɒpʃənl/ *adj.* nicht zwingend; fakultativ; **~ subject** Wahlfach, *das;* **formal dress is ~:** Gesellschaftskleidung ist nicht vorgeschrieben; **~ extra** Extra, *das;* **take an ~ paper** eine freiwillige Klausur schreiben

**optionally** /'ɒpʃənəlɪ/ *adv.* freiwillig

**opulence** /'ɒpjʊləns/ *n., no pl.* Wohlstand, *der*

**opulent** /'ɒpjʊlənt/ *adj.* (*rich*) wohlhabend ‹Person, Aussehen›; (*luxurious*) feudal ‹Auto, Haus, Hotel usw.›

**opulently** /'ɒpjʊləntlɪ/ *adv.* im Luxus ‹leben›; feudal ‹möbliert, eingerichtet›

**opus** /'əʊpəs, 'ɒpəs/ *n., pl.* **opera** /'ɒpərə/ Ⓐ (*Mus.*) Opus, *das;* Ⓑ **magnum ~, ~ [magnum]** (*great work*) großes Werk; (*greatest work*) Hauptwerk, *das*

**OR** *abbr.* **operational research** OR

**or**[1] /ə(r), *stressed* ɔ:(r)/ *conj.* Ⓐ oder; **he cannot read or write** er kann weder lesen noch schreiben; **without food or water** ohne Essen und Wasser; **[either] ... or [else] ...:** entweder ... oder [aber] ...; Ⓑ *introducing synonym* oder [auch]; *introducing explanation* das heißt; **or rather** beziehungsweise; [oder] genauer gesagt; Ⓒ *indicating uncertainty* oder; **15 or 20 minutes** 15 bis 20 Minuten; **in a day or two** in ein, zwei Tagen; **a doctor or something** ein Arzt oder so [was] (*ugs.*); **he must be ill or something** vielleicht ist er krank oder so (*ugs.*); **have you gone out of your mind or something?** bist du übergeschnappt, oder was? (*ugs.*); **he or somebody else** er oder sonst jemand; **in Leeds or somewhere** in Leeds oder irgendwo da; ⇒ *also* **so**[1] 2; Ⓓ *expr. significant afterthought* oder; **he was obviously lying — or was he?** er hat ganz offensichtlich gelogen — oder [doch nicht]?; **they cannot throw you out — or can they?** sie können dich doch nicht hinauswerfen — oder [etwa doch]?

**or**[2] /ɔ:(r)/ (*Her.*) ❶ *n.* Gold, *das.* ❷ *adj.* golden

**oracle** /'ɒrəkl/ *n.* Ⓐ (*infallible guide or indicator*) Orakel, *das* (*fig.*); Ⓑ (*very wise person*) Koryphäe, *die;* Autorität, *die;* Ⓒ (*place or response of deity*) Orakel, *das;* Ⓓ **work the ~** (*Brit. fig.*) [ein wenig] nachhelfen

**oracular** /ə'rækjʊlə(r)/ *adj.* Ⓐ (*of oracle[s]*) Orakel‹stätte, -priester›; Ⓑ (*infallible*) über alle Zweifel erhaben ‹Äußerung, Buch›; Ⓒ (*derog.: obscure or ambiguous*) orakelhaft

**oral** /'ɔ:rl/ ❶ *adj.* Ⓐ (*spoken*) mündlich ‹Prüfung, Vereinbarung›; mündlich überliefert ‹Tradition›; **the agreement was only ~:** die Vereinbarung war nur mündlich getroffen worden; Ⓑ (*done or taken by the mouth*) oral; **~ sex** Oralverkehr, *der;* Ⓒ (*Anat.*) Mund‹höhle, -schleimhaut›. ❷ *n.* (*coll.: examination*) **the ~[s]** das Mündliche

**orally** /'ɔ:rəlɪ/ *adv.* Ⓐ (*in speech*) mündlich; Ⓑ (*by the mouth*) oral; **take ~:** einnehmen

**orange** /'ɒrɪndʒ/ ❶ *n.* Ⓐ (*fruit*) Orange, *die;* Apfelsine, *die;* Ⓑ (*tree*) Orangenbaum, *der;* **mock ~** (*Bot.*) Falscher Jasmin; Blasser Pfeifenstrauch; Ⓒ (*colour*) **~ [colour]** Orange, *das.* ❷ *adj.* orange[farben]; Orangen‹geschmack›; **~ drink** Getränk mit Orangengeschmack

**orange: ~ blossom** *n.* Orangenblüte, *die;* **~ box** *n.* Apfelsinenkiste, *die;* **~ juice** *n.* Orangensaft, *der;* **O~man** /'ɒrɪndʒmən/ *n., pl.* **O~men** /'ɒrɪndʒmən/ (*Polit.*) Orangeman, *der;* Mitglied der Orange Society; **~ peel** *n.* Orangenschale, *die*

**orangery** /ˈɒrɪndʒərɪ/ *n.* Orangerie, *die*

**orange: ~ ˈsquash** ⇒ **squash**[1] 3 A; **~ stick** *n.* Maniküreståbchen, *das*

**orang-utan** /ɔːræŋʊˈtæn/ *n.* (*Zool.*) Orang-Utan, *der*

**orate** /əˈreɪt/ *v.i.* (*joc.*) Reden schwingen (*ugs.*); (*derog.*) salbadern (*ugs. abwertend*)

**oration** /əˈreɪʃn/ *n.* Rede, *die*

**orator** /ˈɒrətə(r)/ *n.* Redner, *der*/Rednerin, *die;* (*eloquent speaker*) Rhetoriker, *der*/Rhetorikerin, *die*

**oratorical** /ɒrəˈtɒrɪkl/ *adj.* ausdrucksstark

**oratorio** /ɒrəˈtɔːrɪəʊ/ *n., pl.* **~s** (*Mus.*) Oratorium, *das*

**oratory** /ˈɒrətərɪ/ *n.* **A** *no pl.* (*art of public speaking*) Redekunst, *die;* Rhetorik, *die;* **B** *no pl.* (*rhetorical language*) Rhetorik, *die;* **C** (*small chapel*) Oratorium, *das*

**orb** /ɔːb/ *n.* **A** (*sphere*) Kugel, *die;* **B** (*part of regalia*) Reichsapfel, *der*

**orbit** /ˈɔːbɪt/ **1** *n.* **A** (*Astron.*) [Umlauf]bahn, *die;* **B** (*Astronaut.*) Umlaufbahn, *die;* Orbit, *der;* (*single circuit*) Umkreisung, *die;* **be in/go into ~ [around the moon]** in der [Mond]umlaufbahn sein/in die [Mond]umlaufbahn eintreten; **put/send into ~:** in die Umlaufbahn bringen/schießen; **C** (*fig.*) Sphäre, *die;* **D** (*Anat.*) Augenhöhle, *die;* Orbita, *die* (*fachspr.*); **E** (*Phys.: of electron*) Orbital, *das.* **2** *v.i.* kreisen. **3** *v.t.* umkreisen

**orbital** /ˈɔːbɪtl/ *adj.* **A** (*Anat.*) Orbital-; **B** (*Astron., Phys.*) Bahn-; **C** Ring‹straße, -linie›; **north ~ route** Nordring, *der*

**Orcadian** /ɔːˈkeɪdɪən/ **1** *adj.* Orkney-; der Orkneyinseln *nachgestellt.* **2** *n.* Bewohner/Bewohnerin der Orkneyinseln

**orchard** /ˈɔːtʃəd/ *n.* Obstgarten, *der;* (*commercial*) Obstplantage, *die;* **cherry ~:** Kirschgarten, *der*

**orchestra** /ˈɔːkɪstrə/ *n.* **A** (*Mus.*) Orchester, *das;* **B** ⇒ **orchestra pit**

**orchestral** /ɔːˈkestrl/ *adj.* Orchester-; (*suggestive of orchestra*) orchestral

**orchestra: ~ pit** *n.* Orchestergraben, *der;* **~ stalls** *n. pl.* Parkett, *das;* **seat in the ~ stalls** Sperrsitz, *der*

**orchestrate** /ˈɔːkɪstreɪt/ *v.t.* (*Mus.; also fig.*) orchestrieren

**orchestration** /ɔːkɪˈstreɪʃn/ *n.* **A** (*Mus.*) Orchesterbearbeitung, *die;* Orchestrierung, *die;* **B** (*fig.*) Orchestrierung, *die*

**orchid** /ˈɔːkɪd/ *n.* Orchidee, *die*

**orchis** /ˈɔːkɪs/ *n.* (*Bot.*) Knabenkraut, *das;* Orchis, *die* (*fachspr.*)

**ordain** /ɔːˈdeɪn/ *v.t.* **A** (*Eccl.*) ordinieren; **be ~ed priest** ordiniert werden; **B** (*destine*) bestimmen; **if fate should so ~ it** wenn es das Schicksal so will *od.* fügt; **C** (*decree*) verfügen

**ordeal** /ɔːˈdiːl/ *n.* **A** Qual, *die;* (*geh.*) Tortur, *die* (**by** durch); **B** (*Hist.*) Ordal, *das* (*fachspr.*); Gottesurteil, *das;* **~ by fire/water** Feuer-/Wasserprobe, *die*

**order** /ˈɔːdə(r)/ **1** *n.* **A** (*sequence*) Reihenfolge, *die;* **~ of words, word ~:** Wortstellung, *die;* **~ of play** (*Tennis etc.*) Spielfolge, *die;* **in ~ of importance/size/age** nach Wichtigkeit/Größe/Alter; **be in subject ~** *or* **~ of subject** nach Gebieten geordnet sein; **put sth. in ~:** etw. [in der richtigen Reihenfolge] ordnen; **keep sth. in ~:** etw. in der richtigen Reihenfolge halten; **answer the questions in ~:** die Fragen der Reihe nach beantworten; **out of ~:** nicht in der richtigen Reihenfolge; durcheinander; **the cards get out of ~:** die Karten geraten in Unordnung *od.* durcheinander; **put sth. back out of ~:** etw. nicht an den richtigen Platz zurückstellen/-legen; **B** (*regular array, normal state*) Ordnung, *die;* **put** *or* **set sth./one's affairs in ~:** Ordnung in etw. bringen/seine Angelegenheiten ordnen; **be/not be in ~:** in Ordnung/nicht in Ordnung sein (*ugs.*); **put sth. in ~** (*repair*) etw. in Ordnung bringen (*ugs.*); **be out of/in ~** (*not in/in working condition*) nicht funktionieren/funktionieren; **'out of ~'** „außer Betrieb"; **the engine is now in running ~:** der Motor läuft jetzt wieder *od.* ist jetzt wieder betriebsbereit; **in good/bad ~:** in gutem/schlechtem Zustand; **in working ~:** betriebsfähig; ⇒ *also* **house** 1 A; **C** *in sing. and pl.* (*command*) Anweisung, *die;* Anordnung, *die;* Weisung, *die* (*geh.*); (*Mil.*) Befehl, *der;* (*Law*) Beschluss, *der;* Verfügung, *die;* **my ~s are to ..., I have ~s to ...:** ich habe Anweisung zu ...; **while following ~s** bei Befolgung der Anweisung/bei der Befehlsausführung; **act on ~s** auf Befehl handeln; **be the one who gives the ~s** das Sagen haben; **I don't take ~s from anyone!** ich lasse mir von keinem etwas befehlen!; **~s are ~s** Befehl ist Befehl; **court ~:** Gerichtsbeschluss, *der;* **by ~ of** auf Anordnung (+ *Gen.*); ⇒ *also* **doctor** 1 A; **further** 1 B; **starter** A; **D in ~ to do sth.** um etw. zu tun; **in ~ that sb. should do sth.** damit jmd. etw. tut; **E** (*Commerc.*) Auftrag, *der* (**for** über + *Akk.*); Bestellung, *die* (**for** *Gen.*); Order, *die* (*Kaufmannsspr.*); (*to waiter, ~ed goods*) Bestellung, *die;* **place an ~ [with sb.]** [jmdm.] einen Auftrag erteilen; **have sth. on ~:** etw. bestellt haben; **put goods on ~:** Waren in Bestellung geben; **to ~:** auf Bestellung; **she could cry to ~** (*fig.*) sie konnte auf Befehl weinen; **made to ~:** nach Maß angefertigt, maßgeschneidert ‹Kleidung›; **a suit made to ~:** ein Maßanzug; **last ~s please** (*Brit.*) die letzten Bestellungen (*vor der Sperrstunde*), bitte!; ⇒ *also* **tall** 1 B; **F** (*law-abiding state*) [öffentliche] Ordnung; **forces of ~:** Ordnungsmächte; **keep ~:** Ordnung [be]wahren; ⇒ *also* **law** B; **G** (*Eccl.: fraternity*) Orden, *der;* **H** (*Eccl.: grade of ministry*) Weihestufe, *die;* **holy ~s** heilige Weihen; **be in [holy] ~s** dem geistlichen Stand angehören; **take [holy] ~s** die [heiligen] Weihen empfangen; **I** (*social class*) [Gesellschafts]schicht, *die;* (*clerical ~, ~ of baronets, etc.*) Stand, *der;* ⇒ *also* **lower**[2] 1 B; **J** (*principles of decorum and rules of procedure*) [Geschäfts]ordnung, *die;* **O~! O~!** zur Ordnung!; Ruhe bitte!; **~ in court** (*Brit.*) *or* (*Amer.*) **the courtroom** Ruhe im Gerichtssaal; **call sb./the meeting to ~:** jmdn./die Versammlung zur Ordnung rufen; **call a meeting to ~** (*open the proceedings*) eine Versammlung für eröffnet erklären; **point of ~:** Verfahrensfrage, *die;* **[on a] point of ~, Mr Chairman** Antrag zur Geschäftsordnung, Herr Vorsitzender; **be in ~:** zulässig sein; (*fig.*) ‹Forderung:› berechtigt sein; ‹Drink, Erklärung:› angebracht sein; **the speaker is in ~:** der Redner hält sich an die Geschäftsordnung; **it is in ~ for him to do that** es ist in Ordnung, wenn er das tut; **be out of ~:** gegen die Geschäftsordnung verstoßen; ‹Verhalten, Handlung:› unzulässig sein; **that's/you're out of ~, mate** (*coll.*) so [gehts] nicht, Kumpel (*ugs.*); **~ of the day** (*lit. or fig.*) Tagesordnung, *die;* **be the ~ of the day** auf der Tagesordnung stehen; (*fig.*) an der Tagesordnung sein; **~ of business** Geschäftsordnung, *die;* (*sequence of matters*) Tagesordnung, *die;* ⇒ *also* **standing orders** b; **K** (*constitution of things*) Ordnung, *die;* **a new ~ of literary criticism** eine neue Art *od.* Gattung von Literaturkritik; **L** (*kind, degree*) Klasse, *die;* Art, *die;* **intelligence of a high ~:** hochgradige Intelligenz; **his work is usually of a high ~:** seine Arbeit ist gewöhnlich erstklassig; **M** (*Archit.*) Säulenordnung, *die;* **N** (*company of distinguished persons, badge or insignia*) Orden, *der;* **O~ of Merit** (*Brit.*) Verdienstorden, *der;* **Masonic O~:** Freimaurerloge, *die;* **O** (*Finance*) Order, *die;* Zahlungsanweisung, *die;* **[banker's] ~:** [Bank]anweisung, *die;* **'pay to the ~ of ...'** „zahlbar an ..." (+ *Akk.*); ⇒ *also* **money order; standing order** a; **P** (*Mil.*) Ordnung, *die;* **marching ~:** Marschordnung, *die;* **in close ~:** in geschlossener Formation; **in battle ~:** in Kampfaufstellung; **Q** (*Math.*) Ordnung, *die;* **~ [of magnitude]** Größenordnung, *die;* **of** *or* **in the ~ of ...:** in der Größenordnung von ...; **of the first ~** ‹Gleichung› ersten Grades; **a scoundrel of the first ~** (*fig. coll.*) ein Schurke ersten Ranges; **R** (*Eccl.: form of service*) Ritual, *das;* **S** (*Biol.*) Ordnung, *die;* ⇒ *also* **natural order.**

**2** *v.t.* **A** (*command*) befehlen; anordnen; ‹Gott, Schicksal:› bestimmen; ‹Richter:› verfügen; verordnen ‹Arznei, Ruhe usw.›; **~ sb. to do sth.** jmdn. anweisen/(*Milit.*) jmdm. befehlen, etw. zu tun; **~ sth. [to be] done** anordnen, dass etw. getan wird; **the dog was ~ed to be destroyed** es wurde die Tötung des Hundes verfügt *od.* angeordnet; ⇒ *also* **doctor** 1 A; **B** (*direct the supply of*) bestellen (**from** bei); ordern ‹Kaufmannsspr.›; **~ in advance** vorbestellen; **C** (*arrange*) ordnen; **~ed** geordnet *od.* geregelt ‹Leben›; **~ arms** (*Mil.*) Gewehr bei Fuß stehen; **D** (*command to go*) schicken; (*Mil.*) beordern; **~ sb. [to go] to Spain** jmdn. nach Spanien schicken/beordern; **~ sb. [to come] home** jmdn. befehlen, nach Hause zu kommen; **~ sb. out of the house** jmdn. aus dem Haus weisen; **~ back** zurückbeordern; **E** (*ordain*) bestimmen

**~ aˈbout, ~ aˈround** *v.t.* herumkommandieren

**~ ˈoff** *v.t.* (*Sport*) **~ sb. off [the pitch/field]** jmdn. vom Platz stellen

**~ ˈout** *v.t.* hinausschicken; ausschicken, einsetzen ‹Truppen usw.›

**order: ~ book** *n.* **A** (*Commerc.*) Auftragsbuch, *das;* **B O~ Book** (*Brit. Parl.*) Buch mit Eintragungen der angemeldeten Anträge; **~ form** *n.* Bestellformular, *das;* Bestellschein, *der;* **O~ in ˈCouncil** *n.* (*Brit.*) Regierungserlass, *der*

**orderly** /ˈɔːdəlɪ/ **1** *adj.* **A** friedlich ‹Demonstration usw.›; diszipliniert ‹Menge›; (*conforming to order*) ordnungsgemäß; (*methodical*) methodisch; geordnet ‹Linie, Leben›; geregelt ‹Leben, Gewohnheiten›; ordentlich ‹Person›; (*tidy*) ordentlich; **B** (*Mil.*) Dienst habend *od.* tuend. **2** **A** *n.* (*Mil.*) [Offiziers]bursche, *der;* **B** **medical ~:** ≈ Krankenpflegehelfer, *der*

**orderly: ~ officer** *n.* (*Brit.*) Offizier vom Dienst, *der;* **~ room** *n.* Schreibstube, *die*

**order: ~ pad** *n.* Bestellblock, *der;* **~ paper** *n.* (*Brit. Parl.*) Tagesordnung, *die*

**ordinal** /ˈɔːdɪnl/ (*Math.*) ▶ **1352** **1** *adj.* **~ number** ⇒ **2. 2** *n.* Ordnungs-, Ordinalzahl, *die*

**ordinance** /ˈɔːdɪnəns/ *n.* **A** (*order, decree*) Verordnung, *die;* **divine ~:** göttliche Bestimmung; **B** (*enactment by local authority*) Verfügung, *die;* Bestimmung, *die;* **C** (*religious rite*) Ritus, *der*

**ordinand** /ˈɔːdɪnænd/ *n.* (*Eccl.*) Weihekandidat, *der*

**ordinarily** /ˈɔːdɪnərɪlɪ/ *adv.* normalerweise; gewöhnlich; in der Regel; (*unexceptionally*) gewöhnlich

**ordinary** /ˈɔːdɪnərɪ/ *adj.* **A** (*regular, normal*) normal ‹Gebrauch›; üblich ‹Verfahren›; (*not exceptional*) gewöhnlich; (*average*) durchschnittlich; **very ~** (*derog.*) ziemlich mittelmäßig; **in the ~ way** (*usually*) normalerweise; **better/worse than ~:** besser/schlechter als sonst; **~ tap water** normales *od.* gewöhnliches Leitungswasser; **in ~ life** im Alltagsleben; **be no ~ thing** kein gewöhnliches Ding sein; **~ people** *or* **folk** einfache Leute; ⇒ *also* **course** 1 A; **B** (*Brit. St. Exch.*) **~ share** Stammaktie, *die;* **~ stock** Stammaktien; **C** **above the ~:** über dem Durchschnitt; überdurchschnittlich ‹Intelligenz usw.›; **out of the ~:** außergewöhnlich; ungewöhnlich; **something/nothing out of the ~:** etwas/nichts Außergewöhnliches

**ordinary: ~ level** ⇒ **O level; ~ ˈseaman** *n.* Leichtmatrose, *der*

**ordination** /ɔːdɪˈneɪʃn/ *n.* **A** (*Eccl.*) Ordination, *die;* Ordinierung, *die;* **B** (*decreeing*) Bestimmung, *die;* **God's ~:** Gottes Wille

**ordnance** /ˈɔːdnəns/ *n.* **A** (*guns*) Artillerie, *die;* Geschütze *Pl.;* **~ factory** Waffenfabrik, *die;* **piece of ~:** Geschütz, *das;* **B** (*service*) Feldzeugwesen, *das;* Feldzeugmeisterei, *die;* *attrib.* Feldzeug-; **O~ Corps** Technische Truppe

**ordnance: ~ map** = **~ survey map; ~ ˈsurvey** *n.* (*Brit.*) amtliche Landesvermessung; **~ survey map** amtliche topographische Karte

O

**ore** /ɔ:(r)/ *n.* Erz, *das*

**oregano** /ɒrɪ'gɑ:nəʊ, ə'regənəʊ/ *n., no pl.* (*Cookery*) Oregano, *der;* Origano, *der*

**organ** /'ɔ:gən/ *n.* Ⓐ (*Mus.*) Orgel, *die;* (*harmonium*) Harmonium, *das;* ⇒ *also* **American organ**; Ⓑ (*Biol.*) Organ, *das;* **speech ~s** Sprechwerkzeuge; **the male ~** (*euphem.*) das männliche Glied; Ⓒ (*medium of communication*) Sprachrohr, *das;* (*of political party etc.*) Organ, *das*

**organdie** (*Amer.:* **organdy**) /'ɔ:gəndɪ, ɔ:'gændɪ/ *n.* (*Textiles*) Organdy, *der*

**'organ donor** *n.* Organspender, *der*/Organspenderin, *die;* **~ card** Organspende[r]ausweis, *der*

**'organ-grinder** *n.* Drehorgelspieler, *der*/-spielerin, *die;* Leierkastenmann, *der*

**organic** /ɔ:'gænɪk/ *adj.* Ⓐ (*also Chem. Physiol.*) organisch; Ⓑ (*constitutional, inherent, structural*) konstitutionell; (*fundamental, vital*) konstitutiv (*geh.*) ‹Teile›; Ⓒ (*without chemicals*) biologisch, biodynamisch ‹Nahrungsmittel›; biologisch-dynamisch ‹Ackerbau usw.›; Ⓓ (*Med.*) organisch, körperlich ‹Leiden›

**organically** /ɔ:'gænɪkəlɪ/ *adv.* Ⓐ (*also Med.*) organisch; Ⓑ (*without chemicals*) biologisch; biodynamisch

**organic 'chemist** *n.* ▶ 1261 Organiker, *der*/Organikerin, *die*

**organisation**, **organise**, **organised**, **organiser** ⇒ **organiz-**

**organism** /'ɔ:gənɪzm/ *n.* Ⓐ (*organized body*) Organismus, *der;* Ⓑ (*Biol.*) Organismus, *der;* (*structure*) Aufbau, *der*

**organist** /'ɔ:gənɪst/ *n.* ▶ 1261 Organist, *der*/Organistin, *die*

**organization** /ɔ:gənaɪ'zeɪʃn/ *n.* Ⓐ (*organizing, systematic arrangement*) Organisation, *die;* (*of material*) Ordnung, *die;* (*of library*) Anordnung, *die;* **~ of time/work** Zeit-/Arbeitseinteilung, *die;* Ⓑ (*organized body, system*) Organisation, *die*

**organizational** /ɔ:gənaɪ'zeɪʃənl/ *adj.* organisatorisch

**organi'zation man** *n., Mensch, der die Belange der Organisation, der er dient, über alles stellt*

**organize** /'ɔ:gənaɪz/ *v.t.* Ⓐ (*give orderly structure to*) ordnen; planen ‹Leben›; einteilen ‹Arbeit, Zeit›; (*frame, establish*) veranstalten ‹Konferenz, Festival›; organisieren ‹Verein, Partei, Firma, Institution›; **organizing ability** Organisationstalent, *das;* **I must get ~d** (*get ready*) ich muss fertig werden; **~ sb.** jmdn. an die Hand nehmen (*fig.*); **as soon as I've got myself ~d** sobald ich so weit bin; Ⓑ (*arrange*) organisieren; **can you ~ the catering?** kümmerst du dich um die Verpflegung?; Ⓒ **~ into groups/teams** in Gruppen/Mannschaften einteilen

**organized** /'ɔ:gənaɪzd/ *adj.* (*systematic, structured*) organisiert; geregelt ‹Leben›; **be well ~ for a trip** für eine Reise gut vorbereitet sein; **~ crime** das organisierte Verbrechen; die organisierte Kriminalität

**organizer** /'ɔ:gənaɪzə(r)/ *n.* Ⓐ Organisator, *der*/Organisatorin, *die;* (*of event, festival*) Veranstalter, *der*/Veranstalterin, *die;* Ⓑ (*bag*) Aktentasche, *die*

**organ:** **~ loft** *n.* Orgelempore, *die;* **~ music** *n.* Orgelmusik, *die;* **~ pipe** *n.* (*Mus.*) Orgelpfeife, *die;* **~ stop** *n.* (*Mus.*) Orgelregister, *das;* (*handle*) Registerzug, *der*

**'organ transplant** *n.* Organverpflanzung, *die;* Organtransplantation, *die* (*fachspr.*)

**orgasm** /'ɔ:gæzəm/ *n.* Orgasmus, *der;* Höhepunkt, *der* (*auch fig.*)

**orgiastic** /ɔ:dʒɪ'æstɪk/ *adj.* orgiastisch

**orgy** /'ɔ:dʒɪ/ *n.* Orgie, *die;* **drunken ~:** Orgie unter Alkoholeinfluss; **an ~ of spending** eine Kauforgie; Kaufexzesse *Pl.;* **an ~ of killing** eine Orgie des Tötens; ein Blutrausch

**oriel** /'ɔ:rɪəl/ *n.* Erkerfenster, *das*

**orient** ❶ /'ɔ:rɪənt/ *n.* **the O~:** der Orient; (*East Asia*) der Ferne Osten. ❷ /'ɔ:rɪent, 'ɒrɪent/ *v.t.* Ⓐ (*set or determine position of*) ausrichten **(towards** nach); Ⓑ (*fig.*) einweisen **(in** in + *Akk.*); ausrichten, abstellen **(towards** auf + *Akk.*) ‹Programm›; **~ oneself** sich orientieren *od.* zurechtfinden; **-~ed** -orientiert; **money-~ed** materiell orientiert; **career-~ed** berufsbezogen; praxisorientiert

**oriental** /ɔ:rɪ'entl, ɒrɪ'entl/ ❶ *adj.* orientalisch; Orient‹teppich›; asiatisch ‹Unergründlichkeit›; **the O~ Church** die Ostkirche; die orientalische Kirche; **O~ studies** Orientalistik, *die;* **~ trade/travel** Orienthandel, *der*/Orientreisen. ❷ *n.* Asiat, *der*/Asiatin, *die*

**orientalist** /ɔ:rɪ'entəlɪst, ɒrɪ'entəlɪst/ *n.* Orientalist, *der*/Orientalistin, *die*

**orientate** /'ɒrɪənteɪt, 'ɔ:rɪənteɪt/ ⇒ **orient** 2

**orientation** /ɒrɪən'teɪʃn, ɔ:rɪən'teɪʃn/ *n.* Ⓐ (*orienting*) Orientierung, *die;* (*of new employees etc.*) Einweisung, *die;* **sense of ~:** Orientierungssinn, *der;* Ⓑ (*relative position*) Ausrichtung, *die;* (*fig.*) Orientierung, *die;* **what is the ~ of ...?** wie ist ... ausgerichtet?; **my ~ was always towards ...:** ich war immer auf ... ausgerichtet

**orien'tation course** *n.* Einführungsveranstaltung, *die*

**orienteering** /ɔ:rɪən'tɪərɪŋ, ɒrɪən'tɪərɪŋ/ *n.* (*Brit.*) Orientierungsrennen, *das*

**orifice** /'ɒrɪfɪs/ *n.* Öffnung, *die;* (*of tube*) Mündung, *die;* **nasal ~:** Nasenloch, *das*

**origami** /ɒrɪ'gɑ:mɪ/ *n.* Origami, *das*

**origin** /'ɒrɪdʒɪn/ *n.* (*derivation*) Abstammung, *die;* Herkunft, *die;* (*beginnings*) Anfänge *Pl.;* (*of world etc.*) Entstehung, *die;* (*source*) Ursprung, *der;* (*of belief, rumour*) Quelle, *die;* **be of humble ~, have humble ~s** bescheidener Herkunft sein; **be Irish by ~:** irischer Herkunft sein; **the ~ of species** die Entstehung der Arten; **country of ~:** Herkunftsland, *das;* **words which are of French ~** *or* **are French in ~:** Wörter französischen Ursprungs; **have its ~ in sth.** seinen Ursprung in etw. (*Dat.*) haben; einer Sache (*Dat.*) seinen Ursprung verdanken

**original** /ə'rɪdʒɪnl/ ❶ *adj.* Ⓐ (*first, earliest*) ursprünglich; **~ edition** Originalausgabe, *die;* **the ~ inhabitants** die Ureinwohner; **~ sin** (*Theol.*) Erbsünde, *die;* Ⓑ (*primary*) original; Original-; Ur‹text, -fassung›; eigenständig ‹Forschung›; (*inventive*) originell; (*creative*) schöpferisch; **an ~ painting** ein Original; **from the ~ German** aus der deutschen Urfassung. ❷ *n.* Ⓐ Original, *das;* Ⓑ (*eccentric person*) Original, *das* (*ugs.*)

**original 'gravity** *n.* Stammwürze, *die*

**originality** /ərɪdʒɪ'nælɪtɪ/ *n.* Originalität, *die*

**originally** /ə'rɪdʒɪnəlɪ/ *adv.* Ⓐ ursprünglich; **be ~ from ...:** [ursprünglich] aus ... stammen; Ⓑ (*in an original way*) originell ‹schreiben usw.›; **think ~:** originelle Gedanken haben

**originate** /ə'rɪdʒɪneɪt/ ❶ *v.i.* **~ from** entstehen aus; **~ in** seinen Ursprung haben in (+ *Dat.*); **~ with sb.** von jmdm. stammen. ❷ *v.t.* schaffen; hervorbringen; kreieren ‹neue Mode›; (*discover*) erfinden; **who ~d the idea?** von wem stammt die Idee?

**origination** /ərɪdʒɪ'neɪʃn/ *n.* Entstehung, *die*

**originator** /ə'rɪdʒɪneɪtə(r)/ *n.* Urheber, *der*/Urheberin, *die;* (*inventor*) Erfinder, *der*/Erfinderin, *die;* **who was the ~ of that idea?** von wem stammt diese Idee?

**Orkney [Islands]** /'ɔ:knɪ (aɪləndz)/ *pr. n.* [*pl.*], **Orkneys** /'ɔ:knɪz/ *pr. n. pl.* Orkneyinseln *Pl.;* Orkneys *Pl.*

**ornament** ❶ /'ɔ:nəmənt/ *n.* Ⓐ (*decorative object*) Schmuck-, Ziergegenstand, *der;* (*on pillar etc.*) Ornament, *das;* (*person*) Zierde, *die;* Ⓑ *no pl.* (*decorating*) Verzierungen *Pl.;* Zierrat, *der* (*geh.*); **for** *or* **by way of ~:** zum Schmuck *od.* zur Zierde; **an altar rich in ~:** ein reich verzierter Altar; Ⓒ *usu. in pl.* (*Eccl.*) Kirchengerät, *das;* liturgisches Gerät; Ⓓ *in pl.* (*Mus.*) Verzierungen *Pl.;* Ornamente *Pl.* ❷ /'ɔ:nəment/ *v.t.* verzieren

**ornamental** /ɔ:nə'mentl/ ❶ *adj.* dekorativ; ornamental (*bes. Kunst*); Zier‹pflanze, -naht usw.›; **purely ~:** nur zum Schmuck *od.* zur Zierde; rein dekorativ; **an ~ lake** ein Zierteich. ❷ *n.* (*plant*) Zierpflanze, *die*

**ornamentally** /ɔ:nə'mentəlɪ/ *adv.* dekorativ

**ornamentation** /ɔ:nəmen'teɪʃn/ *n., no pl.* Ⓐ (*ornamenting*) Ausschmückung, *die;* Ⓑ (*embellishment[s]*) Verzierung, *die*

**ornate** /ɔ:'neɪt/ *adj.* Ⓐ (*elaborately adorned*) reich verziert; prunkvoll ‹Dekoration›; **heavily ~:** überladen; Ⓑ (*style*) blumig (*abwertend*); reich ausgeschmückt ‹Prosa›

**ornery** /'ɔ:nərɪ/ *adj.* (*Amer. coll.*) Ⓐ (*of poor quality*) primitiv (*abwertend*); Ⓑ (*cantankerous*) aggressiv; streitlustig

**ornithological** /ɔ:nɪθə'lɒdʒɪkl/ *adj.* ornithologisch; vogelkundlich

**ornithologist** /ɔ:nɪ'θɒlədʒɪst/ *n.*. Ornithologe, *der*/Ornithologin, *die;* Vogelkundler, *der*/Vogelkundlerin, *die*

**ornithology** /ɔ:nɪ'θɒlədʒɪ/ *n.* Ornithologie, *die;* Vogelkunde, *die*

**orphan** /'ɔ:fn/ ❶ *n.* Waise, *die;* Waisenkind, *das;* **be left an ~:** [zur] Waise werden. ❷ *attrib. adj.* Waisen-. ❸ *v.t.* zur Waise machen; **be ~ed** [zur] Waise werden

**orphanage** /'ɔ:fənɪdʒ/ *n.* Waisenhaus, *das*

**orthodontics** /ɔ:θə'dɒntɪks/ *n., no pl.* Kieferorthopädie, *die*

**orthodontist** /ɔ:θə'dɒntɪst/ *n.* Kieferorthopäde, *der*/Kieferorthopädin, *die*

**orthodox** /'ɔ:θədɒks/ *adj.* orthodox; (*conservative*) konventionell

**Orthodox 'Church** *n.* orthodoxe Kirche

**orthodoxy** /'ɔ:θədɒksɪ/ *n.* Orthodoxie, *die*

**orthography** /ɔ:'θɒgrəfɪ/ *n.* Orthographie, *die;* Rechtschreibung, *die*

**orthopaedic** /ɔ:θə'pi:dɪk/ *adj.* orthopädisch

**orthopaedics** /ɔ:θə'pi:dɪks/ *n., no pl.* (*Med.*) Orthopädie, *die*

**orthopaedist** /ɔ:θə'pi:dɪst/ *n.* ▶ 1261 (*Med.*) Orthopäde, *der*/Orthopädin, *die*

**orthopedic**, **orthopedics**, **orthopedist** (*Amer.*) ⇒ **orthopaed-**

**Orwellian** /ɔ:'welɪən/ *adj.* orwellsch

**OS** *abbr.* Ⓐ (*Brit.*) **Ordnance Survey;** Ⓑ **outsize** übergr.

**Oscar** /'ɒskə(r)/ *n.* (*Cinemat.*) Oscar, *der*

**oscillate** /'ɒsɪleɪt/ *v.i.* Ⓐ (*swing like a pendulum*) schwingen; oszillieren (*fachspr.*); Ⓑ (*move to and fro between points*) pendeln; Ⓒ (*fig.*) schwanken; (*vary between extremes of condition or action*) hin und her gerissen sein; Ⓓ (*Radio*) schwingen

**oscillation** /ɒsɪ'leɪʃn/ *n.* Ⓐ (*action*) ⇒ **oscillate**: Schwingen, *das;* Oszillieren, *das;* Pendeln, *das;* Schwanken, *das;* Hin-und-her-gerissen-Sein, *das;* Schwingung, *die;* Ⓑ (*single ~*) Schwingung, *die;* (*of pendulum*) Pendelausschlag, *der*

**oscillator** /'ɒsɪleɪtə(r)/ *n.* (*Electr.*) Oszillator, *der*

**oscillograph** /ə'sɪləgrɑ:f/ *n.* (*Electr.*) Oszillograph, *der*

**oscilloscope** /ə'sɪləskəʊp/ *n.* (*Electr.*) Oszilloskop, *das*

**osier** /'əʊzɪə(r)/ *n.* Ⓐ (*Bot.*) Korbweide, *die;* Ⓑ *attrib.* Weiden‹korb, -rute›; Korb‹sessel, -möbel›

**osmosis** /ɒz'məʊsɪs/ *n., pl.* **osmoses** /ɒz'məʊsi:z/ Osmose, *die*

**osmotic** /ɒz'mɒtɪk/ *adj.* osmotisch

**osprey** /'ɒspreɪ/ *n.* (*Ornith.*) Fischadler, *der*

**Ossie** ⇒ **Aussie**

**ossify** /'ɒsɪfaɪ/ ❶ *v.i.* ossifizieren (*fachspr.*); verknöchern (*auch fig.*). ❷ *v.t.* (*turn into bone*) ossifizieren (*fachspr.*) *od.* verknöchern lassen

**Ostend** /ɒ'stend/ *pr. n.* ▶ 1626 Ostende (*das*)

**ostensible** /ɒ'stensɪbl/ *adj.* vorgeschoben; Schein-; **~ excuse/reason** Ausrede, *die* (*abwertend*)/Vorwand, *der*

**ostensibly** /ɒ'stensɪblɪ/ *adv.* vorgeblich

**ostentation** /ɒsten'teɪʃn/ *n.* Ostentation, *die* (*geh.*); Prahlerei, *die* (*abwertend*); (*showiness*) Prunk, *der*

**ostentatious** /ɒsten'teɪʃəs/ *adj.* prunkhaft ‹Kleidung, Schmuck›; prahlerisch ‹Art›; auffällig großzügig ‹Spende›; **be ~ about sth.** mit etw. prunken *od.* (*ugs.*) protzen

**ostentatiously** /ɒsten'teɪʃəslɪ/ *adv.* ostentativ (*geh.*), demonstrativ ‹fehlen, schweigen›; prunkhaft ‹leben›; prahlerisch ‹bemerken›; auffällig ‹sich kleiden, sich benehmen›

**osteopath** /'ɒstɪəpæθ/ *n.* ▶ 1261 (*Med.*) Osteopath, *der*/Osteopathin, *die*

O

**osteoporosis** /ɒstɪəʊpəˈrəʊsɪs/ *n., no pl.* ▶ 1232 (*Med.*) Osteoporose, *die*

**ostler** /ˈɒslə(r)/ *n.* (*Brit. Hist.*) Pferdeknecht, *der* (*veralt.*); Reitknecht, *der* (*früher*)

**ostracise** ⇒ **ostracize**

**ostracism** /ˈɒstrəsɪzm/ *n.* Ächtung, *die*

**ostracize** /ˈɒstrəsaɪz/ *v.t.* ächten; ~ **from sth.** ausschließen von etw.

**ostrich** /ˈɒstrɪtʃ/ *n.* **A** Strauß, *der;* **B** *attrib.* Straußen‹ei›; ~ **attitude** Vogel-Strauß-Einstellung, *die*

**ostrich:** ~ **feather** *n.* Straußenfeder, *die;* ~**-like** *adj.* Vogel-Strauß-‹Reaktion, Einstellung›; ~ **plume** *n.* Straußenfedern *Pl.*

**Ostrogoth** /ˈɒstrəgɒθ/ *n.* (*Hist.*) Ostgote, *der*/Ostgotin, *die*

**OT** *abbr.* **Old Testament** A.T.

**OTE** *abbr.* **on-target earnings**

**other** /ˈʌðə(r)/ **1** *adj.* **A** (*not the same*) ander...; **the** ~ **two/three** *etc.* (*the remaining*) die beiden/drei *usw.* anderen; **the** ~ **way round** *or* **about** gerade umgekehrt; ~ **people's property** fremdes Eigentum; **the** ~ **one** der/die/das andere; **the** ~ **thing** (*coll.*) das Gegenteil; **there is no** ~ **way** es geht nicht anders; **I know of no** ~ **way of doing it** ich weiß nicht, wie ich es sonst machen soll; **some** ~ **time** ein andermal; **B** (*further*) **two** ~ **people/questions** noch zwei [andere *od.* weitere] Leute/Fragen; **one** ~ **thing** noch eins; **there's just one** ~ **thing I need to do** ich muss nur noch eines tun; **have you any** ~ **news/questions?** hast du noch weitere *od.* sonst noch Neuigkeiten/Fragen?; **some/six** ~ **people** noch ein paar/noch sechs [andere *od.* weitere] Leute; **no** ~ **questions** keine weiteren Fragen; **do you know of any** ~ **person who ...?** weißt du noch jemand anderen *od.* sonst noch jemanden, der ...?; **C** ~ **than** (*different from*) anders als; (*except*) außer; **never** ~ **than charming** immer charmant; **any person** ~ **than yourself** jeder außer dir; **D** **some writer/charity or** ~: irgendein Schriftsteller/Wohltätigkeitsverein; **some time/way or** ~: irgendwann/-wie; **something/somehow/somewhere/somebody or** ~: irgendetwas/-wie/-wo/-wer. ⇒ *also* **another** 1 D; **every** C; **half** 1 A; **none** 1; **place** 2 B; **side** 1 G; **this** 2 C; **woman** A; **world** A; **E** **the** ~ **day/evening** neulich/neulich abends.

**2** *n.* **A** (~ *person or thing*) anderer/andere/anderes; **there are six** ~**s** es sind noch sechs andere da; **are there any** ~**s who ...?** ist noch jemand da, der ...?; **tell one from the** ~: sie auseinander halten; **one or** ~ **of you/them** irgendwer *od.* -einer/-eine von euch/ihnen; **any** ~: irgendein anderer/-eine andere/-ein anderes; **not any** ~: kein anderer/keine andere/kein anderes; **one after the** ~: einer/eine/eins nach dem/der/dem anderen; **a bit of the** ~ (*sl.*) Sex, *der;* **have a bit of the** ~ (*sl.*) es treiben (*ugs.*); **all he ever wants is a bit of the** ~ (*sl.*) er will immer nur das eine; ⇒ *also* **each** 2 B; **B** (*arch.*) **no** ~ (*person*) kein anderer/keine andere; **he could do no** ~ **than come** er konnte nichts anderes tun als kommen.

**3** *adv.* anders; **I've never seen her** ~ **than with him** ich habe sie immer nur mit ihm zusammen gesehen; ~ **than that, no real news** abgesehen davon, keine echten Neuigkeiten

**otherwise** /ˈʌðəwaɪz/ **1** *adv.* **A** (*in a different way*) anders; **think** ~: anders darüber denken; anderer Meinung sein; **it cannot be** ~: es kann nicht anders sein; **be** ~ **engaged** anderweitige Verpflichtungen haben; **except where** ~ **stated** sofern nicht anders angegeben; **...,** ~ **[known as] Barbarossa** ..., auch als Rotbart bekannt; **B** (*or else*) sonst; anderenfalls; **he would have let me know** ~: sonst *od.* anderenfalls hätte er mich benachrichtigt; **C** (*in other respects*) ansonsten (*ugs.*); im Übrigen; **the merits, or** ~, **of his paintings** die Vorzüge oder Mängel seiner Gemälde; **the probability or** ~ **of sth.** die Wahrscheinlichkeit oder Unwahrscheinlichkeit einer Sache; **workers enjoyed (or** ~**) an enforced holiday** die Arbeiter genossen einen erzwungenen Urlaub (oder auch nicht).

**2** *pred. adj.* anders

**otiose** /ˈəʊtɪəʊs/ *adj.* (*literary: not required*) überflüssig

**otter** /ˈɒtə(r)/ *n.* [Fisch]otter, *der;* (*fur*) [Fisch]otterpelz, *der*

**otter:** ~ **dog,** ~ **hound** *ns.* (*Zool., Hunting*) Otterhund, *der*

**ottoman** *n.* **A** (*seat*) Ottomane, *die;* **B** (*footstool*) Polsterschemel, *der*

**Ottoman** /ˈɒtəmən/ *adj.* osmanisch ‹Reich›

**OU** *abbr.* (*Brit.*) **Open University**

**oubliette** /u:blɪˈet/ *n.* (*Hist.*) Oubliette, *die;* Burgverlies, *das*

**ouch** /aʊtʃ/ *int.* autsch

**ought**[1] /ɔ:t/ *v. aux. only in pres. and past* **ought,** *neg.* (*coll.*) **oughtn't** /ˈɔ:tnt/ **A** **I** ~ **to do/have done it** *expr. moral duty* ich müsste es tun/hätte es tun müssen; *expr. desirability* ich sollte es tun/hätte es tun sollen; **he tries to tell me what I** ~ **to think** er will mir vorschreiben, was ich zu denken habe; **behave as one** ~: sich richtig verhalten *od.* korrekt benehmen; **you** ~ **to see that film** diesen Film solltest du sehen; **she** ~ **to have been a teacher** sie hätte Lehrerin werden sollen; ~ **not** *or* ~**n't you to have left by now?** müsstest du nicht schon weg sein?; hättest du nicht schon gehen müssen?; **one** ~ **not to do it** man sollte es nicht tun; **he** ~ **to be hanged/in hospital** er gehört an den Galgen/ins Krankenhaus; **B** *expr. probability* **that** ~ **to be enough** das dürfte reichen; **there** ~ **to be a signpost soon** jetzt müsste bald ein Wegweiser kommen; **he** ~ **to win** er müsste [eigentlich] gewinnen; **he** ~ **to have reached Paris by now** er müsste *od.* dürfte inzwischen in Paris [angekommen] sein

**ought**[2] *n.* (*coll.*) Null, *die*

**oughtn't** /ˈɔ:tnt/ (*coll.*) = **ought not**

**Ouija [board]** ®, **ouija [board]** /ˈwi:dʒə (bɔ:d)/ *n. Tafel mit Buchstaben und anderen Zeichen für spiritistische Sitzungen;* Oui-ja-board, *das* (*Parapsych.*)

**ounce** /aʊns/ *n.* **A** ▶ 1671, ▶ 1683 (*measure*) Unze, *die;* **fluid** ~ (*Brit.*) ≈ 0,0284 l; (*Amer.*) ≈ 0,0296 l; **B** (*fig.*) **not an** ~ **of common sense** kein Fünkchen Verstand; **there is not an** ~ **of truth in it** daran ist kein Körnchen Wahrheit; **not have an** ~ **of sympathy** nicht für fünf Pfennige Mitgefühl haben (*ugs.*)

**our** /ˈaʊə(r)/ *poss. pron. attrib.* **A** unser; **we bumped** ~ **heads** wir stießen uns (*Dat.*) den Kopf *od.* die Köpfe an; **as soon as we've made** ~ **minds up** sobald wir uns (*Akk.*) entschieden haben; **we have done** ~ **share** wir haben unseren Teil *od.* (*geh.*) das Unsere getan; ~ **Joe** *etc.* (*coll.*) unser *od.* (*ugs.*) uns Joe *usw.;* **B** (*of all people*) unser; ⇒ *also* **father** 1 E; **lady** E; **lord** 1 B; **saviour** B. ⇒ *also* **her**[2]

**ours** /ˈaʊəz/ *poss. pron. pred.* unserer/unsere/unseres; **that car is** ~: das ist unser Wagen; ~ **is a different system** wir haben ein anderes System; unser System ist anders; **in this country of** ~: hierzulande [bei uns]; in diesem unserem Lande (*geh.*); ⇒ *also* **hers**

**ourselves** /aʊəˈselvz/ *pron.* **A** *emphat.* selbst; **B** *refl.* uns. ⇒ *also* **between** 1 B; **herself**

**oust** /aʊst/ *v.t.* **A** (*expel, force out*) ~ **sb. from his job** jmdn. von seinem Arbeitsplatz vertreiben; ~ **sb. from office/his position** jmdn. aus dem Amt/seiner Stellung vertreiben; ~ **the president/king/government from power** den Präsidenten/den König /die Regierung entmachten *od.* stürzen; **B** (*force out and take place of*) verdrängen; ablösen ‹Regierung›; **C** (*Law: deprive*) berauben **(of,** *Gen.*)

**ouster** /ˈaʊstə(r)/ *n.* (*Amer.: dismissal*) Entlassung, *die*

**out** /aʊt/ **1** *adv.* **A** (*away from place*) ~ **here/there** hier/da draußen; **'Out'** „Ausfahrt"/„Ausgang" *od.* „Aus"; **that book is** ~ (*from library*) das Buch ist ausgeliehen; ~ **from under sth.** unter etw. (*Dat.*) hervor; ~ **with him!** raus (*ugs.*) *od.* hinaus mit ihm!; **please keep the dog** ~: lassen Sie bitte den Hund nicht herein; **put the cat** ~: die Katze hinauslassen; **be** ~ **in the garden** draußen im Garten sein; **what's it like** ~**?** wie ist es draußen?; **shut the door to keep the wind** ~: die Tür schließen, damit es nicht zieht; **go** ~ **shopping** *etc.* einkaufen *usw.* gehen; **be** ~ (*not at home, not in one's office, etc.*) nicht da sein; **go** ~ **in the evenings** abends aus- *od.* weggehen; **she was/stayed** ~ **all night** sie war/blieb eine/die ganze Nacht weg; **have a day** ~ **in London/at the beach** einen Tag in London/am Strand verbringen; **would you come** ~ **with me?** würdest du mit mir ausgehen?; **row** ~ **to ...:** hinaus-/herausrudern zu ...; **ten miles** ~ **from the harbour** 10 Meilen vom Hafen entfernt; **be** ~ **at sea** auf See sein; **anchor some way** ~: weit draußen ankern; **the journey** ~: die Hinfahrt; **the goods were damaged on the journey** ~: die Waren wurden auf dem Transport beschädigt; **missionaries were going** ~ **to India** Missionare gingen nach Indien; **he is** ~ **in Africa** er ist in Afrika; ~ **in the fields** [draußen] auf dem Feld; **how long have you been living** ~ **here in Australia?** wie lange lebst du schon hier in Australien?; **the Socialist Party is** ~: die Sozialisten sind nicht mehr an der Regierung *od.* (*ugs.*) am Ruder; **that idea/proposal is** ~: die Idee/der Vorschlag ist indiskutabel; **Tell him that you're married — No, that's** ~: Sag ihm, dass du verheiratet bist. — Nein, das kommt nicht in Frage; **B** (*Sport, Games*) **be** ~ ‹Ball:› aus *od.* im Aus sein; ‹Mitspieler:› ausscheiden; ‹Schlagmann:› aus[geschlagen] sein; **not** ~: nicht aus; **give sb.** ~ ‹Schiedsrichter:› jmdn. für „Aus" erklären; **C** **be** ~ (*asleep*) weg sein (*ugs.*); (*drunk*) hinüber sein (*ugs.*); (*unconscious*) bewusstlos sein; (*Boxing*) aus sein; ~ **on one's feet** (*Boxing*) stehend k. o.; (*fig.*) total erschlagen; ⇒ *also* **count**[1] 1 D; **D** (*no longer burning*) aus[gegangen]; **E** (*no longer visible*) **rub** *etc.* ~: ausradieren *usw.;* **F** (*in error*) **be 3%** ~ **in one's calculations** sich um 3% verrechnet *od.* vertan haben; **his reckoning was** ~: seine Rechnung war falsch; **you're a long way** ~: du hast dich gewaltig geirrt; **this is £5** ~: das stimmt um 5 Pfund nicht *od.* ist um 5 Pfund verkehrt; **my watch is 5 minutes** ~: meine Uhr geht 5 Minuten falsch *od.* verkehrt; ⇒ *also* **far** 1 D; **G** (*not in fashion*) passé (*ugs.*); out (*ugs.*); **H** (*so as to be seen or heard*) heraus; raus (*ugs.*); **there is a warrant** ~ **for his arrest** es liegt ein Haftbefehl gegen ihn vor; **say it** ~ **loud** es laut sagen; **tell sb. sth. right** ~: jmdm. etw. geradeheraus *od.* ohne Umschweife sagen; **with the waterproof side** ~: mit der wasserdichten Seite nach außen; **[come]** ~ **with it!** heraus *od.* (*ugs.*) raus damit *od.* mit der Sprache; **their secret is** ~: ihr Geheimnis ist herausgekommen *od.* bekannt geworden; **[the] truth will** ~: die Wahrheit wird herauskommen *od.* an den Tag kommen; **the moon is** ~: der Mond ist zu sehen; **just** ~ **— the third volume** soeben erschienen — der dritte Band; **is the evening paper** ~ **yet?** ist die Abendausgabe schon erschienen?; **the roses are just** ~: die Rosen fangen gerade an zu blühen; **the apple blossom is** ~: die Apfelbäume stehen in Blüte; **the sun/moon is** ~: die Sonne/der Mond scheint; **I** (*known to exist*) **that is the best car** ~: das ist das beste Auto auf dem Markt; **J** **be** ~ **for sth./to do sth.** auf etw. (*Akk.*) aus sein/darauf aus sein, etw. zu tun; **be** ~ **for all one can get** alles haben wollen, was man bekommen kann; **be** ~ **for trouble** Streit suchen; **he's** ~ **for your money** er hat es auf dein Geld abgesehen; **be** ~ **to pass the exam/capture the market** entschlossen sein, die Prüfung zu bestehen/den Markt zu erobern; **she's** ~ **to get him/find a husband** sie ist hinter ihm her/sucht einen Mann; **they're just** ~ **to make money** sie sind nur aufs Geld aus; ihnen geht es nur ums Geld; **K** (*to or at an end*) **he had it finished before the day/month was** ~: er war noch am selben Tag/vor Ende des Monats damit fertig;

**please hear me ~:** lass mich bitte ausreden; **Eggs? I'm afraid we're ~:** Eier? Die sind leider ausgegangen *od.* (*ugs.*) alle; **school is ~** (*Amer.*) die Schule ist aus; **L** (*to a solution or result*) **work ~:** ausrechnen; ausarbeiten ‹Plan, Strategie›; **M** (*in finished form*) **type ~ a thesis** eine Dissertation [ins Reine] tippen; **do it ~ in rough first** sich (*Dat.*) erst ein Konzept machen; **N** (*in radio communication*) Ende; **O ~ and away** mit Abstand; bei weitem; **a scoundrel ~ and ~, an ~ and ~ scoundrel** ein Schurke durch und durch; **an ~ and ~ disgrace** eine ungeheure *od.* (*ugs.*) bodenlose Schande. ⇒ *also* **about** 1 D; **luck** B; **out of**; **tide** 1 A.

**2** *prep.* aus; **go ~ the door** zur Tür hinausgehen; **throw sth. ~ the window** etw. aus dem Fenster werfen.

**3** *n.* (*way of escape*) Ausweg, *der* (*fig.*); (*excuse*) Alibi, *das.*

**4** *v.t.* (*coll.: expose*) outen (*ugs.*)

**out: ~'act** *v.t.* an die Wand spielen; **~back** *n.* (*esp. Austral.*) Hinterland, *das;* **an ~back farm** eine Farm im Hinterland; **~'bid** *v.t.*, **~'bid A** überbieten; **~bid sb. for sth.** für etw. mehr bieten *od.* ein besseres Angebot machen als jmd.; **B** (*surpass*) übertrumpfen; **~board** (*Naut.*, *Aeronaut.*, *Motor Veh.*) **1** *adj.* **A** Außenbord-; **~board motor** Außenbordmotor, *der;* Außenborder, *der* (*ugs.*); **~board motor boat** Boot mit Außenbordmotor; **B** (*on outside*) sich außenbords befindend; Außenbord-; **2** *n.* Außenborder, *der* (*ugs.*); **~bound** *adj.* auslaufend ‹Schiff›; **~break** *n.* Ausbruch, *der;* **a recent ~break of fire caused ...:** ein Brand verursachte kürzlich ...; **at the ~break of war** bei Kriegsausbruch *od.* Ausbruch des Krieges; **an ~break of flu/smallpox** eine Grippe-/Pockenepidemie; **there will be ~breaks of rain during the afternoon** am Nachmittag wird es zu Regenfällen kommen; **~building** *n.* Nebengebäude, *das;* **~burst** *n.* Ausbruch, *der;* **an ~burst of weeping/laughter** ein Weinkrampf/Lachanfall *od.* -krampf; **an ~burst of anger/temper** ein Zornesausbruch (*geh.*) *od.* Wutanfall; **apologize for one's ~burst** sich für seinen Gefühlsausbruch entschuldigen; **there was an ~burst of applause** Beifall brach los; **~bursts of flame** Auflodern von Flammen; **an ~burst of energy** ein Anfall von Energie; **his ~bursts of violence** seine Anfälle von Gewalttätigkeit; **~cast 1** *n.* Ausgestoßene, *der/die;* **a social ~cast, an ~cast of society** ein Geächteter/eine Geächtete; ein Outcast (*Soziol.*); **2** *adj.* ausgestoßen; verstoßen ‹Familienmitglied›; **~'class** *v.t.* **A** (*belong to higher class than*) überlegen sein (+ *Dat.*); **B** (*defeat easily*) in den Schatten stellen; **he was ~classed in that race** er wurde in diesem Rennen deklassiert; **~come** *n.* Ergebnis, *das;* Resultat, *das;* **what was the ~come of your meeting?** was ist bei eurer Versammlung herausgekommen?; **~crop 1** *n.* **A** (*Geol.: stratum*) Ausgehende, *das;* Ausstreichende, *das;* **a rock ~crop** ausstreichendes Gestein; **B** (*fig.*) Auftreten, *das;* **2** *v.i.* **A** (*Geol.*) ausstreichen (*fachspr.*); **B** (*fig.*) auftauchen; **~cry** *n.* **A** *no pl.* (*clamour*) [Aufschrei der] Empörung; [Sturm der] Entrüstung; **a public/general ~cry about/against sth.** allgemeine Empörung *od.* Entrüstung über etw. (*Akk.*); **the ~cry in the press** die heftigen Proteste in der Presse; **raise an ~cry about sth.** lautstarken Protest gegen etw. erheben; **B** (*crying ~*) Aufschrei, *der;* **~'dated** *adj.* veraltet; überholt; antiquiert (*abwertend*) ‹Ausdrucksweise›; altmodisch ‹Vorstellung, Kleidung›; **~'distance** *v.t.* [weit] hinter sich (*Dat.*) lassen; überflügeln; **John was ~distanced by his brother in the race** John fiel in dem Rennen [weit] hinter seinem Bruder zurück; **~'do** *v.t.*, **~'doing** /aʊt'du:ɪŋ/, **~'did** /aʊt'dɪd/, **~done** /aʊt'dʌn/ übertreffen, überbieten (**in** an + *Dat.*); **not to be ~done [by sb.]** um nicht zurückzustehen [hinter jmdm.]; **~door** *adj.* **~door shoes/things** Straßenschuhe/-kleidung, *die;* **be an ~door type** gern und oft im Freien sein; **lead an ~door life** viel im Freien sein; **~door games/pursuits** Spiele/Beschäftigungen im Freien; **~door shots** (*Photog.*) Außenaufnahmen; **~door swimming pool** Freibad, *das;* **~door ice rink** nicht überdachte Eisbahn; **~'doors 1** *adv.* draußen; **sleep ~doors** draußen *od.* im Freien schlafen; **go ~doors** nach draußen gehen; **2** *n.* **the [great] ~doors** die freie Natur

**outer** /'aʊtə(r)/ *adj.* **A** äußer...; Außen‹fläche, -seite, -wand, -tür, -hafen›; **sb.'s ~ appearance** jmds. äußere Erscheinung; jmds. Äußeres; **~ garments** Oberbekleidung, *die;* **B** (*objective, physical*) äußerlich; **the ~ world** die Außenwelt. ⇒ *also* **bar¹** 1 I

**outermost** /'aʊtəməʊst/ *adj.* äußerst...

**outer 'space** *n.* Weltraum, *der;* All, *das;* **come from ~** (*fig. coll.*) von einem anderen Stern sein

**out: ~'face** *v.t.* [durch Blicke] einschüchtern; zum Schweigen bringen ‹Kritiker›; **~fall** *n.* Ausfluss, *der;* (*in river engineering*) Vorfluter, *der;* **~fall pipe** Abflussrohr, *das;* **~field** *n.* (*Cricket*, *Baseball*) Außenfeld, *das;* **~fit** *n.* **A** (*person's clothes*) Kleider *Pl.;* (*for fancy-dress party*) Kostüm, *das;* **wear the same ~fit** dasselbe tragen *od.* anhaben; **I do like your ~fit!** du bist sehr gut angezogen; **B** (*complete equipment*) Ausrüstung, *die;* Ausstattung, *die;* **C** (*coll.: group of persons*) Haufen, *der* (*ugs.*); Clique, *die* (*abwertend*); (*Mil.*) Haufen, *der* (*Soldatenspr.*); Trupp, *der;* (*jazz band*) Ensemble, *das;* **D** (*coll.: organization*) Laden, *der* (*ugs.*); **a publishing/manufacturing ~fit** ein Verlag/ein Produktionsbetrieb; **~fitter** *n.* ▶ **1261** Ausrüster, *der*/Ausrüsterin, *die;* Ausstatter, *der*/Ausstatterin, *die;* **camping/sports ~fitter** Camping-/Sportgeschäft, *das;* **a gents' ~fitter's** ein Herrenausstatter; **~'flank** *v.t.* **A** (*Mil.: ~manœuvre; also fig.*) überlisten; ausmanövrieren; **B** (*Mil.: extend beyond flank of*) umgehen, umfassen ‹Armee›; **~flanking movement** Umfassungsbewegung, *die;* **~flow** *n.* **A** (*~ward flow*) Austritt, *der;* (*fig.: of gold, capital, etc.*) Abfluss, *der;* **B** (*amount*) Ausfluss, *der;* Abflussmenge, *die;* **C ~flow [pipe *or* channel]** Abfluss, *der;* **~'fox** *v.t.* (*coll.*) austricksen (*ugs.*); **~going 1** *adj.* **A** (*retiring from office*) [aus dem Amt] scheidend ‹Regierung, Präsident, Ausschuss›; **B** (*friendly*) kontaktfreudig ‹Person›; **you should be more ~going** du solltest mehr aus dir herausgehen; **C** (*going ~*) abgehend ‹Zug, Schiff›; ausziehend ‹Mieter›; **~going flights will be delayed** bei den Abflügen wird es zu Verzögerungen kommen; **the ~going post *or* mail** die ausgehende Post; der Postausgang (*Bürow.*); **2** *n. in pl.* (*expenditure*) Ausgaben *Pl.;* **~'grow** *v.t.*, *forms as* **grow A** (*leave behind*) entwachsen (+ *Dat.*); hinauswachsen über (+ *Akk.*); ablegen ‹Interesse, Schüchternheit, Vorliebe›; überwinden ‹Ansicht, Schüchternheit›; **we've ~grown all that** das alles haben wir hinter uns; **B** (*become taller than*) größer werden als; über den Kopf wachsen (+ *Dat.*) ‹älterem Bruder usw.›; (*grow too big for*) herauswachsen aus ‹Kleidung›; **~growth** *n.* Auswuchs, *der;* **~'guess** *v.t.* gedanklich voraus sein (+ *Dat.*); ausrechnen (*Sportjargon*); **~'gun** *v.t.* (*fig.*) **be ~gunned** an Feuerkraft unterlegen sein; **~house** *n.* **A** (*building*) Nebengebäude, *das;* **B** (*Amer.: privy*) Außentoilette, *die*

**outing** /'aʊtɪŋ/ *n.* **A** (*pleasure trip*) Ausflug, *der;* **school/day's ~:** Schul-/Tagesausflug, *der;* **firm's/works ~:** Betriebsausflug, *der;* **go on an ~:** einen Ausflug machen; **go for an ~ in the car** eine Spazierfahrt machen; **B** (*appearance*) (*in athletic contest*) Wettkampf, *der;* (*in race*) Rennen, *das;* (*in game*) Spiel, *das*

**out: ~landish** /aʊt'lændɪʃ/ *adj.* **A** (*looking or sounding foreign*) fremdländisch; **B** (*bizarre*) ausgefallen; seltsam, sonderbar ‹Benehmen›; verschroben ‹Ansichten›; **~'last** *v.t.* überdauern; überleben ‹Person, Jahrhundert›; **~law 1** *n.* **A** (*lawless violent person*) Bandit, *der*/Banditin, *die;* **B** (*person deprived of protection of law*) Geächtete, *der/die* (*hist.*); **2** *v.t.* **A** (*deprive of the protection of law*) ächten (*hist.*); für vogelfrei erklären (*hist.*); **B** (*make illegal*) verbieten ‹Zeitung, Handlung›; **~lay** *n.* **an ~lay** Ausgaben *Pl.* (**on** für); **initial ~lay** Anschaffungskosten *Pl.;* **~lay of capital** Kapitalaufwand, *der;* **recover the ~lay** seine Auslagen zurückbekommen; **~let** /'aʊtlet, 'aʊtlɪt/ **A** (*means of exit*) Ablauf, -fluss, *der;* Auslauf, -lass, *der;* (*of lake*) Abfluss, *der;* **~let valve** Ablassventil, *das;* **B** (*fig.: vent*) Ventil, *das;* **C** (*Commerc.*) (*market*) Absatzmarkt, *der;* (*shop*) Verkaufsstelle, *die;* **D** (*Electr.*) Steckdose, *die;* (*connection*) Stromanschluss, *der;* **~line 1** *n.* **A** *in sing. or pl.* (*line[s]*) Umriss, *der;* Kontur, *die;* Silhouette, *die;* **the ~lines of the trees/drawing** die Umrisse der Bäume/Zeichnung; **visible only in ~line** nur in Umrissen sichtbar; **B** (*short account*) Grundriss, *der;* Grundzüge *Pl.;* (*of topic*) Übersicht, die (**of** über + *Akk.*); (*rough draft for essay, book, play, etc.*) Entwurf, *der* (**of, for** *Gen. od.* zu); Konzept, *das* (**of, for** *Gen.*); **trace the development in ~line** die Entwicklung im Grundriss *od.* in ihren Grundzügen verfolgen; **~line plan** Übersichtsplan, *der;* **C** *in pl.* (*main features*) Grundzüge *Pl.;* **D** (*sketch*) Skizze, *die;* **sketch/draw sth. in ~line** etw. in Umrissen skizzieren/zeichnen; **~line map** Umrisskarte, *die;* **2** *v.t.* **A** (*draw ~line of*) **~line sth.** die Umrisse *od.* Konturen einer Sache zeichnen; **B** (*define ~line of*) **~line sth.** die Umrisse *od.* Konturen einer Sache hervorheben; **the mountain was ~lined against the sky** die Silhouette/Umrisse *od.* Konturen des Berges zeichnete/zeichneten sich gegen den Himmel ab; **C** (*trace or ascertain ~line of*) **~line the limits/boundaries of sth.** den Verlauf der Grenzen von etw. ermitteln; **D** (*describe in general terms*) skizzieren, umreißen ‹Programm, Plan, Projekt›; **~live** /aʊt'lɪv/ *v.t.* überleben; **it's ~lived its usefulness** es ist unbrauchbar geworden; es hat ausgedient; **~look** *n.* **A** (*prospect*) Aussicht, *die* (**over** über + *Akk.*, **on to** auf + *Akk.*); (*fig.*, *Meteorol.*) Aussichten *Pl.;* **the house has a wonderful ~look over ...:** vom Haus aus hat man eine herrliche Aussicht über ... (*Akk.*); **what's the ~look?** wie sind die Aussichten?; **business ~look** Geschäftsaussichten *Pl.;* **B** (*mental attitude*) Haltung, *die* (**on** gegenüber); Einstellung, *die* (**on** zu); Auffassung, *die* (**on** von); **~look on life** Lebensauffassung, *die;* **his whole ~look** seine ganze Einstellung; **adopt a narrow ~look on things** in seinen Anschauungen beschränkt sein; die Dinge zu eng sehen; **C** (*looking out*) Hinaussehen, *das;* **~lying** *adj.* abgelegen, entlegen ‹Gegend, Vorort, Dorf›; **the ~lying suburbs of Tokyo** die Außenbezirke von Tokio; **~ma'nœuvre** *v.t.* überlisten ‹Truppen›; ausstechen, ausmanövrieren ‹Rivalen›; **~moded** /aʊt'məʊdɪd/ *adj.* **A** (*no longer in fashion*) altmodisch; **B** (*obsolete*) antiquiert (*abwertend*) ‹Ausdrucksweise›; **~'number** *v.t.* zahlenmäßig überlegen sein (+ *Dat.*); **they were ~numbered five to one** die anderen waren fünfmal so viele wie sie; **be [vastly] ~numbered [by sb.]** [jmdm.] zahlenmäßig [weit] unterlegen sein

**'out of** *prep.* **A** (*from within*) aus; **go ~ the door** zur Tür hinausgehen; **fall ~ sth.** aus etw. [heraus]fallen; **B** (*not within*) **be ~ the country** im Ausland sein; außer Landes sein (*geh.*); **be ~ town/the room** nicht in der Stadt/im Zimmer sein; **feel ~ it *or* things** sich ausgeschlossen *od.* nicht dazugehörig fühlen; **I'm glad to be ~ it** ich bin froh, dass ich die Sache hinter mir habe; **C** (*outside the limits of*) **marry ~ one's faith** einen Anhänger/eine Anhängerin eines anderen Glaubens heiraten; **born ~ wedlock** unehelich geboren; **be ~ the tournament** aus dem Turnier ausgeschieden sein; ⇒ *also* **order** 1 A, B; **D** (*from among*) **one ~ every three smokers** jeder dritte Raucher; **58 ~ every 100** 58 von hundert; **pick one ~ the pile** einen/eine/eins aus dem Stapel herausgreifen; **eighth ~ ten** als Achter von zehn Teilnehmern *usw.;* **choose ~ what is there** unter dem auswählen, was vorhanden ist; **only one instance ~ several** nur einer von mehreren Fällen; **E** (*beyond range of*) außer ‹Reich-/Hörweite, Sicht, Kontrolle›; **F** (*from*) aus; **get money ~ sb.** Geld aus jmdm. herausholen; **do well ~ sb./sth.** von jmdm./etw. profitieren; **G** (*owing to*) aus ‹Mitleid, Trotz, Furcht, Verehrung, Neugier usw.›; **H** (*no longer in*) **~ danger** außer Gefahr; **I** (*without*) **be ~ luck** kein Glück haben; **~ money** ohne Geld; **~ work** ohne Arbeit; arbeitslos; **we're ~ tea** der Tee ist uns ausgegangen; wir haben keinen Tee mehr; **be ~ a suit** (*Cards*) keine Karten einer Farbe haben; ⇒ *also* **out-of-work**; **J** (*by use of*) aus; **make a profit ~ sth.** mit etw. ein Geschäft machen; **made ~ silver** aus Silber; **what did you make it ~?** woraus hast du es gemacht?; **K** (*away from*) von ... entfernt; **three days ~ port** drei Tage nach dem Auslaufen aus dem Hafen; **ten miles ~ London** 10 Meilen außerhalb von London; **L** (*beyond*) ⇒ **depth** D; **ordinary** C

**out: ~-of-court settlement** *n.* (*Law*) (*agreement*) außergerichtlicher Vergleich; außergerichtliche Einigung; (*payment*) Vergleichssumme, *die;* **~-of-date** *attrib. adj.* (*old, not relevant*) veraltet; (*old-fashioned*) altmodisch; unmodern; antiquiert (*abwertend*) ‹Ausdrucksweise›; (*expired*) ungültig, verfallen ‹Karte›; **~-of-'pocket** *attrib. adj.* Bar‹auslagen›; **~-of-print** *attrib. adj.* vergriffen; **~-of-the-way** *attrib. adj.* (*remote*) abgelegen; entlegen; (*unusual, seldom met with*) ausgefallen; entlegen; **~-of-town** *attrib. adj.* außerhalb der Stadt gelegen ‹Einkaufszentrum›; (*fig.: unsophisticated*) Provinz- (*abwertend*); **~-of-work** *attrib. adj.* arbeitslos; **~'pace** *v.t.* ausstechen ‹Konkurrenten›; (*Sport*) besiegen ‹Läufer›; **be ~paced** ‹Sportler:› überholt werden; **~patient** *n.* ambulanter *od.* poliklinischer Patient/ambulante *od.* poliklinische Patientin; **~patients[' department]** Poliklinik, *die;* **have sth. done as an ~patient** etw. ambulant *od.* in der Ambulanz machen lassen; **be an ~patient** ambulant behandelt werden; **~per'form** *v.t.* überbieten; **~'play** *v.t.* (*Sport*) besser spielen als; **we can ~play them** wir sind ihnen spielerisch überlegen; **be ~played [by sb.]** [jmdm.] unterlegen sein; **~placement** /'aʊtpleɪsmənt/ *n., no pl.* (*Commerc.*) Outplacement, *das* (*fachspr.*); **~'point** *v.t.* (*Sport, esp. Boxing*) auspunkten; **~post** *n.* Außenposten, *der;* (*of civilization etc.; also Mil.*) Vorposten, *der;* **~pouring** *n., usu. in pl.* (*expression of emotion*) Gefühlsäußerung, *die;* (*impetuous, passionate*) Erguss, *der* (*geh. abwertend*); **~put** ❶ *n.* **A** (*amount*) Output, *der* (*fachspr.*); Produktion, *die;* (*of liquid, electricity, etc.*) Leistung, *die;* (*of coal mine etc.*) Förderung, *die;* Fördermenge, *die;* **total/daily/average/literary ~put** Gesamt-/Tages-/Durchschnitts-/literarische Produktion; **the factory has a daily ~put of 200 pairs** in der Fabrik werden pro Tag 200 Paar hergestellt; **B** (*Computing*) Ausgabe, *die;* Output, *der* (*fachspr.*); **~ device** Ausgabegerät, das; **~put capacity/terminal** Ausgabekapazität, *die*/-terminal, *das;* **C** (*Electr.*) (*energy*) [Ausgangs]leistung, *die;* Output, *der* (*fachspr.*); (*signal*) Ausgangssignal, *das;* **~put circuit/current** Ausgangsschaltung, *die*/-strom, *der;* **D** (*place*) Ausgang, *der;* (*recording or printing device*) Ausgabegerät, *das;* ❷ *v.t.*, **-tt-**, **~put** *or* **~putted** /'aʊtpʊtɪd/ (*Computing*) ausgeben ‹Information›

**outrage** ❶ /'aʊtreɪdʒ/ *n.* **A** (*deed of violence, violation of rights*) Verbrechen, *das;* (*during war*) Gräueltat, *die;* (*against good taste or decency*) grober *od.* krasser Verstoß; (*upon dignity*) krasse *od.* grobe Verletzung (**upon** *Gen.*); **be an ~ against good taste/decency/upon dignity** den guten Geschmack/Anstand/die Würde in grober *od.* krasser Weise verletzen; **an ~ against humanity** ein Verbrechen gegen die Menschheit; **an ~ upon decency/justice** eine Verhöhnung des Anstands/der Gerechtigkeit; **a bomb ~:** ein verbrecherischer Bombenanschlag; **B** (*strong resentment*) Empörung, *die* (**at** *gegen*); **react with a sense of ~:** empört sein.
❷ /'aʊtreɪdʒ, aʊt'reɪdʒ/ *v.t.* **A** (*cause to feel resentment, insult*) empören; **be ~d at** *or* **by sth.** über etw. (*Akk.*) empört sein; **B** (*infringe*) in grober *od.* krasser Weise verstoßen gegen ‹Anstand, Moral›

**outrageous** /aʊt'reɪdʒəs/ *adj.* **A** (*immoderate*) unverschämt (*ugs.*) ‹Forderung›; unverschämt hoch ‹Preis, Summe›; grell, schreiend ‹Farbe›; zu auffällig ‹Kleidung›; maßlos ‹Übertreibung›; **it's ~!** das ist unverschämt *od.* eine Unverschämtheit!; **B** (*grossly cruel, offensive*) ungeheuer ‹Grausamkeit›; haarsträubend, (*ugs.*) katastrophal ‹Behandlung, Bedienung›; unverschämt ‹Lüge, Benehmen, Unterstellung›; wüst ‹Schmähung›; geschmacklos ‹Witz›; ungeheuerlich ‹Anklage›; unerhört ‹Frechheit, Unhöflichkeit, Skandal›; unflätig ‹Sprache›; **C** (*violent*) grausam ‹Rache›; **~ deeds** Untaten; Grausamkeiten

**outrageously** /aʊt'reɪdʒəslɪ/ *adv.* **A** (*to an immoderate degree*) zu auffällig, aufdringlich ‹sich kleiden, schminken›; maßlos ‹übertreiben›; **an ~ low neckline** ein herausfordernd tiefer Ausschnitt; **B** (*atrociously, flagrantly*) unverschämt, schamlos ‹lügen, sich benehmen›; fürchterlich ‹fluchen›; **~ bad service** haarsträubend schlechte Bedienung; **he suggested quite ~ that ...:** er war so unverschämt vorzuschlagen, dass ...

**out'rank** *v.t.* (*Mil.*) einen höheren Rang einnehmen als; rangmäßig stehen über (+ *Dat.*); **be ~ed by sb.** einen niedrigeren Rang als jmd. haben; rangmäßig unter jmdm. stehen

**outré** /'u:treɪ/ *adj.* outriert (*geh. veralt.*); überspannt ‹Vorstellung, Geschmack›; absurd ‹Kleidung›

**out: ~rider** *n.* **A** (*mounted attendant*) berittener Begleiter/berittene Begleiterin; **B** (*motorcyclist*) **[motorcycle] ~rider** Kradbegleiter, *der*/-begleiterin, *die;* **C** (*Amer.: herdsman*) berittener Viehhirte; **~rigger** *n.* (*Naut.*) (*beam, spar, framework*) Maststütze, *die;* (*log fixed to canoe*) Schwimmbalken, *der;* Ausleger, *der;* (*iron bracket*) Ausleger, *der;* (*boat*) Auslegerboot, *das;* **~right** ❶ /-'-/ *adv.* **A** (*altogether, entirely*) ganz, komplett ‹kaufen, verkaufen›; (*instantaneously, on the spot*) auf der Stelle; **pay for/purchase/buy sth. ~right** sofort den ganzen Preis für etw. bezahlen; **B** (*openly*) geradeheraus (*ugs.*), freiheraus, rundheraus ‹erzählen, sagen, lachen›; ❷ /'--/ *adj.* ausgemacht ‹Unsinn, Schlechtigkeit, Unehrlichkeit›; offen, direkt ‹Wesensart›; rein, pur (*ugs.*) ‹Arroganz, Unverschämtheit, Irrtum, Egoismus, Unsinn›; glatt (*ugs.*) ‹Ablehnung, Absage, Lüge›; klar ‹Sieg, Niederlage, Sieger›; **~right sale** Verkauf in Bausch und Bogen; **~'run** *v.t., forms as* **run** 3 **A** (*run faster than*) schneller laufen *od.* sein als; **B** (*escape*) entkommen (+ *Dat.*); **~'sell** *v.t., forms as* **sell** 1 **A** (*be sold in greater quantities than*) sich besser verkaufen als; **be ~sold by ...:** sich schlechter verkaufen als ...; **B** (*sell more than*) mehr verkaufen als; **~sell sb. by two to one** zweimal so viel wie jmd. verkaufen; **~set** *n.* Anfang, *der;* Beginn, *der;* **at the ~set** zu Beginn *od.* Anfang; am Anfang; **from the ~set** von Anfang an; **~'shine** *v.t.*, **~shone** /aʊt'ʃɒn/ **A** (*shine brighter than*) heller leuchten als; **B** (*fig.*) in den Schatten stellen

**outside** ❶ /-'-, '--/ *n.* **A** (*external side*) Außenseite, *die;* **the ~ of the car is red** das Auto ist außen rot; **on the ~:** außen; **on the ~ of the door** außen an der Tür; **overtake sb. on the ~** (*in driving*) jmdn. außen überholen; **~ lane** Überholspur, *die;* **B** (*position on outer side*) **to/from the ~:** nach/von außen; **see a problem from the ~:** ein Problem als Außenstehender/Außenstehende sehen; **be kept on the ~:** ausgeschlossen bleiben; **C** (*external appearance*) Äußere, *das;* äußere Erscheinung; **D** (*of path etc.*) Rand, *der;* **E at the [very] ~:** äußerstenfalls; höchstens.
❷ /'--/ *adj.* **A** (*of, on, nearer the ~*) äußer...; Außen‹wand, -mauer, -antenne, -reparatur, -belag, -kajüte, -toilette, -ansicht, -durchmesser›; **B** (*remote*) **have only an ~ chance** nur eine sehr geringe Chance *od.* eine Außenseiterchance haben; **C** (*not coming from or belonging within*) fremd ‹Hilfe›; äußer... ‹Einfluss›; Freizeit‹aktivitäten, -interessen›; **~ pressure** Druck von außen; **some ~ help** (*extra workers*) zusätzliche Arbeitskräfte; **~ investment** Investitionen von außen; **an ~ opinion** die Meinung eines Außenstehenden; **the ex-convict had to adjust to the ~ world** der ehemalige Sträfling musste sich an das Leben draußen gewöhnen; **D** (*greatest possible*) maximal, höchst... ‹Schätzung›; **at an ~ estimate** maximal *od.* höchstens *od.* im Höchstfall.
❸ /-'-/ *adv.* **A** (*on the ~*) draußen; (*to the ~*) nach draußen; **the world ~:** die Außenwelt; **come from ~:** von draußen kommen; **seen from ~ it looks ...:** von [dr]außen sieht es ... aus; **come** *or* **step ~** (*as challenge to fight*) komm mal mit nach draußen *od.* vor die Tür; **who's that ~?** wer ist das da draußen?; **B ~ of** ⇒ **4**; **C** (*sl.: not in prison*) draußen (*ugs.*).
❹ /-'-/ *prep.* **A** (*on outer side of*) außerhalb (+ *Gen.*); **~ the door** vor der Tür; draußen; **prowl about/park ~ the house** ums Haus herumstreichen/vor dem Haus parken; **B** (*beyond*) außerhalb (+ *Gen.*) ‹Reichweite, Festival, Familie›; **it's ~ the terms of the agreement** es gehört nicht zu den Bedingungen der Abmachung; **this falls ~ the scope of ...:** das geht über den Rahmen von ... hinaus; **C** (*to the ~ of*) aus ... hinaus; **go ~ the house** nach draußen gehen

**outside: ~ 'broadcast** *n.* (*Brit.*) Außenübertragung, *die;* **~ 'edge** *n.* (*Skating, Cricket*) Außenkante, *die;* **~ 'forward** *n.* (*Footb., Hockey*) Außenstürmer, *der;* **~ 'half** *n.* (*Rugby*) Flügelhalbspieler, *der;* **~ 'left** *n.* (*Footb., Hockey*) Linksaußen, *der*

**outsider** /aʊt'saɪdə(r)/ *n.* **A** (*non-member, person without special knowledge*) Außenstehende, *der/die;* **B** (*Sport; also fig.*) Außenseiter, *der;* Outsider, *der*

**outside: ~ 'right** *n.* (*Footb., Hockey*) Rechtsaußen, *der;* **~ seat** *n.* Platz am Rand; **~ 'track** *n.* (*Racing*) Außenbahn, *die*

**out: ~size** *adj.* überdimensional; **~size person/clothes** Person mit/Kleidung in Übergröße; **~size shop/department** Geschäft/Abteilung für Übergrößen; **~skirts** *n. pl.* Stadtrand, *der;* **on the ~skirts [of Paris]** am Stadtrand [von Paris]; **the ~skirts of the city** die Außenbezirke der Stadt; **~'smart** *v.t.* (*coll.*) ausschmieren (*ugs.*); reinlegen (*ugs.*); **~source** ❶ *v.t.* extern vergeben ‹Arbeit, Aufträge›; ❷ *v.i.* Arbeiten/Aufträge extern vergeben; **~sourcing** /'aʊtsɔ:sɪŋ/ *n., no pl.* Outsourcing, *das* (*fachspr.*); Fremdbezug, *der* (*fachspr.*); **~'spoken** *adj.* freimütig ‹Person, Kritik, Bemerkung, Kommentar›; **be ~spoken about sth.** sich freimütig über etw. äußern; **the book was ~spoken on the subject** in dem Buch wurde das Thema freimütig *od.* offenherzig *od.* (*ugs.*) unverblümt behandelt; **~spread** *adj.* /'--, *pred.* -'-/ ausgebreitet; **he stood there, [with] arms ~spread** er stand mit ausgebreiteten Armen da; **~'standing** *adj.* **A** (*conspicuous*) hervorstechend ‹Merkmal›; **B** (*exceptional*) hervorragend ‹Leistung, Redner, Künstler, Dienst›; überragend ‹Bedeutung›; außergewöhnlich ‹Person, Mut, Fähigkeit, Geschick›; **not be ~standing** nicht überragend sein; **~standing in courage and skill** außergewöhnlich mutig und geschickt; **of ~standing ability/skill** außergewöhnlich fähig/geschickt; **be ~standing at skating** hervorragend Schlittschuh laufen können; **work of ~standing excellence** ganz hervorragende Arbeit; **C** (*not yet settled*) ausstehend ‹Schuld, Verbindlichkeit, Geldsumme›; offen, unbezahlt ‹Rechnung›; unerledigt ‹Arbeit›; ungelöst ‹Problem›; **there's £5 still ~standing** es stehen noch 5 Pfund aus; **have work still ~standing** noch etwas zu erledigen haben; **~standingly** /aʊt'stændɪŋlɪ/ *adv.* außergewöhnlich ‹intelligent, gut, begabt›; **not ~standingly** nicht besonders; **be ~standingly good at tennis/Latin** hervorragend Tennis spielen/Latein können; **~station** *n.* Außenposten, *der;* **~'stay** *v.t.* **A** (*stay beyond*) überziehen ‹Urlaub›; **B** (*stay longer than*) länger bleiben als; (*surpass in staying power, endurance*) mehr Stehvermögen haben als; ⇒ *also* **welcome** 2 A; **~'step** *v.t.* hinausgehen über (+ *Akk.*); **~stretched** *adj.* ausgestreckt; (*spread out*) ausgebreitet; **~'strip** *v.t.* A (*pass in running*) überholen; B (*surpass in competition*) überflügeln; übersteigen ‹Einsicht, Ressourcen, Ersparnisse›; **~-takes** *n. pl.* (*Cinemat. etc.*) Ausschuss, *der;* **~tray** *n.* Ablage für Ausgänge; **~'vote** *v.t.* überstimmen

**outward** /'aʊtwəd/ ❶ *adj.* A (*external, apparent*) [rein] äußerlich; äußere ‹Erscheinung, Bedingung›; **sb.'s ~ self** jmds. äußere Erscheinung; **with an ~ show of confidence** mit einem Anstrich von Selbstsicherheit; **an ~ display of fear** eine Demonstration der Angst; **~ form** Erscheinungsform, *die;* äußere Form; B (*directed towards outside*) nach außen gerichtet ‹Neigung, Bewegung›; (*going out*) Hin‹reise, -fracht›; **~ flow of money/traffic** Kapitalabfluss, *der*/abfließender Verkehr; **the ~ half of a return ticket** der Hinfahrtabschnitt einer Fahrkarte.

❷ *adv.* nach außen ‹aufgehen, richten›; **be ~ bound [for New York]** ‹Schiff:› [mit Kurs auf New York (*Akk.*)] auslaufen; ‹Person:› [in Richtung New York] abreisen

**outward-'bound** *attrib. adj.* auslaufend (**for** nach) ‹Schiff›; abreisend ‹Passagier›

**outwardly** /'aʊtwədlɪ/ *adv.* nach außen hin ‹Gefühle zeigen›; öffentlich ‹Loyalität erklären›

**outwards** ⇒ **outward** 2

**out: ~'weigh** *v.t.* schwerer wiegen als; überwiegen ‹Nachteile›; [mehr als] wettmachen ‹Verluste›; **~'wit** *v.t.*, **-tt-** überlisten; **~work** *n.* A (*part of fortification*) **~work[s]** Vorfestung, *die;* Vorwerk, *das;* Außenbefestigung, *die;* B (*work*) Arbeit außerhalb des Betriebs; Heimarbeit, *die;* **~worker** *n. jmd., der außerhalb des Betriebs arbeitet;* Heimarbeiter, *der*/-arbeiterin, *die;* **~'worn** *adj.* (*obsolete*) veraltet ‹Brauch, Ansicht, Lehre, Theorie›

**ova** *pl. of* **ovum**

**oval** /'əʊvl/ ❶ *adj.* A oval; länglich rund ‹Form›; eiförmig ‹Ball›; B (*having outline of egg*) oval; **O~ Office** *Büro des US-Präsidenten im Weißen Haus.* ❷ *n.* Oval, *das*

**ovary** /'əʊvərɪ/ *n.* (*Anat.*) Ovarium, *das;* Eierstock, *der;* (*Bot.*) Ovarium, *das;* Fruchtknoten, *der*

**ovation** /əʊ'veɪʃn/ *n.* Ovation, *die;* begeisterter Beifall; **get an ~ for sth.** Ovationen *od.* begeisterten Beifall für etw. bekommen; **a standing ~:** stehende Ovationen

**oven** /'ʌvn/ *n.* [Back]ofen, *der;* **put sth. in the ~ for 40 minutes** etw. 40 Minuten backen; **cook in a hot/moderate/slow ~:** bei starker/mäßiger/schwacher Hitze backen/braten/schmoren; **it's like an ~ in here** hier ist es warm wie in einem Backofen; **have a bun in the ~** (*coll.*) ein Kind kriegen (*ugs.*)

**oven: ~ cloth** *n.* Topflappen, *der;* **~-fresh** *adj.* ofenfrisch; **~ glove** *n.* Topfhandschuh, *der;* **~proof** *adj.* feuerfest; **~-ready** *adj.* backfertig ‹Pommes frites, Pastete›; bratfertig ‹Geflügel›; **~-to-table** *adj.* feuerfest ‹Geschirr›; **~ware** *n., no pl.* feuerfestes Geschirr

**over** /'əʊvə(r)/ ❶ *adv.* A (*outward and downward*) hinüber; **kick ~:** umstoßen; B (*so as to cover surface*) **draw/board/cover ~:** zuziehen/-nageln/-decken; **paint ~:** [an]streichen ‹Raum, Wand›; überstreichen ‹Inschrift›; C (*with motion above sth.*) **climb/look/jump ~:** hinüber- *od.* (*ugs.*) rüberklettern/-sehen/-springen; **boil ~:** überkochen; **this goes under and that goes ~:** dies kommt darunter und das darüber; D (*so as to reverse position etc.*) herum; **change ~:** umschalten ‹Programm, Sender›; austauschen ‹Bilder, Format›; **switch ~:** umschalten ‹Programm, Sender›; **it rolled ~ and ~:** es rollte und rollte; E (*across a space*) hinüber; (*towards speaker*) herüber; **row ~ to a place** an einen Ort hinüberrudern; **he swam ~ to us/the other side** er schwamm zu uns herüber/hinüber zur anderen Seite; **fly ~:** vorüberfliegen; **drive sb. ~ to the other side of town** jmdn. ans andere Ende der Stadt fahren; **be ~** (*have arrived*) drüben [angekommen] sein; **~ here/there** (*direction*) hier herüber/dort hinüber; (*location*) hier/dort; **they are ~ [here] for the day** sie sind einen Tag hier; **ask sb. ~ [for dinner]** jmdn. [zum Essen] einladen; **~ against** (*opposite*) gegenüber; (*in contrast to*) im Gegensatz zu; F (*with change from one to another*) **[come in, please,] ~** (*Radio*) übernehmen Sie bitte; **~ and out** (*Radio*) Ende; **and now, ~ to ...** (*Radio*) wir schalten jetzt um nach ...; **and it's ~ to you** jetzt bist du dran; (*Radio*) ich übergebe an Sie; G ▸912 (*in excess etc.*) **children of 12 and ~:** Kinder im Alter von zwölf Jahren und darüber; **there are two cakes each and one ~:** es sind zwei Kuchen für jeden da und einer übrig; **be [left] ~:** übrig [geblieben] sein; **have ~:** übrig haben ‹Geld›; zu viel haben ‹Spielkarte›; **9 into 28 goes 3 and 1 ~:** 28 geteilt durch neun ist gleich 3, Rest 1; **it's a bit ~** (*in weight*) es ist ein bisschen mehr; **do you want it ~ or under?** darf es mehr oder soll es weniger sein?; **run three minutes ~:** drei Minuten über die Zeit laufen; **£50 ~ and above** obendrein noch *od.* überdies noch 50 Pfund; H (*from beginning to end*) von Anfang bis Ende; **say sth. twice ~:** etw. wiederholen *od.* zweimal sagen; **[all] ~ again,** (*Amer.*) **~:** noch einmal [ganz von vorn]; **~ and ~ [again]** immer wieder; wieder und wieder (*geh.*); **several times ~:** mehrmals; I (*at an end*) vorbei; vorüber; **be ~:** vorbei sein; ‹Aufführung:› zu Ende sein; **the rain is ~:** der Regen hat aufgehört; **get sth. ~ with** etw. hinter sich (*Akk.*) bringen; **be ~ and done with** erledigt sein; J **all ~** (*completely finished*) aus [und vorbei]; (*in or on one's whole body etc.*) überall; (*in characteristic attitude*) typisch; **it is all ~ with him** es ist aus mit ihm (*ugs.*); **I ache all ~:** mir tut alles weh; **be shaking all ~:** am ganzen Körper zittern; **be wet all ~:** völlig nass sein; **the dog licked her all ~:** der Hund leckte sie von oben bis unten ab; **I feel stiff all ~:** ich bin ganz steif; **embroidered all ~ with flowers** ganz mit Blumen bestickt; **it happens all ~** (*Amer.: everywhere*) das kommt überall vor; **that is him/sth. all ~:** das ist typisch für ihn/etw.; K (*overleaf*) umseitig; rückseitig; auf der Rückseite; **see ~:** siehe Rückseite.

❷ *prep.* A (*above*) (*indicating position*) über (+ *Dat.*); (*indicating motion*) über (+ *Akk.*); **bent ~ his books** über seine Bücher gebeugt; **his crime will hang ~ him until he dies** sein Verbrechen wird ihn bis zu seinem Tode verfolgen; B (*on*) (*indicating position*) über (+ *Dat.*); (*indicating motion*) über (+ *Akk.*); **hit sb. ~ the head** jmdm. auf den Kopf schlagen; **carry a coat ~ one's arm** einen Mantel über dem Arm tragen; **tie a piece of paper ~ a jar** ein Stück Papier auf einem Glas befestigen; **~ the page** auf der nächsten Seite; C (*in or across every part of*) [überall] in (+ *Dat.*); (*to and fro upon*) über (+ *Akk.*); (*all through*) durch; **all ~** (*in or on all parts of*) überall in (+ *Dat.*); **sell sth./travel all ~ the country** etw. im ganzen Land verkaufen/das ganze Land bereisen; **all ~ Spain** überall in Spanien; in ganz Spanien; **all ~ everything** überall; **you've got jam all ~ your face** du hast überall im Gesicht Marmelade *od.* dein Gesicht ist ganz voller Marmelade; **she spilt wine all ~ her skirt** sie hat sich (*Dat.*) Wein über den ganzen Rock geschüttet; **all ~ the world** in der ganzen Welt; **be all ~ sb.** (*coll.: be very attentive to*) sich an jmdn. ranschmeißen (*salopp*); **show sb. ~ the house** jmdm. das Haus zeigen; **~ all** ⇒ **overall** 3; D (*round about*) (*indicating position*) über (+ *Dat.*); (*indicating motion*) über (+ *Akk.*); **a sense of gloom hung ~ him** ihn umgab eine gedrückte Stimmung; **doubt hangs ~ the authenticity of the diaries** es besteht *od.* bestehen Zweifel an der Echtheit der Tagebücher; E (*on account of*) wegen; **laugh ~ sth.** über etw. (*Akk.*) lachen; F (*engaged with*) bei; **take trouble ~ sth.** sich (*Dat.*) mit etw. Mühe geben; **be a long time ~ sth.** lange für etw. brauchen; **fall asleep ~ one's work** bei der Arbeit einschlafen; **~ work/dinner/a cup of tea/a bottle** bei der Arbeit/beim Essen/bei einer Tasse Tee/einer guten Flasche; **~ the telephone** am Telefon; G (*superior to, in charge of*) über (+ *Akk.*); **have command/authority ~ sb.** Befehlsgewalt über jmdn./Weisungsbefugnis gegenüber jmdm. haben; **be ~ sb.** (*in rank*) über jmdm. stehen; H (*beyond, more than*) über (+ *Akk.*); **an increase ~ last year's total** eine Zunahme gegenüber der letztjährigen Gesamtmenge; **it's been ~ a month since ...:** es ist über einen Monat her, dass ...; **~ and above** zusätzlich zu; I (*in comparison with*) **a decrease ~ last year** eine Abnahme gegenüber dem letzten Jahr; J (*out and down from etc.*) über (+ *Akk.*); **look ~ a wall** über eine Mauer sehen; **the window looks ~ the street** das Fenster geht zur Straße hinaus *od.* liegt zur Straße; **fall ~ a cliff** von einem Felsen stürzen; **jump ~ a precipice** in einen Abgrund springen; K (*across*) über (+ *Akk.*); **the pub ~ the road** die Wirtschaft auf der anderen Straßenseite *od.* gegenüber; **~ sea and land/hill and dale** über Meer und Land/Berg und Tal; **climb ~ the wall** über die Mauer steigen *od.* klettern; **be safely ~ an obstacle** sicher über ein Hindernis gekommen sein; **be ~ the worst** das Schlimmste hinter sich (*Dat.*) *od.* überstanden haben; **come from ~ the wall** ‹Lärm:› von der anderen Seite der Mauer kommen; **be ~ an illness** eine Krankheit überstanden haben; L (*throughout, during*) über (+ *Akk.*); **stay ~ Christmas/the weekend/Wednesday** über Weihnachten/das Wochenende/bis Donnerstag bleiben; **~ the summer** den Sommer über; **~ the past years** in den letzten Jahren; **mellow ~ the years** ‹Person:› mit den Jahren abgeklärter werden; M (*Math.: divided by*) [geteilt] durch.

❸ *n.* (*Cricket*) Over, *das;* [Anzahl von] 6/(*esp. in Australia*) 8 Würfel[n]; ⇒ *also* **maiden over**

**over: ~-a'bundant** *adj.* überreichlich; **~a'chieve** *v.i.* (*Psych.*) einen Leistungsüberschuss haben; **~'act** ❶ *v.t.* übertrieben spielen ‹Rolle, Theaterstück›; chargieren ‹Nebenrolle›; ❷ *v.i.* übertreiben; **~'active** *adj.* hyperaktiv; **have an ~active thyroid** an Schilddrüsenüberfunktion leiden; **~-'age** *adj.* zu alt; **~all** ❶ *n.* A (*Brit.: garment*) Arbeitsmantel, *der;* Arbeitskittel, *der;* B *in pl.* **[pair of] ~alls** Overall, *der;* (*with a bib and strap top*) Latzhose, *die;* ❷ *adj.* A (*from end to end; total*) Gesamt‹breite, -einsparung, -klassement, -abmessung›; **have an ~all majority** die absolute Mehrheit haben; B (*general*) allgemein ‹Verbesserung, Wirkung›; ❸ /'---, --'-/ *adv.* A (*in all parts*) insgesamt; **a ship dressed ~all** ein über die Toppen geflaggtes Schiff; B (*taken as a whole*) im Großen und Ganzen; **come fourth ~all** (*Sport*) Vierter/Vierte der Gesamtwertung werden; **~am'bitious** *adj.* allzu ehrgeizig ‹Projekt, Plan›; **~an'xiety** *n.* Überängstlichkeit, *die;* übergroße Sorge (**about** um); **~'anxious** *adj.* **be ~-anxious to do sth.** etw. unbedingt tun wollen; **be ~-anxious about making mistakes** übermäßig besorgt sein, Fehler zu machen; **~arm** ❶ *adj.* A (*Cricket*) **~arm bowling** Werfen mit über die Schulter erhobenem Arm; B (*Swimming*) **~arm stroke** Zug, bei dem ein Arm/beide Arme aus dem Wasser gehoben wird/werden; C (*Tennis*) **~arm service** Aufschlag von oben; ❷ *adv.* mit über die Schulter erhobenem Arm ‹werfen, aufschlagen›; **~'awe** *v.t.* Ehrfurcht einflößen (+ *Dat.*); ‹Waffe, Anzahl:› einschüchtern; **they were ~awed by the splendour** die Pracht flößte ihnen Ehrfurcht ein; **~'balance** ❶ *v.i.* A ‹Person:› das Gleichgewicht verlieren, aus dem Gleichgewicht kommen; B (*capsize*) ‹Gegenstand:› umkippen; ‹Boot:› kentern; ❷ *v.t.* A aus dem Gleichgewicht bringen ‹Person›; B (*capsize*) umkippen ‹Gegenstand›; zum Kentern bringen ‹Boot›; **~'bearing** *adj.*, **~bearingly** /əʊvə'beərɪŋlɪ/ *adv.* herrisch; **~bid** ❶ /--'-/ *v.t., forms as* **bid** 1 B überbieten ‹Händler, Gegner, Gebot›; ❷ /--'-/ *v.i., forms as* **bid** 2 (*Bridge*) überrufen; ❸ /'---/ *n.* höheres Angebot; Übergebot, *das;* (*higher than justified*) überhöhtes Angebot; **~blouse** *n.* Überziehbluse, *die;* **~'blown** *adj.* A (*past its prime, lit. or fig.*) verblühend; **be ~blown** [fast] verblüht sein; B (*inflated or pretentious*) geschraubt,

O

gestelzt, gespreizt ‹Stil, Prosa›; **~board** *adv.* über Bord; **fall ~board** über Bord gehen; **go ~board** (*fig. coll.*) ausflippen (*ugs.*) (**about** wegen); **~'book** *v.t.* überbuchen; **~boot** *n.* Überschuh, *der;* **~'burden** *v.t.* (*fig.*) überlasten ‹System, Person› (**by** mit); **I don't want to ~burden you** ich möchte Sie nicht überbeanspruchen; **be ~burdened with care/grief** zu viele Sorgen/zu viel Kummer haben; **~call** (*Bridge*) ❶ /--'-/ *v.t.* überbieten ‹Gegner, Gebot›; ❷ /--'-/ *v.i.* (*Brit.*) überrufen; ein Übergebot *od.* höheres Gebot machen *od.* abgeben; ❸ /'---/ *n.* Übergebot, *das;* höheres Gebot; **~'careful** *adj.* übervorsichtig; **~cast** *adj.* [A] trübe ‹Wetter, Himmel, Tag›; bewölkt ‹Himmel, Nacht›; bedeckt, bezogen ‹Himmel›; [B] (*Sewing*) überwendlich ‹Naht›; **~'cautious** *adj.* übervorsichtig; **~'charge** ❶ *v.t.* [A] (*charge beyond reasonable price*) zu viel abnehmen *od.* abverlangen (+ *Dat.*); **we were ~charged for the eggs** wir haben für die Eier zu viel *od.* einen überhöhten Preis bezahlt; [B] (*charge beyond right price*) zu viel berechnen (+ *Dat.*); **~charge sb. by 25p** jmdm. 25 Pence zu viel berechnen; [C] (*put too much charge into*) überladen ‹Batterie›; über[be]lasten ‹Elektrogerät›; ❷ *v.i.* zu viel berechnen; **~coat** *n.* [A] (*coat*) Mantel, *der;* [B] (*of paint*) Anstrich, *der;* **~'come** ❶ *v.t., forms as* **come** 1 [A] (*prevail ~*) überwinden; bezwingen ‹Feind›; ablegen ‹Angewohnheit›; widerstehen (+ *Dat.*) ‹Versuchung›; ‹Schlaf:› überkommen, übermannen; ‹Dämpfe:› betäuben; [B] *in p.p.* (*exhausted, affected*) **he was ~come by grief/with emotion** Kummer/Rührung übermannte *od.* überwältigte ihn; **she was ~come by fear/shyness** Angst/Schüchternheit überkam *od.* überwältigte sie; **they were too ~come with fatigue** sie waren zu müde; **~come with loneliness** von Einsamkeit übermannt; **they were ~come with remorse** Reue befiel sie; **I'm quite ~come** ich bin ganz überwältigt; ❷ *v.i., forms as* **come** 1 siegen; siegreich sein; **~compen'sation** *n.* (*Psych.*) Überkompensation, *die;* **~'confidence** *n.* übersteigertes Selbstvertrauen; **~'confident** *adj.* übertrieben zuversichtlich; **be ~confident of success** sich (*Dat.*) des Erfolges allzu sicher sein; **~'confidently** *adv.* übertrieben zuversichtlich; **~'cooked** *adj.* verkocht; **~'critical** *adj.* zu kritisch; überkritisch; **be ~critical of sth.** etw. zu sehr kritisieren; **~'crowded** *adj.* überfüllt ‹Zug, Bus, Raum›; übervölkert ‹Stadt›; **~'crowding** *n.* (*of room, bus, train*) Überfüllung, *die;* (*of city*) Übervölkerung, *die;* **~de'velop** *v.t.* (*Photog.*) überentwickeln; **~de'veloped** *adj.* überentwickelt; frühreif ‹Kind, Jugendliche›; **~'do** *v.t.*, **~doing** /əʊvəˈduːɪŋ/, **~'did** /əʊvəˈdɪd/, **~done** /əʊvəˈdʌn/ [A] (*carry to excess*) übertreiben; überladen ‹Geschichte›; übertrieben spielen ‹Rolle, Szene›; **~do one's gratitude/the sympathy** es mit der Dankbarkeit/dem Mitleid übertreiben; **~do the salt** zu großzügig mit dem Salz umgehen; [B] **~do it** *or* **things** (*work too hard*) sich übernehmen; (*exaggerate*) es übertreiben; **~'done** *adj.* [A] (*exaggerated*) übertrieben; [B] (*cooked too much*) verkocht; verbraten ‹Fleisch›; **~dose** ❶ /'---/ *n.* Überdosis, *die;* ❷ /--'-/ *v.t.* eine Überdosis geben (+ *Dat.*); ❸ *v.i.* eine Überdosis nehmen; **~dose on heroin/amphetamines** eine Überdosis Heroin/Amphetamine nehmen; **~draft** *n.* Kontoüberziehung, *die;* **have an ~draft of £50 at the bank** sein Konto um 50 Pfund überzogen haben; **get/pay off an ~draft** einen Überziehungskredit erhalten/abbezahlen; **~'draw** *v.t., forms as* **draw** 1 (*Banking*) überziehen ‹Konto›; **~'drawn** *adj.* überzogen ‹Konto›; **I am ~drawn [at the bank]** mein Konto ist überzogen; **~'dress** *v.i.* sich zu fein anziehen; **~'dressed** *adj.* zu fein angezogen; overdressed (*geh.*); **~drive** *n.* (*Motor Veh.*) Overdrive, *der;* Schongang, *der;* **~'due** *adj.* überfällig; **the train is 15 minutes ~due** der Zug hat schon 15 Minuten Verspätung; **your rent is ~due** Ihre Miete steht noch aus; **~'eager** *adj.* übereifrig; **be ~eager to do sth.** sich übereifrig bemühen, etw. zu tun; **we weren't ~eager to go back** wir waren nicht gerade wild darauf zurückzukehren (*ugs.*); **~'eat** *v.i., forms as* **eat** zu viel essen; **~eating** übermäßiges Essen; **~e'laborate** *adj.* allzu *od.* übertrieben kunstvoll ‹Konstruktion, Frisur, Stil›; allzu ausgefeilt ‹Plan›; allzu ausgeklügelt ‹Plan, Entschuldigung›; **~'emphasis** *n.* Überbetonung, *die;* **~'emphasize** *v.t.* überbetonen; **one cannot ~emphasize the importance of this** man kann nicht genug betonen, wie wichtig das ist; **~-enthusi'astic** *adj.* übertrieben begeistert (**at, about** von); **~estimate** ❶ /əʊvərˈestɪmeɪt/ *v.t.* überschätzen; **~estimate one's own importance** sich zu wichtig nehmen (*ugs.*); ❷ /əʊvərˈestɪmət/ *n.* zu hohe Schätzung; **~ex'cite** *v.t.* zu sehr aufregen ‹Patient›; **~excited** überreizt ‹Zustand, Gemüt›; **become ~excited** ganz aufgeregt werden; **~ex'citement** *n.* Überreizung, *die;* **~ex'ert** *v. refl.* sich überanstrengen; **~ex'pose** *v.t.* [A] (*Photog.*) überbelichten; [B] **be ~exposed to sth.** einer Sache (*Dat.*) im Übermaß ausgesetzt sein; **he is becoming ~exposed** (*on TV*) man sieht sich (*Dat.*) ihn über (*ugs.*); **~ex'posure** *n.* [A] (*Photog.*) Überbelichtung, *die;* [B] (*to radiation*) übermäßige Belastung (**to** durch); (*by the media*) zu häufige Präsentation (**by** durch); **~'feed** *v.t., forms as* **feed** 1 überfüttern ‹Tier, (fam.) Kind›; **~'fill** *v.t.* zu voll machen; **~ 'fish** *v.t.* überfischen; **~fishing** Überfischung, *die;* **~flight** *n.* Überflug, *der;* **~flow** ❶ /--'-/ *v.t.* [A] (*flow ~*) laufen über (+ *Akk.*) ‹Rand›; [B] (*flow ~ brim of*) überlaufen aus ‹Tank›; **a river ~flowing its banks** ein Fluss, der über die Ufer tritt; [C] (*extend beyond limits of*) ‹Menge, Personen:› nicht genug Platz finden in (+ *Dat.*); [D] (*flood*) überschwemmen ‹Feld›; ❷ *v.i.* [A] (*flow ~ edge or limit*) überlaufen; **be filled/full to ~flowing** ‹Raum:› überfüllt sein; ‹Flüssigkeitsbehälter:› zum Überlaufen voll sein; ‹Schublade:› fast überquellen; **~flow into the street** ‹Menge:› bis auf die Straße stehen; [B] (*fig.*) ‹Herz, Person:› überfließen (*geh.*), überströmen (**with** vor + *Dat.*); ❸ /'---/ *n.* [A] (*what flows ~, lit. or fig.*) **the ~flow** was übergelaufen ist; das Übergelaufene; **the ~flow from the cities** die Menschen, für die in den Städten kein Platz ist; **~flow of population** Bevölkerungsüberschuss, *der;* [B] (*outlet*) **~flow [pipe]** Überlauf, *der;* **~flow meeting** *n.* Parallelversammlung, *die;* **~ 'fly** *v.t., forms as* **fly**[2] 2 [A] (*fly ~*) überfliegen; [B] (*fly beyond*) hinausschießen über (+ *Akk.*) ‹Landebahn›; **~'fond** *adj.* **be/not be ~fond of sb./sth.** jmdn./etw. nur zu gern/nicht sonderlich mögen; **be/not be ~fond of doing sth.** etw. nur zu gern/nicht sonderlich gern tun; **~'fondness** *n., no pl.* übertriebene Vorliebe (**for** für); **~ful'fil** (*Amer.:* **~ful'fill**) *v.t.* übererfüllen ‹[Plan]soll, Plan›; **~ful'filment** (*Amer.:* **~ful'fillment**) *n.* Überfüllung, *die;* **~'full** *adj.* zu voll; übervoll; **~'generous** *adj.* zu *od.* übertrieben großzügig ‹Person›; reichlich groß ‹Portion›; **you weren't ~generous with the butter** mit der Butter bist du ja nicht gerade verschwenderisch umgegangen; **~ground** *adj.* oberirdisch ‹Krypta, Pflanzenteil›; oberirdisch verkehrend ‹Bahn›; **~'grow** *v.t., forms as* **grow** 2 überwachsen, überwuchern ‹Beet›; **~'grown** *adj.* [A] überwachsen, überwuchert ‹Beet› (**with** von); [B] **he acts like an ~grown schoolboy** er führt sich auf wie ein großes Kind; **~hand knot** *n.* einfacher Knoten; **~hang** ❶ /--'-/ *v.t.*, **~hung** /əʊvəˈhʌŋ/ ‹Felsen, Stockwerk:› hinausragen über (+ *Akk.*); ❷ /--'-/ *v.i.*, **~hung** ‹Fels, Klippe:› überhängen; ❸ /'---/ *n.* Überhang, *der;* **rock ~hang** Felsvorsprung, *der;* Überhang, *der;* **~'hanging** *adj.* überhängend; **~'hasty** *adj.* vorschnell, übereilt ‹Urteil, Verurteilung, Entschluss, Schluss, Antwort›; **be ~hasty in doing sth.** etw. vorschnell *od.* übereilt tun; **~haul** ❶ /--'-/ *v.t.* [A] (*examine and adjust*) überholen ‹Auto, Schiff, Maschine, Motor›; überprüfen ‹System›; [B] (*~take*) überholen ‹Fahrzeug, Person›; ❷ /'---/ *n.* Überholung, *die;* **need an ~haul** ‹Maschine:› überholt werden müssen; ‹System:› überarbeitet werden müssen; **give sth. an ~haul** etw. überholen; **~head** ❶ /--'-/ *adv.* **high ~head** hoch oben; **the sky ~head** der Himmel darüber; (*above me/him/us etc.*) der Himmel über mir/ihm/uns *usw.;* **the clouds ~head** die Wolken am Himmel; **hear a sound ~head** ein Geräusch über sich (*Dat.*) hören; ❷ /'---/ *adj.* [A] **~head wires** Hochleitung, *die;* **~head cable** Luftkabel, *das;* Freileitung, *die;* **~head railway** Hochbahn, *die;* **~head lighting** Deckenbeleuchtung, *die;* **~head projector** Overheadprojektor, *der;* [B] **~head expenses/charges/costs** (*Commerc.*) Gemeinkosten *Pl.;* ❸ /'---/ *n.* [A] **~heads,** (*Amer.*) **~head** (*Commerc.*) Gemeinkosten *Pl.;* [B] (*Sport*) Überkopfball, *der;* **~'hear** *v.t., forms as* **hear** 1 (*accidentally*) zufällig [mit]hören, mitbekommen ‹Unterhaltung, Bemerkung›; (*intentionally*) belauschen ‹Gespräch, Personen›; **speak quietly, so that we can't be ~heard** sprich leise, damit niemand etwas mitbekommt; *abs.* **not want sb. to ~hear** nicht wollen, dass jmd. mithört; **~'heat** ❶ *v.t.* überhitzen ‹Motor, Metall usw.›; **~heated imagination** überdrehte Fantasie; **~heated economy** überhitzte Konjunktur; ❷ *v.i.* zu heiß werden; ‹Maschine, Lager:› heißlaufen; (*fig.*) ‹Konjunktur:› sich überhitzen; **~-in'dulge** ❶ *v.t.* zu sehr frönen (*geh.*) (+ *Dat.*) ‹Appetit›; **~-indulge a child** einem Kind gegenüber zu nachgiebig sein; **~-indulge oneself** sich allzu sehr gehen lassen; ❷ *v.i.* es übertreiben; **~-indulge in food and drink** sich an Essen und Trinken mehr als gütlich tun; **~in'dulgence** *n.* übermäßiger Genuss (**in** von); (*towards a person*) zu große Nachgiebigkeit; **~indulgence in drink/drugs/sex** übermäßiges Trinken/übermäßiger Drogengenuss/zu viel Sex; **~-in'dulgent** *adj.* unmäßig; (*towards a person*) zu nachgiebig; **~-in'sured** *adj.* zu hoch versichert

**overjoyed** /əʊvəˈdʒɔɪd/ *adj.* überglücklich (**at** über + *Akk.*)

**over: ~kill** *n.* (*Mil.*) Overkill, *das od. der;* **be ~kill** (*fig.*) zu viel des Guten sein; **~land** ❶ /--'-/ *adv.* auf dem Landweg; ❷ /'---/ *adj.* **by the ~land route** auf dem Landweg; **~land transport/journey** Beförderung/Reise auf dem Landweg; **~lap** ❶ /--'-/ *v.t.* überlappen ‹Fläche, Dachziegel›; teilweise überdecken ‹Farbe›; sich überschneiden mit ‹Aufgabe, Datum›; ❷ /--'-/ *v.i.* ‹Flächen, Dachziegel:› sich überlappen; ‹Aufgaben, Daten, Zuständigkeitsbereiche:› sich überschneiden; ‹Farben:› sich teilweise überdecken; ‹Bretter:› teilweise übereinander liegen; ❸ /'---/ *n.* [A] Überlappung, *die;* (*of colours*) teilweise Überdeckung; (*of dates or tasks; between subjects, periods, etc.*) Überschneidung, *die;* **have an ~lap of 4 cm** ‹Bretter usw.:› sich auf einer Breite von 4 cm überdecken; [B] (*~lapping part*) Überlappung, *die;* (*between map-sheets*) sich überschneidende Teile; **~'large** *adj.* übergroß; **~-large for sth.** zu groß für etw.; **~lay** ❶ /--'-/ *v.t., forms as* **lay**[2] 1 [A] (*cover*) bedecken; (*with film, veneer*) überziehen; [B] ⇒ **~lie;** ❷ /'---/ *n.* [A] (*cover*) Überzug, *der;* [B] (*transparent sheet*) Auflegefolie, *die;* **~'leaf** *adv.* auf der Rückseite; **see diagram ~leaf** siehe das umseitige Diagramm; **see ~leaf for details** Details siehe Rückseite; **~'lie** *v.t., forms as* **lie**[2] 2 überlagern; **~load** ❶ /--'-/ *v.t.* überladen (*auch fig.*), überlasten ‹Stromkreis, Lautsprecher usw.›; überbelasten ‹Maschine, Motor, Mechanismus usw.›; ❷ *v.i.* überbelastet werden; ❸ /'---/ *n.* (*Electr.*) Überlastung, *die;* **~'long** *adj.* überlang; **~'look** *v.t.* [A] (*have view of*) ‹Hotel, Zimmer, Haus:› Aussicht haben *od.* bieten auf (+ *Akk.*); **house ~looking the lake** Haus mit Blick auf den See; [B] (*be higher than*) überragen; [C] (*not see, ignore*) übersehen; (*allow to go unpunished*) hinwegsehen über (+ *Akk.*) ‹Vergehen, Beleidigung›; **~lord** *n.* Oberherr, *der*

**overly** /ˈəʊvəlɪ/ *adv.* allzu

**over: ~'man** *v.t.* überbesetzen; **~manning** *n.* [personelle] Überbesetzung; **~mantel** *n.* Kaminaufsatz, *der;* **~'modest** *adj.* zu bescheiden; **~'much** ❶ *adj.* allzu viel; ❷ *adv.* allzu sehr

**overnight** ❶ /--'-/ *adv.* (*also fig.: suddenly*) über Nacht; **stay ~ in a hotel** in einem Hotel übernachten; ❷ /'---/ *adj.* [A] **~ train/bus** Nachtzug, *der*/Nachtbus, *der;* **~ stay**

Übernachtung, *die;* **make an ~ stay** übernachten; Ⓑ (*fig.: sudden*) **be an ~ success** über Nacht Erfolg haben

**overnight: ~ bag** *n.* [kleine] Reisetasche; **~ case** *n.* Handköfferchen, *das*

**over: ~pass** ⇒ **flyover**; **~'pay** *v.t., forms as* **pay** 2 überbezahlen; **~'payment** *n.* Überbezahlung, *die;* **receive an ~payment of £20** 20 Pfund zu viel bekommen; **~'play** *v.t.* Ⓐ (*overact*) übertrieben spielen ‹Rolle›; Ⓑ (*exaggerate*) hochspielen ‹Faktor, Bedeutung›; **~play one's hand** (*Cards*) sich überreizen; (*fig.*) den Bogen überspannen; **~'populated** *adj.* überbevölkert; **~popu'lation** *n.* Übervölkerung, *die;* **~'power** *v.t.* Ⓐ (*subdue, overwhelm*) überwältigen; (*wrestling*) bezwingen; Ⓑ (*render imperceptible*) überdecken (*fig.*); **~'powered** *adj.* (*Motor Veh.*) übermotorisiert; **~powering** /əʊvə'paʊərɪŋ/ *adj.* überwältigend; durchdringend ‹Geruch›; **the heat was ~powering** die Hitze war unerträglich; **I find him a bit ~powering** seine Art ist mir manchmal zu viel; **~'praise** *v.t.* zu sehr loben; **~priced** /əʊvə'praɪst/ *adj.* zu teuer; **~print** ❶ *v.t.* Ⓐ /--'-/ (*print too many/extra copies of*) **~print sth. by 100 copies** 100 Exemplare zu viel/mehr von etw. drucken; Ⓑ /'---/ (*print further matter on, print over*) überdrucken (**with** mit); ❷ /'---/ *n.* [zusätzlicher] Aufdruck; (*on stamp also*) Überdruck, *der;* **~-pro'duce** *v.t.* **~-produce milk/steel** *etc.* zu viel Milch/Stahl *usw.* produzieren; **~pro'duction** *n., no pl., no indef. art.* Überproduktion, *die;* **~pro'tective** *adj.* überfürsorglich (**towards** gegenüber); **~'qualified** *adj.* überqualifiziert; **~'rate** *v.t.* überschätzen; **be ~rated** überschätzt werden; ‹Buch, Film:› überbewertet werden; **~'reach** *v. refl.* sich übernehmen; **~re'act** *v.i.* unangemessen heftig reagieren (**to** auf + *Akk.*); **~re'action** *n.* Überreaktion, *die* (**to** auf + *Akk.*); **~ride** ❶ /--'-/ *v.t., forms as* **ride** 3 sich hinwegsetzen über (+ *Akk.*); **be ~ridden** missachtet werden; ❷ /'---/ *n.* (*control*) **[manual] ~ride** Automatikabschaltung, *die;* **~'riding** *adj.* vorrangig; **be of ~riding importance** wichtiger als alles andere sein; **~ripe** *adj.* überreif; **~'rule** *v.t.* Ⓐ (*set aside*) aufheben ‹Entscheidung›; zurückweisen ‹Einwand, Appell, Forderung, Argument›; Ⓑ (*reject proposal of*) **~rule sb.** jmds. Vorschlag ablehnen; **be ~ruled by the majority** von der Mehrheit überstimmt werden; **objection ~ruled!** Einspruch abgelehnt!; **~'run** *v.t., forms as* **run** 3 Ⓐ **be ~run with** überlaufen sein von ‹Touristen›; überwuchert sein von ‹Unkraut›; wimmeln von ‹Mäusen, Schädlingen›; Ⓑ (*Mil.*) einfallen in (+ *Akk.*) ‹Land›; überrennen ‹Stellungen›; Ⓒ (*exceed*) **~run its allotted time** ‹Programm, Treffen, Diskussion:› länger als vorgesehen dauern; **~run [one's time]** ‹Dozent, Redner:› überziehen; *abs.* **the programme ~ran by five minutes** die vorgesehene Sendezeit wurde um fünf Minuten überzogen; **~'scrupulous** *adj.* übertrieben gewissenhaft; **he is not ~-scrupulous about that** damit nimmt er es nicht allzu genau; **~seas** ❶ /--'-/ *adv.* in Übersee ‹leben, sein, sich niederlassen›; nach Übersee ‹gehen›; **colonies ~seas** überseeische Kolonien; Überseekolonien; ❷ /'---/ *adj.* Ⓐ (*across the sea*) Übersee‹postgebühren, -handel, -telefonat›; **~seas broadcasting** Sendungen für Hörer in Übersee; Ⓑ (*foreign*) Auslands‹hilfe, -zulage, -ausgabe, -nachrichten›; ausländisch ‹Student›; **~seas visitors/ambassadors** Besucher/Botschafter aus dem Ausland; **~'see** *v.t., forms as* **see**[1] 1 überwachen; (*manage*) leiten ‹Abteilung›; **~seer** ⇒ **supervisor**; **~'sell** *v.t.* Ⓐ (*overpraise*) zu sehr anpreisen; Ⓑ (*sell too much of*) **~sell one's goods** mehr Waren verkaufen, als man liefern kann; **~'sensitive** *adj.* überempfindlich; übersensibel; **~sew** *v.t., forms as* **sew** 1 überwendlich nähen; **~-sexed** /əʊvə'sekst/ *adj.* sexbesessen; **~'shadow** *v.t.* (*lit. or fig.*) überschatten; (*fig.: make seem minor*) in den Schatten stellen ‹Leistung, Person›; **~shoe** *n.* Überschuh, *der;* **~'shoot** *v.t., forms as* **shoot** 2 hinausschießen über (+ *Akk.*); vorbeifahren an (+ *Akk.*) ‹Abzweigung›; **~shoot the mark** (*fig.*) über das Ziel hinausschießen; **~shoot [the runway]** ‹Pilot, Flugzeug:› zu weit kommen; **~sight** *n.* Ⓐ Versehen, *das;* **by** *or* **through an ~sight** versehentlich; aus Versehen; Ⓑ ⇒ **supervision**; **~simplifi'cation** *n.* zu starke Vereinfachung; **~'simplify** *v.t.* zu stark vereinfachen; **~size, ~sized** ⇒ **outsize**; **~'sleep** *v.i., forms as* **sleep** 2 verschlafen; **~sleep by half an hour** eine halbe Stunde zu lange schlafen; **~-so'licitous** *adj.* übermäßig *od.* allzu besorgt; **~'spend** ❶ *v.i., forms as* **spend** zu viel [Geld] ausgeben; **~spending** zu hohe Ausgaben; **~spend by £100** 100 Pfund zu viel ausgeben; ❷ *v.t.* überschreiten, überziehen ‹Etat, Budget, Einkommen›; **~spill** *n.* Ⓐ (*surplus population*) Bevölkerungsüberschuss, *der; attrib.* Satelliten‹stadt, -siedlung›; Ⓑ (*overflow*) **the ~spill** [das,] was übergelaufen ist/überläuft; **~'staff** *v.t.* überbesetzen; **~'staffing** *n.* Überbesetzung, *die;* **~'state** *v.t.* übertrieben darstellen; überbetonen ‹Argument›; **~'statement** *n.* Übertreibung, *die;* (*of case, problem*) übertriebene Darstellung; **~'stay** *v.t.* überziehen ‹Urlaub›; **~stay one's time [by three days]** [drei Tage] länger als vorgesehen bleiben; ⇒ *also* **welcome** 2 A; **~steer** (*Motor Veh.*) ❶ /--'-/ *v.i.* übersteuern; ❷ /'---/ *n.* Übersteuern, *das;* **~'step** *v.t.* überschreiten; **~step the mark** (*fig.*) zu weit gehen; **~'stock** *v.t.* überbestücken ‹Lager›; zu stark besetzen (*Fischereiw.*) ‹Teich›; **~'strain** ❶ *n.* Überforderung, die; ❷ *v.t.* überfordern; **~'stretch** *v.t.* überdehnen; (*fig.*) überfordern; **~strung** *adj.* kreuzsaitig ‹Klavier›; (*fig.*) überreizt; **~sub'scribed** *adj.* (*Finance*) überzeichnet

**overt** /'əʊvət, əʊ'vɜ:t/ *adj.* unverhohlen; **their actions were ~:** sie haben mit offenen Karten gespielt *od.* nichts verborgen

**over: ~'take** *v.t.* Ⓐ *also abs.* (*esp. Brit.: pass*) überholen; **'no ~taking'** (*Brit.*) „Überholen verboten"; Ⓑ (*catch up*) einholen; Ⓒ (*fig.*) **be ~taken by events** ‹Plan:› von den Ereignissen überholt werden; Ⓓ (*exceed*) **supply will ~take demand** das Angebot wird die Nachfrage übersteigen; Ⓔ (*befall*) hereinbrechen über (+ *Akk.*); ‹Schicksal:› ereilen (*geh.*); **~'tax** *v.t.* Ⓐ (*demand too much tax from*) überbesteuern; Ⓑ (*~strain*) überstrapazieren, überfordern ‹Verstand, Geduld›; überanstrengen ‹Verstand›; **~tax one's strength** sich übernehmen; **don't ~tax my patience!** stell meine Geduld nicht auf die Probe!; **~-the-top** *adj.* überzogen; **~throw** ❶ /--'-/ *v.t., forms as* **throw** 1 Ⓐ stürzen ‹Regierung, Regime usw.›; aus dem Weg räumen ‹Gegner›; (*defeat*) schlagen, besiegen ‹Feind›; Ⓑ (*subvert*) umstoßen, (*ugs.*) über den Haufen werfen ‹Verfassung, Theorie, Überzeugung›; ❷ /'---/ *n.* Ⓐ (*removal from power*) Sturz, *der;* Ⓑ (*subversion*) Umsturz, *der;* (*of ideas*) Umwälzung, *die;* **~time** ❶ *n.* Überstunden *Pl.;* **work ten hours'/put in a lot of ~time** zehn/eine Menge Überstunden machen; **be on ~time** Überstunden machen; **~time ban/payment** Überstundenstopp, *der*/-zuschlag, *der;* ❷ *adv.* **work ~time** Überstunden machen; (*fig. coll.*) ‹Apparat:› auf Hochtouren laufen; **his brain/imagination was working ~time** er dachte fieberhaft nach/er hatte eine überspannte Fantasie; **~'tire** *v.t.* übermüden; **~tire oneself** sich übernehmen *od.* überanstrengen

**overtly** /'əʊvətlɪ, əʊ'vɜ:tlɪ/ *adv.* unverhohlen

**over: ~tone** *n.* Ⓐ (*fig.: implication*) Unterton, *der;* **the crime had political ~tones** das Verbrechen hatte auch politische Implikationen; Ⓑ (*Mus.*) Oberton, *der;* **~'train** (*Sport*) ❶ *v.t.* übertrainieren; ❷ *v.i.* zu viel trainieren; **~trick** *n.* (*Bridge*) Überstich, *der;* **~'trump** *v.t.* (*Cards*) übertrumpfen

**overture** /'əʊvətjʊə(r)/ *n.* Ⓐ (*Mus.*) Ouvertüre, *die;* Ⓑ (*formal proposal or offer*) Angebot, *das;* **~s of peace** Friedensangebot, *das;* **make ~s [to sb.]** [jmdm.] ein Angebot machen; (*to woman*) [bei jmdm.] Annäherungsversuche machen

**over: ~'turn** ❶ *v.t.* Ⓐ (*upset*) umstoßen; Ⓑ (*overthrow*) umstürzen ‹bestehende Ordnung, Vorstellung, Prinzip›; stürzen ‹Regierung›; beseitigen ‹Institution›; (*reverse*) aufheben ‹Urteil, Entscheid[ung]›; ❷ *v.i.* ‹Auto, Boot, Kutsche:› umkippen; ‹Boot:› kentern; ‹Auto:› sich überschlagen; **~use** ❶ /əʊvə'ju:z/ *v.t.* zu oft verwenden; ❷ /əʊvə'ju:s/ *n.* zu häufiger Gebrauch; **~'value** *v.t.* überbewerten ‹Währung›; **his contribution cannot be ~valued** sein Beitrag kann gar nicht hoch genug bewertet werden; **~view** *n.* Überblick, *der* (**of** über + *Akk.*)

**overweening** /əʊvə'wi:nɪŋ/ *adj.* maßlos ‹Ehrgeiz, Gier, Stolz›

**'overweight** ❶ *adj.* Ⓐ (*obese*) übergewichtig ‹Person›; **be [12 pounds] ~:** [12 Pfund] Übergewicht haben; Ⓑ (*weighing in excess*) zu schwer; (*very heavy*) bleischwer. ❷ *n.* Übergewicht, *das*

**overwhelm** /əʊvə'welm/ *v.t.* Ⓐ (*overpower, lit. or fig.*) überwältigen; **be ~ed with work** die Arbeit kaum bewältigen können; Ⓑ (*crush, destroy*) **be ~ed by the enemy** vom übermächtigen Feind völlig aufgerieben werden; Ⓒ (*bury*) verschütten; ‹Wasser:› überschwemmen, überfluten

**overwhelming** /əʊvə'welmɪŋ/ *adj.* überwältigend; unbändig ‹Wut, Kraft, Verlangen, Zorn›; unermesslich ‹Leid, Kummer›; **against ~ odds** entgegen aller Wahrscheinlichkeit

**over: ~wind** /əʊvə'waɪnd/ *v.t., forms as* **wind**[2] 1, 2 überdrehen; **~'work** ❶ *v.t.* Ⓐ (*make work too hard*) mit Arbeit überlasten; **~work oneself** sich überarbeiten; Ⓑ (*fig.*) überstrapazieren ‹Metapher, Wort usw.›; ❷ *v.i.* sich überarbeiten; ❸ *n.* [Arbeits]überlastung, *die;* **become ill from ~work** sich krank arbeiten; **~'wrought** *adj.* überreizt; **~'zealous** *adj.* übereifrig

**oviduct** /'əʊvɪdʌkt/ *n.* (*Anat., Zool.*) Ovidukt, *der* (*fachspr.*); Eileiter, *der*

**oviparous** /əʊ'vɪpərəs/ *adj.* (*Zool.*) ovipar

**ovulate** /'ɒvjʊleɪt, 'əʊvjʊleɪt/ *v.i.* (*Physiol.*) ovulieren (*fachspr.*); reife *od.* befruchtungsfähige Eizellen abstoßen

**ovulation** /ɒvjʊ'leɪʃn, əʊvjʊ'leɪʃn/ *n.* Ovulation, *die* (*fachspr.*); Eisprung, *der*

**ovum** /'əʊvəm/ *n., pl.* **ova** /'əʊvə/ Ovum, *das* (*fachspr.*); (*Biol.*) Ei, *das*

**ow** /aʊ/ *int.* au

**owe** /əʊ/ *v.t.,* **owing** /'əʊɪŋ/ Ⓐ schulden; **~ sb. sth., ~ sth. to sb.** jmdm. etw. schulden; **~ it to sb. to do sth.** es jmdm. schuldig sein, etw. zu tun; **I ~ you an explanation** ich bin dir eine Erklärung schuldig; **you ~ it to yourself to take a break** du musst dir einfach eine Pause gönnen; **can I ~ you the rest?** kann ich dir den Rest schuldig bleiben?; **money was ~d to them** sie hatten Außenstände; **I hate owing money** ich hasse es, Schulden zu haben; **~ [sb.] for sth.** [jmdm.] etw. bezahlen müssen; **I [still] ~ you for the ticket** du kriegst von mir noch das Geld für die Karte (*ugs.*); Ⓑ (*feel gratitude for, be indebted for*) verdanken; **~ sth. to sb.** jmdm. etw. verdanken *od.* zu verdanken haben

**owing** /'əʊɪŋ/ *pred. adj.* ausstehend; **be ~:** ausstehen; **money is ~ to them** sie haben noch Außenstände; **£10 is ~ on the furniture** für die Möbel müssen noch 10 Pfund bezahlt werden

**'owing to** *prep.* wegen; **~ his foresight** dank seinem Weitblick; **~ unfortunate circumstances** auf Grund unglücklicher Umstände

**owl** /aʊl/ *n.* Ⓐ Eule, *die;* Ⓑ (*fig. person*) **he's a wise ~:** er ist weise wie eine Eule

**owlet** /'aʊlɪt/ *n.* Eulenjunge, *das*

**owlish** /'aʊlɪʃ/ *adj.* eulenhaft

**own** /əʊn/ ❶ *adj.* eigen; **with one's ~ eyes** mit eigenen Augen; **be sb.'s ~ [property]** jmds. Eigentum sein; jmdm. selbst gehören; **look after one's ~ affairs** sich selbst um seine Angelegenheiten kümmern; **this is your ~ responsibility** dafür bist du selbst verantwortlich; **speak from one's ~ experience** aus eigener Erfahrung sprechen; **this is all my ~ work** das habe ich alles selbst *od.* ganz allein gemacht; **reserve sth.**

O

**for one's ~ use** etw. für sich selbst reservieren; **have one's ~ room** [s]ein eigenes Zimmer haben; **one's ~ brother** der eigene Bruder; **sb.'s ~ country** jmds. Heimatland; **do one's ~ cooking/housework** selbst kochen/die Hausarbeit selbst machen; **make one's ~ clothes** seine Kleidung selbst schneidern; **virtue is its ~ reward** die Tugend trägt ihren Lohn in sich selbst; **have a charm all [of] its ~:** einen ganz eigenen Reiz haben; **a house/ideas** *etc.* **of one's ~:** ein eigenes Haus/eigene Ideen *usw.*; **have nothing of one's ~:** kein persönliches Eigentum haben; **have enough problems of one's ~:** selbst genug Probleme haben; **have [got] one of one's ~:** selbst einen/eine/eins haben; **for reasons of his ~ ...:** aus nur ihm selbst bekannten Gründen ...; **come into one's ~** (*Law.: inherit property*) sein Erbe antreten; **that's where he/it comes into his/its ~** (*fig.*) da kommt er/es voll zur Geltung; **on one's/its ~** (*alone*) allein; **drink whisky on its ~:** Whisky pur trinken; **get better on its ~:** von selbst besser werden; **start up on one's ~:** sich selbstständig machen; **he's on his ~** *or* **in a class of his ~** (*fig.*) er ist eine Klasse für sich; **be on one's ~** (*without outside help*) auf sich (*Akk.*) selbst gestellt sein; ⇒ *also* **business** C; **call** 2 J; **flesh** 1 A; **get back** 2 B; **hold²** 1 K; **man** 1 B; **master** 1 A; **right** 3 A.
❷ *v.t.* Ⓐ (*possess*) besitzen; **be ~ed by sb.** jmdm. gehören; **who ~s that house?** wem gehört das Haus?; **be privately ~ed** sich in Privatbesitz befinden; **they behaved as if they ~ed the place** sie benahmen sich, als ob der Laden ihnen gehörte (*ugs.*); Ⓑ (*acknowledge*) anerkennen; Ⓒ ⇒ **admit** 1 C.
❸ *v.i.* **~ to** eingestehen; **~ to doing sth./to being ashamed** [ein]gestehen *od.* zugeben, dass man etw. tut/dass man sich schämt
**~ 'up** *v.i.* ‹Schuldiger, Täter:› gestehen; **~ up to sth.** etw. [ein]gestehen *od.* zugeben; **~ up to having done sth.** [ein]gestehen *od.* zugeben, dass man etw. getan hat; **Come on, ~ up! Who did it?** Na los, raus mit der Sprache! Wer ist es gewesen?

**'own-brand, 'own-label** ❶ *attrib. adjs.* Eigenmarken-. ❷ *n.* Hausmarke, *die*

O

**owned** /əʊnd/ *adj.* **publicly ~:** gemeinde-/staatseigen; **company-~:** firmeneigen; **privately ~:** in Privatbesitz *nachgestellt;* **English/American-~:** in englischem/amerikanischem Besitz befindlich ‹Firma, Bank›

**owner** /ˈəʊnə(r)/ *n.* Besitzer, *der*/Besitzerin, *die;* Eigentümer, *der*/Eigentümerin, *die;* (*of car also*) Halter, *der*/Halterin, *die;* (*of shop, hotel, firm, etc.*) Inhaber, *der*/Inhaberin, *die;* **at ~'s risk** auf eigene Gefahr; **dog/property-~s** Hunde-/Grundbesitzer

**owner-'driver** *n.* (*Brit.*) *Halter/Halterin eines Autos, der/die das Auto selbst fährt*

**ownerless** /ˈəʊnəlɪs/ *adj.* herrenlos

**owner-'occupier** *n.* (*Brit.*) Eigenheimbesitzer, *der*/-besitzerin, *die*

**ownership** /ˈəʊnəʃɪp/ *n., no pl.* Besitz, *der;* **~ is disputed** die Besitzverhältnisse sind umstritten; **the ~ of the land was disputed** es war umstritten, wem das Land gehörte; **be under new ~** ‹Firma, Laden, Restaurant:› einen neuen Inhaber/eine neue Inhaberin haben

**own 'goal** *n.* (*lit. or fig.*) Eigentor, *das*

**ox** /ɒks/ *n., pl.* **oxen** /ˈɒksn/ Ochse, *der;* ⇒ *also* **strong** 1 B

**oxalic acid** /ɒksælɪk ˈæsɪd/ *n.* (*Chem.*) Oxalsäure, *die* (*fachspr.*); Kleesäure, *die*

**'oxbow** *n.* Ⓐ (*of yoke*) Brustholz, *das;* Ⓑ (*Geog.: river bend*) Flussschleife, *die;* (*one of several*) Mäander, *der*

**ox-bow 'lake** *n.* (*Geog.*) Altwasser, *das*

**Oxbridge** /ˈɒksbrɪdʒ/ *n.* (*Brit.*) die Universitäten Oxford und Cambridge; *attrib.* **~ graduate/education** Absolvent[in] der/Ausbildung an der Universität Oxford oder Cambridge

**Oxfam** /ˈɒksfæm/ *pr. n.* Oxforder Hungerhilfekomitee

**Oxford** /ˈɒksfəd/ ⇒ **Oxford shoe**

**Oxford: ~ 'accent** *n.* Oxford-Akzent, *der;* **~ 'blue** *n.* Dunkelblau, *das;* **~ shoe** *n.* Schnürhalbschuh, *der*

**'oxhide** *n.* (*skin*) Rindshaut, *die;* (*leather*) Rindsleder, *das*

**oxidant** /ˈɒksɪdənt/ *n.* (*Chem.*) Oxidationsmittel, *das*

**oxidation** /ɒksɪˈdeɪʃn/ *n.* (*Chem.*) Oxidation, *die*

**oxide** /ˈɒksaɪd/ *n.* (*Chem.*) Oxid, *das*

**oxidize (oxidise)** /ˈɒksɪdaɪz/ *v.t. & i.* (*Chem.*) oxidieren

**oxlip** *n.* Primel, *die;* Schlüsselblume, *die*

**Oxon.** /ˈɒksn/ *abbr.* Ⓐ **Oxfordshire;** Ⓑ **of Oxford University**

**Oxonian** /ɒkˈsəʊnɪən/ ❶ *adj.* der Universität Oxford *nachgestellt.* ❷ *n.* Mitglied der Universität Oxford

**'oxtail** *n.* Ochsenschwanz, *der*

**oxtail 'soup** *n.* (*Gastr.*) Ochsenschwanzsuppe, *die*

**'ox-tongue** *n.* (*Gastr.*) Ochsenzunge, *die*

**oxyacetylene** /ɒksɪəˈsetɪliːn/ *adj.* **~ welding** Autogenschweißen, *das;* **~ torch** *or* **blowpipe** *or* **burner** Schweißbrenner, *der*

**oxygen** /ˈɒksɪdʒən/ *n.* (*Chem.*) Sauerstoff, *der*

**oxygenate** /ˈɒksɪdʒəneɪt/ *v.t.* (*Chem., Physiol.*) oxygenieren (*fachspr.*)

**oxygenation** /ɒksɪdʒəˈneɪʃn/ *n.* (*Chem., Physiol.*) Oxygenation, *die* (*fachspr.*)

**oxygen: ~ bottle, ~ cylinder** *ns.* Sauerstoffflasche, *die;* **~ mask** *n.* Sauerstoffmaske, *die;* **~ tent** *n.* (*Med.*) Sauerstoffzelt, *das*

**oxymoron** /ɒksɪˈmɔːrɒn/ *n.* (*Rhet.*) Oxymoron, *das*

**oyez (oyes)** /əʊˈjez, əʊˈjes/ *int.* Achtung (*Ruf eines Ausrufers*)

**oyster** /ˈɔɪstə(r)/ *n.* Auster, *die;* **the world's his ~** (*fig.*) ihm liegt die Welt zu Füßen

**oyster: ~ bed** *n.* Austernbank, *die;* **~catcher** *n.* (*Ornith.*) Austernfischer, *der;* **~ farm** *n.* Austernpark, *der;* **~ knife** *n.* Austernmesser, *das*

**Oz** /ɒz/ *n.* (*coll.*) Australien (*das*)

**oz.** *abbr.* ▶ 1683 **ounce[s]**

**ozone** /ˈəʊzəʊn, əʊˈzəʊn/ *n.* Ozon, *das*

**ozone: ~ depletion** *n.* Ozonabbau, *der;* **~-friendly** *adj.* ozonsicher; (*not using CFCs*) FCKW-frei; **~ hole** *n.* Ozonloch, *das* (*ugs.*); **~ layer** *n.* Ozonschicht, *die;* **the hole in the ~ layer** das Ozonloch (*ugs.*); **~ value** *n.* Ozonwert, *der*

# Pp

**P¹, p** /piː/ *n., pl.* **Ps** *or* **P's** P, p, *das;* ⇒ *also* **mind** 2 B

**P²** *abbr.* (*Chess*) **pawn** B

**p.** *abbr.* **A** **page** S.; **B** /piː/ ▶1328 (*Brit.*) **penny/pence** p; **C** (*Mus.*) **piano** p; **D** (*Phys.*) **pico-** p

**PA** *abbr.* **A** ▶1261 **personal assistant** pers. Ass.; **B** **public address: PA [system]** LS-Anlage, *die*

**Pa** *abbr.* (*Phys.*) **Pascal** Pa

**pa** /pɑː/ *n.* (*coll.*) Papa, *der* (*fam.*)

**p.a.** *abbr.* **per annum** p.a.

**pabulum** /ˈpæbjʊləm/ *n.* (*lit. or fig.*) Nahrung, *die*

**pace¹** /peɪs/ ❶ *n.* **A** (*step, distance*) Schritt, *der;* **B** (*speed*) Tempo, *das;* **slacken/quicken one's ~** (*walking*) seinen Schritt verlangsamen/beschleunigen; **at a steady/good ~:** in gleichmäßigem/zügigem Tempo; **at a snail's ~:** im Schneckentempo (*ugs.*); **set the ~:** das Tempo angeben *od.* bestimmen; (*act as pacemaker*) Schrittmacher sein; **keep ~ [with sb./sth.]** [mit jmdm./etw.] Schritt halten; **stay** *or* **stand the ~, stay** *or* **keep with the ~** (*Sport*) das Tempo durchhalten; **be off the ~** (*Sport*) zurückliegen; **he couldn't stand the ~ of life** (*fig.*) ihm war das Leben zu hektisch; **C** (*of horse*) Passgang, *der;* **put sb./a horse through his/its ~s** (*fig.*) jmdn./ein Pferd zeigen lassen, was er/es kann; **show one's ~s** zeigen, was man kann.
❷ *v.i.* **A** schreiten (*geh.*); [gemessenen Schrittes] gehen; **~ up and down [the platform/room]** [auf dem Bahnsteig/im Zimmer] auf und ab gehen *od.* marschieren; **B** (*amble*) ‹Pferd:› im Pass[gang] gehen.
❸ *v.t.* **A** auf und ab gehen in (+ *Dat.*); **B** (*set the ~ for*) Schrittmacher sein für

**~ 'out** *v.t.* abschreiten ‹Entfernung, Weg›

**pace²** /ˈpeɪsɪ, ˈpɑːtʃeɪ/ *prep.* (*formal*) **~ Mr Smith ...:** ohne Mr. Smith (*Dat.*) zu nahe treten zu wollen ...

**pace 'bowler** ⇒ **fast bowler**

**-paced** /peɪst/ *adj. in comb.* **a well-~ performance** eine [rhythmisch] ausgewogene Aufführung; **be even-~:** ein gleichförmiges Tempo haben

**'pacemaker** *n.* **A** (*Sport*) Schrittmacher, *der*/-macherin, *die;* **B** (*Med.*) [Herz]schrittmacher, *der*

**'pacesetter** *n.* Schrittmacher, *der*/-macherin, *die*

**pachyderm** /ˈpækɪdɜːm/ *n.* (*Zool.*) Dickhäuter, *der*

**pacific** /pəˈsɪfɪk/ ❶ *adj.* **A** (*conciliatory, peaceable*) versöhnlich; **B** (*tranquil*) friedlich; **C** (*Geog.*) Pazifik‹küste, -insel›; **P~ Ocean** Pazifischer *od.* Stiller Ozean. ❷ *n.* **the P~:** der Pazifik

**pacification** /pæsɪfɪˈkeɪʃn/ *n.* Befriedung, *die*

**pacifier** /ˈpæsɪfaɪə(r)/ *n.* **A** (*person*) Friedensstifter, *der*/-stifterin, *die;* **B** (*Amer.: baby's dummy*) Schnuller, *der*

**pacifism** /ˈpæsɪfɪzm/ *n., no pl., no art.* Pazifismus, *der*

**pacifist** /ˈpæsɪfɪst/ ❶ *n.* Pazifist, *der*/Pazifistin, *die.* ❷ *adj.* pazifistisch

**pacify** /ˈpæsɪfaɪ/ *v.t.* **A** besänftigen; beruhigen ‹weinendes Kind›; **B** (*bring peace to*) befrieden ‹Land, Provinz›

**pack** /pæk/ ❶ *n.* **A** (*bundle*) Bündel, *das;* (*Mil.*) Tornister, *der;* (*rucksack*) Rucksack, *der;* **B** (*derog.: lot*) (*people*) Bande, *die;* **a ~ of lies/nonsense** ein Sack voll Lügen/eine Menge Unsinn; **what a ~ of lies!** alles erlogen!; **C** (*Brit.*) **~ [of cards]** [Karten]spiel, *das;* **D** (*wolves, wild dogs*) Rudel, *das;* (*grouse*) Schwarm, *der;* (*hounds, beagles*) Meute, *die;* **E** (*Cub Scouts, Brownies*) Gruppe, *die;* **F** (*packet, set*) Schachtel, *die;* Packung, *die;* **~ of ten** Zehnerpackung, *die;* Zehnerpack, *der;* **disc ~** (*Computing*) [Magnet]plattenstapel, *der;* **G** ⇒ **ice pack** C; **H** (*Med.*) Packung, *die;* Kompresse, *die;* (*compress*) Tampon, *der;* Kompresse, *die;* ⇒ *also* **ice pack** A; **I** (*cosmetic*) Packung, *die;* (*for face*) [Gesichts]maske, *die;* **J** (*Rugby*) *die Stürmer einer Mannschaft, die die eine Hälfte des Gedränges bilden;* (*scrum*) Gedränge, *das;* **K** (*Sport: runners*) Feld, *das.*
❷ *v.t.* **A** (*put into container*) einpacken; **~ sth. into sth.** etw. in etw. (*Akk.*) packen; **B** (*fill*) packen; **~ one's bags** seine Koffer packen; **C** (*cram*) voll stopfen (*ugs.*); (*fill with a crowd*) füllen ‹Raum, Stadion usw.›; **he ~ed the jury** er sorgte dafür, dass als Geschworene nur ihm genehme Leute berufen wurden; **D** (*wrap*) verpacken (**in** in + *Dat. od. Akk.*); **~ed in** verpackt in (+ *Dat.*); **E** (*Med.*) tamponieren; **F** (*coll.: carry*) tragen, dabeihaben ‹Waffe›; **G** **~ [quite] a punch** (*coll.*) ganz schön zuschlagen können (*ugs.*); ‹Getränk:› ganz schön reinhauen (*salopp*).
❸ *v.i.* packen; **send sb. ~ing** (*fig.*) jmdn. rausschmeißen (*ugs.*)

**~ a'way** *v.t.* wegpacken

**~ 'in** *v.t.* **A** (*coll.: give up*) aufstecken (*ugs.*); aufhören mit ‹Arbeit, Spiel›; **~ it in!** hör [doch] auf damit!; **B** (*Theatre. coll.*) in Scharen anziehen ‹Publikum›; **the new play is ~ing them in** das neue Stück ist ein Zuschauer- *od.* Publikumsmagnet; **C** (*find time for*) hineinpacken

**~ into** *v.t.* sich drängen in (+ *Akk.*); **we all ~ed into the car** wir quetschten uns alle in das Auto (*ugs.*)

**~ 'off** *v.t.* (*send away*) fortschicken

**~ 'up** ❶ *v.t.* **A** (*package*) zusammenpacken ‹Sachen, Werkzeug›; packen ‹Paket›; **~ up one's luggage** packen; **B** (*coll.: stop*) aufhören *od.* (*ugs.*) Schluss machen mit; **~ up work** Feierabend machen; (*permanently*) aufhören zu arbeiten; **~ it up!** (*coll.*) hör [doch] auf damit! ❷ *v.i.* (*coll.*) **A** (*give up*) aufhören; Schluss machen (*ugs.*); **B** (*break down*) den Geist aufgeben (*ugs.*); **the car ~ed up on me** das Auto ist mir verreckt (*ugs.*)

**package** /ˈpækɪdʒ/ ❶ *n.* **A** (*bundle; fig. coll.: transaction*) Paket, *das;* **B** (*container*) Verpackung, *die.* ❷ *v.t.* (*lit. or fig.*) verpacken; **~d into 1 lb. bags** in 1-Pfund-Tüten abgepackt

**package: ~ deal** *n.* Paket, *das;* **~ holiday, ~ tour** *ns.* Pauschalreise, *die*

**packaging** /ˈpækɪdʒɪŋ/ *n.* **A** (*material*) Verpackung, *die;* **B** (*action*) Verpacken, *das*

**'pack drill** *n.* (*Mil.*) Strafexerzieren in voller Marschausrüstung

**packed** /pækt/ *adj.* **A** gepackt ‹Kiste, Koffer›; **~ meal/lunch** Esspaket, *das*/Lunchpaket, *das;* **B** (*crowded*) [über]voll ‹Theater, Kino, Halle›; **~ to overflowing** völlig überfüllt (**with** von); **~ out** (*coll.*) gerammelt voll (*ugs.*)

**packer** /ˈpækə(r)/ *n.* Packer, *der*/Packerin, *die;* (*in factory*) Abpacker, *der*/Abpackerin, *die*

**packet** /ˈpækɪt/ *n.* **A** (*package*) Päckchen, *das;* (*box*) Schachtel, *die;* **a ~ of cigarettes** eine Schachtel/ein Päckchen Zigaretten; ⇒ *also* **pay packet**; **B** (*coll.: large sum of money*) Haufen Geld (*ugs.*); **cost/earn a ~:** ein Heidengeld kosten (*ugs.*)/Schweinegeld verdienen (*ugs.*) **C** (*Naut.*) **[steam] ~** ⇒ **packet steamer**

**packet: ~ 'soup** *n.* Instantsuppe, *die;* Tütensuppe, *die* (*ugs.*); **~ steamer** *n.* Postschiff, *das*

**pack: ~horse** *n.* Packpferd, *das;* **~ ice** *n.* Packeis, *das*

**packing** /ˈpækɪŋ/ *n.* **A** (*packaging*) (*material*) Verpackungsmaterial, *das;* (*action*) Verpacken, *das;* **including postage and ~:** einschließlich Porto und Verpackung; **B** (*to seal joint*) Dichtungsmaterial, *das;* **C** **do one's ~:** packen

**'packing case** *n.* [Pack]kiste, *die*

**pact** /pækt/ *n.* Pakt, *der;* **make a ~ with sb.** einen Pakt mit jmdm. schließen

**pad¹** /pæd/ ❶ *n.* **A** (*cushioning material*) Polster, *das;* (*to protect wound*) Kompresse, *die;* (*Sport*) (*on leg*) Beinschützer, *der;* (*on shoulder*) Schulterschützer, *der;* (*on knee*) Knieschützer, *der;* **B** (*block of paper*) Block, *der;* **a ~ of notepaper, a [writing] ~:** ein Schreibblock; **C** (*launching surface*) Abschussrampe, *die;* **[helicopter] ~:** [Hubschrauber-]Start-und-Lande-Platz, *der;* **D** (*coll.: house, flat*) Bude, *die* (*ugs.*); **E** (*Zool.*) (*sole*) Ballen, *der;* (*paw*) Pfote, *die;* **F** (*of brake*) Belag, *der.*
❷ *v.t.,* **-dd-** **A** polstern ‹Jacke, Schulter, Stuhl›; **B** (*fig.: lengthen unnecessarily*) auswalzen (*ugs.*) ‹Brief, Aufsatz usw.› (**with** durch)

**~ 'out** ⇒ **pad¹** 2

**pad²** *v.t. & i.,* **-dd-** (*walk softly*) (*in socks, slippers, etc.*) tappen; (*along path etc.*) trotten

**padded** /ˈpædɪd/ *adj.* gepolstert

**padded: ~ 'cell** *n.* Gummizelle, *die;* **~ 'envelope** *n.* wattierter Umschlag

**padding** /ˈpædɪŋ/ *n.* **A** Polsterung, *die;* **be filled/covered with ~:** gepolstert sein; **B** (*fig. superfluous matter*) Füllsel, *das*

**paddle¹** /ˈpædl/ ❶ *n.* **A** (*oar*) [Stech]paddel, *das;* **B** (*paddling*) (*in canoe*) Fahrt im Paddelboot; (*in rowing boat*) Ruderpartie, *die;* **go for a ~:** paddeln/rudern gehen; **C** (*stirring implement*) Paddel, *das;* **D** (*wheel*) Schaufelrad, *das;* (*blade*) Schaufel, *die;* **E** (*on lock gate*) Schütz, *das;* **F** (*Zool.: fin*) Flosse, *die.*
❷ *v.t. & i.* (*in canoe*) paddeln; (*in rowing boat*) gemächlich rudern; **~ one's own canoe** (*fig. coll.*) auf eigenen Beinen stehen

**paddle²** ❶ *v.i.* (*with feet*) planschen. ❷ *n.* **have a/go for a ~:** ein bisschen planschen/planschen gehen

**paddle: ~ boat, ~ steamer** *ns.* [Schaufel]raddampfer, *der;* **~ wheel** *n.* Schaufelrad, *das*

**paddling pool** /ˈpædlɪŋpuːl/ *n.* Planschbecken, *das*

**paddock** /ˈpædək/ *n.* **A** Koppel, *die;* **B** (*Horseracing*) Sattelplatz, *der;* (*Motor racing*) Fahrerlager, *das*

**paddy¹** *n.* (*Brit. coll.: bad temper*) Koller, *der* (*ugs.*); **be in a ~:** einen Koller haben

**paddy², 'paddy field** *ns.* Reisfeld, *das*

**Paddy** /ˈpædɪ/ *n.* (*coll.*) Ire, *der;* Paddy, *der*

**'padlock** ❶ *n.* Vorhängeschloss, *das.* ❷ *v.t.* [mit einem Vorhängeschloss] verschließen

**paean** /ˈpiːən/ *n.* **~ [of praise]** Preislied, *das;* (*fig.*) Lobeshymne, *die*

**paediatric** /piːdɪˈætrɪk/ *adj.* (*Med.*) pädiatrisch; Kinder‹schwester, -station›

**paediatrician** /piːdɪəˈtrɪʃn/ *n.* ▶1261 (*Med.*) Kinderarzt, *der*/-ärztin, *die*

**paediatrics** /piːdɪˈætrɪks/ *n., no pl.* (*Med.*) Pädiatrie, *die* (*fachspr.*); Kinderheilkunde, *die*

**paedophile** /ˈpiːdəfaɪl/ ❶ *n.* Pädophile, *der.* ❷ *adj.* pädophil

**paella** /pɑːˈelə/ *n.* (*Gastr.*) Paella, *die*

**pagan** /ˈpeɪgən/ ❶ *n.* A (*heathen*) Heide, *der*/Heidin, *die;* B (*fig.: irreligious person*) Ungläubige, *der*/*die;* gottloser Mensch. ❷ *adj.* A (*heathen*) heidnisch; ungläubig ‹Person›; B (*fig.: irreligious*) gottlos

**paganism** /ˈpeɪgənɪzm/ *n.* Heidentum, *das;* Paganismus, *der*

**page[1]** /peɪdʒ/ ❶ *n.* Page, *der.* ❷ *v.t. & i.* **~ [for] sb.** (*over loudspeaker*) jmdn. ausrufen; (*by paging-device*) jmdn. anpiepen (*ugs.*); **paging Mr Miller** Herr Miller, bitte!

**page[2]** ❶ *n.* A Seite, *die;* (*leaf, sheet of paper*) Blatt, *das;* **front/sports/fashion ~:** erste Seite/Sport-/Modeseite, *die;* **~ three girl** Pin-up-Girl, *das;* **write on one side of the ~ only** beschreiben Sie das Blatt nur auf einer Seite; **turn to the next ~:** umblättern; *attrib.* **three-/double-~:** drei-/doppelseitig ‹Artikel, Brief›; B (*fig.: episode*) Kapitel, *das;* **go down in the ~s of history** in die Annalen der Geschichte eingehen. ❷ *v.t.* ⇒ **paginate**

**pageant** /ˈpædʒənt/ *n.* A (*spectacle*) Schauspiel, *das;* B (*procession*) [Fest]umzug, *der;* (*play*) **historical ~:** Historienspiel, *das*

**pageantry** /ˈpædʒəntrɪ/ *n.* Prachtentfaltung, *die;* Prunk, *der;* **empty ~:** eitler Pomp

ˈ**pageboy** *n.* A ⇒ **page[1]** 1; B (*hairstyle*) Pagenkopf, der

**page: ~ break** *n.* (*Computing*) Seitenbruch, *der;* **~ number** *n.* Seitenzahl, *die*

ˈ**page proof** *n.* (*Printing*) Umbruch, *der*

**pager** /ˈpeɪdʒə(r)/ *n.* Piepser, *der* (*ugs.*)

**paginate** /ˈpædʒɪneɪt/ *v.t.* paginieren

**pagination** /pædʒɪˈneɪʃn/ *n.* Paginierung, *die*

ˈ**paging device** ⇒ **pager**

**pagoda** /pəˈgəʊdə/ *n.* Pagode, *die*

**pah** /pɑː/ *int. expr. disgust* bah; *expr. contempt* pa

**paid** /peɪd/ ❶ ⇒ **pay** 2, 3. ❷ *adj.* bezahlt ‹Urlaub, Arbeit›; **put ~ to** (*Brit. fig. coll.*) (*terminate*) zunichte machen ‹Hoffnung, Plan, Aussichten›; (*deal with*) kurzen Prozess machen mit (*ugs.*) ‹Person›

ˈ**paid-up** *adj.* bezahlt; **[fully] ~ member** Mitglied, das alle Beträge bezahlt hat; (*fig.*) überzeugtes Mitglied

**pail** /peɪl/ *n.* Eimer, *der*

**pailful** /ˈpeɪlfʊl/ *n.* Eimer, *der;* **a ~ of water** ein Eimer [voll] Wasser

**pain** /peɪn/ ❶ *n.* A *no indef. art.* Schmerzen *Pl.;* (*mental ~*) Qualen *Pl.;* **feel [some] ~, be in ~:** Schmerzen haben; **cause sb. ~** (*lit. or fig.*) jmdm. wehtun; B ▸ 1232 (*instance*) Schmerz, *der;* **I have a ~ in my shoulder/knee/stomach** meine Schulter/mein Knie/Magen tut weh; ich habe Schmerzen in der Schulter/im Knie/habe Magenschmerzen; (*fig.*) **be a ~ in the arse** (*coarse*) einem auf die Eier gehen (*derb*); **be a ~ in the neck** ⇒ **neck** 1 A; C (*coll.: nuisance*) Plage, *die;* (*sb./sth. getting on one's nerves*) Nervensäge, *die* (*ugs.*); **this job/he is a real ~:** diese Arbeit/er kann einem wirklich auf die Nerven *od.* (*ugs.*) den Wecker gehen; D *in pl.* (*trouble taken*) Mühe, *die;* Anstrengung, *die;* **spare no ~s** keine Mühe *od.* Anstrengung scheuen; **take ~s** sich (*Dat.*) Mühe geben (**over** mit, bei); **be at ~s to do sth.** sich sehr bemühen *od.* sich (*Dat.*) große Mühe geben, etw. zu tun; **he got nothing for all his ~s** seine ganze Mühe war umsonst; E (*Law*) **on** *or* **under ~ of death/imprisonment** bei Todesstrafe/unter Androhung (*Dat.*) einer Gefängnisstrafe.
❷ *v.t.* schmerzen

**pained** /peɪnd/ *adj.* gequält

**painful** /ˈpeɪnfl/ *adj.* A (*causing pain*) schmerzhaft ‹Krankheit, Operation, Wunde›; **be/become ~** ‹Körperteil:› wehtun *od.* schmerzen/anfangen, wehzutun; **the glare was ~ to the eyes** das grelle Licht tat in den Augen weh; **suffer from a ~ shoulder** Schmerzen in der Schulter haben; B (*distressing*) schmerzlich ‹Gedanke, Erinnerung›; traurig ‹Pflicht›; **it was ~ to watch him** es tat weh, ihm zuzusehen; C (*troublesome*) schwierig ‹Problem›; (*laborious*) beschwerlich ‹Aufstieg›; **make only ~ progress** nur mühsam weiterkommen

**painfully** /ˈpeɪnfəlɪ/ *adv.* A (*with great pain*) unter großen Schmerzen; **my shoes are ~ tight** meine Schuhe drücken fürchterlich (*ugs.*); B (*fig.*) (*excessively*) über die Maßen (*geh.*); (*laboriously*) quälend ‹langsam›; **~ obvious** nur zu offensichtlich

ˈ**painkiller** *n.* schmerzstillendes Mittel; Schmerzmittel, *das* (*ugs.*)

**painless** /ˈpeɪnlɪs/ *adj.* A (*not causing pain*) schmerzlos; B (*fig.: free of trouble, not causing problems*) unproblematisch

**painlessly** /ˈpeɪnlɪslɪ/ *adv.* A schmerzlos ‹behandeln›; B (*fig.*) mühelos ‹Problem lösen›; problemlos ‹verlaufen›

**painstaking** /ˈpeɪnzteɪkɪŋ/ *adj.* gewissenhaft; **it is ~ work** es ist eine mühsame Arbeit; **with ~ care** mit äußerster Sorgfalt

**paint** /peɪnt/ ❶ *n.* A Farbe, *die;* (*on car*) Lack, *der;* **'wet ~'** „Frisch gestrichen!"; **as clever** *or* **smart as ~:** äußerst intelligent; ⇒ *also* **fresh** 1 A; **luminous** A; **wet** 1 C; B (*joc.: cosmetic*) Schminke, *die;* **put one's ~ on** sich anmalen (*ugs.*).
❷ *v.t.* A (*cover, colour*) [an]streichen; **~ one's body** seinen Körper bemalen; **~ the town red** (*fig. coll.*) auf die Pauke hauen (*ugs.*); **~ oneself into a corner** (*fig. coll.*) sich selbst in die Bredouille bringen (*ugs.*); ⇒ *also* **black** 1 F; B (*make picture of, make by ~ing*) malen; *abs.* **~ for a living** Maler/Malerin sein; **the picture was ~ed by R.** das Bild ist von R.; C (*adorn with ~ing*) bemalen ‹Wand, Vase, Decke›; D (*fig.: describe*) zeichnen ‹Bild›; **~ sth. in glowing/gloomy colours, ~ a glowing/gloomy picture of sth.** etw. in leuchtenden/düsteren Farben malen *od.* schildern; E (*apply cosmetic to*) schminken ‹Augen, Gesicht, Lippen›; lackieren ‹Nägel›; F (*Med.*) pinseln ‹Hals›; bepinseln ‹Verletzung›

**~ ˈin** *v.t.* hineinmalen

**~ ˈon** *v.t.* aufmalen

**~ ˈout** *v.t.* übermalen; **~ sb. out of a picture** jmdn. auf einem Bild übermalen

**paint: ~box** *n.* Malkasten, *der;* Farb[en]kasten, *der;* **~brush** *n.* Pinsel, *der*

**painted**/ˈpeɪntɪd/**: ~ ˈlady** *n.* (*Zool.*) Distelfalter, *der;* **~ ˈwoman** *n.* Dirne, *die*

**painter[1]** /ˈpeɪntə(r)/ *n.* ▸ 1261 A (*artist*) Maler, *der*/Malerin, *die;* B **[house] ~:** Maler, *der*/Malerin, *die;* Anstreicher, *der*/Anstreicherin, *die*

**painter[2]** *n.* (*Naut.: rope*) Fangleine, *die*

**painting** /ˈpeɪntɪŋ/ *n.* A *no pl., no indef. art.* (*art*) Malerei, *die;* B (*picture*) Gemälde, *das;* Bild, *das*

ˈ**painting book** *n.* Malbuch, *das*

ˈ**paint stripper** *n.* Abbeizer, *der;* Abbeizmittel, *das;* **hot-air ~** Heißluftpistole [zum Entfernen alter Farbe]

ˈ**paintwork** *n.* (*on walls etc.*) Anstrich, *der;* (*of car*) Lack, *der*

**pair** /peə(r)/ ❶ *n.* A (*set of two*) Paar, *das;* **a ~ of gloves/socks/shoes** *etc.* ein Paar Handschuhe/Socken/Schuhe *usw.;* **a** *or* **one ~ of hands/eyes** zwei Hände/Augen; **in ~s** paarweise; **the ~ of them** die beiden; **fine ~ [of rascals]** (*iron.*) feines [Gauner]pärchen *od.* [Gauner]gespann; B (*single article*) **a ~ of pyjamas/scissors** *etc.* ein Schlafanzug/eine Schere *usw.;* **a ~ of trousers/jeans** eine Hose/Jeans; ein Paar Hosen/Jeans; C (*married couple*) [Ehe]paar, *das;* (*mated animals*) Paar, *das;* Pärchen, *das;* D (*Cards*) Pärchen, *das;* **a ~ of tens** zwei Zehnen; E **~ [of horses]** Zweiergespann [Pferde], *das;* **carriage** *or* **coach and ~:** Zweispänner, *der;* F (*Parl.*) *zwei Abgeordnete gegnerischer Parteien, die vereinbaren, sich bei einer Abstimmung zu enthalten;* G (*Rowing*) (*crew*) Zweiermannschaft, *die;* **~s** (*race*) Zweierrennen, *das.*
❷ *v.t.* A (*arrange in couples*) paaren; [paarweise] zusammenstellen; B (*marry*) verheiraten (**with** an + *Akk.*, mit).
❸ *v.i.* ‹Tiere:› sich paaren

**~ ˈoff** ❶ *v.t.* zu Paaren *od.* paarweise zusammenstellen; **she was ~ed off with Alan** sie bekam Alan als Partner. ❷ *v.i.* Zweiergruppen bilden

**~ ˈup** ⇒ **~ off** 2

**~ with** *v.t.* (*Parl.*) **~ with sb.** ‹Abgeordneter:› *mit jmdm. von der gegnerischen Fraktion vereinbaren, sich bei einer Abstimmung zu enthalten*

**pairing** /ˈpeərɪŋ/ *n.* (*Parl.*) **~ [arrangement]** *Absprache zwischen Abgeordneten gegnerischer Parteien, sich bei einer Abstimmung zu enthalten*

**Paisley** /ˈpeɪzlɪ/ *adj.* (*Textiles*) Paisley‹schal, -kleid, -samt usw.›; **~ pattern** Paisleymuster, *das*

**pajamas** /pəˈdʒɑːməz/ (*Amer.*) ⇒ **pyjamas**

**Pak** /pæk/, **Paki** /ˈpækɪ/ *n.* (*Brit. sl. derog.: Pakistani*) Pakistaner, *der*/Pakistanerin, *die;* **Paki-bashing** Zusammenschlagen von Pakistanern

**Pakistan** /pɑːkɪˈstɑːn/ *pr. n.* Pakistan (*das*)

**Pakistani** /pɑːkɪˈstɑːnɪ/ ▸ 1340 ❶ *adj.* pakistanisch; **sb. is ~:** jmd. ist Pakistani. ❷ *n.* Pakistani, *der*/*die;* Pakistaner, *der*/Pakistanerin, *die*

**pal** /pæl/ (*coll.*) ❶ *n.* Kumpel, *der* (*ugs.*); (*derog.*) Kumpan, *der* (*ugs. abwertend*); **be a ~ and ...:** sei so nett und ...; ⇒ *also* **old** 1 C. ❷ *v.i.*, **-ll-: ~ up with sb.** sich mit jmdm. anfreunden

**palace** /ˈpælɪs/ *n.* Palast, *der;* (*of bishop or aristocrat also*) Palais, *das;* (*stately mansion*) Schloss, *das;* *attrib.* Schloss‹garten, -park›; Palast‹wache, -truppe usw.›

**palace revoˈlution** *n.* (*lit. or fig.*) Palastrevolution, *die*

**paladin** /ˈpælədɪn/ *n.* A (*Hist.: knight errant*) fahrender Ritter; B (*knightly hero*) Recke, *der*

**Palaeocene** /ˈpælɪəsiːn, ˈpeɪlɪəsiːn/ (*Geol.*) ❶ *adj.* paläozän. ❷ *n.* Paläozän, *das*

**palaeography** /pælɪˈɒgrəfɪ, peɪlɪˈɒgrəfɪ/ *n.* Paläographie, *die*

**palaeolithic** /pælɪəˈlɪθɪk, peɪlɪəˈlɪθɪk/ *adj.* (*Archaeol.*) paläolithisch (*fachspr.*); altsteinzeitlich; **~ man** Paläolithiker, *der*

**palaeontology** /pælɪɒnˈtɒlədʒɪ, peɪlɪɒnˈtɒlədʒɪ/ *n.* Paläontologie, *die*

**Palaeozoic** /pælɪəˈzəʊɪk, peɪlɪəˈzəʊɪk/ (*Geol.*) ❶ *adj.* paläozoisch. ❷ *n.* Paläozoikum, *das*

**palatable** /ˈpælətəbl/ *adj.* A (*acceptable in taste*) genießbar; trinkbar ‹Wein›; (*pleasant*) wohlschmeckend ‹Speise›; B (*fig.*) annehmbar, akzeptabel ‹Gesetz, Erhöhung, Aufführung›; **make sth. ~ to sb.** jmdm. etw. schmackhaft machen (*ugs.*); **not be ~ to sb.** jmdm. nicht schmecken (*ugs.*)

**palatal** /ˈpælətəl/ ❶ *adj.* A (*Anat.*) Gaumen-; B (*Phonet.*) palatal. ❷ *n.* (*Phonet.*) Palatal, *der*

**palate** /ˈpælət/ *n.* A (*Anat.*) Gaumen, *der;* **hard/soft ~:** harter/weicher Gaumen; ⇒ *also* **cleft[2]** 2; B (*taste*) Gaumen, *der* (*geh.*); **be sharp on the ~** ‹Wein:› sauer schmecken; **not be to sb.'s ~** (*fig.*) nicht [nach] jmds. Geschmack sein

**palatial** /pəˈleɪʃl/ *adj.* palastartig; **built in ~ style** wie ein Palast gebaut

**Palatinate** /pəˈlætɪnət/ *pr. n.* **the ~** (*in Germany*) die Pfalz

**Palatine** /ˈpælətaɪn/ *adj.* palatinisch

**palaver** /pəˈlɑːvə(r)/ *n.* A (*coll.: fuss*) Umstand, *der;* Theater, *das* (*ugs.*); B (*conference; derog.: idle talk*) Palaver, *das*

**pale[1]** /peɪl/ *n.* A **be beyond the ~** ‹Verhalten, Benehmen:› unmöglich sein; **regard sb. as beyond the ~:** jmdn. indiskutabel finden; B (*stake*) Pfahl, *der;* (*slat*) [Zaun]latte, *die*

**pale[2]** /peɪl/ ❶ *adj.* A blass, (*esp. in illness*) fahl, (*nearly white*) bleich ‹Gesichtsfarbe, Haut, Gesicht, Aussehen›; **go ~:** blass/bleich werden; **his face was ~:** er war blass/bleich; B (*light in colour*) von blasser Farbe *nachgestellt;* blass ‹Farbe›; hell ‹Sherry›; **a ~ blue/red dress** ein blassblaues/-rotes Kleid; **~ ale** Pale Ale, *das;* C (*faint*) fahl ‹Licht›; D (*fig.: poor*) **~ imitation/reflection** schlechte Nachahmung/schwacher Abglanz. ❷ *v.i.*

P

bleich *od.* blass werden (**at** bei); **his face ~d** er wurde bleich *od.* blass; **~ into insignificance** völlig bedeutungslos werden; **~ in comparison with sth.** neben etw. (*Dat.*) verblassen

**'paleface** *n.* Bleichgesicht, *das*

**'pale-faced** *adj.* blass

**palely** /'peɪllɪ/ *adv.* fahl, bleich ‹scheinen›; matt, schwach ‹erleuchten›

**paleness** /'peɪlnɪs/ *n., no pl.* (*of person*) Blässe, *die*

**paleo-** (*Amer.*) ⇒ **palaeo-**

**Palestine** /'pælɪstaɪn/ *pr. n.* Palästina (*das*)

**Palestinian** /pælɪ'stɪnɪən/ ▶ **1340** ❶ *adj.* palästinensisch; **sb. is ~:** jmd. ist Palästinenser/Palästinenserin. ❷ *n.* Palästinenser, *der*/Palästinenserin, *die*

**palette** /'pælɪt/ *n.* Palette, *die*

**'palette knife** *n.* (*Art*) Palettenmesser, *das*

**palfrey** /'pɔːlfrɪ/ *n.* (*Hist.*) Zelter, *der*

**palimpsest** /'pælɪmpsest/ *n.* Palimpsest, *der od. das*

**palindrome** /'pælɪndrəʊm/ *n.* Palindrom, *das*

**paling** /'peɪlɪŋ/ *n.* [A] (*stake*) [Zaun]pfahl, *der;* (*slat*) [Zaun]latte, *die;* [B] (*fence*) Lattenzaun, *der*

**palisade** /pælɪ'seɪd/ *n.* [A] (*fence*) Palisade, *die;* Palisadenzaun, *der;* [B] *in pl.* (*Amer.: cliffs*) *steile, bes. säulenähnliche Formationen aufweisende Felswand*

**palish** /'peɪlɪʃ/ *adj.* blässlich

**pall[1]** /pɔːl/ *n.* [A] (*over coffin*) Sargtuch, *das;* [B] (*fig.*) Schleier, *der;* **cast a ~ of gloom over sb.** jmdn. in gedrückte Stimmung versetzen

**pall[2]** *v.i.* **~ [on sb.]** [jmdm.] langweilig werden

**Palladian** /pə'leɪdɪən/ *adj.* (*Archit.*) palladianisch

**'pall-bearer** *n.* Sargträger, *der*/-trägerin, *die*

**pallet[1]** /'pælɪt/ *n.* [A] (*bed*) Pritsche, *die;* [B] (*mattress*) Strohsack, *der*

**pallet[2]** *n.* (*platform*) Palette, *die*

**palliasse** /'pælɪæs, pælɪ'æs/ *n.* Strohsack, *der*

**palliate** /'pælɪeɪt/ *v.t.* [A] (*alleviate*) lindern, erträglicher machen ‹Krankheit›; [B] (*excuse*) entschuldigen; (*gloss over*) beschönigen

**palliative** /'pælɪətɪv/ (*Med.*) ❶ *adj.* palliativ (*fachspr.*); lindernd; **~ drug** Palliativ[um], *das* (*fachspr.*); Linderungsmittel, *das.* ❷ *n.* Palliativ[um], *das* (*fachspr.*); Linderungsmittel, *das*

**pallid** /'pælɪd/ *adj.* [A] ⇒ **pale[2]** 1 A; [B] matt, blass ‹Farbe›

**pallor** /'pælə(r)/ *n.* Blässe, *die;* Fahlheit, *die*

**pally** /'pælɪ/ *adj.* (*coll.*) **they are very ~ [with each other]** sie sind dicke Freunde (*ugs.*); **be ~ or on ~ terms with sb.** mit jmdm. dick befreundet sein (*ugs.*); **his ~ manner** seine kumpelhafte Art

**palm[1]** /pɑːm/ *n.* [A] (*tree*) Palme, *die; attrib.* **~ leaf/oil/kernel/frond** Palmblatt, *das*/-öl, *das*/-kern, *der*/-wedel, *der;* **~ [branch]** (*also Eccl.*) Palmzweig, *der;* [B] (*symbol of victory*) Siegespalme, *die;* (*Bibl.*) Palme, *die;* **bear or take the ~** (*fig.*) die Siegespalme davontragen (*geh.*)

**palm[2]** ❶ *n.* [A] ▶ **966** (*of hand*) Handteller, *der;* Handfläche, *die;* **hold/weigh sth. in one's ~ or the ~ of one's hand** etw. in der Hand halten/wiegen; **have sth. in the ~ of one's hand** (*fig.*) etw. in der Hand haben; **on the ~s of one's hands** auf den Handtellern *od.* -flächen; **the ~ of one's right hand** der rechte Handteller; die rechte Handfläche; ⇒ *also* **cross** 2 A; **grease** 2; [B] (*of glove*) Innenfläche, *die.* ❷ *v.t.* in der [hohlen] Hand verschwinden lassen

**~ 'off** *v.t.* **~ sth. off on sb., ~ sb. off with sth.** jmdm. etw. andrehen (*ugs.*); **~ sb. off on sb. else** jmdn. zu jmd. anderem abschieben (*ugs.*); **~ sth. off as sth.** etw. als etw. verkaufen; **~ sb. off with promises** jmdn. mit Versprechungen abspeisen (*ugs.*)

**palm 'court** *adj.* **~ music/orchestra** ≈ Kaffeehausmusik, *die*/-orchester, *das*

**palmist** /'pɑːmɪst/ *n.* Handleser, *der*/-leserin, *die;* Handliniendeuter, *der*/-deuterin, *die*

**palmistry** /'pɑːmɪstrɪ/ *n., no pl.* Handlesekunst, *die;* Handliniendeutung, *die*

**palm: P~ 'Sunday** *n.* (*Eccl.*) Palmsonntag, *der;* **~top** *n.* **~top [computer]** Palmtop, *der;* **~ tree** *n.* Palme, *die*

**palomino** /pælə'miːnəʊ/ *n., pl.* **~s** (*Zool.*) Isabelle, *die*

**palpable** /'pælpəbl/ *adj.* [A] (*tangible*) fühlbar; tastbar; [B] (*perceptible*) spürbar ‹Unterschied›; eindeutig ‹Zeichen›; (*obvious*) offenkundig ‹Lüge, Unwissenheit, Absurdität›

**palpably** /'pælpəblɪ/ *adv.* offenkundig

**palpitate** /'pælpɪteɪt/ *v.i.* [A] (*pulsate*) ‹Herz:› palpitieren (*fachspr.*), pochen, hämmern; [B] (*throb*) beben; zucken; (*tremble*) zittern (**with** vor + *Dat.*)

**palpitation** /pælpɪ'teɪʃn/ *n.* [A] (*throbbing*) Beben, *das;* Zucken, *das;* (*trembling*) Zittern, *das;* [B] *in pl.* (*Med.: of heart*) Palpitation, *die* (*fachspr.*); Herzklopfen, *das;* **suffer from ~s** Herzklopfen haben

**palsy** /'pɔːlzɪ, 'pɒlzɪ/ *n.* (*Med. dated*) Lähmung, *die;* Paralyse, *die* (*fachspr.*); ⇒ *also* **cerebral palsy**

**paltry** /'pɔːltrɪ, 'pɒltrɪ/ *adj.* schäbig; armselig ‹Auswahl›; (*trivial*) belanglos; **~ matters** Belanglosigkeiten; **a ~ £5** schäbige 5 Pfund

**pampas** /'pæmpəz, 'pæmpəs/ *n. pl.* (*Geog.*) Pampas *Pl.*

**'pampas grass** *n.* Pampasgras, *das*

**pamper** /'pæmpə(r)/ *v.t.* verhätscheln; **~ oneself** sich verwöhnen

**pamphlet** /'pæmflɪt/ *n.* (*leaflet*) Prospekt, *der;* (*esp. Polit.*) Flugblatt, *das;* (*booklet*) Broschüre, *die;* (*Polit., Relig.: tract*) Streitschrift, *die*

**pamphleteer** /pæmflɪ'tɪə(r)/ *n.* Verfasser/Verfasserin des Flugblatts/der Streitschrift/der Flugblätter/der Streitschriften

**pan[1]** /pæn/ ❶ *n.* [A] [Koch]topf, *der;* (*for frying*) Pfanne, *die;* **pots and ~s** Kochtöpfe; **a ~ of milk** ein Topf Milch; ⇒ *also* **saucepan;** [B] (*of scales*) Schale, *die;* [C] (*Brit.: of WC*) **[lavatory] ~:** Toilettenschüssel, *die;* [D] (*Amer. coll.: face*) Visage, *die* (*ugs. abwertend*). ⇒ *also* **flash** 1 A. ❷ *v.t.,* **-nn-** (*coll.*) verreißen ‹Theaterstück, Buch, Film usw.›; harte Kritik üben an (+ *Dat.*) ‹Person›

**~ 'out** *v.i.* (*progress*) sich entwickeln

**pan[2]** ❶ *v.t.,* **-nn-** (*Cinemat., Telev.*) schwenken; (*Photog.*) mitziehen. ❷ *v.i.,* **-nn-** (*Cinemat., Telev.*) schwenken (**to** auf + *Akk.*); (*Photog.*) [die Kamera] mitziehen; **~ning shot** [Kamera]schwenk, *der.* ❸ *n.* (*Cinemat., Telev.*) Schwenk, *der*

**pan-** /pæn/ *in comb.* pan‹amerikanisch, -slawistisch, -islamisch, -germanisch usw.›; Pan‹afrikanismus, -slawist usw.›

**panacea** /pænə'siːə/ *n.* Allheilmittel, *das*

**panache** /pə'næʃ/ *n.* Schwung, *der;* Elan, *der*

**Panama** /pænə'mɑː/ ❶ *pr. n.* Panama (*das*). ❷ *n.* **p~ [hat]** Panamahut, *der*

**Panama Ca'nal** *pr. n.* Panamakanal, *der*

**Panamanian** /pænə'meɪnɪən/ ▶ **1340** ❶ *adj.* panamaisch; **sb. is ~:** jmd. ist Panamaer/Panamaerin. ❷ *n.* Panamaer, *der*/Panamaerin, *die*

**panatella** /pænə'telə/ *n.* Panatela, *die*

**pancake** /'pænkeɪk/ *n.* Pfannkuchen, *der;* **be flat as a ~:** platt wie ein Pfannkuchen sein; ‹Gelände:› topfeben sein; (*squashed*) platt wie eine Briefmarke sein; ‹Reifen:› völlig platt sein

**pancake: P~ Day** *n.* (*Brit.*) Fastnachtsdienstag, *der;* **~ 'landing** *n.* (*Aeronaut.*) Bauchlandung, *die;* **~ roll** *n.* gerollter Pfannkuchen mit Füllung

**panchromatic** /pænkrə'mætɪk/ *adj.* (*Photog.*) panchromatisch

**pancreas** /'pæŋkrɪəs/ *n.* (*Anat.*) Bauchspeicheldrüse, *die;* Pankreas, *das* (*fachspr.*)

**pancreatic** /pæŋkrɪ'ætɪk/ *adj.* (*Anat., Physiol.*) Pankreas-; **~ duct** Ausführungsgang des Pankreas

**panda** /'pændə/ *n.* (*Zool.*) Panda, *der*

**'panda car** *n.* (*Brit. Police*) Streifenwagen, *der*

**pandemonium** /pændɪ'məʊnɪəm/ *n.* Chaos, *das;* (*uproar*) Tumult, *der;* **there was ~ in the stadium** das Stadion war ein Hexenkessel; **~ reigned** es herrschte ein einziges Chaos

**pander** /'pændə(r)/ ❶ *n.* (*go-between*) Kuppler, *der*/Kupplerin, *die;* (*procurer*) Zuhälter, *der.* ❷ *v.i.* **~ to** allzu sehr entgegenkommen (+ *Dat.*) ‹Person, Geschmack, Instinkt›; frönen (+ *Dat.*) ‹Laster›

**Pandora's box** /pændɔːrəz 'bɒks/ *n.* (*Mythol.; also fig.*) Büchse der Pandora

**p. & p.** *abbr.* (*Brit.*) **postage and packing** Porto und Verpackung

**pane** /peɪn/ *n.* (*glass*) Scheibe, *die;* **window ~/~ of glass** Fenster-/Glasscheibe, *die*

**panegyric** /pænɪ'dʒɪrɪk/ ❶ *n.* Lobrede, *die* (**on** auf + *Akk.*). ❷ *adj.* panegyrisch (*geh.*)

**panel** /'pænl/ ❶ *n.* [A] (*of door, wall, etc.*) Paneel, *das;* (*of fence*) Bretterzaunelement, *das;* (*of screen, triptych*) Flügel, *der;* [B] (*esp. Telev., Radio, etc.*) (*quiz team*) Rateteam, *das;* (*in public discussion*) Podium, *das;* **~ discussion** Podiumsdiskussion, *die;* [C] (*advisory body*) Gremium, *das;* Kommission, *die;* **~ of experts** Expertengremium, *das;* [D] (*Dressmaking*) Einsatz, *der.* ⇒ *also* **control panel; instrument panel.** ❷ *v.t.,* (*Brit.*) **-ll-** paneelieren ‹Tür, Zimmer, Wand›; täfeln ‹Zimmer, Wand›

**panel: ~ beater** *n.* Autospengler, *der*/-spenglerin, *die;* **~ game** *n.* Ratespiel, *das;* Quiz, *das;* (*Telev., Radio*) Rate-, Quizsendung, *die*

**paneling, panelist** (*Amer.*) ⇒ **panell-**

**panelling** /'pænəlɪŋ/ *n.* Täfelung, *die*

**panellist** /'pænəlɪst/ *n.* (*Telev., Radio*) (*on quiz programme*) Mitglied des Rateteams; (*on discussion panel*) Diskussionsteilnehmer, *der*/-teilnehmerin, *die*

**panel: ~ pin** *n.* Tapeziernagel, *der;* **~ truck** *n.* Lieferwagen, *der*

**'pan-fry** *v.t.* [in der Pfanne] braten

**panful** /'pænfʊl/ *n.* Topf, *der;* **a ~ of water** ein Topf [voll] Wasser

**pang** /pæŋ/ *n.* [A] (*of pain*) Stich, *der;* ⇒ *also* **hunger** 1; [B] (*of distress*) **feel ~s of conscience/guilt** Gewissensbisse haben; **feel ~s of remorse** bittere Reue empfinden

**'panhandle** ❶ *n.* [A] Topfstiel, *der;* (*of frying pan*) Pfannenstiel, *der;* [B] (*of land*) schmaler Landstreifen; (*in US*) Panhandle, *der.* ❷ *v.t.* (*coll.*) anschnorren (*ugs.*) (**for** um). ❸ *v.i.* (*coll.*) schnorren (*ugs.*)

**panic** /'pænɪk/ ❶ *n.* Panik, *die;* **be in a [state of] ~ [over or at having done sth.]** von Panik erfasst *od.* ergriffen sein[, weil man etw. getan hat]; **there was ~ on the stock market** es kam zu einer Börsenpanik. ❷ *v.i.,* **-ck-** in Panik (*Akk.*) geraten; **don't ~!** nur keine Panik! ❸ *v.t.,* **-ck-** in Panik versetzen; **~ sb. into doing sth.** jmdn. so in Panik versetzen, dass er etw. tut. ❹ *attrib. adj.* (*overhasty*) übereilt, überstürzt ‹Maßnahmen›; wild, atemlos ‹Hast›; **~ buying** Hamsterkäufe *Pl.;* **~ selling** Panikverkäufe *Pl.*

**'panic attack** *n.* Angstanfall, *der;* Anfall von Panik; **she suffers from ~s** sie leidet an Angstzuständen

**panic: ~ bolt** *n.* Panikverschluss, *der;* **~ button** *n.* Alarmknopf, *der;* **hit the ~ button** (*fig. coll.*) Alarm schlagen; (**~**) durchdrehen (*ugs.*); die Panik kriegen (*ugs.*)

**panicky** /'pænɪkɪ/ *adj.* von Panik bestimmt ‹Verhalten, Handeln, Rede›; **be ~:** in Panik sein

**panicle** /'pænɪkl/ *n.* (*Bot.*) Rispe, *die*

**panic: ~monger** *n.* Panikmacher, *der*/-macherin, *die;* **~ stations** *n. pl.* (*fig. coll.*) **be at ~ stations** am Rotieren sein (*ugs.*) (**about** wegen); **it was ~ stations** alles war am Rotieren (*ugs.*); **~-stricken, ~-struck** *adjs.* von Panik erfasst *od.* ergriffen

**pannier** /'pænɪə(r)/ *n.* [A] (*basket*) Lastkorb, *der;* [B] (*bag*) Packtasche, *die*

**panoply** /'pænəplɪ/ *n.* Palette, *die* (*fig.*); **the full ~ of a state burial** ein Staatsbegräbnis mit allem, was dazugehört; **a wonderful ~ of colours** eine herrliche Farbenpracht

**panorama** /pænə'rɑːmə/ *n.* Panorama, *das;* (*fig.: survey*) Überblick, *der* (**of** über + *Akk.*); **aerial ~:** Luftaufnahme, *die*

**panoramic** /pænəˈræmɪk/ *adj.* Panorama-; ~ **survey** (*fig.*) umfassender Überblick (**of** über + *Akk.*)

ˈ**pan pipes** *n. pl.* (*Mus.*) Panflöte, *die*

**pansy** /ˈpænzɪ/ *n.* A (*Bot.*) Stiefmütterchen, *das;* B (*coll.: effeminate man*) Schwuchtel, *die* (*ugs.*); Tunte, *die* (*ugs.*)

**pant** /pænt/ ❶ *v.i.* keuchen; ‹Hund:› hecheln. ❷ *v.t.* ~ **[out]** keuchend hervorstoßen ‹Nachricht, Worte›

~ **for** *v.t.* ringen nach ‹Luft, Atem›; schnappen nach ‹Luft›; lechzen nach ‹Getränk›

**pantechnicon** /pænˈteknɪkən/ *n.* ~ **[van]** (*Brit.*) Möbelwagen, *der*

**pantheism** /ˈpænθiːɪzm/ *n., no art.* (*Relig.*) Pantheismus, *der*

**pantheist** /ˈpænθiːɪst/ *n.* (*Relig.*) Pantheist, *der*/Pantheistin, *die*

**pantheistic** /pænθɪˈɪstɪk/, **pantheistical** /pænθɪˈɪstɪkl/ *adj.* (*Relig.*) pantheistisch

**pantheon** /ˈpænθɪən, pænˈθiːən/ *n.* Pantheon, *das*

**panther** /ˈpænθə(r)/ *n.* (*Zool.*) A Panther, *der;* B (*Amer.: puma*) Puma, *der;* Berglöwe, *der*

**pantie-girdle** /ˈpæntɪɡɜːdl/ *n.* (*coll.*) Miederhose, *die*

**panties** /ˈpæntɪz/ *n. pl.* (*coll.*) **[pair of]** ~: Schlüpfer, *der*

**pantihose** /ˈpæntɪhəʊz/ ⇒ **tights** 3 A

**pantile** /ˈpæntaɪl/ *n.* (*Building*) Hohlpfanne, *die*

**panto** /ˈpæntəʊ/ *n., pl.* ~**s** (*Brit. coll.*) ⇒ **pantomime** A

**pantograph** /ˈpæntəɡrɑːf/ *n.* A (*for copying*) Pantograph, *der;* Storchschnabel, *der;* B (*Electr.*) Scherenstromabnehmer, *der*

**pantomime** /ˈpæntəmaɪm/ *n.* A (*Brit.*) *Märchenspiel im Varieteestil, das um Weihnachten aufgeführt wird;* B (*gestures*) Pantomime, *die*

**pantry** /ˈpæntrɪ/ *n.* Speisekammer, *die;* **[butler's]** ~: Anrichtezimmer, *das*

**pants** /pænts/ *n. pl.* A (*esp. Amer.: trousers*) **[pair of]** ~: Hose, *die;* **bore/scare the** ~ **off sb.** (*fig. coll.*) jmdn. zu Tode langweilen/erschrecken; **talk the** ~ **off sb.** (*fig. coll.*) jmdn. voll labern *od.* voll quatschen (*ugs.*); **catch sb. with his** ~ **down** (*fig. coll.*) jmdn. unvorbereitet treffen; ⇒ *also* **kick** 1 A; B (*Brit.: underpants*) Unterhose, *die*

ˈ**pant suit** *n.* Hosenanzug, *der*

**panzer** /ˈpæntsə(r)/ *adj.* (*Mil.*) Panzer-

**pap** /pæp/ *n.* (*food*) Brei, *der;* (*fig. derog.*) Schmarren, *der* (*ugs. abwertend*)

**papa** /pəˈpɑː/ *n.* (*arch. child lang.*) Papa, *der* (*fam.*)

**papacy** /ˈpeɪpəsɪ/ *n.* A *no pl.* (*office*) Papat, *der;* **be elected to the** ~: zum Papst gewählt werden; B (*tenure*) Amtszeit als Papst; C *no pl.* (*papal system*) Papsttum, *das*

**papal** /ˈpeɪpl/ *adj.* päpstlich; ⇒ *also* **infallibility**

**paparazzo** /pæpæˈrɑːtsəʊ/ *n., pl.* **paparazzi** /pæpæˈrɑːtsiː/ Paparazzo, *der*

**papaw** /pəˈpɔː/, **papaya** /pəˈpaɪə/ *n.* (*Bot.*) A (*tree*) ~ **[tree]** Papaya- *od.* Melonenbaum, *der;* B (*fruit*) Papaya[frucht], *die*

**paper** /ˈpeɪpə(r)/ ❶ *n.* A (*material*) Papier, *das;* **put sth. down on** ~: etw. schriftlich festhalten *od.* niederlegen; **it looks all right on** ~ (*in theory*) auf dem Papier sieht es ganz gut aus; **put pen to** ~: zur Feder greifen; **the treaty** *etc.* **isn't worth the** ~ **it's written on** (*coll.*) der Vertrag *usw.* ist nicht das Papier wert, auf dem er geschrieben steht; B *in pl.* (*documents*) Dokumente *Pl.;* Unterlagen *Pl.;* (*to prove identity etc.*) Papiere *Pl.;* C (*in examination*) (*Univ.*) Klausur, *die;* (*Sch.*) Arbeit, *die;* D (*newspaper*) Zeitung, *die;* **daily/weekly** ~: Tages-/Wochenzeitung, *die;* E (*wallpaper*) Tapete, *die;* F (*wrapper*) Stück Papier; **don't scatter the** ~**s all over the floor** wirf das Papier nicht überall auf den Boden; G (*learned article*) Referat, *das;* (*shorter*) Paper, *das;* H *no pl., no indef. art.* (*Commerc.: bills of exchange etc.*) [Wert]papiere *Pl.*

❷ *adj.* A (*made of* ~) aus Papier *nachgestellt;* Papier‹mütze, -taschentuch›; B (*theoretical*) nominell ‹zahlenmäßige Stärke, Profit›. ❸ *v.t.* tapezieren

~ ˈ**over** *v.t.* [mit Tapete] überkleben; ~ **over the cracks** (*fig.: cover up mistakes/differences*) die Fehler/Differenzen übertünchen

**paper:** ~**back** ❶ *n.* Paperback, *das;* (*pocket-size*) Taschenbuch, *das;* **available in** ~**back** als Paperback/Taschenbuch erhältlich; ❷ *adj.* ~**back edition** Paperback-/Taschenbuchausgabe, *die;* ~**back book** Paperback, *das*/Taschenbuch, *das;* ~ ˈ**bag** *n.* Papiertüte, *die;* ~ **boy** *n.* Zeitungsjunge, *der;* ~ **chain** *n.* Papiergirlande, *die;* ~**chase** *n.* Schnitzeljagd, *die;* ~ **clip** *n.* Büroklammer, *die;* (*larger*) Aktenklammer, *die;* ~ ˈ**cup** *n.* Pappbecher, *der;* ~ **currency** ⇒ ~ **money;** ~ **girl** ⇒ **newsgirl;** ~ ˈ**handkerchief** *n.* Papiertaschentuch, *das;* ~**hanger** *n.* Tapezierer, *der*/Tapeziererin, *die;* ~**hanging** *n.* Tapezieren, *das;* ~ ˈ**hanky** *n.* (*coll.*) Papiertaschentuch, *das;* ~**knife** *n.* Brieföffner, *der;* ~**less** /ˈpeɪpəlɪs/ *adj.* papierlos ‹Transaktion, System›; **the** ~**less office** das papierlose Büro; ~**making** *n., no pl.* Papierherstellung, *die;* ~ **mill** *n.* Papierfabrik *od.* -mühle, *die;* ~ **money** *n.* Papiergeld, *das;* ~ ˈ**napkin** *n.* Papierserviette, *die;* ~ ˈ**plate** *n.* Pappteller, *der;* ~ **qualification** *n.* Zeugnis, *das;* ~ **round** *n.* Zeitungenaustragen, *das;* **on one's** ~ **round** beim Zeitungenaustragen; **have/do a** ~ **round** Zeitungen austragen; ~ **serviˈette** ⇒ ~ **napkin;** ~ **shop** *n.* Zeitungsgeschäft, *das;* ~**-thin** *adj.* (*lit. or fig.*) hauchdünn; ~ ˈ**tiger** ⇒ **tiger** A; ~ ˈ**towel** *n.* Papierhandtuch, *das;* ~**weight** *n.* Briefbeschwerer, *der;* ~**work** *n.* A Schreibarbeit, *die;* Papierkram, *der* (*abwertend*); B (*documents*) Unterlagen *Pl.*

**papery** /ˈpeɪpərɪ/ *adj.* papierartig; **be** ~: wie Papier sein

**papier mâché** /pæpjeɪ ˈmæʃeɪ, pæpjeɪ ˈmɑːʃeɪ/ *n.* Papiermaschee, *das;* Pappmaschee, *das*

**papist** /ˈpeɪpɪst/ *n.* (*Relig. derog.*) Papist, *der*/Papistin, *die* (*abwertend*)

**papoose** /pəˈpuːs/ *n.* Kleinkind, *das* (*bei den nordamerikanischen Indianern*)

**paprika** /ˈpæprɪkə, pəˈpriːkə/ *n.* A ⇒ **pepper** 1 B; B (*Cookery: condiment*) Paprika, *der*

**Papua New Guinea** /pɑːpʊə njuː ˈɡɪnɪ/ *pr. n.* Papua-Neuguinea (*das*)

**papyrus** /pəˈpaɪrəs/ *n., pl.* **papyri** /pəˈpaɪraɪ/ Papyrus, *der*

**par** /pɑː(r)/ *n.* A (*average*) **above/below** ~: über/unter dem Durchschnitt; **the work is [well] below** ~: die Arbeit liegt [weit] unter dem üblichen Niveau; **feel rather below** ~, **not feel up to** ~ (*fig.*) nicht ganz auf dem Posten *od.* Damm sein (*ugs.*); B (*equality*) **be on a** ~: vergleichbar sein; **be on a** ~ **with sb./sth.** jmdm./einer Sache gleichkommen; C (*Golf*) Par, *das;* **that's about** ~ **for the course** (*fig. coll.*) das ist so das Übliche; D (*Commerc.: nominal value*) ~ **[of exchange]** Wechselkurs, *der;* **be at/above/below** ~ ‹Aktie, Wert:› al/über/unter pari stehen

**para** /ˈpærə/ *n.* (*coll.*) A (*paratrooper*) Para, *der;* B (*paragraph*) Absatz, der

**para.** *abbr.* **paragraph** Abs.; (*in contract or law*) Paragr.

**parable** /ˈpærəbl/ *n.* Gleichnis, *das;* Parabel, *die* (*bes. Literaturw.*)

**parabola** /pəˈræbələ/ *n.* (*Geom.*) Parabel, *die*

**parabolic** /pærəˈbɒlɪk/ *adj.* (*Geom.*) parabolisch; ~ **antenna** Parabolantenne, *die;* ~ **mirror** Parabolspiegel, *der*

**parachute** /ˈpærəʃuːt/ ❶ *n.* A Fallschirm, *der;* B (*to brake aircraft etc.*) Bremsfallschirm, *der.* ❷ *v.t.* [mit dem Fallschirm] absetzen ‹Person› (**into** über + *Dat.*); mit dem Fallschirm abwerfen ‹Vorräte›. ❸ *v.i.* ‹Truppen:› [mit dem Fallschirm] abspringen (**into** über + *Dat.*). ❹ *adj.* Fallschirm‹absprung, -abwurf›; (*Mil.*) Fallschirmjäger‹truppen, -regiment›

**parachutist** /ˈpærəʃuːtɪst/ *n.* A **[sports]** ~: Fallschirmspringer, *der*/-springerin, *die;* B (*Mil.*) Fallschirmjäger, *der*

**parade** /pəˈreɪd/ ❶ *n.* A (*display*) Zurschaustellung, *die;* **make a** ~ **of** zur Schau stellen ‹Tugend, Eigenschaft›; **make a** ~ **of one's knowledge** mit seinem Wissen paradieren (*geh.*); B (*Mil.: muster*) Appell, *der;* **on** ~: beim Appell; C (*procession*) Umzug, *der;* (*of troops*) Parade, *die;* D (*succession*) Reihe, *die;* E (*promenade, street*) Promenade, *die;* **a** ~ **of shops** eine Reihe Läden.

❷ *v.t.* A (*display*) zur Schau stellen; vorzeigen ‹Person› (**before** bei); B (*march through*) ~ **the streets** durch die Straßen marschieren; C (*Mil.: muster*) antreten lassen.

❸ *v.i.* paradieren; ‹Demonstranten:› marschieren; **the national teams** ~**d round the stadium** die Nationalmannschaften marschierten durch das Stadion

**paˈrade ground** *n.* Exerzierplatz, *der*

**paradigm** /ˈpærədaɪm/ *n.* (*esp. Ling.*) Paradigma, *das*

**paradise** /ˈpærədaɪs/ *n.* Paradies, *das;* **children's/gourmet's** ~: Paradies für Kinder/Gourmets; **an earthly** ~: ein Paradies auf Erden; **this is** ~**!** himmlisch! ⇒ *also* **bird of paradise; fool's paradise**

**paradox** /ˈpærədɒks/ *n.* A Paradox[on], *das;* B *no pl., no indef. art.* (*quality*) Paradoxie, *die;* Widersprüchlichkeit, *die*

**paradoxical** /pærəˈdɒksɪkl/ *adj.* paradox

**paradoxically** /pærəˈdɒksɪkəlɪ/ *adv.* paradox; *as sentence-modifier* paradoxerweise

**paraffin** /ˈpærəfɪn/ *n.* A (*Chem.*) Paraffin, *das;* B (*Brit.: fuel*) Petroleum, *das; attrib.* Petroleum‹lampe, -kocher›; C **liquid** ~ (*Brit.: laxative*) Paraffinöl, *das*

**paraffin:** ~ ˈ**oil** (*Brit.*) ⇒ **paraffin** B; ~ ˈ**stove** *n.* Petroleumkocher, *der;* (*for heating*) Petroleumofen, *der;* ~ ˈ**wax** *n.* Paraffin[-wachs], *das*

**paragliding** /ˈpærəɡlaɪdɪŋ/ *n., no pl.* Paragliding, *das;* Gleitschirmfliegen, *das*

**paragon** /ˈpærəɡən/ Muster, *das* (**of** an + *Dat.*); **a** ~ **of beauty** der Inbegriff der Schönheit; ~ **of virtue** Tugendheld, *der*

**paragraph** /ˈpærəɡrɑːf/ *n.* A (*section of text*) Absatz, *der;* B (*subsection of law etc.*) Paragraph, *der;* C (*Journ.: news item*) Notiz, *die;* D (*symbol*) Absatzzeichen, *das*

**Paraguay** /ˈpærəɡwaɪ/ *pr. n.* Paraguay (*das*)

**Paraguayan** /pærəˈɡwaɪən/ ▶ **1340** ❶ *adj.* paraguayisch; **sb. is** ~: jmd. ist Paraguayer/Paraguayerin. ❷ *n.* Paraguayer, *der*/Paraguayerin, *die*

**parakeet** /ˈpærəkiːt/ *n.* (*Ornith.*) Sittich, *der*

**parallax** /ˈpærəlæks/ *n.* (*Astron., Phys.*) Parallaxe, *die*

**parallel** /ˈpærəlel/ ❶ *adj.* A parallel; **line A is** ~ **to line B** (*Geom.*) Gerade A ist der Geraden B parallel; **the railway ran** ~ **to the river** die Bahnlinie verlief parallel zum Fluss; ~ **bars** (*Gymnastics*) Barren, *der;* B (*fig.: similar*) vergleichbar; **be** ~: sich (*Dat.*) [genau] entsprechen; (*share common features*) Parallelen aufweisen; **there is nothing** ~ **to this in history** dazu gibt es in der Geschichte keine Parallele.

❷ *n.* A Parallele, *die;* **this has no** ~ *or* **is without** ~: dazu gibt es keine Parallele; **there is a** ~ **between x and y** es gibt eine Parallelität zwischen x und y; **the two societies are** ~**s** die beiden Gesellschaften gleichen sich; B (*Electr.*) **in** ~: parallel; **be connected in** ~: parallel geschaltet sein; C (*Geog.*) ~ **[of latitude]** Breitenkreis, *der;* **the 42nd** ~: der 42. Breitengrad; D (*Astron.*) Deklinationskreis, *der.*

❸ *v.t.* A (*match*) gleichkommen (+ *Dat.*); **his arrogance cannot be** ~**ed** seine Arroganz ist beispiellos; B (*find sth. similar to*) **this behaviour may be** ~**ed in human life** eine Parallele zu diesem Verhalten lässt sich beim Menschen feststellen; C (*compare*) vergleichen

**parallelism** /ˈpærəlelɪzm/ *n.* (*lit. or fig.*) Parallelität, *die* (**in** *Gen.*); Übereinstimmung, *die* (**in** *Gen.*)

**parallelogram** /pærəˈleləɡræm/ *n.* (*Geom.*) Parallelogramm, *das*

**parallel ˈprocessing** *n.* (*Computing*) Parallelverarbeitung, *die*

**paralyse** /'pærəlaɪz/ *v.t.* **A** lähmen; paralysieren (*Med.*); **he is ~d in both legs** seine beiden Beine sind gelähmt; **B** (*fig.*) lahm legen ‹Verkehr, Industrie›; zum Erliegen bringen ‹Verkehr›; **be ~d with fright** vor Schreck wie gelähmt sein; **be ~d** ‹Verkehr:› zum Erliegen gekommen sein

**paralysis** /pə'rælɪsɪs/ *n.*, *pl.* **paralyses** /pə'rælɪsi:z/ Lähmung, *die;* Paralyse, *die* (*Med.*); (*fig.*, *of industry, traffic*) Lahmlegung, *die*

**paralytic** /pærə'lɪtɪk/ ❶ *adj.* **A** gelähmt; paralytisch (*Med.*); **B** (*Brit. coll.: very drunk*) stockvoll, sternhagelvoll (*salopp*). ❷ *n.* Gelähmte, *der/die;* Paralytiker, *der*/Paralytikerin, *die* (*Med.*)

**paralyze** (*Amer.*) ⇒ **paralyse**

**paramedic** /pærə'medɪk/ *n.* ▶ **1261** medizinische Hilfskraft; (*ambulance worker*) Sanitäter, *der*/Sanitäterin, *die*

**paramedical** /pærə'medɪkl/ *adj.* **~ personnel/staff** medizinisches Hilfspersonal; (*in hospital*) nichtärztliches Personal; **~ training** Ausbildung zur medizinischen Hilfskraft

**parameter** /pə'ræmɪtə(r)/ *n.* **A** (*defining feature*) Faktor, *der;* **B** (*Math.*) Parameter, *der*

**paramilitary** /pærə'mɪlɪtərɪ/ *adj.* paramilitärisch; halbmilitärisch

**paramount** /'pærəmaʊnt/ *adj.* **A** (*supreme*) höchst... ‹Macht, Autorität›; oberst... ‹Herrscher, Souverän›; **B** (*pre-eminent*) größt..., höchst... ‹Wichtigkeit›; Haupt‹gesichtspunkt, -überlegung›; **be ~** ‹Wunsch:› Vorrang haben

**paramour** /'pærəmʊə(r)/ *n.* (*arch./rhet.*) Buhle, *der/die* (*dichter. veralt.*)

**paranoia** /pærə'nɔɪə/ *n.* **A** (*disorder*) Paranoia, *die* (*Med.*); **B** (*tendency*) **[feeling of] ~:** krankhaftes Misstrauen; Verfolgungswahn, *der*

**paranoiac** /pærə'nɔɪæk/, **paranoic** /pærə'nəʊɪk/ ❶ *n.* (*Med.*) Paranoiker, *der*/Paranoikerin, *die;* **be a ~** (*fig.*) an Verfolgungswahn leiden. ❷ *adj.* (*Med.*) paranoisch; (*fig.*) krankhaft [gesteigert] ‹Misstrauen›

**paranoid** /'pærənɔɪd/ ❶ *adj.* (*Med.*) paranoid (*fachspr.*); (*fig.*) wahnhaft; krankhaft [gesteigert] ‹Misstrauen, Abneigung, Angst›; **be ~:** an Verfolgungswahn leiden; **he's ~ about his boss** er bildet sich ein, dass sein Chef ihn schikanieren will. ❷ *n.* (*Med.*) Paranoiker, *der*/Paranoikerin, *die;* **be a ~:** paranoid sein; an Verfolgungswahn leiden

**paranormal** /pærə'nɔ:ml/ *adj.* paranormal; übersinnlich

**parapet** /'pærəpɪt, 'pærəpet/ *n.* **A** (*low wall or barrier*) Brüstung, *die;* **B** (*Mil.*) Parapett, *das* (*hist.*); Brustwehr, *die*

**paraphernalia** /pærəfə'neɪlɪə/ *n. sing.* **A** (*personal belongings*) Utensilien *Pl.;* **B** (*equipment*) (*of justice, power*) Instrumentarium, *das* (*geh.*); Apparat, *der;* (*of war*) Material, *das;* **equestrian/sporting/photographic ~:** Reit-/Sport-/Fotoausrüstung, *die;* **the whole ~** (*coll.*) alles, was so dazugehört (*ugs.*)

**paraphrase** /'pærəfreɪz/ ❶ *n.* Umschreibung, *die;* Paraphrase, *die* (*fachspr.*). ❷ *v.t.* umschreiben; paraphrasieren (*fachspr.*)

**paraplegia** /pærə'pli:dʒɪə/ *n.* (*Med.*) Paraplegie, *die* (*fachspr.*); ≈ Querschnittslähmung, *die*

**paraplegic** /pærə'pli:dʒɪk/ (*Med.*) ❶ *adj.* doppelseitig gelähmt; paraplegisch (*fachspr.*). ❷ *n.* doppelseitig Gelähmter/Gelähmte; Paraplegiker, *der*/Paraplegikerin, *die* (*fachspr.*)

**parapsychology** /pærəsaɪ'kɒlədʒɪ/ *n.* Parapsychologie, *die*

**paraquat** /'pærəkwɒt/ *n.* (*Agric.*) Paraquat, *das* (*ein Kontaktherbizid*)

**parasailing** /'pæraseɪlɪŋ/ *n.*, *no pl.* Parasailing, *das*

**parascending** /'pærəsendɪŋ/ *n.*, *no pl.* **A** ⇒ **parasailing;** **B** ⇒ **paragliding**

**parasite** /'pærəsaɪt/ *n.* **A** (*Biol.*) Schmarotzer, *der;* Parasit, *der* (*fachspr.*); **B** (*fig. derog.: person*) Schmarotzer, *der;* Parasit, *der;* **be a total ~:** nur schmarotzen

**parasitic** /pærə'sɪtɪk/ *adj.* **A** (*Biol.*) parasitisch; parasitär ‹Pilz›; **be ~ on** schmarotzen in (+ *Dat.*); ‹Pflanze:› schmarotzen *od.* an (+ *Dat.*); **B** (*fig.*) schmarotzerisch; schmarotzerhaft; **be ~ on** als Schmarotzer leben von

**parasitism** /'pærəsaɪtɪzm/ *n.*, *no pl.* **A** (*Biol.*) Parasitismus, *der;* **B** (*fig.*) Schmarotzertum, *das*

**parasol** /'pærəsɒl/ *n.* Sonnenschirm, *der;* Parasol, *der od. das* (*veralt.*)

**parasympathetic** /pærəsɪmpə'θetɪk/ *adj.* (*Anat.*) parasympathisch; **~ nerve** Parasympathikus, *der*

**paratrooper** /'pærətru:pə(r)/ *n.* ▶ **1261** (*Mil.*) Fallschirmjäger, *der*

**paratroops** /'pærətru:ps/ *n. pl.* (*Mil.*) Fallschirmjägertruppe, *die;* Fallschirmjäger *Pl.*

**paratyphoid** /pærə'taɪfɔɪd/ *n.* ▶ **1232** (*Med.*) Paratyphus, *der*

**parboil** /'pɑ:bɔɪl/ *v.t.* (*Cookery*) ankochen

**parcel** /'pɑ:sl/ ❶ *n.* **A** (*package*) Paket, *das;* **send/receive sth. by ~ post** etw. mit der Paketpost *od.* als Postpaket schicken/bekommen; **B** **a ~ of land** ein Stück Land; ⇒ *also* **part** 1 A. ❷ *v.t.*, (*Brit.*) **-ll-** [zu Paketen] verpacken

**~ 'out** *v.t.* aufteilen ‹Land›

**~ 'up** *v.t.* einwickeln

**'parcel: ~ bomb** *n.* Paketbombe, *die;* **~ service** *n.* Paketdienst, *der*

**parch** /pɑ:tʃ/ ❶ *v.t.* **A** (*dry out*) ausdörren, austrocknen ‹Land, Boden›; **B** (*toast*) rösten ‹Kerne›. ❷ *v.i.* ‹Haut:› austrocknen

**parched** /pɑ:tʃt/ *adj.* ausgedörrt ‹Kehle, Land, Boden›; trocken ‹Lippen›; **I am [absolutely] ~ [with thirst]** meine Kehle ist wie ausgetrocknet

**parchment** /'pɑ:tʃmənt/ *n.* **A** (*skin*) Pergament, *das;* **B** (*manuscript*) Pergament, *das;* (*document*) Urkunde, *die*

**pardon** /'pɑ:dn/ ❶ *n.* **A** (*forgiveness*) Vergebung, *die* (*geh.*); Verzeihung, *die;* **ask sb.'s ~ for sth.** jmdn. wegen etw. um Verzeihung bitten; **no ~ will be given** es gibt kein Pardon; Pardon wird nicht gegeben; **B** **beg sb.'s ~:** jmdn. um Entschuldigung *od.* (*geh.*) Verzeihung bitten; **I beg your ~:** entschuldigen *od.* verzeihen Sie bitte; (*please repeat*) wie bitte? (*auch iron.*); **I do beg your ~:** entschuldigen Sie bitte vielmals; **beg ~** (*coll.*) Entschuldigung; Verzeihung; **~?** bitte?; **~!** Entschuldigung!; **C** (*Law*) **[free] ~:** Begnadigung, *die;* **grant sb. a ~:** jmdn. begnadigen.

❷ *v.t.* **A** (*forgive*) **~ sb.'s infidelity** jmdm. seine Untreue verzeihen; **~ sb. [for] sth.** jmdm. etw. verzeihen; **B** (*excuse*) entschuldigen; **~ my saying so, but ...:** entschuldigen Sie bitte, dass ich es so ausdrücke, aber...; **one could be ~ed for thinking ...** es wäre zu entschuldigen, wenn man dächte, ...; **~ 'me!** Entschuldigung!; **C** (*Law*) begnadigen

**pardonable** /'pɑ:dənəbl/ *adj.* verzeihlich; entschuldbar; verständlich ‹Sorge›

**pardonably** /'pɑ:dənəblɪ/ *adv.* verständlicherweise

**pare** /peə(r)/ *v.t.* **A** (*trim*) schneiden ‹Finger-, Zehennägel›; zurichten, beschneiden ‹Hufe›; **B** (*peel*) schälen ‹Apfel, Kartoffel›

**~ a'way** *v.t.* abschälen ‹Rinde›; (*fig.*) beschneiden, schmälern ‹Privileg, Profit usw.›

**~ 'down** *v.t.* (*fig.: reduce*) reduzieren, kürzen ‹Ausgaben, Kosten, Zuschuss›

**parent** /'peərənt/ *n.* **A** Elternteil, *der;* **~s** Eltern *Pl.;* **duties as a ~:** elterliche Pflichten; **B** (*Bot., Zool.*) Elter, *der od. das* (*fachspr.*); (*Bot. also*) Mutterpflanze, *die;* (*Zool. also*) Elterntier, *das;* **C** (*fig.: source*) Quelle, *die;* **D** *attrib.* Mutter‹pflanze, -baum, -zelle, -gesellschaft›; Stamm‹firma, -organisation, -organismus›; **~ ship** (*Naut.*) Mutterschiff, *das*

**parentage** /'peərəntɪdʒ/ *n.* (*lit. or fig.*) Herkunft, *die;* (*fig. also*) Ursprung, *der*

**parental** /pə'rentl/ *adj.* elterlich ‹Gewalt›; Eltern‹pflicht, -haus, -liebe›; ‹Abweisung› durch die Eltern; **~ approval/discipline** Zustimmung/disziplinierende Maßnahmen der Eltern

**parenthesis** /pə'renθɪsɪs/ *n.*, *pl.* **parentheses** /pə'renθɪsi:z/ **A** (*bracket*) runde Klammer; Parenthese, *die* (*fachspr.*); **B** (*word, clause, sentence*) Parenthese, *die* (*geh.*); Einschub, *der;* **in ~:** als Parenthese *od.* Einschub; (*fig.*) nebenbei; am Rande

**parenthetic** /pærən'θetɪk/, **parenthetical** /pærən'θetɪkl/ *adj.* eingeschoben; parenthetisch (*fachspr.*)

**parenthetically** /pærən'θetɪkəlɪ/ *adv.* parenthetisch; in Parenthese (*geh.*); (*fig.*) nebenbei, am Rande ‹hinzufügen, erwähnen, sagen›

**parenthood** /'peərənthʊd/ *n.*, *no pl.* Elternschaft, *die;* **joys of ~:** Elternfreuden *Pl.*

**'parents' evening** *n.* Elternabend, *der*

**parent-'teacher association** *n.* Eltern-Lehrer-Vertretung, *die*

**parer** /'peərə(r)/ *n.* Küchenmesser, *das;* **potato ~:** Kartoffelschälmesser, *das*

**par excellence** /pɑ:r 'eksəlãs/ *adv.* par excellence (*geh.*); schlechthin

**pariah** /pə'raɪə/ **[social] ~:** Paria, *der* (*geh.*); Ausgestoßene, *der/die*

**parietal** /pə'raɪətl/ *adj.* (*Anat.*) parietal (*fachspr.*); seitlich; **~ bone** Scheitelbein, *das*

**paring** /'peərɪŋ/ *n.* **A** (*action*) (*of fruit, vegetables*) Schälen, *das;* (*of nails*) Schneiden, *das;* (*of hoofs*) Zurichten, *das;* Beschneiden, *das;* **B** *usu. in pl.* (*peel, shaving, etc.*) Schalen, *die;* **nail ~s** abgeschnittene Nägel

**'paring knife** ⇒ **parer**

**Paris** /'pærɪs/ *pr. n.* ▶ **1626** Paris (*das*)

**parish** /'pærɪʃ/ *n.* Gemeinde, *die*

**parish: ~ 'church** *n.* Pfarrkirche, *die;* **~ 'council** *n.* (*Brit.*) Gemeinderat, *der;* **~ 'councillor** *n.* (*Brit.*) Gemeinderat, *der*/Gemeinderätin, *die*

**parishioner** /pə'rɪʃənə(r)/ *n.* Gemeinde[mit]glied, *das;* **the ~s** die Gemeinde

**parish: ~ 'priest** *n.* Gemeindepfarrer, *der;* **~-'pump** *adj.* (*Brit.*) krähwinklig (*abwertend*), provinziell (*abwertend*) ‹Angelegenheit›; **~-pump politics** Kirchturmpolitik, *die;* **~ 'register** *n.* Kirchenbuch, *das*

**Parisian** /pə'rɪzɪən/ ▶ **1626** ❶ *n.* Pariser, *der*/Pariserin, *die.* ❷ *adj.* Pariser ‹Mode›; **be ~** ‹Person:› Pariser/Pariserin sein

**parity** /'pærɪtɪ/ *n.* **A** (*equality*) Parität, *die* (*geh.*); Gleichheit, *die;* **have ~ in voting rights** das gleiche Stimmrecht haben; **~ of pay** gleiche Bezahlung; **B** (*Commerc.*) Parität, *die;* **the ~ of sterling against the dollar** die Pfund-Dollar-Parität

**park** /pɑ:k/ ❶ *n.* **A** Park, *der;* (*land kept in natural state*) Natur[schutz]park, *der;* **B** (*sports ground*) Sportplatz, *der;* (*stadium*) Stadion, *das;* (*Baseball, Footb.*) Spielfeld, *das;* **C** **amusement ~:** Vergnügungspark, *der;* **business ~:** Betriebsgelände, *das.* ⇒ *also* **industrial park; science park; theme park.**

❷ *v.i.* parken; **find somewhere to ~:** einen Parkplatz finden; **there's nowhere to ~:** da kann man nicht parken; (*all spaces are occupied*) da ist kein Parkplatz frei.

❸ *v.t.* **A** (*place, leave*) abstellen; parken ‹Kfz›; **the car was ~ed right in front of the house** das Auto parkte genau vor dem Haus; **a ~ed car** ein geparktes *od.* parkendes Auto; **B** (*coll.: leave, put*) deponieren ‹scherzh.›; **~ oneself [down]** (*coll.*) sich [hin]pflanzen (*ugs.*); **~ oneself on sb.** (*coll.*) sich bei jmdm. häuslich niederlassen (*ugs.*)

**parka** /'pɑ:kə/ *n.* Parka, *der*

**park-and-'ride** *n.* Park-and-ride-System, *das;* (*place*) Park-and-ride-Parkplatz, *der*

**parking** /'pɑ:kɪŋ/ *n.*, *no pl.*, *no indef. art.* Parken, *das;* **'No ~'** „Parken verboten"; **there is no ~ in the main street** auf der Hauptstraße ist Parkverbot; **'P~ for 500 cars'** „500 Parkplätze"

**parking: ~ attendant** *n.* ▶ **1261** Parkplatzwächter, *der*/-wächterin, *die;* **~ disc** *n.* Parkscheibe, *die;* **~ fine** *n.* Geldbuße für falsches Parken; **~ light** *n.* Parklicht, *das;* Parkleuchte, *die;* **~ lot** *n.* (*Amer.*) Parkplatz, *der;* **~ meter** *n.* Parkuhr, *die;* Parkometer, *das od. der;* **~ offence** *n.* Verstoß gegen das

P

Parkverbot; ~ **space** *n.* **A** *no pl.* Parkraum, *der;* **B** *(single space)* Platz zum Parken; Parkplatz, *der;* *(between other vehicles)* Parklücke, *die;* ~ **ticket** *n.* Strafzettel [für falsches Parken]

**Parkinson's** /'pɑːkɪnsənz/**:** ~ **disease** *n.* ▶ **1232** *(Med.)* Parkinson-Krankheit, *die;* ~ **law** *n.* *(joc.)* das parkinsonsche Gesetz

**park:** ~**-keeper** *n.* ▶ **1261** Parkwärter, *der*/-wärterin, *die;* ~**land** *n.* Parklandschaft, *die;* ~**way** *n.* *(Amer.)* [*für Lkw gesperrte*] Allee

**parky** /'pɑːkɪ/ *adj.* *(Brit. coll.)* frisch *(ugs.)*; kühl

**parlance** /'pɑːləns/ *n.* Ausdrucksweise, *die;* Sprache, *die;* **in common/legal/modern ~:** im allgemeinen/juristischen/modernen Sprachgebrauch

**parley** /'pɑːlɪ/ **1** *n.* Verhandlungen *Pl.* **2** *v.i.* verhandeln; **meet to ~:** sich zu Verhandlungen treffen

**parliament** /'pɑːləmənt/ *n.* Parlament, *das;* **[Houses of] P~** *(Brit.)* Parlament, *das;* **in P~:** im Parlament; **be before P~** ‹Antrag:› im Parlament beraten werden; **open P~:** das parlamentarische Sitzungsjahr eröffnen; ⇒ *also* **member** B

**parliamentarian** /pɑːləmən'teərɪən/ *n.* Parlamentarier, *der*/Parlamentarierin, *die*

**parliamentary** /pɑːlə'mentərɪ/ *adj.* parlamentarisch; Parlaments‹geschäfte, -wahlen, -reform›; **P~ approval** Zustimmung des Parlaments; ⇒ *also* **privilege** 1 A; **secretary** B

'**parlor car** *n.* *(Amer. Railw.)* Salonwagen, *der*

**parlour** *(Brit.; Amer.:* **parlor**) /'pɑːlə(r)/ *n.* **A** *(dated: sitting room)* Wohnzimmer, *das;* gute Stube *(veralt.)*; **B** *(in mansion, convent, inn)* Salon, *der;* **C** **ice cream ~:** Eisdiele, *die;* **beauty/massage ~:** Schönheits-/Massagesalon, *der*

**parlour:** ~ **game** *n.* Gesellschaftsspiel, *das;* ~**maid** *n.* *(Hist.)* Hausangestellte *od.* -gehilfin, *die;* ~ **tricks** *n. pl.* gesellschaftliche Spielchen

**parlous** /'pɑːləs/ *adj.* *(arch./joc.)* kritisch, bedenklich, Besorgnis erregend ‹Zustand›; kritisch ‹Zeit›

**Parmesan** /'pɑːmɪzæn, pɑːmɪ'zæn/ *adj., n.* ~ **[cheese]** Parmesan[käse], *der*

**parochial** /pə'rəʊkɪəl/ *adj.* **A** *(narrow)* krähwinklig *(abwertend)*; eng ‹Horizont›; **be ~ in one's outlook** einen engen Horizont haben; **B** *(Eccl.)* Gemeinde-; parochial *(fachspr.)*

**parochialism** /pə'rəʊkɪəlɪzm/ *n.* Provinzialismus, *der (abwertend)*; Engstirnigkeit, *die (abwertend)*

**parodist** /'pærədɪst/ *n.* Parodist, *der*/Parodistin, *die;* **be a ~ of sth.** etw. parodieren

**parody** /'pærədɪ/ **1** *n.* **A** *(humorous imitation)* Parodie, *die,* *(geh.)* Persiflage, *die* **(of** auf + *Akk.*); **B** *(feeble imitation)* Abklatsch, *der (abwertend)*; *(of justice)* Verhöhnung, *die.* **2** *v.t.* parodieren; persiflieren *(geh.)*

**parole** /pə'rəʊl/ **1** *n.* *(conditional release)* bedingter Straferlass *(Rechtsw.)*; *(word of honour)* Ehrenwort, *das;* **he was released** *or* **let out on ~/he is on ~:** er wurde auf Bewährung entlassen; **he's on three months' ~:** er hat drei Monate Bewährung. **2** *v.t.* *(Law)* ~ **sb.** jmdm. seine Strafe bedingt erlassen

**paroxysm** /'pærəksɪzm/ *n.* Krampf, *der;* *(fit, convulsion)* Anfall, *der* **(of** von); Paroxysmus, *der (Med., Geol.)*; ~ **of rage/laughter** Wut-/Lachanfall, *der;* **burst into ~s of laughter** einen Lachkrampf bekommen; **in a ~ of grief** außer sich vor Trauer

**parquet** /'pɑːkɪ, 'pɑːkeɪ/ *n.* ~ **[flooring]** Parkett, *das;* ~ **floor** Parkettfußboden, *der*

**parricide** /'pærɪsaɪd/ ⇒ **patricide**

**parrot** /'pærət/ **1** *n.* **A** Papagei, *der;* **I was as sick as a ~** *(coll.)* mir war zum Kotzen zumute *(salopp)*; **B** *(fig.: person)* Nachplapperer, *der*/-plapperin, *die (abwertend)*. **2** *v.t.* nachplappern *(abwertend)*; ~ **sb.** jmdm. alles nachplappern

'**parrot-fashion** *adv.* papageienhaft, wie ein Papagei ‹wiederholen›; stur, mechanisch ‹lernen›; **repeat things ~:** [papageienhaft *od.* wie ein Papagei] nachplappern *od.* nachschwatzen

**parry** /'pærɪ/ **1** *v.t.* *(Boxing)* abwehren ‹Faustschlag›; *(Fencing; also fig.)* parieren ‹Fechthieb, Frage›. **2** *n.* *(Boxing)* Abwehr, *die;* *(Fencing)* Parade, *die;* **make a ~** *(Boxing)* abwehren; *(Fencing)* parieren

**parse** /pɑːz/ *v.t.* *(Ling.)* grammatisch beschreiben ‹Wort›; grammatisch analysieren ‹Satz›

**parsimonious** /pɑːsɪ'məʊnɪəs/ *adj.* sparsam; *(niggardly)* geizig; *(sparing)* sparsam; **be ~ with sth.** mit etw. geizen

**parsimony** /'pɑːsɪmənɪ/ *n.* *(meanness)* Geiz, *der;* *(carefulness)* Sparsamkeit, *die*

**parsley** /'pɑːslɪ/ *n., no pl., no indef. art.* Petersilie, *die*

**parsley:** ~ **butter** *n.* Petersilienbutter, *die;* ~ '**sauce** *n.* Petersiliensauce, *die*

**parsnip** /'pɑːsnɪp/ *n.* Gemeiner Pastinak, *der;* Pastinake, *die;* ⇒ *also* **butter** 2

**parson** /'pɑːsn/ *n.* *(vicar, rector)* Pfarrer, *der;* *(coll.: any clergyman)* Geistliche, *der;* Pfaffe, *der (abwertend)*; ⇒ *also* **nose** 1 A

**parsonage** /'pɑːsənɪdʒ/ *n.* Pfarrhaus, *das*

**part** /pɑːt/ **1** *n.* **A** Teil, *der;* *(element of history, family, character)* Bestandteil, *der;* ~ **of the cake/newspaper** *etc.* ein Teil des Kuchens/der Zeitung *usw.;* **the greater ~:** der größte Teil; der Großteil; **four-~:** vierteilig ‹Serie›; **the hottest ~ of the day** die heißesten Stunden des Tages; **accept ~ of the blame** einen Teil der Schuld auf sich *(Akk.)* nehmen; **he deserves no small ~ of the credit for this achievement** an diesem Erfolg hat er keinen geringen Anteil; **for the most ~:** größtenteils; zum größten Teil; **in ~:** teilweise; **in large ~:** groß[en]teils; **in ~s** zum Teil; ~ **and parcel** wesentlicher Bestandteil; **the funny ~ of it was that he ...:** das Komische daran war, dass er ...; **it's [all] ~ of the fun/job** *etc.* das gehört [mit] dazu; **be** *or* **form ~ of sth.** zu etw. gehören; **be very much a ~ of sth.** wesentlicher Bestandteil von etw. sein; **the affected ~:** die befallene Partie; ⇒ *also* **better** 1; **B** *(of machine or other apparatus)* [Einzel]teil, *das;* **spare/machine ~:** Ersatz-/Maschinenteil, *das;* **C** *(share)* Anteil, *der;* **I want no ~ in this** ich möchte damit nichts zu tun haben; **what's your ~ in all this?** was hast du mit all dem zu tun?; **D** *(duty)* Aufgabe, *die;* **do one's ~:** seinen Teil *od.* seine Pflicht *od.* das Seine tun; **E** *(Theatre: character, words)* Rolle, *die;* Part, *der (geh.)*; *(copy)* Rollentext, *der;* *(fig.)* **dress the ~:** die angemessene Kleidung tragen; **play a noble ~:** nobel handeln; **play a [great/considerable] ~** *(contribute)* eine [wichtige] Rolle spielen; **play a ~** *(act deceitfully)* schauspielern *(abwertend)*; sich verstellen; ⇒ *also* **act** 2 B; **look** 1 E; **F** *(Mus.)* Part, *der;* Partie, *die;* Stimme, *die;* **six-~:** sechsstimmig ‹Fuge, Harmonie›; **G** *usu. in pl.* *(region)* Gegend, *die;* *(of continent, world)* Teil, *der;* **be in foreign ~s** im Ausland sein; **I am a stranger in these ~s** ich kenne mich hier nicht aus; **in this** *or* **our/your ~ of the world** hierzulande/bei Ihnen; **H** *(side)* Partei, *die;* **take sb.'s ~:** jmds. *od.* für jmdn. Partei ergreifen; **for my ~:** für mein[en] Teil; **on the ~ of** seitens (+ *Gen.*) *(Papierdt.)*; vonseiten (+ *Gen.*); **on my/your** *etc.* **~:** meiner-/deinerseits *usw;* **I** *pl.* *(abilities)* **a man of [many] ~s** ein [vielseitig] begabter *od.* befähigter Mann; **J** *(Ling.)* ~ **of speech** Wortart *od.* -klasse, *die;* ⇒ *also* **principal parts**; **K** **take [no] ~ [in sth.]** sich [an etw. *(Dat.)*] [nicht] beteiligen; [bei etw.] [nicht] mitmachen; **those taking ~ were ...:** teilgenommen haben ...; **L** **take sth. in good ~:** etw. nicht übel nehmen; **M** *(Amer.)* ⇒ **parting** 1 B.

**2** *adv.* teils; **an alloy which is ~ copper, ~ zinc** eine Legierung aus Kupfer und Zink; ~ **... [and] ~ ...:** teils ..., teils ...

**3** *v.t.* **A** *(divide into parts)* teilen; scheiteln ‹Haar›; **B** *(separate)* trennen; **a fool and his money are soon ~ed** *(prov.)* wer nicht aufpasst, dem rinnt das Geld durch die Finger; **till death us do ~** *(in marriage vow)* bis dass der Tod uns scheidet; ⇒ *also* **company** A.

**4** *v.i.* **A** *(divide into parts)* ‹Menge:› eine Gasse bilden; ‹Wolken:› sich teilen; ‹Vorhang:› sich öffnen; *(become divided or broken)* ‹Seil, Tau, Kette:› reißen; ‹Lippen:› sich öffnen; **B** *(separate)* ‹Wege, Personen:› sich trennen; ~ **from sb./sth.** sich von jmdm./etw. trennen; **let us ~ friends** wir wollen als Freunde auseinander gehen; ~ **with** sich trennen von ‹Besitz, Geld›; verzichten auf ‹Kontrolle›

**partake** /pɑː'teɪk/ *v.i., forms as* **take** 2 *(formal)* **A** ~ **of** *(eat)* zu sich nehmen, einnehmen *(geh.)* ‹Kost, Mahlzeit›; *(joc.)* sich einverleiben *(scherzh.)*; **B** *(share)* ~ **in** sich *(Dat.)* teilen ‹Beute›; teilhaben an (+ *Dat.*), teilen ‹jmds. Schicksal, Freuden›

**partaken** ⇒ **partake**

**parterre** /pɑː'teə(r)/ *n.* **A** *(Hort.)* Parterreanlage, *die;* **B** *(Amer. Theatre)* Parterre, *das*

**part ex'change** **1** *n.* **accept sth. in ~ for sth.** etw. für etw. in Zahlung nehmen; **sell sth. in ~:** etw. in Zahlung geben. **2** *v.t.* in Zahlung geben

**parthenogenesis** /pɑːθɪnə'dʒenɪsɪs/ *n., no pl.* *(Biol.)* Parthenogenese, *die (fachspr.)*; Jungfernzeugung, *die*

**Parthian shot** /pɑːθɪən 'ʃɒt/ *n.* *(remark)* spitze Schlussbemerkung; *(action)* Abschiedsgeste, *die*

**partial** /'pɑːʃl/ *adj.* **A** *(biased, unfair)* voreingenommen; parteiisch ‹Urteil›; **B** **be/not be ~ to sb./sth.** *(like/dislike)* eine Schwäche/keine besondere Vorliebe für jmdn./etw. haben; **C** *(incomplete)* partiell ‹Lähmung, Sonnen-, Mondfinsternis›; teilweise ‹Verlust, Misserfolg›; Mit‹verantwortung, -eigentümer usw.›; **a ~ success** ein Teilerfolg

**partiality** /pɑːʃɪ'ælɪtɪ/ *n.* **A** *(fondness)* Vorliebe, *die;* *(for alcohol etc.)* Schwäche, *die;* **B** *(bias)* Voreingenommenheit, *die;* Parteilichkeit, *die;* **show ~:** parteiisch *od.* voreingenommen sein

**partially** /'pɑːʃəlɪ/ *adv.* zum Teil; teilweise

**participant** /pɑː'tɪsɪpənt/ *n.* *(actively involved)* Beteiligte, *der/die* **(in** an + *Dat.*); *(in arranged event)* Teilnehmer, *der*/Teilnehmerin, *die* **(in** an + *Dat.*)

**participate** /pɑː'tɪsɪpeɪt/ *v.i.* *(be actively involved)* sich beteiligen **(in** an + *Dat.*); *(in arranged event)* teilnehmen **(in** an + *Dat.*); *(have part or share)* partizipieren *(geh.)*, teilhaben **(in** an + *Dat.*)

**participation** /pɑːtɪsɪ'peɪʃn/ *n.* *(active involvement)* Beteiligung, *die* **(in** an + *Dat.*); *(in arranged event)* Teilnahme, *die* **(in** bei, an + *Dat.*); **worker ~:** industrielle Mitbestimmung; **audience ~:** Publikumsbeteiligung, *die*

**participator** /pɑː'tɪsɪpeɪtə(r)/ *n.* Beteiligte, *der/die;* **be a ~ in sth.** sich an etw. *(Dat.)* beteiligen

**participatory** /pɑː'tɪsɪpeɪtərɪ/ *adj.* ‹Fernsehsendung, Theaterstück› mit Zuschauerbeteiligung; ‹Radiosendung› mit Hörerbeteiligung; *(Polit.)* mit Bürgerbeteiligung *nachgestellt*

**participial** /pɑːtɪ'sɪpɪəl/ *adj.* *(Ling.)* partizipial; Partizipial-

**participle** /'pɑːtɪsɪpl/ *n.* *(Ling.)* Partizip, *das;* Mittelwort, *das;* **present/past ~:** Partizip Präsens/Perfekt; Mittelwort der Gegenwart/Vergangenheit

**particle** /'pɑːtɪkl/ *n.* **A** *(tiny portion; also Phys.)* Teilchen, *das;* *(of sand)* Körnchen, *das;* **B** *(fig.)* Quäntchen, *das (geh.)*; *(of sense, truth)* Fünkchen, *das;* *(of truth also)* Körnchen, *das;* **C** *(Ling.)* Partikel, *die*

**particoloured** *(Brit.; Amer.:* **particolored**) /pɑːtɪ'kʌləd/ *adj.* bunt

**particular** /pə'tɪkjʊlə(r)/ **1** *adj.* **A** *(special; more than ordinary)* besonder...; **which ~ place do you have in mind?** an welchen Ort denkst du speziell?; **here in ~:** besonders hier; **nothing/anything [in] ~:** nichts/irgendetwas Besonderes; **what in ~ made you so angry?** was genau hat dich so geärgert?; **B** *(individual)* **each ~ hair** jedes [einzelne] Haar; **in his ~ case** in seinem [besonderen] Fall; **one ~ example of each type** ein Beispiel für jede Sorte; **C** *(fussy, fastidious)* genau; eigen *(landsch.)*; **I am not ~:** es ist mir gleich; **be ~ about**

**sth.** es mit etw. genau nehmen; in etw. (*Dat.*) eigen sein (*landsch.*); **be ~ in one's habits** in allem genau *od.* (*landsch.*) eigen sein; **be ~ about what one eats** wählerisch im Essen sein; **D** (*detailed*) detailliert, ausführlich ‹Bericht›; eingehend, genau, gründlich ‹Kenntnis›.
❷ *n.* **A** *in pl.* (*details*) Einzelheiten; Details; (*of person*) Personalien *Pl.*; (*of incident*) nähere Umstände; **B** (*detail*) Einzelheit, *die;* Detail, *das;* **describe sth. in every ~:** etw. in allen Einzelheiten beschreiben

**particularize** (**particularise**) /pəˈtɪkjʊləraɪz/ ❶ *v.t.* spezifizieren. ❷ *v.i.* ins Detail gehen

**particularly** /pəˈtɪkjʊləlɪ/ *adv.* **A** (*especially*) besonders; **B** (*specifically*) speziell; insbesondere

**parting** /ˈpɑːtɪŋ/ ❶ *n.* **A** (*leave-taking*) [**final**] **~:** Trennung, *die;* Abschied, *der;* **B** (*Brit.: in hair*) Scheitel, *der;* **side ~:** Seitenscheitel, *der;* **C** **~ of the ways** (*of road*) Gabelung, *die;* (*fig.: critical point*) Scheideweg, *der;* **we came to a ~ of the ways** (*fig.*) unsere Wege trennten sich. ❷ *attrib. adj.* Abschieds-; **~ shot** Schlussbemerkung, *die;* **~ glance/advice** Blick/Ratschlag zum Abschied

**partisan** /pɑːtɪˈzæn, ˈpɑːtɪzæn/ ❶ *n.* **A** (*adherent*) Anhänger, *der*/Anhängerin, *die;* (*of party also*) Parteigänger, *der*/-gängerin, *die* (*oft abwertend*); (*of cause also*) Befürworter, *der*/Befürworterin, *die;* **B** (*Mil.*) Partisan, *der*/Partisanin, *die.* ❷ *adj.* **A** (*often derog.: biased*) voreingenommen, parteiisch ‹Ansatz, Urteil, Versuch›; Partei‹politik, -geist›; **B** (*Mil.*) Partisanen‹gruppe, -krieg, -aktivität›

**partisanship** /pɑːtɪˈzænʃɪp, ˈpɑːtɪzænʃɪp/ *n., no pl.* Parteinahme, *die;* Parteilichkeit, *die;* Voreingenommenheit, *die*

**partita** /pɑːˈtiːtə/ *n.* (*Mus.*) Partita, *die;* Suite, *die*

**partition** /pɑːˈtɪʃn/ ❶ *n.* **A** (*division*) (*of text etc.*) Unterteilung, *die* (**into** in + *Akk.*); (*between subjects*) Trennung, *die;* **B** (*Polit.*) Teilung, *die;* **C** (*room divider*) Trennwand, *die;* **D** (*section of hall or library*) Abteilung, *die;* Bereich, *der;* **E** (*Law: of estate etc.*) Aufteilung, *die.* ❷ *v.t.* **A** (*divide*) aufteilen ‹Land, Zimmer›; [unter]teilen ‹Zimmer›; **B** (*Polit.*) teilen ‹Land›

**~ 'off** *v.t.* abteilen ‹Teil, Raum›

**partitive** /ˈpɑːtɪtɪv/ (*Ling.*) *adj.* partitiv ‹Wort, Nomen›

**partly** /ˈpɑːtlɪ/ *adv.* zum Teil; teilweise; **he was ~ responsible for the accident** er war mitschuldig an dem Unglück; **~ ... [and] ~ ...:** teils ..., teils ...

**partner** /ˈpɑːtnə(r)/ ❶ *n.* Partner, *der*/Partnerin, *die;* **~ in crime** Komplize, *der*/Komplizin, *die* (*abwertend*); **business ~:** Geschäftspartner, *der*/-partnerin, *die;* **be a ~ in a firm** Teilhaber/-haberin einer Firma sein; **junior/senior ~:** Junior, *der*/Senior, *der;* [**dancing**] **~:** Tanzpartner, *der*/-partnerin, *die;* **take your ~s** bitte Aufstellung nehmen; **tennis/croquet ~:** Tennis-/Krocketpartner, *der*/-partnerin, *die;* **~ [in marriage]** Ehepartner, *der*/-partnerin, *die;* ⇒ *also* **sleeping partner**.
❷ *v.t.* **A** (*make a ~*) **~ sb. with sb.** jmdn. mit jmdm. zusammenbringen; **be ~ed with sb.** jmds. Partner/Partnerin sein; **B** (*be ~ of*) **~ sb.** jmds. Partner/Partnerin sein; **~ sb. at tennis/in the dance** mit jmdm. Tennis spielen/tanzen

**partnership** /ˈpɑːtnəʃɪp/ *n.* **A** (*association*) Partnerschaft, *die;* **they were a marvellous ~:** sie waren großartige Partner; **B** (*Commerc.*) **business ~:** [Personen]gesellschaft, *die;* **go** *or* **enter into ~ with sb.** mit jmdm. eine [Personen]gesellschaft gründen; **leave the ~:** aus der Gesellschaft ausscheiden

**partook** ⇒ **partake**

**part: ~-owner** *n.* Mitbesitzer, *der*/-besitzerin, *die;* **~ 'payment** *n.* **A** ⇒ **part exchange** 1; **B** (*sum*) Anzahlung, *die*

**partridge** /ˈpɑːtrɪdʒ/ *n., pl. same or* **~s** Rebhuhn, *das*

**part: ~-song** *n.* mehrstimmiges Lied; **~ 'time** *n.* **some employees were put on ~ time** einige Beschäftigte mussten kurzarbeiten; **~-time** ❶ /ˈ--/ *adj.* Teilzeit‹arbeit, -arbeiter›; **be engaged on a ~-time basis to teach French** als Teilzeitlehrer/-lehrerin für Französisch eingestellt sein; **he is only ~-time** er ist nur eine Teilzeitkraft; ❷ /-ˈ-/ *adv.* stundenweise, halbtags ‹arbeiten, studieren›; **work ~-time** als Teilzeitkraft beschäftigt sein; **~-'timer** *n.* Teilzeitkraft, *die;* **study as a ~-timer** halbtags *od.* stundenweise studieren

**parturition** /pɑːtjʊˈrɪʃn/ *n.* (*Physiol.*) Partus, *der* (*fachspr.*); Geburt, *die*

**part: ~-way** *adv.* **~-way down the slope he slipped** nachdem er ein Stück des Hangs bewältigt hatte, rutschte er aus; **we were ~-way through the tunnel** wir hatten ein Stück des Tunnels hinter uns; **go ~-way towards meeting sb.'s demands** jmds. Forderungen (*Dat.*) teilweise *od.* halbwegs entsprechen; **~-way through her speech** mitten in ihrer Rede; **~-work** *n.* (*Publishing*) Lieferungswerk, *das;* Partwork, *das*

**party** /ˈpɑːtɪ/ *n.* **A** (*group united in a cause etc.; Polit., Law*) Partei, *die; attrib.* Partei‹apparat, -versammlung, -mitglied, -politik, -politiker usw.›; **opposing ~:** Gegenpartei, *die;* gegnerische Partei; **the P~:** die Partei; **~ loyalty** Treue zur Partei; **B** (*group*) Gruppe, *die;* **a ~ of tourists** eine Touristengruppe; **hunting ~:** Jagdgesellschaft, *die;* **tennis ~:** Gruppe von Tennisspielern; **C** (*social gathering*) Party, *die;* Fete, *die* (*ugs.*); (*more formal*) Gesellschaft, *die;* **office ~:** Betriebsfest, *das;* ⇒ *also* **birthday**; **dinner party**; **tea party**; **D** (*participator*) Beteiligte, *der/die;* **be [a] ~ in** *or* **to sth.** sich an etw. (*Dat.*) beteiligen; **parties to an agreement/a dispute** Parteien bei einem Abkommen/streitende Parteien; **the guilty ~:** der/die Schuldige; ⇒ *also* **third party**; **E** (*coll.: person*) Figur, *die* (*salopp*); **he's a funny old ~:** er ist ein komischer Kauz (*ugs.*)

**party: ~-coloured** ⇒ **particoloured**; **~ game** *n.* Gesellschaftsspiel, *das;* **~ line** *n.* **A** /ˈ---/ (*Teleph.*) Gemeinschafts-, Sammelanschluss, *der;* **B** /--ˈ-/ (*Polit.*) Parteilinie, *die;* **what is the ~ line on this problem?** welche Linie verfolgt die Partei bei diesem Problem?; **~-'liner** *n.* (*Polit.*) linientreues Parteimitglied; **~ piece** *n.* **this song was my ~ piece** dieses Lied musste ich auf jeder Gesellschaft zum Besten geben; **~ po'litical** *adj.* parteipolitisch ‹Propaganda, Sendung, Ziele, Fragen etc.›; **~ political broadcast** parteipolitische Sendung; **a Labour ~ political broadcast** eine Sendung der Labour Party; **~ 'politics** *n.* Parteipolitik, *die;* **~ pooper** /ˈpɑːtɪ puːpə(r)/ *n.* (*Amer. coll.*) Partymuffel, *der;* **~ spirit** *n.* **A** /--ˈ--/ (*Polit.*) Parteigeist, *der;* **B** /ˈ----/ (*festive atmosphere*) Partystimmung, *die;* **get the ~ spirit going** die Party in Schwung *od.* Schwung in die Party bringen (*ugs.*); **~ trick** *n.* Trick, der auf Partys Stimmung erzeugt; **~ wall** *n.* Mauer zum Nachbargrundstück/-gebäude; Kommunmauer, *die* (*Rechtsspr.*)

**parvenu** /ˈpɑːvənuː/ ❶ *n.* Parvenü, *der* (*geh.*); Emporkömmling, *der.* ❷ *adj.* arriviert; neureich; parvenühaft ‹Dreistigkeit›

**pascal** /ˈpæskl/ *n.* (*Phys.*) Pascal, *das*

**paschal** /ˈpæskl/ *adj.* **A** (*of Jewish Passover*) Passah-; **~ lamb** Passah[lamm], *das;* (*fig.*) Lamm Gottes; Agnus Dei (*fachspr.*); **B** (*of Easter*) Oster-

**pash** /pæʃ/ *n.* (*dated. coll.*) Schulmädchenschwärmerei, *die;* (*person*) Schwarm, *der* (*ugs.*); **have a ~ for sb.** für jmdn. schwärmen

**pasha** /ˈpɑːʃə/ *n.* (*Hist.*) Pascha, *der*

**paso doble** /pɑːsəʊ ˈdəʊbleɪ/ *n.* (*Dancing*) Paso doble, *der*

**pasque flower** *n.* Kuhschelle, *die*

**pass** /pɑːs/ ❶ *n.* **A** (*passing of an examination*) bestandene Prüfung; **be awarded a ~ with distinction** ein Examen mit Auszeichnung bestehen; **get a ~ in maths** die Mathematikprüfung bestehen; '**~**' (*mark or grade*) Ausreichend, *das;* [Note] Vier, *die;* **B** (*written permission*) Ausweis, *der;* Erlaubnisschein, *der;* (*for going into or out of a place also*) Passierschein, *der;* (*Mil.: for leave*) Urlaubsschein, *der;* (*for free transportation*) Freifahrschein, *der;* (*for free admission*) Freikarte, *die;* **C** (*critical position*) Notlage, *die;* kritische Lage; **things have come to a pretty ~ [when ...]** es muss schon weit gekommen sein[, wenn ...]; **D** (*Football*) Pass, *der* (*fachspr.*); Ballabgabe, *die;* (*Tennis*) ⇒ **passing shot**; (*Fencing*) Ausfall, *der;* **make a ~ to a player** [den Ball] zu einem Spieler passen (*fachspr.*) *od.* abgeben; **make a ~ over** (*Aeronaut.*) überfliegen; **E** (*by conjuror, hypnotist*) **~ [of the hands]** Handbewegung, *die;* **F** **make a ~ at sb.** (*fig. coll.: amorously*) jmdm. gegenüber Annäherungsversuche machen; jmdn. anmachen (*ugs.*); **G** (*in mountains*) Pass, *der;* **H** (*strategic entrance into a country*) strategisch wichtiger Zugang; Schlüsselstellung, *die;* **I** (*Cards*) Passen, *das.*
❷ *v.i.* **A** (*move onward*) ‹Prozession:› ziehen; ‹Wasser:› fließen; ‹Gas:› strömen; (*fig.*) ‹Redner:› übergehen (**to** zu); **~ further along** *or* **down the bus, please!** bitte weiter durchgehen!; **B** (*go*) passieren; **~ through** ‹Blut:› fließen durch ‹Organ›; ‹Zug, Reisender:› fahren durch ‹Land›; ‹Faden:› gehen durch ‹Nadelöhr›; **~ over** (*in plane*) überfliegen ‹Ort›; **a cloud ~ed over the sun** eine Wolke schob sich vor die Sonne; **let sb. ~:** jmdn. durchlassen *od.* passieren lassen; **C** (*be transported, lit. or fig.*) kommen; **~ into history/oblivion** in die Geschichte eingehen/in Vergessenheit geraten; **messages ~ed between them** Nachrichten wurden zwischen ihnen ausgetauscht; **the title/property ~es to sb.** der Titel/Besitz geht auf jmdn. über; **D** (*change*) wechseln; **~ from one state/stage to another** von einem Zustand in einen anderen/von einem Stadium in ein anderes übergehen; **E** (*go by*) ‹Fußgänger:› vorbeigehen; ‹Fahrer, Fahrzeug:› vorbeifahren; ‹Prozession:› vorbeiziehen; ‹Zeit, Sekunde:› vergehen; (*by chance*) ‹Person, Fahrzeug:› vorbeikommen; **let sb./a car ~:** jmdn./ein Auto vorbeilassen (*ugs.*); **make it impossible for sb./sth. to ~:** jmdm./einer Sache den Weg versperren; **he said hello as he ~ed** er grüßte im Vorbeigehen; **~ unheeded** ‹Bemerkung:› keine Beachtung finden; **she would not let this ~ without comment** das wollte sie nicht unkommentiert [im Raum stehen] lassen; **F** (*be accepted as adequate*) durchgehen; hingehen; **let that/it/the matter ~:** das/es/die Sache durch- *od.* hingehen lassen; **G** (*come to an end*) vorbeigehen; ‹Fieber:› zurückgehen, [ab]sinken; ‹Ärger, Zorn, Sturm:› sich legen; ‹Gewitter, Unwetter:› vorüberziehen; ‹Königreich, Volk:› untergehen; **H** (*formal/arch. euphem.: die*) ableben (*veralt. geh.*); **~ out of this world** aus dieser Welt gehen *od.* scheiden (*geh. verhüll.*); **I** (*happen*) passieren; (*between persons*) vorfallen; **bring/come to ~** (*arch.*) bewirken/sich zutragen *od.* begeben (*geh.*); **J** (*be known*) **~ by** *or* **under the name of White** unter dem Namen White bekannt sein; **K** (*be accepted*) durchgehen (**as** als, **for** für); **~ as currency** als Währung akzeptiert werden; **L** (*be sanctioned*) ‹Gesetzentwurf:› angenommen werden, durchgehen; **M** (*satisfy examiner*) bestehen; **let ~** ‹Zensor:› freigeben ‹Film, Buch, Theaterstück›; **N** (*circulate, be current*) im Umlauf sein; **O** (*Chess*) **~ed pawn** Freibauer, *der;* **P** (*Cards*) passen; **[I] ~!** [ich] passe! ⇒ *also* **crowd** 1 A; **ship** 1 A.
❸ *v.t.* **A** (*move past*) ‹Fußgänger:› vorbeigehen an (+ *Dat.*); ‹Fahrer, Fahrzeug:› vorbeifahren an (+ *Dat.*); ‹Prozession:› vorbeiziehen an (+ *Dat.*); (*by chance*) ‹Person, Fahrzeug:› vorbeikommen an (+ *Dat.*); **B** (*overtake*) vorbeifahren an (+ *Dat.*) ‹Fahrzeug, Person›; **C** (*cross*) überschreiten ‹Schwelle, feindliche Linien, Grenze, Marke›; nehmen, überwinden ‹Hindernis›; **D** (*be approved by*) ‹Film:› passieren ‹Zensur›; ‹Gesetzentwurf:› verabschiedet werden von ‹Parlament›; (*reach standard in*) bestehen ‹Prüfung›; (*satisfy requirements of*) kommen durch ‹Kontrolle›; **E** (*approve*) verabschieden ‹Gesetzentwurf›; annehmen ‹Vorschlag›; ‹Zoll:› abfertigen ‹Gepäck›;

P

‹Zensor:› freigeben ‹Film, Buch, Theaterstück›; bestehen lassen ‹Prüfungskandidaten›; ~ **sb. as fit** ‹Arzt:› jmdn. für gesund erklären; **F** (*be too great for*) überschreiten, übersteigen ‹Auffassungsgabe, Verständnis›; **G** (*move*) bringen; ~ **one's hand across one's face** sich mit der Hand über das Gesicht streichen; ~ **a rope/thread through a ring/the eye of a needle** ein Seil/einen Faden durch einen Ring/ein Nadelöhr ziehen *od.* führen; ~ **a duster over the furniture** mit einem Staubtuch über die Möbel wischen; ~ **meat through a mincer/tomatoes through a sieve** Fleisch durch einen Fleischwolf drehen/Tomaten durch ein Sieb streichen; ~ **one's eye over a letter** *etc.* einen Brief *usw.* überfliegen; **H** (*Footb. etc.*) passen (*fachspr.*) (**to** zu); abgeben (**to** an + *Akk.*); zuspielen (**to** *Dat.*); **I** (*spend*) verbringen ‹Leben, Zeit, Tag›; **J** (*hand*) ~ **sb. sth.** jmdm. etw. reichen *od.* geben; **would you ~ the salt, please?** gibst *od.* reichst du mir bitte das Salz?; ~ **sth. to another department** etw. an eine andere Abteilung weitergeben; ⇒ *also* **around** 1 B; **K** (*cause to circulate*) in Umlauf bringen ‹Geld›; **L** (*Mil.*) ~ **in review** defilieren *od.* vorbeimarschieren lassen ‹Truppen›; (*fig.*) Revue passieren lassen; **M** (*utter*) fällen, verkünden ‹Urteil›; machen ‹Bemerkung›; ~ **censure on sth.** etw. tadeln; **N** (*discharge*) lassen ‹Wasser›; ~ **blood** (*from the bowels*) Blut im Stuhl haben; (*by spitting*) Blut spucken; (*by coughing*) Blut husten; (*in urine*) Blut im Urin haben. ⇒ *also* **buck**[2]; **hat** B; **muster** 1 A; **time** 1 B

~ **a'way** ❶ *v.i.* **A** (*cease to exist*) ‹Reich:› untergehen; **B** (*euphem.: die*) verscheiden (*geh.*); ~ **away in one's sleep** im Schlaf dahingehen (*geh. verhüll.*). ❷ *v.t.* verbringen ‹Zeit[raum], Abend›

~ **by** ❶ /'--/ *v.t.* **A** (*go past*) ‹Fußgänger:› vorbeigehen an (+ *Dat.*); ‹Fahrer, Fahrzeug:› vorbeifahren an (+ *Dat.*); ‹Prozession:› vorbeiziehen an (+ *Dat.*); (*by chance*) ‹Person, Fahrzeug:› vorbeikommen an (+ *Dat.*); **B** (*omit, disregard*) übergehen. ❷ /-'-/ *v.i.* ‹Fußgänger:› vorbeigehen; ‹Fahrer, Fahrzeug:› vorbeifahren; ‹Prozession:› vorbeiziehen; (*by chance*) ‹Person, Fahrzeug:› vorbeikommen; ⇒ *also* **side** 1 E

~ **'down** ⇒ **hand down** A, C

~ **for** *v.t.* durchgehen für; gehalten werden für

~ **'off** ❶ *v.t.* **A** (*represent falsely*) ausgeben (**as, for** als); als echt ausgeben ‹Fälschung›; **B** (*turn attention away from*) hinweggehen über (+ *Akk.*). ❷ *v.i.* **A** (*disappear gradually*) ‹Schock, Schmerz, Hochstimmung:› abklingen, sich legen; **B** (*take place, be carried through*) verlaufen

~ **'on** ❶ *v.i.* **A** (*proceed*) fortfahren; weitermachen; ~ **on to sth.** zu etw. übergehen; **B** (*euphem.: die*) die Augen schließen *od.* zumachen (*verhüll.*). ❷ *v.t.* weitergeben (**to** an + *Akk.*); vererben ‹Besitz, Krankheit›

~ **out** ❶ /-'-/ *v.i.* **A** (*faint*) ohnmächtig werden (**with** vor + *Dat.*); **B** (*complete military training*) seine militärische Ausbildung abschließen. ❷ /'--/ *v.t.* bekannt geben, bekannt machen ‹Informationen›

~ **'over** ❶ *v.t.* übergehen; überschreiten ‹Grenze, Schwelle›; ~ **sth. over in silence** etw. stillschweigend übergehen; ⇒ *also* ~ 2 B. ❷ *v.i.* (*euphem.: die*) die Augen schließen *od.* zumachen (*verhüll.*)

~ **through** ❶ /'--/ *v.t.* durchmachen ‹schwierige Zeit, Krankheit›; durchleben ‹Augenblick›; ‹Buch:› gehen durch ‹Hände›; **it ~ed through my mind** es ging mir durch den Sinn; ⇒ *also* ~ 2 B. ❷ /-'-/ *v.i.* durchreisen; **be just ~ing through** nur auf der Durchreise sein

~ **'up** *v.t.* sich (*Dat.*) entgehen lassen, ungenutzt vorübergehen lassen ‹Gelegenheit›; ablehnen, ausschlagen ‹Angebot, Einladung›

**passable** /'pɑ:səbl/ *adj.* **A** (*acceptable*) passabel, annehmbar ‹Versuch, Arbeit, Essen, Porträt›; **B** (*in condition to be crossed, traversed*) passierbar, befahrbar ‹Straße›

**passably** /'pɑ:səblɪ/ *adv.* passabel; annehmbar; einigermaßen ‹höflich, angenehm, gut aussehend›

**passage** /'pæsɪdʒ/ *n.* **A** (*going by, through, etc.*) (*of river*) Überquerung, *die;* (*of time*) [Ab-, Ver]lauf, *der;* Verstreichen, *das;* (*of seasons*) Wechsel, *der;* **erased by the ~ of time** ausgelöscht vom Strom der Zeit; **their ~ was halted by an obstruction** ein Hindernis hemmte ihren Weg; **B** (*transition*) Übergang, *der;* **C** (*voyage*) Überfahrt, *die;* **D** (*way*) Gang, *der;* (*corridor*) Korridor, *der;* (*between houses*) Durchgang, *der;* (*in shopping precinct*) Passage, *die;* (*for ship, boat, car*) Durchfahrt, *die;* **E** *no art., no pl.* (*liberty or right to pass through*) Durchreise, *die;* **guarantee sb. rights of ~ through a territory** jmdm. die Durchreise durch ein Gebiet genehmigen; **F** (*right to travel*) Passage, *die;* **work one's ~:** seine Überfahrt abarbeiten; **G** (*part of book etc.*) Passage, *die;* Textstelle, *die;* **H** (*Mus.*) Passage, *die;* Stelle, *die;* **I** (*of a bill into law*) parlamentarische Behandlung; (*final*) Annahme, *die;* Verabschiedung, *die;* **J** (*duct*) **urinary ~:** Harntrakt, *der;* **ear ~:** Gehörgang, *der;* **air ~s** Luft- *od.* Atemwege. ⇒ *also* **back passage; bird of passage; front passage; purple passage; rite**

**'passageway** *n.* Gang, *der;* (*between houses*) Durchgang, *der*

**pass: ~book** *n.* **A** (*bank book*) Bankbuch, *das;* Kontobuch, *das;* **B** (*S. Afr.*) *Ausweispapier für Farbige;* ~ **degree** *n.* (*Brit. Univ.*) **get a ~ degree** ein Examen ohne Prädikat bestehen

**passé** *adj. masc.,* **passée** *adj. fem.* /'pæseɪ/ **A** (*past prime*) angekratzt (*salopp*); verblüht ‹Frau›; **B** (*outmoded*) überholt; passee *nicht attr.*

**passel** /'pæsl/ *n.* (*Amer. coll.*) Schar, *die*

**passenger** /'pæsɪndʒə(r)/ *n.* **A** (*traveller*) (*on ship*) Passagier, *der;* (*on plane*) Passagier, *der;* Fluggast, *der;* (*on train*) Reisende, *der/die;* (*on bus, in taxi*) Fahrgast, *der;* (*in car, on motorcycle*) Mitfahrer, *der*/Mitfahrerin, *die;* (*in front seat of car*) Beifahrer, *der*/Beifahrerin, *die;* **B** (*coll.: ineffective member*) *Mensch, der/Tier, das von den anderen mit durchgeschleppt wird* (*ugs.*); **feel like a mere ~ in an enterprise** sich bei einem Unternehmen wie das fünfte Rad am Wagen fühlen; **we cannot afford to have ~s in our team** Leute, die nichts leisten, können wir in unserem Team nicht gebrauchen

**passenger: ~ aircraft** *n.* Passagierflugzeug, *das;* ~ **door** *n.* Beifahrertür, *die;* ~ **elevator** (*Amer.*), ~ **lift** (*Brit.*) *ns.* Personenaufzug, *der;* ~ **list** *n.* Passagierliste, *die;* ~ **lounge** *n.* Warteraum, *der;* ~ **mile** *n.* Personenmeile, *die;* Passagiermeile, *die* (*Flugw.*); ~ **plane** *n.* Passagierflugzeug, *das;* ~ **seat** *n.* Beifahrersitz, *der;* ~ **service** *n.* (*train*) Personenzugverbindung, *die;* (*ferry*) Personenfährverbindung, *die;* **all ~ services out of London Victoria Station** alle Personenzüge ab London Victoria Station; ~ **train** *n.* Zug im Personenverkehr

**passer-by** /pɑ:sə'baɪ/ *n.* Passant, *der*/Passantin, *die*

**passim** /'pæsɪm/ *adv.* (*literary*) passim

**passing** /'pɑ:sɪŋ/ ❶ *n.* **A** (*going by*) (*of time, years*) Lauf, *der;* (*of winter*) Vorübergehen, *das;* (*of old year*) Ausklang, *der;* (*death*) Ende, *das;* Hinscheiden, *das* (*geh. verhüll.*); **in ~:** beiläufig ‹bemerken usw.›; flüchtig ‹begrüßen›; **B** ⇒ **passage** I.

❷ *adj.* **A** (*going past*) vorbeifahrend ‹Zug, Auto›; vorbeikommend ‹Person›; vorbeiziehend ‹Schatten›; **they depend on the ~ trade** sie sind von der Laufkundschaft abhängig; **with every ~ moment** von Minute zu Minute; **B** (*fleeting*) flüchtig ‹Blick›; vorübergehend ‹Mode, Laune, Interesse›; **C** (*superficial*) flüchtig ‹Bekanntschaft›; oberflächlich ‹Kenntnisse›; (*cursory*) beiläufig ‹Bemerkung›; schnell vorübergehend ‹Empfindung›.

❸ *adv.* (*arch.*) überaus

**passing: ~ note** *n.* (*Mus.*) Durchgangston, *der;* Durchgangsdissonanz, *die;* **~-'out [ceremony]** *n.* (*Mil. etc.*) Abschlussfeier, *die;* ~ **place** *n.* Ausweichstelle, *die;* ~ **shot** *n.* (*Tennis*) Passierschlag, *der;* Passierschuss, *der;* ~ **tone** (*Amer.*) ⇒ ~ **note**

**passion** /'pæʃn/ *n.* **A** (*emotion*) Leidenschaft, *die;* Leidenschaftlichkeit, *die;* **B** (*outburst*) Gefühlsausbruch, *der;* (*of anger*) Wutanfall, *der;* **fly into a ~:** einen Wutanfall bekommen; **C** (*sexual love*) Leidenschaft, *die;* (*lust*) Begierde, *die;* (*desire*) Verlangen, *das;* **D** (*enthusiasm*) leidenschaftliche Begeisterung; (*object arousing enthusiasm*) Leidenschaft, *die;* **he has a ~ for steam engines** Dampfloks sind seine Leidenschaft; er hat eine Passion für Dampfloks; **have a ~ for lobster/interfering in people's lives** leidenschaftlich gern Hummer essen/sich mit Begeisterung in anderer Leute Angelegenheiten einmischen; **sth. is sb.'s ~/sb.'s ~ is doing sth.** etw./etw. tun ist jmds. Leidenschaft *od.* ist bei jmdm. eine Leidenschaft; **E P~** (*Relig., Mus.*) Passion, *die;* Leiden Christi *Pl.;* (*narrative*) Leidens- *od.* Passionsgeschichte, *die;* **Bach's 'St Matthew P~'** die Matthäuspassion von Bach

**passionate** /'pæʃənət/ *adj.* **A** (*quick-tempered*) hitzig; leidenschaftlich; heftig; **a ~ young man** ein Hitzkopf; **B** (*ardent*) leidenschaftlich ‹Person›; heftig ‹Verlangen›; **have a ~ faith in sb.** mit glühender Begeisterung an jmdn. glauben; **have a ~ belief in sth.** mit unbeirrbarem Eifer von etw. überzeugt sein; **C** (*expressing violent or intense feeling*) leidenschaftlich ‹Rede›; (*unrestrained*) leidenschaftlich; hemmungslos; **make a ~ plea for mercy** inständig um Gnade bitten *od.* flehen

**passionately** /'pæʃənətlɪ/ *adv.* leidenschaftlich; mit Leidenschaft; hemmungslos ‹weinen›; inständig ‹bitten›; **be ~ fond of lobster/cricket** leidenschaftlich gerne Hummer essen/Cricket mögen

**passion: ~ flower** *n.* (*Bot.*) Passionsblume, *die;* ~ **fruit** *n.* Passionsfrucht, *die;* Maracuja, *die;* ~ **play** *n.* Passionsspiel, *das;* **P~ 'Sunday** *n.* Passionssonntag, *der;* **P~ Week** *n.* **A** (*before Palm Sunday*) die Woche nach dem ersten Passionssonntag; **B** (*after Palm Sunday*) die Karwoche

**passive** /'pæsɪv/ ❶ *adj.* **A** (*suffering action, acted upon*) passiv; **B** (*without opposition*) passiv; teilnahmslos; widerstandslos; widerspruchslos ‹Hinnahme, Annahme›; **remain ~:** unbeteiligt bleiben; ~ **smoking** passives Rauchen; ~ **resistance** passiver Widerstand; **C** (*inert*) regungslos ‹Gestalt, Körper, Wasserfläche›; unbewegt ‹Wasserfläche›; passiv ‹Rolle›; **your son is too ~:** Ihr Sohn ist zu passiv *od.* hat zu wenig Initiative; **D** (*not expressed*) unausgesprochen; **E** (*Metallurgy: unreactive*) passiv; **F** (*Ling.*) Passiv-; passivisch; ~ **voice** Passiv, *das;* ~ **vocabulary** passiver Wortschatz. ❷ *n.* (*Ling.*) Passiv, *das*

**passively** /'pæsɪvlɪ/ *adv.* teilnahmslos, unbeteiligt ‹dasitzen, lächeln, hinnehmen›; tatenlos ‹zusehen›; **be ~ involved in sth.** bei etw. eine passive Rolle spielen

**passiveness** /'pæsɪvnɪs/, **passivity** /pæ'sɪvɪtɪ/ *ns., no pl.* Passivität, *die;* Teilnahmslosigkeit, *die*

**pass: ~ key** *n.* **A** (*master key*) Hauptschlüssel, *der;* **B** (*private key*) Hausschlüssel, *der;* ~ **mark** *n.* Mindestpunktzahl, *die;* **the ~ mark was 40%** zum Bestehen [der Klausur *etc.*] mussten mindestens 40% der Punkte erreicht werden; **P~over** *n.* Passah, *das;* **the feast of P~over** das Passahfest; **~port** *n.* **A** [Reise]pass, *der;* *attrib.* Pass-; **B** (*fig.*) Schlüssel, *der* (**to** zu); **~word** *n.* **A** Parole, *die;* Losung, *die;* **B** (*Computing*) Passwort, *das*

**past** /pɑ:st/ ❶ *adj.* **A** *pred.* (*over*) vorbei; vorüber; **B** *attrib.* (*previous*) früher; vergangen; verflossen (*geh.*) ‹Jahre›; früher, ehemalig ‹Präsident, Vorsitzende usw.›; ~ **history** Vorleben, *das;* **she has a ~ history of violence** sie hat ein gewalttätiges Vorleben; **this is all ~ history** das ist alles Vergangenheit; **her ~ behaviour** *or* **conduct** ihr Verhalten in der Vergangenheit; **in centuries ~:** in vergangenen *od.* früheren Jahrhunderten; **C** (*just gone by*) letzt...; vergangen; **for weeks ~:** während der letzten Wochen; **in the ~ few days** während der letzten Tage; **the ~ hour/decade** die letzte *od.* vergangene Stunde/das

letzte *od.* vorige Jahrzehnt; Ⓓ (*Ling.*) ~ **tense** Vergangenheit, *die;* Präteritum, *das;* ~ **definite**, ~ **historic** historisches Perfekt; ~ **perfect** ⇒ **pluperfect**; ⇒ *also* **participle**.
❷ *n.* Ⓐ Vergangenheit, *die;* (*that which happened in the* ~) Vergangene, *das;* Gewesene, *das;* **in the** ~: früher; in der Vergangenheit ‹leben›; **be a thing of the** ~: der Vergangenheit (*Dat.*) angehören; Ⓑ (*previous history*) Vergangenheit, *die;* **a woman with a** ~: eine Frau mit Vergangenheit; Ⓒ (*Ling.*) Vergangenheit, *die;* **be/put in the** ~: in der Vergangenheit stehen/in die Vergangenheit setzen.
❸ *prep.* ▶ 1012 Ⓐ (*beyond in time*) nach; (*beyond in place*) hinter (+ *Dat.*); **half** ~ **three** halb vier; **five [minutes]** ~ **two** fünf [Minuten] nach zwei; **it's** ~ **midnight** es ist schon nach Mitternacht *od.* Mitternacht vorbei; **it's** ~ **the time he said he'd arrive** um diese Zeit wollte er eigentlich schon hier sein; **he is** ~ **sixty** er ist über sechzig; **she's** ~ **the age for having children** sie ist schon zu alt, um Kinder zu bekommen; **gaze/walk** ~ **sb./sth.** an jmdm./etw. vorbeiblicken/vorüber- *od.* vorbeigehen; Ⓑ (*not capable of*) ~ **repair/all comprehension** nicht mehr zu reparieren/völlig unverständlich; **he is** ~ **help/caring** ihm ist nicht mehr zu helfen/es kümmert ihn nicht mehr; **be/be getting** ~ **it** (*coll.*) [ein bisschen] zu alt sein/allmählich zu alt werden; **I wouldn't put it** ~ **her to do that** ich würde es ihr schon zutrauen, dass sie das tut; **I wouldn't put anything** ~ **him** ihm ist alles zuzutrauen.
❹ *adv.* vorbei; vorüber; **hurry** ~: vorüber- *od.* vorbeieilen

**pasta** /ˈpæstə, ˈpɑːstə/ *n.* Nudeln *Pl.;* Teigwaren *Pl.*

**paste** /peɪst/ ❶ *n.* Ⓐ Brei, *der;* (*for cakes*) Teig, *der;* **mix into a smooth/thick** ~: zu einem lockeren/dicken Brei anrühren; zu einem glatten/festen Teig anrühren ‹Backmischung›; Ⓑ (*glue*) Kleister, *der;* Ⓒ (*of meat, fish, etc.*) Paste, *die;* (*sweet doughy confection*) Masse, *die;* **anchovy** ~: Sardellenpaste, *die;* **almond** ~: Marzipanmasse, *die;* Ⓓ *no pl., no indef. art.* (*imitation gems*) Strass, *der;* Similisteine *Pl.;* Ⓔ (*Pottery*) Brei, *der.* ❷ *v.t.* Ⓐ (*fasten with glue*) kleben; ~ **sth. down/into sth.** etw. ankleben/in etw. (*Akk.*) einkleben; Ⓑ (*coll.: beat, thrash, bomb*) in die Pfanne hauen (*ugs.*); Ⓒ (*Computing*) einfügen (**into** in + *Akk.*); ⇒ *also* **cut**

~ **'over** *v.t.* überkleben

~ **'up** *v.t.* ankleben (**on** an + *Akk.*); ⇒ *also* **paste-up**

**'pasteboard** ❶ *n.* Pappe, *die;* Karton, *der;* ❷ *adj.* Papp-; (*fig.*) hohl ‹Glanz›; billig ‹Konstruktion›

**pastel** /ˈpæstl/ ❶ *n.* Ⓐ (*crayon*) Pastellstift, *der;* Pastellkreide, *die;* Ⓑ (*drawing*) Pastellzeichnung, *die;* Ⓒ (*art*) Pastellmalerei, *die;* Pastell, *das.* ❷ *adj.* pastellen; pastellfarben; Pastell‹farben, -töne, -zeichnung, -bild›; ~ **green** Pastellgrün, *das*

**'paste-up** *n.* Klebeumbruch, *der;* Montage, *die*

**pasteurisation, pasteurise** ⇒ **pasteuriz-**

**pasteurization** /pæstʃəraɪˈzeɪʃn, pɑːstʃəraɪˈzeɪʃn/ *n.* Pasteurisation, *die;* Pasteurisierung, *die*

**pasteurize** /ˈpæstʃəraɪz, ˈpɑːstʃəraɪz/ *v.t.* pasteurisieren

**pastille** /ˈpæstɪl/ *n.* Pastille, *die*

**pastime** /ˈpɑːstaɪm/ *n.* Zeitvertreib, *der;* (*person's specific* ~) Hobby, *das;* **my** ~**s are tennis and cricket** in meiner Freizeit spiele ich Tennis und Cricket; **amuse oneself/while away the time with various** ~**s** sich (*Dat.*) die Zeit mit verschiedenen Beschäftigungen vertreiben; **national** ~: Nationalsport, *der* (*auch iron.*); **favourite** ~: Lieblingsbeschäftigung, *die*

**pasting** /ˈpeɪstɪŋ/ *n.* (*coll.*) **give sb. a** ~: jmdm. eins überbraten (*salopp*); **take a** ~: eins übergebraten kriegen (*salopp*); (*from critics*) verrissen werden (*ugs.*)

**past 'master** *n.* (*fig.*) Meister, *der*

**pastor** /ˈpɑːstə(r)/ *n.* ▶ 1261 Pfarrer, *der/*Pfarrerin, *die;* Pastor, *der/*Pastorin, *die*

**pastoral** /ˈpɑːstərl/ ❶ *adj.* Ⓐ Weide-; ländlich ‹Reiz, Idylle, Umgebung›; Ⓑ (*Lit., Art, Mus.*) pastoral; ~ **poetry** Hirten-, Schäferdichtung, *die;* (*ancient*) Bukolik, *die;* ~ **drama** Schäferspiel, *das;* ~ **theme** ländliches Motiv; Ⓒ (*Eccl.*) pastoral; des Pfarrers *nachgestellt;* Hirten‹amt, -brief›; seelsorgerisch ‹Pflicht, Aufgabe, Leitung, Aktivitäten›; ~ **care** Seelsorge, *die;* Ⓓ (*relating to shepherds*) ~ **economy** Weidewirtschaft, *die;* **a** ~ **people** ein Hirtenvolk. ❷ *n.* (*Lit., Art, Mus.*) Pastorale, *das od. die*

**pastorale** /pæstəˈrɑːl/ ⇒ **pastoral** 2

**pastrami** /pæˈstrɑːmɪ/ *n.* (*Amer.*) *geräuchertes, stark gewürztes Rindfleisch* (*vom Schulterstück*)

**pastry** /ˈpeɪstrɪ/ *n.* Ⓐ (*flour paste*) Teig, *der;* Ⓑ (*article of food*) Gebäckstück, *das;* Ⓒ **pastries** *collect.* [Fein]gebäck, *das*

**pastry:** ~ **board** *n.* Backbrett, *das;* ~ **cook** *n.* Konditor, *der/*Konditorin, *die;* ~ **cutter** *n.* Ausstechform, *die;* ~ **wheel** *n.* Kuchenrad, *das*

**pasturage** /ˈpɑːstʃərɪdʒ, ˈpɑːstjʊərɪdʒ/ *n.* Ⓐ (*grazing*) Weide, *die;* **rights of** ~: Weiderecht, *das;* Ⓑ (*grass*) Futter, *das;* Gras, *das;* Ⓒ (*land*) Weideland, *das*

**pasture** /ˈpɑːstʃə(r)/ ❶ *n.* Ⓐ (*grass*) Futter, *das;* Gras, *das;* ~ **for cattle** Viehfutter, *das;* Ⓑ (*land*) Weideland, *das;* (*piece of land*) Weide, *die;* Ⓒ (*fig.*) **home** ~**s** heimatliche Gefilde *Pl.* (*scherzh.*); **in search of** ~**s new** auf der Suche nach etwas Neuem. ❷ *v.t.* (*lead or put to pasture*) weiden [lassen]. ❸ *v.i.* weiden; grasen

**'pastureland** *n.* Weideland, *das*

**pasty**[1] /ˈpæstɪ/ *n.* Pastete, *die*

**pasty**[2] /ˈpeɪstɪ/ *adj.* Ⓐ teigig; zähflüssig; Ⓑ ⇒ **pasty-faced**

**pasty-faced** /ˈpeɪstɪfeɪst/ *adj.* mit teigigem Gesicht *nachgestellt;* **be** ~: ein teigiges Gesicht haben

**pat**[1] /pæt/ ❶ *n.* Ⓐ (*stroke, tap*) Klaps, *der;* leichter Schlag; **give sb./a dog a** ~: jmdn./einen Hund tätscheln; (*once*) jmdm./einem Hund einen Klaps geben; **give sb./a dog a** ~ **on the head** jmdm./einem Hund den Kopf tätscheln; **give sb. a** ~ **on the shoulder** jmdm. auf die Schulter klopfen; **a** ~ **on the back** (*fig.*) eine Anerkennung; **she deserves a** ~ **on the back** (*fig.*) sie verdient Anerkennung *od.* ein Lob; **give oneself/sb. a** ~ **on the back** (*fig.*) sich (*Dat.*) [selbst] auf die Schulter klopfen/jmdm. einige anerkennende Worte sagen; Ⓑ (*of butter*) Stückchen, *das;* (*of mud, clay*) Klümpchen, *das;* ⇒ *also* **cowpat**.
❷ *v.t.*, **-tt-** Ⓐ (*strike gently*) leicht klopfen auf (+ *Akk.*); tätscheln, (*once*) einen Klaps geben (+ *Dat.*) ‹Person, Hund, Pferd›; ~ **sb. on the arm/head/cheek** jmdm. den Arm/Kopf/die Wange tätscheln; ~ **oneself/sb. on the back** (*fig.*) sich (*Dat.*) [selbst]/jmdm. auf die Schulter klopfen; ~ **one's face dry** sein Gesicht trockentupfen; Ⓑ (*flatten*) festklopfen ‹Sand›; andrücken ‹Haare›; ~ **flat** flach klopfen; ~ **one's hair into place** sich (*Dat.*) das Haar zurechtlegen

**pat**[2] ❶ *adv.* (*ready, prepared*) **have sth. off** ~: etw. parat haben; **know sth. off** ~: etw. aus dem Effeff können *od.* beherrschen (*ugs.*); etw. in- und auswendig können; **come** ~ ‹Antwort:› wie aus der Pistole geschossen kommen; (*opportunely*) ‹Geschichte:› wie gerufen kommen; **stand** ~ (*fig.*) keinen Zollbreit nachgeben; unbeirrbar sein. ❷ *adj.* (*ready*) allzu schlagfertig ‹Antwort›; (*opportune*) passend; treffend; **he has some** ~ **phrases for every occasion** er hat für jede Gelegenheit einen Spruch parat (*ugs.*)

**patch** /pætʃ/ ❶ *n.* Ⓐ Stelle, *die;* **inflamed** ~**es of skin** entzündete [Haut]stellen; **a** ~ **of blue sky** ein Stückchen blauer Himmel; **there were still** ~**es of snow** es lag vereinzelt *od.* hier und da noch Schnee; **the dog had a black** ~ **on its ear** der Hund hatte einen schwarzen Fleck am Ohr; **there were** ~**es of black ice on the roads** auf den Straßen war stellenweise Glatteis; **there were** ~**es of sunshine** auf einige Stellen schien die Sonne; ~**es of rain** (*during period of time*) ab und zu Regen; (*in several places*) stellenweise Regen; **fog** ~**es** Nebelfelder; **we went through one or two rough** ~**es on our crossing** während der Überfahrt hatten wir ein- oder zweimal raue See; **in** ~**es** stellenweise; **go through** *or* **strike a bad/good** ~ (*Brit.*) eine Pech-/Glückssträhne haben; **a sticky** ~ **in her life** eine schwierige Phase in ihrem Leben; Ⓑ (*on worn garment*) Flicken, *der;* **be not a** ~ **on sth.** (*fig. coll.*) nichts gegen etw. sein; nicht an etw. (*Akk.*) heranreichen; Ⓒ (*on eye*) Augenklappe, *die;* **wear a** ~ **on one eye** eine Augenklappe tragen; Ⓓ (*piece of ground*) Stück Land, *das;* **every** ~ **of ground** jeder Zentimeter Boden; **potato** ~: Kartoffelacker, *der;* (*in garden*) Kartoffelbeet, *das;* Ⓔ (*area patrolled by police; also fig.*) Revier, *das;* **keep off our** ~ (*fig.*) komm uns ja nicht ins Gehege; Ⓕ (*Mil.: badge*) Schulterklappe, *die;* Schulterstück, *das;* Ⓖ (*Hist.: beauty spot*) Schönheitspflästerchen, *das;* Mouche, *die* (*geh.*).
❷ *v.t.* (*apply* ~ *to*) flicken

~ **to'gether** *v.t.* zusammenstücke[l]n; (*fig.*) zusammenflicken, zusammenstoppeln (*ugs. abwertend*) ‹Buch, Artikel›; zusammenschustern (*ugs. abwertend*) ‹Grundsatzprogramm, Vereinbarung›

~ **'up** *v.t.* reparieren; zusammenflicken ‹Segel, Buch›; notdürftig verbinden ‹Wunde›; zusammenflicken (*scherzh.*) ‹Verletzten›; (*fig.*) beilegen ‹Streit, Differenzen›; kitten ‹Ehe, Freundschaft›; **try to** ~ **the matter up** versuchen, die Sache wieder ins Lot zu bringen

**patch:** ~ **pocket** *n.* aufgesetzte Tasche; ~**work** *n.* Patchwork, *das;* **a** ~**work quilt** eine Patchworkdecke; (*fig.*) **a** ~**work of fields** ein bunter Teppich von Feldern

**patchy** /ˈpætʃɪ/ *adj.* uneinheitlich ‹Qualität›; ungleichmäßig, unterschiedlich ‹Arbeit, Aufführung, Ausstoß›; unausgewogen ‹Darbietung›; fleckig ‹Anstrich›; stellenweise spärlich ‹Ernte›; sehr lückenhaft ‹Wissen›; in der Qualität unterschiedlich ‹Film, Buch, Theaterstück›

**pate** /peɪt/ *n.* (*arch.*) Haupt, *das* (*geh.*); (*coll.*) Birne, *die* (*salopp*); Rübe, *die* (*salopp*); **bald** ~: Glatze, *die*

**pâté** /ˈpæteɪ/ *n.* Pastete, *die;* ~ **de foie gras** /ˈpæteɪ/ˈpɑːteɪ də fwɑ ˈgrɑː/ Gänseleberpastete, *die*

**patella** /pəˈtelə/ *n., pl.* ~**e** /pəˈteliː/ (*Anat.*) Kniescheibe, *die;* Patella, *die* (*fachspr.*)

**paten** /ˈpætn/ *n.* (*Eccl.*) Patene, *die;* Hostienteller, *der*

**patent** /ˈpeɪtənt, ˈpætənt/ ❶ *adj.* Ⓐ patentiert; patentrechtlich geschützt; gesetzlich geschützt; (*fig.: characteristic*) ureigen; ~ **medicine** Markenmedizin, *die;* patentrechtlich geschütztes Arzneimittel; ~ **article** Markenartikel, *der;* ~ **remedy** Spezial- *od.* Patentrezept, *das;* Patentlösung, *die;* Ⓑ (*obvious*) offenkundig; offensichtlich. ❷ *n.* Ⓐ (*licence*) Patent, *das;* ~ **applied for** *or* **pending** Patent angemeldet; **take out a** ~ **for** *or* **on sth.** sich (*Dat.*) etw. patentieren lassen; Ⓑ (*invention or process*) Patent, *das;* Ⓒ (*fig.: exclusive property or claim*) Patent, *das* (**on** auf + *Akk.*). ❸ *v.t.* patentieren lassen; **sth. has been** ~**ed** etw. ist patentrechtlich geschützt

**patentable** /ˈpeɪtəntəbl, ˈpætəntəbl/ *adj.* patentfähig

**patent:** ~ **agent** (*Brit.*), ~ **attorney** (*Amer.*) *ns.* ▶ 1261 Patentanwalt, *der/*-anwältin, *die*

**patentee** /peɪtənˈtiː, pætənˈtiː/ *n.* Patentinhaber, *der/*-inhaberin, *die*

**patent 'leather** *n.* Lackleder, *das;* ~ **shoes** Lackschuhe

**patently** /ˈpeɪtəntlɪ, ˈpætəntlɪ/ *adv.* offenkundig; offensichtlich; ~ **obvious** ganz offenkundig *od.* offensichtlich

**patent:** ~ **office** *n.* Patentamt, *das;* ~ **rights** *n. pl.* Erfinderrecht, *das*

**paterfamilias** /peɪtəfəˈmɪlɪæs, pætəfəˈmɪlɪæs/ *n.* (*often joc.*) Familienoberhaupt, *das;* Paterfamilias, *der* (*geh. scherzh.*)

**paternal** /pəˈtɜːnl/ *adj.* Ⓐ (*fatherly*) väterlich; Ⓑ (*related*) ‹Großeltern, Onkel, Tante› väterlicherseits

**paternalism** /pəˈtɜːnəlɪzm/ *n.* Bevormundung, *die*

**paternalistic** /pətɜːnəˈlɪstɪk/ *adj.* patriarchalisch; paternalistisch

**paternally** /pəˈtɜːnəlɪ/ *adv.* väterlich

**paternity** /pəˈtɜːnɪtɪ/ *n.* Ⓐ (*fatherhood*) Vaterschaft, *die;* **deny ~ of a child** die Vaterschaft an einem Kind bestreiten *od.* leugnen; Ⓑ (*origin*) Abstammung väterlicherseits, *die*

**paternity: ~ leave** *n.* Vaterschaftsurlaub, *der;* **~ suit** *n.* Vaterschaftsklage, *die;* Vaterschaftsprozess, *der;* **~ test** *n.* Vaterschaftsuntersuchung, *die*

**paternoster** /pætəˈnɒstə(r)/ *n.* Ⓐ (*prayer*) Vaterunser, *das;* Paternoster, *das;* Ⓑ (*lift*) Paternoster, *der*

**path** /pɑːθ/ *n., pl.* **~s** /pɑːðz/ Ⓐ (*way*) Weg, *der;* Pfad, *der;* (*merely made by walking*) Trampelpfad, *der;* **keep to the ~:** auf dem Weg bleiben; Ⓑ (*line of motion*) Bahn, *die;* (*of tornado, caravan, etc.*) Weg, *der;* **his ~ led across fields and meadows** sein Weg führte ihn über Felder und Wiesen; **into the ~ of a moving vehicle** vor ein Fahrzeug; ⇒ *also* **flight path**; Ⓒ (*fig.: course of action*) Weg, *der;* **the middle ~:** der Mittelweg; **our ~s crossed/diverged** unsere Wege kreuzten/trennten sich; **the ~ to salvation/of virtue** der Weg des Heils/der Pfad der Tugend

**pathetic** /pəˈθetɪk/ *adj.* Ⓐ (*pitiful*) Mitleid erregend; herzergreifend; **be a ~ sight** ein Bild des Jammers bieten; Ⓑ (*full of pathos*) pathetisch; Ⓒ (*contemptible*) armselig ‹Entschuldigung›; erbärmlich ‹Darbietung, Rede, Person, Leistung›; **you're/it's ~:** du bist ein hoffnungsloser Fall/es ist wirklich ein schwaches Bild (*ugs.*); **are these ~ scribbles meant to be art?** soll dieses jämmerliche Gekritzel vielleicht Kunst sein?; Ⓓ **~ fallacy** Vermenschlichung der Natur, *die*

**pathetically** /pəˈθetɪkəlɪ/ *adv.* Ⓐ (*pitifully*) Mitleid erregend ‹stöhnen›; herzergreifend ‹flehen›; Ⓑ (*contemptibly*) erbärmlich; erschreckend ‹wenig›; **~ bad** miserabel

ˈ**pathfinder** *n.* Ⓐ (*person*) jmd., *der jmdm. den Weg findet/zeigt;* (*fig.*) Wegbereiter, *der*/-bereiterin, *die;* Bahnbrecher, *der*/Bahnbrecherin, *die;* Ⓑ (*aircraft*) Pfadfinder, *der* (*Milit.*)

**pathless** /ˈpɑːθlɪs/ *adj.* weglos

**pathogen** /ˈpæθədʒən/ *n.* (*Med.*) [Krankheits]erreger, *der*

**pathogenic** /pæθəˈdʒenɪk/ *adj.* (*Med.*) pathogen (*fachspr.*); krankheitserregend

**pathological** /pæθəˈlɒdʒɪkl/ *adj.* Ⓐ pathologisch; Pathologie-; Ⓑ (*morbid*) pathologisch; krankhaft; Ⓒ (*fig.: obsessive*) krankhaft; pathologisch

**pathologically** /pæθəˈlɒdʒɪkəlɪ/ *adv.* pathologisch; (*fig.: obsessively*) krankhaft

**pathologist** /pəˈθɒlədʒɪst/ *n.* ▶ 1261 Pathologe, *der*/Pathologin, *die*

**pathology** /pəˈθɒlədʒɪ/ *n.* Ⓐ (*science*) Pathologie, *die;* Ⓑ (*symptoms*) Symptomatik, *die;* **the ~ of a disease** das Krankheitsbild

**pathos** /ˈpeɪθɒs/ *n.* Pathos, *das*

ˈ**pathway** *n.* Ⓐ ⇒ **path** A; Ⓑ (*Physiol.*) Bahn, *die;* Leitung, *die;* **optical ~:** Sehbahn, *die*

**patience** /ˈpeɪʃəns/ *n.* Ⓐ *no pl., no art.* Geduld, *die;* (*perseverance*) Ausdauer, *die;* Beharrlichkeit, *die;* (*forbearance*) Langmut, *die;* **with ~:** geduldig; **have endless ~:** eine Engelsgeduld haben; **my ~ is finally exhausted** meine Geduld ist jetzt am Ende *od.* erschöpft; **lose [one's] ~ [with sth./sb.]** [mit etw./jmdm.] die Geduld verlieren; **I lost my ~:** mir riss der Geduldsfaden (*ugs.*) *od.* die Geduld; **~ is a virtue** (*prov.*) Geduld ist eine Tugend; **it is enough to try the ~ of a saint** das ist eine harte Geduldsprobe; **have the ~ of a saint** eine Engelsgeduld haben; Ⓑ (*Brit. Cards*) Patience, *die.* ⇒ *also* **Job**

**patient** /ˈpeɪʃənt/ ❶ *adj.* geduldig; (*forbearing*) langmütig; (*persevering*) beharrlich; **please be ~:** bitte hab Geduld; gedulde dich bitte; **remain ~:** sich in Geduld fassen. ❷ *n.* ▶ 1232 Patient, *der*/Patientin, *die*

**patiently** /ˈpeɪʃəntlɪ/ *adv.* (*with composure*) geduldig; mit Geduld; (*with forbearance*) geduldig; nachsichtig; (*with calm*) geduldig; (*with perseverance*) beharrlich; ausdauernd

**patina** /ˈpætɪnə/ *n.* (*on bronze*) Patina, *die;* (*on woodwork*) Altersglanz, *der;* (*fig.*) Patina, *die*

**patio** /ˈpætɪəʊ/ *n., pl.* **~s** Ⓐ (*paved area*) Veranda, *die;* Terrasse, *die;* Ⓑ (*inner court*) Innenhof, *der;* Patio, *der*

**patio** ˈ**door** *n.* große Glasschiebetür (*zum Garten*)

**patisserie** /pæˈtɪsərɪ/ *n.* Ⓐ (*shop*) Konditorei, *die;* Ⓑ (*cakes and pastries*) Feingebäck, *das*

**Patna rice** /ˈpætnə raɪs/ *n.* Patnareis, *der*

**patois** /ˈpætwɑː/ *n., pl. same* Ⓐ (*dialect*) Mundart, *die;* Dialekt, *der;* Ⓑ (*jargon*) Jargon, *der*

**patriarch** /ˈpeɪtrɪɑːk/ *n.* Ⓐ (*of family*) Familienoberhaupt, *das;* Patriarch, *der;* (*of tribe*) Stammesoberhaupt, *das;* Häuptling, *der;* Ⓑ (*Relig.*) (*in early and Orthodox Church*) Patriarch, *der;* (*RC Ch.*) Bischof von Rom, *der;* Ⓒ (*founder*) Begründer, *der;* Ⓓ (*old man*) ehrwürdiger Greis

**patriarchal** /peɪtrɪˈɑːkl/ *adj.* Ⓐ patriarchalisch; Ⓑ (*old, venerable*) [alt]ehrwürdig

**patriarchy** /ˈpeɪtrɪɑːkɪ/ *n.* Patriarchat, *das*

**patrician** /pəˈtrɪʃn/ ❶ *n.* (*Hist.*) Patrizier, *der*/Patrizierin, *die.* ❷ *adj.* Ⓐ (*noble*) vornehm; edel; Ⓑ (*Hist.*) patrizisch; Patrizier-; **~ family** Patrizierfamilie, *die;* Patriziergeschlecht, *das*

**patricide** /ˈpætrɪsaɪd/ *n.* Ⓐ (*murder*) Vatermord, *der;* Ⓑ (*murderer*) Vatermörder, *der*/Vatermörderin, *die*

**patrimony** /ˈpætrɪmənɪ/ *n.* Patrimonium, *das;* väterliches Erbe; (*fig.*) Erbe, *das;* (*endowment*) Vermögen, *das*

**patriot** /ˈpætrɪət, ˈpeɪtrɪət/ *n.* Patriot, *der*/Patriotin, *die*

**patriotic** /pætrɪˈɒtɪk, peɪtrɪˈɒtɪk/ *adj.* patriotisch

**patriotism** /ˈpætrɪətɪzm, ˈpeɪtrɪətɪzm/ *n.* Patriotismus, *der;* vaterländische Gesinnung

**patrol** /pəˈtrəʊl/ ❶ *n.* Ⓐ (*of police*) Streife, *die;* (*of watchman*) Runde, *die;* Rundgang, *der;* (*of aircraft, ship*) Patrouille, *die;* (*Mil.*) Patrouille, *die;* **put sb. on ~:** jmdn. auf Streife *od.* (*Milit.*) Patrouille schicken; **policeman on ~:** Streifenpolizist, *der;* **be on** *or* **keep ~** ‹Soldat, Wächter:› patrouillieren; Ⓑ (*person, group*) (*Police*) Streife, *die;* (*Mil.*) Patrouille, *die;* **coast ~:** Küstenwache, *die;* Küstenwacht, *die;* **police ~:** Polizeistreife, *die;* **army ~:** Militärpatrouille, *die;* Militärstreife, *die;* **fire ~:** Brandwache, *die;* Ⓒ (*troops*) Spähtrupp, *der;* Spähpatrouille, *die;* Ⓓ (*unit*) (*of Scouts*) Fähnlein, *das;* (*of Guides*) Gilde, *die.* ❷ *v.i.*, **-ll-** patrouillieren; ‹Polizei:› Streife laufen/fahren; ‹Wachmann:› seine Runde[n] machen; ‹Flugzeug:› Patrouille fliegen. ❸ *v.t.*, **-ll-** patrouillieren durch (+ *Akk.*); abpatrouillieren ‹Straßen, Mauer, Gegend, Lager›; patrouillieren vor (+ *Dat.*) ‹Küste, Grenze›; ‹Polizei:› Streife laufen/fahren in (+ *Dat.*) ‹Straßen, Stadtteil›; ‹Wachmann:› seine Runde[n] machen in (+ *Dat.*)

**patrol: ~ boat** *n.* Patrouillenboot, *das;* **~ car** *n.* Streifenwagen, *der;* **~man** /pəˈtrəʊlmən/ *n., pl.* **~men** /pəˈtrəʊlmən/ ▶ 1261 (*Amer.*) [Streifen]polizist, *der;* **~ wagon** *n.* (*Amer.*) Gefangenenwagen, *der*

**patron** /ˈpeɪtrən/ *n.* Ⓐ (*supporter*) Gönner, *der*/Gönnerin, *die;* (*of institution, campaign*) Schirmherr, *der*/Schirmherrin, *die;* **~ of the arts** Kunstmäzen, *der;* Ⓑ (*customer*) (*of shop*) Kunde, *der*/Kundin, *die;* (*of restaurant, hotel*) Gast, *der;* (*of theatre, cinema*) Besucher, *der*/Besucherin, *die;* '**~s only**' „nur für Kunden/Gäste"; Ⓒ **~ [saint]** Schutzheilige, *der/die;* Schutzpatron, *der*/Schutzpatronin, *die;* Ⓓ (*Brit. Eccl.*) Pfründner, *der*/Pfründnerin, *die*

**patronage** /ˈpætrənɪdʒ/ *n.* Ⓐ (*support*) Gönnerschaft, *die;* Unterstützung, *die;* (*for campaign, institution*) Schirmherrschaft, *die;* Ⓑ (*customer's support*) Kundschaft, *die;* **we thank our customers for their ~:** wir danken unseren Kunden für ihr *od.* das in uns gesetzte Vertrauen; **withdraw one's ~:** ein Geschäft *usw.* nicht mehr betreten; Ⓒ (*dated: condescension*) Gönnerhaftigkeit, *die;* **with an air of ~:** mit Gönnermiene *od.* gönnerhafter Miene; Ⓓ (*Polit.*) Recht der Ämterbesetzung

**patroness** /ˈpeɪtrənes/ *n.* Ⓐ (*supporter*) Gönnerin, *die;* (*of campaign, institution*) Schirmherrin, *die;* Ⓑ (*saint*) Schutzheilige, *die;* Schutzpatronin, *die*

**patronise**, **patronising**, **patronisingly** ⇒ **patroniz-**

**patronize** /ˈpætrənaɪz/ *v.t.* Ⓐ (*frequent*) besuchen; **we hope you will continue to ~ our services** bitte beehren Sie uns bald wieder; bitte schenken Sie uns auch weiterhin Ihr Vertrauen; Ⓑ (*support*) fördern; unterstützen; Ⓒ (*condescend to*) **~ sb.** jmdn. gönnerhaft *od.* von oben herab *od.* herablassend behandeln

**patronizing** /ˈpætrənaɪzɪŋ/ *adj.*, **patronizingly** /ˈpætrənaɪzɪŋlɪ/ *adv.* gönnerhaft; herablassend

**patronymic** /pætrəˈnɪmɪk/ ❶ *n.* Patronymikon, *das;* Vater[s]name, *der.* ❷ *adj.* patronymisch

**patsy** /ˈpætsɪ/ *n.* (*Amer. coll.*) Einfaltspinsel, *der* (*ugs.*)

**patter** /ˈpætə(r)/ ❶ *n.* Ⓐ (*of rain*) Prasseln, *das;* (*of feet, footsteps*) Trappeln, *das;* Getrappel, *das;* **the ~ of tiny feet** (*fig.*) fröhliches Kindertreiben; Ⓑ (*language of salesman or comedian*) Sprüche *Pl.;* **sales ~:** Vertretersprüche *Pl.;* **keep up a ~:** ohne Unterbrechung reden; Ⓒ (*jargon*) Fachjargon, *der.* ❷ *v.i.* Ⓐ (*make tapping sounds*) ‹Regen, Hagel:› prasseln; ‹Schritte:› trappeln; Ⓑ (*run*) trippeln

**pattern** /ˈpætən/ ❶ *n.* Ⓐ (*design*) Muster, *das;* (*on carpet, wallpaper, cloth, etc. also*) Dessin, *das;* **frost ~s** Eisblumen; **a ~ of footprints** Fußspuren *Pl.;* Ⓑ (*form, order*) Muster, *das;* Schema, *das;* **follow a ~:** einem regelmäßigen Muster *od.* Schema folgen; **behaviour ~:** Verhaltensmuster, *das;* **~ of development** Entwicklungsschema, *das;* **~ of thought** Denkmuster, *das;* Denkschema, *das;* **~ of life** Lebensweise, *die;* **~ of events** Ereignisfolge, *die;* Ⓒ (*model*) Vorlage, *die;* (*for sewing*) Schnittmuster, *das;* Schnitt, *der;* (*for knitting*) Strickanleitung, *die;* Strickmuster, *das;* **follow a ~:** nach einer Vorlage arbeiten; (*knitting*) nach einem Strickmuster stricken; **a democracy on the British ~:** eine Demokratie nach britischem Muster; Ⓓ (*sample*) Muster, *das;* Ⓔ (*on target*) [Treffer]bild, *das.* ❷ *v.t.* Ⓐ (*model*) gestalten; **~ sth. after/on sth.** etw. einer Sache (*Dat.*) nachbilden; **she ~ed her behaviour on her father's** sie richtete sich in ihrem Verhalten nach dem Vorbild ihres Vaters; Ⓑ (*decorate*) mustern; **~ sth. with intricate designs** etw. mit verschlungenen Mustern verzieren

ˈ**pattern book** *n.* Musterbuch, *das*

**patty** /ˈpætɪ/ *n.* Ⓐ (*pie, pastry*) Pastetchen, *das;* Ⓑ (*Amer.: of meat*) Frikadelle, *die*

**paucity** /ˈpɔːsɪtɪ/ *n.* (*formal*) Mangel, *der* (**of** an + *Dat.*); **~ of support** geringe *od.* mangelnde Unterstützung; **a growing ~ of ...:** immer weniger ...

**Paul** /pɔːl/ *pr. n.* (*Hist., as name*) (*of ruler etc.*) Paul; (*of saint*) Paulus

**Pauline** /ˈpɔːlaɪn/ *adj.* (*Bibl.*) paulinisch

**paunch** /pɔːntʃ/ *n.* Bauch, *der;* Wanst, *der* (*salopp abwertend*); **develop a ~:** einen Bauch ansetzen

**paunchy** /ˈpɔːntʃɪ/ *adj.* dickbäuchig; **become ~:** einen Bauch ansetzen

**pauper** /ˈpɔːpə(r)/ *n.* Ⓐ Arme, *der/die;* **they were ~s** sie waren arm; **live like ~s** leben wie arme Leute; Ⓑ (*Hist.*) Unterstützungsempfänger, *der*/-empfängerin, *die;* **~'s grave** Armengrab, *das*

p

**pauperism** /ˈpɔːpərɪzm/ *n., no pl.* Armut, *die;* **be reduced to ~:** völlig verarmen

**pauperize** /ˈpɔːpəraɪz/ *v.t.* arm machen; **be ~d** verarmt sein

**pause** /pɔːz/ ❶ *n.* Ⓐ Pause, *die;* **without [a] ~:** ohne Pause; **an anxious ~:** ängstliches Schweigen; **a ~ in the fighting** eine Kampfpause; **give sb. ~:** jmdm. zu denken geben; Ⓑ *(Mus.)* Fermate, *die.* ❷ *v.i.* Ⓐ *(wait)* eine Pause machen; eine Pause einlegen; ‹Redner:› innehalten; *(hesitate)* zögern; **~ for reflection/thought** in Ruhe überlegen; **he ~d to consider his next move** er hielt ein und überlegte, wie er weiter vorgehen solle; **~ for a rest** eine Erholungspause *od.* Ruhepause einlegen; Ⓑ *(linger)* verweilen **(upon, over** bei)

**pavan** /ˈpævən/, **pavane** /pəˈvɑːn/ *n. (Hist./Mus.)* Pavane, *die*

**pave** /peɪv/ *v.t.* Ⓐ *(cover, lit. or fig.)* befestigen; *(with stones)* pflastern; Ⓑ *(fig.: prepare)* **~ the way for** *or* **to sth.** einer Sache *(Dat.)* den Weg ebnen; für etw. den Weg ebnen

**pavement** /ˈpeɪvmənt/ *n.* Ⓐ *(Brit.: footway)* Bürgersteig, *der;* Gehsteig, *der;* Ⓑ *(paved surface)* Belag, *der;* Pflaster, *das;* Ⓒ *(Amer.: roadway)* Fahrbahn, *die*

**ˈpavement café** *n.* Straßencafé, *das*

**pavilion** /pəˈvɪljən/ *n.* Ⓐ *(tent)* Festzelt, *das;* Pavillon, *der;* Ⓑ *(ornamental building)* Pavillon, *der;* Ⓒ *(Brit. Sport)* Klubhaus, *das;* Ⓓ *(stand at exhibition)* [Messe]pavillon, *der*

**paving** /ˈpeɪvɪŋ/ *n.* Ⓐ *(action)* Pflastern, *das;* Ⓑ *(paced surface)* Pflaster, *das*

**ˈpaving stone** *n.* Platte, *die;* Pflasterstein, *der*

**paw** /pɔː/ ❶ *n.* Ⓐ Pfote, *die; (of bear, lion, tiger)* Pranke, *die;* Ⓑ *(coll. derog.: hand)* Pfote, *die (ugs. abwertend);* **keep your ~s off [me]/off my car!** Pfoten weg!/Pfoten weg von meinem Auto! ❷ *v.t.* Ⓐ ‹Hund, Wolf:› mit der Pfote/den Pfoten berühren; ‹Bär, Löwe, Tiger:› mit der Pranke/den Pranken berühren; *(playfully)* tätscheln; **~ the ground** scharren; Ⓑ *(coll. derog.: fondle)* befummeln *(ugs.).* ❸ *v.i.* Ⓐ scharren; **~ at** mit der Pfote/den Pfoten *usw.* berühren; Ⓑ **~ at sb./sth.** *(coll. derog.)* jmdn./etw. befummeln *(ugs.)*

**pawl** /pɔːl/ *n. (Mech. Engin.)* Sperre, *die;* Sperrklinke, *die*

**pawn**[1] /pɔːn/ *n.* Ⓐ *(Chess)* Bauer, *der;* Ⓑ *(fig.)* Schachfigur, *die;* **a ~ in the hands of Fate** ein Spielball des Schicksals

**pawn**[2] ❶ *n.* Pfand, *das;* **in ~:** verpfändet; versetzt; **put sth. in ~:** etw. verpfänden *od.* versetzen; **take sth. out of ~:** etw. einlösen. ❷ *v.t.* Ⓐ verpfänden; versetzen; Ⓑ *(fig.)* verpfänden ‹Leben, Ehre, Wort, Seele›

**pawn: ~broker** *n.* ▶ 1261 Pfandleiher, *der/*-leiherin, *die;* **~broking** *n., no art.* Pfandleihgeschäft, *das;* **~shop** *n.* Leihhaus, *das;* Pfandleihe, *die*

**pawpaw** /pɔːˈpɔː/ ⇒ **papaw**

**pay** /peɪ/ ❶ *n., no pl., no indef. art. (wages)* Lohn, *der; (salary)* Gehalt, *das; (of soldier)* Sold, *der;* **the ~ is good** die Bezahlung ist gut; **be in the ~ of sb./sth.** für jmdn./etw. arbeiten; in jmds. Sold/im Sold einer Sache stehen *(abwertend);* ⇒ *also* **equal** 1 A. ❷ *v.t.,* **paid** /peɪd/ Ⓐ *(give money to)* bezahlen; *(fig.)* belohnen; **I paid him for the tickets** ich habe ihm das Geld für die Karten gegeben; **~ sb. to do sth.** jmdn. dafür bezahlen, dass er etw. tut; ⇒ *also* **coin** 1; Ⓑ *(hand over)* zahlen; *(so as to discharge an obligation)* bezahlen; *(~ back)* zurückbezahlen; *(in instalments)* abbezahlen; **I paid what I owed him** ich habe meine Schulden bei ihm bezahlt; **~ the bill** die Rechnung bezahlen; **~ sb.'s expenses** *(reimburse)* jmds. Auslagen erstatten; **~ sb. £10** jmdm. 10 Pfund zahlen; **~ £10 for sth.** 10 Pfund für etw. [be]zahlen; **you ~s your money and you takes your choice** *(Brit. fig. coll.)* die Wahl steht bei Ihnen; **~ sth. into a bank account** etw. auf ein Konto ein[be]zahlen; Ⓒ *(bestow)* **~ sb. a visit** jmdm. einen Besuch abstatten *(geh.);* ⇒ *also* **attention** 1 A; **compliment** 1 A; **heed** 2; **regard** 2 A; **respect** 1 B, E; **tribute** A; Ⓓ *(yield)* einbringen, abwerfen ‹Dividende usw.›; **this job ~s very little** diese Arbeit bringt sehr wenig ein; Ⓔ *(be profitable to)* **it ~s him to live overseas** er steht sich finanziell besser *(ugs.),* seit er im Ausland lebt; **it would ~ her to do that** *(fig.)* es würde ihr nichts schaden *od.* es würde sich für sie bezahlt machen, das zu tun; Ⓕ **~ the price** den Preis zahlen; **it's too high a price to ~:** das ist ein zu hoher Preis. ⇒ *also* **court** 1 F; **devil** 1 C; **piper** A. ❸ *v.i.,* **paid** Ⓐ zahlen; **~ for sth./sb.** etw./für jmdn. bezahlen; **I'll ~ for you as well** ich bezahle für dich mit; **sth. ~s for itself** etw. macht sich bezahlt; **has this been paid for?** ist das schon bezahlt?; **I'd like to know what I'm ~ing for** ich wüsste gern, wofür ich eigentlich mein Geld ausgebe; Ⓑ *(yield)* sich lohnen; sich auszahlen; ‹Geschäft:› rentabel sein; **it ~s to be careful** es lohnt sich, vorsichtig zu sein; Ⓒ *(fig.: suffer)* büßen müssen; **if you do this you'll have to ~ for it later** wenn du das tust, wirst du später dafür büßen müssen. ⇒ *also* **crime** B; **nose** 1 A; **paid**

**~ aˈway** ⇒ **~ out** 1 B

**~ ˈback** *v.t.* Ⓐ zurückzahlen; **I'll ~ you back later** ich gebe dir das Geld später zurück; Ⓑ *(fig.)* erwidern ‹Kompliment›; sich revanchieren für ‹Beleidigung, Untreue›; **I'll ~ him back** ich werde es ihm heimzahlen; **I'll ~ him back with interest** ich werde es ihm mit Zins und Zinseszins zurückzahlen

**~ ˈin** *v.t. & i.* einzahlen

**~ ˈoff** ❶ *v.t.* Ⓐ auszahlen ‹Arbeiter›; abmustern ‹Schiffsbesatzung›; abbezahlen ‹Schulden›; ablösen ‹Hypothek›; befriedigen ‹Gläubiger›; *(fig.)* abgelten ‹Verpflichtung›; Ⓑ *(coll.: bribe)* schmieren *(salopp abwertend); (pay hush-money to)* Schweigegeld zahlen (+ *Dat.*). ❷ *v.i.* Ⓐ *(coll.)* sich auszahlen; sich bezahlt machen; Ⓑ *(Naut.)* leewärts steuern. ⇒ *also* **pay-off**

**~ ˈout** ❶ *v.t.* Ⓐ auszahlen; *(spend)* ausgeben; **we've already paid out a fortune to these people** wir haben schon ein Vermögen an diese Leute bezahlt *od.* für diese Leute ausgegeben; **~ out large sums on sth.** hohe Beträge für etw. ausgeben; Ⓑ *(Naut.)* ablaufen lassen ‹Seil, Tau›; Ⓒ *(coll.: punish)* **~ sb. out** es jmdm. heimzahlen; **~ sb. out for sth.** jmdm. etw. heimzahlen. ⇒ *also* **pay-out.** ❷ *v.i.* bezahlen

**~ ˈup** ❶ *v.t.* zurückzahlen ‹Schulden›. ❷ *v.i.* zahlen. ⇒ *also* **paid-up**

**payable** /ˈpeɪəbl/ *adj.* Ⓐ *(due)* zahlbar; **be ~ to sb.** jmdm. *od.* an jmdn. zu zahlen sein; Ⓑ *(that may be paid)* zahlbar; **make a cheque ~ to the Post Office/to sb.** einen Scheck auf die Post/auf jmds. Namen ausstellen

**ˈpay and display** ❶ *n.* Parken mit Parkschein; *attrib.* Parkschein-; **park in the ~:** auf dem [gebührenpflichtigen] Parkplatz mit Parkscheinautomat parken. ❷ *n.* **~ car park** Parkplatz mit Parkscheinautomat

**pay: ~-as-you-ˈearn** *attrib. adj. (Brit.)* **~-as-you-earn system/method** Quellenabzugsverfahren, *das;* **~-as-you-earn tax system** *Steuersystem, bei dem die Lohnsteuer direkt einbehalten wird;* **~-as-you-ˈenter** *attrib. adj.* ‹Bus› *in dem man das Fahrgeld beim Einsteigen bezahlt;* **~ award** *n.* Gehaltserhöhung, *die;* **~ bed** *n.* Privatbett, *das;* **~ cheque** *n.* Lohn-/Gehaltsscheck, *der;* **~ claim** *n.* Lohn-/Gehaltsforderung, *die;* **~ day** *n.* Zahltag, *der;* **~ dirt** *n. (Amer.)* abbauwürdiges Erzlager; **hit ~ dirt** *(fig.)* einen Volltreffer landen *(fig. ugs.)*

**PAYE** *abbr. (Brit.)* **pay-as-you-earn**

**payee** /peɪˈiː/ *n.* Zahlungsempfänger, *der/*-empfängerin, *die*

**pay envelope** *(Amer.)* ⇒ **pay packet**

**payer** /ˈpeɪə(r)/ *n.* Zahler, *der/*Zahlerin, *die;* **bad ~:** unzuverlässiger Zahler

**ˈpay increase** ⇒ **pay rise**

**paying**/ˈpeɪɪŋ/: **~ ˈguest** *n.* zahlender Gast; **~-ˈin book** *n. (Brit. Banking) Heft mit Einzahlungsscheinen;* **~-ˈin slip** *n. (Brit. Banking)* Einzahlungsschein, *der;* **~ patient** *n.* Privatpatient, *der/*-patientin, *die*

**pay: ~load** *n.* Nutzlast, *die;* **~master** *n.* Zahlmeister, *der; (fig.)* Geldgeber, *der;* **P~master ˈGeneral** *n. (Brit. Admin.)* Generalzahlmeister des englischen Schatzamts

**payment** /ˈpeɪmənt/ *n.* Ⓐ *(of sum, bill, debt, fine)* Bezahlung, *die; (of interest, instalment, tax, fee)* Zahlung, *die; (paying back)* Rückzahlung, *die; (in instalments)* Abzahlung, *die;* **in ~ [for sth.]** als Bezahlung [für etw.]; **~ on account** Akontozahlung, *die;* **stop ~** ‹Bank:› die Zahlungen einstellen; **stop ~ on a cheque** einen Scheck sperren; **on ~ of ...:** gegen Zahlung von ...; Ⓑ *(amount)* Zahlung, *die;* **make a ~:** eine Zahlung leisten; **by monthly ~s** auf Monatsraten; Ⓒ *(fig.)* Belohnung, *die;* Lohn, *der;* **be fitting ~ for sth.** der gerechte Lohn für etw. sein

**pay: ~ negotiations** *n. pl.* Tarifverhandlungen; **~-off** *n. (coll.) (return)* Lohn, *der; (punishment)* Quittung, *die; (climax)* Clou, *der (ugs.); (bribe)* Bestechungsgeld, *das;* Schmiergeld, *das (ugs. abwertend)*

**payola** /peɪˈəʊlə/ *n. (bribery)* Bestechung, *die; (bribe)* Bestechungsgeld, *das;* Schmiergeld, *das (ugs. abwertend)*

**pay: ~out** *n.* Auszahlung, *die;* **~ packet** *n. (Brit.)* Lohntüte, *die;* **~-per-view** *n.* Pay-per-view, *das;* **~ phone** *n.* Münzfernsprecher, *der;* **~ rise** *n.* Lohn-/Gehaltserhöhung, *die;* **~roll** *n.* Lohnliste, *die;* **have 200 workers/people on the ~roll** 200 Arbeiter beschäftigen/Beschäftigte haben; **be on sb.'s ~roll** für jmdn. *od.* bei jmdm. arbeiten; **a ~roll of about a hundred** etwa hundert Arbeitsplätze; **reduce the ~roll** die Lohn- und Gehaltssumme senken; **~ round** *n.* Tarifrunde, *die;* **~slip** *n.* Lohnstreifen, *der/*Gehaltszettel, *der;* **~ station** *(Amer.)* ⇒ **~ phone;** **~ talks** *n. pl.* Tarifverhandlungen; **~ television** *n.* Münzfernsehen, *das*

**PC** *abbr.* Ⓐ ▶ 1617 *(Brit.)* **police constable** Wachtm.; Ⓑ ▶ 1617 *(Brit.)* **Privy Counsellor** Geh. R.; Geh. Rat; Ⓒ **personal computer** PC; Ⓓ **politically correct** politisch korrekt

**p.c.** *abbr.* **per cent** v. H.

**pct.** *abbr. (Amer.)* **per cent** v. H.

**p.d.q.** /piːdiːˈkjuː/ *abbr. (coll.)* **pretty damn quick** verdammt schnell *(ugs.)*

**PE** *abbr.* **physical education**

**pea** /piː/ *n.* Erbse, *die; (plant)* Erbse[npflanze], *die;* **they are as like as two ~s [in a pod]** sie gleichen sich *(Dat.) od.* einander wie ein Ei dem anderen; ⇒ *also* **chickpea; split pea; sweet pea**

**peace** /piːs/ *n.* Ⓐ *(freedom from war)* Frieden, *der;* Friede, *der (geh.); (treaty)* Frieden, *der;* Friedensschluss, *der;* **these countries are now at ~:** zwischen diesen Ländern herrscht jetzt Frieden; **maintain/restore ~:** den Frieden bewahren/wieder herstellen; **~ talks/treaty** Friedensgespräche *Pl.*/Friedensvertrag, *der;* **make ~ [with sb.]** [mit jmdm.] Frieden schließen; **the P~ of Utrecht** *(Hist.)* der Friede von Utrecht; Ⓑ *(freedom from civil disorder)* Ruhe und Ordnung; öffentliche Ordnung; *(absence of discord)* Frieden, *der;* **in ~ [and harmony]** in [Frieden und] Eintracht; **restore ~:** Ruhe und Ordnung wieder herstellen; **the [King's/Queen's] ~:** die öffentliche Ordnung; **bind sb. over to keep the ~:** jmdn. verwarnen *od.* rechtlich verpflichten, die öffentliche Ordnung zu wahren; **be at ~ [with sb./sth.]** mit jmdm./etw. in Frieden leben; **be at ~ with oneself** mit sich selbst im Reinen sein; **make [one's] ~ [with sb.]** sich [mit jmdm.] aussöhnen *od.* versöhnen; **make one's ~ with God/the world** seinen Frieden mit Gott/der Welt machen; **hold one's ~:** schweigen; ruhig sein; Ⓒ *(tranquillity)* Ruhe, *die; (stillness)* Stille, *die;* Ruhe, *die;* **in ~:** in Ruhe; **leave sb. in ~:** jmdn. in Frieden *od.* in Ruhe lassen; **I get no ~:** ich habe keine ruhige Minute; **give sb. no ~:** jmdm. keine Ruhe lassen; **~ and quiet** Ruhe und Frieden; **the ~ and quiet of the countryside** die friedvolle Ruhe der Landschaft; Ⓓ *(mental state)* Ruhe, *die;* **find ~:** Frieden finden; **~ of mind** Seelenfrieden, *der;* innere Ruhe; **I shall have no ~ of mind until I**

**know it** ich werde keine ruhige Minute haben, bis ich es weiß; **E** (*in or following biblical use*) ~ **be with** *or* **unto you** Friede sei mit dir/euch; **go in ~:** gehe/gehet hin in Frieden; **may his soul rest in ~:** er ruhe in Frieden; **he is at ~** (*literary: is dead*) er ruht in Frieden (*geh.*). ⇒ *also* **breach** 1 A; **justice** C

**peaceable** /'pi:səbl/ *adj.* **A** (*not quarrelsome*) friedfertig; friedliebend ‹Volk›; (*calm*) friedlich; **B** (*quiet, undisturbed*) friedlich

**peaceably** /'pi:səblɪ/ *adv.* **A** (*amicably*) friedlich; **B** (*quietly, in peace*) friedlich; **go ~ about one's business** in Ruhe seinen Geschäften nachgehen

**'Peace Corps** *n.* (*Amer.*) Friedenskorps, *das*

**'peace dividend** *n.* Friedensdividende, *die*

**peaceful** /'pi:sfl/ *adj.* friedlich; friedfertig ‹Person, Volk›; ruhig ‹Augenblick›; ⇒ *also* **coexistence**

**peacefully** /'pi:sfəlɪ/ *adv.* friedlich; **die ~:** sanft entschlafen

**peace: ~keeper** *n.* Friedenswächter, *der;* **~keeping** **1** *adj.* ‹Maßnahmen, Operationen› zur Friedenssicherung; **~keeping force** Friedenstruppe, *die;* **2** *n.* Friedenssicherung, *die;* **~-loving** *adj.* friedliebend; **~maker** *n.* Friedensstifter, *der*/-stifterin, *die;* **blessed are the ~makers** (*Bibl.*) selig sind die Friedfertigen; **~ offer** *n.* Friedensangebot, *das;* **~ offering** *n.* Friedensangebot, *das;* (*fig.*) Versöhnungsgeschenk, *das;* **~ pipe** *n.* Friedenspfeife, *die;* **~ plan** *n.* Friedensplan, *der;* **~ process** *n.* Friedensprozess, *der;* **~time** *n.* Friedenszeiten *Pl.; attrib.* Friedens‹produktion, -wirtschaft, -stärke›; in Friedenszeiten *nachgestellt*

**peach** /pi:tʃ/ *n.* **A** Pfirsich, *der;* **~es-and-cream complexion** Pfirsichhaut, *die;* **B** ⇒ **peach tree**; **C** (*coll.*) **sb./sth. is a ~:** jmd./etw. ist spitze *od.* klasse (*ugs.*); **a ~ of a woman/man/house** eine klasse Frau/ein klasse Kerl *od.* Typ/ein klasse Haus (*ugs.*); **D** (*colour*) Pfirsichton, *der*

**peach: ~ blossom** *n.* Pfirsichblüte, *die;* **~ 'brandy** *n.* Pfirsichbrandy, *der;* Pfirsichlikör, *der;* **~-coloured** *adj.* pfirsichfarben

**'peachick** *n.* Pfauküken, *das*

**peach: ~ 'Melba** *n.* Pfirsich Melba, *der;* **~ tree** *n.* Pfirsichbaum, *der*

**'peacock** *n.* Pfau, *der;* Pfauhahn, *der;* **strut like a ~:** wie ein Pfau einherstolzieren; **proud/vain as a ~:** stolz/eitel wie ein Pfau; **be proud as a ~ of sth.** vor Stolz auf etw. (*Akk.*) fast bersten

**peacock: ~ 'blue** **1** *adj.* pfauenblau; **2** *n.* Pfauenblau, *das;* **~ butterfly** *n.* Tagpfauenauge, *das*

**'peafowl** *n.* Pfau, *der*

**'pea-green** *adj.* erbsengrün; maigrün

**'peahen** *n.* Pfauhenne, *die*

**'pea jacket** *n.* Kolani, *der;* Pijacke, *die* (*Seew. veralt.*)

**peak** /pi:k/ **1** *n.* **A** (*of cap*) Schirm, *der;* Schild, *der;* **B** (*of mountain*) Gipfel, *der;* (*of waves*) Kamm, *der;* Krone, *die;* **C** (*highest point*) Höhepunkt, *der;* **reach/be at/be past its ~:** seinen Höhepunkt erreichen/den Höhepunkt erreicht haben/den Höhepunkt überschritten haben; **his career was at its ~:** er stand auf dem Höhepunkt seiner Laufbahn; **D** (*Naut.*) Piek, *die.* **2** *attrib. adj.* Höchst-, Spitzen‹preise, -werte›; **~ listening/viewing audience** höchste Einschaltquote; **~ listening/viewing period** Hauptsendezeit, *die.* **3** *v.i.* seinen Höhepunkt erreichen; **~ too soon** (*Sport*) vorzeitig in Höchstform sein

**peaked**[1] /pi:kt/ *adj.* **~ cap** Schirmmütze, *die*

**peaked**[2] *adj.* (*pinched*) spitz ‹Gesicht›; abgehärmt, verhärmt ‹Person, Gesicht, Aussehen›

**peak: ~-hour** *attrib. adj.* **~-hour travel** Fahren während der Hauptverkehrszeit; **~-hour traffic** Stoßverkehr, *der;* **~-hour listening period** Hauptsendezeit, *die;* **~ load** *n.* Spitzenlast, *die;* **the ~ load of traffic** der Stoßverkehr; **~ season** *n.* Hochsaison, *die*

**peaky** /'pi:kɪ/ *adj.* kränklich; **look ~:** nicht gut aussehen; angeschlagen aussehen

**peal** /pi:l/ **1** *n.* **A** (*ringing*) Geläut[e], *das;* Läuten, *das;* **~ of bells** Glockengeläut[e], *das;* Glockenläuten, *das;* **B** (*set of bells*) Glockenspiel, *das;* **C** (*loud sound*) **a ~ of laughter** schallendes Gelächter; **a ~ of thunder** ein Donnerschlag. **2** *v.i.* ‹Glocken:› läuten; ‹Donner:› rollen; ‹Trompete:› schmettern. **3** *v.t.* **A** erschallen lassen; **B** (*ring*) läuten ‹Glocken›

**~ 'out** *v.i.* tönen

**peanut** /'pi:nʌt/ *n.* Erdnuss, *die;* **~ butter** Erdnussbutter, *die;* **~s** (*coll.*) (*trivial thing*) ein Klacks (*ugs.*); kleine Fische *Pl.;* (*money*) ein paar Kröten (*salopp*); **this is ~s compared to ...:** das ist ein Klacks gegen ...; **work for ~s** für ein Butterbrot arbeiten (*ugs.*); **sell sth. for ~s** etw. für ein Butterbrot *od.* für einen Apfel und ein Ei verkaufen (*ugs.*); **this costs ~s compared to ...:** das ist [fast] geschenkt im Vergleich zu ... (*ugs.*); **be worth ~s** kaum etw. wert sein

**pear** /peə(r)/ *n.* **A** (*fruit*) Birne, *die;* **B** ⇒ **pear tree.** ⇒ *also* **anchovy pear**; **avocado pear**; **prickly pear**

**'pear drop** *n. hartes Bonbon in Birnenform [mit Birnengeschmack]*

**pearl** /pɜ:l/ *n.* **A** Perle, *die;* **[string of] ~s** (*necklace*) Perlenkette, *die;* **B** (*fig.*) Juwel, *das;* Kleinod, *das;* Perle, *die;* **be a ~ of architecture** ein Juwel der Baukunst sein; **~ of wisdom** (*often iron.*) Weisheit, *die;* **cast ~s before swine** (*fig.*) Perlen vor die Säue werfen (*salopp*); **C** (*~-like thing*) Perle, *die;* **~s of dew** Tautropfen. ⇒ *also* **mother-of-pearl**; **seed pearl**

**pearl: ~ 'barley** *n.* Perlengraupen *Pl.;* **~ 'bulb** *n.* matte Glühbirne; **~ 'button** *n.* Perlmutt[er]knopf, *der;* **~ diver** *n.* Perlentaucher, *der*/-taucherin, *die;* **~ fisher** *n.* Perlenfischer, *der*/-fischerin, *die;* **~-grey** *adj.* perlgrau; **~ oyster** *n.* Perlmuschel, *die*

**pearly** /'pɜ:lɪ/ *adj.* **A** perlmuttern, perlenähnlich, (*geh.*) perlengleich ‹Glanz, Schimmer›; perl[en]förmig ‹Regen-, Tautropfen›; **B** (*set with pearls*) perlenbesetzt; **P~ Gates** Himmelstür, *die;* **~ king/queen** (*Brit.*) *Straßenverkäufer/-verkäuferin in London mit perlenbestickter Kleidung*

**'pear-shaped** *adj.* birnenförmig

**peart** /pɜ:t/ *adj.* (*Amer.*) fröhlich

**'pear tree** *n.* Birnbaum, *der;* Birne, *die*

**peasant** /'pezənt/ *n.* **A** [armer] Bauer, *der;* Landarbeiter, *der;* **~ farmer** Bauer, *der;* **~ uprising** Bauernaufstand, *der;* **~ economy** Agrarwirtschaft, *die;* **~ woman** Bauersfrau, *die;* **B** (*coll. derog.*) (*ignorant or stupid person*) Bauer, *der* (*ugs. abwertend*); (*lower-class person*) Plebejer, *der* (*abwertend*)

**peasantry** /'pezəntrɪ/ *n.* Bauernschaft, *die*

**pease pudding** /pi:z'pʊdɪŋ/ *n.* Erbsenpudding, *der*

**pea: ~-shooter** *n.* Pusterohr, *das;* **~ 'soup** *n.* Erbsensuppe, *die;* **~-stick** *n.* Bohnenstange, *die*

**peat** /pi:t/ *n.* **A** (*substance*) Torf, *der;* **B** (*piece*) Torfstück, *das;* Torfsode, *die;* **cut ~:** Torf stechen

**peat: ~bog,** (*Brit.*) **~moor** *ns.* Torfmoor, *das*

**peaty** /'pi:tɪ/ *adj.* torfig

**pebble** /'pebl/ *n.* Kiesel[stein], *der;* **he is/you are not the only ~ on the beach** es gibt noch andere

**pebble: ~dash** *n.* Kieselrauputz, *der; attrib.* mit Kieselrauputz *nachgestellt;* **~ glasses** *n. pl.* [dicke] Brille; **~ lens** *n.* [dickes] Brillenglas

**pebbly** /'peblɪ/ *adj.* steinig

**pecan** /pɪ'kæn/ *n.* **A** (*nut*) Pekannuss, *die;* **B** (*tree*) Pekannussbaum, *der*

**peccadillo** /pekə'dɪləʊ/ *n., pl.* **~es** *or* **~s** (*small sin*) leichte Verfehlung; (*small fault*) kleiner Fehler

**peccary** /'pekərɪ/ *n.* (*Zool.*) Pekari, *das;* Nabelschwein, *das*

**peck**[1] /pek/ **1** *v.t.* **A** hacken; picken ‹Körner›; **the bird ~ed my finger/was ~ing the bark** der Vogel pickte mir *od.* mich in den Finger/pickte an der Rinde; **B** (*kiss*) flüchtig küssen. **2** *v.i.* picken (**at** nach); **~ at one's food** in seinem Essen herumstochern. **3** *n.* **A** **the hen gave its chick a ~:** die Henne pickte *od.* hackte nach ihrem Küken; **B** (*kiss*) flüchtiger Kuss; Küsschen, *das*

**~ 'out** *v.t.* aushacken; auspicken

**~ 'up** *v.t.* aufpicken

**peck**[2] *n.* (*measure*) Viertelscheffel, *der;* **a ~ of trouble/dirt** (*fig.*) ein gerütteltes Maß an Sorgen/eine Menge Schmutz

**pecker** /'pekə(r)/ *n.* **A** (*Amer. sl.: penis*) Schwanz, *der* (*salopp*); **B** **keep your ~ up** (*Brit. coll.*) halt die Ohren steif (*ugs.*)

**pecking order** /'pekɪŋ ɔ:də(r)/ *n.* Hackordnung, *die*

**peckish** /'pekɪʃ/ *adj.* **A** (*coll.: hungry*) hungrig; **feel/get ~:** Hunger haben/bekommen; **B** (*Amer. coll.: irritable*) gereizt

**pectin** /'pektɪn/ *n.* (*Chem.*) Pektin, *das*

**pectoral** /'pektərl/ **1** *n.* **A** (*Med.*) Hustenmittel, *das;* **B** *in pl.* (*often joc.*) Brustmuskeln. **2** *adj.* (*Anat.*) pektoral (*fachspr.*); Brust‹höhle, -atmung›

**pectoral: ~ 'cross** *n.* (*Eccl.*) Pektorale, *das;* **~ fin** *n.* (*Zool.*) Brustflosse, *die;* **~ muscle** *n.* (*Anat.*) Brustmuskel, *der*

**peculiar** /pɪ'kju:lɪə(r)/ *adj.* **A** (*strange*) seltsam; eigenartig; sonderbar; **what a ~ person he is!** was ist er doch für ein komischer Kauz! (*ugs.*); **I feel [slightly] ~:** mir ist [etwas] komisch; **a ~ incident occurred** es passierte etwas Seltsames; **B** (*especial*) besonder...; **be of ~ interest [to sb.]** [für jmdn.] von besonderem Interesse sein; **C** (*belonging exclusively*) eigentümlich (**to** *Dat.*); **this bird is ~ to South Africa** dieser Vogel kommt nur in Südafrika vor; **she has a ~ style of acting, all her own** sie hat einen ganz eigenen Stil zu spielen

**peculiarity** /pɪkju:lɪ'ærɪtɪ/ *n.* **A** *no pl., no indef. art.* (*unusualness*) Ausgefallenheit, *die;* (*of behaviour, speech*) Sonderbarkeit, *die;* Merkwürdigkeit, *die;* **B** (*odd trait*) Eigentümlichkeit, *die;* **behavioural peculiarities** seltsame Verhaltensweisen; **C** (*distinguishing characteristic*) [charakteristisches] Merkmal; Kennzeichen, *das;* (*special characteristic*) Besonderheit, *die*

**peculiarly** /pɪ'kju:lɪəlɪ/ *adv.* **A** (*strangely*) seltsam; eigenartig; sonderbar; **B** (*especially*) besonders; **C** (*in a way that is one's own*) **be something ~ British** etwas rein Britisches sein; **a treatment ~ his own** eine ganz eigene Behandlung

**pecuniary** /pɪ'kju:nɪərɪ/ *adj.* (*of money*) finanziell, (*geh.*) pekuniär ‹Hilfe, Überlegungen›; **~ award** Geldpreis, *der*

**pedagog** (*Amer.*) ⇒ **pedagogue**

**pedagogic[al]** /pedə'gɒgɪk(l), pedə'gɒdʒɪk(l)/ *adj.* **A** (*arch./derog.: of a pedagogue*) belehrend; schulmeisterlich (*abwertend*); **B** (*of pedagogy*) pädagogisch

**pedagogue** /'pedəgɒg/ *n.* **A** (*arch.: teacher*) Pädagoge, *der*/Pädagogin, *die;* **B** (*derog.: pedantic teacher*) Schulmeister, *der* (*abwertend*)

**pedagogy** /'pedəgɒdʒɪ/ *n.* Pädagogik, *die*

**pedal** /'pedl/ **1** *n.* **A** (*Mus.*) (*organ key, on piano*) Pedal, *das;* (*organ stop control*) Fußtritt, *der;* Fußhebel, *der;* **loud ~:** rechtes Pedal; Fortepedal, *das;* **soft ~:** linkes Pedal; Pianopedal, *das;* **B** (*of bicycle, ~ bin; Mech. Engin., Motor Veh.*) Pedal, *das.* **2** *v.i.,* (*Brit.*) **-ll-:** **A** (*work cycle ~s*) **~ [away]** in die Pedale treten; strampeln (*ugs.*); **B** (*ride*) [mit dem Fahrrad] fahren; radeln (*ugs.*); **~ by/off** vorbeiradeln/losradeln (*ugs.*); **C** (*Mus.*) (*on organ*) das Pedal spielen; (*on piano*) die Pedale benutzen. **3** *v.t.,* (*Brit.*) **-ll-** (*propel*) fahren mit ‹Fahrrad, Dreirad›; **~ one's bike** Rad fahren; radeln (*ugs.*)

**pedal: ~ bin** *n.* Treteimer, *der;* **~ car** *n.* Tretauto, *das*

**pedalo** /'pedələʊ/ *n., pl.* **~s** Tretboot, *das*

**'pedal pushers** *n. pl. dreiviertellange Damen-/Mädchenhose*

**pedant** /'pedənt/ *n.* **A** (*one who overrates learning*) Stubengelehrte, *der/die;* **B**

P

(*stickler for formal detail*) Pedant, *der*/Pedantin, *die* (*abwertend*); Kleinigkeitskrämer, *der*/-krämerin, *die* (*abwertend*)

**pedantic** /pɪˈdæntɪk/ *adj.* Ⓐ (*ostentatiously learned*) schulmeisterlich (*abwertend*); Ⓑ (*unduly concerned with formal detail*) pedantisch (*abwertend*)

**pedantry** /ˈpedəntrɪ/ *n.* Pedanterie, *die;* Kleinlichkeit, *die* (*abwertend*)

**peddle** /ˈpedl/ *v.t.* Ⓐ auf der Straße verkaufen; (*from door to door*) hausieren mit; handeln mit, (*ugs.*) dealen mit ‹Drogen, Rauschgift›; Ⓑ (*fig.: disseminate*) hausieren [gehen] mit ‹Theorie, Vorschlag›; verbreiten ‹Neuigkeiten, Klatsch, Gerücht›

**peddler** /ˈpedlə(r)/ ⇒ **pedlar**

**pederast** /ˈpedəræst/ *n.* Päderast, *der*

**pederasty** /ˈpedəræstɪ/ *n., no pl., no indef. art.* Päderastie, *die*

**pedestal** /ˈpedɪstl/ *n.* Sockel, *der;* **knock sb. off his ~** (*fig.*) jmdn. von seinem Sockel stoßen; **put** *or* **set sb./sth. on a ~** (*fig.*) jmdn./etw. in den Himmel heben (*ugs.*)

**pedestrian** /pɪˈdestrɪən/ ❶ *adj.* (*uninspired*) trocken; langweilig. ❷ *n.* Fußgänger, *der*/-gängerin, *die;* **~-controlled** *or* **~-operated lights** Bedarfsampel, *die*

**pedestrian ˈcrossing** *n.* Fußgängerüberweg, *der*

**pedestrianism** /pɪˈdestrɪənɪzm/ *n., no pl.* (*of style*) Trockenheit, *die;* Langweiligkeit, *die*

**pedestrianize** (**pedestrianise**) /pɪˈdestrɪənaɪz/ *v.t.* zur Fußgängerzone machen

**pedestrian ˈprecinct** ⇒ **precinct** A

**pediatri-** (*Amer.*) ⇒ **paediatri-**

**pediatric** (*Amer.*) ⇒ **paediatric**

**pedicel** /ˈpedɪsl/, **pedicle** /ˈpedɪkl/ *n.* (*Biol.*) Stiel, *der;* (*of flower*) [Blüten]stängel, *der*

**pedicure** /ˈpedɪkjʊə(r)/ *n. no pl., no art.* Pediküre, *die;* Fußpflege, *die;* **give sb. a ~:** jmdn. pediküren

**pedigree** /ˈpedɪgriː/ ❶ *n.* Ⓐ (*genealogical table*) Stammbaum, *der;* Ahnentafel, *die* (*geh.*); Ⓑ (*ancestral line*) Stammbaum, *der;* Ahnenreihe, *die;* (*of animal*) Stammbaum, *der;* Ⓒ (*derivation*) Herkunft, *die;* Ⓓ *no pl., no art.* (*ancient descent*) **have ~, be a man/woman of ~:** von berühmten Ahnen abstammen. ❷ *adj.* (*with recorded line of descent*) mit Stammbaum *nachgestellt*

**pedigreed** /ˈpedɪgriːd/ ⇒ **pedigree** 2

**pediment** /ˈpedɪmənt/ *n.* (*Archit.*) (*in Grecian style*) Giebeldreieck, *das;* (*in Roman or Renaissance style*) Ziergiebel, *der*

**pedlar** /ˈpedlə(r)/ *n.* Ⓐ Straßenhändler, *der*/-händlerin, *die;* (*from door to door*) Hausierer, *der*/Hausiererin, *die;* (*selling drugs*) Rauschgifthändler, *der*/-händlerin, *die;* Dealer, *der*/Dealerin, *die* (*ugs.*); Ⓑ (*fig.: disseminator*) **be a ~ of gossip/scandal** *etc.* Klatsch/Skandalgeschichten *usw.* verbreiten

**pedometer** /pɪˈdɒmɪtə(r)/ *n.* Pedometer, *das* (*fachspr.*); Schrittzähler, *der*

**peduncle** /pɪˈdʌŋkl/ *n.* (*Bot., Zool.*) Stiel, *der*

**pee** /piː/ (*coll.*) ❶ *v.i.* pinkeln (*salopp*); Pipi machen (*Kinderspr.*). ❷ *n.* Ⓐ (*urination*) **need/have a ~:** pinkeln müssen/pinkeln (*salopp*); **I must go for a ~:** ich muss mal eben pinkeln (*salopp*); Ⓑ (*urine*) Pipi, *das* (*Kinderspr.*)

**peek** /piːk/ ❶ *v.i.* gucken (*ugs.*); **no ~ing!** nicht gucken!; **~ at sb./sth.** zu jmdm./etw. hingucken; **~ in at sb.** zu jmdm. hereingucken. ❷ *n.* (*quick*) kurzer Blick; (*sly*) verstohlener Blick; **take a quick ~ round** sich schnell umgucken; **have a ~ through the keyhole** durch das Schlüsselloch gucken (*ugs.*); **take a quick ~ at sb.** kurz zu jmdm. hingucken; **give sb. a ~ at sth.** jmdn. einen Blick auf etw. (*Akk.*) werfen lassen

**peekaboo** /ˈpiːkəbuː/ ❶ *n.* (*Amer.*) ⇒ **peep-bo**. ❷ *adj.* durchsichtig; (*with pattern of small holes*) mit Lochmuster *nachgestellt;* **~ design** Lochmuster, *das*

**peel** /piːl/ ❶ *v.t.* schälen; **~ the shell off an egg/the skin off a banana** ein Ei/eine Banane schälen; ⇒ *also* **eye** 1 A. ❷ *v.i.* Ⓐ ‹Person, Haut:› sich schälen *od.* (*bes. nordd.*) pellen; ‹Rinde, Borke:› sich lösen; ‹Farbe:› abblättern; Ⓑ (*coll.: undress*) sich ausziehen. ❸ *n.* Schale, *die;* ⇒ *also* **candy** 2

**~ aˈway** ❶ *v.t.* abschälen. ❷ *v.i.* Ⓐ ‹Haut:› sich schälen *od.* (*bes. nordd.*) pellen; ‹Rinde, Borke:› sich lösen; ‹Farbe:› abblättern; Ⓑ (*veer away*) ausscheren

**~ ˈback** *v.t.* halb abziehen ‹Kabelmantel, Bananenschale›; zurückziehen ‹Bettdecke›; umschlagen ‹Stoffmuster›

**~ ˈoff** ❶ *v.t.* abschälen; abstreifen, ausziehen ‹Kleider›. ❷ *v.i.* Ⓐ ⇒ **~ away** 2 A; Ⓑ (*veer away*) ausscheren; Ⓒ ⇒ **peel** 2 B

**peeler** /ˈpiːlə(r)/ *n.* Schäler, *der;* Schälmesser, *das*

**peeling** /ˈpiːlɪŋ/ *n.* Stück Schale; **~s** Schalen

**peep¹** /piːp/ ❶ *v.i.* ‹Maus, Vogel:› piep[s]en; (*squeal*) quieken. ❷ *n.* (*shrill sound*) Piepsen, *das;* (*coll.: slight utterance*) Piep[s], *der* (*ugs.*); **one ~ out of you and …:** ein Pieps [von dir], und …

**peep²** ❶ *v.i.* Ⓐ (*look through narrow aperture*) gucken (*ugs.*); spähen (*geh., veralt., noch landsch.*); Ⓑ (*look furtively*) verstohlen gucken; linsen (*ugs.*); **~ round** sich umgucken; **no ~ing!** nicht gucken!; Ⓒ (*come into view*) **~ out** [he]rausgucken; hervorgucken; (*fig.: show itself*) zum Vorschein kommen; durchscheinen. ❷ *n.* kurzer Blick; **steal a ~ at sb.** verstohlen zu jmdm. hingucken; **take a ~ through the curtain** durch die Gardine spähen *od.* (*ugs.*) linsen

**peep-bo** /ˈpiːpbəʊ/ ❶ *n.* Guck-guck-Spiel, *das.* ❷ *int.* guck, guck; kuckuck

**ˈpeephole** *n.* Guckloch, *das*

**peeping Tom** /piːpɪŋ ˈtɒm/ *n.* Spanner, *der* (*ugs.*); Voyeur, *der; attrib.* voyeuristisch

**ˈpeep show** *n.* Ⓐ (*exhibition of small pictures in box*) Guckkastenschau, *die;* Ⓑ (*erotic spectacle*) Peepshow, *die*

**peep-toe[d]** /ˈpiːptəʊ(d)/ *adj.* vorn offen ‹Schuh›; zehenfrei ‹Sandale›; **the shoes had a ~ design** die Schuhe waren vorn offen

**peer¹** /pɪə(r)/ *n.* Ⓐ (*Brit.: member of nobility*) **~ [of the realm]** Peer, *der;* ⇒ *also* **life peer**; Ⓑ (*noble of any country*) hoher Adliger; **the ~s of France** der Hochadel Frankreichs; Ⓒ (*equal in standing*) Gleichgestellte, *der/die;* **be judged by a jury of one's ~s** von seinesgleichen gerichtet werden; **among her social ~s** unter ihresgleichen; Ⓓ (*equal in attainment*) Ebenbürtige, *der/die;* **find sb.'s ~:** jemanden finden, der jmdm. ebenbürtig ist

**peer²** *v.i.* (*look searchingly*) forschend schauen; (*look with difficulty*) angestrengt schauen; **~ at sth./sb.** (*searchingly*) [sich (*Dat.*)] etw. genau ansehen/jmdn. forschend *od.* prüfend ansehen; (*with difficulty*) [sich (*Dat.*)] etw. angestrengt ansehen/jmdn. angestrengt ansehen; **~ into a cave/the distance** in eine Höhle/die Ferne spähen; **~ down at sb.** zu jmdm. hinunter-/herunterspähen

**peerage** /ˈpɪərɪdʒ/ *n.* Ⓐ *no pl.* (*Brit.: body of peers*) **the ~:** die Peers; **be raised to the ~:** in den Adelsstand erhoben werden; Ⓑ (*Brit.: rank of peer*) Peerswürde, *die;* ⇒ *also* **life peerage**; Ⓒ (*nobility of any country*) Adel, *der;* Ⓓ (*book*) Peerskalender, *der; britisches Adelsverzeichnis*

**peeress** /ˈpɪəres/ *n.* Peeress, *die*

**ˈpeer group** *n.* Peergroup, *die* (*Psych., Soziol.*)

**peerless** /ˈpɪəlɪs/ *adj.* beispiellos

**ˈpeer pressure** *n.* Gruppenzwang, *der*

**peeve** /piːv/ (*coll.*) ❶ *n.* Ⓐ (*cause of annoyance*) **it was a bit of a ~:** es war ganz schön ärgerlich; **it was one of his ~s that …:** es wurmte ihn, dass … (*ugs.*); ⇒ *also* **pet¹** 2 C; Ⓑ (*mood*) **be in a [real] ~:** [stock]sauer sein (*ugs.*). ❷ *v.t.* (*irritate*) nerven (*salopp*); **it ~d me that …:** es wurmte *od.* fuchste mich, dass … (*ugs.*)

**peeved** /piːvd/ *adj.* (*coll.*) sauer (*ugs.*); **be/get ~ with sb.** auf jmdn. sauer sein/werden; **be ~ at/get ~ about sth.** über etw. (*Akk.*) sauer sein/wegen etw. sauer werden

**peevish** /ˈpiːvɪʃ/ *adj.* (*querulous*) nörgelig (*abwertend*); quengelig (*ugs.*) ‹Kind›; (*showing vexation*) gereizt

**peevishly** /ˈpiːvɪʃlɪ/ *adv.* missmutig; (*in vexation*) **do sth. ~:** etw. gereizt tun

**peewit** /ˈpiːwɪt/ *n.* Ⓐ (*Ornith.*) Kiebitz, *der;* Ⓑ (*cry*) Kiwitt, *das*

**peg** /peg/ ❶ *n.* (*pin, bolt*) (*for holding together parts of framework*) Stift, *der;* (*for tying things to*) Pflock, *der;* (*for hanging things on*) Haken, *der;* (*clothes ~*) Wäscheklammer, *die;* (*for holding tent ropes*) Hering, *der;* (*for marking cribbage scores etc.*) Stift, *der;* (*Mus.: for adjusting strings*) Wirbel, *der;* **off the ~** (*Brit.: ready-made*) von der Stange (*ugs.*); **take sb. down a ~ [or two]** (*fig.*) jmdm. einen Dämpfer aufsetzen *od.* geben; **be taken down a ~ or two** (*fig.*) einen Dämpfer bekommen; **a ~ to hang sth. on** (*fig.*) ein Aufhänger für etw.; ⇒ *also* **hole** 1 A.

❷ *v.t.,* **-gg-** Ⓐ (*fix with ~*) mit Stiften/Pflöcken befestigen; Ⓑ (*Econ.: stabilize*) stabilisieren; (*support*) stützen; (*freeze*) einfrieren; **~ wages/prices/exchange rates** Löhne/Preise/Wechselkurse stabil halten; Ⓒ (*Cribbage*) durch eingesteckte Holzstifte anzeigen ‹Spielstand›; **~ two holes** den Holzstift zwei Löcher weiter einstecken; **they are level ~ging at school** (*fig.*) sie sind gleich gut in der Schule.

❸ *v.i.,* **-gg-: keep ~ging along** bei der Stange bleiben; **she's still ~ging at her writing** sie schreibt immer noch unverdrossen weiter

**~ aˈway** *v.i.* schuften (*ugs.*); **~ away for four hours** vier Stunden lang ununterbrochen schuften; **[keep] ~[ging] away with sth.** nicht lockerlassen mit etw. (*ugs.*)

**~ ˈdown** *v.t.* Ⓐ (*secure with ~s*) festpflocken; Ⓑ ⇒ **pin down** A

**~ ˈout** ❶ *v.t.* Ⓐ (*spread out and secure*) ausspannen ‹Felle etc.›; (*Brit.: attach to line*) [draußen] aufhängen ‹Wäsche›; Ⓑ (*mark*) abstecken ‹Gebiet, Fläche›. ❷ *v.i.* Ⓐ (*coll.*) (*faint*) zusammenklappen (*ugs.*); (*die*) den Löffel abgeben (*salopp*); (*cease to function*) den Geist aufgeben (*ugs.*); Ⓑ (*Croquet*) den Zielpflock treffen; Ⓒ (*Cribbage*) gewinnen

**peg: ~board** *n.* Ⓐ (*for games*) Lochbrett, *das;* Ⓑ (*board holding hooks*) gelochte Platte; **~ leg** *n.* Ⓐ (*artificial leg*) Holzbein, *das;* Ⓑ (*person*) Stelzfuß, *der* (*ugs.*)

**peignoir** /ˈpeɪnwɑː(r)/ *n.* Negligé, *das*

**pejorative** /pɪˈdʒɒrətɪv/ ❶ *adj.* pejorativ (*Sprachw.*); abwertend; **~ word** Pejorativum, *das* (*Sprachw.*). ❷ *n.* Pejorativum, *das* (*Sprachw.*)

**pejoratively** /pɪˈdʒɒrətɪvlɪ/ *adv.* abwertend

**pekan** /ˈpekən/ *n.* (*Zool.*) Fischermarder, *der*

**peke** /piːk/ (*coll.*) ⇒ **Pekingese** 1 A

**Pekingese** /piːkɪŋˈiːz/ (**Pekinese** /piːkɪˈniːz/) ❶ *n., pl. same* Ⓐ **Pekinese [dog]** Pekinese, *der;* Ⓑ (*person*) Pekinger, *der*/Pekingerin, *die.* ❷ *attrib. adj.* Pekinger; **~ man/woman** Pekinger, *der*/Pekingerin, *die*

**pelican** /ˈpelɪkən/ *n.* (*Ornith.*) Pelikan, *der*

**ˈpelican crossing** *n.* (*Brit.*) Ampelübergang, *der*

**pellagra** /pɪˈlægrə, pɪˈleɪgrə/ *n.* ▶ 1232 (*Med.*) Pellagra, *das*

**pellet** /ˈpelɪt/ *n.* Ⓐ (*small ball*) Kügelchen, *das;* (*mass of food*) Pellet, *das* (*fachspr.*); Ⓑ (*pill*) Pille, *die;* Ⓒ (*regurgitated mass*) Gewölle, *das* (*Zool., Jägerspr.*); (*excreted mass*) Kötel, *der* (*nordd.*); Ⓓ (*small shot*) Schrot, *der od. das;* **peppered with shotgun ~s** mit Schrot[kugeln] gespickt

**pell-mell** /pelˈmel/ ❶ *adv.* Ⓐ (*in disorder*) durcheinander; (*without discrimination*) wahllos; **everything was heaped together ~:** alles wurde durcheinander auf einen Haufen geworfen; Ⓑ (*headlong*) Hals über Kopf. ❷ *adj.* [kunter]bunt; chaotisch

**pellucid** /pɪˈluːsɪd, pɪˈljuːsɪd/ *adj.* Ⓐ (*transparent*) durchsichtig; [glas]klar ‹Wasser›; Ⓑ (*clear in style*) klar; in einem klaren Stil gehalten ‹Schriften›; Ⓒ (*mentally clear*) klar ‹Verstand, Kopf›

**pelmet** /ˈpelmɪt/ *n.* (*of wood*) Blende, *die;* (*of fabric*) Schabracke, *die*

**Peloponnese** /'peləpəni:s/ *pr. n.* **the ~:** der *od.* die Peloponnes

**pelota** /pɪ'ləʊtə/ *n.* (*Sport*) Pelota, *die;* Pelotaspiel, *das*

**pelt**[1] /pelt/ *n.* **A** (*of sheep or goat*) Fell, *das;* (*of fur-bearing animal*) [Roh]fell, *das;* **sheep's ~:** Schaffell, *das;* **B** (*Tanning: raw skin*) enthaartes Fell

**pelt**[2] **1** *v.t.* **A** (*assail with missiles, lit. or fig.*) **~ sb. with sth.** jmdn. mit etw. bewerfen *od.* (*ugs.*) bombardieren; **~ sb. with questions** jmdn. mit Fragen überschütten *od.* (*ugs.*) bombardieren; **B** (*throw a stream of*) **~ sth. at sb.** jmdn. mit etw. bewerfen *od.* (*ugs.*) bombardieren; **they ~ed abuse at each other** (*fig.*) sie warfen sich [gegenseitig] Beschimpfungen an den Kopf. **2** *v.i.* **A** ‹Regen:› prasseln; **it was ~ing down [with rain]** es goss wie aus Kübeln (*ugs.*); **B** (*run fast*) rasen (*ugs.*); pesen (*ugs.*); **he set off as fast as he could ~:** so schnell er konnte, raste *od.* peste er los (*ugs.*). **3** *n., no pl., no indef. art.* **[at] full ~:** mit Karacho (*ugs.*); volle Pulle (*salopp*)

**pelvic** /'pelvɪk/ *adj.* (*Anat.*) Becken-

**pelvis** /'pelvɪs/ *n., pl.* **pelves** /'pelvi:z/ *or* **~es** ▶ **966** (*Anat.*) Becken, *das;* **renal ~:** Nierenbecken, *das*

**pen**[1] /pen/ **1** *n.* **A** (*enclosure*) Pferch, *der;* **B** (*Navy*) Bunker, *der.* **2** *v.t.,* **-nn- A** (*shut up in ~*) einpferchen; **B** (*confine*) **~ sb. in a corner** jmdn. in eine Ecke drängen

**~ 'in** *v.t.* **A** einpferchen; **B** (*fig.: restrict*) einengen; **feel ~ned in by one's life** sein Leben sehr beengend finden

**~ 'up** *v.t.* ⇒ **~ in B**

**pen**[2] **1** *n.* **A** (*for writing*) Federhalter, *der;* (*fountain ~*) Füller, *der;* (*ball ~*) Kugelschreiber, *der;* Kuli, *der* (*ugs.*); (*felt-tip ~*) Filzstift, *der;* (*ball ~ or felt-tip ~*) Stift, *der;* **make one's living by the ~:** vom Schreiben leben; **the ~ is mightier than the sword** (*prov.*) die Feder ist mächtiger als das Schwert; ⇒ *also* **paper 1 A**; **B** (*quill feather*) Feder, *die;* ⇒ *also* **quill pen**. **2** *v.t.,* **-nn-** niederschreiben; **~ a letter to/a note for sb.** jmdm. einen Brief/ein paar Worte schreiben

**pen**[3] *n.* (*female swan*) weiblicher Schwan

**pen**[4] *n.* (*Amer. coll.: penitentiary*) Knast, *der* (*ugs.*); **do eight years in the ~:** acht Jahre [Knast] abreißen (*salopp*) *od.* (*ugs.*) absitzen

**penal** /'pi:nl/ *adj.* **A** (*of punishment*) Straf‹vollzug, -gesetzbuch›; (*concerned with inflicting punishment*) strafrechtlich ‹Bestimmungen, Klauseln›; Straf‹gesetze, -gesetzgebung, -maßnahme›; **~ reform** Strafvollzugsreform, *die;* **B** (*punishable*) strafbar ‹Handlung, Tat›; **~ offence** Straftat, *die;* **C ~ colony** *or* **settlement** Strafkolonie, *die*

**penalize** (**penalise**) /'pi:nəlaɪz/ *v.t.* **A** (*subject to penalty*) bestrafen; pönalisieren (*geh.*); (*Sport*) eine Strafe verhängen gegen; **B** unter Strafe stellen ‹Handlung, Tat›

**penal 'servitude** *n., no pl., no indef. art.* (*Brit. Law. Hist.*) Zwangsarbeit, *die*

**penalty** /'penltɪ/ *n.* **A** (*punishment*) Strafe, *die;* **the ~ for this offence is imprisonment/a fine** auf dieses Delikt steht Gefängnis/eine Geldstrafe; **pay/have paid the ~/the ~ for** *or* **of sth.** (*lit. or fig.*) dafür/für etw. büßen [müssen]/gebüßt haben; **his ~ was a £50 fine** er erhielt eine [Geld]strafe von 50 Pfund; **on** *or* **under ~ of £200/of instant dismissal** bei einer Geldstrafe von 200 Pfund/unter Androhung (*Dat.*) der sofortigen Entlassung; **B** (*disadvantage*) Preis, *der;* **C** (*Sport: disadvantage imposed*) (*Horseracing*) Pönalität, *die;* (*Golf*) **~ [stroke]** Strafschlag, *der;* (*Footb., Rugby*) ⇒ **penalty kick**; (*Hockey*) ⇒ **penalty bully**; **penalty corner**; **penalty shot**; **D** (*Bridge*) Strafpunkte *Pl.*

**penalty: ~ area** *n.* (*Footb.*) Strafraum, *der;* **~ box** *n.* (*Footb.*) Strafraum, *der;* (*Ice Hockey*) Strafbank, *die;* **~ bully** *n.* (*Hockey*) Siebenmeterball, *der;* **~ clause** *n.* Strafklausel, *die;* **~ corner** *n.* (*Hockey*) Strafecke, *die;* **~ goal** *n.* (*Hockey*) Siebenmetertor, *das;* (*Rugby*) durch einen Straftritt erzieltes Tor; **~ kick** *n.* (*Footb.*) Strafstoß, *der;* Elfmeter, *der;* (*Rugby*) Straftritt, *der;* **~ shot** *n.* (*Hockey*) Strafschlag, *der;* **~ spot** *n.* (*Footb.*) Strafstoßmarke, *die;* Elfmeterpunkt, *der;* (*Hockey*) Siebenmeterpunkt, *der*

**penance** /'penəns/ *n., no pl., no art.* Buße, *die;* **act of ~:** Bußübung, *die;* Bußwerk, *das;* **undergo/do ~:** büßen/Buße tun

**'pen-and-ink** *adj.* Feder‹zeichnung, -skizze›

**pence** ⇒ **penny**

**penchant** /'pɑ̃ʃɑ̃/ *n.* Schwäche, *die;* Vorliebe, *die* (**for** für); **have a ~ for doing sth.** dazu neigen, etw. zu tun

**pencil** /'pensɪl/ **1** *n.* **A** Bleistift, *der;* **red/coloured ~:** Rot-/Bunt- *od.* Farbstift, *der;* **write in ~:** mit Bleistift schreiben; **a ~ drawing, a drawing in ~:** eine Bleistiftzeichnung; ⇒ *also* **lead pencil**; **B** (*cosmetic*) Stift, *der;* **eyebrow ~:** Augenbrauenstift, *der.* **2** *v.t.,* (*Brit.*) **-ll- A** (*mark*) mit Bleistift/Farbstift markieren; **B** (*sketch*) mit Bleistift zeichnen *od.* skizzieren; **C** (*write with ~*) mit einem Bleistift/Farbstift schreiben; **D** (*write tentatively*) entwerfen; skizzieren; ⇒ *also* **~ in B**

**~ 'in** *v.t.* **A** (*shade with ~*) mit Bleistift [aus]schraffieren; **B** (*note or arrange provisionally*) vorläufig notieren

**'pencil case** *n.* Griffelkasten, *der;* (*made of a soft material*) Federmäppchen, *das;* Schreibmäppchen, *das*

**pencilled** (*Amer.:* **penciled**) /'pensɪld/ *adj.* mit Bleistift geschrieben; nachgezogen ‹Augenbrauen›

**'pencil sharpener** *n.* Bleistiftspitzer, *der*

**pendant** /'pendənt/ **1** *n.* **A** (*hanging ornament*) Anhänger, *der;* (*light*) Hängelampe, *die;* **B** (*companion*) Pendant, *das* (*geh.*); **C** ⇒ **pennant A**. **2** *adj.* ⇒ **pendent**

**pendent** /'pendənt/ *adj.* **A** (*hanging*) herabhängend; **B** (*overhanging*) überhängend

**pending** /'pendɪŋ/ **1** *adj.* **A** (*undecided*) unentschieden ‹Angelegenheit, Sache›; anhängig (*Rechtsspr.*), schwebend ‹Verfahren›; laufend ‹Verhandlungen›; **be ~** ‹Verfahren:› noch anhängig sein (*Rechtsspr.*), noch schweben; ‹Sache, Angelegenheit:› noch unentschieden sein *od.* in der Schwebe sein; ‹Entscheidung, Probleme:› noch anstehen; ‹Debatte, Verhandlungen:› noch im Gang sein; **a treaty was ~:** es wurde über einen Vertrag verhandelt; **B** (*about to come into existence*) bevorstehend ‹Krieg›; **patent ~:** Patent angemeldet.

**2** *prep.* (*until*) **~ his return** bis zu seiner Rückkehr; **~ the final settlement** bis zur endgültigen Regelung; **~ full discussion of the matter** bis die Angelegenheit ausdiskutiert ist

**'pending tray** *n.* Ablage für noch Unerledigtes

**pendulous** /'pendjʊləs/ *adj.* **A** (*suspended, hanging down*) herabhängend; Hänge‹backen, -brüste, -ohren›; **B** (*oscillating*) pendelnd

**pendulum** /'pendjʊləm/ *n.* Pendel, *das;* **the swing of the ~** (*fig.*) der Umschwung; **according to the swing of the ~:** je nachdem, nach welcher Seite das Pendel ausschlägt (*fig.*)

**penetrable** /'penɪtrəbl/ *adj.* **A** (*capable of being entered*) durchdringlich; **scarcely ~:** fast undurchdringlich; **B** (*fig.: capable of being found out*) ergründbar; **be ~:** sich ergründen lassen; **C** (*permeable*) durchlässig

**penetrate** /'penɪtreɪt/ **1** *v.t.* **A** (*find access into*) eindringen in (+ *Akk.*); vordringen in (+ *Akk.*) ‹unbekannte Regionen›; aufbrechen ‹Safe›; (*pass through*) durchdringen; **get sth. to ~ sb.'s mind** etw. in jmds. Kopf reinkriegen (*ugs.*); **~ sb.'s disguise** (*fig.*) hinter jmds. Maske (*Akk.*) schauen; **B** (*fig.: find out*) ergründen ‹Geheimnis›; durchschauen ‹Plan, Absicht, Gedanken›; herausfinden ‹Wahrheit›; **C** (*permeate*) dringen in (+ *Akk.*); (*fig.*) durchdringen; (*infiltrate*) infiltrieren; unterwandern; ‹Spion:› sich einschleusen in (+ *Akk.*); **D** (*see into*) ‹Augen:› durchdringen ‹Dunkelheit, Nebel›; **E** (*sexually*) eindringen in (+ *Akk.*); penetrieren (*geh.*).

**2** *v.i.* **A** (*make a way*) **~ into/to sth.** in etw. (*Akk.*) eindringen/zu etw. vordringen; **~ through sth.** durch etw. hindurchdringen; **the cold ~d through the whole house** die Kälte durchdrang das ganze Haus; **B** (*be understood or realized*) **my hint did not ~:** mein Wink wurde nicht verstanden; **something's finally ~d!** der Groschen ist endlich gefallen (*ugs.*)

**penetrating** /'penɪtreɪtɪŋ/ *adj.* **A** (*easily heard*) durchdringend; **B** (*gifted with insight*) scharf ‹Verstand›; (*showing insight*) scharfsinnig ‹Bemerkung, Kommentar, Studie›; scharf ‹Beobachtung›; verstehend ‹Blick›

**penetration** /penɪ'treɪʃn/ *n.* **A** (*finding of access into*) Eindringen, *das* (**of** in + *Akk.*); (*of safe*) Aufbrechen, *das;* (*act of passing through*) Durchdringen, *das;* (*passage through*) Durchdringung, *die;* **B** *no pl.* (*fig.: discernment*) Scharfsinn, *der;* Scharfsinnigkeit, *die;* **C** (*act of permeating*) Durchdringen, *das;* Durchdringung, *die;* (*infiltration*) Infiltration, *die;* Unterwanderung, *die;* **D** (*seeing into sth.*) Durchdringen, *das;* **E** (*sexual*) Eindringen [in die Scheide]; Penetration, *die* (*geh.*)

**penetrative** /'penɪtrətɪv/ *adj.* **A** (*acute*) scharf ‹Verstand, Beobachtung›; **B** (*permeating*) eindringend

**'penfriend** *n.* Brieffreund, *der*/-freundin, *die*

**penguin** /'peŋgwɪn/ *n.* Pinguin, *der*

**'penholder** *n.* Federhalter, *der*

**penicillin** /penɪ'sɪlɪn/ *n.* (*Med.*) Penizillin, *das*

**peninsula** /pɪ'nɪnsjʊlə/ *n.* Halbinsel, *die;* **the Lleyn ~:** die Halbinsel Lleyn

**peninsular** /pɪ'nɪnsjʊlə(r)/ *adj.* **A** (*of a peninsula*) peninsular[isch]; Halbinsel-; (*like a peninsula*) halbinselartig; **B** (*Hist.: of Spain and Portugal*) **the P~ War** der Spanische Unabhängigkeitskrieg

**penis** /'pi:nɪs/ *n., pl.* **~es** *or* **penes** /'pi:ni:z/ ▶ **966** (*Anat.*) Penis, *der;* männliches Glied

**'penis envy** *n.* (*Psych.*) Penisneid, *der*

**penitence** /'penɪtəns/ *n., no pl.* Reue, *die*

**penitent** /'penɪtənt/ **1** *adj.* reuevoll (*geh.*); reuig (*geh.*) ‹Sünder›; **be ~:** bereuen; **feel [sincerely] ~:** [echte] Reue empfinden; **be deeply ~ about sth.** tiefe Reue über etw. (*Akk.*) empfinden. **2** *n.* (*repentant sinner*) reuiger Sünder/reuige Sünderin; (*person doing penance*) Büßer, *der*/Büßerin, *die* (*Rel.*)

**penitential** /penɪ'tenʃl/ *adj.* reuevoll; reuig (*geh.*); Buß‹tag, -gebet›; **the ~ psalms** (*Relig.*) die Bußpsalmen

**penitentiary** /penɪ'tenʃərɪ/ **1** *n.* (*Amer.*) Straf[vollzugs]anstalt, *die;* [Justiz]vollzugsanstalt, *die.* **2** *adj.* **A** (*of penance*) **~ pilgrimage** Bußpilgerfahrt, *die;* **B** (*of reformatory treatment*) **~ system** Strafvollzug, *der*

**penitently** /'penɪtəntlɪ/ *adv.* reuevoll (*geh.*); reumütig (*öfter scherzh.*) ‹zurückkehren›; **behave ~:** Reue zeigen

**pen: ~knife** *n.* Taschenmesser, *das;* **~ light** *n.* [Mini]stablampe, *die*

**penmanship** /'penmənʃɪp/ *n., no pl.* **A** (*skill in handwriting*) Schönschreiben, *das;* **a piece of good/bad ~:** ein schön/schlecht geschriebener Text; **B** (*style of writing*) Schrift, *die*

**'pen name** *n.* Schriftstellername, *der*

**pennant** /'penənt/ *n.* **A** (*Naut.: tapering flag*) Stander, *der;* **broad ~:** Doppelstander, *der;* **B** (*Amer.: flag symbolizing championship*) Meisterschaftswimpel, *der;* **C** ⇒ **pennon**

**penniless** /'penɪlɪs/ *adj.* (*having no money*) **be ~:** keinen Pfennig Geld haben; (*fig.: be poor*) mittellos sein; **be left ~:** völlig mittellos *od.* ohne einen Pfennig Geld dastehen

**pennon** /'penən/ *n.* **A** Wimpel, *der;* **B** (*Mil.: long narrow flag*) Fähnchen, *das;* Fähnlein, *das*

**penn'orth** /'penəθ/ ⇒ **pennyworth**

**Pennsylvania Dutch** /pensɪlveɪnɪə 'dʌtʃ/ *n.* **A** *no pl., no indef. art.* (*dialect*) Pennsylvaniadeutsch, *das;* Pennsilfaanisch, *das;* **B** *constr. as pl.* **the ~:** die Pennsylvaniendeutschen

**penny** /'penɪ/ *n., pl. usu.* **pennies** /'penɪz/ (*for separate coins*), **pence** /pens/ (*for *sum of money*) A ▶1328 (*British coin, monetary unit*) Penny, *der;* **fifty pence** fünfzig Pence; **two/five/ten/twenty/fifty pence [piece]** Zwei-/Fünf-/Zehn-/Zwanzig-/Fünfzigpencestück, *das od.* -münze, *die;* ⇒ *also* **halfpenny**; B ▶1328 (*Amer. coll.: one-cent coin*) Cent, *der;* Centstück, *das;* C **keep turning up like a bad ~**: immer wieder auftauchen; **the ~ has dropped** (*fig. coll.*) der Groschen ist gefallen (*ugs.*); **pennies from heaven** ein warmer Regen (*fig. ugs.*); **in for a ~, in for a pound** (*prov.*) wennschon, dennschon (*ugs.*); **a pretty ~**: eine hübsche *od.* schöne Stange Geld (*ugs.*); ein hübsches Sümmchen (*ugs.*); **I was not a ~ the worse** (*fig.*) es hat mich nichts gekostet (*fig.*); **take care of the pence** *or* **pennies** im Kleinen sparen; **take care of the pence** *or* **pennies, and the pounds will look after themselves** spare im Kleinen, dann hast du im Großen; **not have two pennies to rub together** ohne einen Pfennig sein; keinen Pfennig haben; **look twice at every ~**: jeden Pfennig dreimal umdrehen; **a ~ for your thoughts** woran denkst du [gerade]?; **sth. is two** *or* **ten a ~**: etw. gibt es wie Sand am Meer (*ugs.*); **be ~ wise** im Kleinen sparsam sein; **be ~ wise and pound foolish** im Kleinen sparsam und im Großen verschwenderisch sein; am falschen Ende sparen. ⇒ *also* **count**[1] 2 A; **honest** E; **name** 1 A; **spend** A

**penny: ~ 'dreadful** *n.* (*Brit.*) (*cheap story book*) Groschenheft, *das* (*abwertend*); (*cheap novel*) Groschenroman, *der* (*abwertend*); **~ 'farthing [bicycle]** *n.* (*Brit. coll*) Hochrad, *das;* **~-pincher** /'penɪpɪnʃə(r)/ *n.* Pfennigfuchser, *der*/-fuchserin, *die* (*ugs.*); **~-pinching** /'penɪpɪnʃɪŋ/ 1 *n., no pl., no indef. art.* Pfennigfuchserei, *die* (*ugs.*); Knauserei, *die* (*ugs. abwertend*); 2 *adj.* knaus[e]rig (*ugs. abwertend*); **~weight** *n.* Pennyweight, *das;* **~ 'whistle** ⇒ **whistle** 3 B

**pennyworth** /'pen(ɪw)əθ/ *n.* A *pl. same* **a ~ of bread/six ~ of sweets** für einen Penny Brot/für sechs Pence Bonbons; **not a ~ [of]** (*fig.: not even a small amount*) nicht für fünf Pfennig (*ugs.*); B (*bargain*) **a good/bad ~**: ein guter/schlechter Kauf

**penology** /pi:'nɒlədʒɪ/ *n.* Pönologie, *die*

**pen: ~ pal** (*coll.*) ⇒ **penfriend**; **~ portrait** *n.* Charakterbild, *das;* **~-pusher** *n.* (*coll.*) Büromensch, *der;* (*male*) Bürohengst, *der* (*ugs. abwertend*); **~-pushing** *n., no pl., no indef. art.* (*coll.*) Schreibkram, *der* (*ugs. abwertend*)

**pension** /'penʃn/ 1 *n.* A (*given by employer*) Rente, *die;* (*payment to retired civil servant also*) Pension, *die;* Ruhegehalt, *das* (*Amtsspr.*); **retire on a ~**: in *od.* auf Rente gehen (*ugs.*); ‹Beamter:› in Pension gehen; **be on a ~ [from one's company]** eine Rente [von seiner Firma] beziehen; **~ fund** Rentenfonds, *der;* Pensionsfonds, *der;* **~ rights** Renten- *od.* Pensionsansprüche; **~ scheme** Rentenversicherung, *die;* **the company has** *or* **operates a ~ fund/scheme for its employees** die Firma hat eine Pensionskasse/betriebliche Altersversorgung für ihre Beschäftigten; B (*given by State*) Rente, *die;* **disability** *or* **disablement ~**: Erwerbsunfähigkeitsrente, *die;* Invalidenrente, *die* (*ugs.*); **widow's ~**: Witwenrente, *die;* **war ~**: Kriegsopferrente, *die;* **~ book** ≈ Rentenausweis, *der;* **~ day** Rentenzahltag, *der;* ⇒ *also* **old-age**; C /'pɑ̃sjɔ̃/ (*European boarding house*) Pension, *die.*
2 *v.t.* eine Rente zahlen (+ *Dat.*); **be ~ed** eine Rente bekommen
**~ 'off** *v.t.* A (*discharge*) berenten (*Amtsspr.*); auf Rente setzen (*ugs.*); pensionieren ‹Lehrer, Beamten›; B (*fig.: cease to use*) ausmustern; ausrangieren (*ugs.*)

**pensionable** /'penʃənəbl/ *adj.* A (*entitled to a pension*) rentenberechtigt; pensionsberechtigt ‹Beamter›; B (*entitling to a pension*) zu einer Rente berechtigend; **reach ~ age** das Rentenalter erreichen; (*as civil servant*) das Pensionsalter erreichen; **~ salary/earnings** rentenfähiges Gehalt/rentenfähiger Verdienst

**pensioned-off** /penʃnd'ɒf/ *adj.* (*fig.*) ausrangiert (*ugs.*)

**pensioner** /'penʃənə(r)/ *n.* Rentner, *der*/Rentnerin, *die;* (*retired civil servant*) Pensionär, *der*/Pensionärin, *die;* Ruhegehaltsempfänger, *der*/-empfängerin, *die*

**pensive** /'pensɪv/ *adj.* A (*plunged in thought*) nachdenklich; B (*sorrowfully thoughtful*) schwermütig

**pensively** /'pensɪvlɪ/ *adv.* ⇒ **pensive**: nachdenklich; schwermütig

**pent** /pent/ *adj.* A (*literary*) eingedämmt; unterdrückt ‹Atem›; B **~ in** *or* **up** eingedämmt ‹Fluss›; angestaut ‹Wut, Ärger›; ⇒ *also* **pent-up**

**pentagon** /'pentəgən/ *n.* A (*Geom.*) Fünfeck, *das;* Pentagon, *das* (*fachspr.*); B **the P~** (*Amer. Polit.*) das Pentagon

**pentagonal** /pen'tægənl/ *adj.* (*Geom.*) fünfeckig; pentagonal (*fachspr.*); fünfseitig ‹Pyramide, Prisma›

**pentagram** /'pentəgræm/ *n.* Pentagramm, *das;* Drudenfuß, *der*

**pentameter** /pen'tæmɪtə(r)/ *n.* (*Pros.*) Pentameter, *der*

**pentane** /'penteɪn/ *n.* (*Chem.*) Pentan, *das*

**pentaprism** /'pentəprɪzm/ *n.* Penta[dachkant]prisma, *das;* **~ viewfinder** (*Photog.*) Prismensucher, *der*

**Pentateuch** /'pentətju:k/ *n.* (*Bibl.*) **the ~**: die fünf Bücher Mose; der Pentateuch (*fachspr.*)

**pentathlete** /pen'tæθli:t/ *n.* Fünfkämpfer, *der*/-kämpferin, *die*

**pentathlon** /pen'tæθlən/ *n.* (*Sport*) Fünfkampf, *der*

**penta'tonic** *adj.* (*Mus.*) pentatonisch; Fünfton-; **~ scale** fünfstufige Tonleiter

**Pentecost** /'pentɪkɒst/ *n.* (*Relig.*) Pfingsten, *das;* Pfingstfest, *das;* (*Jewish harvest festival*) Ernte[dank]fest, *das*

**pentecostal** /pentɪ'kɒstl/ *attrib. adj.* (*Relig.*) pfingstlich; Pfingst‹gottesdienst, -hymne, -bewegung›

**Pentecostal 'Church** *n.* (*Relig.*) Pfingstkirche, *die*

**pent: ~house** *n.* A (*house, flat*) Penthaus, *das;* Penthouse, *das;* B (*sloping roof*) Schleppdach, *das;* **~-up** *attrib. adj.* angestaut ‹Ärger, Wut›; verhalten ‹Freude›; unterdrückt ‹Sehnsucht, Gefühle›

**penultimate** /pe'nʌltɪmət/ *adj.* vorletzt...

**penumbra** /pɪ'nʌmbrə/ *n., pl.* **~e** /pɪ'nʌmbri:/ *or* **~s** A Halbschatten, *der;* B (*Astron.: of sunspot*) Penumbra, *die*

**penurious** /pɪ'njʊərɪəs/ *adj.* A (*poor*) arm ‹Person›; entbehrungsreich ‹Zeit›; armselig, kümmerlich ‹Verhältnisse›; B (*stingy*) geizig; knauserig (*ugs. abwertend*)

**penury** /'penjʊərɪ/ *n., no pl.* Armut, *die;* Not, *die*

**peon** /'pi:ən, pju:n/ *n.* A (*in Latin America: day labourer*) Tagelöhner, *der;* Peon, *der;* **~ labour** Peonenarbeit, *die;* B (*in India and Pakistan: messenger, attendant*) Bote, *der;* Laufbursche, *der*

**peony** /'pi:ənɪ/ *n.* (*Bot.*) Pfingstrose, *die;* Päonie, *die;* **~ red** päonienrot; tiefrot

**people** /'pi:pl/ 1 *n.* A (*persons composing nation, community, etc.*) Volk, *das;* B *constr. as pl.* (*persons forming class etc.*) Leute *Pl.;* Menschen; **city/country ~** (*inhabitants*) Stadt-/Landbewohner; (*who prefer the city/the country*) Stadt-/Landmenschen; **village ~**: Dorfbewohner; **local ~**: Einheimische; **working ~**: arbeitende Menschen; Werktätige (*bes. DDR*); **coloured/white ~**: Farbige/Weiße; **~ of wealth** reiche *od.* begüterte Leute *Pl.;* **her [own] sort/kind of ~**: ihresgleichen; ⇒ *also* **choose** 1 A; C *constr. as pl.* (*subjects of ruler*) Volk, *das;* (*congregation*) Gemeinde, *die;* D *constr. as pl.* (*persons not of nobility*) **the ~**: das [gemeine] Volk; E *constr. as sing. or pl.* (*voters*) Volk, *das;* **will of the ~**: Volkswille, *der* (*Polit.*); **go to the ~**: Wahlen ausschreiben; F *constr. as pl.* (*persons in general*) Menschen; Leute *Pl.;* (*as opposed to animals*) Menschen; **~ say he's very rich** die Leute sagen *od.* man sagt *od.* es heißt, dass er sehr reich sei; er soll sehr reich sein; **that is quite enough to alarm ~**: das reicht zur Genüge, um einen in Alarm zu versetzen; **a crowd of ~**: eine Menschenmenge; **don't tell ~ about this** erzähle niemandem davon; **~ are like that** so sind die Menschen; **I don't understand ~ any more** ich verstehe die Welt nicht mehr; **'some ~** (*certain persons, usu. with whom the speaker disagrees*) gewisse Leute; (*you*) manche Leute; **some '~!** Leute gibt es!; **honestly, some '~!** also wirklich!; **listen, you ~!** hört mal [zu]!; **what do you ~ think?** was denkt ihr [denn]?; **you of 'all ~ ought ...**: gerade du solltest ...; **who do you think I saw at the party? 'Bill, of all ~!** wen, glaubst du, habe ich auf der Party getroffen? Ausgerechnet Bill!; **no sign of any ~**: keine Menschenseele; G *constr. as pl.* (*relatives*) Familie, *die.*
2 *v.t.* A (*fill with ~ or animals*) bevölkern; B (*inhabit*) bevölkern; (*become inhabitant of*) besiedeln

**'people carrier** *n.* Großraumlimousine, *die;* [Mini]van, *der*

**peopled** /'pi:pld/ *adj.* bevölkert

**People's Re'public** *n.* (*Polit.*) Volksrepublik, *die;* **the ~ of China** die Volksrepublik China

**pep** /pep/ (*coll.*) 1 *n., no pl., no indef. art.* Schwung, *der;* Pep, *der* (*salopp*); **be full of ~**: viel Schwung *od.* (*salopp*) Pep haben.
2 *v.t.*, **-pp-**: **~ [up]** aufpeppen (*ugs.*)

**PEP** /pep/ *abbr.* (*Brit.*) **personal equity plan**

**peplum** /'pepləm/ *n.* (*Fashion*) Schößchen, *das*

**pepper** /'pepə(r)/ 1 *n.* A Pfeffer, *der;* **black/white ~**: schwarzer/weißer Pfeffer; B (*capsicum plant*) Paprika, *der;* (*fruit*) Paprikaschote, *die;* **red/yellow/green ~**: roter/gelber/grüner Paprika; **sweet ~**: Gemüsepaprika, *der.* ⇒ *also* **cayenne**. 2 *v.t.* A (*sprinkle with ~*) pfeffern; B (*besprinkle*) übersäen; C (*pelt with missiles*) bombardieren (*ugs., auch fig.*); **~ the target with shot** das Ziel mit Schrot spicken

**pepper: ~-and-'salt** *n.* (*Textiles*) Pfeffer und Salz; *attrib.* pfeffer- und salzfarben; **~corn** *n.* Pfefferkorn, *das;* **~corn rent** symbolischer Pachtzins; **~ mill** *n.* Pfeffermühle, *die;* **~mint** *n.* A (*plant*) Pfefferminze, *die;* B (*sweet*) Pfefferminz, *das; attrib.* Pfefferminz‹bonbon, -drops, -pastille›; C (*oil*) Pfefferminzöl, *das;* **~ pot** *n.* Pfefferstreuer, *der*

**peppery** /'pepərɪ/ *adj.* pfeff[e]rig; (*spicy*) scharf; (*fig.: pungent*) scharf; (*fig.: hot-tempered*) jähzornig; **the soup is rather ~**: die Suppe schmeckt ziemlich stark nach Pfeffer/die Suppe ist ziemlich scharf

**'pep pill** *n.* (*coll.*) Peppille, *die* (*ugs.*); Aufputschtablette, *die*

**peppy** /'pepɪ/ *adj.* (*coll.*) lebhaft, quirlig (*ugs.*); schwungvoll ‹Tanz›

**pepsin** /'pepsɪn/ *n.* (*Chem.*) Pepsin, *das*

**'pep talk** *n.* (*coll.*) Aufmunterung, *die;* **give sb. a ~**: jmdm. ein paar aufmunternde Worte sagen

**peptic** /'peptɪk/ *adj.* (*Physiol.*) peptisch (*fachspr.*); Verdauungs-

**peptic 'ulcer** *n.* ▶1232 (*Med.*) peptisches Ulkus (*fachspr.*); Magengeschwür, *das*

**peptide** /'peptaɪd/ *n.* (*Chem.*) Peptid, *das*

**per** /pə(r), *stressed* pɜ:(r)/ *prep.* A (*by means of*) per ‹Post, Bahn, Schiff, Bote›; durch ‹Spediteur, Herrn X.›; B (*according to*) **[as] ~ sth.** wie in etw. (*Dat.*) angegeben; laut ‹Anweisung, Preisliste›; **as ~ usual** (*joc.*) wie üblich; C ▶1552 (*for each*) pro; **£50 ~ week** 50 Pfund in der Woche *od.* pro Woche; **fifty kilometres ~ hour** fünfzig Kilometer in der *od.* pro Stunde; **get 11 francs ~ pound** 11 Francs für ein Pfund bekommen

**peradventure** /pərəd'ventʃə(r), pərəd'ventʃə(r)/ (*arch.*) *adv.* vielleicht; **lest ~ ...**: für den Fall, dass ...; **if ~**: im Fall[e], dass ...

**perambulator** /pə'ræmbjʊleɪtə(r)/ (*Brit. formal*) ⇒ **pram**

**per annum** /pər 'ænəm/ *adv.* im Jahr; pro Jahr (*bes. Kaufmannsspr., ugs.*)

**per capita** /pə 'kæpɪtə/ ❶ *adv.* pro Kopf; pro Person; **earnings ~:** Pro-Kopf-Einkommen, *das.* ❷ *adj.* Pro-Kopf-‹Einkommen, Verbrauch usw.›; **~ tax** Kopfsteuer, *die*

**perceivable** /pə'si:vəbl/ ⇒ **perceptible**

**perceive** /pə'si:v/ *v.t.* Ⓐ (*with the mind*) spüren; bemerken; ‹menschlicher Geist:› wahrnehmen; **~ sb.'s thoughts** jmds. Gedanken erraten; Ⓑ (*through the senses*) wahrnehmen; **we ~d a figure in the distance** wir erblickten in der Ferne eine Gestalt; Ⓒ (*regard mentally in a certain way*) wahrnehmen; **~d** vermeintlich ‹Bedrohung, Gefahr, Wert›

**per cent** (*Brit.; Amer.:* **percent**) /pə'sent/ ❶ *adv.* **ninety ~ effective** zu 90 Prozent wirksam; ⇒ *also* **hundred** 1 C. ❷ *adj.* **a 5 ~ increase** ein Zuwachs von 5 Prozent; ein fünfprozentiger Zuwachs. ❸ *n.* Ⓐ ⇒ **percentage**; Ⓑ (*hundredth*) Prozent, *das*

**percentage** /pə'sentɪdʒ/ *n.* Ⓐ (*rate or proportion per cent*) Prozentsatz, *der;* **a high ~ of alcohol** ein hoher Alkoholgehalt; **what ~ of 48 is 11?** wie viel Prozent von 48 sind 11?; **~ lead/improvement** prozentualer Vorsprung/prozentuale Verbesserung; Ⓑ (*proportion*) [prozentualer] Anteil

**per'centage sign** *n.* Prozentzeichen, *das*

**perceptible** /pə'septɪbl/ *adj.* wahrnehmbar; **be quite ~:** ganz offensichtlich sein

**perceptibly** /pə'septɪblɪ/ *adv.* sichtlich; sichtbar, merklich ‹schrumpfen, welken›

**perception** /pə'sepʃn/ *n.* Ⓐ (*act*) Wahrnehmung, *die;* (*result*) Erkenntnis, *die;* **have keen ~s** ein stark ausgeprägtes Wahrnehmungsvermögen haben; Ⓑ *no pl.* (*faculty*) Wahrnehmungsvermögen, *das;* **colour ~:** Farbensinn, *der;* **depth ~:** Tiefensehen, *das* (*Med.*); **~ of sounds** Gehör, *das;* **~ of objects** gegenständliche Wahrnehmung; Ⓒ (*intuitive recognition*) Gespür, *das* (**of** für); (*instance*) Erfassen, *das;* **the direct ~ of truth** das unmittelbare Erfassen der Wahrheit; **have no clear ~ of sth.** keine klare Vorstellung von etw. haben

**perceptive** /pə'septɪv/ *adj.* Ⓐ (*discerning*) scharf ‹Auge›; fein ‹Gehör, Nase, Geruchssinn›; scharfsinnig ‹Person›; Ⓑ (*having intuitive recognition or insight*) einfühlsam ‹Person, Zeitungsartikel, Bemerkung›

**perceptively** /pə'septɪvlɪ/ *adv.* Ⓐ (*discerningly*) mit scharfer Wahrnehmung; Ⓑ (*with intuitive recognition or insight*) einfühlsam

**perceptiveness** /pə'septɪvnɪs/, **perceptivity** /pɜ:sep'tɪvɪtɪ/ *ns., no pl.* Ⓐ (*discernment*) **~ of the senses** scharfes Wahrnehmungsvermögen; Ⓑ (*intuitive recognition, insight*) Einfühlsamkeit, *die*

**perch**[1] /pɜ:tʃ/ *n., pl. same or* **~es** (*Zool.*) Flussbarsch, *der*

**perch**[2] ❶ *n.* Ⓐ (*horizontal bar*) Sitzstange, *die;* (*for hens*) Hühnerstange, *die;* Ⓑ (*place to sit*) Sitzplatz, *der;* Ⓒ (*fig.: elevated or secure position*) guter Posten; **knock sb. off his ~:** jmdn. von seinem hohen Ross herunterholen; **come off one's ~:** von seinem hohen Ross herunterkommen *od.* steigen; Ⓓ (*Brit.: measure*) (*of length*) Perch, *das;* $5\frac{1}{2}$ Yards; (*of area*) **[square] ~** (*Brit.*) Quadratperch, *das.* ❷ *v.i.* Ⓐ sich niederlassen; Ⓑ (*be supported*) sitzen. ❸ *v.t.* setzen/stellen/legen

**perchance** /pə'tʃɑ:ns/ *adv.* (*arch.*) Ⓐ (*possibly*) möglicherweise; vielleicht; Ⓑ ⇒ **peradventure**

**perched** /pɜ:tʃt/ *adj.* **be ~** ‹Vogel:› sitzen; **stand ~ on a cliff** hoch auf einer Klippe stehen; **a village ~ on a hill** ein hoch oben auf einem Berg gelegenes Dorf; **with his hat ~ on the back of his head** mit hinten auf dem Kopf sitzendem Hut

**percipient** /pə'sɪpɪənt/ *adj.* Ⓐ (*conscious*) wahrnehmend; **be ~ of sth.** in der Lage sein, etw. zu erkennen; Ⓑ (*discerning*) scharf ‹Augen›; fein ‹Gehör›; scharfsichtig ‹Kritiker›

**percolate** /'pɜ:kəleɪt/ ❶ *v.i.* Ⓐ (*ooze*) **~ through sth.** durch etw. [durch]sickern; Ⓑ (*fig.: spread gradually*) vordringen; Ⓒ (*be brewed in percolator*) ‹Kaffee:› durchlaufen. ❷ *v.t.* Ⓐ (*permeate*) sickern durch ‹Gestein›; Ⓑ (*fig.: penetrate*) dringen in (+ *Akk.*) ‹Bewusstsein›; Ⓒ (*brew in percolator*) [mit der Kaffeemaschine] machen ‹Kaffee›

**percolation** /pɜ:kə'leɪʃn/ *n.* Ⓐ (*passage of liquid through filter*) [Durch]sickern, *das;* Ⓑ (*fig.: diffusion by spreading*) Vordringen, *das;* Ⓒ (*of coffee*) Filtern, *das*

**percolator** /'pɜ:kəleɪtə(r)/ *n.* Kaffeemaschine, *die*

**percussion** /pə'kʌʃn/ *n.* Ⓐ (*Mus.*) (*playing by striking*) Anschlag, *der;* (*group of instruments*) Schlagzeug, *das; attrib.* Schlagzeug‹gruppe, -band, -begleitung›; **~ instrument** Schlaginstrument, *das;* **~ section** Schlagzeug, *das;* Ⓑ (*forcible striking*) **explode by ~:** bei Erschütterung explodieren; Ⓒ (*Med.*) Perkussion, *die;* (*massage*) Klopfmassage, *die*

**per'cussion cap** *n.* (*Arms*) Zündhütchen, *das;* (*in toy*) Zündblättchen, *das*

**percussionist** /pə'kʌʃənɪst/ *n.* (*Mus.*) Schlagzeuger, *der*/-zeugerin, *die*

**per diem** /pɜ: 'di:em/ ❶ *adv.* pro Tag; täglich. ❷ *adj.* täglich; **on a ~ basis** tageweise. ❸ *n.* (*allowance*) Tagegeld, *das;* (*payment*) Entgelt, *das*

**perdition** /pə'dɪʃn/ *n., no pl., no art.* (*literary: eternal death*) Verdammnis, *die;* **escape ~:** der [ewigen] Verdammnis entkommen; **damn you to ~!** sei auf ewig verdammt!

**peregrination** /perɪgrɪ'neɪʃn/ *n.* (*arch./joc.*) Ⓐ *no pl.* (*travelling*) Reise, *die;* (*joc.*) Umherreisen, *das;* Ⓑ *in pl.* (*travels*) Reisen; **during your ~s** (*joc.*) auf deinen Streifzügen

**peregrine** /'perɪgrɪn/ *n.* **~ [falcon]** (*Ornith.*) Wanderfalke, *der*

**peremptorily** /pə'remptərɪlɪ, 'perɪmptərɪlɪ/ *adv.* Ⓐ (*so as to admit no contradiction*) kategorisch; (*imperiously*) herrisch; gebieterisch (*geh.*); Ⓑ (*dogmatically*) beharrlich, hartnäckig ‹leugnen›; **speak ~ on sth.** sich dogmatisch zu etw. äußern

**peremptory** /pə'remptərɪ, 'perɪmptərɪ/ *adj.* Ⓐ (*admitting no contradiction*) kategorisch; (*imperious*) herrisch; gebieterisch (*geh.*); Ⓑ (*essential*) unbedingt; unerlässlich ‹Vorschrift›; Ⓒ (*dogmatic*) beharrlich; hartnäckig; Ⓓ (*Law*) **~ writ** gerichtliche Verfügung; **~ challenge** Ablehnung [eines Geschworenen] ohne Angabe der Gründe

**perennial** /pə'renjəl/ ❶ *adj.* Ⓐ (*lasting all year*) ganzjährig; perennierend (*fachspr.*) ‹Quelle, Brunnen, Bach›; Ⓑ (*lasting indefinitely*) immer während; ewig ‹Jugend, Mythos, Suche›; immer wieder auftretend ‹Problem›; Ⓒ (*Bot.*) ausdauernd; perennierend (*fachspr.*). ❷ *n.* (*Bot.*) ausdauernde *od.* (*fachspr.*) perennierende Pflanze

**perennially** /pə'renjəlɪ/ *adv.* Ⓐ (*throughout the year*) **flow ~** ‹Fluss:› das ganze Jahr Wasser führen; Ⓑ (*perpetually*) ständig; ewig ‹ungelöst›

**perestroika** /perɪ'strɔɪkə/ *n.* Perestroika, *die*

**perfect** ❶ /'pɜ:fɪkt/ *adj.* Ⓐ (*complete*) vollkommen; umfassend ‹Kenntnisse, Wissen›; Ⓑ (*faultless*) vollkommen; perfekt ‹Englisch, Technik, Timing›; tadellos ‹Zustand›; [absolut] gelungen ‹Aufführung›; lupenrein ‹Diamant›; (*conforming to an abstract concept*) perfekt; **get a technique ~:** eine Technik vollkommen *od.* absolut beherrschen lernen; **~ gas** (*Phys.*) ideales Gas; Ⓒ (*trained, skilled*) **be ~ in the performance of one's duties** seine Aufgaben tadellos erfüllen; **practice makes ~:** Übung macht den Meister; Ⓓ (*very satisfactory*) herrlich; wunderbar; Ⓔ (*exact*) perfekt; getreu ‹Ebenbild, Abbild›; (*fully what the name implies*) perfekt ‹Gentleman, Dame, Ehemann, Gastgeberin›; ⇒ *also* **square** 1 G; Ⓕ (*absolute*) **a ~ stranger** ein völlig Fremder; ein Wildfremder (*ugs.*); **he is a ~ stranger to me** er ist mir völlig unbekannt; **he is a ~ scream** (*coll.*)/**angel** (*coll.*)/**charmer** er ist wirklich zum Schreien [komisch]/ein Engel/charmant; **she looks a ~ little angel** sie sieht wie ein richtiger kleiner Engel aus; **I have a ~ right to stay** ich habe eindeutig *od.* durchaus das Recht zu bleiben; **have ~ freedom to make one's own decision** völlig frei entscheiden können; Ⓖ (*coll.: unmitigated*) absolut; **look a ~ fright/mess** wirklich zum Weglaufen/absolut verboten aussehen (*ugs.*); **a ~ tantrum** ein regelrechter Wutanfall; Ⓗ (*Ling.*) Perfekt-; **the ~ tense** das Perfekt; **future ~ tense** Futur II, *das;* vollendetes Futur; **past ~** ⇒ **pluperfect** 2; **present perfect** ⇒ **present**[1] 1 D; Ⓘ (*Mus.*) **~ interval** reines Intervall. ❷ *n.* (*Ling.*) Perfekt, *das.* ❸ /pə'fekt/ *v.t.* vervollkommnen; perfektionieren

**perfection** /pə'fekʃn/ *n.* Ⓐ *no pl.* (*making perfect*) Vervollkommnung, *die;* Perfektionierung, *die;* Ⓑ *no pl.* (*faultlessness*) Vollkommenheit, *die;* Perfektion, *die;* **~ of detail** Vollkommenheit *od.* Perfektion im Detail; **~ of technique** technische Perfektion; **to ~:** perfekt; **it/he succeeded to ~:** es war ein voller Erfolg/er war absolut erfolgreich; **you cook to ~:** du bist eine perfekte Köchin/ein perfekter Koch; Ⓒ *no pl.* (*perfect person or thing*) **be ~:** perfekt sein; Ⓓ *no pl., no indef. art.* (*most perfect degree*) Inbegriff, *der;* **sth. has reached its ~:** etw. hat seine höchste Vollkommenheit erreicht

**perfectionism** /pə'fekʃənɪzm/ *n., no pl.* Perfektionismus, *der*

**perfectionist** /pə'fekʃənɪst/ *n.* Perfektionist, *der*/Perfektionistin, *die*

**perfectly** /'pɜ:fɪktlɪ/ *adv.* Ⓐ (*completely*) vollkommen; völlig; **I understand that ~:** ich verstehe das vollkommen *od.* völlig; **be ~ entitled to do sth.** durchaus berechtigt sein, etw. zu tun; Ⓑ (*faultlessly*) perfekt; tadellos ‹sich verhalten›; fehlerlos ‹singen›; Ⓒ (*exactly*) vollkommen; exakt, genau ‹vorhersagbar›; Ⓓ (*coll.: to an unmitigated extent*) furchtbar (*ugs.*) ‹schrecklich, schlimm, ekelhaft›

**perfect 'pitch** *n.* (*Mus.*) absolutes Gehör

**perfidious** /pə:'fɪdɪəs/ *adj.* perfid (*geh.*); ⇒ *also* **Albion**

**perfidy** /'pɜ:fɪdɪ/ *n.* Perfidie, *die* (*geh.*)

**perforate** /'pɜ:fəreɪt/ *v.t.* Ⓐ (*make hole[s] through*) perforieren; **suffer from a ~d eardrum/ulcer** ein Loch im Trommelfell/ein durchgebrochenes Magengeschwür haben; Ⓑ (*make an opening into*) durchlöchern

**perforation** /pɜ:fə'reɪʃn/ *n.* Ⓐ (*action of perforating*) Perforierung, *die;* Ⓑ (*hole*) Loch, *das;* **~s** (*line of holes esp. in paper*) Perforation, *die;* (*in sheets of stamps*) Zähnung, *die;* Perforation, *die*

**perforator** /'pɜ:fəreɪtə(r)/ *n.* Perforiermaschine, *die;* (*rock drill*) Bohrer, *der;* (*used in stripping wallpaper*) Tapetenperforator, *der*

**perforce** /pə'fɔ:s/ *adv.* (*arch./formal*) notgedrungen

**perform** /pə'fɔ:m/ ❶ *v.t.* Ⓐ (*fulfil*) ausführen ‹Befehl, Arbeit, Operation›; erfüllen ‹Bitte, Wunsch, Pflicht, Vertrag, Versprechen, Bedingung, Aufgabe›; nachkommen (+ *Dat.*) ‹Verpflichtung›; vollbringen ‹[Helden]tat, Leistung›; durchführen ‹Operation›; einhalten ‹Versprechen, Vertrag›; Ⓑ (*carry out*) ausfüllen ‹Funktion›; vollbringen ‹Wunder›; anstellen ‹Berechnungen›; durchführen ‹Experiment, Sektion›; vornehmen ‹Sektion›; vorführen, zeigen ‹Trick›; (*in formal manner or according to prescribed ritual*) vollziehen ‹Trauung, Taufe, Riten, Rituale, Opfer›; [ab]halten ‹Gottesdienst›; (*render*) aufführen ‹Theaterstück, Scharade›; vortragen, vorsingen ‹Lied›; vorspielen, vortragen ‹Sonate usw.›. ❷ *v.i.* Ⓐ eine Vorführung geben; (*sing*) singen; (*play*) spielen; ‹Jongleur:› Kunststücke zeigen *od.* vorführen; ‹Zauberer:› Zaubertricks ausführen *od.* vorführen; **he ~ed very well** seine Darbietung war sehr gut; **she ~s as soloist** sie ist Solistin; (*occasionally*) sie tritt als Solistin auf; **she ~ed skilfully on the flute/piano** sie spielte mit großer Könnerschaft Flöte/Klavier; Ⓑ (*Theatre*) auftreten; **he ~ed very well** sein Auftritt war sehr gut; Ⓒ (*execute tricks*) ‹Tier:› Kunststücke zeigen *od.* vorführen; **train an animal to ~:** einem Tier Kunststücke beibringen; Ⓓ (*work, function*) ‹Auto:› laufen, fahren; **he ~ed all right/well [in the exam]** er machte seine Sache [in der Prüfung] ordentlich/gut; **E** (*coll. euphem.*) (*accomplish sexual intercourse*) es machen (*ugs. verhüll.*); (*excrete, urinate*) ‹Kind, Haustier:› machen (*ugs. verhüll.*)

**performance** /pəˈfɔːməns/ *n.* **A** (*fulfilment*) (*of promise, duty, task*) Erfüllung, *die;* (*of command*) Ausführung, *die;* **B** (*carrying out*) Durchführung, *die;* **C** (*notable feat*) Leistung, *die;* **put up a good ~:** eine gute Leistung zeigen; seine Sache gut machen; **D** (*performing of play etc.*) Vorstellung, *die;* **the ~s of the gymnasts** die Turnveranstaltungen; **her ~ in the play** ihre [schauspielerische] Leistung in dem Theaterstück; **her ~ as Desdemona** ihre Darstellung *od.* Interpretation der Desdemona; **the ~ of a play/opera** die Aufführung eines Theaterstücks/einer Oper; **give a ~ of a symphony/play** eine Sinfonie/ein Stück spielen *od.* aufführen; **E** (*achievement under test*) Leistung, *die;* **athletic ~:** die Leistung eines Sportlers; **the car has good ~:** der Wagen bringt viel Leistung; **give an engine more ~:** die Leistung eines Motors erhöhen; **are you satisfied with the ~ of your new car?** sind Sie mit ihrem neuen Auto zufrieden?; **the ~ of the equipment, in tests, was somewhat variable** die Anlage hat in Tests nicht immer gleich abgeschnitten; **F** (*coll.: display of anger etc.*) Auftritt, *der;* **G** (*coll.: difficult procedure*) Theater, *das* (*ugs., abwertend*); Umstand, *der;* **it was a hell of a ~ getting my passport** das war vielleicht ein Umstand *od.* Theater, bis ich meinen Pass hatte

**performance: ~ art** *n.* Performance-Art, *die;* **~ artist** *n.* ▶ **1261** Performancekünstler, *der*/-künstlerin, *die* **~-enhancing** *adj.* **~-enhancing drug/substance** leistungsfördernde *od.* -steigernde Droge/Substanz

**performer** /pəˈfɔːmə(r)/ *n.* Künstler, *der*/Künstlerin, *die;* **as a ~ of tricks he was unsurpassed** im Vorführen von Tricks war er unübertroffen

**performing** /pəˈfɔːmɪŋ/ *adj.* **A** (*acting, singing, etc.*) auftretend ‹Künstler›; **~ arts** darstellende Künste; **~ rights** Aufführungsrechte *Pl.;* **B** (*executing tricks*) dressiert ‹Tier›

**performing ˈarts** *n. pl.* darstellende Künste

**perfume** ❶ /ˈpɜːfjuːm/ *n.* **A** (*sweet smell*) Duft, *der;* **B** (*fluid*) Parfüm, *das;* **~ atomizer** *or* **spray** Parfümzerstäuber, *der.* ❷ /pəˈfjuːm, ˈpɜːfjuːm/ *v.t.* (*impart sweet scent to*) mit Wohlgeruch erfüllen; (*impregnate with sweet smell*) parfümieren

**perfumer** /pəˈfjuːmə(r)/ *n.* (*maker of perfume*) Parfümeur, *der*/Parfümeuse, *die;* (*seller of perfume*) Parfümhändler, *der*/Parfümhändlerin, *die*

**perfumery** /pəˈfjuːmərɪ/ *n.* **A** *no pl.* (*preparation of perfumes*) Parfümherstellung, *die;* **B** (*perfumes*) Parfümeriewaren *Pl.; attrib.* Parfümerie-; **C** (*shop*) Parfümerie, *die*

**perfunctorily** /pəˈfʌŋktərɪlɪ/ *adv.* pflichtschuldig; oberflächlich, mechanisch ‹arbeiten›

**perfunctory** /pəˈfʌŋktərɪ/ *adj.* (*done for duty's sake only*) pflichtschuldig; flüchtig ‹Erkundigung, Bemerkung›; (*superficial*) oberflächlich ‹Arbeit, Überprüfung›; **his tidying of his bedroom had been very ~:** er hatte sein Zimmer nur sehr oberflächlich aufgeräumt; **put in a ~ appearance** sich, um seiner Pflicht zu genügen, kurz zeigen

**pergola** /ˈpɜːgələ/ *n.* (*Hort.*) Pergola, *die;* Laubengang, *der*

**perhaps** /pəˈhæps, præps/ *adv.* vielleicht; **I'll go out, ~:** ich gehe vielleicht aus; **~ so** [das] mag [ja] sein; **~ not** (*maybe this is or will not be the case*) vielleicht auch nicht; (*it might be best not to do this*) vielleicht lieber nicht

**perianth** /ˈperɪænθ/ *n.* (*Bot.*) Perianth[ium], *das* (*fachspr.*); Blütenhülle, *die*

**pericardium** /perɪˈkɑːdɪəm/ *n., pl.* **pericardia** /perɪˈkɑːdɪə/ (*Anat.*) Perikard[ium], *das* (*fachspr.*); Herzbeutel, *der*

**pericarp** /ˈperɪkɑːp/ *n.* (*Bot.*) Perikarp, *das* (*fachspr.*); Fruchtwand, *die*

**perigee** /ˈperɪdʒiː/ *n.* (*Astron.*) Perigäum, *das* (*fachspr.*); Erdnähe, *die*

**peril** /ˈperl/ *n.* Gefahr, *die;* **they were in constant ~ from their enemies** sie waren ständig von ihren Feinden bedroht; **be in deadly ~, be in ~ of death** *or* **one's life** in Lebensgefahr sein *od.* schweben; **be in ~ of doing sth.** Gefahr laufen, etw. zu tun; **do sth. at one's ~** (*accepting risk of injury*) etw. auf eigene Gefahr tun

**perilous** /ˈperələs/ *adj.* **A** (*full of danger*) gefahrvoll; **be ~:** gefährlich sein; **B** (*exposed to imminent risk*) gefährdet; anfällig ‹Beziehung›; **a ~ pile of chairs** ein gefährlich hoher Turm aus Stühlen

**perilously** /ˈperələslɪ/ *adv.* gefährlich; **~ ill** todkrank

**perimeter** /pəˈrɪmɪtə(r)/ *n.* **A** (*outer boundary*) [äußere] Begrenzung; Grenze, *die;* **troops were stationed all around the ~ to guard the camp** Truppen waren rundherum postiert, um das Lager zu bewachen; **at the ~ of the racetrack** am Rande der Rennbahn; **B** (*outline of figure*) Umriss, *der;* (*length of outline*) Umfang, *der*

**perinatal** /perɪˈneɪtl/ *adj.* (*Med.*) perinatal

**perineum** /perɪˈniːəm/ *n., pl.* **~s** *or* **perinea** /perɪˈniːə/ (*Anat.*) Damm, *der*

**period** /ˈpɪərɪəd/ ❶ *n.* **A** (*distinct portion of history or life*) Periode, *die;* Zeit, *die;* **~s of history** geschichtliche Perioden; **the modern ~:** die Moderne; das Zeitalter der Moderne; **the Reformation/Tudor/Victorian ~:** die Reformationszeit/die Tudorzeit/die viktorianische Zeit; **during the ~ of his youth** in seiner Jugend[zeit]; **at a later ~ of her life** zu einem späteren Zeitpunkt ihres Lebens *od.* in ihrem Leben; **a ~ of literature/art** eine literarische/kunstgeschichtliche Epoche; **the Classical/Romantic/Renaissance ~:** die Klassik/Romantik/Renaissance; **of the ~** (*of the time under discussion*) der damaligen Zeit; **B** (*any portion of time*) Zeitraum, *der;* Zeitspanne, *die;* **over a ~ [of time]** über einen längeren Zeitraum; **within the agreed ~:** innerhalb der vereinbarten Frist; **showers and bright ~s** (*Meteorol.*) Schauer und Aufheiterungen; **over a longer ~ I changed my mind** im Laufe der Zeit änderte ich meine Meinung; **I've had ~s of anxiety** es gab Zeiten der Angst für mich; **C** (*Sch.: time allocated for lesson*) Stunde, *die;* **teaching/lesson ~:** Unterrichtsstunde, *die;* **geography/chemistry/English ~:** Geographie-/Chemie-/Englischstunde, *die;* **have five ~s a week for French** fünf Stunden Französisch[unterricht] in der Woche haben; **have two chemistry ~s** zwei Stunden Chemie haben; **a detention ~, a ~ of detention** eine Stunde Arrest; **a free ~:** eine Freistunde; **D** (*occurrence of menstruation*) Periode, *die;* Regel[blutung], *die;* **have her/a ~:** ihre Periode *od.* Regel *od.* (*ugs. verhüll.*) Tage haben; **miss one's ~:** ihre Periode nicht bekommen; **~ pains** Menstruationsschmerzen; **E** (*punctuation mark*) Punkt, *der;* **F** (*pause in speech*) Pause, *die;* (*fig.*) Stillstand, *der;* **G** (*appended to statement*) [und damit] basta! (*ugs.*); **we can't pay higher wages, ~:** wir können keine höheren Löhne zahlen, da ist nichts zu machen; **H** (*time taken by recurring process*) Periode, *die;* (*Astron.: time of revolution*) Umlaufzeit, *die;* **I** (*Geol.*) Periode, *die;* **J** (*complete sentence*) Satz, *der;* Satzgefüge, *das* (*Sprachw.*); **K** (*Math.*) (*set of figures*) [Ziffern]gruppe, *die;* (*set of recurring figures*) Periode, *die;* **L** (*Chem.*) Periode, *die.* ❷ *adj.* zeitgenössisch ‹Tracht, Kostüm›; Zeit‹roman, -stück›; antik ‹Möbel›; ‹Zimmer› im Zeitstil; **~ piece** (*play*) Zeitstück, *das;* (*novel*) Zeitroman, *der;* **this Georgian cabinet is a true ~ piece** dieser georgianische Schrank ist ein für die Zeit ausgesprochen typisches Stück

**periodic** /pɪərɪˈɒdɪk/ *adj.* **A** (*recurring at regular intervals*) periodisch *od.* regelmäßig [auftretend *od.* wiederkehrend]; (*intermittent*) gelegentlich [auftretend]; vereinzelt ‹Regenschauer›; **make ~ good resolutions** von Zeit zu Zeit *od.* immer mal wieder gute Vorsätze fassen; **B** (*Astron.*) periodisch; **the ~ time of a planet** die Umlaufzeit eines Planeten

**periodical** /pɪərɪˈɒdɪkl/ ❶ *adj.* **A** ⇒ **periodic**; **B** (*published at regular intervals*) regelmäßig erscheinend; **~ journal/magazine** Zeitschrift, *die.* ❷ *n.* Zeitschrift, *die; attrib.* Zeitschriften-; **weekly/monthly/quarterly ~:** Wochenzeitschrift/Monatsschrift/Vierteljahresschrift, *die*

**periodically** /pɪərɪˈɒdɪkəlɪ/ *adv.* (*at regular intervals*) regelmäßig; (*intermittently*) gelegentlich

**periodic ˈtable** *n.* (*Chem.*) Periodensystem, *das*

**peripatetic** /perɪpəˈtetɪk/ *adj.* **~ teacher** Lehrer, der/Lehrerin, die an mehreren Schulen unterrichtet; **~ teaching** Unterricht durch Lehrer, die an mehreren Schulen arbeiten; **~ lifestyle** Wanderleben, *das*

**peripheral** /pəˈrɪfərl/ ❶ *adj.* **A** (*of the periphery*) ‹Parkraum› in Randlage; **~ road** Ringstraße, *die;* **~ speed** Umfangsgeschwindigkeit, *die;* **B** (*of minor importance*) peripher (*geh.*); marginal (*geh.*); Rand‹problem, -kultur, -erscheinung, -figur, -gebiet, -bemerkung, -lage›; **be merely ~** *or* **of merely ~ importance to sth.** für etw. von nur marginaler (*geh.*) *od.* untergeordneter Bedeutung sein; **C** (*Anat.*) peripher; **D** (*Computing*) peripher. ❷ *n.* (*Computing*) Peripheriegerät, *das*

**peripherally** /pəˈrɪfərəlɪ/ *adv.* **A** (*at the periphery*) außen; **B** (*marginally*) am Rande; peripher (*geh.*); marginal (*geh.*)

**periphery** /pəˈrɪfərɪ/ *n.* **A** ⇒ **circumference**; **B** (*external boundary*) Begrenzung, *die;* (*of surface*) Außenfläche, *die;* **C** (*outer region*) Peripherie, *die* (*geh.*); Rand, *der*

**periphrasis** /pəˈrɪfrəsɪs/ *n., pl.* **periphrases** /pəˈrɪfrəsiːz/ **A** *no pl.* (*roundabout way of speaking*) periphrastischer (*Rhet.*) *od.* umschreibender Stil; **B** (*roundabout phrase*) Periphrase, *die* (*Rhet.*); Umschreibung, *die*

**periphrastic** /perɪˈfræstɪk/ *adj.* periphrastisch (*Rhet.*); umschreibend

**periscope** /ˈperɪskəʊp/ *n.* Periskop, *das*

**periscopic** /perɪˈskɒpɪk/ *adj.* periskopisch

**perish** /ˈperɪʃ/ ❶ *v.i.* **A** (*suffer destruction*) umkommen; ‹Volk, Rasse, Kultur:› untergehen; ‹Kraft, Energie:› versiegen; ‹Pflanze:› eingehen; **his name will never ~:** sein Name wird für alle Zeiten fortleben; **~ by the sword/at the hand of the enemy** durch das Schwert/durch Feindes Hand umkommen; **he ~ed from the cold** er erfror; **... or ~ in the attempt** (*joc.*) ..., koste es, was es wolle; **~ the thought!** Gott behüte *od.* bewahre!; **B** (*rot*) verderben; ‹Fresken, Gemälde:› verblassen; ‹Gummi:› altern. ❷ *v.t.* **A** (*reduce to distress*) **we were ~ed [with cold]** wir waren ganz durchgefroren; **B** (*cause to rot*) [schneller] altern lassen ‹Gummi›; angreifen ‹Reifen›

**perishable** /ˈperɪʃəbl/ ❶ *adj.* (*liable to perish*) vergänglich; (*subject to speedy decay*) [leicht] verderblich. ❷ *n. in pl.* leicht verderbliche Güter *od.* Waren

**perisher** /ˈperɪʃə(r)/ *n.* (*Brit. coll.*) (*annoying person*) Ekel, *das* (*ugs.*); Miststück, *das* (*salopp*); (*unfortunate person*) **poor ~:** armer Hund (*ugs.*); armes Schwein (*ugs.*)

**perishing** /ˈperɪʃɪŋ/ (*coll.*) ❶ *adj.* **A** mörderisch ‹Wind, Kälte›; (*very cold*) eiskalt; **it's/I'm ~:** es ist bitterkalt/ich komme um vor Kälte (*ugs.*); **B** (*Brit.: confounded*) elend; **that child is a ~ nuisance** das Kind kann einem den Nerv töten (*ugs.*). ❷ *adv.* **A** mörderisch ‹kalt›; **B** (*Brit.: confoundedly*) fürchterlich (*ugs.*)

**peristaltic** /perɪˈstæltɪk/ *adj.* (*Physiol.*) peristaltisch

**peritoneum** /perɪtəˈniːəm/ *n., pl.* **~s** *or* **peritonea** /perɪtəˈniːə/ (*Anat.*) Bauchfell, *das*

**peritonitis** /perɪtəˈnaɪtɪs/ *n.* ▶ **1232** (*Med.*) Peritonitis, *die* (*fachspr.*); Bauchfellentzündung, *die*

**periwig** /ˈperɪwɪg/ *n.* (*Hist.*) Perücke, *die*

**periwinkle**[1] /ˈperɪwɪŋkl/ *n.* **A** (*Bot.*) Immergrün, *das;* **B** (*colour*) **~ [blue]** Veilchenblau, *das*

**periwinkle**[2] ⇒ **winkle** 1

**perjure** /ˈpɜːdʒə(r)/ *v. refl.* (*swear to false statement*) einen Meineid leisten; (*Law: give false*

P

*evidence under oath*) [unter Eid] falsch aussagen

**perjured** /'pɜ:dʒəd/ *adj.* **~ testimony** falsche Aussage unter Eid; **be ~:** [unter Eid] falsch ausgesagt haben; meineidig sein

**perjurer** /'pɜ:dʒərə(r)/ *n.* Meineidige, *der/die*

**perjury** /'pɜ:dʒərɪ/ *n.* Ⓐ (*swearing to false statement*) Meineid, *der;* (*Law: giving false evidence while under oath*) eidliche Falschaussage; **commit ~:** einen Meineid leisten/sich der eidlichen Falschaussage schuldig machen; Ⓑ (*breach of oath*) Eidesverletzung, *die;* Eidbruch, *der*

**perk¹** /pɜ:k/ (*coll.*) ❶ *v.i.* **~ up** munter werden; ‹Wirtschaft:› in Gang kommen (*ugs.*); (*cheer up*) aufleben; **life had ~ed up again** das Leben machte wieder Spaß. ❷ *v.t.* Ⓐ **~ up** (*restore liveliness of*) aufmuntern; **I need a drink to ~ me up** ich muss jetzt erst mal zur Aufmunterung was trinken (*ugs.*); **~ up sb.'s spirits** jmdn. aufmuntern; **take pills to ~ oneself up** sich mit Pillen aufputschen; Ⓑ **~ up** (*raise briskly*) aufstellen ‹Schwanz, Ohren›; heben ‹Kopf›; Ⓒ (*smarten*) **~ oneself/sth. up** sich fein machen/etw. verschönern

**perk²** *n.* (*Brit. coll.: perquisite*) [Sonder]vergünstigung, *die*

**perk³** (*coll.*) ❶ *v.i.* ‹Kaffee:› durchlaufen; ‹Kaffeemaschine:› in Gang sein. ❷ *v.t.* machen ‹Kaffee›

**perkily** /'pɜ:kɪlɪ/ *adv.* ⇒ **perky**: lebhaft; munter; keck; selbstbewusst

**perky** /'pɜ:kɪ/ *adj.* Ⓐ (*lively*) lebhaft; munter; Ⓑ (*self-assertive*) keck; selbstbewusst

**perlite** /'pɜ:laɪt/ *n.* Perlit, *der*

**perm¹** /pɜ:m/ ❶ *n.* (*permanent wave*) Dauerwelle, *die.* ❷ *v.t.* **~ sb.'s hair** jmdm. eine Dauerwelle machen; **have one's hair ~ed** sich (*Dat.*) eine Dauerwelle machen lassen; **have ~ed hair** eine Dauerwelle haben

**perm²** (*Brit.*) ❶ *n.* (*permutation*) Tippreihe, *die.* ❷ *v.t.* als Tippreihe ankreuzen

**permafrost** /'pɜ:məfrɒst/ *n.* (*Geog.*) Permafrost, *der;* Dauerfrostboden, *der*

**permanence** /'pɜ:mənəns/ *n., no pl.* Dauerhaftigkeit, *die;* **the place had an air of ~:** die Stätte umgab eine Aura von Unvergänglichkeit

**permanency** /'pɜ:mənənsɪ/ *n.* Ⓐ *no pl.* ⇒ **permanence**; Ⓑ (*condition*) Dauerzustand, *der;* (*job*) Dauerstellung, *die*

**permanent** /'pɜ:mənənt/ *adj.* fest ‹Sitz, Bestandteil, Mitglied›; beständig, ewig ‹Werte›; treu ‹Freund›; ständig ‹Plage, Meckern, Wohnsitz, Adresse, Kampf›; Dauer‹gast, -stellung, -visum›; bleibend ‹Folge, Zahn, Gebiss, Schaden›; **be in ~ residence here** ständig hier wohnen; **of ~ value** von bleibendem Wert; **this time it's ~:** diesmal ist es für immer; **sb./sth. is a ~ fixture** jmd./etw. gehört zum Inventar; **be employed on a ~ basis** fest angestellt sein; **~ magnet** Permanentmagnet, *der*

**permanently** /'pɜ:mənəntlɪ/ *adv.* dauernd; auf Dauer ‹verhindern, bleiben›; fest ‹anstellen, einstellen›; (*repeatedly*) ständig; dauernd; **they live in France ~ now** sie leben jetzt ganz (*ugs.*) *od.* ständig in Frankreich; **she was ~ disabled in the accident** sie hat bei dem Unfall eine bleibende Behinderung davongetragen; **she was ~ affected by the shock** der Schock hatte für sie bleibende Folgen

**permanent: ~ 'wave** *n.* Dauerwelle, *die;* **~ 'way** *n.* (*Brit. Railw.*) Oberbau, *der*

**permeable** /'pɜ:mɪəbl/ *adj.* durchlässig; **~ by water** wasserdurchlässig; **be ~ to sth.** etw. durchlassen

**permeate** /'pɜ:mɪeɪt/ ❶ *v.t.* (*get into*) dringen in (+ *Akk.*); (*pass through*) dringen durch; (*saturate*) erfüllen; **~ sb.'s consciousness** jmdm. ins Bewusstsein dringen; **be ~d with** *or* **by sth.** (*fig.*) von etw. durchdrungen sein. ❷ *v.i.* **~ through sth.** etw. durchdringen; **~ through to sb.** zu jmdm. durchdringen

**permissible** /pə'mɪsɪbl/ *adj.* zulässig; **be ~ to** *or* **for sb.** jmdm. erlaubt sein; **~ under the law** nicht gesetzeswidrig; **~ dose** (*Med.*) zulässige Dosis; (*of radiation*) zulässige Belastung

**permission** /pə'mɪʃn/ *n., no indef. art.* Erlaubnis, *die;* (*given by official body*) Genehmigung, *die;* **ask [sb.'s] ~:** [jmdn.] um Erlaubnis bitten; **who gave you ~ to do this?** wer hat dir erlaubt, das zu tun?; **by whose ~?** mit wessen Erlaubnis?; **with your ~:** wenn Sie gestatten; mit Ihrer Erlaubnis; **written ~:** eine schriftliche Genehmigung

**permissive** /pə'mɪsɪv/ *adj.* Ⓐ (*giving permission*) **~ legislation** permissive Gesetzgebung; Ⓑ (*tolerant*) tolerant; großzügig; (*in relation to moral matters*) freizügig; permissiv (*geh.*); **the ~ society** die permissive Gesellschaft

**permissiveness** /pə'mɪsɪvnɪs/ *n., no pl.* Freizügigkeit, *die;* Toleranz, *die*

**permit** ❶ /pə'mɪt/ *v.t.*, **-tt-** zulassen ‹Berufung, Einspruch usw.›; **~ sb. sth.** jmdm. etw. erlauben *od.* (*geh.*) gestatten; **~ me to offer my congratulations** (*formal*) gestatten Sie mir, Ihnen meine Glückwünsche auszusprechen (*geh.*); **sb. is ~ted to do sth.** es ist jmdm. erlaubt *od.* (*geh.*) gestattet, etw. zu tun. ❷ *v.i.*, **-tt-** Ⓐ (*give opportunity*) es zulassen; **weather ~ting** bei entsprechendem Wetter; wenn das Wetter mitspielt (*ugs.*); Ⓑ (*admit*) **~ of sth.** etw. erlauben *od.* gestatten; **not ~ of sth.** etw. verbieten. ❸ /'pɜ:mɪt/ *n.* (*written order*) Genehmigung, *die;* (*for entering premises*) Passierschein, *der;* (*for using car park*) Parkausweis, *der;* **fishing ~:** Fischereischein, *der;* Angelschein, *der;* **be a ~-holder** einen Passierschein/Parkausweis/Angelschein *usw.* haben

**permutation** /pɜ:mjʊ'teɪʃn/ *n.* Ⓐ (*varying of order*) Umstellung, *die;* Ⓑ (*result of variation of order*) Anordnung, *die;* (*of series of items*) Reihenfolge, *die;* Permutation, *die* (*Math.*); Ⓒ (*selection of items*) Auswahl, *die;* (*Brit.: in football pools*) Tippreihe, *die;* **make a ~:** eine Auswahl treffen/eine Tippreihe ankreuzen

**permute** /pə'mju:t/ *v.t.* umstellen; (*Math.*) permutieren

**pernicious** /pə'nɪʃəs/ *adj.* ▶ 1232 verderblich; bösartig ‹Krankheit, Person›; schlimm, übel ‹Angewohnheit›; (*fatal*) fatal; **be a ~ influence on sb.** einen schlimmen *od.* üblen Einfluss auf jmdn. ausüben; **be ~ to sb./sth.** jmdm./einer Sache abträglich sein (*geh.*) *od.* schaden; **~ anaemia** (*Med.*) perniziöse Anämie

**pernickety** /pə'nɪkɪtɪ/ *adj.* (*coll.*) Ⓐ (*fastidious, meticulous*) pingelig (*ugs.*) (**about** in Bezug auf + *Akk.*); Ⓑ (*tricky*) heikel ‹Frage, Thema›; kitzelig ‹Aufgabe, Job›; fummelig (*ugs.*) ‹Arbeitsvorgang›

**peroration** /perə'reɪʃn/ *n.* Schlusswort, *das*

**peroxide** /pə'rɒksaɪd/ ❶ *n.* Ⓐ (*Chem.*) Peroxid, *das;* Ⓑ **[hydrogen] ~:** Wasserstoffperoxid, *das;* **~ blonde** Wasserstoffblondine, *die.* ❷ *v.t.* [mit Wasserstoffperoxid] bleichen

**perpendicular** /pɜ:pən'dɪkjʊlə(r)/ ❶ *adj.* Ⓐ senkrecht; lotrecht; Ⓑ (*very steep*) [fast] senkrecht ‹Aufstieg, Abstieg›; senkrecht abfallend/aufragend ‹Kliff, Felswand usw.›; **~ drop/slope/rock face** Steilabfall, *der*/-hang, *der*/-wand, *die;* Ⓒ (*erect, upright*) aufrecht; (*joc.: standing*) stehend; **be/remain ~** (*joc.*) stehen/stehen bleiben; Ⓓ (*Geom.*) senkrecht (**to** zu); **two ~ planes/lines** zwei zueinander senkrechte Ebenen/Linien; Ⓔ (*Archit.*) ‹Bauwerk, Fenster› im Perpendikularstil; **P~ style** Perpendikularstil, *der.*
❷ *n.* Ⓐ (*line*) Senkrechte, *die* (**to** zu); Lot, *das* (**to** auf + *Dat.*); Ⓑ (*position*) **the ~:** die Senkrechte; das Lot; **be [slightly] out of [the] ~:** [etwas] aus dem Lot sein; nicht [ganz] senkrecht sein; Ⓒ (*instrument*) Lot, *das*

**perpendicularly** /pɜ:pən'dɪkjʊləlɪ/ *adv.* Ⓐ (*vertically*) senkrecht; lotrecht; Ⓑ (*steeply*) [beinahe] senkrecht; Ⓒ (*Geom.*) senkrecht

**perpetrate** /'pɜ:pɪtreɪt/ *v.t.* begehen; anrichten ‹Blutbad, Schaden›; verüben ‹Gemetzel, Gräuel›; ausführen ‹Streich›; (*joc.*) zum Besten geben (*ugs.*) ‹Witz, Lied›

**perpetration** /pɜ:pɪ'treɪʃn/ *n.* (*of crime, blunder*) Begehen, *das;* (*of atrocity, outrage*) Verübung, *die*

**perpetrator** /'pɜ:pɪtreɪtə(r)/ *n.* [Übel]täter, *der*/-täterin, *die;* **be the ~ of a crime/fraud/atrocity/massacre** ein Verbrechen/einen Betrug begangen haben/eine Gräueltat verübt haben/ein Blutbad angerichtet haben

**perpetual** /pə'petjʊəl/ *adj.* Ⓐ (*eternal*) ewig; Ⓑ (*continuous*) ständig; Ⓒ (*repeated*) ständig; [an]dauernd; **she has ~ crises** sie hat [an]dauernd *od.* ständig Krisen; Ⓓ (*applicable or valid for ever*) immer während; ewig

**perpetual 'calendar** *n.* Ⓐ (*table*) ewiger *od.* immer währender Kalender; Ⓑ (*device*) Dauerkalender, *der*

**perpetually** /pə'petjʊəlɪ/ *adv.* Ⓐ (*eternally*) ewig; Ⓑ (*continuously*) ständig; Ⓒ (*repeatedly*) ständig; [an]dauernd

**perpetual: ~ 'motion** *n., no pl., no art.* ewige Bewegung; **~-'motion machine** *n.* Perpetuum mobile, *das*

**perpetuate** /pə'petjʊeɪt/ *v.t.* Ⓐ (*preserve from oblivion*) lebendig erhalten ‹Andenken›; unsterblich machen ‹Namen›; aufrechterhalten ‹Tradition›; Ⓑ (*make perpetual*) aufrechterhalten; erhalten ‹Art, Macht›

**perpetuation** /pəpetjʊ'eɪʃn/ *n.* Ⓐ (*preservation from oblivion*) **~ of sb.'s memory** Bewahrung jmds. Andenkens; **in ~ of sb.'s memory** zu jmds. Gedächtnis; Ⓑ (*action of making perpetual*) Aufrechterhaltung, *die;* (*of species, power*) Erhaltung, *die*

**perpetuity** /pɜ:pɪ'tju:ɪtɪ/ *n., no pl., no indef. art.* ewiger Bestand; **in** *or* **to** *or* **for ~:** für alle Ewigkeit *od.* alle Zeiten

**perplex** /pə'pleks/ *v.t.* Ⓐ (*bewilder*) verwirren; **~ sb.'s mind** jmdn. verwirren; **such questions have ~ed men since time began** solche Fragen haben die Menschheit seit Anbeginn (*geh.*) beunruhigt; Ⓑ (*make [more] complicated*) [noch] verwickelter machen; komplizieren

**perplexed** /pə'plekst/ *adj.* Ⓐ (*bewildered*) verwirrt; (*puzzled*) ratlos; Ⓑ (*complicated*) kompliziert

**perplexedly** /pə'pleksɪdlɪ/ *adv.* ⇒ **perplexed** A: verwirrt; ratlos

**perplexity** /pə'pleksɪtɪ/ *n., no pl.* (*bewilderment*) Verwirrung, *die;* (*puzzlement*) Ratlosigkeit, *die;* **look at sb. in ~:** jmdn. voller Verwirrung ansehen; **cause sb. ~:** jmdn. verwirren

**perquisite** /'pɜ:kwɪzɪt/ *n.* Ⓐ (*incidental benefit*) Vergünstigung, *die;* Ⓑ (*customary gratuity*) Trinkgeld, *das;* Ⓒ (*fig.: thing to which person has sole right*) Vorrecht, *das;* Privileg, *das*

**Perrier** ® /'perɪeɪ/ *n.* **~ [water]** Perrier[wasser], *das*

**perry** /'perɪ/ *n.* (*Brit.*) Birnenmost, *der*

**per se** /pɜ: 'seɪ/ *adv.* an sich; per se (*geh.*); **considered ~:** für sich genommen

**persecute** /'pɜ:sɪkju:t/ *v.t.* Ⓐ verfolgen; Ⓑ (*harass, worry*) plagen; zusetzen (+ *Dat.*); **~ sb. with sth.** jmdm. mit etw. zusetzen; **stop persecuting me** lass mich in Ruhe

**persecution** /pɜ:sɪ'kju:ʃn/ *n.* Ⓐ Verfolgung, *die;* **suffer ~:** verfolgt werden; Ⓑ (*harassment*) Plagerei, *die*

**persecution: ~ complex, ~ mania** *ns.* (*Psych.*) Verfolgungswahn, *der*

**persecutor** /'pɜ:sɪkju:tə(r)/ *n.* Ⓐ Verfolger, *der*/Verfolgerin, *die;* Ⓑ (*who harasses*) Peiniger, *der*/Peinigerin, *die*

**perseverance** /pɜ:sɪ'vɪərəns/ *n.* Beharrlichkeit, *die;* Ausdauer, *die*

**persevere** /pɜ:sɪ'vɪə(r)/ *v.i.* ausharren; **~ with** *or* **at** *or* **in sth.** bei etw. dabeibleiben; **~ in doing sth.** darauf beharren, etw. zu tun

**Persia** /'pɜ:ʃə/ *pr. n.* (*Hist.*) Persien (*das*)

**Persian** /'pɜ:ʃn/ ▶ 1275, ▶ 1340 ❶ *adj.* persisch; ⇒ *also* **English** 1. ❷ *n.* Ⓐ (*person*) Perser, *der*/Perserin, *die;* Ⓑ (*language*) Persisch, *das;* ⇒ *also* **English** 2 A; Ⓒ ⇒ **Persian cat**

**Persian: ~ 'carpet** *n.* Perser[teppich], *der;* **~ 'cat** *n.* Perserkatze, *die;* **~ 'lamb** *n.* Persianer, *der;* **~ lamb coat** Persianermantel, *der*

**persiflage** /ˈpɜ:sɪflɑ:ʒ/ *n.* **[piece of] ~:** Spöttelei, *die;* Persiflage, *die*

**persimmon** /pəˈsɪmən/ *n.* Persimone, *die*

**persist** /pəˈsɪst/ *v.i.* **A** *(continue firmly)* beharrlich sein Ziel verfolgen; nicht nachgeben; **~ in sth.** an etw. *(Dat.)* [beharrlich] festhalten; **~ in doing sth.** etw. weiterhin [beharrlich] tun; **~ in one's efforts to do sth.** in seinen Anstrengungen, etw. zu tun, nicht nachlassen; **B** *(continue in existence)* anhalten

**persistence** /pəˈsɪstəns/ *n., no pl.* **A** *(continuance in particular course)* Hartnäckigkeit, *die;* Beharrlichkeit, *die;* **~ in a habit/a course of action** hartnäckiges *od.* beharrliches Festhalten an einer Gewohnheit/Vorgehensweise; **B** *(quality of perseverance)* Ausdauer, *die;* Zähigkeit, *die;* **C** *(continued existence)* Fortbestehen, *das*

**persistency** /pəˈsɪstənsɪ/ ⇒ **persistence**

**persistent** /pəˈsɪstənt/ *adj.* **A** *(continuing firmly or obstinately)* hartnäckig; **be ~ in one's beliefs** hartnäckig an seinen Überzeugungen festhalten; **be ~ in continuing to do sth.** etw. hartnäckig weiterhin tun; **she was ~ in her efforts to ...:** sie gab ihre Versuche, ... zu ..., nicht auf; **B** *(constantly repeated)* dauernd; hartnäckig ‹Gerüchte›; nicht nachlassend ‹Anstrengung, Bemühung›; **~ showers** anhaltende Schauertätigkeit; **suffer ~ attacks of nausea** dauernd *od.* immer wieder Anfälle von Übelkeit haben; **C** *(enduring)* anhaltend

**persistently** /pəˈsɪstəntlɪ/ *adv.* **A** *(so as to continue firmly or obstinately)* hartnäckig; beharrlich; **B** *(repeatedly)* hartnäckig ‹sich weigern›; **C** *(enduringly)* ständig; **she has ~ made a nuisance of herself** sie hat die ganze Zeit Ärger gemacht

**persnickety** /pəˈsnɪkɪtɪ/ *(Amer. coll.)* ⇒ **pernickety**

**person** /ˈpɜ:sn/ *n.* **A** Mensch, *der;* Person, *die (oft abwertend);* **a rich/sick/unemployed ~:** ein Reicher/Kranker/Arbeitsloser/eine Reiche *usw.;* **the first ~ to leave was ...:** der/die Erste, der/die wegging, war ...; **if any ~ ...:** wenn jemand ...; **what sort of ~ do you think I am?** Wofür halten Sie mich eigentlich?; **in the ~ of sb.** in jmdm. *od.* jmds. Person; **in ~** *(personally)* persönlich; selbst; **B** *(living body)* Körper, *der;* *(appearance)* [äußere] Erscheinung; Äußere, *das;* **C** *(euphem.: genitals)* **expose one's ~:** sich entblößen; **D** *(Ling.)* Person, *die;* **first/second/third ~:** erste/zweite/dritte Person; **E** *(Law)* Person, *die;* **natural/artificial ~:** natürliche/juristische Person

**persona** /pəˈsəʊnə/ *n., pl.* **~e** /pəˈsəʊni:/ **A** *(character assumed by author)* Person, *die;* **B** *(aspect of personality shown to others)* Rolle, *die*

**personable** /ˈpɜ:sənəbl/ *adj.* sympathisch

**personage** /ˈpɜ:sənɪdʒ/ *n.* **A** *(person of rank)* Persönlichkeit, *die;* **B** *(person not known to speaker)* Person, *die*

**persona grata** /pəsəʊnə ˈgrɑ:tə/ *n., pl.* **personae gratae** /pəsəʊni: ˈgrɑ:ti:/ Persona grata, *die*

**personal** /ˈpɜ:sənl/ *adj.* **A** *(one's own)* persönlich; Privat‹angelegenheit, -leben›; **be ~ to sb.** an jmds. Person gebunden sein; ‹Sache:› jmdm. persönlich gehören; ⇒ *also* **touch** 3 F; **B** *(of the body)* persönlich; **~ appearance** äußere Erscheinung; **~ hygiene** Körperpflege, *die;* **~ contact** *(Sport)* Körperkontakt, *der;* **~ foul** *(Sport)* persönliches Foul; **C** *(done in person)* persönlich; **~ audience** Privataudienz, *die;* **he gave us a ~ tour of his estate** er zeigte uns persönlich seinen Besitz; **D** *(directed or referring to the individual)* persönlich; **~ call** *(Brit. Teleph.)* Anruf mit Voranmeldung; **~ stereo** Walkman, *der;* **pay sb. a ~ call** jmdn. privat aufsuchen; **a letter marked 'P~'** ein Brief mit der Aufschrift „Persönlich"; **do you have to make ~ remarks?** musst du unbedingt persönlich *od.* anzüglich werden?; **it's nothing ~, but ...:** nimm es bitte nicht persönlich, aber ...; **E** *(given to or making ~ remarks)* persönlich; anzüglich; **F** *(of a person as opposed to an abstraction)* persönlich; menschlich; *(existing as a person)* persönlich; personal; **G** *(Ling.)* persönlich; Personal‹endung, -pronomen›

**personal: ~ ad** *n.* Privatanzeige, *die;* *(seeking friendship, romance)* Kontaktanzeige, *die;* **~ asˈsistant** *n.* **▶ 1261** persönlicher Referent/persönliche Referentin; **~ ˈbest** *n.* *(Sport)* persönliche Bestleistung; **~ column** *n.* Rubrik für private [Klein]anzeigen; **~ comˈputer** *n.* Personalcomputer, *der;* PC, *der;* **~ ˈequity plan** *n.* *(Brit.)* *persönlicher Vermögensplan auf Aktienbasis;* **~ esˈtate** *n.* *(Law)* bewegliches Vermögen; **~ identiˈfiˈcation number** *n.* persönliche Identifikationsnummer; Geheimnummer, *die*

**personalise** ⇒ **personalize**

**personality** /pɜ:səˈnælɪtɪ/ *n.* **A** *(distinctive personal character)* Persönlichkeit, *die;* Wesen, *das;* *(of inanimate objects)* spezifischer Charakter; **have a strong ~,** *(coll.)* **have lots of ~:** eine starke Persönlichkeit sein *od.* haben; **be lacking in ~:** keine [starke] Persönlichkeit sein; **there was a [strong] ~ clash between them** sie passten [absolut] nicht zusammen; **B** *(noted person)* Persönlichkeit, *die;* **she's quite a ~ in the theatre world** sie ist jemand *od.* hat einen Namen in der Welt des Theaters; **C** *usu. in pl. (personal remark)* persönlicher Angriff; Anzüglichkeit, *die.* ⇒ *also* **split personality**

**persoˈnality cult** *n.* Personenkult, *der;* Persönlichkeitskult, *der*

**personalize** /ˈpɜ:sənəlaɪz/ *v.t.* **A** *(make personal)* persönlich gestalten; eine persönliche Note geben (+ *Dat.*); *(mark with owner's name etc.)* als persönliches Eigentum kennzeichnen; **~d writing paper** persönliches Briefpapier; **B** *(personify)* personifizieren

**ˈpersonal loan** *n.* Personal- *od.* Privatdarlehen, *das;* Personal- *od.* Privatkredit, *der*

**personally** /ˈpɜ:sənəlɪ/ *adv.* persönlich; **~, I see no objection** ich persönlich sehe keine Einwände

**personal: ~ ˈorganizer** *n.* Terminplaner, *der;* **~ ˈpension plan** *n.* persönlicher Renten[vorsorge]plan; persönliche Rentenvorsorge; **~ ˈproperty** *n.* **A** persönliches Eigentum; **abolish ~ property** das Privateigentum abschaffen; **B** ⇒ **personal estate;** **~ ˈservice** *n.* individueller Service; **get ~ service** individuell *od.* persönlich bedient werden

**personalty** /ˈpɜ:sənltɪ/ *n.* *(Law)* bewegliches Vermögen

**persona non grata** /pəsəʊnə nɒn ˈgrɑ:tə/ *n., pl.* **personae non gratae** /pəsəʊni: nɒn ˈgrɑ:ti:/ Persona non grata, *die;* unerwünschte Person

**personification** /pəsɒnɪfɪˈkeɪʃn/ *n.* Verkörperung, *die;* **be the [very] ~ of kindness** die Freundlichkeit selbst *od.* in Person sein

**personify** /pəˈsɒnɪfaɪ/ *v.t.* **be kindness personified, ~ kindness** die Freundlichkeit in Person sein

**personnel** /pɜ:səˈnel/ *n.* **A** *constr. as sing. or pl.* Belegschaft, *die;* *(of shop, restaurant, etc.)* Personal, *das;* **military ~:** Militärangehörige; *attrib.* Personal-; **~ carrier** *(Mil.)* Schützenpanzer, *der;* **~ manager ▶ 1261** Personalchef, *der*/-chefin, *die;* **~ office** Personalbüro, *das;* **~ officer ▶ 1261** Personalsachbearbeiter, *der*/-sachbearbeiterin, *die;* **B** *no pl., no art. (department of firm)* Personalabteilung, *die*

**person-to-ˈperson** *adj.* *(Amer. Teleph.)* **~ call** Anruf mit Voranmeldung

**perspective** /pəˈspektɪv/ ❶ *n.* **A** Perspektive, *die;* *(picture drawn)* perspektivische Zeichnung; **in ~:** perspektivisch richtig; **[do] keep things in ~:** das darfst du nicht so eng sehen; *(don't get too excited)* bleib mal auf dem Teppich; **B** *(fig.)* Blickwinkel, *der;* **throw sth. into ~:** etw. ins rechte Licht rücken; **put a different ~ on events** ein neues Licht auf die Ereignisse werfen; **in/out of ~, in the *or* its right/wrong ~:** unter dem/nicht unter dem richtigen Blickwinkel; **C** *(view)* Aussicht, *die;* *(fig.: mental view)* Ausblick, *der.* ❷ *adj.* perspektivisch

**Perspex** ® /ˈpɜ:speks/ *n.* Plexiglas ⓌⓏ, *das*

**perspicacious** /pɜ:spɪˈkeɪʃəs/ *adj.* scharfsinnig

**perspicacity** /pɜ:spɪˈkæsɪtɪ/ *n., no pl.* Scharfsinnigkeit, *die*

**perspicuity** /pɜ:spɪˈkju:ɪtɪ/ *n., no pl.* Klarheit, *die;* Verständlichkeit, *die*

**perspicuous** /pəˈspɪkjʊəs/ *adj.* **A** *(easily understood)* [klar] verständlich; leicht zu verstehen; **B** *(expressing things clearly)* sich klar ausdrückend; **be ~:** sich klar ausdrücken

**perspiration** /pɜ:spɪˈreɪʃn/ *n.* **A** Schweiß, *der;* **B** *(action of perspiring)* Schwitzen, *das;* Transpiration, *die (geh.)*

**perspire** /pəˈspaɪə(r)/ *v.i.* schwitzen; transpirieren *(geh.)*

**persuadable** /pəˈsweɪdəbl/ *adj.* leicht zu überreden; **be easily ~:** sich leicht überreden lassen; **he might be ~:** vielleicht lässt er sich überreden

**persuade** /pəˈsweɪd/ *v.t.* **A** *(cause to have belief)* überzeugen (**of** von); **~ oneself of sth.** sich *(Dat.)* etw. einreden; **~ oneself [that] ...:** sich *(Dat.)* einreden, dass ...; **~ sb. into believing otherwise** jmdm. etwas anderes einreden *od.* *(ugs.)* weismachen; **B** *(induce)* überreden; **~ sb. into/out of doing sth.** jmdn. [dazu] überreden, etw. zu tun/nicht zu tun

**persuaded** /pəˈsweɪdɪd/ *adj.* überzeugt (**of** von)

**persuader** /pəˈsweɪdə(r)/ *n.* *(coll.: gun)* Kanone, *die (salopp)*

**persuasible** /pəˈsweɪzɪbl/ ⇒ **persuadable**

**persuasion** /pəˈsweɪʒn/ *n.* **A** *(action of persuading)* Überzeugung, die; *(persuasiveness)* Überzeugungskraft, *die;* **it didn't take much ~:** es brauchte nicht viel Überredungskunst; **he didn't need much ~ [to have another drink]** man brauchte ihn nicht lange dazu überreden[, noch etwas zu trinken]; **convince sb. by ~:** jmdn. überzeugen; **have considerable powers of ~, be good at ~:** große Überzeugungskraft haben; **B** *(belief)* Überzeugung, *die;* **C** *(religious belief)* Glaubensrichtung, *die;* Glaube, *der;* *(sect)* Glaubensgemeinschaft, *die*

**persuasive** /pəˈsweɪsɪv/ *adj.*, **persuasively** /pəˈsweɪsɪvlɪ/ *adv.* überzeugend

**persuasiveness** /pəˈsweɪsɪvnɪs/ *n., no pl.* Überzeugungskraft, *die*

**pert** /pɜ:t/ *adj.* **A** *(saucy, impudent)* unverschämt; frech; **B** *(neat)* keck ‹Hut, Anzug usw.›; hübsch ‹Körper, Nase, Hinterteil›; **C** *(Amer.)* ⇒ **peart**

**pertain** /pəˈteɪn/ *v.i.* **A** *(belong as part)* **~ to** [dazu]gehören zu; verbunden sein mit, einhergehen mit ‹Ereignis, Katastrophe›; **B** *(be relevant)* ‹Kriterien usw.:› gelten; **~ to** von Bedeutung sein für; ‹Verhalten:› anstehen *(geh.)* (+ *Dat.*); ‹Begeisterung:› typisch sein für; **C** *(have reference)* **~ to sth.** etw. betreffen; mit etw. zu tun haben

**pertinacious** /pɜ:tɪˈneɪʃəs/ *adj.* *(resolute)* unbeirrbar; *(stubbornly inflexible)* starrsinnig ‹Person›; starr ‹Ansichten›; hartnäckig ‹Weigerung, Beharren›; unüberwindlich ‹Abneigung›

**pertinacity** /pɜ:tɪˈnæsɪtɪ/ *n., no pl.* ⇒ **pertinacious:** Starrsinnigkeit, *die;* Hartnäckigkeit, *die*

**pertinence** /ˈpɜ:tɪnəns/ *n., no pl.* Relevanz, *die;* **of/of no *or* without ~:** von/ohne Bedeutung *od.* Belang

**pertinent** /ˈpɜ:tɪnənt/ *adj.* relevant (**to** für); **there are some ~ notes in the appendix** im Anhang stehen einige diesbezügliche Bemerkungen *od.* Bemerkungen hierzu

**pertinently** /ˈpɜ:tɪnəntlɪ/ *adv.* *(relevantly)* zum passenden Zeitpunkt; *(so as to be to the point)* sachbezogen

**pertly** /ˈpɜ:tlɪ/ *adv.* **A** *(saucily, impudently)* unverschämt; frech; herausfordernd ‹gehen, blicken›; **B** *(neatly)* keck

**perturb** /pə'tɜ:b/ *v.t.* Ⓐ (*throw into confusion*) stören; durchkreuzen ‹Plan›; Ⓑ (*disturb mentally*) beunruhigen; **get ~ed** unruhig werden; Ⓒ (*Astron., Phys.*) stören

**perturbation** /pɜ:tə'beɪʃn/ *n.* Ⓐ (*throwing into confusion*) Störung, *die;* (*of plans*) Durchkreuzung, *die;* Ⓑ (*agitation*) Beunruhigung, *die;* Ⓒ (*Astron., Phys.*) Störung, *die;* Perturbation, *die* (*fachspr.*)

**Peru** /pə'ru:/ *pr. n.* Peru (*das*)

**perusal** /pə'ru:zl/ *n.* Lektüre, *die;* (*of documents*) sorgfältiges Studium; (*fig.: action of examining*) (*of documents*) sorgfältige Durchsicht; **give sth. a careful ~:** etw. genau durchlesen *od.* studieren

**peruse** /pə'ru:z/ *v.t.* genau durchlesen; (*fig.: examine*) untersuchen; unter die Lupe nehmen (*ugs.*)

**Peruvian** /pə'ru:vɪən/ ▶ **1340** ❶ *adj.* peruanisch; **sb. is ~:** jmd. ist Peruaner/Peruanerin. ❷ *n.* Peruaner, *der*/Peruanerin, *die*

**pervade** /pə'veɪd/ *v.t.* Ⓐ (*spread throughout*) durchdringen; ‹Licht:› durchfluten; **be ~d with** *or* **by** durchdrungen sein von; Ⓑ (*be rife among*) ‹Seuche:› wüten in (+ *Dat.*); ‹Ansicht:› weit verbreitet sein in (+ *Dat.*)

**pervasion** /pə'veɪʒn/ *n.* (*action of spreading throughout sth.*) Durchdringung, *die*

**pervasive** /pə'veɪsɪv/ *adj.* (*pervading*) durchdringend ‹Geruch, Feuchtigkeit, Kälte›; weit verbreitet ‹Ansicht›; sich ausbreitend ‹Gefühl›; (*able to pervade*) alles durchdringend

**pervasively** /pə'veɪsɪvlɪ/ *adv.* alles durchdringend; **spread ~:** um sich greifen

**perverse** /pə'vɜ:s/ *adj.* Ⓐ (*persistent in error*) uneinsichtig, verstockt ‹Person›; borniert ‹Person, Argument›; Ⓑ (*different from what is reasonable*) verrückt; Ⓒ (*peevish*) grimmig; bockig ‹Kind›; Ⓓ (*perverted, wicked*) schlecht, verdorben; Ⓔ (*Law: contrary to evidence or judge's direction*) abweichend

**perversely** /pə'vɜ:slɪ/ *adv.* Ⓐ (*with persistence in error*) uneinsichtig; verstockt; Ⓑ (*contrary to what is reasonable*) verrückt; Ⓒ (*peevishly*) grimmig; (*of child's behaviour*) bockig

**perverseness** /pə'vɜ:snɪs/ ⇒ **perversity**

**perversion** /pə'vɜ:ʃn/ *n.* Ⓐ (*turning aside from proper use*) Missbrauch, *der;* (*misconstruction*) Pervertierung, *die;* (*of words, statement*) Verdrehung, *die;* (*leading astray*) Verführung, *die;* **~ of justice** Rechtsbeugung, *die;* Ⓑ (*perverted form of sth.*) Pervertierung, *die;* Ⓒ (*sexual*) Perversion, *die*

**perversity** /pə'vɜ:sɪtɪ/ *n.* Ⓐ (*persistence in error*) Uneinsichtigkeit, *die;* Verstocktheit, *die;* Ⓑ (*difference from what is reasonable*) Verrücktheit, *die*

**pervert** ❶ /pə'vɜ:t/ *v.t.* Ⓐ (*turn aside from proper use or nature*) pervertieren (*geh.*); beugen ‹Recht›; untergraben ‹Staatsform, Demokratie›; vereiteln ‹Absicht›; **~ [the course of] justice** die Justiz behindern; Ⓑ (*misconstrue*) verfälschen; Ⓒ (*lead astray*) verderben. ❷ /'pɜ:vɜ:t/ *n.* Ⓐ (*sexual*) Perverse, *der/die;* perverser Mensch; **he must be a ~:** er muss pervers sein; Ⓑ (*apostate*) Renegat, *der*/Renegatin, *die*

**perverted** /pə'vɜ:tɪd/ *adj.* Ⓐ (*turned aside from proper use*) pervertiert (*geh.*); Ⓑ (*misconstrued*) verdreht; Ⓒ (*led astray*) schlecht; verdorben; Ⓓ (*sexually*) pervers

**peseta** /pə'seɪtə/ *n.* ▶ **1328** Peseta, *die*

**pesky** /'peskɪ/ *adj.* (*Amer. coll.*) verdammt (*ugs.*)

**peso** /'peɪsəʊ/ *n., pl.* **~s** ▶ **1328** Peso, *der*

**pessary** /'pesərɪ/ *n.* (*Med.*) Ⓐ Pessar, *das;* Ⓑ (*vaginal suppository*) Vaginalzäpfchen, *das;* Vaginatorium, *das* (*fachspr.*)

**pessimism** /'pesɪmɪzm/ *n., no pl.* Pessimismus, *der*

**pessimist** /'pesɪmɪst/ *n.* Pessimist, *der*/Pessimistin, *die*

**pessimistic** /pesɪ'mɪstɪk/ *adj.*, **pessimistically** /pesɪ'mɪstɪkəlɪ/ *adv.* pessimistisch

**pest** /pest/ *n.* Ⓐ (*troublesome thing*) Ärgernis, *das;* Plage, *die;* (*troublesome person*) Nervensäge, *die* (*ugs.*); (*destructive or annoying animal*) Schädling, *der;* **~s** (*insects*) Schädlinge; Ungeziefer, *das;* **I know it's a ~, but ...** (*a nuisance*) ich weiß, es ist lästig, aber ...; **he's a real ~:** er ist einfach unausstehlich; **~ officer** Schädlingsbekämpfer, *der;* Kammerjäger, *der* (*veralt.*); **~ control** Schädlingsbekämpfung, *die;* Ⓑ (*arch.*) (*disease*) Seuche, *die;* (*plague*) Pest, *die*

**pester** /'pestə(r)/ *v.t.* belästigen; nerven (*ugs.*); **~ sb. for sth.** jmdm. wegen etw. in den Ohren liegen; **~ sb. to do sth.** jmdm. in den Ohren liegen, etw. zu tun; **~ sb. for money** jmdn. [um Geld] anbetteln; **~ sb. for an interview** jmdn. wegen eines Interviews bedrängen *od.* (*ugs.*) nerven

**pesticide** /'pestɪsaɪd/ *n.* Pestizid, *das*

**pestilence** /'pestɪləns/ *n.* Pestilenz, *die;* Seuche, *die;* (*bubonic plague*) Pest, *die*

**pestilent** /'pestɪlənt/ *adj.* Ⓐ tödlich; todbringend; Ⓑ (*fig. coll.: troublesome*) unausstehlich; lästig ‹Ansinnen›; Ⓒ (*pernicious*) verderblich; zersetzend ‹Lehre›

**pestilential** /pestɪ'lenʃl/ *adj.* Ⓐ pestilenzartig; Ⓑ (*fig. coll.: troublesome*) unausstehlich; **he's a ~ nuisance** er ist unausstehlich; **these ~ flies** diese elenden Fliegen; Ⓒ (*pernicious*) verderblich; zersetzend ‹Lehre›

**pestle** /'pesl/ *n.* Stößel, *der;* Pistill, *das* (*fachspr.*)

**pet**[1] /pet/ ❶ *n.* Ⓐ (*tame animal*) Haustier, *das;* Ⓑ (*darling, favourite*) Liebling, *der;* (*sweet person; also as term of endearment*) Schatz, *der;* **make a ~ of sb.** jmdn. verhätscheln; **mother's** *or* **mummy's ~** (*derog.*) Mamas Liebling; (*male*) Muttersöhnchen, *das* (*abwertend*); **teacher's ~** (*derog.*) Liebling des Lehrers/der Lehrerin; **you have been a ~:** du bist ein Schatz; **[do] be a ~ and do sth.** sei so lieb und tue etw.
❷ *adj.* Ⓐ (*kept as ~*) zahm; Ⓑ (*of or for ~ animals*) Haustier-; **~ accessories** Zoobedarf, *der;* Ⓒ (*favourite*) Lieblings-; **sth./sb. is sb.'s ~ aversion** *or* **hate** jmd. kann etw./jmdn. auf den Tod nicht ausstehen (*ugs.*); **be sb.'s ~ peeve** jmdm. ein Dorn im Auge sein; Ⓓ (*expressing fondness*) Kose‹form, -name›.
❸ *v.t.*, **-tt-** Ⓐ (*treat as favourite*) bevorzugen; verwöhnen; (*indulge*) verhätscheln; Ⓑ (*fondle*) streicheln; liebkosen.
❹ *v.i.*, **-tt-** knutschen (*ugs.*); zärtlich sein (*verhüll.*)

**pet**[2] *n.* (*bad temper*) **in a ~:** verstimmt; beleidigt; eingeschnappt (*ugs.*); **she is in one of her ~s** sie hat mal wieder schlechte Laune

**petal** /'petl/ *n.* Blütenblatt, *das*

**-petal[l]ed** /'petld/ *adj. in comb.* -blättrig ‹Blüte›

**petard** /pɪ'tɑ:d/ *n.* (*Hist.*) Petarde, *die;* ⇒ *also* **hoist** 3

**Pete** /pi:t/ *n.* **for ~'s sake** ≈ **for Heaven's sake** ⇒ **sake**[1]

**peter** *v.i.* **~ out** [allmählich] zu Ende gehen; ‹Wasserlauf:› versickern; ‹Weg:› sich verlieren; ‹Briefwechsel:› versanden; ‹Angriff:› sich totlaufen

**Peter** /'pi:tə(r)/ *pr. n.* Peter; Petrus (*hist., im MA. u. früher*); **Saint ~:** Sankt Petrus *od.* Peter; **rob ~ to pay Paul** ein Loch mit etwas stopfen, was dann woanders fehlt (*fig.*); ⇒ *also* **Blue Peter**

**Peter 'Pan** *n.* Peter Pan; **be a ~:** ein Kindskopf sein; **~ collar** Bubikragen, *der*

**petersham** /'pi:təʃəm/ *n.* Gurtband, *das*

**'pet food** *n.* Tierfutter, *das*

**petiole** /'petɪəʊl/ *n.* (*Bot.*) Blattstängel, *der*

**petit** /'petɪ/ (*Law*) ⇒ **petty** D

**petit bourgeois** /pəti: 'bʊəʒwɑ:/ *n., pl.* **petits bourgeois** /pəti: 'bʊəʒwɑ:/ (*usu. derog.*) Kleinbürger, *der; attrib.* Kleinbürger-; kleinbürgerlich

**petite** /pə'ti:t/ *adj. fem.* zierlich

**petite bourgeoisie** /pəti:t bʊəʒwɑ:'zi:/ *n., no pl., no indef. art.* Kleinbürgertum, *das*

**petit four** /pəti: 'fɔə(r)/ *n., pl.* **petits fours** /pəti: 'fɔə(r)/ Petit Four, *das*

**petition** /pə'tɪʃn/ ❶ *n.* Ⓐ (*formal written supplication*) Petition, *die;* Eingabe, *die;* **get together** *or* **up a ~ for/against sth.** Unterschriften für/gegen etw. sammeln; Ⓑ (*Law: application for writ etc.*) [förmlicher] Antrag; (*for divorce*) Klage, *die.* ❷ *v.t.* eine Eingabe richten an (+ *Akk.*); eine Eingabe machen bei; **~ sb. for sth.** jmdn. um etw. ersuchen. ❸ *v.i.* **~ for** ersuchen um (*geh.*); nachsuchen um (*geh.*); (*present ~ for*) eine Unterschriftenliste einreichen für; einkommen um (*geh.*); **~ for divorce** die Scheidung einreichen; **~ against** eine Eingabe machen gegen

**petitioner** /pə'tɪʃənə(r)/ *n.* Antragsteller, *der*/Antragstellerin, *die;* (*for divorce*) Kläger, *der*/Klägerin, *die*

**petit point** /pəti: 'pwæ̃/ *n.* Ⓐ (*embroidery*) Petit Point, *das;* Ⓑ (*stitch*) Perlstich, *der*

**petits pois** /pəti: 'pwɑ/ *n. pl.* feine Erbsen

**Petrarch** /'petrɑ:k/ *pr. n.* Petrarca (*der*)

**petrel** /'petrl/ *n.* (*Ornith.*) Sturmvogel, *der*

**petrifaction** /petrɪ'fækʃn/ *n.* Versteinerung, *die*

**petrify** /'petrɪfaɪ/ ❶ *v.t.* Ⓐ (*change into stone*) petrifizieren (*geh.*); versteinern lassen; **become petrified** versteinern; petrifizieren (*geh.*); Ⓑ (*fig.: cause to become inert*) erstarren lassen; **be petrified with fear/shock** starr vor Angst/Schrecken sein; vor Angst/Schrecken [wie] versteinert sein (*geh.*); **be petrified by sb./sth.** vor jmdm./etw. erstarren; sich vor jmdm. panisch fürchten; **she looked quite petrified** sie schien entsetzliche Angst zu haben. ❷ *v.i.* (*turn to stone*) versteinern; (*fig.: become inert*) erstarren

**petrochemical** /petrəʊ'kemɪkl/ ❶ *n.* Petrochemikalie, *die.* ❷ *adj.* Ⓐ (*of chemistry of rocks*) petrochemisch; Ⓑ (*of chemistry of petroleum*) petro[l]chemisch

**petrochemistry** /petrəʊ'kemɪstrɪ/ *n.* Ⓐ (*chemistry of rocks*) Petrochemie, *die;* Ⓑ (*chemistry of petroleum*) Petro[l]chemie, *die*

**petrodollar** /'petrəʊdɒlə(r)/ *n.* Petrodollar, *der*

**petrol** /'petrl/ *n.* (*Brit.*) Benzin, *das;* **fill up with ~:** tanken

**petrolatum** /petrə'leɪtəm/ *n.* (*Amer.*) ⇒ **petroleum jelly**

**petrol: ~ bomb** *n.* Benzinbombe, *die;* **~ can** *n.* (*Brit.*) Benzinkanister, *der;* **~ cap** *n.* (*Brit.*) Tankverschluss, *der;* **~ engine** *n.* Benzinmotor, *der*

**petroleum** /pɪ'trəʊlɪəm/ *n.* Erdöl, *das*

**petroleum 'jelly** *n.* Vaseline, *die*

**'petrol gauge** *n.* (*Brit.*) Benzinuhr, *die;* Kraftstoffanzeiger, *der* (*Technik*)

**petrology** /pɪ'trɒlədʒɪ/ *n.* Petrologie, *die*

**petrol: ~ pump** *n.* (*Brit.*) Ⓐ (*in ~ station*) Zapfsäule, *die;* Tanksäule, *die;* **~ pump attendant** Tankwart, *der*/Tankwartin, *die;* Ⓑ (*in car, aircraft, etc.*) Benzin- *od.* Kraftstoffpumpe, *die;* **~ station** *n.* (*Brit.*) Tankstelle, *die;* **~ tank** *n.* (*Brit.*) (*in car, aircraft, etc.*) Benzintank, *der;* **~ tanker** *n.* (*Brit.*) Benzintankwagen, *der*

**'pet shop** *n.* Tierhandlung, *die;* Zoohandlung, *die*

**petticoat** /'petɪkəʊt/ ❶ *n.* Unterrock, *der.* ❷ *adj.* weiblich; Frauen-; **~ government** Frauenherrschaft, *die;* Weiberregiment, *das* (*abwertend*)

**pettifogging** /'petɪfɒgɪŋ/ *adj.* kleinkariert, kleinlich ‹Person›; belanglos ‹Detail›; kleinlich ‹Einwand›; **his ~ mind** seine Kleinkariertheit

**petting** /'petɪŋ/ *n.* Petting, *das*

**pettish** /'petɪʃ/ *adj.*, **pettishly** /'petɪʃlɪ/ *adv.* übellaunig; grantig (*ugs.*)

**petty** /'petɪ/ *adj.* Ⓐ (*trivial*) belanglos ‹Detail, Sorgen›; kleinlich ‹Einwand, Vorschrift›; Ⓑ (*minor*) Klein‹staat, -unternehmer, -landwirt›; klein ‹Geschäftsmann›; Duodez‹fürst, -fürstentum, -staat›; **~ criminal** Kleinkriminelle, *der/die;* **~ theft** Bagatelldiebstahl, *der;* **~ thief** kleiner Dieb/kleine Diebin; Ⓒ (*small-minded*) kleinlich; kleinkariert; Ⓓ (*Law*) geringfügig; Bagatell-; ⇒ *also* **session** G

**petty: ~ 'cash** *n.* kleine Kasse; Portokasse, *die;* **~-minded** ⇒ **small-minded**; **~ 'officer** *n.* (*Navy*) ≈ [Ober]maat, *der*

**petulance** /'petjʊləns/ *n., no pl.* Bockigkeit, *die*

**petulant** /'petjʊlənt/ *adj.*, **petulantly** /'petjʊləntlɪ/ *adv.* bockig

**petunia** /pɪ'tju:nɪə/ *n.* (*Bot.*) Petunie, *die*

**pew** /pju:/ *n.* **A** (*Eccl.*) Kirchenbank, *die;* **B** (*coll.: seat*) [Sitz]platz, *der;* **have** *or* **take a ~:** sich platzen (*ugs. scherzh.*)

**pewit** ⇒ **peewit**

**pewter** /'pju:tə(r)/ **1** *n., no pl., no indef. art.* (*substance, vessels*) Pewter, *der;* [Hart]zinn, *das.* **2** *attrib. adj.* Zinn‹becher, -geschirr›

**PG** *abbr.* (*Brit. Cinemat.*) **Parental Guidance** ≈ bedingt jugendfrei

**PGCE** *abbr.* (*Brit.*) **Postgraduate Certificate in Education**

**pH** /pi:'eɪtʃ/ *n.* (*Chem.*) pH-Wert, *der*

**phalanx** /'fælæŋks/ *n., pl.* **~es** *or* **phalanges** /fæ'lændʒi:z/ **A** (*of troops, police, etc.*) Phalanx, *die;* **B** (*Anat.*) Phalanx, *die;* (*of finger*) Fingerglied, *das;* (*of toe*) Zehenglied, *das*

**phallic** /'fælɪk/ *adj.* phallisch; **~ symbol** Phallussymbol, *das*

**phallus** /'fæləs/ *n., pl.* **~es** *or* **phalli** /'fælaɪ/ Phallus, *der*

**phantasmagoria** /fæntæzmə'gɔ:rɪə/ *n.* Trugbild, *das;* Phantasmagorie, *die* (*geh.*)

**phantasy** ⇒ **fantasy** A, B

**phantom** /'fæntəm/ **1** *n.* **A** (*spectre*) Phantom, *das;* (*image*) Phantom, *das;* Trugbild, *das;* **B** (*mental illusion*) Fantasiegebilde, *das.* **2** *adj.* Phantom-

**phantom: ~ 'limb** *n.* (*Med.*) Phantomglied, *das;* **~ 'pregnancy** *n.* (*Med.*) Scheinschwangerschaft, *die*

**Pharaoh** /'feərəʊ/ *n.* Pharao, *der*

**Pharisaic[al]** /færɪ'seɪɪk(l)/ *adj.* pharisäerhaft

**Pharisee** /'færɪsi:/ *n.* **A** Pharisäer, *der;* **B** **p~** (*self-righteous person*) Pharisäer, *der*

**pharmaceutical** /fɑ:mə'sju:tɪkl/ **1** *adj.* pharmazeutisch; Arzneimittel-, Pharma‹industrie, -konzern, -hersteller›; **~ chemist** Arzneimittelchemiker, *der*/-chemikerin, *die.* **2** *n. in pl.* Pharmaka

**pharmacist** /'fɑ:məsɪst/ *n.* ▶ **1261** Apotheker, *der*/Apothekerin, *die;* (*in research*) Pharmazeut, *der*/Pharmazeutin, *die*

**pharmacological** /fɑ:məkə'lɒdʒɪkl/ *adj.* pharmakologisch

**pharmacologist** /fɑ:mə'kɒlədʒɪst/ *n.* Pharmakologe, *der*/Pharmakologin, *die*

**pharmacology** /fɑ:mə'kɒlədʒɪ/ *n.* Pharmakologie, *die*

**pharmacopoeia** /fɑ:məkə'pi:ə/ *n.* Pharmakopöe, *die;* amtliches Arzneibuch

**pharmacy** /'fɑ:məsɪ/ *n.* **A** *no pl., no art.* (*preparation of drugs*) Pharmazie, *die;* Arzneimittelkunde, *die;* **B** (*dispensary*) Apotheke, *die*

**pharyngeal** /fæ'rɪndʒɪəl/ *adj.* (*Anat., Med.*) Rachen‹katarrh, -entzündung, -mandel, -höhle usw.›; Schlund‹tasche, -krampf›

**pharyngitis** /færɪn'dʒaɪtɪs/ *n.* ▶ **1232** (*Med.*) Rachenkatarrh, *der;* Pharyngitis, *die* (*fachspr.*)

**pharynx** /'færɪŋks/ *n., pl.* **pharynges** /fə'rɪndʒi:z/ (*Anat.*) Schlund, *der;* Rachen, *der;* Pharynx, *der* (*fachspr.*)

**phase** /feɪz/ **1** *n.* **A** Phase, *die;* (*of project, construction, history also*) Abschnitt, *der;* (*of illness, development also*) Stadium, *das;* **it's only** *or* **just a ~ [he's/she's going through]** das gibt sich [mit der Zeit] wieder (*ugs.*); **B** (*Phys., Astron., Chem.*) Phase, *die;* **in ~:** phasengleich; in [gleicher] Phase; **out of ~:** phasenverschoben; **have got out of ~** (*fig.*) nicht mehr koordiniert sein. **2** *v.t.* stufenweise durchführen

**~ 'in** *v.t.* stufenweise einführen

**~ 'out** *v.t.* **A** (*eliminate gradually*) nach und nach auflösen ‹Abteilung›; allmählich abschaffen ‹Verfahrensweise, Methode›; **B** (*discontinue production of*) [langsam] auslaufen lassen

**Ph.D.** /pi:eɪtʃ'di:/ *abbr.* **Doctor of Philosophy** Dr. phil.; **he/she is studying for a ~:** er ist Doktorand/sie ist Doktorandin; er/sie promoviert; **John Clarke ~:** Dr. phil. John Clarke; **do one's ~:** seinen Doktor machen; **~ thesis** Doktorarbeit, *die;* Dissertation, *die*

**pheasant** /'fezənt/ *n.* Fasan, *der*

**phenobarbitone** /fi:nəʊ'bɑ:bɪtəʊn/ (*Brit.; Amer.:* **phenobarbital** /fi:nəʊ'bɑ:bɪtl/) *n.* (*Med.*) Phenobarbital, *das*

**phenol** /'fi:nɒl/ *n.* (*Chem.*) Phenol, *das;* Karbolsäure, *die*

**phenomenal** /fɪ'nɒmɪnl/ *adj.* **A** (*remarkable*) phänomenal; sagenhaft (*ugs.*); unwahrscheinlich (*ugs.*) ‹Spektakel, Radau›; **B** (*Philos.*) phänomenal; wahrnehmbar

**phenomenalism** /fɪ'nɒmɪnəlɪzm/ *n.* (*Philos.*) Phänomenalismus, *der*

**phenomenally** /fɪ'nɒmɪnəlɪ/ *adj.* phänomenal; unglaublich; unwahrscheinlich (*ugs.*) ‹schlecht, langweilig, laut›

**phenomenon** /fɪ'nɒmɪnən/ *n., pl.* **phenomena** /fɪ'nɒmɪnə/ Phänomen, *das*

**phew** /fju:/ *int.* puh

**phial** /'faɪəl/ *n.* [Medizin]fläschchen, *das;* Phiole, *die*

**philander** /fɪ'lændə(r)/ *v.i.* (*flirt*) schäkern; flirten; (*with heavier sexual overtones*) nachstellen (**with** *Dat.*)

**philanderer** /fɪ'lændərə(r)/ *n.* Schürzenjäger, *der* (*spött.*)

**philanthropic** /fɪlən'θrɒpɪk/ *adj.* philanthropisch (*geh.*); menschenfreundlich; Wohltätigkeits‹organisation, -verein usw.›

**philanthropically** /fɪlən'θrɒpɪkəlɪ/ *adv.* philanthropisch (*geh.*)

**philanthropist** /fɪ'lænθrəpɪst/ *n.* Philanthrop, *der*/Philanthropin, *die* (*geh.*); Menschenfreund, *der*/Menschenfreundin, *die*

**philanthropy** /fɪ'lænθrəpɪ/ *n.* Philanthropie, *die* (*geh.*); (*love of mankind also*) Menschenliebe, *die;* Menschenfreundlichkeit, *die*

**philatelic** /fɪlə'telɪk/ *adv.* philatelistisch

**philatelist** /fɪ'lætəlɪst/ *n.* Philatelist, *der*/Philatelistin, *die;* (*collector also*) Briefmarkensammler, *der*/-sammlerin, *die*

**philately** /fɪ'lætəlɪ/ *n.* Philatelie, *die;* Briefmarkenkunde, *die*

**philharmonic** /fɪlhɑ:'mɒnɪk, fɪlɑ:'mɒnɪk/ **1** *adj.* philharmonisch. **2** *n.* Philharmonie, *die*

**Philip** /'fɪlɪp/ *pr. n.* Philipp; (*Bibl.*) Philippus

**philippic** /fɪ'lɪpɪk/ *n.* Philippika, *die* (*geh.*)

**Philippine** /'fɪlɪpi:n/ *adj.* **A** (*Geog.*) philippinisch; **B** ⇒ **Filipino**

**Philippines** /'fɪlɪpi:nz/ *pr. n. pl.* Philippinen *Pl.*

**philistine** /'fɪlɪstaɪn/ **1** *n.* **A** (*uncultured person*) [Kultur]banause, *der*/-banausin, *die;* **B** **P~** (*native of ancient Philistia*) Philister, *der.* **2** *adj.* banausisch; kulturlos

**philistinism** /'fɪlɪstɪnɪzm/ *n., no pl.* Banausentum, *das;* (*bourgeois narrow-mindedness*) Philistertum, *das* (*geh.*)

**Phillips** /'fɪlɪps/ *n.* **~ screw** ® Kreuz[schlitz]schraube, *die;* **~ screwdriver** ® Kreuz[schlitz]schraubenzieher, *der*

**philological** /fɪlə'lɒdʒɪkl/ *adj.* philologisch

**philologist** /fɪ'lɒlədʒɪst/ *n.* Philologe, *der*/Philologin, *die*

**philology** /fɪ'lɒlədʒɪ/ *n.* **A** (*science of language*) [historische] Sprachwissenschaft; **B** (*Amer.: study of literature*) Philologie, *die;* Literaturwissenschaft, *die*

**philosopher** /fɪ'lɒsəfə(r)/ *n.* ▶ **1261** Philosoph, *der*/Philosophin, *die*

**philosopher: ~'s stone, ~s' stone** *n.* Stein der Weisen

**philosophic** /fɪlə'sɒfɪk/, **philosophical** /fɪlə'sɒfɪkl/ *adj.* **A** philosophisch; philosophisch gebildet *od.* geschult ‹Person›; **B** (*resigned, calm*) abgeklärt; gelassen

**philosophically** /fɪlə'sɒfɪkəlɪ/ *adv.* **A** **~ [speaking]** philosophisch betrachtet; vom philosophischen Standpunkt gesehen; **B** (*calmly*) gelassen

**philosophize** (**philosophise**) /fɪ'lɒsəfaɪz/ *v.i.* philosophieren (**about, on** über + *Akk.*)

**philosophy** /fɪ'lɒsəfɪ/ *n.* Philosophie, *die;* **~ of life** Lebensphilosophie, *die;* **~ of education** Erziehungsphilosophie, *die*

**phlebitis** /flɪ'baɪtɪs/ *n.* ▶ **1232** (*Med.*) Venenentzündung, *die;* Phlebitis, *die* (*fachspr.*)

**phlegm** /flem/ *n., no pl., no indef. art.* **A** (*Physiol.*) Schleim, *der;* Mucus, *der* (*Med.*); **B** (*coolness*) stoische Ruhe; Gleichmut, *der;* **C** (*stolidness*) Phlegma, *das*

**phlegmatic** /fleg'mætɪk/ *adj.* **A** (*cool*) gleichmütig; **B** (*stolid*) phlegmatisch

**phlegmatically** /fleg'mætɪkəlɪ/ *adv.* ⇒ **phlegmatic**: gleichmütig; phlegmatisch

**phloem** /'fləʊem/ *n.* (*Bot.*) Phloem, *das*

**phlox** /flɒks/ *n.* (*Bot.*) Phlox, *der;* Flammenblume, *die*

**phobia** /'fəʊbɪə/ *n.* Phobie, *die* (*Psychol.*); [krankhafte] Angst

**-phobia** /'fəʊbɪə/ *n. in comb.* -phobie, *die*

**phobic** /'fəʊbɪk/ *adj.* phobisch; **be ~ about sth.** krankhafte Angst *od.* (*bildungsspr.*) eine Phobie vor etw. haben

**-phobic** /'fəʊbɪk/ *adj. in comb.* -phob

**Phoenician** /fə'ni:ʃn/ **1** *adj.* phönizisch; phönikisch. **2** *n.* Phönizier, *der*/Phönizierin, *die;* Phöniker, *der*/Phönikerin, *die*

**phoenix** /'fi:nɪks/ *n.* (*Mythol.*) Phönix, *der;* **~-like** wie ein Phönix

**phone** /fəʊn/ **1** *n.* Telefon, *das;* **pick up/put down the ~:** [den Hörer] abnehmen/auflegen; **by ~:** telefonisch; **speak to sb. by ~** *or* **on the ~:** mit jmdm. telefonieren; **be on the ~ for hours** stundenlang telefonieren; **I'm not on the ~:** ich habe kein Telefon. **2** *v.i.* anrufen; **can we ~ from here?** können wir von hier aus telefonieren? **3** *v.t.* anrufen; **~ the office/home** im Büro/zu Hause anrufen; **~ a message through to sb.** jmdm. eine Nachricht telefonisch übermitteln *od.* durchgeben. ⇒ *also* **telephone**

**~ a'round** **1** *v.i.* herumtelefonieren. **2** *v.t.* [nacheinander] anrufen

**~ 'back** *v.t. & i.* (*make a return ~ call* [*to*]) zurückrufen; (*make a further ~ call* [*to*]) wieder *od.* nochmals anrufen

**~ 'in** **1** *v.i.* anrufen. **2** *v.t.* telefonisch mitteilen *od.* durchgeben. ⇒ *also* **phone-in**

**~ 'up** *v.t. & i.* anrufen

**phone: ~ book** *n.* Telefonbuch, *das;* **~ booth, ~ box** *ns.* Telefonzelle, *die;* **~ call** *n.* Anruf, *der;* ⇒ *also* **telephone call**; **~card** *n.* Telefonkarte, *die;* **~-in** *n.* **~-in [programme]** (*Radio*) Hörersendung, *die;* (*Telev.*) Phone-in-Sendung, *die* (*Jargon*); Sendung mit Zuschaueranrufen

**phoneme** /'fəʊni:m/ *n.* (*Phonet.*) Phonem, *das*

**phone: ~ number** *n.* Telefonnummer, *die;* **~-tapping** *n.* Anzapfen von Telefonleitungen

**phonetic** /fə'netɪk/ *adj.* phonetisch; ⇒ *also* **alphabet**

**phonetically** /fə'netɪkəlɪ/ *adv.* phonetisch

**phonetician** /fəʊnɪ'tɪʃn/ *n.* ▶ **1261** Phonetiker, *der*/Phonetikerin, *die*

**phonetics** /fə'netɪks/ *n.* **A** *no pl.* Phonetik, *die;* **B** *no pl.* (*phonetic script*) phonetische Umschrift; **C** *constr. as pl.* (*phonetic transcription*) phonetische Angaben

**phoney** /'fəʊnɪ/ (*coll.*) **1** *adj.*, **phonier** /'fəʊnɪə(r)/, **phoniest** /'fəʊnɪɪst/ **A** (*sham*) falsch; gefälscht ‹Brief, Dokument›; **there's something a bit ~ about the whole thing** irgendetwas an der ganzen Sache ist faul (*ugs.*); **B** (*fictitious*) falsch ‹Name›; erfunden ‹Geschichte›; **C** (*fraudulent*) Schein‹firma, -geschäft, -krieg›; falsch, scheinbar ‹Doktor, Diplomat, Geschäftsmann›. **2** *n.* **A** (*person*) Blender, *der*/Blenderin, *die;* **this doctor is just a ~:** dieser Arzt ist ein Scharlatan; **B** (*sham*) Fälschung, *die*

**phonograph** /'fəʊnəgrɑ:f/ *n.* (*Amer.*) ⇒ **gramophone**

**phonology** /fə'nɒlədʒɪ/ *n.* Phonologie, *die*

**phony** ⇒ **phoney**

**phooey** /'fu:ɪ/ *int.* pah

**phosphate** /'fɒsfeɪt/ *n.* (*Chem.*) Phosphat, *das*

**phosphor** /'fɒsfə(r)/ *n.* Phosphor, *der*

**phosphorescence** /fɒsfə'resəns/ *n.* Phosphoreszenz, *die*

**phosphorescent** /fɒsfə'resənt/ *adj.* phosphoreszierend

**phosphorus** /'fɒsfərəs/ *n.* (*Chem.*) Phosphor, *der*

P

**photo** /ˈfəʊtəʊ/ *n., pl.* **~s** Foto, *das;* ⇒ *also* **photograph** 1

**photo-** /fəʊtəʊ/ *in comb.* Ⓐ(*light*) photo-/Photo-; Ⓑ(*photography*) foto-/Foto-

**photo: ~ album** *n.* Fotoalbum, *das;* **~call** *n.* Fototermin, *der;* **~cell** *n.* Photozelle, *die;* **~ˈchemical** *adj.* photochemisch; **~ˈchemistry** *n.* Photochemie, *die;* **~composition** ⇒ **filmsetting**; **~copier** *n.* Fotokopiergerät, *das;* **~copy** ❶ *n.* Fotokopie, *die;* ❷ *v.t.* fotokopieren; **~electric** *adj.* photoelektrisch; **~electric cell** Photozelle, *die;* **~ finish** *n.* Fotofinish, *das;* (*fig.*) Kopf-an-Kopf-Rennen, *das;* **~fit** *n.* Phantombild, *das;* Phantomfoto, *das;* **~genic** /fəʊtəˈdʒenɪk, fəʊtəˈdʒiːnɪk/ *adj.* fotogen

**photograph** /ˈfəʊtəgrɑːf/ ❶ *n.* Fotografie, *die;* Foto, *das;* **take a ~ [of sb./sth.]** [jmdn./etw.] fotografieren; ein Foto [von jmdm./etw.] machen. ❷ *v.t. & i.* fotografieren; **he ~s well/badly** (*as subject*) er lässt sich gut/schlecht fotografieren

**ˈphotograph album** *n.* Fotoalbum, *das*

**photographer** /fəˈtɒgrəfə(r)/ *n.* ▸ 1261 Fotograf, *der*/Fotografin, *die*

**photographic** /fəʊtəˈgræfɪk/ *adj.* fotografisch; Foto‹ausrüstung, -club, -papier, -apparat, -ausstellung, -zeitschrift›; **~ memory** (*fig.*) fotografisches Gedächtnis

**photographically** /fəʊtəˈgræfɪkəlɪ/ *adv.* fotografisch

**photography** /fəˈtɒgrəfɪ/ *n., no pl., no indef. art.* Fotografie, *die*

**photogravure** /fəʊtəgrəˈvjʊə(r)/ *n.* Photogravüre, *die*

**photometer** /fəʊˈtɒmɪtə(r)/ *n.* Photometer, *der*

**photomonˈtage** *n.* Fotomontage, *die*

**photon** /ˈfəʊtɒn/ *n.* (*Phys.*) Photon, *das*

**photo: ~ opportunity** *n.* Ⓐ ⇒ **~call**; Ⓑ (*Brit.: opportunity for a good photograph*) [Foto]motiv, *das;* **~ˈsensitive** *adj.* lichtempfindlich; **~sensiˈtivity** *n.* Lichtempfindlichkeit, *die;* **~ session, ~ shoot** *ns.* Shooting, *das;* **~setting** ⇒ **filmsetting**; **P~stat** ® /ˈfəʊtəstæt/ (*Brit.*) ❶ *n.* ⇒ **photocopy** 1; ❷ *v.t.*, **-tt-** ⇒ **photocopy** 2; **~ˈsynthesis** *n.* (*Bot.*) Photosynthese, *die;* **~voltaic** *adj.* (*Phys.*) photovoltaisch

**phrasal ˈverb** *n.* (*Ling.*) mehrgliedriges Verb

**phrase** /freɪz/ ❶ *n.* Ⓐ(*Ling.*) Phrase, *die* (*fachspr.*); (*idiomatic expression*) idiomatische Wendung; [Rede]wendung, *die;* **set ~:** feste [Rede]wendung; **noun/verb ~:** Nominal-/Verbalphrase, *die;* Ⓑ(*brief expression*) kurze Formel; **be good at turning a ~:** ausgezeichnet formulieren können; **hackneyed ~:** abgegriffene *od.* (*ugs.*) abgedroschene Phrase; ⇒ *also* **turn** 1 J; Ⓒ(*Mus.*) Phrase, *die.* ❷ *v.t.* Ⓐ(*express in words*) formulieren; **~ one's idea** seinen Gedanken in Worte fassen; Ⓑ(*Mus.*) phrasieren

**ˈphrase book** *n.* Sprachführer, *der*

**phraseology** /freɪzɪˈɒlədʒɪ/ *n.* Ausdrucksweise, *die;* (*technical terms*) Terminologie, *die*

**phrasing** /ˈfreɪzɪŋ/ *n.* Ⓐ(*style of expression*) Ausdrucksweise, *die;* Ⓑ(*Mus.*) Phrasierung, *die*

**phrenetic** ⇒ **frenetic**

**phrenology** /frɪˈnɒlədʒɪ/ *n.* Phrenologie, *die*

**phut** /fʌt/ ❶ *adv.* (*coll.*) **go ~:** kaputtgehen (*ugs.*); (*fig.*) ‹Plan, Projekt:› in die Binsen gehen (*ugs.*); ‹Geschäft, Firma:› kaputtgehen (*ugs.*). ❷ *n.* Knall, *der;* **~!** peng!

**phylloxera** /fɪˈlɒksərə/ *n.* (*Zool.*) Reblaus, *die*

**phylum** /ˈfaɪləm/ *n., pl.* **phyla** /ˈfaɪlə/ (*Biol.*) [Tier-/Pflanzen]stamm, *der;* Phylum, *das* (*fachspr.*)

**physic** /ˈfɪzɪk/ (*arch.*) ❶ *n.* Ⓐ(*art of healing*) Heilkunde, *die;* Ⓑ(*medicine*) Arznei, *die* (*veralt.*); Heilmittel, *das.* ❷ *v.t.*, **-ck-** mit Arzneimitteln behandeln

**physical** /ˈfɪzɪkl/ ❶ *adj.* Ⓐ(*material*) physisch ‹Gewalt›; stofflich, dinglich ‹Welt, Universum›; Ⓑ(*of physics*) physikalisch; **it's a ~ impossibility** (*fig.*) es ist absolut unmöglich; Ⓒ(*bodily*) körperlich; physisch; **you need to take more ~ exercise** du brauchst mehr Bewegung; **~ check-up** *or* **examination** ärztliche Untersuchung; **get/be ~** (*coll.*) rabiat werden/sein; Ⓓ(*carnal, sensual*) körperlich ‹Liebe›; sinnlich ‹Person, Ausstrahlung›. ❷ *n.* ärztliche [Vorsorge]untersuchung; (*for joining the army*) Musterung, *die*

**physical: ~ ˈchemistry** *n.* physikalische Chemie; Physikochemie, *die;* **~ eduˈcation** *n.* Sportunterricht, *der;* (*school subject*) Sport, *der;* **~ geˈography** *n.* physische Geographie; **~ ˈjerks** *n. pl.* (*coll.*) Gymnastikübungen

**physically** /ˈfɪzɪkəlɪ/ *adv.* Ⓐ(*in accordance with physical laws*) physikalisch; **~ impossible** (*fig.*) absolut unmöglich; Ⓑ(*relating to the body*) körperlich; physisch; **they had to be ~ removed** sie mussten mit [physischer] Gewalt entfernt werden; **be ~ sick** einen physischen Ekel empfinden; **~ disabled** körperbehindert

**physical: ~ ˈscience** *n.* exakte Naturwissenschaften; **~ ˈtraining** *n.* Sport, *der;* (*in school*) Sport[unterricht], *der*

**ˈphysic garden** *n.* (*arch.*) [Heil]kräutergarten, *der*

**physician** /fɪˈzɪʃn/ *n.* ▸ 1261 Arzt, *der*/Ärztin, *die*

**physicist** /ˈfɪzɪsɪst/ *n.* ▸ 1261 Physiker, *der*/Physikerin, *die*

**physics** /ˈfɪzɪks/ *n., no pl.* Physik, *die*

**physio** /ˈfɪzɪəʊ/ *n., pl.* **~s** ▸ 1261 (*coll.*) Physiotherapeut, *der*/Physiotherapeutin, *die*

**physiognomy** /fɪzɪˈɒnəmɪ/ *n.* Physiognomie, *die;* Gesichtszüge; (*study*) Physiognomik, *die;* (*fig.: of mountain, country, city, etc.*) Physiognomie, *die* (*geh.*); Gestalt, *die*

**physiological** /fɪzɪəˈlɒdʒɪkl/ *adj.* physiologisch

**physiologist** /fɪzɪˈɒlədʒɪst/ *n.* ▸ 1261 Physiologe, *der*/Physiologin, *die*

**physiology** /fɪzɪˈɒlədʒɪ/ *n.* Physiologie, *die*

**physiotherapist** /fɪzɪəʊˈθerəpɪst/ *n.* ▸ 1261 Physiotherapeut, *der*/-therapeutin, *die*

**physiotherapy** /fɪzɪəʊˈθerəpɪ/ *n.* Physiotherapie, *die*

**physique** /fɪˈziːk/ *n.* Körperbau, *der;* **be small in ~:** von geringer Körpergröße *od.* kleinem Wuchs sein

**pi** /paɪ/ *n.* (*Math., Greek letter*) Pi, *das*

**pianissimo** /pɪəˈnɪsɪməʊ/ (*Mus.*) ❶ *adj.* pianissimo *nicht attr.;* Pianissimo-. ❷ *adv.* pianissimo. ❸ *n., pl.* **~s** *or* **pianissimi** /pɪəˈnɪsɪmiː/ Pianissimo, *das*

**pianist** /ˈpiːənɪst/ *n.* ▸ 1261 Klavierspieler, *der*/Klavierspielerin, *die;* (*professional*) Pianist, *der*/Pianistin, *die*

**piano¹** /pɪˈænəʊ/ *n., pl.* **~s** (*Mus.*) (*upright*) Klavier, *das;* (*grand*) Flügel, *der;* *attrib.* Klavier-; **play the ~:** Klavier spielen; ⇒ *also* **grand piano**; **player-piano**; **upright** 1 A

**piano²** /pɪˈɑːnəʊ/ (*Mus.*) ❶ *adj.* piano *nicht attr.;* piano gespielt/gesungen; Piano-. ❷ *adv.* piano. ❸ *n., pl.* **~s** *or* **piani** /pɪˈɑːniː/ (*passage*) Piano, *das*

**piano acˈcordion** *n.* Akkordeon, *das*

**pianoforte** /pɪænəˈfɔːtɪ/ *n.* (*Mus. formal/arch.*) Pianoforte, *das* (*veralt.*)

**Pianola** ® /piːəˈnəʊlə/ *n.* Pianola, *das*

**piano**/pɪˈænəʊ/: **~ music** *n.* Klaviermusik, *die;* (*score*) Klaviernoten *Pl.;* **~ player** *n.* Klavierspieler, *der*/-spielerin, *die;* **~ stool** *n.* Klavierschemel, *der;* **~ tuner** *n.* ▸ 1261 Klavierstimmer, *der*/-stimmerin, *die*

**piazza** /pɪˈætsə/ *n.* Ⓐ*pl.* **piazze** /pɪˈætseɪ/ (*public square*) Piazza, *die;* Ⓑ*pl.* **~s** (*Amer.: veranda*) Veranda, *die*

**picador** /ˈpɪkədɔː(r)/ *n.* Picador, *der;* Lanzenreiter, *der*

**picaresque** /pɪkəˈresk/ *adj.* pikaresk; pikarisch; **~ novel** Schelmenroman, *der*

**picayune** /pɪkəˈjuːn/ *adj.* (*Amer. coll.*) Ⓐ(*petty*) kleinlich; Ⓑ(*paltry*) unbedeutend; unerheblich

**piccalilli** /pɪkəˈlɪlɪ/ *n.* Piccalilli, *das;* *scharf gewürztes eingelegtes Senfgemüse*

**piccaninny** /ˈpɪkənɪnɪ/ (*Brit.*) *n.* [kleines] Negerkind

**piccolo** /ˈpɪkələʊ/ *n., pl.* **~s** (*Mus.*) Pikkoloflöte, *die;* Pikkolo, *das*

**pick¹** /pɪk/ *n.* Ⓐ(*for breaking up hard ground, rocks, etc.*) Spitzhacke, *die;* (*for breaking up ice*) [Eis]pickel, *der;* Ⓑ ⇒ **toothpick**; Ⓒ(*Mus.*) Plektrum, *das*

**pick²** ❶ *n.* Ⓐ(*choice*) Wahl, *die;* **take your ~:** du hast die Wahl; **you can take your ~ of the rooms** du kannst dir ein Zimmer aussuchen; **she had the ~ of several jobs** sie konnte zwischen mehreren Jobs [aus]wählen; **have [the] first ~ of sth.** als Erster aus etw. auswählen dürfen; Ⓑ(*best part*) Elite, *die;* **the ~ of the herd/fruit** *etc.* die besten Tiere aus der Herde/die besten Früchte *usw.;* ⇒ *also* **bunch** 1 B. ❷ *v.t.* Ⓐ pflücken ‹Blumen›; [ab]ernten, [ab]pflücken ‹Äpfel, Trauben usw.›; **'~ your own strawberries'** „Erdbeeren zum Selbstpflücken“; Ⓑ(*select*) auswählen; aufstellen ‹Mannschaft›; **~ the** *or* **a winner/the winning horse** auf den Sieger/das richtige *od.* siegreiche Pferd setzen; **~ a winner** (*fig.*) eine gute Wahl treffen; das große Los ziehen; **~ one's words** seine Worte mit Bedacht wählen; **~ one's way** *or* **steps** sich (*Dat.*) vorsichtig [s]einen Weg suchen; **~ one's way through the rules and regulations** sich (*Dat.*) seinen Weg durch das Dickicht der Vorschriften und Bestimmungen suchen; **~ and choose** sich (*Dat.*) aussuchen; **you can't ~ and choose which laws to obey** du kannst dir nicht aussuchen, welche Gesetze du befolgen willst [und welche nicht]; **~ one's time [for sth.]** den Zeitpunkt [für etw.] festlegen; **you certainly ~ your times!** (*iron.*) du suchst dir aber auch immer die unmöglichsten Zeiten aus!; **~ sides [for the game]** abwechselnd einen Spieler/eine Spielerin [für das Spiel] auswählen; Ⓒ(*clear of flesh*) **~ the bones [clean]** ‹Hund:› die Knochen [sauber] abnagen; **~ the carcass** ‹Geier, Hyäne usw.:› den Kadaver abfressen; Ⓓ **~ sb.'s brains [about sth.]** jmdn. [über etw. (*Akk.*)] ausfragen *od.* (*ugs.*) ausquetschen; Ⓔ **~ one's nose/teeth** in der Nase bohren/in den Zähnen [herum]stochern; Ⓕ **~ sb.'s pocket** jmdn. bestehlen; **he had his pocket ~ed** er wurde von einem Taschendieb bestohlen; Ⓖ **~ a lock** ein Schloss knacken (*salopp*); Ⓗ **~ to pieces** (*fig.: criticize*) kein gutes Haar lassen an (+ *Dat.*) (*ugs.*); Ⓘ(*Amer. Mus.*) zupfen ‹Saiten›; **~ a banjo/guitar** Banjo/Gitarre spielen. ⇒ *also* **bone** 1 D; **hole** 1 A; **quarrel** 1 A. ❸ *v.i.* **~ and choose [too much]** [zu] wählerisch sein

**~ at** *v.t.* Ⓐ(*eat without interest*) herumstochern in (+ *Dat.*) ‹Essen›; Ⓑ(*criticize*) herumhacken auf (+ *Dat.*) (*ugs.*); Ⓒ herumspielen an, (*landsch.*) knaupeln an (+ *Dat.*) ‹Pickel›

**~ off** *v.t.* Ⓐ /ˈ--/ (*pluck off*) abrupfen ‹Blüten, Blumen›; abzupfen, ablesen ‹Haare, Fusseln›; **the helicopter ~ed him off his boat** der Hubschrauber holte ihn aus seinem Boot heraus; Ⓑ /-ˈ-/ (*shoot one by one*) [einzeln] abschießen *od.* (*ugs.*) abknallen

**~ on** *v.t.* Ⓐ(*victimize*) es abgesehen haben auf (+ *Akk.*); **he's constantly being ~ed on to do the dirty jobs** ihm wird immer die Dreckarbeit aufgehalst; **why ~ on me every time?** warum immer gerade *od.* ausgerechnet ich?; **~ on someone your own size!** leg dich doch wenigstens mit einem Gleichstarken an! (*ugs.*); Ⓑ(*select*) sich (*Dat.*) aussuchen

**~ ˈout** *v.t.* Ⓐ(*choose*) auswählen; (*for oneself*) sich (*Dat.*) aussuchen ‹Kleid, Blume›; heraussuchen, [her]aussortieren ‹rote Kugeln, kleine Bälle, defekte Ware, [un]reife Früchte›; (*from text*) herausgreifen ‹Beispiel, Passage›; Ⓑ(*distinguish*) ausmachen, entdecken ‹Detail, jmds. Gesicht in der Menge›; **the spotlight ~ed out a child in the audience** der Scheinwerfer erfasste ein Kind im Publikum; **~ out sth. from sth.** etw. von etw. unterscheiden; Ⓒ(*highlight*) hervorheben ‹Buchstaben, Inschrift›; Ⓓ(*play by ear etc.*) sich (*Dat.*) zusammensuchen ‹Melodie›

**~ ˈover** *v.t.* durchstöbern; **the tomatoes have been well ~ed over** die besten Tomaten sind schon herausgesucht worden

**~ up** ❶ /ˈ--/ *v.t.* Ⓐ(*take up*) [in die Hand] nehmen ‹Brief, Buch usw.›; hochnehmen ‹Baby›;

[wieder] aufnehmen ‹Handarbeit›; aufnehmen ‹Masche›; auffinden ‹Fehler›; (*after dropping*) aufheben; **~ sth. up from the table** etw. vom Tisch nehmen; **~ a child up in one's arms** ein Kind auf den Arm nehmen; **~ up the telephone** den [Telefon]hörer abnehmen; **~ up the pieces** (*lit. or fig.*) die Scherben aufsammeln; **~ up your feet** heb die Füße hoch; ⇒ *also* **thread** 1 B; Ⓑ (*collect*) mitnehmen; (*by arrangement*) abholen (**at, from** von); (*obtain*) holen; **~ up sth. on the way home** etw. auf dem Nachhauseweg abholen; Ⓒ (*become infected by*) sich (*Dat.*) einfangen *od.* holen (*ugs.*) ‹Virus, Grippe›; Ⓓ (*take on board*) ‹Bus, Autofahrer:› mitnehmen; **~ sb. up at** *or* **from the station** jmdn. vom Bahnhof abholen; Ⓔ (*rescue from the sea*) [aus Seenot] bergen; Ⓕ (*coll.: earn*) einstreichen (*ugs.*); Ⓖ (*coll.: make acquaintance of*) aufreißen (*ugs.*); Ⓗ (*find and arrest*) festnehmen; Ⓘ (*receive*) empfangen ‹Signal, Funkspruch usw.›; Ⓙ (*hear*) aufschnappen (*ugs.*); **he'd ~ed up some tale that ...:** er hatte davon läuten gehört, dass ...; Ⓚ (*obtain casually*) sich (*Dat.*) aneignen; bekommen ‹Sache›; **things we ~ed up on our holidays/journeys** Dinge, die wir aus dem Urlaub/von unseren Reisen mitgebracht haben; **~ up languages easily** mühelos Sprachen lernen; **~ up odd habits** seltsame Gewohnheiten annehmen; **where do you ~ up such expressions?** wo hast du denn diese Ausdrücke her?; Ⓛ (*obtain*) auftreiben (*ugs.*); Ⓜ (*resume*) wieder aufnehmen ‹Erzählung, Gespräch›; Ⓝ (*succeed in seeing*) ausmachen; Ⓞ (*regain*) wieder finden ‹Spur, Fährte›; wieder aufnehmen ‹Witterung›; **you cross the field and ~ up the path on the other side** du überquerst das Feld und stößt *od.* kommst auf der anderen Seite wieder auf den Weg; Ⓟ (*pay*) **~ up the bill** *etc.* **for sth.** die Kosten *od.* die Rechnung *usw.* für etw. übernehmen. ⇒ *also* **pick-me-up**; **pick-up**; **speed** 1 A. ❷ /-'-/ *v.i.* Ⓐ (*improve, recover*) ‹Gesundheitszustand, Befinden, Stimmung, Laune, Wetter:› sich bessern; ‹Person:› sich erholen, wieder auf die Beine kommen; ‹Markt, Geschäft:› sich erholen *od.* beleben; ‹Gewinne:› steigen, zunehmen; Ⓑ (*gain speed*) beschleunigen; ‹Wind:› auffrischen.
❸ *v. refl.* **~ oneself up** wieder aufstehen; (*with difficulty*) sich wieder aufrappeln (*ugs.*); (*fig.*) sich aufrappeln (*ugs.*)

**~ 'up with** *v.t.* (*coll.: make the acquaintance of*) kennen lernen

**pick-a-back** /'pɪkəbæk/ ⇒ **piggyback**

**pickaninny** (*Amer.*) ⇒ **piccaninny**

**'pickaxe** (*Amer.:* **'pickax**) ⇒ **pick**[1] A

**picker** /'pɪkə(r)/ *n.* (*of fruit, hops, cotton, etc.*) Pflücker, *der*/Pflückerin, *die*

**picket** /'pɪkɪt/ ❶ *n.* Ⓐ (*Industry*) Streikposten, *der;* **mount a ~ [at** *or* **on a gate]** [an einem Tor] Streikposten aufstellen; ⇒ *also* **flying picket**; Ⓑ (*pointed stake*) Pfahl, *der;* Ⓒ (*Mil.: small body of troops*) Feldposten, *der;* **advanced ~:** vorgeschobener Posten; Vorposten, *der;* Ⓓ (*Mil.: camp policeman*) Feldjäger, *der.* ❷ *v.t.* Streikposten aufstellen vor (+ *Dat.*) ‹Fabrik, Büro usw.›. ❸ *v.i.* Streikposten stehen

**'picket duty** *n.* **be on/do ~:** Streikposten stehen

**picketer** /'pɪkɪtə(r)/ *n.* Streikposten, *der*

**'picket fence** *n.* Palisadenzaun, *der*

**picketing** /'pɪkɪtɪŋ/ *n.* Aufstellen von Streikposten; **secondary ~** *Streikpostenstehen bei einem Betrieb, dem man selbst nicht angehört*

**'picket line** *n.* Streikpostenkette, *die;* **be on the ~:** Streikposten stehen; in der Streikpostenkette stehen

**picking** /'pɪkɪŋ/ *n.* Ⓐ Ernten, *das;* (*of fruit, hops, cotton also*) Pflücken, *das;* (*of grapes also*) Lesen, *das;* Ⓑ (*fruit picked*) Ernte, *die;* [Ernte]ertrag, *der;* **a large ~ of apples** eine reiche Apfelernte; Ⓒ *in pl.* (*gleanings*) Reste *Pl.;* (*things stolen*) [Aus]beute, *die;* (*things allowed*) zusätzliche Vergünstigungen; (*yield*) Ausbeute, *die;* **it's easy ~s** das ist ein einträgliches Geschäft; ⇒ *also* **slim** 1 B

**pickle** /'pɪkl/ ❶ *n.* Ⓐ (*preservative*) *Konservierungsmittel enthaltende Flüssigkeit;* (*brine*) Salzlake, *die;* (*vinegar solution*) Marinade, *die;* Ⓑ *usu. in pl.* (*food*) [Mixed] Pickles *Pl.;* Essiggemüse, *das;* Ⓒ (*coll.: predicament*) **be in a ~:** in der Klemme sitzen (*ugs.*); **get into a ~:** in die Klemme geraten (*ugs.*); **be in a sorry** *or* (*iron.*) **nice** *etc.* **~:** ganz schön in der Klemme sitzen (*ugs.*); Ⓓ (*acid solution*) Beize, *die.* ❷ *v.t.* Ⓐ (*preserve*) [in Essig *od.* sauer] einlegen ‹Gurken, Zwiebeln, Eier›; marinieren ‹Hering›; Ⓑ (*treat*) beizen ‹Leder, Metall›

**pickled** /'pɪkld/ *adj.* Ⓐ (*coll.: drunk*) betrunken; besoffen (*derb*); **get [thoroughly] ~:** sich [richtig] voll laufen lassen (*ugs.*); Ⓑ (*preserved*) eingelegt ‹Eier usw.›; mariniert ‹Hering›; (*in brine*) gepökelt ‹Fleisch›; **~ onions/gherkins** eingelegte Zwiebeln/saure Gurken

**pick: ~lock** *n.* Ⓐ (*person*) Einbrecher, *der*/Einbrecherin, *die;* Ⓑ (*tool*) Dietrich, *der;* **~-me-up** *n.* Stärkungsmittel, *das;* **the holiday/hearing that good news was a real ~-me-up** der Urlaub/diese gute Nachricht hat mir richtig gut getan; **~pocket** *n.* Taschendieb, *der*/-diebin, *die;* **~up** *n.* Ⓐ (*of goods*) Laden, *das;* Ⓑ (*improvement*) Anstieg, *der;* **a ~up in sales/quality** ein Anstieg der Verkaufszahlen/eine Verbesserung der Qualität; Ⓒ (*coll.: person*) Zufallsbekanntschaft, *die;* **is that his latest ~up?** ist das seine neueste Errungenschaft? (*ugs.*); Ⓓ (*truck*) **~up [truck/van]** Kleinlastwagen, *der;* Ⓔ (*of record player, guitar*) Tonabnehmer, *der;* Pick-up, *der;* **~up point** *n.* Ⓐ (*for person*) Zusteigepunkt, *der;* Ⓑ (*for goods*) Warenausgabe, *die*

**picky** /'pɪkɪ/ *adj.* (*Amer. coll.*) pingelig (*ugs.*)

**picnic** /'pɪknɪk/ ❶ *n.* Ⓐ Picknick, *das;* **go for** *or* **on a ~:** ein Picknick machen; picknicken gehen; **have a ~:** ein Picknick machen; picknicken; Ⓑ (*coll.: easy task, pleasant experience*) Kinderspiel, *das;* **be no ~:** kein Zuckerlecken *od.* Honig[sch]lecken sein; **the Korean War was a ~ in comparison** der Koreakrieg war dagegen ein Spaziergang. ❷ *v.i.*, **-ck-** picknicken; Picknick machen

**'picnic basket** *n.* Picknickkorb, *der*

**picnicker** /'pɪknɪkə(r)/ *n.* **there were a lot of ~s on the beach** viele Menschen machten Picknick am Strand; **the ~s cleared up their litter** die Ausflügler räumten nach dem Picknick ihre Abfälle weg

**picnic: ~ 'lunch** *n.* Ⓐ Picknick, *das* (*als Mittagessen*); Ⓑ (*packed up*) Lunchpaket, *das;* **~ site** *n.* Picknickplatz, *der*

**Pict** /pɪkt/ *n.* (*Hist.*) Pikte, *der*/Piktin, *die*

**pictogram** /'pɪktəgræm/, **pictograph** /'pɪktəgrɑ:f/ *ns.* Piktogramm, *das*

**pictorial** /pɪk'tɔ:rɪəl/ ❶ *adj.* illustriert ‹Bericht, Zeitschrift, Wochenmagazin›; bildlich ‹Darstellung›; Bild‹journalismus, -band, -bericht›; **give a ~ record of sth.** etw. im Bild festhalten. ❷ *n.* (*magazine, newspaper, etc.*) Illustrierte, *die*

**pictorially** /pɪk'tɔ:rɪəlɪ/ *adv.* in illustrierter Form; bildhaft ‹darstellen›

**picture** /'pɪktʃə(r)/ ❶ *n.* Ⓐ Bild, *das;* ⇒ *also* **pretty** 1 A; **tell** 1 B; Ⓑ (*portrait*) Porträt, *das;* (*photograph*) Porträtfoto, *das;* **have one's ~ painted** sich malen *od.* porträtieren lassen; Ⓒ (*mental image*) Vorstellung, *die;* Bild, *das;* **get a ~ of sth.** sich (*Dat.*) von etw. ein Bild machen; von etw. eine Vorstellung bekommen; **give a ~ of sth.** von etw. einen Eindruck vermitteln; **the employment ~** (*fig.*) das Bild der Arbeitsmarktlage; **present a sorry ~** (*fig.*) ein trauriges *od.* jämmerliches Bild abgeben; **look the [very] ~ of health/misery/innocence** wie das blühende Leben aussehen/ein Bild des Jammers sein/wie die Unschuld in Person aussehen; **be the ~ of delight** die Freude in Person sein; **get the ~** (*coll.*) verstehen[, worum es geht]; **I'm beginning to get the ~:** langsam *od.* allmählich verstehe *od.* (*ugs.*) kapiere ich; **[do you] get the ~?** verstehst du?; **get the whole ~:** den Gesamtzusammenhang erkennen; **put sb. in the ~:** jmdn. ins Bild setzen; **be in the ~** (*be aware*) im Bilde sein; **keep out of the ~:** sich raushalten; **keep sb. in the ~:** jmdn. auf dem Laufenden halten; **come** *or* **enter into the ~:** [dabei] eine Rolle spielen; Ⓓ (*film*) Film, *der;* Ⓔ *in pl.* (*Brit.: cinema*) Kino, *das;* **go to the ~s** ins Kino gehen; **what's on at the ~s?** was gibts *od.* läuft im Kino?; **is there anything on at the ~s?** läuft etwas [Interessantes] im Kino?; Ⓕ (*delightful object*) **be a ~:** wunderschön *od.* (*ugs.*) ein Gedicht sein; **her face was a ~:** ihr Gesicht sprach Bände; **she looked a ~:** sie sah bildschön aus.
❷ *v.t.* Ⓐ (*represent*) abbilden; Ⓑ (*imagine*) **~ [to oneself]** sich (*Dat.*) vorstellen; Ⓒ (*describe graphically*) anschaulich schildern

**picture: ~ book** ❶ *n.* Bilderbuch, *das;* ❷ *adj.* Bilderbuch-; **~ card** *n.* Figurenkarte, *die;* Bild, *das;* **~ frame** *n.* Bilderrahmen, *der;* **~-framer** ▸ **1261** ⇒ **framer**; **~ gallery** *n.* Gemäldegalerie, *die;* **~ hook** *n.* Bilderhaken, *der;* **~ palace** *n.* (*dated*) Filmpalast, *der* (*veralt.*); **~ 'postcard** *n.* Ansichtskarte, *die;* **~ rail** *n.* Bilderleiste, *die*

**picturesque** /pɪktʃə'resk/ *adj.* malerisch; pittoresk (*geh.*); (*vivid*) anschaulich, bildhaft ‹Beschreibung, Erzählung›

**picturesquely** /pɪktʃə'resklɪ/ *adv.* malerisch; (*graphically*) anschaulich

**picture: ~ window** *n.* Panoramafenster, *das;* **~-writing** *n.* Bilderschrift, *die*

**piddle** /'pɪdl/ (*coll.*) ❶ *v.i.* Ⓐ (*act in trifling way*) **~ about** *or* **around** herummachen (*ugs.*); Ⓑ (*urinate*) Pipi machen (*Kinderspr.*); pinkeln (*ugs.*). ❷ *n.* Ⓐ **have a/do one's ~:** Pipi machen (*Kinderspr.*); pinkeln (*ugs.*); **he needs to have a ~:** er muss mal (*ugs.*); Ⓑ (*urine*) Pipi, *das* (*Kinderspr.*)

**piddling** /'pɪdlɪŋ/ *adj.* (*coll.*) lächerlich (*abwertend*)

**pidgin** /'pɪdʒɪn/ *n.* Pidgin, *das*

**pidgin 'English** *n.* Pidgin-Englisch, *das*

**pie** /paɪ/ *n.* (*of meat, fish, etc.*) Pastete, *die;* (*of fruit etc.*) ≈ Obstkuchen, *der;* **as sweet/nice** *etc.* **as ~** (*coll.*) superfreundlich (*ugs.*); scheißfreundlich (*salopp*); **as easy as ~** (*coll.*) kinderleicht (*ugs.*); **have a finger in every ~** (*coll.*) überall die Finger drin haben (*ugs.*); **that's all just ~ in the sky** (*coll.*) das sind alles nur Luftschlösser; das ist alles völlig unrealistisch

**piebald** /'paɪbɔ:ld/ ❶ *adj.* gescheckt, scheckig ‹Pferd, Kuh, Pony›. ❷ *n.* Schecke, *die*/*der*

**piece** /pi:s/ ❶ *n.* Ⓐ Stück, *das;* (*of broken glass or pottery*) Scherbe, *die;* (*of jigsaw puzzle, crashed aircraft, etc.*) Teil, *der;* (*Amer.: distance*) [kleines] Stück; **a ~ of meat** ein Stück Fleisch; **[all] in one ~:** unbeschädigt; (*fig.*) heil; wohlbehalten; **in ~s** (*broken*) kaputt (*ugs.*); zerbrochen; (*taken apart*) [in Einzelteile] zerlegt; **break into ~s, fall to ~s** zerbrechen; kaputtgehen (*ugs.*); **break sth. to ~s** etw. zerbrechen *od.* (*ugs.*) kaputtmachen; **go [all] to ~s** (*fig.*) [völlig] die Fassung verlieren; **[all] of a ~:** aus einem Guss; **be [all] of a ~ with sth.** [ganz] genau zu etw. passen; **say one's ~** (*fig.*) sagen, was man zu sagen hat; Ⓑ (*part of set*) **~ of furniture/clothing/luggage** Möbel-/Kleidungs-/Gepäckstück, *das;* **a 21-~ teaset** ein 21teiliges Teeservice; **a five-~ band** eine fünfköpfige Band *od.* Kapelle; **a three-/four-~ suite** eine drei-/vierteilige Sitzgarnitur; **a three-~ suit** ein dreiteiliger Anzug; Ⓒ (*enclosed area*) **a ~ of land/property** ein Stück Land/Grundstück; **a ~ of water** ein kleines Gewässer; Ⓓ (*example*) **a ~ of impudence [like that]** eine [solche] Unverschämtheit; **~ of luck** Glücksfall, *der;* **by a ~ of good luck** durch eine glückliche Fügung; **a fine ~ of pottery/Victorian literature** eine sehr schöne Töpferarbeit/ein hervorragendes Werk der viktorianischen Literatur; **fine ~ of work** hervorragende Arbeit; **he's an unpleasant ~ of work** (*fig.*) er ist ein unangenehmer Vertreter (*ugs.*); ⇒ *also* **nasty** 1 A; Ⓔ (*item*) **~ of news/gossip/information** Nachricht, *die*/Klatsch, *der*/Information, *die;* **be paid by the ~** ‹Arbeiter:› Akkord- *od.* Stücklohn erhalten; **the work is paid by the ~:** für die Arbeit wird Akkord- *od.* Stücklohn gezahlt; ⇒ *also* **advice** A; Ⓕ (*Chess*) Figur, *die;* (*Draughts, Backgammon, etc.*) Stein, *der;* Ⓖ ▸ **1328** (*coin*) **gold ~:** Goldstück, *das;* **~ of silver** Silbermünze, *die;* **a 10p ~:** ein 10-Pence-Stück; eine 10-Pence-Münze; **~ of eight** mexikanischer *od.* spanischer Dollar; Achterstück, *das (veralt.)*; (H) *(article in newspaper, magazine, etc.)* Beitrag, *der;* (I) *(literary or musical composition)* Stück, *das;* **~ of music** Musikstück, *das;* ⇒ *also* **villain** B; (J) *(coll.: woman)* Mieze, *die (ugs.)*; (K) *(Mil.: weapon) (firearm)* Schusswaffe, *die; (of artillery)* Geschütz, *das;* (L) *(picture)* Stück, *das;* Werk, *das.* ❷ *v.t.* **~ together** *(lit. or fig.)* zusammenfügen (**from** aus); **~ together what happened** rekonstruieren, was passiert ist

**pièce de résistance** /pi:eɪs də reɪzɪ'stɑ̃s/ *n., pl.* **pièces de résistance** /pi:eɪs də reɪzɪ'stɑ̃s/ (A) *(dish)* Hauptgericht, *das;* Pièce de résistance, *das (veralt.)*; (B) *(item)* Krönung, *die;* **and now for my ~!** und nun die Krönung!

**'piecemeal** *adv., adj.* stückweise

**piece: ~ rate** *n.* Akkordsatz, *der;* **be paid at** *or* **be on ~ rates** ‹Arbeiter:› Akkord- *od.* Stücklohn erhalten; **the work is paid at ~ rates** für die Arbeit wird Akkord- *od.* Stücklohn gezahlt; **~work** *n., no pl.* Akkordarbeit, *die;* **put sb. on ~work** jmdn. im Akkord beschäftigen; **be on ~work** im Akkord arbeiten; **~work system** Akkordlohnsystem, *das;* **~worker** *n.* Akkordarbeiter, *der*/ -arbeiterin, *die*

**pie: ~ chart** *n.* Kreisdiagramm, *das;* **~crust** *n.* Teigmantel, *der*

**pied** /paɪd/ *adj.* gescheckt ‹Pferd, Kuh usw.›; [bunt] gefleckt ‹Schmetterling, Vogel›

**pied-à-terre** /pjeɪdɑ:'teə(r)/ *n., pl.* **pieds-à-terre** /pjeɪdɑ:'teə(r)/ Zweitwohnung, *die*

**'pie dish** *n.* Pastetenform, *die*

**Pied 'Piper** *n.* Rattenfänger, *der;* **the ~ of Hamelin** der Rattenfänger von Hameln

**pie: ~-eyed** *adj. (coll.)* sternhagelvoll *(ugs.)*; **~man** /'paɪmən/ *n., pl.* **~men** /'paɪmən/ *(arch.)* Pastetenverkäufer, *der*

**pier** /pɪə(r)/ *n.* (A) *(for landing place, as promenade)* Pier, *der od. (Seemannsspr.) die;* (B) *(to protect or form harbour)* [Hafen]mole, *die;* Hafendamm, *der;* (C) *(support of bridge)* Pfeiler, *der;* (D) *(Archit.)* Trumeau, *der*

**pierce** /pɪəs/ *v.t.* (A) *(prick)* durchbohren, durchstechen ‹Hülle, Verkleidung, Ohrläppchen›; *(penetrate)* sich bohren in, [ein]dringen in (+ *Akk.*) ‹Körper, Fleisch, Herz›; **~ a hole in sth.** ein Loch in etw. *(Akk.)* stechen; **have one's ears ~d** sich *(Dat.)* Löcher in die Ohrläppchen machen *od.* stechen lassen; (B) *(fig.)* **the cold ~d him to the bone** die Kälte drang ihm bis ins Mark; **a scream ~d the night/silence** ein Schrei gellte durch die Nacht/zerriss die Stille; (C) *(force one's way through)* durchbrechen ‹feindliche Linien›; *(fig.)* erschüttern ‹Gleichgültigkeit›

**piercing** /'pɪəsɪŋ/ *adj.* durchdringend ‹Stimme, Schrei, Blick›; schneidend ‹Sarkasmus, Kälte›

**pierrot** /'pɪərəʊ/ *n.* Pierrot, *der*

**pietà** /pjer'tɑ:/ *n. (Art)* Pieta, *die*

**piety** /'paɪətɪ/ *n.* (A) *no pl. (quality)* Frömmigkeit, *die;* (B) *(act)* fromme Handlung

**piffle** /'pɪfl/ *(coll.) n.* (A) *(nonsense)* Quatsch, *der (ugs.)*; (B) *(empty talk)* Geschwafel, *das (ugs.)*; Blabla, *das (ugs.)*

**piffling** /'pɪflɪŋ/ *adj. (coll.)* lächerlich

**pig** /pɪg/ ❶ *n.* (A) Schwein, *das;* **the sow is in ~:** die Sau ist trächtig; **bleed like a [stuck] ~:** wie ein Schwein bluten *(derb)*; heftig bluten; **~s might fly** *(iron.)* da müsste schon ein Wunder geschehen; **buy a ~ in a poke** *(fig.)* die Katze im Sack kaufen; (B) *(coll.) (greedy person)* Vielfraß, *der (ugs.)*; Fresssack, *der (salopp)*; *(obstinate person)* Dickschädel, *der (ugs.)*; *(dirty person)* Ferkel, *das (ugs.)*; [Dreck]schwein, *das (derb)*; *(unpleasant thing)* Scheißding, *das (salopp)*; *(unpleasant person)* Ekel, *das (ugs.)*; Schwein, *das (derb)*; **make a ~ of oneself** *(overeat)* sich *(Dat.)* den Bauch *od.* Wanst voll schlagen *(salopp)*; **live like ~s** hausen wie die Schweine *(ugs.)*; (C) *(sl. derog.: policeman)* Bulle, *der (salopp abwertend)*; (D) *(metal)* Massel, *die (Metall.)*; (E) *(Amer.: young swine)* Ferkel, *das.* ⇒ *also* **chauvinist.** ❷ *v.t.*, **-gg-: ~ it** *(coll.)* hausen *(ugs.)*

**pigeon¹** /'pɪdʒɪn/ *n.* Taube, *die;* **cock ~:** Tauber, *der;* Täuber[ich], *der*

**pigeon²** *n.* (A) ⇒ **pidgin;** (B) *(coll.: business)* **be sb.'s ~:** jmdn. angehen; **that's not my ~:** das ist nicht mein Bier *(ugs.)*

**pigeon: ~ fancier** *n.* Taubenfreund, *der*/ -freundin, *die;* **~hole** ❶ *n.* (A) *(in cabinet etc.)* [Ablage]fach, *das; (for letters)* Postfach, *das;* **put people in ~holes** *(fig.)* Menschen in Schubladen einordnen *od.* stecken; (B) *(for pigeon)* [Tauben]flugloch, *das;* ❷ *v.t.* (A) *(deposit)* [in die Fächer] sortieren; (B) *(put aside)* auf Eis legen; **get ~holed** in die Schublade wandern; auf Eis gelegt werden; (C) *(categorize)* einordnen; in eine Schublade/in Schubladen stecken; **~ loft** *n.* Taubenschlag, *der;* **~-toed** ❶ *adj.* **a ~-toed man** ein Mann, der mit einwärts gerichteten Füßen geht; **be ~-toed** mit einwärts gerichteten Füßen *od. (ugs.)* über den großen Onkel gehen; ❷ *adv.* mit einwärts gerichteten Füßen; über den großen Onkel *(ugs.)*

**piggery** /'pɪgərɪ/ *n.* (A) *(pig-breeding establishment)* Schweinezucht, *die;* (B) ⇒ **pigsty;** (C) *(coll.: gluttony)* Gefräßigkeit, *die (ugs.)*

**piggish** /'pɪgɪʃ/ *adj. (coll.)* (A) *(gluttonous)* gefräßig *(ugs.)*; verfressen *(salopp)*; (B) *(dirty)* schmuddelig *(ugs.)*; dreckig *(ugs.)*; (C) *(stubborn)* dickschädelig; stur

**piggy** /'pɪgɪ/ *(coll.)* ❶ *n.* Schweinchen, *das;* Ferkel, *das.* ❷ *adj.* **~ face** Schweinchengesicht, *das;* **~ eyes** Schweinsäuglein *Pl.*

**piggy: ~back** ❶ *n.* **give sb. a ~back** jmdn. huckepack nehmen *od.* tragen; **ask for a ~back** huckepack getragen werden wollen; ❷ *adv.* huckepack; ❸ *adj.* **give a child a ~back ride** ein Kind huckepack tragen; **~ bank** *n.* Sparschwein[chen], *das;* **~ in the middle** *n.* (A) *(game)* Schweinchen in der Mitte; (B) *(fig.: person)* **I don't want to be** *or* **play ~ in the middle** ich möchte nicht zwischen die Fronten geraten

**pig: ~'headed** *adj.* dickschädelig *(ugs.)*; stur; **~headedness** /pɪg'hedɪdnɪs/ *n., no pl.* Dickschädeligkeit, *die (ugs.)*; Sturheit, *die;* **~ iron** *n.* Roheisen, *das;* Masseleisen, *das (Metall.)*

**piglet** /'pɪglɪt/ *n.* Ferkel, *das*

**'pig meat** *n.* Schweinefleisch, *das*

**pigment** /'pɪgmənt/ ❶ *n.* Pigment, *das.* ❷ *v.t.* pigmentieren

**pigmentation** /pɪgmən'teɪʃn/ *n.* Pigmentierung, *die;* Pigmentation, *die*

**pigmy** ⇒ **pygmy**

**pig: ~pen** *(Amer.)* ⇒ **pigsty; ~'s 'ear** *n. (Brit. coll.)* **make a ~'s ear of sth.** etw. verpfuschen *od. (ugs.)* vermurksen; **~skin** *n.* (A) Schweinehaut, *die;* (B) *(leather)* Schweinsleder, *das; attrib.* schweinsledern; Schweinsleder-; (C) *(Amer. coll.: football)* Leder, *das (ugs.)*; **~sty** *n. (lit. or fig.)* Schweinestall, *der;* **~swill** *n.* Schweinefutter, *das; (fig. coll.) (food)* Schweinefraß, *der (derb)*; *(drink, soup, etc.)* Spülwasser, *das (salopp)*; **~tail** *n. (plaited)* Zopf, *der;* **~tails** *(worn loose, at either side of head)* Rattenschwänzchen *Pl. (ugs.)*

**pike¹** /paɪk/ *n., pl. same (Zool.)* Hecht, *der*

**pike²** *n. (Arms Hist.)* Pike, *die;* Spieß, *der*

**pike³** *n. (Brit. Hist., Amer.)* (A) *(toll bar)* Zahlstelle, *die;* Mautstelle, *die (bes. südd. u. österr.)*; (B) *(road)* gebührenpflichtige Straße; Mautstraße, *die (bes. südd. u. österr.)*

**pike: ~perch** *n. (Zool.)* Zander, *der;* **~staff** *n.* **plain as a ~staff** sonnenklar *(ugs.)*

**pilaff** /pɪ'læf/ *n.* Pilaw, *der (Kochk.)*

**pilaster** /pɪ'læstə(r)/ *n. (Archit.)* Pilaster, *der*

**pilchard** /'pɪltʃəd/ *n.* Sardine, *die*

**pile¹** /paɪl/ ❶ *n.* (A) *(heap) (of dishes, plates)* Stapel, *der; (of paper, books, letters)* Stoß, *der; (of clothes)* Haufen, *der;* (B) *(coll.: large quantity)* Masse, *die (ugs.)*; Haufen, *der (ugs.)*; **a ~ of troubles/letters/people** eine *od. (ugs.)* jede Menge Sorgen/Briefe/Leute; **a great ~ of work/problems** eine Unmenge Arbeit/Probleme; **a ~ of difficult problems awaited her** eine Menge schwierige Probleme erwartete sie; (C) *(coll.: fortune)* **make a** *or* **one's ~:** ein Vermögen machen; **he's made his ~:** er hat sein Schäfchen im Trockenen *(ugs.)*; (D) *(large building)* Bauwerk, *das;* (E) *(Electr.)* voltasche Säule. ❷ *v.t.* (A) *(load)* [voll] beladen; **~ a table with dishes** einen Tisch mit [Stapeln von] Geschirr vollstellen; (B) *(heap up)* aufstapeln ‹Holz, Steine›; aufhäufen ‹Abfall, Schnee›; (C) **~ furniture into a van/lorry** *etc.* Möbel in einen Liefer-/Lastwagen *usw.* laden

**~ 'in** ❶ *v.i.* (A) *(get in) (seen from outside)* hineindrängen; *(seen from inside)* hereindrängen; **~ in!** [kommt] nur *od.* immer herein!; quetscht euch rein! *(ugs.)*; (B) *(coll.: begin) (to eat)* reinhauen *(ugs.)*; zulangen *(ugs.)*; *(to work)* mit anpacken; *(to fight)* mitmischen *(ugs.)*; mit von der Partie sein *(ugs.)*. ❷ *v.t.* hineinquetschen *(ugs.)*

**~ into** *v.t.* drängen in (+ *Akk.*) ‹Stadion, Halle›; drängen auf (+ *Akk.*) ‹Platz, Wiese›; sich zwängen in (+ *Akk.*) ‹Auto, Zimmer, Zugabteil, Telefonzelle›

**~ off** *(coll.)* ❶ /-'-/ *v.i. (seen from inside)* hinausdrängen; *(seen from outside)* herausdrängen. ❷ /'--/ *v.t.* drängen *od.* strömen aus ‹Bus usw.›

**~ 'on** ❶ *v.i.* ⇒ **pile in a.** ❷ *v.t. (fig.)* **~ on the work/praise** massiv mit Arbeit/Lob kommen; **~ on the pressure** Druck machen; **~ on the agony, ~ it on** *(coll.)* dick auftragen *(ugs.)*

**~ on to** *v.t.* (A) *(heap on to)* **~ logs on to the fire** Holzscheite auf das Feuer legen; **he ~d food on to my plate** er häufte mir Essen auf den Teller; **~ work on to sb.** *(fig.)* jmdm. Arbeit aufbürden *od.* aufladen; (B) *(enter)* drängen in (+ *Akk.*) ‹Bus usw.›

**~ 'out** *v.i.* nach draußen strömen *od.* drängen

**~ 'out of** *v.t.* strömen *od.* drängen aus

**~ 'up** ❶ *v.i.* (A) *(accumulate)* ‹Waren, Post, Aufträge, Arbeit, Schnee:› sich auftürmen; ‹Verkehr:› sich stauen; ‹Schulden:› sich vermehren; ‹Verdacht, Eindruck, Beweise:› sich verdichten; (B) *(crash)* aufeinander auffahren. ❷ *v.t.* aufstapeln ‹Steine, Bücher usw.›; auftürmen ‹Haar, Frisur›; aufhäufen ‹Abfall, Schnee›; *(fig.)* zusammentragen ‹Beweise usw.›; **~ up debts** sich immer mehr verschulden. ⇒ *also* **pile-up**

**pile²** *n.* (A) *(soft surface)* Flor, *der;* (B) *(soft hair, down)* Flaum, *der*

**pile³** *n. (stake)* Pfahl, *der*

**pile: ~driver** *n.* [Pfahl]ramme, *die;* **~ dwelling** *n.* Pfahlbau, *der*

**piles** /paɪlz/ *n. pl. (Med.)* Hämorrhoiden *Pl.*

**'pile-up** *n.* Massenkarambolage, *die*

**pilfer** /'pɪlfə(r)/ *v.t.* stehlen; klauen *(ugs.)*

**pilferage** /'pɪlfərɪdʒ/ *n.* Diebstahl, *der*

**pilferer** /'pɪlfərə(r)/ *n.* Dieb, *der*/Diebin, *die;* Langfinger, *der (oft scherzh.)*

**'pilfer-proof** *adj.* einbruch-/diebstahlsicher

**pilgrim** /'pɪlgrɪm/ *n.* Pilger, *der*/Pilgerin, *die;* Wallfahrer, *der*/Wallfahrerin, *die*

**pilgrimage** /'pɪlgrɪmɪdʒ/ *n.* Pilgerfahrt, *die;* Wallfahrt, *die*

**Pilgrim 'Fathers** *n. pl. (Hist.)* Pilgerväter *Pl.*

**pill** /pɪl/ *n.* (A) Tablette, *die;* Pille, *die (ugs.)*; **be on ~s** Tabletten einnehmen müssen; (B) *(coll.: contraceptive)* **the ~** *or* **P~:** die Pille *(ugs.)*; **be on the ~:** die Pille nehmen *(ugs.)*; **come off the ~:** die Pille absetzen *od.* nicht mehr nehmen *(ugs.)*; **go on the ~:** mit der Pille anfangen *(ugs.)*; (C) *(fig.: unpleasant thing)* **swallow the ~:** die [bittere] Pille schlucken *(ugs.)*; **sweeten the ~:** die bittere Pille versüßen *(ugs.)*; **be a bitter ~ [to swallow]** eine bittere Pille *od.* bitter sein; (D) *(coll./joc.: ball)* Pille, *die (salopp)*

**pillage** /'pɪlɪdʒ/ ❶ *n.* Plünderung, *die.* ❷ *v.t.* [aus]plündern; **the abbey was ~d of its treasures** die Schätze der Abtei wurden geraubt. ❸ *v.i.* plündern

**pillar** /'pɪlə(r)/ *n.* (A) *(vertical support)* Säule, *die; (with angular cross-section)* Pfeiler, *der; (of bed, door)* Pfosten, *der;* **a ~ of strength** *(fig.)* eine Stütze; **from ~ to post** *(fig.)* hin und her; (B) *(fig.: supporter) (of church, family, party, society, etc.)* Stütze, *die; (of science,* *alliance, faith, etc.*) Säule, *die;* Ⓒ (*upright mass*) ~ **of dust/cloud/water** Staub-/Wolken-/Wassersäule, *die;* Ⓓ (*Mining*) [Abbau]pfeiler, *der*

**'pillar box** *n.* (*Brit.*) Briefkasten, *der; attrib.* ~ **red** knallrot (*ugs.*)

**'pillbox** *n.* Ⓐ Pillenschachtel, *die;* Ⓑ ~ **[hat]** Pillbox, *die; flacher runder Hut ohne Krempe;* (*of bell-boy*) Pagenkappe, *die;* Ⓒ (*Mil.*) MG-Unterstand, *der*

**pillion** /'pɪljən/ *n.* Soziussitz, *der;* Beifahrersitz, *der;* **ride** ~: als Beifahrer/Beifahrerin *od.* auf dem Soziussitz mitfahren

**pillock** /'pɪlək/ *n.* (*sl.*) Schwachkopf, *der* (*ugs.*)

**pillory** /'pɪlərɪ/ ❶ *v.t.* (*lit. or fig.*) an den Pranger stellen. ❷ *n.* (*Hist.*) Pranger, *der*

**pillow** /'pɪləʊ/ ❶ *n.* [Kopf]kissen, *das.* ❷ *v.t.* **her arm ~ed the sleeping child** das schlafende Kind lag in ihrem Arm gebettet; **he was like a baby, ~ed in her arms** wie ein Baby lag er in ihren Armen

**pillow:** ~**case** *n.* [Kopf]kissenbezug, *der;* ~ **fight** *n.* Kissenschlacht, *die;* ~ **lace** *n.* Klöppelspitze, *die;* ~ **lava** *n.* (*Geol.*) Kissenlava, *die;* Pillowlava, *die;* ~**slip** ⇒ ~**case**; ~ **talk** *n.* Bettgeflüster, *das*

**'pill-popping** *n.* (*coll.*) Pillenschluckerei, *die* (*ugs.*)

**pilot** /'paɪlət/ ❶ *n.* ▶ **1261** Ⓐ (*Aeronaut.*) Pilot, *der*/Pilotin, *die;* Flugzeugführer, *der*/-führerin, *die;* ~**'s licence** Flug- *od.* Pilotenschein, *der;* Ⓑ (*Naut.; also fig.: guide*) Lotse, *der.* ❷ *adj.* Pilot‹programm, -studie, -projekt usw.›. ❸ *v.t.* Ⓐ (*Aeronaut.*) fliegen; Ⓑ (*Naut.*) lotsen; ~ **sb. into/out of the harbour** jmdn. einlotsen *od.* in den Hafen lotsen/auslotsen *od.* aus dem Hafen lotsen; Ⓒ (*fig.: guide*) lotsen; ~ **a bill through the House** (*Parl.*) einen Gesetzentwurf durch das Parlament bringen

**pilot:** ~ **boat** *n.* Lotsenboot, *das;* ~**fish** *n.* Lotsenfisch, *der;* Pilotfisch, *der*

**pilotless** /'paɪlətlɪs/ *adj.* unbemannt; führerlos

**pilot:** ~ **light** *n.* Ⓐ (*gas burner*) Zündflamme, *die;* Ⓑ (*electric light*) Kontrolllampe, *die od.* -lämpchen, *das;* ~ **officer** *n.* (*Brit. Air Force*) ≈ [Flieger]leutnant, *der*

**pimento** /pɪ'mentəʊ/ *n., pl.* ~**s** (*berry*) Piment, *der od. das;* Nelkenpfeffer, *der;* (*tree*) Pimentbaum, *der;* Nelkenpfefferbaum, *der*

**pimp** /pɪmp/ ❶ *n.* Zuhälter, *der.* ❷ *v.i.* Zuhälterei betreiben; ~ **for sb.** jmds. Zuhälter sein

**pimpernel** /'pɪmpənel/ *n.* (*Bot.*) **[scarlet]** ~: Ackergauchheil, *der;* Roter Gauchheil

**pimple** /'pɪmpl/ *n.* Ⓐ (*spot*) Pickel, *der;* Pustel, *die;* **he/his face had come out in ~s** er hat Pickel/Pickel im Gesicht bekommen; Ⓑ (*slight swelling*) Erhebung, *die;* (*on table tennis bat*) Noppe, *die*

**pimpled** /'pɪmpld/ *adj.* pick[e]lig; genoppt ‹Tischtennisschläger›

**pimply** /'pɪmplɪ/ *adj.* pick[e]lig

**pin** ❶ *n.* Ⓐ Stecknadel, *die;* **you could have heard a ~ drop** man hätte eine Stecknadel fallen hören können; **as clean as a new ~:** blitzblank (*ugs.*); ~**s and needles** (*fig.*) Kribbeln, *das;* **I had ~s and needles in my legs** (*fig.*) meine Beine kribbelten *od.* waren eingeschlafen; Ⓑ (*peg*) Stift, *der;* **split** ~: Splint, *der;* Ⓒ (*Electr.*) Kontaktstift, *der;* **a two-/three-~ plug** ein zwei-/dreipoliger Stecker; Ⓓ **I don't give** *or* **care a ~:** es ist mir völlig egal; **for two ~s I'd resign** es fehlt nicht mehr viel, dann kündige ich; Ⓔ (*Golf*) Flaggenstock, *der;* Ⓕ (*Mus.: for string of instrument*) Wirbel, *der;* Ⓖ (*half-firkin cask*) ≈ Zwanzigliterfass, *das;* Ⓗ (*in grenade*) Zündring, *der;* Ⓘ *in pl.* (*coll.: legs*) Stelzen (*salopp*); Ⓙ (*skittle*) Kegel, *der;* (*scoring point*) Punkt, *der;* Pin, *der* (*Kegelsport*); Ⓚ (*Amer.: brooch*) Anstecknadel, *die;* **[lapel]** ~ (*of society, club, etc.*) Abzeichen, *das;* Ⓛ (*Med.*) Stift, *der;* Pin, *der* (*fachspr.*). ❷ *v.t.*, **-nn-** Ⓐ nageln ‹Knochen, Bein, Hüfte›; ~ **a badge to one's lapel** sich (*Dat.*) ein Abzeichen ans Revers heften *od.* stecken; ~ **a notice on the board** einen Zettel ans schwarze Brett hängen *od.* (*ugs.*) pinnen; ~ **together** mit einer Stecknadel zusammenhalten; (*Dressm.*) zusammenstecken; Ⓑ (*fig.*) ~ **one's ears back** die Ohren spitzen (*ugs.*); ~ **one's hopes on sb./sth.** seine [ganze] Hoffnung auf jmdn./etw. setzen; ~ **the blame/responsibility for sth. on sb.** jmdm. die Schuld an etw. (*Dat.*)/die Verantwortung für etw. zuschieben; **you won't ~ it on him** das wirst du ihm nicht unterschieben *od.* (*ugs.*) anhängen können; ⇒ *also* **faith** A; Ⓒ (*seize and hold fast*) ~ **sb. against the wall** jmdn. an *od.* gegen die Wand drängen *od.* drücken; ~ **sb.'s arms to his sides** jmdm. die Arme an den Körper pressen; ~ **sb. to the ground** jmdn. auf den Boden drücken; ~ **sb.'s arm behind his back** jmdm. den Arm auf den Rücken drehen

~ **'down** *v.t.* Ⓐ (*fig.: bind*) festlegen, festnageln (**to** *or* **on** auf + *Akk.*); **he's a difficult man to ~ down** man kann ihn nur schwer dazu bringen, sich [auf etwas] festzulegen; **he's difficult to ~ down on policies** es ist schwer, ihn auf eine konkrete Politik festzulegen; Ⓑ (*trap*) festhalten; ~ **sb. down [to the ground]** jmdn. auf den Boden drücken; Ⓒ (*define exactly*) ~ **sth. down in words** etw. in Worte fassen; **I can't quite ~ it down** ich kann es nicht richtig ausmachen; ~ **the fault down to the carburettor** feststellen, dass der Fehler im Vergaser liegt; ~ **down the exact meaning of a word** die Bedeutung eines Wortes genau bestimmen

~ **'up** *v.t.* aufhängen ‹Bild, Foto›; anschlagen ‹Bekanntmachung, Hinweis, Liste›; aufstecken, hochstecken ‹Haar, Frisur›; heften ‹Saum, Naht›; ⇒ *also* **pin-up**

**PIN** /pɪn/ *abbr.* **PIN [number]** ⇒ **personal identification number**

**pinafore** /'pɪnəfɔ:(r)/ *n.* [Träger]schürze, *die*

**'pinafore dress** *n.* Trägerrock, *der;* Trägerkleid, *das*

**'pinball** *n.* Flippern, *das; attrib.* Flipper‹spiel, -automat›; **play** ~: flippern; **have a game of** ~: [eine Runde] flippern

**pince-nez** /'pænsneɪ/ *n., pl. same* Kneifer, *der;* Pincenez, *das* (*veralt.*)

**'pincer movement** /'pɪnsə mu:vmənt/ *n.* (*Mil.*) Zangenbewegung, *die*

**pincers** /'pɪnsəz/ *n. pl.* Ⓐ **[pair of]** ~: Beißod. Kneifzange, *die;* Ⓑ (*of crab etc.*) Schere, *die;* Zange, *die* (*ugs.*)

**pinch** /pɪnʃ/ ❶ *n.* Ⓐ (*squeezing*) Kniff, *der;* **give sb. a ~:** jmdn. kneifen *od.* (*bes. südd., österr.*) zwicken; **give sb. a ~ on the arm/cheek** *etc.* jmdn. *od.* jmdm. in den Arm/die Backe (*usw.*) kneifen *od.* (*bes. südd., österr.*) zwicken; Ⓑ (*fig.*) **feel the ~:** knapp bei Kasse sein (*ugs.*); **the firm is feeling the ~:** der Firma geht es finanziell nicht gut; **at a ~:** zur Not; wenn es [unbedingt] sein muss; **if it comes to a** *or* **the ~:** wenn es zum Äußersten *od.* Schlimmsten kommt; Ⓒ (*small amount*) Prise, *die;* ⇒ *also* **salt** 1 A. ❷ *v.t.* Ⓐ (*grip tightly*) kneifen; zwicken (*bes. südd., österr.*); ~ **sb.'s cheek/bottom** jmdn. in die Wange/den Hintern (*ugs.*) kneifen; **I had to ~ myself** ich musste mich erst mal in den Arm kneifen (*ugs.*); ~**ed with cold** (*fig.*) [völlig] durchgefroren; starr vor Kälte; Ⓑ (*coll.: steal*) klauen (*salopp*); Ⓒ (*coll.: arrest*) sich (*Dat.*) schnappen (*ugs.*); **get ~ed** geschnappt werden (*ugs.*); Ⓓ (*Hort.*) ~ **back** *or* **down** *or* **out** abzwicken; abknipsen (*ugs.*). ❸ *v.i.* Ⓐ ‹Schuh:› drücken; **that's where the shoe ~es** (*fig.*) da liegt der Hase im Pfeffer *od.* der Hund begraben (*ugs.*); Ⓑ (*be niggardly*) knapsen (*ugs.*), knausern (*ugs. abwertend*) (**on** mit)

**pinchbeck** /'pɪntʃbek/ ❶ *n.* Tombak, *der.* ❷ *adj.* Ⓐ aus Tombak *nachgestellt;* Ⓑ (*fig.: counterfeit*) **be ~:** Talmi sein

**'pinch-hitter** *n.* (*Baseball*) Ersatzspieler, *der*/-spielerin, *die*

**'pincushion** *n.* Nadelkissen, *das*

**pine**[1] /paɪn/ *n.* Ⓐ (*tree*) Kiefer, *die; attrib.* Kiefern-; Ⓑ (*wood*) Kiefernholz, *das;* Kiefer, *die; attrib.* Kiefer[nholz]-; **a kitchen in ~:** eine Küche aus Kiefer[nholz]

**pine**[2] *v.i.* Ⓐ (*languish*) (**over, about** wegen) sich [vor Kummer] verzehren (*geh.*); Ⓑ (*long eagerly*) ~ **for sb./sth.** sich nach jmdm./etw. sehnen *od.* (*geh.*) verzehren

~ **a'way** *v.i.* dahinkümmern

**pineal** /'pɪnɪəl/ *adj.* (*Anat.*) ~ **body** *or* **gland** Zirbeldrüse, *die;* Epiphyse, *die*

**pineapple** /'paɪnæpl/ *n.* Ananas, *die;* ~ **juice** Ananassaft, *der;* ~ **rings/chunks** Ananasringe *od.* -scheiben/-stücke

**pine:** ~ **cone** *n.* (*Bot.*) Kiefernzapfen, *der;* ~ **marten** *n.* (*Zool.*) (*American*) Fichtenmarder, *der;* (*European*) Edelmarder, *der;* ~ **needle** *n.* Kiefernnadel, *die*

**pinetum** /paɪ'ni:təm/ *n., pl.* **pineta** /paɪ'ni:tə/ Kiefernarboretum, *das*

**'pine wood** *n.* Ⓐ (*material*) Kiefernholz, *das;* Ⓑ (*forest*) Kiefernwald, *der*

**ping** /pɪŋ/ ❶ *n.* (*of bullet*) Pfeifen, *das;* (*of bell*) Klingeln, *das;* **the stone made a ~ as it hit the glass** es machte klick, als der Stein gegen das Glas flog. ❷ *v.i.* ‹Kugel:› pfeifen, peitschen; ‹Glocke, Schreibmaschine:› klingeln

**pinger** /'pɪŋə(r)/ *n.* Kurzzeitwecker, *der;* (*in kitchen*) Küchenwecker, *der*

**ping-pong** (*Amer.:* **Ping-Pong** ®) /'pɪŋpɒŋ/ *n.* Tischtennis, *das;* Pingpong, *das* (*ugs. veralt.*)

**ping-pong:** ~**-pong ball** *n.* Tischtennisball, *der;* Pingpongball, *der* (*ugs. veralt.*); ~**-pong table** *n.* Tischtennisplatte, *die*

**pin:** ~**head** *n.* Ⓐ Stecknadelkopf, *der; attrib.* (*fig.*) winzig; stecknadelkopfgroß; Ⓑ (*coll.: fool*) Dummkopf, *der;* Strohkopf, *der* (*ugs.*); ~**-headed** *adj.* blöd (*ugs.*); dämlich (*ugs.*); ~**-'high** *adj.* (*Golf*) auf Flaggenstockhöhe *nachgestellt;* ~**hole** *n.* [nadelfeines] Loch; ~**hole camera** *n.* (*Photog.*) Lochkamera, *die;* Camera obscura, *die*

**pinion**[1] /'pɪnjən/ *n.* (*cogwheel*) Ritzel, *das* (*Technik*); kleines Zahnrad

**pinion**[2] ❶ *v.t.* ~ **sb.**, ~ **sb.'s arms** jmdm. die Arme [an den Körper] fesseln *od.* binden; ~ **sb. to sth.** jmdn. an etw. (*Dat.*) festbinden. ❷ *n.* Ⓐ (*Ornith.*) (*terminal segment of wing*) Hand[schwinge], *die;* (*flight feather*) Schwungfeder, *die;* Ⓑ (*poet.: wing*) Schwinge, *die* (*geh.*); Fittich, *der* (*dichter.*)

**pink**[1] /pɪŋk/ ❶ *n.* Ⓐ Rosa, *das;* Ⓑ **in the ~ of condition** in hervorragendem Zustand; **be in the ~** (*coll.*) kerngesund sein; Ⓒ (*Bot.*) [Garten]nelke, *die;* Ⓓ ⇒ **hunting pink.** ❷ *adj.* Ⓐ rosa ‹Kleid, Wand›; rosig, rosarot ‹Himmel, Gesicht, Haut, Wangen›; Ⓑ (*Polit. coll.*) rosa[rot]; rot angehaucht. ⇒ *also* **elephant**; **gin**[1]; **rose-pink**; **salmon pink**; **tickle** 1 B

**pink**[2] *v.i.* (*Motor Veh.*) klingeln

**pink**[3] *v.t.* Ⓐ (*pierce slightly*) piksen; Ⓑ (*Sewing*) auszacken

**pinkie** /'pɪŋkɪ/ *n.* (*Amer., Scot.*) kleiner Finger

**pinking** /'pɪŋkɪŋ/: ~ **scissors**, ~ **shears** *ns. pl.* **[pair of]** ~ **scissors** *or* **shears** Zackenschere, *die*

**pinko** /'pɪŋkəʊ/ *n., pl.* ~**s** (*Polit. coll.*) Rosarote, *der/die*

**'pin money** *n.* (*for private expenditure*) Taschengeld, *das;* (*for dress expenses*) Nadelgeld, *das* (*veralt.*); (*coll.: small sum*) Taschen- *od.* Trinkgeld, *das* (*ugs.*)

**pinnace** /'pɪnəs/ *n.* (*Naut.*) Pinasse, *die;* Beiboot, *das*

**pinnacle** /'pɪnəkl/ *n.* Ⓐ (*Archit.*) Fiale, *die;* Ⓑ (*natural peak*) Gipfel, *der;* Ⓒ (*fig.: climax*) Höhepunkt, *der;* Gipfel, *der;* **at the ~ of his fame** auf dem Gipfel *od.* Höhepunkt seines Ruhmes

**pinnate** /'pɪnət/ *adj.* (*Bot.*) gefiedert

**pinny** /'pɪnɪ/ *n.* (*child lang./coll.*) Schürze, *die*

**pin:** ~**point** ❶ *v.t.* (*locate, define*) genau bestimmen; (*determine*) genau festlegen; ❷ *n.* [Steck]nadelspitze, *die;* ~**points of light** winzige Lichter; ❸ *adj.* ~**point accuracy** höchste Genauigkeit; ~**prick** *n.* Nadelstich, *der;* (*fig.*) [harmlose] Stichelei; ~**stripe** *n.* Nadelstreifen, *der;* (*suit*) Nadelstreifenanzug, *der; attrib.* Nadelstreifen‹anzug, -kostüm›

**pint** /paɪnt/ *n.* Ⓐ ▶ **1671** (*one-eighth of a gallon*) Pint, *das;* ≈ halber Liter; Ⓑ (*Brit.:*

P

*quantity of liquid*) Pint, *das;* **a ~ of milk/beer** ≈ ein halber Liter Milch/Bier; **have a ~:** ein Bier trinken; **go to the pub for a couple of ~s** auf ein paar Bier[chen] in die Kneipe gehen; **he likes his ~:** er trinkt gern ein Bier[chen]

**pinta** /ˈpaɪntə/ *n.* (*Brit. coll.*) ≈ halber Liter [Milch/Bier *usw.*]; **drink one's daily ~:** täglich seine Milch/sein Bier *usw.* trinken

**pin: ~-table** *n.* Flipper[automat], *der;* **~tail** *n.* (*Ornith.*) Spießente, *die*

**pint 'mug** *n.* ≈ Halbliterglas, *das od.* -humpen, *der*

**pinto** /ˈpɪntəʊ/ *adj., n., pl.* **~s** (*Amer.*) ⇒ **piebald**

**pint: ~ pot** *n.* ≈ Halbliterhumpen, *der;* ⇒ *also* **quart** A; **~size[d]** *adj.* (*fig. coll.*) winzig; mick[e]rig (*ugs.*) ‹Person›

**pin: ~-tuck** *n.* (*Sewing*) Biese, *die;* **~-up** ❶ *n.* Ⓐ (*picture*) (*of beautiful girl*) Pin-up-[-Foto], *das;* (*of famous person*) Prominentenfoto, *das;* (*esp. of sports, film or pop star*) Starfoto, *das;* Ⓑ (*beautiful girl*) Schönheit, *die;* (*in photograph*) Pin-up-Girl, *das;* ❷ *adj.* Pin-up-‹Foto, Girl›; **~-up-girl/~-up-man** Fotomodell, *das;* **~wheel** *n.* Ⓐ (*firework*) Feuerrad, *das;* Ⓑ (*Amer.: toy*) Windrädchen, *das*

**pioneer** /paɪəˈnɪə(r)/ ❶ *n.* Pionier, *der;* (*fig. also*) Wegbereiter, *der*/Wegbereiterin, *die.* ❷ *v.i.* Pionierarbeit leisten; bahnbrechend sein; **~ing settlers/studies/work** Pioniere *od.* erste Siedler/bahnbrechende Untersuchungen/Pionierarbeit, *die.* ❸ *v.t.* Ⓐ (*originate*) Pionierarbeit leisten für ‹Entwicklung, Technologie, Nutzung›; Ⓑ (*open up as ~*) erkunden

**pious** /ˈpaɪəs/ *adj.* Ⓐ (*devout*) fromm; **a ~ hope** (*lit. or fig.*) ein frommer Wunsch; Ⓑ (*hypocritically virtuous*) heuchlerisch; scheinheilig; Ⓒ (*dutiful*) ehrfurchtsvoll; heilig ‹Pflicht›. ⇒ *also* **fraud** B

**piously** /ˈpaɪəslɪ/ *adv.* Ⓐ (*devoutly*) **kneel ~:** in frommer Andacht knien; Ⓑ (*marked by sham*) scheinheilig; Ⓒ (*dutifully*) ehrfurchtsvoll

**pip**[1] /pɪp/ ❶ *n.* (*seed*) Kern, *der.* ❷ *v.t.*, **-pp-** entkernen

**pip**[2] *n.* Ⓐ (*on cards, dominoes, etc.*) Auge, *das;* Punkt, *der;* Ⓑ (*Brit. Mil.*) Stern, *der;* Ⓒ (*on radar screen*) Echosignal, *das;* (*spot of light also*) Leuchtpunkt, *der;* Echosignal, *das*

**pip**[3] *n.* (*Brit.: sound*) [kurzer] Piepston; (*time signal also*) Zeitzeichen, *das;* **when the ~s go** (*during telephone call*) wenn die Piepstöne anzeigen, dass eine neue Münze eingeworfen werden muss

**pip**[4] *n.* (*coll.*) **give sb. the ~:** jmdm. auf den Wecker gehen (*ugs.*); **sb. has [got] the ~:** jmd. ist sauer (*ugs.*)

**pip**[5] *v.t.*, **-pp-** (*Brit.*) (*defeat*) besiegen; schlagen; **~ sb. at the post** (*coll.*) jmdn. im Ziel abfangen; (*fig.*) jmdn. im letzten Moment ausbooten (*ugs.*)

**pipe** /paɪp/ ❶ *n.* Ⓐ (*tube*) Rohr, *das;* Ⓑ (*Mus.*) Pfeife, *die;* (*flute*) Flöte, *die;* (*in organ*) [Orgel]pfeife, *die;* Ⓒ *in pl.* (*bagpipes*) Dudelsack, *der;* Ⓓ **[tobacco] ~:** [Tabaks]pfeife, *die;* **light/smoke a ~:** eine Pfeife anzünden/rauchen; **put that in your ~ and smoke it** (*fig. coll.*) lass dir das gesagt sein; schreib dir das hinter die Ohren (*ugs.*); ⇒ *also* **clay pipe**; **peace pipe**; Ⓔ (*cask*) Pipe, *das od. die;* 105-Gallonen-Fass, *das;* Ⓕ (*Geol.*) Schlot, *der.* ❷ *v.t.* Ⓐ (*convey by ~*) [durch ein Rohr/durch Rohre] leiten; **be ~d** ‹Öl, Wasser:› [durch eine Rohrleitung] fließen; ‹Gas:› [durch eine Rohrleitung] strömen; Ⓑ (*transmit by wire etc.*) leiten ‹Strom›; übertragen ‹Sendung›; [ab]spielen ‹[Tonband-, Schallplatten]musik›; **~d music** Hintergrundmusik, *die;* Musikberieselung, *die;* Ⓒ (*Mus.*) [auf der Flöte/dem Dudelsack] spielen ‹Melodie, Lied›; mit Pfeifenklang geleiten *od.* führen ‹Soldaten›; Ⓓ (*utter shrilly*) ‹Vogel:› piepsen, pfeifen; ‹Kind:› piepsen; Ⓔ (*Sewing*) paspel[iere]n; Ⓕ (*Cookery*) spritzen; Ⓖ (*Naut.*) **~ sb. aboard** jmdn. mit Pfeifenklängen an Bord empfangen. ❸ *v.i.* Ⓐ (*whistle*) pfeifen; Ⓑ ‹Stimme:› hell klingen, schrillen; ‹Person:› piepsen, mit heller *od.* schriller Stimme sprechen; ‹Vogel:› pfeifen, piepsen; ‹kleiner, junger Vogel:› piepsen; Ⓒ (*Mus.*) [Flöte/Pfeife] spielen

**~ 'down** *v.i.* (*coll.: be less noisy*) ruhig sein; **~ down, will you!** sei/seid doch mal ruhig!

**~ 'up** *v.i.* (*begin to speak*) etwas sagen; **~ up with the answer** die Antwort geben

**pipe: ~ band** *n.* Pfeifer; **~clay** *n.* Pfeifenton, *der;* **~-cleaner** *n.* Pfeifenreiniger, *der;* **~ dream** *n.* Wunschtraum, *der;* Hirngespinst, *das* (*abwertend*); **~line** *n.* Pipeline, *die;* **in the ~line** (*fig.*) in Vorbereitung; **pay rises are in the ~line** (*fig.*) Gehaltserhöhungen stehen bevor; **have some ideas in the ~line** (*fig.*) ein paar Ideen auf Lager haben (*ugs.*); **~ organ** *n.* (*Mus.*) [Pfeifen]orgel, *die*

**piper** /ˈpaɪpə(r)/ *n.* Ⓐ Pfeifer, *der*/Pfeiferin, *die;* (*flautist*) Flötenspieler, *der*/-spielerin, *die;* **pay the ~** (*fig.*) die Kosten tragen; **he who pays the ~ calls the tune** (*prov.*) wes Brot ich ess, des Lied ich sing (*Spr.*); Ⓑ (*bagpiper*) Dudelsackspieler, *der*/-spielerin, *die*

**pipe: ~ rack** *n.* Pfeifenständer, *der;* **~ smoker** *n.* Pfeifenraucher, *der*/-raucherin, *die;* **~ tobacco** *n.* Pfeifentabak, *der*

**pipette** /pɪˈpet/ *n.* (*Chem.*) Pipette, *die*

**piping** /ˈpaɪpɪŋ/ ❶ *n.* Ⓐ (*system of pipes*) Rohrleitungssystem, *das;* Ⓑ (*quantity of pipes*) Rohrmaterial, *das;* Ⓒ (*Sewing*) Paspel, *die;* (*on furniture*) Kordel, *die;* Ⓓ (*Cookery*) Spritzgussverzierung, *die;* Ⓔ (*Mus.*) Pfeifen, *das;* (*of flute*) Flöten, *das;* Ⓕ (*shrill sound*) Pfeifen, *das.* ❷ *adj.* piepsend

**piping 'hot** *adj.* kochend heiß

**pipistrelle** /pɪpɪˈstrel/ *n.* (*Zool.*) Zwergfledermaus, *die*

**pipit** /ˈpɪpɪt/ *n.* (*Ornith.*) Pieper, *der*

**pippin** /ˈpɪpɪn/ *n.* Tafelapfel, *der*

**'pipsqueak** *n.* (*coll. derog.*) Würstchen, *das* (*ugs.*)

**piquancy** /ˈpiːkənsɪ/ *n.* Ⓐ (*sharpness*) Würze, *die;* pikanter Geschmack; Ⓑ (*fig.*) Pikanterie, *die* (*geh.*)

**piquant** /ˈpiːkənt, ˈpiːkɑːnt/ *adj.*, **piquantly** /ˈpiːkəntlɪ, ˈpiːkɑːntlɪ/ *adv.* (*lit. or fig.*) pikant

**pique** /piːk/ ❶ *v.t.* Ⓐ (*irritate*) verärgern; **be ~d at sb./sth.** über jmdn./etw. verärgert sein; Ⓑ (*wound the pride of*) kränken; **be ~d at sth.** wegen etw. gekränkt sein. ❷ *n.* **in a [fit of] ~:** verstimmt; eingeschnappt (*ugs.*)

**piqué** /ˈpiːkeɪ/ *n.* (*Textiles*) Pikee, *der*

**piracy** /ˈpaɪrəsɪ/ *n.* Seeräuberei, *die;* Piraterie, *die;* (*fig.*) Piraterie, *die;* **the ~ of books/records/video tapes** der illegale Nachdruck von Büchern/die illegale Pressung von Schallplatten/die illegale Vervielfältigung von Videobändern

**piranha** /pɪˈrɑːnə, pɪˈrɑːnjə/ *n.* (*Zool.*) Piranha, *der*

**pirate** /ˈpaɪrət/ ❶ *n.* Ⓐ Pirat, *der;* Seeräuber, *der;* (*fig.*) Schwindler, *der;* (*of book etc.*) Raubdrucker, *der*/-druckerin, *die;* (*of record*) Raubpresser, *der*/Raubpresserin, *die;* Hersteller/Herstellerin von Raubpressungen; (*of video*) Hersteller/Herstellerin von unerlaubten Kopien; Ⓑ (*Radio*) [Rundfunk]pirat, *der; attrib.* **~ radio station** Piratensender, *der;* **~ broadcast[ing]** Piratensendung, *die;* Ⓒ (*ship*) Piratenschiff, *das;* Seeräuberschiff, *das.* ❷ *v.t.* ausplündern ‹Schiff›; rauben ‹Waren usw.›; (*fig.*) illegal nachdrucken ‹Buch›; illegal pressen ‹Schallplatte›; illegal vervielfältigen ‹Videoband›; **~d edition** Raubdruck, *der*

**piratical** /paɪˈrætɪkl/ *adj.* Piraten-; Seeräuber-; seeräuberisch ‹Praktiken, Umtriebe›

**pirouette** /pɪrʊˈet/ ❶ *n.* Pirouette, *die.* ❷ *v.i.* pirouettieren; Pirouetten/eine Pirouette ausführen *od.* drehen

**Piscean** /ˈpaɪsɪən/ (*Astrol.*) *n.* Fisch, *der;* Fischemann, *der*/-frau, *die*

**Pisces** /ˈpaɪsiːz, ˈpɪskiːz/ *n., pl. same* (*Astrol., Astron.*) Fische *Pl.;* Pisces *Pl.;* ⇒ *also* **Aries**

**piss** /pɪs/ (*coarse*) ❶ *n.* Ⓐ (*urine*) Pisse, *die* (*derb*); Ⓑ (*act*) Pissen, *das* (*derb*); **need a ~:** pissen müssen (*derb*); **have a/go for a ~:** pissen/pissen gehen (*derb*); Ⓒ **take the ~ out of sb.** jmdn. verarschen (*salopp*); **stop taking the ~!** lass die Verarscherei! (*salopp*). ❷ *v.i.* Ⓐ (*urinate*) pissen (*derb*); Ⓑ ⇒ **piss down.** ❸ *v.t.* pissen (*derb*); **~ oneself** in die Hose pissen (*derb*)

**~ a'bout, ~ a'round** (*sl.*) ❶ *v.i.* Ⓐ (*spend time lazily*) rumhängen (*ugs.*); Ⓑ (*behave in foolish way*) rummachen (*ugs.*); Ⓒ (*work in disorganized way*) sich (*Dat.*) einen abbrechen (*salopp*); **~ around with sth.** mit etw. rummachen (*ugs.*). ❷ *v.t.* **~ sb. about or around** jmdn. wie [den letzten] Dreck behandeln (*salopp*)

**~ down** *v.i.* (*sl.*) **~ down [with rain]** schiffen (*salopp*)

**~ 'off** (*Brit. sl.*) ❶ *v.i.* sich verpissen (*salopp*). ❷ *v.t.* ankotzen (*derb*); ⇒ *also* **pissed off**

**'piss artist** *n.* (*sl.*) Suffkopp, *der* (*salopp*)

**pissed** /pɪst/ *adj.* (*sl.*) Ⓐ (*drunk*) voll (*salopp*); besoffen (*derb*); **~ as a lord** *or* **newt** voll wie eine Strandhaubitze (*ugs.*); **~ out of one's mind** *or* **head** *or* **brain** sturzbesoffen (*derb*); hackevoll (*salopp*); Ⓑ (*Amer.: angry*) [stock]sauer (**with** auf + *Akk.*) (*salopp*)

**pissed 'off** *adj.* (*sl.*) stocksauer (**with** auf + *Akk.*) (*salopp*); **get ~ [with sb./sth.]** langsam die Schnauze voll haben [von jmdm./etw.] (*salopp*)

**'piss-up** *n.* (*sl.*) Sauferei, *die* (*salopp*)

**pistachio** /pɪˈstɑːʃɪəʊ/ *n., pl.* **~s** Ⓐ Pistazie, *die;* Ⓑ (*colour*) Pistaziengrün, *das*

**piste** /piːst/ *n.* Piste, *die*

**pistil** /ˈpɪstɪl/ *n.* (*Bot.*) Stempel, *der*

**pistol** /ˈpɪstl/ *n.* (*small firearm*) Pistole, *die;* **hold a ~ to sb.'s head** jmdm. die Pistole an die Schläfe *od.* den Kopf setzen; (*fig.*) jmdm. die Pistole auf die Brust setzen

**pistol: ~ grip** *n.* Pistolengriff, *der;* **~ shot** *n.* Pistolenschuss, *der;* **~-whip** *v.t.* mit der Pistole schlagen

**piston** /ˈpɪstən/ *n.* Kolben, *der*

**piston: ~ engine** *n.* Kolbenmotor, *der;* **~ ring** *n.* Kolbenring, *der;* **~ rod** *n.* Kolbenstange, *die;* Pleuelstange, *die*

**pit**[1] /pɪt/ ❶ *n.* Ⓐ (*hole, mine*) Grube, *die;* (*natural*) Vertiefung, *die;* (*as trap*) Fallgrube, *die;* (*for cockfighting*) Kampfplatz, *der;* **[work] down the ~:** unter Tage [arbeiten] (*Bergmannsspr.*); **dig a ~ for sb.** (*fig.*) jmdm. eine Falle stellen; **this really is the ~s** (*coll.*) das ist wirklich das Letzte (*ugs.*); Ⓑ **~ of the stomach** Magengrube, *die;* Ⓒ (*scar*) [vertiefte] Narbe; (*after smallpox*) Pockennarbe, *die;* Ⓓ (*Brit. Theatre*) Parkett, *das;* (*for orchestra*) Orchestergraben, *der;* Ⓔ (*in garage*) Grube, *die;* (*Motor racing*) Box, *die;* Ⓕ (*Amer. St. Exch.*) Maklerstand, *der.* ❷ *v.t.*, **-tt-** Ⓐ (*set to fight*) kämpfen lassen; Ⓑ (*fig.: match*) **~ sth. against sth.** etw. gegen etw. einsetzen; **~ one's wits/skill etc. against sth.** seinen Verstand/sein Können *usw.* an etw. (*Dat.*) messen; Ⓒ **be ~ted** (*have ~s*) voller Vertiefungen sein; **the ~ted surface of the moon** die mit Kratern bedeckte Mondoberfläche

**pit**[2] (*Amer.*) ❶ *n.* (*stone in fruit*) Kern, *der.* ❷ *v.t.*, **-tt-** (*remove ~s from*) entkernen

**pit-a-pat** /ˈpɪtəpæt/ ❶ *adv.* **go ~** ‹Herz:› schneller schlagen; ‹Regen:› [sanft] klopfen. ❷ *n.* (*of heart*) Pochen, *das;* (*of hoofs, feet*) Getrappel, *das;* (*of rain etc.*) Klopfen, *das*

**'pit bull terrier** *n.* Pitbullterrier, *der*

**pitch**[1] /pɪtʃ/ ❶ *n.* Ⓐ (*Brit.: usual place*) [Stand]platz, *der;* (*stand*) Stand, *der;* (*Sport: playing area*) Feld, *das;* Platz, *der;* **artificial ~:** Spielfeld mit künstlichem Rasen; ⇒ *also* **queer** 3; Ⓑ (*Mus.*) Tonhöhe, *die;* (*of voice*) Stimmlage, *die;* (*of instrument*) Tonlage, *die;* **have perfect ~:** absolutes Gehör haben; ⇒ *also* **concert pitch**; Ⓒ (*slope*) Neigung, *die;* **the ~ of the roof** die Dachneigung; Ⓓ (*fig.: degree, intensity*) **the children were at a high ~ of excitement** die Kinder waren wahnsinnig aufgedreht (*ugs.*); **reach such a ~ that ...:** sich so zuspitzen, dass...; ⇒ *also* **fever pitch**; Ⓔ ⇒ **pitching**; Ⓕ (*Baseball: delivery*) Pitch, *der;* Wurf, *der;* (*Golf*) ⇒ **pitch shot**; Ⓖ (*Mech.: distance*) (*between cogwheel teeth or screw ridges*) Teilung, *die;* (*in one turn* *of propeller*) Steigung, *die;* **H** (*Mountaineering*) Seillänge, *die;* **I** (*sales talk*) Verkaufsargumentation, *die;* **make one's ~** (*lit. or fig.*) seine Vorstellung geben; **get one's ~ in early** (*fig.*) seine Sache frühzeitig vorbringen.

**2** *v.t.* **A** (*erect*) aufschlagen; **~ camp** ein/das Lager aufschlagen; **B** (*throw*) werfen; **the horse ~ed its rider over its head** das Pferd warf den Reiter vornüber; **the car overturned and the driver was ~ed out** der Wagen überschlug sich, und der Fahrer wurde herausgeschleudert; **~ sb. out of sth.** jmdn. aus etw. hinauswerfen; **C** (*Mus.*) anstimmen ‹Melodie›; stimmen ‹Instrument›; **~ one's voice too high/at the right level** eine zu hohe/die richtige Stimmlage wählen; **D** (*fig.*) **~ a programme at a particular level** ein Programm auf ein bestimmtes Niveau abstimmen; **our expectations were ~ed too high** unsere Erwartungen waren zu hoch gesteckt; **E ~ed battle** offene [Feld]schlacht; **the debate became a ~ed battle** (*fig.*) aus der Debatte wurde eine Redeschlacht.

**3** *v.i.* (*fall*) [kopfüber] stürzen; ‹Schiff, Fahrzeug, Flugzeug:› mit einem Ruck nach vorn kippen; (*Cricket*) ‹Ball:› aufschlagen; (*repeatedly*) ‹Schiff:› stampfen; ‹Fahrzeug, Flugzeug:› ruckartig schwingen; **~ forward** vornüberstürzen; ‹Fahrzeug:› ruckartig anfahren

**~ 'in** *v.i.* (*coll.*) loslegen (*ugs.*); (*begin*) sich daranmachen (*ugs.*); **~ in [and *or* to help]** zupacken (*ugs.*) [und helfen]; mit anpacken

**~ into** *v.t.* (*coll.*) herfallen über (+ *Akk.*); sich hermachen über (+ *Akk.*) (*ugs.*) ‹Essen›

**pitch**[2] *n.* (*substance*) Pech, *das;* **as black as ~:** pechschwarz

**pitch: ~-'black** *adj.* pechschwarz; stockdunkel (*ugs.*), pechfinster ‹Nacht, Raum›; **~blende** /'pɪtʃblend/ *n.* (*Min.*) Pechblende, *die;* **~-'dark** *adj.* stockdunkel (*ugs.*); pechfinster; **~-'darkness** *n.* tiefste Finsternis

**pitched 'roof** *n.* schräges Dach

**pitcher**[1] /'pɪtʃə(r)/ *n.* **A** (*vessel*) [Henkel]krug, *der;* (*in bedroom etc.*) Wasserkanne, *die;* **B** (*Bot.*) Kanne, *die*

**pitcher**[2] *n.* (*Baseball*) Werfer, *der;* Pitcher, *der*

**'pitcher plant** *n.* (*Bot.*) Kannenpflanze, *die*

**'pitchfork 1** *n.* (*for hay*) Heugabel, *die;* (*for manure*) Mistgabel, *die.* **2** *v.t.* gabeln; **~ sb. into sth.** (*fig.*) jmdn. in etw. ‹Akk.› katapultieren

**pitching** /'pɪtʃɪŋ/ *n.* (*of ship*) Stampfen, *das;* (*of vehicle, aircraft*) ruckartiges Schwingen

**pitch: ~ pine** *n.* Pechkiefer, *die;* (*wood*) Pitchpine, *das;* Pechkiefernholz, *das;* **~-pipe** *n.* (*Mus.*) Stimmpfeife, *die;* **~ shot** *n.* (*Golf*) kurzer Annäherungsschlag; Pitchshot, *der*

**piteous** /'pɪtɪəs/ *adj.* erbärmlich; (*causing pity*) Mitleid erregend; kläglich ‹Schrei›

**piteously** /'pɪtɪəslɪ/ *adv.* erbärmlich

**'pitfall** *n.* **A** Fallstrick, *der;* (*risk*) Gefahr, *die;* **avoid all ~s** alle Klippen umgehen; **B** (*animal trap*) Fallgrube, *die*

**pith** /pɪθ/ *n.* **A** (*in plant*) Mark, *das;* (*of orange etc.*) weiße Haut; Albedo, *die* (*Bot.*); **B** (*fig.: essential part*) Kern, *der;* **C** (*fig.*) (*strength*) Kraft, *die;* (*force of words etc.*) Überzeugungskraft, *die;* **men of ~:** starke Männer; **of ~ and moment** gewichtig

**'pithead** *n.* ≈ Zechengelände, *das;* **at the ~:** am Schachteingang; **~ baths** Waschkauen (*Bergmannsspr.*); **~ ballot** Abstimmung der Bergleute auf der Zeche

**'pith helmet** *n.* Tropenhelm, *der*

**pithily** /'pɪθɪlɪ/ *adv.* prägnant

**pithy** /'pɪθɪ/ *adj.* **A** markhaltig; reich an Mark *nicht attr.;* ‹Orange usw.› mit dicker weißer Haut; **B** (*fig.*) (*full of meaning*) prägnant; (*vigorous*) markig

**pitiable** /'pɪtɪəbl/ ⇒ **pitiful**

**pitiably** /'pɪtɪəblɪ/ *adv.* jämmerlich

**pitiful** /'pɪtɪfl/ *adj.* **A** Mitleid erregend; (*with strong emotional appeal*) erbärmlich; jämmerlich; kläglich ‹Versuch›; **B** (*contemptible*) jämmerlich (*abwertend*)

**pitifully** /'pɪtɪfəlɪ/ *adv.* erbärmlich; jämmerlich

**pitiless** /'pɪtɪlɪs/ *adj.*, **pitilessly** /'pɪtɪlɪslɪ/ *adv.* unbarmherzig (*auch fig.*); erbarmungslos

**pitman** /'pɪtmən/ *n.* **A** *pl.* **pitmen** /'pɪtmən/ (*miner*) Bergmann, *der;* **B** *pl.* **~s** (*Amer.: connecting-rod*) Pleuelstange, *die*

**piton** /'pi:tɒn/ *n.* (*for rock*) Felshaken, *der;* (*for ice*) Eishaken, *der*

**pit: ~ pony** *n.* (*Brit.*) Grubenpferd, *das;* **~ prop** *n.* [Gruben]stempel, *der;* (*of wood also*) Grubenholz, *das;* **~ saw** *n.* Schrot- *od.* Zugsäge, *die;* **~ stop** *n.* (*Motor racing*) Boxenstopp, *der*

**pitta** /'pɪtə/ *n.* **~ [bread]** Pittabrot, *das;* Fladenbrot, *das*

**pittance** /'pɪtəns/ *n.* **A** Hungerlohn, *der* (*abwertend*); (*small allowance*) [magere] Beihilfe; **B** (*small amount of money*) **a ~:** ein paar Pfennige

**pitter-patter** /pɪtə'pætə(r)/ ⇒ **pit-a-pat**

**pituitary** /pɪ'tju:ɪtərɪ/ *n.* **~ [body *or* gland]** (*Anat., Zool.*) Hirnanhangdrüse, *die;* Hypophyse, *die* (*fachspr.*)

**'pit viper** *n.* Grubenotter, *die*

**pity** /'pɪtɪ/ **1** *n.* **A** (*sorrow*) Mitleid, *das;* Mitgefühl, *das;* **feel ~ for sb.** Mitgefühl für jmdn. *od.* mit jmdm. empfinden; **have you no ~?** hast du [denn] kein Mitleid?; **be moved to ~:** Mitleid empfinden; **have/take ~ on sb./an animal** Erbarmen mit jmdm./einem Tier haben; **for ~'s sake!** um Gottes *od.* Himmels willen!; **B** (*cause for regret*) **[what a] ~!** [wie] schade!; **it's a ~ about sb./sth.** es ist ein Jammer mit jmdm./etw. (*ugs.*); **it's a [great] ~/a thousand pities [that] …:** es ist [sehr *od.* zu] schade/jammerschade (*ugs.*) *od.* ein Jammer (*ugs.*), dass …; **the ~ of it is [that] …:** das Traurige daran ist, dass …; **more's the ~** leider!

**2** *v.t.* bedauern; bemitleiden; **I ~ you** (*also contemptuously*) du tust mir Leid

**pitying** /'pɪtɪɪŋ/ *adj.*, **pityingly** /'pɪtɪɪŋlɪ/ *adv.* mitleidig

**pivot** /'pɪvət/ **1** *n.* **A** [Dreh]zapfen, *der;* (*of a hinge*) Angelzapfen, *der;* **B** (*fig.*) [Dreh- und] Angelpunkt, *der;* (*crucial point*) springender Punkt. **2** *v.t.* (*provide with ~[s]*) mit Zapfen/mit einem Zapfen versehen; (*mount on ~[s]*) drehbar lagern. **3** *v.i.* sich drehen; **the guns ~ easily** die Geschütze lassen sich leicht schwenken; **~ on sth.** (*fig.*) von etw. abhängen

**pivotal** /'pɪvətl/ *adj.* (*fig.: crucial*) zentral; **~ figure/position** Schlüsselfigur, *die*/Schlüsselstellung, *die*

**pix** /pɪks/ *n. pl.* (*coll.*) Bilder

**pixel** /'pɪksel/ *n.* (*Computing etc.*) Bildpunkt, *der;* Pixel, *das*

**pixie** /'pɪksɪ/ *n.* Kobold, *der*

**pixie: ~ hat, ~ hood** *ns. spitz zulaufendes Käppchen*

**pixy** ⇒ **pixie**

**pizza** /'pi:tsə/ *n.* Pizza, *die*

**pizzazz** /pɪ'zæz/ *n.* Klasse, *die;* (*showiness*) Glamour, *der*

**pizzeria** /pi:tsə'ri:ə/ *n.* Pizzeria, *die*

**pizzicato** /pɪtsɪ'kɑ:təʊ/ (*Mus.*) **1** *adj.* **~ accompaniment** Pizzikatobegleitung; **a series of ~ notes** eine pizzicato gespielte Tonfolge. **2** *adv.* pizzicato. **3** *n., pl.* **~s** *or* **pizzicati** /pɪtsɪ'kɑ:ti:/ Pizzicato, *das*

**pl.** *abbr.* **A plate 1 g; B plural** Pl.

**placard** /'plækɑ:d/ **1** *n.* Plakat, *das;* **a ~ announcing the date of the next meeting** ein Anschlag *od.* Aushang mit dem nächsten Sitzungstermin. **2** *v.t.* **A** (*post up ~s on*) mit Plakaten bekleben ‹Wand usw.›; **the town is ~ed with posters** überall in der Stadt kleben Plakate; **B** (*advertise*) plakatieren

**placate** /plə'keɪt/ *v.t.* beschwichtigen, besänftigen ‹Person›

**placatory** /plə'keɪtərɪ/ *adj.* beschwichtigend; besänftigend; Versöhnungs‹opfer, -gabe›

**place** /pleɪs/ **1** *n.* **A** Ort, *der;* (*spot*) Stelle, *die;* Platz, *der;* **put it in a ~ where you can find it** tun Sie es an einen Platz, wo Sie es wieder finden; **I left it in a safe ~:** ich habe es an einem sicheren Ort gelassen; **it was still in the same ~:** es war noch an derselben Stelle *od.* am selben Platz; **the [exact] ~ where …:** die [genaue] Stelle, wo *od.* an der …; **this was the 'last ~ I expected to find you** hier hätte ich dich am allerwenigsten erwartet; **a ~ in the queue** ein Platz in der Schlange; **all over the ~:** überall; (*coll.: in a mess*) ganz durcheinander (*ugs.*); **I can't be in two ~s at once** ich kann nicht an zwei Orten gleichzeitig sein *od.* (*ugs.*) alles auf einmal machen; **from ~ to ~:** von Ort zu Ort; **in ~s** hier und da; (*in parts*) stellenweise; **the animal does still exist in ~s** das Tier kommt noch vereinzelt vor; **find a ~ in sth.** (*be included*) in etw. (*Akk.*) eingehen; ⇒ *also* **take 1 D; B** (*fig.: rank, position*) Stellung, *die;* **as a critic, his ~ is in the front rank** als Kritiker rangiert er ganz vorn; **keep/put sb. in his/her ~:** jmdn. immer wieder/jmdn. in seine/ihre Schranken weisen; jmdm. immer wieder/jmdm. einen Dämpfer aufsetzen (*ugs.*); **know one's ~:** wissen, was sich für einen gehört; **it's not my ~ to do that** es kommt mir nicht zu, das zu tun; **C** (*building or area for specific purpose*) **a [good] ~ to park/to stop** ein [guter] Platz zum Parken/eine [gute] Stelle zum Halten; **do you know a good/cheap ~ to eat?** weißt du, wo man gut/billig essen kann?; **We couldn't get into the café. The ~ was full** Wir kamen gar nicht erst in das Café. Es war alles voll *od.* besetzt; **~ of residence *or* domicile** Wohnort, *der;* **~ of work** Arbeitsplatz, *der;* Arbeitsstätte, *die;* **~ of worship** Andachtsort, *der;* **~ of amusement** Vergnügungsstätte, *die;* ⇒ *also* **another 2 C; D** (*country, town*) Ort, *der;* **the best hotel in the ~:** das beste Hotel am Platz; **Paris/Italy is a great ~:** Paris ist eine tolle Stadt/Italien ist ein tolles Land (*ugs.*); **~ of birth** Geburtsort, *der;* **know the ~:** sich [hier/dort] auskennen; **'go ~s** (*coll.*) herumkommen (*ugs.*); (*fig.*) es [im Leben] zu was bringen (*ugs.*); **E** (*coll.: premises*) Bude, *die* (*ugs.*); (*hotel, restaurant, etc.*) Laden, *der* (*ugs.*); **liven the ~ up** Leben in die Bude bringen (*ugs.*); **she is at his/John's ~:** sie ist bei ihm/John; **[shall we go to] your ~ or mine?** [gehen wir] zu dir oder zu mir?; **I called at your ~:** ich bin bei dir [zu Hause] vorbeigegangen; **a ~ in the country** ein Haus auf dem Lande; **F** (*seat etc.*) [Sitz]platz, *der;* **change ~s [with sb.]** [mit jmdm.] die Plätze tauschen; (*fig.*) [mit jmdm.] tauschen; **lay a/another ~:** ein/noch ein Gedeck auflegen; **take one's ~ at table** am Tisch Platz nehmen; **is this anyone's ~?** ist dieser Platz noch frei?; **G** (*particular spot on surface*) Stelle, *die;* **H** (*in book etc.*) Stelle, *die;* **lose one's ~:** die Seite verschlagen *od.* verblättern; (*on page*) nicht mehr wissen, an welcher Stelle man ist; **keep one's ~:** die Stelle markieren, an der man ist/war; **find one's ~:** die Stelle wieder finden; **I** (*step, stage*) **in the first ~:** zuerst; **why didn't you say so in the first ~?** warum hast du das nicht gleich gesagt?; **they should never have got married in the first ~:** sie hätten von vornherein nicht heiraten sollen; **I objected to it in the first ~:** ich war von Anfang an dagegen; **in the first/second/third** *etc.* **~:** erstens/zweitens/drittens *usw.*; **J** (*proper ~*) Platz, *der;* **everything fell into ~** (*fig.*) alles wurde klar; **take your ~s for the next dance** stellen Sie sich zum nächsten Tanz auf; **he likes to have everything in [its] ~:** bei ihm muss alles an seinem Platz sein; **a woman's ~ is in the home** eine Frau gehört ins Haus; **this is no ~ for a child** das ist kein Ort für ein Kind; **give ~ to sb./sth.** jmdm./einer Sache Platz machen; **winter gave ~ to spring** der Winter räumte dem Frühling das Feld; **the clamp is properly in ~:** die Klammer sitzt richtig; **her hat was held in ~ by a hatpin** ihr Hut wurde von einer Hutnadel festgehalten; **into ~:** fest‹nageln, -schrauben, -kleben›; **out of ~:** nicht am richtigen Platz; (*several things*) in Unordnung; (*fig.*) fehl am Platz; **your suggestion is rather out of ~** (*fig.*) dein Vorschlag ist nicht ganz angebracht *od.* passend; **with not**

P

**a hair out of ~:** makellos frisiert; **in ~ of** anstelle *od.* an Stelle (+ *Gen.*); **I'll go in ~ of you/in your ~:** ich werde an deiner Stelle gehen; **take the ~ of sb./sth.** jmds. Platz *od.* den Platz von jmdm./den Platz von etw. einnehmen; ⇒ *also* **sun** 1; **K** *(position in competition)* Platz, *der;* **drop/go up two ~s in the charts** [um] zwei Plätze in der Hitparade fallen/steigen; **first ~ went to ...:** der erste Platz ging an ... (+ *Akk.*); **take first/second** *etc.* **~:** den ersten/zweiten *usw.* Platz belegen; *(fig.: have priority)* an erster/zweiter *usw.* Stelle kommen; **in second ~:** auf dem zweiten Platz; **beat sb. into second ~:** jmdn. auf den zweiten Platz verweisen; **get a ~** *(Racing)* eine Platzierung erreichen; *(Amer.: second ~)* den zweiten Platz belegen; **L** *(Math.: position of figure in series)* Stelle, *die;* ⇒ *also* **decimal place**; **M** *(job, position, etc.)* Stelle, *die;* *(as pupil; in team, crew)* Platz, *der;* **university ~:** Studienplatz, *der;* **N** *(personal situation)* **what would you do in my ~?** was würden Sie an meiner Stelle tun?; **put yourself in my ~:** versetzen Sie sich in meine Lage.

❷ *v.t.* **A** *(put)* *(vertically)* stellen; *(horizontally)* legen; **he ~d himself where ...:** er stellte sich dahin, wo ...; **~ a foot on a chair** einen Fuß auf einen Stuhl setzen; **~ the ball on the penalty spot** den Ball auf den Elfmeterpunkt legen; **~ in position** richtig hinstellen/hinlegen; **~ an announcement/advertisement in a paper** eine Anzeige/ein Inserat in eine Zeitung setzen; **~ a bet/~ money on a horse** auf ein Pferd wetten/Geld auf ein Pferd setzen; **B** *(fig.)* **~ one's trust in sb./sth.** sein Vertrauen auf *od.* in jmdn./etw. setzen; **he ~s happiness above all other things** Glück steht für ihn an erster Stelle; ⇒ *also* **emphasis** A, C; **C** *in p.p.* *(situated)* gelegen; **a badly ~d window** ein Fenster an einer ungünstigen Stelle; **be well ~d to watch sth.** einen guten Platz *od.* Standort haben, um bei etw. zuzusehen; **he was not well ~d to return the shot** *(Tennis)* er stand ungünstig zum Ball; **we are well ~d for buses/shops** *etc.* wir haben es nicht weit zur Bushaltestelle/zum Einkaufen *usw.*; **how are you ~d for time/money?** *(coll.)* wie stehts mit deiner Zeit/deinem Geld?; **how are you ~d [for lending me a fiver]?** *(coll.)* wie siehts bei dir aus[, kannst du mir einen Fünfer leihen]? *(ugs.)*; **be well ~d financially** sich [finanziell] gut stehen *(ugs.)*; **D** *(find situation or home for)* unterbringen (**with** bei); **~ sb. in command of a company** jmdm. das Kommando über eine Kompanie erteilen; **~ sb. under sb.'s care** jmdn. in jmds. Obhut geben; **E** *(invest)* anlegen ‹Geld›; *(Commerc.)* absetzen ‹Waren›; **~ an order with a firm** einer Firma *(Dat.)* einen Auftrag erteilen; **F** *(class, identify)* einordnen; einstufen; **~ sb. among the greatest statesmen** jmdn. zu den größten Staatsmännern zählen; **~ an artefact in the Neolithic period** ein Artefakt der Jungsteinzeit zuordnen; **I've seen him before but I can't ~ him** ich habe ihn schon einmal gesehen, aber ich weiß nicht, wo ich ihn unterbringen *od.* *(ugs.)* hintun soll; **G** *(Sports etc.)* **be ~d** sich platzieren; *(Brit.: in first three)* unter den ersten drei sein; *(Amer.: second)* Zweiter sein; **be ~d second in the race/charts** im Rennen/in der Hitliste den zweiten Platz belegen

**'place bet** *n.* Platzwette, *die*

**placebo** /plə'si:bəʊ/ *n., pl.* **~s** *(Med.)* Placebo, *das*

**place: ~ card** *n.* Tischkarte, *die;* **~ kick** *n.* *(Footb.)* Platztritt, *der;* **~ mat** *n.* Set, *der od. das*

**placement** /'pleɪsmənt/ *n.* Platzierung, *die*

**'place name** *n.* Ortsname, *der*

**placenta** /plə'sentə/ *n., pl.* **~e** /plə'senti:/ *or* **~s** *(Anat., Zool.)* Plazenta, *die (fachspr.)*; Mutterkuchen, *der*

**placer** /'pleɪsə(r), 'plæsə(r)/ *n.* *(Geol.)* Seife, *die;* *(place)* [Seifen]lagerstätte, *die*

**'place setting** *n.* Gedeck, *das*

**placid** /'plæsɪd/ *adj.* ruhig, gelassen ‹Person›; ruhig ‹Wasser, Wesensart›; *(peaceable)* friedlich, friedfertig ‹Person›

**placidity** /plə'sɪdɪtɪ/ *n., no pl.* ⇒ **placid**: Ruhe, *die;* Gelassenheit, *die;* Friedfertigkeit, *die*

**placidly** /'plæsɪdlɪ/ *adv.* ⇒ **placid**: ruhig; gelassen; friedlich

**placket** /'plækɪt/ *n.* *(Dressm.)* Schlitz, *der*

**plagiarism** /'pleɪdʒərɪzm/ *n.* Plagiat, *das*

**plagiarist** /'pleɪdʒərɪst/ *n.* Plagiator, *der*

**plagiarize** (**plagiarise**) /'pleɪdʒəraɪz/ *v.t.* plagiieren

**plague** /pleɪg/ ❶ *n.* **A** *(esp. Hist.: epidemic)* Seuche, *die;* **the ~** *(bubonic)* die Pest; **spread like the ~:** sich wie eine Seuche ausbreiten; **avoid/hate sb./sth. like the ~:** jmdn./etw. wie die Pest meiden/hassen; **a ~ on it/you!** *(arch.)* hols/hol dich die Pest!; **a ~ on both your houses!** *(fig. arch.)* hol euch beide die Pest! ; **B** *(esp. Bibl.: punishment; coll.: nuisance)* Plage, *die;* **C** *(infestation)* **~ of rats/insects** Ratten-/Insektenplage, *die.*

❷ *v.t.* **A** *(afflict)* plagen; quälen; **~d with** *or* **by sth.** von etw. geplagt; **a disease that ~s mankind** eine Krankheit, die die Menschheit heimsucht; **B** *(bother)* **~ sb. [with sth.]** jmdm. [mit etw.] auf die Nerven gehen *(ugs.)*; **be ~d with sth.** von etw. geplagt werden; **be ~d by bad weather** unter schlechtem Wetter zu leiden haben

**plaice** /pleɪs/ *n., pl. same* **A** Scholle, *die;* **B** *(Amer.: summer flounder)* Sommerflunder, *die*

**plaid** /plæd/ ❶ *n.* Plaid, *das od. der.* ❷ *adj.* [bunt] kariert; **~ blanket** Plaid, *das od. der*

**plain** /pleɪn/ ❶ *adj.* **A** *(clear)* klar; *(obvious)* offensichtlich; **He didn't like us. That was ~ enough** Er mochte uns nicht. Das war ganz klar *od.* offenkundig; **make sth. ~ [to sb.]** [jmdm.] etw. klarmachen; **make it ~ that ...:** klarstellen, dass ...; **make oneself/one's meaning ~:** sich verständlich machen; sich klar ausdrücken; **make one's views/intentions ~:** seine Ansichten/Absichten klar zum Ausdruck bringen; **do I make myself ~?** ist das klar?; habe ich mich klar ausgedrückt?; **the reason is ~ [to see]** der Grund liegt auf der Hand; **the consequences of the act were not ~ at the time** die Folgen dieses Schrittes waren zu dieser Zeit nicht absehbar *od.* klar zu erkennen; ⇒ *also* **English** 2 A; **pikestaff**; **B** *(frank, straightforward)* ehrlich; offen; schlicht ‹Wahrheit›; **be ~ with sb.** mit jmdm. *od.* jmdm. gegenüber offen sein; **there was some ~ speaking** es fielen einige offene Worte; **be [all] ~ sailing** *(fig.)* [ganz] einfach sein; **~ dealing** Redlichkeit, *die;* **C** *(unsophisticated)* einfach; schlicht ‹Kleidung, Frisur›; klar ‹Wasser›; einfach, bescheiden ‹Lebensstil›; *(not lined)* unliniert ‹Papier›; *(not patterned)* ‹Stoff› ohne Muster; **she is a ~ cook** sie kocht einfach; **~ cooking** gutbürgerliche Küche; **~ stitch** rechte Masche; **~ text** *(without notes)* [unkommentierter] Originaltext; *(decoded)* Klartext, *der;* ⇒ *also* **cover** 1 C; **~ clothes**; **D** *(unattractive)* wenig attraktiv ‹Mädchen›; **she's rather a ~ Jane** *(coll.)* sie ist nicht gerade eine Schönheit; **E** *(sheer)* rein; **that's ~ bad manners** das ist einfach schlechtes Benehmen; **that's just ~ common sense** das sagt einem doch der gesunde Menschenverstand.

❷ *adv.* **A** *(clearly)* deutlich; **B** *(simply)* einfach; **I'm just ~ tired** ich bin einfach nur müde.

❸ *n.* **A** Ebene, *die;* **the P~s** *(of North America)* die Prärie; **B** *(Knitting)* rechte Masche; **two ~, two purl** zwei rechts, zwei links

**plain: ~chant** ⇒ **plainsong**; **~ 'chocolate** *n.* halbbittere Schokolade; *(without any sweetness)* bittere Schokolade; **~ 'clothes** *n. pl.* **in ~ clothes** in Zivil; **~clothes detective** *etc.* Kriminalbeamter *usw.* in Zivil

**plainly** /'pleɪnlɪ/ *adv.* **A** *(clearly)* deutlich; verständlich ‹erklären›; **B** *(obviously)* offensichtlich; *(undoubtedly)* eindeutig; **C** *(frankly)* offen; **D** *(simply, unpretentiously)* einfach; schlicht; bescheiden ‹leben›

**plainness** /'pleɪnnɪs/ *n., no pl.* **A** *(clearness)* Klarheit, *die;* **B** *(frankness)* Offenheit, *die;* **his ~ of speech** seine Offenheit; **C** *(simplicity)* Schlichtheit, *die;* **D** *(ugliness)* Unattraktivität, *die;* Unansehnlichkeit, *die*

**plainsman** /'pleɪnzmən/ *n., pl.* **plainsmen** /'pleɪnzmən/ Flachländer, *der;* *(in North America)* Präriebewohner, *der*

**plain: ~song** *n.* *(Mus., Eccl.)* Cantus planus, *der (fachspr.)*; gregorianischer Gesang; **~-'spoken** *adj.* freimütig

**plaint** /pleɪnt/ *n.* **A** *(literary: lamentation)* [Weh]klage, *die;* **B** *(Brit. Law)* Klage, *die*

**plaintiff** /'pleɪntɪf/ *n.* *(Law)* Kläger, *der*/Klägerin, *die*

**plaintive** /'pleɪntɪv/ *adj.* klagend; traurig, leidend ‹Blick›

**plaintively** /'pleɪntɪvlɪ/ *adv.* klagend; in klagendem Ton ‹sprechen usw.›; traurig, leidend ‹blicken›

**plain: ~ weave** *n.* Leinwandbindung, *die;* **~ weaving** *n.* Gewebe in Leinwandbindung

**plait** /plæt/ ❶ *n.* *(of hair)* Zopf, *der;* Flechte, *die (geh.)*; *(of straw, ribbon, etc.)* geflochtenes Band. ❷ *v.t.* flechten

**plan** /plæn/ ❶ *n.* Plan, *der;* *(for story etc.)* Konzept, *das;* Entwurf, *der;* *(intention)* Absicht, *die;* **~ of action** Aktionsprogramm, *das;* **what is your ~ of action?** wie willst du vorgehen?; **have great ~s for sb.** große Pläne mit jmdm. haben; **~ of campaign** Strategie, *die;* **make ~s for sth.** Pläne für etw. machen *od.* schmieden; **what are your ~s for tomorrow?** was hast du morgen vor?; **your best ~ is to stay on at school** am besten bleibst du auf der Schule; **[go] according to ~:** nach Plan [gehen]; planmäßig [verlaufen *od.* laufen]; ⇒ *also* **five-year plan**.

❷ *v.t.*, **-nn- A** planen; *(design)* entwerfen ‹Gebäude, Maschine›; **~ to do sth.** planen *od.* vorhaben, etw. zu tun; **as ~ned** plangemäß; wie geplant; ⇒ *also* **obsolescence**; **B** *(make plan of)* **~ sth.** einen [Lage]plan einer Sache *(Gen.)* *od.* von etw. anfertigen.

❸ *v.i.*, **-nn-** planen; **~ [weeks] ahead** [Wochen] im Voraus planen *od.* vorausplanen; **~ for sth.** Pläne für etw. machen; **we hadn't ~ned on that** damit hatten wir nicht gerechnet; **~ on doing sth.** *(coll.)* vorhaben, etw. zu tun; **what do you ~ on doing today?** was hast du heute vor?

**planchette** /plæn'ʃet/ *n.* Planchette, *die*

**plane**[1] /pleɪn/ *n.* **~ [tree]** Platane, *die*

**plane**[2] ❶ *n.* *(tool)* Hobel, *der.* ❷ *v.t.* hobeln

**plane**[3] ❶ *n.* **A** *(Geom.)* Ebene, *die;* *(flat surface)* Fläche, *die;* ⇒ *also* **inclined plane**; **B** *(fig.)* Ebene, *die;* *(moral, intellectual)* Niveau, *das;* **~ of thought/attainment/knowledge** Denk-/Leistungs-/Wissensniveau, *das;* **C** *(aircraft)* Flugzeug, *das;* Maschine, *die (ugs.)*; *(Aeronaut.: supporting surface)* Tragfläche, *die.* ❷ *v.i.* gleiten

**'planeload** *n.* Flugzeugladung, *die*

**planet** /'plænɪt/ *n.* Planet, *der;* **major ~:** Riesenplanet, *der;* **minor ~:** kleiner Planet

**planetarium** /plænɪ'teərɪəm/ *n., pl.* **~s** *or* **planetaria** /plænɪ'teərɪə/ Planetarium, *das*

**planetary** /'plænɪtərɪ/ *adj.* planetarisch; Planeten‹forscher, -system, -bewegung›

**planetoid** /'plænətɔɪd/ *n.* *(Astron.)* Planetoid, *der*

**plangent** /'plændʒənt/ *adj.* **A** *(resounding)* klangvoll; **B** *(plaintive)* schwermütig und ergreifend; getragen ‹Melodie usw.›

**planish** /'plænɪʃ/ *v.t.* glätten; glatt hämmern ‹Blech›

**plank** /plæŋk/ ❶ *n.* **A** *(piece of timber)* Brett, *das;* *(thicker)* Bohle, *die;* *(on ship)* Planke, *die;* **be as thick as two [short] ~s** *(coll.)* dumm wie Bohnenstroh sein *(ugs.)*; **be made to walk the ~** *(Hist.)* über die Planke laufen müssen *(fig.)*; **B** *(fig.: item of political programme)* Programmpunkt, *der.* ❷ *v.t.* **A** mit Brettern/Bohlen/Planken versehen; beplanken ‹Schiff›; **~ sth. over** etw. mit Brettern abdecken; **B** *(coll.: put down)* knallen *(ugs.)*; **C** *(Amer.)* *auf einem Holzbrett garen und servieren;* **~ed steak** Steak auf dem Holzbrett

**planking** /ˈplæŋkɪŋ/ *n.* (*planks*) ⇒ **plank** 1 A: Bretter *Pl.;* Bohlen *Pl.;* Planken *Pl.;* (*of ship*) Beplankung, *die*

**plankton** /ˈplæŋktn/ *n.* (*Biol.*) Plankton, *das*

**planned eˈconomy** *n.* (*Econ.*) Planwirtschaft, *die*

**planner** /ˈplænə(r)/ *n.* Planer, *der*/Planerin, *die*

**planning** /ˈplænɪŋ/ *n.* Planen, *das;* Planung, *die;* **at the ~ stage** im Planungsstadium; **~ permission** Baugenehmigung, *die*

**plant** /plɑːnt/ ❶ *n.* Ⓐ (*Bot.*) Pflanze, *die;* Ⓑ (*machinery*) *no indef. art.* Maschinen *Pl.;* (*single complex*) Anlage, *die;* **earth-moving ~** *no indef. art.* Maschinen für Erdarbeiten; **generating ~** *no indef. art.* Generatoren *Pl.;* **a generating ~:** eine Generatorenanlage; Ⓒ (*factory*) Fabrik, *die;* Werk, *das;* Ⓓ (*coll.: undercover agent*) Spitzel, *der;* Ⓔ (*coll.: thing concealed*) Untergeschobene, *das;* **he said the heroin was a ~:** er sagte, das Heroin sei ihm untergeschoben worden.
❷ *v.t.* Ⓐ (*put in ground*) pflanzen; aussäen ‹Samen›; anlegen ‹Garten usw.›; anpflanzen ‹Beet›; bepflanzen ‹Land›; **~ a field with barley** auf einem Feld Gerste anpflanzen; Ⓑ (*fix*) setzen; **~ stakes [in the ground]** Pfähle setzen; **he ~ed his feet wide apart** er stellte seine Füße weit auseinander; **~ oneself** sich hinstellen *od.* (*ugs.*) aufpflanzen; Ⓒ (*in mind*) **~ an idea** *etc.* **in sb.'s mind/in sb.** jmdm. eine Idee *usw.* einimpfen (*ugs.*) *od.* (*geh.*) einpflanzen; Ⓓ (*deliver etc.*) **~ a blow** *etc.* **on sb.'s nose** *etc.* jmdm. einen Schlag *usw.* auf die Nase *usw.* verpassen; **~ a kiss on sb.'s forehead** *etc.* jmdm. einen Kuss auf die Stirn *usw.* drücken; Ⓔ (*coll.: conceal*) schmuggeln (*ugs.*); anbringen ‹Wanze›; legen ‹Bombe›; **~ sth. on sb.** jmdm. etw. unterschieben; Ⓕ (*station as spy etc.*) einschmuggeln

**~ ˈout** *v.t.* auspflanzen ‹Setzlinge›

**Plantagenet** /plænˈtædʒɪnɪt/ (*Brit. Hist.*) ❶ *n.* Plantagenet, *der/die.* ❷ *attrib. adj.* Plantagenet-

**plantain**[1] /ˈplæntɪn/ *n.* (*Bot.: in temperate regions, Plantago*) Wegerich, *der*

**plantain**[2] (*Bot.: in tropics, Musa*) Kochbanane, *die;* Mehlbanane *die;* Plante, *die* (*fachspr.*)

**plantain ˈlily** *n.* (*Bot.*) Funkie, *die*

**plantation** /plænˈteɪʃn, plɑːnˈteɪʃn/ *n.* Ⓐ (*estate*) Pflanzung, *die;* Plantage, *die;* Ⓑ (*group of plants*) Anpflanzung, *die*

**ˈplant breeding** *n.* Pflanzenzucht, *die*

**planter** /ˈplɑːntə(r)/ *n.* Ⓐ Pflanzer, *der*/Pflanzerin, *die;* Ⓑ (*machine*) Pflanzmaschine, *die;* (*for seeds*) Sämaschine, *die;* Ⓒ (*container*) Pflanzgefäß, *das*

**plant: ~ food** *n.* Pflanzennahrung, *die;* (*naturally occurring*) Nährstoffe *Pl.;* **~ hire** *n.* Baumaschinenverleih, *der;* **~ kingdom** *n.* Pflanzenreich, *das;* **~-louse** *n.* (*Zool.*) Pflanzenlaus, *die*

**plaque** /plɑːk, plæk/ *n.* Ⓐ (*ornamental tablet*) [Schmuck]platte, *die;* (*commemorating sb.*) [Gedenk]tafel, *die;* Plakette, *die* (*Kunstwiss.*); Ⓑ (*Dent.*) Plaque, *die* (*fachspr.*); [weißer] Zahnbelag

**plasma** /ˈplæzmə/ *n.* Ⓐ (*Anat., Zool., Phys.*) Plasma, *das;* Ⓑ (*Biol.*) ⇒ **protoplasm**

**plaster** /ˈplɑːstə(r)/ ❶ *n.* Ⓐ (*for walls etc.*) [Ver]putz, *der;* Ⓑ **~ [of Paris]** Gips, *der;* **have one's leg in ~:** ein Gipsbein *od.* sein Bein in Gips haben; **put sb.'s leg in ~:** jmds. Bein in Gips legen; Ⓒ ⇒ **sticking plaster.** ❷ *v.t.* Ⓐ verputzen ‹Wand›; vergipsen, zugipsen ‹Loch, Riß›; Ⓑ (*daub*) **~ sth. on sth.** etw. dick auf etw. (*Akk.*) auftragen; **~ make-up on one's face, ~ one's face with make-up** sich (*Dat.*) Make-up ins Gesicht kleistern (*ugs.*); **~ed with mud** mit Schlamm bedeckt; Ⓒ (*stick on*) kleistern (*ugs.*) ‹Plakate, Briefmarken› (**on** auf + *Akk.*); **~ posters all over the wall/the wall with posters** die Wand mit Plakaten zukleistern (*salopp*); Ⓓ (*coll.: shell, bomb*) bepflastern (*Soldatenspr.*)

**~ ˈdown** *v.t.* **~ sb.'s/one's hair down** jmdm./sich das Haar anklatschen

**~ ˈover** *v.t.* vergipsen ‹Loch, Riss›

**plaster: ~board** *n.* Gipsplatte, *die;* **~ cast** *n.* Ⓐ (*model in plaster*) Gipsabguss *od.* -abdruck, *der;* Ⓑ (*Med.*) Gipsverband, *der*

**plastered** /ˈplɑːstəd/ *pred. adj.* (*sl.: drunk*) voll (*salopp*); **get ~:** sich voll laufen lassen (*salopp*)

**plasterer** /ˈplɑːstərə(r)/ *n.* ▶ 1261 Gipser, *der*

**plaster ˈsaint** *n.* Heiligenfigur aus Gips; (*fig., usu. iron.*) Heilige, *der/die* (*ugs.*)

**plastic** /ˈplæstɪk/ ❶ *n.* Ⓐ Plastik, *das;* Kunststoff, *der;* Plast, *der* (*DDR*); *in pl., attrib.* Plastik-; Kunststoff-; Plast- (*DDR*); Ⓑ (*coll.: credit cards etc.*) Plastikgeld, *das.* ❷ *adj.* Ⓐ (*made of plastic*) Plastik-; Kunststoff-; Plast- (*DDR*); aus Plastik/Kunststoff/Plast *nachgestellt;* (*coll. derog.: synthetic*) Plastik-; **~ bag** Plastiktüte, *die;* **~ money** (*joc.*) Kreditkarten *Pl.;* Plastikgeld, *das;* Ⓑ (*produced by moulding*) plastisch; **~ figure** Plastik, *die;* Ⓒ (*malleable, lit. or fig.*) formbar; bildbar; **the ~ qualities of wax** die plastischen Eigenschaften von Wachs; Ⓓ **the ~ arts** die Plastik; (*including painting etc.*) die bildende Kunst

**plastic: ~ ˈbullet** *n.* Plastikgeschoss, *das;* **~ ˈsurgeon** *n.* ▶ 1261 Facharzt für plastische Chirurgie; **~ ˈsurgery** *n.* plastische Chirurgie; **undergo** *or* **have ~ surgery** sich einer plastischen *od.* kosmetischen Operation unterziehen

**Plasticine** ® /ˈplæstɪsiːn/ *n.* Plastilin, *das*

**plasticise** ⇒ **plasticize**

**plasticity** /plæˈstɪsɪtɪ/ *n., no pl.* (*lit. or fig.*) Formbarkeit, *die;* Plastizität, *die*

**plasticize** /ˈplæstɪsaɪz/ *v.t.* geschmeidig machen; plasti[fi]zieren (*fachspr.*)

**plasticizer** /ˈplæstɪsaɪzə(r)/ *n.* Weichmacher, *der;* Plasti[fi]kator, *der* (*Chemie*)

**plasticky** /ˈplæstɪkɪ/ *adj.* (*coll. derog.*) plastikartig; **be very ~:** billiges Plastikzeug sein

**plate** /pleɪt/ ❶ *n.* Ⓐ (*for food*) Teller, *der;* (*large ~ for serving food*) Platte, *die;* (*Amer.: main course on one ~*) Tellergericht, *das;* (*Amer.: food for one person*) Gedeck, *das;* **a ~ of soup/sandwiches** ein Teller Suppe/belegte Brote *od.* mit belegten Broten; **have sth. handed to one on a ~** (*fig. coll.*) etw. auf silbernem Tablett serviert bekommen (*fig.*); **have a lot** *etc.* **on one's ~** (*fig. coll.*) viel *usw.* am Hals *od.* um die Ohren haben (*ugs.*); Ⓑ (*for collection in church*) Teller für die Kollekte; Ⓒ (*sheet of metal etc.*) Platte, *die;* Ⓓ (*metal ~ with name etc.*) Schild, *das;* **[number] ~:** Nummernschild, *das;* **put up one's ~** (*fig.*) seine eigene Praxis eröffnen; Ⓔ (*Photog.*) [fotografische] Platte; Ⓕ *no pl., no indef. art.* (*Brit.: tableware*) [Tafel]silber, *das;* (*gold*) Gold[geschirr], *das;* (*pewter*) Zinn, *das;* Silber-/Gold-/Zinnsachen *Pl.;* (*plated*) **[made of] real silver, not ~:** aus echtem Silber, nicht nur versilbert; Ⓖ (*for engraving, printing*) Platte, *die;* (*impression*) Stich, *der;* (*illustration*) [Bild]tafel, *die* (*Druckw.*); **printing ~:** Druckplatte, *die;* Ⓗ (*Sport*) (*trophy*) Pokal, *der;* (*race*) Pokal[wettbewerb], *der;* Ⓘ (*Dent.*) Gaumenplatte, *die;* (*coll.: denture*) [Zahn]prothese, *die;* Gebiss, *das;* Ⓙ (*Amer. Electronics*) Anode, *die;* Ⓚ (*Geol.*) Platte, *die;* Ⓛ (*Baseball*) Wurfmal, *das;* **home ~:** Schlagmal, *das.* ⇒ *also* **tracery** A.
❷ *v.t.* Ⓐ (*coat*) plattieren; **~ sth. [with gold/silver/chromium]** etw. vergolden/versilbern/verchromen; Ⓑ panzern ‹Schiff›

**plateau** /ˈplætəʊ/ *n., pl.* **~x** /ˈplætəʊz/ *or* **~s** Ⓐ Hochebene, *die;* Plateau, *das;* Ⓑ (*fig.*) **a price ~:** eine Stabilisierung der Preise; **reach/be on a ~** ‹Preise, Produktion usw.:› sich einpendeln/sich eingependelt haben

**plated** /ˈpleɪtɪd/ *adj.* plattiert; **[gold-]~:** dubliert; vergoldet; **[silver-/chromium-/nickel-]~:** versilbert/verchromt/vernickelt

**plateful** /ˈpleɪtfʊl/ *n.* Teller, *der;* **a ~ of rice** ein Teller [voll] Reis; **I've already had two ~s** ich habe schon zwei Teller voll gegessen; **I've had a ~** (*fig. coll.*) ich habe die Nase voll davon (*ugs.*)

**plate: ~ ˈglass** *n.* Flachglas, *das;* **~-holder** *n.* (*Photogr.*) [Platten]kassette, *die;* **~layer** *n.* (*Brit. Railw.*) Streckenarbeiter, *der*

**platelet** /ˈpleɪtlət/ *n.* (*Physiol.*) Blutplättchen, *das*

**platen** /ˈplætn/ *n.* (*Printing*) Drucktiegel, *der;* (*on typewriter*) [Schreib]walze, *die*

**plate: ~ rack** *n.* (*Brit.*) Abtropfständer, *der;* Geschirrablage, *die;* **~-warmer** *n.* Tellerwärmer, *der*

**platform** /ˈplætfɔːm/ *n.* Ⓐ (*Brit. Railw.*) Bahnsteig, *der;* **the train leaves from/will arrive at ~ 4** der Zug fährt von Gleis 4 ab/in Gleis 4 ein; **edge of the ~:** Bahnsteigkante, *die;* Ⓑ (*stage*) Podium, *das;* Ⓒ (*Polit.*) Wahlplattform, *die;* Ⓓ (*Geol.*) Strandterrasse, *die;* Ⓔ (*in bus etc.*) Plattform, *die;* Ⓕ (*of shoe*) Plateausohle, *die; attrib.* Plateau‹schuh, -sohle›; Ⓖ (*Computing*) Plattform, *die*

**ˈplatform ticket** *n.* (*Brit.*) Bahnsteigkarte, *die*

**plating** /ˈpleɪtɪŋ/ *n.* (*process*) Plattierung, *die;* (*coat*) Plattierung, *die;* Auflage, *die;* **gold/silver/chromium ~:** Vergoldung/Versilberung/Verchromung, *die*

**platinum** /ˈplætɪnəm/ *n.* Platin, *das*

**platinum ˈblonde** ❶ *n.* Platinblonde, *die.* ❷ *adj.* platinblond

**platitude** /ˈplætɪtjuːd/ *n.* Ⓐ (*trite remark*) Plattitüde, *die* (*geh.*); Gemeinplatz, *der;* Ⓑ *no pl.* (*triteness*) Banalität, *die*

**platitudinous** /plætɪˈtjuːdɪnəs/ *adj.* banal; platt (*abwertend*)

**Plato** /ˈpleɪtəʊ/ *pr. n.* Plato[n] (*der*)

**Platonic** /pləˈtɒnɪk/ *adj.* Ⓐ (*of Plato*) platonisch; Ⓑ **p~** (*not sexual*) platonisch ‹Liebe, Freundschaft›

**platonically** /pləˈtɒnɪkəlɪ/ *adv.* platonisch

**Platonist** /ˈpleɪtənɪst/ *n.* Platoniker, *der*

**platoon** /pləˈtuːn/ *n.* (*Mil.*) Zug, *der*

**platter** /ˈplætə(r)/ *n.* (*Amer./arch.*) Platte, *die;* (*arch.: plate*) Teller, *der;* **have sth. handed to one on a ~** (*fig. coll.*) etw. auf silbernem Tablett serviert bekommen (*fig.*)

**platypus** /ˈplætɪpəs/ *n.* (*Zool.*) Schnabeltier, *das*

**plaudits** /ˈplɔːdɪts/ *n. pl.* Beifall, *der*

**plausibility** /plɔːzɪˈbɪlɪtɪ/ *n., no pl.* Plausibilität, *die;* Glaubwürdigkeit, *die;* (*of person*) Glaubwürdigkeit, *die;* **this version has more ~:** diese Version ist glaubwürdiger *od.* plausibler

**plausible** /ˈplɔːzɪbl/ *adj.* plausibel; einleuchtend; glaubwürdig ‹Person›

**plausibly** /ˈplɔːzɪblɪ/ *adv.* plausibel; einleuchtend; **as long as she ~ could** so lange es sich vertreten ließ

**play** /pleɪ/ ❶ *n.* Ⓐ (*Theatre*) [Theater]stück, *das;* **television ~:** Fernsehspiel, *das;* **put on a ~:** ein Stück aufführen; **go to [see] a ~:** ins Theater gehen; **a ~ within a ~:** ein Spiel im Spiel; **it was as good as a ~:** dafür hätte man Eintrittsgeld verlangen können; Ⓑ (*recreation*) Spielen, *das;* Spiel, *das;* **time for ~:** Zeit zum Spielen; **at ~:** beim Spielen; **say/do sth. in ~:** etw. aus *od.* im *od.* zum Spaß sagen/tun; **~ [up]on words** Wortspiel, *das;* Ⓒ (*Sport*) Spiel, *das;* (*Amer.: manœuvre*) Spielzug, *der;* **abandon ~:** das Spiel abbrechen; **~ is impossible because of the weather** wegen des Wetters kann nicht gespielt werden; **start/close of ~:** Spielbeginn, *der/*-ende, *das;* **in the last minute of ~:** in der letzten Spielminute; **forward ~:** Angriffsspiel, *das;* **a good piece of ~:** ein guter Spielzug; **be in/out of ~** ‹Ball:› im Spiel/aus [dem Spiel] sein; **keep the ball in ~:** den Ball im Spiel halten; **make a ~ for sb./sth.** (*fig. coll.*) hinter jmdm./etw. her sein (*ugs.*); es auf jmdn./etw. abgesehen haben; ⇒ *also* **child's play**; **fair**[2] 1 A; **foul** 1 E; Ⓓ (*gambling*) Spiel, *das;* Ⓔ **sb.'s imagination is brought** *or* **called into ~:** jmds. Fantasie wird angeregt; **come into ~, be brought** *or* **called into ~:** ins Spiel kommen; **put into ~:** ins Spiel bringen; **make great ~ of sth.** etw. demonstrativ zur Schau stellen; **make [great] ~ with**

sth. viel Wesen um etw. machen; (F) (*freedom of movement*) Spiel, *das* (*Technik*); (*fig.*) Spielraum, *der*; **some/2 mm of/too much ~:** etwas/2 mm/zu viel Spiel; **the knot has too much ~:** der Knoten ist zu locker; **give the rope more ~:** das Seil lockern; **give full ~ to one's emotions/imagination** *etc.*, **allow one's emotions/imagination** *etc.* **full ~** (*fig.*) seinen Gefühlen/seiner Fantasie *usw.* freien Lauf lassen; (G) (*rapid movement*) **the ~ of light on water** das Spiel des Lichts auf Wasser; (H) (*turn, move*) **it's your ~:** du bist dran *od.* an der Reihe (*ugs.*); (*in board game*) du bist am Zug.

**2** *v.i.* (A) spielen; **~ for money** um Geld spielen; **~ with sb./sth.** (*lit. or fig.*) mit jmdm./etw. spielen; **have no one to ~ with** niemanden zum Spielen haben; **he won't ~** (*coll.: won't do what sb. wants*) er will nicht mitspielen; **~ with oneself** (*euphem.: sexually*) an sich (*Dat.*) herumspielen (*ugs. verhüll.*); **~ [up]on words** Wortspiele/ein Wortspiel machen; **~ fair [with sb.]** fair [gegen jmdn.] spielen; (*fig.*) [jmdm. gegenüber] fair sein; sich [jmdm. gegenüber] fair verhalten; **not have much time** *etc.* **to ~ with** (*coll.*) zeitlich *usw.* nicht viel Spielraum haben; **~ into sb.'s hands** (*fig.*) jmdm. in die Hand *od.* Hände arbeiten; **~ safe** sichergehen; auf Nummer Sicher gehen (*ugs.*); **~ing safe, she took an umbrella** sicherheits- *od.* vorsichtshalber nahm sie einen Schirm mit; **~ for time** Zeit gewinnen wollen; [ver]suchen, Zeit zu gewinnen; ⇒ *also* **fire** 1 B; (B) (*be suitable for ~*) **the pitch is ~ing well/badly** auf dem Platz spielt es sich gut/schlecht; (C) (*Mus.*) spielen (**on** auf + *Dat.*); **~ by ear** nach dem Gehör spielen; (D) (*Theatre*) spielen; **what is ~ing at the theatre?** was wird im Theater gespielt *od.* gegeben?; ⇒ *also* **gallery** B; (E) (*move about*) spielen; **a smile ~ed on/about her lips** ein Lächeln spielte um ihre Lippen; (F) ‹Springbrunnen:› in Betrieb sein; (G) (*fiddle about*) spielen; herumspielen (*ugs.*) (**with** mit, an + *Dat.*).

**3** *v.t.* (A) (*Mus.: perform on*) spielen; **~ the violin** *etc.* Geige *usw.* spielen; **~ sth. on the piano** *etc.* etw. auf dem Klavier *usw.* spielen; **~ sb. in/out** jmdn. musikalisch begrüßen/verabschieden; **~ sth. by ear** etw. nach dem Gehör spielen; **~ it by ear** (*fig.*) es dem Augenblick/der Situation überlassen; (B) spielen ‹Grammophon, Tonbandgerät›; abspielen ‹Schallplatte, Tonband›; spielen lassen ‹Radio›; **~ sb. a record** jmdm. eine [Schall]platte vorspielen; (C) (*Theatre; also fig.*) spielen; **~ a town** in einer Stadt spielen; **~ a theatre** an einem Theater spielen; **~ the fool/innocent** den Clown/Unschuldigen spielen; ⇒ *also* **man** 1 B; (D) (*execute, practise*) **~ a trick/joke on sb.** jmdn. hereinlegen (*ugs.*)/jmdm. einen Streich spielen; (E) (*Sport, Cards*) spielen ‹Fußball, Karten, Schach usw.›; spielen *od.* antreten gegen ‹Mannschaft, Gegner›; (*include in team*) einsetzen, aufstellen ‹Stürmer, Verteidiger›; **~ a match** einen Wettkampf bestreiten; (*in team games*) ein Spiel machen; **he ~ed me at chess/squash** er war im Schach/Squash mein Gegner; **~ it cool** (*fig. coll.*) auf cool machen (*salopp*); **~ it right/safe/straight** es geschickt anstellen/auf Nummer Sicher gehen/es sachlich behandeln; **~ oneself in** (*esp. Cricket*) sich einspielen; (*fig.*) sich einarbeiten; ⇒ *also* **ball¹** 1 B; **duck¹** 1 A; **fast²** 1 A; **game¹** 1 A, B, D; **hand** 1 P; **hell** B; **hookey**; (F) (*Sport: execute*) ausführen ‹Schlag›; (*Cricket etc.*) schlagen ‹Ball›; (G) (*Chess etc.: move*) ziehen; (*Cards*) spielen; **~ one's last card** (*fig.*) alle seine Karten ausspielen; **have ~ed all one's cards** (*fig.*) seinen letzten Trumpf ausgespielt haben; **~ one's cards right** (*fig.*) es richtig anfassen (*fig.*); ⇒ *also* **trump¹** 1; (H) (*Angling*) drillen; (I) (*gamble on*) **~ the market** spekulieren (**in** mit *od. Wirtsch.* in + *Dat.*); **~ the stock market** an der Börse spekulieren

**~ a'bout** ⇒ **~ around**

**~ a'long** *v.i.* mitspielen; **~ along with sb./sth.** sich mit jmdm./etw. arrangieren

**~ a'round** *v.i.* (*coll.*) spielen; **~ around with sb./sb.'s affections/sth.** mit jmdm./jmds. Zuneigung spielen/mit etw. herumspielen (*ugs.*); **stop ~ing around!** hör [doch] auf mit dem Blödsinn!

**~ at** *v.t.* spielen; **what do you think you're ~ing at?** was soll denn das?; **~ at being sb.** jmdn. spielen

**~ 'back** *v.t.* abspielen ‹Tonband, Aufnahme›; **he ~ed part of the discussion back to them** er spielte ihnen einen Teil der Diskussion vor; ⇒ *also* **playback**

**~ 'down** *v.t.* herunterspielen

**~ 'off** **1** *v.i.* zum Entscheidungsspiel antreten; ⇒ *also* **play-off**. **2** *v.t.* ausspielen; **~ one person/firm** *etc.* **off against another** eine Person/Firma *usw.* gegen eine andere ausspielen

**~ on** **1** /'--/ *v.t.* ⇒ **~ upon**. **2** /-'-/ *v.i.* (*Cricket*) auf das eigene Mal schlagen

**~ 'up** **1** *v.i.* (A) (*play vigorously*) **~ up!** los, vorwärts!; (B) ‹Kinder:› nichts als Ärger machen; ‹Auto:› verrückt spielen; ‹Rücken, Bein usw.:› Schwierigkeiten *od.* Ärger machen. **2** *v.t.* (A) (*annoy, torment*) ärgern; ‹Krankheit:› zu schaffen machen (+ *Dat.*); (B) (*exploit*) hochspielen; Wesen machen von (*ugs.*) ‹Krankheit›; hervor-, herauskehren ‹Eigenschaft usw.›

**~ upon** *v.t.* sich (*Dat.*) zunutze machen ‹Gefühle, Ängste usw.›; **~ upon sb.'s sympathies** auf jmds. Mitgefühl (*Akk.*) spekulieren (*ugs.*)

**~ 'up to** *v.t.* (A) (*Theatre coll.*) gut in Szene setzen ‹Schauspieler›; (B) (*fig.: flatter*) **~ up to sb.** sich bei jmdm. beliebt machen

**playable** /'pleɪəbl/ *adj.* (A) (*able to be played*) spielbar; (B) (*Sport: able to be played on*) bespielbar ‹Spielfeld›

**play: ~-acting** *n.* Schauspielkunst, *die*; Schauspielerei, *die* (*ugs.*); (*fig.*) Theater, *das* (*ugs.*); **~-actor** *n.* (*fig., usu. derog.*) **he's just a ~-actor** er spielt immer nur Theater (*ugs.*); **~ area** *n.* Spielplatz, *der*; **~back** *n.* Wiedergabe, *die*; **listen to the ~back** die Aufnahme anhören; **~bill** *n.* (A) (*poster*) Theaterplakat, *das*; (B) (*Amer.: theatre programme*) Theaterprogramm, *das*; **~boy** *n.* Playboy, *der*

**played 'out** *adj.* verbraucht; erschöpft ‹Person, Tier›; **this idea is ~:** diese Idee hat sich überlebt

**player** /'pleɪə(r)/ *n.* (A) Spieler, *der*/Spielerin, *die*; **amateur/professional ~:** Amateur, *der*/Profi[spieler], *der*; (B) (*Mus.*) Musiker, *der*/Musikerin, *die*; Spieler, *der*/Spielerin, *die*; **orchestral ~:** Orchestermusiker, *der*/-musikerin, *die*; **organ-~:** Orgelspieler, *der*/-spielerin, *die*; (C) (*actor*) Schauspieler, *der*/Schauspielerin, *die*; (D) ⇒ **record player**

**'player-piano** *n.* automatisches Klavier; Pianola, *das*

**'playfellow** *n.* Spielkamerad, *der*/Spielkameradin, *die*

**playful** /'pleɪfl/ *adj.* (A) (*fond of playing*) spielerisch; (*frolicsome*) verspielt; (B) (*teasing*) neckisch; (*joking*) scherzhaft

**playfully** /'pleɪfəlɪ/ *adv.* (A) (*gaily*) spielerisch; ausgelassen; (B) (*teasingly*) neckisch; (*jokingly*) aus *od.* im *od.* zum Scherz

**play: ~goer** *n.* Theaterbesucher, *der*/-besucherin, *die*; **be a regular ~goer** regelmäßig ins Theater gehen; **~ground** *n.* Spielplatz, *der*; (*Sch.*) Schulhof, *der*; **the ~ground of the rich** (*fig.*) der Tummelplatz der Reichen; **~group** *n.* Spielgruppe, *die*; **~house** *n.* (A) (*theatre*) Schauspielhaus, *das*; (B) (*toy house*) Spielhaus, *das*

**playing** /'pleɪɪŋ/ *n.* Spiel, *das*

**playing: ~ card** *n.* Spielkarte, *die*; **~ field** *n.* Sportplatz, *der*; **they are not competing on a level ~ field** (*fig.*) zwischen ihnen besteht keine Chancengleichheit; **~ time** *n.* Spieldauer, *die*; Spielzeit, *die*

**playlet** /'pleɪlɪt/ *n.* Dramolett, *das*

**play: ~mate** *n.* Spielkamerad, *der*/Spielkameradin, *die*; **~off** *n.* Entscheidungsspiel, *das*; **~pen** *n.* Laufgitter, *das*; Laufstall, *der*; **~ school** *n.* Kindergarten, *der*; **~suit** *n.* Spielanzug, *der*; **~thing** *n.* (*lit. or fig.*) Spielzeug, *das*; **~things** Spielzeug, *das*; Spielsachen *Pl.*; **~time** *n.* Zeit zum Spielen; **during ~time** (*Sch.*) in der [großen] Pause; **~wright** /'pleɪraɪt/ *n.* ▶ 1261 Dramatiker, *der*/Dramatikerin, *die*; Stückeschreiber, *der*/-schreiberin, *die*

**plaza** /'plɑːzə/ *n.* Piazza, *die*

**PLC, plc** *abbr.* (*Brit.*) **public limited company** ≈ GmbH

**plea** /pliː/ *n.* (A) (*appeal, entreaty*) Appell, *der* (**for** zu); **make a ~ for sth.** zu etw. aufrufen; (B) (*pleading*) Begründung, *die*; (*excuse*) Entschuldigung, *die*; **excuse oneself on the ~ of sth.** sich mit etw. entschuldigen; (C) (*Law*) Verteidigungsrede, *die*; **special ~:** besondere Einrede; **~ bargaining** *Praktik, bei der Verteidigung und Anklage übereinkommen, dass der Angeklagte ein [Teil]geständnis ablegt und dafür bestimmte Zusicherungen (milderes Strafmaß o. Ä.) erhält*

**plead** /pliːd/ **1** *v.i.*, **~ed** *or* (*esp. Amer., Scot., dial.*) **pled** /pled/ (A) (*make appeal*) inständig bitten (**for** um); (*imploringly*) flehen (**for** um); **~ with sb. for sth./to do sth.** jmdn. inständig um etw. bitten/jmdn. inständig [darum] bitten, etw. zu tun; (*imploringly*) jmdn. um etw. anflehen/jmdn. anflehen, etw. zu tun; (B) (*Law: put forward plea; also fig.*) plädieren; **I'd get a lawyer to ~ for me** ich würde mich von einem Anwalt vertreten lassen; (C) (*Law*) **how do you ~?** bekennen Sie sich schuldig?

**2** *v.t.*, **~ed** *or* (*esp. Amer., Scot., dial.*) **pled** (A) (*beg*) inständig bitten; (*imploringly*) flehen; (B) (*Law: offer in mitigation*) sich berufen auf (+ *Akk.*); geltend machen; (*as excuse*) sich entschuldigen mit; **he ~ed insanity** er plädierte auf Unzurechnungsfähigkeit; **~ guilty/not guilty** (*lit. or fig.*) sich schuldig/nicht schuldig bekennen; **~ guilty to [having committed] the crime** sich des Verbrechens schuldig bekennen; (C) (*present in court*) **~ sb.'s case** *or* **~ the case for sb.** jmds. Sache vor Gericht vertreten

**pleading** /'pliːdɪŋ/ **1** *adj.* flehend. **2** *n.* (A) Bitten, *das*; (*imploring*) Flehen, *das*; (B) *usu. in pl.* (*Law*) Plädoyer, *das*; Vortrag, *der*; (*written*) Schriftsatz, *der*; ⇒ *also* **special pleading**

**pleadingly** /'pliːdɪŋlɪ/ *adv.* flehentlich

**pleasant** /'plezənt/ *adj.*, **~er** /'plezəntə(r)/, **~est** /'plezəntɪst/ (*agreeable*) angenehm; schön ‹Tag, Zeit›; nett ‹Gesicht, Lächeln›; **be ~ with** *or* **to sb.** nett zu jmdm. sein

**pleasantly** /'plezəntlɪ/ *adv.* angenehm; schön ‹singen›; freundlich ‹sprechen, lächeln usw.›

**pleasantry** /'plezəntrɪ/ *n.* (A) (*agreeable remark*) Nettigkeit, *die*; (*humorous remark*) Scherz, *der*; (B) (*jocularity*) Humor, *der*

**please** /pliːz/ **1** *v.t.* (A) (*give pleasure to*) gefallen (+ *Dat.*); Freude machen (+ *Dat.*); **there's no pleasing her** man kann ihr nichts *od.* es ihr nicht recht machen; **she's easy to ~** *or* **easily ~d/hard to ~:** sie ist leicht/nicht leicht zufrieden zu stellen; **[just] to ~ you** [nur] dir zu Gefallen; **one can't ~ everybody** man kann es nicht allen recht machen; **~ the eye** das Auge erfreuen; **~ oneself** tun, was man will; **~ yourself** ganz wie du willst; (B) (*[may it] be the will of*) gefallen; **~ God** das gebe Gott; so Gott will; **may it ~ your Honour** (*to a judge*) mit Ihrer Erlaubnis, Hohes Gericht.

**2** *v.i.* (A) (*think fit*) **what he ~s** was ihm gefällt; was er will; **they come and go as they ~:** sie kommen und gehen, wie es ihnen gefällt; **do as one ~s** tun, was man will; **take as much as you ~:** nimm, so viel[, wie] du willst *od.* möchtest; (B) (*give pleasure*) gefallen; **anxious** *or* **eager to ~:** bemüht, gefällig zu sein; **the poem is sure to ~:** das Gedicht kommt garantiert gut an (*ugs.*) *od.* wird bestimmt gefallen; (C) *in requests* bitte; **may I have the bill, ~?** kann ich bitte zahlen?; **~ do!** aber bitte *od.* gern!; **~ don't** bitte nicht; (D) **if you ~:** bitte schön; (*iron.: believe it or not*) stell dir vor

**pleased** /pliːzd/ *adj.* (*satisfied*) zufrieden (**by** mit); (*glad, happy*) erfreut (**by** über + *Akk.*); **he'll be ~ when he sees that** (*iron.*) er wird seine Freude haben, wenn er das sieht; **be ~ at** *or* **about sth.** sich über etw. (*Akk.*) freuen; **be ~ with sth./sb.** mit etw./jmdm. zufrieden sein; **~ with oneself** mit sich selbst zufrieden; **don't look so ~ with yourself** guck nicht so selbstzufrieden *od.* selbstgefällig (*ugs.*); **be ~ to do sth.** sich freuen, etw. zu tun; (*formal/iron.: with condescension*) belieben, etw. zu tun (*geh./iron.*); **I am [only too] ~ to be of assistance** es ist mir [wirklich] eine Freude, Ihnen zu helfen; **I shall be ~ to [come]** [ich komme] gerne; ⇒ *also* **meet¹** 1 C

**pleasing** /ˈpli:zɪŋ/ *adj.* gefällig; ansprechend; nett ‹Person, Ausblick›; **it is ~ to see how well ...:** es ist eine Freude zu sehen, wie gut ...; **be ~ to the eye/ear** *etc.* das Auge/Ohr *usw.* erfreuen

**pleasurable** /ˈpleʒərəbl/ *adj.*, **pleasurably** /ˈpleʒərəblɪ/ *adv.* angenehm

**pleasure** /ˈpleʒə(r)/ ❶ *n.* Ⓐ (*feeling of joy*) Freude, *die;* (*usu. derog.: sensuous enjoyment*) Vergnügen, *das;* **sth. gives sb. ~:** etw. macht jmdm. Freude; **for ~:** zum Vergnügen; **it's no ~ to do sth.** es macht keinen Spaß, etw. zu tun; **get a lot of ~ from** *or* **out of sb./sth.** viel Freude *od.* Spaß an jmdm./etw. haben; Ⓑ (*gratification*) **have the ~ of doing sth.** das Vergnügen haben, etw. zu tun; **it's a ~ to talk to him** es ist ein Vergnügen, mit ihm zu reden; **may I have the ~ [of the next dance]?** darf ich [Sie um den nächsten Tanz] bitten?; **do me the ~ of dining with me** machen Sie mir das Vergnügen *od.* die Freude, mit mir zu speisen; **he had the ~ of knowing that he was always welcome** er war in der glücklichen Lage zu wissen, dass er immer willkommen war; **I don't think I've had the ~:** wir kennen uns noch nicht; **take [a] ~ in** Vergnügen finden *od.* Spaß haben an (+ *Dat.*); **he takes ~ in teasing me** es macht ihm Spaß *od.* bereitet ihm Vergnügen, mich zu necken; **my ~, it's a ~:** gern geschehen; es war mir ein Vergnügen; **the ~ is all mine** das Vergnügen ist ganz meinerseits *od.* auf meiner Seite; **it gives me great ~ to inform you that ..., I have much ~ in informing you that ...** (*formal*) ich freue mich, Ihnen mitteilen zu können, dass ...; **Mrs P. requests the ~ of your company** (*formal*) Frau P. gibt sich (*Dat.*) die Ehre, Sie einzuladen; **Mr F. has great ~ in accepting the invitation** (*formal*) Herr F. nimmt die Einladung mit dem größten Vergnügen an; **with ~:** mit Vergnügen; gern[e]; **with the greatest of ~:** mit dem größten Vergnügen; Ⓒ (*will, desire*) **what is your ~?** (*formal*) Sie wünschen?; **at ~:** nach Wunsch *od.* Belieben; **come and go at one's ~:** kommen und gehen, wie es einem beliebt (*geh.*) *od.* wann immer man will; **consult sb.'s ~** (*formal*) fragen, was jmdm. genehm ist (*geh.*); **we await your ~** (*formal*) wir warten auf Ihren Bescheid; **be detained during Her Majesty's ~:** eine Haftstrafe auf unbestimmte Zeit verbüßen.

❷ *v.t.* (*give ~ to*) erfreuen; (*sexually*) beglücken (*scherzh.*)

**pleasure: ~ boat** *n.* Vergnügungsboot, *das;* **~ craft** *n., pl. same* Vergnügungsboot, *das;* **~ cruise** *n.* Vergnügungsfahrt, *die;* **~ ground** *n.* Vergnügungspark, *der;* **~-loving** *adj.* lebenslustig; (*~-seeking*) vergnügungssüchtig; **~ principle** *n.* (*Psych.*) Lustprinzip, *das;* **~-seeking** ❶ *adj.* vergnügungssüchtig; ❷ *n.* Vergnügungssucht, *die*

**pleat** /pli:t/ ❶ *n.* Falte, *die;* **inverted ~:** Kellerfalte, *die;* ⇒ *also* **box-pleat**; **knife pleat**. ❷ *v.t.* in Falten legen; fälteln

**pleated** /ˈpli:tɪd/ *adj.* gefältelt; Falten‹rock›

**pleb** /pleb/ *n.* (*coll.*) Prolet, *der* (*ugs.*)

**plebby** /ˈplebɪ/ *adj.* (*coll.*) primitiv (*abwertend*)

**plebeian** /plɪˈbi:ən/ ❶ *adj.* Ⓐ proletarisch; Ⓑ (*coarse*) plebejisch; gewöhnlich. ❷ *n.* Ⓐ (*in ancient Rome*) Plebejer, *der*/Plebejerin, *die;* Ⓑ (*commoner*) Bürgerliche, *der/die;* **the ~s** das [einfache] Volk

**plebiscite** /ˈplebɪsɪt, ˈplebɪsaɪt/ *n.* Plebiszit, *das*

**plectrum** /ˈplektrəm/ *n., pl.* **plectra** /ˈplektrə/ *or* **~s** (*Mus.*) Plektrum, *das*

**pled** ⇒ **plead**

**pledge** /pledʒ/ ❶ *n.* Ⓐ (*promise, vow*) Versprechen, *das;* Gelöbnis, *das* (*geh.*); **under the ~ of secrecy** unter dem Siegel der Geheimhaltung; **take** *or* **sign the ~:** sich zur Abstinenz verpflichten; dem Alkohol abschwören; Ⓑ (*as security*) Pfand, *das;* Sicherheit, *die;* Ⓒ (*token*) [Unter]pfand, *das* (*geh.*); Ⓓ (*state of being ~d*) Verpfändung, *die;* **put sth. in ~:** etw. verpfänden; **take sth. out of ~:** etw. auslösen.

❷ *v.t.* Ⓐ (*promise solemnly*) versprechen; geloben ‹Treue›; **~ one's word/honour** sein Wort/seine Ehre verpfänden (*geh.*); **~ one's service[s]** seine Dienste zusichern; Ⓑ (*bind by promise*) verpflichten; Ⓒ (*deposit, pawn*) verpfänden (**to** *Dat.*); Ⓓ (*drink to health of*) einen Trinkspruch *od.* Toast ausbringen auf (+ *Akk.*); **they ~d each other** sie tranken auf ihr gegenseitiges Wohl

**Pleiades** /ˈplaɪədi:z/ *n. pl.* (*Astron.*) Plejaden *Pl.*

**plein air** /plenˈeə(r)/ *adj.* (*Art*) Pleinair-

**Pleistocene** /ˈplaɪstəsi:n/ (*Geol.*) ❶ *adj.* pleistozän; Pleistozän-. ❷ *n.* Pleistozän, *das*

**plenary** /ˈpli:nərɪ/ *adj.* Ⓐ (*entire, absolute*) uneingeschränkt; **~ powers** uneingeschränkte Vollmacht; Ⓑ (*of all members*) Plenar‹sitzung›; Voll‹versammlung›

**plenipotentiary** /plenɪpəˈtenʃərɪ/ ❶ *adj.* Ⓐ (*invested with full power*) [general]bevollmächtigt ‹Gesandte›; absolut ‹Herrscher›; allmächtig ‹Parlament›; Ⓑ (*absolute*) uneingeschränkt. ❷ *n.* [General]bevollmächtigte, *der*

**plenitude** /ˈplenɪtju:d/ *n., no pl.* (*abundance*) Fülle, *die* (**of** von)

**plenteous** /ˈplentɪəs/ *adj.* (*rhet.*) reichlich; reich ‹Ernte›

**plentiful** /ˈplentɪfl/ *adj.* Ⓐ (*abundant, copious*) reichlich; häufig ‹Element, Rohstoff›; **be ~** *or* **in ~ supply** reichlich vorhanden sein; **there was a ~ supply of food** es gab reichlich zu essen; Ⓑ (*yielding abundance*) fruchtbar ‹Land›; ertragreich ‹Jahr›

**plentifully** /ˈplentɪfəlɪ/ *adv.* reichlich

**plenty** /ˈplentɪ/ ❶ *n., no pl.* **~ of** viel; eine Menge; (*coll.: enough*) genug; **have you all got ~ of meat?** habt ihr alle reichlich Fleisch?; **take ~ of exercise** sich viel bewegen; **time[s] of ~:** Zeit[en] des Überflusses; **that's ~** (*coll.*) das ist genug *od.* reichlich; das reicht; **take ~!** nimm dir reichlich *od.* (*ugs.*) ordentlich!; **we gave him ~ of warning** wir haben ihn früh genug gewarnt; ⇒ *also* **horn** 1 F. ❷ *adj.* (*coll.*) reichlich vorhanden. ❸ *adv.* (*coll.*) **it's ~ large enough** es ist groß genug; **there's ~ more where this/those** *etc.* **came from** es ist noch genug da (*ugs.*)

**pleonasm** /ˈpli:ənæzm/ *n.* (*Ling.*) Pleonasmus, *der*

**pleonastic** /pli:əˈnæstɪk/ *adj.* (*Ling.*) pleonastisch

**plethora** /ˈpleθərə/ *n.* Ⓐ (*fig.: excess*) Unmenge, *die* (**of** von); Ⓑ (*Med.*) Plethora, *die* (*fachspr.*); Blutandrang, *der*

**plethoric** /plɪˈθɒrɪk/ *adj.* (*Med.*) vollblütig; plethorisch (*fachspr.*)

**pleura** /ˈplʊərə/ *n., pl.* **~e** /ˈplʊəri:/ (*Anat.*) Pleura, *die* (*fachspr.*); Brustfell, *das*

**pleural** /ˈplʊərl/ *adj.* (*Anat.*) pleural; **~ cavity** Brusthöhle, *die;* **~ inflammation** Brustfellentzündung, *die*

**pleurisy** /ˈplʊərɪsɪ/ *n.* ▶ **1232** (*Med.*) Pleuritis, *die* (*fachspr.*); Brustfellentzündung, *die*

**Plexiglas** (*Amer.* ®), **plexiglass** /ˈpleksɪglɑ:s/ *n.* (*Amer.*) Plexiglas, *das* Ⓦⓩ

**plexus** /ˈpleksəs/ *n.* (*Anat.*) Plexus, *der;* ⇒ *also* **solar plexus**

**pliability** /plaɪəˈbɪlɪtɪ/ *n., no pl.* Biegsamkeit, *die;* (*of leather etc.*) Geschmeidigkeit, *die;* (*fig.: of person, disposition*) Fügsamkeit, *die;* Nachgiebigkeit, *die*

**pliable** /ˈplaɪəbl/ *adj.* (*flexible, yielding*) biegsam; geschmeidig ‹Ton, Leder›; (*fig.*) nachgiebig ‹Charakter›; **be ~ to sb.'s wishes** jmds. Wünschen nachgeben

**pliant** /ˈplaɪənt/ *adj.* biegsam ‹Ast, Körper›; geschmeidig ‹Körper›; (*fig.*) formbar

**pliers** /ˈplaɪəz/ *n. pl.* **[pair of] ~:** Zange, *die*

**plight¹** /plaɪt/ *n.* Notlage, *die;* **hopeless/miserable ~:** trostloser/jämmerlicher Zustand; **what a ~ to find yourself in!** was für eine verzweifelte Lage!

**plight²** *v.t., esp. in p.p.* (*arch.*) geloben (*geh.*) ‹Treue›; schwören ‹Eid›; **~ one's word [that ...]** sein Wort [dafür] verpfänden[, dass ...]; ⇒ *also* **troth** B

**plimsoll** /ˈplɪmsl/ *n.* (*Brit.*) Turnschuh, *der*

**Plimsoll: ~ line, ~ mark** *ns.* (*Naut.*) Freibordmarke, *die;* Plimsollmarke, *die*

**plinth** /plɪnθ/ *n.* Ⓐ (*for vase, statue, etc.; of wall*) Sockel, *der;* Ⓑ (*of column*) Plinthe, *die* (*fachspr.*)

**Pliocene** /ˈplaɪəsi:n/ (*Geol.*) ❶ *adj.* pliozän; Pliozän-. ❷ *n.* Pliozän, *das*

**PLO** *abbr.* **Palestine Liberation Organization** PLO, *die*

**plod** /plɒd/ ❶ *v.i.*, **-dd-** trotten; **~ along** dahintrotten; **~ [on] through the snow** [weiter] durch den Schnee stapfen; **~ through a book/one's work** (*fig.*) sich durch ein Buch kämpfen/sich mit seiner Arbeit abplagen. ❷ *v.t.*, **-dd-** entlangtrotten; **~ one's way home** nach Hause trotten. ❸ *n.* (*laborious walk*) Stapfen, *das;* (*laborious work*) Plackerei, *die* (*ugs.*)

**~ aˈway** *v.i.* (*fig.*) sich abmühen; **~ away at sth.** sich mit etw. abmühen

**~ ˈon** *v.i.* (*fig.*) sich weiterkämpfen; **~ on with sth.** sich weiter durch etw. kämpfen

**plodder** /ˈplɒdə(r)/ *n.* (*worker*) Arbeitstier, *das;* (*walker*) Fußlahme, *der/die* (*ugs.*); **he is a ~:** er arbeitet schwerfällig/hat einen schwerfälligen Gang; (*Sch.*) er ist ein bisschen langsam

**plonk¹** /plɒŋk/ *v.t.* (*coll.*) **~ sth. [down]** etw. hinknallen (*ugs.*) *od.* hinwerfen; **~ sth. down in a corner** etw. in eine Ecke knallen (*ugs.*); **~ oneself [down] in an armchair** sich in einen Sessel knallen *od.* hauen (*ugs.*)

**plonk²** *n.* (*coll.: wine*) [billiger] Wein

**plop** /plɒp/ ❶ *v.i.*, **-pp-** plumpsen (*ugs.*); ‹Regen:› klatschen, platschen. ❷ *v.t.*, **-pp-** plumpsen lassen (*ugs.*). ❸ *n.* Plumpsen, *das;* **with a ~:** mit einem Plumps. ❹ *adv.* plumps

**plosive** /ˈpləʊsɪv/ (*Ling.*) ❶ *adj.* plosiv; Verschluss-. ❷ *n.* Plosiv, *der;* Verschlusslaut, *der*

**plot** /plɒt/ ❶ *n.* Ⓐ (*conspiracy*) Komplott, *das;* Verschwörung, *die;* Ⓑ (*of play, film, novel*) Handlung, *die;* Fabel, *die;* Plot, *der* (*Literaturw.*); Ⓒ (*of ground*) Stück Land; **vegetable ~:** Gemüsebeet, *das;* **building ~:** Baugrundstück, *das;* Bauplatz, *der;* Ⓓ (*curve etc.*) Diagramm, *das;* Ⓔ (*Amer.: ground plan*) Plan, *der.*

❷ *v.t.*, **-tt-** Ⓐ (*plan secretly*) [heimlich] planen; **~ treason** auf Verrat sinnen (*geh.*); **~ to do sth.** [heimlich] planen, etw. zu tun; Ⓑ (*make plan or map of*) kartieren, kartographieren ‹Gebiet usw.›; einen Plan zeichnen (+ *Gen.*) ‹Gebäude usw.›; (*make by ~ing*) zeichnen ‹Karte, Plan›; (*fig.*) entwerfen ‹Roman›; Ⓒ (*mark on map, diagram*) **~ [down]** eintragen; einzeichnen.

❸ *v.i.*, **-tt-: ~ against sb.** sich gegen jmdn. verschwören; ein Komplott gegen jmdn. schmieden

**plotter** /ˈplɒtə(r)/ *n.* Ⓐ (*conspirator*) Verschwörer, *der*/Verschwörerin, *die;* Ⓑ (*instrument*) Plotter, *der;* Planzeichner, *der*

**plough** /plaʊ/ ❶ *n.* (*Agric.*) Pflug, *der;* **put one's hand to the ~** (*fig.*) eine Sache in Angriff nehmen; **the P~** (*Astron.*) der Große Wagen *od.* Bär. ❷ *v.t.* Ⓐ pflügen; **~ the sand[s]** (*fig.*) Wasser mit einem Sieb schöpfen; Ⓑ (*cut furrows in*) zerpflügen; Ⓒ **~ furrows** Furchen ziehen *od.* pflügen; **~ a lonely furrow** (*fig.*) allein auf weiter Flur sein *od.* stehen (*geh.*); Ⓓ (*fig.*) ‹Schiff:› [durch]pflügen ‹Wasserfläche›; Ⓔ (*Brit. coll.: reject in examination*) durchrasseln lassen (*salopp*). ❸ *v.i.* (*Brit. coll.: fail in examination*) durchrasseln (*salopp*)

**~ ˈback** *v.t.* Ⓐ unterpflügen; Ⓑ (*Finance*) reinvestieren; **~ profits** *etc.* **back into the business** *etc.* Gewinne *usw.* wieder in die Firma *usw.* stecken

**~ ˈin** *v.t.* unterpflügen

**~ into** *v.t.* (*move violently*) rasen *od.* (*salopp*) rasseln in (+ *Akk.*)

P

~ **through** *v.t.* (*advance laboriously in*) sich kämpfen durch; ‹Schiff:› sich pflügen durch; (*move violently through*) rasen durch

~ **'up** *v.t.* auspflügen ‹Kartoffeln, Rüben usw.›; zerpflügen ‹Boden›

**plough:** ~**man** /'plaʊmən/ *n.*, *pl.* ~**men** /'plaʊmən/ Pflüger, *der;* ~**man's [lunch]** (*Brit.*) *Imbiss aus Käse, Brot und Mixedpickles;* ~**share** *n.* Pflugschar, *die*

**plover** /'plʌvə(r)/ *n.* (*Ornith.*) Regenpfeifer, *der*

**plow** (*Amer./arch.*) ⇒ **plough** 1, 2 A, B, C, D

**ploy** /plɔɪ/ *n.* Trick, *der;* (*tactical approach*) Taktik, *die;* (*gambit*) Manöver, *das;* (*method*) Masche, *die* (*ugs.*)

**PLR** *abbr.* (*Brit.*) **Public Lending Right**

**pluck** /plʌk/ ❶ *v.t.* Ⓐ (*pull off, pick*) pflücken ‹Blumen, Obst›; ~ **[out]** auszupfen ‹Federn, Haare›; Ⓑ (*pull at, twitch*) zupfen an (+ *Dat.*); zupfen ‹Saite, Gitarre›; **he** ~**ed his mother's skirt** er zupfte seine Mutter am Rock; Ⓒ (*strip of feathers*) rupfen. ❷ *v.i.* ~ **at sth.** an etw. (*Dat.*) zupfen; **he** ~**ed at his mother's skirt** er zupfte seine Mutter am Rock. ❸ *n.* Ⓐ (*courage*) Mut, *der;* Schneid, *der* (*ugs.*); Ⓑ (*heart, liver, lungs of animal as food*) Innereien *Pl.*

~ **'up** *v.t.* ~ **up [one's] courage** all seinen Mut zusammennehmen; ~ **up courage to do sth.** den Mut finden, etw. zu tun; **he** ~**ed up [enough] courage to ask her out** er fasste sich (*Dat.*) ein Herz und bat sie, mit ihm auszugehen

**pluckily** /'plʌkɪlɪ/ *adv.*, **plucky** /'plʌkɪ/ *adj.* tapfer

**plug** /plʌg/ ❶ *n.* Ⓐ (*filling hole*) Pfropfen, *der;* (*in cask*) Spund, *der;* Zapfen, *der;* (*stopper for basin, vessel, etc.*) Stöpsel, *der;* (*of wax etc.*) Pfropf, *der;* Ⓑ (*Electr.*) Stecker, *der;* (*coll.: socket*) Stecker, *der* (*ugs.*); **pull the** ~ **on sb./sth.** (*coll.*) jmdn./einer Sache den Hahn zudrehen (*ugs.*); ⇒ *also* **sparking plug**; Ⓒ (*coll.: of water closet*) Stöpsel, *der;* **pull the** ~: [ab]ziehen; Ⓓ (*of tobacco*) Plug, *der* (*fachspr.*); (*piece of chewing tobacco*) Priem, *der;* Ⓔ (*coll.: piece of good publicity*) **give sth. a** ~: Werbung für etw. machen; **give sb. a** ~: jmdm. [etwas] Publicity verschaffen.

❷ *v.t.*, **-gg-** Ⓐ ~ **[up]** zustopfen, verstopfen ‹Loch usw.›; Ⓑ (*coll.: advertise*) Schleichwerbung machen für; (*by presenting sth. repeatedly*) pushen (*ugs.*)

~ **a'way** *v.i.* (*coll.*) vor sich hin schuften (*ugs.*); ~ **away at sth.** sich mit etw. abschuften (*ugs.*)

~ **'in** *v.t.* anschließen; **is it** ~**ged in?** ist der Stecker in der Steckdose *od.* (*ugs.*) drin?; ⇒ *also* **plug-in**

**plug:** ~ **hat** *n.* (*Amer. coll.*) Angströhre, *die* (*ugs. scherzh.*); ~**hole** *n.* Abfluss, *der;* **go down the** ~**hole** (*fig. coll.*) im Eimer sein (*salopp*); ~**-in** *adj.* anschließbar

**plum** /plʌm/ *n.* Ⓐ (*tree*) Pflaumenbaum, *der;* Pflaume, *die;* (*fruit*) Pflaume, *die;* **speak with a** ~ **in one's mouth** (*Brit. coll.*) affektiert sprechen; Ⓑ (*fig.*) Leckerbissen, *der;* **a** ~ **job/position** ein Traumjob (*ugs.*); **his job is a real** ~: sein Job ist einfach traumhaft; Ⓒ (*colour*) Pflaumenblau, *das*

**plumage** /'plu:mɪdʒ/ *n.* Gefieder, *das*

**plumb¹** /plʌm/ ❶ *v.t.* (*sound, measure*) [aus]loten; (*fig.*) ergründen ‹Geheimnis›; ~ **the depths of loneliness/sorrow** die tiefsten Tiefen der Einsamkeit/Trauer erleben. ❷ *adv.* Ⓐ (*vertically*) senkrecht; lotrecht; Ⓑ (*fig.: exactly*) genau; Ⓒ (*Amer. coll.: utterly*) total (*ugs.*); **you get** ~ **out of here!** raus hier, aber 'n bisschen plötzlich! (*ugs.*). ❸ *adj.* Ⓐ (*vertical*) senkrecht; lotrecht; Ⓑ (*fig.: downright, sheer*) völlig; absolut. ❹ *n.* Lot, *das;* Senkblei, *das;* **off** *or* **out of** ~: außer *od.* nicht im Lot

**plumb²** *v.t.* ~ **in** (*connect*) fest anschließen

**plumbago** /plʌm'beɪgəʊ/ *n.*, *pl.* ~**s** Ⓐ (*Min.*) Graphit, *der;* Ⓑ (*Bot.*) Bleiwurz, *die*

**plumber** /'plʌmə(r)/ *n.* Klempner, *der;* Installateur, *der*

**plumbing** /'plʌmɪŋ/ *n.* Ⓐ (*plumber's work*) Klempnerarbeiten *Pl.;* Installationsarbeiten *Pl.;* Ⓑ (*water pipes*) Wasserrohre *Pl.;* Wasserleitungen *Pl.;* **a cottage without** ~: ein Häuschen ohne Wasseranschluss; Ⓒ (*coll.: lavatory*) Klo, *das* (*ugs.*); **go and inspect the** ~: die Örtlichkeit aufsuchen

**'plumb line** *n.* Ⓐ (*for measuring*) Lot, *das;* Ⓑ (*fig.*) Maßstab, *der*

**'plum cake** *n.* Rosinenkuchen, *der*

**plume** /plu:m/ ❶ *n.* Ⓐ (*feather*) Feder, *die;* (*ornamental bunch*) Federbusch, *der;* ~ **of white feathers** weißer Federbusch; **borrowed** ~**s** (*fig.*) fremde Federn; Ⓑ ~ **of smoke/steam/snow** Rauchwolke *od.* -fahne/Dampfwolke/Schneefahne, *die.* ❷ *v.t.* Ⓐ (*furnish, decorate with* ~*s*) mit Federn schmücken; befiedern ‹Pfeil›; Ⓑ ~ **oneself on sth.** sich mit etw. brüsten; Ⓒ (*preen etc.*) ‹Vogel:› ordnen ‹Federn›; **the swan** ~**d itself** der Schwan ordnete sein Gefieder

**plummet** /'plʌmɪt/ ❶ *v.i.* stürzen. ❷ *n.* Ⓐ (*weight*) Lotblei, *das;* (*plumb line*) Lot, *das;* Ⓑ (*sounding lead*) Lot, *das;* Senkblei, *das;* Ⓒ (*Angling*) Bleigewicht, *das;* Blei, *das*

**plummy** /'plʌmɪ/ *adj.* Ⓐ (*coll.*) sonor ‹Stimme›; (*derog.: affected*) affektiert; Ⓑ (*coll.: desirable, good*) bombig (*ugs.*); Bomben‹stelle, -job› (*ugs.*)

**plump¹** /plʌmp/ *adj.* mollig; rundlich; stämmig ‹Arme, Beine›; fleischig ‹Brathuhn usw.›; ~ **cheeks** Pausbacken *Pl.* (*fam.*); runde *od.* volle Backen

~ **'out** ❶ *v.i.* sich runden; rund werden. ❷ *v.t.* runden; rund werden lassen

~ **'up** ❶ *v.t.* aufschütteln ‹Kissen›; (*fatten up*) mästen. ❷ *v.i.* Fett ansetzen

**plump²** ❶ *v.t.* ~ **sb./oneself/sth. down** jmdn./sich/etw. fallen lassen; **he** ~**ed the cases in the hall** er setzte die Koffer schwungvoll in der Halle ab. ❷ *v.i.* Ⓐ (*drop*) fallen; Ⓑ (*Amer.: move abruptly*) stürmen; stürzen

~ **for** *v.t.* Ⓐ (*Brit.: vote for*) stimmen für; Ⓑ (*choose*) sich entscheiden für

**plumpness** /'plʌmpnɪs/ *n.*, *no pl.* ⇒ **plump¹**: Molligkeit, *die;* Rundlichkeit, *die;* Stämmigkeit, *die;* Fleischigkeit, *die*

**plum:** ~ **'pudding** *n.* Plumpudding, *der;* (*suet pudding*) *mit Nierenfett zubereiteter Pudding mit Rosinen;* ≈ Rosinenpudding, *der;* ~ **tree** *n.* Pflaumenbaum, *der*

**plunder** /'plʌndə(r)/ ❶ *v.t.* [aus]plündern ‹Gebäude, Gebiet›; ausplündern ‹Person›; rauben ‹Sache›; **the church was** ~**ed of its holy relics** die heiligen Reliquien wurden aus der Kirche geraubt. ❷ *n.* Ⓐ (*action*) Plünderung, *die;* (*spoil, booty*) Beute, *die;* Ⓑ (*coll.: profit*) Profit, *der*

**plunderer** /'plʌndərə(r)/ *n.* Plünd[e]rer, *der*

**plunge** /plʌndʒ/ ❶ *v.t.* Ⓐ (*thrust violently*) stecken; (*into liquid*) tauchen; ~ **a knife into sb.'s back** jmdm. ein Messer in den Rücken stoßen; Ⓑ (*fig.*) ~**d in thought** in Gedanken versunken; **be** ~**d into sth.** in etw. (*Akk.*) gestürzt werden; ~ **oneself into sth.** sich in etw. (*Akk.*) stürzen; **be** ~**d into darkness** in Dunkelheit getaucht sein (*geh.*). ❷ *v.i.* Ⓐ ~ **into sth.** (*lit. or fig.*) in etw. (*Akk.*) stürzen; **he** ~**d into the crowd** er tauchte in die Menge ein; ~ **in** sich hineinstürzen; **they** ~**d into a political discussion** sie stürzten sich in eine politische Diskussion; Ⓑ (*descend suddenly*) ‹Straße usw.:› steil abfallen; **plunging neckline** tiefer Ausschnitt; [tiefes] Dekolleté; ~ **down the stairs** die Treppe hinunterstürzen; Ⓒ (*enter impetuously*) stürzen; Ⓓ (*start violently forward*) ‹Pferd:› durchgehen; (*pitch*) ‹Schiff:› eintauchen; Ⓔ (*coll.: gamble*) spielen. ❸ *n.* Sprung, *der;* **take the** ~ (*fig. coll.*) den Sprung wagen; **they have decided to take the** ~ **and do it** sie haben sich dazu durchgerungen, es zu tun

**plunger** /'plʌndʒə(r)/ *n.* Ⓐ (*part of mechanism*) [Tauch]kolben, *der;* Plunger[kolben], *der;* Ⓑ (*rubber suction cup*) Stampfer, *der*

**plunk** /plʌŋk/ ⇒ **plonk¹**

**pluperfect** /plu:'pɜ:fɪkt/ (*Ling.*) ❶ *n.* Plusquamperfekt, *das.* ❷ *adj.* ~ **tense** Plusquamperfekt, *das*

**plural** /'plʊərl/ (*Ling.*) ❶ *adj.* pluralisch; Plural-; ~ **noun** Substantiv im Plural; ~ **form** Pluralform, *die;* **third person** ~: dritte Person Plural. ❷ *n.* Mehrzahl, *die;* Plural, *der*

**pluralise** ⇒ **pluralize**

**pluralism** /'plʊərəlɪzm/ *n.* Ⓐ (*holding of more than one office*) Ämterhäufung, *die;* Ⓑ (*Polit., Sociol.*) Pluralismus, *der*

**pluralist** /'plʊərəlɪst/ *n.* Ⓐ (*holder of more than one office*) Inhaber mehrerer [Kirchen]ämter; Ⓑ (*Polit., Sociol.*) Pluralist, *der*

**pluralistic** /plʊərə'lɪstɪk/ *adj.* pluralistisch

**plurality** /plʊə'rælɪtɪ/ *n.* Ⓐ (*being plural*) Pluralität, *die;* Ⓑ (*large number*) Vielzahl, *die;* Ⓒ (*majority*) Majorität, *die;* Mehrheit, *die;* ~ **of sth.** Mehrheit einer Sache (*Gen.*); Ⓓ (*Amer. Polit.*) [Stimmen]vorsprung, *der* (**over** vor + *Dat.*)

**pluralize** /'plʊərəlaɪz/ *v.t.* pluralisieren (*Sprachw.*); in den Plural setzen

**plural:** ~ **'number** ⇒ **plural** 2; ~ **so'ciety** *n.* plurale Gesellschaft; ~ **'vote** *n.* Mehrstimmenrecht, *das;* ~ **'voting** *n.* Pluralwahlrecht, *das*

**plus** /plʌs/ ❶ *prep.* Ⓐ (*with the addition of*) plus (+ *Dat.*); (*and also*) und [zusätzlich]; Ⓑ (*above zero*) plus; ~ **ten degrees** plus zehn Grad; zehn Grad plus; Ⓒ (*coll.*); **he returned from America** ~ **a wife and child** er kam aus Amerika zurück — mit Frau und Kind; **a** ~ **one** *etc.* **player** (*Golf*) ein Spieler mit einer Vorgabe von eins *usw.* ❷ *adj.* Ⓐ (*additional, extra*) zusätzlich; Ⓑ (*at least*) **fifteen** *etc.* ~: über fünfzehn *usw.;* **alpha** *etc.* ~: Eins *usw.* plus; Ⓒ (*Math.: positive*) positiv ‹Wert, Menge, Größe›; Ⓓ (*Electr.*) ~ **pole/terminal** Pluspol, *der.* ❸ *n.* Ⓐ (*symbol*) Plus[zeichen], *das;* Ⓑ (*additional quantity*) Plus, *das;* Ⓒ (*advantage*) Pluspunkt, *der.* ❹ *conj.* (*coll.*) und außerdem

**plus-'fours** *n. pl.* Überfallhose, *die*

**plush** /plʌʃ/ ❶ *n.* Plüsch, *der.* ❷ *adj.* Ⓐ (*made of plush*) Plüsch-; plüschen; Ⓑ (*covered in plush*) mit Plüsch bezogen; Ⓒ (*coll.: luxurious*) feudal (*ugs.*)

**plushy** /'plʌʃɪ/ *adj.* Ⓐ (*of, like plush*) plüschig; Ⓑ ⇒ **plush** 2 C

**Pluto** /'plu:təʊ/ *pr. n.* Ⓐ (*Astron.*) Pluto, *der;* Ⓑ (*Roman Mythol.*) Pluto (*der*)

**plutocracy** /plu:'tɒkrəsɪ/ *n.* Ⓐ (*rule by the rich; state*) Plutokratie, *die;* Ⓑ (*rich ruling class*) Plutokraten *Pl.*

**plutocrat** /'plu:təkræt/ *n.* Plutokrat, *der*

**plutocratic** /plu:tə'krætɪk/ *adj.* plutokratisch

**plutonic** /plu:'tɒnɪk/ *adj.* (*Geol.*) plutonisch; ~ **theory** Plutonismus, *der*

**plutonium** /plu:'təʊnɪəm/ *n.* (*Chem.*) Plutonium, *das*

**pluvial** /'plu:vɪəl/ *adj.* Regen-

**ply¹** /plaɪ/ ❶ *v.t.* Ⓐ (*use, wield*) gebrauchen; führen; **they plied their oars** sie legten sich in die Ruder; Ⓑ (*work at*) nachgehen (+ *Dat.*) ‹Handwerk, Arbeit›; Ⓒ (*sell*) verkaufen; Ⓓ (*supply*) ~ **sb. with sth.** jmdn. mit etw. versorgen; Ⓔ (*assail*) überhäufen; ~ **sb. with questions** jmdn. mit Fragen überschütten; Ⓕ (*sail over*) befahren. ❷ *v.i.* Ⓐ (*go to and fro*) ~ **between** zwischen ‹Orten› [hin- und her]pendeln; (*operate on regular services*) zwischen ‹Orten› verkehren; Ⓑ (*attend regularly for custom*) seine Dienste anbieten; ~ **for customers** auf Kunden *od.* Kundschaft warten; **a taxi** ~**ing for hire** ein auf Kundschaft wartendes Taxi

**ply²** *n.* Ⓐ (*of yarn, wool, etc.*) [Einzel]faden, *der;* (*of rope, cord, etc.*) Strang, *der;* (*of plywood, cloth, etc.*) Lage, *die;* Schicht, *die;* ⇒ *also* **three-ply; two-ply;** Ⓑ ⇒ **plywood**

**'plywood** *n.* Sperrholz, *das*

**PM** *abbr.* Ⓐ **postmortem;** Ⓑ **Prime Minister**

**p.m.** /pi:'em/ ▶ **1012** ❶ *adv.* nachmittags; **one** ~: ein Uhr mittags; **two/five** ~: zwei/fünf Uhr nachmittags; **six/eleven** ~: sechs/

elf Uhr abends. ❷ *n.* Nachmittag, *der;* **Monday/this ~:** Montag/heute Nachmittag

**PMT** *abbr.* **premenstrual tension**

**pneumatic** /njuːˈmætɪk/ *adj.* pneumatisch; mit Druckluft betrieben *od.* arbeitend ‹Maschine›; Druckluft‹werkzeug, -hammer›

**pneumatically** /njuːˈmætɪkəlɪ/ *adv.* pneumatisch; mit Druckluft *nachgestellt*

**pneumatic: ~ ˈblonde** *n.* (*joc.*) üppige Blondine; **~ ˈdrill** *n.* Pressluftbohrer, *der;* **~ ˈtyre** *n.* Luftreifen, *der;* Pneumatik, *der*

**pneumoconiosis** /njuːməʊkɒnɪˈəʊsɪs/ *n., no pl.* **▶ 1232** (*Med.*) Pneumokoniose, *die* (*fachspr.*); Staublunge, *die*

**pneumonia** /njuːˈməʊnɪə/ *n.* **▶ 1232** Lungenentzündung, *die;* Pneumonie, *die* (*Med.*); **double/single ~:** doppelseitige/einseitige Lungenentzündung

**PO** *abbr.* **A** **postal order** PA; **B** **Post Office** PA; **C** (*Brit. Navy*) **Petty Officer;** **D** (*Brit. Air Force*) **Pilot Officer** LT

**po** /pəʊ/ *n., pl.* **pos** (*coll.*) [Nacht]topf, *der;* Pott, *der* (*ugs., bes. nordd.*)

**poach¹** /pəʊtʃ/ ❶ *v.t.* **A** (*catch illegally*) wildern; illegal fangen ‹Fische›; **~ pupils away from other teachers** anderen Lehrern die Schüler abspenstig machen; **B** (*obtain unfairly*) stehlen, (*ugs.*) klauen ‹Idee›; sich (*Dat.*) erschleichen ‹Vorteil›. ❷ *v.i.* **A** (*catch animals illegally*) wildern; **B** (*encroach*) **~ [on sb.'s territory]** jmdm. ins Handwerk pfuschen; (*Sport*) dazwischengehen

**poach²** *v.t.* (*Cookery*) pochieren ‹Ei›; dünsten, pochieren ‹Fisch, Fleisch, Gemüse›; **~ed eggs** pochierte *od.* verlorene Eier

**poacher¹** /ˈpəʊtʃə(r)/ *n.* Wilderer, *der;* Wilddieb, *der;* **the ~ turns gamekeeper** aus einem Saulus wird ein Paulus

**poacher²** *n.* (*Cookery*) Dünster, *der;* **[egg] ~:** Eierkocher für pochierte Eier

**PO box** ⇒ **post office box**

**pochard** /ˈpəʊtʃəd/ *n.* (*Ornith.*) Tafelente, *die*

**pock** /pɒk/ *n.* Pickel, *der;* Pustel, *die* (*Med.*); (*of smallpox*) Pocke, *die*

**pocked** /pɒkt/ *adj.* durchlöchert (**with** von)

**pocket** /ˈpɒkɪt/ ❶ *n.* **A** Tasche, *die;* (*in suitcase etc.*) Seitentasche, *die;* (*in handbag*) [Seiten]fach, *das;* (*on rucksack etc.*) [Außen]tasche, *die;* (*Billiards etc.*) Loch, *das;* Tasche, *die;* **be in sb.'s ~** (*fig.*) von jmdm. abhängig sein; **the business is virtually in his ~:** in der Firma ist er praktisch der Boss (*ugs.*); **have [got] sb. in one's ~:** jmdn. in der Tasche haben (*ugs.*); **make a hole in sb.'s ~** (*fig.*) ein Loch in jmds. Geldbeutel (*Akk.*) reißen; **B** (*fig.: financial resources*) **with an empty ~, with empty ~s** mit leeren Taschen; **pay for sth. out of one's own ~:** etw. aus eigener *od.* der eigenen Tasche bezahlen; **it is beyond my ~:** es übersteigt meine finanziellen Möglichkeiten; **put one's hand in one's ~:** in die Tasche greifen (*ugs.*); **be in ~:** Geld verdient haben; **be £100 in ~:** 100 Pfund gutgemacht haben; **be out of ~** (*have lost money*) draufgelegt haben (*ugs.*); zugesetzt haben; **I don't want you to be out of ~ because of me** ich möchte nicht, dass du meinetwegen drauflegst (*ugs.*) *od.* zusetzt; ⇒ *also* **out-of-pocket**; **C** (*Mil.*) (*area*) Kessel, *der;* **enemy ~:** [versprengte] feindliche Einheit; **~ of resistance** Widerstandsnest, *das;* **D** (*isolated group*) ≈ Schwerpunkt, *der;* **~ of unemployment** schwerpunktmäßiges Auftreten von Arbeitslosigkeit; **E** (*Mining, Geol.*) Nest, *das.* ⇒ *also* **line²**.
❷ *adj.* Taschen‹rechner, -uhr, -ausgabe›.
❸ *v.t.* **A** (*put in one's pocket*) einstecken; **B** (*steal*) in die eigene Tasche stecken (*ugs.*); **C** (*fig.: submit to*) wegstecken; einstecken; **D** (*fig.: conceal*) verbergen, hinunterschlucken (*ugs.*) ‹Zorn, Gefühlsregung›; **E** (*Billiards etc.*) einlochen

**ˈpocketbook** *n.* **A** (*wallet*) Brieftasche, *die;* **B** (*notebook*) Notizbuch, *das;* **C** (*Amer.: paperback*) Taschenbuch, *das;* **in ~:** als Taschenbuch; **D** (*Amer.: handbag*) Handtasche, *die*

**pocketful** /ˈpɒkɪtfʊl/ *n.* **a ~ of loose change** eine Tasche voll Kleingeld

**pocket: ~ ˈhandkerchief** *n.* **A** Taschentuch, *das;* **B** (*fig.: very small area*) **a ~ handkerchief of a garden** ein winziger Garten; **~ knife** *n.* Taschenmesser, *das;* **~ money** *n.* Taschengeld, *das;* **~-size[d]** *adj.* **A** im Taschenformat *nachgestellt;* **~-sized edition** Taschenausgabe, *die;* **B** (*fig.: small scale*) Westentaschen- (*ugs. scherzh.*); im [Westen]taschenformat *nachgestellt* (*ugs. scherzh.*); **~ ˈveto** *n.* (*Amer. Polit.*) *durch Nichtunterzeichnung einer Gesetzesvorlage ausgeübtes Veto*

**pock: ~mark** *n.* **A** (*Med.*) Pockennarbe, *die;* **B** Delle, *die;* (*from bullet*) Einschuss, *der;* **~marked** *adj.* **A** pockennarbig ‹Gesicht, Haut›; **B** **a wall ~marked with bullets** eine mit Einschüssen übersäte Wand

**pod** /pɒd/ ❶ *n.* **A** (*seed case*) Hülse, *die;* (*of pea*) Schote, *die;* Hülse, *die;* **B** (*in aircraft etc.*) (*for engine*) Gondel, *die;* (*for fuel*) Außentank, *der;* (*for missile etc.*) Behälter, *der;* Pod, *der;* (*radome*) Radom, *das.* ❷ *v.t.*, **-dd-** aus- *od.* enthülsen. ❸ *v.i.*, **-dd-** (*form pods*) [Früchte] ansetzen; (*bear pods*) [Früchte] tragen

**podge** /pɒdʒ/ *n.* (*coll.*) Pummel, *der* (*ugs.*)

**podgy** /ˈpɒdʒɪ/ *adj.* dicklich; pummelig (*ugs.*), rundlich (*fam.*), mollig ‹Frau›; pausbäckig, (*fam.*) rundlich ‹Gesicht›; **~ cheek** Pausbacke, *die* (*fam.*); **~ fingers** Wurstfinger (*ugs.*)

**podium** /ˈpəʊdɪəm/ *n., pl.* **podia** /ˈpəʊdɪə/ *or* **-s** Podium, *das*

**podzol** /ˈpɒdzɒl/ *n.* (*Soil Sci.*) Podsol, *der*

**poem** /ˈpəʊɪm/ *n.* Gedicht, *das;* **symphonic ~** (*Mus.*) sinfonische Dichtung

**poesy** /ˈpəʊɪsɪ, ˈpəʊɪzɪ/ *n.* (*arch./poet.*) (*poetry*) Poesie, *die;* (*art*) Dichtkunst, *die;* (*poems collectively*) Dichtung, *die*

**poet** /ˈpəʊɪt/ *n.* **▶ 1261** (*writer of poems*) Dichter, *der;* Poet, *der* (*geh.*); (*sb. with great creativity*) Künstler, *der;* **P~s' Corner** die Dichterecke *od.* der Dichterwinkel (*in der Westminsterabtei*); ⇒ *also* **laureate**

**poetaster** /pəʊɪˈtæstə(r)/ *n.* (*dated derog.*) Dichterling, *der* (*abwertend*); Poetaster, *der* (*geh. abwertend*)

**poetess** /ˈpəʊɪtes/ *n.* **▶ 1261** Dichterin, *die;* Poetin, *die* (*geh.*)

**poetic** /pəʊˈetɪk/ *adj.* dichterisch; poetisch (*geh.*); anmutig ‹Bewegung›; ‹Bild, Anblick› voller Poesie; **in ~ form** in Versen; ⇒ *also* **justice** A; **licence** 1 D

**poetical** /pəʊˈetɪkl/ *adj.* **A** ⇒ **poetic**; **B** (*written in verse*) in Gedichtform *nachgestellt;* **~ drama** Versdrama, *das;* **his ~ works** seine Gedichte

**poetically** /pəʊˈetɪkəlɪ/ *adv.* dichterisch; poetisch (*geh.*)

**poetry** /ˈpəʊɪtrɪ/ *n.* [Vers]dichtung, *die;* Lyrik, *die;* (*fig.*) Poesie, *die* (*geh.*); **prose ~:** Prosadichtung, *die;* **~ reading** ≈ Dichterlesung, *die*

**ˈpo-faced** /ˈpəʊfeɪst/ *adj.* mit unbewegter Miene *nachgestellt;* (*smug, priggish*) blasiert (*abwertend*); (*narrow-minded*) borniert; **sound ~:** abweisend klingen

**pogo** /ˈpəʊgəʊ/ *n., pl.* **~s: ~ [stick]** Springstab, *der*

**pogrom** /ˈpɒgrəm/ *n.* Pogrom, *das od. der*

**poignancy** /ˈpɔɪnjənsɪ/ *n., no pl.* [schmerzliche] Intensität; (*of words, wit, etc.*) Schärfe, *die*

**poignant** /ˈpɔɪnjənt/ *adj.* tief ‹Bedauern, Trauer, Schmerz, Verzweiflung›; überwältigend ‹Schönheit›; quälend ‹Hunger›; (*causing sympathy*) ergreifend, herzzerreißend ‹Anblick, Geschichte›

**poignantly** /ˈpɔɪnjəntlɪ/ *adv.* (*touchingly*) ergreifend; in bewegenden Worten ‹sprechen, schreiben›; (*regretfully*) wehmütig; (*pungently*) beißend

**poinsettia** /pɔɪnˈsetɪə/ *n.* (*Bot.*) Weihnachtsstern, *der*

**point** /pɔɪnt/ ❶ *n.* **A** (*tiny mark, dot*) Punkt, *der;* **nought ~ two** null Komma zwei; ⇒ *also* **decimal point**; **full point**; **B** (*sharp end of tool, weapon, pencil, etc.*) Spitze, *die;* **come to a [sharp] ~:** spitz zulaufen; **at gun~/knife~:** mit vorgehaltener [Schuss]waffe/vorgehaltenem Messer; **hold sb. at gun~/knife~:** jmdn. mit vorgehaltener Pistole/vorgehaltenem Messer bedrohen; **not to put too fine a ~ on it** (*fig.*) um nichts zu beschönigen; **C** (*single item*) Punkt, *der;* **the ~ under dispute** der strittige Punkt; die strittige Frage; **~ of conscience** Gewissensfrage, *die;* **agree on a ~:** in einem Punkt *od.* einer Frage übereinstimmen; **Are you an experienced cook? — No, in ~ of fact I've never cooked a meal before** Sind Sie ein erfahrener Koch? — Nein, ganz im Gegenteil. Ich habe [bisher] noch nie gekocht; **You haven't met him, have you? — Yes, in ~ of fact, I have** Du kennst ihn nicht, oder? — Doch, wir kennen uns; **be a ~ of honour with sb.** für jmdn. [eine] Ehrensache sein; **possession is nine ~s of the law** das Gesetz ist meistens auf der Seite des Besitzers; ⇒ *also* **law** A; **order** 1 J; **stretch** 1 D; **D** (*unit of scoring*) Punkt, *der;* **win by 100 ~s** mit 100 Punkten Vorsprung gewinnen; **give ~s to sb.** jmdm. eine Vorgabe geben; **score ~s off sb.** (*fig.*) jmdn. an die Wand spielen; **win on ~s** (*Boxing; also fig.*) nach Punkten gewinnen; **a win on ~s** ein Sieg nach Punkten; ein Punktsieg; **E** (*stage, degree*) **things have reached a ~ where** *or* **come to such a ~ that …:** die Sache ist dahin *od.* so weit gediehen, dass …; (*negatively*) es ist so weit gekommen, dass …; **the shares reached their highest ~:** die Aktien erreichten ihren höchsten Stand *od.* Höchststand; **up to a ~:** bis zu einem gewissen Grad; **beyond a certain ~:** über einen bestimmten Punkt hinaus; **he gave up at this ~:** an diesem Punkt gab er auf; **she was abrupt to the ~ of rudeness** sie war in einer Weise barsch, die schon an Unverschämtheit grenzte; ⇒ *also* **boiling point**; **freezing point**; **melting point**; **F** (*moment*) Zeitpunkt, *der;* **when it comes/came to the ~:** wenn es so weit ist/als es so weit war; wenn es ernst wird/als es ernst wurde; **be at/on the ~ of sth.** kurz vor etw. (*Dat.*) sein; einer Sache (*Dat.*) nahe sein; **be at the ~ of death** im Sterben liegen; **be on the ~ of doing sth.** im Begriff sein, etw. zu tun; etw. gerade tun wollen; **G** (*distinctive trait*) Seite, *die;* (*feature in animal*) [Rassen]merkmal, *das;* **best/strong ~:** starke Seite; Stärke, *die;* **good/bad ~:** gute/schlechte Seite; **getting up early has its ~s** frühes Aufstehen hat auch seine Vorzüge; **the ~** (*essential thing*) das Entscheidende; **the ~ is, what am I to do if I can't get a job?** fragt sich nur: was mache ich, wenn ich keinen Job finde?; (*thing to be discussed*) **that is just the ~** *or* **the whole ~:** das ist genau der springende Punkt; **come to** *or* **get to the ~:** zur Sache *od.* zum Thema kommen; **keep** *or* **stick to the ~:** beim Thema bleiben; **keep sb. to the ~:** verhindern, dass jmd. [vom Thema] abschweift; **be beside the ~:** unerheblich sein; keine Rolle spielen; **that's beside the ~:** darum geht es nicht; **~ taken** habe verstanden; **carry** *or* **make one's ~:** sich durchsetzen; sein Ziel erreichen; **right, I agree with you, you've made your ~:** also gut, ich gebe dir Recht, ich habe verstanden; **in ~:** relevant (*geh.*); **not in ~:** irrelevant (*geh.*); **a case in ~:** ein typisches Beispiel; **that's not in ~:** das gehört nicht zur Sache *od.* hierher; **make a ~ of doing sth.** [großen] Wert darauf legen, etw. zu tun; **… and I shall make a ~ of telling him so …** und ich werde ihm das jetzt auch mal sagen; **make a ~ of it** Wert darauf legen; **make** *or* **prove a ~:** etw. beweisen; **make** *or* **prove a ~ against sth.** ein Argument gegen etw. anführen *od.* (*geh.*) ins Feld führen; **be always making** *or* **proving a ~ of some kind** ständig etwas beweisen wollen; **to the ~:** sachbezogen; **more to the ~:** wichtiger; **a topic that is not strictly to the ~:** ein Punkt, der nicht direkt zum Thema gehört; **he was very brief and to the ~:** seine Ausführungen waren sehr knapp und sachbezogen; **you have a ~ there** da hast du Recht; da ist [et]was dran (*ugs.*); ⇒ *also* **take** 1 T; **H** (*tip*) Spitze, *die;* (*Boxing*) Kinnspitze, *die;* Kinn, *das;* (*Ballet*) Spitze, *die;* *in pl.* (*of horse, dog, etc.*) (*extremities*) Extremitäten

p

*Pl.;* (*area of contrasting colour in an animal's fur*) Abzeichen *Pl.;* **the ~ of his jaw** seine Kinnspitze; **the ~s of his ears** seine Ohrläppchen; **dance on the ~s of one's toes** auf den Zehen- *od.* Fußspitzen tanzen; **on ~, on one's ~s, on the ~s** (*Ballet*) auf Spitzen; **a ~ [of land]** eine Landspitze *od.* -zunge; **I** (*of story, joke, remark*) Pointe, *die;* (*pungency, effect*) (*of literary work*) Eindringlichkeit, *die;* (*of remark*) Durchschlagskraft, *die;* Überzeugungskraft, *die;* **see** *or* **get/miss the ~:** die Pointe verstehen/nicht verstehen; **miss the ~ of a joke** die Pointe eines Witzes nicht verstehen *od.* (*ugs.*) mitkriegen; **J** (*purpose, value*) Zweck, *der;* Sinn, *der;* **what's the ~ of worrying?** was für einen Sinn *od.* Zweck hat es, sich (*Dat.*) Sorgen zu machen?; wozu sich (*Dat.*) Sorgen machen? (*ugs.*); **there's no ~ in protesting** es hat keinen Sinn *od.* Zweck zu protestieren; es ist sinnlos *od.* zwecklos zu protestieren; **K** (*precise place, spot*) Punkt, *der;* Stelle, *die;* (*Geom.*) Punkt, *der;* **fire broke out at several ~s** an mehreren Punkten *od.* Stellen brach Feuer aus; **Bombay and ~s east** Bombay und Orte östlich davon; **~ of contact** Berührungspunkt, *der;* **~ of no return** Punkt, an dem es kein Zurück mehr gibt; **~ of view** (*fig.*) Standpunkt, *der;* **from my/a money/an atheistic ~ of view** (*fig.*) aus meiner/finanzieller/atheistischer Sicht; von meinem/von einem finanziellen/atheistischen Standpunkt aus; ⇒ *also* **departure** D; **L** (*Brit.*) **[power** *or* **electric] ~:** Steckdose, *die;* **M** (*Brit. Railw.*) *usu in pl.* Weiche, *die;* **N** (*sharp-pointed tool*) spitzes Werkzeug; (*in engraving, etching, etc.*) Grabstichel, *der;* (*in masonry*) Grabmeißel, *der;* Punktiereisen, *das;* **O** (*of deer*) Ende, *das* (*Jägerspr.*); Sprosse, *die* (*Jägerspr.*); **P** *usu in pl.* (*Motor Veh.: contact device*) Kontakt, *der;* **contact breaker ~:** Unterbrecherkontakt, *der;* **Q** (*unit in Bridge, competition, rationing, stocks, shares, etc.*) Punkt, *der;* (*unit of weight for precious stones*) ein Hundertstel Karat; 0,01 Karat; **prices/the cost of living went up three ~s** die Preise/Lebenshaltungskosten sind um drei [Prozent]punkte gestiegen; **R** (*on compass*) Strich, *der;* ⇒ *also* **cardinal points; S** (*Printing*) Punkt, *der;* **eight-~:** Achtpunkt, *der;* **T** (*Cricket*) *Feldspieler, der einige Meter seitlich vom Torwächter steht;* (*Lacrosse*) *dem Torwart am nächsten stehender Verteidiger.*

❷ *v.i.* **A** zeigen, weisen, ‹Person auch:› deuten (**to, at** auf + *Akk.*); **it's rude to ~:** es gehört sich nicht, mit dem Finger auf jemanden zu zeigen; **she ~ed through the window** sie zeigte aus dem Fenster; **the compass needle ~ed to the north** die Kompassnadel zeigte *od.* wies nach Norden; **B ~ towards** *or* **to** (*fig.*) [hin]deuten *od.* hinweisen auf (+ *Akk.*).

❸ *v.t.* **A** (*direct*) richten ‹Waffe, Kamera› (**at** auf + *Akk.*); **~ one's finger at sth./sb.** mit dem Finger auf etw./jmdn. deuten *od.* zeigen *od.* weisen; **~ me in the right direction** zeige mir den richtigen Weg; **B** (*Building*) aus-, verfugen ‹Mauer, Steine›; ausfüllen ‹Fugen›; **C** (*give force to*) Nachdruck verleihen (+ *Dat.*), unterstreichen ‹Bemerkung›; würzen ‹Erzählung, Rede›; verstärken ‹Gefühl›; **D** (*sharpen*) [an]spitzen ‹Bleistift›; **E** (*show presence of*) ‹Hund:› vorstehen (*Jägerspr.*); **F** (*punctuate*) mit Satzzeichen versehen; mit Deklamationszeichen versehen ‹Psalm usw.›; (*in Hebrew etc.*) mit diakritischen Zeichen versehen

**~ 'out** *v.t.* hinweisen auf (+ *Akk.*); **~ sth./sb. out to sb.** jmdn. auf etw./jmdn. hinweisen *od.* aufmerksam machen; **I ~ed him out to the others** ich zeigte ihn den anderen; **he ~ed out the house** er zeigte das Haus; **he ~ed out my mistake** er zeigte meinen Fehler auf

**~ 'up** *v.t.* (*emphasize*) herausstellen; (*make clear*) verdeutlichen

**point-'blank** ❶ *adj.* (*direct, flat*) direkt; (*fig.*) direkt ‹Frage, Art›; glatt ‹Weigerung›; **~ shot** Schuss aus kürzester Entfernung; Kern- *od.* Fleckschuss, *der* (*Jägerspr.*); **~ distance** *or* **range** kürzeste Entfernung; Kernschussweite, *die* (*Jägerspr.*); **give a ~ denial** alles leugnen. ❷ *adv.* **A** (*at very close range*) aus kürzester Entfernung ‹schießen›; **B** (*in direct line*) direkt; (*fig.: directly*) rundheraus, (*ugs.*) geradeheraus ‹fragen, sagen›; **tell sb. ~ that ...:** jmdm. direkt ins Gesicht *od.* unverblümt *od.* (*ugs.*) geradeheraus sagen, dass ...

**'point-by-point** *adj.* Punkt für Punkt *nachgestellt*

**'point duty** *n.* (*Brit.*) *Einsatz zur Verkehrsregelung;* **policeman on ~:** Verkehrspolizist, *der*

**pointed** /ˈpɔɪntɪd/ *adj.* **A** spitz; **~ arch** Spitzbogen, *der;* **B** (*fig.: sharply expressed*) unmissverständlich; deutlich; **C** (*emphasized*) ostentativ (*geh.*); betont ‹Interesse, Aufmerksamkeit›

**pointedly** /ˈpɔɪntɪdlɪ/ *adv.* (*explicitly, significantly*) demonstrativ; ostentativ (*geh.*)

**pointer** /ˈpɔɪntə(r)/ *n.* **A** (*indicator*) Zeiger, *der;* (*rod*) Zeigestock, *der;* **B ~ [dog]** Pointer, *der;* englischer Vorstehhund; **C** (*coll.*) (*hint*) Fingerzeig, *der;* Tipp, *der* (*ugs.*); (*indication*) Hinweis, *der* (**to** auf + *Akk.*); **D** *in pl.* (*Astron.*) (*in Great Bear*) *die vorderen Kastensterne (des Großen Wagens); (in Southern Cross) die beiden die Längsachse des Kreuzes markierenden Sterne (im Kreuz des Südens)*

**pointillism** /ˈpwæntɪlɪzm/ *n.* (*Art*) Pointillismus, *der*

**pointing** /ˈpɔɪntɪŋ/ *n.* (*of brickwork*) Fugung, *die;* (*action*) Ausfugen, *das;* Verfugen, *das;* (*material*) [Fugen]mörtel, *der*

**pointless** /ˈpɔɪntlɪs/ *adj.* (*without purpose or meaning, useless*) sinnlos; (*without force, meaningless*) belanglos ‹Bemerkung, Geschichte›

**pointlessly** /ˈpɔɪntlɪslɪ/ *adv.* sinnlos; unnötig ‹sich Sorgen machen›; unmotiviert ‹lachen›; ohne Zweck und Ziel ‹herumlungern›

**point-to-'point [race]** *n.* (*Horseracing*) Kirchturmrennen, *das*

**poise** /pɔɪz/ ❶ *n.* **A** (*composure*) Haltung, *die;* (*self-confidence*) Selbstsicherheit, *die;* Selbstvertrauen, *das;* **have ~:** beherrscht sein/selbstsicher sein; **keep one's ~:** Haltung/Selbstsicherheit behalten; **lose one's ~:** die Haltung *od.* Beherrschung *od.* Fassung/sein Selbstvertrauen verlieren; **B** (*good carriage*) Haltung, *die;* (*of body*) Körperhaltung, *die.*

❷ *v.t.* **A** *in p.p.* (*in readiness*) **sit ~d on the edge of one's chair** auf der Stuhlkante balancieren; **be ~d for action** einsatzbereit sein; **hang ~d** ‹Vogel, Insekt:› schweben; ⇒ *also* **poised; B** (*balance*) balancieren; **C** (*hold suspended, carry in a particular way*) **~ the spear ready to hurl it** den Speer wurfbereit in der Hand halten; **~ oneself on one's toes** auf den Zehen stehen

**poised** /pɔɪzd/ *adj.* selbstsicher; ⇒ *also* **poise** 2 A

**poison** /ˈpɔɪzn/ ❶ *n.* (*harmful substance; lit. or fig.*) Gift, *das;* **slow ~:** langsam wirkendes Gift; **hate sb./sth. like ~:** jmdn./etw. wie die Pest hassen; **what's your ~?** (*coll.*) was trinkst du?

❷ *v.t.* **A** vergiften; (*cause disease in*) infizieren; (*contaminate*) verseuchen ‹Boden, Luft, Wasser›; verpesten (*abwertend*) ‹Luft›; (*smear with poison*) vergiften ‹Pfeil›; **die of ~ing** an einer Vergiftung sterben; **~ed hand** infizierte Hand; **~ed arrow** Giftpfeil, *der;* **B** (*fig.*) (*corrupt*) vergiften ‹Gedanken, Seele›; (*injure, destroy*) zerstören, ruinieren ‹Ehe, Leben›; vergällen ‹Freude›; verderben ‹Speisen, Feldfrüchte usw.›; **~ sb.'s mind** jmdn. verderben *od.* (*geh.*) korrumpieren; **she ~ed his mind** *or* **caused his thoughts to be ~ed against me** sie hat ihn gegen mich aufgebracht

**poisoner** /ˈpɔɪzənə(r)/ *n.* Giftmörder, *der*/Giftmörderin, *die*

**poison 'gas** *n.* Giftgas, *das*

**poisoning** /ˈpɔɪzənɪŋ/ *n.* Vergiftung, *die;* (*contamination*) Verseuchung, *die*

**poison 'ivy** *n.* Giftefeu, *der;* Kletternder Giftsumach (*Bot.*)

**poisonous** /ˈpɔɪzənəs/ *adj.* **A** giftig; tödlich ‹Dosis›; **~ snake/mushroom/substance** Giftschlange, *die*/-pilz, *der*/-stoff, *der;* **B** (*fig.*) verderblich ‹Lehre, Wirkung›; giftig ‹Blick, Zunge›

**poke**[1] /pəʊk/ *n.* (*dial.: bag*) Beutel, *der;* Sack, *der;* ⇒ *also* **pig** 1 A

**poke**[2] ❶ *v.t.* **A ~ sth. [with sth.]** [mit etw.] gegen etw. stoßen; **she ~d the hedgehog to see if it was dead** sie stieß den Igel an, um zu sehen, ob er tot war; **~ sth. into sth.** etw. in etw. (*Akk.*) stoßen; **~ one's finger up one's nose** den Finger in die Nase stecken; **~ the fire** das Feuer schüren; **he accidentally ~d me in the eye** er stieß mir versehentlich ins Auge; **~ sb. in the ribs** jmdm. einen Rippenstoß geben *od.* versetzen; ⇒ *also* **fun** 1; **B** (*thrust forward*) stecken ‹Kopf›; **~ one's head in through the window** den Kopf zum Fenster hin-/hereinstecken; **~ one's head round the corner/door** um die Ecke gucken (*ugs.*)/den Kopf in die Türöffnung stecken; **~ one's head in** reingucken (*ugs.*); **~ one's finger at sb.** mit dem Finger nach jmdm. stoßen; **C** (*pierce*) bohren; **D** (*coarse: have sexual intercourse with*) stoßen (*derb*).

❷ *v.i.* **A** (*in pond, at food, among rubbish*) [herum]stochern (**at, in, among** in + *Dat.*); **~ at sth. with a stick** *etc.* mit einem Stock *usw.* nach etw. stoßen; **B** (*thrust itself*) sich schieben; **his elbows were poking through the sleeves** seine Ärmel hatten Löcher, aus denen die Ellbogen hervorguckten; **C** (*pry*) schnüffeln (*ugs. abwertend*); **~ into things that don't concern one** seine Nase in Dinge stecken, die einen nichts angehen (*ugs.*).

❸ *n.* **A** (*thrust*) Stoß, *der;* **give sb. a ~ [in the ribs]** jmdm. einen [Rippen]stoß versetzen *od.* geben; **give sb. a ~ in the eye** jmdn. ins Auge stoßen; **give the fire a ~:** das Feuer [an]schüren; **better than a ~ in the eye [with a pointed stick]** (*coll.*) besser als gar nichts *od.* (*derb*) als in die hohle Hand geschissen; **B have a ~ around a shop** *etc.* in einem Laden *usw.* herumstöbern; **have a ~ around in sb.'s writing desk** in jmds. Schreibtisch herumstöbern *od.* -wühlen; **C** (*coarse: sexual intercourse*) Fick, *der* (*vulg.*); **have a ~:** stoßen (*derb*)

**~ a'bout, ~ a'round** *v.i.* **A** herumschnüffeln (*ugs. abwertend*); **B** (*rummage*) herumsuchen (*ugs.*); herumkramen (*ugs.*); **~ about in sth. for sth.** etw. nach etw. durchwühlen

**~ 'out** ❶ *v.t.* rausstrecken; **you nearly ~d my eye out** du hast mir fast das Auge ausgestochen; **~ the dirt out of sth.** den Schmutz aus etw. kratzen; **~ one's head out** rausgucken (*ugs.*). ❷ *v.i.* rausgucken (*ugs.*)

**'poke bonnet** *n.* Schutenhut, *der*

**poker**[1] /ˈpəʊkə(r)/ *n.* (*for fire*) Schürstange, *die;* Schüreisen, *das;* **as stiff as a ~:** stocksteif (*ugs.*)

**poker**[2] *n.* (*Cards*) Poker, *das od. der;* **have a game of ~:** eine Runde pokern

**poker: ~ dice** *n. pl. Würfel mit Spielkartensymbolen;* ≈ Skatwürfel; **~ face** *n.* Pokerface, *das;* Pokergesicht, *das;* **~-faced** *adj.* mit unbewegter Miene *nachgestellt;* **remain ~-faced** keine Miene verziehen

**poky** /ˈpəʊkɪ/ *adj.* winzig; **~ little** winzig klein; **it's so ~ in here** es ist so eng hier drinnen

**Poland** /ˈpəʊlənd/ *pr. n.* Polen (*das*)

**polar** /ˈpəʊlə(r)/ *adj.* **A** (*of pole*) polar ‹Kaltluft, Kälte, Fauna, Klima, Gewässer›; Polar‹eis, -gebiet, -luft, -meer, -nacht, -fuchs, -hase›; **B** (*Magn.*) polar; **C** (*fig.: central*) zentral; **D** (*directly opposite*) [diametral] entgegengesetzt; polar (*geh.*); äußerst ‹Extrem›; grundlegend ‹Unterschied›

**polar: ~ bear** *n.* Eisbär, *der;* **~ 'cap** *n.* (*Geog.*) Polkappe, *die;* **~ 'circles** *n. pl.* (*Geog.*) Polarkreise; **~ 'front** *n.* (*Meteorol.*) Polarfront, *die*

**Polaris** /pəˈlɑːrɪs/ *pr. n.* **A** (*missile*) Polaris, *die;* **B** (*Astron.*) Polaris (*die*)

**polarisation, polarise** ⇒ **polariz-**

**polarity** /pəˈlærɪtɪ/ *n.* **A** (*Magn.*) Polung, *die;* Polarität, *die;* **B** (*direction of axis; having two poles*) Polarität, *die;* **C** (*fig.: contrary* *qualities*) Gegensatz, *der;* Polarität, *die* (*geh.*); **D** (*Electr.*) Polung, *die;* **change of ~:** Polwechsel, *der*

**polarization** /pəʊləraɪˈzeɪʃn/ *n.* (*Phys.*) Polarisation, *die;* (*fig.*) Polarisierung, *die;* Polarisation, *die*

**polarize** /ˈpəʊləraɪz/ ❶ *v.t.* **A** (*Phys.*) polarisieren; **B** (*fig.: divide*) spalten; polarisieren (*geh.*); **~ political life** eine Polarisierung des politischen Lebens bewirken. ❷ *v.i.* sich [auf]spalten; sich polarisieren (*geh.*)

**Polaroid** ® /ˈpəʊlərɔɪd/ *n.* **A** (*material*) Polaroidfolie, *die* Wz; **B ~s** (*sunglasses*) Polaroidbrille, *die* Wz; **C ~ [camera]** Polaroidkamera, *die* Wz

**polar ˈstar** ⇒ **pole star**

**polder** /ˈpəʊldə(r)/ *n.* Polder, *der*

**pole**[1] *n.* **A** (*support*) Stange, *die;* (*for ~ vaulter*) Stab, *der;* (*for large tent, house in lake*) Pfahl, *der;* **be up the ~** (*Brit. coll.*) (*in difficulty*) in der Klemme sitzen (*ugs.*); (*crazy*) nicht ganz dicht sein (*ugs. abwertend*); **drive sb. up the ~** (*Brit. coll.*) jmdn. zum Wahnsinn treiben (*ugs.*); **climb the greasy ~** (*fig.*) sich hocharbeiten; **B** (*for propelling boat*) Stake, *die* (*nordd.*); **C** (*of horse-drawn vehicle*) Deichsel, *die;* **~s** [Gabel]deichsel, *die;* **D** (*measure*) Rute, *die*

**pole**[2] *n.* **A** (*Astron., Geog., Magn., Electr., Geom., Biol.*) Pol, *der;* **positive/negative ~:** positiver/negativer Pol; Plus-/Minuspol, *der;* **they are ~s apart** (*coll.*) zwischen ihnen liegen Welten; ⇒ *also* **magnetic pole**; **North Pole**; **South Pole**; **B** (*fig.*) Pol, *der;* **be at opposite ~s** sich (*Dat.*) als Pol und Gegenpol gegenüberstehen; einander entgegengesetzte Pole bilden

**Pole** /pəʊl/ *n.* ▶ 1340 Pole, *der*/Polin, *die*

**pole-axed** /ˈpəʊlækst/ *adj.* **as if ~:** wie vor den Kopf geschlagen

**ˈpolecat** *n.* (*Zool.*) **A** (*Brit.*) Iltis, *der;* **B** (*Amer.*) ⇒ **skunk** A

**polemic** /pəˈlemɪk/ ❶ *adj.* polemisch. ❷ *n.* **A** (*discussion*) Polemik, *die;* (*written also*) Streitschrift, *die;* **B** *in pl.* (*practice*) Polemik, *die*

**polemical** /pəˈlemɪkl/ *adj.*, **polemically** /pəˈlemɪkəlɪ/ *adv.* polemisch

**pole: ~ position** *n.* (*Motor racing*) Poleposition, *die;* **~ star** *n.* (*Astron.*) Polarstern, *der;* **~ vault** *n.* Stabhochsprung, *der;* **~ vaulter** *n.* Stabhochspringer, *der*/-springerin, *die;* **~-vaulting** *n.* Stabhochsprung, *der;* Stabhochspringen, *das*

**police** /pəˈliːs/ ❶ *n. pl.* **A** Polizei, *die;* **be in the ~:** bei der Polizei sein; **river ~:** Wasserschutzpolizei, *die; attrib.* Polizei‹wagen, -hund, -schutz, -eskorte, -staat›; **B** (*members*) Polizisten *Pl.;* Polizeibeamte *Pl.; attrib.* Polizei-; **whole squads of ~:** ein gewaltiges Polizeiaufgebot; **the ~ are on his trail** die Polizei ist ihm auf der Spur; **extra ~ were called in** zusätzliche Polizeikräfte wurden hinzugezogen; **help the ~ with their enquiries** von der Polizei vernommen werden.
❷ *v.t.* **A** [polizeilich] überwachen ‹Gebiet, Verkehr, Fußballspiel›; kontrollieren ‹Gebiet, Grenze, Gewässer›; **B** (*fig.: check on*) überwachen; kontrollieren; **C** (*provide with ~*) Polizeibeamte einsetzen in (+ *Dat.*) ‹Gebiet, Stadt usw.›; **the inadequate policing of the district** die unzureichende Polizeipräsenz in dem Bezirk

**police: ~ constable** *n.* ▶ 1261 Polizist, *der*/Polizistin, *die;* (*rank*) Polizeihauptwachtmeister, *der;* **~ force** *n.* Polizeitruppe, *die;* **the ~ force** die Polizei; **~man** /pəˈliːsmən/ *n., pl.* **-men** /pəˈliːsmən/ ▶ 1261 Polizist, *der;* Polizeibeamte, *der;* ⇒ *also* **sleeping policeman**; **~ notice** *n.* polizeilicher Hinweis; **'P~ Notice: No Parking'** „Parken polizeilich verboten"; **~ officer** *n.* ▶ 1261 Polizeibeamte, *der*/-beamtin, *die;* **~ record** ⇒ **record** 3 E; **~ state** *n.* Polizeistaat, *der;* **~ station** *n.* Polizeiwache, *die;* Polizeirevier, *das;* **~woman** *n.* ▶ 1261 Polizistin, *die;* Polizeibeamtin, *die*

**policy**[1] /ˈpɒlɪsɪ/ *n.* **A** (*method*) Handlungsweise, *die;* Vorgehensweise, *die;* (*overall plan*) Politik, *die;* **it is company ~ to ...:** es ist Firmenpolitik, ... zu ...; **adopt** *or* **pursue a wise/cautious/foolish ~:** klug/vorsichtig/töricht vorgehen; **it is the store's ~ to prosecute shoplifters** der Laden erstattet grundsätzlich Anzeige gegen Ladendiebe; **it is not our ~ to do that, our ~ is not to do that** wir machen das grundsätzlich nicht; **government ~:** Regierungspolitik, *die;* **~ on immigration** Einwanderungspolitik, *die;* **party ~:** Parteikurs, *der;* **the firm's policies** die Politik der Firma; **~ decision/document** Grundsatzentscheidung, *die*/-papier, *das;* **~ statement** programmatische Erklärung; Grundsatzerklärung, *die;* **it's bad ~ to ...:** es ist unvernünftig, ... zu ...; ⇒ *also* **honesty** B; **B** *no pl., no art.* (*prudent conduct*) **~ demands occasional compromise** manchmal sind Kompromisse das einzig Vernünftige

**policy**[2] *n.* (*Insurance*) Police, *die;* Versicherungsschein, *der;* **take out a ~ on sth.** eine Versicherung für etw. abschließen; **the ~ on my car** meine Autoversicherung

**ˈpolicy: ~ holder** *n.* Versicherte, *der/die;* Versicherungsnehmer, *der*/-nehmerin, *die* (*fachspr.*); **~-making** *attrib. adj.* richtungsweisend

**polio** /ˈpəʊlɪəʊ/ *n., no pl., no art.* ▶ 1232 Polio, *die;* [spinale] Kinderlähmung; *attrib.* Polio-; **~ vaccine** Polioimpfstoff, *der*

**poliomyelitis** /pəʊlɪəʊmaɪəˈlaɪtɪs/ *n.* ▶ 1232 (*Med.*) Poliomyelitis, *die;* [spinale] Kinderlähmung

**polish** /ˈpɒlɪʃ/ ❶ *v.t.* **A** (*make smooth*) polieren; bohnern ‹Fußboden›; putzen ‹Schuhe›; **highly ~ed** auf Hochglanz poliert; **B** (*fig.*) ausfeilen ‹Text, Theorie, Technik, Stil›; polieren ‹Text›; Schliff beibringen (+ *Dat.*) ‹Person›; **~ed** geschliffen ‹Stil, Manieren, Sprache, Auftreten, Weltmann›; ausgefeilt ‹Technik, Taktik, Plan, Satz›; **a highly ~ed piece of prose** ein bis ins Kleinste ausgefeiltes Stück Prosa.
❷ *n.* **A** (*smoothness*) Glanz, *der;* **put a ~ on** polieren; **a table with a high ~:** ein auf Hochglanz polierter Tisch; **take off** *or* **spoil the ~** ‹Person:› die Politur beschädigen; ‹Substanz:› die Politur angreifen; **B** (*substance*) Poliermittel, *das;* Politur, *die;* **C** (*fig.*) Geschliffenheit, *die;* Schliff, *der;* **D** (*action*) **my shoes could do with a ~:** meine Schuhe müssten mal geputzt werden; **give sth. a ~:** etw. polieren; **give the floor a ~:** den Fußboden bohnern; **give the shoes a ~:** die Schuhe putzen; ⇒ *also* **spit**[1] 3 B

**~ ˈoff** *v.t.* (*coll.*) **A** (*consume*) verdrücken (*ugs.*); wegputzen (*ugs.*) ‹Essen›; aussüffeln (*ugs.*) ‹Getränk›; **B** (*complete quickly*) durchziehen (*ugs.*); **C** (*defeat*) erledigen; abservieren (*salopp, bes. Sport*)

**~ ˈup** *v.t.* **A** (*make shiny*) polieren; **B** (*improve*) ausfeilen ‹Stil, Technik›; aufpolieren ‹[Sprach]kenntnisse›

**Polish** /ˈpəʊlɪʃ/ ▶ 1275, ▶ 1340 ❶ *adj.* polnisch; **sb. is ~:** jmd. ist Pole/Polin; ⇒ *also* **English** 1. ❷ *n.* Polnisch, *das;* ⇒ *also* **English** 2 A

**polisher** /ˈpɒlɪʃə(r)/ *n.* **A** (*person*) ▶ 1261 Polierer, *der*/Poliererin, *die;* **B** (*tool*) Poliergerät, *das;* (*for floors*) Bohnerklotz, *der;* (*machine*) Poliermaschine, *die;* (*for floors*) Bohnermaschine, *die;* (*cloth*) Poliertuch, *das*

**politburo** /ˈpɒlɪtbjʊərəʊ/ *n., pl.* **~s** Politbüro, *das*

**polite** /pəˈlaɪt/ *adj.*, **~r** /pəˈlaɪtə(r)/, **~st** /pəˈlaɪtɪst/ **A** (*courteous*) höflich; **the ~ form of address** die höfliche Anredeform; **be ~ about her dress** mach ihr ein paar Komplimente zu ihrem Kleid; **he was just being ~:** er wollte nur höflich sein; **B** (*cultured*) kultiviert; **C** (*well-mannered*) schicklich (*geh.*) ‹Verhalten›; wohlerzogen, artig ‹Kind›; **it's not [considered] ~:** es gehört sich *od.* (*geh.*) schickt sich nicht; **in some circles it is considered ~ to ...** in manchen Kreisen gehört es zum guten Ton, zu ...

**politely** /pəˈlaɪtlɪ/ *adv.* höflich

**politeness** /pəˈlaɪtnɪs/ *n., no pl.* Höflichkeit, *die*

**politic** /ˈpɒlɪtɪk/ ❶ *adj.* **A** (*prudent*) klug ‹Person, Handlung›; opportun (*geh.*) ‹Handlung›; **it would be ~ to make some changes** es wäre klug *od.* (*geh.*) opportun, einiges zu ändern; **it's not ~ to do sth.** es ist unklug *od.* nicht ratsam, etw. zu tun; **B body ~** (*State*) das Staatswesen. ❷ *v.i.*, **-ck-** sich politisch betätigen *od.* engagieren

**political** /pəˈlɪtɪkl/ *adj.* politisch; **~ animal** politischer *od.* politisch engagierter Mensch

**political: ~ aˈsylum** ⇒ **asylum**; **~ ecoˈnomy** *n.* politische Ökonomie; **~ geˈography** *n.* politische Geographie; **a map of the ~ geography of Britain** eine politische Karte von Großbritannien

**politically** /pəˈlɪtɪkəlɪ/ *adv.* politisch; **be ~ aware** *or* **conscious** politisches Bewusstsein haben; **~ correct** politisch korrekt; *von „richtigem" politischem Bewusstsein zeugend;* **~ speaking** politisch gesehen; vom politischen Standpunkt betrachtet

**political: ~ ˈprisoner** *n.* politischer Gefangener/politische Gefangene; **~ ˈscience** *n.* Politologie, *die*

**politician** /pɒlɪˈtɪʃn/ *n.* **A** ▶ 1261 Politiker, *der*/Politikerin, *die;* **B** (*Amer. derog.: one seeking gain*) Politiker/Politikerin aus Eigennutz

**politicize (politicise)** /pəˈlɪtɪsaɪz/ *v.t.* politisieren

**politicking** /ˈpɒlɪtɪkɪŋ/ *n.* (*derog.*) politischer Aktionismus (*abwertend*)

**politico** /pəˈlɪtɪkəʊ/ *n., pl.* **~s** (*coll.*) Politiker, *der*/Politikerin, *die*

**politics** /ˈpɒlɪtɪks/ *n., no pl.* **A** *no art.* (*political administration*) Politik, *die;* (*Univ.: subject*) Politik[wissenschaft], *die;* Politologie, *die;* **B** *no art., constr. as sing. or pl.* (*political affairs*) Politik, *die;* **~ is a dirty business** die Politik ist ein schmutziges Geschäft; **interested/involved in ~:** politisch interessiert/engagiert; **enter ~:** in die Politik gehen; **C** *as pl.* (*political principles*) Politik, *die;* (*of individual*) politische Einstellung; **world ~ are complex** die Weltpolitik ist eine komplizierte Angelegenheit; **what are his ~?** wo steht er politisch?; **the ~ of the decision** der politische Hintergrund der Entscheidung; **it is not good ~ to do sth.** es ist politisch unklug, etw. zu tun; **practical ~:** Realpolitik, *die*

**polity** /ˈpɒlɪtɪ/ *n.* **A** (*form of government*) politisches System; politische Ordnung; **B** (*formal/arch.: State*) Staat, *der;* Gemeinwesen, *das*

**polka** /ˈpɒlkə, ˈpəʊlkə/ *n.* Polka, *die*

**ˈpolka dot** *n.* [großer] Tupfen; **the blouse is patterned with ~s** die Bluse hat ein Muster aus großen Tupfen; **a polka-dot scarf** ein Halstuch mit großen Tupfen

**poll** /pəʊl/ ❶ *n.* **A** (*voting*) Abstimmung, *die;* (*to elect sb.*) Wahl, *die;* (*result of vote*) Abstimmungsergebnis, *das*/Wahlergebnis, *das;* (*number of votes*) Wahlbeteiligung, *die;* **take a ~:** abstimmen lassen; eine Abstimmung durchführen; **day of the ~:** Wahltag, *der;* **at the ~[s]** bei den Wahlen; **the result of the ~:** das Abstimmungsergebnis/Wahlergebnis; **a defeat at the ~s** eine Wahlniederlage; **go to the ~:** seine Stimme abgeben; wählen [gehen]; **Britain goes to the ~s** Großbritannien wählt; in Großbritannien wird gewählt; **be at the head of the ~:** die meisten Stimmen erhalten [haben]; **the declaration of the ~:** die Bekanntgabe des Wahlergebnisses; **a heavy/light** *or* **low ~:** eine starke/geringe *od.* niedrige Wahlbeteiligung; **B** (*survey of opinion*) Umfrage, *die;* **~ findings** Umfrageergebnis, *das;* **C** (*human head*) Kopf, *der;* Schädel, *der;* (*part of head*) [Hinter]kopf, *der.*
❷ *v.t.* **A** (*take vote[s] of*) abstimmen/wählen lassen; **be ~ed** seine Stimme abgeben; **B** (*take opinion of*) befragen; (*take survey of*) [demoskopisch] erforschen; **those ~ed** die Befragten; **C** (*obtain in poll*) erhalten ‹Stimmen›; **D** (*cut off top of*) kappen ‹Baum, Baumkrone›.
❸ *v.i.* wählen; seine Stimme abgeben

**pollack** /ˈpɒlək/ *n.* (*Zool.*) Köhler, *der;* (*Commerc.*) Seelachs, *der*

**pollard** /ˈpɒləd/ ❶ *n.* (*Bot.*) gekappter Baum. ❷ *v.t.* (*Bot.*) kappen

P

**pollen** /'pɒlən/ *n.* (*Bot.*) Pollen, *der;* Blütenstaub, *der*

**pollen:** ~ **analysis** *n.* Pollenanalyse, *die;* ~ **count** *n.* Pollenmenge, *die;* ~ **sac** *n.* Pollensack, *der*

**pollinate** /'pɒlɪneɪt/ *v.t.* (*Bot.*) bestäuben

**pollination** /pɒlɪ'neɪʃn/ *n.* (*Bot.*) Bestäubung, *die;* Pollination, *die* (*fachspr.*)

**polling** /'pəʊlɪŋ/: ~ **booth** *n.* Wahlkabine, *die;* ~ **day** *n.* Wahltag, *der;* ~ **district** *n.* Wahlbezirk, *der;* ~ **station** *n.* (*Brit.*) Wahllokal, *das*

**pollock** ⇒ **pollack**

**pollster** /'pəʊlstə(r)/ *n.* Meinungsforscher, *der*/Meinungsforscherin, *die;* Demoskop, *der*/Demoskopin, *die*

**'poll tax** *n.* Kopfsteuer, *die*

**pollutant** /pə'lu:tənt/ ❶ *n.* (*substance*) [Umwelt]schadstoff, *der.* ❷ *adj.* [umwelt]schädlich; ~ **substance** [Umwelt]schadstoff, *der*

**pollute** /pə'lu:t/ *v.t.* Ⓐ (*contaminate*) verschmutzen, verunreinigen ‹Luft, Boden, Wasser›; verpesten (*abwertend*) ‹Luft›; **the most ~d cities** die am stärksten mit [Umwelt]schadstoffen belasteten Städte; Ⓑ (*make foul*) verseuchen; Ⓒ (*fig.*) verderben ‹Jugend, Menschen, Charakter›

**pollution** /pə'lu:ʃn/ *n.* Ⓐ (*contamination*) [Umwelt]verschmutzung, *die;* **atmospheric ~:** atmosphärische Verschmutzung; Verschmutzung der Atmosphäre; **water ~:** Gewässerverschmutzung, *die;* **noise ~:** Lärmbelästigung, *die;* Ⓑ (*polluting substance[s]*) Verunreinigungen *Pl.;* Schadstoffe *Pl.;* Ⓒ (*fig.*) Verderben, *das*

**Pollyanna** /pɒlɪ'ænə/ *n.* (*Amer. derog.*) unverbesserlicher Optimist/unverbesserliche Optimistin; *attrib.* [übertrieben *od.* grundlos] optimistisch

**polo** /'pəʊləʊ/ *n., no pl.* Polo, *das*

**polonaise** /pɒlə'neɪz/ *n.* (*dance, music*) Polonaise, *die;* Polonäse, *die*

**'polo neck** *n.* Rollkragen, *der;* **~[ed]** *attrib.* Rollkragen-; ~ **[jumper]** Rollkragenpulli, *der* (*ugs.*); Rolli, *der* (*Mode Jargon*)

**polo:** ~ **shirt** *n.* Polohemd, *das;* ~ **stick** *n.* Polostock, *der*

**poltergeist** /'pɒltəgaɪst/ *n.* Klopfgeist, *der;* Poltergeist, *der*

**poltroon** /pɒl'tru:n/ *n.* (*derog.*) Angsthase, *der* (*ugs. abwertend*)

**poly** /'pɒlɪ/ *n., pl.* **~s** (*coll.*) Polytechnikum, *das;* ≈ TH, *die*

**polyanthus** /pɒlɪ'ænθəs/ *n.* (*Bot.*) [Garten]primel, *die*

**polychromatic** /pɒlɪkrə'mætɪk/ *adj.* Ⓐ (*many-coloured*) vielfarbig; polychrom (*fachspr.*); Ⓑ (*Phys.*) polychromatisch

**polyclinic** /'pɒlɪklɪnɪk/ *n.* Poliklinik, *die*

**polyester** /pɒlɪ'estə(r)/ *n.* Polyester, *der*

**polyethylene** /pɒlɪ'eθɪli:n/ (*Amer.*) ⇒ **polythene**

**polygamist** /pə'lɪgəmɪst/ *n.* Polygamist, *der* (*geh.*); **be a ~:** polygam leben (*geh.*); (*in disposition*) polygam sein (*geh.*)

**polygamous** /pə'lɪgəməs/ *adj.* polygam (*geh., fachspr.*)

**polygamy** /pə'lɪgəmɪ/ *n.* Polygamie, *die* (*geh., fachspr.*); Mehrehe, *die;* Vielehe, *die*

**polyglot** /'pɒlɪglɒt/ ❶ *adj.* Ⓐ polyglott (*geh., fachspr.*); mehrsprachig; Ⓑ (*speaking several languages*) polyglott (*geh.*). ❷ *n.* Polyglotte, *der/die* (*geh.*)

**polygon** /'pɒlɪgən/ *n.* (*Geom.*) Vieleck, *das;* Polygon, *das* (*fachspr.*)

**polygraph** /'pɒlɪgrɑ:f/ *n.* (*lie detector*) Lügendetektor, *der;* Polygraph, *der* (*fachspr.*)

**polyhedron** /pɒlɪ'hi:drən/ *n., pl.* **~s** *or* **polyhedra** /pɒlɪ'hi:drə/ (*Geom.*) Polyeder, *das* (*fachspr.*); Vielflächner, *der*

**polymath** /'pɒlɪmæθ/ *n.* universell Gebildeter/Gebildete

**polymer** /'pɒlɪmə(r)/ *n.* (*Chem.*) Polymer[e], *das*

**polymeric** /pɒlɪ'merɪk/ *adj.* (*Chem.*) polymer

**polymerisation**, **polymerise** ⇒ **polymeriz-**

**polymerization** /pɒlɪmərаɪ'zeɪʃn/ *n.* (*Chem.*) Polymerisation, *die*

**polymerize** /'pɒlɪməraɪz/ *v.t. & i.* (*Chem.*) polymerisieren

**Polynesia** /pɒlɪ'ni:ʒə/ *pr. n.* Polynesien (*das*)

**Polynesian** /pɒlɪ'ni:ʒən/ ▶ 1340 ❶ *adj.* polynesisch. ❷ *n.* Polynesier, *der*/Polynesierin, *die*

**polynomial** /pɒlɪ'nəʊmɪəl/ *n.* (*Math.*) Polynom, *das*

**polyp** /'pɒlɪp/ *n.* (*Zool., Med.*) Polyp, *der*

**polyphonic** /pɒlɪ'fɒnɪk/, **polyphonous** /pə'lɪfənəs/ *adjs.* (*Mus.*) polyphon

**polyphony** /pə'lɪfənɪ/ *n.* (*Mus.*) Polyphonie, *die*

**polystyrene** /pɒlɪ'staɪri:n/ *n.* Polystyrol, *das;* ~ **foam** Styropor Ⓦz, *das*

**polysyllabic** /pɒlɪsɪ'læbɪk/ *adj.* vielsilbig

**polytechnic** /pɒlɪ'teknɪk/ *n.* (*Brit.*) ≈ technische Hochschule *od.* Universität; ~ **student/teacher/term** Student/Lehrer/Semester am Polytechnikum

**polytheism** /'pɒlɪθi:ɪzm/ *n.* Polytheismus, *der*

**polythene** /'pɒlɪθi:n/ *n.* Polyäthylen, *das;* Polyethylen, *das* (*fachspr.*); (*coll.: plastic*) Plastik, *das;* ~ **bag/sheet** Plastikbeutel, *der*/-folie, *die*

**polyunsaturated** /pɒlɪʌn'sætʃəreɪtɪd/ *adj.* mehrfach ungesättigt

**polyunsaturates** /pɒlɪʌn'sætjʊrəts/ *pl. n.* mehrfach ungesättigte Fettsäuren

**polyurethane** /pɒlɪ'jʊərɪθeɪn/ *n.* Polyurethan, *das*

**polyvinyl chloride** /pɒlɪvaɪnɪl 'klɔ:raɪd/ *n.* Polyvinylchlorid, *das*

**pom** /pɒm/ *n.* Ⓐ (*dog*) Spitz, *der;* Ⓑ (*Austral. and NZ coll.: Briton*) Brite, *der*/Britin, *die*

**pomade** /pə'mɑ:d/ *n.* Pomade, *die*

**pomaded** /pə'meɪdɪd/ *adj.* pomadig ‹Haar›

**pomander** /pə'mændə(r)/ *n.* Duftkugel, *die*

**pome** /pəʊm/ *n.* (*Bot.*) Sammelbalgfrucht, *die*

**pomegranate** /'pɒmɪgrænɪt/ *n.* Ⓐ (*fruit*) Granatapfel, *der;* Ⓑ (*tree*) Granatapfel[baum], *der;* Granatbaum, *der*

**Pomerania** /pɒmə'reɪnɪə/ *pr. n.* Pommern (*das*)

**Pomeranian** /pɒmə'reɪnɪən/ *n.* (*dog*) Spitz, *der*

**pommel** /'pʌml, 'pɒml/ ❶ *n.* Ⓐ (*on sword*) [Schwert]knauf, *der;* Ⓑ (*on saddle*) Sattelknopf, *der;* Ⓒ (*Gymnastics*) Pausche, *die.* ❷ *v.t.,* (*Brit.*) **-ll-** ⇒ **pummel**

**'pommel horse** *n.* Seitpferd, *das*

**pommy** (**pommie**) /'pɒmɪ/ *n.* (*Austral. and NZ sl. derog.*) Brite, *der*/Britin, *die;* ~ **bastard** Scheißbrite, *der*/-britin, *die* (*salopp abwertend*)

**pomp** /pɒmp/ *n.* Pomp, *der* (*abwertend*); Prunk, *der;* Gepränge, *das* (*geh.*); ~ **and circumstance** festliches Gepränge (*geh.*)

**Pompeii** /pɒm'peɪi:/ *pr. n.* ▶ 1626 Pompeji (*das*)

**pompom** /'pɒmpɒm/, **pompon** /'pɒmpɒn/ *n.* Ⓐ (*tuft*) Pompon, *der;* Troddel, *die;* ~ **hat** Pudelmütze, *die;* Ⓑ (*Bot.*) ~ **[dahlia]** Pompondahlie, *die*

**pom-pom** /'pɒmpɒm/ *n.* (*Arms*) Maschinenkanone, *die*

**pomposity** /pɒm'pɒsɪtɪ/ *n., no pl.* Großspurigkeit, *die;* Aufgeblasenheit, *die;* ~ **of language** geschwollene *od.* gespreizte Sprache

**pompous** /'pɒmpəs/ *adj.* (*self-important*) großspurig; aufgeblasen; geschwollen (*abwertend*); gespreizt (*abwertend*) ‹Sprache›; **don't be so ~!** blas dich nicht so auf!

**pompously** /'pɒmpəslɪ/ *adv.* großspurig, aufgeblasen ‹auftreten, sich benehmen›; geschwollen (*abwertend*), gespreizt (*abwertend*) ‹schreiben, reden›

**'pon** /pɒn/ (*poet./arch.*) ⇒ **upon**

**ponce** /pɒns/ (*Brit. sl.*) ❶ *n.* Ⓐ (*pimp*) Zuhälter, *der;* Ⓑ (*derog.: homosexual*) Schwule, *der* (*ugs.*); Homo, *der* (*ugs.*); **be a ~:** schwul sein. ❷ *v.i.* Zuhälterei betreiben; ~ **for sb.** jmds. Zuhälter sein

~ **a'bout**, ~ **a'round** *v.i.* (*derog.*) herumtänzeln (*ugs.*)

~ **'up** *v.t.* (*derog.*) [tuntenhaft] auftakeln (*ugs. abwertend*); **what are you all ~d up for?** wozu hast du dich denn so aufgedonnert? (*salopp*)

**poncho** /'pɒntʃəʊ/ *n., pl.* **~s** Poncho, *der;* Umhang, *der*

**pond** /pɒnd/ *n.* Teich, *der;* **the [big] ~** (*joc.: Atlantic*) der große Teich (*ugs. scherzh.*); **a big fish in a small ~** (*fig.*) eine Lokalgröße; ein Lokalmatador (*ugs.*)

**ponder** /'pɒndə(r)/ ❶ *v.t.* nachdenken über (+ *Akk.*) ‹Frage, Problem, Ereignis›; bedenken ‹Folgen›; abwägen ‹Vorteile, Worte›; ~ **whether/how to do sth.** sich (*Dat.*) überlegen, ob man etw. tun soll/wie man etw. tun kann. ❷ *v.i.* nachdenken (**over, on** über + *Akk.*); **careful ~ing** sorgfältige Überlegung; sorgfältiges Nachdenken

**ponderous** /'pɒndərəs/ *adj.* Ⓐ (*heavy*) schwer; Ⓑ (*unwieldy, laborious*) schwerfällig; umständlich ‹Ausdrucksweise›; Ⓒ (*dull*) ermüdend

**ponderously** /'pɒndərəslɪ/ *adv.* schwerfällig; umständlich ‹sich ausdrücken›

**pond:** ~ **life** *n.* (*Zool.*) Teichfauna, *die;* ~ **skater** *n.* (*Zool.*) Wasserläufer, *der;* **~weed** *n.* (*Bot.*) Laichkraut, *das*

**pong** /pɒŋ/ (*Brit. coll.*) ❶ *n.* Gestank, *der* (*abwertend*); Mief, *der* (*ugs. abwertend*). ❷ *v.i.* stinken (*abwertend*); miefen (*ugs. abwertend*)

**pontiff** /'pɒntɪf/ *n.* Papst, *der*

**pontifical** /pɒn'tɪfɪkl/ *adj.* Ⓐ (*of pontiff*) päpstlich; Ⓑ (*fig.: dogmatic*) pastoral

**pontificate** /pɒn'tɪfɪkeɪt/ *v.i.* dozieren; in dozierendem Ton sprechen

**pontoon**[1] /pɒn'tu:n/ *n.* Ⓐ (*boat*) Ponton, *der;* Prahm, *der;* Ⓑ (*support*) Ponton, *der*

**pontoon**[2] *n.* (*Brit. Cards*) Siebzehnundvier, *das*

**pontoon 'bridge** *n.* Pontonbrücke, *die*

**pony** /'pəʊnɪ/ ❶ *n.* Ⓐ Pony, *das;* ⇒ *also* **shank** A; Ⓑ (*Amer. coll.: small glass*) kleines Glas; (*of beer*) Kleine, *das;* Ⓒ (*Amer. coll.: dancer*) kleine Tänzerin; Ⓓ (*Amer. coll.: crib*) Klatsche, *die* (*Schülerspr. landsch.*); Schmierer, *der* (*österr.*); Ⓔ (*Brit. coll.: £25*) 25 Pfund. ❷ *v.t.* (*Amer. coll.*) ~ **up** löhnen (*salopp*); blechen (*ugs.*)

**pony:** ~ **ex'press** *n.* Ponyexpress, *der;* **~tail** *n.* Pferdeschwanz, *der;* **wear one's hair in a ~tail** einen Pferdeschwanz tragen *od.* haben; **~-trekking** /'pəʊnɪtrekɪŋ/ *n.* (*Brit.*) Ponyreiten, *das*

**pooch** /pu:tʃ/ *n.* (*Amer. coll.*) Köter, *der* (*abwertend*)

**poodle** /'pu:dl/ *n.* Pudel, *der;* **be sb.'s ~** (*fig.*) immer nach jmds. Pfeife tanzen

**poof** /pʊf/ *n.* (*Brit. coll. derog.*), **poofter** /'pʊftə(r)/ *n.* (*Austral. coll. derog.*) Schwule, *der* (*ugs.*); Schwuchtel, *die* (*salopp abwertend*); Tunte, *die* (*salopp abwertend*)

**pooh** /pu:/ *int.* Ⓐ *expr. disgust* bah; bäh; pfui [Teufel]; Ⓑ *expr. disdain* pah

**pooh-'pooh** *v.t.* [als läppisch] abtun

**pool**[1] /pu:l/ *n.* Ⓐ (*permanent*) Tümpel, *der;* Wasserloch, *das;* Ⓑ (*temporary*) Pfütze, *die;* Lache, *die;* ~ **of blood** Blutlache, *die;* ~ **of sunlight/shade** (*fig.*) sonnige/schattige Stelle; Ⓒ (*swimming ~*) Schwimmbecken, *das;* (*public swimming ~*) Schwimmbad, *das;* (*in house or garden*) [Swimming]pool, *der;* **sit at the edge of the ~:** am Beckenrand sitzen; **go to the ~:** ins Schwimmbad gehen; Ⓓ (*in river*) tiefe Stelle (*in einem Fluss od. Bach*); Kolk, *der* (*fachspr.*); **the P~ [of London]** (*Brit.*) *Themseabschnitt unterhalb der London Bridge*

**pool**[2] ❶ *n.* Ⓐ (*Gambling*) [gemeinsame Spiel]kasse; **the ~s** (*Brit.*) das Toto; **do the ~s** Toto spielen; **win the ~s** im Toto gewinnen; **have a big win on the ~s** einen großen Gewinn im Toto haben; Ⓑ (*common supply*) Fonds, *der;* Topf, *der;* **that goes into the common ~:** das kommt in den großen Topf (*ugs.*); **a [great] ~ of experience** ein [großer] Fundus von *od.* an Erfahrung; ein [umfangreicher] Erfahrungsschatz; Ⓒ (*group of people*) Reservoir, *das;* Potenzial, *das;* **typing** *or* **typists' ~:** Schreibzentrale, *die;* Ⓓ

p

(*Commerc.*) Kartell, *das;* **E** (*game*) Pool[billard], *das.*
❷ *v.t.* zusammenlegen ‹Geld, Ersparnisse, Mittel, Besitz›; bündeln ‹Anstrengungen›; **they ~ed their experience** sie nutzten ihre Erfahrung gemeinsam

**pool: ~hall, ~room** *ns.* Billardzimmer, *das;* **~side** *n.* [Schwimm]beckenrand, *der; attrib.* ‹Bar, Tisch› am [Schwimm]beckenrand; **~ table** *n.* Pool[billard]tisch, *der*

**poop**[1] /pu:p/ *n.* (*Naut.*) **A** (*stern*) Heck, *das;* Hinterschiff, *das;* **B** **~ [deck]** Poop, *die* (*fachspr.*); Hütte, *die* (*fachspr.*)

**poop**[2] (*coll.*) ❶ *v.t.* schlauchen (*ugs.*). ❷ *v.i.* **~ out** schlappmachen (*ugs.*); ‹Maschine usw.:› streiken (*ugs.*)

**poor** /pʊə(r)/ ❶ *adj.* **A** arm; **I am the ~er by £10** *or* **£10 the ~er** ich bin um 10 Pfund ärmer; ⇒ *also* **church mouse**; **B** (*inadequate*) schlecht; schwach ‹Rede, Spiel, Gedächtnis, Beteiligung, Besuch, Leistung, Witz, Gesundheit›; dürftig ‹Essen, Kleidung, Unterkunft, Ausrede, Entschuldigung›; **of ~ quality** minderer Qualität; **he's a ~ speller** er ist schlecht in Rechtschreibung; **I'm a ~ traveller** ich vertrage das Reisen nicht gut; **be ~ at maths** *etc.* schlecht *od.* schwach in Mathematik *usw.* sein; **sb. is ~ at games** Ballspiele liegen jmdm. nicht; **have a ~ sense of responsibility** zu wenig Verantwortungsgefühl haben; **have a ~ grasp of sth.** etw. nur unzureichend beherrschen; **I only came a ~ second** bei mir hat es nur für einen schlechten zweiten Platz gereicht; **compared with Joe he comes a ~ second** gegen Joe hat er absolut nichts drin (*ugs.*); **C** (*paltry*) schwach ‹Trost›; schlecht ‹Aussichten, Situation›; (*disgusting*) mies (*ugs. abwertend*); **it's very ~ of them not to have replied** es ist sehr schäbig von ihnen *od.* (*ugs.*) es ist ein schwaches Bild, dass sie nicht geantwortet haben; **have** *or* **stand a ~ chance of success** kaum Aussicht auf Erfolg haben; **that's pretty ~!** das ist reichlich dürftig *od.* (*ugs.*) ganz schön schwach; ⇒ *also* **show** 1 E; **D** (*unfortunate*) arm (*auch iron.*); **~ you!** du Armer/Arme!; du Ärmster/Ärmste!; **~ thing/creature!** armes Ding!; das arme Ding!; **~ things!** die Armen *od.* Ärmsten!; **she's all alone, ~ woman** die Ärmste ist ganz allein; sie ist ganz allein, die arme Frau; **~ old Joe** der arme Joe; **~ Joe** (*dead*) der gute Joe; **E** (*infertile*) karg, schlecht ‹Boden, Land›; **F** (*spiritless, pathetic*) arm ‹Teufel, Dummkopf›; armselig, (*abwertend*) elend ‹Kreatur, Stümper›; **cut a ~ figure** eine schlechte *od.* klägliche Figur abgeben; **G** (*iron./joc.: humble*) **in my ~ opinion** nach meiner unmaßgeblichen Meinung; **my ~ self** meine Wenigkeit (*scherzh.*); **H** (*deficient*) arm (**in** an + *Dat.*); **~ in content/ideas/vitamins** inhalts-/ideen-/vitaminarm; **~ in minerals** ‹Land› arm an Bodenschätzen; **I take a ~ view of** nicht [sehr] viel halten von; für gering halten ‹Aussichten, Chancen›; **have a ~ opinion of** eine schlechte *od.* keine [sehr] hohe Meinung haben von ‹Person›; gering einschätzen ‹jmds. Fähigkeit›.
❷ *n. pl.* **the ~:** die Armen; **respected by both rich and ~:** geachtet von *od.* bei Arm und Reich

**poor: ~ box** *n.* Almosenbüchse, *die;* **~house** *n.* (*Hist.*) Armenhaus, *das;* **~ law** *n.* (*Hist.*) Armengesetz, *das*

**poorly** /ˈpʊəlɪ/ ❶ *adv.* **A** (*scantily*) schlecht; unzureichend; **they're ~ off** es geht ihnen [finanziell] schlecht; **sb. is ~ off for sth.** es fehlt *od.* mangelt jmdm. an etw. (*Dat.*); **B** (*badly*) schlecht; unbeholfen ‹schreiben, sprechen›; **he did ~ in his exams** er war in seinen Prüfungen schlecht; **the team is doing ~:** die Mannschaft spielt schlecht; **exports are doing ~:** das Exportgeschäft geht schlecht; **C** (*meanly*) schlecht ‹leben›. ❷ *pred. adj.* schlecht ‹aussehen, sich fühlen›; **he has been ~ lately** ihm geht es in letzter Zeit schlecht

**ˈpoor: ~ man's** *adj.* (*coll.*) des kleinen Mannes *nachgestellt;* **a kind of ~ man's Marlon Brando** ein Marlon-Brando-Verschnitt; ein Westentaschen-Marlon-Brando; **~ reˈlation** *n.* arme Verwandte, *der/die;* (*fig.*) Stiefkind, *das;* **be the ~ relation** (*fig.*) im Vergleich zu etw. schlecht abschneiden; **feel like a ~ relation** sich (*Dat.*) wie ein Stiefkind vorkommen; **~-relief** *n.* (*Hist.*) Armenpflege, *die;* **~ ˈwhite** *n.* (*Amer. Black derog.*) armer Weißer/arme Weiße; **~ white trash** weißer Pöbel (*abwertend*); weißes Gesindel (*abwertend*)

**poove** /pu:v/ ⇒ **poof**

**pop**[1] /pɒp/ ❶ *v.i.*, **-pp-:** **A** (*make sound*) ‹Korken:› knallen; ‹Schote, Samenkapsel:› aufplatzen, aufspringen; **a faint ~ping sound** ein leises Knacken; **his buttons ~ped open** seine Knöpfe sprangen auf; (*fig.*) **his eyes ~ped with amazement** er guckte wie ein Auto (*ugs.*); **prices that would make your eyes ~:** Preise, bei denen Sie staunen würden; **B** (*coll.: move, go quickly*) **let's ~ round to Fred's** komm, wir gehen mal eben *od.* schnell *od.* kurz bei Fred vorbei (*ugs.*); **I'll just ~ upstairs and see granny** ich gehe *od.* (*ugs.*) springe nur mal eben hoch zu Oma; **~ down to London** mal eben *od.* schnell nach London fahren; **you must ~ round and see us** du musst mal vorbeikommen und uns besuchen *od.* musst mal bei uns reingucken (*ugs.*); **she ~ped back for her book** sie lief *od.* (*ugs.*) flitzte noch mal zurück, um ihr Buch zu holen; **C** (*fire gun*) ballern (*ugs.*) (**at** auf + *Akk.*).
❷ *v.t.*, **-pp-:** **A** (*coll.: put*) **~ the meat in the fridge** das Fleisch in den Kühlschrank tun; **~ a cake into the oven** einen Kuchen in den Ofen schieben; **~ a peanut into one's mouth** [sich (*Dat.*)] eine Erdnuss in den Mund stecken; **~ one's head in at the door** den Kopf zur Tür reinstecken; mal eben hereinschauen; **~ one's head out [of the window]** den Kopf [zum Fenster] rausstrecken; **~ the kettle on** den Kessel aufsetzen; **~ a letter in the post** einen Brief einwerfen; einen Brief in den Briefkasten werfen; **~ sth. into a bag** etw. in eine Tasche tun *od.* stecken; **B** (*cause to burst*) enthülsen ‹Erbsen, Bohnen›; platzen *od.* (*ugs.*) knallen lassen ‹Luftballon›; zerknallen ‹Papiertüte›; **C** (*sl.: take as drug*) nehmen; schlucken, (*Jargon*) schmeißen ‹Pillen, Trips›; (*by injection*) schießen (*Jargon*); drücken (*Jargon*); **D** (*cause to burst*) puffen; **~ corn** Popcorn machen; **E** **~ the question [to sb.]** (*coll.*) jmdm. einen [Heirats]antrag machen.
❸ *n.* **A** (*sound*) Knall, *der;* Knallen, *das;* **B** (*coll.: drink*) Sprudel, *der;* (*flavoured*) Brause, *die* (*ugs.*); **soda ~:** Selter[s], *das.*
❹ *adv.* **go ~:** knallen; peng machen (*ugs.*)

**~ ˈoff** *v.i.* **A** (*coll.: die*) abnibbeln (*ugs., bes. nordd.*); den Löffel weglegen *od.* abgeben (*salopp*); **B** (*move or go away*) ‹Person:› verschwinden, (*ugs.*) abdampfen

**~ ˈout** *v.i.* hervorschießen aus; **~ one's head out of the window** den Kopf zum Fenster herausstrecken; **~ out from behind a bush** hinter einem Busch hervorspringen; **~ out for a newspaper/to the shops** schnell *od.* eben mal eine Zeitung holen gehen/einkaufen gehen (*ugs.*); **~ out for a beer** eben mal ein Bier[chen] trinken gehen (*ugs.*); **he's just ~ped out for a moment** er ist nur mal kurz weggegangen (*ugs.*)

**~ ˈout of** *v.t.* hervorschieben aus; **~ one's head out of the window** den Kopf zum Fenster herausstrecken; **sb.'s eyes nearly** *or* **almost ~ out of his head** *or* **skull** (*coll.*) (*with surprise*) jmdm. fallen fast die Augen aus dem Kopf; (*with excitement*) jmd. (*bes. Kind*) macht große Augen

**~ ˈup** *v.i.* **A** (*fig.: appear*) auftauchen; **sb./sth. keeps ~ping up** (*fig.*) jmd./etw. begegnet einem immer wieder (*fig.*); **B** (*rise up*) sich aufstellen; (*spring up*) hochspringen; ⇒ *also* **pop-up**

**pop**[2] (*coll.*) ❶ *n.* (*popular music*) Popmusik, *die;* Pop, *der;* **be top of the ~s** an der Spitze der Charts *od.* Hitlisten stehen. ❷ *adj.* Pop‹star, -musik usw.›

**pop**[3] *n.* (*Amer. coll.: father*) Pa[pa], *der* (*fam.*)

**pop.** *abbr.* **population** Einw.

**pop: ~ art** *n., no pl., no indef. art.* Pop-Art, *die; attrib.* Pop-Art-; **~ concert** *n.* Popkonzert, *das;* **~corn** *n.* Popcorn, *das*

**pope** /pəʊp/ *n.* **A** (*RC Ch.; also fig.*) Papst, *der*/Päpstin, *die;* **B** (*Coptic Ch.*) Patriarch, *der;* **C** (*Orthodox Ch.*) Pope, *der.* ⇒ *also* **nose** 1 A

**popery** /ˈpəʊpərɪ/ *n., no pl., no art.* (*derog.*) Pfaffentum, *das* (*abwertend*); Papismus, *der* (*abwertend*)

**pop: ~-eyed** /ˈpɒpaɪd/ *adj.* (*coll.*) **A** (*wide-eyed*) großäugig; **they were ~-eyed with amazement** sie staunten Bauklötze (*salopp*); **B** (*having bulging eyes*) glotzäugig; glupschäugig (*nordd.*); **~ festival** *n.* Popfestival, *das;* **~ group** *n.* Popgruppe, *die;* **~gun** *n.* Spielzeuggewehr, *das*/Spielzeugpistole, *die*

**popish** /ˈpəʊpɪʃ/ *adj.* (*arch./derog.*) papistisch (*abwertend*); **the ~ religion** der Papismus (*abwertend*)

**poplar** /ˈpɒplə(r)/ *n.* Pappel, *die*

**poplin** /ˈpɒplɪn/ *n.* (*Textiles*) Popelin, *der;* Popeline, *der od. die*

**pop: ~ music** *n.* Popmusik, *die;* **~over** *n.* (*Amer.*) **A** *stark aufgehendes Backwerk aus Eiern, Milch, Mehl und Butter;* **B** (*garment*) weites Kleidungsstück (*das über den Kopf gezogen wird*)

**poppadam, poppadum** /ˈpɒpədəm/ *n.* (*Ind. Gastr.*) *knuspriger, hauchdünner frittierter Fladen*

**popper** /ˈpɒpə(r)/ *n.* (*Brit. coll.*) Druckknopf, *der*

**poppet** /ˈpɒpɪt/ *n.* (*Brit. coll.*) Schätzchen, *das;* Schatz, *der*

**poppy** /ˈpɒpɪ/ *n.* **A** (*Bot.*) Mohn, *der;* **a field of poppies** ein Mohnfeld; **Californian ~:** Goldmohn, *der;* **opium ~:** Schlafmohn, *der;* **Welsh ~:** Scheinmohn, *der;* **B** (*Brit.: emblem*) [künstliche] Mohnblume (*als Zeichen des Gedenkens am 'Poppy Day'*)

**poppycock** /ˈpɒpɪkɒk/ *n., no pl., no art.* (*coll.*) Mumpitz, *der* (*ugs. abwertend*)

**poppy: P~ Day** (*Brit.*) ⇒ **Remembrance Sunday**; **~ head** *n.* Mohnkapsel, *die;* **~ seed** *n.* Mohnsamen, *der;* **~ seeds** (*Cookery*) Mohn, *der*

**Popsicle** ® /ˈpɒpsɪkl/ *n.* (*Amer.*) [Wasser]eis am Stiel

**pop: ~ singer** *n.* Popsänger, *der*/-sängerin, *die;* Schlagersänger, *der*/-sängerin, *die;* **~ song** *n.* Popsong, *der;* Schlager, *der;* **~ star** *n.* Popstar, *der;* Schlagerstar, *der*

**popsy (popsie)** /ˈpɒpsɪ/ *n.* (*coll.*) (*young woman*) Mieze, *die* (*salopp*); (*young girl*) Maus, *die;* (*as form of address*) Schätzchen, *das*

**populace** /ˈpɒpjʊləs/ *n., no pl.* **A** (*common people*) [breite] Masse; Volk, *das;* **the Roman ~:** das Volk von Rom; **B** (*derog.: rabble*) Pöbel, *der* (*abwertend*)

**popular** /ˈpɒpjʊlə(r)/ *adj.* **A** (*well liked*) beliebt; populär ‹Entscheidung, Maßnahme›; **I know I shan't be ~ if I suggest that** ich weiß, dass ich mich mit diesem Vorschlag nicht gerade beliebt mache; **he was a very ~ choice** mit ihm hatte man sich für einen sehr beliebten *od.* populären Mann entschieden; **be ~ with sb.** bei jmdm. beliebt sein; **he's ~ with the girls** die Mädchen mögen ihn; **I'm not very ~ in the office just now** im Büro ist man zurzeit nicht gut auf mich zu sprechen; **prove ~:** gut ankommen; **B** (*suited to the public*) volkstümlich; populär (*geh.*); **at ~ prices** zu günstigen Preisen; **~ edition** Volksausgabe, *die;* **~ journal/newspaper** Massenblatt, *das;* **a ~ romance** ein Liebesroman; **~ science** die Populärwissenschaft; **C** (*prevalent*) landläufig; allgemein ‹Unzufriedenheit›; **~ etymology** Volksetymologie, *die;* **D** (*of the people*) Volks-; verbreitet ‹Aberglaube, Irrtum, Meinung›; allgemein ‹Wahl, Zustimmung, Unterstützung›; **~ remedy** Hausmittel, *das;* **by ~ request** auf allgemeinen Wunsch

**popular: ~ ˈart** *n.* Volkskunst, *die;* **~ ˈfront** *n.* (*Polit.*) Volksfront, *die*

**popularise** ⇒ **popularize**

**popularity** /pɒpjʊˈlærɪtɪ/ *n., no pl.* Popularität, *die;* Beliebtheit, *die;* (*of decision, measure*) Popularität, *die;* **that won her ~ with her classmates** das machte sie bei ihren Klassenkameradinnen beliebt

P

**popularize** /ˈpɒpjʊləraɪz/ *v.t.* **A** (*make popular*) populär machen; ~ **sth.** einer Sache (*Dat.*) Popularität verschaffen; **B** (*make known*) bekannt machen; **C** (*make understandable*) breiteren Kreisen zugänglich machen; popularisieren (*geh.*)

**popularly** /ˈpɒpjʊləlɪ/ *adv.* **A** (*generally*) allgemein; landläufig; **it is ~ believed that ...:** es ist ein im Volk verbreiteter Glaube, dass ...; **B** (*for the people*) volkstümlich; allgemein verständlich

**popular ˈmusic** *n.* Unterhaltungsmusik, *die;* Populärmusik, *die* (*fachspr.*)

**populate** /ˈpɒpjʊleɪt/ *v.t.* bevölkern ‹Land, Gebiet›; bewohnen ‹Insel, Gebiet›; **the characters that ~ his novel** die Charaktere, die seinen Roman bevölkern; **thickly** *or* **heavily** *or* **densely/sparsely ~d** dicht/dünn besiedelt ‹Land, Gebiet usw.›; dicht/dünn bevölkert ‹Stadt›

**population** /pɒpjʊˈleɪʃn/ *n.* **A** Bevölkerung, *die;* **Britain has a ~ of 56 million** Großbritannien hat 56 Millionen Einwohner; **the growing immigrant ~ of London** der wachsende Einwandereranteil an der Londoner Bevölkerung; **the seal ~ of Greenland** der Seehundbestand *od.* (*fachspr.*) die Seehundpopulation Grönlands; **B** (*Statistics*) Grundgesamtheit, *die*

**popuˈlation explosion** *n.* Bevölkerungsexplosion, *die*

**populism** /ˈpɒpjʊlɪzm/ *n.* Populismus, *der*

**populist** /ˈpɒpjʊlɪst/ **1** *n.* Populist, *der*/Populistin, *die.* **2** *adj.* populistisch

**populous** /ˈpɒpjʊləs/ *adj.* dicht bevölkert

**ˈpop-up** *adj.* Stehauf‹buch, -illustration›; ~ **toaster** Toaster mit Auswerfmechanismus; ~ **menu** (*Computing*) Pop-up-Menü, *das*

**porcelain** /ˈpɔːslɪn/ *n.* **A** Porzellan, *das; attrib.* Porzellan-; **Meissen ~:** Meißner Porzellan; **B** (*article*) Porzellangegenstand, *der;* **~s** Porzellan, *das*

**porch** /pɔːtʃ/ *n.* **A** (*Archit.*) Vordach, *das;* (*with side walls*) Vorbau, *der;* (*enclosed*) Windfang, *der;* (*of church etc.*) Vorhalle, *die;* **B** (*Amer.: veranda*) [offene] Veranda

**porcine** /ˈpɔːsaɪn/ *adj.* Schweine-; (*fig.*) schweineähnlich; wie ein Schwein *nachgestellt*

**porcupine** /ˈpɔːkjʊpaɪn/ *n.* (*Zool.*) **A** (*Brit.: Hystricidae*) Stachelschwein, *das;* **B** (*Amer.: Erethizontidae*) Baumstachler, *der*

**pore¹** /pɔː(r)/ *n.* Pore, *die*

**pore²** *v.i.* ~ **over sth.** etw. [genau] studieren; (*think deeply*) ~ **over** *or* **on sth.** über etw. (*Akk.*) [gründlich] nachdenken

**pork** /pɔːk/ *n.* Schweinefleisch, *das; attrib.* Schweine-; Schweins- (*bes. südd.*); **a leg of ~:** eine Schweinekeule

**pork: ~ barrel** *n.* (*Amer. coll.*) *aus politischen Gründen bewilligte staatliche Zuschüsse;* ~ **butcher** *n.* Schweinemetzger, *der* (*bes. südd.*); Schweineschlachter, *der* (*bes. nordd.*); ~ **ˈchop** *n.* Schweinekotelett, *das*

**porker** /ˈpɔːkə(r)/ *n.* Mastschwein, *das;* (*young pig*) Mastferkel, *das*

**pork: ~ ˈpie** *n.* Schweinepastete, *die;* **~-pie ˈhat** *n.* flacher [Herren]hut; ~ **ˈsausage** *n.* Schweinswürstchen, *das*

**porn** /pɔːn/ *n., no pl.* (*coll.*) Pornographie, *die;* Pornos, *Pl.* (*ugs.*); **write ~:** Pornos schreiben (*ugs.*); ~ **film** Pornofilm, *der* (*ugs.*)

**porno** /ˈpɔːnəʊ/ (*coll.*) **1** *n., no pl.* ⇒ **porn.** **2** *adj.* Porno- (*ugs.*)

**pornographic** /pɔːnəˈgræfɪk/ *adj.* pornographisch; Porno- (*ugs.*)

**pornography** /pɔːˈnɒgrəfɪ/ *n.* Pornographie, *die*

**porosity** /pɔːˈrɒsɪtɪ/ *n., no pl.* Porosität, *die*

**porous** /ˈpɔːrəs/ *adj.* porös ‹Fels, Gestein, Stoff›; porenreich ‹Haut, Holz›

**porpoise** /ˈpɔːpəs/ *n.* (*Zool.*) Schweinswal, *der*

**porridge** /ˈpɒrɪdʒ/ *n., no pl.* **A** (*food*) Porridge, *der;* Haferbrei, *der;* **B** (*sl.: imprisonment*) Knast, *der* (*ugs.*); **do ~:** Knast schieben (*salopp*); im Knast sitzen (*ugs.*)

**porridge ˈoats** *n. pl.* Haferflocken *Pl.*

**port¹** /pɔːt/ **1** *n.* **A** (*harbour*) Hafen, *der;* **come** *or* **put into ~:** [in den Hafen] einlaufen; **leave ~:** [aus dem Hafen] auslaufen; **reach ~:** den Hafen erreichen; ankommen; **out of ~:** auf See; **naval ~:** Kriegshafen, *der;* **any ~ in a storm** (*fig. coll.*) manchmal kann man sichs eben nicht aussuchen (*ugs.*); ≈ in der Not frisst der Teufel Fliegen (*ugs.*); ~ **of call** Anlaufhafen, *der;* (*fig.*) Ziel, *das;* **where's your next ~ of call?** (*fig.*) wo willst du als Nächstes hin?; ~ **of entry** Zoll-[abfertigungs]hafen, *der;* (*for goods*) Einfuhrhafen, *der;* (*for persons*) Einreisehafen, *der;* ⇒ *also* **free port**; **B** (*town*) Hafenstadt, *die;* Hafen, *der;* **C** (*Naut., Aeronaut.: left side*) Backbord, *das;* **land to ~!** Land an Backbord!; **turn** *or* **put the helm to ~:** nach Backbord drehen. **2** *adj.* (*Naut., Aeronaut.: left*) Backbord-; backbordseitig; **on the ~ bow/quarter** Backbord voraus/Backbord achteraus; ⇒ *also* **beam** 1 E; **tack¹** 1 C; **watch** 1 C

**port²** *n.* **A** (*Naut.: opening*) Pforte, *die;* **B** (*Naut.: porthole*) Seitenfenster, *das;* (*circular*) Bullauge, *das;* **C** (*aperture*) Öffnung, *die;* **D** (*gun aperture*) Schießscharte, *die;* (*on ship*) Geschützpforte, *die*

**port³** *n.* (*wine*) Portwein, *der;* Port, *der* (*ugs.*)

**portable** /ˈpɔːtəbl/ **1** *adj.* tragbar; portabel (*Werbespr.*). **2** *n.* (*television*) Portable, *der;* (*radio*) Portable, *der;* Koffergerät, *das;* (*typewriter*) Portable, *die;* Koffermaschine, *die*

**portage** /ˈpɔːtɪdʒ/ *n.* **A** (*carrying*) Transport über Land; **B** (*place*) Portage, *die*

**Portakabin** ® /ˈpɔːtəkæbɪn/ *n.* Container, *der;* (*as temporary office etc.*) Bürocontainer, *der;* (*as temporary living accommodation*) Wohncontainer, *der*

**portal** /ˈpɔːtl/ *n.* Eingang, *der;* Pforte, *die* (*geh.*); (*of church, palace, etc.*) Portal, *das;* **pass through the ~s of a place** (*fig.*) einen Ort besuchen; **the ~s of heaven** die Pforten des Himmels *od.* Himmelspforten (*dichter.*)

**port auˈthority** *n.* Hafenbehörde, *die*

**portcullis** /pɔːtˈkʌlɪs/ *n.* (*Archit.*) Fallgitter, *das;* Fallgatter, *das*

**portend** /pɔːˈtend/ *v.t.* hindeuten auf (+ *Akk.*); **what does this ~?** was hat das zu bedeuten?

**portent** /ˈpɔːtent/ *n.* (*literary*) Vorzeichen, *das;* Omen, *das;* **a ~ of doom** ein schlimmes [Vor]zeichen; ein böses Omen; **~s of war** Vorzeichen *od.* Vorboten des Krieges; **a ~ of the project's success** ein gutes Omen für den Erfolg des Vorhabens

**portentous** /pɔːˈtentəs/ *adj.* bedeutungsvoll; schicksalhaft ‹Bedeutung›; (*ominous*) unheilvoll

**porter¹** /ˈpɔːtə(r)/ *n.* ▶ **1261** (*Brit.: doorman*) Pförtner, *der;* (*of hotel etc.*) Portier, *der*

**porter²** *n.* **A** ▶ **1261** (*luggage handler*) [Gepäck]träger, *der*/-trägerin, *die;* (*in hotel*) Hausdiener, *der;* **B** (*Amer., Ir./Hist.: beer*) Porter, *der od. das;* **C** (*Amer. Railw.*) Schlafwagenschaffner, *der*/-schaffnerin, *die*

**porterage** /ˈpɔːtərɪdʒ/ *n.* (*charge*) Trägerlohn, *der*

**porterhouse ˈsteak** *n.* Porterhousesteak, *das*

**porter's ˈlodge** ⇒ **lodge** 1 B

**portfolio** /pɔːtˈfəʊlɪəʊ/ *n., pl.* **~s** **A** (*list*) Portefeuille, *das;* **B** (*Polit.*) Geschäftsbereich, *der;* Portefeuille, *das* (*geh.*); **C** (*case, contents*) Mappe, *die*

**ˈporthole** ⇒ **port²** B

**portico** /ˈpɔːtɪkəʊ/ *n., pl.* **~es** *or* **~s** (*Archit.*) Säulenvorbau, *der;* Portikus, *der* (*fachspr.*)

**portière** /pɔːˈtjeə(r)/ *n.* [schwerer] Türvorhang; Portiere, *die*

**portion** /ˈpɔːʃn/ **1** *n.* **A** (*part*) Teil, *der;* (*of ticket*) Abschnitt, *der;* (*of inheritance*) Anteil, *der;* **B** (*amount of food*) Portion, *die;* **C** (*arch./literary: destiny*) Los, *das;* Schicksal, *das;* **D** (*quantity*) gewisses Maß (**of** an + *Dat.*). **2** *v.t.* aufteilen (**among** unter + *Akk.*, **into** in + *Akk.*)

~ **ˈout** *v.t.* aufteilen (**among, between** unter + *Akk.*); **she ~ed out the food** sie verteilte das Essen

**Portland** /ˈpɔːtlənd/: ~ **ceˈment** *n.* Portlandzement, *der;* ~ **ˈstone** *n.* Portland[kalk]stein, *der*

**portly** /ˈpɔːtlɪ/ *adj.* beleibt; korpulent; **have a ~ frame** beleibt *od.* korpulent sein

**portmanteau** /pɔːtˈmæntəʊ/ *n., pl.* **~s** *or* **~x** /pɔːtˈmæntəʊz/ Reisekoffer, *der*

**portˈmanteau word** *n.* Port[e]manteauform, *die* (*fachspr.*); (*fig.: generalized term*) weiter Begriff

**portrait** /ˈpɔːtrɪt/ *n.* **A** (*picture*) Porträt, *das;* Bildnis, *das* (*geh.*); *attrib.* Porträt-; **sit for one's ~ [to sb.]** [jmdm.] Porträt sitzen; sich [von jmdm.] porträtieren lassen; **have one's ~ painted** sich porträtieren lassen; **full-length ~:** Ganzporträt, *das;* **B** (*description*) Porträt, *das;* Bild, *das;* **give/convey an unflattering ~ of sb./sth.** ein wenig schmeichelhaftes Bild von jmdm./etw. zeichnen

**portraitist** /ˈpɔːtrɪtɪst/ *n.* ▶ **1261** Porträtist, *der*/Porträtistin, *die;* (*painter also*) Porträtmaler, *der*/-malerin, *die;* (*photographer also*) Porträtfotograf, *der*/-fotografin, *die*

**portraiture** /ˈpɔːtrɪtʃə(r)/ *n.* Porträtieren, *das;* (*painting also*) Porträtmalerei, *die;* (*photographing also*) Porträtfotografie, *die;* **he is known for his ~:** er ist für *od.* durch seine Porträts bekannt

**portray** /pɔːˈtreɪ/ *v.t.* **A** (*describe*) darstellen; schildern; **B** (*make likeness of*) porträtieren ‹Person›; darstellen, wiedergeben ‹Atmosphäre usw.›; ‹Schauspieler:› darstellen ‹Rolle, Person›

**portrayal** /pɔːˈtreɪəl/ *n.* **A** (*description*) Darstellung, *die;* Schilderung, *die;* (*esp. of person*) Porträt, *das;* **B** (*acting*) Darstellung, *die;* **C** (*portrait*) Darstellung, *die;* Porträt, *das*

**Portugal** /ˈpɔːtjʊgl/ *pr. n.* Portugal (*das*)

**Portuguese** /pɔːtjʊˈgiːz/ ▶ **1275**, ▶ **1340** **1** *adj.* portugiesisch; **sb. is ~:** jmd. ist Portugiese/Portugiesin; ⇒ *also* **English** 1. **2** *n., pl. same* **A** (*person*) Portugiese, *der*/Portugiesin, *die;* **B** (*language*) Portugiesisch, *das;* ⇒ *also* **English** 2 A

**Portuguese man-of-ˈwar** *n.* (*Zool.*) Portugiesische Galeere

**pose** /pəʊz/ **1** *v.t.* **A** (*be cause of*) aufwerfen ‹Frage, Problem›; darstellen ‹Bedrohung, Problem›; bedeuten ‹Bedrohung›; mit sich bringen ‹Schwierigkeiten›; **B** (*propound*) vorbringen; aufstellen ‹Theorie›; **C** (*place*) Aufstellung nehmen lassen, sich aufstellen lassen ‹Gruppe, Kinder, Mannschaft, Gesellschaft›; Positur einnehmen lassen, posieren lassen ‹Modell›. **2** *v.i.* **A** (*assume attitude*) posieren; (*fig.*) sich geziert benehmen *od.* geben (*abwertend*); ~ **[in the] nude** für einen Akt posieren; **B** ~ **as** sich geben als; **he likes to ~ as an expert** er spielt gern den Experten. **3** *n.* Haltung, *die;* Pose, *die;* (*fig.*) Pose, *die;* Gehabe, *das* (*abwertend*); **strike a ~:** eine Pose einnehmen; **she's always striking ~s** (*fig.*) sie benimmt sich immer so geziert; **hold a ~:** eine Pose beibehalten; in einer Haltung verharren (*geh.*); **hold that ~!** bleib so!; **it's just a [big] ~** (*fig.*) es ist reine Pose

**poser** /ˈpəʊzə(r)/ *n.* (*question*) knifflige Frage; (*problem*) schwieriges Problem; **that's a real ~:** das ist eine harte Nuss (*ugs.*); **set some ~s for sb.** jmdm. manche harte Nuss zu knacken geben (*ugs.*)

**poseur** /pəʊˈzɜː(r)/ *n.* Blender, *der* (*abwertend*); Poseur, *der* (*geh. abwertend*)

**poseuse** /pəʊˈzɜːz/ *n. fem.* Blenderin, *die* (*abwertend*)

**posh** /pɒʃ/ **1** *adj.* (*coll.*) vornehm; nobel (*spött.*); stinkvornehm (*salopp*); ~ **hotel/newspaper** Nobelhotel, *das*/Nobelgazette, *die* (*spött.*); **the ~ people** die Schickeria (*ugs.*). **2** *adv.* **talk ~:** hochgestochen reden/mit vornehmem Akzent sprechen. **3** *v.t.* ~ **up** aufmotzen (*ugs.*)

**posit** /ˈpɒzɪt/ *v.t.* postulieren (*geh.*)

**position** /pəˈzɪʃn/ **1** *n.* **A** (*place occupied*) Platz, *der;* (*of player in team or line-up, of* *actor, of plane, ship, etc.*) Position, *die;* (*of hands of clock, words, stars*) Stellung, *die;* (*of building etc., of organ in body*) Lage, *die;* (*of river*) [Ver]lauf, *der;* **find one's ~ on a map** seinen Standort auf einer Karte finden; **take [up] one's ~:** seinen Platz einnehmen; **they took their ~ at the end of the queue** sie stellten sich ans Ende der Schlange; **after the second lap he was in fourth ~:** nach der zweiten Runde lag er an vierter Stelle; **he finished in second ~:** er belegte den zweiten Platz; **what ~ do you play [in]?** (*Sport*) in welcher Position spielst du?; **in the starting ~:** auf Startposition; **B** (*proper place*) **be in/out of ~:** an seinem Platz/nicht an seinem Platz sein; **put sth. into ~:** etw. an seinen Platz stellen; **C** (*Mil.*) Stellung, *die;* **D** (*Chess*) Position, *die;* Stellung, *die;* **~ play** Positionsspiel, *das;* Stellungsspiel, *das;* **leave the pieces in ~:** die Figuren aufgestellt *od.* stehen lassen; **E** (*fig.: mental attitude*) Standpunkt, *der;* Haltung, *die;* **take up a ~ on sth.** einen Standpunkt *od.* eine Haltung zu etw. einnehmen; **take the ~ that ...:** auf dem Standpunkt stehen *od.* sich auf den Standpunkt stellen, dass ...; **F** (*fig.: situation*) **be in a good ~ [financially]** [finanziell] gut gestellt sein *od.* dastehen; **be in a ~ of strength** eine starke Position haben; **negotiate from a ~ of strength** aus einer Position der Stärke heraus verhandeln; **what's the ~?** wie stehen *od.* liegen die Dinge?; **what would you do if you were in my ~?** was würdest du in meiner Lage tun?; **put yourself in my ~!** versetz dich [einmal] in meine Lage!; **be in a/no ~ to do sth.** in der Lage/nicht in der Lage sein, etw. zu tun; **he's in no ~ to criticize us** es steht ihm nicht zu, uns zu kritisieren; ⇒ *also* **jockey** 2; **G** (*rank*) Stellung, *die;* Position, *die;* **a person of ~:** eine hoch gestellte Persönlichkeit; **a high ~ in society** eine hohe gesellschaftliche Stellung; **a pupil's ~ in class** die Stellung eines Schülers innerhalb der Klasse; **social ~:** gesellschaftliche *od.* soziale Stellung; **H** (*employment*) [Arbeits]stelle, *die;* Stellung, *die;* **the ~ of ambassador in Bogotá** die Position des Botschafters in Bogotá; **permanent ~:** Dauerstellung, *die;* **the ~ of assistant manager** die Stelle *od.* Position des stellvertretenden Geschäftsführers; **rise to a ~ of responsibility** in eine verantwortliche Stellung aufsteigen; **~ of trust** Vertrauensstellung, *die;* Vertrauensposten, *der;* **I** (*posture*) Haltung, *die;* (*during sexual intercourse*) Stellung, *die;* Position, *die;* (*ballet*) Position, *die;* (*yoga*) Stellung, *die;* **in a reclining ~:** zurückgelehnt; **in a sitting ~:** in sitzender Position *od.* Stellung; sitzend; **in an uncomfortable ~:** in unbequemer Stellung *od.* Haltung.

**2** *v.t.* **A** platzieren; positionieren ‹Lautsprecherboxen, Leuchten usw.›; aufstellen, postieren ‹Polizisten, Wachen›; **~ oneself near the exit** sich in die Nähe des Ausgangs stellen/setzen; ‹Wache, Posten usw.:› sich in der Nähe des Ausgangs aufstellen; **B** (*Mil.: station*) stationieren

**positional** /pəˈzɪʃənl/ *adj.* **A** (*Ling.*) isolierend ‹Sprache›; **B** (*Sport*) positionell (*fachspr.*); **~ play** Stellungsspiel, *das;* **C** (*Mil.*) **~ war** Stellungskrieg, *der*

**positive** /ˈpɒzɪtɪv/ **1** *adj.* **A** (*definite*) eindeutig; entschieden ‹Weigerung›; positiv ‹Recht›; **in a ~ tone of voice** in bestimmtem *od.* entschiedenem Ton; **to my ~ knowledge ...:** wie ich ganz sicher weiß, ...; **B** (*convinced*) sicher; **Are you sure? — P~!** Bist du sicher? — Absolut [sicher]!; **he is ~ that he is right** er ist sich (*Dat.*) völlig sicher, dass er Recht hat; **I'm ~ of it** ich bin [mir] [dessen] ganz sicher; **C** (*affirmative*) positiv; **D** (*optimistic*) positiv; **regard sth. in a ~ light** etw. in positivem Licht sehen; **E** (*showing presence of sth.*) positiv ‹Ergebnis, Befund, Test›; **F** (*constructive*) konstruktiv ‹Kritik, Vorschlag, Anregung, Rat, Hilfe›; positiv ‹Philosophie, Erfahrung, Denken›; **she's the most ~ of the group** sie hat von allen in der Gruppe die positivste Einstellung; **G** (*Math.*) positiv; **H** (*Ling.*) ungesteigert; **I** (*Electr.*) positiv ‹Elektrode, Platte, Ladung, Ion›; Plus‹platte, -leiter›; ⇒ *also* **feedback** B; **J** *as intensifier* (*coll.*) echt; **it would be a ~ miracle** es wäre ein echtes Wunder *od.* (*ugs.*) echt ein Wunder; **K** (*Photog.*) positiv; Positiv-.

**2** *n.* **A** (*Ling.*) Positiv, *der;* Grundstufe [des Adjektivs], *die;* **B** (*Photog.*) Positiv, *das;* Positivbild, *das*

**positive discrimiˈnation** *n.* positive Diskriminierung (*fachspr.*); Bevorzugung, *die*

**positively** /ˈpɒzɪtɪvlɪ/ *adv.* **A** (*constructively*) konstruktiv ‹kritisieren›; positiv ‹denken›; **B** (*Electr.*) positiv; **C** (*definitely*) eindeutig, entschieden ‹sich weigern›; **D** *as intensifier* (*coll.*) echt (*ugs.*); **it's ~ marvellous that ...:** es ist echt Spitze, dass ...

**ˈpositive: ~ sign** *n.* (*Math.*) positives Vorzeichen; (*symbol*) Pluszeichen, *das;* **~ vetting** *n., no indef. art.* (*Brit.*) Sicherheitsüberprüfung, *die*

**positivism** /ˈpɒzɪtɪvɪzm/ *n.* (*Philos., Relig.*) Positivismus, *der;* ⇒ *also* **logical positivism**

**positivist** /ˈpɒzɪtɪvɪst/ **1** *n.* Positivist, *der*/Positivistin, *die.* **2** *adj.* positivistisch

**positron** /ˈpɒzɪtrɒn/ *n.* (*Phys.*) Positron, *das*

**posse** /ˈpɒsɪ/ *n.* **A** (*Amer.: force with legal authority*) [Polizei]trupp, *der;* [Polizei]aufgebot, *das;* **B** (*crowd*) Schar, *die;* **~ of advisers** Beraterstab, *der*

**possess** /pəˈzes/ *v.t.* **A** (*own*) besitzen; verfügen über (+ *Akk.*) (*geh.*); **be ~ed of** gesegnet sein mit (*geh.*); **~ed of money/wealth** bemittelt/begütert; **~ed of reason** vernunftbegabt; **B** (*have as faculty or quality*) haben; **~ great passion** sehr leidenschaftlich sein; **C** (*dominate*) ‹Furcht usw.:› ergreifen, Besitz nehmen von ‹Person›; **what ~ed you/him?** was ist in dich/ihn gefahren?; was für ein Teufel hat dich/ihn geritten? (*ugs.*); **D** (*dated: copulate with*) besitzen (*geh. verhüll.*); **E** (*arch./formal*) **~ oneself of sth.** sich einer Sache (*Gen.*) bemächtigen; sich (*Dat.*) etw. aneignen

**possessed** /pəˈzest/ *adj.* (*dominated*) besessen; **he's a man ~:** er ist ein Besessener; **~ by the devil/by** *or* **with an idea** vom Teufel/von einer Idee besessen; **be ~ by** *or* **with fear/horror** von Angst/Schrecken ergriffen sein; **be ~ by** *or* **with greed/ambition** von Gier/Ehrgeiz besessen sein; **be ~ by** *or* **with envy/rage** von Neid erfüllt sein/rasen; **like one ~:** wie ein Besessener/eine Besessene

**possession** /pəˈzeʃn/ *n.* **A** (*thing possessed*) Besitz, *der;* **some of my ~s** einige meiner Sachen; **B** *in pl.* (*property*) Besitz, *der;* (*territory*) Besitzungen; **worldly ~s** irdische Güter; **all his ~s** sein ganzer Besitz; all seine Habe; **C** (*controlling*) **take ~ of** (*Mil.*) einnehmen ‹Festung, Stadt usw.›; besetzen ‹Gebiet›; **the enemy's ~ of the town** die feindliche Herrschaft *od.* Herrschaft des Feindes über die Stadt; **~ by the devil** Besessensein vom Teufel; **D** (*possessing*) Besitz, *der;* **~ of land/firearms** Landbesitz, *der*/Waffenbesitz, *der;* **be in ~ of sth.** im Besitz einer Sache (*Gen.*) sein; **come into** *or* **get ~ of sth.** in den Besitz einer Sache (*Gen.*) gelangen; **regain** *or* **resume ~ of sth.** wieder in den Besitz einer Sache (*Gen.*) gelangen; **be in ~ of a high income** über ein hohes Einkommen verfügen; **put sb. in ~ of sth./of the facts** jmdn. in den Besitz einer Sache (*Gen.*) bringen/jmdn. ins Bild setzen; **in full ~ of one's senses** im Vollbesitz seiner geistigen Kräfte; **be in full ~ of the facts** voll im Bilde sein; **the information in my ~:** die mir vorliegenden Informationen; **have sth. in one's ~:** im Besitz einer Sache (*Gen.*) sein; **take ~ of** in Besitz nehmen; beziehen ‹Haus, Wohnung›; **E** (*Sport*) **win ~ of the ball** in Ballbesitz gelangen; **lose ~:** den Ball verlieren; **in ~:** im Ballbesitz; **F** (*Law*) Besitz, *der;* **enter into ~ of sth.** etw. in Besitz nehmen; ⇒ *also* **point** 1 C; **vacant** A

**possessive** /pəˈzesɪv/ **1** *adj.* **A** (*jealously retaining possession*) besitzergreifend; **be ~ about sth.** etw. eifersüchtig hüten; **be ~ about** *or* **towards sb.** an jmdn. Besitzansprüche stellen; **B** (*Ling.*) possessiv; **~ adjective** Possessivadjektiv, *das;* ⇒ *also* **pronoun.** **2** *n.* (*Ling.*) Possessivum, *das*

**posˈsessive case** *n.* Possessiv[us], *der*

**possessively** /pəˈzesɪvlɪ/ *adv.* besitzergreifend

**possessor** /pəˈzesə(r)/ *n.* Besitzer, *der*/Besitzerin, *die;* **be the ~ of a fine singing voice** eine schöne Singstimme besitzen

**posset** /ˈpɒsɪt/ *n.* (*Hist.*) *heiße Milch mit Bier od. Wein und Gewürzen*

**possibility** /pɒsɪˈbɪlɪtɪ/ *n.* **A** Möglichkeit, *die;* **be within the range** *or* **bounds of ~:** im Bereich des Möglichen liegen; **there's no ~ of his coming/agreeing** es ist ausgeschlossen, dass er kommt/zustimmt; **there's not much ~ of success** die Erfolgschancen sind nicht groß; **the constant ~ of failure** die ständige Gefahr des Scheiterns; **if by any ~ ...:** falls tatsächlich ...; (*if without taking any trouble*) falls zufällig ...; **is there any ~ of our being able to do it?** gibt es für uns irgendeine Möglichkeit, es zu tun?; **it's a distinct ~ that ...:** es ist gut möglich, dass ...; **accept that sth. is a ~:** es akzeptieren, dass etw. möglich ist *od.* nicht auszuschließen ist; **he is a ~ for the job** er ist ein möglicher Anwärter auf die Stelle; er kommt für die Stelle in Betracht; **what are the possibilities?** welche Möglichkeiten gibt es?; **B** *in pl.* (*potential*) Möglichkeiten *Pl.;* **the house/subject has possibilities** aus dem Haus/Thema lässt sich etwas machen; **the scheme has possibilities** in dem Plan stecken Möglichkeiten

**possible** /ˈpɒsɪbl/ **1** *adj.* **A** möglich; **if ~:** wenn *od.* falls möglich; wenn es geht; **as ... as ~:** so ... wie möglich; möglichst ...; **the greatest ~ assistance** die größtmögliche Unterstützung; **all the assistance ~:** alle denkbare Unterstützung; **anything is ~:** alles ist möglich; es ist alles möglich; **at the earliest ~ time** so früh wie möglich; (*formal*) zum frühestmöglichen Termin/Zeitpunkt; **they made it ~ for me to be here** sie haben es mir ermöglicht, hier zu sein; **the worst ~ solution** die denkbar schlechteste Lösung; die schlechteste der möglichen Lösungen; **if it's at all ~:** wenn es irgend geht *od.* möglich ist; **would it be ~ for me to ...?** könnte ich vielleicht ...?; **it is not ~ to do more** mehr kann man unmöglich tun; **for ~ emergencies** für eventuelle Notfälle; **all ~ risks** alle denkbaren Risiken; **I'll do everything ~ to help you** ich werde mein Möglichstes *od.* alles nur Erdenkliche tun, um dir zu helfen; **be as kind to her as ~:** sei so nett zu ihr, wie [nur irgend] möglich; **we will help as far as ~:** wir werden helfen, so weit wir können; **B** (*likely*) [durchaus *od.* gut] möglich; **few thought his election was ~:** nur wenige glaubten an seine Wahl; **C** (*acceptable*) möglich; **there's no ~ excuse for it** dafür gibt es keine Entschuldigung; **the only ~ man for the position** der einzige Mann, der für die Stellung infrage kommt.

**2** *n.* Anwärter, *der*/Anwärterin, *die;* Kandidat, *der*/Kandidatin, *die;* **presidential ~:** Präsidentschaftsanwärter, *der*

**possibly** /ˈpɒsɪblɪ/ *adv.* **A** (*by possible means*) **I cannot ~ commit myself** ich kann mich unmöglich festlegen; **how can I ~?** wie könnte ich?; **how could I ~ have come?** wie hätte ich denn kommen können?; **can that ~ be true?** kann das überhaupt wahr sein *od.* stimmen?; **they did all they ~ could** sie haben alles Menschenmögliche *od.* alles in ihrer Macht Stehende getan; **if I ~ can** wenn es mir irgendwie möglich ist; **as often as I ~ can** sooft ich irgend kann; **I'll come as soon as I ~ can** ich komme so früh, wie es nur irgend geht; **can you ~ lend me £10?** kannst du mir vielleicht *od.* wohl 10 Pfund leihen?; **B** (*perhaps*) möglicherweise; vielleicht; **he might ~ be related to them** er ist vielleicht *od.* möglicherweise mit ihnen verwandt; **Do you think ...? — P~:** Glaubst du ...? — Möglich[erweise] *od.* Vielleicht

**possum** /ˈpɒsəm/ *n.* (*coll.*) **A** ⇒ **opossum** A; **B play ~** (*pretend to be asleep*) sich schlafend stellen; (*pretend to be dead*) sich tot stellen; **C** (*Austral., NZ*) Fuchskusu, *der*

**post**[1] /pəʊst/ ❶ *n.* Ⓐ *(as support)* Pfosten, *der;* Ⓑ *(stake)* Pfahl, *der;* **deaf as a ~** *(coll.)* stocktaub *(ugs.)*; ⇒ *also* **pillar** A; Ⓒ *(Racing)* *(starting/finishing ~)* Start-/Zielpfosten, *der;* **be left at the ~:** [hoffnungslos] abgehängt werden *(ugs.)*; weit zurückbleiben; *(fig.)* von Anfang an keine Chancen haben; **be first past the ~:** als Erster durchs Ziel gehen; **the 'first past the ~' system** das Mehrheitswahlsystem; **be beaten at the ~** *(lit. or fig.)* im letzten Moment noch geschlagen werden; ⇒ *also* **pip**[5]; Ⓓ *(Sport: of goal)* Pfosten, *der.*
❷ *v.t.* Ⓐ *(stick up)* anschlagen, ankleben ‹Plakat, Aufruf, Notiz, Zettel›; **~ something on the noticeboard** einen Anschlag am schwarzen Brett machen; **'~ no bills'** „Plakate ankleben verboten"; Ⓑ *(make known)* [öffentlich] anschlagen *od.* bekannt geben; ausschreiben ‹Belohnung›; ausweisen ‹Ansteigen, Gewinn, Verlust›; öffentlich ankündigen, bekannt machen ‹Veranstaltung›; **~ [as] missing** als vermisst melden; Ⓒ *(Amer.: achieve)* erreichen; schaffen; erringen ‹Sieg›
**~ 'up** *v.t.* anschlagen; ankleben; **~ up a notice** einen Anschlag machen

**post**[2] ❶ *n.* Ⓐ *(Brit.: one dispatch of letters)* Postausgang, *der;* **by the same ~:** mit gleicher Post; **by return of ~:** postwendend; **sort the ~:** die Postausgänge sortieren; Ⓑ *(Brit.: one collection of letters)* [Briefkasten]leerung, *die;* Ⓒ *(Brit.: one delivery of letters)* Post[zustellung], *die;* **in the ~:** bei der Post (⇒ *also* **d**); **the ~ has come** die Post ist da *od.* ist schon gekommen; **the arrival of the ~:** das Eintreffen der Briefpost; **sort the ~:** die Posteingänge sortieren; **is there a second ~ in this area?** gibt es hier eine zweite Postzustellung?; **there is no ~ on Sundays** sonntags kommt keine Post; **there has been no ~ today** heute ist keine Post gekommen; **is there any ~ for me?** habe ich Post?; **have a heavy ~:** viel Post bekommen; **the morning's ~:** die Morgenpost; **you'll get it in tomorrow's ~:** du bekommst es mit der morgigen Post; Ⓓ *no pl., no indef. art.* *(Brit.: official conveying)* Post, *die;* **by ~:** mit der Post; per Post; **in the ~:** in der Post (⇒ *also* **c**); Ⓔ *(~ office)* Post, *die;* *(~box)* Briefkasten, *der;* **take sth. to the ~:** etw. zur Post bringen/*(to ~box)* etw. einwerfen *od.* in den Briefkasten werfen; **drop sth. in the ~:** etw. einwerfen *od.* in den Briefkasten werfen.
❷ *v.t.* Ⓐ *(dispatch)* abschicken; *(take to ~ office)* zur Post bringen; *(put in ~box)* einwerfen; **~ sb. sth.** jmdm. etw. schicken; **~ sth. off** etw. abschicken; Ⓑ *(Bookk.)* übertragen; **~ up** auf den letzten Stand bringen ‹Bücher›; verbuchen ‹Verkäufe, Abschlüsse›; Ⓒ *(fig. coll.)* **keep sb. ~ed [about *or* on sth.]** jmdn. [über etw. *(Akk.)*] auf dem Laufenden halten

**post**[3] ❶ *n.* Ⓐ *(job)* Stelle, *die;* Posten, *der;* **in ~:** im Amt; **a teaching ~:** eine Stelle als Lehrer *od.* Lehrerstelle; **a ~ as director** ein Posten als Direktor *od.* Direktorenposten; **the ~ of driver** die Stelle des Fahrers; **a diplomatic ~:** ein diplomatischer Posten; Ⓑ *(Mil.: place of duty)* Posten, *der;* *(fig.)* Platz, *der;* Posten, *der;* **the sentries are at/took up their ~s** die Wachen sind auf ihren/bezogen ihre Posten; **take up one's ~** *(fig.)* seinen Platz einnehmen; **all workers must be at their ~s by 8.30** alle Arbeiter müssen um 8.30 Uhr an ihren Arbeitsplätzen sein; **last/first ~** *(Brit. Mil.)* letzter/erster Zapfenstreich; Ⓒ *(Mil.: position of unit)* Garnison, *die;* Standort, *der;* Ⓓ *(Mil.: fort)* Fort, *das;* Ⓔ *(trading-~)* Niederlassung, *die.*
❷ *v.t.* Ⓐ *(place)* postieren; aufstellen; Ⓑ *(appoint)* einsetzen; **~ sb. overseas/to Abu Dhabi/to a ship** jmdn. in Übersee/in Abu Dhabi/auf einem Schiff einsetzen; **be ~ed to an embassy** an eine Botschaft versetzt werden; **~ an officer to a unit** einen Offizier einer Einheit *(Dat.)* zuweisen; **be ~ed away** versetzt *od.* *(Mil.)* abkommandiert werden; **where's he being ~ed to?** wo wird er eingesetzt?; *(to new place)* wohin wird er versetzt?

**post-** /pəʊst/ *pref.* nach-/Nach-; post-/Post- *(mit Fremdwörtern)*

**postage** /ˈpəʊstɪdʒ/ *n.* Porto, *das*

**postage: ~ 'due** *n.* Nachgebühr, *die;* **~-due stamp** Portomarke, *die;* **~ meter** *n.* *(Amer.)* Frankiermaschine, *die;* [Post]freistempler, *der;* **~ stamp** *n.* Briefmarke, *die;* Postwertzeichen, *das* *(Postw.)*

**postal** /ˈpəʊstl/ *adj.* Ⓐ *(of the post)* Post-; postalisch ‹Aufgabe, Einrichtung›; Ⓑ *(by post)* per Post *nachgestellt;* **~ tuition** Fernunterricht, *der*

**postal: ~ card** *(Amer.)* ⇒ **postcard**; **~ code** ⇒ **postcode**; **~ district** *n.* Zustellbezirk, *der;* **~ meter** *n.* *(Amer.)* ⇒ **postage meter**; **~ order** *n.* ≈ Postanweisung, *die;* **~ rate** *n.* Postgebühr, *die;* **P~ Union** *n.* Postverein, *der;* **~ vote** *n.* Briefwahl, *die*

**post: ~bag** *(Brit.)* ⇒ **mailbag**; **~box** *n.* *(Brit.)* Briefkasten, *der;* **~card** *n.* Postkarte, *die;* **~-chaise** *n.* *(Hist.)* Postchaise, *die*

**post-'classic[al]** *adj.* nachklassisch

**'postcode** *n.* *(Brit.)* Postleitzahl, *die*

**post'date** *v.t.* Ⓐ *(give later date to)* vordatieren; Ⓑ *(belong to later date than)* späteren *od.* jüngeren Datums sein als (+ *Nom.*); von einem späteren Zeitpunkt/aus einer späteren Zeit datieren als (+ *Nom.*)

**post-'doctoral** *adj.* **~ thesis/grant** Habilitationsschrift, *die*/-stipendium, *das;* **~ research** *Forschungen im Anschluss an die Promotion*

**poster** /ˈpəʊstə(r)/ *n.* Ⓐ *(placard)* Plakat, *das;* *(notice)* Anschlag, *der;* Ⓑ *(printed picture)* Plakat, *das;* Poster, *das*

**'poster colour** ⇒ **poster paint**

**poste restante** /pəʊst reˈstɑ̃t/ *n.* Abteilung/Schalter für postlagernde Sendungen; **write to sb. [at the] ~ in Rome** jmdm. postlagernd nach Rom schreiben

**posterior** /pɒˈstɪərɪə(r)/ ❶ *adj.* Ⓐ *(formal: later)* später; **~ to** nach; Ⓑ *(placed behind)* hinter... ❷ *n.* *(joc.)* Hinterteil, *das* *(ugs.)*

**posterity** /pɒˈsterɪtɪ/ *n., no pl., no art.* *(future generations)* die Nachwelt; **go down to ~ [as sth.]** [als etw.] in die Geschichte eingehen

**'poster paint** *n.* Plakatfarbe, *die*

**post: ~ exchange** *n.* *(Amer. Mil.)* PX, *das;* *Kaufhaus für Angehörige der amerikanischen Truppen;* **~-'free** *(Brit.)* ❶ *adj.* Ⓐ *(free of charge)* portofrei; Ⓑ *(with postage prepaid)* freigemacht; frankiert; ❷ *adv.* portofrei

**postgrad** /pəʊstˈgræd/ *(coll.)*, **post'graduate** ❶ *adj.* Graduierten-; ‹College, Studiengang› für Graduierte; postgraduell *(fachspr.)*; **~uate study** ≈ Aufbaustudium, *das;* ≈ *weiterführendes Studium;* **~uate student** Graduierte, *der/die;* **~uate degree** höherer akademischer Grad. ❷ *n.* Graduierte, *der/die*

**post: ~'haste** *adv.* schnellstens; **~ horn** *n.* *(Hist.)* Posthorn, *das;* **~ horse** *n.* *(Hist.)* Postpferd, *das;* **~ house** *n.* *(Hist.)* Poststation, *die*

**posthumous** /ˈpɒstjʊməs/ *adj.* Ⓐ nachgelassen, *(geh.)* postum ‹Buch usw.›; Ⓑ *(occurring after death)* nachträglich; post[h]um *(geh.)*; **~ fame** Nachruhm, *der;* Ⓒ nach dem Tode des Vaters geboren, post[h]um *(geh.)* ‹Kind›

**posthumously** /ˈpɒstjʊməslɪ/ *adv.* postum *(geh.)*, nach dem Tode ‹veröffentlicht werden›; postum *(geh.)*, nachträglich ‹rehabilitieren, verleihen›; nach dem Tode des Vaters ‹geboren›

**postil[l]ion** /pəˈstɪljən/ *n.* *(Hist.)* Postillion, *der*

**post-im'pressionism** *n.* Postimpressionismus, *der*

**post-im'pressionist** *n.* Postimpressionist, *der*/Postimpressionistin, *die*

**post-impression'istic** *adj.* postimpressionistisch

**post-in'dustrial** *adj.* postindustriell

**posting** /ˈpəʊstɪŋ/ *n.* *(appointment)* Versetzung, *die;* *(post)* Stelle, *die;* Posten, *der;* **he's got a new ~:** er ist versetzt worden

**post: ~man** /ˈpəʊstmən/, *pl.* **~men** /ˈpəʊstmən/ *n.* ▶ 1261 Briefträger, *der;* Postbote, *der* *(ugs.)*; **~man's 'knock** *n.* *(Brit.)* *Gesellschaftsspiel, bei dem der 'Postbote' Briefe gegen einen Kuss aushändigt;* **~mark** ❶ *n.* Poststempel, *der;* **'date as ~mark'** „Datum des Poststempels"; ❷ *v.t.* abstempeln; **the letter was ~marked 'Brighton'** der Brief war in Brighton abgestempelt; **~master** *n.* ▶ 1261 Postamtvorsteher, *der;* Postmeister, *der* *(veralt.)*; **P~master 'General** *n., pl.* **P~masters General** *(Hist.)* Postminister, *der*/-ministerin, *die;* **~ mill** *n.* Bockmühle, *die;* **~mistress** *n.* ▶ 1261 Postamtvorsteherin, *die;* Postmeisterin, *die* *(veralt.)*; **~'modern** ⇒ **~modernist** 1; **~'modernism** *n.* Postmodernismus, *der;* Postmoderne, *die;* **~'modernist** ❶ *adj.* postmodernistisch; postmodern; ❷ *n.* Postmodernist, *der*/Postmodernistin, *die;* Vertreter, *der*/Vertreterin, *die* der Postmoderne

**postmortem** /pəʊstˈmɔːtəm/ ❶ *adv.* nach dem Tode; post mortem *(fachspr.)*. ❷ *adj.* Ⓐ *(after death)* nach dem Tode eintretend, *(fachspr., geh.)* postmortal ‹Veränderung›; **~ examination** Leichenschau, *die;* *(with dissection)* Obduktion, *die;* Ⓑ *(fig.: after an event)* nachträglich. ❸ *n.* Ⓐ *(examination)* Obduktion, *die;* Ⓑ *(fig.)* nachträgliche Bewertung *od.* Analyse; Manöverkritik, *die* *(fig.)*; **hold *or* have a ~ on sth.** etw. einer nachträglichen Bewertung *od.* Analyse unterziehen; **hold a ~ on the election** eine Wahlanalyse durchführen; das Wahlergebnis einer Analyse *(Dat.)* unterziehen

**post'natal** *adj.* nach der Geburt *nachgestellt;* nachgeburtlich *(fachspr.)*; postnatal *(fachspr.)*

**post: ~ office** *n.* Ⓐ *(organization)* **the P~ Office** die Post; *attrib.* **P~ Office** Post-; **work for the P~ Office** bei der Post arbeiten; Ⓑ *(place)* Postamt, *das;* Post, *die;* Ⓒ *(Amer.)* ⇒ **postman's knock**; **~ office box** *n.* ▶ 1286 Postfach, *das;* **~paid** ❶ /'--/ *adj.* frankiert; freigemacht; **~paid envelope** Freiumschlag, *der;* ❷ /-'-/ *adv.* portofrei; franko *(fachspr. veralt.)*; **£6.50 ~paid** 6,50 Pfund einschließlich Porto; **reply ~paid** mit vorfrankiertem Umschlag/mit vorfrankierter Postkarte antworten

**postpone** /pəʊstˈpəʊn, pəˈspəʊn/ *v.t.* verschieben; *(for an indefinite period)* aufschieben; **~ sth. until next week** etw. auf nächste Woche verschieben; **~ sth. for a year** etw. um ein Jahr verschieben; **~ further discussion of a matter** die weitere Diskussion einer Angelegenheit zurückstellen

**postponement** /pəʊstˈpəʊnmənt, pəˈspəʊnmənt/ *n.* Verschiebung, *die;* *(for an indefinite period)* Aufschub, *der;* **a 30-day ~:** eine Verschiebung um 30 Tage

**postpositive** /pəʊstˈpɒzɪtɪv/ *adj.* *(Ling.)* nachgestellt; postpositiv *(fachspr.)*

**postprandial** /pəʊstˈprændɪəl/ *adj.* *(formal/joc.)* Verdauungs‹schläfchen, -spaziergang, -schnaps› *(ugs.)*; ‹Rede, Gespräch, Schwatz› nach dem Essen, nach Tisch

**'post room** *n.* Poststelle, *die*

**postscript** /ˈpəʊstskrɪpt, ˈpəʊskrɪpt/ *n.* Nachschrift, *die;* Postskript, *das;* *(fig.)* Nachtrag, *der;* **the ~ was that ...** *(fig.)* das Ende vom Lied war, dass ... *(ugs.)*; **add a ~** *(fig.)* einen Nachtrag machen, etwas nachtragen (**to** zu)

**post-'tax** *adj.* nach Abzug der Steuern *(nachgestellt)*

**'post town** *n.* Postort, *der*

**'post-traumatic stress disorder** *n.* *(Med.)* posttraumatische Belastungsstörung

**postulate** ❶ /ˈpɒstjʊleɪt/ *v.t.* *(claim as true, existent, necessary)* postulieren; ausgehen von; *(depend on)* voraussetzen; *(put forward)* aufstellen ‹Theorie›. ❷ /ˈpɒstjʊlət/ *n.* *(fundamental condition)* Postulat, *das* *(geh.)*; *(prerequisite)* Voraussetzung, *die;* Postulat, *das* *(geh.)*; *(Math.)* Axiom, *das*

**posture** /ˈpɒstʃə(r)/ ❶ *n.* *(relative position)* [Körper]haltung, *die;* *(fig.: mental, political, military)* Haltung, *die;* **have poor/good ~:** eine schlechte/gute Haltung haben. ❷ *v.i.* posieren; *(strike a pose)* sich in Positur werfen *(ugs., leicht spött.)*

**'post-war** *adj.* Nachkriegs-; der Nachkriegszeit *nachgestellt;* **~ credits** Kriegsanleihen

**'postwoman** *n.* ▶ **1261** Briefträgerin, *die;* Postbotin, *die* (*ugs.*)

**posy** /ˈpəʊzɪ/ *n.* Sträußchen, *das*

**pot¹** /pɒt/ ❶ *n.* Ⓐ (*cooking vessel*) [Koch]topf, *der;* **it's [a case of] the ~ calling the kettle black** (*coll.*) ein Esel schimpft *od.* (*geh.*) schilt den andern Langohr; der soll/die soll/die sollen sich an die eigene Nase fassen (*ugs.*); **go to ~** (*coll.*) den Bach runtergehen (*ugs.*); **let oneself go to ~** (*coll.*) sich hängen lassen [und den Bach runtergehen] (*ugs.*); ⇒ *also* **boil¹** 1 A; **pan¹** 1 A; Ⓑ (*container, contents*) Topf, *der;* (*tea~, coffee ~*) Kanne, *die;* **a ~ of tea** eine Kanne Tee; (*in café etc.*) ein Kännchen Tee; ⇒ *also* **gold** 1 B; Ⓒ (*drinking vessel*) Becher, *der;* (*with handle*) Krug, *der;* Ⓓ (*coll.: as prize*) Pott, *der* (*ugs.*); Ⓔ (*coll.: prize*) Preis, *der;* Ⓕ (*coll.: ~belly*) Schmerbauch, *der* (*ugs.*); Wampe, *die* (*ugs. abwertend*); Ⓖ (*coll.: large sum*) **a ~ of/~s of** massenweise; jede Menge; Ⓗ (*amount bet*) [Gesamt]einsatz, *der;* Pot, *der;* **contribute to the ~:** [ein]setzen.

❷ *v.t.*, **-tt-** Ⓐ (*put in container[s]*) in einen Topf/in Töpfe füllen; Ⓑ (*put in plant ~*) **~ [up]** eintopfen; **~ out** austopfen; Ⓒ (*kill*) abschießen; abknallen (*ugs. abwertend*); Ⓓ (*Brit. Billiards, Snooker*) einlochen. ⇒ *also* **potted**.

❸ *v.i.*, **-tt-** ballern (*ugs.*) (**at** auf + *Akk.*)

**pot²** *n.* (*sl.: marijuana*) Pot, *das* (*Jargon*)

**potable** /ˈpəʊtəbl/ *adj.* (*formal*) trinkbar

**potash** /ˈpɒtæʃ/ *n.* Kaliumkarbonat, *das;* Pottasche, *die* (*veralt.*); **~ fertilizer** Kalidünger, *der*

**potassium** /pəˈtæsɪəm/ *n.* (*Chem.*) Kalium, *das*

**potato** /pəˈteɪtəʊ/ *n., pl.* **~es** Ⓐ Kartoffel, *die;* **a hot ~** (*fig. coll.*) ein heißes Eisen (*ugs.*); **drop sb./sth. like a hot ~** (*coll.*) jmdn./etw. fallen lassen wie eine heiße Kartoffel; ⇒ *also* **bake** 1 A; **boil** 2 A; **chip** 2 B; **crisp** 2 A; **fry¹** 2; **mash** 1 D, 2; Ⓑ (*plant*) Kartoffel[pflanze], *die*

**potato 'salad** *n.* Kartoffelsalat, *der*

**pot: ~belly** *n.* Ⓐ (*bulging belly*) Schmerbauch, *der* (*ugs.*); Wampe, *die* (*ugs. abwertend*); (*from malnutrition*) Blähbauch, *der;* Ⓑ (*person*) Dickbauch, *der* (*scherzh.*); Dickwanst, *der* (*salopp abwertend*); **~boiler** *n.* (*derog.*) (*novel etc.*) Fließbandprodukt, *das* (*abwertend*); (*film, theatre production*) Fließbandproduktion, *die* (*abwertend*)

**potency** /ˈpəʊtənsɪ/ *n.* Ⓐ (*of drug*) Wirksamkeit, *die;* (*of alcoholic drink*) Stärke, *die;* (*Mil.*) Schlagkraft, *die;* (*of reason, argument*) Gewichtigkeit, *die;* (*influence*) Einfluss, *der;* Potenz, *die* (*geh.*); **the ~ to do sth.** die Fähigkeit, etw. zu tun; Ⓑ (*of male*) **[sexual] ~:** [sexuelle] Potenz

**potent** /ˈpəʊtənt/ *adj.* Ⓐ [hoch]wirksam ‹Droge, Medizin›; stark ‹Schnaps, Kaffee, Tee usw.›; schlagkräftig ‹Mannschaft, Truppe, Waffe›; gewichtig, schwerwiegend ‹Grund, Argument›; wichtig, entscheidend ‹Faktor›; stark ‹Motiv›; (*influential*) einflussreich; potent (*geh.*); Ⓑ (*sexually*) potent ‹Mann›

**potentate** /ˈpəʊtənteɪt/ *n.* Herrscher, *der/* Herrscherin, *die;* Potentat, *der*/Potentatin, *die* (*geh. abwertend*)

**potential** /pəˈtenʃl/ ❶ *adj.* potenziell (*geh.*); möglich; **~ energy** potenzielle Energie. ❷ *n.* Ⓐ (*possibility*) Potenzial, *das* (*geh.*); Möglichkeiten *Pl.;* **~ for growth/development** Wachstums-/Entwicklungspotenzial, *das;* **acting ~:** schauspielerisches Talent; **leadership ~:** Führungsqualitäten; **realize/reach one's ~:** seine Möglichkeiten ausschöpfen; **develop one's ~:** seine Fähigkeiten [weiter]entwickeln; Ⓑ (*Phys.*) Potenzial, *das*

**potentiality** /pətenʃɪˈælɪtɪ/ *n.* Ⓐ (*capacity*) Möglichkeiten *Pl.;* **have great growth ~:** ein großes Wachstumspotenzial haben; Ⓑ (*possibility*) Möglichkeit, *die*

**potentially** /pəˈtenʃəlɪ/ *adv.* potenziell (*geh.*); **he's ~ dangerous** er kann gefährlich werden; **a ~ useful invention** eine Erfindung mit Anwendungsmöglichkeiten; **he's ~ capable of it** er wäre dazu fähig; **a ~ rich country** ein Land, das reich sein könnte

**potentilla** /pəʊtənˈtɪlə/ *n.* (*Bot.*) Fingerkraut, *das*

**pot: ~head** *n.* (*sl.*) Kiffer, *der*/Kifferin, *die* (*ugs.*); **~ herb** *n.* Küchenkraut, *das;* **~hole** ❶ *n.* Ⓐ (*in road*) Schlagloch, *das;* Ⓑ (*deep cave*) [tiefe] Höhle; ❷ *v.i.* Höhlen erkunden; **~holer** /ˈpɒthəʊlə(r)/ *n.* [Hobby]höhlenforscher, *der/*-forscherin, *die;* **~holing** /ˈpɒthəʊlɪŋ/ *n.* Erkundung von Höhlen; **go ~holing** Höhlen erkunden gehen; Höhlenfahrten/eine Höhlenfahrt machen (*fachspr.*); **~-hunter** *n.* Ⓐ (*hunter*) Jäger, der alles abschießt[, was ihm vor die Flinte kommt] (*abwertend*); Ⓑ (*athlete*) Pokalsammler, *der/* -sammlerin, *die*

**potion** /ˈpəʊʃn/ *n.* Trank, *der*

**pot: ~'luck** *n.* **take ~luck [with sb.]** sich überraschen lassen; **there are so many to choose from; I'll just take ~luck** die Auswahl ist so groß; ich greife einfach mal aufs Geratewohl *od.* blind einen/eine/eins raus; **~ plant** *n.* Topfpflanze, *die*

**potpourri** /pəʊpʊəˈriː, pəʊˈpʊərɪ/ *n.* Ⓐ Duftmischung, *die;* Ⓑ (*fig.*) (*of music*) Potpourri, *das;* (*of literary writings*) Sammlung, *die;* Anthologie, *die* (*Literaturw.*); (*mixture*) Sammelsurium, *das;* buntes Allerlei

**pot: ~ roast** ❶ *n.* Schmorbraten, *der;* ❷ *v.t.* schmoren; **~sherd** /ˈpɒtʃɜːd/ *n.* (*Archaeol.*) [Ton]scherbe, *die;* **~shot** *n.* Ⓐ (*random shot*) Schuss aufs Geratewohl; **take a ~shot [at sb./sth.]** aufs Geratewohl [auf jmdn./ etw.] schießen; Ⓑ (*fig.: critical remark*) Attacke, *die;* **take a ~shot at sth.** etw. attackieren; Ⓒ (*fig.: random attempt*) Versuch auf gut Glück; Schuss ins Blaue [hinein]

**pottage** /ˈpɒtɪdʒ/ ⇒ **mess** 1 E

**potted** /ˈpɒtɪd/ *adj.* Ⓐ (*preserved*) eingemacht; **~ meat/fish** Fleisch-/Fischkonserven; Ⓑ (*planted*) Topf-; Ⓒ kurz gefasst; (*derog.: easily assimilated*) für schlichtere Gemüter *nachgestellt;* **a ~ biography/history of England** eine Kurzbiografie/ein Abriss der Geschichte Englands

**potter¹** /ˈpɒtə(r)/ *n.* ▶ **1261** Töpfer, *der*/Töpferin, *die*

**potter²** *v.i.* [he]rumwerkeln (*ugs.*); **~ round the shops** durch die Geschäfte bummeln; **~ along the road** ‹Autofahrer:› gemütlich die Straße entlangzuckeln; **~ [about] in the garden** sich (*Dat.*) im Garten zu schaffen machen

**~ a'bout, ~ a'round** *v.i.* herumwerkeln (*ugs.*) (**with** an + *Dat.*); **~ about in a canoe** in einem Kanu herumpaddeln; **~ about in the garden** ⇒ **~²**

**potter's 'wheel** *n.* Töpferscheibe, *die*

**pottery** /ˈpɒtərɪ/ *n.* Ⓐ *no pl., no indef. art.* (*vessels*) Töpferware, *die;* Keramik, *die; attrib.* Ton-; Keramik-; Ⓑ (*workshop*) Töpferei, *die;* Ⓒ *no pl., no indef. art.* (*craft*) Töpferei, *die*

**'potting compost** *n.* Blumenerde, *die*

**potting-shed** /ˈpɒtɪŋʃed/ *n.* (*Brit.*) Gewächshaus [zum Vorziehen von Pflanzen]

**potty¹** /ˈpɒtɪ/ *adj.* (*Brit. coll.: crazy*) verrückt (*ugs.*) (**about, on** nach); **he's driving me ~:** er macht mich wahnsinnig (*ugs.*); **they've gone ~:** sie sind [völlig] übergeschnappt (*ugs.*)

**potty²** *n.* (*Brit. coll.*) Töpfchen, *das;* **be ~-trained** aufs Töpfchen gehen

**'potty-train** *v.t.* **~ a baby** ein Baby an den Topf *od.* ans Töpfchen gewöhnen; **the baby is ~ed** das Baby ist sauber *od.* geht aufs Töpfchen

**pouch** /paʊtʃ/ *n.* Ⓐ (*small bag*) Tasche, *die;* Täschchen, *das;* (*worn on belt*) Gürteltasche, *die;* (*drawstring bag*) Beutel, *der;* Ⓑ (*under eye*) [Tränen]sack, *der;* Ⓒ (*ammunition bag*) [Patronen]tasche, *die;* Ⓓ (*mailbag*) Postsack, *der;* Postbeutel, *der;* (*diplomatic bag*) Kuriertasche, *die;* Ⓔ (*Zool.*) (*of marsupial*) Beutel, *der;* (*of pelican*) Kehlsack, *der*

**pouffe** /puːf/ *n.* (*cushion*) Sitzpolster, *das;* Puff, *der*

**poulterer** /ˈpəʊltərə(r)/ *n.* Geflügelhändler, *der*/-händlerin, *die;* ⇒ *also* **baker**

**poultice** /ˈpəʊltɪs/ ❶ *n.* Breiumschlag, *der;* Breipackung, *die.* ❷ *v.t.* einen Breiumschlag auflegen auf (+ *Akk.*)

**poultry** /ˈpəʊltrɪ/ *n.* Ⓐ *constr. as pl.* (*birds*) Geflügel, *das;* Ⓑ *no pl., no indef. art.* (*as food*) Geflügel, *das.* ⇒ *also* **farm** 1 A; **farmer**

**pounce** /paʊns/ ❶ *v.i.* Ⓐ sich auf sein Opfer stürzen; **~ [up]on** sich stürzen auf (+ *Akk.*); ‹Raubvogel:› herabstoßen auf (+ *Akk.*); **be ~d upon by sb.** von jmdm. angefallen werden; Ⓑ (*fig.*) **~ [up]on/at** sich stürzen auf (+ *Akk.*); **then we'll ~!** dann schlagen wir zu!. ❷ *n.* Sprung, *der;* Satz, *der;* **make a ~ on sb.** sich auf jmdn. stürzen

**pound¹** /paʊnd/ *n.* Ⓐ ▶ **1683** (*unit of weight*) [britisches] Pfund (*453,6 Gramm*); **two ~s of apples** 2 Pfund Äpfel; **by the ~:** pfundweise; **it's 20 pence a ~:** es kostet 20 Pence das Pfund; **two-~:** Zwei-Pfund-‹Dose, Brot, Packung›; zweipfündig, zwei Pfund schwer ‹Kugel, Kohlkopf›; **exact** *or* **demand one's ~ of flesh** (*fig.*) sein Recht rücksichtslos verlangen; Ⓑ ▶ **1328** (*unit of currency*) Pfund, *das;* **five-~note** Fünfpfundnote, *die;* Fünfpfundschein, *der;* **it must have cost ~s** das muss eine schöne Stange Geld gekostet haben (*ugs.*); **[it's] a ~ to a penny** (*fig. coll.*) es ist so gut wie sicher; ich wette hundert zu eins

**pound²** *n.* (*enclosure*) Pferch, *der;* (*for stray dogs*) Zwinger [für eingefangene Hunde]; (*for cars*) Abstellplatz [für polizeilich abgeschleppte Fahrzeuge]

**pound³** ❶ *v.t.* Ⓐ (*crush*) zerstoßen; zerdrücken ‹Tomaten›; Ⓑ (*thump*) einschlagen auf (+ *Akk.*) ‹Person›; herumhämmern auf (+ *Dat.*) (*ugs.*) ‹Klavier, Tisch, Schreibmaschine›; klopfen ‹Fleisch›; ‹Sturm:› heimsuchen ‹Gebiet, Insel›; ‹Wellen:› klatschen auf (+ *Akk.*) ‹Strand, Ufer,› gegen *od.* an (+ *Akk.*) ‹Felsen, Schiff›; ‹Geschütz:› unter Beschuss (*Akk.*) nehmen ‹Ziel›; ‹Bombenflugzeug:› bombardieren ‹Ziel›; **~ sb./sth. with one's fists** jmdn./etw. mit den Fäusten bearbeiten *od.* traktieren; **the ship was ~ed by the waves** die Wellen klatschten gegen das Schiff; **~ the beat** (*coll.*) ‹Polizist:› zu Fuß seine Runde machen; Ⓒ (*knock*) **~ to pieces** ‹Wellen:› zertrümmern, zerschmettern ‹Schiff›; ‹Geschütz, Bomben:› in Trümmer legen ‹Stadt, Mauern›; Ⓓ (*compress*) **~ [down]** feststampfen ‹Erde, Boden›; (*by treading*) festtreten.

❷ *v.i.* Ⓐ (*make one's way heavily*) stampfen; Ⓑ (*beat rapidly*) ‹Herz:› heftig schlagen *od.* klopfen *od.* (*geh.*) pochen; Ⓒ (*strike*) ‹See, Brandung:› donnern; **~ away** ‹Artillerie:› donnern; **~ at/on** herumhämmern auf (+ *Dat.*) (*ugs.*) ‹Klavier, Tisch, Schreibmaschine›

**~ a'way at** *v.t.* unter schweren [ständigen] Beschuss nehmen ‹Feind, Stadt›; (*fig.*) herumhämmern auf (+ *Dat.*) (*ugs.*) ‹Klavier, Schreibmaschine usw.›; (*work at*) ackern an (+ *Dat.*) (*ugs.*)

**~ 'out** *v.t.* (*on typewriter*) herunterhämmern (*ugs.*) ‹Brief, Aufsatz›; (*on piano*) hämmern (*ugs.*) ‹Lied, Stück›; **~ out sth. on the typewriter** etw. in die [Schreib]maschine hämmern

**poundage** /ˈpaʊndɪdʒ/ *n.* Ⓐ (*per pound of weight*) Gebühr [pro Pfund]; Ⓑ (*per pound sterling*) (*charge, fee*) Gebühr, *die;* (*commission*) Provision [pro Pfund]

**-pounder** /ˈpaʊndə(r)/ *n. in comb.* -pfünder, *der*

**pounding** /ˈpaʊndɪŋ/ *n.* Ⓐ (*striking*) (*of hammer etc.*) Schlagen, *das;* Klopfen, *das;* (*of artillery*) [schwerer] Beschuss; (*of waves*) Klatschen, *das;* **the ship took a ~ from the waves** das Schiff wurde von den Wellen kräftig durchgeschüttelt; **our team took a ~:** unsere Mannschaft musste eine Schlappe einstecken (*ugs.*); **his play took a ~ from the critics** sein Stück wurde von den Kritikern verrissen; Ⓑ (*of hooves, footsteps*) Stampfen, *das;* (*of train*) Rumpeln, *das;* Ⓒ (*beating*) (*of heart*) Klopfen, *das;* Pochen, *das* (*geh.*); (*of music, drums*) Dröhnen, *das*

**pound 'note** *n.* (*Hist.*) Pfundnote, *die;* Pfundschein, *der*

P

**'pound[s] sign** *n.* Pfundzeichen, *das*

**pour** /pɔ:(r)/ ❶ *v.t.* Ⓐ gießen, schütten ‹Flüssigkeit›; schütten ‹Sand, Kies, Getreide usw.›; (*into drinking vessel*) einschenken; eingießen; **~ a bucket of water over sb.'s head** jmdm. einen Eimer Wasser über den Kopf gießen *od.* schütten; **~ water over the flowers** die Blumen wässern *od.* [mit Wasser] gießen; **they ~ed beer all over him** sie übergossen ihn mit Bier; **~ scorn** *or* **ridicule on sb./sth.** jmdn. mit Spott übergießen *od.* überschütten/über etw. (*Akk.*) spotten; **~ oil on the flames** (*fig.*) Öl ins Feuer gießen; **~ oil on troubled waters** *or* **the water** (*fig.*) Öl auf die Wogen gießen; ⇒ *also* **water** 1 A; Ⓑ (*discharge*) ‹Fluss:› ergießen (*geh.*) ‹Wasser›; (*fig.*) pumpen ‹Geld, Geschosse›.
❷ *v.i.* Ⓐ (*flow*) strömen; ‹Rauch:› hervorquellen (**from** aus); **sweat was ~ing off the runners** den Läufern lief der Schweiß in Strömen herunter; **~ [with rain]** in Strömen regnen; [in Strömen] gießen (*ugs.*); **it never rains but it ~s** (*fig.*) da kommt aber auch alles zusammen; Ⓑ (*fig.*) strömen; **~ in** herein-/hineinströmen; **~ out** heraus-/hinausströmen; **tourists/refugees ~ into the city** Touristen/Flüchtlinge strömen in Scharen in die Stadt; **~ out of** strömen aus; (*fig.*) ‹Menge, Personen:› strömen aus ‹Gebäude, Halle›; ‹Musik:› schallen aus ‹Musikbox›; ‹Propaganda:› tönen aus ‹Lautsprecher›; **the crowd ~ed out of the doors** die Menge strömte durch die Türen hinaus; **cars ~ed along the road** ein [endloser] Strom von Autos flutete über die Straße; **letters/protests ~ed in** eine Flut von Briefen/Protesten brach herein

**~ 'down** *v.i.* **it's ~ing down** es gießt [in Strömen] (*ugs.*); **the rain ~ed down** es regnete in Strömen

**~ 'forth** ❶ *v.t.* von sich geben; erklingen lassen ‹Lied›; ausschütten ‹Kummer›; erzählen ‹Geschichte›. ❷ *v.i.* ‹Gesang, Musik usw.:› ertönen, erklingen; ‹Menge, Personen:› herausströmen

**~ 'off** *v.t.* abgießen

**~ 'out** ❶ *v.t.* eingießen, einschenken ‹Getränk›; ‹Fabrik:› ausstoßen ‹Produkte›; ‹Sender:› in den Äther schicken ‹Musik usw.›; **the chimney was ~ing out smoke** aus dem Schornstein quoll Rauch; **~ out one's thanks** sich überschwänglich bedanken; **~ out a torrent of words** eine Flut von Worten von sich geben *od.* hervorsprudeln lassen; **~ out one's woes** *or* **troubles/heart to sb.** jmdm. seinen Kummer/sein Herz ausschütten; **~ out one's feelings** seinen Gefühlen Luft machen *od.* Ausdruck geben; **~ out one's story to sb.** [jmdm.] seine Geschichte erzählen. ❷ *v.i.* ⇒ ~ 2 B

**pouring** /'pɔ:rɪŋ/ *adj.* Ⓐ strömend ‹Regen›; **a ~ wet day** ein völlig verregneter Tag; Ⓑ (*for dispensing*) Gieß-; (*for being poured*) flüssig

**pout** /paʊt/ ❶ *v.i.* Ⓐ einen Schmollmund machen *od.* ziehen; **~ing lips** Schmolllippen *Pl.*; **his mouth ~ed** er zog einen Schmollmund; Ⓑ (*sulk*) schmollen. ❷ *v.t.* Ⓐ (*protrude*) aufwerfen, schürzen ‹Lippen›; Ⓑ (*say*) schmollend sagen; schmollen. ❸ *n.* Schmollmund, *der;* **have the** *or* **be in the ~s** schmollen; im Schmollwinkel sitzen (*ugs.*)

**poverty** /'pɒvətɪ/ *n.* Ⓐ Armut, *die;* **plead ~:** behaupten, kein Geld zu haben; **fall into ~:** in Armut (*Akk.*) geraten; **be reduced to ~:** verarmt sein; Ⓑ (*Relig.*) Armut, *die;* Ⓒ (*fig.: deficiency*) Armut, *die* (**in** an + *Dat.*); **~ of ideas** Ideenarmut, *die;* gedankliche Armut; **~ of the soil/the region** Kargheit des Bodens/der Gegend; **spiritual ~:** seelische Verelendung; Ⓓ (*inferiority*) (*of language, vocabulary*) Armut, *die;* **~ of imagination/intellect** Fantasielosigkeit, *die*/geistige Unzulänglichkeit

**poverty: ~ line** *n.* Armutsgrenze, *die;* **be on the ~ line** an der Armutsgrenze liegen; **~-stricken** *adj.* Not leidend; verarmt; (*fig.*) armselig; kümmerlich; **~ trap** *n. soziale Situation, die dadurch gekennzeichnet ist, dass die Aufnahme einer Erwerbstätigkeit für den Betroffenen zu einer Verschlechterung seiner wirtschaftlichen Lage führen kann, weil er durch sie seinen Anspruch auf staatliche Sozialhilfe verlieren würde*

**pow** /paʊ/ *int.* peng

**POW** *abbr.* **prisoner of war**

**powder** /'paʊdə(r)/ ❶ *n.* Ⓐ Pulver, *das;* Ⓑ (*cosmetic*) Puder, *der;* **put ~ on one's face** sich (*Dat.*) das Gesicht pudern; Ⓒ (*medicine*) Pulver, *das;* **take a ~** (*Amer. fig. coll.*) die Flatter machen (*salopp*); Ⓓ (*gun~*) Pulver, *das;* **keep one's ~ dry** (*fig.*) sein Pulver trocken halten; **he/it is not worth ~ and shot** (*fig.*) er ist keinen Schuss Pulver wert (*ugs.*)/es ist die Mühe nicht wert. ❷ *v.t.* Ⓐ pudern; **I'll just go and ~ my nose** (*euphem.*) ich muss [nur] mal verschwinden (*ugs. verhüll.*); Ⓑ (*reduce to ~*) pulverisieren; zu Pulver verarbeiten ‹Milch, Eier›; **~ed milk** Milchpulver, *das;* Trockenmilch, *die;* **~ed eggs** Eipulver, *das;* Trockenei, *das;* **~ed sugar** Puderzucker, *der*

**powder: ~ 'blue** *n.* Ⓐ (*for laundry*) Waschblau, *das;* Ⓑ (*colour*) Himmelblau, *das;* **~ compact** ⇒ **compact²** A

**powdering** /'paʊdərɪŋ/ *n.* Ⓐ (*act*) [Ein]pudern, *das;* Ⓑ **a ~ of snow** eine dünne Schicht Schnee

**powder: ~ keg** *n.* (*lit. or fig.*) Pulverfass, *das;* **~ magazine** *n.* Pulvermagazin, *das;* **~ puff** *n.* Puderquaste, *die;* **~ room** *n.* [Damen]toilette, *die;* **~ snow** *n.* Pulverschnee, *der*

**powdery** /'paʊdərɪ/ *adj.* Ⓐ (*like powder*) pulv[e]rig; (*in powder form*) pulverförmig; (*finer*) pud[e]rig/puderförmig; Ⓑ (*crumbly*) bröckelig; bröselig

**power** /paʊə(r)/ ❶ *n.* Ⓐ (*ability*) Kraft, *die;* **if they had the ~:** wenn sie könnten *od.* die Möglichkeit hätten; **do all in one's ~ to help sb.** alles in seiner Macht *od.* seinen Kräften Stehende tun, um jmdm. zu helfen; **be beyond** *or* **outside** *or* **not be within sb.'s ~:** nicht in jmds. Macht (*Dat.*) liegen; Ⓑ (*faculty*) Fähigkeit, *die;* Vermögen, *das* (*geh.*); (*talent*) Begabung, *die;* Talent, *das;* **~ of smell** Riechvermögen, *das;* Geruchssinn, *der;* **tax sb.'s ~s to the utmost** ‹Arbeit, Aufgabe:› jmdn. bis an die Grenzen seiner Leistungsfähigkeit beanspruchen; **psychic ~s** übersinnliche Kräfte; **~s of observation** Beobachtungsgabe, *die;* **~s of persuasion** Überredungskünste; Ⓒ (*vigour, intensity*) (*of sun's rays*) Kraft, *die;* (*of sermon, performance*) Eindringlichkeit, *die;* (*solidity, physical strength*) Kraft, *die;* (*of a blow*) Wucht, *die;* **more ~ to you** *or* **your elbow!** viel Erfolg!; **have no ~** ‹Schuss, Schlag:› schwach *od.* kraftlos sein; Ⓓ (*authority*) Macht, *die,* Herrschaft, *die* (**over** über + *Akk.*); **have sth. in one's ~** ‹Diktator:› etw. in seiner Gewalt haben; die Herrschaft über etw. (*Akk.*) haben; **she was in his ~:** sie war in seiner Gewalt; er hatte sie in seiner Gewalt; **~ corrupts** Macht korrumpiert; Ⓔ (*personal ascendancy*) **[exercise/get] ~:** Einfluss [ausüben/gewinnen] (**over** auf + *Akk.*); Ⓕ (*political or social ascendancy*) Macht, *die;* **student/worker ~:** ≈ Mitbestimmung der Studenten/Arbeiter; **hold ~:** an der Macht sein; **fall from ~:** die Macht verlieren; ‹Präsident:› gestürzt werden; **come into ~:** an die Macht kommen; **the party in ~:** die herrschende Partei; die Partei an der Macht; **~ politics** Machtpolitik, *die;* **balance of ~:** Kräftegleichgewicht, *das;* **hold the balance of ~:** das Zünglein an der Waage sein; Ⓖ (*authorization*) Vollmacht, *die;* Befugnis, *die;* **~ to negotiate** Verhandlungsvollmacht, *die;* **exceed one's ~s** seine Kompetenzen *od.* Befugnisse überschreiten; ⇒ *also* **attorney** A; Ⓗ (*influential person*) Autorität, *die;* (*influential thing*) Machtfaktor, *der;* **be a real ~ in these circles** in diesen Kreisen großen Einfluss haben; **a ~ in the land** eine einflussreiche Macht; **be the ~ behind the throne** (*Polit.*) die graue Eminenz sein; **the ~s that be** die maßgeblichen Stellen; die da oben (*ugs.*); Ⓘ (*State*) Macht, *die;* **four-~ conference** Viermächtekonferenz, *die;* **a sea/world ~:** eine See-/Weltmacht; ⇒ *also* **Great Power**; Ⓙ (*coll.: large amount*) Menge, *die* (*ugs.*); **do sb. a ~ of good** jmdm. außerordentlich gut tun; Ⓚ ▶ **1352** (*Math.*) Potenz, *die;* **3 to the ~ of 4** 3 hoch 4; Ⓛ (*mechanical, electrical*) Kraft, *die;* (*electric current*) Strom, *der;* (*of loudspeaker, transmitter*) Leistung, *die;* **under one's/its own ~:** mit eigener Kraft; **steam ~:** Dampfkraft, *die;* **turn off the ~:** den Strom ausschalten *od.* abstellen; Ⓜ (*capacity for force*) Leistung, *die;* ⇒ *also* **horsepower**; Ⓝ (*Optics*) **[magnifying] ~:** Vergrößerungskraft, *die;* [Brenn]stärke, *die;* Ⓞ (*deity*) Macht, *die;* **the ~s of darkness** die Mächte der Finsternis; Ⓟ (*of drug*) Wirkung, *die.*
❷ *v.t.* ‹Treibstoff, Dampf, Strom, Gas:› antreiben; ‹Person:› betreiben ‹Maschine›; ‹Batterie:› mit Energie versehen *od.* versorgen; **he ~ed the ball past the goalkeeper** (*fig.*) er hämmerte den Ball ins Netz.
❸ *v.i.* (*coll.*) rasen

**power: ~-assisted** *adj.* **~-assisted steering/brakes** Servolenkung, *die*/-bremsen *Pl.*; **~ base** *n.* **the unions are the party's ~ base** die Gewerkschaften sind die Stützen der Partei; **have one's ~ base in the Middle West** seine treueste Anhängerschaft im Mittelwesten haben; **~ boat** *n.* Motorboot, *das;* **~ brakes** *n. pl.* Servobremsen *Pl.*; **~ cable** *n.* Hochspannungsleitung, *die;* **~ cut** *n.* Stromsperre, *die;* Stromabschaltung, *die;* (*failure*) Stromausfall, *der;* **~ dive** ❶ *n.* Sturzflug mit Vollgas, *der;* ❷ *v.i.* einen Sturzflug machen, ohne den Motor zu drosseln; **~ dressing** *n.: das Tragen betont streng wirkender Kleidung;* **~ drill** *n.* elektrische Bohrmaschine; **~-driven** *adj.* motorbetrieben; **~ failure** *n.* Stromausfall, *der*

**powerful** /'paʊəfl/ *adj.* Ⓐ (*strong*) stark; kräftig ‹Tritt, Schlag, Tier, Geruch, Körperbau, Statur›; heftig ‹Gefühl, Empfindung›; hell, strahlend ‹Licht›; scharf ‹Verstand, Geist›; überzeugend ‹Redner, Schauspieler›; eindringlich ‹Buch, Rede›; beeindruckend ‹Film, Darstellung›; Ⓑ (*influential*); mächtig ‹Clique, Person, Stadt, Herrscher›; wesentlich ‹Faktor›

**powerfully** /'paʊəfəlɪ/ *adv.* kräftig ‹gebaut›; eindringlich ‹predigen›; **he was ~ attracted to her** sie übte eine starke Anziehungskraft auf ihn aus

**power: ~house** *n.* Ⓐ ⇒ **power station**; Ⓑ (*fig.*) treibende Kraft; **be an intellectual ~house** intellektuell stets produktiv sein; **be a ~house of ideas and energy** ‹Person:› ein einfallsreiches Energiebündel sein

**powerless** /'paʊəlɪs/ *adj.* Ⓐ (*wholly unable*) machtlos; **be ~ to do sth.** nicht die Macht haben, etw. zu tun; **be ~ to help** nicht helfen können; Ⓑ (*without power*) machtlos; **~ in the hands of the enemy** hilflos in den Händen des Feindes; **leave sb. ~ against sth.** ‹Gesetz:› jmdn. machtlos gegen etw. machen; **leave sb. ~ to do sth.** ‹Gesetz:› jmdn. daran hindern *od.* es jmdm. unmöglich machen, etw. zu tun

**powerlessly** /'paʊəlɪslɪ/ *adv.* machtlos ‹zusehen, den Kopf schütteln›

**power: ~ line** *n.* Stromleitung, *die;* **overhead ~ line** Freileitung, *die;* **~ pack** *n.* Netzteil, *das;* Netzgerät, *das;* (*for camera flash*) Generatorteil, *das od. der;* **~ plant** *n.* Ⓐ ⇒ **~ station**; Ⓑ (*engine*) Triebwerk, *das;* **~ point** *n.* (*Brit.*) Steckdose, *die;* **~ saw** *n.* Motorsäge, *die;* **~ station** *n.* Kraftwerk, *das;* Elektrizitätswerk, *das;* **~ steering** *n.* Servolenkung, *die;* **~ stroke** *n.* Arbeitstakt, *der;* Arbeitshub, *der;* **~ supply** *n.* Energieversorgung, *die* (**to** *Gen.*)

**powwow** /'paʊwaʊ/ ❶ *n.* Pow-Wow, *das* (*Völkerk.*); (*fig.*) Besprechung, *die.* ❷ *v.i.* (*fig.*) sich beraten

**pox** /pɒks/ *n.* ▶ **1232** Ⓐ (*disease with pocks*) Pocken *Pl.*; Blattern *Pl.* (*veralt.*); **a ~ on him!** (*arch.*) dass ihn die Pest hole! (*veralt.*); Ⓑ (*coll.: syphilis*) Syphilis, *die;* Syph, *die od. der* (*salopp*)

**pp** *abbr.* **pianissimo** pp

**pp.** *abbr.* **pages**

**p.p.** /pi:'pi:/ *abbr.* **by proxy** pp[a].

**p.p.m.** *abbr.* **parts per million** (*by volume*) mm³/l; (*by weight*) mg/kg

p

**PPS** *abbr.* **second postscript** PPS

**PR** *abbr.* A **proportional representation;** B **public relations** PR; Public Relations; **PR man** Werbefachmann, *der;* PR-Mann, *der*

**pr.** *abbr.* **pair** P.

**practicable** /'præktɪkəbl/ *adj.* A *(feasible)* durchführbar ‹Projekt, Idee, Plan›; praktikabel ‹Lösung, Vorschlag, Plan, Methode›; B *(usable)* befahrbar, passierbar ‹Straße, Gelände›

**practical** /'præktɪkl/ ❶ *adj.* A praktisch; **for all ~ purposes** praktisch; **be true for all ~ purposes** in der Praxis Gültigkeit haben; B *(inclined to action)* praktisch veranlagt ‹Person›; praktisch ‹Denkweise, Veranlagung, Einstellung›; **~ man** Praktiker, *der;* **have a ~ approach/mind** praktisch an die Dinge herangehen; C *(virtual)* tatsächlich ‹Freiheit, Organisator›; D *(feasible)* möglich ‹Alternative›; praktikabel ‹Alternative, Möglichkeit›; ⇒ *also* **politics** C.
❷ *n.* praktische Prüfung

**practicality** /præktɪ'kælɪtɪ/ *n.* A *no pl.* *(of plan)* Durchführbarkeit, *die;* *(of person)* praktische Veranlagung; B *in pl.* *(practical details)* **the practicalities of the situation are that ...:** die Situation sieht praktisch so aus, dass ...; **deal in practicalities** sich mit praktischen Dingen befassen

**practical: ~ 'joke** *n.* Streich, *der;* **play ~ jokes on sb.** jmdm. Streiche spielen; **~ 'joker** *n.* Witzbold, *der*

**practically** /'præktɪkəlɪ/ *adv.* A *(almost)* praktisch *(ugs.)*; so gut wie; beinahe; B *(in a practical manner)* praktisch; **~ orientated course** praxisbezogener Kurs; **~ speaking, I see no way out** ich sehe praktisch keinen Ausweg

**'practical nurse** *n.* *(Amer.)* praktisch ausgebildete, nicht examinierte Krankenschwester; Hilfsschwester, *die*

**practice¹** /'præktɪs/ *n.* A *(repeated exercise)* Praxis, *die;* Übung, *die;* **years of ~:** Jahre der Praxis; jahrelange Übung; **put in** *or* **do some/a lot of ~:** üben/viel üben; **after all the ~ he has had, he should ...:** nach so viel Übung sollte er ...; **it's all good ~** *(means of improving)* es ist alles Übung; **~ makes perfect** *(prov.)* Übung macht den Meister; **be out of ~, not be in ~:** außer Übung sein; **be in ~:** in der Übung sein; B *(spell)* Übungen *Pl.;* **piano ~:** Klavierüben, *das;* **do one's piano ~:** Klavier üben; C *(work or business of doctor, lawyer, etc.)* Praxis, *die;* ⇒ *also* **general practice**; D *(habitual action)* übliche Praxis; Gewohnheit, *die;* **~ shows that ...:** die Erfahrung zeigt *od.* lehrt, dass ...; **make a ~ of doing sth.** es sich *(Dat.)* zur [An]gewohnheit machen, etw. zu tun; **good ~** *(satisfactory procedure)* gutes Vorgehen; gute Vorgehensweise; E *(action)* Praxis, *die;* **the ~ tends to be different** in der Praxis sieht es gewöhnlich *od.* die Praxis sieht gewöhnlich anders aus; **actual ~:** Praxis, *die;* **in ~:** in der Praxis; in Wirklichkeit; **be quite useless in ~:** in der Praxis nutzlos sein; praktisch nutzlos sein; **put sth. into ~:** etw. in die Praxis umsetzen; F *(custom)* Gewohnheit, *die;* **don't make a ~ of it** lass es nicht zur Gewohnheit werden; **regular ~:** Brauch, *der;* **it is the regular ~ to do sth.** es ist Brauch *od.* üblich, etw. zu tun; G *(legal procedures)* **[legal] ~:** Gerichtspraxis, *die.* ⇒ *also* **sharp** 1 F

**practice²**, **practiced**, **practicing** *(Amer.)* ⇒ **practis-**

**practise** /'præktɪs/ ❶ *v.t.* A *(apply)* anwenden; praktizieren; B *(be engaged in)* ausüben ‹Beruf, Tätigkeit, Religion›; **~ gymnastics** Gymnastik treiben; **~ medicine** [als Arzt] praktizieren; C *(exercise oneself in)* trainieren in (+ *Dat.*) ‹Sportart›; **~ the bicycle kick** den Fallrückzieher trainieren; **~ the piano/flute** Klavier/Flöte üben. ❷ *v.i.* üben

**practised** /'præktɪst/ *adj.* geübt ‹Person, Auge, Blick›; erfahren, versiert, routiniert ‹Person›; **with [a] ~ eye** mit geübtem Blick; **with ~ skill** routiniert

**practising** /'præktɪsɪŋ/ *adj.* praktizierend ‹Arzt, Katholik, Anglikaner usw.›; **~ homosexual** aktiv Homosexueller; **~ barrister** niedergelassener Anwalt

**practitioner** /præk'tɪʃənə(r)/ *n.* Fachmann, *der;* Praktiker, *der*/Praktikerin, *die;* **~ of the law, legal ~:** Anwalt, *der*/Anwältin, *die;* ⇒ *also* **general practitioner**; **medical practitioner**

**praesidium** /praɪ'sɪdɪəm/ ⇒ **presidium**

**pragmatic** /præg'mætɪk/ *adj.* pragmatisch

**pragmatically** /præg'mætɪkəlɪ/ *adv.* pragmatisch; *as sentence-modifier* pragmatisch betrachtet

**pragmatism** /'prægmətɪzm/ *n.* Pragmatismus, *der*

**pragmatist** /'prægmətɪst/ *n.* Pragmatiker, *der*/Pragmatikerin, *die*

**Prague** /prɑ:g/ *pr. n.* ▶ **1626** Prag *(das)*

**prairie** /'preərɪ/ *n.* Grasland, *das;* Grassteppe, *die;* *(in North America)* Prärie, *die;* **animal of the ~s** Steppentier, *das;* **out on the ~:** in der Grassteppe

**prairie: ~ 'chicken** *n.* Präriehuhn, *das;* **~ dog** *n.* Präriehund, *der;* **~ fire** *n.* *(fig.)* Lauffeuer, *das;* **~ 'hen** ⇒ **~ chicken**; **~ 'oyster** *n.* Prärieauster, *die;* **~ 'schooner** *n.* *(Amer. Hist.)* Planwagen, *der;* **~ 'wolf** *n.* Kojote, *der;* Präriewolf, *der*

**praise** /preɪz/ ❶ *v.t.* A *(commend)* loben; *(more strongly)* rühmen; **~ sb. for sth.** jmdn. für *od.* wegen etw. loben; *(more strongly)* jmdn. wegen etw. rühmen; **~ sb. for doing sth.** jmdn. dafür loben, dass er etw. tut/getan hat; B *(glorify)* preisen *(geh.)*, *(dichter.)* lobpreisen ‹Gott›.
❷ *n.* A *(approval)* Lob, *das;* **win high ~:** großes *od.* hohes Lob erhalten *od.* ernten; **be loud in one's ~s of sth.** des Lobes voll sein über etw. *(geh.)*; **a speech in ~ of sb.** eine Lobrede auf jmdn.; **sing one's own/sb.'s ~s** ein Loblied auf sich/jmdn. singen; B *(worship)* Lobpreisung, *die (dichter.)*; **offer ~ to God for sth.** Gott für etw. preisen *(geh.) od.* *(dichter.)* lobpreisen; **~ be!** Gott dem Herrn sei Lob und Preis! ⇒ *also* **damn** 1 A

**praiseworthy** /'preɪzwɜ:ðɪ/ *adj.* lobenswert; löblich *(oft iron.)*

**praline** /'prɑ:li:n/ *n.* gebrannte Nuss; gebrannte Mandel

**pram** /præm/ *n.* *(Brit.)* Kinderwagen, *der;* *(for dolls)* Puppenwagen, *der*

**prance** /prɑ:ns/ *v.i.* A ‹Pferd:› tänzeln; B *(fig.)* stolzieren; ‹Tänzer:› tänzeln; **~ about** *or* **around** ‹Kind, Tänzer:› herumhüpfen

**prang** /præŋ/ *(Brit. coll.)* ❶ *v.t.* A *(bomb)* bombardieren; bepflastern *(Soldatenspr.)*; B *(crash)* zu Bruch fahren ‹Fahrzeug›; bruchlanden mit ‹Flugzeug›; kaputtfahren *(ugs.)* ‹Auto›; C *(damage)* ramponieren *(ugs.)*. ❷ *n.* *(of aircraft)* Absturz, *der;* *(of vehicle)* Unfall, *der;* **have a ~:** Bruch machen *(Fliegerspr.)*; einen Unfall bauen *(ugs.)*

**prank** /præŋk/ *n.* Streich, *der;* Schabernack, *der;* **play a ~ on sb.** jmdm. einen Streich *od.* Schabernack spielen

**prankster** /'præŋkstə(r)/ *n.* Witzbold, *der* *(ugs. abwertend)*

**prat** /præt/ *n.* *(coll.)* Trottel, *der (ugs. abwertend)*

**prate** /preɪt/ *v.i.* A *(chatter)* daherreden *(abwertend)*; sabbeln *(salopp abwertend)*; **~ about sth.** sich lang und breit über etw. *(Akk.)* auslassen; B *(talk foolishly)* dumm daherreden; schwafeln *(ugs. abwertend)*; labern *(ugs. abwertend)*

**prating** /'preɪtɪŋ/ *adj.* geschwätzig *(abwertend)*; schwatzhaft *(abwertend)*

**prattle** /'prætl/ ❶ *v.i.* schwafeln *(ugs. abwertend)*; ‹Kleinkind:› plappern *(ugs.)*; **~ on about sth.** ohne Pause über etw. *(Akk.)* plappern; **~ away to sb.** zu jmdm. drauflosplappern. ❷ *n.* Geplapper, *das (ugs. abwertend)*; Geschwafel, *das (ugs. abwertend)*

**prawn** /prɔ:n/ *n.* Garnele, *die*

**prawn 'cocktail** *n.* Krabbencocktail, *der*

**pray** /preɪ/ ❶ *v.i.* beten **(for** um); **let us ~:** lasset uns beten; **~ [to God] for sb.** für jmdn. beten; **~ to God for help** Gott um Hilfe anflehen; **~ to God to do sth.** zu Gott beten, dass er etw. tue; **he is past ~ing for** ihm ist nicht mehr zu helfen. ❷ *v.t.* A *(beseech)* anflehen, flehen zu ‹Gott, Heiligen, Jungfrau Maria› **(for** um); **~ God for sth.** etw. von Gott erflehen; B **(~** *to***)** beten zu; **~ God she is safe** bitte, lieber Gott, lass sie in Sicherheit sein; C *(ellipt.: I ask)* bitte; **~ consider what ...:** überlegen Sie doch bitte, was ...; **what is the use of that, ~?** wozu, bitte [schön], soll das gut sein? ⇒ *also* **mantis**

**prayer** /preə(r)/ *n.* A Gebet, *das;* **make/offer up a ~ for sb.** für jmdn. beten; ein Gebet für jmdn. sprechen; **offer ~s for** beten für; **offer up a quick ~:** schnell ein Gebet sprechen; **say one's ~s** beten; **say your ~s!** *(iron.)* jetzt hast du Grund zum Beten *(iron.)*; **lead the ~s** die Gebete vorsprechen; ⇒ *also* **lord** 1 B; B *no pl., no art.* *(praying)* Beten, *das;* **gather in ~:** sich zum Gebet versammeln; **what's the use of ~?** was nützt es zu beten?; C *(service)* Andacht, *die;* **family ~s** Familienandacht, *die;* D *(entreaty)* inständige *od.* eindringliche Bitte; E *(Amer. coll.: slight chance of success)* Hauch einer Chance; **without a ~ of doing sth.** ohne die geringste Chance *od.* Aussicht, etw. erfolgreich zu tun

**prayer: ~ book** *n.* A Gebetbuch, *das;* B **the ~ book = the Book of Common Prayer** ⇒ **Common Prayer**; **~ mat** *n.* Gebetsteppich, *der;* **~ meeting** *n.* Gebetsversammlung, *die;* **~ wheel** *n.* Gebetsmühle, *die*

**preach** /pri:tʃ/ ❶ *v.i.* A *(deliver sermon)* predigen **(to** zu, vor + *Dat.*; **on** über + *Akk.*); **~ to the converted** *(fig.)* offene Türen einrennen *(ugs.)*; B *(fig.: give moral advice)* eine Predigt halten *(ugs.)*; *(abwertend)* Moralpredigten halten **(at, to** *Dat.*). ❷ *v.t.* A *(deliver)* halten ‹Predigt, Ansprache›; B *(proclaim)* predigen ‹Evangelium, Botschaft›; verkündigen ‹Glauben, Lehre, Evangelium, Botschaft›; C *(advocate)* predigen *(ugs.)*; **practice what one ~es** *(fig.)* was man [anderen] predigt, selbst auch tun

**preacher** /'pri:tʃə(r)/ *n.* A Prediger, *der*/Predigerin, *die;* B *(fig.)* **be a ~ of privatization** die Privatisierung predigen *(ugs.)*

**preachify** /'pri:tʃɪfaɪ/ *v.i.* predigen

**preachy** /'pri:tʃɪ/ *adj.* *(coll.)* predigerhaft

**preamble** /pri:'æmbl/ *n.* A *(preliminary statement)* Vorbemerkung, *die;* Einleitung, *die;* *(to a book)* Geleitwort, *das;* B *(Law)* Präambel, *die*

**pre-arrange** /pri:ə'reɪndʒ/ *v.t.* vorher absprechen; vorher ausmachen *od.* verabreden ‹Treffpunkt, Zeichen›

**pre-arrangement** /pri:ə'reɪndʒmənt/ *n.* vorherige Absprache; **by ~:** nach vorheriger Absprache

**prebend** /'prebənd/ *n.* Pfründe, *die*

**prebendary** /'prebəndərɪ/ *n.* A *(honorary canon)* ehrenamtlicher Pfründner/ehrenamtliche Pfründnerin; B *(holder of prebend)* Pfründner, *der*/Pfründnerin, *die*

**precarious** /prɪ'keərɪəs/ *adj.* A *(uncertain)* labil, prekär ‹Gleichgewicht, Situation›; gefährdet ‹Friede, Ernte›; **make a ~ living** eine unsichere Existenz haben; B *(insecure)* gefährlich ‹Weg, Pfad›; riskant, gefährlich ‹Politik, Leben, Balanceakt›; instabil *(geh.)* ‹Bauwerk›; kritisch, bedenklich ‹Gesundheitszustand›; unsicher ‹Koalition›

**precariously** /prɪ'keərɪəslɪ/ *adv.* **live ~:** eine unsichere Existenz haben; **be perched ~ on the edge of a steep slope** ‹Haus:› gefährlich nahe am Rand eines Steilhangs stehen

**pre-cast** /'pri:kɑ:st/ ❶ *v.t.*, **pre-cast** vorfabrizieren, vorfertigen ‹Beton›. ❷ *adj.* vorgefertigt; vorfabriziert

**precaution** /prɪ'kɔ:ʃn/ *n.* A *(action)* Vorsichts-, Schutzmaßnahme, *die;* **take ~s against sth.** Vorsichts- *od.* Schutzmaßnahmen gegen etw. treffen; **do sth. as a ~:** vorsichts- *od.* sicherheitshalber etw. tun; **do you take ~s?** *(euphem.)* nimmst du Verhütungsmittel?; B *no pl.* *(foresight)* Vorsicht, *die*

**precautionary** /prɪ'kɔ:ʃənərɪ/ *adj.* vorsorglich; vorbeugend; prophylaktisch *(geh.,*

*Med.*); präventiv (*geh.*); **~ measure** Vorsichts- *od.* Schutzmaßnahme, *die;* **as a ~ measure** vorsichts- *od.* sicherheitshalber

**precede** /prɪ'si:d/ *v.t.* Ⓐ (*in rank*) rangieren vor (+ *Dat.*); (*in importance*) wichtiger sein als; Vorrang haben vor (+ *Dat.*); **be ~d by sth.** hinter etw. (*Dat.*) rangieren; Ⓑ (*in order or time*) vorangehen (+ *Dat.*); (*in vehicle*) voranfahren (+ *Dat.*); (*in time also*) vorausgehen (+ *Dat.*); **the words that ~ [this paragraph]** die [diesem Absatz] vorangehenden Worte; Ⓒ (*preface, introduce*) **~ X with Y** X (*Dat.*) Y vorausschicken *od.* voranstellen; **~ an address with a welcome** einer Ansprache einen Willkommensgruß vorausschicken *od.* voranstellen

**precedence** /'presɪdəns/, **precedency** /'presɪdənsɪ/ *n., no pl.* Ⓐ (*in rank*) Priorität, *die* (*geh.*) (**over** vor + *Dat.*, gegenüber); Vorrang, *der* (**over** vor + *Dat.*); Ⓑ (*in time*) Priorität, *die* (*geh.*) (**over** vor + *Dat.*, gegenüber); zeitliches Vorhergehen; **have [the] ~ over all the others** Priorität vor *od.* gegenüber allen anderen haben; Ⓒ (*in ceremonies*) Rangordnung, *die*

**precedent** ❶ /'presɪdənt/ *n.* Ⓐ (*example*) Präzedenzfall, *der;* [vorangegangenes] exemplarisches Beispiel; **there is no ~ for this** so ein Fall ist noch nicht vorgekommen; **it is without ~ [that ...]** es ist noch nie da gewesen[, dass ...]; **set** *or* **create** *or* **establish a ~:** einen Präzedenzfall schaffen; Ⓑ (*Law*) Präzedenzfall, *der;* Präjudiz, *das* (*fachspr.*). ❷ /prɪ'si:dənt/ *adj.* Ⓐ (*in order*) vorangestellt; vorangehend; Ⓑ (*in time*) voran-, vorausgehend; vorhergehend

**precept** /'pri:sept/ *n.* Ⓐ (*command*) Grundsatz, *der;* Prinzip, *das;* Ⓑ (*moral instruction*) moralischer Grundsatz; Moralprinzip, -gesetz, *das*

**precession** /prɪ'seʃn/ *n.* (*Phys.*) Präzession, *die;* **~ of the equinoxes** (*Astron.*) Präzession, *die*

**pre-Christian** /pri:'krɪstjən/ *adj.* vorchristlich

**precinct** /'pri:sɪŋkt/ *n.* Ⓐ (*traffic-free area*) **[pedestrian] ~:** Fußgängerzone, *die;* **[shopping] ~:** für den Verkehr weitgehend gesperrtes Einkaufsviertel; Ⓑ (*enclosed area*) Areal, *das;* Bereich, *der;* Bezirk, *der;* **temple/cathedral ~:** Tempel-/Dombereich, *der;* **in the hospital ~s** auf dem Krankenhausgelände; Ⓒ (*boundary*) Grenze, *die;* **within the ~s of the school** auf dem Schulgelände; Ⓓ (*Amer.: police or electoral district*) Bezirk, *der*

**preciosity** /preʃɪ'ɒsɪtɪ/ *n., no pl.* Affektiertheit, *die*

**precious** /'preʃəs/ ❶ *adj.* Ⓐ (*costly*) wertvoll, kostbar ‹Schmuckstück›; Edel‹metall, -stein›; Ⓑ (*highly valued*) wertvoll, kostbar ‹Zeit, Eigenschaft, Trostwort, Privileg›; **be ~ to sb.** jmdm. lieb und wert sein; Ⓒ (*beloved*) teuer (*geh.*), lieb ‹Freund›; **my ~ one!** mein Schatz; Ⓓ (*affected*) affektiert; Ⓔ (*coll.: considerable*) beträchtlich; erheblich; **do a ~ sight more work/cost a ~ sight more than ...:** beträchtlich *od.* erheblich mehr tun/kosten als ... ❷ *adv.* (*coll.*) herzlich ‹wenig›; **~ few of them** herzlich wenige von ihnen

**precipice** /'presɪpɪs/ *n.* Abgrund, *der;* **we are on the edge of a ~** (*fig.*) wir stehen am Rande einer Katastrophe

**precipitant** /prɪ'sɪpɪtənt/ ⇒ **precipitate 1**

**precipitate** ❶ /prɪ'sɪpɪtət/ *adj.* Ⓐ (*hurried*) eilig ‹Flucht, Entbindung›; hastig ‹Abreise›; **make a ~ exit** hastig *od.* eilig hinausgehen; Ⓑ (*rash*) übereilt, überstürzt ‹Tat, Entschluss, Maßnahme›; groß, fliegend ‹Eile›; **be ~ in doing sth.** etw. übereilt tun; **do nothing ~:** nichts übereilt tun. ❷ /prɪ'sɪpɪteɪt/ *v.t.* Ⓐ (*throw down*) hinunterschleudern; **be ~d into a chasm** in eine Spalte stürzen; **~ a nation into war** ‹Nachricht, Aggression:› ein Volk in einen Krieg stürzen; Ⓑ (*hasten*) beschleunigen; (*trigger*) auslösen; Ⓒ (*Chem.*) ‹Säure:› ausfällen; Ⓓ (*Phys.*) kondensieren. ❸ /prɪ'sɪpɪtət/ *n.* Ⓐ (*Chem.*) Niederschlag, *der;* Ⓑ (*Phys.*) Niederschlag, *der;* Kondensat, *das*

**precipitately** /prɪ'sɪpɪtətlɪ/ *adv.* übereilt, überstürzt ‹fliehen, flüchten›; unüberlegt, voreilig ‹handeln, sich in etw. stürzen›; hastig ‹hetzen, eilen, stürzen›

**precipitation** /prɪsɪpɪ'teɪʃn/ *n.* Ⓐ (*Meteorol.*) Niederschlag, *der;* Ⓑ Voreiligkeit, *die;* Unüberlegtheit, *die*

**precipitous** /prɪ'sɪpɪtəs/ *adj.* Ⓐ (*very steep*) sehr steil ‹Schlucht, Abhang, Treppe, Weg›; schroff ‹Abhang, Felswand›; abschüssig ‹Straße›; steilwandig ‹Cañon›; **~ slope/drop** Steilhang, *der*/[steiler] Absturz; Ⓑ ⇒ **precipitate 1**

**precipitously** /prɪ'sɪpɪtəslɪ/ *adv.* Ⓐ sehr steil ‹[an]steigen sich erheben, abfallen›; schroff ‹ansteigen, abfallen›; jäh (*geh.*) ‹abfallen›; Ⓑ ⇒ **precipitately**

**précis** /'preɪsi:/ ❶ *n., pl. same* /preɪsi:z/ Inhaltsangabe, *die;* Zusammenfassung, *die;* Précis, *der* (*fachspr.*); **~ of German history** Abriss der deutschen Geschichte; **do** *or* **make a ~ of sth.** eine Inhaltsangabe einer Sache (*Gen.*) anfertigen. ❷ *v.t.* zusammenfassen

**precise** /prɪ'saɪs/ *adj.* genau; präzise; fein ‹Instrument›; groß ‹Genauigkeit›; förmlich ‹Art›; **be very ~ about sth.** es mit etw. sehr genau nehmen; **put sth. in more ~ terms** etw. präzisieren *od.* präziser ausdrücken; **be [more] ~:** sich präzise[r] ausdrücken; **what are your ~ intentions?** was genau hast du vor?; **..., to be ~ ...,** um genau zu sein; ..., genauer gesagt; **be the ~ opposite of sth.** genau das Gegenteil von etw. sein; **this is the ~ design/colour/shade that ...:** das ist genau das Muster/die Farbe/der Ton, das/die/der ...; **the ~ moment at which ...:** genau der Augenblick, in dem ...; **at that ~ moment** genau in dem Augenblick

**precisely** /prɪ'saɪslɪ/ *adv.* genau; präzise ‹antworten›; **speak ~:** sich präzise ausdrücken; **the date is not ~ known** das genaue Datum ist nicht bekannt; **that is ~ what/why ...:** genau das/deswegen ...; **what ~ do you want/mean?** was willst/meinst du eigentlich genau?; **do ~ the opposite** genau das Gegenteil tun; **it is ~ because ...:** gerade weil ...; **it will be 5.21 ~:** es wird genau 5 Uhr 21; **at ~ 1.30, at 1.30 ~:** Punkt 1 Uhr 30; genau um 1 Uhr 30

**precision** /prɪ'sɪʒn/ *n., no pl.* Genauigkeit, *die;* **with[out] a great deal of ~:** [nicht] sehr präzise ‹sich ausdrücken›; *attrib.* **a ~ landing** eine Präzisionslandung

**precision:** **~ 'bombing** *n.* (*Mil.*) Punktzielbombardement, *das;* **~ 'instrument** *n.* Präzisions[mess]gerät, *das;* Feinmessgerät, *das;* **~ 'tool** *n.* Präzisionswerkzeug, *das*

**pre-classical** /pri:'klæsɪkl/ *adj.* vorklassisch

**preclude** /prɪ'klu:d/ *v.t.* ausschließen ‹Zweifel›; **~ sb. from a duty/taking part** jmdn. von einer Pflicht/der Teilnahme entbinden; **so as to ~ all doubt** um jeden Zweifel auszuschließen

**precocious** /prɪ'kəʊʃəs/ *adj.* frühreif ‹Kind, Jugendlicher, Genie›; altklug ‹Äußerung›; verfrüht ‹Wachstum, Erfolg›; **at the ~ age of 25** schon mit 25 Jahren; **a ~ interest in sth.** frühzeitiges Interesse an etw. (*Dat.*)

**precociously** /prɪ'kəʊʃəslɪ/ *adv.* frühreif ‹sich benehmen›; altklug ‹reden›

**precognition** /pri:kɒg'nɪʃn/ *n.* vorherige Kenntnis (**of** von); (*Parapsych.*) Präkognition, *die*

**preconceived** /pri:kən'si:vd/ *adj.* vorgefasst ‹Ansicht, Vorstellung›

**preconception** /pri:kən'sepʃn/ *n.* vorgefasste Meinung (**of** über + *Akk.*); **with too many ~s** allzu voreingenommen

**precondition** /pri:kən'dɪʃn/ *n.* Vorbedingung, *die* (**of** für)

**pre-cook** /pri:'kʊk/ *v.t.* vorkochen

**pre-cooked** /pri:'kʊkt/ *adj.* vorgekocht

**precursor** /pri:'kɜ:sə(r)/ *n.* Ⓐ (*of revolution, movement, etc.*) Wegbereiter, *der*/-bereiterin, *die;* (*of illness*) Vorbote, *der*/Vorbotin, *die;* Ⓑ (*predecessor*) Vorgänger, *der*/-gängerin, *die*

**pre-date** /pri:'deɪt/ *v.t.* Ⓐ (*precede in date*) **~ sth.** ‹Ereignis:› einer Sache (*Dat.*) vorausgehen; ‹Sache:› aus der Zeit vor etw. (*Dat.*) stammen; Ⓑ (*give earlier date to*) zurückdatieren ‹Brief, Scheck›

**pre-dated** /pri:'deɪtɪd/ *adj.* zurückdatiert ‹Brief, Scheck›

**predator** /'predətə(r)/ *n.* Raubtier, *das;* (*fish*) Raubfisch, *der*

**predatory** /'predətərɪ/ *adj.* Ⓐ (*plundering, robbing*) räuberisch; Raub‹instinkte, -krieg›; beutegierig ‹Gesellschaftsschicht, Charakter›; Ⓑ (*preying upon others*) räuberisch; **~ animal** Raubtier, *das*

**predecease** /pri:dɪ'si:s/ *v.t.* **~ sb.** vor jmdm. sterben

**predecessor** /'pri:dɪsesə(r)/ *n.* Ⓐ (*former holder of position*) Vorgänger, *der*/-gängerin, *die;* **~ in office/title** Amts-/Rechtsvorgänger, *der;* Ⓑ (*preceding thing*) Vorläufer, *der;* **his second novel is better than its ~:** sein zweiter Roman ist besser als sein erster; Ⓒ (*ancestor*) Vorfahr[e], *der*/-fahrin, *die;* Ahn, *der* (*geh.*)/Ahne, *die* (*geh.*)

**predestination** /prɪdestɪ'neɪʃn/ *n., no pl.* Vorherbestimmung, *die;* Prädestination, *die* (*geh.*)

**predestine** /prɪ'destɪn/ *v.t.* von vornherein bestimmen (**to** zu); prädestinieren (**to** zu) (*geh.*)

**predetermination** /pri:dɪtɜ:mɪ'neɪʃn/ *n., no pl.* Ⓐ (*predestination*) Vorherbestimmung, *die;* Prädestination, *die* (*geh.*); Ⓑ (*intention*) Vorsatz, *der;* Absicht, *die;* **with a ~ to do sth.** mit dem Vorsatz *od.* in der Absicht, etw. zu tun

**predetermine** /pri:dɪ'tɜ:mɪn/ *v.t.* Ⓐ im Voraus *od.* von vornherein bestimmen; ‹Gott, Schicksal:› vorherbestimmen; Ⓑ (*impel*) zwingen (**to** zu)

**predicament** /prɪ'dɪkəmənt/ *n.* Dilemma, *das;* Zwangslage, *die;* **he found himself in a ~:** er befand sich in einem Dilemma

**predicate** ❶ /'predɪkət/ *n.* Ⓐ (*Ling.*) Prädikat, *das;* Ⓑ (*Logic*) Prädikat, *das;* Prädikator, *der.* ❷ /'predɪkeɪt/ *v.t.* Ⓐ (*affirm*) **~ sth. of sb./sth.** jmdm./einer Sache etw. zuschreiben; **~ of sb./sth. that ...:** von jmdm./etw. behaupten *od.* sagen, dass ...; Ⓑ (*found, base*) gründen (**on** auf + *Dat.*); **be ~d on** basieren (*geh.*) *od.* sich gründen auf (+ *Dat.*); Ⓒ (*Logic*) zusprechen (**of** *Dat.*)

**predicative** /prɪ'dɪkətɪv/ *adj.* Ⓐ (*making a predication*) eine Aussage beinhaltend (**of, about** über + *Akk.*); Ⓑ (*Ling.*) prädikativ

**predicatively** /prɪ'dɪkətɪvlɪ/ *adv.* (*Ling.*) prädikativ

**predict** /prɪ'dɪkt/ *v.t.* voraus-, vorhersagen; prophezeien; voraus-, vorhersehen ‹Folgen›; **what do you ~ will be the result?** wie glaubst du, wird das Ergebnis aussehen?

**predictable** /prɪ'dɪktəbl/ *adj.* voraus-, vorhersagbar; voraus-, vorhersehbar ‹Folgen, Reaktion, Ereignis›; berechenbar ‹Person›

**predictably** /prɪ'dɪktəblɪ/ *adv.* wie voraus- *od.* vorherzusehen war; **he was ~ annoyed** wie voraus- *od.* vorherzusehen [war], war er verärgert

**prediction** /prɪ'dɪkʃn/ *n.* Voraus-, Vorhersage, *die*

**predigest** /pri:dɪ'dʒest, pri:daɪ'dʒest/ *v.t.* vorverdauen

**predilection** /pri:dɪ'lekʃn/ *n.* Vorliebe, *die*

**predispose** /pri:dɪ'spəʊz/ *v.t.* **~ sb. to do sth.** jmdn. etw. tun lassen; **be ~d to do sth.** (*be willing to do sth.*) geneigt sein, etw. zu tun; (*tend to do sth.*) dazu neigen, etw. zu tun; **~ sb. to sth.** jmdn. zu etw. neigen lassen; **~ sb. to an illness** jmdn. für eine Krankheit anfällig machen; **~ sb. in favour of sb./sth.** jmdn. für jmdn./etw. einnehmen

**predisposition** /pri:dɪspə'zɪʃn/ *n.* Neigung, *die* (**to** zu); (*Med.*) Anfälligkeit, *die* (**to** für); Prädisposition, *die* (*fachspr.*)

**predominance** /prɪ'dɒmɪnəns/ *n.* Ⓐ (*control*) (*of country*) Vorherrschaft, *die* (**over** über + *Akk.*); Vorrangstellung, *die* (**over** gegenüber); (*of person*) Überlegenheit, *die* (**over** gegenüber); Ⓑ (*majority*) Überzahl, *die* (**of** von); **there is a ~ of newcomers** die Neulinge sind in der Überzahl

**predominant** /prɪˈdɒmɪnənt/ *adj.* Ⓐ (*having more power*) dominierend ‹Interesse, Partei, Macht, Persönlichkeit›; Ⓑ (*prevailing*) vorherrschend; **the ~ desire expressed by them** der von ihnen über- *od.* vorwiegend zum Ausdruck gebrachte Wunsch

**predominantly** /prɪˈdɒmɪnəntlɪ/ *adv.* überwiegend

**predominate** /prɪˈdɒmɪneɪt/ *v.i.* (*be more powerful*) dominierend sein; (*be more important*) vorherrschen; überwiegen; (*be more numerous*) in der Überzahl sein

**pre-eminence** /priːˈemɪnəns/ *n., no pl.* Vorrangstellung, *die;* **achieve ~:** eine herausragende Stellung erlangen; **her ~ in this field** ihre herausragende Stellung auf diesem Gebiet

**pre-eminent** /priːˈemɪnənt/ *adj.* herausragend; **be ~:** eine herausragende Stellung einnehmen

**pre-eminently** /priːˈemɪnəntlɪ/ *adv.* herausragend; überaus ‹gelehrt›; (*mainly*) vor allem; in erster Linie; **figure ~:** an herausragender Stelle stehen

**pre-empt** /priːˈempt/ *v.t.* (*forestall*) zuvorkommen (+ *Dat.*) (**on** bei); **she had been ~ed** man war ihr zuvorgekommen

**pre-emptive** /priːˈemptɪv/ *adj.* Ⓐ Vorkaufs‹preis, -recht›; **~ right** (*of shareholder*) Bezugsrecht, *das;* **he made a ~ bid to gain power** er machte im Vorfeld seine Machtansprüche geltend; Ⓑ (*Mil.*) Präventiv‹krieg, -maßnahme, -schlag›; Ⓒ (*Bridge*) **~ bid** Sperrgebot, *das*

**preen** /priːn/ ❶ *v.t.* ‹Vogel:› putzen ‹Federn, Gefieder›. ❷ *v. refl.* ‹Vogel:› sich putzen; ‹Person:› sich herausputzen; **~ oneself on sth.** sich (*Dat.*) etwas auf etw. (*Akk.*) einbilden; **he is always ~ing himself on ...:** er brüstet sich dauernd mit ...

**prefab** /ˈpriːfæb/ *n.* (*coll.*) (*house*) Fertighaus, *das;* (*building*) Gebäude aus Fertigteilen; Fertigbau, *der*

**prefabricate** /priːˈfæbrɪkeɪt/ *v.t.* vorfertigen ‹Produkt, Teil, Gebäude usw.›

**prefabricated** *adj.* /priːˈfæbrɪkeɪtɪd/ vorgefertigt; **~ house/building** Fertighaus, *das*/Fertigbau, *der;* **a ~ garage** eine in Fertigbauweise errichtete Garage; **a ~ system/scheme** (*fig.*) ein vorfabriziertes System/Schema

**prefabrication** /priːfæbrɪˈkeɪʃn/ *n.* Vorfabrikation, *die;* Vorfertigung, *die*

**preface** /ˈprefəs/ ❶ *n.* Ⓐ (*of book*) Vorwort, *das* (**to** *Gen.*); Vorbemerkung, *die* (**to** zu); Ⓑ (*of speech*) Vorrede, *die;* Einleitung, *die.* ❷ *v.t.* Ⓐ (*introduce*) einleiten; Ⓑ (*furnish with a ~*) mit einem Vorwort *od.* einer Vorbemerkung versehen

**prefatory** /ˈprefətərɪ/ *adj.* einleitend ‹Hinweise, Worte›; **be ~ to sth.** etw. einleiten

**prefect** /ˈpriːfekt/ *n.* (*Sch.*) *die Aufsicht führender älterer Schüler/führende ältere Schülerin;* **form ~** *Schüler/Schülerin einer Klasse, der/die die Aufsicht führt*

**prefer** /prɪˈfɜː(r)/ *v.t.*, **-rr-** Ⓐ (*like better*) vorziehen; **~ to do sth.** etw. lieber tun; es vorziehen, etw. zu tun; **~ sth. to sth.** etw. einer Sache (*Dat.*) vorziehen; **I ~ skiing to skating** ich fahre lieber Ski als Schlittschuh; **I ~ not to talk about it** darüber möchte ich lieber nicht sprechen; **I should ~ to wait** ich würde lieber warten; **I'd ~ it if ...:** mir wäre es lieb, wenn ...; **~ to go to prison rather than pay** eher *od.* lieber ins Gefängnis gehen als zu bezahlen; **I ~ that we should wait rather than act now** ich meine, wir sollten lieber warten, als jetzt handeln; **this plant ~s cool conditions** diese Pflanze bevorzugt einen kühlen Standort; **they ~ blondes** sie bevorzugen Blondinen; **I ~ water to wine** ich trinke lieber Wasser als Wein; **which of them do you ~, John or Peter?** wer ist dir lieber, John oder Peter?; **there is tea or coffee, which do you ~?** es gibt Tee oder Kaffee, was ist Ihnen lieber?; **I should ~ something more elegant** ich hätte gerne etwas Eleganteres; Ⓑ (*submit*) erheben ‹Anklage, Anschuldigungen› (**against** gegen, **for** wegen); vorbringen ‹Beschwerde›; Ⓒ (*promote*) befördern; **be ~red to a post** auf einen Posten berufen werden; **he was ~red to the See of Chichester** er wurde zum Bischof von Chichester ernannt

**preferable** /ˈprefərəbl/ *adj.* vorzuziehen *präd.;* vorzuziehend *attr.;* besser (**to** als); **which do you think ~, x or y?** was ist Ihrer Meinung nach vorzuziehen, x oder y?; **he felt it ~ to be silent** er fand, dass es besser war zu schweigen; **the cold was ~ to the smoke** die Kälte war noch erträglicher als der Rauch

**preferably** /ˈprefərəblɪ/ *adv.* am besten; (*as best liked*) am liebsten; **a piano, ~ not too expensive** ein möglichst nicht zu teures Klavier; **Wine or beer? — Wine, ~!** Wein oder Bier? — Lieber Wein!

**preference** /ˈprefərəns/ *n.* Ⓐ (*greater liking*) Vorliebe, *die;* **for ~** ⇒ **preferably; have a ~ for sth. [over sth.]** etw. [einer Sache (*Dat.*)] vorziehen; **he has a ~ for tea over coffee** er mag *od.* trinkt lieber Tee als Kaffee; **do sth. in ~ to sth. else** etw. lieber als etw. anderes tun; Ⓑ (*thing preferred*) **of the three skirts the blue one is my ~:** von den drei Röcken gefällt mir der blaue am besten; **his ~ is a holiday abroad** ein Urlaub im Ausland ist ihm am liebsten; **what are your ~s?** was wäre dir am liebsten?; **I have no ~:** mir ist alles gleich recht; **have you any ~ among his novels?** magst du einen seiner Romane besonders?; Ⓒ (*prior right*) Vorrecht, *das* (**for** auf + *Akk.*); **give a creditor ~ over sb.** einen Gläubiger gegenüber jmdm. begünstigen; Ⓓ (*favouring of one person or country*) Präferenzbehandlung, *die;* (*Econ.*) Präferenz, *die;* **give [one's] ~ to sb.** jmdn. bevorzugen; **give sb. ~ over others** jmdm. anderen gegenüber Vergünstigungen einräumen; Ⓔ *attrib.* (*Brit. Finance*) Vorzugs-, Prioritäts‹obligation, -aktie›

**preferential** /prefəˈrenʃl/ *adj.* bevorzugt ‹Behandlung›; bevorrechtigt ‹Ansprache, Stellung›; **[a] ~ status** eine Vorzugsstellung; **give sb. ~ treatment** jmdn. bevorzugt behandeln; **~ customs duties** Präferenz- *od.* Vorzugszölle

**preferentially** /prefəˈrenʃəlɪ/ *adv.* Ⓐ bevorzugt ‹behandeln›; Ⓑ (*to a greater extent*) vorwiegend

**preferment** /prɪˈfɜːmənt/ *n.* Ⓐ (*promotion*) Beförderung, *die;* (*advancement*) Voran-, Vorwärtskommen, *das;* **receive ~:** befördert werden; Ⓑ (*post*) höhere *od.* gehobene Stellung; (*Eccl.*) höheres Amt; Ⓒ (*Law*) **~ of charges** Anklageerhebung, *die*

**preferred** /prɪˈfɜːd/ *adj.* Ⓐ bevorzugt; **my ~ conclusion/solution** *etc.* die Schlussfolgerung/Lösung *usw.,* der ich den Vorzug gebe; Ⓑ **~ share** *etc.* = **preference share** *etc.* ⇒ **preference** E

**prefigure** /priːˈfɪgə(r)/ *v.t.* Ⓐ (*represent beforehand*) ankünd[ig]en; hindeuten auf (+ *Akk.*); Ⓑ (*picture to oneself*) sich (*Dat.*) [vorher] vorstellen; sich (*Dat.*) ausmalen

**prefix** ❶ /ˈpriːfɪks, priːˈfɪks/ *v.t.* Ⓐ (*add*) voranstellen (**to** *Dat.*); **~ a title to a name** einen Titel vor einen Namen setzen; Ⓑ (*Ling.*) als Präfix setzen (**to** vor + *Akk.*); **~ the definite article to sth.** den bestimmten Artikel vor etw. (*Akk.*) setzen. ❷ /ˈpriːfɪks/ *n.* Ⓐ (*Ling.*) Präfix, *das;* Vorsilbe, *die;* Ⓑ (*title*) [Namens]zusatz, *der;* **the ~ 'Mr' before a name** der Zusatz „Mr." vor einem Namen

**preflight** /ˈpriːflaɪt/ *attrib. adj.* ‹Informationen, Kontrollen› vor dem Flug

**preform** /priːˈfɔːm/ *v.t.* vorbilden; **~ed ideas** vorgeformte Ideen

**preggers** /ˈpregəz/ (*Brit.*), **preggy** /ˈpregɪ/ *adj.* (*coll.*) dick (*derb*); schwanger

**pregnancy** /ˈpregnənsɪ/ *n.* Ⓐ (*of woman*) Schwangerschaft, *die;* (*of animal*) Trächtigkeit, *die;* **her advanced state of ~:** ihre fortgeschrittene Schwangerschaft; **in the fourth week of ~:** in der vierten Woche der Schwangerschaft *od.* Schwangerschaftswoche; Ⓑ (*fig.: of speech, words*) Bedeutungsgehalt, *der;* Bedeutungsschwere, *die* (*geh.*)

ˈ**pregnancy test** *n.* Schwangerschaftstest, *der*

**pregnant** /ˈpregnənt/ *adj.* Ⓐ schwanger ‹Frau›; trächtig ‹Tier›; **be six months ~:** im siebten Monat schwanger sein; **she is ~ with her second child** sie erwartet ihr zweites Kind; **heavily** *or* (*coll.*) **very ~:** hoch schwanger; Ⓑ (*fig.: momentous*) bedeutungsschwer (*geh.*); **~ with consequences/meaning** folgenschwer/bedeutungsschwanger

**preheat** /priːˈhiːt/ *v.t.* vorheizen ‹Backofen›; vorwärmen ‹Geschirr, Essen›; vorher erwärmen ‹Gas, Werkzeug›

**prehensile** /prɪˈhensaɪl/ *adj.* (*Zool.*) Greif‹vermögen, -fuß, -schwanz›

**prehistoric** /priːhɪˈstɒrɪk/ *adj.* Ⓐ vorgeschichtlich; prähistorisch; **tools dating from ~ times** vorgeschichtliche *od.* prähistorische Werkzeuge; Ⓑ (*coll.*) (*ancient*) uralt (*ugs.*); (*out of date*) vorsintflutlich (*ugs.*)

**prehistory** /priːˈhɪstərɪ/ *n.* Ⓐ Vorgeschichte, *die;* Prähistorie, *die;* Ⓑ (*of a situation etc.*) Vorgeschichte, *die*

**pre-ignition** /priːɪgˈnɪʃn/ *n.* (*Motor Veh.*) Frühzündung, *die*

**pre-industrial** /priːɪnˈdʌstrɪəl/ *adj.* vorindustriell

**prejudge** /priːˈdʒʌdʒ/ *v.t.* Ⓐ (*form premature opinion about*) vorschnell *od.* voreilig urteilen über (+ *Akk.*); Ⓑ (*judge before trial*) im Voraus beurteilen, vorverurteilen ‹Person›; im Voraus entscheiden ‹Fall›

**prejudg[e]ment** /priːˈdʒʌdʒmənt/ *n.* vorschnelles Urteil (**of** über + *Akk.*); **we must avoid any ~ of the case/accused** wir dürfen den Fall nicht im Voraus entscheiden/den Angeklagten nicht vorverurteilen

**prejudice** /ˈpredʒʊdɪs/ ❶ *n.* Ⓐ (*bias*) Vorurteil, *das;* **colour ~:** Vorurteil aufgrund der Hautfarbe; **overcome ~:** Vorurteile ablegen; **this is mere ~!** das sind bloße Vorurteile!; Ⓑ (*injury*) Schaden, *der;* Nachteil, *der;* **to sb.'s ~:** zu jmds. Nachteil *od.* Schaden; **without ~ [to court action]** (*Law*) ohne Schaden für die eigenen Rechte [bei gerichtlichem Vorgehen]; **without ~ to sth.** unbeschadet einer Sache (*Gen.*); **be without ~ to sth.** etw. unberührt lassen. ❷ *v.t.* Ⓐ (*bias*) beeinflussen; **~ sb.** *or* **sb.'s mind in sb.'s favour/against sb.** jmdn. für/gegen jmdn. einnehmen; jmdn. zu jmds. Gunsten/Ungunsten beeinflussen; Ⓑ (*injure*) beeinträchtigen

**prejudiced** /ˈpredʒʊdɪst/ *adj.* voreingenommen (**about** gegenüber, **against** gegen); **the most ~ passages in this book** die einseitigsten Passagen dieses Buches; **~ opinion** Vorurteil, *das;* **be racially ~:** Rassenvorurteile haben; **be totally ~ against women** Frauen gegenüber völlig voreingenommen *od.* voller Vorurteile sein

**prejudicial** /predʒʊˈdɪʃl/ *adj.* abträglich (*geh.*) (**to** *Dat.*); nachteilig (**to** für); **be ~ to** beeinträchtigen ‹Anspruch, Chance, Recht›; schaden (+ *Dat.*) ‹Interesse›

**prejudicially** /predʒʊˈdɪʃəlɪ/ *adv.* nachteilig; **affect ~:** beeinträchtigen ‹Anspruch, Recht›; schaden (+ *Dat.*) ‹Interesse›

**prelate** /ˈprelət/ *n.* Prälat, *der*

**prelim** /ˈpriːlɪm/ *n.* Ⓐ (*coll.: exam*) Vorprüfung, *die;* Ⓑ *in pl.* (*Printing*) Titelei, *die*

**preliminarily** /prɪˈlɪmɪnərɪlɪ/ *adv.* vorher

**preliminary** /prɪˈlɪmɪnərɪ/ ❶ *adj.* Vor-; vorbereitend ‹Forschung, Schritt, Maßnahme›; einleitend ‹Kapitel, Vertragsbestimmungen›; **~ inquiry/request/search** erste Nachforschung/Bitte/Suche; **~ draft** Rohentwurf, *der.*
❷ *n., usu. in pl.* **preliminaries** Präliminarien *Pl.;* (*Sports*) Ausscheidungskämpfe; **as a ~ to sth.** (*as a preparation*) als Vorbereitung auf etw. (*Akk.*); **just a ~:** nur ein Vorspiel (**to** zu); **we have now completed the preliminaries** wir haben die Vorbereitungen jetzt abgeschlossen; **dispense with the preliminaries** ohne Umschweife *od.* direkt zur Sache kommen; in medias res gehen (*geh.*); **without any further preliminaries** ohne [weitere] Umschweife.
❸ *adv.* ⇒ **preparatory** 2

**prelude** /ˈpreljuːd/ ❶ *n.* Ⓐ (*introduction*) Anfang, *der* (**to** *Gen.*); Auftakt, *der* (**to** zu); Ⓑ (*of play*) Vorspiel, *das* (**to** zu); (*of poem*) Einleitung, *die* (**to** zu *od. Gen.*); Ⓒ (*Mus.*) Präludium, *das;* Vorspiel, *das.* ❷ *v.t.* Ⓐ (*foreshadow*) ankündigen; Ⓑ (*start*) ~ **sth. by** *or* **with sth.** etw. mit etw. einleiten

**premarital** /priːˈmærɪtl/ *adj.* vorehelich; ~ **sex** Geschlechtsverkehr vor der Ehe; vorehelicher Geschlechtsverkehr

**premature** /ˈprematjʊə(r)/ *adj.* Ⓐ (*hasty*) voreilig, übereilt ‹Entscheidung, Handeln›; Ⓑ (*early*) früh-, vorzeitig ‹Altern, Ankunft, Haarausfall›; verfrüht ‹Bericht, Eile, Furcht›; ~ **baby** Frühgeburt, *die;* **the baby was five weeks ~:** das Baby wurde fünf Wochen zu früh geboren

**prematurely** /ˈpremətjʊəlɪ/ *adv.* (*early*) vorzeitig; zu früh ‹geboren werden›; (*hastily*) voreilig, übereilt ‹entscheiden, handeln›

**premedical** /prɪːˈmedɪkl/ *adj.* (*Amer.*) auf das Medizinstudium vorbereitend

**premedication** /priːmedɪˈkeɪʃn/ *n.* (*Med.*) Prämedikation, *die*

**premeditated** /priːˈmedɪteɪtɪd/ *adj.* vorsätzlich

**premeditation** /priːmedɪˈteɪʃn/ *n.* Vorsatz, *der;* **with ~:** nach vorheriger Planung; vorsätzlich ‹ermorden, ein Verbrechen begehen›

**premenstrual** /priːˈmenstrʊəl/ *adj.* (*Med.*) prämenstruell; ~ **tension** prämenstruelle Spannung

**premier** /ˈpremɪə(r)/ ❶ *adj.* (*first*) erst...; (*best*) best... ‹Qualität›; (*most important*) bedeutendst..., wichtigst... ‹Position, Stellung›. ❷ *n.* Premier[minister], *der*/Premierministerin, *die*

**première** /ˈpremjeə(r)/ ❶ *n.* (*of production*) Premiere, *die;* Erstaufführung, *die;* (*of work*) Uraufführung, *die.* ❷ *v.t.* erst-/uraufführen

**premiership** /ˈpremɪəʃɪp/ *n.* Amtsperiode als Premierminister/-ministerin; (*office*) Amt des Premier[minister]s/der Premierministerin

**premise** /ˈpremɪs/ *n.* Ⓐ *in pl.* (*building*) Gebäude, *das;* (*buildings and land of factory or school*) Gelände, *das;* (*rooms*) Räumlichkeiten *Pl.;* **on the ~s** hier/dort; (*of public house, restaurant, etc.*) im Lokal; **all repairs are done on the ~s** alle Reparaturen werden an Ort und Stelle erledigt; Ⓑ ⇒ **premiss**

**premiss** /ˈpremɪs/ *n.* (*Logic*) Prämisse, *die*

**premium** /ˈpriːmɪəm/ *n.* Ⓐ (*Insurance*) Prämie, *die;* Ⓑ (*reward*) Preis, *der;* Prämie, *die;* **put a ~ on sth.** (*make advantageous*) etw. belohnen; (*attach special value to*) etw. [hoch ein]schätzen; großen Wert auf etw. (*Akk.*) legen; Ⓒ (*bonus*) Zusatzzahlung, *die;* (*additional to fixed price/wage*) Aufgeld, *das*/Prämie, *die;* Ⓓ (*Amer.: charge for loan*) Kreditgebühr, *die;* Ⓔ (*St. Exch.*) Agio, *das;* Aufgeld, *das;* **be at a ~:** über pari stehen; (*fig.: be highly valued*) sehr gefragt sein; hoch im Kurs stehen; **those shares are on offer at a ~:** diese Aktien werden über pari *od.* mit einem Agio angeboten

ˈ**Premium [Savings] Bond** *n.* (*Brit.*) Prämienanleihe, *die;* Losanleihe, *die*

**premolar** /priːˈməʊlə(r)/ *n.* (*Anat.*) vorderer Backenzahn; Prämolar, *der* (*fachspr.*)

**premonition** /priːməˈnɪʃn/ *n.* Ⓐ (*forewarning*) Vorwarnung, *die;* **falling leaves gave a ~ of coming winter** fallendes Laub gemahnte an den kommenden Winter; Ⓑ (*presentiment*) Vorahnung, *die;* **feel/have a ~ of sth.** eine Vorahnung von etw. haben

**premonitory** /prɪˈmɒnɪtərɪ/ *adj.* warnend ‹An-, Vorzeichen›; ungut ‹Gefühl›

**pre-natal** /priːˈneɪtl/ *adj.* (*Med.*) pränatal (*fachspr.*); vor der Geburt *nachgestellt;* ~ **care** Schwangerschaftsfürsorge, *die*

**preoccupation** /prɪɒkjʊˈpeɪʃn/ *n.* Sorge, *die* (**with** um); **his ~ with his work left little time for his family** er war so sehr mit seiner Arbeit beschäftigt, dass wenig Zeit für die Familie blieb; **first** *or* **greatest** *or* **main ~:** Hauptanliegen, *das;* Hauptsorge, *die*

**preoccupied** /prɪˈɒkjʊpaɪd/ *adj.* (*lost in thought*) gedankenverloren; (*concerned*) besorgt (**with** um); (*absorbed*) beschäftigt (**with** mit)

**preoccupy** /prɪˈɒkjʊpaɪ/ *v.t.* beschäftigen; **my mind is preoccupied** meine Gedanken sind beschäftigt

**pre-ordain** /priːɔːˈdeɪn/ *v.t.* vorherbestimmen

**prep** /prep/ *n.* (*Brit. Sch. coll.*) Ⓐ (*homework*) [Haus-, Schul]aufgaben *Pl.;* Schularbeiten *Pl.;* Ⓑ (*homework period*) Hausaufgabenvorbereitung, *die*

**pre-packaged** /priːˈpækɪdʒd/, **pre-packed** /priːˈpækt/ *adjs.* abgepackt; (*fig.*) vorgefertigt ‹Ideen, Meinung›

**prepaid** ⇒ **prepay**

**preparation** /prepəˈreɪʃn/ *n.* Ⓐ Vorbereitung, *die;* **be in a state of ~ for combat** kampfbereit sein; **be in ~** ‹Publikation:› in Vorbereitung sein; **be in ~ for sth.** der Vorbereitung einer Sache (*Gen.*) dienen; **in ~ for the new baby/term** als Vorbereitung auf das neue Baby/Semester; Ⓑ *in pl.* (*things done to get ready*) Vorbereitungen *Pl.* (**for** für); **~s for war/the funeral/the voyage/the wedding** Kriegs-/Begräbnis-/Reise-/Hochzeitsvorbereitungen; **make ~s for sth.** Vorbereitungen für etw. treffen; Ⓒ (*Chem., Med., Pharm.*) Präparat, *das;* **herbal ~:** Kräuterpräparat, *das;* (*Cookery*) Kräutermischung, *die;* Ⓓ (*Brit. Sch.*) [Haus-, Schul]aufgaben *Pl.;* Schularbeiten *Pl.*

**preparative** /prɪˈpærətɪv/ ⇒ **preparatory 1 A**

**preparatory** /prɪˈpærətərɪ/ ❶ *adj.* Ⓐ (*introductory*) vorbereitend, einleitend ‹Maßnahme, Schritt›; einleitend ‹Ermittlung, Geste, Untersuchung›; Vor‹ermittlung, -untersuchung›; ~ **work** Vorarbeiten *Pl.;* Ⓑ (*Sch., Univ.*) für die Aufnahme an einer Public School/einem College vorbereitend; ‹Ausbildung, Stunden, Unterricht› an einer privaten Vorbereitungsschule. ❷ *adv.* ~ **to sth.** vor etw. (*Dat.*); ~ **to doing sth.** bevor man etw. tut; **I am packing ~ to departure** *or* **departing** ich packe vor meiner Abreise

**preˈparatory school** *n.* Ⓐ (*Brit. Sch.*) *für die Aufnahme an einer Public School vorbereitende Privatschule;* Ⓑ (*Amer. Univ.*) *meist private, für die Aufnahme an einem College vorbereitende Schule*

**prepare** /prɪˈpeə(r)/ ❶ *v.t.* Ⓐ (*make ready*) vorbereiten; entwerfen, ausarbeiten ‹Plan, Rede›; herrichten (*ugs.*), fertig machen ‹Gästezimmer›; (*make mentally ready, equip with necessary knowledge*) vorbereiten ‹Person› (**for** auf + *Akk.*); **~ the ground** *or* **way for sb./sth.** (*fig.*) für jmdn./etw. die nötige Vorarbeit leisten; jmdm. die Steine aus dem Weg räumen; **~ oneself for a shock/the worst** sich auf einen Schock/das Schlimmste gefasst machen; **be ~d for anything** auf alles gefasst sein; **be ~d to do sth.** (*be willing*) bereit sein, etw. zu tun; Ⓑ (*make*) herstellen ‹Chemikalie, Metall usw.›; zubereiten ‹Essen›. ❷ *v.i.* sich vorbereiten (**for** auf + *Akk.*); ~ **for battle/war** ‹Land:› zum Kampf/Krieg rüsten; **~ to do sth.** sich bereit machen *od.* (*geh.*) anschicken, etw. zu tun; **~ to advance/retreat** sich zum Vorstoß/Rückzug bereit machen

**preparedness** /prɪˈpeərɪdnɪs/ *n., no pl.* (*willingness*) Bereitschaft, *die* (**for** zu); **[state of] ~** (*readiness*) Vorbereitetsein, *das* (**for** für, auf + *Akk.*); **be in a state of ~ for action** (*Amer.*) sich in Alarmbereitschaft befinden

**prepay** /priːˈpeɪ/ *v.t.*, **prepaid** /priːˈpeɪd/ im Voraus [be]zahlen; (*pay postage of*) frankieren, freimachen ‹Brief, Paket usw.›; **send a parcel carriage prepaid** ein Paket frachtfrei versenden; **prepaid envelope** frankierter Umschlag; Freiumschlag, *der*

**prepayment** /priːˈpeɪmənt/ *n.* [Be]zahlung im Voraus; Voraus[be]zahlung, *die;* (*of letters, parcels, etc.*) Frankierung, *die;* Freimachung, *die*

**preponderance** /prɪˈpɒndərəns/ *n.* Überlegenheit, *die* (**over** über + *Akk.*, gegenüber); Übergewicht, *das;* **[numerical] ~, ~ in numbers** zahlenmäßige Überlegenheit; zahlenmäßiges Übergewicht

**preponderant** /prɪˈpɒndərənt/ *adj.* überlegen; **~ in numbers** zahlenmäßig überlegen

**preponderantly** /prɪˈpɒndərəntlɪ/ *adv.* überwiegend

**preponderate** /prɪˈpɒndəreɪt/ *v.i.* überwiegen (**over** gegenüber)

**preposition** /prepəˈzɪʃn/ *n.* (*Ling.*) Präposition, *die;* Verhältniswort, *das*

**prepositional** /prepəˈzɪʃənl/ *adj.* (*Ling.*) präpositional; Präpositional‹attribut, -fall, -objekt›

**prepossess** /priːpəˈzes/ *v.t.* Ⓐ (*preoccupy mentally*) erfüllen; beherrschen; Ⓑ (*prejudice*) beeinflussen; **~ sb. in sb.'s favour/against sb.** jmdn. zu jmds. Gunsten/Ungunsten beeinflussen

**prepossessing** /priːpəˈzesɪŋ/ *adj.* einnehmend, anziehend ‹Äußeres, Erscheinung, Person, Lächeln usw.›

**preposterous** /prɪˈpɒstərəs/ *adj.* absurd; grotesk ‹Äußeres, Kleidung›

**preposterously** /prɪˈpɒstərəslɪ/ *adv.* absurd; absurderweise ‹etw. tun›; **suggest, quite ~, that ...:** absurderweise vorschlagen, dass ...

**preppy** /ˈprepɪ/ (*Amer.*) ❶ *n. Schüler/Schülerin einer „preparatory school", der/die sich teuer und gepflegt kleidet, aus wohlhabendem Elternhaus stammt, eher konservativ eingestellt ist.* ❷ *adj.* für einen „Preppy" typisch ‹Kleidung, Meinung usw.›

**preprandial** /priːˈprændɪəl/ *adj.* (*formal/joc.*) ‹Drink usw.› vor dem Essen, vor Tisch

**preprint** /ˈpriːprɪnt/ *n.* Vorabdruck, *der*

ˈ**pre-program** *v.t.*, **-mm-** [vor]programmieren

ˈ**prep school** (*coll.*) ⇒ **preparatory school**

**prepuce** /ˈpriːpjuːs/ *n.* (*Anat.*) Vorhaut, *die*

**Pre-Raphaelite** /priːˈræfəlaɪt/ (*Art*) ❶ *n.* Präraffaelit, *der*/-raffaelitin, *die.* ❷ *adj.* präraffaelitisch

**pre-record** /priːrɪˈkɔːd/ *v.t.* vorher aufnehmen; **~ed tape** bespieltes Band

**prerequisite** /priːˈrekwɪzɪt/ ❶ *n.* [Grund]voraussetzung, *die.* ❷ *adj.* unbedingt erforderlich

**prerogative** /prɪˈrɒgətɪv/ *n.* Ⓐ Privileg, *das;* Vorrecht, *das;* **the ~ of mercy** das Begnadigungsrecht; Ⓑ (*of sovereign*) **[royal] ~:** [königliche] Prärogative

**Pres.** *abbr.* **President** Präs.

**presage** ❶ /ˈpresɪdʒ/ *n.* Ⓐ (*omen*) Vorzeichen, *das;* **a ~ of worse to come** ein schlechtes Omen; Ⓑ (*foreboding*) Vorahnung, *die.* ❷ /ˈpresɪdʒ, prɪˈseɪdʒ/ *v.t.* (*foreshadow*) ankündigen; (*give warning of*) ankünden

**Presbyterian** /prezbɪˈtɪərɪən, presbɪˈtɪərɪən/ ❶ *adj.* presbyterianisch. ❷ *n.* Presbyterianer, *der*/Presbyterianerin, *die*

**Presbyterianism** /prezbɪˈtɪərɪənɪzm, presbɪˈtɪərɪənɪzm/ *n.* Presbyterianismus, *der*

**presbytery** /ˈprezbɪtərɪ, ˈpresbɪtərɪ/ *n.* Presbyterium, *das*

**preschool** /ˈpriːskuːl/ *adj.* Vorschul-; ~ **years** Vorschulalter, *das*

**prescience** /ˈpresɪəns/ *n.* Voraussschau, *die*

**prescient** /ˈpresɪənt/ *adj.* weitblickend

**pre-scientific** /priːsaɪənˈtɪfɪk/ *adj.* vorwissenschaftlich

**prescribe** /prɪˈskraɪb/ ❶ *v.t.* Ⓐ (*impose*) vorschreiben; **~d book** ⇒ **set 4 B**; Ⓑ (*Med.; also fig.*) verschreiben; verordnen. ❷ *v.i.* Vorschriften machen

**prescript** /ˈpriːskrɪpt/ *n.* Vorschrift, *die*

**prescription** /prɪˈskrɪpʃn/ *n.* Ⓐ (*prescribing*) Anordnung, *die;* Vorschreiben, *das;* Ⓑ (*Med.*) Rezept, *das;* Verschreibung, *die;* (*medicine*) [verordnete *od.* verschriebene] Medizin; Verordnung, *die* (*fachspr.*); **be available only on ~:** nur auf Rezept *od.* Verschreibung erhältlich sein; rezept- *od.* verschreibungspflichtig sein

**preˈscription charge** *n.* Rezeptgebühr, *die*

**prescriptive** /prɪˈskrɪptɪv/ *adj.* (*Ling.*) präskriptiv

**pre-select** /priːsɪˈlekt/ *v.t.* vorwählen

**presence** /ˈprezəns/ *n.* Ⓐ (*being present*) (*of person*) Gegenwart, *die;* Anwesenheit, *die;* (*of things*) Vorhandensein, *das;* **in the ~ of his**

**friends** in Gegenwart *od.* Anwesenheit seiner Freunde; **in the ~ of danger** angesichts von Gefahren; **make one's ~ felt** sich bemerkbar machen; **be admitted to/be banished from the King's ~:** zum König vorgelassen werden/aus der Umgebung des Königs verbannt werden; **B** (*appearance*) Äußere, *das;* (*bearing*) Auftreten, *das;* **[stage] ~:** Ausstrahlung [auf der Bühne]; **she has ~:** sie stellt etwas dar *od.* strahlt etwas aus; **C** (*being represented*) Präsenz, *die;* **police ~:** Polizeipräsenz, *die;* **the British ~ east of Suez** die britische Präsenz östlich von Suez; **D** (*person or thing*) Erscheinung, *die;* **feel an invisible ~ in the room** die Anwesenheit von etwas Unsichtbarem im Zimmer spüren; **E ~ of mind** Geistesgegenwart, *die*

**present¹** /ˈprezənt/ **1** *adj.* **A** anwesend, (*geh.*) zugegen (**at** bei); **be ~ in the air/water/in large amounts** in der Luft/im Wasser/in großen Mengen vorhanden sein; **all ~ and correct** (*joc.*) alle sind da; **all those ~:** alle Anwesenden; **~ company excepted** Anwesende ausgenommen; **be ~ to sb.** *or* **sb.'s mind** jmdm. gegenwärtig sein; **B** (*being dealt with*) betreffend; **it's not relevant to the ~ matter** es ist für diese Angelegenheit nicht von Bedeutung; **in the ~ connection** in diesem Zusammenhang; **in the ~ case** im vorliegenden Fall; **C** (*existing now*) gegenwärtig; jetzig, derzeitig ‹Dekan, Bischof, Chef usw.›; **during the ~ month** im laufenden Monat; **the ~ writer/author** *etc.* der Autor des vorliegenden Textes; **D** (*Ling.*) **~ tense** Präsens, *das;* Gegenwart, *die;* **~ perfect** Perfekt, *das;* vollendete Gegenwart; ⇒ *also* **participle**; **E a very ~ help in trouble** (*arch.*) eine allgegenwärtige Hilfe in der Not.
**2** *n.* **A the ~:** die Gegenwart; **up to the ~:** bis jetzt; bisher; **at ~:** zur Zeit; **I can't help you/say more at ~:** im Augenblick kann ich dir nicht helfen/kann ich nicht mehr sagen; **for the ~:** vorläufig; **[there is] no time like the ~:** die Gelegenheit ist günstig; jetzt ist der beste Augenblick; **B** (*Ling.*) Präsens, *das;* Gegenwart, *die*

**present²** **1** /ˈprezənt/ *n.* (*gift*) Geschenk, *das;* Präsent, *das* (*geh.*); **parting ~:** Abschiedsgeschenk, *das;* **make a ~ of sth. to sb., make sb. a ~ of sth.** jmdm. etw. zum Geschenk machen; ⇒ *also* **give** 1 B. **2** /prɪˈzent/ *v.t.* **A** schenken; überreichen ‹Preis, Medaille, Geschenk›; **~ sth. to sb.** *or* **sb. with sth.** jmdm. etw. schenken *od.* zum Geschenk machen; **~ sb. with gifts** jmdm. Geschenke machen; **~ sb. with difficulties/a problem** jmdn. vor Schwierigkeiten/ein Problem stellen; **he was ~ed with an opportunity that ...:** ihm bot sich eine Gelegenheit, die ...; **B** (*express*) **~ one's compliments to sb.** sich jmdm. empfehlen; **~ one's regards to sb.** jmdm. Grüße bestellen *od.* ausrichten; jmdm. seine Grüße entbieten (*geh.*); **C** (*deliver*) überreichen ‹Gesuch› (**to** bei); vorlegen ‹Scheck, Bericht, Rechnung› (**to** *Dat.*); **~ one's case** seinen Fall darlegen; **D** (*exhibit*) zeigen; bereiten ‹Schwierigkeit›; aufweisen ‹Aspekt›; **~ a ragged appearance** einen zerlumpten Anblick bieten; **~ a bold front** *or* **brave face to the world** sich nach außen hin unerschrocken geben; **E** (*introduce*) vorstellen (**to** *Dat.*); **F** (*to the public*) geben, aufführen ‹Theaterstück›; zeigen ‹Film›; moderieren ‹Sendung›; bringen ‹Fernsehserie, Schauspieler in einer Rolle›; vorstellen ‹Produkt usw.›; vorlegen ‹Abhandlung›; darlegen ‹Theorie usw.›; **G** (*Parl.*) vorlegen ‹Gesetzentwurf›; **H ~ arms!** (*Mil.*) präsentiert das Gewehr!; **I** (*aim, hold horizontally*) anlegen ‹Gewehr usw.›; **he ~ed his weapon** er legte an.
**3** *v. refl.* ‹Problem:› auftreten; ‹Möglichkeit:› sich ergeben; **~ itself to sb.** ‹Möglichkeit:› jmdm. vor Augen stehen; ‹Erinnerung usw.:› sich bei jmdm. einstellen; ‹Gedanke:› jmdm. kommen; **~ oneself to sb.** sich jmdm. vorstellen; **~ oneself for interview/an examination** zu einem Gespräch/einer Prüfung erscheinen

**presentable** /prɪˈzentəbl/ *adj.* ansehnlich; **she is quite a ~ young lady** man kann sie gut vorzeigen *od.* sich gut mit ihr sehen lassen; **the flat is not very ~ at the moment** die Wohnung ist im Augenblick nicht besonders präsentabel; **I'm not ~:** ich kann mich nicht so zeigen; **make oneself/sth. ~:** sich/etw. zurechtmachen; **his most ~ jacket** sein bestes Jackett

**presentably** /prɪˈzentəblɪ/ *adv.* ansehnlich; angemessen ‹sich kleiden›; ganz ordentlich ‹Klavier spielen, malen usw.›

**presentation** /prezənˈteɪʃn/ *n.* **A** (*giving*) Schenkung, *die;* (*of prize, medal, gift*) Überreichung, *die;* **make sb. a ~ of sth.** jmdm. etw. schenken/überreichen; **B** (*ceremony*) Verleihung, *die;* **~ of the awards/medals** Preis-/Ordensverleihung, *die;* **C** (*delivering*) (*of petition*) Überreichung, *die;* (*of cheque, report, account*) Vorlage, *die;* (*of case, position, thesis*) Darlegung, *die;* (*manner of putting forward, presenting*) Präsentation, *die* (*geh.*); Darbietung, *die;* **on ~ of** gegen Vorlage (+ *Gen.*); **D** (*exhibition*) Darstellung, *die;* **E** (*Theatre, Radio, Telev.*) Darbietung, *die;* (*Theatre also*) Inszenierung, *die;* (*Radio, Telev. also*) Moderation, *die;* **F** (*introduction*) Vorstellung, *die;* **G** (*Med.*) Lage, *die;* **head/breech ~:** Kopf-/Steißlage, *die*

**presenˈtation: ~ copy** *n.* Dedikationsexemplar, *das;* **~ skills** *n. pl.* Presentationsfähigheiten *Pl.*

**present-ˈday** *adj.* heutig; zeitgemäß ‹Einstellungen, Ansichten›; **by ~ standards** nach heutigen *od.* gegenwärtigen Maßstäben

**presenter** /prɪˈzentə(r)/ *n.* **A** (*of cheque*) Überbringer, *der*/Überbringerin, *die;* **be the ~ of a petition/report** eine Petition überreichen/einen Bericht vorlegen; **B** ▸ **1261** (*Radio, Telev.*) Moderator, *der*/Moderatorin, *die*

**presentiment** /prɪˈzentɪmənt/ *n.* Vorahnung, *die;* **I have a ~ about the opening night** ich habe das Gefühl, dass bei der Premiere irgendetwas passiert; **have a ~ that ...:** vorausahnen, dass ...

**presently** /ˈprezəntlɪ/ *adv.* **A** (*soon*) bald; **see you ~:** bis gleich; **B** (*Amer., Scot.: now*) zurzeit; derzeit

**present: ~ ˈvalue, ~ ˈworth** *ns.* (*Econ.*) jetziger Wert; Tageswert, *der*

**preservation** /prezəˈveɪʃn/ *n., no pl.* **A** (*action*) Erhaltung, *die;* (*of leather, wood, etc.*) Konservierung, *die;* **the ~ of peace** die Erhaltung des Friedens; **B** (*state*) Erhaltungszustand, *der;* **be in an excellent state of ~:** außerordentlich gut erhalten sein; ‹Person:› sich außerordentlich gut gehalten haben

**preserˈvation order** *n.* *Verordnung, die etw. unter Denkmalschutz stellt;* **put a ~ on sth.** etw. unter Denkmalschutz stellen

**preservative** /prɪˈzɜːvətɪv/ **1** *n.* Konservierungsmittel, *das.* **2** *adj.* konservierend; Konservierungs-; konservativ ‹Lösung›

**preserve** /prɪˈzɜːv/ **1** *n.* **A** *in sing. or pl.* (*fruit*) Eingemachte, *das;* **strawberry/quince ~s** eingemachte Erdbeeren/Quitten; **B** (*jam*) Konfitüre, *die;* **C** (*fig.: special sphere*) Domäne, *die* (*geh.*); (*of political power*) Einflussbereich, *der;* **D** (*for wildlife*) [Natur]schutzgebiet, *das;* Reservat, *das;* (*water*) [Fisch]gehege, *das;* **wildlife/game ~:** Tierschutzgebiet, *das*/Wildpark *der.*
**2** *v.t.* **A** (*keep safe*) schützen (**from** vor + *Dat.*); **~ sth. from destruction** etw. vor der Zerstörung bewahren; **B** (*maintain*) aufrechterhalten ‹Disziplin›; bewahren ‹Sehfähigkeit, Brauch, Würde›; behalten ‹Stellung›; wahren ‹Anschein, Reputation›; **~ the peace** den Frieden bewahren *od.* erhalten; **C** (*retain*) speichern ‹Hitze›; bewahren ‹Haltung, Distanz, Humor›; **D** (*prepare, keep from decay*) konservieren; (*bottle*) einmachen ‹Obst, Gemüse›; präparieren; ‹Leiche, Kadaver›; **E** (*keep alive*) erhalten; (*fig.*) bewahren ‹Erinnerung, Andenken›; **Heaven ~ us!** [Gott] bewahre!; **F** (*care for and protect*) hegen ‹Tierart, Wald›; unter Schutz stellen ‹Gewässer, Gebiet›

**preset** /priːˈset/ *v.t., forms as* **set** 1: vorher einstellen

**pre-shrink** /priːˈʃrɪŋk/ *v.t., forms as* **shrink** 2 (*Textiles*) vorschrumpfen; vorwaschen ‹Jeans›

**pre-shrunk** /priːˈʃrʌŋk/ *adj.* (*Textiles*) vorgeschrumpft, vorgewaschen ‹Jeans›

**preside** /prɪˈzaɪd/ *v.i.* **A** (*at meeting etc.*) den Vorsitz haben (**at** bei); präsidieren, vorsitzen (**over** *Dat.*); **B** (*at meal*) den Vorsitz haben; **~ at dinner** bei Tisch vorsitzen; **C** (*exercise control*) **~ over** leiten ‹Abteilung, Organisation, Programm›; lenken ‹Geschick›; vorstehen (+ *Dat.*) ‹Familie›; bestimmen ‹Bildung, Gründung›

**presidency** /ˈprezɪdənsɪ/ *n.* **A** Präsidentschaft, *die;* **B** (*of legislative body*) Vorsitz, *der;* **C** (*Univ., esp. Amer.*) Präsidentschaft, *die;* Rektorat, *das;* **D** (*of society etc.*) Vorsitz, *der;* Präsidentschaft, *die;* **E** (*of council, board, etc.*) Vorsitz, *der;* **F** (*Amer.: of bank or company*) Vorstandsvorsitz, *der*

**president** /ˈprezɪdənt/ *n.* ▸ **1261**, ▸ **1617** **A** Präsident, *der*/Präsidentin, *die;* **B** (*of legislative body*) Vorsitzende, *der/die;* **C** (*Univ., esp. Amer.*) Präsident, *der*/Präsidentin, *die;* Rektor, *der*/Rektorin, *die;* **D** (*of society etc.*) Vorsitzende, *der/die;* Präsident, *der*/Präsidentin, *die;* **E** (*of council, board, etc.*) Vorstand, *der;* Vorsitzende, *der/die;* **Lord P~ of the Council** (*Brit.*) *Titel des dem Privy Council präsidierenden Kabinettsmitglieds;* **F** (*Amer.: of bank or company*) Vorstandvorsitzende, *der/die;* Generaldirektor, *der*/-direktorin, *die*

**presidential** /prezɪˈdenʃl/ *adj.* Präsidenten-; **~ campaign** Präsidentschaftswahlkampf, *der;* **~ address** Ansprache des Präsidenten; **~ ambitions** Streben nach der Präsidentschaft

**presidium** /prɪˈsɪdɪəm, prɪˈzɪdɪəm/ *n.* Präsidium, *das*

**press¹** /pres/ **1** *n.* **A** (*newspapers etc.*) Presse, *die;* *attrib.* Presse-; der Presse *nachgestellt;* **get/have a good/bad ~** (*fig.*) eine gute/schlechte Presse bekommen/haben; ⇒ *also* **freedom** A; **B** ⇒ **printing press**; **C** (*printing house*) Druckerei, *die;* **at** *or* **in [the] ~:** im Druck; **send to [the] ~:** in Druck geben; **go to [the] ~:** in Druck gehen: **D** (*publishing firm*) Verlag, *der;* **E** (*for flattening, compressing, etc.*) Presse, *die;* (*for sports racket*) Spanner, *der;* **F** (*crowding*) Gedränge, *das;* **G** (*crowd*) Menge, *die;* **a ~ of people** eine Menschenmenge, *die;* **H** (*in battle*) Getümmel, *das;* Gewühl, *das;* **I** (*~ing*) Druck, *der;* **give sth. a ~:** etw. drücken; **your trousers could do with a ~:** deine Hosen sollten wieder einmal gebügelt werden; **with a ~ of the button** mit einem Knopfdruck *od.* Druck auf den Knopf; **J** (*Weightlifting*) Drücken, *das.*
**2** *v.t.* **A** drücken; pressen; drücken auf (+ *Akk.*) ‹Klingel, Knopf›; treten auf (+ *Akk.*) ‹Gas-, Brems-, Kupplungspedal usw.›; **~ the trigger** abdrücken; den Abzug betätigen; **B** (*urge*) drängen ‹Person›; (*force*) aufdrängen (**[up]on** *Dat.*); (*insist on*) nachdrücklich vorbringen ‹Forderung, Argument, Vorschlag›; verfechten ‹Standpunkt›; **~ sb. for an answer** jmdn. zu einer Antwort drängen; **he did not ~ the point** er ließ die Sache auf sich beruhen; **~ the analogy too far** die Analogie zu weit treiben; **C** (*exert force on*) drücken; pressen; **D** (*squeeze*) drücken; **~ sb.'s hand** jmdm. die Hand drücken; **E** (*compress*) pressen; auspressen ‹Orangen, Saft›; keltern ‹Trauben, Äpfel›; **F** (*iron*) bügeln; **G** (*bear heavily on*) bedrängen; **be hard ~ed** (*by enemy*) hart bedrängt werden; (*experience great difficulty*) unter großem Druck stehen; **H be ~ed for space/time/money** (*have barely enough*) zu wenig Platz/Zeit/Geld haben; **I** (*Weightlifting*) drücken; **J** (*make*) pressen ‹Schallplatte›.
**3** *v.i.* **A** (*exert pressure*) drücken; **the child ~ed against the railings** das Kind drückte sich gegen das Geländer; **B** (*weigh*) **~ [up]on sb.'s mind/heart** jmdn. bedrücken; **C** (*be urgent*) drängen; **time/sth. ~es** die Zeit drängt/etw. eilt *od.* ist dringend; **D** (*make demand*) **~ for sth.** auf etw. (*Akk.*) drängen; **E** (*crowd*) [sich] drängen; **~ up** sich herandrängen; **~ in upon sb.** ‹Gedanken:› auf jmdn. eindringen

**~ aˈhead, ~ ˈforward, ~ ˈon** *v.i.* (*continue activity*) [zügig] weitermachen; (*continue travelling*) [zügig] weitergehen/-fahren; **~**

P

on with one's work sich mit der Arbeit ranhalten (*ugs.*)
~ 'out *v.t.* auspressen; (*out of cardboard*) herausdrücken

**press²** *v.t.* ~ **into service/use** in Dienst nehmen; einsetzen

**press:** ~ **agent** *n.* ▶ 1261 Presseagent, *der*/-agentin, *die*; ~ **attaché** ⇒ attaché; ~ **box** *n.* Pressekabine, *die*; ~**-button** ⇒ push-button; ~ **campaign** *n.* Pressefeldzug, *der*; Pressekampagne, *die*; ~ **card** *n.* Presseausweis, *der*; ~ **clipping** (*Amer.*) ⇒ ~ cutting; ~ **conference** *n.* Pressekonferenz, *die*; ~ **coverage** *n.* Berichterstattung in der Presse; ~ **cutting** *n.* (*Brit.*) Zeitungsausschnitt, *der*; ~ **gallery** *n.* Pressetribüne, *die*; ~ **gang** ❶ *n.* (*Hist.*) Pressgang, *der* (*veralt.*); ❷ *v.t.* (*Hist.*) pressen; zwangsrekrutieren; (*fig.*) zwingen, pressen (**into** zu)

**pressing** /'presɪŋ/ ❶ *adj.* Ⓐ (*urgent*) dringend; **the danger was** ~: Gefahr war im Verzug; Ⓑ (*persistent*) dringlich; nachdrücklich. ❷ *n.* Ⓐ (*exertion of pressure*) Drücken, *das*; (*of apples, grapes*) Keltern, *das*; (*of cheese, olives*) Pressen, *das*; (*of clothes*) Bügeln, *das*; Ⓑ (*product, esp. record*) Pressung, *die*

**pressingly** /'presɪŋlɪ/ *adv.* dringend

**press:** ~**man** *n.* ▶ 1261 (*Brit.*: *journalist*) Journalist, *der*; Pressemann, *der* (*ugs.*); ~ **office** *n.* Pressebüro, *das*; ~ **officer** *n.* ▶ 1261 Pressereferent, *der*/-referentin, *die*; Pressesprecher, *der*/-sprecherin, *die*; ~ **photographer** *n.* ▶ 1261 Pressefotograf, *der*/-fotografin, *die*; ~ **release** *n.* Presseinformation, *die*; ~ **report** *n.* Pressebericht, *der*; ~ **stud** *n.* (*Brit.*) Druckknopf, *der*; ~-**up** *n.* Liegestütz, *der*

**pressure** /'preʃə(r)/ ❶ *n.* Ⓐ (*exertion of force, amount*) Druck, *der*; **apply firm ~ to the joint** die Verbindung fest zusammendrücken; **atmospheric** ~: Luftdruck, *der*; Ⓑ (*oppression*) Last, *die*; Belastung, *die*; **mental** ~: psychische Belastung; Ⓒ (*trouble*) Druck, *der*; **under financial** ~: finanziell unter Druck; **~s at [one's] work** berufliche Belastungen; **the finances of the company were under** ~: die Firma stand [finanziell] unter Druck; Ⓓ (*urgency*) Druck, *der*; (*of affairs*) Dringlichkeit, *die*; **the ~ was on him** er stand unter Zeitdruck; **he [positively] thrives under** ~: er braucht den Druck [geradezu]; Ⓔ (*constraint*) Druck, *der*; Zwang, *der*; **put ~ on sb.** jmdn. unter Druck setzen; **be under a lot of ~ to do sth.** stark unter Druck gesetzt werden, etw. zu tun; **put the ~ on** die Daumenschrauben anlegen *od.* -setzen. ⇒ *also* **high pressure**; **low pressure**. ❷ *v.t.* Ⓐ (*coerce*) ~ **sb. into doing sth.** jmdn. [dazu] drängen, etw. zu tun; Ⓑ (*fig.*: *apply ~ to*) unter Druck setzen

**pressure:** ~ **cooker** *n.* Schnellkochtopf, *der*; ~ **gauge** *n.* (*Motor Veh.*) Druckluftmesser, *der*; Manometer, *das*; (*Railw.*) Druckanzeige, *die*; ~ **group** *n.* Pressuregroup, *die*; ~ **point** *n.* (*Med.*) Ⓐ (*where sore may develop*) Druckstelle, *die*; Ⓑ (*where bleeding can be stopped*) Druckpunkt, *der*; ~ **suit** *n.* (*Astronaut.*) Druckanzug, *der*

**pressurize** (**pressurise**) /'preʃəraɪz/ *v.t.* Ⓐ ⇒ **pressure** 2 A; Ⓑ (*raise to high pressure*) unter Druck setzen; Ⓒ (*maintain normal pressure in*) druckfest machen, auf Normaldruck halten ‹Flugzeugkabine›; **~d cabin/suit** Druckkabine, *die*/-anzug, *der*

**prestige** /pre'sti:ʒ/ ❶ *n.* Prestige, *das*; Renommee, *das*. ❷ *adj.* renommiert; Nobel‹hotel, -gegend›; ~ **value** Prestigewert, *der*

**prestigious** /pre'stɪdʒəs/ *adj.* angesehen

**presto** /'prestəʊ/ ⇒ **hey**

**pre-stressed** /pri:'strest/ *adj.* (*Building*) vorgespannt; ~ **concrete** Spannbeton, *der*

**presumable** /prɪ'zju:məbl/ *adj.* mutmaßlich

**presumably** /prɪ'zju:məblɪ/ *adv.* vermutlich; ~ **he knows what he is doing** er wird schon wissen, was er tut; ~ **something must have delayed them** etwas muss sie aufgehalten haben

**presume** /prɪ'zju:m/ ❶ *v.t.* Ⓐ (*venture*) ~ **to do sth.** sich (*Dat.*) anmaßen, etw. zu tun; (*take the liberty*) sich (*Dat.*) erlauben, etw. zu tun; Ⓑ (*suppose*) annehmen; **be ~d innocent** als unschuldig gelten *od.* angesehen werden; **missing ~d dead** vermisst, wahrscheinlich *od.* mutmaßlich tot. ❷ *v.i.* sich (*Dat.*) anmaßen; ~ **[up]on sth.** etw. ausnützen

**presumption** /prɪ'zʌmpʃn/ *n.* Ⓐ (*arrogance*) Anmaßung, *die*; Vermessenheit, *die*; **have the ~ to do sth.** die Vermessenheit besitzen, etw. zu tun; sich (*Dat.*) anmaßen, etw. zu tun; Ⓑ (*assumption*) Annahme, *die*; Vermutung, *die*; **the ~ is that he lost it** vermutlich hat er es verloren; es ist zu vermuten, dass er es verloren hat; **we are working on the ~ that ...:** wir gehen von der Annahme aus, dass ...; **the ~ of innocence** die Unschuldsvermutung; Ⓒ (*ground for belief*) **there is a strong ~ against its truth** es besteht hinreichend Grund zu der Annahme, dass es nicht stimmt

**presumptive** /prɪ'zʌmptɪv/ *adj.* ~ **evidence** Indizienbeweis, *der*; **heir** ~: mutmaßlicher Erbe/mutmaßliche Erbin

**presumptuous** /prɪ'zʌmptjʊəs/ *adj.* anmaßend; überheblich; (*impertinent*) aufdringlich

**presumptuously** /prɪ'zʌmptjʊəslɪ/ *adv.* überheblich; (*impertinently*) aufdringlich

**presuppose** /pri:sə'pəʊz/ *v.t.* Ⓐ (*assume*) voraussetzen; Ⓑ (*imply*) voraussetzen; zur Voraussetzung haben

**presupposition** /pri:sʌpə'zɪʃn/ *n.* Ⓐ (*presupposing*) Annahme, *die*; Voraussetzung, *die*; Ⓑ (*thing assumed*) Prämisse, *die* (*bes. Philos.*, *Rechtsw.*); Voraussetzung, *die*; **work on a** ~: von einer Prämisse/Voraussetzung ausgehen

**pre-tax** /'pri:tæks/ *adj.* vor Steuern *nachgestellt*; ~ **profits** Gewinn vor Steuern

**pre-teen** /'pri:ti:n/ *adj.* ≈ zehn- bis zwölfjährig

**pretence** /prɪ'tens/ *n.* (*Brit.*) Ⓐ (*pretext*) Vorwand, *der*; **under [the] ~ of helping** unter dem Vorwand zu helfen; ⇒ *also* **false pretences**; Ⓑ *no art.* (*make-believe, insincere behaviour*) Verstellung, *die*; Ⓒ (*piece of insincere behaviour*) **it is all** *or* **just a** ~: das ist alles nicht echt; Ⓓ (*affectation*) Affektiertheit, *die* (*abwertend*); Unnatürlichkeit, *die*; Ⓔ (*claim*) Anspruch, *der*; **make the/no ~ of** *or* **to sth.** Anspruch/keinen Anspruch auf etw. (*Akk.*) erheben

**pretend** /prɪ'tend/ ❶ *v.t.* Ⓐ vorgeben; **she ~ed to be asleep** sie tat, als ob sie schlief[e]; Ⓑ (*imagine in play*) ~ **to be sth.** so tun, als ob man etw. sei; **let's ~ that we are king and queen** lass uns König und Königin spielen; Ⓒ (*profess falsely*) vortäuschen; simulieren, vorschützen ‹Krankheit›; (*say falsely*) vorgeben, fälschlich beteuern (**to** gegenüber); ~ **illness** krank spielen (*ugs.*); Ⓓ (*claim*) **not ~ to do sth.** nicht behaupten wollen, etw. zu tun. ❷ *v.i.* Ⓐ sich verstellen; **she's only ~ing** sie tut nur so; ~ **to sb.** jmdm. etwas vormachen; Ⓑ (*presume*) sich unterfangen (*geh.*); wagen; Ⓒ ~ **to** (*claim*) für sich in Anspruch nehmen; Anspruch erheben auf (+ *Akk.*) (*Titel, Amt*)

**pretender** /prɪ'tendə(r)/ *n.* Prätendent, *der* (*geh.*)/Prätendentin, *die* (*geh.*) (**to** auf + *Akk.*); ~ **to the throne** Thronanwärter *od.* -prätendent, *der*/Thronanwärterin *od.* -prätendentin, *die*; **Old/Young P~** *Sohn/Enkel von Jakob II. als britischer Thronanwärter*

**pretense** (*Amer.*) ⇒ **pretence**

**pretension** /prɪ'tenʃn/ *n.* Ⓐ (*claim*) Anspruch, *der*; **have/make ~s to great wisdom** vorgeben *od.* den Anspruch erheben, sehr klug zu sein; Ⓑ (*justifiable claim*) Anspruch, *der* (**to** auf + *Akk.*); **a country estate of some ~s** ein Landsitz, der sich sehen lassen kann; **people with ~s to taste and culture** Menschen, die Geschmack und Kultur für sich in Anspruch nehmen können; Ⓒ (*pretentiousness*) Überheblichkeit, *die*; Anmaßung, *die*; (*of things: ostentation*) Protzigkeit, *die*

**pretentious** /prɪ'tenʃəs/ *adj.* Ⓐ prätentiös (*geh.*); hochgestochen; wichtigtuerisch ‹Person›; Ⓑ (*ostentatious*) protzig (*abwertend*); großspurig (*abwertend*) ‹Person, Verhalten, Art›

**pretentiously** /prɪ'tenʃəslɪ/ *adv.* Ⓐ prätentiös (*geh.*); hochgestochen; **speak** ~: wichtigtuerische Reden führen; Ⓑ (*ostentatiously*) protzig (*abwertend*); großspurig (*abwertend*) ‹sich benehmen›

**preterite** (*Amer.*: **preterit**) /'pretərɪt/ (*Ling.*) ❶ *adj.* Präteritums-; ~ **tense** Präteritum, *das*. ❷ *n.* Präteritum, *das*

**preternatural** /pri:tə'nætʃərl/ *adj.* Ⓐ (*non-natural*) außergewöhnlich; Ⓑ (*supernatural*) übernatürlich; übersinnlich

**pretext** /'pri:tekst/ *n.* Vorwand, *der*; Ausrede, *die*; **make illness the ~ for staying at home** Krankheit vorschützen, um zu Hause zu bleiben; **[up]on** *or* **under the ~ of doing sth./being ill** unter dem Vorwand *od.* mit der Entschuldigung, etw. tun zu wollen/krank zu sein; **on the slightest** ~: mit *od.* unter dem fadenscheinigsten Vorwand

**prettify** /'prɪtɪfaɪ/ *v.t.* verschönern; (*in an insipid way*) verkitschen

**prettily** /'prɪtɪlɪ/ *adv.* hübsch; sehr schön ‹singen, tanzen›; **curtsy** ~: einen graziösen Knicks machen; **thank sb.** ~: sich [bei jmdm.] sehr nett bedanken

**pretty** /'prɪtɪ/ ❶ *adj.* Ⓐ (*attractive*) hübsch; nett ‹Art›; niedlich ‹Geschichte, Liedchen›; **she's not just a ~ face!** sie ist nicht nur hübsch[, sie kann auch was]!; **as ~ as a picture** bildhübsch; **not a ~ sight** (*iron.*) kein schöner Anblick; Ⓑ (*iron.*) hübsch, schön (*ugs. iron.*); **a ~ state of affairs** eine schöne Geschichte; **a ~ mess** eine schöne Bescherung. ❷ *adv.* ziemlich; **I am ~ well** es geht mir ganz gut; ~ **much** *or* **well as ...:** so ziemlich wie ...; **we have ~ nearly finished** wir sind so gut wie fertig; **be ~ well over/exhausted** so gut wie vorbei/erschöpft sein; ~ **much the same** ziemlich unverändert; ~ **much the same thing** so ziemlich *od.* fast das Gleiche; **be sitting** ~ (*coll.*) sein Schäfchen im Trockenen haben (*ugs.*); ausgesorgt haben; **~-~** (*coll.*) kitschig (*abwertend*)

**pretzel** /'pretsl/ *n.* Brezel, *die*

**prevail** /prɪ'veɪl/ *v.i.* Ⓐ (*gain mastery*) siegen, die Oberhand gewinnen (**against, over** über + *Akk.*); ~ **[up]on sb.** auf jmdn. einwirken; jmdn. überreden; ~ **[up]on sb. to do sth.** jmdn. dazu bewegen *od.* überreden, etw. zu tun; **be ~ed [up]on to do sth.** sich bewegen *od.* überreden lassen, etw. zu tun; Ⓑ (*predominate*) ‹Zustand, Bedingung:› vorherrschen; Ⓒ (*be current*) herrschen; **this type of approach ~ed for many years** dieser Ansatz war jahrelang gängig *od.* üblich

**prevailing** /prɪ'veɪlɪŋ/ *adj.* Ⓐ (*common*) [vor]herrschend; aktuell ‹Mode›; Ⓑ (*most frequent*) **the ~ wind is from the West** der Wind kommt vorwiegend von Westen

**prevalence** /'prevələns/ *n.*, *no pl.* Vorherrschen, *das*; (*of crime, corruption, etc.*) Überhandnehmen, *das*; (*of disease, malnutrition, etc.*) weite Verbreitung; **gain** ~ ‹Standpunkt:› sich durchsetzen

**prevalent** /'prevələnt/ *adj.* Ⓐ (*existing*) herrschend; gängig, geläufig ‹Schreibweise›; weit verbreitet ‹Krankheit›; aktuell ‹Trend›; Ⓑ (*predominant*) vorherrschend; **be/become** ~: vorherrschen/sich durchsetzen

**prevaricate** /prɪ'værɪkeɪt/ *v.i.* Ausflüchte machen (**over** wegen)

**prevarication** /prɪværɪ'keɪʃn/ *n.* Ⓐ (*prevaricating*) Ausflüchte *Pl.*; Ⓑ (*statement*) Ausflucht, *die*

**prevent** /prɪ'vent/ *v.t.* (*hinder*) verhindern; verhüten; (*forestall*) vorbeugen; verhüten; ~ **sb. from doing sth.**, ~ **sb.'s doing sth.**, (*coll.*) ~ **sb. doing sth.** jmdn. daran hindern *od.* davon abhalten, etw. zu tun; **there is nothing to ~ me** nichts hindert mich daran; ~ **sb. from coming** jmdn. am Kommen hindern; **catch sb.'s arm to ~ him [from] falling** jmdn. am Arm fassen, damit er nicht fällt; **do everything to ~ it from happening** *or* ~ **its happening** alles tun, um es zu verhindern *od.* damit es nicht geschieht

**preventable** /prɪˈventəbl/ *adj.* vermeidbar

**preventative** /prɪˈventətɪv/ ⇒ **preventive**

**prevention** /prɪˈvenʃn/ *n.* Verhinderung, *die;* Verhütung, *die;* (*forestalling*) Vorbeugung, *die;* Verhütung, *die;* **~ of crime** Verbrechensverhütung, *die;* **society for the ~ of cruelty to children/animals** Kinderschutzbund/Tierschutzverein, *der;* **~ is better than cure** (*prov.*) Vorbeugen ist besser als Heilen (*Spr.*)

**preventive** /prɪˈventɪv/ ❶ *adj.* vorbeugend; präventiv (*geh.*); Präventiv‹maßnahme, -krieg›; **~ treatment** (*Med.*) Präventivbehandlung, *die.* ❷ *n.* Vorbeugungsmaßnahme, *die;* Präventivmittel, *das* (*Med.*); **as a ~:** zur/als Vorbeugung

**preventive: ~ deˈtention** *n.* (*Brit. Law*) Sicherungsverwahrung, *die;* **~ ˈmedicine** *n.* Präventivmedizin, *die*

**preview** /ˈpriːvjuː/ ❶ *n.* Ⓐ (*of film, play*) Voraufführung, *die;* (*of exhibition*) Vernissage, *die* (*geh.*); (*of book*) Vorbesprechung, *die;* **give a ~:** eine Voraufführung geben/Vernissage veranstalten/Vorbesprechung geben; Ⓑ (*Amer.: trailer of film*) Vorschau, *die.* ❷ *v.t.* eine Vorschau sehen von ‹Film›

**previous** /ˈpriːvɪəs/ ❶ *adj.* Ⓐ (*coming before*) früher ‹Anstellung, Gelegenheit›; ‹Tag, Morgen, Abend, Nacht› vorher; vorherig ‹Abend›; vorig ‹Besitzer, Wohnsitz›; **the ~ page** die Seite davor; **no ~ experience necessary** keine Berufserfahrung nötig; **no ~ convictions** keine Vorstrafen; Ⓑ (*prior*) **~ to** vor (+ *Dat.*); Ⓒ (*hasty*) verfrüht; voreilig. ❷ *adv.* **~ to** vor (+ *Dat.*); **~ to being a nurse, she was ...:** bevor sie Krankenschwester wurde, war sie ...

**previously** /ˈpriːvɪəslɪ/ *adv.* vorher; **two years ~:** zwei Jahre zuvor

**pre-war** /ˈpriːwɔː(r)/ *adj.* Vorkriegs-; **these houses are all ~:** diese Häuser stammen alle aus der Zeit vor dem Krieg

**prey** /preɪ/ ❶ *n., pl. same* Ⓐ (*animal[s]*) Beute, *die;* Beutetier, *das;* **beast/bird of ~:** Raubtier, *das*/-vogel, *der;* **easy ~** (*lit. or fig.*) leichte Beute; Ⓑ (*victim*) Beute, *die* (*geh.*); Opfer, *das;* **fall [a] ~ to sth.** einer Sache (*Dat.*) zum Opfer fallen; **be a ~ to sth.** eine Beute *od.* ein Opfer von etw. werden. ❷ *v.i.* **~ [up]on** ‹Raubtier, Raubvogel:› schlagen; (*take as ~*) erbeuten; (*plunder*) ausplündern ‹Person›; (*exploit*) ausnutzen; **~ [up]on sb.'s mind** jmdm. keine Ruhe lassen; ‹Krankheit:› jmdm. sehr zusetzen; ‹Kummer, Angst:› an jmdm. nagen

**prezzie** /ˈprezɪ/ *n.* (*coll.*) Geschenk, *das*

**price** /praɪs/ ❶ *n.* Ⓐ ▶ 1328 (*money etc.*) Preis, *der;* **the ~ of wheat/a pint** der Weizenpreis/der Preis für ein Bier; **what is the ~ of this?** was kostet das?; **at a ~ of** zum Preis von; **for the ~ of a few drinks** für ein paar Drinks; **~s and incomes policy** Preis- und Einkommenspolitik, *die;* Lohn-Preis-Politik, *die;* **sth. goes up/down in ~:** der Preis von etw. steigt/fällt; etw. steigt/fällt im Preis; **what sort of ~ do they charge for a meal?** was verlangen *od.* berechnen sie für eine Mahlzeit?; **at a ~:** zum entsprechenden Preis; **set a ~ on sth.** einen Preis für etw. festsetzen; **set a ~ on sb.'s head** *or* **life** einen Preis *od.* eine Belohnung auf jmds. Kopf (*Akk.*) aussetzen; Ⓑ (*betting odds*) Eventualquote, *die;* Ⓒ (*value*) **be without/beyond ~:** [mit Geld] nicht zu bezahlen sein; Ⓓ (*fig.*) Preis, *der;* **be achieved at a ~:** seinen Preis haben; **he succeeded, but at a great ~:** er hatte Erfolg, musste aber einen hohen Preis dafür bezahlen; **every man has his ~:** jeder Mensch hat seinen Preis *od.* ist käuflich; **at/not at any ~:** um jeden/keinen Preis; **at the ~ of ruining his marriage/health** auf Kosten seiner Ehe/Gesundheit; **what ~ ...?** (*Brit. coll.*) (*what is the chance of ...*) wie wärs mit ...?; (*... has failed*) wie stehts jetzt mit ...? ⇒ *also* **pay** 2 F.
❷ *v.t.* (*fix ~ of*) kalkulieren ‹Ware›; (*label with ~*) auszeichnen; **modestly ~d** zu niedrigem Preis *nachgestellt;* **favourably ~d** preisgünstig

**price: ~ bracket** ⇒ **price range; ~ control** *n.* Preiskontrolle, *die;* **~ cut** *n.* Preissenkung, *die;* **~-cutting** *n.* Preisschleuderei, *die;* **~-fixing** *n.* Preisabsprache, *die;* **~ freeze** *n.* Preisstopp, *der*

**priceless** /ˈpraɪslɪs/ *adj.* Ⓐ (*invaluable*) unbezahlbar; unschätzbar ‹Gut›; Ⓑ (*coll.: amusing*) köstlich

**price: ~ list** *n.* Preisliste, *die;* **~ range** *n.* Preisspanne, *die;* **it's within/outside my ~ range** das kann ich mir leisten/nicht leisten; **~ ring** *n.* (*Econ.*) Preiskartell, *das;* **~ rise** *n.* Preisanstieg, *der* (**on** bei); **constant ~ rises** ständig steigende Preise; ständige Preiserhöhungen; **~ tag** *n.* Preisschild, *das;* (*fig.*) Kosten *Pl.;* **~ war** *n.* Preiskrieg, *der*

**pricey** /ˈpraɪsɪ/ *adj.*, **pricier** /ˈpraɪsɪə(r)/, **priciest** /ˈpraɪsɪɪst/ (*Brit. coll.*) teuer

**prick** /prɪk/ ❶ *v.t.* Ⓐ (*pierce*) stechen; stechen in ‹Ballon›; aufstechen ‹Blase›; **he ~ed his finger with the needle** er stach sich (*Dat.*) mit der Nadel in den Finger; **~ the bubble** (*fig.*) die Illusion zerstören; **~ out** auspflanzen ‹Setzlinge›; Ⓑ (*fig.*) quälen; plagen; **my conscience ~ed me** ich hatte Gewissensbisse; Ⓒ (*mark*) **~ [off *or* out]** vorstechen ‹Stickmuster, Linie usw.›; Ⓓ (*mark off*) markieren.
❷ *v.i.* Ⓐ (*hurt*) stechen; Ⓑ (*thrust*) stechen; **~ at sb.'s conscience** jmdm. Gewissensbisse verursachen.
❸ *n.* Ⓐ **I felt a little ~:** ich fühlte einen leichten Stich; **give sb.'s finger a ~ with the needle** jmdn. mit der Nadel in den Finger stechen; **~s of conscience** Gewissensbisse *Pl.;* Ⓑ (*mark*) Punkt, *der;* Ⓒ (*coarse: penis*) Pimmel, *der* (*fam.*); Schwanz, *der* (*derb*); Ⓓ (*coarse derog.: man*) Wichser, *der* (*derb*); Ⓔ (*arch.: goad*) Stachel, *der;* **kick against the ~s** (*fig.*) wider den Stachel löcken (*geh.*)

**~ up** ❶ *v.t.* aufrichten ‹Ohren›; **~ up one's/its ears** (*listen*) die Ohren spitzen. ❷ *v.i.* ‹Ohren:› sich aufrichten

**prickle** /ˈprɪkl/ ❶ *n.* Ⓐ (*thorn*) Dorn, *der;* Ⓑ (*Zool., Bot.*) Stachel, *der.* ❷ *v.t.* stechen; ‹Wolle:› kratzen auf (+ *Dat.*), ‹Hitze, Wind:› prickeln auf (+ *Dat.*) ‹Haut›. ❸ *v.i.* kratzen

**prickly** /ˈprɪklɪ/ *adj.* Ⓐ (*with prickles*) ⇒ **prickle** 1: dornig; stachelig; **be ~** ‹Pflanze:› Stacheln/Dornen haben; Ⓑ (*fig.*) empfindlich; Ⓒ (*tingling*) kratzig; **a ~ sensation in the limbs** ein Kribbeln *od.* Prickeln in den Gliedern

**prickly: ~ ˈheat** *n.* (*Med.*) rote Frieseln; **~ ˈpear** *n.* Ⓐ (*cactus*) Feigenkaktus, *der;* Ⓑ (*fruit*) Kaktusfeige, *die*

**pricy** ⇒ **pricey**

**pride** /praɪd/ ❶ *n.* Ⓐ Stolz, *der;* (*arrogance*) Hochmut, *der* (*abwertend*); **~ goes before a fall** (*prov.*) Hochmut kommt vor dem Fall (*Spr.*); **take *or* have ~ of place** die Spitzenstellung einnehmen *od.* innehaben; (*in collection etc.*) das Glanzstück sein; **proper ~:** gesunder Stolz; **a proper ~ in oneself** ein gesundes Selbstwertgefühl; **she has a lot of ~:** sie ist sehr stolz; **his own ~ prevented him from doing that** sein Ehrgefühl verbot ihm, das zu tun; **false ~:** falscher Stolz; **take [a] ~ in sb./sth.** auf jmdn./etw. stolz sein; Ⓑ (*object, best one*) Stolz, *der;* **sb.'s ~ and joy** jmds. ganzer Stolz; **give sth. ~ of place** einer Sache einen Ehrenplatz einräumen; Ⓒ (*of lions*) Rudel, *das.*
❷ *v. refl.* **~ oneself [up]on sth.** (*congratulate oneself*) auf etw. (*Akk.*) stolz sein; (*plume oneself*) sich mit etw. brüsten (*abwertend*)

**priest** /priːst/ *n.* Priester, *der;* ⇒ *also* **high priest**

**priestess** /ˈpriːstɪs/ *n.* Priesterin, *die*

**priesthood** /ˈpriːsthʊd/ *n.* (*office*) geistliches Amt; (*order of priests; priests*) Geistlichkeit, *die;* **go into the ~:** Priester werden

**priestlike** /ˈpriːstlaɪk/ *adv.* priesterlich

**priestly** /ˈpriːstlɪ/ *adj.* priesterlich; Priester‹kaste, -rolle›

**prig** /prɪg/ *n.* (*didactic*) Besserwisser, *der*/-wisserin, *die* (*abwertend*); (*smug*) selbstgefälliger Mensch; (*self-righteous*) Tugendbold, *der* (*ugs., iron.*)

**priggish** /ˈprɪgɪʃ/ *adj.* (*didactic*) besserwisserisch (*abwertend*); (*smug*) selbstgefällig (*abwertend*); (*self-righteous*) übertrieben tugendhaft

**prim** /prɪm/ *adj.* Ⓐ spröde, steif ‹Person›; streng ‹Kleidung›; **~ and proper** etepetete (*ugs.*); Ⓑ (*prudish*) zimperlich; prüde

**prima ballerina** /priːmə bæləˈriːnə/ *n.* Primaballerina, *die*

**primacy** /ˈpraɪməsɪ/ *n.* Ⓐ (*pre-eminence*) Vorrang, *der;* Primat, *der od. das* (*geh.*); **position of ~:** Vorrangstellung, *die;* Ⓑ (*Eccl.: office*) Primat, *der od. das*

**prima donna** /priːmə ˈdɒnə/ *n.* (*Theatre; also fig.*) Primadonna, *die*

**primaeval** ⇒ **primeval**

**prima facie** /praɪmə ˈfeɪʃiː/ ❶ *adv.* auf den ersten Blick. ❷ *adj.* glaubhaft klingend; **~ evidence** (*Law*) Anscheinsbeweis, *der;* **I don't see a ~ reason for it** ich sehe keinen einleuchtenden Grund dafür

**primal** /ˈpraɪml/ *adj.* ursprünglich; primitiv; **~ forces** Urkräfte *Pl.*

**primarily** /ˈpraɪmərɪlɪ/ *adv.* in erster Linie

**primary** /ˈpraɪmərɪ/ ❶ *adj.* Ⓐ (*first in sequence*) primär (*geh.*); grundlegend; **the ~ meaning of a word** die Grundbedeutung eines Wortes; **~ source** Primärquelle, *die* (*geh.*); Ⓑ (*chief*) Haupt‹rolle, -sorge, -ziel, -zweck›; **of ~ importance** von höchster Bedeutung. ❷ *n.* (*Amer.: election*) Vorwahl, *die*

**primary: ~ ˈbattery** *n.* (*Electr.*) Primärbatterie, *die;* **~ ˈcell** *n.* (*Electr.*) Primärelement, *das;* **~ ˈcoil** *n.* (*Electr.*) Primärspule, *die;* **~ ˈcolour** ⇒ **colour** 1 A; **~ eduˈcation** *n.* Grundschulerziehung, *die;* **~ eˈlection** *n.* (*Amer.*) Vorwahl, *die;* **~ ˈfeather** *n.* (*Ornith.*) Schwungfeder, *die;* **~ ˈplanet** *n.* (*Astron.*) Hauptplanet, *der;* **~ school** *n.* Grundschule, *die; attrib.* **~-school teacher** ▶ 1261 Grundschullehrer, *der*/-lehrerin, *die;* **~ stress** *n.* (*Ling.*) Hauptakzent, *der*

**primate** /ˈpraɪmeɪt/ *n.* Ⓐ (*Eccl.*) Primas, *der;* **P~ of England** Primas von England; *Titel des Erzbischofs von York;* **P~ of all England** Primas von ganz England; *Titel des Erzbischofs von Canterbury;* Ⓑ (*Zool.*) Primat, *der*

**prime**[1] /praɪm/ ❶ *n.* Ⓐ (*perfection*) Höhepunkt, *der;* Krönung, *die;* **in the ~ of life/youth/manhood** in der Blüte seiner/ihrer Jahre/der Jugend (*geh.*)/im besten Mannesalter; **be in/past one's ~:** in den besten Jahren sein/die besten Jahre überschritten haben; Ⓑ (*best part*) Beste, *das;* Ⓒ (*Math.*) Primzahl, *die.* ❷ *adj.* Ⓐ (*chief*) Haupt-; hauptsächlich; **~ motive** Hauptmotiv, *das;* **be of ~ importance** von höchster Wichtigkeit sein; Ⓑ (*excellent*) erstklassig; vortrefflich ‹Beispiel›; **~ ham/lamb/pork** Schinken/Lamm/Schweinefleisch erster Güteklasse; **in ~ condition** ‹Sportler, Tier› in bester Verfassung; voll ausgereift ‹Obst›

**prime**[2] *v.t.* Ⓐ (*equip*) vorbereiten; **~ sb. with sth.** jmdn. mit etw. vertraut machen; **~ sb. with information/advice** jmdn. instruieren/jmdm. Ratschläge erteilen; **well ~d** gut vorbereitet; Ⓑ (*ply with liquor*) betrunken machen; abfüllen (*ugs.*); **be well ~d** voll sein (*salopp*); Ⓒ grundieren ‹Wand, Decke›; Ⓓ füllen ‹Pumpe›; Ⓔ (*inject petrol into*) Anlasskraftstoff einspritzen in (+ *Akk.*) ‹Motor, Zylinder›; Ⓕ schärfen ‹Sprengkörper›

**prime: ~ ˈcost** *n.* (*Econ.*) Selbstkosten *Pl.;* **~ meˈridian** *n.* (*Geog.*) Nullmeridian, *der;* **~ ˈminister** *n.* ▶ 1261, ▶ 1617 Premierminister, *der*/-ministerin, *die;* **~ ˈnumber** *n.* (*Math.*) Primzahl, *die*

**primer**[1] /ˈpraɪmə(r)/ *n.* (*book*) Fibel, *die*

**primer**[2] *n.* Ⓐ (*explosive*) Zündvorrichtung, *die;* Ⓑ (*paint etc.*) Grundierlack, *der*

**prime: ~ rate** *n.* (*Econ.*) Prime rate, *die;* **~ ˈribs** *n. pl.* Hochrippen *Pl.;* **~ time** *n.* Hauptsendezeit, *die;* **~-time TV** Hauptsendezeit im Fernsehen

**primeval** /praɪˈmiːvl/ *adj.* urzeitlich; **~ times/forests** Urzeiten/Urwälder

**priming** /ˈpraɪmɪŋ/ *n.* (*paint*) Grundanstrich, *der;* Grundierung, *die*

**primitive** /ˈprɪmɪtɪv/ ❶ *adj.* Ⓐ primitiv; (*original*) ursprünglich; (*prehistoric*) urzeitlich ‹Mensch›; frühzeitlich ‹Ackerbau, Technik›; Ⓑ (*Ling.*) **~ word** Stammwort, *das;* Primitivum, *das* (*fachspr.*). ❷ *n.* (*painter*) *Maler der Zeit vor der Renaissance;* (*in modern art*) Primitive, *der/die*

**primitively** /ˈprɪmɪtɪvlɪ/ *adv.* primitiv

**primly** /ˈprɪmlɪ/ *adv.* steif; streng ‹sich kleiden›

**primness** /ˈprɪmnɪs/ *n. no pl.* Steifheit, *die;* (*of dress*) Strenge, *die*

**primogeniture** /praɪməˈdʒenɪtʃə(r)/ *n.* (*Law*) **[right of] ~:** Primogenitur, *die;* **rights of ~:** Erstgeburtsrechte *Pl.*

**primordial** /praɪˈmɔːdɪəl/ *adj.* ursprünglich; Ur‹masse, -zustand, -zeiten›; primordial (*bes. Philos.*); **~ soup** Urschleim, *der*

**primp** /prɪmp/ *v.t.* zurechtstreichen, zurechtzupfen ‹Haar, Kleid›; **~ oneself** sich zurecht- *od.* schönmachen (*ugs.*)

**primrose** /ˈprɪmrəʊz/ *n.* Ⓐ (*plant, flower*) gelbe Schlüsselblume; Himmelsschlüsselchen, *das;* **the ~ path** (*fig.*) der Pfad des Vergnügens; (*path of least resistance*) der Weg des geringsten Widerstandes; ⇒ *also* **evening primrose;** Ⓑ (*colour*) schlüsselblumengelb

**primula** /ˈprɪmjʊlə/ *n.* (*Bot.*) Primel, *die*

**Primus** ® /ˈpraɪməs/ *n.* **~ [stove]** Primuskocher, *der*

**prince** /prɪns/ *n.* ▶ 1617 Ⓐ (*ruler*) Fürst, *der;* Ⓑ (*member of royal family*) **~ [of the blood]** Prinz [von Geblüt]; **P~ of Wales** Prinz von Wales; Ⓒ (*rhet.: sovereign ruler*) Fürst, *der;* Monarch, *der;* **the P~ of Peace** der Friedensfürst; **the P~ of Darkness** der Fürst der Finsternis *od.* der Hölle; Ⓓ (*fig.: greatest one*) König, *der* (**of** unter + *Dat.*); **a ~ among men** ein Fürst unter den Sterblichen (*geh.*)

**Prince: ~ Albert** /prɪns ˈælbət/ *n.* (*Amer. coll.*) Gehrock, *der;* Bratenrock, *der* (*veralt., scherzh.*); **~ 'Charming** *n.* (*fig.*) Märchenprinz, *der;* **p~ 'consort** *n.* Prinzgemahl, *der*

**princely** /ˈprɪnslɪ/ *adj.* (*lit. or fig.*) fürstlich; **~ houses** Fürstenhäuser

**Prince 'Regent** *n.* Prinzregent, *der*

**princess** /ˈprɪnses, prɪnˈses/ *n.* ▶ 1617 Ⓐ Prinzessin, *die;* **~ [of the blood]** Prinzessin [von Geblüt]; Ⓑ (*wife of prince*) Fürstin, *die*

**princess: ~ dress** *n.* Prinzesskleid, *das;* **~ line** *n.* Prinzessform, *die;* **~ 'royal** *n.* [*Titel für*] *älteste Tochter eines Monarchen*

**principal** /ˈprɪnsɪpl/ ❶ *adj.* Ⓐ Haupt-; (*most important*) wichtigst...; bedeutendst...; **the ~ cause of lung cancer** die häufigste Ursache für Lungenkrebs; Ⓑ (*Mus.*) **~ horn/bassoon** *etc.* erstes Horn/Fagott *usw.* ❷ *n.* Ⓐ ▶ 1617 (*head of school or college*) Rektor, *der*/Rektorin, *die;* Ⓑ (*performer*) Hauptdarsteller, *der*/-darstellerin, *die* (*Theater, Film*); Ⓒ (*leader*) Vorsitzende, *der/die;* Ⓓ (*employer of agent*) Auftraggeber, *der*/-geberin, *die;* Ⓔ (*in duel*) Duellant, *der;* Ⓕ (*Finance*) (*invested*) Kapitalbetrag, *der;* (*lent*) Kreditsumme, *die;* Ⓖ (*Law*) (*for whom another is surety*) Hauptschuldner, *der*/-schuldnerin, *die;* (*directly responsible for crime*) Hauptschuldige, *der/die*

**principal: ~ 'boy** *n.* (*Brit. Theatre*) [*gewöhnlich von einer Frau gespielte*] *männliche Hauptrolle im britischen Weihnachtsmärchen;* **~ clause** *n.* (*Ling.*) Hauptsatz, *der;* **~ 'girl** *n.* (*Brit. Theatre*) *weibliche Hauptrolle im britischen Weihnachtsmärchen*

**principality** /prɪnsɪˈpælɪtɪ/ *n.* Fürstentum, *das;* **the P~** (*Brit.*) Wales

**principally** /ˈprɪnsɪpəlɪ/ *adv.* in erster Linie

**principal 'parts** *n. pl.* (*Ling.*) Stammformen

**principle** /ˈprɪnsɪpl/ *n.* Ⓐ Prinzip, *das;* **on the ~ that ...:** nach dem Grundsatz, dass ...; **be based on the ~ that ...:** auf dem Grundsatz basieren, dass ...; **basic ~:** Grundprinzip, *das;* **go back to first ~s** zu den Grundlagen zurückgehen; **in ~:** im Prinzip; **it's the ~ [of the thing]** es geht [dabei] ums Prinzip; **make it a ~ to do sth.** es sich (*Dat.*) zum Prinzip machen, etw. zu tun; **a man of high ~** *or* **strong ~s** ein Mann von *od.* mit hohen Prinzipien; **a matter of ~:** eine Prinzipfrage; **do sth. on ~** *or* **as a matter of ~:** etw. prinzipiell *od.* aus Prinzip tun; **operate by** *or* **work on the same ~:** nach demselben Prinzip funktionieren; **work on the ~ of 'first come, first served'** nach dem Prinzip „wer zuerst kommt, mahlt zuerst" vorgehen; Ⓑ (*Phys.*) Lehrsatz, *der;* Ⓒ (*Chem.*) Komponente, *die*

**principled** /ˈprɪnsɪpld/ *adj.* von Prinzipien geleitet

**prink** /prɪŋk/ *v.t.* zurechtmachen (*ugs.*) ‹Person, Haar›; schmücken ‹Kleid, Haus›; **~ oneself [up]** sich herausputzen; sich zurechtmachen (*ugs.*)

**print** /prɪnt/ ❶ *n.* Ⓐ (*impression*) Abdruck, *der;* (*finger~*) Fingerabdruck, *der;* (*foot~*) Fußabdruck, *der;* Ⓑ (*~ed lettering*) Gedruckte, *das;* (*typeface*) Druck, *der;* **clear/large ~:** deutlicher/großer Druck; **this ~ is too small** das ist zu klein gedruckt; **editions in large ~:** Großdruckbücher; ⇒ *also* **small print;** Ⓒ (*handwriting*) **write [sth.] in ~:** [etw.] in Druckschrift schreiben; Ⓓ (*published or ~ed state*) **be in/out of ~** ‹Buch:› erhältlich/vergriffen sein; **appear in/get into ~:** gedruckt werden; ⇒ *also* **rush into a;** Ⓔ (*~ed picture or design*) Druck, *der;* Ⓕ (*Photog.*) Abzug, *der;* (*Cinemat.*) Kopie, *die;* **black and white/colour ~:** Schwarzweiß-/Farbabdruck, *der*/-kopie, *die;* Ⓖ (*Textiles*) (*cloth with design*) bedruckter Stoff; (*design*) Druckmuster, *das;* Ⓗ (*~ed publication*) Publikation, *die;* **~s** (*Amer. Post*) Druckschriften; **the ~s** (*Amer. Journ.*) die Presse.

❷ *v.t.* Ⓐ drucken ‹Buch, Zeitschrift, Geldschein usw.›; Ⓑ (*write*) in Druckschrift schreiben; Ⓒ (*cause to be published*) veröffentlichen ‹Artikel, Roman, Ansichten usw.›; Ⓓ (*Photog.*) abziehen; (*Cinemat.*) kopieren; Ⓔ (*Textiles*) bedrucken ‹Stoff›; Ⓕ (*impress*) eindrücken; **~ sth. with sth.** etw. mit etw. bedrucken; **~ sth. on** etw. drücken in (+ *Akk.*) ‹Haut›; etw. aufdrucken auf (+ *Akk.*) ‹Papier, Holz›.

❸ *v.i.* Ⓐ (*Printing*) drucken; Ⓑ (*write*) in Druckschrift schreiben

**~ 'out** *v.t.* (*Computing*) ausdrucken; ⇒ *also* **printout**

**printable** /ˈprɪntəbl/ *adj.* druckbar; **be ~** (*Photog.*) einen guten Abzug ermöglichen; **what he replied is not ~** (*fig.*) was er geantwortet hat, kann man [hier] nicht wiederholen

**printed** /ˈprɪntɪd/ *adj.* Ⓐ (*Printing*) gedruckt; **~ characters** *or* **letters** Druckbuchstaben; **on the ~ page** gedruckt; Ⓑ (*written like print*) in Druckschrift; Ⓒ (*published*) veröffentlicht ‹Artikel, Roman, Ansichten usw.›; Ⓓ (*Textiles*) bedruckt ‹Stoff›; **~ design** Druckmuster, *das*

**printed: ~ 'circuit** *n.* (*Electronics*) gedruckte Schaltung; **~ matter** *n., no pl., no indef. art.* Gedruckte, *das;* (*Post*) Drucksachen *Pl.;* **[item of] ~ matter** Drucksache, *die;* **~ 'papers** (*Brit. Post*) ⇒ **~ matter**

**printer** /ˈprɪntə(r)/ *n.* Ⓐ (*Printing*) (*worker*) Drucker, *der*/Druckerin, *die;* **firm of ~s** Druckerei, *die;* **send sth. off to the ~'s** etw. in die Druckerei schicken; **at the ~'s** in der Druckerei; Ⓑ (*Computing*) Drucker, *der*

**printer: ~'s 'devil** *n.* (*Hist.*) Setzerjunge, *der;* **~'s 'error** *n.* Druckfehler, *der;* **~'s 'ink** *n.* Druckfarbe, *die*

**printing** /ˈprɪntɪŋ/ *n.* Ⓐ Drucken, *das;* **[the] ~ [trade]** das Druckgewerbe; Ⓑ (*writing like print*) Druckschrift, *die;* Ⓒ (*edition*) Auflage, *die;* Ⓓ (*Photog.*) Abziehen, *das;* Ⓔ (*Textiles*) Bedrucken, *das*

**printing: ~ error** *n.* Druckfehler, *der;* **~ house** *n.* Druckerei, *die;* **~ ink** *n.* Druckfarbe, *die;* **~ machine** *n.* (*Brit.*) Druckmaschine, *die;* **~ press** *n.* Druckerpresse, *die*

**print: ~maker** *n.* (*Graph. Arts*) Grafiker, *der*/Grafikerin, *die;* **~out** *n.* (*Computing*) Ausdruck, *der;* **~ run** *n.* (*Publishing*) Auflage, die; **what is the ~ run?** wie hoch ist die Auflage?; **~ seller** *n.* Grafikhändler, *der*/-händlerin, *die;* **~shop** *n.* Ⓐ (*shop*) Grafikhandlung, *die;* Ⓑ (*~ing establishment*) [kleinere] Druckerei

**prior** /ˈpraɪə(r)/ ❶ *adj.* vorherig ‹Warnung, Zustimmung, Vereinbarung usw.›; früher ‹Verabredung, Ehe›; vorrangig ‹Bedeutung, Interesse›; Vor‹geschichte, -kenntnis, -warnung›; **give a matter ~ consideration** eine Angelegenheit vorher überdenken *od.* überprüfen; **have a** *or* **the ~ claim to sth.** ältere Rechte an etw. (*Dat.*) *od.* auf etw. (*Akk.*) haben. ❷ *adv.* **~ to** vor (+ *Dat.*); **~ to doing sth.** bevor man etw. tut/tat; **~ to that** vorher. ❸ *n.* (*Eccl.*) Prior, *der*

**prioritize (prioritise)** /praɪˈɒrɪtaɪz/ *v.t.* nach Vordringlichkeit ordnen

**priority** /praɪˈɒrɪtɪ/ *n.* Ⓐ (*precedence*) Vorrang, *der; attrib.* vorrangig; **have** *or* **take ~:** Vorrang haben (**over** vor + *Dat.*); (*on road*) Vorfahrt haben; **give ~ to sb./sth.** jmdm./einer Sache den Vorrang geben; **give top ~ to sth.** einer Sache (*Dat.*) höchste Priorität einräumen; **what is the order of ~ for those jobs?** in welcher Reihenfolge sollen die Arbeiten erledigt werden?; **be listed in order of ~:** der Vorrangigkeit nach aufgeführt sein; **according to ~:** der Vorrangigkeit nach; Ⓑ (*matter*) vordringliche Angelegenheit; **our first ~ is to ...:** zuallererst müssen wir ...; **be high/low on the list of priorities** oben/unten auf der Prioritätenliste stehen; **get one's priorities right/wrong** seine Prioritäten richtig/falsch setzen; **it depends on one's** *or* **your priorities** es kommt darauf an, was einem wichtig ist

**priory** /ˈpraɪərɪ/ *n.* (*Eccl.*) Priorat, *das*

**prise** ⇒ **prize²**

**prism** /ˈprɪzm/ *n.* (*Optics, Geom.*) Prisma, *das*

**prismatic** /prɪzˈmætɪk/ *adj.* Ⓐ (*in shape*) prismenförmig; Ⓑ **~ colours** Spektralfarben

**prismatic: ~ bi'noculars** *n. pl.* Prismenglas, *das;* **~ 'compass** *n.* (*Surv.*) Patentbussole, *die*

**prison** /ˈprɪzn/ *n.* Ⓐ (*lit. or fig.*) Gefängnis, *das; attrib.* Gefängnis-; **~ without bars** offene [Vollzugs]anstalt; **stone walls do not a ~ make [nor iron bars a cage]** (*prov.*) ≈ die Gedanken sind frei; Ⓑ *no pl., no art.* (*custody*) Haft, *die;* **10 years' ~:** eine zehnjährige Gefängnisstrafe; **in ~:** im Gefängnis; **go to ~:** ins Gefängnis gehen *od.* (*ugs.*) wandern; **send sb. to ~:** jmdn. ins Gefängnis schicken; **escape/be released from ~:** aus dem Gefängnis ausbrechen/entlassen werden; **put sb. in ~:** jmdn. verhaften *od.* (*ugs.*) einsperren; **let sb. out of ~:** jmdn. aus der Haft entlassen

**'prison camp** *n.* Gefangenenlager, *das*

**prisoner** /ˈprɪznə(r)/ *n.* (*lit. or fig.*) Gefangene, *der/die;* **~ [at the bar]** (*accused person*) Angeklagte, *der/die;* **~ of conscience** *aus politischen od. religiösen Gründen Inhaftierter/Inhaftierte;* **a ~ of circumstance** (*fig.*) ein Opfer der Umstände; **hold** *or* **keep sb. ~** (*lit. or fig.*) jmdn. gefangen halten; **take sb. ~:** jmdn. gefangen nehmen

**prisoner of 'war** *n.* Kriegsgefangene, *der/die;* **prisoner-of-war camp** [Kriegs]gefangenenlager, *das*

**prison: ~ 'guard** *n.* ▶ 1261 Gefängniswärter, *der*/-wärterin, *die;* **~ life** *n., no art.* Gefängnisleben, *das;* **~ service** Strafvollzugsbehörde, *die;* **~ 'visitor** *n.* ≈ Gefangenenfürsorger, *der*/-fürsorgerin, *die*

**prissy** /ˈprɪsɪ/ *adj.* (*coll.*) zickig (*ugs.*); piepsig (*ugs.*) ‹Stimme›

**pristine** /ˈprɪstiːn, ˈprɪstaɪn/ *adj.* unberührt; ursprünglich ‹Glanz, Weiße, Schönheit›; **in ~ condition** in tadellosem Zustand

**privacy** /ˈprɪvəsɪ, ˈpraɪvəsɪ/ *n.* Ⓐ (*seclusion*) Zurückgezogenheit, *die;* **guard one's ~:** seine Privatsphäre abschirmen; **in the ~ of one's [own] home/living room** in den eigenen vier Wänden (*ugs.*); **invasion of ~/sb.'s ~:** Eindringen in die/jmds. Privatsphäre; **I have** *or* **get no ~ in this house** ich habe keine Ruhe in diesem Haus; **allow**

**sb. no ~:** jmdm. kein Privatleben erlauben; [B] *(confidentiality)* **in the strictest ~:** unter strengster Geheimhaltung

**private** /'praɪvət/ ❶ *adj.* [A] *(outside State system)* privat; Privat‹unterricht, -schule, -industrie, -klinik, -patient, -station usw.›; **a doctor working in ~ medicine** ein Arzt, der Privatpatienten hat; **have a ~ education** auf eine Privatschule gehen; [B] *(belonging to individual, not public, not business)* persönlich ‹Dinge›; nicht öffentlich ‹Versammlung, Sitzung›; privat ‹Telefongespräch, Schriftverkehr›; Privat‹flugzeug, -strand, -parkplatz, -leben, -konto›; '~' *(on door)* „Privat"; *(in public building)* „kein Zutritt"; *(on ~ land)* „Betreten verboten"; **for [one's own] ~ use** für den persönlichen Gebrauch; **do some ~ studying in the holidays** in den Ferien allein lernen; **the funeral was ~:** die Beisetzung hat in aller Stille stattgefunden; **they were married in a ~ ceremony** ihre Hochzeit wurde im engen Familien- und Freundeskreis gefeiert; **in a ~ capacity** als Privatperson; [C] *(personal, affecting individual)* persönlich ‹Meinung, Interesse, Überzeugung, Rache›; privat ‹Vereinbarung, Zweck›; **~ joke** Witz, den nur Eingeweihte verstehen; **~ war** Privatkrieg, *der;* [D] *(not for public disclosure)* geheim ‹Verhandlung, Geschäft, Tränen›; still ‹Gebet, Nachdenken, Grübeln›; persönlich ‹Gründe›; *(confidential)* vertraulich; **have a ~ word with sb.** jmdn. unter vier Augen sprechen; [E] *(secluded)* still ‹Ort›; *(undisturbed)* ungestört; **we can be ~ here** hier sind wir ungestört; [F] *(not in public office)* nicht beamtet *(Amtsspr.)*; **~ citizen** *or* **individual** Privatperson, *die.*

❷ *n.* [A] *(Brit. Mil.)* einfacher Soldat; *(Amer. Mil.)* Gefreite, *der;* **~ first 'class** *(Amer.)* Obergefreite, *der;* **P~ X** Soldat/Gefreiter X; [B] **in ~:** privat; in kleinem Kreis ‹feiern›; *(confidentially)* ganz im Vertrauen; **speak to sb. in ~:** jmdn. unter vier Augen sprechen; **make a deal in ~:** ein privates Geschäft abschließen; **you should do it in ~:** du solltest das nicht in der Öffentlichkeit tun; [C] *in pl. (coll.: genitals)* Geschlechtsteile *Pl.*

**private: ~ 'army** *n.* Privatarmee, *die;* **~ 'bed** *n.* Bett für Privatpatienten; **~ 'car** *n.* Privatwagen, *der;* **~ 'company** *n. (Brit. Commerc.)* Privatgesellschaft, *die;* **~ de'tective** *n.* ▶ **1261** [Privat]detektiv, *der*/-detektivin, *die;* **~ 'enterprise** *n. (Commerc.)* das freie *od.* private Unternehmertum; **[spirit of] ~ enterprise** *(fig.)* Unternehmungsgeist, *der*

**privateer** /praɪvə'tɪə(r)/ *n.* [A] Kaperschiff, *das;* [B] *(person)* Kaper, *der*

**private: ~ 'eye** *n. (coll.)* [Privat]detektiv, *der*/-detektivin, *die;* **~ ho'tel** *n.* Pension, *die;* **~ 'income** *n.* private Einkünfte; **~ investigator** *n.* Privatdetektiv, *der*/-detektivin, *die*

**privately** /'praɪvətlɪ/ *adv.* privat ‹erziehen, zugeben, korrespondieren›; vertraulich ‹jmdn. sprechen›; insgeheim ‹denken, glauben, verhandeln›; **study ~:** private Studien betreiben; **~ owned** in Privatbesitz; **~ held opinion** persönliche Meinung

**private: ~ 'means** *n. pl.* ⇒ **private income;** **~ 'member** *n. (Brit. Parl.) nicht der Regierung angehörender/angehörende Abgeordnete;* **~ 'member's bill** *n. (Brit. Parl.) Gesetzesvorlage eines/einer nicht der Regierung angehörenden Abgeordneten;* **~ 'parts** *n. pl.* Geschlechtsteile *Pl.;* **~ 'practice** *n.* [A] *(Med.)* Privatpraxis, *die; (patients)* Stamm von Privatpatienten; **he is now in ~ practice** er hat jetzt eine Privatpraxis; [B] *(of architect/lawyer)* eigenes Büro/eigene Kanzlei; **be in ~ practice** ein eigenes Büro/eine eigene Kanzlei haben; **~ 'press** *n.* Privatdruckerei, *die;* **~ 'property** *n.* Privateigentum, *das;* **~ 'secretary** *n.* Privatsekretär, *der*/-sekretärin, *die;* **~ sector** *n.* **the ~ sector [of industry]** die Privatwirtschaft; **~ 'soldier** *n.* [A] *(Brit. Mil.)* einfacher Soldat; [B] *(Amer. Mil.)* Gefreite, *der;* **~ 'treaty** *n.* privater Vertrag; **sold by ~ treaty** auf privater Basis verkauft; **~ 'view[ing]** *n. (Art)* Vernissage, *die; (Cinemat.) Aufführung eines Films für geladene Zuschauer vor der öffentlichen Erstaufführung*

**privation** /praɪ'veɪʃn/ *n. (lack of comforts)* Not, *die;* **suffer many ~s** viele Entbehrungen erleiden

**privatisation, privatise** ⇒ **privatiz-**

**privatization** /praɪvətaɪ'zeɪʃn/ *n.* Privatisierung, *die*

**privatize** /'praɪvətaɪz/ *v.t.* privatisieren

**privet** /'prɪvɪt/ *n. (Bot.)* Liguster, *der*

**privilege** /'prɪvɪlɪdʒ/ ❶ *n.* [A] *(right, immunity)* Privileg, *das; collect.* Privilegien *Pl.;* **tax ~s** Steuervorteile *Pl.;* **that's a lady's ~:** das ist das Vorrecht einer Dame; **Parliamentary ~:** Immunität des Abgeordneten; [B] *(special benefit)* Sonderrecht, *das; (honour)* Ehre, *die;* **it was a ~ to listen to him** es war ein besonderes Vergnügen, ihm zuzuhören; **we were expected to pay for the ~** *(iron.)* wir hatten auch noch die Ehre, dafür bezahlen zu dürfen; [C] *(monopoly)* Vorrecht, *das; (sole right of selling sth.)* Alleinverkaufsrecht, *das;* [D] *(Amer. St. Exch.)* Termingeschäft, *das;* **buy ~s** Optionsrechte erwerben.

❷ *v.t.* **~ sb. to do sth.** jmdm. das Recht einräumen, etw. zu tun

**privileged** /'prɪvɪlɪdʒd/ *adj.* privilegiert; **the ~ classes** die privilegierten Schichten; **a/the ~ few** einige wenige Privilegierte/die kleine Gruppe von Privilegierten; **sb. is ~ to do sth.** jmd. hat die Ehre, etw. zu tun; **I am [greatly] ~ to introduce sb./sth.** es ist mir eine [große] Ehre, Ihnen jmdn./etw. vorstellen zu können; **have a** *or* **be in a ~ position** eine bevorzugte Position innehaben

**privy** /'prɪvɪ/ ❶ *adj.* **be ~ to sth.** in etw. *(Akk.)* eingeweiht sein. ❷ *n. (arch./Amer.)* Abtritt, *der (veralt.)*; Häuschen, *das (ugs.)*

**privy: P~ 'Council** *n. (Brit.)* Geheimer [Staats]rat; **~ 'counsellor (~ 'councillor)** *n. (Brit.: member of Privy Council)* Geheimer Rat; **~ 'seal** *n. (Brit.)* Geheimsiegel, *das;* Kleines Siegel; **Lord P~ Seal** Lordsiegelbewahrer, *der*

**prize**[1] /praɪz/ ❶ *n.* [A] *(reward, money)* Preis, *der;* **win** *or* **take first/second/third ~:** den ersten/zweiten/dritten Preis gewinnen; **for sheer impudence he takes the ~!** *(fig.)* für seine Frechheit müsste er einen Preis bekommen *(iron.)*; **there are no ~s for doing sth.** *(iron.)* es ist kinderleicht, etw. zu tun; **cash** *or* **money ~:** Geldpreis, *der;* [B] *(in lottery)* Gewinn, *der; (got by buying goods)* Werbegeschenk, *das;* **win sth. as a ~:** etw. gewinnen; **I won a ~ of £1,000** ich habe 1000 Pfund gewonnen; [C] *(fig.: something worth striving for)* Lohn, *der;* **glittering ~s** verlockender Lohn.

❷ *v.t. (value)* **~ sth. [highly]** etw. hoch schätzen; **gold is one of the most ~d [of] metals** Gold ist eines der begehrtesten Metalle; **we ~ liberty more than life** wir lieben die Freiheit mehr als das Leben; **sb.'s most ~d possessions** jmds. wertvollster Besitz.

❸ *attrib. adj.* [A] *(~winning)* preisgekrönt; [B] *(awarded as ~)* **~ medal/trophy** Siegesmedaille, *die*/Siegestrophäe, *die;* [C] *(iron.)* **~ idiot** Vollidiot, *der*/-idiotin, *die (ugs.)*; **~ muddle** Durcheinander erster Güte; **~ example** Musterbeispiel, *das (iron.)*

**prize**[2] *v.t. (force)* **~ [open]** aufstemmen; **~ up** abheben ‹Diele›; **~ the lid off a crate** eine Kiste aufstemmen; **~ sth. out of sth.** etw. aus etw. herausbekommen; **~ information/a secret out of sb.** Informationen/ein Geheimnis aus jmdm. herauspressen

**~ a'part** *v.t.* auseinander stemmen

**~ 'out** *v.t.* herausbrechen

**prize**[3] *n.* [A] *(captured ship)* Prise, *die;* [B] *(chance find)* [zufälliger] Fund; **this is a rare ~!** das ist ein seltener Fund!

**prize: ~ day** *n. (Sch.)* Tag der Preisverleihung; **~-day speech** Rede zur Preisverleihung; **~fight** *n. (Boxing)* Preisboxkampf, *der;* **enter a ~fight** an einem Preisboxen teilnehmen; **~fighter** *n. (Boxing)* Preisboxer, *der;* **~fighting** *n. (Boxing)* Preisboxen, *das;* **~-giving** *n. (Sch.)* Preisverleihung, *die;* **~ money** *n.* Geldpreis, *der; (Sport)* Preisgeld, *das;* **offer £5,000 in ~ money** Geldpreise in Höhe von insgesamt 5 000 Pfund anbieten; **~winner** *n.* Preisträger, *der*/-trägerin, *die; (in lottery)* Gewinner, *der*/Gewinnerin, *die;* **~winning** *adj.* preisgekrönt; *(in lottery)* Gewinner-

**pro**[1] /prəʊ/ ❶ *n. in pl.* **the ~s and cons** das Pro und Kontra; **there are more ~s than cons** die Sache hat mehr Vorteile als Nachteile. ❷ *adv.* **~ and con** pro und kontra. ❸ *prep.* für; **~ and con** für und gegen

**pro**[2] ❶ *n. (coll.)* [A] *(Sport, Theatre)* Profi, *der;* [B] *(prostitute)* Nutte, *die (derb).* ❷ *adj.* Profi-

**pro-**[3] *pref.* pro-; **~Communist** prokommunistisch; **be ~hanging** für die Todesstrafe [durch den Strang] sein

**PRO** *abbr.* [A] **public relations officer** PR-Manager, *der*/-Managerin, *die;* [B] **public relations office** PR-Abteilung, *die*

**proactive** /prəʊ'æktɪv/ *adj.* aktiv ‹Haltung, Rolle›; **be ~** ‹Person:› [selbst] die Initiative ergreifen; Eigeninitiative zeigen

**pro-am** /prəʊ'æm/ *adj. (Sport)* **~ competition** Wettbewerb für Profis und Amateure

**probability** /prɒbə'bɪlɪtɪ/ *n.* [A] *(likelihood; also Math.)* Wahrscheinlichkeit, *die;* **exceed the bounds of ~:** die Grenzen des Wahrscheinlichen übersteigen; **against all ~:** entgegen aller Wahrscheinlichkeit; **in all ~:** aller Wahrscheinlichkeit nach; **there is little/a strong ~ that ...:** die Wahrscheinlichkeit, dass ..., ist gering/groß; **there's every ~ of a victory** höchstwahrscheinlich wird es zu einem Sieg kommen; [B] *(likely event)* **the ~ is that ...:** es ist zu erwarten, dass ...; **war is becoming a ~:** der Ausbruch eines Krieges wird immer wahrscheinlicher; **it is more than a possibility, it is a ~:** es ist nicht nur möglich, es ist wahrscheinlich

**probable** /'prɒbəbl/ ❶ *adj.* wahrscheinlich; **highly ~:** höchstwahrscheinlich; **his explanation did not sound very ~:** seine Erklärung klang nicht sehr glaubhaft; **another wet summer looks ~:** es sieht ganz nach einem weiteren verregneten Sommer aus; **he seems the most ~ winner** er scheint die besten Aussichten auf einen Sieg zu haben. ❷ *n. (participant)* wahrscheinlicher Teilnehmer/wahrscheinliche Teilnehmerin (**for** an + *Dat.*); *(candidate)* wahrscheinlicher Kandidat/wahrscheinliche Kandidatin (**for** für)

**probably** /'prɒbəblɪ/ *adv.* wahrscheinlich

**probate** /'prəʊbeɪt/ *n. (Law)* [A] gerichtliche Testamentsbestätigung; [B] *(copy)* beglaubigte Testamentsabschrift

**probation** /prə'beɪʃn/ *n.* [A] Probezeit, *die;* **a year's ~:** eine einjährige Probezeit; **[be put] on ~:** auf Probe [eingestellt werden]; **be on ~:** Probezeit haben; **while on ~:** während der Probezeit; [B] *(Law)* Bewährung, *die;* **give sb. [two years'] ~, put sb. on ~ [for two years]** jmdm. [zwei Jahre] Bewährung geben; **be on ~:** auf Bewährung sein

**probationary** /prə'beɪʃənərɪ/ *adj.* Probe-; **~ period** Probezeit, *die;* **~ appointment** Einstellung auf Probe

**probationer** /prə'beɪʃənə(r)/ *n.* [A] *(employee)* Angestellter/Angestellte auf Probe; *(nurse)* Lernschwester, *die*/-pfleger, *der; (candidate)* Probekandidat, *der*/-kandidatin, *die;* [B] *(Law: offender)* auf Bewährung Freigelassener/Freigelassene

**pro'bation officer** *n.* ▶ **1261** Bewährungshelfer, *der*/-helferin, *die*

**probe** /prəʊb/ ❶ *n.* [A] *(investigation)* Untersuchung, *die* (**into** *Gen.*); **a ~ is being conducted** Nachforschungen werden angestellt; [B] *(Med., Electronics, Astron.)* Sonde, *die;* [C] *(pointed instrument)* Tastgerät, *das.* ❷ *v.t.* [A] *(investigate)* erforschen; untersuchen; [B] *(with pointed instrument)* stechen in (+ *Akk.*); sondieren *(Med.)*; [C] *(reach deeply into)* gründlich untersuchen ‹Tasche usw.›; gründlich erforschen ‹Kontinent, Weltall›.

❸ *v.i.* [A] *(make investigation)* forschen; **he**

**kept probing** er bohrte weiter (*ugs.*); **~ into a matter** einer Angelegenheit (*Dat.*) auf den Grund gehen; **B** (*with pointed instrument*) herumstochern; (*Med.*) sondieren; **C** (*reach deeply*) vordringen (**into** in + *Akk.*)

**probing** /ˈprəʊbɪŋ/ *adj.* (*penetrating*) gründlich; durchdringend ‹Blick›; **~ question** Testfrage, *die*

**probity** /ˈprəʊbɪtɪ/ *n.*, *no pl.* Rechtschaffenheit, *die*

**problem** /ˈprɒbləm/ *n.* **A** (*difficult matter*) Problem, *das; attrib.* Problem‹gebiet, -fall, -familie, -stück›; **~ child** Problemkind, *das;* (*fig.: cause of difficulties*) Sorgenkind, *das;* **I find it a ~ to start** *or* **have a ~ [in] starting the car** ich habe Probleme, das Auto anzulassen; **[I see] no ~** (*coll.*) kein Problem; **what's the ~?** (*coll.*) wo fehlts denn?; **the ~ about** *or* **with sb./sth.** das Problem mit jmdm./bei etw.; **the ~ of how to do sth.** das Problem *od.* die Frage, wie man etw. tun soll; **the Northern Ireland ~:** die Nordirlandfrage; **he has a drink ~:** er hat ein Alkoholproblem; **that presents a ~:** das ist ein Problem; **the least of her ~s** ihre geringste Sorge; **you think 'you've got ~s!** (*coll. iron.*) deine Sorgen möchte ich haben! (*ugs. iron.*); **B** (*puzzle*) Rätsel, *das;* **C** (*Chess, Bridge, Math., Phys., Geom.*) Problem, *das*

**problematic** /prɒbləˈmætɪk/, **problematical** /prɒbləˈmætɪkl/ *adj.* problematisch; (*doubtful*) fragwürdig

**problematically** /prɒbləˈmætɪkəlɪ/ *adv.* auf problematische Weise

**proboscis** /prəˈbɒsɪs/ *n.*, *pl.* **~es** *or* **proboscides** /prəˈbɒsɪdiːz/ (*Zool.*) Rüssel, *der;* (*of monkey*) Nase, *die*

**procedural** /prəˈsiːdjʊrl/ *adj.* verfahrensmäßig; (*Law*) verfahrensrechtlich

**procedure** /prəˈsiːdjə(r)/ *n.* **A** (*particular course of action*) Verfahren, das; Prozedur, *die* (*meist abwertend*); **~s are under way** es sind Maßnahmen im Gange; **B** (*way of doing sth.*) Verfahrensweise, *die;* (*Parl.*) [parlamentarisches] Verfahren; (*Law*) Verfahrensordnung, *die;* **according to democratic ~s** gemäß den Spielregeln der Demokratie; **what is the normal ~?** wie wird das normalerweise gehandhabt?

**proceed** /prəˈsiːd/ *v.i.* (*formal*) **A** (*go*) (*on foot*) gehen; (*as or by vehicle*) fahren; (*on horseback*) reiten; (*after interruption*) weitergehen/-fahren/-reiten; **~ somewhere** sich irgendwohin begeben; **~ on one's way** seinen Weg fortsetzen; **as the evening ~ed** im [weiteren] Verlauf des Abends; **~ to business** sich geschäftlichen Dingen zuwenden; **~ to the next item on the agenda** zum nächsten Punkt der Tagesordnung übergehen; **~ [from Rome] to Venice** (*continue*) [von Rom] nach Venedig weiterreisen; **B** (*begin and carry on*) beginnen; (*after interruption*) fortfahren; **~ to talk/eat** *etc.* (*begin and carry on*) beginnen, zu sprechen/essen *usw.;* (*after interruption*) weitersprechen/-essen *usw.;* **~ in** *or* **with sth.** (*begin*) [mit] etw. beginnen; (*continue*) etw. fortsetzen; **C** (*adopt course*) vorgehen; **we must ~ carefully in this case** wir müssen in diesem Fall umsichtig vorgehen; **~ harshly** *etc.* **with sb.** hart *usw.* mit jmdm. umgehen; **~ discreetly with sth.** etw. diskret behandeln; **D** (*be carried on*) ‹Rennen:› verlaufen; (*be under way*) ‹Verfahren:› laufen; (*be continued after interruption*) fortgesetzt werden; **how is the project ~ing?** wie geht das Projekt voran?; **E** (*go on to say*) fortfahren; **F** (*originate*) **~ from** (*issue from*) kommen von; (*be caused by*) herrühren von

**~ against** *v.t.* (*Law*) gerichtlich vorgehen gegen

**proceeding** /prəˈsiːdɪŋ/ *n.* **A** (*action*) Vorgehensweise, *die;* **B** *in pl.* (*events*) Vorgänge; **lose control of the ~s** nicht mehr Herr der Lage sein; **I'll go along to watch the ~s** ich geh mal gucken, was da läuft; **be involved in questionable ~s** in eine fragwürdige Sache verwickelt sein; **C** *in pl.* (*Law*) Verfahren, *das;* **court ~s** Gerichtsverhandlung, *die;* **court ~s can be lengthy** eine Gerichtsverhandlung kann sich in die Länge ziehen; **legal ~s** Gerichtsverfahren, *das;* **start/take [legal] ~s [against sb.]** gerichtlich [gegen jmdn.] vorgehen; **civil/criminal ~s** Zivil-/Strafprozess, *der;* **take criminal/divorce ~s against sb.** ein Strafverfahren gegen jmdn. einleiten/einen Scheidungsprozess gegen jmdn. anstrengen; **D** *in pl.* (*report*) Tätigkeitsbericht, *der;* (*of single meeting*) Protokoll, *das*

**proceeds** /ˈprəʊsiːdz/ *n. pl.* Erlös, *der* (**from** aus)

**pro-ceˈlebrity** *adj.* (*Sport*) Schau‹wettkampf, -turnier› (*mit Prominenten und Profis*)

**process**[1] /ˈprəʊses/ ❶ *n.* **A** (*of time or history*) Lauf, *der;* **he learnt a lot in the ~:** er lernte eine Menge dabei; **in the ~ of the operation** *or* **being operated on** im Verlauf der Operation; **in the ~ of teaching his children** bei der Erziehung seiner Kinder; **be in the ~ of doing sth.** gerade etw. tun; **be in ~:** in Gang sein; **sth. is in ~ of formation** etw. wird gerade gebildet; **B** (*proceeding*) Vorgang, *der;* Prozedur, *die;* **undergo** *or* **be subjected to a ~ of interrogation** mehrfach verhört werden; **by due ~ of law** nach rechtsmäßigem Verfahren; **the democratic ~:** das demokratische Verfahren; **C** (*method*) Verfahren, *das;* **~es of communication** Kommunikationsprozesse; **by a ~ of elimination** durch Eliminierung; **D** (*natural operation*) Prozess, *der;* Vorgang, *der;* **~ of evolution/natural selection** Evolutionsprozess, *der*/natürliche Auslese; **E** (*Anat., Bot., Zool.: protuberance*) Fortsatz, *der.*

❷ *v.t.* verarbeiten ‹Rohstoff, Signal, Daten›; bearbeiten ‹Antrag, Akte, Darlehen›; aufbereiten ‹Abwasser, Abfall›; (*for conservation*) behandeln ‹Leder, Lebensmittel›; (*Photog.*) entwickeln ‹Film›

**process**[2] /prəˈses/ *v.i.* ziehen

**ˈprocess cheese** (*Amer.*), **ˈprocessed cheese** *ns.* Schmelzkäse, *der*

**processer** ⇒ **processor**

**procession** /prəˈseʃn/ *n.* **A** Zug, *der;* (*religious*) Prozession, *die;* (*festive*) Umzug, *der;* **go/march/move** *etc.* **in ~:** ziehen; **funeral ~:** Trauerzug, *der;* **B** (*fig.: series*) Reihe, *die;* **his life was an endless ~ of parties** sein Leben war eine endlose Folge von Partys; **there has been a ~ of people in and out of my office all day** heute war in meinem Büro ein ständiges Kommen und Gehen

**processional** /prəˈseʃənl/ ❶ *adj.* Prozessions-; **at a ~ pace** im Schritttempo. ❷ *n.* (*hymn*) Prozessionshymne, *die*

**processor** /ˈprəʊsesə(r)/ *n.* (*machine*) Prozessor, *der;* **central ~** (*Computing*) Zentralprozessor, *der*

**proclaim** /prəˈkleɪm/ *v.t.* **A** erklären ‹Absicht›; bekannt geben ‹Fakten, Einzelheiten›; beteuern ‹Unschuld›; geltend machen ‹Recht, Anspruch›; (*declare officially*) verkünden ‹Amnestie›; ausrufen ‹Republik›; **~ sb./oneself King/Queen** jmdn./sich zum König/zur Königin ausrufen; **~ a country [to be] a republic** in einem Land die Republik ausrufen; **~ 1 January a public holiday** den 1. Januar zum Feiertag erklären; **~ sb./oneself heir to the throne** jmdn./sich zum Thronfolger ernennen; **B** (*reveal*) verraten; **~ sb./sth. [to be] sth.** verraten, dass jmd./etw. etw. ist

**proclamation** /prɒkləˈmeɪʃn/ *n.* **A** (*act of proclaiming*) Verkündung, *die;* Proklamation, *die* (*geh.*); **the ~ of a new sovereign** die Ausrufung *od.* Proklamation eines neuen Herrschers; **by ~:** durch Bekanntmachung; **B** (*notice*) Bekanntmachung, *die;* (*edict, decree*) Erlass, *der;* **issue** *or* **make a ~:** eine Bekanntmachung/einen Erlass herausgeben

**proclivity** /prəˈklɪvɪtɪ/ *n.* Neigung, *die;* **have/show a ~** *or* **proclivities for** *or* **towards sth.** einen Hang zu etw. haben/zeigen

**procrastinate** /prəˈkræstɪneɪt/ *v.i.* zaudern (*geh.*); **~ in doing sth.** es hinauszögern, etw. zu tun; **I ought to start but I keep procrastinating** ich müsste anfangen, aber ich schiebe es immer vor mir her

**procrastination** /prəkræstɪˈneɪʃn/ *n.* Saumseligkeit, *die* (*geh.*); **there is no time for ~:** die Sache duldet keinen Aufschub; **~ is the thief of time** (*prov.*) ≈ was du heute kannst besorgen, das verschiebe nicht auf morgen (*Spr.*)

**procreate** /ˈprəʊkrɪeɪt/ ❶ *v.t.* **A ~ children** Kinder bekommen; **B** (*fig.: produce*) hervorbringen. ❷ *v.i.* sich fortpflanzen

**procreation** /prəʊkrɪˈeɪʃn/ *n.* Fortpflanzung, *die;* (*fig.: production*) Erzeugung, *die*

**Procrustean** /prəˈkrʌstɪən/ *adj.* starr ‹Gesetze, Regeln, Prinzipien, Einstellung›; unnachgiebig ‹Strenge, Entschlossenheit›

**proctor** /ˈprɒktə(r)/ *n.* **A** (*Brit. Univ.*) *Aufsichtsbeamter der Universität;* **B** (*Amer. Univ.*) ⇒ **invigilator**

**procurator** /ˈprɒkjʊəreɪtə(r)/ *n.* Stellvertreter, *der*/Stellvertreterin, *die;* Bevollmächtigte, *der/die*

**procurator ˈfiscal** *n.* (*Scot. Law*) Staatsanwalt, *der*

**procure** /prəˈkjʊə(r)/ ❶ *v.t.* **A** (*obtain*) beschaffen; **~ for sb./oneself** jmdm./sich verschaffen ‹Arbeit, Unterkunft, Respekt, Reichtum›; jmdm./sich beschaffen ‹Arbeit, Ware›; **B** (*bring about*) herbeiführen ‹Ergebnis, Wechsel, Frieden›; bewirken ‹Freilassung›; **C** (*for sexual gratification*) beschaffen. ❷ *v.i.* Kuppelei betreiben; **procuring** Kuppelei, *die;* **~ for a prostitute** einer Prostituierten (*Dat.*) Kunden beschaffen

**procurement** /prəˈkjʊəmənt/ *n.* ⇒ **procure** 1: Beschaffung, *die;* Herbeiführung, *die;* Bewirkung, *die*

**procurer** /prəˈkjʊərə(r)/ *n.* (*for sexual purposes*) Kuppler, *der;* **act as a ~ of girls/boys for sb.** jmdm. Mädchen/Jungen besorgen

**procuress** /prəˈkjʊrɪs/ *n.* Kupplerin, *die*

**prod** /prɒd/ ❶ *v.t.*, **-dd- A** (*poke*) stupsen (*ugs.*); stoßen mit ‹Stock, Finger usw.›; **he ~ded the map with his finger** er stieß mit dem Finger auf die Karte; **~ sb. gently** jmdn. anstupsen *od.* leicht anstoßen; **~ the fire/pile of leaves** im Feuer stochern/im Blätterhaufen herumstochern; **~ sb. in the ribs** jmdm. einen Rippenstoß versetzen; jmdn. in die Rippen stoßen; **B** (*fig.: rouse*) antreiben; nachhelfen (+ *Dat.*) ‹Gedächtnis›; **he needs ~ding before he will do anything** man muss ihn zu allem erst antreiben; **~ sb. to do sth.** *or* **into doing sth.** jmdn. drängen, etw. zu tun. ❷ *v.i.*, **-dd-** stochern.

❸ *n.* Stupser, *der;* **a ~ in the/my** *etc.* **ribs** ein Rippenstoß; **give sb. a ~:** jmdm. einen Stupser geben; (*fig.*) jmdn. auf Touren bringen; **this sight gave my memory a ~** (*fig.*) dieser Anblick half meinem Gedächtnis auf die Sprünge

**~ aˈbout, ~ aˈround** *v.i.* (*lit. or fig.*) herumstochern

**~ at** *v.t.* anstupsen

**Prod** /prɒd/ *n.* (*Ir. coll.*) Protestant, *der*/Protestantin, *die;* Evangele, *der* (*ugs.*)

**prodigal** /ˈprɒdɪgl/ ❶ *adj.* verschwenderisch; **be ~ with sth.** verschwenderisch mit etw. umgehen; **be ~ of sth.** (*literary*) freigebig mit etw. sein. ❷ *n.* Verschwender, *der*/Verschwenderin, *die*

**prodigality** /prɒdɪˈgælɪtɪ/ *n.*, *no pl.* **A** (*extravagance*) Verschwendungssucht, *die;* **B** (*liberality*) Großzügigkeit, *die*

**prodigal ˈson** *n.* (*Bibl.; also fig. iron.*) verlorener Sohn; **the return of the ~:** die Heimkehr des verlorenen Sohnes

**prodigious** /prəˈdɪdʒəs/ *adj.* ungeheuer; unglaublich ‹Lügner, Dummkopf›; wunderbar ‹Ereignis, Anblick, Taten›; außerordentlich ‹Begabung, Können›; gewaltig ‹Fortschritt, Kraft, Energie›; **to a ~ degree** über alle Maßen

**prodigiously** /prəˈdɪdʒəslɪ/ *adv.* ungeheuer; außerordentlich ‹begabt, dumm›

**prodigy** /ˈprɒdɪdʒɪ/ *n.* **A** (*gifted person*) [außergewöhnliches] Talent; **musical ~:** musikalisches Wunderkind; ⇒ *also* **child prodigy**; **infant prodigy**; **B** (*marvel*) Wunder, *das;* **C be a ~ of sth.** ein Wunder/(*derog.*) ein Ausbund an etw. (*Dat.*) sein

**produce** ❶ /ˈprɒdju:s/ *n.* **A** (*things produced*) Produkte *Pl.;* '**~ of Spain**' „spanisches Erzeugnis"; **B** (*yield*) Ertrag, *der;* (*Mining*) Ausbeute, *die.*
❷ /prəˈdju:s/ *v.t.* **A** (*bring forward*) erbringen ‹Beweis›; vorlegen ‹Beweismaterial›; beibringen ‹Zeugen›; angeben ‹Grund›; geben ‹Erklärung›; vorzeigen ‹Pass, Fahrkarte, Papiere›; herausholen ‹Brieftasche, Portemonnaie, Pistole›; **~ sth. from one's pocket** etw. aus der Tasche ziehen; **he ~d a splendid shot** ihm gelang ein großartiger Schuss; **~ a rabbit out of a hat** ein Kaninchen aus einem Zylinder hervorzaubern; **he ~d a few coins from his pocket** er holte einige Münzen aus seiner Tasche; **B** produzieren ‹Show, Film›; inszenieren ‹Theaterstück, Hörspiel, Fernsehspiel›; herausgeben ‹Schallplatte, Buch›; **well-~d** gut gemacht ‹Film, Theaterstück, Programm›; **C** (*manufacture*) herstellen; zubereiten ‹Mahlzeit›; (*in nature; Agric.*) produzieren; **D** (*create*) schreiben ‹Roman, Gedichte, Artikel, Aufsatz, Symphonie›; schaffen ‹Gemälde, Skulptur, Meisterwerk›; aufstellen ‹Theorie›; **E** (*cause*) hervorrufen; bewirken ‹Änderung›; herbeiführen ‹Reformen›; **F** (*bring into being*) erzeugen; führen zu ‹Situation, Lage, Zustände›; **chemical reactions producing poisonous gases** chemische Reaktionen, bei denen giftige Gase entstehen; **G** (*yield*) erzeugen ‹Ware, Produkt›; geben ‹Milch›; tragen ‹Wolle›; legen ‹Eier›; liefern ‹Ernte›; fördern ‹Metall, Kohle›; abwerfen ‹Ertrag, Gewinn›; hervorbringen ‹Dichter, Denker, Künstler›; führen zu ‹Resultat›; **H** (*bear*) gebären; ‹Säugetier:› werfen; ‹Vogel, Reptil:› legen ‹Eier›; ‹Fisch, Insekt:› ablegen ‹Eier›; ‹Bäume, Blumen:› tragen ‹Früchte, Blüten›; entwickeln ‹Triebe›; bilden ‹Keime›; **~ offspring** Nachwuchs bekommen (*fam.*).
❸ *v.i.* **A** (*manufacture goods*) produzieren; **producing nation** Erzeugerland, *das;* **B** (*Brit. Theatre/Radio/Telev.*) Stücke/Hörspiele/Fernsehspiele inszenieren; (*Cinemat.*) Filme produzieren; **C** (*yield*) Ertrag bringen; **the mine has stopped producing** das Bergwerk fördert nicht mehr *od.* hat die Förderung eingestellt; **D** (*joc.: bear offspring*) ein Kind/Kinder kriegen (*ugs.*)

**producer** /prəˈdju:sə(r)/ *n.* **A** ▶ **1261** (*Cinemat., Theatre, Radio, Telev.*) Produzent, *der*/Produzentin, *die;* **B** ▶ **1261** (*Brit. Theatre/Radio/Telev.*) Regisseur, *der*/Regisseurin, *die;* **C** (*Econ.*) Produzent, *der*/Produzentin, *die*

**product** /ˈprɒdʌkt/ *n.* **A** (*thing produced*) Produkt, *das;* (*of industrial process*) Erzeugnis, *das;* (*of art or intellect*) Werk, *das;* **beauty ~s** Kosmetika; **food ~:** Nahrungsmittelprodukt, *das;* **what is your company's ~?** was stellt Ihre Firma her?; **the ~ of a fertile imagination** das Produkt einer lebhaften Fantasie; **carbon dioxide is a ~ of respiration** Kohlendioxid entsteht bei der Atmung; **B** (*result*) Folge, *die;* **be the ~ of one's age** ein Kind seiner Zeit sein; **C** (*Math.*) Produkt, *das* (**of** aus); **D** (*total produced*) Produktion, *die;* **the national ~:** das Sozialprodukt; ⇒ *also* **gross**[1] 1 D

**production** /prəˈdʌkʃn/ *n.* **A** (*bringing forward*) (*of evidence*) Erbringung, *die;* (*in physical form*) Vorlage, *die;* (*of witness*) Beibringung, *die;* (*of reason*) Angabe, *die;* (*of explanation*) Abgabe, *die;* (*of passport etc.*) Vorzeigen, *das;* **on ~ of your passport** gegen Vorlage Ihres Passes; **B** (*public presentation*) (*Cinemat.*) Produktion, *die;* (*Theatre*) Inszenierung, *die;* (*of record, book*) Herausgabe, *die;* **C** (*action of making*) Produktion, *die;* (*manufacturing*) Herstellung, *die;* (*thing produced*) Produkt, *das;* **cease ~:** die Produktion einstellen; **be in/go into ~:** in Produktion sein/gehen; **be** *or* **have gone out of ~:** nicht mehr hergestellt werden; **have a play in ~** ‹Theater:› ein Stück inszenieren; ⇒ *also* **mass production**; **D** (*thing created*) Werk, *das;* (*Brit. Theatre: show produced*) Inszenierung, *die;* **E** (*causing*) Hervorrufen, *das;* **F** (*bringing into being*) Hervorbringung, *die;* **the ~ of crystals/toxic gases** die Kristallbildung/die Bildung giftiger Gase; **G** (*process of yielding*) Produktion, *die;* (*Mining*) Förderung, *die;* **the mine has ceased ~:** das Bergwerk hat die Förderung eingestellt; **H** (*yield*) Ertrag, *der;* **~ of eggs, egg ~:** Legeleistung, *die;* **[the] annual/total ~ from the mine** die jährliche/gesamte Förderleistung des Bergwerks

**production: ~ control** *n.* Produktionssteuerung, *die;* **~ cost** *n.* Herstellungskosten *Pl.;* **~ engineer** *n.* Betriebsingenieur, *der;* **~ line** *n.* Fertigungsstraße, *die;* **~ manager** *n.* Produktionsleiter, *der*/-leiterin, *die*

**productive** /prəˈdʌktɪv/ *adj.* **A** (*producing*) **be ~** ‹Fabrik:› produzieren; **the writer's ~ period** die produktive *od.* schöpferische Periode des Schriftstellers; **be ~ of** produzieren ‹Ware, Getreide›; hervorbringen ‹Ideen, Kunstwerke›; zutage bringen ‹Ergebnis, Information›; **B** (*producing abundantly*) ertragreich ‹Land, Boden, Obstbaum, Mine›; leistungsfähig ‹Betrieb, Bauernhof›; produktiv ‹Künstler, Komponist, Schriftsteller, Geist›; **C** (*yielding favourable results*) fruchtbar ‹Gespräch, Verhandlungen, Forschungsarbeit›; ergiebig ‹Nachforschungen›; **it's not very ~ arguing about it** es bringt nichts, darüber zu streiten

**productivity** /prɒdʌkˈtɪvɪtɪ/ *n.* Produktivität, *die;* **~ agreement** *or* **deal** Produktivitätsvereinbarung, *die;* **~ bonus** Leistungszulage, *die*

**prof** *n.* (*coll.*) Prof, *der* (*ugs.*)

**Prof.** /prɒf/ *abbr.* ▶ **1617** **Professor** Prof.

**profanation** /prɒfəˈneɪʃn/ *n.* **A** (*desecration*) Entweihung, *die;* Profanierung, *die* (*geh.*); **B** (*disrespectful treatment*) Verunglimpfung, *die* (*geh.*)

**profane** /prəˈfeɪn/ ❶ *adj.* **A** (*irreligious*) gotteslästerlich; **B** (*irreverent*) respektlos ‹Bemerkung, Person›; profan ‹Humor, Sprache›; **C** (*secular*) weltlich; profan. ❷ *v.t.* entweihen

**profanity** /prəˈfænɪtɪ/ *n.* **A** (*irreligiousness, irreligious act*) Gotteslästerung, *die;* **B** (*irreverent behaviour, act, or utterance*) Respektlosigkeit, *die;* **C** (*indecent remark*) Fluch, *der*

**profess** /prəˈfes/ *v.t.* **A** (*declare openly*) bekunden ‹Vorliebe, Abneigung, Interesse›; **~ to be/do sth.** erklären, etw. zu sein/tun; **~ oneself satisfied** sich zufrieden erklären; **B** (*claim*) vorgeben; geltend machen ‹Recht, Anspruch›; **~ to be/do sth.** behaupten, etw. zu sein/tun; **he ~ed regret that ...:** er behauptete, es tue ihm leid, dass ...; **C** (*affirm faith in*) sich bekennen zu

**professed** /prəˈfest/ *adj.* **A** (*self-acknowledged*) erklärt ‹Marxist, Bewunderer, Absicht›; ausdrücklich ‹Zweck›; **be a ~ Christian** ein bekennender Christ sein; **B** (*alleged*) angeblich; **C** (*Relig.*) **be ~:** die [Ordens]gelübde *od.* (*fachspr.*) die Profess abgelegt haben; **~ monk/nun** Mönch, der/Nonne, die die [Ordens]gelübde abgelegt hat

**professedly** /prəˈfesɪdlɪ/ *adv.* **A** (*avowedly*) erklärtermaßen; **B** (*allegedly*) angeblich

**profession** /prəˈfeʃn/ *n.* **A** Beruf, *der;* **what is your ~?** was sind Sie von Beruf?; **medicine/teaching/the law is a ~ requiring great dedication** der Beruf des Mediziners/Lehrers/Juristen erfordert große Hingabe; **he is training** *or* **studying for the ~ of doctor/banker** er wird Arzt/geht ins Bankfach; **take up/go into** *or* **enter a ~:** einen Beruf ergreifen/in einen Beruf gehen; **be in a ~:** einen Beruf ausüben; **she is in the legal ~:** sie ist Juristin; **be a pilot by ~:** von Beruf Pilot sein; **the teaching/medical ~:** der Lehr-/Arztberuf; **the idea has been rejected by the medical ~** die Idee ist von der Ärzteschaft abgelehnt worden; **his career in the teaching ~:** seine Karriere als Lehrer; **the [learned] ~s** Theologie, Jura und Medizin; **the oldest ~** (*joc. euphem.*) das älteste Gewerbe der Welt (*verhüll. scherzh.*); **B** (*body of people*) Berufsstand, *der;* **the ~** (*Theatre coll.*) die Bühne; **C** (*declaration*) **~ of faith/love/loyalty** Glaubensbekenntnis, *das*/Liebeserklärung, *die*/Treuegelöbnis, *das;* **~ of friendship/sympathy** Freundschafts-/Sympathiebekundung, *die;* **make a ~ of, make ~s of** erklären ‹Liebe›; geloben ‹Treue›; **D** (*Relig.: affirmation of faith*) Bekenntnis, *das* (**of** zu); (*faith affirmed*) Glaube, *der;* **make ~ of a faith** sich zu einem Glauben bekennen; **E** (*Relig.*) (*vow*) [Ordens]gelübde, *das;* (*entrance into order*) Profess, *die* (*fachspr.*); **make one's ~:** die Gelübde ablegen

**professional** /prəˈfeʃənl/ ❶ *adj.* **A** (*of profession*) Berufs‹ausbildung, -leben›; beruflich ‹Qualifikation, Laufbahn, Tätigkeit, Stolz, Ansehen›; **~ body** Berufsorganisation, *die;* **on ~ business/for ~ reasons/on a ~ matter** geschäftlich; **~ advice** fachmännischer Rat; **~ jealousy** Konkurrenzneid, *der;* **~ standards** Leistungsniveau, *das;* **B** (*worthy of profession*) (*in technical expertise*) fachmännisch; (*in attitude*) professionell; (*in experience*) routiniert; **make a ~ job of sth.** etw. fachmännisch erledigen; **C** (*engaged in profession*) **~ people** Angehörige hoch qualifizierter Berufe; '**apartment to let to ~ woman**' „Wohnung an berufstätige Dame zu vermieten"; **the ~ class[es]** die gehobenen Berufe; **D** (*by profession*) gelernt; mit abgeschlossener Berufsausbildung *nachgestellt;* (*not amateur*) Berufs‹musiker, -sportler, -soldat, -fotograf›; Profi‹sportler›; (*fig.*) notorisch ‹Unruhestifter, Schnorrer›; **a ~ killer/spy** (*derog.*) ein professioneller Killer/Agent; **E** (*paid*) Profi‹sport, -boxen, -fußball, -tennis›; **go** *or* **turn ~:** Profi werden; **be in the ~ army** Berufssoldat sein; **be in the ~ theatre/on the ~ stage** beruflich am Theater/als Schauspieler arbeiten; **make a career in ~ dancing** Berufstänzer werden.
❷ *n.* (*trained person, lit. or fig.*) Fachmann, *der*/Fachfrau, *die;* (*paid worker*) Berufstätige, *der/die;* (*non-amateur; also Sport, Theatre*) Profi, *der;* **better leave it to a ~/the ~s** überlass das lieber einem Fachmann/den Fachleuten

**professional 'foul** *n.* (*Footb.*) absichtliches Foul

**professionalism** /prəˈfeʃənəlɪzm/ *n., no pl.* **A** (*of work*) fachmännische Ausführung; (*of person*) fachliche Qualifikation; (*in artistic field*) technisches Können; (*attitude*) professionelle Einstellung; (*ethical quality*) Berufsethos, *das;* **B** (*paid participation*) Professionalismus, *der;* Profitum, *das;* **~ in one's attitude to the game** eine profihafte Einstellung zum Spiel

**professionally** /prəˈfeʃənəlɪ/ *adv.* **A** (*in professional capacity*) geschäftlich ‹beraten, besuchen, konsultieren›; beruflich ‹erfolgreich›; (*in manner worthy of profession*) professionell; (*ethically*) dem Berufsethos entsprechend; **I'm here ~:** ich bin geschäftlich hier; **be ~ trained/qualified** eine Berufsausbildung/abgeschlossene Berufsausbildung haben; **B** (*as paid work*) berufsmäßig; **she plays tennis/the piano ~:** sie ist Tennisprofi/von Beruf Pianistin; **she acts ~:** sie ist Berufsschauspielerin; **C** (*by professional*) fachmännisch ‹leiten, betreiben›; von einem Fachmann/von Fachleuten ‹erledigen lassen›; **the play was performed ~:** das Stück wurde an einem professionellen Theater aufgeführt

**professor** /prəˈfesə(r)/ *n.* **A** ▶ **1261**, ▶ **1617** (*Univ.: holder of chair*) Professor, *der*/Professorin, *die;* **the mathematics ~:** der Professor/die Professorin für Mathematik; **~ of ...** (*title*) Professor/Professorin für ...; **P~ Smith** Herr/Frau Professor Smith; **how do you do, P~?** guten Tag, Herr/Frau Professor!; **B** ▶ **1261**, ▶ **1617** (*Amer.: teacher at university*) Dozent, *der*/Dozentin, *die;* **C** (*one who professes a religion*) Bekenner, *der*/Bekennerin, *die;* **be a ~ of sth.** sich zu etw. bekennen

**professorial** /prɒfɪˈsɔ:rɪəl/ *adj.* **A** (*Univ.*) professoral; **his ~ duties** seine Pflichten als Professor; **~ chair** Professur, *die;* **B** (*characteristic of professor*) ‹Wissen, Autorität, Art› eines Professors; (*pedagogic, dogmatic*) professoral (*abwertend*) ‹Stil, Ton›; (*fig.*) professorhaft ‹Aussehen›

**professorship** /prəˈfesəʃɪp/ *n.* Professur, *die;* **she has been appointed to a ~:** sie ist auf einen Lehrstuhl berufen worden; **hold the P~ of History** den Lehrstuhl für Geschichte innehaben

**proffer** /ˈprɒfə(r)/ *v.t.* (*literary*) darbieten ‹Hand, Krone, Geschenk›; anbieten ‹Frieden, Hilfe,

Dienstleistung, Arm, Freundschaft›; aussprechen ‹Dank›; vorbringen ‹Vorschlag›

**proficiency** /prəˈfɪʃənsɪ/ *n.* Können, *das;* **degree** *or* **standard of ~:** Fertigkeit, *die;* **his ~ in mathematics/horsemanship** seine Mathematikkenntnisse/sein reiterliches Können; **achieve great ~ in sth.** große Fertigkeiten in etw. (*Dat.*) erlangen

**proficiency: ~ certificate** *n.* Leistungsnachweis, *der;* **~ test** *n.* Leistungstest, *der*

**proficient** /prəˈfɪʃənt/ *adj.* fähig; gut ‹Pianist, Reiter, Skiläufer usw.›; geschickt ‹Radfahrer, Handwerker, Lügner›; (*in field of knowledge*) bewandert **(at, in** in + *Dat.*); **be ~ at** *or* **in cooking/maths/French** gut kochen können/viel von Mathematik verstehen/gute Französischkenntnisse haben; **he soon became ~:** er beherrschte die Sache bald

**profile** /ˈprəʊfaɪl/ ❶ *n.* Ⓐ (*side aspect*) Profil, *das;* **in ~:** im Profil; **a drawing in ~:** eine Profilzeichnung; Ⓑ (*representation*) Profilbild, *das;* (*outline*) Umriss, *der;* Ⓒ (*biographical sketch*) Porträt, *das* **(of,** on *Gen.*); Ⓓ (*personal record*) [Personal]akte, *die;* **interest ~:** Interessenprofil, *das;* Ⓔ (*vertical cross-section*) Längsschnitt, *der;* (*Archit., Geol., Palaeont.*) Profil, *das;* (*Archaeol.*) Schnitt, *der;* Ⓕ (*graph, curve*) Kurve, *die;* Ⓖ (*fig.*) **low ~ [attitude]** Zurückhaltung, *die;* **keep** *or* **maintain a low ~:** sich zurückhalten; **adopt a low ~ approach [to sth.]** sich [in einer Sache] zurückhalten; **high ~ [tactics]** starkes Engagement.

❷ *v.t.* Ⓐ (*represent from side*) im Profil darstellen; Ⓑ (*outline*) im Umriss abbilden; Ⓒ (*sketch biographically*) porträtieren

**profit** /ˈprɒfɪt/ ❶ *n.* Ⓐ (*Commerc.*) Gewinn, *der;* Profit, *der;* **at a ~:** mit Gewinn ‹verkaufen›; **at a 10% ~:** mit einem Gewinn von 10%; **run sth. at a ~:** mit etw. Gewinne erzielen; **run at a ~** ‹Geschäft:› Gewinn abwerfen; **make a ~ from** *or* **out of sth.** mit etw. Geld verdienen; **make [a few pence] ~ on sth.** [ein paar Pfennige] an etw. (*Dat.*) verdienen; **show a ~:** einen Gewinn verzeichnen; **yield a ~:** Gewinn abwerfen; **~ and loss** Gewinn und Verlust; **~-and-loss account** Gewinn-und-Verlust-Rechnung, *die;* Ⓑ (*advantage*) Nutzen, *der;* **there is no ~ in sth.** etw. ist zwecklos; **be to sb.'s ~:** von Nutzen für jmdn. sein; **find ~ in sth./doing sth.** von etw. profitieren/davon profitieren, dass man etw. tut.

❷ *v.t.* **~ sb.** für jmdn. von Nutzen sein; **it ~s me nothing to do that** es nützt mir nichts, das zu tun; **it did not ~ them in the end** es hat ihnen letzten Endes gar nichts gebracht.

❸ *v.i.* (*derive benefit*) profitieren

**~ by** *v.t.* profitieren von; Nutzen ziehen aus ‹Fehler, Erfahrung›; ausnützen ‹Verwirrung›

**~ from** *v.t.* profitieren von ‹Reise, Studium, Ratschlag›; nutzen ‹Gelegenheit›

**profitability** /prɒfɪtəˈbɪlɪtɪ/ *n., no pl.* Rentabilität, *die*

**profitable** /ˈprɒfɪtəbl/ *adj.* Ⓐ (*lucrative*) rentabel; einträglich; Ⓑ (*beneficial*) lohnend ‹Unternehmung, Zeitvertreib, Kauf›; nützlich ‹Studium, Diskussion, Verhandlung, Nachforschungen›

**profitably** /ˈprɒfɪtəblɪ/ *adv.* Ⓐ (*lucratively*) Gewinn bringend; **run ~** ‹Geschäft:› Gewinn abwerfen; Ⓑ (*beneficially*) nutzbringend

**profiteer** /prɒfɪˈtɪə(r)/ ❶ *n.* Profitmacher, *der*/-macherin, *die.* ❷ *v.i.* sich bereichern

**profiteering** /prɒfɪˈtɪərɪŋ/ *n., no pl,* Wucher, *der*

**profiterole** /prəˈfɪtərəʊl/ *n.* (*Gastr.*) Profiterole, *die* (*Kochk.*)

**profitless** /ˈprɒfɪtlɪs/ *adj.* Ⓐ (*useless*) nutzlos; Ⓑ (*yielding no profit*) unrentabel

**profit: ~-making** *adj.* gewinnorientiert; **it was intended to be ~-making** es sollte Gewinn bringen; **~ margin** *n.* Gewinnspanne, *die;* **~-sharing** *n.* Gewinnbeteiligung, *die; attrib.* Gewinnbeteiligungs-; **~taking** *n.* (*St. Exch.*) Gewinnmitnahme, *die*

**profligacy** /ˈprɒflɪgəsɪ/ *n., no pl.* Ⓐ (*extravagance*) Verschwendung, *die* **(with** von); Ⓑ (*dissipation*) Sittenlosigkeit, *die;* **a life of ~:** ein ausschweifendes Leben

**profligate** /ˈprɒflɪgət/ ❶ *adj.* Ⓐ (*extravagant*) verschwenderisch; **be ~ in spending money** das Geld mit vollen Händen ausgeben; **be ~ of** *or* **with sth.** verschwenderisch umgehen mit etw.; **~ squandering of sth.** allzu bereitwillige Vergeudung von etw.; Ⓑ (*dissipated*) hemmungslos ‹Lust, Trunkenheit, Gier›; ausschweifend ‹Person›. ❷ *n.* Ⓐ (*spendthrift*) Verschwender, *der*/Verschwenderin, *die;* Ⓑ (*rake*) Wüstling, *der* (*abwertend*)

**pro forma** /prəʊ ˈfɔːmə/ ❶ *adv.* pro forma. ❷ *adj.* Ⓐ (*as formality*) Pro-Forma-; Ⓑ (*Commerc.*) Muster-. ❸ *n.* ⇒ **pro forma invoice**

**pro forma 'invoice** *n.* (*Commerc.*) Pro-Forma-Rechnung, *die*

**profound** /prəˈfaʊnd/ *adj.*, **~er** /prəˈfaʊndə(r)/, **~est** /prəˈfaʊndɪst/ Ⓐ (*extreme*) tief; heftig ‹Erregung, Verlangen›; nachhaltig ‹Wirkung, Einfluss, Eindruck›; tief greifend ‹Wandel, Veränderung›; lebhaft ‹Interesse›; tief empfunden ‹Beileid, Mitgefühl›; tief sitzend ‹Angst, Misstrauen›; völlig ‹Unwissenheit›; gespannt ‹Aufmerksamkeit›; verborgen ‹Geheimnis, Tiefe›; tödlich ‹Langeweile›; hochgradig ‹Schwerhörigkeit›; **it is a matter of ~ indifference to me** es ist mir völlig gleichgültig; Ⓑ (*penetrating*) tief; profund (*geh.*) ‹Wissen, Erkenntnis, Werk, Kenner›; tiefgründig ‹Untersuchung, Abhandlung, Betrachtung›; tief schürfend ‹Essay, Vortrag, Analyse, Forscher›; tiefsinnig ‹Gedicht, Buch, Schriftsteller›; scharfsinnig ‹Politiker, Denker, Forscher›; **that's a very ~ remark** (*also iron.*) das ist sehr tiefsinnig; Ⓒ (*demanding thought*) tief ‹Geheimnis, Bedeutung, Sinn›; unergründlich ‹Rätsel, Geheimnis›; schwierig ‹Lektüre, Problem, Theorie›; inhaltsschwer ‹Symbolik, Worte›; Ⓓ (*rhet./fig.: deep*) tief

**profoundly** /prəˈfaʊndlɪ/ *adv.* Ⓐ (*extremely*) zutiefst; tief ‹schlafen›; stark ‹interessiert, beeinflusst, mitgenommen›; überaus ‹friedlich, verschlossen, geheimnisvoll›; völlig ‹unbedarft, gleichgültig, versunken, rätselhaft›; hochgradig ‹schwerhörig›; **I am ~ indifferent about it** es ist mir völlig gleichgültig; Ⓑ (*penetratingly*) ungemein ‹scharfsinnig, beschlagen, feinfühlig›; hoch‹intelligent, -gelehrt, -gebildet›; **a ~ wise man** ein Mann von tiefer Weisheit; **..., she said ~:** ..., sagte sie tiefsinnig

**profundity** /prəˈfʌndɪtɪ/ *n.* Ⓐ *no pl.* (*extremeness*) (*of feelings, silence, sleep, respect*) Tiefe, *die;* (*of joy, sorrow, concern, change*) [großes] Ausmaß; Ⓑ *no pl.* (*depth of intellect*) Tiefsinnigkeit, *die;* (*of analysis, book*) Tiefe, *die;* Ⓒ (*depth of meaning*) Tiefgründigkeit, *die; in pl.* tiefgründige Gedanken

**profuse** /prəˈfjuːs/ *adj.* Ⓐ (*giving freely*) überschwänglich; großzügig ‹Schenkender, Gebender›; **be ~ in one's thanks/praise** überschwänglich danken/loben; **be ~ in one's apologies** sich wieder und wieder entschuldigen; Ⓑ (*abundant*) verschwenderisch ‹Fülle, Üppigkeit, Vielfalt›; reichlich ‹Beifall›; reich ‹Ernte›; massenhaft ‹Wachstum, Vorkommen›; groß ‹Dankbarkeit›; überschwänglich ‹Entschuldigung, Lob›; **~ bleeding** starke Blutung

**profusely** /prəˈfjuːslɪ/ *adv.* Ⓐ (*liberally*) großzügig ‹spenden, schenken›; übermäßig ‹loben›; Ⓑ (*abundantly*) massenhaft ‹wachsen, vorkommen›; heftig ‹bluten, erröten, schwitzen›; überaus ‹dankbar›; üppig ‹beladen, gedeihen›; überschwänglich ‹sich entschuldigen›

**profusion** /prəˈfjuːʒn/ *n.* Ⓐ (*abundance*) ungeheure *od.* überwältigende Menge; **a ~ of choice** *or* **in the choice offered** eine überreiche Auswahl; **in ~:** in Hülle und Fülle; **in gay/chaotic ~:** in bunter/chaotischer Vielfalt; Ⓑ (*large amount*) [Über]fülle, *die;* **a ~ of flowers/debts** eine verschwenderische Fülle von Blumen/große Menge Schulden

**progenitor** /prəˈdʒenɪtə(r)/ *n.* Ⓐ (*ancestor*) Vorfahr[e], *der*/Vorfahrin, *die;* Ⓑ (*fig.: predecessor*) Vorläufer, *der*/Vorläuferin, *die;* (*intellectual ancestor*) geistiger Vater

**progeny** /ˈprɒdʒənɪ/ *n., no pl.* Nachkommenschaft, *die;* **they are the ~ of transported convicts** sie sind die Nachkommen deportierter Sträflinge

**progesterone** /prəˈdʒestərəʊn/ *n.* (*Physiol., Pharm.*) Gelbkörperhormon, *das;* Progesteron, *das* (*fachspr.*)

**prognosis** /prɒgˈnəʊsɪs/ *n., pl.* **prognoses** /prɒgˈnəʊsiːz/ Ⓐ (*Med.*) (*forecast*) Prognose, *die;* **what is the doctor's ~?** welche Prognose stellt der Arzt?; **make a ~ of sth.** eine Prognose über etw. (*Akk.*) stellen; Ⓑ (*prediction*) Vorhersage, *die;* Prognose, *die;* **give** *or* **make a ~ of sth.** einen Ausblick auf etw. (*Akk.*) geben

**prognostic** /prɒgˈnɒstɪk/ *adj.* (*also Med.*) prognostisch

**prognosticate** /prɒgˈnɒstɪkeɪt/ ❶ *v.t.* Ⓐ (*foretell; also Med.*) prognostizieren; Ⓑ (*indicate*) deuten auf (+ *Akk.*). ❷ *v.i.* eine Prognose stellen

**prognostication** /prɒgnɒstɪˈkeɪʃn/ *n.* Ⓐ (*predicting, forecast*) Prognose, *die;* **make a ~ [about sth.]** [über etw. (*Akk.*)] eine Prognose stellen; Ⓑ (*indication*) Vorzeichen, *das* **(of** für)

**program** /ˈprəʊgræm/ ❶ *n.* Ⓐ (*Amer.*) ⇒ **programme** 1; Ⓑ (*Computing, Electronics*) Programm, *das.* ❷ *v.t.*, **-mm-** Ⓐ (*Amer.*) ⇒ **programme** 2; Ⓑ (*Computing, Electronics*) programmieren; **~ a computer to do sth.** einen Computer so programmieren, dass er etw. tut; **~ming language** Programmiersprache, *die*

**programer** (*Amer.*) ⇒ **programmer**

**programmatic** /prəʊgrəˈmætɪk/ *adj.* Ⓐ programmatisch ‹Politik, Ansatz, Werk, Autor›; klar umrissen ‹Plan, System, Stufen, Projekt›; genau festgelegt ‹Zeitplan›; Ⓑ (*Mus.*) programmatisch ‹Komposition, Trend›

**programme** /ˈprəʊgræm/ ❶ *n.* Ⓐ ([*notice of*] *events*) Programm, *das;* **the evening's ~:** das Abendprogramm; **a ~ of Schubert songs** ein Programm mit *od.* aus Schubertliedern; eine Darbietung von Schubertliedern; **what is the ~ for today?** was steht heute auf dem Programm?; **my ~ for today** mein [heutiges] Tagesprogramm; Ⓑ (*Radio, Telev.*) (*presentation*) Sendung, *die;* (*Radio: service*) Sender, *der;* Programm, *das;* **the ~ is on at 6 o'clock** die Sendung läuft um 6 Uhr; Ⓒ (*plan, instructions for machine*) Programm, *das;* **a five-year ~:** ein Fünfjahresprogramm; **a ~ of study** ein Studienprogramm.

❷ *v.t.* Ⓐ (*make ~ for*) ein Programm zusammenstellen für; Ⓑ (*plan*) festlegen ‹Soll›; planen, vorbereiten ‹Maßnahmen›; durchplanen ‹Leben, Tagesablauf›; **the tumble-drier can be ~d to operate for between 10 and 60 minutes** der Trockner kann auf 10-60 Minuten Betriebszeit eingestellt werden; Ⓒ (*print in ~*) **be ~d** auf dem Programm stehen; **an event not officially ~d** ein Ereignis, das nicht offiziell angekündigt war/ist; Ⓓ (*fig.*) **~ sb. to do sth.** jmdn. darauf drillen, etw. zu tun (*ugs.*)

**programme: ~ music** *n.* (*Mus.*) Programmmusik, *die;* **~ note** *n.* Erläuterung zum Programm

**programmer** /ˈprəʊgræmə(r)/ *n.* (*Computing, Electronics*) Ⓐ ▶ **1261** (*operator*) Programmierer, *der*/Programmiererin, *die;* Ⓑ (*component*) Programmiergerät, *das;* Programmspeicher, *der*

**progress** ❶ /ˈprəʊgres/ *n.* Ⓐ *no pl., no indef. art.* (*onward movement*) [Vorwärts]bewegung, *die;* **our ~ has been slow** wir sind nur langsam vorangekommen; **he continued his ~ across the fields** er setzte seinen Weg durch die Felder fort; **make ~:** vorankommen; **I saw how much ~ I had made** ich sah, wie weit ich vorangekommen war; **in ~:** im Gange; Ⓑ *no pl., no indef. art.* (*advance*) Fortschritt, *der;* **~ of science/civilization** wissenschaftlicher/kultureller Fortschritt; **there has been some ~ towards peace** man ist dem Frieden etwas näher gekommen; **make ~:** vorankommen; ‹Student, Patient:› Fortschritte machen; **make good ~ [towards recovery]** ‹Patient:› sich gut erholen; **some ~ was made** es wurden einige Fortschritte erzielt; **that's ~ [for you]** (*iron.*) [und] das nennt man nun Fortschritt!; **you can't stand in the way of ~:** man kann den Fortschritt nicht aufhalten; Ⓒ (*Brit. Hist.*) (*royal journey*) Rundreise, *die;* (*state procession*) prunkvolle Prozession.

**2** /prəˈgres/ *v.i.* **A** (*move forward*) vorankommen; **the concert had not ~ed very far** das Konzert war noch nicht weit fortgeschritten; **~ to the next point of discussion** zum nächsten Diskussionspunkt übergehen; **B** (*be carried on, develop*) Fortschritte machen; ‹Krankheit:› fortschreiten; **my novel is ~ing nicely** ich komme mit meinem Roman gut voran; **~ towards sth.** einer Sache (*Dat.*) näher kommen.
**3** /ˈprəʊgres/ *v.t.* vorantreiben

**progress** /ˈprəʊgres/**: ~ chart** *n.* Arbeitsdiagramm, *das;* **~ chaser** *n.* ≈ Kontrolleur, *der*/Kontrolleurin, *die* (*verantwortlich für die Einhaltung von Produktionszeitplänen*)

**progression** /prəˈgreʃn/ *n.* **A** (*progressing*) Fortbewegung, *die;* (*of career*) Verlauf, *der;* **his ~ through life** sein Lebensweg; **his ~ from office clerk to head of department** sein Aufstieg vom Büroangestellten zum Abteilungsleiter; **B** (*development*) Fortschritt, *der* (**in** bei); **C** (*succession*) Folge, *die;* **D** (*Mus.*) Fortschreitung, *die;* Progression, *die;* **E** (*Math.*) Reihe, *die;* ⇒ *also* **arithmetical; geometrical**

**progressive** /prəˈgresɪv/ **1** *adj.* **A** (*moving forward*) fortschreitend; **~ motion** *or* **movement** Vorwärtsbewegung, *die;* **B** (*gradual*) fortschreitend ‹Verbesserung, Verschlechterung›; schrittweise ‹Reform›; aufeinander folgend ‹Ereignisse›; allmählich ‹Veränderung, Herannahen, Fortschreiten, Prozess, Besserung›; **in ~ stages** Schritt für Schritt; **C** (*improving*) sich [weiter] entwickelnd; **D** (*worsening*) schlimmer werdend; (*Med.*) progressiv; **E** (*favouring reform; in culture*) fortschrittlich; progressiv; **~ music** progressive Musik; **F** (*informal; also Educ.*) progressiv; **G** (*Taxation*) gestaffelt; progressiv (*fachspr.*); **~ tax** Progressivsteuer, *die;* **H** (*Ling.*) **~ tense** Verlaufsform, *die.*
**2** *n.* Progressive, *der/die;* **the ~s** die fortschrittlichen Kräfte

**progressively** /prəˈgresɪvlɪ/ *adv.* **A** (*continuously*) immer ‹weiter, schlechter›; (*gradually*) stetig; Schritt für Schritt ‹reformieren›; (*successively*) [chronologisch] fortschreitend; **move ~ towards sth.** sich immer weiter auf etw. zubewegen; **~ approach bankruptcy** sich Schritt für Schritt auf den Bankrott zubewegen; **B** (*with progressive views, informally; also Educ., Taxation*) progressiv

**ˈprogress report** *n.* Tätigkeitsbericht, *der;* (*fig.: news*) Lagebericht, *der*

**prohibit** /prəˈhɪbɪt/ *v.t.* **A** (*forbid*) verbieten; **~ sb.'s doing sth., ~ sb. from doing sth.** jmdm. verbieten, etw. zu tun; **it is ~ed to do sth.** es ist verboten, etw. zu tun; **B** (*prevent*) verhindern; **~ sb.'s doing sth., ~ sb. from doing sth.** jmdn. daran hindern, etw. zu tun

**prohibition** /prəʊhɪˈbɪʃn, prəʊɪˈbɪʃn/ *n.* **A** (*forbidding*) Verbot, *das;* **B** (*edict*) [gesetzliches] Verbot (**against** *Gen.*); **C** *no pl., no art.* (*Amer. Hist.*) [gesetzliches] Alkoholverbot; **P~** (*1920-33*) die Prohibition; *attrib.* Prohibitions-

**prohibitionist** /prəʊhɪˈbɪʃənɪst, prəʊɪˈbɪʃənɪst/ *n.* (*Amer. Hist.: person supporting prohibition*) (*19th century*) Mitglied der Prohibitionspartei; (*20th century*) **P~:** Prohibitionist, *der*/Prohibitionistin, *die*

**prohibitive** /prəˈhɪbɪtɪv/ *adj.* **A** (*prohibiting*) prohibitiv (*geh.*); Verbots‹zeichen, -gesetz›; **B** (*too high*) unerschwinglich ‹Preis, Miete›; untragbar ‹Kosten›

**prohibitively** /prəˈhɪbɪtɪvlɪ/ *adv.* (*excessively*) unerschwinglich ‹hoch, teuer›

**prohibitory** /prəˈhɪbɪtərɪ/ ⇒ **prohibitive**

**project 1** /prəˈdʒekt/ *v.t.* **A** (*throw*) schleudern; abfeuern ‹Kugel, Geschoss›; abschießen ‹Rakete›; **~ one's voice to the very back of the auditorium** seine Stimme so erheben, dass sie auch ganz hinten im Zuschauerraum zu hören ist; **B** werfen ‹Schatten, Schein, Licht›; senden ‹Strahl›; (*Cinemat.*) projizieren; **~ against** *or* **on to sth.** gegen *od.* auf etw. (*Akk.*) projizieren ‹Schatten, Umriss›; **C** (*make known*) vermitteln; **~ the product more favourably** ein positiveres Bild des Produkts vermitteln; **~ one's own personality** seine eigene Person in den Vordergrund stellen; **D** (*plan*) planen; **E** (*extrapolate*) übertragen (**to** auf + *Akk.*); **F** (*Psych.*) projizieren; **~ sth. [on] to** *or* **on sb./sth.** etw. auf jmdn./etw. projizieren; **G** (*Geom., Cartography*) projizieren.
**2** *v.i.* **A** (*jut out*) ‹Felsen:› vorspringen; ‹Zähne, Brauen:› vorstehen; **~ into the sea** ‹Felsen:› ins Meer hinausragen; **~ over the street** ‹Balkon:› über die Straße ragen; **B** (*Theatre*) laut und deutlich sprechen.
**3** *v. refl.* (*transport oneself*) **~ oneself into sth.** sich in etw. (*Akk.*) [hinein]versetzen; **~ oneself back in time** sich in eine frühere Zeit/in frühere Zeiten zurückversetzen.
**4** /ˈprɒdʒekt/ *n.* **A** (*plan*) Plan, *der;* **B** (*enterprise*) Projekt, *das;* **~ manager** Projektmanager, *der*/-managerin, *die;* Projektleiter, *der*/-leiterin, *die*

**projectile** /prəˈdʒektaɪl/ *n.* Geschoss, *das;* Projektil, *das* (*Waffent.*)

**projection** /prəˈdʒekʃn/ *n.* **A** (*throwing*) Schleudern, *das;* (*of missile*) Abschuss, *der;* (*of bullet, shell*) Abfeuern, *das;* **B** (*protruding*) Vorstehen, *das;* (*protruding thing*) Vorsprung, *der;* **C** (*making of visible image*) Projektion, *die;* (*of film*) Vorführung, *die;* **D** (*making known*) (*of image or character*) Darstellung, *die;* (*of product or invention*) Präsentation, *die;* **the ~ of his own personality** seine Selbstdarstellung; **E** (*planning*) Planung, *die;* (*thing planned*) Plan, *der;* **make a ~ [for sth.]** einen Plan [für etw.] machen *od.* aufstellen; **F** (*extrapolation*) Übertragung, *die;* Hochrechnung, *die* (*Statistik*); (*estimate of future possibilities*) Voraussage, *die* (**of** über + *Akk.*); **G** (*Psych.*) Projektion, *die;* **~ of sth. on [to] sb./sth.** Projektion einer Sache (*Gen.*) auf jmdn./etw.; **H** (*Geom.*) Projektion, *die;* **I** (*Cartography*) [Karten]projektion, *die;* **conical ~:** Kegelprojektion, *die;* **cylindrical ~:** Zylinderprojektion, *die;* ⇒ *also* **Mercator**

**projectionist** /prəˈdʒekʃənɪst/ *n.* ▶ 1261 (*Cinemat.*) Filmvorführer, *der*/-vorführerin, *die*

**proˈjection room** *n.* (*Cinemat.*) Vorführraum, *der*

**projector** /prəˈdʒektə(r)/ *n.* Projektor, *der;* (*for slides*) Diaprojektor, *der*

**prolapse** (*Med.*) **1** /prəʊˈlæps/ *v.i.* prolabieren (*fachspr.*); vorfallen. **2** /ˈprəʊlæps/ *n.* Prolaps[us], *der* (*fachspr.*); Vorfall, *der*

**prole** /prəʊl/ (*Brit. coll. derog.*) *n.* Prolet, *der*/Proletin, *die* (*abwertend*)

**proletarian** /prəʊlɪˈteərɪən/ **1** *adj.* proletarisch. **2** *n.* Proletarier, *der*/Proletarierin, *die*

**proletarianism** /prəʊlɪˈteərɪənɪzm/ *n., no pl.* Proletariertum, *das*

**proletariat, proletariate** /prəʊlɪˈteərɪət/ *n.* **A** (*Roman Hist.*) Proletariat, *das;* **B** (*derog.: lowest class*) Proleten *Pl.* (*abwertend*); **C** (*Econ., Polit.*) Proletariat, *das*

**ˈpro-life** *adj.* Lebensschutz-; **a ~ movement/position** eine Pro-Leben-Bewegung; **a ~ activist** ein aktiver Befürworter des Rechts auf Leben

**ˈpro-lifer** *n.* Verfechter, *der*/Verfechterin, *die* des Rechts auf Leben

**proliferate** /prəˈlɪfəreɪt/ *v.i.* **A** (*Biol.*) sich stark vermehren; (*Med.*) proliferieren (*fachspr.*); wuchern; **B** (*increase, lit. or fig.*) sich ausbreiten

**proliferation** /prəlɪfəˈreɪʃn/ *n.* **A** (*Biol.*) starke Vermehrung; (*Med.*) Proliferation, *die* (*fachspr.*); Wucherung, *die;* **B** (*increase, lit. or fig.*) starke Zunahme; (*of nuclear weapons*) Proliferation, *die;* (*abundance, lit. or fig.*) Unmenge, *die*

**prolific** /prəˈlɪfɪk/ *adj.* **A** (*fertile*) fruchtbar; **B** (*productive*) produktiv; **be ~ in sth.** reich an etw. (*Dat.*) sein; **be ~ of sth.** etw. in großen Mengen hervorbringen; **C** (*abundant*) reich

**prolifically** /prəˈlɪfɪkəlɪ/ *adv.* **A** (*productively*) reichlich; **B** (*abundantly*) in Hülle und Fülle

**prolix** /ˈprəʊlɪks, prəˈlɪks/ *adj.* weitschweifig

**prolixity** /prəˈlɪksɪtɪ/ *n., no pl.* Weitschweifigkeit, *die*

**prologue** (*Amer.:* **prolog**) /ˈprəʊlɒg/ *n.* **A** (*introduction*) Prolog, *der* (**to** zu); **B** (*fig.*) Vorspiel, *das* (**to** zu)

**prolong** /prəˈlɒŋ/ *v.t.* **A** (*extend in duration or length*) verlängern; **~ the agony** (*fig. coll.*) die Qual [unnötig] in die Länge ziehen; **don't ~ the agony!** (*fig. coll.*) mach es nicht so spannend! (*ugs.*); **B** (*Phonet.*) dehnen

**prolongation** /prəʊlɒŋˈgeɪʃn/ *n.* **A** Verlängerung, *die;* (*fig.*) Weiterführung, *die;* **B** (*Phonet.*) Dehnung, *die;* **C** (*Mus.*) Aushalten, *das*

**prolonged** /prəˈlɒŋd/ *adj.* lang; lang anhaltend ‹Beifall›; lang gezogen ‹Schrei›

**prom** /prɒm/ *n.* (*coll.*) **A** (*Brit.: seaside walkway*) [Strand]promenade, *die;* **B** (*Brit.: concert*) Promenadenkonzert, *das;* **the P~s** *Konzerte, die alljährlich im Sommer in der Royal Albert Hall in London stattfinden;* **C** (*Amer.: dance*) **school/college ~:** Schul-/Studentenball, *der*

**promenade** /prɒməˈnɑːd/ **1** *n.* **A** (*walkway*) Promenade, *die;* (*Brit.: at seaside*) [Strand]promenade, *die;* **B** (*leisured walk*) Spaziergang, *der;* Promenade, *die* (*veralt.*); **go for** *or* **make** *or* **take a ~:** einen Spaziergang machen; **C** (*Amer.: dance*) ⇒ **prom** C. **2** *v.i.* promenieren (*geh.*). **3** *v.t.* (*lead*) führen

**promenade: ~ concert** *n.* Promenadenkonzert, *das;* **~ deck** *n.* (*Naut.*) Promenadendeck, *das*

**promenader** /prɒməˈnɑːdə(r)/ *n.* **A** (*one who promenades*) Spaziergänger, *der*/Spaziergängerin, *die;* **B** (*Brit.: concert-goer*) Konzertbesucher, *der*/-besucherin, *die* (*auf Stehplätzen bei einem Promenadenkonzert*)

**Promethean** /prəˈmiːθɪən/ *adj.* prometheisch (*geh.*)

**prominence** /ˈprɒmɪnəns/ *n.* **A** (*conspicuousness*) Auffälligkeit, *die;* **the continual ~ of his name in the newspapers** das ständige [auffällige] Auftauchen seines Namens in den Zeitungen; **B** (*distinction*) Bekanntheit, *die;* **come into** *or* **rise to ~:** bekannt werden; **fade from ~:** in Vergessenheit geraten; **give ~ to sth.** etw. in den Vordergrund stellen; **C** (*projecting part*) Vorsprung, *der*

**prominent** /ˈprɒmɪnənt/ *adj.* **A** (*conspicuous*) auffallend; **B** (*foremost*) herausragend; **become very ~ as a singer** als Sänger/Sängerin sehr bekannt werden; **he was ~ in politics** er war ein prominenter Politiker; **a ~ topic of discussion** ein viel diskutiertes Thema; **C** (*projecting*) vorspringend; vorstehend ‹Backenknochen, Brauen›

**prominently** /ˈprɒmɪnəntlɪ/ *adv.* **A** (*conspicuously*) auffallend; **B** (*in forefront*) in einer führenden Rolle; **he figured ~ in the case** er spielte in dem Fall eine wichtige Rolle

**promiscuity** /prɒmɪˈskjuːɪtɪ/ *n., no pl.* **A** (*in sexual relations*) Promiskuität, *die* (*geh.*); **B** (*indiscriminate action*) Wahllosigkeit, *die*

**promiscuous** /prəˈmɪskjʊəs/ *adj.* **A** (*in sexual relations*) promiskuitiv (*geh.*); promisk; **be ~:** ‹Person:› den [Sexual]partner/die [Sexual]partnerin häufig wechseln; **a ~ man** ein Mann, der häufig die Partnerin wechselt; **~ behaviour** häufige Partnerwechsel; **B** (*mixed*) bunt gemischt; **C** (*indiscriminate*) wahllos; **D** (*coll.: casual*) nachlässig

**promiscuously** /prəˈmɪskjʊəslɪ/ *adv.* **A** (*in sexual relations*) promiskuitiv (*geh.*); promisk; **B** (*indiscriminately*) wahllos

**promise** /ˈprɒmɪs/ **1** *n.* **A** (*assurance*) Versprechen, *das;* **sb.'s ~s** jmds. Versprechungen; **give** *or* **make a ~ [to sb.]** [jmdm.] ein Versprechen geben; **give** *or* **make a ~ [to sb.] to do sth.** [jmdm.] versprechen, etw. zu tun; **I'm not making any ~s** ich kann nichts versprechen; **give** *or* **make a ~ [to sb.] that sth. will happen** [jmdm.] versprechen, dass etw. geschehen wird; **you have my ~:** ich verspreche es dir; **give** *or* **make a ~ of sth. [to sb.]** [jmdm.] etw. versprechen; **~s of love/reform** Liebes-/Reformversprechungen; **it's a ~:** ganz bestimmt; **~s, ~s!** (*coll. iron.*) Versprechungen, nichts

p

als Versprechungen!; **is that a threat or a ~?** (*coll. iron.*) soll das eine Drohung oder ein Versprechen sein?; Ⓑ (*guarantee*) Zusicherung, *die;* **they gave me a ~ that the work would be ready on time** sie sicherten mir zu, dass die Arbeit rechtzeitig fertig sein werde; Ⓒ (*fig.: reason for expectation*) Hoffnung, *die;* **he never fulfilled his early ~:** er enttäuschte die Erwartungen, die man zunächst in ihn gesetzt hatte; **land of ~:** Land der Verheißung (*geh.*); **a painter of** *or* **with ~:** ein viel versprechender Maler; **~ of sth.** Aussicht auf etw. (*Akk.*); **show [great] ~:** zu großen Hoffnungen berechtigen. ⇒ *also* **breach** 1 A.
❷ *v.t.* Ⓐ (*give assurance of*) versprechen; **~ sth. to sb., ~ sb. sth.** jmdm. etw. versprechen; **~ revenge** Rache schwören; Ⓑ (*fig.: give reason for expectation of*) verheißen (*geh.*); **~ sb. sth.** jmdm. etw. in Aussicht stellen; **~ to do/be sth.** versprechen, etw. zu tun/zu sein; Ⓒ **~ oneself sth./that one will do sth.** sich (*Dat.*) etw. vornehmen/sich vornehmen, etw. zu tun; Ⓓ (*coll.: assure*) **I ~ you** das sage ich dir; **I ~** *or* **let me ~ you this/that** das verspreche ich dir.
❸ *v.i.* Ⓐ **~ well** *or* **favourably [for the future]** viel versprechend [für die Zukunft] sein; **he ~s well as a teacher** er ist ein viel versprechender Lehrer; Ⓑ (*give assurances*) Versprechungen machen; **I can't ~:** ich kann es nicht versprechen

**promised land** /prɒmɪst 'lænd/ *n.* Ⓐ **the ~** (*Bibl.*) das Gelobte Land; Ⓑ (*fig.: ideal state*) Paradies, *das*

**promising** /'prɒmɪsɪŋ/ *adj.*, **promisingly** /'prɒmɪsɪŋlɪ/ *adv.* viel versprechend

**'promissory note** *n.* (*Finance*) Schuldschein, *der*

**promontory** /'prɒməntərɪ/ *n.* Vorgebirge, *das*

**promote** /prə'məʊt/ *v.t.* Ⓐ (*advance*) befördern; Ⓑ (*encourage*) fördern; **a lifestyle which does not ~ health** ein Lebensstil, der der Gesundheit nicht förderlich ist; **~ the success of the firm** der Firma zu mehr Erfolg verhelfen; Ⓒ (*publicize*) Werbung machen für; Ⓓ (*initiate*) in Angriff nehmen ‹Projekt›; gründen ‹Tochtergesellschaft›; **~ a bill** (*Parl.*) einen Gesetzentwurf einbringen; Ⓔ (*Chess*) umwandeln; Ⓕ (*Footb.*) **be ~d** aufsteigen

**promoter** /prə'məʊtə(r)/ *n.* Ⓐ (*who organizes and finances event*) Veranstalter, *der*/Veranstalterin, *die;* (*of ballet tour, pop festival, boxing match, cycle race also*) Promoter, *der*/Promoterin, *die;* Ⓑ (*furtherer*) Förderer, *der*/Förderin, *die;* Ⓒ (*publicizer*) Promoter, *der*/Promoterin, *die;* Ⓓ (*initiator*) Begründer, *der*/Begründerin, *die;* (*Parl.*) *jmd., der einen Gesetzentwurf einbringt und unterstützt;* **[company] ~:** Firmengründer, *der*/-gründerin, *die*

**promotion** /prə'məʊʃn/ *n.* Ⓐ (*advancement*) Beförderung, *die;* **win** *or* **gain ~:** befördert werden; **he is due for ~:** er dürfte bald befördert werden; **~ to [the rank of] sergeant** *etc.* Beförderung zum Unteroffizier *usw.;* Ⓑ (*furtherance*) Förderung, *die;* Ⓒ (*Sport, Theatre: event*) Veranstaltung, *die;* Ⓓ (*publicization*) Werbung, *die;* (*instance*) Werbekampagne, *die;* **sales ~:** Werbung, *die;* Ⓔ (*initiation*) Begründung, *die;* (*Parl.: of bill*) Einbringung, *die;* Ⓕ (*of a company*) Gründung, *die;* Ⓖ (*Chess*) Umwandlung, *die;* Ⓗ (*Footb.*) Aufstieg, *der;* **be sure of ~:** mit Sicherheit aufsteigen

**promotional** /prə'məʊʃənl/ *adj.* Ⓐ (*of advancement*) Beförderungs‹aussichten, -möglichkeiten›; Ⓑ (*of publicity*) Werbe‹kampagne, -broschüre, -strategie usw.›

**prompt** /prɒmpt/ ❶ *adj.* Ⓐ (*ready to act*) bereitwillig; **be a ~ helper/volunteer** bereitwillig helfen/sich bereitwillig zur Verfügung stellen; **be ~ in doing sth.** *or* **to do sth.** etw. unverzüglich tun; **he was ~ in his reply** er antwortete prompt; Ⓑ (*done readily*) sofortig; **her ~ answer/reaction** ihre prompte Antwort/Reaktion; **take ~ action** sofort handeln; **make a ~ decision** sich sofort entschließen; Ⓒ (*punctual*) pünktlich.
❷ *adv.* pünktlich; **at 6 o'clock ~:** Punkt 6 Uhr.
❸ *v.t.* Ⓐ (*incite*) veranlassen; **~ sb. to sth./to do sth.** jmdn. zu etw. veranlassen/dazu veranlassen, etw. zu tun; Ⓑ (*supply with words; also Theatre*) soufflieren (+ *Dat.*); (*supply with answers*) vorsagen (+ *Dat.*); (*give suggestion to*) weiterhelfen (+ *Dat.*); **~ sb. with sth.** jmdm. etw. soufflieren/vorsagen/jmdm. mit etw. weiterhelfen; **he had to be ~ed** man musste ihm soufflieren/vorsagen/weiterhelfen; Ⓒ (*inspire*) hervorrufen ‹Kritik, Eifersucht usw.›; provozieren ‹Antwort›; **this ~s the question ...:** hierbei drängt sich die Frage auf: ...
❹ *v.i.* soufflieren.
❺ *n.* Ⓐ Soufflieren, *das;* **give a ~:** soufflieren; **I'll give you a ~ if you need one** (*a suggestion*) wenn nötig, werde ich dir weiterhelfen; Ⓑ (*Computing*) Bereitschaftsmeldung, *die;* Prompt, *der* (*fachspr.*)

**prompt: ~ box** *n.* (*Theatre*) Souffleurkasten, *der;* **~ copy** *n.* (*Theatre*) Rollenheft, *das*

**prompter** /'prɒmptə(r)/ *n.* (*Theatre*) Souffleur, *der*/Souffleuse, *die*

**prompting** /'prɒmptɪŋ/ *n.* Ⓐ **the ~s of his heart/conscience** die Stimme seines Herzens/Gewissens; Ⓑ **he never needs ~:** man muss ihn nicht zweimal bitten; Ⓒ (*Theatre*) Soufflieren, *das*

**promptitude** /'prɒmptɪtju:d/ ⇒ **promptness**

**promptly** /'prɒmptlɪ/ *adv.* Ⓐ (*quickly*) prompt; **he ~ went and did the opposite** (*iron.*) er hat natürlich prompt [genau] das Gegenteil getan; Ⓑ (*punctually*) pünktlich; **at 8 o'clock ~, ~ at 8 o'clock** Punkt 8 Uhr; pünktlich um 8 Uhr

**promptness** /'prɒmptnɪs/ *n., no pl.* Promptheit, *die;* **be carried out with ~:** prompt durchgeführt werden; **the public's ~ in responding to the appeal** die Geschwindigkeit, mit der die Öffentlichkeit auf den Aufruf reagierte

**'prompt side** *n.* (*Brit. Theatre*) *Bühnenseite links vom Schauspieler;* (*Amer. Theatre*) *Bühnenseite rechts vom Schauspieler*

**promulgate** /'prɒməlgeɪt/ *v.t.* Ⓐ (*disseminate*) verbreiten; Ⓑ (*announce officially*) verkünden

**promulgation** /prɒməl'geɪʃn/ *n.* ⇒ **promulgate**: Verbreitung, *die;* Verkündung, *die*

**prone** /prəʊn/ *adj.* Ⓐ (*liable*) **be ~ to** anfällig sein für ‹Krankheiten, Depressionen›; neigen zu ‹Faulheit, Meditation›; **be ~ to do sth.** dazu neigen, etw. zu tun; *in comb.* **strike-~:** streikanfällig; **a disaster-~ country** ein Land, in dem es häufig zu Katastrophen kommt; ⇒ *also* **accident-prone**; Ⓑ (*down-facing*) **assume a ~ position on the floor** sich in Bauchlage auf den Boden legen; **fall/throw oneself ~ to** *or* **on the ground** sich flach auf den Boden fallen lassen/werfen; **slumped ~ over her typewriter** vornüber über ihre Schreibmaschine gesunken; Ⓒ (*prostrate*) lang gestreckt

**prong** /prɒŋ/ ❶ *n.* Ⓐ (*of fork*) Zinke, *die;* Ⓑ (*of antler*) Ende, *das.* ❷ *v.t.* aufspießen

**-pronged** /prɒŋd/ *adj. in comb.* -zinkig; **three-~ attack** (*Mil.; also fig.*) Angriff von drei Seiten

**pronominal** /prə'nɒmɪnl/ *adj.* (*Ling.*) pronominal; Pronominal‹adjektiv, -adverb›

**pronoun** /'prəʊnaʊn/ *n.* (*Ling.*) (*word replacing noun*) Pronomen, *das;* Fürwort, *das;* (*pronominal adjective*) Pronominaladjektiv, *das;* **demonstrative ~:** Demonstrativpronomen, *das;* **distributive ~:** Distributivum, *das;* **impersonal** *or* **indefinite ~:** Indefinitpronomen, *das;* **possessive ~:** Possessivpronomen, *das;* besitzanzeigendes Fürwort; **reflexive ~:** Reflexivpronomen, *das*

**pronounce** /prə'naʊns/ ❶ *v.t.* Ⓐ (*declare formally*) verkünden; **~ a curse [up]on sb.** jmdn. verfluchen; **~ excommunication [up]on sb.** die Exkommunikation über jmdn. verhängen; **~ judgement** das Urteil verkünden; **~ judgement on sb./sth.** über jmdn./etw. das Urteil sprechen; **~ sb./sth. [to be] sth.** jmdn./etw. für etw. erklären; **he was ~d [to be] a traitor** er wurde zum Verräter erklärt; **~ sb. fit for work** jmdn. für arbeitsfähig erklären; Ⓑ (*declare as opinion*) erklären für; **he has been ~d an excellent actor** es heißt, er sei ein ausgezeichneter Schauspieler; **he ~d himself [to be]** *or* **~d that he was disgusted with it** er erklärte, er sei empört darüber; Ⓒ (*speak*) aussprechen ‹Wort, Buchstaben usw.›.
❷ *v.i.* **~ on sth.** zu etw. Stellung nehmen; **~ for** *or* **in favour of/against sth.** sich für/gegen etw. aussprechen

**pronounceable** /prə'naʊnsəbl/ *adj.* aussprechbar

**pronounced** /prə'naʊnst/ *adj.* Ⓐ (*declared*) erklärt; ausgesprochen ‹Gegner, Autorität›; Ⓑ (*spoken*) ausgesprochen; **the h is not ~:** das h wird nicht gesprochen; Ⓒ (*marked*) ausgeprägt; **walk with a ~ limp** stark hinken

**pronouncement** /prə'naʊnsmənt/ *n.* Erklärung, *die;* **make a ~ [about sth.]** eine Erklärung [zu etw.] abgeben; **make the ~ that ...:** erklären, dass ...

**pro'nouncing dictionary** *n.* Aussprachewörterbuch, *das*

**pronto** /'prɒntəʊ/ *adv.* (*coll.*) dalli (*ugs.*); **and [do it] ~!** aber fix! (*ugs.*); aber [ein bisschen] dalli! (*ugs.*)

**pronunciation** /prənʌnsɪ'eɪʃn/ *n.* Aussprache, *die;* **error of ~:** Aussprachefehler, *der;* **what is the ~ of this word?** wie wird dieses Wort ausgesprochen?; **this word has two ~s** dieses Wort kann auf zwei Arten ausgesprochen werden

**proof** /pru:f/ ❶ *n.* Ⓐ (*fact, evidence*) Beweis, *der;* **very good ~:** sehr gute Beweise; **~ positive** eindeutige Beweise; ⇒ *also* **burden** 1 A; Ⓑ *no pl., no indef. art.* (*Law*) Beweismaterial, *das;* Ⓒ *no pl.* (*proving*) **in ~ of** zum Beweis (+ *Gen.*); **be capable of experimental ~:** sich experimentell beweisen lassen; Ⓓ *no pl.* (*test, trial*) Beweis, *der;* **put a theory to the ~:** eine Theorie unter Beweis stellen; **the ~ of the pudding is in the eating** (*prov.*) Probieren geht über Studieren (*Spr.*); Ⓔ *no pl., no art.* (*standard of strength*) Proof *o. Art.;* **100 ~** (*Brit.*), **128 ~** (*Amer.*) 64 Vol.-% Alkohol; **above/below ~:** über/unter 57,27 Vol.-% Alkohol; Ⓕ (*Printing*) Abzug, *der;* **first ~:** Erstsatz, *der;* ⇒ *also* **galley** C; **page proof**; **read** 1 A; Ⓖ (*Photog., Art*) [Probe]abzug, *der.*
❷ *adj.* Ⓐ (*impervious*) **be ~ against sth.** unempfindlich gegen etw. sein; (*fig.*) gegen etw. immun sein; **~ against wind/bullets/the weather** winddurchlässig/kugelsicher/wetterfest; Ⓑ *in comb.* (*resistant to*) ‹kugel-, bruch-, einbruch-, diebes-, idioten›sicher; ‹schall-, wasser›dicht; Ⓒ hochprozentig ‹Alkohol›; **this liqueur is 67.4°** (*Brit.*) *or* (*Amer.*) **76.8° ~:** dieser Likör hat 38,4 Vol.-% Alkohol.
❸ *v.t.* Ⓐ (*Printing*) (*take ~ of*) andrucken; (*proof-read*) Korrektur lesen; Ⓑ (*Photog., Art*) einen [Probe]abzug herstellen von; Ⓒ (*make resistant*) **~ [against sth.]** [gegen etw.] imprägnieren ‹Stoff, Gewebe›; [gegen etw.] abdichten ‹Wand›; *in comb.* **sound/water-~:** schall-/wasserdicht machen; **flame-~ sth.** etw. nicht brennbar machen; Ⓓ (*in baking*) gehen lassen

**proof: ~-read** *v.t.* (*Printing*) Korrektur lesen; **~-reader** *n.* ▶ **1261** (*Printing*) Korrektor, *der*/Korrektorin, *die;* **~-reading** *n.* (*Printing*) Korrekturlesen, *das;* **~ sheet** *n.* (*Printing*) Korrekturfahne, *die;* **~ 'spirit** *n.* *Alkohol-Wasser-Gemisch mit einem bestimmten Alkoholanteil;* Proofspirit, *der*

**prop**[1] /prɒp/ ❶ *n.* Ⓐ (*support, lit. or fig.*) Stütze, *die;* (*Mining*) Strebe, *die;* Ⓑ (*Rugby*) *Spieler außen in der vorderen Reihe des Gedränges.* ❷ *v.t.*, **-pp-** Ⓐ (*support*) stützen; **the ladder was ~ped against the house** die Leiter war gegen das Haus gelehnt; **the door was ~ped open with a brick** die Tür wurde von einem Ziegelstein offen gehalten; Ⓑ (*fig.*) ⇒ **~ up** B

**~ 'up** *v.t.* Ⓐ (*support*) stützen; **~ oneself up on one's elbows** sich auf die Ellbogen stützen; **sit ~ped up against the wall** [mit dem Rücken] an die Wand gelehnt sitzen; **~ up the bar** (*joc./iron.*) an der Theke rumhängen (*ugs.*); Ⓑ (*fig.*) aufrichten ‹Person›;

vor dem Konkurs bewahren ‹Firma›; stützen ‹Regierung, Währung›

**prop²** *n.* (*coll.*) **A** (*Theatre, Cinemat.: also fig.*) Requisit, *das;* **B** *in pl.* ⇒ **property man**

**prop³** *n.* (*Aeronaut. coll.*) Propeller, *der*

**propaganda** /prɒpəˈgændə/ *n., no pl., no indef. art.* Propaganda, *die*

**propagandist** /prɒpəˈgændɪst/ **1** *n.* Propagandist, *der*/Propagandistin, *die* (**of, for** *Gen.*). **2** *adj.* propagandistisch; Propaganda‹schrift, -blatt›

**propagate** /ˈprɒpəgeɪt/ **1** *v.t.* **A** (*Hort., Bacteriol.*) vermehren (**from, by** durch); (*Breeding, Zool.*) züchten; **B** (*hand down*) vererben ‹Eigenschaft, Merkmal› (**to** auf + *Akk.*); **C** (*spread*) verbreiten; **D** (*Phys.*) **be** ~**d** sich fortpflanzen. **2** *v.i.* **A** (*Bot., Zool., Bacteriol.*) sich vermehren; **B** (*spread, extend, travel*) sich ausbreiten. **3** *v. refl.* (*Bot., Zool., Bacteriol.*) sich vermehren

**propagation** /prɒpəˈgeɪʃn/ *n.* **A** (*Hort., Breeding, Bacteriol.: causing to propagate*) Züchtung, *die;* **B** (*Bot., Zool., Bacteriol.: reproduction*) Vermehrung, *die;* **C** (*handing down*) Vererbung, *die* (**to** auf + *Akk.*); **D** (*spreading*) Verbreitung, *die;* **E** (*Phys.*) Fortpflanzung, *die*

**propagative** /ˈprɒpəgeɪtɪv/ *adj.* **A** (*Hort.*) Vermehrungs-; **B** (*reproductive*) Fortpflanzungs-

**propagator** /ˈprɒpəgeɪtə(r)/ *n.* **A** (*Hort.*) (*person*) Züchter, *der*/Züchterin, *die;* (*device*) [beheizbare] Saatkiste; **B** (*disseminator*) Propagator, *der*/Propagatorin, *die* (*geh.*)

**propane** /ˈprəʊpeɪn/ *n.* (*Chem.*) Propan, *das*

**propel** /prəˈpel/ *v.t.*, **-ll-** (*lit. or fig.*) antreiben; **the boat was** ~**led through the water by the oarsmen** die Ruderer trieben das Boot durchs Wasser; **the rider was** ~**led over the horse's head** der Reiter wurde über den Kopf des Pferdes geschleudert

**propellant** /prəˈpelənt/ *n.* **A** Treibstoff, *der;* **B** (*of aerosol spray*) Treibgas, *das;* **C** (*explosive charge*) Treibladung, *die*

**-propelled** /prəˈpeld/ *adj. in comb.* -getrieben

**propellent** /prəˈpelənt/ *adj.* Antriebs‹kraft, -energie, -leistung, -mittel, -system›

**propeller** /prəˈpelə(r)/ *n.* Propeller, *der*

**propeller:** ~ **shaft** *n.* (*Aeronaut.*) Propellerwelle, *die;* (*Motor Veh.*) Kardanwelle, *die;* ~ **turbine** *n.* (*Aeronaut.*) Propellerturbine, *die*

**propelling 'pencil** *n.* (*Brit.*) Drehbleistift, *der*

**propensity** /prəˈpensɪtɪ/ *n.* Neigung, *die;* **[have] a** ~ **to** *or* **towards sth.** einen Hang zu etw. [haben]; **have a** ~ **to do sth.** *or* **for doing sth.** dazu neigen, etw. zu tun

**proper** /ˈprɒpə(r)/ **1** *adj.* **A** (*accurate*) richtig; wahrheitsgetreu ‹Bericht›; zutreffend ‹Beschreibung›; eigentlich ‹Wortbedeutung›; ursprünglich ‹Fassung›; **in the** ~ **sense** im wahrsten Sinne des Wortes; **B** *postpos.* (*strictly so called*) im engeren Sinn *nachgestellt;* **within the sphere of architecture** ~**:** auf dem Gebiet der Architektur an sich; **in London** ~**:** in London selbst; **C** (*genuine*) echt; richtig ‹Wirbelsturm, Schauspieler›; **D** (*satisfactory*) richtig; zufrieden stellend ‹Antwort›; hinreichend ‹Grund›; **E** (*suitable*) angemessen; (*morally fitting*) gebührend; **do sth. the** ~ **way** etw. richtig machen; **we must do the** ~ **thing by him** wir müssen ihn fair behandeln; **he did not know which was the** ~ **knife to use** er wusste nicht, welches Messer er benutzen sollte; **do as you think** ~**:** tu, was du für richtig hältst; **that's not a** ~ **attitude to take towards ...:** so verhält man sich nicht gegenüber ...; **F** (*conventionally acceptable*) gehörig; **have no notion of what is** ~**:** nicht wissen, was sich gehört; **language not** ~ **for a lady's ears** eine Ausdrucksweise, die nicht für die Ohren einer Dame bestimmt ist; **it would not be** ~ **for me to ...:** es gehört sich nicht, dass ich ...; **the conduct** ~ **to a gentleman** das Benehmen, das sich für einen Gentleman gehört; **G** (*conventional, prim*) förmlich; **H** *attrib.* (*coll.: thorough*) richtig; **she gave him a** ~ **hiding** sie gab ihm eine ordentliche Tracht Prügel; **you gave me a** ~ **turn** du hast mir einen ganz schönen Schrecken eingejagt.
**2** *adv.* (*coll.*) **good and** ~**:** gehörig; nach Strich und Faden (*ugs.*)

**proper 'fraction** *n.* (*Math.*) echter Bruch

**properly** /ˈprɒpəlɪ/ *adv.* **A** richtig; (*rightly*) zu Recht; (*with decency*) anständig; ~ **speaking** genau genommen; **he is** ~ **considered to be a great artist** er wird mit Recht als ein großer Künstler angesehen; **he is not** ~ **a captain at all** er ist eigentlich gar kein Kapitän; **I'm not** ~ **authorized to do it** ich bin eigentlich nicht dazu berechtigt; **he very** ~ **went to see the doctor** er tat das einzig Richtige und ging zum Arzt; **B** (*primly*) förmlich; **C** (*coll.: thoroughly*) total (*ugs.*)

**proper:** ~ **'motion** *n.* (*Astron.*) Eigenbewegung, *die;* ~ **'name**, ~ **'noun** *ns.* (*Ling.*) Eigenname, *der*

**propertied** /ˈprɒpətɪd/ *adj.* begütert; **the** ~ **class[es]** die besitzende[n] Klasse[n]

**property** /ˈprɒpətɪ/ *n.* **A** (*possession[s], ownership*) Eigentum, *das;* **the** ~**-owning classes** die besitzenden Klassen; ~ **speculator/dealer** Immobilienspekulant, *der*/-händler, *der* ; **make sth. sb.'s** ~**:** jmdm. etw. übereignen; **lost** ~**:** Fundsachen *Pl.;* **lost** ~ **[department** *or* **office]** Fundbüro, *das;* **man of** ~**:** begüterter Mann; **common** ~**:** Gemeingut, *das;* (*fig.*) ⇒ **common knowledge**; **B** (*estate*) Besitz, *der;* Immobilie, *die* (*fachspr.*); ~ **in London is expensive** die Immobilienpreise in London sind hoch; ⇒ *also* **personal property a**; **real property**; **C** (*attribute*) Eigenschaft, *die;* (*effect, special power*) Wirkung, *die;* **D** (*Cinemat., Theatre*) Requisit, *das*

**property:** ~ **developer** *n.* ≈ Bauunternehmer, *der*/-unternehmerin, *die;* ~ **man** *n.* (*Cinemat., Theatre*) Requisiteur, *der;* ~ **market** *n.* Immobilienmarkt, *der;* ~ **master** ⇒ ~ **man**; ~ **owner** *n.* Grundbesitzer, *der*/-besitzerin, *die;* ~ **qualification** *n. Eigentumsnachweis als Voraussetzung für ein Amt od. Recht;* ~ **tax** *n.* Vermögenssteuer, *die*

**prop 'forward** ⇒ **prop¹** 1 B

**prophecy** /ˈprɒfɪsɪ/ *n.* **A** (*prediction*) Vorhersage, *die;* **make the** ~ **that ...:** vorhersagen, dass ...; **B** (*prophetic utterance*) Prophezeiung, *die;* **C** (*prophetic faculty*) **[the power** *or* **gift of]** ~**:** die Gabe der Prophetie (*geh.*)

**prophesy** /ˈprɒfɪsaɪ/ **1** *v.t.* (*predict*) vorhersagen; (*fig.*) prophezeien ‹Unglück›; (*as fortune teller*) weissagen; **what do you** ~ **will happen?** was wird deiner Vorhersage nach geschehen? **2** *v.i.* **A** (*foretell future*) Vorhersagen machen; ~ **of sth.** (*lit. or fig.*) etw. ankündigen; **B** (*speak as prophet*) Prophezeiungen machen

**prophet** /ˈprɒfɪt/ *n.* **A** (*lit. or fig.*) Prophet, *der;* **be the** ~ **of sth.** etw. prophezeien; ~ **of doom** Schwarzseher, *der;* **B** (*advocate*) Vorkämpfer, *der*

**prophetess** /ˈprɒfɪtɪs/ *n.* **A** Prophetin, *die;* **B** (*advocate*) Vorkämpferin, *die*

**prophetic** /prəˈfetɪk/ *adj.* prophetisch; **be** ~ **of sth.** ein Vorzeichen für etw. sein

**prophetically** /prəˈfetɪkəlɪ/ *adv.* prophetisch

**prophylactic** /prɒfɪˈlæktɪk/ **1** *adj.* prophylaktisch (*Med., geh.*); vorbeugend. **2** *n.* **A** Prophylaxe, *die* (*Med.*); Vorbeugung, *die;* (*preventive measure*) Vorbeugungsmaßnahme, *die;* **B** (*contraceptive*) Verhütungsmittel, *das*

**prophylaxis** /prɒfɪˈlæksɪs/ *n., pl.* **prophylaxes** /prɒfɪˈlæksiːz/ (*Med.*) Prophylaxe, *die*

**propinquity** /prəˈpɪŋkwɪtɪ/ *n., no pl.* (*formal*) **A** (*nearness*) Nähe, *die* (**to** zu); **in close** ~ **[to each other]** nah beieinander; **B** (*kinship*) [nahe] Verwandtschaft (**to** mit, **between** zwischen)

**propitiate** /prəˈpɪʃɪeɪt/ *v.t.* (*formal*) (*appease*) besänftigen; (*make favourably inclined*) günstig stimmen

**propitiation** /prəpɪʃɪˈeɪʃn/ *n.* (*formal*) Besänftigung, *die*

**propitiatory** /prəˈpɪʃɪətərɪ/ *adj.* (*formal*) (*of propitiation*) Besänftigungs-; besänftigend ‹Wort, Lächeln, Geste›

**propitious** /prəˈpɪʃəs/ *adj.* **A** (*auspicious*) verheißungsvoll; **B** (*favouring, benevolent*) günstig; ~ **for** *or* **to sth.** günstig für etw.; ~ **for** *or* **to doing sth.** dafür geeignet, etw. zu tun; **be hardly** ~ **to sth.** einer Sache (*Dat.*) kaum förderlich sein

**propitiously** /prəˈpɪʃəslɪ/ *adv.* (*auspiciously, favourably*) günstig

**'prop jet** *n.* (*Aeronaut.*) (*aircraft*) Turbo-Prop-Flugzeug, *das;* (*engine*) Turbo-Prop-Triebwerk, *das*

**proponent** /prəˈpəʊnənt/ *n.* Befürworter, *der*/Befürworterin, *die*

**proportion** /prəˈpɔːʃn/ **1** *n.* **A** (*portion*) Teil, *der;* (*in recipe*) Menge, *die;* **the** ~ **of deaths is high** der Anteil der Todesfälle ist hoch; **what** ~ **of candidates pass the exam?** wie groß ist der Anteil der erfolgreichen Prüfungskandidaten?; **B** (*ratio*) Verhältnis, *das;* **the** ~ **of sth. to sth.** das Verhältnis von etw. zu etw.; **the high** ~ **of imports to exports** der hohe Anteil der Importe im Vergleich zu den Exporten; **in** ~ **[to sth.]** [einer Sache (*Dat.*)] entsprechend; **our excitement grew in** ~ **as the ship came closer** je näher das Schiff kam, desto aufgeregter wurden wir; **C** (*correct relation*) Proportion, *die;* (*fig.*) Ausgewogenheit, *die;* **the design lacks** ~**:** der Entwurf ist schlecht proportioniert; **sense of** ~**:** Sinn für Proportionen; **be in** ~ **[to** *or* **with sth.]** (*lit. or fig.*) im richtigen Verhältnis [zu *od.* mit etw.] stehen; **try to keep things in** ~ (*fig.*) versuchen Sie, die Dinge im richtigen Licht zu sehen; **be out of** ~**/all** *or* **any** ~ **[to** *or* **with sth.]** (*lit. or fig.*) in keinem/keinerlei Verhältnis zu etw. stehen; **get things out of** ~ (*fig.*) die Dinge zu wichtig nehmen; (*worry unnecessarily*) sich (*Dat.*) zu viele Sorgen machen; **D** *in pl.* (*size*) Dimension, *die;* **the** ~**s of each room were modest** die Räume waren von bescheidener Größe; **of mountainous** ~**s** riesenhaften Ausmaßes; **E** (*Math.*) **[geometric]** ~**:** Proportion, *die;* **in direct/inverse** ~**:** direkt/umgekehrt proportional; **rule of** ~ = **rule of three** ⇒ **rule** 1 A. ⇒ *also* **direct proportion**; **inverse proportion**.
**2** *v.t.* (*make proportionate*) proportionieren; (*harmonize*) aufeinander abstimmen; ~ **sth. to sth.** etw. einer Sache (*Dat.*) anpassen; **the architect has** ~**ed the whole building** der Architekt hat das ganze Gebäude ausgewogen gestaltet; ⇒ *also* **proportioned**

**proportional** /prəˈpɔːʃənl/ *adj.* **A** (*in proportion*) entsprechend; **be** ~ **to sth.** einer Sache (*Dat.*) entsprechen; **B** (*in correct relation*) ausgewogen; **be** ~ **to sth.** (*lit. or fig.*) einer Sache (*Dat.*) entsprechen; **C** (*Math.*) ~ **[to sth.]** proportional [zu etw.]; **be directly/indirectly** ~ **to sth.** einer Sache (*Dat.*) direkt/umgekehrt proportional sein; **D** (*of proportions*) proportional

**proportionality** /prəpɔːʃəˈnælɪtɪ/ *n., no pl.* **A** (*being in proportion*) Verhältnismäßigkeit, *die;* **there is a** ~ **between A and B** A und B verhalten sich proportional zueinander; **B** (*harmony*) Ausgewogenheit, *die;* ~ **to sth.** ausgewogenes Verhältnis zu etw.

**proportionally** /prəˈpɔːʃənəlɪ/ *adv.* **A** (*in proportion*) [dem]entsprechend; **B** (*in correct relation*) proportional gesehen; **correspond/not correspond** ~ **to sth.** im richtigen/in keinem Verhältnis zu etw. stehen

**proportional:** ~ **represen'tation** *n.* (*Polit.*) Verhältniswahlsystem, *das;* ~ **tax** *n.* Proportionalsteuer, *die*

**proportionate** /prəˈpɔːʃənət/ *adj.* **A** (*in proportion*) entsprechend; ~ **to sth.** proportional zu etw.; **B** (*in correct relation*) ausgewogen; ~ **to sth.** einer Sache (*Dat.*) entsprechend; **the length of the room is not** ~ **to its breadth** die Länge des Zimmers steht in keinem Verhältnis zu seiner Breite

**proportionately** /prəˈpɔːʃənətlɪ/ *adv.* **A** (*in proportion*) entsprechend; **B** (*in correct relation*) angemessen

**proportioned** /prəˈpɔːʃnd/ *adj.* proportioniert; **well-/ill-**~**:** wohlproportioniert/schlecht proportioniert

P

**proposal** /prə'pəʊzl/ *n.* Ⓐ (*thing proposed*) Vorschlag, *der;* (*offer*) Angebot, *das;* **make ~s for peace** Friedensvorschläge unterbreiten; **make a ~ for doing sth.** *or* **to do sth.** einen Vorschlag machen, etw. zu tun; **his ~ for improving the system** sein Vorschlag zur Verbesserung des Systems; **draw up ~s/a ~:** Pläne/einen Plan aufstellen; Ⓑ **~ [of marriage]** [Heirats]antrag, *der;* Ⓒ (*act of proposing*) Unterbreitung, *die;* **he was interrupted in the middle of his ~ to her/the committee** er wurde unterbrochen, während er ihr einen Heiratsantrag machte/dem Ausschuss seinen Vorschlag unterbreitete

**propose** /prə'pəʊz/ ❶ *v.t.* Ⓐ (*put forward for consideration*) vorschlagen; **~ sth. to sb.** jmdm. etw. vorschlagen; **~ marriage [to sb.]** [jmdm.] einen Heiratsantrag machen; **~ a truce** einen Waffenstillstand anbieten *od.* vorschlagen; Ⓑ (*nominate*) **~ sb. as/for sth.** jmdn. als/für etw. vorschlagen; Ⓒ (*for drinking of toast*) **~ a toast to sb./sth.** einen Trinkspruch auf jmdn./etw. ausbringen; **~ sb.'s health** sein Glas erheben, um auf jmds. Gesundheit zu trinken; **I [should like to] ~: 'The bride and groom!'** trinken wir auf das Brautpaar!; Ⓓ (*intend*) **~ doing** *or* **to do sth.** beabsichtigen, etw. zu tun; Ⓔ (*set up as aim*) planen; **~ sth. to oneself** sich (*Dat.*) etw. vornehmen; **he ~s their destruction** sein Ziel ist ihre Vernichtung.
❷ *v.i.* Ⓐ (*offer marriage*) **~ [to sb.]** jmdm. einen Heiratsantrag machen; Ⓑ ⇒ **dispose** 2

**proposer** /prə'pəʊzə(r)/ *n.* (*of motion*) Antragsteller, *der*/-stellerin, *die;* (*of candidate*) Vorschlagende, *der/die*

**proposition** /prɒpə'zɪʃn/ ❶ *n.* Ⓐ (*proposal*) Vorschlag, *der;* **make** *or* **put a ~ to sb.** jmdm. einen Vorschlag machen; Ⓑ (*statement*) Aussage, *die;* **Galileo's ~ that the Earth revolves around the Sun** Galileis These, dass die Erde sich um die Sonne dreht; Ⓒ (*coll.: undertaking, problem*) Sache, *die* (*ugs.*); **paying ~:** lohnendes Geschäft; **it's not a ~:** das kommt nicht infrage; **the project is no longer a practical/viable ~:** das Projekt ist nicht mehr durchführbar/rentabel; **he looks a tough/nasty ~:** er scheint ein zäher/widerlicher Typ zu sein (*ugs.*); Ⓓ (*Logic*) Satz, *der;* Proposition, *die* (*fachspr.*); Ⓔ (*Math.*) Satz, *der.*
❷ *v.t.* (*coll.*) jmdn. anmachen (*ugs.*)

**propositional** /prɒpə'zɪʃənl/ *adj.* Ⓐ (*Logic*) propositional; Ⓑ (*Math.*) lehrsatzartig

**propound** /prə'paʊnd/ *v.t.* darlegen; **~ a question** eine Frage aufwerfen; **~ sth. to sb.** jmdm. etw. vortragen

**proprietary** /prə'praɪətərɪ/ *adj.* Ⓐ (*belonging to private owner*) Eigentums-; ‹Pflichten› als Eigentümer; **~ rights/claims** Eigentumsrechte/-ansprüche; Ⓑ (*characteristic of a proprietor*) **have a ~ attitude to sb.** jmdn. als seinen Besitz betrachten; Ⓒ (*holding property*) Eigentümer-; **~ owner** Eigenbesitzer, *der*/-besitzerin, *die* (*Wirtsch.*); Ⓓ (*privately owned*) privat; Ⓔ (*patented*) Marken-; **~ brand** *or* **make of washing powder** Markenwaschmittel, *das*

**proprietary: ~ 'company** *n.* (*Brit. Commerc.*) Privatfirma, *die;* **~ 'medicine** *n.* Markenmedikament, *das;* **~ 'name, ~ 'term** *ns.* (*Commerc.*) Markenname, *der*

**proprietor** /prə'praɪətə(r)/ *n.* Inhaber, *der*/Inhaberin, *die;* (*of newspaper*) Besitzer, *der*/Besitzerin, *die*

**proprietorial** /prəpraɪə'tɔ:rɪəl/ *adj.* Ⓐ (*of proprietor*) Inhaber-; ‹Pflichten› als Inhaber; Ⓑ (*characteristic of proprietor*) **have a ~ attitude to sb.** jmdn. als seinen Besitz betrachten; **~ pride** Besitzerstolz, *der*

**proprietorship** /prə'praɪətəʃɪp/ *n.* (*ownership*) Eigentum, *das;* (*of newspaper*) Besitz, *der;* **under sb.'s ~:** während jmd. Inhaber ist/war

**proprietress** /prə'praɪətrɪs/ *n.* Inhaberin, *die;* (*of newspaper*) Besitzerin, *die*

**propriety** /prə'praɪətɪ/ *n.* Ⓐ *no pl.* (*decency*) Anstand, *der;* **with ~:** anständig; **breach of ~:** Verstoß gegen die guten Sitten; Ⓑ *in pl.* **the proprieties** die Regeln des Anstands; **observe the proprieties** Anstand und Sitte bewahren; Ⓒ *no pl.* (*fitness*) Angemessenheit, *die;* Ⓓ *no pl.* (*accuracy*) Richtigkeit, *die;* **with perfect ~:** völlig zu Recht

**propulsion** /prə'pʌlʃn/ *n.* Antrieb, *der;* (*driving force, lit. or fig.*) Antriebskraft, *die;* ⇒ *also* **jet propulsion**

**propulsive** /prə'pʌlsɪv/ *adj.* Antriebs-; (*fig.*) mobilisierend

**pro rata** /prəʊ 'rɑ:tə/ ❶ *adv.* anteilmäßig. ❷ *adj.* anteilmäßig; **be paid on a ~ basis** anteilmäßig bezahlt werden

**prorogation** /prəʊrə'geɪʃn/ *n.* Vertagung, *die* (**to** auf + *Akk.*); (*Parl.: interval between sessions*) Parlamentsferien *Pl.*

**prorogue** /prə'rəʊg/ ❶ *v.t.* (*also Parl.*) vertagen. ❷ *v.i.* (*also Parl.*) sich vertagen

**prosaic** /prə'zeɪɪk, prəʊ'zeɪɪk/ *adj.,* **prosaically** /prə'zeɪɪkəlɪ, prəʊ'zeɪɪkəlɪ/ *adv.* prosaisch (*geh.*); nüchtern

**proscenium** /prə'si:nɪəm/ *n., pl.* **~s** *or* **proscenia** /prə'si:nɪə/ (*Theatre*) (*front of stage*) Proszenium, *das;* (*framework*) Bühnenrahmen, *der*

**proscenium 'arch** *n.* (*Theatre*) Bühnenrahmen, *der*

**proscribe** /prə'skraɪb/ *v.t.* Ⓐ (*Hist.: outlaw*) für vogelfrei erklären; Ⓑ (*exile*) verbannen; (*fig.*) ächten; Ⓒ (*prohibit*) verbieten

**proscription** /prə'skrɪpʃn/ *n.* Ⓐ (*Hist.: outlawing*) Ächtung, *die;* Ⓑ (*exile*) Verbannung, *die;* **issue a ~ against sb.** jmdn. in die Verbannung schicken; Ⓒ (*prohibition*) Verbot, *das*

**prose** /prəʊz/ *n.* Ⓐ (*form of language*) Prosa, *die; attrib.* Prosa‹werk, -stil›; Ⓑ (*Sch., Univ.*) **~ [translation]** Übersetzung in die Fremdsprache; **a ~ passage for translation** ein Text zur Übersetzung in die Fremdsprache. ⇒ *also* **idyll** A; **poetry**

**prosecute** /'prɒsɪkju:t/ ❶ *v.t.* Ⓐ (*Law*) strafrechtlich verfolgen; **~ sb. for sth./doing sth.** jmdn. wegen etw. strafrechtlich verfolgen/jmdn. strafrechtlich verfolgen, weil er etw. tut/getan hat; Ⓑ (*pursue*) verfolgen; Ⓒ (*carry on*) ausüben. ❷ *v.i.* Anzeige erstatten; **as a barrister, he preferred defending to prosecuting** als Rechtsanwalt zog er die Verteidigung der Anklage vor

**prosecuting**/'prɒsɪkju:tɪŋ/: **~ at'torney** *n.* (*Amer. Law*), **~ 'counsel** *n.* (*Brit. Law*) Staatsanwalt, *der*/-anwältin, *die*

**prosecution** /prɒsɪ'kju:ʃn/ *n.* Ⓐ (*Law*) (*bringing to trial*) [strafrechtliche] Verfolgung; (*court procedure*) Anklage, *die;* **start a ~ against sb.** Anklage gegen jmdn. erheben; Ⓑ (*Law: prosecuting party*) Anklage[vertretung], *die;* **the [case for the] ~:** die Anklage; **witness for the ~, ~ witness** Zeuge/Zeugin der Anklage; **~ lawyer** Staatsanwalt, *der*/-anwältin, *die;* Ⓒ (*pursuing*) Verfolgung, *die;* Ⓓ (*carrying on*) Ausübung, *die*

**prosecutor** /'prɒsɪkju:tə(r)/ *n.* (*Law*) Ankläger, *der*/Anklägerin, *die;* **public ~:** ≈ Generalstaatsanwalt, *der*/-anwältin, *die*

**proselyte** /'prɒsɪlaɪt/ *n.* (*convert; also Jewish Relig.*) Proselyt, *der*/Proselytin, *die*

**proselytize (proselytise)** /'prɒsɪlɪtaɪz/ *v.i.* missionieren

**prose: ~ writer** *n.* Prosaschriftsteller, *der*/-schriftstellerin, *die;* **~ writing** *n.* Prosa, *die*

**prosodic** /prə'sɒdɪk/ *adj.* prosodisch

**prosodist** /'prɒsədɪst/ *n.* Prosodiker, *der*/Prosodikerin, *die*

**prosody** /'prɒsədɪ/ *n.* Ⓐ Verslehre, *die;* Ⓑ (*Ling.*) Prosodie, *die*

**prospect** ❶ /'prɒspekt/ *n.* Ⓐ (*extensive view*) Aussicht, *die* (**of** auf + *Akk.*); (*spectacle*) Anblick, *der;* (*mental view*) Einsicht, *die* (**of** in + *Akk.*); **open [up] new ~s to sb.'s mind** jmds. geistigen Horizont erweitern; Ⓑ (*expectation*) Erwartung, *die* (**of** hinsichtlich); **[at the] ~ of sth./doing sth.** (*mental picture, likelihood*) [bei der] Aussicht auf etw.(*Akk.*)/[darauf], etw. zu tun; **what are the ~s of your coming?** wie sind die Aussichten, dass du kommst?; **have the ~ of sth., have sth. in ~:** etw. in Aussicht haben; Ⓒ *in pl.* (*hope of success*) Zukunftsaussichten; **a man with [good] ~s** ein Mann mit Zukunft; **a job with no ~s** eine Stelle ohne Zukunft; **sb.'s ~s of sth./doing sth.** jmds. Chancen auf etw. (*Akk.*)/darauf, etw. zu tun; **what are his ~s of being accepted?** wie stehen seine Chancen, angenommen zu werden?; **~s of survival** Überlebenschancen; **the ~s for sb./sth.** die Aussichten für jmdn./etw.; Ⓓ (*possible customer*) [möglicher] Kunde/[mögliche] Kundin; (*possible candidate*) Anwärter, *der*/Anwärterin, *die;* (*possible winner*) Kandidat, *der*/Kandidatin, *die;* **be a good ~ for a race/the job** bei einem Rennen gute Chancen haben/ein aussichtsreicher Kandidat für den Job sein.
❷ /prə'spekt/ *v.i.* (*explore for mineral*) prospektieren (*Bergw.*); nach Bodenschätzen suchen; (*fig.*) Ausschau halten (**for** nach); **~ for gold** nach Gold suchen.
❸ /prə'spekt/ *v.t.* Ⓐ (*Mining*) erkunden; prospektieren (*fachspr.*); **~ sth. for sth.** in etw. (*Dat.*) nach etw. suchen; Ⓑ (*investigate*) untersuchen

**prospective** /prə'spektɪv/ *adj.* Ⓐ (*expected*) voraussichtlich; zukünftig ‹Erbe, Braut›; potenziell ‹Käufer, Kandidat›; Ⓑ (*referring to the future*) zukünftig; **make ~ enquiries** sich vorab informieren; **take a ~ view of sth.** etw. vorausschauend betrachten

**prospectively** /prə'spektɪvlɪ/ *adv.* Ⓐ (*with foresight*) vorsorglich; Ⓑ (*with future effectiveness*) in der Zukunft

**prospector** /prə'spektə(r)/ *n.* Prospektor, *der* (*Bergw.*); (*for gold*) Goldsucher, *der*

**prospectus** /prə'spektəs/ *n.* Ⓐ (*of enterprise*) Prospekt, *der* (*Wirtsch.*); Ⓑ (*of book*) Prospekt, *der;* Ⓒ (*Brit. Sch.*) Lehrprogramm, *das;* (*Brit. Univ.*) Studienführer, *der*

**prosper** /'prɒspə(r)/ *v.i.* gedeihen; ‹Geschäft:› florieren; ‹Kunst usw.:› eine Blütezeit erleben; ‹Berufstätiger:› Erfolg haben; **how is he ~ing in that business of his/in his career?** läuft sein Geschäft gut?/was macht seine Karriere?; **cheats never ~:** ≈ unrecht Gut gedeihet nicht (*Spr.*)

**prosperity** /prɒ'sperɪtɪ/ *n., no pl.* Wohlstand, *der*

**prosperous** /'prɒspərəs/ *adj.* Ⓐ (*flourishing*) wohlhabend; gut gehend, florierend ‹Unternehmen›; (*blessed with good fortune*) erfolgreich; **~ years/time** Jahre/Zeit des Wohlstands; Ⓑ (*auspicious*) günstig

**prostate** /'prɒsteɪt/ *n.* **~ [gland]** (*Anat., Zool.*) Prostata, *die;* Vorsteherdrüse, *die*

**prosthesis** /prɒs'θi:sɪs/ *n., pl.* **prostheses** /prɒs'θi:si:z/ Ⓐ (*Med.*) (*artificial part*) Prothese, *die;* (*branch of surgery*) Prothetik, *die;* Ⓑ (*Ling., Pros.*) Prothese, *die*

**prosthetic** /prɒs'θetɪk/ *adj.* (*Med., Ling., Pros.*) prothetisch; **~ leg** Beinprothese, *die;* **~ surgery** Prothetik, *die*

**prosthetics** /prɒs'θetɪks/ *n., no pl.* (*Med.*) Prothetik, *die*

**prostitute** /'prɒstɪtju:t/ ❶ *n.* Ⓐ (*woman*) Prostituierte, *die;* Ⓑ (*man*) Strichjunge, *der* (*salopp*). ❷ *v.t.* zur Prostitution anbieten; (*fig.*) prostituieren ‹Talent, Integrität›; **~ oneself** (*lit. or fig.*) sich prostituieren

**prostitution** /prɒstɪ'tju:ʃn/ *n.* (*lit. or fig.*) Prostitution, *die*

**prostrate** ❶ /'prɒstreɪt/ *adj.* Ⓐ [auf dem Bauch] ausgestreckt; **she lay ~ before him** sie lag ihm zu Füßen; **~ with grief/shame** von Schmerz/Trauer übermannt; Ⓑ (*exhausted*) erschöpft; **be ~ with fever** vom Fieber geschwächt sein; Ⓒ (*Bot.*) kriechend.
❷ /prɒ'streɪt, prə'streɪt/ *v.t.* Ⓐ (*lay flat*) zu Boden werfen ‹Person›; Ⓑ (*make submissive, lay low*) zermürben; (*overcome emotionally*) übermannen; Ⓒ (*exhaust*) erschöpfen; **be ~d by exhaustion** vor Erschöpfung ganz kraftlos sein. ❸ *v. refl.* (*throw oneself down*) **~ oneself [at sth./before sb.]** sich [vor etw./jmdm.] niederwerfen; **~ oneself at sb.'s feet** sich jmdm. zu Füßen werfen; **~**

**oneself [before sb.]** (*humble oneself*) sich [vor jmdm.] demütigen

**prostration** /prɒ'streɪʃn, prə'streɪʃn/ *n.* Ⓐ (*prostrating oneself*) Fußfall, *der;* **in ~:** [demütig] ausgestreckt; Ⓑ (*submission*) Unterwürfigkeit, *die;* (*subjugation*) Unterdrückung, *die;* Ⓒ (*being emotionally overcome*) Erschütterung, *die;* Ⓓ (*reduction to powerlessness*) (*of country or party*) Entmachtung, *die;* (*of business*) Ruin, *der;* **reduce a country to economic ~:** ein Land wirtschaftlich ruinieren; Ⓔ (*exhaustion*) Erschöpfung, *die*

**prosy** /'prəʊzɪ/ *adj.* langatmig

**Prot** /prɒt/ ⇨ **Prod**

**protagonist** /prəʊ'tægənɪst/ *n.* Ⓐ (*advocate*) Vorkämpfer, *der*/Vorkämpferin, *die;* (*spokesperson*) Wortführer, *der*/-führerin, *die;* Ⓑ (*Lit./Theatre: chief character*) Protagonist, *der*/Protagonistin, *die;* (*fig.*) Hauptakteur, *der*/-akteurin, *die*

**protean** /'prəʊtɪən, prəʊ'ti:ən/ *adj.* proteisch (*geh.*)

**protect** /prə'tekt/ *v.t.* Ⓐ (*defend*) schützen (**from** vor + *Dat.*, **against** gegen); **~ed by law** gesetzlich geschützt; **they led happy ~ed lives** sie führten ein glückliches, behütetes Leben; **~ sb. against** *or* **from himself/herself** jmdn. vor sich (*Dat.*) selbst schützen; **~ one's/sb.'s interests** seine/jmds. Interessen wahren; **~ the peace** den Frieden sichern; Ⓑ (*preserve*) unter [Natur]schutz stellen ‹Pflanze, Tier, Gebiet›; **~ed plants/animals** geschützte Pflanzen/Tiere; **the golden eagle is a ~ed bird** der Steinadler steht unter Naturschutz; Ⓒ (*give legal immunity to*) schützen; **the law ~s foreign diplomats** ausländische Diplomaten genießen den Schutz der Immunität; **be a ~ed tenant** mietrechtlich geschützt sein; Ⓓ (*Econ.*) durch Protektionismus schützen; Ⓔ (*render safe*) sichern ‹Gerät, Leitung›

**protected**/prə'tektɪd/: **~ 'species** *n.* geschützte Art; **~ 'state** *n.* (*Polit.*) Schutzstaat, *der*

**protection** /prə'tekʃn/ *n.* Ⓐ (*defence*) Schutz, *der* (**from** vor + *Dat.*, **against** gegen); **under the ~ of sb./sth.** unter jmds. Schutz/dem Schutz einer Sache (*Gen.*); **[under] police ~:** [unter] Polizeischutz; Ⓑ (*immunity from molestation*) Schutz, *der;* (*money paid*) Schutzgeld, *das;* Ⓒ (*of wildlife etc.*) Schutz, *der;* Ⓓ (*legal immunity*) Immunität, *die;* Ⓔ (*Econ.*) Schutz, *der;* (*system*) Protektionismus, *der;* Ⓕ (*protective agent*) Schutz, *der;* **as a ~ against** zum *od.* als Schutz gegen

**protectionism** /prə'tekʃənɪzm/ *n.* (*Econ.*) Protektionismus, *der*

**protectionist** /prə'tekʃənɪst/ (*Econ.*) ❶ *n.* Protektionist, *der*/Protektionistin, *die.* ❷ *adj.* protektionistisch

**protection: ~ money** *n.* Schutzgeld, *das;* **~ racket** *n.* Erpresserorganisation, *die;* **run a ~ racket** die Erpressung von Schutzgeldern organisieren

**protective** /prə'tektɪv/ *adj.* Ⓐ (*protecting*) schützend; Schutz‹hülle, -anstrich, -vorrichtung, -maske›; **be ~ towards sb.** fürsorglich gegenüber jmdm. sein; **~ instinct** Beschützerinstinkt, *der;* **be ~ against sth.** vor etw. (*Dat.*) schützen; **butterflies/tigers have ~ camouflage/colouring** Schmetterlinge/Tiger haben eine Tarntracht/Tarn- *od.* Schutzfärbung; **the soldiers wore ~ camouflage** die Soldaten trugen Tarnanzüge; **~ clothing** Schutzkleidung, *die;* Ⓑ (*Econ.*) protektionistisch; Schutz‹zoll›

**protective: ~ ar'rest, ~ 'custody** *ns.* Schutzgewahrsam, *der* (*Amtsspr.*); Schutzhaft, *die*

**protectively** /prə'tektɪvlɪ/ *adv.* schützend; **she brought up her children too ~:** sie hat ihre Kinder zu behütet aufgezogen; **these insects are ~ coloured** diese Insekten haben eine Schutz- *od.* Tarnfärbung; **a vaccine acts** *or* **works ~:** ein Impfstoff hat eine Schutzwirkung

**protector** /prə'tektə(r)/ *n.* Ⓐ (*person*) Beschützer, *der*/Beschützerin, *die;* Ⓑ (*thing*) Schutz, *der; in comb.* -schutz, *der;* Ⓒ (*regent*) Regent, *der;* **P~ of the Realm** (*Brit. Hist.*) Regent des Königreiches

**protectorate** /prə'tektərət/ *n.* (*Int. Law, Brit. Hist.*) Protektorat, *das*

**protégé** /'prɒteʒeɪ/ *n.* Protegé, *der* (*geh.*); Schützling, *der*

**protégée** /'prɒteʒeɪ/ *n.* Schützling, *der*

**protein** /'prəʊti:n/ *n.* (*Chem.*) Protein, *das* (*fachspr.*); Eiweiß, *das;* **a high-~ diet** eine eiweißreiche Kost

**pro tem** /prəʊ 'tem/ (*coll.*) ❶ *adj.* befristet; ‹Vorsitzender› auf Zeit. ❷ *adv.* vorübergehend

**pro tempore** /prəʊ 'tempərɪ/ ❶ *adj.* befristet; (*temporary*) vorübergehend. ❷ *adv.* vorübergehend

**protest** ❶ /'prəʊtest/ *n.* Ⓐ (*remonstrance*) Beschwerde, *die;* (*Sport*) Protest, *der;* **make** *or* **lodge a ~ [against sb./sth.]** eine Beschwerde [gegen jmdn./etw.] einreichen; Ⓑ (*show of unwillingness, gesture of disapproval*) **~[s]** Protest, *der;* **under ~:** unter Protest; **in ~ [against sth.]** aus Protest [gegen etw.]; Ⓒ *no pl., no art.* (*dissent*) Protest, *der;* **the right of ~:** das Recht zu protestieren; **literature/song of ~:** Protestliteratur, *die*/Protestsong, *der;* Ⓓ (*Brit. Commerc.: written declaration*) Protest, *der.*
❷ /prə'test/ *v.t.* Ⓐ (*affirm*) beteuern; **I ~, I have never seen you before** ich versichere, dass ich Sie noch niemals zuvor gesehen habe; Ⓑ (*Amer.: object to*) protestieren gegen; Ⓒ (*Commerc.*) protestieren; zu Protest gehen lassen; **be ~ed** zu Protest gehen.
❸ /prə'test/ *v.i.* protestieren; (*make written or formal ~*) Protest einlegen (**to** bei); **~ about sb./sth.** gegen jmdn./etw. protestieren; **~ against being/doing sth.** dagegen protestieren, dass man etw. ist/tut

**Protestant** /'prɒtɪstənt/ (*Relig.*) ❶ *n.* Protestant, *der*/Protestantin, *die;* Evangelische, *der/die.* ❷ *adj.* protestantisch; evangelisch

**Protestantism** /'prɒtɪstəntɪzm/ *n., no pl., no art.* (*Relig.*) Protestantismus, *der*

**protestation** /prɒtɪ'steɪʃn/ *n.* Ⓐ (*affirmation*) Beteuerung, *die;* **a formal ~ that ...:** eine formelle Erklärung, dass ...; **~s of innocence** Unschuldsbeteuerungen *Pl.;* Ⓑ (*protest*) Protest, *der*

**protester** /prə'testə(r)/ *n.* (*dissenter*) Protestierende, *der/die;* (*at demonstration*) Demonstrant, *der*/Demonstrantin, *die*

**protest**/'prəʊtest/: **~ march** *n.* Protestmarsch, *der;* **~ marcher** ⇨ **marcher;** **~ song** *n.* Protestsong, *der;* **~ vote** *n.* Proteststimme, *die*

**proto-** /prəʊtə/ *in comb.* proto-/Proto-; **~ Germanic** urgermanisch

**protocol** /'prəʊtəkɒl/ *n.* Protokoll, *das;* **observe/defy ~:** das Protokoll befolgen/sich über das Protokoll hinwegsetzen

**proton** /'prəʊtɒn/ *n.* (*Phys.*) Proton, *das*

**protoplasm** /'prəʊtəplæzəm/ *n.* (*Biol.*) Protoplasma, *das*

**prototype** /'prəʊtətaɪp/ *n.* Prototyp, *der;* **a ~ aeroplane/machine** der Prototyp eines Flugzeugs/einer Maschine

**protozoa** /prəʊtə'zəʊə/ *n. pl.* (*Zool.*) Protozoen *Pl.*

**protozoan** /prəʊtə'zəʊən/ (*Zool.*) ❶ *adj.* protozoisch. ❷ *n.* Protozoon, *das*

**protract** /prə'trækt/ *v.t.* verlängern; **a ~ed argument/visit/illness/period of idleness** ein langwieriger Streit/ein längerer Besuch/eine längere Krankheit/eine längere Untätigkeit; **delays became more and more ~ed** die Verzögerungen wurden immer gravierender

**protraction** /prə'trækʃn/ *n.* Verlängerung, *die*

**protractor** /prə'træktə(r)/ *n.* (*Geom.*) Winkelmesser, *der*

**protrude** /prə'tru:d/ ❶ *v.i.* herausragen (**from** aus); ‹Zähne:› vorstehen; **~ above/beneath/from behind sth.** etw. überragen/unter/hinter etw. (*Dat.*) hervorragen; **~ beyond sth.** über etw. (*Akk.*) hinausragen. ❷ *v.t.* ausstrecken ‹Fühler›; vorstülpen ‹Lippen›

**protrusion** /prə'tru:ʒn/ *n.* Ⓐ (*projection*) (*of jaw or teeth*) Vorstehen, *das;* Ⓑ (*projecting thing*) Vorsprung, *der*

**protuberance** /prə'tju:bərəns/ *n.* Ⓐ (*state*) Vorstehen, *das;* Ⓑ (*thing*) Auswuchs, *der*

**protuberant** /prə'tju:bərənt/ *adj.* vorstehend; hervortretend ‹Augen›

**proud** /praʊd/ ❶ *adj.* Ⓐ stolz; **it made me [feel] really ~:** es erfüllte mich mit Stolz; **I'm ~ to say I'm never late** ich kann mit Stolz behaupten, nie zu spät zu kommen; **~ to do sth.** *or* **to be doing sth.** stolz darauf, etw. zu tun; **~ of sb./sth./doing sth.** stolz auf jmdn./etw./darauf, etw. zu tun; **he is far too ~ of himself/his house** er bildet sich (*Dat.*) zu viel ein/zu viel auf sein Haus ein; **she answered his offer with a ~ refusal** sie lehnte sein Angebot stolz ab; Ⓑ (*arrogant*) hochmütig; stolz ‹Tier›; **I'm not too ~ to scrub floors** ich bin mir nicht zu gut zum Fußbodenschrubben; Ⓒ (*Brit.: projecting*) herausstehend; **stand** *or* **be ~ of sth.** (*vertically*) über etw. (*Akk.*) herausragen; **stand out too ~:** zu weit herausragen; Ⓓ **~ flesh** (*Med.*) wildes Fleisch.
❷ *adv.* (*Brit. coll.*) **do sb. ~** (*treat generously*) jmdn. verwöhnen; (*honour greatly*) jmdm. eine Ehrung bereiten; **do oneself ~:** sich (*Dat.*) etwas Gutes tun

**proud-hearted** /praʊd'hɑ:tɪd/ *adj.* stolz

**proudly** /'praʊdlɪ/ *adv.* Ⓐ stolz; **remain ~ silent/loyal** stolz schweigen/seine Loyalität bewahren; Ⓑ (*arrogantly*) hochmütig

**provable** /'pru:vəbl/ *adj.* beweisbar; nachweisbar

**prove** /pru:v/ ❶ *v.t., p.p.* **~d** *or* **~n** /'pru:vn/ Ⓐ beweisen; nachweisen ‹Identität›; **~ one's ability** sein Können unter Beweis stellen; **an expert of ~n ability** ein ausgewiesener Fachmann; **his guilt/innocence was ~d, he was ~d [to be] guilty/innocent** er wurde überführt/seine Unschuld wurde bewiesen; **~ sb. right/wrong** ‹Ereignis:› jmdm. Recht/Unrecht geben; **be ~d wrong** *or* **to be false** ‹Theorie, System:› widerlegt werden; **~ sth. to be true** beweisen, dass etw. wahr ist; **~ one's/sb.'s case** *or* **point** beweisen, dass man Recht hat/jmdm. Recht geben; **it was ~d that ...:** es stellte sich heraus *od.* erwies *od.* zeigte sich, dass ...; **not ~** (*Scot. Law*) Schuldbeweis nicht erbracht; ⇨ *also* **exception** A; **point** 1 G; Ⓑ (*establish validity of*) beglaubigen ‹Testament›; Ⓒ (*Cookery: cause to rise*) ‹Hefe:› gehen lassen ‹Teig›.
❷ *v. refl., p.p.* **~d** *or* **~n: ~ oneself** sich bewähren; **~ oneself intelligent/a good player** sich als intelligent/als [ein] guter Spieler erweisen.
❸ *v.i., p.p.* **~d** *or* **~n:** Ⓐ (*be found to be*) sich erweisen als; **~ [to be] unnecessary/interesting/a failure** sich als unnötig/interessant/[ein] Fehlschlag erweisen; Ⓑ (*Cookery: rise*) [auf]gehen

**proven** /'pru:vn/ ⇨ **prove**

**provenance** /'prɒvɪnəns/ *n.* Herkunft, *die*

**Provençal** /prɒvɑ̃'sɑ:l/ ❶ *adj.* provenzalisch; ⇨ *also* **English** 1. ❷ *n.* Ⓐ (*language*) Provenzalisch, *das;* Ⓑ (*person*) Provenzale, *der*/Provenzalin, *die.* ⇨ *also* **English** 2 A

**Provence** /prɒ'vɑ̃s/ *pr. n.* die Provence

**provender** /'prɒvɪndə(r)/ *n.* Futter, *das;* (*joc.: food for humans*) Futter, *das* (*salopp*)

**proverb** /'prɒvɜ:b/ *n.* Sprichwort, *das;* **be a ~** (*fig.*) ‹Eigenschaft:› sprichwörtlich sein; **[Book of] P~s** *sing.* (*Bibl.*) [Buch der] Sprüche; Sprüche Salomos

**proverbial** /prə'vɜ:bɪəl/ *adj.,* **proverbially** /prə'vɜ:bɪəlɪ/ *adv.* sprichwörtlich

**provide** /prə'vaɪd/ *v.t.* Ⓐ (*supply*) besorgen; sorgen für; liefern ‹Beweis›; bereitstellen ‹Dienst, Geld›; **instructions are ~d with every machine** mit jeder Maschine wird eine Anleitung mitgeliefert; **~ homes/materials/a car for sb.** jmdm. Unterkünfte/Materialien/ein Auto [zur Verfügung] stellen; **~ shade for sb.** ‹Baum usw.:› jmdm. Schatten spenden; **~ sb. with money** jmdn. unterhalten; (*for journey etc.*) jmdm. Geld zur Verfügung stellen; **be [well] ~d with sth.** mit etw. [wohl] versorgt *od.* [wohl] versehen

P

sein; ~ **oneself with sth.** sich (*Dat.*) etw. besorgen; [B] (*stipulate*) ‹Vertrag, Gesetz:› vorsehen; [C] **providing that** ⇒ **provided**

~ **against** *v.t.* sich wappnen gegen; **have ~d against sth.** gegen etw. gewappnet sein

~ **for** *v.t.* [A] (*make provision for*) vorsorgen für; Vorsorge treffen für; ‹Plan, Gesetz:› vorsehen ‹Maßnahmen, Steuern›; ‹Schätzung:› berücksichtigen ‹Inflation›; **has everybody been ~d for?** sind alle versorgt?; [B] (*maintain*) sorgen für, versorgen ‹Familie, Kind›

**provided** /prəˈvaɪdɪd/ *conj.* ~ **[that] ...** vorausgesetzt, [dass] ...

**providence** /ˈprɒvɪdəns/ *n.* [A] (*care of God etc.*) Vorsehung, *die;* **[divine]** ~: die [göttliche] Vorsehung; **a special** ~: eine besondere Fügung [des Schicksals]; [B] **P~** (*God*) der Himmel; [C] (*foresight*) Weitblick, *der;* **have the ~ to do sth.** so vorausschauend sein, etw. zu tun; [D] (*thrift*) Sparsamkeit, *die*

**provident** /ˈprɒvɪdənt/ *adj.* [A] (*having foresight*) weitblickend; vorausschauend; [B] (*thrifty*) sparsam; haushälterisch; **P~ Society** (*Brit.*) ⇒ **Friendly Society**

**providential** /prɒvɪˈdenʃl/ *adj.* [A] (*opportune*) **it was ~ that ...:** es war ein Glück, dass ...; **your arrival was quite ~:** es war wirklich ein Glück, dass du [dazu] kamst; [B] (*of divine providence*) durch die [göttliche] Vorsehung bewirkt ‹Befreiung, Rettung›

**providentially** /prɒvɪˈdenʃəlɪ/ *adv.* [A] (*opportunely*) durch einen glücklichen Zufall; **help came quite ~:** die Hilfe kam wie eine glückliche Fügung; **work out ~:** sich glücklich fügen; [B] (*by divine providence*) durch die [göttliche] Vorsehung

**providently** /ˈprɒvɪdəntlɪ/ *adv.* [A] (*with foresight*) vorausschauend ‹handeln›; **he had ~ equipped himself with ...:** er hatte sich vorsorglich mit ... ausgestattet; [B] (*thriftily*) sparsam, haushälterisch ‹mit etw. umgehen›

**provider** /prəˈvaɪdə(r)/ *n.* [A] **he was the chief ~ of money/work** er war der Hauptgeldgeber/der größte Arbeitgeber; **the principal ~ of subsidies** der Hauptsubventionsträger; [B] (*breadwinner*) Ernährer, *der*/Ernährerin, *die;* Versorger, *der*/Versorgerin, *die;* **be the ~ for sb.** jmdn. ernähren *od.* versorgen

**province** /ˈprɒvɪns/ *n.* [A] (*administrative area*) Provinz, *die;* [B] **the ~s** (*regions outside capital*) die Provinz (*oft abwertend*); [C] (*sphere of action*) [Arbeits-, Tätigkeits-, Wirkungs]bereich, *der;* [Arbeits-, Tätigkeits]gebiet, *das;* (*area of responsibility*) Zuständigkeitsbereich, *der;* **that is not my ~:** da kenne ich mich nicht aus; (*not my responsibility*) dafür bin ich nicht zuständig

**provincial** /prəˈvɪnʃl/ ❶ *adj.* Provinz-; (*of the provinces*) Provinz-; (*typical of the provinces*) provinziell. ❷ *n.* Provinzbewohner, *der*/-bewohnerin, *die* (*oft abwertend*); (*of the provinces also*) Provinzler, *der*/Provinzlerin, *die* (*abwertend*)

**provincialism** /prəˈvɪnʃəlɪzm/ *n.* [A] (*mode of thought*) Provinzialismus, *der* (*abwertend*); [B] (*Ling.*) Provinzialismus, *der*

**provincially** /prəˈvɪnʃəlɪ/ *adv.* provinziell; ~ **narrow-minded** provinziell und engstirnig

**proving ground** /ˈpru:vɪŋgraʊnd/ *n.* Versuchsgelände, *das*

**provision** /prəˈvɪʒn/ *n.* [A] (*providing*) Bereitstellung, *die;* **as a** *or* **by way of ~ against ...:** zum Schutz gegen ...; ~ **of medical care** medizinische Versorgung; **make ~ for** vorsorgen *od.* Vorsorge treffen für ‹Notfall›; berücksichtigen ‹Inflation›; **make ~ for sb. in one's will** jmdn. in seinem Testament bedenken; **make ~ against sth.** Vorkehrungen zum Schutz gegen etw. treffen; [B] (*amount available*) Vorrat, *der;* [C] *in pl.* (*food*) Lebensmittel; (*for expedition also*) Proviant, *der;* **stock up with ~s** Lebensmittelvorräte anlegen; [D] (*legal statement*) Verordnung, *die;* (*clause*) Bestimmung, *die*

**provisional** /prəˈvɪʒənl/ ❶ *adj.* vorläufig; provisorisch; ~ **government** provisorische Regierung; ~ **arrangement** Provisorium, *das.* ❷ *n. in pl.* **the P~s** die provisorische IRA

**provisional: P~ IRˈA** *n.* provisorische IRA; ~ **licence** *n.* vorläufige Fahrerlaubnis

**provisionally** /prəˈvɪʒənəlɪ/ *adv.* vorläufig; provisorisch

**proviso** /prəˈvaɪzəʊ/ *n., pl.* **~s** Vorbehalt, *der*

**provisory** /prəˈvaɪzərɪ/ *adj.* [A] (*conditional*) vorbehaltlich; ~ **clause** Vorbehaltsklausel, *die;* [B] (*provisional*) vorläufig; provisorisch

**provocation** /prɒvəˈkeɪʃn/ *n.* Provokation, *die;* Herausforderung, *die;* **be under severe ~:** stark provoziert werden; **he hit him without ~:** er hat ihn ohne jeden Anlass geschlagen; **he loses his temper at** *or* **on the slightest** *or* **smallest ~:** er verliert die Beherrschung beim geringsten Anlass

**provocative** /prəˈvɒkətɪv/ *adj.* provozierend; herausfordernd; (*sexually*) aufreizend; **his actions were felt to be ~:** seine Aktionen wurden als Provokation empfunden; **be ~ of** hervorrufen; provozieren; **be ~** (*be intentionally annoying*) provozieren

**provoke** /prəˈvəʊk/ *v.t.* [A] (*annoy, incite*) provozieren ‹Person›; reizen ‹Person, Tier›; (*sexually*) aufreizen; **be easily ~d** leicht reizbar sein; sich leicht provozieren lassen; ~ **sb. to anger/fury** jmdn. in Wut (*Akk.*)/zur Raserei bringen; ~ **sb. into doing sth.** jmdn. so sehr provozieren *od.* reizen, dass er etw. tut; **he was finally ~d into taking action** er ließ sich schließlich dazu hinreißen *od.* provozieren, etwas zu unternehmen; [B] (*give rise to*) hervorrufen; erregen ‹Ärger, Neugier, Zorn›; auslösen ‹Kontroverse, Krise›; herausfordern ‹Widerstand›; verursachen ‹Zwischenfall›; Anlass geben zu ‹Klagen, Kritik›; **what ~d the incident?** wie kam es zu dem Zwischenfall?

**provoking** /prəˈvəʊkɪŋ/ *adj.* provozierend; herausfordernd; **his behaviour/refusal was [very] ~:** sein Benehmen/seine Weigerung war eine [große] Provokation

**provost** /ˈprɒvəst/ *n.* [A] (*Scot.: mayor*) Bürgermeister, *der*/-meisterin, *die;* **Lord P~:** Oberbürgermeister, *der;* [B] (*Eccl.*) Propst, *der*/Pröpstin, *die;* [C] (*Univ.*) Provost, *der;* [D] /prəˈvəʊ/ ⇒ ~ **marshal**

**provost** /prəˈvəʊ/: ~ **guard** *n.* (*Amer. Mil.*) *Sondertrupp der Militärpolizei;* ~ **ˈmarshal** *n.* (*Mil.*) *Kommandeur der Militärpolizei*

**prow** /praʊ/ *n.* (*Naut.*) Bug, *der*

**prowess** /ˈpraʊɪs/ *n.* [A] (*valour*) Tapferkeit, *die;* [B] (*skill*) Fähigkeiten *Pl.;* Können, *das;* ~ **at sports** [große] Sportlichkeit; **sexual ~:** sexuelle Leistungsfähigkeit

**prowl** /praʊl/ ❶ *v.i.* streifen; ~ **about/around sth.** etw. durchstreifen; ~ **about** *or* **around** herumschleichen (*ugs.*). ❷ *v.t.* durchstreifen. ❸ *n.* Streifzug, *der;* **be on the ~:** auf einem Streifzug sein; (*fig. in search of sexual contact*) was zum Vernaschen suchen (*salopp*)

**ˈprowl car** *n.* (*Amer.*) Streifenwagen, *der*

**prowler** /ˈpraʊlə(r)/ *n.* **the police have warned of ~s in the area** die Polizei warnt vor verdächtigen Personen, die in der Gegend herumstreifen; **see a ~ in the back yard** sehen, wie jmd. im Hinterhof herumschleicht (*ugs.*)

**prox.** /prɒks/ *abbr.* **proximo** n. M.

**proximate** /ˈprɒksɪmət/ *adj.* unmittelbar ‹Ursache, Zukunft›; nächst... ‹Zukunft›

**proximity** /prɒkˈsɪmɪtɪ/ *n., no pl.* Nähe, *die* (**to** zu); **a house with equal ~ to the shops and to the beach** ein Haus, das gleichermaßen nah zu den Geschäften und zum Strand liegt

**proxˈimity fuse** *n.* (*Mil.*) [An]näherungszünder, *der*

**proximo** /ˈprɒksɪməʊ/ *adj.* (*Commerc.*) [des] nächsten Monats

**proxy** /ˈprɒksɪ/ *n.* [A] (*agency, document*) Vollmacht, *die;* Bevollmächtigung, *die;* **by ~:** durch einen Bevollmächtigten/eine Bevollmächtigte; **give one's ~ to sb.** jmdn. bevollmächtigen; **marriage by ~:** ≈ Ferntrauung, *die;* ⇒ *also* **stand** 1 G; [B] (*person*) Bevollmächtigte, *der/die;* (*vote*) durch einen Bevollmächtigten/eine Bevollmächtigte abgegebene Stimme; **make sb. one's ~:** jmdn. bevollmächtigen

**prude** /pru:d/ *n.* prüder Mensch

**prudence** /ˈpru:dəns/ *n., no pl.* Besonnenheit, *die;* Überlegtheit, *die;* **act with ~:** besonnen *od.* überlegt handeln

**prudent** /ˈpru:dənt/ *adj.* [A] (*careful*) besonnen ‹Person›; besonnen, überlegt ‹Verhalten›; [B] (*circumspect*) vorsichtig; **think it more ~ to do sth.** es für klüger halten, etw. zu tun

**prudently** /ˈpru:dəntlɪ/ *adv.* [A] (*in a prudent manner*) besonnen, überlegt ‹handeln, sich verhalten›; **they ~ waited for more information before acting** sie warteten klugerweise ab, bis sie mehr wussten, ehe sie handelten; [B] (*circumspectly*) vorsichtig

**prudery** /ˈpru:dərɪ/ *n., no pl.* Prüderie, *die*

**prudish** /ˈpru:dɪʃ/ *adj.* prüde

**prune¹** /pru:n/ *n.* [A] (*fruit*) **[dried] ~:** Backod. Dörrpflaume, *die;* [B] (*coll.: simpleton*) Trottel, *der* (*ugs. abwertend*)

**prune²** *v.t.* [A] (*trim*) [be]schneiden; ~ **back** zurückschneiden; [B] (*lop off*) ~ **[away/off]** ab- *od.* wegschneiden; ~ **[out]** herausschneiden; [C] (*fig.: reduce*) reduzieren; ~ **back** Abstriche machen an (+ *Dat.*) ‹Projekt›

**pruning shears** /ˈpru:nɪŋʃɪəz/ *n. pl.* Gartenschere, *die;* Rosenschere, *die*

**prurience** /ˈprʊərɪəns/ *n., no pl.* Lüsternheit, *die*

**prurient** /ˈprʊərɪənt/ *adj.* lüstern

**pruritus** /prʊəˈraɪtəs/ *n.* (*Med.*) Pruritus, *der* (*fachspr.*); Hautjucken, *das*

**Prussia** /ˈprʌʃə/ *pr. n.* (*Hist.*) Preußen (*das*)

**Prussian** /ˈprʌʃən/ ❶ *adj.* preußisch. ❷ *n.* [A] (*person*) Preuße, *der*/Preußin, *die;* [B] (*language*) **Old ~:** Altpreußisch, *das*

**Prussian ˈblue** ❶ *n.* Preußischblau, *das.* ❷ *adj.* preußischblau

**prussic** /ˈprʌsɪk/ *adj.* (*Chem.*) ~ **acid** Blausäure, *die*

**pry¹** /praɪ/ *v.i.* neugierig sein

~ **aˈbout** *v.i.* herumschnüffeln (*ugs. abwertend*) *od.* -spionieren

~ **into** *v.t.* seine Nase stecken in (+ *Akk.*) (*ugs.*) ‹Angelegenheit›; herumschnüffeln in (+ *Dat.*) (*ugs. abwertend*) ‹Buch, Brief›

**pry²** *v.t.* (*Amer.*) [A] (*get with effort*) ~ **sth. open** etw. aufbrechen; ~ **a secret** *etc.* **out of sb.** jmdm. ein Geheimnis *usw.* abringen; [B] ⇒ **prize²**

**prying** /ˈpraɪɪŋ/ *adj.* neugierig

**PS** *abbr.* **postscript** PS

**psalm** /sɑ:m/ *n.* (*Eccl.*) Psalm, *der;* **the Book of P~s** (*Bibl.*) das Buch der Psalmen; **the P~s** (*Bibl.*) die Psalmen

**ˈpsalm book** *n.* (*Eccl.*) Psalter, *der*

**psalter** /ˈsɔ:ltə(r), ˈsɒltə(r)/ *n.* Psalter, *der*

**psaltery** /ˈsɔ:ltərɪ, ˈsɒltərɪ/ *n.* (*Mus.*) Psalterium, *das*

**PSBR** *abbr.* (*Brit.*) **public sector borrowing requirement** ⇒ **public sector**

**psephologist** /seˈfɒlədʒɪst/ *n.* Psephologe, *der*/Psephologin, *die* (*fachspr.*); Wahlanalytiker, *der*/-analytikerin, *die*

**psephology** /seˈfɒlədʒɪ/ *n, no pl., no art.* (*Polit.*) Psephologie, *die* (*fachspr.*); Wahlanalytik, *die*

**pseud** /sju:d/ (*coll.*) ❶ *adj.* [A] (*pretentious*) pseudointellektuell; [B] ⇒ **pseudo** 1 A. ❷ *n.* ⇒ **pseudo** 2

**pseudo** /ˈsju:dəʊ/ ❶ *adj.* [A] (*sham, spurious*) unecht; **intellectuals, real or ~:** Intellektuelle, seien es richtige oder solche, die gern welche wären; [B] (*insincere*) verlogen. ❷ *n., pl.* **~s** [A] (*pretentious person*) Möchtegern, *der* (*ugs. spött.*); [B] (*insincere person*) Heuchler, *der*/Heuchlerin, *die*

**pseudo-** /sju:dəʊ/ *in comb.* pseudo-/Pseudo- (*fachspr., geh.*)

**pseudonym** /ˈsju:dənɪm/ *n.* Pseudonym, *das*

**pshaw** /pʃɔ:, ʃɔ:/ *int.* (*arch.*) *expr. contempt* pah; *expr. impatience* heieiei

**psoriasis** /səˈraɪəsɪs/ *n., pl.* **psoriases** /səˈraɪəsi:z/ ▶ **1232** (*Med.*) Psoriasis, *die* (*fachspr.*); Schuppenflechte, *die*

**psst, pst** /pst/ *int.* st

**PST** *abbr.* **Pacific Standard Time** pazifische Standardzeit

P

**psych** /saɪk/ *v.t.* (*coll.*) ~ **sb. out** jmdn. durchschauen; ~ **sb./oneself up** jmdn./sich einstimmen

**psyche** /'saɪkɪ/ *n.* Psyche, *die*

**psychedelic** /saɪkɪ'delɪk/ ❶ *adj.* psychedelisch. ❷ *n.* Psychedelikum, *das;* psychedelische Substanz

**psychiatric** /saɪkɪ'ætrɪk/ *adj.* psychiatrisch

**psychiatrist** /saɪ'kaɪətrɪst/ *n.* ▶ **1261** Psychiater, *der*/Psychiaterin, *die;* ⇒ *also* **couch¹** 1 B

**psychiatry** /saɪ'kaɪətrɪ/ *n.* Psychiatrie, *die*

**psychic** /'saɪkɪk/ ❶ *adj.* Ⓐ ⇒ **psychical** A; Ⓑ ⇒ **psychical** B; Ⓒ (*having occult powers*) **be** ~: übernatürliche Fähigkeiten haben; **you must be** ~ (*fig.*) du kannst wohl Gedanken lesen. ❷ *n.* (*medium*) Medium, *das;* (*clairvoyant*) Hellseher, *der*/-seherin, *die*

**psychical** /'saɪkɪkl/ *adj.* Ⓐ (*of the soul*) psychisch; seelisch; ~ **life** Seelenleben, *das;* Ⓑ (*of paranormal phenomena*) parapsychisch; ~ **research** Parapsychologie, *die*

**psycho** /'saɪkəʊ/ (*coll.*) ❶ *adj.* verrückt (*ugs.*). ❷ *n., pl.* ~**s** Verrückte, *der/die* (*ugs.*)

**psycho'analyse** *v.t.* psychoanalysieren (*fachspr.*); psychoanalytisch behandeln

**psychoa'nalysis** *n.* Psychoanalyse, *die*

**psycho'analyst** *n.* ▶ **1261** Psychoanalytiker, *der*/-analytikerin, *die*

**psychoana'lytic**, **psychoana'lytical** *adj.* psychoanalytisch

**psychological** /saɪkə'lɒdʒɪkl/ *adj.* Ⓐ (*of the mind*) psychisch ‹Problem›; psychologisch ‹Wirkung, Druck›; ⇒ *also* **block** 1 L; Ⓑ (*of psychology*) psychologisch

**psychologically** /saɪkə'lɒdʒɪkəlɪ/ *adv.* Ⓐ (*mentally*) psychisch; Ⓑ (*in relation to psychology*) psychologisch

**psychological 'warfare** *n.* psychologische Kriegführung

**psychologist** /saɪ'kɒlədʒɪst/ *n.* ▶ **1261** (*also fig.*) Psychologe, *der*/Psychologin, *die*

**psychology** /saɪ'kɒlədʒɪ/ *n.* Ⓐ Psychologie, *die;* Ⓑ (*characteristics*) Psychologie, *die* (*ugs.*); **I can't make out his** ~: ich werde aus ihm nicht schlau (*ugs.*)

**psychopath** /'saɪkəpæθ/ *n.* Psychopath, *der*/Psychopathin, *die*

**psychopathic** /saɪkə'pæθɪk/ *adj.* psychopathisch

**psychopathology** /saɪkəʊpə'θɒlədʒɪ/ *n.* Psychopathologie, *die*

**psychosis** /saɪ'kəʊsɪs/ *n., pl.* **psychoses** /saɪ'kəʊsiːz/ Psychose, *die*

**psychosomatic** /saɪkəʊsə'mætɪk/ *adj.* (*Med.*) psychosomatisch

**psychotherapist** /saɪkəʊ'θerəpɪst/ *n.* ▶ **1261** Psychotherapeut, *der*/-therapeutin, *die*

**psycho'therapy** *n., no pl.* (*Med.*) Psychotherapie, *die;* **treat sth. by** ~: etw. psychotherapeutisch behandeln

**psychotic** /saɪ'kɒtɪk/ ❶ *adj.* psychotisch; ~ **illness** Psychose, *die.* ❷ *n.* Psychotiker, *der*/Psychotikerin, *die*

**PT** *abbr.* **physical training**

**pt.** *abbr.* Ⓐ **part** T.; Ⓑ **pint** pt.; Ⓒ **point** Pkt.; **pts.** Pkte.

**PTA** *abbr.* **parent-teacher association**

**ptarmigan** /'tɑːmɪgən/ *n.* (*Ornith.*) Schneehuhn, *das*

**Pte.** *abbr.* (*Mil.*) **Private**

**pterodactyl** /terə'dæktɪl/ *n.* (*Palaeont.*) Pterodaktylus, *der;* Flugfinger, *der*

**PTO** *abbr.* **please turn over** b. w.

**pub** /pʌb/ *n.* (*Brit.*) Kneipe, *die* (*ugs.*); (*esp. in British Isles*) Pub, *das; attrib.* Kneipen-; **go to the** ~: in die Kneipe gehen

**'pub crawl** *n.* (*Brit. coll.*) Zechtour, *die;* Bierreise, *die* (*ugs. scherzh.*); Zug durch die Gemeinde (*ugs. scherzh.*)

**puberty** /'pjuːbətɪ/ *n., no pl., no art.* Pubertät, *die;* **at** ~: in *od.* während der Pubertät; **age of** ~: Pubertätsalter, *das*

**pubescent** /pjuː'besənt/ *adj.* heranreifend

**'pub grub** *n.* (*Brit. coll.*) Kneipenessen, *das* (*ugs.*)

**pubic** /'pjuːbɪk/ *adj.* (*Anat.*) Scham-

**pubis** /'pjuːbɪs/ *n., pl.* **pubes** /'pjuːbiːz/ (*Anat.*) Schambein, *das*

**public** /'pʌblɪk/ ❶ *adj.* öffentlich; ~ **assembly** Volksversammlung, *die;* ~ **confidence** das Vertrauen der Öffentlichkeit; **a** ~ **danger/service** eine Gefahr für die/ein Dienst an der Allgemeinheit; **the** ~ **good** das allgemeine Wohl; **be a matter of** ~ **knowledge** allgemein bekannt sein; **in the** ~ **eye** im Blickpunkt der Öffentlichkeit; **make a** ~ **announcement of sth.** etw. öffentlich bekannt geben *od.* machen; **make a** ~ **protest** öffentlich protestieren; **make sth.** ~: etw. publik (*geh.*) od. bekannt machen; **go** ~ (*Econ.*) in eine Aktiengesellschaft umgewandelt werden; (*fig.*) an die Öffentlichkeit treten; ⇒ *also* **image** F.

❷ *n., no pl.; constr. as sing. or pl.* Ⓐ (*the people*) Öffentlichkeit, *die;* Allgemeinheit, *die;* **the general** ~: die Allgemeinheit; die breite Öffentlichkeit; **member of the** ~: Bürger, *der*/Bürgerin, *die;* **be open to the** ~: für den Publikumsverkehr geöffnet sein; Ⓑ (*section of community*) Publikum, *das;* (*author's readers also*) Leserschaft, *die;* **the reading** ~: das Lesepublikum; Ⓒ **in** ~ (*publicly*) öffentlich; (*openly*) offen; **behave oneself in** ~: sich in der Öffentlichkeit benehmen; **make a fool of oneself in** ~: sich in aller Öffentlichkeit lächerlich machen

**public-ad'dress system** *n.* Lautsprecheranlage, *die*

**publican** /'pʌblɪkən/ *n.* Ⓐ (*Brit.*) ▶ **1261** [Gast]wirt, *der*/-wirtin, *die;* Ⓑ (*Roman Hist., Bibl.*) Zöllner, *der*/Zöllnerin, *die*

**public as'sistance** *n.* (*Amer.*) staatliche Fürsorge

**publication** /pʌblɪ'keɪʃn/ *n.* Ⓐ (*making known*) Bekanntmachung, *die;* Bekanntgabe, *die;* Ⓑ (*issuing of book etc.; book etc. issued*) Veröffentlichung, *die;* Publikation, *die;* **the magazine is a weekly** ~: die Zeitschrift erscheint wöchentlich

**public:** ~ **'bar** *n.* (*Brit.*) ≈ Ausschank, *der;* ~ **'building** *n.* öffentliches Gebäude; ~ **'company** *n.* (*Brit. Econ.*) Aktiengesellschaft, *die;* ~ **convenience** ⇒ **convenience** E; ~ **do'main** *n.* **in the** ~ **domain** gemeinfrei ‹Werk›; **be in the** ~ **domain** Allgemeingut sein; frei sein; (*not protected by patent/copyright*) patentrechtlich/urheberrechtlich nicht [mehr] geschützt sein; ~ **'enemy** *n.* Staatsfeind, *der;* ~ **'figure** *n.* Persönlichkeit des öffentlichen Lebens; ~ **'footpath** *n.* öffentlicher Fußweg; ~ **'health** *n., no pl., no art.* [öffentliches] Gesundheitswesen; ~ **'holiday** *n.* gesetzlicher Feiertag; ~ **'house** *n.* (*Brit.*) Gastwirtschaft, *die;* Gaststätte, *die;* **the 'Lion'** ~ **house** die Gaststätte „The Lion"; ~ **in'quiry** *n.* öffentliche Untersuchung; ~ **'interest** *n.* Interesse der Allgemeinheit

**publicise** ⇒ **publicize**

**publicist** /'pʌblɪsɪst/ *n.* Ⓐ (*writer*) Publizist, *der*/Publizistin, *die;* Ⓑ (*publicity agent*) Publicity-Manager, *der*/-Managerin, *die*

**publicity** /pʌb'lɪsɪtɪ/ *n., no pl., no indef. art.* Ⓐ Publicity, *die;* (*advertising*) Werbung, *die;* ~ **campaign** Werbekampagne, *die;* ~ **material** Werbematerial, *das;* **get** ~ **for sth.** [es] erreichen, dass etw. in der Öffentlichkeit bekannt wird; Ⓑ (*being public*) Öffentlichkeit, *die;* Ⓒ (*attention*) Publicity, *die;* Publizität, *die* (*geh.*); **in the full glare of** ~: im grellen Licht der Öffentlichkeit; **attract** ~ ‹Vorfall:› Aufsehen erregen

**pub'licity agent** *n.* ▶ **1261** Publicitymanager, *der*/-managerin, *die*

**publicize** /'pʌblɪsaɪz/ *v.t.* publik machen ‹Ungerechtigkeit›; werben für, Reklame machen für ‹Produkt, Veranstaltung›; **well-~d** ausreichend publik gemacht

**public:** ~ **'law** *n., no pl.* (*branch of law*) öffentliches Recht; ~ **'lending right** *n.* Anspruch (*der Autoren u. Verleger*) auf eine Bibliotheksabgabe; ~ **'libel** ⇒ **libel** 1 A; ~ **'library** *n.* öffentliche Bücherei; ~ **limited company** *n.* (*Brit.*) ≈ Aktiengesellschaft, *die*

**publicly** /'pʌblɪklɪ/ *adv.* Ⓐ (*in public*) öffentlich; Ⓑ (*by the public*) mit öffentlichen Geldern ‹finanzieren, subventionieren›; ~ **owned** staatseigen; staatlich

**public:** ~ **'nuisance** *n.* Ⓐ (*Law*) Störung der öffentlichen [Sicherheit und] Ordnung; Ⓑ (*coll.*) **make a** ~ **nuisance of oneself** sich danebenbenehmen (*ugs.*); **be a** ~ **nuisance** ein allgemeines Ärgernis sein; ~ **o'pinion** ⇒ **opinion** B; ~ **'order offence** *n.* Störung der öffentlichen Sicherheit und Ordnung; ~ **'ownership** *n., no pl.* Staatseigentum, *das* (**of** an + *Dat.*); Gemeineigentum, *das* (**of** an + *Dat.*); **be taken into** ~ **ownership** verstaatlicht werden; ~ **property** *n.* Staatsbesitz, *der;* **sth. is** ~ **property** (*fig.*) etw. ist allgemein bekannt; ~ **'prosecutor** *n.* ▶ **1261** (*Law*) Staatsanwalt, *der*/-anwältin, *die;* ~ **'purse** ⇒ **purse** 1 A; **P~ 'Record Office** *n.* ≈ Bundesarchiv, *das* (*Bundesrepublik Deutschland*); ≈ Deutsches Zentralarchiv (*DDR*); ~ **re'lations** *n. pl., constr. as sing. or pl.* Public Relations *Pl.;* Öffentlichkeitsarbeit, *die; attrib.* Public-Relations-‹Abteilung, Berater›; ~ **relations officer** Öffentlichkeitsreferent, *der*/-referentin, *die;* ~ **school** *n.* Ⓐ (*Brit.*) Privatschule, *die; attrib.* Privatschul-; Ⓑ (*Scot., Amer.: school run by public authorities*) staatliche *od.* öffentliche Schule; ~ **'sector** *n.* **the** ~ **sector** der öffentliche *od.* staatliche Sektor; ~ **sector borrowing requirement** Kreditbedarf der öffentlichen Hand; ~ **'servant** *n.* Inhaber/Inhaberin eines öffentlichen Amtes; ~ **'service industry** *n.* öffentlicher Dienstleistungsbetrieb; ~ **'service vehicle** *n.* öffentliches Verkehrsmittel; ~ **'speaking** *n.* Sprechen vor einem [größeren] Publikum; **take lessons in** ~ **speaking** Rhetorikunterricht nehmen; ~ **'spirit** *n.* Gemeinsinn, *der;* ~**-'spirited** *adj.* von Gemeinsinn zeugend ‹Verhalten›; **be a** ~**-spirited person** Gemeinsinn haben; **it was** ~**-spirited of him to ...:** es zeugt von Gemeinsinn, dass er ...; ~ **'transport** *n.* öffentlicher Personenverkehr; **travel by** ~ **transport** mit öffentlichen Verkehrsmitteln fahren; ~ **u'tility** *n.* öffentlicher Versorgungsbetrieb; ~ **'works** *n. pl.* staatliche Bauvorhaben *od.* -projekte

**publish** /'pʌblɪʃ/ *v.t.* Ⓐ (*issue*) ‹Verleger, Verlag:› verlegen ‹Buch, Zeitschrift, Musik usw.›; ‹Autor:› publizieren, veröffentlichen ‹Text›; **we will** ~ **his novel** wir werden seinen Roman verlegen *od.* herausbringen; **be** ~**ed** erscheinen; **the book has been** ~**ed by a British company** das Buch ist in *od.* bei einem britischen Verlag erschienen; **he has had a novel** ~**ed** von ihm ist ein Roman erschienen; Ⓑ (*announce publicly*) verkünden; (*read out*) verlesen ‹Aufgebot›; Ⓒ (*make generally known*) publik machen ‹Ergebnisse, Einzelheiten›

**publishable** /'pʌblɪʃəbl/ *adj.* zur Veröffentlichung geeignet

**publisher** /'pʌblɪʃə(r)/ *n.* ▶ **1261** Verleger, *der*/Verlegerin, *die;* ~**[s]** (*company*) Verlag, *der;* **who are the** ~**s of this book?** in welchem Verlag ist dieses Buch erschienen?; ~**s of children's books** Kinderbuchverlag, *der;* **music/scientific/magazine** ~**s** Musikverlag, *der*/wissenschaftlicher Verlag/Zeitschriftenverlag, *der*

**publishing** /'pʌblɪʃɪŋ/ *n., no pl., no art.* Verlagswesen, *das; attrib.* Verlags-; **be in** ~: im Verlagswesen [tätig] sein; ~ **firm/company** Verlag, *der;* **the** ~ **business** das Verlagswesen

**'publishing house** *n.* Verlag, *der*

**puce** /pjuːs/ ❶ *n.* Flohbraun, *das.* ❷ *adj.* flohbraun; **go** ~ **in the face** puterrot werden

**puck** /pʌk/ *n.* (*Ice Hockey*) Puck, *der*

**pucker** /'pʌkə(r)/ ❶ *v.t.* ~ **[up]** runzeln ‹Brauen, Stirn›; krausen, kraus ziehen ‹Stirn›; kräuseln ‹Lippen›; (*sewing*) kräuseln ‹Stoff›; ~**ed** runzlig, faltig ‹Haut›. ❷ *v.i.* ~ **[up]** ‹Gesicht:› sich in Falten legen; ‹Stoff:› sich kräuseln. ❸ *n.* Knitter, *der;* (*in face*) Falte, *die*

P

**puckish** /ˈpʌkɪʃ/ *adj.* koboldhaft

**pud** /pʊd/ (*coll.*) ⇒ **pudding** A, B

**pudding** /ˈpʊdɪŋ/ *n.* [A] Pudding, *der;* [B] (*dessert*) süße Nachspeise; [C] (*person or thing like* ~) Kloß, *der* (*ugs.*)

**pudding:** ~ **basin**, ~ **bowl** *ns.* Puddingform, *die;* ~ **club** *n.* (*coll.*) **be in the** ~ **club** 'n dicken Bauch haben (*ugs.*); ~ **face** *n.* [Voll]mondgesicht, *das* (*ugs.*); ~**-head** *n.* Gipskopf, *der* (*ugs. abwertend*)

**puddle** /ˈpʌdl/ *n.* Pfütze, *die*

**pudendum** /pju:ˈdendəm/ *n.*, *pl.* **pudenda** /pju:ˈdendə/ *in sing. or pl.* (*Anat.*) Scham, *die*

**pudge** /pʌdʒ/ ⇒ **podge**

**pudgy** /ˈpʌdʒɪ/ ⇒ **podgy**

**puerile** /ˈpjʊəraɪl/ *adj.* kindisch (*abwertend*); infantil (*abwertend*)

**puerility** /pjʊəˈrɪlɪtɪ/ *n.*, *no pl.* Infantilität, *die* (*abwertend*)

**puerperal** /pju:ˈɜ:pərl/ *adj.* (*Med.*) puerperal (*fachspr.*); ~ **fever** Kindbettfieber, *das*

**Puerto Rican** /pwɜ:təʊ ˈri:kən/ ▶ **1340** ❶ *adj.* puerto-ricanisch; **sb. is** ~: jmd. ist Puerto-Ricaner/Puerto-Ricanerin. ❷ *n.* Puerto-Ricaner, *der*/Puerto-Ricanerin, *die*

**Puerto Rico** /pwɜ:təʊ ˈri:kəʊ/ *pr. n.* Puerto Rico (*das*)

**puff** /pʌf/ ❶ *n.* [A] Stoß, *der;* ~ **of breath/wind** Atem-/Windstoß, *der;* [B] (*sound of escaping vapour*) Zischen, *das;* [C] (*quantity*) ~ **of smoke** Rauchstoß, *der;* ~ **of steam** Dampfwolke, *die;* [D] (*in dress etc.*) Bausch, *der;* Puff, *der* (*veralt.*); [E] (*pastry*) Blätterteigteilchen, *das;* ⇒ *also* **cream puff**; [F] (*advertisement*) Reklame, *die;* **give sth. a** ~: Reklame für etw. machen; [G] ⇒ **powder puff**; [H] **sb. runs out of** ~ (*lit. or fig. coll.*) jmdm. geht die Puste aus (*ugs.*). ❷ *v.i.* [A] ‹Blasebalg:› blasen; ~ **[and blow]** pusten (*ugs.*) *od.* schnaufen [und keuchen]; [B] (~ *cigarette smoke etc.*) paffen (*ugs.*) (**at** an + *Dat.*); [C] (*move with* ~*ing*) ‹Person:› keuchen; ‹Zug, Lokomotive, Dampfer:› schnaufend fahren; [D] (*be emitted*) ‹Dampf, Luft, Rauch:› stoßweise entweichen, (*ugs.*) puffen; [E] (*swell*) ~ **up** ‹Frosch:› sich aufblähen; ~ **out** ‹Finger:› [an]schwellen. ❸ *v.t.* [A] (*blow*) pusten (*ugs.*), blasen ‹Rauch›; stäuben ‹Puder›; [B] (*smoke in* ~*s*) paffen (*ugs.*); [C] (*put out of breath*) ⇒ ~ **out** 1 B; [D] (*utter pantingly*) keuchen; [E] (*advertise*) hochjubeln (*ugs.*); [F] ~**ed sleeve** ⇒ **puff sleeve**

~ ˈ**out** ❶ *v.t.* [A] (*inflate*) ‹Wind:› blähen, bauschen ‹Segel›; **he** ~**ed out his chest** er blähte seine Brust; [B] (*put out of breath*) außer Puste (*salopp*) *od.* Atem bringen ‹Person›; **be** ~**ed out** außer Puste (*salopp*) *od.* Atem sein; [C] (*utter pantingly*) heraus-, hervorstoßen; [D] (*extinguish*) ausblasen; auspusten (*ugs.*). ❷ *v.i.* ‹Segel, Fahne:› sich bauschen, sich [auf]blähen

~ ˈ**up** ❶ *v.t.* [A] (*inflate*) aufblasen; aufpusten (*ugs.*); [B] **be** ~**ed up** (*proud*) aufgeblasen sein (**by** infolge). ❷ *v.i.* sich [auf]blähen

**puff:** ~ **adder** *n.* (*Zool.*) Puffotter, *die;* ~**ball** *n.* (*Bot.*) Bovist, *der*

ˈ**puffer [train]** ⇒ **puff-puff**

**puffin** /ˈpʌfɪn/ *n.* (*Ornith.*) Papageientaucher, *der*

ˈ**puffin crossing** *n.* (*Brit.*) *Fußgängerüberweg mit elektronisch gesteuerter Ampel*

**puff:** ~ ˈ**pastry** *n.* (*Cookery*) Blätterteig, *der;* ~-~ *n.* (*Brit. child. lang.*) Puffzug, *der* (*Kinderspr.*); ~ ˈ**sleeve** *n.* Puffärmel, *der*

**puffy** /ˈpʌfɪ/ *adj.* verschwollen

**pug** /pʌg/ *n.* ~**[ dog]** Mops, *der*

**pugilism** /ˈpju:dʒɪlɪzm/ *n.*, *no pl.*, *no art.* (*formal*) Pugilismus, *der* (*veralt.*); Faustkampf, *der* (*geh.*)

**pugilist** /ˈpju:dʒɪlɪst/ *n.* (*formal*) Pugilist, *der* (*veralt.*); Faustkämpfer, *der* (*geh.*)

**pugilistic** /pju:dʒɪˈlɪstɪk/ *adj.* (*formal*) pugilistisch (*veralt.*)

**pugnacious** /pʌgˈneɪʃəs/ *adj.* (*literary*) kampflustig

**pugnaciously** /pʌgˈneɪʃəslɪ/ *adv.* (*literary*) mit großem Einsatz ‹kämpfen›

**pugnacity** /pʌgˈnæsɪtɪ/ *n.*, *no pl.* Kampflust, *die*

**pug:** ~ **nose** *n.* Stumpfnase, *die;* ~**-nosed** *adj.* stumpfnasig

**puissance** /ˈpju:ɪsəns, pwɪsəns/ *n.* (*Showjumping*) Mächtigkeitsspringen, *das*

**puke** /pju:k/ (*coarse*) ❶ *v.i.* kotzen (*salopp*); **the smell nearly made me** ~: von dem Geruch musste ich beinahe kotzen. ❷ *v.t.* ~ **up** auskotzen (*salopp*); ausspucken (*ugs.*); ~ **one's guts up** kotzen wie ein Reiher (*derb*). ❸ *n.* Kotze, *die* (*salopp*); Ausgespuckte, *das* (*ugs.*)

**pukka** /ˈpʌkə/ *adj.* (*Anglo-Ind.*) richtig; **it's** ~ **information** es ist Tatsache

**pulchritude** /ˈpʌlkrɪtju:d/ *n.* (*literary*) Lieblichkeit, *die* (*geh.*)

**pull** /pʊl/ ❶ *v.t.* [A] (*draw, tug*) ziehen an (+ *Dat.*); ziehen ‹Hebel›; ~ **aside** beiseite ziehen; ~ **sb.'s** *or* **sb. by the hair/ears/sleeve** jmdn. an den Haaren/Ohren/am Ärmel ziehen; ~ **shut** zuziehen ‹Tür›; ~ **sth. over one's ears/head** sich (*Dat.*) etw. über die Ohren/den Kopf ziehen; ~ **the other one** *or* **leg[, it's got bells on]** (*fig. coll.*) das kannst du einem anderen erzählen; ~ **sth. out of the fire** (*fig.*) etw. [doch] noch retten; ~ **to pieces** in Stücke reißen; (*fig.: criticize severely*) zerpflücken ‹Argument, Artikel›; [B] (*extract*) [her]ausziehen; [heraus]ziehen ‹Zahn›; zapfen ‹Bier›; [C] (*coll.: accomplish*) bringen (*ugs.*); ~ **a stunt** *or* **trick** etwas Wahnsinniges tun; ~ **a dirty trick** ein linkes Ding drehen (*ugs.*); ⇒ *also* **fast**[2] 1 D; [D] (*strain*) sich (*Dat.*) zerren ‹Muskel, Sehne, Band›; [E] ~ **a long/wry** *etc.* **face** ein langes/ironisches *usw.* Gesicht machen; ⇒ *also* **face** 1 A; [F] (*draw from sheath etc.*) ziehen ‹Waffe›; ~ **a knife/gun on sb.** ein Messer/eine Pistole ziehen und jmdn. damit bedrohen; [G] (*Rowing*) pullen (*Seemannsspr.*); rudern; ~ **one's weight** (*do one's fair share*) sich voll einsetzen; [H] (*hold back*) parieren, verhalten ‹Pferd›; ~ **one's punches** ‹Boxer:› verhalten schlagen; (*fig.: be gentle or lenient*) sich zurückhalten; **not** ~ **one's punches** (*fig.*) nicht zimperlich sein; [I] (*Printing*) machen ‹Abzug›.

❷ *v.i.* [A] ziehen; **'Pull'** „Ziehen"; [B] ~ **[to the left/right]** ‹Auto, Boot:› [nach links/rechts] ziehen; [C] (*move with effort*) sich schleppen; [D] (*pluck*) ~ **at** ziehen an (+ *Dat.*); ~ **at sb.'s sleeve** jmdn. am Ärmel ziehen; [E] (*draw*) ~ **at** ziehen an (+ *Dat.*) ‹Pfeife›.

❸ *n.* [A] Zug, *der;* Ziehen, *das;* (*of the moon, sun, etc.*) Anziehungskraft, *die;* (*of tide*) Sog, *der;* (*of conflicting emotions*) Widerstreit, *der;* **give a** ~ **at sth.** an etw. (*Dat.*) ziehen; **feel a** ~ **on** *or* **at sth.** ein Ziehen an etw. (*Dat.*) spüren; [B] *no pl.* (*influence*) Einfluss, *der* (**with** auf + *Akk.*, bei); [C] ⇒ **bell pull**; [D] (*drink*) Zug, *der* (**at** aus); [E] (*Rowing*) Ruderfahrt, *die;* [F] (*Printing*) Abzug, *der*

~ **aˈbout** *v.t.* (*treat roughly*) zurichten

~ **aˈhead** *v.i.* in Führung gehen; sich an die Spitze setzen; ~ **ahead of** sich setzen vor (+ *Akk.*); ~ **ahead by a few metres** mit einigen Metern Vorsprung in Führung gehen; **the firm is beginning to** ~ **ahead of its competitors** die Firma überholt die Konkurrenz allmählich

~ **aˈpart** *v.t.* [A] (*take to pieces*) auseinander nehmen; zerlegen; [B] (*fig.: criticize severely*) zerpflücken ‹Interpretation, Argumentation usw.›; verreißen ‹Buch, [literarisches] Werk›

~ **aˈway** ❶ *v.t.* wegziehen. ❷ *v.i.* anfahren; (*with effort*) anziehen; ~ **away from the kerb/platform** anfahren

~ ˈ**back** ❶ *v.i.* [A] (*retreat*) zurücktreten; ‹Truppen:› sich zurückziehen; [B] (*Sport*) [wieder] aufholen (**to** bis auf + *Akk.*). ❷ *v.t.* [A] zurückziehen; [B] (*Sport*) aufholen. ⇒ *also* ~**-back**

~ ˈ**down** *v.t.* [A] herunterziehen; [B] (*demolish*) abreißen; [C] (*make less*) drücken ‹Preis›; (*weaken*) mitnehmen ‹Person›; [D] (*in exam*) ~ **sb. down** jmds. [Gesamt]note drücken

~ ˈ**in** ❶ *v.t.* [A] hereinziehen; zurückziehen ‹Beine›; [B] (*earn*) kriegen (*ugs.*); [C] (*attract*) anziehen; [D] (*coll.: detain in custody*) einkassieren (*salopp*): kassieren (*ugs.*). ❷ *v.i.* [A] ‹Zug:› einfahren; [B] (*move to side of road*) an die Seite fahren; (*stop*) anhalten; ~ **in to the side of the road** an den Straßenrand fahren; **a good place to** ~ **in** eine gute Stelle zum [An]halten; [C] ~ **in to the bank** ‹Boot:› ans Ufer fahren. ⇒ *also* **pull-in**

~ **into** *v.t.* [A] ‹Zug:› einfahren in (+ *Akk.*); [B] (*move off road into*) fahren in (+ *Akk.*)

~ ˈ**off** *v.t.* [A] (*remove*) abziehen; (*violently*) abreißen; ausziehen ‹Kleidungsstück›; ausziehen, abstreifen ‹Handschuhe›; [B] (*accomplish*) an Land ziehen (*ugs.*) ‹Geschäft, Knüller›; einfahren (*ugs.*) ‹Sieg›; abziehen (*salopp*) ‹Raubüberfall›

~ ˈ**on** *v.t.* [sich (*Dat.*)] an- *od.* überziehen; (*in a hurry*) sich werfen in (+ *Akk.*)

~ ˈ**out** ❶ *v.t.* [A] (*extract*) herausziehen; [heraus]ziehen ‹Zahn›; [B] (*take out of pocket etc.*) aus der Tasche ziehen; herausziehen ‹Messer, Pistole›; [heraus]ziehen, (*scherzh.*) zücken ‹Brieftasche›; [C] (*detach*) heraustrennen ‹Zeitungsbeilage, Foto›; [D] (*withdraw*) abziehen ‹Truppen›; herausnehmen ‹Spieler, Mannschaft›. ⇒ *also* **stop** 3 E. ❷ *v.i.* [A] (*depart*) ‹Zug:› abfahren; ~ **out of the station** aus dem Bahnhof ausfahren; [B] (*away from roadside*) ausscheren; [C] (*withdraw*) ‹Truppen:› abziehen (**of** aus); (*from deal, project, competition, etc.*) aussteigen (*ugs.*) (**of** aus); **the first country to** ~ **out of the negotiations** das erste Land, das seine Teilnahme an den Verhandlungen eingestellt hat; [D] ~ **out of a dive** ‹Flugzeug:› aus dem Sturzflug abgefangen werden; ‹Pilot:› die Maschine aus dem Sturzflug abfangen. ⇒ *also* **pull-out**

~ ˈ**over** ❶ *v.i.* ⇒ ~ **in** 2 B. ❷ *v.t.* ~ **one's car over to the side of the road** seinen Wagen an den Straßenrand *od.* an die Seite fahren

~ ˈ**round** ❶ *v.i.* (*regain health*) wieder auf die Beine kommen; (*regain former success*) wieder Tritt fassen. ❷ *v.t.* wieder auf die Beine bringen ‹Patienten›; (*fig.: put into a better condition*) herausreißen (*ugs.*)

~ ˈ**through** ❶ *v.t.* durchziehen; ~ **sb. through** (*cause to recover or succeed*) jmdn. durchbringen; ~ **through sth.** etw. überstehen. ❷ *v.i.* ‹Patient:› durchkommen; ‹Firma:› überleben

~ **toˈgether** ❶ *v.i.* an einem *od.* am selben Strang ziehen. ❷ *v.t.* näher zusammenziehen; zusammenschweißen ‹Partei, Allianz›; in Schuss bringen (*ugs.*) ‹Firma›; ~ **sb. together** jmdn. auf die Beine helfen. ❸ *v. refl.* sich zusammennehmen

~ ˈ**up** ❶ *v.t.* [A] hochziehen; [B] ~ **up a chair** einen Stuhl heranziehen; [C] [he]rausziehen ‹Unkraut, Pflanze usw.›; (*violently*) [he]rausreißen; [D] (*stop*) anhalten, zum Stehen bringen ‹Auto›; [E] (*reprimand*) zurechtweisen; rügen. ❷ *v.i.* [A] (*stop*) anhalten; [B] (*improve*) sich verbessern *od.* vorarbeiten. ❸ *v. refl.* sich hocharbeiten. ⇒ *also* **bootstraps**; **pull-up**; **sock**[1] A

ˈ**pull:** ~**-back** *n.* (*withdrawal*) Abzug, *der;* ~**-down menu** *n.* (*Computing*) Pull-down-Menü, *das* (*fachspr.*)

**pullet** /ˈpʊlɪt/ *n.* Junghenne, *die*

**pulley** /ˈpʊlɪ/ *n.* Rolle, *die;* (*for drive belt*) Riemenscheibe, *die;* **set of** ~**s** (*tackle*) Flaschenzug, *der*

ˈ**pull-in** *n.* [A] (*place at the side of the road for vehicles*) Haltebucht, *die;* [B] (*Brit.: transport café*) Fernfahrerlokal, *das*

**Pullman** /ˈpʊlmən/ *n.* ~ **[car** *or* **coach]** Pullman[wagen], *der*

ˈ**pull-out** *n.* [A] (*folding portion of book etc.*) ausfaltbarer Teil; (*map*) Faltkarte, *die;* (*detachable section*) heraustrennbarer Teil; [B] (*withdrawal*) Abzug, *der;* ~ **of troops** Truppenabzug, *der*

**pullover** /ˈpʊləʊvə(r)/ *n.* Pullover, *der;* Pulli, *der* (*ugs.*)

ˈ**pull-up** *n.* [A] (*stopping place*) Platz zum Haltmachen; [B] (*Gymnastics*) Klimmzug, *der*

**pulmonary** /ˈpʌlmənərɪ/ *adj.* (*Anat.*, *Physiol.*) Lungen-

**pulp** /pʌlp/ ❶ *n.* [A] (*of fruit*) Fruchtfleisch, *das;* [B] (*soft mass*) Brei, *der;* **beat sb. to a** ~: jmdn. zu Brei schlagen (*salopp*); [C] (*Anat., Zool.: fleshy or soft part*) Mark, *das;* [D] (*ore*) Trübe, *die.* ❷ *v.t.* zerdrücken, zerstampfen ‹Rübe›; einstampfen ‹Druckerzeugnis›

**pulpit** /'pʊlpɪt/ *n.* (*Eccl.*) Kanzel, *die*

**pulp:** ~ **magazine** *n.* Groschenheft, *das;* ~**wood** *n.* (*Papermaking etc.*) Industrieholz, *das*

**pulpy** /'pʌlpɪ/ *adj.* **A** (*soft and moist*) fleischig ‹Frucht›; **B** (*consisting of a soft mass*) breiig

**pulsar** /'pʌlsɑ:(r)/ *n.* (*Astron.*) Pulsar, *der*

**pulsate** /pʌl'seɪt, 'pʌlseɪt/ *v.i.* **A** (*beat, throb*) pulsieren; ‹Herz:› schlagen; (*fig. literary*) pulsieren; **B** (*fig.: vibrate*) schwingen; ‹Land:› pulsieren

**pulsation** /pʌl'seɪʃn/ *n.* **A** (*beating, throbbing*) Schlagen, *das;* (*of artery; also fig.*) Pulsieren, *das;* **B** (*fig.: vibration*) Schwingen, *das*

**pulse**[1] /pʌls/ **1** *n.* **A** (*lit. or fig.*) Puls, *der;* (*single beat*) Pulsschlag, *der;* **have/keep one's finger on the ~ of sth.** die Hand am Puls einer Sache (*Gen.*) haben/auf dem Laufenden über etw. (*Akk.*) bleiben; ⇒ *also* **feel** 1 A; **B** (*rhythmical recurrence*) Rhythmus, *der;* **C** (*single vibration*) Schwingung, *die;* (*Mus.*) Betonung, *die;* (*Electronics*) Impuls, *der.* **2** *v.i.* ⇒ **pulsate** A, B

**pulse**[2] *n.* **A** *no pl., constr. as sing. or pl.* (*seeds*) Hülsenfrüchte *Pl.;* **B** (*variety of edible seed*) Hülsenfrucht, *die*

'**pulse rate** *n.* Pulsfrequenz, *die;* **push up sb's ~:** jmds. Puls hochtreiben

**pulverize (pulverise)** /'pʌlvəraɪz/ *v.t.* **A** (*to powder or dust*) pulverisieren; **B** (*into spray*) zerstäuben; **C** (*fig.: crush*) aufreiben ‹Truppen›; abservieren (*Sport*) ‹Gegner›; **I'll ~ you!** ich schlag dich zu Brei! (*derb*)

**puma** /'pju:mə/ *n.* (*Zool.*) Puma, *der*

**pumice** /'pʌmɪs/ **1** *n.* (*Min.*) ~ **[stone]** Bimsstein, *der.* **2** *v.t.* bimsen; mit Bimsstein abreiben

**pummel** /'pʌml/ *v.t.*, (*Brit.*) **-ll-** einschlagen auf (+ *Akk.*)

**pump**[1] /pʌmp/ **1** *n.* (*machine; also fig.*) Pumpe, *die.* **2** *v.i.* pumpen. **3** *v.t.* **A** pumpen; ~ **sb. full of lead** jmdn. mit Blei voll pumpen (*salopp*); ~ **bullets into sth.** Kugeln in etw. (*Akk.*) jagen (*ugs.*); ~ **information into sb.** jmdn. mit Wissen voll stopfen (*ugs.*); **B** ~ **sth. dry** etw. leer pumpen *od.* auspumpen *od.* (*Seemannsspr.*) lenzen; ~ **sb. for information** Auskünfte aus jmdm. herausholen; **C** ~ **up** (*inflate*) aufpumpen ‹Reifen, Fahrrad›

**pump**[2] *n.* **A** (*shoe*) Turn-, Sportschuh, *der;* **[dancing] ~:** Tanzschuh, *der;* **B** (*Amer.: court shoe*) Pumps, *der*

'**pump-action** *adj.* ~ **shotgun** Pumpgun, *das;* ~ **spray** Pumpspray, *das od. der*

**pumpernickel** /'pʌmpənɪkl, 'pʊmpənɪkl/ *n.* Pumpernickel, *der*

**pumping station** /'pʌmpɪŋsteɪʃn/ *n.* Pumpwerk, *das*

**pumpkin** /'pʌmpkɪn/ *n.* (*Bot.*) Kürbis, *der; attrib.* Kürbis-

'**pump room** *n.* Pumpenhaus, *das;* (*in spa*) Brunnenhaus, *das*

**pun** /pʌn/ **1** *n.* Wortspiel, *das;* **the sentence is a ~ on the words 'bread' and 'bred'** in dem Satz wird mit den Worten „bread" und „bred" gespielt. **2** *v.i.*, **-nn-** ein Wortspiel/Wortspiele *Pl.* machen (**on** mit)

**punch**[1] **1** *v.t.* **A** (*strike with fist*) boxen; mit der Faust schlagen; **the boxer ~ed his opponent with his left fist** der Boxer traf seinen Gegner mit der Linken; **B** (*pierce, open up*) lochen; ~ **a hole** ein Loch stanzen; ~ **a hole/holes in sth.** etw. lochen; **C** (*prod*) stoßen; **D** (*Amer.: drive*) vorwärts treiben ‹Vieh›.
**2** *n.* **A** (*blow*) Faustschlag, *der;* **a ~ on the head/chin/chest** ein Faustschlag an den Kopf/an das Kinn/vor die Brust; **give sb. a ~ on the jaw/in the ribs** jmdm. einen Kinnhaken/Rippenstoß versetzen; **a ~ with the left fist** ein Schlag mit der linken Faust; **B** *no pl.* (*ability to deliver blow*) Punch, *der* (*Boxen*); Schlagkraft, *die;* **have a good/strong ~** ‹Boxer:› einen guten/harten Schlag haben; **C** (*coll.: vigour*) Pep, *der* (*ugs.*); **have [a] ~:** Pep haben; **put ~ into sth.** einer Sache (*Dat.*) Pep geben; **D** (*device for making holes*) (*in leather, tickets*) Lochzange, *die;* (*in paper*) Locher, *der;* (*in leather*) Locheisen, *das;* (*Printing*) Stempel, *der.* ⇒ *also* **pack** 2 G; **pull** 1 H

**punch**[2] *n.* (*drink*) Punsch, *der*

**Punch** /pʌntʃ/ *n.* Punch, *der;* Hanswurst, *der;* ~ **and Judy show** Kasperletheater, *das;* **be as proud/pleased as ~:** stolz wie ein Pfau *od.* Spanier sein/(*ugs.*) sich freuen wie ein Schneekönig

**punch:** ~**ball** *n.* (*Brit.*) (*ball*) Punchingball, *der;* (*bag*) Sandsack, *der;* ~**bowl** *n.* Bowlengefäß, *das;* Bowle, *die;* ~ **card** *n.* (*Computing*) Lochkarte, *die;* ~**-drunk** *adj.* **A** an einem Boxersyndrom leidend; **be ~-drunk** ein Boxersyndrom haben; punchdrunk sein (*Boxen*); **B** (*fig.*) benommen; **the troops were ~-drunk** die Truppen waren schwer angeschlagen

**punched** /pʌntʃt/**:** ~ **card/tape** ⇒ **punch card/tape**

**punching bag** /'pʌntʃɪŋ bæg/ (*Amer.*) ⇒ **punchball**

**punch:** ~ **line** *n.* Pointe, *die;* ~ **tape** *n.* (*Computing*) Lochstreifen, *der;* ~**-up** *n.* (*Brit. coll.*) (*fist fight, brawl*) Prügelei, *die*

**punchy** /'pʌntʃɪ/ *adj.* (*forceful*) ausdrucksstark ‹Sprache›; zündend ‹Rede›; schwungvoll ‹Handlung›

**punctilious** /pʌŋk'tɪlɪəs/ *adj.* [peinlich] korrekt; peinlich ‹Genauigkeit›

**punctiliously** /pʌŋk'tɪlɪəslɪ/ *adv.* [peinlich] korrekt ‹arbeiten›; peinlich ‹genau›

**punctual** /'pʌŋktʃʊəl/ *adj.* pünktlich

**punctuality** /pʌŋktʃʊ'ælɪtɪ/ *n., no pl.* Pünktlichkeit, *die*

**punctually** /'pʌŋktʃʊəlɪ/ *adv.* pünktlich

**punctuate** /'pʌŋktʃʊeɪt/ *v.t.* interpunktieren (*fachspr.*); mit Satzzeichen versehen; (*fig.: interrupt*) unterbrechen (**with** durch)

**punctuation** /pʌŋktʃʊ'eɪʃn/ *n., no pl.* Interpunktion, *die* (*fachspr.*); Zeichensetzung, *die*

**punctu'ation mark** *n.* Satzzeichen, *das*

**puncture** /'pʌŋktʃə(r)/ **1** *n.* **A** (*flat tyre*) Reifenpanne, *die;* Platte, *der* (*ugs.*); **B** (*hole*) Loch, *das;* (*in skin*) Einstich, *der;* ~ **[repair] kit** Flickzeug, *das;* Pannenset, *das;* ⇒ *also* **lumbar. 2** *v.t.* durchstechen; (*fig.*) verletzen ‹Würde›; kratzen an (+ *Dat.*) ‹Mythos›; lädieren ‹Ruf›; **be ~d** ‹Reifen:› ein Loch haben, platt sein; ‹Haut:› einen Einstich aufweisen. **3** *v.i.* ‹Reifen:› ein Loch bekommen, platt werden

**pundit** /'pʌndɪt/ *n.* **A** (*expert*) Experte, *der*/Expertin, *die;* (*iron.*) Augur, *der;* **B** (*learned Hindu*) Pandit, *der*

**punditry** /'pʌndɪtrɪ/ *n.* Expertentum, *das*

**pungency** /'pʌndʒənsɪ/ *n., no pl.* (*lit. or fig.*) [beißende od. ätzende] Schärfe

**pungent** /'pʌndʒənt/ *adj.* **A** beißend, ätzend ‹Rauch, Dämpfe›; scharf ‹Soße, Gewürz usw.›; stechend riechend ‹Gas›; **B** (*fig.: biting*) beißend; ätzend

**punish** /'pʌnɪʃ/ *v.t.* **A** bestrafen ‹Person, Tat›; strafen (*geh.*) ‹Person›; **he has been ~ed enough** (*fig.*) er ist gestraft genug; **B** (*Boxing coll.: inflict severe blows on*) schwer zusetzen (+ *Dat.*); **C** (*Sport coll.: take advantage of*) kein Pardon kennen bei ‹schwachen Würfen, Schlägen des Gegners›; **the bowlers were ~ed by the batsmen** die Werfer bekamen ihre Quittung von den Schlagmännern; **D** (*coll.: tax*) auf eine harte Probe stellen; **E** (*coll.: put under stress*) strapazieren ‹Nerven, Bauwerk›

**punishable** /'pʌnɪʃəbl/ *adj.* strafbar; **it is a ~ offence to ...:** es ist strafbar, ... zu ...; **be ~ by sth.** mit etw. bestraft werden

**punishing** /'pʌnɪʃɪŋ/ *adj.* **A** (*Boxing coll.*) mörderisch ‹Haken›; **B** (*Sport coll.*) tödlich (*Sportjargon*) ‹Schuss, Schlag, Volley›; **he is a ~ hitter** wenn der Gegner ihm eine Blöße bietet, schlägt er gnadenlos zu; **C** (*taxing*) mörderisch (*ugs.*) ‹Rennen, Zeitplan, Kurs›; aufreibend ‹Wahlkampf›

**punishment** /'pʌnɪʃmənt/ *n.* **A** *no pl.* (*punishing*) Bestrafung, *die;* **inflict ~ on sb.** jmdn. bestrafen; **undergo ~:** bestraft werden; eine Strafe erhalten; **deserve ~:** [eine] Strafe verdient haben; **crime and ~:** Verbrechen und Strafe; **B** (*penalty*) Strafe, *die;* **the ~ for cheating is disqualification** Betrug wird mit Disqualifikation bestraft; **make the ~ fit the crime** (*lit. or fig.*) Gleiches mit Gleichem vergelten; **as a ~ for sth.** zur Strafe für etw.; **C** (*coll.: rough treatment*) **take a lot of ~:** ganz schön getriezt *od.* gezwiebelt werden (*ugs.*). ⇒ *also* **take** 1 W

**punitive** /'pju:nɪtɪv/ *adj.* **A** (*penal*) Straf-; **B** (*severe*) [allzu] rigoros ‹finanzielle Maßnahmen, Besteuerung›; unzumutbar ‹Steuersatz›; **C** (*Law*) ~ **damages** verschärfter Schadenersatz

**Punjab** /pʌn'dʒɑ:b/ *pr. n.* **the ~:** das Pandschab

**punk** /pʌŋk/ **1** *n.* **A** (*Amer. sl.: worthless person*) Dreckskerl, der (*salopp*); **B** (*Amer. coll.: young ruffian*) Rabauke, *der* (*ugs.*); **C** (*admirer of ~ rock*) Punk, *der;* (*performer of ~ rock*) Punk[rock]er, *der*/-rockerin, *die;* **D** (*music*) ⇒ **punk rock. 2** *adj.* **A** (*coll.: worthless*) mies (*abwertend*); **B** (*of or playing ~ rock*) Punk-

**punk 'rock** *n.* Punkrock, *der*

**punnet** /'pʌnɪt/ *n.* (*Brit.*) Körbchen, *das*

**punt**[1] /pʌnt/ **1** *n.* Stechkahn, *der.* **2** *v.t.* **A** (*propel*) staken ‹Boot›; **B** (*convey*) in einem Stechkahn fahren ‹Person›. **3** *v.i.* staken

**punt**[2] (*Footb.*) **1** *v.t.* aus der Hand schießen; ‹Torwart:› abschlagen. **2** *n.* Schuss aus der Hand; (*by goalkeeper*) Abschlag, *der*

**punt**[3] *v.i.* (*Brit. coll.: bet*) wetten; (*speculate*) spekulieren

**punt**[4] /pʊnt/ *n.* (*Finance*) Irisches Pfund

**punter**[1] /'pʌntə(r)/ *n.* (*coll.*) **A** (*gambler*) Zocker, *der*/Zockerin, *die* (*salopp*); **B** (*client of prostitute*) Freier, *der* (*verhüll.*); **C** **the ~s** (*customers*) die Leutchen (*ugs.*)

**punter**[2] *n.* (*in punt*[1]) Stechkahnfahrer, *der*/-fahrerin, *die*

**puny** /'pju:nɪ/ *adj.* **A** (*undersized*) zu klein ‹Baby, Junge›; **B** (*feeble*) gering ‹Kraft›; schwach ‹Waffe, Person›; **C** (*petty*) belanglos, unerheblich ‹Leistung, Einwand›

**pup** /pʌp/ **1** *n.* **A** (*young dog or wolf*) Welpe, *der;* **be in ~** ‹Hündin:› trächtig sein; **B** (*young animal*) Junge, *das;* **C** (*objectionable young man*) Schnösel, *der* (*ugs. abwertend*). **2** *v.i.*, **-pp-** ‹Hündin:› werfen

**pupa** /'pju:pə/ *n., pl.* ~**e** /'pju:pi:/ (*Zool.*) Puppe, *die*

**pupal** /'pju:pl/ *adj.* (*Zool.*) Puppen-

**pupate** /pju:'peɪt/ *v.i.* (*Zool.*) sich verpuppen

**pupil** /'pju:pɪl/ *n.* **A** (*schoolchild, disciple*) Schüler, *der*/Schülerin, *die;* **B** (*Anat.*) Pupille, die

**puppet** /'pʌpɪt/ *n.* **A** Puppe, *die;* (*marionette*) Marionette, *die;* ⇒ *also* **glove puppet**; **B** (*person*) Marionette, *die; attrib.* Marionetten- ‹regime, -regierung›

**puppetry** /'pʌpɪtrɪ/ *n., no pl., no art.* (*making of puppets*) Puppenmachen, *das;* (*production of puppet shows*) Puppenspiel, *das*

'**puppet show** *n.* Puppenspiel, *das;* (*with marionettes*) Marionettenspiel, *das*

**puppy** /'pʌpɪ/ *n.* Hundejunge, *das;* Welpe, *der;* **the dog is still only a ~:** der Hund ist noch ganz jung

'**puppy dog** *n.* (*child lang.*) Hündchen, *das;* kleiner Hund

**puppy:** ~ **fat** *n., no pl.* (*Brit.*) Babyspeck, *der;* ~ **love** *n.* Jugendschwärmerei, *die*

**purblind** /'pɜ:blaɪnd/ *adj.* (*literary*) halb blind; (*fig.*) kurzsichtig

**purchasable** /'pɜ:tʃəsəbl/ *adj.* käuflich; (*available on the market*) [im Handel] erhältlich

**purchase** /'pɜ:tʃəs/ **1** *n.* **A** (*buying*) Kauf, *der;* **make several ~s/a ~:** Verschiedenes/etwas kaufen; **B** (*thing bought*) Kauf, *der;* **carry one's ~s home** seine Einkäufe nach Hause tragen *od.* bringen; **C** *no pl.* (*hold*) Halt, *der;* (*leverage*) Hebelwirkung, *die;* Hebelkraft, *die;* **get a ~:** guten *od.* festen Halt finden. **2** *v.t.* **A** kaufen; erwerben (*geh.*); **purchasing power** Kaufkraft, *die;* **B** (*acquire*) erkaufen

P

**'purchase price** *n.* Kaufpreis, *der*

**purchaser** /'pɜ:tʃəsə(r)/ *n.* Käufer, *der*/Käuferin, *die*

**'purchase tax** *n.* (*Brit. Hist.*) ≈ Verbrauchssteuer, *die*

**'purchasing power** *n.* Kaufkraft, *die*

**purdah** /'pɜ:də/ *n.* (*seclusion of women*) Absonderung der Frauen; **they were kept in ~:** sie durften nicht in Erscheinung treten; (*fig.*) sie wurden kaltgestellt (*ugs.*)

**pure** /pjʊə(r)/ ❶ *adj.* Ⓐ (*unmixed*) rein; rein, pur ‹Gold, Silber›; (*not discordant*) rein ‹Ton, Note›; Ⓑ (*of unmixed descent*) reinblütig ‹Mensch›; rein ‹Blut›; Ⓒ (*mere*) pur; rein; **it is madness ~ and simple** es ist schlicht *od.* ganz einfach Wahnsinn; Ⓓ (*Phonet.*) einfach ‹Vokal›; Ⓔ (*not corrupt*) rein; **blessed are the ~ in heart** (*Bibl.*) selig sind, die reinen Herzens sind; Ⓕ (*chaste*) rein. ⇒ *also* **mathematics** A; **science** A.
❷ *adv.* **a ~ blue sky** ein klarer blauer Himmel

**pure: ~-blooded** *adj.* reinblütig; **~-bred** *adj.* reinrassig

**purée** /'pjʊəreɪ/ ❶ *n.* Püree, *das;* **tomato ~:** Tomatenmark, *das.* ❷ *v.t.* pürieren

**purely** /'pjʊəlɪ/ *adv.* Ⓐ (*solely*) rein; Ⓑ (*merely*) lediglich

**pureness** /'pjʊənɪs/ ⇒ **purity**

**purgative** /'pɜ:gətɪv/ ❶ *adj.* Ⓐ (*laxative*) [stark] abführend; Abführ(mittel, -tablette); purgativ (*fachspr.*); Ⓑ (*purifying*) läuternd (*geh.*). ❷ *n.* (*medicine*) [starkes] Abführmittel; Purgativum, *das* (*fachspr.*)

**purgatory** /'pɜ:gətərɪ/ *n.* (*Relig.*) Fegefeuer, *das;* Purgatorium, das (*fachspr.*); **undergo ~:** durchs Fegefeuer gehen; **it was ~** (*fig.*) es war eine Strafe *od.* die Hölle

**purge** /pɜ:dʒ/ ❶ *v.t.* Ⓐ (*cleanse*) reinigen (**of** von); **~ me from my sin** (*Relig.*) reinige mich von meiner Sünde; Ⓑ (*remove*) entfernen; **~ away** *or* **out** beseitigen; Ⓒ (*rid*) säubern ‹Partei› (**of** von); (*remove*) entfernen ‹Person›; Ⓓ (*Med.*) abführen lassen ‹Patienten›; **use sth. to ~ the bowels** etw. zum Abführen verwenden; Ⓔ (*Law: atone for*) sühnen [für]. ❷ *n.* Ⓐ (*clearance*) Säuberung[saktion], *die;* (*Polit.*) Säuberung, *die;* **a ~ of writers** eine gegen Schriftsteller gerichtete Säuberung[saktion]; Ⓑ (*Med.*) [starkes] Abführmittel

**purification** /pjʊərɪfɪ'keɪʃn/ *n.* Ⓐ Reinigung, *die;* Ⓑ (*spiritual cleansing*) Läuterung, *die;* Ⓒ (*ceremonial cleansing*) Reinigung, *die;* **the P~ [of Our Lady** *or* **the Virgin Mary]** (*Relig.*) Mariä Reinigung; (*feast*) [Mariä] Lichtmess; Mariä Reinigung

**purifier** /'pjʊərɪfaɪə(r)/ *n.* Reiniger, *der;* Reinigungsmittel, *das;* (*machine*) Reinigungsapparat, *der;* Reinigungsanlage, *die*

**purify** /'pjʊərɪfaɪ/ *v.t.* Ⓐ (*make pure or clear*) reinigen; Ⓑ (*spiritually*) reinigen; läutern; Ⓒ (*ceremonially*) reinigen

**purism** /'pjʊərɪzm/ *n., no pl.* Purismus, *der*

**purist** /'pjʊərɪst/ *n.* Purist, *der*/Puristin, *die*

**puritan** /'pjʊərɪtn/ ❶ *n.* Ⓐ Puritaner, *der*/Puritanerin, *die;* Ⓑ **P~** (*Hist.*) Puritaner, *der*/Puritanerin, *die.* ❷ *adj.* Ⓐ puritanisch; Ⓑ **P~** (*Hist.*) puritanisch

**puritanic** /pjʊərɪ'tænɪk/, **puritanical** /pjʊərɪ'tænɪkl/ *adj.* puritanisch; moralinsauer (*abwertend*)

**puritanism** /'pjʊərɪtənɪzm/ *n., no pl.* Ⓐ Puritanismus, *der;* puritanische Einstellung; Ⓑ **P~** (*Hist.*) Puritanismus, *der*

**purity** /'pjʊərɪtɪ/ *n., no pl.* Ⓐ Reinheit, *die;* Ⓑ (*chastity*) Keuschheit, *die*

**purl** /pɜ:l/ ❶ *n.* linke Masche. ❷ *v.t.* links stricken; **~ three stitches** drei linke Maschen stricken

**purler** /'pɜ:lə(r)/ *n.* (*Brit. coll.*); **come** *or* **take a ~:** längelang hinknallen (*ugs.*)

**purlieus** /'pɜ:lju:z/ *n. pl.* Außenbezirke *Pl.;* Weichbild, *das;* **within the ~ of A** innerhalb des Stadtgebietes *od.* Weichbildes von A

**purlin** /'pɜ:lɪn/ *n.* (*Building*) Pfette, *die*

**purloin** /pə'lɔɪn/ *v.t.* (*literary*) entwenden (*geh.*)

**purple** /'pɜ:pl/ ❶ *adj.* lila; violett; (*crimson*) purpurn; (*fig.*) überfrachtet, überladen ‹Prosa›; **his face went ~ with rage** vor Zorn bekam er ein hochrotes Gesicht. ❷ *n.* Ⓐ Lila, *das;* Violett, *das;* (*crimson*) Purpur, *das;* Ⓑ (*dress of cardinal*) Purpur, *der;* **the ~** (*fig.*) das Kardinalskollegium. ❸ *v.i.* ‹Gesicht:› dunkelrot anlaufen

**purple: ~ 'heart** *n.* (*Brit.*) Purple Heart, *das* (*Drogenjargon*); **P~ 'Heart** *n.* (*Amer. Mil.*) *US-amerikanisches Verwundetenabzeichen;* **~ passage, ~ patch** *ns.* [über]reich ausgeschmückte Passage

**purplish** /'pɜ:plɪʃ/ *adj.* ins Violette spielend; **be ~:** ins Violette spielen

**purport** ❶ /pə'pɔ:t/ *v.t.* Ⓐ **~ to do sth.** (*profess*) [von sich] behaupten, etw. zu tun; (*be intended to seem*) den Anschein erwecken sollen, etw. zu tun; **the ~ed intention/object** die angebliche Absicht/der angebliche Zweck; **a letter ~ing to be written by the president** ein angeblich vom Präsidenten geschriebener Brief; **the document ~s to be official** die Urkunde soll angeblich amtlich sein; **the law ~s to protect morality** das Gesetz soll angeblich die Moral schützen; Ⓑ (*convey*) beinhalten; **~ that ...:** besagen, dass ... . ❷ /'pɜ:pɔ:t/ *n.* Inhalt, *der*

**purportedly** /pə'pɔ:tɪdlɪ/ *adv.* angeblich

**purpose** /'pɜ:pəs/ ❶ *n.* Ⓐ (*object*) Zweck, *der;* (*intention*) Absicht, *die;* **what is the ~ of doing that?** was hat es für einen Zweck, das zu tun?; **he never did anything without a ~:** er tat nie etwas ohne eine bestimmte Absicht; **you must have had some ~ in mind** du musst irgendetwas damit bezweckt haben; **wander around with no particular ~:** ziellos *od.* ohne Ziel umherwandern; **answer** *or* **suit sb.'s ~:** jmds. Zwecken dienen *od.* entsprechen; **for a ~:** zu einem bestimmten Zweck; **I did it for a ~:** ich habe damit einen bestimmten Zweck verfolgt; **for the ~ of discussing sth.** um etw. zu besprechen; **on ~:** mit Absicht; absichtlich; **for ~s of** zum Zwecke (+ *Gen.*); ⇒ *also* **cross purposes; serve** 1 C; Ⓑ (*effect*) **to no ~:** ohne Erfolg; **to some/little/good ~:** mit einigem/wenig/gutem Erfolg; Ⓒ (*determination*) Entschlossenheit, *die;* **have a ~ in life** in seinem Leben einen Sinn sehen; **give sb. a ~ in life** jmds. Leben (*Dat.*) einen Sinn geben; Ⓓ (*intention to act*) Absicht, *die.*
❷ *v.t.* beabsichtigen

**'purpose-built** *adj.* [eigens] zu diesem Zweck errichtet ‹Gebäude›; [eigens] zu diesem Zweck hergestellt, speziell angefertigt ‹Gerät, Bauteil›

**purposeful** /'pɜ:pəsfl/ *adj.* Ⓐ zielstrebig; (*with specific aim*) entschlossen; Ⓑ (*with intention*) absichtsvoll

**purposefully** /'pɜ:pəsfəlɪ/ *adv.* Ⓐ entschlossen; Ⓑ (*intentionally*) absichtsvoll

**purposeless** /'pɜ:pəslɪs/ *adj.* sinnlos

**purposely** /'pɜ:pəslɪ/ *adv.* absichtlich; mit Absicht

**'purpose-made** *adj.* spezialgefertigt; eigens angelegt ‹Straße›

**purposive** /'pɜ:pəsɪv/ *adj.* ⇒ **purposeful** A

**purr** /pɜ:(r)/ ❶ *v.i.* schnurren; (*fig.: be in satisfied mood*) strahlen. ❷ *v.t.* durch Schnurren zum Ausdruck bringen; (*fig.*) säuseln; **the cat ~ed her contentment** die Katze schnurrte zufrieden. ❸ *n.* Schnurren, *das*

**purse** /pɜ:s/ ❶ *n.* Ⓐ (*lit. or fig.*) Portemonnaie, *das;* Geldbeutel, *der* (*bes. südd.*); **the public ~:** die Staatskasse; **light ~** (*fig.*) kleiner Geldbeutel (*fig.*); ⇒ *also* **silk** 2; Ⓑ (*prize*) Geldpreis *der;* Börse, *die* (*Boxen*); Ⓒ (*Amer.: handbag*) Handtasche, *die.* ❷ *v.t.* kräuseln, schürzen ‹Lippen›

**purser** /'pɜ:sə(r)/ *n.* ▶ 1261 Zahlmeister, *der*/-meisterin, *die*

**'purse strings** *n. pl.* Schnüre *od.* Bänder [zum Verschließen des Geldbeutels]; **hold the ~** (*fig.*) über das Geld bestimmen; **tighten/loosen the ~** (*fig.*) sparen/mehr ausgeben

**pursuance** /pə'sju:əns/ *n., no pl.* **in ~ of [one's] duties/instructions** pflichtgemäß/auftragsgemäß; **in [the] ~ of his ends** bei der Verfolgung seiner Ziele; **in ~ of the act/decree** gemäß dem Gesetz/der Verfügung

**pursuant** /pə'sju:ənt/ *adv.* **~ to sth.** gemäß einer Sache

**pursue** /pə'sju:/ *v.t.* Ⓐ (*literary: chase, lit. or fig.*) verfolgen; **bad luck ~d him** er war vom Pech verfolgt; Ⓑ (*seek after*) streben nach; suchen nach; verfolgen ‹Ziel›; Ⓒ (*look into*) nachgehen (+ *Dat.*); Ⓓ (*engage in*) betreiben; **~ a career as an accountant** als Buchhalter tätig sein; **~ one's studies** seinem Studium nachgehen; Ⓔ (*carry out*) durchführen ‹Plan›

**pursuer** /pə'sju:ə(r)/ *n.* Verfolger, *der*/Verfolgerin, *die*

**pursuit** /pə'sju:t, pə'su:t/ *n.* Ⓐ (*pursuing*) (*of person, animal, aim*) Verfolgung, *die;* (*of knowledge, truth, etc.*) Streben, *das* (**of** nach); (*of pleasure*); Jagd, *die* (**of** nach); **the ~ of his studies** die Beschäftigung mit seinen Studien; **in ~ of** auf der Jagd nach ‹Wild, Dieb usw.›; in Ausführung (+ *Gen.*) ‹Beschäftigung, Tätigkeit, Hobby›; **with the police in [full] ~** mit der Polizei [dicht] auf den Fersen; ⇒ *also* **hot** 1 J; Ⓑ (*pastime*) Beschäftigung, *die;* Betätigung, *die*

**pursuit: ~ plane** (*Amer.*) ⇒ **fighter** B; **~ race** *n.* (*Cycling*) Verfolgungsrennen, *das*

**purulent** /'pjʊərʊlənt/ *adj.* (*Med.*) (*consisting of pus, full of pus*) eitrig; (*discharging pus*) eiternd; **be ~:** eitern

**purvey** /pə'veɪ/ *v.t.* (*lit. or fig.*) liefern

**purveyor** /pə'veɪə(r)/ *n.* Lieferant, *der*/Lieferantin, *die;* **a ~ of [wild] rumours** ein Kolporteur [wilder Gerüchte]

**purview** /'pɜ:vju:/ *n.* (*of act, document*) Geltungsbereich, *der;* (*of scheme, book, occupation*) Rahmen, *der;* **fall within sb.'s ~:** in jmds. Aufgaben- *od.* Zuständigkeitsbereich fallen

**pus** /pʌs/ *n., no indef. art.* (*Med.*) Eiter, *der*

**push** /pʊʃ/ ❶ *v.t.* Ⓐ schieben; (*make fall*) stoßen; schubsen (*ugs.*); **don't ~ me like that!** schieb *od.* drängel [doch] nicht so!; **~ a car** (*to start the engine*) ein Auto anschieben; **~ the door to/open** die Tür zu-/aufstoßen; **she ~ed the door instead of pulling** sie drückte gegen die Tür, statt zu ziehen; **did he/you** *etc.* **fall** *or* **jump or was he/were you** *etc.* **~ed?** (*fig.*) freiwillig oder unfreiwillig?; **~ sb. about in a wheelchair** jmdn. im Rollstuhl herumfahren; **~ one's hair back** sich (*Dat.*) das Haar zurückstreichen; **the policemen ~ed the crowd back** die Polizisten drängten die Menge zurück; **~ sth. between sth.** etw. zwischen etw. (*Akk.*) schieben; (*to pass right through*) etw. zwischen etw. (*Dat.*) hindurchschieben; **~ sth. under the bottom of the door** etw. unter der Tür [hin]durchschieben; **~ sth. up the hill** etw. den Berg hinaufschieben; **~ one's way through/into/on to** *etc.* **sth.** sich (*Dat.*) einen Weg durch/in/auf *usw.* etw. (*Akk.*) bahnen; Ⓑ (*fig.: impel*) drängen; **~ sb. into doing sth.** jmdn. dahin bringen, dass er etw. tut; Ⓒ (*tax*) **~ sb. [hard]** jmdn. [stark] fordern; **~ sb. too hard/too far** jmdn. überfordern; **he ~es himself very hard** er verlangt sich (*Dat.*) sehr viel ab; **be ~ed for sth.** (*coll.: find it difficult to provide sth.*) mit etw. knapp sein; **be ~ed for money** *or* **cash** knapp bei Kasse sein (*ugs.*); **be ~ed to do sth.** (*coll.*) Mühe haben, etw. zu tun; **~ one's luck** (*coll.*) übermütig werden; **~ one's luck with sth.** sich mit etw. auf ein gefährliches Spiel einlassen; Ⓓ (*press for sale of*) die Werbetrommel rühren für; pushen (*Werbejargon*); Ⓔ (*sell illegally, esp. drugs*) dealen; pushen (*Drogenjargon*); Ⓕ (*advance*) **~ sth. a step/stage further** etw. einen Schritt vorantreiben; **not ~ the point** die Sache auf sich beruhen lassen; **~ sth. too far** mit etw. zu weit gehen; es mit etw. zu weit treiben; **~ things to extremes** die Dinge *od.* es zum Äußersten *od.* auf die Spitze treiben; **~ one's claims** auf seine Ansprüche pochen.
❷ *v.i.* Ⓐ schieben; (*in queue*) drängeln; (*at door*) drücken; **'Push'** (*on door etc.*) „Drücken"; **~ and shove** schubsen und drängeln;

**~ at sth.** gegen etw. drücken; Ⓑ (*make demands*) **~ for sth.** etw. fordern; Ⓒ (*make one's way*) **he ~ed between us** er drängte sich zwischen uns; **~ through the crowd** sich durch die Menge drängeln; **~ past** *or* **by sb.** sich an jmdm. vorbeidrängeln *od.* -drücken; **~ by** (*not stop*) weiterrennen (*ugs.*); Ⓓ (*assert oneself for one's advancement*) sich in den Vordergrund spielen. ❸ *n.* Ⓐ Stoß, *der;* Schubs, *der* (*ugs.*); **give sth. a ~:** etw. schieben *od.* stoßen; **give sb. a ~:** jmdm. einen Schubs geben (*ugs.*); jmdm. einen Stoß versetzen; **My car won't start; can you give me a ~?** Mein Auto springt nicht an. Kannst du mich anschieben?; **give sth. a gentle ~:** etw. leicht anstoßen; **we gave a great ~:** wir haben gewaltig gedrückt; Ⓑ (*effort*) Anstrengungen *Pl.;* (*Mil.: attack*) Vorstoß, *der;* Offensive, *die;* **a ~ forward** (*Mil.*) ein Vorstoß; **make a ~:** sich ins Zeug legen (*ugs.*); (*Mil.*) einen Vorstoß unternehmen; eine Offensive durchführen; Ⓒ (*determination*) Tatkraft, *die;* Initiative, *die;* Ⓓ (*crisis*) **when it comes/came to the ~,** (*Amer. coll.*) **when ~ comes/came to shove** wenn es ernst wird/als es ernst wurde; **at a ~:** wenn es sein muss; Ⓔ (*Brit. coll.: dismissal*) **get the ~:** rausfliegen (*ugs.*); **give sb. the ~:** jmdn. rausschmeißen (*ugs.*); Ⓕ (*influence*) Förderung, *die;* Protektion, *die;* Ⓖ ⇒ **~-button**

**~ a'bout** *v.t.* herumschieben; (*bully*) herumkommandieren

**~ a'head** *v.i.* ‹Armee:› [weiter] vorstoßen *od.* -rücken; (*with [regard to] plans etc.*) weitermachen; **~ ahead with sth.** etw. vorantreiben

**~ a'long** ❶ *v.t.* [vor sich (*Dat.*) her]schieben. ❷ *v.i.* (*coll.*) sich [wieder] auf den Weg machen

**~ a'round** ⇒ **~ about**

**~ a'side** *v.t.* (*lit. or fig.*) beiseite schieben

**~ a'way** *v.t.* wegschieben

**~ 'forward** ❶ *v.i.* ⇒ **~ ahead.** ❷ *v.t.* vorschieben; (*Mil.*) vorstoßen; **~ oneself forward** sich in den Vordergrund schieben

**~ 'in** ❶ /-'-/ *v.t.* eindrücken; (*make fall into the water*) hineinstoßen *od* (*ugs.*) -schubsen. ❷ /'--/ *v.i.* sich hineindrängen

**~ 'off** ❶ *v.i.* Ⓐ (*Boating*) abstoßen; Ⓑ (*coll.: leave*) abhauen (*salopp*); abschieben (*salopp*). ❷ *v.t.* Ⓐ abdrücken ‹Deckel, Verschluss usw.›; Ⓑ (*Boating*) abstoßen

**~ 'on** ❶ ⇒ **~ ahead.** ❷ *v.t.* draufdrücken ‹Deckel, Verschluss usw.›

**~ 'out** ❶ *v.t.* hinausschieben; ‹Pflanzen:› [aus]treiben ‹Wurzeln›; ⇒ *also* **boat** 1 A. ❷ *v.i.* hinausragen

**~ 'out of** *v.t.* (*force to leave*) hinausdrängen aus

**~ 'over** *v.t.* (*make fall*) umstoßen; ⇒ *also* **pushover**

**~ 'through** *v.t.* (*fig.*) durchpeitschen (*ugs.*) ‹Gesetzesvorlage›; durchdrücken (*ugs.*) ‹Vorschlag›; **we ~ed it through successfully** wir haben es durchgekriegt (*ugs.*)

**~ 'up** *v.t.* hochschieben; (*fig.*) hochtreiben; ⇒ *also* **daisy; push-up**

**push: ~-ball** *n.* (*game, ball*) Pushball, *der;* **~bike** *n.* (*Brit. coll.*) Fahrrad, *das;* **~-button** ❶ *adj.* Drucktasten‹telefon, -radio›; **~-button warfare** Krieg per Knopfdruck; automatisierte Kriegführung; ❷ *n.* [Druck]knopf, *der;* Drucktaste, *die;* **~cart** *n.* Ⓐ ⇒ **handcart;** Ⓑ (*Amer.: trolley*) Einkaufswagen, *der;* **~chair** *n.* (*Brit.*) Sportwagen, *der*

**pusher** /'pʊʃə(r)/ *n.* Ⓐ (*seller of drugs*) Dealer, *der* (*Drogenjargon*); Pusher, *der* (*Drogenjargon*); Ⓑ (*pushy person*) Streber, *der*/Streberin, *die* (*abwertend*); Ehrgeizling, *der* (*ugs. abwertend*)

**pushing** /'pʊʃɪŋ/ *adj.* Ⓐ [übermäßig] ehrgeizig; Ⓑ (*coll.*) **be ~ sixty** auf die Sechzig zugehen

**push: ~over** *n.* (*coll.*) Kinderspiel, *das;* **he'll be a ~ for her** sie steckt ihn [glatt] in die Tasche (*ugs.*); **the match should be a ~over for Leeds** das Spiel dürfte für Leeds ein Spaziergang werden (*Sportjargon*); **~-start** ❶ *n.* Schubstart, *der;* **give sb. a ~-start** jmdn. *od.* jmds. Auto anschieben; ❷ *v.t.* anschieben

**'push-up** (*Amer.*) ⇒ **press-up**

**pushy** /'pʊʃɪ/ *adj.* (*coll.*) [übermäßig] ehrgeizig ‹Person›

**pusillanimity** /pju:sɪlə'nɪmɪtɪ/ *n., no pl.* Ängstlichkeit, *die;* Zaghaftigkeit, *die;* (*lack of courage*) Feigheit, *die*

**pusillanimous** /pju:sɪ'lænɪməs/ *adj.*, **pusillanimously** /pju:sɪ'lænɪməslɪ/ *adv.* ängstlich; zaghaft; (*without courage*) feige

**puss** /pʊs/ *n.* (*coll.*) Mieze, *die* (*fam.*); **~, ~, ~!** Miez, Miez, Miez!; **P~ in Boots** der Gestiefelte Kater

**pussy** /'pʊsɪ/ *n.* Ⓐ (*child lang.: cat*) Miezekatze, *die* (*fam.*); Muschi, *die* (*Kinderspr.*); Ⓑ (*coarse*) (*vulva*) Kätzchen, *das* (*salopp*); Muschi, *die* (*vulg.*); (*sexual intercourse*) Sex, *der*

**pussy: ~ cat** ⇒ **pussy** A; **~foot** *v.i.* [herum]schleichen; (*act cautiously*) überängstlich sein; **stop ~footing!** hör auf, wie die Katze um den heißen Brei zu schleichen!; **~ willow** *n.* Salweide, *die;* Palmweide, *die*

**pustule** /'pʌstju:l/ *n.* (*Med.*) (*pimple*) Pustel, *die*

**put**[1] /pʊt/ ❶ *v.t.*, **-tt-, put** Ⓐ (*place*) tun; (*vertically*) stellen; (*horizontally*) legen; (*through or into narrow opening*) stecken; **~ plates on the table** Teller auf den Tisch stellen; **~ books on the shelf/on top of the pile** Bücher ins Regal stellen/auf den Stapel legen; **~ clean sheets on the bed** das Bett frisch beziehen; **don't ~ your elbows on the table** lass deine Ellbogen vom Tisch; **I ~ my hand on his shoulder** ich legte meine Hand auf seine Schulter; **~ a stamp on the letter** eine Briefmarke auf den Brief kleben; **~ salt on one's food** Salz auf sein Essen tun *od.* streuen; **~ some more coal on the fire** Kohle nachlegen; **~ antiseptic on one's finger** sich (*Dat.*) Antiseptikum auf den Finger tun; **~ the letter in an envelope/the letter box** den Brief in einen Umschlag/in den Briefkasten stecken; **~ sth. in one's pocket** etw. in die Tasche stecken; etw. einstecken; **~ the shopping in the car** die Einkäufe ins Auto tun *od.* legen; **~ one's hands in one's pockets** die Hände in die Taschen stecken; **~ sugar in one's tea** sich (*Dat.*) Zucker in den Tee tun; **~ petrol in the tank** Benzin in den Tank tun *od.* füllen; **~ the car in[to] the garage** das Auto in die Garage stellen; **~ rubbish in the waste-paper basket** Abfall in den Papierkorb tun *od.* werfen; **~ the cork in the bottle** den Korken in die Flasche stecken; **~ the plug in the socket** den Stecker in die Steckdose stecken; **~ paper in the typewriter** Papier in die Schreibmaschine tun *od.* einspannen; **~ tobacco in the pipe** Tabak in die Pfeife tun; die Pfeife stopfen; **~ a new pane of glass in the window** eine neue Glasscheibe in das Fenster [ein]setzen; **~ a new engine in the car** einen neuen Motor in das Auto einbauen; **~ the letters in the file** die Briefe in den Ordner tun *od.* [ein]heften; **~ documents in the safe** Urkunden in den Safe tun *od.* legen; **~ fish into a pond** Fische in einen Teich setzen; **~ the cat into a basket** die Katze in einen Korb setzen *od.* stecken; **~ the ball into the net/over the bar** den Ball ins Netz befördern *od.* setzen/über die Latte befördern; **~ one's arm round sb.'s waist** den Arm um jmds. Taille legen; **~ a bandage round one's wrist** sich (*Dat.*) einen Verband ums Handgelenk legen; **~ one's hands over one's eyes** sich (*Dat.*) die Hände auf die Augen legen; **~ one's finger to one's lips** den *od.* seinen Finger auf die Lippen legen; **~ one's foot through the rotten floorboards/on a chair** den Fuß durch die morschen Dielen stecken/auf einen Stuhl setzen; **~ the letter at the bottom of the pile** den Brief unter den Stapel legen; **~ the boxes one on top of the other** die Kisten übereinander stellen; **~ the jacket on its hanger** die Jacke auf den Bügel tun *od.* hängen; **where shall I ~ it?** wohin soll ich es tun (*ugs.*)/stellen/legen *usw.?;* wo soll ich es hintun (*ugs.*)/-stellen/-legen *usw.?;* **~ sb. into a taxi** jmdn. in ein Taxi setzen; **~ a child on a swing** ein Kind auf eine Schaukel setzen; **we ~ our guest in Peter's room** wir haben unseren Gast in Peters Zimmer (*Dat.*) untergebracht; **~ the baby in the pram** das Baby in den Kinderwagen legen *od.* (*ugs.*) stecken; **not know where to ~ oneself** (*fig.*) sehr verlegen sein/werden; **~ it there!** (*coll.*) lass mich deine Hand schütteln!; Ⓑ (*cause to enter*) stoßen; **~ a knife into sb.** jmdm. ein Messer in den Leib stoßen; **~ a satellite into orbit** einen Satelliten in eine Umlaufbahn bringen; **~ a bullet** *etc.* **through sb./sth.** (*coll.*) jmdm. eine Kugel verpassen/etw. zerballern (*ugs.*); Ⓒ (*bring into specified state*) setzen; **~ through Parliament** im Parlament durchbringen ‹Gesetzentwurf usw.›; **~ one's proposals through the committee** seine Vorschläge im Ausschuss durchbringen; **~ sb. in a difficult** *etc.* **position** jmdn. in eine schwierige *usw.* Lage bringen; **be ~ in a difficult** *etc.* **position** in eine schwierige *usw.* Lage geraten; **be ~ in a position of trust** eine Vertrauensstellung erhalten; **~ sb. in[to] a job** jmdm. eine Arbeit[sstellung] *od.* (*ugs.*) einen Job geben; **be ~ into power** an die Macht kommen; **~ sb. on the committee** jmdn. in den Ausschuss schicken; **~ sth. above** *or* **before sth.** (*fig.*) einer Sache (*Dat.*) den Vorrang vor etw. (*Dat.*) geben; **~ sth. out of order** etw. kaputtmachen (*ugs.*); etw. funktionsuntüchtig machen; **be ~ out of order** kaputtgehen (*ugs.*); defekt werden; **~ sb. on to sth.** (*fig.*) jmdn. auf etw. (*Akk.*) hinweisen *od.* aufmerksam machen; jmdm. etw. zeigen; **~ sb. on to a job** (*assign*) jmdm. eine Arbeit zuweisen; Ⓓ (*impose*) **~ a limit/an interpretation on sth.** etw. begrenzen *od.* beschränken/interpretieren; ⇒ *also* **end** 1 A; **stop** 3 A; **veto** 1 B; Ⓔ (*submit*) unterbreiten (**to** *Dat.*) ‹Vorschlag, Plan usw.›; **~ the situation to sb.** jmdm. die Situation darstellen; **~ sth. to the vote** über etw. (*Akk.*) abstimmen lassen; etw. zur Abstimmung bringen (*Papierdt.*); **I ~ it to you that you never saw him** ich behaupte *od.* sage, dass Sie ihn nie gesehen haben; Ⓕ (*cause to go or do*) **~ sb. to work** jmdn. arbeiten lassen; **~ sb. on the job** jmdn. damit *od.* mit der Arbeit beauftragen; **~ sb. out of contention for sth.** jmdn. aus dem Rennen um etw. werfen; jmdm. sämtliche Chancen auf etw. nehmen; **be ~ out of the game by an injury** wegen einer Verletzung nicht mehr spielen können; **~ sb. out of the championship** jmdm. den Titel abnehmen; **they were ~ out of the cup by Liverpool** sie scheiterten an Liverpool und mussten aus dem Cupwettbewerb ausscheiden; **~ the troops on full alert** die Streitkräfte in volle Alarm- *od.* Gefechtsbereitschaft versetzen; **~ sb. on antibiotics** jmdn. auf Antibiotika setzen; **~ sb. on the stage** jmdn. zur Bühne schicken; ⇒ *also* **pace**[1] 1 C; Ⓖ (*impose*) **~ taxes** *etc.* **upon sth.** etw. mit Steuern *usw.* belegen; Steuern *usw.* für etw. erheben; Ⓗ (*express*) ausdrücken; **let's ~ it like this: ...:** sagen wir so: ...; **that's one way of ~ting it** (*also iron.*) so kann man es [natürlich] auch ausdrücken; **I don't quite know how to ~ this, but ...:** ich weiß nicht recht, wie ich es sagen soll, aber ...; Ⓘ (*render*) **~ sth. into English** *etc.* etw. ins Englische übertragen *od.* übersetzen; **~ sth. into words** etw. in Worte fassen; **~ sth. into one's own words** etw. mit seinen eigenen Worten sagen; Ⓙ (*write*) schreiben; **~ one's name on the list** seinen Namen auf die Liste setzen; **~ a tick in the box** ein Häkchen in das Kästchen machen; **~ a cross against sth.** etw. ankreuzen; **~ one's signature to sth.** seine Unterschrift unter etw. setzen; **~ a black mark against a name** einen Namen schwarz markieren *od.* anstreichen; **~ sth. on the bill** etw. auf die Rechnung setzen; **~ sth. on the list** (*fig.*) sich (*Dat.*) etw. [fest] vornehmen; etw. vormerken; Ⓚ (*imagine*) **~ oneself in sb.'s place** *or* **situation** sich in jmdn. *od.* in jmds. Lage versetzen; Ⓛ (*substitute*) setzen; Ⓜ (*invest*) **~ money** *etc.* **into sth.** Geld *usw.* in etw. (*Akk.*) stecken; **~ work/time/effort into**

p

**sth.** Arbeit/Zeit/Energie in etw. (*Akk.*) stecken *od.* auf etw. (*Akk.*) verwenden; **N** (*stake*) setzen (**on** auf + *Akk.*); **~ money on a horse/on sth. happening** auf ein Pferd setzen/darauf wetten, dass etw. passiert; **O** (*estimate*) **~ sb./sth. at** jmdn./etw. schätzen auf (+ *Akk.*); **to ~ it no higher** um das Wenigste zu sagen; ⇒ *also* **past** 3 B; **P** (*subject*) **~ sb. to** jmdm. ‹Unkosten, Mühe, Umstände› verursachen *od.* machen; ⇒ *also* **shame** 1 B; **test** 1 A; **Q** (*drive*) **~ sb. to sth.** jmdn. zu etw. treiben *od.* zwingen; ⇒ *also* **flight²** A; **hard** 2 D; **rout¹** 1 A; **R** (*harness*) **~ to sth.** vor etw. (*Akk.*) spannen; **S** (*Athletics: throw*) stoßen ‹Kugel›; **~ the shot** kugelstoßen.

❷ *v.i.*, **-tt-**, **~** (*Naut.*) **~ [out] to sea** in See stechen; auslaufen; **~ into port** [in den Hafen] einlaufen; **~ across/over to** übersetzen nach; **~ out from England** von England aus in See stechen; England verlassen; **~ off** ablegen; **they had to ~ in at Valetta** sie mussten Valetta anlaufen.

❸ *n.* (*Sport*) Stoß, *der*

**~ a'bout** ❶ *v.t.* **A** (*circulate*) verbreiten; in Umlauf bringen; **it was ~ about that ...:** man munkelte (*ugs.*) *od.* es hieß, dass ...; **B** (*Naut.*) **~ the ship** *etc.* **about** den Kurs [des Schiffes *usw.*] ändern; (*cause to change tack*) [das Schiff *usw.*] wenden; **C** (*cause to turn about*) wenden ‹Pferd usw.›; **D** (*Scot., N. Engl.*) (*disconcert*) beunruhigen; (*upset*) verärgern; **don't ~ yourself about** (*inconvenience*) mach keine Umstände. ❷ *v.i.* (*Naut.*) den Kurs ändern

**~ a'cross** *v.t.* **A** (*communicate*) vermitteln (**to** *Dat.*); **B** (*make acceptable*) ankommen mit; (*make effective*) durchsetzen; **~ sth. across to sb.** mit etw. bei jmdm. ankommen/etw. bei jmdm. durchsetzen; **C** (*Amer.*) **sb. ~s across a fraud** jmdm. gelingt ein Betrug; **he ~ that tale across them** sie haben ihm diese Geschichte abgenommen; **D ~ one across sb.** (*coll.*) (*get the better of*) es jmdm. zeigen; (*deceive*) jmdn. reinlegen (*ugs.*) *od.* (*salopp*) linken. ⇒ *also* **~** 2

**~ a'side** *v.t.* **A** (*disregard*) absehen von; **~ting aside the fact that ...:** wenn man von der Tatsache *od.* davon absieht, dass ...; von der Tatsache *od.* davon abgesehen, dass ...; **B** (*save*) beiseite *od.* auf die Seite legen

**~ a'sunder** *v.t.* (*arch.*) scheiden

**~ a'way** *v.t.* **A** wegräumen; reinstellen ‹Auto›; (*in file*) wegheften; abheften; **B** (*abandon*) ablegen, aufgeben ‹Gewohnheiten, Vorurteile›; **C** (*save*) beiseite *od.* auf die Seite legen; **D** (*coll.*) (*eat*) verdrücken (*ugs.*); (*drink*) runterkippen (*ugs.*); **E** (*confine*) einsperren (*ugs.*); in eine Anstalt stecken (*ugs.*); **F** (*coll.: kill*) einschläfern ‹Tier›; um die Ecke bringen (*ugs.*) ‹Person›

**~ 'back** *v.t.* **A ~ the book back** das Buch zurücktun; **~ the book back on the shelf** das Buch wieder ins Regal stellen *od.* ins Regal zurückstellen; **B ~ the clock back [one hour]** die Uhr [eine Stunde] zurückstellen; ⇒ *also* **clock** 1 A; **C** (*delay*) zurückwerfen; verzögern ‹Ernte, Lieferung›; **D** (*postpone*) verschieben

**~ 'by** *v.t.* beiseite *od.* auf die Seite legen; **I've got a few hundred pounds ~ by** ich habe ein paar hundert Pfund auf der hohen Kante (*ugs.*)

**~ 'down** ❶ *v.t.* **A** (*set down*) (*vertically*) hinstellen; (*horizontally*) hinlegen; auflegen ‹Hörer›; **~ sth. down on sth.** etw. auf etw. (*Akk.*) stellen/legen; **~ down a deposit** eine Anzahlung machen; **B** (*suppress*) niederwerfen, -schlagen ‹Revolte, Rebellion, Aufruhr›; **C** (*humiliate*) herabsetzen; (*snub*) eine Abfuhr erteilen (+ *Dat.*); abfahren lassen (*salopp*); ⇒ *also* **put-down**; **D** (*kill painlessly*) töten; **E** (*write*) notieren; aufschreiben; **~ sth. down in writing** etw. schriftlich niederlegen; **he ~ it all down on paper** er schrieb alles auf; **~ sb.'s name down on a list** jmdn. *od.* jmds. Namen auf eine Liste setzen; **~ sb. down for** für jmdn. reservieren ‹Lose›; jmdn. notieren für ‹Dienst, Arbeit›; jmdn. anmelden bei ‹Schule, Verein usw.›; **I ~ him down for a £5 subscription** ich habe ihn mit einem Beitrag von 5 Pfund notiert; **F** (*Parl.*) einbringen; stellen ‹Antrag›; **G** (*allow to alight*) aussteigen lassen; absetzen; **H ~ sb. down as ...:** jmdn. eintragen als ...; **~ sth. down as ...:** etw. angeben als ...; **he ~ himself down as 'unemployed'** er gab als Beschäftigung „arbeitslos" an; (*fig.: classify*) **~ sb./sth. down as ...:** jmdn./etw. halten für *od.* einschätzen als ...; **I** (*attribute*) **~ sth. down to sth.** etw. auf etw. (*Akk.*) zurückführen; **J** (*store*) einlagern; (*in cellar*) einkellern; **K** (*to bed*) hinlegen ‹Baby›; **L** (*cease to read*) weglegen, aus der Hand legen ‹Buch›; **M** (*land*) aufsetzen. ⇒ *also* **down³** 1 F.

❷ *v.i.* (*land*) niedergehen; **look for a place to ~ down** nach einem geeigneten Landeplatz suchen

**~ 'forth** *v.t.* (*sprout*) hervorbringen ‹neue Triebe, Knospen›; treiben ‹Knospen›

**~ 'forward** *v.t.* **A** (*propose*) aufwarten mit; **the explanation ~ forward by him** die Erklärung, mit der er aufwartete; **several theories have been ~ forward to account for this** darüber gibt es verschiedene Theorien; **B** (*nominate*) vorschlagen; **C ~ the clock forward [one hour]** die Uhr [eine Stunde] vorstellen

**~ 'in** ❶ *v.t.* **A** (*install*) einbauen; einstellen ‹Arbeiter, Hausmeister, Leiter usw.›; **B** (*elect*) an die Regierung *od.* Macht bringen; **be ~ in** an die Regierung *od.* Macht kommen; **C** (*enter*) melden ‹Person›; **D** (*submit*) stellen ‹Forderung, Antrag›; einreichen ‹Bewerbung, Antrag›; **~ in a claim for damages** eine Schadensersatzforderung stellen; **~ in a plea of not guilty** sich nicht schuldig bekennen; **E** (*devote*) aufwenden ‹Mühe, Kraft›; (*perform*) einlegen ‹Sonderschicht, Überstunden›; (*spend*) einschieben ‹eine Stunde usw.›; **F** (*interpose*) einwerfen ‹Bemerkung›; **I ~ in a word of warning** ich mischte mich ein und warnte sie/ihn *usw.*; **~ in a blow** zuschlagen; **G** (*plant*) einpflanzen ‹Setzlinge, Stecklinge›; setzen ‹Salat, Tomaten, Saatpflanzen›; stecken ‹Bohnen, Kartoffeln, Zwiebeln›; [ein]säen ‹Samen›; **H** (*Cricket*) schlagen lassen ‹gegnerische Mannschaft›; spielen lassen, einsetzen ‹eigenen Spieler›; **they ~ us in [to bat]** sie ließen uns schlagen. ⇒ *also* **~** 2.

❷ *v.i.* **~ in for** sich bewerben um ‹Stellung, Posten, Vorsitz›; beantragen ‹Urlaub, Versetzung›

**~ in'side** *v.t.* (*sl.: imprison*) einlochen (*salopp*)

**~ 'off** *v.t.* **A** (*postpone*) verschieben (**until** auf + *Akk.*); (*postpone engagement with*) vertrösten (**until** auf + *Akk.*); **can't you ~ her off?** kannst du ihr nicht [erst einmal] absagen?; **B** (*switch off*) ausmachen; **C** (*repel*) abstoßen; **don't be ~ off by his rudeness** lass dich von seiner Grobheit nicht abschrecken; **~ sb. off sth.** jmdm. etw. verleiden; **D** (*distract*) stören; **the noise ~ him off his game** bei dem Lärm konnte er sich nicht mehr auf sein Spiel konzentrieren; **E** (*fob off*) abspeisen; **F** (*dissuade*) **~ sb. off doing sth.** jmdn. davon abbringen *od.* jmdm. ausreden, etw. zu tun; **G** (*remove*) ausziehen, ablegen ‹Kleidungsstücke›. ⇒ *also* **~** 2

**~ 'on** *v.t.* **A** anziehen ‹Kleidung, Hose usw.›; aufsetzen ‹Hut, Brille›; draufsetzen, (*ugs.*) draufmachen ‹Deckel, Verschluss usw.›; (*fig.: assume*) aufsetzen ‹Miene, Lächeln, Gesicht›; **~ on a disguise** sich verkleiden; **~ sb.'s clothes on [for him]** jmdn. anziehen; **~ sb.'s shoes on [for him]** jmdm. die Schuhe anziehen; **~ it on** (*coll.*) [nur] Schau machen (*ugs.*); **he does ~ it on, doesn't he?** er übertreibt doch, oder?; **his modesty is all ~ on** seine Bescheidenheit ist nur gespielt *od.* (*ugs.*) ist reine Schau; **the town had ~ on a holiday look** die Stadt gab sich festlich; **B** (*switch or turn on*) anmachen ‹Radio, Motor, Heizung, Licht usw.›; aufmachen ‹Hahn›; (*cause to heat up*) aufsetzen ‹Wasser, Essen, Kessel, Topf›; (*fig.: apply*) ausüben ‹Druck›; ⇒ *also* **screw** 1 A; **C** (*gain*) **~ on weight/two pounds** zunehmen/zwei Pfund zunehmen; **~ it on** (*coll.: gain weight*) Speck ansetzen (*ugs.*); **D** (*add*) **~ on speed** beschleunigen; **~ 8p on [to] the price** den Preis um 8 Pence erhöhen; 8 Pence auf den Preis aufschlagen; **E** (*stage*) spielen ‹Stück›; zeigen ‹Show, Film›; veranstalten ‹Ausstellung›; ⇒ *also* **act** 1 E; **F** (*arrange*) einsetzen ‹Sonderzug, -bus›; **G** ⇒ **~ forward c**; **H** (*coll.: tease*) veräppeln (*ugs.*); verarschen (*salopp*); ⇒ *also* **put-on**; **I** (*Cricket*) die Punktzahl erhöhen um ‹Läufe›; [als Werfer] einsetzen ‹Spieler›; **be ~ on [to bowl]** als Werfer eingesetzt werden. ⇒ *also* **~** 1 A

**~ 'out** *v.t.* **A** rausbringen; auslegen ‹Futter›; **~ one's hand out** die Hand ausstrecken; ⇒ *also* **tongue** A; **B** (*extinguish*) ausmachen ‹Licht, Lampe›; löschen ‹Feuer, Brand›; **C** (*issue*) [he]rausgeben ‹Buch, Zeitschrift, Broschüre, Anweisung, Erlass›; abgeben ‹Stellungnahme, Erklärung›; (*broadcast*) senden; bringen; **D** (*produce*) produzieren; ausstoßen ‹Warenmenge›; **E** (*annoy*) verärgern; **be ~ out** verärgert *od.* entrüstet sein; **F** (*inconvenience*) in Verlegenheit bringen; **~ oneself out to do sth.** die Mühe auf sich nehmen, etw. zu tun; **G** (*make inaccurate*) verfälschen ‹Ergebnis, Berechnung›; **H** (*dislocate*) verrenken; ausrenken ‹Schulter›; **~ one's thumb/ankle out** sich (*Dat.*) den Daumen/Knöchel verrenken; **I** (*give to outside worker*) außer Haus geben; **~ sth. out to sb.** jmdn. mit etw. beauftragen; **J** (*sprout*) hervorbringen; [aus]treiben; **K** ausstechen ‹Augen›. ⇒ *also* **~** 2

**~ 'over** ⇒ **~ across**

**~ 'through** *v.t.* **A** (*carry out*) durchführen ‹Plan, Programm, Kampagne, Sanierung›; durchbringen ‹Gesetz, Vorschlag›; (*complete*) zum Abschluss bringen, abschließen ‹Geschäft usw.›; **B** (*Teleph.*) verbinden (**to** mit); durchstellen ‹Gespräch› (**to** zu); **~ a call through to New York** nach New York telefonieren. ⇒ *also* **~** 1 C

**~ to'gether** *v.t.* zusammensetzen ‹Bauteile, Scherben, Steine, Einzelteile, Maschine usw.›; ordnen ‹Gedanken›; erstellen, ausarbeiten ‹Begründung, Argumentation, Beweisführung›; ⇒ *also* **head** 1 A; **two** 2

**~ 'under** *v.t.* (*make unconscious*) betäuben

**~ 'up** ❶ *v.t.* **A** heben ‹Hand›; (*erect*) errichten ‹Gebäude, Denkmal, Gerüst, Zaun usw.›; bauen ‹Haus›; aufstellen ‹Denkmal, Gerüst, Verkehrsschilder, Leinwand, Zelt›; aufbauen ‹Zelt, Verteidigungsanlagen›; anbringen ‹Schild, Notiz usw.› (**on** an + *Dat.*); ‹Igel:› aufstellen ‹Stacheln›; (*fig.*) aufbauen ‹Fassade›; abziehen ‹Schau›; ⇒ *also* **put-up**; **B** (*display*) anschlagen; aushängen; **C** (*offer as defence*) hochnehmen ‹Fäuste›; leisten ‹Widerstand, Gegenwehr›; **~ up a struggle** sich wehren *od.* zur Wehr setzen; **~ up a bold front** sich tapfer wehren; tapfer Widerstand leisten; **~ up a defence** sich verteidigen; **D** (*present for consideration*) einreichen ‹Petition, Gesuch, Vorschlag›; sprechen ‹Gebet›; (*propose*) vorschlagen; (*nominate*) aufstellen; **~ sb. up for election** jmdn. als Kandidaten aufstellen; **~ sb. up for secretary** jmdn. für das Amt des Sekretärs vorschlagen; **E** (*incite*) **~ sb. up to sth.** jmdn. zu etw. anstiften; **F** (*accommodate*) unterbringen; **G** (*increase*) [he]raufsetzen, anheben ‹Preis, Miete, Steuer, Zins›; **H** (*provide*) zur Verfügung stellen; *abs.* **~ up or shut up** (*coll.*) steh zu deinem Wort, oder halt gefälligst den Mund!; **I ~ sth. up for sale** etw. zum Verkauf anbieten; **~ sth. up for auction** etw. versteigern lassen; **~ sth. up for competition** etw. [öffentlich] ausschreiben; **J** (*Hunting*) aufscheuchen; auftun (*fachspr.*); **K** (*arch.: sheathe*) in die Scheide stecken. ⇒ *also* **back** 1 A; **fight** 3 A.

❷ *v.i.* **A** (*be candidate*) kandidieren; sich aufstellen lassen; **B** (*lodge*) übernachten; sich einquartieren

**~ upon** *v.t.* ausnutzen; **let oneself be ~ upon by sb.** sich von jmdm. ausnutzen lassen

**~ 'up with** *v.t.* sich (*Dat.*) gefallen *od.* bieten lassen ‹Beleidigung, Benehmen, Unhöflichkeit›; sich abfinden mit ‹Lärm, Elend, Ärger, Bedingungen›; sich abgeben mit ‹Person›

**put²** ⇒ **putt**

**putative** /ˈpjuːtətɪv/ *adj.* mutmaßlich; (*erroneously*) vermeintlich

**put: ~-down** *n.* Herabsetzung, *die*; (*snub*) Abfuhr, *die*; **~-on** *n.* (*coll.*) Veräppelung, *die* (*ugs.*); Verarschung, *die* (*salopp*)

**put-put** /ˈpʌtpʌt/ ❶ *n.* Tuckern, *das.* ❷ *v.i.*, **-tt-** tuckern

**putrefaction** /pjuːtrɪˈfækʃn/ *n., no pl., no indef. art.* Zersetzung, *die*

**putrefy** /ˈpjuːtrɪfaɪ/ *v.i.* sich zersetzen

**putrid** /ˈpjuːtrɪd/ *adj.* Ⓐ (*rotten*) faul; **become ~:** sich zersetzen; Ⓑ (*of putrefaction*) faulig; **~ smell** Fäulnisgeruch, *der;* Ⓒ (*fig.: corrupt*) verdorben; verworfen (*geh.*); Ⓓ (*coll.*) (*dreadful*) scheußlich; (*stupid*) blödsinnig ‹Ansichten›

**putsch** /pʊtʃ/ *n.* Putsch, *der;* **army ~:** Militärputsch, *der*

**putt** /pʌt/ (*Golf*) ❶ *v.i. & t.* putten. ❷ *n.* Putt, *der*

**puttee** /ˈpʌtɪ/ *n.* Ⓐ Wickelgamasche, *die;* Ⓑ (*Amer.: leather legging*) Ledergamasche, *die*

**putter** /ˈpʌtə(r)/ (*Golf*) Putter, *der*

**putting green** /ˈpʌtɪŋɡriːn/ *n.* (*Golf*) Ⓐ Grün, *das;* Ⓑ (*miniature golf course*) *kleiner Golfplatz nur zum Putten*

**putty** /ˈpʌtɪ/ ❶ *n.* Ⓐ Kitt, *der;* **glaziers' ~:** Fensterkitt, *der;* Glaserkitt, *der;* Ⓑ **[jewellers'] ~:** Zinnasche, *die;* Polierasche, *die.* ❷ *v.t.* Ⓐ (*fix with glaziers' ~*) einkitten ‹Fensterscheibe›; (*fill with ~*) auskitten ‹Risse›; Ⓑ (*cover with plasterers' ~*) verputzen ‹Wand›; ausgipsen ‹Fugen›

**'putty knife** *n.* Kittmesser, *das*

**'put-up** *adj.* **a ~ thing/job** eine abgekartete Sache/ein abgekartetes Spiel

**puzzle** /ˈpʌzl/ ❶ *n.* Ⓐ (*problem*) Rätsel, *das;* (*brainteaser*) Denksportaufgabe, *die;* (*toy*) Geduldsspiel, *das;* Ⓑ (*enigma*) Rätsel, *das;* **be a ~ to sb.** jmdm. ein Rätsel sein; **be a ~:** rätselhaft sein. ❷ *v.t.* rätselhaft *od.* ein Rätsel sein (+ *Dat.*); vor ein Rätsel stellen; **he would have been ~d to explain it** er hätte nicht gewusst, wie er es hätte erklären sollen; **he was ~d what to do** er wusste nicht, was er tun sollte. ❸ *v.i.* **~ over** *or* **about sth.** sich (*Dat.*) über etw. den Kopf zerbrechen; über etw. rätseln; **we ~d over what had happened** wir rätselten, was wohl passiert war

**~ 'out** *v.t.* herausfinden; **~ out an answer to a question** eine Antwort auf eine Frage finden

**puzzled** /ˈpʌzld/ *adj.* ratlos

**puzzlement** /ˈpʌzlmənt/ *n., no pl.* Verwirrung, *die*

**puzzling** /ˈpʌzlɪŋ/ *adj.* rätselhaft

**PVC** *abbr.* **polyvinyl chloride** PVC, *das*

**PX** *abbr.* (*Amer.*) **Post Exchange**

**pygmy** /ˈpɪɡmɪ/ ❶ *n.* Ⓐ Pygmäe, *der;* Ⓑ (*dwarf; also fig.*) Zwerg, *der*/Zwergin, *die.* ❷ *attrib. adj.* Ⓐ pygmäisch; **the ~ people** die Pygmäen; Ⓑ (*dwarf*) Zwerg-

**pyjama** /pɪˈdʒɑːmə/ *adj.* Pyjama-; Schlafanzug-; **~ suit** Pyjama, *der;* Schlafanzug, *der*

**pyjamas** /pɪˈdʒɑːməz/ *n. pl.* **[pair of] ~:** Schlafanzug, *der;* Pyjama, *der*

**pylon** /ˈpaɪlən/ *n.* Mast, *der*

**pyramid** /ˈpɪrəmɪd/ *n.* Pyramide, *die*

**pyramidal** /pɪˈræmɪdl/ *adj.* pyramidenförmig

**'pyramid selling** *n., no pl., no indef. art. Verkauf von Vertriebsrechten nach dem Schneeballsystem*

**pyre** /paɪə(r)/ *n.* Scheiterhaufen, *der*

**Pyrenean** /pɪrəˈniːən/ *adj.* pyrenäisch; **~ mountain dog** Pyrenäenhund, *der*

**Pyrenees** /pɪrəˈniːz/ *pr. n. pl.* **the ~:** die Pyrenäen

**pyrethrum** /paɪˈriːθrəm/ *n.* Ⓐ (*flower*) Chrysantheme, *die;* Pyrethrum, *das* (*veralt.*); Ⓑ (*insecticide*) Pyrethrum, *das*

**Pyrex** ® /ˈpaɪreks/ *n.* ≈ Jenaer Glas, *das* Ⓦⓩ; *attrib.* **~ dish** feuerfeste Glasschüssel

**pyrites** /paɪˈraɪtiːz/ *n., no pl.* (*Min.*) **[iron] ~:** Pyrit, *der;* Eisenkies, *der*

**pyrotechnic** /paɪrəʊˈteknɪk/ ❶ *adj.* pyrotechnisch; Feuerwerks-; (*fig.: brilliant*) brillant. ❷ *n. in pl.* Feuerwerk, *das;* (*fig.*) Brillanz, *die*

**pyrotechnics** /paɪərəʊˈteknɪks/ *n. pl.* Feuerwerk, *das;* (*fig.*) Brillanz, *die*

**Pyrrhic** /ˈpɪrɪk/ *adj.* **~ victory** Pyrrhussieg, *der*

**Pythagoras** /paɪˈθæɡərəs/ *pr. n.* Pythagoras, *der;* **~' theorem** (*Geom.*) der Satz des Pythagoras

**python** /ˈpaɪθən/ *n.* Python[schlange], *die*

# Qq

**Q¹, q** /kju:/ *n., pl.* **Qs** *or* **Q's** Q, q, *das;* ⇒ *also* **mind** 2 B

**Q²** *abbr.* **question** F

**Q.** *abbr.* Ⓐ **Queen** Kgn.; Ⓑ **Queen's** kgl.; Ⓒ (*Chess*) **queen** D

**QC** *abbr.* (*Brit.*) **Queen's Counsel**

**QED** *abbr.* **quod erat demonstrandum** q. e. d.; w. z. b. w.

**qr.** *abbr.* **quarter[s]** qr.

**qt.** *abbr.* **quart[s]** qt

**qua** /kweɪ, kwɑ:/ *conj.* (*literary*) qua (*geh.*)

**quack¹** /kwæk/ ❶ *v.i.* ‹Ente:› quaken. ❷ *n.* Quaken, *das*

**quack²** (*derog.*) ❶ *n.* Quacksalber, *der* (*abwertend*). ❷ *attrib. adj.* Ⓐ ~ **doctor** Quacksalber, *der;* Ⓑ Quacksalber‹kur, -tropfen, -pillen› (*abwertend*); ~ **remedy** Mittelchen, *das* (*ugs. abwertend*)

**'quack-quack** *n.* (*child lang.*) Quakente, *die* (*Kinderspr.*)

**quad** /kwɒd/ *n.* Ⓐ (*coll.: quadrangle*) Innenhof, *der;* Ⓑ (*quadraphonic*) ~ **[sound system]** Quadroanlage, *die;* Ⓒ (*coll.: quadruplet*) Vierling, *der;* Ⓓ (*Print.: quadrat*) **[em]** ~/**en** ~: Geviert/Halbgeviert, *das*

**'quad bike** *n.* Quad, *das*

**quadrangle** /'kwɒdræŋgl/ *n.* Ⓐ (*enclosed court*) viereckiger Innenhof; (*with buildings*) Block, *der;* Karree, *das;* Ⓑ (*Geom.*) Viereck, *das*

**quadrant** /'kwɒdrənt/ *n.* Ⓐ (*Geom., Astron., Naut.*) Quadrant, *der;* (*of sphere*) Viertelkugel, *die;* Ⓑ (*object shaped like quarter-circle*) viertelkreisförmiger Gegenstand

**quadraphonic** /kwɒdrə'fɒnɪk/ *adj.* quadrophon; Quadro‹anlage, -sound usw.›

**quadratic** /kwə'drætɪk/ *adj.* (*Math.*) quadratisch; zweiten Grades *nachgestellt*

**quadrilateral** /kwɒdrɪ'lætərl/ *n.* (*Geom.*) Viereck, *das*

**quadrille** /kwə'drɪl/ *n.* Quadrille, *die*

**quadriplegia** /kwɒdrɪ'pli:dʒɪə/ *n.* (*Med.*) Quadri-, Tetraplegie, *die* (*fachspr.*); gleichzeitige Lähmung aller vier Gliedmaßen

**quadriplegic** /kwɒdrɪ'pli:dʒɪk/ (*Med.*) ❶ *n.* Quadri-, Tetraplegiker, *der*/-plegikerin, *die.* ❷ *adj.* quadri-, tetraplegisch; **be** ~: an allen vier Gliedmaßen gelähmt sein

**quadruped** /'kwɒdrʊped/ *n.* Vierfüßler, *der*

**quadruple** /'kwɒdrʊpl/ ❶ *adj.* Ⓐ vierfach; Ⓑ (*four times*) viermal; **be** ~ **today's value** viermal so hoch sein wie der heutige Wert; ~ **the amount** die vierfache Menge; Ⓒ (*Mus.*) ~ **time** Vierertakt, *der.* ❷ *v.t.* mit vier malnehmen ‹Zahl›; vervierfachen ‹Einkommen, Produktion, Profit›. ❸ *v.i.* sich vervierfachen

**quadruplet** /'kwɒdrʊplɪt, kwɒ'dru:plɪt/ *n.* Vierling, *der*

**quadruplicate** /kwɒ'dru:plɪkət/ *n.* vierfache Ausfertigung; **in** ~: in vierfacher Ausfertigung *nachgestellt*

**quaff** /kwɑ:f, kwɒf/ (*literary*) ❶ *v.i.* zechen (*veralt., scherzh.*); pokulieren (*veralt., scherzh.*). ❷ *v.t.* [mit langen, kräftigen Schlucken] leeren *od.* austrinken ‹Glas›; [mit langen, kräftigen Schlucken] trinken ‹Getränk›

**quag** /kwæg, kwɒg/ *n.* (*marshy spot*) sumpfige *od.* morastige Stelle; (*quaking bog*) Schwingmoor, *das*

**quagmire** /'kwægmaɪə(r), kwɒgmaɪə(r)/ *n.* Sumpf, *der;* Morast, *der;* (*quaking bog*) Schwingmoor, *das;* (*fig.: complex or difficult situation*) Sumpf, *der;* **be in a** ~ (*lit. or fig.*) in einem Sumpf stecken; **a** ~ **of details/problems** ein Wust von Einzelheiten/Problemen

**quail¹** /kweɪl/ *n., pl. same or* ~**s** (*Ornith.*) Wachtel, *die*

**quail²** *v.i.* ‹Person:› [ver]zagen, den Mut sinken lassen; ‹Blick, Mut, Hoffnung, Vertrauen:› sinken; **make sb.'s courage/spirit** ~: jmdn. entmutigen; ~ **at the prospect of sth.** bei der Aussicht auf etw. (*Akk.*) verzagen

**quaint** /kweɪnt/ *adj.* drollig; putzig (*ugs.*) ‹Häuschen, Einrichtung›; malerisch, pittoresk ‹Ort›; (*odd, strange*) kurios, seltsam ‹Bräuche, Anblick, Begebenheit›; schnurrig ‹alter Kauz›

**quaintly** /'kweɪntlɪ/ *adv.* putzig (*ugs.*); drollig ‹bemerken›

**quake** /kweɪk/ ❶ *n.* (*coll.*) [Erd]beben, *das.* ❷ *v.i.* beben; ‹Sumpfboden:› schwingen; ~ **with fear/fright** vor Angst/Schreck zittern *od.* beben

**Quaker** /'kweɪkə(r)/ *n.* Quäker, *der*/Quäkerin, *die*

**quaking** /'kweɪkɪŋ/: ~ **bog** *n.* Schwingmoor, *das;* ~ **grass** *n.* (*Bot.*) Zittergras, *das*

**qualification** /kwɒlɪfɪ'keɪʃn/ *n.* Ⓐ (*ability*) Qualifikation, *die;* (*condition to be fulfilled*) Voraussetzung, *die;* **secretarial** ~**s** Ausbildung als Sekretärin; Ⓑ (*on paper*) Zeugnis, *das;* Ⓒ (*limitation*) Vorbehalt, *der;* **without** ~: vorbehaltlos; ohne Vorbehalt; **the offer was subject to one** ~: das Angebot hatte eine Einschränkung

**qualified** /'kwɒlɪfaɪd/ *adj.* Ⓐ qualifiziert; (*by training*) ausgebildet; (*entitled, having right to*) berechtigt; **be** ~ **for a job/to vote** die Qualifikation für eine Stelle besitzen/wahlberechtigt sein; **you are better** ~ **to judge that** du kannst das besser beurteilen; **I am not** ~ **to speak on that** ich kann darüber nichts sagen; **be** ~ **to vote** wahlberechtigt sein; Ⓑ (*restricted*) nicht uneingeschränkt; **a** ~ **success** kein voller Erfolg; ~ **approval/reply** Zustimmung/Antwort unter Vorbehalt; ~ **acceptance** bedingte Annahme

**qualifier** /'kwɒlɪfaɪə(r)/ *n.* Ⓐ (*restriction*) Einschränkung, *die* (**of, on** *Gen.*); Ⓑ (*person*) **be among the** ~**s** zu denen gehören, die sich qualifiziert haben; Ⓒ (*Sport: match*) Qualifikationsspiel, *das*

**qualify** /'kwɒlɪfaɪ/ ❶ *v.t.* Ⓐ (*make competent, make officially entitled*) berechtigen (**for** zu); Ⓑ (*modify*) einschränken; modifizieren ‹Meinung, Feststellung›; Ⓒ (*describe*) bewerten; bezeichnen; Ⓓ (*moderate*) abschwächen; ~ **justice with mercy** Gnade vor Recht ergehen lassen; Ⓔ (*Ling.*) näher bestimmen.
❷ *v.i.* Ⓐ ~ **in law/medicine/education/chemistry** seinen [Studien]abschluss in Jura/Medizin/Pädagogik/Chemie machen; ~ **as a doctor/lawyer/teacher/chemist** sein Examen als Arzt/Anwalt/Lehrer/Chemiker machen; Ⓑ (*fulfil a condition*) infrage kommen (**for** für); ~ **for the vote/a pension** wahl-/rentenberechtigt sein; ~ **for admission to a university/club** die Aufnahmebedingungen einer Universität/eines Vereins erfüllen; ~ **for a post** für eine Stelle qualifiziert sein; ~ **for membership** die Bedingungen für die Mitgliedschaft erfüllen; Ⓒ (*Sport*) sich qualifizieren

**qualifying** /'kwɒlɪfaɪɪŋ/ *adj.* Ⓐ ~ **statement** einschränkende Aussage; Ⓑ (*Sport*) ~ **match** Qualifikationsspiel, *das;* ~ **round/heat** Ausscheidungs- *od.* Qualifikationsrunde, *die;* Ⓒ ~ **examination** Zulassungsprüfung, *die*

**qualitative** /'kwɒlɪtətɪv/ *adj.*, **qualitatively** /'kwɒlɪtətɪvlɪ/ *adv.* qualitativ

**quality** /'kwɒlɪtɪ/ ❶ *n.* Ⓐ Qualität, *die;* **of good/poor** *etc.* ~: von guter/schlechter *usw.* Qualität; **of the best** ~: bester Qualität; ~ **rather than quantity** Qualität, nicht Quantität; **clothes of** ~: Qualitätskleidung, *die;* **the** ~ **of her writing/craftsmanship** ihre schriftstellerischen Leistungen/handwerklichen Fähigkeiten; Ⓑ (*characteristic*) Eigenschaft, *die;* **the melodious** ~ **of her voice** die Melodie ihrer Stimme; **possess the qualities of a ruler/leader** eine Führernatur sein; **have the** ~ **of inspiring others with confidence** die Gabe haben, andere mit Zuversicht zu erfüllen; ⇒ *also* **defect** 1 B; Ⓒ (*of sound, voice*) Klang, *der;* Ⓓ (*arch.: rank*) Rang, *der;* **people of** ~: Leute von Rang [und Namen].
❷ *adj.* Ⓐ (*excellent*) Qualitäts-; Ⓑ (*maintaining* ~) Qualitäts‹prüfung, -kontrolle›; (*denoting* ~) Güte‹grad, -klasse, -zeichen›

**quality:** ~ **control** *n.* Qualitätskontrolle, *die;* ~ **controller** *n.* ▶ 1261 Qualitätsprüfer, *der;* ~ **time** *n.: ganz dem Miteinander gewidmete Zeit;* **spend** ~ **time with sb.** einen Teil seiner Zeit ganz jmdm. widmen

**qualm** /kwɑ:m, kwɔ:m/ *n.* Ⓐ (*sudden misgiving*) ungutes Gefühl; Ⓑ (*scruple*) Bedenken, *das* (*meist Pl.*) (**over, about** gegen); **he had no** ~**s about borrowing money** er hatte keine Bedenken, sich (*Dat.*) Geld zu leihen; Ⓒ (*sick feeling*) Übelkeit, *die*

**quandary** /'kwɒndərɪ/ *n.* Dilemma, *das;* **this demand put him in a** ~: diese Forderung brachte ihn in eine verzwickte Lage; **he was in a** ~ **about what to do next** er wusste nicht, was er als Nächstes tun sollte

**quango** /'kwæŋgəʊ/ *n., pl.* ~**s** (*Brit.*) *halböffentliche Verwaltungseinrichtung*

**quanta** *pl. of* **quantum**

**quantifiable** /'kwɒntɪfaɪəbl/ *adj.* quantifizierbar

**quantify** /'kwɒntɪfaɪ/ *v.t.* quantifizieren

**quantitative** /'kwɒntɪtətɪv/ *adj.*, **quantitatively** /'kwɒntɪtətɪvlɪ/ *adv.* quantitativ

**quantity** /'kwɒntɪtɪ/ *n.* Ⓐ Quantität, *die;* Ⓑ (*amount, sum*) Menge, *die;* **what** ~ **of flour do you need for this recipe?** wie viel Mehl braucht man für dieses Rezept?; ~ **of heat** Wärmemenge, *die;* Ⓒ (*large amount*) [Un]menge, *die;* **coal/gold in quantities** Kohle/Gold in Unmengen *od.* (*ugs.*) rauen Mengen; **buy in quantities** in großen Mengen einkaufen; ⇒ *also* **bill³** 1 H; Ⓓ (*Math.*) Größe, *die;* Ⓔ (*fig.*) **negligible** ~: Quantité négligeable, *die* (*geh.*); **he is a negligible** ~: er ist völlig unwichtig; **an unknown** ~: eine unbekannte Größe; Ⓕ (*Phonet., Pros.*) Quantität, *die*

**quantity:** ~ **mark** *n.* (*Pros.*) Quantitätszeichen, *das;* ~ **surveyor** *n.* ▶ 1261 Baukostenkalkulator, *der*/-kalkulatorin, *die*

**quantum** /'kwɒntəm/ *n., pl.* **quanta** /'kwɒntə/ Ⓐ (*literary*) (*amount*) Menge, *die;* (*share, portion*) Anteil, *der;* (*required, desired, or allowed amount*) Quantum, *das;* Ⓑ (*Phys.*) Quant, *das*

**quantum:** ~ **jump,** ~ **leap** *ns.* (*Phys.; also fig.*) Quantensprung, *der;* ~ **me'chanics** *n.* (*Phys.*) Quantenmechanik, *die;* ~ **theory** *n.* (*Phys.*) Quantentheorie, *die*

**quarantine** /'kwɒrənti:n/ ❶ *n.* Quarantäne, *die; attrib.* Quarantäne‹bestimmungen, -zeit, -flagge›; **put under** ~: unter Quarantäne stellen; **be in** ~: unter Quarantäne stehen. ❷ *v.t.* unter Quarantäne stellen

**quark** /kwɑ:k, kwɔ:k/ *n.* (*Phys.*) Quark, *das*

**quarrel** /'kwɒrl/ ❶ *n.* Ⓐ Streit, *der;* **have a** ~ **with sb. [about/over sth.]** sich mit

jmdm. [über etw. (*Akk.*) *od.* wegen etw./um etw.] streiten; **let's not have a ~ about it** wir wollen uns nicht darüber streiten; **I don't want to have a ~ with you** ich will mich mit dir nicht streiten *od.* will keinen Streit mit dir; **pick a ~ [with sb. over sth.]** [mit jmdm. wegen etw.] Streit anfangen; B (*cause of complaint*) Einwand, *der* (**with** gegen); **I have no ~ with you** ich habe nichts gegen dich.
2 *v.i.*, (*Brit.*) **-ll-** A [sich] streiten (**over** um, **about** über + *Akk.*, wegen); **~ with each other** [sich] [miteinander] streiten; (*fall out, dispute*) sich [zer]streiten (**over** um, **about** über + *Akk.*, wegen); B (*find fault*) etwas auszusetzen haben (**with** an + *Dat.*); **I really can't ~ with that** daran habe ich wirklich nichts auszusetzen

**quarrelsome** /'kwɒrlsəm/ *adj.* streitsüchtig; **his ~ nature** seine Streitsucht

**quarry**[1] /'kwɒrɪ/ 1 *n.* Steinbruch, *der;* **marble/slate ~:** Marmor-/Schieferbruch, *der;* (*fig.*) Fundgrube, *die* (**of** für); **~ of information** Informationsquelle, *die.* 2 *v.t.* brechen ‹Steine, Marmor›; (*fig.*) zutage fördern. 3 *v.i.* (*fig.*) herumstöbern

**quarry**[2] *n.* (*prey*) Beute, *die;* (*fig.*) Opfer, *das*

**quarry: ~man** /'kwɒrɪmən/ *n., pl.* **~men** /'kwɒrɪmən/ ▶ 1261 Steinbrucharbeiter, *der;* **~ tile** *n.* unglasierte Steinfliese

**quart** /kwɔːt/ *n.* A ▶ 1671 Quart, *das;* **try to put a ~ into a pint pot** (*fig.*) mehr in etwas unterbringen wollen als hineinpasst; B (*vessel*) Quartgefäß, *das*

**'quart bottle** *n.* Quartflasche, *die*

**quarter** /'kwɔːtə(r)/ 1 *n.* A ▶ 1352, ▶ 1683 Viertel, *das;* **a** *or* **one ~ of** ein Viertel (+ *Gen.*); **a ~ [of] the price** ein Viertel des Preises; **divide/cut sth. into ~s** etw. in vier Teile teilen/schneiden; etw. vierteln; **six and a ~:** sechseinviertel; **an hour and a ~:** eineinviertel Stunden; **a ~ [of a pound] of cheese** ein Viertel[pfund] Käse; **~ of lamb/beef** Lamm-/Rinderviertel, *das;* **a ~ of a mile/an hour/a century** eine Viertelmeile/-stunde/ein Vierteljahrhundert; **three ~s of an hour** eine Dreiviertelstunde; B (*of year*) Quartal, *das;* Vierteljahr, *das;* C ▶ 1012 (*point of time*) **[a] ~ to/past six** Viertel vor/nach sechs; drei Viertel sechs/viertel sieben (*landsch.*); **there are buses at ~ to and ~ past [the hour]** es fahren Busse um Viertel vor und Viertel nach jeder vollen Stunde *od.* (*ugs.*) eine Viertelstunde vor und nach voll; D (*direction*) Richtung, *die;* **blow from all ~s** ‹Wind:› aus allen Richtungen wehen; **flock in from all ~s** aus allen Himmelsrichtungen zusammenströmen; **from every ~ of the globe** von überall her; E (*source of supply or help*) Seite, *die;* **from this ~:** von dieser Stelle; **secret information from a high ~:** Geheiminformationen von höchster Stelle; **turn for support to other ~s** sich woanders *od.* anderweitig um Unterstützung bemühen; F (*area of town*) [Stadt]viertel, *das;* Quartier, *das;* **in some ~s** (*fig.*) in gewissen Kreisen; G *in pl.* (*lodgings*) Quartier, *das* (*bes. Milit.*); Unterkunft, *die;* **take up [one's] ~s** Quartier beziehen; ⇒ *also* **close** 1 A; H (*Brit.: measure*) (*of volume*) Quarter, *der;* (*of weight*) ≈ Viertelzentner, *der;* I (*Amer.*) (*school term*) Viertelschuljahr, *das;* (*university term*) halbes Semester; J (*Astron.*) Viertel, *das;* **the moon is in its last ~:** der Mond steht im letzten Viertel; K (*mercy*) Schonung, *die;* **give/receive ~:** Schonung *od.* (*veralt.*) Pardon gewähren/gewährt bekommen; **give no ~ to sb.** jmdm. keinen Pardon (*veralt.*) gewähren *od.* geben; L ▶ 1328 (*Amer., Can.: amount, coin*) Vierteldollar, *der;* 25-Cent-Stück, *das;* **the bus fare was a ~:** die Busfahrt hat 25 Cent *od.* einen Vierteldollar gekostet; M (*Naut.*) Achterschiff, *das;* Hinterschiff, *das;* N (*in shoemaking*) Seitenteil, *das;* Quartier, *das* (*fachspr.*).
2 *v.t.* A (*divide*) vierteln ‹Apfel, Tomate usw.›; in vier Teile teilen ‹Stück Fleisch›; durch vier teilen ‹Zahl, Summe›; B (*lodge*) einquartieren ‹Soldaten›; C (*Hist.*) vierteilen ‹Verbrecher›

**quarter: ~back** *n.* (*Amer. Football*) Quarterback, *der;* **~ binding** *n.* (*Bookbinding*) Halbfranz, *das;* **~ day** *n.* Quartalsende, *das;* **~deck** *n.* (*Naut.*) A (*of ship*) Quarterdeck, *das;* B (*officers*) Marineoffiziere *Pl.;* **~-'final** *n.* Viertelfinale, *das;* **in the ~-finals** im Viertelfinale; **~-'finalist** *n.* Viertelfinalist, *der*/-finalistin, *die;* **~-'hour** *n.* A Viertelstunde, *die;* B **on the ~-hour** (*fifteen minutes before*) um Viertel vor; (*fifteen minutes after*) um Viertel nach

**quartering** /'kwɔːtərɪŋ/ *n.* A (*dividing*) Vierteln, *das;* B (*lodging*) Einquartierung, *die*

**'quarter-light** *n.* (*Brit. Motor Veh.*) (*bes. ausstellbares*) Teil des Fond-/Türfensters

**quarterly** /'kwɔːtəlɪ/ 1 *adj.* vierteljährlich. 2 *n.* Vierteljahr[e]sschrift, *die.* 3 *adv.* vierteljährlich; alle Vierteljahre

**quarter: ~master** *n.* A (*Naut.*) Quartermeister, *der;* B (*Mil.*) Quartiermeister, *der* (*veralt.*); **~ 'mile** *n.* Viertelmeile, *die;* **~ note** (*Amer. Mus.*) ⇒ **crotchet**; **~-pounder** *n.* Viertelpfünder, *der;* **~ 'sessions** *n. pl.* (*Brit. Hist.*) *vierteljährliche Gerichtssitzungen*

**quartet, quartette** /kwɔː'tet/ *n.* (*also Mus.*) Quartett, *das;* **piano/string ~:** Klavier-/Streichquartett, *das*

**quarto** /'kwɔːtəʊ/ *n., pl.* **~s** A (*book*) Quartband, *der;* B (*size*) Quart[format], *das;* **~ paper** Papier im Quartformat

**quartz** /kwɔːts/ *n.* Quarz, *der*

**quartz: ~ clock** *n.* Quarzuhr, *die;* **~ lamp** *n.* Quarzlampe, *die;* **~ watch** *n.* Quarzuhr, *die*

**quasar** /'kweɪsɑː(r), 'kweɪzɑː(r)/ *n.* (*Astron.*) Quasar, *der*

**quash** /kwɒʃ/ *v.t.* A (*annul, make void*) aufheben ‹Urteil, Entscheidung›; zurückweisen ‹Einspruch, Klage›; B (*suppress, crush*) unterdrücken ‹Opposition›; niederschlagen ‹Aufstand, Generalstreik›

**quasi** /'kweɪzaɪ, 'kwɑːzɪ/ *adv.* quasi

**quasi-** *pref.* A (*not real, seeming*) Schein-; B (*half-*) Quasi-; quasi; **~official** halbamtlich

**Quaternary** /kwə'tɜːnərɪ/ (*Geol.*) 1 *adj.* quartär. 2 *n.* Quartär, *das*

**quatrain** /'kwɒtreɪn/ *n.* (*Pros.*) Vierzeiler, *der;* Quatrain, *das od. der* (*fachspr.*)

**quatrefoil** /'kætrəfɔɪl/ *n.* (*Archit.*) Vierpass, *der*

**quaver** /'kweɪvə(r)/ 1 *n.* A (*Brit. Mus.*) Achtelnote, *die;* B (*Mus.: trill*) Tremolo, *das;* C (*in speech*) Zittern, *das;* Beben, *das* (*geh.*); **admit with a ~ [in one's voice] that ...:** mit zitternder Stimme zugeben, dass ... 2 *v.i.* (*vibrate, tremble*) zittern; beben (*geh.*)

**quavering** /'kweɪvərɪŋ/, **quavery** /'kweɪvərɪ/ *adjs.* zitternd, bebend ‹Stimme›

**quay** /kiː/, **'quayside** *ns.* Kai, *der;* Kaje, *die* (*nordd.*)

**queasiness** /'kwiːzɪnɪs/ *n., no pl.* Übelkeit, *die*

**queasy** /'kwiːzɪ/ *adj.* unwohl; (*uneasy*) mulmig (*ugs.*); **a ~ feeling** ein Gefühl der Übelkeit; **just the thought of it makes me [feel] ~:** schon beim Gedanken daran wird mir ganz schlecht *od.* übel; **my stomach is in such a ~ state** mir ist so komisch im Magen

**queen** /kwiːn/ *n.* A ▶ 1617 Königin, *die;* **Q~ of [the] May** Maikönigin, *die;* B (*bee, ant, wasp*) Königin, *die;* C (*personified best example of sth.*) Juwel, *das;* Perle, *die;* D (*Chess, Cards*) Dame, *die;* **~'s bishop/knight/pawn/rook** Damenläufer/-springer/-bauer/-turm, *der;* **~ of hearts** Herzdame, *die;* E (*sl.: male homosexual*) Tunte, *die* (*salopp*). ⇒ *also* **bench** D; **colour** 1 J; **counsel** 1 C; **English** 2 A; **evidence** 1 B; **guide** 1 E; **highway** A; **messenger** B; **peace** B; **save** 1 C; **scout** 1 A; **shilling**

**queen: ~ 'bee** *n.* Bienenkönigin, *die;* **~ 'consort** *n.* Königin, *die;* Gemahlin des Königs

**queenly** /'kwiːnlɪ/ *adj.* königlich; (*majestic*) majestätisch

**queen 'mother** *n.* Königinmutter, *die*

**queer** /kwɪə(r)/ 1 *adj.* A (*strange*) sonderbar; seltsam; (*eccentric*) komisch; verschroben; **a ~ feeling** ein komisches Gefühl; ⇒ *also* **fish** 1 C; B (*shady, suspect*) merkwürdig; seltsam; **there's something ~ about this whole business** die ganze Sache ist nicht ganz hasenrein; C (*out of sorts, faint*) unwohl; **I feel ~:** mir ist komisch *od.* (*ugs.*) flau; **you are looking a bit ~:** du siehst ein bisschen angegriffen aus; D (*coll.: mad, insane*) verrückt (*salopp*); **~ in the head** plemplem (*salopp*); E (*sl. derog.: homosexual*) schwul (*ugs.*).
2 *n.* (*sl. derog.: homosexual*) Schwule, *der* (*ugs.*).
3 *v.t.* (*coll.: spoil*) vermasseln (*salopp*); **~ the pitch for sb., ~ sb.'s pitch** jmdm. einen Strich durch die Rechnung machen

**queerly** /'kwɪəlɪ/ *adv.* sonderbar; seltsam

**'Queer Street** *n.* **be in ~** (*in difficulties, trouble, debt*) in der Tinte sitzen (*ugs.*); in Schwulitäten sein (*ugs.*)

**quell** /kwel/ *v.t.* (*literary*) niederschlagen ‹Aufstand, Rebellion›; bezwingen; zügeln ‹Leidenschaft, Furcht›; überwinden ‹Ängste, Befürchtungen›

**quench** /kwentʃ/ *v.t.* A (*extinguish*) löschen; (*fig.*) auslöschen (*geh.*); B (*satisfy*) **~ one's thirst** seinen Durst löschen *od.* stillen; C (*cool*) löschen ‹Koks›; abschrecken ‹Metall›; D (*stifle, suppress*) unterdrücken; dämpfen ‹Begeisterung›

**quern** /kwɜːn/ *n.* Handmühle, *die*

**querulous** /'kwerʊləs/ *adj.* gereizt; (*by nature*) reizbar

**querulously** /'kwerʊləslɪ/ *adv.* gereizt; **discuss sth. ~:** in gereiztem Ton über etw. (*Akk.*) diskutieren

**query** /'kwɪərɪ/ 1 *n.* A (*question*) Frage, *die;* **put/raise a ~:** eine Frage stellen/aufwerfen; **that raises the ~ whether we ...:** das wirft die Frage auf *od.* damit stellt sich die Frage, ob wir ...; B (*question mark*) Fragezeichen, *das.* 2 *v.t.* A (*call in question*) infrage stellen ‹Anweisung, Glaubwürdigkeit, Ergebnis usw.›; beanstanden ‹Rechnung, Kontoauszug›; B (*ask, inquire*) **~ whether/if ...:** fragen, ob ...

**quest** /kwest/ *n.* Suche, *die* (**for** nach); (*for happiness, riches, knowledge, etc.*) Streben, *das* (**for** nach); **in ~ of sth.** auf der Suche nach etw.; **man's ~ for happiness** das menschliche Glücksstreben

**question** /'kwestʃn/ 1 *n.* A Frage, *die;* **ask sb. a ~:** jmdm. eine Frage stellen; **put a ~ to sb.** an jmdn. eine Frage richten; **don't ask so many ~s!** frag nicht so viel!; **ask ~s** Fragen stellen; **ask me no ~s and I'll tell you no lies** wenn du nicht willst, dass ich lüge, stell mir keine Fragen; **ask a silly ~ and you get a silly answer** (*prov.*) wie die Frage, so die Antwort (*Spr.*); **and no ~s asked** ohne dass groß gefragt wird/worden ist (*ugs.*); **[that's a] good ~!** [das ist eine] gute Frage!; ⇒ *also* **leading question**; **pop**[1] 2 E; B (*doubt, objection*) Zweifel, *der* (**about** an + *Dat.*); **there is no ~ about sth.** es besteht kein Zweifel an (*Dat.*) etw.; **there is no ~ [but] that ...:** es besteht kein Zweifel, dass ...; **accept/follow sth. without ~:** etwas kritiklos akzeptieren/befolgen; **not be in ~:** außer [allem] Zweifel stehen; außer Frage sein *od.* stehen; **your honesty is/is not in ~:** man zweifelt/niemand zweifelt an deiner Ehrlichkeit; **beyond all** *or* **without ~:** zweifellos; ohne Frage *od.* Zweifel; **be beyond all** *or* **be without ~:** außer allem Zweifel stehen; außer Frage sein *od.* stehen; ⇒ *also* **call** 1 C; C (*problem, concern, subject*) Frage, *die;* **sth./it is only a ~ of time** etw./es ist [nur] eine Frage der Zeit; **it is [only] a ~ of doing sth.** es geht [nur] darum, etw. zu tun; **a ~ of money** eine Geldfrage; **there is no/some ~ of his doing that** es kann keine Rede davon sein/es ist die Rede davon, dass er das tut; **the ~ of sth. arises** es erhebt sich die Frage von etw.; **the person/thing in ~:** die fragliche *od.* betreffende Person/Sache; **sth./it is out of the ~:** etw./es ist ausgeschlossen; etw./es kommt nicht in Frage (*ugs.*); **the ~ is**

**whether ...:** es geht darum, ob ...; **that is not the ~:** darum geht es nicht; **beside the ~:** belanglos; **put the ~:** zur Abstimmung aufrufen (**to** *Akk.*); **come into ~:** infrage kommen; ⇨ *also* **beg** 1 D; **hour** E; **open** 1 F, G ❷ *v.t.* Ⓐ befragen; ‹Polizei, Gericht usw.:› vernehmen; **he started ~ing me about where I had been** er fing an, mich danach auszufragen, wo ich gewesen war; Ⓑ (*throw doubt upon, raise objections to*) bezweifeln; **her goodwill cannot be ~ed** an ihrem guten Willen kann nicht gezweifelt werden

**questionable** /ˈkwestʃənəbl/ *adj.* fragwürdig

**questionably** /ˈkwestʃənəblɪ/ *adv.* fragwürdig ‹sich benehmen›; auf fragwürdige Weise ‹erwerben›

**questioner** /ˈkwestʃənə(r)/ *n.* Fragesteller, *der*/Fragestellerin, *die*

**questioning** /ˈkwestʃənɪŋ/ ❶ *adj.* fragend; forschend ‹Geist›. ❷ *n.* Fragen, *das;* (*at examination*) Befragung, *die;* (*by police etc.*) Vernehmung, *die;* **brought in for ~:** ins Verhör genommen

**questioningly** /ˈkwestʃənɪŋlɪ/ *adv.* fragend

**question: ~ mark** *n.* (*lit. or fig.*) Fragezeichen, *das;* **a ~ mark hangs over sth.** etw. muss mit einem [großen] Fragezeichen versehen werden; **~ master** *n.* Quizmaster, *der*

**questionnaire** /kwestʃəˈneə(r)/ *n.* Fragebogen, *der*

**ˈquestion time** *n.* Diskussionszeit, *die;* (*Parl.*) Fragestunde, *die;* **at ~ time** während der Diskussionszeit/Fragestunde

**queue** /kju:/ ❶ *n.* Ⓐ (*line*) Schlange, *die;* **a ~ of people/cars** eine Menschen-/Autoschlange; **a long ~ of people** eine lange Schlange; **stand** *or* **wait in a ~:** Schlange stehen; anstehen; **join the ~:** sich anstellen; **take one's place in a ~:** sich in eine Schlange einreihen; ⇨ *also* **jump** 3 G; Ⓑ (*of hair*) Zopf, *der.* ❷ *v.i.* **~ [up]** Schlange stehen; anstehen; (*join ~*) sich anstellen; **~ to buy admission tickets** nach Eintrittskarten anstehen; **~ for a bus** an der Bushaltestelle Schlange stehen; **~ for vegetables** nach Gemüse anstehen

**queue: ~-jumper** *n.* (*Brit.*) *jmd., der sich vordrängt;* **~-jumping** *n.* (*Brit.*) Vordrängen, *das;* Vordrängeln, *das* (*ugs.*)

**quibble** /ˈkwɪbl/ ❶ *n.* Ⓐ (*argument*) spitzfindiges Argument; Ⓑ (*petty objection*) Spitzfindigkeit, *die.* ❷ *v.i.* streiten; **~ over** *or* **about sth.** über etw. (*Akk.*) streiten; **~ about the quality of sb.'s work** die Qualität von jmds. Arbeit bekritteln

**quibbler** /ˈkwɪblə(r)/ *n.* Kritt[e]ler, *der;* Nörgler, *der*

**quibbling** /ˈkwɪblɪŋ/ *adj.* spitzfindig

**quiche** /ki:ʃ/ *n.* Quiche, *die;* **bacon ~:** Speckkuchen, *der*

**quick** /kwɪk/ ❶ *adj.* Ⓐ schnell; kurz ‹Rede, Zusammenfassung, Pause›; flüchtig ‹Kuss, Blick usw.›; **it's ~er by train** mit dem Zug geht es schneller; **ˈthat was/ˈyou were ~!** das ging aber schnell!; **could I have a ~ word with you?** kann ich Sie kurz einmal sprechen?; **he had a ~ bite to eat** er hat schnell etwas gegessen; **how about a ~ drink?** wollen wir kurz einen trinken gehen? (*ugs.*); **write sb. a ~ note** jmdm. schnell ein paar Zeilen schreiben; **be ~!** mach schnell! (*ugs.*); beeil[e] dich!; **be ~ about it!** mach ein bisschen dalli! (*ugs.*); **please try to be ~ [about it]** (*in discussion, on telephone*) bitte fassen Sie sich kurz; Ⓑ (*ready, sensitive, prompt to act or understand*) schnell ‹Person›; wach ‹Verstand›; aufgeweckt ‹Kind›; **he is very ~:** er ist sehr schnell von Begriff (*ugs.*); **be ~ to do sth.** etw. schnell tun; **be ~ to take offence** schnell *od.* leicht beleidigt sein; **she is ~ to criticise** mit Kritik ist sie schnell bei der Hand; **be ~ at figures/repartee** schnell rechnen können/schlagfertig sein; **he's too ~ for me** mit ihm komme ich nicht mit; **have a ~ ear/eye** ein feines Ohr/scharfes Auge haben; **he has a ~ eye/ear for ...:** er hat ein Auge/Ohr für ...; **[have] a ~ temper** ein aufbrausendes Wesen [haben]; **have ~ wits** Köpfchen haben (*ugs.*); Ⓒ (*arch.: living, alive*) lebendig; **the ~ and the dead** die Lebenden und die Toten. ❷ *adv.* schnell; **~!** [mach] schnell! ❸ *n.* empfindliches Fleisch; **bite one's nails to the ~:** die Nägel bis zum Fleisch abkauen; **be cut** *or* **hurt** *or* **stung** *etc.* **to the ~** (*fig.*) tief getroffen *od.* verletzt sein

**quick: ~-acting** *attrib. adj.* schnell wirkend; **~-change** *attrib. adj.* (*Theatre*) Verwandlungs‹künstler, -nummer›

**quicken** /ˈkwɪkn/ ❶ *v.t.* Ⓐ (*make quicker*) beschleunigen; Ⓑ (*animate*) lebendig machen; erwecken; Ⓒ (*stimulate, rouse, inspire*) beflügeln ‹Fantasie, Begeisterung›. ❷ *v.i.* Ⓐ (*become quicker*) sich beschleunigen; schneller werden; ‹Herz:› schneller schlagen; **her breath/steps ~ed** sie atmete/ging schneller; Ⓑ (*be stimulated, roused*) ‹Hoffnung:› sich regen (*geh.*)

**quick: ~ fire** *n.* (*Mil.*) Schnellfeuer, *das;* **~-fire questions** (*fig.*) Fragen wie aus dem Maschinengewehr; **~-firing** *adj.* (*Mil.*) Schnellfeuer-; **~-freeze** *v.t.* schnell gefrieren

**quickie** /ˈkwɪkɪ/ *n.* (*coll.*) im Schnellverfahren hergestellte Sache; (*drink*) Schluck auf die Schnelle (*ugs.*); (*sexual intercourse*) eine Nummer auf die Schnelle (*salopp*); **be a ~:** im Schnellverfahren hergestellt sein

**ˈquicklime** *n.* ungelöschter Kalk

**quickly** /ˈkwɪklɪ/ *adv.* schnell

**ˈquick march** *n.* (*Mil.*) Eilmarsch, *der*

**quickness** /ˈkwɪknɪs/ *n., no pl.* Ⓐ (*speed*) Schnelligkeit, *die;* **the ~ of the hand deceives the eye** die Geschicklichkeit der Hand täuscht das Auge; **~ of action** schnelles Handeln; Ⓑ (*acuteness of perception*) Schärfe, *die;* **~ of the mind** schnelle Auffassungsgabe; Ⓒ (*hastiness*) **~ of temper** Hitzigkeit, *die;* aufbrausendes Wesen

**quick: ~ one** *n.* (*coll.*) Schluck auf die Schnelle (*ugs.*); **have a ~ one** schnell einen trinken [gehen]; (*sexually*) eine schnelle Nummer machen (*salopp*); **~-release** *adj.* **~-release buckle** Schnellverschluss, *der;* **~-release hub** Schnellspannnabe, *die;* **~-release front wheel** Vorderrad, *das* mit Schnellspannnabe; **~sand** *n.* Treibsand, *der;* Mahlsand, *der* (*Seemannsspr.*); **~set** *n.* Heckenpflanze, *die;* (*hedge*) Hecke, *die;* **~-setting** *adj.* schnell trocknend ‹Klebstoff›; schnell bindend ‹Zement›; schnell gelierend ‹Konfitüre usw.›; **~silver** *n.* Ⓐ Quecksilber, *das;* Ⓑ *attrib.* (*fig.*) lebhaft; quecksilbrig; **have a ~silver temperament** Quecksilber im Leib haben (*ugs.*); **~ step** *n.* Ⓐ (*Mil.*) Eilschritt, *der;* Ⓑ (*Dancing*) Quickstep, *der;* **~tempered** *adj.* hitzig; **be ~-tempered** leicht aufbrausen; **~thorn** *n.* (*Bot.*) Weißdorn, *der;* **~-witted** *adj.* geistesgegenwärtig; schlagfertig ‹Antwort›; **~-wittedness** /kwɪkˈwɪtɪdnɪs/ *n., no pl.* Geistesgegenwart, *die;* (*of answer*) Schlagfertigkeit, *die*

**quid[1]** /kwɪd/ *n.* (*Brit. coll.*) Ⓐ *pl. same* (*one pound*) Pfund, *das;* **a few ~:** ein paar Möpse *od.* Flöhe (*salopp*); **fifty ~:** fünfzig Kugeln (*salopp*); Ⓑ **be ~s in** auf sein Geld kommen (*ugs.*)

**quid[2]** *n.* (*tobacco*) Priem, *der*

**quid pro quo** /kwɪd prəʊ ˈkwəʊ/ *n.* Gegenleistung, *die;* Quidproquo, *das* (*geh.*)

**quiescence** /kwɪˈesəns/ *n.* Ruhe, *die*

**quiescent** /kwɪˈesənt/ *adj.* still; untätig ‹Vulkan›

**quiet** /ˈkwaɪət/ ❶ *adj.*, **~er** /ˈkwaɪətə(r)/, **~est** /ˈkwaɪətɪst/ Ⓐ (*silent*) still; (*not loud*) leise ‹Schritte, Musik, Stimme, Motor, Fahrzeug›; **be ~!** (*coll.*) sei still *od.* ruhig!; **~!** Ruhe!; **keep ~:** still sein; **keep sth. ~, keep ~ about sth.** (*fig.*) etw. geheim halten; **I want the matter to be kept ~:** ich möchte, dass darüber Stillschweigen bewahrt wird; **keep sb./a child ~:** dafür sorgen, dass jmd. schweigt/ein Kind ruhig ist; **go ~:** still werden; Ⓑ (*peaceful, not busy*) ruhig; **a ~ evening at home** ein geruhsamer Abend zu Hause; **let's go for a ~ drink** gehen wir in aller Ruhe einen trinken; **have a ~ mind** beruhigt sein; **all was ~ on the border** an der Grenze herrschte Ruhe *od.* war alles ruhig; Ⓒ (*gentle*) sanft; ruhig ‹Kind, Person›; Ⓓ (*not overt, disguised*) versteckt; heimlich ‹Groll›; **have a ~ word with sb.** mit jmdm. unter vier Augen reden; **have a ~ laugh about sth.** im Stillen über etw. (*Akk.*) lachen; **on the ~:** still und heimlich; Ⓔ (*not formal*) zwanglos; klein ‹Feier›; Ⓕ (*not showy*) dezent ‹Farben, Muster›; schlicht ‹Eleganz, Stil›. ❷ *n.* Ruhe, *die;* (*silence, stillness*) Stille, *die;* **in the ~ of the night** in der Stille der Nacht; ⇨ *also* **peace** C. ❸ *v.t.* ⇨ **quieten** 1

**quieten** /ˈkwaɪətn/ (*Brit.*) ❶ *v.t.* Ⓐ beruhigen; zur Ruhe bringen ‹Kind, Schulklasse›; Ⓑ zerstreuen ‹Bedenken, Angst, Verdacht›. ❷ *v.i.* sich beruhigen

**~ ˈdown** ❶ *v.t.* ⇨ **~** 1 A. ❷ *v.i.* sich beruhigen; **since her marriage she has ~ed down** seit sie geheiratet hat, ist sie viel ruhiger geworden

**quietism** /ˈkwaɪətɪzm/ *n.* Quietismus, *der*

**quietly** /ˈkwaɪətlɪ/ *adv.* Ⓐ (*silently*) still; (*not loudly*) leise; **die ~:** eines sanften Todes sterben (*geh.*); Ⓑ (*peacefully, tranquilly*) ruhig; **be ~ drinking one's tea** in [aller] Ruhe seinen Tee trinken; **I'll come ~** (*said by person being arrested*) ich werde ohne Widerstand mitkommen; Ⓒ (*gently*) sanft; **be ~ spoken** eine ruhige Art zu sprechen haben; Ⓓ (*not overtly*) insgeheim; **they settled the affair ~:** sie haben die Angelegenheit unter sich (*Dat.*) ausgemacht; Ⓔ (*not formally*) zwanglos; **get married ~:** im kleinen Rahmen heiraten; Ⓕ (*not showily*) dezent; schlicht

**quietness** /ˈkwaɪətnɪs/ *n., no pl.* Ⓐ (*absence of noise or motion*) Stille, *die;* (*of reply*) Ruhe, *die;* (*of car, engine*) Geräuscharmut, *die;* (*of footsteps*) Geräusch-, Lautlosigkeit, *die;* Ⓑ (*peacefulness, gentleness*) Ruhe, *die*

**quietude** /ˈkwaɪətju:d/ *n.* (*literary*) Stille, *die;* Frieden, *der* (*geh.*)

**quiff** /kwɪf/ *n.* (*Brit.*) Ⓐ (*curl*) Stirnlocke, *die;* Schmachtlocke, *die* (*ugs.*); Ⓑ (*tuft of hair*) [Haar]tolle, *die* (*ugs.*)

**quill** /kwɪl/ *n.* Ⓐ ⇨ **quill feather**; Ⓑ ⇨ **quill pen**; Ⓒ (*stem of feather*) [Feder]kiel, *der;* Ⓓ (*of porcupine*) Stachel, *der*

**quill: ~ feather** *n.* Kielfeder, *die;* **~ pen** *n.* [Feder]kiel, *der*

**quilt** /kwɪlt/ ❶ *n.* Ⓐ (*padded bed coverlet*) Schlafdecke, *die;* **continental ~:** Steppdecke, *die;* Ⓑ (*bedspread*) Tagesdecke, *die;* ⇨ *also* **crazy** D; **patchwork**. ❷ *v.t.* Ⓐ (*cover or line with padded material*) wattieren; Ⓑ (*make or join like ~*) steppen

**quilting** /ˈkwɪltɪŋ/ *n.* Ⓐ (*process*) Steppen, *das;* Ⓑ (*material*) gesteppter Stoff

**quin** /kwɪn/ *n.* (*coll.*) Fünfling, *der*

**quince** /kwɪns/ *n.* Ⓐ (*fruit*) Quitte, *die;* Ⓑ (*tree*) Quittenbaum, *der;* ⇨ *also* **Japanese quince**

**quince ˈjelly** *n.* Quittengelee, *das*

**quinine** /ˈkwɪni:n, kwɪˈni:n/ *n.* Chinin, *das*

**quinquennial** /kwɪŋˈkwenɪəl/ *adj.* (*lasting five years*) fünfjährig; (*once every five years*) fünfjährlich

**quinquennium** /kwɪŋˈkwenɪəm/ *n., pl.* **~s** *or* **quinquennia** /kwɪŋˈkwenɪə/ Jahrfünft, *das*

**quinsy** /ˈkwɪnzɪ/ *n.* (*Med.*) Mandelentzündung, *die*

**quintessence** /kwɪnˈtesəns/ *n.* Ⓐ (*most perfect form*) Quintessenz, *die;* (*embodiment*) Inbegriff, *der;* Ⓑ (*essence, extract of substance*) Extrakt, *der*

**quintessential** /kwɪntɪˈsenʃl/ *adj.* typisch; wesentlich

**quintet, quintette** /kwɪnˈtet/ *n.* (*also Mus.*) Quintett, *das;* **piano/clarinet ~:** Klavier-/Klarinettenquintett, *das*

**quintuple** /ˈkwɪntjʊpl/ ❶ *adj.* fünffach. ❷ *n.* Fünffache, *das.* ❸ *v.t.* verfünffachen. ❹ *v.i.* sich verfünffachen

**quintuplet** /ˈkwɪntjʊplɪt, kwɪnˈtju:plɪt/ *n.* Fünfling, *der*

**quip** /kwɪp/ ❶ *n.* Ⓐ (*clever saying*) Witzelei, *die;* Geistreichelei, *die* (*scherzh. abwertend*); Ⓑ (*sarcastic remark*) Bissigkeit, *die.*

**2** *v.i.*, **-pp-** (*make quips*) witzeln (**at** über + *Akk.*); geistreicheln (*scherzh. abwertend*)

**quire** /ˈkwaɪə(r)/ *n.* (*Bookbinding: collection of sheets*) Lage, *die;* (*24/25 sheets*) 24/25 Bögen Papier; (*4 sheets*) *4 zu 8 Blättern gefaltete Bögen;* **in ~s** ungebunden

**quirk** /kwɜːk/ *n.* Marotte, *die;* Schrulle, *die* (*ugs.*); **[by a] ~ of nature/fate/history** *etc.* [durch eine] Laune der Natur/des Schicksals/der Geschichte *usw.*

**quirky** /ˈkwɜːkɪ/ *adj.* schrullig (*ugs.*)

**quisling** /ˈkwɪzlɪŋ/ *n.* Quisling, *der* (*abwertend*)

**quit** /kwɪt/ **1** *pred. adj.* **be ~ of sb./sth.** jmds./einer Sache ledig sein (*geh.*). **2** *v.t.*, **-tt-**, (*Amer.*) **quit** **A** (*give up*) aufgeben; (*cease, stop*) aufhören mit; **~ doing sth.** aufhören, etw. zu tun; **B** (*depart from*) verlassen; (*leave occupied premises*) ausziehen aus; *abs.* ausziehen; **they were given** *or* **had notice to ~ [the flat** *etc.***]** ihnen wurde [die Wohnung *usw.*] gekündigt; **~ hold of sth.** etw. loslassen; **C** *also abs.* (*from job*) kündigen

**quitch [grass]** /ˈkwɪtʃ (grɑːs)/ ⇒ **couch²**

**quite** /kwaɪt/ *adv.* **A** (*entirely*) ganz; völlig; vollkommen; gänzlich ‹unnötig›; fest ‹entschlossen›; **not ~** (*almost*) nicht ganz; (*noticeably not*) nicht gerade; **I'm sorry — That's ~ all right** Entschuldigung — Schon gut *od.* in Ordnung; **not ~ five o'clock** noch nicht ganz 5 Uhr; **I don't need any help; I'm ~ all right, thank you** danke, es geht schon, ich komme allein zurecht; **I've had ~ enough of it** jetzt habe ich aber genug davon; **how can you be ~ so sure?** wie kannst du so sicher sein?; **I've never known anyone who was ~ so stubborn** ich kenne niemanden, der so stur wie er/sie ist; **I ~ agree/understand** ganz meine Meinung/ich verstehe schon; **~ [so]!** [ja,] genau *od.* richtig!; **be ~ a hero** wirklich ein Idol sein; **that is ~ a different matter** das ist etwas ganz anderes *od.* schon etwas anderes; **we drove at ~ a speed** wir sind vielleicht schnell gefahren (*ugs.*); **they had ~ a party** sie haben vielleicht gefeiert (*ugs.*); **be ~ other than sth.** ‹Wahrheit, Ansicht:› sich deutlich von etw. unterscheiden; **~ another story/case** eine ganz andere Geschichte/ein ganz anderer Fall; **B** (*somewhat, to some extent*) ziemlich; recht; ganz ‹gern›; **it was ~ an effort** es war ziemlich *od.* recht anstrengend; **that is ~ a shock/surprise** das ist ein ziemlicher Schock/eine ziemliche Überraschung; **I'd ~ like to talk to him** ich würde ganz gern mit ihm sprechen; **~ a few** ziemlich viele *od.* eine ganze Menge ‹Bücher, Preise, Urteile›; **they had ~ a lot of applicants/a run of success** sie hatten eine ziemlich große Anzahl von Bewerbern/sie waren ziemlich lange [Zeit] erfolgreich

**quits** /kwɪts/ *pred. adj.* **be ~ [with sb.]** [mit jmdm.] quitt sein (*ugs.*); **call it ~** ‹Einzelperson:› zustimmen *od.* Ruhe geben; ‹mehrere Personen:› sich vertragen; **let's call it ~!** wollen wir die Sache auf sich beruhen lassen!; (*nothing owed*) sagen wir, wir sind quitt; ⇒ *also* **double** 3 C

**quitter** /ˈkwɪtə(r)/ *n.* Drückeberger, *der*/Drückebergerin, *die* (*ugs. abwertend*)

**quiver¹** /ˈkwɪvə(r)/ **1** *v.i.* zittern (**with** vor + *Dat.*); ‹Stimme, Lippen:› beben (*geh.*); ‹Lid:› zucken; ‹Stimme:› vibrieren; **her legs ~ed** ihr zitterten die Beine; ihre Beine zitterten. **2** *n.* Zittern, *das;* (*of lips, voice also*) Beben, *das* (*geh.*); (*of eyelid*) Zucken, *das;* **there was a ~ in her voice** ihre Stimme zitterte *od.* (*geh.*) bebte; **be all in a ~:** am ganzen Körper zittern

**quiver²** *n.* (*for arrows*) Köcher, *der*

**qui vive** /kiː ˈviːv/ *n.* **be on the ~:** auf dem Quivive sein (*ugs.*); wachsam sein

**quixotic** /kwɪkˈsɒtɪk/ *adj.* lebensfremd ‹Person, Ideal›; idealistisch ‹Verhalten›; **a ~ act** eine Donquichotterie; **a ~ person** ein Don Quichotte *od.* Quixote *od.* Quijote

**quiz** /kwɪz/ **1** *n., pl.* **~zes** **A** (*Radio, Telev., etc.*) Quiz, *das;* Ratespiel, *das;* **contestants in/guests on the ~:** Quizteilnehmer *Pl.;* **B** (*interrogation, questionnaire, test*) Prüfung, *die;* (*for pupils*) Aufgabe, *die.* **2** *v.t.*, **-zz-** ausfragen (**about sth.** nach etw., **about sb.** über jmdn.), fragen (**about** nach); ‹Polizei:› verhören, vernehmen ‹Verdächtige›

**quiz: ~master** *n.* (*Radio, Telev.*) Quizmaster, *der;* Spielleiter, *der;* **~ programme, ~ show** *ns.* (*Radio, Telev.*) Quizsendung, *die*

**quizzical** /ˈkwɪzɪkl/ *adj.* fragend ‹Blick, Miene›; (*mocking*) spöttisch ‹Lächeln›

**quizzically** /ˈkwɪzɪkəlɪ/ *adv.* fragend ‹blicken›; (*mocking*) spöttisch ‹lächeln›

**quoin** /kɔɪn/ *n.* **A** (*angle*) Ecke, *die;* **B** (*cornerstone*) Eckstein, *der*

**quoit** /kɔɪt/ *n.* (*Games*) [Gummi]ring, *der*

**quoits** /kɔɪts/ *n., no pl.* (*Games*) Ringtennis, *das*

**quorate** /ˈkwɔːreɪt/ *adj.* beschlussfähig

**quorum** /ˈkwɔːrəm/ *n.* Quorum, *das*

**quota** /ˈkwəʊtə/ *n.* **A** (*share*) Anteil, *der;* **B** (*maximum quantity*) Höchstquote, *die;* (*of goods to be produced/imported*) maximale Produktions-/Einfuhrquote; (*quantity of goods to be produced*) Produktionsmindestquote, *die;* (*of work*) [Arbeits]pensum, *das;* **C** (*maximum number*) Höchstquote, *die;* (*of immigrants/students permitted*) maximale Einwanderungs-/Zulassungsquote

**quotation** /kwəʊˈteɪʃn/ *n.* **A** Zitieren, *das;* Zitate *Pl.;* (*passage*) Zitat, *das;* **dictionary of ~s** Zitatenlexikon, *das;* **B** (*amount stated as current price*) [Börsen]kurs, *der;* Quotation, *die* (*fachspr.*); [Börsen-, Kurs]notierung, *die;* **C** (*contractor's estimate*) Kosten[vor]anschlag, *der;* Kalkulation, *die*

**quoˈtation marks** *n. pl.* Anführungszeichen *Pl.*

**quote** /kwəʊt/ **1** *v.t.* **A** *also abs.* zitieren (**from** aus); zitieren aus ‹Buch, Text, Klassiker, Übersetzung›; (*appeal to*) sich berufen auf (+ *Akk.*) ‹Person, Buch, Text, Quelle›; (*mention*) anführen ‹Vorkommnis, Beispiel›; **he is ~d as saying that ...:** er soll gesagt haben, dass ...; **don't ~ me on it** sagen Sie nicht, dass Sie das von mir haben; **~ an earlier case to sb.** jmdm. einen früheren Fall nennen; **~ sth. as the reason/an example** etw. als Grund/Beispiel anführen; **..., and I ~, ...:** ..., ich zitiere, ...; **B** (*state price of*) angeben, nennen ‹Preis›; quotieren (*fachspr.*); **wheat/the £ is ~d at ...:** der Weizenpreis/Pfundkurs wird mit ... angegeben; **~ sb. a price** jmdm. einen Preis nennen; **C** (*St. Exch.*) notieren ‹Aktie›; **be ~d at a lower price** niedriger notiert werden; **D** (*enclose in quotation marks*) in Anführungszeichen (*Akk.*) setzen; **..., ~, ...:** ..., Zitat, ...
**2** *n.* (*coll.*) **A** (*passage*) Zitat, *das;* **B** (*commercial quotation*) Kosten[vor]anschlag, *der;* Kalkulation, *die;* **C** *usu. in pl.* (*quotation mark*) Anführungszeichen, *das;* Gänsefüßchen, *das* (*ugs.*)

**quoth** /kwəʊθ/ *v.t. 1st & 3rd pers. p. t.* (*arch.*) *in sing./pl.* sprach/sprachen (*geh.*)

**quotient** /ˈkwəʊʃnt/ *n.* (*Math.*) Quotient, *der;* ⇒ *also* **intelligence quotient**

**q.v.** /kjuːˈviː/ *abbr.* **quod vide** s. d.

# Rr

**R, r** /ɑ:(r)/ *n., pl.* **Rs** *or* **R's** A (*letter*) R, r, *das;* B **the three Rs** Lesen, Schreiben und Rechnen; C **the R months** die Monate mit r

**R.** *abbr.* A ▶1480| **River** Fl.; **R. Thames** die Themse; B **Regina/Rex** Königin, *die*/König, *der;* **in the case R. v. Smith** in der Sache der Königin/des Königs gegen Smith; C ® **registered as trademark** ®; Wz; D (*Amer.*) **Republican;** E (*Chess*) **rook** T

**r.** *abbr.* **right** re.

**RA** *abbr.* A **Royal Academician** Mitglied der „Royal Academy"; B **Royal Academy** ⇒ **academy** A; C **Royal Artillery** Königl. Art.

**rabbet** /ˈræbɪt/ *n.* (*groove*) Falz, *der;* (*to receive edge of door or window*) Anschlag, *der*

**rabbi** /ˈræbaɪ/ *n.* Rabbi[ner], *der;* (*as title*) Rabbi, *der;* **Chief R~:** Oberrabbiner, *der*

**rabbit** /ˈræbɪt/ ❶ *n.* A Kaninchen, *das;* B (*Brit. coll.: poor player*) Flasche, *die* (*ugs.*); Niete, *die* (*ugs.*); C (*Amer.: hare*) Hase, *der.* ⇒ *also* **breed** 2 A; **Welsh rabbit.** ❷ *v.i.* (*Brit. coll.: talk*) ~ [**on**] sülzen (*salopp*); quatschen (*salopp*)

**rabbit:** ~ **burrow** *n.* Kaninchenbau, *der;* Kaninchenhöhle, *die;* ~ **food** *n.* Kaninchenfutter, *das;* (*fig. joc.*) Grünzeug, *das;* Kaninchenfutter, *das* (*scherzh.*); ~ **fur** *n.* Kaninchenfell, *das;* Kanin, *das* (*fachspr.*); (*coat*) Kaninmantel, *der;* ~ **hole** ⇒ ~ **burrow;** ~ **hutch** *n.* (*lit. or fig. joc.*) Kaninchenstall, *der;* ~ **punch** *n.* Rabbitpunch, *der* (*Boxen*); Genickschlag, *der;* ~ **warren** *n.* Kaninchengehege, *das;* **this building is a ~ warren** dieses Gebäude ist das reinste Labyrinth

**rabble** /ˈræbl/ *n.* Mob, *der* (*abwertend*); Pöbel, *der* (*abwertend*)

**rabble:** ~**-rouser** /ˈræblraʊzə(r)/ *n.* Aufwiegler, *der*/Aufwieglerin, *die;* [Auf]hetzer, *der*/[Auf]hetzerin, *die;* ~**-rousing** ❶ *adj.* aufwieglerisch, [auf]hetzerisch ‹Rede, Wort›; ❷ *n.* [Auf]hetzerei, *die;* Aufwiegelei, *die*

**Rabelaisian** /ræbəˈleɪzjən/ *adj.* rabelaissch ‹Stil, Sprachreichtum›

**rabid** /ˈræbɪd/ *adj.* A ([*Vet.*] *Med.*) tollwütig ‹Tier, Person›; Tollwut‹symptom, -erreger, -virus›; B (*furious, violent*) wild ‹Hass, Wut›; (*unreasoning, extreme*) fanatisch ‹Demokrat, Reformer, Anhänger, Befürworter, Antisemitismus›

**rabies** /ˈreɪbi:z/ *n.* ([*Vet.*] *Med.*) Tollwut, *die;* Rabies, *die* (*fachspr.*)

**RAC** *abbr.* (*Brit.*) **Royal Automobile Club** Königlicher Britischer Automobilklub

**raccoon** ⇒ **racoon**

**race¹** /reɪs/ ❶ *n.* A Rennen, *das;* **have a ~ [with** *or* **against sb.]** mit jmdm. um die Wette laufen/schwimmen/reiten *usw.;* **100 metres ~:** 100-m-Rennen/-Schwimmen, *das;* **be in the ~** (*lit. or fig.*) gut im Rennen liegen; **be out of the ~** ‹Läufer, Schwimmer, Reiter usw.:› ausgeschieden sein; (*fig.*) ‹Bewerber:› nicht mehr im Rennen sein; B *in pl.* (*series*) (*for horses*) Pferderennen, *das;* (*for dogs*) Hunderennen, *das;* **go to the ~s** zum Rennen gehen; **a day at the ~s** ein Tag auf der Rennbahn; C (*fig.*) **a ~ against time** ein Wettlauf mit der Zeit; **sb.'s** *or* **the ~ is [nearly] run** (*after pursuit*) jmd. ist verloren; (*after severe illness, euphem.*) jmds. Zeit ist gekommen (*geh. verhüll.*); **the ~ for governor/nomination** das Rennen um den Gouverneursposten/die Nominierung; **it will be a mad ~ to get the work finished in time** es wird eine wahnsinnige Hetze werden, die Arbeit rechtzeitig fertig zu bekommen; D (*channel of stream*) Gerinne, *das* (*veralt.*); ⇒ *also* **mill race;** E (*Mech. Engin.: of ball bearing*) Ring, *der.*
❷ *v.i.* A (*in swimming, running, walking, sailing, etc.*) um die Wette schwimmen/laufen/gehen/segeln *usw.* (**with, against** mit); ~ **against time** ‹Läufer:› gegen die Uhr laufen; (*fig.*) gegen die Uhr *od.* Zeit arbeiten; B (*indulge in horseracing*) dem Pferderennsport frönen; (*Sports: in car*) Autorennen fahren; ~ **at a meeting** (*own or train horses for it*) bei einem Rennen Pferde laufen lassen; C (*go at full or excessive speed*) ‹Motor:› durchdrehen; ‹Puls:› jagen, rasen; D (*rush*) sich sehr beeilen; hetzen; ‹Wolken:› jagen; (*on foot also*) rennen; jagen; ~ **after sb.** jmdm. hinterherhetzen; ~ **[a]round** *or* **about** herumhetzen; hin und her hetzen; ~ **to finish sth.** sich beeilen, um etw. fertig zu kriegen (*ugs.*); ~ **ahead with sth.** (*hurry*) etw. im Eiltempo vorantreiben (*ugs.*); (*make rapid progress*) bei etw. mit Riesenschritten vorankommen (*ugs.*).
❸ *v.t.* A (*have ~ with*) (*in swimming, riding, walking, running, etc.*) um die Wette schwimmen/reiten/gehen/laufen *usw.* mit; **I'll ~ you** ich mache mit dir einen Wettlauf; B (*cause to ~*) ‹Fahrer:› rasen mit (*ugs.*) ‹Auto, Kajak usw.›; ‹Steuermann:› sehr schnell fahren mit ‹Schiff›; C hochjagen (*salopp*) ‹Motor›; ~ **sb. along** jmdn. vorwärts hetzen (*ugs.*)

**race²** *n.* A (*Anthrop., Biol.*) Rasse, *die;* **be of mixed ~:** gemischtrassig *od.* -rassisch sein; B (*class of persons*) Klasse, *die;* (*esp. Relig.*) Kaste, *die;* C (*group with common descent*) Geschlecht, *das;* Sippe, *die;* (*nation*) Volk, *das;* (*tribe*) Volk, *das;* Stamm, *der;* **the human ~:** die Menschheit; die Menschen; **be of noble ~:** vornehmer Abkunft (*geh.*) *od.* Abstammung sein

**race:** ~**card** *n.* Rennprogramm, *das;* ~**course** *n.* Rennbahn, *die;* ~**goer** *n.* Rennbesucher, *der*/-besucherin, *die;* ~ **hatred** *n.* Rassenhass, *der;* ~**horse** *n.* Rennpferd, *das*

**raceme** /rəˈsi:m/ *n.* (*Bot.*) Blütentraube, *die*

ˈ**race meeting** *n.* (*Sport*) Renntag, *der;* (*on successive days*) Renntage *Pl.*

**racer** /ˈreɪsə(r)/ *n.* (*person*) Läufer, *der*/Läuferin, *die;* (*horse*) Rennpferd, *das;* Renner, *der;* (*yacht*) Rennjacht, *die;* (*bicycle*) Rennrad, *das;* Rennmaschine, *die;* (*car*) Rennwagen, *der;* (*plane*) Sportflugzeug, *das*

**race:** ~ **relations** *n. pl.* Beziehung zwischen den Rassen; **R~ Relations Act** (*Brit.*) Gesetz gegen Rassendiskriminierung; ~ **riot** *n.* Rassenkrawall, *der;* ~**track** *n.* Rennbahn, *die;* ~**way** *n.* (*Amer.*) Trabrennbahn, *die*

**rachitic** /rəˈkɪtɪk/ *adj.* (*Med.*) rachitisch

**rachitis** /rəˈkaɪtɪs/ *n.* (*Med.*) Rachitis, *die*

**racial** /ˈreɪʃl/ *adj.* Rassen‹diskriminierung, -konflikt, -gleichheit, -vorurteil, -unruhen, -stolz›; rassisch ‹Gruppe, Minderheit›; ~ **attack/assault** rassistischer Angriff/Überfall; ~ **harmony** Eintracht unter den Rassen; **Commission for R~ Equality** (*Brit.*) Kommission für Rassengleichheit

**racialism** /ˈreɪʃəlɪzm/ *n., no pl.* Rassismus, *der*

**racialist** /ˈreɪʃəlɪst/ ❶ *n.* Rassist, *der*/Rassistin, *die.* ❷ *adj.* rassistisch

**racially** /ˈreɪʃəlɪ/ *adv.* rassisch; **be ~ prejudiced** Rassenvorurteile haben

**racily** /ˈreɪsɪlɪ/ *adv.* A flott ‹erzählen, schreiben›; pikant ‹gewürzt›; kraftvoll ‹gestaltet›; B (*Amer.: in a risqué manner*) gewagt ‹erzählen, sich kleiden›

**racing** /ˈreɪsɪŋ/ *n., no pl., no indef. art.* A (*profession, sport*) Rennsport, *der;* (*with horses*) Pferdesport, *der;* B (*races*) Rennen *Pl.;* **go ~** (*attend horse/motor races*) zum Rennen gehen; **it is a ~ certainty that he will ...:** mit größter Wahrscheinlichkeit wird er ...

**racing:** ~ **bicycle** *n.* Rennrad, *das;* Rennmaschine, *die;* ~ **car** *n.* Rennwagen, *der;* ~ **colours** *n. pl.* Rennfarben *Pl.;* ~ **driver** *n.* Rennfahrer, *der*/-fahrerin, *die;* ~ **track** *n.* Rennbahn, *die*

**racism** /ˈreɪsɪzm/ *n.* Rassismus, *der*

**racist** /ˈreɪsɪst/ ❶ *n.* Rassist, *der*/Rassistin, *die.* ❷ *adj.* rassistisch

**rack¹** /ræk/ ❶ *n.* A (*for luggage in bus, train, etc.*) Ablage, *die;* (*for pipes, hats, spectacles, toast, plates*) Ständer, *der;* (*for tools*) Regal, *das;* (*on bicycle, motorcycle*) Gepäckträger, *der;* (*on car*) Dachgepäckträger, *der;* B (*for fodder*) Raufe, *die;* C (*instrument of torture*) Folter[bank], *die;* **put sb. on the ~:** jmdn. auf die Folter legen; (*fig.*) ‹Problem, Ungewissheit:› jmdn. quälen; **be on the ~** (*lit. or fig.*) Folterqualen leiden; D (*Mech. Engin.*) Zahnstange, *die;* ~ **and pinion** Zahntrieb, *der.*
❷ *v.t.* A (*lit. or fig.: torture*) quälen, plagen; **be ~ed by** *or* **with pain** *etc.* von Schmerzen *usw.* gequält und geplagt werden; B (*shake violently*) ‹Husten, Vibration:› erschüttern, heftig schütteln ‹Körper›; C ~ **one's brain[s]** (*fig.*) sich (*Dat.*) den Kopf zerbrechen *od.* das Hirn zermartern (*ugs.*) (**for** über + *Akk.*)
~ ˈ**up** *v.t.* (*Amer.: achieve*) machen (*ugs.*), erzielen ‹Punkte›; kriegen (*ugs.*) ‹Preis›

**rack²** *n.* (*joint of lamb etc.*) vorderes Rippenstück [vom Lamm *usw.*]

**rack³** ⇒ **ruin** 1 A

**rack⁴** *v.t.* ~ **[off]** abziehen ‹Wein, Bier› (**into** auf + *Akk.*)

**racket¹** /ˈrækɪt/ *n.* A (*Sport*) Schläger, *der;* (*Tennis also*) Racket, *das;* B *in pl., usu. constr. as sing.* (*ball game*) Racquets, *das;* Racquetball, *der*

**racket²** *n.* A (*disturbance, uproar*) Lärm, *der;* Krach, *der;* **make a ~:** Krach *od.* Lärm machen; **they kicked up no end of a ~** (*coll.*) sie machten einen Höllenlärm (*ugs.*); B (*dishonest scheme*) Schwindelgeschäft, *das* (*ugs.*); **a narcotics** *or* **drug ~:** krimineller Drogenhandel; C (*coll.: line of business*) Job, *der* (*ugs.*); **I'm in the insurance ~:** ich mache in Versicherungen (*salopp*)

**racketeer** /rækɪˈtɪə(r)/ *n.* Ganove, *der;* (*profiteer*) Wucherer, *der;* **drug ~:** Drogenhändler, *der*/-händlerin, *die;* Dealer, *der*/Dealerin, *die* (*ugs.*)

**racketeering** /rækɪˈtɪərɪŋ/ *n.* kriminelle Geschäfte *Pl.;* Schwindel, *der;* (*profiteering*) Wucher, *der*

ˈ**racket press** *n.* (*Sport*) Spanner, *der*

**racking** /ˈrækɪŋ/ *attrib. adj.* quälend

**rack:** ~ **railway** *n.* Zahnrad-, Zahnstangenbahn, *die;* ~ **rent** *n.* (*excessive rent*) überhöhte Miete; Wuchermiete, *die* (*abwertend*)

**raconteur** /rækɒnˈtɜ:(r)/ *n.* Geschichten-, Anekdotenerzähler, *der*/-erzählerin, *die*

**racoon** /rəˈku:n/ *n.* (*Zool.*) Waschbär, *der*

**racquet** ⇒ **racket¹**

**racy** /ˈreɪsɪ/ *adj.* A flott (*ugs.*), schwungvoll ‹Erzählweise, Stil, Sprache›; schwungvoll ‹Rede›; pikant ‹Aroma›; saftig (*ugs.*) ‹Humor›; rassig ‹Traubensorte, Wein›; B (*Amer.: risqué*) gewagt, pikant ‹Geschichte, Anekdote›

**rad** /ræd/ *n.* (*Phys.*) Rad, *das*

**RADA** /ɑ:reɪdi:ˈeɪ, (*coll.*) ˈrɑ:də/ *abbr.* (*Brit.*) **Royal Academy of Dramatic Art** RADA; Königliche Schauspielakademie

**radar** /ˈreɪdɑ:(r)/ *n.* Radar, *das od. der*

**radar: ~ operator** *n.* ▶ 1261 Radartechniker, *der*/-technikerin, *die;* **~ scanner** *n.* Radarantenne, *die;* **~ screen** *n.* Radarschirm, *der;* **~ trap** *n.* Radarfalle, *die* (*ugs.*)

**radial** /ˈreɪdɪəl/ ❶ *adj.* Ⓐ (*arranged like rays or radii*) strahlenförmig angeordnet; radiär (*fachspr.*); strahlig, strahlenförmig ‹Muster›; Ⓑ (*acting or moving from centre*) radial ‹Durchfluss, Dispersion, Bahn›; Radial‹bohrmaschine, -beschleunigung›; Ⓒ (*having spokes or radiating lines*) strahlenförmig ‹Bauform›; **~ wheel** Radialrad, *das;* Ⓓ (*Anat.*) Speichen‹nerv, -vene›; **~ artery** Speichenarterie, *die;* Puls[schlag]ader, *die* (*volkst.*). ❷ *n.* Radial-, Gürtelreifen, *der*

**ˈradial engine** *n.* Sternmotor, *der*

**radially** /ˈreɪdɪəlɪ/ *adv.* strahlenförmig; radial (*fachspr.*)

**radial: ~[-ply] tyre** *n.* Radial-, Gürtelreifen, *der*

**radian** /ˈreɪdɪən/ *n.* (*Geom.*) Radiant, *der*

**radiance** /ˈreɪdɪəns/, **radiancy** /ˈreɪdɪənsɪ/ *n.* Ⓐ (*emission of light rays etc.*) Leuchten, *das;* (*of sun, stars, lamp also*) Strahlen, *das;* Ⓑ (*joyful, hopeful, etc. appearance*) Strahlen, *das;* **~ of joy/hope** freudiges/hoffnungsvolles Strahlen

**radiant** /ˈreɪdɪənt/ ❶ *adj.* Ⓐ strahlend, leuchtend ‹Himmelskörper, Dämmerung›; leuchtend ‹Lichtstrahl›; **~ colours** leuchtende Farben; Ⓑ (*fig.*) strahlend; fröhlich ‹Stimmung›; **be ~** ‹Person, Augen:› strahlen (**with** vor + *Dat.*). ❷ *n.* Ⓐ (*on electric or gas heater*) Heizfläche, *die;* Ⓑ (*Astron.*) Radiant, *der*

**radiant: ~ heat** *n.* Strahlungswärme, *die;* **~ heater** *n.* Heizstrahler, *der*

**radiantly** /ˈreɪdɪəntlɪ/ *adv.* Ⓐ leuchtend; strahlend; **shine ~** ‹Sonne, Sterne:› leuchten; ‹Lichtquelle:› strahlen; Ⓑ (*fig.*) strahlend; **be ~ beautiful** von strahlender Schönheit sein

**radiate** /ˈreɪdɪeɪt/ ❶ *v.i.* Ⓐ ‹Sonne, Sterne:› scheinen, strahlen; ‹Glas, Metall:› leuchten, glänzen; ‹Kerze:› scheinen; ‹Hitze, Wärme:› ausstrahlen, sich verbreiten; ‹Schein, Radiowellen:› ausgesendet werden, ausgehen (**from** von); ‹Lichtstrahl:› leuchten; Ⓑ (*diverge or spread from central point*) strahlenförmig ausgehen (**from** von). ❷ *v.t.* Ⓐ verbreiten, ausstrahlen ‹Licht, Wärme, Klang›; aussenden ‹Strahlen, Wellen›; Ⓑ ausstrahlen ‹Glück, Liebe, Hoffnung, Gesundheit, Fröhlichkeit›; (*spread as from centre*) verbreiten ‹Liebe, Heiterkeit usw.› (**around** um … herum)

**radiation** /reɪdɪˈeɪʃn/ *n.* Ⓐ (*emission of energy*) Emission, *die;* (*of signals*) Ausstrahlung, *die;* Ⓑ (*energy transmitted*) Strahlung, *die;* Strahlenemission, *die;* **solar ~:** Sonneneinstrahlung, *die;* **~ from a coal fire** Wärmestrahlung eines Kohleofens; **contaminated by ~:** strahlenverseucht; Ⓒ *attrib.* Strahlen‹behandlung, -therapie, -krankheit, -belastung, -dosis, -verseuchung, -zählrohr, -chemie›; Strahlungs‹intensität, -leistung, -messgerät, -energie, -verbrennung, -niveau›; **~ leak[age]** Leckstrahlung, *die*

**radiator** /ˈreɪdɪeɪtə(r)/ *n.* Ⓐ (*for heating a room*) [Rippen]heizkörper, *der;* Radiator, *der;* (*portable*) Heizgerät, *das;* Heizstrahler, *der;* Ⓑ (*for cooling engine*) Kühler, *der*

**radiator: ~ cap** *n.* Kühlverschraubung, *die;* Kühlerverschlussdeckel, *der;* **~ grille** *n.* Kühlergrill, *der;* Kühlerschutzgitter, *das;* **~ mascot** *n.* Kühlerfigur, *die*

**radical** /ˈrædɪkl/ ❶ *adj.* Ⓐ (*thorough, drastic; also Polit.*) radikal; drastisch, radikal ‹Maßnahme›; umwälzend ‹Auswirkungen›; durchgreifend ‹Umstrukturierung, Veränderung usw.›; (*Brit. Hist.*) radikal; extrem liberal; (*Amer. Hist.*) radikal [republikanisch]; **a ~ cure** eine Radikalkur; Ⓑ (*progressive, unorthodox*) radikal; revolutionär ‹Stil, Design, Sprachgebrauch›; Ⓒ (*inherent, fundamental*) grundlegend ‹Fehler, Unterschied›; Ⓓ (*Med.*) **~ surgery** Radikaloperation, *die;* Ⓔ (*Bot., Ling., Math.*) Wurzel-.
❷ *n.* Ⓐ (*Polit.*) Radikale, *der/die;* Ⓑ (*Math.*) (*quantity*) Wurzelausdruck, *der;* Radikal, *das* (*fachspr.*); (*radical sign*) Wurzelzeichen, *das;* Ⓒ (*Chem.*) Radikal, *das*

**radical ˈchic** *n.* linke Schickeria

**radicalism** /ˈrædɪkəlɪzm/ *n.*, *no pl.* (*Polit.*) Radikalismus, *der*

**radically** /ˈrædɪkəlɪ/ *adv.* Ⓐ (*thoroughly, drastically*) radikal; von Grund auf; Ⓑ (*Polit.*) radikal; Ⓒ (*originally, basically*) prinzipiell; Ⓓ (*inherently, fundamentally*) von Grund auf

**radicchio** /rəˈdɪkjəʊ/ *n.*, *no pl.* Radicchio, *der*

**radicle** /ˈrædɪkl/ *n.* (*Bot.*) (*part of embryo*) Keimwurzel, *die;* Radicula, *die* (*fachspr.*); (*rootlet*) Würzelchen, *das*

**radio** /ˈreɪdɪəʊ/ ❶ *n.*, *pl.* **~s** Ⓐ *no pl.*, *no indef. art.* Funk, *der;* (*for private communication*) Sprechfunk, *der;* **over the/by ~:** über/per Funk; Ⓑ *no pl.*, *no indef. art.* (*Broadcasting*) Rundfunk, *der;* Hörfunk, *der;* **listen to the ~:** Radio hören; **on the ~:** im Radio *od.* Rundfunk; **commercial ~:** Werbefunk, *der;* **work in ~:** beim Rundfunk arbeiten; Ⓒ (*apparatus*) Radio, *das;* **~ [equipment]** Funk[sprech]gerät, *das;* Ⓓ (*broadcasting station*) Rundfunk- *od.* Radiosender, *der;* **R~ Luxembourg** Radio Luxemburg; **R~ One** Erstes [Rundfunk]programm.
❷ *attrib. adj.* Ⓐ (*Broadcasting*) Rundfunk‹antenne, -gerät, -empfänger, -sender, -sendung, -sprecher, -interview, -programm, -übertragung, -techniker, -technik›; Radio‹gerät, -sendung, -programm, -welle›; Sende‹antenne, -mast, -erlaubnis›; Funk‹mast, -turm, -frequenz, -verbindung, -verkehr, -netz, -taxi, -gerät, -wagen›; **~ beam** Leitfunkstrahl, *der;* Richtstrahl, *der;* **~ frequency** Hochfrequenz, *die;* **~ drama** *or* **play** Hörspiel, *das;* Ⓑ (*Astron.*) Radio‹astronomie, -galaxis, -teleskop›. ⇒ *also* **fix** 4 B; **ham** 1 C.
❸ *v.t.* funken ‹Meldung, Nachricht›; durch *od.* per Funk übermitteln; **~ sb. for sth.** von jmdm. über Funk etw. anfordern.
❹ *v.i.* funken; eine Funkmeldung *od.* einen Funkspruch übermitteln *od.* durchgeben; **the ship ~ed for help** das Schiff bat über Funk um Hilfe

**radio: ~ˈactive** *adj.* radioaktiv; **~acˈtivity** *n.* Radioaktivität, *die;* **~ beacon** *n.* Funkfeuer, *das;* **~biˈology** *n.* Strahlenbiologie, *die;* Radiobiologie, *die;* **~ˈcarbon** *n.* Radiokohlenstoff, *der;* Karbon-14, *das;* **~carbon dating** *n.* Radiokarbondatierung, *die;* **~ casˈsette player** *n.* Kassettenradio, *das;* Radio mit Kassettenteil; **~ˈchemistry** *n.* Radiochemie, *die;* Strahlenchemie, *die;* **~ control** *n.* Funk[fern]steuerung, *die;* **~-controlled** *adj.* funkgesteuert; ferngesteuert; **~ frequency** *n.* Hochfrequenz, *die; attrib.* **~-frequency** Hochfrequenz-

**radiogram** /ˈreɪdɪəʊgræm/ *n.* Ⓐ (*Brit.*) ≈ Musiktruhe, *die;* Ⓑ ⇒ **radiograph** 1

**radiograph** /ˈreɪdɪəgrɑ:f/ ❶ *n.* Röntgenaufnahme, *die;* Radiogramm, *das* (*fachspr.*). ❷ *v.t.* eine Röntgenaufnahme/ein Radiogramm machen von

**radiographer** /reɪdɪˈɒgrəfə(r)/ *n.* ▶ 1261 Röntgenologe, *der*/Röntgenologin, *die;* (*instrument-operator*) Röntgenassistent, *der*/-assistentin, *die*

**radiographic** /reɪdɪəˈgræfɪk/ *adj.* röntgenographisch; radiographisch

**radiography** /reɪdɪˈɒgrəfɪ/ *n.* Radiographie, *die;* Röntgenographie, *die*

**ˈradio ham** *n.* Funkamateur, *der*

**radio: ~ˈisotope** *n.* Radioisotop, *das;* radioaktives Isotop; **~ loˈcation** *n.* Funkortung, *die;* Radar, *der od. das*

**radiological** /reɪdɪəˈlɒdʒɪkl/ *adj.* radiologisch; röntgenologisch

**radiologist** /reɪdɪˈɒlədʒɪst/ *n.* ▶ 1261 Radiologe, *der*/Radiologin, *die;* Röntgenologe, *der*/Röntgenologin, *die*

**radiology** /reɪdɪˈɒlədʒɪ/ *n.*, *no pl.* Radiologie, *die;* Röntgenologie, *die*

**radiometer** /reɪdɪˈɒmɪtə(r)/ *n.* Radiometer, *das;* Strahlungsmesser, *der*

**radio: ~ star** *n.* (*Astron.*) [punktförmige] Radioquelle; **~ station** *n.* Rundfunkstation, *die;* Rundfunk- *od.* Radiosender, *der;* **~-telegram** *n.* Funktelegramm, *das;* Radiotelegramm, *das;* **~-teˈlegraphy** *n.* Funktelegrafie, *die;* **~-ˈtelephone** *n.* Funktelefon, *das;* **~ ˈtelescope** *n.* Radioteleskop, *das;* **~ˈtherapy** *n.* Strahlentherapie, *die;* Radiotherapie, *die* (*fachspr.*)

**radish** /ˈrædɪʃ/ *n.* Rettich, *der;* (*small, red*) Radieschen, *das*

**radium** /ˈreɪdɪəm/ *n.* (*Chem.*) Radium, *das*

**radius** /ˈreɪdɪəs/ *n.*, *pl.* **radii** /ˈreɪdɪaɪ/ *or* **~es** Ⓐ (*Math.*) Radius, *der;* Halbmesser, *der;* **~ of action** [Aktions]radius, *der;* Wirkungsbereich, *der;* (*of missile*) Reichweite, *die;* (*fig.*) Umkreis, *der;* **within a ~ of 20 miles** im Umkreis von 20 Meilen; Ⓑ (*Anat.*) Speiche, *die;* Ⓒ (*line from centre*) Strahl, *der;* (*spoke of wheel*) Speiche, *die;* Ⓓ (*Bot.*) [Blüten-, Dolden]strahl, *der*

**radome** /ˈreɪdəʊm/ *n.* Radom, *das*

**radon** /ˈreɪdɒn/ *n.* (*Chem.*) Radon, *das*

**RAF** /ɑ:reɪˈef, (*coll.*) ræf/ *abbr.* **Royal Air Force**

**raffia** /ˈræfɪə/ *n.* Ⓐ (*fibre*) Raphia-, Raffiabast, *der;* **~ mat** Bastmatte, *die;* Ⓑ (*tree*) Raphia[palme], *die*

**raffish** /ˈræfɪʃ/ *adj.* Ⓐ liederlich; verkommen; Ⓑ (*unconventional*) flott

**raffle** /ˈræfl/ ❶ *n.* Tombola, *die;* **~ ticket** Los, *das.* ❷ *v.t.* **~ [off]** verlosen

**raft** /rɑ:ft/ ❶ *n.* Ⓐ Floß, *das;* Ⓑ (*floating trees, ice, etc.*) Drift, *die.* ❷ *v.t.* (*transport*) flößen; mit dem Floß befördern

**rafter** /ˈrɑ:ftə(r)/ *n.* (*Building*) Sparren, *der*

**rag**[1] /ræg/ *n.* Ⓐ [Stoff]fetzen, *der;* [Stoff]lappen, *der;* **[all] in ~s** [ganz] zerrissen; **feel like a wet ~** (*coll.*) wie ausgelaugt sein; **sb. loses his ~** (*coll.*) jmdm. reißt die Geduld; Ⓑ *in pl.* (*old and torn clothes*) Lumpen *Pl.;* **[dressed] in ~s [and tatters]** abgerissen; in Lumpen *nachgestellt;* **go from ~s to riches** vom armen Schlucker zum Millionär/zur Millionärin werden; ⇒ *also* **chew** 1; **glad rags;** Ⓒ (*derog.: newspaper*) Käseblatt, *das* (*salopp abwertend*); Ⓓ (*material for paper*) Lumpen, *der;* Hader, *der* (*fachspr.*); **~ paper/fibres** Hadernpapier, *das*/Haderstoff, *der* (*fachspr.*)

**rag**[2] ❶ *v.t.*, **-gg-** (*tease, play jokes on*) aufziehen; necken. ❷ *v.i.*, **-gg-** Ⓐ (*Brit.: engage in rough play*) herumtoben; Ⓑ (*be noisy and riotous*) Radau *od.* Rabatz machen (*ugs.*). ❸ *n.* Ⓐ (*Brit. Univ.*) spaßige studentische [Wohltätigkeits]veranstaltung; **the university's Rag Week** *die alljährliche Wohltätigkeitswoche der Universität [mit komischen Darbietungen];* Ⓑ (*prank*) Ulk, *der;* Streich, *der;* *in pl.* Ulkerei, *die*

**rag**[3] *n.* (*Mus.*) Rag, *der*

**ragamuffin** /ˈrægəmʌfɪn/ *n.* [zerlumptes] Gassenkind; **look a proper ~:** ziemlich abgerissen aussehen

**rag: ~-and-ˈbone man** *n.* (*Brit.*) Lumpensammler, *der;* **~bag** *n.* Ⓐ Lumpen-, Flickensack, *der;* Ⓑ (*fig.: collection*) Sammelsurium, *das* (*abwertend*); Ⓒ (*fig. coll.: sloppily-dressed woman*) Schlampe, *die* (*ugs. abwertend*); **~ book** *n.* Kinderbuch aus unzerreißbarem Material; **~ doll** *n.* Stoffpuppe, *die*

**rage** /reɪdʒ/ ❶ *n.* Ⓐ (*violent anger*) Wut, *die;* (*fit of anger*) Wutausbruch, *der;* **be in/fly into a ~:** in Wut *od.* (*ugs.*) Rage sein/geraten; **in a fit of ~:** in einem Anfall von Wut; in einem plötzlichen Wutausbruch; Ⓑ (*vehement desire or passion*) Besessenheit, *die;* **sth. is [all] the ~:** etw. ist [ganz] groß in Mode *od.* (*ugs.*) ist der letzte Schrei. ❷ *v.i.* Ⓐ (*rave*) toben; **~ at** *or* **against sth./sb.** gegen etw./jmdn. wüten *od.* (*ugs.*) wettern; Ⓑ (*be violent, operate unchecked*) toben; ‹Krankheit:› wüten; ‹Fieber:› rasen

**ragged** /ˈrægɪd/ *adj.* Ⓐ zerrissen; kaputt (*ugs.*); ausgefranst ‹Saum, Manschetten, Wundränder›; Ⓑ (*rough, shaggy*) zottig ‹Pferd, Schaf, Haar, Bart›; Ⓒ (*jagged*) zerklüftet ‹Felsen, Küste, Klippe, Landschaft›; zerzaust ‹Baum, Strauch›; (*in tattered clothes*) abgerissen; zerlumpt; Ⓓ (*imperfect, lacking finish*) stümperhaft (*abwertend*) ‹Arbeit, Ausführung›; holprig ‹Reim, Rhythmus›; Ⓔ (*tired*) ermattet; ausgelaugt; **they were run ~:** sie waren völlig erledigt (*ugs.*) *od.* total groggy (*salopp*)

**raggedly** /ˈrægɪdlɪ/ *adv.* Ⓐ abgerissen ‹gekleidet›; Ⓑ (*shaggily*) zottig ‹wachsen›; Ⓒ

(*jaggedly*) zerklüftet ‹verlaufen›; Ⓓ (*imperfectly*) stümperhaft (*abwertend*) ‹musizieren, arbeiten›

**ragged 'robin** *n.* (*Bot.*) Kuckuckslichtnelke, *die*

**raglan sleeve** /ræglən 'sliːv/ *n.* Raglanärmel, *der*

**ragout** /ræ'guː/ *n.* (*Gastr.*) Ragout, *das*

**rag: ~ paper** *n.* Hadernpapier, *das* (*fachspr.*); **~stone** *n.* [Kalk-, Kiesel]sandstein, *der;* **~tag [and bobtail]** *n.* Pöbel, *der* (*abwertend*); Plebs, *der* (*abwertend*); **~time** *n.* Ragtime, *der; attrib.* Ragtime‹band, -musik, -sänger›; **~ trade** *n.* (*coll.*) Modebranche, *die* (*ugs.*); **~weed** *n.* (*Bot.*) Ⓐ ⇒ **ragwort**; Ⓑ (*Amer.: Ambrosia*) Ambrosienkraut, *das;* **~wort** *n.* (*Bot.*) Greiskraut, *das;* Kreuzkraut, *das*

**raid** /reɪd/ ❶ *n.* Ⓐ Einfall, *der;* Überfall, *der;* (*Mil.*) Überraschungsangriff *der;* **~ on a bank** Banküberfall, *der;* **make a ~ on sb.'s orchard/the larder** (*joc.*) jmds. Obstgarten heimsuchen/die Speisekammer plündern (*scherzh.*); ⇒ *also* **air raid**; Ⓑ (*by police*) Razzia, *die* (**on** in + *Dat.*); Ⓒ (*St. Exch.*) ≈ aggressive Unternehmensaufkäufe. ❷ *v.t.* ‹Polizei:› eine Razzia machen auf (+ *Akk.*); ‹Bande/Räuber/Soldaten:› überfallen ‹Bank/Viehherde/Land›; ‹Trupp, Kommando:› stürmen ‹feindliche Stellung›; ‹Kinder:› heimsuchen, plündern (*scherzh.*) ‹Obstgarten›; **~ the larder** (*joc.*) die Speisekammer plündern (*scherzh.*)

**raider** /'reɪdə(r)/ *n.* (*on bank, farm*) Räuber, *der*/Räuberin, *die;* (*looter*) Plünderer, *der*/Plünderin, *die;* (*burglar*) Einbrecher, *der*/Einbrecherin, *die*

**rail**[1] /reɪl/ ❶ *n.* Ⓐ ‹Kleider-, Gardinen›stange, *die;* (*as part of fence*) (*wooden*) Latte, *die;* (*metal*) Stange, *die;* (*on ship*) Reling, *die;* (*as protection against contact*) Barriere, *die;* **the ~s** (*Horseracing*) die Innenumzäunung; die Bande; Ⓑ (*Railw.: of track*) Schiene, *die;* **go off the ~s** (*lit.*) entgleisen; (*fig.*) (*depart from what is accepted*) auf die schiefe Bahn geraten; (*go mad*) durchdrehen (*ugs.*); (*get out of control or order*) aus dem Ruder laufen; Ⓒ (*~way*) [Eisen]bahn, *die; attrib.* Bahn-; **by ~:** mit der Bahn; mit dem Zug; **~ union** Eisenbahnergewerkschaft, *die.* ❷ *v.t.* **~ in** einzäunen ‹Grundstück, Gebäudeteil›; mit einem Geländer *od.* einer Absperrung umgeben ‹Altar, Denkmal›; **~ off** abzäunen; mit einem [Schutz]geländer versehen

**rail**[2] *n.* (*Ornith.*) Ralle, *die*

**rail**[3] *v.i.* **~ at/against sb./sth.** auf/über jmdn./etw. schimpfen; **~ at fate** mit dem Schicksal hadern

**rail: ~car** *n.* Triebwagen, *der;* Schienenbus, *der;* **~ card** *n.* Bahnkarte, *die;* (*for senior citizens*) ≈ Seniorenpass, *der;* **~ fence** *n.* (*Amer.*) (*wooden*) Lattenzaun, *der;* (*metal*) Stangenzaun, *der;* **~head** *n.* Ⓐ (*farthest point during construction*) Ende einer im Bau befindlichen Bahnstrecke; Baustellenende, *das;* Ⓑ (*terminal*) Ausladebahnhof, *der;* Verladebahnhof, *der*

**railing** /'reɪlɪŋ/ *n.* (*round garden, park*) Zaun, *der;* (*on sides of staircase*) Geländer, *das*

**raillery** /'reɪlərɪ/ *n.* Neckerei, *die;* Spöttelei, *die*

**rail: ~ link** *n.* Bahn[strecke], *die;* **~road** ❶ *n.* (*Amer.*) ⇒ **railway**; ❷ *v.t.* Ⓐ (*send or push through in haste*) **~road sb. into doing sth.** jmdn. dazu antreiben, etw. zu tun; **~road a bill through parliament** einen Gesetzentwurf im Parlament durchpeitschen (*ugs.*); Ⓑ (*send to prison by fraud*) unrechtmäßig einsperren (*ugs.*); **~ strike** *n.* Eisenbahnerstreik, *der;* **R~track** *n., no pl., no art.* (*Brit.*) *Betreibergesellschaft des britischen Schienennetzes*

**railway** /'reɪlweɪ/ *n.* Ⓐ (*track*) Bahnlinie, *die;* Bahnstrecke, *die;* Ⓑ (*system*) [Eisen]bahn, *die;* **work on the ~:** bei der Bahn arbeiten; **what a way to run a ~!** (*fig.*) komisches Verfahren!; ⇒ *also* **cable railway**

**railway: ~ carriage** *n.* Eisenbahnwagen, *der;* Reisezugwagen, *der* (*fachspr.*); **~ crossing** *n.* Bahnübergang, *der;* **~ engine** *n.* Lokomotive, *die;* **~ engineer** *n.* Eisenbahningenieur, *der;* **~ guide** *n.* Fahrplan, *der;* (*book*) Kursbuch, *das;* **~ line** *n.* [Eisen]bahnlinie, *die;* [Eisen]bahnstrecke, *die;* **~man** /'reɪlweɪmən/ *n., pl.* **~men** /'reɪlweɪmən/ ▶ **1261** Eisenbahner, *der;* **~ network** *n.* [Eisen]bahnnetz, *das;* **~station** *n.* Bahnhof, *der;* (*smaller*) [Eisen]bahnstation, *die;* **~ worker** *n.* ▶ **1261** Bahnarbeiter, *der;* **~ yard** *n.* Abstellbahnhof, *der;* Rangierbahnhof, *der*

**raiment** /'reɪmənt/ *n.* (*arch./literary*) Gewand, *das* (*geh.*)

**rain** /reɪn/ ❶ *n.* Ⓐ Regen, *der;* **it looks like ~:** es sieht nach Regen aus; **out in the ~:** draußen im Regen ‹sein, lassen›; hinaus in den Regen ‹gehen›; **come ~ or shine** bei jedem Wetter; (*fig.*) unter allen Umständen; ⇒ *also* **right** 1 D; Ⓑ (*fig.: of arrows, blows, etc.*) Hagel, *der;* Ⓒ *in pl.* (*falls of ~*) **the ~s** die Regenzeit.
❷ *v.i.* Ⓐ *impers.* **it ~s** *or* **is ~ing** es regnet; **it starts ~ing** *or* **to ~:** es fängt an zu regnen; ⇒ *also* **cat** A; **pour** 2 A; Ⓑ ‹Tränen:› strömen; ‹Konfetti, Reis:› regnen, niedergehen (**on** auf + *Akk.*); ‹Schläge:› niederprasseln (**on** auf + *Akk.*); **bombs ~ed on many cities** auf viele Städte regnete es Bomben.
❸ *v.t.* prasseln *od.* hageln lassen ‹Schläge, Hiebe›; regnen lassen ‹Reis, Konfetti›; **~ abuse on sb.** eine Schimpfkanonade gegen jmdn. loslassen (*ugs.*)

**~ 'down** *v.i.* ‹Schläge, Steine, Flüche usw.:› niederprasseln; ‹Schüsse, Kugeln usw.:› niederhageln

**~ 'off,** (*Amer.*) **~ 'out** *v.t.* **be ~ed off** *or* **out** (*be terminated*) wegen Regen abgebrochen werden; (*be cancelled*) wegen Regen ausfallen; ins Wasser fallen (*ugs. scherzh.*)

**rainbow** /'reɪnbəʊ/ ❶ *n.* Regenbogen, *der;* **secondary ~:** Nebenregenbogen, *der;* **all the colours of the ~:** alle Regenbogenfarben; ⇒ *also* **gold** 1 B. ❷ *adj.* Regenbogen‹farben, -streifen›; regenbogenfarbig, -farben ‹Kleid, Blumen, Federkleid›

**'rainbow coalition** *n.* Regenbogenkoalition, *die*

**rainbow 'trout** *n.* Regenbogenforelle, *die*

**rain: ~ check** *n.* (*Amer.*) Eintrittskarte für Ersatzveranstaltung; **take a ~ check on sth.** (*fig.*) auf etw. (*Akk.*) später wieder zurückkommen; **~ cloud** *n.* Regenwolke, *die;* **~coat** *n.* Regenmantel, *der;* **~drop** *n.* Regentropfen, *der;* **~fall** *n.* (*shower*) [Regen]schauer, *der;* (*quantity*) Niederschlag, *der;* **~forest** *n.* Regenwald, *der;* **~ gauge** *n.* Regenmesser, *der;* **~making** *n.* Erzeugung von künstlichem Regen *od.* Niederschlag; künstliche Niederschlagsauslösung; **~proof** ❶ *adj.* regendicht; wasserdicht; ❷ *v.t.* appretieren; **~ shower** *n.* Regenschauer, *der;* **~storm** *n.* stürmisches Regenwetter; heftiger Regenguss; **~water** *n.* Regenwasser, *das;* **~wear** *n.* Regenkleidung, *die*

**rainy** /'reɪnɪ/ *adj.* regnerisch ‹Tag, Wetter›; regenreich ‹Klima, Gebiet, Sommer, Winter›; regenverhangen ‹Himmel›; **~ season** Regenzeit, *die;* **keep sth. for a ~ day** (*fig.*) sich (*Dat.*) etw. für schlechte Zeiten aufheben

**raise** /reɪz/ ❶ *v.t.* Ⓐ (*lift up*) heben; erhöhen ‹Note, Pulsfrequenz, Temperatur, Steuern, Miete, Lohn, Gehalt, Kosten›; hochziehen ‹Rollladen, Fahne, Schultern›; aufziehen ‹Vorhang›; hochheben ‹Koffer, Arm, Hand›; hochschieben ‹Schiebefenster›; höher machen, aufhöhen (*fachspr.*) ‹Mauer usw.› (**by** um); (*Cookery*) gehen lassen ‹Brot, Teig›; **~ one's eyes** den Blick *od.* die Augen heben; hinaufblicken (**to** zu); aufblicken (**from** von); **~ one's eyes to heaven** die Augen zum Himmel erheben (*geh.*); **~ one's glass to sb.** das Glas auf jmdn. erheben; auf jmdn. anstoßen; **~ one's hand/fist to sb.** die Hand/Faust gegen jmdn. erheben; **~ one's voice** die Stimme heben; **they ~d their voices** (*in anger*) sie *od.* ihre Stimmen wurden lauter; **don't you ~ your voice at me** schrei mich nicht an!; **war ~d its [ugly] head** der Krieg erhob sein [hässliches] Haupt; **be ~d to the peerage/priesthood** in den Stand eines Peers/in den Priesterstand erhoben werden; ⇒ *also* **finger** 1 A; **hat** A; **roof** 1 A; Ⓑ (*set upright, cause to stand up*) aufrichten; erheben ‹Banner›; aufstellen ‹Fahnenstange, Zaun, Gerüst›; **~ the people to revolt** das Volk zum Aufstand mobilisieren; **~ the country against an invader** den Widerstand der Bevölkerung gegen einen Eindringling mobilisieren; **be ~d from the dead** von den Toten [auf]erweckt werden; **~ the dust** (*fig.: cause turmoil*) Ärger machen; **~ sb.'s spirits** jmds. Stimmung heben; Ⓒ (*build up, construct*) errichten ‹Gebäude, Statue›; verursachen ‹Blutblase usw.›; (*create, start*) auslösen ‹Kontroverse›; schaffen ‹Probleme›; erheben ‹Forderungen, Einwände, Ansprüche, Bedenken, Protest›; entstehen lassen ‹Vorurteile›; (*introduce*) aufwerfen ‹Frage›; zur Sprache bringen, anschneiden ‹Angelegenheit, Thema, Problem›; (*utter*) erschallen lassen ‹Ruf, Schrei, Beifallgeschrei, Jubel›; Ⓓ (*grow, produce, breed, rear*) anbauen ‹Gemüse, Getreide›; aufziehen ‹Vieh, [Haus]tiere›; großziehen ‹Familie, Kinder›; **[be born and] ~d in ...** (*Amer.*) [geboren und] aufgewachsen [sein] in ... (*Dat.*); Ⓔ (*bring together, procure*) aufbringen ‹Geld, Betrag, Summe›; aufstellen ‹Armee, Flotte, Truppen›; aufnehmen ‹Hypothek, Kredit, Darlehen›; Ⓕ (*end, cause to end*) aufheben, beenden ‹Belagerung, Blockade›; (*remove*) aufheben ‹Aufnahme-, Einstellungsstopp, Embargo, Verfügung, Anordnung, Verbot›; Ⓖ (*cause to appear*) [herbei]rufen, beschwören ‹Geist, Verstorbenen, Teufel›; **~ [merry] hell** (*coll.*) Krach schlagen (*ugs.*) (**over** wegen); Ⓗ (*Math.*) **~ to the fourth power** in die 4. Potenz erheben; mit 4 potenzieren; Ⓘ (*Cards*) erhöhen (**to** auf); **~ sb.** jmdn. überbieten; **~ [one's] partner** seinen Mitspieler mit derselben Farbe überbieten *od.* überrufen; Ⓙ (*coll.: find*) **~ sb.** jmdn. aufstöbern *od.* (*ugs.*) auftreiben.
❷ *n.* Ⓐ (*Cards*) Erhöhen, *das;* Ⓑ (*Amer.*) (*in wages*) Lohnerhöhung, *die;* (*in salary*) Gehaltserhöhung, *die*

**~ 'up** Ⓐ (*cause to stand up*) aufstellen; Ⓑ (*build up*) errichten ‹Mauer, Gebäude›; aufstapeln ‹Haufen›; aufbauen, gestalten ‹Struktur›

**raised** /reɪzd/ *adj.* Ⓐ erhoben ‹Arm, Augen, Blick, Stimme›; Ⓑ (*Amer. Cookery*) aufgegangen ‹Teig, Brot, Kuchen›; Ⓒ [auf]geraut ‹Gewebe, Stoff›; Ⓓ (*having pattern or design in relief*) erhaben

**raisin** /'reɪzn/ *n.* Rosine, *die*

**raison d'être** /reɪzɔ̃ 'detr/ *n., pl.* **raisons d'être** /reɪzɔ̃ 'detr/ Existenzberechtigung, *die;* **his happiness was her ~:** sie lebte nur für sein Wohlergehen

**raj** /rɑːdʒ/ *n.* (*Ind. Hist.*) Herrschaft, *die;* **the British ~:** die britische Oberherrschaft (*in Indien vor 1947*)

**raja[h]** /'rɑːdʒə/ *n.* (*Hist.*) Radscha, *der*

**rake**[1] /reɪk/ ❶ *n.* Ⓐ (*Hort.*) Rechen, *der* (*bes. südd. u. md.*); Harke, *die* (*bes. nordd.*); Ⓑ (*Agric.: wheeled implement*) Rechwender, *der;* Ⓒ (*croupier's*) Rateau, *das;* Geldharke, *die.* ⇒ *also* **thin** 1 B. ❷ *v.t.* Ⓐ harken ‹Laub, Erde, Fußboden, Kies, Oberfläche›; **~ together** (*fig.*) zusammentragen ‹Beweise, Hinweise, Anklagepunkte›; Ⓑ **~ the fire** die Asche entfernen; Ⓒ (*sweep*) (*with eyes*) bestreichen; (*with shots*) bestreichen; beharken (*Soldatenspr.*). ❸ *v.i.* **~ among** *or* **into** *or* **[around] in** herumstöbern in (+ *Dat.*)

**~ 'in** *v.t.* (*coll.*) scheffeln (*ugs.*) ‹Geld›; **~ in the money, ~ it in** Geld scheffeln (*ugs.*)

**~ over** *v.t.* Ⓐ harken; Ⓑ (*fig.*) wieder ausgraben; **~ over old ashes** (*fig.*) alte Geschichten wieder ausgraben

**~ 'up** *v.t.* Ⓐ zusammenharken; Ⓑ (*fig.*) wieder ausgraben ‹Vergangenes›

**rake**[2] *n.* Ⓐ (*sloping position,* [*amount of*] *slope*) Neigung, *die;* Ⓑ (*in theatre*) Schräge, *die;* **there is a ~ on this stage** diese Bühne hat eine Schräge

**rake**[3] *n.* (*person*) Lebemann, *der*

**raked** /reɪkt/ *adj.* ‹Bühne, Zuschauerraum› mit einer Schräge

**'rake-off** *n.* (*coll.*) [Gewinn]anteil, *der*

**rakish**[1] /'reɪkɪʃ/ *adj.* Ⓐ (*dissolute*) ausschweifend; Ⓑ (*jaunty*) flott; kess; **wear one's hat at a ~ angle** seinen Hut frech *od.* keck aufgesetzt haben

r

**rakish²** *adj.* (*smartly designed*) schnittig

**rakishly** /ˈreɪkɪʃlɪ/ *adv.* Ⓐ (*dissolutely*) wie ein Lebemann; Ⓑ (*jauntily*) kess; keck

**rally¹** /ˈrælɪ/ ❶ *v.i.* Ⓐ (*come together*) sich versammeln; ~ **to the support of** *or* **the defence of**, ~ **behind** *or* **to sb.** (*fig.*) sich hinter jmdn. stellen; **the banks rallied to the support of the pound** die Banken versuchten gemeinsam, das Pfund zu stützen; ~ **round** sich zusammentun; Ⓑ (*regain health*) sich wieder [ein wenig] erholen; Ⓒ (*reassemble*) sich [wieder] sammeln; Ⓓ (*increase in value after fall*) ‹Aktie, Kurs:› wieder anziehen, sich wieder erholen.

❷ *v.t.* Ⓐ (*reassemble*) wieder zusammenrufen; Ⓑ (*bring together*) einigen ‹Partei, Kräfte›; sammeln ‹Anhänger›; Ⓒ (*rouse*) aufmuntern; (*revive*) ~ **one's strength** seine [ganze] Kraft zusammennehmen; ~ **support for sb./sth.** um Unterstützung für jmdn./etw. werben.

❸ *n.* Ⓐ (*mass meeting*) Versammlung, *die;* **Scout** ~: [großes] Pfadfindertreffen; **peace** ~: Friedenskundgebung, *die;* Ⓑ (*competition*) **[motor]** ~: Rallye, *die;* **Monte Carlo R~/Isle of Man TT R~:** Rallye Monte Carlo/Tourist Trophy, *die;* Ⓒ (*Tennis*) Ballwechsel, *der;* Ⓓ **a** ~ **in prices/shares** ein Anziehen der Preise/Aktienkurse

**rally²** *v.t.* (*tease*) aufziehen (*ugs.*); necken

ˈ**rallycross** *n.* (*Sport*) Rallyecross, *das*

**ram** /ræm/ ❶ *n.* Ⓐ (*Zool.*) Schafbock, *der;* Widder, *der;* Ⓑ **the Ram** (*Astrol.*) der Widder; ⇒ *also* **archer** B; Ⓒ ⇒ **battering ram**; Ⓓ (*Naut.: projecting beak*) Rammsporn, *der;* Ⓔ (*hydraulic lifting-machine*) hydraulischer Widder; Ⓕ (*weight*) Rammklotz, *der;* Bär, *der;* Ⓖ (*tool*) Stampfer, *der;* Ⓗ (*piston*) Plunger, *der.*

❷ *v.t.*, **-mm-** Ⓐ (*force*) stopfen; ~ **a post into the ground** einen Pfosten in die Erde rammen; ~ **in** in etw. (*Akk.*) rammen; **he** ~**med his hat down on his head** er knallte sich (*Dat.*) seinen Hut auf den Kopf (*ugs.*); ~ **sth. into sb.** *or* **sb.'s head** (*fig.*) jmdm. etw. einhämmern; ~ **sth. home to sb.** jmdm. etw. deutlich vor Augen führen; ⇒ *also* **throat** A; Ⓑ (*collide with*) rammen ‹Fahrzeug, Pfosten›; Ⓒ ~ **[down]** (*beat down*) feststampfen ‹Erde, Ton, Kies›

**RAM** /ræm/ *abbr.* (*Computing*) **random access memory** RAM, *das;* ~ **facility** Randomspeicher, *der*

**Ramadan** /ræməˈdɑːn/ *n.* (*Muslim Relig.*) **[month of]** ~: Ramadan, *der*

**ramble** /ˈræmbl/ ❶ *n.* **[nature]** ~: Wanderung, *die.* ❷ *v.i.* Ⓐ (*walk*) umherstreifen (**through, in** in + *Dat.*); Ⓑ (*wander in discourse*) zusammenhangloses Zeug reden (*abwertend*); **keep rambling on about sth.** sich endlos über etw. (*Akk.*) auslassen

**rambler** /ˈræmblə(r)/ *n.* Ⓐ Wanderer, *der*/Wanderin, *die;* Ⓑ (*Bot.*) Kletterrose, *die*

**rambling** /ˈræmblɪŋ/ ❶ *n.* Wandern, *das;* ~ **club** Wanderverein, *der.* ❷ *adj.* Ⓐ (*irregularly arranged*) verschachtelt; verwinkelt ‹Straßen›; Ⓑ (*incoherent*) unzusammenhängend ‹Erklärung, Brief›; zerstreut ‹Professor›; Ⓒ (*Bot.*) ~ **rose** Kletterrose, *die*

**rambunctious** /ræmˈbʌŋkʃəs/ *adj.* (*Amer. coll.*) nicht zu bändigend; **be** ~: nicht zu bändigen sein

**ramekin** /ˈræmɪkɪn/ Ⓐ (*Gastr.*) Käsewindbeutel, *der;* Ramequin, *der* (*fachspr.*); Ⓑ ⇒ ~ **case**

**ramekin:** ~ **case**, ~ **dish** *ns.* kleine Auflaufform

**ramification** /ræmɪfɪˈkeɪʃn/ *n.* Ⓐ (*of river, railway, business; Bot., Anat.*) Verzweigung, *die;* Ⓑ *usu. in pl.* (*consequence*) Auswirkungen; **what would be the** ~**s of this?** wie würde sich das auswirken?

**ramify** /ˈræmɪfaɪ/ *v.i.* sich verzweigen; ~**ing network** verzweigtes Netz

ˈ**ramjet** *n.* (*Aeronaut.*) ~ **[engine]** Staustrahltriebwerk, *das*

**rammer** /ˈræmə(r)/ *n.* Stampfer, *der*

**ramp** /ræmp/ ❶ *n.* Ⓐ (*slope*) Rampe, *die;* **'beware** *or* **caution,** ~**!'** „Vorsicht, unebene Fahrbahn!"; Ⓑ (*Aeronaut.*) Gangway, *die.* ❷ *v.t.* mit einer Rampe versehen

**rampage** ❶ /ˈræmpeɪdʒ, ræmˈpeɪdʒ/ *n.* Randale, *die* (*ugs.*); **be/go on the** ~ ‹Rowdys:› randalieren; ‹verärgerte Person:› toben. ❷ /ræmˈpeɪdʒ/ *v.i.* ‹Rowdys:› randalieren; ~ **about** ‹verärgerte Person:› toben

**rampant** /ˈræmpənt/ *adj.* Ⓐ (*unchecked*) zügellos ‹Gewalt, Rassismus, Randalieren›; schreiend ‹soziale Ungerechtigkeit›; steil ansteigend ‹Verbrechensrate, Inflation›; üppig ‹Wachstum›; **cholera was** ~: die Cholera grassierte; Ⓑ *postpos.* (*Her.*) zum Grimmen geschickt ‹Löwe›; Ⓒ (*rank*) **make too** ~, **cause the** ~ **growth of** wuchern lassen ‹Pflanzen›

**rampart** /ˈræmpɑːt/ *n.* Ⓐ (*walk*) Wehrgang, *der;* Ⓑ (*protective barrier*) Wall, *der;* (*fig.*) Schutzschild, *der*

**rampion** /ˈræmpɪən/ *n.* (*Bot.*) Rapunzelglockenblume, *die*

**ram:** ~ **raid** ❶ *v.t.* [durch Rammen mit einem Fahrzeug] einbrechen in (+ *Akk.*); ❷ *n.* [durch Rammen eines Gebäudes verübter] Einbruch; ~**-raider** *n.: Einbrecher, der sich durch Einrammen bes. eines Schaufensters mit einem Fahrzeug Zutritt verschafft*

ˈ**ramrod** *n.* Ladestock, *der;* **[with one's back] as straight** *or* **stiff as a** ~ (*fig.*) so steif, als ob man einen Besenstiel verschluckt hätte; stocksteif

ˈ**ramshackle** *adj.* klapprig ‹Auto›; verkommen ‹Gebäude›

**ran** ⇒ **run** 2, 3

**ranch** /rɑːntʃ/ ❶ *n.* Ranch, *die;* **[mink/poultry]** ~: [Nerz-/Geflügel]farm, *die;* **livestock** ~: Viehbetrieb, *der;* **meanwhile, back at the** ~ (*joc. coll.*) inzwischen ... zu Hause; ⇒ *also* **dude ranch**. ❷ *v.i.* Viehwirtschaft treiben

**rancher** /ˈrɑːntʃə(r)/ *n.* (*owner, operator*) Rancher, *der*/Rancherin, *die;* (*employee*) Farmarbeiter, *der*/-arbeiterin, *die;* **be a** ~: eine Ranch haben/auf einer Ranch arbeiten

**ranch:** ~ **hand** *n.* Farmarbeiter, *der*/-arbeiterin, *die;* ~ **house** *n.* Wohnhaus auf einer/der Ranch

**rancid** /ˈrænsɪd/ *adj.* ranzig

**rancor** (*Amer.*) ⇒ **rancour**

**rancorous** /ˈræŋkərəs/ *adj.* bitter; **feel** ~ **towards sb.** über jmdn. verbittert sein

**rancour** /ˈræŋkə(r)/ *n.* (*Brit.*) [tiefe] Verbitterung; **she bore him no** ~: sie hegte keinen Groll gegen ihn (*geh.*)

**rand** /rænd, rɑːnt/ *n.* ▶ **1328** (*S. Afr. monetary unit*) Rand, *der*

**R&B** *abbr.* **rhythm and blues** R&B

**R&D** *abbr.* **research and development** F&E

**randiness** /ˈrændɪnɪs/ *n.*, *no pl.* Lüsternheit, *die* (*geh.*); Geilheit, *die*

**random** /ˈrændəm/ ❶ *n.* **at** ~: wahllos; willkürlich; (*aimlessly*) ziellos; **speak/choose at** ~: ins Blaue hinein reden/aufs Geratewohl wählen. ❷ *adj.* Ⓐ (*unsystematic*) willkürlich ‹Auswahl›; **make a** ~ **guess** raten aufs Geratewohl; Ⓑ (*Statistics*) Zufalls-

**random:** ~ ˈ**access memory** *n.* (*Computing*) Schreib-Lese-Speicher, *der;* ~ **distribution** *n.* (*Statistics*) Zufallsverteilung, *die*

**randomize** (**randomise**) /ˈrændəmaɪz/ *v.t.* randomisieren (*fachspr.*); willkürlich anordnen

**random:** ~ ˈ**sample** *n.* (*Statistics*) [Zufalls]stichprobe, *die;* ~ ˈ**variable** *n.* (*Statistics*) Zufallsvariable, *die*

**randy** /ˈrændɪ/ *adj.* geil; scharf (*ugs.*); **feel** ~: geil sein

**rang** ⇒ **ring²** 2, 3

**range** /reɪndʒ/ ❶ *n.* Ⓐ (*row*) ~ **of mountains/ cliffs** Berg-/Felsenkette, *die;* Ⓑ (*of subjects, interests, topics*) Palette, *die;* (*of musical instrument*) Tonumfang, *der;* (*of knowledge, voice*) Umfang, *der;* (*of income, department, possibility*) Bereich, *der;* ~ **of influence** Einflussbereich, *der;* **a** ~ **of options** verschiedene Möglichkeiten; **the annual** ~ **of temperature** die Temperaturunterschiede im Verlauf des Jahres; **be outside the** ~ **of a department** nicht in ein Ressort gehören; **sth. is out of** *or* **beyond sb's** ~ (*lit. or fig.*) etw. ist außerhalb jmds. Reichweite; Ⓒ (*Bot., Zool.: area of distribution*) Verbreitungsgebiet, *das;* Ⓓ (*of telescope, missile, aircraft, etc.*) Reichweite, *die;* (*distance between gun and target*) Schussweite, *die;* **flying** ~: Flugbereich, *der;* **at a** ~ **of 200 metres** auf eine Entfernung von 200 Metern; **up to a** ~ **of 5 miles** bis zu einem Umkreis von 5 Meilen; **shoot at close** *or* **short/long** ~: aus kurzer/großer Entfernung schießen; **[with]in/out of** *or* **beyond [firing]** ~: in/außer Schussweite; **within** ~ **of a sound** in Hörweite eines Geräuschs; **experience sth. at close** ~: etw. in unmittelbarer Nähe erleben; Ⓔ (*series, selection*) Kollektion, *die;* Ⓕ **[shooting]** ~: Schießstand, *der;* (*at funfair*) Schießbude, *die;* Ⓖ (*testing site*) Versuchsgelände, *das;* Ⓗ (*grazing ground*) Weide[fläche], *die;* **cattle** ~: Viehweide, *die;* Ⓘ **give free** ~ **to** (*freedom to roam*) frei herumlaufen lassen ‹Tier›; umherschweifen lassen ‹Gedanken›; Ⓙ (*direction*) Verlauf, *der;* Ⓚ (*cooking stove*) Herd, *der.*

❷ *v.i.* Ⓐ (*vary within limits*) ‹Preise, Temperaturen:› schwanken, sich bewegen (**from ... to** zwischen [+ *Dat.*] ... und); **they** ~ **in age from 3 to 12** sie sind zwischen 3 und 12 Jahre alt; Ⓑ (*extend*) ‹Klippen, Gipfel, Häuser:› sich hinziehen; **her hobbies** ~ **from x to y** die Palette ihrer Hobbys reicht von x bis y; Ⓒ (*Bot., Zool.: occur over wide area*) **the plant/animal** ~**s from ... to ...:** das Verbreitungsgebiet der Pflanze/des Tieres erstreckt sich von ... bis ...; Ⓓ (*roam*) umherziehen (**around, about** in + *Dat.*); (*fig.*) ‹Gedanken:› umherschweifen; **the discussion** ~**d over ...:** die Diskussion erstreckte sich auf (+ *Akk.*) ...; **the speaker** ~**d far and wide** der Redner sprach viele verschiedene Themen an.

❸ *v.t.* Ⓐ (*arrange*) aufreihen ‹Bücher, Tische›; antreten lassen ‹Soldaten›; **they** ~**d themselves in lines** sie stellten sich in Reih und Glied auf; **several enemy platoons were** ~**d against us** wir standen einer Reihe feindlicher Züge gegenüber; ~ **oneself with sb.** (*fig.*) sich auf jmds. Seite schlagen; ~ **oneself against sb./sth.** (*fig.*) sich gegen jmdn./etw. zusammenschließen; ~ **oneself behind sth.** (*fig.*) sich hinter etw. (*Akk.*) stellen; Ⓑ richten ‹Teleskop, Geschütz› (**on** auf + *Akk.*); Ⓒ (*roam*) umherstreifen in (+ *Dat.*); durchstreifen ‹Landschaft, Berge, Wälder›; befahren ‹Meere›

ˈ**rangefinder** *n.* Entfernungsmesser, *der*

**ranger** /ˈreɪndʒə(r)/ *n.* Ⓐ (*keeper*) Aufseher, *der*/Aufseherin, *die;* (*of forest*) Förster, *der*/Försterin, *die;* Ⓑ (*Amer.: law officer*) Ranger, *der;* *Angehöriger der berittenen Polizeitruppe;* Ⓒ (*Brit.: Girl Guide*) Pfadfinderin (*zwischen 14 und 18 Jahren*); Ⓓ (*Amer. Mil.*) Ranger, *der*

r

**ranging** /ˈreɪndʒɪŋ/: ~ **pole**, ~ **rod** *ns.* (*Surv.*) Bake, *die*

**rangy** /ˈreɪndʒɪ/ *adj.* langgliedrig

**rank¹** /ræŋk/ ❶ *n.* Ⓐ (*position in hierarchy*) Rang, *der;* (*Mil. also*) Dienstgrad, *der;* **be above/below sb. in** ~: einen höheren/niedrigeren Rang/Dienstgrad haben als jmd.; **pull** ~: den Vorgesetzten herauskehren (**on** gegenüber); **of high** ~: hochrangig; **be in the front** *or* **top** ~ **of performers** ein Künstler der Spitzenklasse sein; **of the first** ~: erstklassig; Ⓑ (*social position*) [soziale] Stellung; **people of all** ~**s** Menschen aus allen [Gesellschafts]schichten; **persons of** ~: hoch gestellte Persönlichkeiten; **belong to a high** ~ **of society** zur oberen Gesellschaftsschicht gehören; Ⓒ (*row*) Reihe, *die;* Ⓓ (*Brit.: taxi stand*) [Taxen]stand, *der;* Ⓔ (*line of soldiers*) Reihe, *die;* **step forward from the** ~: vortreten; **the** ~**s** (*enlisted men*) die Mannschaften und Unteroffiziere; **the** ~ **and file** die Mannschaften und Unteroffiziere; (*fig.*) die breite Masse; **close [our/their]** ~**s** die Reihen schließen; (*fig.*) sich zusammenschließen; **other** ~**s** Mannschaften und Unteroffiziere; **rise from the** ~**s** sich [aus dem Mannschaftsstand] zum Offizier hochdienen;

(*fig.*) sich hocharbeiten; Ⓕ (*order*) **keep/break ~[s]** in Reih und Glied stehen/aus dem Glied treten.
❷ *v.t.* Ⓐ (*classify*) **~ among** *or* **with** zählen *od.* rechnen zu; **his achievement was ~ed with hers** seine Leistung wurde mit ihrer auf eine Stufe gestellt; **be ~ed second in the world** an zweiter Stelle in der Welt stehen; **~ sth. highly** etw. hoch einstufen; Ⓑ (*arrange*) aufstellen ‹Schachfiguren›; in Reih und Glied antreten lassen ‹Kompanie›; Ⓒ (*Amer.: take precedence of*) rangmäßig stehen über (+ *Dat.*); **who ~s whom?** wie ist die Rangordnung?
❸ *v.i.* Ⓐ (*have position*) **~ among** *or* **with** gehören *od.* zählen zu; **~ above/next to sb.** rangmäßig über/direkt unter jmdm. stehen; **~ high/low** eine hohe/niedere Stellung einnehmen; viel/nicht viel gelten; **it ~s as his best book** es gilt als sein bestes Buch; Ⓑ (*Amer.: have senior position*) **~ing executive** übergeordneter Manager

**rank²** *adj.* Ⓐ (*complete*) blank ‹Unsinn, Frechheit›; krass ‹Außenseiter, Illoyalität›; Ⓑ (*foul-smelling*) stinkend; **~ odour** Gestank, *der;* **smell ~:** stinken; Ⓒ (*vile*) ordinär; unflätig; Ⓓ (*rampant*) überwuchert ‹Garten›; **~ weeds** [wild] wucherndes Unkraut

**'rank-and-file** *adj.* einfach ‹Mitglied, Mann usw.›

**ranker** /'ræŋkə(r)/ *n.* (*Mil.*) Ⓐ (*commissioned officer*) aus dem Mannschaftsstand aufgestiegener Offizier; Ⓑ (*soldier*) einfacher *od.* gemeiner Soldat

**rankings** /'ræŋkɪŋz/ *n. pl.* (*Sport*) Rangliste, *die;* **the team has fallen in the ~:** die Mannschaft ist in der Tabelle nach unten gerutscht

**rankle** /'ræŋkl/ ❶ *v.i.* **it/sb.'s success** *etc.* **~s [with sb.]** es/jmds. Erfolg *usw.* wurmt jmdn. (*ugs.*). ❷ *v.t.* wurmen (*ugs.*)

**ransack** /'rænsæk/ *v.t.* Ⓐ (*search*) durchsuchen (**for** nach); (*fig.*) kramen in (+ *Dat.*) (*ugs.*) ‹Erinnerung, Gedächtnis›; erforschen ‹Gewissen›; Ⓑ (*pillage*) plündern

**ransom** /'rænsəm/ ❶ *n.* **~ [money]** Lösegeld, *das;* **hold to ~:** als Geisel festhalten; (*fig.*) erpressen, unter Druck (*Akk.*) setzen ‹Regierung›; **jewels worth a king's ~:** Juwelen, die ein Vermögen wert sind. ❷ *v.t.* Ⓐ (*redeem*) Lösegeld bezahlen für; auslösen; Ⓑ (*hold to ransom*) als Geisel festhalten

**'ransom note** *n.* Erpresserbrief, *der*

**rant** /rænt/ ❶ *v.i.* wettern (*ugs.*); **~ at** anschnauzen (*ugs.*); **~ on about** herumzetern wegen (*ugs.*); **~ and rave about sth.** über etw. (*Akk.*) wettern (*ugs.*). ❷ *n.* Ⓐ (*tirade*) Tirade, *die* (*abwertend*); Redeschwall, *der;* Ⓑ *no pl.* (*empty talk*) Schwulst, *der;* leeres Geschwätz (*ugs.*)

**ranunculus** /rə'nʌŋkjʊləs/ *n., pl.* **~es** *or* **ranunculi** /rə'nʌŋkjʊlaɪ/ (*Bot.*) Hahnenfußgewächs, *das*

**rap¹** /ræp/ ❶ *n.* Ⓐ (*sharp knock*) [energisches] Klopfen; **there was a ~ on** *or* **at the door** es klopfte [laut]; **I heard a ~ on** *or* **at the door** ich hörte es [laut] klopfen; **give sb. a ~ on** *or* **over the knuckles** jmdm. auf die Finger schlagen; (*fig.*) jmdm. auf die Finger klopfen; **get a ~ on** *or* **over the knuckles** (*lit. or fig.*) eins auf die Finger bekommen; Ⓑ (*coll.: blame*) **take the ~ [for sth.]** [für etw.] den Kopf hinhalten (*ugs.*); **leave sb. behind to take the ~:** jmdn. die Suppe auslöffeln lassen (*ugs.*); Ⓒ (*Amer. coll.: prison sentence*) Kittchen, *das* (*ugs.*); Knast, *der* (*ugs.*); Ⓓ (*Amer. coll.: criminal charge*) Anklage, *die;* Ⓔ (*Amer. coll.*) (*conversation*) Unterhaltung, *die;* (*discussion*) Palaver, *das* (*ugs.*); (*in pop music*) rhythmischer Sprechgesang; Rap, *der.*
❷ *v.t.,* **-pp-** Ⓐ (*strike smartly*) klopfen; **~ sb. on the knuckles** jmdm. auf die Finger klopfen; **~ sth. on sth.** mit etw. gegen etw. klopfen; Ⓑ (*criticize*) attackieren.
❸ *v.i.,* **-pp-** Ⓐ (*make sound*) klopfen (**on** an + *Akk.*); **~ on the table** auf den Tisch klopfen; Ⓑ (*Amer. coll.: talk*) quatschen (*ugs.*)
**~ 'out** *v.t.* ausstoßen ‹Befehl, Fluch›; **~ out a message** melden

**rap²** *n.* **I don't care** *or* **give a ~:** es ist mir völlig egal (*ugs.*)

**rapacious** /rə'peɪʃəs/ *adj.* (*greedy*) habgierig; (*predatory*) räuberisch

**rapaciously** /rə'peɪʃəslɪ/ *adv.* (*greedily*) habgierig; (*in predatory manner*) raublustig

**rapacity** /rə'pæsɪtɪ/ *n., no pl.* Habgier, *die;* (*being predatory*) Raublust, *die*

**rape¹** /reɪp/ ❶ *n.* Vergewaltigung, *die* (*auch fig.*); Notzucht, *die* (*Rechtsspr.*); **statutory ~** (*Amer.*) Geschlechtsverkehr mit einer Minderjährigen; **homosexual ~:** Vergewaltigung einer gleichgeschlechtlichen Person. ❷ *v.t.* vergewaltigen; notzüchtigen (*Rechtsspr.*); (*fig.: despoil*) vergewaltigen ‹Landschaft›

**rape²** *n.* (*Bot., Agric.*) Raps, *der*

**rape: ~ cake** *n.* Rapskuchen, *der;* **~ oil** ⇒ **~-seed oil**; **~seed** *n.* Rapssamen, *der;* **~seed oil** *n.* Rapsöl, *das*

**Raphael** /'ræfeɪəl/ *pr. n.* Ⓐ (*archangel*) Raphael (*der*); Ⓑ (*artist*) Raffael (*der*)

**rapid** /'ræpɪd/ ❶ *adj.* schnell ‹Bewegung, Wachstum, Puls›; rasch ‹Folge, Bewegung, Fortschritt, Ausbreitung, Änderung›; rapide ‹Niedergang›; steil ‹Abstieg›; reißend ‹Gewässer, Strömung›; stark ‹Gefälle, Strömung›; **give ~ results** schnell Ergebnisse bringen; **there has been a ~ decline** es ging rapide abwärts. ❷ *n. in pl.* Stromschnellen

**rapid-'fire** *adj.* Schnellfeuer‹waffe, -schießen›; (*fig.*) schnell aufeinander folgend ‹Wiederholung›; Schnellfeuer‹witze, -fragen›

**rapidity** /rə'pɪdɪtɪ/ *n., no pl.* Schnelligkeit, *die*

**rapidly** /'ræpɪdlɪ/ *adv.* schnell; **descend ~** ‹Hang:› steil abfallen

**rapid 'transit** (*Amer.*) *n.* Schnellverkehr, *der*

**rapier** /'reɪpɪə(r)/ *n.* (*Fencing*) Rapier, *das*

**rapine** /'ræpaɪn, 'ræpɪn/ *n.* (*poet./literary*) Plünderung, *die*

**rapist** /'reɪpɪst/ *n.* Vergewaltiger, *der*

**rapport** /ræ'pɔ:(r)/ *n.* [harmonisches] Verhältnis; **have a great ~ with sb.** ein ausgezeichnetes Verhältnis zu jmdm. haben; **establish a ~ with sb.** eine Beziehung zu jmdm. aufbauen; **lack of ~:** fehlende Übereinstimmung

**rapprochement** /ræ'prɒʃmã/ *n.* (*Polit., Diplom.*) Rapprochement, *das* (*fachspr.*); Wiederannäherung, *die*

**rapscallion** /ræp'skæljən/ *n.* (*joc.*) Spitzbube, *der* (*scherzh.*); Schlingel, *der* (*scherzh.*)

**rapt** /ræpt/ *adj.* gespannt ‹Aufmerksamkeit, Miene›; **in ~ contemplation** in Betrachtungen versunken

**raptly** /'ræptlɪ/ *adv.* gespannt ‹zuhören›

**rapture** /'ræptʃə(r)/ *n.* Ⓐ (*ecstatic delight*) **[state of] ~:** Verzückung, *die;* Ⓑ *in pl.* (*enthusiasm*) **be in ~s** entzückt sein (**over, about** über + *Akk.*); **go into ~s** [überschwänglich] schwärmen (**over, about** von); **be sent into ~s by sth.** über etw. (*Akk.*) in Verzückung geraten

**rapturous** /'ræptʃərəs/ *adj.* begeistert ‹Applaus, Menge, Willkommen›; verzückt ‹Miene›

**rare¹** /reə(r)/ *adj.* Ⓐ (*uncommon*) selten; **~ occurrence** Seltenheit, *die;* **it's ~ for him to do that** es kommt selten vor, dass er so etwas tut; Ⓑ (*thin*) dünn ‹Luft, Atmosphäre›; Ⓒ (*extreme*) **have ~ fun with sb.** mit jmdm. einen Heidenspaß haben; **have a ~ old time** sich köstlich amüsieren

**rare²** *adj.* (*Cookery*) englisch gebraten; nur schwach gebraten; **medium ~:** halb durchgebraten

**rarebit** /'reəbɪt/ ⇒ **Welsh rarebit**

**rare: ~ 'book** *n.* Rarität, *die;* Rarum, *das* (*Buchw.*); **~ 'earth** (*Chem.*) *n.* seltene Erde

**rarefaction** /reərɪ'fækʃn/ *n.* Verdünnung, *die*

**rarefied** /'reərɪfaɪd/ *adj.* dünn ‹Luft›; (*fig.*) exklusiv

**rarefy** /'reərɪfaɪ/ *v.t.* Ⓐ verdünnen ‹Feuchtigkeit, Luft›; Ⓑ (*make subtle*) verfeinern

**rare 'gas** ⇒ **noble gas**

**rarely** /'reəlɪ/ *adv.* Ⓐ selten; Ⓑ (*to an unusual degree*) außergewöhnlich

**raring** /'reərɪŋ/ *adj.* (*coll.*) **be ~ to go** kaum abwarten können, bis es losgeht

**rarity** /'reərɪtɪ/ *n.* Ⓐ Seltenheit, *die;* Rarität, *die;* **a collection of rarities** eine Sammlung von Raritäten; **be an object of great ~:** eine große Seltenheit sein; **such people are a ~:** solche Leute sind rar; Ⓑ **the ~ of the atmosphere** die dünne Luft

**'rarity value** *n.* Seltenheitswert, *der*

**rascal** /'rɑ:skl/ *n.* Ⓐ (*dishonest person*) Halunke, *der;* Schuft, *der;* Ⓑ (*joc.: mischievous person*) Schlingel, *der* (*scherzh.*); Spitzbube, *der* (*scherzh.*)

**rascally** /'rɑ:skəlɪ/ *adj.* Ⓐ (*dishonest*) schurkisch; Ⓑ (*joc.: mischievous*) schlimm ‹Junge, Streich›

**rase** ⇒ **raze**

**rash¹** /ræʃ/ *n.* (*Med.*) [Haut]ausschlag, *der;* **develop a** *or* **break out** *or* **come out in a ~:** einen Ausschlag bekommen; **bring sb. out in a ~:** einen Ausschlag bei jmdm. hervorrufen; **a ~ of burglaries/strikes** (*fig.*) eine Serie von Einbrüchen/Streiks

**rash²** *adj.* voreilig ‹Urteil, Entscheidung, Entschluss›; überstürzt ‹Versprechungen, Handlung, Erklärung›; (*impetuous*) ungestüm ‹Person›

**rasher** /'ræʃə(r)/ *n.* **~ [of bacon]** Speckscheibe, *die;* **bacon sliced into ~s** in [dünne] Scheiben geschnittener Speck

**rashly** /'ræʃlɪ/ *adv.* voreilig ‹handeln, etw. versprechen, zustimmen›

**rashness** /'ræʃnɪs/ *n., no pl.* Voreiligkeit, *die;* **regret one's ~ in doing sth.** bedauern, dass man etw. voreilig getan hat

**rasp** /rɑ:sp/ ❶ *n.* Ⓐ (*tool*) Raspel, *die;* Ⓑ (*sound*) (*of metal on wood*) schneidendes Geräusch; (*of a cricket*) Zirpen, *das;* (*of breathing*) Rasseln, *das.* ❷ *v.i.* kratzen. ❸ *v.t.* Ⓐ (*scrape with ~*) raspeln ‹Blech, Kante›; Ⓑ (*say gratingly*) schnarren

**raspberry** /'rɑ:zbərɪ/ *n.* Ⓐ Himbeere, *die;* (*plant also*) Himbeerstrauch, *der; attrib.* Himbeer‹marmelade, -torte, -rosa, -eis›; Ⓑ (*coll.: rude noise*) **blow a ~:** verächtlich prusten

**'raspberry-cane** *n.* Himbeerrute, *die;* Himbeerstrauch, *der*

**rasping** /'rɑ:spɪŋ/ *adj.* krächzend ‹Husten, Stimme›; rasselnd ‹Geräusch›

**Rasta** /'ræstə/ *n.* Rasta, *der;* **the ~ people** die Rastas

**Rastafarian** /ræstə'feərɪən/ (*Relig.*) ❶ *n.* Rastafari, *der.* ❷ *adj.* Rasta-

**raster** /'ræstə(r)/ *n.* (*Telev.*) Raster, *das*

**rat** /ræt/ ❶ *n.* Ⓐ Ratte, *die;* **brown** *or* **sewer ~:** Wanderratte, *die;* **look like a drowned ~** (*coll.*) wie eine gebadete Maus aussehen (*ugs.*); **~s!** (*coll.*) (*drat it!*) verflixt! (*ugs.*); verdammt! (*salopp*); (*nonsense!*) Quatsch! (*ugs.*); **smell a ~** (*fig. coll.*) Lunte *od.* den Braten riechen (*ugs.*); **~s leaving** *or* **deserting the [sinking] ship** (*fig.*) Ratten, die das sinkende Schiff verlassen; ⇒ *also* **musk-rat**; **water rat**; Ⓑ (*coll. derog.: unpleasant person*) Ratte, *die* (*derb*); Ⓒ (*Polit.*) Abtrünnige, *der/die.*
❷ *v.i.,* **-tt-** Ratten jagen; **be out ~ting** auf Rattenfang sein
**~ on** *v.t.* (*coll.*) Ⓐ (*inform on*) verpfeifen (*ugs.*); Ⓑ (*go back on*) nicht halten ‹Versprechen›; Verrat üben an (+ *Dat.*) ‹Politik›; sitzen lassen (*ugs.*) ‹Person›

**'rat-arsed** /'rætɑ:st/ *adj.* (*Brit. sl.*) stock- *od.* stinkbesoffen (*derb*)

**ratatouille** /rætə'tu:ɪ/ *n.* (*Gastr.*) Ratatouille, *die*

**rat: ~bag** *n.* (*coll.*) Knallkopf, *der/*[dumme] Kuh (*ugs.*); **~-catcher** *n.* Rattenfänger, *der/* -fängerin, *die*

**ratchet** /'rætʃɪt/ *n.* (*Mech. Engin.*) Ⓐ (*set of teeth*) Zahnkranz, *der;* Ⓑ **~ [wheel]** Klinkenrad, *das*

**'ratchet screwdriver** *n.* Drillschraubenzieher, *der*

**rate¹** /reɪt/ ❶ *n.* Ⓐ (*proportion*) Rate, *die;* **increase at a ~ of 50 a week** [um] 50 pro Woche anwachsen; **lose at the ~ of two minutes a day** ‹Uhr:› zwei Minuten pro Tag nachgehen; **~ of inflation/absentee ~:** Inflations-/Abwesenheitsrate, *die;* Ⓑ (*tariff*) Satz, *der;* **interest/taxation ~, ~ of interest/taxation** Zins-/Steuersatz, *der;* **lending/premium ~s** Lombardsatz, *der*/Prämientarif, *der;* ⇒ *also* **bank rate**; **exchange** 3 D;

**water rate**; Ⓒ (*amount of money*) Gebühr, *die;* ~ **[of pay]** Lohnsatz, *der;* **the ~ for the job** die festgelegte Vergütung für diese Arbeit; **letter/parcel ~:** Briefporto, *das*/Paketgebühr, *die;* **at reduced ~:** gebührenermäßigt ‹Drucksache›; Ⓓ (*speed*) Geschwindigkeit, *die;* Tempo, *das;* **at a** *or* **the ~ of 50 mph** mit [einer Geschwindigkeit von] 80 km/h; **at a good/fast/moderate/dangerous ~:** zügig/mit hoher/mäßiger Geschwindigkeit/gefährlich schnell; Ⓔ (*Brit.: local authority levy*) Gemeindeabgabe, *die;* Realsteuer, *die;* **county/district ~:** Grafschafts-/Bezirksabgabe, *die;* **[local** *or* **council] ~s** Gemeindeabgaben; Ⓕ (*coll.*) **at any ~** (*at least*) zumindest; wenigstens; (*whatever happens*) auf jeden Fall; **at this ~ we won't get any work done** so kommen wir zu nichts; **at the ~ you're going, ...** (*fig.*) wenn du so weitermachst, ...; **we can't afford to spend money at this ~:** wir können es uns (*Dat.*) nicht leisten, so mit unserem Geld umzugehen; **you'll always be hard up at that ~:** so wirst du immer knapp bei Kasse sein. ⇒ *also* **knot**[1] 1 F.
❷ *v.t.* Ⓐ (*estimate worth of*) schätzen ‹Vermögen›; einschätzen ‹Intelligenz, Leistung, Fähigkeit›; **~ sb./sth. highly** jmdn./etw. hoch einschätzen; Ⓑ (*consider*) betrachten; rechnen **(among** zu); **be ~d the top tennis player in Europe** als der beste Tennisspieler Europas gelten; Ⓒ (*assign value to*) beurteilen, bewerten ‹schulische Leistung, Lesefertigkeit›; angeben ‹Lebensdauer, Schubkraft› **(at** mit); Ⓓ (*Brit.: subject to payment of local authority levy*) Gemeindeabgaben auferlegen (+ *Dat.*); Ⓔ (*Brit.: value*) **the house is ~d at £800 a year** die Grundlage für die Berechnung der Gemeindeabgaben für das Haus beträgt 800 Pfund pro Jahr; Ⓕ (*merit*) verdienen ‹Auszeichnung, Erwähnung›; **does his work ~ a pass?** soll man ihn mit dieser Arbeit bestehen lassen?; **he didn't ~ an invitation** (*coll.*) er war nicht wichtig genug, [um] eingeladen zu werden; Ⓖ (*coll.: think much of*) viel halten von ‹Person›; **~/not ~ one's chances** sich (*Dat.*) große/keine großen Chancen ausrechnen.
❸ *v.i.* zählen **(among** zu); **~ as** gelten als; **~ high in a team/low on a test** in einer Mannschaft viel gelten/bei einem Test schlecht abschneiden

**rate**[2] *v.t.* (*scold*) beschimpfen

**rateable** /ˈreɪtəbl/ *adj.* (*Brit.*) [real]steuerpflichtig ‹Eigentum, Gebäude›; **~ value** steuerbarer Wert

**rate-capping** /ˈreɪtkæpɪŋ/ *n.* (*Brit.*) *gesetzliches Recht der Regierung, durch Entzug den Etat einer Kommunalverwaltung zu kürzen, wenn diese zu hohe Abgaben erhebt oder im vorangegangenen Haushaltsjahr zu viel Geld ausgegeben hat*

**ˈratepayer** *n.* (*Brit.*) Realsteuerpflichtige, *der/die;* ≈ Steuerzahler, *der*/-zahlerin, *die*

**rather** /ˈrɑːðə(r)/ *adv.* Ⓐ (*by preference*) lieber; **he wanted to appear witty ~ than brainy** er wollte lieber geistreich als klug erscheinen; **~ than accept bribes, he decided to resign** ehe er sich bestechen ließ, trat er lieber zurück; **I had ~ die than ...:** ich würde lieber sterben, als ...; **no, thanks, I'd ~ not** nein danke, lieber nicht; **I would ~ you ...:** es wäre mir lieber, wenn du ...; Ⓑ (*somewhat*) ziemlich ‹gut, gelangweilt, unvorsichtig, nett, warm›; **I ~ think that ...:** ich bin ziemlich sicher, dass ...; **be a ~ good one** ziemlich gut sein; **be ~ better/more complicated than expected** um einiges besser/komplizierter sein als erwartet; **fall ~ flat** ein ziemlicher Reinfall sein; **be ~ a nice person** ziemlich nett sein; **it is ~ too early** ich fürchte, es ist zu früh; **it looks ~ like a banana** es sieht ungefähr wie eine Banane aus; **I ~ like beans/him** ich esse Bohnen ganz gern/ich mag ihn recht gern; Ⓒ (*more truly*) vielmehr; **or ~:** beziehungsweise; [oder] genauer gesagt; **he was careless ~ than wicked** er war eher nachlässig als böswillig; Ⓓ (*Brit. dated coll.: certainly*) aber gewiss doch; na klar (*ugs.*)

**rathskeller** /ˈrɑːtskelə(r)/ *n.* (*Amer.*) Kellerlokal, *das*

**ratification** /rætɪfɪˈkeɪʃn/ *n.* ⇒ **ratify**: Ratifizierung, *die;* Bestätigung, *die;* Sanktionierung, *die*

**ratify** /ˈrætɪfaɪ/ *v.t.* ratifizieren ‹völkerrechtlichen Vertrag›; bestätigen ‹Ernennung›; sanktionieren ‹Vertrag, Gesetzentwurf›

**rating**[1] /ˈreɪtɪŋ/ *n.* Ⓐ (*estimated standing*) Einschätzung, *die;* **security ~:** Geheimhaltungsstufe, *die;* **have a high/low ~:** hoch/niedrig eingeschätzt werden; Ⓑ (*Radio, Telev.*) **[popularity] ~:** Einschaltquote, *die;* **be high/low in the ~s** eine hohe/niedrige Einschaltquote haben; Ⓒ (*Navy: rank*) Dienstgrad, *der;* Ⓓ (*Brit. Navy: sailor*) **[naval] ~:** Mannschaftsdienstgrad, *der;* **deck ~s** Angehörige der Decksmannschaften; Ⓔ (*of racing yacht*) Rennwert, *der*

**rating**[2] *n.* (*scolding*) Schimpfe, *die* (*ugs.*); **get a ~:** Schimpfe bekommen (*ugs.*); ausgeschimpft werden; **give sb. a ~:** jmdn. ausschimpfen

**ratio** /ˈreɪʃɪəʊ/ *n., pl.* **~s** Verhältnis, *das;* **in a** *or* **the ~ of 1 to 5** im Verhältnis 1 : 5; **in direct ~ to** *or* **with** im gleichen Verhältnis wie; **the teacher-student ~:** das Verhältnis von Lehrern zu Schülern; **what is the ~ of men to women?** wie hoch ist der Männeranteil im Vergleich zu dem der Frauen?

**ratiocination** /rætɪɒsɪˈneɪʃn, ræʃɪɒsɪˈneɪʃn/ *n.* Reflexion, *die* **(on** über + *Akk.*)

**ration** /ˈræʃn/ ❶ *n.* Ⓐ (*daily food allowance*) [Tages]ration, *die;* **put sb. on short ~s** jmdn. auf halbe Ration setzen (*ugs.*); Ⓑ (*fixed allowance of food etc. for civilians*) **~[s]** Ration, *die* **(of** an + *Dat.*); **sugar/petrol/meat/sweet ~:** Zucker-/Benzin-/Fleisch-/Süßigkeitenration, *die;* Ⓒ (*single portion*) Ration, *die;* **be given [out] with the ~s** (*fig. coll.*) automatisch vergeben werden (*ugs.*). ❷ *v.t.* rationieren ‹Benzin, Autos›; Rationen zuteilen (+ *Dat.*) ‹Person›; (*allocate systematically*) einteilen ‹Zeit›; **be ~ed to one glass of spirits per day** nur ein Glas Alkohol pro Tag trinken dürfen; **~ oneself to ten cigarettes a day** sich (*Dat.*) nur zehn Zigaretten pro Tag erlauben

**~ ˈout** *v.t.* zuteilen **(to** *Dat.*); in Rationen austeilen **(to** an + *Akk.*)

**rational** /ˈræʃənl/ *adj.* Ⓐ (*having reason*) rational, vernunftbegabt ‹Wesen›; (*sensible*) vernünftig ‹Person, Art, Politik usw.›; Ⓑ (*based on reason; also Math.*) rational ‹Erklärung, Analyse, Zahl›

**rationale** /ræʃəˈnɑːl/ *n.* Ⓐ (*statement of reasons*) rationale Erklärung **(of** für); Ⓑ (*fundamental reason*) logische Grundlage

**rationalisation, rationalise** ⇒ **rationaliz-**

**rationalism** /ˈræʃənəlɪzm/ *n.* (*Theol., Philos.*) Rationalismus, *der*

**rationalist** /ˈræʃənəlɪst/ *n.* (*Theol., Philos.*) Rationalist, *der*/Rationalistin, *die*

**rationalistic** /ræʃənəˈlɪstɪk/ *adj.* rationalistisch

**rationality** /ræʃəˈnælɪtɪ/ *n., no pl.* Ⓐ ⇒ **rational** A: Rationalität, *die;* Vernunftbegabtheit, *die;* Vernünftigkeit, *die;* Vernunft, *die;* Ⓑ (*of explanation, analysis, etc.*) Rationalität, *die*

**rationalization** /ræʃənəlaɪˈzeɪʃn/ *n.* (*Econ., Psych.*) Rationalisierung, *die*

**rationalize** /ˈræʃənəlaɪz/ ❶ *v.t.* Ⓐ (*Econ., Psych.*) rationalisieren; Ⓑ (*explain by rationalism*) **~ away** rationalistisch erklären. ❷ *v.i.* Ⓐ Scheinbegründungen finden; Ⓑ (*be a rationalist*) rational denken/handeln

**rationally** /ˈræʃənəlɪ/ *adv.* rational; (*sensibly*) vernünftig

**ration:** ~ **book** *n.* Bezugsscheinheft, *das;* ~ **card,** ~ **coupon** *ns.* Bezugsschein, *der*

**rationing** /ˈræʃənɪŋ/ *n.* Rationierung, *die*

**ratline (ratlin)** /ˈrætlɪn/, **ratling** /ˈrætlɪŋ/ *n.* (*Naut.*) Webeleine, *die*

**rat:** ~ **poison** *n.* Rattengift, *das;* ~ **race** *n.* erbarmungsloser Konkurrenzkampf; ~ **run** *n.* (*Brit. coll.*) Schleichweg, *der;* **~'s-tail** *n.* Rattenschwanz, *der*

**rattan** /rəˈtæn/ *n.* Ⓐ (*cane*) Peddigrohr, *das;* Rattan, *das; attrib.* Rattan‹möbel, -matte, -tau›; Ⓑ (*Bot.*) Rotangpalme, *die*

**rat-tat** /rætˈtæt/, **rat-tat-tat** /rætæˈtæt/ *ns.* Klopfen, *das*

**ˈratted** /ˈrætɪd/ *adj.* ⇒ **rat-arsed**

**ratter** /ˈrætə(r)/ *n.* Rattenjäger, *der*

**rattle** /ˈrætl/ ❶ *v.i.* Ⓐ (*clatter*) ‹Fenster, Maschinenteil, Schlüssel:› klappern; ‹Hagel:› prasseln; ‹Flaschen:› klirren; ‹Kette:› rasseln; ‹Münzen:› klingen; **~ at the door** an der Tür rütteln; Ⓑ (*move*) ‹Zug, Bus:› rattern; ‹Kutsche:› rumpeln.
❷ *v.t.* Ⓐ (*make ~*) klappern mit ‹Würfel, Geschirr, Dose, Münzen, Schlüsselbund›; klirren lassen ‹Fenster[scheiben]›; rasseln mit ‹Kette›; Ⓑ (*coll.: disconcert*) **~ sb., get sb. ~d** jmdn. durcheinander bringen; **don't get ~d!** reg dich nicht auf!; **they tried to ~ the performer** sie versuchten, den Künstler aus dem Konzept zu bringen. ⇒ *also* **sabre.**
❸ *n.* Ⓐ (*of baby, musician*) Rassel, *die;* (*of sports fan*) Ratsche, *die;* Klapper, *die;* Ⓑ (*sound*) Klappern, *das;* (*of hail*) Prasseln, *das;* (*of drums*) Schnarren, *das;* (*of machine gun*) Rattern, *das;* (*of chains*) Rasseln, *das;* (*of bottles*) Klirren, *das;* Ⓒ (*of ~snake*) Rassel, *die;* Klapper, *die*

**~ aˈway** *v.i.* (*coll.*) (*talk*) schnattern (*ugs.*); (*on typewriter*) klappern (*ugs.*); **~ away at** *or* **on** klappern auf (+ *Dat.*) ‹Schreibmaschine›

**~ ˈoff** *v.t.* (*coll.*) herunterrasseln (*ugs.*); **~ sth. off like a machine gun** etw. herunterrattern wie ein Maschinengewehr

**~ ˈon** *v.i.* (*coll.*) plappern (*ugs.*)

**~ through** *v.t.* (*fig.*) herunterrasseln

**rattler** /ˈrætlə(r)/ *n.* (*Amer. coll.*) Klapperschlange, *die*

**rattle: ~snake** *n.* Klapperschlange, *die;* **~trap** *n.* (*coll.*) Klapperkasten, *der* (*ugs.*)

**rattling** /ˈrætlɪŋ/ ❶ *adj.* flott ‹Tempo›. ❷ *adv.* (*coll.*) verdammt (*ugs.*) ‹gut›

**ˈrat trap** *n.* Rattenfalle, *die*

**ratty** /ˈrætɪ/ *adj.* (*coll.: irritable*) gereizt; **don't get ~ with me!** lass deinen Ärger nicht an mir aus!

**raucous** /ˈrɔːkəs/ *adj.* Ⓐ rau ‹Stimme, Lachen›; Ⓑ (*boisterous, disorderly*) wild ‹Benehmen›; wüst ‹Gesänge›; roh ‹Zuruf›

**raucously** /ˈrɔːkəslɪ/ *adv.* Ⓐ mit rauer Stimme; Ⓑ (*boisterously*) **they sang/laughed/shouted ~:** sie sangen wüste Gesänge/lachten roh/stießen wilde Rufe aus

**raunchy** /ˈrɔːntʃɪ/ *adj.* (*lewd*) vulgär; (*suggestive*) scharf (*salopp*)

**ravage** /ˈrævɪdʒ/ ❶ *v.t.* heimsuchen ‹Gebiet, Stadt›; so gut wie vernichten ‹Ernte›; schwer zeichnen ‹Gesichtszüge›. ❷ *n. in pl.* verheerende Wirkung; **the ~s of time/war** die Zeichen der Zeit/die Wunden des Krieges; **be marked by the ~s of famine** vom Hunger schwer gezeichnet sein

**rave** /reɪv/ ❶ *v.i.* Ⓐ (*talk wildly*) irrereden; **he's just raving** er redet nur irres Zeug (*ugs.*); **~ at** [wüst] beschimpfen; ⇒ *also* **rant** 1; Ⓑ (*speak with admiration*) schwärmen **(about, over** von); Ⓒ (*howl*) ‹Wind, Sturm, Meer:› brausen. ❷ *adj.* (*coll.*) [hellauf] begeistert ‹Kritik›. ❸ *n.* Ⓐ (*Brit. coll.: fad, fashion*) **the latest ~:** der letzte Schrei; **it's all the ~:** es ist der letzte Schrei; Ⓑ *n.* (*coll.: dancing party*) Rave, *der od. das*

**ravel** /ˈrævl/ ❶ *v.t.,* (*Brit.*) **-ll-** Ⓐ (*entangle*) verheddern ‹Wollstrang›; **~ into knots** verwickeln und verknoten; Ⓑ ⇒ **unravel** 1. ❷ *v.i.,* (*Brit.*) **-ll-** Ⓐ (*become entangled*) sich verwickeln; Ⓑ ⇒ **unravel** 2

**~ ˈout** ⇒ **unravel** 1

**raven** /ˈreɪvn/ ❶ *n.* Rabe, *der;* Kolkrabe, *der* (*Zool.*). ❷ *adj.* **~-black** [kohl]rabenschwarz ‹Haar›; **~-haired** mit kohlrabenschwarzem Haar *nachgestellt*

**ravening** /ˈrævənɪŋ/ *adj.* beutegierig

**ravenous** /ˈrævənəs/ *adj.* Ⓐ ausgehungert; **I'm ~:** ich habe einen Bärenhunger (*ugs.*); **have a ~ hunger/appetite** einen richtigen Heißhunger haben; Ⓑ (*greedy*) räuberisch

**ravenously** /ˈrævənəslɪ/ *adv.* heißhungrig; **be ~ hungry** einen Riesenhunger haben (*ugs.*); ausgehungert sein

**raver** /ˈreɪvə(r)/ *n.* Ⓐ (*uninhibited person*) Lebemensch, *der;* (*man also*) Lebemann, *der;* Ⓑ (*person who goes to raves*) Raver, *der*/Raverin, *die*

**ˈrave-up** *n.* (*Brit. coll.*) [wilde] Fete (*ugs.*)

**ravine** /rəˈviːn/ *n.* Schlucht, *die;* (*produced by river also*) Klamm, *die*

**raving** /ˈreɪvɪŋ/ ❶ *n. in pl.* irres Gerede. ❷ *adj.* Ⓐ (*talking madly*) irre redend ‹Wahnsinniger, Idiot›; Ⓑ (*outstanding*) fantastisch (*ugs.*) ‹Erfolg›; **be a ~ beauty** hinreißend schön sein. ❸ *adv.* **be ~ mad** (*insane*) hochgradig schwachsinnig sein; (*stupid*) völlig verrückt sein (*ugs.*)

**ravioli** /rævɪˈəʊlɪ/ *n.* (*Gastr.*) Ravioli *Pl.*

**ravish** /ˈrævɪʃ/ *v.t.* Ⓐ (*charm*) entzücken; bezaubern; **be ~ed** hingerissen *od.* bezaubert sein (**by, with** von); Ⓑ (*rape*) schänden (*veralt.*); Gewalt antun (*geh.* + *Dat.*)

**ravishing** /ˈrævɪʃɪŋ/ *adj.* bildschön ‹Anblick, Person›; hinreißend ‹Schönheit›; **~ sight** Augenweide, *die*

**raw** /rɔː/ ❶ *adj.* Ⓐ (*uncooked*) roh; Ⓑ (*inexperienced*) unerfahren; frisch gebacken ‹Akademiker›; blutig ‹Anfänger›; ⇨ *also* **recruit** 1 A, D; Ⓒ (*unbound*) ungesäumt ‹Kante, Stoff›; Ⓓ (*stripped of skin*) blutig ‹Fleisch›; offen ‹Wunde›; (*sore*) wund ‹Füße›; **touch** *or* **hit a ~ nerve** einen wunden Punkt *od.* eine empfindliche Stelle treffen; Ⓔ (*chilly*) nasskalt; Ⓕ (*untreated*) Roh‹haut, -holz, -seide, -zucker, -erz, -leder›; (*undiluted*) rein ‹Alkohol›; Ⓖ (*fig.: unpolished*) grob; Ⓗ (*Statistics*) unaufbereitet. ⇨ *also* **deal**[1] 3 A; **sienna**; **umber**.
❷ *n.* **nature in the ~:** unverfälschte Natur; **life in the ~:** das Leben, wie es wirklich ist; **in the ~** (*fig.*) unbekleidet ‹schlafen›; **touch sb. on the ~** (*Brit.*) jmdn. an [s]einer verwundbaren Stelle treffen

**raw: ~-boned** /ˈrɔːbəʊnd/ *adj.* knochig; **~hide** *n.* Ⓐ (*leather*) Rohleder, *das;* Ⓑ (*whip*) Peitsche aus Rohleder

**Rawlplug** ® /ˈrɔːlplʌg/ *n.* Dübel, *der*

**raw maˈterial** *n.* Rohstoff, *der*

**ray**[1] /reɪ/ *n.* Ⓐ (*lit. or fig.*) Strahl, *der;* **~ of sunshine/light** Sonnen-/Lichtstrahl, *der;* **~ of sunshine** (*fig.*) Sonnenschein, *der;* **~ of hope** Hoffnungsstrahl, *der;* **give sb. a ~ of hope** jmdm. Hoffnung machen; **provide a ~ of comfort** etwas Trost spenden; Ⓑ *in pl.* (*radiation*) Strahlen; Strahlung, *die;* ⇨ *also* **cosmic**; **gamma rays**; **X-ray** 1; Ⓒ (*Zool.*) (*of fish's fin*) Flossenstrahl, *der;* Radius, *der* (*fachspr.*); (*of starfish*) Arm, *der*

**ray**[2] *n.* (*fish*) Rochen, *der*

**ray**[3] *n.* (*Mus.*) re

**ˈray gun** *n.* (*Science Fiction*) Strahlenpistole, *die*

**rayon** /ˈreɪɒn/ *n.* (*Textiles*) Reyon, *das od. der; attrib.* Reyon‹kleid, -hemd›

**raze** /reɪz/ *v.t.* (*completely destroy*) völlig zerstören; (*pull down*) abreißen; **~ to the ground** dem Erdboden gleichmachen

**razor** /ˈreɪzə(r)/ *n.* Rasiermesser, *das;* **[electric] ~:** [elektrischer] Rasierapparat; [Elektro- *od.* Trocken]rasierer, *der* (*ugs.*); ⇨ *also* **safety razor**

**razor: ~bill** *n.* (*Ornith.*) Tordalk, *der;* **~ blade** *n.* Rasierklinge, *die;* **~ edge** *n.* Rasierschneide, *die;* **sharpen to a ~ edge** rasiermesserscharf machen; **be** *or* **stand on a ~ edge** *or* **~'s edge** (*fig.*) sich auf einer Gratwanderung befinden; **~fish** *n.* (*Zool.*) Scheidenmuschel, *die;* **~-sharp** *adj.* sehr scharf ‹Messer›; (*fig.*) messerscharf ‹Verstand, Intellekt›; scharfsinnig ‹Person›; **~ shell** ⇨ **~-fish**; **~ wire** *n. wie Stacheldraht verwendeter, dünner, scharfkantiger Draht*

**razzamatazz** /ˈræzəmətæz/ ⇨ **razzmatazz**

**razzle** /ˈræzl/ *n.* (*coll.*) **be/go on the ~:** einen draufmachen (*ugs.*)

**razzle-dazzle** /ˈræzldæzl/, **razzmatazz** /ˈræzmətæz/ *ns.* (*coll.*) Ⓐ (*excitement*) Trubel, *der;* **add ~ to sth.** etwas aufmotzen (*salopp*); Ⓑ (*extravagant show*) Rummel, *der* (*ugs.*)

**RC** *abbr.* **Roman Catholic** r.-k.; röm.-kath.

**Rd.** *abbr.* **road** Str.

**RDA** *abbr.* **recommended daily** *or* **dietary allowance** *empfohlene Tagesmenge od. Tageszufuhr*

**RE** *abbr.* (*Brit.*) Ⓐ **Royal Engineers** Pionierkorps der britischen Armee; Ⓑ **Religious Education** Religionslehre, *die*

**re**[1] ⇨ **ray**[3]

**re**[2] /riː/ *prep.* Ⓐ (*coll.*) über (+ *Akk.*); Ⓑ (*Law*) in Sachen; Ⓒ (*Commerc.*) betreffs

**'re** /ə(r)/ = **are;** ⇨ **be**

**reach** /riːtʃ/ ❶ *v.t.* Ⓐ (*arrive at*) erreichen; ankommen *od.* eintreffen in (+ *Dat.*) ‹Stadt, Land›; ankommen an (+ *Dat.*) ‹Reiseziel›; erzielen ‹Übereinstimmung, Übereinkunft›; kommen zu ‹Entscheidung, Entschluss, Ausgang, Eingang›; **be easily ~ed** leicht erreichbar *od.* zu erreichen sein (**by** mit); **not a sound ~ed our ears** kein Laut drang an unsere Ohren; **your letter ~ed me today** dein Brief hat mich heute erreicht; **have you ~ed page 45 yet?** bist du schon auf Seite 45 [angelangt]?; **you can ~ her at this number/by radio** du kannst sie unter dieser Nummer/über Funk erreichen; Ⓑ (*extend to*) ‹Straße:› führen bis zu; ‹Leiter, Haar:› reichen bis zu; Ⓒ (*pass*) **~ me that book** reich mir das Buch herüber.
❷ *v.i.* Ⓐ (*stretch out hand*) **~ for sth.** nach etw. greifen; **~ across the table/through the window** über den Tisch/durchs Fenster langen; **how high can you ~?** wie hoch kannst du langen?; Ⓑ (*be long/tall enough*) **sth. will/won't ~:** etw. ist/ist nicht lang genug; **will it ~ as far as …?** wird es bis zu … reichen? **I can't ~:** ich komme nicht daran; **he can't ~ up to the top shelf** er kann das oberste Regal nicht [mit der Hand] erreichen; **can you ~?** kannst *od.* kommst du dran? (*ugs.*); Ⓒ (*go as far as*) ‹Wasser, Gebäude, Besitz:› reichen (**[up] to** bis [hinauf] zu); ‹Betrag:› erreichen (**to** *Akk.*); ‹Stimme:› zu hören sein (**to** bis); **his influence ~es beyond the limits of the town** sein Einfluss reicht über die Stadtgrenzen hinaus.
❸ *n.* Ⓐ (*extent of ~ing*) Reichweite, *die;* **be within easy ~ [of a place]** [von einem Ort aus] leicht erreichbar sein; **live within ~ of sb.** in jmds. Nähe leben; **be out of ~ [of a place]** [von einem Ort aus] nicht erreichbar sein; **be above sb.'s ~:** zu hoch für jmdn. sein; **keep sth. out of ~ of sb.** etw. unerreichbar für jmdn. aufbewahren; **keep sth. within easy ~:** etw. in greifbarer Nähe aufbewahren; **move sth. beyond sb.'s ~:** etw. aus jmds. Reichweite entfernen; **be within/beyond the ~ of sb.** in/außer jmds. Reichweite sein; (*fig.*) für jmdn. im/nicht im Bereich des Möglichen liegen; (*financially*) für jmdn. erschwinglich/unerschwinglich sein; Ⓑ (*act of stretching out hand*) **make a ~ for sth.** nach etw. greifen; **it was a long ~ from the bed to the light switch** der Lichtschalter war vom Bett aus schwer zu erreichen; Ⓒ (*expanse*) Abschnitt, *der;* **a ~ of woodland** ein Waldgebiet; **the upper/lower ~es [of the river]** die oberen/unteren [Fluss]abschnitte; Ⓓ (*Naut.*) Segelstrecke zwischen zwei Wendungen; **be on a ~:** raumen Kurs segeln

**~ aˈcross** *v.i.* die Hand ausstrecken

**~ ˈback** *v.i.* zurückreichen (**over** *Akk.;* **to** bis in + *Akk.*)

**~ ˈdown** ❶ *v.i.* den Arm nach unten ausstrecken; **~ down to sth.** (*be long enough*) bis zu etw. [hinunter]reichen. ❷ *v.t.* hinunterholen; (*to receiving speaker*) herunterreichen

**~ ˈout** ❶ *v.t.* (*stretch out*) ausstrecken ‹Fuß, Bein, Hand, Arm› (**for** nach). ❷ *v.i.* die Hand ausstrecken (**for** nach); **~ out for, ~ out to grasp** ‹Person, Hand:› greifen nach; **~ out to sb.** (*fig.*) jmdn. zu erreichen versuchen

**~ ˈover** *v.i.* die Hand ausstrecken

**reachable** /ˈriːtʃəbl/ *adj.* erreichbar

**ˈreach-me-down** (*Brit.*) ⇨ **hand-me-down** 1 B

**react** /rɪˈækt/ ❶ *v.i.* Ⓐ (*respond*) reagieren (**to** auf + *Akk.*); **be quick to ~ to sth.** auf etw. schnell reagieren; Ⓑ (*act in opposition*) sich widersetzen (**against** *Dat.*); Ⓒ (*produce reciprocal effect*) zurückwirken (**upon** auf + *Akk.*); seine Wirkung haben (**upon** auf + *Akk.*); Ⓓ (*Chem., Phys.*) reagieren. ❷ *v.t.* (*Chem.*) reagieren lassen

**reaction** /rɪˈækʃn/ *n.* Ⓐ Reaktion, *die* (**to** auf + *Akk.*); **~ against sth.** Widerstand gegen etw.; **action and ~:** Wirkung und Gegenwirkung; **what was his ~?** wie hat er reagiert?; **there was a favourable ~ to the proposal** der Vorschlag ist positiv aufgenommen worden; **chemical/nuclear ~:** chemische Reaktion/Kernreaktion, *die;* **I had a bad ~ after the injection** mein Körper hat die Injektion schlecht vertragen; Ⓑ (*opposite physical action*) Gegenreaktion, *die;* Ⓒ (*Polit.*) Reaktion, *die;* **forces of ~:** reaktionäre Kräfte

**reactionary** /rɪˈækʃənərɪ/ (*Polit.*) ❶ *adj.* reaktionär. ❷ *n.* Reaktionär, *der*/Reaktionärin, *die*

**reactivate** /rɪˈæktɪveɪt/ *v.t.* reaktivieren; wieder in Gang bringen ‹Motor, Generator›; wieder einrichten ‹Stützpunkt›

**reactive** /rɪˈæktɪv/ *adj.* Ⓐ (*showing reaction*) auf eine Reaktion hindeutend ‹Symptom›; **~ response** Gegenreaktion, *die;* Ⓑ (*Chem., Phys.*) reaktiv

**reactivity** /rɪækˈtɪvɪtɪ/ *n.* (*Chem., Phys.*) Reaktionsfähigkeit, *die*

**reactor** /rɪˈæktə(r)/ *n.* Ⓐ **[nuclear] ~:** Kernreaktor, *der;* **pressurized-water ~:** Druckwasserreaktor, *der;* Ⓑ (*Chem.*) Reaktor, *der;* Reaktionsapparat, *der*

**read** /riːd/ ❶ *v.t.*, **read** /red/ Ⓐ lesen; **~ sb. sth., ~ sth. to sb.** jmdm. etwas vorlesen; **~ a Bill for the first/second/third time** (*Parl.*) einen Gesetzentwurf in erster/zweiter/dritter Lesung beraten; **for 'white' ~ 'black'** statt „weiß" muss es „schwarz" heißen; **~ proof[s]** (*Print.*) Korrektur[en] lesen; **~ the electricity/gas meter** den Strom/das Gas ablesen; **~ all about it!** lesen Sie selbst!; Ⓑ (*show a ~ing of*) anzeigen; Ⓒ (*interpret*) deuten; **~ terror in sb.'s eyes** Schrecken an jmds. Augen (*Dat.*) ablesen können; **~ sb. like a book** (*fig.*) in jmdm. lesen können wie in einem Buch; **~ the cards/sb.'s hand** Karten lesen/jmdm. aus der Hand lesen; **~ sb.'s mind** *or* **thoughts** jmds. Gedanken lesen; **~ sth. into sth.** etw. in etw. (*Akk.*) hineinlesen; **~ between the lines** zwischen den Zeilen lesen; Ⓓ (*understand*) hören; **do you ~ me?** können Sie mich hören?; Ⓔ (*Brit. Univ.: study*) studieren; Ⓕ (*Computing*) abtasten ‹Lochkarte›; lesen ‹Band, Information›; **~ into** einlesen in (+ *Akk.*); **~ out of** entnehmen aus. ⇨ *also* **take** 1 U.
❷ *v.i.*, **read** Ⓐ lesen; **~ to sb.** jmdm. vorlesen; **~ [a]round a subject** Hintergrundmaterial zu einem Thema lesen; Ⓑ (*convey meaning*) lauten; **the contract ~s as follows** der Vertrag hat folgenden Wortlaut; **Arabic ~s from right to left** die arabische Schrift wird von rechts nach links gelesen; Ⓒ (*affect ~er*) sich lesen; **the play ~s better than it acts** das Stück wirkt besser beim Lesen als auf der Bühne.
❸ *n.* Ⓐ (*time spent in ~ing*) **have a quiet ~:** in Ruhe lesen; **have a ~ of sth.** (*coll.*) mal in etw. (*Akk.*) gucken (*ugs.*); Ⓑ (*Brit. coll.: ~ing matter*) **be a good ~:** sich gut lesen.
❹ [red] *adj.* **widely** *or* **deeply ~:** sehr belesen ‹Person›; **a widely ~/little-~ book/author** ein viel/wenig gelesenes Buch/gelesener Autor; **the most widely ~ book/author** das meistgelesene Buch/der meistgelesene Autor

**~ ˈback** *v.t.* wiederholen; noch einmal vorlesen

**~ ˈin** *v.t.* (*Computing*) einlesen; ⇨ *also* **read-in**

**~ ˈoff** *v.t.* durchlesen; (*from meter, board*) ablesen ‹Zahl, Stand›

**~ ˈout** *v.t.* Ⓐ (*aloud*) laut vorlesen; Ⓑ (*Computing*) ausgeben; ⇨ *also* **read-out**; Ⓒ (*Amer.: expel*) ausschließen (**of** aus)

**~ ˈover, ~ ˈthrough** *v.t.* durchlesen

**~ ˈup** *v.t.* sich informieren (**on** über + *Akk.*)

**readability** /riːdəˈbɪlɪtɪ/ *n., no pl.* Lesbarkeit, *die;* **improve the ~ of sth.** etw. lesbarer machen

**readable** /'ri:dəbl/ *adj.* Ⓐ *(pleasant to read)* lesenswert; Ⓑ *(legible)* leserlich

**readdress** /ri:ə'dres/ *v.t.* umadressieren

**reader** /'ri:də(r)/ *n.* Ⓐ Leser, *der*/Leserin, *die;* **be a slow/good/great ∼ [of sth.]** [etw.] langsam/gut/gern lesen; Ⓑ *(who reads aloud)* Vorlesende, *der/die;* Ⓒ *(Publishing)* **[publisher's] ∼:** [Verlags]lektor, *der*/-lektorin, *die;* Ⓓ *(textbook)* Lehrbuch, *das;* *(to learn to read, containing original texts)* Lesebuch, *das;* **Latin/poetry ∼:** Latein[lehr]buch, *das*/Gedichtbuch, *das;* Ⓔ *(Printing)* ⇒ **proof-reader**; Ⓕ *(Brit. Univ.)* ≈ Assistenzprofessor, *der*/-professorin, *die* **(in** für); Ⓖ *(machine)* Lesegerät, *das*

**readership** /'ri:dəʃɪp/ *n.* Ⓐ *(number or type of readers)* Leserschaft, *die;* Leserkreis, *der;* **what is the ∼ of the paper?** wie groß ist die Leserschaft der Zeitung?; Ⓑ *(Brit. Univ.)* ≈ Assistenzprofessur, *die* **(in** für)

**readies** /'redɪz/ *n. pl. (coll.)* Knete, *die (ugs.);* **short of the ∼:** knapp bei Kasse *(ugs.)*

**readily** /'redɪlɪ/ *adv.* Ⓐ *(willingly)* bereitwillig; Ⓑ *(without difficulty)* ohne weiteres

**read-in** /'ri:dɪn/ *n. (Computing)* Eingabe, *die; attrib.* Eingabe-

**readiness** /'redɪnɪs/ *n., no pl.* Ⓐ Bereitschaft, *die;* **show [a] ∼ to do sth.** Bereitschaft zeigen, etw. zu tun; **∼ to learn** Lernbereitschaft, *die;* **have/be in ∼ [for sth.]** [für etw.] bereithalten/bereit sein; Ⓑ *(quickness)* Schnelligkeit, *die;* **∼ of wit** Schlagfertigkeit, *die*

**reading** /'ri:dɪŋ/ *n.* Ⓐ Lesen, *das;* **help sb. with his ∼:** jmdm. beim Lesen helfen; **do some ∼:** [ein wenig] lesen; **on [a] second ∼:** beim zweiten Lesen; **a man of vast** *or* **wide/little ∼:** ein sehr/wenig belesener Mann; Ⓑ *(matter to be read)* Lektüre, *die;* **plenty of ∼:** viel zu lesen; **make interesting/be good/dull ∼:** interessant/gut/langweilig zu lesen sein; **a book of ∼s from the Bible** ein Buch mit ausgewählten Bibeltexten *od.* Auszügen aus der Bibel; Ⓒ *(figure shown)* Anzeige, *die;* **the temperature ∼s for last month** die Temperaturwerte des letzten Monats; Ⓓ *(recital)* Lesung, *die* **(from** aus); **give a poetry ∼:** Gedichte vorlesen; **give a ∼ from** lesen aus; Ⓔ *(interpretation)* [Aus]deutung, *die;* **my ∼ of the sentence was ...:** ich habe den Satz so verstanden: ...; **our ∼ of the law is that ...:** wir legen das Recht so aus, dass ...; Ⓕ *(particular form)* Version, *die;* Fassung, *die;* Ⓖ *(Parl.)* **[first/second/third] ∼:** [erste/zweite/dritte] Lesung; **have its first ∼:** in erster Lesung beraten werden; **be thrown out on the second ∼** *(Brit.)* in zweiter Lesung verworfen werden; **give the bill its second ∼** *(Amer.)* den Gesetzentwurf in zweiter Lesung beraten

**reading: ∼ age** *n.* **a child with a ∼ age of 10** ein Kind mit der Lesefertigkeit eines Zehnjährigen; **have a ∼ age of 10** wie ein zehnjähriges Kind lesen können; **∼ desk** *n.* Lesepult, *das;* **∼ glasses** *n. pl.* Lesebrille, *die;* **∼ knowledge** *n.* **have a ∼ knowledge of a language** Texte in einer Sprache lesen können; **∼ lamp, ∼ light** *ns.* Leselampe, *die;* **∼ list** *n.* Literaturliste, *die;* **∼ matter** *n., no pl., no indef. art.* Lesestoff, *der;* Lektüre, *die;* **∼ room** *n.* Lesesaal, *der*

**readjust** /ri:ə'dʒʌst/ ❶ *v.t.* neu einstellen; neu anpassen ‹Gehalt, Zinssatz›. ❷ *v. refl. & i.* **∼ [oneself] to** sich wieder gewöhnen an (+ *Akk.*) ‹Leben›

**readjustment** /ri:ə'dʒʌstmənt/ *n.* Änderung, *die;* **period of ∼:** Zeit der Neuorientierung

**read** /ri:d/: **∼-'only memory** *n. (Computing)* Fest[wert]speicher, *der;* **∼-out** *n. (Computing)* Ausgabe, *die;* **∼-write** *n. attrib. (Computing)* Schreib-Lese-; **∼-write head** Schreib-Lese-Kopf, *der*

**ready** /'redɪ/ ❶ *adj.* Ⓐ *(prepared)* fertig; **be ∼ for the fight** *or* **to fight** kampfbereit sein; **be ∼ to do sth.** bereit sein, etw. zu tun; **the troops are ∼ to march/for battle** die Truppen sind marsch-/gefechtsbereit; **be ∼ for work/school** zur Arbeit/für die Schule bereit sein; *(about to leave)* für die Arbeit/Schule fertig sein; **be ∼ to leave** aufbruchsbereit sein; **be ∼ for sb.** bereit sein, sich jmdm. zu stellen; **be ∼ for anything** auf alles vorbereitet sein; **make ∼:** Vorbereitungen treffen **(for** für); **make ∼ to go** sich zum Aufbruch bereitmachen; Ⓑ *(willing)* bereit; **I'm ∼ to believe it** ich glaube es gerne; Ⓒ *(prompt)* schnell; **have ∼, be ∼ with** parat haben, nicht verlegen sein um ‹Antwort, Ausrede, Vorschlag›; **be too ∼ to suspect others** allzu schnell bereit sein, andere zu verdächtigen; Ⓓ *(likely)* im Begriff; **be ∼ to burst** ‹Knospe:› kurz vor dem Aufbrechen sein; **be ∼ to cry** den Tränen nahe sein; Ⓔ *(within reach)* griffbereit ‹Waffe, Fahrkarte, Taschenlampe›; **have your tickets ∼!** halten Sie Ihre Fahrkarten bitte bereit!; **a ∼ source of supplies** eine sofort zugängliche Bezugsquelle; Ⓕ *(not reluctant)* bereitwillig ‹Zustimmung, Anerkennung›; willig ‹Arbeiter›; Ⓖ *(easy)* leicht ‹Löslichkeit, Zugänglichkeit›; **she has a ∼ smile** sie lächelt gern.

❷ *adv.* fertig; **∼ cooked** vorgekocht.

❸ *n.* Ⓐ **at the ∼:** schussbereit, im Anschlag ‹Schusswaffe›; Ⓑ ⇒ **readies**

**ready: ∼ 'cash** ⇒ **∼ money**; **∼-cooked** *adj.* vorgekocht; **∼-cooked meal** Fertiggericht, *das;* Fertigmahlzeit, *die;* **∼-made** *adj.* Ⓐ Konfektions‹anzug, -kleidung›; **∼-made curtains** Fertiggardinen; Ⓑ *(fig.)* vorgefertigt; **∼ meal** *n.* Fertiggericht, *das;* **∼ 'money** *n.* Ⓐ *(cash)* Bargeld, *das;* Ⓑ *(immediate payment)* **for ∼ money** gegen bar; **∼ 'reckoner** *n.* Berechnungstabelle, *die;* *(for conversion)* Umrechnungstabelle, *die;* **∼, set** *or* **steady, 'go!** *int.* Achtung, fertig, los!; **∼-to-eat** *adj.* Fertig‹mahlzeit, -dessert›; **∼-to-serve** *adj.* tischfertig; **∼-to-wear** *adj.* Konfektions‹anzug, -kleidung›

**reaffirm** /ri:ə'fɜ:m/ *v.t.* [erneut] bekräftigen

**reaffirmation** /ri:æfə'meɪʃn/ *n.* [erneute] Bekräftigung

**reafforest** /ri:ə'fɒrɪst/ *(Brit.)* ⇒ **reforest**

**reafforestation** /ri:əfɒrɪ'steɪʃn/ *n.* Wiederaufforstung, *die*

**reagent** /ri:'eɪdʒənt/ *n. (Chem.)* Reagens, *das;* Reagenz, *das*

**real** /rɪəl/ ❶ *adj.* Ⓐ *(actually existing)* real ‹Gestalt, Ereignis, Lebewesen›; wirklich ‹Macht›; Ⓑ *(genuine)* echt ‹Interesse, Gold, Seide›; **very ∼** *(coll.)* wirklich groß ‹Vergnügen, Ehre›; Ⓒ *(complete)* total *(ugs.)* ‹Desaster, Bauernfängerei, Wucher, Enttäuschung›; Ⓓ *(true)* wahr ‹Grund, Freund, Name, Glück›; echt ‹Mitleid, Vergnügen, Sieg›; **the ∼ thing** *(genuine article)* der/die/das Echte; *(fig.: true love)* [die] wahre Liebe; **look like the ∼ thing** wie echt aussehen; **be [not] the ∼ thing** [un]echt sein; **have experienced the ∼ thing** das Echte kennen; **feel a ∼ fool** sich *(Dat.)* wie ein richtiger Idiot vorkommen; Ⓔ *(Econ.)* real; Real-; **in ∼ terms** real ‹sinken, steigen›; **salaries decreased in ∼ terms** die Realgehälter sind gesunken; Ⓕ **be for ∼** *(coll.)* echt sein; ‹Angebot, Drohung:› ernst gemeint sein; ‹Person:› aufrichtig sein; **fight for ∼:** richtig kämpfen; Ⓖ *(Philos.)* real; Ⓗ *(Math., Optics)* reell ‹Zahl, Bild, Analyse›. ⇒ *also* **tennis**.

❷ *adv. (Scot. and Amer. coll. as intensifier)* echt *(ugs.)* ‹gut, schön, usw.›; recht ‹bald›

**real: ∼ 'ale** *n. (Brit.)* echtes Ale; **∼ 'coffee** *n.* Bohnenkaffee, *der;* **∼ estate** *n. (Law)* Immobilien *Pl.;* **be in ∼ estate** Immobilienhandel betreiben; **∼-estate** *adj.* Immobilien‹büro, -makler›

**realign** /ri:ə'laɪn/ *v.t.* neu ordnen ‹Text, Daten›; neu aufeinander abstimmen ‹Währungen›

**realignment** /ri:ə'laɪnmənt/ *n.* Neuordnung, *die;* *(of currency)* Realignment, *das (Finanzw.)*

**realisable, realisation, realise** ⇒ **realiz-**

**realism** /'rɪəlɪzm/ *n.* Realismus, *der;* **[sense of] ∼:** Wirklichkeitssinn, *der*

**realist** /'rɪəlɪst/ *n.* Realist, *der*/Realistin, *die*

**realistic** /rɪə'lɪstɪk/ *adj.* realistisch; **be ∼ about sth.** etw. realistisch sehen

**realistically** /rɪə'lɪstɪkəlɪ/ *adv.* realistisch

**reality** /rɪ'ælɪtɪ/ *n.* Ⓐ *no pl.* Realität, *die;* **appearance and ∼:** Schein und Sein; **bring sb. back to ∼:** jmdn. in die Realität zurückholen; **in ∼:** in Wirklichkeit; Ⓑ *no pl. (resemblance to original)* Naturtreue, *die;* **with [startling] ∼:** [erstaunlich] naturgetreu; Ⓒ *(real fact)* Gegebenheit, *die;* **the realities of the situation** die tatsächliche Situation

**realizable** /'rɪəlaɪzəbl/ *adj.* realisierbar

**realization** /rɪəlaɪ'zeɪʃn/ *n.* Ⓐ *(understanding)* Erkenntnis, *die;* Ⓑ *(becoming real)* Verwirklichung, *die;* Ⓒ *(Finance: act of selling)* Realisierung, *die*

**realize** /'rɪəlaɪz/ *v.t.* Ⓐ *(be aware of)* bemerken; realisieren; erkennen ‹Fehler›; **they've ∼d the importance of tact** sie merkten, wie wichtig Taktgefühl ist; **I never ∼d how much I depend on him** erst jetzt wird mir bewusst, wie sehr ich auf ihn angewiesen bin; **∼ [that] ...:** merken, dass ...; **I hardly ∼d what was happening** ich habe kaum mitbekommen, was da vor sich ging; **I didn't ∼** *(abs.)* ich habe es nicht gewusst/*(had not noticed)* bemerkt; Ⓑ *(make happen)* verwirklichen; **be ∼d** wahr werden; Ⓒ *(Finance: sell for cash)* realisieren *(fachspr.)*; in Geld *(Akk.)* umsetzen; Ⓓ *(fetch as price or profit)* erbringen ‹Summe, Gewinn, Preis›; Ⓔ *(gain)* erwerben ‹Vermögen›; machen ‹Gewinn›

**real: ∼ 'life** *n.* das wirkliche Leben; die Realität; **∼-life** *attrib. adj.* real

**really** /'rɪəlɪ/ *adv.* wirklich; **it's a ∼ good film** es ist ein wirklich guter Film; **I don't ∼/∼ don't know what to do now** ich weiß eigentlich/wirklich nicht, was ich jetzt tun soll; **I ∼ think you ought to apologize** ich finde wirklich, dass du dich entschuldigen solltest; **not ∼:** eigentlich nicht; **that's not ∼ a problem** das ist eigentlich kein Problem; **he didn't ∼ mean it** er hat es nicht so gemeint; **I ∼ don't know** ich weiß es wirklich nicht; **[well,] ∼!** [also] so was!; **∼, I would never have expected that of you** also wirklich, das hätte ich nie von dir erwartet; **∼?** wirklich?; tatsächlich?; **∼ and truly** wirklich

**realm** /relm/ *n.* [König]reich, *das;* **be in the ∼[s] of fancy** ins Reich der Fantasie gehören; **be within/beyond the ∼s of possibility** *or* **the possible** im/nicht im Bereich des Möglichen liegen

**real: ∼ 'man** *n.* richtiger Mann; **∼ 'money** *n.* Bargeld, *das;* **pay in ∼ money** bar bezahlen; **∼ 'property** *n. (Law)* Grundvermögen, *das;* **∼ time** *n. (Computing)* Realzeit, *die;* Echtzeit, *die*

**realtor** /'ri:əltə(r)/ *(Amer.)* ⇒ **estate agent a**

**real 'world** *n. (beyond school)* Arbeitswelt, *die;* *(as opposed to film etc.)* Realität, *die;* **the ∼ outside** die [reale] Außenwelt

**ream** /ri:m/ *n.* Ⓐ *(quantity)* 500 Blatt; halbes [Neu]ries; **three ∼s** 1 500 Blatt; anderthalb [Neu]ries; Ⓑ *in pl. (fig.)* ein ganzer Roman; **write ∼s [and ∼s] of poetry** ganze Bände von Gedichten schreiben

**reanimate** /rɪ'ænɪmeɪt/ *v.t.* wieder beleben

**reap** /ri:p/ *v.t.* Ⓐ *(cut)* schneiden ‹Getreide›; Ⓑ *(gather in)* einfahren ‹Getreide, Ernte›; Ⓒ *(harvest)* abernten ‹Feld›; Ⓓ *(fig.)* ernten ‹Ruhm, Lob›; erhalten ‹Belohnung›; erzielen ‹Gewinn›; **∼ what one has sown** ernten, was man gesät hat; **∼ the benefits of sth.** die Früchte einer Sache ernten; ⇒ *also* **whirlwind A**

**reaper** /'ri:pə(r)/ *n.* Ⓐ ⇒ **harvester**; Ⓑ **the [grim] R∼** *(fig.)* der Sensenmann *(verhüll.)*; der Schnitter [Tod]

**reaping**/'ri:pɪŋ/: **∼ hook** *n.* Sichel, *die;* **∼ machine** ⇒ **harvester A**

**reappear** /ri:ə'pɪə(r)/ *v.i.* wieder auftauchen; *(come back)* [wieder] zurückkommen; ‹Sonne:› wieder zum Vorschein kommen

**reappearance** /ri:ə'pɪərəns/ *n.* Wiederauftauchen, *das*

**reapply** /ri:ə'plaɪ/ ❶ *v.i.* sich erneut bewerben **(for** um). ❷ *v.t.* noch einmal auftragen ‹Kleister›

**reappoint** /ri:ə'pɔɪnt/ *v.t.* wieder einstellen

**reappointment** /ri:ə'pɔɪntmənt/ *n.* Wiedereinstellung, *die*

**reappraisal** /riːəˈpreɪzl/ *n.* Neubewertung, *die*

**reappraise** /riːəˈpreɪz/ *v.t.* neu bewerten

**rear¹** /rɪə(r)/ ❶ *n.* Ⓐ *(back part)* hinterer Teil; **at** *or (Amer.)* **in the ~ of** im hinteren Teil (+ *Gen.*); **please move to the ~:** bitte nach hinten durchgehen; Ⓑ *(back)* Rückseite, *die;* **bring up the ~, be in the ~:** den Schluss bilden; **to the ~ of the house there is ...:** hinter dem Haus ist ...; **go round to the ~ of the house** hinter das Haus gehen; **in the ~ of the procession** am Schluss der Prozession; **the spectators at the ~:** die hinten sitzenden/stehenden Zuschauer; Ⓒ *(Mil.)* Rücken, *der;* rückwärtiger Teil; **attack in the ~:** von hinten angreifen; Ⓓ *(coll.: buttocks)* Hintern, *der (ugs.).* ❷ *adj.* hinter ... ‹Eingang, Tür, Blinklicht›; **~ axle** Hinterachse, *die*

**rear²** ❶ *v.t.* Ⓐ *(bring up)* großziehen ‹Kind, Familie›; halten ‹Vieh›; hegen ‹Wild›; Ⓑ *(lift up)* heben ‹Kopf›; aufrichten ‹Leiter›; **~ its ugly head** *(fig.)* seine hässliche Fratze zeigen. ❷ *v.i.* Ⓐ *(raise itself on hind legs)* **~ [up]** ‹Pferd:› sich aufbäumen; Ⓑ *(extend to great height)* ‹Gebäude, Berg:› sich erheben **(over, above** über + *Akk.*)

**rear: ~ 'admiral** *n. (Navy)* Konteradmiral, *der;* **~ 'door** *n. (Motor Veh.)* Fondtür, *die;* Hintertür, *die; (to boot)* Hecktür, *die;* **~ 'end** *n. (coll.: buttocks)* Hinterteil, *das (ugs.);* **~-engined** *adj. (Motor Veh.)* mit Heckantrieb *nachgestellt;* **be ~-engined** Heckantrieb haben; **~guard** *n. (Mil.)* Nachhut, *die;* **~guard action** *n. (Mil.)* Nachhutgefecht, *das; (fig.)* Rückzugsgefecht, *das;* **~ lamp, ~ light** *ns.* Rücklicht, *das*

**rearm** /riːˈɑːm/ ❶ *v.i.* wieder aufrüsten. ❷ *v.t.* wieder aufrüsten ‹Land›; wieder bewaffnen ‹Truppen›; *(give more modern arms to)* neu bewaffnen *od.* ausrüsten ‹Truppen›; **~ sb./oneself** jmdn./sich wieder bewaffnen

**rearmament** /riːˈɑːməmənt/ *n.* Wiederbewaffnung, *die; (of country also)* Wiederaufrüstung, *die*

**rearmost** /ˈrɪəməʊst/ *adj.* hinterst ...

**rearrange** /riːəˈreɪndʒ/ *v.t. (alter plan of)* umräumen ‹Möbel, Zimmer›; verlegen ‹Treffen, Spiel› **(for** auf + *Akk.*); ändern ‹Anordnung, Programm›

**rearrangement** /riːəˈreɪndʒmənt/ *n.* ⇒ **rearrange**: Umräumen, *das;* Verlegung, *die;* Änderung, *die*

**rear: ~-view 'mirror** *n.* Rückspiegel, *der;* **~ward** /ˈrɪəwəd/ ❶ *n.* **be to ~ward of the troops** sich im Rücken der Truppen befinden; ❷ *adj.* hinter ... ‹Teil›; nach hinten gerichtet ‹Bewegung›; **in a ~ward direction** nach hinten; ❸ *adv.* nach hinten; **~-wheel drive** ❶ *n.* Hinterradantrieb, *der;* Heckantrieb, *der;* ❷ *adj.* **a ~-wheel drive vehicle** ein Fahrzeug mit Hinterrad- *od.* Heckantrieb; **the car is ~-wheel drive** das Auto hat Hinterrad- *od.* Heckantrieb

**reason** /ˈriːzn/ ❶ *n.* Ⓐ *(cause)* Grund, *der;* **what is your ~ for doing that?** aus welchem Grund tust du das/hast du das getan?; **there is [no/every] ~ to assume** *or* **believe that ...:** es besteht [kein/ein guter] Grund zu der Annahme, dass ...; **have every ~ to suppose that ...:** allen Grund zu der Annahme haben, dass ...; **have no ~ to complain** *or* **for complaint** sich nicht beklagen können; **for that [very] ~:** aus [eben] diesem Grund; **for no ~:** grundlos; **no particular ~** *(as answer)* einfach so; **see ~ to do sth.** es für gerechtfertigt halten, etw. zu tun; **all the more ~ for doing sth.** ein Grund mehr, etw. zu tun; **for ~s best known to himself** aus Gründen, die er allein kennt; **for some ~, for one ~ or another** aus irgendeinem Grund; **for ~s of health** aus gesundheitlichen Gründen; **for obvious ~s** aus gutem Grund; **for no obvious ~:** aus keinem ersichtlichen Grund; **for the [simple] ~ that ...:** [einfach,] weil ...; **by ~ of** wegen; aufgrund; **with ~:** aus gutem Grund; Ⓑ *no pl., no art. (power to understand; sense; Philos.)* Vernunft, *die; (sanity)* gesunder Verstand; **lose one's ~:** den Verstand verlieren; **regain one's ~:** wieder normal werden; *(fig.)* wieder zur Vernunft kommen; **contrary to ~:** unsinnig; absurd; **be out of all ~:** völlig unsinnig sein; **be** *or* **go beyond all ~:** völlig überzogen sein; **I can't see the ~ of it** ich sehe keinen Sinn darin; **in** *or* **within ~:** innerhalb eines vernünftigen Rahmens; **you can have anything within ~:** du kannst alles haben, solange es im Rahmen bleibt; **stand to ~:** unzweifelhaft sein; **not listen to ~:** sich *(Dat.)* nichts sagen lassen; **see ~:** zur Einsicht kommen; **make sb. see ~, bring sb. to ~:** jmdn. zur Einsicht bringen; **Age of R~** *(Hist.)* Zeitalter der Aufklärung *od.* Vernunft; **for ~s of State** aus Gründen der Staatsräson.
❷ *v.i.* Ⓐ schlussfolgern **(from** aus); **ability to ~:** logisches Denkvermögen; **he can ~ clearly** er hat einen klaren Verstand; Ⓑ **~ with** diskutieren mit **(about, on** über + *Akk.*); **you can't ~ with her** mit ihr kann man nicht vernünftig reden.
❸ *v.t.* Ⓐ *(conclude)* schlussfolgern; Ⓑ *(persuade)* **~ sb. into doing sth.** jmdn. dazu überreden, etw. zu tun; **~ sb. out of sth.** jmdm. etw. ausreden; Ⓒ *(question)* **ours not to ~ why** es ist nicht unsere Sache, nach dem Warum zu fragen

**~ 'out** *v.t.* sich *(Dat.)* überlegen; **he could ~ out the result** *(knew in advance)* er konnte sich *(Dat.)* das Ergebnis schon denken; **it's easy to ~ out what ...:** man kann sich leicht denken, was ...

**reasonable** /ˈriːzənəbl/ *adj.* Ⓐ vernünftig; angemessen, vernünftig ‹Forderung›; **be ~!** sei [doch] vernünftig!; **not be ~ in one's demands** überzogene Forderungen stellen; **beyond ~ doubt** unzweifelhaft; Ⓑ *(inexpensive)* günstig; **it's a ~ price** das ist ein vernünftiger Preis; Ⓒ *(fair)* passabel ‹Leistung, Wein›; **with a ~ amount of luck** mit ein bisschen Glück; Ⓓ *(within limits)* realistisch ‹Chancen, Angebot›

**reasonably** /ˈriːzənəblɪ/ *adv.* Ⓐ *(within reason)* vernünftig; **no one could ~ believe that ...:** niemand kann ernsthaft glauben, dass ...; Ⓑ *(moderately)* **~ priced** preisgünstig; Ⓒ *(fairly)* ganz ‹gut›; ziemlich ‹gesund›

**reasoned** /ˈriːznd/ *adj.* durchdacht

**reasoner** /ˈriːzənə(r)/ *n.* **skilful** *or* **clever ~:** kluger *od.* heller Kopf

**reasoning** /ˈriːzənɪŋ/ *n.* logisches Denken; *(argumentation)* Argumentation, *die;* **a brilliant piece of ~:** eine brillante Argumentation; **power of ~:** logisches Denkvermögen; **there's no ~ with her** mit ihr kann man nicht vernünftig reden

**reassemble** /riːəˈsembl/ ❶ *v.i.* sich wieder versammeln; ‹Streitkräfte, Truppen:› sich wieder sammeln. ❷ *v.t.* Ⓐ *(bring together again)* wieder versammeln ‹Anhänger›; [wieder] sammeln ‹Truppen›; Ⓑ *(put together again)* wieder zusammenbauen

**reassert** /riːəˈsɜːt/ *v.t.* [erneut] bekräftigen

**reassertion** /riːəˈsɜːʃn/ *n.* [erneute] Bekräftigung

**reassess** /riːəˈses/ *v.t.* neu bewerten ‹Situation›; überdenken ‹Vorschlag›; überprüfen ‹Argument, Beweis, Anspruch›; *(for taxation)* neu veranlagen ‹Besitz›

**reassessment** /riːəˈsesmənt/ *n. (of evidence, argument, claim)* Überprüfung, *die; (of proposal)* Überdenken, *das; (of situation)* Neubewertung, *die; (for taxation)* Neuveranlagung, *die*

**reassign** /riːəˈsaɪn/ *v.t.* neu zuweisen

**reassignment** /riːəˈsaɪnmənt/ *n. (of personnel)* Versetzung, *die; (of resources, money)* Übertragung, *die*

**reassurance** /riːəˈʃʊərəns/ *n.* Ⓐ *(calming)* **give sb. ~:** jmdn. beruhigen; Ⓑ *(confirmation in opinion)* Bestätigung, *die; in pl.* [wiederholte] Versicherungen

**reassure** /riːəˈʃʊə(r)/ *v.t.* Ⓐ *(calm fears of)* beruhigen; Ⓑ *(confirm in opinion)* bestätigen; **he needs to be constantly ~d that ...:** man muss ihm dauernd aufs Neue bestätigen *od.* versichern, dass ...; **~ sb. about his health** jmdm. versichern, dass er gesund ist

**reassuring** /riːəˈʃʊərɪŋ/ *adj.,* **reassuringly** /riːəˈʃʊərɪŋlɪ/ *adv.* beruhigend

**reawaken** /riːəˈweɪkn/ ❶ *v.t. (lit. or fig.)* wieder erwecken. ❷ *v.i. (lit. or fig.)* wieder erwachen

**reawakening** /riːəˈweɪknɪŋ/ *n. (fig.)* Wiedererwachen, *das*

**rebate¹** /ˈriːbeɪt/ *n.* Ⓐ *(refund)* Rückzahlung, *die;* **~ on tax** Steuerrückzahlung, *die;* **get a ~ on the gas bill** Geld von den Gaswerken zurückbekommen; Ⓑ *(discount)* Preisnachlass, *der* **(on** auf + *Akk.*); Rabatt, *der* **(on** auf + *Akk.*); **rate ~** *(Brit.)* Ermäßigung der Gemeindeabgaben

**rebate²** /ˈræbɪt/ ⇒ **rabbet**

**rebel** ❶ /ˈrebl/ *n.* Rebell, *der*/Rebellin, *die.* ❷ *attrib. adj.* Ⓐ *(of rebels)* Rebellen-; Ⓑ *(refusing obedience to ruler)* rebellisch; aufständisch. ❸ /rɪˈbel/ *v.i.,* **-ll-** rebellieren

**rebellion** /rɪˈbeljən/ *n.* Rebellion, *die;* **rise [up] in ~:** sich erheben; rebellieren

**rebellious** /rɪˈbeljəs/ *adj.* Ⓐ *(defiant)* rebellisch; aufsässig; Ⓑ *(in rebellion)* rebellierend ‹Sklave, Untertan›

**rebind** /riːˈbaɪnd/ *v.t.,* **rebound** /riːˈbaʊnd/ neu [ein]binden

**rebirth** /riːˈbɜːθ/ *n.* Ⓐ Wiedergeburt, *die;* Ⓑ *(revival)* Wiederaufleben, *das*

**reboot** /riːˈbuːt/ *(Computing)* ❶ *v.t. & i* neu booten. ❷ *n.* Neubooten, *das;* Reboot, *das*

**reborn** /riːˈbɔːn/ *adj.* wieder geboren; **feel ~:** sich wie neugeboren fühlen; **be ~:** wieder geboren werden

**rebound¹** ❶ /rɪˈbaʊnd/ *v.i.* Ⓐ *(spring back)* abprallen **(from** von); Ⓑ *(have reactive effect)* zurückfallen **(upon** auf + *Akk.*); **the plan ~ed on her** *or* **on her head** der Plan schadete ihr nur selbst. ❷ /ˈriːbaʊnd/ *n.* Ⓐ *(recoil)* Abprall, *der;* Rebound, *der (Basketball);* **catch the ball on the ~:** den Abpraller *od. (Basketball)* Rebound fangen; Ⓑ *(fig.: emotional reaction)* **marry/turn to sb. on the ~:** in seiner Enttäuschung jmdn. heiraten/sich jmdm. zuwenden

**rebound²** ⇒ **rebind**

**rebroadcast** /riːˈbrɔːdkɑːst/ ❶ *n.* Wiederholung, *die.* ❷ *v.t., forms as* **broadcast** 2 wiederholen

**rebuff** /rɪˈbʌf/ ❶ *n.* [schroffe] Abweisung; **be met with a ~:** auf Ablehnung stoßen; **suffer a ~:** abgelehnt werden. ❷ *v.t.* [schroff] zurückweisen

**rebuild** /riːˈbɪld/ *v.t.,* **rebuilt** /riːˈbɪlt/ *(lit. or fig.)* wieder aufbauen; *(make extensive changes to)* umbauen

**rebuke** /rɪˈbjuːk/ ❶ *v.t.* tadeln, rügen **(for** wegen); **~ sb. for doing sth.** jmdn. zurechtweisen, weil er etwas tut/getan hat. ❷ *n.* Rüge, *die;* Zurechtweisung, *die*

**rebus** /ˈriːbəs/ *n.* Bilderrätsel, *das*

**rebut** /rɪˈbʌt/ *v.t.,* **-tt-** *(formal)* widerlegen

**rebuttal** /rɪˈbʌtl/ *n. (Law)* Widerlegung, *die;* **call evidence in ~ of it** den Gegenbeweis dafür antreten

**recalcitrant** /rɪˈkælsɪtrənt/ ❶ *adj.* aufsässig ‹Person›; schwergängig ‹Hebel, Mechanismus›. ❷ *n.* Unruhestifter, *der*/-stifterin, *die*

**recall** ❶ /rɪˈkɔːl/ *v.t.* Ⓐ *(remember)* sich erinnern an (+ *Akk.*); **~ what/how ...:** sich daran erinnern, was/wie ...; Ⓑ *(serve as reminder of)* erinnern an (+ *Akk.*); **~ sth. to sb.** jmdn. an etw. *(Akk.)* erinnern; Ⓒ *(summon back)* zurückrufen ‹Soldat, fehlerhaftes Produkt›; zurückfordern ‹Buch›; **~ Parliament** das Parlament zurückrufen; **the noise ~ed her to the present** der Lärm brachte sie in die Wirklichkeit zurück; Ⓓ *(suspend appointment of)* abberufen ‹Botschafter, Delegation› **(from** aus).
❷ /rɪˈkɔːl, ˈriːkɔːl/ *n.* Ⓐ *(ability to remember)* **[powers of] ~:** Erinnerungsvermögen, *das;* Gedächtnis, *das;* ⇒ *also* **total recall**; Ⓑ *(possibility of annulling)* **beyond** *or* **past ~:** unwiderruflich; Ⓒ *(summons back)* Rückruf, *der; (to active duty)* Wiedereinberufung, *die;* Ⓓ *(suspension of appointment abroad)* Abberufung, *die*

**recant** /riːˈkænt/ ❶ *v.i.* [öffentlich] widerrufen. ❷ *v.t.* widerrufen

**recantation** /ri:kæn'teɪʃn/ *n.* Widerruf, *der;* **make a ~ of sth.** etw. widerrufen

**recap¹** /ri:'kæp/ *v.t.*, **-pp-** (*Amer.*) A (*replace cap on*) wieder verschließen ‹Flasche›; B (*retread*) runderneuern ‹Reifen›

**recap²** /'ri:kæp/ (*coll.*) ❶ *v.t. & i.*, **-pp-** rekapitulieren; kurz zusammenfassen. ❷ *n.* Zusammenfassung, *die;* **let's just have a quick ~:** fassen wir kurz zusammen

**recapitulate** /ri:kə'pɪtjʊleɪt/ *v.t. & i.* rekapitulieren; kurz zusammenfassen

**recapitulation** /ri:kəpɪtjʊ'leɪʃn/ *n.* A (*summing up*) Zusammenfassung, *die;* Rekapitulation, *die;* B (*Mus.*) Reprise, *die*

**recapture** /ri:'kæptʃə(r)/ ❶ *v.t.* A (*capture again*) wieder ergreifen ‹Gefangenen›; wieder einfangen ‹Tier›; zurückerobern ‹Stadt›; B (*recreate*) wieder lebendig werden lassen ‹Atmosphäre›; (*experience again*) noch einmal durchleben ‹Aufregung, Vergangenheit, Jugend, Glück›. ❷ *n.* (*retaking*) Rückeroberung, *die*

**recast** /ri:'kɑ:st/ *v.t.*, **recast** A (*remould*) neu gießen; B (*refashion*) revidieren ‹Vorstellung, Einstellung›; C (*rewrite*) umschreiben

**recce** /'rekɪ/ (*Brit. coll.*) *n.* Erkundung, *die;* **make a ~:** die Lage peilen (*ugs.*)

**recede** /rɪ'si:d/ *v.i.* A ‹Hochwasser, Flut:› zurückgehen; ‹Küste:› zurückweichen; **his hair is beginning to ~:** er bekommt eine Stirnglatze; B (*be left at increasing distance*) **~ [into the distance]** in der Ferne verschwinden; C (*decline*) ‹Preis:› fallen; **~ in importance** an Bedeutung verlieren

**receding** /rɪ'si:dɪŋ/ *adj.* fliehend ‹Kinn, Stirn›; zurückweichend ‹Küste›; zurückgehend ‹Flut, Hochwasser›; ⇒ *also* **hairline** A

**receipt** /rɪ'si:t/ ❶ *n.* A Empfang, *der;* **please acknowledge ~ of this letter/order** bestätigen Sie bitte den Empfang dieses Briefes/dieser Bestellung; **be in ~ of** (*formal*) erhalten haben ‹Brief›; **those in ~ of a pension** Rentenempfänger; **[up]on ~ of the news/your remittance** (*formal*) nach Eingang der Nachricht/Ihrer Überweisung; B (*written acknowledgement*) Empfangsbestätigung, *die;* Quittung, *die;* **~ for payment** Quittung, *die;* C *in pl.* (*amount received*) Einnahmen (**from** aus). ❷ *v.t.* quittieren

**receivable** /rɪ'si:vəbl/ *adj.* (*Commerc.*) offen; ausstehend

**receive** /rɪ'si:v/ *v.t.* A (*get*) erhalten; beziehen ‹Gehalt, Rente›; verliehen bekommen ‹akademischen Grad›; **~ a cordial welcome** herzlich begrüßt werden; **~ one's education at a private school** eine Privatschule besuchen; **she ~d a lot of attention/sympathy [from him]** es wurde ihr [von ihm] viel Aufmerksamkeit/Verständnis entgegengebracht; **~ [fatal] injuries** [tödlich] verletzt werden; **'payment ~d with thanks'** „Betrag dankend erhalten"; **your letter will ~ our immediate attention** wir werden Ihren Brief umgehend bearbeiten; **~ insults/praise** beschimpft/gelobt werden; **~ much unfavourable comment** stark kritisiert werden; **~ 30 days [imprisonment]** 30 Tage Gefängnis bekommen; **~ the sacraments/holy communion** (*Relig.*) das Abendmahl/die heilige Kommunion empfangen; B (*accept*) entgegennehmen ‹Bukett, Lieferung›; (*submit to*) über sich (*Akk.*) ergehen lassen; **be convicted for receiving [stolen goods]** (*Law*) der Hehlerei überführt werden; C (*serve as receptacle for*) aufnehmen; D (*greet*) reagieren auf (*Akk.*), aufnehmen ‹Angebot, Nachricht, Theaterstück, Roman›; empfangen ‹Person›; E (*entertain*) empfangen ‹Botschafter, Delegation, Nachbarn, Gast›; F (*consent to hear*) abnehmen ‹Beichte, Eid›; entgegennehmen ‹Gesuch› (**from** *Gen.*); **~ sb.'s confession/oath** jmdm. die Beichte/den Eid abnehmen; G (*Radio, Telev.*) empfangen ‹Sender, Signal›; **are you receiving me?** können Sie mich hören?; H tragen ‹Last, Gewicht›; I (*accept as true*) anerkennen ‹Theorie, Lehre›; J (*Tennis*) **~ the serve** den Aufschlag nehmen; **Hingis to ~:** Hingis nimmt den Aufschlag. ⇒ *also* **end** 1 D

**~ into** *v.t.* aufnehmen in (+ *Akk.*)

**received** /rɪ'si:vd/ *adj.* landläufig ‹Vorstellung, Weisheit, Meinung›; gültig ‹Version, Text›

**received pronunci'ation** (*Amer.:* **Received 'Standard**) *ns.* (*Ling.*) englische Standardaussprache

**receiver** /rɪ'si:və(r)/ *n.* A Empfänger, *der*/Empfängerin, *die;* B ([*Table*]*Tennis*) Rückschläger, *der*/-schlägerin, *die;* C (*Teleph.*) [Telefon]hörer, *der;* D (*Radio, Telev.*) Empfänger, *der;* Receiver, *der* (*Technik*); E **[official] ~** (*Law*) (*for property of bankrupt*) [gerichtlich bestellter/bestellte] Konkursverwalter/-verwalterin; (*for insane person*) Pfleger, *der*/Pflegerin, *die;* F (*who receives stolen goods*) Hehler, *der*/Hehlerin, *die;* G (*Chem.: vessel*) Vorlage, *die*

**receivership** /rɪ'si:vəʃɪp/ *n.* (*Law: being in hands of receiver*) Konkursverwaltung, *die;* **put sth. in** *or* **into ~:** etw. unter Konkursverwaltung stellen

**recension** /rɪ'senʃn/ *n.* Überarbeitung, *die;* Rezension, *die* (*fachspr.*)

**recent** /'ri:sənt/ *adj.* A (*not long past*) jüngst ‹Ereignisse, Wahlen, Vergangenheit usw.›; **the ~ closure of the factory** die kürzlich erfolgte Schließung der Fabrik; **at our ~ meeting** als wir uns kürzlich *od.* vor kurzem trafen; **a ~/more ~ survey** eine neuere Untersuchung; **the most ~ survey** die neueste Untersuchung; **at our most ~ meeting** bei unserer letzten Begegnung; B (*not long established*) Neu‹auflage, -anschaffung, -erscheinung›; **~ additions to the library's holdings** Neuerwerbungen der Bibliothek; C **R~** (*Geol.*) Holozän, *das*

**recently** /'ri:səntlɪ/ *adv.* (*a short time ago*) neulich; kürzlich; vor kurzem; (*in the recent past*) in der letzten Zeit; **until ~/until quite ~:** bis vor kurzem/bis vor ganz kurzer Zeit; **~ we've been following a different policy** seit kurzem verfolgen wir eine andere Politik; **as ~ as last year** (*last year still*) noch letztes Jahr; **as ~ as this morning** (*not until this morning*) [gerade] erst heute Morgen; **one morning ~:** neulich morgens; **I haven't seen him ~:** ich habe ihn in letzter Zeit nicht gesehen

**receptacle** /rɪ'septəkl/ *n.* A (*container*) Behälter, *der;* Gefäß, *das;* B (*Bot.*) Blütenboden, *der;* Receptaculum, *das* (*fachspr.*)

**reception** /rɪ'sepʃn/ *n.* A (*welcome*) (*of person*) Empfang, *der;* Aufnahme, *die;* (*of play, speech*) Aufnahme, *die;* **meet with a cool ~:** kühl aufgenommen werden; **give sb. a warm ~:** jmdn. herzlich empfangen; **give a favourable ~ to** positiv aufnehmen ‹Theaterstück, Rede›; B (*formal party, welcome*) Empfang, *der;* **hold** *or* **give a ~:** einen Empfang geben; C *no art.* (*Brit.: foyer*) die Rezeption; D *no art.* (*Radio, Telev.*) der Empfang; **get good ~:** guten Empfang haben

**reception: ~ class** *n.* (*Brit.*) Vorschul- *od.* Anfängerklasse, *die;* **~ committee** *n.* Empfangskomitee, *das*

**re'ception desk** *n.* Rezeption, *die*

**receptionist** /rɪ'sepʃənɪst/ *n.* ▶ 1261 (*in hotel*) Empfangschef, *der*/-dame, *die;* (*at doctor's, dentist's*) Sprechstundenhilfe, *die;* (*at hairdresser's, solarium, etc.*) *Angestellter, der*/*Angestellte, die die Kunden empfängt und mit ihnen die Termine vereinbart;* (*with firm*) Empfangssekretärin, *die*

**reception: ~ office** (*Amer.*) ⇒ **reception** C; **~ room** *n.* A Empfangsraum, *der;* B (*esp. Brit.: in private house*) Wohnzimmer, *das*

**receptive** /rɪ'septɪv/ *adj.* A aufgeschlossen, empfänglich (**to** für); paarungsbereit ‹Tier›; **have a ~ mind** aufgeschlossen sein; B (*Biol.*) Rezeptor-; rezeptorisch

**receptively** /rɪ'septɪvlɪ/ *adv.* rezeptiv

**receptor** /rɪ'septə(r)/ *n.* (*Biol.*) Rezeptor, *der;* **~ organ** Rezeptionsorgan, *das*

**recess** /rɪ'ses, 'ri:ses/ ❶ *n.* A (*alcove*) Nische, *die;* B (*Brit. Parl.; Amer.: short vacation*) Ferien *Pl.;* (*Amer. Sch.: between classes*) Pause, *die;* **be in ~** ‹Parlament:› in den Ferien sein; **adjourn for summer ~** (*Amer.*) sich bis nach der Sommerpause vertagen; C (*lit. or fig.: remote place*) Winkel, *der.* ❷ *v.t.* A (*set back*) [in die Wand] einlassen ‹Schrank, Fenster›; B (*provide with ~*) eine Nische aussparen in (+ *Dat.*) ‹Wand, Mauer›; C (*Amer.: end sitting of*) unterbrechen ‹Verhandlung, Sitzung›. ❸ *v.i.* (*Amer.: end a sitting*) sich vertagen

**recession** /rɪ'seʃn/ *n.* A (*Econ.: decline*) Rezession, *die* (*fachspr.*); Konjunkturrückgang, *der;* **period of ~:** Rezession[sphase], *die;* B (*receding*) Zurückgehen, *das*

**recessional** /rɪ'seʃənl/ (*Eccl.*) ❶ *adj.* Schluss‹hymne, -musik›. ❷ *n.* [*während des Auszugs der Geistlichen und des Chors gesungene*] Schlusshymne, *die*

**recessive** /rɪ'sesɪv/ *adj.* (*Genetics, Phonet.*) rezessiv

**recharge** ❶ /ri:'tʃɑ:dʒ/ *v.t.* aufladen ‹Batterie›; nachladen ‹Waffe›; **~ one's batteries** (*fig.*) neue Kräfte auftanken. ❷ /'ri:tʃɑ:dʒ/ *n.* Nachfüllen, *das;* **the battery needs a ~:** die Batterie muss aufgeladen werden

**rechargeable** /ri:'tʃɑ:dʒəbl/ *adj.* wieder aufladbar

**recherché** /rə'ʃeəʃeɪ/ *adj.* ausgefallen ‹Vorstellungen, Ansichten›; gesucht ‹Ausdruck, Formulierung›

**rechristen** /ri:'krɪsn/ *v.t.* A (*christen again*) noch einmal taufen; B ⇒ **rename**

**recidivism** /rɪ'sɪdɪvɪzm/ *n.* Rückfälligkeit, *die*

**recidivist** /rɪ'sɪdɪvɪst/ ❶ *n.* Rückfällige, *der*/*die;* (*habitual criminal*) Rückfalltäter, *der*/-täterin, *die.* ❷ *adj.* rückfällig

**recipe** /'resɪpɪ/ *n.* (*lit. or fig.*) Rezept, *das;* **~ for success** Erfolgsrezept, *das;* **it's a ~ for disaster** damit ist die Katastrophe vorprogrammiert

**recipient** /rɪ'sɪpɪənt/ *n.* Empfänger, *der*/Empfängerin, *die;* **she was the unwilling ~ of his attention** sie war das unfreiwillige Opfer seiner Aufmerksamkeit

**reciprocal** /rɪ'sɪprəkl/ ❶ *adj.* A gegenseitig ‹Abkommen, Zuneigung, Hilfe›; B (*Ling.*) reziprok ‹Pronomen›. ❷ *n.* (*Math.*) Kehrwert, *der*

**reciprocally** /rɪ'sɪprəkəlɪ/ *adv.* gegenseitig

**reciprocate** /rɪ'sɪprəkeɪt/ ❶ *v.t.* A austauschen ‹Versprechen›; erwidern ‹Gruß, Lächeln, Abneigung, Annäherungsversuch›; sich revanchieren für ‹Hilfe›; B (*Mech. Engin.*) hin- und herbewegen. ❷ *v.i.* A (*respond*) sich revanchieren; B (*Mech. Engin.*) sich hin- und herbewegen; **reciprocating engine/saw** Kolbenmaschine, *die*/Gattersäge, *die;* **reciprocating motion** Hin- und Herbewegung, *die*

**reciprocity** /resɪ'prɒsɪtɪ/ *n.* A (*mutual action*) **there is deep ~ of feeling** es besteht eine innige wechselseitige Gefühlsbindung; **~ of influence** gegen- *od.* wechselseitige Beeinflussung; B (*interchange of privileges*) Wechselseitigkeit, *die;* Reziprozität, *die* (*fachspr.*); **~ in trade** Handelsreziprozität, *die*

**recital** /rɪ'saɪtl/ *n.* A (*performance*) [Solisten]konzert, *das;* (*of literature also*) Rezitation, *die;* **piano/poetry ~:** Klavierkonzert, *das*/Gedichtrezitation, *die;* **give one's first solo ~:** seinen ersten Soloauftritt haben; B (*detailed account*) Schilderung, *die;* **give a ~ of sth.** etw. eingehend schildern

**recitation** /resɪ'teɪʃn/ *n.* Rezitation, *die;* **give ~s from Shakespeare** Shakespeare rezitieren; **a ~ of her grievances/my faults** eine detaillierte Aufzählung ihrer Probleme/meiner Fehler

**recitative** /resɪtə'ti:v/ *n.* (*Mus.*) Rezitativ, *das*

**recite** /rɪ'saɪt/ ❶ *v.t.* A (*speak from memory*) rezitieren ‹Passage, Gedicht›; B (*give list of*) aufzählen. ❷ *v.i.* rezitieren

**reckless** /'reklɪs/ *adj.* unbesonnen; rücksichtslos ‹Fahrweise›; tollkühn ‹Fluchtversuch›; **~ of the dangers/consequences** ungeachtet der Gefahren/Folgen

**recklessly** /'reklɪslɪ/ *adv.* unbesonnen; (*without concern for others*) rücksichtslos

**reckon** /'rekn/ ❶ *v.t.* A (*work out*) ausrechnen ‹Kosten, Lohn, Ausgaben›; bestimmen ‹Position›; B (*conclude*) schätzen; **what do you ~ are his chances?** wie beurteilst du seine Chancen?; **I ~ you're lucky to be alive** ich glaube, du kannst von Glück sagen, dass du

r

noch lebst!; **I ~ to arrive** *or* **I shall arrive there by 8.30** ich nehme an, dass ich [spätestens] halb neun dort bin; **I usually ~ to arrive there by 8.30** in der Regel bin ich [spätestens] halb neun dort; Ⓒ (*consider*) halten (**as** für); **be ~ed as** *or* **to be sth.** als etw. gelten; **~ sb./sth. [to be] among the best** jmdn./etw. zu den Besten zählen *od.* rechnen; **be ~ed among sth.** zu etw. zählen; Ⓓ (*arrive at as total*) kommen auf (+ *Akk.*); **I ~ 53 of them** ich komme auf 53.
❷ *v.i.* rechnen; **~ from 1 April** vom 1. April an rechnen

**~ 'in** *v.t.* [mit] einrechnen

**~ on** ⇨ **~ upon**

**~ 'up** ❶ *v.t.* zusammenzählen; **~ up the bill** die Rechnungsposten zusammenzählen. ❷ *v.i.* **~ up with sb.** mit jmdm. abrechnen

**~ upon** *v.t.* Ⓐ (*rely on*) zählen auf (+ *Akk.*); **I was ~ing upon doing that this morning** ich hatte gedacht, ich könnte das heute früh tun; Ⓑ (*expect*) rechnen mit

**~ with** *v.i.* Ⓐ (*take into account*) rechnen mit ‹Hindernis, Möglichkeit›; **he is a man to be ~ed with** er ist ein Mann, den man nicht unterschätzen sollte; Ⓑ (*deal with*) abrechnen mit; **you'll have me/the police to ~ with** du bekommst es mit mir/der Polizei zu tun

**~ without** *v.i.* nicht rechnen mit; **we had ~ed without the weather** das Wetter hat uns einen Strich durch die Rechnung gemacht

**reckoner** /'rekənə(r)/ ⇨ **ready reckoner**

**reckoning** /'reknɪŋ/ *n.* Ⓐ (*calculation*) Berechnung, *die;* **by my ~:** nach meiner Rechnung; **day of ~** (*fig.*) Tag der Abrechnung; (*moment of truth*) Stunde der Wahrheit; **be [wildly] out in one's ~:** sich [gehörig] verrechnet haben; Ⓑ (*bill*) Rechnung, *die.* ⇨ *also* **dead**

**reclaim** /rɪ'kleɪm/ ❶ *v.t.* Ⓐ urbar machen ‹Land, Wüste›; **~ land from the sea** dem Meer Land abgewinnen; Ⓑ (*recover possession of*) zurückbekommen ‹Steuern›; zurückerlangen ‹Recht›; Ⓒ (*for reuse*) zur Wiederverwertung sammeln; wieder verwenden ‹Rohstoff›; regenerieren (*Technik*).
❷ *n.* **be past** *or* **beyond ~:** unwiederbringlich verloren sein; ⇨ *also* **baggage reclaim**

**reclamation** /reklə'meɪʃn/ *n.* Urbarmachung, *die;* **land ~:** Landgewinnung, *die*

**recline** /rɪ'klaɪn/ ❶ *v.i.* Ⓐ (*lean back*) sich zurücklehnen; **the chair ~s** die Rückenlehne des Sessels lässt sich [nach hinten] verstellen; **reclining seat** (*in car*) Liegesitz, *der;* Ⓑ (*be lying down*) liegen. ❷ *v.t.* [nach hinten] lehnen; **~ the seat** die Rückenlehne des Sitzes nach hinten verstellen

**recliner** /rɪ'klaɪnə(r)/ *n.* Lehnsessel, *der;* **~ seat** Liegesitz, *der*

**recluse** /rɪ'klu:s/ *n.* Einsiedler, *der*/Einsiedlerin, *die*

**reclusive** /rɪ'klu:sɪv/ *adj.* einsiedlerisch

**recognisability, recognisable, recognisably, recognisance, recognise** ⇨ **recogniz-**

**recognition** /rekəg'nɪʃn/ *n.* Ⓐ *no pl., no art.* Wiedererkennen, *das;* **he's changed beyond all ~:** er ist nicht mehr wieder zu erkennen; **escape ~:** unerkannt bleiben; Ⓑ (*acceptance, acknowledgement*) Anerkennung, *die;* **achieve/receive ~:** Anerkennung finden; **in ~ of** als Anerkennung für

**recognizability** /rekəgnaɪzə'bɪlɪtɪ/ *n., no pl.* Erkennbarkeit, *die*

**recognizable** /'rekəgnaɪzəbl/ *adj.* erkennbar; deutlich ‹Unterschied›; **be ~:** wieder zu erkennen sein

**recognizably** /'rekəgnaɪzəblɪ/ *adv.* erkennbar; **be not ~ different from sth.** sich kaum von etw. unterscheiden

**recognizance** /rɪ'kɒgnɪzəns/ *n.* Ⓐ (*bond*) Verpflichtung, *die;* **enter into ~s to do sth.** (*Law*) sich vor Gericht dazu verpflichten, etw. zu tun; Ⓑ (*sum*) Kaution, *die*

**recognize** /'rekəgnaɪz/ *v.t.* Ⓐ (*know again*) wieder erkennen (**by** an + *Dat.*, **from** durch); Ⓑ (*acknowledge*) erkennen; anerkennen ‹Gültigkeit, Land, Methode, Leistung, Bedeutung, Dienst›; **be ~d as** angesehen werden *od.* gelten als; Ⓒ (*admit*) zugeben; **~ sth. as valid** etw. als gültig anerkennen; **~ sb. as heir** jmdn. als Erben anerkennen; **~ sb. to be cleverer** *or* **that sb. is cleverer** zugeben, dass jmd. klüger ist; Ⓓ (*identify nature of*) erkennen; **~ sb. to be a fraud** erkennen, dass jmd. ein Betrüger ist; Ⓔ (*Amer.: allow to speak*) das Wort erteilen (+ *Dat.*)

**recoil** ❶ /rɪ'kɔɪl/ *v.i.* Ⓐ (*shrink back*) zurückfahren; **he ~ed visibly** er zuckte sichtbar zurück; **~ from an idea** vor einem Gedanken zurückschrecken; Ⓑ ‹Waffe:› einen Rückstoß haben. ❷ /'ri:kɔɪl, rɪ'kɔɪl/ *n.* (*of gun*) Rückstoß, *der* (**from** *Gen.*)

**~ [up]on** *v.i.* zurückfallen auf (+ *Akk.*); **~ upon sb.'s [own] head** *or* **upon sb.** auf jmdn. [selbst] zurückfallen

**recollect** /rekə'lekt/ ❶ *v.t.* Ⓐ sich erinnern an (+ *Akk.*); **~ meeting sb.** sich daran erinnern, jmdn. getroffen zu haben; Ⓑ **~ oneself** wieder zu sich selbst finden. ❷ *v.i.* sich erinnern

**recollection** /rekə'lekʃn/ *n.* Erinnerung, *die;* **to the best of my ~ ...:** soweit ich mich erinnern kann, ...; **have a/no ~ of sth.** sich an etw. (*Akk.*) erinnern/nicht erinnern können

**recombinant** /ri:'kɒmbɪnənt/ *adj.* (*Genetics*) rekombinant

**recombination** /ri:kɒmbɪ'neɪʃn/ *n.* (*Phys., Genetics*) Rekombination, *die*

**recombine** /ri:kəm'baɪn/ ❶ *v.t.* neu kombinieren. ❷ *v.i.* sich neu kombinieren

**recommence** /ri:kə'mens/ ❶ *v.i.* wieder beginnen. ❷ *v.t.* wieder beginnen mit

**recommencement** /ri:kə'mensmənt/ *n.* Wiederbeginn, *der*

**recommend** /rekə'mend/ *v.t.* Ⓐ empfehlen; **~ sb. to do sth.** jmdm. empfehlen, etw. zu tun; Ⓑ (*make acceptable*) sprechen für; **the plan has little/nothing to ~ it** es spricht wenig/nichts für den Plan

**recommendable** /rekə'mendəbl/ *adj.* empfehlenswert; **it is [not] ~ to do sth.** es empfiehlt sich [nicht], etw. zu tun

**recommendation** /rekəmen'deɪʃn/ *n.* Empfehlung, *die;* **speak in ~ of sth./sb.** etw./jmdn. empfehlen; **on sb.'s ~:** auf jmds. Empfehlung (*Akk.*); **letter of ~:** Empfehlungsschreiben, *das;* **make ~s to sb.** jmdn. beraten; **be a ~ for sth.** für etw. sprechen

**recompense** /'rekəmpens/ (*formal*) ❶ *v.t.* Ⓐ (*reward*) belohnen; Ⓑ (*make amends to*) entschädigen. ❷ *n., no art., no pl.* Ⓐ (*reward*) Lohn, *der;* Anerkennung, *die;* **in ~ for** als Dank für; **work without ~:** unentgeltlich arbeiten; Ⓑ (*compensation*) Entschädigung, *die*

**reconcilable** /'rekənsaɪləbl/ *adj.* versöhnbar ‹Personen›; überbrückbar ‹Differenzen›; miteinander vereinbar ‹Unterschiede, Standpunkte›

**reconcile** /'rekənsaɪl/ *v.t.* Ⓐ (*restore to friendship*) versöhnen; **become ~d** sich versöhnen; Ⓑ (*resign oneself*) **~ oneself** *or* **become/be ~d to sth.** sich mit etw. versöhnen; Ⓒ (*make compatible*) in Einklang bringen ‹Vorstellungen, Überzeugungen›; (*show to be compatible*) miteinander vereinen; **one cannot ~ dictatorship and freedom of speech** Diktatur und Redefreiheit sind miteinander unvereinbar; Ⓓ (*settle*) beilegen ‹Meinungsverschiedenheit›

**reconciliation** /rekənsɪlɪ'eɪʃn/ *n.* Ⓐ (*restoring to friendship*) Versöhnung, *die;* **bring about a ~ between persons** Personen miteinander versöhnen; **try for a ~:** einen Versöhnungsversuch unternehmen; Ⓑ (*making compatible*) Harmonisierung, *die*

**recondite** /'rekəndaɪt, rɪ'kɒndaɪt/ *adj.* (*formal*) abstrus

**recondition** /ri:kən'dɪʃn/ *v.t.* [general]überholen; **~ed engine** Austauschmotor, *der*

**reconnaissance** /rɪ'kɒnɪsəns/ *n., no pl., no def. art.* (*Mil.*) Aufklärung, *die;* (*of area*) Erkundung, *die;* **after ~:** nach Erkundung der Lage; **the plane was on ~:** das Flugzeug war auf einem Aufklärungsflug; **make a ~ [of the area]** (*lit. or fig.*) das Terrain sondieren; *attrib.* **~ aircraft** Aufklärungsflugzeug, *das;* **~ party** Spähtrupp, *der*

**reconnoitre** (*Brit.; Amer.:* **reconnoiter**) /rekə'nɔɪtə(r)/ ❶ *v.t.* (*esp. Mil.*) auskundschaften; erkunden ‹Gelände›; (*fig.*) erkunden; in Augenschein nehmen ‹Hotel, Restaurant›. ❷ *v.i.* (*esp. Mil.*) auf Erkundung [aus]gehen; (*fig.*) sich umsehen

**reconquer** /ri:'kɒŋkə(r)/ *v.t.* zurückerobern

**reconsider** /ri:kən'sɪdə(r)/ *v.t.* [noch einmal] überdenken; **~ a case** einen Fall von neuem aufrollen; *abs.* **there is still time to ~:** du kannst es dir/wir können es uns *usw.* immer noch überlegen

**reconsideration** /ri:kənsɪdə'reɪʃn/ *n.* Überdenken, *das;* **put a case before the court for ~:** einen Fall zur neuerlichen Beratung vor ein Gericht bringen

**reconstitute** /ri:'kɒnstɪtju:t/ *v.t.* Ⓐ (*build up again*) wieder aufbauen; rekonstruieren; Ⓑ (*restore to natural state*) **~ [with water]** [mit Wasser] anrühren; [in Wasser] einweichen ‹Trockenobst›; Ⓒ (*piece together*) rekonstruieren ‹Ereignisse›; Ⓓ (*reorganize*) umbauen ‹Anlage›; umbilden ‹Komitee, Kabinett›; Ⓔ (*bring back into existence*) wieder einrichten

**reconstitution** /ri:kɒnstɪ'tju:ʃn/ *n.* Ⓐ (*building up again*) Rekonstruktion, *die;* Ⓑ (*restoration to natural state*) Anrühren, *das;* (*of dried fruit*) Einweichen, *das;* Ⓒ (*reorganization*) Umbildung, *die;* Ⓓ (*bringing back into existence*) Wiedereinrichtung, *die*

**reconstruct** /ri:kən'strʌkt/ *v.t.* Ⓐ (*build again*) wieder aufbauen ‹Stadt, Gebäude›; neu errichten ‹Gerüst›; rekonstruieren ‹Anlage›; (*fig.*) rekonstruieren; Ⓑ (*reorganize*) umstrukturieren

**reconstruction** /ri:kən'strʌkʃn/ *n.* Ⓐ (*process*) Wiederaufbau, *der;* (*reorganization*) Umstrukturierung, *die;* Ⓑ (*thing reconstructed*) Rekonstruktion, *die*

**record** ❶ /rɪ'kɔ:d/ *v.t.* Ⓐ aufzeichnen; **~ a new CD** eine neue CD aufnehmen; **~ sth. in a book/painting** etw. in einem Buch/auf einem Gemälde festhalten; **be ~ed for ever in sb.'s memory** auf ewig in jmds. Gedächtnis eingegraben sein; **history ~s that ...:** es ist geschichtlich belegt, dass ...; Ⓑ (*register officially*) dokumentieren; protokollieren ‹Verhandlung›; **~ one's vote** seine Stimme abgeben; **count and ~ the votes** die Stimmen auszählen [und das Ergebnis schriftlich festhalten].
❷ *v.i.* aufzeichnen; (*on tape*) Tonbandaufnahmen/eine Tonbandaufnahme machen; **the tape recorder isn't ~ing properly** das Tonbandgerät nimmt nicht richtig auf.
❸ /'rekɔ:d/ *n.* Ⓐ **be on ~** ‹Prozess, Verhandlung, Besprechung:› protokolliert sein; **there is no such case on ~:** ein solcher Fall ist nicht dokumentiert; **it is on ~ that ...:** es ist dokumentiert, dass ...; **have sth. on ~:** etw. dokumentiert haben; **there is nothing on ~ to prove that ...:** es gibt keine Aufzeichnungen, die beweisen, dass ...; **put sth. on ~:** etw. schriftlich festhalten; **I am quite happy to go on ~ as having said that** man kann ruhig festhalten, dass ich das gesagt habe; **it is a matter of ~ that ...:** es ist eine verbürgte Tatsache, dass ...; Ⓑ (*report*) Protokoll, *das;* (*Law: official report*) [Gerichts]akte, *die;* Ⓒ (*document*) Dokument, *das;* (*piece of evidence*) Zeugnis, *das;* Beleg, *der;* **medical ~s** medizinische Unterlagen; **criminal ~s** Strafregister, *das;* **~ of attendance** Anwesenheitsliste, *die;* **keep a ~ of sth.** über etw. (*Akk.*) Buch führen; (*listing persons*) eine Liste von etw. führen; **for the ~:** für das Protokoll; **just for the ~:** der Vollständigkeit halber; (*iron.*) nur der Ordnung halber; **[strictly] off the ~:** [ganz] inoffiziell; **get** *or* **keep** *or* **put** *or* **set the ~ straight** keine Missverständnisse aufkommen lassen; **let me put the ~ straight** ich möchte es einmal ganz unmissverständlich sagen; Ⓓ (*disc for gramophone*) [Schall]platte, *die;* **make a ~:** eine Platte machen (*ugs.*); Ⓔ (*facts of sb.'s/sth.'s past*) Ruf, *der;* **have a good ~ [of achievements]** gute Leistungen vorweisen können; **the aircraft has an excellent ~ for reliability/a good safety ~:** das Flugzeug hat sich als höchst

zuverlässig/sehr sicher erwiesen; **have a [criminal/police] ~:** vorbestraft sein; **keep a clean ~:** sich (*Dat.*) nichts zuschulden kommen lassen; **F** (*best performance*) Rekord, *der;* **set a ~:** einen Rekord aufstellen; **break** *or* **beat the ~:** den Rekord brechen.
❹ *attrib. adj.* Rekord-

**record** /ˈrekɔːd/**: ~ album** *n.* [Schall]plattenalbum, *das;* **~-breaking** *adj.* Rekord-; **~ deck** *n.* Plattenspieler, *der*

**recorded** /rɪˈkɔːdɪd/ *adj.* aufgezeichnet ‹Film, Konzert, Rede›; überliefert ‹Ereignis, Geschichte›; bespielt ‹Band›; **~ music** Musikaufnahmen

**recorded deˈlivery** *n.* (*Brit. Post*) eingeschriebene Sendung (*ohne Versicherung*); **send sth. by ~ delivery** etw. per Einschreiben schicken

**recorder** /rɪˈkɔːdə(r)/ *n.* **A** (*instrument/apparatus*) Aufzeichnungsgerät, *das;* **earthquake ~:** Seismograph, *der;* **B** ⇒ **tape recorder**; **C** (*Mus.*) Blockflöte, *die;* **D** (*Brit. Law*) nebenamtlicher Richter (*beim Crown Court usw.*)

**ˈrecord holder** *n.* (*Sport*) Rekordhalter, *der*/-halterin, *die*

**recording** /rɪˈkɔːdɪŋ/ *n.* **A** (*process*) Aufzeichnung, *die;* **B** (*what is recorded*) Aufnahme, *die;* (*to be heard or seen later*) Aufzeichnung, *die*

**recording: ~ ˈangel** *n.* (*Theol.*) Engel der Gerechtigkeit; **~ head** *n.* Aufnahmekopf, *der;* **~ session** *n.* Aufnahme, *die;* **~ studio** *n.* Tonstudio, *das;* **~ van** *n.* Aufnahmewagen, *der*

**recordist** /rɪˈkɔːdɪst/ *n.* **[sound] ~:** Tonmeister, *der*/-meisterin, *die*

**record** /ˈrekɔːd/**: ~ library** *n.* Phonothek, *die;* **R~ Office** ⇒ **Public R~ Office**; **~ player** *n.* Plattenspieler, *der;* **~ shop** *n.* [Schall]plattengeschäft, *das;* **~ sleeve** *n.* Plattenhülle, *die;* Plattencover, *das;* **~ token** *n.* [Schall]plattengutschein, *der*

**recount** /rɪˈkaʊnt/ *v.t.* (*tell*) erzählen

**re-count** ❶ /riːˈkaʊnt/ *v.t.* (*count again*) [noch einmal] nachzählen. ❷ /ˈriːkaʊnt/ *n.* Nachzählung, *die;* **have a ~:** nachzählen

**recoup** /rɪˈkuːp/ *v.t.* **A** (*regain*) ausgleichen ‹Verlust›; [wieder] hereinbekommen ‹[Geld]einsatz›; wiedergewinnen ‹Stärke, Gesundheit›; **B** (*reimburse*) wieder einbringen ‹Auslagen›; **~ oneself** seine Ausgaben ausgleichen

**recourse** /rɪˈkɔːs/ *n.* **A** (*resort*) Zufluchtnahme, *die;* **have ~ to sb./sth.** bei jmdm./zu etw. Zuflucht nehmen; **B** (*person or thing resorted to*) Zuflucht, *die;* **your only ~ is legal action** das Einzige, was dir bleibt, ist vor Gericht zu gehen; **C** (*Finance*) Regress, *der;* Rückgriff, *der*

**recover** /rɪˈkʌvə(r)/ ❶ *v.t.* **A** (*regain*) zurückerobern; **B** (*find again*) wieder finden ‹Verlorenes, Fährte, Spur›; **C** (*retrieve*) zurückbekommen; bergen ‹Wrack›; **D** (*make up for*) aufholen ‹verlorene Zeit›; **E** (*acquire again*) wiedergewinnen ‹Vertrauen›; wieder finden ‹Gleichgewicht, innere Ruhe usw.›; **have ~ed one's lost appetite/normal colour** wieder Appetit/Farbe haben; **~ consciousness** das Bewusstsein wiedererlangen; **~ one's senses** (*lit. or fig.*) wieder zur Besinnung kommen; **~ the use of one's hands/feet** seine Hände/Füße wieder gebrauchen können; **~ one's sight** sein Sehvermögen wiedergewinnen; **~ one's voice** seine Stimme wieder finden; **~ one's breath** wieder zu Atem kommen; **~ oneself** sich fangen; **F** (*reclaim*) **~ land from the sea** dem Meer Land abgewinnen; **~ metal from scrap** Metall aus Schrott gewinnen; **G** (*Law*) erheben ‹Steuer, Abgabe›; erhalten ‹Schadenersatz, Schmerzensgeld›; *abs.* Schadenersatz erhalten.
❷ *v.i.* ▶ **1232** **~ from sth.** sich von etw. [wieder] erholen; **how long will it take him to ~?** wann wird er wieder gesund sein?; **be [completely** *or* **totally** *or* **fully** *or* **quite] ~ed** [völlig] wiederhergestellt sein

**re-cover** /riːˈkʌvə(r)/ *v.t.* neu beziehen ‹Sessel, Schirm usw.›

**recoverable** /rɪˈkʌvərəbl/ *adj.* **A** (*capable of being regained*) erstattungsfähig ‹Unkosten›; ersetzbar ‹Schaden, Verlust›; rückzahlbar ‹Kaution, Geldeinlage›; **the cost was ~ through his insurance policy** die Kosten konnten durch seine Versicherung ersetzt werden; **B** (*capable of being restored*) wieder herstellbar; wieder gewinnbar ‹Brauchwasser›; **C** (*Law*) eintreibbar ‹Geldstrafe, Schulden usw.›; **D** (*extractable*) abbaufähig; abbaubar; förderbar ‹Öl-, Gasreserven›

**recovery** /rɪˈkʌvərɪ/ *n.* **A** ▶ **1232** (*restoration*) Erholung, *die;* **be on the road to ~:** auf dem Wege der Besserung sein; **make a quick/good ~:** sich schnell/gut erholen; **he is past ~:** für ihn gibt es keine Hoffnung mehr; **B** (*regaining of sth. lost*) Wiederfinden, *das;* Fund, *der;* **C** (*Law*) (*of debts*) Eintreibung, *die;* **~ of damages** Erfüllung des Anspruchs auf Schadenersatz; **D** (*Swimming, Rowing*) Rückkehr in die Grundstellung; **E** (*extraction, reclamation*) Rückgewinnung, *die*

**recovery: ~ position** *n.* (*Med.*) stabile Seitenlage; **~ room** *n.* (*Med.*) Aufwachraum, *der;* **~ vehicle** *n.* Bergungsfahrzeug, *das*

**recreant** /ˈrekrɪənt/ (*literary*) ❶ *adj.* **A** (*cowardly*) kleinmütig (*geh.*); verzagt (*geh.*); **B** (*treacherous*) verräterisch; (*apostate*) abtrünnig. ❷ *n.* **A** (*coward*) Feigling, *der;* **B** (*betrayer*) Verräter, *der*/Verräterin, *die;* (*apostate*) Abtrünnige, *der/die*

**recreate** /riːkrɪˈeɪt/ *v.t.* **A** (*create over again*) [wieder] neu [er]schaffen; wieder aufleben lassen ‹Industrie›; **B** (*simulate, reenact*) nachempfinden, nachbilden ‹Kunstwerk, Gegenstand›; reproduzieren (*geh.*) ‹Atmosphäre, Klänge›; nachstellen ‹Szene›

**recreation** /rekrɪˈeɪʃn/ *n.* **A** (*act of relaxing*) Ausruhen, *das;* **B** (*means of entertainment*) Freizeitbeschäftigung, *die;* Hobby, *das;* **for** *or* **as a ~:** zur Freizeitbeschäftigung *od.* Entspannung; **he enjoys driving as a ~:** Fahren bedeutet für ihn Entspannung

**recreational** /rekrɪˈeɪʃənl/ *adj.* Freizeit‹wert, -möglichkeiten, -gelände›; Erholungs‹gebiet›; **~ drug** Freizeitdroge, *die;* Droge zum Entspannen; **~ vehicle** (*Amer.*) Wohnmobil, *das*

**recreation: ~ centre** *n.* Freizeitzentrum, *das;* **~ ground** *n.* Freizeitgelände, *das;* (*for children*) Spielplatz, *der;* **~ period** *n.* Pause, *die;* **~ room** *n.* **A** (*playroom*) Spielzimmer, *das;* (*hobbyroom*) Hobbyraum, *der;* **B** (*public room*) Aufenthaltsraum, *der;* **~ time** *n.* Freizeit, *die;* (*in school*) Pause, *die*

**recriminate** /rɪˈkrɪmɪneɪt/ *v.i.* Gegenbeschuldigungen erheben

**recrimination** /rɪkrɪmɪˈneɪʃn/ *n.* Gegenbeschuldigung, *die;* (*counter-accusation*) **[mutual] ~s** [gegenseitige] Beschuldigungen

**recrudescence** /riːkruːˈdesəns/ *n.* (*of symptoms, disease*) erneutes Auftreten; (*of epidemic, aggression, violence*) Wiederaufflackern, *das*

**recruit** /rɪˈkruːt/ ❶ *n.* **A** (*Mil.*) Rekrut, *der;* **a raw ~:** ein frisch Eingezogener; **B** (*Amer.*) (*soldier of lowest rank*) einfacher Soldat; (*sailor of lowest rank*) Matrose, *der;* **C** (*new member*) neues Mitglied; **D** **[raw] ~** (*fig.: novice*) blutiger Anfänger. ❷ *v.t.* **A** (*Mil.: enlist*) anwerben; (*into society, party, etc.*) werben ‹Mitglied›; **B** (*select for appointment*) einstellen; **staff were ~ed once a year** einmal im Jahr wurden neue Mitarbeiter eingestellt. ❸ *v.i.* **A** (*Mil.: enlist*) Rekruten anwerben; ‹Partei, Klub:› neue Mitglieder finden; **B** (*select for appointment*) Neueinstellungen vornehmen; **~ for staff** neue Mitarbeiter einstellen; **~ from one's own staff** freie Stellen aus den eigenen Reihen besetzen

**recruitment** /rɪˈkruːtmənt/ *n.* **A** (*Mil.*) Anwerbung, *die;* (*for membership*) **~ of members** Mitgliederwerbung, *die;* **~ has been good this year** die Mitgliederwerbung war dieses Jahr sehr erfolgreich; **~ for evening classes** Werbung für Abendkurse; **B** (*process of selecting for appointment*) Neueinstellung, *die*

**recta** *pl. of* **rectum**

**rectal** /ˈrektl/ *adj.* (*Anat.*) rektal

**rectangle** /ˈrektæŋgl/ *n.* Rechteck, *das*

**rectangular** /rekˈtæŋgjʊlə(r)/ *adj.* **A** **~ [shaped]** rechteckig; **B** (*placed at right angles*) rechtwinklig

**rectifiable** /ˈrektɪfaɪəbl/ *adj.* korrigierbar ‹Fehler›; **do you think the situation is ~?** glauben Sie, dass noch etwas zu machen ist?

**rectification** /rektɪfɪˈkeɪʃn/ *n.* **A** (*correction of error*) Berichtigung, *die;* Korrektur, *die;* **B** (*Electr.*) Gleichrichtung, *die*

**rectifier** /ˈrektɪfaɪə(r)/ *n.* (*Electr.*) Gleichrichter, *der*

**rectify** /ˈrektɪfaɪ/ *v.t.* **A** korrigieren ‹Fehler, Berechnung, Kurs›; richtig stellen ‹Bemerkung, Sachverhalt›; Abhilfe schaffen (+ *Dat.*) ‹Mangel, Missstand›; **~ the situation** die Sache wieder ins Lot bringen; **B** (*Electr.*) gleichrichten

**rectilineal** /rektɪˈlɪnɪəl/, **rectilinear** /rektɪˈlɪnɪə(r)/ *adj.* geradlinig ‹Bewegung, Strecke, Anordnung›; aus Geraden gebildet ‹Winkel›; geradlinig begrenzt ‹Figur, Garten›

**rectitude** /ˈrektɪtjuːd/ *n.* **A** (*with regard to morality*) Rechtschaffenheit, *die;* **a life of ~:** ein rechtschaffenes Leben; **B** (*with regard to correctness*) Richtigkeit, *die*

**recto** /ˈrektəʊ/ *n., pl.* **~s** (*Printing, Bibliog.*) **A** (*right-hand page*) rechte Seite; **B** (*front of leaf*) Rekto, *das* (*fachspr.*); Vorderseite, *die*

**rector** /ˈrektə(r)/ *n.* **A** Pfarrer, *der;* **B** (*Univ.*) Rektor, *der*/Rektorin, *die*

**rectory** /ˈrektərɪ/ *n.* Pfarrhaus, *das*

**rectum** /ˈrektəm/ *n., pl.* **~s** *or* **recta** /ˈrektə/ (*Anat.*) Mastdarm, *der;* Rektum, *das* (*fachspr.*)

**recumbent** /rɪˈkʌmbənt/ *adj.* ruhend; liegend ‹Skulptur›; **be [lying] ~:** ruhen

**recuperate** /rɪˈkjuːpəreɪt/ ❶ *v.i.* sich erholen. ❷ *v.t.* wieder herstellen ‹Gesundheit›; **~ one's strength/health** wieder zu Kräften kommen/gesund werden

**recuperation** /rɪkjuːpəˈreɪʃn/ *n.* Erholung, *die;* **in rest and ~:** in Ruhe und Entspannung

**recuperative** /rɪˈkjuːpərətɪv/ *adj.* stärkend; **~ remedies/powers** Heilmittel/-kräfte

**recur** /rɪˈkɜː(r)/ *v.i.*, **-rr-** **A** sich wiederholen; ‹Beschwerden, Krankheit usw.:› wiederkehren; ‹Problem, Symptom:› wieder auftreten; **B** (*return to one's mind*) ‹Gedanke, Furcht, Gefühl:› wiederkehren; **C** (*Math.*) **~ring decimal** periodischer Dezimalbruch; **2.3 ~ring** 2 Komma 3 Periode

**recurrence** /rɪˈkʌrəns/ *n.* **A** Wiederholung, *die;* (*of illness, complaint*) Wiederkehr, *die;* (*of problem, symptom*) Wiederauftreten, *das;* **there's to be no ~ of this type of behaviour** dieses Verhalten darf sich nicht wiederholen; **B** (*to mind*) Wiederkehr, *die*

**recurrent** /rɪˈkʌrənt/ *adj.* immer wiederkehrend; wiederholt ‹Hinweis, Bezugnahme›; **have ~ problems with sth.** häufig Probleme mit etw. haben

**recyclable** /riːˈsaɪkləbl/ *adj.* recycelbar

**recycle** /riːˈsaɪkl/ *v.t.* (*reuse*) wieder verwerten ‹Papier, Glas, Abfall›; (*convert*) wieder aufbereiten ‹Metall, Brauchwasser, Abfall›; **~d paper** Recyclingpapier, *das*

**recycling** /riːˈsaɪklɪŋ/ *n.* Recycling, *das;* Wiederaufbereitung, *die; attrib.* **~ plant** Recyclingwerk, *das*

**red** /red/ ❶ *adj.* **A** rot; Rot‹wild, -buche›; rot glühend ‹Feuer, Lava usw.›; **the ~ colour of the setting sun** das Rot der untergehenden Sonne; **go ~ with shame** rot vor Scham werden; **go ~ in the face** rot werden; **as ~ as a beetroot** puterrot; rot wie eine Tomate (*ugs. scherzh.*); **her eyes were ~ with crying** sie hatte rot geweinte Augen; ⇒ *also* **paint** 2 A; **see¹** 2 A; **B** (*anarchistic*) rot; **C** **R~** (*Hist.: Soviet Russian*) rot, kommunistisch ‹Soldat, Propaganda›; **the R~ Army** die Rote Armee; **better R~ than dead** lieber rot als tot.
❷ *n.* **A** (*colour*) Rot, *das;* (*in roulette*) Rouge, *das;* (*redness*) Röte, *die;* **the ~s** die

r

Rottöne; **underline sth. in ~:** etw. rot unterstreichen; Ⓑ (*debt*) **get out of the ~:** aus den roten Zahlen kommen; **[be] in the ~:** in den roten Zahlen [sein]; Ⓒ **R~** (*communist*) Rote, *der/die;* **Reds under the bed scare** Angst vor kommunistischer Unterwanderung; Ⓓ (*ball*) rote Kugel; Ⓔ (*red clothes*) **dressed in ~:** rot gekleidet; Ⓕ (*traffic light*) Rot, *das;* **the traffic light is at ~:** die Ampel steht auf Rot; **we drove straight through on ~:** wir fuhren bei Rot durch (*ugs.*)

**red: ~ admiral** ⇨ **admiral** B; **~ alert** *n.* [höchste] Alarmbereitschaft; **be on ~ alert** sich in Alarmzustand befinden; **~-blooded** /ˈredblʌdɪd/ *adj.* heißblütig; **~breast** *n.* (*Ornith.*) Rotkehlchen, *das;* **~brick** *adj.* (*Brit.*) weniger traditionsreich ‹Universität›; **~cap** *n.* Ⓐ (*Brit.: military policeman*) Militärpolizist, *der;* Ⓑ (*Amer.: railway porter*) Gepäckträger, *der;* **~ ˈcard** *n.* (*Footb.*) rote Karte; **he was shown the ~ card** er bekam die rote Karte; **~ ˈcarpet** *n.* (*lit. or fig.*) roter Teppich; **~-carpet** *adj.*; **give sb. the ~-carpet treatment** *or* **a ~-carpet reception** jmdn. mit großem Bahnhof (*ugs.*) *od.* mit allen Ehren empfangen; **~ cell** *n.* (*Anat., Zool.*) rotes Blutkörperchen; **~ ˈcent** *n.* (*Amer.*) roter Heller; **~-cheeked** *adj.* rotwangig (*geh.*); **Red ˈChina** *n.* Rotchina, *das;* **~coat** *n.* (*Brit. Hist.*) Rotrock, *der; britischer Soldat;* **~ corpuscle** ⇨ **red cell**; **Red ˈCrescent** *n.* Roter Halbmond; **Red ˈCross** *n.* Rotes Kreuz; **~ˈcurrant** *n.* [rote] Johannisbeere

**redden** /ˈredn/ ❶ *v.i.* ‹Gesicht, Himmel:› sich röten; ‹Person:› rot werden, erröten; ‹Blätter, Wasser:› sich rot färben; **his face ~ed [with shame** *etc.*] er lief rot an *od.* bekam einen roten Kopf [vor Scham *usw.*]. ❷ *v.t.* rot färben; röten (*geh.*)

**reddish** /ˈredɪʃ/ *adj.* rötlich; **~ brown** rotbraun

**redecorate** /riːˈdekəreɪt/ *v.t.* renovieren; (*with wallpaper*) neu tapezieren; (*with paint*) neu streichen

**redecoration** /riːdekəˈreɪʃn/ *n.* Renovierung, *die;* (*with wallpaper*) Neutapezieren, *das;* (*with paint*) Neuanstrich, *der*

**redeem** /rɪˈdiːm/ *v.t.* Ⓐ (*regain*) wieder herstellen ‹Ehre, Gesundheit›; wiedergewinnen ‹Position›; Ⓑ (*buy back*) tilgen ‹Hypothek›; [wieder] einlösen ‹Pfand›; abzahlen ‹Grundstück›; Ⓒ (*convert*) einlösen ‹Gutschein, Coupon›; Ⓓ (*make amends for*) ausgleichen, wettmachen ‹Fehler, Schuld usw.›; **he has one ~ing feature** man muss ihm eins zugute halten; Ⓔ (*repay*) abzahlen ‹Schuld, Kredit›; **~ one's obligation to sb.** seine Schuld jmdm. gegenüber begleichen; Ⓕ (*fulfil*) einlösen, halten ‹Versprechen›; Ⓖ (*save*) retten; **~ sb. from his sins/from hell** jmdn. von seinen Sünden/aus der Hölle erlösen; Ⓗ (*make less bad*) retten ‹Situation, Beziehung, Party usw.›; **~ oneself** sich freikaufen; **he ~ed himself in their eyes by apologizing** er fand Gnade vor ihren Augen, indem er sich entschuldigte

**redeemable** /rɪˈdiːməbl/ *adj.* einlösbar ‹Gutschein, Pfand, Aktien usw.›; tilgbar ‹Schuld›; kündbar ‹Obligation›

**redeemer** /rɪˈdiːmə(r)/ *n.* Ⓐ Retter, *der;* Ⓑ **R~** (*Relig.*) Erlöser, *der;* Heiland, *der*

**redefine** /riːdɪˈfaɪn/ *v.t.* neu bestimmen *od.* festlegen ‹Aufgaben, Bedingungen›; neu formulieren ‹These, Vertrag[spunkte]›

**redemption** /rɪˈdempʃn/ *n.* Ⓐ (*of pawned goods*) Einlösen, *das;* Rückkauf, *der;* Ⓑ (*of tokens, trading stamps, stocks, etc.*) Einlösen, *das;* Ⓒ (*of mortgage, debt*) Tilgung, *die;* (*of land*) Abzahlung, *die;* Ⓓ (*of promise, pledge*) Erfüllung, *die;* Ⓔ (*of person, country*) Befreiung, *die;* **he's past** *or* **beyond ~:** für ihn gibt es keine Rettung mehr; **the situation is beyond ~:** die Lage ist hoffnungslos verfahren *od.* völlig ausweglos; Ⓕ (*deliverance from sin*) Erlösung, *die;* Ⓖ (*thing that redeems*) Rettung, *die*

**redeploy** /riːdɪˈplɔɪ/ *v.t.* umstationieren ‹Truppen, Raketen›; woanders einsetzen ‹Arbeitskräfte›; **~ from ... to ...:** von ... nach ... verlegen

**redeployment** /riːdɪˈplɔɪmənt/ *n.* (*of troops, missiles*) Umstationierung, *die;* (*of labour force, workers, staff*) Einsatz an anderer Stelle; **~ from ... to ...:** Verlegung von ... nach ...

**redesign** /riːdɪˈzaɪn/ *v.t.* umgestalten ‹Raum, Mechanismus, Verpackung, Modell›; überarbeiten ‹Plan, Design›

**red: ~-eyed** *adj.* **be ~-eyed** rote Augen haben; **~-faced** *adj.* rotgesichtig; **be ~-faced** (*with rage/embarrassment*) ein [hoch]rotes Gesicht haben/vor Verlegenheit rot werden; **go ~-faced with rage** vor Wut rot anlaufen; **~ ˈflag** ⇨ **flag**[1] 1; **Red ˈGuard** *n.* Rote Garde; (*member*) Rotgardist, *der/-gardistin, die;* **~-haired** *adj.* rothaarig; **~-handed** /redˈhændɪd/ *adj.* **catch sb. ~-handed** jmdn. auf frischer Tat ertappen; **~head** *n.* Rotschopf, *der* (*ugs.*); Rothaarige, *der/die;* **~-headed** /ˈredhedɪd/ *adj.* rothaarig; **be ~-headed** rote Haare haben; **~ heat** *n.* Rotglut, *die;* (*fig.*) Glut, *die;* **bring to a ~ heat** auf Rotglut erhitzen; **~ ˈherring** *n.* Ⓐ (*fish*) Räucherhering, *der;* Ⓑ (*fig.*) Ablenkungsmanöver, *das;* (*in thriller, historical research*) falsche Fährte; **~-hot** *adj.* Ⓐ [rot] glühend; Ⓑ (*fig.*) glühend ‹Anhänger, Gläubiger, Liebhaber, Zorn›; heiß ‹Blondine, Thema, Musik›; brandaktuell ‹Nachricht›; **this new film is ~-hot stuff** dieser neue Film ist heiß

**redial** ❶ /riːˈdaɪəl/ *v.t.* noch einmal wählen ‹Telefonnummer›; *abs.* noch einmal wählen; **to ~, just press the button** zur Wahlwiederholung einfach diese Taste drücken. ❷ /ˈriːdaɪəl/ *n.* Wahlwiederholung, *die;* **last number ~:** Wahlwiederholung, *die;* **~ button** Wahlwiederholungstaste, *die*

**redid** ⇨ **redo**

**Red ˈIndian** (*Brit. dated*) ❶ *n.* Indianer, *der/*Indianerin, *die.* ❷ *adj.* Indianer-

**redirect** /riːdaɪˈrekt, riːdɪˈrekt/ *v.t.* nachsenden ‹Post, Brief usw.›; umleiten ‹Verkehr›; weiterleiten (**to** an + *Akk.*) ‹Anfrage›; richten (**to** auf + *Akk.*) ‹Aufmerksamkeit›

**redirection** /riːdaɪˈrekʃn, riːdɪˈrekʃn/ *n.* (*of mail*) Nachsendung, *die;* (*of traffic*) Umleitung, *die;* (*of question*) Weiterleitung, *die* (**to** an + *Akk.*)

**rediscover** /riːdɪˈskʌvə(r)/ *v.t.* wieder entdecken

**rediscovery** /riːdɪˈskʌvərɪ/ *n.* Wiederentdeckung, *die*

**redistribute** /riːdɪˈstrɪbjuːt/ *v.t.* umverteilen ‹Besitz, Einkommen›; versetzen ‹Arbeitskräfte›; (*reorganize*) neu aufteilen

**redistribution** /riːdɪstrɪˈbjuːʃn/ *n.* (*of land, wealth*) Umverteilung, *die;* (*of labour etc.*) Versetzung, *die,* (*reorganization*) Neuaufteilung, *die*

**red: ~ lead** /red ˈled/ *n.* Mennige, *die;* **~-ˈletter day** *n.* Ⓐ (*memorable day*) im Kalender rot anzustreichender Tag; großer Tag; Ⓑ (*Relig.*) Feiertag, *der;* **~ ˈlight** *n.* Ⓐ [rotes] Warnlicht; (*of traffic lights*) rote [Verkehrs]ampel; **drive straight through the ~ light** bei Rot über die Ampel fahren; Ⓑ (*fig.*) Warnzeichen, *das;* **they saw the** *or* **a ~ light** bei ihnen leuchtete ein [rotes] Warnsignal auf; **~-ˈlight district** *n.* Amüsierviertel, *das;* Strich, *der* (*salopp*); **~ meat** *n.* dunkles Fleisch (*z. B. vom Rind*); **~neck** *n.* (*Amer.*) armer weißer Landbewohner aus den Südstaaten; (*derog.*) weißer Rassist *od.* Reaktionär

**redness** /ˈrednɪs/ *n., no pl.* (*of face, skin, eyes, sky*) Röte, *die;* (*of blood, fire, rose, dress, light*) rote Farbe

**redo** /riːˈduː/ *v.t.*, **redoes** /riːˈdʌz/, **redoing** /riːˈduːɪŋ/, **redid** /riːˈdɪd/, **redone** /riːˈdʌn/ Ⓐ (*do again*) wiederholen ‹Prüfung, Spiel, Test›; neu frisieren ‹Haare›; erneuern ‹Make-up, Lidschatten›; noch einmal machen ‹Bett, Hausaufgabe›; überarbeiten ‹Aufsatz, Übersetzung, Komposition›; **~ one's face** sein Make-up erneuern; Ⓑ (*redecorate*) [gründlich] renovieren; (*repaper*) neu tapezieren; (*repaint*) neu streichen

**redolent** /ˈredələnt/ *adj.* Ⓐ duftend; **~ odours** Düfte *Pl.;* **~ of** *or* **with sth.** nach etw. duftend; Ⓑ (*fig.*) **be ~ of sth.** stark an etw. (*Akk.*) erinnern

**redone** ⇨ **redo**

**redouble** /riːˈdʌbl/ ❶ *v.t.* Ⓐ verdoppeln; Ⓑ (*Bridge*) rekontrieren. ❷ *v.i.* sich verdoppeln. ❸ *n.* (*Bridge*) Rekontra, *das*

**redoubt** /rɪˈdaʊt/ *n.* (*Mil.*) Redoute, *die*

**redoubtable** /rɪˈdaʊtəbl/ *adj.* Ehrfurcht gebietend ‹Person›; gewaltig, enorm ‹Aufgabe, Pflicht usw.›; gefürchtet ‹Gegner, Krieger›; glänzend ‹Anwalt›

**redound** /rɪˈdaʊnd/ *v.i.* **~ to sb.'s advantage/disadvantage/honour** *or* **credit/fame** jmdm. Vorteile/Nachteile/Ehre/Ruhm einbringen; **~ to sb.'s reputation/good name** zu jmds. Ruf/gutem Namen beitragen

**red ˈpepper** *n.* Ⓐ ⇨ **cayenne**; Ⓑ (*vegetable*) rote Paprika[schote]

**redraft** /riːˈdrɑːft/ *v.t.* neu entwerfen; neu aufsetzen ‹Vertrag›; neu abfassen ‹Schriftstück›

**red ˈrag** *n.* (*fig.*) rotes Tuch (**to** für); **be like a ~ to a bull [to sb.]** wie ein rotes Tuch [auf jmdn.] wirken

**redraw** /riːˈdrɔː/ *v.t., forms as* **draw** neu zeichnen

**redress** /rɪˈdres/ ❶ *n.* (*reparation, correction*) Entschädigung, *die;* **seek ~ for sth.** eine Entschädigung für etw. verlangen; **seek [legal] ~:** auf Schadenersatz klagen; **have no ~:** keine Entschädigung erhalten; (*Law*) keinen Rechtsanspruch auf Entschädigung haben. ❷ *v.t.* Ⓐ (*adjust again*) ins Gleichgewicht bringen; **~ the balance** das Gleichgewicht wieder herstellen; Ⓑ (*set right, rectify*) wieder gutmachen ‹Unrecht›; ausgleichen ‹Ungerechtigkeiten›; beseitigen ‹Missstand, Übel, Despotie›; abhelfen (+ *Dat.*) ‹Beschwerden, Missbrauch›

**Red: ~ ˈRiding Hood** *pr. n.* Rotkäppchen, *das;* **~ ˈSea** *pr. n.* Rote Meer, *das*

**red: ~shank** *n.* (*Ornith.*) Rotschenkel, *der;* **~ shift** *n.* (*Astron.*) Rotverschiebung, *die;* **~skin** (*dated/derog.*) ⇨ **Red Indian** 1; **~ ˈsquirrel** *n.* Eichhörnchen, *das;* **Red ˈStar** *n.* Roter Stern; **~start** *n.* (*Ornith.*) Rotschwanz, *der;* **~ ˈtape** *n.* (*fig.*) [unnötige] Bürokratie; **cut through the ~ tape** die Bürokratie umgehen; **Red ˈTerror** ⇨ **terror** A

**reduce** /rɪˈdjuːs/ ❶ *v.t.* Ⓐ (*diminish*) senken ‹Preis, Gebühr, Fieber, Aufwendungen, Blutdruck usw.›; verbilligen ‹Ware›; reduzieren ‹Geschwindigkeit, Gewicht, Anzahl, Menge, Preis›; **at ~d prices** zu herabgesetzten Preisen; **~ one's weight** abnehmen; Ⓑ **~ to order/despair/silence/tears/submission** auf Vordermann bringen (*ugs.*)/in Verzweiflung stürzen/verstummen lassen/zum Weinen bringen/ zum Aufgeben zwingen; **~ sb. to begging** jmdn. an den Bettelstab bringen; **be ~d to starvation** hungern müssen; **be ~d to borrowing money/pawning sth.** sich (*Dat.*) Geld leihen müssen/etw. versetzen müssen; **live in ~d circumstances** in verarmten Verhältnissen leben; **~ sb. to the ranks** jmdn. in den Mannschaftsstand degradieren; Ⓒ (*convert to other form*) **~ wood to pulp** Holz zu einem Brei verarbeiten; **~ yards to inches** Yards in Inches umwandeln; Ⓓ (*Photog.*) abschwächen; Ⓔ (*Med.*) einrenken ‹Gliedmaße, Gelenk›; einrichten ‹Bruch›; Ⓕ (*Chem.*) reduzieren.
❷ *v.i.* abnehmen

**reducer** /rɪˈdjuːsə(r)/ *n.* Ⓐ (*Photog.*) Abschwächer, *der;* Ⓑ (*Chem.*) Reduktionsmittel, *das*

**reducible** /rɪˈdjuːsɪbl/ *adj.* Ⓐ reduzierbar (**to** auf + *Akk.*); **be ~:** reduziert werden können (**to** auf + *Akk.*); Ⓑ (*Chem.*) reduzierbar

**reducing**/rɪˈdjuːsɪŋ/**: ~ agent** *n.* (*Chem.*) Reduktionsmittel, *das;* **~ diet** *n.* Schlankheitskur, *die*

**reductio ad absurdum** /rɪdʌktɪəʊ æd əbˈsɜːdəm/ *n., no pl.* Reductio ad absurdum, *die* (*geh.*)

**reduction** /rɪˈdʌkʃn/ *n.* Ⓐ (*amount, process*) (*in price, costs, wages, rates, speed, etc.*) Senkung, *die* (**in** *Gen.*); (*in numbers, output, etc.*) Verringerung, *die* (**in** *Gen.*); **~ in prices/wages/weight** Preis-/Lohnsenkung, *die*/Gewichtsabnahme, *die;* **there is a ~ on all**

**furniture** alle Möbel sind im Preis heruntergesetzt; **a ~ of £10** ein Preisnachlass von 10 Pfund; **B** *(smaller copy)* Verkleinerung, *die;* **C** *(conversion to other form)* Verarbeitung, *die;* **~ of yards to metres** Umwandlung von Yards in Meter; **D** *(Photog.)* Abschwächung, *die;* **E** *(Chem.)* Reduktion, *die*

**reductionism** /rɪˈdʌkʃənɪzm/ *n.* *(Philos.)* Reduktionismus, *der*

**reductive** /rɪˈdʌktɪv/ *adj.* *(Philos.)* reduktiv

**redundancy** /rɪˈdʌndənsɪ/ *n.* **A** *(Brit.)* Arbeitslosigkeit, *die;* **redundancies** Entlassungen; **take** *or* **accept voluntary ~:** seiner betriebsbedingten Kündigung zustimmen; **B** *(being more than needed)* Überfluss, *der;* *(of materials, capital)* Überschuss, *der;* *(being more than suitable)* Redundanz, *die;* *(of style)* Überladenheit, *die*

**re'dundancy payment** *n.* Abfindung, *die*

**redundant** /rɪˈdʌndənt/ *adj.* **A** *(Brit.: now unemployed)* arbeitslos; **be made** *or* **become ~:** den Arbeitsplatz verlieren; **make ~:** entlassen; **B** *(more than needed)* überflüssig; überschüssig ‹Kapital, Material›; *(more than suitable)* redundant; überflüssig ‹Absatz, Kapitel, Wort›; überladen ‹Stil›

**reduplicate** /rɪˈdjuːplɪkeɪt/ **1** *v.t.* **A** verdoppeln; *(repeat)* wiederholen; **B** *(Ling.)* verdoppeln. **2** *v.i.* *(Ling.)* reduplizieren

**reduplication** /rɪdjuːplɪˈkeɪʃn/ *n.* **A** *(act of doubling)* Verdopplung, *die;* *(repetition)* Wiederholung, *die;* **B** *(Ling.)* Reduplikation, *die*

**red: ~ 'wine** *n.* Rotwein, *der;* **~wood** *n.* *(Bot.)* Mammutbaum, *der*

**re-echo** /riːˈekəʊ/ *v.i.* **A** widerhallen (**with** von); **the cry echoed and ~ed round the cave** der Ruf wurde in dem Gewölbe wieder und wieder zurückgeworfen; **B** *(fig.)* **these words ~ through the book** an diese Worte wird man in dem Buch immer wieder erinnert

**reed** /riːd/ *n.* **A** *(Bot.)* Schilf[rohr], *das;* Ried, *das;* **the tall ~s by the river's edge** das hohe Schilf *od.* Ried am Flussufer; **prove to be a broken ~** *(fig.)* sich als unzuverlässig erweisen; **B** *(Mus.)* *(part of instrument)* Rohrblatt, *das;* *(instrument)* Rohrblattinstrument, *das*

**reed: ~ bunting** *n.* *(Ornith.)* Rohrammer, *die;* **~ instrument** *n.* *(Mus.)* Rohrblattinstrument, *das;* **~ mace** *n.* *(Bot.)* Breitblättriger Rohrkolben; **~ organ** *n.* *(Mus.)* Harmonium, *das*

**re-educate** /riːˈedjʊkeɪt/ *v.t.* umerziehen

**re-education** /riːedjʊˈkeɪʃn/ *n., no pl.* Umerziehung, *die*

**reed warbler, reed wren** *ns.* *(Ornith.)* Teichrohrsänger, *der*

**reedy** /ˈriːdɪ/ *adj.* **A** schnarrend ‹Musik, Singen›; dünn ‹Stimme›; **B** *(full of reeds)* schilfig

**reef**[1] /riːf/ *(Naut.)* **1** *n.* *(on sail)* Reff, *das* *(Seemannsspr.)*; **take in a ~:** die Segel reffen. **2** *v.t.* reffen *(Seemannsspr.)*

**reef**[2] *n.* **A** *(ridge)* Riff, *das;* **~ of sand/rocks/coral** Sand-/Fels-/Korallenriff, *das;* **B** *(fig.)* Klippe, *die;* **C** *(lode)* Erzgang, *der*

**reefer** /ˈriːfə(r)/ *n.* *(sl.: marijuana cigarette)* Joint, *der* *(Drogenjargon)*

**'reef knot** *n.* Kreuzknoten, *der*

**reek** /riːk/ **1** *n.* Geruch, *der;* Gestank, *der* *(abwertend)*. **2** *v.i.* **A** riechen, *(abwertend)* stinken (**of** nach); **B** *(fig.)* riechen *(ugs.)* (**of, with** nach)

**reel** /riːl/ **1** *n.* **A** *(roller, cylinder)* ‹Papier-, Schlauch-, Garn-, Angel›rolle, *die;* ‹Film-, Tonband-, Garn›spule, *die;* **B** *(quantity)* Rolle, *die;* **steel rope in ~s of 1800 feet** Stahlseil auf Rollen zu 1 800 Fuß; **~ of film** Filmrolle, *die;* **C** *(dance, music)* Reel, *der.* **2** *v.t.* **~ [up]** *(wind on)* aufspulen. **3** *v.i.* **A** *(be in a whirl)* sich drehen; **his head was ~ing** in seinem Kopf drehte sich alles; **her mind ~ed with all the facts** ihr schwirrte der Kopf von all den Daten; **B** *(sway)* torkeln; *(fig.: be shaken)* taumeln; **begin to ~:** ins Wanken geraten; **his mind ~ed when he heard the news** als er die Nachricht hörte, drehte sich ihm alles

**~ 'in** *v.t.* an Land ziehen ‹Fisch›

**~ 'off** *v.t.* **A** *(say rapidly)* herunterleiern *(ugs. abwertend)*, hersagen ‹Geschichte›; *(without apparent effort)* abspulen *(ugs.)* ‹Gedicht, Namen, Einzelheiten›; **B** *(take off)* abwickeln

**re-elect** /riːɪˈlekt/ *v.t.* wieder wählen

**re-election** /riːɪˈlekʃn/ *n.* Wiederwahl, *die*

**re-eligible** /riːˈelɪdʒɪbl/ *adj.* wieder wählbar; **be ~:** wieder gewählt werden können

**re-embark** /riːɪmˈbɑːk/ **1** *v.t.* wieder einschiffen ‹Ladung, Passagiere›. **2** *v.i.* sich wieder einschiffen (**for** nach); **~ on sth.** *(fig.)* bei etw. wieder einsteigen

**re-emerge** /riːɪˈmɜːdʒ/ *v.i.* **A** *(out of liquid)* wieder auftauchen; **B** *(into view; crop up)* wieder auftauchen; ‹Mond, Sonne usw.:› wieder hervorkommen; **C** *(return)* zurückkehren (**in** nach, **from** aus)

**re-emergent** /riːɪˈmɜːdʒənt/ *adj.* wieder auftauchend ‹Frage, Idee›; wiederkehrend ‹Glaube›; wieder erstehend *(geh.)* ‹Nation›

**re-enact** /riːɪˈnækt/ *v.t.* **A** wieder in Kraft setzen ‹Gesetz, Erlass usw.›; **B** *(perform)* wiederholen ‹Tatsachen, Einzelheiten›; nachstellen ‹Szene, Schlacht›; **~ a role** noch einmal in einer Rolle auftreten; **~ a crime** den Hergang eines Verbrechens nachspielen

**re-enlist** *(Mil.)* **1** *v.i.* wieder [in die Armee/Marine] eintreten. **2** *v.t.* wieder anwerben

**re-enter** /riːˈentə(r)/ **1** *v.i.* **A** wieder eintreten; *(come on stage)* die Bühne [wieder] betreten; *(as stage direction)* **~ Hamlet from left** Auftritt Hamlet von links; **B** *(for race, exam, etc.)* wieder antreten; **C** *(penetrate)* wieder eindringen. **2** *v.t.* wieder betreten ‹Raum, Gebäude›; wieder eintreffen in (+ *Dat.*) ‹Ortschaft›; wieder einreisen in (+ *Akk.*) ‹Land›; wieder eintreten in (+ *Akk.*) ‹Erdatmosphäre›

**re-entry** /riːˈentrɪ/ *n.* **A** Wiedereintreten, *das;* *(into country)* Wiedereinreise, *die;* *(for exam)* Wiederantreten, *das;* nochmaliges Antreten (**for** zu); *(of spacecraft)* **[atmospheric] ~:** Wiedereintritt [in die Erdatmosphäre]; **B** *(Law: taking possession again)* Wiederinbesitznahme, *die*

**re-erect** /riːɪˈrekt/ *v.t.* wieder aufbauen

**re-establish** /riːɪˈstæblɪʃ/ *v.t.* wieder herstellen ‹Kontakt, Demokratie, Beziehungen, Frieden, Ordnung›; wieder beleben ‹Brauch, Mode›; wieder aufbauen ‹Organisation, Stützpunkt›; wieder einsetzen ‹Regierung›; beweisen ‹Unschuld usw.›; **~ sb. as ruler** jmdn. als Herrscher wieder einsetzen; **~ oneself as sth./in a position** sich erneut als etw./in einer Position etablieren

**reeve**[1] /riːv/ *n.* **A** *(Hist.)* *(magistrate)* Vogt, *der;* *(manorial supervisor)* Aufseher, *der;* **B** *(minor official)* Gemeindebeamte, *der/*-beamtin, *die*

**reeve**[2] *v.t.,* **rove** /rəʊv/ *or* **~d** *(Naut.)* scheren ‹Tau›; *(fasten)* festzurren

**re-examination** /riːɪgzæmɪˈneɪʃn/ *n.* **A** *(Law)* erneute [Zeugen]vernehmung; **B** *(investigation)* erneute Untersuchung; **C** *(act of testing knowledge or ability)* Wiederholungsprüfung, *die;* **D** *(act of scrutinizing again)* nochmalige [Über]prüfung

**re-examine** /riːɪgˈzæmɪn/ *v.t.* **A** *(Law)* erneut vernehmen; **B** *(investigate)* [erneut] untersuchen; **C** *(test knowledge or ability of)* von neuem *od.* wieder prüfen; **D** *(scrutinize)* erneut überprüfen

**re-export** /riːɪkˈspɔːt/ *v.t.* reexportieren; wieder ausführen

**ref** /ref/ *n.* *(Sport coll.)* Schiri, *der* *(Sportjargon)*; *(Boxing)* Ringrichter, *der*

**ref.** *abbr.* **reference** Verw.; **with ref. to** mit Bz. *od.* unter Bezugn. auf (+ *Akk.*); **your/our ref.** Ihr/unser Zeichen

**reface** /riːˈfeɪs/ *v.t.* **~ sth.** die Fassade einer Sache *(Gen.)* restaurieren

**refashion** /riːˈfæʃn/ *v.t.* umgestalten

**refectory** /rɪˈfektərɪ/ *n.* *(in college, university)* Mensa, *die;* *(in convent, monastery)* Refektorium, *das*

**refer** /rɪˈfɜː(r)/ **1** *v.i.,* **-rr-** **A** **~ to** *(allude to)* sich beziehen auf (+ *Akk.*) ‹Buch, Person usw.›; *(speak of)* sprechen von ‹Person, Problem, Ereignis usw.›; **B** **~ to** *(apply to, relate to)* betreffen; ‹Beschreibung:› sich beziehen auf (+ *Akk.*); **does that remark ~ to me?** gilt diese Bemerkung mir?; **C** **~ to** *(consult, cite as proof)* konsultieren *(geh.)*; nachsehen in (+ *Dat.*); **~ to sb./a case** sich auf jmdn./einen Fall berufen.
**2** *v.t.,* **-rr-** **A** *(send on to)* **~ sb./sth. to sb./sth.** jmdn./etw. an jmdn./auf etw. *(Akk.)* verweisen; **~ a patient to a specialist** einen Patienten an einen Facharzt überweisen; **the dispute was ~red to the UN** der Streitfall wurde vor die UNO gebracht; **~ sb. to a paragraph/an article** jmdn. auf einen Absatz/Artikel aufmerksam machen; **~ to drawer** *(Banking)* zurück an Aussteller; **B** **~ to** *(assign to)* zurückführen auf (+ *Akk.*); **~ sth. to sb.** jmdm. etw. zuschreiben; **~red pain** *(Med.)* ausstrahlender Schmerz; **C** *(after examination)* zurückstellen ‹Prüfling›; [zur Überarbeitung] zurückgeben ‹Dissertation›

**~ 'back** **1** *v.t.* **~ back to** zurückverweisen an (+ *Akk.*). **2** *v.i.* **A** *(to past event)* **~ back to** sich beziehen auf (+ *Akk.*); **B** *(to source of information)* **~ back to sb./sth.** Rücksprache halten mit jmdm./auf etw. *(Akk.)* zurückgreifen

**referee** /refəˈriː/ **1** *n.* **A** *(Sport: umpire)* Schiedsrichter, *der/*-richterin, *die;* *(Boxing)* Ringrichter, *der;* *(Wrestling)* Kampfrichter, *der;* **B** *(Brit.: person willing to testify)* Referenz, *die;* **C** *(arbitrator)* Schlichter, *der;* **D** *(person who assesses)* Gutachter, *der/*Gutachterin, *die.* **2** *v.t.* **A** *(Sport: umpire)* als Schiedsrichter/-richterin leiten; **~ a football match** ein Fußballspiel pfeifen *od.* leiten; **B** *(arbitrate)* schlichten; **C** *(assess, evaluate)* begutachten. **3** *v.i.* **A** *(Sport: umpire)* Schiedsrichter/-richterin sein; **B** *(arbitrate)* schlichten; Schlichter sein; **C** *(assess or evaluate work)* als Gutachter/Gutachterin tätig sein

**reference** /ˈrefrəns/ *n.* **A** *(allusion)* Hinweis, *der* (**to** auf + *Akk.*); **make [several] ~[s] to sth.** sich [mehrfach] auf etw. *(Akk.)* beziehen; **make no ~ to sth.** etw. nicht ansprechen; **omit all ~ to sth.** etw. völlig verschweigen; **put a ~ to sth. in the introduction of the book** in der Einleitung des Buches auf etw. *(Akk.)* hinweisen; **B** *(note directing reader)* Verweis, *der* (**to** auf + *Akk.*); **C** *(cited book, passage)* Quellenangabe, *die;* **D** *(testimonial)* Zeugnis, *das;* Referenz, *die;* **character ~:** persönliche Referenzen; **give sb. a good ~:** jmdm. ein gutes Zeugnis ausstellen; **E** *(person willing to testify)* Referenz, *die;* **quote sb. as one's ~:** jmdn. als Referenz angeben; **F** *(act of referring)* Konsultation, *die* (**to** *Gen.*) *(geh.)*; **~ to a dictionary/map** Nachschlagen in einem Wörterbuch/Nachsehen auf einer Karte; **work of ~:** Nachschlagewerk, *das;* **without ~ to sb.** ohne jmdn. zu fragen; **speak without ~ to one's notes** sprechen, ohne seine Aufzeichnungen zu Hilfe zu nehmen; **G** *(relation, correspondence)* **have ~ to sth.** in Beziehung zu etw. stehen; **in** *or* **with ~ to sth.** mit Bezug auf etw. *(Akk.)*; unter Bezugnahme auf etw. *(Akk.)*; **with ~ to your suggestion** was deinen Vorschlag anbetrifft. ⇒ *also* **cross reference; library** A; **term** 1 B

**reference: ~ book** *n.* Nachschlagewerk, *das;* **~ mark** *n.* Verweiszeichen, *das;* **~ number** *n.* [Kenn]nummer, *die;* **~ point** *n.* Bezugspunkt, *der*

**referendum** /refəˈrendəm/ *n., pl.* **~s** *or* **referenda** /refəˈrendə/ Volksentscheid, *der;* Referendum, *das*

**referral** /rɪˈfɜːrl/ *n.* **A** *(for advice)* Überweisung, *die* (**to** an + *Akk.*); **B** *(for action)* Weiterleitung, *die* (**to** an + *Akk.*)

**refill** **1** /riːˈfɪl/ *v.t.* nachfüllen ‹Glas, Feuerzeug›; neu füllen ‹Kissen›; mit einer neuen Füllung versehen ‹Zahn›; **~ the glasses** nachschenken; **~ a pen with ink** einen Füller mit Tinte füllen. **2** /ˈriːfɪl/ *n.* **A** *(cartridge)* [Nachfüll]patrone, *die;* *(for ball pen)* Ersatzmine, *die;* *(pad of paper)* Nachfüllpackung, *die;* **B** *(with drink)* Nachgießen, *das;* **can I have a ~?** *(coll.)* gießt du mir noch einmal nach?

r

**refine** /rɪˈfaɪn/ ❶ *v.t.* Ⓐ *(purify)* raffinieren; Ⓑ *(make cultured)* kultivieren; verfeinern ‹Stil, Ausdrucksweise›; stilistisch verbessern ‹Rede, Aufsatz›; Ⓒ *(improve)* verbessern; verfeinern ‹Stil, Technik›. ❷ *v.i.* Ⓐ *(become pure)* rein werden; Ⓑ *(become more cultured)* sich verfeinern

~ **[up]on** *v.t.* [weiter] verfeinern; weiterentwickeln

**refined** /rɪˈfaɪnd/ *adj.* Ⓐ *(purified)* raffiniert; Fein‹kupfer, -silber usw.›; ~ **sugar** [Zucker]raffinade, *die;* Ⓑ *(cultured)* kultiviert; Ⓒ *(precise)* scharfsinnig, differenziert ‹Argumentation›; ausgeklügelt ‹Technik, Maschine[rie]›; kompliziert ‹Rechnung›

**refinement** /rɪˈfaɪnmənt/ *n.* Ⓐ *(purifying)* Raffination, *die;* Ⓑ *(fineness of feeling, elegance)* Kultiviertheit, *die;* **person of** ~: kultivierter Mensch; ~ **of feeling** verfeinertes Gefühl; Ⓒ *(subtle manifestation)* Verfeinerung, *die;* Ⓓ *(improvement)* Verbesserung, *die;* Weiterentwicklung, *die* (**[up]on** *Gen.*); **introduce** ~**s into a machine** eine Maschine weiterentwickeln; Ⓔ *(piece of reasoning)* Spitzfindigkeit, *die* *(abwertend)*

**refinery** /rɪˈfaɪnərɪ/ *n.* Raffinerie, *die*

**refit** ❶ /riːˈfɪt/ *v.t.*, **-tt-** überholen; reparieren; *(equip with new things)* neu ausstatten. ❷ *v.i.*, **-tt-** überholt werden; repariert werden; *(renew supplies or equipment)* sich neu ausrüsten. ❸ /ˈriːfɪt/ *n.* Überholung, *die;* *(with supplies or equipment)* Neuausstattung, *die*

**refitment** /riːˈfɪtmənt/ ⇒ **refit** 3

**reflate** /riːˈfleɪt/ *v.t.* *(Econ.)* ankurbeln ‹Wirtschaft, Konjunktur›

**reflation** /riːˈfleɪʃn/ *n.* *(Econ.)* Reflation, *die*

**reflationary** /riːˈfleɪʃənərɪ/ *adj.* *(Econ.)* reflationär

**reflect** /rɪˈflekt/ ❶ *v.t.* Ⓐ *(throw back)* reflektieren; **bask in sb.'s** ~**ed glory** sich in jmds. Ruhm sonnen; Ⓑ *(reproduce)* spiegeln; *(fig.)* widerspiegeln ‹Ansichten, Gefühle, Werte›; **be** ~**ed** sich spiegeln; Ⓒ *(contemplate)* nachdenken über (+ *Akk.*); ~ **what/how ...:** überlegen, was/wie .... ❷ *v.i.* *(meditate)* nachdenken

~ **[up]on** *v.t.* Ⓐ *(consider, contemplate)* nachdenken über (+ *Akk.*); abwägen ‹Konsequenzen›; Ⓑ ~ **credit/discredit [up]on sb./sth.** ein gutes/schlechtes Licht auf jmdn./etw. werfen; Ⓒ *(bring discredit on)* diskreditieren; ~ **[up]on sb.'s sincerity** an jmds. Aufrichtigkeit *(Dat.)* zweifeln lassen; ~ **badly [up]on sb./sth.** auf jmdn./etw. ein schlechtes Licht werfen; Ⓓ *(bring credit on)* ~ **well [up]on sb./sth.** jmdn./etw. in einem guten Licht erscheinen lassen; Ⓔ *(cast doubt or reproach on)* in Zweifel ziehen

**re'flecting telescope** ⇒ **reflector** B

**reflection** /rɪˈflekʃn/ *n.* Ⓐ *(of light etc.)* Reflexion, *die;* *(by surface of water etc.)* Spiegelung, *die;* **angle of** ~: Reflexionswinkel, *der;* Ⓑ *(reflected light, heat, or colour)* Reflexion, *die;* *(image; lit. or fig.)* Spiegelbild, *das;* Ⓒ *(meditation, consideration)* Nachdenken, *das* (**upon** über + *Akk.*); **be lost in** ~: in Gedanken versunken sein; **on** ~: bei weiterem Nachdenken; **on** ~, **I think ...:** wenn ich mir das recht überlege, [so] glaube ich ...; Ⓓ *(censure)* ~ **on** Kritik an (+ *Dat.*); **be a** ~ **[up]on sb./sth.** an jmdm./etw. zweifeln lassen; **cast** ~**s on sth.** etw. in Zweifel ziehen; Ⓔ *(idea)* Vorstellung, *die;* Ⓕ *(remark)* Reflexion, *die* *(geh.)*, Betrachtung, *die* (**on** über + *Akk.*); Ⓖ *(Philos.)* Nachdenken, *das;* Reflexion, *die* *(fachspr.)*

**reflective** /rɪˈflektɪv/ *adj.* Ⓐ reflektierend; **be** ~: reflektieren; ~ **power** Reflexionsvermögen, *das;* Ⓑ *(thoughtful)* nachdenklich; Ⓒ *(reflected)* reflektiert; Ⓓ *(concerned in reflection)* gedanklich ‹Fähigkeiten, Kraft›

**reflectively** /rɪˈflektɪvlɪ/ *adv.* nachdenklich

**reflector** /rɪˈflektə(r)/ *n.* Ⓐ Rückstrahler, *der;* Ⓑ *(telescope)* Reflektor, *der*

**reflex** /ˈriːfleks/ ❶ *n.* *(Physiol.)* Reflex, *der;* **conditioned** ~: bedingter Reflex. ❷ *adj.* *(by reflection)* Reflex-

**reflex:** ~ **action** *n.* *(Physiol.)* Reflexhandlung, *die;* ~ **angle** *n.* überstumpfer Winkel; ~ **camera** *n.* *(Photog.)* Spiegelreflexkamera, *die*

**reflexion** *(Brit.)* ⇒ **reflection**

**reflexive** /rɪˈfleksɪv/ *(Ling.)* *adj.* reflexiv; ⇒ *also* **pronoun**

**reflexively** /rɪˈfleksɪvlɪ/ *adv.* *(Ling.)* reflexiv

**reflex re'action** *n.* *(Physiol.; also fig.)* Reflexreaktion, *die*

**refloat** /riːˈfləʊt/ *v.t.* [wieder] flottmachen ‹Schiff›; *(fig.)* wieder flüssig machen *(ugs.)*

**reflux** /ˈriːflʌks/ *n.* Ⓐ Rückfluss, *der;* Ⓑ *(Chem.)* Rückfluss, *der*

**reforest** /riːˈfɒrɪst/ *v.t.* wieder aufforsten

**reforestation** /riːfɒrɪˈsteɪʃn/ *n.*, *no pl.* Wiederaufforstung, *die*

**reform** /rɪˈfɔːm/ ❶ *v.t.* Ⓐ *(make better)* reformieren ‹Institution›; bessern ‹Person›; Ⓑ *(abolish)* ~ **sth.** mit etw. aufräumen. ❷ *v.i.* sich bessern. ❸ *n.* Ⓐ *(of person)* Besserung, *die;* *(in a system)* Reform, *die* (**in** *Gen.*); Ⓑ *(removal)* Beseitigung, *die* ; **R**~ **Bill** *(Hist.)* Reformgesetz, *das*

**re-form** /riːˈfɔːm/ ❶ *v.t.* Ⓐ neu gründen ‹Gesellschaft usw.›; Ⓑ *(Mil.)* neu formieren. ❷ *v.i.* Ⓐ sich neu bilden; ‹Band, Gesellschaft:› neu gegründet werden; Ⓑ *(Mil.)* sich neu formieren

**reformation** /refəˈmeɪʃn/ *n.* *(of attitude)* Änderung, *die* (**in** *Gen.*); *(of society, procedure, practice)* Neugestaltung, *die* (**in** *Gen.*); *(of person, character)* Wandlung, *die* (**in** *Gen.*); **the R**~ *(Hist.)* die Reformation

**re-formation** /riːfɔːˈmeɪʃn/ *n.* Ⓐ Wiederaufbau, *der;* Ⓑ *(Mil.)* Neuformierung, *die*

**reformatory** /rɪˈfɔːmətərɪ/ ❶ *adj.* reformatorisch; ~ **measures** Reformmaßnahmen. ❷ *n.* *(Hist./Amer.)* Besserungsanstalt, *die* *(veralt.)*

**reformed** /rɪˈfɔːmd/ *adj.* gewandelt; **he's a** ~ **character** *or* **man** er hat sich positiv verändert; **R**~ **Church** Reformierte Kirche

**reformer** /rɪˈfɔːmə(r)/ *n.* **[political]** ~: Reformpolitiker, *der*/-politikerin, *die*

**reformism** /rɪˈfɔːmɪzm/ *n.* Reformismus, *der*

**reformist** /rɪˈfɔːmɪst/ ❶ *n.* Reformist, *der*/Reformistin, *die.* ❷ *adj.* reformistisch

**re'form school** *n.* Fürsorge[erziehungs]heim, *das*

**refract** /rɪˈfrækt/ *v.t.* *(Phys.)* brechen

**re'fracting telescope** *n.* Linsenfernrohr, *das;* Refraktor, *der* *(fachspr.)*

**refraction** /rɪˈfrækʃn/ *n.* *(Phys.)* Brechung, *die;* Refraktion, *die* *(fachspr.)*; **angle of** ~: Brechungswinkel, *der*

**refractive** /rɪˈfræktɪv/ *adj.* *(Phys.)* brechend; ⇒ *also* **index** 1 B

**refractor** /rɪˈfræktə(r)/ *n.* *(telescope)* Refraktor, *der*

**refractory** /rɪˈfræktərɪ/ ❶ *adj.* Ⓐ *(stubborn)* störrisch; widerspenstig; Ⓑ *(Med.)* hartnäckig; Ⓒ *(heat-resistant)* hitzebeständig; schwer schmelzbar ‹Metalle usw.›. ❷ *n.* hitzebeständiges Material

**refrain**[1] /rɪˈfreɪn/ *n.* Refrain, *der*

**refrain**[2] *v.i.* ~ **from doing sth.** es unterlassen, etw. zu tun; **could you kindly** ~? würden Sie das bitte unterlassen?; **I think I'd better** ~: ich glaube, ich lasse das besser [sein]; **'please** ~ **from smoking'** „bitte nicht rauchen"; **he** ~**ed from comment** er enthielt sich jeden Kommentars *(geh.)*

**refresh** /rɪˈfreʃ/ *v.t.* Ⓐ *(reanimate)* erquicken *(geh.)*; erfrischen; *(with food and/or drink)* stärken; ~ **oneself** *(with rest)* sich ausruhen; *(with food and/or drink)* sich stärken; Ⓑ *(freshen up)* auffrischen ‹Wissen›; **let me** ~ **your memory** lassen Sie mich Ihrem Gedächtnis nachhelfen

**refresher** /rɪˈfreʃə(r)/ *n.* Ⓐ *(Brit. Law)* Sonderhonorar, *das;* Ⓑ Erfrischung, *die;* **have a** ~: etwas trinken

**re'fresher course** *n.* Auffrischungskurs, *der*

**refreshing** /rɪˈfreʃɪŋ/ *adj.* Ⓐ wohltuend ‹Ruhe›; erfrischend ‹Brise, Getränk, Schlaf›; Ⓑ *(interesting)* erfrischend

**refreshment** /rɪˈfreʃmənt/ *n.* Erfrischung, *die*

**refreshment:** ~ **room** *n.* Imbissstube, *die;* ~ **stall** *n.* Erfrischungsstand, *der*

**refrigerant** /riːˈfrɪdʒərənt/ *n.* Kühlmittel, *das*

**refrigerate** /rɪˈfrɪdʒəreɪt/ *v.t.* Ⓐ kühl lagern ‹Lebensmittel›; Ⓑ *(chill)* kühlen; *(freeze)* einfrieren; Ⓒ *(make cool)* abkühlen ‹Luft›

**refrigeration** /rɪfrɪdʒəˈreɪʃn/ *n.* kühle Lagerung; *(chilling)* Kühlung, *die;* *(freezing)* Einfrieren, *das*

**refrigerator** /rɪˈfrɪdʒəreɪtə(r)/ *n.* Kühlschrank, *der*

**refuel** /riːˈfjuːəl/, *(Brit.)* **-ll-** ❶ *v.t.* auftanken. ❷ *v.i.* [auf]tanken

**refuge** /ˈrefjuːdʒ/ *n.* Ⓐ Zuflucht, *die;* **find [a]** ~ **from the storm** Schutz vor dem Sturm finden; **take** ~ **in** Schutz *od.* Zuflucht suchen in (+ *Dat.*) (**from** vor + *Dat.*); *(fig.)* Zuflucht nehmen zu ‹Alkohol, Religion, Lüge›; **be a** ~ **to sb.** jmds. Zuflucht sein; **women's** ~: Frauenhaus, *das;* Ⓑ *(traffic island)* Verkehrsinsel, *die*

**refugee** /refjʊˈdʒiː/ *n.* Flüchtling, *der;* ~**s from the earthquake** Menschen, die Schutz vor dem Erdbeben suchen; **economic** ~: Wirtschaftsflüchtling, *der*

**refu'gee camp** *n.* Flüchtlingslager, *das*

**refulgent** /rɪˈfʌldʒənt/ *adj.* *(literary)* strahlend ‹Licht, Tag›; leuchtend ‹Farbe, Sonnenuntergang›

**refund** ❶ /riːˈfʌnd/ *v.t.* Ⓐ *(pay back)* zurückzahlen ‹Geld, Schulden›; erstatten ‹Kosten›; *abs.* die Schulden zurückzahlen; **your satisfaction guaranteed or your money** ~**ed** bei Nichtgefallen [bekommen Sie Ihr] Geld zurück; Ⓑ *(reimburse)* das Geld zurückzahlen (+ *Dat.*); ~ **sb. for** jmdm. [zurück]erstatten ‹Kosten›; jmdm. ersetzen ‹Verlust, Schaden›. ❷ /ˈriːfʌnd/ *n.* Rückzahlung, *die;* *(of expenses)* [Rück]erstattung, *die;* **get a** ~ **of ten pence on a bottle** zehn Pence [Pfand] für eine Flasche zurückbekommen; **obtain a** ~ **of sth.** etw. zurückbekommen

**refundable** /riːˈfʌndəbl/ *adj.* **be** ~: zurückerstattet werden

**refurbish** /riːˈfɜːbɪʃ/ *v.t.* renovieren ‹Haus›; aufarbeiten ‹Kleidung›; aufpolieren ‹Möbel›

**refurnish** /riːˈfɜːnɪʃ/ *v.t.* neu einrichten

**refusal** /rɪˈfjuːzl/ *n.* Ablehnung, *die;* *(after a period of time)* Absage, *die;* *(of admittance, entry, permission)* Verweigerung, *die;* ~ **to do sth.** Weigerung, etw. zu tun; **her** ~ **of food** ihre Weigerung, etwas zu essen; **have/get [the] first** ~ **on sth.** das Vorkaufsrecht für etw. haben/eingeräumt bekommen; **give sb. [the] first** ~: jmdm. das Vorkaufsrecht einräumen

**refuse**[1] /rɪˈfjuːz/ ❶ *v.t.* Ⓐ ablehnen; abweisen ‹Heiratsantrag›; verweigern ‹Nahrung, Befehl, Bewilligung, Zutritt, Einreise, Erlaubnis›; ~ **sb. admittance/entry/permission** jmdm. den Zutritt/die Einreise/die Erlaubnis verweigern; ~ **to do sth.** sich weigern, etw. zu tun; Ⓑ *(not oblige)* abweisen ‹Person›; Ⓒ ‹Pferd:› verweigern ‹Hindernis›. ❷ *v.i.* Ⓐ ablehnen; *(after request)* sich weigern; Ⓑ ‹Pferd:› verweigern

**refuse**[2] /ˈrefjuːs/ ❶ *n.* Abfall, *der;* Müll, *der;* **the** ~ **is collected once a week** einmal in der Woche ist Müllabfuhr. ❷ *adj.* ~ **chemicals/water** Chemieabfälle/Abwasser, *das*

**refuse**/ˈrefjuːs/: ~ **collection** *n.* Müllabfuhr, *die;* ~ **collector** *n.* ▶ **1261** Müllwerker, *der;* ~ **disposal** *n.* Abfallbeseitigung, *die;* ~ **heap** *n.* Müllhaufen, *der*

**refusenik** /rɪˈfjuːznɪk/ *n.* *(Hist.)* *sowjetischer Jude, dem die Ausreise [nach Israel] verweigert wurde*

**refutation** /refjʊˈteɪʃn/ *n.* Widerlegung, *die;* **the book was a** ~ **of the theory** in dem Buch wurde die Theorie widerlegt

**refute** /rɪˈfjuːt/ *v.t.* widerlegen

**regain** /rɪˈgeɪn/ *v.t.* Ⓐ *(recover possession of)* zurückgewinnen ‹Zuversicht, Vertrauen, Achtung, Augenlicht›; zurückerobern ‹Gebiet›; ~ **one's health/strength** wieder gesund werden/zu Kräften kommen; ~ **control of sth.** etw. wieder unter Kontrolle bringen; ⇒ *also* **consciousness** A; Ⓑ *(reach)* wieder erreichen ‹Küste, Land›; wieder bekommen ‹Platz›; ~ **firm**

**ground again** wieder festen Boden unter den Füßen haben; **C** (*recover*) ~ **one's balance/footing** das Gleichgewicht/den Halt wiedergewinnen; ~ **one's feet** wieder auf die Beine kommen

**regal** /'ri:gl/ *adj.* **A** (*magnificent, stately*) majestätisch ‹Person, Baum, Art, Tier, Würde›; prachtvoll ‹Villa, Zustand›; groß ‹Luxus›; **B** (*royal*) königlich; ~ **office/power** Amt/Macht des Königs/der Königin

**regale** /rɪ'geɪl/ *v.t.* **A** verwöhnen (**with, on** mit); ~ **sb. with stories** jmdn. mit Geschichten unterhalten; **B** (*give delight to*) erfreuen ‹Auge, Ohr, Sinne, Person›; **be ~d** ‹Auge, Ohr, Sinne:› sich laben (*geh.*); ‹Person:› sich erquicken (*geh.*) (**by** an + *Dat.*)

**regalia** /rɪ'geɪlɪə/ *n. pl.* **A** (*of royalty*) Krönungsinsignien; **B** (*of order*) Ordensinsignien

**regally** /'ri:gəlɪ/ *adv.* wie ein König/eine Königin

**regard** /rɪ'gɑ:d/ **1** *v.t.* **A** (*gaze upon*) betrachten; ~ **sb. fixedly** jmdn. anstarren; **B** (*give heed to*) beachten ‹jmds. Worte, Rat›; Rücksicht nehmen auf (+ *Akk.*) ‹Wunsch, Gesundheit, jmds. Recht›; **C** (*fig.: look upon, contemplate*) betrachten; ~ **sb. kindly/warmly** jmdm. freundlich gesinnt/herzlich zugetan sein; ~ **sb. unfavourably** jmdm. ablehnend gegenüberstehen; ~ **sth. with suspicion/horror** misstrauisch gegen/entsetzt über etw. (*Akk.*) sein; ~ **sb. with envy/scorn** neidisch auf jmdn. sein/jmdn. verachten; ~ **sb. with respect/dislike** Respekt vor jmdm./eine Abneigung gegen jmdn. haben; ~ **sb. as a friend/fool/genius** jmdn. als Freund betrachten/für einen Dummkopf/ein Genie halten; **be ~ed as** gelten als; ~ **sth. as wrong** etw. für falsch halten; **D** (*concern, have relation to*) betreffen; berücksichtigen ‹Tatsachen›; **as ~s sb./sth., ~ing sb./sth.** was jmdn./etw. angeht *od.* betrifft. **2** *n.* **A** (*attention*) Beachtung, *die;* **pay ~ to/have ~ to** *or* **for sb./sth.** jmdm./etw. Beachtung schenken; **pay due ~ to sb.** jmdm. die nötige Beachtung erweisen; **having ~ to these facts ...:** unter Berücksichtigung dieser Tatsachen ...; **without ~ to** ohne Rücksicht auf (+ *Akk.*); **B** (*esteem, kindly feeling*) Achtung, *die;* **hold sb./sth. in high/low ~, have** *or* **show a high/low ~ for sb./sth.** jmdn./etw. sehr schätzen/gering schätzen; **show one's high ~ for sth.** seine Wertschätzung für etw. zum Ausdruck bringen; **C** ▶ **1286** *in pl.* Grüße; **send one's ~s** grüßen lassen; **give her my ~s** grüße sie von mir; **with kind[est] ~s** mit herzlich [st]en Grüßen; **D** (*relation, respect*) Beziehung, *die;* **in this ~:** in dieser Beziehung *od.* Hinsicht; **in** *or* **with ~ to sb./sth.** in Bezug auf jmdn./etw.; **E** (*gaze*) Blick, *der*

**regardful** /rɪ'gɑ:dfl/ *adj.* aufmerksam; **be ~ of** im Auge behalten ‹Gefahr, Schwierigkeit›; Beachtung schenken (+ *Dat.*) ‹Interesse, Problem, Gefühl›

**regarding** /rɪ'gɑ:dɪŋ/ ⇒ **regard** 1 D

**regardless** /rɪ'gɑ:dlɪs/ **1** *adj.* ~ **of sth.** ungeachtet *od.* trotz einer Sache (*Gen.*); ~ **of the consequences/cost** ohne Rücksicht auf die Folgen/Kosten. **2** *adv.* trotzdem; **carry on ~:** trotzdem weitermachen

**regatta** /rɪ'gætə/ *n.* Regatta, *die;* **sailing ~:** Segelregatta, *die*

**regd.** *abbr.* **registered** (*Law*) ges. gesch.

**regency** /'ri:dʒənsɪ/ *n.* **A** Regentschaft, *die* (**of** über + *Akk.*); **B** (*commission*) Regentschaftsrat, *der;* (*fig.*) [stellvertretendes] Führungsgremium; **C the R~** (*in England*) die Regentschaft Georgs IV (1810–20); **R~** *attrib.* Regency‹möbel, -stil›

**regenerate** **1** /rɪ'dʒenəreɪt/ *v.t.* **A** (*generate again, recreate*) regenerieren (*bes. Chemie, Biol.*); neu beleben ‹Hass, Angst, Liebe›; **B** (*improve, reform*) erneuern ‹Kirche, Gesellschaft›; ~ **sb.** aus jmdm. einen neuen Menschen machen; **feel ~d** sich wie neugeboren fühlen; **C** (*Biol.: form afresh*) regenerieren (*fachspr.*), neu bilden ‹Gewebe, verlorenen Körperteil›. **2** /rɪ'dʒenərət/ *adj.* **A** (*Relig.: reborn*) wieder geboren; **B** (*improved*) gewandelt ‹Person›; (*reformed*) umgestaltet ‹Gesellschaft, Institution›

**regeneration** /rɪdʒenə'reɪʃn/ *n.* **A** (*recreation, re-formation*) Neuentstehung, *die;* (*fig.: revival, renaissance*) Wiederbelebung, *die;* (*of church, society*) Erneuerung, *die;* **B** (*Relig.: spiritual rebirth*) Wiedergeburt, *die;* **C** (*Biol.: regrowth*) Regeneration, *die* (*fachspr.*); Neubildung, *die*

**regenerative** /rɪ'dʒenərətɪv/ *adj.* regenerativ

**regent** /'ri:dʒənt/ **1** *n.* **A** Regent, *der*/Regentin, *die;* **B** (*Amer. Univ.*) Mitglied des Verwaltungsrates; **the R~s** der Verwaltungsrat. **2** *adj.* **Prince R~:** Prinzregent, *der*

**reggae** /'regeɪ/ *n.* (*Mus.*) Reggae, *der*

**regicide** /'redʒɪsaɪd/ *n.* **A** (*murder*) Königsmord, *der;* **B** (*murderer*) Königsmörder, *der*/-mörderin, *die*

**regime, régime** /reɪ'ʒi:m/ *n.* **A** (*system*) [Regierungs]system, *das;* (*derog.*) Regime, *das;* (*fig.*) bestehende Ordnung; ⇒ *also* **ancien régime**; **B** (*process*) Methode, *die;* **working ~** Funktionsweise, *die;* **C** (*Med.*) ⇒ **regimen**

**regimen** /'redʒɪmən/ *n.* (*Med.*) Heilprogramm, *das;* (*diet*) Diätplan, *der*

**regiment** **1** /'redʒɪmənt, 'redʒmənt/ *n.* **A** (*Mil.: organizational unit*) Regiment, *das;* **parachute/Highland ~:** Luftlande-/Hochlandregiment, *das;* **B** (*Mil.: operational unit*) Abteilung, *die;* **artillery/tank ~:** Artillerie-/Panzerabteilung, *die;* **Royal R~ [of Artillery]** (*Brit.*) Königliche Artillerie; **C** (*fig.: large number*) (*of persons, animals*) Heer, *das;* (*of books etc.*) Masse, *die.* **2** /'redʒɪmənt, 'redʒɪment/ *v.t.* (*organize*) reglementieren

**regimental** /redʒɪ'mentl/ (*Mil.*) **1** *adj.* Regiments‹kleidung, -vorräte›; **the ~ officers** die Offiziere des Regiments; ⇒ *also* **colour** 1 J. **2** *n. in pl.* [Militär]uniform, *die;* (*of particular regiment*) Regimentsuniform, *die*

**regimentation** /redʒɪmən'teɪʃn, redʒɪmen'teɪʃn/ *n.* Reglementierung, *die*

**Regina** /rɪ'dʒaɪnə/ *n.* (*Law*) ~ **v. Jones** die Königin gegen Jones

**region** /'ri:dʒn/ *n.* **A** (*area*) Gebiet, *das;* **the north-western ~:** der Nordwesten; **B** (*administrative division*) Bezirk, *der;* (*Brit. Radio*) Sendegebiet, *das;* **administrative ~:** Verwaltungsbezirk, *der;* **Strathclyde/North-West R~:** Bezirk Strathclyde/Nordwest; **C** (*fig.: sphere*) Bereich, *der;* Gebiet, *das;* **in the ~ of two tons** ungefähr zwei Tonnen; **D** (*layer*) Schicht, *die;* Region, *die;* **E** (*Anat.*) Region, *die;* ~ **of the eyes/mouth** Augen-/Mundpartie, *die;* ⇒ *also* **lower regions**

**regional** /'ri:dʒənl/ *adj.* regional ‹System, Akzent, Förderung›; Regional‹planung, -fernsehen, -programm, -ausschuss›; ~ **dialect** Regiolekt, *der* (*Sprachw.*); regionaler Dialekt; ~ **wines of France** Weine aus französischen Anbaugebieten

**regionalism** /'ri:dʒənəlɪzm/ *n.* (*Polit., Ling.*) Regionalismus, *der*

**regionalize** /'ri:dʒənəlaɪz/ *v.t.* regionalisieren

**register** /'redʒɪstə(r)/ **1** *n.* **A** (*book, list*) Register, *das;* (*at school*) Klassenbuch, *das;* **parish/hotel/marriage ~:** Kirchen-/Fremden-/Heiratsbuch, *das;* ~ **of births, deaths and marriages** Personenstandsbuch, *das;* **medical ~:** Ärzteregister, *das;* **electoral** *or* **parliamentary ~, ~ of voters** Wählerliste, *die;* Wählerverzeichnis, *das;* ~ **of members/patients** Mitgliederverzeichnis, *das*/Patientenkartei, *die;* **civil service ~:** Verzeichnis der Beamten; **call** *or* **mark the ~** (*at school*) die Anwesenheit der Schüler überprüfen; **B** (*Mus.*) (*in organ*) Registerzug, *der;* (*in harpsichord*) Rechen, *der;* (*set of pipes*) Register, *das;* **C** (*Mus.: range of tones*) Tonumfang, *der;* (*part of voice-compass*) Register, *das* (*fachspr.*); Tonlage, *die;* **middle ~:** Mittellage, *die;* **head/chest ~:** Kopf-/Brustregister, *das;* **D** (*Mech.*) Klappe, *die;* Schieber, *der;* **E** (*recording device*) Zählwerk, *das;* ⇒ *also* **cash register**; **F** (*Printing*) Register, *das;* **be in ~:** Register halten; **G** (*Photog.*) Register, *das;* Passer, *der;* **H** (*Ling.*) Register, *das.*

**2** *v.t.* **A** (*set down*) schriftlich festhalten ‹Name, Zahl, Experiment, Detail›; (*on file; fig.: make mental note of*) registrieren (**on** in + *Dat.*) ‹Name, Faktum, Rat›; **B** (*enter*) registrieren ‹Geburt, Heirat, Todesfall, Patent›; (*cause to be entered*) registrieren lassen; eintragen ‹Warenzeichen, Firma, Verein›; anmelden ‹Auto, Patent›; (*at airport*) einchecken ‹Gepäck›; *abs.* (*at hotel*) sich ins Fremdenbuch eintragen; ~ **[oneself] with the police** sich polizeilich anmelden; **C** (*enrol*) anmelden; (*Univ.*) einschreiben, immatrikulieren; (*as voter*) eintragen (**on** in + *Akk.*) ‹Person›; *abs.* (*as student*) sich einschreiben *od.* immatrikulieren; (*in list of voters*) sich ins Wählerverzeichnis eintragen lassen; ~ **[oneself] with a doctor** sich bei einem praktischen Arzt eintragen lassen; **D** (*record*) anzeigen, registrieren ‹Temperatur›; **E** (*Post*) eingeschrieben versenden; **have sth. ~ed** etw. einschreiben lassen; **F** (*express*) zeigen ‹Gefühlsregung, Freude›; widerspiegeln ‹Angst›; zum Ausdruck bringen ‹Entsetzen, Überraschung›; ~ **a protest** Protest anmelden.

**3** *v.i.* (*make impression*) einen Eindruck machen (**on, with** auf + *Akk.*); **it didn't ~ with him** er hat das nicht registriert

**registered** /'redʒɪstəd/ *adj.* [ins Standesregister] eingetragen ‹Taufe, Heirat›; [ins Handelsregister] eingetragen ‹Firma›; eingeschrieben, immatrikuliert ‹Student›; schriftlich festgehalten ‹Fakten, Zahlen›; eingeschrieben ‹Brief, Post, Päckchen›; ~ **disabled** ≈ Behinderter/Behinderte mit Schwerbehindertenausweis; **State R~ Nurse** (*Brit.*) staatlich geprüfte Krankenschwester/staatlich geprüfter Krankenpfleger; ~ **trade mark** eingetragenes Warenzeichen; **by ~ post** per Einschreiben

**'register office** *n.* (*Brit.*) Standesamt, *das*

**registrar** /'redʒɪstrɑ:(r), redʒɪ'strɑ:(r)/ *n.* ▶ **1261** **A** (*official recorder*) (*at university*) ≈ Kanzler, *der*/Kanzlerin, *die;* (*local official*) Standesbeamte, *der*/-beamtin, *die;* **B** (*Brit.: in court of law*) ≈ Rechtspfleger, *der*/-pflegerin, *die;* **C** (*Med.*) *Arzt/Ärztin in der klinischen Fachausbildung*

**Registrar 'General** *n. Leiter/Leiterin des Amtes für Bevölkerungsstatistik*

**registration** /redʒɪ'streɪʃn/ *n.* **A** (*act of registering*) Registrierung, *die;* (*enrolment*) Anmeldung, *die;* (*of students*) Einschreibung, *die;* Immatrikulation, *die;* (*of voters*) Eintragung ins Wählerverzeichnis; (*Post*) Einschreiben, *das;* **cost of ~** (*of letter, parcel*) Einschreibegebühr, *die;* **B** (*entry*) [Register]eintrag, *der;* **make a ~ of** registrieren; ~ **fee** Anmeldegebühr, *die;* (*for educational course*) Kursgebühr, *die*

**registration:** ~ **document** *n.* (*Brit.*) Kraftfahrzeugbrief, *der;* ~ **mark,** ~ **number** *ns.* (*Motor Veh.*) amtliches *od.* polizeiliches Kennzeichen; ~ **plate** *n.* (*Motor Veh.*) Nummernschild, *das*

**registry** /'redʒɪstrɪ/ *n.* **A** ~ **[office]** Standesamt, *das; attrib.* standesamtlich ‹Trauung›; **be married in a ~ [office]** sich standesamtlich trauen lassen; **B** (*place for registers*) Registratur, *die;* **C** (*registration*) Registrierung, *die;* Eintragung, *die;* (*of students*) Einschreibung, *die;* Immatrikulation, *die*

**Regius** /'ri:dʒɪəs/ *adj.* ~ **professor** (*Brit. Univ.*) *Inhaber/Inhaberin eines von einem Monarchen errichteten od. durch Berufung der Krone besetzten Lehrstuhls*

**regress** /rɪ'gres/ *v.i.* **A** (*in development*) sich zurückentwickeln; (*in career*) Rückschritte machen; **a sign of society ~ing** ein Zeichen gesellschaftlichen Rückschritts; **B** (*Psych.*) regredieren (**to** in + *Akk.*)

**regression** /rɪ'greʃn/ *n.* **A** (*return to previous state*) rückläufige Entwicklung; **a ~ to less civilized standards** ein Rückfall in weniger zivilisierte Normen; **B** (*Psych.*) Regression, *die;* **C** (*Med.: decline*) Rückbildung, *die;* **D** (*backward movement*) Rückkehr, *die*

**re'gression curve** *n.* (*Statistics*) Regressionskurve, *die*

**regressive** /rɪ'gresɪv/ *adj.* **A** (*Psych., Med., Logic*) regressiv; **B** (*tending to go back in development*) rückschrittlich

r

**regret** /rɪ'gret/ ❶ *v.t.*, **-tt-:** [A] (*feel sorrow for loss of*) nachtrauern (+ *Dat.*); [B] ▶924 (*be sorry for*) bedauern; **~ having done sth.** es bedauern, dass man etw. getan hat; **~ being unable to do sth.** *or* **that one cannot do sth.** es bedauern, dass man etw. nicht tun kann; **it is to be ~ted that ...:** es ist bedauerlich, dass ...; **I ~ to say that ...:** ich muss leider sagen, dass ...; **we ~ to hear that ...:** wir hören mit Bedauern, dass ...
❷ *n.* Bedauern, *das;* **feel ~ at sb.'s doing sth.** bedauern, dass jmd. etw. tut; **feel ~ for having done sth.** es bedauern, dass man etw. getan hat; **there's no point in having ~s** es hat keinen Sinn, sich jetzt noch darüber Gedanken zu machen; **much to my ~:** zu meinem großen Bedauern; **have no ~s** nichts bereuen; **send one's ~s** (*polite refusal*) sich entschuldigen lassen; **please accept my ~s at having to refuse** seien Sie mir bitte nicht böse, aber ich muss leider ablehnen

**regretful** /rɪ'gretfl/ *adj.* bedauernd ‹Blick›; **be ~ that one has done sth.** bedauern, dass man etw. getan hat

**regretfully** /rɪ'gretfəlɪ/ *adv.* mit Bedauern

**regrettable** /rɪ'gretəbl/ *adj.* bedauerlich

**regrettably** /rɪ'gretəblɪ/ *adv.* bedauerlicherweise; bedauerlich ‹teuer›

**regroup** /ri:'gru:p/ ❶ *v.t.* [A] umgruppieren; (*into classes*) neu einteilen (**into** in + *Akk.*); [B] (*Mil.: reorganize*) neu formieren ‹Truppen›. ❷ *v.i.* [A] (*form a new group*) sich neu gruppieren; (*meet again*) wieder zusammenkommen; [B] (*Mil.*) sich neu formieren

**regular** /'regjʊlə(r)/ ❶ *adj.* [A] (*recurring uniformly, habitual, orderly*) regelmäßig; geregelt ‹Arbeit›; fest ‹Anstellung, Reihenfolge›; **~ customer** Stammkunde, *der*/-kundin, *die;* **~ staff** Stammpersonal, *das;* **~ doctor** Hausarzt, *der;* **our ~ postman** unser [gewohnter] Briefträger; **get ~ work** ‹Freiberufler:› regelmäßig Aufträge bekommen; **my bowels are ~, I am ~:** ich habe regelmäßig Stuhlgang; **what's the ~ procedure for opening a deposit account?** wie richtet man normalerweise ein Sparkonto ein?; **her periods are always ~:** sie bekommt ihre Periode immer regelmäßig; **have** *or* **lead a ~ life** ein geregeltes Leben führen; ⇒ *also* **hour** C; [B] (*evenly arranged, symmetrical*) regelmäßig; [C] (*correct*) angemessen ‹Verhalten, Verfahren›; [D] (*properly qualified*) ausgebildet; **~ army** reguläre Armee; **~ soldiers** Berufssoldaten; [E] (*Ling.*) regelmäßig; [F] (*coll.: thorough*) richtig (*ugs.*); [G] (*Geom.*) regelmäßig; regulär (*fachspr.*); [H] (*Eccl.*) Regular‹kleriker, -geistlicher›.
❷ *n.* [A] (*coll.: ~ customer, visitor, etc.*) Stammkunde, *der*/-kundin, *die;* (*in pub*) Stammgast, *der;* [B] (*coll.: permanently employed person*) Festangestellte, *der/die;* [C] (*soldier*) Berufssoldat, *der;* [D] (*Amer.: gasoline*) Normal, *das* (*ugs.*); [E] (*Eccl.*) Regularkleriker, *der*

**regularise** ⇒ **regularize**

**regularity** /regjʊ'lærɪtɪ/ *n.* [A] Regelmäßigkeit, *die;* [B] (*Ling.*) regelmäßige Flexion

**regularize** /'regjʊləraɪz/ *v.t.* [A] (*make regular*) regeln; (*by law*) gesetzlich regeln *od.* festlegen; **~ the proceedings** vorschriftsmäßig verfahren; [B] (*make steady*) stabilisieren ‹Atmung, Puls, Spannung›

**regularly** /'regjʊləlɪ/ *adv.* [A] (*at fixed times*) regelmäßig; (*constantly*) ständig; [B] (*steadily*) gleichmäßig; [C] (*symmetrically*) regelmäßig ‹bauen, anlegen›; [D] (*in an orderly manner*) korrekt

**regulate** /'regjʊleɪt/ *v.t.* [A] (*control*) regeln; (*subject to restriction*) begrenzen; [B] (*adjust*) regulieren; einstellen ‹Apparat, Maschine, Zeit›; [richtig ein]stellen ‹Uhr›; **she ~s her hours to fit in with his** sie passt sich ihm in ihrer Zeiteinteilung an; [C] (*moderate*) senken ‹Ausgaben›; (*adapt*) anpassen ‹Lebensstil, Verhalten, Gewohnheit›; **~ one's lifestyle to fit in with sth.** seinen Lebensstil an etw. (*Akk.*) anpassen

**regulation** /regʊ'leɪʃn/ *n.* [A] (*regulating*) Regelung, *die;* (*of quantity, speed*) Regulierung, *die;* (*of machine*) Einstellen, *das;* (*of lifestyle, conduct, habit, mind*) Anpassung, *die;* (*of expenses*) Senkung, *die;* [B] (*rule*) Vorschrift, *die;* **be against ~s** vorschriftswidrig sein; **school/safety/fire ~s** Schulordnung, *die*/Sicherheits-/Brandschutzvorschriften; [C] *attrib.* (*according to rule*) vorgeschrieben ‹Geschwindigkeit›; vorschriftsmäßig ‹Kleidung›; (*usual*) üblich ‹Größe, Kleidung, Frisur›

**regulative** /'regjʊlətɪv/ *adj.* regulativ; **~ mechanism** Regelmechanismus, *der*

**regulator** /'regjʊleɪtə(r)/ *n.* [A] (*device*) Regler, *der;* (*of clock, watch*) Gangregler, *der;* [B] (*clock*) Normaluhr, *die;* Regulator, *der* (*veralt.*)

**regulatory** /'regjʊlətərɪ/ *adj.* regulativ (*geh.*); **~ body/authority** Aufsichtsgremium, *das*/-behörde, *die*

**regurgitate** /ri:'gɜ:dʒɪteɪt/ *v.t.* [A] ‹Person:› erbrechen ‹Essen›; ‹Tier:› herauswürgen ‹Beute›; (*Med.*) zurückpumpen ‹Blut›; [B] (*fig.*) ausspucken

**rehabilitate** /ri:hə'bɪlɪteɪt/ *v.t.* rehabilitieren; renovieren, wieder herrichten ‹altes Gebäude›; **~ [back into society]** wieder [in die Gesellschaft] eingliedern

**rehabilitation** /ri:həbɪlɪ'teɪʃn/ *n.* Rehabilitation, *die;* (*of building*) Renovierung, *die;* Instandsetzung, *die;* **~ [in society]** Wiedereingliederung [in die Gesellschaft]

**rehash** ❶ /ri:'hæʃ/ *v.t.* aufwärmen; **just ~ a text** einen Text ein bisschen aufpolieren (*ugs.*). ❷ /'ri:hæʃ/ *n.* [A] (*restatement*) Aufguss, *der* (*abwertend*); [B] (*act or process of restating*) (*of old arguments*) Aufwärmen, *das;* **do a ~ of the text** den Text ein bisschen aufpolieren (*ugs.*)

**rehearsal** /rɪ'hɜ:sl/ *n.* [A] (*Theatre, Mus., etc.*) Probe, *die;* **have a ~/~s** proben (**of** *Akk.*); **the play is now in ~:** das Stück wird jetzt geprobt; ⇒ *also* **dress rehearsal**; [B] (*recounting*) Aufzählung, *die;* (*recital*) Vortrag, *der;* **give a ~ of** aufzählen ‹Ereignisse›

**rehearse** /rɪ'hɜ:s/ *v.t.* [A] (*Theatre, Mus., etc.*) proben; [B] (*recite*) sprechen ‹Gebet›; rezitieren ‹Gedicht, Stück›; (*repeat*) wiederholen; **~ sth. again to sb.** jmdm. etw. noch einmal erzählen; [C] (*enumerate*) aufzählen; [D] (*train*) proben mit ‹Schauspieler, Musiker›; **be ~d in the correct use of sth.** in den korrekten Gebrauch von etw. eingeübt werden

**reheat** /ri:'hi:t/ *v.t.* wieder erwärmen; aufwärmen ‹Essen›

**rehouse** /ri:'haʊz/ *v.t.* umquartieren

**rehousing** /ri:'haʊzɪŋ/ *n.* Umquartierung, *die*

**Reich** /raɪk, raɪx/ *n.* (*Hist.*) [Deutsches] Reich; **the First/Second ~:** das Heilige Römische/Deutsche Reich; **the Third ~:** das Dritte Reich

**reign** /reɪn/ ❶ *n.* Herrschaft, *die;* (*of monarch also*) Regentschaft, *die;* **in the ~ of King Charles** während der Regentschaft König Karls; ⇒ *also* **terror** A. ❷ *v.i.* [A] (*hold office*) herrschen (**over** über + *Akk.*); **~ing champion** amtierender Meister/amtierende Meisterin; ⇒ *also* **supreme** 1 B; [B] (*prevail*) herrschen; **silence ~s** es herrscht Ruhe

**reignite** /ri:ɪg'naɪt/ ❶ *v.t.* wieder anzünden; wieder entzünden ‹Gas›. ❷ *v.i.* sich wieder entzünden

**Reilly** ⇒ **Riley**

**reimburse** /ri:ɪm'bɜ:s/ *v.t.* [zurück]erstatten ‹[Un]kosten, Spesen›; entschädigen ‹Person›; **~ sb. for** jmdm. [zurück]erstatten ‹[Un]kosten, Spesen›; jmdm. ersetzen ‹Verlust›

**reimbursement** /ri:ɪm'bɜ:smənt/ *n.* Rückzahlung, *die;* (*of expenses*) Erstattung, *die*

**reimport** /ri:ɪm'pɔ:t/ *v.t.* reimportieren (**into** nach)

**reimpose** /ri:ɪm'pəʊz/ *v.t.* erneuern; wieder erheben ‹Zoll, Steuer›; erneut verhängen ‹Kriegsrecht, Sanktionen›; wieder anordnen ‹Rationierung›

**rein** /reɪn/ ❶ *n.* [A] Zügel, *der;* **keep a child on ~s** ein Kind am Laufgurt führen; **draw ~:** die Zügel anziehen; **give one's horse the ~[s]** [seinem Pferd] die Zügel schießen lassen; [B] (*fig.*) Zügel, *der;* **hold the ~s** die Zügel in der Hand haben; **give [full] ~ to sth.** einer Sache (*Dat.*) die Zügel schießen lassen; **keep a tight ~ on** an der Kandare halten ‹Person›; im Zaum halten ‹Gefühle›; in Schranken halten ‹Ausgaben›; **assume/drop the ~s of government/power** die Amtsgeschäfte/Macht übernehmen/abgeben; ⇒ *also* **free** 1 C.
❷ *v.t.* [A] (*check, guide*) lenken ‹Pferd›; **~ to a halt** zum Stehen bringen ‹Pferd›; [B] (*restrain*) im Zaum halten ‹Zunge›

**~ 'back** ❶ *v.t.* zügeln ‹Pferd›. ❷ *v.i.* die Zügel anziehen

**~ 'in** ❶ *v.t.* (*check, lit. or fig.*) zügeln. ❷ *v.i.* Halt machen

**~ 'up** ❶ *v.t.* zügeln ‹Pferd›. ❷ *v.i.* die Zügel anziehen

**reincarnate** /ri:ɪn'kɑ:neɪt/ *v.t.* (*Relig.*) reinkarnieren; **be ~d** wieder geboren werden

**reincarnation** /ri:ɪnkɑ:'neɪʃn/ *n.* (*Relig.*) Reinkarnation, *die;* Wiedergeburt, *die*

**reindeer** /'reɪndɪə(r)/ *n., pl. same* Ren[tier], *das*

**'reindeer moss** *n.* (*Bot.*) Rentierflechte, *die*

**reinforce** /ri:ɪn'fɔ:s/ *v.t.* verstärken ‹Truppen, Mauer, Festung, Stoff›; aufstocken ‹Vorräte›; stärken ‹Partei, Gesundheit›; erhöhen ‹Anzahl›; untermauern ‹Argument›; bestätigen ‹Behauptung›; **~ sb.'s opinion/determination** jmdn. in seiner Meinung/Entschlossenheit bestärken; **~d concrete** Stahlbeton, *der;* **~ the message** was man zu verstehen geben wollte, unterstreichen *od.* bekräftigen

**reinforcement** /ri:ɪn'fɔ:smənt/ *n.* [A] (*of bridge etc.*) Verstärkung, *die;* (*of provisions*) Aufstockung, *die;* (*of numbers*) Zunahme, *die;* (*of argument*) Untermauerung, *die;* (*of determination*) Bestärkung, *die;* [B] **~[s]** (*additional men etc.*) Verstärkung, *die;* [C] (*on punch holes*) Verstärkungsring, *der;* (*for elbow of garment*) Schoner, *der;* (*for buckled girder*) Armierung, *die*

**reinsert** /ri:ɪn'sɜ:t/ *v.t.* noch einmal einwerfen ‹Münze›; ‹Arzt:› noch einmal einstechen ‹Nadel›; noch einmal setzen ‹Inserat›

**reinstate** /ri:ɪn'steɪt/ *v.t.* wieder herstellen ‹Recht und Ordnung›; wieder einstellen ‹Arbeiter›; (*in position*) wieder einsetzen; **be ~d in sb.'s favour** jmds. Gunst wiedergewonnen haben; **be ~d on the throne** wieder auf den Thron gehoben werden

**reinstatement** /ri:ɪn'steɪtmənt/ *n.* (*of law and order*) Wiederherstellung, *die;* **his ~ in the job** seine Wiedereinstellung

**reinsurance** /ri:ɪn'ʃʊərəns/ *n.* Rückversicherung, *die;* (*extension*) Verlängerung der Versicherung

**reinsure** /ri:ɪn'ʃʊə(r)/ *v.t.* rückversichern; (*extend*) die Versicherung verlängern für

**reinter** /ri:ɪn'tɜ:(r)/ *v.t.*, **-rr-** wieder begraben

**reinterpret** /ri:ɪn'tɜ:prɪt/ *v.t.* (*interpret afresh*) noch einmal interpretieren; (*give different interpretation*) neu interpretieren

**reinvent** /ri:ɪn'vent/ *v.t.* ⇒ **wheel** 1 A

**reinvest** /ri:ɪn'vest/ *v.t.* reinvestieren (*fachspr.*); wieder anlegen ‹Kapital›

**reinvestment** /ri:ɪn'vestmənt/ *n.* (*fresh investment*) Reinvestition, *die* (*fachspr.*); Wiederanlage, *die*

**reinvigorate** /ri:ɪn'vɪgəreɪt/ *v.t.* neu beleben; **feel ~d** sich gestärkt fühlen

**reissue** /ri:'ɪʃu:, ri:'ɪsju:/ ❶ *v.t.* neu herausbringen. ❷ *n.* Neuauflage, *die;* (*of film*) Wiederveröffentlichung, *die*

**reiterate** /ri:'ɪtəreɪt/ *v.t.* wiederholen

**reiteration** /ri:ɪtə'reɪʃn/ *n.* Wiederholung, *die*

**reject** ❶ /rɪ'dʒekt/ *v.t.* [A] ablehnen; abweisen ‹Freier›; verweigern ‹Nahrung›; zurückweisen ‹Bitte, Annäherungsversuch›; [B] (*Med.*) nicht vertragen ‹Bluttransfusion, Nahrung, Medizin›; abstoßen ‹Transplantat›. ❷ /'ri:dʒekt/ *n.* (*person*) Ausgestoßene, *der/die;* (*Mil.*) Untaugliche, *der/die;* (*thing*) Ausschuss, *der*

**rejection** /rɪ'dʒekʃn/ *n.* [A] ⇒ **reject** 1 A: Ablehnung, *die;* Abweisung, *die;* Verweigerung, *die;* Zurückweisung, *die;* **parental ~:** Ablehnung durch die Eltern; [B] (*Med.*) Abstoßung, *die;* **~ of food indicates that ...:** dass der Körper Nahrung nicht verträgt, lässt erkennen, dass ...

**re'jection slip** *n.* Absage, *die*

**rejig** /ri:'dʒɪg/ *v.t.*, **-gg-** umrüsten (**with** auf + *Akk.*); (*coll.: rearrange*) ummodeln

**rejoice** /rɪˈdʒɔɪs/ *v.i.* **A** (*feel great joy*) sich freuen (**over, at** über + *Akk.*); **~ in the Lord!** freut euch im Herrn!; **B** (*make merry*) feiern
**~ in** *v.i.* **A** (*joc.: be called by*) **~ in a name/title** sich mit einem Namen/Titel schmücken (*scherzh.*); **B** (*joc.: have*) sich erfreuen (+ *Gen.*); gesegnet sein mit (*oft spött.*)

**rejoicing** /rɪˈdʒɔɪsɪŋ/ *n.* **A** **[sounds of] ~:** Jubel, *der;* **B** *in pl.* (*celebrations*) Feier, *die*

**rejoin**[1] /rɪˈdʒɔɪn/ *v.t.* (*reply*) erwidern (**to** auf + *Akk.*)

**rejoin**[2] /riːˈdʒɔɪn/ **1** *v.t.* **A** (*join again*) wieder stoßen zu ‹Regiment›; wieder eintreten in (+ *Akk.*) ‹Partei, Verein›; **~ each other** sich wieder treffen; **~ one's ship** wieder an Bord gehen; **B** (*reunite*) wieder zusammenfügen ‹Bruchstücke›; ‹Verkehrsteilnehmer:› wieder kommen auf (+ *Akk.*) ‹Straße, Autobahn›; ‹Straße:› wieder [ein]münden in (+ *Akk.*) ‹Straße, Autobahn›. **2** *v.i.* ‹Personen:› sich wieder treffen; ‹Straßen:› wieder zusammentreffen

**rejoinder** /rɪˈdʒɔɪndə(r)/ *n.* Erwiderung, *die* (**to** auf + *Akk.*)

**rejuvenate** /rɪˈdʒuːvəneɪt/ *v.t.* verjüngen ‹Person, Haut›; neu beleben ‹Institution, wirtschaftliches/gesellschaftliches Leben›

**rejuvenation** /rɪdʒuːvəˈneɪʃn/ *n.* Verjüngung, *die;* (*of institutions, economic life, social life*) Neubelebung, *die*

**rekindle** /riːˈkɪndl/ **1** *v.t.* **A** (*relight*) wieder anfachen; **B** (*fig.: reawaken*) wieder entfachen ‹Liebe, Leidenschaft›; wieder aufleben lassen ‹Sehnsucht, Verlangen, Hoffnung›. **2** *v.i.* sich wieder entzünden; (*fig.*) wieder aufflammen

**relapse** /rɪˈlæps/ **1** *v.i.* ‹Kranker:› einen Rückfall bekommen; **~ into** zurückfallen in (+ *Akk.*) ‹Götzendienst, Barbarei›; **~ into drug-taking/shoplifting** rückfällig werden [und wieder Drogen nehmen/Ladendiebstähle begehen]; **~ into silence/lethargy** wieder in Schweigen/Lethargie verfallen. **2** *n.* Rückfall, *der* (**into** in + *Akk.*)

**relate** /rɪˈleɪt/ **1** *v.t.* **A** (*tell*) erzählen ‹Geschichte›; erzählen von ‹Abenteuer›; **B** (*bring into relation*) in Zusammenhang bringen (**to, with** mit); **~ two things** eine Verbindung zwischen zwei Dingen herstellen; **C** (*establish relation or connection between*) einen Zusammenhang herstellen zwischen. **2** *v.i.* **A** **~ to** (*have reference*) ‹Vorlesung:› handeln von; ‹Behauptung, Frage, Angelegenheit:› in Zusammenhang stehen mit; betreffen ‹Person›; **B** **~ to** (*feel involved or connected with*) eine Beziehung haben zu

**related** /rɪˈleɪtɪd/ *adj.* **A** (*by kinship or marriage*) verwandt (**to** mit); **~ by marriage** verschwägert; **they are all ~ [to one another]** sie sind alle miteinander verwandt; **B** (*connected*) miteinander in Zusammenhang stehend; verwandt ‹Sprache, Begriff, Art, Spezies, Fach›

**relation** /rɪˈleɪʃn/ *n.* **A** (*connection*) Beziehung, *die* (**of** ... **and** zwischen ... und); Zusammenhang, *der* (**of** ... **and** zwischen ... und); **be out of all ~ to** in keinem Verhältnis stehen zu ‹Kosten, geleisteter Arbeit›; **have some ~ to** in einem gewissen Zusammenhang stehen zu ; **in** *or* **with ~ to** in Bezug auf (+ *Akk.*); **the ~s expressed by prepositions** die durch Präpositionen ausgedrückten Bezüge; ⇒ *also* **bear**[2] 1 C; **B** *in pl.* (*dealings*) (*with parents, police*) Verhältnis, *das* (**with** zu); (*with country*) Beziehungen (**with** zu, mit); (*sexual intercourse*) intime Beziehungen (**with** zu); **trading ~s** Handelsbeziehungen; **C** (*kin, relative*) Verwandte, *der/die;* **what ~ is he to you?** wie ist er mit dir verwandt?; **is she any ~ [to you]?** ist sie mit dir verwandt?; **D** (*narrative, account*) Erzählung, *die;* (*of details*) Aufzählung, *die;* **E** (*Law*) Anzeige, *die;* **at the** *or* **by ~ of** auf Anzeige (*Akk.*) von

**relationship** /rɪˈleɪʃnʃɪp/ *n.* **A** (*mutual tie*) Beziehung, *die* (**with** zu); **have a good/bad ~ with sb.** zu jmdm. ein gutes/schlechtes Verhältnis haben; **doctor-patient ~:** Verhältnis zwischen Arzt und Patient; **B** (*kinship*) Verwandtschaftsverhältnis, *das;* **what is your ~ to him?** in welchem Verwandtschaftsverhältnis stehst du zu ihm?; **C** (*connection*) Beziehung, *die;* (*between cause and effect*) Zusammenhang, *der;* **D** (*sexual*) Verhältnis, *das*

**relative** /ˈrelətɪv/ **1** *n.* **A** (*family connection*) Verwandte, *der/die;* **have many ~s** eine große Verwandtschaft haben; **B** (*related species*) Verwandte, *der/die;* **C** (*Ling.*) Relativ[um], *das.*
**2** *adj.* **A** (*corresponding*) relativ; **the ~ value of British and German currency is ...:** das Wertverhältnis von der englischen zur deutschen Währung beträgt ...; **B** (*comparative*) jeweilig; **the ~ costs of a and b** die Kostenrelation zwischen a und b; **with ~ calmness** relativ gelassen; **C** (*defined in relation to sth. else*) relativ ‹Dichte, Feuchtigkeit›; **~ positions of troops** Truppenkonstellation, *die;* **~ densities/heights** Dichte-/Höhenrelation, *die;* **~ majority** (*Brit. Polit.*) relative Mehrheit; **D** (*proportioned to sth. else*) **be ~ to sth.** sich nach etw. richten; **a large population ~ to the town's size** eine im Verhältnis zur Größe der Stadt beachtliche Einwohnerzahl; **E** (*implying comparison with sth. else*) relativ ‹Begriff›; **F** (*conditioned by relation to sth. else*) abhängig (**to** von); **be ~ to sth./sb.** ‹Geschmack, Größe:› durch etw./jmdn. relativiert werden; **G** (*correlative*) sich gegenseitig bedingend; **'parents' and 'children' are ~ terms** die Begriffe „Eltern" und „Kinder" bedingen sich gegenseitig; **H** (*having reference to sth.*) **~ to** in Zusammenhang mit; **give me the grid references ~ to your location** geben Sie mir die Koordinaten Ihres Standorts; **I** (*Mus.*) parallel ‹Dur-, Molltonart›

**relative: ~ 'adjective** *n.* (*Ling.*) Relativadjektiv, *das;* **~ 'adverb** *n.* (*Ling.*) Relativadverb, *das;* **~ 'clause** *n.* (*Ling.*) Relativsatz, *der*

**relatively** /ˈrelətɪvlɪ/ *adv.* relativ; verhältnismäßig

**relative 'pronoun** *n.* Relativpronomen, *das*

**relativise** ⇒ **relativize**

**relativism** /ˈrelətɪvɪzm/ *n.* (*Philos.*) Relativismus, *der*

**relativist** /ˈrelətɪvɪst/ *n.* (*Philos.*) Relativist, *der*/Relativistin, *die*

**relativistic** /relətɪˈvɪstɪk/ *adj.* **A** relativistisch; **B** (*Phys.*) Relativitäts‹theorie, -korrektion›

**relativity** /reləˈtɪvɪtɪ/ *n.* **A** (*fact of being relative*) Abhängigkeit, *die* (**to** von); **B** (*Phys.*) Relativität, *die;* **~ theory, the theory of ~:** die Relativitätstheorie; **C** (*Econ.*) (*of posts*) Stellenstaffelung, *die;* (*of salaries*) Gehaltsstaffelung, *die;* **campaign for ~ in pay with men** ‹Frauen:› sich für die tarifliche Gleichstellung mit den Männern einsetzen

**relativize** /ˈrelətɪvaɪz/ *v.t.* relativieren

**relax** /rɪˈlæks/ **1** *v.t.* **A** (*make less tense*) entspannen ‹Muskel, Körper[teil]›; lockern ‹Muskel, Feder, Griff›; (*fig.*) lockern; **winter ~ed its grip on the landscape** (*fig.*) der Winter ließ die Landschaft aus seiner Umklammerung; **B** (*make less strict*) lockern ‹Gesetz, Disziplin, Sitten›; **C** (*slacken*) nachlassen in (+ *Dat.*) ‹Bemühungen, Aufmerksamkeit›; verlangsamen ‹Tempo›; **he began to ~ his attention** seine Aufmerksamkeit ließ allmählich nach.
**2** *v.i.* **A** (*become less tense*) sich entspannen; **his face** *or* **features ~ed into a smile** sein Gesicht entspannte sich zu einem Lächeln; **B** (*slacken*) nachlassen (**in** in + *Dat.*); **C** (*become less stern*) sich mäßigen (**in** in + *Dat.*); **D** (*cease effort*) sich entspannen; ausspannen; (*stop worrying, calm down*) sich beruhigen; **let's just ~!** (*stop worrying!*) nur ruhig Blut!

**relaxant** /riːˈlæksənt/ *n.* (*Med.*) Relaxans, *das*

**relaxation** /riːlækˈseɪʃn/ *n.* **A** (*recreation*) Freizeitbeschäftigung, *die;* **play tennis as a** *or* **for ~:** zur Entspannung Tennis spielen; **B** (*cessation of effort*) Erholung, *die* (**from** von); **find time for ~:** Zeit für Muße finden; **C** (*reduction of physical tension; also fig.*) Lockerung, *die;* **D** (*Phys.*) Relaxation, *die*

**relaxed** /rɪˈlækst/ *adj.* **A** (*informal, not anxious*) entspannt, gelöst ‹Atmosphäre, Lächeln, Gefühl, Person›; **she's a very ~ person** she ist ein sehr gelassener Mensch *od.* die Gelassenheit in Person; **at a ~ pace** gemächlich; **B** (*not strict or exact*) gelockert ‹Regel, Beschränkung›; locker ‹Moral›

**relaxing** /rɪˈlæksɪŋ/ *adj.* entspannend; erholsam; **have a ~ bath** zur Entspannung ein Bad nehmen

**relay** **1** /ˈriːleɪ/ *n.* **A** (*gang*) Schicht, *die;* **work in ~s** schichtweise arbeiten; **B** (*race*) Staffel, *die;* **C** (*vehicles*) **~ [of cars]** [Fahrzeug]stafette, *die;* **D** (*driving operation*) Fahrzeugstafette, *die;* **E** (*Electr.*) Relais, *das;* **protective ~:** Schutzrelais, *das;* **F** (*Radio, Telev.*) **radio ~:** Richtfunkverbindung, *die;* **~ station** Relaisstation, *die;* **G** (*transmission*) Übertragung, *die;* **direct ~:** Direktübertragung, *die.*
**2** /riːˈleɪ, ˈriːleɪ/ *v.t.* **A** (*pass on*) weiterleiten; **~ a message to sb. that ...:** jmdm. ausrichten *od.* mitteilen, dass ...; **B** (*Radio, Telev., Teleph.*) übertragen; **C** (*transport*) [in einer Stafette] befördern; **form a chain to ~ water to the scene of the fire** eine Kette bilden, um Wasser zur Brandstelle durchzureichen

**re-lay** /riːˈleɪ/ *v.t.*, **re-laid** /riːˈleɪd/ wieder verlegen ‹Teppich, Fliesen›; neu belegen ‹Fußboden, Straße›; (*after damage*) neu [ver]legen ‹Rohr, Leitung›

**'relay race** *n.* (*Running, Hurdling*) Staffellauf, *der;* (*Swimming*) Staffelschwimmen, *das;* **the 4 × 100 metres ~:** die 4 × 100-Meter-Staffel; **hurdles ~:** Hürdenstaffel, *die*

**release** /rɪˈliːs/ **1** *v.t.* **A** (*free*) freilassen ‹Tier, Häftling, Sklaven›; (*from imprisonment, jail*) entlassen (**from** aus); (*from bondage, trap*) befreien (**from** aus); (*from pain*) erlösen (**from** von); (*from promise, obligation, vow*) entbinden (**from** von); (*from work*) freistellen (**from** von); **B** (*let go, let fall*) loslassen; lösen ‹Handbremse, Sprungfeder›; ausklinken ‹Bombe›; **~ one's hold** *or* **grip on sth.** etw. loslassen; **~ the shutter** (*Photog.*) den Verschluss auslösen; **~ the pressure** den Druck verringern; **C** (*make known*) veröffentlichen ‹Erklärung, Nachricht›; (*issue*) herausbringen ‹Film, Schallplatte, Produkt›; **D** (*emit*) ablassen ‹Dampf›; freisetzen ‹Energie, Strahlung›.
**2** *n.* **A** (*act of freeing*) ⇒ **1** A: Freilassung, *die;* Entlassung, *die;* Befreiung, *die;* Erlösung, *die;* Entbindung, *die;* Freistellung, *die;* **B** (*of published item*) Veröffentlichung, *die;* **when does the film go out on general ~?** wann kommt der Film in die Kinos?; **the film/album is scheduled for ~ in the autumn** der Film/das Album soll im Herbst herausgebracht werden *od.* herauskommen; **a new ~ by Bob Dylan** eine neue Platte *od.* eine Neuveröffentlichung von Bob Dylan; **the film is a recent ~:** der Film ist erst vor kurzem herausgekommen; **C** (*handle, lever, button*) Auslöser, *der;* **carriage ~:** Wagenrücklauf, *der;* **D** (*of steam*) Ablassen, *das;* (*of pressure*) Verringerung, *die;* (*of energy, radiation*) Freisetzung, *die*

**relegate** /ˈrelɪgeɪt/ *v.t.* **A** (*dismiss, consign*) **~ sb. to the position** *or* **status of ...:** jmdn. zu ... degradieren; **~ sth. to the rubbish bin** etw. in den Mülleimer wandern lassen; **B** (*Sport*) absteigen lassen; **be ~d** absteigen (**to** in + *Akk.*); **C** (*hand over*) weiterleiten (**to** an + *Akk.*); **D** (*banish*) verbannen

**relegation** /relɪˈgeɪʃn/ *n.* **A** (*action of dismissing, consigning*) Degradierung, *die;* **her ~ to the position of ...:** ihre Degradierung zu ...; **B** (*Sport*) Abstieg, *der;* **C** (*action or state of banishment*) Verbannung, *die*

**relent** /rɪˈlent/ *v.i.* nachgeben; (*yield to compassion*) Mitleid zeigen; ‹Wetter:› besser werden

**relentless** /rɪˈlentlɪs/ *adj.* unerbittlich; erbarmungslos ‹Necken›; schonungslos ‹Kritik, Heftigkeit›

**relentlessly** /rɪˈlentlɪslɪ/ *adv.* unerbittlich; erbarmungslos ‹necken›; schonungslos ‹kritisieren›

**relevance** /ˈrelɪvəns/, **relevancy** /ˈrelɪvənsɪ/ *n.* Relevanz, die (**to** für); **what ~ does it have to this?** inwiefern ist es dafür

r

relevant?; **be of ~ to sth.** für etw. relevant sein

**relevant** /ˈrelɪvənt/ *adj.* relevant (**to** für); wichtig ‹Information, Dokument›; entsprechend ‹Formular›; zuständig ‹Person›; **~ to the case** sachdienlich (*Amtsspr.*); **is this question ~ to the argument?** tut diese Frage etwas zur Sache?

**reliability** /rɪlaɪəˈbɪlɪtɪ/ *n., no pl.* Zuverlässigkeit, *die*

**reliable** /rɪˈlaɪəbl/ *adj.* zuverlässig

**reliableness** /rɪˈlaɪəblnɪs/ ⇒ **reliability**

**reliably** /rɪˈlaɪəblɪ/ *adv.* zuverlässig; **I am ~ informed that ...:** ich habe aus zuverlässiger Quelle erfahren, dass ...

**reliance** /rɪˈlaɪəns/ *n.* (*trust, confidence*) Vertrauen, *das* (**in** zu, **on** auf + *Akk.*); (*dependence*) Abhängigkeit, *die* (**on** von); **she resented her ~ on his money** es ärgerte sie, dass sie auf sein Geld angewiesen war; **have ~ on** *or* **in sb./sth.** zu jmdm./etw. Vertrauen haben; **place much ~ [up]on sb.** großes Vertrauen in jmdn. setzen; **there is little ~ to be placed on sth./sb.** auf etw./jmdn. ist kaum Verlass

**reliant** /rɪˈlaɪənt/ *adj.* (*dependent*) **be ~ on sb./sth.** von jmdm./etw. abhängig sein; (*for help also*) auf jmdn./etw. angewiesen sein

**relic** /ˈrelɪk/ *n.* **A** (*Relig.*) Reliquie, *die;* **B** (*surviving trace or memorial*) Überbleibsel, *das* (*ugs.*); Relikt, *das;* **C** (*remains, residue*) Überrest, *der;* **D** (*derog./joc.: old or old-fashioned person or thing*) Fossil, *das* (*fig.*); **he is a ~ from the Sixties** er ist noch aus den Sechzigerjahren übrig geblieben

**relict** /ˈrelɪkt/ *n.* **A** (*arch.: widow*) Witib, *die* (*veralt.*); **B** (*Biol., Geog., Geol.*) Relikt, *das*

**relief**[1] /rɪˈliːf/ *n.* **A** (*alleviation, deliverance*) Erleichterung, *die;* **give** *or* **bring [sb.] ~ [from pain]** [jmdm.] [Schmerz]linderung verschaffen *od.* bringen; **it was with great ~ that I heard the news of ...:** mit großer Erleichterung habe ich die Nachricht vom ... vernommen; **breathe** *or* **heave a sigh of ~:** erleichtert aufatmen; **it was a ~ to take off his tight shoes/to bump into somebody he knew** es war eine Wohltat für ihn, die engen Schuhe auszuziehen/dass ihm ein Bekannter über den Weg lief; **what a ~!, that's a ~!** da bin ich aber erleichtert!; **B** (*that which makes a change from monotony*) Abwechslung, *die;* ; ⇒ *also* **comic** 1 C; **light**[2] 1 A; **C** (*assistance*) Hilfe, *die;* (*financial state assistance*) Sozialhilfe, *die; attrib.* Hilfs‹fond, -organisation, -komitee›; **~ party** *or* **team** Rettungsmannschaft, *die;* **~ worker** Rettungshelfer, *der*/-helferin, *die;* (*in disaster*) Katastrophenhelfer, *der*/-helferin, *die;* **go/live on ~:** Fürsorge beantragen/von der Fürsorge leben; **go** *or* **come to sb.'s ~:** jmdm. zu Hilfe eilen *od.* kommen; **D** (*Brit. Hist.: assistance*) Fürsorge, *die;* **E** (*replacement of person*) Ablösung, *die; attrib.* **~ watchman/driver/troops** ablösender Wachmann/Fahrer/ablösende Truppen; **~ sentry** Wachablösung, *die;* **F** (*Mil.*) (*reinforcement*) Verstärkung, *die;* (*raising of siege*) Entsatz, *der;* **G** (*Law: redress*) Entschädigung, *die*

**relief**[2] *n.* **A** (*Art*) **works in ~:** Reliefarbeiten; **high/low ~:** Hoch-/Flachrelief, *das;* **B** (*piece of sculpture*) Relief, *das;* **C** (*appearance of being done in ~*) reliefartiges Aussehen; **stand out in strong ~ against sth.** sich scharf gegen etw. abheben; (*fig.*) in krassem Gegensatz zu etw. stehen; **bring out in [full] ~** (*lit. or fig.*) deutlich herausarbeiten

**relief: ~ agency** *n.* Hilfsorganisation, *die;* Hilfswerk, *das;* **~ bus, ~ coach** *ns.* (*additional*) Entlastungsbus, *der;* (*as replacement*) Ersatzbus, *der;* **~ map** *n.* Reliefkarte, *die;* **~ road** *n.* Entlastungsstraße, *die;* **~ supplies** *n. pl.* Hilfsgüter *Pl.;* **~ worker** *n.* Helfer, *der*

**relieve** /rɪˈliːv/ *v.t.* **A** (*lessen, mitigate*) lindern; helfen (+ *Dat.*) ‹Notleidenden›; verringern ‹Dampfdruck, Anspannung›; unterbrechen ‹Eintönigkeit›; erleichtern ‹Gewissen›; (*remove*) abbauen ‹Anspannung›; stillen ‹Schmerzen›; (*remove or lessen monotony of*) auflockern; **I am** *or* **feel ~d to hear that ...:** es erleichtert mich zu hören, dass ...; **B** (*release from duty*) ablösen ‹Wache, Truppen›; **C ~ sb.** (*of task, duty*) jmdn. entbinden (**of** von); (*of responsibility, load*) jmdm. abnehmen (**of** *Akk.*); (*from debt*) jmdm. erlassen (**from** *Akk.*); (*of burden, duty, from sorrow, worry*) jmdn. befreien (**of, from** von); **~ sb.'s mind of doubt** jmdm. die Zweifel nehmen; **D ~ sb. of sth.** (*joc.: steal from*) jmdn. um etw. erleichtern (*scherzh.*); **E ~ one's feelings** seinen Gefühlen Luft machen; **F ~ oneself** (*empty the bladder or bowels*) sich erleichtern (*verhüll.*); **G** (*release from a post*) entbinden (**of, from** von); (*dismiss*) entheben (*geh.*) (**of, from** *Gen.*); **~ sb. from duty** *or* **of his post** *or* **office** *or* **duties** jmdn. ablösen; **H** (*Mil.: free from siege*) entsetzen (*bes. Mil.*); befreien

**religion** /rɪˈlɪdʒn/ *n.* **A** Religion, *die;* **freedom of ~:** Glaubensfreiheit, *die;* **what is your ~?** welcher Religion gehörst du an?; **that's against my ~:** das verstößt gegen meinen Glauben; **no thanks, I won't have a cigarette; it's against my ~** (*joc.*) nein danke, ich möchte keine Zigarette, ich bin überzeugter Nichtraucher; ⇒ *also* **established** C; **B** (*recognition of God*) Glaube, *der;* **get ~** (*coll./joc.*) fromm werden; **C** (*object of devotion or obligation*) **he makes a ~ of snooker** Snooker ist ihm heilig; **she makes a ~ of keeping her house clean** es ist ihr eine heilige Pflicht, ihr Haus sauber zu halten (*iron.*)

**religious** /rɪˈlɪdʒəs/ ❶ *adj.* **A** (*pious*) religiös; fromm; **B** (*concerned with religion*) Glaubens‹freiheit, -eifer›; Religions‹freiheit, -unterricht, -kenntnisse›; religiös ‹Überzeugung, Zentrum›; **C** (*of monastic order*) religiös ‹Orden›; **~ community** Ordensgemeinschaft, *die;* **~ house** Kloster, *das;* **D** (*scrupulous*) peinlich ‹Sorgfalt, Genauigkeit, Ordnung›; **with ~ care** *or* **exactitude** sehr gewissenhaft ‹arbeiten›; **pay ~ attention to details** peinlich genau auf Details achten. ❷ *n., pl. same* Ordensmitglied, *das*

**religiously** /rɪˈlɪdʒəslɪ/ *adv.* **A** (*piously, reverently*) inbrünstig ‹beten›; ehrfürchtig ‹verehren, niederknien›; **B** (*conscientiously, scrupulously*) gewissenhaft ‹beachten, durchsehen, verbessern›; peinlich genau ‹sauber machen, verbessern›

**reline** /riːˈlaɪn/ *v.t.* neu [aus]füttern ‹Kleidungsstück›; neu belegen ‹Bremse›; doublieren ‹Gemälde›; **~ a hat with a silk lining** einen Hut mit Seide neu ausfüttern

**relinquish** /rɪˈlɪŋkwɪʃ/ *v.t.* **A** (*give up, abandon*) aufgeben; ablassen von ‹Gewohnheit, Glaube›; zurückziehen ‹Klage›; verzichten auf (+ *Akk.*) ‹Recht, Anspruch, Macht›; aufgeben ‹Anspruch, Stelle, Arbeit, Besitz›; **~ the right/one's claim to sth.** auf sein Recht/seinen Anspruch auf etw. verzichten; **~ sth. to sb.** etw. an jmdn. abtreten; zugunsten von jmdm. auf etw. (*Akk.*) verzichten; **B ~ one's hold** *or* **grip on sb./sth.** jmdn./etw. loslassen; **C** (*fig.*) **~ one's hold on reality** den Bezug zur Realität verlieren; **he has ~ed his hold over** *or* **on her** er hat aufgehört, sie zu bevormunden

**relinquishment** /rɪˈlɪŋkwɪʃmənt/ *n.* Aufgabe, *die;* (*of belief*) Ablassen, *das* (**of** von); (*of right, power, claim, territory*) Verzicht, *der* (**of** auf + *Akk.*)

**reliquary** /ˈrelɪkwərɪ/ *n.* Reliquiar, *das*

**relish** /ˈrelɪʃ/ ❶ *n.* **A** (*liking*) Vorliebe, *die;* **show a real ~ for doing sth.** etw. mit Vorliebe tun; **have a great/no ~ for sth.** viel/nichts für eine Sache übrig haben; **do sth. with [great] ~:** etw. mit [großem] Genuss tun; **he takes [great] ~ in doing sth.** es bereitet ihm [große] Freude, etw. zu tun; **B** (*condiment*) Relish, *das* (*Kochk.*); **C** (*attractive quality*) Reiz, *der;* **have no/great ~:** reizlos/sehr verlockend sein; **meat has no ~ when one is ill** man hat keine Lust auf Fleisch, wenn man krank ist.
❷ *v.t.* genießen; reizvoll finden ‹Gedanke, Vorstellung›; **I should ~ a lobster and a bottle of wine** was ich jetzt gern hätte, wäre ein Hummer und eine Flasche Wein

**relive** /riːˈlɪv/ *n.* noch einmal durchleben; **~ one's life** noch einmal leben

**reload** /riːˈləʊd/ *v.t.* nachladen ‹Schusswaffe›; wieder beladen ‹Lastwagen›; wieder aufladen ‹Waren›; **~ the camera** einen neuen Film einlegen

**relocate** /riːləˈkeɪt/ ❶ *v.t.* **A** (*move to another place*) verlegen ‹Fabrik, Büro›; versetzen ‹Angestellten, Fenster, Ventil›; **B** (*find again*) wieder ausfindig machen ‹Aufenthaltsort›; wieder finden ‹Eingang, Gleise›. ❷ *v.i.* (*settle*) sich niederlassen

**relocation** /riːləˈkeɪʃn/ *n.* (*of factory, office*) Verlegung, *die;* (*of employee*) Versetzung, *die;* **~ expenses** Umzugskosten *Pl.*

**reluctance** /rɪˈlʌktəns/ *n., no pl.* Widerwille, *der;* Abneigung, *die;* **have a [great] ~ to do sth.** etw. nur mit Widerwillen tun; **show some ~ at doing sth.** etw. nur ungern tun

**reluctant** /rɪˈlʌktənt/ *adj.* unwillig; **be ~ to do sth.** etw. nur ungern *od.* widerstrebend tun; **give sb. ~ assistance** jmdm. nur widerstrebend helfen

**reluctantly** /rɪˈlʌktəntlɪ/ *adv.* nur ungern; widerstrebend

**rely** /rɪˈlaɪ/ *v.i.* **A** (*have trust*) sich verlassen (**[up]on** auf + *Akk.*); **you can always ~ on him to turn up too early** (*iron.*) du kannst dich darauf verlassen, dass er immer zu früh kommt; **B** (*be dependent*) angewiesen sein (**[up]on** auf + *Akk.*); **[have to] ~ on sb. to help** darauf angewiesen sein, dass jmd. hilft

**remade** ⇒ **remake** 1

**remain** /rɪˈmeɪn/ *v.i.* **A** (*be left over*) übrig bleiben; **all that ~ed for me to do was to ...:** ich musste *od.* brauchte nur noch ...; **nothing ~s but to thank you all** es bleibt mir nur, Ihnen allen zu danken; **only one match still ~s to be played** es muss nur noch ein Spiel ausgetragen werden; **the few pleasures that ~ to an old man** die wenigen Freuden, die einem alten Mann [noch] bleiben; **B** (*stay*) bleiben; **~ behind** noch dableiben; **~ in sb.'s memory** jmdm. im Gedächtnis bleiben; **C** (*continue to be*) bleiben; **~ true to sb.'s memory** jmdm. ein treues Andenken bewahren; **that** *or* **it ~s to be seen** das bleibt abzuwarten *od.* wird sich zeigen; **the fact ~s that ...:** das ändert nichts an der Tatsache *od.* daran, dass ...; **I ~, yours faithfully, J. Smith** ich verbleibe mit freundlichen Grüßen Ihr J. Smith

**remainder** /rɪˈmeɪndə(r)/ ❶ *n.* **A** (*sb. or sth. left over; also Math.*) Rest, *der;* **the ~ of the guests** die übrigen Gäste; **B** (*remaining stock*) Restposten, *der;* **[publisher's] ~:** Restauflage, *die;* **C** (*Law*) Anwartschaft auf die Nacherbschaft; **D** (*right to succeed to a title or position*) Anwartschaft auf die Nachfolge. ❷ *v.t.* (*Publishing*) [als Restauflage] zu herabgesetztem Preis verkaufen

**remaining** /rɪˈmeɪnɪŋ/ *adj.* restlich; übrig; **spend one's ~ years ...:** seinen Lebensabend ... verbringen

**remains** /rɪˈmeɪnz/ *n. pl.* **A** (*left-over part*) Reste; **B** (*corpse*) sterbliche [Über]reste (*verhüll.*); **C** (*relics*) Relikte; Reste; **Roman ~:** Relikte aus der Römerzeit

**remake** ❶ /riːˈmeɪk/ *v.t.*, **remade** /riːˈmeɪd/ wieder machen ‹Bett›; neu vereinbaren ‹Verabredung›; wieder herrichten ‹Kleidung›; **~ the booking** neu buchen. ❷ /ˈriːmeɪk/ *n.* (*Cinemat.*) Remake, *das* (*fachspr.*); Neuverfilmung, *die;* **do a ~ of sth.** etw. neu verfilmen

**remand** /rɪˈmɑːnd/ ❶ *v.t.* **~ sb. [in** *or* **into custody]** jmdn. in Untersuchungshaft behalten; **be ~ed in custody/on bail** in Untersuchungshaft bleiben müssen/gegen Kaution aus der Untersuchungshaft entlassen werden. ❷ *n.* **[period of] ~:** Untersuchungshaft, *die;* **place sb. on ~:** jmdn. in Untersuchungshaft nehmen; **be on ~:** in Untersuchungshaft sein; **be held on ~:** in Untersuchungshaft bleiben müssen; *attrib.* **~ prisoner** Untersuchungsgefangene, *der/die*

**remand: ~ centre** *n.* (*Brit.*) *Untersuchungsgefängnis für jugendliche Straftäter zwischen 14 und 21 Jahren;* **~ home** *n.* (*Brit. Hist.*) *Untersuchungsgefängnis für jugendliche Straftäter unter 17 Jahren*

**remark** /rɪˈmɑːk/ ❶ *v.t.* Ⓐ (*say*) bemerken (**to** gegenüber); Ⓑ (*arch.: observe*) gewahr werden. ❷ *v.i.* eine Bemerkung machen (**[up]on** zu, über + *Akk.*). ❸ *n.* Ⓐ (*comment*) Bemerkung, *die* (**on** über + *Akk.*); **make a ~:** eine Bemerkung machen (**about, at** über + *Akk.*); **I have a few ~s to make about that** ich habe dazu einiges zu sagen; Ⓑ *no art.* (*commenting*) Kommentar, *der;* **without ~:** kommentarlos; **be worthy of special ~** (*formal*) besondere Beachtung verdienen; **nothing worthy of ~** (*formal*) nichts Bemerkenswertes

**remarkable** /rɪˈmɑːkəbl/ *adj.* Ⓐ (*notable*) bemerkenswert; Ⓑ (*extraordinary*) außergewöhnlich; **a boy who is ~ for his stupidity** ein Junge von ganz außergewöhnlicher Dummheit

**remarkably** /rɪˈmɑːkəblɪ/ *adv.* Ⓐ (*notably*) bemerkenswert; Ⓑ (*exceptionally*) außergewöhnlich

**remarriage** /riːˈmærɪdʒ/ *n.* Wiederverheiratung, *die*

**remarry** /riːˈmærɪ/ *v.i. & t.* wieder heiraten

**rematch** /ˈriːmætʃ/ *n.* Rückkampf, *der*

**remediable** /rɪˈmiːdɪəbl/ *adj.* behebbar; **be ~:** beseitigt werden können; **is the situation ~?** gibt es einen Ausweg aus der Situation?

**remedial** /rɪˈmiːdɪəl/ *adj.* Ⓐ (*affording a remedy*) Heil‹behandlung, -wirkung›; (*intended to remedy deficiency etc.*) rehabilitierend ‹Maßnahme›; **take ~ action** Hilfsmaßnahmen ergreifen; **be ~ rather than preventive** eher therapeutischer als vorbeugender Natur sein; Ⓑ (*Educ.*) Förder-; **classes in ~ reading** Förderunterricht im Lesen; **~ education** Förderunterricht, *der*

**remedy** /ˈremɪdɪ/ ❶ *n.* Ⓐ (*cure*) [Heil]mittel, *das* (**for** gegen); **cough/herbal ~:** Husten-/Kräutermittel, *das;* **cold/flu ~:** Mittel gegen Erkältung/Grippe; **be past** *or* **beyond ~:** unheilbar sein; Ⓑ (*means of counteracting*) [Gegen]mittel, *das* (**for** gegen); Ⓒ (*Law: redress*) (*through civil proceedings*) Rechtsbehelf, *der;* (*through self-help*) Entschädigung, *die.* ❷ *v.t.* beheben ‹Sprachfehler, Problem›; ausgleichen ‹Kurzsichtigkeit›; retten ‹Situation›; **the problem/situation cannot be remedied** das Problem kann nicht behoben werden/die Situation ist nicht zu retten

**remember** /rɪˈmembə(r)/ *v.t.* Ⓐ (*keep in memory*) denken an (+ *Akk.*); (*bring to mind*) sich erinnern an (+ *Akk.*); **I've just ~ed what I wanted to tell you** mir ist gerade [wieder] eingefallen, was ich dir sagen wollte; **don't you ~ me?** erinnern Sie sich nicht an mich?; **~ who/where you are!** vergiss nicht, wer/wo du bist; **I can't ~ the word I want** das Wort, das ich brauche, fällt mir gerade nicht ein; **she gave him something to ~ her by** sie gab ihm etwas, das ihn an sie erinnern sollte; (*fig.*) sie gab ihm einen Denkzettel; **I ~ed to bring the book** ich habe daran gedacht, das Buch mitzubringen; **I can't ~ how to put it back together** ich weiß nicht mehr, wie es wieder zusammengesetzt wird; **do you ~ when the bus leaves?** weißt du noch, wann der Bus abfährt?; **I can never ~ her name** ich kann mir ihren Namen einfach nicht merken; **I distinctly ~ posting the letter** ich erinnere mich genau, dass ich den Brief eingeworfen habe; **if I ~ correctly** (*abs.*) wenn ich mich recht erinnere; **an evening to ~:** ein unvergesslicher Abend; Ⓑ (*convey greetings from*) grüßen; **~ me to them** grüße sie von mir; **she asked to be ~ed to you** sie lässt dich grüßen; Ⓒ **~ oneself** sich zusammennehmen; Ⓓ **~ sb. in one's will/prayers** jmdn. in seinem Testament bedenken/in sein Gebet einschließen

**remembrance** /rɪˈmembrəns/ *n.* Gedenken, *das;* **in ~ of sb.** zu jmds. Gedächtnis; zum Gedenken an jmdn.

**Remembrance: ~ Day** *n.* (*Brit.*) Ⓐ (*Hist.: 11 Nov.*) Gedenktag für die Gefallenen der beiden Weltkriege; Ⓑ ⇨ **~ Sunday**; **~ Sunday** *n.* (*Brit.*) ≈ Volkstrauertag, *der*

**remind** /rɪˈmaɪnd/ *v.t.* erinnern (**of** an + *Akk.*); **~ sb. to do sth.** jmdn. daran erinnern, etw. zu tun; **can you ~ me how to do it?** kannst du mal meinem Gedächtnis nachhelfen, wie man das macht?; **that ~s me, ...:** dabei fällt mir ein, ...; **you are ~ed that ...:** beachten Sie bitte, dass ...; **travellers are ~ed that ...:** Reisende werden darauf hingewiesen, dass ...

**reminder** /rɪˈmaɪndə(r)/ *n.* Erinnerung, *die* (**of** an + *Akk.*); (*mnemonic*) Gedächtnishilfe *od.* -stütze, *die;* (*photo etc.*) Andenken, *das* (**of** an + *Akk.*); **give sb. a ~ that ...:** jmdn. daran erinnern, dass ...; **serve as/be a ~ of sth.** an etw. (*Akk.*) erinnern; **~ [letter]** Mahnung, *die;* Mahnbrief, *der;* **a gentle ~:** ein zarter Wink

**reminisce** /remɪˈnɪs/ *v.i.* sich in Erinnerungen (*Dat.*) ergehen (**about** an + *Akk.*)

**reminiscence** /remɪˈnɪsəns/ *n.* Ⓐ Erinnerung, *die* (**of** an + *Akk.*); Ⓑ *in pl.* (*memoirs*) [Lebens]erinnerungen *Pl.;* Memoiren *Pl.*

**reminiscent** /remɪˈnɪsənt/ *adj.* Ⓐ **~ of sth.** an etw. (*Akk.*) erinnernd; **be ~ of sth.** an etw. (*Akk.*) erinnern; Ⓑ (*nostalgic*) **~ mood** nostalgische Stimmung

**remiss** /rɪˈmɪs/ *adj.* nachlässig (**of** von)

**remission** /rɪˈmɪʃn/ *n.* Ⓐ (*of sins*) Vergebung, *die;* Ⓑ (*of debt, punishment*) Erlass, *der;* Ⓒ (*prison sentence*) Straferlass, *der;* **he gained one year's ~:** ihm ist ein Jahr erlassen worden; Ⓓ (*Med.*) Remission, *die;* **go into ~:** remittieren

**remit** ❶ /rɪˈmɪt/ *v.t.*, **-tt-** Ⓐ (*pardon*) vergeben ‹Sünde, Beleidigung usw.›; Ⓑ (*cancel*) erlassen ‹Steuer, Gebühr usw.›; **~ sb.'s punishment** jmdm. seine Strafe erlassen; Ⓒ (*refer*) weiterleiten ‹Frage, Angelegenheit› (**to** an + *Akk.*); (*Law*) zurückverweisen ‹Fall, Bericht›; Ⓓ (*postpone*) verschieben, vertagen (**until** bis, **to** auf + *Akk.*); Ⓔ (*send*) überweisen ‹Geld›. ❷ /ˈriːmɪt, rɪˈmɪt/ *n.* Aufgabe, *die;* Auftrag, *der*

**remittance** /rɪˈmɪtəns/ *n.* Überweisung, *die*

**remnant** /ˈremnənt/ *n.* Ⓐ Rest, *der;* **only a ~ of the family survives** nur noch wenige Mitglieder der Familie leben; **~s of carpet/wood** Teppich-/Holzreste *Pl.;* **sale of ~s** Resteverkauf, *der;* Ⓑ (*trace*) Überrest, *der;* **salvage the ~s of sth.** retten, was von etw. übrig geblieben ist

**remodel** /riːˈmɒdl/ *v.t.*, (*Brit.*) **-ll-** (*lit. or fig.*) umgestalten

**remold** (*Amer.*) ⇨ **remould**

**remonstrance** /rɪˈmɒnstrəns/ *n.* Protest, *der* (**with, against** gegen)

**remonstrate** /ˈremənstreɪt, rɪˈmɒnstreɪt/ *v.i.* protestieren (**against** gegen); **~ with sb.** jmdm. Vorhaltungen machen (**on** wegen)

**remonstration** ⇨ **remonstrance**

**remonstrative** /ˈremənstreɪtɪv, rɪˈmɒnstrətɪv/ *adv.* protestierend; Protest‹brief usw.›

**remorse** /rɪˈmɔːs/ *n.* Reue, *die* (**for, about** über + *Akk.*); **without ~:** erbarmungslos

**remorseful** /rɪˈmɔːsfl/ *adj.* reuig, reuevoll (*geh.*); reumütig (*öfter scherzh.*); Reue‹gefühl›; **feel ~:** Reue empfinden

**remorseless** /rɪˈmɔːslɪs/ *adj.* Ⓐ (*merciless*) erbarmungslos ‹Grausamkeit, Barbarei›; Ⓑ (*relentless*) unerbittlich ‹Schicksal, Logik›

**remorselessly** /rɪˈmɔːslɪslɪ/ *adv.* ⇨ **remorseless:** erbarmungslos; unerbittlich

**remote** /rɪˈməʊt/ *adj.*, **~r** /rɪˈməʊtə(r)/, **~st** /rɪˈməʊtɪst/ Ⓐ (*far apart*) entfernt; **be very ~ from each other** sehr weit voneinander entfernt sein; **nations as ~ in culture as X and Y** Völker mit so verschiedenen *od.* unterschiedlichen Kulturen wie X und Y; Ⓑ (*far off*) fern ‹Vergangenheit, Zukunft, Zeit›; früh ‹Altertum›; abgelegen, (*geh.*) entlegen ‹Ort, Gebiet›; **~ from** (*lit. or fig.*) weit entfernt von; **~ from the road** weitab von der Straße; Ⓒ (*not closely related*) entfernt, weitläufig ‹Vorfahr, Nachkomme, Verwandte›; Ⓓ (*aloof*) unnahbar, distanziert ‹Person, Art›; Ⓔ (*slight*) gering ‹Auswirkung, Chance, Möglichkeit, Vorstellung›; **I don't have the ~st idea what you're talking about** ich habe nicht die geringste *od.* leiseste Ahnung, wovon du sprichst

**remote: ~ conˈtrol** *n.* (*of vehicle*) Fernlenkung, *die;* Fernsteuerung, *die;* (*of apparatus*) Fernbedienung, *die;* **~-control[led]** *adj.* ferngesteuert; ferngelenkt; fernbedient ‹Anlage›

**remotely** /rɪˈməʊtlɪ/ *adv.* Ⓐ (*distantly*) entfernt, weitläufig ‹verwandt›; **~ controlled** ⇨ **remote-control[led]**; Ⓑ (*aloofly*) distanziert, unnahbar ‹lächeln, antworten›; Ⓒ (*slightly*) **they are not [even] ~ alike** sie haben [aber auch] nicht die entfernteste Ähnlichkeit [miteinander]; **it is not [even] ~ possible that ...:** es besteht [aber auch] nicht die geringste Möglichkeit, dass ...; **it is ~ conceivable that ...:** es ist nicht völlig auszuschließen, dass ...

**remoteness** /rɪˈməʊtnɪs/ *n., no pl.* Ⓐ (*seclusion*) Abgeschiedenheit, *die;* Abgelegenheit, *die;* (*distance*) große Entfernung (**from** von); Ⓑ (*of relationship*) Weitläufigkeit, *die;* Ⓒ (*separateness*) fehlender Zusammenhang (**of ... from** zwischen ... und); **~ from everyday life** Lebensfremdheit, *die*

**remould** ❶ /riːˈməʊld/ *v.t.* (*refashion*) ummodeln, umgestalten (**into** zu); (*Motor Veh.*) runderneuern ‹Reifen›. ❷ /ˈriːməʊld/ *n.* (*Motor Veh.*) runderneuerter Reifen

**remount** /riːˈmaʊnt/ ❶ *v.t.* Ⓐ (*ascend again*) wieder hinaufsteigen ‹Leiter›; **~ one's horse/bicycle** wieder aufs Pferd/Fahrrad steigen; Ⓑ (*put in fresh mount*) wieder aufziehen ‹Bild›. ❷ *v.i.* (*on horse*) wieder aufsitzen; (*on bicycle*) wieder aufs Fahrrad steigen

**removable** /rɪˈmuːvəbl/ *adj.* abnehmbar; entfernbar ‹Fleck, Trennwand›; herausnehmbar ‹Futter›; **be ~:** sich entfernen lassen

**removal** /rɪˈmuːvl/ *n.* Ⓐ (*taking away*) Entfernung, *die;* (*of passage from book*) Streichung, *die* (**from** aus); (*of traces*) Beseitigung, *die;* (*taking off*) **the ~ of the valve from the tyre proved difficult** es war schwierig, das Ventil aus dem Reifen herauszunehmen; Ⓑ (*dismissal*) Entlassung, *die;* **the minister's ~ from office** die Entfernung des Ministers aus dem Amt; Ⓒ ⇨ **remove** 1 C: Beseitigung, *die;* Vertreibung, *die;* Zerstreuung, *die;* Ⓓ (*transfer*) **his ~ to another school** seine Umschulung; **the ~ of the books to the next room** die Umräumung *od.* das Umräumen der Bücher in das andere Zimmer; **his ~ to another department** seine Versetzung in eine andere Abteilung; **his ~ to hospital** seine Einlieferung ins Krankenhaus; Ⓔ (*transfer of furniture*) Umzug, *der;* **'Smith & Co., R~s'** „Smith & Co., Spedition"; **office/factory ~:** Büro-/Werksverlegung, *die*

**removal: ~ expenses** *n. pl.* Umzugskosten *Pl.;* **~ firm** *n.* Spedition, *die;* **~ man** *n.* Möbelpacker, *der;* **~ van** *n.* Möbelwagen, *der*

**remove** /rɪˈmuːv/ ❶ *v.t.* Ⓐ (*take away*) entfernen; streichen ‹Buchpassage›; wegnehmen, wegräumen ‹Papiere, Ordner usw.›; abräumen ‹Geschirr›; beseitigen ‹Spur›; (*take off*) abnehmen; ausziehen ‹Kleidungsstück›; **she ~d her/the child's coat** sie legte ihren Mantel ab/sie zog dem Kind den Mantel aus; **~ a book from the shelf/the valve from a tyre** ein Buch vom Regal nehmen/das Ventil aus einem Reifen [heraus]nehmen; **~ one's make-up** sich abschminken; **~ the papers/dishes from the table** die Papiere/das Geschirr vom Tisch räumen; **the parents ~d the child from the school** die Eltern nahmen das Kind von der Schule; Ⓑ (*dismiss*) entlassen; **~ sb. from office/his post** jmdn. aus dem Amt/von seinem Posten entfernen; Ⓒ (*eradicate*) beseitigen ‹Gefahr, Hindernis, Problem, Zweifel›; vertreiben ‹Angst›; zerstreuen ‹Verdacht, Befürchtungen›; Ⓓ (*transfer*) **~ a pupil to another school** einen Schüler auf eine andere Schule schicken; **we ~d the books to another room** wir haben die Bücher in ein anderes Zimmer umgeräumt; **~ an employee to another department** einen Angestellten in eine andere Abteilung versetzen; Ⓔ (*euphem.: kill*) beseitigen (*verhüll.*); Ⓕ *in p.p.* ⇨ **cousin**; Ⓖ *in p.p.* (*remote*) **be entirely ~d from politics/everyday life** gar nichts mit Politik zu tun haben/völlig lebensfremd sein.
❷ *v.i.* [um]ziehen; **~ to the country** aufs Land ziehen; **they ~d from here** sie sind

r

[von hier] weggezogen. ❸ *n.* Ⓐ (*degree*) Schritt, *der;* **be only a few ~s/but one ~ from** nicht mehr weit/nur noch einen Schritt entfernt sein von; **at one ~:** auf Distanz (**from** gegenüber); Ⓑ (*distance*) Abstand, *der* (**from** zu); **be a far ~ from sth.** weit entfernt von etw. sein

**remover** /rɪˈmuːvə(r)/ *n.* Ⓐ (*of paint/varnish/hair/rust*) Farb-/Lack-/Haar-/Rostentferner, *der;* Ⓑ (*removal man*) Möbelpacker, *der;* **[firm of] ~s** Spedition[sfirma], *die*

**remunerate** /rɪˈmjuːnəreɪt/ *v.t.* bezahlen; entlohnen; (*recompense*) belohnen

**remuneration** /rɪmjuːnəˈreɪʃn/ *n.* Bezahlung, *die;* Entlohnung, *die;* (*reward*) Belohnung, *die*

**remunerative** /rɪˈmjuːnərətɪv/ *adj.* lohnend; einträglich

**Renaissance** /rəˈneɪsəns, rəˈneɪsɑ̃s, rɪˈneɪsəns/ *n.* Ⓐ *no pl.* (*Hist.*) Renaissance, *die;* **~ man** der Renaissancemensch; Ⓑ **r~** (*rebirth*) Renaissance, *die;* Wiedergeburt, *die* (*geh.*)

**renal** /ˈriːnl/ *adj.* (*Anat., Med.*) Nieren-

**rename** /riːˈneɪm/ *v.t.* umbenennen; umtaufen ‹Schiff›

**renascence** ⇨ **Renaissance** B

**rend** /rend/ **rent** /rent/ *v.t.* (*literary*) Ⓐ (*tear*) reißen (**from** aus); Ⓑ (*split*) spalten ‹Baum, Gruppe, Land›; ‹Schrei:› zerreißen ‹Stille›

**render** /ˈrendə(r)/ *v.t.* Ⓐ (*make*) machen; **the tone ~ed the statement an insult** der Ton machte die Feststellung zu einer Beleidigung; Ⓑ (*show, give*) leisten ‹Gehorsam, Hilfe›; erweisen ‹Ehre, Achtung, Respekt, Dienst›; bieten, gewähren ‹Schutz›; **~ a service to sb., ~ sb. a service** jmdm. einen Dienst erweisen; **~ thanks [un]to God** Gott Dank sagen; **~ [un]to Caesar the things that are Caesar's** (*Bibl.*) gebet dem Kaiser, was des Kaisers ist; Ⓒ (*pay*) entrichten ‹Tribut, Steuern, Abgaben›; Ⓓ (*represent, reproduce*) wiedergeben, spielen ‹Musik, Szene, Rolle›; (*translate*) übersetzen (**by** mit); **~ a text into another language** einen Text in eine andere Sprache übertragen; Ⓔ (*present*) **~ a report to sb.** jmdm. Bericht erstatten; **~ an annual account [to sb.]** [jmdm.] einen Jahresbericht vorlegen; **account ~ed** (*Commerc.*) ausgestellte Rechnung; Ⓕ (*Building: plaster*) berappen (*fachspr.*), verputzen ‹Mauer›; Ⓖ **~ [down]** auslassen ‹Fett›

**~ 'up** *v.t.* (*formal*) übergeben (**to** *Dat.*) ‹Festung, Fort, Stadt›

**rendering** /ˈrendərɪŋ/ *n.* Ⓐ Wiedergabe, *die;* (*translation*) Übersetzung, *die* (**into** in + *Akk.*); (*of play also*) Aufführung, *die;* (*of musical piece, poem also*) Vortrag, *der;* (*of historical events also*) Darstellung, *die;* **give a [superb] ~ of sth.** etw. [meisterhaft] wiedergeben / aufführen / vortragen / darstellen; Ⓑ (*Building: plastering*) Berapp, *der* (*fachspr.*); Putz, *der*

**rendezvous** /ˈrɒndɪvuː, ˈrɒndeɪvuː/ ❶ *n., pl. same* /ˈrɒndɪvuːz, ˈrɒndeɪvuːz/ Ⓐ (*meeting place*) Treffpunkt, *der;* Ⓑ (*meeting*) Rendezvous, *das* (*veralt., meist noch scherzh.*); Verabredung, *die;* Ⓒ (*Astronaut.*) Rendezvous, *das.* ❷ *v.i., pres.* **~es** /ˈrɒndɪvuːz, ˈrɒndeɪvuːz/, *p.t. & p.p.* **~ed** /ˈrɒndɪvuːd, ˈrɒndeɪvuːd/, *pres. p.* **~ing** /ˈrɒndɪvuːɪŋ, ˈrɒndeɪvuːɪŋ/ sich treffen

**rendition** /renˈdɪʃn/ ⇨ **rendering** A

**renegade** /ˈrenɪgeɪd/ ❶ *n.* Abtrünnige, *der/die;* Renegat, *der*/Renegatin, *die* (*abwertend*). ❷ *adj.* abtrünnig

**renege, renegue** /rɪˈniːg, rɪˈneɪg/ *v.i.* Ⓐ (*Amer. Cards*) nicht bedienen; Ⓑ **~ [on an agreement/a promise]** [eine Vereinbarung/ein Versprechen] nicht einhalten

**renegotiate** /riːnɪˈgəʊʃɪeɪt/ *v.t.* neu aushandeln; erneut verhandeln über (+ *Akk.*)

**renew** /rɪˈnjuː/ *v.t.* Ⓐ (*restore, regenerate, recover*) erneuern; wieder wecken *od.* wachrufen ‹Gefühle›; wiederherstellen ‹Kraft›; **~ sb.'s energy** jmdm. neue Energie geben; **feel spiritually ~ed** sich wie neugeboren fühlen; Ⓑ (*replace*) erneuern; auffüllen ‹Vorrat›; ausbessern ‹Kleidungsstück›; Ⓒ (*begin again*) erneuern ‹Bekanntschaft›; wieder aufnehmen ‹Kampf, Korrespondenz›; fortsetzen ‹Angriff, Bemühungen›; **~ed exhortations/outbreaks of rioting** erneute Ermahnungen/Krawalle; Ⓓ (*repeat*) wiederholen ‹Aussage, Beschuldigung›; Ⓔ (*extend*) erneuern, verlängern ‹Vertrag, Genehmigung, Ausweis etc.›; **~ a library book** ‹Bibliothekar/Benutzer:› ein Buch [aus der Bücherei] verlängern/verlängern lassen

**renewable** /rɪˈnjuːəbl/ *adj.* regenerationsfähig ‹Energiequelle›; verlängerbar ‹Vertrag, Genehmigung, Ausweis›

**renewal** /rɪˈnjuːəl/ *n.* Ⓐ Erneuerung, *die;* (*of contract, passport, etc. also*) Verlängerung, *die;* (*of attack*) Wiederaufnahme, *die;* (*of library book*) Verlängerung der Leihfrist; Ⓑ **[urban] ~:** [Stadt]sanierung, *die*

**rennet** /ˈrenɪt/ *n.* Lab, *das*

**renounce** /rɪˈnaʊns/ ❶ *v.t.* Ⓐ (*abandon*) verzichten auf (+ *Akk.*); Ⓑ (*refuse to recognize*) aufkündigen ‹Vertrag, Freundschaft›; aufgeben ‹Grundsatz, Plan, Versuch›; leugnen ‹jmds. Autorität›; verstoßen ‹Person›; **~ the world** der Welt (*Dat.*) entsagen (*geh.*); **~ the devil/one's faith** dem Teufel/seinem Glauben abschwören. ❷ *v.i.* Ⓐ (*Law*) offiziell seinen Verzicht erklären; Ⓑ (*Cards*) nicht bedienen

**renouncement** /rɪˈnaʊnsmənt/ ⇨ **renunciation** A

**renovate** /ˈrenəveɪt/ *v.t.* renovieren ‹Gebäude›; restaurieren ‹Möbel, Gemälde›

**renovation** /renəˈveɪʃn/ *n.* Renovierung, *die;* (*of furniture etc.*) Restaurierung, *die*

**renown** /rɪˈnaʊn/ Renommee, *das;* Ansehen, *das;* **of [great] ~:** von hohem Ansehen; sehr berühmt ‹Stadt›

**renowned** /rɪˈnaʊnd/ *adj.* berühmt (**for** wegen, für); **he is ~ as a portrait painter** er hat als Porträtmaler einen großen Namen

**rent**[1] ⇨ **rend**

**rent**[2] /rent/ *n.* (*tear, cleft*) Riss, *der* (*auch fig.*); (*cleft also*) Spalte, *die;* **~ in the clouds** Wolkenspalt, *der*

**rent**[3] /rent/ ❶ *n.* (*for house, flat, etc.*) Miete, *die;* (*for land*) Pacht, *die;* **have a house free of ~:** ein Haus mietfrei bewohnen; **for ~** (*Amer.*) ‹Haus, Wohnung etc.› zu vermieten; ‹Land› zu verpachten; ‹Kostüme› zu verleihen. ❷ *v.t.* Ⓐ (*use*) mieten ‹Haus, Wohnung usw.›; pachten ‹Land›; mieten ‹Auto, Gerät›; Ⓑ (*let*) vermieten ‹Haus, Wohnung, Auto etc.› (**to** *Dat.*, an + *Akk.*); verpachten ‹Land› (**to** *Dat.*, an + *Akk.*). ❸ *v.i.* ‹Haus, Wohnung, Auto usw.:› vermietet werden; ‹Land:› verpachtet werden

**~ 'out** *v.t.* ⇨ **rent**[3] 2 B

**rentable** /ˈrentəbl/ *adj.* ⇨ **rent**[3] 2: zu [ver]mieten/[ver]pachten *präd.;* zu [ver]mietend/[ver]pachtend *attr.*

**rent: ~-a-car** *attrib. adj.* **~-a-car business/company/service** Autoverleih, *der;* **~-a-crowd** *n.* bestellter Haufen; (*claque*) Claque, *die*

**rental** /ˈrentl/ *n.* Ⓐ (*from houses etc.*) Miete, *die;* (*from land*) Pacht, *die;* Ⓑ ⇨ **rent**[3] 2: Mietung, *die;* Pachtung, *die;* (*letting*) Vermietung, *die;* Verpachtung, *die;* **car ~:** Autoverleih, *der;* **the property is on ~:** der Besitz ist verpachtet *od.* in Pacht; Ⓒ (*Amer.: thing rented*) Mietgegenstand, *der;* Mietsache, *die* (*Rechtsw.*)

**ˈrental library** *n.* (*Amer.*) (*kommerzielle*) Leihbücherei

**rent: ~-a-mob** *n.* bestellter Haufen von Randalierern; **~-a-van** *attrib. adj.* **~-a-van business/company/service** Transportervermietung, *die;* **~ boy** *n.* (*coll.*) Strichjunge, *der* (*salopp*); **~ collector** *n. jmd., der für den Hausbesitzer die Miete kassiert;* **~ control** *n.* ≈ Mietpreisbindung, *die;* **~-controlled** *adj.* mietpreisgebunden; **~-free** *adj.* mietfrei; **~ officer** *n. Beamter/Beamtin der kommunalen Beratungsstelle für mietrechtliche Fragen;* **~ rebate** *n.* Mietermäßigung, *die;* **~ tribunal** *n.* Mietgericht, *das*

**renumber** /riːˈnʌmbə(r)/ *v.t.* umnummerieren; neu beziffern *od.* benummern

**renunciation** /rɪnʌnsɪˈeɪʃn/ *n.* Ⓐ ⇨ **renounce** 1 A, B: Verzicht, *der;* Aufkündigung, *die;* Aufgabe, *die;* Leugnung, *die;* Verstoßung, *die;* Ⓑ (*self-denial*) Selbstverleugnung, *die*

**reoccupation** /riːɒkjʊˈpeɪʃn/ *n.* Wiederbesetzung, *die;* (*of house etc.*) Wiederübernahme, *die*

**reoccupy** /riːˈɒkjʊpaɪ/ *v.t.* wieder besetzen (*Milit.*) ‹Ort, Stellung›; wieder übernehmen ‹Haus, Wohnung›

**reopen** /riːˈəʊpn/ ❶ *v.t.* Ⓐ (*open again*) wieder öffnen; wieder aufmachen; wieder eröffnen ‹Geschäft, Lokal usw.›; Ⓑ (*return to*) wieder aufnehmen ‹Diskussion, Verhandlung, Feindseligkeiten›; wieder aufnehmen, wieder aufrollen ‹Fall›; zurückkommen auf (+ *Akk.*) ‹Angelegenheit›. ❷ *v.i.* ‹Geschäft, Lokal usw.:› wieder öffnen; wieder eröffnet werden; ‹Verhandlungen, Unterricht:› wieder beginnen

**reorder** /riːˈɔːdə(r)/ ❶ *v.t.* Ⓐ (*Commerc.: order again*) nachbestellen ‹Ware›; (*after theft, loss*) neu bestellen; Ⓑ (*rearrange*) umordnen; neu ordnen; (*on list*) umstellen ‹Namen›; neu festlegen ‹Reihenfolge›. ❷ *n.* (*Commerc.*) Nachbestellung, *die*

**reorganisation, reorganise** ⇨ **reorganiz-**

**reorganization** /riːɔːgənaɪˈzeɪʃn/ *n.* Umorganisation, *die;* (*of text*) Neugliederung, *die;* (*of time, work*) Neueinteilung, *die*

**reorganize** /riːˈɔːgənaɪz/ *v.t.* umorganisieren; neu einteilen ‹Zeit, Arbeit›; neu gliedern ‹Aufsatz, Referat›

**reorient** /riːˈɔːrɪent, riːˈɒrɪent/, **reorientate** /riːˈɒrɪənteɪt, riːˈɔːrɪənteɪt/ *v.t.* neu ausrichten ‹Programm, Politik, Denken, Handeln›; **~** *or* **reorientate a person** einem Menschen eine neue Orientierung geben

**reorientation** /riːɒrɪənˈteɪʃn, riːɔːrɪənˈteɪʃn/ *n.* Neuorientierung, *die*

**rep**[1] /rep/ *n.* (*Textiles*) Rips, *der*

**rep**[2] *n.* **▶ 1261** (*coll.: representative*) Vertreter, *der*/Vertreterin, *die*

**rep**[3] *n.* (*Theatre coll.*) Repertoiretheater, *das;* **be in ~:** an einem Repertoiretheater spielen

**Rep.** *abbr.* (*Amer.*) Ⓐ **Representative** Abg.; Ⓑ **Republican** Rep.

**repaid** ⇨ **repay**

**repaint** ❶ /riːˈpeɪnt/ *v.t.* neu streichen ‹Gebäude, Wand, Tür usw.›; neu lackieren ‹Auto›. ❷ /ˈriːpeɪnt/ *n.* **the door needs a ~:** die Tür braucht einen neuen Anstrich; **give sth. a ~:** etw. neu streichen/lackieren

**repair**[1] /rɪˈpeə(r)/ ❶ *v.t.* Ⓐ (*restore, mend*) reparieren; ausbessern ‹Kleidung, Straße›; Ⓑ (*remedy*) wieder gutmachen ‹Schaden, Fehler›; beheben ‹Schaden, Mangel›. ❷ *n.* Ⓐ (*restoring, renovation*) Reparatur, *die;* **be beyond ~:** sich nicht mehr reparieren lassen; **be in need of ~:** reparaturbedürftig sein; ‹Schuhe:› repariert werden müssen; **be under ~** ‹Maschine, Gerät, Fahrzeug:› in Reparatur sein; **the road is under ~:** an der Straße werden gerade Bauarbeiten ausgeführt; **closed for ~s** wegen Reparaturarbeiten geschlossen; **'~s [done] while you wait'** „Reparaturschnelldienst"; Ⓑ *no pl., no art.* (*condition*) **be in good/bad ~** *or* **in a good/bad state of ~:** in gutem/schlechtem Zustand sein

**repair**[2] *v.i.* (*formal: go*) sich begeben (**to** nach/zu/in + *Akk.*) (*Papierdt.*)

**repairable** /rɪˈpeərəbl/ *adj.* reparabel; **be ~** *or* **in a ~ state** zu reparieren sein

**repairer** /rɪˈpeərə(r)/ *n.* (*of watches/shoes*) Uhr-/Schuhmacher, *der;* **take sth. to the ~'s** etw. zur Reparatur bringen

**repair: ~man** *n.* (*of mechanism*) Mechaniker, *der;* (*in house*) Handwerker, *der;* **~ shop** *n.* Reparaturwerkstatt, *die*

**repaper** /riːˈpeɪpə(r)/ *v.t.* neu tapezieren

**reparation** /repəˈreɪʃn/ *n.* Ⓐ (*making amends*) Wiedergutmachung, *die;* Ⓑ (*compensation*) Entschädigung, *die;* **~s** (*for war damage*) Reparationen; **make ~ [for sth.]** [für etw.] Ersatz leisten

**repartee** /repɑːˈtiː/ *n.* Ⓐ (*skill in making retorts*) Schlagfertigkeit, *die;* Ⓑ (*conversation*) von [Geist und] Schlagfertigkeit sprühende Unterhaltung

**repast** /rɪˈpɑːst/ *n.* (*formal*) Mahl, *das* (*geh.*)

**repatriate** /riːˈpætrɪeɪt/ *v.t.* repatriieren

**repatriation** /riːpætrɪˈeɪʃn/ *n.* Repatriierung, *die*

r

**repay** /riːˈpeɪ/ ❶ *v.t.*, **repaid** /riːˈpeɪd/ **A** (*pay back*) zurückzahlen ‹Schulden usw.›; erstatten ‹Spesen›; **if you'll lend me £1, I'll ~ you next week** wenn du mir ein Pfund leihst, zahle ich es dir nächste Woche zurück; **B** (*return*) erwidern ‹Besuch, Gruß, Freundlichkeit›; **C** (*give in recompense*) **be ~ sb. for sth.** jmdm. etw. vergelten; **D** (*requite*) **~ efforts** *etc.* für Bemühungen *usw.* entschädigen. ❷ *v.i.*, **repaid** Rückzahlungen leisten

**repayable** /riːˈpeɪəbl/ *adj.* rückzahlbar; **be ~ at the end of the year** zum Jahresende zurückgezahlt werden müssen

**repayment** /riːˈpeɪmənt/ *n.* **A** (*paying back*) Rückzahlung, *die;* **she's having trouble with the ~s** sie hat Schwierigkeiten mit der Rückzahlung; **B** (*reward*) Lohn, *der* (**for** für)

**reˈpayment mortgage** *n.* Tilgungshypothek, *die*

**repeal** /rɪˈpiːl/ ❶ *v.t.* aufheben ‹Gesetz, Erlass usw.›. ❷ *n.* Aufhebung, *die*

**repeat** /rɪˈpiːt/ ❶ *n.* **A** Wiederholung, *die;* (*Radio, TV also*) Wiederholungssendung, *die;* **do a ~ of sth.** etw. wiederholen; **there will be a ~ of this programme** diese Sendung wird wiederholt; **B** (*Commerc.*) Nachbestellung, *die;* **C** (*Mus.*) (*passage*) Wiederholung, *die;* (*sign*) Wiederholungszeichen, *das;* **D** (*repeated pattern*) Rapport, *der* (*bes. Kunstwiss.*).

❷ *v.t.* **A** (*say, do, broadcast again*) wiederholen; **ˈnot, ~ ˈnot** auf [gar] keinen Fall; unter [gar] keinen Umständen; **ˈnobody, [I] ~ ˈnobody** niemand, ich betone, niemand; (*Radio*) niemand, ich wiederhole, niemand; **please ~ after me: ...:** sprich/sprecht/sprechen Sie mir bitte nach: ...; **B** (*recite*) aufsagen ‹Gedicht, Strophe, Text›; **C** (*report*) weitererzählen (**to** *Dat.*); **do you want me to ~ the conversation?** soll ich dir das Gespräch wiedergeben?. ❸ *v.i.* **A** (*Math.: recur*) ‹Zahl:› periodisch sein; **B** (*Amer.: vote more than once*) seine Stimme mehrmals abgeben. ❹ *v. refl.* **~ oneself/itself** sich wiederholen

**repeated** /rɪˈpiːtɪd/ *adj.* wiederholt; (*several*) mehrere; **make ~ efforts to...:** wiederholt *od.* mehrfach versuchen, zu...

**repeatedly** /rɪˈpiːtɪdlɪ/ *adv.* mehrmals

**repeater** /rɪˈpiːtə(r)/ *n.* **A** (*Horol.*) Repetieruhr, *die;* **B** (*Arms*) Repetiergewehr, *das;* Mehrlader, *der*

**repeating ˈdecimal** *n.* (*Math.*) periodische Dezimalzahl

**repeat: ~ ˈorder** *n.* (*Commerc.*) Nachbestellung, *die;* **~ perˈformance** *n.* Wiederholungsvorstellung, *die* (*Theater*); (*of music*) Wiederholungskonzert, *das*

**repêchage** /ˈrepəʃɑːʒ/ *n.* (*esp. Rowing*) Hoffnungslauf, *der;* (*Fencing*) Trostrunde, *die*

**repel** /rɪˈpel/ *v.t.*, **-ll-** **A** (*drive back*) abwehren ‹Feind, Angriff, Annäherungsversuch, Schlag usw.›; widerstehen (+ *Dat.*) ‹Versuchung›; abstoßen ‹Feuchtigkeit, elektrische Ladung, Magnetpol›; **B** (*be repulsive to*) abstoßen

**repellent** /rɪˈpelənt/ ❶ *adj.* **A** (*repugnant*) abstoßend; **B** (*repelling*) **water-~:** Wasser abstoßend *od.* (*seltener*) abweisend; **mosquito ~:** Mückenschutz‹mittel usw.›. ❷ *n.* **[insect] ~:** Insektenschutzmittel, *das*

**repent** /rɪˈpent/ ❶ *v.i.* bereuen (**of** *Akk.*). ❷ *v.t.* bereuen

**repentance** /rɪˈpentəns/ *n.* Reue, *die*

**repentant** /rɪˈpentənt/ *adj.* reuig, reuevoll (*geh.*); reumütig (*öfter scherzh.*); **a ~ sinner** ein reuiger Sünder

**repercussion** /riːpəˈkʌʃn/ *n. usu. in pl.* Auswirkung, *die* (**[up]on** auf + *Akk.*)

**repertoire** /ˈrepətwɑː(r)/ *n.* **A** (*Mus., Theatre*) Repertoire, *das* (**of** an + *Dat.*, von); **B** (*complete list*) Spektrum, *das*

**repertory** /ˈrepətərɪ/ *n.* **A** ⇒ **repertoire; B** (*Theatre*) Repertoiretheater, *das;* **play/be in ~:** an einem Repertoiretheater spielen

**ˈrepertory company** *n.* Repertoiretheater, *das*

**répétiteur** /repetɪˈtɜː(r)/ *n.* (*Mus., Theatre*) [Kor]repetitor, *der*

**repetition** /repɪˈtɪʃn/ *n.* Wiederholung, *die*

**repetitious** /repɪˈtɪʃəs/ *adj.* sich immer wiederholend *attr.;* **his style is ~:** er wiederholt sich immer

**repetitive** /rɪˈpetɪtɪv/ *adj.* eintönig; **sth. is ~:** etw. bietet keine Abwechslung

**repetitive ˈstrain injury** *n.* chronisches Überlastungssyndrom

**rephrase** /riːˈfreɪz/ *v.t.* umformulieren; **I'll ~ that** ich will es anders ausdrücken

**repine** /rɪˈpaɪn/ *v.i.* (*literary*) hadern (*geh.*) (**at** mit)

**replace** /rɪˈpleɪs/ *v.t.* **A** (*put back in place*) (*vertically*) zurückstellen; wieder einordnen ‹Karteikarte›; (*horizontally*) zurücklegen; [wieder] auflegen ‹Telefonhörer›; **I ~d the key in the lock** ich steckte den Schlüssel wieder ins Schloss; **he ~d the fish in the tank** er setzte den Fisch wieder in den Tank; **B** (*take place of, provide substitute for*) ersetzen; **~ A with** *or* **by B** A durch B ersetzen; **C** (*renew*) ersetzen ‹Gestohlenes usw.›; austauschen, auswechseln ‹Maschinen[teile] usw.›; auswechseln ‹Glühbirne›; auffüllen ‹Vorrat›

**replaceable** /rɪˈpleɪsəbl/ *adj.* ersetzbar ‹Person, Verlorenes usw.›; austauschbar, auswechselbar ‹Maschinenteil usw.›

**replacement** /rɪˈpleɪsmənt/ *n.* **A** (*putting back*) ⇒ **replace** A: Zurückstellen, *das;* Zurücklegen, *das;* Wiedereinordnen, *das;* Auflegen, *das;* **B** (*provision of substitute for*) Ersatz, *der;* Ersetzen, *das; attrib.* Ersatz-; **the ~ of the blood loss** der Ausgleich des Blutverlusts; **C** (*substitute*) Ersatz, *der;* **~ [part]** Ersatzteil, *das;* **~s** (*staff, troops*) Ersatz, *der;* **my ~:** mein Nachfolger/meine Nachfolgerin

**replant** /riːˈplɑːnt/ *v.t.* **A** (*plant again*) umpflanzen; **B** (*provide with new plants*) neu bepflanzen

**replay** ❶ /riːˈpleɪ/ *v.t.* wiederholen ‹Spiel›; nochmals abspielen ‹Tonband usw.›. ❷ /ˈriːpleɪ/ *n.* Wiederholung, *die;* (*match*) Wiederholungsspiel, *das*

**replenish** /rɪˈplenɪʃ/ *v.t.* [wieder] auffüllen

**replenishment** /rɪˈplenɪʃmənt/ *n.* **A** (*renewing*) (*of supplies*) Auffüllung, *die;* Wiederauffüllen, *das;* (*of stocks*) Ergänzung, *die;* **B** (*fresh supply*) **~s** Nachschub, *der*

**replete** /rɪˈpliːt/ *adj.* **A** (*filled*) reich (**with** an + *Dat.*); **a story ~ with drama** eine Geschichte voller Dramatik; **B** (*gorged*) satt

**repleteness** /rɪˈpliːtnɪs/ *n., no pl.* Sattheit, *die;* **feeling of ~:** Völlegefühl, *das*

**repletion** /rɪˈpliːʃn/ *n.* Sättigung, *die;* **eat to ~:** sich satt essen

**replica** /ˈreplɪkə/ *n.* Nachbildung, *die;* (*of work of art*) Kopie, *die;* (*by original artist*) Replik, *die;* (*esp. on smaller scale*) Modell, *das;* **he is a ~ of his brother** er ist das Ebenbild (*geh.*) seines Bruders

**replicate** /ˈreplɪkeɪt/ ❶ *v.t.* nachbilden; replizieren (*Kunstwiss.*); (*Biol.*) replizieren. ❷ *v.i.* (*Biol.*) sich reproduzieren

**replication** /replɪˈkeɪʃn/ *n.* **A** Nachbildung, *die;* **B** (*Biol.*) Replikation, *die*

**reply** /rɪˈplaɪ/ ❶ *v.i.* **~ [to sb./sth.]** [jmdm./auf etw. (*Akk.*)] antworten; **~ [to the gunfire]** das Feuer erwidern. ❷ *v.t.* **~ that ...** antworten, dass ... ❸ *n.* **A** Antwort, *die* (**to** auf + *Akk.*); **my ~ to him** die Antwort, die ich ihm gegeben habe/geben werde *usw.*; **in/by way of ~:** als Antwort; **in ~ to your letter** in Beantwortung Ihres Schreibens (*Amtsspr.*); **what did he say in ~?** was hat er darauf geantwortet?; **make [a] ~** (*formal*) [eine] Antwort geben; **B** (*Law*) Replik, *die*

**reply: ~ coupon** *n.* (*Post*) internationaler Antwortschein; **~-paid** *adj.* **~-paid telegram** RP-Telegramm, *das;* **~-paid envelope** Freiumschlag, *der*

**repoint** /riːˈpɔɪnt/ *v.t.* (*Building*) neu ausfugen *od.* verfugen

**repopulate** /riːˈpɒpjʊleɪt/ *v.t.* neu besiedeln

**report** /rɪˈpɔːt/ ❶ *v.t.* **A** (*relate*) berichten/ (*in writing*) einen Bericht schreiben über (+ *Akk.*) ‹Ereignis usw.›; (*state formally also*) melden; **sb. is/was ~ed to be ...:** jmd. soll ... sein/gewesen sein; **she ~ed all the details to me** sie berichtete mir [über] alle Einzelheiten; **it is ~ed from Buckingham Palace that ...:** aus dem Buckingham-Palast wird gemeldet *od.* berichtet, dass ...; **nothing to ~:** keine besonderen Vorkommnisse; **~ sb. missing** jmdn. als vermisst melden; **the papers ~ed him [as] dead** laut Zeitungsberichten war er tot; **~ progress on** (*Brit.*) einen Tätigkeitsbericht abgeben über (+ *Akk.*); **B** (*repeat*) übermitteln (**to** *Dat.*) ‹Botschaft›; wiedergeben (**to** *Dat.*) ‹Worte, Sinn›; **he is ~ed as having said that ...:** er soll gesagt haben, dass ...; **C** (*name or notify to authorities*) melden (**to** *Dat.*); (*for prosecution*) anzeigen (**to** bei); **D** (*present*) **~ oneself [to sb.]** sich [bei jmdm.] melden; **~ oneself present** (*Mil.*) sich zur Stelle melden.

❷ *v.i.* **A** Bericht erstatten (**on** über + *Akk.*); berichten (**on** über + *Akk.*); **he ~s on financial affairs for the 'Guardian'** er schreibt für den Wirtschaftsteil des „Guardian"; **B** (*present oneself*) sich melden (**to** bei); **~ for duty** sich zum Dienst melden; **~ sick** sich krankmelden; **C** (*be responsible*) **~ to sb.** jmdm. unterstehen; **D** (*give report*) **~ well/badly of sb./sth.** Gutes/Schlechtes *od.* nichts Gutes über jmdn./etw. berichten; (*Radio/Telev.*) **Mark Tally ~ing [from Delhi]** Mark Tally berichtet [aus Delhi].

❸ *n.* **A** (*account*) Bericht, *der* (**on, about** über + *Akk.*); (*in newspaper etc. also*) Reportage, *die* (**on** über + *Akk.*); **make a ~:** einen Bericht abfassen; **an official ~ on price trends** ein Gutachten über die Preisentwicklung; **B** (*Sch.*) Zeugnis, *das;* **C** (*sound*) Knall, *der;* **D** (*rumour*) Gerücht, *das;* **the ~ goes that ...:** man sagt, dass ...; **know sth. only by ~:** etw. nur vom Hörensagen kennen/wissen

**~ ˈback** *v.i.* **A** (*present oneself again*) sich zurückmelden (**for** zu); **B** (*give a report*) Bericht erstatten (**to** *Dat.*)

**reportage** /repɔːˈtɑːʒ/ *n.* Reportage, *die*

**reˈport card** *n.* (*Amer.*) Zeugnis, *das*

**reportedly** /rɪˈpɔːtɪdlɪ/ *adv.* wie verlautet; **they have ~ made huge profits** sie sollen sehr große Gewinne gemacht haben

**reported ˈspeech** *n.* (*Ling.*) indirekte Rede

**reporter** /rɪˈpɔːtə(r)/ *n.* ▶ **1261** (*Radio, Telev., Journ.*) Reporter, *der*/Reporterin, *die;* Berichterstatter, *der*/-erstatterin, *die*

**reˈport stage** *n.* (*Brit. Parl.*) *Unterhausdebatte über Gesetzentwurf nach dessen Beratung im Ausschuss*

**repose** /rɪˈpəʊz/ (*literary*) ❶ *n.* **A** (*rest, respite*) Ruhe, *die;* **in ~:** ruhend; **B** (*composure*) Gelassenheit, *die.* ❷ *v.i.* **A** (*lie*) ruhen; (*joc.: be situated*) liegen; sich befinden; **B** (*be supported*) beruhen (**[up]on** auf + *Dat.*). ❸ *v.t.* (*rest*) ausruhen

**reposition** /riːpəˈzɪʃn/ *v.t.* umstellen; verstellen ‹Teil›

**repository** /rɪˈpɒzɪtərɪ/ *n.* **A** (*receptacle*) Behälter, *der;* **B** (*store*) Lager, *das;* (*fig.*) (*book etc.*) Fundgrube, *die* (**of** für); (*person*) Quelle, *die* (**of** für)

**repossess** /riːpəˈzes/ *v.t.* wiedergewinnen ‹Gebiet usw.›; wieder in Besitz nehmen ‹Waren›; ‹Bausparkasse:› beschlagnahmen lassen ‹Haus›

**repossession** /riːpəˈzeʃn/ *n.* (*of territories etc.*) Wiedergewinnung, *die;* (*of goods*) Wiederinbesitznahme, *die;* (*of house*) Erwirkung der Beschlagnahme

**repot** /riːˈpɒt/ *v.t.*, **-tt-** umtopfen

**repp** ⇒ **rep**[1]

**reprehend** /reprɪˈhend/ *v.t.* tadeln; rügen

**reprehensible** /reprɪˈhensɪbl/ *adj.* tadelnswert; sträflich; **be morally ~:** moralisch zu verurteilen sein

**reprehensibly** /reprɪˈhensɪblɪ/ *adv.* tadelnswert; sträflich

**represent** /reprɪˈzent/ *v.t.* **A** (*symbolize*) verkörpern; **B** (*denote, depict, present*) darstellen (**as** als); (*Theatre also*) spielen; **the symbol x ~s guttural sounds** das Zeichen x steht für Gutturallaute; **I am not what you ~ me as** *or* **to be** ich bin nicht so, wie

r

du mich hinstellst; Ⓒ (*correspond to*) entsprechen (+ *Dat.*); Ⓓ (*be specimen of, act for*) vertreten

**re-present** /riːprɪˈzent/ *v.t.* erneut vorlegen

**representation** /reprɪzenˈteɪʃn/ *n.* Ⓐ (*depicting, image*) Darstellung, *die;* Ⓑ (*acting for sb.*) Vertretung, *die;* Ⓒ (*protest*) Protest, *der;* **make ~s to sb.** bei jmdm. Protest einlegen

**representational** /reprɪzenˈteɪʃənl/ *adj.* Ⓐ gegenständlich ‹Kunst›; Ⓑ ⇒ **representative** 2 C

**representative** /reprɪˈzentətɪv/ ❶ *n.* Ⓐ ▶ **1261** (*member, successor, agent, deputy*) Vertreter, *der*/Vertreterin, *die;* (*firm's agent, deputy also*) Repräsentant, *der*/Repräsentantin, *die;* **there were no ~s of the family at the funeral** die Familie war bei der Beerdigung nicht vertreten; Ⓑ **R~** (*Amer. Polit.*) Abgeordneter/Abgeordnete im Repräsentantenhaus; **House of R~s** Repräsentantenhaus, *das.*
❷ *adj.* Ⓐ (*typical*) repräsentativ (**of** für); **a ~ modern building** ein typisches modernes Gebäude; **Charles II was fully ~ of his age** Charles II war ein typischer Vertreter seiner Zeit; Ⓑ (*consisting of deputies*) Abgeordneten‹versammlung, -kammer usw.›; Ⓒ (*Polit.: based on representation*) repräsentativ; Repräsentativ‹system, -verfassung›; **~ government/institutions** parlamentarische Regierung/Institution; Ⓓ **be ~ of** (*portray*) darstellen; (*symbolize*) symbolisieren; ‹Person:› verkörpern; Ⓔ (*that presents sth. to the mind*) **~ faculty/power** Vorstellungsvermögen, *das*/-kraft, *die*

**representatively** /reprɪˈzentətɪvlɪ/ *adv.* repräsentativ

**representativeness** /reprɪˈzentətɪvnɪs/ *n., no pl.* Repräsentanz, *die*

**repress** /rɪˈpres/ *v.t.* Ⓐ unterdrücken ‹Aufruhr, Gefühle, Lachen usw.›; Ⓑ (*Psych.*) verdrängen ‹Gefühle› (**from** aus)

**repressed** /rɪˈprest/ *adj.* unterdrückt; (*Psych.*) verdrängt

**repression** /rɪˈpreʃn/ *n.* Unterdrückung, *die;* (*Psych.*) Verdrängung, *die*

**repressive** /rɪˈpresɪv/ *adj.* repressiv; **~ measures** Repressivmaßnahmen

**reprieve** /rɪˈpriːv/ ❶ *v.t.* **~ sb.** (*postpone execution*) jmdm. Strafaufschub gewähren; (*remit execution*) jmdn. begnadigen; (*fig.*) verschonen. ❷ *n.* Strafaufschub, *der* (**of** für); Begnadigung, *die;* (*fig.*) Gnadenfrist, *die*

**reprimand** /ˈreprɪmɑːnd/ ❶ *n.* Tadel, *der;* Verweis, *der.* ❷ *v.t.* tadeln; einen Verweis erteilen (+ *Dat.*)

**reprint** ❶ /riːˈprɪnt/ *v.t.* Ⓐ (*print again*) wieder abdrucken; Ⓑ (*make reprint of*) nachdrucken. ❷ /ˈriːprɪnt/ *n.* Ⓐ (*book reprinted*) Nachdruck, *der;* Ⓑ **how big was the ~?** wie viel Exemplare wurden nachgedruckt?; **it has had ten ~s** es ist zehnmal nachgedruckt worden; Ⓒ (*article printed separately*) Sonderdruck, *der*

**reprisal** /rɪˈpraɪzl/ *n.* Vergeltungsakt, *der* (**for** gegen)

**reprise** /rəˈpriːz/ *n.* (*Mus.*) Reprise, *die*

**repro** /ˈriːprəʊ/ ❶ *n.* (*Printing*) Repro, *das;* **~ [proof]** Reproabzug, *der.* ❷ *adj.* **it's only ~:** es ist nur eine Reproduktion

**reproach** /rɪˈprəʊtʃ/ ❶ *v.t.* **~ sb.** jmdm. Vorwürfe machen; **~ sb. with** *or* **for sth.** jmdm. etw. vorwerfen *od.* zum Vorwurf machen; **~ sb. bitterly for having done sth.** jmdm. bittere Vorwürfe machen, dass er etw. getan hat; **have nothing to ~ oneself for** *or* **with** sich (*Dat.*) nichts vorzuwerfen haben. ❷ *n.* Ⓐ (*rebuke*) Vorwurf, *der;* **be above** *or* **beyond ~:** über jeden Vorwurf erhaben sein; **be used as a term of ~:** abwertend gebraucht werden; **look of ~:** vorwurfsvoller Blick; Ⓑ (*disgrace*) Schande, *die* (**to** für)

**reproachful** /rɪˈprəʊtʃfl/ *adj.*, **reproachfully** /rɪˈprəʊtʃfəlɪ/ *adv.* vorwurfsvoll

**reprobate** /ˈreprəbeɪt/ ❶ *n.* Halunke, *der.* ❷ *adj.* verkommen

**reprocess** /riːˈprəʊses/ *v.t.* wieder aufbereiten; **~ing plant** Wiederaufbereitungsanlage, *die*

**reproduce** /riːprəˈdjuːs/ ❶ *v.t.* Ⓐ wiedergeben; reproduzieren (*Druckw.*) ‹Bilder usw.›; Ⓑ **~ oneself** sich fortpflanzen; sich vermehren; Ⓒ (*Biol.: form afresh*) neu bilden ‹Organe, Gliedmaßen usw.›. ❷ *v.i.* Ⓐ (*multiply*) sich fortpflanzen; sich vermehren; Ⓑ (*give copy*) sich reproduzieren lassen

**reproducible** /riːprəˈdjuːsɪbl/ *adj.* reproduzierbar; **be ~:** sich reproduzieren lassen

**reproduction** /riːprəˈdʌkʃn/ *n.* Ⓐ Wiedergabe, *die;* Reproduktion, *die* (*Druckw.*); **~ of sound** Tonwiedergabe, *die;* Ⓑ (*producing offspring*) Fortpflanzung, *die;* Ⓒ (*copy*) Reproduktion, *die;* **printed ~:** Druck, *der; attrib.* **~ furniture** Stilmöbel *Pl.;* **a ~ Chippendale chair** ein Stuhl im Chippendalestil; Ⓓ (*Biol.: forming afresh*) Regeneration, *die*

**reproductive** /riːprəˈdʌktɪv/ *adj.* Fortpflanzungs-

**reprographic** /riːprəˈgræfɪk/ *adj.* reprographisch (*Druckw.*)

**reproof** /rɪˈpruːf/ *n.* Tadel, *der;* **a glance/word of ~:** ein tadelnder Blick/ein tadelndes Wort; **deserving of ~:** tadelnswert

**reprove** /rɪˈpruːv/ *v.t.* tadeln ‹Verhalten usw.›; tadeln, zurechtweisen ‹Person›

**reproving** /rɪˈpruːvɪŋ/ *adj.* tadelnd

**reprovingly** /rɪˈpruːvɪŋlɪ/ *adv.* tadelnd

**reptile** /ˈreptaɪl/ *n.* Reptil, *das;* Kriechtier, *das;* (*fig. derog.*) Ekel, *das* (*ugs. abwertend*)

**reptilian** /repˈtɪljən/ ❶ *adj.* reptilartig; (*of the Reptilia*) Reptilien‹knochen, -schädel›. ❷ *n.* Reptil, *das;* Kriechtier, *das*

**republic** /rɪˈpʌblɪk/ *n.* Republik, *die*

**republican** /rɪˈpʌblɪkən/ ❶ *adj.* Ⓐ republikanisch; Ⓑ (*Amer. Polit.*) **R~ Party** Republikanische Partei. ❷ *n.* **R~** (*Amer. Polit.*) Republikaner, *der*/Republikanerin, *die*

**republicanism** /rɪˈpʌblɪkənɪzm/ *n.* Republikanismus, *der*

**republication** /riːpʌblɪˈkeɪʃn/ *n.* Wiederveröffentlichung, *die*

**republish** /riːˈpʌblɪʃ/ *v.t.* wieder veröffentlichen

**repudiate** /rɪˈpjuːdɪeɪt/ *v.t.* Ⓐ (*deny*) zurückweisen ‹Anschuldigung usw.›; (*reject*) nicht anerkennen ‹Autorität, Vertrag usw.›; Ⓑ (*disown*) verstoßen ‹Person›

**repudiation** /rɪpjuːdɪˈeɪʃn/ *n.* ⇒ **repudiate**: Zurückweisung, *die;* Nichtanerkennung, *die;* Verstoßung, *die*

**repugnance** /rɪˈpʌgnəns/ *n.* (*strong dislike*) [starke] Abneigung (**to[wards]** gegen); Abscheu, *der* (**to[wards]** vor + *Dat.*)

**repugnant** /rɪˈpʌgnənt/ *adj.* (*distasteful*) widerlich; abstoßend; **be ~ to sb.** jmdm. widerlich sein

**repulse** /rɪˈpʌls/ ❶ *v.t.* abwehren (*auch fig.*); zurückweisen ‹Unterstellung›. ❷ *n.* Abwehr, *die;* **suffer a ~:** eine Niederlage erleiden

**repulsion** /rɪˈpʌlʃn/ *n.* Ⓐ (*disgust*) Widerwille, *der* (**towards** gegen); Ⓑ (*Phys.*) Repulsion, *die*

**repulsive** /rɪˈpʌlsɪv/ *adj.* Ⓐ (*disgusting*) abstoßend; widerwärtig; Ⓑ (*Phys.*) repulsiv

**repulsively** /rɪˈpʌlsɪvlɪ/ *adv.* abstoßend

**repurchase** /riːˈpɜːtʃɪs/ ❶ *v.t.* zurückkaufen. ❷ *n.* Rückkauf, *der*

**reputable** /ˈrepjʊtəbl/ *adj.* angesehen ‹Person, Familie, Beruf, Zeitung usw.›; anständig ‹Verhalten›; seriös ‹Firma›

**reputably** /ˈrepjʊtəblɪ/ *adv.* anständig

**reputation** /repjʊˈteɪʃn/ *n.* Ⓐ Ruf, *der;* **have a ~ for** *or* **of doing/being sth.** in dem Ruf stehen, etw. zu tun/sein; **he has a ~ for integrity/stealing** er gilt als integer/man sagt, dass er stiehlt; **what sort of ~ do they have?** wie ist ihr Ruf?; Ⓑ (*good name*) Name, *der;* Renommee, *das;* **men with a ~ as scientists** Männer, die sich als Wissenschaftler einen Namen gemacht haben; **make one's** *or* **gain a ~:** sich (*Dat.*) einen Namen machen (**as** als); Ⓒ (*bad name*) schlechter Ruf; **get oneself** *or* **acquire quite a ~:** sich in Verruf bringen

**repute** /rɪˈpjuːt/ ❶ *v.t. in pass.* **be ~d [to be] sth.** als etw. gelten; **she is ~d to have/make ...:** man sagt, dass sie ... hat/macht; **be very highly ~d [as a doctor]** einen sehr guten Ruf [als Arzt] haben. ❷ *n.* Ruf, *der;* Ansehen, *das;* **hold sb./sth. in high ~:** von jmdm./etw. eine hohe Meinung haben; jmdn./etw. hoch schätzen (*geh.*); **of ill ~:** von schlechtem Ruf; **a house of ill ~:** ein Haus von zweifelhaftem Ruf; **know sb. by ~:** von jmdm. schon viel gehört haben; **a philosopher of ~:** ein angesehener Philosoph

**reputed** /rɪˈpjuːtɪd/ *adj.* angeblich; **the ~ father** der mutmaßliche Vater

**reputedly** /rɪˈpjuːtɪdlɪ/ *adv.* angeblich; vermeintlich

**request** /rɪˈkwest/ ❶ *v.t.* bitten; **~ sth. of** *or* **from sb.** jmdn. um etw. bitten; **~ sb.'s presence** um jmds. Anwesenheit bitten; **~ silence** um Ruhe bitten; **~ a record** einen Plattenwunsch äußern; **~ that ...:** darum bitten, dass ...; **~ sb. to do sth.** jmdn. [darum] bitten, etw. zu tun; **the essay I am ~ed to write** der Essay, den ich schreiben soll; **'You are ~ed not to smoke'** „Bitte nicht rauchen".
❷ *n.* Bitte, *die* (**for** um); **at sb.'s ~:** auf jmds. Bitte *od.* Wunsch (*Akk.*) [hin]; **make a ~ for sth.** um etw. bitten; **I have one ~ to make of** *or* **to you** ich habe eine Bitte an Sie; **by** *or* **on ~:** auf Wunsch; **have one's ~:** seine Bitte *od.* seinen Wunsch erfüllt bekommen; **record ~s** (*Radio*) Plattenwünsche *Pl.;* **we do not receive many ~s for it** dafür haben wir keine große Nachfrage; *no art., no pl.* (*demand*) **be much in ~** sehr gefragt sein

**request: ~ programme** *n.* (*Radio*) Wunschkonzert, *das;* **~ stop** *n.* (*Brit.*) Bedarfshaltestelle, *die*

**requiem** /ˈrekwɪem/ *n.* Requiem, *das*

**requiem 'mass** *n.* (*Eccl.*) Requiem, *das* (*kath. Kirche*); Totenmesse, *die*

**require** /rɪˈkwaɪə(r)/ *v.t.* Ⓐ (*need, wish to have*) brauchen; benötigen; erfordern ‹Tun, Verhalten›; **a catalogue/guide is available if ~d** bei Bedarf ist ein Katalog erhältlich/auf Wunsch steht ein Führer zur Verfügung; **is there anything else you ~?** brauchen/ (*want*) wünschen Sie außerdem noch etwas?; **I have all I ~:** ich habe alles, was ich brauche; **it ~d all his authority ...:** es bedurfte seiner ganzen Autorität ... (*geh.*); Ⓑ (*order, demand*) verlangen (**of** von); **~ sb. to do sth., ~ of sb. that he does sth.** von jmdm. verlangen, dass er etw. tut; **be ~d to do sth.** etw. tun müssen *od.* sollen; **~d reading** Pflichtlektüre, *die*

**requirement** /rɪˈkwaɪəmənt/ *n.* Ⓐ (*need*) Bedarf, *der;* **meet the ~s** den Bedarf decken; **meet sb.'s ~s** jmds. Wünschen entsprechen; **what are your ~s?** was brauchen Sie?; **borrowing ~:** Kreditbedarf, *der;* Ⓑ (*condition*) Erfordernis, *das;* (*for a job*) Voraussetzung, *die;* **fulfil sb.'s ~s** jmds. Anforderungen (*Dat.*) genügen; **there are certain language ~s for this job** diese Stelle setzt [bestimmte] Sprachkenntnisse voraus

**requisite** /ˈrekwɪzɪt/ ❶ *adj.* notwendig (**to, for** für); erforderlich ‹Voraussetzung, Kenntnisse›. ❷ *n.* Erfordernis, *das* (**for** für); **be a ~ for sth.** für etw. erforderlich sein; **toilet/travel ~s** Toiletten-/Reiseartikel *Pl.*

**requisition** /rekwɪˈzɪʃn/ ❶ *n.* Ⓐ (*esp. Law: demand*) Aufforderung, *die;* Ⓑ (*order for sth.*) Anforderung, *die* (**for** *Gen.*); (*by force if necessary*) Beschlagnahmung, *die* (**for** *Gen.*); **make a ~ on sb. for sth.** etw. bei jmdm. anfordern; **be put under ~:** beschlagnahmt werden. ❷ *v.t.* anfordern; (*by force if necessary*) beschlagnahmen

**requital** /rɪˈkwaɪtl/ *n.* Vergeltung, *die*

**requite** /rɪˈkwaɪt/ *v.t.* vergelten; **~ sb. for sth.** jmdm. etw. vergelten; (*avenge*) jmdm. etw. heimzahlen

**reran** ⇒ **rerun** 1

**reread** /riːˈriːd/ *v.t.*, **reread** /riːˈred/ wieder *od.* nochmals lesen; **~ sth. several times** etw. mehrmals *od.* wiederholt lesen

**reredos** /ˈrɪədɒs/ *n.* (*Eccl.*) Altaraufsatz, *der;* Retabel, *das*

**re-route** /riːˈruːt/ *v.t.*, **~ing** umleiten

**rerun** ❶ /riːˈrʌn/ *v.t.*, *forms as* **run** wiederholen ‹Rennen›; wieder auf- *od.* vorführen ‹Film›; wieder abspielen ‹Tonband›. ❷ /ˈriːrʌn/ *n.* ⇒ **1**: Wiederholung, *die;* Wiederaufführung, *die;* Wiederabspielen, *das*

**resale** /riːˈseɪl/ *n.* Weiterverkauf, *der* (*Wirtsch.*) (**to** an + *Akk.*); **'not for ~'** „nicht zum Wiederverkauf bestimmt"; (*on free samples*) „unverkäufliches Muster"; **~ price maintenance** Preisbindung, *die*

**resat** ⇒ **resit** 1, 2

**reschedule** /riːˈʃedjuːl/ *v.t.* **A** zeitlich neu festlegen ‹Veranstaltung, Flug, Programm usw.›; **the flight will be ~d for 5 o'clock** der Flug wird auf 5 Uhr verlegt; **B** (*Fin.*) umschulden, refinanzieren ‹Kredit, Darlehen›; refinanzieren ‹Schulden›

**rescind** /rɪˈsɪnd/ *v.t.* für ungültig erklären

**rescue** /ˈreskjuː/ ❶ *v.t.* retten (**from** aus); (*set free*) befreien (**from** aus); **~ sb. from drowning** jmdn. vorm Ertrinken retten. ❷ *n.* ⇒ **1**: Rettung, *die;* Befreiung, *die; attrib.* Rettungs‹dienst, -versuch, -mannschaft, -aktion›; **go/come to the/sb.'s ~:** jmdm. zu Hilfe kommen; **once again it was Margaret to the ~:** es war wieder mal Margaret, die die Situation gerettet hat

**rescuer** /ˈreskjuːə(r)/ *n.* Retter, *der*/Retterin, *die*

**'rescue worker** *n.* [Einsatz]helfer, *der*/-helferin, *die*

**research** /rɪˈsɜːtʃ, ˈriːsɜːtʃ/ ❶ *n.* **A** (*scientific study*) Forschung, *die* (**into, on** über + *Akk.*); **do ~ in biochemistry** auf dem Gebiet der Biochemie forschen; **carry out/be engaged in ~ into sth.** wissenschaftliche Untersuchungen über etw. (*Akk.*) durchführen/sich in seiner Forschungsarbeit mit etw. befassen; **piece of ~:** Forschungsarbeit, *die;* (*investigation*) Untersuchung, *die;* **B** (*inquiry*) Nachforschung, *die* (**into** über + *Akk.*). ❷ *v.i.* forschen; **~ into sth.** etw. erforschen *od.* untersuchen; (*esp. Univ.*) über etw. (*Akk.*) forschen. ❸ *v.t.* erforschen; untersuchen; recherchieren ‹Buch usw.›

**research assistant** /-ˈ- ---, ˈ-- ---/ *n.* ▶ **1261** wissenschaftlicher Assistent/wissenschaftliche Assistentin

**researcher** /rɪˈsɜːtʃə(r), ˈriːsɜːtʃə(r)/ *n.* ▶ **1261** Forscher, *der*/Forscherin, *die*

**research: ~ fellow** *n.* Forschungsstipendiat, *der*/-stipendiatin, *die;* **~ fellowship** *n.* Forschungsstipendium, *das;* **~ student** *n.* ≈ Doktorand, *der*/Doktorandin, *die;* **~ work** *n.* Recherchen *Pl.;* **~ worker** *n.* ▶ **1261** *mit Nachforschungen beauftragte Person;* ≈ Rechercheur, *der*/Rechercheurin, *die*

**resection** /rɪˈsekʃn/ *n.* (*Med.*) Resektion, *die*

**reselect** /riːsɪˈlekt/ *v.t.* (*Parl.*) wieder aufstellen ‹Abgeordneten›

**reselection** /riːsɪˈlekʃn/ *n.* (*Parl.*) Wiederaufstellung, *die*

**resell** /riːˈsel/ *v.t.*, **resold** /riːˈsəʊld/ weiterverkaufen (**to** an + *Akk.*)

**resemblance** /rɪˈzembləns/ *n.* Ähnlichkeit, *die* (**to** mit, **between** zwischen + *Dat.*); **bear a faint/strong/no ~ to ...:** eine geringe/starke/keine Ähnlichkeit mit ... haben

**resemble** /rɪˈzembl/ *v.t.* ähneln, gleichen (+ *Dat.*); **they ~ each other** sie ähneln *od.* gleichen sich (*Dat.*) *od.* einander

**resent** /rɪˈzent/ *v.t.* übel nehmen; **she ~ed his familiarity/success** sie nahm ihm seine Vertraulichkeit übel/missgönnte ihm seinen Erfolg; **I ~ the way you take my help for granted** es gefällt mir nicht, wie du meine Hilfe als selbstverständlich hinnimmst; **she ~ed his having won** sie ärgerte sich darüber, dass er gewonnen hatte

**resentful** /rɪˈzentfl/ *adj.* übelnehmerisch, nachtragend ‹Person, Art, Verhalten›; grollend (*geh.*) ‹Blick›; **be ~ of** *or* **feel ~ about sth.** etw. übel nehmen; **be ~ of sb.'s criticism/success** jmdm. seine Kritik übel nehmen/seinen Erfolg missgönnen

**resentfully** /rɪˈzentfəlɪ/ *adv.* grollend (*geh.*); voller Groll *nachgestellt* (*geh.*)

**resentment** /rɪˈzentmənt/ *n., no pl.* Groll, *der* (*geh.*); **feel ~ towards** *or* **against sb.** einen Groll auf jmdn. haben

**reservation** /rezəˈveɪʃn/ *n.* **A** Reservierung, *die;* **[seat] ~:** [Platz]reservierung, *die;* **have a ~ [for a room]** ein Zimmer reserviert haben; **B** (*doubt, objection*) Vorbehalt, *der* (**about** gegen); Bedenken (**about** bezüglich + *Gen.*); **without ~:** ohne Vorbehalt; vorbehaltlos; **with ~s** mit [gewissen] Vorbehalten; ⇒ *also* **mental reservation**; **C central ~** (*Brit. Road Constr.*) Mittelstreifen, *der;* **D** (*Amer.: land reserved for Indians*) Reservat, *das;* Reservation, *die*

**reserve** /rɪˈzɜːv/ ❶ *v.t.* **A** (*secure*) reservieren lassen ‹Zimmer, Tisch, Platz›; (*set aside*) reservieren; **~ the right to do sth.** sich (*Dat.*) [das Recht] vorbehalten, etw. zu tun; **all seats ~d** Plätze nur auf Vorbestellung; **all rights ~d** alle Rechte vorbehalten; **B** *in pass.* (*be kept*) **be ~d for sb.** ‹Funktion, Tätigkeit:› jmdm. vorbehalten sein; **C** (*postpone*) aufheben ‹Überraschung, Neuigkeit›; **~ judgement** sein Urteil aufschieben; **~ oneself for sth.** sich für etw. schonen; **~ one's strength** seine Kräfte schonen.
❷ *n.* **A** (*extra amount*) Reserve, *die* (**of** an + *Dat.*) (*Banking also*) Rücklage, *die;* **~s of energy/strength** Energie-/Kraftreserven; **hidden ~:** stille Reserve; **have/hold** *or* **keep sth. in ~:** etw. in Reserve haben/halten; **B** *in sing. or pl.* (*Mil.*) (*troops*) Reserve, *die;* **the ~s** die Reservetruppen *od.* -einheiten; **C** ⇒ **reservist**; **D** (*Sport*) Reservespieler, *der*/-spielerin, *die;* **the Reserves** die Reserve; **E** (*place set apart*) Reservat, *das;* **F** (*restriction*) Vorbehalt, *der;* **without ~:** ohne Vorbehalt; vorbehaltlos; **G** ⇒ **~ price**; **H** (*self-restraint, reticence*) Reserve, *die;* Zurückhaltung, *die*

**reserve 'currency** *n.* Reservewährung, *die*

**reserved** /rɪˈzɜːvd/ *adj.* **A** (*reticent*) reserviert; zurückhaltend; **B** (*booked*) reserviert

**reserve: ~ list** *n.* (*Mil.*) **be on the ~ list** Reservist sein; **~ player** *n.* Reservespieler, *der*/-spielerin, *die;* **~ price** *n.* Mindestgebot, *das*

**reservist** /rɪˈzɜːvɪst/ *n.* (*Mil.*) Reservist, *der*

**reservoir** /ˈrezəvwɑː(r)/ *n.* **A** ([*artificial*] *lake*) Reservoir, *das;* **B** (*container*) Behälter, *der;* Speicher, *der;* (*of fountain pen*) Tintenraum, *der;* **C** (*reserve supply*) Vorrat, *der* (**of** an + *Dat.*); (*fig.*) Reservoir, *das*

**reset** /riːˈset/ *v.t.*, **-tt-**, **reset** **A** neu [ein]fassen ‹Schmuck-, Edelstein›; neu stellen ‹Uhr, Timer›; umstellen ‹Uhr› (**for, to** auf + *Akk.*); **B** (*Med.*) wieder einrichten ‹Gliedmaße, Knochen›; wieder einrenken ‹ausgerenktes Gelenk›; **C** (*Printing*) neu setzen

**resettle** /riːˈsetl/ *v.t.* **A** umsiedeln ‹Flüchtlinge usw.› (**in** in + *Akk.*); **B** (*repopulate*) wieder besiedeln ‹Gebiet›

**resettlement** /riːˈsetlmənt/ *n.* **A** (*of refugees*) Umsiedlung, *die;* **B** (*repopulating*) Neubesiedlung, *die*

**reshape** /riːˈʃeɪp/ *v.t.* **A** (*give new form to*) umgestalten; umstellen ‹Politik›; **B** (*remould*) umformen

**reshuffle** /riːˈʃʌfl/ ❶ *v.t.* **A** (*reorganize*) umbilden ‹Kabinett usw.›; **B** (*Cards*) neu mischen. ❷ *n.* Umbildung, *die;* **Cabinet ~:** Kabinettsumbildung, *die*

**reside** /rɪˈzaɪd/ *v.i.* (*formal*) **A** (*dwell*) wohnen; wohnhaft sein (*Amtsspr.*); ‹Monarch, Präsident usw.:› residieren; **B** (*be vested, present, inherent*) liegen (**in** bei)

**residence** /ˈrezɪdəns/ *n.* **A** (*abode*) Wohnsitz, *der;* (*house*) Wohnhaus, *das;* (*mansion*) Villa, *die;* (*of a head of state or church, an ambassador*) Residenz, *die;* **the President's official ~:** der offizielle Wohnsitz des Präsidenten; **have one's ~ in London/in Victoria Street** seinen Wohnsitz in London haben/seine Privatwohnung in der Victoria Street haben; **B** (*residing*) Aufenthalt, *der;* **take up [one's] ~ in Rome** seinen Wohnsitz in Rom nehmen; **be in ~** ‹König, Präsident usw.:› [an seinem offiziellen Wohnsitz] anwesend sein; ‹Student:› im College sein; **we have a doctor in ~:** wir haben einen Arzt im Hause; **writer** *etc.* **in ~** *von einer Gemeinde od. einer Institution geförderter, am Ort lebender Schriftsteller usw.*

**'residence permit** *n.* Aufenthaltsgenehmigung, *die*

**residency** /ˈrezɪdənsɪ/ *n.* (*Amer. Med.*) Zeit als Assistenzarzt/-ärztin im Krankenhaus

**resident** /ˈrezɪdənt/ ❶ *adj.* **A** (*residing*) wohnhaft; **~ population** [orts]ansässige Bevölkerung; **he is ~ in England** er hat seinen Wohnsitz in England; **B** (*living in*) im Haus wohnend ‹Haushälterin›; Anstalts‹arzt, -geistlicher›; **~ tutor** Hauslehrer, *der.* ❷ *n.* **A** (*inhabitant*) Bewohner, *der*/Bewohnerin, *die;* (*in a town etc. also*) Einwohner, *der*/Einwohnerin, *die;* (*at hotel*) Hotelgast, *der;* **'access/parking for ~s only'** „Anlieger frei"/„Parken nur für Anlieger"; **local ~:** Anwohner, *der*/Anwohnerin, *die;* **~s association** *Interessengemeinschaft von* [*benachbarten*] *Anwohnern eines bestimmten Gebiets;* **B** (*Amer. Med.*) ≈ Assistenzarzt, *der*/-ärztin, *die*

**residential** /rezɪˈdenʃl/ *adj.* **A** Wohn‹gebiet, -siedlung, -straße›; **for ~ purposes** zu Wohnzwecken; **~ hotel** Hotel für Dauergäste; **B ~ course** *Kurs, dessen Teilnehmer am Ort wohnen;* **the ~ qualification for voters** *Nachweis des Wohnsitzes als Voraussetzung zur Ausübung des Wahlrechts*

**residential 'care** *n.* stationäre Pflege

**resident's 'parking** *n.* Parken nur für Anlieger

**residual** /rɪˈzɪdjʊəl/ *adj.* zurückgeblieben; noch vorhanden; ungeklärt ‹Problem, Frage›

**residue** /ˈrezɪdjuː/ *n.* **A** (*remainder*) Rest, *der;* **B** (*Law*) restlicher Nachlass (*nach Abzug aller Nachlassverbindlichkeiten*); **C** (*Chem.*) Rückstand, *der*

**residuum** /rɪˈzɪdjʊəm/ *n., pl.* **residua** /rɪˈzɪdjʊə/ (*Chem.*) Rückstand, *der*

**resign** /rɪˈzaɪn/ ❶ *v.t.* (*hand over*) zurücktreten von ‹Amt›; verzichten auf (+ *Akk.*) ‹Recht, Anspruch›; **~ the leadership to sb.** jmdm. die Führung überlassen *od.* -geben; **~ one's commission** (*Mil.*) seinen Abschied nehmen; **~ one's job/post** seine Stelle/Stellung kündigen. ❷ *v. refl.* **~ oneself to sth./to doing sth.** sich mit etw. abfinden/sich damit abfinden, etw. zu tun. ❸ *v.i.* **A** ‹Arbeitnehmer:› kündigen; ‹Regierungsbeamter:› zurücktreten (**from** von); ‹Geistlicher, Richter:› sein Amt niederlegen; ‹Vorsitzender:› zurücktreten, sein Amt niederlegen; **~ from one's post** ‹Beamter:› seine Stellung kündigen; **B** (*Chess*) aufgeben

**resignation** /rezɪgˈneɪʃn/ *n.* **A** ⇒ **resign** 3 A: Kündigung, *die;* Verzicht, *der* (**of** auf + *Akk.*); Rücktritt, *der;* Amtsniederlegung, *die;* **give** *or* **send in** *or* **tender one's ~:** seinen Rücktritt/seine Kündigung einreichen/sein Amt niederlegen; **B** (*being resigned*) Resignation, *die;* **with ~:** resigniert

**resigned** /rɪˈzaɪnd/ *adj.* resigniert; **become/be ~ to sth.** sich mit etw. abfinden/abgefunden haben

**resignedly** /rɪˈzaɪnɪdlɪ/ *adv.* resigniert

**resilience** /rɪˈzɪlɪəns/, **resiliency** /rɪˈzɪlɪənsɪ/ *n., no pl.* **A** (*elasticity*) Elastizität, *die;* **B** (*fig.*) Unverwüstlichkeit, *die*

**resilient** /rɪˈzɪlɪənt/ *adj.* **A** (*elastic*) elastisch; **B** (*fig.*) unverwüstlich; **be ~:** sich nicht [so leicht] unterkriegen lassen

**resin** /ˈrezɪn/ *n.* **A** (*Bot.*) Harz, *das;* **B [synthetic] ~:** Kunstharz, *das*

**resinous** /ˈrezɪnəs/ *adj.* (*like resin*) harzartig; (*containing resin*) harzig; harzhaltig

**resist** /rɪˈzɪst/ ❶ *v.t.* **A** (*withstand action of*) standhalten (+ *Dat.*) ‹Frost, Hitze, Feuchtigkeit usw.›; **be unable to ~ an infection/a disease** keine Abwehrkräfte gegen eine Infektion/Krankheit haben; **B** (*oppose, repel*) sich widersetzen (+ *Dat.*) ‹Maßnahme, Festnahme, Plan usw.›; widerstehen (+ *Dat.*) ‹Versuchung, jmds. Charme›; Widerstand leisten gegen ‹Angriff, Feind›; sich wehren gegen ‹Veränderung, Einfluss›. ❷ *v.i.* ⇒ **1** B: sich widersetzen; widerstehen; Widerstand leisten; sich wehren

r

**resistance** /rɪˈzɪstəns/ *n.* Ⓐ (*resisting, opposing force; also Phys., Electr.*) Widerstand, *der* (**to** gegen); **make** *or* **offer no ~ [to sb./sth.]** [jmdm./einer Sache] keinen Widerstand leisten; **take the line of least ~** (*fig.*) den Weg des geringsten Widerstandes gehen; ⇒ *also* **passive** 1 B; Ⓑ (*power of resisting*) Widerstandsfähigkeit, *die* (**to** gegen); **~ to wear and tear** Strapazierfähigkeit, *die;* **~ to heat/cold** Hitze-/Kältebeständigkeit, *die;* Ⓒ (*Biol., Med.*) Widerstandskraft, *die* (**to** gegen); Ⓓ (*against occupation*) Widerstand, *der;* **the French R~:** die Résistance

**resistance: ~ fighter** *n.* Widerstandskämpfer, *der*/-kämpferin, *die;* **~ movement** *n.* Widerstandsbewegung, *die*

**resistant** /rɪˈzɪstənt/ *adj.* Ⓐ (*opposed*) **be ~ to** sich widersetzen (+ *Dat.*); sich entgegenstellen (+ *Dat.*); Ⓑ (*having power to resist*) widerstandsfähig (**to** gegen); **highly ~ to wear and tear** sehr strapazierfähig; **heat-/water-/rust-~:** hitze-/wasser-/rostbeständig; Ⓒ (*Med., Biol.*) resistent (**to** gegen)

**resistor** /rɪˈzɪstə(r)/ *n.* (*Electr.*) Widerstand, *der*

**resit** ❶ /riːˈsɪt/ *v.t.*, **-tt-**, **resat** /riːˈsæt/ wiederholen ‹Prüfung›. ❷ *v.i.*, **-tt-**, **resat** die Prüfung wiederholen. ❸ /ˈriːsɪt/ *n.* Wiederholungsprüfung, *die*

**reskill** /riːˈskɪl/ *v.t.* fort- *od.* weiterbilden; umschulen ‹Arbeitslose›

**resold** ⇒ **resell**

**resole** /riːˈsəʊl/ *v.t.* neu besohlen

**resolute** /ˈrezəluːt/ *adj.* resolut, energisch ‹Person›; entschlossen ‹Tat›; entschieden ‹Antwort, Weigerung›

**resolutely** /ˈrezəluːtlɪ/ *adv.* entschlossen

**resolution** /rezəˈluːʃn/ *n.* Ⓐ (*decision*) Entschließung, *die;* (*Polit. also*) Resolution, *die;* **a ~ of sympathy/solidarity** eine Sympathie-/Solidaritätserklärung; Ⓑ (*resolve*) Vorsatz, *der;* **make a ~:** einen Vorsatz fassen; **make a ~ to do sth.** den Vorsatz fassen, etw. zu tun; **break one's ~:** seinem Vorsatz untreu werden; **good ~s** gute Vorsätze; **New Year['s] ~s** gute Vorsätze fürs neue Jahr; Ⓒ *no pl.* (*firmness*) Entschlossenheit, *die;* Ⓓ *no pl.* (*solving*) ⇒ **resolve** 1 A, B: Beseitigung, *die;* Ausräumung, *die;* Lösung, *die;* Ⓔ (*separation; also Phys., Mus.*) Auflösung, *die*

**resolve** /rɪˈzɒlv/ ❶ *v.t.* Ⓐ (*dispel*) beseitigen, ausräumen ‹Schwierigkeit, Zweifel, Unklarheit›; Ⓑ (*explain*) lösen ‹Problem, Rätsel›; Ⓒ (*decide*) beschließen; **they ~d that they must part** sie beschlossen, sich zu trennen; **this discovery made me ~ to leave** diese Entdeckung hat mich zu dem Entschluss gebracht, fortzugehen; Ⓓ (*settle*) beilegen ‹Streit›; klären ‹Streitpunkt›; regeln ‹Angelegenheit›; Ⓔ (*separate; also Phys., Mus.*) auflösen (**into** in + *Akk.*); Ⓕ (*analyse, divide; also Mech.*) zerlegen (**into** in + *Akk.*).

❷ *v.i.* Ⓐ (*decide*) **~ [up]on sth./doing sth.** sich zu etw. entschließen/sich [dazu] entschließen, etw. zu tun; Ⓑ (*dissolve*) sich auflösen (**into** in + *Akk.*).

❸ *n.* Ⓐ Vorsatz, *der;* **make a/keep one's ~:** einen Vorsatz fassen/bei seinem Vorsatz bleiben; **make a ~ to do sth.** den Vorsatz fassen, etw. zu tun; Ⓑ (*Amer.*) ⇒ **resolution** A; Ⓒ (*resoluteness*) Entschlossenheit, *die*

**resolved** /rɪˈzɒlvd/ *pred. adj.* **~ [to do sth.]** entschlossen[, etw. zu tun]; **he was ~ that ...:** es stand für ihn fest, dass ...

**reˈsolving power** *n.* (*Phys.*) Auflösungsvermögen, *das*

**resonance** /ˈrezənəns/ *n.* Resonanz, *die;* (*of voice*) voller Klang; (*fig.*) Widerhall, *der*

**resonant** /ˈrezənənt/ *adj.* Ⓐ (*resounding*) hallend ‹Echo, Ton, Klang›; volltönend ‹Stimme›; Ⓑ (*tending to reinforce sounds*) ‹Raum, Körper:› mit viel Resonanz

**resonate** /ˈrezəneɪt/ *v.i.* mitschwingen; resonieren (*Physik, Musik*)

**resonator** /ˈrezəneɪtə(r)/ *n.* (*Phys., Mus.*) Resonator, *der*

**resorption** /rɪˈsɔːpʃn/ *n.* (*Biol., Med.*) Resorption, *die*

**resort** /rɪˈzɔːt/ ❶ *n.* Ⓐ (*resource, recourse*) Ausweg, *der* ; **have ~ to force** Gewalt anwenden; **without ~ to force** ohne Gewaltanwendung; **you were my last ~:** du warst meine letzte Rettung (*ugs.*); **as a** *or* **in the last ~:** als letzter Ausweg; **in the last ~** (*in the end*) letzten Endes; Ⓑ (*place frequented*) Aufenthalt[sort], *der;* **[holiday] ~:** Urlaubsort, *der;* Ferienort, *der;* **ski/health ~:** Skiurlaubs-/Kurort, *der;* **mountain/coastal ~:** Ferienort im Gebirge/an der Küste; **seaside ~:** Seebad, *das;* Ⓒ (*frequenting*) häufiger Besuch.

❷ *v.i.* **~ to sth./sb.** zu etw. greifen/sich an jmdn. wenden (**for** um); **~ to violence** *or* **force** Gewalt anwenden; **~ to stealing/shouting** *etc.* sich aufs Stehlen/Schreien *usw.* verlegen; **~ to crime** kriminell werden

**resound** /rɪˈzaʊnd/ *v.i.* Ⓐ (*ring*) widerhallen (**with** von); Ⓑ (*produce echo*) hallen; **his fame ~ed through Greece** (*fig.*) sein Ruhm hallte durch [ganz] Griechenland

**resounding** /rɪˈzaʊndɪŋ/ *adj.* hallend ‹Lärm, Schreie, Schritte›; schallend ‹Gelächter, Stimme›; überwältigend ‹Mehrheit, Sieg, Erfolg›; gewaltig ‹Niederlage, Misserfolg›

**resoundingly** /rɪˈzaʊndɪŋlɪ/ *adv.* schallend ‹ertönen, erklingen›; **be ~ successful** ein durchschlagender Erfolg sein

**resource** /rɪˈsɔːs, rɪˈzɔːs/ *n.* Ⓐ *usu. in pl.* (*stock*) Mittel *Pl.;* Ressource, *die;* **have no inner ~s** keine inneren Reserven haben; **financial/mineral ~s** Geldmittel *Pl.*/Bodenschätze *Pl.;* **~s in** *or* **of men and money** Reserven an Menschen und Geldmitteln; Ⓑ *usu. pl.* (*Amer.: asset*) Aktivposten, *der;* Ⓒ (*expedient*) Ausweg, *der;* **be at the end of one's ~s** am Ende seiner Möglichkeiten sein; **be left to one's own ~s** sich (*Dat.*) selbst überlassen sein; **as a last ~:** als letzter Ausweg; Ⓓ *no art., no pl.* (*ingenuity*) Findigkeit, *die;* **be full of ~:** sich (*Dat.*) immer zu helfen wissen

**resourceful** /rɪˈsɔːsfl, rɪˈzɔːsfl/ *adj.* findig ‹Person›; einfallsreich ‹Plan›

**resourcefully** /rɪˈsɔːsfəlɪ, rɪˈzɔːsfəlɪ/ *adv.* findig

**resourcefulness** /rɪˈsɔːsflnɪs, rɪˈzɔːsflnɪs/ *n., no pl.* (*of person*) Findigkeit, *die;* (*of plan etc.*) Einfallsreichtum, *der*

**respect** /rɪˈspekt/ ❶ *n.* Ⓐ (*esteem*) Respekt, *der* (**for** vor + *Dat.*); Achtung, *die* (**for** vor + *Dat.*); **show ~ for sb./sth.** Respekt vor jmdm./etw. zeigen; **hold sb. in [high** *or* **great] ~:** jmdn. [sehr] achten; **command ~:** Respekt einflößen; **treat sb./sth. with ~:** jmdm./etw. mit Respekt *od.* Achtung begegnen/etw. mit Vorsicht behandeln; **with [all due] ~, ...:** bei allem Respekt, ...; mit Verlaub, ... (*geh.*); Ⓑ (*consideration*) Rücksicht, *die* (**for** auf + *Akk.*); **have** *or* **pay [no] ~ to sth.** etw. [nicht] berücksichtigen; Ⓒ (*aspect*) Beziehung, *die;* Hinsicht, *die;* **in ~ of style** hinsichtlich des Stils; in stilistischer Hinsicht; **in all/many/some ~s** in jeder/vieler/mancher Beziehung *od.* Hinsicht; Ⓓ (*reference*) Bezug, *der;* **with ~ to ...:** in Bezug auf ... (*Akk.*); was ... [an]betrifft; **have ~ to sth.** etw. betreffen; sich auf etw. (*Akk.*) beziehen; Ⓔ *in pl.* **give him my ~s** grüße ihn von mir; **pay one's ~s to sb.** (*formal*) jmdm. seine Aufwartung machen (*veralt.*); **pay one's last ~s** jmdm. die letzte Ehre erweisen (*geh.*).

❷ *v.t.* respektieren; achten; **he doesn't ~ his teachers much** er hat nicht viel Respekt vor seinen Lehrern; **much ~ed** sehr angesehen ‹Politiker, Firma›; **~ sb.'s feelings** auf jmds. Gefühle Rücksicht nehmen; **~ the rules of the road** die Verkehrsregeln beachten

**respectability** /rɪspektəˈbɪlɪtɪ/ *n., no pl.* ⇒ **respectable** A: Ansehen, *das;* Ehrbarkeit, *die* (*geh.*); **I do not doubt the ~ of his motives** ich zweifle nicht daran, dass seine Motive ehrenwert sind

**respectable** /rɪˈspektəbl/ *adj.* Ⓐ (*of good character*) angesehen ‹Bürger usw.›; ehrenwert ‹Motive›; (*decent*) ehrbar (*geh.*) ‹Leute, Kaufmann, Hausfrau›; Ⓑ (*presentable*) anständig, respektabel ‹Beschäftigung usw.›; vornehm, gut ‹Adresse›; ordentlich, (*that one can be seen in*) vorzeigbar (*ugs.*) ‹Kleidung›; **are you ~?** (*joc.*) hast du was an? (*ugs.*); Ⓒ (*considerable*) beachtlich ‹Summe›; Ⓓ (*passable*) passabel

**respectably** /rɪˈspektəblɪ/ *adv.* Ⓐ anständig ‹sich benehmen›; ordentlich ‹gekleidet›; **be ~ employed** eine anständige Beschäftigung haben; Ⓑ (*passably*) passabel

**respecter** /rɪˈspektə(r)/ *n.* **be no ~ of persons** alle ohne Ansehen der Person gleich behandeln

**respectful** /rɪˈspektfl/ *adj.* respektvoll (**to [wards]** gegenüber)

**respectfully** /rɪˈspektfəlɪ/ *adv.* respektvoll; **~ yours, X** (*formal*) Ihr sehr ergebener X

**respecting** /rɪˈspektɪŋ/ *prep.* bezüglich; hinsichtlich

**respective** /rɪˈspektɪv/ *adj.* jeweilig; **you must go to your ~ places** jeder von euch muss auf seinen Platz gehen; **he and I contributed ~ amounts of £10 and £1** er und ich steuerten Beträge von 10 bzw. 1 Pfund bei

**respectively** /rɪˈspektɪvlɪ/ *adv.* beziehungsweise; **the two cars were red and white ~:** die beiden Autos waren rot bzw. weiß; **he and I contributed £10 and £1 ~:** er und ich steuerten 10 bzw. 1 Pfund bei

**respell** /riːˈspel/ *v.t.*, **respelt** (*Brit.*) /riːˈspelt/ *or* **respelled** noch einmal buchstabieren

**respiration** /respɪˈreɪʃn/ *n.* (*one breath*) Atemzug, *der;* (*breathing*) Atmung, *die;* **she was finding ~ difficult** das Atmen fiel ihr schwer

**respirator** /ˈrespɪreɪtə(r)/ *n.* Ⓐ (*protecting device*) Atemschutzgerät, *das;* Ⓑ (*Med.*) Respirator, *der*

**respiratory** /ˈrespərətərɪ, rɪˈspɪrətərɪ/ *adj.* Atem‹geräusch, -wege›; Atmungs‹system, -organ, -funktion›; **~ infection** Infektion der Atemwege

**respire** /rɪˈspaɪə(r)/ *v.t. & i.* atmen

**respite** /ˈrespaɪt/ *n.* Ⓐ (*delay*) Aufschub, *der;* Ⓑ (*interval of relief*) Ruhepause, *die;* **~ from sth.** Erholung von etw.; **without ~:** ohne Pause *od.* Unterbrechung

**resplendent** /rɪˈsplendənt/ *adj.* prächtig; **~ in his uniform** in der vollen Pracht seiner Uniform

**resplendently** /rɪˈsplendəntlɪ/ *adv.* prächtig

**respond** /rɪˈspɒnd/ ❶ *v.i.* Ⓐ (*answer*) antworten (**to** auf + *Akk.*); **~ to sb.'s greeting** jmds. Gruß erwidern; Ⓑ (*react*) reagieren (**to** auf + *Akk.*); ‹Patient, Bremsen, Lenkung usw.:› ansprechen (**to** auf + *Akk.*); **[not] ~ to kindness** [nicht] empfänglich für Freundlichkeit sein; **they ~ed very generously to this appeal** der Aufruf fand bei ihnen ein großes Echo; **the illness ~s to treatment** die Krankheit lässt sich behandeln. ❷ *v.t.* antworten; erwidern. ❸ *n.* (*Archit.*) Wandpfeiler, *der;* Pilaster, *der* (*fachspr.*)

**respondent** /rɪˈspɒndənt/ *n.* (*Law*) Beklagte, *der/die;* (*in divorce case*) Scheidungsbeklagte, *der/die*

**response** /rɪˈspɒns/ *n.* Ⓐ (*answer*) Antwort, *die* (**to** auf + *Akk.*); **in ~ [to]** als Antwort [auf (+ *Akk.*)]; **in ~ to your letter** in Beantwortung Ihres Schreibens (*Papierdt.*); **make no ~:** nicht antworten; Ⓑ (*reaction*) Reaktion, *die;* **make no ~ to sth.** auf etw. (*Akk.*) nicht reagieren; **his ~ was to resign** er reagierte mit seinem Rücktritt; **meet with no/a large ~:** kein Echo/großes Echo finden; **£20,000 was raised in ~ to the appeal** der Aufruf brachte Spenden in Höhe von 20 000 Pfund ein; Ⓒ (*Eccl.*) Responsorium, *das*

**responsibility** /rɪspɒnsɪˈbɪlɪtɪ/ *n.* Ⓐ *no pl., no indef. art.* (*being responsible*) Verantwortung, *die;* **take** *or* **bear** *or* **accept** *or* **assume/claim [full] ~ [for sth.]** die [volle] Verantwortung [für etw.] übernehmen; **'the management accepts no ~ for garments left here'** „die Geschäftsleitung übernimmt keine Haftung für die Garderobe"; **lay** *or* **put** *or* **place the ~ for sth. on sb.['s shoulders]** jmdn. für etw. verantwortlich machen; **claim ~ for a bombing** sich zu einem Bombenanschlag bekennen; **do sth.**

**on one's own ~:** etw. in eigener Verantwortung tun; (*at one's own risk*) etw. auf eigene Verantwortung tun; B (*duty*) Verpflichtung, *die;* **the responsibilities of office** die Dienstpflicht; **that's 'your ~:** dafür bist du verantwortlich

**responsible** /rɪ'spɒnsɪbl/ *adj.* A verantwortlich (**for** für); **hold sb. ~ for sth.** jmdn. für etw. verantwortlich machen; **be ~ to sb. [for sth.]** jmdm. gegenüber [für etw.] verantwortlich sein; **be ~ for sth.** ‹Person:› für etw. verantwortlich sein; ‹Sache:› die Ursache für etw. sein; **what's ~ for the breakdown?** woran liegt die Betriebsstörung?; **I've made you ~ for the travel arrangements** ich habe dir die Verantwortung für die Reisevorbereitungen übertragen; B verantwortlich, verantwortungsvoll ‹Stellung, Tätigkeit, Aufgabe›; C (*trustworthy*) verantwortungsvoll, verantwortungsbewusst ‹Person›

**responsibly** /rɪ'spɒnsɪblɪ/ *adv.* verantwortungsbewusst ‹handeln, sich verhalten›

**responsive** /rɪ'spɒnsɪv/ *adj.* (*reacting positively*) aufgeschlossen ‹Person›; gut ansprechend ‹Bremsen, Motor usw.›; **the audience was very ~, it was a very ~ audience** das Publikum ging sehr gut mit; **be ~ to sth.** auf etw. (*Akk.*) reagieren *od.* eingehen

**respray** 1 /ri:'spreɪ/ *v.t.* neu spritzen ‹Auto›. 2 /'ri:spreɪ/ *n.* neue Lackierung; **give the car a ~:** den Wagen neu spritzen

**rest¹** /rest/ 1 *v.i.* A (*lie, lit. or fig.*) ruhen; **~ on** ruhen auf (+ *Dat.*); ‹Schatten, Licht:› liegen auf (+ *Dat.*); (*fig.*) ‹Argumentation:› sich stützen auf (+ *Akk.*); ‹Ruf:› beruhen auf (+ *Dat.*); **~ against sth.** an etw. (*Dat.*) lehnen; **sit with one's back ~ing against sth.** mit dem Rücken an etw. (*Akk.*) gelehnt sitzen; **her head is ~ing against his shoulder** ihr Kopf liegt an seiner Schulter; B (*take repose*) ruhen; sich ausruhen (**from** von); (*pause*) eine Pause machen *od.* einlegen; **never let one's enemy ~:** seinem Feind keine Ruhepause gönnen; **she never ~s** ihre Hände ruhen nie; **I won't ~ until ...:** ich werde nicht ruhen noch rasten, bis ...; **tell sb. to ~** ‹Arzt:› jmdn. Ruhe verordnen; **be ~ing** (*Brit. Theatre*) ‹Schauspieler:› ohne Engagement sein; C (*euphem.: lie in death*) ruhen (*geh.*); **let her/may she ~ in peace** lass sie/möge sie in Frieden ruhen; D (*be left*) **let the matter ~:** die Sache ruhen lassen; **... and there the matter ~ed** ... und dabei blieb es; **~ assured that ...:** seien Sie versichert, dass ...; E **~ with sb.** ‹Verantwortung, Entscheidung, Schuld:› bei jmdn. liegen; F (*Agric.: lie fallow*) ruhen; brachliegen; G (*Amer. Law*) ‹Verteidigung:› die Beweiserhebung abschließen. ⇒ *also* **laurel** A; **oar** A.

2 *v.t.* A (*place for support*) **~ sth. against sth.** etw. an etw. (*Akk.*) lehnen; **~ sth. on sth.** (*lit. or fig.*) etw. auf etw. (*Akk.*) stützen; **she was ~ing all her hopes on her son** sie setzte ihre ganze Hoffnung auf ihren Sohn; **he ~ed the load on the ground [for a moment]** er setzte die Last [für einen Augenblick] ab; B (*give relief to*) ausruhen lassen ‹Pferd, Person›; ausruhen ‹Augen›; schonen ‹Stimme, Körperteil›; **~ oneself** sich ausruhen; C (*Agric.: allow to lie fallow*) brachlegen (*fachspr.*); ruhen lassen; D (*Law*) **~ one's case** sein Plädoyer beschließen; E **[may] God ~ his soul!** Gott hab ihn selig!

3 *n.* A (*repose*) Ruhe, *die;* **need nine hours' ~:** neun Stunden Schlaf brauchen; **go** *or* **retire to ~:** sich zur Ruhe legen *od.* begeben (*geh.*); **get a good night's ~:** sich ordentlich ausschlafen; **be at ~** (*euphem.: be dead*) ruhen (*geh.*); **go to one's ~** (*euphem.: die*) zur ewigen Ruhe eingehen (*geh. verhüll.*); **lay to ~** (*euphem.: bury*) zur letzten Ruhe betten (*geh. verhüll.*); B (*freedom from exertion*) Ruhe[pause], *die;* Erholung, *die* (**from** von); **take a ~:** sich ausruhen (**from** von); **tell sb. to take a ~** ‹Arzt:› jmdm. Ruhe verordnen; **set sb.'s mind at ~:** jmdn. beruhigen (**about** hinsichtlich); C (*pause*) **~ period** [Ruhe]pause, *die;* **have** *or* **take a ~:** [eine] Pause machen; **give sb./sth. a ~:** ausruhen lassen ‹Person, Nutztier›; ruhen lassen ‹Maschine›; (*fig.*) ruhen lassen ‹Thema, Angelegenheit›; **give it a ~!** (*coll.*) hör jetzt mal auf damit!; D (*stationary position*) **at ~:** in Ruhe; **come to ~:** zum Stehen kommen; (*have final position*) landen; **bring to ~:** zum Stehen bringen; E (*support*) (*for telephone receiver*) Gabel, *die;* (*for billiard cue, telescope, firearm*) Auflage, *die;* (*for neck*) Stütze, *die;* F (*Mus.*) Pause, *die*

**~ 'up** *v.i.* sich ausruhen

**rest²** *n.* (*remainder*) **the ~:** der Rest; **we'll do the ~:** alles Übrige erledigen wir; **the ~ of her clothes** ihre übrigen Kleider; **the ~ of the butter** die restliche *od.* übrige Butter; **she's no different from the ~:** sie ist nicht besser als die anderen; **and [all] the ~ of it** und so weiter; **for the ~:** im Übrigen; sonst

**restart** 1 /ri:'stɑ:t/ *v.t.* A (*start again*) wieder anstellen ‹Maschine›; wieder anlassen ‹Auto, Motor›; B (*resume*) wieder aufnehmen ‹Verhandlungen, Berufstätigkeit›; fortsetzen ‹Spiel›; neu starten ‹Rennen›; **~ work** wieder anfangen zu arbeiten. 2 /ri:'stɑ:t/ *v.i.* A ‹Motor:› wieder anspringen; B (*resume*) wieder anfangen; ‹Verhandlungen:› wieder aufgenommen werden. 3 /'ri:stɑ:t/ *n.* ⇒ **1** B: Wiederaufnahme, *die;* Fortsetzung, *die*

**restate** /ri:'steɪt/ *v.t.* (*express again*) noch einmal darlegen; (*express differently*) anders darlegen; (*Mus.: repeat*) wieder aufnehmen ‹Thema›

**restatement** /ri:'steɪtmənt/ *n.* (*repetition*) nochmalige Darlegung; nochmalige Feststellung; (*reformulation*) Neuformulierung, *die;* (*Mus.*) Wiederaufnahme, *die*

**restaurant** /'restərɔ̃, 'restərɒnt/ *n.* Restaurant, *das*

**'restaurant car** *n.* (*Brit. Railw.*) Speisewagen, *der*

**restaurateur** /restərə'tɜ:(r)/ *n.* ▶ **1261** Gastwirt, *der*

**rest: ~ cure** *n.* (*Med.*) Erholungskur, *die;* **~ day** *n.* Ruhetag, *der*

**rested** /'restɪd/ *adj.* ausgeruht

**restful** /'restfl/ *adj.* A (*free from disturbance*) ruhig ‹Tag, Woche, Ort›; B (*conducive to rest*) beruhigend; **be a ~ person to be with** Ruhe ausstrahlen

**restfully** /'restfəlɪ/ *adv.* ruhig ‹schlafen›; geruhsam ‹Zeit verbringen›

**restfulness** /'restflnɪs/ *n., no pl.* Entspanntheit, *die;* Gelöstheit, *die*

**rest home** *n.* Pflegeheim, *das*

**'resting place** *n.* Rastplatz, *der;* **last ~** (*euphem.*) letzte Ruhestätte (*geh.*)

**restitution** /restɪ'tju:ʃn/ *n.* Rückgabe, *die;* (*of sth. lost*) Erstattung, *die;* Ersatz, *der;* **make ~:** Ersatz leisten; **make ~ of sth. to sb.** jmdm. etw. zurückgeben/erstatten

**restive** /'restɪv/ *adj.* A (*stubborn*) störrisch ‹Pferd, Person›; **become ~** ‹Pferd:› bocken; B (*unmanageable*) aufsässig ‹Einwohner, Bevölkerung›; C (*restless*) unruhig

**restively** /'restɪvlɪ/ *adv.* A (*stubbornly*) störrisch; B (*in fidgety manner*) unruhig

**restless** /'restlɪs/ *adj.* A (*affording no rest*) unruhig ‹Nacht, Schlaf, Bewegung›; B (*uneasy*) ruhelos ‹Person, Sehnsucht›; C (*taking no rest*) rastlos ‹Person, Lebensstil›

**restlessly** /'restlɪslɪ/ *adv.* ⇒ **restless** A, B: unruhig; ruhelos

**restlessness** /'restlɪsnɪs/ *n., no pl.* ⇒ **restless** B, C: Ruhelosigkeit, *die;* Rastlosigkeit, *die*

**restock** /ri:'stɒk/ 1 *v.t.* A **~ a shop** das Lager eines Geschäfts wieder auffüllen; B wieder besetzen ‹Fluss, Teich›; wieder aufforsten ‹Wald›; **~ a farm** einen [landwirtschaftlichen] Betrieb wieder mit Vieh besetzen. 2 *v.i.* (*Commerc.*) das Lager auffüllen

**restoration** /restə'reɪʃn/ *n.* A (*restoring*) (*of peace, health*) Wiederherstellung, *die;* (*of a work of art, building, etc.*) Restaurierung, *die;* Restauration, *die* (*fachspr.*); **her ~ to health** ihre [gesundheitliche] Wiederherstellung; B (*giving back*) Rückgabe, *die;* C (*reestablishment*) Wiedereinführung, *die;* **the R~** (*Brit. Hist.*) die Restauration

**restorative** /rɪ'stɒrətɪv, rɪ'stɔ:rətɪv/ 1 *adj.* stärkend; aufbauend; Stärkungs-, Aufbau‹mittel›; Aufbau-, Kräftigungs‹kost›. 2 *n.* Stärkungs- *od.* Aufbaumittel, *das*

**restore** /rɪ'stɔ:(r)/ *v.t.* A (*give back*) zurückgeben; B (*bring to original state*) restaurieren ‹Bauwerk, Kunstwerk usw.›; konjizieren ‹Text, Satz› (*Literaturw.*); **~ sb. to health, ~ sb.'s health** jmds. Gesundheit *od.* jmdn. wieder herstellen; **his strength was ~d** er kam wieder zu Kräften; **~ sb. to better spirits** jmdn. aufheitern; C (*reinstate*) wieder einsetzen (**to** in + *Akk.*); **~ sb. to the throne/to power** jmdn. als König/Königin wieder einsetzen/jmdn. wieder an die Macht bringen; **her success ~d her to her place as leading actress** der Erfolg hat sie wieder zur führenden Schauspielerin gemacht; D (*reestablish*) wiederherstellen ‹Ordnung, Ruhe, Vertrauen›; E (*put back*) **~ the book to its place [on the shelf]** das Buch wieder an seinen Platz [im Regal] zurückstellen

**restorer** /rɪ'stɔ:rə(r)/ *n.* A (*Art, Archit.: person*) Restaurator, *der*/Restauratorin, *die;* B (*agent*) ≈ Pflegemittel, *das;* ⇒ *also* **hair-restorer**

**restrain** /rɪ'streɪn/ *v.t.* zurückhalten ‹Gefühl, Lachen, Drang, Person›; bändigen ‹unartiges Kind, Tier›; **~ sb./oneself from doing sth.** jmdn. davon abhalten/sich zurückhalten, etw. zu tun; **~ yourself!** beherrsch dich!

**restrained** /rɪ'streɪnd/ *adj.* zurückhaltend ‹Wesen, Kritik›; verhalten ‹Blick, Geste, Gefühl›; beherrscht ‹Reaktion, Worte›; unaufdringlich ‹Stil›

**restraint** /rɪ'streɪnt/ *n.* A (*restriction*) Einschränkung, *die;* **without ~:** ungehindert; B (*reserve*) Zurückhaltung, *die;* C (*moderation*) Unaufdringlichkeit, *die;* (*self-control*) Selbstbeherrschung, *die;* **with ~:** unaufdringlich; **without ~:** ungehemmt; **his style shows a lack of ~:** er hat einen aufdringlichen Stil

**restrict** /rɪ'strɪkt/ *v.t.* beschränken (**to** auf + *Akk.*); ‹Kleidung:› be-, einengen; **the trees ~ed our view** die Bäume nahmen uns die freie Sicht

**restricted** /rɪ'strɪktɪd/ *adj.* A (*limited*) beschränkt; begrenzt; **~ diet** Diät, *die;* **I feel ~ in these clothes** ich fühle mich in dieser Kleidung beengt *od.* eingeengt; B (*subject to restriction*) Sperr‹gebiet›; begrenzt ‹Zulassung, Aufnahme, Anwendbarkeit›; **be ~ to 30 m.p.h.** nicht schneller als 30 Meilen in der Stunde fahren dürfen; **be ~ to doing sth.** sich darauf beschränken müssen, etw. zu tun; **be ~ within narrow limits** ‹Freiheit:› stark eingeschränkt sein; C (*not for disclosure*) geheim ‹Dokument, Information›

**restricted 'area** *n.* A Sperrgebiet, *das;* B (*Brit.: with speed limit*) *Gebiet mit Geschwindigkeitsbeschränkung*

**restriction** /rɪ'strɪkʃn/ *n.* Be-, Einschränkung, *die* (**on** *Gen.*); (*of persons*) Einengung, *die;* **without ~:** ohne Einschränkung; uneingeschränkt; **put** *or* **place** *or* **impose ~s on sth.** etw. einschränken *od.* Einschränkungen (*Dat.*) unterwerfen; **speed/weight/price ~:** Geschwindigkeits-/Gewichts-/Preisbeschränkung, *die*

**restrictive** /rɪ'strɪktɪv/ *adj.* restriktiv; einschränkend *nicht präd.;* beengend ‹Kleidung›

**restrictively** /rɪ'strɪktɪvlɪ/ *adv.* restriktiv; einschränkend

**restrictive 'practice** *n.* (*Commerc.*) wettbewerbsbeschränkende Geschäftspraktik

**'restroom** *n.* (*esp. Amer.*) Toilette, *die*

**restructure** /ri:'strʌktʃə(r)/ *v.t.* umstrukturieren

**'rest stop** *n.* (*Amer.*) Raststätte, *die*

**restyle** /ri:'staɪl/ *v.t.* neu stylen; **~ sb.'s hair** jmdm. eine neue Frisur machen

**result** /rɪ'zʌlt/ 1 *v.i.* A (*follow*) **~ from sth.** die Folge einer Sache (*Gen.*) sein; von etw. herrühren; (*future*) aus etw. resultieren; B (*end*) **~ in sth.** in etw. (*Dat.*) resultieren; zu etw. führen; **the game ~ed in a draw** das Spiel endete mit einem Unentschieden; **~ in sb.'s doing sth.** zur Folge haben, dass jmd. etw. tut.

2 *n.* Ergebnis, *das;* Resultat, *das;* **be the ~ of sth.** die Folge einer Sache (*Gen.*) sein; **as a ~ [of this]** infolgedessen; **he knows how**

**to get ~s** er weiß, wie man Ergebnisse *od.* Erfolg erzielt; **without ~:** ergebnislos; **What was the ~? — Leeds won 3-2** Wie ist es ausgegangen? — Leeds hat 3 : 2 gewonnen; **when you add up the figures, what is the ~?** was kommt heraus, wenn du die Zahlen zusammenzählst?

**resultant** /rɪˈzʌltənt/ ❶ *adj.* daraus resultierend; sich daraus ergebend. ❷ *n.* (*Phys.*) Resultante, *die;* Resultierende, *die*

**resume** /rɪˈzjuːm/ ❶ *v.t.* [A] (*begin again*) wieder aufnehmen; fortsetzen ‹Reise›; wieder annehmen ‹Gewohnheit›; [B] (*get back*) wieder-, zurückgewinnen; wieder übernehmen ‹Kommando›; **~ possession of sth.** etw. wieder in Besitz nehmen; ⇒ *also* **seat** 1 B. ❷ *v.i.* weitermachen; ‹Parlament:› die Sitzung fortsetzen; ‹Unterricht:› wieder beginnen

**résumé** /ˈrezʊmeɪ/ *n.* [A] (*summary*) Zusammenfassung, *die;* [B] (*Amer.: curriculum vitae*) Lebenslauf, *der*

**resumption** /rɪˈzʌmpʃn/ *n.* [A] ⇒ **resume** 1 A: Wiederaufnahme, *die;* Fortsetzung, *die;* Wiederannahme, *die;* [B] ⇒ **resume** 1 B: Wieder-, Zurückgewinnung, *die;* Wiederübernahme, *die;* Wiedereinnahme, *die*

**resurface** /riːˈsɜːfɪs/ ❶ *v.t.* **~ a road** den Belag einer Straße erneuern. ❷ *v.i.* (*lit. or fig.*) wieder auftauchen

**resurgence** /rɪˈsɜːdʒəns/ *n.* Wiederaufleben, *das*

**resurgent** /rɪˈsɜːdʒənt/ *adj.* wieder auflebend; wieder erwachend ‹Leben›; **be ~:** wieder aufleben

**resurrect** /rezəˈrekt/ *v.t.* [A] (*raise from the dead*) wieder zum Leben erwecken; [B] (*revive*) wieder beleben; wieder aufleben lassen ‹Vorstellungen, Bräuche›; (*coll.: dig out*) wieder ausgraben ‹alte Kleider usw.›

**resurrection** /rezəˈrekʃn/ *n.* [A] (*Relig.*) Auferstehung, *die;* **the R~:** die Auferstehung Christi; [B] (*revival*) Wiederbelebung, *die;* Wiederaufleben, *das*

**resuscitate** /rɪˈsʌsɪteɪt/ *v.t.* (*lit. or fig.*) wieder beleben

**resuscitation** /rɪsʌsɪˈteɪʃn/ *n.* (*lit. or fig.*) Wiederbelebung, *die*

**ret.** *abbr.* **retired** a. D.; i. R.

**retail** ❶ /ˈriːteɪl/ *n.* Einzelhandel, *der.* ❷ *adj.* Einzel‹handel›; Einzelhandels‹geschäft, -preis›; [End]verkaufs‹preis›. ❸ *adv.* **buy/sell ~:** en détail kaufen/verkaufen (*Kaufmannsspr.*). ❹ *v.t.* [A] /ˈriːteɪl, rɪˈteɪl/ (*sell*) [im Einzelhandel] verkaufen; [B] /rɪˈteɪl/ (*relate*) weitererzählen ‹Klatsch›; **~ a conversation to sb.** jmdm. ein Gespräch wiedererzählen. ❺ /ˈriːteɪl, rɪˈteɪl/ *v.i.* im Einzelhandel verkauft werden (**at, for** für)

**retailer** /ˈriːteɪlə(r), rɪˈteɪlə(r)/ *n.* Einzelhändler, *der*/-händlerin, *die*

**retailing** /ˈriːteɪlɪŋ/ *n., no pl., no art.* Einzelhandel, *der; attrib.* Einzelhandels-

**retail ˈprice index** *n.* (*Brit.*) Preisindex des Einzelhandels

**retain** /rɪˈteɪn/ *v.t.* [A] (*keep*) behalten; sich (*Dat.*) bewahren ‹Witz, Einfallsreichtum, Fähigkeit›; ein-, zurückbehalten ‹Gelder›; gespeichert lassen ‹Information›; **~ power** ‹Partei:› an der Macht bleiben; **~ possession of sth.** etw. im Besitz behalten; **~ control [of sth.]** die Kontrolle [über etw. (*Akk.*)] behalten; [B] (*continue to practise*) festhalten an (*Dat.*), beibehalten ‹Gewohnheit, Tradition, Brauch›; [C] (*keep in place*) ‹Damm:› stauen/‹Deich:› zurückhalten/‹Boden:› speichern/‹Gefäß:› halten ‹Wasser›; **~ sth. in position** etw. in der richtigen Position halten; [D] (*secure services of*) beauftragen ‹Anwalt›; [E] (*not forget*) behalten, sich (*Dat.*) merken ‹Gedanke, Tatsache›

**retainer** /rɪˈteɪnə(r)/ *n.* [A] (*Hist.: follower*) Trabant, *der;* **old ~** (*joc.*) altes Faktotum; [B] (*fee*) Honorarvorschuss, *der*

**retaining: ~ fee** *n.* Honorarvorschuss, *der;* **~ wall** *n.* Böschungsmauer, *die*

**retake** ❶ /riːˈteɪk/ *v.t., forms as* **take** 1, 2 [A] (*recapture*) wieder einnehmen ‹Stadt, Festung›; [B] (*take again*) wiederholen ‹Prüfung, Strafstoß›; [C] (*Cinemat.*) nachdrehen ‹Szene›. ❷ /ˈriːteɪk/ *n.* [A] (*of exam*) Wiederholung, *die;* [B] (*Cinemat.*) Retake, *das;* Neuaufnahme, *die*

**retaliate** /rɪˈtælɪeɪt/ *v.i.* Vergeltung üben (**against** an + *Dat.*); sich revanchieren (*ugs.*); ‹Truppen:› zurückschlagen; kontern (**against** *Akk.*) ‹Maßnahme, Kritik›; **~ by doing sth.** sich revanchieren, indem man etw. tut

**retaliation** /rɪtælɪˈeɪʃn/ *n.* (*in war, fight*) Vergeltung, *die;* Gegenschlag, *der;* (*in argument etc.*) Konter, *der* (*ugs.*); Konterschlag, *der;* **in ~ for** als Vergeltung für; **she did that in ~ for his cruelty** sie revanchierte sich damit für seine Grausamkeit

**retaliatory** /rɪˈtæljətərɪ/ *adj.* Vergeltungs‹maßnahme, -angriff›

**retard** /rɪˈtɑːd/ *v.t.* verzögern; retardieren (*bes. Physiol., Psych.*)

**retardant** /rɪˈtɑːdənt/ ❶ *adj.* hemmend; **flame-/rust-~:** feuer-/rosthemmend. ❷ *n.* Hemmstoff, *der*

**retardation** /riːtɑːˈdeɪʃn/ *n.* Verzögerung, *die;* Retardation, *die* (*bes. Physiol., Psych.*); (*braking*) Bremswirkung, *die*

**retarded** /rɪˈtɑːdɪd/ *adj.* [A] (*Psychol.*) **[mentally] ~:** [geistig] zurückgeblieben; [B] (*Motor Veh.*) **~ ignition** Spätzündung, *die*

**retarder** /rɪˈtɑːdə(r)/ *n.* (*Motor Veh.*) Dauerbremse, *die*

**retch** /retʃ, riːtʃ/ ❶ *v.i.* würgen. ❷ *n.* Würgen, *das*

**retd.** *abbr.* **retired** a. D.; i. R.

**retell** /riːˈtel/ *v.t.*, **retold** /riːˈtəʊld/ nacherzählen; (*tell again*) noch einmal erzählen

**retention** /rɪˈtenʃn/ *n.* [A] (*keeping*) (*of power*) Erhaltung, *die;* (*of money*) Einbehaltung, *die;* [B] ⇒ **retain** B: Festhalten, *das* (**of** an + *Dat.*); Beibehaltung, *die;* [C] **~ of water** (*by soil, plant*) Speicherung von Wasser; [D] ⇒ **retain** D: Beauftragung, *die;* [E] (*Med.*) Retention, *die;* (*of urine*) Verhaltung, *die;* [F] **powers of ~:** Merkfähigkeit, *die*

**retentive** /rɪˈtentɪv/ *adj.* [A] gut ‹Gedächtnis›; **a memory ~ of details** ein gutes Gedächtnis für Details; [B] (*holding moisture*) Feuchtigkeit speichernd *nicht präd.* ‹Boden›; **soil ~ of moisture** Boden, der Feuchtigkeit speichert

**rethink** /riːˈθɪŋk/ ❶ *v.t.*, **rethought** /riːˈθɔːt/ noch einmal überdenken. ❷ *n.* **have a ~ about sth.** etw. noch einmal überdenken

**reticence** /ˈretɪsəns/ *n., no pl.* Zurückhaltung, *die* (**on** in Bezug auf + *Akk.*)

**reticent** /ˈretɪsənt/ *adj.* [A] (*reserved*) zurückhaltend (**on, about** in Bezug auf + *Akk.*); [B] (*restrained*) schlicht ‹Stil›

**retina** /ˈretɪnə/ *n., pl.* **~s** *or* **~e** /ˈretɪniː/ (*Anat.*) Retina, *die* (*fachspr.*); Netzhaut, *die*

**retinitis** /retɪˈnaɪtɪs/ *n.* (*Med.*) Netzhautentzündung, *die;* Retinitis, *die* (*fachspr.*)

**retinue** /ˈretɪnjuː/ *n.* Gefolge, *das*

**retiracy** /rɪˈtaɪərəsɪ/ *n., no pl.* (*Amer.*) Abgeschiedenheit, *die*

**retiral** /rɪˈtaɪərl/ *n.* (*Scot.*) Rücktritt, *der* (**from** von); Ausscheiden, *das* (**from** aus)

**retire** /rɪˈtaɪə(r)/ ❶ *v.i.* [A] (*give up work or position*) ausscheiden (**from** aus); aufhören [zu arbeiten]; ‹Angestellter, Arbeiter:› in Rente (*Akk.*) gehen; ‹Beamter, Militär:› in Pension *od.* den Ruhestand gehen; ‹Selbstständiger:› sich zur Ruhe setzen; **~ on a pension** ‹Angestellter, Arbeiter:› auf *od.* in Rente (*Akk.*) gehen; ‹Beamter, Militär:› in Pension (*Akk.*) gehen; [B] (*withdraw*) sich zurückziehen (**to** in + *Akk.*); (*Sport*) aufgeben; **~ [to bed]** sich [zum Schlafen] zurückziehen; **~ from the world/into oneself** sich von der Welt/in sich (*Akk.*) selbst zurückziehen.
❷ *v.t.* (*compel to leave*) aus Altersgründen entlassen; pensionieren, in den Ruhestand versetzen ‹Beamten, Militär›; **be ~d early** in den vorzeitigen Ruhestand versetzt werden

**retired** /rɪˈtaɪəd/ *adj.* [A] (*no longer working*) aus dem Berufsleben ausgeschieden ‹Angestellter, Arbeiter, Selbstständiger›; ‹Beamter, Soldat:› im Ruhestand, pensioniert; **be ~:** nicht mehr arbeiten; ‹Angestellter, Arbeiter:› Rentner/Rentnerin *od.* in Rente (*Akk.*) sein; ‹Beamter, Soldat:› im Ruhestand *od.* pensioniert sein; [B] (*withdrawn*) zurückgezogen ‹Leben›

**retired list** *n.* (*Mil.*) Liste der aus dem aktiven Dienst Ausgeschiedenen

**retiree** /rɪtaɪəˈriː/ *n.* (*Amer.*) Ruheständler, *der*/-ständlerin, *die;* (*ex-employee also*) Rentner, *der*/Rentnerin, *die;* (*ex-civil servant/serviceman also*) Pensionär, *der*/Pensionärin, *die*

**retirement** /rɪˈtaɪəmənt/ *n.* [A] (*leaving work*) Ausscheiden aus dem Arbeitsleben; [B] *no art.* (*period*) Ruhestand, *der;* **go into ~** ‹Selbstständiger:› sich zur Ruhe setzen; ‹Angestellter, Arbeiter:› in Rente (*Akk.*) gehen; ‹Beamter, Militär:› in Pension *od.* den Ruhestand gehen; **take early ~** ‹Selbstständiger:› sich vorzeitig zur Ruhe setzen; ‹Angestellter, Arbeiter:› vorzeitig in Rente (*Akk.*) gehen; ‹Beamter, Militär:› sich vorzeitig pensionieren lassen; **how will you spend your ~?** was machen Sie, wenn Sie einmal nicht mehr arbeiten/in Rente/im Ruhestand sind?; [C] (*withdrawing*) Rückzug, *der* (**to, into** in + *Akk.*); [D] (*seclusion*) Zurückgezogenheit, *die;* **live in ~:** zurückgezogen leben

**retirement: ~ age** *n.* Altersgrenze, *die;* (*of employees also*) Rentenalter, *das;* (*of civil servants, servicemen also*) Pensionsalter, *das;* **~ home** *n.* [A] (*house, flat*) Alters- *od.* Ruhesitz, *der;* [B] (*institution*) Alters- *od.* Altenheim, *das;* **~ pay, ~ pension** *ns.* (*for employees*) [Alters]rente, *die;* (*for civil servants, servicemen*) Pension, *die*

**retiring** /rɪˈtaɪərɪŋ/ *adj.* (*shy*) zurückhaltend

**retiring: ~ age** ⇒ **retirement age**; **~ collection** *n.* (*at church service*) Kollekte, *die;* (*at concert*) Spendensammlung, *die*

**retold** ⇒ **retell**

**retook** ⇒ **retake** 1

**retool** /riːˈtuːl/ *v.t.* umrüsten (**for** auf + *Akk.*)

**retort**[1] /rɪˈtɔːt/ ❶ *n.* Entgegnung, *die,* Erwiderung, *die* (**to** auf + *Akk.*). ❷ *v.t.* entgegnen. ❸ *v.i.* scharf antworten

**retort**[2] *n.* (*Chem., Industry*) Retorte, *die*

**retouch** /riːˈtʌtʃ/ *v.t.* (*Art, Photog., Printing*) retuschieren

**retrace** /rɪˈtreɪs/ *v.t.* [A] (*trace back*) zurückverfolgen; [B] (*trace again*) nachvollziehen ‹Entwicklung›; [C] (*go back over*) zurückgehen; **~ one's steps/path** denselben Weg noch einmal zurückgehen

**retract** /rɪˈtrækt/ ❶ *v.t.* [A] (*withdraw*) zurücknehmen; *abs.* **he refused to ~:** er weigerte sich, es zurückzunehmen; [B] (*Aeronaut.*) einziehen, einfahren ‹Fahrgestell›; [C] (*draw back*) zurückziehen; einziehen ‹Fühler, Krallen›. ❷ *v.i.* [A] (*Aeronaut.*) ‹Fahrgestell:› einziehbar *od.* einfahrbar sein; [B] (*be drawn back*) ‹Fühler, Krallen:› eingezogen werden

**retractable** /rɪˈtræktəbl/ *adj.* (*Aeronaut.*) einziehbar, einfahrbar ‹Fahrgestell›

**retraction** /rɪˈtrækʃn/ *n.* [A] (*withdrawing*) Zurücknahme, *die;* **make a ~ of sth.** etw. zurücknehmen; [B] (*drawing-back of undercarriage, claws, etc.*) Einziehen, *das*

**retrain** /riːˈtreɪn/ ❶ *v.i.* [sich] umschulen [lassen]. ❷ *v.t.* umschulen ‹Person›

**retraining** /riːˈtreɪnɪŋ/ *n.* Umschulung, *die; attrib.* Umschulungs‹programm›

**retranslate** /riːtrænsˈleɪt/ *v.t.* [zu]rückübersetzen

**retranslation** /riːtrænsˈleɪʃn/ *n.* Rückübersetzung, *die*

**retransmit** /riːtrænsˈmɪt/ *v.t.*, **-tt-** [A] (*transmit again*) noch einmal übermitteln ‹Nachricht›; noch einmal senden ‹Signal›; [B] (*transmit further*) weiterübermitteln ‹Nachricht›; weitersenden ‹Signal›

**retread** (*Motor Veh.*) ❶ /ˈriːtred/ *n.* runderneuerter Reifen. ❷ /riːˈtred/ *v.t.* runderneuern ‹Reifen›

**retreat** /rɪˈtriːt/ ❶ *n.* [A] (*withdrawal; also Mil. or fig.*) Rückzug, *der;* **their ~ from the territory/position** ihr Rückzug aus dem Gebiet/von der Stellung; **beat a ~:** den Rückzug antreten; (*fig.*) das Feld räumen; **make good one's ~:** sich in Sicherheit (*Akk.*) bringen; (*fig.*) sich aus dem Staub machen (*ugs.*); ⇒ *also* **hasty**; [B] (*place of seclusion*) Zuflucht, *die;* Zufluchtsort, *der;* (*hiding place*

*also*) Unterschlupf, *der;* **country ~:** Refugium auf dem Lande; **C** (*Relig.: for prayer*) Exerzitien *Pl.;* **D** (*Mil.: bugle-call*) (*for return to barracks*) Zapfenstreich, *der;* (*for withdrawal*) **sound/give the ~:** zum Rückzug blasen.
❷ *v.i.* **A** (*withdraw; also Mil. or fig.*) sich zurückziehen; (*in fear*) zurückweichen; **~ within oneself** sich in sich (*Akk.*) selbst zurückziehen; **~ from a territory/position** sich aus einem Gebiet/von einer Stellung zurückziehen; **~ from an aggressive stance** eine aggressive Haltung aufgeben; **B** (*recede*) ‹Überschwemmung, Gletscher usw.:› zurückgehen

**retrench** /rɪˈtrenʃ/ ❶ *v.t.* senken ‹Ausgaben, Lohn›. ❷ *v.i.* sich einschränken

**retrenchment** /rɪˈtrenʃmənt/ *n.* Senkung, *die;* **policy of ~:** Sparpolitik, *die*

**retrial** /riːˈtraɪəl/ *n.* (*Law*) Wiederaufnahmeverfahren, *das;* **he asked for a ~:** er verlangte eine Wiederaufnahme des Verfahrens

**retribution** /retrɪˈbjuːʃn/ *n.* Vergeltung, *die;* **in ~ for** zur Vergeltung für

**retributive** /rɪˈtrɪbjʊtɪv/ *adj.* vergeltend; ausgleichend ‹Gerechtigkeit›

**retrievable** /rɪˈtriːvəbl/ *adj.* **A** (*able to be set right*) noch nicht ausweglos *od.* völlig verfahren ‹Situation›; wieder gutzumachend *nicht präd.* ‹Fehler›; **be ~** ‹Situation:› zu retten sein; ‹Fehler:› wieder gutzumachen sein; **B** (*able to be rescued*) zu rettend/(*from wreckage*) zu bergend *nicht präd.;* **be ~:** zu retten/bergen sein; **C** (*able to be recovered*) **the ball/money is ~:** den Ball/das Geld kann man wiederholen/-bekommen; **D** (*Computing*) wieder auffindbar ‹Information›

**retrieval** /rɪˈtriːvl/ *n.* **A** (*setting right*) (*of situation*) Rettung, *die;* (*of mistake*) Wiedergutmachung, *die;* **beyond** *or* **past ~:** hoffnungslos; **B** (*rescue*) Rettung, *die;* (*from wreckage*) Bergung, *die* (**from** aus); **C** (*recovery*) ⇒ **retrieve** 1 C: Zurückholen, *das;* Wiederholen, *das;* Wiedergewinnung, *die;* **the ~ of the money was difficult** es war schwierig, das Geld wiederzubekommen; **the money/chance was lost beyond ~:** das Geld/die Gelegenheit war unwiederbringlich verloren; **D** (*Computing*) Wiederauffinden, *das*

**retrieve** /rɪˈtriːv/ *v.t.* **A** (*set right*) wieder gutmachen ‹Fehler›; retten ‹Situation›; **B** (*rescue*) retten (**from** aus); (*from wreckage*) bergen (**from** aus); **timber ~d from the beach** als Strandgut aufgelesenes Holz; **C** (*recover*) zurückholen ‹Brief›; wiederholen ‹Ball›; wiedergewinnen ‹Ansehen, Würde›; wiederbekommen ‹Geld›; **~ sth. from the depths of one's subconscious** etw. aus den Tiefen seines Unterbewusstseins hervorholen; **D** (*Computing*) wieder auffinden ‹Information›; **E** (*fetch*) ‹Hund:› apportieren

**retriever** /rɪˈtriːvə(r)/ *n.* Apportierhund, *der;* (*breed*) Retriever, *der*

**retroactive** /retrəʊˈæktɪv/ *adj.* rückwirkend; **~ effect** Rückwirkung, *die*

**retrochoir** /ˈretrəʊkwaɪə(r)/ *n.* (*Eccl. Archit.*) Retrochor, *der*

**retrograde** /ˈretrəgreɪd/ *adj.* **A** (*retreating*) **~ motion** Rückwärtsbewegung, *die;* **~ step** (*fig.*) Rückschritt, *der;* **B** (*reverting to the past*) rückschrittlich ‹Idee, Politik, Maßnahme›; **C** (*inverse*) umgekehrt ‹Reihenfolge›

**retrogress** /retrəˈgres/ *v.i.* **A** sich zurückbewegen; **B** (*fig.: deteriorate*) ‹Gesundheitszustand:› sich verschlechtern

**retrogression** /retrəˈgreʃn/ *n.* **A** Rückwärtsbewegung, *die;* **B** (*Biol.*) Rückentwicklung, *die*

**retrogressive** /retrəˈgresɪv/ *adj.* **A** ⇒ **retrograde** A, B; **B** (*Biol.*) rückläufig ‹Entwicklung›

**retro-rocket** /ˈretrəʊrɒkɪt/ *n.* (*Astronaut.*) Bremsrakete, *die*

**retrospect** /ˈretrəspekt/ *n.* **in ~:** im Nachhinein; **in ~, I think ...:** rückblickend *od.* im Nachhinein glaube ich, ...

**retrospection** /retrəˈspekʃn/ *n.* Rückschau, *die*

**retrospective** /retrəˈspektɪv/ ❶ *adj.* **A** retrospektiv (*geh.*); **~ exhibition** Retrospektive, *die* (*geh.*); **take a ~ look at sth.** Rückschau auf etw. (*Akk.*) halten (*geh.*); **B** (*applying to the past*) rückwirkend ‹Lohnerhöhung, Gesetz, Vertragsänderung›; **be ~:** Rückwirkung haben. ❷ *n.* (*Art*) Retrospektive, *die* (*geh.*)

**retrospectively** /retrəˈspektɪvlɪ/ *adv.* **A** (*by retrospection*) im Nachhinein, rückblickend ‹betrachten›; **B** (*so as to apply to the past*) rückwirkend; **a law operating ~:** ein rückwirkendes Gesetz; ein Gesetz mit Rückwirkung

**retroussé** /rəˈtruːseɪ/ *adj.* **~ nose** Stupsnase, *die*

**retrovirus** /ˈretrəʊvaɪrəs/ *n.* (*Biol.*) Retrovirus, *das od. der*

**retry** /riːˈtraɪ/ *v.t.* (*Law*) neu verhandeln ‹Fall›; neu verhandeln gegen ‹Person›

**retsina** /reˈtsiːnə/ *n.* Retsina, *der*

**retune** /riːˈtjuːn/ *v.t.* **A** neu stimmen ‹Musikinstrument›; **B** neu einstellen ‹Radio›

**returf** /riːˈtɜːf/ *v.t.* neuen Rasen verlegen auf (+ *Dat.*) ‹Platz, Spielfeld usw.›

**return** /rɪˈtɜːn/ ❶ *v.i.* **A** (*come back*) zurückkommen; zurückkehren (*geh.*); ‹Jahreszeit:› wiederkehren; (*go back*) zurückgehen; zurückkehren (*geh.*); (*go back by vehicle*) zurückfahren; zurückkehren (*geh.*); **~ home** wieder nach Hause kommen/gehen/fahren/zurückkehren; **~ to work** (*after holiday or strike*) die Arbeit wieder aufnehmen; **she had gone never to ~:** sie war für immer gegangen; **~ to health** wieder gesund werden; **his good spirits quickly ~ed** seine gute Laune stellte sich rasch wieder ein; **B** (*revert*) **~ to a subject/one's old habits** auf ein Thema zurückkommen/in seine alten Gewohnheiten zurückfallen; **unto dust thou shalt ~** (*Relig.*) zu Staub sollst du wieder werden.
❷ *v.t.* **A** (*bring back*) zurückbringen; zurückgeben ‹geliehenen/gestohlenen Gegenstand, gekaufte Ware›; [wieder] zurückschicken ‹unzustellbaren Brief›; (*to original position*) zurückstellen ‹Hebel›; (*hand back, refuse*) zurückweisen ‹Scheck›; (*put back*) (*vertically*) [wieder] zurückstellen ‹Buch, Ordner›; (*horizontally*) [wieder] zurücklegen ‹Geld, Buch, Ordner›; (*to file*) wieder einheften ‹Brief›; **~ed with thanks** mit Dank zurück; **'~ to sender'** (*on letter*) „zurück an Absender"; **he ~ed his purse to his pocket** er steckte sein Portemonnaie wieder ein; **he ~ed the fish to the water** er setzte den Fisch wieder ins Wasser; **B** (*restore*) **~ sth. to its original state** *or* **condition** etw. wieder in seinen ursprünglichen Zustand versetzen; **C** (*yield*) abwerfen ‹Gewinn›; **D** (*give back sth. similar*) erwidern ‹Besuch, Gruß, Liebe, Gewehrfeuer›; sich revanchieren für (*ugs.*) ‹Freundlichkeit, Gefallen›; zurückgeben ‹Schlag›; **E** (*elect*) wählen ‹Kandidaten›; **~ sb. to Parliament** jmdn. ins Parlament wählen; **F** (*Sport*) zurückschlagen ‹Ball›; (*throw back*) zurückwerfen; **G** (*answer*) erwidern; entgegnen; **H** (*declare*) **~ a verdict of guilty/not guilty** ‹Geschworene:› auf „schuldig"/„nicht schuldig" erkennen; **~ sb. guilty** jmdn. schuldig sprechen.
❸ *n.* **A** **▶ 1191** (*coming back*) Rückkehr, *die;* (*to home*) Heimkehr, *die;* (*of illness*) Wiederauftreten, *das;* **his ~ to work/school had to be delayed** er musste die Wiederaufnahme seiner *od.* der Arbeit verschieben/er konnte erst später [als vorgesehen] wieder zur Schule gehen; **point of no ~** ⇒ **point** 1 K; **~ to health** Genesung, *die* (*geh.*); **many happy ~s [of the day]!** herzlichen Glückwunsch [zum Geburtstag]!; **wish sb. many happy ~s [of the day]** jmdm. [zum Geburtstag] alles Gute wünschen; **B** **by ~ [of post]** postwendend; **C** (*ticket*) Rückfahrkarte, *die;* (*for flight*) Rückflugschein, *der;* **single or ~?** einfach oder hin und zurück?; **D** (*proceeds*) **~[s]** Ertrag, Gewinn, *der* (**on, from** aus); **~ on capital** Kapitalgewinn, *der;* ⇒ *also* **diminishing**; **E** (*bringing back*) Zurückbringen, *das;* (*of property, goods, book*) Rückgabe, *die* (**to** an + *Akk.*); (*of cheque*) Zurückweisung, *die;* (*of loan*) Rückzahlung, *die;* **F** (*giving back of sth. similar*) Erwiderung, *die;* **receive/get sth. in ~ [for sth.]** etw. [für etw.] bekommen; **G** (*Sport: striking back*) Rückschlag, *der;* (*throw back*) Rückwurf, *der;* **pick up the ~** (*Footb. etc.*) den zurückgespielten Ball annehmen; **H** (*report*) Bericht, *der;* (*set of statistics*) statistischer Bericht; Statistik, *die;* **income-tax ~:** Einkommenssteuererklärung, *die;* **election ~s** Wahlergebnisse; **I** (*Brit. Parl.: electing*) Wahl, *die;* **J** *attrib.* (*Archit.*) Flügel‹mauer, -wand›; **K** (*Computing*) **press ~:** Return *od.* die Returntaste drücken; **~ key** Returntaste, *die*

**returnable** /rɪˈtɜːnəbl/ *adj.* Mehrweg‹behälter, -flasche usw.›; rückzahlbar ‹Gebühr, Kaution›; **~ bottle** Pfandflasche, *die;* **~ deposit** Pfand, *der*

**returned** /rɪˈtɜːnd/ *adj.* heimgekehrt; **~ emigrant** Rückwanderer, *der*

**return: ~ 'fare** *n.* Preis für eine Rückfahrkarte/(*for flight*) einen Rückflugschein; **what is the ~ fare?** wie viel kostet eine Rückfahrkarte/ein Rückflugschein?; **~ 'flight** *n.* Rückflug, *der;* (*both ways*) Hin- und Rückflug, *der;* **~ 'game** *n.* Rückspiel, *das*

**re'turning officer** *n.* (*Brit. Parl.*) Wahlleiter, *der*/-leiterin, *die*

**return: ~ 'journey** *n.* Rückreise, *die;* Rückfahrt, *die;* (*both ways*) Hin- und Rückfahrt, *die;* **~ 'match** *n.* Rückspiel, *das;* **~ 'ticket** *n.* (*Brit.*) Rückfahrkarte, *die;* (*for flight*) Rückflugschein, *der;* **~ 'trip** *n.* **A** (*trip back*) Rückweg, *der;* Rückfahrt, *die;* **B** (*trip out and back*) Hin- und Rückfahrt, *die;* Hin- und Rückreise, *die;* (*by plane*) Hin- und Rückflug, *der;* **~ 'visit** *n.* **A** (*further visit*) nochmaliger Besuch; **make a ~ visit to a place** einen Ort noch einmal besuchen; **B** (*visit in reciprocation*) Gegenbesuch, *der*

**retype** /riːˈtaɪp/ *v.t.* neu tippen

**reunification** /riːjuːnɪfɪˈkeɪʃn/ *n.* Wiedervereinigung, *die*

**reunion** /riːˈjuːnjən/ *n.* **A** (*gathering*) Treffen, *das;* **B** (*reuniting*) Wiedersehen, *das;* **C** (*reunited state*) Wiedervereinigung, *die*

**reunite** /riːjʊˈnaɪt/ ❶ *v.t.* wieder zusammenführen; **a ~d Germany** ein wieder vereinigtes Deutschland. ❷ *v.i.* sich wieder zusammenschließen; ‹Kirchen:› sich wieder vereinigen

**reusable** /riːˈjuːzəbl/ *adj.* wieder verwendbar

**reuse** ❶ /riːˈjuːz/ *v.t.* wieder verwenden. ❷ /riːˈjuːs/ *n.* Wiederverwendung, *die*

**rev** /rev/ (*coll.*) ❶ *n., usu. in pl.* Umdrehung, *die;* Tour, *die* (*Technikjargon*); **~ counter** (*Brit.*) Tourenzähler, *der* (*ugs.*). ❷ *v.i.*, **-vv-** mit hoher Drehzahl *od.* hochtourig laufen. ❸ *v.t.*, **-vv-** hochdrehen (*Technikjargon*); (*noisily*) aufheulen lassen ‹Motor›

**~ 'up** ❶ *v.i.* ‹Motor:› hochgejagt werden (*Technikjargon*); **I heard [the sound of] a car ~ving up** ich hörte den Motor eines Autos aufheulen. ❷ *v.t.* hochjagen (*Technikjargon*); aufheulen lassen ‹Motor[rad]›

**Rev.** /ˈrevərənd, (*coll.*) rev/ *abbr.* **▶ 1617** **Reverend** Rev.

**revaluation** /riːvæljʊˈeɪʃn/ *n.* **A** (*of object*) Neubewertung, *die;* **B** (*Econ.: of currency*) Aufwertung, *die*

**revalue** /riːˈvæljuː/ *v.t.* **A** neu bewerten; **B** (*Econ.*) aufwerten ‹Währung›

**revamp** /riːˈvæmp/ *v.t.* renovieren ‹Zimmer, Gebäude›; [wieder] aufmöbeln *od.* aufpolieren ‹Schrank, Auto usw.›; neu bearbeiten ‹Stück, Musical usw.›; auf Vordermann bringen (*ugs.*) ‹Firma›

**Revd.** /ˈrevərənd, (*coll.*) rev/ *abbr.* **▶ 1617** **Reverend** Rev.

**reveal** /rɪˈviːl/ ❶ *v.t.* enthüllen (*geh.*); verraten; offenbaren (*geh., Theol.*), [offen] zeigen ‹Gefühle›; **be ~ed** ‹Wahrheit:› ans Licht kommen; **all will be ~ed** (*joc.*) es kommt alles ans Licht (*scherzh.*); **~ one's identity** seine Identität preisgeben (*geh.*); **~ oneself/itself to be** *or* **as being sth.** sich als etw. erweisen; **~ sb. to be sth.** jmdn. als etw. enthüllen (*geh.*); **the rising curtain ~ed a street scene** der sich hebende Vorhang gab den Blick auf eine Straßenszene frei; **there was not much that the dress did not ~:** das

Kleid verhüllte nur wenig. ❷ *n.* (*Archit.*) Laibung, *die*

**revealed religion** /rɪviːld rɪˈlɪdʒn/ *n.* Offenbarungsreligion, *die*

**revealing** /rɪˈviːlɪŋ/ *adj.* aufschlussreich ‹Darstellung, Dokument›; verräterisch ‹Bemerkung, Versprecher›; offenherzig (*scherzh.*) ‹Kleid, Bluse usw.›; **be ~ about sth.** etwas *od.* einiges über etw. (*Akk.*) verraten

**reveille** /rɪˈvælɪ, rɪˈvelɪ/ *n.* (*Mil.*) Reveille, *die* (*fachspr. veralt.*); Wecksignal, *das;* **sound [the] ~:** das Wecksignal geben; **~ was at 6 a. m.** Wecken war um sechs Uhr morgens

**revel** /ˈrevl/ ❶ *v.i.*, (*Brit.*) **-ll-** Ⓐ (*take delight*) genießen (**in** *Akk.*); **~ in doing sth.** es [richtig] genießen, etw. zu tun; Ⓑ (*carouse*) feiern; **~ the night away, ~ till dawn** die Nacht durchfeiern (*ugs.*). ❷ *n. usu pl.* Feiern, *das;* Feierei, *die* (*ugs.*)

**revelation** /revəˈleɪʃn/ *n.* Ⓐ Enthüllung, *die* (*geh.*); **be a ~:** einem die Augen öffnen; **the dessert/concert was a ~:** das Dessert/Konzert war eine Offenbarung (*scherzh.*); **what a ~!** unglaublich!; **be a ~ to sb.** jmdm. die Augen öffnen; Ⓑ (*Relig.*) Offenbarung, *die;* **[the** *or* **the Book of] R~[s]** die Offenbarung [des Johannes]; **R~[s] 3:14** Offenbarung 3,14

**reveller** /ˈrevələ(r)/ *n.* Feiernde, *der/die*

**revelry** /ˈrevəlrɪ/ *n.* Feiern, *das;* Feierei, *die* (*ugs.*); **spend the whole night in ~:** die ganze Nacht durchfeiern (*ugs.*); **hear sounds of ~:** hören, wie gefeiert wird

**revenge** /rɪˈvendʒ/ ❶ *v.t.* rächen ‹Person, Tat›; sich rächen für ‹Tat›; **~ oneself** *or* **be ~d [on sb.] [for sth.]** sich [für etw.] [an jmdm.] rächen. ❷ *n.* Ⓐ (*action*) Rache, *die;* **[desire for] ~:** Rachsucht, *die* (*geh.*); **take ~** *or* **have** *or* (*literary*) **exact one's ~ [on sb.] [for sth.]** Rache [an jmdm.] [für etw.] nehmen *od.* (*geh.*) üben; **~ is sweet** Rache ist süß; **in ~ for sth.** als Rache für etw.; Ⓑ (*Sport, Games*) Revanche, *die;* **give sb. his ~:** jmdm. Revanche geben

**revengeful** /rɪˈvendʒfl/ *adj.* rachsüchtig (*geh.*); **~ act** Racheakt, *der*

**revenue** /ˈrevənjuː/ *n.* Ⓐ (*State's income*) **[national/state] ~:** Staatseinnahmen; öffentliche Einnahmen; Ⓑ **~[s]** (*income*) Einnahmen; Einkünfte *Pl.;* **source of ~:** Einnahmequelle, *die;* Ⓒ **R~** (*department*) *oberste Finanzbehörde*

**revenue: ~ officer** *n.* ≈ Zollbeamter, *der*/-beamtin, *die;* **~ stamp** *n.* Steuerzeichen, *das;* (*paper strip on cigarette packet etc.*); [Steuer]banderole, *die*

**reverberate** /rɪˈvɜːbəreɪt/ ❶ *v.i.* ‹Geräusch, Musik:› widerhallen. ❷ *v.t.* zurückwerfen; reflektieren

**reverberation** /rɪvɜːbəˈreɪʃn/ *n.* **~[s]** Widerhall, *der;* **~ of sound** Schallreflexion, *die;* **the ~s of that episode** (*fig.*) der Nachhall dieser Begebenheit

**revere** /rɪˈvɪə(r)/ *v.t.* verehren

**reverence** /ˈrevərəns/ *n.* Ⓐ (*revering*) Verehrung, *die;* Ehrfurcht, *die;* **hold sb. in** *or* **regard sb. with ~:** jmdn. verehren; **hold sth. in ~:** etw. heilig halten; **pay ~ to sb.** jmdm. Verehrung entgegenbringen; **have/show ~ for sth./sb.** vor etw./jmdm. Ehrfurcht haben/zeigen; Ⓑ **Your/His R~** (*arch./Ir./joc.*) Euer/Seine Hochwürden

**reverend** /ˈrevərənd/ ▶ **1617** ❶ *adj.* ehrwürdig; **the R~ John Wilson, the R~ Mr Wilson** Hochwürden [John] Wilson; **the Very/Right R~ Donald Todd** Hochwürden [Donald] Todd; **the Most R~ Archbishop of York** Seine Exzellenz der Hochwürdigste Erzbischof von York; **the R~ Father [O'Higgins]** Hochwürden [O'Higgins]; **the ~ gentleman** Hochwürden; **R~ Mother** Ehrwürdige Schwester Oberin *od.* Frau Oberin. ❷ *n.* (*coll.*) Pfarrer, *der;* (*form of address*) Hochwürden

**reverent** /ˈrevərənt/ *adj.* ehrfürchtig; **have a ~ attitude to sb., be ~ towards sb.** Ehrfurcht vor jmdm. haben; **in hushed and ~ tones** mit ehrfurchtsvoll gedämpfter Stimme

**reverential** /revəˈrenʃl/ *adj.* ehrfürchtig

**reverently** /ˈrevərəntlɪ/ *adv.* ehrfürchtig; ehrerbietig ‹sich verneigen›

**reverie** /ˈrevərɪ/ *n.* Träumerei, *die;* **be deep** *or* **lost** *or* **sunk in [a] ~:** in Träumereien (*Akk.*) versunken sein; **fall into a ~:** in Träumereien (*Akk.*) versinken

**reversal** /rɪˈvɜːsl/ *n.* Ⓐ Umkehrung, *die;* **~ [colour] film** Umkehrfilm, *der;* Ⓑ (*Law*) Aufhebung, *die*

**reverse** /rɪˈvɜːs/ ❶ *adj.* entgegengesetzt ‹Richtung›; Rück‹seite›; umgekehrt ‹Reihenfolge›; **the ~ side of the coin** (*fig.*) die Kehrseite der Medaille.

❷ *n.* Ⓐ (*contrary*) Gegenteil, *das;* **quite the ~!** ganz im Gegenteil!; **in ~:** rückwärts ‹schreiben, drucken›; Ⓑ (*Motor Veh.*) Rückwärtsgang, *der;* **in ~:** im Rückwärtsgang; **put the car into ~, go into ~:** den Rückwärtsgang einlegen; Ⓒ (*defeat*) Rückschlag, *der;* **~s of fortune** Schicksalsschläge *Pl.;* Ⓓ (*back side of coin etc.*) Rückseite, *die;* Revers, *der* (*Münzk.*); (*design*) Rückseitenbild, *das;* Ⓔ (*back of page*) Rückseite, *die;* Verso, *das* (*Buchw.*).

❸ *v.t.* Ⓐ (*turn around*) umkehren ‹Reihenfolge, Wortstellung, Bewegung, Richtung›; grundlegend revidieren ‹Politik›; **~ the charge[s]** (*Brit.*) ein R-Gespräch anmelden; **make a ~d-charge call** (*Brit.*) ein R-Gespräch führen; **~ arms** (*Mil.*) die Gewehre mit dem Kolben nach oben halten; Ⓑ (*cause to move backwards*) zurücksetzen; **~ a car into sth.** ein Auto rückwärts in etw. (*Akk.*) fahren; Ⓒ (*revoke*) aufheben ‹Urteil, Anordnung›; kassieren (*Rechtsspr.*) ‹Urteil›; rückgängig machen ‹Maßnahme›.

❹ *v.i.* zurücksetzen; rückwärts fahren; **~ into sth.** rückwärts in etw. (*Akk.*) fahren

**reverse: ~-charge** *adj.* (*Brit.*) **make a ~-charge call** ein R-Gespräch führen; **~ 'gear** *n.* (*Motor Veh.*) Rückwärtsgang, *der;* ⇒ *also* **gear** 1 A

**reversible** /rɪˈvɜːsɪbl/ *adj.* Ⓐ umkehrbar, (*fachspr.*) reversibel ‹Vorgang›; (*capable of being revoked*) aufhebbar ‹Entscheidung, Anordnung›; Ⓑ (*having two usable sides*) beidseitig verwendbar, (*Textilw.*) beidrecht ‹Stoff›; beidseitig tragbar ‹Kleidungsstück›; Wende‹mantel, -jacke›

**re'versing light** *n.* Rückfahrscheinwerfer, *der*

**reversion** /rɪˈvɜːʃn/ *n.* Ⓐ (*return*) Rückkehr, *die* (**to** zu); **~ to type** (*Biol.*) Rückschlag auf eine frühere Ahnenform; (*fig.*) atavistischer Rückfall; Ⓑ (*Law: return of estate*) Rückfall, *der;* Heimfall, *der* (*Rechtsspr.*)

**revert** /rɪˈvɜːt/ *v.i.* Ⓐ (*recur, return*) zurückkommen (**to** auf + *Akk.*), wieder aufgreifen (**to** *Akk.*) ‹Thema, Angelegenheit, Frage›; ‹Gedanken:› zurückkehren (*geh.*) (**to** zu); **to ~ to ...:** um wieder auf ... (*Akk.*) zurückzukommen; **she has ~ed to using her maiden name** sie hat wieder ihren Mädchennamen angenommen; **~ to type** (*Biol.*) auf eine frühere Ahnenform zurückschlagen; **he has ~ed to type** (*fig.*) er geht jetzt wieder seinen alten Gewohnheiten nach; **~ to its natural state** in den Naturzustand zurückkehren; **~ to savagery** ‹Menschen:› in den Zustand der Wildheit zurückfallen; **~ to desert** *etc.* ‹Land:› wieder verwüsten *usw.;* Ⓑ (*Law*) ‹Eigentum:› zurückfallen, (*Rechtsspr.*) heimfallen (**to** an + *Akk.*)

**revetment** /rɪˈvetmənt/ *n.* Futtermauer, *die* (*Archit.*)

**review** /rɪˈvjuː/ ❶ *n.* Ⓐ (*survey*) Übersicht, *die* (**of** über + *Akk.*); Überblick, *der* (**of** über + *Akk.*); (*of past events*) Rückschau, *die* (**of** auf + *Akk.*); **be a ~ of sth.** einen Überblick *od.* eine Übersicht über etw. (*Akk.*) geben; Ⓑ (*re-examination*) [nochmalige] Überprüfung; nochmalige Prüfung; (*of salary*) Revision, *die;* **be under ~** ‹Vereinbarung, Lage:› nochmals geprüft werden; Ⓒ (*account*) Besprechung, *die;* Kritik, *die;* Rezension, *die;* **~ copy** (*Publishing*) Rezensionsexemplar, *das;* Ⓓ (*periodical*) Zeitschrift, *die;* Ⓔ (*Mil.*) Inspektion, *die;* (*march*) Parade, *die;* **naval ~:** Flottenparade, *die;* **pass in ~:** [vorbei]defilieren; **pass sth. in ~** (*fig.*) etw. Revue passieren lassen.

❷ *v.t.* Ⓐ (*survey*) untersuchen; prüfen; Ⓑ (*re-examine*) überprüfen; Ⓒ (*Mil.*) inspizieren; mustern; Ⓓ (*write a criticism of*) besprechen; rezensieren; Ⓔ (*Law*) überprüfen

**reviewer** /rɪˈvjuːə(r)/ *n.* Rezensent, *der*/Rezensentin, *die;* Kritiker, *der*/Kritikerin, *die*

**revile** /rɪˈvaɪl/ *v.t.* schmähen (*geh.*)

**revise** /rɪˈvaɪz/ ❶ *v.t.* Ⓐ (*amend*) revidieren ‹Urteil, Gesetz, Vorschlag›; **R~d Version** (*Brit.*) *revidierte Fassung der „Authorized Version" der Bibel (im 19. Jh.)*; Ⓑ (*check over*) durchsehen ‹Manuskript, Text, Notizen›; Ⓒ (*reread*) noch einmal durchlesen ‹Notizen›; *abs.* lernen; **~ one's maths** Mathe (*ugs.*) wiederholen. ❷ *n.* (*Printing*) Revisionsbogen, *der*

**reviser** /rɪˈvaɪzə(r)/ *n.* Bearbeiter, *der*/Bearbeiterin, *die;* (*of printer's proof*) Korrektor, *der*/Korrektorin, *die*

**revision** /rɪˈvɪʒn/ *n.* Ⓐ (*amending*) Revision, *die;* **in need of ~:** revisionsbedürftig; Ⓑ (*checking over*) Durchsicht, *die;* Ⓒ (*amended version*) [Neu]bearbeitung, *die;* überarbeitete *od.* revidierte Fassung; Ⓓ (*rereading*) Wiederholung, *die;* **~ exercises** Wiederholungsübungen

**revisionism** /rɪˈvɪʒənɪzm/ *n.* Revisionismus, *der*

**revisionist** /rɪˈvɪʒənɪst/ ❶ *n.* Revisionist, *der*/Revisionistin, *die.* ❷ *adj.* revisionistisch

**revisit** /riːˈvɪzɪt/ *v.t.* wieder besuchen

**revitalize (revitalise)** /riːˈvaɪtəlaɪz/ *v.t.* neu beleben

**revival** /rɪˈvaɪvl/ *n.* Ⓐ (*making active again, bringing back into use*) Wieder- *od.* Neubelebung, *die;* **~ of learning/letters** neue geistige/literarische Blüte; Ⓑ (*Theatre*) Wiederaufführung, *die;* Revival, *das;* Ⓒ (*Relig.: awakening*) Erweckung, *die;* **~ meeting** Erweckungsversammlung, *die;* Ⓓ (*restoration*) Wiederherstellung, *die;* Regenerierung, *die* (*geh.*); (*to consciousness or life; also fig.*) Wiederbelebung, *die*

**revivalism** /rɪˈvaɪvəlɪzm/ *n.* Erweckungsglaube, *der;* Revivalism, *der*

**revivalist** /rɪˈvaɪvəlɪst/ *n.* Erwecker, *der*/Erweckerin, *die;* (*evangelist*) Erweckungsprediger, *der*

**revive** /rɪˈvaɪv/ ❶ *v.i.* Ⓐ (*come back to consciousness*) wieder zu sich kommen; Ⓑ (*be reinvigorated*) wieder aufleben; zu neuem Leben erwachen; ‹Geschäft:› sich wieder beleben; **his spirits/hopes ~d** er lebte wieder auf/schöpfte neue Hoffnung.

❷ *v.t.* Ⓐ (*restore to consciousness*) wieder beleben; Ⓑ (*restore to healthy state*) wieder auf die Beine bringen ‹Person›; wieder aufleben lassen ‹Blume›; (*reinvigorate*) wieder zu Kräften kommen lassen; Ⓒ (*strengthen, reawaken*) wieder wecken ‹Lebensgeister, Ehrgeiz, Interesse, Wunsch›; **~ sb.'s hopes** jmdn. neue Hoffnung schöpfen lassen; Ⓓ (*make active again, bring back into use*) wieder aufleben lassen; **the mini-skirt was ~d** der Minirock kam wieder in Mode (*Akk.*); Ⓔ (*Theatre*) wieder auf die Bühne bringen; Ⓕ (*renew memory of*) wieder lebendig werden lassen

**revocable** /ˈrevəkəbl/ *adj.* widerrufbar

**revocation** /revəˈkeɪʃn/ *n.* ⇒ **revoke** 1: Aufhebung, *die;* Widerrufung, *die;* Zurückziehen, *das;* Zurücknahme, *die*

**revoke** /rɪˈvəʊk/ ❶ *v.t.* Ⓐ (*cancel*) aufheben ‹Erlass, Privileg, Entscheidung›; widerrufen ‹Befehl›; zurückziehen ‹Auftrag›; Ⓑ (*withdraw*) widerrufen ‹Erlaubnis, Genehmigung›; zurücknehmen ‹Versprechen›. ❷ *v.i.* (*Cards*) [unzulässigerweise] nicht bedienen. ❸ *n.* (*Cards*) Revoke, *die*

**revolt** /rɪˈvəʊlt/ ❶ *v.i.* Ⓐ (*rebel*) revoltieren, aufbegehren (*geh.*) (**against** gegen); Ⓑ (*feel revulsion*) sich sträuben (**at, against, from** gegen); ‹Magen:› revoltieren, rebellieren (**from** bei). ❷ *v.t.* mit Abscheu erfüllen; **she was ~ed by their brutality** ihre Brutalität erfüllte sie mit Abscheu. ❸ *n.* (*rebelling*) Aufruhr, *der;* Rebellion, *die;* (*rising*) Revolte, *die* (*auch fig.*); Aufstand, *der;* **a spirit of ~:** eine rebellische Stimmung; **be** *or* **rise in ~:** revoltieren; aufbegehren (*geh.*)

**revolting** /rɪˈvəʊltɪŋ/ *adj.* (*repulsive*) abscheulich; scheußlich ‹Gedanke, Wetter›; widerlich ‹Person›; **be ~ to sb.'s sense of decency** jmds. Anstandsgefühl verletzen

**revoltingly** /rɪˈvəʊltɪŋlɪ/ *adv.* abstoßend ‹hässlich, grausam›

**revolution** /revəˈluːʃn/ *n.* **A** (*lit. or fig.*) Revolution, *die;* **the American R~:** die Amerikanische Revolution; der Nordamerikanische Unabhängigkeitskrieg; **B** (*single turn*) Umdrehung, *die;* **number of ~s** Drehzahl, *die;* **C** (*Astron.: movement in orbit*) Umlauf, *der*

**revolutionary** /revəˈluːʃənərɪ/ **1** *adj.* **A** (*Polit.*) revolutionär; **B** (*involving great changes*) revolutionär; umwälzend; (*pioneering*) bahnbrechend; **C** **R~** (*Amer. Hist.*) des Nordamerikanischen Unabhängigkeitskrieges *nachgestellt;* der Amerikanischen Revolution *nachgestellt.* **2** *n.* Revolutionär, *der*/Revolutionärin, *die*

**revoˈlution counter** *n.* Drehzahlmesser, *der*

**revolutionize** (**revolutionise**) /revəˈluːʃənaɪz/ *v.t.* grundlegend verändern; revolutionieren ‹Gesellschaft, Technik›

**revolve** /rɪˈvɒlv/ **1** *v.t.* **A** (*turn round*) drehen; **B** **~ sth. in one's mind** (*ponder*) etw. erwägen. **2** *v.i.* sich drehen (**round, about, on** um); **everything ~s around her** sie ist der Mittelpunkt[, um den sich alles dreht]

**revolver** /rɪˈvɒlvə(r)/ *n.* [Trommel]revolver, *der*

**revolving** /rɪˈvɒlvɪŋ/ *attrib. adj.* drehbar; Dreh‹stuhl, -tür, -bühne›; **~ credit** (*Finance*) Revolvingkredit, *der*

**revue** /rɪˈvjuː/ *n.* Kabarett, *das;* (*musical show*) Revue, *die*

**revulsion** /rɪˈvʌlʃn/ *n.* **A** (*feeling*) Abscheu, *der* (**at** vor + *Dat.*, gegen); **have a sense of ~ about sth.** von etw. angewidert sein; **B** (*recoiling*) Distanzierung, *die* (**from** von)

**reward** /rɪˈwɔːd/ **1** *n.* Belohnung, *die;* (*for kindness*) Dank, *der;* Lohn, *der;* (*recognition of merit etc.*) Auszeichnung, *die;* **get very little ~:** kaum belohnt werden; **offer a ~ of £100** 100 Pfund Belohnung aussetzen. **2** *v.t.* belohnen; **is that how you ~ me for my help?** ist das der Dank für meine Hilfe?

**rewarding** /rɪˈwɔːdɪŋ/ *adj.* lohnend ‹Zeitvertreib, Beschäftigung›; **be ~/financially ~:** sich lohnen/einträglich sein; **bringing up a child can be very ~:** das Großziehen eines Kindes kann einem sehr viel geben

**rewind** /riːˈwaɪnd/ *v.t.*, **rewound** /riːˈwaʊnd/ **A** (*wind again*) wieder aufziehen ‹Uhr›; **B** (*wind back*) zurückspulen ‹Film, Band›

**ˈrewind button** *n.* (*on camera*) Rückspulknopf, *der;* (*on tape recorder etc.*) Rücklauftaste, *die*

**rewire** /riːˈwaɪə(r)/ *v.t.* mit neuen Leitungen versehen; **~ a house/car** in einem Haus/Auto die Leitungen erneuern

**reword** /riːˈwɜːd/ *v.t.* umformulieren; neu formulieren

**rework** /riːˈwɜːk/ *v.t.* neu bearbeiten ‹Theaterstück, Szene usw.›; neu formulieren ‹Satz, Absatz, Text›

**rewound** ⇒ **rewind**

**rewrite** **1** /riːˈraɪt/ *v.t.*, **rewrote** /riːˈrəʊt/, **rewritten** /riːˈrɪtn/ (*write again*) noch einmal [neu] schreiben; (*write differently*) umschreiben. **2** /ˈriːraɪt/ *n.* Neufassung, *die;* **a complete ~:** eine völlig neue Fassung

**ˈrewrite man** *n.* (*Amer.*) Rewriter, *der* (*fachspr.*); Bearbeiter, *der*

**Reynard** /ˈrenəd, ˈreɪnəd/ **~[, the fox]** Reineke [Fuchs]

**r. h.** *abbr.* **right hand** r.

**rhapsodic** /ræpˈsɒdɪk/ *adj.* **A** (*Mus.*) rhapsodisch; **B** (*fig.: ecstatic*) ekstatisch

**rhapsodize** (**rhapsodise**) /ˈræpsədaɪz/ *v.i.* schwärmen (**about, on** von; **over** über + *Akk.*)

**rhapsody** /ˈræpsədɪ/ *n.* **A** (*Mus.*) Rhapsodie, *die;* **B** (*ecstatic utterance*) Schwärmerei, *die;* **go into rhapsodies over sth.** über etw. (*Akk.*) in Ekstase geraten

**rhea** /ˈriːə/ *n.* (*Ornith.*) Nandu, *der*

**Rhenish** /ˈriːnɪʃ, ˈrenɪʃ/ (*arch.*) *adj.* rheinisch; **~ wine** Rheinwein, *der;* **~ Confederation** (*Hist.*) Rheinbund, *der*

**rheostat** /ˈriːəstæt/ *n.* (*Electr.*) Rheostat, *der*

**rhesus**/ˈriːsəs/: **~ baby** *n.* (*Med.*) Rh-geschädigtes Baby; **~ factor** *n.* (*Med.*) Rhesusfaktor, *der;* **~ monkey** *n.* Rhesusaffe, *der;* **~ ˈnegative** *n.* (*Med.*) Rhesusfaktor negativ; **~ ˈpositive** *n.* (*Med.*) Rhesusfaktor positiv

**rhetoric** /ˈretərɪk/ *n.* **A** (*art of discourse*) **[art of] ~:** Redekunst, *die;* Rhetorik, *die;* **B** (*derog.*) Phrasen (*abwertend*) *Pl.*

**rhetorical** /rɪˈtɒrɪkl/ *adj.* **A** rhetorisch ‹Frage, Diskurs›; **B** (*derog.: designed to impress*) phrasenhaft (*abwertend*)

**rheumatic** /ruːˈmætɪk/ **1** *adj.* rheumatisch. **2** *n.* **A** *in pl.* (*coll.*) Rheuma, *das* (*ugs.*); **B** (*person*) Rheumatiker, *der*/Rheumatikerin, *die;* Rheumakranke, *der/die*

**rheumatism** /ˈruːmətɪzm/ *n.* ▶ **1232** (*Med.*) Rheumatismus, *der;* Rheuma, *das* (*ugs.*)

**rheumatoid arthritis** /ruːmətɔɪd ɑːˈθraɪtɪs/ *n.* ▶ **1232** (*Med.*) chronischer Gelenkrheumatismus

**Rhine** /raɪn/ *pr. n.* ▶ **1480** Rhein, *der*

**ˈRhineland** *pr. n.* Rheinland, *das*

**Rhineland-Paˈlatinate** /raɪnlænd pəˈlætɪnət/ *pr. n.* Rheinland-Pfalz (*das*)

**Rhine ˈwine** *n.* Rheinwein, *der*

**rhino** /ˈraɪnəʊ/ *n., pl. same or* **~s** (*coll.*), **rhinoceros** /raɪˈnɒsərəs/ *n., pl. same or* **~ceroses** Nashorn, *das;* Rhinozeros, *das*

**rhizome** /ˈraɪzəʊm/ *n.* (*Bot.*) Rhizom, *das* (*fachspr.*); Wurzelstock, *der*

**Rhodes** /rəʊdz/ *pr. n.* Rhodos (*das*)

**Rhodesia** /rəʊˈdiːʒə/ *pr. n.* (*Hist.*) Rhodesien (*das*)

**Rhodesian** /rəʊˈdiːʒən/ ▶ **1340** (*Hist.*) **1** *adj.* rhodesisch. **2** *n.* Rhodesier, *der*/Rhodesierin, *die*

**rhododendron** /rəʊdəˈdendrən/ *n.* (*Bot.*) Rhododendron, *der;* Alpenrose, *die*

**rhombic** /ˈrɒmbɪk/ *adj.* rhombisch

**rhombus** /ˈrɒmbəs/ *n., pl.* **~es** *or* **rhombi** /ˈrɒmbaɪ/ (*Geom.*) Rhombus, *der;* Raute, *die*

**rhubarb** /ˈruːbɑːb/ *n.* **A** Rhabarber, *der;* (*root, purgative*) Rhabarberwurzel, *die;* **B** (*Theatre coll.*) **~, ~, ~ ...:** Rhabarber, Rhabarber, Rhabarber ...

**rhyme** /raɪm/ **1** *n.* **A** Reim, *der;* **find no ~ or reason in sth.** sich (*Dat.*) auf etw. (*Akk.*) keinen Reim machen können; **without ~ or reason** ohne Sinn und Verstand; **B** (*short poem*) Reim, *der;* (*rhyming verse*) gereimte Verse; **put sth. into ~:** etw. in Reime setzen; **C** (*rhyming word*) Reimwort, *das;* **'honey' is a ~ for** *or* **to 'money'** „honey" reimt sich auf „money". **2** *v.i.* **A** sich reimen (**with** auf + *Akk.*); **B** (*versify*) reimen. **3** *v.t.* reimen

**ˈrhyme scheme** *n.* (*Pros.*) Reimschema, *das*

**rhyming**/ˈraɪmɪŋ/: **~ ˈcouplet** *n.* (*Pros.*) Reimpaar, *das;* **~ dictionary** *n.* Reimwörterbuch, *das;* **~ slang** *n.* Rhyming Slang, *der; Slang, bei dem das eigentliche Wort durch eine sich darauf reimende Phrase oder einen Teil einer solchen ersetzt wird*

**rhythm** /rɪðm/ *n.* Rhythmus, *der;* **~ and blues** (*Mus.*) Rhythm and Blues, *der*

**rhythmic** /ˈrɪðmɪk/, **rhythmical** /ˈrɪðmɪkl/ *adj.* rhythmisch; gleichmäßig

**rhythmic gymˈnastics** *n.* rhythmische Sportgymnastik

**rhythm: ~ method** *n.* Knaus-Ogino-Methode, *die;* **~ section** *n.* Rhythmusgruppe, *die*

**RI** *abbr.* (*Sch.*) **religious instruction**

**rib** /rɪb/ **1** *n.* **A** ▶ **966** (*Anat.*) Rippe, *die;* **bruised ~s** Rippenprellung, *die;* **dig in the ~s** Rippenstoß, *der;* **B** **~[s]** (*joint of meat*) Rippenstück, *das;* **C** (*supporting piece*) (*of insect's wing*) Ader, *die;* (*of feather*) Kiel, *der;* Schaft, *der;* (*of boat, ship*) Spant, *das;* (*of bridge, leaf, ceiling, in knitting, fabric*) Rippe, *die;* (*of umbrella*) Speiche, *die;* **D** (*Amer. coll.: joke*) Witz, *der;* Flachs, *der* (*ugs.*). **2** *v.t.*, **-bb-** (*coll.*) aufziehen (*ugs.*)

**ribald** /ˈrɪbəld/ *adj.* zotig; schmutzig ‹Lachen›; unanständig ‹Ausdrücke›; (*irreverent*) anzüglich; rüde ‹Gesellschaft›

**ribaldry** /ˈrɪbəldrɪ/ *n.* Derbheit, *die;* Zotigkeit, *die;* (*irreverence*) Anzüglichkeit, *die*

**riband** /ˈrɪbənd/ ⇒ **ribbon A**

**ribbed** /rɪbd/ *adj.* gerippt

**ribbon** /rɪbn/ *n.* **A** (*band for hair, dress, etc.*) Band, *das;* (*on typewriter*) [Farb]band, *das;* (*on medal*) [Ordens]band, *das;* **campaign/service ~:** Kriegs-/Dienstauszeichnung, *die;* ⇒ *also* **blue ribbon**; **B** (*fig.: strip*) Streifen, *der;* **~ of light** Lichtstreifen, *der;* **C** *in pl.* (*ragged strips*) Fetzen *Pl.;* **tear to ~s** zerfetzen; (*fig.: condemn*) fertig machen (*ugs.*); in der Luft zerreißen ‹Buch, Stück usw.›

**ribbon: ~ building, ~ development** *ns., no pl.* Bandbebauung, *die*

**ˈribcage** *n.* (*Anat.*) Brustkorb, *der*

**ribonucleic acid** /raɪbənjuːkliːɪk ˈæsɪd/ *n.* (*Biol.*) Ribonukleinsäure, *die*

**rice** /raɪs/ *n.* Reis, *der*

**rice: ~ field** *n.* Reisfeld, *das;* **~ paper** *n.* Reispapier, *das;* **~ ˈpudding** *n.* Milchreis, *der*

**ricer** /ˈraɪsə(r)/ *n.* (*Amer.*) ≈ Kartoffelpresse, *die*

**ˈrice wine** *n.* Reiswein, *der*

**rich** /rɪtʃ/ **1** *adj.* **A** reich; ⇒ *also* **get-~-quick**; **B** (*having great resources*) reich (**in** an + *Dat.*); (*fertile*) fruchtbar ‹Land, Boden›; **oil-~:** ölreich; **~ in vitamins/lime/forests** vitamin-/kalk-/waldreich; **a play ~ in new ideas** ein Stück voll neuer Ideen; **strike it ~:** das große Geld machen; **C** (*splendid*) prachtvoll; prächtig; reich ‹Ausstattung›; **D** (*containing much fat, oil, eggs, etc.*) gehaltvoll; (*indigestible*) schwer ‹Essen›; **E** (*deep, full*) voll[tönend] ‹Stimme›; voll ‹Ton›; satt ‹Farbe, Farbton›; schwer ‹Geruch›; voll ‹Geschmack›; **F** (*ample*) reichlich; **G** (*valuable*) wertvoll; reich (*geh.*) ‹Geschenke, Opfergaben›; **H** (*amusing*) köstlich; **that's ~!** köstlich!; (*iron.*) das ist stark! (*ugs.*); **I** (*Motor Veh.*) fett ‹Gemisch›.
**2** *n. pl.* **the ~:** die Reichen; **~ and poor** Arm und Reich

**riches** /ˈrɪtʃɪz/ *n. pl.* Reichtum, *der*

**richly** /ˈrɪtʃlɪ/ *adv.* **A** (*splendidly*) reich; üppig ‹ausgestattet›; prächtig ‹gekleidet›; **~ ornamented** reich verziert; reich geschmückt; **~ coloured** farbenprächtig; **~ endowed** reichlich ausgestattet; **B** (*fully*) voll und ganz; **~ deserved** wohlverdient

**richness** /ˈrɪtʃnɪs/ *n., no pl.* **A** (*elaborateness*) Pracht, *die;* Prächtigkeit, *die;* **the ~ of ornamentation** der Reichtum der Ornamentik; die reiche Ornamentik; **B** (*of food*) Reichhaltigkeit, *die;* (*indigestibility*) Schwere, *die;* **C** (*fullness*) (*of voice*) voller Klang; Vollheit, *die;* (*of colour*) Sattheit, *die;* **D** (*great resources*) Reichtum, *der* (**in** an + *Dat.*); (*of soil*) Fruchtbarkeit, *die*

**Richter scale** /ˈrɪktə skeɪl/ *n.* (*Geol.*) Richter-Skala, *die*

**rick**[1] /rɪk/ *n.* (*stack of hay*) Dieme, *die* (*bes. nordd.*); Schober, *der* (*bes. südd., österr.*)

**rick**[2] (*Brit.*) **1** *n.* (*slight sprain or strain*) Verrenkung, *die;* **have a ~ in one's neck** einen verrenkten Hals haben. **2** *v.t.* verrenken; **~ one's neck** sich (*Dat.*) den Hals verrenken

**rickets** /ˈrɪkɪts/ *n. constr. as sing. or pl.* ▶ **1232** (*Med.*) Rachitis, *die*

**rickety** /ˈrɪkɪtɪ/ *adj.* **A** wack[e]lig ‹Tisch, Stuhl usw.›; klapp[e]rig ‹Auto›; **B** (*feeble*) hinfällig, gebrechlich, (*ugs.*) wack[e]lig ‹alter Mensch›

**rickshaw** /ˈrɪkʃɔː/ *n.* Rikscha, *die*

**ricochet** /ˈrɪkəʃeɪ/ **1** *n.* **A** Abprallen, *das;* **B** (*hit*) Abpraller, *der.* **2** *v.i.*, **~[t]ing** /ˈrɪkəʃeɪɪŋ/, **~[t]ed** /ˈrɪkəʃeɪd/ abprallen (**off** von)

**rictus** /ˈrɪktəs/ *n.* **A** (*Anat., Zool.*) Mund-/Maul-/Schnabelöffnung, *die;* **B** (*fig.*) weit aufgerissener Mund

**rid** /rɪd/ *v.t.*, **-dd-, rid: ~ sth. of sth.** etw. von etw. befreien; **~ oneself of sb./sth.** sich von jmdm./etw. befreien; sich jmds./einer Sache entledigen (*geh.*); **be ~ of sb./sth.** jmdn./etw. los sein (*ugs.*); **get ~ of sb./**

r

**sth.** jmdn./etw. loswerden; **we are well ~ of him** wir sind froh, dass wir ihn los sind (*ugs.*)

**riddance** /ˈrɪdəns/ *n.* **good ~ [to bad rubbish]** zum Glück *od.* Gott sei Dank ist er/es *usw.* weg!; **he's left at last — and good ~ to him!** er ist endlich gegangen — Gott sei Dank!

**ridden** ⇒ ride 2, 3

**riddle¹** /ˈrɪdl/ *n.* Rätsel, *das;* **talk** *or* **speak in ~s** in Rätseln sprechen; **tell sb. a ~:** jmdm. ein Rätsel aufgeben

**riddle²** ❶ *n.* (*sieve*) [Schüttel]sieb, *das.* ❷ *v.t.* Ⓐ (*fill with holes*) durchlöchern; **~d with bullets** von Kugeln durchsiebt *od.* durchlöchert; **~d with corruption/mistakes** (*fig.*) von Korruption durchsetzt/mit *od.* von Fehlern übersät; Ⓑ (*sift*) sieben

**ride** /raɪd/ ❶ *n.* Ⓐ (*journey*) (*on horseback*) [Aus]ritt, *der;* (*in vehicle, at fair*) Fahrt, die; **~ in a train/coach** Zug-/Busfahrt, *die;* **go for a ~:** ausreiten; **go for a [bi]cycle ~:** Rad fahren; (*longer distance*) eine Radtour machen; **go for a ~ [in the car]** [mit dem Auto] wegfahren; **have a ~ in a train/taxi/on the merry-go-round** mit dem Zug/Taxi/Karussell fahren; **can I have a ~ on your bike/pony?** darf ich mal mit deinem Rad fahren/auf deinem Pony reiten?; **give sb. a ~:** jmdn. mitnehmen; **give sb. a ~ on one's back** jmdn. auf seinen Schultern reiten lassen; **be/come along for the ~** (*coll.*) nur so (*ugs.*) *od.* nur aus Interesse dabei sein/mitkommen; **take sb. for a ~:** jmdn. spazieren fahren; (*fig. coll.: deceive*) jmdn. reinlegen (*ugs.*); Ⓑ (*quality of ~*) Fahrkomfort, *der;* **the car gives [you] a bumpy/smooth** *etc.* **~:** das Auto fährt holprig/sanft *usw.;* **give sb. a rough/an easy ~** (*fig.*) es jmdm. schwer/leicht machen; **have a rough/an easy ~:** es schwer/leicht haben; Ⓒ (*path*) Reitweg, *der.*

❷ *v.i.*, **rode** /rəʊd/, **ridden** /ˈrɪdn/ Ⓐ (*travel*) (*on horse*) reiten; (*on bicycle, in vehicle; Amer.: in elevator*) fahren; **~ to town on one's bike/in one's car/on the train** mit dem Rad/Auto/Zug in die Stadt fahren; Ⓑ (*float*) **~ at anchor** vor Anker liegen *od.* (*Seemannsspr.*) reiten; **~ high [in the sky]** (*fig.*) ‹Mond:› hoch am Himmel schweben; Ⓒ (*be carried*) reiten; rittlings sitzen; **'X ~s again'** (*fig.*) „X ist wieder da"; **be riding on sth.** (*fig.*) von etw. abhängen; **be riding for a fall** halsbrecherisch reiten; (*fig.*) in sein Unglück rennen (*ugs.*); **be riding high** (*fig.*) Oberwasser haben (*ugs.*); **let sth. ~** (*fig.*) etw. auf sich beruhen lassen; ⇒ *also* **forth** C; **hound** 1 A; **roughshod**.

❸ *v.t.*, **rode, ridden** Ⓐ (*~ on*) reiten ‹Pferd usw.›; fahren mit ‹Fahrrad›; **learn to ~ a bicycle** Rad fahren lernen; **~ the waves** sich auf den Wellen wiegen; Ⓑ (*oppress*) plagen; **ridden by fears/guilt** von Ängsten/von Schuldgefühlen geplagt *od.* heimgesucht; Ⓒ (*traverse*) (*on horseback*) reiten; (*on cycle*) fahren; Ⓓ (*yield to*) reiten (*Boxsport*), ausweichen (+ *Dat.*) ‹Schlag›; Ⓔ (*Amer. coll.: harass*) fertig machen (*ugs.*); **I guess I've been riding you pretty hard** ich hab dir wohl ziemlich zugesetzt

**~ a'way** *v.i.* wegreiten/wegfahren

**~ 'down** *v.t.* umreiten

**~ 'off** ⇒ **~ away**

**~ 'out** *v.t.* abreiten (*Seemannsspr.*) ‹Sturm›; (*fig.*) überstehen

**~ 'up** *v.i.* Ⓐ **~ up [to sth.]** ‹Reiter:› an etw. (*Akk.*) heranreiten; ‹Fahrer:› an etw. (*Akk.*) heranfahren; Ⓑ **the skirt rode up over her knees** (*fig.*) der Rock rutschte über ihr Knie

**rider** /ˈraɪdə(r)/ *n.* Ⓐ Reiter, *der*/Reiterin, *die;* (*of cycle*) Fahrer, *der*/Fahrerin, *die;* Ⓑ (*addition*) Zusatz, *der;* **add a ~:** einen Zusatz machen; (*Brit. Law*) eine zusätzliche Erklärung *od.* Feststellung abgeben

**riderless** /ˈraɪdəlɪs/ *adj.* reiterlos

**ridge** /rɪdʒ/ ❶ *n.* Ⓐ (*of roof*) First, *der;* (*of nose*) Rücken, *der;* Ⓑ (*long hilltop*) Grat, *der;* Kamm, *der;* **~ of hills** Höhenrücken, *der;* **~ of mountains** Gebirgskamm, *der;* Ⓒ (*Agric.*) Kamm, *der;* Rücken, *der;* Ⓓ (*Meteorol.*) **~ [of high pressure]** lang gestrecktes Hoch; (*connecting two highs*) Hochdruckbrücke, *die.* ❷ *v.t.* häufeln

**ridge: ~ piece** *n.* Firstbalken, *der;* **~ pole** *n.* Firststange, *die;* **~ tent** *n.* Hauszelt, *das;* **~ tile** *n.* Firstziegel, *der;* **~way** *n.* Gratweg, *der*

**ridicule** /ˈrɪdɪkjuːl/ ❶ *n.* Spott, *der;* **object of ~:** Zielscheibe des Spotts; Gespött, *das;* **hold sb./sth. up to ~:** jmdn./etw. der Lächerlichkeit preisgeben; **lay oneself open to ~:** sich dem Gespött aussetzen. ❷ *v.t.* verspotten; spotten über (+ *Akk.*)

**ridiculous** /rɪˈdɪkjʊləs/ *adj.* lächerlich; **don't be ~!** sei nicht albern!; **make oneself [look] ~:** sich lächerlich machen

**ridiculously** /rɪˈdɪkjʊləslɪ/ *adv.* lächerlich

**riding** /ˈraɪdɪŋ/ *n.* Reiten, *das*

**riding: ~ breeches** *n. pl.* Reithose, *die;* **~ crop** *n.* Reitgerte, *die;* **~ habit** *n.* Reitkleid, *das;* **~ lamp** *n.* (*Naut.*) Ankerlaterne, *die;* **~ lesson** *n.* Reitstunde, *die;* **~ light** ⇒ **~ lamp**; **~ school** *n.* Reitschule, *die*

**Riesling** /ˈriːzlɪŋ, ˈriːslɪŋ/ *n.* Riesling, *der*

**rife** /raɪf/ *pred. adj.* Ⓐ (*widespread*) weit verbreitet; **rumours were ~:** es gingen Gerüchte um; Ⓑ **~ with** (*full of*) voller; voll von; **the country was ~ with rumours of war** im ganzen Land gab es Kriegsgerüchte

**riff-raff** /ˈrɪfræf/ *n.* Gesindel, *das*

**rifle** /ˈraɪfl/ ❶ *n.* (*firearm*) Gewehr, *das;* (*hunting ~*) Büchse, *die.* ❷ *v.t.* Ⓐ (*ransack*) durchwühlen; (*pillage*) plündern; **~ sth. of its contents** etw. ausplündern; Ⓑ (*make grooves in*) ziehen (*fachspr.*) ‹Gewehrlauf›. ❸ *v.i.* **~ through sth.** etw. durchwühlen

**rifle: ~ barrel** *n.* Gewehrlauf, *der;* (*of hunting ~*) Büchsenlauf, *der;* **~ butt** *n.* Gewehrkolben, *der;* **~man** /ˈraɪflmən/ *n.*, *pl.* **~men** /ˈraɪflmən/ Schütze, *der;* **~ range** *n.* Schießstand, *der;* Schießplatz, *der;* **~ shot** *n.* Gewehrschuss, *der*

**rift** /rɪft/ *n.* Ⓐ (*dispute*) Unstimmigkeit, *die;* Ⓑ (*cleft*) Spalte, *die;* (*in cloud*) Riss, *der*

**'rift valley** *n.* (*Geog.*) Graben[bruch], *der*

**rig¹** /rɪg/ ❶ *n.* Ⓐ (*Naut.*) Takelung, *die;* Ⓑ (*for oil well*) [Öl]förderturm, *der;* (*off shore*) Förderinsel, *die;* **drilling ~:** Bohrturm, *der;* (*off shore*) Bohrinsel, *die;* Ⓒ (*outfit*) Kluft, *die;* **in full ~:** in Schale (*ugs.*); **in full climbing ~:** in voller Klettermontur (*ugs.*). ❷ *v.t.*, **-gg-** Ⓐ (*Naut.*) auftakeln; Ⓑ (*Aeronaut.*) (*assemble*) montieren; (*fit out*) ausrüsten ‹Flugzeug›

**~ 'out** *v.t.* ausstaffieren

**~ 'up** *v.t.* aufbauen

**rig²** *v.t.*, **-gg-** (*falsify*) fälschen ‹Wahl›; verfälschen, (*geh.*) manipulieren ‹[Wahl]ergebnis›; **~ the market** die Preise/(*St. Exch.*) die Kurse manipulieren (*geh.*) *od.* künstlich beeinflussen; **the whole thing was ~ged** das war alles Schiebung (*ugs.*)

**rigger** /ˈrɪgə(r)/ *n.* ▶ **1261** Ⓐ (*Naut.*) Takler, *der*/Taklerin, *die;* Ⓑ (*Aeronaut.*) [Rüst]mechaniker, *der*/[Rüst]mechanikerin, *die*

**rigging¹** /ˈrɪgɪŋ/ *n.* Ⓐ (*Naut.*) Takelung, *die;* (*ropes and chains also*) Gut, *das;* Takelage, *die;* Ⓑ (*Aeronaut.*) Ausrüstung, *die*

**rigging²** *n.* (*illicit manipulation*) Manipulation, *die* (*geh.*); Schiebung, *die* (*ugs.*)

**right** /raɪt/ ❶ *adj.* Ⓐ (*just, morally good*) richtig; **it's not ~ for sb. to do sth.** es ist nicht richtig *od.* recht von jmdm., dass er etw. tut; **it is only ~ [and proper] to do sth./that sb. should do sth.** es ist nur recht und billig, etw. zu tun/dass jmd. etw. tut; **do the ~ thing by sb.** sich jmdm. gegenüber anständig verhalten; Ⓑ (*correct, true*) richtig; **~ enough** völlig richtig; **~ enough!** in Ordnung!; okay! (*ugs.*); **you're [quite] ~:** du hast [völlig] Recht; **too ~** (*coll.*) allerdings!; **how ~ you are!** wie Recht du hast!; **you are ~ to do** *or* **in doing it** du tust recht daran, es zu tun; **be ~ in sth.** Recht mit etw. haben; **let's get it ~ this time!** machen wir es diesmal besser!; **let's get this ~!** das wollen wir doch mal klarstellen!; **is that clock ~?** geht die Uhr da richtig?; **have you got the ~ fare?** haben Sie das Fahrgeld passend?; **put** *or* **set ~:** richtig stellen ‹Irrtum, Behauptung›; wieder gutmachen ‹Unrecht›; berichtigen ‹Fehler›; bereinigen ‹Missverständnis, Angelegenheit›; beheben ‹Missstand, Mangel›; wieder in Ordnung bringen ‹Situation, Angelegenheit, Maschine, Gerät›; richtig stellen ‹Uhr›; **put** *or* **set sb. ~:** jmdn. berichtigen *od.* korrigieren; **~ [you are]!**, (*Brit.*) **~ oh!** (*coll.*) ja, gut!; okay! (*ugs.*); **that's ~:** ja [wohl]; so ist es; **that's ~, smash the place up!** (*iron.*) recht so, hau nur immer auf den Putz (*ugs. iron.*); **is that ~?** stimmt das?; (*indeed?*) aha!; **[am I] ~?** nicht [wahr]?; oder [nicht]? (*ugs.*); ⇒ *also* **all** 3; **road** B; **track** 1 A; Ⓒ (*preferable, most suitable*) richtig; recht; **the ~ man for the job** der richtige Mann [dafür]; **do sth. the ~ way** etw. richtig machen; **say/do the ~ thing** das Richtige sagen/tun; **know how to say the ~ thing** die richtigen *od.* passenden Worte finden; **I did the ~ thing when I ...:** es war richtig, dass ich ...; ⇒ *also* **Mr**; **whale** A; Ⓓ (*sound, sane*) richtig; **all's ~ with the world** die Welt *od.* alles ist in Ordnung; **not be quite ~ in the head** nicht ganz bei Verstand sein; nicht ganz richtig [im Kopf] sein; **as ~ as rain** (*coll.*) (*in health*) gesund wie ein Fisch im Wasser; (*satisfactory*) in bester Ordnung; **put** *or* **set sb. ~** (*restore to health*) jmdn. [wieder] in Ordnung *od.* auf die Beine bringen; **she'll be ~** (*Austral. coll.*) das geht [schon] in Ordnung (*ugs.*); **I'll/we'll** *etc.* **see you ~:** es soll dein Schaden nicht sein; ⇒ *also* **mind** 1 G; Ⓔ (*coll./arch.: real, properly so called*) richtig; recht (*veralt.*); **you're a ~ one!** du bist mir der/die Richtige!; **your room's in a ~ mess** in deinem Zimmer sieht es wüst aus; **he made a ~ mess of that job/of it** er hat die Sache/es total vermurkst (*ugs.*); Ⓕ ▶ **1679** (*opposite of left*) recht...; ⇒ *also* **turn** 1 C; **be sb.'s ~ arm** (*fig.*) jmds. rechte Hand sein; Ⓖ **R~** (*Polit.*) recht... ⇒ *also* **~ side**.

❷ *v.t.* Ⓐ (*avenge*) aus der Welt schaffen ‹Unrecht›; Ⓑ (*correct*) berichtigen; richtig stellen; Ⓒ (*restore to upright position*) [wieder] aufrichten; ‹Boot usw.:› **~ itself** sich [von selbst] [wieder] aufrichten; (*fig.: come to proper state*) ‹Mangel:› sich [von selbst] geben; ‹Körper, Organismus:› (*ugs.*) von selbst in Ordnung kommen.

❸ *n.* Ⓐ (*fair claim, authority*) Recht, *das;* Anrecht, *das;* **have a/no ~ to sth.** ein/kein Anrecht *od.* Recht auf etw. (*Akk.*) haben; **have a** *or* **the/no ~ to do sth.** das/kein Recht haben, etw. zu tun; **as of ~:** kraft Gesetzes; **by ~ of** aufgrund (+ *Gen.*); **belong to sb. as of** *or* **by ~:** jmds. rechtmäßiges Eigentum sein; **what ~ has he [got] to do that?** mit welchem Recht tut er das?; **in one's own ~:** aus eigenem Recht; **an authoress in her own ~:** eine eigenständige Autorin; **the ~ to worke** das Recht auf Arbeit; **~-to-work** *attrib.* (*Amer.*) gegen Gewerkschaftszwang gerichtet ‹Gesetz, Politik›; **~-to-work state** Staat ohne Gewerkschaftszwang; **the ~ to life** das Recht auf Leben (*des ungeborenen Kindes*); **film ~s** Filmrechte *Pl.;* **grazing ~s** Weiderechte *Pl.;* **~ of way** (*~ to pass across*) Wegerecht, *das;* (*path*) öffentlicher Weg; (*precedence*) Vorfahrtsrecht, *das;* **who has the ~ of way?** wer hat Vorfahrt?; **Bill of R~s** Bill of Rights, *die;* **Black R~s** Rechte der Schwarzen; **be within one's ~s to do sth.** etw. mit [Fug und] Recht tun können; ⇒ *also* **right-to-life**; Ⓑ (*what is just*) Recht, *das;* **~ is on our side** das Recht ist auf unserer Seite; **understand the ~s and wrongs of a situation** beurteilen können, was [bei einer Sache] richtig und was falsch ist; **by ~[s]** von Rechts wegen; **do ~ by sb.** jmdn. anständig behandeln; **do ~:** sich richtig verhalten; richtig handeln; **do ~ to do sth.** recht daran tun, etw. zu tun; **in the ~:** im Recht; Ⓒ ▶ **1679** (*~-hand side*) rechte Seite; **move to the ~:** nach rechts rücken; **on** *or* **to the ~ [of the door]** rechts [von der Tür]; **on** *or* **to my ~, to the ~ of me** rechts von mir; zu meiner Rechten; **from ~ and left** von rechts und links; **drive on the ~:** rechts fahren; Ⓓ (*Polit.*) **the R~:** die

Rechte; (*radicals*) die Rechten; **be on the R~ of the party** dem rechten Flügel der Partei angehören; [E] *in pl.* (*proper state*) **set** *or* **put sth. to ~s** etw. in Ordnung bringen; **set** *or* **put the world to ~s** die Welt verbessern; [F] (*Boxing*) Rechte, *die;* [G] **get sb. bang to ~s** (*Brit. coll.*) *or* (*Amer. coll.*) **dead to ~s** jmdn. auf frischer Tat ertappen; [H] (*Theatre* [*stage*] *right:*) linke Bühnenseite; [I] (*in marching*) ⇒ **left²** 3 E.

❹ *adv.* [A] (*properly, correctly, justly*) richtig ‹machen, raten, halten›; **go ~** (*succeed*) klappen (*ugs.*); **nothing is going ~ for** *or* **with me today** bei mir klappt heute nichts (*ugs.*); **if I remember ~:** wenn ich mich recht *od.* richtig erinnere; [B] ▶ **1679** (*to the side opposite left*) nach rechts; **~ of the road** rechts von der Straße; **~, left, and centre, left, ~, and centre** (*fig. coll.*) überall; (*repeatedly*) immer wieder; [C] (*all the way*) bis ganz; (*completely*) ganz; völlig; **windows coming ~ down to the floor** Fenster, die bis ganz auf den Fußboden herunterreichen; **~ through the summer** den ganzen Sommer hindurch; **turn ~ round** sich ganz umdrehen; ‹Zeiger:› eine ganze Umdrehung machen; **~ round the house** ums ganze Haus [herum]; **rotten ~ through** durch und durch verfault; [D] (*exactly*) genau; **~ in the middle of sth.** mitten in etw. (*Dat./Akk.*); **~ now** im Moment; jetzt sofort, gleich ‹handeln›; **~ on the chin** direkt *od.* genau am/ans Kinn; **he was '~ next to me** (*coll.*) er war direkt *od.* genau neben mir; **~ at the beginning** gleich am Anfang; **~ on!** (*coll.*) (*approving*) recht so!; so ists recht!; (*agreeing*) genau!; ganz recht!; [E] (*straight*) direkt; genau; **go ~ on [the way one is going]** [weiter] geradeaus gehen *od.* fahren; **I'm going ~ home now** ich gehe jetzt direkt nach Hause; [F] (*coll.: immediately*) **~ [away/off]** sofort; gleich; **I'll be ~ 'with you** ich bin gleich [wieder] da; **things went wrong ~ at** *or* **from the beginning** es ging schon am Anfang *od.* von Anfang an schief; [G] (*very*) sehr; **~ royal** [wahrhaft] fürstlich ‹Mahl, Empfang›; **a ~ royal dressing down** eine Standpauke, die sich gewaschen hat (*ugs.*); ⇒ *also* **honourable** D; **reverend** 1

**right: ~ a'bout ['turn** *or* (*Amer.*) **'face]** *n.* (*Mil.*) Rechtsummachen, *das;* Kehrtwendung nach rechts; (*as command*) rechtsum!; (*fig.*) Kehrtwendung, *die;* **~ angle** *n.* rechter Winkel; **at ~ angles to ...:** rechtwinklig zu ...; im rechten Winkel zu ...; **~-angled** *adj.* rechtwinklig; **~ 'back** *n.* (*Footb.*) rechter Verteidiger/rechte Verteidigerin

**righteous** /'raɪtʃəs/ ❶ *adj.* [A] (*upright*) rechtschaffen, (*bibl.*) gerecht ‹Person›; gerecht ‹Gott, Staat, Herr›; [B] (*morally justifiable*) gerecht ‹Zorn, Sache›; gerechtfertigt ‹Maßnahme, Tat›. ❷ *n. pl.* **the ~:** die Gerechten

**'right-footed** *adj.* mit dem rechten Fuß geschickter; rechtsfüßig ‹Fußballspieler›

**rightful** /'raɪtfl/ *adj.* [A] (*fair*) gerecht ‹Sache, Strafe›; berechtigt ‹Forderung, Anspruch›; [B] (*entitled*) rechtmäßig ‹Besitzer, Eigentümer, Herrscher, Erbe, Anteil›

**rightfully** /'raɪtfəlɪ/ *adv.* [A] (*fairly*) rechtmäßig; [B] (*correctly*) mit *od.* zu Recht

**right: ~ 'hand** *n.* [A] rechte Hand; Rechte, *die;* [B] (**~ *side***) **on** *or* **at sb.'s ~ hand** zu jmds. Rechten; rechts von jmdm.; [C] (*fig.: chief assistant*) rechte Hand; **~-hand** *adj.* recht...; rechtsgängig, rechtsdrehend ‹Schraube, Gewinde›; **~-hand bend** Rechtskurve, *die;* **on the/your ~-hand side you see ...:** rechts *od.* auf der rechten Seite sehen Sie ...; ⇒ *also* **drive** 1 I; **~-handed** /raɪt'hændɪd/ ❶ *adj.* [A] rechtshändig; ‹Schlag› mit der Rechten; ‹Werkzeug› für Rechtshänder; **be ~-handed** Rechtshänder/Rechtshänderin sein; [B] (*turning to* ~) rechts angeschlagen ‹Tür›; Rechts‹gewinde, -drehung›; rechtsgängig, rechtsdrehend ‹Schraube, Gewinde›; ❷ *adv.* rechtshändig; mit der rechten Hand; **~-handedness** /raɪt'hændɪdnɪs/ *n.* Rechtshändigkeit, *die;* **~-hander** /raɪt'hændə(r)/ *n.* [A] (*person*) Rechtshänder, *der*/-händerin, *die;* [B] (*blow*) Schlag mit der Rechten; (*Boxing*) Rechte, *die;* **~-hand 'man** *n.* (*chief assistant*) rechte Hand

**rightism** /'raɪtɪzm/ *n., no pl.* (*Polit.*) Konservativismus, *der*

**rightist** /'raɪtɪst/ (*Polit.*) ❶ *adj.* rechtsorientiert. ❷ *n.* Rechte, *der/die*

**rightly** /'raɪtlɪ/ *adv.* [A] (*fairly, correctly*) richtig; **do ~:** richtig handeln; **..., and ~ so ...,** und zwar zu Recht; **~ or wrongly, ...:** ob es nun richtig ist/war oder nicht, ...; [B] (*fitly*) zu Recht

**right-'minded** *adj.* gerecht denkend

**rightness** /'raɪtnɪs/ *n., no pl.* Richtigkeit, *die*

**righto** /'raɪtəʊ, raɪ'təʊ/ *int.* (*Brit.*) okay (*ugs.*); alles klar (*ugs.*)

**'right side** *n.* [A] (*of fabric*) Oberseite, *die;* [B] **be on the ~ of fifty** noch keine fünfzig sein; **[the] ~ out/up** richtig herum; **get on the ~ of sb.** (*fig.*) sich mit jmdm. gut stellen

**'rights issue** *n.* (*Finance*) Bezugsangebot, *das*

**'right-thinking** *adj.* billig denkend

**right-to-'life** *attrib. adj.* Recht-auf-Leben-; **~ advocate** Befürworter des Rechts auf Leben

**rightward** /'raɪtwəd/ ❶ *adv.* [nach] rechts ‹abbiegen›; nach rechts ‹blicken, sich wenden›; **lie ~ of sth.** rechts von etw. liegen. ❷ *adj.* rechter Hand *nachgestellt*

**rightwards** /'raɪtwədz/ ⇒ **rightward** 1

**right: ~-wing** *adj.* [A] (*Sport*) Rechtsaußen‹spieler, -position›; [B] (*Polit.*) recht...; rechtsgerichtet; Rechts‹intellektueller, -extremist, -radikalismus›; **~-winger** *n.* [A] (*Sport*) Rechtsaußen, *der;* [B] (*Polit.*) Rechte, *der/die;* **extreme ~-winger** Rechtsaußen, *der/die* (*Jargon*); Rechtsradikale, *der/die*

**rigid** /'rɪdʒɪd/ *adj.* [A] starr; (*stiff*) steif; (*hard*) hart; (*firm*) fest; **~ airship** Starrluftschiff, *das;* [B] (*fig.: harsh, inflexible*) streng ‹Person›; unbeugsam ‹Haltung, System›

**rigidity** /rɪ'dʒɪdɪtɪ/ *n., no pl.* ⇒ **rigid**: [A] Starrheit, *die;* Steifheit, *die;* Härte, *die;* Festigkeit, *die;* [B] Strenge, *die*

**rigidly** /'rɪdʒɪdlɪ/ *adv.* [A] starr; [B] (*harshly, inflexibly*) [allzu] streng; peinlich ‹korrekt›; rigoros ‹vernichten, beschränken›

**rigmarole** /'rɪgmərəʊl/ *n.* (*derog.*) [A] (*long story*) langatmiges Geschwafel (*ugs. abwertend*); [B] (*complex procedure*) Zirkus, *der* (*ugs. abwertend*)

**rigor** /'rɪgə(r)/ (*Amer.*) ⇒ **rigour**

**rigor mortis** /rɪgə 'mɔ:tɪs/ *n.* (*Med.*) Totenstarre, *die;* Rigor mortis, *der* (*fachspr.*)

**rigorous** /'rɪgərəs/ *adj.* [A] (*strict*) streng; rigoros ‹Methode, Maßnahme, Beschränkung, Strenge›; **~ tests** strenge Prüfungen; [B] (*marked by extremes*) hart ‹Leben, Bedingungen, Winter›; extrem ‹Klima›; [C] (*precise*) peinlich ‹Genauigkeit, Beachtung›; exakt ‹Analyse›; streng ‹Beurteilung, Maßstab›; scharf ‹Auge›; genau ‹Arbeit›; schlüssig ‹Argumentation›

**rigorously** /'rɪgərəslɪ/ *adv.* [A] (*strictly*) streng; rigoros ‹durchführen, ausschließen›; [B] (*precisely*) exakt ‹berechnen›

**rigour** /'rɪgə(r)/ *n.* (*Brit.*) [A] (*strictness*) Strenge, *die;* [B] (*extremeness*) Härte, *die;* Strenge, *die;* **the ~s of sth.** die Unbilden (*geh.*) einer Sache (*Gen.*); [C] (*precision*) Stringenz, *die* (*geh.*); (*of argument*) Schlüssigkeit, *die*

**rile** /raɪl/ *v.t.* (*coll.*) ärgern; **get/feel ~d** sich ärgern; **it ~s me when ...:** es fuchst mich, wenn ... (*ugs.*)

**Riley** /'raɪlɪ/ *n.* **live** *or* **lead the life of ~** (*coll.*) wie die Made im Speck leben (*ugs.*)

**rill** /rɪl/ *n.* Bächlein, *das*

**rim** /rɪm/ *n.* Rand, *der;* (*of wheel*) Felge, *die*

**rime** /raɪm/ *n.* (*frost*) [Rau]reif, *der*

**rimless** /'rɪmlɪs/ *adj.* randlos

**-rimmed** /rɪmd/ *adj. in comb.* -randig

**rind** /raɪnd/ *n.* (*of fruit*) Schale, *die;* (*of cheese*) Rinde, *die;* (*of bacon*) Schwarte, *die*

**ring¹** /rɪŋ/ ❶ *n.* [A] Ring, *der;* [B] (*Horseracing, Boxing*) Ring, *der;* (*bull~*) Arena, *die;* (*in circus*) Manege, *die;* **the ~** (*bookmakers*) der Ring; die Buchmacher; [C] (*group*) Ring, *der;* (*gang*) Bande, *die;* (*controlling prices*) Kartell, *das;* [D] (*circle*) Kreis, *der;* **make** *or* **run ~s [a]round sb.** (*fig.*) jmdn. in die Tasche stecken (*ugs.*); [E] (*halo round moon*) Hof, *der;* [F] (*Chem.*) Ring, *der.* ❷ *v.t.* [A] (*surround*) umringen; einkreisen ‹Wort, Buchstaben usw.›; [B] (*Brit.: put ~ on leg of*) beringen ‹Vogel›

**ring²** ❶ *n.* [A] (*act of sounding bell*) Läuten, *das;* Klingeln, *das;* **there's a ~ at the door** es hat geklingelt; **give two ~s** zweimal läuten *od.* klingeln; [B] (*Brit. coll.: telephone call*) Anruf, *der;* **give sb. a ~:** jmdn. anrufen; [C] (*resonance; fig.: impression*) Klang, *der;* (*fig.*) **have the ~ of plausibility/truth** einleuchtend/glaubhaft klingen; (*fig.*) **a ~ of insistence in her tone** ein nachdrücklicher Ton in ihrer Stimme.

❷ *v.i.*, **rang** /ræŋ/, **rung** /rʌŋ/ [A] (*sound clearly*) [er]schallen; ‹Hammer:› [er]dröhnen; **oaths rang across the yard** Flüche hallten über den Hof; [B] (*be sounded*) ‹Glocke, Klingel, Telefon:› läuten; ‹Wecker, Telefon, Kasse:› klingeln; **the doorbell rang** die Türklingel ging; es klingelte; [C] (**~ *bell***) läuten (**for** nach); **please ~ for attention** bitte läuten; [D] (*Brit.: make telephone call*) anrufen; [E] (*resound*) ‹Wald, Raum, Halle:› [wider]hallen (**with** von); **~ in sb.'s ears** jmdm. in den Ohren klingen; **~ true/false** ‹Münze:› echt/falsch klingen; (*fig.*) glaubhaft/unglaubhaft klingen; [F] (*hum*) summen; (*loudly*) dröhnen; **my ears are ~ing** mir dröhnen die Ohren.

❸ *v.t.*, **rang, rung** [A] läuten ‹Glocke›; **~ the [door]bell** läuten; klingeln; **~ a peal** die Glocken läuten; **it ~s a bell** (*fig. coll.*) es kommt mir [irgendwie] bekannt vor; **~ the bell [with sb.]** (*fig.*) [bei jmdm.] ankommen (*ugs.*); ⇒ *also* **change** 1 H; **knell** B; [B] (*Brit.: telephone*) anrufen

**~ 'back** *v.t. & i.* (*Brit.*) [A] (*again*) wieder anrufen; [B] (*in return*) zurückrufen

**~ down** *v.t.* (*Theatre*) fallen lassen, herunterlassen ‹Vorhang›; **~ the curtain down on a project/a love affair** (*fig.*) unter ein Vorhaben/Liebesverhältnis einen Schlussstrich ziehen

**~ 'in** ❶ *v.i.* (*Brit.*) anrufen. ❷ *v.t.* einläuten

**~ 'off** *v.i.* (*Brit.*) auflegen; abhängen

**~ 'out** ❶ *v.i.* ertönen. ❷ *v.t.* ausläuten

**~ round** (*Brit.*) ❶ /-'-/ *v.i.* herumtelefonieren. ❷ /'--/ *v.t.* herumtelefonieren bei

**~ 'up** *v.t.* [A] (*Brit.: telephone*) anrufen; [B] (*record on cash register*) [ein]tippen; bongen (*ugs.*); [C] (*Theatre*) **~ up the curtain** den Vorhang hochziehen

**ring: ~-a-~-o'-'roses** *n.* Ringelreihen, *der;* **~ binder** *n.* Ringbuch, *das;* **~ circuit** *n.* (*Electr.*) Ringschaltung, *die;* **~dove** *n.* Ringeltaube, *die*

**ringed** /rɪŋd/ *adj.* beringt; **the ~ planet** der Ringplanet

**ringer** /'rɪŋə(r)/ *n.* [A] (*bell-~*) [Glocken]läuter, *der;* [B] **be a [dead] ~ for sb./sth.** (*coll.: very similar*) für jmdn. durchgehen [können]/einer Sache (*Dat.*) [aufs Haar] gleichen

**ring: ~ fence** *n.* Umzäunung, *die;* **~-fence** *v.t.* [ab]sichern ‹Gelder›; **~ finger** *n.* Ringfinger, *der*

**ringing** /'rɪŋɪŋ/ ❶ *adj.* [A] (*clear and full*) schallend ‹Stimme, Gelächter›; (*sonorous*) klangvoll, volltönend ‹Stimme, Lachen, Lied›; (*resounding*) dröhnend ‹Schlag›; [B] (*decisive*) eindringlich ‹Appell›. ❷ *n.* [A] (*sounding, sound*) Läuten, *das;* [B] (*Brit. Teleph.*) **~ tone** Freiton, *der;* [C] (*sensation*) **~ in the** *or* **one's ears** Ohrensausen, *das*

**'ringleader** *n.* Rädelsführer, *der* (*abwertend*); Anführer, *der*/Anführerin, *die*

**ringlet** /'rɪŋlɪt/ *n.* [Ringel]löckchen, *das*

**ring: ~ main** *n.* (*Electr.*) Ringnetz, *das;* **~master** *n.* Dresseur, *der;* **~ pull** *adj.* **~ pull can** Aufreißdose, *die;* Ring-Pull-Dose, *die;* **~ road** *n.* Ringstraße, *die;* **~side** ❶ *n.* **at (the) ~side** [direkt] am Ring; ❷ *adj.* **~side seat** (*Boxing*) Ringplatz, *der;* (*in circus*) Manegenplatz, *der;* Logenplatz, *der* (*auch fig.*); **~sider** /'rɪŋsaɪdə(r)/ *n.* Zuschauer mit Ring-/Manegenplatz; **~way** *n.* Ringstraße, *die;* **~worm** *n.* (*Med.*) Kopfgrind, *der;* Flechtengrind, *der*

r

**rink** /rɪŋk/ *n.* (*for ice skating*) Eisbahn, *die;* (*for curling*) Eisschießbahn, *die;* (*for roller skating*) Rollschuhbahn, *die;* (*bowling green*) Bowlingfläche, *die*

**rinse** /rɪns/ ❶ *v.t.* **A** (*wash out*) ausspülen ‹Mund, Gefäß usw.›; *abs.* **please ~** (*said by dentist*) bitte mal [aus]spülen; **B** (*wash lightly*) durchspülen ‹Wäsche›; **C** (*put through water*) [aus]spülen ‹Wäsche usw.›; abspülen ‹Hände, Geschirr›. ❷ *n.* **A** (*rinsing*) Spülen, *das;* Spülung, *die;* **give sth. a [good/quick] ~:** etw. [gut/schnell] abspülen/ausspülen/spülen; **after several ~s** nach mehrmaligem Spülen; **have a ~** (*said by dentist*) bitte [aus]spülen; **B** (*solution*) [Haar]tönung, *die;* [Haar]töner, *der*

**~ a'way** *v.t.* wegspülen

**~ 'out** *v.t.* **A** (*wash with clean water*) ausspülen ‹Wäsche, Mund, Behälter›; **B** (*remove by washing*) [her]ausspülen

**'rinse aid** *n.* Klarspülmittel, *das*

**riot** /'raɪət/ ❶ *n.* **A** (*violent disturbance*) Aufruhr, *der;* **~s** Unruhen *Pl.;* Aufstand, *der;* **there'll be a ~** (*fig.*) es wird Ärger *od.* einen Aufstand geben (*ugs.*); **B** (*noisy or uncontrolled behaviour*) Krawall, *der;* Tumult, *der;* **run ~:** randalieren; (*in protest*) auf die Barrikaden gehen (*ugs.*); **run ~ [all over sth.]** ‹Pflanze:› [etw. völlig über]wuchern; **let one's imagination run ~:** seiner Fantasie freien Lauf lassen; **C** (*unrestrained indulgence*) Orgie, *die;* **D** (*coll.: amusing thing or person*) **be a ~:** zum Piepen sein (*ugs.*). ❷ *v.i.* randalieren; **the mob had been ~ing all night** der Mob hatte während der ganzen Nacht gewütet; **the ~ing** der Aufruhr; die Unruhen

**'Riot Act** *n.* (*Hist.*) Aufruhrgesetz, *das;* **read sb. the ~** (*fig. coll.*) jmdm. die Leviten lesen

**rioter** /'raɪətə(r)/ *n.* Randalierer, *der*

**'riot gear** *n.* (*bei Krawallen von Polizeibeamten getragene*) Schutzkleidung *od.* -ausrüstung

**riotous** /'raɪətəs/ *adj.* **A** (*violent*) gewalttätig; tumultartig ‹Vorgang›; **B** (*dissolute*) ausschweifend; **C** (*unrestrained*) wild; schallend ‹Gelächter›; **a ~ display of colour** eine reiche Farbenpracht

**riotously** /'raɪətəslɪ/ *adv.* **A** (*dissolutely*) ausschweifend; **B ~ funny** (*coll.*) urkomisch; zum Schreien *präd.* (*ugs.*)

**riot: ~ police** *n.* Bereitschaftspolizei, *die;* **~ shield** *n.* Schutzschild, *der;* **~ squad** *n.* Einsatzkommando, *das od.* -truppe, *die* (*der Bereitschaftspolizei*)

**rip**[1] /rɪp/ ❶ *n.* **A** (*tear*) Riss, *der;* **B** (*act of ripping*) Reißen, *das.* ❷ *v.t.*, **-pp- A** (*make tear in*) zerreißen; **~ open** aufreißen; (*with knife*) aufschlitzen; **~ one's skirt on sth.** sich (*Dat.*) an etw. (*Dat.*) das Kleid einreißen *od.* zerreißen; **~ sth. down the middle/to pieces** etw. in der Mitte *od.* etw. mitten durchreißen/in Stücke zerreißen; **B** (*make by tearing*) reißen ‹Loch›. ❸ *v.i.*, **-pp- A** (*split*) [ein]reißen; **B** (*coll.*) **let ~:** loslegen (*ugs.*); **he let ~ down the motorway** er bretterte volles Rohr über die Autobahn (*ugs.*); **let ~ at sb.** jmdn. zur Minna machen (*ugs.*)

**~ a'part** *v.t.* (*tear apart*) auseinander reißen; zerreißen; (*destroy*) demolieren

**~ a'way** *v.t.* abreißen; **~ sth. away from sth.** etw. von etw. reißen

**~ 'down** *v.t.* abreißen; herunterreißen

**~ into** *v.t.* **~ into sb.** (*attack*) über jmdn. herfallen; (*fig.: attack verbally*) jmdm. ins Gesicht springen (*ugs.*)

**~ 'off** *v.t.* **A** (*remove from*) reißen von; (*remove*) abreißen; herunterreißen ‹Maske, Kleidungsstück›; **B** (*coll.: defraud*) übers Ohr hauen (*ugs.*); bescheißen (*derb*); **C** (*coll.: steal*) klauen (*salopp*). ⇒ *also* **rip-off**

**~ 'out** *v.t.* herausreißen (**of** aus)

**~ 'up** *v.t.* zerreißen; kaputtreißen (*ugs.*); **~ up an agreement** (*fig.*) aus einer Vereinbarung einfach wieder aussteigen (*ugs.*)

**rip**[2] *n.* **A** (*roué*) Windhund, *der* (*abwertend*); **B** (*rascal*) Halunke, *der* (*scherzh.*)

**RIP** *abbr.* **rest in peace** R.I.P.

**'ripcord** *n.* Reißleine, *die*

**ripe** /raɪp/ *adj.* reif (**for** zu); ausgereift ‹Käse, Wein, Plan›; vollkommen, vollendet ‹Gelehrsamkeit›; reich ‹Erfahrung›; groß ‹Verständnis›; **the time is ~ for doing sth.** es ist an der Zeit, etw. zu tun; **be ~ for development** ‹Land:› entwicklungsreif sein; **~ old age** hohes Alter

**ripen** /'raɪpn/ ❶ *v.t.* zur Reife bringen; (*fig.*) reifen lassen (*geh.*). ❷ *v.i.* (*lit. or fig.*) reifen; **~ into sth.** (*fig.*) zu etw. reifen (*geh.*)

**ripeness** /'raɪpnɪs/ *n., no pl.* (*lit. or fig.*) Reife, *die*

**rip-off** *n.* (*coll.*) Nepp, *der* (*ugs. abwertend*); **that place is a ~:** das ist ein Neppladen (*ugs. abwertend*)

**riposte** /rɪ'pɒst/ ❶ *n.* **A** (*retort*) [rasche] Entgegnung *od.* (*geh.*) Replik; **B** (*Fencing*) Riposte, *die.* ❷ *v.i.* **A** (*retort*) [rasch] antworten; **B** (*Fencing*) ripostieren

**ripper** /'rɪpə(r)/ *n.* Lustmörder, *der;* **the Yorkshire R~:** der Ripper von Yorkshire

**ripping** /'rɪpɪŋ/ *adj.* (*Brit. dated coll.*) famos (*ugs. veralt.*)

**ripple** /'rɪpl/ ❶ *n.* **A** (*small wave*) kleine Welle; **the breeze sent ~s along the surface** die Brise kräuselte die Oberfläche; **B** (*sound*) **a ~ of applause/laughter** kurzer Beifall/ein perlendes Lachen; **C** (*Electr.*) leichte [Strom]schwankung. ❷ *v.i.* **A** (*form ~s*) ‹See:› sich kräuseln; ‹Muskeln:› spielen; **B** (*flow*) ‹Welle:› plätschern; ‹Bach:› in kleinen Wellen fließen; **C** (*sound*) erklingen. ❸ *v.t.* kräuseln

**'ripple mark** *n.* Rippelmarke, *die*

**rip: ~-roaring** *adj.* wahnsinnig (*ugs.*); Wahnsinns- (*ugs.*); **~saw** *n.* Längsschnittsäge, *die;* **~snorter** /'rɪpsnɔːtə(r)/ *n.* (*coll.*) (*person*) Teufelskerl, *der* (*ugs.*); (*thing*) **a ~snorter of a storm/match** *etc.* ein mordsmäßiger Sturm/mordsmäßiges Spiel *usw.;* **~ tide** *n.* (*turbulence*) Kabbelung, *die;* (*current*) Brandungsrückströmung, *die*

**rise** /raɪz/ ❶ *n.* **A** (*going up*) (*of sun etc.*) Aufgang, *der;* (*Theatre: of curtain*) Aufgehen, *das;* (*advancement*) Aufstieg, *der;* **~ and ~** (*joc.*) unaufhaltsamer Aufstieg; **B** (*emergence*) Aufkommen, *das;* **C** (*increase*) (*in value, price, cost*) Steigerung, *die;* (*St. Exch.: in shares*) Hausse, *die;* (*in population, temperature*) Zunahme, *die;* **be on the ~:** steigen; zunehmen; **D** (*Brit.*) **[pay] ~** (*in wages*) Lohnerhöhung, *die;* (*in salary*) Gehaltserhöhung, *die;* **E** (*hill*) Anhöhe, *die;* Erhebung, *die;* **a ~ in the road** eine Steigung; **F** (*origin*) Ursprung, *der;* **give ~ to** führen zu; ‹Ereignis:› Anlass geben zu ‹Spekulation›; **what has given ~ to this bizarre idea?** woher kommt denn diese seltsame Idee?; **G** (*Angling*) Steigen, *das;* (*fish*) steigender Fisch; **H get** *or* **take a ~ out of sb.** (*fig.*) (*make fun of*) sich über jmdn. lustig machen; (*annoy, provoke*) jmdn. reizen; **I** (*height of step*) [Stufen]höhe, *die.* ❷ *v.i.*, **rose** /rəʊz/, **risen** /'rɪzn/ **A** (*go up*) aufsteigen; **~ [up] into the air** ‹Rauch:› aufsteigen, in die Höhe steigen; ‹Ballon, Vogel, Flugzeug:› sich in die Luft erheben; **B** (*come up*) ‹Sonne, Mond:› aufgehen; ‹Blase:› aufsteigen; **indignation rose in him** Unmut stieg in ihm hoch; **C** (*reach higher level*) steigen; ‹Stimme:› höher werden; **her pleading rose to heights of passionate eloquence** ihr inständiges Bitten steigerte sich zu leidenschaftlicher Beredtheit; **D** (*extend upward*) aufragen; sich erheben; ‹Weg, Straße:› ansteigen; **~ to 2,000 metres** ‹Berg:› 2000 m hoch aufragen; **~ [a storey] higher than sth.** etw. [um ein Stockwerk] überragen; **E** (*advance*) ‹Person:› aufsteigen, aufrücken; **~ to a rank/to be the director** in einen Rang/zum Direktor aufsteigen; **~ in one's profession** in seinem Beruf voran- *od.* vorwärts- *od.* weiterkommen; **~ in the world** voran- *od.* weiterkommen; ⇒ *also* **fame**; **rank**[1] 1 E; **F** (*increase*) steigen; ‹Interesse:› wachsen; ‹Stimme:› lauter werden; (*blow more strongly*) ‹Wind, Sturm:› auffrischen, stärker werden; **~ to a gale** zum Sturm werden; **G** (*Cookery*) ‹Teig, Kuchen:› aufgehen; **H** (*become more cheerful*) ‹Stimmung, Moral:› steigen; **I** (*come to surface*) ‹Fisch:› steigen; **~ to the bait** (*fig.*) sich ködern lassen (*ugs.*); **~ to sb.'s taunts** sich von jmdm. herausfordern lassen; **J** (*Theatre*) ‹Vorhang:› aufgehen, sich heben; **~ on a scene** *or* **to reveal a scene** [aufgehen *od.* sich heben und] den Blick auf eine Szene freigeben; **K** (*rebel, cease to be quiet*) ‹Person:› aufbegehren (*geh.*), sich erheben; **~ as one man** wie ein Mann aufstehen; **~ in arms** einen bewaffneten Aufstand machen; **my whole soul ~s against it** mein ganzes Inneres sträubt sich dagegen; ⇒ *also* **gorge** 1 B; **L** (*get up*) **~ [to one's feet]** aufstehen; (*from sitting or lying also; after accolade*) sich erheben; **he fell, never to ~ again** er stürzte und kam nicht wieder auf die Beine; **~ on its hind legs** ‹Pferd:› steigen; **~ and shine!** (*coll.*) aufstehen!; raus aus den Federn! (*ugs.*); ⇒ *also* **sun** 1; **M** (*adjourn*) ‹Parlament:› in die Ferien gehen, die Sitzungsperiode beenden; (*end a session*) die Sitzung beenden; **N** (*come to life again*) auferstehen; **Christ is ~n** Christus ist auferstanden *od.* (*geh.*) erstanden; **~ from the ashes** (*fig.*) ‹Industrie:› aus den Trümmern wiedererstehen; **look as though one had ~n from the grave** wie eine lebende Leiche aussehen (*salopp*); **O** (*have origin*) ‹Fluss:› entspringen

**~ above** *v.t.* überragen; (*fig.*) hinauskommen über (+ *Akk.*) ‹Niveau›; (*morally*) erhaben sein über (+ *Akk.*)

**~ to** *v.t.* ⇒ **challenge** 1 B; **occasion** 1 A

**~ 'up** *v.i.* **A** (*get up*) aufstehen; sich erheben; **B** (*advance*) aufsteigen; (*in level*) ansteigen; **C** (*rebel*) **~ up [in revolt]** aufbegehren (*geh.*); sich erheben; **D** (*extend upward*) ‹Berg:› aufragen; **~ up to 2,000 metres** 2000 m hoch aufragen

**risen** ⇒ **rise** 2

**riser** /'raɪzə(r)/ *n.* **A** (*one who gets up*) **early ~:** Frühaufsteher, *der*/Frühaufsteherin, *die;* **late ~:** Spätaufsteher, *der*/Spätaufsteherin, *die;* **B** (*of stair, step*) Setzstufe, *die;* **C** (*vertical pipe*) Steigrohr, *das;* Steigleitung, *die*

**risible** /'rɪzɪbl/ *adj.* (*literary*) lächerlich

**rising** /'raɪzɪŋ/ ❶ *n.* **A** (*appearance above the horizon*) Aufgang, *der;* **B** (*increase in height*) Steigen, *das;* **he waited for the ~ of the tide** er wartete auf die Flut; **C** (*getting up*) Aufstehen, *das;* **D** (*revolt*) Aufstand, *der;* **E** (*resurrection*) Auferstehung, *die.* ❷ *adj.* **A** (*appearing above the horizon*) aufgehend; **B** (*increasing*) steigend ‹Kosten, Temperatur›; (*fig.*) wachsend ‹Entrüstung, Wut, Ärger, Bedeutung›; **C** (*mounting*) steigend ‹Wasser, Flut›; hochgehend ‹Welle›; **D the ~ generation** die heranwachsende Generation; **E** (*advancing in standing*) aufstrebend; **F** (*sloping upwards*) ansteigend; **G** (*approaching the age of*) **be ~ forty** auf die Vierzig zugehen; **be ~ sixteen** sechzehn werden; **the ~ fives** die fast fünfjährigen Kinder

**rising: ~ butt** ⇒ **~ hinge**; **~ 'damp** *n.* aufsteigende Feuchtigkeit; **~ hinge** *n.* Hebescharnier, *das*

**risk** /rɪsk/ ❶ *n.* **A** (*hazard*) Gefahr, *die;* (*chance taken*) Risiko, *das;* **~ of infection/loss** Ansteckungsgefahr, *die*/Verlustrisiko, *das;* **there is a/no ~ of sb.'s doing sth.** *or* **that sb. will do sth.** es besteht die/keine Gefahr, dass jmd. etw. tut; **at the ~ of one's life** unter Lebensgefahr; **be at ~** ‹Zukunft, Plan:› in Gefahr sein, gefährdet sein; **at one's own ~:** auf eigene Gefahr *od.* eigenes Risiko; **at owner's ~:** auf Gefahr *od.* Risiko des Eigentümers; **'coats/luggage** *etc.* **left at owner's ~'** „keine Haftung für Garderobe/Gepäck *usw.*"; **put at ~:** gefährden; in Gefahr bringen; **run** *or* **take a ~:** ein Risiko *od.* Wagnis eingehen *od.* auf sich (*Akk.*) nehmen; **run** *or* **take ~s/a lot of ~s** etwas/viel riskieren; **take ~s with one's life** sein Leben in Gefahr bringen *od.* riskieren; **run the ~ of doing sth.** Gefahr laufen, etw. zu tun; (*knowingly*) es riskieren, etw. zu tun; **take the ~ of doing sth.** es riskieren, etw. zu tun; das Risiko eingehen *od.* in Kauf nehmen, etw. zu tun; **B** (*Insurance*) **he is a poor/good ~:** bei ihm ist das Risiko groß/gering.

❷ *v.t.* riskieren; wagen ‹Sprung, Kampf›; **you'll ~ losing your job** du riskierst es, deinen Job zu verlieren; **I'll ~ it!** ich lasse es drauf ankommen; ich riskiere es; **~ one's life/neck** sein Leben/seinen Hals riskieren; (*thoughtlessly*) sein Leben aufs Spiel setzen

**riskily** /ˈrɪskɪlɪ/ *adv.* riskant; gewagt

**ˈrisk-money** *n.* Fehlgeld, *das*

**risky** /ˈrɪskɪ/ *adj.* gefährlich; riskant, gewagt ‹Experiment, Unternehmen, Projekt›

**risotto** /rɪˈzɒtəʊ/ *n., pl.* **~s** (*Cookery*) Risotto, *der od. das*

**risqué** /ˈrɪskeɪ/ *adj.* gewagt; nicht ganz salonfähig

**rissole** /ˈrɪsəʊl/ *n.* (*Cookery*) Rissole, *die*

**rite** /raɪt/ *n.* Ritus, *der;* **~ of passage** Rite de passage (*Völkerk.*); Übergangsritus, *der*

**ritual** /ˈrɪtʃʊəl/ ❶ *adj.* (*of* ~) rituell; Ritual‹mord, -tötung›; (*done as* ~) ritualisiert; **~ object** Kultgegenstand, *der.* ❷ *n.* Ⓐ (*act*) Ritual, *das;* Ⓑ *no pl.* (*prescribed procedure*) Ritus, *der;* Ritual, *das;* **he likes ~:** er mag Rituale

**ritualistic** /rɪtʃʊəˈlɪstɪk/ *adj.* ritualistisch

**ritually** /ˈrɪtʃʊəlɪ/ *adv.* rituell; in einem rituellen Akt ‹töten›

**ritzy** /ˈrɪtsɪ/ *adj.* (*coll.*) Ⓐ (*high-class*) feudal, nobel ‹Hotel, Restaurant, Wohnung usw.›; smart ‹Mann, Kleidung›; Ⓑ (*derog.: ostentatiously smart*) stinkfein ‹Vorort, Schule›; (*pretentious-looking*) protzig (*ugs. abwertend*)

**rival** /ˈraɪvl/ ❶ *n.* Ⓐ (*competitor*) Rivale, *der/*Rivalin, *die;* **they were ~s for her affection** sie rivalisierten um ihre Zuneigung; **~s in love** Nebenbuhler; **business ~s** Konkurrenten; Ⓑ (*equal*) **have no ~/~s** seines-/ihresgleichen suchen; **without ~s** konkurrenzlos. ❷ *v.t.,* (*Brit.*) **-ll-** gleichkommen (+ *Dat.*); nicht nachstehen (+ *Dat.*); **he can't ~ that** da kann er nicht mithalten; **I cannot ~ him for speed** an Geschwindigkeit kann ich es nicht mit ihm aufnehmen. ❸ *adj.* rivalisierend ‹Gruppen›; konkurrierend ‹Forderungen›; Konkurrenz‹unternehmen usw.›; **~ applicant** Mitbewerber, *der/*-bewerberin, *die*

**rivalry** /ˈraɪvlrɪ/ *n.* Rivalität, *die* (*geh.*); **business ~:** Wettbewerb, *der;* **friendly ~:** freundschaftlicher Wettstreit

**riven** /ˈrɪvn/ *adj.* (*dated, literary*) zerrissen; **~ by grief** vom Gram zerfressen

**river** /ˈrɪvə(r)/ ❶ *n.* Ⓐ ▶ 1480 Fluss, *der;* (*large*) Strom, *der;* **the ~ Thames** (*Brit.*), **the Thames ~** (*Amer.*) die Themse; **sell sb. down the ~** (*fig. coll.*) jmdn. verschaukeln (*ugs.*); **go up the ~** (*Amer. fig. coll.*) ins Kittchen wandern (*ugs.*); Ⓑ (*fig.*) Strom, *der;* **~ of lava** Lavastrom, *der;* **~s of tears/blood** Ströme von Tränen/Blut. ❷ *attrib. adj.* Ⓐ (*Biol.*) Fluss‹delphin, -aal, -krebs›; Ⓑ (*of* ~) Fluss‹tal, -ufer, -gott usw.›

**river: ~ bank** *n.* Flussufer, *das;* **~ basin** *n.* Stromgebiet, *das;* Einzugsgebiet [eines Flusses]; **~ bed** *n.* Flussbett, *das;* **~ bottom** *n.* (*Amer.*) Flussebene, *die;* **~ head** *n.* Flussquelle, *die;* **~ police** *n. pl.* Wasser[schutz]polizei, *die;* **~side** ❶ *n.* Flussufer, *das;* **on** *or* **by the ~side** am Fluss; ❷ *attrib. adj.* am Fluss gelegen; am Fluss *nachgestellt*

**rivet** /ˈrɪvɪt/ ❶ *n.* Niete, *die;* Niet, *der od. das* (*Technik*). ❷ *v.t.* Ⓐ [ver]nieten; **~ sth. down/together** etw. annieten *od.* festnieten/zusammennieten; Ⓑ (*fig.: hold firmly*) fesseln ‹Person, Aufmerksamkeit, Blick›; **be ~ed to the spot** wie angenagelt [da]stehen (*ugs.*); **be ~ed on sth.** ‹Aufmerksamkeit:› durch etw. gefesselt werden; **his eyes were ~ed on** *or* **to the screen** seine Augen waren auf den Bildschirm geheftet (*geh.*)

**riveter** /ˈrɪvɪtə(r)/ *n.* Nieter, *der/*Nieterin, *die;* (*machine*) Nietmaschine, *die*

**riveting** /ˈrɪvɪtɪŋ/ *adj.* fesselnd

**Riviera** /rɪvɪˈeərə/ *n.* Riviera, *die*

**rivulet** /ˈrɪvjʊlɪt/ *n.* (*lit. or fig.*) Bach, *der*

**rly.** *abbr.* **railway** Eisenb.

**rm.** *abbr.* **room** Zi.

**RM** *abbr.* (*Brit.*) Ⓐ **Royal Mail;** Ⓑ **Royal Marines**

**RN** *abbr.* (*Brit.*) **Royal Navy** Königl. Mar.

**RNA** *abbr.* **ribonucleic acid** RNS

**RNIB** *abbr.* (*Brit.*) **Royal National Institute for the Blind** *Königliches Blindeninstitut*

**RNLI** *abbr.* (*Brit.*) **Royal National Lifeboat Institution** *Königliches Institut für Rettungsboote*

**RNR, RNVR** *abbrs.* (*Brit. Hist.*) **Royal Navy [Volunteer] Reserve** [*Freiwillige*] *Reserve der Königlichen Marine*

**roach**[1] /rəʊtʃ/ *n., pl. same* (*fish*) Plötze, *die;* Rotauge, *das*

**roach**[2] (*Amer.*) ⇒ **cockroach**

**road** /rəʊd/ *n.* Ⓐ Straße, *die;* **the Birmingham/London ~:** die Straße nach Birmingham/London; (*name of ~/street*) **London/Shelley R~:** Londoner Straße/Shelleystraße; **'~ up'** „Straßenarbeiten"; **'~ narrows'** „Fahrbahnverengung"; **across** *or* **over the ~ [from us]** [bei uns *od.* (*geh.*) uns (*Dat.*)] gegenüber; **by ~** (*by car/bus*) per Auto/Bus; (*by lorry/truck*) per LKW; **off the ~** (*on the verge etc.*) neben der Straße *od.* Fahrbahn; (*across country*) im Gelände ‹ein Fahrzeug benutzen›; durchs Gelände ‹fahren›; (*being repaired*) in der Werkstatt; in Reparatur; **take a vehicle off the ~** (*no longer use it*) ein Fahrzeug stilllegen; **one for the ~** (*coll.*) ein Glas zum Abschied; **be a danger on the ~:** eine Gefahr für den Straßenverkehr sein; **be on the ~:** auf Reisen *od.* unterwegs sein; ‹Theaterensemble usw.:› auf Tournee *od.* (*ugs.*) Tour (*Dat.*) sein; **put a vehicle on the ~:** ein Fahrzeug in Betrieb nehmen; **take the ~:** sich auf den Weg machen; aufbrechen; (*become tramp*) ein Tramp werden; **the rule of the ~:** die Verkehrsregeln; Ⓑ (*means of access*) Weg, *der;* **set sb. on the ~ to ruin** jmdn. ins Verderben führen; **be on the right ~:** auf dem richtigen Weg sein; **be on the ~ to success/ruin** auf dem Weg zum Erfolg sein/in sein Verderben rennen; **change one's mind somewhere along the ~** (*fig.*) es sich (*Dat.*) irgendwo unterwegs anders überlegen; **end of the ~** (*destination*) Ziel, *das;* (*limit*) Ende, *das;* **it's the end of the ~ for us** (*fig.*) mit uns ist es jetzt vorbei; Ⓒ (*one's way*) Weg, *der;* **get in sb.'s ~** (*coll.*) jmdm. in die Quere kommen (*ugs.*); **get out of my ~!** (*coll.*) geh mir aus dem Weg!; Ⓓ (*Amer.*) ⇒ **railway;** Ⓔ (*Mining*) Strecke, *die;* Ⓕ *usu. in pl.* (*Naut.*) Reede, *die;* **lie in the ~s** auf der Reede liegen

**road: ~ accident** *n.* Verkehrsunfall, *der; attrib.* **~ accident victims** Verkehrsopfer; **~ atlas** *n.* Autoatlas, *der;* **~bed** *n.* Ⓐ (*foundation of ~, railway*) Unterbau, *der;* Ⓑ (*Amer.: part of ~ on which vehicles travel*) Fahrbahn, *die;* **~block** *n.* Straßensperre, *die;* **~ book** *n.* Autoreiseführer, *der;* **~ bridge** *n.* Straßenbrücke, *die;* **~ fund licence** *n.* (*Brit.*) Kfz-Steuerbeleg, *der;* **~ haulage** *n.* Gütertransport auf der Straße; **~ hog** *n.* Verkehrsrowdy, *der* (*abwertend*); **~holding** *n.* (*Brit. Motor Veh.*) Straßenlage, *die;* **~ house** *n.* Rasthaus, *das;* **~ hump** ⇒ **speed hump**

**roadie** /ˈrəʊdɪ/ *n.* (*coll.*) Roadie, *der*

**road: ~ manager** *n.* ▶ 1261 Roadmanager, *der;* **~ map** *n.* Straßenkarte, *die;* **~mender** *n.* ▶ 1261 Straßen[bau]arbeiter, *der/*-arbeiterin, *die;* **~ metal** *n.* Schotter, *der;* (*smaller pieces*) Splitt, *der;* **~ rage** *n.: häufig zu gewalttätigen Ausbrüchen führende Wut eines Autofahrers;* **~ roller** *n.* Straßenwalze, *die;* **~runner** *n.* (*Ornith.*) (*Geococcyx californianus*) Erdkuckuck, *der;* (*G. velox*) Rennkuckuck, *der;* **~ safety** *n.* Verkehrssicherheit, *die;* **~ sense** *n.* Gespür für Verkehrssituationen; **~ show** *n.* (*promotional*) [Werbe]tour, *die;* Roadshow, *die;* (*political*) [Wahlkampf]tour, *die;* **'Radio One R~show'** 'Radio One unterwegs *od.* vor Ort'; **~side** ❶ *n.* Straßenrand, *der;* **at** *or* **by/along the ~side** am Straßenrand; an/entlang der Straße; ❷ *adj.* ‹Gasthaus usw.› am Straßenrand, an der Straße; **~side inn** Rasthaus, *das;* **~ sign** *n.* Straßenschild, *das* (*ugs.*); Verkehrszeichen, *das*

**roadster** /ˈrəʊdstə(r)/ *n.* Ⓐ (*open car*) Roadster, *der;* Sportkabrio[lett], *das;* Ⓑ (*bicycle*) Tourenrad, *das*

**road: ~ sweeper** *n.* Ⓐ ▶ 1261 (*person*) Straßenkehrer, *der/*-kehrerin, *die* (*bes. südd.*); Straßenfeger, *der/*-fegerin, *die* (*bes. nordd.*); Ⓑ (*machine*) [Straßen]kehrmaschine, *die;* **~ tax** *n.* (*Brit.*) Kraftfahrzeugsteuer, *die;* Kfz-Steuer, *die;* **~ test** *n.* Fahrtest, *der;* **~-test** *v.t.* einem Fahrtest unterziehen; **~ transport** *n.* Ⓐ **form of ~ transport** Verkehrsmittel der Straße; Ⓑ (*process*) Personen- und Güterbeförderung auf der Straße; **~ user** *n.* Verkehrsteilnehmer, *der/*-teilnehmerin, *die;* **~way** *n.* Ⓐ (*road*) Straße, *die;* Ⓑ (*central part of road*) Fahrbahn, *die;* **~works** *n. pl.* Straßenbauarbeiten *Pl.;* **'~works'** „Baustelle"; **~worthy** *adj.* fahrtüchtig ‹Fahrzeug›

**roam** /rəʊm/ ❶ *v.i.* umherstreifen; herumstreifen (*ugs.*); ‹Nomade:› wandern; (*stray*) ‹Tier:› streunen; **~ through the town** durch die Stadt streifen; **be free to ~** ‹Tier:› frei herumlaufen dürfen; **tendency to ~:** Hang zum Streunen. ❷ *v.t.* streifen durch; durchstreifen (*geh.*). ❸ *n.* Streifzug, *der*

**~ aˈbout, ~ aˈround** ❶ *v.i.* herumstreifen (*ugs.*); umherstreifen; **he ~s about all over the place** er zieht überall in der Gegend herum (*ugs.*). ❷ *v.t.* herumstreifen in (+ *Dat.*) (*ugs.*); durchstreifen (*geh.*)

**roamer** /ˈrəʊmə(r)/ *n.* (*person*) Herumtreiber, *der* (*ugs.*); (*animal*) streunendes Tier

**roaming** /ˈrəʊmɪŋ/ *adj.* wandernd ‹Herde›; (*fig.*) schweifend, wandernd ‹Gedanke›

**roan**[1] /rəʊn/ ❶ *adj.* stichelhaarig ‹Fell, Tier›. ❷ *n.* (*horse*) stichelhaariges Pferd; (*cow*) stichelhaarige Kuh; **be a ~:** stichelhaarig sein

**roan**[2] *n.* (*Bookbinding*) Schafleder, *das*

**roar** /rɔː(r)/ ❶ *n.* (*of wild beast*) Brüllen, *das;* Gebrüll, *das;* (*of water*) Tosen, *das;* Getose, *das;* (*of avalanche, guns*) Donner, *der;* (*of applause*) Tosen, *das;* (*of machine, traffic*) Dröhnen, *das;* Getöse, *das;* **a ~ of applause** tosender Beifall; **~s/a ~ [of laughter]** dröhnendes *od.* brüllendes Gelächter. ❷ *v.i.* Ⓐ (*cry loudly*) brüllen (**with** vor + *Dat.*); **~ [with laughter]** [vor Lachen] brüllen; Ⓑ (*make loud noise*) ‹Motor:› dröhnen; ‹Artillerie:› donnern; (*blaze up*) ‹Feuer:› bullern (*ugs.*); Ⓒ (*travel fast*) ‹Fahrzeug:› donnern. ❸ *v.t.* brüllen; **~ [one's] approval [of sth.]** [einer Sache (*Dat.*)] lautstark zustimmen

**roaring** /ˈrɔːrɪŋ/ ❶ *adj.* Ⓐ (*making loud noise*) dröhnend ‹Motor, Donner›; tosend ‹Meer›; brüllend ‹Löwe›; Ⓑ (*blazing loudly*) bullernd (*ugs.*) ‹Feuer›; **a ~ inferno** ein tosendes Inferno; Ⓒ (*riotous*) **a ~ success** ein Bombenerfolg (*ugs.*); **the ~ twenties** die wilden Zwanzigerjahre; die Roaring Twenties; Ⓓ (*brisk*) **do a ~ business** *or* **trade** ein Bombengeschäft machen; ⇒ *also* **forty** 2. ❷ *adv.* **~ drunk** sternhagelvoll (*salopp*)

**roast** /rəʊst/ ❶ *v.t.* Ⓐ (*cook by radiant heat*) braten; (*prepare by heating*) rösten ‹Kaffeebohnen, Erdnüsse, Mandeln, Kastanien›; Ⓑ (*expose to heat*) **~ oneself in front of the fire/in the sun** sich am Feuer rösten lassen/in der Sonne braten lassen (*scherzh.*); Ⓒ (*Metallurgy*) rösten ‹Erz›; Ⓓ (*coll.*) (*tell off*) zusammenstauchen (*ugs.*) ‹Person›; (*esp. Amer.: criticize*) abqualifizieren; heruntermachen (*salopp*); geißeln, anprangern ‹Vorgehensweise›; verreißen ‹Buch usw.›.

❷ *attrib. adj.* gebraten ‹Fleisch, Ente usw.›; Brat‹hähnchen, -kartoffeln›; Röst‹kastanien›; **eat ~ duck/pork/beef** Enten-/Schweine-/Rinderbraten essen; **~ [sirloin of] beef** Roastbeef, *das.*

❸ *n.* Ⓐ (~ *meat, meat for ~ing*) Braten, *der;* Ⓑ ⇒ **1** A: Braten, *das;* Rösten, *das;* **give sth. a ~:** etw. braten/rösten; Ⓒ (*Amer.: social gathering*) Grillparty, *die;* Grillfest, *das.*

❹ *v.i.* Ⓐ ‹Fleisch:› braten; Ⓑ (*bask in warmth of sun/fire*) sich braten/rösten lassen (*scherzh.*)

**roaster** /ˈrəʊstə(r)/ *n.* Ⓐ (*oven*) Bratofen, *der;* (*dish*) Bratentopf, *der;* (*for coffee*) Röstmaschine, *die;* Ⓑ (*chicken*) Brathähnchen,

r

# Rivers

German has two words for *river*. The usual one is **der Fluss**, which applies to any river, while **der Strom** is only used for a really large river such as the Rhine (**der Rhein**), the Danube (**die Donau**), the Volga (**die Wolga**), the Zambezi (**der Sambesi**), the Amazon (**der Amazonas**), and so on. Most rivers are masculine, but there are quite a number of exceptions (including of course the two already mentioned). All French rivers are feminine for a start, since they are feminine in French. The following German and most Austrian rivers are also feminine:

> die Weser, die Elbe, die Saar, die Mosel, die Ruhr, die Isar, die Spree, die Havel, die Oder, die Neiße; (and in Austria) die Salzach, die Enns, die Etsch, die Drau and many others.

In addition there are a couple of rivers in neighbouring countries:

> die Maas, die Amstel in Holland;
>
> die Moldau (the Vltava) in the Czech Republic;
>
> die Weichsel (the Vistula) in Poland.

Virtually all rivers in the rest of the world are masculine, with the one exception of the Thames (die Themse).

German does not insert a word for river before the name as does English:

| ***the river Main*** | ***the river Seine*** |
|---|---|
| = der Main | = die Seine |

When rivers occur in place names, the preposition used is **an**. Such mentions often distinguish between places with the same name:

> Frankfurt am Main ↔ Frankfurt an der Oder
>
> Linz am Rhein ↔ Linz an der Donau

**am** can be abbreviated as **a.** and **an der** as **a.d.**, and the names of the rivers can be reduced to the initial letter where these are familiar, giving e.g.

> Frankfurt a.M. ↔ Frankfurt a.d.O.
>
> Bruck a.d. Mur

## Some river phrases

***to go upstream/downstream*** or ***up/down the river***
= flussaufwärts/flussabwärts fahren

***to go up/down the Rhine***
= rheinaufwärts/rheinabwärts fahren

Similar adverbs can be formed with the name of any river (**donauaufwärts, themseabwärts** etc.).

***a house by or on the river***
= ein Haus am Fluss

***on the right bank of the Weser***
= am rechten Weserufer

***He was carried along by the current***
= Er wurde von der Strömung mitgerissen

***The river is in flood or in full spate***
= Der Fluss führt Hochwasser

***The river is very low***
= Der Fluss führt sehr wenig Wasser

***The Rhine rises in Switzerland and flows into the North Sea***
= Der Rhein entspringt in der Schweiz und mündet in die Nordsee

***The ship sank in the mouth of the Elbe or the Elbe estuary***
= Das Schiff ist in der Elbmündung gesunken

---

*das;* Ⓒ (*Metallurgy: furnace*) Röstofen, *der;* Ⓓ (*coll.: hot day*) knallheißer Tag (*ugs.*)

**roasting** /ˈrəʊstɪŋ/ ❶ *n.* Ⓐ (*cooking*) Braten, *das;* (*of coffee, ore*) Rösten, *das; attrib.* ‹Fleisch, Huhn› zum Braten; Brat‹spieß, -zeit›; Braten‹wender, -gabel›; Ⓑ (*severe criticism*) (*by parent, boss, etc.*) Standpauke, *die* (*ugs.*); (*by critic*) Verriss, *der* (*ugs.*); **get a ~:** eins auf den Deckel kriegen (*ugs.*); **give sb. a ~:** jmdn. zusammenstauchen (*ugs.*); **give sth. a ~** ‹Kritiker:› etw. verreißen (*ugs.*). ❷ *adj.* (*coll.: hot*) knallheiß (*ugs.*); **I am ~:** ich komme um vor Hitze

**rob** /rɒb/ *v.t.*, **-bb-** ausrauben ‹Bank, Safe, Kasse›; berauben ‹Person›; *abs.* rauben; **~ sth. of sth.** einer Sache (*Dat.*) etw. nehmen; **~ sb. of sth.** jmdm. etw. rauben *od.* stehlen; (*deprive of what is due*) jmdn. um etw. bringen *od.* betrügen; (*withhold sth. from*) jmdm. etw. vorenthalten; **~ a bird of its eggs** einem Vogel die Eier wegnehmen; **be ~bed** bestohlen werden; (*by force*) beraubt werden; **we wuz ~bed** (*Sport coll.*) das war Schiebung! (*ugs.*); ⇒ *also* **Peter**

**robber** /ˈrɒbə(r)/ *n.* Räuber, *der*/Räuberin, *die;* **band of ~s** Räuberbande, *die*

**robbery** /ˈrɒbərɪ/ *n.* Raub, *der;* **robberies** Raubüberfälle; **it's sheer ~!** das ist ja die reinste Halsabschneiderei (*ugs. abwertend*)

**robe** /rəʊb/ ❶ *n.* Ⓐ (*ceremonial garment*) Gewand, *das* (*geh.*); (*of judge, vicar*) Talar, *der;* **coronation ~s** Krönungsornat, *der;* **~ of office** Amtstracht, *die;* Ⓑ (*long garment*) [langes Über]gewand; Ⓒ (*dressing gown*) Morgenrock, *der;* **beach ~:** Bademantel, *der;* Ⓓ **christening ~:** Taufkleid, *das;* Ⓔ (*Amer.: blanket*) [Reise]decke, *die;* Ⓕ (*Amer.: wardrobe*) [Kleider]schrank, *der.* ❷ *v.t.* (*formal*) **~ sb. in sth.** jmdn. in etw. (*Akk.*) kleiden; jmdm. etw. anlegen (*geh.*); **the vicar/judge ~d himself** der Pfarrer/Richter legte (*geh.*) *od.* zog einen/seinen/den Talar an. ❸ *v.i.* (*formal*) sich ankleiden (*geh.*)

**robin** /ˈrɒbɪn/ *n.* (*Ornith.*) Ⓐ **~ [redbreast]** Rotkehlchen, *das;* Ⓑ (*Amer.: thrush*) Wanderdrossel, *die*

**robing room** /ˈrəʊbɪŋruːm, ˈrəʊbɪŋrʊm/ *n.* Ankleideraum, *der*

**Robin 'Hood** *n.* Robin Hood (*der*)

**robinia** /rəˈbɪnɪə/ *n.* (*Bot.*) Robinie, *die;* falsche Akazie

**robot** /ˈrəʊbɒt/ *n.* Roboter, *der*

**robotics** /rəʊˈbɒtɪks/ *n., no pl.* Robotertechnik, *die;* Robotik, *die*

**robust** /rəʊˈbʌst/ *adj.* Ⓐ (*strong*) robust ‹Person, Gesundheit, Nervenkostüm›; kräftig ‹Person, Wein›; (*not delicate*) unempfindlich, widerstandsfähig ‹Pflanze›; Ⓑ (*strongly built*) kräftig ‹Gestalt, Körperbau›; robust ‹Fahrzeug, Maschine, Konstruktion, Möbel›; stabil ‹Haus›; Ⓒ (*fig.: straightforward*) unerschütterlich ‹Skepsis›; nüchtern ‹Verstand›; fest ‹Glaube›

**robustly** /rəʊˈbʌstlɪ/ *adv.* stabil, solide ‹bauen›; energisch ‹sich entgegenstellen›

**rock¹** /rɒk/ *n.* Ⓐ (*piece of ~*) Fels, *der;* **come to grief on the ~s** ‹Schiff:› auf Felsen *od.* Klippen auflaufen; **be as solid as a ~** (*fig.*) absolut zuverlässig sein; **be as steady as a ~:** bombenfest sein; (*fig.*) durch nichts zu erschüttern sein; Ⓑ (*large ~, hill*) Felsen, *der;* Fels, *der* (*geh.*); **the R~ [of Gibraltar]** [der Felsen von] Gibraltar; Ⓒ (*substance*) Fels, *der;* (*esp. Geol.*) Gestein, *das;* **mass of ~:** Felsmasse, *die;* Ⓓ (*boulder*) Felsbrocken, *der;* (*Amer.: stone*) Stein, *der;* Steinbrocken, *der;* **'danger, falling ~s'** „Achtung *od.* Vorsicht, Steinschlag!"; „Steinschlaggefahr!"; **be caught between a ~ and a hard place** (*fig.*) in einer Zwickmühle stizen (*ugs.*); Ⓔ *no pl., no indef. art.* (*hard sweet*) **stick of ~:** Zuckerstange, *die;* **sell ~:** Zuckerstangen verkaufen; Ⓕ (*fig.: support*) Stütze, *die;* Rückhalt, *der;* (*of society*) Fundament, *das;* Ⓖ (*fig.: source of danger or destruction*) **a ~ on which others have foundered** eine Klippe, an der schon andere gescheitert sind; **be heading for the ~s** ‹Ehe:› zu scheitern drohen; **be on the ~s** (*fig. coll.*) (*be short of/without money*) knapp bei Kasse/pleite sein (*ugs.*); (*have failed*) ‹Ehe, Firma:› kaputt sein (*ugs.*); Ⓗ **on the ~s** (*with ice cubes*) mit Eis *od.* on the rocks; Ⓘ *in pl.* (*Amer. coll.: money*) Kies, *der* (*salopp*); Ⓙ (*coll.: gem*) Klunker, *der* (*ugs.*)

**rock²** ❶ *v.t.* Ⓐ (*move to and fro*) wiegen; (*in cradle*) schaukeln; wiegen; **~ oneself** (*in chair*) schaukeln; sich wiegen; Ⓑ (*shake*) erschüttern; (*fig.*) erschüttern ‹Person›; **~ sth. to its foundations** (*fig.*) etw. in seinen Grundfesten erschüttern; **~ the boat** (*fig. coll.*) Trouble machen (*ugs.*).
❷ *v.i.* Ⓐ (*move to and fro*) sich wiegen; schaukeln; Ⓑ (*sway*) schwanken; wanken; **~ with laughter** sich vor Lachen (*Dat.*) schütteln; Ⓒ (*dance*) rocken; Rock tanzen; **~ and roll** Rock and Roll tanzen.
❸ *n.* Ⓐ (*~ing motion, spell of ~ing*) Schaukeln, *das;* **give the cradle a ~:** die Wiege schaukeln; Ⓑ (*beat music or dance*) Rock, *der; attrib.* Rock-; **~ and** *or* **'n' roll [music]** Rock and Roll, *der;* Rock 'n' Roll, *der;* **do the ~ and roll** Rock and Roll tanzen

**rock: ~-'bottom** (*coll.*) ❶ *adj.* **~-bottom prices** Schleuderpreise (*ugs.*); **at a ~-bottom price/rent** spottbillig (*ugs.*); ❷ *n.* **reach** *or* **hit** *or* **touch ~-bottom** ‹Handel, Währung, Nachfrage, Preis usw.:› in den Keller fallen *od.* sinken (*ugs.*); **her spirits reached ~-bottom** ihre Stimmung war auf dem Tiefpunkt [angelangt]; **~ cake** *n.: Rosinengebäck mit rauher Oberfläche;* **~ climber** *n.* Kletterer, *der*/Kletterin, *die;* **~ climbing** *n.* [Fels]klettern, *das*

**rocker** /ˈrɒkə(r)/ *n.* Ⓐ (*Brit.: gang member*) Rocker, *der;* Ⓑ (*curved bar of chair, cradle, etc.*) Kufe, *die;* **be/go off one's ~** (*fig. coll.*) übergeschnappt *od.* durchgedreht sein (*ugs.*)/überschnappen (*ugs.*) *od.* durchdrehen (*ugs.*); Ⓒ (*rocking chair*) Schaukelstuhl, *der;* Ⓓ (*Electr.*) **~ [switch]** Wippschalter, *der;* Ⓔ (*Mech. Engin.*) Kipphebel, *der*

**rockery** /ˈrɒkərɪ/ *n.* Steingarten, *der*

**rocket¹** /ˈrɒkɪt/ ❶ *n.* Ⓐ Rakete, *die;* **~ range** (*place*) Raketenversuchsgelände, *das;* Ⓑ (*Brit. coll.: reprimand*) **give sb. a ~:** jmdm. eine Zigarre verpassen (*ugs.*); **get a**

**~:** eine Zigarre bekommen (*ugs.*). ❷ *v.i.* (A) ‹Preise:› in die Höhe schnellen; (B) **~ into the air** wie eine Rakete in die Luft schießen

**rocket²** *n.* (*Bot.*) (A) **[sweet] ~:** Nachtviole, *die;* (B) (*used in salad*) [Öl]rauke, *die*

**rocket: ~ base** *n.* (*Mil.*) Raketen[abschuss]basis, *die;* **~ bomb** *n.* (A) (*air-to-ground*) [Flieger]rakete, *die;* Luft-Boden-Rakete, *die;* (B) (*ground-to-ground*) [Artillerie]rakete, *die;* Boden-Boden-Rakete, *die;* **~ engine** *n.* Raketentriebwerk, *das;* **~-firing** *adj.* mit Raketen bewaffnet *nachgestellt;* **~ flight** *n.* Raketenflug, *der;* **~ launcher** *n.* Raketenwerfer, *der;* **~ plane** *n.* Raketenflugzeug, *das;* **~-powered**, **~-propelled** *adjs.* raketengetrieben; **~ propulsion** *n.* Raketenantrieb, *der;* **~ range** *n.* Raketenversuchsgelände, *das*

**rocketry** /ˈrɒkɪtrɪ/ *n., no pl.* Raketentechnik, *die*

**rock: ~ face** *n.* Felswand, *die;* **~fall** *n.* Steinschlag, *der;* **~ formation** *n.* Gesteinsformation, *die;* **~ garden** *n.* Steingarten, *der;* **~-hard** *adj.* steinhart

**Rockies** /ˈrɒkɪz/ *pr. n. pl.* **the ~:** die Rocky Mountains

**rocking**/ˈrɒkɪŋ/: **~ chair** *n.* Schaukelstuhl, *der;* **~ horse** *n.* Schaukelpferd, *das*

**rock: ~like** *adj.* felsartig; felsenfest ‹Glaube usw.›; **~ plant** *n.* Felsenpflanze, *die;* (*Hort.*) Steingartengewächs, *das;* **~ salmon** *n.* (A) (*Brit.: dogfish*) Katzenhai, *der;* (B) (*Amer.: Seriola*) Gelbschwanzmakrele, *die;* **~ salt** *n.* Steinsalz, *das*

**rocky** /ˈrɒkɪ/ *adj.* (A) (*coll.: unsteady*) wackelig (*ugs.*); (B) (*full or consisting of rocks*) felsig; (C) **the R~ Mountains** ⇒ **Rockies**

**rococo** /rəˈkəʊkəʊ/ ❶ *adj.* Rokoko-; (*florid*) schwülstig. ❷ *n., pl.* **~s** Rokoko, *das*

**rod** /rɒd/ *n.* (A) Stange, *die;* **ride the ~s** (*Amer. coll.*) [im Gestänge unter Eisenbahnwaggons] schwarzfahren; (B) (*shorter*) Stab, *der;* **~ of office** Amtsstab, *der;* (C) (*for punishing*) Stock, *der;* Rute, *die;* **the ~** (*punishment*) die Prügelstrafe; **make a ~ for one's own back** (*fig.*) sich (*Dat.*) selbst eine Rute aufbinden (*veralt.*); **a ~ to beat sb. with** (*fig.*) Sanktionen gegen jmdn.; **rule with a ~ of iron** (*fig.*) mit eiserner Faust *od.* Rute regieren; **spare the ~ and spoil the child** wer die Rute schont, verdirbt das Kind; (D) (*for fishing*) [Angel]rute, *die;* (E) (*measure*) Rute, *die* (*veralt.*); (F) (*Amer. coll.: gun*) Schießeisen, *das* (*ugs.*); (G) (*Anat.*) Stäbchen, *das*

**rode** ⇒ **ride** 2, 3

**rodent** /ˈrəʊdənt/ *n.* Nagetier, *das*

**ˈrodent officer** *n.* (*Brit.*) Rattenfänger, *der*

**rodeo** /ˈrəʊdɪəʊ, rəʊˈdeɪəʊ/ *n., pl.* **~s** Rodeo, *der od. das*

**roe¹** /rəʊ/ *n.* (*of fish*) **[hard] ~:** Rogen, *der;* **[soft] ~:** Milch, *die*

**roe²** *n.* (*deer*) Reh, *das*

**roe: ~buck** *n.* Rehbock, *der;* **~-deer** *n.* Reh, *das*

**roentgen** /ˈrʌntjən/ *n.* (*Phys.*) Röntgen, *das*

**rogation** /rəˈgeɪʃn/ *n.* (*Eccl.*) Bittlitanei, *die;* **R~ Days** Bittage *Pl.;* **R~ Sunday** [der Sonntag] Rogate; **R~ Week** Bittwoche, *die*

**roger** /ˈrɒdʒə(r)/ *int.* (A) (*message received*) verstanden; (B) (*coll.: I agree*) okay (*ugs.*)

**rogue** /rəʊg/ ❶ *n.* (A) Gauner, *der* (*abwertend*); **~s' gallery** (*Police*) Verbrecheralbum, *das;* (B) (*joc.: mischievous child*) Spitzbube, *der* (*scherzh.*); (C) (*dangerous animal*) **~ [buffalo/elephant** *etc.*] bösartiger Einzelgänger. ❷ *attrib. adj.* defekt; fehlerhaft; **~ car** Montagsauto, *das;* **~ result** Ausreißer, *der;* **~ firms** schwarze Schafe unter den Firmen

**roguery** /ˈrəʊgərɪ/ *n., no pl., no indef. art.* Gaunerei, *die;* (*mischief*) Spitzbüberei, *die*

**roguish** /ˈrəʊgɪʃ/ *adj.* (A) gaunerhaft; (B) (*mischievous*) spitzbübisch

**roguishly** /ˈrəʊgɪʃlɪ/ *adv.* ⇒ **roguish**: gaunerhaft; spitzbübisch

**roisterer** /ˈrɔɪstərə(r)/ *n.* Krakeeler, *der* (*ugs. abwertend*)

**role, rôle** /rəʊl/ *n.* Rolle, *die*

**role: ~ model** *n.* Leitbild, *das;* **~ playing** *n.* Rollenspiel, *das;* Rollenverhalten, *das;* **~ reversal** *n.* Rollentausch, *der*

**roll¹** /rəʊl/ *n.* (A) Rolle, *die;* (*of cloth, tobacco, etc.*) Ballen, *der;* (*of fat on body*) Wulst, *der;* **~ of film** Rolle Film; (B) (*of bread etc.*) **[bread] ~:** Brötchen, *das;* **egg/ham ~:** Eier-/Schinkenbrötchen, *das;* **jam ~:** [Biskuit]rolle mit Marmelade; (C) (*document*) [Schrift]rolle, *die;* (D) (*register, catalogue*) Liste, *die;* Verzeichnis, *das;* **~ of honour** Gedenktafel [für die Gefallenen]; (E) (*Brit.: list of solicitors*) Anwaltsliste, *die;* **strike sb. off the ~s** jmdm. die Zulassung entziehen; (F) (*Mil., Sch.: list of names*) Liste, *die;* **schools with falling ~s** Schulen mit sinkenden Schülerzahlen; **call the ~:** die Anwesenheit feststellen; (G) (*Amer.: of paper money*) Geldbündel, *das;* (H) **be on a ~** (*coll.*) eine Glückssträhne haben

**roll²** ❶ *n.* (A) (*of drum*) Wirbel, *der;* (*of thunder*) Rollen, *das;* (B) (*motion*) Rollen, *das;* (C) (*single movement*) Rolle, *die;* (*of dice*) Wurf, *der;* (D) (*gait*) wiegender Gang.

❷ *v.t.* (A) (*move, send*) rollen; (*between surfaces*) drehen; (B) (*shape by ~ing*) rollen; **~ a cigarette** eine Zigarette rollen *od.* drehen; **~ one's own** [selbst] drehen; **~ snow/wool into a ball** einen Schneeball formen/Wolle zu einem Knäuel aufwickeln; **[all] ~ed into one** (*fig.*) in einem; **~ oneself/itself into a ball** sich zusammenrollen; **~ed in blankets** in Decken eingewickelt; (C) (*flatten*) walzen ‹Rasen, Metall usw.›; ausrollen ‹Teig›; (D) **~ one's eyes** die Augen rollen; **~ one's eyes at sb.** (*amorously*) jmdm. schöne Augen machen; **~ one's shoulders/head** die Schultern/den Kopf kreisen; (E) **~ one's r's** das r rollen; (F) (*Amer.*) **~ dice** würfeln; (G) (*Amer. coll.: rob*) ausrauben.

❸ *v.i.* (A) (*move by turning over*) rollen; **heads will ~** (*fig.*) es werden Köpfe rollen; (B) (*operate*) ‹Maschine:› laufen; ‹Presse:› sich drehen; rotieren; (*on wheels*) rollen; **let it ~** (*start the machine etc.*) lass laufen; **be ready to ~** ‹Kamera:› aufnahmebereit sein; **get sth. ~ing** (*fig.*) etw. ins Rollen bringen; **keep things ~ing** (*fig.*) die Dinge am Laufen halten; ⇒ *also* **aisle**; **ball¹** 1 A, B; (C) (*wallow, sway, walk*) sich wälzen; (*walk also*) schwanken; **the way he ~s along** sein wiegender Gang; (D) (*Naut.*) ‹Schiff:› rollen, schlingern; (E) (*revolve*) ‹Augen:› sich [ver]drehen; (F) (*flow, go forward*) sich wälzen (*fig.*); ‹Wolken:› ziehen; ‹Tränen:› rollen; **~ off** *or* **from sb.'s tongue** (*fig.*) ‹Worte:› jmdm. von den Lippen fließen; (G) (*make deep sound*) ‹Donner:› rollen; ‹Trommel:› dröhnen

**~ aˈbout** *v.i.* herumrollen; ‹Schiff:› schlingern, rollen; ‹Kind, Hund usw.:› sich wälzen; **be ~ing about with laughter** sich vor Lachen wälzen

**~ aˈlong** ❶ *v.i.* (A) [dahin]rollen; ‹Fahrzeug:› [dahin]rollen, [dahin]fahren; **things are ~ing along nicely** (*fig.*) die Dinge laufen gut; (B) (*coll.: turn up*) eintrudeln (*ugs.*); aufkreuzen (*salopp*). ❷ *v.t.* entlangrollen

**~ aˈway** ❶ *v.i.* ‹Ball:› wegrollen; ‹Nebel, Wolken:› sich verziehen. ❷ *v.t.* wegrollen

**~ ˈback** ❶ *v.t.* (A) zurückrollen; (B) (*cause to retreat*) zurückschlagen ‹Feinde, Truppen›; (C) **~ back the years/centuries** das Rad der Zeit [um Jahre/Jahrhunderte] zurückdrehen. ❷ *v.i.* ‹Wagen, Wellen:› zurückrollen

**~ ˈby** *v.i.* vorbeirollen; ‹Zeit:› vergehen; **the years ~ed by** die Jahre zogen ins Land

**~ ˈin** ❶ *v.i.* (*coll.*) ‹Briefe, Geschenke, Geldbeträge:› eingehen; ‹Personen, Kunden:› hereinströmen; **~ in an hour late** mit einer Stunde Verspätung aufkreuzen (*salopp*). ❷ *v.t.* herein-/hineinrollen

**~ ˈoff** *v.i.* (A) (*fall off*) herunterrollen; (B) (*start*) sich in Bewegung setzen

**~ ˈon** ❶ *v.t.* mit einer Rolle auftragen ‹Farbe›. ❷ *v.i.* (A) (*pass by*) ‹Jahre:› vergehen; (B) (*Brit. coll.*) **~ on Saturday!** wenn doch schon Samstag wäre! ⇒ *also* **roll-on**

**~ ˈout** ❶ *v.t.* (A) (*make flat and smooth*) auswalzen ‹Metall›; ausrollen ‹Teig, Teppich›; (B) (*bring out*) herausbringen; **~ out the barrel** (*fig. coll.*) ein paar Flaschen den Hals brechen (*ugs.*). ❷ *v.i.* heraus-/hinausrollen

**~ ˈover** ❶ *v.i.* ‹Person:› sich umdrehen, (*to make room*) sich zur Seite rollen; **~ over [and over]** ‹Auto:› sich [immer wieder] überschlagen; **the dog ~ed over on to its back** der Hund rollte sich auf den Rücken. ❷ *v.t.* herumdrehen; (*with effort*) herumwälzen

**~ ˈpast** ⇒ **~ by**

**~ ˈup** ❶ *v.t.* (A) aufrollen ‹Teppich, Maßband›; zusammenrollen ‹Regenschirm, Landkarte, Dokument usw.›; hochkrempeln ‹Hose›; ⇒ *also* **sleeve** A; (B) (*Mil.*) aufrollen ‹feindliche Stellung›. ❷ *v.i.* (A) (*curl up*) sich zusammenrollen; (B) (*arrive*) aufkreuzen (*salopp*); **~ up! ~ up!** hereinspaziert!; **they ~ed up in their new car** sie fuhren in ihrem neuen Auto vor

**roll: ~away [bed]** *n.* Raumsparbett auf Rollen; **~ bar** *n.* (*Motor Veh.*) Überrollbügel, *der;* **~-call** *n.* Aufrufen aller Namen; (*Mil.*) Zählappell, *der*

**rolled**/rəʊld/: **~ ˈgold** *n.* Goldauflage, *die;* **~ ˈoats** *n. pl.* Haferflocken *Pl.*

**roller** /ˈrəʊlə(r)/ *n.* (A) (*heavy, for pressing, smoothing road, lawn, etc.*) Walze, *die;* (*smaller, for towel, painting, pastry*) Rolle, *die;* (B) (*Med.*) **~ [bandage]** Binde, *die;* (C) (*for hair*) Lockenwickler, *der;* **put one's hair in ~s** sich (*Dat.*) die Haare aufdrehen; (D) (*wave*) Roller, *der* (*Meeresk.*)

**roller: ~ bearing** *n.* Rollenlager, *das* (*Technik*); **R~blade** ® *n.* Rollerblade, *der;* **[a pair of] R~blades** [ein Paar] Rollerblades; **~blade** *v.i.* Rollerblades fahren; **~ blind** *n.* Rouleau, *das;* Rollo, *das;* **~ coaster** *n.* Achterbahn, *die;* **~ skate** *n.* Rollschuh, *der;* **~-skate** *v.i.* Rollschuh laufen; **~ skater** *n.* Rollschuhläufer, *der*/-läuferin, *die;* **~ skating** *n.* Rollschuhlaufen, *das; attrib.* **~-skating rink** Rollschuhbahn, *die;* **~ towel** *n.: auf einer Rolle hängendes endloses Handtuch*

**ˈroll film** *n.* Rollfilm, *der*

**rollick** /ˈrɒlɪk/ *v.i.* ausgelassen spielen; **~ [about]** [herum]tollen

**rollicking** /ˈrɒlɪkɪŋ/ ❶ *adj.* (*unrestrained*) ausgelassen. ❷ *n.* **give sb. a ~** (*coll.*) jmdm. den Marsch blasen (*salopp*)

**rolling** /ˈrəʊlɪŋ/ *adj.* (A) (*moving from side to side*) rollend ‹Augen›; schwankend ‹Gang›; schlingernd ‹Schiff›; (B) (*undulating*) wogend ‹See›; wellig ‹Gelände›; **~ hills** sanfte Hügel; (C) (*resounding*) rollend ‹Donner›; hochtrabend (*abwertend*) ‹Phrasen›; (D) (*coll.: rich*) **be ~ [in it** *or* **in money]** im Geld schwimmen (*ugs.*)

**rolling: ~ mill** *n.* Walzwerk, *das;* **~ pin** *n.* (*Cookery*) Teigrolle, *die;* Nudelholz, *das;* **~ stock** *n.* (A) (*Brit. Railw.*) Fahrzeugbestand, *der;* rollendes Material (*fachspr.*); (B) (*Amer.: road vehicles*) Fahrzeugpark, *der;* **~ ˈstone** *n.* (*fig.*) unsteter Mensch; **a ~ stone gathers no moss** (*prov.*) wer ein unstetes Leben führt, bringt es zu nichts

**roll: ~mop[s]** *n.* (*Gastr.*) Rollmops, *der;* **~-neck** ❶ *n.* Rollkragen, *der;* ❷ *adj.* Rollkragen-; **~-on** *n.* (A) (*corset*) elastischer Hüfthalter; (B) (*deodorant*) Deoroller, *der;* **~-on ~-off** *adj.* **~-on ~-off ship/ferry** Roll-on-roll-off-Schiff, *das*/-Fähre, *die;* **~over** *n.* (*von Auslosung zu Auslosung*) aufgestockter Jackpot; **~-top** *n.* Rollverschluss, *der;* **~-top desk** *n. Schreibtisch mit Rollverschluss;* **~-up** (*Brit. coll.*), **~-your-own** (*esp. Amer. coll.*) *ns.* Selbstgedrehte, *die*

**roly-poly** /rəʊlɪˈpəʊlɪ/ ❶ *n.* (A) **~ [pudding]** ≈ Strudel, *der;* (B) (*Amer.: toy*) Stehaufmännchen, *das.* ❷ *adj.* (*coll.*) kugelrund

**ROM** /rɒm/ *abbr.* (*Computing*) **read-only memory** ROM, *das*

**Roman** /ˈrəʊmən/ ❶ *n.* (A) ▶ 1626 Römer, *der*/Römerin, *die;* (B) **r~** (*Printing*) Antiqua, *die.* ❷ *adj.* (A) römisch; **~ road** Römerstraße, *die;* (B) ⇒ **Roman Catholic** 1. ⇒ *also* **snail**

**roman à clef** /rəʊmɑːn ɑː ˈkleɪ/ *n.* (*Lit.*) Schlüsselroman, *der*

**Roman: ~ ˈalphabet** *n.* lateinisches Alphabet; **~ ˈcandle** *n.* ≈ Goldregen, *der;* **~ ˈCatholic** ❶ *adj.* römisch-katholisch; ❷ *n.*

r

Katholik, *der*/Katholikin, *die;* **sb. is a ~ Catholic** jmd. ist römisch-katholisch; **~ Ca'tholicism** *n., no pl.* Katholizismus, *der*

**romance** /rəˈmæns/ ❶ *n.* **A** (*love affair*) Romanze, *die;* **B** (*love story*) [romantische] Liebesgeschichte; **C** (*romantic quality*) Romantik, *die;* **there was an air of ~ about the place** der Ort hatte etwas Romantisches; **D** (*Lit.*) (*medieval tale*) Romanze, *die;* (*improbable tale*) fantastische Geschichte; **E** (*make-believe*) Fantasterei, *die;* **F** (*Mus.*) Romanze, *die;* **G** **R~** (*Ling.*) Romanisch, *das.* ❷ *adj.* **R~** (*Ling.*) romanisch; **R~ languages and literature** (*subject*) Romanistik, *die.* ❸ *v.i.* fantasieren

**romancer** /rəʊˈmænsə(r)/ *n.* Fantast, *der* (*abwertend*)

**Roman 'Empire** *n.* (*Hist.*) Römisches Reich; **Holy ~:** Heiliges Römisches Reich [Deutscher Nation]

**Romanesque** /rəʊməˈnesk/ *n.* (*Art, Archit.*) Romanik, *die*

**Romania** /rəʊˈmeɪnɪə/ *pr. n.* Rumänien (*das*)

**Romanian** /rəʊˈmeɪnɪən/ ▶ 1275, ▶ 1340 ❶ *adj.* rumänisch; **sb. is ~:** jmd. ist Rumäne/Rumänin; ⇨ *also* **English** 1. ❷ *n.* **A** (*person*) Rumäne, *der*/Rumänin, *die;* **B** (*language*) Rumänisch, *das;* ⇨ *also* **English** 2 A

**romanize (romanise)** /ˈrəʊmənaɪz/ *v.t.* **A** (*Hist.*) romanisieren (*veralt.*); **B** (*Relig.*) katholisieren

**Roman: ~ law** *n.* römisches Recht; **~ 'nose** *n.* Römernase, *die;* **~ 'numeral** *n.* römische Ziffer

**Romansh** /rəˈmænʃ, rəˈmɑːnʃ/ ❶ *n.* Romantsch, *das.* ❷ *adj.* Romantsch-

**romantic** /rəʊˈmæntɪk/ ❶ *adj.* **A** (*emotional, fantastic*) romantisch; **~ fiction** (*love stories*) Liebesromane; **B** **R~** (*Lit., Art*) romantisch; der Romantik *nachgestellt.* ❷ *n.* **R~** (*Lit., Art, Mus.*) Romantiker, *der*/Romantikerin, *die*

**romantically** /rəʊˈmæntɪkəlɪ/ *adv.* romantisch

**Romanticism** /rəʊˈmæntɪsɪzm/ *n.* (*Lit., Art, Mus.*) Romantik, *die*

**Romanticist** /rəʊˈmæntɪsɪst/ *n.* (*Lit., Art, Mus.*) Romantiker, *der*

**romanticize** /rəʊˈmæntɪsaɪz/ *v.t.* romantisieren

**'roman type** *n.* (*Printing*) Antiquaschrift, *die*

**Romany** /ˈrəʊmənɪ/ ❶ *n.* **A** (*gypsy*) Rom, *der;* **the Romanies** die Roma; **B** ▶ 1275 (*language*) Romani, *das.* ❷ *adj.* **A** Roma-; **B** (*Ling.*) Romani-

**Rome** /rəʊm/ *pr. n.* ▶ 1626 Rom (*das*); **all roads lead to ~** (*prov.*) alle Wege führen nach Rom (*Spr.*); **~ was not built in a day** (*prov.*) Rom ist nicht an einem Tag erbaut worden (*Spr.*); **when in ~ do as the Romans [do]** man muss sich den örtlichen Gegebenheiten anpassen

**Romeo** /ˈrəʊmɪəʊ/ *n., pl.* **~s** Casanova, *der*

**romp** /rɒmp/ ❶ *v.i.* **A** [herum]tollen; **B** (*coll.: win, succeed, etc. easily*) **~ home** *or* **in** spielend gewinnen; **~ through sth.** etw. spielend schaffen; **~ along** dahinflitzen (*ugs.*). ❷ *n.* Tollerei, *die;* **have a ~** ⇨ **1** A

**rompers** /ˈrɒmpəz/ *n. pl.* Spielhöschen, *das*

**'romper suit** *n.* Spielanzug, *der*

**rondo** /ˈrɒndəʊ/ *n., pl.* **~s** (*Mus.*) Rondo, *das*

**roo** /ruː/ *n.* (*Austral. coll.*) Känguru, *das*

**rood** /ruːd/ *n.* (*crucifix*) Kruzifix, *das*

**rood: ~ loft** *n.* Empore des Lettners; **~ screen** *n.* Lettner, *der*

**roof** /ruːf/ ❶ *n.* **A** Dach, *das;* **under one ~:** unter einem Dach; **live under the same ~ [as sb.]** [mit jmdm.] unter einem Dach wohnen (*ugs.*); **have a ~ over one's head** ein Dach über dem Kopf haben; **go through the ~** ‹Preise:› krass in die Höhe steigen; **sb. goes through** *or* **hits the ~** (*fig. coll.*) jmd. geht an die Decke (*ugs.*); **raise the ~** (*fig. coll.: make much noise*) die Wände zum Beben bringen; **B** (*Anat.*) **~ of the mouth** Gaumen, *der.* ❷ *v.t.* bedachen; **~ in** *or* **over** überdachen

**'roof garden** *n.* Dachgarten, *der*

**roofing** /ˈruːfɪŋ/ *n.* **A** (*action*) Bedachung, *die;* **B** (*material for roof*) Deckung, *die*

**'roofing felt** *n.* Dachpappe, *die*

**roofless** /ˈruːflɪs/ *adj.* dachlos

**roof: ~ rack** *n.* Dachgepäckträger, *der;* **~ timbers** *n. pl.* Dachstuhl, *der;* **~top** *n.* Dach, *das;* **shout sth. from the ~tops** (*fig.*) etw. in die Welt hinausrufen

**rook**[1] /rʊk/ ❶ *n.* (*Ornith.*) Saatkrähe, *die.* ❷ *v.t.* **A** (*charge extortionately*) neppen (*ugs. abwertend*); **B** (*in gambling*) ausnehmen; **~ sb. of £10** jmdm. 10 Pfund abnehmen

**rook**[2] *n.* (*Chess*) Turm, *der*

**rookery** /ˈrʊkərɪ/ *n.* **A** Saatkrähenkolonie, *die;* **B** (*of penguins or seals*) Kolonie, *die*

**rookie** /ˈrʊkɪ/ *n.* **A** (*Mil. coll.*) Rekrut, *der;* **B** (*Amer.: new member etc.*) Neuling, *der*

**room** /ruːm, rʊm/ ❶ *n.* **A** (*in building*) Zimmer, *das;* (*esp. without furniture*) Raum, *der;* (*large ~, for function*) Saal, *der;* **leave the ~** (*coll.: go to lavatory*) austreten (*ugs.*); **B** *no pl., no indef. art.* (*space*) Platz, *der;* **we have no ~ for idlers** für Müßiggänger ist bei uns kein Platz; **give sb. ~:** jmdm. Platz machen; **give sb. ~ to do sth.** (*fig.*) jmdm. die Freiheit lassen, etw. zu tun; **~ and to spare** Platz genug; **make ~ [for sb./sth.]** [jmdm./einer Sache] Platz machen; **C** (*scope*) **there is no ~ for dispute/doubt about that** darüber kann es keine Diskussion/keinen Zweifel geben; **there is still ~ for improvement in his work** seine Arbeit ist noch verbesserungsfähig; **this did not leave us much ~ for manœuvre** das ließ uns wenig Spielraum; **D** *in pl.* (*apartments, lodgings*) Wohnung, *die;* '**~s to let**' „Zimmer zu vermieten"; **E** (*persons in a ~*) Raum, *der;* Zimmer, *das.* ⇨ *also* **cat** A.
❷ *v.i.* (*Amer.: lodge*) wohnen; **~ with sb.** (*be tenant of*) bei jmdm. wohnen; (*share with*) mit jmdm. zusammenwohnen

**'room divider** *n.* Raumteiler, *der*

**-roomed** /ruːmd, rʊmd/ *adj. in comb.* **a three-~ flat** eine Dreizimmerwohnung; **a one-~/four-~ building** ein Haus mit einem Zimmer/vier Zimmern

**roomette** /ruːˈmet, rʊˈmet/ *n.* (*Amer. Railw.*) Schlafwagenkabine, *die*

**roomful** /ˈruːmfʊl, ˈrʊmfʊl/ *n.* **a ~ of people** *etc.* ein Zimmer voll[er] Leute *usw.*

**rooming house** /ˈruːmɪŋhaʊs/ *n.* Pension, *die*

**room: ~-mate** *n.* Zimmergenosse, *der*/-genossin, *die;* Stubenkamerad, *der* (*Milit.*); **~ service** *n.* Zimmerservice, *der;* **~ temperature** *n.* Zimmertemperatur, *die*

**roomy** /ˈruːmɪ/ *adj.* geräumig

**roost** /ruːst/ ❶ *n.* Schlafplatz, *der;* (*perch*) [Sitz]stange, *die;* **come home to ~** (*fig.*) jmdm. heimgezahlt werden; ⇨ *also* **rule** 2 B. ❷ *v.i.* sich [zum Schlafen] niederlassen

**rooster** /ˈruːstə(r)/ *n.* (*Amer.*) Hahn, *der*

**root**[1] /ruːt/ ❶ *n.* **A** Wurzel, *die;* **pull sth. up by the ~/~s** etw. mit der Wurzel/den Wurzeln ausreißen; (*fig.*) etw. mit der Wurzel ausrotten; **put down ~s/strike** *or* **take ~** (*lit. or fig.*) Wurzeln schlagen; (*fig.*) **strike at the ~[s] of sth.** etw. in seinem Lebensnerv treffen; **have ~s** verwurzelt sein; **without ~s** wurzellos; **B** (*source*) Wurzel, *die;* (*basis*) Grundlage, *die;* **have its ~s in sth.** einer Sache (*Dat.*) entspringen; **get at** *or* **to the ~[s] of things** den Dingen auf den Grund kommen; **be at the ~ of the matter** der Kern der Sache sein; **the ~ cause** der wirkliche Grund; **C** (*Ling.*) Wurzel, *die;* **D** (*Mus.*) Grundton, *der;* **E** (*Math.: square ~*) [Quadrat]wurzel, *die* (**of** aus).
❷ *v.t.* **~ a plant firmly** eine Pflanze fest einpflanzen; **have ~ed itself in sth.** (*fig.*) in etw. (*Dat.*) verwurzelt sein; **stand ~ed to the spot** wie angewurzelt dastehen.
❸ *v.i.* ‹Pflanze:› wurzeln, anwachsen

**~ 'out** *v.t.* ausrotten; ausmerzen

**~ 'up** *v.t.* mit den Wurzeln ausreißen; ausroden ‹Baum[stumpf], Busch›

**root**[2] *v.i.* **A** (*turn up ground*) wühlen (**for** nach); **B** (*coll.*) **~ for** (*cheer*) anfeuern; (*wish for success of*) Stimmung machen für

**~ a'bout, ~ a'round** *v.i.* herumwühlen

**~ 'out** *v.t.* (*find by search*) zu Tage fördern

**root: ~ and 'branch** ❶ *adj.* radikal; ‹Reform› an Haupt und Gliedern; ❷ *adv.* radikal; an Haupt und Gliedern ‹reformieren›; **~ beer** *n.* (*Amer.*) Rootbeer, *das* (*schäumendes Getränk aus Wurzeln und Kräutern*); **~ crop[s]** *n.* [*pl.*] Hackfrüchte *Pl.*

**rooted** /ˈruːtɪd/ *adj.* eingewurzelt

**rootless** /ˈruːtlɪs/ *adj.* wurzellos

**root: ~ mean 'square** *n.* (*Math.*) quadratisches Mittel; **~ sign** ⇨ **radical sign** 2 B; **~stock** *n.* **A** (*rhizome*) Wurzelstock, *der;* **B** (*for grafting*) Unterlage, *die;* **~ vegetable** *n.* Wurzelgemüse, *das;* **~ word** *n.* (*Ling.*) Wurzelwort, *das*

**rope** /rəʊp/ ❶ *n.* **A** (*cord*) Seil, *das;* Tau, *das;* **~'s end** (*short piece*) Tauende, *das;* **B** (*Amer.: lasso*) Lasso, *das;* **C** (*for hanging sb.*) **the ~:** der Strang; (*fig.: death penalty*) die Todesstrafe; **D** *in pl.* (*Boxing*) **the ~s** die Seile; **be on the ~s** (*lit., or fig.: near defeat*) in den Seilen hängen; **E** *in pl.* **learn the ~s** lernen, sich zurechtzufinden; (*at work*) sich einarbeiten; **know the ~s** sich auskennen; **show sb. the ~s** jmdn. mit allem vertraut machen; **F** **give sb. some ~** (*fig.*) jmdm. eine gewisse Freiheit lassen; **give him enough ~ and he'll hang himself** (*fig.*) lass ihn alleine machen, dann schaufelt er sich sein eigenes Grab; **G** (*Mount.*) **on the ~:** am Seil.
❷ *v.t.* **A** festbinden; **~ sb. to a tree** jmdn. an einen Baum binden; **B** (*Mount.*) anseilen

**~ 'in** *v.t.* **A** mit einem Seil/mit Seilen absperren ‹Gebiet›; **B** (*fig.*) einspannen (*ugs.*); (*for membership*) anheuern (*ugs.*); **how did you get ~d in to that?** warum hast du dich dazu breitschlagen lassen? (*ugs.*)

**~ 'off** *v.t.* [mit einem Seil/mit Seilen] absperren

**~ to'gether** *v.t.* (*Mount.*) aneinander seilen

**rope: ~-dancer** *n.* Seiltänzer, *der*/-tänzerin, *die;* **~ 'ladder** *n.* Strickleiter, *die;* **~ 'sole** *n.* Kordelsohle, *die;* **~-walker** *n.* Seilakrobat, *der*/-akrobatin, *die;* **~way** *n.* Seilbahn, *die*

**ropy** /ˈrəʊpɪ/ *adj.* (*coll.*) (*poor*) schäbig; (*in a bad state*) mitgenommen; **be a bit ~:** nicht viel taugen; **you look a bit ~:** du siehst ziemlich kaputt aus

**Roquefort** /ˈrɒkfɔː(r)/ *n.* Roquefort, *der*

**ro-ro** /ˈrəʊrəʊ/ *adj.* Ro-Ro-‹Schiff, Fähre›

**rorqual** /ˈrɔːkwəl/ *n.* (*Zool.*) Finnwal, *der*

**Rorschach test** /ˈrɔːʃɑːk test/ *n.* (*Psych.*) Rorschachtest, *der*

**rosary** /ˈrəʊzərɪ/ *n.* (*Relig.*) Rosenkranz, *der*

**rose**[1] /rəʊz/ ❶ *n.* **A** (*plant, flower*) Rose, *die;* **~ of Jericho/Sharon** Jerichorose, *die*/Johanniskraut, *das;* **no bed of ~s** (*fig.*) kein Honigschlecken; **~s[, ~s,] all the way** (*fig.*) der Himmel auf Erden; **it's not all ~s** es ist nicht alles [so] rosig; **everything's [coming up] ~s** alles ist bestens; **[there's] no ~ without a thorn** (*prov.*) keine Rose ohne Dornen (*Spr.*); **Wars of the R~s** (*Brit. Hist.*) Rosenkriege *Pl.;* **~s in one's cheeks** rosige Wangen; **B** (*colour*) Rosa, *das;* **C** (*nozzle*) Brause, *die.*
❷ *adj.* rosa[farben]

**rose**[2] ⇨ **rise** 2

**rosé** /rəʊˈzeɪ, ˈrəʊzeɪ/ *n.* Rosé, *der*

**roseate** /ˈrəʊzɪət/ *adj.* rosenrot

**rose: ~ bed** *n.* Rosenbeet, *das;* **~bud** *n.* Rosenknospe, *die;* **~bud mouth** Kirschenmund, *der* (*dichter.*); **~ bush** *n.* Rosenstrauch, *der;* **~-coloured** *adj.* (*lit. or fig.*) rosarot; **see things through ~-coloured spectacles** die Dinge durch eine rosarote Brille sehen; **~fish** *n.* Rotbarsch, *der;* **~ garden** *n.* Rosengarten, *der;* **~ hip** *n.* (*Bot.*) Hagebutte, *die;* **~ hip tea** Hagebuttentee, *der;* **~ leaf** *n.* Rosenblatt, *das*

**rosemary** /ˈrəʊzmərɪ/ *n.* (*Bot.*) Rosmarin, *der*

**rose: ~ petal** *n.* Rosen[blüten]blatt, *das;* **~-pink** ❶ *adj.* rosarot; ❷ *n.* Rosarot, *das;* **~-red** ❶ *adj.* rosenrot; ❷ *n.* Rosenrot, *das;* **~-tinted** ⇨ **rose-coloured**; **~ tree** *n.* Rosenstock, *der*

**rosette** /rəʊ'zet/ *n.* Rosette, *die*

**rose:** ~ **water** *n.* Rosenwasser, *das;* ~ **window** *n.* (*Archit.*) Fensterrose, *die;* ~**wood** *n.* Rosenholz, *das*

**Rosicrucian** /rəʊzɪ'kru:ʃn/ ❶ *n.* Rosenkreuzer, *der*/-kreuzerin, *die.* ❷ *adj.* Rosenkreuzer-

**rosin** /'rɒzɪn/ *n.* Harz, *das;* (*for violin bow*) Kolophonium, *das*

**RoSPA** /'rɒspə/ *abbr.* (*Brit.*) **Royal Society for the Prevention of Accidents**

**roster** /'rɒstə(r)/ ❶ *n.* Dienstplan, *der.* ❷ *v.t.* einteilen ‹Arbeitskraft›; **call for flexible** ~**ing** flexible Dienstpläne fordern

**rostrum** /'rɒstrəm/ *n., pl.* **rostra** /'rɒstrə/ *or* ~**s** (*platform*) Podium, *das;* (*desk*) Rednerpult, *das*

**rosy** /'rəʊzɪ/ *adj.* Ⓐ rosig; Ⓑ (*fig.*) rosig ‹Zukunft, Aussichten›; **paint a** ~ **picture of sth.** etw. in den rosigsten Farben schildern

**rot** /rɒt/ ❶ *n.* Ⓐ ⇒ 2 A: Verrottung, *die;* Fäulnis, *die;* Verwesung, *die;* Vermoderung, *die;* (*rust*) Rost, *der;* (*fig.: deterioration*) Verfall, *der;* **stop the** ~ (*fig.*) dem Verfall Einhalt gebieten; **the** ~ **has set in** (*fig.*) der Verfall hat eingesetzt; ⇒ *also* **dry rot**; Ⓑ (*coll.: nonsense*) Quark, *der* (*salopp*); ~**!** Blödsinn! (*ugs.*).

❷ *v.i.*, **-tt-** Ⓐ (*decay*) verrotten; ‹Fleisch, Gemüse, Obst:› verfaulen; ‹Leiche:› verwesen; ‹Metall:› verrosten; ‹Laub:› vermodern, verrotten; ‹Holz:› faulen; ‹Zähne:› schlecht werden; Ⓑ (*fig.: go to ruin*) verrotten; **leave sb. to** ~**:** jmdn. verrotten lassen (*ugs.*).

❸ *v.t.*, **-tt-** Ⓐ (*make rotten*) verrotten lassen; verfaulen lassen ‹Fleisch, Gemüse, Obst›; vermodern *od.* verrotten lassen ‹Laub›; faulen lassen ‹Holz›; verwesen lassen ‹Leiche›; zerstören ‹Zähne›; **that stuff will** ~ **your guts** (*coll.*) das Zeug bringt dich um (*ugs.*); Ⓑ (*Brit. coll.: tease*) aufziehen (*ugs.*)

~ **a'way** *v.i.* verfaulen; ‹Leiche:› verwesen; ‹Holz:› faulen; (*moulder away*) vermodern

**rota** /'rəʊtə/ *n.* (*Brit.*) Ⓐ (*order of rotation*) Turnus, *der;* **draw up the cleaning** ~**:** den Putzplan aufstellen; **she has a regular** ~ **of visitors** sie bekommt in regelmäßigem Turnus Besuch; Ⓑ (*list of persons*) [Arbeits]plan, *der*

**Rotarian** /rəʊ'teərɪən/ ❶ *n.* Rotarier, *der.* ❷ *adj.* rotarisch; Rotarier-

**rotary** /'rəʊtərɪ/ ❶ *adj.* Ⓐ (*acting by rotation*) rotierend; Rotations-; ~ **engine** Drehkolbenmotor, *der;* ~ **press** (*Printing*) Rotationsmaschine, *die;* ~ **pump** Kreiselpumpe, *die;* ~ **mower** Rasenmäher mit rotierenden Messern; Ⓑ **R**~**:** Rotarier-; **R**~ **Club** Rotary-Club, *der.* ❷ *n.* Ⓐ **The R**~, **R**~ **International** der Rotary-Club; Rotary International; Ⓑ (*Amer.: roundabout*) Verkehrskreisel, *der*

**rotate** /rəʊ'teɪt/ ❶ *v.i.* Ⓐ (*revolve*) rotieren; sich drehen; ~ **on an axis** sich um eine Achse drehen; Ⓑ (*alternate*) **these posts** ~ **regularly** diese Stellen werden in einem regelmäßigen Turnus neu besetzt. ❷ *v.t.* Ⓐ (*cause to revolve*) in Rotation versetzen; Ⓑ (*alternate*) abwechselnd erledigen ‹Aufgaben›; abwechselnd erfüllen ‹Pflichten›; ~ **[the] crops** Fruchtwechselwirtschaft betreiben; **change the way one** ~**s the crops** die Fruchtfolge ändern

**rotation** /rəʊ'teɪʃn/ *n.* Ⓐ Rotation, *die,* Drehung, *die* (**about** um); Ⓑ (*succession*) turnusmäßiger Wechsel; (*in political office*) Rotation, *die;* ~ **of crops** Fruchtfolge, *die;* **the** ~ **of the seasons** der Wechsel der Jahreszeiten; **by** ~**:** im Turnus; ~ **in office** turnusmäßiger Amtswechsel; **take office in** *or* **by** ~**:** ein Amt nach dem Rotationsprinzip ausüben

**rotatory** /'rəʊtətərɪ/ *adj.* Dreh-; drehend

**rotavate** /'rəʊtəveɪt/ *v.t.* mit der Fräse bearbeiten ‹Boden›

**Rotavator** ® /'rəʊtəveɪtə(r)/ *n.* [Boden]fräse, *die*

**rote** /rəʊt/ *n.* **by** ~**:** auswendig ‹lernen, aufsagen›; **teach sth. by** ~**:** etw. durch Auswendiglernen einüben

**'rote-learning** *n.* Auswendiglernen, *das*

**'rotgut** (*coll.*) ❶ *n.* Fusel, *der* (*ugs., abwertend*). ❷ *adj.* fuselig

**rotisserie** /rəʊ'tɪsərɪ/ *n.* Ⓐ (*restaurant*) Rotisserie, *die;* Ⓑ (*appliance*) Grill, *der*

**rotor** /'rəʊtə(r)/ *n.* Rotor, *der* (*Technik*)

**rotten** /'rɒtn/ ❶ *adj.*, ~**er** /'rɒtənə(r)/, ~**est** /'rɒtənɪst/ Ⓐ (*decayed*) verrottet; verwest ‹Leiche›; vermodert, verrottet ‹Laub, Holz›; verfault ‹Obst, Gemüse, Fleisch›; faul ‹Ei, Zähne›; (*rusted*) verrostet; ~ **to the core** (*fig.*) verdorben bis ins Mark; völlig verrottet ‹System, Gesellschaft›; Ⓑ (*corrupt*) verdorben; verkommen; Ⓒ (*coll.: bad*) mies (*ugs.*); **feel** ~ (*ill*) sich mies fühlen (*ugs.*); (*have a bad conscience*) ein schlechtes Gewissen haben; **it's a** ~ **shame** so ein Mist (*ugs.*); ~ **luck** saumäßiges Pech (*salopp*).

❷ *adv.* (*coll.*) saumäßig (*salopp*); **hurt/stink something** ~**:** saumäßig wehtun/stinken (*salopp*); **spoilt** ~**:** ganz schön verwöhnt (*ugs.*)

**rottenly** /'rɒtnlɪ/ *adv.* (*coll.*) saumäßig (*salopp*)

**rotter** /'rɒtə(r)/ *n.* (*coll.*) mieser Typ (*salopp abwertend*); Halunke, *der*

**rotund** /rəʊ'tʌnd/ *adj.* Ⓐ (*round*) rund; Ⓑ (*plump*) rundlich

**rotunda** /rə'tʌndə/ *n.* Rotunde, *die* (*Archit.*)

**rotundity** /rəʊ'tʌndɪtɪ/ *n., no pl.* Ⓐ (*roundness*) Rundheit, *die;* Ⓑ (*plumpness*) Rundlichkeit, *die*

**rouble** /'ru:bl/ *n.* ▶ **1328** Rubel, *der*

**roué** /'ru:eɪ/ *n.* Roué, *der* (*veralt.*)

**rouge** /ru:ʒ/ ❶ *n.* Ⓐ (*cosmetic powder*) Rouge, *das;* Ⓑ (*polishing agent*) Englischrot, *das;* ⇒ *also* **jeweller**. ❷ *v.t.* ~ **one's cheeks** *or* **face** Rouge auflegen

**rough** /rʌf/ ❶ *adj.* Ⓐ (*coarse, uneven*) rau; holp[e]rig ‹Straße usw.›; uneben ‹Gelände›; aufgewühlt ‹Wasser›; unruhig ‹Überfahrt›; (*shaggy*) haarig ‹Lebewesen›; stopp[e]lig ‹Bart›; Ⓑ (*violent*) rau, roh, grob (*abwertend*) ‹Person, Worte, Behandlung, Benehmen›; rau ‹Gegend›; **the** ~ **element [of the population]** die Rowdys [unter der Bevölkerung]; **the remedy was** ~ **but effective** die Behandlung war eine Rosskur, aber sie hat gewirkt; Ⓒ (*harsh to the senses*) rau; kratzig ‹Geschmack, Getränk›; sauer ‹Apfelwein›; Ⓓ (*trying*) hart; **this is** ~ **on him** das ist hart für ihn; **sth. is** ~ **going** etw. ist nicht einfach; **have a** ~ **time** es schwer haben; **give sb. a** ~ **time** es jmdm. schwer machen; **have a** ~ **tongue** einen rauen Ton am Leibe haben (*ugs.*); ⇒ *also* **edge** 1 A; Ⓔ (*fig.: lacking finish, polish*) derb; rau ‹Empfang›; unbeholfen ‹Stil›; ungeschliffen ‹Benehmen, Sprache›; Ⓕ (*rudimentary*) primitiv ‹Unterkunft, Leben›; (*approximate*) grob ‹Skizze, Schätzung, Einteilung, Übersetzung›; vag ‹Vorstellung›; ~ **notes** stichwortartige Notizen; ~ **attempt** erster Versuch; ~ **draft** Rohentwurf, *der;* **in a somewhat** ~ **state** in einem einigermaßen unfertigen Zustand; **a** ~ **circle** ein ungefährer Kreis; ~ **paper/notebook** Konzeptpapier, *das*/Kladde, *die;* Ⓖ (*coll.: ill*) angeschlagen (*ugs.*). ⇒ *also* **deal**[1] 3 A.

❷ *n.* Ⓐ (*hooligan*) Schläger, *der* (*abwertend*); Rowdy, *der* (*abwertend*); Ⓑ (*Golf*) Rough, *das;* Ⓒ **take the** ~ **with the smooth** die Dinge nehmen, wie sie kommen; Ⓓ (*unfinished state*) **[be] in** ~**:** [sich] im Rohzustand [befinden].

❸ *adv.* rau ‹spielen›; scharf ‹reiten›; **sleep** ~**:** im Freien schlafen.

❹ *v.t.* ~ **it** primitiv leben; **he had to** ~ **it for a while** er musste eine Zeit lang auf den gewohnten Komfort verzichten

~ **'in** *v.t.* skizzenhaft einzeichnen; [mit wenigen Strichen] andeuten

~ **'out** *v.t.* [grob] entwerfen

~ **'up** *v.t.* Ⓐ (*coll.: deal roughly with*) zusammenschlagen; Ⓑ (*ruffle*) gegen den Strich streichen ‹Haare›

**roughage** /'rʌfɪdʒ/ *n.* Ⓐ (*for people*) Ballaststoffe *Pl.* (*Med.*); Ⓑ (*for animals*) Raufutter, *das* (*Landw.*)

**rough:** ~**-and-ready** *adj.* Ⓐ (*not elaborate*) provisorisch; skizzenhaft ‹Beschreibung›; behelfsmäßig ‹Hütte, Methode›; grob ‹Schätzung›; **a** ~**-and-ready method for calculating sth.** eine Faustformel für die Berechnung von etw.; Ⓑ (*not refined*) raubeinig (*ugs.*) ‹Person›; ~ **and 'tumble** ❶ *adj.* wild; turbulent ‹Atmosphäre›; ❷ *n.* [wildes] Handgemenge; [wilde] Rauferei; (*fig.: turbulent life*) Catch-as-catch-can, *das* (*ugs. abwertend*); ~**cast** (*Building*) ❶ *adj.* mit Grobmörtel verputzt; ❷ *n.* Grobmörtel, *der;* ❸ *v.t.* mit Grobmörtel verputzen; ~ **'copy** *n.* Ⓐ (*original draft*) [erster] Entwurf; Konzept, *das;* Ⓑ (*simplified copy*) grobe Skizze; ~ **'diamond** *n.* (*fig.*) ungehobelter, aber guter Mensch; **he's a** ~ **diamond** er ist rau, aber herzlich; ~**-dry** *v.t.* [nur] trocknen ‹Wäsche›; ~ **'edges** *n. pl.* (*in book*) unbeschnittene Kanten; **he has a few** ~ **edges** (*fig.*) er ist ein wenig ungeschliffen

**roughen** /'rʌfn/ ❶ *v.t.* aufrauhen ‹Oberfläche›; rau machen ‹Hände›. ❷ *v.i.* rau werden

**rough:** ~ **'grazing** *n.* (*Brit.*) natürliche Weide; ~ **house** *n.* (*coll.*) Keilerei, *die* (*ugs.*); ~ **'justice** *n.* ziemlich willkürliche Urteile; ~ **'luck** *n.* Pech, *das*

**roughly** /'rʌflɪ/ *adv.* Ⓐ (*violently*) roh; grob; Ⓑ (*crudely*) leidlich; grob ‹skizzieren, bearbeiten, bauen›; Ⓒ (*approximately*) ungefähr; grob ‹geschätzt›; ⇒ *also* **speaking** 2

**'roughneck** *n.* (*coll.*) Ⓐ (*Amer.: rowdy*) Raufbold, *der* (*abwertend*); Ⓑ (*driller on oil rig*) Bohrarbeiter, *der*

**roughness** /'rʌfnɪs/ *n.* Ⓐ *no pl.* Rauheit, *die;* (*unevenness*) Unebenheit, *die;* Ⓑ *no pl.* (*sharpness*) (*of wine, fruit juice*) Säure, *die;* (*of voice*) Rauheit, *die;* Ⓒ *no pl.* (*violence*) Rohheit, *die;* **the** ~ **of the area** die Häufigkeit von Gewalttaten in der Gegend; Ⓓ (*rough place or part*) unausgefeilte Stelle

**rough:** ~ **'passage** *n.* Ⓐ (*Naut.*) raue [Über]fahrt; Ⓑ (*fig.*) **get a** ~ **passage** ‹Gesetzentwurf:› nur mit Mühe durchkommen; **the interview board gave him a** ~ **passage** die Prüfungskommission hat es ihm nicht leicht gemacht; ~ **'ride** ⇒ **ride** 1 B; ~**-rider** *n.* Ⓐ (*horsebreaker*) Zureiter, *der;* Ⓑ (*Mil.*) irregulärer Kavallerist; ~**shod** *adj.* **ride** ~**shod over sb./sth.** jmdn./etw. mit Füßen treten; ~ **stuff** *n.* (*coll.*) Zoff, *der* (*salopp*); ~ **'work** *n.* Ⓐ (*needing force*) Knochenarbeit, *die* (*ugs.*); Ⓑ (*preliminary*) Vorbereitungsarbeit, *die*

**roulette** /ru:'let/ *n.* Roulette, *das*

**Roumania** /ru'meɪnɪə/ ⇒ **Romania**

**Roumanian** /ru'meɪnɪən/ ⇒ **Romanian**

**round** /raʊnd/ ❶ *adj.* Ⓐ rund; rundlich ‹Arme›; ~ **cheeks** Pausbacken *Pl.* (*fam.*); **in** ~ **figures, it will cost £1,000** rund gerechnet wird es 1 000 Pfund kosten; **a** ~ **dozen** ein volles *od.* ganzes Dutzend; Ⓑ (*plain*) **in the** ~**est manner, in** ~ **terms** ohne Umschweife; rundheraus; Ⓒ (*considerable*) stattlich ‹Summe, Preis›; **a good** ~ **sum** eine hübsche Summe; Ⓓ (*semicircular*) ~ **arch** Rundbogen, *der;* Ⓔ (*Phonet.*) gerundet; Ⓕ (*full-toned and mellow*) voll ‹Ton›; volltönend ‹Stimme›.

❷ *n.* Ⓐ (*recurring series*) Serie, *die;* ~ **of talks/negotiations** Gesprächs-/Verhandlungsrunde, *die;* **the daily** ~**:** der Alltag; **the daily** ~ **of chores** die täglichen Pflichten; Ⓑ (*charge of ammunition*) Ladung, *die;* **50** ~**s [of ammunition]** 50 Schuss Munition; **put five** ~**s in a magazine** fünf Kugeln in ein Magazin stecken; **fire five** ~**s** fünf Schüsse abfeuern; Ⓒ (*division of game or contest*) Runde, *die;* Ⓓ (*burst*) ~ **of applause** Beifallssturm, *der;* ~**s of cheers** Hochrufe; Ⓔ ~ **[of drinks]** Runde, *die;* Ⓕ (*regular calls*) Runde, *die;* Tour, *die;* **be on sb.'s** ~**:** auf jmds. Tour liegen; **the doctor is on her** ~ **at present** Frau Doktor macht gerade Hausbesuche; **go [on]** *or* **make one's** ~**s** ‹Posten, Wächter usw.:› seine Runde machen *od.* gehen; ‹Krankenhausarzt:› Visite machen; **make the** ~ **of the wards** Visite machen; **do** *or* **go the** ~**s** ‹Person, Gerücht usw.:› die Runde machen (*ugs.*); **do the** ~**s of all the second-hand shops/one's relatives** alle Gebrauchtwarenläden/seine Verwandtschaft abklappern (*ugs.*); **she is certainly doing the** ~**s** (*is promiscuous*) sie macht bei den Männern die Runde (*ugs.*); Ⓖ (*Golf*) Runde,

r

*die;* **a ∼ of golf** eine Runde Golf; Ⓗ (*Mus.*) Round, *der* (*fachspr.*); einfacher Zirkelkanon; Ⓘ (*slice*) **a ∼ of bread/toast** eine Scheibe Brot/Toast; **a ∼ of cucumber sandwiches** ein Gurkensandwich (*in 2 od. 4 Stücke geschnitten*); Ⓙ **in the ∼** *postpos.* (*Art*) als Vollplastik; vollplastisch; (*fig.: as a whole*) ganzheitlich; **theatre in the ∼:** Arenabühne, *die;* Rundtheater, *das;* Ⓚ (*Archery*) Runde, *die.*

❸ *adv.* Ⓐ **all the year ∼:** das ganze Jahr hindurch; **the third time ∼:** beim dritten Mal; **have a wall all ∼:** von einer Mauer eingeschlossen sein; **have a look ∼:** sich umsehen; Ⓑ (*in girth*) **be [all of] ten feet ∼:** einen Umfang von [mindestens] zehn Fuß haben; Ⓒ (*from one point, place, person, etc. to another*) **tea was handed ∼:** es wurde Tee herumgereicht; **he asked ∼ among his friends** er fragte seine Freunde; **the room was hung ∼ with portraits** in dem Zimmer hingen ringsum Portraits; **for a mile ∼:** im Umkreis einer Meile; Ⓓ (*by indirect way*) herum; **walk ∼:** außen herum gehen; **go a/the long way ∼:** einen weiten Umweg machen; Ⓔ (*here*) hier; (*there*) dort; **I'll go ∼ tomorrow** ich gehe morgen hin; **call ∼ any time!** kommen Sie doch jederzeit vorbei!; **ask sb. ∼ [for a drink]** jmdn. [zu einem Gläschen zu sich] einladen; **order a car** *etc.* **∼:** nach einem Wagen *usw.* schicken; **send a car ∼:** einen Wagen vorbeischicken; ⇒ *also* **clock** 1 A.

❹ *prep.* Ⓐ um [... herum]; **a tour ∼ the world** eine Weltreise; **travel ∼ England** durch England reisen; **she had a blanket ∼ her** sie hatte eine Decke um sich geschlungen; **the box had a band ∼ it** um die Schachtel war ein Band gebunden; **right ∼ the lake** um den ganzen See herum; **be ∼ the back of the house** hinter dem Haus sein; **run ∼ the back of the house** hinten ums Haus rennen; (*to position there*) hinter das Haus rennen; **run ∼ the streets** durch die Straßen rennen; **walk** *etc.* **∼ and ∼ sth.** immer wieder um etw. herumgehen *usw.;* **she ran ∼ and ∼ the park** sie lief Runde um Runde durch den Park; Ⓑ (*with successive visits to*) **he hawks them ∼ the cafés** er hausiert mit ihnen in den Cafés; **he sings ∼ the pubs** er singt in den Kneipen; **we looked ∼ the shops** wir sahen uns in den Geschäften um; Ⓒ (*in various directions from*) um [... herum]; rund um ‹einen Ort›; **look ∼ one** um sich schauen; **in Chelsea and ∼ it** in und um Chelsea; **do you live ∼ here?** wohnst du [hier] in der Nähe?; **if you're ever ∼ this way** wenn du hier in der Nähe bist; Ⓓ **argue ∼ and ∼ a matter/problem** *etc.* um eine Sache/ein Problem *usw.* herumreden (*ugs.*).

❺ *v.t.* Ⓐ (*give ∼ shape to*) rund machen; runden ‹Lippen, Rücken›; Ⓑ (*state as ∼ number*) runden (**to** auf + *Akk.*); Ⓒ (*go ∼*) umfahren/umgehen *usw.;* **∼ a turn/bend** um eine Kurve fahren/gehen/kommen *usw.;* **∼ a cape** um ein Kap fahren; Ⓓ (*Phonet.*) mit Rundung der Lippen sprechen; labialisieren (*Sprachw.*)

**∼ 'down** *v.t.* abrunden ‹Zahl› (**to** auf + *Akk.*)

**∼ 'off** *v.t.* (*also fig.: complete*) abrunden

**∼ on** *v.t.* anfahren

**∼ 'out** *v.t.* vervollständigen

**∼ 'up** *v.t.* Ⓐ (*gather, collect together*) verhaften ‹Verdächtige›; zusammentreiben ‹Vieh›; beschaffen, (*ugs.*) auftreiben ‹Geld›; ⇒ *also* **round-up**; Ⓑ (*to ∼ figure*) aufrunden (**to** auf + *Akk.*)

**round: ∼ a'bout** ❶ *adv.* Ⓐ (*on all sides*) ringsum; **the villages ∼ about** die umliegenden Dörfer; Ⓑ (*indirectly*) auf Umwegen; Ⓒ (*approximately*) rund; **∼ about 2,500 people** um die *od.* rund 2 500 Leute; ❷ *prep.* rund um; **∼about** ❶ *n.* Ⓐ (*Brit.: road junction*) Verkehrskreisel, *der;* Ⓑ (*Brit.: merry-go-round*) Karussell, *das;* **what you lose on the swings you gain on the ∼abouts** (*prov.*) was man auf der einen Seite verliert, gewinnt man auf der anderen; **it is swings and ∼abouts** es gleicht sich aus; ❷ *adj.* Ⓐ (*meandering*) **a [very] ∼about way** *or* **road** *or* **route** *etc.* ein [sehr] umständlicher Weg; **∼about journey** Reise mit Umwegen; **the taxi took us/went a ∼ about way** das Taxi brachte uns auf einem Umweg zum Ziel/machte einen Umweg; Ⓑ (*fig.: indirect*) umständlich; **a more ∼about method** eine weniger direkte Methode; **∼ 'brackets** *n. pl.* runde Klammern; **∼ dance** *n.* Rundtanz, *der*

**rounded** /'raʊndɪd/ *adj.* Ⓐ rund; abgerundet ‹Kante›; Ⓑ (*perfected*) abgerundet; harmonisch ‹Person›; Ⓒ (*fig.: polished*) ausgefeilt; Ⓓ (*sonorous*) voll

**roundel** /'raʊndl/ *n.* Ⓐ (*disc*) [kleine runde] Scheibe; Ⓑ (*mark*) Kreiszeichen, *das*

**roundelay** /'raʊndɪleɪ/ *n.* (*Mus.*) einfaches Liedchen mit Refrain

**rounders** /'raʊndəz/ *n. sing.* (*Brit.*) Rounders, *das;* Rundball, *das* (*dem Baseball ähnliches Spiel*)

**round: ∼-eyed** *adj.* mit großen Augen *nachgestellt;* **be ∼-eyed with amazement** große Augen machen; **∼-faced** *adj.* pausbäckig (*fam.*); **∼ game** *n. Spiel für beliebig viele Mitspieler, bei dem jeder gegen jeden spielt;* **R∼head** *n.* (*Brit. Hist.*) Rundkopf, *der*

**roundly** /'raʊndlɪ/ *adv.* entschieden

**'round-neck** *adj.* ‹Pullover, Bluse usw.› mit rundem Halsausschnitt

**roundness** /'raʊndnɪs/ *n., no pl.* Rundheit, *die;* (*of figure*) Rundlichkeit, *die*

**round: ∼ 'number** *n.* runde Zahl; **∼ 'robin** *n.* Ⓐ (*petition*) Petition, *die* (*mit kreisförmig angeordneten Unterschriften*); Ⓑ (*Amer.: tournament*) Round-Robin-Turnier, *das* (*Sport*); **∼-'shouldered** *adj.* ‹Person› mit einem Rundrücken; **be ∼-shouldered** einen Rundrücken haben

**roundsman** /'raʊndzmən/ *n., pl.* **roundsmen** /'raʊndzmən/ Ⓐ (*Brit.*) Austräger, *der;* **milk ∼:** Milchmann, *der* (*ugs.*); Ⓑ (*Amer.: police officer*) ≈ Polizeimeister, *der*

**round: R∼ 'Table** *n.* runde Tafel des Königs Artus; **[King Arthur and the] Knights of the R∼ Table** [König Artus und die] Ritter der Tafelrunde; **∼-table 'conference** *n.* Roundtablekonferenz, *die;* **∼-the-'clock** *adj.* rund um die Uhr *nachgestellt;* ⇒ *also* **clock** 1 A; **∼-the-world** *attrib. adj.* **∼-the-world flight/cruise** *etc.* Flug/Kreuzfahrt *usw.* um die [ganze] Welt; **∼-the-world voyage/trip** Weltreise, *die;* **∼-the-world yachtsman/yachtswoman** Weltumsegler, *der*/Weltumseglerin, *die;* **∼ 'trip** *n.* Ⓐ Rundreise, *die;* Ⓑ (*Amer.: return trip*) Hin- und Rückfahrt, *die;* **the ∼ trip to the island** die Fahrt zu der Insel und zurück; *attrib.* **∼-trip ticket** Rückfahrkarte, *die;* **∼-up** *n.* Ⓐ (*gathering-in*) (*of persons*) Einfangen, *das;* (*arrest*) Verhaftung, *die;* (*of animals*) Zusammentreiben, *das;* Ⓑ (*summary*) Zusammenfassung, *die;* **∼worm** *n.* (*Zool., Med.*) Spulwurm, *der*

**rouse** /raʊz/ ❶ *v.t.* Ⓐ (*awaken, lit. or fig.*) wecken (**from** aus); **∼ oneself** aufwachen; (*overcome indolence*) sich aufraffen; **∼ sb./oneself to action** jmdn. zur Tat anstacheln/sich zur Tat aufraffen; Ⓑ (*provoke*) reizen; **he is terrible when ∼d** er ist furchtbar, wenn man ihn reizt; **∼ sb. to anger** jmdn. in Wut bringen; Ⓒ (*cause*) wecken; hervorrufen, auslösen ‹Empörung, Beschuldigungen›; Ⓓ (*startle from cover*) aufscheuchen. ❷ *v.i.* **∼ [up]** aufwachen

**rousing** /'raʊzɪŋ/ *adj.* mitreißend ‹Lied›; leidenschaftlich ‹Rede›; stürmisch ‹Beifall›

**roustabout** /'raʊstəbaʊt/ *n.* Ⓐ (*Amer.: labourer*) Hilfsarbeiter, *der;* Handlanger, *der;* (*dockhand*) Schauermann, *der;* Ⓑ (*labourer on oil rig*) Bohrarbeiter, *der*

**rout**[1] /raʊt/ ❶ *n.* (*disorderly retreat*) [wilde] Flucht; (*disastrous defeat*) verheerende Niederlage; **put to ∼:** in die Flucht schlagen; (*arch., Law: mob*) Horde, *die.* ❷ *v.t.* aufreiben ‹Feind, Truppen›; vernichtend schlagen ‹Gegner›

**rout**[2] *v.i.* (*root*) wühlen

**∼ 'out** *v.t.* herausjagen; **∼ sb. out of sth.** jmdn. aus etw. jagen

**route** /ru:t, *Mil. also:* raʊt/ ❶ *n.* Ⓐ (*course*) Route, *die;* Weg, *der;* **a [very] circuitous ∼** (*lit. or fig.*) ein [großer] Umweg; **shipping ∼:** Schifffahrtsstraße, *die;* **bus/air ∼:** Bus-/Fluglinie, *die;* Ⓑ (*Amer.: delivery round*) Bezirk, *der.* ❷ *v.t.,* **∼ing** fahren lassen ‹Fahrzeug›; führen ‹Linie›; **the train is ∼d through** *or* **via Crewe** der Zug fährt über Crewe

**route: ∼man** /'ru:tmən/ *n., pl.* **∼men** /'ru:tmən/ (*Amer.*) (*delivery-man*) Austräger, *der;* (*salesman*) Vertreter, *der;* **∼ march** *n.* (*Mil.*) Übungsmarsch, *der*

**router** /'raʊtə(r)/ *n.* (*tool*) Nuthobel, *der*

**routine** /ru:'ti:n/ ❶ *n.* Ⓐ (*regular procedure*) Routine, *die;* **strict ∼s must be kept to** ein genau festgelegter Ablauf muss eingehalten werden; **creature of ∼:** Gewohnheitsmensch, *der;* **establish a new ∼ after retirement** nach der Pensionierung einen neuen Lebensrhythmus finden; Ⓑ (*coll.*) (*set speech*) Platte, *die* (*ugs.*); (*formula*) Spruch, *der;* Ⓒ (*Theatre*) Nummer, *die;* (*Dancing, Skating*) Figur, *die;* (*Gymnastics*) Übung, *die;* Ⓓ (*Computing*) Routine, *die.* ❷ *adj.* routinemäßig; Routine‹arbeit, -untersuchung usw.›; **the investigation was purely ∼:** die Untersuchung verlief absolut routinemäßig

**routinely** /ru:'ti:nlɪ/ *adv.* routinemäßig

**roux** /ru:/ *n., pl. same* (*Cookery*) Mehlschwitze, *die*

**rove**[1] /rəʊv/ ❶ *v.i.* ziehen; ‹Blick:› schweifen (*geh.*); **∼ [about]** herumziehen. ❷ *v.t.* streifen durch; durchstreifen (*geh.*); ‹Blick:› durchschweifen ‹Raum›

**rove**[2] ⇒ **reeve**

**rover**[1] /'rəʊvə(r)/ *n.* (*wanderer*) Vagabund, *der* (*veralt.*); **R∼ Scout** (*Hist.*) Rover, *der*

**rover**[2] *n.* (*pirate*) Pirat, *der*

**roving**/'rəʊvɪŋ/: **∼ com'mission** *n.* Reiseauftrag, *der;* **have a ∼ commission** einen Aufgabenbereich haben, bei dem man viel herumkommt; **∼ 'eye** *n.* **have a ∼ eye** den Frauen/Männern schöne Augen machen

**row**[1] /raʊ/ (*coll.*) ❶ *n.* Ⓐ (*noise*) Krach, *der;* **make a ∼:** Krach machen; (*protest*) Rabatz machen (*ugs.*); Ⓑ (*quarrel*) Krach, *der* (*ugs.*); **have/start a ∼:** Krach haben/anfangen (*ugs.*); **they're always having** *or* **they keep having ∼s** sie streiten dauernd; sie haben ständig Krach (*ugs.*); Ⓒ **get into a ∼ over sth.** (*be reprimanded*) wegen etw. Ärger kriegen (*ugs.*). ❷ *v.i.* sich streiten

**row**[2] /rəʊ/ *n.* Ⓐ Reihe, *die;* **in a ∼:** in einer Reihe; (*coll.: in succession*) nacheinander; hintereinander; Ⓑ (*line of numbers etc.*) Zeile, *die;* Ⓒ (*terrace*) **∼ [of houses]** [Häuser]zeile, *die;* [Häuser]reihe, *die*

**row**[3] /rəʊ/ ❶ *v.i.* (*move boat with oars etc.*) rudern; **∼ out/back** hinaus-/zurückrudern. ❷ *v.t.* rudern; **∼ sb. across** jmdn. hinüberrudern. ❸ *n.* **go for a ∼:** rudern gehen; **after a long ∼:** nach langem Rudern

**rowan** /'rəʊən, 'raʊən/ ⇒ **rowan-tree**

**rowan: ∼ berry** *n.* Vogelbeere, *die;* **∼ tree** *n.* Ⓐ (*Scot., N.Engl.*) Eberesche, *die;* Ⓑ (*Amer.*) amerikanische Eberesche

**rowboat** /'rəʊbəʊt/ *n.* Ruderboot, *das*

**rowdiness** /'raʊdɪnɪs/ *n., no pl.* Rabaukenhaftigkeit, *die;* (*behaviour*) rabaukenhaftes Benehmen

**rowdy** /'raʊdɪ/ ❶ *adj.* rowdyhaft (*abwertend*); **∼ adolescents** jugendliche Rowdys (*abwertend*); **the ∼ element in the audience** die Rüpel (*abwertend*) unter den Zuhörern; **∼ scenes** tumultartige Szenen; **the party was ∼:** auf der Party ging es laut zu. ❷ *n.* Krawallmacher, *der;* Rabauke, *der*

**rowdyism** /'raʊdɪɪzm/ *n., no pl.* Rabaukentum, *das* (*abwertend*)

**rower** /'rəʊə(r)/ *n.* Ruderer, *der*/Ruderin, *die;* **be a ∼:** rudern

**row house** /'rəʊhaʊs/ *n.* (*Amer.*) Reihenhaus, *das*

**rowing** /'rəʊɪŋ/ *n., no pl.* Rudern, *das;* **do a lot of/like ∼:** viel/gern rudern

**rowing: ∼ boat** *n.* (*Brit.*) Ruderboot, *das;* **∼ club** *n.* Ruderklub, *der;* **∼ machine** *n.* Rudergerät, *das*

**rowlock** /ˈrɒlək/ *n.* (*Brit.*) Dolle, *die*

**royal** /ˈrɔɪəl/ ❶ *adj.* königlich; **the ~ plural** der Pluralis majestatis; ⇒ *also* **academy** A; **assent** 2; **blood** 1 C; **commission** 1 D; **duke** A; **Highness; regiment** 1 B; **right** 4 G; **tennis; we.** ❷ *n.* (*coll.*) Mitglied der Königsfamilie; **the ~s** die Königsfamilie

**royal: R~ 'Air Force** *n.* (*Brit.*) Königliche Luftwaffe; **~ 'blue** *n.* (*Brit.*) Königsblau, *das;* **~ 'burgh** *n.* (*in Schottland*) grafschaftsfreie Stadt; **R~ Engi'neers** *n. pl. Pioniertruppe der britischen Armee;* **~ 'family** *n.* königliche Familie; **~ 'icing** *n.* (*Cookery*) Zuckerguss, *der*

**royalism** /ˈrɔɪəlɪzm/ *n.* Royalismus, *der*

**royalist** /ˈrɔɪəlɪst/ *n.* Royalist, *der*/Royalistin, *die; attrib.* Royalisten-; royalistisch

**royal 'jelly** *n.* Gelée royale, *das*

**royally** /ˈrɔɪəlɪ/ *adv.* königlich

**royal: R~ Ma'rine** *n.* (*Brit.*) *britischer Marineinfanterist;* **R~ 'Navy** *n.* (*Brit.*) Königliche Kriegsmarine; **~ 'oak** *n. Eichenzweig, der zum Gedenken der Wiedereinsetzung Charles II. als König getragen wird;* **~ stag** *n.* (*Hunting*) Kapitalhirsch, *der;* **~ 'standard** *n.* königliche Standarte

**royalty** /ˈrɔɪəltɪ/ *n.* Ⓐ (*payment*) Tantieme, *die* (**on** für); Ⓑ *collect.* (*royal persons*) Mitglieder des Königshauses; Ⓒ *no pl., no art.* (*member of royal family*) ein Mitglied der königlichen Familie; **she's ~:** sie gehört zur königlichen Familie

**royal 'warrant** *n. Recht, den königlichen Hof zu beliefern*

**rozzer** /ˈrɒzə(r)/ *n.* (*Brit. sl.*) Polyp, *der* (*salopp*)

**RPI** *abbr.* (*Brit.*) **retail price index**

**r.p.m.** /ɑːpiːˈem/ *abbr.* Ⓐ **resale price maintenance;** Ⓑ **revolutions per minute** U.p.M.

**RSI** *abbr.* **repetitive strain injury**

**RSPCA** *abbr.* (*Brit.*) **Royal Society for the Prevention of Cruelty to Animals** *britischer Tierschutzverein*

**RSVP** *abbr.* **répondez s'il vous plaît** R.S.V.P.; U.A.w.g.

**rt.** *abbr.* **right**

**Rt. Hon.** *abbr.* ▶ 1617 (*Brit.*) **Right Honourable**

**Rt. Rev[d].** *abbr.* ▶ 1617 **Right Reverend; the Rt. Rev[d].** S./Sr. E[xz].

**rub** /rʌb/ ❶ *v.t.*, **-bb-:** Ⓐ reiben (**on, against** an + *Dat.*); (*with ointment etc.*) einreiben; (*to remove dirt etc.*) abreiben; (*to dry*) trockenreiben; (*with sandpaper*) [ab]schmirgeln; **~ sth. off sth.** etw. von etw. reiben; **~ sth. dry** etw. trockenreiben; **~ one's hands** sich (*Dat.*) die Hände reiben; **~ noses** die Nasen aneinander reiben; **~ shoulders** *or* **elbows with sb.** (*fig.*) Tuchfühlung mit jmdm. haben; **~ a hole in sth.** ein Loch in etw. (*Akk.*) scheuern; **~ one's feet on sth.** sich (*Dat.*) die Füße an etw. (*Dat.*) reiben; **~ two things together** zwei Dinge aneinander reiben; **~ sth. through a sieve** etw. durch ein Sieb streichen; **he ~bed liniment over his chest** er rieb sich (*Dat.*) die Brust mit einem Einreibemittel ein; ⇒ *also* **nose** 1 A; **penny** C; Ⓑ (*reproduce by ~bing*) *kopieren, indem man auf ein Relief Papier legt und mit Malkreide, Bleistift o. ä. darüber reibt.*
❷ *v.i.*, **-bb-** Ⓐ (*exercise friction*) reiben (**[up]on, against** an + *Dat.*); Ⓑ (*get frayed*) sich abreiben; **~ bare** sich blank reiben *od.* scheuern.
❸ *n.* Reiben, *das;* **give it a quick ~:** reib es kurz ab; **there's the ~** (*fig.*) da liegt der Haken [dabei] (*ugs.*)

**~ a'long** *v.i.* Ⓐ **~ along [together]** [gut] miteinander auskommen; Ⓑ (*financially*) auskommen

**~ a'way** *v.t.* abreiben ‹Farbe, Schmutz›; wegmassieren ‹Schmerzen›

**~ 'down** *v.t.* Ⓐ (*prepare*) abschmirgeln; Ⓑ (*dry*) abreiben. ⇒ *also* **rub-down**

**~ 'in** *v.t.* einreiben; **there's no need to** *or* **don't ~ it in** (*fig.*) reib es mir nicht [dauernd] unter die Nase (*ugs.*)

**~ 'off** ❶ *v.t.* wegreiben; wegwischen. ❷ *v.i.* (*lit. or fig.*) abfärben (**on** auf + *Akk.*); **a lot of dirt/oil ~bed off on my hands** ich bekam sehr schmutzige/ölige Hände

**~ 'out** ❶ *v.t.* ausreiben; (*from paper*) ausradieren. ❷ *v.i.* sich ausreiben/(*from paper*) sich ausradieren lassen

**~ 'up** *v.t.* Ⓐ (*polish*) blank reiben; wienern (*ugs.*); Ⓑ (*revise*) auffrischen; aufpolieren (*ugs.*); Ⓒ **~ sb. up the right/wrong way** (*fig.*) jmdm. um den Bart gehen (*ugs.*)/auf den Schlips treten (*ugs.*)

**rubber**[1] /ˈrʌbə(r)/ *n.* Ⓐ Gummi, *das od. der; attrib.* Gummi-; Ⓑ (*eraser*) Radiergummi, *der;* Ⓒ (*sl.: condom*) Gummi, *der* (*salopp*); Ⓓ *in pl.* (*Amer.: galoshes*) Galoschen *Pl.*

**rubber**[2] *n.* (*Cards*) Robber, *der*

**rubber: ~ 'band** *n.* Gummiband, *das;* **~ 'bullet** *n.* Gummigeschoss, *das;* **~ 'cheque** *n.* (*coll.*) ungedeckter Scheck; **~ 'glove** *n.* Gummihandschuh, *der;* **~ goods** *n. pl.* Gummiwaren *Pl.*; (*condoms*) Gummis *Pl.* (*ugs.*)

**rubberize** /ˈrʌbəraɪz/ *v.t.* gummieren

**rubber: ~neck** (*Amer.*) ❶ *n.* Gaffer, *der*/Gafferin, *die* (*abwertend*); ❷ *v.i.* gaffen (*abwertend*); **~ plant** *n.* (*Bot.*) Gummibaum, *der;* **~ solution** *n.* Gummilösung, *die;* **~ 'stamp** *n.* Ⓐ Gummistempel, *der;* Ⓑ (*fig.: one who endorses uncritically*) Jasager, *der*/Jasagerin, *die* (*abwertend*); **the council is a ~ stamp body** die Ratsversammlung sagt zu allem Ja und Amen (*ugs.*); **~-'stamp** *v.t.* (*fig.: approve*) absegnen (*ugs. scherzh.*)

**rubbery** /ˈrʌbərɪ/ *adj.* gummiartig; (*tough*) zäh; **be tough and ~:** zäh wie Gummi sein

**rubbing** /ˈrʌbɪŋ/ *n.: Kopie, die entsteht, wenn man auf ein Relief Papier legt und mit Malkreide, Bleistift o. ä. darüber reibt*

**rubbish** /ˈrʌbɪʃ/ ❶ *n., no pl., no indef. art.* Ⓐ (*refuse*) Abfall, *der;* Abfälle; (*to be collected and dumped*) Müll, *der;* Ⓑ (*worthless material*) Plunder, *der* (*ugs. abwertend*); **be ~:** nichts taugen; Ⓒ (*nonsense*) Quatsch, *der* (*ugs.*); Blödsinn, *der* (*ugs.*); **talk a lot of ~:** eine Menge Blödsinn reden; **what ~!** was für ein Quatsch *od.* Schmarren! ❷ *int.* Quatsch (*ugs. abwertend*). ❸ *v.t.* verreißen

**rubbish: ~ bin** *n.* Abfall-/Mülleimer, *der;* (*in factory*) Abfall-/Mülltonne, *die;* **~ chute** *n.* Müllschlucker, *der;* **~ dump** *n.* Müllkippe, *die;* **~ heap** *n.* Müllhaufen, *der;* (*in garden*) Abfallhaufen, *der;* **~ tip** *n.* Müllabladeplatz, *der*

**rubbishy** /ˈrʌbɪʃɪ/ *adj.* mies (*ugs.*); **~ newspaper** Käseblatt, *das* (*salopp abwertend*)

**rubble** /ˈrʌbl/ *n.* Ⓐ (*from damaged building*) Trümmer *Pl.*; (*Geol. also*) Schutt, *der;* **reduce sth. to ~:** etw. in Schutt und Asche legen; Ⓑ (*water-worn stones*) Geröll, *das*

**'rub-down** *n.* **give sb./sth. a [quick] ~:** jmdn./etw. [kurz *od.* schnell] abreiben

**rube** /ruːb/ *n.* (*Amer. coll.*) Bauer, *der* (*ugs.*)

**rubella** /rʊˈbelə/ *n.* ▶ 1232 (*Med.*) Röteln *Pl.*

**Rubicon** /ˈruːbɪkən/ *n.* **cross the ~** (*fig.*) den Rubikon überschreiten (*geh.*)

**rubicund** /ˈruːbɪkʌnd/ *adj.* (*literary*) rosig; rotgesichtig ‹Person›

**Rubik cube** /ruːbɪk ˈkjuːb/ *n.* Zauberwürfel, *der;* Rubik-Würfel, *der*

**rubric** /ˈruːbrɪk/ *n.* Ⓐ Rubrik, *die;* Ⓑ (*commentary*) Glosse, *die*

**ruby** /ˈruːbɪ/ ❶ *n.* Ⓐ (*precious stone*) Rubin, *der;* (*Horol.*) Stein, *der;* Ⓑ (*colour*) Rubinrot, *das.* ❷ *adj.* Ⓐ (*red*) rubinfarben; rubinrot; Ⓑ (*containing stone*) Rubin‹ring, -brosche usw.›

**ruby: ~-red** *adj.* rubinrot; **~ 'wedding** *n.* Rubinhochzeit, *die*

**RUC** *abbr.* **Royal Ulster Constabulary** nordirische Polizei

**ruche** /ruːʃ/ *n.* Rüsche, *die*

**ruched** /ruːʃt/ *adj.* Rüschen-

**ruck**[1] /rʌk/ *n.* Ⓐ (*Sport: main body of competitors*) Feld, *das;* Ⓑ (*fig.: crowd, mass*) Masse, *die;* Ⓒ (*Rugby*) offenes Gedränge

**ruck**[2], (*Brit.*) **ruckle** /ˈrʌkl/ ❶ *n.* (*crease*) Falte, *die.* ❷ *v.i.* **~ up** hochrutschen

**rucksack** /ˈrʌksæk, ˈrʊksæk/ *n.* Rucksack, *der*

**ruckus** /ˈrʌkəs/ *n.*, (*coll.*) **ructions** /ˈrʌkʃnz/ *n. pl.* Rabatz, *der* (*ugs.*)

**rudder** /ˈrʌdə(r)/ *n.* Ruder, *das*

**rudderless** /ˈrʌdəlɪs/ *adj.* ruderlos; ohne Ruder *nachgestellt;* (*fig.*) richtungslos

**ruddy** /ˈrʌdɪ/ *adj.* Ⓐ (*reddish*) rötlich; Ⓑ (*rosy*) rosig; Ⓒ (*Brit. coll. euphem.: bloody*) verdammt (*salopp*)

**rude** /ruːd/ *adj.* Ⓐ (*impolite*) unhöflich; (*stronger*) rüde; **say ~ things** *or* **be ~ about sb.** in ungehöriger Weise von jmdm. sprechen; **be ~ to sb.** zu jmdm. grob unhöflich sein; jmdn. rüde behandeln; **be ~ to a teacher** zu einem Lehrer frech *od.* unverschämt sein; Ⓑ (*abrupt*) unsanft; **~ awakening** böses *od.* (*geh.*) jähes Erwachen; Ⓒ (*hearty*) **in ~ health** (*dated*) kerngesund; Ⓓ (*simple*) primitiv; Ⓔ (*obscene*) unanständig

**rudely** /ˈruːdlɪ/ *adv.* Ⓐ (*impolitely*) unhöflich; rüde; Ⓑ (*abruptly*) jäh (*geh.*); **be ~ reminded of sth.** unsanft an etw. (*Akk.*) erinnert werden; Ⓒ (*roughly*) primitiv; **a ~ constructed hut** eine grob gezimmerte Hütte; Ⓓ (*obscenely*) unanständig; **gesture ~ at sb.** jmdm. eine unanständige Geste zeigen

**rudeness** /ˈruːdnɪs/ *n., no pl.* (*bad manners*) ungehöriges *od.* rüdes Benehmen

**rudiment** /ˈruːdɪmənt/ *n.* Ⓐ *in pl.* (*first principles*) Grundzüge *Pl.;* Grundlagen *Pl.;* **know the ~s of law** über juristische Grundkenntnisse verfügen; Ⓑ *in pl.* (*imperfect beginning*) [erster] Ansatz

**rudimentary** /ruːdɪˈmentərɪ/ *adj.* Ⓐ (*elementary*) elementar; primitiv ‹Gebäude›; **~ knowledge** Grundkenntnisse *Pl.;* Ⓑ (*Anat., Zool.*) rudimentär

**rue** /ruː/ *v.t.*, **~ing** *or* **ruing** /ˈruːɪŋ/ (*literary: repent of*) bereuen; **you'll live to ~ it** es wird dich noch gereuen (*geh., veralt.*); **~ the day/hour when …:** den Tag/die Stunde verwünschen, da …

**rueful** /ˈruːfl/ *adj.*, **ruefully** /ˈruːfəlɪ/ *adv.* reumütig; reuig

**ruff**[1] /rʌf/ *n.* Halskrause, *die*

**ruff**[2] *n.* (*sandpiper*) Kampfläufer, *der*

**ruff**[3] (*Cards*) ❶ *n.* Trumpfen, *das.* ❷ *v.i.* trumpfen. ❸ *v.t.* mit einem Trumpf stechen

**ruffian** /ˈrʌfɪən/ *n.* Rohling, *der* (*abwertend*); **gang of ~s** Schlägerbande, *die;* **the little ~** (*joc.*) der kleine Strolch

**ruffianly** /ˈrʌfɪənlɪ/ *adj.* roh; rau ‹Bursche›

**ruffle** /ˈrʌfl/ ❶ *v.t.* Ⓐ (*disturb smoothness of*) kräuseln; **~ sb.'s hair** jmdm. durch die Haare fahren; ⇒ *also* **feather** 1 A; Ⓑ (*upset*) aus der Fassung bringen; **her composure was not ~d** sie verlor ihre Fassung nicht; **be easily ~d** leicht aus der Fassung geraten; Ⓒ (*gather*) kräuseln. ❷ *n.* (*frill*) Rüsche, *die*

**~ 'up** *v.t.* sträuben ‹Gefieder›

**rug** /rʌg/ *n.* Ⓐ (*for floor*) [kleiner, dicker] Teppich; **Persian ~:** Perserbrücke, *die;* **pull the ~ [out] from under sb.** (*fig.*) jmdm. den Boden unter den Füßen wegziehen; Ⓑ (*wrap, blanket*) [dicke] Wolldecke

**Rugby** /ˈrʌgbɪ/ *n.* Rugby, *das;* ⇒ *also* **fives**

**Rugby: ~ ball** *n.* Rugbyball, *der;* **~ 'football** *n.* Ⓐ (*game*) ⇒ **Rugby;** Ⓑ (*ball*) ⇒ **Rugby ball; ~ 'footballer** *n.* Rugbyspieler, *der;* **~ 'League** *n.* (*Brit.*) *Rugby mit 13 Spielern pro Mannschaft;* **~ player** ⇒ **~ footballer; ~ tackle** *n.* tiefes Fassen (*Rugby*); **the policeman brought him down with a ~ tackle** der Polizist warf sich auf ihn und riss ihn zu Boden; **~ 'Union** *n.* (*Brit.*) *Rugby mit 15 Spielern pro Mannschaft*

**rugged** /ˈrʌgɪd/ *adj.* Ⓐ (*sturdy*) robust; Ⓑ (*involving hardship*) hart ‹Test›; Ⓒ (*unpolished*) rau; unverfälscht ‹Ehrlichkeit, Freundlichkeit usw.›; **with ~ good looks** gut aussehend mit markanten Gesichtszügen; Ⓓ (*uneven*) zerklüftet; unwegsam ‹Land, Anstieg›; zerfurcht ‹Gesicht›

**ruggedize** /ˈrʌgɪdaɪz/ *v.t.* (*Amer.*) armieren

**ruggedly** /ˈrʌgɪdlɪ/ *adv.* **~ constructed** robust gebaut; **~ handsome** gut aussehend mit markanten Gesichtszügen

r

**rugger** /'rʌgə(r)/ *n.* (*Brit. coll.*) Rugby, *das*

**Ruhr** /rʊə(r)/ *pr. n.* **the ~:** das Ruhrgebiet

**ruin** /'ru:ɪn/ ❶ *n.* **A** *no pl., no indef. art.* (*decay*) Verfall, *der;* **bring about one's own ~:** sich selbst ruinieren; **be reduced to a state of ~:** völlig verfallen sein; **the ~ of his hopes** das Ende seiner Hoffnungen; **go to** *or* **fall into rack and ~** ‹Gebäude:› völlig verfallen; ‹Garten:› völlig verwahrlosen; ‹Pläne:› zunichte werden; **B** *no pl., no indef. art.* (*downfall*) Ruin, *der;* **his business was facing ~:** sein Geschäft stand am Rande des Ruins; **~ stared her in the face** sie stand vor dem Ruin; **C** *in sing. or pl.* (*remains*) Ruine, *die;* **in ~s** in Trümmern; **he is a ~** (*fig.*) er ist eine Ruine (*ugs.*) *od.* ein Wrack; **rise from the ~s of sth.** aus den Trümmern einer Sache entstehen; **D** (*cause of ~*) Ruin, *der;* Untergang, *der;* **you'll be the ~ of me** du ruinierst mich [noch].
❷ *v.t.* ruinieren; verderben ‹Urlaub, Abend›; zunichte machen ‹Aussichten, Möglichkeiten usw.›

**ruination** /ru:ɪ'neɪʃn/ *n., no pl.* ⇒ **ruin** 1 D

**ruined** /'ru:ɪnd/ *adj.* **A** (*reduced to ruins*) verfallen; **~ town** Ruinenstadt, *die;* **a ~ castle/palace/church** eine Burg-/Palast-/Kirchenruine; **B** (*brought to ruin*) ruiniert; **his speculations left him a ~ man** seine Spekulationen ruinierten ihn; **C** (*spoilt*) verdorben

**ruinous** /'ru:ɪnəs/ *adj.* **A** (*in ruins*) verfallen; **B** (*disastrous*) ruinös; katastrophal ‹Wirkung›; **be ~ to sb./sth.** jmdn./etw. ruinieren

**ruinously** /'ru:ɪnəslɪ/ *adv.* ruinös; katastrophal ‹teuer, hoch usw.›

**rule** /ru:l/ ❶ *n.* **A** (*principle*) Regel, *die;* **~ of conduct/decorum/cricket/life** Verhaltens-/Anstands-/Kricket-/Lebensregel, *die;* **the ~s of the game** (*lit. or fig.*) die Spielregeln; **stick to** *or* **play by the ~s** (*lit. or fig.*) sich an die Spielregeln halten; **~s and regulations** Regeln und Vorschriften; **[always] make it a ~ to do sth.** (*fig.*) es sich (*Dat.*) zur Regel machen, etw. zu tun; **be against the ~s** regelwidrig sein; (*fig.*) gegen die Spielregeln verstoßen; **bend** *or* **stretch the ~s** (*fig.*) ein Auge zudrücken (*ugs.*); **R~** (*Austral. Footb.*) *Fußball nach den australischen Regeln;* **as a ~:** in der Regel; **~ of three** (*Math.*) Dreisatz, *der;* **~ of thumb** Faustregel, *die;* **the usual ~ of thumb is ...:** als Faustregel gilt ...; **~ of thumb estimate** grobe Schätzung; **B** (*custom*) Regel, *die;* **the ~ of the house is that ...:** in diesem Haus ist es üblich, dass ...; **suits are the ~ on such an occasion** bei einem solchen Anlass trägt man normalerweise einen Anzug; **C** *no pl.* (*government*) Herrschaft, *die* (**over** über + *Akk.*); **the ~ of law** die Autorität des Gesetzes; **D** (*Eccl.: code*) [Ordens]regel, *die;* **E** (*graduated measure*) Maß, *das;* (*tape*) Bandmaß, *das;* (*folding*) Zollstock, *der;* **F** (*Printing*) Linie, *die.* ⇒ *also* **road** A; **work** 2 A.
❷ *v.t.* **A** (*control*) beherrschen; **B** (*be the ruler of*) regieren; ‹Monarch, Diktator usw.:› herrschen über (+ *Akk.*); **~ the roost [in the house]** Herr im Hause sein; ⇒ *also* **rod** C; **C** (*give as decision*) entscheiden; **he ~d the ball out** er entschied, dass der Ball aus war; **~ a motion out of order** einen Antrag nicht zulassen; **~ sb. out of order** jmdm. [unter Hinweis auf die Geschäftsordnung] das Wort entziehen; **D** (*draw*) ziehen ‹Linie›; (*draw lines on*) linieren ‹Papier›.
❸ *v.i.* **A** (*govern*) herrschen; **~ by fear** eine Schreckensherrschaft führen; **X ~s** (*coll.*) X ist der/die Größte; **B** (*decide, declare formally*) entscheiden (**against** gegen; **in favour of** für); **~ on a matter** in einer Sache entscheiden

**~ 'off** ❶ *v.t.* mit einem Strich abtrennen; **~ off a margin** am Rand einen Strich ziehen
❷ *v.i.* einen Schlussstrich ziehen

**~ 'out** *v.t.* **A** (*exclude, eliminate*) ausschließen; **B** (*prevent*) unmöglich machen

**'rule book** *n.* (*lit. or fig.*) Regeln; Regelbuch, *das*

**ruled** /ru:ld/ *adj.* liniert ‹Papier›

**ruler** /'ru:lə(r)/ *n.* **A** (*person*) Herrscher, *der*/Herrscherin, *die;* **B** (*for drawing or measuring*) Lineal, *das*

**ruling** /'ru:lɪŋ/ ❶ *n.* **A** (*decision*) Entscheidung, *die;* **B** (*using a ruler*) Linierung, *die.*
❷ *adj.* **A** (*predominating*) herrschend ‹Meinung›; vorherrschend ‹Charakterzug›; **sb.'s ~ ambition/passion** jmds. größter Ehrgeiz/größte Leidenschaft; **B** (*current*) **[the] ~ prices** die geltenden Preise; **C** (*governing, reigning*) herrschend ‹Klasse›; regierend ‹Partei›; amtierend ‹Regierung›

**rum**[1] /rʌm/ *n.* Rum, *der*

**rum**[2] *adj.* (*Brit. coll.*) (*odd*) seltsam

**Rumania** /ru:'meɪnɪə/ ⇒ **Romania**

**Rumanian** /ru:'meɪnɪən/ ⇒ **Romanian**

**rumba** /'rʌmbə/ ❶ *n.* Rumba, *die,* (*österr.*) *der;* **dance the ~:** Rumba tanzen. ❷ *v.i.*, **~ed** *or* **~'d** /'rʌmbəd/ Rumba tanzen

**rumble**[1] /'rʌmbl/ ❶ *n.* **A** (*sound*) Grollen, *das;* (*of heavy vehicle*) Rumpeln, *das* (*ugs.*); **B** (*Amer. coll.: street fight*) Straßenschlacht, *die;* Schlacht, *die* (*fig.*); **C** (*Amer. coll.: rumour*) Gerücht, *das;* **the ~ is that ...:** man munkelt, dass ... ❷ *v.i.* **A** (*make low, heavy sound*) grollen; ‹Magen:› knurren; **B** (*go with rumbling noise*) rumpeln (*ugs.*)

**rumble**[2] *v.t.* (*coll.: understand*) spitzkriegen (*ugs.*) ‹Sache›; auf die Schliche kommen (+ *Dat.*) ‹Person›

**'rumble: ~ seat** *n.* (*Amer. dated*) Notsitz, *der;* **~ strip** *n.* Signalschwelle, *die;* akustische Schwelle

**rumbustious** /rʌm'bʌstʃəs/ *adj.* (*coll.*) wild

**ruminant** /'ru:mɪnənt/ (*Zool.*) ❶ *n.* Wiederkäuer, *der.* ❷ *adj.* wiederkäuend

**ruminate** /'ru:mɪneɪt/ *v.i.* **A ~ over** *or* **about** *or* **on sth.** über etw. (*Akk.*) nachsinnen (*geh.*) *od.* grübeln; **she sat ruminating for a moment** sie saß einen Augenblick nachdenklich da; **B** (*Zool.*) wiederkäuen

**rumination** /ru:mɪ'neɪʃn/ *n.* **A** Nachsinnen, *das* (*geh.*); Grübeln, *das;* **his ~s were interrupted** seine Gedanken wurden unterbrochen; **B** (*Zool.*) Wiederkäuen, *das*

**ruminative** /'ru:mɪnətɪv/ *adj.* beschaulich ‹Stimmung›; grüblerisch ‹Person›

**rummage** /'rʌmɪdʒ/ ❶ *v.i.* wühlen (*ugs.*); kramen (*ugs.*); **~ among old clothes** in alten Kleidungsstücken herumwühlen *od.* -stöbern; **~ through sth.** etw. durchwühlen (*ugs.*); **~ about** *or* **around** herumkramen (*ugs.*). ❷ *n.* **have a ~ through sth.** etw. durchwühlen *od.* durchstöbern; **enjoy a good ~ around bookshops** gern in Buchhandlungen herumstöbern (*ugs.*)

**~ 'out** *v.t.* hervorkramen (*ugs.*)

**'rummage sale** (*esp. Amer.*) ⇒ **jumble sale**

**rummy** /'rʌmɪ/ *n.* (*Cards*) Rommé, *das*

**rumour** (*Brit.; Amer.:* **rumor**) /'ru:mə(r)/ ❶ *n.* **A** (*unverified story*) Gerücht, *das;* **there is a ~ that ...:** es geht das Gerücht, dass ...; **there is a persistent ~ that ...:** das Gerücht hält sich hartnäckig, dass ...; **B** *no pl., no art.* (*common talk*) Gerücht, *das;* **~ puts the number of casualties at around 5,000** Gerüchten zufolge liegt die Zahl der Opfer bei 5 000; **~ has it that ...:** es geht das Gerücht, dass ... ❷ *v.t.* **sb. is ~ed to have done sth., it is ~ed that sb. has done sth.** man munkelt (*ugs.*) *od.* es geht das Gerücht, dass jmd. etw. getan hat; **the ~ed earthquake** das Erdbeben, das sich [Gerüchten zufolge] ereignet haben soll

**rump** /rʌmp/ *n.* **A** (*buttocks*) Hinterteil, *das* (*ugs.*); **meat from the ~:** Fleisch aus der Keule; **B** (*remnant*) Rest, *der;* **sth. is only a ~:** von etw. ist nur noch der Rumpf übrig; **the R~** (*Brit. Hist.*) das Rumpfparlament

**rumple** /'rʌmpl/ *v.t.* **A** (*crease*) zerknittern; **B** (*tousle*) zerzausen

**'rump steak** *n.* Rumpsteak, *das*

**rumpus** /'rʌmpəs/ *n., no pl.* (*coll.*) Krach, *der* (*ugs.*); Spektakel, *der* (*ugs.*); **kick up** *or* **make a ~:** einen Spektakel veranstalten (*ugs.*)

**'rumpus room** *n.* (*Amer.*) Spielzimmer, *das*

**run** /rʌn/ ❶ *n.* **A** Lauf, *der;* **let the dogs out for a ~:** die Hunde hinauslassen, damit sie Auslauf haben; **go for a ~ before breakfast** vor dem Frühstück einen Lauf machen; **make a late ~** (*Sport or fig.*) zum Endspurt ansetzen; **come towards sb./take a hurdle/start off at a ~:** jmdm. entgegenlaufen/eine Hürde im Lauf nehmen/losrennen; **I've had a good ~ for my money** ich bin auf meine Kosten gekommen; **we'll give our opponents a good ~ for their money** wir werden es unseren Gegnern nicht leicht machen; **on the ~:** auf der Flucht; **keep the enemy on the ~:** den Feind nicht zur Ruhe kommen lassen; **B** (*trip in vehicle*) Fahrt, *die;* (*for pleasure*) Ausflug, *der;* **on the ~ down to Cornwall** auf der Fahrt nach Cornwall; **a two-hour/a day's ~:** eine Fahrt von zwei Stunden/eine Tagesreise; **go for a ~ [in the car]** einen [Auto]ausflug machen; **C** (*continuous stretch*) Länge, *die;* **a 500 ft. ~ of pipe** eine Rohrleitung von 500 Fuß Länge; **D** (*spell*) **have a ~ of fine weather** eine Schönwetterperiode haben; **she has had a long ~ of success** sie war lange [Zeit] erfolgreich; **have a long ~** ‹Stück, Show:› viele Aufführungen erleben; **a successful [West End] ~:** eine erfolgreiche Spielzeit [im Westend]; **E** (*succession*) Serie, *die;* (*Cards*) Sequenz, *die;* **a ~ of victories** eine Siegesserie; **F** (*tendency*) Ablauf, *der;* **~ of [the] play** (*Sport*) Spielverlauf, *der;* **the general ~ of things/events** der Lauf der Dinge/der Gang der Ereignisse; **G** (*regular route*) Strecke, *die;* **do a regular ~ between London and Edinburgh** regelmäßig die Strecke London-Edinburgh fahren; **he is on** *or* **he does the Glasgow ~:** er fährt die Glasgower Strecke; **H** (*Cricket, Baseball*) Lauf, *der;* Run, *der;* **I** ⇒ **ladder** 1 B; **J** (*Mus.*) Lauf, *der;* **K** (*quantity produced*) (*of book*) Auflage, *die;* **production ~:** Ausstoß, *der* (*Wirtsch.*); **L** (*demand*) Run, *der* (**on** auf + *Akk.*); **M** (*general type*) **the common** *or* **general ~ of people** der Durchschnittsmensch; **he's not like the usual ~ of disc jockeys** er ist anders als die üblichen Diskjockeys; **N the ~s** (*coll.: diarrhoea*) Durchmarsch, *der* (*salopp*); **O** (*unrestricted use*) **give sb. the ~ of sth.** jmdm. etw. zu seiner freien Verfügung überlassen; **have the ~ of sth.** etw. zu seiner freien Verfügung haben; **P** (*animal enclosure*) Auslauf, *der;* (*regular track of animals*) Wildwechsel, *der.* ⇒ *also* **long** 1 C; **short** 1 A; **ski run.**
❷ *v.i.*, **-nn-, ran** /ræn/, **run A** laufen; (*fast also*) rennen; **~ for all one is worth** rennen so schnell man kann; **~ for the bus** laufen *od.* rennen, um den Bus zu kriegen (*ugs.*); **~ to help sb.** jmdm. zu Hilfe eilen; **~ at sb.** auf jmdn. losstürzen; **the horse ran at the fence** das Pferd lief auf den Zaun zu; **B** (*compete*) laufen; **he ran sixth/a poor third** er wurde sechster/erreichte einen mäßigen dritten Platz; **C** (*hurry*) laufen; **don't ~ to me when things go wrong** komm mir nicht angelaufen, wenn etwas schief geht (*ugs.*); **~ to meet sb.** jmdm. entgegenlaufen; **he ran to meet her at the gate** er lief ihr bis ans Tor entgegen; **D** (*roll*) laufen; ‹Ball, Kugel:› rollen, laufen; **the wheels ran into a rut** die Räder gerieten in eine Furche; **E** (*slide*) laufen; ‹Schlitten, [Schiebe]tür:› gleiten; **F** (*revolve*) ‹Rad, Maschine:› laufen; **G** (*Naut.*) **~ for Plymouth** Plymouth anlaufen; **~ into port** in den Hafen einlaufen; **~ aground** auf Grund laufen; ⇒ *also* **foul** 1 F; **H** (*flee*) davonlaufen; **~ for it** sich aus dem Staub machen (*ugs.*); **~ for cover** schnell in Deckung gehen; ⇒ *also* **life** A; **I** (*travel*) **~ over** *or* **across** hinüberfahren; **~ down/up [to London]** [nach London] runter-/rauffahren (*ugs.*); **~ into town** in die Stadt fahren; **J** (*operate on a schedule*) fahren; **~ between two places** ‹Zug, Bus:› zwischen zwei Orten verkehren; **the train is ~ning late** der Zug hat Verspätung; **we're ~ning late** (*fig.*) wir sind spät dran (*ugs.*); **~ on time** pünktlich sein; keine Verspätung haben; **the train doesn't ~ on Sundays** der Zug verkehrt nicht an Sonntagen; **K** (*pass cursorily*) **~ through** überfliegen ‹Text›; **~ through one's head** *or* **mind** ‹Gedanken, Ideen:› einem durch den Kopf gehen; **~ through the various possibilities** die

verschiedenen Möglichkeiten durchspielen; **his eyes ran over the article/photo** er ließ die Augen über den Artikel/das Foto wandern; **her fingers ran over the keys** ihre Finger liefen über die Tasten; **the tune is ~ning in my head** die Melodie geht mir im Kopf herum; **L** (*flow*) laufen; ‹Fluss:› fließen; ‹Augen:› tränen; **your bath is ~ning** dein Bad läuft ein; **till the blood ran** bis es blutete; **the child's nose was ~ning** dem Kind lief die Nase; **the walls are ~ning with moisture** die Wände triefen vor Nässe (*Dat.*); **~ dry** ‹Fluss:› austrocknen; ‹Quelle:› versiegen; **the taps had ~ dry** es lief kein Wasser mehr aus der Leitung; **~ low** *or* **short** knapp werden; ausgehen; **we ran short of** *or* **low on fruit** unsere Obstvorräte wurden knapp *od.* gingen aus; **M** (*flow rapidly*) **a heavy sea was ~ning** es herrschte starker Seegang; **the tide ran strong/out** die Flutwellen schlugen hoch/die Flut ging zurück; **N** (*be current*) ‹Vertrag, Theaterstück:› laufen; **O** (*be present*) **~ through sth.** sich durch etw. ziehen; **~ in the family** ‹Eigenschaft, Begabung:› in der Familie liegen; **P** (*function*) laufen; **keep/leave the engine ~ning** den Motor laufen lassen/nicht abstellen; **the machine ~s on batteries/oil** *etc.* die Maschine läuft mit Batterien/Öl *usw.*; **things aren't ~ning too smoothly in their marriage** (*fig.*) in ihrer Ehe läuft es [zur Zeit] nicht besonders gut (*ugs.*); **Q** (*have a course*) ‹Straße, Bahnlinie:› verlaufen; **R** (*have wording*) lauten; ‹Geschichte:› gehen (*fig.*); **S** (*have tendency*) **my inclination does not ~ that way** meine Neigung geht nicht in diese Richtung; **T** (*have certain level*) **inflation is ~ning at 5%** die Inflationsrate beläuft sich auf *od.* beträgt 5%; **interest rates are ~ning at record levels** die Zinsen bewegen sich auf Rekordhöhe; **U** (*seek election*) kandidieren; **~ for mayor** für das Amt des Bürgermeisters kandidieren; **V** (*spread quickly*) **a cheer ran down** *or* **along the lines of soldiers** ein Hurra ging durch die Reihen der Soldaten; **a shiver ran down my spine** ein Schau[d]er (*geh.*) lief mir den Rücken hinunter; **W** (*spread undesirably*) ‹Butter, Eis:› zerlaufen; ‹Farben:› (*in washing*) auslaufen; (*on painting etc.*) ineinander laufen; **X** (*Cricket*) einen Lauf *od.* Run machen; **Y** (*ladder*) Laufmaschen bekommen; **stockings guaranteed not to ~:** garantiert laufmaschensichere Strümpfe. ⇒ *also* **also**; **blood** 1 A; **cut** 2 E; **feeling** 1 C; **riot** 1 B; **wild** 1 C; **writ**[1] A.

❸ *v.t.*, **-nn-, ran, run** **A** (*cause to move*) laufen lassen; (*drive*) fahren; **~ the ship aground** das Schiff auf Grund laufen lassen *od.* (*Seemannsspr.*) auflaufen lassen; **~ the boat into the water** das Boot zu Wasser lassen; **~ the car into the garage** das Auto in die Garage fahren; **~ one's hand/fingers through/along** *or* **down** *or* **over sth.** mit der Hand/den Fingern durch etw. fahren/über etw. (*Akk.*) streichen; **~ an** *or* **one's eye along** *or* **down** *or* **over sth.** (*fig.*) etw. überfliegen; **~ one's finger down a list** mit dem Finger eine Liste entlangfahren; **~ a rope through sth.** ein Seil durch etw. führen; **B** (*cause to flow*) [ein]laufen lassen; **~ a bath** ein Bad einlaufen lassen; **C** (*organize, manage*) führen, leiten ‹Geschäft usw.›; durchführen ‹Experiment›; veranstalten ‹Wettbewerb›; führen ‹Leben›; **the people who ~ things [in this city]** die maßgeblichen Leute [dieser Stadt]; **~ the show** (*fig. coll.*) das Sagen haben (*ugs.*); **D** (*operate*) bedienen ‹Maschine›; verkehren lassen ‹Verkehrsmittel›; einsetzen ‹Sonderbus, -zug›; laufen lassen ‹Motor›; abspielen ‹Tonband›; **~ a train service** eine Schienenverbindung unterhalten; **~ a taxi** Taxi fahren; **~ forward/back** vorwärts-/zurückspulen ‹Film, Tonband›; **E** (*own and use*) sich (*Dat.*) halten ‹Auto›; **a Jaguar is expensive to ~:** ein Jaguar ist im Unterhalt sehr teuer; **~ning a freezer saves money** mit einer Tiefkühltruhe spart man Geld; **~ a car with defective brakes** ein Auto mit defekten Bremsen fahren; **F** (*take for journey*) fahren; **I'll ~ you into town** ich fahre *od.* bringe dich in die Stadt; **G** (*pursue*) jagen; ‹Tier›; (*fig.*) aufspüren; **~ sb. hard** *or* **close** jmdm. auf den Fersen sein *od.* sitzen (*ugs.*); **be ~ off one's feet** alle Hände voll zu tun haben (*ugs.*); (*in business*) Hochbetrieb haben (*ugs.*); ⇒ *also* **earth** 1 E; **H** (*complete*) laufen ‹Rennen, Marathon, Strecke›; **~ messages/errands** Botengänge machen; **the race will be ~ tomorrow** das Rennen wird morgen gelaufen/gefahren; **I** (*smuggle*) schmuggeln ‹Waffen, Drogen, Personen›; schleusen ‹Personen›; **J** (*enter for race or election*) laufen lassen ‹Pferd›; aufstellen ‹Kandidaten›; **K** (*publish*) bringen (*ugs.*) ‹Bericht, Artikel usw.›; in die Zeitung setzen ‹Anzeige›; **L** **~ a fever/a temperature** Fieber/erhöhte Temperatur haben. ⇒ *also* **course** 1 A; **fine**[2] 1 G; **gauntlet**[2]; **ground** 1 B; **ragged** E; **risk** 1 A

**~ a'bout** *v.i.* **A** (*bustle*) hin- und herlaufen; **B** (*play without restraint*) herumtollen; herumspringen (*ugs.*). ⇒ *also* **runabout**

**~ a'cross** *v.t.* **~ across sb.** jmdn. treffen; jmdm. über den Weg laufen; **~ across sth.** auf etw. (*Akk.*) stoßen

**~ after** *v.t.* **A** (**~** *to catch, follow persistently*) hinterherlaufen (+ *Dat.*); **B** nachlaufen (+ *Dat.*) ‹Mode usw.›

**~ a'long** *v.i.* (*coll.: depart*) sich trollen (*ugs.*)

**~ a'round** ❶ *v.i.* **A** **~ around with sb.** sich mit jmdm. herumtreiben; **B** ⇒ **run about a**; **C** ⇒ **run about b**. ❷ *v.t.* herumfahren

**~ a'way** *v.i.* **A** (*flee*) weglaufen; fortlaufen; **B** (*abscond*) **~ away [from home/from the children's home]** [von zu Hause/aus dem Kinderheim] weglaufen; **C** (*elope*) **~ away with sb./together** mit jmdm./zusammen durchbrennen (*ugs.*); **D** (*bolt*) ‹Pferd:› durchgehen; **E** ‹Wasser:› ablaufen; **F** (*get ahead*) **~ away from the rest of the field** dem übrigen Feld davonlaufen. ⇒ *also* **runaway**

**~ a'way with** *v.t.* **A** (*coll.: steal*) abhauen mit (*salopp*); **B** (*fig.: win*) **~ away with the top prize/all the trophies** den 1. Preis/alle Trophäen erringen; **C** (*fig.: be misled by*) **~ away with the idea** *or* **notion that ...:** irrtümlich annehmen, dass ...; **don't ~ away with the idea that ...:** glaub bloß nicht, dass ...; **he let his imagination/enthusiasm ~ away with him** seine Fantasie/Begeisterung ist mit ihm durchgegangen; **D** (*fig.: consume*) verbrauchen; verschlingen ‹Geld›; fressen (*ugs.*) ‹Benzin›. ⇒ *also* **run away c**

**~ 'back over** *v.t.* sich (*Dat.*) in Erinnerung rufen; **her thoughts ran back over the past** sie dachte an die vergangenen Zeiten

**~ 'down** ❶ *v.t.* **A** (*collide with*) überfahren; **B** (*find after search*) aufspüren; **C** (*criticize*) heruntermachen (*ugs.*); herabsetzen; **don't ~ yourself down all the time** mach dich nicht immer selbst so schlecht; **D** (*cause to diminish*) abbauen; verringern ‹Produktion›; **E** (*cause to lose power*) leer machen ‹Batterie›. ❷ *v.i.* **A** hin-/herunterlaufen/-rennen/-fahren; **B** (*decline*) sich verringern; ‹Schienennetz:› schrumpfen; **C** (*lose power*) ausgehen; ‹Batterie:› leer werden; ‹Uhr, Spielzeug:› ablaufen. ⇒ *also* **rundown**

**~ 'in** ❶ *v.t.* **A** (*prepare for use*) einfahren ‹Auto›; sich einlaufen lassen ‹Maschine›; **B** (*coll.: arrest*) hoppnehmen (*salopp*). ❷ *v.i.* hin-/hereinlaufen/-rennen

**~ into** *v.t.* **A** **~ into a telegraph pole/tree** gegen einen Telegrafenmast/Baum fahren; **~ into a sandbank** auf eine Sandbank geraten *od.* (*Seemannsspr.*) auflaufen; **B** (*cause to collide with*) **~ one's car into a tree** seinen Wagen gegen einen Baum fahren; **C** (*cause to incur*) **~ the family into debt** die Familie in Schulden stürzen; **D** (*fig.: meet*) **~ into sb.** jmdm. in die Arme laufen (*ugs.*); **E** (*be faced with*) stoßen auf (+ *Akk.*) ‹Schwierigkeiten, Widerstand, Probleme usw.›; **F** (*enter*) geraten in (+ *Akk.*) ‹Sturm, schlechtes Wetter, Schulden›; **his debts ~ into thousands** seine Schulden gehen in die Tausende; **G** (*merge with*) **~ into one another** ‹Seen, Tage:› ineinander übergehen

**~ 'off** ❶ *v.i.* ⇒ **~ away** A, C. ❷ *v.t.* **A** (*compose rapidly*) hinwerfen ‹ein paar Zeilen, Verse, Notizen›; zu Papier bringen ‹Brief›; **B** (*produce on machine*) abziehen ‹Kopien, Handzettel usw.›; **C** (*cause to drain away*) ablaufen lassen; **D** (*recite fluently*) ⇒ **rattle off**; **E** (*decide by run-off*) durch Stechen entscheiden; ⇒ *also* **run-off**

**~ 'off with** *v.t.* (*coll.: steal*) abhauen mit (*salopp*); ⇒ *also* **~ away c**; **~ away with b**

**~ 'on** ❶ *v.i.* **A** (*continue without a break*) weitergehen; ‹Krankheit:› fortschreiten; ‹Redner:› weiterreden; **B** (*Printing: continue on same line*) '**~ on'** „ohne Absatz"; **C** (*elapse*) ‹Zeit:› verstreichen; **D** (*join up*) **let the letters ~ on** (*beim Schreiben*) die Buchstaben miteinander verbinden; **E** (*talk incessantly*) reden wie ein Wasserfall (*ugs.*); **her tongue ~s on** ihr Mundwerk steht nicht still (*ugs.*). ❷ *v.t.* **A** (*Printing*) als fortlaufenden Text setzen; **B** /'--/ (*be concerned with*) sich befassen mit; **his mind was ~ning on this subject** seine Gedanken kreisten um dieses Thema

**~ 'out** ❶ *v.i.* **A** hin-/herauslaufen/-rennen; **he ran out a deserved winner** er ging aus dem Kampf als verdienter Sieger hervor; ⇒ *also* **~** 2 M; **B** (*become exhausted*) ‹Vorräte, Bestände:› zu Ende gehen; ‹Geduld:› sich erschöpfen; **we have ~ out** wir haben keinen/keine/keines mehr; (*sold everything*) wir sind ausverkauft; **C** (*expire*) ‹Vertrag:› ablaufen; **time is ~ning out** die Zeit wird knapp; **D** (*jut out*) ‹Land:› vorspringen; ‹Pier:› ins Meer hinausreichen. ⇒ *also* **sand** 1 C. ❷ *v.t.* (*Cricket*) **~ a batsman out** *einen Schlagmann zum Ausscheiden bringen, indem man mit dem Ball das Tor zerstört, bevor er die Schlagmallinie erreicht*

**~ 'out of** *v.t.* **A** (*exhaust stock of*) **sb. ~s out of sth.** jmdm. geht etw. aus; **I'm ~ning out of patience** meine Geduld geht zu Ende; **we're ~ning out of time** uns wird die Zeit [allmählich] knapp; **B** (*flow out of*) auslaufen aus

**~ 'out on** *v.t.* (*desert*) im Stich lassen

**~ over** ❶ /'---/ *v.t.* **A** ⇒ **go over** 2 A; **B** (*knock down*) überfahren. ⇒ *also* **~** 2 K. ❷ /-'--/ *v.i.* **A** (*overflow*) überlaufen; **B** (*exceed limit*) [die Zeit] überziehen

**~ through** *v.t.* **A** ⇒ **get through** 2 H; **B** abspielen ‹Tonband, Film›; **C** (*rehearse*) durchspielen ‹Theaterstück›; **D** /-'-/ (*pierce right through*) **~ sb. through with sth.** jmdn. mit etw. durchbohren. ⇒ *also* **~** 2 K, O; **run-through**

**~ to** *v.t.* **A** (*amount to*) umfassen; ‹Geldsumme, Kosten:› sich belaufen auf (+ *Akk.*); **B** (*be sufficient for*) **sth. will ~ to sth.** etw. reicht für etw.; **C** (*afford*) **sb. can ~ to sth.** jmd. kann sich (*Dat.*) etw. leisten; **D** (*show inclination towards*) **~ to fat** [zu] dick werden; **his style ~s too easily to sentiment** sein Stil gleitet allzu leicht ins Sentimentale ab; ⇒ *also* **seed** 1 B

**~ 'up** ❶ *v.i.* **A** hinlaufen; (*Sport*) Anlauf nehmen; **he ran up to where they were standing** er lief *od.* rannte zu ihnen hin; **come ~ning along** herangelaufen kommen; **B** (*amount to*) **~ up to** sich belaufen auf (+ *Akk.*). ❷ *v.t.* **A** (*hoist*) hissen ‹Fahne›; **B** (*make quickly*) rasch nähen ‹Kleidungsstück›; zusammenzimmern ‹Schuppen›; hochziehen (*ugs.*) ‹Gebäude›; **C** (*allow to accumulate*) **~ up debts/a [big] bill** Schulden/eine hohe Rechnung zusammenkommen lassen. ⇒ *also* **run-up**

**~ 'up against** *v.t.* stoßen auf (+ *Akk.*) ‹Probleme, Widerstand usw.›

**run: ~about** *n.* (*coll.*) [**little**] **~about** Kleinwagen, *der*; **~around** *n.* (*coll.*) **give sb. the ~around** jmdn. an der Nase herumführen (*ugs.*); **~away** ❶ *n.* Ausreißer, *der*/Ausreißerin, *die* (*ugs.*); ❷ *attrib. adj.* **A** (*fleeing*) flüchtig; **she was a ~away schoolgirl** sie war aus der Schule weggelaufen; **have a ~away wedding** weglaufen und heiraten; **B** (*out of control*) durchgegangen ‹Pferd›; außer Kontrolle geraten ‹Fahrzeug, Preise›; (*fig.*) galoppierend ‹Inflation›; **C** (*outstanding*) überwältigend ‹Erfolg›; triumphal ‹Sieg›; **~down** *n.* **A** (*coll.: briefing*) Übersicht, *die* (**on** über + *Akk.*); **B** (*reduction*) Abbau, *der*; **~-down** *adj.* **A** (*tired*) mitgenommen; **in a**

r

completely **~-down condition** völlig erschöpft; **B** (*neglected*) heruntergekommen (*ugs.*) ‹Gegend, Stadt, Gewerbe›

**rune** /ru:n/ *n.* Rune, *die*

**rung¹** /rʌŋ/ *n.* **A** (*of ladder*) Sprosse, *die;* **B** (*fig.*) **start on the bottom** *or* **lowest/reach the top** *or* **highest ~:** auf der ersten Sprosse beginnen/die oberste Sprosse erreichen

**rung²** ⇨ **ring²** 2, 3

**runic** /'ru:nɪk/ *adj.* Runen-; runisch

**runnel** /'rʌnl/ *n.* **A** (*brook*) Wasserlauf, *der;* Rinnsal, *das* (*geh.*); **B** (*gutter*) Rinne, *die*

**runner** /'rʌnə(r)/ *n.* **A** Läufer, *der*/Läuferin, *die;* **B** (*horse in race*) **eight ~s were in the race** acht Pferde liefen beim Rennen; **C** (*messenger*) Bote, *der;* Laufbursche, *der;* **D** (*Bot.: creeping stem*) Ausläufer, *der;* **E** (*twining plant*) Kletterpflanze, *die;* **F** **curtain ~:** Gardinenröllchen, *das;* **G** (*part on which sth. slides*) Kufe, *die;* (*for curtains*) Gardinenleiste, *die;* (*groove*) Laufschiene, *die;* **H** (*cloth*) Tischläufer, *der;* (*carpet*) Läufer, *der;* **I** (*who handles illegal goods*) Schieber, *der* (*ugs.*); **[drug] ~:** [Drogen]kurier, *der* (*ugs.*); **J** (*who runs a blockade*) Blockadebrecher, *der;* **K** (*car*) **'good ~'** „fährt *od.* läuft einwandfrei"; **L** **do a ~** (*Brit. coll.*) abhauen (*salopp*); türmen (*salopp*)

**runner: ~ bean** *n.* (*Brit.*) Stangenbohne, *die;* **~-'up** *n.* Zweite, *der/die;* **the ~s-up** die Platzierten; **they were joint ~s-up** sie teilten sich den zweiten Platz

**running** /'rʌnɪŋ/ ❶ *n.* **A** (*management*) Leitung, *die;* **B** (*action*) Laufen, *das;* (*jogging*) Jogging, *das;* **make the ~** (*in competition*) an der Spitze liegen; (*fig.: have the initiative*) den Ton angeben; **take up the ~:** sich an die Spitze setzen; **in/out of the ~:** im/aus dem Rennen; **be out of the ~ for the Presidency** keine Aussichten [mehr] auf die Präsidentschaft haben; **C** (*ability to run*) **have a lot of ~ left** noch gute Laufkondition haben; **D** (*Horseracing: condition of surface*) **the ~ is good/soft** es lässt sich gut laufen/die Laufbahn ist weich; **E** (*of engine, machine*) Laufen, *das.*
❷ *adj.* **A** (*continuous*) ständig; fortlaufend ‹Erklärungen›; **have** *or* **fight a ~ battle** (*fig.*) ständig im Streit liegen; ⇨ *also* **fire** 1 G; **B** (*in succession*) hintereinander; **win for the third year ~:** schon drei Jahre hintereinander gewinnen; **C** (*Motor Veh.*) **in ~ order** in fahrbereitem Zustand

**running: ~-board** *n.* Trittbrett, *das;* **~ 'commentary** *n.* (*Broadcasting; also fig.*) Livekommentar, *der;* **~ costs** *n. pl.* Betriebskosten *Pl.;* **~ dog** *n.* (*Polit. derog.*) Kettenhund, *der* (*abwertend*); **~ 'head[line]** *n.* (*Printing*) Kolumnentitel, *der;* **~ 'jump** *n.* **you can [go and] take a ~ jump [at yourself]** (*fig. coll.*) du kannst mir den Buckel runterrutschen (*ugs.*); **~ knot** *n.* Knoten einer Schlinge; **~ mate** *n.* (*Amer.*) **A** Mitkandidat, *der*/Mitkandidatin, *die* [*als Vizepräsidentschaftskandidat*]; **B** (*horse as pacesetter*) Pacemacher, *der;* **~ re'pairs** *n. pl.* laufende Reparaturen; **~ shoe** *n.* Rennschuh, *der;* **~ shorts** *n. pl.* Sporthose, *die;* **~ 'sore** *n.* nässende Wunde; (*fig.*) schwärende Wunde; **~ stitch** *n.* (*Needlework*) Vorstich, *der;* **~ 'title** ⇨ **~ head;** **~ 'total** *n.* fortlaufende Summe; **~ track** *n.* Aschenbahn, *die;* **~ 'water** *n.* **A** (*in stream*) fließendes Gewässer; **B** (*available through pipe*) fließendes Wasser; **hot and cold ~ water** fließend warm und kalt Wasser

**runny** /'rʌnɪ/ *adj.* **A** (*secreting mucus*) laufend ‹Nase›; **B** (*excessively liquid*) zerlaufend; zu dünn ‹Farbe, Marmelade›

**'run-off** *n.* (*Sport*) Stechen, *das*

**run-of-the-'mill** *adj.* ganz gewöhnlich

**runt** /rʌnt/ *n.* **A** (*weakling pig*) Kümmerer, *der* (*Landw.*); **B** (*fig. derog.*) Kümmerling, *der* (*abwertend*)

**run: ~-through** *n.* **A** (*cursory reading*) **give a text a [quick] ~-through, have a [brief] ~-through of a text** einen Text [kurz] überfliegen; **B** (*rapid summary*) Überblick, *der* (**of** über + *Akk.*); **C** (*rehearsal*) Durchlaufprobe, *die;* **~-up** *n.* **A** (*approach to an event*) **during** *or* **in the ~-up to an event** im Vorfeld (*fig.*) eines Ereignisses; **B** (*Sport*) Anlauf, *der;* **take a ~-up** Anlauf nehmen

**runway** /'rʌnweɪ/ *n.* (*for take-off*) Startbahn, *die;* (*for landing*) Landebahn, *die*

**rupee** /ru:'pi:/ *n.* ▶ **1328** Rupie, *die*

**rupture** /'rʌptʃə(r)/ ❶ *n.* **A** (*lit. or fig.*) Bruch, *der;* **B** (*Med.*) Ruptur, *die.* ❷ *v.t.* **A** (*burst*) aufreißen; **a ~d appendix/spleen** ein geplatzter Blinddarm/eine gerissene Milz; **B** **~ oneself** sich (*Dat.*) einen Bruch zuziehen *od.* heben; **C** (*sever*) auseinander brechen lassen ‹Beziehungen, Einheit›. ❸ *v.i.* reißen; ‹Blutgefäß, Blinddarm:› platzen

**rural** /'rʊərl/ *adj.* ländlich; **~ life** Landleben, *das*

**rural: ~ 'dean** *n.* (*Eccl.*) ≈ Dekan, *der;* **~ 'district** *n.* (*Brit. Admin. Hist.*) ≈ Landkreis, *der*

**Ruritania** /rʊərɪ'teɪnɪə/ *n. fiktionales mitteleuropäisches Königreich;* Ruritanien (*das*); ≈ Operettenstaat, *der*

**ruse** /ru:z/ *n.* List, *die*

**rush¹** /rʌʃ/ *n.* (*Bot.*) Binse, *die*

**rush²** ❶ *n.* **A** (*rapid moving forward*) **be swept away by the ~ of the current** von der Gewalt der Strömung mitgerissen werden; **make a ~ for sth.** sich auf etw. (*Akk.*) stürzen; **the ~ to the coast** der Ansturm auf die Küste; **the holiday ~:** der [hektische] Urlaubsverkehr; **B** (*hurry*) Eile, *die;* **what's all the ~?** wozu diese Hast?; **be in a [great] ~:** in [großer] Eile sein; es [sehr] eilig haben; **everything happened in such a ~:** es ging alles so schnell; **have a ~ to get somewhere** sich abhetzen, um irgendwohin zu kommen; **C** (*surging*) Anwandlung, *die* (**of** von); **a ~ of blood [to the head]** (*fig. coll.*) eine [plötzliche] Anwandlung; **D** (*period of great activity*) Hochbetrieb, *der;* (**~ hour**) Stoßzeit, *die;* **there is a ~ on** es herrscht Hochbetrieb (*ugs.*); **a ~ of new orders** eine Flut von neuen Aufträgen; **E** *in pl.* (*Cinemat. coll.*) [Bild]muster; Musterkopien; **F** (*heavy demand*) Ansturm, *der* (**for, on** auf + *Akk.*); **G** (*Footb.*) Sturmangriff, *der;* **H** (*Amer. Footb.*) Durchbruch, *der.*
❷ *v.t.* **A** (*convey rapidly*) **~ sb./sth. somewhere** jmdn./etw. auf schnellstem Wege irgendwohin bringen; **~ sb. supplies** jmdn. schnell mit Vorräten versorgen; **~ sb. round the sights** jmdn. von einer Sehenswürdigkeit zur anderen hetzen; **~ through Parliament** im Parlament durchpeitschen (*ugs. abwertend*) ‹Gesetz›; **~ a regiment to the front** ein Regiment an die Front werfen; **be ~ed** (*have to hurry*) in Eile sein; **B** (*cause to act hastily*) **~ sb. into doing sth.** jmdn. dazu drängen, etw. zu tun; **~ sb. into danger/trouble/marriage** jmdn. in Gefahr/Schwierigkeiten bringen/zur Heirat drängen; **she hates to be ~ed** sie kann es nicht ausstehen, wenn sie sich [ab]hetzen muss; **C** (*perform quickly*) auf die Schnelle erledigen; (*perform too quickly*) **~ it** zu schnell machen; **D** (*Mil. or fig.: charge*) stürmen; überrumpeln ‹feindliche Gruppe›; **~ one's fences** (*fig.*) überstürzt handeln; **E** (*coll.: swindle*) **~ sb.** jmdn. neppen (*ugs. abwertend*); **how much did they ~ you for that sherry?** wie viel haben sie dir für den Sherry abgeknöpft? (*salopp*); **F** (*Amer.*) (*entertain*) keilen (*ugs.*); umwerben; (*date*) umwerben. ⇨ *also* **foot** 1 A.
❸ *v.i.* **A** (*move quickly*) eilen; ‹Hund, Pferd:› laufen; **she ~ed into the room** sie stürzte ins Zimmer; **~ through Customs/the exit** durch den Zoll/Ausgang stürmen; **~ to help sb.** jmdm. zu Hilfe eilen; **B** (*hurry unduly*) sich zu sehr beeilen; **don't ~!** nur keine Eile!; **don't be tempted to ~!** lass dir Zeit [dabei]!; **there is no need to ~:** es gibt keinen Grund zur Eile; **C** (*flow rapidly*) stürzen; **~ past** vorbeistürzen; **~ down** hinunterstürzen; **D** (*surge up rapidly*) **the blood ~ed to his face** das Blut schoss ihm ins Gesicht

**~ a'bout, ~ a'round** *v.i.* herumhetzen

**~ at** *v.t.* sich stürzen auf (+ *Akk.*); (*Mil.: charge*) anstürmen gegen ‹Stellung usw.›

**~ 'in** *v.i.* hin-/hereinstürzen; (*fig.*) **~ in with new solutions** vorschnell neue Lösungen präsentieren; **fools ~ in [where angels fear to tread]** (*prov.*) blinder Eifer schadet nur (*Spr.*)

**~ into** *v.t.* **~ into sth.** in etw. (*Akk.*) hin-/hereinstürzen; (*fig.*) sich in etw. (*Akk.*) stürzen/etw. überstürzt tun; **~ into print with sth.** etw. schnellstens veröffentlichen; **you shouldn't ~ into it** das sollte man nicht übereilen

**~ 'up** *v.i.* angestürzt kommen; **~ up to sb.** zu jmdm. stürzen

**rush: ~ hour** *n.* Stoßzeit, *die;* Hauptverkehrszeit, *die;* **~-hour traffic** Berufsverkehr, *der;* **~ job** *n.* eilige Arbeit; **~ mat** *n.* Binsenmatte, *die;* **~ order** *n.* Eilauftrag, *der;* dringende Bestellung

**rusk** /rʌsk/ *n.* Zwieback, *der*

**russet** /'rʌsɪt/ ❶ *n.* **A** (*reddish-brown*) Rotbraun, *das;* **B** (*apple*) *Apfel mit rot- od. gelbbrauner od. braun gesprenkelter rauer Schale.* ❷ *adj.* rotbraun

**Russia** /'rʌʃə/ *pr. n.* Russland (*das*)

**Russian** /'rʌʃn/ ▶ **1275**, ▶ **1340** ❶ *adj.* russisch; **sb. is ~:** jmd. ist Russe/Russin; ⇨ *also* **English** 1. ❷ *n.* **A** (*person*) Russe, *der*/Russin, *die;* **B** (*language*) Russisch, *das;* **Little ~:** Ukrainisch, *das;* ⇨ *also* **English** 2 A

**Russian: ~ 'boot** *n.* Russenstiefel, *der;* **~ Fede'ration** *pr. n.* Russische Föderation; **~ 'mafia** *n.* Russenmafia, *die;* **~ rou'lette** *n.* russisches Roulett[e]; **~ 'salad** *n.* russischer Salat

**Russki** /'rʌskɪ/ *n., pl.* **~s** *or* **~es** (*joc./derog.*) Russki, *der* (*salopp*)

**Russo-** /rʌsəʊ/ *in comb.* russisch-/Russisch-

**rust** /rʌst/ ❶ *n., no pl., no indef. art.* **A** Rost, *der;* **protection against ~:** Rostschutz, *der;* **B** (*Bot.*) Rost, *der.* ❷ *v.i.* **A** rosten; **B** (*fig.: become impaired*) ‹Fähigkeiten, Gedächtnis:› einrosten (*fig.*).
❸ *v.t.* [ver]rosten lassen; **badly ~ed** stark verrostet; **~ed up** festgerostet

**~ 'through** *v.i.* durchrosten

**'Rust Belt** *n.* Rostgürtel, *der;* **a ~ town** eine Stadt im Rostgürtel

**'rust-coloured** *adj.* rostfarben

**rustic** /'rʌstɪk/ ❶ *adj.* **A** (*of the country*) ländlich; **~ life** Landleben, *das;* **B** (*unrefined*) bäurisch (*abwertend*); **C** (*roughly built*) rustikal ‹Mobiliar›; grob gezimmert ‹Bank, Brücke usw.›. ❷ *n.* Bauer, *der*/Bäuerin, *die* (*abwertend*)

**rustically** /'rʌstɪkəlɪ/ *adv.* rustikal

**rusticate** /'rʌstɪkeɪt/ *v.t.* zeitweilig von der Universität relegieren

**rusticity** /rʌ'stɪsɪtɪ/ *n.* Ländlichkeit, *die*

**'rustic-work** *n.* (*Archit.*) Rustika, *die*

**rustle** /'rʌsl/ ❶ *n.* Rascheln, *das.* ❷ *v.i.* rascheln. ❸ *v.t.* **A** rascheln lassen; rascheln mit ‹Papieren›; **B** (*Amer.: steal*) stehlen; **C** (*Amer. coll.*) ⇨ **rustle up**

**~ 'up** *v.t.* (*coll.: produce*) auftreiben (*ugs.*); zusammenzaubern (*fig.*) ‹Mahlzeit›

**rustler** /'rʌslə(r)/ *n.* (*Amer.*) Viehdieb, *der;* **sheep ~:** Schafdieb, *der*

**rustless** /'rʌstlɪs/ *adj.* rostfrei

**'rustproof** ❶ *adj.* rostfrei. ❷ *v.t.* rostfrei *od.* rostbeständig machen

**rusty** /'rʌstɪ/ *adj.* **A** (*rusted*) rostig; **B** (*fig.: impaired by neglect*) eingerostet; **I am a bit ~:** ich bin ein bisschen aus der Übung; **C** (*rust-coloured*) rostfarben; rostfarbig; rost‹braun, -rot›

**rut¹** /rʌt/ ❶ *n.* **A** (*track*) Spurrille, *die;* **B** (*fig.: established procedure*) **get into a ~:** in einen gewissen Trott verfallen; **be in a ~:** aus dem [Alltags]trott nicht mehr herauskommen. ❷ *v.t.*, **-tt-** durchfurchen

**rut²** ❶ *n.* (*sexual excitement*) Brunst, *die;* (*of roe-deer, stag, etc.*) Brunft, *die* (*Jägersprache*). ❷ *v.i.*, **-tt-** in der Brunst sein; ‹Schalenwild:› brunften (*Jägerspr.*)

**rutabaga** /ru:tə'beɪgə/ ⇒ **swede**
**ruthless** /'ru:θlɪs/ *adj.*, **ruthlessly** /'ru:θlɪslɪ/ *adv.* rücksichtslos
**ruthlessness** /'ru:θlɪsnɪs/ *n.*, *no pl.* Rücksichtslosigkeit, *die*
**rutted** /'rʌtɪd/, **rutty** /'rʌtɪ/ *adjs.* zerfurcht
**RV** *abbr.* (*Amer.*) **recreational vehicle**
**Rwanda** /rʊ'ændə/ *pr. n.* Ruanda (*das*)
**rye** /raɪ/ *n.* **A** (*cereal*) Roggen, *der;* **B** ~ [**whisky**] Roggenwhisky, *der;* Rye, *der;* **C** (*Amer.*) ⇒ **rye bread**
**rye:** ~ **bread** *n.* Roggenbrot, *das;* ~**grass** *n.* Raigras, *das*

r

# S s

**S**[1], **s** /es/ *n., pl.* **Ss** *or* **S's** /ˈesɪs/ Ⓐ (*letter*) S, s, *das;* Ⓑ (*curve*) **S bend** S-Biegung, *die*

**S**[2] *abbr.* Ⓐ ▶ 1024 **south** S; Ⓑ ▶ 1024 **southern** s.; Ⓒ **Saint** St.

**'s** (*coll.*) = **is, has, does; let's** /lets/ = **let us**

**s.** *abbr.* Ⓐ **second[s]** Sek.; Ⓑ **singular** Sg.; Ⓒ **son** S.

**SA** *abbr.* Ⓐ **South America;** Ⓑ **South Africa**

**Saar** /zɑː(r)/ *pr. n.* Saar, *die*

**Saarland** /ˈzɑːlænd/ *pr. n.* Saarland, *das*

**Saarlander** /ˈzɑːlændə(r)/ *n.* Saarländer, *der*/-länderin, *die*

**sabbath** /ˈsæbəθ/ *n.* Ⓐ (*Jewish*) Sabbat, *der;* Ⓑ (*Christian*) Sonntag, *der;* Ⓒ **witches' ~:** Hexensabbat, *der*

**sabbatical** /səˈbætɪkl/ ❶ *adj.* Ⓐ (*Jewish Relig.*) **~ year** Sabbatjahr, *das:* Ⓑ **~ term/year** Forschungssemester/-jahr, *das.* ❷ *n.* Forschungsurlaub, *der*

**saber** (*Amer.*) ⇒ **sabre**

**sable** /ˈseɪbl/ *n.* Ⓐ (*Zool., also fur*) Zobel, *der;* Ⓑ **[American] ~:** Fichtenmarder, *der* (*Zool.*); Amerikanischer Zobel

**sabotage** /ˈsæbətɑːʒ/ ❶ *n.* (*lit. or fig.*) Sabotage, *die;* **act of ~:** Sabotageakt, *der;* **industrial ~:** Wirtschaftssabotage, *die.* ❷ *v.t.* einen Sabotageakt verüben auf (+ *Akk.*); (*fig.*) sabotieren ‹Pläne usw.›; **vehicles were ~d** es wurden Sabotageakte auf Fahrzeuge verübt

**saboteur** /sæbəˈtɜː(r)/ *n.* Saboteur, *der*

**sabre** /ˈseɪbə(r)/ *n.* (*Brit.*) Säbel, *der;* **rattle the ~** (*fig.*) mit dem Säbel rasseln (*abwertend*)

**sabre: ~ cut** *n.* Ⓐ (*blow*) Säbelhieb, *der;* Ⓑ (*wound*) Säbelverletzung, *die;* **~-rattling** ❶ *n.* Säbelrasseln, *das* (*abwertend*); ❷ *adj.* säbelrasselnd (*abwertend*)

**sac** /sæk/ *n.* (*Biol.*) **air ~:** Luftsack, *der* (*Zool.*); **foetal ~:** Fruchtblase, *die* (*Med.*)

**saccharin** /ˈsækərɪn/ *n.* Saccharin, *das*

**saccharine** /ˈsækəriːn/ *adj.* (*lit. or fig.*) süßlich

**sacerdotal** /sæsəˈdəʊtl/ *adj.* (*priestly*) priesterlich; Priester‹gewand, -amt›

**sachet** /ˈsæʃeɪ/ *n.* Ⓐ (*small packet*) (*for shampoo etc.*) Beutel, *der;* (*cushion-shaped*) Kissen, *das;* **a ~ of shampoo** ein Beutel/Kissen Shampoo; Ⓑ (*bag for scenting clothes*) Duftkissen, *das*

**sack**[1] /sæk/ ❶ *n.* Ⓐ Sack, *der;* **buy sth. by the ~:** etw. sackweise kaufen; **a ~ of potatoes** ein Sack Kartoffeln; **three ~s of mail** drei Säcke mit Post; Ⓑ (*coll.: dismissal*) Rausschmiss, *der* (*ugs.*); **threaten sb. with the ~:** jmdm. mit Entlassung drohen; **get the ~:** rausgeschmissen werden (*ugs.*); **give sb. the ~:** jmdn. rausschmeißen (*ugs.*); Ⓒ **hit the ~** (*coll.*) sich in die Falle hauen (*salopp*). ❷ *v.t.* Ⓐ (*coll.: dismiss*) rausschmeißen (*ugs.*) (**for** wegen); Ⓑ (*put into ~[s]*) einsacken

**sack**[2] ❶ *v.t.* (*loot*) plündern. ❷ *n.* Plünderung, *die*

**'sackcloth** *n.* Sackleinen, *das;* (*mourning*) Trauergewand, *das;* (*penitential*) Büßergewand, *das;* **in ~ and ashes** in Sack und Asche (*geh.*)

**sackful** /ˈsækfʊl/ *n.* Sack, *der;* **three ~s of potatoes/cement** drei Sack Kartoffeln/Zement; **by the ~:** sackweise

**sacking**[1] /ˈsækɪŋ/ *n.* Ⓐ (*coll.: dismissal*) Rausschmiss, *der* (*ugs.*); Ⓑ (*coarse fabric*) Sackleinen, *das*

**sacking**[2] ⇒ **sack**[2] 2

**'sack race** *n.* Sackhüpfen, *das*

**sacral** /ˈseɪkrl/ *adj.* Ⓐ (*Anat.*) Sakral-; **the ~ vertebrae** die Kreuzbeinwirbel; Vertebrae sacrales (*Med.*); Ⓑ (*Anthrop.*) sakral

**sacrament** /ˈsækrəmənt/ *n.* Sakrament, *das;* **the last ~s** die Sterbesakramente; **the ~ [of the altar], the Blessed** *or* **Holy S~:** das Altarsakrament; **administer/receive the ~** (*the Eucharist*) das Sakrament austeilen/empfangen; **the Holy S~** (*the Host*) das Allerheiligste

**sacramental** /sækrəˈmentl/ *adj.* sakramental; **~ doctrine** Lehre von den Sakramenten

**sacred** /ˈseɪkrɪd/ *adj.* heilig; geheiligt ‹Tradition›; geistlich ‹Musik, Dichtung›; **nothing is ~ to him, he holds nothing ~** (*lit. or fig.*) ihm ist nichts heilig; **is nothing ~?** (*iron.*) scheut man denn vor nichts mehr zurück?

**sacred: ~ 'cow** *n.* (*lit. or fig.*) heilige Kuh; **S~ 'Heart** *n.* **the S~ Heart [of Jesus]** das Herz Jesu

**sacredness** /ˈseɪkrɪdnɪs/ *n., no pl.* Heiligkeit, *die*

**sacrifice** /ˈsækrɪfaɪs/ ❶ *n.* Ⓐ (*giving up valued thing*) Opferung, *die;* (*of principles*) Preisgabe, *die;* (*of pride, possessions*) Aufgabe, *die;* **make ~s** Opfer bringen; Ⓑ (*offering to deity*) Opfer, *das;* **~s to the gods** den Göttern dargebrachte Opfer; (*fig.*) **fall [a] ~ to sth.** einer Sache (*Dat.*) zum Opfer fallen; Ⓒ (*Games: deliberate incurring of loss*) Opfern, *das;* (*Baseball*) *Schlag ins Aus, wobei der Läufer weiterkommt;* (*Bridge*) Opfer, *das* (**against** für). ❷ *v.t.* Ⓐ (*give up, offer as ~*) opfern; **~ oneself/sth. to sth.** sich/etw. einer Sache (*Dat.*) opfern; Ⓑ (*sell at a loss*) zu einem Schleuderpreis verkaufen (*ugs.*). ❸ *v.i.* opfern

**sacrificial** /sækrɪˈfɪʃl/ *adj.* Opfer-; **~ victim** Opfer, *das;* **~ price** (*fig.*) Schleuderpreis, *der*

**sacrilege** /ˈsækrɪlɪdʒ/ *n., no pl.* **[act of] ~:** Sakrileg, *das;* **be little short of ~:** an ein Sakrileg grenzen

**sacrilegious** /sækrɪˈlɪdʒəs/ *adj.* sakrilegisch; (*fig.*) frevelhaft

**sacristan** /ˈsækrɪstən/ *n.* (*Eccl.*) Küster, *der;* Kirchendiener, *der* (*bes. ev. Kirche*); Sakristan, *der* (*bes. kath. Kirche*)

**sacristy** /ˈsækrɪstɪ/ *n.* (*Eccl.*) Sakristei, *die*

**sacrosanct** /ˈsækrəsæŋkt/ *adj.* (*lit. or fig.*) sakrosankt

**sacrum** /ˈseɪkrəm/ *n.* (*Anat.*) Kreuzbein, *das;* Sakrum, *das* (*fachspr.*)

**sad** /sæd/ *adj.* Ⓐ (*sorrowful*) traurig (**at, about** über + *Akk.*); **he was ~ at** *or* **about not getting the job** er war traurig, weil er die Stelle nicht bekam; **feel ~, be in a ~ mood** traurig sein; **it left him a ~der and a wiser man** er hat dabei viel Lehrgeld zahlen müssen; durch Schaden ist er klug geworden; Ⓑ (*causing grief*) traurig; schmerzlich ‹Tod, Verlust›; **it's ~ about Jim** es ist schade um Jim; **~ to say, ...:** bedauerlicherweise ...; **I am ~ to say that ...:** leider *od.* zu meinem Bedauern muss ich sagen, dass ...; leider ...; Ⓒ (*derog./joc.: deplorably bad*) traurig

**SAD** *abbr.* **seasonal affective disorder**

**sadden** /ˈsædn/ *v.t.* traurig stimmen; **be deeply ~ed** tieftraurig sein; **his old age was ~ed by ...:** sein Alter war überschattet von ...; **I was ~ed to see that ...:** es betrübte mich zu sehen, dass ...

**saddle** /ˈsædl/ ❶ *n.* Ⓐ (*seat for rider*) Sattel, *der;* **be in the ~** (*fig.*) das Heft in der Hand haben (*geh.*); Ⓑ (*ridge between summits*) [Berg]sattel, *der;* Ⓒ (*support for cable*) Kabelsattel, *der;* Ⓓ (*Gastr.*) Rücken, *der;* Rückenstück, *das;* **~ of lamb/mutton** Lamm-/Hammelrücken, *der.* ❷ *v.t.* Ⓐ satteln ‹Pferd usw.›; Ⓑ (*fig.*) **~ sb. with sth.** jmdm. etw. aufbürden (*geh.*); **~ debts/responsibility [up]on sb.** Schulden/Verantwortung auf jmdn. abwälzen

**~ 'up** *v.t. & i* aufsatteln

**saddle: ~back** *n.* Ⓐ (*Archit.*) Satteldach, *das;* Ⓑ (*hill*) Hügel mit sattelförmigem Rücken; Ⓒ (*pig*) Sattelschwein, *das;* **~backed** *adj.* sattelförmig; **~bag** *n.* Satteltasche, *die;* **~ blanket** *n.* Satteldecke, *die;* Woilach, *der;* **~ bow** /ˈsædlbəʊ/ *n.* Zwiesel, *der;* **~cloth** ⇒ **~ blanket**

**saddler** /ˈsædlə(r)/ *n.* ▶ 1261 Sattler, *der*

**saddlery** /ˈsædlərɪ/ *n.* Ⓐ (*work, place*) Sattlerei, *die;* Ⓑ (*saddles etc.*) Sattlerwaren *Pl.*

**saddle: ~ soap** *n.* Sattelseife, *die;* **~ sore** *n.* Sattelwunde, *die;* **~-sore** *adj.* **be ~-sore** wund vom Reiten/Radfahren sein; **~ stitch** *n.* Ⓐ (*Bookbinding*) Heftstich, *der;* Ⓑ (*Needlework*) Vorstich, *der*

**sadism** /ˈseɪdɪzm/ *n.* Sadismus, *der*

**sadist** /ˈseɪdɪst/ *n.* Sadist, *der*/Sadistin, *die*

**sadistic** /səˈdɪstɪk/ *adj.*, **sadistically** /səˈdɪstɪkəlɪ/ *adv.* sadistisch

**sadly** /ˈsædlɪ/ *adv.* Ⓐ (*with sorrow*) traurig; Ⓑ (*unfortunately*) leider; Ⓒ (*deplorably*) erbärmlich (*abwertend*); **they are ~ lacking in common sense** sie haben erbärmlich wenig [gesunden Menschen]verstand

**sadness** /ˈsædnɪs/ *n., no pl.* Traurigkeit, *die* (**at, about** über + *Akk.*)

**sadomasochism** /seɪdəʊˈmæsəkɪzm/ *n.* Sadomasochismus, *der*

**sadomasochist** /seɪdəʊˈmæsəkɪst/ *n.* Sadomasochist, *der*/Sadomasochistin, *die*

**'sad sack** *n.* (*Amer. coll.*) trübe Tasse (*ugs. abwertend*)

**s.a.e.** /eseɪˈiː/ *abbr.* **stamped addressed envelope** adressierter Freiumschlag

**safari** /səˈfɑːrɪ/ *n.* Safari, *die;* **be/go on ~:** auf Safari sein/gehen

**sa'fari park** *n.* Safaripark, *der*

**safe** /seɪf/ ❶ *n.* Ⓐ Safe, *der;* Geldschrank, *der;* Ⓑ (*Amer. coll.: contraceptive*) Präser, *der* (*salopp*); Ⓒ ⇒ **meat safe**.
❷ *adj.* Ⓐ (*out of danger*) sicher (**from** vor + *Dat.*); **he's ~:** er ist in Sicherheit; **the bullfighter was ~:** der Stierkämpfer war nicht in Gefahr; **make sth. ~ from sth.** etw. gegen etw. sichern; **~ and sound** sicher und wohlbehalten; Ⓑ (*free from danger*) ungefährlich; sicher ‹Ort, Hafen›; **she's a ~ driver** sie fährt sicher; **better ~ than sorry** Vorsicht ist besser als Nachsicht (*ugs.*); **is the water ~ to drink?** kann man das Wasser ohne Risiko trinken?; **wish sb. a ~ journey** jmdm. eine gute Reise wünschen; **is the car ~ to drive?** ist der Wagen verkehrssicher?; **the maximum ~ load** das zulässige Ladegewicht; **a ~ margin** eine Sicherheitsmarge; **the beach is ~ for bathing** es ist ungefährlich, am Strand zu baden; **to be on the ~ side** zur Sicherheit; **we had better be on the ~ side** wir sollten lieber sichergehen; Ⓒ (*unlikely to produce controversy*) sicher; bewährt (*iron.*) ‹Klischee›; **it is ~ to say [that ...]** man kann mit einiger Sicherheit sagen[, dass ...]; **it is not ~ to generalize in such a matter** in einer solchen Frage kann man nicht einfach verallgemeinern; Ⓓ (*reliable*) sicher ‹Methode, Investition, Stelle›; nahe liegend ‹Vermutung›; **in ~**

S

hands in guten Händen; a ~ Conservative seat (*Polit.*) eine Hochburg der Konservativen Partei; E (*secure*) be ~ in prison, be in ~ custody in sicherem Gewahrsam sein; your secrets will be ~ with me deine Geheimnisse sind bei mir gut aufgehoben

**safe:** ~ **'bet** *n.* it is a ~ bet he will be there man kann darauf wetten, dass er dort ist; he is a ~ bet to win/for Prime Minister man kann darauf wetten, dass er gewinnt/dass er der nächste Premierminister wird; ~-**breaker** *n.* Geldschrankknacker, *der* (*ugs.*); ~ **'conduct** *n.* A (*privilege*) freies *od.* sicheres Geleit; B (*document*) Schutzbrief, *der* (*Politik, Dipl.*); ~-**cracker** ⇒ ~-breaker; ~ **de'posit** *n.* Tresor, *der; attrib.* ~-**deposit box** (*at the bank*) Banksafe, *der;* ~**guard** ❶ *n.* Schutz, *der;* as a ~guard against infection zum Schutz gegen Infektionen; ❷ *v.t.* schützen; ~guard sb.'s future/interests jmds. Zukunft sichern/Interessen wahren; ~ **'haven** *n.* A (*safe place*) Zuflucht, *die;* Zufluchtsort, *der;* B (*Polit.: protected zone*) Schutzzone, *die;* ~ **house** *n.* geheimer Unterschlupf (*von Terroristen, Agenten usw.*); ~ **'keeping** *n.* sichere Obhut (*geh.*); (*of thing*) [sichere] Aufbewahrung

**safely** /'seɪflɪ/ *adv.* A (*without harm*) sicher; did the parcel arrive ~? ist das Paket heil angekommen?; B (*securely*) sicher; the children are ~ tucked up in bed die Kinder liegen friedlich im Bett; be ~ behind bars [in sicherem Gewahrsam] hinter Schloss und Riegel sein; C (*with certainty*) one can ~ say [that] she will come man kann mit ziemlicher Sicherheit sagen, dass sie kommt

**safe:** ~ **period** *n.* unfruchtbare Tage; ~ **'seat** *n.* (*Polit.*) Hochburg, *die;* ≈ sicherer Wahlkreis; ~ **'sex** *n.* Safer Sex, *der;* geschützter Sex

**safety** /'seɪftɪ/ *n.* A (*being out of danger*) Sicherheit, *die;* cross the river in ~: sicher über den Fluss fahren; B (*lack of danger*) Ungefährlichkeit, *die;* (*of a machine*) Betriebssicherheit, *die;* do sth. with ~: etw. tun, ohne sich einer Gefahr (*Dat.*) auszusetzen; there is ~ in numbers zu mehreren ist man sicherer; a ~ first policy eine Politik der Vorsicht; one can say with ~ that ...: man kann mit Sicherheit behaupten, dass ...; C *attrib.* Sicherheits‹netz, -kette, -faktor, -maßnahmen, -vorrichtungen›

**safety:** ~ **belt** *n.* Sicherheitsgurt, *der;* ~ **catch** *n.* (*of door*) Sicherheitsverriegelung, *die;* (*of gun*) Sicherungshebel, *der;* ~ **curtain** *n.* (*Theatre*) eiserner Vorhang; ~ **fuse** *n.* (*Electr.*) Sicherung, *die;* ~ **glass** *n.* Sicherheitsglas, *das;* ~ **helmet** *n.* Schutzhelm, *der;* ~ **margin** *n.* Spielraum, *der;* ~ **match** *n.* Sicherheitszündholz, *das;* ~ **pin** *n.* Sicherheitsnadel, *die;* ~ **play** *n.* (*Bridge*) Auf-sicher-Spielen, *das; Spiel, bei dem geringe Verluste hingenommen werden, um größere zu vermeiden;* ~ **razor** *n.* Rasierapparat, *der;* ~ **valve** *n.* Sicherheitsventil, *das* (*Technik*); (*fig.*) Ventil, *das* (*fig.*); ~ **zone** *n.* (*Amer.: traffic island*) Verkehrsinsel, *die*

**'safe zone** *n.* (*Polit.*) Schutzzone, *die*

**saffron** /'sæfrən/ ❶ *n.* Safran, *der;* ⇒ *also* **meadow saffron**. ❷ *adj.* safrangelb

**sag** /sæg/ ❶ *v.i.,* **-gg-** A (*have downward bulge*) durchhängen; B (*sink*) sich senken; absacken (*ugs.*); ‹Gebäude:› [in sich (*Akk.*)] zusammensacken (*ugs.*); ‹Schultern:› herabhängen; ‹Brüste:› hängen; (*fig.: decline*) ‹Mut, Stimmung:› sinken; the interest/storyline ~s halfway through the book die Spannung/Geschichte lässt in der Mitte des Buches [spürbar] nach; ~ging breasts Hängebusen, *der* (*ugs.*); C (*hang lopsidedly*) the gate ~ged half off its hinges das Tor hing schief in den Angeln; the bridge ~s on one side die Brücke ist auf einer Seite abgesackt (*ugs.*).
❷ *n.* A (*amount that rope etc. ~s*) Durchhang, *der;* B (*sinking*) there was a ~ in the seat/mattress der Sitz war durchgesessen/die Matratze war durchgelegen

**saga** /'sɑːgə/ *n.* A (*story of adventure*) Heldenepos, *das* (*fig.*); (*medieval narrative*) Saga, *die* (*Literaturw.*); knightly ~: ≈ Ritterroman, *der;* the ~ of a family die Geschichte einer Familie; B (*long involved story*) [ganzer] Roman (*fig.*); the ~ of our holiday in Spain die Geschichte unseres Spanienurlaubs

**sagacious** /sə'geɪʃəs/ *adj.* klug; ~ mind scharfer Verstand

**sagaciously** /sə'geɪʃəslɪ/ *adv.* klug

**sagacity** /sə'gæsɪtɪ/ *n., no pl.* Klugheit, *die*

**sage**[1] /seɪdʒ/ *n.* (*Bot.*) Salbei, *der od. die;* ~-and-onion stuffing Salbei-und-Zwiebel-Füllung, *die*

**sage**[2] ❶ *n.* Weise, *der.* ❷ *adj.* weise

**sage:** ~**brush** *n.* (*Bot.*) Beifuß, *der* (*in nordamerikanischen Steppen*); ~ **'cheese**, ~ **'Derby** *ns.* Käse mit Salbeigewürz; ~-**'green** ❶ *adj.* salbeigrün; ❷ *n.* Salbeigrün, *das*

**sagely** /'seɪdʒlɪ/ *adv.* weise

**sage 'tea** *n.* Salbeitee, *der*

**Sagittarian** /sædʒɪ'teərɪən/ *n.* (*Astrol.*) Schütze, *der*

**Sagittarius** /sædʒɪ'teərɪəs/ *n.* (*Astrol., Astron.*) der Schütze; der Sagittarius; ⇒ *also* **Aries**

**sago** /'seɪgəʊ/ *n., pl.* ~**s** Sago, *der*

**Sahara** /sə'hɑːrə/ *pr. n.* the ~ [Desert] die [Wüste] Sahara

**sahib** /sɑːb, 'sɑːɪb/ *n.* A (*arch.: title*) Sahib, *der;* B (*gentleman*) Herr, *der*

**said** ⇒ **say** 1, 2

**sail** /seɪl/ ❶ *n.* A (*voyage in ~ing vessel*) Segelfahrt, *die;* go for a ~: eine Segelfahrt machen; the island is ten days' ~ from Plymouth von Plymouth aus erreicht man die Insel [mit dem Segelschiff] in zehn Tagen; B (*piece of canvas*) Segel, *das;* in *or* under full ~: mit vollen Segeln; under ~: unter Segel (*Seemannsspr.*); C *pl. same* (*ship*) Segelschiff, *das;* D (*of windmill*) [Windmühlen]flügel, *der.* ⇒ *also* **make** 1 S; **set** 1 L; **shorten** 2 B; **strike** 2 T; **wind**[1] 1 A.
❷ *v.i.* A (*travel on water*) fahren; (*in sailing boat*) segeln; a lovely boat to ~ in ein schönes Boot zum Segeln; B (*start voyage*) auslaufen (for nach); in See stechen; C (*glide in air*) segeln; D (*fig.: be thrown*) segeln (*ugs.*); the bottle which ~ed past his ear die Flasche, die an seinem Ohr vorbeisegelte (*ugs.*); E (*walk in stately manner*) segeln (*ugs.*); ~ by vorübersegeln (*salopp*); F (*move smoothly*) gleiten; ~ through hindurchgleiten; G (*fig. coll.: pass easily*) ~ through an examination eine Prüfung spielend schaffen. ⇒ *also* **colour** 1 J; **wind**[1] 1 A.
❸ *v.t.* A steuern ‹Boot, Schiff›; segeln mit ‹Segeljacht, -schiff›; B (*travel across*) durchfahren, befahren ‹Meer›; ‹Segelschiff:› durchsegeln
~ **'in** *v.i.* (*coll.: enter*) hereinsegeln (*ugs.*)
~ **into** *v.t.* (*coll.*) A ~ into a room in ein Zimmer hereingesegelt kommen (*ugs.*); B (*attack*) ~ into sb. über jmdn. herfallen

**sail:** ~**board** *n.* Surfbrett, *das* (*zum Windsurfen*); ~**boarding** ⇒ **windsurfing**; ~**boat** *n.* (*Amer.*) Segelboot, *das;* ~**cloth** *n.* Segeltuch, *das*

**sailing** /'seɪlɪŋ/ *n.* A (*handling a boat*) Segeln, *das;* weather for ~: Segelwetter, *das;* B (*departure from a port*) Abfahrt, *die;* there are regular ~s from here across to the island von hier fahren regelmäßig Schiffe hinüber zur Insel

**sailing:** ~ **boat** *n.* Segelboot, *das;* ~ **orders** *n. pl.* Order zum Auslaufen; ~ **ship**, ~ **vessel** *ns.* Segelschiff, *das*

**'sailmaker** *n.* ▶ 1261 Segelmacher, *der*

**sailor** /'seɪlə(r)/ *n.* Seemann, *der;* (*in navy*) Matrose, *der;* be a good/bad ~ (*not get seasick/get seasick*) seefest/nicht seefest sein

**'sailor suit** *n.* Matrosenanzug, *der*

**sainfoin** /'sænfɔɪn, 'seɪnfɔɪn/ *n.* (*Bot.*) Esparsette, *die*

**saint** ❶ /sənt/ *adj.* S~ Michael/Helena der heilige Michael/die heilige Helena; Sankt Michael/Helena; *as voc.* heiliger Michael/heilige Helena; ~ Michael's [Church] die Michaelskirche; ~ Andrew's/George's cross Andreas-/Georgskreuz, *das.* ❷ /seɪnt/ *n.* Heilige, *der/die;* make *or* declare sb. a ~ (*RC Ch.*) jmdn. heilig sprechen; be as patient as a ~: eine Engelsgeduld haben; ⇒ *also* **aunt**, **patron** C

**Saint Bernard** /sənt 'bɜːnəd/ *n.* ~ [dog] Bernhardiner, *der*

**sainthood** /'seɪnthʊd/ *n.* Heiligkeit, *die*

**Saint:** ~ **James** /sənt 'dʒeɪmz/ *n.* Court of ~ James *der britische Hof;* ~ **John's wort** /sənt 'dʒɒnz wɜːt/ *n.* (*Bot.*) Johanniskraut, *das;* ~ **Lawrence** /sənt 'lɒrəns/ *n.* (*Geog.*) Sankt-Lorenz-Strom, *der*

**saintly** /'seɪntlɪ/ *adj.* heilig; ~ patience Engelsgeduld, *die*

**Saint:** ~ **Peter's** /sənt 'piːtəz/ *pr. n.* (*in Rome*) die Peterskirche; **s~'s day** *n.* Tag eines/einer Heiligen; ⇒ *also* **all** 1 B; ~ **Swithin's day** /sənt 'swɪðɪnz deɪ/ *n. 15. Juli, der nach britischem Volksglauben wetterbestimmend für die folgenden vierzig Tage ist;* ≈ Siebenschläfer, *der;* ~ **Vitus's dance** /sənt vaɪtəsɪz 'dɑːns/ ⇒ **dance** 3 D

**sake**[1] /seɪk/ *n.* for the ~ of um ... (*Gen.*) willen; for my *etc.* ~: um meinetwillen *usw.;* mir *usw.* zuliebe; for all our ~s uns allen zuliebe; for your/its own ~: um deiner/seiner selbst willen; art for art's ~: Kunst um ihrer selbst willen; for the ~ of a few pounds wegen ein paar Pfund; for Christ's *or* God's *or* goodness' *or* Heaven's *or* (*coll.*) Pete's *etc.* ~: um Gottes *od.* Himmels willen; for old times' ~: um der schönen Erinnerung willen; ⇒ *also* **appearance** B; **argument** B; **convenience** B

**sake**[2] /'sɑːkɪ/ *n.* (*drink*) Sake, *der*

**salaam** /sə'lɑːm/ *n.* Salam [alaikum] (*veralt., noch scherzh.*); *in pl.* (*respects*) Komplimente (*veralt.*)

**salable** ⇒ **saleable**

**salacious** /sə'leɪʃəs/ *adj.* A (*lustful*) lüstern; B (*inciting sexual desire*) pornographisch

**salaciously** /sə'leɪʃəslɪ/ *adv.* lüstern

**salad** /'sæləd/ *n.* Salat, *der;* ham/tomato ~: Schinken-/Tomatensalat, *der*

**salad:** ~ **cream** *n.* ≈ Mayonnaise, *die;* ~ **days** *n. pl.* in my ~ days als ich noch nicht trocken hinter den Ohren war (*ugs.*); ~ **dressing** *n.* Dressing, *das;* Salatsoße, *die;* ~ **oil** *n.* Salatöl, *das;* ~ **servers** *n. pl.* Salatbesteck, *das*

**salamander** /'sæləmændə(r)/ *n.* A (*Zool.*) Salamander, *der;* B (*Amer.*) ⇒ **gopher** A

**salami** /sə'lɑːmɪ/ *n.* Salami, *die*

**sal ammoniac** /sæl ə'məʊnɪæk/ *n.* Salmiak, *der od. das*

**salaried** /'sælərɪd/ *adj.* A (*receiving salary*) Gehalt beziehend; ~ employee Angestellte, *der/die;* the ~ class die Gehaltsempfänger; B (*having salary attached to it*) ~ post Stelle mit festem Gehalt

**salary** /'sælərɪ/ *n.* Gehalt, *das;* (*Amer.: weekly*) Lohn, *der;* ~ increase Gehaltserhöhung, *die;* what is your ~? wie hoch ist dein Gehalt?; draw a ~: ein Gehalt beziehen

**sale** /seɪl/ *n.* A (*selling*) Verkauf, *der;* [up] for ~: zu verkaufen; put up *or* offer for ~: zum Verkauf anbieten; on ~: im Handel; on ~ at your chemist's in Ihrer Apotheke erhältlich; go on ~: in den Handel kommen; offer *etc.* sth. on a ~ or return basis etw. auf Kommissionsbasis anbieten *usw.;* B (*instance of selling*) Verkauf, *der;* make a ~: einen Verkauf tätigen (*Kaufmannsspr.*); find a ready ~ for sth. etw. gut verkaufen; sth. finds a ready ~: etw. verkauft sich gut; C *in pl., no art.* (*amount sold*) Verkaufszahlen *Pl.* (of für); Absatz, *der;* D [jumble *or* rummage] ~: [Wohltätigkeits]basar, *der;* ~ of work Wohltätigkeitsbasar mit eigenen Bastel-, Handarbeiten; E (*disposal at reduced prices*) Ausverkauf, *der;* clearance/end-of-season/summer ~: Räumungs-/Schluss-/Sommerschlussverkauf, *der;* at the ~s im Ausverkauf; F (*public auction*) [Verkauf durch] Versteigerung; put sth. up for

S

~ **[by auction]** etw. zur Versteigerung anbieten

**saleable** /'seɪləbl/ *adj.* verkäuflich; **be [highly] ~:** sich [gut] verkaufen lassen

**sale: ~ ring** *n.* Käuferring bei einer Auktion; **~room** *n.* (*Brit.*) Auktionsraum, *der*

**sales: ~ assistant** (*Brit.*), **~ clerk** (*Amer.*) *ns.* ▶ 1261 Verkäufer, *der*/Verkäuferin, *die;* **~ department** *n.* Verkaufsabteilung, *die;* **~ desk** ⇒ **desk** B; **~ force** *n.* Vertreterstab, *der;* **~girl**, **~lady** *ns.* ▶ 1261 Verkäuferin, *die;* **~man** /'seɪlzmən/ *n., pl.* **~men** /'seɪlzmən/ ▶ 1261 Verkäufer, *der;* **~ manager** *n.* ▶ 1261 Verkaufsleiter, *der*/-leiterin, *die;* Salesmanager, *der*

**salesmanship** /'seɪlzmənʃɪp/ *n., no pl., no indef. art.* Kunst des Verkaufens

**sales: ~ patter**, **~ pitch** *ns.* Verkaufsargumentation, *die;* **~ rep** (*coll.*), **~ representative** *ns.* ▶ 1261 [Handels]vertreter, *der*/-vertreterin, *die;* **~ resistance** *n.* Kaufunlust, *die;* **~ talk** ⇒ **~ patter**; **~ tax** *n.* Umsatzsteuer, *die;* **~woman** *n.* ▶ 1261 Verkäuferin, *die*

**salient** /'seɪlɪənt/ ❶ *adj.* Ⓐ (*striking*) auffallend; ins Auge springend; hervorstechend ‹Charakterzug›; **the ~ points of a speech** die herausragenden Punkte einer Rede; Ⓑ (*pointing outwards*) vorspringend. ❷ *n.* (*Mil.*) vorgeschobene Stellung

**saline** /'seɪlaɪn/ *adj.* salzig; Salz‹ablagerung›; **~ solution** Salzlösung, *die;* (*Med.*) [physiologische] Kochsalzlösung; **~ drip** (*Med.*) Tropfinfusion, *die*

**salinity** /sə'lɪnɪtɪ/ *n.* Salzgehalt, *der;* **be high in ~:** stark salzhaltig sein

**saliva** /sə'laɪvə/ *n.* Speichel, *der*

**salivary** /'sælɪvərɪ, sə'laɪvərɪ/ *adj.* (*Anat.*) **~ gland** Speicheldrüse, *die*

**salivate** /'sælɪveɪt/ *v.i.* speicheln

**sa'liva test** *n.* Speicheltest, *der* (*bes. Med.*)

**sallow[1]** /'sæləʊ/ *adj.* blassgelb

**sallow[2]** *n.* (*Bot.*) Salweide, *die*

**sallowness** /'sæləʊnɪs/ *n., no pl.* gelbliche Blässe

**sally** ❶ *n.* Ⓐ (*Mil.: sortie*) Ausfall, *der;* Ⓑ (*excursion*) Ausflug, *der;* Ⓒ (*verbal attack*) **his sallies against the authorities** seine Ausfälle gegen die Obrigkeit; Ⓓ (*witty remark*) Geistesblitz, *der* (*ugs.*). ❷ *v.i.* Ⓐ **~ out** (*Mil.: make sortie/sorties*) einen Ausfall/Ausfälle machen; Ⓑ **~ forth** aufbrechen, sich aufmachen (**for** zu)

**Sally** /'sælɪ/ ⇒ **aunt**

**salmon** /'sæmən/ ❶ *n., pl. same* Lachs, *der.* ❷ *adj.* (*colour*) lachsfarben; lachsrosa ‹Farbton›

**'salmon-coloured** *adj.* lachsfarben

**salmonella** /sælmə'nelə/ *n.* ▶ 1232 Salmonelle, *die;* **~ poisoning** Salmonellenvergiftung, *die*

**salmon: ~ ladder**, **~ leap** *ns.* Lachstreppe, *die;* **~ pink** ❶ *n.* lachsrosa Farbton; ❷ *adj.* lachsfarben; **~ 'trout** *n.* Lachsforelle, *die*

**salon** /'sælɒ̃/ *n.* Salon, *der*

**'salon music** *n.* Salonmusik, *die*

**saloon** /sə'lu:n/ *n.* Ⓐ (*public room in ship, hotel, etc.*) Salon, *der;* **dining ~:** Speisesaal, *der;* **billiard ~** (*Brit.*) Billardraum, *der;* Ⓑ (*Brit.: motor car*) Limousine, *die;* Ⓒ (*Amer.: bar*) Saloon, *der*

**saloon: ~ 'bar** *n.* (*Brit.*) *separater Teil eines Pubs mit mehr Komfort;* **~ 'car** ⇒ **saloon** B; **~ deck** *n.* Salondeck, *das*

**salsify** /'sælsɪfɪ/ *n.* (*Bot.*) Haferwurz, *die*

**salt** /sɔ:lt, sɒlt/ ❶ *n.* Ⓐ (*for food etc.; also Chem.*) **[common] ~:** [Koch]salz, *das;* **above/below the ~** (*Hist.*) oben/unten an der Tafel; **rub ~ in[to] the wound** (*fig.*) Salz in die Wunde streuen; **take sth. with a grain** *or* **pinch of ~** (*fig.*) etw. cum grano salis (*geh.*) *od.* nicht ganz wörtlich nehmen; **be the ~ of the earth** (*fig.*) anständig und rechtschaffen sein; das Salz der Erde sein (*bibl.*); **be worth one's ~:** etwas taugen; (*worth the money one is paid*) sein Geld wert sein; Ⓑ *in pl.* (*medicine*) Salz, *das;* **like a dose of ~s** (*coll.*) in null Komma nichts (*ugs.*); **he went through the department like a dose of ~s** (*fig.*) er kehrte in der Abteilung mit eisernem Besen [aus]; Ⓒ (*fig.: zest*) Salz, *das* (*fig.*); Würze, *die* (*fig.*); Ⓓ **[old] ~** (*sailor*) [alter] Seebär (*ugs. scherzh.*).
❷ *adj.* Ⓐ (*containing or tasting of ~*) salzig; (*preserved with ~*) gepökelt ‹Fleisch›; gesalzen ‹Butter›; Ⓑ (*bitter*) salzig ‹Tränen›; Ⓒ (*biting*) scharf, ätzend ‹Witz›.
❸ *v.t.* Ⓐ (*add ~ to*) salzen; (*fig.*) würzen; Ⓑ (*preserve with ~ or brine*) [ein]pökeln; **~ed beef/pork** gepökeltes Rind-/Schweinefleisch; Ⓒ (*spread ~ on*) **~ the roads** Salz auf die Straßen streuen
**~ a'way**, **~ 'down** *v.t.* (*coll.*) auf die hohe Kante legen (*ugs.*)

**SALT** /sɔ:lt, sɒlt/ *abbr.* **Strategic Arms Limitation Talks/Treaty** SALT

**salt: ~ cellar** *n.* (*open*) Salzfass, *das;* (*sprinkler*) Salzstreuer, *der;* **~ 'lake** *n.* Salzsee, *der;* **~ lick** *n.* Salzlecke, *die* (*Jägerspr.*); **~ marsh** *n.* Salzwiesengebiet, *das;* (*formed by evaporation*) Salzsumpf, *der;* **~ mine** *n.* Salzbergwerk, *das;* **~ pan** *n.* Salzpfanne, *die*

**saltpetre** (*Amer.:* **saltpeter**) /'sɔ:ltpi:tə(r), 'sɒltpi:tə(r)/ *n.* Salpeter, *der*

**salt: ~ shaker** *n.* (*Amer.*) Salzstreuer, *der;* **~ spoon** *n.* Salzlöffelchen, *das;* **~ sprinkler** *n.* Salzstreuer, *der;* **~ 'water** *n.* Salzwasser, *das;* **~water** *adj.* Salzwasser-; **~ works** *n. sing., pl. same* Saline, *die*

**salty** /'sɔ:ltɪ, 'sɒltɪ/ *adj.* salzig; (*fig.*) scharf ‹Witz›

**salubrious** /sə'lu:brɪəs/ *adj.* gesund; **not a very ~ area** (*fig.*) ein etwas zweifelhaftes Viertel

**saluki** /sə'lu:kɪ/ *n.* Saluki, *der;* Persischer Windhund

**salutary** /'sæljʊtərɪ/ *adj.* heilsam ‹Wirkung, Einfluss, Schock›; heilkräftig ‹Medizin›

**salutation** /sæljʊ'teɪʃn/ *n.* (*formal*) Gruß, *der;* Begrüßung, *die;* **form of ~:** Begrüßungsformel, *die;* **raise one's hat [to sb.] in ~:** [vor jmdm.] zum Gruß den Hut ziehen

**salute** /sə'lu:t/ ❶ *v.t.* Ⓐ (*Mil., Navy*) **~ sb.** jmdn. [militärisch] grüßen; (*fig.: pay tribute to*) sich vor jmdm. verneigen; Ⓑ (*greet*) grüßen. ❷ *v.i.* (*Mil., Navy*) [militärisch] grüßen. ❸ *n.* Ⓐ (*Mil., Navy*) Salut, *der;* militärischer Gruß; **fire a seven-gun ~:** sieben Schuss Salut abfeuern; **give a ~:** militärisch grüßen; **take the ~** ‹Vorgesetzter:› den militärischen Gruß entgegennehmen; ‹Staatsoberhaupt usw.:› die Parade abnehmen; Ⓑ (*gesture of greeting*) Gruß, *der;* Ⓒ (*Fencing*) [Fecht]gruß, *der*

**Salvadorean** /sælvə'dɔ:rɪən/ ▶ 1340 ❶ *n.* Salvadorianer, *der*/Salvadorianerin, *die.* ❷ *adj.* salvadorianisch

**salvage** /'sælvɪdʒ/ ❶ *n.* Ⓐ (*rescue of property*) Bergung, *die; attrib.* Bergungs‹arbeiten, -aktion›; Ⓑ (*payment*) Bergelohn, *der* (*Seew.*); Ⓒ (*rescued property*) Bergegut, *das;* (*for recycling*) Sammelgut, *das;* **collect bottles for ~:** Flaschen zur Wiedergewinnung von Glas sammeln. ❷ *v.t.* Ⓐ (*rescue*) bergen; retten (*auch fig.*) (**from** von); **~ one's valuables from the flames** seine Wertsachen aus den Flammen retten; Ⓑ (*save for recycling*) für die Wiederverwendung sammeln

**'salvage operation** *n.* Bergungsaktion, *die*

**salvation** /sæl'veɪʃn/ *n.* Ⓐ *no art.* (*Relig.*) Erlösung, *die;* **doctrine of ~:** Heilslehre, *die;* **find ~:** zum Heil gelangen; **work out one's own ~** (*fig.*) auf eigene Weise ans Ziel gelangen; Ⓑ (*means of preservation*) Rettung, *die;* **those biscuits were my ~** (*joc.*) diese Kekse haben mir das Leben gerettet (*scherzh.*)

**Salvation 'Army** *n.* Heilsarmee, *die*

**Salvationist** /sæl'veɪʃənɪst/ *n.* (*member of Salvation Army*) Heilsarmist, *der*/-armistin, *die*

**salve[1]** /sælv/ ❶ *n.* Balsam, *der* (*geh.*) (**to** für); **his apology was merely a ~ for his conscience** mit der Entschuldigung wollte er nur sein Gewissen beruhigen. ❷ *v.t.* (*soothe*) besänftigen; beruhigen ‹Gewissen›

**salve[2]** /sælv/ *v.t.* ⇒ **salvage** 2 A

**salver** /'sælvə(r)/ *n.* Tablett, *das*

**salvo** /'sælvəʊ/ *n., pl.* **~es** *or* **~s** Ⓐ (*of guns*) Salve, *die;* Ⓑ **~ of applause/laughter** Beifalls-/Lachsalve, *die*

**sal volatile** /sæl vɒ'lætɪlɪ/ *n.* Riechsalz, *das*

**Samaritan** /sə'mærɪtən/ *n.* **good ~:** [barmherziger] Samariter; **I decided to be a good ~:** ich beschloss, ein gutes Werk zu tun; **the ~s** (*organization*) ≈ die Telefonseelsorge

**samba** /'sæmbə/ *n.* Samba, *der*

**Sam Browne** /sæm 'braʊn/ *n.* Ⓐ (*von brit. Offizieren getragenes*) Koppel mit Schulterriemen; Ⓑ (*cyclist's*) Leuchtgurt, *der*

**same** /seɪm/ ❶ *adj.* **the ~:** der/die/das gleiche; **the ~ [thing]** (*identical*) der-/die-/dasselbe; **the ~ afternoon/evening** (*of ~ day*) schon am Nachmittag/Abend; **she seemed just the ~ [as ever] to me** sie schien mir unverändert *od.* immer noch die Alte; **my parents are much the ~** (*not much changed*) meine Eltern haben sich kaum geändert; **he was no longer the ~ man** er war nicht mehr derselbe; **one and the ~ person/man** ein und dieselbe Person/ein und derselbe Mann; **the very ~:** genau der/die/das; ebenderselbe/-dieselbe/-dasselbe; **much the ~ as** fast genauso wie; **this/that/these** *or* **those ~:** ebender-/ebendie-/ebendasselbe/ebendieselben; genau der-/die-/dasselbe/dieselben; ⇒ *also* **token** 1 D.
❷ *pron.* **the ~**, (*coll.*) **~** (*the ~ thing*) der-/die-/dasselbe; **he ran up big bills but was not strong at paying ~** (*coll.*) er machte große Schulden, machte aber keine Anstalten, sie zu bezahlen; **an actual banana or a photo of the ~:** eine echte Banane oder ein Foto davon; **things haven't been the ~ since you left** seit du nicht mehr da bist, haben sich die Dinge geändert; **they look [exactly] the ~:** sie sehen gleich aus; **more of the ~:** noch mehr davon; **and the ~ to you!** (*also iron.*) danke gleichfalls; **[the] ~ again** das Gleiche noch einmal; **I feel bored — S~ here** (*coll.*) Ich langweile mich — dito.
❸ *adv.* **[the] ~ as you do** genau wie du; **the ~ as before** genau wie vorher; **be pronounced the ~:** gleich ausgesprochen werden; **all** *or* **just the ~:** trotzdem; nichtsdestotrotz (*ugs., oft scherzh.*); **think the ~ of/feel the ~ towards** dasselbe halten von/empfinden für

**'same-day** *adj.* ‹Dienst› noch am gleichen Tag

**sameness** /'seɪmnɪs/ *n., no pl.* Gleichheit, *die*

**Samoa** /sə'məʊə/ *pr. n.* Samoa (*das*)

**Samoan** /sə'məʊən/ ▶ 1275, ▶ 1340 ❶ *adj.* samoanisch. ❷ *n.* Samoaner, *der*/Samoanerin, *die*

**samovar** /'sæməvɑ:(r)/ *n.* Samowar, *der*

**sampan** /'sæmpæn/ *n.* Sampan, *der*

**sample** /'sɑ:mpl/ ❶ *n.* Ⓐ (*representative portion*) Auswahl, *die;* (*in opinion research, statistics*) Querschnitt, *der;* Sample, *das;* Ⓑ (*example*) [Muster]beispiel, *das;* (*specimen*) Probe, *die;* **[commercial] ~:** Muster, *das; attrib.* Probe‹exemplar, -seite›; **~ of air/blood** Luft-/Blutprobe, *die.* ❷ *v.t.* probieren; **~ the pleasures of country life** die Freuden des Landlebens kosten (*geh.*)

**sampler** /'sɑ:mplə(r)/ *n.* Ⓐ (*piece of needlework*) Stickarbeit, *die;* Stickerei, *die;* Ⓑ (*trial pack*) Probe[packung], *die;* Ⓒ (*Mus.*) Sampler, *der*

**Samson** /'sæmsn/ *pr. n.* Samson, *der;* (*fig.: strong man*) Herkules, *der*

**samurai** /'sæmʊəraɪ/ *n., pl. same or* **~s** (*Hist.*) Samurai, *der*

**sanatarium** /sænə'teərɪəm/ (*Amer.*) ⇒ **sanatorium**

**sanatorium** /sænə'tɔ:rɪəm/ *n., pl.* **~s** *or* **sanatoria** /sænə'tɔ:rɪə/ Ⓐ (*clinic*) Sanatorium, *das;* Ⓑ (*sickbay*) Krankenzimmer, *das*

**sanctification** /sæŋktɪfɪ'keɪʃn/ *n.* Heiligung, *die* (*geh.*)

**sanctify** /'sæŋktɪfaɪ/ *v.t.* Ⓐ heiligen; Ⓑ (*consecrate*) weihen; heiligen (*bes. bibl.*)

S

**sanctimonious** /sæŋktɪˈməʊnɪəs/ *adj.*, **sanctimoniously** /sæŋktɪˈməʊnɪəslɪ/ *adv.* scheinheilig

**sanction** /ˈsæŋkʃn/ ❶ *n.* Ⓐ (*official approval*) Sanktion, *die;* **give one's ~ to sth.** seine Erlaubnis für etw. geben; Ⓑ (*Polit.: penalty; Law: punishment*) Sanktion, *die.* ❷ *v.t.* sanktionieren

**sanctity** /ˈsæŋktɪtɪ/ *n.*, *no pl.* Heiligkeit, *die*

**sanctuary** /ˈsæŋktʃʊərɪ/ *n.* Ⓐ (*holy place*) Heiligtum, *das;* Ⓑ (*part of church*) Altarraum, *der;* Sanktuarium, *das* (*kath. Kirche*); Ⓒ (*place of refuge*) Zufluchtsort, *der;* (*Hist.: guaranteeing safety*) Freistatt, *die;* Ⓓ (*for animals or plants*) Naturschutzgebiet, *das;* **bird/animal ~:** Vogel-/Tierschutzgebiet, *das;* Ⓔ (*asylum*) Asyl, *das;* Freiung, *die* (*hist.*); **take ~:** Zuflucht suchen

**sanctum** /ˈsæŋktəm/ *n.* (*joc.: private retreat*) **[inner] ~:** Allerheiligste, *das* (*fig.*)

**sanctus** /ˈsæŋktəs/ *n.* Sanctus, *das* (*kath. Kirche*)

ˈ**sanctus bell** *n.* Sakristeiglocke, *die*

**sand** /sænd/ ❶ *n.* Ⓐ Sand, *der;* **the beach has four miles of ~:** der Sandstrand ist 4 Meilen lang; **built on ~** (*fig.*) auf Sand gebaut; **have** *or* **keep** *or* **bury one's head in the ~** (*fig.*) den Kopf in den Sand stecken; Ⓑ *in pl.* (*expanse*) Sandbank, *die;* (*beach*) Sandstrand, *der;* Ⓒ *in pl.* **the ~s [of time] are running out** (*fig.*) die Zeit läuft ab; Ⓓ (*Amer. coll.: determination*) **have not got ~ enough to do sth.** nicht den Mumm (*ugs.*) haben, etw zu tun; **he loses his ~:** ihm rutscht das Herz in die Hose (*ugs.*, *oft scherzh.*). ⇒ *also* **plough** 2 A. ❷ *v.t.* Ⓐ (*sprinkle*) **~ the road** die Straße mit Sand streuen; Ⓑ (*bury*) **be ~ed up** *or* **over** versandet sein; Ⓒ (*polish*) **~ sth. down** etw. [ab]schmirgeln

**sandal** /ˈsændl/ *n.* Sandale, *die*

**sandal: ~-tree** *n.* Sandelbaum, *der;* **~wood** *n.* **[red] ~wood** Sandelholz, *das;* **~wood oil** Sandel[holz]öl, *das*

**sand: ~bag** ❶ *n.* Sandsack, *der;* ❷ *v.t.* Ⓐ (*barricade*) mit Sandsäcken schützen; Ⓑ (*Amer.: coerce*) **~bag sb. into sth.** jmdn. zu etw. zwingen; **~bag sb. into doing sth.** jmdn. so lange bearbeiten, bis er etw. tut; **~bank** *n.* Sandbank, *die;* **~ bar** *n.* Sandbank, *die* (*an Flussmündungen, Häfen*); **~ bath** *n.* (*Chem.*) Sandbad, *das;* **~blast** *v.t.* sandstrahlen (*Technik*); **~box** *n.* (*Amer.*) Sandkasten, *der;* **~boy** *n.* **be happy as a ~boy** glücklich und zufrieden sein; **~castle** *n.* Sandburg, *die;* **~ dollar** *n.* (*Amer.: Zool.*) Sanddollar, *der;* **~ dune** *n.* Düne, *die*

**sander** /ˈsændə(r)/ *n.* Sandpapierschleifmaschine, *die*

**sand: ~glass** *n.* Sanduhr, *die;* **~hill** *n.* Düne, *die;* **~lot** *n.* (*Amer.*) Spielplatz, *der;* (*for older children*) Bolzplatz, *der* (*ugs.*); **~man** /ˈsændmæn/ *n.* Sandmann, *der;* **~ martin** *n.* (*Brit. Ornith.*) Uferschwalbe, *die;* **~paper** ❶ *n.* Sandpapier, *das;* ❷ *v.t.* [mit Sandpapier] [ab]schmirgeln; **~piper** *n.* (*Ornith.*) Wasserläufer, *der;* **~pit** *n.* Sandkasten, *der;* **~stone** *n.* Sandstein, *der;* **~storm** *n.* Sandsturm, *der;* **~ trap** *n.* (*Amer. Golf*) Bunker, *der*

**sandwich** /ˈsænwɪdʒ, ˈsænwɪtʃ/ ❶ *n.* Ⓐ Sandwich, *der od. das;* ≈ [zusammengeklapptes] belegtes Brot; **cheese ~:** Käsebrot, *das;* **open ~:** belegtes Brot; Ⓑ ⇒ **sandwich cake**. ❷ *v.t.* einschieben (**between** zwischen + *Akk.;* **into** in + *Akk.*); **be ~ed between other people/cars** zwischen andere Personen gequetscht werden/Autos eingeklemmt sein

**sandwich: ~ board** *n. von einem Sandwichmann getragenes Reklameplakat;* **~ cake** *n. ein- od. mehrschichtig gefüllter Kuchen;* **~ course** *n. Ausbildung mit abwechselnd theoretischem und praktischem Unterricht;* **~ man** *n.* Sandwichmann, *der;* **~ tin** *n.* Brotbüchse, *die*

**sandy** /ˈsændɪ/ *adj.* Ⓐ (*consisting of sand*) sandig; Sand‹boden, -strand›; Ⓑ (*yellowish-red*) rotblond ‹Haar›

ˈ**sand yacht** *n.* Strandsegler, *der*

**sane** /seɪn/ *adj.* Ⓐ geistig gesund; **they do not think him entirely ~:** sie halten ihn nicht für ganz normal; **not ~:** geistesgestört; Ⓑ (*sensible*) vernünftig

**sanely** /ˈseɪnlɪ/ *adv.* Ⓐ normal; Ⓑ (*sensibly*) vernünftig

**sang** ⇒ **sing** 1, 2

**sang-froid** /sɑ̃ˈfrwɑː/ *n.* Kaltblütigkeit, *die;* Sang-froid, *das* (*veralt.*)

**sangria** /sæŋˈgriːə/ *n.* Sangria, *die*

**sanguinary** /ˈsæŋgwɪnərɪ/ *adj.* Ⓐ (*delighting in bloodshed*) blutrünstig; Ⓑ (*bloody*) blutig

**sanguine** /ˈsæŋgwɪn/ *adj.* Ⓐ (*confident*) zuversichtlich (**about** was ... betrifft); heiter ‹Temperament›; Ⓑ (*florid*) blühend ‹Gesichtsfarbe›

**sanguinely** /ˈsæŋgwɪnlɪ/ *adv.* zuversichtlich

**sanitarium** /sænɪˈteərɪəm/ (*Amer.*) ⇒ **sanatorium**

**sanitary** /ˈsænɪtərɪ/ *adj.* sanitär ‹Verhältnisse, Anlagen›; gesundheitlich ‹Gesichtspunkt, Problem›; Gesundheits‹behörde›; hygienisch ‹Küche, Krankenhaus, Gewohnheit›; Sanitär‹fliesen, -abflussrohr›

**sanitary: ~ engiˈneer** *n.* Sanitärtechniker, *der*/-technikerin, *die;* **~ engiˈneering** *n.* Sanitärtechnik, *die;* **~ inspector** *n.* Gesundheitsinspektor, *der*/-inspektorin, *die;* **~ napkin** (*Amer.*), **~ towel** (*Brit.*) *ns.* Damenbinde, *die;* **~ ware** *n.*, *no pl.* Sanitärkeramik, *die*

**sanitation** /sænɪˈteɪʃn/ *n.*, *no pl.* Ⓐ (*drainage, refuse disposal*) Kanalisation und Abfallbeseitigung; Ⓑ (*hygiene*) Hygiene, *die*

**sanitize (sanitise)** /ˈsænɪtaɪz/ *v.t.* keimfrei machen ‹Luft, Toilettensitz, Besteck›; (*fig.*) entschärfen ‹Dokument, Protokoll, Film›

**sanity** /ˈsænɪtɪ/ *n.* Ⓐ (*mental health*) geistige Gesundheit; **lose one's ~:** den Verstand verlieren; **cause sb. to lose his ~:** jmdn. um den Verstand bringen; **fear for/doubt sb.'s ~:** um jmds. Zurechnungsfähigkeit fürchten/an jmds. Verstand (*Dat.*) zweifeln; Ⓑ (*good sense*) Vernünftigkeit, *die;* **restore ~ to the proceedings** die Veranstaltung wieder in vernünftige Bahnen lenken

**sank** ⇒ **sink** 2, 3

**sans** /sænz/ *prep.* (*arch./joc.*) ohne

**sanserif** /sænˈserɪf/ (*Printing*) ❶ *n.* Grotesk[schrift], *die.* ❷ *adj.* serifenlos; Grotesk‹buchstabe, -ziffer›

**Sanskrit** /ˈsænskrɪt/ ▶ 1275 ❶ *adj.* sanskritisch; Sanskrit‹text, -inschrift, -literatur›; ‹Grammatik› des Sanskrits; ⇒ *also* **English** 1. ❷ *n.* Sanskrit, *das;* ⇒ *also* **English** 2 A

**Santa** /ˈsæntə/ (*coll.*), **Santa Claus** /ˈsæntə klɔːz/ *n.* der Weihnachtsmann

**sap**[1] /sæp/ ❶ *n.* Ⓐ (*Bot.*) Saft, *der;* (*fig.: vital spirit*) belebende Kraft; **in the spring the ~ rises** im Frühling steigen die Säfte; Ⓑ (*Amer. coll.: club*) Knüppel, *der.* ❷ *v.t.*, **-pp-** Ⓐ (*drain*) den Saft entziehen (+ *Dat.*) ‹Holz›; (*for sugar, rubber*) anzapfen (**for** zur Gewinnung von); Ⓑ (*fig.: exhaust vigour of*) zehren an (+ *Dat.*); **~ sb. of [all] his/her strength** jmdn. [völlig] entkräften; **her strength had been ~ped by disease/hunger** Krankheit/Hunger hatte an ihren Kräften gezehrt; Ⓒ (*Amer. coll.: hit*) mit einem Knüppel/mit Knüppeln schlagen

**sap**[2] ❶ *v.t.*, **-pp-** unterhöhlen ‹Fundament, Mauer›. ❷ *n.* (*Mil.*) (*trench*) Sappe, *die;* (*under enemy's fortification*) Tunnel, *der*

**sap**[3] *n.* (*coll.: fool*) Trottel, *der* (*ugs. abwertend*); **find some ~ to do sth.** einen Dummen finden, der etw. tut

**sapele** /səˈpiːlɪ/ *n.* Ⓐ (*tree*) Sapelli[baum], *der;* Ⓑ (*wood*) Sapelli[holz], *das*

ˈ**sap-green** ❶ *n.* Saftgrün, *das.* ❷ *adj.* saftgrün

**sapling** /ˈsæplɪŋ/ *n.* junger Baum

**sapper** /ˈsæpə(r)/ *n.* (*Brit. Mil.*) Pionier, *der*

**Sapphic** /ˈsæfɪk/ (*Pros.*) ❶ *adj.* sapphisch. ❷ *n.* sapphischer Vers

**sapphire** /ˈsæfaɪə(r)/ *n.* Saphir, *der; attrib.* **~ blue** saphirblau; **~ ring** Saphirring, *der;* **~ wedding** 45. Hochzeitstag

**sappy** /ˈsæpɪ/ *adj.* saftig ‹Gras›; (*fig.: full of vitality*) voll Saft und Kraft *nachgestellt*

ˈ**sapwood** *n.* (*Bot.*) Splintholz, *das*

**saraband[e]** /ˈsærəbænd/ *n.* (*Mus.*, *Dancing*) Sarabande, *die*

**Saracen** /ˈsærəsn/ (*Hist.*, *Ethnol.*) ❶ *n.* Sarazene, *der*/Sarazenin, *die* (*veralt.*). ❷ *adj.* sarazenisch; Sarazenen‹führer, -frau›

**sarcasm** /ˈsɑːkæzəm/ *n.* Sarkasmus, *der;* (*remark*) sarkastische Bemerkung; **with heavy ~:** mit beißendem Sarkasmus

**sarcastic** /sɑːˈkæstɪk/ *adj.*, **sarcastically** /sɑːˈkæstɪkəlɪ/ *adv.* sarkastisch

**sarcoma** /sɑːˈkəʊmə/ *n.*, *pl.* **~ta** /sɑːˈkəʊmətə/ (*Med.*) Sarkom, *das*

**sarcophagus** /sɑːˈkɒfəgəs/ *n.*, *pl.* **sarcophagi** /sɑːˈkɒfəgaɪ/ Sarkophag, *der*

**sardine** /sɑːˈdiːn/ *n.* (*Zool.*) Sardine, *die;* (*Gastr.*) [Öl]sardine, *die;* **like ~s** (*fig.*) wie die Ölsardinen

**Sardinia** /sɑːˈdɪnɪə/ *pr. n.* Sardinien (*das*)

**Sardinian** /sɑːˈdɪnɪən/ ▶ 1275, ▶ 1340 ❶ *n.* Ⓐ (*person*) Sarde, *der*/Sardin, *die;* Sardinier, *der*/Sardinierin, *die;* Ⓑ (*language*) Sardisch, *das.* ❷ *adj.* sardisch

**sardonic** /sɑːˈdɒnɪk/ *adj.* höhnisch ‹Bemerkung›; sardonisch ‹Lachen, Lächeln›; **he can be very ~:** er kann sehr bissig sein

**sardonically** /sɑːˈdɒnɪkəlɪ/ *adv.* höhnisch ‹bemerken›; sardonisch ‹lächeln, lachen›

**sarge** /sɑːdʒ/ *n.* (*coll.*) Sergeant, *der;* (*Mil.*) ≈ Hauptfeld, *der* (*Militärjargon*)

**sari** /ˈsɑːrɪ/ *n.* Sari, *der*

**sarky** /ˈsɑːkɪ/ *adj.* (*Brit. coll.*) ätzend (*ugs.*)

**sarnie** /ˈsɑːnɪ/ (*Brit. coll.*) ⇒ **sandwich** 1 A

**sarong** /səˈrɒŋ/ *n.* Sarong, *der*

**sartorial** /sɑːˈtɔːrɪəl/ *adj.* **he has high ~ standards** er stellt hohe Ansprüche, was seine Kleidung betrifft; **~ fashion** Herrenmode, *die;* **he was the height of ~ elegance** er war der Inbegriff des elegant gekleideten Herrn

**SAS** *abbr.* (*Brit. Mil.*) **Special Air Service** *auf Geheimoperationen spezialisiertes Regiment der britischen Armee*

**sash**[1] /sæʃ/ *n.* Schärpe, *die*

**sash**[2] *n.* Ⓐ (*of window*) Fensterrahmen, *der;* Ⓑ (*window*) Schiebefenster, *das*

**sashay** /ˈsæʃeɪ/ *v.i.* (*Amer.*) Ⓐ (*walk casually*) schlendern; Ⓑ (*ostentatiously*) stolzieren; Ⓒ (*diagonally*) **~ through a crowd** sich durch eine Menschenmenge schlängeln

**sash: ~ cord**, **~ line** *ns.* Gewichtsschnur, *die;* **~ ˈwindow** *n.* Schiebefenster, *das*

**sass** /sæs/ (*Amer. coll.*) ❶ *n.* Frechheit, *die.* ❷ *v.t.* frech sein zu

**Sassenach** /ˈsæsənæx, ˈsæsənæk/ (*Scot.*, *Ir.;* *usu. derog.*) ❶ *n.* Engländer, *der*/Engländerin, *die.* ❷ *adj.* englisch

**sassy** /ˈsæsɪ/ *adj.* (*Amer. coll.*) Ⓐ (*cheeky*) frech; Ⓑ (*stylish*) schick

**sat** ⇒ **sit**

**Sat.** *abbr.* ▶ 1056 **Saturday** Sa.

**Satan** /ˈseɪtən/ *pr. n.* Satan, *der*

**satanic** /səˈtænɪk/ *adj.* satanisch; teuflisch

**Satanism** /ˈseɪtənɪzm/ *n.*, *no pl.*, *no art.* Satanismus, *der;* Satanskult, *der*

**satchel** /ˈsætʃl/ *n.* [Schul]ranzen, *der*

**sate** /seɪt/ *v.t.* (*literary*) Ⓐ (*gratify*) stillen ‹Hunger, Durst, Verlangen, Zorn›; zufrieden stellen ‹Person›; **feel pleasantly ~d** ein angenehmes Sättigungsgefühl empfinden; **~ oneself on sth.** sich an etw. (*Dat.*) sättigen (*geh.*); Ⓑ (*cloy*) übersättigen ‹Lust, Verlangen›; **become ~d with/be ~d by sth.** einer Sache (*Gen.*) überdrüssig werden/sein

**sateen** /səˈtiːn/ *n.* (*Textiles*) Baumwollsatin, *der*

**satellite** /ˈsætəlaɪt/ ❶ *n.* Ⓐ (*Astronaut.*, *Astron.;* *also country*) Satellit, *der;* **by ~:** über Satellit; Ⓑ (*fig.*) (*object associated with another*) Ableger, *der* (*fig.*); (*follower*) Trabant, *der* (*fig.*). ❷ *attrib. adj.* Satelliten‹film, -bild, -fernsehen, -regierung›; **~ industries** Zulieferindustrie, *die*

S

**satellite: ~ 'broadcasting** *n., no pl., no art.* Satellitenfunk, *der;* **~ dish** *n.* Satellitenschüssel, *die;* **~ receiver** *n.* Satellitenempfänger, *der;* Satellitenreceiver, *der* (*fachspr.*); **~ state** *n.* Satellitenstaat, *der;* **~ 'television** *n.* Satellitenfernsehen, *das;* **~ town** *n.* Satelliten- *od.* Trabantenstadt, *die*

**satiate** /'seɪʃɪeɪt/ ⇒ **sate**

**satiation** /seɪʃɪ'eɪʃn/ *n.* Ⓐ (*gratification*) Sättigung, *die;* Ⓑ (*cloying*) Übersättigung, *die*

**satiety** /sə'taɪətɪ/ *n.* Übersättigung, *die;* **to [the point of] ~:** bis zum Überdruss

**satin** /'sætɪn/ ❶ *n.* Satin, *der.* ❷ *attrib. adj.* Ⓐ (*made of ~*) Satin-; Ⓑ (*like ~*) seidig

**'satinwood** *n.* (*tree*) [ostindischer] Satinholzbaum; (*wood*) [ostindisches] Satinholz

**satiny** /'sætɪnɪ/ *adj.* seidig

**satire** /'sætaɪə(r)/ *n.* Satire, *die* (**on** auf + *Akk.*); **element/tone of ~:** satirisches Element/satirischer Ton; **gift** *or* **talent for ~:** satirische Begabung

**satirical** /sə'tɪrɪkl/ *adj.*, **satirically** /sə'tɪrɪkəlɪ/ *adv.* satirisch

**satirise** ⇒ **satirize**

**satirist** /'sætɪrɪst/ *n.* Satiriker, *der*/Satirikerin, *die;* **be a ~ of sb./sth.** jmdn./etw. mit satirischen Mitteln angreifen

**satirize** /'sætɪraɪz/ *v.t.* Ⓐ (*write satire on*) satirisch darstellen; Ⓑ (*describe satirically*) ‹Buch, Film usw.:› eine Satire sein auf (+ *Akk.*); **be brutally ~d** ‹Person:› das Opfer gnadenloser Satire werden

**satisfaction** /sætɪs'fækʃn/ *n.* Ⓐ *no pl.* (*act*) Befriedigung, *die;* **we strive for the ~ of our clients** wir bemühen uns, unsere Kunden zufrieden zu stellen; Ⓑ *no pl.* (*feeling of gratification*) Befriedigung, *die* (**at, with** über + *Akk.*); Genugtuung, *die* (**at, with** über + *Akk.*); **job ~:** Befriedigung in der Arbeit; **it is with [great] ~ that I .../it gives me [great] ~ to ...:** es erfüllt mich mit [großer] Befriedigung, zu ...; **get ~ out of one's work** in seiner Arbeit Befriedigung finden; **there's a lot of ~ [to be had] in doing sth.** es ist sehr befriedigend, etw. zu tun; **what ~ can it give you?** was befriedigt dich daran?; **I can't get any ~ from him** er stellt mich nicht zufrieden; Ⓒ *no pl.* (*gratified state*) **meet with sb.'s** *or* **give sb. [complete] ~:** jmdn. [in jeder Weise] zufrieden stellen; **~ guaranteed** Sie werden garantiert zufrieden sein; **fail to give ~** ‹Arbeit:› nicht zufrieden stellend ausfallen; ‹Angestellte:› nicht zufrieden stellend arbeiten; **to sb.'s ~, to the ~ of sb.** zu jmds. Zufriedenheit; Ⓓ (*instance of gratification*) Befriedigung, *die;* **it is a great ~ to me that ...:** es erfüllt mich mit großer Befriedigung, dass ...; **give every ~:** in jeder Hinsicht befriedigend sein; **have the ~ of doing sth.** das Vergnügen haben, etw. zu tun; **one of the ~s of the job** eine der Befriedigungen, die die Arbeit gewährt; Ⓔ (*Hist.: revenge in duel*) Satisfaktion, *die*

**satisfactorily** /sætɪs'fæktərɪlɪ/ *adv.* zufriedenstellend; richtig ‹passen›; **progress ~:** befriedigende Fortschritte machen

**satisfactory** /sætɪs'fæktərɪ/ *adj.* zufriedenstellend; angemessen ‹Bezahlung›; **'~'** (*as school mark*) „ausreichend"

**satisfied** /'sætɪsfaɪd/ *adj.* Ⓐ (*contented*) zufrieden; (*replete*) satt; **be ~ with doing sth.** sich damit begnügen, etw. zu tun; **be ~ to do sth.** damit zufrieden sein, etw. zu tun; Ⓑ (*convinced*) überzeugt (**of** von); **be ~ that ...:** [davon] überzeugt sein, dass ...

**satisfy** /'sætɪsfaɪ/ ❶ *v.t.* Ⓐ (*content*) befriedigen; zufrieden stellen ‹Kunden, Publikum›; entsprechen (+ *Dat.*) ‹Vorliebe, Empfinden, Meinung, Zeitgeist›; erfüllen ‹Hoffnung, Erwartung›; **~/fail to ~ the examiners** die Prüfung bestehen/nicht bestehen; Ⓑ (*rid of want*) befriedigen; (*put an end to*) stillen ‹Hunger, Durst›; (*make replete*) sättigen; **that meal wouldn't ~ a sparrow** davon würde nicht einmal ein Spatz satt; Ⓒ (*convince*) **~ sb. [of sth.]** jmdn. [von etw.] überzeugen; **~ sb. that ...:** jmdn. [davon] überzeugen, dass ...; **~ oneself of** *or* **as to** sich überzeugen von ‹Wahrheit, Ehrlichkeit›; sich (*Dat.*) Gewissheit verschaffen über (+ *Akk.*) ‹Motiv›; **~ oneself as to what happened** sich (*Dat.*) Klarheit *od.* Gewissheit darüber verschaffen, was geschehen ist; Ⓓ (*adequately deal with*) ausräumen ‹Einwand, Zweifel›; Ⓔ (*pay*) begleichen ‹Bitte, Forderung, Bedingung›; befriedigen ‹Gläubiger, Forderung›; Ⓕ (*fulfil*) erfüllen ‹Vertrag, Verpflichtung, Forderung›; Ⓖ (*Math.*) erfüllen ‹Gleichung›.

❷ *v.i.* Ⓐ (*make replete*) sättigen; Ⓑ (*be convincing*) ‹Argument:› überzeugen

**satisfying** /'sætɪsfaɪɪŋ/ *adj.* befriedigend; sättigend ‹Gericht, Speise›; zufrieden stellend ‹Antwort, Lösung, Leistung›

**satsuma** /sæt'suːmə/ *n.* Satsuma, *die*

**saturate** /'sætʃəreɪt, 'sætjʊreɪt/ *v.t.* Ⓐ (*soak*) durchnässen; [mit Feuchtigkeit durch]tränken ‹Boden, Erde›; **cake ~d in** *or* **with liqueur** mit Likör getränkter Kuchen; Ⓑ (*fill to capacity*) auslasten; sättigen ‹Markt›; Ⓒ (*Mil.: bomb intensively*) mit einem Bombenteppich belegen; Ⓓ (*Phys., Chem.*) sättigen

**saturated** /'sætʃəreɪtɪd, 'sætjʊreɪtɪd/ *adj.* Ⓐ (*soaked*) durchnässt; völlig nass ‹Boden›; Ⓑ (*imbued*) durchdrungen (**with, in** von); **be ~ with** durchdrungen sein von; ganz erfüllt sein von ‹Duft›; **be ~ in history/tradition** sehr geschichtsträchtig/traditionsreich sein; Ⓒ (*filled to capacity*) ausgelastet; gesättigt ‹Markt›; Ⓓ (*Phys., Chem.*) gesättigt ‹Lösung, Verbindung, Fett›; Ⓔ (*Art*) satt ‹Farbe, Farbton›

**saturation** /sætʃə'reɪʃn, sætjʊ'reɪʃn/ *n.* Ⓐ (*soaking, being soaked*) Durchnässung, *die;* Ⓑ (*filling to capacity*) Auslastung, *die* (**by, with** mit); (*of market*) Sättigung, *die;* Ⓒ (*Mil.*) **~ [bombing]** Flächenbombardierung, *die;* Ⓓ (*Phys., Chem.*) Sättigung, *die;* Ⓔ (*colour intensity*) Sattheit, *die*

**satu'ration point** *n.* Ⓐ (*limit of capacity*) [Ober]grenze, *die;* (*of market*) Sättigungspunkt, *der;* (*limit of response*) Grenze der Aufnahmefähigkeit; (*of harmful effect*) Grenze der Belastbarkeit; Ⓑ (*Phys.*) Sättigungspunkt, *der*

**Saturday** /'sætədeɪ, 'sætədɪ/ ▶ **1056** ❶ *n.* Sonnabend, *der;* Samstag, *der.* ❷ *adv.* (*coll.*) **he comes ~s** er kommt sonnabends *od.* samstags. ⇒ *also* **Friday**

**Saturn** /'sætən/ *pr. n.* Ⓐ (*Astron.*) Saturn, *der;* Ⓑ (*Roman Mythol.*) Saturn (*der*)

**Saturnalia** /sætə'neɪlɪə/ *n. pl.* (*Roman Ant.*) Saturnalien *Pl.*

**saturnine** /'sætənaɪn/ *adj.* melancholisch; düster ‹Einstellung›; (*sinister*) finster

**satyr** /'sætə(r)/ *n.* (*Mythol.*) Satyr, *der*

**sauce** /sɔːs/ ❶ *n.* Ⓐ Soße, *die;* **be served with the same ~** (*fig.*) es mit *od.* in gleicher Münze heimgezahlt bekommen; ⇒ *also* **gander** A; Ⓑ (*fig.: sth. that adds piquancy*) Würze, *die;* Ⓒ (*Amer.: stewed fruit*) Kompott, *das;* Ⓓ (*Amer. coll.*) **the ~:** Alkohol; **in the ~:** alkoholisiert; Ⓔ (*Amer.: vegetables*) Beilage, *die;* Ⓕ (*impudence*) Frechheit, *die;* **he's got a lot of ~!** der ist ganz schön frech!; **don't give me any of your ~!** sei nicht so frech! ❷ *v.t.* (*coll.*) frech sein zu

**sauce: ~ boat** *n.* Sauciere, *die;* **~box** *n.* (*coll.*) Frechdachs, *der* (*fam.*); **~pan** /'sɔːspən/ *n.* Kochtopf, *der;* (*with straight handle*) [Stiel]kasserolle, *die*

**saucer** /'sɔːsə(r)/ *n.* Untertasse, *die;* **their eyes were like ~s** (*fig.*) sie machten große Augen (*ugs.*); **with eyes like ~s** (*fig.*) mit großen Augen; ⇒ *also* **flying saucer**

**saucerful** /'sɔːsəfʊl/ *n.* **a ~ [of milk]** eine Untertasse [Milch *od.* voll Milch]

**saucily** /'sɔːsɪlɪ/ *adv.* Ⓐ (*rudely*) frech; Ⓑ (*pertly*) keck

**sauciness** /'sɔːsɪnɪs/ *n., no pl.* Ⓐ (*rudeness*) Frechheit, *die;* Ⓑ (*pertness, jauntiness*) Keckheit, *die*

**saucy** /'sɔːsɪ/ *adj.* Ⓐ (*rude*) frech; Ⓑ (*pert, jaunty*) keck

**Saudi** /'saʊdɪ/ ❶ *adj.* Ⓐ ⇒ **Saudi-Arabian** 1; Ⓑ (*of dynasty*) saudisch ‹Prinz, Palast›. ❷ *n.* Ⓐ ⇒ **Saudi-Arabian** 2; Ⓑ (*member of dynasty*) Saudi, *der*

**Saudi Arabia** /saʊdɪ ə'reɪbɪə/ *pr. n.* Saudi-Arabien (*das*)

**Saudi-Arabian** /saʊdɪə'reɪbɪən/ ▶ **1340** ❶ *adj.* saudi-arabisch. ❷ *n.* Saudi[-Araber], *der*/-Araberin, *die*

**sauerkraut** /'saʊəkraʊt/ *n.* (*Gastr.*) Sauerkraut, *das*

**sauna** /'sɔːnə, 'saʊnə/ *n.* Sauna, *die;* **have** *or* **take a ~:** saunieren; ein Saunabad nehmen

**saunter** /'sɔːntə(r)/ ❶ *v.i.* schlendern; **I think I will ~ [down/over/up] to the village** ich werde wohl ins Dorf runter-/rüber-/raufschlendern (*ugs.*). ❷ *n.* (*stroll*) Bummel, *der* (*ugs.*); (*leisurely pace*) Schlenderschritt, *der;* **at a ~:** im Schlenderschritt; **go for a** *or* **have a ~:** schlendern

**saurian** /'sɔːrɪən/ ❶ *n.* (*Zool.*) Echse, *die;* (*Palaeont.*) Saurier, *der.* ❷ *adj.* (*Zool.: of the Sauria*) der Echsen *nachgestellt;* (*lizard-like*) echsenartig; **~ reptile** Echse, *die*

**sausage** /'sɒsɪdʒ/ *n.* Wurst, *die;* (*smaller*) Würstchen, *das;* **not a ~** (*fig. coll.*) gar nix (*ugs.*)

**sausage: ~ dog** *n.* (*Brit. coll.*) Dackel, *der;* **~ machine** *n.* Wurstfüllmaschine, *die;* (*Educ. fig.*) Bildungsfabrik, *die* (*abwertend*); **~ meat** *n.* Wurstmasse, *die;* **~ 'roll** *n.* *Blätterteig mit Wurstfüllung*

**sauté** /'səʊteɪ/ (*Cookery*) ❶ *adj.* sautiert (*fachspr.*); kurz [an]gebraten; **~ potatoes** ≈ Bratkartoffeln. ❷ *n.* Sauté, *das.* ❸ *v.t.*, **~d** *or* **~ed** /'səʊteɪd/ sautieren (*fachspr.*); kurz [an]braten

**Sauterne[s]** /səʊ'tɜːn/ *n.* Sauternes[wein], *der*

**savage** /'sævɪdʒ/ ❶ *adj.* Ⓐ (*uncivilized*) primitiv; wild ‹Volksstamm›; unzivilisiert ‹Land›; Ⓑ (*fierce*) brutal; wild ‹Tier›; scharf ‹Hund›; jähzornig ‹Temperament›; schonungslos ‹Kritiker, Satiriker›; **have a wild, ~ look in one's eye** wild und brutal aussehen; **make a ~ attack on sb.** brutal über jmdn. herfallen; (*fig.*) jmdn. schonungslos angreifen.

❷ *n.* Ⓐ (*uncivilized person*) Wilde, *der/die* (*veralt.*); **behave like ~s** sich wie die Wilden aufführen (*abwertend*); Ⓑ (*barbarous or uncultivated person*) Barbar, *der*/Barbarin, *die* (*abwertend*).

❸ *v.t.* Ⓐ ‹Hund usw.:› anfallen ‹Kind usw.›; (*lacerate*) zerfleischen; Ⓑ (*fig.*) ‹Kritiker, Journalist:› herfallen über (+ *Akk.*) ‹Politiker usw.›; ‹Kritiker, Zeitung:› schonungslos verreißen ‹Theaterstück usw.›

**savagely** /'sævɪdʒlɪ/ *adv.* (*fiercely*) brutal; wild ‹brüllen›; wüst ‹beschimpfen›; schonungslos ‹kritisieren›

**savagery** /'sævɪdʒrɪ/ *n., no pl.* Ⓐ (*uncivilized condition*) Unzivilisiertheit, *die;* Ⓑ (*ferocity*) Brutalität, *die*

**savannah (savanna)** /sə'vænə/ *n.* (*Geog.*) Savanne, *die*

**save** /seɪv/ ❶ *v.t.* Ⓐ (*rescue*) retten (**from** vor + *Dat.*); **please, ~ me!** bitte helfen Sie mir!; **~ sb. from the clutches of the enemy/from making a mistake** jmdn. aus den Klauen des Feindes retten/davor bewahren, dass er einen Fehler macht; **alcoholics must be ~d from themselves** Alkoholiker müssen vor sich (*Dat.*) selbst geschützt werden; **he ~d my reputation** er rettete meinen guten Ruf; **~ oneself from falling** sich [beim Hinfallen] fangen; **be ~d by the bell** (*fig. coll.*) gerade noch mal davonkommen (*ugs.*); **~ the day** die Situation retten; **sb. can't do sth. to ~ his/her life** (*coll.*) jmd. kann etw. [ganz] einfach nicht tun; ⇒ *also* **bacon**; **face** 1 A; **life** A; **skin** 1 A; Ⓑ (*keep undamaged*) schonen ‹Kleidung, Möbelstück›; Ⓒ **God ~ the King/Queen** *etc.* Gott behüte *od.* beschütze den König/die Königin *usw.;* **[God] ~ sb. from sb./sth.** Gott bewahre jmdn. vor jmdm./etw.; Ⓓ (*Theol.*) retten ‹Sünder, Seele, Menschen›; **be past saving** nicht mehr zu retten sein; **~ oneself** ‹Sünder:› seine Seele retten; **Jesus ~s!** Jesus ist der Retter!; Ⓔ (*put aside*) aufheben; sparen ‹Geld›; sammeln ‹Rabattmarken, Briefmarken›; (*conserve*) sparsam umgehen mit ‹Geldmitteln, Kräften, Wasser›; **~ money for a rainy day** (*fig.*) einen Notgroschen zurücklegen; **~ water for the drought** Wasser für die Trockenzeit sammeln; **~ oneself** sich schonen; seine Kräfte

S

sparen; ~ **one's breath** sich (*Dat.*) seine Worte sparen; **you can ~ your pains** *or* **trouble/apologies** die Mühe/deine Entschuldigungen kannst du dir sparen; ~ **a seat for sb.** jmdm. einen Platz freihalten; Ⓕ (*make unnecessary*) sparen ‹Geld, Zeit, Energie›; ~ **sb./oneself sth.** jmdm./sich etw. ersparen; ~ **oneself money/half the cost** Geld/die Hälfte des Preises [ein]sparen; ~ **sb./oneself doing sth.** *or* **having to do sth.** es jmdm./sich ersparen, etw. tun zu müssen; **a stitch in time ~s nine** (*prov.*) was du heute kannst besorgen, das verschiebe nicht auf morgen; Vorsorge ist besser als Nachsorge; Ⓖ (*avoid losing*) nicht verlieren ‹Satz, Karte, Stich›; (*prevent from making a score*) abwehren ‹Schuss, Ball›; verhindern ‹Tor›; (*Cricket*) ‹Fänger:› verhindern ‹Lauf›; **his goal ~d the match for his team** sein Tor rettete seine Mannschaft vor der Niederlage; Ⓗ (*Computing*) speichern; sichern; ~ **sth. on [to a] disk** etw. auf Diskette abspeichern.
❷ *v.i.* Ⓐ (*put money by*) sparen; ~ **with a building society** bei einer Bausparkasse sparen; Ⓑ (*avoid waste*) sparen (**on** *Akk.*); ~ **on food** am Essen sparen; Ⓒ (*Sport*) ‹Torwart:› halten.
❸ *n.* (*Sport*) Abwehr, *die;* Parade, *die* (*fachspr.*); **make a ~** ‹Torwart:› halten.
❹ *prep.* (*arch./poet./rhet.*) mit Ausnahme (+ *Gen.*).
❺ *conj.* (*arch.*) außer; ~ **for sth.** von etw. abgesehen
~ **'up** ❶ *v.t.* sparen; sammeln, sparen ‹Marken, Gutscheine usw.›. ❷ *v.i.* sparen (**for** für, auf + *Akk.*)

**save-as-you-'earn** *n.* (*Brit.*) *Sparen durch regelmäßige Abbuchung eines bestimmten Betrages vom Lohn-/Gehaltskonto*

**saveloy** /'sævəlɔɪ/ *n.* Zervelatwurst, *die*

**saver** /'seɪvə(r)/ *n.* Ⓐ (*of money*) Sparer, *der*/Sparerin, *die;* Ⓑ *in comb.* (*device*) **sth. is a time-~/labour-~/money-~:** etw. spart Zeit/Arbeit/Geld; Ⓒ ~ **of souls** Seelenretter, *der*/-retterin, *die*

**saving** /'seɪvɪŋ/ ❶ *n.* Ⓐ *in pl.* (*money saved*) Ersparnisse *Pl.;* **have money put by in ~s** Geld zurückgelegt haben; **how much have you got in your ~s?** wie viel Geld hast du [an]gespart?; Ⓑ (*rescue; also Theol.*) Rettung, *die;* Ⓒ (*instance of economy*) Ersparnis, *die;* ~ **in** *or* **of** *or* **on time/money/fuel/effort** Zeit-/Geld-/Brennstoff-/Arbeitsersparnis, *die;* **make a ~ in** *or* **of money/on equipment/in** *or* **of time** Geld/Ausrüstung/Zeit [ein]sparen; **there's no ~ at all** es wird überhaupt nichts eingespart; **there are ~s to be made on clothes** man kann beim Kleiderkauf einiges sparen.
❷ *adj.* Ⓐ *in comb.* ‹Kosten, Benzin› sparend; Ⓑ (*redeeming*) **the only ~ feature of the play** das einzig Versöhnliche an dem Stück.
❸ *prep.* (*except*) bis auf (+ *Akk.*)

**saving: ~ clause** *n.* einschränkende Klausel; Vorbehaltsklausel, *die;* ~ **'grace** *n.* versöhnender Zug; **her only ~ grace was her honesty** das Einzige, was einen mit ihr versöhnte, war ihre Ehrlichkeit

**savings: ~ account** *n.* Sparkonto, *das;* ~ **account and loan association** (*Amer.*) ⇒ **building society**; ~ **bank** *n.* Sparkasse, *die;* ~ **certificate** *n.* (*Brit.*) Staatspapier, *das*

**saviour** (*Amer.:* **savior**) /'seɪvjə(r)/ *n.* Ⓐ Retter, *der*/Retterin, *die;* (*thing*) Rettung, *die;* Ⓑ (*Relig.*) **our/the S~:** unser/der Heiland

**savoir-faire** /sævwɑ:'feə(r)/ *n.* Gewandtheit, *die*

**savor** (*Amer.*) ⇒ **savour**

**savory**[1] (*Amer.*) ⇒ **savoury**

**savory**[2] /'seɪvərɪ/ *n.* (*Bot.*) Bohnenkraut, *das*

**savour** /'seɪvə(r)/ (*Brit.*) ❶ *n.* Ⓐ (*flavour*) Geschmack, *der;* (*fig.*) Charakter, *der;* Ⓑ (*trace*) **a ~ of sth.** ein Hauch *od.* Anflug von etw.; Ⓒ (*enjoyable quality*) Reiz, *der.* ❷ *v.t.* (*lit. or fig., literary*) genießen; **that is a dish/perfume I particularly ~:** das Gericht/Parfüm ist ein ganz besonderer Genuss für mich. ❸ *v.i.* **sth. ~s of sth.** (*fig.*) etw. schmeckt nach etw. (*fig.*)

**savoury** /'seɪvərɪ/ (*Brit.*) ❶ *adj.* Ⓐ (*not sweet*) pikant; (*having salt flavour*) salzig; Ⓑ (*appetizing*) appetitanregend. ❷ *n.* [pikantes] Häppchen

**savoy** /sə'vɔɪ/ *n.* ~ **[cabbage]** Wirsing[kohl], *der*

**Savoy** *pr. n.* Savoyen (*das*)

**savvy** /'sævɪ/ (*coll.*) ❶ *v.t.* kapieren (*ugs.*); **I don't ~ French** Französisch hab ich nicht drauf (*salopp*). ❷ *v.i.* **..., ~?** ..., kapiert? (*ugs.*); **no ~** (*I don't know*) keine Ahnung (*ugs.*); (*I don't understand*) nix capito (*salopp*). ❸ *n.* Durchblick, *der* (*ugs.*). ❹ *adj.* (*Amer.*) ausgebufft (*salopp*)

**saw**[1] /sɔ:/ ❶ *n.* Säge, *die;* **musical ~:** singende Säge. ❷ *v.t., p.p.* **sawn** /sɔ:n/ *or* **sawed** [zer]sägen; (*make with ~*) sägen; ~ **across** *or* **through** durchsägen; ~ **in half** in der Mitte durchsägen; ~ **the air [with one's hands/arms]** [mit den Händen/Armen] in der Luft herumfuchteln (*ugs.*). ❸ *v.i., p.p.* **sawn** *or* **sawed** Ⓐ sägen; ~ **through sth.** etw. durchsägen; Ⓑ (*fig.*) ~ **away [at the violin]** [auf der Geige] drauflossägen (*ugs.*)
~ **'down** *v.t.* umsägen ‹Baum›
~ **'off** *v.t.* absägen
~ **'up** *v.t.* zersägen (**into** in + *Akk.*)

**saw**[2] *n.* (*saying*) Sprichwort, *das*

**saw**[3] ⇒ **see**[1]

**sawder** /'sɔ:də(r)/ *n.* (*coll.*) **soft ~:** Schmus, *der* (*ugs.*); **give sb. a load of soft ~:** jmdm. ordentlich Honig um den Bart schmieren (*ugs.*)

**saw: ~dust** *n.* Sägemehl, *das;* **~-edged** *adj.* gezähnt ‹Klinge›; **a ~-edged knife** ein Sägemesser

**saw: ~fish** *n.* Sägerochen, *der;* Sägefisch, *der;* **~mill** *n.* Sägemühle, *die*

**sawn** ⇒ **saw**[1] 2, 3

**'sawn-off** *adj.* (*Brit.*) Ⓐ abgesägt; ‹Gewehr› mit abgesägtem Lauf; Ⓑ (*coll.: undersized*) mickrig (*ugs. abwertend*)

**saw: ~-pit** *n.* Sägegrube, *die;* **~tooth[ed]** /'sɔ:tu:θ(t)/ *adj.* Ⓐ gezackt ‹Berge›; Sägе‹dach›; Ⓑ (*Electr.*) Sägezahn‹generator, -schwingung, -spannung›

**sawyer** /'sɔ:jə(r)/ *n.* Säger, *der;* Sägemüller, *der*

**sax** /sæks/ *n.* (*Mus. coll.*) Saxophon, *das*

**saxe** /sæks/ *n.* ~ **[blue]** Sächsischblau, *das*

**saxifrage** /'sæksɪfrɪdʒ, 'sæksɪfreɪdʒ/ *n.* (*Bot.*) Steinbrech, *der*

**Saxon** /'sæksn/ ❶ *n.* Ⓐ Sachse, *der*/Sächsin, *die;* Ⓑ (*Ling.*) Sächsisch, *das;* **[Old] ~:** Westsächsisch, *das.* ❷ *adj.* Ⓐ sächsisch; Ⓑ (*Ling.*) sächsisch; (*of Old ~*) westsächsisch

**Saxony** /'sæksənɪ/ *pr. n.* Sachsen (*das*)

**saxophone** /'sæksəfəʊn/ *n.* (*Mus.*) Saxophon, *das*

**saxophonist** /sæk'sɒfənɪst, 'sæksəfəʊnɪst/ *n.* ▸ 1261 Saxophonist, *der*/Saxophonistin, *die*

**say** /seɪ/ ❶ *v.t., pres. t.* **he says** /sez/, *p.t. & p.p.* **said** /sed/ Ⓐ sagen; ~ **sth. out loud** etw. aussprechen *od.* laut sagen; ~ **sth. to oneself** sich (*Dat.*) etw. sagen; **he said something about going out** er hat etwas von Ausgehen gesagt; **please ~ something** bitte sag doch etwas; (*make a short speech*) sage bitte ein paar Worte; **all I can ~ is ...:** ich kann nur sagen ...; **what more can I ~?** was soll ich da noch [groß] sagen?; **I don't know 'what to ~:** ich weiß nicht, was ich [dazu] sagen soll; **I wouldn't [go so far as to] ~ that, but ...:** das würde ich nicht [unbedingt] sagen, aber ...; **..., not to ~ ...:** ..., um nicht zu sagen ...; **it ~s a lot** *or* **much** *or* **something for sb./sth. that ...:** es spricht sehr für jmdn./etw., dass ...; **have a lot/not much to ~ for oneself** viel reden/nicht viel von sich geben; ~ **no 'more!** (*I understand*) schon gut; **we'll** *or* **let's ~ no more about it** reden wir nicht mehr davon; **there is no** *or* **nothing more to be said** es erübrigt sich jedes weitere Wort (**on** zu); **to ~ nothing of** (*quite apart from*) ganz zu schweigen von; mal ganz abgesehen von; **that is to ~:** das heißt; **as much as to ~:** als wollte er/sie *usw.* sagen ...; **as you might ~:** wie man sagen könnte; **having said that, that said** (*nevertheless*) abgesehen davon; **when all is said and done** letzten Endes; ~ **what you 'like** du kannst sagen, was du willst; **though I ~ it myself ...:** wenn ich es mal selbst so sagen darf; **you can ~ 'that again, you 'said it** (*coll.*) das kannst du laut sagen (*ugs.*); **you don't '~ [so]** (*coll.*) was du nicht sagst (*ugs.*); **~s** *or* **said he** *etc.*/**said I** *or* (*coll.*) **~s I** sagt er/(*ugs.*) sag ich; **~s you** (*coll.*) wers glaubt, wird selig (*ugs. scherzh.*); **~s who?** (*coll.*) wer sagt das?; **I'll ~ [it is]!** (*coll.: it certainly is*) und wie!; **don't let** *or* **never let it be said [that] ...:** niemand soll sagen können, [dass] ...; **they** *or* **people ~** *or* **it is said [that] ...:** man sagt, [dass] ...; **..., they ~:** ..., sagt man *od.* heißt es; **I can't ~ [that] I like cats/the idea** ich kann nicht gerade sagen *od.* behaupten, dass ich Katzen mag/die Idee gut finde; **what I [always] ~ is ...:** also, ich sage immer, ...; **[well,] I 'must ~:** also, ich muss schon sagen; **I should ~ so/not** ich glaube schon/nicht; (*emphatic*) bestimmt/bestimmt nicht; **Is it true that ...? — So she ~s** Stimmt es, dass ...? — Das sagt sie [jedenfalls]; **what have you got to ~ for yourself?** was haben Sie zu Ihren Gunsten zu sagen?; **there's a lot to be said for** *or* **in favour of/against sth.** es spricht viel für/gegen etw.; **there's something to be said on both sides/either side** man kann für beide Seiten/jede Seite Argumente anführen; **who can** *or* **who is to ~?** (*rhet.*) wer weiß das schon *od.* kann das schon sagen?; **I cannot** *or* **could not ~:** das kann ich nicht sagen; **I can't ~ fairer than that** ein besseres Angebot kann ich nicht machen; **he didn't ~:** er hat dazu *od.* darüber nichts gesagt; **I'd rather not ~:** ich möchte es lieber nicht sagen; **and so ~ all of us** der Meinung sind wir auch; **what do** *or* **would you ~ to sb./sth.?** (*think about*) was hältst du von jmdm./etw.?; was würdest du zu jmdm./etw. sagen?; **how ~ you?** (*Law*) wie lautet Ihr Urteil?; **[let us** *or* **shall we] ~:** sagen wir mal; ~ **it were true, what then?** angenommen es stimmt, was dann?; ⇒ *also* **dare** 1 A; **hearsay; no** 2 B; **so**[1] 2; **when** 1 A; **word** 1 B; **yes** 1; Ⓑ (*recite, repeat, speak words of*) sprechen ‹Gebet, Text›; aufsagen ‹Einmaleins, Gedicht›; lesen ‹Messe›; Ⓒ (*have specified wording or reading*) sagen; ‹Zeitung:› schreiben; ‹Uhr:› zeigen ‹Uhrzeit›; **the Bible ~s** *or* **it ~s in the Bible [that] ...:** in der Bibel heißt es, dass ...; die Bibel sagt, dass ...; **a sign ~ing ...:** ein Schild mit der Aufschrift ...; **what does it ~ here?** was steht hier?; Ⓓ (*express, convey information*) sagen; ~ **things well/eloquently** sich gut/gewandt ausdrücken; **what I'm trying to ~ is this** was ich sagen will, ist Folgendes; **his expression said it all** sein Gesichtsausdruck sagte alles; **a novel that really ~s something** ein Roman, der wirklich eine Aussage hat; ~ **nothing to sb.** (*fig.*) ‹Musik, Kunst:› jmdm. nichts bedeuten; **which/that is not ~ing much** *or* **a lot** was nicht viel heißen will/das will nicht viel heißen; ⇒ *also* **soon** B; Ⓔ (*order*) sagen; **do as** *or* **what I ~:** tun Sie, was ich sage; **he said [to us] to be ready at ten** er hat gesagt, wir sollten um zehn fertig sein; Ⓕ *in pass.* **she is said to be clever/have done it** man sagt, sie sei klug/habe es getan; **a horse is said to be a pony when ...:** man bezeichnet ein Pferd als Pony, wenn ...; **the said Mr Smith** (*Law/joc.*) besagter Mr. Smith (*Papierdt., scherzh.*); Ⓖ **215, ~ two hundred and fifteen** 215, in Worten: zweihundert[und]fünfzehn.
❷ *v.i., forms as* 1 Ⓐ (*speak*) sagen; **I ~!** (*Brit.*) (*seeking attention*) Entschuldigung!; (*admiring*) Donnerwetter!; (*dismayed*) ich fürchte; (*reproachful*) ich muss schon sagen!; Ⓑ *in imper.* (*poet.: tell*) sag an! (*veralt.*); Ⓒ *in imper.* (*Amer.*) Mensch!
❸ *n.* Ⓐ (*share in decision*) **have a** *or* **some ~:** ein Mitspracherecht haben (**in** bei); **have no ~:** nichts zu sagen haben; Ⓑ (*power of decision*) **the [final] ~:** das letzte Wort (**in** bei); Ⓒ (*what one has to say*) **have one's ~:**

S

seine Meinung sagen; (*chance to speak*) **get one's** *or* **have a ~:** zu Wort kommen

**SAYE** *abbr.* (*Brit.*) **save-as-you-earn**

**saying** /ˈseɪɪŋ/ *n.* [A] (*maxim*) Redensart, *die;* **there is a ~ that ...:** wie es [im Sprichwort/in der Maxime] heißt, ...; **as the ~ goes** wie es so schön heißt; [B] (*remark*) Ausspruch, *der;* **the ~s of Chairman Mao** die Worte des Vorsitzenden Mao; [C] **there is no ~ what/why ...:** man kann nicht sagen, was/warum ...; **go without ~:** sich von selbst verstehen

**ˈsay-so** *n.* [A] (*power of decision*) **on/without sb.'s ~:** auf/ohne jmds. Anweisung (*Akk.*); **the final ~:** das letzte Wort; [B] (*assertion*) **I won't believe it just on your ~:** das glaube ich dir nicht einfach so

**sc.** /ˈsaɪlɪset/ *abbr.* **scilicet** sc.; d.h.

**scab** /skæb/ *n.* [A] (*over wound, sore*) [Wund]schorf, *der;* **form a ~:** verschorfen; **be covered in ~s** mit Schorf bedeckt sein; [B] *no pl.* (*skin disease*) Räude, *die;* (*plant disease*) Schorf, *der;* [C] (*derog.: strikebreaker*) Streikbrecher, *der*/-brecherin, *die;* **use ~ labour** Streikbrecher einsetzen

**scabbard** /ˈskæbəd/ *n.* Scheide, *die*

**scabies** /ˈskeɪbiːz/ *n.* ▶ **1232** (*Med.*) Krätze, *die;* Skabies, *die* (*fachspr.*)

**scabious** /ˈskeɪbɪəs/ *n.* (*Bot.*) Krätz[en]kraut, *das;* Skabiose, *die* (*fachspr.*)

**scabrous** /ˈskeɪbrəs/ *adj.* [A] (*requiring tact*) heikel ‹Thema›; [B] (*indecent*) geschmacklos; [C] (*Bot., Physiol., Zool.*) rau

**scads** /skædz/ *n. pl.* (*Amer. coll.*) **~ of money** *etc.* haufenweise Geld *usw.* (*ugs.*)

**scaffold** /ˈskæfəld/ *n.* [A] (*for execution*) Schafott, *das;* **go to the ~:** auf das Schafott kommen; [B] (*for building*) Gerüst, *das*

**scaffolding** /ˈskæfəldɪŋ/ *n., no pl.* Gerüst, *das;* (*materials*) Gerüstmaterial, *das;* **be surrounded by ~:** eingerüstet sein (*Bauw.*); **erect [a] ~ around** einrüsten (*Bauw.*)

**ˈscaffolding pole** *n.* Gerüststange, *die*

**scalar** /ˈskeɪlə(r)/ (*Math.*) ❶ *n.* Skalar, *der.* ❷ *adj.* skalar; Skalar-

**scald** /skɔːld, skɒld/ ❶ *n.* Verbrühung, *die.* ❷ *v.t.* [A] verbrühen; **~ oneself** *or* **one's skin** sich verbrühen; **be ~ed to death** tödliche Verbrühungen erleiden; **cry ~ing tears** heiße Tränen weinen; **~ing hot** brühheiß; **like a ~ed cat** wie von der Tarantel gestochen; [B] (*Cookery*) erhitzen ‹Milch›; [C] (*clean with boiling water*) auskochen; [D] (*remove hair or feathers from*) [ab]brühen ‹Schwein, Geflügel›; (*remove skin from*) überbrühen ‹Gemüse, Obst›

**scale¹** /skeɪl/ ❶ *n.* [A] Schuppe, *die;* (*of rust*) Flocke, *die;* **the ~s fall from sb.'s eyes** (*fig.*) es fällt jmdm. wie Schuppen von den Augen; [B] *no pl.* (*deposit in kettles, boilers, etc.*) Kesselstein, *der;* (*on teeth*) Zahnstein, *der.* ❷ *v.t.* [A] (*remove scales from*) [ab]schuppen ‹Fisch›; [B] (*remove deposit from*) von Kesselstein befreien ‹Kessel, Boiler›; von Zahnstein befreien ‹Zähne›

**scale²** ❶ *n.* [A] *in sing. or pl.* (*weighing instrument*) **~[s]** Waage, *die;* **a pair** *or* **set of ~s** eine Waage; **bathroom/kitchen/letter ~[s]** Personen-/Küchen-/Briefwaage, *die;* **the ~s are evenly balanced** (*fig.*) die Chancen sind ausgewogen; [B] (*dish of balance*) Waagschale, *die;* **tip** *or* **turn the ~[s]** (*fig.*) den Ausschlag geben; **tip** *or* **turn the ~[s] at 65 kilos** 65 Kilo wiegen *od.* auf die Waage bringen; [C] (*Astrol.*) **the S~s** die Waage; ⇒ *also* **archer** B. ❷ *v.t.* wiegen

**scale³** ❶ *n.* [A] (*series of degrees*) Skala, *die;* **the social ~:** die gesellschaftliche Stufenleiter; [B] (*Mus.*) Tonleiter, *die;* [C] (*dimensions*) Ausmaß, *das;* (*standard*) Richtschnur, *die;* **be on a small ~:** bescheidenen Umfang haben; **on a grand ~:** im großen Stil; **on a commercial ~:** gewerbsmäßig; **plan on a large ~:** in großem Rahmen planen; **on an international ~:** auf internationaler Ebene; ‹Katastrophe› von internationalem Ausmaß; **economies of ~:** Einsparungen durch Produktionserweiterung; [D] (*ratio of reduction*) Maßstab, *der; attrib.* maßstab[s]gerecht ‹Modell, Zeichnung›; **what is the ~ of the map?** welchen Maßstab hat diese Karte?; **a map with a ~ of 1 : 250,000** eine Karte im Maßstab 1 : 250 000; **on a large/small ~:** in großem/kleinem Maßstab; **to ~:** maßstab[s]gerecht; **be drawn on** *or* **to a ~ of 1 : 2** im Maßstab 1 : 2 gezeichnet sein; **be in ~:** maßstab[s]getreu sein; **be in ~ with sth.** im Maßstab zu etw. passen; **be out of ~:** im Maßstab nicht passen (**with** zu); [E] (*indication*) (*on map, plan*) Maßstab, *der;* (*on thermometer, ruler, exposure meter*) [Anzeige]skala, *die;* (*instrument*) Messstab, *der;* **what ~ are these temperatures measured in?** nach welcher [Einheiten]skala werden diese Temperaturen gemessen?; **a ruler marked off in the metric ~:** ein Lineal mit Zentimeterskala; [F] (*Math.*) **~ [of notation]** Positionssystem, *das;* **decimal ~:** Dezimalsystem, *das;* **binary ~:** Dualsystem, *das;* Binärsystem, *das.*
❷ *v.t.* [A] (*climb, clamber up*) ersteigen ‹Festung, Mauer, Leiter, Gipfel›; erklettern ‹Felswand, Leiter, Gipfel›; [B] (*represent in proportion*) [ab]stufen, staffeln ‹Fahrpreise›; maßstab[s]gerecht anfertigen ‹Zeichnung›; **~ production/prices to demand** die Produktion/Preise an die Nachfrage anpassen

**~ ˈdown** *v.t.* [entsprechend] drosseln ‹Produktion›; [entsprechende] Abstriche machen an (+ *Dat.*) ‹Ideen›; **we ~d down our plans** wir haben bei unseren Planungen Abstriche gemacht; **a ~d down version** eine kleinere Version

**~ ˈup** *v.t.* [entsprechend] vergrößern ‹Umfang, Ausmaß›; **we ~d up our plans** wir haben im größeren Maßstab neu geplant; **a ~d up version** eine größere Version

**scalene** /ˈskeɪliːn/ *adj.* (*Geom.*) ungleichseitig ‹Dreieck›

**ˈscale pan** *n.* Waagschale, *die*

**scaling ladder** /ˈskeɪlɪŋlædə(r)/ *n.* Sturmleiter, *die;* (*of fire engine*) Feuer[wehr]leiter, *die*

**scallion** /ˈskæljən/ *n.* (*Bot.*) [A] ⇒ **shallot**; [B] (*spring onion*) Frühlingszwiebel, *die*

**scallop** /ˈskæləp, ˈskɒləp/ ❶ *n.* [A] *in pl.* (*ornamental edging*) Feston, *das;* Bogenkante, *die;* [B] (*Zool.*) Kammmuschel, *die;* (*Gastr.*) Jakobsmuschel, *die;* [C] (*Cookery: pan*) muschelförmige Schale. ❷ *v.t.* festonieren

**scallop-ˈedge** *n.* Bogenkante, *die*

**scalloping** /ˈskæləpɪŋ, ˈskɒləpɪŋ/ *n.* Feston, *das;* **be decorated with ~:** festoniert sein

**ˈscallop shell** *n.* Kammmuschel[schale], *die*

**scallywag** /ˈskælɪwæg/ *n.* Schlingel, *der* (*scherzh.*); Tunichtgut, *der*

**scalp** /skælp/ ❶ *n.* [A] ▶ **966** Kopfhaut, *die;* [B] (*war trophy*) Skalp, *der;* (*fig.*) Trophäe, *die;* **be after sb.'s ~** (*fig.*) jmdm. an den Kragen wollen; **the newspapers call for ~s** (*fig.*) die Zeitungen wollen Köpfe rollen sehen. ❷ *v.t.* [A] skalpieren; [B] (*criticize*) kein gutes Haar lassen an (+ *Dat.*) (*ugs.*) ‹Person, Buch›; [C] (*Amer.*) (*defeat*) vernichtend schlagen, fertig machen (*ugs.*) ‹Partei, Gegner›; [D] (*Amer. coll.: sell*) mit hohem Gewinn weiterverkaufen ‹Aktien, Eintrittskarte›; **get ~ed tickets** Karten auf dem Schwarzmarkt bekommen

**scalpel** /ˈskælpl/ *n.* (*Med.*) Skalpell, *das*

**scalper** /ˈskælpə(r)/ *n.* (*Amer. coll.*) kleiner Spekulant/kleine Spekulantin; (*ticket tout*) [Karten]schwarzhändler, *der*/-händlerin, *die*

**scaly** /ˈskeɪlɪ/ *adj.* [A] schuppig; abblätternd ‹Farbe, Rost›; **be ~** ‹Schlange:› eine schuppige Haut haben; [B] (*covered in deposit*) mit Kesselstein überzogen; (*covered in tartar*) mit Zahnstein überzogen; [C] (*forming deposit*) **~ substance** *or* **incrustation** Kesselstein, *der;* Wasserstein, *der*

**scam** /skæm/ *n.* (*Amer. coll.*) Masche, *die* (*ugs.*)

**scamp** /skæmp/ ❶ *n.* (*derog./joc.*) Spitzbube, *der* (*abwertend/fam.*). ❷ *v.t.* ⇒ **skimp** 1

**scamper** /ˈskæmpə(r)/ ❶ *v.i.* ‹Person:› flitzen; ‹Tier:› huschen; (*hop*) hoppeln; **the mice ~ed to and fro** die Mäuse huschten hin und her; **~ down the stairs** die Treppe hinunterflitzen; (*romp*) **~ through the woods/park** durch die Wälder/den Park tollen. ❷ *n.* **have a ~** (*romp*) herumtollen

**scampi** /ˈskæmpɪ/ *n. pl.* Scampi *Pl.*

**scan** /skæn/ ❶ *v.t.*, **-nn-** [A] (*examine intensely*) [genau] studieren; (*search thoroughly, lit. or fig.*) absuchen (**for** nach); [B] (*look over cursorily*) flüchtig ansehen; überfliegen ‹Zeitung, Liste usw.› (**for** auf der Suche nach); [C] (*Computing*) scannen; **~ in** einscannen; [D] (*examine for radioactivity*) auf Radioaktivität (*Akk.*) untersuchen; [E] (*examine with beam*) durchleuchten ‹Gepäck›; ‹Radar:› [mittels Strahlen] abtasten ‹Luftraum›; ‹Flugsicherung:› [mittels Radar] überwachen ‹Luftraum›; [F] (*Med.*) szintigraphisch untersuchen ‹Körper, Organ›; [G] (*Pros.*) das Metrum bestimmen von ‹Vers[zeile]›; [H] (*Telev.*) abtasten ‹Ziel, Bild›.
❷ *v.i.*, **-nn-** ‹Vers[zeile]:› das richtige Versmaß haben; **make sth. ~:** etw. in das richtige Versmaß bringen.
❸ *n.* [A] (*thorough search*) Absuchen, *das;* [B] (*quick look*) **[cursory] ~:** flüchtiger Blick; **do a quick ~ of** *or* **through** überfliegen, flüchtig durchblättern ‹Zeitung›; [C] (*examination for radioactivity*) Untersuchung auf Radioaktivität (*Akk.*); [D] (*examination by beam*) Durchleuchtung, *die;* **check the radar ~ for sth.** den Radarschirm nach etw. absuchen; [E] (*Med.*) szintigraphische Untersuchung; **body/brain ~:** Ganzkörper-/Gehirnscan, *der;* **have a ~:** sich szintigraphisch untersuchen lassen

**scandal** /ˈskændl/ *n.* [A] Skandal, *der* (**about/of** um); (*story*) Skandalgeschichte, *die;* **cause** *or* **create a ~:** einen Skandal verursachen; [B] (*outrage*) Empörung, *die;* **arouse a feeling** *or* **sense of ~ in sb.** jmdn. mit Empörung erfüllen; [C] *no art.* (*damage to reputation*) Schande, *die;* **be untouched by ~:** einen makellosen Ruf haben; **be ruined by ~:** durch einen Skandal ruiniert werden; [D] (*malicious gossip*) Klatsch, *der* (*ugs.*); (*in newspapers etc.*) Skandalgeschichten *Pl.*

**scandalize** (**scandalise**) /ˈskændəlaɪz/ *v.t.* schockieren

**scandalmonger** /ˈskændlmʌŋgə(r)/ *n.* Klatschmaul, *das* (*salopp abwertend*); (*in the press*) Schreiber/Schreiberin von Skandalgeschichten

**scandalmongering** /ˈskændlmʌŋgərɪŋ/ *n.* Verbreitung von Skandalgeschichten

**scandalous** /ˈskændələs/ *adj.* skandalös; schockierend ‹Bemerkung›; Skandal‹blatt, -presse, -geschichte, -bericht›; **how ~!** unerhört!; **this is ~:** das ist ein Skandal

**ˈscandal sheet** *n.* (*derog.*) Skandalblatt, *das* (*abwertend*); Klatschblatt, *das* (*ugs. abwertend*)

**Scandinavia** /skændɪˈneɪvɪə/ *pr. n.* Skandinavien (*das*)

**Scandinavian** /skændɪˈneɪvɪən/ ❶ *adj.* skandinavisch; **sb. is ~:** jmd. ist Skandinavier/Skandinavierin. ❷ *n.* [A] (*person*) Skandinavier, *der*/Skandinavierin, *die;* [B] (*Ling.*) skandinavische Sprachen

**scanner** /ˈskænə(r)/ *n.* [A] (*to detect radioactivity*) Geigerzähler, *der;* [B] (*radar aerial*) Radarantenne, *die;* [C] (*Computing, Med.*) Scanner, *der;* [D] (*Telev.*) Bildabtaster, *der*

**scansion** /ˈskænʃn/ *n.* (*Pros.*) metrische Gliederung; (*rhythm analysis*) Bestimmung des Versmaßes

**scant** /skænt/ *adj.* (*arch./literary*) karg (*geh.*) ‹Lob, Lohn›; wenig ‹Rücksicht›; **pay sb./sth. ~ attention** jmdn./etw. kaum beachten; **a ~ two hours** knappe zwei Stunden

**scantily** /ˈskæntɪlɪ/ *adv.* kärglich; spärlich ‹bekleidet›

**scanty** /ˈskæntɪ/ *adj.* spärlich; knapp ‹Bikini›; nur wenig ‹Vergnügen, Spaß›

**scapegoat** /ˈskeɪpgəʊt/ *n.* Sündenbock, *der;* **make sb. a ~:** jmdn. zum Sündenbock machen; **act as** *or* **be a ~ for sth.** als Sündenbock für etw. herhalten müssen

**scapegrace** /ˈskeɪpgreɪs/ *n.* Taugenichts, *der*

**scapula** /ˈskæpjʊlə/ *n., pl.* **~e** /ˈskæpjʊliː/ (*Anat.*) Schulterblatt, *das*

S

**scar** /skɑ:(r)/ ❶ *n.* (*lit. or fig.*) Narbe, *die;* **duelling ~:** Schmiss, *der;* **battle ~:** Kriegsnarbe, *die;* **bear the ~s of sth.** (*fig.*) von etw. gezeichnet sein; **be a ~ on the landscape** (*fig.*) ein Schandfleck in der Landschaft sein. ❷ *v.t.*, **-rr-: ~ sb./sb.'s face** bei jmdm./in jmds. Gesicht (*Dat.*) Narben hinterlassen; **~ sb. for life** (*fig.*) jmdn. für sein ganzes Leben zeichnen; **leave sb. [badly] ~red** (*lit. or fig.*) [schlimme] Narben bei jmdm. hinterlassen. ❸ *v.i.* **~ over** vernarben

**scarab** /'skærəb/ *n.* (*Zool., gem*) Skarabäus, *der*

**scarce** /skeəs/ ❶ *adj.* Ⓐ (*insufficient*) knapp; Ⓑ (*rare*) selten; **make oneself ~** (*coll.*) sich aus dem Staub machen (*ugs.*). ❷ *adv.* (*arch./literary*) kaum

**scarcely** /'skeəslɪ/ *adv.* kaum; **there was ~ a drop of wine left** es war fast kein Tropfen Wein mehr da; **~ [ever]** kaum [jemals]; **it is ~ likely** es ist wenig wahrscheinlich; **she will ~ be pleased** (*iron.: by no means*) sie wird sich nicht gerade freuen

**scarceness** /'skeəsnɪs/ *n., no pl.* Knappheit, *die* (**of** an + *Dat.*)

**scarcity** /'skeəsɪtɪ/ *n.* Ⓐ (*short supply*) Knappheit, *die* (**of** an + *Dat.*); **there is a ~ of sugar** es herrscht Zuckerknappheit; **~ of teachers** Lehrermangel, *der;* **food ~:** Lebensmittelknappheit, *die;* Ⓑ *no pl.* (*rareness*) Seltenheit, *die;* **have [a] ~ value** Seltenheitswert haben

**scare** /skeə(r)/ ❶ *n.* Ⓐ (*sensation of fear*) Schreck[en], *der;* **give sb. a ~:** jmdm. einen Schreck[en] einjagen; **I had/it gave me a [nasty] ~:** ich bekam einen [bösen] Schrecken; Ⓑ (*general alarm; panic*) [allgemeine] Hysterie; **bomb ~:** Bombendrohung, *die;* **food poisoning ~:** Alarm wegen Lebensmittelvergiftung; *attrib.* **~ story** Schauergeschichte, *die.*
❷ *v.t.* Ⓐ (*frighten*) Angst machen (+ *Dat.*); (*startle*) erschrecken; **he/hard work/your threat doesn't ~ me** ich habe keine Angst vor ihm/harter Arbeit/deiner Drohung; **~ sb. into doing sth.** jmdn. dazu bringen, etw. [aus Angst] zu tun; **~ sb. out of his mind** *or* **skin** *or* **wits** (*fig.*), **~ sb. rigid** *or* **silly** *or* **stiff** (*fig.*), **~ the wits** *or* (*coarse*) **the shit out of sb.** (*fig.*) jmdm. eine wahnsinnige Angst einjagen (*ugs.*); (*startle*) jmdn. zu Tode erschrecken; **horror films ~ the pants off me** (*coll.*) bei Horrorfilmen habe ich immer eine wahnsinnige Angst (*ugs.*); Ⓑ (*drive away*) verscheuchen ‹Vögel›. ❸ *v.i.* erschrecken (**at** bei); ‹Pferd:› scheuen (**at** vor + *Dat.*); **~ easily** sich leicht erschrecken lassen

**~ a'way** *v.t.* verscheuchen

**~ 'off** *v.t.* verscheuchen

**~ 'out, ~ 'up** *v.t.* (*Amer.: Hunting, fig.*) aufstöbern ‹Wild, Gegenstand›; auftreiben (*ugs.*) ‹etw. zu essen, Informationen›

**scare: ~ buying** *n.* (*Amer.*) Hamsterkäufe *Pl.;* **~crow** *n.* (*lit. or fig.*) Vogelscheuche, *die*

**scared** /skeəd/ *adj.* verängstigt ‹Gesicht, Stimme›; **be/feel [very] ~:** [große] Angst haben; **be ~ of sb./sth.** vor jmdm./etw. Angst haben; **be ~ of doing/to do sth.** sich nicht [ge]trauen, etw. zu tun; **be ~ [that] sth. might happen** befürchten, dass etw. passieren könnte

**scaremonger** /'skeəmʌŋgə(r)/ *n.* Panikmacher, *der*/-macherin, *die* (*abwertend*)

**scaremongering** /'skeəmʌŋgərɪŋ/ *n., no pl.* Panikmache, *die*

**'scare tactics** *n. pl.* ≈ Panikmache, *die* (*ugs.*)

**scarf** /skɑ:f/ *n., pl.* **~s** *or* **scarves** /skɑ:vz/ Schal, *der;* (*triangular/square piece of fine material*) Halstuch, *das;* (*worn over hair*) Kopftuch, *das;* (*worn over shoulders*) Schultertuch, *das*

**scarf: ~ pin** *n.* (*Brit.*) Vorstecknadel, *die;* Halstuchnadel, *die;* **~ ring** *n.* (*Brit.*) Halstuchring, *der*

**scarify**[1] /'skærɪfaɪ, 'skeərɪfaɪ/ *v.t.* Ⓐ (*Med.*) skarifizieren (*fachspr.*); anritzen; Ⓑ (*fig.: by criticism*) geißeln; Ⓒ (*Agric.*) auflockern ‹Boden›; (*Constr.*) aufreißen ‹Straße›

**scarify**[2] /'skeərɪfaɪ/ *v.t.* (*coll.: frighten*) Angst machen (+ *Dat.*); **~ing** beängstigend

**scarlatina** /skɑ:lə'ti:nə/ ▶ 1232 ⇒ **scarlet fever**

**scarlet** /'skɑ:lɪt/ ❶ *n.* Scharlach, *der;* Scharlachrot, *das.* ❷ *adj.* scharlachrot; **I turned ~:** ich wurde puterrot; ⇒ *also* **pimpernel**

**scarlet: ~ 'fever** *n.* ▶ 1232 (*Med.*) Scharlach, *der;* **~ 'runner** *n.* (*Bot.*) Feuerbohne, *die*

**scarp** /skɑ:p/ *n.* Steilhang, *der*

**scarper** /'skɑ:pə(r)/ *v.i.* (*Brit. coll.*) abhauen (*salopp*); sich aus dem Staub machen (*ugs.*)

**'scar tissue** *n.* (*Med.*) Narbengewebe, *das*

**scarves** *pl. of* **scarf**

**scary** /'skeərɪ/ *adj.* (*coll.*) Ⓐ (*frightening*) Furcht erregend ‹Anblick›; schaurig ‹Film, Geschichte›; Angst einflößend ‹Person, Gesicht›; **a ~ moment** eine Schrecksekunde; **it was ~ to listen to** beim Zuhören konnte man richtig Angst kriegen (*ugs.*); Ⓑ (*easily frightened*) schreckhaft ‹Kind, Tier›; (*timid*) ängstlich

**scathing** /'skeɪðɪŋ/ *adj.* beißend ‹Spott, Kritik›; scharf ‹Angriff›; bissig ‹Person, Humor, Bemerkung›; **be ~ about sth.** etw. bissig herabsetzen *od.* (*ugs.*) heruntermachen

**scathingly** /'skeɪðɪŋlɪ/ *adv.* scharf ‹kritisieren›; bissig ‹sagen, bemerken›

**scatological** /skætə'lɒdʒɪkl/ *adj.* Ⓐ (*obscene*) obszön; **~ language** Fäkalsprache, *die;* Ⓑ (*Med., Palaeont.*) skatologisch

**scatter** /'skætə(r)/ ❶ *v.t.* Ⓐ vertreiben; zerstreuen, auseinander treiben ‹Menge›; zunichte machen ‹Hoffnungen›; **he slammed his fist on the table, ~ing china everywhere** er schlug mit der Faust auf den Tisch, dass das Porzellan in alle Richtungen flog; Ⓑ (*distribute irregularly*) verstreuen; ausstreuen ‹Samen›; **ice cream with nuts ~ed on top** mit Nüssen bestreutes Eis; Ⓒ (*partly cover*) [be]streuen ‹Straße›; **~ a field with seeds** Samen auf einem Feld ausstreuen.
❷ *v.i.* sich auflösen; ‹Menge:› sich zerstreuen; (*in fear*) auseinander stieben.
❸ *n.* Ⓐ ⇒ **~ing** A; Ⓑ (*Arms*) Streuung, *die*

**scatter: ~brain** *n.* zerstreuter Mensch; Schussel, *der* (*ugs.*); **~brained** *adj.* zerstreut; schusselig (*ugs.*); **~ cushion** *n.* Sofakissen, *das*

**scattered** /'skætəd/ *adj.* verstreut; vereinzelt ‹Fälle, Anzeichen, Regenschauer›; **thinly ~ population** verstreut lebende Bevölkerung

**scattering** /'skætərɪŋ/ *n.* Ⓐ (*small amount*) **a ~ of people/customers/letters** ein paar vereinzelte Leute/Kunden/Briefe; **add a ~ of nuts to sth.** Nüsse auf etw. (*Akk.*) streuen; **a thin ~ of snow** eine dünne Schneedecke; Ⓑ (*Phys.*) Streuung, *die*

**scatter: ~ rug** *n.* Brücke, *die;* **~shot** (*Amer.*) ❶ *n.* Streupatrone, *die;* ❷ *adj.* willkürlich

**scatty** /'skætɪ/ *adj.* (*Brit. coll.*) dusslig (*salopp*); **drive sb. ~:** jmdn. verrückt machen (*ugs.*)

**scavenge** /'skævɪndʒ/ ❶ *v.t.* Ⓐ sich (*Dat.*) holen; **~ sth. from a jumble sale** etw. auf einem Trödelmarkt ergattern; Ⓑ (*search*) durchstöbern (**for** nach); absuchen ‹Strand›; fleddern ‹Leiche›. ❷ *v.i.* **~ for sth.** nach etw. suchen; **live by scavenging** ‹Geier:› Aasfresser sein; **~ through** durchstöbern (*ugs.*) ‹Abfallhaufen›

**scavenger** /'skævɪndʒə(r)/ *n.* (*animal*) Aasfresser, *der;* (*fig. derog.: person*) Aasgeier, *der* (*ugs. abwertend*)

**scenario** /sɪ'nɑ:rɪəʊ, sɪ'neərɪəʊ/ *n., pl.* **~s** (*Theatre, Cinemat.; also fig.*) Szenario, *das*

**scene** /si:n/ *n.* Ⓐ (*place of event*) Schauplatz, *der;* (*in novel, play, etc.*) Ort der Handlung; **the ~ of the novel is set in Venice** der Roman spielt in Venedig; **~ of the crime** Ort des Verbrechens; Tatort, *der;* Ⓑ (*portion of play, film, or book*) Szene, *die;* (*division of act*) Auftritt, *der;* **love/trial ~:** Liebes-/Gerichtsszene, *die;* **steal the ~** ‹Schauspieler:› die Szene beherrschen; (*fig.*) sich in den Vordergrund spielen; Ⓒ (*display of passion, anger, jealousy*) Szene, *die;* **create** *or* **make a ~:** eine Szene machen; **there were ~s of rejoicing** es spielten sich Freudenszenen ab; **end in violent ~s** mit Gewalttätigkeiten enden; Ⓓ (*view*) Anblick, *der;* (*as depicted*) Aussicht, *die;* **present a ~ of horror** ein Bild des Schreckens bieten (*geh.*); **change of ~:** Tapetenwechsel, *der* (*ugs.*); Ⓔ (*place of action*) Ort des Geschehens; **arrive** *or* **come on the ~:** auftauchen; **a new political party has appeared on the ~:** eine neue Partei ist auf den Plan getreten; **he got into a bad ~** (*coll.*) er ist ins Schleudern gekommen (*salopp*); **leave** *or* **quit the ~:** abtreten; Ⓕ (*field of action*) **the political/drug/artistic ~:** die politische/Drogen-/Kunstszene; **the fashion/sporting ~:** die Modewelt/die Welt des Sports; **the social ~:** das gesellschaftliche Leben; Ⓖ (*coll.: area of interest*) **what's your ~?** worauf stehst du? (*ugs.*); worauf fährst du ab? (*salopp*); **that's not my ~:** das ist nicht mein Fall (*ugs.*); Ⓗ (*Theatre: set*) Bühnenbild, *das;* **change the ~:** die Kulissen auswechseln; **behind the ~s** (*lit. or fig.*) hinter den Kulissen; **behind-the-~s investigation** (*fig.*) geheime Untersuchung; **give a behind-the-~s glimpse [of sth.]** einen Blick hinter die Kulissen [einer Sache (*Gen.*)] gewähren; **set the ~ [for sb.]** (*fig.*) [jmdm.] die Ausgangssituation darlegen

**'scene: ~ change** *n.* (*Theatre*) Kulissenwechsel, *der;* **~-painter** *n.* ▶ 1261 Kulissenmaler, *der*/-malerin, *die*

**scenery** /'si:nərɪ/ *n., no pl.* Ⓐ (*Theatre*) Bühnenbild, *das;* Ⓑ (*landscape*) Landschaft, *die;* (*picturesque*) [malerische] Landschaft; **mountain ~:** Gebirgslandschaft, *die;* **some beautiful ~:** einige schöne Landstriche; **change of ~:** Tapetenwechsel, *der* (*ugs.*)

**scene: ~-shifter** *n.* ▶ 1261 (*Theatre*) Bühnenarbeiter, *der*/-arbeiterin, *die;* **~-shifting** *n.* (*Theatre*) Kulissenwechsel, *der*

**scenic** /'si:nɪk/ *adj.* Ⓐ (*with fine natural scenery*) landschaftlich schön; **a ~ drive** eine Fahrt durch schöne Landschaft; **~ beauty** *or* **qualities** landschaftliche Schönheit; **~ railway** Berg-und-Tal-Bahn, *die;* Ⓑ (*Theatre*) Bühnen-; **be a ~ designer** Bühnenbildner/-bildnerin sein; Ⓒ (*Art: in painting etc.*) szenisch

**scent** /sent/ ❶ *n.* Ⓐ (*smell*) Duft, *der;* (*fig.*) [Vor]ahnung, *die;* **catch the ~ of sth.** den Duft von etw. in die Nase bekommen; Ⓑ (*Hunting; also fig.: trail*) Fährte, *die;* **get/be on the [right] ~** (*lit. or fig.*) die richtige Fährte finden/auf der richtigen Fährte sein; **be on the ~ of sb./sth.** (*fig.*) jmdm./einer Sache auf der Spur sein; **[lay** *or* **set] a false ~** (*lit. or fig.*) eine falsche Fährte [legen]; **put the hounds on/off the ~:** die Hunde auf die Fährte setzen/von der Fährte abbringen; **put** *or* **throw sb. off the ~** (*fig.*) jmdn. auf eine falsche Fährte bringen; **put sb. on the ~ of sb./sth.** (*fig.*) jmdn. auf jmds. Spur bringen/einer Sache (*Dat.*) auf die Spur bringen; ⇒ *also* **cold** 1 K; **hot** 1 I; Ⓒ (*Brit.: perfume*) Parfüm, *das;* Ⓓ (*sense of smell*) Geruchssinn, *der;* (*fig.: power to detect*) Spürsinn, *der.*
❷ *v.t.* Ⓐ (*lit. or fig.*) wittern; spüren ‹Heuchelei›; ‹Tier:› beriechen (*ugs.*), beschnuppern ‹Boden›; Ⓑ (*apply perfume to*) parfümieren

**~ 'out** *v.t.* (*lit. or fig.*) aufspüren

**'scent bottle** *n.* (*Brit.*) Parfümfläschchen, *das*

**scented** /'sentɪd/ *adj.* Ⓐ (*having smell*) duftend; **be ~** ‹Blume:› duften; **~ air** von Düften erfüllte Luft; Ⓑ (*perfumed*) parfümiert

**'scent gland** *n.* (*Zool.*) Duftdrüse, *die*

**scentless** /'sentlɪs/ *adj.* geruchlos; ‹Blume› ohne Duft; **be ~:** nicht duften

**scepsis** /'skepsɪs/ *n., no pl.* (*Philos.*) Skepsis, *die*

**scepter** (*Amer.*) ⇒ **sceptre**

**sceptic** /'skeptɪk/ *n.* Skeptiker, *der*/Skeptikerin, *die;* (*with religious doubts*) [Glaubens]zweifler, *der*/-zweiflerin, *die*

S

**sceptical** /ˈskeptɪkl/ *adj.* skeptisch; **be ~ about** *or* **of sb./sth.** jmdm./einer Sache skeptisch gegenüberstehen

**sceptically** /ˈskeptɪkəlɪ/ *adv.* skeptisch

**scepticism** /ˈskeptɪsɪzm/ *n.* Skepsis, *die;* (*Philos.*) Skeptizismus, *der;* (*religious doubt*) Glaubenszweifel *Pl.*

**sceptre** /ˈseptə(r)/ *n.* (*Brit.; lit. or fig.*) Zepter, *das*

**schedule** /ˈʃedjuːl/ ❶ *n.* A (*list*) Tabelle, *die;* (*for event, festival*) Programm, *das;* B (*plan of procedure*) Zeitplan, *der;* **filming ~:** Drehplan, *der;* **we are working to a tight ~:** unsere Termine sind sehr eng; **go** *or* **happen [according] to ~:** nach Plan laufen; C (*set of tasks*) Terminplan, *der;* Programm, *das;* **work/study ~:** Arbeits-/Studienplan, *der;* **a heavy work ~:** ein umfangreiches Arbeitspensum; D (*tabulated statement*) Aufstellung, *die;* (*appendix*) tabellarischer Anhang; (*blank form*) Formblatt, *das;* **[tax] ~:** Steuertabelle, *die;* E (*timetable*) Fahrplan, *der;* F (*time stated in plan*) **on ~:** programmgemäß; **arrive on ~:** pünktlich ankommen; **flight ~s** Ankunfts- und Abflugzeiten; **bus/train ~s** Ankunfts- und Abfahrtszeiten der Busse/Züge; ⇒ *also* **ahead** C; **behind** 2 E.
❷ *v.t.* A (*make plan of*) zeitlich planen; (*appoint to be done*) anberaumen ‹Sitzung›; **be ~d for Thursday** für Donnerstag geplant sein; **we are ~d to start next week** laut Plan sollen wir nächste Woche anfangen; **they have ~d the building for demolition** nach ihren Plänen soll das Gebäude abgerissen werden; B (*make timetable of*) einen Fahrplan aufstellen für; (*include in timetable*) in den Fahrplan aufnehmen; **trains which are ~d to run at a given time** Züge, die zu einer bestimmten Zeit fahren sollen; C (*make list of*) auflisten; (*include in list*) aufführen (**in** in + *Dat.*); (*Brit.: to be preserved*) unter Denkmalschutz stellen ‹Gebäude›

**scheduled** /ˈʃedjuːld/ *adj.* A (*according to timetable*) [fahr]planmäßig ‹Zug, Halt›; flugplanmäßig ‹Zwischenlandung›; Linien‹flugzeug, -dienst, -maschine›; **~ flight** Linienflug, *der;* **make a ~ stop** ‹Flugzeug:› planmäßig zwischenlanden; B (*Brit.: in list of protected buildings*) unter Denkmalschutz stehend

**schematic** /skɪˈmætɪk, skiːˈmætɪk/ *adj.*, **schematically** /skɪˈmætɪkəlɪ, skiːˈmætɪkəlɪ/ *adv.* schematisch

**schematize (schematise)** /ˈskiːmətaɪz/ *v.t.* schematisieren (**into** zu)

**scheme** /skiːm/ ❶ *n.* A (*arrangement*) Anordnung, *die;* **general ~ of things** allgemeine Gegebenheiten; ⇒ *also* **colour scheme**; B (*table of classification, outline*) Schema, *das;* **~ [of study]** (*syllabus*) Studienprogramm, *das;* C (*plan*) Programm, *das;* (*project*) Projekt, *das;* **pension ~:** Altersversorgung, *die;* D (*dishonest plan*) Intrige, *die;* **~ of revenge** Racheplan, *der;* **what ~ are you plotting?** was führst du im Schilde? ❷ *v.i.* Pläne schmieden; **~ for sb.'s downfall/to assassinate sb.** jmds. Sturz/ein Attentat auf jmdn. planen. ❸ *v.t.* im Schilde führen

**schemer** /ˈskiːmə(r)/ *n.* Intrigant, *der*/Intrigantin, *die;* **your sister is a real little ~:** deine Schwester ist ein raffiniertes kleines Biest (*ugs.*)

**scheming** /ˈskiːmɪŋ/ ❶ *n., no pl., no indef. art.* Winkelzüge *Pl.;* Machenschaften *Pl.;* **be given to ~:** gern intrigieren. ❷ *adj.* intrigant; **be a ~ person, have a ~ nature** gern intrigieren

**scherzo** /ˈskeətsəʊ/ *n., pl.* **~s** (*Mus.*) Scherzo, *das*

**schilling** /ˈʃɪlɪŋ/ *n.* ▸ **1328** Schilling, *der*

**schism** /ˈsɪzm, ˈskɪzm/ *n.* A (*Eccl.*) Schisma, *das;* B (*in any group*) Spaltung, *die*

**schismatic** /sɪzˈmætɪk, skɪzˈmætɪk/ *adj.* (*Eccl.*) schismatisch

**schist** /ʃɪst/ *n.* (*Geol.*) Schiefer, *der*

**schizo** /ˈskɪtsəʊ/ (*coll.*) ❶ *n., pl.* **~s** Schizophrene, *der/die.* ❷ *adj.* schizophren

**schizoid** /ˈskɪtsɔɪd/ (*Psych.*) ❶ *adj.* schizoid. ❷ *n.* Schizoide, *der/die;* **be a ~:** schizoid sein

**schizophrenia** /skɪtsəˈfriːnɪə/ *n.* (*Psych.*) Schizophrenie, *die*

**schizophrenic** /skɪtsəˈfrenɪk, skɪtsəˈfriːnɪk/ (*Psych.; also fig. coll.*) ❶ *adj.* schizophren; ‹Symptom› der Schizophrenie. ❷ *n.* Schizophrene, *der/die*

**schlock** /ʃlɒk/ *n.* (*coll.*) Mist, *der* (*fig.*)

**schmaltz** /ʃmɔːlts/ *n.* (*coll.*) Schmalz, *der* (*ugs. abwertend*)

**schmaltzy** /ˈʃmɔːltsɪ/ *adj.* (*coll.*) schmalzig (*abwertend*)

**schmuck** /ʃmʌk/ *n.* (*esp. Amer. coll.*) Schwachkopf, *der* (*abwertend*)

**schnapps** /ʃnæps/ *n.* Schnaps, *der*

**schnauzer** /ˈʃnaʊtsə(r)/ *n.* Schnauzer, *der*

**schnitzel** /ˈʃnɪtsl/ *n.* (*Gastr.*) [Kalbs]schnitzel, *das*

**schnorkel** /ˈʃnɔːkl/ ⇒ **snorkel**

**scholar** /ˈskɒlə(r)/ *n.* A (*learned person*) Gelehrte, *der/die;* **literary/linguistic/musical ~:** Literatur-/Sprach-/Musikwissenschaftler *der*/-wissenschaftlerin, *die;* **Shakespeare[an] ~:** Shakespeare-Forscher, *der*/-Forscherin, *die;* **be a ~ in one's field** Experte/Expertin auf seinem/ihrem Gebiet sein; B (*one who learns*) Schüler, *der*/Schülerin, *die;* **be no ~:** kein guter Schüler/keine gute Schülerin sein; C (*holder of scholarship*) Stipendiat, *der*/Stipendiatin, *die*

**scholarly** /ˈskɒləlɪ/ *adj.* wissenschaftlich; gelehrt ‹Person›; **a ~ life** ein Gelehrtenleben; **he has a ~ appearance** er hat das Aussehen eines Gelehrten

**scholarship** /ˈskɒləʃɪp/ *n.* A (*payment for education*) Stipendium, *das;* **closed ~** *Stipendium, das nur bestimmten Bewerbern gewährt wird;* **open ~** *Stipendium, um das sich jeder bewerben kann;* B *no pl.* (*scholarly work*) Gelehrsamkeit, *die* (*geh.*); (*methods*) Wissenschaftlichkeit, *die;* **a work full of ~:** ein hochwissenschaftliches Werk; C *no pl.* (*body of learning*) **literary/linguistic/historical ~:** Literatur-/Sprach-/Geschichtswissenschaft, *die;* **contribute to Shakespearean/Romance ~:** einen Beitrag zur Shakespeareforschung/Romanistik leisten

**scholastic** /skəˈlæstɪk/ *adj.* A akademisch; Akademiker‹familie, -milieu›; wissenschaftlich ‹Buchhandlung, Leistung, Standard›; B (*Philos., Theol.*) scholastisch

**scholasticism** /skəˈlæstɪsɪzm/ *n.* A Scholastizismus, *der;* B (*Philos., Theol.*) Scholastik, *die*

**school¹** /skuːl/ ❶ *n.* A Schule, *die;* (*Amer.: university, college*) Hochschule, *die; attrib.* Schul-; **what do they teach them in ~s?** was lernen sie in der Schule?; **be at** *or* **in ~:** in der Schule sein; (*attend ~*) zur Schule gehen; **be kept in ~ [late]** nachsitzen müssen; **to/from ~:** zur/von *od.* aus der Schule; **go to ~:** zur Schule gehen; **leave ~:** die Schule verlassen; **have ~:** Schule *od.* Unterricht haben; **have time off ~:** schulfrei haben; **be absent from ~:** in der Schule fehlen; **one hour before/after ~:** eine Stunde vor Unterrichtsbeginn/nach Schulschluss; **there will be no ~ today** heute ist keine Schule; **the ~ of life** (*fig.*) die Schule des Lebens; **~ is fun/boring** Schule macht Spaß/ist langweilig; **my first day of ~, the day I started ~:** mein erster Schultag; B *attrib.* Schul‹arzt, -aufsatz, -bus, -bibliothek, -gebäude, -jahr, -orchester, -system›; **~ holidays** Schulferien *Pl.;* **~ exchange** Schüleraustausch, *der;* **the ~ term** die Schulzeit; **take ~ meals** in der Schule [zu Mittag] essen; **the ~ caretaker** der Hausmeister der Schule; **my rusty ~ French** mein eingerostetes Schulfranzösisch; C (*disciples*) Schule, *die;* **~ of thought** Lehrmeinung, *die;* ⇒ *also* **old** 1 C, F; D (*Brit.: group of gamblers*) Runde, *die;* E (*Univ.: department*) Institut, *das;* **~ of history** Institut für Zeitgeschichte; **law/medical ~:** juristische/medizinische Fakultät.
❷ *v.t.* A (*send to ~*) einschulen; B (*train*) erziehen; dressieren ‹Pferd›; **~ sb. in sth.** jmdn. in etw. (*Akk.*) unterweisen (*geh.*)

**school²** *n.* (*of fish*) Schwarm, *der;* Schule, *die* (*Zool.*)

**school: ~ age** *n.* Schulalter, *das;* **children of ~ age** Kinder im schulpflichtigen Alter; **~bag** *n.* Schultasche, *die;* **~ board** *n.* (*Amer./Hist.*) [örtliche] Schulbehörde; **~ book** *n.* Schulbuch, *das;* **~boy** *n.* Schüler, *der;* (*with reference to behaviour*) Schuljunge, *der;* **every ~boy knows that** das weiß jeder Schuljunge; **~boyish** *adj.* schuljungenhaft; **~child** *n.* Schulkind, *das;* **~days** *n. pl.* Schulzeit, *die*

**schooled** /skuːld/ *adj.* geschult ‹Pferd›; **be [highly] ~ in sth.** [ausgezeichnet] Bescheid wissen über etw. (*Akk.*)

**school: ~ fees** *n. pl.* Schulgeld, *das;* **~fellow** *n.* Mitschüler, *der*/-schülerin, *die;* Schulkamerad, *der*/-kameradin, *die;* **~ friend** *n.* Schulfreund, *der*/-freundin, *die;* **~girl** *n.* Schülerin, *die;* (*with reference to behaviour*) Schulmädchen, *das;* **~girlish** *adj.* schulmädchenhaft; **~house** *n.* Schulhaus, *das*

**schooling** /ˈskuːlɪŋ/ *n.* A Schulbildung, *die;* **he has had little ~:** er hat keine richtige Schulbildung gehabt; **have one's ~:** zur Schule gehen; **I received my ~ at his hands** er war mein Lehrmeister; B (*Horse riding*) Ausbildung, *die*

**school: ~kid** *n.* (*coll.*) Schulkind, *das;* **~ leaver** *n.* (*Brit.*) Schulabgänger, *der*/-abgängerin, *die;* **~-ˈleaving age** *n.* (*Brit.*) Schulabgangsalter, *das;* **~maʼam** *n.* (*coll.*) ⇒ **~marm**; **~man** /ˈskuːlmən/ *n., pl.* **~men** /ˈskuːlmən/ A (*medieval teacher*) Magister, *der;* (*Philos., Theol.*) Scholastiker, *der;* B (*Amer.: teacher*) Lehrer, *der;* **~marm** /ˈskuːlmɑːm/ *n.* (*coll.*) Gouvernante, *die* (*ugs.*); **~marmish** /ˈskuːlmɑːmɪʃ/ *adj.* (*coll.*) gouvernantenhaft; altjüngferlich; **~master** *n.* ▸ **1261** Lehrer, *der;* **~mastering** /ˈskuːlmɑːstərɪŋ/ *n.* Schuldienst, *der;* **~mate** ⇒ **schoolfellow**; **~mistress** *n.* ▸ **1261** Lehrerin, *die;* **~room** *n.* Schulzimmer, *das;* **~teacher** *n.* ▸ **1261** Lehrer, *der*/Lehrerin, *die;* **~ time** *n.* A (*lesson-time*) Schule, *die;* Unterricht, *der;* **in** *or* **during ~ time** während des Unterrichts; B (*~days*) Schulzeit, *die;* **~ work** *n.* Schularbeiten *Pl.*

**schooner** /ˈskuːnə(r)/ *n.* A (*Naut.*) Schoner, *der;* B (*Brit.: sherry glass*) [hohes] Sherryglas; C (*Amer.: beer glass*) [großes] Bierglas

**schottische** /ʃɒˈtiːʃ/ *n.* (*Mus.*) Schottisch, *der*

**schuss** /ʃʊs/ (*Skiing*) ❶ *n.* (*downhill run*) Schuss, *der;* (*course*) Schusspiste, *die.* ❷ *v.i.* Schuss fahren. ❸ *v.t.* in Schussfahrt (*Dat.*) hinunterfahren

**schwa** /ʃwɑː/ *n.* (*Phonet.*) Schwa, *das*

**sciatic** /saɪˈætɪk/ *adj.* (*Med.*) ischiadisch; Ischias‹schmerzen, -symptom›; **have a ~ hip** Ischiasbeschwerden in der Hüfte haben

**sciatica** /saɪˈætɪkə/ *n.* ▸ **1232** (*Med.*) Ischias, *die* (*fachspr. der od. das*)

**sciatic nerve** /saɪætɪk ˈnɜːv/ *n.* (*Anat.*) Ischiadikus, *der* (*fachspr.*); Ischiasnerv, *der*

**science** /ˈsaɪəns/ *n.* A *no pl., no art.* Wissenschaft, *die;* **applied/pure ~:** angewandte/reine Wissenschaft; **the ~ of medicine, medical ~:** Medizin, *die;* B (*branch of knowledge*) Wissenschaft, *die;* **moral ~:** Sittenlehre, *die;* C **[natural] ~:** Naturwissenschaften; *attrib.* naturwissenschaftlich ‹Buch, Labor›; D (*technique, expert's skill*) Kunst, *die*

**science: ~ ˈfiction** *n.* Sciencefiction, *die;* **~ park** *n.* Technologiepark, *der*

**scientific** /saɪənˈtɪfɪk/ *adj.* A wissenschaftlich; (*of natural science*) naturwissenschaftlich; B (*using technical skill*) technisch gut ‹Boxer, Schauspieler, Tennis›

**scientifically** /saɪənˈtɪfɪkəlɪ/ *adv.* A wissenschaftlich; (*with relation to natural science*) naturwissenschaftlich; nach wissenschaftlichen Methoden ‹Vieh züchten›; B (*using technical skill*) technisch gut ‹boxen›

**scientist** /ˈsaɪəntɪst/ *n.* ▸ **1261** Wissenschaftler, *der*/Wissenschaftlerin, *die;* (*in physical or natural science*) Naturwissenschaftler, *der*/-wissenschaftlerin, *die;* (*student of a science*)

Student/Studentin der Naturwissenschaften; **biological/social/computer ~s** Biologen/Soziologen/Informatiker

**Scientologist** /saɪən'tɒlədʒɪst/ *n.* Anhänger/Anhängerin der Scientology [Kirche]

**Scientology** /saɪən'tɒlədʒɪ/ *n.* Scientology, *die*

**sci-fi** /'saɪfaɪ/ *n.* (*coll.*) Sciencefiction, *die*

**scilla** /'sɪlə/ *n.* (*Bot.*) Szilla, *die;* Blaustern, *der*

**Scillies** /'sɪlɪz/, **Scilly Isles** /'sɪlɪ aɪlz/ *pr. n. pl.* Scillyinseln *Pl.*

**scimitar** /'sɪmɪtə(r)/ *n.* Krummsäbel, *der*

**scintillate** /'sɪntɪleɪt/ *v.i.* (*fig.*) vor Geist sprühen

**scintillating** /'sɪntɪleɪtɪŋ/ *adj.* (*fig.*) geistsprühend

**scintillation** /sɪntɪ'leɪʃn/ *n.* **A** *no pl.* (*sparkling*) Funkeln, *das;* **B** (*spark*) Funke, *der;* **C** (*Astron., Phys.*) Szintillation, *die*

**scion** /'saɪən/ *n.* **A** (*Hort.*) Schössling, *der;* (*for grafting*) Edelreis, *das;* **B** (*descendant*) Spross, *der*

**scissors** /'sɪzəz/ *n. pl.* **[pair of] ~:** Schere, *die;* **any/some ~:** eine Schere; **be a ~-and-paste job** [aus anderen Werken] zusammengeschrieben sein

**'scissors kick** *n.* (*Swimming*) Scherenschlag, *der*

**sclerosis** /sklə'rəʊsɪs/ *n., pl.* **scleroses** /sklə'rəʊsi:z/ **A** ▶ **1232** (*Med.*) Sklerose, *die;* **disseminated** *or* **multiple ~:** multiple Sklerose; **B** (*Bot.*) Verholzung, *die*

**sclerotic** /sklə'rɒtɪk/ *adj.* **A** (*Med.*) sklerotisch; **be a ~ patient** an Sklerose leiden; **B** (*Bot.*) verholzt; **C** (*Anat.*) skleral (*fachspr.*)

**scoff**[1] /skɒf/ *v.i.* (*mock*) spotten; **~ing remarks** spöttische Bemerkungen; **~ at sb./sth.** sich über jmdn./etw. lustig machen; **he ~ed at danger** er spottete der Gefahr (*geh.*)

**scoff**[2] (*coll.*) ❶ *v.t.* (*eat greedily*) verschlingen. ❷ *v.i.* sich [(*Dat.*) den Bauch] voll schlagen (*salopp*)

**scoffer** /'skɒfə(r)/ *n.* Spötter, *der*/Spötterin, *die*

**scold** /skəʊld/ ❶ *v.t.* schelten (*geh.*); ausschimpfen (**for** wegen); **she ~ed him for coming late** sie schimpfte ihn aus *od.* schalt ihn, weil er zu spät kam. ❷ *v.i.* schimpfen; **~ing wife** zänkische Ehefrau. ❸ *n.* Xanthippe, *die* (*abwertend*)

**scolding** /'skəʊldɪŋ/ *n.* Schimpfen, *das;* (*instance*) Schelte, *die* (*geh.*); Schimpfe, *die* (*ugs.*); **give sb. a ~ [for sth.]** jmdn. [wegen etw.] schelten *od.* ausschimpfen; **get a ~:** ausgeschimpft werden

**scollop** /'skɒləp/ ⇒ **scallop**

**sconce** /skɒns/ *n.* **A** (*flat candlestick*) flacher Kerzenständer; (*candlestick fixed to wall*) Wandleuchter, *der;* **B** (*socket*) [Kerzen]halterung, *die*

**scone** /skɒn, skəʊn/ *n. weicher, oft zum Tee gegessener kleiner Kuchen*

**scoop** /sku:p/ ❶ *n.* **A** (*shovel*) Schaufel, *die;* **a ~ of coal** eine Schaufel Kohlen; **B** (*ladle; ladleful*) Schöpflöffel, *der;* [Schöpf]kelle, *die;* **C** (*for ice cream, mashed potatoes*) Portionierer, *der;* (*quantity taken by ~*) Portion, *die;* (*of ice cream*) Kugel, *die;* **D** **apple ~:** Apfelausschneider, *der;* **cheese ~:** Käsestecher, *der;* **E** (*large profit*) Fischzug, *der* (*fig.*); **make a [considerable] ~:** einen beachtlichen Schnitt machen (*ugs.*); **F** (*Journ.*) Knüller, *der* (*ugs.*); Scoop, *der* (*fachspr.*).
❷ *v.t.* **A** (*lift*) schaufeln ‹Kohlen, Zucker›; (*with ladle*) schöpfen ‹Flüssigkeit, Schaum›; (*out of fruit, cheese*) ausstechen ‹Kerngehäuse, Probe›; **B** (*secure*) erzielen ‹Gewinn›; hereinholen (*ugs.*) ‹Auftrag›; (*in a lottery, bet*) gewinnen ‹Vermögen›; **~ the pool** den ganzen Einsatz gewinnen; **C** (*Journ.*) ausstechen
**~ 'out** *v.t.* **A** (*hollow out*) aushöhlen; schaufeln ‹Loch, Graben›; **B** (*remove*) [her]ausschöpfen ‹Flüssigkeit›; auslöffeln ‹Fruchtfleisch›; schöpfen ‹Mousse, Brei›; (*with a knife*) herausschneiden ‹Fruchtfleisch, Gehäuse›; (*excavate*) ausbaggern ‹Erde›
**~ 'up** *v.t.* schöpfen ‹Wasser, Suppe›; schaufeln ‹Erde›; aufschaufeln ‹Kohlen, Kies›; **he ~ed the child up in his arms** er hob das Kind in seine Arme

**'scoop neck** *n.* U-Ausschnitt, *der;* **a ~ dress** ein Kleid mit U-Ausschnitt

**scoot** /sku:t/ *v.i.* (*coll.*) rasen; (*to escape*) die Kurve kratzen (*ugs.*); **off you go, ~!** verschwinde/verschwindet!

**scooter** /'sku:tə(r)/ *n.* **A** (*toy*) Roller, *der;* **B** **[motor] ~:** [Motor]roller, *der*

**scope**[1] /skəʊp/ *n., no indef. art.* **A** Bereich, *der;* (*of person's activities*) Betätigungsfeld, *das;* (*of person's job*) Aufgabenbereich, *der;* (*of law*) Geltungsbereich, *der;* (*of department etc.*) Zuständigkeitsbereich, *der;* Zuständigkeit, *die;* (*of discussion, meeting, negotiations, investigations, etc.*) Rahmen, *der;* **that is a subject within my ~:** davon verstehe ich etwas; **that is a subject beyond my ~:** das fällt nicht in meine Sparte; (*beyond my grasp*) das ist mir zu hoch; **that is beyond the ~ of my essay** das sprengt den Rahmen meines Aufsatzes; **B** (*opportunity*) Entfaltungsmöglichkeiten *Pl.;* **give ample ~ for new ideas** weiten Raum für neue Ideen bieten

**scope**[2] *n.* (*coll.*) (*telescope*) Fernrohr, *das;* (*microscope*) Mikroskop, *das*

**scorch** /skɔ:tʃ/ ❶ *v.t.* verbrennen; versengen. ❷ *v.i.* **A** (*become damaged by heat*) versengt werden; verbrennen; **B** (*coll.: run or travel quickly*) flitzen. ❸ *n.* versengte Stelle; Brandfleck, *der*

**scorched earth policy** /skɔ:tʃt 'ɜ:θ pɒlɪsɪ/ *n.* (*Mil.*) Politik der verbrannten Erde

**scorcher** /'skɔ:tʃə(r)/ *n.* (*Brit. coll.*) **today's a [real] ~:** heute ist [wirklich] eine Affenhitze (*salopp*); **what a ~!** ist das eine Affenhitze heute!

**scorching** /'skɔ:tʃɪŋ/ ❶ *adj.* **A** glühend heiß; sengend, glühend ‹Hitze›; **B** (*coll.*) affenartig (*ugs.*) ‹Geschwindigkeit›. ❷ *adv.* **~ hot** glühend heiß ‹Tag, Wetter›

**score** /skɔ:(r)/ ❶ *n.* **A** (*points*) [Spiel]stand, *der;* (*made by one player*) Punktzahl, *die;* (*Golf*) Score, *der;* **What's the ~? — The ~ was 4-1 at half-time** Wie steht es? — Der Halbzeitstand war 4 : 1; **final ~:** Endstand, *der;* **keep [the] ~:** zählen; (*in written form*) aufschreiben; anschreiben; **know the ~** (*fig. coll.*) wissen, was Sache ist *od.* was läuft (*salopp*); **B** (*Mus.*) Partitur, *die;* (*Film*) [Film]musik, *die;* **in ~:** in Partitur; **C** *pl.* **~** *or* **~s** (*group of 20*) zwanzig; **a ~ of people** [ungefähr] zwanzig Leute; **three ~ years and ten** siebzig Jahre; **D** *in pl.* (*great numbers*) **~s [and ~s] of** zig (*ugs.*); Dutzende [von]; **~s of times** zigmal (*ugs.*); **E** (*notch*) Kerbe, *die;* (*scratch*) Kratzer, *der;* Schramme, *die;* (*weal*) Striemen, *der;* (*crack in skin*) Schrunde, *die;* **make a ~ on the cardboard** die Pappe [ein]ritzen; **F** (*dated: running account*) Rechnung, *die;* (*in bar, restaurant also*) Zeche, *die;* **pay off** *or* **settle an old ~** (*fig.*) eine alte Rechnung begleichen; **G** (*reason*) Grund, *der;* **on one/this ~:** aus einem/diesem Grund; **on the ~ of** wegen; **on that ~:** was das betrifft *od.* angeht; diesbezüglich.
❷ *v.t.* **A** (*win*) erzielen ‹Erfolg, Punkt, Treffer usw.›; **~ a direct hit on sth.** ‹Person:› einen Volltreffer landen; ‹Bombe:› etw. voll treffen; **the play ~d a success** das Stück war *od.* wurde ein Erfolg; **they ~d a success** sie hatten Erfolg *od.* konnten einen Erfolg [für sich] verbuchen; **you've ~d a success there** das ist ein Erfolg für dich; **~ a goal** ein Tor schießen/werfen; **we ~d 13** wir haben 13 Punkte gemacht/Tore geschossen/Tore geworfen; **~ points off** (*coll.*) ⇒ **score off**; **B** (*make notch/notches in*) einkerben; (*carve in*) [ein]ritzen; **~ grooves in sth.** Rillen in etw. (*Akk.*) kratzen; **the wood was deeply ~d** (*with notches/grooves*) in dem Holz waren tiefe Kerben/Rillen; **C** (*be worth*) zählen; **the ace ~s ten [points]** das Ass zählt zehn [Punkte]; **D** (*allot ~ to*) ‹Punktrichter, Juror:› Punkte geben (+ *Dat.*); **E** (*dated: mark up*) ankreiden (**to** *or* **against** *Dat.*) (*veralt.*); **~ sth. against** *or* **to sb.** (*fig.*) jmdm. etw. negativ anrechnen; **F** (*Mus.*) setzen; (*orchestrate*) orchestrieren ‹Musikstück›; (*compose music for*) die Musik komponieren *od.* schreiben für ‹Film, Theaterstück›; **G** (*make record of*) aufschreiben ‹Punkte›; **H** (*Amer.: criticize severely*) heftig angreifen; schwere Vorwürfe erheben gegen.
❸ *v.i.* **A** (*make ~*) Punkte/einen Punkt erzielen *od.* (*ugs.*) machen; punkten (*bes. Boxen*); (**~ goal/goals**) ein Tor/Tore schießen/werfen; **~ high** *or* **well** (*in test etc.*) eine hohe Punktzahl erreichen *od.* erzielen; **do you know how to ~?** weißt du, wie gezählt wird?; **B** (*keep ~*) aufschreiben; anschreiben; **C** (*secure advantage*) die besseren Karten haben (**over** gegenüber, im Vergleich zu); (*be a hit*) ‹Schauspieler:› gut ankommen (*ugs.*); **D** (*sl.: obtain drugs*) Stoff auftreiben (*ugs.*); **E** (*sl.: have sex*) zum Schuss kommen (*salopp*) (**with** bei); **I'd like to ~ with her** ich würde sie gerne [mal] aufs Kreuz legen *od.* vernaschen (*salopp*)
**~ off** *v.t.* (*coll.*) als dumm hinstellen
**~ 'out, ~ 'through** *v.t.* durchstreichen; ausstreichen
**~ 'up** *v.t.* anschreiben; verbuchen ‹Erfolg, Sieg usw.›; **~ up the amount I owe you for these goods** setzen Sie den Betrag für die Waren auf mein Konto

**score: ~board** *n.* Anzeigetafel, *die;* **~book** *n.* (*Sport*) Anschreibebögen; **~card** *n.* (*Sport*) Anschreibekarte, *die;* (*Golf*) Scorekarte, *die*

**scorer** /'skɔ:rə(r)/ *n.* **A** (*recorder of score*) Anschreiber, *der*/Anschreiberin, *die;* **B** (*Footb.*) Torschütze, *der*/-schützin, *die;* **he was the top** *or* **highest ~:** er hat die meisten Tore/Punkte/Treffer *usw.* erzielt

**'scoresheet** *n.* Anschreibebogen, *der*

**scoring** /'skɔ:rɪŋ/ *n.* **A** (*Mus.*) Instrumentierung, *die;* (*for orchestra*) Orchestrierung, *die;* **B** (*keeping score*) Aufschreiben, *das;* Anschreiben, *das*

**scorn** /skɔ:n/ ❶ *n., no pl., no indef. art.* Verachtung, *die;* **with ~:** mit *od.* voll[er] Verachtung; verachtungsvoll; **be the ~ of sb.** von jmdm. verachtet werden; ⇒ *also* **pour** 1 A. ❷ *v.t.* **A** (*hold in contempt*) verachten; **B** (*refuse*) in den Wind schlagen ‹Rat›; ausschlagen ‹Angebot›; verschmähen (*geh.*); **~ doing** *or* **to do sth.** es für unter seiner Würde halten, etw. zu tun

**scornful** /'skɔ:nfl/ *adj.* verächtlich ‹Lächeln, Blick›; **with ~ disdain** voll[er] Verachtung; verachtungsvoll; **be ~ of sth.** für etw. nur Verachtung haben

**scornfully** /'skɔ:nfəlɪ/ *adv.* verächtlich; voll[er] Verachtung

**Scorpian** /'skɔ:pɪən/ *n.* (*Astrol.*) Skorpion, *der*

**Scorpio** /'skɔ:pɪəʊ/ *n.* (*Astrol., Astron.*) der Skorpion; der Scorpius; ⇒ *also* **Aries**

**scorpion** /'skɔ:pɪən/ *n.* **A** (*Zool.*) Skorpion, *der;* **B** (*Astrol.*) **the S~:** der Skorpion; ⇒ *also* **archer** B

**Scot** /skɒt/ *n.* ▶ **1340** Schotte, *der*/Schottin, *die*

**scotch** *v.t.* **A** (*frustrate*) zunichte machen ‹Plan›; **B** (*put an end to*) den Boden entziehen (+ *Dat.*) ‹Gerücht, Darstellung›

**Scotch** /skɒtʃ/ ❶ *adj.* **A** (*of Scotland*) ⇒ **Scottish**; **B** (*Ling.*) ⇒ **Scots** 1 B. ❷ *n.* **A** (*whisky*) Scotch, *der;* schottischer Whisky; **B** (*Ling.*) ⇒ **Scots** 2; **C** *constr. as pl.* **the ~:** die Schotten

**Scotch: ~ 'broth** *n.* (*Gastr.*) *Hammelfleisch- od. Rindfleischsuppe mit Gemüse und Perlgraupen;* **~ 'egg** *n.* (*Gastr.*) *hart gekochtes Ei in Wurstbrät;* **~ 'fir** *n.* [Gemeine] Kiefer; Waldkiefer, *die;* **~man** /'skɒtʃmən/ ⇒ **Scotsman**; **~ 'mist** *n.* dichter Nieselregen; **~ 'pine** ⇒ **~ fir**; **~ tape** ® *n.* (*Amer.*) ≈ Tesafilm, *der* (Wz); **~ 'terrier** *n.* Scotch[terrier], *der;* **~ 'whisky** *n.* schottischer Whisky; **~woman** ⇒ **Scotswoman**

**scot-'free** *pred. adj.* ungeschoren; **get off/go/escape ~:** ungeschoren davonkommen *od.* bleiben

S

**Scotland** /'skɒtlənd/ *pr. n.* Schottland (*das*)

**Scotland 'Yard** *n.* (*Brit.*) Scotland Yard (*der*)

**Scots** /skɒts/ ▶ 1275 ❶ *adj.* [A] (*esp. Scot.*) ⇒ **Scottish**; [B] (*Ling.*) schottisch. ❷ *n.* (*dialect*) Schottisch, *das*

**Scots: ~man** /'skɒtsmən/ *n., pl.* **~men** /'skɒtsmən/ Schotte, *der;* **~woman** *n.* Schottin, *die*

**Scottie** /'skɒtɪ/ *n.* (*coll.*) [A] ⇒ **Scotch terrier**; [B] (*man*) Schotte, *der*

**Scottish** /'skɒtɪʃ/ *adj.* ▶ 1340 schottisch; **he/she is ~:** er ist Schotte/sie ist Schottin

**scoundrel** /'skaʊndrl/ *n.* Schuft, *der* (*abwertend*); (*villain*) Schurke, *der* (*abwertend*)

**scoundrelly** /'skaʊndrəlɪ/ *adj.* schurkisch (*abwertend*); schuftig (*abwertend*)

**scour**[1] /skaʊə(r)/ *v.t.* [A] (*cleanse by friction*) scheuern ‹Topf, Metall›; **~ out** ausscheuern ‹Topf›; [B] (*clear out*) **~ [out]** durchspülen ‹Rohr›; [C] (*remove by rubbing*) [ab]scheuern; **~ away/off** ab-/wegscheuern

**scour**[2] *v.t.* (*search*) durchkämmen (**for** nach)

**scourer** /'skaʊərə(r)/ *n.* Topfreiniger, *der;* Topfkratzer, *der*

**scourge** /skɜːdʒ/ ❶ *n.* (*lit. or fig.*) Geißel, *die;* **they were the ~ of the English coast** sie suchten die englische Küste immer wieder heim. ❷ *v.t.* [A] (*whip*) geißeln; [B] (*afflict*) heimsuchen

**scouse** /skaʊs/ (*Brit. coll.*) ❶ *n.* [A] (*dialect*) Liverpooler Dialekt; [B] (*person*) Liverpooler, *der*/Liverpoolerin, *die.* ❷ *adj.* Liverpooler

**scout**[1] /skaʊt/ ❶ *n.* [A] **[Boy] S~:** Pfadfinder, *der;* **King's/Queen's S~** (*im Britischen Commonwealth*) *Pfadfinder der höchsten Rangstufe;* ⇒ *also* **girl scout**; [B] (*Mil. etc.: sent to get information*) Späher, *der*/Späherin, *die;* Kundschafter, *der*/Kundschafterin, *die;* (*aircraft*) Aufklärer, *der;* [C] (*Brit. Univ.: college servant*) Collegediener, *der;* [D] (*coll.: helpful person*) **be a good ~:** immer bereit sein zu helfen; [E] (*act of looking*) Erkundung, *die;* (*Mil.*) Aufklärung, *die;* **take a ~ around** sich umsehen.
❷ *v.i.* auf Erkundung gehen; **~ for sb./sth.** nach jmdm./etw. Ausschau halten: **be ~ing for talent** auf Talentsuche sein

**~ a'bout, ~ a'round** *v.i.* sich umsehen (**for** nach); Ausschau halten (**for** nach)

**~ 'out** *v.t.* auskundschaften; erkunden

**scout**[2] *v.t.* (*reject*) ablehnen; zurückweisen; aus der Welt schaffen ‹Gerücht›

**'scout car** *n.* (*Mil.*) Panzerspähwagen, *der*

**scouting** /'skaʊtɪŋ/ *n.* [A] (*reconnaissance*) Erkundung, *die;* Aufklärung, *die* (*Milit.*); [B] **S~:** Pfadfindertum, *das;* Pfadfinderei, *die* (*ugs.*); (*Scout movement*) Pfadfinderbewegung, *die*

**scout: ~ leader**, (*Hist.*) **~master** *ns.* Pfadfinderführer, *der;* **S~ movement** *n.* Pfadfinderbewegung, *die*

**scowl** /skaʊl/ ❶ *v.i.* ein mürrisches *od.* verdrießliches Gesicht machen; **~ at sb.** jmdn. mürrisch *od.* verdrießlich ansehen. ❷ *n.* mürrischer *od.* verdrießlicher [Gesichts]ausdruck

**SCR** *abbr.* (*Brit. Univ.*) [A] **Senior Common Room;** [B] **Senior Combination Room**

**scrabble** /skræbl/ ❶ *v.i.* (*scratch*) ‹Maus, Hund:› scharren, kratzen; **~ about** ‹Maus:› herumkratzen *od.* -scharren; (*for missing object*) ‹Person:› wühlen (**for** nach); **the child was scrabbling in the sand** das Kind buddelte (*ugs.*) im Sand. ❷ *n.* **S~** ® Scrabble, *das*

**scrag[-end]** /skræg('end)/ *n.* (*Gastr.*) Hals, *der;* Halsstück, *das*

**scraggy** /'skrægɪ/ *adj.* (*derog.*) mager ‹Person, Tier›; dürr ‹Arme, Beine›; hager ‹Hals›

**scram** /skræm/ *v.i.*, **-mm-** (*coll.*) abhauen (*salopp*); verschwinden (*ugs.*)

**scramble** /'skræmbl/ ❶ *v.i.* [A] (*clamber*) klettern; kraxeln (*ugs.*); **~ through a hedge** sich durch eine Hecke zwängen; [B] (*move hastily*) hasten (*geh.*); rennen (*ugs.*); **~ for sth.** um etw. rangeln; ‹Kinder:› sich um etw. balgen; [C] (*Air Force*) [im Alarmfalle] aufsteigen.
❷ *v.t.* [A] (*Cookery*) **~ some eggs** Rührei[er] machen; **would you like your eggs ~d?** möchtest du deine Eier als Rührei?; ⇒ *also* **scrambled egg**; [B] (*Teleph., Radio*) verschlüsseln ‹Botschaft, Nachricht›; an ein Verschlüsselungsgerät anschließen ‹Telefon›; [C] (*mix together*) [ver]mischen; [D] (*deal with hastily*) **~ a bill through Parliament** einen Gesetzentwurf durchs Parlament peitschen (*ugs.*); **~ the ball away** (*Footb.*) den Ball [irgendwie] wegschlagen.
❸ *n.* [A] (*struggle*) Gerangel, *das* (**for** um); (*on roads*) [Verkehrs]gewühl, *das;* [Verkehrs]chaos, *das;* [B] (*climb*) Kletterpartie, *die* (*ugs.*)

**scrambled egg** /skræmbld 'eg/ *n.* (*Gastr.*) Rührei, *das*

**scrambler** /'skræmblə(r)/ *n.* (*Teleph., Radio*) [elektronisches] Verschlüsselungsgerät

**scrap**[1] /skræp/ ❶ *n.* [A] (*fragment*) (*of paper, conversation*) Fetzen, *der;* (*of food*) Bissen, *der;* **~ of paper** Stück Papier; (*small, torn*) Papierfetzen, *der;* [B] (*odds and ends*) (*of food*) Reste *Pl.;* (*of language*) Brocken *Pl.;* **a few ~s of information/news** ein paar bruchstückhafte Informationen/Nachrichten; **a few ~s of French** ein paar Brocken Französisch; [C] (*smallest amount*) **not a ~ of** kein bisschen; (*of sympathy, truth also*) nicht ein Fünkchen; (*of truth also*) nicht ein Körnchen; **not a ~ of evidence** nicht die Spur eines Beweises; [D] *no pl., no indef. art.* (*waste metal*) Schrott, *der;* **~ metal** Schrott, *der;* Altmetall, *das;* **~ iron** Eisenschrott, *der;* Alteisen, *das;* [E] *no pl., no indef. art.* (*rubbish*) Abfall, *der;* **they are ~:** das ist Abfall *od.* sind Abfälle.
❷ *v.t.*, **-pp-** wegwerfen; wegschmeißen (*ugs.*); (*send for ~*) verschrotten; (*fig.*) aufgeben ‹Plan, Projekt usw.›; **you can ~ that idea right away** die Idee kannst du gleich vergessen (*ugs.*)

**scrap**[2] (*coll.*) ❶ *n.* (*fight*) Rauferei, *die;* Klopperei, *die* (*ugs.*); (*verbal*) Kabbelei, *die* (*ugs.*); **get into a ~ with sb.** sich mit jmdm. in die Wolle kriegen (*ugs.*); **have a ~:** sich in der Wolle haben (*ugs.*). ❷ *v.i.*, **-pp-** sich raufen (**with** mit); (*verbally*) sich kabbeln

**'scrapbook** *n.* [Sammel]album, *das*

**scrape** /skreɪp/ ❶ *v.t.* [A] (*make smooth*) schaben ‹Häute, Möhren, Kartoffeln usw.›; abziehen ‹Holz›; (*damage*) verkratzen, verschrammen ‹Fußboden, Auto›; schürfen ‹Körperteil›; **~ one's knee/the skin off one's knee** sich (*Dat.*) das Knie schürfen/sich (*Dat.*) am Knie die Haut abschürfen; [B] (*remove*) [ab]schaben, [ab]kratzen (**off, from** von) ‹Farbe, Schmutz, Rost›; [C] (*draw along*) schleifen; **~ the bow across the fiddle** mit dem Bogen über die Geige kratzen; [D] (*remove dirt from*) abstreifen ‹Schuhe, Stiefel›; [E] (*draw back*) straff kämmen ‹Haar›; [F] (*excavate*) scharren ‹Loch›; [G] (*accumulate by care with money*) **~ together/up** (*raise*) zusammenkratzen (*ugs.*); (*save up*) zusammensparen; [H] **~ together/up** (*amass by scraping*) zusammenscharren ‹Sand, Kies›; (*rake together*) zusammenharken ‹Laub usw.›; (*amass with difficulty*) zusammenkriegen (*ugs.*) ‹Geld›; **~ [an] acquaintance with sb.** sich bei jmdm. anbiedern (*abwertend*); [I] (*leave no food on or in*) abkratzen ‹Teller›; auskratzen ‹Schüssel›; [J] (*Naut.*) von Bewuchs befreien *od.* reinigen ‹Schiff›. ⇒ *also* **barrel** A.
❷ *v.i.* [A] (*pass along with sound*) schleifen; **the chalk ~d along the blackboard** die Kreide kratzte über die Tafel; [B] (*emit scraping noise*) ein schabendes Geräusch machen; [C] (*rub*) streifen (**against, over** *Akk.*); [D] (*very nearly graze or be grazed*) **~ over sth.** ‹Flugzeug:› haarscharf über etw. (*Akk.*) hinwegfliegen; **~ past each other** ‹Autos:› haarscharf aneinander vorbeifahren; **~ into second place** (*fig.*) mit Hängen und Würgen (*ugs.*) auf den zweiten Platz kommen; [E] **bow and ~:** katzbuckeln (*abwertend*); [F] (*be careful with money*) sein Geld zusammenhalten; ⇒ *also* **scrimp**.
❸ *n.* [A] (*act, sound*) Kratzen, *das* (**against** an + *Dat.*); Schaben, *das* (**against** an + *Dat.*); **give the potatoes a ~:** die Kartoffeln schaben; [B] (*predicament*) Schwulitäten *Pl.* (*ugs.*); **be in a/get into a ~:** in Schwulitäten sein/kommen; **get sb. out of a ~:** jmdm. aus der Bredouille *od.* Patsche helfen (*ugs.*); [C] (*~d place*) Kratzer, *der* (*ugs.*); Schramme, *die*

**~ a'long** *v.i.* (*fig.*) sich über Wasser halten (**on** mit)

**~ a'way** *v.t.* abkratzen, abschaben

**~ 'by** ⇒ **~ along**

**~ 'out** *v.t.* [A] (*excavate*) buddeln (*ugs.*); scharren; [B] (*clean*) auskratzen, -schaben

**~ through** ❶ /'--/ *v.t.* [A] sich zwängen durch; [B] (*fig.: just succeed in passing*) mit Hängen und Würgen kommen durch ‹Prüfung›. ❷ /-'-/ *v.i.* [A] sich durchzwängen; [B] (*fig.: just succeed in passing examination*) mit Hängen und Würgen durchkommen

**scraper** /'skreɪpə(r)/ *n.* [A] (*for shoes*) Kratzeisen, *das;* (*grid*) Abtreter, *der;* Abstreifer, *der;* [B] (*hand tool, kitchen utensil*) Schaber, *der;* (*for clearing snow*) Schneescharre, *die;* Schneeschieber, *der;* (*for clearing mud or dung*) [Schmutz]kratzer, *der;* (*decorator's*) Spachtel, *der;* (*for removing ice from car windows*) [Eis]kratzer, *der*

**'scraperboard** *n.* (*Art*) Schabpapier, *das*

**'scrap heap** *n.* Schutthaufen, *der;* Müllhaufen, *der;* (*for scrap metal*) Schrotthaufen, *der;* **the scheme has been thrown/is on the ~** (*fig.*) der Plan ist zu Makulatur gemacht worden/ist Makulatur; **sb. is on the ~:** jmd. wird nicht mehr gebraucht; (*because of age*) jmd. gehört zum alten Eisen (*fig. ugs.*)

**scrapings** /'skreɪpɪŋz/ *n. pl.* Schabsel; Geschabsel, *das*

**scrap: ~ merchant** *n.* ▶ 1261 Schrotthändler, *der*/-händlerin, *die;* **~ 'paper** *n.* Schmierpapier, *das*

**scrappily** /'skræpɪlɪ/ *adv.* unzulänglich; (*without unity*) uneinheitlich; (*unsystematically*) unsystematisch

**scrappy** /'skræpɪ/ *adj.* [A] (*not complete*) lückenhaft ‹Bericht, Bildung usw.›; (*not unified*) uneinheitlich; [B] (*lacking consistency*) inkonsistent (*geh.*), unausgewogen ‹Aufsatz, Bericht›; [C] (*made up of bits or scraps*) zusammengestoppelt (*abwertend*); **a ~ meal, consisting of leftovers** ein aus Resten zusammengestoppeltes Essen

**'scrapyard** *n.* Schrottplatz, *der;* **be sent to the ~:** verschrottet werden

**scratch** /skrætʃ/ ❶ *v.t.* [A] (*score surface of*) zerkratzen; verkratzen; (*score skin of*) kratzen; **~ the surface [of sth.]** ‹Geschoss usw.:› [etw.] streifen; **he has only ~ed the surface [of the problem]** er hat das Problem nur oberflächlich gestreift; **~ an A and find a B** (*fig.*) in jedem A steckt ein B; [B] (*get ~[es] on*) **~ oneself/one's hands** *etc.* sich schrammen/sich (*Dat.*) die Hände *usw.* zerkratzen *od.* [zer]schrammen *od.* ritzen; [C] (*scrape without marking*) kratzen; kratzen an (+ *Dat.*) ‹Insektenstich usw.›; **~ oneself/one's arm** *etc.* sich kratzen/sich (*Dat.*) den Arm *usw. od.* am Arm *usw.* kratzen; *abs.* ‹Person:› sich kratzen; **~ one's head** sich am Kopf kratzen; **~ one's head [over sth.]** (*fig.*) sich (*Dat.*) den Kopf über etw. (*Akk.*) zerbrechen; **you ~ my back and I'll ~ yours** (*fig. coll.*) eine Hand wäscht die andere (*Spr.*); [D] (*form*) kratzen, ritzen ‹Buchstaben etc.›; (*excavate in ground*) kratzen, scharren ‹Loch› (**in** in + *Akk.*); (*scribble*) kritzeln ‹Zeilen›; **~ a living** sich schlecht und recht ernähren (**from** von); [E] (*erase from list*) streichen (**from** aus); (*withdraw from competition*) von der Starter- *od.* Teilnehmerliste streichen ‹Rennpferd, Athleten›; (*Amer. Polit.*) [von der Kandidatenliste] streichen ‹Kandidat›; *abs.* ‹Rennfahrer:› [seine Meldung *od.* Nennung] zurückziehen.
❷ *v.i.* [A] (*make wounds, cause itching, make grating sound*) kratzen; [B] (*scrape*) ‹Huhn:› kratzen, scharren.
❸ *n.* [A] (*mark, wound; coll.: trifling wound*) Kratzer, *der* (*ugs.*); Schramme, *die;* **be covered in ~es** zer- *od.* verkratzt sein; zer- *od.* verschrammt sein; **without a ~:** ohne eine Schramme; [B] (*sound*) Kratzen, *das* (**at** an + *Dat.*); Kratzgeräusch, *das;* **there was a ~ at the door** es kratzte an der Tür; [C]

*(spell of scratching)* **have a [good] ~:** sich [ordentlich] kratzen; Ⓓ *(Sport) hinterste Startlinie (bei Handicaprennen)*; **on ~:** ohne Vorgabe; Ⓔ **start from ~** *(fig.)* bei null anfangen *(ugs.)*; **be up to ~** ‹Arbeit, Leistung:› nichts zu wünschen übrig lassen; ‹Person:› in Form *od. (ugs.)* auf Zack sein; **not be up to ~:** [einiges] zu wünschen übrig lassen; ‹Mensch:› nicht in Form *od. (ugs.)* auf Zack sein; **bring sth. up to ~:** etw. auf Vordermann *(scherzh.) od. (ugs.)* auf Zack bringen; **bring sb.'s performance up to ~:** jmdn. in Form *od. (ugs.)* auf Zack bringen; Ⓕ *no pl., no indef. art. (sl.: money)* Kohle, *die (salopp)*; Knete, *die (salopp)*.
❹ *adj.* Ⓐ *(Sport)* ohne Vorgabe *nachgestellt;* **~ player** *(Golf)* Scratchspieler, *der;* Ⓑ *(collected haphazardly)* bunt zusammengewürfelt; improvisiert ‹Mahlzeit›

**~ a'bout, ~ a'round** *v.i.* scharren; *(fig.: search)* suchen (**for** nach)

**~ 'off** *v.t.* abkratzen; *(delete)* streichen ‹Person, Name›

**~ 'out** *v.t.* Ⓐ *(score out)* aus-, durchstreichen ‹Name, Wort›; Ⓑ *(gouge out)* auskratzen ‹Auge›

**~ 'through** ⇒ **~ out a**

**~ to'gether, ~ 'up** *v.t.* zusammenstoppeln *(ugs.)* ‹Mahlzeit›; zusammenkratzen *(ugs.)* ‹Geld›

**'scratch: ~board** ⇒ **scraperboard**; **~ card** *n.* Rubbellos, *das;* **~ card game** Rubbellos-Gewinnspiel, *das*

**scratchily** /'skrætʃɪlɪ/ *adv.* kratzend

**scratchy** /'skrætʃɪ/ *adj.* Ⓐ *(making sound of scratching)* kratzig [klingend] ‹Schallplatte›; **this is a ~ nib** diese Feder kratzt; Ⓑ *(causing itching)* kratzig ‹Wolle, Kleidungsstück›; Ⓒ *(careless)* kritzlig *(ugs.)* ‹Handschrift, Zeichnung›; Ⓓ *(irritable)* kratzbürstig; kratzig *(ugs.)*

**scrawl** /skrɔ:l/ ❶ *v.t.* hinkritzeln; **~ sth. on sth.** etw. auf etw. *(Akk.)* kritzeln. ❷ *v.i.* kritzeln. ❸ *n.* Ⓐ *(piece of writing)* Gekritzel, *das; (handwriting)* Klaue, *die (salopp abwertend)*; Ⓑ *(note)* hingekritzelte Zeilen

**~ 'out** *v.t.* wegstreichen ‹Wort›

**~ 'over** *v.t.* voll kritzeln, voll schmieren ‹Seite, Buch›

**scrawny** /'skrɔ:nɪ/ *adj. (derog.)* hager, dürr ‹Hals, Person›; mager ‹Vieh›

**scream** /skri:m/ ❶ *v.i.* Ⓐ *(utter cry)* schreien (**with** vor + *Dat.*); **~ at sb.** jmdn. anschreien; Ⓑ *(give shrill cry)* ‹Vogel, Affe:› schreien; Ⓒ *(whistle or hoot shrilly)* ‹Sirene, Triebwerk:› heulen; ‹Reifen:› quietschen; ‹Säge:› kreischen; **the car ~ed past** das Auto kam mit heulendem Motor vorbeigerast; Ⓓ *(laugh)* schreien (**with** vor + *Dat.*); Ⓔ *(speak or write excitedly)* **~ about sth.** um etw. ein großes Geschrei machen *(ugs.)*; **the shipyards are ~ing for work** die Werften schreien nach Aufträgen *(geh.)*; Ⓕ *(be blatantly obvious)* ‹Schlagzeile:› in die Augen springen, einem entgegenspringen.
❷ *v.t.* schreien; **~ sth. at sb.** jmdm. etw. ins Gesicht schreien.
❸ *n.* Ⓐ *(cry)* Schrei, *der; (of siren or jet engine)* Heulen, *das;* **~s of pain/laughter** Schmerzensschreie/gellendes Gelächter; Ⓑ *(coll.: comical person or thing)* **be a ~:** zum Schreien sein *(ugs.)*

**screaming** /'skri:mɪŋ/ *adj.* Ⓐ schreiend; quietschend ‹Reifen›; heulend ‹Sirene, Wind, Triebwerk›; Ⓑ *(funny)* urkomisch

**screamingly** /skri:mɪŋlɪ/ *adv.* **~ funny** urkomisch

**scree** /skri:/ *n.* **~[s]** Ⓐ *(stones)* Schutt, *der;* Geröll, *das;* Schotter, *der;* Ⓑ *(mountain slope)* Schutthalde, *die*

**screech** /skri:tʃ/ ❶ *v.i.* *(utter cry)* ‹Kind, Eule:› kreischen, schreien; *(make sound like cry)* ‹Bremsen:› quietschen, kreischen; **~ to a halt, come to a ~ing halt** ‹Auto:› quietschend *od.* kreischend zum Stehen kommen. ❷ *v.t.* kreischen. ❸ *n. (cry)* Schrei, *der;* Kreischen, *das; (sound like cry)* Quietschen, *das;* Kreischen, *das;* **give a ~ of laughter** gellend auflachen

**'screech owl** *n.* Ⓐ *(Brit.: barn owl)* Schleiereule, *die;* Ⓑ *(Amer.: of genus Otus)* Zwergohreule, *die; (Otus asio)* Kreischeule, *die*

**screed** /skri:d/ *n.* Ⓐ *(lengthy writing)* Roman, *der (ugs.)*; Ⓑ *(harangue)* Strafpredigt, *die;* Ⓒ *(Building)* Estrich, *der*

**screen** /skri:n/ ❶ *n.* Ⓐ *(partition)* Trennwand, *die; (piece of furniture)* Wandschirm, *der; (fire ~)* [Ofen]schirm, *der;* ⇒ *also* **rood screen**; Ⓑ *(sth. that conceals from view)* Sichtschutz, *der; (Hunting)* [Jagd]schirm, *der; (of trees, persons, fog)* Wand, *die; (of persons)* Mauer, *die; (expression of face or measure adopted for concealment)* Maske, *die; (of indifference, secrecy also)* Wand, *die;* Mauer, *die;* Ⓒ *(surface on which pictures are projected)* Leinwand, *die;* Projektionswand, *die; (in cathode-ray tube)* Schirm, *der;* **[TV] ~:** [Fernseh]schirm, *der;* Bildschirm, *der;* **the ~** *(Cinemat.)* die Leinwand; **stage and ~:** Bühne und Leinwand; **the small ~:** der Bildschirm; Ⓓ *(vertical display surface) (for exhibits)* Stellwand, *die; (for notices)* Pinnwand, *die;* Anschlagtafel, *die;* Ⓔ *(Phys.)* [Schutz]schirm, *der; (Electr.)* Abschirmung, *die;* Ⓕ *(Motor Veh.)* ⇒ **windscreen**; Ⓖ *(Amer.: netting to exclude insects)* Fliegendraht, *der;* Fliegengitter, *das;* Ⓗ *(sieve)* [Wurf]sieb, *das;* Durchwurf, *der;* Ⓘ *(Cricket)* ⇒ **sight screen**; Ⓙ *(Photog.)* Mattscheibe, *die;* Ⓚ *(Printing)* [Bild]raster, *der.*
❷ *v.t.* Ⓐ *(shelter)* schützen (**from** vor + *Dat.*); *(conceal)* verdecken; **~ one's eyes from the sun** seine Augen vor der Sonne schützen *od. (geh.)* gegen die Sonne beschirmen; **be ~ed from view** vor Einblicken geschützt sein; **~ sth. from sb.** etw. jmds. Blicken entziehen; Ⓑ *(show)* vorführen, zeigen ‹Dias, Film›; Ⓒ *(test)* durchleuchten (**for** auf ... [*Akk.*] hin); Ⓓ *(fig.: protect)* decken ‹Straftäter›; *(from blame)* in Schutz nehmen (**from** gegen); *(from justice)* bewahren (**from** vor + *Dat.*); Ⓔ *(sieve)* [durch]sieben; Ⓕ *(Electr. Phys., Nucl. Engin.)* abschirmen

**~ 'off** *v.t.* abteilen ‹Teil eines Raums›; [mit einem Wandschirm] abtrennen ‹Bett›

**screening** /'skri:nɪŋ/ *n.* Ⓐ *(in cinema)* Vorführung, *die; (on TV)* Sendung, *die;* Ausstrahlung, *die;* Ⓑ *(Med.)* Untersuchung, *die;* **mass ~** Reihenuntersuchung, *die*

**screen: ~play** *n. (Cinemat.)* Drehbuch, *das;* **~ printing** *n. (Textiles)* Gewebefilmdruck, *der;* **~ saver** *n. (Computing)* Bildschirmschoner, *der;* **~ test** *n. (Cinemat.)* Probeaufnahmen *Pl.*; **~writer** *n.* ▶ **1261** *(Cinemat.)* Filmautor, *der/*-autorin, *die*

**screw** /skru:/ ❶ *n.* Ⓐ Schraube, *die;* **he has a ~ loose** *(coll. joc.)* bei ihm ist eine Schraube locker *od.* lose *(salopp)*; **put the ~[s] on sb.** *(fig. coll.)* jmdm. [die] Daumenschrauben anlegen *(ugs.)*; Ⓑ *(Naut., Aeronaut.)* Schraube, *die;* Ⓒ *(sl.: prison warder)* Wachtel, *die (salopp)*; Schien, *der (Gaunerspr. veralt.)*; Ⓓ *(coarse) (copulation)* Fick, *der (vulg.)*; Nummer, *die (derb)*; *(partner in copulation)* Ficker, *der/*Fickerin, *die (vulg.)*; **have a ~:** ficken *(vulg.)*; vögeln *(vulg.)*; **be a good ~:** gut ficken *od.* vögeln *(vulg.)*; Ⓔ *(Brit. sl.: wages)* **they're/he's** *etc.* **paid a good ~:** die Kohlen stimmen [bei ihnen/ihm] *(ugs.)*; Ⓕ *(turn of ~)* [Um]drehung, *die;* **give the bolt another ~:** dreh die Schraube noch eine Umdrehung weiter.
❷ *v.t.* Ⓐ *(fasten)* schrauben (**to** an + *Akk.*); **~ together** zusammenschrauben; verschrauben; **~ down** festschrauben; **have one's head ~ed on [straight** *or* **the right way** *or* **properly]** *(coll.)* ein vernünftiger Mensch sein; Ⓑ *(turn)* schrauben ‹Schraubverschluss usw.›; **~ one's head round** den Kopf verdrehen; **~ a piece of paper into a ball** ein Stück Papier zu einer Kugel zusammendrehen; Ⓒ *(sl.: extort)* [raus]quetschen *(salopp)* ‹Geld, Geständnis› (**out of** aus); **can't you ~ a bit more money out of your parents?** kannst du deinen Eltern nicht noch ein bisschen mehr Geld aus dem Kreuz leiern? *(salopp)*; **~ sb. for a loan/for repayment** ein Darlehen/die Rückzahlung aus jmdm. rausquetschen *(salopp)*; Ⓓ *(coarse: copulate with)* ‹Mann:› ficken *(vulg.)*, vögeln *(vulg.)*; ‹Frau:› ficken mit *(vulg.)*, vögeln mit *(vulg.)*; **~ you!** *(coarse)* leck mich am Arsch! *(salopp)*; **~ you and your ...!** *(coarse)* leck mich am Arsch mit deinem/deiner/deinen ...! Ⓔ *(sl.: burgle)* knacken *(salopp)* ‹Tresor›; einen Bruch machen bei *(salopp)* ‹Bank usw.›.
❸ *v.i.* Ⓐ *(revolve)* sich schrauben lassen; sich drehen lassen; **~ to the right** ein Rechtsgewinde haben; **~ out/together** sich herausschrauben/zusammenschrauben lassen; Ⓑ *(coarse: copulate)* ficken *(vulg.)*; vögeln *(vulg.)*

**~ 'up** *v.t.* Ⓐ *(make tenser)* spannen ‹Saite›; **~ up one's courage** sich *(Dat.)* ein Herz fassen; Ⓑ *(crumple up)* zusammenknüllen ‹Blatt Papier›; Ⓒ *(make grimace with)* verziehen ‹Gesicht›; *(contract the outer parts of)* zusammenkneifen ‹Augen, Mund›; Ⓓ *(sl.: bungle)* vermurksen *(ugs.)*; vermasseln *(salopp)*; **~ it/things up** Mist bauen *(salopp)*

**screw: ~ball** *(Amer. coll.)* ❶ *n.* Spinner, *der/*Spinnerin, *die (ugs. abwertend)*; **be a ~:** spinnen; ❷ *adj.* spleenig; **~ cap** *n.* Schraubdeckel, *der;* Schraubverschluss, *der;* **~ coupling** *n. (Mech. Engin.)* Gewindemuffe, *die;* **~driver** *n.* Ⓐ Schraubenzieher, *der;* Schraubendreher, *der (fachspr.)*; Ⓑ *(cocktail)* Wodka-Orange, *der;* Screwdriver, *der*

**screwed** /skru:d/ *adj. (sl.: drunk)* besoffen *(salopp)*

**'screwed-up** *adj. (fig. coll.)* neurotisch; **get [all] ~ about sth.** wegen etw. ausflippen *(ugs.)*

**screw top** ⇒ **screw cap**

**screwy** /'skru:ɪ/ *adj. (coll.: eccentric)* spinnig *(ugs. abwertend)*; spleenig; *(crazy)* verrückt ‹Humor, Idee, Plan›

**scribble** /'skrɪbl/ ❶ *v.t.* Ⓐ *(write hastily)* hinkritzeln ‹Zeilen, Nachricht›; Ⓑ *(draw carelessly or meaninglessly)* kritzeln ‹Skizze, Muster›; Ⓒ *(joc. derog.: write)* absondern *(salopp abwertend)* ‹Gedicht, Artikel›. ❷ *v.i.* Ⓐ *(write hurriedly, draw carelessly)* kritzeln; Ⓑ *(joc. derog.: be journalist etc.)* schreiben; **are you still scribbling?** machst du [immer] noch auf Schreiberling? *(ugs. abwertend)*. ❸ *n.* Gekritzel, *das (abwertend)*; *(handwriting)* Klaue, *die (salopp abwertend)*

**~ 'out, ~ 'over** *v.t.* aus-, durchstreichen; überkritzeln

**scribbler** /'skrɪblə(r)/ *n. (joc. derog.)* Schreiberling, *der (abwertend)*; *(of poems also)* Dichterling, *der (abwertend)*

**scribbling**/'skrɪblɪŋ/**: ~ pad** *n. (Brit.)* Notizblock, *der;* **~ paper** *n. (Brit.)* Schmierpapier, *das (ugs.)*

**scribe** /skraɪb/ *n.* Ⓐ *(producer of manuscripts)* Schreiber, *der;* Skriptor, *der; (copyist)* Abschreiber, *der;* Kopist, *der;* Ⓑ *(Bibl.: theologian)* Schriftgelehrte, *der*

**scrimmage** /'skrɪmɪdʒ/ ❶ *n.* Gerangel, *das.* ❷ *v.i.* rangeln; ‹spielende Kinder:› sich balgen

**scrimp** /skrɪmp/ *v.i.* knausern *(ugs.)*; knapsen *(ugs.)*; **~ and save** *or* **scrape** knapsen und knausern *(ugs.)*; **~ on sth.** mit etw. knausern

**scrip** /skrɪp/ *n. (Finance)* Ⓐ *(certificate)* Scrip, *der;* Zwischenschein, *der;* Ⓑ *(extra share[s])* Gratisaktie, *die/*Gratisaktien *Pl.*

**script** /skrɪpt/ ❶ *n.* Ⓐ *(handwriting)* Handschrift, *die;* **in ~:** handgeschrieben; handschriftlich; Ⓑ *(of play)* Regiebuch, *das; (of film)* [Dreh]buch, *das;* Skript, *das (fachspr.)*; Ⓒ *(for broadcaster)* Skript, *das;* Manuskript, *das;* Ⓓ *(system of writing)* Schrift, *die;* Ⓔ *(Printing)* Schreibschrift, *die;* Ⓕ *(Brit. Educ.)* [Prüfungs]arbeit, *die.* ❷ *v.t.* schriftlich ausarbeiten ‹Rede›; das [Dreh]buch schreiben zu ‹Film, Fernsehspot usw.›; das Storyboard machen zu ‹Fernsehspot›

**'script girl** *n.* ▶ **1261** Skriptgirl, *das*

**scriptorium** /skrɪp'tɔ:rɪəm/ *n., pl.* **scriptoria** /skrɪp'tɔ:rɪə/ *or* **~s** Skriptorium, *das;* [Kloster]schreibstube, *die*

**scriptural** /'skrɪptʃərl, 'skrɪptʃʊrl/ *adj.* Ⓐ *(of the Bible)* biblisch ‹Geschichte›; Bibel‹kenntnis›; Schrift‹lesung›; Ⓑ *(founded on doctrines of the Bible)* schriftgemäß

**scripture** /'skrɪptʃə(r)/ *n.* Ⓐ *(Relig.: sacred book)* heilige Schrift; **[Holy] S~, the [Holy] S~s** *(Christian Relig.)* die [Heilige]

Schrift; *attrib.* Bibel‹text, -stunde›; **B** (*Christian Relig.: Bible text*) Bibeltext, *der;* **C** *no pl., no art.* (*Sch.*) Religion, *die*

**'scriptwriter** *n.* ▶ 1261 (*of film*) Drehbuchautor, *der*/-autorin, *die;* (*for radio*) Hörspielautor, *der*/-autorin, *die*

**scrofula** /'skrɒfjʊlə/ *n.* ▶ 1232 (*Med.*) Skrofulose, *die;* Skrofeln *Pl.*

**scroll** /skrəʊl/ ❶ *n.* **A** (*roll*) Rolle, *die;* **B** (*design*) (*Archit.*) Volute, *die;* Schnecke, *die;* (*Mus.: on violin*) Schnecke, *die;* (*flourish in writing*) Schnörkel, *der.* ❷ *v.t.* (*Computing*) verschieben; scrollen (*fachspr.*); **~ a few pages** ein paar Seiten durchlaufen lassen

**scrollable** /'skrəʊləbl/ *adj.* (*Computing*) scrollbar

**'scroll: ~ bar** *n.* Rollbalken, *der;* **~work** *n., no pl.* (*Art*) Schneckenverzierung, *die*

**Scrooge** /skru:dʒ/ *n.* (*coll.: derog.*) Geizkragen, *der* (*ugs. abwertend*); **don't be such a ~:** sei nicht so geizig

**scrotum** /skrəʊtəm/ *n., pl.* **scrota** /'skrəʊtə/ *or* **~s** (*Anat.*) Hodensack, *der;* Skrotum, *das* (*fachspr.*)

**scrounge** /skraʊndʒ/ (*coll.*) ❶ *v.t.* **A** (*cadge*) schnorren (*ugs.*) (**off, from** von); **~ things** schnorren; **B** (*take illicitly*) mitgehen lassen (*ugs.*); sich (*Dat.*) unter den Nagel reißen (*salopp*). ❷ *v.i.* **A** (*cadge things*) schnorren (*ugs.*) (**from** bei); **B** (*take things illicitly*) klauen (*salopp*); **C ~ [around]** herumsuchen; herumstöbern (*ugs.*); **~ for sth.** nach etw. suchen. ❸ *n.* **be on the ~ [for sth.]** [etw.] schnorren wollen (*ugs.*)

**scrounger** /'skraʊndʒə(r)/ *n.* (*coll.*) (*cadger*) Schnorrer, *der*/Schnorrerin, *die* (*ugs. abwertend*)

**scrub**[1] /skrʌb/ ❶ *v.t.*, **-bb-: A** (*rub*) schrubben (*ugs.*); scheuern; **B** (*coll.: cancel, scrap*) zurücknehmen ‹Befehl›; sausen lassen, schießen lassen (*salopp*) ‹Plan, Projekt›; wegschmeißen (*ugs.*) ‹Brief›; **the project had to be ~bed** das Projekt musste abgeblasen werden (*ugs.*). ❷ *v.i.*, **-bb- A** (*use brush*) schrubben (*ugs.*); scheuern; **B** ⇒ **~ up.** ❸ *n.* **give sth. a ~:** etw. schrubben (*ugs.*) *od.* scheuern

**~ 'out** *v.t.* **A** (*clean thoroughly*) schrubben (*ugs.*), [aus]scheuern ‹Pfanne›; schrubben (*ugs.*), scheuern ‹Zimmer›; **B** (*remove*) ausbürsten ‹Fleck›; **C** ⇒ **~** 1 B

**~ 'up** *v.i.* (*Med.*) sich (*Dat.*) die Hände [und Unterarme] desinfizieren

**scrub**[2] *n.* **A** (*brushwood*) Buschwerk, *das;* Strauchwerk, *das;* Gesträuch, *das;* (*area of brushwood*) Buschland, *das;* **B** (*stunted person, animal, or plant*) Kümmerling, *der*

**scrubber** /'skrʌbə(r)/ *n.* **A** (*sl.: immoral woman*) Flittchen, *das* (*ugs. abwertend*); Nutte, *die* (*abwertend*); (*sluttish woman*) Schlampe, *die* (*ugs. abwertend*); **B** (*Chem.*) Wascher, *der*

**'scrub brush** (*Amer.*), **'scrubbing-brush** *ns.* Scheuerbürste, *die*

**scrubby** /'skrʌbɪ/ *adj.* **A** (*bristly*) stoppelig ‹Kinn›; stachelig, borstig ‹Bart›; **B** (*with stunted bushes*) mit [niedrigem] Busch- *od.* Strauchwerk bewachsen ‹Gebiet›; **C** (*stunted*) krüppelhaft ‹Büsche, Sträucher›

**scruff**[1] /skrʌf/ *n.* **by the ~ of the neck** beim *od.* am Genick

**scruff**[2] *n.* (*Brit. coll.*) (*scruffy man*) vergammelter Typ (*ugs.*); (*scruffy woman, girl*) Schlampe, *die* (*abwertend*)

**scruffily** /'skrʌfɪlɪ/ *adv.* (*coll.*) gammelig (*ugs. abwertend*) ‹angezogen›

**scruffy** /'skrʌfɪ/ *adj.* vergammelt (*ugs. abwertend*); heruntergekommen ‹Haus, Restaurant, Gegend›; ungepflegt ‹Haar›

**scrum** /skrʌm/ *n.* **A** (*Rugby*) Gedränge, *das;* **B** (*coll.: milling crowd*) Gedränge, *das;* Gewimmel, *das;* **a ~ of press photographers** ein Schwarm von Pressefotografen

**scrum 'half** *n.* (*Rugby*) Gedrängehalb[spieler], *der*

**scrummage** /'skrʌmɪdʒ/ ⇒ **scrum** A

**scrump** /skrʌmp/ *v.t. & i.* stehlen

**scrumptious** /'skrʌmʃəs/ *adj.* (*coll.*) lecker ‹Essen›; **she's/she looks ~:** sie ist zum Anbeißen/sie sieht zum Anbeißen aus (*ugs.*)

**scrumpy** /'skrʌmpɪ/ *n.* (*esp. dial.*) ≈ saurer Apfelmost (*bes. südd.*)

**scrunch** /skrʌntʃ/ ⇒ **crunch**

**scruple** /'skru:pl/ ❶ *n.* **A** *in sing. or pl.* Skrupel, *der;* Bedenken, *das;* **be [totally] without ~:** keine[rlei] Bedenken *od.* Skrupel haben; **a person with no ~s** ein gewissen- *od.* skrupelloser Mensch; **have no ~s about doing sth.** keine Bedenken *od.* Skrupel haben, etw. zu tun; **B** (*Brit. Hist.: unit of weight*) Skrupel, *das.* ❷ *v.i.* Bedenken *od.* Skrupel haben; **[not] ~ to do sth./about doing sth.** [keine] Bedenken *od.* Skrupel haben, etw. zu tun

**scrupulous** /'skru:pjʊləs/ *adj.* **A** (*conscientious*) gewissenhaft ‹Person›; unbedingt ‹Ehrlichkeit›; peinlich ‹Sorgfalt›; **pay ~ attention to sth.** peinlich auf etw. (*Akk.*) achten; **B** (*over-attentive to detail*) penibel (*geh.*); pingelig (*ugs.*); [übermäßig] streng ‹Eltern›; **be ~ about sth./in sth.** es mit etw. übertrieben genau nehmen

**scrupulously** /'skru:pjʊləslɪ/ *adv.* **A** (*conscientiously*) peinlich ‹sauber, genau›; **~ honest** auf unbedingte Ehrlichkeit bedacht; **B** (*with undue attention to detail*) penibel (*geh.*); pingelig (*ugs.*)

**scrutineer** /skru:tɪ'nɪə(r)/ *n.* (*Brit. Admin.*) ≈ Wahlvorstand, *der*

**scrutinize** (**scrutinise**) /'skru:tɪnaɪz/ *v.t.* [genau] untersuchen ‹Gegenstand, Forschungsgegenstand›; [über]prüfen ‹Rechnung, Pass, Fahrkarte›; mustern ‹Miene, Person›

**scrutiny** /'skru:tɪnɪ/ *n., no pl.* **A** (*critical gaze*) musternder Blick; prüfender Blick; (*close examination*) (*of recruit*) Musterung, *die;* (*of bill, passport, ticket*) [Über]prüfung, *die;* **bear ~:** einer [genauen] Prüfung standhalten; **B** (*Brit.: examination of votes*) Stimmenauszählung, *die*

**scuba** /'skju:bə, 'sku:bə/ *n.* (*Sport*) Regenerationstauchgerät, *das; attrib.* Geräte‹tauchen›; [Geräte]tauch‹ausrüstung›

**scud** /skʌd/ *v.i.*, **-dd- A** (*skim along*) ‹Wolke:› jagen; **B** (*Naut.*) **~ before the wind** vor dem Wind laufen *od.* (*fachspr.*) lenzen

**scuff** /skʌf/ ❶ *v.t.* **A** (*graze*) streifen; **~ one's shoe against sth.** etw. mit dem Schuh streifen; **B** (*mark by grazing*) verkratzen, verschrammen ‹Schuhe, Fußboden›. ❷ *n.* **A** Kratzer, *der;* Kratzspur, *die;* Schramme, *die;* **B** (*slipper*) Pantoffel, *der*

**scuffle** /'skʌfl/ ❶ *n.* Handgreiflichkeiten *Pl.;* Tätlichkeiten *Pl.;* **a ~ broke out** es kam zu Handgreiflichkeiten *od.* Tätlichkeiten. ❷ *v.i.* **A** handgreiflich *od.* tätlich werden (**with** gegen); **B** (*shuffle*) schlurfen; (*scurry*) ‹Mäuse:› rascheln

**scull** /skʌl/ ❶ *n.* **A** (*oar*) Skull, *das;* **B** (*boat*) Skullboot, *das.* ❷ *v.t.* skullen; rudern. ❸ *v.i.* skullen

**scullery** /'skʌlərɪ/ *n.* Spülküche, *die*

**sculpt** /skʌlpt/ ❶ *v.t.* bildhauern (*ugs.*) ❷ *v.i.* (*coll.*) bildhauern (*ugs.*); **make a living from ~ing** vom Bildhauern leben

**sculptor** /'skʌlptə(r)/ *n.* ▶ 1261 Bildhauer, *der*/-hauerin, *die*

**sculptress** /'skʌlptrɪs/ *n.* ▶ 1261 Bildhauerin, *die*

**sculptural** /'skʌlptʃərl/ *adj.* **A** plastisch; **B** (*resembling sculpture*) skulptural (*geh.*) ‹Gesichtszüge, Form›; plastisch

**sculpture** /'skʌlptʃə(r)/ ❶ *n.* **A** (*art*) Bildhauerei, *die;* **B** (*piece of work*) Skulptur, *die;* Plastik, *die;* (*pieces collectively*) Skulpturen; Plastiken. ❷ *v.t.* **A** (*represent*) skulpt[ur]ieren (*geh.*); bildhauerisch darstellen; **~d in marble/stone/bronze** in Marmor/Stein gehauen/in Bronze gegossen; **B** (*shape*) formen (**into** zu); **a finely ~d nose** eine schön *od.* fein modellierte Nase. ❸ *v.i.* bildhauern (*ugs.*); skulpt[ur]ieren (*geh.*); (*in plastic material*) modellieren

**scum** /skʌm/ *n.* **A** Schmutzschicht, *die;* (*film*) Schmutzfilm, *der;* (*on soup etc.*) oben schwimmende Schicht; (*greasy*) Fettschicht, *die;* **a ring of ~ around the bath** ein Schmutzrand in der Badewanne; **B** *no pl., no indef. art.* (*fig. derog.*) Abschaum, *der* (*abwertend*); Auswurf, *der* (*abwertend*); **the ~ of the earth/of humanity** der Abschaum der Menschheit

**'scumbag** *n.* (*sl. derog.*) Schwein, *das* (*salopp*)

**scupper**[1] /'skʌpə(r)/ *n.* (*Naut.*) Speigatt, *das*

**scupper**[2] *v.t.* (*Brit. coll.*) **A** (*defeat*) über den Haufen werfen (*ugs.*) ‹Plan›; **we're ~ed if the police arrive** wenn die Polizei kommt, sind wir erledigt; **B** (*sink*) versenken ‹Schiff, Mannschaft›; **be ~ed** ‹Mannschaft:› absaufen (*salopp*)

**scurf** /skɜ:f/ *n.* Schuppen *Pl.*

**scurfy** /'skɜ:fɪ/ *adj.* schuppig ‹Haar, Fell›

**scurrilous** /'skʌrɪləs/ *adj.* **A** (*abusive*) niederträchtig; **B** (*gross, obscene*) unflätig

**scurrilously** /'skʌrɪləslɪ/ *adv.* **A** (*abusively*) in niederträchtiger Weise; **B** (*grossly, obscenely*) in unflätiger Weise

**scurry** /'skʌrɪ/ ❶ *v.i.* huschen; flitzen (*ugs.*). ❷ *n.* **A** (*bustle*) Geschäftigkeit, *die;* **B** (*act*) Hetze, *die;* **a ~ for the best seats** ein Sturm auf die besten Plätze; **C** (*sound*) (*of feet*) Getrappel, *das*

**scurvy** /'skɜ:vɪ/ ❶ *n.* (*Med.*) Skorbut, *der.* ❷ *adj.* (*arch.*) niederträchtig

**'scuse** /skju:z/ *v.t.* (*coll.*) **~ me** 'tschuldigung; **~ fingers** 'tschuldigung, dass *od.* wenn ich die Finger nehme

**scut** /skʌt/ *n.* (*of deer*) Wedel, *der* (*Jägerspr.*); (*of rabbit, hare*) Blume, *die* (*Jägerspr.*)

**scuttle**[1] /'skʌtl/ *n.* **A** (*coal box*) Kohlenfüller, *der;* **B** (*Brit. Motor Veh.*) *Teil der Karosserie zwischen Motorhaube und unterem Rand der Windschutzscheibe*

**scuttle**[2] (*Naut.*) ❶ *v.t.* versenken. ❷ *n.* Luke, *die*

**scuttle**[3] *v.i.* (*scurry*) rennen; flitzen (*ugs.*); ‹Maus, Krabbe:› huschen; **she ~d off** sie huschte davon

**Scylla and Charybdis** /sɪlə ənd kə'rɪbdɪs/ *n., no pl.* **between ~:** zwischen Szylla und Charybdis

**scythe** /saɪð/ ❶ *n.* Sense, *die.* ❷ *v.t.* [mit der Sense] mähen ‹Wiese, Gras, usw.›; [mit der Sense] abmähen ‹Gras usw.›

**SDI** *abbr.* **strategic defence initiative** SDI

**SDLP** *abbr.* **Social Democratic and Labour Party** sozialistische Partei Nordirlands

**SDP** *abbr.* (*Brit. Polit.*) **Social Democratic Party**

**SDR** *abbr.* (*Econ.*) **special drawing right** SZR

**SE** *abbr.* ▶ 1024 **A** /saʊθ'i:st/ **south-east** SO; **B** /saʊθ'i:stən/ **south-eastern** sö.

**sea** /si:/ *n.* **A** Meer, *das;* **the ~:** das Meer; die See; **by ~:** mit dem Schiff; **by the ~:** am Meer; an der See; **at ~:** auf See (*Dat.*); **be all at ~** (*fig.*) nicht mehr weiter wissen; **when it comes to maths I'm all at ~:** von Mathe hab ich nicht die geringste Ahnung; **worse things happen at ~** (*joc.*) davon geht die Welt nicht unter (*ugs.*); **beyond [the] ~[s]** (*literary*) ⇒ **overseas** A; **go to ~:** in See stechen; (*become sailor*) zur See gehen (*ugs.*); **on the ~** (*in ship*) auf See (*Dat.*); (*on coast*) am Meer; an der See; **put [out] to ~:** in See (*Akk.*) gehen *od.* stechen; auslaufen; ⇒ *also* **high seas; inland sea; B** (*specific tract of water*) Meer, *das;* **the seven ~s** (*literary/poet.*) die sieben [Welt]meere; **C** (*freshwater lake*) See, *der;* **the S~ of Galilee** der See Genezareth; **D** *in sing. or pl.* (*state of ~*) See, *die;* (*wave*) Welle, *die;* Woge, *die* (*geh.*); See, *die* (*Seemannsspr.*); **there was a heavy ~:** es herrschte schwere See (*Seemannsspr.*); **run into heavy ~s** in schwere See kommen (*Seemannsspr.*); ⇒ *also* **half-seas-over; ship** 2 D; **E** (*fig.: vast quantity*) Meer, *das;* (*of drink*) Strom, *der;* **F** *attrib.* (*of or on the ~*) See‹klima, -wind, -wasser, -schlacht, -karte, -weg›; Meer‹gott, -ungeheuer, -wasser, -salz usw.›; Meeres‹grund, -küste, -niveau, -spiegel usw.›; (*in names of marine fauna or flora*) See‹maus, -gurke, -anemone, -löwe, -schildkröte usw.›; Meer‹brasse, -neunauge, -gurke usw.›

**sea: ~ 'air** *n.* Seeluft, *die;* **~ a'nemone** *n.* (*Zool.*) Seeanemone, *die;* Seerose, *die;*

**~ bass** *n.* (*Zool.*) [Schwarzer] Sägebarsch; **~'bed** *n.* Meeresboden *der;* Meeresgrund, *der;* **~bird** *n.* Seevogel, *der;* **~board** *n.* Küste, *die;* **~boot** *n.* Seestiefel, *der;* **~ breeze** *n.* (*Meteorol.*) Seewind, *der;* Seebrise, *die;* **~ captain** *n.* [Schiffs]kapitän, *der;* **~ change** *n.* (*esp. literary: unexpected or notable transformation*) erstaunliche Metamorphose (*geh.*); **~ chest** *n.* (*Naut.*) Seekiste, *die;* **~ coast** *n.* Meeresküste, *die;* **~ 'cucumber** *n.* (*Zool.*) Seegurke, *die;* Meergurke, *die;* **~ dog** *n.* Ⓐ (*Zool.*) Seehund, *der;* Ⓑ (*literary/joc.: experienced sailor*) Seebär, *der* (*ugs. scherzh.*); **~ eagle** *n.* Seeadler, *der;* **~farer** /'si:feərə(r)/ *n.* (*formal*) Matrose, *der;* **~faring** /'si:feərɪŋ/ ❶ *adj.* **~faring man** Seemann, *der;* **~faring nation** Seefahrernation, *die;* seefahrende Nation; **his ~faring days** die Zeit, als er zur See fuhr; ❷ *n., no pl., no indef. art.* Seefahrt, *die;* **~ fish** *n.* Seefisch, *der;* **~ fog** *n.* Seenebel, *der;* **~food** *n.* Meeresfrüchte *Pl.; attrib.* Fisch‹restaurant›; **~food cocktail** Cocktail aus Meeresfrüchten; **~ fowl** ⇒ **~bird**; **~front** *n. unmittelbar am Meer gelegene Straße[n] einer Seestadt;* **a walk along the ~front** ein Spaziergang am Wasser *od.* auf der Uferpromenade; **the hotels on the ~front** die Hotels direkt am Wasser *od.* an der Uferpromenade; **~ god** *n.* Meergott, *der;* **~going** *adj.* (*for crossing sea*) seegehend; **~going yacht** Hochseejacht, *die;* **~ green** ❶ /-'-/ *n.* Seegrün, *das;* Meergrün, *das;* ❷ /'--/ *adj.* seegrün; meergrün; **~gull** *n.* [See]möwe, *die;* **~ horse** *n.* (*Zool.*) Seepferdchen, *das;* **~kale** *n.* (*Bot.*) Meerkohl, *der;* Seekohl, *der;* Englischer Kohl

**seal¹** /si:l/ *n.* Ⓐ (*Zool.*) Robbe, *die;* **[common] ~:** [Gemeiner] Seehund; Ⓑ ⇒ **~skin**

**seal²** ❶ *n.* Ⓐ (*piece of wax, lead, etc., stamp, impression*) Siegel, *das;* (*lead ~ also*) Plombe, *die;* (*stamp also*) Siegelstempel, *der;* Petschaft, *das;* (*impression also*) Siegelabdruck, *der;* **fix a ~ on** versiegeln; (*using lead*) verplomben; plombieren; **put [lead] ~s on** verplomben, plombieren ‹Tür›; **~s of office** (*Brit.*) Dienstsiegel; Amtssiegel; Ⓑ (*adhesive stamp*) Julmarke, *die* (*Philat.*); Ⓒ **set the ~ on** (*fig.*) zementieren (+ *Akk.*); **set one's ~ to sth.** (*fig.*) grünes Licht für etw. geben; etw. absegnen (*ugs.*); Ⓓ (*guarantee*) **gain the ~ of respectability** sich (*Dat.*) großes Ansehen erwerben; **have the ~ of official approval** offiziell gebilligt werden; Ⓔ (*to close aperture*) Abdichtung, *die;* (*odour trap*) Geruchsverschluss, *der.* ⇒ *also* **privy seal**.
❷ *v.t.* Ⓐ (*stamp with ~, affix ~ to*) siegeln ‹Dokument›; (*fasten with ~*) verplomben, plombieren ‹Tür, Stromzähler›; Ⓑ (*close securely*) abdichten ‹Behälter, Rohr usw.›; zukleben ‹Umschlag, Paket›; [zum Verschließen der Poren] kurz anbraten ‹Fleisch›; **my lips are ~ed** (*fig.*) meine Lippen sind versiegelt; **be a ~ed book to sb.** (*fig.*) ein Buch mit sieben Siegeln für jmdn. sein; **~ed orders** versiegelte Order; Ⓒ (*stop up*) verschließen; abdichten ‹Leck›; verschmieren ‹Riss›; Ⓓ (*decide*) besiegeln ‹Geschäft, Abmachung, jmds. Schicksal›; Ⓔ (*provide with water ~*) mit einem Geruchsverschluss versehen ‹Rohr›; Ⓕ (*Road Constr.*) befestigen; mit einer [Fahrbahn]decke versehen

**~ 'in** *v.t.* bewahren ‹Geschmack›; am Austreten hindern ‹Fleischsaft›

**~ 'off** *v.t.* abriegeln

**~ 'up** ⇒ **~** 2 B, C

**'sea lane** *n.* (*Naut.*) See[schifffahrts]straße, *die*

**sealant** /'si:lənt/ *n.* Dichtungsmaterial, *das*

**sea: ~ legs** *n. pl.* Seebeine *Pl.* (*Seemannsspr.*); **get** *or* **find one's ~ legs** sich (*Dat.*) Seebeine wachsen lassen (*Seemannsspr.*); **~level** *n.* Meeresspiegel, *der* (*fachspr.*); **200 feet above/below ~level** 200 Fuß über/unter dem Meeresspiegel *od.* über/unter Meereshöhe *od.* (*fachspr.*) Normalnull; **at ~level** auf Meereshöhe (*Dat.*)

**sealing wax** /'si:lɪŋwæks/ *n.* Siegellack, *der;* Siegelwachs, *das*

**'sea lion** *n.* (*Zool.*) Seelöwe, *der*

**'Sea Lord** *n.* (*Brit.*) Seelord, *der*

**'sealskin** *n.* Robbenfell, *das;* (*garment*) Robbenfelljacke, *die*/Robbenfellmantel, *der usw.*

**Sealyham [terrier]** /'si:lɪəm (terɪə[r])/ *n.* Sealyhamterrier, *der*

**seam** /si:m/ *n.* Ⓐ (*line of joining*) Naht, *die;* (*Carpentry*) Verbindung, *die;* **come apart at the ~s** aus den Nähten gehen; (*fig. coll.: fail*) zusammenbrechen; **burst at the ~s** (*fig.*) aus den *od.* allen Nähten platzen (*ugs.*); ⇒ *also* **fall** 2 T; Ⓑ (*fissure*) Spalt, *der;* Spalte, *die;* (*in ship*) Naht, die (*fachspr.*); Ⓒ (*Mining*) Flöz, *das;* (*Geol.*) (*stratum*) Schicht, *die;* (*line between strata*) [Schicht]fuge, *die;* Ⓓ (*wrinkle*) Runzel, *die;* Falte, *die*

**seaman** /'si:mən/ *n., pl.* **seamen** /'si:mən/ Ⓐ (*sailor*) Matrose, *der;* ⇒ *also* **able seaman**; **ordinary seaman**; Ⓑ (*expert in navigation etc.*) Seemann, *der*

**seamanlike** /'si:mənlaɪk/ *adj.* seemännisch

**seamanship** /'si:mənʃɪp/ *n., no pl.* seemännisches Geschick; Seemannschaft, *die* (*fachspr.*)

**'seamark** *n.* (*Naut.*) Seezeichen, *das*

**seamed** /si:md/ *adj.* Ⓐ (*having seam*) **~ stockings** Strümpfe mit Naht; Ⓑ (*wrinkled*) faltig; runzlig; zerfurcht; Ⓒ (*Geol.: having seams*) geschiefert

**sea: ~mew** *n.* [See]möwe, *die;* **~ mile** ⇒ **nautical mile**; **~ mist** *n.* Küstennebel, *der*

**seamless** /'si:mlɪs/ *adj.* nahtlos

**sea: ~ monster** *n.* (*Mythol.*) Seeungeheuer, *das;* Meerungeheuer, *das;* **~mount** *n.* (*Geog.*) Tiefseeberg, *der*

**seamstress** /'semstrɪs/ *n.* ▶ **1261** Näherin, *die*

**seamy** /'si:mɪ/ *adj.* Ⓐ (*having wrinkles*) faltig, runzlig; Ⓑ (*run down*) heruntergekommen ‹Stadtteil›; **the ~ side [of life** *etc.*] (*fig.*) die Schattenseite[n] [des Lebens *usw.*]

**seance** /'seɪɑ̃s/, **séance** /'seɪɑ̃s/ *n.* Séance, *die* (*fachspr.*); spiritistische Sitzung

**sea: ~ pink** *n.* (*Bot.*) Grasnelke, *die;* Strandnelke, *die;* **~plane** *n.* Wasserflugzeug, *das;* **~port** *n.* Seehafen, *der;* **~ power** *n.* Seemacht, *die;* **~ quake** *n.* Seebeben, *das*

**sear** /sɪə(r)/ *v.t.* verbrennen, versengen; (*Med.: cauterize*) ausbrennen ‹Wunde›

**search** /sɜ:tʃ/ ❶ *v.t.* durchsuchen (**for** nach); absuchen ‹Gebiet, Fläche› (**for** nach); prüfen *od.* musternd blicken in (+ *Akk.*) ‹Gesicht›; (*fig.: probe*) erforschen ‹Herz, Gewissen›; suchen in (+ *Dat.*), durchstöbern (*ugs.*) ‹Gedächtnis› (**for** nach); **~ me** (*coll.*) keine Ahnung! ❷ *v.i.* suchen; **~ after sth.** etw. *od.* nach etw. suchen. ❸ *n.* Suche, *die* (**for** nach); (*of building, room, etc.*) Durchsuchung, *die;* **make a ~ for** suchen nach ‹Waffen, Drogen, Diebesgut›; **in ~ of sb./sth.** auf der Suche nach jmdm./etw.; **go off in ~ of sth.** sich auf die Suche nach etw. machen; **right of ~:** Durchsuchungsrecht, *das*

**~ for** *v.t.* suchen [nach]

**~ 'out** *v.t.* heraussuchen; aufspüren ‹Person mit unbekanntem Aufenthalt›

**~ through** *v.t.* durchsuchen; durchsehen ‹Buch›

**'search engine** *n.* (*Computing*) Suchmaschine, *die;* Suchroboter, *der*

**searcher** /'sɜ:tʃə(r)/ *n.* Sucher, *der*/Sucherin, *die;* Suchende, *der/die;* **the ~s returned with the missing child** die Suchmannschaft kehrte mit dem vermissten Kind zurück

**searching** /'sɜ:tʃɪŋ/ *adj.* prüfend, forschend ‹Blick›; bohrend ‹Frage›; (*thorough*) eingehend ‹Untersuchung›

**searchingly** /'sɜ:tʃɪŋlɪ/ *adv.* prüfend, forschend ‹jmdn. ansehen›; eingehend ‹befragen›

**search: ~light** *n.* Ⓐ (*lamp*) Suchscheinwerfer, *der;* Ⓑ (*beam of light*) Scheinwerferlicht, *das* (*auch fig.*); (*fig.*) Rampenlicht, *das;* **the ~light is on him** (*fig.*) er steht im Scheinwerfer- *od.* Rampenlicht; **~ party** *n.* Suchtrupp, *der;* Suchmannschaft, *die;* **~ warrant** *n.* (*Law*) Durchsuchungsbefehl, *der*

**searing** /'sɪərɪŋ/ *adj.* sengend ‹Hitze›; brennend ‹Schmerz›; (*fig.: intense*) bohrend, stechend ‹Blick›

**sea: ~ salt** *n.* Meersalz, *das;* Seesalz, das; **~scape** *n.* Ⓐ (*Art: picture*) Seestück, *das;* Marine, *die;* Ⓑ (*view*) Meerespanorama, *das;*

**S~ Scout** *n.* (*Brit.*) Seepfadfinder, *der*/-pfadfinderin, *die;* **~ serpent** *n.* Seeschlange, *die;* **~ shanty** ⇒ **shanty²**; **~shell** *n.* Muschel[schale], *die;* **~shore** *n.* (*land near ~*) [Meeres]küste, *die;* (*beach*) Strand, *der;* **walk along the ~shore** am Meer/Strand entlanggehen; **~sick** *adj.* seekrank; **~sickness** *n., no pl.* Seekrankheit, *die;* **~side** *n., no pl.* [Meeres]küste, *die;* **by/to/at the ~side** am/ans/am Meer; an der/an die/an der See; *attrib.* **~side town** Seestadt, *die;* **the usual ~side attractions** die Vergnügungen, die die Küste gemeinhin bietet

**season** /'si:zn/ ❶ *n.* Ⓐ ▶ **1504** (*time of the year*) Jahreszeit, *die;* **dry/rainy ~:** Trocken-/Regenzeit, *die;* Ⓑ (*time of breeding*) (*for mammals*) Tragezeit, *die;* (*for birds*) Brutzeit, *die;* (*time of flourishing*) Blüte[zeit], *die;* (*time when animal is hunted*) Jagdzeit, *die;* **blackberry ~:** Brombeerzeit, *die;* **nesting ~:** Nistzeit, *die;* Brut[zeit], *die;* ⇒ *also* **close season**; **open season**; Ⓒ (*time devoted to specified, social activity*) Saison, *die;* **harvest/opera ~:** Erntezeit, die/Opernsaison, *die;* **football ~:** Fußballsaison, *die;* **holiday** *or* (*Amer.*) **vacation ~:** Urlaubszeit, *die;* Ferienzeit, *die;* **tourist ~:** Touristensaison, *die;* Reisezeit, *die;* **the ~ of goodwill** (*Christmas*) die Zeit der Nächstenliebe; **'compliments of the ~'** (*formal*), **'the ~'s greetings'** „ein frohes Weihnachtsfest und ein glückliches neues Jahr"; Ⓓ **raspberries are in/out of** *or* **not in ~:** jetzt ist die/nicht die Saison *od.* Zeit für Himbeeren; **be in ~** (*on heat*) brünstig sein; **a word in ~** (*literary*) ein Rat[schlag] zur rechten Zeit; **in and out of ~:** zu jeder passenden oder unpassenden Zeit; (*again and again*) immer wieder; Ⓔ (*ticket*) ⇒ **season ticket**; Ⓕ (*period of time*) Zeit, *die;* (*Theatre, Cinemat.*) Spielzeit, *die;* **for a ~** (*dated*) eine Zeit lang; **they are doing a ~ in Oxford** sie gastieren [zurzeit] in Oxford; **put on a Shakespeare/Russian ~:** ≈ Shakespeare-/russische Wochen veranstalten. ⇒ *also* **high season**; **low season**; **off-season**; **silly** 1 A.
❷ *v.t.* Ⓐ (*make palatable, lit. or fig.*) würzen ‹Fleisch, Rede›; Ⓑ (*mature*) ablagern lassen ‹Holz›; **~ed** erfahren ‹Wahlkämpfer, Soldat, Reisender›; Ⓒ (*temper*) mäßigen (*geh.*) ‹Impulsivität›.
❸ *v.i.* ‹Holz:› ablagern; ‹Whisky:› lagern, reifen

**seasonable** /'si:zənəbl/ *adj.* Ⓐ (*suitable to the time of the year*) der Jahreszeit gemäß; Ⓑ (*opportune*) willkommen ‹Angebot›; (*meeting needs of occasion*) geboten ‹Vorsicht›; passend ‹Worte›

**seasonably** /'si:zənəblɪ/ *adv.* Ⓐ (*in a way typical of the season*) der Jahreszeit entsprechend; Ⓑ (*so as to be opportune*) zur rechten Zeit

**seasonal** /'si:zənl/ *adj.* Saison‹arbeit, -geschäft›; saisonabhängig ‹Preise›

**seasonal af'fective disorder** /si:zənl ə'fektɪv dɪsɔ:də(r)/ *n.* (*Med.*) saisonabhängige Depression

**seasonally** /'si:zənəlɪ/ *adv.* saisonal, saisonbedingt ‹schwanken›; **~ adjusted** (*Statistics*) saisonbereinigt ‹Arbeitslosenzahlen›

**seasoning** /'si:zənɪŋ/ *n.* Ⓐ (*Cookery*) Gewürze *Pl.;* Würze, *die;* Ⓑ (*fig.*) Würze, *die;* **have a ~ of wit** ‹Unterhaltung:› witzig *od.* geistreich *od.* mit Witz gewürzt sein

**'season ticket** *n.* Dauerkarte, *die;* (*for one year/month*) Jahres-/Monatskarte, *die*

**seat** /si:t/ ❶ *n.* Ⓐ (*thing for sitting on*) Sitzgelegenheit, *die;* (*in vehicle, cinema, etc.*) Sitz, *der;* (*of toilet*) [Klosett]brille, *die* (*ugs.*); **use sth. for a ~:** sich auf etw. (*Akk.*) setzen; (*be sitting*) auf etw. (*Dat.*) sitzen; Ⓑ (*place*) Platz, *der;* (*in vehicle*) [Sitz]platz, *der;* **have** *or* **take a ~:** sich [hin]setzen; Platz nehmen (*geh.*); **take one's ~ at table** sich zu Tisch setzen; **keep one's ~:** sitzen bleiben; ‹Reiter:› im Sattel bleiben, sich im Sattel halten; **resume one's ~:** sich wieder [hin]setzen; (*after the interval etc.*) seinen Platz wieder einnehmen; wieder Platz nehmen (*geh.*); ⇒ *also* **back seat**; Ⓒ (*part of chair*) Sitzfläche, *die;* Ⓓ (*buttocks*) Gesäß, *das;* (*part of clothing*) Gesäßpartie, *die;* (*of trousers*) Sitz, *der;* Hosenboden, *der;* **by the ~ of one's pants** (*coll. fig.*) nach Gefühl; Ⓔ (*site*) Sitz, *der;* (*of*

S

# Seasons

In German, the seasons are always written with an article, whether there is one in English or not:

***in spring, in the spring***
= im Frühling *or* Frühjahr

***in summer, in the summer***
= im Sommer

***in autumn, in the autumn*** (esp. Brit.), ***in the fall*** (Amer.)
= im Herbst

***in winter, in the winter***
= im Winter

All four words for the seasons in German are masculine, with the exception of the alternative term for *spring*, **das Frühjahr**. Generally this refers simply to the time of year, whereas **der Frühling** has all the connotations of rebirth etc. associated with spring, while also being the term used in astronomical contexts (there is even a third term, **der Lenz**, which occurs only in poetry).

***Spring came early***
= Der Frühling ist früh eingetroffen

***in early/late spring***
= zu Anfang/Ende des Frühjahrs

***It's going to be a hard winter***
= Der Winter wird hart werden

***He is staying [for] the whole summer***
= Er bleibt den ganzen Sommer

***It lasted all summer*** or ***throughout the summer***
= Es dauerte den ganzen Sommer

***She was here last winter***
= Sie war letzten Winter hier

***They are coming this/next autumn***
= Sie kommen diesen/nächsten Herbst

## Seasonal adjectives

The four adjectives in German derived from the names of the seasons are **frühlingshaft, sommerlich, herbstlich** and **winterlich**. They have the sense "typical or appropriate for the season", like the English *springlike*, *summery*, *autumnal* and *wintry* respectively, although they will also equate to some attributive uses of the noun:

***winter clothing***
= (*worn in winter*) Winterkleidung; (*warm and thus suitable for winter*) winterliche Kleidung

***summer clothing***
= (*worn in summer*) Sommerkleidung; (*light and thus suitable for summer*) sommerliche Kleidung

***winter/summer temperatures***
= winterliche/sommerliche Temperaturen

***a winter landscape***
= (*seen in winter*) eine Winterlandschaft; (*typical of winter, wintry*) eine winterliche Landschaft

*disease also*) Herd, *der* (*Med.*); (*of learning*) Stätte, *die* (*geh.*); (*of trouble*) Quelle, *die;* **~ of the fire** Brandherd, *der;* **F** (*right to sit in Parliament etc.*) Sitz, *der;* Mandat, *das;* **be elected to a ~ in Parliament** ins Parlament gewählt werden; **be appointed to a ~ on a committee** in einen Ausschuss berufen werden; **G [country] ~** (*mansion*) Landsitz, *der;* **H** (*on horseback*) Sitz, *der;* [Sitz]haltung, *die;* **I** (*Mech. Engin.*) Sitz, *der;* **valve ~:** Ventilsitz, *der.* **2** *v.t.* **A** (*cause to sit*) setzen; (*accommodate at table etc.*) unterbringen; (*ask to sit*) ‹Platzanweiser:› einen Platz anweisen (+ *Dat.*); **~ oneself** sich setzen; **B** (*have ~s for*) Sitzplätze bieten (+ *Dat.*); **~ 500 people** 500 Sitzplätze haben; **the car ~s five comfortably** in dem Auto haben fünf Personen bequem Platz; **C** (*fit with seats*) bestuhlen ‹Saal usw.›; **D** (*Mech. Engin.*) in [die richtige] Position bringen

**'seat belt** *n.* (*Motor Veh., Aeronaut.*) Sicherheitsgurt, *der;* **fasten one's ~:** sich anschnallen; den Gurt anlegen; **wear a ~:** angeschnallt sein; (*during journey*) angeschnallt fahren

**'seat-belt tensioner** /'tenʃnə(r)/*n.* Gurtstraffer, *der*

**seated** /'si:tɪd/ *adj.* sitzend; **remain ~:** sitzen bleiben; **take 50 ~ passengers** 50 Sitzplätze haben; **be ~** (*formal*) Platz nehmen (*geh.*)

**-seater** /'si:tə(r)/ *adj. in comb.* -sitzig; **two-~ [car]** Zweisitzer, *der*

**seating** /'si:tɪŋ/ *n., no pl., no indef. art.* **A** (*seats*) Sitzplätze; Sitzgelegenheiten; **B** (*act*) Platzierung, *die;* Versorgung mit Sitzplätzen; **C** *attrib.* Sitz‹ordnung, -plan›; **~ accommodation** Sitzgelegenheiten; Sitzplätze; **the ~ arrangements** die Sitzordnung

**SEATO** /'si:təʊ/ *abbr.* **South-East-Asia Treaty Organisation** SEATO, *die*

**sea: ~ urchin** *n.* (*Zool.*) Seeigel, *der;* **~ wall** *n.* Strandmauer, *die;* (*dike*) Deich, *der*

**seaward** /'si:wəd/ **1** *adj.* seewärtig ‹Kurs, Wind›; **the ~ side** die Seeseite; **the ~ view** die Aussicht aufs Meer *od.* auf die See. **2** *adv.* seewärts; nach See zu. **3** *n.* **to [the] ~:** zur Seeseite hin

**seawards** /'si:wədz/ ⇒ **seaward 2**

**sea: ~ water** *n.* Meerwasser, *das;* Seewasser, *das;* **~weed** *n.* [See]tang, *der;* **~worthy** *adj.* seetüchtig

**sebaceous** /sɪ'beɪʃəs/ *adj.* talgig; **~ duct/gland** (*Anat.*) Talgdrüsenausführungsgang, *der*/Talgdrüse, *die*

**seborrhoea** (*Amer.:* **seborrhea**) /sebə'ri:ə/ *n.* (*Med.*) Seborrhö[e], *die* (*fachspr.*); Talgfluss, *der*

**sec** /sek/ (*coll.*) ⇒ **second 2 B**

**sec.** *abbr.* **second[s]** Sek.

**Sec.** *abbr.* **Secretary** Sekr.

**secant** /'si:kənt, 'sekənt/ *n.* (*Math.*) Sekante, *die;* (*of angle*) Sekans, *der*

**secateurs** /sekə'tɜ:z, 'sekətɜ:z/ *n. pl.* (*Brit. Hort.*) Gartenschere, *die;* Rosenschere, *die*

**secede** /sɪ'si:d/ *v.i.* (*Polit./Eccl./formal*) sich abspalten (**from** von); ‹Mitglied:› austreten (**from** aus)

**secession** /sɪ'seʃn/ *n.* (*Polit./Eccl./formal*) Abspaltung, *die;* (*of member*) Austritt, *der;* **the ~ of some southern states** die Sezession einiger Südstaaten

**seclude** /sɪ'klu:d/ *v.t.* absondern; **~ oneself** (*from society*) sich abkapseln *od.* absondern; (*into a room*) sich zurückziehen (**into** in + *Akk.*)

**secluded** /sɪ'klu:dɪd/ *adj.* **A** (*hidden from view*) versteckt; (*somewhat isolated*) abgelegen; **B** (*solitary*) zurückgezogen ‹Leben›

**seclusion** /sɪ'klu:ʒn/ *n.* **A** (*keeping from company*) Absonderung, *die;* (*being kept from company*) Abgesondertheit, *die;* **in ~ from** abgesondert von; **B** (*privacy*) (*of life*) Zurückgezogenheit, *die;* (*of room*) Abgeschiedenheit, *die;* **in ~:** zurückgezogen ‹leben›; **C** *no pl.* (*remoteness*) Abgelegenheit, *die*

**second** /'sekənd/ **1** *adj.* ▶ **1352** zweit...; zweitwichtigst... ‹Stadt, Hafen usw.›; **~ largest/highest** *etc.* zweitgrößt.../-höchst... *usw.;* **come in/be ~:** Zweiter/Zweite werden/sein; **every ~ week** jede zweite Woche; **~ to none** unübertroffen. **2** *n.* **A** ▶ **1012** (*unit of time or angle*) Sekunde, *die;* **B** (*coll.: moment*) Sekunde, *die* (*ugs.*); **wait a few ~s** einen Moment warten; **in a ~** (*immediately*) sofort (*ugs.*); (*very quickly*) im Nu (*ugs.*); **just a ~!** (*coll.*) einen Moment!; **C** (*additional person or thing*) **a ~:** noch einer/eine/eins; **D the ~** (*in sequence, rank*) der/die/das Zweite; **be the ~ to arrive** als Zweiter/Zweite ankommen; **be a good ~:** einen guten zweiten Platz belegen; **E** (*in duel, boxing*) Sekundant, *der*/Sekundantin, *die;* **~s out [of the ring]** (*Boxing*) Ring frei!; **F** *in pl.* (*helping of food*) zweite Portion; (**~** *course*) zweiter Gang; **are there any ~s?** kann man eine zweite Portion bekommen?; **G** ▶ **1055** (*day*) **the ~ of May** der zweite Mai; **the ~ [of the month]** der Zweite [des Monats]; **H** (**~** *form*) zweite [Schul]klasse; Zweite, *die* (*Schuljargon*); **I** *in pl.* (*goods of ~ quality*) Waren zweiter Wahl; **be ~s** zweite Wahl sein; **J** (*Motor Veh.*) zweiter Gang; **in ~:** im zweiten [Gang]; **change into ~:** in den zweiten [Gang] schalten; **K** (*Brit. Univ.*) ≈ Gut, *das;* ≈ Zwei, *die;* **she got a ~ in mathematics** sie hat in Mathematik mit [einem] Gut *od.* [einer] Zwei abgeschlossen; **L** (*Mus.*) Sekunde, *die.* **3** *v.t.* **A** (*support in debate*) unterstützen ‹Antrag, Nominierung›; sekundieren (*geh.*); **I'll ~ that!** (*coll.*) dem schließe ich mich an!; **B** /sɪ'kɒnd/ (*transfer*) vorübergehend versetzen; **C** /'sekənd/ (*support*) unterstützen; **D** /sɪ'kɒnd/ (*Brit. Mil.*) abstellen

**secondarily** /'sekəndərɪlɪ/ *adv.* **A** in zweiter Linie; an zweiter Stelle; **B** (*indirectly*) mittelbar; indirekt

**secondary** /'sekəndərɪ/ *adj.* **A** (*of less importance*) zweitrangig; sekundär (*geh.*); Neben‹akzent, -sache›; (*derived from sth. primary*) weiterverarbeitend ‹Industrie›; **~ literature** Sekundärliteratur, *die;* **be ~ to sth.** einer Sache (*Dat.*) untergeordnet sein; **B** (*indirectly caused*) sekundär (*geh., Med., Biol.*); ⇒ *also* **picketing**; **C** (*supplementary*) zusätzlich; **D S~** (*Geol.*) ⇒ **Mesozoic 1**

**secondary: ~ coil** *n.* (*Electr.*) Sekundärspule, *die;* **~ colour** ⇒ **colour 1 A**; **~ education** *n.* höhere Schule; (*result*) höhere Schulbildung; **~ 'modern [school]** *n.* (*Brit. Hist.*) ≈ Mittelschule, *die* (*veralt.*); Realschule, *die;* **~ school** *n.* höhere *od.* weiterführende Schule

**second: ~ 'base** ⇒ **base[1] 1 C**; **~-best 1** /'---/ *adj.* zweitbest...; **2** /--'-/ *adv.* **come off ~-best** den Kürzeren ziehen (*ugs.*); **3** /--'-/ *n., no pl.* Zweitbeste, *der/die/das;* **don't settle for [the] ~-best!** gib dich nicht mit halben Sachen zufrieden; **~ 'chamber** *n.*

(*Parl.*) zweite Kammer; ~ **'childhood** ⇒ **childhood**; ~ **'class** *n.* (A) (*set ranking after others*) zweite Kategorie; (B) (*Transport, Post*) zweite Klasse; **travel in the ~ class** zweiter Klasse reisen; (C) (*Brit. Univ.*) ⇒ **second** 2 K; **~-class** ❶ /'---/ *adj.* (A) (*of lower class*) zweiter Klasse *nachgestellt;* Zweite[r]-Klasse-‹Post, Passagier, Fahrkarte usw.›; **~-class stamp** *Briefmarke für langsamere Postzustellung;* **get a ~-class degree** (*Brit. Univ.*) mit der Note Zwei *od.* Gut abschließen; (B) (*of inferior class*) zweitklassig (*abwertend*); **~-class citizen** Bürger zweiter Klasse; ❷ /--'-/ *adv.* zweiter Klasse ‹reisen, fahren›; **send a letter ~-class** einen Brief mit Zweiter-Klasse-Post schicken; ~ **'coming** *n., no pl.* (*Relig.*) zweite Ankunft; Wiederkunft, *die;* [zweite] Parusie (*fachspr.*); ~ **'cousin** ⇒ **cousin**

**seconder** /'sekəndə(r)/ *n.* Befürworter, *der*/-worterin, *die;* Sekundant, *der*/Sekundantin, *die* (*geh.*)

**second:** ~ **'fiddle** ⇒ **fiddle** 1 A; ~ **'floor** ⇒ **floor** 1 B; ~ **form** ⇒ **form** 1 D; ~ **'gear** *n., no pl.* (*Motor Veh.*) zweiter Gang; ⇒ *also* **gear** 1 A; **~-generation** *adj.* der zweiten Generation *nachgestellt;* **~-guess** *v.t.* (*Amer.*) (A) im Nachhinein kritisieren; (B) (*anticipate*) voraussehen; **~-guess sb.** voraussehen, was jmd. tun wird; ~ **hand** *n.* (*Horol.*) Sekundenzeiger, *der;* **~-hand** ❶ /'---/ *adj.* (A) (*used*) gebraucht ‹Kleidung, Auto usw.›; antiquarisch ‹Buch›; Secondhand‹buch, -schallplatte, -kleidung usw.›; **~-hand car** Gebrauchtwagen, *der;* (B) (*selling used goods*) Gebrauchtwaren-; Secondhand‹laden, -shop›; (C) (*taken on another's authority*) ‹Nachrichten, Bericht› aus zweiter Hand; ❷ /--'-/ *adv.* aus zweiter Hand (*auch fig.*); gebraucht; **get a book ~-hand** ein Buch antiquarisch kaufen; ~ **'home** *n.* Zweitwohnung, *die;* (*holiday house*) Ferienhaus, *das;* ~ **in com'mand** *n.* (*Mil.*) stellvertretender Kommandeur; (*of ship*) stellvertretender Kommandant; (*fig. coll.*) stellvertretender Leiter; ~ **lieu'tenant** *n.* (*Mil.*) ≈ Leutnant, *der*

**secondly** /'sekəndlɪ/ *adv.* zweitens

**secondment** /sɪ'kɒndmənt/ *n.* (*Brit.*) (A) (*of official*) vorübergehende Versetzung; **be on [a] ~:** vorübergehend versetzt sein; (B) (*Mil.*) Abstellung, *die*

**second:** ~ **name** *n.* Nachname, *der;* Zuname, *der;* ~ **'nature** *n., no pl., no art.* (*coll.*) zweite Natur; **become/be ~ nature to sb.** jmdm. zur zweiten Natur werden/geworden sein; jmdm. in Fleisch und Blut (*Akk.*) übergehen/übergegangen sein; ~ **'officer** *n.* (*Naut.*) zweiter Offizier; ~ **'person** ⇒ **person** D; **~-'rate** *adj.* zweitklassig; **very/rather ~-rate** sehr/ziemlich mittelmäßig; **~-'rater** *n.* (*coll.*) **be a ~-rater** zweitklassig sein; ~ **'reading** ⇒ **reading** G; **~s hand** ⇒ **second hand;** ~ **sight** ⇒ **sight** 1 A; ~ **'string** ⇒ **string** 1 B; ~ **'thoughts** *n. pl.* **have ~ thoughts** es sich (*Dat.*) anders überlegen (**about** mit); **we've had ~ thoughts about buying the house** wir wollen das Haus nun doch nicht kaufen; **we've had ~ thoughts about the house** wir haben uns das mit dem Haus doch noch einmal überlegt; **there's no time for ~ thoughts** es ist zu spät, es sich noch einmal anders zu überlegen; **but on ~ thoughts I think I will** wenn ich mirs [noch mal] überlege, werde ich es doch tun; ~ **wind** ⇒ **wind**[1] 1 F

**secrecy** /'si:krɪsɪ/ *n.* (A) (*keeping of secret*) Geheimhaltung, *die;* **with great ~:** in aller Heimlichkeit *od.* ganz im Geheimen; (B) (*secretiveness*) Heimlichtuerei, *die* (*abwertend*); (C) (*unrevealed state*) Heimlichkeit, *die;* **be shrouded in ~:** geheim gehalten werden; **in ~:** im Geheimen

**secret** /'si:krɪt/ ❶ *adj.* (A) (*kept private, not to be made known*) geheim; Geheim‹fach, -tür, -abkommen, -kode›; **keep sth. ~:** etw. geheim halten (**from** vor + *Dat.*); (B) (*acting in ~*) heimlich ‹Trinker, Liebhaber, Bewunderer›. ❷ *n.* (A) Geheimnis, *das;* **make no ~ of sth.** kein Geheimnis aus etw. machen; (*not conceal feelings, opinion*) kein[en] Hehl aus etw. machen; **keep the ~:** es für sich behalten; **keep ~s/a ~:** schweigen (*fig.*); den Mund halten (*ugs.*); **can you keep a ~?** kannst du schweigen?; **make sth. a ~:** etw. geheim halten; **keep ~s from sb.** Geheimnisse vor jmdm. haben; **let sb. in on a ~:** jmdn. in ein Geheimnis einweihen; **be in the ~:** eingeweiht sein; **open ~:** offenes Geheimnis; **the ~ of health/success** *etc.* das Geheimnis der Gesundheit/des Erfolgs *usw.;* der Schlüssel zur Gesundheit/zum Erfolg *usw.;* (B) **in ~:** im Geheimen; heimlich

**secret 'agent** *n.* Geheimagent, *der*/-agentin, *die*

**secretaire** /sekrɪ'teə(r)/ ⇒ **escritoire**

**secretarial** /sekrə'teərɪəl/ *adj.* Sekretariats‹personal›; Sekretärinnen‹kursus, -tätigkeit›; ‹Arbeit› als Sekretärin; ~ **skills** Steno- und Schreibmaschinenkenntnisse

**secretariat** /sekrə'teərɪət/ *n.* Sekretariat, *das*

**secretary** /'sekrətərɪ/ *n.* ▶ **1261** (A) (*official of organization*) Sekretär, *der*/Sekretärin, *die;* (*of company*) Schriftführer, *der*/-führerin, *die;* **honorary ~:** ehrenamtlicher Sekretär; (B) (*personal assistant*) Sekretär, *der*/Sekretärin, *die;* **Parliamentary [Private] S~** (*Brit. Parl.*) ≈ parlamentarischer Staatssekretär/parlamentarische Staatssekretärin; **Permanent S~** (*Brit. Admin.*) ≈ Staatssekretär, *der*/-sekretärin, *die;* ⇒ *also* **private secretary**

**secretary:** ~ **bird** *n.* Sekretär, *der;* **S~ 'General** *n., pl.* **Secretaries General** Generalsekretär, *der*/-sekretärin, *die;* **S~ of 'State** *n.* (A) (*Brit. Polit.*) Minister, *der*/Ministerin, *die;* **S~ of State for Defence** Verteidigungsminister, *der*/-ministerin, *die;* (B) (*Amer. Polit.*) Außenminister, *der*/-ministerin, *die;* (C) (*Amer. Admin.: head of records department*) *Leiter/Leiterin des Archivs eines Bundesstaates*

**secretaryship** /'sekrətərɪʃɪp/ *n.* (A) (*office*) Amt des Sekretärs/der Sekretärin; (B) (*tenure*) Amtszeit als Sekretär/Sekretärin

**secret 'ballot** *n.* geheime Abstimmung

**secrete** /sɪ'kri:t/ *v.t.* (A) (*Physiol.*) absondern; sezernieren (*fachspr.*); (B) (*formal/literary: hide*) verbergen; ~ **oneself** sich verbergen

**secretion** /sɪ'kri:ʃn/ *n.* (A) (*Physiol.*) Absonderung, *die;* (*process also*) Sekretion, *die* (*fachspr.*); (*substance also*) Sekret, *das* (*fachspr.*); (B) (*formal/literary: concealing*) Verbergen, *das*

**secretive** /'si:krɪtɪv/ *adj.* verschlossen ‹Person›; geheimnisvoll ‹Lächeln›; **be ~:** heimlich tun (*abwertend*) *od.* geheimnisvoll tun (**about** mit); **she was being very ~ about something** sie versuchte, irgendetwas zu verheimlichen

**secretively** /'si:krɪtɪvlɪ, sɪ'kri:tɪvlɪ/ *adv.* geheimnisvoll ‹lächeln›; **behave ~:** geheimnisvoll *od.* (*abwertend*) heimlich tun

**secretly** /'si:krɪtlɪ/ *adv.* heimlich; insgeheim ‹etw. glauben›

**secretory** /sɪ'kri:tərɪ/ *adj.* (*Physiol.*) sekretorisch

**Secret:** ~ **Police** *n.* Geheimpolizei, *die;* ~ **'Service** *n.* Geheimdienst, *der;* **s~ so'ciety** *n.* Geheimbund, *der*

**sect** /sekt/ *n.* (A) Sekte, *die;* (B) (*religious denomination*) Religionsgemeinschaft, *die;* (C) (*followers of school of thought*) Schule, *die*

**sectarian** /sek'teərɪən/ ❶ *adj.* konfessionell; konfessionell motiviert ‹Handlungen›; konfessionell ausgerichtet ‹Erziehung›; Konfessions‹krieg, -streit›. ❷ *n.* Sektenanhänger *der*/-anhängerin, *die;* Sektierer, *der*/Sektiererin, *die*

**sectarianism** /sek'teərɪənɪzm/ *n., no pl.* Sektierertum, *das*

**section** /'sekʃn/ *n.* (A) (*part cut off*) Abschnitt, *der;* Stück, *das;* (*part of divided whole*) Teil, *der;* (*of railway track*) [Strecken]abschnitt, *der;* Teilstück, *das;* (B) (*of firm*) Abteilung, *die;* (*of organization etc.*) Sektion, *die;* (*of orchestra or band*) Gruppe, *die;* **accounts ~** (*Econ.*) Buchhaltung, *die;* **business ~** (*in newspaper*) Wirtschaftsteil, *der;* (C) (*component part*) [Einzel]teil, *das;* [Bau]element, *das;* (*of ship, bridge, etc. also*) Sektion, *die* (*Technik*); (D) (*of chapter, book*) Abschnitt, *der;* (*of statute, act*) Paragraph, *der;* (E) (*part of community*) Gruppe, *die;* (F) (*Amer.: area of country*) [Landes]teil, *der;* Gebiet, *das;* (G) (*representation*) Schnitt, *der;* **vertical/horizontal/longitudinal/oblique ~:** Vertikal-/Horizontal-/Längs-/Schrägschnitt, *der;* (H) (*Amer.: square mile*) Sektion, *die;* (I) (*Geom.*) (*cutting of solid*) Schnitt, *der;* ([*area of*] *figure*) Schnitt, *der;* Schnittfläche, *die;* (*shape or area of cross-section*) Querschnitt, *der;* ⇒ *also* **conic;** (J) (*Amer.: district*) Bezirk, *der;* **the business/residential ~:** die City/die Wohngebiete; (K) (*Med.*) Schnitt, *der;* **abdominal ~:** Bauchdeckenschnitt, *der*

**sectional** /'sekʃənl/ *adj.* (A) (*pertaining to a representation*) Schnitt-; (B) (*pertaining to part of community*) Gruppen‹interessen›; partikular ‹Interessen›; ‹Auseinandersetzung› zwischen den Bevölkerungsgruppen; (C) (*made in parts*) zum Zusammenbauen *nachgestellt*

**sectionalism** /'sekʃənəlɪzm/ *n.* Partikularismus, *der* (*meist abwertend*)

**sector** /'sektə(r)/ *n.* (A) (*of activity*) Sektor, *der;* Bereich, *der;* **the leisure/industrial ~:** der Freizeitsektor/der Bereich der Industrie; ⇒ *also* **private sector; public sector;** (B) (*Geom.*) Sektor, *der;* (*of circle also*) Kreisausschnitt, *der;* (C) (*Mil.*) (*area*) Kampfabschnitt, *der;* Gefechtsabschnitt, *der*

**secular** /'sekjʊlə(r)/ *adj.* (*not sacred*) säkular (*geh.*); weltlich ‹Angelegenheit, Schule, Musik, Gericht›; profan (*geh.*) ‹Musik›; ~ **buildings** Profanbauten (*fachspr.*)

**secular 'clergy** *n. pl.* (*Eccl.*) Weltgeistlichkeit, *die;* Weltklerus, *der*

**secularism** /'sekjʊlərɪzm/ *n.* Säkularismus, *der*

**secularize (secularise)** /'sekjʊləraɪz/ *v.t.* säkularisieren; verweltlichen; **become ~d (secularised)** verweltlichen

**secure** /sɪ'kjʊə(r)/ ❶ *adj.* (A) (*safe*) sicher; ~ **against burglars/fire** gegen Einbruch/Feuer geschützt; einbruch-/feuersicher; **make sth. ~ from attack/enemies** etw. gegen Angriffe/Feinde sichern; (B) (*firmly fastened*) fest; **be ~** ‹Ladung:› gesichert sein; ‹Riegel, Tür:› fest zu sein; ‹Tür:› ver- *od.* zugeriegelt sein; ‹Schraube:› fest sein *od.* sitzen; **make sth. ~:** etw. sichern; (C) (*untroubled*) sicher, gesichert ‹Existenz›; **feel ~:** sich sicher *od.* geborgen fühlen; ~ **in the knowledge that ...:** in dem sicheren Bewusstsein, dass ...; **emotionally ~:** emotional stabil. ❷ *v.t.* (A) (*obtain*) sichern (**for** *Dat.*); beschaffen ‹Auftrag› (**for** *Dat.*); (*for oneself*) sich (*Dat.*) sichern; (B) (*confine*) fesseln ‹Gefangenen›; (*in container*) einschließen ‹Wertsachen›; (*fasten firmly*) sichern, fest zumachen ‹Fenster, Tür›; festmachen ‹Boot› (**to** an + *Dat.*); (C) (*guarantee*) absichern ‹Darlehen›; ~ **oneself [against sth.]** sich [gegen etw.] absichern; (D) (*fortify*) sichern

**securely** /sɪ'kjʊəlɪ/ *adv.* (A) (*firmly*) fest ‹verriegeln, zumachen›; sicher ‹befestigen›; (B) (*safely*) sicher ‹untergebracht sein›; ~ **locked up** unter sicherem Verschluss

**security** /sɪ'kjʊərɪtɪ/ *n.* (A) (*safety*) Sicherheit, *die;* (*of knot*) sicherer Halt; (B) (*safety of State or organization*) Sicherheit, *die;* ~ **[measures]** Sicherheitsmaßnahmen; Sicherheitsvorkehrungen; ~ **reasons** Sicherheitsgründe; **national ~:** nationale Sicherheit; Staatssicherheit, *die;* (C) (*thing that guarantees*) Sicherheit, *die;* Gewähr, *die;* Garantie, *die;* (*object of value*) Pfand, *das;* **as** *or* **in ~ for sth.** als Sicherheit/Pfand für etw.; **obtain a loan on [the] ~ of sth.** auf etw. (*Akk.*) ein Darlehen bekommen; (D) *usu. in pl.* (*Finance*) Wertpapier, *das;* **securities** Wertpapiere; Effekten *Pl.;* (E) **emotional ~:** emotionale Sicherheit; **he needs the ~ of a good home** er braucht die Geborgenheit eines guten Zuhauses; (F) (*assured freedom from want*) Sicherheit, *die*

**security:** ~ **check** *n.* Sicherheitskontrolle, *die;* **S~ Council** *n.* (*Polit.*) Sicherheitsrat, *der;* ~ **forces** *n. pl.* Sicherheitskräfte *Pl.;* ~ **guard** *n.* ▶ **1261** Wächter, *der*/Wächterin,

S

*die;* ~ **man** *n.* ▶1261 Wachmann, *der;* ~ **officer** *n.* ▶1261 Sicherheitsbeauftragte, *der/die;* ~ **risk** *n.* Sicherheitsrisiko, *das;* ~ **van** *n.* gepanzerter Transporter; (*for transporting money*) Geldtransporter, *der*

**sedan** /sɪ'dæn/ *n.* **A** (*Hist.: chair*) Sänfte, *die;* **B** (*Amer. Motor Veh.*) Limousine, *die*

**se'dan chair** ⇒ **sedan** A

**sedate** /sɪ'deɪt/ ❶ *adj.* **A** bedächtig; gesetzt ‹alte Dame›; ruhig ‹Kind›; gemächlich ‹Tempo, Leben, Auto›; **in a ~ manner** in aller Ruhe; **B** (*fig.*) schlicht; gemächlich ‹altes Pferd›. ❷ *v.t.* (*Med.*) sedieren (*fachspr.*); ruhig stellen

**sedately** /sɪ'deɪtlɪ/ *adv.* bedächtig; gemächlich ‹fahren›

**sedation** /sɪ'deɪʃn/ *n.* (*Med.*) Sedation, *die* (*fachspr.*); Ruhigstellung, *die;* **be under ~:** sediert sein (*fachspr.*); ruhig gestellt sein

**sedative** /'sedətɪv/ ❶ *n.* (*Med.*) Sedativum, *das* (*fachspr.*); Beruhigungsmittel, *das.* ❷ *adj.* **A** (*Med.*) sedativ (*fachspr.*); ~ **agent** ⇒ **1**; **B** (*fig.: calming*) beruhigend ‹Wirkung›

**sedentary** /'sedəntərɪ/ *adj.* sitzend ‹Haltung, Lebensweise, Tätigkeit›; **lead a ~ life** eine sitzende Lebensweise haben; viel sitzen

**sedge** /sedʒ/ *n.* (*Bot.*) **A** (*plant*) Segge, *die;* **B** *no pl.* (*bed*) Seggenried, *das*

**'sedge warbler**, **'sedge wren** *ns.* (*Ornith.*) Schilfrohrsänger, *der*

**sediment** /'sedɪmənt/ *n.* **A** (*matter*) Ablagerung, *die;* Ablagerungen *Pl.;* **B** (*lees*) Bodensatz, *der;* (*of wine also*) Depot, *das* (*fachspr.*); **C** (*Geol.*) Sediment, *das*

**sedimentary** /sedɪ'mentərɪ/ *adj.* (*Geol.*) sedimentär; Sediment‹gestein›

**sedimentation** /sedɪmən'teɪʃn/ *n.* Sedimentation, *die* (*fachspr.*); Bildung von Ablagerungen

**sedition** /sɪ'dɪʃn/ *n.* Aufruhr, *der;* **[incitement to] ~:** Anstiftung zum Aufruhr

**seditious** /sɪ'dɪʃəs/ *adj.* aufrührerisch; staatsgefährdend ‹Delikt›

**seduce** /sɪ'dju:s/ *v.t.* **A** (*sexually*) verführen; **B** (*lead astray*) verführen; (*distract*) ablenken (**away from** von); ~ **sb. into doing sth.** jmdn. dazu verführen *od.* verleiten, etw. zu tun

**seducer** /sɪ'dju:sə(r)/ *n.* Verführer, *der*

**seduction** /sɪ'dʌkʃn/ *n.* **A** (*sexual*) Verführung, *die;* **B** (*leading astray*) Verführung, *die* (**into** zu); Verleitung, *die* (**into** zu); **C** (*thing that tempts*) Verlockung, *die;* Versuchung, *die*

**seductive** /sɪ'dʌktɪv/ *adj.* verführerisch; verlockend ‹Angebot›

**seductively** /sɪ'dʌktɪvlɪ/ *adv.* verführerisch

**sedulous** /'sedʒʊləs/ *adj.* (*formal*) unermüdlich; eifrig ‹Sammler›; (*painstaking*) akkurat (*geh.*) ‹Sorgfalt, Arbeiter›

**sedulously** /'sedʒʊləslɪ/ *adv.* (*formal*) unermüdlich; (*painstakingly*) akkurat; geflissentlich ‹etw. vermeiden, überhören›

**see**[1] /si:/ ❶ *v.t.*, **saw** /sɔ:/, **seen** /si:n/ **A** sehen; **let sb. ~ sth.** (*show*) jmdm. etw. zeigen; **let me ~:** lass mich mal sehen; **I saw her fall** *or* **falling** ich habe sie fallen sehen; **he was ~n to fall down the stairs** man hat gesehen, wie er die Treppe hinunterfiel; **he was ~n to leave** *or* **~n leaving the building** er ist beim Verlassen des Gebäudes gesehen worden; **I'll believe it when I ~ it** das will ich erst mal sehen; **they saw it happen** sie haben gesehen, wie es passiert ist; sie haben es gesehen; **can you ~ that house over there?** siehst du das Haus da drüben?; **for all [the world] to ~:** für jedermann sichtbar; (*fig.: in public*) in aller Öffentlichkeit; vor aller Welt; **be worth ~ing** sehenswert sein; sich lohnen (*ugs.*); ~ **the light** (*fig.: undergo conversion*) das Licht schauen (*geh.*); **I saw the light** (*I realized my error etc.*) mir ging ein Licht auf (*ugs.*); **he'll ~ the light eventually** (*he'll realize the truth*) ihm werden die Augen noch aufgehen; ~ **the light [of day]** (*be born*) das Licht der Welt erblicken (*geh.*); (*fig.: be published or produced*) herauskommen; '~ **things** Halluzinationen haben; **I must be ~ing things** (*joc.*) ich glaub, ich seh nicht richtig; ~ **stars** Sterne sehen (*ugs.*); ~ **the sights/town** sich (*Dat.*) die Sehenswürdigkeiten/Stadt ansehen; ~ **visions** Visionen *od.* Gesichte haben; ~ **one's way [clear] to do** *or* **to doing sth.** es einrichten, etw. zu tun; **we cannot ~ our way [clear] to do it** es ist uns [zurzeit] nicht möglich, es zu tun; ⇒ *also* **back** 1 A; **something** C, G; **world** A; **B** (*watch*) sehen; **let's ~ a film** sehen wir uns (*Dat.*) einen Film an!; **C** (*meet [with]*) sehen; treffen; (*meet socially*) zusammenkommen mit; sich treffen mit; **I'll ~ you there/at 5** wir sehen uns dort/um 5; ~ **you!** (*coll.*), **[I'll] be ~ing you!** (*coll.*) bis bald (*ugs.*); ~ **you on Saturday/soon** bis Samstag/bald; ⇒ *also* **long**[1] 1 C; **D** (*speak to*) sprechen ‹Person› (**about** wegen); (*pay visit to*) gehen zu, (*geh.*) aufsuchen ‹Arzt, Anwalt usw.›; (*receive*) empfangen; **the doctor will ~ you now** Herr Doktor lässt bitten; **whom would you like to ~?** wen möchten Sie sprechen?; zu wem möchten Sie?; **E** (*discern mentally*) sehen; **I ~ it all!** jetzt ist mir alles klar; **I can ~ it's difficult for you** ich verstehe, dass es nicht leicht für dich ist; **I ~ what you mean** ich verstehe [was du meinst]; ~ **what I mean?** siehst du?; **I saw that it was a mistake** mir war klar, dass es ein Fehler war; **I don't ~ the point of it** ich sehe keinen Sinn darin; **I can't ~ the good/advantage of doing it** ich kann keinen Sinn/Vorteil darin sehen, es zu tun; **he didn't ~ the joke** er fand es [gar] nicht lustig; (*did not understand*) er hat den Witz nicht verstanden; **I can't think what she ~s in him** ich weiß nicht, was sie an ihm findet; **I saw myself [being] obliged to ...:** ich sah mich gezwungen, zu...; **F** (*consider*) sehen; **let me ~ what I can do** [ich will] mal sehen, was ich tun kann; **G** (*foresee*) sehen; **I can ~ I'm going to be busy** ich sehe [es] schon [kommen], dass ich beschäftigt sein werde; **I can ~ it won't be easy** ich sehe schon *od.* weiß jetzt schon, dass es nicht einfach sein wird; **H** (*find out*) feststellen; (*by looking*) nachsehen; **that remains to be ~n** das wird man sehen; ~ **if you can read this** guck mal, ob du das hier lesen kannst (*ugs.*); **I** (*take view of*) sehen; betrachten; ~ **things as sb. does** jmds. Ansichten teilen; **try to ~ it my way** versuche es doch mal aus meiner Sicht zu sehen; **as I ~ it** meines Erachtens; meiner Ansicht *od.* Meinung nach; ⇒ *also* **eye** 1 A; **fit**[2] 1 C; **J** (*learn*) sehen; **I ~ from your letter that ...:** ich entnehme Ihrem Brief, dass ...; **as we have ~n** wie wir schon gesehen haben; **K** (*make sure*) ~ **[that] ...:** zusehen *od.* darauf achten, dass ...; **L** *usu. in imper.* (*look at*) einsehen ‹Buch›; ~ **below/p. 15** siehe unten/S. 15; **M** (*experience*) erleben; **live to ~ sth.** etw. miterleben; **1936 saw him in India/a revolution in that country** 1936 hielt er sich in Indien auf/kam es in dem Land zu einer Revolution; **I've ~n it all** mir ist nichts unbekannt; **I've ~n it all before** das kenne ich; **now I've ~n everything!** (*iron.*) hat man so etwas schon erlebt *od.* gesehen!; **N** (*be witness of*) erleben; (*be the scene of*) Schauplatz (+ *Gen.*) sein; **we shall ~:** wir werden [ja/schon] sehen; **~/have ~n life** das Leben kennen lernen/kennen; **he will not** *or* **never ~ 50 again** er ist [bestimmt] über 50; ⇒ *also* **day** C; **service** 1 A, P; **O** (*imagine*) sich (*Dat.*) vorstellen; ~ **sb./oneself doing sth.** sich vorstellen, dass jmd./man etw. tut; ~ **oneself as a star** sich schon als Star sehen; **I can ~ it now — ...:** ich sehe es schon bildhaft vor mir — ...; **P** (*contemplate*) mit ansehen; zusehen bei; **[stand by and] ~ sb. doing sth.** [tatenlos] zusehen *od.* es [tatenlos] mit ansehen, wie jmd. etw. tut; **I'll ~ him damned** *or* **dead** *or* **hanged** *or* **in hell [first]** das wäre das Letzte[, was ich täte]!; nie im Leben!; **Q** (*escort*) begleiten, bringen (**to [bis]** zu); **R** (*supervise*) ~ **the doors locked/the book through the press** das Abschließen der Türen/den Druck des Buches überwachen; **I'll stay and ~ you on the bus** ich bleibe noch, bis du im Bus sitzt; **S** (*consent willingly to*) einsehen; **not ~ oneself doing sth.** es nicht einsehen, dass man etw. tut; **he couldn't ~ it** er konnte sich nicht damit anfreunden; **T** (*Gambling*) mithalten mit.

❷ *v.i.*, **saw, seen** **A** (*discern objects*) sehen; ~ **for yourself!** sieh doch selbst!; ~ **red** rotsehen (*ugs.*); **sth. makes sb. ~ red** jmd. sieht bei etw. rot (*ugs.*); etw. bringt jmdn. zur Weißglut; **B** (*make sure*) nachsehen; **C** (*reflect*) überlegen; **let me ~:** lass mich überlegen; warte mal ['n Moment] (*ugs.*); **D** **I ~:** ich verstehe; aha (*ugs.*); ach so (*ugs.*); **you ~:** weißt du/wisst ihr/wissen Sie; **there you are, you ~!** Siehst du? Ich habs doch gesagt!; **well, you ~, ...** (*in apologies*) es tut mir Leid, aber ...; **she used to be a nurse, you ~:** sie war nämlich mal Krankenschwester; **~?** (*coll.*) verstanden? (*salopp*); klar? (*salopp*); **as far as I can ~:** soweit ich das *od.* es beurteilen kann; ~ **here!** na hör/hören Sie mal!

~ **about** *v.t.* sich kümmern um; **I'll ~ about getting the car repaired** ich werde mich darum kümmern, dass das Auto repariert wird; **I've come to ~ about the room/cooker** ich komme wegen des Zimmers/des Herdes; **I'll ~ about it** (*consider it*) [ich will] mal sehen (*ugs.*); **we'll ~ about that!** (*you may well be wrong*) das werden wir ja sehen!

~ **into** *v.t.* **A** (*gain view into*) [hinein]sehen in (+ *Akk.*); [rein]gucken (*ugs.*) in (+ *Akk.*); ~ **into it** hineinsehen; reingucken (*ugs.*); **B** (*fig.: investigate*) nachgehen, auf den Grund gehen (+ *Dat.*) ‹Angelegenheit, Klage›

~ **'off** *v.t.* **A** (*say farewell to*) verabschieden; **B** (*chase away*) vertreiben; ~ **him off, Rover!** mach ihm Beine, Rover! (*ugs.*); **C** (*defeat*) erledigen; abservieren (*Sportjargon*)

~ **'out** ❶ *v.i.* hinaussehen; rausgucken (*ugs.*). ❷ *v.t.* **A** (*remain till end of*) ‹Zuschauer:› sich (*Dat.*) zu Ende ansehen ‹Spiel›; ableisten ‹Amtsperiode›; ‹Patient:› überleben ‹Zeitraum›; **enough fuel to ~ the winter out** genug Heizmaterial, um über den Winter zu kommen; ~ **sb. out** (*be present at sb.'s death*) bei jmds. Tod bei ihm/ihr sein; (*live or last until sb.'s death*) ‹Person, Gegenstand:› jmdn. überleben; **B** (*escort from premises*) hinausbegleiten (**of** aus); hinausbringen (**of** aus); ~ **oneself out** allein hinausfinden; **C** ⇒ ~ **through** c

~ **over**, ~ **round** *v.t.* besichtigen

~ **through** *v.t.* **A** /'--/ (*penetrate with vision*) hindurchsehen durch; durchgucken (*ugs.*) durch; ⇒ *also* **see-through**; **B** /'--/ (*fig.: penetrate nature of*) durchschauen; **C** /-'-/ (*not abandon*) zu Ende *od.* zum Abschluss bringen; ~ **things through** bei der Stange bleiben; **D** /-'-/ (*be sufficient for*) ~ **sb. through** jmdm. reichen; **we have enough food to ~ us through the weekend** wir haben für das Wochenende genug zu essen; **E** ~ **sb. through his difficulties** jmdm. über seine Schwierigkeiten hinweghelfen

~ **to** *v.t.* sich kümmern um; **I'll ~ to that** dafür werde ich sorgen; ~ **to it that ...:** dafür sorgen, dass ...; **well, ~ to it you do!** gut, dann sieh mal zu!

**see**[2] *n.* (*Eccl.*) [erz]bischöflicher Stuhl; **the Holy See** *or* **See of Rome** (*RC Ch.*) der Heilige *od.* Apostolische Stuhl

**seed** /si:d/ ❶ *n.* **A** (*grain*) Samen, *der;* Samenkorn, *das;* (*of grape etc.*) Kern, *der;* (*for birds*) Korn, *das;* **B** *no pl., no indef. art.* (~*s collectively*) Samen[körner] *Pl.;* (*as collected for sowing*) Saatgut, *das;* Saat, *die;* (*of various plants also*) Sämereien *Pl.;* **grass ~:** Grassamen *Pl.;* **go** *or* **run to ~:** Samen bilden; ‹Salat:› [in Samen] schießen; (*fig.*) herunterkommen (*ugs.*); **C** (*fig.: beginning*) Saat, *die;* Samen, *der* (*geh.*); **sow [the] ~s of doubt/a conflict/discord** für Zweifel/Konflikt sorgen/Zwietracht säen; **D** (*Sport coll.*) gesetzter Spieler/gesetzte Spielerin; **fourth ~/number one ~:** als Nummer vier/eins gesetzter Spieler/gesetzte Spielerin; **E** *no pl.* (*arch.*) (*semen*) Samen, *der;* **F** *no pl.* (*Bibl.: descendants*) Same, *der.*

❷ *v.t.* **A** (*place ~s in*) besäen; **B** (*Sport*)

setzen ‹Spieler›; **be ~ed number one** als Nummer eins gesetzt werden/sein; **C** (*lit. or fig.: sprinkle* [*as*] *with* ~) besäen; **D** (*place crystal*[*s*] *in*) impfen ‹Wolken, chemische Lösung›. **3** *v.i.* **A** (*produce* ~*s*) Samen bilden; **B** (*go to* ~) [in Samen] schießen; **C** (*sow* ~*s*) säen

**seed: ~bed** *n.* **A** (*Hort.*) [Saat]beet, *das;* **B** (*fig.: place of development*) Grundlage, *die;* (*of evil*) Brutstätte, *die;* **prepare the ~bed of sth.** einer Sache (*Dat.*) den Boden bereiten; **~ cake** *n.* Kümmelkuchen, *der;* **~corn** *n.* Saatgetreide, *das;* Saatkorn, *das;* **~ crystal** *n.* (*Chem.*) [Kristallisations]keim, *der;* Impfkristall, *der*

**seedless** /ˈsiːdlɪs/ *adj.* kernlos ‹Trauben, Rosinen›

**seedling** /ˈsiːdlɪŋ/ *n.* Sämling, *der*

**seed: ~ money** *n.* Anfangs-, Startkapital, *das;* **~ packet** *n.* Samentüte, *die;* **~ pearl** *n.* Samenperle, *die;* Saatperle, *die;* **~ potato** *n.* (*Hort.*) Saatkartoffel, *die;* **~sman** /ˈsiːdzmən/ *n., pl.* **~smen** /ˈsiːdzmən/ *n.* Samenhändler, *der;* **~time** *n.* [Aus]saatzeit, *die*

**seedy** /ˈsiːdɪ/ *adj.* **A** (*coll.: unwell*) **feel ~:** sich [leicht] angeschlagen fühlen; **B** (*shabby*) schäbig, (*ugs. abwertend*) vergammelt ‹Aussehen, Kleidung›; heruntergekommen ‹Stadtteil›; **C** (*disreputable*) zweifelhaft ‹Person›

**seeing** /ˈsiːɪŋ/ **1** *conj.* **~ [that] ...** da ...; wo ... (*ugs.*). **2** *n., no pl., no indef. art.* (*faculty or power of sight*) Sehvermögen, *das;* **~ is believing** so was glaubt man erst, wenn man es gesehen hat

**seeing ˈeye** *n.* (*dog*) Blindenhund, *der*

**seek** /siːk/ *v.t.*, **sought** /sɔːt/ **A** suchen; anstreben ‹Posten, Amt›; sich bemühen um ‹Anerkennung, Freundschaft, Interview, Einstellung›; (*try to reach*) aufsuchen; **~ shelter/help/one's fortune/sb.'s advice** Schutz/Hilfe/sein Glück/jmds. Rat suchen; **scientists are ~ing the solution** Wissenschaftler suchen nach der Lösung; **B** (*literary/formal: attempt*) suchen (*geh.*); versuchen; **~ to do sth.** suchen, etw. zu tun (*geh.*); **I'm only ~ing to establish a fact** es ist mir nur darum zu tun, eine Tatsache festzustellen (*geh.*); ⇒ *also* **level 1 A**

**~ after** *v.t.* suchen nach; **be much sought after** sehr gesucht sein

**~ for** *v.t.* suchen nach; **~ing for information** auf der Suche nach Informationen

**~ ˈout** *v.t.* ausfindig machen ‹Sache, Ort›; aufsuchen, kommen zu ‹Personen›

**seeker** /ˈsiːkə(r)/ *n.* Sucher, *der*/Sucherin, *die;* **~ after the Truth** Wahrheitssucher, *der*/-sucherin, *die* (*geh.*); **bargain-~s** Leute, die Jagd auf günstige Angebote machen/machten *usw.*

**seem** /siːm/ *v.i.* **A** (*appear* [*to be*]) scheinen; **you ~ tired** du wirkst müde; **she ~s nice** sie scheint nett zu sein; **it's not quite what it ~s** es ist nicht ganz das, was es [zunächst] zu sein scheint; **it ~s like only yesterday** es ist, als wäre es erst gestern gewesen; **he ~s certain to win** es sieht ganz so aus, als würde er gewinnen; **she ~s younger than 45** sie wirkt jünger als 45; **what ~s to be the trouble?** wo fehlts denn? (*ugs.*); wo drückt denn der Schuh? (*ugs.*); **it ~s a pity** es ist doch schade; **I ~ to recall having seen him before** ich glaube mich zu erinnern, ihn schon einmal gesehen zu haben; **it just ~s as if it were** es scheint nur so *od.* kommt einem nur so vor; **doing such a thing just doesn't ~ right somehow** es ist doch irgendwie nicht richtig, so etwas zu tun; **it ~s [that] ...:** anscheinend ...; **it ~s to me that it's silly to do that** ich finde es töricht *od.* es kommt mir töricht vor, das zu tun; **it ~s that we had better decide quickly** wir sollten uns wohl besser schnell entscheiden; **it ~s you were lying** du hast ja wohl gelogen; **it ~s [as if] there will be war** es sieht nach Krieg aus; es sieht so aus, als ob es Krieg geben wird; **it would** *or* (*arch.*) **should ~ to be ...:** es scheint ja wohl ... zu sein; **you know everything, it would ~:** du scheinst ja wohl alles zu wissen; **it would ~ that he is ...:** er scheint ja wohl ... zu sein; **so it ~s** *or* **would ~:** so will es scheinen; **Dead? — So it would ~:** Tot? — Allem Anschein nach; **so it ~s!** (*iron.*) was Sie nicht sagen! (*iron.*); **B sb. can't ~ to do sth.** (*coll.*) jmd. scheint etw. nicht tun zu können; **I just can't ~ to do it** (*coll.*) ich kann es einfach irgendwie nicht [tun] (*ugs.*); **she doesn't ~ to notice such things** (*coll.*) so was merkt sie irgendwie nicht (*ugs.*); **~ good to sb.** jmdm. das Beste [zu sein] scheinen

**seeming** /ˈsiːmɪŋ/ *adj.* scheinbar

**seemingly** /ˈsiːmɪŋlɪ/ *adv.* **A** (*evidently*) offensichtlich; **B** (*to outward appearance*) scheinbar

**seemly** /ˈsiːmlɪ/ *adj.* anständig; **it isn't ~ to praise oneself** es gehört sich nicht, sich selbst zu loben

**seen** ⇒ **see**[1]

**seep** /siːp/ *v.i.* **~ [away]** [ab]sickern; **~ in through** durch etw. hineinsickern; **~ out of sth.** aus etw. heraussickern; **[gradually] ~ through to sb.'s consciousness** (*fig.*) jmdm. [langsam] dämmern (*ugs.*) *od.* bewusst werden

**seepage** /ˈsiːpɪdʒ/ *n.* **A** Versickern, *das;* (*into sth.*) Hineinsickern, *das;* **B** (*quantity*) Lache, *die;* (*of oil*) Ölausbiss, *der* (*Geol.*); (*of gas*) Austritt, *der*

**seer** /sɪə(r)/ *n.* (*prophet*) Seher, *der*/Seherin, *die*

**seersucker** /ˈsɪəsʌkə(r)/ *n.* (*Textiles*) Seersucker, *der;* *Baumwoll- od. Leinengewebe mit Kreppstreifen; attrib.* ‹Kleid, Tagesdecke› aus Seersucker

**ˈsee-saw** **1** *n.* **A** (*plank*) Wippe, *die;* **B** *no art.* (*game*) Wippen, *das;* **let's have a game of ~:** komm, wir gehen auf die Wippe *od.* wippen; **C** (*fig.: contest*) Auf und Ab, *das.* **2** *v.i.* **A** (*move up and down*) ‹Weg, Straße:› auf und ab führen; ‹Deck:› [auf und ab] schaukeln; **B** (*vacillate*) schwanken; **C** (*play on ~*) wippen

**seethe** /siːð/ *v.i.* **A** (*surge*) ‹Wellen, Meer:› branden; ‹Straßen usw.:› wimmeln (**with** von); (*bubble or foam as if boiling*) schäumen; **B** (*fig.: be agitated*) schäumen; **~ [with anger/inwardly]** vor Wut/innerlich schäumen

**ˈsee-through** *adj.* durchsichtig

**segment** **1** /ˈsegmənt/ *n.* **A** (*of orange, pineapple*) Scheibe, *die;* Schnitz, *der* (*bes. südd.*); (*of cake, pear*) Stück, *das;* (*of worm, skull, limb*) Segment, *das;* (*of bowel*) Abschnitt, *der;* Segment, *das* (*Med.*); (*of economy, market*) Bereich, *der;* **B** (*Ling., Geom., Sociol.*) Segment, *das;* **~ of a circle** Kreissegment, *das.* **2** /segˈment, ˈsegmənt/ *v.t.* untergliedern; [in Gruppen] aufteilen ‹Menschen›. **3** *v.i.* (*Biol.*) sich teilen

**segmentation** /segmənˈteɪʃn/ *n.* Untergliederung, *die;* (*Biol.*) Zellteilung, *die*

**segregate** /ˈsegrɪgeɪt/ *v.t.* **A** trennen; isolieren ‹Kranke›; aussondern ‹Forschungsgebiet›; **B** (*racially*) segregieren (*geh.*); absondern

**segregation** /segrɪˈgeɪʃn/ *n., no pl.* **A** Trennung, *die;* **B [racial] ~:** Rassentrennung, *die*

**segregationist** /segrɪˈgeɪʃənɪst/ *n.* Befürworter/Befürworterin der Rassentrennung

**seine** /seɪn/ *n.* (*Fishing*) **~[ net]** Treibnetz, *das*

**seismic** /ˈsaɪzmɪk/ *adj.* seismisch; **~ area** *or* **region** Erdbebengebiet, *das;* **of ~ proportions** (*fig.*) von verheerenden Ausmaßen

**seismically** /ˈsaɪzmɪkəlɪ/ *adv.* seismisch

**seismograph** /ˈsaɪzməgrɑːf/ *n.* Seismograph, *der;* Seismometer, *das*

**seize** /siːz/ **1** *v.t.* **A** ergreifen; **~ power** die Macht ergreifen; **~ sb. by the arm/collar/shoulder** jmdn. am Arm/Kragen/an der Schulter packen; **~ the opportunity** *or* **occasion/moment [to do sth.]** die Gelegenheit ergreifen/den günstigen Augenblick nutzen [und etw. tun]; **~ any/a** *or* **the chance [to do sth.]** jede/die Gelegenheit nutzen[, um etw. zu tun]; **be ~d with remorse/panic** von Gewissensbissen geplagt/von Panik ergriffen werden; **she ~d it with both hands** (*fig.*) sie griff mit beiden Händen zu (*fig.*); **B** (*capture*) gefangen nehmen ‹Person›; kapern ‹Schiff›; mit Gewalt übernehmen ‹Flugzeug, Gebäude›; einnehmen ‹Festung, Brücke›; **C** (*understand*) erfassen; **D** (*confiscate*) beschlagnahmen.
**2** *v.i.* ⇒ **~ up**

**~ on** *v.t.* sich (*Dat.*) vornehmen ‹Einzelheit, Aspekt, Schwachpunkt›; aufgreifen ‹Idee, Vorschlag›; ergreifen ‹Chance›

**~ ˈup** *v.i.* sich festfressen; ‹Verkehr:› zusammenbrechen, zum Erliegen kommen

**~ upon** ⇒ **~ on**

**seizure** /ˈsiːʒə(r)/ *n.* **A** (*capturing*) Gefangennahme, *die;* (*of ship*) Kapern, *das;* (*of aircraft, building*) Übernahme, *die;* (*of fortress, bridge*) Einnahme, *die;* **~ of power** Machtergreifung, *die;* **B** (*confiscation*) Beschlagnahme, *die;* **C** (*Med.: attack*) Anfall, *der*

**seldom** /ˈseldəm/ **1** *adv.* selten; **~ or never** so gut wie nie; **~, if ever** fast nie; äußerst selten. **2** *adj.* selten; **a ~ thing** eine Seltenheit; etwas Seltenes

**select** /sɪˈlekt/ **1** *adj.* **A** (*carefully chosen*) ausgewählt; **only the most ~ company** nur eine kleine Gruppe Auserwählter; **B** (*exclusive*) exklusiv. **2** *v.t.* auswählen; **~ one's own apples** sich (*Dat.*) die Äpfel selbst aussuchen

**select comˈmittee** *n.* Sonderkommission, *die*

**selectee** /sɪlekˈtiː/ *n.* (*Amer.*) Einberufene, *der*

**selection** /sɪˈlekʃn/ *n.* **A** (*what is selected* [*from*]) Auswahl, *die* (**of** an + *Dat.*, **from** aus); (*person*) Wahl, *die;* **a ~ from ...** (*Mus.*) eine Auswahl aus ...; **make a ~** (*one*) eine Wahl treffen; (*several*) eine Auswahl treffen; **~s from the best writers** ausgewählte Werke der besten Schriftsteller; **what is your ~ for the Derby?** was ist dein Tipp für das Derby?; **B** (*act of choosing*) [Aus]wahl, *die;* **~ committee** Auswahlkomitee, *das;* **C** (*being chosen*) Wahl, *die;* **his ~ as president** seine Wahl zum Präsidenten; **D** (*Biol.: in evolution*) Selektion, *die;* Auslese, *die*

**selective** /sɪˈlektɪv/ *adj.* **A** (*using selection*) selektiv; (*careful in one's choice*) wählerisch; **B** (*Electr.*) selektiv; trennscharf

**selectively** /sɪˈlektɪvlɪ/ *adv.* selektiv; **not read ~ enough** [viel] zu wahllos lesen; **shop ~:** gezielt einkaufen

**selectiveness** /sɪˈlektɪvnɪs/ *n., no pl.* Eingrenzung, *die*

**selectivity** /sɪlekˈtɪvɪtɪ, selekˈtɪvɪtɪ, siːlekˈtɪvɪtɪ/ *n., no pl.* **have a high degree of ~** ‹Insektizid:› nur spezifisch wirksam sein; **show ~:** wählerisch sein

**selectman** /sɪˈlektmən/, *pl.* **selectmen** /sɪˈlektmən/ *n.* (*Amer.*) Stadtrat, *der*

**selectness** /sɪˈlektnɪs/ *n., no pl.* Exklusivität, *die*

**selector** /sɪˈlektə(r)/ *n.* **A** (*person who selects*) (*of team*) Mannschaftsaufsteller, *der*/-aufstellerin, *die;* (*of merchandise*) Einkäufer, *der*/Einkäuferin, *die;* **B** (*device that selects*) (*knob*) Schaltknopf, *der;* (*lever*) Schaltgriff, *der;* (*switch*) Wahlschalter, *der;* (*for selecting programmes*) Programmtaste, *die;* (*of computer*) Selektor, *der*

**self** /self/ *n., pl.* **selves** /selvz/ **A** (*person's essence*) Selbst, *das* (*geh.*); Ich, *das;* **be one's usual ~:** man selbst sein; **not be one's usual cheerful ~:** nicht so fröhlich wie sonst sein; **be back to one's former** *or* **old ~ [again]** wieder der/die Alte sein; **one's better ~:** sein besseres Ich; **my humble ~/your good selves** (*joc.*) meine Wenigkeit/die werten Herrschaften (*scherzh.*); **how is your good ~?** (*arch.*) wie ist das werte Befinden? (*veralt.*); **B** (*one's own interest*) die eigene Person; **she cares for nothing but ~:** sie nimmt nur sich selbst wichtig; **she has no thoughts of ~:** sie ist sehr selbstlos; **C** (*Commerc.*) **drawn to ~:** auf selbst ausgestellt ‹Scheck›; **pay to ~:** zahlbar an Aussteller *od.* selbst

**self-** *in comb.* **A** *expr. direct reflexive action* selbst‹anklagend, -schließend›; Selbst‹ankläger,

S

-anzeige›); **stand ~accused** sich selbst angeklagt haben; Ⓑ *expr. action or condition* selbst-; **~acting** automatisch; selbsttätig

**self:** **~-ab'sorbed** *adj.* mit sich selbst beschäftigt; **~-ab'sorption** *n.* Mit-sich-selbst-beschäftigt-Sein, *das;* **~-ad'dressed** *adj.* **a ~-addressed envelope** ein adressierter Rückumschlag; **~-ad'hesive** *adj.* selbstklebend; **~-ad'vertisement** *n.* Selbstreklame, *die;* **~-ag'grandizement** *n.* Vergrößerung der eigenen Macht; **~-a'nalysis** *n.* Selbstanalyse, *die;* **~-ap'pointed** *adj.* selbst ernannt; **~-as'sertion** *n.* Durchsetzungsvermögen, *das* (**over** gegenüber); **~-as'sertive** *adj.*, **~-assertively** /selfəˈsɜːtɪvlɪ/ *adv.* selbstbewusst; **~-as'sertiveness** *n., no pl.* Durchsetzungsvermögen, *das;* **a ~-assertiveness training course** ein Trainingskurs in Durchsetzungsvermögen; **~-as'surance** *n., no pl.* Selbstbewusstsein, *das;* Selbstsicherheit, *die;* **~-as'sured** *adj.* selbstsicher; selbstbewusst; **~-a'wareness** *n.* Selbsterkenntnis, *die;* **~-'catering** ❶ *adj.* mit Selbstversorgung *nachgestellt;* ❷ *n.* Selbstversorgung, *die;* **~-'centred** *adj.* egozentrisch; ichbezogen; **~-'closing** *adj.* selbstschließend; **~-coloured** *adj.* (*with uniform colouring*) einfarbig; **~-com'mand** *n., no pl.* Selbstbeherrschung, *die;* **~-con'demned** *adj.* **be** *or* **stand ~-condemned** sich selbst überführt haben; **~-con'fessed** *adj.* erklärt; **~-'confidence** *n., no pl.* Selbstvertrauen, *das;* **~-'confident** *adj.*, **~-'confidently** *adv.* selbstsicher; **~-'conscious** *adj.* Ⓐ (*ill at ease*) unsicher; Ⓑ (*deliberate*) reflektiert ‹Prosa, Stil›; **~-'consciousness** *n.* Ⓐ Unsicherheit, *die;* Ⓑ (*deliberateness*) Reflektiertheit, *die;* **~-con'tained** *adj.* Ⓐ (*not dependent*) selbstgenügsam; (*not communicative*) verschlossen; Ⓑ (*having no parts in common*) unabhängig ‹Maschine, Anlage›; einzeln stehend ‹Haus›; Ⓒ (*Brit.: complete in itself*) abgeschlossen ‹Wohnung›; **~-contra'dictory** *adj.* mit sich selbst in Widerspruch; **~-con'trol** *n., no pl.* Selbstbeherrschung, *die;* **~-con'trolled** *adj.* voller Selbstbeherrschung *nachgestellt;* **~-'critical** *adj.* selbstkritisch; **~-de'ception** *n.* Selbsttäuschung, *die;* Selbstbetrug, *der;* **~-de'feating** *adj.* unsinnig; zwecklos; **~-de'fence** *n., no pl., no indef. art.* Notwehr, *die;* Selbstverteidigung, *die;* **in ~-defence** aus Notwehr; **~-defence classes** Selbstverteidigungskurs, *der;* **~-de'lusion** *n.* Selbsttäuschung, *die;* **~-de'nial** *n.* Selbstverleugnung, *die;* **~-deprecating** /selfˈdeprɪkeɪtɪŋ/ *adj.* bescheiden; **~-de'struct** *v.i.* sich selbst zerstören; **~-de'struction** *n.* Selbstzerstörung, *die;* **~-de'structive** *adj.*, **~-de'structively** *adv.* selbstzerstörerisch; **~-'discipline** *n., no pl.* Selbstdisziplin, *die;* **~-drive** *adj.* **~-drive hire [company]** Autovermietung, *die;* **~-drive vehicle** Mietwagen, *der;* **~-'educated** *adj.* autodidaktisch; **be ~-educated, be a ~-educated person** Autodidakt/Autodidaktin sein; **~-ef'facing** *adj.* zurückhaltend; **~-em'ployed** *adj.* selbstständig; **~-employed man/woman** Selbstständige, *der/die;* **~-e'steem** *n.* Ⓐ (*~-respect*) Selbstachtung, *die;* Ⓑ (*~-conceit*) Selbstgefälligkeit, *die;* **~-'evident** *adj.*, **~-'evidently** *adv.* offenkundig; **~-ex'planatory** *adj.* ohne weiteres verständlich; **be ~-explanatory** für sich selbst sprechen; **~-ex'pression** *n., no pl., no indef. art.* Selbstdarstellung, *die;* **~-fertili'zation** *n.* (*Biol.*) Selbstbefruchtung, *die;* **~-financing** *adj.* sich selbst tragend; kostenneutral ‹Tarifvertrag›; **~-ful'filling** *adj.* zur eigenen Bestätigung mit beitragend; **~-fulfilling prophecy** zur Bestätigung ihrer selbst mit beitragende Voraussage; Selffulfilling Prophecy, *die* (*Soziol.*); **~-'governing** *adj.* selbst verwaltet; **~-'government** *n., no pl., no indef. art.* Selbstverwaltung, *die;* **~-'help** *n., no pl.* Selbsthilfe, *die;* **~-'image** *n.* Selbstbild, *das;* **~-im'portance** *n., no pl.* Selbstgefälligkeit, *die;* (*arrogant and pompous bearing*) Selbstherrlichkeit, *die;* **~-im'portant** *adj.* selbstgefällig; (*arrogant and pompous*) selbstherrlich; **~-im'posed** *adj.* selbst auferlegt; **~-im'provement** *n.* selbstständige Weiterbildung; **~-in'duced** *adj.* Ⓐ selbst verursacht; Ⓑ (*Electr.*) selbstinduziert; **~-in'duction** *n.* (*Electr.*) Selbstinduktion, *die;* **~-in'dulgence** *n.* Maßlosigkeit, *die;* **a little ~-indulgence never hurt anyone** sich ein bisschen zu verwöhnen, hat noch keinem geschadet; **this novel is a piece of pure ~-indulgence** dieser Roman ist weiter nichts als Selbstbefriedigung des Autors; **~-in'dulgent** *adj.* maßlos; **I've been very ~-indulgent lately** ich habe mich in der letzten Zeit sehr gehen lassen; **~-in'flicted** *adj.* selbst beigebracht ‹Wunde›; selbst auferlegt ‹Strafe›; **~-'interest** *n.* Eigeninteresse, *das;* **~-in'vited** *adj.* **a ~-invited guest** ein Gast, der sich selbst eingeladen hat

**selfish** /ˈselfɪʃ/ *adj.* egoistisch; selbstsüchtig

**selfishly** /ˈselfɪʃlɪ/ *adv.* egoistisch; selbstsüchtig; **do sth. ~:** etw. aus Egoismus tun

**selfishness** /ˈselfɪʃnɪs/ *n., no pl.* Egoismus, *der;* Selbstsucht, *die*

**self:** **~-justifi'cation** *n.* Rechtfertigung, *die;* **attempt at ~-justification** Versuch, sich zu rechtfertigen; **~-'knowledge** *n.* Selbsterkenntnis, *die*

**selfless** /ˈselflɪs/ *adj.*, **selflessly** /ˈselflɪslɪ/ *adv.* selbstlos

**self:** **~-'loading** *adj.* mit Selbstladevorrichtung *nachgestellt;* **~-'loathing** *n.* Selbstverachtung, *die;* **be consumed by deep ~-loathing** eine tiefe Abscheu gegen sich selbst empfinden; **~-'locking** *adj.* selbstschließend; **~-'love** *n., no pl.* Selbstliebe, *die;* Eigenliebe, *die;* **~-made** *adj.* selbst gemacht; **a ~-made man** ein Selfmademan; **she is a ~-made woman** sie hat sich aus eigener Kraft hochgearbeitet; **~-'mockery** *n.* Selbstverspottung, *die;* **~-'mocking** *adj.* selbstspöttisch; **~-'motivated** *adj.* von sich aus motiviert; selbstmotiviert ‹Lernen›; **~-moti'vation** *n.* Motiviertheit, *die;* [innere] Motivation; **~-ob'sessed** *adj.* ichbesessen; **~-o'pinionated** *adj.* Ⓐ (*conceited*) eingebildet; von sich eingenommen; Ⓑ (*obstinate*) starrköpfig; rechthaberisch; **~-per'petuating** *adj.* sich selbst erhaltend; **be ~-perpetuating** sich selbst erhalten; **~-'pity** *n., no pl.* Selbstmitleid, *das;* **~-'pitying** *adj.* selbstmitleidig; **~-'portrait** *n.* Selbstporträt, *das;* **~-pos'sessed** *adj.* selbstbeherrscht; **remain ~-possessed** die Selbstbeherrschung behalten; **be ~-possessed** sich beherrschen *od.* zusammennehmen; **~-pos'session** *n., no pl.* Selbstbeherrschung, *die;* **~-preser'vation** *n., no pl., no indef. art.* Selbsterhaltung, *die;* **~-'propagating** *adj.* (*Bot.*) selbstbefruchtend; **be ~-propagating** Selbstbefruchter sein; (*fig.*) sich selbst vermehren; **~-pro'pelled** *adj.* mit Eigenantrieb *nachgestellt;* **~-'raising flour** *n.* (*Brit.*) mit Backpulver versetztes Mehl; **~-re'gard** *n., no pl.* Selbstachtung, *die;* **~-'regulating** *adj.* sich selbst steuernd ‹Maschine›; autonom ‹Institution›; **~-re'liance** *n., no pl.* Selbstvertrauen, *das;* Selbstsicherheit, *die;* **~-re'liant** *adj.* selbstbewusst; selbstsicher; **~-re'spect** *n., no pl.* Selbstachtung, *die;* **~-re'specting** *adj.* mit Selbstachtung *nachgestellt;* **no ~-respecting person ...:** niemand, der etwas auf sich hält, ...; **~-re'straint** *n., no pl.* Selbstbeherrschung, *die;* **~-'righteous** *adj.* selbstgerecht; **~-'righteousness** *n., no pl.* Selbstgerechtigkeit, *die;* **~-'righting** *adj.* selbstaufrichtend; **~-'rising flour** (*Amer.*) ⇒ **~-raising flour;** **~-'sacrifice** *n.* Selbstaufopferung, *die;* **~-'sacrificing** *adj.* [sich] aufopfernd ‹Mutter, Vater›; aufopfernd ‹Liebe›; **~same** *adj.* **the ~same** der-/die-/dasselbe; **~-satis'faction** *n., no pl.* Selbstzufriedenheit, *die;* (*smugness*) Selbstgefälligkeit, *die;* **~-'satisfied** *adj.* selbstzufrieden; (*smug*) selbstgefällig; **~-'sealing** *adj.* Ⓐ (*automatically sealing*) selbstdichtend; Ⓑ (*~-adhesive*) selbstklebend; **~-seeking** ❶ *adj.* selbstsüchtig; ❷ *n., no pl.* Selbstsucht, *die;* **~-'service** ❶ *n.* Ⓐ (*operation*) Selbstbedienung, *die; attrib.* Selbstbedienungs-; Ⓑ (*shop*) Selbstbedienungsladen, *der;* (*petrol station*) Tankstelle zum Selbsttanken; (*restaurant*) Selbstbedienungsrestaurant, *das;* ❷ *pred. adj.* **the petrol station is/has become ~-service** die Tankstelle hat Selbstbedienung/hat auf Selbstbedienung umgestellt; **~-sown** *adj.* selbst ausgesät; **~-'starter** *n.* (*Motor Veh.*) Selbststarter, *der;* **~-'study** *n.* Selbststudium, *das;* **~-styled** *adj.* selbst ernannt; von eigenen Gnaden *nachgestellt;* **~-suf'ficiency** *n.* Unabhängigkeit, *die;* (*of country*) Autarkie, *die;* **~-suf'ficient** *adj.* (*independent*) unabhängig; autark ‹Land›; selbstständig ‹Person›; **be ~-sufficient in food** seinen Nahrungsbedarf selbst decken; **~-sup'porting** *adj.* Ⓐ sich selbst tragend ‹Unternehmen, Verein›; finanziell unabhängig ‹Person›; **the club/firm is ~-supporting** der Verein/die Firma trägt sich selbst; Ⓑ (*not requiring support*) frei-, selbsttragend ‹Konstruktion, Gebäude›; **~-'tapping** *adj.* selbstschneidend ‹Schraube›; **~-'taught** *adj.* autodidaktisch; selbst erlernt ‹Fertigkeiten›; **~-taught person** Autodidakt, *der*/Autodidaktin, *die;* **be a ~-taught painter/be ~-taught in German** sich (*Dat.*) das Malen/Deutsch selbst beigebracht haben; **she is ~-taught** sie ist Autodidaktin; **~-'will** *n., no pl.* Eigensinn, *der;* **~-'willed** *adj.* eigensinnig; **~-winding** *adj.* automatisch; **a ~-winding watch** eine Uhr mit Selbstaufzug

**sell** /sel/ ❶ *v.t.*, **sold** /səʊld/ Ⓐ verkaufen; **the shop ~s groceries** in dem Laden gibt es Lebensmittel [zu kaufen]; **~ sth. to sb., ~ sb. sth.** jmdm. etw. verkaufen; **~ one's life** *etc.* **dear** *or* **dearly** (*fig.*) sein Leben *usw.* teuer verkaufen; **it is the advertising that ~s the product** die Werbung sorgt für den Absatz des Produkts; **~ by ...** (*on package*) ≈ mindestens haltbar bis ...; Ⓑ (*betray*) verraten; Ⓒ (*offer dishonourably*) verkaufen; verhökern (*ugs. abwertend*); **~ oneself/one's soul** sich/seine Seele verkaufen (**to** *Dat.*); Ⓓ (*coll.: cheat, disappoint*) verraten; anschmieren (*salopp*); **I've been sold!, sold again!** ich bin [wieder] der/die Dumme! (*ugs.*); Ⓔ (*gain acceptance for*) **~ sb. as ...:** jmdn. als ... verkaufen (*ugs.*); **~ sth. to sb.** jmdn. für etw. gewinnen; **~ sb. the idea of doing sth.** jmdn. für den Gedanken gewinnen, etw. zu tun; Ⓕ **~ sb. on sth.** (*coll.: make enthusiastic*) jmdn. für etw. begeistern *od.* erwärmen; **be sold on sth.** (*coll.*) von etw. begeistert sein. ⇒ *also* **dummy** 1 E; **river** 1 A; **short** 1 I.

❷ *v.i.*, **sold** Ⓐ sich verkaufen [lassen]; ‹Person:› verkaufen; **the book sold 5,000 copies in a week** in einer Woche wurden 5 000 Exemplare des Buches verkauft; Ⓑ **~ at** *or* **for** kosten. ⇒ *also* **cake** 1 B.

❸ *n.* Ⓐ **be a tough ~:** ein Ladenhüter (*abwertend*) sein; sich schlecht verkaufen; **be an easy ~:** ein Verkaufsschlager sein; sich gut verkaufen; Ⓑ (*coll.: deception*) Schwindel, *der* (*abwertend*). ⇒ *also* **hard sell**; **soft sell**

**~ 'off** *v.t.* verkaufen; abstoßen ‹Anteile, Aktien›

**~ 'out** ❶ *v.t.* Ⓐ ausverkaufen; restlos verkaufen; **the play/performance was sold out** das Stück/die Aufführung war ausverkauft; Ⓑ (*coll.: betray*) verpfeifen (*ugs.*).
❷ *v.i.* Ⓐ **we have** *or* **are sold out** wir sind ausverkauft; **sth. ~s out quickly** etw. verkauft sich schnell; **~ out to another firm** durch Verkauf in eine andere Firma übergehen; Ⓑ (*coll.: betray one's cause*) **~ out to sb./sth.** zu jmdm./etw. überlaufen. ⇒ *also* **sell-out**

**~ 'out of** *v.t.* **we have** *or* **are sold out of sth.** etw. ist ausverkauft

**~ 'up** *v.t.* (*Brit.*) verkaufen; *abs.* sein Hab und Gut verkaufen

**'sell-by date** *n.* ≈ Mindesthaltbarkeitsdatum, *das*

**seller** /ˈselə(r)/ *n.* Ⓐ Verkäufer, *der*/Verkäuferin, *die;* **be a ~ of sth.** etw. verkaufen; **a ~'s** *or* **~s' market** ein Verkäufermarkt; Ⓑ (*product*) **be a slow/bad ~:** sich nur langsam/schlecht verkaufen; **be a fast** *or* **strong** *or* **big ~:** ein Renner *od.* Verkaufsschlager sein; **be a good ~:** sich gut verkaufen

**selling** /ˈselɪŋ/ ❶ *n.* Ⓐ (*act, occupation*) Verkaufen, *das;* Ⓑ (*salesmanship*) Verkauf, *der;* **training in ~:** Verkaufsschulung, *die.* ❷ *adj. in comb.* **a fast- *or* good-~ book** ein Buch, das sich gut verkauft

**selling:** **~ point** *n.* **a [good] ~ point** ein Verkaufsargument; (*fig.*) ein Pluspunkt; **~ price** *n.* Verkaufspreis, *der*

**sellotape** *v.t.* mit Klebeband kleben

**Sellotape** ® /'seləʊteɪp/ *n., no pl., no indef. art.* ≈ Tesafilm, *der* Ⓦⓩ

**'sell-out** *n.* Ⓐ (*event*) **be a ~:** ausverkauft sein; Ⓑ (*coll.: betrayal*) Verrat, *der*

**selvage, selvedge** /'selvɪdʒ/ *n.* Webkante, *die*

**selves** *pl. of* **self**

**semantic** /sɪ'mæntɪk/ *adj.* semantisch

**semantically** /sɪ'mæntɪkəlɪ/ *adv.* semantisch

**semantics** /sɪ'mæntɪks/ *n., no pl.* Semantik, *die;* **only argue about ~:** sich um Worte streiten

**semaphore** /'seməfɔ:(r)/ ❶ *n.* Ⓐ (*apparatus*) Signalmast, *der;* Semaphor, *das od. der;* Ⓑ (*system*) Winken, *das;* **~ alphabet** Winkeralphabet, *das.* ❷ *v.i.* **~ to sb.** jmdm. ein Winksignal übermitteln. ❸ *v.t.* [durch Winksignale] übermitteln

**semblance** /'sembləns/ *n.* Ⓐ (*outward appearance*) Anschein, *der;* **without a ~ of regret/a smile** ohne das geringste Zeichen von Bedauern/den Anflug eines Lächelns; **without even the ~ of a trial** ohne auch nur die geringste Verhandlung; **bring some ~ of order to sth.** wenigstens den Anschein von Ordnung in etw. (*Akk.*) bringen; Ⓑ (*resemblance*) Ähnlichkeit, *die*

**semeiology** /si:maɪ'ɒlədʒɪ/, **semeiotics** /si:maɪ'ɒtɪks/ ⇒ **semiology**

**semen** /'si:men/ *n.* (*Physiol.*) Samen, *der;* Sperma, *das*

**semester** /sɪ'mestə(r)/ *n.* (*Univ.*) Semester, *das*

**semi** /'semɪ/ *n.* (*coll.*) Ⓐ (*Brit.: house*) Doppelhaushälfte, *die;* Ⓑ (*Amer.: vehicle*) Sattelanhänger, *der*

**semi-** *in comb.* halb-/Halb-

**semi: ~-auto'matic** ❶ *adj.* halbautomatisch; ❷ *n.* halbautomatische Feuerwaffe; **~-basement** *n.* Halbsouterrain, *das;* **~bold** *adj.* (*Printing*) halbfett; **~breve** *n.* (*Brit. Mus.*) ganze Note; **~circle** *n.* Halbkreis, *der;* **~'circular** *adj.* halbkreisförmig; **~-'colon** *n.* Semikolon, *das;* **~con'ductor** *n.* (*Phys.*) Halbleiter, *der;* **~-'conscious** *adj.* halb bewusstlos; **be only ~-conscious** nicht bei vollem Bewusstsein sein; **~-'darkness** *n.* Halbdunkel, *das;* **in ~-darkness** im Halbdunkel; **~-de'tached** ❶ *adj.* **the house is ~-detached** es ist eine Doppelhaushälfte; **a ~-detached house** eine Doppelhaushälfte; ❷ *n.* (*Brit.: house*) Doppelhaushälfte, *die;* **~-'final** *n.* Halbfinale, *das;* Semifinale, *das;* **in the ~-finals** im Halbfinale; **~-'finalist** *n.* Halbfinalteilnehmer, *der*/-teilnehmerin, *die;* Halbfinalist, *der*/-finalistin, *die;* **~-'finished** *adj.* halb fertig; **~-'invalid** *n.* Teilinvalide, *der/die;* **~-literate** *adj.* **be ~-literate** kaum lesen und schreiben können

**seminal** /'semɪnl, 'si:mɪnl/ *adj.* Ⓐ (*having originative power*) schöpferisch; (*embryonic*) keimhaft; Ⓑ (*reproductive*) Samen‹leiter, -flüssigkeit›

**seminar** /'semɪnɑ:(r)/ *n.* Ⓐ (*small class*) Seminar, *das;* Ⓑ (*Amer.: conference*) Konferenz, *die;* Ⓒ (*study-course*) Kurs[us], *der;* Seminar, *das*

**seminarian** /semɪ'neəriən/, **seminarist** /'semɪnərɪst/ *ns.* Seminarist, *der*

**seminary** /'semɪnərɪ/ *n.* Priesterseminar, *das*

**semiology** /si:mɪ'ɒlədʒɪ/, **semiotics** /si:mɪ'ɒtɪks/ *ns.* Semiotik, *die;* Semiologie, *die*

**semi: ~-'permanent** *adj.* fast permanent; **~-'precious** *adj.* **~-precious stone** Halbedelstein, *der;* Schmuckstein, *der;* **be ~-precious** ein Halbedelstein sein; **~quaver** *n.* (*Brit. Mus.*) Sechzehntelnote, *die;* **~-'skilled** *adj.* angelernt; **~-skimmed** ❶ *adj.* teilentrahmt; ❷ *n.* teilentrahmte Milch; **~-'sweet** *adj.* halbsüß ‹Sekt, Wein›; [nur] leicht gesüßt ‹Kuchen, Schokolade›

**Semite** /'si:maɪt, 'semaɪt/ ❶ *n.* Semit, *der*/Semitin, *die.* ❷ *adj.* semitisch

**Semitic** /sɪ'mɪtɪk/ *adj.* semitisch

**'semitone** *n.* (*Mus.*) Halbton, *der*

**'semi-trailer** *n.* Sattelanhänger, *der*

**semolina** /semə'li:nə/ *n.* Ⓐ Grieß, *der;* Ⓑ (*pudding*) Grießpudding, *der*

**sempstress** ⇒ **seamstress**

**Sen.** *abbr.* Ⓐ **Senator** Sen.; Ⓑ **Senior** sen.

**SEN** *abbr.* (*Brit.*) **State Enrolled Nurse**

**senate** /'senət/ *n.* Senat, *der*

**senator** /'senətə(r)/ *n.* ▶ 1617 Senator, *der*/Senatorin, *die*

**send** /send/ ❶ *v.t.,* **sent** /sent/ Ⓐ (*cause to go*) schicken; senden (*geh.*); **~ sb. to Africa** jmdn. nach Afrika schicken; **~ sb. to university/boarding school** jmdn. auf die Universität/ins Internat schicken; **~ sb. on a course/tour** jmdn. in einen Kurs/auf eine Tour schicken; **~ a dog after sb.** einen Hund auf jmdn. hetzen; **she ~s her best wishes/love** sie lässt grüßen/herzlich grüßen; **~ [sb.] apologies/congratulations** sich [bei jmdm.] entschuldigen lassen/[jmdm.] seine Glückwünsche übermitteln; **she sent him congratulations on ...:** sie schickte ihm Glückwünsche zu ...; **~ sb. home/to bed** jmdn. nach Hause/ins Bett schicken; **~ sb. to his death** jmdn. in den Tod schicken; ⇒ *also* **word** 1 F; Ⓑ (*grant*) schicken; **~ her victorious!** (*arch.*) [Herr,] lass sie siegreich sein!; **God ~s the rain on the just and the unjust** (*prov.*) Gott lässt regnen über Gerechte und Ungerechte; Ⓒ (*propel*) **~ a rocket into space** eine Rakete in den Weltraum schießen; **~ a ball over the wall** einen Ball über die Mauer schießen; **~ up clouds of dust** Staubwolken aufwirbeln; **~ sth. to the ground/hurtling through the air** etw. zu Boden werfen/durch die Luft sausen lassen; **~ sb. sprawling/reeling** jmdn. zu Boden strecken/ins Wanken bringen; **~ sb. running for cover** jmdn. schnell Deckung suchen lassen; **~ sth. off course** etw. vom Kurs abkommen lassen; ⇒ *also* **fly²** 1 D; Ⓓ (*drive into condition*) **~ sb. mad** *or* **crazy** jmdn. verrückt machen (*ugs.*); **~ sb. into raptures/a temper/fits of laughter** jmdn. ins Schwärmen geraten lassen/in Wut bringen/dazu bringen, dass er sich totlacht (*ugs.*); **~ sb. to sleep** jmdn. zum Einschlafen bringen; **that loud music ~s me round the bend** (*fig. coll.*) bei dieser lauten Musik könnte ich verrückt *od.* wahnsinnig werden (*ugs.*); Ⓔ (*dismiss*) **~ sb. about his/her** *etc.* **business** jmdn. vor die Tür setzen; ⇒ *also* **Coventry**; **pack** 3; Ⓕ (*coll.: put into ecstasy*) begeistern; **she really ~s me** sie macht mich total an (*salopp*). ❷ *v.i.,* **sent: ~ to sb. for sth.** (*by letter*) jmdn. um etw. anschreiben; **we'll ~ to Germany for that** wir werden nach Deutschland schreiben, dass sie uns das schicken

**~ a'head** *v.t.* vorausschicken; **he was sent ahead of the main group** er wurde dem Haupttrupp vorausgeschickt

**~ a'way** ❶ *v.t.* wegschicken; fortschicken (*landsch., geh.*); **we like to ~ our guests away with pleasant memories** wir möchten unseren Gästen angenehme Erinnerungen mitgeben; ⇒ *also* **flea.** ❷ *v.i.* **~ away [to sb.] for sth.** etw. [bei jmdm.] anfordern

**~ 'back** *v.t.* Ⓐ (*return*) zurückschicken; Ⓑ (*because of dissatisfaction*) zurückgehen lassen ‹Speise, Getränk›; (*by post*) zurückschicken ‹Ware›

**~ 'down** ❶ *v.t.* Ⓐ [hinunter]schicken; Ⓑ (*Brit. Univ.*) relegieren (*geh.*); von der Hochschule verweisen; Ⓒ (*put in prison*) hinter Schloss und Riegel bringen (*ugs.*); Ⓓ (*Cricket*) werfen ‹Ball›; Ⓔ nach unten treiben ‹Preis, Kosten, Temperatur›. ❷ *v.i.* **~ down [to the store] for sth.** etw. aus dem Lager holen lassen

**~ for** *v.t.* Ⓐ (*tell to come*) holen lassen; rufen ‹Polizei, Arzt, Krankenwagen›; Ⓑ (*order from elsewhere*) anfordern

**~ 'in** *v.t.* einschicken

**~ 'off** ❶ *v.t.* Ⓐ (*dispatch*) abschicken ‹Sache›; losschicken (*ugs.*) ‹Person›; **~ one's children off to boarding school** seine Kinder ins Internat schicken; Ⓑ (*bid farewell to*) verabschieden; ⇒ *also* **send-off**; Ⓒ (*Sport*) vom Platz stellen (**for** wegen); ❷ *v.i.* **~ off for sth. [to sb.]** etw. [von jmdm.] anfordern

**~ 'on** *v.t.* Ⓐ (*forward*) nachsenden ‹Post›; **they sent me on to you** ich wurde an Sie verwiesen; Ⓑ (*cause to go ahead*) **~ on [ahead]** vorausschicken; Ⓒ (*cause to participate*) **~ a player on** einen Spieler einsetzen

**~ 'out** ❶ *v.t.* Ⓐ (*issue*) verschicken; Ⓑ (*emit*) aussenden ‹Hilferuf, Nachricht›; abgeben ‹Hitze›; senden ‹Lichtstrahlen›; ausstoßen ‹Rauch›; verströmen ‹Geruch›; Ⓒ (*dispatch*) schicken; **~ sb. out to Africa** jmdn. nach Afrika schicken; **~ sb. out for sth.** jmdn. schicken, um etw. zu besorgen; Ⓓ (*order to leave*) hinausschicken. ❷ *v.i.* **~ out for sth.** etw. besorgen *od.* holen lassen

**~ 'up** *v.t.* Ⓐ (*Brit. coll.: ridicule*) (*in play, sketch, song*) parodieren; (*in cartoon*) karikieren; ⇒ *also* **send-up**; Ⓑ (*Amer. coll.: put in prison*) in den Knast stecken (*ugs.*); einbuchten (*salopp*); Ⓒ (*transmit to higher authority*) weiterleiten (**to** an + *Akk.*); Ⓓ (*cause to rise*) steigen lassen ‹Ballon›; hochtreiben ‹Preis, Kosten, Temperatur›; **~ sb.'s temperature up** (*fig. joc.*) jmdn. zum Kochen bringen (*ugs.*); Ⓔ (*destroy*) in die Luft jagen (*ugs.*) *od.* sprengen

**sender** /'sendə(r)/ *n.* ▶ 1286 (*of goods*) Lieferant, *der*/Lieferantin, *die;* (*of letter*) Absender, *der*/Absenderin, *die*

**send: ~-off** *n.* Verabschiedung, *die;* **give sb. a good ~-off** jmdn. groß verabschieden; **~-up** *n.* (*Brit. coll.: parody*) Parodie, *die;* (*in cartoon*) Karikatur, *die;* **do a ~-up of sb./sth.** jmdn./etw. parodieren

**Senegal** /senɪ'gɔ:l/ *pr. n.* Senegal (*das*) *od. der*

**Senegalese** /senɪgə'li:z/ ▶ 1340 ❶ *adj.* senegalesisch; **sb. is ~:** jmd. ist Senegalese/Senegalesin. ❷ *n., pl. same* Senegalese, *der*/Senegalesin, *die*

**senescent** /sɪ'nesənt/ *adj.* alternd

**senile** /'si:naɪl/ *adj.* senil; (*physically*) altersschwach; (*caused by old age*) altersbedingt ‹Apathie, Schwatzhaftigkeit›; **~ decay** Altersabbau, *der*

**senile de'mentia** *n.* (*Med.*) senile Demenz

**senility** /sɪ'nɪlɪtɪ/ *n., no pl.* Senilität, *die;* (*physical infirmity*) Altersschwäche, *die*

**senior** /'si:nɪə(r)/ ❶ *adj.* Ⓐ ▶ 912 (*older*) älter; **be ~ to sb.** älter als jmd. sein; **~ team** Seniorenmannschaft, *die;* Ⓑ ▶ 1261 (*of higher rank*) höher ‹Rang, Beamter, Stellung›; leitend ‹Angestellter, Stellung›; (*longest-serving*) ältest ...; **someone ~:** jemand in höherer Stellung; **~ management** Geschäftsleitung, *die;* **~ consultant/nurse** (*in hospital*) ≈ Oberarzt, *der*/Oberschwester, *die;* **be ~ to sb.** eine höhere Stellung als jmd. haben; **she is ~/not very ~:** sie hat einen/keinen gehobenen Posten; **~ manager** obere Führungskraft; **~ management** oberer Führungskreis; Ⓒ *appended to name* (*the elder*) **Mr Smith S~:** Mr. Smith senior; Ⓓ (*Brit. Sch.*) **~ school** *or* **section** Oberstufe, *die;* Ⓔ (*Brit. Univ.*) **~ combination** *or* **common room** Gemeinschaftsraum für Dozenten; Ⓕ (*Amer. Sch., Univ.*) **~ class** Abschlussklasse, *die;* **~ year** letztes Jahr vor der Abschlussprüfung.
❷ *n.* Ⓐ ▶ 912 (*older person*) Ältere, *der/die;* (*person of higher rank*) Vorgesetzte, *der/die;* **be sb.'s ~ [by six years]** *or* **[six years] sb.'s ~:** [sechs Jahre] älter als jmd. sein; Ⓑ (*Brit. Sch.*) Schüler/Schülerin einer höheren Schule; (*in the last three years*) Oberstufenschüler, *der*/-schülerin, *die;* Ⓒ (*Amer.*) (*Sch.*) Schüler/Schülerin im letzten Schuljahr; (*Univ.*) Student/Studentin im letzten Studienjahr

**senior: ~ 'citizen** *n.* Senior, *der*/Seniorin, *die;* **~ college** *n.* (*Amer.*) höhere Schule; ≈ [Gymnasial]oberstufe, *die*

**seniority** /si:nɪ'ɒrɪtɪ/ *n.* Ⓐ (*superior age*) Alter, *das;* Ⓑ (*priority in length of service*) höheres Dienstalter; Ⓒ (*superior rank*) höherer Rang

**senior: ~ 'officer** *n.* ▶ 1261 höherer Beamter/höhere Beamtin; (*Mil.*) ranghöchster Offizier; **sb.'s ~ officer** jmds. Vorgesetzter; **~ 'partner** *n.* Seniorpartner, *der*/-partnerin, *die;* **~ service** *n.* (*Brit.*) Marine, *die*

**senna** /'senə/ *n.* Ⓐ (*Bot.*) Sennespflanze, *die;* Kassie, *die;* Ⓑ (*drug*) Sennesblätter; Senna, *die*

S

**sensation** /sen'seɪʃn/ *n.* A (*feeling*) Gefühl, *das;* ~ **of hunger/thirst/giddiness** Hunger-/Durst-/Schwindelgefühl, *das;* **have a ~ of falling** das Gefühl haben zu fallen; B (*person, event, etc. causing intense excitement*) Sensation, *die;* **a great ~:** ein großes Ereignis; C (*excitement*) Aufsehen, *das*

**sensational** /sen'seɪʃənl/ *adj.* A (*spectacular*) aufsehenerregend; sensationell; B (*arousing intense response*) reißerisch (*abwertend*); Sensations‹blatt, -presse›; C (*phenomenal*) phänomenal

**sensationalise** ⇒ **sensationalize**

**sensationalism** /sen'seɪʃənəlɪzm/ *n.* Sensationshascherei, *die* (*abwertend*); **[desire for] ~:** Sensationsgier, *die* (*abwertend*)

**sensationalist** /sen'seɪʃənəlɪst/ *adj.* sensationslüstern (*abwertend*); sensationsgeil (*ugs. abwertend*); Sensations‹blatt, -presse, usw.›; **~ nonsense** um der Sensation willen verbreiteter Unsinn

**sensationalize** /sen'seɪʃənəlaɪz/ *v.t.* **~ sth.** etw. zur Sensation aufbauschen

**sensationally** /sen'seɪʃənəlɪ/ *adv.* sensationell

**sense** /sens/ ❶ *n.* A (*faculty of perception*) Sinn, *der;* **~ of smell/touch/taste** Geruchs-/Tast-/Geschmackssinn, *der;* **come to one's ~s** das Bewusstsein wiedererlangen; B *in pl.* (*normal state of mind*) Verstand, *der;* **in full possession of one's ~s** im Vollbesitz seiner geistigen Kräfte; **no one in his ~s would do that** niemand mit einem Funken Verstand würde so etwas tun; **have taken leave of** *or* **be out of one's ~s** den Verstand verloren haben; **frighten sb. out of his ~s** jmdm. einen furchtbaren Schrecken einjagen; **come to one's ~s** zur Vernunft kommen; **bring sb. to his ~s** jmdn. zur Vernunft *od.* Besinnung bringen; C (*consciousness*) Gefühl, *das;* **~ of responsibility/guilt** Verantwortungs-/Schuldgefühl, *das;* **out of a ~ of duty** aus Pflichtgefühl; **~ of gratitude** Gefühl der Dankbarkeit; **a keen ~ of honour** ein ausgeprägtes Ehrgefühl; **have a ~ of one's own importance** sich sehr wichtig nehmen; ⇒ *also* **direction** C; **humour** 1 A; **road sense**; D (*ability to perceive*) Gespür, *das;* (*instinct*) [instinktives] Gespür; **~ of the absurd** Gespür für das Absurde; E (*practical wisdom*) Verstand, *der;* **there's a lot of ~ in what he's saying** was er sagt, klingt sehr vernünftig; **sound** *or* **good ~:** [gesunder Menschen]verstand; **not have the ~ to do sth.** nicht so schlau sein, etw. zu tun; **there is no ~ in doing that** es hat keinen Sinn, das zu tun; **what is the ~ of** *or* **in doing that?** was hat man davon *od.* wozu soll es gut sein, das zu tun?; **have more ~ than to do sth.** genug Verstand haben, etw. nicht zu tun; **talk ~:** vernünftig reden; **now you are talking ~:** jetzt wirst du vernünftig; **you're just not talking ~:** du redest einfach Unsinn; **see ~:** zur Vernunft kommen; **make sb. see ~:** jmdn. zur Vernunft bringen; **be a man/woman of ~:** wissen, was man tut; **she hasn't the ~ she was born with** sie hat keinen Funken Verstand; ⇒ *also* **common sense**; F (*meaning*) Sinn, *der;* (*of word*) Bedeutung, *die;* **in the strict** *or* **literal ~:** im strengen *od.* wörtlichen Sinn; **in every ~ [of the word]** in jeder Hinsicht; **there is a ~ in which ...:** man könnte durchaus die Ansicht vertreten, dass ...; **in some ~:** irgendwie; **in a** *or* **one ~:** in gewisser Hinsicht *od.* Weise; **make ~:** einen Sinn ergeben; **her arguments do not make ~ to me** ihre Argumente leuchten mir nicht ein; **it does not make ~ to do that** es ist Unsinn *od.* unvernünftig, das zu tun; **it makes [a lot of] ~** (*is [very] reasonable*) es ist [sehr] sinnvoll; **it makes good** *or* **sound financial ~:** es ist in finanzieller Hinsicht sinnvoll; **it all makes ~ to me now** jetzt verstehe ich alles; **it just doesn't make ~:** es ergibt einfach keinen Sinn; **now you're making ~:** jetzt verstehe ich, was du sagen willst; **make ~ of sth.** etw. verstehen; aus etw. schlau werden; G (*prevailing sentiment*) **take the ~ of the meeting** die Meinung der Versammlung einholen.

❷ *v.t.* spüren; ‹Tier:› wittern; ‹Gerät:› wahrnehmen

**senseless** /'senslɪs/ *adj.* A (*unconscious*) bewusstlos; B (*foolish*) unvernünftig; dumm; **what a ~ thing to do/say!** wie kann man nur so etwas Dummes machen/sagen!; C (*purposeless*) unsinnig ‹Argument›; sinnlos ‹Diskussion, Vergeudung›

**'sense organ** *n.* Sinnesorgan, *das*

**sensibility** /sensɪ'bɪlɪtɪ/ *n.* A *in pl.* (*susceptibility*) Empfindlichkeit, *die;* **her sensibilities are easily wounded** sie ist sehr schnell verletzt *od.* gekränkt; B (*openness to emotional impressions*) Sensibilität, *die* (**to** in Bezug auf + *Akk.*); **~ to pain/beauty** Schmerzempfindlichkeit, *die*/Empfänglichkeit für Schönheit; C (*delicacy of feeling*) Feingefühl, *das* (**to** gegenüber; **of** für); Einfühlungsvermögen, *das* (**of** in + *Akk.*); D (*oversensitiveness*) Empfindsamkeit, *die*

**sensible** /'sensɪbl/ *adj.* A (*reasonable*) vernünftig; **he was ~ enough to do it** er war so vernünftig, es zu tun; **be ~ [about it]!** sei doch vernünftig!; B (*practical*) praktisch; zweckmäßig; fest ‹Schuhe›; C (*appreciable*) gravierend ‹Fehler›; beachtlich, merklich ‹Anstieg, Rückgang, Unterschied›; D (*literary: aware*) **be ~ of** *or* **to sth.** etw. spüren

**sensibly** /'sensɪblɪ/ *adv.* A (*reasonably*) vernünftig; besonnen; **~ enough, he refused** er war so vernünftig abzulehnen; B (*practically*) zweckmäßig; C (*appreciably*) merklich

**sensitisation, sensitise** ⇒ **sensitiz-**

**sensitive** /'sensɪtɪv/ *adj.* A (*recording slight changes*) empfindlich; **be ~ to sth.** empfindlich auf etw. (*Akk.*) reagieren; **~ to light** lichtempfindlich; B (*touchy*) empfindlich (**about** wegen); **be ~ to sth.** empfindlich auf etw. (*Akk.*) reagieren; C heikel ‹Thema, Diskussion›; D (*perceptive*) einfühlsam

**sensitively** /'sensɪtɪvlɪ/ *adv.* empfindlich ‹reagieren›; einfühlsam ‹darstellen›

**'sensitive plant** *n.* (*Bot.; also fig.: person*) Mimose, *die*

**sensitivity** /sensɪ'tɪvɪtɪ/ *n.* A (*capacity to respond emotionally*) Sensibilität, *die;* Empfindlichkeit, *die* (**to** gegen); **offend sb.'s sensitivities** jmds. Feingefühl verletzen; B (*responsiveness*) Empfindlichkeit, *die;* **~ to light** Lichtempfindlichkeit, *die*

**sensitization** /sensɪtaɪ'zeɪʃn/ *n.* Sensibilisierung, *die*

**sensitize** /'sensɪtaɪz/ *v.t.* sensibilisieren (**to** für)

**sensor** /'sensə(r)/ *n.* Sensor, *der*

**sensory** /'sensərɪ/ *adj.* sensorisch; Sinnes‹wahrnehmung, -organ›

**sensual** /'sensjʊəl, 'senʃʊəl/ *adj.* sinnlich; lustvoll ‹Leben›; Sinnen‹freude, -genuss›

**sensuality** /sensjʊ'ælɪtɪ, senʃʊ'ælɪtɪ/ *n.* Sinnlichkeit, *die*

**sensually** /'sensjʊəlɪ, 'senʃʊəlɪ/ *adv.* sinnlich; genussvoll ‹essen›

**sensuous** /'sensjʊəs/ *adj.* sinnlich

**sensuously** /'sensjʊəslɪ/ *adv.* sinnlich; **~ beautiful** von sinnlicher Schönheit *nachgestellt*

**sent** ⇒ **send**

**sentence** /'sentəns/ ❶ *n.* A (*decision of law-court*) [Straf]urteil, *das;* (*fig.*) Strafe, *die;* **give sb. a three-year ~:** jmdn. zu drei Jahren Haft verurteilen; **pass ~ [on sb.]** [jmdm.] das Urteil verkünden; **be under ~ of death** zum Tode verurteilt sein; (*fig.*) zum Untergang verurteilt sein; B (*Ling.*) Satz, *der;* ⇒ *also* **complex** 1 C; **compound**[1] 1 F; **simple** E.

❷ *v.t.* (*lit. or fig.*) verurteilen (**to** zu)

**'sentence-modifier** *n.* (*Ling.*) Satzpartikel, *die*

**sententious** /sen'tenʃəs/ *adj.* A (*pithy*) prägnant; sentenziös (*geh.*); B (*affectedly formal*) salbungsvoll (*abwertend*); C (*given to pompous moralizing*) moralistisch; schulmeisterhaft

**sententiously** /sen'tenʃəslɪ/ *adv.* A (*pithily*) kurz und prägnant; B (*pompously*) schulmeisterhaft

**sentient** /'senʃənt/ *adj.* empfindungsfähig

**sentiment** /'sentɪmənt/ *n.* A (*mental feeling*) Gefühl, *das;* **noble ~s** edle Gesinnung; **~ unchecked by reason** nicht vernunftgesteuerte Gefühle; **those are** *or* (*coll.*) **them's my ~s** so denke ich darüber; B (*emotion conveyed in art*) Empfindung, *die;* C *no pl.* (*emotional weakness*) Sentimentalität, *die;* Rührseligkeit, *die;* D (*expression of view*) Gedanke, *der*

**sentimental** /sentɪ'mentl/ *adj.* A (*motivated by feeling*) sentimental; **sth. has ~ value [for sb.]** jmd. hängt an etw. (*Dat.*); **~ attachment to sth.** gefühlsmäßige Bindung an etw. (*Akk.*); **for ~ reasons** aus Sentimentalität; B (*appealing to sentiment*) rührselig; sentimental; **a ~ song** eine Schnulze

**sentimentalism** /sentɪ'mentəlɪzm/ *n., no pl.* Sentimentalität, *die*

**sentimentalist** /sentɪ'mentəlɪst/ *n.* sentimentaler Mensch

**sentimentality** /sentɪmen'tælɪtɪ/ *n.* Sentimentalität, *die*

**sentimentalize** /sentɪ'mentəlaɪz/ ❶ *v.i.* sich sentimentalen Gefühlen hingeben. ❷ *v.t.* sentimental darstellen

**sentimentally** /sentɪ'mentəlɪ/ *adv.* sentimental; gefühlsmäßig ‹verbunden›

**sentinel** /'sentɪnl/ *n.* (*lit. or fig.*) Wache, *die;* **stand ~ over sth.** (*fig.*) über etw. (*Akk.*) wachen

**sentry** /'sentrɪ/ *n.* (*lit. or fig.*) Wache, *die;* **stand ~ at the door** an der Tür Wache halten

**sentry: ~ box** *n.* Wachhäuschen, *das;* **~ duty** *n.* **be on ~ duty** Wachdienst haben

**sepal** /'sepl, 'si:pl/ *n.* (*Bot.*) Kelchblatt, *das*

**separability** /sepərə'bɪlɪtɪ/ *n., no pl.* Trennbarkeit, *die*

**separable** /'sepərəbl/ *adj.* A trennbar; zerlegbar ‹Werkzeug, Gerät›; B (*Ling.*) trennbar ‹Vorsilbe, Verb›

**separate** ❶ /'sepərət/ *adj.* verschieden ‹Fragen, Probleme, Gelegenheiten›; getrennt ‹Konten, Betten›; gesondert ‹Teil›; separat ‹Eingang, Toilette, Blatt Papier, Abteil›; Sonder‹vereinbarung›; (*one's own, individual*) eigen ‹Zimmer, Identität, Organisation›; **lead ~ lives** getrennt leben; **go ~ ways** getrennte Wege gehen; **the ~ volumes** die einzelnen Bände; **one is quite ~ from the other** das eine ist ganz unabhängig von dem anderen/(*different*) ganz anders als das andere; **keep two things ~:** zwei Dinge auseinander halten; **keep issue A ~ from issue B** Frage A und Frage B getrennt behandeln; **keep one's chequebook ~ from one's bank card** Scheckbuch und Scheckkarte getrennt aufbewahren.

❷ /'sepəreɪt/ *v.t.* A trennen; **they are ~d** (*no longer live together*) sie leben getrennt; B (*Amer.: discharge*) entlassen (**from** aus).

❸ *v.i.* A (*disperse*) sich trennen; B ‹Ehepaar› sich trennen; C (*secede*) sich abspalten; D ⇒ **separate out** 1. ⇒ *also* **separates**

**~ 'out** ❶ *v.i.* sich entmischen (*fachspr.*); sich trennen. ❷ *v.t.* (*distinguish*) auseinander halten; (*extract*) trennen

**separately** /'sepərətlɪ/ *adv.* getrennt; **they had, quite ~, reached the same conclusion** sie waren — ganz unabhängig voneinander — zum gleichen Schluss gekommen

**separate 'maintenance** *n.* (*Law*) Unterhalt, *der*

**separates** /'sepərəts/ *n. pl.* (*Fashion*) Separates; einzelne Kleidungsstücke [die man kombinieren kann]

**separation** /sepə'reɪʃn/ *n.* A Trennung, *die;* **judicial** *or* **legal ~:** gerichtliche Trennung; B (*Amer.: resignation, discharge*) Entlassung, *die* (**from** aus)

**sepa'ration order** *n.* gerichtliche Anordnung des Getrenntlebens

**separatism** /'sepərətɪzm/ *n.* A (*advocacy of separation*) Separatismus, *der;* B (*segregation*) **[racial/class] ~:** [Rassen-/Klassen]trennung, *die*

**separatist** /'sepərətɪst/ *n.* Separatist, *der*/Separatistin, *die; attrib.* ~ **movement** Separatistenbewegung, *die*

**separator** /'sepəreɪtə(r)/ *n.* Separator, *der*

**sepia** /'si:pɪə/ *n.* **A** (*pigment*) Sepia, *die;* **B** (*colour*) Sepiabraun, *das;* ~ **photograph/drawing** sepiafarbenes Foto/Sepiazeichnung, *die;* **C** (*drawing*) Sepiazeichnung, *die*

**sepsis** /'sepsɪs/ *n., pl.* **sepses** /'sepsi:z/ (*Med.*) Sepsis, *die* (*fachspr.*); Blutvergiftung, *die*

**Sept.** *abbr.* **September** Sept.

**septa** *pl. of* **septum**

**September** /sep'tembə(r)/ *n.* ▶ **1055** September, *der;* ⇒ *also* **August**

**septet, septette** /sep'tet/ *n.* (*Mus.*) Septett, *das*

**septic** /'septɪk/ *adj.* septisch

**septicaemia** (*Amer.:* **septicemia**) /septɪ'si:mɪə/ *n.* ▶ **1232** (*Med.*) Sepsis, *die;* Septikämie, *die* (*fachspr.*)

**septic 'tank** *n.* Faulraum, *der*

**septuagenarian** /septjʊədʒɪ'neərɪən/ **1** *adj.* siebzigjährig; (*more than 70 years old*) in den Siebzigern *nachgestellt.* **2** *n.* Siebziger, *der*/Siebzigerin, *die*

**septum** /'septəm/ *n., pl.* **septa** /'septə/ (*Anat., Bot., Zool.*) Septum, *das*

**sepulcher** (*Amer.*) ⇒ **sepulchre**

**sepulchral** /sɪ'pʌlkrl/ *adj.* **A** (*of burial*) Grab-; Bestattungs‹brauch, -ritus›; **B** (*fig.: funereal*) düster

**sepulchre** /'seplkə(r)/ *n.* (*Brit.*) Grab, *das;* **the Holy S~:** das Heilige Grab

**sequel** /'si:kwl/ *n.* **A** (*consequence, result*) Folge, *die* (**to** von); **B** (*continuation*) Fortsetzung, *die;* **there was a tragic ~:** es gab ein tragisches Nachspiel; **in the ~:** in der Folge

**sequence** /'si:kwəns/ *n.* **A** (*succession*) Reihenfolge, *die;* **rapid/logical ~:** rasche/logische Abfolge; **a ~ of musicals** eine Reihe von Musicals; **B** (*part of film; set of poems, also Cards; Mus., Eccl.*) Sequenz, *die;* **C** (*succession without cause*) Aufeinanderfolge, *die;* **D** ~ **of tenses** (*Ling.*) Zeitenfolge, *die*

**sequential** /sɪ'kwenʃl/ *adj.* (*forming a sequence*) aufeinander folgend; **be ~ to** *or* **upon sth.** auf etw. (*Akk.*) folgen

**sequester** /sɪ'kwestə(r)/ **1** *v.t.* **A** (*set apart*) abtrennen ‹Teil›; absondern ‹Person›; **B** (*Law: seize*) sequestrieren; **C** (*confiscate*) beschlagnahmen. **2** *v. refl.* sich fern halten; ~ **oneself from the world** sich von der Welt abkapseln

**sequestered** /sɪ'kwestəd/ *adj.* abgelegen; ‹Leben› in Abgeschiedenheit

**sequestrate** /'si:kwɪstreɪt/ ⇒ **sequester** 1 B, C

**sequestration** /si:kwɪ'streɪʃn/ *n.* **A** (*Law: appropriation*) Sequestration, *die;* **B** (*confiscation*) Beschlagnahme, *die*

**sequestrator** /'si:kwɪstreɪtə(r)/ *n.* Sequester, *der*

**sequin** /'si:kwɪn/ *n.* Paillette, *die*

**sequined, sequinned** /'si:kwɪnd/ *adj.* paillettenbesetzt ‹Kleid›

**sequoia** /sɪ'kwɔɪə/ *n.* (*Bot.*) Mammutbaum, *der;* Sequoia, *die* (*fachspr.*)

**sera** *pl. of* **serum**

**seraglio** /sə'rɑ:ljəʊ/ *n., pl.* **~s** Harem, *der;* Serail, *das* (*veralt.*)

**seraph** /'serəf/ *n., pl.* **seraphim** /'serəfɪm/ *or* **~s** Seraph, *der*

**seraphic** /sə'ræfɪk/ *adj.* seraphisch (*geh.*)

**Serb** /sɜ:b/ ▶ **1340** ⇒ **Serbian**

**Serbia** /'sɜ:bɪə/ *pr. n.* Serbien, (*das*)

**Serbian** /'sɜ:bɪən/ ▶ **1275**, ▶ **1340** **1** *adj.* serbisch; **sb. is ~:** jmd. ist Serbe/Serbin; ⇒ *also* **English** 1. **2** *n.* **A** (*dialect*) serbischer Dialekt; **B** (*person*) Serbe, *der*/Serbin, *die.* ⇒ *also* **English** 2 A

**Serbo-Croat** /sɜ:bəʊ'krəʊæt/, **Serbo-Croatian** /sɜ:bəʊkrəʊ'eɪʃn/ ▶ **1275** **1** *adj.* serbokroatisch; ⇒ *also* **English** 1. **2** *n.* Serbokroatisch, *das;* ⇒ *also* **English** 2 A

**serenade** /serə'neɪd/ **1** *n.* (*Mus.*) **A** Ständchen, *das;* **sing** *or* **play sb. a ~:** jmdm. ein Ständchen bringen; **B** (*cantata*) Serenade, *die.* **2** *v.t.* (*Mus.*) ~ **sb.** jmdm. ein Ständchen bringen

**serendipity** /serən'dɪpɪtɪ/ *n.* glücklicher Zufall

**serene** /sɪ'ri:n/ *adj.*, **~r** /sɪ'ri:nə(r)/, **~st** /sɪ'ri:nɪst/ **A** (*calm*) klar ‹Wetter, Himmel›; **B** (*unruffled*) unbewegt ‹Wasser, See usw.›; **C** (*placid*) ruhig; gelassen; **calm and ~:** ruhig und gelassen

**serenely** /sɪ'ri:nlɪ, sə'ri:nlɪ/ *adv.* gelassen; ~ **indifferent** gleichmütig und gelassen

**serenity** /sɪ'renɪtɪ, sə'renɪtɪ/ *n., no pl.* **A** (*placidity*) Gelassenheit, *die;* **B** (*of clear weather*) Klarheit, *die*

**serf** /sɜ:f/ *n.* **A** (*villein*) Leibeigene, *der*/*die;* **B** (*fig.: drudge*) Sklave, *der*

**serfdom** /'sɜ:fdəm/ *n.* Leibeigenschaft, *die;* (*fig.*) Sklaverei, *die;* Plackerei, *die* (*ugs.*)

**serge** /sɜ:dʒ/ *n.* (*Textiles*) Serge, *die*

**sergeant** /'sɑ:dʒənt/ *n.* ▶ **1617** **A** (*Mil.*) Unteroffizier, *der;* **B** (*police officer*) ≈Polizeimeister, *der*

**sergeant:** ~ **'major** ▶ **1617** (*Amer.*), **[regimental]** ~ **major** (*Brit.*) ≈ [Ober]stabsfeldwebel, *der;* ⇒ *also* **company** G

**serial** /'sɪərɪəl/ **1** *adj.* **A** (*forming a series*) aufeinander folgend; ~ **production** Serienproduktion, *die;* **publish sth. in ~ form** etw. in Serienform veröffentlichen; **B** (*issued in instalments*) Fortsetzungs‹geschichte, -roman›; ~ **radio/TV play** Radio-/Fernsehserie, *die;* **C** (*periodical*) periodisch erscheinend; **a monthly ~ publication** eine Monatsschrift; **D** (*Mus., Computing*) seriell. **2** *n.* **A** (*story*) Fortsetzungsgeschichte, *die;* (*on radio, television*) Serie, *die;* **B** (*periodical*) [periodisch erscheinende] Zeitschrift; Periodikum, *das* (*geh.*)

**serialize** /'sɪərɪəlaɪz/ *v.t.* in Fortsetzungen veröffentlichen; (*on radio, television*) in Fortsetzungen *od.* als Serie senden

**serial 'killer** *n.* Serienmörder, *der*

**serially** /'sɪərɪəlɪ/ *adv.* in Fortsetzungen, als Serie ‹senden›; ~ **numbered** fortlaufend nummeriert

**serial:** ~ **mo'nogamy** *n.* serielle Monogamie; ~ **number** *n.* Seriennummer, *die;* ~ **rights** *n. pl.* Rechte zur Veröffentlichung als Serie

**series** /'sɪəri:z, 'sɪərɪz/ *n., pl. same* **A** (*sequence*) Reihe, *die;* **a ~ of events/misfortunes** eine Folge von Ereignissen/Missgeschicken; **B** (*set of successive issues*) Serie, *die;* **radio/TV ~:** Hörfunkreihe/Fernsehserie, *die;* ~ **of programmes** Sendereihe, *die;* **first ~:** erste Folge; **C** (*set of books*) Reihe, *die;* **D** (*group of stamps etc.*) Serie, *die;* **E** (*group of games etc.*) Serie, *die;* **a lecture ~:** eine Vortragsreihe; **F** (*Chem.: set of elements*) homologe Reihe; **G** (*Electr.*) **in ~:** in Reihe; hintereinander; **H** (*Mus., Math.*) Reihe, *die;* **I** (*Geol.: set of strata*) Schichtenfolge, *die*

**serif** /'serɪf/ *n.* (*Printing*) Serife, *die*

**serio-comic** /sɪərɪəʊ'kɒmɪk/ *adj.* tragikomisch

**serious** /'sɪərɪəs/ *adj.* **A** (*earnest*) ernst; ~ **music** ernste Musik; **a ~ play** ein ernstes Stück; **B** (*important, grave*) ernst ‹Angelegenheit, Lage, Problem, Zustand›; ernsthaft ‹Frage, Einwand, Kandidat›; gravierend ‹Änderung›; schwer ‹Krankheit, Unfall, Fehler, Überschwemmung, Niederlage›; ernst zu nehmend ‹Rivale›; ernstlich ‹Gefahr, Bedrohung›; bedenklich ‹Verschlechterung, Mangel›; **things are/sth. is getting ~:** die Lage spitzt sich zu/ etw. nimmt ernste Ausmaße an; **there is a ~ danger that ...:** es besteht ernste Gefahr, dass ...; ~ **charge/offence** schwerwiegender Vorwurf/schwerer Verstoß; **C** (*in earnest*) **are you ~:** ist das dein Ernst?; **but now to be ~:** aber jetzt mal im Ernst; **you cannot be ~:** das kann doch nicht dein Ernst sein; **he is a ~ worker** er nimmt seine Arbeit ernst; **be ~ about sth./doing sth.** etw. ernst nehmen/ernsthaft tun wollen; **is he ~ about her?** meint er es ernst mit ihr?; **give sth. ~ thought** ernsthaft über etw. (*Akk.*) nachdenken

**seriously** /'sɪərɪəslɪ/ *adv.* **A** (*earnestly*) ernst[haft]; **speak ~ to sb.** mit jmdm. ein ernstes Wort sprechen; **quite ~, ...:** ganz im Ernst, ...; **take sth./sb. ~:** etw./jmdn. ernst nehmen; **B** (*severely*) ernstlich; schwer ‹verletzt, überflutet›; **go ~ wrong** ‹Person:› sich schwer täuschen; ‹Sache:› völlig missglücken *od.* fehlschlagen

**seriousness** /'sɪərɪəsnɪs/ *n., no pl.* **A** (*earnestness*) Ernst, *der;* Ernsthaftigkeit, *die;* **in all ~:** ganz im Ernst; **B** (*gravity*) Schwere, *die;* (*of situation*) Ernst, *der*

**sermon** /'sɜ:mən/ *n.* **A** (*Relig.*) Predigt, *die;* **the S~ on the Mount** die Bergpredigt; **give a ~:** eine Predigt halten; **B** (*moral reflections*) Mahnrede, *die;* **C** (*lecture, scolding*) [Moral]predigt, *die*

**sermonize** /'sɜ:mənaɪz/ **1** *v.t.* ~ **sb.** jmdm. eine [Moral]predigt halten. **2** *v.i.* **A** (*lecture*) ‹Person:› dozieren; ‹Buch, Film:› moralisieren; **B** (*preach*) predigen

**serpent** /'sɜ:pənt/ *n.* **A** (*snake*) Schlange, *die;* **B** (*fig.: treacherous person*) falsche Schlange; **C** (*Mus.*) Serpent, *der*

**serpentine** /'sɜ:pəntaɪn/ **1** *adj.* **A** (*tortuous*) Serpentinen-; gewunden ‹Fluss›; **B** (*of serpent*) Schlangen-; (*resembling a snake*) schlangengleich. **2** *n.* (*Min.*) Serpentin, *der*

**SERPS** /sɜ:ps/ *abbr.* (*Brit.*) **State earnings-related pension scheme**

**serrated** /se'reɪtɪd/ *adj.* gezackt; ~ **knife** Sägemesser, *das*

**serration** /se'reɪʃn/ *n.* gezackter Rand; (*one tooth*) Zacke, *die;* **in ~s** gezackt

**serried** /'serɪd/ *adj.* dicht ‹Reihen›

**serum** /'sɪərəm/ *n., pl.* **sera** /'sɪərə/ *or* **~s** (*Physiol.*) Serum, *das*

**servant** /'sɜ:vənt/ *n.* **A** (*wage-earning employee*) Angestellte, *der*/*die;* **a faithful ~ of the company** ein treuer Diener der Firma; **B** (*domestic attendant*) Diener, *der*/Dienerin, *die;* (*female also*) Dienstmädchen, *das;* **keep** *or* **have ~s** Bedienstete haben; **C** (*in letter*) **your humble** (*arch.*) *or* **obedient ~** (*Brit.*) Ihr ergebenster *od.* untertänigster Diener (*veralt.*). ⇒ *also* **civil servant; domestic** 1 A; **public servant**

**'servant girl** *n.* Dienstmädchen, *das*

**'servants' hall** *n.* Dienstbotenzimmer, *das*

**serve** /sɜ:v/ **1** *v.t.* **A** (*work for*) dienen (+ *Dat.*); **she had ~d the family well for ten years** sie hatte der Familie zehn Jahre lang gute Dienste geleistet; ~ **two masters** (*fig.*) auf beiden Schultern Wasser tragen; **B** (*be useful to*) dienlich sein (+ *Dat.*); **this car ~d us well** dieses Auto hat uns gute Dienste getan; **if my memory ~s me right** wenn mich mein Gedächtnis nicht täuscht; **C** (*meet needs of*) nutzen (+ *Dat.*); **in order to ~ some private ends** für Privatzwecke; **that excuse will not ~ you** die Entschuldigung wird dir nichts nützen; **one packet ~s him for a week** eine Packung reicht ihm für eine Woche; ~ **a/no purpose** einen Zweck erfüllen/keinen Zweck haben *od.* zwecklos sein; ~ **sb.'s needs** *or* **purpose[s]** *or* **turn** jmds. Zweck (*Dat.*) genügen; ~ **its purpose** *or* **turn** seinen Zweck erfüllen; ~ **the purpose of doing sth.** den Zweck erfüllen *od.* dem Zweck genügen, etw. zu tun; **D** (*go through period of*) durchlaufen ‹Lehre›; absitzen, verbüßen ‹Haftstrafe›; ~ **a four-year term as Prime Minister** vier Jahre lang Premierminister sein; ~ **one's time** (*hold office*) seine Amtszeit ableisten; ~ **[one's] time** (*undergo apprenticeship*) seine Lehrzeit durchmachen; (*perform military service*) seinen Wehrdienst ableisten; (*undergo imprisonment*) seine Zeit absitzen; **E** (*dish up*) servieren; (*pour out*) einschenken (**to** *Dat.*); **dinner is ~d** das Essen ist aufgetragen; ~ **tea in china cups** Tee in Porzellantassen reichen; **F** (*render obedience to*) dienen (+ *Dat.*) ‹Gott, König, Land›; **G** (*attend*) bedienen; **are you being ~d?** werden Sie schon bedient?; **H** (*supply*) versorgen; **~s three** (*in recipe*) für drei Personen *od.* Portionen; **I** (*provide with food*) bedienen; **has everyone been ~d?** sind alle bedient?; **J** (*make legal delivery of*) zustellen; ~ **a summons on sb.**

S

jmdn. vorladen; **he has been ~d notice to quit** ihm ist gekündigt worden; **~ sb. with a writ, ~ a writ on sb.** jmdm. eine Verfügung zustellen; **K** (*Tennis etc.*) aufschlagen; **~ many double faults** viele Doppelfehler machen; **~ an ace** ein As schlagen; **L** (*arch./literary: treat*) behandeln; **~ sb. ill/well** jmdm. einen schlechten/guten Dienst erweisen; **M** **~[s]** *or* **it ~s him right!** [das] geschieht ihm recht!; **N** (*copulate with*) ‹Tier:› decken.

**2** *v.i.* **A** (*do service*) dienen; **~ as chairman** das Amt des Vorsitzenden innehaben; **~ as a Member of Parliament** Mitglied des Parlaments sein; **~ on a jury** Geschworener/Geschworene sein; **~ on a board** Mitglied des Aufsichtsrates sein; **B** (*be employed; be soldier etc.*) dienen; Dienst tun; **he ~d against the Russians** er hat gegen die Russen gekämpft; **C** (*be of use*) **~ to do sth.** dazu dienen, etw. zu tun; **~ to show sth.** etw. zeigen; **if memory ~s** wenn mein Gedächtnis mich nicht trügt; **for him nothing would ~ but ...:** er war nur mit ... zufrieden zu stellen; **~ for** *or* **as** dienen als; **it will ~:** das geht schon; das tuts (*ugs.*); **D** (*~ food*) **be employed to ~ at table** zum Auftragen eingestellt sein; **shall I ~?** soll ich auftragen?; **E** (*attend in shop etc.*) bedienen; **F** (*Eccl.*) ministrieren; **G** (*Tennis etc.*) aufschlagen; **it's your turn to ~:** du hast Aufschlag.

**3** *n.* ⇒ **service** 1 H

**~ 'out** *v.t.* **A** (*distribute*) austeilen; ausgeben; **B** (*work*) ableisten ‹Dienst›; beenden ‹Lehrzeit›; **C** (*punish in return*) **~ sb. out** es jmdm. heimzahlen

**~ 'up** *v.t.* **A** (*put before eaters*) servieren; **B** (*offer for consideration*) auftischen (*ugs.*)

**server** /'sɜːvə(r)/ *n.* (*Computing*) Server, *der*

**service** /'sɜːvɪs/ **1** *n.* **A** (*doing of work for employer etc.*) Dienst, *der;* **give good ~:** gute Dienste leisten; **do ~ as sth.** als etw. dienen; **see ~** ‹Gerät:› seine Dienste tun; **he has seen ~ in the tropics** er hat in den Tropen Dienst getan; **sth. has seen long ~:** etw. hat lange Zeit gute Dienste geleistet; **he died in the ~ of his country** er starb in Pflichterfüllung für sein Vaterland; **have thirty years' ~ behind one** dreißig Jahre Dienstzeit hinter sich (*Dat.*) haben; **B** (*sth. done to help others*) **do sb. a ~:** jmdm. einen guten Dienst erweisen; **~s** Dienste; (*Econ.*) Dienstleistungen; **ask for sb.'s ~s** jmdn. um Unterstützung bitten; **do you need the ~s of a doctor?** brauchen Sie einen Arzt?; **[in recognition of her] ~s to the hospital/state** [in Anerkennung ihrer] Verdienste um das Krankenhaus/den Staat; **C** (*Eccl.*) Gottesdienst, *der;* **D** (*act of attending to customer*) Service, *der;* (*in shop, garage, etc.*) Bedienung, *die;* **E** (*system of transport*) Verbindung, *die;* **airline ~:** Flugverbindung, *die;* **there is no bus ~ on Sundays** sonntags verkehren keine Busse; **the number 325 bus ~:** die Buslinie Nr. 325; **when does the Oxford ~ leave?** wann fährt der Zug/Bus nach Oxford ab?; **F** (*provision of maintenance*) **[after-sale** *or* **follow-up] ~:** Kundendienst, *der;* **ask for a ~:** den Kundendienst kommen lassen; **take one's car in for a ~:** sein Auto zur Inspektion bringen; **G** *no pl., no art.* (*operation*) Betrieb, *der;* **bring into ~:** in Betrieb nehmen; **out of ~:** außer Betrieb; **take out of ~:** außer Betrieb setzen; **go** *or* **come into ~:** in Betrieb genommen werden; **H** (*Tennis etc.*) Aufschlag, *der;* **whose ~ is it?** wer hat Aufschlag?; **I** (*crockery set*) Service, *das;* **dessert/tea ~:** Dessert-/Tee-Service, *das;* **J** (*legal delivery*) Zustellung, *die;* **K** (*assistance*) **can I be of ~ [to you]?** kann ich Ihnen behilflich sein?; **will it be of ~ to you?** wird es Ihnen helfen?; **L** (*payment*) Bedienung, *die;* Bedienungsgeld, *das;* ⇒ *also* **service charge**; **M** (*person's behalf*) **in his ~:** in seinem Auftrag; **I'm at your ~:** ich stehe zu Ihren Diensten; **'on His/Her Majesty's ~'** (*Brit.*) „[gebührenfreie] Dienstsache"; **N** (*department of public employ*) **the consular ~:** der Konsulatsdienst; **the rail-way/telephone ~:** das Eisenbahnwesen/der Telefondienst; **BBC World S~:** BBC Weltsender; **public ~:** öffentlicher Dienst; ⇒ *also* **Civil Service**; **Secret Service**; **O** *in pl.* (*Brit.: public supply*) Versorgungseinrichtungen; **cut off all the ~s** Gas, Wasser und Strom abstellen; **P** (*Mil.*) **the [armed** *or* **fighting] ~s** die Streitkräfte; **in the ~s** beim Militär; **be on ~:** dienen; **see ~:** im Einsatz sein; **Q** (*being servant*) **be in/go into ~:** in Stellung sein/gehen (*veralt.*) (**with** bei); **R** (*employ*) Stellung, *die;* **enter the ~ of sb.** bei jmdm. in Stellung gehen (*veralt.*); **take sb. into one's ~:** jmdn. in seine Dienste nehmen.

**2** *v.t.* **A** (*provide maintenance for*) warten ‹Wagen, Waschmaschine, Heizung›; **take one's car to be ~d** sein Auto zur Inspektion bringen; **B** (*perform business function for*) versorgen; **C** (*pay interest on*) Zinsen zahlen für ‹Schulden›; **D** (*copulate with*) ‹Tier:› decken.

**3** *adj.* militärisch; Militär‹fahrzeug, -flugzeug›; **a ~ family** die Familie eines Militärangehörigen

**serviceable** /'sɜːvɪsəbl/ *adj.* **A** (*useful*) nützlich; **B** (*durable*) haltbar; **the shoes are ~ rather than fashionable** die Schuhe sind eher praktisch als modisch

**service: ~ area** *n.* **A** (*for motorists' needs*) Raststätte, *die;* **B** (*Radio, Telev.*) Sendebereich, *der;* **~ book** *n.* (*Eccl.*) Gesangbuch, *das;* **~ charge** *n.* (*in restaurant*) Bedienungsgeld, *das;* (*of bank*) Bearbeitungsgebühr, *die;* **~ court** *n.* (*Tennis etc.*) Aufschlagfeld, *das;* **~ dress** *n., no pl.* Dienstkleidung, *die;* **~ engineer** *n.* Servicetechniker, *der*/-technikerin, *die;* **~ flat** *n.* (*Brit.*) Wohnung mit Betreuung; **~ hatch** *n.* Durchreiche, *die;* **~ industry** *n.* Dienstleistungsbetrieb, *der;* **~ lift** *n.* Lastenaufzug, *der;* **~man** /'sɜːvɪsmən/ *n., pl.* **~men** /'sɜːvɪsmən/ (*in armed ~s*) Militärangehörige, *der;* **~ provider** *n.* **A** (*Computing*) Provider, *der;* **Internet ~ provider** Internetanbieter, *der;* **B** (*person or firm providing service*) Dienstleister, *der*/Dienstleisterin, *die;* **~ road** *n.* Zufahrtsstraße, *die;* **~ sector** *n.* Dienstleistungssektor, *der;* **~ station** *n.* Tankstelle, *die;* **~woman** *n.* Militärangehörige, *die*

**serviette** /sɜːvɪ'et/ *n.* (*Brit.*) Serviette, *die*

**servi'ette ring** *n.* (*Brit.*) Serviettenring, *der*

**servile** /'sɜːvaɪl/ *adj.* unterwürfig; erbärmlich ‹Unterwürfigkeit, Furcht›

**servilely** /'sɜːvaɪlɪ/ *adv.* unterwürfig

**servility** /sɜː'vɪlɪtɪ/ *n., no pl.* Unterwürfigkeit, *die*

**serving** /'sɜːvɪŋ/ **1** *n.* (*quantity*) Portion, *die.* **2** *adj.* dienend

**serving: ~ dish** *n.* Servierschüssel, *die;* **~ hatch** *n.* Durchreiche, *die;* **~ spoon** *n.* Vorlegelöffel, *der*

**servitude** /'sɜːvɪtjuːd/ *n., no pl.* (*lit. or fig.*) Knechtschaft, *die;* ⇒ *also* **penal servitude**

**servo** /'sɜːvəʊ/ *n., pl.* **~s** Servoeinrichtung, *die*

**servo: ~-assisted** *adj.* **~-assisted brakes** Servobremsen; **~mechanism** *n.* Servomechanismus, *der;* **~motor** *n.* Servomotor, *der*

**sesame** /'sesəmɪ/ *n.* **A** (*herb*) Sesam, *der;* **B** (*seed*) **~ [seed]** Sesamkorn, *das;* **C** **open ~!** Sesam, öffne dich!; **an open ~:** ein Sesam-öffne-dich

**sessile** /'sesaɪl/ *adj.* (*Bot., Zool.*) sessil (*fachspr.*); festsitzend

**'sessile oak** *n.* Traubeneiche, *die*

**session** /'seʃn/ *n.* **A** (*meeting*) Sitzung, *die;* **discussion ~:** Diskussionsrunde, *die;* **be in ~:** tagen; **B** (*period spent*) Sitzung, *die;* (*by several people*) Treffen, *das;* **have daily tennis ~s with sb.** mit jmdm. täglich Tennis spielen; **let's have a cleaning ~ tomorrow** lass/lasst uns morgen [mal] groß reinemachen; **recording ~:** Aufnahme, *die;* **have a card ~:** zusammen Karten spielen; **C** (*Brit.: academic year*) Studienjahr, *das;* **D** (*Amer.: university term*) Vorlesungsperiode, *die;* **the summer ~:** die Sommervorlesungen; **E** (*time for meeting*) Sitzung, *die;* **summer ~s** Sommersitzungsperiode, *die;* **F** (*Eccl.*) Kirchenvorstand, *der;* **G** (*Law*) **Court of S~** *oberstes schottisches Zivilgericht;* **petty ~s** *summarisches Schnellverfahren vor mehreren Friedensrichtern;* ⇒ *also* **quarter sessions**

**sestet** /ses'tet/ *n.* **A** ⇒ **sextet**; **B** (*Pros.*) Sextett, *das*

**sestina** /ses'tiːnə/ *n.* (*Pros.*) Sestine, *die*

**set** /set/ **1** *v.t.*, **-tt-, set** **A** (*put*) (*horizontally*) legen; (*vertically*) stellen; **~ sb. ashore** jmdn. an Land setzen; **~ food before sb.** jmdm. Essen hinstellen; **~ one brick on another** einen Stein auf den anderen setzen; **~ the proposals before the board** (*fig.*) dem Vorstand die Vorschläge unterbreiten *od.* vorlegen; **~ sth. against sth.** (*balance*) etw. einer Sache (*Dat.*) gegenüberstellen; **B** (*apply*) setzen; **~ pen to paper** etwas zu Papier bringen; **~ a match to sth.** ein Streichholz an etw. halten; ⇒ *also* **fire** 1 A; **hand** 1 A; **light**[1] 1 E; **seal**[2] 1 C; **shoulder** 1 A; **C** (*adjust*) einstellen (**at** auf + *Akk.*); aufstellen ‹Falle›; stellen ‹Uhr›; **~ your watch by mine** stell deine Uhr nach meiner; **~ the alarm for 5.30 a.m.** den Wecker auf 5.30 Uhr stellen; **D** **be ~** (*have location of action*) ‹Buch, Film:› spielen; **~ a book/film in Australia/a brothel** ein Buch/einen Film in Australien/in einem Bordell spielen lassen; **E** (*specify*) festlegen ‹Bedingungen›; festsetzen ‹Termin, Ort usw.› (**for** auf + *Akk.*); **~ the interest rate at 10%** die Zinsen auf 10% festsetzen; **~ limits** Grenzen setzen; **F** (*bring into specified state*) **~ sth./things right** *or* **in order** etw./die Dinge in Ordnung bringen; **~ sb. laughing** jmdn. zum Lachen bringen; **~ a dog barking** einen Hund anschlagen lassen; **~ sb. thinking that ...:** jmdn. auf den Gedanken bringen, dass ...; **the news ~ me thinking** die Nachricht machte mich nachdenklich; ⇒ *also* **cap** 1 A; **defiance**; **ease** 1 A; **edge** 1 A; **fire** 1 B; **foot** 1 A; **free** 1 A; **go**[1] 1 F; **house** 1 A; **motion** 1 A; **rest**[1] 3 B; **right** 1 D, 3 E; **G** (*put forward*) stellen ‹Frage, Aufgabe›; aufgeben ‹Hausaufgabe›; vorschreiben ‹Textbuch, Lektüre›; (*compose*) zusammenstellen ‹Rätsel, Fragen, Prüfungsaufgaben›; **~ sb. an example, ~ an example to sb.** jmdm. ein Beispiel geben; **~ sb. a task/problem** jmdm. eine Aufgabe stellen/jmdn. vor ein Problem stellen; **~ [sb./oneself] a target** [jmdm./sich] ein Ziel setzen; **H** (*turn to solid*) fest werden lassen; **is the jelly ~ yet?** ist das Gelee schon fest?; **I** (*put in ground to grow*) einpflanzen, setzen ‹Pflanzen›; säen ‹Samen›; **J** (*lay for meal*) decken ‹Tisch›; auflegen ‹Gedeck›; **K** (*place for visitor*) aufstellen ‹Stuhl, Tisch›; **L** **~ sail** (*hoist sail*) die Segel setzen *od.* hissen; (*begin voyage*) losfahren (**for** nach); **M** **~ a watch** (*guard*) eine Wache aufstellen; **~ the watch** (*Naut.*) die Wache aufstellen; **N** (*establish*) aufstellen ‹Rekord, Richtlinien›; **~ the fashion for sth.** etw. in Mode bringen; **~ the pace** das Tempo bestimmen; **O** (*Med.: put into place*) [ein]richten; einrenken ‹verrenktes Gelenk›; **P** (*fix*) legen ‹Haare›; **~ eyes on sb./sth.** jmdn./etw. sehen; **~ one's teeth** (*lit. or fig.*) die Zähne zusammenbeißen; ⇒ *also* **face** 1 A; **heart** 1 B; **hope** 1; **mind** 1 C; **price** 1 A; **scene** H; **store** 1 F; **value** 1 A; **Q** (*Printing*) setzen; **~ close/out** *or* **wide** eng/breit setzen; **R** **~ sb. to sth./doing sth.** jmdn. zu etw. anhalten/jmdn. veranlassen, etw. zu tun; **~ sb. wood-chopping** jmdn. Holz hacken schicken; **~ oneself to sth./do sth.** sich an etw. (*Akk.*) machen/daran machen, etw. zu tun; **~ sb. in charge of sth.** jmdn. mit etw. betrauen; **~ a dog on sb.** einen Hund auf jmdn. hetzen; **~ a dog/the police after sb.** einen Hund/die Polizei auf jmdn. hetzen; **they ~ their thugs/detectives on him** sie setzten ihre Schläger/Detektive auf ihn an; **~ sb. against sb.** jmdn. gegen jmdn. aufbringen; **~ father against son** Zwietracht säen zwischen Vater und Sohn; ⇒ *also* **work** 1 A; **S** **~ sth. to music** *or* **a tune** etw. vertonen; **T** (*ornament*) besetzen; [ein]fassen ‹Edelstein, Ränder›; bepflanzen ‹Beet›; **the lid was ~ with gems** der Deckel war mit Edelsteinen besetzt; **a sky ~ with stars** ein sternenbesetzter Himmel; **U** **be ~ on a hill** ‹Haus:› auf einem Hügel stehen; **V** (*make fast*) fixieren ‹Farbe, Färbemittel›.

❷ *v.i.*, **-tt-, set** [A] (*solidify*) fest werden; **has the jelly ~ yet?** ist das Gelee schon fest?; [B] (*go down*) ‹Sonne, Mond:› untergehen; **sb.'s star ~s** (*fig.*) jmds. Stern ist im Sinken begriffen; [C] (*flow along*) **the current ~s eastwards** die Strömung geht nach Osten; **~ against sth.** (*fig.*) sich gegen etw. richten; [D] (*Bot.*) (*form into or develop fruit*) ‹Blüte, Pflanze:› Frucht ansetzen; (*develop out of blossom*) ‹Frucht:› sich entwickeln; [E] ‹Gesicht:› sich verhärten (**with** vor + *Dat.*); [F] (*take rigid attitude*) **~ [rigidly]** ‹Jagdhund:› [fest] vorstehen.

❸ *n.* [A] (*group*) Satz, *der;* **~ [of two]** Paar, *das;* **a ~ of chairs** eine Sitzgruppe; eine Stuhlgarnitur; **a ~ of stamps** ein Satz Briefmarken; **a complete ~ of Dickens' novels** eine Gesamtausgabe der Romane von Dickens; **a ~ of lectures** eine Vortragsreihe; **chess ~:** Schachspiel, *das;* [B] ⇒ **service** 1 I; [C] (*section of society*) Kreis, *der;* **racing ~:** Rennsportfreunde *od.* -fans; **the younger ~:** die Jüngeren; **the fast ~:** die Lebewelt; ⇒ *also* **jet set; smart** 1 C; [D] (*Math.*) Menge, *die;* **theory of ~s** Mengenlehre, *die;* [E] **~ [of teeth]** Gebiss, *das;* [F] (*radio or TV receiver*) Gerät, *das;* Apparat, *der;* [G] (*Tennis*) Satz, *der;* [H] (*of hair*) Frisieren, *das;* Einlegen, *das;* **have a shampoo and ~:** sich (*Dat.*) die Haare waschen und legen lassen; [I] (*Theatre: built-up scenery*) Szenenaufbau, *der;* [J] (*area of performance*) (*of film*) Drehort, *der;* (*of play*) Bühne, *die;* **on the ~** (*for film*) bei den Dreharbeiten; (*for play*) bei den Proben; [K] (*granite paving block*) Pflasterstein, *der;* [L] (*burrow*) Bau, *der;* [M] (*of dog*) **[dead] ~:** Vorstehen, *das;* **make a dead ~ at sb.** (*fig.*) (*try to win affections of*) sich an jmdn. heranmachen; (*attack*) über jmdn. herfallen; [N] (*Hort.*) (*shoot, cutting*) Setzling, *der;* (*bulb*) Knolle, *die;* Zwiebel, *die;* [O] (*literary: sunset*) **at ~ of sun** bei Sonnenuntergang; [P] *no pl.* (*posture*) Haltung, *die;* **the ~ of his head** seine Kopfhaltung; [Q] (*way dress etc. sits or flows*) Sitz, *der.*

❹ *adj.* [A] (*fixed*) starr ‹Linie, Gewohnheit, Blick, Lächeln›; fest ‹Absichten, Zielvorstellungen, Zeitpunkt›; **be ~ in one's ways** *or* **habits** in seinen Gewohnheiten festgefahren sein; **deep-~ eyes** tief liegende Augen; [B] (*assigned for study or discussion*) vorgeschrieben ‹Buch, Text›; bestimmt, festgelegt ‹Thema›; **be a ~ book** Pflichtlektüre sein; [C] (*according to fixed menu*) **~ meal** *or* **menu** Menü, *das;* [D] (*ready*) **sth. is ~ to increase** etw. wird bald steigen; **be/get ~ for sth.** zu etw. bereit sein/sich zu etw. fertig machen; **be/get ~ to leave** bereit sein/sich fertig machen zum Aufbruch; **all ~?** (*coll.*) alles klar *od.* fertig?; **be all ~ for sth.** zu etw. bereit sein; **be all ~ to do sth.** bereit sein, etw. zu tun; **are we all ~?** alle startklar? (*ugs.*); [E] (*determined*) **be ~ on sth./doing sth.** zu etw. entschlossen sein/entschlossen sein, etw. zu tun; **be [dead] ~ against sth.** [absolut] gegen etw. sein; **of ~ purpose** mit Absicht; absichtlich; ⇒ *also* **close-set**

**~ about** *v.t.* [A] (*begin purposefully*) **~ about sth.** sich an etw. (*Akk.*) machen; etw. in Angriff nehmen; **~ about doing sth.** sich daranmachen, etw. zu tun; [B] (*spread*) verbreiten ‹Gerücht, Geschichte›; [C] (*coll.: attack*) herfallen über (+ *Akk.*)

**~ a'part** *v.t.* [A] (*reserve*) reservieren; einplanen ‹Zeit›; [B] (*make different*) abheben (**from** von); **his strength ~s him apart from others** durch seine Kraft zeichnet er sich gegenüber anderen aus

**~ a'side** *v.t.* [A] (*put to one side*) beiseite legen ‹Buch, Zeitung, Strickzeug›; beiseite stellen ‹Stuhl, Glas usw.›; unterbrechen ‹Arbeit, Tätigkeit›; außer Acht lassen ‹Frage›; unberücksichtigt lassen ‹Angebot›; (*postpone*) aufschieben ‹Arbeit›; [B] (*cancel*) aufheben ‹Urteil, Entscheidung›; [C] (*pay no attention to*) außer Acht lassen ‹Unterschiede, Formalitäten›; begraben ‹Feindschaft›; vergessen ‹Bitterkeit, Stolz, Eifersucht›; abschaffen ‹Recht›; [D] (*reserve*) aufheben ‹Essen, Zutaten›; einplanen ‹Minute, Zeit›; beiseite legen ‹Geld›; (*save for customer*) zurücklegen ‹Ware›; **why don't you ~ aside a day to come and visit me?** halt dir doch [einfach] einen Tag frei, an dem du mich besuchen kommst!

**~ 'back** *v.t.* [A] (*hinder progress of*) behindern ‹Fortschritt›; aufhalten ‹Entwicklung›; zurückwerfen ‹Projekt, Programm›; [B] (*coll.: be an expense to*) **~ sb. back a fair amount/sum** jmdn. eine hübsche Summe kosten; [C] (*place at a distance*) zurücksetzen; **the house is ~ back some distance from the road** das Haus steht in einiger Entfernung von der Straße; [D] (*postpone*) verschieben ‹Termin› (**to** auf + *Akk.*). ⇒ *also* **setback**

**~ 'by** ⇒ **~ aside** A, D

**~ 'down** *v.t.* [A] (*allow to alight*) absetzen ‹Fahrgast, Ladung›; **the bus will ~ you down there** der Bus hält dort; du kannst dort aus dem Bus aussteigen; [B] (*record on paper*) niederschreiben; [C] (*place on surface*) absetzen; abstellen; [D] (*fix*) anberaumen ‹Sitzung, Treffen, Anhörung usw.›; [E] (*attribute*) zuschreiben (**to** *Dat.*); [F] **~ down as** *or* **for** *or* **to be** (*judge*) halten für; (*record*) eintragen als

**~ 'forth** ❶ *v.i.* (*begin journey*) aufbrechen; **~ forth on a journey** eine Reise antreten. ❷ *v.t.* (*present*) darstellen ‹Zahlen, Kosten›; darlegen ‹Programm, Ziel, Politik›

**~ 'forward** *v.t.* [A] (*move further in front*) weiter nach vorn stellen *od.* setzen; [B] (*present*) darlegen ‹Programm, Plan usw.›; [C] (*bring forward in time*) voranbringen ‹Ernte, Entwicklung usw.›; [D] vorstellen ‹Uhr›

**~ 'in** ❶ *v.i.* (*gain a hold*) ‹Dunkelheit, Regen, Reaktion, Verfall:› einsetzen; ‹Mode:› aufkommen. ❷ *v.t.* (*insert*) einsetzen

**~ 'off** ❶ *v.i.* (*begin journey*) aufbrechen; (*start to move*) loslaufen; ‹Zug:› losfahren; **~ off for work** sich auf den Weg zur Arbeit machen. ❷ *v.t.* [A] (*show to advantage*) hervorheben; [B] (*start*) führen zu; auslösen ‹Reaktion, Alarmanlage›; einleiten ‹Entwicklung›; in Umlauf setzen ‹Gerücht›; **~ sb. off into hysterics** jmdn. hysterisch werden lassen; **~ sb. off thinking/laughing** jmdn. zum Nachdenken anregen/zum Lachen bringen; [C] (*cause to explode*) explodieren lassen; abbrennen ‹Feuerwerk›; [D] (*counterbalance*) ausgleichen; **~ sth. off against sth.** etw. einer Sache (*Dat.*) gegenüberstellen; (*use as compensatory item*) etw. als Ausgleich für etw. nehmen

**~ on** *v.t.* (*attack*) überfallen

**~ 'out** ❶ *v.i.* [A] (*begin journey*) aufbrechen; [B] (*begin with intention*) **~ out to do sth.** sich (*Dat.*) vornehmen, etw. zu tun; **~ out in business** sein eigenes Geschäft aufmachen; **~ out on a career as ...:** eine Laufbahn als ... einschlagen. ❷ *v.t.* [A] (*present*) darlegen ‹Gedanke, Argument›; auslegen ‹Waren›; ausbreiten ‹Geschenke›; aufstellen ‹Schachfiguren›; setzen ‹Pflanzen›; [B] (*state, specify*) darlegen ‹Bedingungen, Einwände, Vorschriften›; [C] (*mark out*) entwerfen. ⇒ *also* **set-out**

**~ over** *v.t.* stellen über (+ *Akk.*)

**~ 'to** *v.i.* [A] (*begin vigorously*) sich daranmachen; (*begin eating hungrily*) es sich (*Dat.*) schmecken lassen; [B] (*begin to fight*) loslegen (*ugs.*); ⇒ *also* **set-to**

**~ 'up** ❶ *v.t.* [A] (*erect*) errichten ‹Straßensperre, Denkmal›; aufstellen ‹Kamera›; aufbauen ‹Zelt, Klapptisch›; **~ up the type** setzen; **~ up a column in type** eine Spalte setzen; [B] (*establish*) bilden ‹Regierung usw.›; gründen ‹Gesellschaft, Organisation, Orden›; aufbauen ‹Kontrollsystem, Verteidigung›; einleiten ‹Untersuchung›; einrichten ‹Büro›; **~ oneself up as a dentist/in business** sich als Zahnarzt niederlassen/ein Geschäft aufmachen; **~ sb. up in business** jmdm. die Gründung eines eigenen Geschäfts ermöglichen; [C] (*begin to utter*) anstimmen; **the class ~ up such a din** die Klasse veranstaltete einen solchen Lärm; [D] (*cause*) auslösen ‹Infektion, Reaktion›; [E] (*coll.: make stronger*) stärken; **a good breakfast should ~ you up for the day** ein gutes Frühstück gibt dir Kraft für den ganzen Tag; **well ~ up** kerngesund; kraftstrotzend; [F] (*achieve*) aufstellen ‹Rekord, Zeit›; [G] (*provide adequately*) **~ sb. up with sth.** jmdn. mit etw. versorgen *od.* (*ugs.*) eindecken; [H] (*place in view*) anbringen ‹Schild, Warnung›; hissen ‹Flagge›; [I] (*prepare*) vorbereiten ‹Experiment›; betriebsbereit machen ‹Maschine›; [J] (*propound*) aufstellen ‹Theorie›; [K] **~ sb. up** (*coll.: frame*) jmdm. die Schuld in die Schuhe schieben. ⇒ *also* **house** 1 A; **set-up; shop** 1 B. ❷ *v.i.* **~ up in business/in the fashion trade** ein Geschäft aufmachen/sich in der Modebranche etablieren; **~ up as a dentist** sich als Zahnarzt niederlassen. ❸ *v. refl.* **~ oneself up as** *or* **to be sb./sth.** (*coll.*) sich als jmd./etw. aufspielen

**set: ~back** *n.* [A] (*checking of progress*) Rückschlag, *der;* [B] (*defeat*) Niederlage, *die;* **~-off** *n.* [A] (*counterbalance*) Ausgleich, *der* (**against** für); [B] (*Commerc., Law*) Ausgleich, *der* (**to, against** für); **by ~-off against other cheques** durch Verrechnung mit anderen Schecks; [C] (*start*) Aufbruch, *der;* [D] (*adornment*) Zier, *die;* **~-out** *n.* (*commencement*) Start, *der;* **~ phrase** *n.* feste Wendung; Phrase, *die;* **~ 'piece** *n.* [A] (*design formed with fireworks*) Bild aus Feuerwerkskörpern; [B] (*Footb.*) Standardsituation, *die;* **~ point** *n.* (*Tennis etc.*) Satzball, *der;* **~ 'screw** *n.* (*Mech. Engin.*) Stellschraube, *die;* **~ 'scrum** *n.* (*Rugby*) Gedränge, *das;* **~ 'speech** *n.* fertige Rede; **~ square** *n.* Zeichendreieck, *das*

**sett** /set/ ⇒ **set** 3 K, L, N

**settee** /se'ti:/ *n.* Sofa, *das*

**setter** /'setə(r)/ *n.* (*dog*) Setter, *der*

**'set theory** *n.* (*Math.*) Mengenlehre, *die*

**setting** /'setɪŋ/ *n.* [A] (*Mus.*) Vertonung, *die;* [B] (*frame for jewel*) Fassung, *die;* [C] (*surroundings*) Rahmen, *der;* (*of novel etc.*) Schauplatz, *der;* **a cottage in a pleasant ~:** ein Häuschen in schöner Umgebung; [D] (*Theatre*) Bühnendekoration, *die;* [E] (*plates and cutlery*) Gedeck, *das*

**'setting lotion** *n.* Haarfestiger, *der*

**settle** /'setl/ ❶ *v.t.* [A] (*place*) (*horizontally*) [sorgfältig] legen; (*vertically*) [sorgfältig] stellen; (*at an angle*) [sorgfältig] lehnen; **~ a patient in his bed/an armchair** einen Patienten richtig ins Bett legen/im Sessel zurechtsetzen; **he ~d himself comfortably on the couch** er machte es sich (*Dat.*) auf der Couch bequem; [B] (*establish*) (*in house or business*) unterbringen; (*in country or colony*) ansiedeln ‹Volk›; **we got them ~d in their new house** wir haben ihnen geholfen, sich in ihrem neuen Haus einzurichten; [C] (*determine, resolve*) aushandeln, sich einigen auf ‹Preis›; beilegen ‹Streit, Konflikt, Meinungsverschiedenheit›; beseitigen, ausräumen ‹Zweifel, Bedenken›; entscheiden ‹Frage, Spiel›; regeln, in Ordnung bringen ‹Angelegenheit›; entscheiden über (+ *Akk.*) ‹Sieger›; festlegen, planen ‹Urlaub›; **nothing has been ~d as yet** es ist noch nichts entschieden; **that should ~ the match** damit dürfte das Spiel entschieden sein; **~ the matter among yourselves!** macht das unter euch aus!; **that ~s it** dann ist ja alles klar (*ugs.*); *expr. exasperation* jetzt reicht's! (*ugs.*); **~ a case out of court** sich außergerichtlich vergleichen; **~ one's affairs** seine Angelegenheiten in Ordnung bringen; seinen Nachlass regeln; **~ the day/date/place** den Tag/Termin/Ort festsetzen *od.* festlegen; **is the date ~d yet?** steht der Termin schon fest?; [D] (*deal with, dispose of*) fertig werden mit; ⇒ *also* **hash**[1] 1; [E] (*pay money owed according to*) bezahlen, (*geh.*) begleichen ‹Rechnung, Betrag›; erfüllen ‹Forderung, Anspruch›; ausgleichen ‹Konto›; ⇒ *also* **score** 1 F; [F] (*cause to sink*) sich absetzen lassen ‹Bodensatz, Sand, Sediment›; **a shower will ~ the dust** ein Schauer wird den Staub binden; [G] (*calm*) beruhigen ‹Nerven, Magen›; (*aid digestion of*) verdauen ‹Essen›; [H] (*colonize*) besiedeln; [I] (*bestow*) **~ money/property on sb.** jmdm. Geld/Besitz übereignen; **~ an annuity on sb.** jmdm. eine Rente aussetzen. ❷ *v.i.* [A] (*become established*) sich niederlassen; (*as colonist*) sich ansiedeln; [B] (*end dispute*) sich einigen; [C] (*pay what is owed*) abrechnen; [D] (*in chair, in front of the fire, etc.*) sich niederlassen; (*to work etc.*) sich konzentrieren (**to** auf + *Akk.*); (*into way of life, retirement, middle age, etc.*) sich gewöhnen (**into** an + *Akk.*); **it took a long time to ~ in our new house** es dauerte lange, bis wir uns

S

in unserem neuen Haus richtig eingelebt hatten; **the cold ~d on her chest** die Erkältung hat sich ihr auf die Bronchien gelegt; **the snow/dust ~d on the ground** der Schnee blieb liegen/der Staub setzte sich [am Boden] ab; **darkness/silence/fog ~d over the village** Dunkelheit/Stille/Nebel legte *od.* senkte sich über das Dorf; ⇒ *also* **dust** 1 A; Ⓔ (*subside*) ‹Haus, Fundament, Boden:› sich senken; (*sink*) ‹Schiff:› sinken; ‹Sediment:› sich ablagern; ‹Kristalle:› sich absetzen (**at, on** auf + *Dat.*); Ⓕ (*be digested*) ‹Essen:› sich setzen; (*become calm*) ‹Magen:› sich beruhigen; Ⓖ (*become clear*) ‹Wein, Bier:› sich klären

~ **'back** *v.i.* Ⓐ (*relax*) sich zurücklehnen (**in** in + *Dat.*); Ⓑ ~ **back into one's routine** sich wieder in die Alltagsroutine hineinfinden

~ **'down** ❶ *v.i.* Ⓐ (*make oneself comfortable*) sich niederlassen (**in** in + *Dat.*); ~ **down for the night** sich schlafen *od.* zur Ruhe legen; Ⓑ (*become established in a place*) (*in town or house*) sesshaft *od.* heimisch werden; (*in school*) sich eingewöhnen (**in** in + *Akk.*); ~ **down in a job** (*find permanent work*) eine feste Anstellung finden; (*get used to a job*) sich einarbeiten; Ⓒ (*marry*) **it's about time he ~d down** er sollte allmählich häuslich werden [und heiraten]; ~ **down to married life** ein häusliches Eheleben beginnen; Ⓓ (*calm down*) ‹Person:› sich beruhigen; ‹Lärm, Aufregung:› sich legen; ~ **down to work** richtig mit der Arbeit anfangen. ❷ *v.t.* Ⓐ (*make comfortable*) ~ **oneself down** sich [gemütlich] hinsetzen; ~ **oneself down in a chair** sich [gemütlich] auf einen Stuhl setzen; ~ **the baby down for the night/to sleep** das Baby schlafen legen; Ⓑ (*calm down*) beruhigen

~ **for** *v.t.* Ⓐ (*agree to*) sich zufrieden geben mit; Ⓑ (*decide on*) sich entscheiden für

~ **'in** ❶ *v.i.* (*in new home*) sich einleben; (*in new job or school*) sich eingewöhnen. ❷ *v.t.* **we all helped to ~ them in** wir trugen alle dazu bei, dass sie heimisch wurden

~ **on** *v.t.* Ⓐ (*decide on*) sich entscheiden für; Ⓑ (*agree on*) sich einigen auf (+ *Akk.*)

~ **'up** *v.i.* abrechnen; ~ **up with the waiter** beim Kellner bezahlen

~ **with** *v.t.* ~ **with sb.** (*pay agreed amount to sb.*) jmdm. eine Abfindung zahlen; (*pay all the money owed to sb.*) bei jmdm. seine Rechnung begleichen; (*fig.*) mit jmdm. abrechnen; **now to ~ with 'you!** jetzt bist du dran! (*ugs.*)

**settled** /'setld/ *adj.* fest ‹Meinung, Überzeugung, Grundsätze, Gewohnheit›; festgelegt ‹Verfahren›; vorausbestimmt ‹Zukunft›; beständig ‹Wetter›; geregelt ‹Lebensweise›; **I don't feel ~ in this house/job** ich kann mich in diesem Haus nicht heimisch fühlen/in diese Arbeit nicht hineinfinden; **we can now expect ~ weather** jetzt ist eine Wetterberuhigung zu erwarten

**settlement** /'setlmənt/ *n.* Ⓐ Entscheidung, *die;* (*in relation to price*) Einigung, *die;* (*of argument, conflict, dispute, differences, troubles*) Beilegung, *die;* (*of problem*) Lösung, *die;* (*of question*) Klärung, *die;* (*of affairs*) Regelung, *die;* (*of court case*) Vergleich, *der;* **reach a ~:** zu einer Einigung kommen; **reach a ~ out of court** sich außergerichtlich vergleichen; **terms of ~** (*Law*) Vergleichsbedingungen; Ⓑ (*of bill, account, etc.*) Bezahlung, *die;* Begleichung, *die;* **a cheque in ~ of a bill** ein Scheck zur Begleichung einer Rechnung; Ⓒ (*Law: bestowal*) Zuwendung, *die;* (*in will*) Legat, *das* (*fachspr.*); Vermächtnis, *das;* ⇒ *also* **marriage settlement**; Ⓓ (*colony*) Siedlung, *die;* (*colonization*) Besiedlung, *die;* **penal ~:** Strafkolonie, *die;* Ⓔ (*subsidence*) [Ab]senkung, *die*

**settler** /'setlə(r)/ *n.* Ⓐ (*colonist*) Siedler, *der*/Siedlerin, *die;* Ⓑ (*coll.: decisive blow or argument*) entscheidender Schlag

**settling day** /'setlɪŋ deɪ/ *n.* (*Brit. St. Exch.*) Abrechnungstermin, *der*

**set: ~-to** /'settu:/ *n., pl.* **~s** Streit, *der;* **~-tos** Streitereien; (*with fists*) Prügeleien; **have a ~-to** Streit haben; (*with fists*) sich prügeln; **~-up** *n.* (*coll.*) Ⓐ (*organization*) System, *das;* (*structure*) Aufbau, *der;* Ⓑ (*situation*) Zustand, *der;* **isn't it a rather strange ~-up?** ist das nicht ein bisschen seltsam?; **what's the ~-up here?** wie läuft das hier? (*ugs.*)

**seven** /'sevn/ ▶ 912 , ▶ 1012 , ▶ 1352 ❶ *adj.* sieben; **the S~ Years War** der Siebenjährige Krieg; ⇒ *also* **eight** 1; **sea** B; **wonder** 1 B. ❷ *n.* (*number, symbol*) Sieben, *die;* ⇒ *also* **eight** 2 A, C, D

**'sevenfold** *adj., adv.* siebenfach; ⇒ *also* **eightfold**

**'seven-league boots** *n. pl.* Siebenmeilenstiefel

**seventeen** /sevn'ti:n/ ▶ 912 , ▶ 1012 , ▶ 1352 ❶ *adj.* siebzehn; **sweet ~:** süße siebzehn [Jahre alt]; ⇒ *also* **eight** 1. ❷ *n.* Siebzehn, *die;* ⇒ *also* **eight** 2 A; **eighteen** 2

**seventeenth** /sevn'ti:nθ/ ▶ 1055 ❶ *adj.* ▶ 1352 siebzehnt...; ⇒ *also* **eighth** 1. ❷ *n.* (*fraction*) Siebzehntel, *das;* ⇒ *also* **eighth** 2

**seventh** /'sevnθ/ ❶ *adj.* ▶ 1352 sieb[en]t...; ⇒ *also* **eighth** 1; **heaven** A. ❷ *n.* Ⓐ (*in sequence, rank*) Sieb[en]te, *der/die/das;* (*fraction*) Sieb[en]tel, *das;* Ⓑ (*Mus.*) Septime, *die;* Ⓒ ▶ 1055 (*day*) **the ~ of May** der sieb[en]te Mai; **the ~ [of the month]** der Sieb[en]te [des Monats]; **S~-day Adventists** Siebenten-Tags-Adventisten

**seventieth** /'sevntɪɪθ/ ❶ *adj.* ▶ 1352 siebzigst...; ⇒ *also* **eighth** 1. ❷ *n.* (*fraction*) Siebzigstel, *das;* ⇒ *also* **eighth** 2

**seventy** /'sevntɪ/ ▶ 912 , ▶ 1352 ❶ *adj.* siebzig; **one-and-~** (*arch.*) ⇒ **seventy-one** 1; ⇒ *also* **eight** 1. ❷ *n.* Siebzig, *die;* **one-and-~** (*arch.*) ⇒ **seventy-one** 2; ⇒ *also* **eight** 2 A; **eighty** 2

**seventy: ~-eight** *n.* ▶ 1352 (*record*) Achtundsiebziger[platte], *die;* **~-first** *etc. adj.* ▶ 1352 einundsiebzigst... *usw.;* ⇒ *also* **eighth** 1; **~-one** *etc.* ❶ *adj.* einundsiebzig *usw.;* ⇒ *also* **eight** 1; ❷ *n.* ▶ 1352 Einundsiebzig *usw., die;* ⇒ *also* **eight** 2 A

**seven-year 'itch** *n.* **the ~:** ≈ das verflixte sieb[en]te Jahr

**sever** /'sevə(r)/ ❶ *v.t.* Ⓐ (*cut*) durchtrennen; (*fig.: break off*) abbrechen ‹Beziehungen, Verbindung›; **some cables were ~ed in the storm** einige Kabel sind bei dem Sturm gerissen; Ⓑ (*separate with force*) abtrennen; (*with axe etc.*) abhacken; **the axe ~ed his head from his body** die Axt trennte seinen Kopf vom Rumpf; Ⓒ (*divide*) **the sea ~s England and** *or* **from France** das Meer trennt England und *od.* von Frankreich. ❷ *v.i.* (*tear*) reißen; (*be torn off*) abreißen

**several** /'sevrl/ ❶ *adv.* Ⓐ (*a few*) mehrere; einige; **~ times** mehrmals; mehrere *od.* einige Male; **~ more copies** noch einige Exemplare mehr; Ⓑ (*separate, diverse*) verschieden; **joint and ~** (*Law*) gesamtschuldnerisch ‹Haftung›. ❷ *pron.* einige; **~ of us** einige von uns; **~ of the buildings** einige *od.* mehrere [der] Gebäude

**severally** /'sevrəlɪ/ *adv.* gesondert; **jointly and ~** (*Law*) gesamtschuldnerisch

**severance** /'sevərəns/ *n.* (*of diplomatic relations*) Abbruch, *der;* (*of communications*) Unterbrechung, *die;* (*of contract*) Lösung, *die;* *attrib.* **~ pay** Abfindung, *die*

**severe** /sɪ'vɪə(r)/ *adj.,* **~r** /sɪ'vɪərə(r)/, **~st** /sɪ'vɪərɪst/ Ⓐ (*strict*) streng; hart ‹Urteil, Strafe, Kritik›; **be ~ on** *or* **with sb.** streng mit jmdm. sein *od.* umgehen; Ⓑ (*violent, extreme*) streng ‹Frost, Winter›; schwer ‹Sturm, Dürre, Verlust, Behinderung, Verletzung›; rau ‹Wetter›; heftig ‹Anfall, Schmerz›; Ⓒ (*making great demands*) hart ‹Test, Prüfung, Konkurrenz›; scharf ‹Tempo›; Ⓓ (*serious, not slight*) bedrohlich ‹Mangel, Knappheit›; heftig, stark ‹Blutung›; schwer ‹Krankheit›; Ⓔ (*unadorned*) streng ‹Stil, Schönheit, Dekor›

**severely** /sɪ'vɪəlɪ/ *adv.* hart; hart, streng ‹bestrafen›; schwer ‹verletzt, behindert›; **leave sth. ~ alone** unbedingt die Finger von etw. lassen (*ugs.*); **be ~ critical of sth.** etw. scharf kritisieren

**severeness** /sɪ'vɪənɪs/, **severity** /sɪ'verɪtɪ/ *ns.* Strenge, *die;* (*of drought, shortage*) großes Ausmaß; (*of criticism*) Schärfe, *die;* **with severity** streng ‹bestrafen›; **the severities of army life** die Härte des Soldatenlebens

**Seville** /sə'vɪl/ *pr. n.* ▶ 1626 Sevilla (*das*)

**Seville orange** /sevɪl 'ɒrɪndʒ/ *n.* Pomeranze, *die;* Sevillaorange, *die*

**sew** /səʊ/ ❶ *v.t., p.p.* **sewn** /səʊn/ *or* **sewed** /səʊd/ nähen ‹Kleid, Naht, Wunde›; heften, broschieren ‹Buch usw.›; zunähen ‹Loch, Riss›; **~ together** zusammennähen ‹Stoff, Leder usw.›; **~ money into one's coat** Geld in seinen Mantel einnähen. ❷ *v.i., p.p.* **sewn** *or* **sewed** nähen

~ **'down** *v.t.* aufnähen

~ **'in** *v.t.* einsetzen ‹Flicken›

~ **'on** *v.t.* annähen ‹Knopf›; aufnähen ‹Abzeichen, Band›

~ **'up** *v.t.* Ⓐ nähen ‹Saum, Naht, Wunde›; **they ~ed me up after the operation** (*coll.*) nach der Operation haben sie mich wieder zugenäht; Ⓑ (*Brit. fig. coll.: settle, arrange*) **be ~n up** unter Dach und Fach sein; (*completely organized*) durchorganisiert sein; **we've got the match all ~n up** wir haben den Sieg schon in der Tasche (*ugs.*)

**sewage** /'sju:ɪdʒ, 'su:ɪdʒ/ *n.* Abwasser, *das*

**sewage: ~ disposal** *n.* Abwasserbeseitigung, *die;* **~ farm** *n.,* **~ works** *n. sing., pl. same* Kläranlage, *die*

**sewer**[1] /'sju:ə(r), 'su:ə(r)/ *n.* (*tunnel*) Abwasserkanal, *der;* (*pipe*) Abwasserleitung, *die*

**sewer**[2] /'səʊə(r)/ *n.* (*person*) Näher, *der*/Näherin, *die*

**sewerage** /'sju:ərɪdʒ, 'su:ərɪdʒ/ *n.* Ⓐ (*system of sewers*) Kanalisation, *die;* Ⓑ *no pl.* (*removal of sewage*) Abwasserbeseitigung, *die;* Ⓒ (*sewage*) Abwasser, *das*

**sewing** /'səʊɪŋ/ *n.* Näharbeit, *die*

**sewing: ~ basket** *n.* Nähkorb, *der;* **~ machine** *n.* Nähmaschine, *die*

**sewn** ⇒ **sew**

**sex** /seks/ ❶ *n.* Ⓐ Geschlecht, *das;* **what ~ is the baby/puppy?** welches Geschlecht hat das Baby/der Welpe?; Ⓑ (*sexuality; coll.: intercourse*) Sex, *der* (*ugs.*); **have ~ with sb.** (*coll.*) mit jmdm. schlafen (*verhüll.*); Sex mit jmdm. haben (*salopp*). ❷ *attrib. adj.* Geschlechts‹organ, -trieb›; Sexual‹verbrechen, -trieb, -instinkt›. ❸ *v.t.* Ⓐ (*determine sex of*) **~ a rabbit/chicken** das Geschlecht eines Kaninchens/Kükens bestimmen; Ⓑ **be highly ~ed** einen starken Sexualtrieb haben

**'sex act** *n.* Geschlechtsakt, *der*

**sexagenarian** /seksədʒɪ'neərɪən/ ❶ *adj.* sechzigjährig; (*more than 60 years old*) in den Sechzigern *nachgestellt.* ❷ *n.* Sechziger, *der*/Sechzigerin, *die*

**sex: ~ aid** *n.* Mittel zur sexuellen Stimulation; **~ appeal** *n.* Sex-Appeal, *der;* **~ bomb** ⇒ **~pot**; **~ change** *n.* Geschlechtsumwandlung, *die;* **~-change operation** *n.* operative Geschlechtsumwandlung; **~ chromosome** *n.* (*Biol.*) Geschlechtschromosom, *das;* **~ discrimination** *n.* sexuelle Diskriminierung; **~ education** *n.* Sexualerziehung, *die*

**sexily** /'seksɪlɪ/ *adv.* aufreizend, (*ugs.*) sexy ‹sprechen, lächeln›; **walk ~:** einen aufreizenden *od.* (*ugs.*) sexy Gang haben

**sexism** /'seksɪzm/ *n., no pl.* Sexismus, *der*

**sexist** /'seksɪst/ ❶ *n.* Sexist, *der*/Sexistin, *die.* ❷ *adj.* sexistisch

**'sex kitten** *n.* Sexbiene, *die* (*salopp*)

**sexless** /'sekslɪs/ *adj.* geschlechtslos

**sex: ~ life** *n.* Geschlechtsleben, *das;* Sexualleben, *das;* **~-linked** *adj.* (*Biol.*) geschlechtsgebunden; **~ maniac** *n.* Triebverbrecher, *der;* **you ~ maniac!** (*coll.*) du geiler Bock (*ugs.*); **he behaves like a ~ maniac** (*coll.*) er benimmt sich, als habe er nur Sex im Kopf; **~ offender** *n.* Sexual[straf]täter, *der*/-täterin, *die*

**sexology** /sek'sɒlədʒɪ/ *n.* Sexologie, *die;* Sexualwissenschaft, *die*

**sexploitation** /seksplɔɪ'teɪʃn/ *n.* [kommerzielle] Ausbeutung der Sexualität; Geschäft mit dem Sex; **~ film** [kommerzieller] Sexfilm

**sex: ~pot** *n.* (*coll.*) Sexbombe, *die* (*salopp*); **~ shop** *n.* Sexshop, *der;* **~-starved** *adj.* sexuell ausgehungert; **~ symbol** *n.* Sexidol, *das*

S

**sextant** /ˈsekstənt/ *n.* Sextant, *der*

**sextet, sextette** /sekˈstet/ *n.* (*Mus.*) Sextett, *das*

**sexton** /ˈsekstən/ *n.* Küster, *der;* Kirchendiener, *der*

**ˈsexton beetle** *n.* (*Zool.*) Totengräber, *der*

**sextuplet** /ˈsekstjuːplɪt, seksˈtjuːplɪt/ *n.* Sechsling, *der*

**sexual** /ˈseksjʊəl, ˈsekʃʊəl/ *adj.* Ⓐ sexuell; geschlechtlich, sexuell ‹Anziehung, Erregung, Verlangen, Diskriminierung›; **~ maturity/behaviour** Geschlechtsreife, *die*/Sexualverhalten, *das;* Ⓑ (*Biol.*) Geschlechts-; geschlechtlich ‹Fortpflanzung›

**sexual: ~ aˈbuse** *n.* sexueller Missbrauch; **suffer ~ abuse:** sexuell missbraucht werden; **~ ˈharassment** *n.* sexuelle Belästigung; **~ ˈintercourse** *n., no pl., no indef. art.* Geschlechtsverkehr, *der*

**sexuality** /seksjʊˈælɪtɪ, sekʃʊˈælɪtɪ/ *n., no pl.* Sexualität, *die;* Geschlechtlichkeit, *die*

**sexually** /ˈseksjʊəlɪ, ˈsekʃʊəlɪ/ *adv.* Ⓐ sexuell; **~ mature** geschlechtsreif; **~ transmitted disease** durch Geschlechtsverkehr übertragbare Krankheit; Geschlechtskrankheit, *die;* Ⓑ (*Biol.*) geschlechtlich

**sexual ˈorgans** *n. pl.* Geschlechtsorgane

**sexy** /ˈseksɪ/ *adj.* sexy (*ugs.*); erotisch ‹Film, Buch, Gemälde›

**Seychelles** /seɪˈʃelz/ *pr. n.* Seychellen *Pl.*

**sez** /sez/ *v.i.* **~ ˈyou = says you** ⇒ **say** 1 A

**SF** *abbr.* **science fiction** SF

**Sgt.** *abbr.* **Sergeant** Uffz.

**sh** /ʃ/ *int.* sch; pst

**shabbily** /ˈʃæbɪlɪ/ *adv.*, **shabby** /ˈʃæbɪ/ *adj.* schäbig

**shabby-genˈteel** *adj.* von schäbiger Eleganz *nachgestellt*

**shack** /ʃæk/ ❶ *n.* Hütte, *die.* ❷ *v.i.* (*coll.*) **~ up with sb.** mit jmdm. zusammenziehen

**shackle** /ˈʃækl/ ❶ *n.* Ⓐ *usu. in pl.* (*lit. or fig.*) Fessel, *die;* (*fetter*) Fußfessel, *die;* Ⓑ (*coupling link*) Schäkel, *der* (*Technik*). ❷ *v.t.* (*lit. or fig.*) anketten (**to** an + *Akk.*); **the chain is ~d to the anchor** die Kette ist mit einem Schäkel am Anker befestigt

**shade** /ʃeɪd/ ❶ *n.* Ⓐ Schatten, *der;* **the ~s of night/evening** (*literary*) die Schatten der Nacht/des Abends (*dichter.*); **put sb./sth. in[to] the ~** (*fig.*) jmdn./etw. in den Schatten stellen; **38 [°C] in the ~:** 38° im Schatten; Ⓑ (*colour*) Ton, *der;* (*fig.*) Schattierung, *die;* **the newest ~s of lipstick** die neuesten Lippenstiftfarben; **various ~s of purple** verschiedene Violetttöne; **~s of meaning** Bedeutungsnuancen *od.* -schattierungen; **all ~s of opinion** Standpunkte der verschiedensten Schattierungen; Ⓒ (*small amount*) Spur, *die;* Ⓓ (*ghost*) Geist, *der;* **~s of the past** die Schatten der Vergangenheit; **the ~s** (*Mythol.*) das Schattenreich; das Reich der Schatten; **~s of ...!** das erinnert an ...!; Ⓔ (*eye shield*) [Augen]schirm, *der;* (*lamp~*) [Lampen]schirm, *der;* (*window blind*) Jalousie, *die;* Ⓕ *in pl.* (*coll.: sunglasses*) Sonnenbrille, *die.*

❷ *v.t.* Ⓐ (*screen*) beschatten (*geh.*); Schatten geben (+ *Dat.*); **be ~d from the sun** vor Sonneneinstrahlung geschützt sein; **~ one's eyes with one's hand** die Hand schützend über die Augen halten; Ⓑ abdunkeln ‹Fenster, Lampe, Licht›; Ⓒ (*darken with lines*) **~ [in]** [ab]schattieren; Ⓓ (*just defeat*) knapp überbieten.

❸ *v.i.* (*lit. or fig.*) übergehen (**into** in + *Akk.*); **~ [off] into another** *or* **each other** ineinander übergehen

**~ ˈin** *v.t.* [ab]schattieren

**shading** /ˈʃeɪdɪŋ/ *n.* Schattierung, *die;* (*protection from light*) Lichtschutz, *der*

**shadow** /ˈʃædəʊ/ ❶ *n.* Ⓐ Schatten, *der;* **his life was lived in the ~s** (*fig.*) er lebte sein Leben im Verborgenen; **cast a ~ over** (*lit. or fig.*) einen Schatten werfen auf (+ *Akk.*); **cast a long ~** (*fig.*) großen *od.* nachhaltigen Einfluss haben; **be in sb.'s ~** (*fig.*) in jmds. Schatten stehen; **have deep ~s under one's eyes** tiefe Schatten unter den Augen haben; **be afraid of one's own ~** (*fig.*) sich vor seinem eigenen Schatten fürchten; **be sb.'s ~** (*fig.*) jmds. Schatten sein; Ⓑ (*slightest trace*) **without a ~ of doubt** ohne den Schatten eines Zweifels; **catch at** *or* **chase after ~s** einem Phantom *od.* (*geh.*) Schatten nachjagen; Ⓒ (*ghost, lit. or fig.*) Schatten, *der;* **be worn to a ~** (*fig.*) sich völlig aufgerieben haben; **he is only a ~ of his former self** (*fig.*) er ist nur noch ein *od.* der Schatten seiner selbst; Ⓓ **S~** *attrib.* (*Brit. Polit.*) ‹Minister, Kanzler› im Schattenkabinett; **S~ Cabinet** Schattenkabinett, *das.*

❷ *v.t.* Ⓐ (*darken*) überschatten; Ⓑ (*follow secretly*) beschatten

**ˈshadow boxing** *n.* Schattenboxen, *das*

**shadowy** /ˈʃædəʊɪ/ *adj.* Ⓐ (*not distinct*) schattenhaft; schemenhaft (*geh.*); Ⓑ (*full of shade*) schattig

**shady** /ˈʃeɪdɪ/ *adj.* Ⓐ (*giving shade*) Schatten spendend (*geh.*); (*situated in shade*) schattig; Ⓑ (*disreputable*) zwielichtig

**shaft** /ʃɑːft/ *n.* Ⓐ (*of tool, golf club, feather, spear, lance*) Schaft, *der;* Ⓑ (*Archit.*) [Säulen]schaft, *der;* Ⓒ (*Mech. Engin.*) Welle, *die;* Ⓓ (*of cart or carriage*) Deichsel, *die:* **pair of ~s** Gabeldeichsel, *die;* Ⓔ (*of mine, blast furnace, tunnel, drain, lift, etc.*) Schacht, *der;* Ⓕ (*arrow*) Pfeil, *der;* (*stem of arrow*) Schaft, *der;* Ⓖ (*of light or lightning*) Strahl, *der*

**shag**[1] /ʃæg/ *n.* Ⓐ (*tobacco*) Shag[tabak], *der;* Feinschnitt, *der;* Ⓑ (*Ornith.*) Krähenscharbe, *die*

**shag**[2] (*sl*) ❶ *v.t.*, **-gg-** bumsen (*salopp*). ❷ *n.* **have a ~ [with sb.]** es [mit jmdm.] treiben (*ugs.*)

**shagged** /ʃægd/ *adj.* (*sl.*) **be ~ [out]** fix und fertig sein (*ugs.*)

**shaggy** /ˈʃægɪ/ *adj.* Ⓐ (*hairy*) zottelig; Ⓑ (*unkempt*) struppig

**shaggy-ˈdog story** *n.* *endlos langer Witz ohne richtige Pointe*

**Shah** /ʃɑː/ *n.* Schah, *der*

**shake** /ʃeɪk/ ❶ *n.* Ⓐ Schütteln, *das;* **give sb./sth. a ~:** jmdn./etw. schütteln; **with a ~ of the head** mit einem Kopfschütteln; **be all of a ~:** am ganzen Körper zittern; **be no great ~s** (*coll.*) nicht gerade umwerfend sein (*ugs.*); **get the ~s** (*coll.*) (*due to alcoholism*) einen Tatterich kriegen (*ugs.*); (*with fear*) das große Zittern kriegen (*ugs.*); Ⓑ ⇒ **milk shake;** Ⓒ (*Amer., NZ: earthquake*) Erdbeben, *das;* Ⓓ **in [half] a ~, in two** *etc.* **~s [of a lamb's tail], in a brace of ~s** (*coll.*) in einer Sekunde.

❷ *v.t.*, **shook** /ʃʊk/, **shaken** /ˈʃeɪkn/ *or* (*arch./coll.*) **shook** Ⓐ (*move violently*) schütteln; **the dog shook itself** der Hund schüttelte sich; **be ~n to pieces** völlig durchgeschüttelt werden; **~ one's fist/a stick at sb.** jmdm. mit der Faust/einem Stock drohen; **~ salt/pepper over one's food** [sich (*Dat.*)] Salz/Pfeffer aufs *od.* über das Essen streuen; '**~ [well] before using'** „vor Gebrauch [gut] schütteln!"; **~ hands** sich (*Dat.*) *od.* einander die Hand geben *od.* schütteln; **they shook hands to conclude the deal** sie besiegelten das Geschäft durch Handschlag; **she won't ~ hands with me** sie gibt mir nicht die Hand; **let's ~ hands** gib mir deine Hand; **~ sb. by the hand** jmdm. die Hand schütteln *od.* drücken; Ⓑ (*cause to tremble*) erschüttern ‹Gebäude usw.›; **~ one's head [over sth.]** [über etw. (*Akk.*)] den Kopf schütteln; ⇒ *also* **leg** A; Ⓒ (*weaken*) erschüttern; **~ sb.'s faith in sth./sb.** jmds. Glauben an etw./jmdn. erschüttern; Ⓓ (*agitate*) erschüttern; **she was badly ~n by the news of his death** die Nachricht von seinem Tod erschütterte sie sehr; **she was not hurt, only badly ~n** sie wurde nicht verletzt, sondern erlitt nur einen schweren Schock; **he failed his exam — that shook him!** er hat die Prüfung nicht bestanden — das war ein Schock für ihn!; **~ sb.'s composure** jmdn. aus dem Gleichgewicht bringen; **~ sb. rigid** (*coll.*) jmdn. umhauen (*salopp*).

❸ *v.i.*, **shook, shaken** *or* (*arch./coll.*) **shook** Ⓐ (*tremble*) wackeln; ‹Boden, Stimme:› beben; ‹Hand:› zittern; ‹Baum:› schwanken; **~ [all over] with cold/fear** [am ganzen Leib] vor Kälte/Angst schlottern; **~ like a leaf** wie Espenlaub zittern; **~ with emotion** vor Erregung beben; **~ in one's shoes** vor Angst schlottern; Ⓑ (*coll.: ~ hands*) sich (*Dat.*) die Hand geben; **let's ~ on it!** schlag ein!; Hand drauf!; **~ on sth.** etw. durch Handschlag besiegeln

**~ ˈdown** ❶ *v.t.* Ⓐ (*get down by shaking*) herunterschütteln; Ⓑ (*Amer. sl.: extort money from*) ausnehmen (*salopp*); **~ sb. down for £50** jmdn. um 50 Pfund erleichtern (*ugs.*). ❷ *v.i.* Ⓐ (*sleep*) kampieren (*ugs.*); ⇒ *also* **shake-down;** Ⓑ (*settle*) ‹Maschine, Motor:› sich einlaufen; ‹Person:› sich eingewöhnen, sich akklimatisieren

**~ ˈoff** *v.t.* (*lit. or fig.*) abschütteln; ⇒ *also* **dust** 1 A

**~ ˈout** *v.t.* ausschütteln; (*spread out*) ausbreiten; ⇒ *also* **shake-out**

**~ ˈup** *v.t.* Ⓐ (*mix*) schütteln; Ⓑ aufschütteln ‹Kissen›; Ⓒ (*make uncomfortable by shaking*) durchschütteln; Ⓓ (*discompose*) einen Schrecken einjagen (+ *Dat.*); **she felt pretty ~n up** sie hatte einen ziemlichen Schrecken bekommen; Ⓔ (*rouse to activity*) aufrütteln; Ⓕ (*reorganize*) umkrempeln (*ugs.*). ⇒ *also* **shake-up**

**ˈshake-down** *n.* [improvisiertes] Nachtlager

**shaken** ⇒ **shake** 2, 3

**ˈshake-out** *n.* radikale Umorganisation; (*making workers redundant*) Rationalisierung, *die*

**shaker** /ˈʃeɪkə(r)/ *n.* Ⓐ (*vessel*) Mixbecher, *der;* Shaker, *der;* Ⓑ **S~** (*Relig.*) Shaker, *der;* Ⓒ (*implement*) Streuer, *der*

**Shakespe[a]rean, Shakespe[a]rian** /ʃeɪkˈspɪərɪən/ *adj.* shakespearesch ‹Sonett, Stil›; ‹Zeit, Zeitalter› Shakespeares

**ˈshake-up** *n.* Ⓐ (*mixing*) **get a [good] ~:** [gut] geschüttelt werden; Ⓑ (*restoring to shape*) **give the pillows a good ~:** die Kissen tüchtig aufschütteln; Ⓒ (*reorganization*) **give sth. a [good] ~:** etw. [total] umkrempeln (*ugs.*); **sth. needs a ~:** etw. muss [mal] umgekrempelt werden (*ugs.*); **government ~:** Regierungsumbildung, *die;* Ⓓ (*rousing to activity*) Neubelebung, *die*

**shakily** /ˈʃeɪkɪlɪ/ *adv.* unsicher ‹stehen, lachen›; wack[e]lig (*ugs.*) ‹gehen, stehen›; mit zittriger Stimme ‹sprechen›; mit zittriger Hand ‹gießen›

**shaky** /ˈʃeɪkɪ/ *adj.* Ⓐ (*unsteady*) wack[e]lig ‹Möbelstück, Leiter, Haus›; zittrig ‹Hand, Stimme, Bewegung, Greis›; **feel ~:** sich zittrig fühlen; **be ~ on one's legs** wacklig auf den Beinen sein (*ugs.*); Ⓑ (*unreliable*) auf wackligen Füßen stehend (*ugs.*); **his German is rather ~:** sein Deutsch steht auf wackligen Füßen (*ugs.*)

**shale** /ʃeɪl/ *n.* Schiefer, *der*

**ˈshale oil** *n.* Schieferöl, *das*

**shall** /ʃl, *stressed* ʃæl/ *v. aux. only in pres.* **shall**, *neg.* (*coll.*) **shan't** /ʃɑːnt/, *past* **should** /ʃəd, *stressed* ʃʊd/, *neg.* (*coll.*) **shouldn't** /ˈʃʊdnt/ Ⓐ *expr. simple future* werden; Ⓑ **should** *expr. conditional* würde/würdest/würden/würdet; **he should not have gone if I could have prevented it** er wäre nicht gegangen, wenn ich es hätte verhindern können; **I should have been killed if I had let go** ich wäre getötet worden, wenn ich losgelassen hätte; Ⓒ *expr. command* **any person found in possession of such weapons ~ be guilty of an offence** (*Law*) jeder, der im Besitz solcher Waffen angetroffen wird, macht sich strafbar *od.* eines Vergehens schuldig; **the committee ~ not be disturbed** der Ausschuss darf nicht gestört werden; **thou shalt not steal** (*Bibl.*) du sollst nicht stehlen; Ⓓ *expr. will or intention* **what ~ we do?** was sollen wir tun?; **let's go in, ~ we?** gehen wir doch hinein, oder?; **I'll buy six, ~ I?** ich kaufe 6 [Stück], ja?; **you ~ pay for this!** das sollst du mir büßen!; **we should be safe now** jetzt dürften wir in Sicherheit sein; **he shouldn't do things like that!** er sollte so etwas nicht tun!; **oh, you shouldn't have!** das wäre doch nicht nötig gewesen!; **you should be more careful** du solltest vorsichtiger *od.*

sorgfältiger sein; ⇒ *also* **worry** 2; **E** *in conditional clause* **if we should be defeated** falls wir unterliegen [sollten]; **should I be there, I will tell her** sollte ich dort sein, werde ich es ihr sagen; **I should hope so** ich hoffe es; (*indignant*) das möchte ich hoffen!; **F** *in tentative assertion* **I should like to disagree with you on that point** in dem Punkt *od.* da möchte ich dir widersprechen; **I should say it is time we went home** ich würde sagen *od.* ich glaube, es ist Zeit, dass wir nach Hause gehen; **G** *forming question* **~ you be going to church?** gehst du in die Kirche?; **H** *expr. purpose* **in order that he ~** *or* **should be able to go** damit er gehen kann; **I gave him £10 so that he should have enough money for the journey** ich habe ihm 10 Pfund gegeben, sodass er genug Geld für die Reise hat/hatte. ⇒ *also* **seem** A

**shallot** /ʃəˈlɒt/ *n.* Schalotte, *die*

**shallow** /ˈʃæləʊ/ ❶ *adj.* ▶ **1210**, ▶ **1480** seicht ‹Wasser, Fluss›; flach ‹Schüssel, Teller, Wasser›; (*fig.*) seicht (*abwertend*) ‹Unterhaltung, Gerede, Roman›; flach (*abwertend*) ‹Person, Denker, Geist›; platt (*abwertend*) ‹Argument, Verallgemeinerung›; **~ breathing** flache Atmung. ❷ *n. in pl.* Flachwasser, *das*

**shalom** /ʃəˈlɒm/ ❶ *int.* Schalom. ❷ *n.* Schalom, *das*

**sham** /ʃæm/ ❶ *adj.* unecht; imitiert ‹Leder, Holz, Pelz, Stein›. ❷ *n.* (*pretence*) Heuchelei, *die;* (*person*) Heuchler, *der*/Heuchlerin, *die;* **it is all a mere ~:** das ist alles bloße Heuchelei; **their marriage is only a ~:** ihre Ehe besteht nur auf dem Papier; **his life is a ~:** sein Leben ist eine einzige Lüge. ❸ *v.t.*, **-mm-** vortäuschen, simulieren; **~ dead/ill/stupid** sich tot/krank/dumm stellen. ❹ *v.i.*, **-mm-** simulieren; sich verstellen

**shaman** /ˈʃæmən/ *n.* Schamane, *der*

**shamble** /ˈʃæmbl/ ❶ *v.i.* schlurfen; **a shambling gait** ein schlurfender Gang. ❷ *n.* Schlurfen, *das;* **move along at a ~:** sich [schwerfällig] schlurfend vorwärts bewegen

**shambles** /ˈʃæmblz/ *n. sing.* (*coll.: mess*) Chaos, *das;* **the house/room was a ~:** das Haus/Zimmer glich einem Schlachtfeld; **the economy is in a ~:** in der Wirtschaft herrschen chaotische Zustände; **she made a ~ of her job** sie hat bei ihrer Arbeit ein heilloses Durcheinander angerichtet

**shambolic** /ʃæmˈbɒlɪk/ *adj.* (*coll.*) chaotisch

**shame** /ʃeɪm/ ❶ *n.* **A** Scham, *die;* **feel ~/no ~ for what one did** sich schämen/sich nicht schämen für das, was man getan hat; **hang one's head in** *or* **for ~:** beschämt den Kopf senken; **blush with ~:** vor Scham erröten; schamrot werden; **be without ~:** schamlos sein; **have no [sense of] ~:** kein[erlei] Schamgefühl besitzen; **have you no ~?** schämst du dich nicht?; **to my ~ I must confess ...:** ich muss zu meiner Schande gestehen ...; **for ~!** du solltest dich/er sollte sich *usw.* schämen!; **B** (*state of disgrace*) Schande, *die;* **~ on you!** du solltest dich schämen; **put sb./sth. to ~:** jmdn. beschämen/etw. in den Schatten stellen; **bring ~ on the family name, be a ~ to one's family** seiner Familie (*Dat.*) Schande machen; **C what a ~!** (*disgrace*) es ist eine Schande!; (*bad luck*) so ein Pech!; (*pity*) wie schade!; **it is a crying** *or* **terrible** *or* **great ~:** es ist eine wahre Schande.
❷ *v.t.* beschämen; **~ sb. into doing/out of doing sth.** jmdn. dazu bringen, dass er sich schämt und etw. tut/nicht tut; **~ one's family** seiner Familie (*Dat.*) Schande machen

ˈ**shamefaced** *adj.* betreten; **have a ~ look, look ~:** betreten dreinblicken

**shamefacedly** /ˈʃeɪmfeɪsɪdlɪ/ *adv.* betreten

**shameful** /ˈʃeɪmfl/ *adj.* beschämend

**shamefully** /ˈʃeɪmfəlɪ/ *adv.* beschämend; **she is ~ ignorant** sie weiß beschämend wenig; es ist eine Schande, wie wenig sie weiß

**shameless** /ˈʃeɪmlɪs/ *adj.* schamlos; **are you completely ~?** hast du denn gar kein Schamgefühl?

**shamelessly** /ˈʃeɪmlɪslɪ/ *adv.* schamlos

**shammy** /ˈʃæmɪ/ *n.* **~ [leather]** (*coll.*) Putzleder *das;* (*for windows*) Fensterleder, *das*

**shampoo** /ʃæmˈpuː/ ❶ *v.t.* schamponieren ‹Haar, Teppich, Polster, Auto›; **shall I ~ your hair for you?** soll ich dir die Haare waschen? ❷ *n.* Shampoo[n], *das;* **carpet ~:** Teppichschaum, *der;* **medicated ~:** medizinisches Shampoo; **car ~:** Autoshampoo, *das;* **have a ~ and set** sich (*Dat.*) die Haare waschen und [ein]legen lassen; **give one's hair a ~:** sich (*Dat.*) die Haare [mit Shampoo] waschen *od.* schamponieren

**shamrock** /ˈʃæmrɒk/ *n.* Klee, *der;* (*emblem of Ireland*) Shamrock, *der*

**shandy** /ˈʃændɪ/ *n.* Bier mit Limonade; Radlermaß, *die* (*bes. südd.*)

**Shangri-La** /ʃæŋgrɪˈlɑː/ *n.* Paradies, *das*

**shank** /ʃæŋk/ *n.* **A** (*of person*) Unterschenkel, *der;* **[go] on S~s's mare** *or* **pony** auf Schusters Rappen [reisen] (*scherzh.*); **B** (*of horse*) Vordermittelfuß, *der;* Röhrbein, *das;* (*cut of meat*) [Hinter]hesse, *die;* **C** (*Bot.*) Stiel, *der;* **D** (*of pillar*) [Säulen]schaft, *der;* (*of key, anchor, nail, fish-hook*) Schaft, *der;* (*of spoon*) [Löffel]stiel, *der*

**shan't** /ʃɑːnt/ (*coll.*) ... **shall not**

**shantung** /ʃænˈtʌŋ/ *n.* Shantung, *der* (*Textilw.*); Schantungseide, *die*

**shanty**[1] /ˈʃæntɪ/ *n.* (*hut*) [armselige] Hütte

**shanty**[2] *n.* (*song*) Shanty, *das;* Seemannslied, *das*

ˈ**shanty town** *n.* Elendsviertel, *das*

**shape** /ʃeɪp/ ❶ *v.t.* **A** (*create, form*) formen; bearbeiten ‹Holz, Stein› (**into** zu); **~ a dress at the waist** ein Kleid taillieren; **you can ~ plastic when it is hot** erwärmter Kunststoff lässt sich [ver]formen; **B** (*adapt, direct*) prägen, formen ‹Charakter, Person›; nehmen ‹Kurs› (**for** auf + *Akk.*); [entscheidend] beeinflussen ‹Gang der Geschichte, Leben, Zukunft, Gesellschaft›. ❷ *v.i.* sich entwickeln; **the way things are shaping, we should be able to come** so wie sich die Dinge entwickeln, werden wir wohl kommen können. ❸ *n.* **A** (*external form, outline*) Form, *die;* **spherical/rectangular in ~:** kugelförmig/rechteckig; **in the ~ of a circle** kreisförmig; in der Form eines Kreises; **she is the right ~ for a dancer** sie hat die richtige Figur für eine Tänzerin; **take ~** ‹Konstruktion, Skulptur:› Gestalt annehmen (⇒ *also* **c**); **B** (*appearance*) Gestalt, *die;* **a monster in human ~:** ein Ungeheuer in Menschengestalt; **in the ~ of a woman** in Gestalt einer Frau; **a paperweight in the ~ of a lizard** ein Briefbeschwerer in Form einer Eidechse; **C** (*specific form*) Form, *die;* Gestalt, *die;* **a surprise in the ~ of an invitation/a holiday** eine Überraschung in Form einer Einladung/Ferienreise; **nothing in the ~ of ...:** nichts in der Art ... (+ *Gen.*); **take ~** ‹Plan, Vorhaben:› Gestalt *od.* feste Formen annehmen (⇒ *also* **a**); **get one's ideas into ~:** seine Gedanken sammeln; Ordnung in seine Gedanken bringen; **knock sth. out of ~:** etw. verbeulen *od.* demolieren; **knock sth. into ~:** etw. wieder in Form bringen; **we have knocked the plans into ~:** wir haben die Pläne jetzt im Wesentlichen fertig; **in all ~s and sizes, in every ~ and size** in allen Formen und Größen; **the ~ of things to come** die Dinge, die da kommen sollen/sollten; **this may be the ~ of things to come** so könnte das in Zukunft aussehen; ⇒ *also* **lick** 1 A; **D** (*condition*) Form, *die* (*bes. Sport*); **do yoga to keep in ~:** Yoga machen, um in Form zu bleiben; **be in good/bad ~:** gut/schlecht in Form sein; **be in poor ~ mentally/physically** geistig/körperlich in schlechter Verfassung sein; **what sort of ~ is the business in?** wie steht es um die Firma?; **be in no ~ to do sth.** nicht in der Lage sein, etw. zu tun; **E** (*person seen, ghost*) Gestalt, *die;* **F** (*mould*) (*for hats*) Hutform, *die;* (*for puddings, jellies, etc.*) Form, *die*

**~ ˈup** *v.i.* sich entwickeln; **how's the new editor shaping up?** wie macht sich der neue Redakteur?

**SHAPE** /ʃeɪp/ *abbr.* **Supreme Headquarters Allied Powers Europe** oberstes Hauptquartier der Nato-Streitkräfte in Europa

**shaped** /ʃeɪpt/ *adj.* geformt; **be ~ like a pear** die Form einer Birne haben; **this is an oddly ~ cake** dieser Kuchen hat eine ungewöhnliche *od.* eigentümliche Form

**shapeless** /ˈʃeɪplɪs/ *adj.* formlos; unförmig ‹Kleid, Person›; unstrukturiert ‹Theaterstück›

**shapely** /ˈʃeɪplɪ/ *adj.* wohlgeformt ‹Beine, Busen›; gut ‹Figur›; formschön ‹Auto, Design›

**shard** /ʃɑːd/ ⇒ **sherd**

**share** /ʃeə(r)/ ❶ *n.* **A** (*portion*) Teil, *der od. das;* (*part one is entitled to*) **[fair] ~:** Anteil, *der;* **he had a large ~ in bringing it about** er hatte großen Anteil daran, dass es zustande kam; **come in for one's full ~ of criticism** seinen Teil Kritik einstecken müssen *od.* abbekommen; **pay one's ~ of the bill** seinen Teil der Rechnung bezahlen; **have a ~ in the profits** am Gewinn beteiligt sein; **fair ~s** gerechte Teile; **do more than one's [fair] ~ of the work** mehr als seinen Teil zur Arbeit beitragen; **each had his ~ of the cake** jeder bekam seinen Teil vom Kuchen ab; **have more than one's [fair] ~ of the blame/attention** mehr Schuld zugewiesen bekommen/mehr Beachtung finden, als man verdient; **she had her ~ of luck/bad luck** sie hat aber auch Glück/Pech gehabt; **take one's ~ of the responsibility** seinen Teil Verantwortung tragen; **take one's ~ of the blame** seinen Teil Schuld auf sich (*Akk.*) nehmen; **go ~s** teilen; **let me go ~s with you in the taxi fare** ich möchte mich an den Kosten für das Taxi beteiligen; **it was ~ and ~ alike** es wurde brüderlich geteilt; ⇒ *also* **lion** A; **B** (*part-ownership of property*) [Geschäfts]anteil, *der;* (*part of company's capital*) Aktie, *die;* **have a ~ in a business** an einem Geschäft beteiligt sein; **hold ~s in a company** (*Brit.*) Anteile *od.* Aktien einer Gesellschaft besitzen; ⇒ *also* **defer**[1] A; **ordinary** B.
❷ *v.t.* teilen; gemeinsam tragen ‹Verantwortung›; **~ the same birthday/surname** am gleichen Tag Geburtstag/den gleichen Nachnamen haben.
❸ *v.i.* **~ in** teilnehmen an (+ *Dat.*); beteiligt sein an (+ *Dat.*) ‹Gewinn, Planung›; teilen ‹Freude, Erfahrung›; **there are no single rooms left, so I'll have to ~:** es sind keine Einzelzimmer mehr frei, sodass ich mit jemandem ein Zimmer teilen muss

**~ ˈout** *v.t.* aufteilen (**among** unter + *Akk.*); ⇒ *also* **share-out**

**share: ~ certificate** *n.* Aktienurkunde, *die;* Mantel, *der* (*Finanzw.*); **~cropper** *n.* (*Amer.*) Teilpächter, *der;* **~holder** *n.* Aktionär, *der*/Aktionärin, *die;* **~ index** *n.* (*Econ.*) Aktienindex, *der;* **~-out** *n.* Aufteilung, *die;* **~ware** *n., no pl.* (*Computing*) Shareware, *die*

**shariah** /ʃəˈriːə/ *n.* (*Islamic Law*) Scharia, *die*

**shark** /ʃɑːk/ *n.* **A** Hai[fisch], *der;* **B** (*fig.: swindler*) gerissener Geschäftemacher; **property ~:** Grundstückshai, *der* (*ugs. abwertend*)

ˈ**sharkskin** *n.* **A** (*skin*) Haut des Haifischs; (*tanned*) Haifischleder, *das;* **B** (*fabric*) Haifischhaut, *die* (*Textilw.*)

**sharp** /ʃɑːp/ ❶ *adj.* **A** (*with fine edge*) scharf; (*with fine point*) spitz ‹Nadel, Bleistift, Giebel, Gipfel›; **~ sand** scharfer Sand (*Bauw.*); **B** (*clear-cut*) scharf ‹Umriss, Kontrast, Bild, Gesichtszüge, Linie›; deutlich ‹Unterscheidung›; präzise ‹Eindruck›; scharf umrissen ‹Schatten›; **C** (*abrupt, angular*) scharf ‹Kurve, Winkel›; eng, scharf ‹Kurve›; spitz ‹Winkel›; steil, schroff ‹Abhang›; stark ‹Gefälle›; **a ~ rise/fall in prices** ein jäher Preisanstieg/Preissturz; **D** (*intense*) groß ‹Appetit, Hunger[gefühl]›; (*acid, pungent*) scharf ‹Würze, Geschmack, Sauce, Käse›; sauer ‹Apfel›; herb ‹Wein›; (*shrill, piercing*) schrill ‹Schrei, Pfiff›; (*biting*) scharf ‹Wind, Frost, Luft›; (*sudden, severe*) heftig ‹Schmerz, Anfall, Krampf, Kampf›; (*harsh, acrimonious*) scharf ‹Protest, Tadel, Ton, Stimme, Zunge, Worte›; **a short ~ struggle** ein kurzer, heftiger Kampf; **a short ~ shock** ein kräftiger Schock; **E** (*acute, quick*) scharf ‹Augen, Verstand, Gehör, Ohr, Beobachtungsgabe, Intelligenz, Geruchssinn›; aufgeweckt ‹Kind›; scharfsinnig ‹Bemerkung›; begabt ‹Schüler,

S

Student›; raffiniert ‹Schachzug›; **be ~ at maths** gut in Mathe sein (*ugs.*); **be as ~ as a needle** schlagfertig sein; **that was pretty ~!** das war ganz schön clever!; **keep a ~ lookout for the police!** halt die Augen offen, falls die Polizei kommt!; **keep a ~ watch** scharf aufpassen; **her mind is as ~ as a needle** sie hat einen messerscharfen Verstand; Ⓕ (*derog.: artful, dishonest, quick to take advantage*) gerissen; **~ practice** unlautere Praktiken; Ⓖ (*vigorous, brisk*) flott (*ugs.*); **that was ~ work** das ging schnell; **~'s the word!, be ~ about it!** mach schnell!; Ⓗ (*Mus.*) [um einen Halbton] erhöht ‹Note›; **F/G/C** *etc.* **~:** fis, Fis/gis, Gis/cis, Cis *usw.*, *das;* Ⓘ (*coll.: stylish*) scharf (*ugs.*); todschick (*ugs.*); **she is a ~ dresser** sie ist [immer] todschick angezogen (*ugs.*).
➋ *adv.* Ⓐ (*punctually*) **at six o'clock ~:** Punkt sechs Uhr; **on the hour ~, ~ on the hour** genau zur vollen Stunde; Ⓑ (*suddenly*) scharf ‹bremsen›; plötzlich ‹anhalten›; **turn ~ right** scharf nach rechts abbiegen; Ⓒ **look ~!** halt dich ran! (*ugs.*); Ⓓ (*Mus.*) zu hoch ‹singen, spielen›.
➌ *n.* (*Mus.*) erhöhter Ton; (*symbol*) Kreuz, *das;* Erhöhungszeichen, *das*

**'sharp-edged** *adj.* scharfkantig; scharf ‹Messer›

**sharpen** /ˈʃɑːpn/ *v.t.* schärfen (*auch fig.*); [an]spitzen ‹Bleistift›; (*fig.*) anregen ‹Appetit›; verstärken ‹Schmerz›

**'sharp end** *n.* (*coll.*) Ⓐ (*Naut.*) Bug, *der;* **be at the ~:** im vorderen Teil des Schiffes sein; Ⓑ (*fig.: place of direct action or decision*) vorderste Linie *od.* Front; **at the ~:** in vorderster Front

**sharpener** /ˈʃɑːpnə(r)/ *n.* (*for pencil*) Bleistiftspitzer, *der;* Spitzer, *der* (*ugs.*); (*for tools*) Abziehstein, *der;* Schleifstein, *der*

**sharper** /ˈʃɑːpə(r)/ *n.* (*at cards*) Falschspieler, *der;* (*swindler*) Betrüger, *der*

**sharp: ~-eyed** *adj.* scharfäugig; **be ~-eyed** scharfe Augen haben; **be as ~-eyed as a hawk/lynx** Augen wie ein Adler/Luchs haben; **it was ~-eyed of you to spot the fault** dass du den Fehler entdeckt hast, zeigt, dass du ein scharfes Auge hast; **~featured** *adj.* scharf geschnitten ‹Gesicht›; ‹Person› mit scharfen Gesichtszügen

**sharpish** /ˈʃɑːpɪʃ/ *adv.* (*coll.*) (*quickly*) rasch; (*promptly*) unverzüglich; sofort

**sharply** /ˈʃɑːplɪ/ *adv.* Ⓐ (*acutely*) spitz; **~ angled** spitzwinklig; **come ~ to a point** spitz[winklig] zu *od.* in einem Punkt zusammenlaufen; Ⓑ (*clearly*) scharf ‹voneinander unterschieden, kontrastierend, umrissen›; Ⓒ (*abruptly*) scharf ‹bremsen, abbiegen›; steil, schroff ‹abfallen›; Ⓓ (*acidly*) scharf ‹gewürzt›; (*harshly*) in scharfem Ton ‹antworten›; **~ contested** hart umkämpft; **~ worded letter** Brief in scharfem Ton; Ⓔ (*quickly*) schnell, rasch ‹denken, handeln›

**sharpness** /ˈʃɑːpnɪs/ *n., no pl.* Schärfe, *die;* (*fineness of point*) Spitzheit, *die*

**sharp: ~shooter** *n.* Scharfschütze, *der;* **~-witted** *adj.* scharfsinnig

**shat** ⇒ **shit**1,2

**shatter** /ˈʃætə(r)/ ➊ *v.t.* Ⓐ (*smash*) zertrümmern; Ⓑ (*destroy*) zerschlagen ‹Hoffnungen›; ruinieren ‹Gesundheit›; Ⓒ (*coll.: greatly upset*) schwer mitnehmen. ➋ *v.i.* zerbrechen; zerspringen

**shattered** /ˈʃætəd/ *adj.* Ⓐ zerbrochen, zersprungen ‹Scheibe, Glas, Fenster›; (*fig.*) zerstört ‹Hoffnungen›; zerrüttet ‹Nerven, Gesundheit›; Ⓑ (*coll.: greatly upset*) **she was ~ by the news** die Nachricht hat sie schwer mitgenommen; **I'm ~!** ich bin ganz erschüttert!; Ⓒ (*Brit. coll.: exhausted*) **I'm ~:** ich bin [völlig] kaputt (*ugs.*); **I feel/she looks ~:** ich bin [völlig] kaputt/sie sieht [ziemlich] kaputt aus (*ugs.*)

**shattering** /ˈʃætərɪŋ/ *adj.* Ⓐ (*ruinously destructive*) verheerend ‹Wirkung, Explosion›; vernichtend ‹Schlag, Niederlage›; Ⓑ (*coll.: very upsetting*) erschütternd; **it must have been ~ for you** es muss dich schwer mitgenommen haben; Ⓒ (*coll.: exhausting*) wahnsinnig anstrengend (*ugs.*)

**'shatter-proof** *adj.* splitterfrei; **~ glass** Sicherheitsglas, *das*

**shave** /ʃeɪv/ ➊ *v.t.* Ⓐ rasieren; abrasieren ‹Haare›; **he ~d his beard** er hat sich (*Dat.*) den Bart abrasiert; Ⓑ (*pare surface of*) abhobeln; Ⓒ (*fig.*) **~ a few hundredths of a second off the record** den Rekord um ein paar Hundertstelsekunden verbessern; Ⓓ (*graze*) ‹Auto:› streifen. ➋ *v.i.* Ⓐ sich rasieren; Ⓑ (*scrape*) **~ past sth.** etw. [leicht] streifen. ➌ *n.* Ⓐ Rasur, *die;* **have** *or* **get a ~:** sich rasieren; **have** *or* **get a ~ at the barber's** sich beim Friseur rasieren lassen; **this razor gives a good ~:** dieser Rasierapparat rasiert gut; **a clean** *or* **close ~:** eine Glattrasur; Ⓑ **close ~** (*fig.*) ⇒ **close** 1 F; Ⓒ (*tool*) Schabmesser, *das*

**~ 'off** *v.t.* abrasieren ‹Bart, Haare›

**shaven** /ˈʃeɪvn/ *adj.* rasiert; [kahl]geschoren ‹Kopf›

**shaver** /ˈʃeɪvə(r)/ *n.* Ⓐ Rasierapparat, *der;* Rasierer, *der* (*ugs.*); Ⓑ (*dated coll.: lad*) **[young] ~:** junger Spund (*ugs.*)

**'shaver point** *n.* Anschluss *od.* Steckdose für den Rasierapparat

**Shavian** /ˈʃeɪvɪən/ *adj.* Shawsch

**shaving** /ˈʃeɪvɪŋ/ *n.* Ⓐ (*action*) Rasieren, *das;* Ⓑ *in pl.* (*of wood, metal, etc.*) Späne

**shaving: ~ brush** *n.* Rasierpinsel, *der;* **~ cream** *n.* Rasiercreme, *die;* **~ foam** *n.* Rasierschaum, *der;* **~ mug** *n.* Rasierbecken, *das;* **~ soap** *n.* Rasierseife, *die;* **~ stick** *n.* Stangenrasierseife, *die*

**shawl** /ʃɔːl/ *n.* Schultertuch, *das;* (*light blanket*) Umschlagtuch, *das*

**she** /ʃɪ, *stressed* ʃiː/ ➊ *pron.* sie; *referring to personified things or animals which correspond to German masculines/neuters* er/es; **it was ~** (*formal*) sie war es; ⇒ *also* **her**[1,2]; **hers; herself.** ➋ *n., pl.* **~s** /ʃiːz/ Sie, *die* (*ugs.*); **is it a he or a ~?** ist es ein Er oder eine Sie?

**she-** /ʃiː/ *in comb.* weiblich; **~ass/-bear** Eselin, *die*/Bärin, *die;* **~cat, ~devil** (*fig. derog.: malignant woman*) Drachen, *der* (*salopp abwertend*)

**sheaf** /ʃiːf/ *n., pl.* **sheaves** /ʃiːvz/ (*of corn etc.*) Garbe, *die;* (*of paper, arrows, etc.*) Bündel, *das*

**shear** /ʃɪə(r)/ ➊ *v.t., p. p.* **shorn** /ʃɔːn/ *or* **sheared** Ⓐ (*clip*) scheren; **be shorn of sth.** (*fig.*) einer Sache (*Gen.*) beraubt sein/werden; Ⓑ (*Mech., Geol.: break*) abscheren. ➋ *v.i., p. p.* **shorn** *or* **sheared** ‹Bolzen, Metallteil:› abscheren (*Technik*); **the motor boat ~ed through the water** (*fig.*) das Motorboot durchschnitt das Wasser (*fig.*); **the cutter blades ~ed through the metal** die Schneiden der Schere zerschnitten das Metall. ➌ *n.* (*Mech., Geol.*) Scherung, *die*

**~ 'off** ➊ *v.t.* abtrennen. ➋ *v.i.* abscheren (*Technik*)

**shearer** /ˈʃɪərə(r)/ *n.* Ⓐ ▶ **1261** (*of sheep*) Scherer, *der;* Ⓑ (*metalworker*) ▶ **1261** Metallschneider, *der;* Ⓒ (*machine*) Schneidemaschine, *die*

**shearing** /ˈʃɪərɪŋ/ *n.* Scheren, *das*

**shears** /ʃɪəz/ *n. pl.* **[pair of] ~** (*große*) Schere, *die;* **garden ~:** Heckenschere, *die*

**'shearwater** *n.* (*Ornith.*) Sturmtaucher, *der*

**sheath** /ʃiːθ/ *n., pl.* **~s** /ʃiːðz, ʃiːθs/ Ⓐ (*for knife, dagger, sword, etc.*) Scheide, *die;* Ⓑ (*Zool.*) (*of insect*) Elytron, *das;* Schutzdecke, *die;* Ⓒ (*Electr.*) Mantel, *der;* Ⓓ (*condom*) Gummischutz, *der*

**sheathe** /ʃiːð/ *v.t.* Ⓐ (*put into sheath*) in die Scheide stecken ‹Messer, Schwert, Dolch›; Ⓑ (*protect*) ummanteln (**in, with** mit)

**sheathing** /ˈʃiːðɪŋ/ *n.* Ummantelung, *die*

**'sheath knife** *n.* Fahrtenmesser, *das*

**sheave**[1] /ʃiːv/ *n.* Rolle, *die*

**sheave**[2] *v.t.* zu Garben binden ‹Getreide›

**sheaves** *pl. of* **sheaf**

**shebang** /ʃɪˈbæŋ/ *n.* (*Amer. coll.*) **the whole ~:** der ganze Kram (*ugs.*); **who runs the whole ~?** wer ist der Boss vom Ganzen? (*ugs.*)

**shed**[1] /ʃed/ *v.t.*, **-dd-, shed** Ⓐ (*part with*) verlieren; abwerfen, verlieren ‹Laub, Geweih›; abstreifen ‹Haut, Hülle, Badehose›; ausziehen ‹Kleidung›; **a duck's back ~s water** vom Rücken einer Ente läuft das Wasser ab; **the snake is ~ding its skin** die Schlange häutet sich; **dogs/cats ~ hairs** Hunde/Katzen haaren; **you should ~ a few pounds** du solltest ein paar Pfund abspecken (*salopp*); Ⓑ vergießen ‹Blut, Tränen›; **~ tears over sth.** wegen einer Sache Tränen vergießen; **don't ~ any tears over him** seinetwegen solltest du keine Tränen vergießen; **without ~ding blood** ohne Blutvergießen; Ⓒ (*dispense*) verbreiten ‹Wärme, Licht›; ⇒ *also* **light**[1] 1 H; Ⓓ (*fig.: cast off*) abschütteln ‹Sorgen, Bürde›; ablegen ‹Gewohnheit›

**shed**[2] *n.* Schuppen, *der;* **wooden ~:** Holzschuppen, *der*

**she'd** /ʃɪd, *stressed* ʃiːd/ Ⓐ = **she had;** Ⓑ = **she would**

**sheen** /ʃiːn/ *n.* Glanz, *der*

**sheep** /ʃiːp/ *n., pl. same* Ⓐ Schaf, *das;* **separate the ~ from the goats** (*fig.*) die Böcke von den Schafen trennen; **count ~** (*fig.*) Schäfchen zählen (*fam.*); **follow sb. like ~:** jmdm. wie eine Schafherde folgen; ⇒ *also* **black sheep; eye** 1 A; **lamb** 1 A; **wolf** 1 A; Ⓑ (*person*) Schäfchen, *das* (*fam.*); Schäflein, *das* (*fam.*)

**sheep: ~ dip** *n.* Desinfektionsbad für Schafe; **~dog** *n.* Hütehund, *der;* Schäferhund, *der;* **Old English S~dog** Bobtail, *der;* **~ farm** *n.* (*Brit.*) Schaffarm, *die;* **~ farmer** *n.* ▶ **1261** (*Brit.*) Schafzüchter, *der*/-züchterin, *die;* **~fold** *n.* Ⓐ (*pen*) Schafhürde, *die;* Pferch, *der;* Ⓑ (*shelter*) Schafstall, *der*

**sheepish** /ˈʃiːpɪʃ/ *adj.* (*awkwardly self-conscious*) verlegen; (*embarrassed*) kleinlaut; **he felt a bit ~** (*foolish*) es war ihm ein bisschen peinlich

**sheepishly** /ˈʃiːpɪʃlɪ/ *adv.* ⇒ **sheepish**: verlegen; kleinlaut

**sheep: ~meat** *n.* Schaffleisch, *das;* **~ pen** ⇒ **sheepfold** A; **~shank** *n.* (*knot*) lange Trompete (*Seemannsspr.*); **~ shearer** /ˈʃiːp ʃɪərə(r)/ *n.* ▶ **1261** Schafscherer, *der;* **~-shearing** *n.* Schafschur, *die;* **~skin** *n.* Ⓐ Schaffell, *das;* **~skin [jacket]** Schaffelljacke, *die;* Ⓑ (*leather*) Schafleder, *das;* **~ walk** *n.* (*Brit.*) Schafweide, *die*

**sheer**[1] /ʃɪə(r)/ ➊ *adj.* Ⓐ *attrib.* (*mere, absolute*) rein; blank ‹Unsinn, Gewalt›; **by ~ chance** rein zufällig; **it is a ~ impossibility to do it** es ist schier unmöglich, es zu tun; **that's ~ robbery!** das ist ja der reinste Wucher!; **the ~ insolence of it!** so eine Frechheit!; **only by ~ hard work** nur durch harte Arbeit; Ⓑ (*perpendicular*) schroff ‹Felsen, Abfall›; steil ‹Felsen, Abfall, Aufstieg›; Ⓒ (*finely woven*) hauchfein. ➋ *adv.* (*perpendicularly*) schroff; steil

**sheer**[2] *v.i.* (*Naut.*) [aus]scheren

**~ a'way** *v.i.* Ⓐ (*Naut.*) abscheren; Ⓑ **~ away from** (*fig.: avoid*) ausweichen (+ *Dat.*) ‹Person, Thema›

**sheet**[1] /ʃiːt/ ➊ *n.* Ⓐ Laken, *das;* (*for covering mattress*) Betttuch, *das;* Laken, *das;* **put clean ~s on the bed** das Bett frisch beziehen; **between the ~s** (*in bed*) im Bett; ⇒ *also* **white** 1 B; Ⓑ (*of thin metal, plastic*) Folie, *die;* (*of iron, tin*) Blech, *das;* (*of glass, of thicker metal, plastic*) Platte, *die;* (*of stamps*) Bogen, *der;* (*of paper*) Bogen, *der;* Blatt, *das;* **a ~ of iron/plastic** ein Eisenblech/eine Plastikfolie; **a ~ of paper** ein Papierbogen; ein Bogen *od.* Blatt Papier; **five ~s of wrapping paper** 5 Bögen Einwickelpapier; **a 250-~ roll of toilet paper** eine 250-Blatt-Rolle Toilettenpapier; **~ of music** Notenblatt, *das; attrib.* **~ glass/metal/iron** Flachglas, *das*/Blech, *das*/Eisenblech, *das;* ⇒ *also* **clean** 1 B; Ⓒ (*wide expanse*) ‹Eis-, Lava-, Nebel›decke, *die;* **a ~ of water covered the lawn** der Rasen stand unter Wasser; **a huge ~ of flame** ein Flammenmeer; **the rain was coming down in ~s** es regnete in Strömen; Ⓓ (*Printing*) Druckbogen, *der;* **a book in ~s** ein Rohexemplar.
➋ *v.i.* **the rain was ~ing down** es regnete in Strömen

**sheet**[2] *n.* A (*of sail*) Schot, *die;* B **be three ~s in** *or* **to the wind** (*coll.*) voll wie eine Strandhaubitze sein (*ugs.*)

**'sheet anchor** *n.* (*Naut.*) Notanker, *der;* (*fig.*) Rettungsanker, *der*

**sheeting** /'ʃi:tɪŋ/ *n.* A (*cloth for making bedsheets*) Bettzeugstoff, *der;* Haustuch, *das;* B (*of thin metal, plastic, etc.*) Folie, *die;* (*of iron, tin*) Blech, *das;* (*of thicker metal, plastic*) Platte, *die*

**sheet: ~ lightning** *n.* (*Meteorol.*) Flächenblitz, *der;* **~ music** *n.* Notenblätter

**sheik, sheikdom** ⇒ **sheikh, sheikhdom**

**sheikh** /ʃeɪk, ʃi:k/ *n.* Scheich, *der*

**sheikhdom** /ʃeɪkdəm, ʃi:kdəm/ *n.* Scheichtum, *das*

**sheila** /'ʃi:lə/ *n.* (*Austral. and NZ coll.: young woman*) Puppe, *die* (*salopp*)

**shekel** /'ʃekl/ *n.* A ▶ **1328** Schekel, *der;* B *in pl.* (*coll.: money, riches*) Moneten *Pl.* (*ugs.*)

**sheldrake** /'ʃeldreɪk/ *n.*, *fem. and pl.* **shelduck** *or* **sheld duck** /'ʃeldʌk/ (*Ornith.*) Brandente, *die;* Brandgans, *die*

**shelf** /ʃelf/ *n.*, *pl.* **shelves** /ʃelvz/ A (*flat board*) Brett, *das;* Bord, *das;* (*compartment*) Fach, *das;* (*set of shelves*) Regal, *das;* **~ of books** Bücherbrett, *das;* **be left on the ~** (*fig.*) sitzen geblieben sein (*ugs.*); **be put on the ~** (*fig.*) aufs Abstellgleis geschoben werden (*ugs.*); B (*Geol.*) Riff, *das;* ⇒ *also* **continental shelf**

**shelf-ful** /'ʃelfful/ *n.* **a ~ of books** *etc.* ein Bord voll Bücher *usw.*

**shelf: ~ life** *n.* Lagerfähigkeit, *die;* **~ mark** *n.* Standortnummer, *die;* **~ room, ~ space** *ns.* Stellfläche [im Regal]; **give ~ room** *or* **space to sth.** sich (*Dat.*) etw. ins Regal stellen

**shell** /ʃel/ ❶ *n.* A (*casing*) Schale, *die;* (*of turtle, tortoise*) Panzer, *der;* (*of pupa*) Hülle, *die;* (*of snail*) Haus, *das;* (*of pea*) Schote, *die;* Hülse, *die;* (*of insect's wing*) Flügeldecke, *die;* **collect ~s on the beach** am Strand Muscheln sammeln; **bring sb. out of his ~** (*fig.*) jmdn. aus der Reserve locken (*ugs.*); **come out of one's ~** (*fig.*) aus sich herausgehen; **retire** *or* **go into one's ~** (*fig.*) sich in sein Schneckenhaus zurückziehen (*ugs.*); B (*frame*) Gerippe, das (*fig.*); (*of unfinished building*) Rohbau, *der;* (*of building needing to be refurbished*) Außenmauern und Dach; (*of ruinous building*) Ruine, *die;* C (*pastry case*) Teighülle, *die;* D (*racing boat*) Rennruderboot, *das;* E (*Motor Veh.*) [**body**] **~:** Aufbau, *der;* Karosserie, *die;* (*after fire, at breaker's, etc.*) [Karosserie]gerippe, *das;* F (*Mil.*) (*bomb*) Granate, *die;* (*Amer.: cartridge*) Patrone, *die.*

❷ *v.t.* A (*take out of ~*) schälen; knacken, schälen ‹Nuss›; öffnen ‹Auster›; enthülsen, (*nordd.*) palen ‹Erbsen›; **as easy as ~ing peas** kinderleicht; **~ed nuts** Nusskerne; B (*Mil.*) [mit Artillerie] beschießen

**~ 'out** *v.t. & i.* (*coll.*) blechen (*ugs.*) (**on** für)

**she'll** /ʃɪl, *stressed* ʃi:l/ ... **she will**

**shellac** /ʃə'læk/ ❶ *n.* Schellack, *der.* ❷ *v.t.*, **-ck-** A (*varnish*) mit Schellack überziehen; B (*Amer. coll.: defeat, thrash*) vermöbeln (*ugs.*); fertig machen (*ugs.*)

**shell: ~fish** *n.*, *pl. same* A Schal[en]tier, *das;* (*oyster, clam*) Muschel, *die;* (*crustacean*) Krebstier, *das;* B *in pl.* (*Gastr.*) Meeresfrüchte *Pl.;* **~-pink** *adj.* muschelrosa; **~proof** *adj.* bombensicher; **~ shock** *n.* (*Psych.*) Kriegsneurose, *die;* **~-shocked** *adj.* **be ~-shocked** eine Kriegsneurose haben; (*fig.*) niedergeschmettert sein; **~ suit** *n.* Trilobalanzug, *der*

**shelter** /'ʃeltə(r)/ ❶ *n.* A (*shield*) Schutz, *der* (**against** vor + *Dat.*, gegen); **bomb** *or* **air-raid ~:** Luftschutzraum, *der;* **get under ~:** sich unterstellen; **under the ~ of the rocks/of night** im Schutz der Felsen/der Nacht; **wooden/mountain ~:** Holz-/Berg- *od.* Schutzhütte, *die;* B *no pl.* (*place of safety*) Zuflucht, *die;* **we needed food and ~:** wir brauchten etwas zu essen und eine Unterkunft; **look for ~ for the night** eine Unterkunft für die Nacht suchen; **offer** *or* **give sb. ~, provide ~ for sb.** jmdm. Zuflucht gewähren *od.* bieten; **in the ~ of one's home** im Schutz *od.* in der Geborgenheit seines Heims; **take ~ [from a storm]** [vor einem Sturm] Schutz suchen; **seek/reach ~:** Schutz *od.* Zuflucht suchen/finden.

❷ *v.t.* schützen (**from** vor + *Dat.*); Unterschlupf gewähren (+ *Dat.*) ‹Flüchtling›; **~ sb. from blame/harm** jmdn. decken/gegen alle Gefahren schützen.

❸ *v.i.* Schutz *od.* Zuflucht suchen (**from** vor + *Dat.*); **this is a good place to ~:** hier ist man gut geschützt

**sheltered** /'ʃeltəd/ *adj.* geschützt ‹Platz, Tal›; behütet ‹Leben›; **~ workshops** beschützende Werkstätten; **~ employment** Beschäftigung in beschützenden Werkstätten; **live in ~ housing** in einer Altenwohnung/in Altenwohnungen leben

**shelve** /ʃelv/ ❶ *v.t.* A (*put on shelves*) ins Regal stellen; (*fig.*) (*abandon*) ad acta *od.* (*ugs.*) zu den Akten legen; (*defer*) auf Eis legen (*ugs.*); B (*fit with shelves*) ein Regal einbauen (+ *Akk.*) ‹Nische›; ausfachen (*fachspr.*), mit Fächern versehen ‹Schrank›; mit Borden versehen ‹Wand›. ❷ *v.i.* **~ away/off/out into** ‹Berg, Boden, Ebene:› abfallen nach

**shelves** *pl. of* **shelf**

**shelving** /'ʃelvɪŋ/ *n.*, *no pl.* Regale *Pl.*

**shemozzle** /ʃɪ'mɒzl/ *n.* (*coll.*) A (*rumpus, brawl*) Keilerei, *die* (*ugs.*); B (*muddle*) Schlamassel, *der* (*ugs.*)

**shenanigans** /ʃɪ'nænɪgənz/ *n. pl.* (*coll.*) (*trickery*) Tricks; (*nonsense*) Fez, *der* (*ugs.*); (*high-spirited behaviour*) Klamauk, *der* (*ugs. abwertend*)

**shepherd** /'ʃepəd/ ❶ ▶ **1261** *n.* Schäfer, *der;* Schafhirt, *der;* (*Relig. fig.*) Hirt[e], *der* (*geh.*); **the Good S~:** der Gute Hirte. ❷ *v.t.* hüten; (*fig.*) führen

**'shepherd dog** *n.* Hütehund, *der;* Schäferhund, *der;* ⇒ *also* **German shepherd [dog]**

**shepherdess** /'ʃepədɪs/ *n.* ▶ **1261** Schäferin, *die;* Schafhirtin, *die*

**shepherd: ~'s 'crook** *n.* Schäferstock, *der;* Hirtenstab, *der* (*geh.*); **~'s 'pie** *n.* (*Gastr.*) *Auflauf aus Hackfleisch mit einer Schicht Kartoffelbrei darüber;* **~'s 'purse** *n.* (*Bot.*) Hirtentäschelkraut, *das*

**sherbet** /'ʃɜ:bət/ n. A (*fruit juice; also Amer.: water ice*) Sorbet[t], *der od. das;* B (*effervescent drink*) Brauselimonade, *die;* (*powder*) Brausepulver, *das*

**sherd** /ʃɜ:d/ *n.* Scherbe, *die*

**sheriff** /'ʃerɪf/ *n.* ▶ **1261** Sheriff, *der*

**'sheriff court** *n.* (*Scot. Law*) *Grafschaftsgericht mit Zuständigkeit in Zivil- und Strafsachen*

**Sherpa** /'ʃɜ:pə/ *n.* (*Ethnol.*) Sherpa, *der*/Sherpani, *die*

**sherry** /'ʃerɪ/ *n.* Sherry, *der;* **~ glass** Sherryglas, *das;* ≈ Südweinglas, *das*

**she's** /ʃɪz, *stressed* ʃi:z/ A = **she is;** B = **she has**

**Shetland** /'ʃetlənd/ *pr. n.* ⇒ **Shetland Islands**

**Shetlander** /'ʃetləndə(r)/ *n.* Shetländer, *der*/-länderin, *die*

**Shetland Islands** *pr. n. pl.* Shetlandinseln *Pl.;* Shetlands *Pl.*

**Shetland: ~ 'jumper** *n.* Pullover aus Shetlandwolle; **~ 'pony** *n.* Shetlandpony, *das*

**Shetlands** /'ʃetləndz/ *pr. n. pl.* Shetlands *Pl.*

**Shetland: ~ 'sheepdog** *n.* Sheltie, *der;* **~ 'wool** *n.* Shetlandwolle, *die*

**shew** (*arch.*) ⇒ **show** 2, 3

**shh** /ʃ/ *int.* pst; sch

**Shiah** /'ʃi:ə/ *n.* (*Muslim Relig.*) Schia, *die*

**shibboleth** /'ʃɪbəleθ/ *n.* Schibboleth, *das* (*geh.*); (*catchword*) Schlagwort, *das*

**shield** /ʃi:ld/ ❶ *n.* A (*piece of armour*) Schild, *der;* B (*in machinery etc.*) Schutz, *der;* (*protective plate*) Schutzplatte, *die;* (*protective screen*) Schutzschirm, *der;* **radiation ~:** Strahlenschutz, *der;* C (*fig.: person or thing that protects*) Schild, *der* (*geh.*); D (*Zool.*) Schild, *der;* E (*Geol.*) Schild, *der;* F (*Her.*) [Wappen]schild, *der;* G (*Sport: trophy*) Trophäe, *die* (*in Form eines Schildes*); H (*Amer.: policeman's badge*) Dienstmarke, *die.*

❷ *v.t.* A (*protect*) schützen (**from** vor + *Dat.*); B (*conceal*) decken ‹Schuldigen›; **~ sb. from the truth** die Wahrheit von jmdn. fern halten

**shier, shiest** ⇒ **shy**[1] 1

**shift** /ʃɪft/ ❶ *v.t.* A (*move*) verrücken, umstellen ‹Möbel›; wegnehmen ‹Arm, Hand, Fuß›; wegräumen ‹Schutt›; entfernen ‹Schmutz, Fleck›; (*to another floor, room, or place*) verlegen ‹Büro, Patienten, Schauplatz›; bringen ‹Gerümpel›; (*to another town*) versetzen ‹Person›; **~ one's weight to the other foot** sein Gewicht auf den anderen Fuß verlagern; **~ the responsibility/blame on to sb.** (*fig.*) die Verantwortung/Schuld auf jmdn. schieben; ⇒ *also* **ground**[1] 1 B; B (*Amer. Motor Veh.*) **~ gears** schalten; C (*coll.: consume*) verkonsumieren (*ugs.*); D (*coll.: sell*) loswerden (*ugs.*).

❷ *v.i.* A ‹Wind:› drehen (**to** nach); ‹Ladung:› verrutschen; (*in drama, novel, etc.*) ‹Szene:› wechseln (**to** nach); ‹Schauplatz:› sich verlagern (**to** nach); **~ uneasily in one's chair** unruhig auf dem Stuhl hin und her rutschen; B (*manage*) **~ for oneself** selbst für sich sorgen; C (*coll.: move quickly*) rasen; **this new Porsche really ~s** der neue Porsche geht ab wie eine Rakete (*ugs.*); D (*Amer. Motor Veh.: change gear*) schalten; **~ down into second gear** in den zweiten Gang runterschalten (*ugs.*).

❸ *n.* A **a ~ in emphasis** eine Verlagerung des Akzents; **a ~ in values/public opinion** ein Wandel der Wertvorstellungen/ein Umschwung der öffentlichen Meinung; **a ~ towards/away from liberalism** eine Hinwendung zum/Abwendung vom Liberalismus; B (*for work*) Schicht, *die;* **eight-hour/late ~:** Achtstunden-/Spätschicht, *die;* **do** *or* **work the late ~:** Spätschicht haben; **work in ~s** Schichtarbeit machen; C (*stratagem, dodge*) Kunstgriff, *der;* D **make ~ with/without sth.** sich (*Dat.*) mit/ohne etw. behelfen; E (*of typewriter*) Umschaltung, *die; attrib.* **~ key** Umschalttaste, *die;* Umschalter, *der;* F (*Amer. Motor Veh.: gear change*) Schaltung, *die;* **manual/automatic ~:** Hand-/Automatikschaltung, *die;* G (*dress*) Hängekleid, *das;* Hänger, *der;* H (*Phys.*) Verschiebung, *die;* I (*Ling.*) **sound ~:** Lautverschiebung, *die*

**shifting 'sands** *n. pl.* (*lit. or fig.*) Flugsand, *der*

**shift: ~less** /'ʃɪftlɪs/ *adj.* (*lacking resourcefulness*) unbeholfen; (*incapable*) unfähig; **~ work** *n.* Schichtarbeit, *die*

**shifty** /'ʃɪftɪ/ *adj.* verschlagen (*abwertend*)

**Shiite** /'ʃi:aɪt/ (*Muslim Relig.*) ❶ *n.* Schiit, *der*/Schiitin, *die.* ❷ *adj.* schiitisch

**shillelagh** /ʃɪ'leɪlə, ʃɪ'leɪlɪ/ *n.* Knüppel, *der* (*aus Schlehdorn- oder Eichenholz*)

**shilling** /'ʃɪlɪŋ/ *n.* Shilling, *der;* **take the King's/Queen's ~** (*arch.*) sich als Rekrut [gegen Handgeld] anwerben lassen; ⇒ *also* **cut off f**

**shilly-shally** /'ʃɪlɪʃælɪ/ *v.i.* zaudern; **stop ~ing!** entschließ dich endlich!

**shimmer** /'ʃɪmə(r)/ ❶ *v.i.* schimmern. ❷ *n.* Schimmer, *der*

**shimmery** /'ʃɪmərɪ/ *adj.* schimmernd

**shin** /ʃɪn/ ❶ *n.* ▶ **966** Schienbein, *das;* **~ of beef** (*Cookery*) [Vorder]hesse, *die.* ❷ *v.i.*, **-nn-: ~ up/down a tree** *etc.* einen Baum *usw.* hinauf-/hinunterklettern

**'shin bone** *n.* Schienbein, *das*

**shindig** /'ʃɪndɪg/ *n.* (*coll.*) A ⇒ **shindy;** B (*party*) Fete, *die* (*ugs.*)

**shindy** /'ʃɪndɪ/ *n.* (*brawl*) Rauferei, *die;* (*row*) Streit, *der;* (*noise*) Krach, *der;* ⇒ *also* **kick up b**

**shine** /ʃaɪn/ ❶ *v.i.*, **shone** /ʃɒn/ A ‹Lampe, Licht, Stern:› leuchten; ‹Sonne:› scheinen; (*reflect light*) glänzen; ‹Mond:› scheinen; **his face shone with happiness/excitement** (*fig.*) er strahlte vor Glück/sein Gesicht glühte vor Aufregung; **a fine morning with the sun shining** ein schöner Morgen mit [strahlendem] Sonnenschein; B (*fig.: be brilliant*) glänzen; **a shining example/light** ein leuchtendes Beispiel/eine Leuchte; **~ at sport** im Sport glänzen; **he does not exactly ~ at maths** er ist nicht gerade eine Leuchte in Mathe (*ugs.*).

❷ *v.t.* Ⓐ *p.t. & p.p.* **shone** leuchten lassen; **~ a light on sth./in sb.'s eyes** etw. anleuchten/jmdm. in die Augen leuchten; **~ the torch this way** leuchte einmal hierher; Ⓑ *p.t. & p.p.* **~d** (*clean and polish*) putzen; (*make shiny*) polieren.

❸ *n., no pl.* Ⓐ (*brightness*) Schein, *der;* Licht, *das;* ⇒ *also* **rain** 1 A; Ⓑ (*polish*) Glanz, *der;* **give your shoes a good ~:** bring deine Schuhe auf Hochglanz; **have a ~** ‹Oberfläche:› glänzen; **put a ~ on sth.** etw. zum Glänzen bringen; **take the ~ off sth.** (*fig.: spoil sth.*) einen Schatten auf etw. (*Akk.*) werfen; Ⓒ **take a ~ to sb./sth.** (*coll.*) Gefallen an jmdm./etw. finden

**shingle**[1] /ˈʃɪŋgl/ ❶ *n.* Ⓐ (*Building*) Schindel, *die;* Ⓑ (*Amer.: signboard*) [Praxis]schild, *das;* Ⓒ (*Hairdressing*) Bubikopf, *der.* ❷ *v.t.* Ⓐ (*Building*) schindeln; Ⓑ (*Hairdressing*) zu einem Bubikopf schneiden ‹Haar›; **~d hair** Bubikopf, *der*

**shingle**[2] *n., no pl., no indef. art.* (*pebbles*) Kies, *der; attrib.* **~ beach** Kiesstrand, *der*

**shingles** /ˈʃɪŋglz/ *n. sing.* ▶ 1232 (*Med.*) Gürtelrose, *die*

**shingly** /ˈʃɪŋglɪ/ *adj.* kiesig; **~ beach** Kiesstrand, *der*

**shin: ~ guard, ~ pad** *ns.* Schienbeinschutz, *der*

**Shinto** /ˈʃɪntəʊ/, **Shintoism** /ˈʃɪntəʊɪzm/ *ns., no pl., no indef. art.* (*Relig.*) Schintoismus, *der*

**Shintoist** /ˈʃɪntəʊɪst/ *n.* (*Relig.*) Schintoist, *der*/Schintoistin, *die*

**shiny** /ˈʃaɪnɪ/ *adj.* Ⓐ (*glistening, polished*) glänzend; Ⓑ (*worn*) blank

**ship** /ʃɪp/ ❶ *n.* Ⓐ Schiff, *das;* **take ~:** sich einschiffen (**for** nach); **when my ~ comes home** *or* **in** (*fig.*) wenn ich zu Geld komme; **~ of the desert** (*fig.*) Wüstenschiff, *das* (*geh. scherzh.*); Schiff der Wüste (*geh.*); **we were just ~s that pass in the night** (*fig.*) nur einmal kreuzten sich unsere Wege; **the ~ of state** das Staatsschiff (*geh.*); **run a tight ~** (*fig.*) ein strenges Regiment führen; ⇒ *also* **break**[1] 1 G; **company** A, H; **tar**[1] 1; Ⓑ (*Amer.: aircraft*) Flugzeug, *das;* Maschine, *die;* Ⓒ (*coll.: spacecraft*) Raumschiff, *das.*

❷ *v.t.*, **-pp-:** Ⓐ (*take on board*) einschiffen, an Bord bringen ‹Vorräte, Ladung, Passagiere›; (*transport by sea*) verschiffen ‹Auto, Truppen›; (*send by train, road, or air*) verschicken, versenden ‹Waren›; Ⓑ (*Naut.: position*) setzen ‹Ruderpinne, Mast, Positionslichter›; Ⓒ **~ oars** (*bring them into the boat*) die Riemen einlegen *od.* -ziehen; Ⓓ **~ water/a sea** Wasser/eine See übernehmen (*Seemansspr.*).

❸ *v.i.*, **-pp-:** Ⓐ (*embark*) sich einschiffen; Ⓑ (*take service on ~*) anheuern, anmustern (*Seemannsspr.*)

**~ 'off** *v.t.* versenden, verschicken ‹Waren›; schicken ‹Person›

**~ 'out** *v.t.* verschiffen ‹Ladung, Güter›

**ship: ~board** ❶ *adj.* ‹Romanze usw.› an Bord; ❷ *n., no pl., no art.* **on ~board** an Bord; **~breaker** *n.* Abwrackfirma, *die;* **~broker** *n.* Schiffsmakler, *der;* **~builder** *n.* ▶ 1261 Schiff[s]bauer, *der;* **firm of ~builders** Schiffbaufirma, *die;* **~building** *n., no pl., no indef. art.* Schiffbau, *der;* **~ canal** *n.* Schifffahrtskanal, *der;* **~load** *n.* Schiffsladung, *die;* **~mate** *n.* Schiffskamerad, *der*

**shipment** /ˈʃɪpmənt/ *n.* Ⓐ Versand, *der;* (*by sea*) Verschiffung, *die;* Ⓑ (*amount*) Sendung, *die;* **a ~ of bananas** eine Ladung Bananen

**'shipowner** *n.* Schiffseigentümer, *der*/-eigentümerin, *die;* Schiffseigner, *der*/-eignerin, *die;* (*of several ships*) Reeder, *der*/Reederin, *die*

**shipper** /ˈʃɪpə(r)/ *n.* (*merchant*) Spediteur, *der*/Spediteurin, *die;* (*company*) Spedition, *die*

**shipping** /ˈʃɪpɪŋ/ *n.* Ⓐ *no pl., no indef. art.* (*ships*) Schiffe *Pl.;* (*traffic*) Schifffahrt, *die;* Schiffsverkehr, *der;* **all ~:** alle Schiffe/der ganze Schiffsverkehr; **closed to ~:** für Schiffe/für die Schifffahrt gesperrt; Ⓑ (*transporting*) Versand, *der*

**shipping: ~ agent** *n.* Schiffsagent, *der;* **~ forecast** *n.* Seewetterbericht, *der;* **~ lane** *n.* Schifffahrtsweg, *der;* (*fairway*) Fahrrinne, *die;* **~ line** ⇒ **line**[1] 1 I; **~ office** *n.* Ⓐ (*of ~ agent*) Schiffsagentur, *die;* Ⓑ (*hiring seamen*) Heuerbüro, *das*

**ship: ~'s 'biscuit** *n.* Schiffszwieback, *der;* **~'s chandler** *n.* Schiffsausrüster, *der;* **~shape** *pred. adj.* in bester Ordnung; **get sth. ~shape** etw. in Ordnung bringen; **find everything ~shape and Bristol fashion** (*coll.*) alles picobello *od.* tipptopp (*ugs.*) vorfinden; **~'s 'papers** *n. pl.* Schiffspapiere *Pl.;* **~way** *n.* Helling, *die* (*Schiffbau*); **~wreck** ❶ *n.* (*lit. or fig.*) Schiffbruch, *der;* **suffer ~wreck** Schiffbruch erleiden; **end in ~wreck** (*fig.*) scheitern; ❷ *v.t.* **be ~wrecked** Schiffbruch erleiden; (*fig.: be ruined*) ‹Hoffnung:› sich zerschlagen haben; ‹Karriere:› gescheitert sein; **be ~wrecked on an island** bei einem Schiffbruch auf eine Insel verschlagen werden; **~wright** *n.* (*~ builder*) Schiff[s]bauer, *der;* (*~'s carpenter*) Schiffszimmermann, *der;* **~yard** *n.* [Schiffs]werft, *die*

**shire** /ˈʃaɪə(r)/ *n.* Ⓐ (*county*) Grafschaft, *die;* Ⓑ **the Shires** (*group of counties*) *die auf -shire endenden englischen Grafschaften;* (*midland counties*) die Grafschaften in Mittelengland; Ⓒ ⇒ **shire-horse**

**'shire horse** *n. bes. in Mittelengland gezüchtetes schweres Zugpferd*

**shirk** /ʃɜːk/ *v.t.* sich entziehen (+ *Dat.*) ‹Pflicht, Verantwortung›; ausweichen (+ *Dat.*) ‹Blick, Kampf›; **~ one's job/doing sth.** sich vor der Arbeit drücken/sich davor drücken (*ugs.*), etw. zu tun; **you're ~ing!** [du bist ein] Drückeberger! (*ugs. abwertend*)

**shirker** /ˈʃɜːkə(r)/ *n.* Drückeberger, *der* (*ugs. abwertend*)

**shirring** /ˈʃɜːrɪŋ/ *n.* Kräusel[ung], *die*

**shirt** /ʃɜːt/ *n.* **[man's] ~:** [Herren- *od.* Ober]hemd, *das;* **[woman's** *or* **lady's] ~:** Hemdbluse, *die;* **sports/rugby/football ~:** Trikot/Rugby-/Fußballtrikot, *das;* **keep your ~ on!** (*fig. coll.*) [nur] ruhig Blut! (*ugs.*); **have the ~ off sb.'s back** (*fig.*) jmdm. das Hemd über den Kopf ziehen (*fig. ugs.*); **lose the ~ off one's back** alles bis aufs Hemd verlieren (*ugs.*); **put one's ~ on sth.** (*fig. coll.*) sein letztes Hemd für etw. verwetten (*ugs.*)

**shirt: ~ blouse** *n.* Hemdbluse, *die;* **~ dress** *n.* Hemdblusenkleid, *das;* **~ front** *n.* Hemdbrust, *die;* (*separate or detachable*) Vorhemd, *das*

**shirting** /ˈʃɜːtɪŋ/ *n.* Hemdenstoff, *der*

**shirt: ~sleeve** ❶ *n.* Hemdsärmel, *der;* **work in one's ~sleeves** in Hemdsärmeln arbeiten; ❷ *adj.* hemdsärmelig; körperlich ‹Arbeit›; **it is real ~sleeve weather** bei diesem Wetter kann man ohne Jacke gehen; **~ tail** ⇒ **tail** 1 D; **~waist** (*Amer.*) ⇒ **shirt blouse**; **~waister** /ˈʃɜːtweɪstə(r)/ (*Brit.*) ⇒ **shirt dress**

**shirty** /ˈʃɜːtɪ/ *adj.* (*coll.*) sauer (*salopp*); **get ~ with sb./about sth.** auf jmdn./wegen etw. sauer werden; **be ~ with sb.** rotzig (*salopp abwertend*) zu jmdm. sein

**shish kebab** /ˈʃɪʃ kɪbæb, ˈʃɪʃ kɪbɑːb/ *n.* (*Gastr.*) Kebab, *der*

**shit** /ʃɪt/ (*coarse*) ❶ *v.i.*, **-tt-, shitted** *or* **shit** *or* **shat** /ʃæt/ scheißen (*derb*); **~ in one's pants** sich (*Dat.*) in die Hose[n] scheißen.

❷ *v. refl.*, **-tt-, shitted** *or* **shit** *or* **shat** sich (*Dat.*) in die Hose[n] scheißen (*derb*).

❸ *int.* Scheiße (*derb*).

❹ *n.* Ⓐ (*excrement*) Scheiße, *die* (*derb*); **have** (*Brit.*) *or* (*Amer.*) **take a ~:** scheißen (*derb*); **have/get the ~s** die Scheißerei (*derb*) haben/kriegen; **when the ~ hits the fan** wenn die Kacke am Dampfen ist (*derb*); Ⓑ (*hashish*) Shit, *der od. das* (*Drogenjargon*); Ⓒ (*person*) Scheißkerl, *der;* (*nonsense*) Scheiß, *der* (*salopp abwertend*); **don't give me that ~:** erzähl mir nicht so einen Scheiß! (*salopp*); **I don't give a ~ [about it]** das ist mir scheißegal (*salopp*); **who gives a ~!** ist doch scheißegal! (*salopp*); **it's not worth a ~:** es ist einen Dreck wert (*salopp abwertend*); **beat** *or* **kick** *or* **knock the ~ out of sb.** (*fig.*) jmdn. gehörig verdreschen (*ugs.*); **I'll beat the ~ out of you!** ich mach' Hackfleisch aus dir! (*ugs.*); **be up ~ creek [without a paddle]** (*fig.*) bis zum Hals in der Scheiße stecken (*derb*); **have/get the ~s** (*fig.*) Schiss haben/kriegen (*salopp*)

**shite** /ʃaɪt/ (*coarse*) ❶ *int.* Scheibenkleister (*ugs. verhüll.*). ❷ *n.* Scheiß, *der* (*salopp*); **not give a ~ for sb./sth.** sich einen [Scheiß]dreck um jmdn./etw. kümmern (*salopp*)

**shitless** /ˈʃɪtlɪs/ *adj.* (*coarse*) **be scared ~:** sich (*Dat.*) vor Angst in die Hose[n] scheißen (*derb*)

**'shit-scared** *pred. adj.* (*coarse*) **be ~:** Schiss haben (*salopp*)

**shitty** /ˈʃɪtɪ/ *adj.* (*coarse*) beschissen (*derb*); Scheiß- (*salopp*)

**shiver**[1] /ˈʃɪvə(r)/ ❶ *v.i.* (*tremble*) zittern (**with** vor + *Dat.*); **~ all over** am ganzen Leib *od.* Körper zittern; **~ like a leaf** wie Espenlaub zittern (*geh.*). ❷ *n.* (*trembling, lit. or fig.*) Schau[d]er, *der* (*geh.*); **~ of cold/fear** Kälte-/Angstschauer, *der;* **send ~s** *or* **a ~ up** *or* **[up and] down sb.'s back** *or* **spine** jmdm. [einen] Schauder über den Rücken jagen; **give sb. the ~s** (*fig.*) jmdn. schaudern lassen; **get/have the ~s** (*fig.*) eine Gänsehaut (*fig.*) *od.* (*bei Krankheit*) Schüttelfrost bekommen/haben

**shiver**[2] ❶ *n. in pl.* (*fragments*) **break/burst into ~s** in Stücke zerbrechen *od.* zerspringen. ❷ *v.t.* zersplittern lassen; **~ me timbers** potz Blitz! (*veralt.*). ❸ *v.i.* zerspringen

**shivery** /ˈʃɪvərɪ/ *adj.* verfroren ‹Person›; **I feel all ~:** mich fröstelt

**shoal**[1] /ʃəʊl/ *n.* Ⓐ (*shallow place*) Untiefe, *die;* (*sandbank*) Sandbank, *die;* Ⓑ *in pl.* (*fig.: hidden danger*) Klippen

**shoal**[2] *n.* (*of fish*) Schwarm, *der;* (*fig.*) Schar, *die;* **~s of letters/complaints** Unmengen von Briefen/Beschwerden

**shock**[1] /ʃɒk/ ❶ *n.* Ⓐ Schock, *der;* **I got the ~ of my life** ich erschrak zu Tode; **the general feeling is one of ~:** man ist allgemein erschüttert; **come as a ~ to sb.** ein Schock für jmdn. sein; **give sb. a ~:** jmdm. einen Schock versetzen; **he's in for a [nasty] ~!** er wird eine böse Überraschung erleben!; **~ horror!** (*joc.*) Schreck, lass nach! (*ugs. scherzh.*); ⇒ *also* **sharp** 1 D; Ⓑ (*violent impact*) Erschütterung, *die* (**of** durch); Ⓒ (*Electr.*) Schlag, *der;* Ⓓ (*Med.*) Schock, *der;* **die of/be suffering from ~:** an einem Schock sterben/unter Schock[wirkung] stehen; **~ is dangerous** ein Schock kann gefährlich sein; **be in [a state of] ~:** unter Schock[wirkung] stehen; **[electric] ~:** Elektroschock, *der.*

❷ *v.t.* Ⓐ **~ sb. [deeply]** ein [schwerer] Schock für jmdn. sein; **sb. is [terribly] ~ed by/at sth.** etw. ist ein [schwerer] Schock für jmdn.; Ⓑ (*scandalize*) schockieren; **I'm not easily ~ed** mich schockiert so leicht nichts; **be ~ed by sth.** über etw. (*Akk.*) schockiert sein.

❸ *v.i.* schockieren

**shock**[2] *n.* (*of corn sheaves*) Hocke, *die* (*meist aus zwölf Garben*)

**shock**[3] *n.* **a ~ of red hair** ein roter Haarschopf; **an untidy ~ of thick grey hair** eine dichte graue Mähne (*scherzh.*)

**'shock absorber** *n.* Stoßdämpfer, *der*

**shocker** /ˈʃɒkə(r)/ *n.* (*coll.*) Ⓐ **he is a ~ for gambling/drink/the girls** er ist ein hemmungsloser Zocker/Säufer/Weiberheld (*salopp*); Ⓑ (*novel etc.*) Schocker, *der* (*ugs.*)

**shock-headed** /ˈʃɒkhedɪd/ *adj.* **be ~:** eine Mähne haben (*ugs.*); **a ~ little boy/girl** ein kleiner Strubbelkopf (*ugs.*)

**shocking** /ˈʃɒkɪŋ/ ❶ *adj.* Ⓐ schockierend; Ⓑ (*coll.: very bad*) fürchterlich (*ugs.*); **what a ~ thing to say** wie kann man nur so etwas sagen! (*ugs.*). ❷ *adv.* (*coll.*) **~ bad** fürchterlich (*ugs.*)

S

**shockingly** /ˈʃɒkɪŋlɪ/ *adv.* [A] (*badly*) schockierend [schlecht] ‹behandeln, sich benehmen›; [B] (*extremely*) sündhaft (*ugs.*) ‹teuer›; erbärmlich ‹schlecht›

**shocking ˈpink** *adj.* pinkfarben; grellrosa

**shock:** ~ **jock** *n.* (*coll.*) Skandal-DJ, *der;* ~**proof** *adj.* stoßfest ‹Uhr, Kiste›; erschütterungsfest ‹Gebäude›; ~ **tactics** *n. pl.* (*Mil.*) *taktischer Einsatz von Stoßtruppen;* (*fig.*) Überrumpelungstaktik, *die;* ~ **therapy,** ~ **treatment** *ns.* (*Med.*) Schocktherapie, *die;* Schockbehandlung, *die;* ~ **troops** *n. pl.* (*Mil.*) Stoßtruppen (*veralt.*); ~ **wave** *n.* Druckwelle, *die* (**from** *Gen.*); (*of earthquake*) Erschütterungswelle, *die* (**from** *Gen.*)

**shod** ⇒ **shoe** 2

**shoddily** /ˈʃɒdɪlɪ/ *adv.* schludrig (*ugs. abwertend*); **treat sb.** ~**:** jmdn. schäbig behandeln (*abwertend*)

**shoddy** /ˈʃɒdɪ/ ❶ *n.* Shoddy, *das od. der* (*Textilw.*); Reißwolle, *die.* ❷ *adj.* schäbig (*abwertend*); (*poorly done, poor in quality*) minderwertig ‹Arbeit, Stoff, Artikel›

**shoe** /ʃuː/ ❶ *n.* [A] Schuh, *der;* **I shouldn't like to be in his** ~**s** (*fig.*) ich möchte nicht in seiner Haut stecken (*ugs.*); **put oneself into sb.'s** ~**s** (*fig.*) sich in jmds. Lage (*Akk.*) versetzen; **sb. shakes in his** ~**s** jmdm. schlottern die Knie; **if the** ~ **fits** (*Amer.*) = **if the cap fits** ⇒ **cap** 1 A; ⇒ *also* **pinch** 3 A; [B] (*of horse*) [Huf]eisen, *das;* [C] (*of brake*) Backe, *die.* ❷ *v.t.,* ~**ing** /ˈʃuːɪŋ/, **shod** /ʃɒd/ beschlagen ‹Pferd›; (*protect with iron tip*) beschuhen ‹Pfahl›; **be well shod** ‹Person:› gut beschuht sein

**shoe:** ~ **bar** *n.* Schnellschusterei, *die;* ~**black** *n.* Schuhputzer, *der;* ~**box** ⇒ **box**[2] 1 A; ~ **brush** *n.* Schuhbürste, *die;* ~ **buckle** *n.* Schuhschnalle, *die;* ~**cream** *n.* Schuhcreme, *die;* ~**horn** *n.* Schuhlöffel, *der;* ~**lace** *n.* Schnürsenkel, *der;* Schuhband, *das;* ~ **leather** *n.* Schuhleder, *das;* **you can save your** ~ **leather** den Weg kannst du dir sparen

**shoeless** /ˈʃuːlɪs/ *adj.* ohne Schuhe

**shoe:** ~**maker** *n.* ▶ **1261** Schuhmacher, *der;* Schuster, *der;* ~**making** *n., no pl.* Schuhmacherei, *die;* ~ **polish** *n.* Schuhcreme, *die;* ~ **repairer** *n.* Flickschuster, *der* (*veralt.*); Schuster, *der;* ~**shine** *n.* (*Amer.*) **have** *or* **get a** ~**shine** sich (*Dat.*) die Schuhe putzen lassen; ~**shine boy** *n.* (*Amer.*) Schuhputzer, *der;* ~ **shop** *n.* Schuhgeschäft, *das;* ~ **spray** *n.* Schuhspray, *der od. das;* ~**string** *n.* [A] ⇒ **shoelace**; [B] (*coll.: small amount*) **on a** ~**string** mit ganz wenig Geld; *attrib.* **a** ~**string budget** ein minimaler Etat; ~**string financing** Finanzierung mit ganz wenig Geld; ~**string ˈtie** *n. wie eine Krawatte getragene, durch einen Ring oder eine Schleife gehaltene Schnur;* ~ **tree** *n.* Schuhspanner, *der*

**shone** ⇒ **shine** 1, 2

**shoo** /ʃuː/ ❶ *int.* sch. ❷ *v.t.* scheuchen; ~ **away** fort- *od.* wegscheuchen

**shook** ⇒ **shake** 2, 3

**shoot** /ʃuːt/ ❶ *v.i.,* **shot** /ʃɒt/ [A] schießen (**at** auf + *Akk.*); ~ **to kill** ‹Polizei:› scharf schießen; **have sth. to** ~ **at** (*fig.*) ein Ziel vor Augen *od.* eine Zielvorstellung haben; ⇒ *also* **hip**[1] A; [B] (*move rapidly*) schießen (*ugs.*); ~ **past sb./down the stairs** an jmdm. vorbeischießen/die Treppe hinunterschießen (*ugs.*); **come** ~**ing in** hereingeschossen kommen (*ugs.*); **pain shot through/up his arm** ein Schmerz schoss durch seinen Arm/seinen Arm hinauf; [C] (*Bot.*) austreiben; [D] (*Sport*) schießen; [E] (*coll.: speak out*) ~**!** schieß los! (*ugs.*). ❷ *v.t.,* **shot** [A] (*wound*) anschießen; (*kill*) erschießen; (*hunt*) schießen; ~ **sb. dead** jmdn. erschießen *od.* (*ugs.*) totschießen; ~ **an animal and kill it** ein Tier tödlich treffen; **he was fatally shot in the head** ihn traf ein tödlicher Kopfschuss; **you'll get shot for this** (*fig.*) du kannst dein Testament machen (*ugs.*); **he ought to be shot** (*fig.*) der gehört aufgehängt (*ugs.*); ~ **oneself in the foot** (*fig. coll.*) sich (*Dat.*) selbst ein Bein stellen; **stop** ~**ing oneself in the foot** aufhören, sich selbst Knüppel zwischen die Beine zu werfen; [B] schießen mit ‹Bogen, Munition, Pistole›; abschießen ‹Pfeil, Kugel› (**at** auf + *Akk.*); [C] (*sl.: inject*) schießen (*Drogenjargon*) ‹Heroin, Kokain›; [D] (*send out*) zuwerfen ‹Lächeln, Blick› (**at** *Dat.*); [aus]treiben ‹Knospen, Schösslinge›; **the volcano shot lava high into the air** der Vulkan schleuderte Lava hoch in die Luft; ~ **a line** (*fig. coll.*) angeben (*ugs.*) (**about** mit); ~ **the moon** (*Brit. coll.*) bei Nacht und Nebel abhauen (*ugs.*); ⇒ *also* **bolt**[1] 1 C; [E] (*Sport*) schießen ‹Tor, Ball, Puck›; (*Basketball*) werfen ‹Korb›; ~ **dice** würfeln; ~ **a hole in one** (*Golf*) ein Loch mit einem Schlag spielen; ⇒ *also* **craps**; [F] (*push, slide*) vorschieben ‹Riegel›; herausziehen ‹Manschetten›; schütten ‹Mehl, Kohle›; [G] (*Cinemat.*) drehen ‹Film, Szene›; [H] (*pass swiftly over*) schießen über (+ *Akk.*) ‹Brücke, Stromschnelle, Wasserfall›; ~ **the lights** (*coll.*) eine rote Ampel überfahren. ❸ *n.* [A] (*Bot.*) Trieb, *der;* [B] ⇒ **chute** A; [C] (~*ing-party, -expedition, -practice, -land*) Jagd, *die;* **a duck** ~**:** eine Entenjagd; **the whole [bang]** ~ (*coll.*) der ganze Kram *od.* Krempel (*ugs.*)

~ **aˈhead** *v.i.* vorpreschen; ~ **ahead of sb.** jmdn. blitzschnell hinter sich (*Dat.*) lassen

~ **aˈlong** *v.i.* dahinschießen

~ **ˈdown** *v.t.* abschießen ‹Flugzeug›; niederschießen ‹Person›; (*fig.*) entkräften ‹Argument›; **be shot down in flames** ‹Flugzeug:› in Brand geschossen werden und abstürzen; (*fig.*) ‹Person, Argument:› in der Luft zerrissen werden

~ **ˈoff** ❶ *v.t.* abschießen ‹Gewehr›; ~ **one's mouth off** (*sl.*) das Maul aufreißen (*derb*). ❷ *v.i.* losschießen (*ugs.*)

~ **ˈout** ❶ *v.i.* hervorschießen; **the dog shot out of the gate** der Hund schoss aus dem Tor heraus (*ugs.*). ❷ *v.t.* herausschleudern; ~ **it out** (*coll.*) sich schießen; ⇒ *also* **shoot-out**

~ **ˈup** ❶ *v.i.* [A] in die Höhe schießen; ‹Preise, Temperatur, Kosten, Pulsfrequenz:› in die Höhe schnellen [B] (*coll.: inject drug*) sich (*Dat.*) einen Schuss setzen (*ugs.*) ❷ *v.t.* herumschießen in (+ *Dat.*) (*ugs.*); **be badly shot up** schwer beschossen werden

**shooter** /ˈʃuːtə(r)/ *n.* (*coll.: gun*) Ballermann, *der* (*ugs.*)

**shooting** /ˈʃuːtɪŋ/ *n.* [A] Schießerei, *die;* **new outbreaks of** ~ **were reported** ein erneutes Aufflammen der Schießereien wurde gemeldet; **two more** ~**s were reported** Meldungen zufolge wurden erneut zwei Menschen von Schüssen getroffen; [B] (*Sport*) Schießen, *das;* **rifle** ~**:** Gewehrschießen, *das;* [C] (*Hunting*) **go** ~**:** auf die Jagd gehen; [D] (*Cinemat.*) Dreharbeiten *Pl.*

**shooting:** ~ **box** *n.* (*Brit. Hunting*) Jagdhütte, *die;* ~ **brake,** ~ **break** *n.* (*Brit. Motor Veh.*) Kombiwagen, *der;* ~ **gallery** *n.* Schießstand, *der;* (*at funfair*) Schießbude, *die;* ~ **iron** *n.* (*coll.*) Schießeisen, *das* (*ugs.*); Schießprügel, *der* (*salopp*); ~ **match** *n.* [A] Wettschießen, *das;* [B] **the whole** ~ **match** (*coll.*) der ganze Kram *od.* Krempel (*ugs. abwertend*); ~ **party** *n.* Jagdgesellschaft, *die;* ~ **range** *n.* Schießstand, *der;* ~ **ˈstar** *n.* Sternschnuppe, *die;* ~ **stick** *n.* Jagdstock, *der;* ~ **war** *n.* offener Krieg

**ˈshoot-out** *n.* Schießerei, *die*

**shop** /ʃɒp/ ❶ *n.* [A] (*premises*) Laden, *der;* Geschäft, *das;* **go to the** ~**s** einkaufen gehen; **keep a** ~**:** einen Laden *od.* ein Geschäft haben; **keep [the]** ~ **for sb.** jmdn. im Laden *od.* Geschäft vertreten; **all over the** ~ (*fig. coll.*) überall; **look for sth. all over the** ~ (*fig. coll.*) in jedem Winkel nach etw. suchen; **my books are all over the** ~ (*fig. coll.*) meine Bücher liegen wie Kraut und Rüben durcheinander (*ugs.*); [B] (*business*) **set up** ~**:** ein Geschäft eröffnen; (*as a lawyer, dentist, etc.*) eine Praxis aufmachen; **shut up** ~**:** das Geschäft schließen; **talk** ~**:** fachsimpeln (*ugs.*); **no [talking]** ~**, please!** keine Fachsimpelei, bitte! (*ugs.*); [C] (*coll.: institution, establishment*) Laden, *der* (*ugs.*); [D] (*workshop*) Werkstatt, *die;* **engineering** ~**:** Maschinenbauhalle, *die;* **pattern/machine** ~**:** Modell-/Maschinenwerkstatt, *die;* [E] (*action*) Einkauf, *der.* ⇒ *also* **closed shop.** ❷ *v.i.,* **-pp-** einkaufen; **go** ~**ping** einkaufen gehen; ~ *or* **go** ~**ping for shoes** Schuhe kaufen gehen. ❸ *v.t.* **-pp-** (*Brit. coll.*) verpfeifen

~ **aˈround** *v.i.* sich umsehen (**for** nach)

**shopaholic** /ʃɒpəˈhɒlɪk/ *n.* Kaufsüchtige, *der/die*

**shop:** ~ **assistant** *n.* ▶ **1261** (*Brit.*) Verkäufer, *der*/Verkäuferin, *die;* ~ **boy** *n.* Ladenbursche, *der* (*veralt.*); ~**fitter** *n.* Ladenbauer, *der;* **firm of** ~**fitters** Ladenbaufirma, *die;* ~**fittings** *n. pl.* Ladeneinrichtung, *die;* ~ **floor** *n.* [A] (*place*) Produktion, *die* (*ugs.*); **the worker on the** ~ **floor** der einfache Arbeiter; **what is the feeling on the** ~ **floor?** was ist die Meinung der Arbeiter?; [B] (*workers*) **the** ~ **floor** die Arbeiter; *attrib.* Arbeiter-; ~ **floor democracy** Demokratie am Arbeitsplatz; ~**front** *n.* Schaufensterfront, *die;* ~ **girl** *n.* Ladenmädchen, *das* (*veralt.*); ~**keeper** *n.* ▶ **1261** Ladenbesitzer, *der*/-besitzerin, *die;* ~**lifter** *n.* Ladendieb, *der*/-diebin, *die;* ~**lifting** *n., no pl., no indef. art.* Ladendiebstahl, *der;* ~**owner** ⇒ ~**keeper**

**shopper** /ˈʃɒpə(r)/ *n.* [A] (*person*) Käufer, *der*/Käuferin, *die;* [B] (*wheeled bag*) Einkaufsroller, *der*

**shopping** /ˈʃɒpɪŋ/ *n.* [A] (*buying goods*) Einkaufen, *das;* **do the/one's** ~**:** einkaufen/[seine] Einkäufe machen; [B] (*items bought*) Einkäufe *Pl.*

**shopping:** ~ **bag** *n.* Einkaufstasche, *die;* ~ **basket** *n.* Einkaufskorb, *der;* ~ **centre** *n.* Einkaufszentrum, *das;* ~ **day** *n.* Einkaufstag, *der;* ~ **list** *n.* Einkaufszettel, *der;* (*fig.*) Wunschliste, *die;* ~ **mall** *n.* (*Amer.*) Einkaufszentrum, *das;* ~ **precinct** *n.* Einkaufs- *od.* Geschäftsviertel, *das;* ~ **street** *n.* Geschäftsstraße, *die;* ~ **trolley** *n.* Einkaufswagen, *der*

**shop:** ~**-soiled** *adj.* (*Brit.*) (*slightly damaged*) leicht beschädigt; (*slightly dirty*) angeschmutzt; ~ **steward** *n.* ▶ **1261** [gewerkschaftlicher] Vertrauensmann; ~ **talk** *n., no pl.* Fachsimpelei, *die* (*ugs.*); ~**walker** *n.* (*Brit.*) ≈ Abteilungsleiter, *der*/-leiterin, *die;* ~ **ˈwindow** *n.* Schaufenster, *das;* ~**-worn** ⇒ ~**-soiled**

**shore**[1] /ʃɔː(r)/ *n.* Ufer, *das;* (*coast*) Küste, *die;* (*beach*) Strand, *der;* **on the** ~**:** am Ufer/an der Küste/am Strand; **on the** ~**[s] of Lake Garda** am Ufer des Gardasees; **off** ~**:** vor der Küste; **a mile off [the]** ~**:** eine Meile vom Ufer entfernt/vor der Küste/vom Strand entfernt; **be on** ~ ‹Seemann:› an Land sein; **these** ~**s** dieses Land; diese Gestade (*dichter.*)

**shore**[2] ❶ *n.* (*prop, beam*) Stützbalken, *der;* Stütze, *die.* ❷ *v.t.* (*support*) abstützen ‹Tunnel›

~ **ˈup** *v.t.* (*support*) abstützen ‹Mauer, Haus›; (*fig.*) stützen ‹Währung, Wirtschaft›

**shore:** ~**-based** /ˈʃɔːbeɪst/ *adj.* landgestützt ‹Rakete›; ~ **leave** *n.* (*Naut.*) Landurlaub, *der;* ~**line** *n.* (*Geog.*) Uferlinie, *die*

**shoring** /ˈʃɔːrɪŋ/ *n.* Abstützung, *die*

**shorn** ⇒ **shear** 1,2

**short** /ʃɔːt/ ❶ *adj.* [A] kurz; **a** ~ **time** *or* **while ago/later** vor kurzem/kurze Zeit später; **for a** ~ **time** *or* **while** eine kleine Weile; ein [kleines] Weilchen; **a** ~ **time before he left** kurz bevor er ging; **a** ~ **time** *or* **while before/after sth.** kurz vor/nach etw. (*Dat.*); **in a** ~ **time** *or* **while** (*soon*) bald; in Kürze; **within a** ~ **[space of] time** innerhalb kurzer Zeit; **a few** ~ **years of happiness** einige wenige Jahre des Glücks; **in the** ~ **run** *or* **term** kurzfristig; kurzzeitig; **there is only a** ~ **haul ahead of us** (*fig.*) wir haben es bald geschafft; **wear one's hair/skirts** ~**:** seine Haare kurz tragen/kurze Röcke tragen; **be** ~ **in the arm/leg** ‹Person:› kurzarmig/kurzbeinig sein; ‹Kleidungsstück:› im Arm/Bein kurz sein; **have/get sb. by the** ~ **hairs** *or* (*sl.*) **by the** ~ **and curlies** jmdn. in der Hand haben/in die Hand kriegen (*ugs.*); ~ **back and sides** kurzer Haarschnitt; **make** ~ **work of sb./sth.** mit jmdm./etw. kurzen Prozess machen (*ugs.*); **he made** ~ **work of the puzzle** er hatte das

Rätsel im Handumdrehen gelöst; ⇒ *also* **neck** 1 B; **notice** 1 B; **range** 1 D; **shrift**; **straw** B; **B** (*not tall*) klein ‹Person, Wuchs›; niedrig ‹Gebäude, Baum, Schornstein›; **C** (*not far-reaching*) kurz ‹Wurf, Schuss, Gedächtnis›; **take a ~ view of things** kurzsichtig sein; **D** (*deficient, scanty*) knapp; **be in ~ supply** knapp sein; **good doctors are in ~ supply** gute Ärzte sind rar *od.* (*ugs.*) sind Mangelware; **give sb. ~ weight** jmdn. beim Abwiegen übervorteilen; (*inadvertently*) sich zu jmds. Ungunsten beim Abwiegen versehen; **be [far/not far] ~ of a record** einen Rekord [bei weitem] nicht erreichen/[knapp] verfehlen; **his jump was 4 cm. ~ of the record** sein Sprung verfehlte den Rekord um 4 cm; **sb./sth. is so much/so many ~:** jmdm./einer Sache fehlt soundso viel/fehlen soundso viele; **sb. is ~ of sth.** jmdm. fehlt es an etw. (*Dat.*); **he is [rather] ~ on talent** er ist nicht besonders talentiert; **time is getting/is ~:** die Zeit wird/ist knapp; **the poor harvest has left them ~ of food** wegen der schlechten Ernte fehlt es ihnen an Nahrung; **don't leave yourself ~ [of money/food]** pass auf, dass du selbst noch genug [Geld/zu essen] hast; **keep sb. ~ [of sth.]** jmdn. [mit etw.] kurz halten; **[have to] go ~ [of sth.]** [an etw. (*Dat.*)] Mangel leiden [müssen]; **she is ~ of milk today** sie hat heute nicht genug Milch; **the firm is ~ of staff** die Firma hat zu wenig Arbeitskräfte; **be ~ [of cash]** knapp [bei Kasse] sein (*ugs.*); **be ~ of sth.** ‹Preis, Temperatur, Leistung usw.:› unter etw. (*Dat.*) liegen; **he is just ~ of six feet/not far ~ of 60** er ist knapp sechs Fuß [groß]/sechzig [Jahre alt]; **a few inches ~ of the line** nur wenige Zoll vor der Linie; **she is three months ~ of retirement** sie steht 3 Monate vor ihrer Pensionierung; **be still far ~ of one's target** von seinem Ziel noch weit entfernt sein; **his behaviour has been little** *or* **not far ~ of criminal** sein Verhalten war beinahe kriminell; **if it was not fraud, it was not far ~ of it** wenn es auch kein ausgesprochener Betrug war, so war es doch nicht weit davon entfernt; **it is nothing ~ of miraculous** es ist ein ausgesprochenes Wunder; ⇒ *also* **hundredweight** C; **measure** 1 A; **ration** 1 A; **run** 2 L; **ton** A; **E** (*brief, concise*) kurz; **a ~ history of Wales** eine kurz gefasste Geschichte von Wales; **the ~ answer is ...:** um es kurz zu machen: die Antwort ist ...; **~ and sweet** (*iron.*) kurz und schmerzlos (*ugs.*); **~ and to the point** kurz und geradeheraus (*ugs.*) *od.* direkt; **something ~** (*drink*) ein Schnaps; **in ~, ...:** kurz, ... ; **his name is Robert, [but he is called] Bob for ~:** er heißt Robert, [wird aber] kurz Bob [genannt]; **Dick is ~ for Richard** Dick ist eine Kurzform von Richard *od.* kurz für Richard; **F** (*curt, uncivil*) kurz angebunden; barsch; **G** (*Cookery*) mürbe ‹Teig›; **H** (*Pros., Phonet.*) kurz; **I** (*St. Exch.*) **~ sale** Leerverkauf, *der;* **make a ~ sale** fixen; **sell sth. ~:** etw. leer verkaufen; **sell oneself ~** (*fig.*) sein Licht unter den Scheffel stellen; **sell sb./sth. ~** (*fig.*) jmdn./etw. unterschätzen; **J** (*Cricket*) *relativ nahe beim Schlagmann [stehend];* **~ ball** kurzer Ball; **K** (*cards*) **~ suit** kurze Farbe.

❷ *adv.* **A** (*abruptly*) plötzlich; **stop ~:** plötzlich abbrechen; ‹Musik, Gespräch:› jäh (*geh.*) abbrechen; **stop ~ at sth.** über etw. (*Akk.*) nicht hinausgehen; **stop sb. ~:** jmdm. ins Wort fallen; **pull up ~:** plötzlich anhalten; **bring** *or* **pull sb. up ~:** jmdn. stutzen lassen; ⇒ *also* **cut** 1 C; **B** (*curtly*) kurz angebunden; barsch; **C** (*before the expected place or time*) **jump/land ~:** zu kurz springen/zu früh landen (*ugs.*); **~ of sth.** vor etw. (*Dat.*); **stop ~ of the line** vor der Linie stehen/liegen bleiben; **the bomb dropped/landed ~ [of its target]** die Bombe fiel vor das/landete (*ugs.*) vor dem Ziel; **fall** *or* **come ~** (*fig.*) ‹Leistung, Vorstellung usw.:› enttäuschen; **fall** *or* **come [far/considerably] ~ of sth.** etw. [bei weitem] nicht erreichen; **stop ~ of sth.** (*fig.*) nicht so weit gehen, etw. zu tun; **stop ~ of doing sth.** davor zurückschrecken, etw. zu tun; **be caught** *or* **taken ~** (*at a disadvantage*) in Bedrängnis geraten; (*coll.: need to go to toilet*) plötzlich dringend müssen (*fam.*); **D** **nothing ~ of a catastrophe/miracle can ...:** nur eine Katastrophe/ein Wunder kann ...; **~ of locking him in, how can I keep him from going out?** wie kann ich ihn daran hindern auszugehen — es sei denn ich schlösse ihn ein?

❸ *n.* **A** (*Electr. coll.*) Kurze, *der* (*ugs.*); **B** (*coll.: drink*) Schnaps, *der* (*ugs.*); **C** (*Cinemat.*) Kurzfilm, *der.* ⇒ *also* **long**[1] 2 B; **shorts**.

❹ *v.t.* (*Electr. coll.*) kurzschließen.

❺ *v.i.* (*Electr. coll.*) einen Kurzschluss kriegen (*ugs.*)

**shortage** /ˈʃɔːtɪdʒ/ *n.* Mangel, *der* (**of** an + *Dat.*); **~ of fruit/teachers** Obstknappheit, *die*/Lehrermangel, *der*

**short: ~bread** *n.* Shortbread, *das; Keks aus Butterteig;* **~cake** *n.* **A** ⇒ **~bread**; **B** (*cake served with fruit*) *Obstkuchen mit Mürbeteigboden;* **a strawberry ~cake** ein Erdbeerkuchen aus Mürbeteig; **~-'change** *v.t.* zu wenig [Wechselgeld] herausgeben (+ *Dat.*); (*fig.*) übers Ohr hauen (*ugs.*); prellen; **~ 'circuit** *n.* (*Electr.*) Kurzschluss, *der;* **~-'circuit** (*Electr.*) ❶ *v.t.* kurzschließen; (*fig.*) umgehen; ❷ *v.i.* einen Kurzschluss bekommen; **~coming** *n., usu. in pl.* Unzulänglichkeit, *die;* **he has only one ~coming** er hat nur einen Fehler; **~ 'commons** *n. pl.* **be on ~ commons** zu wenig zu essen haben; **~ 'cut** *n.* Abkürzung, *die;* **take a ~ cut** (*lit. or fig.*) eine Abkürzung machen; **be a ~ cut to sth.** (*fig.*) den Weg zu etw. abkürzen; **there is no ~ cut to success** (*fig.*) der Weg zum Erfolg lässt sich nicht abkürzen; **~ division** ⇒ **division** G; **~ 'drink** *n.* hochprozentiges Getränk; **have a ~ drink** etwas Hochprozentiges trinken

**shorten** /ˈʃɔːtn/ ❶ *v.i.* **A** (*become shorter*) kürzer werden; **B** (*decrease*) sich verkleinern; ‹Preis, Gewinnquote:› sinken. ❷ *v.t.* **A** (*make shorter*) kürzen; (*curtail*) verkürzen ‹Besuch, Wartezeit, Inkubationszeit›; **B** (*decrease*) senken; reduzieren; **~ sail** (*Naut.*) die Segel reffen; **C** (*Cookery*) mürbe machen

**shortening** /ˈʃɔːtnɪŋ/ *n.* **A** (*making shorter*) [Ver]kürzung, *die;* (*growing shorter*) Kürzerwerden, *das;* **B** (*Cookery*) Ziehfett, *das* (*zum Mürbemachen des Teigs*)

**short: ~fall** *n.* Fehlmenge, *die;* (*in budget, financial resources*) Defizit, *das;* **~-haired** *adj.* kurzhaarig; Kurzhaar‹dackel, -katze›; **~hand** *n.* Kurzschrift, *die;* Stenografie, *die;* **write ~hand** stenografieren; **~hand writer** Stenograf, *der*/Stenografin, *die;* **that's ~hand for ...** (*fig.*) das ist eine Kurzformel für ...; ⇒ *also* **typist**; **~-handed** /ʃɔːtˈhændɪd/ *adj.* zu klein ‹Team›; **we are terribly ~-handed** wir haben furchtbar wenig Leute; **~ haul** *n.* Kurzstreckentransport, *der;* [Güter]nahtransport, *der;* **~-haul** *adj.* Kurzstrecken‹flug, -flugzeug›; ‹Lastwagen, Bus› für den Nahverkehr; **~-haul route** Kurzstrecke, *die;* **~-haul transport** Güternahverkehr, *der;* **~ 'head** *n.* (*Brit. Horseracing*) kurzer Kopf (*fachspr.*); **win by a ~ head** mit einem kurzen Kopf Vorsprung gewinnen; **win an election by a ~ head** eine Wahl knapp gewinnen; **~hold** *adj.* kurzzeitig ‹Mietverhältnis›; **~horn** *n.* (*Agric.*) Shorthornrind, *das; attrib.* Shorthorn-

**shortie** /ˈʃɔːtɪ/ *n.* (*coll.*) **A** ⇒ **shorty** A; **B** (*garment*) Shorty, *das;* **~ nightdress/dress** kurzes Nachthemd/kurzes Kleid

**shortish** /ˈʃɔːtɪʃ/ *adj.* ziemlich kurz; ziemlich klein ‹Person›

**short: ~-legged** *adj.* kurzbeinig; **~list** *n.* (*Brit.*) engere Auswahl; **be on/put sb. on the ~list** in der engeren Auswahl sein/jmdn. in die engere Auswahl nehmen; **~-list** *v.t.* in die engere Auswahl nehmen; **~-lived** /ˈʃɔːtlɪvd/ *adj.* kurzlebig

**shortly** /ˈʃɔːtlɪ/ *adv.* **A** (*soon*) in Kürze; gleich (*ugs.*); **~ before/after sth.** kurz vor/nach etw.; **~ before/after arriving, he phoned us** kurz vor/nach seiner Ankunft rief er uns an; (*outside cinema, theatre*) **'coming ~'** „demnächst“; „Voranzeige“; **B** (*briefly*) kurz; **C** (*curtly*) kurz angebunden; in barschem Ton

**shortness** /ˈʃɔːtnɪs/ *n., no pl.* **A** (*short extent or duration*) Kürze, *die;* **despite the ~ of his life** trotz seines kurzen Lebens; **B** (*smallness of person*) Kleinheit, *die;* geringe Körpergröße; **C** (*scarcity, lack*) Knappheit, *die* (**of** an + *Dat.*); **~ of breath** Kurzatmigkeit; **D** (*briefness*) Kürze, *die;* **E** (*curtness*) Barschheit, *die;* **F** (*of pastry*) Mürbheit, *die*

**short: ~ 'odds** *n. pl.* (*Racing, also fig.*) **it's/I would give you ~ odds on X winning** es ist so gut wie sicher, dass X gewinnt; **~ 'order** *n.* (*Amer.*) **A** (*for food*) Schnellgericht, *das;* **B** **in ~ order** auf der Stelle; **~-order** *adj.* (*Amer.*) Schnell-; **~-order counter** Selbstbedienungsbüfett, *das;* **~ 'pastry** *n.* (*Cookery*) Mürbeteig, *der;* **~-range** *adj.* **A** (*with ~ range*) Kurzstrecken‹flugzeug, -rakete usw.›; **B** (*relating to ~ future period*) kurzfristig

**shorts** /ʃɔːts/ *n. pl.* **A** (*trousers*) kurze Hose[n]; Shorts *Pl.;* (*in sports*) Sporthose, *die;* **football ~:** Fußballshorts; **B** (*Amer.: underpants*) Unterhose, *die*

**short: ~ 'sight** *n., no pl., no art.* Kurzsichtigkeit, *die;* **have ~ sight** kurzsichtig sein; **~-sighted** /ʃɔːtˈsaɪtɪd/ *adj.,* **~-sightedly** /ʃɔːtˈsaɪtɪdlɪ/ *adv.* (*lit. or fig.*) kurzsichtig; **~-sightedness** /ʃɔːtˈsaɪtɪdnɪs/ *n., no pl.* (*lit. or fig.*) Kurzsichtigkeit, *die;* **~-sleeved** /ˈʃɔːtsliːvd/ *adj.* kurzärm[e]lig; **~ 'sleeves** *n. pl.* kurze Ärmel; **~-staffed** /ʃɔːtˈstɑːft/ *adj.* **be [very] ~-staffed** [viel] zu wenig Personal haben; **~ stop** *n.* (*Baseball*) **A** *no pl., no art.* (*position*) Shortstopposition, *die;* **B** (*player*) Shortstop, *der;* **~ 'story** *n.* (*Lit.*) Short Story, *die;* Kurzgeschichte, *die;* **short ~ story** Short short Story, *die;* **~ 'suit** *n.* (*Cards*) kurze Farbe; **have a ~ suit in hearts** wenig Herz haben; **~ 'temper** *n.* aufbrausendes *od.* cholerisches Temperament; **have a ~ temper** aufbrausend *od.* cholerisch sein; **~-'tempered** *adj.* aufbrausend; cholerisch; **be ~-tempered with sb.** ungehalten zu jmdm. sein; **~-term** *adj.* kurzfristig; (*provisional*) vorläufig ‹Lösung, Antwort›; **~ 'time** *n.* (*Industry*) Kurzarbeit, *die;* **be on** *or* **work ~ time** kurzarbeiten; **~-time** *adj.* **~-time working** Kurzarbeit, *die;* **~ 'title** *n.* Kurztitel, *der;* **~ 'trousers** *n. pl.* kurze Hose[n]; **~ 'wave** *n.* (*Radio*) Kurzwelle, *die;* **~-wave** *adj.* (*Radio*) Kurzwellen-; **~winded** /ʃɔːtˈwɪndɪd/ *adj.* kurzatmig

**shorty** /ˈʃɔːtɪ/ *n.* (*coll.*) **A** (*person*) Kleine, *der/die* (*ugs.*); **he/she is a ~:** er ist so'n Kleiner/sie ist so'ne Kleine (*ugs.*); **B** ⇒ **shortie** B

**shot** /ʃɒt/ ❶ *n.* **A** *pl. same* (*single projectile for cannon or gun*) Geschoss, *das;* Kugel, *die* (*ugs.*); *collect.* Munition, *die;* **B** (*Athletics*) Kugel, *die;* **put the ~:** die Kugel stoßen; kugelstoßen; **[putting] the ~:** Kugelstoßen, *das;* **C** *pl. same* (*lead pellet*) [Schrot]kugel, *die; collect.* Schrot, *der od. das;* ⇒ *also* **lead shot**; **D** (*discharge of gun*) Schuss, *der;* (*firing of rocket*) Abschuss, *der;* Start, *der;* **the ~ had gone home** (*fig.*) das hatte gesessen (*ugs.*); **fire a ~ [at sb./sth.]** einen Schuss [auf jmdn./etw.] abgeben; **like a ~** (*fig.*) wie der Blitz (*ugs.*); **I'd do it like a ~:** ich würde es auf der Stelle tun; **call the ~s** (*fig.*) das Sagen haben (*ugs.*); **let sb. call the ~s** nach jmds. Pfeife tanzen (*ugs.*); **have a ~ at sth./at doing sth.** (*fig.*) etw. versuchen/versuchen, etw. zu tun; **the answer is not correct, but it is a good ~:** die Antwort ist nicht richtig, aber es war [für den Anfang] schon ganz gut (*ugs.*); ⇒ *also* **dark** 2 C; **long shot**; **Parthian shot**; **parting** 2; **snap shot**; **E** (*Sport: stroke, kick, throw*) Schuss, *der;* (*Archery, Shooting*) Schuss, *der;* **F** (*Photog.*) Aufnahme, *die;* (*Cinemat.*) Einstellung, *die;* **do** *or* **film interior/exterior/location ~s** (*Cinemat.*) Innenaufnahmen machen/Außenaufnahmen machen/am Originalschauplatz drehen; **out of/in ~** (*Photog.*) außerhalb des Bildes/im Bild; **G** (*person who shoots in specified way*) Schütze, *der;* **H** (*injection*) Spritze, *die;* (*of drug*) Schuss, *der* (*Jargon*); **be a ~ in the arm for sb./sth.** (*fig.*) jmdm./einer Sache Aufschwung geben; **I** (*coll.: dram of spirits*) Schluck, *der*

S

# Should

## Conditional

In the first person singular and plural, *should* is used for *would* to form the conditional, and so is translated by the conditional in German:

***I should be surprised if he wins***
= Es würde mich wundern, wenn er gewänne

***I should have gone if I had been invited***
= Ich wäre hingegangen, wenn ich eingeladen gewesen wäre

***I should have thought it was obvious***
= Ich hätte gedacht, es liegt auf der Hand

***We should welcome more opportunity for contact***
= Wir würden es begrüßen, wenn wir mehr Kontaktmöglichkeiten hätten

***We should like to help you***
= Wir möchten Ihnen helfen

Where *should* occurs in the conditional clause (with any person), the translation is **sollte, sollten** etc., and like the English *should* this can stand at the beginning of the clause:

***If they should be delayed*** or ***Should they be delayed, ...***
= Falls sie aufgehalten werden sollten *or* Sollten sie aufgehalten werden, ...

***Should he turn up after all, let me know***
= Sollte er doch noch auftauchen, sagen Sie mir Bescheid

## Meaning ought to

In most cases expressing obligation, this is also translated by **sollte** (and **hätte sollen** in the past):

***You should tell her***
= Du solltest es ihr sagen

***They shouldn't really be here***
= Eigentlich sollten *or* dürften sie nicht hier sein

***We should have gone earlier***
= Wir hätten früher hingehen sollen

***He shouldn't have come***
= Er hätte nicht kommen sollen

Note that unlike *should*, **sollte** does not normally stand on its own:

***I don't think you should***
= Ich finde, du solltest es nicht tun

With an impersonal subject, **müsste** is used.

***It should be banned***
= Das müsste man verbieten

Also expressing a surmise or estimate, **dürfte** or **müsste** can be used:

***They should be there by now***
= Jetzt dürften *or* müssten sie dort angekommen sein

***That should be enough***
= Das dürfte *or* müsste genügen

***That should have been enough***
= Das hätte genügen müssen

## After that

In clauses beginning with *that* preceded by an adjective, the *should* is not translated:

***It is strange that he should never have told you***
= Es ist seltsam, dass er es dir nie gesagt hat

***It is important that they should be warned***
= Es ist wichtig, dass sie gewarnt werden

Much the same applies to clauses with *in order that* or *so that*:

***She gave me a cushion in order that*** or ***so that I should sit more comfortably***
= Sie gab mir ein Kissen, damit ich bequemer saß

***In order that they should all be able to hear, I used a megaphone***
= Damit sie alle hören konnten, verwendete ich ein Megaphon

(*fig.*); **a ~ of whisky/rum** *etc.* ein Schluck Whisky/Rum *usw.*
❷ *v.t. & i.* ⇒ **shoot** 1, 2.
❸ *adj.* [A] (*iridescent*) durchschossen; **~ [through] with sth.** mit etw. durchschossen; **hair ~ with grey** grau meliertes Haar; [B] **get ~ of sb./sth.** (*coll.*) jmdn./etw. loswerden; **I wish I could get ~ of him** ich würde ihn am liebsten auf den Mond schießen (*salopp*); [C] (*coll.*) **be ~** (*exhausted, finished*) im Eimer sein (*salopp*); **my nerves are ~ [to pieces]** ich bin mit den Nerven [völlig] fertig (*ugs.*)

**shot: ~-blasting** /ˈʃɒtblɑːstɪŋ/ *n.* Kugelstrahlen, *das* (*Technik*); **~-firer** /ˈʃɒt faɪərə(r)/ *n.* Sprengmeister, *der;* Schießmeister, *der;* **~gun** *n.* [Schrot]flinte, *die; attrib.* **~gun wedding/marriage** (*fig. coll.*) Mussheirat/Mussehe, *die* (*ugs.*); **ride ~gun** zur Bewachung als Beifahrer mitfahren; **~-put** *n., no pl., no indef. art.* (*Athletics*) Kugelstoßen, *das;* **~-putter** /ˈʃɒtpʊtə(r)/ *n.* (*Athletics*) Kugelstoßer, *der*/-stoßerin, *die*

**should** *see box*, ⇒ **shall**

**shoulder** /ˈʃəʊldə(r)/ ❶ *n.* [A] ▶966 Schulter, *die;* **~ to ~** (*lit. or fig.*) Schulter an Schulter; **put** *or* **set one's ~ to the wheel** (*fig.*) sich ins Geschirr legen; **straight from the ~** (*fig.*) unverblümt; **cry on sb.'s ~** (*fig.*) sich bei jmdm. ausweinen; **give sb. the cold ~ :** jmdn. schneiden; **get the cold ~ from sb.** von jmdm. geschnitten werden; ⇒ *also* **chip** 1 A; **head** 1 A; **rub** 1 A; [B] *in pl.* (*upper part of back*) Schultern *Pl.;* (*of garment*) Schulterpartie, *die;* **lie** *or* **rest/fall on sb.'s ~s** (*fig.*) auf jmds. Schultern (*Dat.*) lasten/jmdm. aufgebürdet werden; **he has broad ~s** (*fig.: is able to take responsibility*) er hat einen breiten Rücken; **have** *or* **be an old head on young ~s** (*fig.*) reif für sein Alter sein; **have a good head on one's ~s** (*fig.*) Köpfchen haben (*ugs.*); [C] ⇒ **~ joint** A; [D] (*Gastr.*) Bug, *der;* Schulter, *die;* **~ of lamb/veal** Lamm-/Kalbsschulter, *die;* [E] (*Road Constr.*) Randstreifen, *der;* Seitenstreifen, *der;* ⇒ *also* **hard ~**.
❷ *v.t.* [A] (*push with ~*) rempeln; **~ one's way through the crowd** sich rempelnd einen Weg durch die Menge bahnen; [B] (*take on one's ~s*) schultern; (*fig.*) übernehmen ‹Verantwortung, Aufgabe›; auf sich (*Akk.*) nehmen ‹Schuld, Bürde›; **~ arms** (*Mil.*) das Gewehr schultern

**~ a'side** *v.t.* beiseite rempeln; (*fig.*) beiseite schieben

**shoulder: ~ bag** *n.* Umhängetasche, *die;* **~ belt** *n.* Schulterband, *das;* **~ blade** *n.* Schulterblatt, *das*

**-shouldered** /ˈʃəʊldəd/ *adj. in comb.* -schult[e]rig; **square-/straight-~:** mit eckigen/geraden Schultern *nachgestellt*

**shoulder: ~-high** ❶ /ˈ---/ *adj.* schulterhoch; ❷ /--ˈ-/ *adv.* **lift/carry sb. ~-high** jmdn. auf die Schultern heben/auf den Schultern tragen; **they carried him through the streets, ~-high** sie trugen ihn auf den Schultern durch die Straßen; **~ holster** *n.* Schulterhalfter, *die;* **~ joint** *n.* [A] (*Anat.*) Schultergelenk, *das;* [B] (*Gastr.*) Schulterstück, *das;* Bugstück, *das;* **~-length** *adj.* schulterlang; **~ pad** *n.* Schulterpolster, *das;* **~ strap** *n.* [A] (*on ~ of garment*) Schulterklappe, *die;* [B] (*on bag*) Tragriemen, *der;* (*suspending a garment*) Träger, *der*

**shouldn't** /ˈʃʊdnt/ (*coll.*) = **should not;** ⇒ **shall**

**shout** /ʃaʊt/ ❶ *n.* [A] Ruf, *der;* (*inarticulate*) Schrei, *der;* **warning ~, ~ of alarm** Warnruf, *der*/-schrei, *der;* **~ of joy/rage** Freuden-/Wutschrei, *der;* **~ of encouragement/approval** Anfeuerungs-/Beifallsruf, *der;* **give sb. a ~:** jmdn. rufen; (*fig. coll.: let sb. know*) jmdm. Bescheid sagen; [B] (*coll.: turn to pay for drinks*) Runde, *die;* **stand sb. a ~:** jmdm. einen ausgeben (*ugs.*).
❷ *v.i.* [A] schreien; **~ with laughter/pain** vor Lachen/Schmerzen schreien; **~ with** *or* **for joy** vor Freude schreien; **~ at sb.** (*be loudly abusive to sb.*) jmdn. anschreien; **you don't have to ~ [at me] — I can hear you** Du brauchst nicht zu schreien. Ich höre dich auch so; **don't ~!** schrei nicht so!; **she ~ed for him to come** sie schrie *od.* rief, er solle kommen; **he ~ed to me to be careful/help him** er schrie *od.* rief mir zu, ich solle vorsichtig sein/ihm helfen; **~ for sb./sth.** nach jmdm./etw. schreien; **~ for help** um Hilfe schreien *od.* rufen; **it's nothing to ~ about** (*fig.*) darauf braucht er/sie/man *usw.* sich (*Dat.*) nichts einzubilden; [B] (*Austral. and NZ coll.: stand drinks etc.*) einen ausgeben (*ugs.*) (**for** *Dat.*).
❸ *v.t.* [A] schreien; **~ abuse at sb.** jmdn. anpöbeln; **~ oneself hoarse** sich heiser schreien; [B] (*Austral. and NZ coll.*) **~ a drink/a beer for sb., ~ sb. to a drink/a beer** jmdm. einen/ein Bier ausgeben (*ugs.*)

**~ 'down** *v.t.* [A] runterrufen; [B] **~ sb. down** (*prevent from being heard*) jmdn. niederschreien

**~ 'out** ❶ *v.i.* aufschreien; **if you know the answer, don't ~ out — wait till ...:** wenn ihr die Antwort wisst, schreit nicht einfach los — wartet, bis ... ❷ *v.t.* [laut] rufen; schreien

**shouting** /ˈʃaʊtɪŋ/ ❶ *adj.* schreiend. ❷ *n.* (*act*) Schreien, *das;* Schreierei, *die* (*abwertend*); (*shouts*) Geschrei, *das;* **it's all over**

**but** *or* **bar the ~** (*fig.*) das Rennen ist im Grunde schon gelaufen (*ugs.*)

**shove** /ʃʌv/ ❶ *n.* Stoß, *der;* **little ~:** Schubs, *der* (*ugs.*); **a ~ with one's foot** ein Tritt [mit dem Fuß]; ein Fußtritt; **get the ~** (*coll.*) rausfliegen (*ugs.*); **give sb. the ~** (*coll.*) jmdn. rausschmeißen (*ugs.*). ❷ *v.t.* Ⓐ stoßen; schubsen (*ugs.*); Ⓑ (*use force to propel*) schieben; Ⓒ (*coll.: put*) tun. ⇒ *also* **throat** A. ❸ *v.i.* drängen; drängeln (*ugs.*); **~ past the vehicles/through the crowd** (*coll.*) sich an den Fahrzeugen vorbei/durch die Menge drängeln (*ugs.*). ⇒ *also* **push** 2 A, 3 D

**~ a'bout** ⇒ **~ around**

**~ a'long** (*coll.*) ❶ *v.t.* schieben. ❷ *v.i.* sich vorwärts schieben; (*fig. coll.: depart*) abschieben (*ugs.*)

**~ a'round** *v.t.* (*coll.*) herumschieben; (*fig.*) herumschubsen (*ugs.*)

**~ a'way** *v.t.* (*coll.*) wegschubsen (*ugs.*)

**~ 'off** ❶ *v.t.* (*coll.*) Ⓐ (*away*) wegschubsen (*ugs.*); Ⓑ (*down*) runterschubsen (*ugs.*). ❷ *v.i.* Ⓐ (*coll.: move boat from shore*) abstoßen; Ⓑ (*coll.: depart*) abschieben (*ugs.*)

**~ 'over** (*coll.*) ❶ *v.t.* rüberschieben (*ugs.*). ❷ *v.i.* rüberrücken (*ugs.*)

**~ 'past** *v.i.* (*coll.*) sich vorbeidrängeln *od.* -quetschen (*ugs.*)

**shove-'halfpenny** *n. Spiel, bei dem Münzen in die Felder des Spielbretts gestoßen werden müssen*

**shovel** /'ʃʌvl/ ❶ *n.* Ⓐ (*implement, part of machine*) Schaufel, *die;* (*machine*) Bagger, *der;* ⇒ *also* **spade** A; Ⓑ (*quantity*) ⇒ **shovelful**. ❷ *v.t.*, (*Brit.*) **-ll-** Ⓐ schaufeln; Ⓑ (*fig.*) **~ food into one's mouth** Essen in sich reinschaufeln *od.* -stopfen (*ugs.*)

**shovelful** /'ʃʌvlfʊl/ *n.* **a ~ of earth** *etc.* eine Schaufel Erde *usw.;* **~s of earth** schaufelweise Erde

**show** /ʃəʊ/ ❶ *n.* Ⓐ (*act of making visible*) Zeigen, *das;* **without any ~ of anger/emotion/grief** ohne jedes Zeichen des Ärgers/von Gefühl/der Trauer; **~ of generosity** Geste der Großzügigkeit; **~ of knowledge** Zurschaustellung von Wissen; **make a ~ of sth.** etw. zur Schau stellen; **~ of force/strength** *etc.* Demonstration der Macht/Stärke *usw.;* Ⓑ (*display*) Pracht, *die;* (*spectacle, pageant*) Schauspiel, *das* (*geh.*); **a ~ of flowers/colour** eine Blumen-/Farbenpracht; **the trees make a wonderful ~:** die Bäume entfalten eine wunderbare Pracht; **be on ~:** ausgestellt sein; **put sth. on ~:** etw. ausstellen; Ⓒ (*exhibition*) Ausstellung, *die;* Schau, *die;* **dog ~:** Hundeschau, *die;* **~ animal** ausgestelltes Tier; Ⓓ (*entertainment, performance*) Show, *die;* (*Theatre*) Vorstellung, *die;* (*Radio, Telev.*) [Unterhaltungs]sendung, *die;* **summer ~:** Sommerprogramm, *das;* **the ~ must go on** die Show geht weiter; (*fig.*) das Leben geht weiter; ⇒ *also* **steal** 1 A; **stop** 1 B; Ⓔ (*coll.: effort*) **that's a very good ~:** das kann sich sehen lassen; **it's a poor ~:** das ist ein schwaches Bild; **put up a good/poor ~:** eine gute/schlechte Figur machen; **good ~!** gut [gemacht]!; **bad** *or* **poor ~!** schwaches Bild!; Ⓕ (*coll.: undertaking, business*) **it's his ~:** er ist der Boss (*ugs.*); **who is running this ~?** wer ist hier der Boss? (*ugs.*); **give the [whole] ~ away** alles ausquatschen (*salopp*); ⇒ *also* **run** 3 C; Ⓖ (*outward appearance*) Anschein, *der;* **make a great ~ of friendliness** ungeheuer freundlich tun; **make** *or* **put on a [great] ~ of doing sth.** sich (*Dat.*) [angestrengt] den Anschein geben, etw. zu tun; **she puts on a brave ~ of being able to cope** sie gibt sich (*Dat.*) tapfer den Anschein, als käme sie immer gut zurecht; **be for ~:** reine Angeberei sein (*ugs.*); **do sth. just for ~:** etw. nur aus Prestigegründen tun; Ⓗ (*pomp*) **the pomp and ~ of great State occasions** der Pomp und Prunk großer Staatsakte; Ⓘ (*Med.: discharge*) (*at onset of labour*) *leichte Blutung als erstes Anzeichen der beginnenden Geburt;* (*at beginning of menstrual period*) *Vorzeichen der beginnenden Menstruation.*

❷ *v.t.*, *p.p.* **~n** /ʃəʊn/ *or* **~ed** Ⓐ (*allow or cause to be seen*) zeigen; (*produce*) vorzeigen ‹Pass, Fahrschein usw.›; **~ one's cards** *or* **hand** (*Cards*) seine Karten aufdecken; (*fig.: reveal one's intentions*) die Karten auf den Tisch legen; **have nothing/something to ~ for it** [dabei] nichts/etwas zum Vorzeigen haben; ⇒ *also* **cause** 1 C; **face** 1 A; **feather** 1 A; **flag**[1] 1; **tooth** A; Ⓑ (*reveal, disclose*) zeigen; **~ sb. sth.**, **~ sth. to sb.** jmdm. etw. zeigen; **~ me an A and I will ~ you a B** jedes A ist ein B; **that dress ~s your petticoat** bei diesem Kleid sieht man deinen Unterrock; **this material does not ~ the dirt** auf diesem Material sieht man den Schmutz nicht; **~ oneself** sich zeigen; **~ itself** (*become visible*) zum Vorschein kommen; (*reveal itself*) sich zeigen; erkennbar sein; **~ itself at its best/in all its glory** sich von der besten Seite/in all seiner Herrlichkeit zeigen; **the task has been ~n to be difficult** die Aufgabe hat sich als schwierig erwiesen; **this episode ~s him to be honest/a liar** dieser Vorfall zeigt, dass er ehrlich/ein Lügner ist; **~ oneself/itself to be sth.** sich als etw. erweisen; ⇒ *also* **heel**[1] 1 A; **colour** 1 H; **sign** 1 E; Ⓒ (*manifest, give evidence of*) zeigen; beweisen ‹Mut, Entschlossenheit, Urteilsvermögen usw.›; **~ hesitation** zaudern; **he is ~ing his age** man sieht ihm sein Alter an; ⇒ *also* **fight** 3 C; **mettle** A; **willing** 2; Ⓓ **~ [sb.] kindness/mercy** freundlich [zu jmdm.] sein/Erbarmen [mit jmdm.] haben; **~ mercy on** *or* **to sb.** Erbarmen mit jmdm. haben; Ⓔ (*indicate*) zeigen ‹Gefühl, Freude usw.›; ‹Thermometer, Uhr usw.:› anzeigen; **as ~n in the illustration** wie die Abbildung zeigt; **frontiers are ~n by blue lines and towns are ~n in red** Grenzen sind durch blaue Linien und Städte sind rot gekennzeichnet; **the accounts ~ a profit** die Bücher weisen einen Gewinn aus; **the firm ~s a profit/loss** die Firma macht Gewinn/Verlust; Ⓕ (*offer for viewing*) zeigen; (*exhibit in a show*) ausstellen; Ⓖ (*demonstrate, prove*) zeigen; **~ sb. that ...:** jmdm. beweisen, dass ...; **it all/just goes to ~ that ...:** das beweist nur, dass ...; **it all goes to ~, doesn't it?** das beweist es doch, oder?; **I'll ~ you/him** *etc.*! ich werds dir/ihm *usw.* schon zeigen!; **~ sb. who's boss** jmdm. zeigen, wer das Sagen hat; ⇒ *also* **door**; Ⓗ (*conduct*) führen; **~ sb. over the house/to his place** jmdn. durchs Haus/an seinen Platz führen.

❸ *v.i.*, *p.p.* **~n** *or* **~ed** Ⓐ (*be visible*) sichtbar *od.* zu sehen sein; (*come into sight*) sich zeigen; zum Vorschein kommen; **he was angry/bored, and it ~ed** er war wütend/langweilte sich, und man sah es [ihm an]; **his age is beginning to ~:** man sieht ihm sein Alter allmählich an; **your slip is ~ing** dein Unterrock guckt raus; Ⓑ (*coll.: arrive*) sich blicken lassen (*ugs.*); auftauchen; Ⓒ (*be shown*) ‹Film:› laufen; ‹Künstler:› ausstellen; **'Gandhi' — now ~ing in the West End** „Gandhi" — Jetzt im West End; Ⓓ (*make sth. known*) **time will ~:** man wird es [ja] sehen; **only time will ~:** das wird sich erst im Laufe der Zeit herausstellen; Ⓔ (*Amer. Horseracing*) sich [unter den ersten drei] platzieren

**~ 'in** *v.t.* hineinführen/hereinführen

**~ 'off** ❶ *v.t.* Ⓐ (*display*) **~ sth./sb. off** etw./jmdn. vorführen *od.* vorzeigen; (*in order to impress*) mit etw./jmdm. prahlen *od.* (*ugs.*) angeben; Ⓑ (*display to advantage*) zur Geltung bringen. ❷ *v.i.* angeben (*ugs.*); prahlen; ⇒ *also* **show-off**

**~ 'out** *v.t.* hinausführen

**~ 'round** *v.t.* herumführen

**~ 'through** *v.i.* durchscheinen

**~ 'up** ❶ *v.t.* Ⓐ (*conduct upstairs*) hinaufführen/heraufführen; Ⓑ (*make visible*) deutlich sichtbar machen; aufdecken ‹Betrug›; **this incident has ~n him up as** *or* **for a coward** *or* **to be a coward** dieser Vorfall hat gezeigt, dass er [in Wirklichkeit *od.* eigentlich] ein Feigling ist; Ⓒ (*coll.: embarrass*) blamieren. ❷ *v.i.* Ⓐ (*be easily visible*) [deutlich] zu sehen *od.* erkennen sein; (*fig.*) sich zeigen; **it will not ~ up on the photocopy** das kommt auf der Fotokopie nicht heraus; Ⓑ (*coll.: arrive*) sich blicken lassen (*ugs.*); auftauchen

**show:** **~ biz** (*coll.*), **~ business** *ns.*, *no pl.*, *no art.* Schaugeschäft, *das;* Showbusiness, *das;* **~ business personalities/connections** Persönlichkeiten aus dem/Verbindungen zum Schaugeschäft *od.* Showbusiness; **~case** *n.* Vitrine, *die;* Schaukasten, *der;* (*fig.*) Schaufenster, *das;* **~down** *n.* (*fig.*) Kraftprobe, *die;* **have a ~down [with sb.]** sich [mit jmdm.] auseinander setzen

**shower** /'ʃaʊə(r)/ ❶ *n.* Ⓐ Schauer, *der;* **~ of rain/sleet/hail** Regen-/Schneeregen-/Hagelschauer, *der;* **a ~ of confetti/sparks/stones/petals** ein Konfettiregen/Funkenregen/Steinhagel/Regen von Blütenblättern; **a ~ of letters/curses** eine Flut von Briefen/Flüchen; Ⓑ (**~-bath**) Dusche, *die; attrib.* Dusch-; **have** *or* **take a [cold/quick/daily] ~:** [kalt/schnell/täglich] duschen; **be under the ~:** unter der Dusche stehen; **the ~s** der Duschraum; Ⓒ (*Amer.: party*) **~ [party]** Geschenkparty, *die* (*für eine Braut, bei der sie Aussteuergegenstände geschenkt bekommt*); **baby ~** *Geschenkparty für eine werdende Mutter, bei der sie Babyartikel geschenkt bekommt;* Ⓓ (*Brit. coll.: contemptible persons*) Sauhaufen, *der* (*salopp*).

❷ *v.t.* Ⓐ **~ sth. over** *or* **on sb.**, **~ sb. with sth.** jmdn. mit etw. überschütten; Ⓑ (*fig.: lavish*) **~ sth. [up]on sb.**, **~ sb. with sth.** jmdn. mit etw. überhäufen.

❸ *v.i.* Ⓐ (*fall in ~s*) **~ down [up]on sb.** ‹Wasser, Konfetti:› auf jmdn. herabregnen; ‹Steine, Verwünschungen:› auf jmdn. niederhageln; Ⓑ (*have a ~-bath*) duschen

**shower:** **~ bath** *n.* Dusche, *die;* **~ cap** *n.* Duschhaube, *die;* **~ curtain** *n.* Duschvorhang, *der;* **~ gel** *n.* Duschgel, *das;* **~proof** *adj.* [bedingt] regendicht

**showery** /'ʃaʊərɪ/ *adj.* **the weather is ~:** es herrscht Schauerwetter; **outlook ~:** weitere Aussichten: schauerartige Regenfälle; **a cold and ~ day** ein kalter Tag mit häufigen Schauern

**show:** **~ flat** *n.* (*Brit.*) Musterwohnung, *die;* **~girl** *n.* Showgirl, *das;* **~ground** *n.* Ausstellungsgelände, *das;* **~ house** *n.* Musterhaus, *das*

**showily** /'ʃəʊɪlɪ/ *adv.* angeberisch; **behave ~:** eine Schau machen (*ugs.*); angeben

**showing** /'ʃəʊɪŋ/ *n.* Ⓐ (*of film*) Vorführung, *die;* (*of television programme*) Sendung, *die;* **at the film's first ~:** bei der Premiere des Films; Ⓑ (*evidence*) **on this ~:** demnach; **on any ~:** wie man es auch [dreht und] wendet; **on** *or* **by sb.'s own ~:** nach jmds. eigener Darstellung; **on present ~:** wie es sich im Augenblick darstellt; Ⓒ (*quality of performance*) Leistung, *die;* **make a good/poor** *etc.* **~:** eine gute/schwache *usw.* Leistung zeigen; **on this ~:** bei dieser Leistung

**show:** **~jumper** *n.* (*Sport*) Ⓐ (*person*) Springreiter, *der*/-reiterin, *die;* Ⓑ (*horse*) Springpferd, *das;* **~jumping** *n.* (*Sport*) Springreiten, *das;* **~man** /'ʃəʊmən/ *n.*, *pl.* **~men** /'ʃəʊmən/ Ⓐ (*proprietor of fairground booth etc.*) Schausteller, *der;* Ⓑ (*effective presenter*) Showman, *der*

**showmanship** /'ʃəʊmənʃɪp/ *n.*, *no pl.* schauspielerisches Talent; **it's nothing but ~:** es ist reine Schauspielerei

**shown** ⇒ **show** 2, 3

**show:** **~-off** *n.* Aufschneider, *der*/Aufschneiderin, *die;* Angeber, *der*/Angeberin, *die* (*ugs.*); **don't be such a ~-off** gib nicht so an!; **~piece** *n.* Renommierstück, *das* (*geh.*); (*of exhibition, collection*) Schaustück, *das;* (*highlight*) Paradestück, *das;* **a real ~piece** ein richtiges Prachtexemplar *od.* -stück (*ugs.*); **~place** *n.* Attraktion, *die;* **~room** *n.* Ausstellungsraum, *der;* **~room price** Endverbraucherpreis, *der;* **~-stopper** *n.* (*coll.*) **be a ~-stopper** Furore machen; **~ trial** *n.* Schauprozess, *der*

**showy** /'ʃəʊɪ/ *adj.* Ⓐ (*gaudy, ostentatious*) protzig (*ugs.*); Ⓑ (*striking*) großartig; prächtig ‹Farben›; [farben]prächtig ‹Blumen, Blüten›

**shrank** ⇒ **shrink** 1, 2

**shrapnel** /'ʃræpnl/ *n.* (*Mil.*) Ⓐ (*fragments*) Bomben-/Granatsplitter; **piece of ~:**

S

Bomben-/Granatsplitter, *der;* **B** (*projectile*) Schrapnell, *das; collect.* Schrapnelle

**shred** /ʃred/ **1** *n.* Fetzen, *der;* **without a ~ of clothing on him/her** ohne einen Fetzen [Kleidung] am Leib; **not a ~ of evidence/truth** keine Spur eines Beweises/kein Fünkchen Wahrheit; **cut/tear** *etc.* **sth. to ~s** etw. in Fetzen schneiden/reißen *usw.;* **tear sb.'s reputation to ~s** jmds. Ruf ruinieren; **tear sb.['s character] to ~s** kein gutes Haar an jmdm. lassen; **tear a theory/an argument to ~s** eine Theorie/eine Argumentation zerpflücken; **in ~s** in Fetzen; **our clothes were in ~s** unsere Kleidung war zerfetzt; **sb.'s nerves are in ~s** (*fig.*) jmd. ist mit den Nerven am Ende; **sb.'s reputation is in ~s** jmds. guter Ruf ist ruiniert.
**2** *v.t.*, **-dd-** [im Reißwolf] zerkleinern ‹Papier, Textilien›; raspeln ‹Gemüse›

**shredder** /ˈʃredə(r)/ *n.* (*for paper, clothes*) Reißwolf, *der;* (*kitchen aid*) Raspel, *die;* **~ [attachment]** Schnitzelwerk, *das*

**shrew** /ʃruː/ *n.* **A** (*Zool.*) Spitzmaus, *die;* **B** (*woman*) Beißzange, *die* (*salopp*)

**shrewd** /ʃruːd/ *adj.* scharfsinnig ‹Person›; klug ‹Entscheidung, Investition, Schritt, Geschäftsmann›; genau ‹Schätzung, Einschätzung›; treffsicher ‹Urteilsvermögen›; **I had a pretty ~ idea** *or* **suspicion what his next move would be** mir war ziemlich klar, was er als Nächstes tun würde; **have a ~ mind** scharfsinnig sein

**shrewdly** /ˈʃruːdlɪ/ *adv.* klug; **he ~ decided to take the job** er entschloss sich klugerweise dazu, die Stelle anzunehmen

**shrewdness** /ˈʃruːdnɪs/ *n., no pl.* ⇒ **shrewd**: Scharfsinnigkeit, *die;* Klugheit, *die;* Genauigkeit, *die* Treffsicherheit, *die*

**shrewish** /ˈʃruːɪʃ/ *adj.*, **shrewishly** /ˈʃruːɪʃlɪ/ *adv.* zänkisch

**'shrew-mouse** ⇒ **shrew A**

**shriek** /ʃriːk/ **1** *n.* **A** (*shrill cry*) [Auf]schrei, *der;* **give a ~:** [auf]schreien; **give a ~ of horror/fear** *etc.* einen Schrei des Entsetzens/der Angst *usw.* ausstoßen; **there were ~s of laughter from the children** die Kinder kreischten vor Lachen; **B** (*high-pitched sound*) Kreischen, *das.* **2** *v.i.* **A** (*give shrill cry*) [auf]schreien; **~ with horror/fear** *etc.* vor Entsetzen/Angst *usw.* [auf]schreien; **~ [with laughter]** vor Lachen kreischen; **B** (*make high-pitched sound*) kreischen. **3** *v.t.* schreien

**~ 'out** **1** *v.i.* aufschreien. **2** *v.t.* schreien

**shrift** /ʃrɪft/ *n.* **give sb. short ~:** jmdn. kurz abfertigen (*ugs.*); **get short ~ [from sb.]** [von jmdm.] kurz abgefertigt werden (*ugs.*)

**shrike** /ʃraɪk/ *n.* (*Ornith.*) Würger, *der*

**shrill** /ʃrɪl/ **1** *adj.* schrill; (*fig.*) lautstark. **2** *v.i.* schrillen. **3** *v.t.* gellend schreien

**shrillness** /ˈʃrɪlnɪs/ *n., no pl.* Schrillheit, *die*

**shrilly** /ˈʃrɪlɪ/ *adv.* schrill; (*fig.*) lautstark ‹fordern, protestieren›

**shrimp** /ʃrɪmp/ **1** *n.* **A** *pl.* **~s** *or* **~** (*Zool.*) Garnele, *die;* Krabbe, *die* (*ugs.*); (*Gastr.*) Krabbe, *die; attrib.* Garnelen-/Krabben-; **B** (*derog.: small person*) Knirps, *der* (*abwertend*). **2** *v.i.* Krabben/Garnelen fangen

**shrine** /ʃraɪn/ *n.* **A** Heiligtum, *das;* (*tomb*) Grab, *das;* (*casket*) Schrein, *der* (*veralt.*); (*casket holding sacred relics*) Reliquienschrein, *der;* **be a sacred ~ of Christendom** ‹Altar, Kapelle:› eines der größten Heiligtümer der Christenheit sein; **B** (*fig.: place hallowed by memory*) Gedenkstätte, *die;* **~ to sb./sth.** Gedenkstätte für jmdn./etw.

**shrink** /ʃrɪŋk/ **1** *v.i.*, **shrank** /ʃræŋk/, **shrunk** /ʃrʌŋk/ **A** (*grow smaller*) schrumpfen; ‹Mensch:› kleiner werden; ‹Kleidung, Stoff:› einlaufen; ‹Metall, Holz:› sich zusammenziehen; ‹Handel, Einkünfte:› zurückgehen; **B** (*recoil*) sich zusammenkauern; **~ from sb./sth.** vor jmdm. zurückweichen/vor etw. (*Dat.*) zurückschrecken; **~ from doing sth.** sich scheuen, etw. zu tun; ⇒ *also* **violet 1 A**. **2** *v.t.*, **shrank, shrunk** sich zusammenziehen lassen ‹Metall, Holz›; einlaufen lassen ‹Textilien›. **3** *n.* **A** (*act*) Schrumpfen, *das;* (*of fabric*) Einlaufen, *das;* **B** (*degree*) ⇒ **shrinkage B**; **C** (*coll.: psychiatrist*) Seelendoktor, *der*

**~ a'way** *v.i.* **A** (*recoil*) zurückweichen (**from** vor + *Dat.*); **B** (*grow smaller*) zusammenschrumpfen

**~ 'back** *v.i.* zurückweichen (**from** vor + *Dat.*); **~ back from sth./doing sth.** (*fig.*) vor etw. (*Dat.*) zurückschrecken/sich scheuen, etw. zu tun

**shrinkage** /ˈʃrɪŋkɪdʒ/ *n.* **A** (*act*) (*of clothing, material*) Einlaufen, *das;* (*of income, trade, etc.*) Rückgang, *der;* **B** (*degree*) Schrumpfung, *die*

**shrink:** **~-proof**, **~-resistant** *adjs.* schrumpffrei; **be ~-proof** nicht einlaufen; **~-wrap** *v.t.* in einer Schrumpffolie verpacken

**shrive** /ʃraɪv/ *v.t.*, **shrove** /ʃrəʊv/, **shriven** /ʃrɪvn/ (*RC Ch. arch.*) **~ sb.** jmdm. die Beichte abnehmen

**shrivel** /ˈʃrɪvl/ **1** *v.t.*, (*Brit.*) **-ll-:** **~ [up]** schrump[e]lig machen; runzlig machen ‹Haut, Gesicht›; welk werden lassen ‹Pflanze, Blume›; **2** *v.i.*, (*Brit.*) **-ll-:** **~ [up]** verschrumpeln; ‹Haut, Gesicht:› runzlig werden; ‹Pflanze, Blume:› welk werden; ‹Ballon:› zusammenschrumpfen

**~ up** **1** *v.t.* ⇒ **~ 1**. **2** *v.i.* **A** ⇒ **~ 2**; **B** (*fig.: from fear or nervousness*) verschüchtert werden; **I just wanted to ~ up when ...:** ich wäre am liebsten in den Erdboden versunken, als ...

**shrivelled** (*Amer.:* **shriveled**) /ˈʃrɪvld/ *adj.* schrump[e]lig; verschrumpelt; **a ~ old lady** eine verhutzelte alte Frau

**shriven** ⇒ **shrive**

**shroud** /ʃraʊd/ **1** *n.* **A** Leichentuch, *das* (*veralt.*); **B** (*fig.*) (*of fog, mystery, etc.*) Schleier, *der;* (*of snow*) Decke, *die;* **C** *in pl.* (*of ship*) Wanten *Pl.;* (*of parachute*) Fangleine, *die.* **2** *v.t.* (*cover and conceal*) einhüllen; **~ sth. in sth.** etw. in etw. (*Akk.*) hüllen; **mystery ~s their fate** ein Geheimnis umgibt ihr Schicksal (*geh.*)

**shrove** ⇒ **shrive**

**Shrove**/ʃrəʊv/: **~tide** *n.* Fastnacht, *die;* **~ 'Tuesday** *n.* Fastnachtsdienstag, *der*

**shrub** /ʃrʌb/ *n.* Strauch, *der*

**shrubbery** /ˈʃrʌbərɪ/ *n.* **A** Gesträuch, *das;* **B** (*shrubs collectively*) Sträucher

**shrubby** /ˈʃrʌbɪ/ *adj.* **A** (*like a shrub*) strauchartig; **B** (*covered with shrubs*) mit Strauchwerk bewachsen

**shrug** /ʃrʌg/ **1** *n.* **~ [of one's** *or* **the shoulders]** Achselzucken, *das;* **give a ~ [of one's** *or* **the shoulders]** die/mit den Achseln zucken; **give a ~ of resignation/indifference** *etc.* resigniert/gleichgültig *usw.* mit den Achseln zucken. **2** *v.t. & i.* **-gg-:** **~ [one's shoulders]** die *od.* mit den Achseln zucken

**~ 'off** *v.t.* in den Wind schlagen; **~ sth. off as unimportant** etw. als unwichtig abtun

**shrunk** ⇒ **shrink 1, 2**

**shrunken** /ˈʃrʌŋkn/ *adj.* verhutzelt (*ugs.*) ‹Mensch›; schrump[e]lig, verschrumpelt ‹Äpfel›; (*fig.*) geschrumpft ‹Reserven, Gewinn, Ressourcen›; **~ head** Schrumpfkopf, *der*

**shuck** /ʃʌk/ (*Amer.*) **1** *n.* **A** Schale, *die;* (*pea pod*) Hülse, *die;* **B** *in pl.* (*slightest amount*) **I don't care ~s about it** es kümmert mich nicht die Bohne (*ugs.*); **~s!** *expr. annoyance, regret* verdammt! (*salopp*). **2** *v.t.* ausschälen

**shudder** /ˈʃʌdə(r)/ **1** *v.i.* **A** (*shiver*) zittern (**with** vor + *Dat.*); **sb. ~s to think of sth.** jmdn. schaudert bei dem Gedanken an etw. (*Akk.*); **B** (*vibrate*) zittern; **~ to a halt** zitternd zum Stehen kommen. **2** *n.* **A** (*shivering*) Zittern, *das;* Schauder, *der;* **sb. has/gets the ~s** (*coll.*) jmdn. schaudert; **it gives me the ~s to think of it** (*coll.*) mich schaudert, wenn ich daran denke; **B** (*vibration*) Zittern, *das;* **a ~ went through the building** das Gebäude erzitterte

**shuffle** /ˈʃʌfl/ **1** *n.* **A** Schlurfen, *das;* **walk with a ~:** schlurfend gehen; schlurfen; **B** (*Cards*) Mischen, *das;* **give the cards a [good] ~:** die Karten [gut] mischen; **it is his ~:** er ist an der Reihe zu mischen; er muss mischen; **C** (*fig.: change*) Umbildung, *die;* **cabinet/ministerial ~:** Kabinettsumbildung, *die;* **D** (*Dancing*) (*movement*) Schlurfschritt, *der;* (*dance*) *schlurfender Tanz;* ≈ Schleifer, *der.*
**2** *v.t.* **A** (*rearrange*) umbilden ‹Kabinett›; neu verteilen ‹Aufgaben›; sortieren ‹Schriftstücke usw.›; (*mix up*) durcheinander bringen; **B** (*Cards*) mischen; **C** **~ one's feet in embarrassment** verlegen von einem Fuß auf den anderen treten; **he ~s his feet when he walks** er schlurft beim Gehen.
**3** *v.i.* **A** (*Cards*) mischen; **B** (*move, walk*) schlurfen; **C** (*shift one's position*) herumrutschen

**~ a'long** *v.i.* dahinschlurfen

**~ 'off** **1** *v.t.* abstreifen ‹Kleidungsstück›; **~ the responsibility off [on to sb.]** die Verantwortung auf jmdn. abwälzen. **2** *v.i.* wegschlurfen (*ugs.*)

**shuffling** /ˈʃʌflɪŋ/ *adj.* schlurfend

**shufti** /ˈʃʊftɪ, ˈʃʌftɪ/ *n.* (*Brit. coll.*) **have a ~ at sth.** sich (*Dat.*) etw. angucken (*ugs.*)

**shun** /ʃʌn/ *v.t.*, **-nn-** meiden

**'shun** /ʃʌn/ *int.* (*Brit. Mil.*) stillgestanden!

**shunt** /ʃʌnt/ **1** *v.t.* **A** (*Railw.*) rangieren; **~ off** (*fig.*) abschieben; **B** (*Electr.*) shunten. **2** *v.i.* (*Brit. Railw.*) rangieren. **3** *n.* **A** (*Railw.*) Rangieren, *das;* **B** (*Electr.*) Neben[schluss]widerstand, *der;* Shunt, *der;* **C** (*Med.*) Shunt, *der;* **D** (*coll.: collision*) Karambolage, *die* (*ugs.*); **have a ~:** eine Karambolage haben (*ugs.*)

**shunter** /ˈʃʌntə(r)/ *n.* (*Railw.*) Rangierer, *der*

**shush** /ʃʊʃ/ **1** *int.* ⇒ **hush 3**. **2** *v.i.* **A** (*call for silence*) um Ruhe bitten; **B** (*be silent*) still *od.* ruhig sein. **3** *v.t.* zum Schweigen bringen

**shut** /ʃʌt/ **1** *v.t.*, **-tt-**, **shut** **A** zumachen; schließen; **~ sth. to sb./sth.** etw. für jmdn./etw. schließen; **~ a road to traffic** eine Straße für den Verkehr sperren; **the strike ~ the factory for a month** der Streik hat die Fabrik für einen Monat lahm gelegt; **~ the door on sb.** jmdm. die Tür vor der Nase zuschlagen (*ugs.*); **~ the door on sth.** (*fig.*) die Möglichkeit einer Sache (*Gen.*) verbauen; **~ one's eyes to sth.** (*fig.*) seine Augen vor etw. (*Dat.*) verschließen; (*choose to ignore*) über etw. (*Akk.*) hinwegsehen; **~ one's ears to sth.** (*fig.*) die Ohren vor etw. (*Dat.*) verschließen; **~ one's heart to sb./mind to sth.** (*fig.*) sich jmdm./einer Sache verschließen; **~ your mouth** *or* **trap** *or* **face** *or* **gob** *or* (*Amer.*) **head!** (*sl.: stop talking*) halt den Mund (*ugs.*) *od.* die Klappe (*salopp*) *od.* die Fresse (*derb*) *od.* Schnauze (*derb*)!; **~ it!** (*sl.: stop talking*) halt die Klappe! (*salopp*); **B** (*confine*) **~ sb./an animal in[to] sth.** jmdn./ein Tier in etw. (*Akk.*) sperren; **~ oneself in[to] a room** sich in einem Zimmer einschließen; **~ sth. in a safe** etw. in einen Safe schließen; **C** (*exclude*) **~ sb./an animal out of sth.** jmdn./ein Tier aus etw. aussperren; **D** (*catch*) **~ one's finger/coat in a door** sich (*Dat.*) den Finger/den Mantel in einer Tür einklemmen; **E** (*fold up*) schließen, zumachen ‹Buch, Hand›; zusammenklappen ‹Klappmesser, Fächer›.
**2** *v.i.*, **-tt-**, **~** schließen; ‹Laden:› schließen, zumachen; ‹Blüte:› sich schließen; **the door/case won't ~:** die Tür/der Koffer geht nicht zu *od.* schließt nicht; **the door ~ on/after him** die Tür schloss sich vor/hinter ihm.
**3** *adj.* zu; geschlossen; **bang/kick sth. ~:** etw. zuknallen/mit einem Fußtritt zuschlagen; **bang/swing ~** ‹Tür:› zuknallen/zufallen; **we are ~ for lunch/on Saturdays** wir haben über Mittag/samstags geschlossen *od.* zu; **remain** *or* **stay ~:** geschlossen bleiben; zu bleiben; **keep sth. ~:** etw. geschlossen halten *od.* zu lassen; **be** *or* **get ~ of sb./sth.** (*coll.*) = **get shot of sb./sth.** ⇒ **shot 3 B**

**~ a'way** *v.t.* wegschließen; **keep sth. ~ away safely** etw. unter sicherem Verschluss halten

**~ 'down** **1** *v.t.* **A** zumachen, schließen ‹Deckel, Fenster›; **B** (*shut off*) absperren; **C** (*terminate operation of*) stilllegen; abschalten ‹Kernreaktor›; einstellen ‹Aktivitäten›; (*Radio, Telev.*) einstellen ‹Sendebetrieb›; **the strike has ~ down the factory/newspaper** der Streik hat die Fabrik lahm gelegt/hat das Erscheinen der Zeitung verhindert. **2** *v.i.* (*cease working*) ‹Laden, Fabrik:› geschlossen werden; ‹Zeitung, Sendebetrieb:› eingestellt werden; **the winter resorts/ski lifts ~ down during**

S

**the summer** die Einrichtungen der Winterkurorte sind im Sommer geschlossen/die Skilifte sind im Sommer außer Betrieb; **the radio/television ~s down after midnight** der Rundfunk/das Fernsehen stellt den Sendebetrieb nach Mitternacht ein; ⇒ *also* **shutdown**

**~ 'in** *v.t.* **A** (*keep in*) einschließen; ‹Damm:› zurückhalten ‹Wasser›; **B** (*encircle*) umschließen; **feel ~ in** sich eingeschlossen fühlen

**~ 'off** ❶ *v.t.* **A** (*stop*) unterbrechen ‹Strom, Fluss›; abstellen ‹Motor, Maschine, Gerät›; **B** (*isolate*) absperren; **~ sb. off from sb./sth.** jmdn. von jmdm./etw. abschneiden; **~ sb. off from society** jmdn. aus der Gesellschaft ausschließen; **~ oneself off from sb./sth.** sich gegen jmdn./etw. abkapseln. ❷ *v.i.* (*stop working*) sich abstellen

**~ 'out** *v.t.* **A** (*keep out*) aussperren; versperren ‹Aussicht›; (*exclude from view*) verdecken; (*prevent*) ausschließen ‹Gefahr, Möglichkeit›; **the skyscraper/tree ~s out the light** der Wolkenkratzer/Baum nimmt das Licht weg; **B** (*fig.: exclude*) **~ sb. out from sth.** jmdn. von etw. ausschließen; **~ out all thoughts/memories of sb./sth.** alle Gedanken/Erinnerungen an jmdn./etw. beiseite schieben; **C** (*Amer. Sport*) **~ sb. out** jmdn. nicht zum Zuge kommen lassen. ⇒ *also* **shutout**

**~ 'to** ❶ *v.t.* [ganz] schließen. ❷ *v.i.* ‹Tür:› zufallen

**~ 'up** ❶ *v.t.* **A** (*close*) abschließen; zuschließen; **~ up [the/one's] house** das/sein Haus [sicher] abschließen; ⇒ *also* **shop** 1 B; **B** (*put away*) einschließen ‹Dokumente, Wertsachen usw.›; einsperren ‹Tier, Menschen›; **~ sth. up in sth.** etw. in etw. (*Akk.*) schließen; **~ sb. up in an asylum/a prison** jmdn. in eine Anstalt/ein Gefängnis sperren; **C** (*reduce to silence*) zum Schweigen bringen. ❷ *v.i.* **A** (*coll.: be quiet*) den Mund halten (*ugs.*); **~ up!** halt den Mund! (*ugs.*); **B** (*lock up premises*) abschließen

**shut: ~down** *n.* **A** (*stoppage*) Schließung, *die;* (*of newspaper, operations*) Einstellung, *die;* **B** (*Radio, Telev.*) Sendeschluss, *der;* (*period*) Sendepause, *die;* **~-eye** *n.* (*coll.*) Nickerchen, *das* (*fam.*); **get some** *or* **a bit of ~-eye** ein Nickerchen halten (*fam.*); **~out** *n.* **A** (*Amer. Sport*) Zu-null-Spiel, *das;* **B** (*in industrial dispute*) ⇒ **lockout**

**shutter** /'ʃʌtə(r)/ *n.* **A** Laden, *der;* (*of window*) Fensterladen, *der;* **put up the ~s** (*fig.: cease business*) zumachen; schließen; **B** (*Photog.*) Verschluss, *der;* **~ release** Auslöser, *der;* **~ setting** [eingestellte] Verschlusszeit, *die;* **~ speed** Verschlusszeit, *die*

**shuttle** /'ʃʌtl/ ❶ *n.* **A** (*in loom*) [Web]schützen, *der;* Schiffchen, *das;* (*in sewing machine*) Schiffchen, *das;* **B** (*Transport*) (*service*) Pendelverkehr, *der;* Pendelservice, *der;* (*bus*) Pendelbus, *der;* (*aircraft*) Pendelmaschine, *die;* (*train*) Pendelzug, *der;* ⇒ *also* **space ~**; **C** ⇒ **shuttlecock**. ❷ *v.t.* **A** (*cause to move to and fro*) **~ sth. backwards and forwards** etw. hin- und herschicken; **~ passengers about** Passagiere hin- und herfahren; **B** (*transport*) im Pendelverkehr transportieren. ❸ *v.i.* pendeln; **~ backwards and forwards** *or* **to and fro** *or* **back and forth** hin- und herpendeln

**shuttle: ~cock** *n.* Federball, *der;* **be tossed backwards and forwards like a ~cock** wie ein Pingpongball hin- und hergehen; **~ diplomacy** *n.* ≈ Reisediplomatie, *die;* **~ service** *n.* Pendelverkehr, *der;* Pendelservice, *der*

**shy**[1] /ʃaɪ/ ❶ *adj.*, **~er** *or* **shier** /'ʃaɪə(r)/, **~est** *or* **shiest** /'ʃaɪɪst/ **A** scheu; (*diffident*) schüchtern; **don't be ~:** sei nicht [so] schüchtern!; **feel ~ about doing sth.** sich genieren, etw. zu tun; **feel ~ in sb.'s presence/with sb.** sich in jmds. Gegenwart/bei jmdm. gehemmt fühlen; **be ~ of strangers** eine Scheu vor Fremden haben; **be ~ of doing sth.** Hemmungen haben, etw. zu tun; ⇒ *also* **bite** 1; **fight** 1 A; **B** (*coll.: short*) **be ~ of sth.** knapp mit etw. sein; **he is six months ~ of his retirement** ihm fehlt noch ein halbes Jahr, bis er pensioniert wird (*ugs.*).
❷ *v.i.* scheuen (**at** vor + *Dat.*)

**~ a'way** *v.i.* **~ away from sth.** ‹Pferd:› vor etw. (*Dat.*) scheuen; **~ away from sth./doing sth.** (*fig.*) etw. scheuen/sich scheuen, etw. zu tun

**shy**[2] ❶ *v.t.* (*throw*) **~ sth. at sth./sb.** etw. auf etw./jmdn. schmeißen (*ugs.*). ❷ *v.i.* schmeißen (*ugs.*) (**at** nach). ❸ *n.* Wurf, *der;* **have a ~ at sth.** nach etw. schmeißen (*ugs.*); ⇒ *also* **coconut shy**

**shyly** /'ʃaɪlɪ/ *adv.* scheu; (*diffidently*) schüchtern

**shyness** /'ʃaɪnɪs/ *n.*, *no pl.* Scheuheit, *die;* (*diffidence*) Schüchternheit, *die*

**shyster** /'ʃaɪstə(r)/ *n.* (*Amer. coll.*) Ganove, *der;* (*lawyer*) Winkeladvokat, *der* (*abwertend*)

**SI** /es'aɪ/ *adj.* (*Phys.*) SI-; **SI units** SI-Einheiten

**si** /si:/ ⇒ **te**

**Siamese** /saɪə'mi:z/ ❶ *adj.* siamesisch. ❷ *n.*, *pl. same* **A** (*Hist.: native of Siam*) Siamese, *der*/Siamesin, *die;* **B** (*Ling. Hist.*) ⇒ **Thai** 2 B; **C** (*Zool.*) Siamese, *der*

**Siamese: ~ 'cat** *n.* Siamkatze, *die;* **~ 'twins** *n. pl.* siamesische Zwillinge

**Siberia** /saɪ'bɪərɪə/ *pr. n.* Sibirien (*das*)

**Siberian** /saɪ'bɪərɪən/ ▶1340 ❶ *adj.* sibirisch. ❷ *n.* Sibirjake, *der*/Sibirjakin, *die*

**sibilant** /'sɪbɪlənt/ ❶ *adj.* zischend; **~ sound** ⇒ **2.** ❷ *n.* (*Phonet.*) Zischlaut, *der;* Sibilant, *der* (*fachspr.*)

**sibling** /'sɪblɪŋ/ *n.* (*male*) Bruder, *der;* (*female*) Schwester, *die; in pl.* Geschwister *Pl.*; *attrib.* Geschwister-

**sibyl** /'sɪbɪl/ *n.* Sibylle, *die*

**sic** /sɪk/ *adv.* sic

**Sicilian** /sɪ'sɪljən, sɪ'sɪlɪən/ ▶1340 ❶ *adj.* sizil[ian]isch. ❷ *n.* Sizilianer, *der*/Sizilianerin, *die*

**Sicily** /'sɪsɪlɪ/ *pr. n.* Sizilien (*das*)

**sick** /sɪk/ ▶1232 ❶ *adj.* **A** (*ill*) krank; **mentally ~:** geisteskrank; **be ~ with** *or* (*arch.*) **of sth.** an etw. (*Dat.*) erkrankt sein; etw. haben; **go ~, fall** *or* (*coll.*) **take ~:** krank werden; **be off ~:** krank [gemeldet] sein; **sb. is ~ at** *or* **to his/her stomach** (*Amer.*) jmdm. ist [es] schlecht *od.* übel; ⇒ *also* **report** 2 B; **B** (*Brit.: vomiting or about to vomit*) **be ~:** sich erbrechen; **be ~ over sb./sth.** sich über jmdn./etw. erbrechen; **I think I'm going to be ~:** ich glaube, ich muss mich erbrechen *od.* ich muss brechen; **a ~ feeling** ein Übelkeitsgefühl; **sb. gets/feels ~:** jmdm. wird/ist [es] übel *od.* schlecht; **he felt ~ with fear** ihm war vor Angst [ganz] übel; **[as] ~ as a cat** *or* **dog** (*coll.*) speiübel; kotzübel (*derb*); **I get ~ in cars** beim Autofahren wird mir immer schlecht; **sth. makes sb. ~:** von etw. wird [es] jmdm. schlecht *od.* übel (⇒ *also* **d**); **C** (*sickly*) elend ‹Aussehen›; leidend ‹Blick›; matt ‹Lächeln›; ungesund ‹Blässe›; **D** (*fig.*) **~ at heart** niedergeschlagen; **worried ~:** krank vor Sorgen; **the team was ~ at losing** (*coll.*) es hat der Mannschaft schwer zu schaffen gemacht, dass sie verloren hat; **be ~ for home** Heimweh haben; **[as] ~ as a parrot** (*coll.*) völlig fertig (*ugs.*); **be/get ~ of sb./sth.** jmdn./etw. satt haben/allmählich satt haben; **be ~ and tired** *or* **~ to death of sb./sth.** (*coll.*) von jmdm./etw. die Nase [gestrichen] voll haben (*ugs.*); **be ~ of the sight/sound of sb./sth.** (*coll.*) jmdn./etw. nicht mehr sehen/hören können; **be ~ of doing sth.** es satt haben, etw. zu tun; **make sb. ~** (*disgust*) jmdn. anekeln; (*coll.: make envious*) jmdn. ganz neidisch machen; **look ~** (*coll.*) (*be discomfited, upset*) dumm dastehen (*ugs.*); (*be unimpressive*) ‹Leistung, Ergebnis, Bilanz usw.:› ein schwaches Bild sein (*ugs.*); ‹Aktie, Währung usw.:› mies stehen (*ugs.*); ‹Firma:› mies dastehen (*ugs.*) (⇒ *also* **b**); ⇒ *also* **enough** 2; **E** (*deranged*) pervers; (*morally corrupt*) krank ‹Gesellschaft›; (*morbid*) makaber ‹Witz, Humor, Fantasie›.
❷ *n.* **A** *pl.* **the ~:** die Kranken; **B** (*Brit. coll.: vomit*) Erbrochene, *das;* Kotze, *die* (*salopp*).
❸ *v.t.* (*coll.*) **~ [up]** erbrechen; ausspucken (*ugs.*)

**sick: ~bay** ⇒ **bay**[3] C; **~bed** *n.* Krankenbett, *das;* **~ benefit** *n.* (*Brit.*) Krankengeld, *das;* **~ 'building syndrome** *n.* Sickbuildingsyndrom, *das*

**sicken** /'sɪkn/ ▶1232 ❶ *v.i.* **A** (*become ill*) krank werden; erkranken (*geh.*); **be ~ing for something** (*Brit.*) krank werden; etwas ausbrüten (*ugs.*); **be ~ing for the measles** (*Brit.*) [die] Masern bekommen; **B** (*feel nausea or disgust*) **~ at sth.** sich vor etw. (*Dat.*) ekeln; **~ of sth./of doing sth.** einer Sache (*Gen.*) überdrüssig sein/es überdrüssig sein, etw. zu tun. ❷ *v.t.* **A** (*cause to feel ill*) **sth. ~s sb.** bei etw. wird jmdm. übel; **B** (*disgust*) **you ~/your behaviour ~s me** du widerst mich an/dein Benehmen widert mich an; **doesn't it ~ you?** findest du es nicht auch widerlich?

**sickening** /'sɪknɪŋ/ *adj.* **A** Ekel erregend; widerlich ‹Anblick, Geruch›; **with a ~ thud** mit einem entsetzlichen dumpfen Geräusch; **B** (*coll.: infuriating*) unerträglich; **it's really ~:** es kann einen krank machen

**sickeningly** /'sɪknɪŋlɪ/ *adv.* **A** Ekel erregend; **his ~ unctuous manner** seine widerliche salbungsvolle Art; **B** (*coll.: infuriatingly*) unverschämt (*ugs.*)

**sick 'headache** *n.* Migräne, *die*

**sickle** /'sɪkl/ *n.* Sichel, *die;* ⇒ *also* **hammer** 1 A

**'sick leave** *n.* Urlaub wegen Krankheit, *der;* Genesungsurlaub, *der* (*Milit.*); **be on ~:** ≈ krank geschrieben sein

**sickle: ~ cell** *n.* ▶1232 (*Med.*) Sichelzelle, *die;* **~-cell anaemia** Sichelzellenanämie, *die;* **~-shaped** *adj.* sichelförmig

**'sick list** *n.* Liste der Kranken, *die;* **on the ~:** krank [gemeldet/geschrieben]

**sickly** /'sɪklɪ/ *adj.* **A** (*ailing*) kränklich; **B** (*weak, faint*) schwach; matt ‹Lächeln›; kraftlos ‹Sonne›; fahl ‹Licht›; blass ‹Hautfarbe, Gesicht›; **a ~ grey dawn/light** eine fahlgraue Dämmerung/ein fahlgraues Licht; **C** (*nauseating*) ekelhaft; widerlich; (*mawkish*) süßlich; **~-sweet** ekelhaft süßlich; (*fig.: over-sentimental*) zuckersüß (*abwertend*)

**'sick-making** *adj.* (*coll.*) **A** **sth. is ~:** von etw. wird einem schlecht; **B** (*fig.: annoying*) unverschämt (*ugs.*)

**sickness** /'sɪknɪs/ *n.* ▶1232 **A** *no art.* (*being ill*) Krankheit, *die;* **in ~ and in health** in Gesundheit und in Krankheit; ⇒ *also* **bed** 1 A; **benefit** 1 B; **B** (*disease; also fig.*) Krankheit, *die;* **childhood ~:** Kinderkrankheit, *die;* **C** (*nausea*) Übelkeit, *die;* (*vomiting*) Erbrechen, *das;* **bout of ~:** Anfall von Erbrechen; ⇒ *also* **morning sickness**

**sick: ~ nurse** ⇒ **nurse** 1; **~ pay** *n.* Entgeltfortzahlung im Krankheitsfalle; (*paid by insurance*) Krankengeld, *das;* **~room** *n.* Krankenzimmer, *das*

**side** /saɪd/ ❶ *n.* **A** Seite, *die;* **another car rammed the ~ of ours** ein anderer Wagen rammte unseren an der Seite; **this ~ up** oben; **lie on its ~:** auf der Seite liegen; **put** *or* **lay sth. on its ~:** etw. auf die Seite legen; **over the ~** (*over gunwale of ship/boat*) über Bord (*Akk.*); **lean over the ~** (*Naut.*) sich über die Reling lehnen; **B** (*Geom.*) Seite, *die;* **C** (*of flat object*) Seite, *die;* **on both ~s** auf beiden Seiten; ⇒ *also* **bread** 1 A; **coin** 1; **right ~;** **wrong ~;** **D** (*of animal or person*) Seite, *die;* **be hit in the ~:** in die Seite getroffen werden; **sleep on one's right/left ~:** auf der rechten/linken Seite schlafen; **paralysed in/on/down one ~:** halbseitig gelähmt; **~ of mutton/beef/pork** Hammel-/Rinder-/Schweinehälfte, *die;* **~ of bacon** Speckseite, *die;* **split** (*fig.*) *or* **burst** (*fig.*)/**shake one's ~s [laughing** *or* **with laughter]** vor Lachen platzen/sich vor Lachen nicht mehr halten können; **walk/stand ~ by ~:** nebeneinander gehen/stehen; **work/fight** *etc.* **~ by ~ [with sb.]** Seite an Seite [mit jmdm.] arbeiten/kämpfen *usw.*; **live ~ by ~ [with sb.]** in [jmds.] unmittelbarer Nachbarschaft leben; **live ~ by ~ with death/poverty** in der ständigen Gegenwart des Todes/der Armut leben; ⇒ *also* **blind ~;**

S

thorn C; Ⓔ *(part away from the centre)* Seite, *die;* **the eastern ~ of the town** der Ostteil der Stadt; **the ~s of sb.'s mouth** jmds. Mundwinkel; **right[-hand]/left[-hand] ~:** rechte/linke Seite; **on the right[-hand]/left[-hand] ~ of the road** auf der rechten/linken Straßenseite; **from ~ to ~** *(right across)* quer hinüber; *(alternately each way)* von einer Seite auf die andere *od.* zur anderen; **to one ~:** zur Seite; **on one ~:** an der Seite; **on one ~ of his face** auf einer Seite seines Gesichts; **stand on** *or* **to one ~:** an *od.* auf der Seite stehen; **take sb. to** *or* **on one ~:** jmdn. zur Seite nehmen; **leave a question to** *or* **on one ~:** eine Frage beiseite lassen; **put** *or* **set** *or* **place sth. on one ~ [for sb./sth.]** etw. [für jmdn./etw.] beiseite legen; **put sth. on one ~** *(fig.) (postpone dealing with sth.)* etw. beiseite legen; **on the ~** *(fig.) (in addition to regular work or income)* nebenbei; nebenher; *(as a ~ bet)* als zusätzliche Wette; *(secretly)* insgeheim; *(Amer.: as a ~ dish)* als Beilage; **tell sb. sth. on the ~:** jmdm. etw. im Vertrauen erzählen/sagen; **she is his/he has a bit on the ~** *(coll.)* mit ihr treibt ers noch nebenbei *(ugs.)*/er hat nebenbei noch 'ne andere *(ugs.)*; **pass by on the other ~** *(fig.)* so tun, als ginge es einen nichts an; ⇒ *also* **laugh** 2; Ⓕ *(space beside person or thing)* Seite, *die;* **he never left her ~:** er wich nie von ihrer Seite; **at** *or* **by sb.'s ~:** an jmds. Seite; neben jmdm.; **at** *or* **by the ~ of the car** beim *od.* am Auto; **at** *or* **by the ~ of the road/lake/grave** an der Straße/am See/am Grab; **look tiny by the ~ of sb./sth.** neben jmdm./etw. winzig wirken; **on all ~s** *or* **every ~:** von allen Seiten ‹umzingelt, kritisiert›; **look on all ~s** sich nach allen Seiten umsehen; **from all ~s** *or* **every ~:** von allen Seiten; Ⓖ *(in relation to dividing line)* Seite, *die;* **[on] either ~ of** beiderseits, auf beiden Seiten (+ *Gen.*); **[to** *or* **on] one ~ of** neben (+ *Dat.*); **this/the other ~ of** *(with regard to space)* diesseits/jenseits (+ *Gen.*); *(with regard to time)* vor/nach (+ *Dat.*); **he is this ~ of fifty** er ist unter fünfzig; **what he did was only just this ~ of fraud/perfection** was er tat, war hart an der Grenze zum Betrug/war schon fast perfekt; **this ~ [of] the grave** im Diesseits; **on the other ~** *(fig.: after death)* im Jenseits; ⇒ *also* **grass** 1 A; **right ~**; **wrong ~**; Ⓗ *(aspect)* Seite, *die; (department)* Bereich, *der;* **see both ~s [of the question]** beide Seiten verstehen; **there are two ~s to every question** alles hat seine zwei Seiten; **look on the bright/gloomy ~ [of things]** die Dinge von der angenehmen/düsteren Seite sehen; **see the funny ~ of sth.** etw. von der komischen Seite sehen; **be on the high/flat/expensive** *etc.* **~:** [etwas] hoch/flach/teuer *usw.* sein; ⇒ *also* **err**; **safe** 2 B; **seamy** B; Ⓘ *(opposing group or position)* Seite, *die;* Partei, *die; (Sport: team)* Mannschaft, *die;* **put sb.'s ~:** jmds. Seite vertreten; **be on the winning ~** *(fig.)* auf der Seite der Gewinner stehen; **let the ~ down** *(fig.)* versagen; **change ~s** zur anderen Seite überwechseln; **time is on sb.'s ~:** die Zeit arbeitet für jmdn.; **whose ~ are you/is he on?** auf wessen Seite stehst du/steht er?; **take sb.'s ~:** sich auf jmds. Seite stellen; **take ~s [with/against sb.]** [für/gegen jmdn.] Partei ergreifen; **keep one's ~ of a bargain** seinen Teil einer Abmachung einhalten; ⇒ *also* **no ~**; Ⓙ *(of family)* Seite, *die;* **on one's/sb.'s father's/mother's ~:** väterlicher-/mütterlicherseits; **the Welsh ~ of the family** der walisische Teil der Familie; Ⓚ *(Brit. Billiards/Snooker)* Effet, *der;* **put ~ on** *or* **apply ~ to the ball** dem Ball Effet geben; Ⓛ *(Math.: of equation)* Seite, *die.* ❷ *v.i.* **~ with sb.** sich auf jmds. Seite *(Akk.)* stellen; **~ against sb.** sich gegen jmdn. stellen.

❸ *adj.* seitlich; Seiten-

**side: ~ arms** *n. pl. (Mil.)* Seitengewehre; **~band** *n. (Radio)* Seitenband, *das;* **~ bet** *n. (Gambling)* zusätzliche Wette; **~board** *n.* Anrichte, *die;* Sideboard, *das;* **~boards** *(coll.),* **~burns** *ns. pl.* Ⓐ *(hair on cheeks)* Backenbart, *der;* Ⓑ *(hair in front of the ears)* Koteletten *Pl.;* **~car** *n.* Beiwagen, *der*

**-sided** /'saɪdɪd/ *adj. in comb.* -seitig; **a high-~ enclosure/box** eine hohe Einfriedung/Schachtel; **a glass-~ showcase** ein Schaukasten mit gläsernen Seitenwänden; **a steep-~ mountain** ein steiler Berg; **an open-~ structure** eine seitlich offene Konstruktion

**side: ~ dish** *n.* Beilage, *die;* **~ door** *n.* Seitentür, *die;* **by a ~ door** *(fig.)* durch eine Hintertür; **~ drum** *n. (Mus.)* kleine Trommel; **~ effect** *n.* Nebenwirkung, *die;* **~ entrance** *n.* Seiteneingang, *der;* **~ exit** *n.* Seitenausgang, *der;* **~ glance** *n. (lit. or fig.)* Seitenblick, *der* **(at** auf + *Akk.*); **~ issue** *n.* Randproblem, *das;* **~kick** *n. (coll.)* Kumpan, *der;* **~light** *n.* Ⓐ *(Motor Veh.)* Begrenzungsleuchte, *die;* **drive on ~lights** mit Standlicht fahren; Ⓑ *(Naut.)* Seitenlaterne, *die;* Ⓒ *(light from the ~)* Seitenlicht, *das;* Ⓓ *(fig.: incidental information)* Streiflicht, *das;* **~line** ❶ *n.* Ⓐ *(goods)* Nebensortiment, *das;* Ⓑ *(occupation)* Nebenbeschäftigung, *die;* Ⓒ *in pl. (Sport)* Begrenzungslinien; **on the ~lines** *(outside play area/track etc.)* am Spielfeldrand/am Rande der Bahn *(usw.)*; **be content to sit on the ~lines** *(fig.)* sich mit einer Zuschauerrolle begnügen; **remain on the ~lines** *(fig.)* sich [aus allem] heraushalten; ❷ *v.t. (Amer. Sport)* **be ~-lined because of injury/with a broken arm** wegen einer Verletzung/eines gebrochenen Arms ausfallen; **~-line sb. for foul play** jmdn. wegen eines Fouls vom Platz stellen; **~long** ❶ *adj. (directed to one ~)* **a ~long look/glance** ein Seitenblick; ❷ *adv.* seitwärts; **look/glance ~long at sb.** einen Seitenblick auf jmdn. werfen; **~-on** ❶ *adj.* seitlich; ❷ *adv.* seitlich; **look at sth. ~-on** etw. von der Seite ansehen; **~ piece** *n.* Seitenteil, *das; (of ladder)* Holm, *der; (of spectacles)* Bügel, *der;* **~ plate** *n.* kleiner Teller *(neben dem Teller für das Hauptgericht)*

**sidereal** /saɪ'dɪərɪəl/ *adj.* siderisch; **~ time** siderische [Umlauf]zeit; ⇒ *also* **year** A

**side: ~ road** *n.* Seitenstraße, *die;* **~-saddle** ❶ *n.* Damensattel, *der;* ❷ *adv.* **ride ~-saddle** im Damensitz reiten; **~ salad** *n.* Salat [als Beilage]; **steak with chips and a ~ salad** Steak mit Pommes frites und dazu ein Salat; **~ shoot** *n. (Bot.)* Seitenspross, *der;* **~show** *n.* Nebenattraktion, *die;* **~slip** ❶ *n.* Ⓐ *(Aeronaut.)* seitliches Abrutschen; Ⓑ *(sideways skid)* seitliches Wegrutschen; ❷ *v.i.* Ⓐ *(Aeronaut.)* seitlich abrutschen; Ⓑ *(skid sideways)* seitlich wegrutschen; **~sman** /'saɪdzmən/ *n., pl.* **~smen** /'saɪdzmən/ *(Eccl.)* Kirchendiener, *der;* **~ spin** ⇒ **side** 1 K; **~-splitting** *adj.* zwerchfellerschütternd; **be ~-splitting** zum Brüllen sein *(ugs.)*; **~-splittingly** /'saɪdsplɪtɪŋlɪ/ *adv.* **be ~-splittingly funny** zum Brüllen sein *(ugs.)*; **~step** ❶ *n.* Schritt zur Seite, *der; (in dancing)* Seitenschritt, *der;* ❷ *v.t. (lit. or fig.)* ausweichen (+ *Dat.*); ❸ *v.i.* zur Seite treten; *(fig.)* ausweichen; **~ street** *n.* Seitenstraße, *die;* **~swipe** *n.* Seitenhieb, *der;* **take a ~swipe at sb./sth.** *(fig.)* einen Seitenhieb auf jmdn./etw. austeilen; **~ table** *n.* Beistelltisch, *der;* **~track** ❶ *n. (Railw.)* ⇒ **siding**; ❷ *v.t.* Ⓐ *(Railw.)* auf ein Nebengleis schieben; Ⓑ *(fig.)* **get ~tracked** abgelenkt werden; **~ trip** *n.* kleiner Ausflug; Abstecher, *der;* **~ view** *n.* Seitenansicht, *die;* **~walk** *(Amer.)* ⇒ **pavement** A; **~wall** *n.* Seitenwand, *die;* **~ways** /'saɪdweɪz/ ❶ *adv.* seitwärts; **look at sb./sth. ~ways** jmdn./etw. von der Seite ansehen; **look ~ways at sb.** *(fig.)* jmdn. von der Seite ansehen; jmdn. schief ansehen *(ugs.)*; **be knocked ~ways** *(fig. coll.) (be devastated)* am Boden zerstört sein *(ugs.)* **(by** von); *(be very amazed)* [ganz] von den Socken sein *(ugs.)* **(by** über + *Akk.*); **~ways on** von der Seite; **~ways on to sth.** quer zu etw.; ❷ *adj.* seitlich; **~ways view/look** *or* **glance** Seitenansicht, *die*/Seitenblick, *der;* **~ whiskers** *n. pl.* Backenbart, *der;* **~ wind** *n.* Seitenwind, *der*

**siding** /'saɪdɪŋ/ *n. (Railw.)* Abstellgleis, *das;* Rangiergleis, *das*

**sidle** /'saɪdl/ *v.i.* schleichen; **~ up to sb.** [sich] zu jmdm. schleichen

**siege** /siːdʒ/ *n. (Mil.)* Belagerung, *die; (by police)* Umstellung, *die;* **be under ~** *(lit. or fig.)* belagert sein; *(by police)* umstellt sein; **lay ~ to sth.** *(lit. or fig.)* etw. belagern

**sienna** /sɪ'enə/ *n. (Art)* **raw/burnt ~:** Siena natur/gebrannte Siena

**sierra** /sɪ'erə/ *n. (Geog.)* Sierra, *die*

**siesta** /sɪ'estə/ *n.* Siesta, *die;* **have** *or* **take a ~:** [eine] Siesta halten *od.* machen

**sieve** /sɪv/ ❶ *n.* Sieb, *das;* **have a head** *or* **memory like a ~** *(coll.)* ein Gedächtnis wie ein Sieb haben *(ugs.)*. ❷ *v.t.* sieben; *(fig.: select by examining)* [aus]sieben

**~ 'out** *v.t.* aussieben

**sift** /sɪft/ ❶ *v.t.* sieben; *(fig.: examine closely)* unter die Lupe nehmen; **~ together the flour, salt, and baking powder** Mehl, Salz und Backpulver [zusammen] in ein Gefäß sieben; **~ sth. from sth.** etw. von etw. trennen. ❷ *v.i.* **~ through** durchsehen ‹Briefe, Dokumente usw.›; durchsuchen ‹Trümmer, Asche, Habseligkeiten usw.›

**~ 'out** *v.t. (lit. or fig.)* aussieben; **~ out sth. from sth.** etw. aus etw. heraussieben; *(fig.)* etw. von etw. trennen

**sifter** /'sɪftə(r)/ *n. (Cookery)* Sieb, *das*

**sigh** /saɪ/ ❶ *n.* Seufzer, *der;* **give** *or* **breathe** *or* **utter** *or* **heave a ~:** einen Seufzer ausstoßen *od.* tun; **~ of relief/sadness/contentment** Seufzer der Erleichterung/trauriger Seufzer/Seufzer der Zufriedenheit. ❷ *v.i.* seufzen; **~ with relief/despair/contentment** *etc.* vor Erleichterung/Verzweiflung/Zufriedenheit *usw. od.* erleichtert/verzweifelt/zufrieden *usw.* seufzen; **~ for sth./sb.** *(fig.)* sich nach etw./jmdm. sehnen; nach etw./jmdm. seufzen *(geh.)*. ❸ *v.t.* seufzen

**sight** /saɪt/ ❶ *n.* Ⓐ *(faculty)* Sehvermögen, *das;* **loss of ~:** Verlust des Sehvermögens; **spoil** *or* **ruin one's ~:** sich *(Dat.)* die Augen verderben; **second ~:** das zweite Gesicht; **near ~** ⇒ **short sight**; **by sight:** mit dem Gesichtssinn *od.* den Augen; **know sb. by ~:** jmdn. vom Sehen kennen; ⇒ *also* **long sight**; **short sight**; Ⓑ *(act of seeing)* Anblick, *der;* **at [the] ~ of sb./of blood** bei jmds. Anblick/beim Anblick von Blut; **it was our first ~ of the sea** es war das erste Mal, dass wir das Meer sahen; **catch ~ of sb./sth.** *(lit. or fig.)* jmdn./etw. erblicken; **lose ~ of sb./sth.** *(lit. or fig.)* jmdn./etw. aus dem Auge *od.* den Augen verlieren; **be lost to ~:** den Blicken entschwunden sein *(geh.)*; **disappear from ~:** [den Blicken] entschwinden *(geh.)*; **have** *or* **get a good/quick ~ of sth.** etw. gut/kurz sehen können; **keep ~ of sth.** *(lit. or fig.)* etw. im Auge behalten; **read music at ~:** Noten vom Blatt lesen; **play sth. at ~:** etw. vom Blatt spielen; **translate a text at ~:** einen Text aus dem Stegreif übersetzen; **shoot sb. at** *or* **on ~:** jmdn. gleich [bei seinem Erscheinen] erschießen; **the guards had orders to shoot at** *or* **on ~:** die Wachen hatten Befehl, [auf jeden] sofort zu schießen; ; **buy sth. ~ unseen** etw. unbesehen kaufen; **at first ~:** auf den ersten Blick; **love at first ~:** Liebe auf den ersten Blick; ⇒ *also* **line**[1] 1 C; Ⓒ *(opinion)* **in sb.'s ~:** in jmds. Augen *(Dat.)*; **in the ~ of God/of the law** vor Gott/vor dem Gesetz; Ⓓ *(spectacle)* Anblick, *der;* **be a sorry ~:** einen traurigen Anblick *od.* ein trauriges Bild bieten; **it is a ~ to see** *or* **to behold** *or* **worth seeing** das muss man gesehen haben; **a ~ for sore eyes** eine Augenweide; **be/look a [real] ~** *(coll.) (amusing)* [vollkommen] unmöglich aussehen *(ugs.)*; *(horrible)* böse *od.* schlimm aussehen; Ⓔ *in pl. (noteworthy features)* Sehenswürdigkeiten *Pl.;* **see the ~s** sich *(Dat.)* die Sehenswürdigkeiten ansehen; Ⓕ *(range)* Sichtweite, *die;* **in ~** *(lit. or fig.)* in Sicht; **in sb.'s ~, in ~ of sb.** vor jmds. Augen *(Dat.)*; **come into ~:** in Sicht kommen; **keep sb./sth. in ~** *(lit. or fig.)* jmdn./etw. im Auge behalten; **victory/our goal is now within** *or* **in [our] ~** *(fig.)* der Sieg/unser Ziel ist jetzt in Sicht; **within** *or* **in ~ of sb./sth.** *(able to see)* in jmds. Sichtweite *(Dat.)*/in Sichtweite einer Sache;

S

**come/get within ~ of sb./sth.** in jmds. Sichtweite (*Akk.*)/in Sichtweite einer Sache kommen; **keep** *or* **stay within** *or* **in ~ of sth./sb.** in Sichtweite (*Dat.*) einer Sache/in jmds. Sichtweite (*Dat.*) bleiben; **out of sb.'s ~:** außerhalb jmds. Sichtweite; **be out of ~:** außer Sicht sein; (*coll.: be excellent*) wahnsinnig sein (*ugs.*); **drop out of ~** (*fig.*) aus dem Blickfeld verschwinden; **vanish out of ~:** verschwinden; **keep** *or* **stay out of [sb.'s] ~:** sich [von jmdm.] nicht sehen lassen; sich [jmdm.] nicht zeigen; **I thought it best to keep out of his ~:** ich hielt es für das Beste, ihm nicht unter die Augen zu kommen; **keep sb./sth. out of ~:** jmdn./etw. niemanden sehen lassen; **keep sth./sb. out of sb.'s ~:** jmdn. etw./jmdn. nicht sehen lassen; **put sth. out of [sb.'s] ~:** etw. [vor jmdm.] verstecken; **not let sb./sth. out of one's ~:** jmdn./etw. nicht aus den Augen lassen; **[get] out of my ~!** geh mir aus den Augen!; verschwinde! (*ugs.*); **out of ~, out of mind** (*prov.*) aus den Augen, aus dem Sinn; Ⓖ (*aim, observation*) **take a ~:** zielen; **take a ~ at sth.** etw. anvisieren; (*with gun*) auf etw. (*Akk.*) zielen; Ⓗ (*device for aiming*) Visier, *das;* **~s** Visiervorrichtung, *die;* **telescopic ~:** Zielfernrohr, *das;* **line sth./sb. up in one's ~s** auf etw./jmdn. zielen; etw./jmdn. anvisieren; **have sth./sb. [lined up] in one's ~s** etw./jmdn. im Visier haben; (*fig.*) es auf etw./jmdn. abgesehen haben; **set/have [set] one's ~s on sth.** (*fig.*) etw. anpeilen; **his ~s were set on doing it** er hatte es sich (*Dat.*) zum Ziel gesetzt, es zu tun; **set one's ~s [too] high** (*fig.*) seine Ziele [zu] hoch stecken; **lower/raise one's ~s** (*fig.*) zurückstecken/sich (*Dat.*) ein höheres Ziel setzen; Ⓘ *no pl., no def. art.* (*coll.: great deal*) **a ~ too clever/expensive** *etc.* entschieden zu schlau/teuer *usw.*; **a [long** *or* **damn** *or* **damned] ~ better/more expensive** *etc.* entschieden besser/teurer *usw.*; **not by a long ~:** lange *od.* längst nicht.

❷ *v.t.* Ⓐ sichten ‹Land, Schiff, Flugzeug, Wrack›; sehen ‹Entflohenen, Vermissten›; antreffen ‹seltenes Tier, seltene Pflanze›; Ⓑ (*take ~ of*) anvisieren

**sighted** /'saɪtɪd/ *adj.* sehend; **partially ~:** [hochgradig] sehbehindert; **the blind and the partially ~:** Blinde und [hochgradig] Sehbehinderte

**sighting** /'saɪtɪŋ/ *n.* Beobachtung, *die;* **there have been several ~s of the escaped prisoner** der entflohene Häftling wurde mehrfach gesehen

**sightless** /'saɪtlɪs/ *adj.* blind

**sight: ~-read** (*Mus.*) *v.t. & i.* ‹Pianist usw.:› vom Blatt spielen; ‹Sänger:› vom Blatt singen; **~-reader** *n.* (*Mus.*) **be a good/poor ~-reader** ‹Pianist usw.:› gut/schlecht vom Blatt spielen; ‹Sänger:› gut/schlecht vom Blatt singen; **~-reading** *n., no pl.* (*Mus.*) **be good/bad** *or* **poor at ~-reading** ‹Pianist usw.:› gut/schlecht vom Blatt spielen [können]; ‹Sänger:› gut/schlecht vom Blatt singen [können]; **~ screen** *n.* (*Cricket*) Kontrastschirm, *der;* **~seeing** *n.* Sightseeing, *das* (*Touristikjargon*); **go ~seeing** Besichtigungen machen; **do a lot of ~seeing** viele Sehenswürdigkeiten besichtigen; **~seeing bus** Sightseeingbus, *der;* **~seeing tour/trip** Besichtigungsfahrt, *die;* Sightseeingtour, *die* (*Touristikjargon*); (*in town*) Stadtrundfahrt, *die;* **~seer** *n.* Tourist (*der die Sehenswürdigkeiten besichtigt*); **~-testing** *n.* Durchführung von Sehtests; **~-testing is free** Sehtests sind kostenlos

**sigma** /'sɪgmə/ *n.* Sigma, *das*

**sign** /saɪn/ ❶ *n.* Ⓐ (*symbol*) Zeichen, *das;* **chemical/mathematical ~:** chemisches/mathematisches Zeichen; Ⓑ (*Astrol.*) **~ [of the zodiac]** [Tierkreis]zeichen, *das;* Sternzeichen, *das;* **what ~ are you?** welches Tierkreiszeichen *od.* Sternzeichen bist du?; **sb.'s birth ~:** jmds. Tierkreiszeichen; Ⓒ (*notice*) Schild, *das;* **direction ~:** Wegweiser, *der;* **[advertising] ~:** Reklameschild, *das;* Reklame, *die;* (*illuminated, flashing*) Leuchtreklame, *die;* **danger ~** (*lit. or fig.*) Gefahrenzeichen, *das;* Ⓓ (*outside shop etc.*) ⇒ **signboard**; Ⓔ (*indication*) Zeichen, *das;* (*of future event*) Anzeichen, *das;* **his behaviour is a ~ that he is unhappy** sein Verhalten ist ein Zeichen dafür, dass er unglücklich ist; **there is little/no/every ~ of a quick settlement of the strike** *or* **that the strike will be settled quickly** wenig/nichts/alles deutet auf eine baldige Beendigung des Streiks hin *od.* deutet darauf hin, dass der Streik bald beendet wird; **this is a ~ of his intelligence** das zeugt von seiner Intelligenz; **she gave** *or* **showed no ~ of having heard** *or* **that she had heard me** (*did not reveal*) sie ließ durch nichts erkennen, dass sie mich gehört hatte; (*there was no indication*) es deutete nichts darauf hin, dass sie mich gehört hatte; **if he was angry, he gave no ~ of it** wenn er ärgerlich war, so zeigte er es doch nicht; **show [no] ~s of fear/fatigue/strain/improvement** *etc.* [keine] Anzeichen der Angst/Müdigkeit/Anstrengung/Besserung *usw.* zeigen *od.* erkennen lassen; **the carpet showed little/some ~[s] of wear** der Teppich wirkte kaum/etwas abgenutzt; **the cave shows ~s of having been inhabited** in der Höhle gibt es Anzeichen dafür, dass sie bewohnt war; **the window shows no ~[s] of having been forced** das Fenster zeigt keine Spuren von Gewaltanwendung; **as a ~ of** als Zeichen (+ *Gen.*); **do sth. as a ~ of sth.** etw. zum Zeichen einer Sache (*Gen.*) tun; **at the first** *or* **slightest ~ of sth.** schon beim geringsten Anzeichen von etw.; **there was no ~ of him/the car anywhere** er/der Wagen war nirgends zu sehen; **there was no ~ of life** keine Menschenseele war zu sehen; **~ of the times** Zeichen der Zeit; Ⓕ (*gesture, signal*) Zeichen, *das;* **give sb. a ~ to do sth., make a ~ to** *or* **for sb. to do sth.** jmdm. ein Zeichen geben, etw. zu tun; ⇒ *also* **V-sign**; Ⓖ (*mark*) Zeichen, *das;* Ⓗ (*Math.*) Vorzeichen, *das.*

❷ *v.t.* Ⓐ (*write one's name etc. on*) unterzeichnen; unterschreiben; ‹Künstler, Autor:› signieren ‹Werk›; **~ the guest book** sich ins Gästebuch eintragen; **a ~ed copy [of a book]** ein [hand]signiertes Exemplar [eines Buches]; **~ed, sealed, and delivered** (*Law*) unterschrieben, gesiegelt und ausgehändigt; (*fig.*) unter Dach und Fach; Ⓑ **~ one's name** [mit seinem Namen] unterzeichnen *od.* unterschreiben; **~ oneself R. A. Smith** mit R. A. Smith unterschreiben; Ⓒ ⇒ **sign up** 1; Ⓓ (*indicate*) zeigen.

❸ *v.i.* Ⓐ (*write one's name*) unterschreiben; **~ for sth.** (*acknowledge receipt of sth.*) den Empfang einer Sache (*Gen.*) bestätigen; (**~** *a contract etc. for sth.*) [einen Vertrag über] etw. (*Akk.*) unterschreiben; Ⓑ (*signal*) **~ to sb. to do sth.** jmdm. ein Zeichen geben, etw. zu tun; Ⓒ ⇒ **sign on** 2 A

**~ a'way** *v.t.* abtreten ‹Eigentum›; verzichten auf ‹Recht, Freiheit usw.›

**~ 'in** ❶ *v.t.* **~ sb./sth. in [on arrival]** jmds. Eintreffen/das Eintreffen einer Sache schriftlich vermerken *od.* registrieren. ❷ *v.i.* sich [bei der Ankunft] eintragen

**~ 'off** ❶ *v.i.* Ⓐ (*cease employment*) kündigen; ‹Seemann:› abheuern, abmustern (*Seemannsspr.*); Ⓑ (*at end of shift etc.*) sich [zum Feierabend *usw.*] abmelden; Ⓒ (*Radio*) sich verabschieden; ‹Pilot:› die Frequenz verlassen (*Funkw.*); Ⓓ (*at end of letter*) Schluss machen. ❷ *v.t.* kündigen; abheuern, abmustern ‹Seemann› (*Seemannsspr.*)

**~ 'on** ❶ *v.t.* einstellen ‹Arbeitskräfte›; verpflichten ‹Fußballspieler›; anwerben ‹Soldaten›; anheuern, anmustern ‹Seeleute›. ❷ *v.i.* Ⓐ (**~** *an engagement*) sich verpflichten (**with** bei); Ⓑ (*at start of shift etc.*) **~ on for the night shift** sich [per Unterschrift] zur Nachtschicht anmelden; Ⓒ (*Radio*) ‹Rundfunkstation:› seine Sendungen aufnehmen; ‹Funker:› sich melden; Ⓓ **~ on [for the dole]** (*coll.*) sich arbeitslos melden; stempeln gehen (*ugs. veralt.*)

**~ 'out** ❶ *v.t.* **~ books out from the library** Bücher als [aus der Bibliothek] entliehen eintragen. ❷ *v.i.* sich [schriftlich] abmelden; ‹Hotelgast:› abreisen

**~ 'over** *v.t.* überschreiben ‹Immobilien›; übertragen ‹Rechte›

**~ 'up** ❶ *v.t.* (*engage*) [vertraglich] verpflichten; einstellen ‹Arbeiter›; aufnehmen ‹Mitglied›; einschreiben ‹Kursteilnehmer›. ❷ *v.i.* sich [vertraglich] verpflichten (**with** bei); (*join a course etc.*) sich einschreiben

**signal** /'sɪgnl/ ❶ *n.* Ⓐ Signal, *das;* **a ~ for sth./to sb.** ein Zeichen zu etw./für jmdn.; **at a ~ from the headmaster** auf ein Zeichen des Direktors; **the ~ was against us/at red** (*Railw.*) das Signal zeigte „halt"/stand auf Rot; **alarm** *or* **danger/warning ~:** Gefahr-/Warnsignal, *das;* **hand ~s** (*Motor Veh.*) Handzeichen; **sound/light/flag ~:** akustisches Signal/Lichtsignal, *das*/Flaggensignal, *das;* **radio** *or* **wireless ~:** Funkspruch, *der;* **distress ~:** Notsignal, *das;* **code of ~s** ⇒ **signal book**; **the Royal Corps of S~s,** (*coll.*) **the S~s** (*Brit. Mil.*) *die Fernmeldetruppe der britischen Armee;* Ⓑ (*occasion, cause*) Signal, *das;* Zeichen, *das;* **the ~ for rioting/pandemonium** das Zeichen zum Aufruhr/Chaos; Ⓒ (*Electr., Radio, etc.*) Signal, *das.*

❷ *v.i.,* (*Brit.*) **-ll-** signalisieren; Signale geben; ‹Kraftfahrer:› blinken; (*using hand etc.* **~s**) anzeigen; **~ for assistance** ein Hilfesignal geben; **~ to sb. [to do sth.]** jmdm. ein Zeichen geben[, etw. zu tun].

❸ *v.t.,* (*Brit.*) **-ll-** Ⓐ (*lit. or fig.*) signalisieren; **~ sb. [to do sth.]** jmdm. ein Zeichen geben[, etw. zu tun]; **the driver ~led a right turn/that he was turning right** der Fahrer zeigte an, dass er [nach] rechts abbiegen wollte; Ⓑ (*Radio etc.*) funken; [über Funk] durchgeben.

❹ *adj.* außergewöhnlich

**signal: ~ book** *n.* (*Mil., Navy*) Signalbuch, *das;* **~ box** *n.* (*Railw.*) Stellwerk, *das*

**signaler** (*Amer.*) ⇒ **signaller**

**signal: ~ flag** *n.* (*Mil., Navy, Railw.*) Signalflagge, *die;* **~ lamp** *n.* (*Naut., Railw.*) Signallampe, *die*

**signaller** /'sɪgnələ(r)/ *n.* (*Mil.*) Blinker, *der;* (*with flags*) Signalgast, *der* (*Seew.*)

**signally** /'sɪgnəlɪ/ *adv.* ungeheuer; unerhört; **~ ineffective** bemerkenswert ineffektiv; **not ~ successful** nicht übermäßig erfolgreich

**signal: ~man** /'sɪgnlmən/ *n., pl.* **~men** /'sɪgnlmən/ ▶ **1261** Ⓐ (*Brit. Railw.*) Bahnwärter, *der;* Ⓑ ⇒ **signaller**; **~ tower** (*Amer.*) ⇒ **signal box**

**signatory** /'sɪgnətərɪ/ ❶ *adj.* unterzeichnend; vertragschließend ‹Partei, Land›; Signatar‹macht, -staat› (*Politik*). ❷ *n.* (*person*) Unterzeichner, *der;* (*party*) vertragschließende Partei; (*state*) Signatarstaat, *der;* **~ to a petition** Unterzeichner einer Petition; **~ to the treaty/agreement** (*state*) Signatarstaat des Abkommens

**signature** /'sɪgnətʃə(r)/ *n.* Ⓐ Unterschrift, *die;* (*on painting*) Signatur, *die;* **put one's ~ to sth.** seine Unterschrift unter etw. (*Akk.*) setzen; Ⓑ (*Mus.*) ⇒ **key signature**; **time signature**; Ⓒ (*Printing*) (*figure or letter*) Signatur, *die* (*Buchw.*); (*folded sheet*) Bogen, *der;* Ⓓ (*Amer. Med.*) Signatur, *die*

**'signature tune** *n.* (*Radio, Telev.*) Erkennungsmelodie, *die*

**'signboard** *n.* Schild, *das;* (*advertising*) Reklameschild, *das*

**signet** /'sɪgnɪt/ *n.* Petschaft, *das;* Signet, *das* (*veralt.*)

**'signet ring** *n.* Siegelring, *der*

**significance** /sɪg'nɪfɪkəns/ *n.* Ⓐ (*meaning, importance*) Bedeutung, *die;* **be of [no] ~:** [nicht] von Bedeutung sein; **a matter of great/little/no ~:** eine [sehr] wichtige/ziemlich unwichtige/völlig unwichtige Angelegenheit; Ⓑ (*meaningfulness*) Bedeutsamkeit, *die*

**significant** /sɪg'nɪfɪkənt/ *adj.* Ⓐ (*noteworthy, important*) bedeutend; Ⓑ (*full of meaning*) bedeutsam; **be ~ of sth.** etw. verraten; etwas über etw. (*Akk.*) aussagen; Ⓒ (*having a meaning*) bedeutungstragend (*Sprachw.*); **be ~:** etwas bedeuten; Ⓓ (*Statistics*) signifikant

**significant 'figure** *n.* (*Math.*) signifikante Ziffer

S

**significantly** /sɪg'nɪfɪkəntlɪ/ *adv.* Ⓐ (*meaningfully*) bedeutungsvoll; *as sentence-modifier* ~ **[enough]** bedeutsamerweise; Ⓑ (*notably*) bedeutend; signifikant (*geh., fachspr.*)

**signification** /sɪgnɪfɪ'keɪʃn/ *n.* Bedeutung, *die*

**signify** /'sɪgnɪfaɪ/ ❶ *v.t.* Ⓐ (*indicate, mean*) bedeuten; Ⓑ (*communicate, make known*) kundtun (*geh.*); zum Ausdruck bringen. ❷ *v.i.* **it does not** ~: es hat nichts zu bedeuten *od.* (*ugs.*) zu sagen

**signing** /'saɪnɪŋ/ *n.* Ⓐ Unterschreiben, *das;* (*formal*) Unterzeichnung, *die;* Ⓑ (~ *up*) Verpflichtung, *die*

'**sign language** *n.* Zeichensprache, *die*

**sign:** ~ **painter** ⇒ ~**writer**; ~**post** ❶ *n.* (*lit. or fig.*) Wegweiser, *der;* ❷ *v.t.* ausschildern ‹Route, Umleitungsstrecke usw.›; mit Wegweisern versehen ‹Straße›; ~**writer** *n.* ▶ **1261** Schildermaler, *der*

**Sikh** /si:k, sɪk/ *n.* Sikh, *der;* **she is a** ~: sie gehört der Sikhreligion an

**Sikhism** /'si:kɪzm, 'sɪkɪzm/ *n., no pl.* Sikhreligion, *die*

**silage** /'saɪlɪdʒ/ (*Agric.*) ❶ *n.* Silage, *die;* Gärfutter, *das.* ❷ *v.t.* silieren

**silence** /'saɪləns/ ❶ *n.* Schweigen, *das;* (*keeping a secret*) Verschwiegenheit, *die;* (*taciturnity*) Schweigsamkeit, *die;* (*stillness*) Stille, *die;* **there was** ~: es herrschte Schweigen/Stille; **there was a sudden/** (*iron.*) **deafening** ~: es trat plötzlich Stille ein/es herrschte Totenstille; **an awkward** ~**/awkward** ~**s** ein betretenes Schweigen/peinliche [Gesprächs]pausen; **his story was punctuated by long** ~**s** lange Sprechpausen unterbrachen seine Erzählung; ~**!** Ruhe!; '~ — **recording in progress**' „Bitte Ruhe — Aufnahme"; ~ **on sth.** Schweigen zu etw.; **in** ~: schweigend; **suffer in** ~: schweigend leiden; **call for** ~: um Ruhe bitten; **keep** ~ (*lit. or fig.*) schweigen; **break the** ~: die Stille unterbrechen; (*be the first to speak*) das Schweigen brechen; **break one's** ~ (*lit. or fig.*) sein Schweigen brechen; **reduce sb. to** ~ (*lit. or fig.*) jmdn. zum Schweigen *od.* Verstummen bringen; **a minute's** ~: eine Schweigeminute; **the [two minutes']** ~ (*Brit.: on Remembrance Sunday*) die zwei Schweigeminuten (*am Heldengedenktag*); ~ **is golden** Schweigen ist Gold; ⇒ *also* **pass over** 1.
❷ *v.t.* Ⓐ (*make silent*) zum Schweigen *od.* Verstummen bringen; (*fig.*) ersticken ‹Zweifel, Ängste, Proteste›; mundtot machen ‹Gegner, Zeugen›; (*coll.: kill*) zum Schweigen bringen (*verhüllend*); Ⓑ (*make quieter*) leiser machen ‹Motor, Maschine, Auspuff, Bohrmaschine usw.›

**silencer** /'saɪlənsə(r)/ *n.* (*for door*) Türschließer, *der;* (*Brit. Motor Veh.*) Schalldämpfer, *der;* Auspufftopf, *der;* (*Arms*) Schalldämpfer, *der*

**silent** /'saɪlənt/ *adj.* Ⓐ stumm; (*noiseless*) unhörbar; (*still*) still; **as** ~ **as the grave** *or* **tomb** totenstill; **deaf people live in a** ~ **world** Taube leben in einer lautlosen Welt; **be** ~ (*say nothing*) schweigen; (*be still*) still sein; (*not be working*) ‹Maschine:› stillstehen; ‹Waffen:› schweigen; **fall** ~: verstummen; **keep** *or* **remain** ~ (*lit. or fig.*) schweigen; ‹jmd., der verhört wird:› beharrlich schweigen; Ⓑ (*taciturn*) schweigsam; **the strong,** ~ **type** der starke, tatkräftige Typ, der nicht viel Worte macht; Ⓒ (*Ling.*) stumm; Ⓓ (*Cinemat.*) ~ **film** Stummfilm, *der;* **the early motion pictures were** ~: die ersten Filme waren Stummfilme *od.* waren ohne Ton

**silently** /'saɪləntlɪ/ *adv.* schweigend; stumm ‹weinen, beten›; (*noiselessly*) lautlos

**silent:** ~ **ma'jority** *n.* schweigende Mehrheit; ~ **'partner** (*Amer.*) ⇒ **sleeping partner**

**Silesia** /saɪ'lɪ:ʃə/ *pr. n.* Schlesien (*das*)

**Silesian** /saɪ'lɪ:ʃn/ ❶ *adj.* schlesisch; **sb. is** ~: jmd. ist Schlesier/Schlesierin. ❷ *n.* Ⓐ (*person*) Schlesier, *der*/Schlesierin, *die;* Ⓑ (*dialect*) Schlesisch, *das;* **speak** ~: schlesischen Dialekt sprechen

**silhouette** /sɪlʊ'et/ ❶ *n.* Ⓐ (*picture*) Schattenriss, *der;* Ⓑ (*appearance against the light*) Silhouette, *die;* **in** ~: als Silhouette. ❷ *v.t.* **be** ~**d against sth.** sich als Silhouette gegen etw. abheben

**silica** /'sɪlɪkə/ *n.* Kieselerde, *die*

**silicate** /'sɪlɪkeɪt/ *n.* (*Chem.*) Silikat, *das*

**siliceous** /sɪ'lɪsɪəs/ *adj.* Kiesel-

**silicon** /'sɪlɪkən/ *n.* (*Chem.*) Silicium, *das;* Silizium, *das;* ~ **chip** Siliciumchip, *der;* Siliziumchip, *der*

**silicone** /'sɪlɪkəʊn/ *n.* (*Chem.*) Silikon, *das;* ~ **[breast] implant** Silikon[brust]implantat, *das*

**silicosis** /sɪlɪ'kəʊsɪs/ *n., pl.* **silicoses** /sɪlɪ'kəʊsi:z/ ▶ **1232** (*Med.*) Silikose, *die*

**silk** /sɪlk/ ❶ *n.* Ⓐ Seide, *die;* **sewing/embroidery** ~: Näh-/Stickseide, *die;* **take** ~ (*Brit. Law*) Kronanwalt werden; Ⓑ *in pl.* (*kinds of* ~ *material*) Seidenstoffe; (*garments*) seidene Kleider *od.* Kleidungsstücke; (*Horseracing*) Rennfarben *Pl.;* Ⓒ (*of spider etc.*) [Spinnen]faden, *der;* Ⓓ (*Bot.*) Seide, *die;* Ⓔ (*Brit. Law coll.*) Kronanwalt, *der.* ❷ *attrib. adj.* seiden; Seiden-; **you can't make a** ~ **purse out of a sow's ear** (*prov.*) aus einem Schweinsohr lässt sich kein seidener Beutel machen

**silken** /'sɪlkn/ *adj.* Ⓐ seiden; Seiden-; Ⓑ (*lustrous*) seidig; Ⓒ ⇒ **silky** B

**silk:** ~ **'finish** *n.* Seidenglanz, *der;* ~ **'hat** *n.* Zylinder, *der*

**silkily** /'sɪlkɪlɪ/ *adv.* Ⓐ (*lustrously*) seiden; seidig; Ⓑ (*suavely*) **speak** ~: mit samtener Stimme sprechen

**silk:** ~ **mill** *n.* Seidenspinnerei, *die;* ~**-screen printing** ⇒ **screen printing**; ~**worm** *n.* (*Zool.*) Seidenraupe, *die*

**silky** /'sɪlkɪ/ *adj.* Ⓐ seidig; **have a** ~ **feel** sich wie Seide anfühlen; Ⓑ (*suave*) glatt; samten, samtig ‹Stimme›

**sill** /sɪl/ *n.* Ⓐ (*of door*) [Tür]schwelle, *die;* (*of window*) Fensterbank, *die;* Ⓑ (*Geol.*) [schichtparalleler] Lagergang; Sill, *der* (*fachspr.*)

**sillabub** ⇒ **syllabub**

**silliness** /'sɪlɪnɪs/ *n.* Ⓐ *no pl.* Dummheit, *die;* Blödheit, *die* (*ugs.*); Ⓑ *usu. in pl.* (*instance*) Dummheit, *die;* (*piece of childishness*) Albernheit, *die*

**silly** /'sɪlɪ/ ❶ *adj.* dumm; blöd[e] (*ugs.*); (*imprudent, unwise*) töricht; unklug; (*childish*) albern; **only a** ~ **little cut [in the finger]** bloß ein läppischer (*ugs.*) kleiner Schnitt [im Finger]; **with a** ~ **little hammer like this one** mit so einem albernen kleinen Hammer wie diesem; **the** ~ **season** (*Journ.*) die Sauregurkenzeit; **[you]** ~ **child/thing!** [du] dummes Kind/dummes Ding!; **the** ~ **thing** (*inanimate object*) das dumme *od.* (*ugs.*) blöde Ding; **a** ~ **thing** (*a foolish action*) etwas Dummes *od.* (*ugs.*) Blödes; (*a trivial matter*) eine blödsinnige Kleinigkeit (*ugs.*); (*a stupid person*) ein dummes Ding; **it/that was a** ~ **thing to do** es/das war dumm *od.* (*ugs.*) blöd; ~ **fool** Dummkopf, *der* (*ugs.*); **not do anything** ~ (*lit. or fig.*) keine Dummheit[en] machen; **knock sb.** ~: jmdn. bewusstlos schlagen; **I was scared** ~: mir rutschte das Herz in die Hose (*ugs.*); **laugh oneself** ~: sich halb totlachen; ⇒ *also* **me**[1].
❷ *n.* (*coll.*) Dummchen, *das;* Dummerchen, *das* (*fam.*)

'**sillybilly** *n.* (*coll.*) Kindskopf, *der;* **be a** ~ **[about sth.]** sich [bei etw.] dumm *od.* kindisch anstellen

**silo** /'saɪləʊ/ *n., pl.* ~**s** Ⓐ (*Agric.*) Silo, *der;* Ⓑ (*Brit.*) **[grain/cement]** ~: [Getreide-/Zement]silo, *der;* Ⓒ (*Mil.*) **[missile]** ~: [Raketen]silo, *der*

**silt** /sɪlt/ ❶ *n.* Schlamm, *der;* Schlick, *der.* ❷ *v.t.* ~ **up** verschlämmen. ❸ *v.i.* ~ **up** verschlammen

**siltation** /sɪl'teɪʃn/ *n.* Ⓐ (*process*) Verschlämmung, *die;* Ⓑ (*state*) Verschlammung, *die*

**Silurian** /saɪ'ljʊərɪən, sɪ'ljʊərɪən/ (*Geol.*) ❶ *adj.* silurisch. ❷ *n.* Silur, *das*

**silver** /'sɪlvə(r)/ ❶ *n.* Ⓐ *no pl., no indef. art.* Silber, *das;* **the price of** ~: der Silberpreis; Ⓑ (*colour*) Silber, *das;* Ⓒ *no pl., no indef. art.* (*coins*) Silbermünzen *Pl.;* Silber, *das* (*ugs.*); **for thirty pieces** *or* **a handful of** ~ (*fig.*) für einen Judaslohn; Ⓓ (*vessels, cutlery*) Silber, *das;* (*cutlery of other material*) Besteck, *das;* Ⓔ (*medal*) Silber, *das;* **win two** ~**s** zweimal Silber gewinnen. ❷ *attrib. adj.* silbern; Silber‹pokal, -münze›; **have a** ~ **tongue** zungenfertig sein; ⇒ *also* **spoon**[1] 1 A; **standard** 1 H. ❸ *v.t.* Ⓐ (*coat with* ~) versilbern; (*coat with amalgam*) verspiegeln ‹Glas›; Ⓑ ergrauen lassen ‹Haar›. ❹ *v.i.* ergrauen

**silver:** ~ **'band** *n.* (*Mus.*) Blaskapelle (*deren Instrumente versilbert sind*); ~ **'birch** *n.* (*Bot.*) Weißbirke, *die;* ~ **collection** *n.* Sammlung, *die* (*bei der Silbermünzen gespendet werden*); ~**-coloured** *adj.* silberfarben; silberfarbig; ~ **'fir** *n.* (*Bot.*) Weißtanne, *die;* Silbertanne, *die;* ~**fish** *n.* (*Zool.*) Ⓐ (*insect*) Silberfischchen, *das;* Ⓑ (*fish*) Silberfisch, *der;* (*variety of goldfish*) weißer Goldfisch; ~ **'foil** *n.* Ⓐ Silberfolie, *die;* (*aluminium foil*) Alufolie, *die;* Ⓑ (*tin foil*) Stanniol, *das;* ~ **'fox** *n.* (*Zool.; also fur*) Silberfuchs, *der;* ~ **'gilt** *n.* Ⓐ (*gilded* ~) vergoldetes Silber; ~ **gilt dish/tray** Teller/Tablett aus vergoldetem Silber; Ⓑ (*imitation gilt*) Goldimitation, *die;* ~**-grey** *adj.* silbergrau; silbrig grau; ~**-haired** *adj.* silberhaarig (*geh.*); ~ **'jubilee** *n.* silbernes Jubiläum; ~ **'leaf** *n.* Blattsilber, *das;* ~ **'medal** *n.* Silbermedaille, *die;* ~ **'medallist** *n.* Silbermedaillengewinner, *der*/-gewinnerin, *die;* ~ **mine** *n.* Silbermine, *die;* ~ **'paper** *n.* Silberpapier, *das;* ~ **'plate** *n., no pl., no indef. art.* Ⓐ versilberte Ware; (*coating*) Silberauflage, *die;* Ⓑ (*vessels, tableware*) Silbergeschirr, *das;* **be** ~ **plate** versilbert sein; ~**-plate** *v.t.* versilbern; ~**-plated** *adj.* versilbert; ~ **sand** *n. feiner, reiner Sand;* ~ **'screen** *n.* **the** ~ **screen** die Leinwand; ~ **service** *n.* Ⓐ (*set of* ~*ware*) silbernes Service; Ⓑ *no pl.* (*method of restaurant service*) englisches Service; Rundservice, *das;* ~**side** *n.* (*Brit. Gastr.*) Schwanzstück, *das;* ~**smith** *n.* ▶ **1261** Silberschmied, *der*/-schmiedin, *die;* ~**-tongued** *adj.* (*fig.*) zungenfertig; ~**ware** *n., no pl.* Silber, *das;* ~ **'wedding** *n.* Silberhochzeit, *die;* silberne Hochzeit

**silvery** /'sɪlvərɪ/ *adj.* (*silver-coloured*) silbrig; (*clear-sounding*) silbern (*dichter.*); silbrig (*geh.*)

**silviculture** /'sɪlvɪkʌltʃə(r)/ *n.* Waldbau, *der*

**simian** /'sɪmɪən/ ❶ *adj.* Ⓐ (*apelike*) affenähnlich; Ⓑ (*Zool.*) ‹Gehirn usw.› des/der Affen. ❷ *n.* Ⓐ (*ape or monkey*) Affe, *der;* Ⓑ (*Zool.*) Menschenaffe, *der*

**similar** /'sɪmɪlə(r)/ *adj.* (*also Geom.*) ähnlich (**to** *Dat.*); **some flour and a** ~ **amount of sugar** etwas Mehl und ungefähr die gleiche Menge Zucker; **our tastes are very** ~: wir haben einen sehr ähnlichen Geschmack; **of** ~ **size/colour** *etc.* von ähnlicher Größe/Farbe *usw.;* **be** ~ **in size/appearance** *etc.* **[to sb./sth.]** eine ähnliche Größe/ein ähnliches Aussehen haben [wie jmd./etw.]; **look/taste/smell** *etc.* ~ **[to sth.]** ähnlich aussehen/schmecken/riechen *usw.* [wie etw.]; **the two brothers look very** ~: die beiden Brüder sehen sich (*Dat.*) sehr ähnlich

**similarity** /sɪmɪ'lærɪtɪ/ *n.* Ähnlichkeit, *die* (**to** mit); **point of** ~: Ähnlichkeit, *die;* **there the** ~ **ends** sonst gibt es keine Gemeinsamkeiten

**similarly** /'sɪmɪləlɪ/ *adv.* ähnlich; (*to the same degree*) ebenso; *as sentence-modifier* ebenso gut; ~ **effective/costly** *etc.* ähnlich/ebenso effektiv/teuer *usw.*

**simile** /'sɪmɪlɪ/ *n.* (*Lit.*) Vergleich, *der;* Simile, *das* (*geh., veralt.*)

**similitude** /sɪ'mɪlɪtju:d/ *n.* (*literary*) Ähnlichkeit, *die*

**simmer** /'sɪmə(r)/ ❶ *v.i.* Ⓐ (*Cookery*) ‹Flüssigkeit:› sieden; **put the fish in the water and allow to** ~ **for ten minutes** den Fisch ins Wasser legen und zehn Minuten ziehen lassen; Ⓑ (*fig.*) gären; **let things** ~: die Dinge sich entwickeln lassen; ~ **with rage/excitement** eine Wut haben/innerlich ganz aufgeregt sein. ❷ *v.t.* (*Cookery*) köcheln lassen ‹Suppe, Soße usw.›; ziehen lassen ‹Fisch, Klöße usw.›. ❸ *n.* (*Cookery*) **keep at a** *or* **on the** ~:

S

sieden lassen ‹Wasser›; köcheln lassen ‹Suppe, Soße usw.›

~ **'down** *v.i.* sich abregen (*ugs.*); **let things/the situation ~ down** abwarten, bis sich die Wogen geglättet haben

**simnel cake** /'sɪmnl keɪk/ *n.* (*Brit.*) ≈ Rosinenkuchen, *der*

**simper** /'sɪmpə(r)/ ❶ *v.i.* affektiert *od.* gekünstelt lächeln. ❷ *v.t.* mit einem affektierten *od.* gekünstelten Lächeln sagen. ❸ *n.* affektiertes *od.* gekünsteltes Lächeln

**simpering** /'sɪmpərɪŋ/ *adj.* affektiert, gekünstelt ‹Lächeln, Art›; affektiert ‹Frau›

**simple** /'sɪmpl/ *adj.* Ⓐ (*not compound, not complicated*) einfach; (*not elaborate*) schlicht ‹Mobiliar, Schönheit, Kunstwerk, Kleidung›; **the ~ life** das einfache Leben; ⇒ *also* **simple interest**; Ⓑ (*unqualified, absolute*) einfach; simpel; **it was a ~ misunderstanding** es war [ganz] einfach ein Missverständnis; **it is a ~ fact that ...:** es ist [ganz] einfach eine Tatsache *od.* eine simple Tatsache, dass ...; ⇒ *also* **pure** 1 C; Ⓒ (*easy*) einfach; **the ~st thing would be** *or* **it would be the ~st if ...:** es wäre das Einfachste *od.* am einfachsten, wenn ...; **as ~ as ABC** kinderleicht; **it's/it isn't as ~ as that** so einfach ist das/ist das nicht; **it would make things so ~ if ...:** es wäre alles so einfach, wenn ...; **'Electronics made ~'** „Elektronik leicht gemacht"; **it would make my job/task much ~r** es würde mir meine Arbeit sehr erleichtern/meine Aufgabe sehr vereinfachen; Ⓓ (*unsophisticated*) schlicht; (*foolish*) dumm; einfältig; (*feeble-minded*) debil; (*humble*) einfach ‹Person, Arbeiter, Bauer, Leute›; **the ~ pleasures of life** die kleinen Freuden des Lebens; Ⓔ (*Ling.*) **~ tense** einfache Zeitform; **~ past** Präteritum, *das;* **~ sentence** einfacher Satz

**simple: ~-hearted** /'sɪmplhɑ:tɪd/ *adj.* schlicht; **~ 'interest** Kapitalzins, *der;* **~-minded** *adj.* Ⓐ (*unsophisticated*) schlicht; Ⓑ (*feeble-minded*) debil

**'simple time** *n.* (*Mus.*) nicht zusammengesetzte Taktart

**simpleton** /'sɪmpltən/ *n.* Einfaltspinsel, *der* (*ugs.*)

**simplex** /'sɪmpleks/ *n.* (*Ling.*) Simplex, *das*

**simplicity** /sɪm'plɪsɪtɪ/ *n., no pl.* Einfachheit, *die;* (*unpretentiousness, lack of sophistication*) Schlichtheit, *die;* **be ~ itself** ein Kinderspiel sein

**simplification** /sɪmplɪfɪ'keɪʃn/ *n.* Ⓐ *no pl.* Vereinfachung, *die;* Simplifizierung, *die* (*geh.*); Ⓑ (*instance*) Vereinfachung, *die;* Simplifikation, *die* (*geh.*)

**simplify** /'sɪmplɪfaɪ/ *v.t.* vereinfachen; simplifizieren (*geh.*); **it would ~ matters if ...:** es würde die Sache vereinfachen, wenn ...

**simplistic** /sɪm'plɪstɪk/ *adj.* [all]zu simpel

**simply** /'sɪmplɪ/ *adv.* Ⓐ (*in an uncomplicated manner*) einfach; (*in an unsophisticated manner*) schlicht; **live/eat ~:** einfach leben/essen; **speak ~:** in schlichten Worten sprechen; Ⓑ (*absolutely*) einfach; **he's ~ wonderful** er ist einfach großartig; Ⓒ (*categorically, without good reason, without asking*) einfach; (*merely*) nur; **it ~ isn't true** es ist einfach nicht wahr; **you ~ must see that film** du musst den Film einfach sehen; **I was ~ trying to help** ich wollte nur helfen; **quite ~:** ganz einfach; **~ because ...:** einfach weil ...; nur weil ...; **he ~ didn't feel like working** er hatte ganz einfach keine Lust zu arbeiten

**simulate** /'sɪmjʊleɪt/ *v.t.* Ⓐ (*feign*) vortäuschen; heucheln ‹Reue, Tugendhaftigkeit, Entrüstung, Begeisterung›; simulieren, vortäuschen ‹Krankheit›; Ⓑ (*mimic*) nachahmen; (*resemble*) aussehen wie (+ *Nom.*); Ⓒ simulieren ‹Bedingungen, Wetter, Umwelt usw.›

**simulated** /'sɪmjʊleɪtɪd/ *adj.* Ⓐ (*feigned*) vorgetäuscht; geheuchelt; Ⓑ (*artificial*) imitiert ‹Leder, Pelz usw.›; Ⓒ simuliert ‹Bedingungen, Wetter, Umwelt usw.›

**simulation** /sɪmjʊ'leɪʃn/ *n.* Ⓐ (*feigning*) Vortäuschung, *die;* (*of illness*) Vortäuschung, *die;* Simulation, *die;* Ⓑ (*imitation of conditions*) Simulation, *die;* Ⓒ (*simulated object*) Imitation, *die*

**simulator** /'sɪmjʊleɪtə(r)/ *n.* Simulator, *der*

**simultaneity** /sɪmltə'ni:ɪtɪ/ *n., no pl.* Gleichzeitigkeit, *die*

**simultaneous** /sɪml'teɪnɪəs/ *adj.* gleichzeitig (**with** mit); simultan (*fachspr., geh.*); **be ~:** gleichzeitig/simultan erfolgen

**simultaneous: ~ display** *n.* (*Chess*) Simultanvorstellung, *die;* **~ equations** *n. pl.* (*Math.*) Gleichungssystem, *das;* **~ interpretation** *n.* Simultandolmetschen, *das*

**simultaneously** /sɪml'teɪnɪəslɪ/ *adv.* gleichzeitig; simultan (*fachspr., geh.*)

**sin** /sɪn/ ❶ *n.* Sünde, *die;* **a life of ~:** ein Leben in Sünde; ein sündiges Leben; **live in ~** (*coll.*) in Sünde leben (*veralt., scherzh.*); **[as] miserable as ~:** todunglücklich; **for my ~s** (*joc.*) um meiner Missetaten willen (*scherzh.*); **the ~s of the fathers** die Missetat[en] der Väter; ⇒ *also* **beset** B; **find out** B; **multitude** A; **omission** B; **original** 1 A; **wage** 1. ❷ *v.i.*, **-nn-** sündigen; **~ against sb./God** an jmdm./Gott *od.* gegen jmdn./Gott sündigen; sich an jmdm./Gott versündigen (*geh.*); **~ against the rules** gegen die Regeln verstoßen; **he is more ~ned against than ~ning** man sündigt mehr an ihm, als dass er selbst sündigt

**Sinai Peninsula** /saɪnɪaɪ pɪ'nɪnsjʊlə/ *pr. n.* Halbinsel Sinai

**'sin bin** *n.* (*Sport coll.*) Strafbank, *die*

**since** /sɪns/ ▶ 1530 ❶ *adv.* seitdem; **he has ~ remarried, he has remarried ~:** er hat danach wieder geheiratet; **she had not eaten anything so delicious before or ~:** sie hatte weder vorher noch nachher je etwas so Köstliches gegessen; **long ~:** vor langer Zeit; **not long ~:** vor nicht allzu langer Zeit; **he is long ~ dead** er ist seit langem tot; **a long time/many years/six weeks ~:** vor langer Zeit/vielen Jahren/sechs Wochen.

❷ *prep.* seit; **~ seeing you ...:** seit ich dich gesehen habe; **~ then/that time** inzwischen; **he joined the firm 16 years ago and has been with them ~ then** er ist vor 16 Jahren in die Firma eingetreten und ist heute noch dort; **~ when?** seit wann?; **her mother died in 1980, ~ when/~ which time she has been looking after her father** ihre Mutter starb 1980, und seitdem/seit dieser Zeit versorgt sie ihren Vater. ❸ *conj.* Ⓐ seit; **it is a long time/so long/not so long ~ ...:** es ist lange/so lange/gar nicht lange her, dass ...; **how long is it ~ he left you?** wie lange ist es her, dass er dich verlassen hat?; Ⓑ (*seeing that, as*) da

**sincere** /sɪn'sɪə(r)/ *adj.*, **~r** /sɪn'sɪərə(r)/, **~st** /sɪn'sɪərɪst/ aufrichtig; herzlich ‹Grüße, Glückwünsche usw.›; wahr ‹Freund›

**sincerely** /sɪn'sɪəlɪ/ *adv.* ▶ 1286 aufrichtig; **I [most] ~ hope so** (*coll.*) das will ich schwer hoffen (*ugs.*); **yours ~** (*in letter*) mit freundlichen Grüßen

**sincerity** /sɪn'serɪtɪ/ *n., no pl.* Aufrichtigkeit, *die;* **in all ~:** in aller Aufrichtigkeit; **have the ring of ~:** aufrichtig klingen

**sine** /saɪn/ *n.* (*Math.*) Sinus, *der*

**sinecure** /'sɪnɪkjʊə(r), 'saɪnɪkjʊə(r)/ *n.* Pfründe, *die;* Sinekure, *die;* **this job is no ~:** diese Arbeit ist kein reines Honiglecken (*ugs.*)

**sine die** /saɪnɪ 'daɪi:, sɪneɪ 'di:eɪ/ *adv.* auf unbestimmte Zeit

**sine qua non** /saɪnɪ kweɪ 'nɒn, sɪneɪ kwɑ: 'nəʊn/ *n.* notwendige Bedingung; Conditio sine qua non (*geh.*)

**sinew** /'sɪnju:/ *n.* Ⓐ (*Anat.*) Sehne, *die;* **strain every nerve and ~ [to do sth.]** (*fig.*) alle Muskeln anspannen[, um etw. zu tun]; Ⓑ (*strength*) Kraft, *die*

**'sine wave** *n.* (*Math.*) Sinuswelle, *die*

**sinewy** /'sɪnju:ɪ/ *adj.* sehnig; (*fig.: vigorous*) kraftvoll; **the ~ vigour/strength of his style** sein kraftvoller Stil

**sinfonia** /sɪn'fəʊnɪə/ *n.* (*Mus.*) Sinfonia, *die;* (*in name of orchestra*) Sinfonieorchester, *das;* Sinfoniker *Pl.*

**sinfonietta** /sɪnfəʊnɪ'etə/ *n.* (*Mus.*) Ⓐ Sinfonietta, *die;* Ⓑ (*orchestra*) kleines Sinfonieorchester; (*string orchestra*) Streichorchester, *das*

**sinful** /'sɪnfl/ *adj.* sündig; (*reprehensible*) sündhaft; **it is ~ to ...:** es ist eine Sünde, ... zu ...

**sing** /sɪŋ/ ❶ *v.i.*, **sang** /sæŋ/, **sung** /sʌŋ/ singen; (*fig.*) ‹Kessel, Wind:› singen; ‹Geschoss:› sirren, pfeifen; (*sl.: turn informer*) singen (*salopp*); **~ to sb.** jmdm. [etw.] vorsingen; **~ to the guitar/piano** zur Gitarre/zum Klavier singen; **his ears are ~ing** seine Ohren sausen; **~ of sb./sth.** (*celebrate in verse*) jmdn./etw. besingen (*geh.*); von jmdm./etw. singen (*dichter. veralt.*). ❷ *v.t.*, **sang, sung** singen; **~ [the] alto** [den] Alt singen; **~ sb. a song** *or* **a song for sb.** jmdm. ein Lied vorsingen; **~ sb. to sleep** jmdn. in den Schlaf singen; ⇒ *also* **praise** 2 A; **tune** 1 A, B. ❸ *n.* (*Amer.*) **have a ~:** [gemeinsam] singen

~ **a'long** *v.i.* mitsingen

~ **'out** ❶ *v.i.* Ⓐ (*~ loudly*) [laut *od.* aus voller Kehle] singen; **~ out merrily** fröhlich singen; Ⓑ (*call out*) [laut] rufen; **~ out for sb./sth.** nach jmdm./etw. rufen. ❷ *v.t.* (*shout*) rufen; schreien

~ **'up** *v.i.* lauter singen

**singable** /'sɪŋəbl/ *adj.* singbar; (*easily ~*) sangbar; kantabel (*geh.*)

**Singapore** /sɪŋgə'pɔ:(r)/ *pr. n.* ▶ 1626 Singapur (*das*)

**singe** /sɪndʒ/ ❶ *v.t.*, **~ing** ansengen; versengen; absengen ‹Geflügel, Schwein›; **~ sb.'s hair** (*Hairdressing*) jmdm. die Haarspitzen abbrennen. ❷ *v.i.*, **~ing** [ver]sengen. ❸ *n.* Brandfleck, *der*

**singer** /'sɪŋə(r)/ *n.* Sänger, *der*/Sängerin, *die;* **this canary is a good ~:** dieser Kanarienvogel singt schön

**singing** /'sɪŋɪŋ/ *n., no pl.* Ⓐ Singen, *das;* (*fig.*) ⇒ **sing** 1: Singen, *das;* Sirren, *das;* Pfeifen, *das;* **beautiful/loud ~:** schöner/lauter Gesang; **the ~ of the birds** der Gesang der Vögel; **his ~ is terrible** er singt furchtbar; **have a ~ in one's ears** Ohrensausen haben; Ⓑ *no art.* (*Art*) Gesang, *der; attrib.* Gesangs-; **~ voice** Singstimme, *die*

**single** /'sɪŋgl/ ❶ *adj.* Ⓐ einfach; einzig ‹Ziel, Hoffnung›; (*for one person*) Einzel‹bett, -zimmer›; einfach ‹Größe›; (*without the other one of a pair*) einzeln; **~ flower/stem** *etc.* einzelne Blume/einzelner Stamm *usw.;* **speak with a ~ voice** (*fig.*) mit einer Stimme sprechen; **~ sheet/cover** Betttuch/Bettbezug für ein Einzelbett; **~ ticket** (*Brit.*) einfache Fahrkarte; **~ fare** (*Brit.*) Preis für [die] einfache Fahrt; ⇒ *also* **combat** 1; **entry** H; **file**[3] 1 A; **track** 1 B, D; Ⓑ (*one by itself*) einzig; (*isolated*) einzeln; **one ~ ...:** ein einziger/eine einzige/ein einziges ...; **at a** *or* **one ~ blow** *or* **stroke** mit einem Schlag; **two minds with but a ~ thought** zwei Seelen und ein Gedanke; Ⓒ (*unmarried*) ledig; **a ~ man/woman/~ people** ein Lediger/eine Ledige/Ledige; **~ parent** allein erziehender Elternteil; **he/she is a ~ parent** er/sie ist allein erziehend; **~ mother** allein erziehende *od.* stehende Mutter; Ⓓ (*separate, individual*) einzeln; **can a ~ argument be advanced for it?** läßt sich dafür überhaupt irgendein Argument vorbringen?; **every ~ one** jeder/jede/jedes einzelne; **every ~ time/day** aber auch jedes Mal/jeden Tag; **not a ~ one** kein Einziger/keine Einzige/kein Einziges; **not a ~ word/dress/soul** kein einziges Wort/Kleid/keine Menschenseele; **she did not see a ~ thing she liked** sie hat aber auch nichts gesehen, was ihr gefiel; **not/never for a ~ minute** *or* **moment** keinen [einzigen] Augenblick [lang].

❷ *n.* Ⓐ (*Brit.: ticket*) einfache Fahrkarte; **[a] ~/two ~s to Manchester, please** einmal/zweimal einfach nach Manchester, bitte; Ⓑ (*record*) Single, *die;* Ⓒ *in pl.* (*Golf*) Single, *das;* (*Tennis*) Einzel, *das;* **women's** *or* **ladies'/men's ~s** Damen-/Herreneinzel, *das;* Ⓓ (*Brit. Hist.: pound note*) Einpfundschein, *der;* (*Amer.: dollar note*) Eindollarschein, *der;* Ⓔ (*Cricket*) *Schlag für einen Lauf.*

# Since

## As a preposition

The translation of *since* is not a problem — it is always **seit** — but it is important to note that the tense of the verb is often different in German. Whereas English uses the perfect and particularly the perfect continuous (*have been ...ing*), German uses the present:

***I have been waiting since 8 o'clock***
= Ich warte [schon] seit 8 Uhr

***He has lived here since his childhood***
= Er wohnt seit seiner Kindheit hier

Similarly an English verb in the past continuous is translated by a German verb in the imperfect:

***I had been waiting since 8 o'clock***
= Ich wartete [schon] seit 8 Uhr

Particularly with **warten, schon** is often added to stress the length of time.

However in the negative and in other cases where there is no sense of a continuous process the same tense is used in both languages:

***We haven't seen her since the wedding***
= Wir haben sie seit der Hochzeit nicht gesehen

***I have only seen her once since the wedding***
= Ich habe sie seit der Hochzeit nur einmal gesehen

In such cases, **mehr** is often added for emphasis.

***I hadn't been there since 1980***
= Ich war seit 1980 nicht [mehr] dort gewesen

## As an adverb

This is simply the phrase *since then* (= **seitdem**) minus the *then*:

***I haven't seen her since***
= Ich habe sie seitdem nicht gesehen

It often has the sense of *in the meantime* and can be translated by **inzwischen**:

***We have since got to know them better***
= Wir haben sie inzwischen näher kennen gelernt

## As a conjunction

■ **IN TIME EXPRESSIONS**

As in the case of the preposition, the English perfect continuous describing a continuous process is translated by the German present:

***since she has been living in Germany***
= seit sie in Deutschland wohnt

***since they had been in London***
= seit sie in London waren

Referring to the time since a specific event, a different construction is used:

***How long is it since he left?***
= Wie lange ist es her, dass er weggezogen ist?

***It's a year since he left***
= Es ist ein Jahr her, dass er weggezogen ist

■ **MEANING BECAUSE**

In the sense of because, since is translated by **da**:

***Since she was ill, I had to do it***
= Da sie krank war, musste ich es tun

❸ *v.t.* ~ **out** aussondern; (*be distinctive quality of*) auszeichnen (**from** vor + *Dat.*); ~ **sb./sth. out as/for sth.** jmdn./etw. als etw./für etw. auswählen; ~ **sb. out for promotion/special attention** jmdn. für eine Beförderung vorsehen/sich mit jmdm. besonders befassen

**single:** ~**-barrelled** (*Amer.:* ~**-barreled**) /ˈsɪŋglbærəld/ *adj.* (*Arms*) einläufig; ~**-bedded room** /ˈsɪŋglbedɪd ruːm/ *n.* Einzelzimmer, *das;* ~**-breasted** /ˈsɪŋglbrestɪd/ *adj.* (*Tailoring*) einreihig; ~ **cream** *n.* [einfache] Sahne; ~ **ˈcurrency** *n.* Einheitswährung, *die;* ~**-decker** ❶ *n.* **be a** ~**-decker** ‹Bus, Straßenbahn:› nur ein Deck haben; ❷ *adj.* ~**-decker bus/tram** Bus/Straßenbahn mit [nur] einem Deck; ~**-engined** /ˈsɪŋglendʒɪnd/ *adj.* einmotorig; ~ **[European] ˈmarket** *n.* [europäischer] Binnenmarkt; ~**-handed** ❶ /ˈ----/ *adj.* Ⓐ Einhand‹segeln, -segler›; ~**-handed attempt to row across the Atlantic** Versuch, allein über den Atlantik zu rudern; **his** ~**-handed efforts to get a new hospital** seine einsamen Bemühungen um ein neues Krankenhaus; Ⓑ (*for one hand*) ~**-handed weapon/fishing rod** Waffe/Angelrute für eine Hand; ❷ /-ˈ--/ *adv.* Ⓐ allein; **sail round the world** ~**-handed** als Einhandsegler um die Welt fahren; **root out corruption** ~**-handed** im Alleingang die Korruption ausrotten; Ⓑ (*with one hand*) mit einer Hand; einhändig; ~**-lens ˈreflex camera** *n.* (*Photog.*) einäugige Spiegelreflexkamera; ~**-line** *adj.* einspurig; ~**-minded** *adj.* zielstrebig; **be** ~**-minded in one's aim** unbeirrbar sein Ziel verfolgen; ~**-mindedly** /sɪŋglˈmaɪndɪdlɪ/ *adv.* zielstrebig

**singleness** /ˈsɪŋglnɪs/ *n., no pl.* ~ **of purpose** Zielstrebigkeit, *die*

**ˈsingle-phase** *adj.* (*Electr.*) einphasig; ~ **current** Einphasenstrom, *der*

**ˈsingles bar** *n.* Singlekneipe, *die*

**single:** ~**-seater** *n.* Einsitzer, *der;* ~**-seater aircraft** einsitziges Flugzeug; **-sex** *adj.* ~**-sex school** reine Mädchen-/Jungenschule; ~**-sex accommodation** nach Geschlecht getrennte Unterbringung; ~**-storey** *adj.* eingeschossig

**singlet** /ˈsɪŋglɪt/ *n.* (*Brit.: vest*) Unterhemd, *das;* (*Sport*) Trikot, *das*

**singleton** /ˈsɪŋgltən/ *n.* (*Cards*) blanke Karte; **a** ~ **in hearts, a** ~ **heart** ein blankes Herz

**ˈsingle-track** *adj.* eingleisig ‹Bahnlinie›; einspurig ‹Straße›

**singly** /ˈsɪŋglɪ/ *adv.* Ⓐ einzeln; Ⓑ (*by oneself*) allein

**ˈsingsong** ❶ *adj.* leiernd (*ugs.*); **say/recite sth. in a** ~ **manner/voice** etw. herunterleiern (*ugs.*); **his** ~ **accent** sein Singsang. ❷ *n.* Ⓐ (*monotonous tone or rhythm*) leiernder Ton; **recite sth./say sth. in a** ~**:** etw. herunterleiern (*ugs.*); **speak in a** ~**:** leiernd sprechen; Ⓑ (*Brit.: singing*) gemeinschaftliches Singen; **have a** ~**:** gemeinsam singen

**singular** /ˈsɪŋgjʊlə(r)/ ❶ *adj.* Ⓐ (*Ling.*) singularisch; Singular-; ~ **noun** Substantiv im Singular; ~ **form** Singularform, *die;* **first person** ~**:** erste Person Singular; ~ **number** ⇒ **2**; Ⓑ (*individual*) einzeln; (*unique*) einmalig; einzigartig; Ⓒ (*extraordinary*) einmalig; einzigartig; (*odd*) eigenartig; sonderbar; **how very** ~**!** wie eigenartig *od.* sonderbar! ❷ *n.* (*Ling.*) Einzahl, *die;* Singular, *der;* **I said you could have ˈan apple — in the** ~ (*coll.*) ich habe gesagt, du kannst einen Apfel haben — von Äpfeln war nicht die Rede

**singularity** /sɪŋgjʊˈlærɪtɪ/ *n., no pl.* Eigenartigkeit, *die;* Sonderbarkeit, *die*

**singularly** /ˈsɪŋgjʊləlɪ/ *adv.* (*extraordinarily*) außerordentlich; einmalig ‹schön›; (*strangely*) seltsam

**Sinhalese** /sɪnhəˈliːz, sɪnəˈliːz/ ▶ **1275**, ▶ **1340** ❶ *adj.* singhalesisch; **sb. is** ~**:** jmd. ist Singhalese/Singhalesin. ❷ *n.* Ⓐ *pl. same* (*person*) Singhalese, *der*/Singhalesin, *die;* Ⓑ *no pl.* (*language*) Singhalesisch, *das*

**sinister** /ˈsɪnɪstə(r)/ *adj.* Ⓐ (*of evil omen*) Unheil verkündend; Ⓑ (*suggestive of malice*) finster; (*wicked*) übel; Ⓒ (*Her.*) link...; sinister (*fachspr.*); ⇒ *also* **baton** E; **bend²** B

**sink** /sɪŋk/ ❶ *n.* Ⓐ Spülbecken, *das;* Spüle, *die;* **pour sth. down the** ~**:** etw. in den Ausguss schütten; ⇒ *also* **kitchen** ~; Ⓑ (*cesspool*) Senkgrube, *die;* Kloake, *die;* (*fig.: place of vice etc.*) Kloake, *die;* Pfuhl, *der;* Ⓒ (*Geog.: pool*) Senke, *die;* Vertiefung, *die;* Ⓓ (*Geol.*) ⇒ ~**-hole**; Ⓔ (*Phys.*) Feldsenke, *die.* ❷ *v.i.*, **sank** /sæŋk/ *or* **sunk** /sʌŋk/, **sunk** Ⓐ sinken; **we shall** ~ **or swim together** (*fig.*) wir werden gemeinsam untergehen oder gemeinsam überleben; **leave sb. to** ~ **or swim** (*fig.*) jmdn. seinem Schicksal überlassen; Ⓑ ~ **into** (*become immersed in*) sinken in (+ *Akk.*); versinken in (+ *Dat.*); (*penetrate*) eindringen in (+ *Akk.*); (*fig.: be absorbed into*) dringen in (+ *Akk.*) ‹Bewusstsein›; ~ **into an armchair/the cushions** in einen Sessel/die Kissen sinken; ~ **into sb.'s/each other's arms** jmdm./sich in die Arme sinken; ~ **into a deep sleep/a coma/trance/reverie** in einen tiefen Schlaf/in ein Koma/in Trance/in Träumerei sinken (*geh.*); ~ **into depression/despair** in Schwermut/Verzweiflung (*Akk.*) versinken; ~ **into crime/poverty** *etc.* dem Verbrechen/der Armut *usw.* verfallen; **be sunk in thought/despair** in Gedanken/in Verzweiflung (*Akk.*) versunken sein; ⇒ *also* **oblivion**; Ⓒ (*come to lower level or pitch*) sinken; (*suffer subsidence*) absinken; (*slope down*) sich senken; (*be turned downwards*) ‹Augen:› sich senken; (*shrink inwards*) ‹Augen, Wangen:› einfallen; (*subside, abate*) ‹Flut, Wasser, Fluss:› sinken; (*fig.: fail*) ‹Moral, Hoffnung:› sinken; **the patient is** ~**ing [fast]** mit dem Patienten geht es zu

Ende (*verhüll.*); **sb.'s heart ∼s/spirits ∼** jmds. Stimmung sinkt; **sb.'s heart/courage ∼s into his/her boots** (*coll.*) jmdm. rutscht *od.* fällt das Herz in die Hose[n] (*ugs.*); **∼ to one's knees** auf die *od.* seine Knie sinken; Ⓓ (*fall*) ‹Preis, Temperatur, Währung, Produktion usw.:› sinken; **∼ in value** im Wert sinken. ❸ *v.t.*, **sank** *or* **sunk**, **sunk** Ⓐ versenken; (*cause failure of*) zunichte machen; **be sunk** (*fig. coll.: have failed*) aufgeschmissen sein (*ugs.*); **∼ one's differences** seine Streitigkeiten begraben; **enough luggage/make-up to ∼ a battleship** (*fig. joc.*) tonnenweise (*ugs.*) Gepäck/pfundweise (*ugs.*) Make-up; Ⓑ (*lower*) senken; (*Golf*) ins Loch schlagen ‹Ball›; Ⓒ (*dig*) niederbringen; (*inlay*) einlegen; (*recess*) versenken; (*embed*) stoßen ‹Messer, Schwert›; graben (*geh.*) ‹Zähne, Klauen›; **∼ a pole into the ground** einen Pfahl in den Boden senken; ⇒ *also* **fence** 1 A

**∼ 'back** *v.i.* zurücksinken; **∼ back into crime/poverty** (*fig.*) wieder dem Verbrechen/der Armut verfallen

**∼ 'down** *v.i.* hinabsinken; niedersinken; **∼ down to the floor/ground** auf den/zu Boden sinken; **∼ down into the mud** im Schlamm versinken; **his head sank down on to his chest** der Kopf sank ihm auf die Brust; **she sank down [on her knees] before him** sie sank vor ihm [auf die Knie] nieder

**∼ 'in** ❶ *v.i.* Ⓐ (*become immersed*) einsinken; (*penetrate*) eindringen; Ⓑ (*fig.: be absorbed into the mind*) jmdm. ins Bewusstsein dringen; ‹Warnung, Lektion:› verstanden werden. ❷ *v.t.* einsenken ‹Stütze, Pfahl›

**sinker** /ˈsɪŋkə(r)/ *n.* (*Fishing*) Senker, *der;* (*of drift-net*) Grundgewicht, *das;* ⇒ *also* **hook** 1 A

**'sinkhole** *n.* (*Geol.*) Schluckloch, *das*

**sinking** /ˈsɪŋkɪŋ/ ❶ *adj.* Ⓐ sinkend; **[the] rats desert a ∼ ship** die Ratten verlassen das sinkende Schiff; Ⓑ (*declining*) untergehend ‹Sonne›; Ⓒ (*falling in value*) sinkend; Ⓓ **with a ∼ heart** (*fig.*) beklommen; resigniert. ❷ *n.* Ⓐ (*of ship*) (*deliberate*) Versenkung, *die;* (*accidental*) Sinken, *das;* Untergang, *der;* (*of well*) Niederbringung, *die;* Ⓑ **∼ of the heart** (*fig.*) Beklommenheit, *die; attrib.* **a ∼ feeling** (*fig.*) ein flaues Gefühl [im Magen]

**'sinking fund** *n.* (*Finance*) Tilgungsfonds, *der*

**'sink unit** *n.* Spüle, *die*

**sinless** /ˈsɪnlɪs/ *adj.* sündenfrei, sündlos ‹Mensch, Leben›; untad[e]lig ‹Verhalten›

**sinner** /ˈsɪnə(r)/ *n.* Sünder, *der*/Sünderin, *die*

**Sinn Fein** /ʃɪn ˈfeɪn/ *n.*, *no pl.*, *no indef. art.* Sinn Fein, *die* (*nationalistische irische Partei*)

**Sino-** /ˈsaɪnəʊ/ *in comb.* sino-/Sino-; **a ∼Russian war** ein chinesisch-russischer Krieg

**sinter** /ˈsɪntə(r)/ ❶ *v.t.* sintern (*Technik*). ❷ *v.i.* sintern

**sinuous** /ˈsɪnjʊəs/ *adj.* gewunden; sich schlängelnd ‹Schlange›; (*lithe*) geschmeidig ‹Körper, Bewegungen›

**sinus** /ˈsaɪnəs/ *n.* (*Anat.*) Sinus, *der* (*fachspr.*); **[paranasal] ∼:** Nebenhöhle, *die*

**sinusitis** /saɪnəˈsaɪtɪs/ *n.* ▶1232 (*Med.*) Nebenhöhlenentzündung, *die;* Sinusitis, *die* (*fachspr.*)

**Sioux** /suː/ *n.*, *pl. same* (*Ethnol.*) Sioux, *der*/*die; attrib.* Sioux-

**sip** /sɪp/ ❶ *v.t.*, **-pp-: ∼ [up]** schlürfen. ❷ *v.i.*, **-pp-: ∼ at/from sth.** an etw. (*Dat.*) nippen. ❸ *n.* Schlückchen, *das;* **have** *or* **take a ∼ [of sth.]** ein Schlückchen [von etw.] nehmen; **in ∼s** schlückchenweise

**siphon** /ˈsaɪfn/ ❶ *n.* Ⓐ (*bottle*) Siphon, *der;* Ⓑ (*pipe*) Saugheber, *der.* ❷ *v.t.* [durch einen Saugheber] laufen lassen; **∼ sth. from a tank** etw. [mit einem Saugheber] aus einem Tank ablassen. ❸ *v.i.* [durch einen Saugheber] laufen; (*fig.: flow as if through a ∼*) laufen

**∼ 'off** *v.t.* [mit einem Saugheber] ablassen; (*fig.: transfer*) abzweigen

**∼ 'out** *v.t.* [mit einem Saugheber] ablassen

**sir** /sɜː(r)/ *n.* ▶1617 Ⓐ (*formal address*) der Herr; (*to teacher*) Herr Meier/Schmidt *usw.;* Herr Lehrer/Studienrat *usw.* (*veralt.*); **no '∼!** keinesfalls!; von wegen! (*ugs.*); **yes '∼!** allerdings; **Sir!** (*Mil.*) Herr Oberst/Leutnant *usw.!;* (*yes*) jawohl, Herr Oberst/Leutnant *usw.!;* Ⓑ ▶1286 (*in letter*) **Dear Sir:** Sehr geehrter Herr; **Dear Sirs** Sehr geehrte [Damen und] Herren; **Dear Sir or Madam** Sehr geehrte Dame/Sehr geehrter Herr; Ⓒ **S∼** /sə(r)/ (*title of knight etc.*) Sir; Ⓓ /sɜː(r)/ (*person addressed as 'Sir'*) Sir, *der;* Ⓔ *no art.* (*Sch. coll.: teacher*) der [Herr] Lehrer; **I shall tell ∼:** das sag' ich (*ugs.*)

**sire** /ˈsaɪə(r)/ ❶ *n.* Ⓐ Vatertier, *das;* Ⓑ (*poet.*) (*father*) Vater, *der;* (*ancestor*) Ahnherr, *der* (*geh. veralt.*); Ⓒ ▶1617 (*arch.*) **yes, ∼:** ja, Herr. ❷ *v.t.* zeugen

**siren** /ˈsaɪrən/ ❶ *n.* Ⓐ Sirene, *die;* **factory/ship's ∼:** Fabrik-/Schiffssirene, *die;* **air-raid ∼:** Luftschutzsirene, *die;* Ⓑ (*temptress*) Sirene, *die* (*geh.*); Circe, *die* (*geh.*); Ⓒ (*Greek Mythol.*) Sirene, *die.* ❷ *adj.* sirenenhaft; **∼ song** Sirenengesang, *der*

**sirloin** /ˈsɜːlɔɪn/ *n.* Ⓐ (*Brit.: upper part of loin of beef*) Roastbeef, *das;* **a ∼ of beef** ein Stück Roastbeef; **∼ steak** Rumpsteak, *das;* Ⓑ (*Amer.*) Rumpsteak, *das*

**sirocco** /sɪˈrɒkəʊ/ *n.*, *pl.* **∼s** Schirokko, *der*

**sirup** (*Amer.*) ⇒ **syrup**

**sis** /sɪs/ *n.* (*coll.*) Schwesterherz, *das* (*scherzh.*)

**sisal** /ˈsaɪsl/ *n.* Ⓐ (*fibre*) Sisal, *der; attrib.* Sisal-; Ⓑ (*Bot.*) Sisalagave, *die; attrib.* Sisal-

**siskin** /ˈsɪskɪn/ *n.* (*Ornith.*) [Erlen]zeisig, *der*

**sissified** /ˈsɪsɪfaɪd/ *adj.* weibisch (*abwertend*); (*cowardly*) feige (*abwertend*)

**sissy** /ˈsɪsɪ/ ❶ *n.* (*effeminate man*) weibischer Typ; (*cowardly person*) Waschlappen, *der* (*ugs. abwertend*). ❷ *adj.* weibisch (*abwertend*); (*cowardly*) feige (*abwertend*)

**sister** /ˈsɪstə(r)/ *n.* Ⓐ Schwester, *die;* **she has been a ∼ to him/her** (*fig.*) sie war für ihn/sie wie eine Schwester; **the Robinson ∼s** die Robinson-Schwestern; Ⓑ (*friend, associate fellow member*) Schwester, *die;* (*in trade union*) Kollegin, *die;* **∼ company** Schwesterfirma, *die;* Ⓒ (*Eccl.*) Schwester, *die;* **S∼ of Mercy** Barmherzige Schwester; Ⓓ (*Brit.: senior nurse*) Oberschwester, *die;* **ward ∼:** Stationsschwester, *die;* **theatre ∼:** Operationsschwester, *die;* Ⓔ (*Brit. coll.: nurse*) Schwester, *die*

**sisterhood** /ˈsɪstəhʊd/ *n.* Ⓐ *no pl.* Schwesterschaft, *die;* schwesterliches Verhältnis; Ⓑ (*religious society*) Schwesternschaft, *die*

**'sister-in-law** *n.*, *pl.* **sisters-in-law** Schwägerin, *die*

**sisterly** /ˈsɪstəlɪ/ *adj.* schwesterlich; **∼ love** Schwesterliebe, *die*

**'sister ship** *n.* (*Naut.*) Schwesterschiff, *das*

**Sistine Chapel** /sɪstiːn ˈtʃæpl, sɪstaɪn ˈtʃæpl/ *n.* **the ∼:** die Sixtinische Kapelle

**sit** /sɪt/ ❶ *v.i.*, **-tt-**, **sat** /sæt/ Ⓐ (*become seated*) sich setzen; **∼ on** *or* **in a chair/in an armchair** sich auf einen Stuhl/in einen Sessel setzen; **∼!** (*to dog*) sitz!; **∼ by** *or* **with sb.** sich zu jmdm. setzen; **∼ over there!** setz dich dort drüben hin!; Ⓑ (*be seated*) sitzen; **don't just ∼ there!** sitz nicht einfach rum (*ugs.*); **∼ at home** (*fig.*) zu Hause sitzen; **∼ in judgement on** *or* **over sb./sth.** über jmdn./etw. zu Gericht sitzen; **∼ on one's hands** (*fig.*) sich nicht rühren; **∼ still!** sitz ruhig *od.* still!; **∼ tight** (*coll.*) ruhig sitzen bleiben; (*fig.: stay in hiding*) sich nicht fortrühren; (*fig.: persevere in a course of action*) sich nicht beirren lassen; **∼ well [in the saddle/on one's horse]** einen guten Sitz haben; ⇒ *also* **fence** 1 A; **foot** 1 A; **pretty** 2; Ⓒ **∼ for one's portrait/to a painter** *etc.* Porträt sitzen/einem Maler *usw.* Modell sitzen; Ⓓ ⇒ **babysit**; Ⓔ (*take a test*) **∼ for sth.** die Prüfung für etw. machen; Ⓕ (*be in session*) tagen; Ⓖ (*be on perch or nest*) sitzen; Ⓗ (*be situated*) sich befinden; **the sewing machine sat in the attic** die Nähmaschine stand auf dem Dachboden herum; **∼ well on sb.** (*fit*) jmdm. gut passen; (*suit*) jmdm. gut stehen; (*fig.*) gut zu jmdm. passen; Ⓘ (*be member of elected body*) **∼ at Westminster** Mitglied des [britischen] Parlaments sein; **∼ for** (*Brit. Parl.*) vertreten; Abgeordneter/Abgeordnete sein für. ❷ *v.t.*, **-tt-**, **sat** Ⓐ (*cause to be seated, place*) setzen; Ⓑ (*Brit.*) **∼ an examination** eine Prüfung machen; (*have space for*) ⇒ **seat** 2 B

**∼ a'bout, ∼ a'round** *v.i.* herumsitzen (*ugs.*)

**∼ 'back** *v.i.* Ⓐ sich zurücklehnen; Ⓑ (*fig.: do nothing*) sich im Sessel zurücklehnen (*fig.*); **the government is ∼ting back and letting the situation worsen** die Regierung sieht tatenlos zu, wie sich die Lage verschlechtert

**∼ 'by** *v.i.* tatenlos zusehen

**∼ 'down** ❶ *v.i.* Ⓐ (*become seated*) sich setzen (**on/in** auf/in + *Akk.*); **∼ you down** (*coll.*) setz dich hin; Ⓑ (*be seated*) sitzen; **take sth. ∼ting down** (*fig.*) etw. auf sich (*Dat.*) sitzen lassen. ❷ *v.t.* **∼ sb. down** (*invite to ∼*) jmdn. Platz nehmen lassen; (*help to ∼*) jmdm. helfen, sich zu setzen. ⇒ *also* **sit-down**

**∼ 'in** *v.i.* Ⓐ (*occupy place as protest*) ein Sit-in veranstalten; Ⓑ (*stay in*) zu Hause bleiben; Ⓒ (*participate*) mitspielen; **∼ in on** (*be present at*) teilnehmen an (+ *Dat.*); dabei sein bei; Ⓓ ⇒ **stand in a.** ⇒ *also* **sit-in**

**∼ on** *v.t.* Ⓐ (*serve as member of*) sitzen in (+ *Dat.*) ‹Ausschuss usw.›; **∼ on the jury** (*Law*) Geschworener sein; Ⓑ (*coll.: delay*) in der Schublade liegen lassen (*fig. ugs.*); auf die lange Bank schieben (*ugs.*) ‹Entscheidung›; Ⓒ (*coll.: repress*) unterdrücken; nicht aufkommen lassen ‹Wunsch, Gedanken›; **people like her want ∼ting on/ought to be sat on** Leute wie sie muss/sollte man an der kurzen Leine halten (*ugs.*); Ⓓ (*fig.: hold on to*) festhalten

**∼ 'out** ❶ *v.i.* draußen *od.* im Freien sitzen. ❷ *v.t.* Ⓐ (*take no part in*) aussetzen; **∼ out a dance** einen Tanz auslassen; Ⓑ (*endure*) durchstehen

**∼ 'through** ⇒ **∼ out** 2 B

**∼ 'up** ❶ *v.i.* Ⓐ (*rise*) sich aufsetzen; Ⓑ (*be sitting erect*) [aufrecht] sitzen; Ⓒ (*not slouch*) gerade sitzen; **∼ up straight!** sitz gerade!; **make sb. ∼ up** (*fig. coll.*) jmdn. aufhorchen lassen; **∼ up and take notice** (*fig. coll.*) aufhorchen; Ⓓ (*delay going to bed*) aufbleiben; **∼ up [waiting] for sb.** aufbleiben und auf jmdn. warten; **∼ up with sb.** bei jmdm. Nachtwache halten. ❷ *v.t.* aufsetzen. ⇒ *also* **sit-up**

**∼ 'upon** ⇒ **∼ on**; ⇒ *also* **sit-upon**

**sitar** /ˈsɪtɑː(r), sɪˈtɑː(r)/ *n.* (*Mus.*) Sitar, *der*

**sitcom** /ˈsɪtkɒm/ (*coll.*) ⇒ **situation comedy**

**'sit-down** ❶ *n.* **have a ∼:** sich setzen; **enjoy a ∼:** sich gern einmal hinsetzen. ❷ *adj.* **∼ demonstration** Sitzblockade, *die;* **∼ meal** (*im Sitzen eingenommenes*) Essen; **∼ strike** Sitzstreik, *der*

**site** /saɪt/ ❶ *n.* Ⓐ (*land*) Grundstück, *das;* **archaeological/prehistoric burial ∼:** archäologische Grabungsstätte/vorgeschichtliche Grabstätte; **exhibition ∼:** Ausstellungsgelände, *das;* **∼ of a battle** Kampfplatz, *der;* Ⓑ (*location*) Sitz, *der;* (*of new factory etc.*) Standort, *der;* Ⓒ ⇒ **building site.** ❷ *v.t.* (*locate*) stationieren ‹Raketen›; **∼ a factory in London** London als Standort einer Fabrik wählen; **be ∼d** gelegen sein

**'sit-in** *n.* Sit-in, *das*

**siting** /ˈsaɪtɪŋ/ *n.* Standortwahl, *die* (**of** für); (*position*) Lage, *die;* (*of missiles*) Stationierung, *die;* **the ∼ of the new exhibition centre in Leeds** die Wahl von Leeds als Standort des neuen Ausstellungszentrums

**sitter** /ˈsɪtə(r)/ *n.* Ⓐ (*Sport coll.*) (*easy catch*) leicht zu fangender Ball; (*easy shot*) idiotensichere Vorlage (*ugs. scherzh.*); Ⓑ (*artist's model*) Modell, *das;* Ⓒ (*hen*) Glucke, *die;* Bruthenne, *die;* Ⓓ ⇒ **babysitter**

**sitting** /ˈsɪtɪŋ/ ❶ *n.* Ⓐ (*session*) Sitzung, *die;* **lunch is served in two ∼s** es wird in zwei Schichten Mittag gegessen; **when is the first ∼ [for lunch]?** wann geht der erste Schub [zum Mittagessen]?; **in one** *or* **at a ∼** (*fig.*) in einem Zug[e]; Ⓑ (*Law*) Sitzungsperiode, *die.* ❷ *adj.* Ⓐ (*not flying or running*) sitzend; Ⓑ (*hatching*) sitzend; brütend; **these are ∼ hens** das sind Bruthennen

S

**sitting:** ~ **'duck** *n.* (*fig.*) leichtes Ziel; ~ **'member** *n.* (*Brit. Parl.*) **she is/was the ~ member** sie ist/war die derzeitige/damalige Abgeordnete; ~ **room** *n.* **A** (*lounge*) Wohnzimmer, *das;* (*in public buildings*) Aufenthaltsraum, *der;* **B** (*space*) Sitzplatz, *der;* ~ **'target** ⇒ ~ **duck**; ~ **'tenant** *n.* **he is/was the ~ tenant** er ist/war der jetzige/damalige Mieter; **there is a ~ tenant** es ist ein Mieter vorhanden

**situate** ❶ /'sɪtjʊeɪt/ *v.t.* legen; einrichten ‹Büro›. ❷ /'sɪtjʊət/ *adj.* (*Law*) ⇒ **situated**

**situated** /'sɪtjʊeɪtɪd/ *adj.* **A** gelegen; **be ~:** liegen; **a badly ~ house** ein Haus in schlechter *od.* ungünstiger Lage; **the house is well ~ for the shops** in der Nähe des Hauses gibt es gute Einkaufsmöglichkeiten; **B be well/badly ~ financially** finanziell gut/schlecht gestellt sein

**situation** /sɪtjʊ'eɪʃn/ *n.* **A** (*location*) Lage, *die;* **B** (*circumstances*) Situation, *die;* **a ~ of some delicacy** eine ziemlich heikle Situation; **be in the happy ~ of being able to do sth.** in der glücklichen Lage sein, etw. tun zu können; **his ~ is as follows: ...:** seine Lage stellt sich folgendermaßen dar: ...; **what's the ~?** wie stehts?; **lead to a compromise ~:** zu einem Kompromiss führen; **the firm is in a profit ~:** die Firma schreibt Gewinne; **C** (*job*) Stelle, *die;* **~s vacant/wanted** Stellenangebote/-gesuche

**situational** /sɪtjʊ'eɪʃənl/ *adj.* Situations-; ~ **drama** Handlungsdrama, *das* (*Literaturw.*)

**situation 'comedy** *n.* Situationskomödie, *die* (*Serie von Radio- oder Fernsehkomödien mit unverbundenen Episoden bei gleich bleibenden Rollen*)

**sit:** **~-up** *n.* *Bewegung aus der Rückenlage in den Langsitz* (*als gymnastische Übung*); **do twenty ~-ups** sich zwanzigmal aufsetzen; **~-upon** *n.* (*coll.*) Sitzfläche, *die* (*ugs. scherzh.*)

**six** /sɪks/ ▶ **912**, ▶ **1012**, ▶ **1352** ❶ *adj.* sechs; **be ~ feet** *or* **foot under** (*coll.*) unter der Erde liegen; **it is ~ of one and half-a-dozen of the other** (*coll.*) das ist Jacke wie Hose (*ugs.*); ⇒ *also* **eight** 1. ❷ *n.* **A** (*number, symbol*) Sechs, *die;* **be at ~es and sevens** sich in einem heillosen Durcheinander befinden; (*on an issue or matter*) heillos zerstritten sein (**on** über + *Akk.*); ⇒ *also* **best** 3 D; **eight** 2 A, C, D; **B** (*Cricket*) *Schlag, mit dem man sechs Punkte gewinnt;* ⇒ *also* **hit** 1 K

**Six 'Counties** *n. pl.* **the ~:** Nordirland (*das*) (*mit Londonderry, Antrim, Down, Armagh, Tyrone, Fermanagh*)

**six:** **~fold** *adj., adv.* sechsfach; ⇒ *also* **eightfold**; **~-'footer** *n.* (*person*) Zwei-Meter-Mann, *der*/-Frau, *die;* **most of them are ~-footers** die meisten sind fast zwei Meter groß; **~-pack** *n.* Sechserpack, *der;* **~pence** /'sɪkspəns/ *n.* (*Brit. Hist.: coin*) Sixpence, *der;* **~penny** /'sɪkspənɪ/ *adj.* (*Brit.*) zu sechs Pennies *nachgestellt;* ⇒ *also* **bit²** G; **~-shooter** *n.* sechsschüssiger Revolver

**sixteen** /sɪks'ti:n/ ▶ **912**, ▶ **1012**, ▶ **1352** ❶ *adj.* sechzehn; **sweet ~:** süße sechzehn [Jahre alt]; ⇒ *also* **eight** 1. ❷ *n.* Sechzehn, *die;* ⇒ *also* **eight** 2 A, D; **eighteen** 2

**sixteenth** /sɪks'ti:nθ/ ▶ **1055** ❶ *adj.* ▶ **1352** sechzehnt...; ⇒ *also* **eighth** 1. ❷ *n.* (*fraction*) Sechzehntel, *das;* ⇒ *also* **eighth** 2

**six'teenth note** *n.* (*Amer. Mus.*) Sechzehntelnote, *die*

**sixth** /sɪksθ/ ❶ *adj.* ▶ **1352** sechst...; ⇒ *also* **eighth** 1. ❷ *n.* **A** (*in sequence, rank*) Sechste, *der/die/das;* (*fraction*) Sechstel, *das;* **B** ⇒ **sixth form**; **C** (*Mus.*) Sexte, *die;* **D** ▶ **1055** (*day*) **the ~ of May** der sechste Mai; **the ~ [of the month]** der Sechste [des Monats]. ⇒ *also* **eighth** 2

**sixth:** ~ **form** *n.* (*Brit. Sch.*) ≈ zwölfte/dreizehnte Klasse; **~-form college** *n.* (*Brit. Sch.*) ≈ Oberstufenzentrum, *das; College, das nur Schüler der zwölften/dreizehnten Klasse aufnimmt;* **~-former** *n.* (*Brit. Sch.*) Schüler/Schülerin der zwölften/dreizehnten Klasse; ~ **'sense** *n.* sechster Sinn

**sixtieth** /'sɪkstɪɪθ/ ❶ *adj.* ▶ **1352** sechzigst...; ⇒ *also* **eighth** 1. ❷ *n.* (*fraction*) Sechzigstel, *das;* ⇒ *also* **eighth** 2

**sixty** /'sɪkstɪ/ ▶ **912**, ▶ **1352** ❶ *adj.* sechzig; ⇒ *also* **eight** 1; **one-and-~** (*arch.*) ⇒ **sixty-one** 1. ❷ *n.* Sechzig, *die;* **one-and-~** (*arch.*) ⇒ **sixty-one** 2; ⇒ *also* **eight** 2 A; **eighty** 2

**sixty:** **~-'first** *etc. adj.* ▶ **1352** einundsechzigst... *usw.;* ⇒ *also* **eighth** 1; **~-'one** *etc.* ❶ *adj.* einundsechzig *usw.;* ⇒ *also* **eight** 1; ❷ *n.* ▶ **1352** Einundsechzig *usw., die;* ⇒ *also* **eight** 2 A

**size¹** /saɪz/ ❶ *n.* **A** Größe, *die;* (*fig. of problem, project*) Umfang, *der;* Ausmaß, *das;* **reach full ~:** auswachsen; **be quite a ~:** ziemlich groß sein; **what a ~ he is!** wie groß er ist!; **be twice the ~ of sth.** zweimal so groß wie etw. sein; **who can afford a car that ~?** wer kann sich (*Dat.*) einen so großen Wagen leisten?; **what ~ [of] box do you want?** welche Größe soll die [gewünschte] Schachtel haben?; **take the ~ of sth.** etw. [aus]messen; **be small in ~:** klein sein; **be of great/small ~:** groß/klein sein; **a car of some ~:** ein ziemlich großes Auto; **be of a ~:** gleich groß sein; **be the ~ of sth.** so groß wie etw. sein; **be the ~ of a pea** erbsengroß sein; **a house the ~ of a palace** ein Haus so groß wie ein Palast; **that's [about] the ~ of it** (*fig. coll.*) so sieht die Sache aus (*ugs.*); **try sth. for ~:** etw. [wegen der Größe] anprobieren; (*fig.*) es einmal mit etw. versuchen; **what ~?** wie groß?; ⇒ *also* **cut down** 1 C; **B** (*graded class*) Größe, *die;* (*of paper*) Format, *das;* **collar/waist ~:** Kragen-/Taillenweite, *die;* **take a ~ 7 shoe/~ 7 in shoes** Schuhgröße 7 haben; **what ~ is Madam?** welche Größe hat die Dame?; **A 5 ~ paper** A5-Papier; **E 10 ~:** Größe E 10.

❷ *v.t.* nach der Größe sortieren

~ **'up** *v.t.* taxieren ‹Lage›; **I can't ~ her up** ich werde aus ihr nicht schlau (*ugs.*)

**size²** ❶ *n.* Leim, *der;* (*for textiles*) Schlichte, *die.* ❷ *v.t.* leimen; schlichten ‹Textilfaser›

**-size** /saɪz/ *adj. in comb.* **average-~:** durchschnittlich groß; **small-/medium-/large-~:** klein/mittelgroß/groß; ⇒ *also* **full-size**

**sizeable** /'saɪzəbl/ *adj.* ziemlich groß; beträchtlich ‹Summe, Schwierigkeiten, Wissen, Einfluss, Unterschied›; ansehnlich ‹Betrag›

**-sized** /saɪzd/ *adj. in comb.* ⇒ **-size**; **good-~** größer

**sizzle** /'sɪzl/ ❶ *v.i.* **A** zischen; **B** (*coll.: be hot or excited*) schmoren (*ugs.*); **be sizzling with anger** vor Wut kochen (*ugs.*). ❷ *n.* Zischen, *das*

**sizzling** /'sɪzlɪŋ/ ❶ *adj.* **A** zischend; **B** (*very hot*) brütend heiß; ~ **heat/weather** Gluthitze, *die;* **C** (*very fast*) blitzschnell (*ugs.*). ❷ *adv.* ~ **hot** brütend heiß ‹Wetter›; zischend heiß ‹Steak›

**skat** /skæt/ *n.* (*Cards*) Skat, *der*

**skate¹** /skeɪt/ *n.* (*Zool.*) Rochen, *der*

**skate²** ❶ *n.* (*ice ~*) Schlittschuh, *der;* (*roller ~*) Rollschuh, *der;* **get one's ~s on** (*Brit. fig. coll.*) sich sputen. ❷ *v.i.* (*ice-~*) Schlittschuh laufen; (*roller-~*) Rollschuh laufen; **he ~d over to her/in circles** er lief zu ihr hinüber/drehte Kreise; **the insects ~ on the water** (*fig.*) die Insekten gleiten über das Wasser; ~ **on thin ice** (*fig.*) sich auf dünnem Eis bewegen; (*put oneself in danger*) sich auf dünnes Eis begeben

~ **over,** ~ **round** *v.t.* (*fig.*) (*avoid*) hinweggehen über (+ *Akk.*) ‹Frage, Problem›; (*touch lightly on*) [nur] streifen

**skate³** *n.* (*coll.: contemptible person*) **[cheap] ~:** mieser Kerl (*ugs. abwertend*); **you dirty ~:** du Dreckskerl (*derb abwertend*)

**skate:** **~board** ❶ *n.* Skateboard, *das;* Rollerbrett, *das;* ❷ *v.i.* Skateboard fahren; **~boarder** *n.* Skateboardfahrer, *der*/-fahrerin, *die;* **~boarding** *n., no pl.* Skateboardfahren, *das*

**skater** /'skeɪtə(r)/ *n.* (*ice ~*) Eisläufer, *der*/-läuferin, *die;* (*roller ~*) Rollschuhläufer, *der*/-läuferin, *die*

**skating** /'skeɪtɪŋ/ *n., no pl.* (*ice ~*) Schlittschuhlaufen, *das;* (*roller ~*) Rollschuhlaufen, *das*

**'skating rink** *n.* **A** (*ice*) Eisbahn, *die;* Eisfläche, *die;* **B** (*for roller skating*) Rollschuhbahn, *die*

**skedaddle** /skɪ'dædl/ *v.i.* (*coll.*) türmen (*salopp*)

**skeet** /ski:t/ *n.* (*Sport*) ~ **[shooting]** Skeetschießen, *das*

**skein** /skeɪn/ *n.* **A** (*of wool etc.*) Strang, *der;* Docke, *die;* **B** (*fig.: tangle*) Knäuel, *das;* (*of lies*) Netz, *das;* **C a ~ of wild geese** eine Schar Wildgänse

**skeletal** /'skelɪtl/ *adj.* **A** (*relating to the skeleton*) Skelett-; **B** (*emaciated*) knochendürr ‹Körper, Hand›; **have a ~ appearance, look ~:** wie ein Skelett *od.* Gerippe aussehen

**skeleton** /'skelɪtn/ *n.* **A** Skelett, *das;* Gerippe, *das;* **have a ~ in the cupboard** (*Brit.*) *or* (*Amer.*) **closet** (*fig.*) eine Leiche im Keller haben (*ugs.*); **B** (*framework*) Skelett, *das* (*Bauw.*); (*of ship*) Gerippe, *das;* **C** (*outline*) Gerüst, *das;* **D** (*fig.: thin person or animal*) Gerippe, *das;* **she was reduced to a ~:** sie magerte fast bis zum Gerippe ab

**skeleton:** ~ **'crew** *n.* Stammbesatzung, *die;* ~ **'key** *n.* Dietrich, *der;* ~ **'service** *n.* **provide a ~ service** den Betrieb notdürftig aufrechterhalten; **there were buses running, but it was only a ~ service** es fuhren zwar Busse, aber nur einige wenige; ~ **'staff** *n.* Minimalbesetzung, *die*

**skepsis, skeptic** (*Amer.*) ⇒ **scep-**

**sketch** /sketʃ/ ❶ *n.* **A** (*drawing*) Skizze, *die;* **do** *or* **make a ~:** eine Skizze anfertigen; **B** (*fig.: outline*) **give** *or* **deliver a ~ of the situation** die Lage skizzieren; **the plan is only a ~ at the moment** der Plan existiert zur Zeit nur in [groben] Umrissen; **C** (*play*) Sketch, *der;* **D** (*Lit., Mus.*) Skizze, *die.* ❷ *v.t.* (*lit. or fig.*) skizzieren. ❸ *v.i.* skizzieren

~ **'in** *v.t.* **A** (*draw*) einzeichnen; **B** (*fig.: outline*) skizzieren

~ **'out** *v.t.* (*lit. or fig.*) [in groben Umrissen] skizzieren

**sketch:** **~-block** *n.* Skizzenblock, *der;* **~book** *n.* Skizzenbuch, *das*

**sketcher** /'sketʃə(r)/ *n.* Skizzenmaler, *der*/-malerin, *die* (**of** für)

**sketchily** /'sketʃɪlɪ/ *adv.* skizzenhaft; flüchtig ‹vorbereiten, berichten, aufzeichnen›

**sketching** /'sketʃɪŋ/ *n.* Skizzieren, *das*

**sketch:** ~ **map** *n.* Faustskizze, *die;* ~ **pad** ⇒ **sketch-block**

**sketchy** /'sketʃɪ/ *adj.* **A** skizzenhaft; **B** (*incomplete*) lückenhaft ‹Information, Bericht›; **C** (*inadequate*) unzureichend

**skew** /skju:/ ❶ *adj.* schräg; schief ‹Gesicht›. ❷ *n.* **on the ~:** schräg ‹überqueren›; schief ‹tragen, aufsetzen›; **the picture is [hanging] on the ~:** das Bild hängt schief. ❸ *v.t.* abschrägen; verzerren ‹Gesicht, Gestalt, Sachverhalt›. ❹ *v.i.* ~ **round** sich drehen

**skewer** /'skju:ə(r)/ ❶ *n.* [Brat]spieß, *der.* ❷ *v.t.* aufspießen

**skew-'whiff** (*Brit. coll.*) ⇒ **askew**

**ski** /ski:/ ❶ *n.* **A** Ski, *der;* **B** (*on vehicle*) Kufe, *die.* ❷ *v.i.* Ski laufen *od.* fahren; ~ **down the hill** [auf Skiern] den Berg hinabfahren; ~ **cross-country** Skilanglauf machen

**ski:** **~-bob** *n.* Skibob, *der;* **~-bobbing** *n.* Skibobfahren, *das;* ~ **boot** *n.* Skistiefel, *der;* ~ **cap** *n.* Skimütze, *die*

**skid** /skɪd/ ❶ *v.i.,* **-dd-** **A** schlittern; (*from one side to the other; spinning round*) schleudern; ~ **to a halt** schlitternd/schleudernd zum Stehen kommen; **B** (*on foot*) rutschen. ❷ *n.* **A** Schlittern, *das;* (*from one side to the other; spinning round*) Schleudern, *das;* **go into a ~:** ins Schlittern/Schleudern geraten; **get out of the ~, correct the ~:** das Schlittern/Schleudern abfangen; **steer into the ~:** gegenlenken; **B** (*Aeronaut.*) Gleitkufe, *die;* **tail/wing ~:** Gleitkufe unter dem Leitwerk/Flügel; **C** (*braking device*) Radschuh, *der;* Hemmschuh, *der;* **D** (*support*) Stützbalken, *der;* **E** (*slideway*) Schrotbaum,

S

der; (*used in pairs or sets*) Schrotleiter, *die;* (*roller*) Rolle, *die;* **be on the ~s** (*fig. coll.*) auf dem absteigenden Ast sein; **the plan/ project is on the ~s** (*fig. coll.*) der Plan/ das Projekt droht zu scheitern; **put the ~s under sb./sth.** (*fig. coll.*) jmdn./etw. zu Fall bringen

**skid: ~ chains** ⇒ **snow chains**; **~ lid** *n.* (*coll.*) Sturzhelm, *der;* **~ marks** *n. pl.* Schleuderspur, *die;* **~pad** *n.* (*Amer.*), **~pan** *n.* (*Brit.*) *Gelände, auf dem ein Schleudertraining durchgeführt wird;* **~ row** /skɪd'rəʊ/ *n.* (*Amer.*) Pennerviertel, *das* (*salopp abwertend*); **end up on ~ row** (*coll.*) als Penner enden (*salopp abwertend*)

**skier** /'ski:ə(r)/ *n.* Skiläufer, *der*/-läuferin, *die;* Skifahrer, *der*/-fahrerin, *die*

**skiff** /skɪf/ *n.* Skiff, *das;* (*racing boat also*) Einer, *der*

**skiffle** /'skɪfl/ *n.* Skiffle, *der od. das; attrib.* Skiffle-

**'ski goggles** *n. pl.* Skibrille, *die*

**skiing** /'ski:ɪŋ/ *n., no pl.* Skilaufen, *das;* Skifahren, *das;* (*Sport*) Skisport, *der*

**ski: ~ jump** *n.* A (*slope*) Sprungschanze, *die;* B (*leap*) Skisprung, *der;* **~ jumper** *n.* Skispringer, *der*/-springerin, *die;* **~ jumping** *n., no pl.* Skispringen, *das*

**skilful** /'skɪlfl/ *adj.* A (*having skill*) geschickt; gewandt ‹Redner›; gut ‹Beobachter, Lehrer›; B (*well executed*) geschickt; kunstvoll ‹Gemälde, Plastik, Roman, Komposition›; (*expert*) fachgerecht ‹Beurteilung›; kunstgerecht ausgeführt ‹Operation›

**skilfully** /'skɪlfəlɪ/ *adv.* geschickt; kunstvoll ‹malen, dichten, komponieren›; fachgerecht ‹urteilen›; kunstgerecht ‹operieren›

**skilfulness** /'skɪlflnɪs/ *n., no pl.* ⇒ **skill** A

**'ski lift** *n.* Skilift, *der*

**skill** /skɪl/ *n.* A (*expertness*) Geschick, *das;* Fertigkeit, *die;* (*of artist*) Können, *das;* **have ~ at** *or* **in sth.** Geschick/Fertigkeit in etw. (*Dat.*) haben; B (*technique*) Fertigkeit, *die;* (*of weaving, bricklaying*) Technik, *die;* Kunst, *die;* **the ~ of making guests feel at home** die Kunst, Gäste sich wie zu Hause fühlen zu lassen; C *in pl.* (*abilities*) Fähigkeiten; **office ~s** Büroerfahrung, *die;* **language ~s** Sprachkenntnisse, *die;* D (*dexterity*) Geschicklichkeit, *die;* (*of speech*) Gewandtheit, *die;* (*of painting*) Kunstfertigkeit, *die*

**skilled** /skɪld/ *adj.* A ⇒ **skilful** A; B (*requiring skill*) qualifiziert ‹Arbeit, Tätigkeit›; **~ trade** Ausbildungsberuf, *der;* Lehrberuf, *der* (*veralt.*); C (*trained*) ausgebildet; (*experienced*) erfahren; **be ~ in diplomacy/sewing** ein guter Diplomat sein/gut nähen können

**skillet** /'skɪlɪt/ *n.* A (*Brit.: cooking pot*) Tiegel, *der* (*mit Füßen*); B (*Amer.: frying pan*) Bratpfanne, *die*

**skillful, skillfully, skillfulness** (*Amer.*) ⇒ **skilful** *etc.*

**skim** /skɪm/ ❶ *v.t.*, **-mm-:** A (*remove*) abschöpfen; abrahmen ‹Milch›; B (*touch in passing*) streifen; C (*pass closely over*) **~ sth.** dicht über etw. (*Akk.*) fliegen; D (*throw*) segeln lassen; hüpfen lassen ‹Stein›; E (*scan briefly*) ⇒ **skim through**. ❷ *v.i.*, **-mm-:** segeln; **a bullet ~med past** *or* **by my arm** eine Kugel schwirrte an meinem Arm vorbei

**~ 'off** *v.t.* A abschöpfen; B (*fig.*) ⇒ **cream off**

**~ through** *v.t.* überfliegen ‹Buch, Zeitung›

**skimmed 'milk, skim 'milk** *n.* entrahmte Milch

**skimp** /skɪmp/ ❶ *v.t.* sparen an (+ *Dat.*); **he did the work badly, ~ing it** er schluderte bei seiner Arbeit (*ugs.*). ❷ *v.i.* sparen (**with, on** an + *Dat.*); **he had to ~ on food/ clothes** er musste am Essen/an der Kleidung sparen

**skimpily** /'skɪmpɪlɪ/ *adv.* sparsam ‹bekleidet›; kärglich ‹essen›; knapp ‹geschneidert›

**skimpy** /'skɪmpɪ/ *adj.* sparsam; karg ‹Mahl›; kärglich ‹Leben›; winzig ‹Badeanzug›; [zu] knapp ‹Anzug›; spärlich ‹Wissen›

**skin** /skɪn/ ❶ *n.* A ▶966 Haut, *die;* **be all** *or* **just ~ and bone** (*fig.*) nur Haut und Knochen sein (*ugs.*); **be soaked** *or* **wet to the ~:** bis auf die Haut durchnässt sein; **change one's ~** (*fig.*) sich völlig verwandeln; **by** *or* **with the ~ of one's teeth** mit knapper Not; **get under sb.'s ~** (*fig. coll.*) (*irritate sb.*) jmdm. auf die Nerven gehen *od.* fallen (*ugs.*); (*fascinate or enchant sb.*) jmdm. unter die Haut gehen (*ugs.*); **have a thick/ thin ~** (*fig.*) ein dickes Fell haben (*ugs.*)/ dünnhäutig sein; **jump out of one's ~** (*fig.*) aus dem Häuschen geraten (*ugs.*); **save one's ~** (*fig.*) seine Haut retten (*ugs.*); **it's no ~ off my/his** *etc.* **nose** (*coll.*) das braucht mich/ihn *usw.* nicht zu jucken (*ugs.*); **wear sth. next to one's ~:** etw. auf der [bloßen] Haut tragen; **we are all brothers under the ~:** wir sind uns im Grunde alle sehr ähnlich; B (*hide*) Haut, *die;* C (*fur*) Fell, *das;* D (*peel*) Schale, *die;* (*of onion, peach also*) Haut, *die;* E (*sausage-casing*) Haut, *die;* Pelle, *die* (*landsch., bes. nordd.*); F (*on milk*) Haut, *die;* G (*leather*) Leder, *das;* H (*Brit. coll.*) ⇒ **skinhead** A; I (*vessel*) Schlauch, *der;* J (*Naut., Aeronaut.*) Außenhaut, *die;* K (*stencil*) Matrize, *die.* ❷ *v.t.*, **-nn-** (*remove ~ from*) häuten; schälen ‹Frucht›; **~ one's knee** *etc.* sich (*Dat.*) das Knie *usw.* [auf]schürfen (**on** an, auf + *Dat.*, **against** an + *Dat.*); **~ sb. alive** (*fig. coll.*) Hackfleisch aus jmdm. machen (*ugs.*); ⇒ *also* **eye** 1 A

**skin: ~ cancer** *n.* ▶1232 Hautkrebs, *der;* **~ cream** *n.* Hautcreme, *die;* **~-'deep** *adj.* (*fig.*) oberflächlich; ⇒ *also* **beauty** A; **~ disease** *n.* Hautkrankheit, *die;* **~-dive** *v.i.* tauchen; **~ diver** *n.* Taucher, *der*/Taucherin, *die;* **~ diving** *n., no pl.* Tauchen, *das;* **~ flick** *n.* (*coll.*) Pornofilm, *der* (*ugs.*); **~flint** *n.* Geizhals, *der* (*abwertend*); **~ food** *n.* Nährcreme, *die*

**skinful** /'skɪnfʊl/ *n.* (*coll.*) **have had a ~:** voll sein (*salopp*)

**skin: ~ game** *n.* (*Amer. coll.*) [betrügerisches] Glücksspiel; **~ graft** *n.* Hauttransplantation, *die;* **~head** *n.* A (*Brit.*) Skinhead, *der;* B (*Amer. coll.: naval recruit*) Marinerekrut, *der*

**-skinned** /skɪnd/ *adj. in comb.* -häutig

**skinny** /'skɪnɪ/ *adj.* mager

**'skinny-dipping** *n.* (*Amer. coll.*) Nacktbaden, *das*

**skint** /skɪnt/ *adj.* (*Brit. coll.*) bankrott; **be ~:** blank *od.* pleite sein (*ugs.*)

**skin: ~ test** *n.* Hauttest, *der;* **~tight** *adj.* hauteng

**skip**[1] /skɪp/ ❶ *v.i.*, **-pp-** A hüpfen; B (*use skipping rope*) seilspringen; C (*change quickly*) springen (*fig.*); D (*make omissions*) überspringen; E (*coll.: flee*) abhauen (*ugs.*). ❷ *v.t.*, **-pp-** A (*omit*) überspringen; (*in mentioning names*) übergehen; **~ it!** (*coll.*) vergiss es (*ugs.*); **my heart ~ped a beat** (*fig.*) mir stockte das Herz; B (*coll.: miss*) schwänzen (*ugs.*) ‹Schule usw.›; liegen lassen ‹Hausarbeit›; **~ breakfast/lunch** *etc.* das Frühstück/ Mittagessen *usw.* auslassen; C (*coll.: flee from*) abhauen aus (*ugs.*); ⇒ *also* **bail**[1] 1 A; D **~ rope** (*Amer.*) seilspringen. ❸ *n.* Hüpfer, *der;* Hopser, *der* (*ugs.*); **give a ~ of delight** vor Freude hüpfen

**~ a'bout** *v.i.* A herumhüpfen; B **he did not stay with his subject but ~ped about** er hielt sich nicht an sein Thema, sondern sprang von einem Gegenstand zum anderen *od.* nächsten

**~ a'cross** *v.i.* hinüberspringen; rüberspringen (*ugs.*); **~ across to France** (*fig.*) kurz nach Frankreich hinüberfahren *od.* (*ugs.*) rüberfahren

**~ a'round** ⇒ **~ about**

**~ 'off** *v.i.* A ⇒ **pop off** b; B (*flee*) sich absetzen (*ugs.*)

**~ over** ❶ /-'--/ *v.i.* ⇒ **~ across**. ❷ /'---/ *v.t.* ⇒ **~** 2 A

**~ through** *v.t.* A ⇒ **skim through**; B (*make short work of*) [rasch] durchziehen (*ugs.*); herunterschnurren (*ugs.*) ‹Vorlesung›

**skip**[2] *n.* A (*Building*) Container, *der;* B (*Mining*) Skip, *der;* Fördergefäß, *das*

**skip**[3] (*Sport coll.*) ⇒ **skipper** 1 C

**ski: ~ pass** *n.* Skipass, *der;* **~-plane** *n.* Kufenflugzeug, *das;* **~ pole** *n.* Skistock, *der*

**skipper** /'skɪpə(r)/ ❶ *n.* A (*Naut.*) Kapitän, *der;* (*of yacht*) Skipper, *der* (*Seglerjargon*); B (*Aeronaut.*) [Flug]kapitän, *der;* C (*Sport*) [Mannschafts]kapitän, *der.* ❷ *v.t.* **~ a yacht** *etc.* Kapitän einer Jacht *usw.* sein; **~ the team to victory** die Mannschaft zum Sieg führen

**skipping rope** /'skɪpɪŋrəʊp/ (*Brit.*), **'skip-rope** (*Amer.*) *ns.* Sprungseil, *das;* Springseil, *das*

**'ski resort** *n.* Skiurlaubsort, *der*

**skirl** /skɜ:l/ *n.* durchdringendes *od.* gellendes Pfeifen

**skirmish** /'skɜ:mɪʃ/ ❶ *n.* A (*fight*) Rangelei, *die* (*ugs.*); (*of troops, armies*) Gefecht, *das* (*Milit.*); B (*fig.: argument*) Auseinandersetzung, *die.* ❷ *v.i.* A (*fight*) miteinander rangeln (*ugs.*); ‹Armeen, Truppen:› sich (*Dat.*) Gefechte (*Milit.*) liefern; B (*fig.: argue*) [sich] streiten

**skirt** /skɜ:t/ ❶ *n.* A Rock, *der;* B (*of coat*) Schoß, *der;* C (*border*) Rand, *der;* Saum, *der* (*geh.*); D (*on hovercraft*) Schürze, *die;* E (*Riding*) Seitenblatt, *das;* F (*Brit.: cut of meat*) **~ of beef** Rindfleisch vom Unterbauch; G (*sl.: woman*) **[a bit of]** ~: [eine] Mieze (*salopp*). ❷ *v.t.* A (*go past edge of*) herumgehen um; B (*border on*) ‹Straße, Weg:› entlangführen an (+ *Dat.*). ❸ *v.i.* **~ along sth.** an etw. (*Dat.*) entlanggehen/-fahren/-reiten *usw.*

**~ round** *v.t.* herumgehen um; (*fig.*) umgehen; ausweichen (+ *Dat.*)

**skirting** /'skɜ:tɪŋ/ *n.* **~[board]** (*Brit.*) Fußleiste, *die*

**ski: ~ run** *n.* Skihang, *der;* (*prepared*) [Ski]piste, *die;* **~stick** *n.* Skistock, *der;* **~ suit** *n.* Skianzug, *der*

**skit** /skɪt/ *n.* parodistischer Sketch (**on** über + *Akk.*)

**'ski tow** *n.* Schlepplift, *der*

**skittish** /'skɪtɪʃ/ *adj.* A (*nervous*) nervös ‹Pferd›; (*inclined to shy*) schreckhaft ‹Pferd›; B (*lively*) ausgelassen; aufgekratzt (*ugs.*)

**skittishly** /'skɪtɪʃlɪ/ *adv.* ⇒ **skittish**: nervös; schreckhaft; ausgelassen; aufgekratzt (*ugs.*)

**skittle** /'skɪtl/ *n.* A Kegel, *der;* B *in pl., constr. as sing.* (*game*) Kegeln, *das;* **play [at] ~s** kegeln; ⇒ *also* **beer**

**~ 'out** *v.t.* (*Cricket*) in schneller Folge ausscheiden lassen ‹die gegnerischen Schlagmänner›

**'skittle alley** *n.* Kegelbahn, *die*

**skive** /skaɪv/ ❶ *v.t.* A (*pare*) schaben ‹Leder, Fell›; B (*Brit. coll.: evade*) sich drücken vor (+ *Dat.*) (*ugs.*); schwänzen (*ugs.*) ‹Schule usw.›. ❷ *v.i.* (*Brit. coll.*) sich drücken (*ugs.*)

**~ 'off** (*Brit. coll.*) ❶ *v.i.* sich verdrücken (*ugs.*). ❷ *v.t.* schwänzen (*ugs.*)

**skiver** /'skaɪvə(r)/ *n.* (*Brit. coll.*) Drückeberger, *der*/Drückebergerin, *die*

**skivvy** /'skɪvɪ/ *n.* (*Brit. coll. derog.*) Dienstmädchen, *das* (*fig. ugs.*); Dienstbolzen, *der* (*salopp abwertend*)

**skua** /'skju:ə/ *n.* (*Ornith.*) Skua[raubmöwe], *die*

**skulduggery** /skʌl'dʌgərɪ/ *n.* (*joc.*) Hinterlist, *die;* (*Polit.*) Intrige, *die;* **a piece/an act of ~:** eine Hinterlist/Intrige; **what ~ got you the job?** mit welchen Tricks hast du die Stelle bekommen?

**skulk** /skʌlk/ *v.i.* A (*lurk*) lauern; B (*move stealthily*) schleichen; C (*be cowardly*) sich verkriechen; D (*shirk duty*) krankfeiern (*ugs.*)

**~ 'off** *v.i.* sich fortschleichen

**skull** /skʌl/ *n.* A (*Anat.*) Schädel, *der;* B (*as object*) Totenschädel, *der;* (*representation*) Totenkopf, *der;* C (*fig.: seat of intelligence*) Schädel, *der;* **can't you/when will you get it into** *or* **through your thick ~?** (*coll.*) geht das nicht/wann geht das endlich in deinen Schädel [hinein]? (*ugs.*)

**skull: ~ and crossbones** /skʌl ən'krɒsbəʊnz/ *n.* Totenkopf, *der* (*mit gekreuzten Knochen*); (*flag*) Totenkopfflagge, *die;*

S

**~cap** *n.* [A] *(hat)* Scheitelkäppchen, *das;* [B] *(Anat.)* Schädeldach, *das*

**skullduggery** ⇒ **skulduggery**

**-skulled** /skʌld/ *adj. in comb.* -schädelig

**skunk** /skʌŋk/ *n.* [A] *(Zool.)* Stinktier, *das;* Skunk, *der;* [B] *(coll.: contemptible person)* Stinktier, *das (derb);* [C] *(fur)* Skunk, *der*

**'skunk-bear** *(Amer.)* ⇒ **wolverine**

**sky** /skaɪ/ ❶ *n.* Himmel, *der;* **in the ~:** am Himmel; **out of a clear [blue] ~** *(fig.)* aus heiterem Himmel *(ugs.);* **praise sb./sth. to the skies** jmdn./etw. in den Himmel heben *(ugs.);* **there is not a cloud in the ~** *(lit. or fig.)* es zeigt sich kein Wölkchen am Himmel; **the ~'s the limit** *(fig.)* da gibt es [praktisch] keine Grenze; **for a man with his qualifications the ~'s the limit** *(fig.)* einem so hoch qualifizierten Mann stehen alle Möglichkeiten offen; **under the open ~:** unter freiem Himmel. ❷ *v.t.* *(Sport)* hoch in die Luft schlagen

**sky: ~-blue** ❶ *adj.* himmelblau; ❷ *n.* Himmelblau, *das;* **~diver** *n.* Fallschirmspringer, *der/*-springerin, *die;* **~diving** *n.* Fallschirmspringen, *das* *(als Sport);* Fallschirmsport, *der;* **~-high** ❶ *adj.* himmelhoch; astronomisch *(ugs.)* ‹Preise usw.›; ❷ *adv.* hoch in die Luft ‹werfen, steigen usw.›; **go ~-high** ‹Preise usw.:› in astronomische Höhen klettern *(ugs.);* **blow a building/a theory ~-high** ein Gebäude in die Luft jagen *(ugs.)*/eine Theorie völlig umwerfen; **~jack** *(Journ. coll.)* ❶ *v.t.* entführen; ❷ *n.* Flugzeugentführung, *die;* **~jacker** /'skaɪdʒækə(r)/ *n.* *(Journ. coll.)* Flugzeugentführer, *der/*-entführerin, *die;* **~lark** ❶ *n.* *(Ornith.)* [Feld]lerche, *die;* ❷ *v.i.* **~lark [about** *or* **around]** herumalbern *(ugs.);* **~light** *n.* Dachfenster, *das;* **~line** *n.* Silhouette, *die;* *(characteristic of certain town)* Skyline, *die;* **~rocket** ❶ *n.* Rakete, *die;* ❷ *v.i.* *(fig. coll.)* ‹Preise usw.:› in die Höhe schnellen; ‹Beliebtheit:› ungeheuer *(ugs.)* wachsen; **~sail** /'skaɪseɪl, 'skaɪsl/ *n.* *(Naut.)* Skysegel, *das;* **~scraper** *n.* Wolkenkratzer, *der*

**skyward** /'skaɪwəd/ ❶ *adj.* zum Himmel gerichtet; **in a ~ direction/on a ~ path** himmelwärts *(geh.).* ❷ *adv.* himmelwärts *(geh.);* zum *od.* *(veralt.)* gen Himmel

**skywards** ⇒ **skyward** 2

**sky: ~way** *n.* *(Aeronaut.)* Fluglinie, *die;* **~writing** *n.* Himmelsschrift, *die*

**slab** /slæb/ *n.* [A] *(flat stone etc.)* Platte, *die;* **mortuary ~:** Totenbank, *die;* [B] *(thick slice)* [dicke] Scheibe; *(of cake)* [dickes] Stück; *(of chocolate, toffee)* Tafel, *die*

**'slab cake** *n.* Kastenkuchen, *der*

**slack**[1] /slæk/ ❶ *adj.* [A] *(lax)* nachlässig; schlampig *(ugs. abwertend);* **his ~ attendance** sein unregelmäßiges Erscheinen; **be ~ about** *or* **in** *or* **with sth.** in Bezug auf etw. *(Akk.)* nachlässig sein; **not be ~ about** *or* **in** *or* **at doing sth.** nicht lange zögern, etw. zu tun; [B] *(loose)* schlaff; locker ‹Schraube, Verband, Strumpfband›; [C] *(sluggish)* schlaff; schwach ‹Wind, Flut›; [D] *(Commerc.: not busy)* flau; **a ~ three weeks** eine dreiwöchige Flaute. ❷ *n.* [A] **there's too much ~ in the rope** das Seil ist zu locker *od.* ist nicht straff genug; **take in** *or* **up the ~:** das Seil/die Schnur *usw.* straffen; [B] *(lull)* Flaute, *die.* ❸ *v.i.* *(coll.)* bummeln *(ugs.)*

**~ 'off** ⇒ **slacken off**

**~ 'up** ⇒ **slacken up**

**slack**[2] *n.* *(coal dust)* Grus, *der*

**slacken** /'slækn/ ❶ *v.i.* [A] *(loosen)* sich lockern; ‹Seil:› schlaff werden; [B] *(diminish)* nachlassen; ‹Geschwindigkeit:› sich verringern; ‹Schritt:› sich verlangsamen. ❷ *v.t.* [A] *(loosen)* lockern; [B] *(diminish)* verringern; verlangsamen ‹Schritt›; **~ one's efforts/attempts** in seinen Anstrengungen/Bemühungen nachlassen

**~ 'off** ❶ *v.i.* [A] *(loosen)* ⇒ ~ 1 A; [B] *(diminish)* ⇒ ~ 1 B; [C] *(relax)* es etwas langsamer angehen lassen *(ugs.).* ❷ *v.t.* [A] *(loosen)* ⇒ ~ 2 A; [B] *(diminish)* ⇒ ~ 2 B

**~ 'up** *v.i.* [A] *(reduce speed)* ‹Zug, Auto:› die Fahrt verlangsamen; ‹Schritt:› sich verlangsamen; [B] ⇒ **~ off** 1 C

**slacker** /'slækə(r)/ *n.* *(derog.)* [A] Faulenzer, *der;* [B] *(Amer.: young adult)* Hänger, *der* *(ugs.);* Durchhänger, *der (ugs.)*

**slackly** /'slæklɪ/ *adv.* [A] *(negligently)* nachlässig; schlampig *(ugs. abwertend);* [B] *(loosely)* locker; schlaff ‹hängen›

**slackness** /'slæknɪs/ *n., no pl.* [A] *(negligence)* Nachlässigkeit, *die;* [B] *(idleness)* Bummelei, *die (ugs.);* [C] *(looseness)* Schlaffheit, *die;* [D] *(of market, trade)* Flaute, *die*

**slacks** /slæks/ *n. pl.* **[pair of] ~:** lange Hose; Slacks *Pl.* *(Mode)*

**slack 'water** *n.* Stauwasser, *das*

**slag** /slæg/ ❶ *n.* [A] *(Metallurgy, Geol.)* Schlacke, *die;* ⇒ *also* **basic slag;** [B] *(sl.: slattern)* Schlampe, *die (salopp).* ❷ *v.t.* **~ [off]** herziehen über (+ *Akk.*) *(ugs.)*

**'slag heap** *n.* *(Mining)* Schlackenhalde, *die*

**slain** ⇒ **slay**

**slake** /sleɪk/ *v.t.* [A] stillen; löschen, stillen ‹Durst›; [B] *(Chem.)* löschen

**slaked lime** /sleɪkt 'laɪm/ ⇒ **lime**[1] A

**slalom** /'slɑːləm/ *n.* *(Skiing; Motor-/Canoe-racing)* Slalom, *der;* ⇒ *also* **giant slalom**

**slam**[1] /slæm/ ❶ *v.t.,* **-mm-** [A] *(shut)* zuschlagen; zuknallen *(ugs.);* **~ the door in sb.'s face** jmdm. die Tür vor der Nase zuschlagen; [B] *(put violently)* knallen *(ugs.);* **~ sb. in[to] prison** *(coll.)* jmdn. einbuchten *(salopp);* **~ one's foot on the brake** *(coll.)* auf die Bremse steigen *(ugs.);* [C] *(coll.: criticize)* ⇒ **slate** 3 A; [D] *(coll.: hit with force)* knallen *(ugs.)* ‹Ball›. ❷ *v.i.,* **-mm-** [A] zuschlagen; zuknallen *(ugs.);* [B] *(move violently)* stürmen; **the car ~med against** *or* **into the wall** das Auto knallte *(ugs.)* gegen die Mauer. ❸ *n.* *(sound)* Knall, *der;* **hear the ~ of the door** die Tür zuknallen hören *(ugs.)*

**~ 'down** *v.t.* [hin]knallen *(ugs.);* **~ sth. down on sth.** etw. auf etw. *(Akk.)* knallen *(ugs.);* **~ down a window** ein Fenster zuknallen *(ugs.)*

**~ 'on** *v.t.* *(coll.)* **~ on the brakes** auf die Bremse latschen *(salopp)*

**~ 'to** ❶ *v.i.* zuschlagen; zuknallen *(ugs.).* ❷ *v.t.* zuschlagen; zuknallen *(ugs.)*

**slam**[2] *n.* [A] *(Cards)* Schlemm, *der;* **grand/little** *or* **small ~:** großer/kleiner Schlemm; [B] *(Sport)* **achieve the grand ~:** alle [wichtigen] Meistertitel gewinnen; *(Tennis)* den Grand Slam gewinnen

**slam'bang** *adv.* mit einem Knall

**slammer** /'slæmə(r)/ *n.* *(sl.)* Kittchen, *das* *(ugs.)*

**slander** /'slɑːndə(r)/ ❶ *n.* [A] *(false report, defamation)* Verleumdung, *die* **(on** *Gen.*); [B] *(Law)* [mündliche] Verleumdung. ❷ *v.t.* verleumden; schädigen ‹Ruf›

**slanderer** /'slɑːndərə(r)/ *n.* Verleumder, *der/*Verleumderin, *die*

**slanderous** /'slɑːndərəs/ *adj.* verleumderisch

**slang** /slæŋ/ ❶ *n.* Slang, *der;* ‹Theater-, Soldaten-, Juristen›jargon, *der; attrib.* Slang‹wort, -ausdruck›. ❷ *v.t.* **~ sb.** jmdn. übel beschimpfen; **~ sth.** etw. zerreißen *(ugs.)*

**'slanging match** *n.* gegenseitige [lautstarke] Beschimpfung; **I had a ~ with her** wir warfen uns gegenseitig Beschimpfungen an den Kopf

**slangy** /'slæŋɪ/ *adj.* Slang‹ausdruck, -wort›; salopp ‹Wortwahl, Redeweise›

**slant** /slɑːnt/ ❶ *v.i.* ‹Fläche:› sich neigen; ‹Linie:› schräg verlaufen; **the roof ~s at an angle of 45°** das Dach hat eine Neigung von 45°; **green hills ~ing down to the sea** grüne Hügel, die schräg zum Meer abfallen; **his writing ~s from left to right** seine Schrift ist nach rechts geneigt; er schreibt nach rechts; **the desktop ~s** die Schreibtischplatte ist geneigt.
❷ *v.t.* [A] abschrägen; schräg zeichnen ‹Linie›; [B] *(fig.: bias)* [so] hinbiegen *(ugs.)* ‹Meldung, Bemerkung›.
❸ *n.* [A] Schräge, *die;* **have a ~ to the right** ‹Handschrift:› nach rechts geneigt sein; **cut sth. on a** *or* **the ~:** etw. schräg abschneiden; **be on a** *or* **the ~:** schräg sein; **write on the ~:** schräg schreiben; [B] *(fig.: bias)* Tendenz, *die;* Färbung, *die;* **have a left-wing ~** ‹Bericht:› links gefärbt sein; **put a right-wing ~ on sth.** von etw. eine rechts gefärbte Darstellung geben; **give an unfair ~ to events** die Vorfälle schief darstellen

**slanted** /'slɑːntɪd/ *adj.* *(fig.)* gefärbt; **a ~ question** eine Suggestivfrage

**'slant-eyed** *adj.* *(also derog.)* schlitzäugig

**slanting** /'slɑːntɪŋ/ *adj.* schräg

**'slantways** /'slɑːntweɪz/, **slantwise** /'slɑːnt waɪz/ *adv.* schräg

**slap** /slæp/ ❶ *v.t.,* **-pp-:** [A] schlagen; **~ sb. on the face/arm/hand** jmdn. ins Gesicht/auf den Arm/auf die Hand schlagen; **~ sb.'s face** *or* **sb. in** *or* **on the face** jmdn. ohrfeigen; **I'll ~ your face!** du bekommst eine Ohrfeige; **~ one's thigh[s]** sich *(Dat.)* auf die Schenkel schlagen; **~ sb. on the back** jmdm. auf die Schulter klopfen; **she deserves to be ~ped on the back** *(fig.)* sie verdient Beifall; Hut ab vor ihr! *(ugs.);* [B] *(put forcefully)* knallen *(ugs.);* **he ~ped the handcuffs on the prisoner** er ließ die Handschellen an den Armen des Gefangenen zuschnappen; **~ sb. in jail** *(coll.)* jmdn. ins Gefängnis stecken *(ugs.);* [C] *(put hastily or carelessly)* klatschen *(ugs.);* **~ a fine on sb.** jmdm. eine Geldstrafe aufbrummen *(ugs.);* **~ a ban on sth.** etw. [kurzerhand] verbieten.
❷ *v.i.,* **-pp-:** schlagen; klatschen.
❸ *n.* Schlag, *der;* **give sb. a ~:** jmdn. [mit der flachen Hand] schlagen; **give sth. a ~:** [mit der flachen Hand] auf etw. *(Akk.)* schlagen; **a ~ in the face** *(lit. or fig.)* ein Schlag ins Gesicht; **give sb. a ~ on the back** *(lit. or fig.)* jmdm. auf die Schulter klopfen; **a ~ on the back for sb./sth.** *(fig.)* eine Anerkennung für jmdn./etw.; **the judge gave him more than just a ~ on the wrist** *(fig.)* der Richter verpasste ihm einen ordentlichen Denkzettel *(ugs.).*
❹ *adv.* voll; **run ~ into sb.** *(lit. or fig.)* mit jmdm. zusammenprallen; **hit sb. ~ in the eye/face** *etc.* jmdn. mit voller Wucht ins Auge/Gesicht treffen; **~ in the middle** genau in der Mitte; **he arrived ~ on time** er kam auf die Minute pünktlich

**~ 'down** *v.t.* [A] *(lay forcefully)* hinknallen *(ugs.);* **~ sth. down on sth.** etw. auf etw. *(Akk.)* knallen *(ugs.);* [B] *(coll.: check, suppress, reprimand)* **~ sb. down** jmdm. eins auf den Deckel geben *(ugs.);* **be ~ ped down** eins auf den Deckel kriegen *(ugs.)*

**~ 'on** *v.t.* [A] *(coll.: apply hastily)* draufklatschen *(ugs.)* ‹Farbe, Tapete, Make-up›; zuschnappen lassen ‹Handschellen›; [B] *(coll.: impose)* draufschlagen *(ugs.).* ⇒ *also* ~ 1 A

**slap: ~ and 'tickle** *n.* *(Brit. coll.)* Fummelei, *die (salopp);* **~ bang** *adv.* **the table was ~ bang in the middle of the room** der Tisch stand einfach mitten im Zimmer; **~dash** ❶ *adv.* ruck, zuck *(ugs.);* ❷ *adj.* schludrig *(ugs. abwertend);* **in a ~dash way/fashion/manner** im Schnellverfahren; *(carelessly)* schludrig *(ugs. abwertend);* **her essay is ~dash** ihr Aufsatz ist hingeschludert *(ugs. abwertend);* **he is a ~dash sort** er ist ein schludriger Typ; **be ~dash in one's work** bei der Arbeit schludern *(ugs. abwertend);* **~-happy** *adj.* *(coll.)* [A] *(punch-drunk, lit. or fig.)* taumelig; [B] *(cheerfully casual)* unbekümmert; **~stick** *n.* *(Theatre: comedy style)* Slapstick, *der;* **~stick comedy/humour** Slapstickkomödie, *die/*-humor, *der;* **~-up** *attrib. adj.* *(coll.)* ‹Essen, Diner› mit allen Schikanen *(ugs.)*

**slash** /slæʃ/ ❶ *v.i.* **~ with one's sword** sein Schwert schwingen; **~ at sb./sth. with a knife/stick** auf jmdn./etw. mit einem Messer losgehen/mit einem Stock ausholen.
❷ *v.t.* [A] *(make gashes in)* aufschlitzen; **~ one's wrists** sich *(Dat.)* die Pulsadern aufschneiden; **~ sth. to ribbons** *or* **shreds** etw. zerfetzen; [B] *(Dressm., Tailoring)* [auf]schlitzen; [C] *(fig.: reduce sharply)* [drastisch] reduzieren; [drastisch] kürzen ‹Etat, Gehalt, Umfang›; **~ costs by one million** die Kosten um eine Million reduzieren; **~ a book to half its original length** ein Buch auf die Hälfte der ursprünglichen Länge zusammenstreichen; **he ~ed five seconds off the world record** er hat die Weltrekordmarke

S

um [beachtliche] fünf Sekunden unterboten; (D)(*clear by slashing*) **he ~ed his way through the undergrowth** er schlug sich (*Dat.*) einen Weg durch das Unterholz frei. ❸ *n.* (A) (*~ing stroke*) Hieb, *der;* (B) (*wound*) Schnitt, *der;* **give sb. a ~ on the arm** jmdm. den Arm aufschlitzen; (C) (*slit; Dressm., Tailoring*) Schlitz, *der;* (D) (*Amer.: tree debris*) Holzabfall, *der* (*nach Waldbränden, Naturkatastrophen oder Holzschlag*); (E) **go for a** *or* **have a ~** (*sl.: urinate*) sich auspissen gehen (*derb*)

**slash-and-'burn** *attrib. adj.* (*Agric.*) **~ method** Brandrodung, *die*

**slashed** /slæʃt/ *adj.* (*Dressm., Tailoring*) geschlitzt; **~ sleeves** Schlitzärmel

**slashing** /'slæʃɪŋ/ *adj.* vernichtend ‹Angriff, Kritik›

**slat** /slæt/ *n.* Leiste, *die;* (*of wood in bedstead, fence*) Latte, *die;* (*in Venetian blind*) Lamelle, *die*

**slate** /sleɪt/ ❶ *n.* (A) (*Geol.*) Schiefer, *der;* (B) (*Building*) Schieferplatte, *die;* (C) (*writing surface*) Schiefertafel, *die;* **put sth. on the ~** (*Brit. coll.*) etw. anschreiben (*ugs.*); **wipe the ~ clean** (*fig.*) einen Schlussstrich ziehen; (D) (*Amer. Polit.: list of candidates*) Kandidatenliste, *die.* ❷ *attrib. adj.* Schiefer-; **~ roof** Schieferdach, *das.* ❸ *v.t.* (A) (*Brit. coll.: criticize*) in der Luft zerreißen (*ugs.*) (**for** wegen); (B) (*Amer.: schedule*) ansetzen ‹Treffen, Besprechung›

**slate: ~ colour** *n.* Schieferfarbe, *die;* **~-coloured** *adj.* schieferfarben; **~ grey** ❶ *n.* Schiefergrau, *das;* ❷ *adj.* schiefergrau; **~ pencil** *n.* Schiefergriffel, *der*

**slating** /'sleɪtɪŋ/ *n.* (*Brit. coll.*) **get** *or* **take a ~:** in der Luft zerrissen werden (*ugs.*) (**for** wegen); **give sb./sth. a ~:** jmdn./etw. in der Luft zerreißen (*ugs.*) (**for** wegen)

**slattern** /'slætən/ *n.* Schlampe, *die* (*ugs. abwertend*)

**slatternly** /'slætənlɪ/ *adj.* schlampig (*ugs. abwertend*)

**slaughter** /'slɔ:tə(r)/ ❶ *n.* (A) (*killing for food*) Schlachten, *das;* Schlachtung, *die;* ⇒ *also* **lamb** 1 A; (B) (*massacre*) Abschlachten, *das;* (*in battle, war*) Gemetzel, *das;* **the wholesale ~ of birds** der Vogelmord im großen Stil. ❷ *v.t.* (A) (*kill for food*) schlachten; (B) (*massacre*) abschlachten; niedermetzeln (*abwertend*); (C) (*coll.: defeat utterly*) fertig machen (*salopp*); (D) (*coll.: severely criticize*) verreißen

**'slaughterhouse** ⇒ **abattoir**

**Slav** /slɑ:v/ ❶ *n.* Slawe, *der*/Slawin, *die.* ❷ *adj.* slawisch

**slave** /sleɪv/ ❶ *n.* (A) Sklave, *der*/Sklavin, *die;* ⇒ *also* **white slave;** (B) (*fig.*) **be a ~ of** *or* **to sth.** Sklave von etw. sein; **be a ~ to sb.** jmdm. verfallen sein; (C) (*drudge*) Kuli, *der;* **work like a ~:** wie ein Kuli *od.* Brunnenputzer schuften (*ugs.*). ❷ *v.i.* schuften (*ugs.*); **~ at sth.** sich mit etw. abplagen; **~ over a hot stove all day** den ganzen Tag am Herd stehen (*ugs.*)

**~ a'way** *v.i.* sich abplagen; sich abrackern (*salopp*); **~ away at sth.** sich mit etw. abplagen

**slave: ~-drive** *v.t.* schinden; **~ driver** *n.* (A) Sklavenaufseher, *der;* (B) (*fig.: taskmaster*) Sklaventreiber, *der*/-treiberin, *die* (*abwertend*); **~ 'labour** *n.* Sklavenarbeit, *die;* (*fig.*) Ausbeutung, *die*

**slaver**[1] /'slævə(r)/ ❶ *v.i.* sabbern (*ugs.*); ‹Tier:› geifern; **he was ~ing at the mouth** ihm rann Speichel aus dem Mund; **~ over sb./sth.** (*fig. derog.*) nach jmdm./etw. gieren. ❷ *n., no indef. art.* Geifer, *der*

**slaver**[2] /'sleɪvə(r)/ *n.* Sklavenhändler, *der*/-händlerin, *die*

**slavery** /'sleɪvərɪ/ *n., no pl.* (A) Sklaverei, *die;* (B) (*drudgery*) Sklavenarbeit, *die;* Sklaverei, *die*

**slave: ~ trade** *n.* Sklavenhandel, *der;* **~ trader** *n.* Sklavenhändler, *der*/-händlerin, *die*

**Slavic** /'slɑ:vɪk/ ❶ *adj.* slawisch. ❷ *n.* Slawisch, *das*

**slavish** /'sleɪvɪʃ/ *adj.* sklavisch

**slavishly** /'sleɪvɪʃlɪ/ *adv.* sklavisch

**Slavonia** /slə'vəʊnɪə/ *pr. n.* Slawonien (*das*)

**Slavonic** /slə'vɒnɪk/ ▶ **1275** ❶ *adj.* slawisch. ❷ *n.* Slawisch, *das;* **Church** *or* **Old [Church] ~:** Altkirchenslawisch, *das*

**slay** /sleɪ/ *v.t.*, **slew** /slu:/, **slain** /sleɪn/ (⇒ *also* C) (A) (*literary*) ermorden; (*with sword, club also*) erschlagen; vernichtend schlagen ‹Armee›; (B) (*coll.: defeat utterly*) in die Pfanne hauen (*ugs.*); (C) *p.t., p.p.* **~ed** (*coll.: amuse greatly*) **he/his jokes ~ed me** über ihn/seine Witze hätte ich mich totlachen können (*ugs.*)

**SLD** *abbr.* (*Brit. Polit.*) **Social and Liberal Democrats** Sozial-Liberaldemokratische Partei

**sleaze** /sli:z/ *n., no pl.* (*derog.*) Korruption, *die*

**'sleazebag, 'sleazeball** *ns.* (*sl. derog.*) Drecksack, *der* (*derb abwertend*)

**sleazily** /'sli:zɪlɪ/ *adv.* schäbig (*abwertend*); in schäbigen Verhältnissen ‹leben›; **dress ~:** schäbig angezogen gehen

**sleazy** /'sli:zɪ/ *adj.* (*squalid*) schäbig (*abwertend*); heruntergekommen (*ugs.*) ‹Person›; (*disreputable*) anrüchig

**sled** /sled/ (*Amer.*) ❶ *v.i.*, **-dd-** ⇒ **sledge**[1] 2. ❷ *n.* Schlitten, *der*

**sledge**[1] /sledʒ/ ❶ *n.* Schlitten, *der.* ❷ *v.i.* Schlitten fahren; rodeln. ❸ *v.t.* mit dem Schlitten fahren

**sledge**[2] ⇒ **sledgehammer**

**'sledgehammer** ❶ *n.* Vorschlaghammer, *der;* **[take/use] a ~ to crack a nut** mit Kanonen auf Spatzen schießen. ❷ *adj.* schlagend ‹Argument›; wuchtig ‹Schlag›; **~ style** Holzhammermethode, *die* (*ugs.*)

**sleek** /sli:k/ ❶ *adj.* (A) (*glossy*) seidig ‹Fell, Haar, Pelz›; ‹Tier› mit seidigem Fell; (B) (*well-fed*) wohlgenährt; (C) (*polished*) glatt; (*glossy*) seidig glänzend; **the ~ lines of the car** die schnittige Form des Wagens. ❷ *v.t.* glätten

**~ 'back** ⇒ **slick back**

**~ 'down** ⇒ **slick down**

**sleep** /sli:p/ ❶ *n.* Schlaf, *der;* **get some ~:** schlafen; **it's time we got some ~:** es ist Zeit zum Schlafengehen; **get three hours' ~:** drei Stunden schlafen; **get/go to ~:** einschlafen; **go to ~!** schlaf jetzt!; **not lose [any] ~ over sth.** (*fig.*) wegen etw. keine schlaflose Nacht haben; **some cocoa should put him to ~:** etwas Kakao, und er müsste einschlafen; **put an animal to ~** (*euphem.*) ein Tier einschläfern; **he put** *or* **sent me to ~ with his stories** (*coll.*) bei seinen Geschichten bin ich fast eingeschlafen; **talk in one's ~:** im Schlaf sprechen; **one's last ~** (*fig.*) der ewige Schlaf; **walk in one's ~:** schlafwandeln; **I can/could do it in my ~** (*fig.*) ich kann/könnte es im Schlaf; **be in a deep ~:** fest schlafen; **get** *or* **have a good night's ~:** [sich] gründlich ausschlafen; **have a ~:** schlafen; **have a short ~:** ein [kurzes] Schläfchen machen. ❷ *v.i.*, **slept** [slept] (A) schlafen; **~ late** lange schlafen; ausschlafen; **~ like a log** *or* **top** wie ein Stein schlafen (*ugs.*); **~ tight!** (*coll.*) schlaf gut!; **~ at sb.'s** bei jmdm. schlafen; ⇒ *also* **rough** 3; (B) (*fig.: be dormant*) schlafen (*fig.*); ‹Vulkan, Hass:› ruhen, schlafen; (C) (*fig.: lie in grave*) ruhen (*geh.*). ❸ *v.t.*, **slept** (A) **~ the ~ of the just** *or* **dead** (*joc.*) den Schlaf des Gerechten schlafen (*scherzh.*); (B) (*accommodate*) schlafen lassen; **the hotel ~s 80** das Hotel hat 80 Betten. ⇒ *also* **wink** 3 B

**~ a'round** *v.i.* (*coll.*) herumschlafen (*ugs.*)

**~ a'way** *v.t.* verschlafen

**~ 'in** *v.i.* (A) (**~ late**) im Bett bleiben; (B) (*live in*) im Hause wohnen

**~ 'off** *v.t.* ausschlafen; **~ it off** seinen Rausch ausschlafen; **~ off one's lunch** [nach dem Mittagessen] einen Verdauungsschlaf halten

**~ on** ❶ *v.i.* /-'-/ weiterschlafen. ❷ *v.t.* /'--/ überschlafen

**~ 'out** *v.i.* (A) (**~ in the open**) im Freien schlafen; (B) (*live out*) nicht im Hause wohnen

**~ through** *v.t.* **~ through the noise/alarm** trotz des Lärms/Weckerklingelns [weiter]schlafen

**~ together** *v.i.* (*also coll. euphem.*) miteinander schlafen

**~ with** *v.t.* **~ with sb.** (*coll. euphem.*) mit jmdm. schlafen

**sleeper** /'sli:pə(r)/ *n.* (A) Schläfer, *der;* **be a heavy/light ~:** einen tiefen/leichten Schlaf haben; (B) (*Brit. Railw.: support*) Schwelle, *die;* (C) (*Railw.*) (*coach*) Schlafwagen, *der;* (*berth*) Schlafwagenplatz, *der;* (*overnight train*) **[night] ~:** Nachtzug mit Schlafwagen; (D) (*earring*) [medizinischer] Ohrstecker; (E) (*slow starter*) **the novel/film was a ~:** dem Roman/Film gelang erst spät der Durchbruch (*fig.*); (F) (*Amer.*) ⇒ **sleepsuit**

**sleepily** /'sli:pɪlɪ/ *adv.* (A) (*drowsily*) schläfrig; (B) (*sluggishly*) schwerfällig; (*unobservantly*) schlafmützig (*ugs. abwertend*)

**sleepiness** /'sli:pɪnɪs/ *n., no pl.* (*drowsiness*) Schläfrigkeit, *die*

**sleeping** /'sli:pɪŋ/ *adj.* (*lit. or fig.*) schlafend; schlummernd ‹Leidenschaft›; **let ~ dogs lie** (*fig.*) keine schlafenden Hunde wecken

**sleeping: ~ accommodation** *n.* Übernachtungsmöglichkeit, *die;* **the price includes ~ accommodation** im Preis ist die Übernachtung inbegriffen; **~ bag** *n.* Schlafsack, *der;* **S~ 'Beauty** *pr. n.* Dornröschen (*das*); **~ car[riage]** *n.* (*Railw.*) Schlafwagen, *der;* **~ draught** *n.* Schlaftrunk, *der;* **~ drug** *n.* Schlafmittel, *das;* **~ 'partner** *n.* (*Commerc.*) stiller Teilhaber; **~ pill** *n.* Schlaftablette, *die;* **~ po'liceman** *n.* (*Brit.*) Bodenschwelle, *die;* **~ sickness** *n.* ▶ **1232** (*Med.*) Schlafkrankheit, *die;* **~ suit** ⇒ **sleepsuit;** **~ tablet** ⇒ **~ pill**

**sleepless** /'sli:plɪs/ *adj.* schlaflos

**sleeplessness** /'sli:plɪsnɪs/ *n., no pl.* Schlaflosigkeit, *die*

**sleep: ~over** *n.* Übernachtung außer Haus; **~suit** *n.* [Baby]schlafanzug, *der;* **~walk** *v.i.* schlafwandeln; **~walker** *n.* Schlafwandler, *der*/-wandlerin, *die;* **~walking** *n.* Schlafwandeln, *das*

**sleepy** /'sli:pɪ/ *adj.* (A) (*drowsy*) schläfrig; (B) (*sluggish*) schwerfällig; (*unobservant*) schlafmützig (*ugs. abwertend*); (C) (*peaceful*) verschlafen ‹Dorf, Stadt usw.›

**sleepy: ~head** *n.* Schlafmütze, *die* (*ugs.*); **~ sickness** *n.* (*Med.*) Kopfgrippe, *die;* europäische Schlafkrankheit

**sleet** /sli:t/ ❶ *n., no indef. art.* Schneeregen, *der.* ❷ *v.i. impers.* **it was ~ing** es gab Schneeregen

**sleeve** /sli:v/ *n.* (A) Ärmel, *der;* **have sth. up one's ~** (*fig.*) etw. in petto haben (*ugs.*); **roll up one's ~s** (*lit. or fig.*) die Ärmel hochkrempeln (*ugs.*); ⇒ *also* **heart** 1 B; **laugh;** (B) (*record cover*) Hülle, *die;* (C) (*Mech.*) Muffe, *die* (*Technik*); (D) (*Aeronaut.*) (*windsock*) Windsack, *der*

**-sleeved** /sli:vd/ *adj. in comb.* -ärmelig

**sleeveless** /'sli:vlɪs/ *adj.* ärmellos

**'sleeve note** *n.* Covertext, *der*

**sleigh** /sleɪ/ ❶ *n.* Schlitten, *der.* ❷ *v.i. & t.* mit dem Schlitten fahren

**sleigh: ~ bell** *n.* Schlittenschelle, *die;* **~ ride** *n.* Schlittenfahrt, *die*

**sleight of hand** /slaɪt əv 'hænd/ *n.* Fingerfertigkeit, *die*

**slender** /'slendə(r)/ *adj.* (A) (*slim*) schlank; schmal ‹Buch, Band›; (B) (*meagre*) mager ‹Einkommen, Kost›; gering ‹Chance, Mittel, Vorräte, Hoffnung, Kenntnis›; schwach ‹Entschuldigung, Argument, Grund›; **be a person of ~ means** *or* **resources** wenig Geld haben; einen schmalen (*geh.*) Geldbeutel haben

**slenderize** /'slendəraɪz/ ❶ *v.t.* **~ [the figure]** schlank machen. ❷ *v.i.* abnehmen

**slenderly** /'slendəlɪ/ *adv.* **~ built/made** von schlankem Wuchs *nachgestellt;* **be ~ provided for** schlecht versorgt sein

**slept** ⇒ **sleep** 2, 3

**sleuth** /slu:θ/ ❶ *n.* Detektiv, *der.* ❷ *v.i.* **go ~ing** sich detektivisch betätigen

**slew**[1] /slu:/ ❶ *v.i.* **~ to the left/right** sich [schnell] nach links/rechts drehen; ‹Kran:›

S

nach links/rechts schwenken. ❷ *v.t.* herumschleudern; schwenken ‹Kran›

~ **[a]'round** ❶ *v.i.* sich [schnell] drehen; ~ **around to the left** ‹Kran:› nach links schwenken. ❷ *v.t.* [schnell] drehen; schwenken ‹Kran›

**slew²** ⇒ **slay** A,B

**slew³** *n.* (*Amer. coll.*) Haufen, *der* (*ugs.*); **a ~ of people/things** ein Haufen (*ugs.*) Leute/Dinge; **~s of spectators/snow** massenhaft (*ugs.*) Zuschauer/Schnee; **~s of work** Berge von Arbeit

**slice** /slaɪs/ ❶ *n.* Ⓐ (*cut portion*) Scheibe, *die;* (*of apple, melon, peach, apricot, cake, pie*) Stück, *das;* **a ~ of life** ein Ausschnitt aus dem Leben; ⇒ *also* **cake** 1 A, B; Ⓑ (*share*) Teil, *der;* (*allotted part of profits, money*) Anteil, *der;* **a ~ of land** ein Stück Land; **have a ~ of luck** Glück haben; Ⓒ (*utensil*) [Braten]wender, *der;* Ⓓ (*Golf, Tennis: stroke*) Slice, *der.*

❷ *v.t.* Ⓐ (*cut into portions*) in Scheiben schneiden; in Stücke schneiden ‹Bohnen, Apfel, Pfirsich, Kuchen usw.›; **~ sth. thick/thin/into pieces** etw. dick/dünn/in Stücke schneiden; Ⓑ (*Golf*) slicen; (*Tennis*) unterschneiden; slicen.

❸ *v.i.* schneiden; **~ through** durchschneiden; durchpflügen ‹Wellen, Meer›

~ **'off** *v.t.* abschneiden

~ **'up** *v.t.* aufschneiden; (*fig.: divide*) aufteilen

**sliced** /slaɪst/ *adj.* (*cut into slices*) aufgeschnitten; klein geschnitten ‹Gemüse›; **~ bread** Schnittbrot, *das;* **the greatest thing since ~ bread** (*coll. joc.*) der/die/das Größte seit der Erfindung der Bratkartoffel (*ugs. scherzh.*)

**-slicer** /slaɪsə(r)/ *n. in comb.* -schneidemaschine, *die;* **egg-~:** Eierschneider, *der*

**slick** /slɪk/ ❶ *adj.* Ⓐ (*dextrous*) professionell; Ⓑ (*pretentiously dextrous*) clever (*ugs.*); Ⓒ (*slippery*) glatt ‹Fußboden›; rutschig ‹Straße, Weg›; Ⓓ (*glossy*) seidig glänzend; Ⓔ (*glib*) glatt; glattzüngig (*geh. abwertend*); **have a ~ tongue** glattzüngig sein (*geh. abwertend*). ❷ *n.* **[oil] ~:** Ölteppich, *der.* ❸ *v.t.* ⇒ **sleek** 2

~ **'back** *v.t.* **~ back one's hair** sich (*Dat.*) die Haare anklatschen (*salopp*)

~ **'down** *v.t.* **~ down one's hair** sich (*Dat.*) die Haare anklatschen (*salopp*)

**slicker** /'slɪkə(r)/ *n.* (*Amer.*) Ⓐ (*swindler*) Trickbetrüger, *der*/-betrügerin, *die;* Ⓑ ⇒ **city slicker**; Ⓒ (*raincoat*) Regenmantel, *der;* (*oilskin*) [gelbe] Öljacke

**slid** ⇒ **slide** 1, 2

**slide** /slaɪd/ ❶ *v.i.*, **slid** /slɪd/ Ⓐ rutschen; ‹Kolben, Schublade, Feder› gleiten; **the bolt slid home** der Riegel glitt ins Schloss; **~ down sth.** etw. hinunterrutschen; Ⓑ (*glide over ice*) schlittern; Ⓒ (*move smoothly*) gleiten; **everything slid into place** (*fig.*) alles fügte sich zusammen; Ⓓ (*fig.: take its own course*) **let sth./things ~:** etw./die Dinge schleifen lassen (*fig.*); Ⓔ (*fig.: go imperceptibly*) **~ into** hineinschlittern in (+ *Akk.*) (*ugs.*); **~ from one note to another** ‹Sänger, Stimme, Musik:› von einem Ton zum nächsten gleiten.

❷ *v.t.*, **slid** Ⓐ schieben; **~ the bolt across on a door** an einer Tür den Riegel vorschieben; **~ the envelope under the door** den Brief unter der Tür durchschieben; Ⓑ (*place unobtrusively*) gleiten lassen.

❸ *n.* Ⓐ (*Photog.*) Dia[positiv], *das;* Ⓑ (*track on ice*) Rutschbahn, *die* (*ugs.*); Schlitterbahn, *die* (*landsch.*); Ⓒ (*toboggan slope*) **[toboggan] ~:** Rodelbahn, *die;* Ⓓ (*chute*) (*in children's playground*) Rutschbahn, *die;* (*for goods etc.*) Rutsche, *die;* Ⓔ (*Mech. Eng.*) Gleitbahn, *die;* (*moving part*) Gleitstück, *das;* Schieber, *der;* Ⓕ ⇒ **hairslide**; Ⓖ (*act of sliding*) Ausrutscher, *der* (*ugs.*); **go for** *or* **have a ~** (*on chute*) rutschen [gehen]; (*on ice*) schlittern [gehen]; Ⓗ (*fig.: decline*) **be on the ~:** auf dem absteigenden Ast sein; **the ~ in the value of the pound** das Abgleiten des Pfundes; Ⓘ (*Mus.*) Zug, *der;* Ⓙ (*for microscope*) Objektträger, *der*

**slide:** ~ **control** *n.* Flachbahnregler, *der* (*Technik*); ~ **fastener** (*Amer.*) ⇒ **zip** 1 A; ~ **film** *n.* (*Photog.*) Diafilm, *der;* ~ **lecture** *n.* Diavortrag, *der;* ~ **projector** *n.* Diaprojektor, *der;* ~ **rule** *n.* (*Math.*) Rechenschieber, *der;* ~ **show** *n.* Diashow, *die;* ~ **valve** *n.* (*Mech. Engin.*) [Absperr]schieber, *der* (*Technik*)

**sliding**/'slaɪdɪŋ/: ~ **'door** *n.* Schiebetür, *die;* ~ **'keel** *n.* (*Naut.*) Schwert, *das;* ~ **'roof** *n.* Schiebedach, *das;* ~ **'scale** *n.* **~ scale [of fees]** gleitende [Gebühren]skala; ~ **seat** *n.* (*Rowing*) Rollsitz, *der*

**slight** /slaɪt/ ❶ *adj.* Ⓐ leicht; schwach ‹Hoffnung, Aussichten, Wirkung›; gedämpft ‹Optimismus›; gering ‹Bedeutung›; **have only a ~ acquaintance with sth.** etw. nur oberflächlich kennen; **on the ~est pretext** unter dem geringsten Vorwand; **the ~est thing makes her nervous** die kleinste Kleinigkeit macht sie nervös; Ⓑ (*scanty*) oberflächlich; **with but ~ inconvenience** ohne größere Unannehmlichkeiten; **pay sb. ~ attention** jmdn. kaum beachten; Ⓒ (*slender*) zierlich; (*weedy*) schmächtig; (*flimsy*) zerbrechlich; Ⓓ **not in the ~est** nicht im Geringsten; **not the ~est ...:** nicht der/die/das Geringste ...; **I haven't the ~est idea** ich habe nicht die leiseste Ahnung.

❷ *v.t.* (*disparage*) herabsetzen; (*fail in courtesy or respect to*) brüskieren; (*ignore*) ignorieren.

❸ *n.* (*on sb.'s character, reputation, good name*) Verunglimpfung, *die* (**on** *Gen.*); (*on sb.'s abilities*) Herabsetzung, *die* (**on** *Gen.*); (*lack of courtesy*) Affront, *der* (**on** gegen); (*neglect*) Nichtachtung, *die*

**slightly** /'slaɪtlɪ/ *adv.* Ⓐ ein bisschen; leicht ‹verletzen, riechen nach, gewürzt sein, ansteigen›; flüchtig ‹jmdn. kennen›; oberflächlich ‹etw. kennen›; Ⓑ **~ built** (*slender*) zierlich; (*weedy*) schmächtig

**slily** ⇒ **slyly**

**slim** /slɪm/ ❶ *adj.* Ⓐ schlank; schmal ‹Band, Buch›; Ⓑ (*meagre*) mager; schwach ‹Entschuldigung, Aussicht, Hoffnung›; gering ‹Gewinn, Chancen›; **the profit/the supper was ~ pickings** der Gewinn/das Abendessen war ziemlich mickrig; **there were only ~ pickings left** da war nicht mehr viel zu holen. ❷ *v.i.*, **-mm-** abnehmen. ❸ *v.t.*, **-mm-** schlanker machen; (*fig.: decrease*) kürzen ‹Budget›; verschlanken (*Jargon*) ‹Produktion›; reduzieren ‹Nachfrage, Anzahl›

~ **'down** ❶ *v.i.* abnehmen; schlanker werden; **the ~med-down state** der schlanke Staat. ❷ *v.t.* ⇒ ~ 3

**slime** /slaɪm/ ❶ *n.* Schlick, *der;* (*mucus, viscous matter*) Schleim, *der.* ❷ *v.t.* mit Schlick/Schleim bedecken

**'slime mould** *n.* (*Bot.*) Schleimpilz, *der*

**'slimline** *adj.* schlank; schlank geschnitten ‹Kleid›; kalorienarm ‹Lebensmittel›

**slimmer** /'slɪmə(r)/ *n.* (*Brit.*) *jmd., der etwas für die schlanke Linie tut;* **advice/a diet for ~s** Ratschläge/eine Diät zum Abnehmen

**slimming** /'slɪmɪŋ/ ❶ *n.* Ⓐ Abnehmen, *das; attrib.* Schlankheits-; **be in need of ~:** abnehmen müssen; Ⓑ (*fig.: reduction*) (*of budget*) Kürzung, *die;* (*of number*) Reduzierung, *die.* ❷ *adj.* schlank machend ‹Lebensmittel›; **be ~:** schlank machen

**slimness** /'slɪmnɪs/ *n., no pl.* (*slenderness*) Schlankheit, *die;* (*of book*) geringer Umfang

**slimy** /'slaɪmɪ/ *adj.* Ⓐ schleimig; schlickig ‹Schlamm›; Ⓑ (*slippery*) glitschig (*ugs.*); Ⓒ (*fig.: obsequious*) schleimig (*abwertend*); schmierig (*abwertend*)

**sling¹** /slɪŋ/ ❶ *n.* Ⓐ (*weapon*) Schleuder, *die;* Ⓑ (*Med.*) Schlinge, *die;* Ⓒ (*carrying-belt*) Tragriemen, *der;* (*for carrying babies*) Tragehöschen, *das;* Ⓓ (*hoist*) Anschlagseil, *das* (*Technik*); (*belt*) Anschlagband, *das* (*Technik*); (*chain*) Anschlagkette, *die* (*Technik*). ❷ *v.t.*, **slung** /slʌŋ/ Ⓐ (*hurl from ~*) schleudern; Ⓑ (*coll.: throw*) schmeißen (*ugs.*); **she slung him his coat** sie schmiss ihm seinen Mantel zu (*ugs.*); ⇒ *also* **mud** C; Ⓒ (*suspend*) hängen; (*put in ~ ready for hoisting*) anhängen ‹Last›; **she slung the bag over her arm** sie hängte sich (*Dat.*) die Tasche über den Arm

~ **a'way** *v.t.* (*coll.*) wegschmeißen (*ugs.*)

~ **'out** *v.t.* (*coll.*) Ⓐ (*throw out*) **~ sb. out** jmdn. rausschmeißen *od.* -werfen (*ugs.*); Ⓑ ⇒ ~ **away**

**sling²** *n.* (*drink*) Sling, *der* (*Mischgetränk mit Brandy od. Rum*); ⇒ *also* **gin sling**

**sling:** ~**back** *n.* ~**back [shoe]** Slingpumps, *der;* ~**shot** (*Amer.*) ⇒ **catapult** 1

**slink** /slɪŋk/ *v.i.*, **slunk** /slʌŋk/ schleichen

~ **a'way,** ~ **off** *v.i.* davonschleichen; sich fortstehlen

**slinkily** /'slɪŋkɪlɪ/ *adv.* aufreizend

**slinky** /'slɪŋkɪ/ *adj.* Ⓐ aufreizend; Ⓑ hauteng ‹Kleidung›

**slip** /slɪp/ ❶ *v.i.*, **-pp-:** Ⓐ (*slide*) rutschen; ‹Messer:› abrutschen; (*and fall*) ausrutschen; **he ~ped and broke his leg** er rutschte aus und brach sich (*Dat.*) das Bein; Ⓑ (*escape*) schlüpfen; **money ~s through my fingers like water** Geld zerrinnt mir zwischen den Fingern; **let the reins ~ out of one's hands** (*lit. or fig.*) sich (*Dat.*) die Zügel entgleiten lassen; **let a chance/opportunity ~:** sich (*Dat.*) eine Chance/Gelegenheit entgehen lassen; **let [it] ~ that ...:** verraten, dass ...; **let ~ the dogs of war** (*rhet.*) die Kriegsfurie loslassen; Ⓒ (*go*) **~ to the butcher's** [rasch] zum Fleischer rüberspringen (*ugs.*); **~ from the room/~ behind a curtain** aus dem Zimmer/hinter einen Vorhang schlüpfen; Ⓓ (*move smoothly*) gleiten; **everything ~ped into place** (*fig.*) alles fügte sich zusammen; Ⓔ (*make mistake*) [Flüchtigkeits]fehler machen; Ⓕ (*deteriorate*) nachlassen; ‹Moral, Niveau, Ansehen:› sinken.

❷ *v.t.*, **-pp-** Ⓐ stecken; **~ the dress over one's head** das Kleid über den Kopf streifen; **~ sb. sth.** jmdm. etw. zustecken; **~ sb. a glance** jmdm. einen verstohlenen Blick zuwerfen; Ⓑ (*escape from*) entwischen (+ *Dat.*); **the dog ~ped its collar** der Hund streifte sein Halsband ab; **the boat ~ped its mooring** das Boot löste sich aus seiner Verankerung; **~ sb.'s attention** jmds. Aufmerksamkeit (*Dat.*) entgehen; **~ sb.'s memory** *or* **mind** jmdm. entfallen; Ⓒ (*release*) loslassen; **~ a dog from its chain** einen Hund von der Kette lassen; Ⓓ (*Naut.*) slippen; **~ anchor** den Anker lichten; Ⓔ (*Motor Veh.*) schleifen lassen ‹Kupplung›; Ⓕ (*Knitting*) **~ a stitch** eine Masche abheben; Ⓖ (*Med.*) **~ a disc** einen Bandscheibenvorfall erleiden; ⇒ *also* **slipped disc**.

❸ *n.* Ⓐ (*fall*) **after his ~:** nachdem er ausgerutscht [und gestürzt] war; **a ~ on these steps could be nasty** auf diesen Stufen auszurutschen könnte schlimme Folgen haben; **have a [bad] ~:** [sehr unglücklich] ausrutschen; Ⓑ (*mistake*) Versehen, *das;* Ausrutscher, *der* (*ugs.*); **there's been a ~ in the accounts** bei der Berechnung ist ein Fehler unterlaufen; **a ~ of the tongue/pen** ein Versprecher/Schreibfehler; **I'm sorry, it was a ~ of the tongue/pen** Entschuldigung, ich habe mich versprochen/verschrieben; **make a ~:** einen Fehler machen; ⇒ *also* **cup** 1 A; Ⓒ (*underwear*) Unterrock, *der;* Ⓓ (*pillowcase*) [Kopf]kissenbezug, *der;* Ⓔ (*strip*) **~ of metal/plastic** Metall-/Plastikstreifen, *der;* **~ of wood** Holzleiste, *die;* **~ of glass** langes, schmales Stück Glas; Ⓕ (*piece of paper*) ‹Einzahlungs-, Wett›schein, *der;* **~ [of paper]** Zettel, *der;* Ⓖ **give sb. the ~** (*escape*) jmdm. entwischen (*ugs.*); (*avoid*) jmdm. ausweichen; Ⓗ (*Naut.: landing stage*) Aufschleppe, *die;* Slip, *der;* Ⓘ *in pl.* (*Shipb.*) Helling, *die od. der;* Ⓙ **a ~ of a boy/girl** ein zierlicher Junge/ein zierliches Mädchen; eine halbe Portion (*ugs.*); Ⓚ (*Cricket*) *Feldspieler, der seitlich hinter dem Tor aufgestellt ist;* **he was caught at ~** *or* **in the ~s** sein Ball wurde seitlich hinter dem Tor gefangen; Ⓛ (*Ceramics*) geschlämmter Ton. ⇒ *also* **gymslip**

~ **a'cross** *v.i.* rüberspringen (*ugs.*)

~ **a'way** *v.i.* Ⓐ (*leave quietly*) ‹Person:› sich fortschleichen; Ⓑ (*pass quickly*) ‹Zeit, Tage, Wochen usw.:› verfliegen

~ **'back** *v.i.* zurückschleichen; (*very quickly*) zurücksausen; **~ back into unconsciousness** wieder das Bewusstsein verlieren

~ **be'hind** *v.i.* zurückfallen; (*with one's work*) in Rückstand geraten

~ **'by** *v.i.* Ⓐ (*pass unnoticed*) vorbeischleichen; ‹Fehler:› durchrutschen (*ugs.*); Ⓑ ⇒ ~ **away** B

~ **'down** *v.i.* runterrutschen (*ugs.*); ‹Getränk:› die Kehle runterlaufen (*ugs.*)

~ **'in** ❶ *v.i.* sich hineinschleichen; (*enter briefly*) [kurz] reinkommen (*ugs.*); (*enter unnoticed*) ‹Fehler:› sich einschleichen. ❷ *v.t.* einfließen lassen ‹Bemerkung›

~ **into** *v.t.* Ⓐ (*put on*) schlüpfen in (+ *Akk.*) ‹Kleidungsstück›; Ⓑ (*lapse into*) verfallen in (+ *Akk.*)

~ **'off** ❶ *v.i.* Ⓐ (*slide down*) runterrutschen (*ugs.*); Ⓑ ⇒ ~ **away** A. ❷ *v.t.* abstreifen ‹Schmuck, Bezug, Handschuh›; schlüpfen aus ‹Kleid, Hose, Schuh›; ausziehen ‹Strumpf, Handschuh›

~ **'on** *v.t.* überstreifen ‹Bezug, Handschuh, Ring›; schlüpfen in (+ *Akk.*) ‹Kleid, Hose, Schuh›; anziehen ‹Strumpf, Handschuh›; anlegen ‹Schmuck›; ⇒ *also* **slip-on**

~ **'out** *v.i.* Ⓐ (*leave*) sich hinausschleichen; ~ **out to the butcher's** zum Fleischer rüberspringen (*ugs.*); ~ **out to have a cigarette** hinausschlüpfen, um eine Zigarette zu rauchen; Ⓑ (*be revealed*) **it ~ped out** es ist mir/dir/ihm *usw.* herausgerutscht

~ **'over** *v.i.* Ⓐ (*fall*) ausrutschen; Ⓑ ⇒ ~ **across**

~ **'past** ⇒ ~ **by**

~ **'round** *v.i.* rübergehen (*ugs.*); (*towards speaker*) rüberkommen (*ugs.*)

~ **'through** *v.i.* durchschlüpfen; ‹Fehler:› durchrutschen (*ugs.*)

~ **'up** *v.i.* (*coll.*) einen Schnitzer machen (*ugs.*) (**on, over** bei); ⇒ *also* **slip-up**

**slip:** ~ **case** *n.* Schuber, *der;* ~ **cover** *n.* Ⓐ (*for unused furniture*) Schutzüberzug, *der;* Ⓑ (*Amer.: loose cover*) Überzug, *der;* Ⓒ (*protective book jacket*) Schutzhülle, *die;* Buchhülle, *die;* Ⓓ ⇒ ~ **case**; ~ **knot** *n.* Ⓐ (*easily undone knot*) Slipstek, *der;* Ⓑ ⇒ **running knot**; **~-on** ❶ *adj.* **~-on shoes** Slipper; ❷ *n.* (*shoe*) Slipper, *der;* **~over** *n.* Pullunder, *der*

**slippage** /ˈslɪpɪdʒ/ *n.* Ⓐ (*Mech.*) Schlupf, *der;* Ⓑ (*Commerc.*) Rückstand, *der*

**slipped 'disc** *n.* (*Med.*) Bandscheibenvorfall, *der*

**slipper** /ˈslɪpə(r)/ *n.* Hausschuh, *der;* ⇒ *also* **hunt** 2 B

**'slipper bath** *n.* (*Brit.*) *teilweise abgedeckte Badewanne;* (*individual bath in public baths*) Wannenbad, *das*

**slippered** /ˈslɪpəd/ *adj.* in Hausschuhen *nachgestellt*

**slippery** /ˈslɪpərɪ/ *adj.* Ⓐ (*causing slipping*) schlüpfrig; glitschig; **the shoes are ~:** die Schuhe haben [sehr] glatte Sohlen; **be on a ~ path** *or* **slope** (*fig.*) auf einem verhängnisvollen Weg sein; Ⓑ (*elusive*) schlüpfrig; glitschig; wendig ‹Spieler›; (*shifty*) aalglatt (*abwertend*); (*unreliable*) windig (*ugs.*); **he is a ~ customer** er ist aalglatt (*abwertend*); **as ~ as an eel** aalglatt (*abwertend*); Ⓒ (*fig.: delicate*) heikel ‹Thema, Fall›

**slippy** /ˈslɪpɪ/ *adj.* Ⓐ (*coll.*) ⇒ **slippery**; Ⓑ (*Brit. coll.*) **be** *or* **look ~:** sich sputen (*veralt.*); sich ranhalten (*ugs.*)

**slip:** ~ **ring** *n.* (*Electr.*) Schleifring, *der;* ~ **road** *n.* (*Brit.*) (*for approach*) Zufahrtsstraße, *die;* (*to motorway*) Auffahrt, *die;* (*to estate*) Einfahrt, *die;* (*for leaving*) Ausfahrt, *die;* **~shod** *adj.* schlampig (*ugs. abwertend*); abgetreten ‹Schuh›; (*fig.: careless, unsystematic*) schlud[e]rig (*ugs. abwertend*); **~stream** *n.* Ⓐ (*of car, motorcycle*) Fahrtwind, *der;* (*Racing*) Windschatten, *der;* Ⓑ (*of propeller*) Propellerwind, *der;* (*of ship; also Brit. fig.*) Kielwasser, *das;* **~-up** *n.* (*coll.*) Schnitzer, *der* (*ugs.*); **there's been a ~-up somewhere** irgendwo hat jemand einen Schnitzer gemacht (*ugs.*); **~way** ⇒ **slip** 3 H, I

**slit** /slɪt/ ❶ *n.* Schlitz, *der;* **the sleeves have ~s in them** die Ärmel haben Schlitze *od.* sind geschlitzt; **make ~s in the fat of the pork** die Schwarte des Schweinebratens einritzen. ❷ *v.t.*, **-tt-**, **slit** Ⓐ aufschlitzen; ~ **sb.'s throat** jmdm. die Kehle durchschneiden; Ⓑ (*Dressmaking*) schlitzen ‹Rock, Ärmel›

**'slit-eyed** *adj.* schlitzäugig

**slither** /ˈslɪðə(r)/ *v.i.* rutschen; (*on ice, polished floor also*) schlittern

**slit:** ~ **'pocket** *n.* Durchgrifftasche, *die;* ~ **trench** *n.* (*Mil.*) Schützenloch, *das*

**sliver** /ˈslɪvə(r)/ *n.* Ⓐ (*slip*) (*of wood*) Span, *der;* (*of paper*) Streifen, *der;* (*of food*) dünne Scheibe; Ⓑ (*splinter*) Splitter, *der;* ~ **of wood/glass/bone** Holz-/Glas-/Knochensplitter, *der;* Ⓒ (*Textiles*) Kammzug, *der*

**slivovitz** /ˈslɪvəvɪts/ *n.* Slibowitz, *der*

**slob** /slɒb/ *n.* (*coll.*) Schwein, *das* (*derb*); **lazy ~:** fauler Sack (*salopp abwertend*); **fat ~:** Fettsack, *der* (*salopp abwertend*)

**slobber** /ˈslɒbə(r)/ ❶ *v.i.* sabbern (*ugs.*); ~ **over sb./sth.** jmdn./etw. besabbern; (*fig.*) von jmdm./etw. schwärmen. ❷ *v.t.* voll sabbern (*ugs.*). ❸ *n.* ⇒ **slaver**[1] 2

**slobbery** /ˈslɒbərɪ/ *adj.* **the bib is all ~:** das Lätzchen ist ganz vollgesabbert (*ugs.*); **a ~ kiss** ein [feuchter] Schmatz (*ugs.*)

**sloe** /sləʊ/ *n.* (*Bot.*) Schlehe, *die*

**sloe:** **~-eyed** *adj.* Ⓐ (*with ~-coloured eyes*) mit schwarzblauen Augen *nachgestellt;* Ⓑ (*slant-eyed*) schlitzäugig; ~ **gin** *n.* ≈ Schlehenlikör, *der;* Sloe-Gin, *der*

**slog** /slɒg/ ❶ *v.t.*, **-gg-** dreschen (*ugs.*) ‹Ball›; (*in boxing, fight*) voll treffen; (*with several blows*) eindreschen auf (+ *Akk.*) (*ugs.*). ❷ *v.i.*, **-gg-** Ⓐ (*hit*) draufschlagen (*ugs.*); Ⓑ (*fig.: work doggedly*) sich abplagen; schuften (*ugs.*); (*for school, exams*) büffeln (*ugs.*); Ⓒ (*walk doggedly*) sich schleppen; ~ **along** sich dahinschleppen. ❸ *n.* Ⓐ (*hit*) [wuchtiger] Schlag; **give sb./sth. a ~:** jmdm./einer Sache einen wuchtigen Schlag versetzen; Ⓑ (*hard work*) Plackerei, *die* (*ugs.*); **it took me a good two hours' ~:** ich musste mich gut zwei Stunden abplagen; Ⓒ (*tiring walk, hike*) [auf die Knochen gehender] Fußmarsch

~ **at** *v.t.* Ⓐ (*hit*) ~ **at sb./sth.** auf jmdn./etw. eindreschen (*ugs.*); Ⓑ (*work hard at*) sich abplagen mit

~ **a'way** *v.i.* sich abplagen; ~ **away at sth.** sich mit etw. abplagen; **keep ~ging away!** streng dich weiter an!

~ **'out** *v.t.* (*coll.*) ~ **it out** es [bis zum Ende] durchstehen; ~ **one's guts out** sich kaputtarbeiten (*ugs.*)

**slogan** /ˈsləʊgən/ *n.* Ⓐ (*striking phrase*) Slogan, *der;* (*advertising* ~) Werbeslogan, *der;* Werbespruch, *der;* Ⓑ (*motto*) Wahlspruch, *der;* (*in political campaign*) [Wahl]slogan, *der*

**slogger** /ˈslɒgə(r)/ *n.* Ⓐ (*hitter*) **be a [real] ~:** immer nur draufschlagen (*ugs.*); Ⓑ (*hard worker*) Arbeitstier, *das* (*fig.*)

**sloop** /sluːp/ *n.* (*Naut.*) Slup, *die*

**'sloop-rigged** *adj.* (*Naut.*) mit Sluptakelung *nachgestellt;* **be ~:** Sluptakelung haben

**slop** /slɒp/ ❶ *v.i.*, **-pp-** schwappen (**out of, from** aus). ❷ *v.t.*, **-pp-** Ⓐ (*spill*) (*unintentionally*) schwappen; (*intentionally*) kippen; klatschen (*ugs.*) ‹Farbe an die Wand›; Ⓑ (*make mess on*) voll schütten. ❸ *n.* Ⓐ (*liquid food*) Schleim, *der;* Geschlabber, *das* (*ugs.*); Ⓑ (*spilt liquid*) Lache, *die;* Ⓒ (*fig. derog.: gush*) Geseire, *das* (*ugs.*). ⇒ *also* **slops** A

~ **a'bout**, ~ **a'round** *v.i.* Ⓐ (*splash about*) herumschwappen (*ugs.*); Ⓑ (*move in slovenly manner*) herumschlurfen (*ugs.*)

~ **'out** *v.i.* die Toiletteneimer leeren

~ **'over** *v.i.* (*splash over*) überschwappen

**'slop basin** *n.* (*Brit.*) *Schale für den Bodensatz aus der* [*Tee*]*tasse*

**slope** /sləʊp/ ❶ *n.* Ⓐ (*slant*) Neigung, *die;* (*of river*) Gefälle, *das;* **there is a downward/upward ~ to the garden** der Garten fällt ab/steigt an; **the house is built on a steep/gentle ~:** das Haus steht an einem steilen/sanften Hang; **the roof was at a ~ of 45°** das Dach hatte eine Neigung von 45°; **be on a** *or* **the ~:** geneigt sein; Ⓑ (*slanting ground*) Hang, *der;* Ⓒ (*Skiing*) Piste, *die.* ❷ *v.i.* (*slant*) sich neigen; ‹Wand, Mauer:› schief sein; ‹Boden, Garten:› abschüssig sein; ~ **upwards/downwards** ‹Straße:› ansteigen/abfallen. ❸ *v.t.* abschrägen; ~ **arms** (*Mil.*) das Gewehr schultern; ~ **arms!** (*Mil.*) Gewehr über!

~ **a'way** *v.i.* Ⓐ (*slant*) abfallen; Ⓑ ⇒ ~ **off**

~ **down** *v.i.* sich hinabneigen

~ **'off** *v.i.* (*coll.*) sich verdrücken (*ugs.*)

~ **'up** *v.i.* Ⓐ (*rise*) ansteigen; Ⓑ (*approach casually*) daherkommen; ~ **up to sb.** auf jmdn. zugehen/zukommen

**'slop pail** *n.* Toiletteneimer, *der;* (*for kitchen slops*) Abfalleimer, *der*

**sloppily** /ˈslɒpɪlɪ/ *adv.* Ⓐ (*carelessly*) schlud[e]rig (*ugs. abwertend*); **she speaks English rather ~:** sie spricht ein ziemlich schlud[e]riges Englisch (*ugs. abwertend*); Ⓑ (*untidily*) unordentlich; schlampig (*ugs. abwertend*); Ⓒ (*sentimentally*) voller Rührseligkeit

**sloppy** /ˈslɒpɪ/ *adj.* Ⓐ (*careless*) schlud[e]rig (*ugs. abwertend*); Ⓑ (*untidy*) unordentlich; schlampig (*ugs. abwertend*); Ⓒ (*splashed*) voll geschwappt; Ⓓ (*sentimental*) rührselig; **it's ~ to kiss Grandma at my age** ich bin schon zu erwachsen, um Großmama einen Kuss zu geben

**sloppy Joe** /slɒpi ˈdʒəʊ/ *n. langer, weiter Pullover für Mädchen;* Schlabberpulli, *der* (*ugs.*)

**slops** /slɒps/ *n. pl.* Ⓐ Schmutzwasser, *das;* (*contents of bedroom or prison vessels*) Fäkalien *Pl.;* **empty the ~:** die Nachttöpfe leeren und das Schmutzwasser beseitigen; Ⓑ ⇒ **slop** 3 A

**slosh** /slɒʃ/ ❶ *v.i.* platschen (*ugs.*); ‹Flüssigkeit:› schwappen. ❷ *v.t.* Ⓐ (*coll.: pour clumsily*) schwappen; Ⓑ (*coll.: pour liquid on*) übergießen; Ⓒ (*Brit. coll.: hit*) verdreschen (*ugs.*). ❸ *n.* Ⓐ ⇒ **slush**; Ⓑ (*Brit. coll.: heavy blow*) [wuchtiger] Schlag

~ **a'bout**, ~ **a'round** ❶ *v.i.* Ⓐ (*splash about playfully*) herumspritzen (*ugs.*); Ⓑ (*slop about*) herumschwappen (*ugs.*). ❷ *v.t.* verspritzen

**sloshed** /slɒʃt/ *adj.* (*Brit. coll.*) blau (*ugs.*)

**slot** /slɒt/ ❶ *n.* Ⓐ (*hole*) Schlitz, *der;* Ⓑ (*groove*) Nut, *die;* **the ~ for a tenon** das Zapfenloch (*Technik*); Ⓒ (*coll.: position*) Platz, *der;* Ⓓ (*coll.: in schedule*) Termin, *der;* (*Radio, Telev.*) Sendezeit, *die;* **the news will go out in its usual ~ at 10 o'clock** die Nachrichten werden wie üblich um 10 Uhr gesendet. ❷ *v.t.*, **-tt-** Ⓐ (*provide with holes*) schlitzen; (*provide with grooves*) nuten; Ⓑ (*insert*) ~ **sth. into place/sth.** etw. einfügen/in etw. (*Akk.*) einfügen. ❸ *v.i.*, **-tt-:** ~ **into place/sth.** (*lit. or fig.*) sich einfügen/in etw. (*Akk.*) einfügen; **everything ~ted into place** (*fig.*) alles fügte sich zusammen

~ **'in** ❶ *v.t.* einfügen; **can you ~ me in at 10 o'clock?** (*fig.*) können Sie mich um 10 Uhr dazwischenschieben?. ❷ *v.i.* (*lit. or fig.*) sich einfügen

~ **to'gether** ❶ *v.t.* zusammenfügen. ❷ *v.i.* (*lit. or fig.*) sich zusammenfügen

**sloth** /sləʊθ/ *n.* Ⓐ *no pl.* (*lethargy*) Trägheit, *die;* Ⓑ (*Zool.*) Faultier, *das*

**'sloth bear** *n.* (*Zool.*) Lippenbär, *der*

**slothful** /ˈsləʊθfl/ *adj.* träge; schwerfällig ‹Anstrengungen, Versuche›; **a life of ~ ease** ein Leben träger Bequemlichkeit; **develop ~ habits** ziemlich träge werden

**slot:** ~ **machine** *n.* Ⓐ (*vending machine*) Automat, *der;* Ⓑ (*Amer.*) ⇒ **fruit machine**; ~ **meter** *n.* Münzzähler, *der*

**slouch** /slaʊtʃ/ ❶ *n.* Ⓐ (*posture*) schlaffe Haltung; **walk with a ~:** einen nachlässigen Gang haben; Ⓑ (*coll.: lazy person*) Faulpelz, *der;* **be no ~ at sth.** etwas loshaben in etw. (*Dat.*); **he's no ~ at billiards/at geography** er ist verdammt gut im Billard/in Geographie (*ugs.*). ❷ *v.i.* Ⓐ sich schlecht halten; **don't ~!** halte dich gerade!; Ⓑ (*be ungainly*) sich herumflegeln (*ugs. abwertend*); **sit ~ed over one's desk** schlaff über seinem Schreibtisch hängen

~ **a'bout**, ~ **a'round** *v.i.* herumlungern (*salopp*)

**'slouch hat** *n.* Schlapphut, *der*

**slough**[1] /slaʊ/ *n.* (*literary*) Sumpf, *der;* ⇒ *also* **despond** 2

**slough**[2] /slʌf/ ❶ *n.* Ⓐ (*Zool.*) abgestreifte Haut; (*whole skin of snake*) Natternhemd,

S

das; Ⓑ (*Med.*) Schorf, *der.* ❷ *v.t.* (*Zool.; fig.: abandon*) abstreifen

~ **'off** ⇒ **slough² 2**

**Slovak** /'sləʊvæk/ ▶1275, ▶1340 ❶ *adj.* slowakisch; **sb. is ~:** jmd. ist Slowake/Slowakin; ⇒ *also* **English** 1. ❷ *n.* Ⓐ (*person*) Slowake, *der*/Slowakin, *die;* Ⓑ (*language*) Slowakisch, *das;* ⇒ *also* **English** 2 A

**Slovakia** /slə'vɑ:kɪə/ *pr. n.* Slowakei, *die*

**sloven** /'slʌvn/ *n.* (*female*) Schlampe, *die* (*ugs. abwertend*); (*male*) Liederjan, *der* (*ugs. abwertend*)

**Slovene** /'sləʊvi:n/ ▶1275, ▶1340 ❶ *adj.* slowenisch. ❷ *n.* Ⓐ (*person*) Slowene, *der*/Slowenin, *die;* Ⓑ (*language*) Slowenisch, *das*

**Slovenia** /slə'vi:nɪə/ *pr. n.* Slowenien (*das*)

**Slovenian** /slə'vi:nɪən/ ⇒ **Slovene**

**slovenliness** /'slʌvnlɪnɪs/ *n., no pl.* Schlampigkeit, *die* (*ugs. abwertend*)

**slovenly** /'slʌvnlɪ/ ❶ *adj.* schlampig (*ugs.*); schlud[e]rig (*ugs.*); **be a ~ dresser** sich schlampig *od.* schlud[e]rig anziehen (*ugs.*). ❷ *adv.* schlampig (*ugs.*); schlud[e]rig (*ugs.*)

**slow** /sləʊ/ ❶ *adj.* Ⓐ langsam; **~ and steady wins the race, ~ and sure does it** eile mit Weile! (*Spr.*); **~ but sure** langsam, aber zuverlässig; Ⓑ (*gradual*) langsam; langwierig ‹Suche, Arbeit›; **make a ~ recovery from one's illness** sich nur langsam von seiner Krankheit erholen; **be ~ in doing sth.** etw. langsam tun; **get off to a ~ start** beim Start langsam wegkommen; ‹Aufruf, Produkt:› zunächst nur wenig Anklang finden; **make ~ progress [in** *or* **at** *or* **with sth.]** nur langsam [mit etw.] vorankommen; ⇒ *also* **going** 1 B; Ⓒ ▶1012 **be ~ [by ten minutes], be [ten minutes] ~** ‹Uhr:› [zehn Minuten] nachgehen; Ⓓ (*preventing quick motion*) nur langsam befahrbar ‹Strecke, Straße, Belag›; Ⓔ (*tardy*) **[not] be ~ to do sth.** [nicht] zögern, etw. zu tun; Ⓕ (*not easily roused*) **be ~ to anger/to take offence** sich nicht leicht ärgern/beleidigen lassen; Ⓖ (*dull-witted*) schwerfällig; langsam; **be ~ at mathematics** sich in Mathematik schwer tun (*ugs.*); **be ~ [to understand]** schwer *od.* langsam von Begriff sein (*ugs.*); **be ~ of speech** schwerfällig *od.* unbeholfen sprechen; ⇒ *also* **uptake**; Ⓗ (*burning feebly*) schwach; Ⓘ (*uninteresting*) langweilig; Ⓙ (*Commerc.*) flau ‹Geschäft›; Ⓚ (*not hot*) **bake in a ~ oven** bei schwacher Hitze backen; Ⓛ (*Photog.*) niedrigempfindlich ‹Film›; lichtschwach ‹Objektiv›; Ⓜ **~ court** (*Tennis*)/**~ wicket** (*Cricket*) langsamer Platz.

❷ *adv.* langsam; '**~**' „langsam fahren!"; **go ~:** langsam fahren; (*Brit. Industry*) langsam arbeiten.

❸ *v.i.* langsamer werden; **we ~ed to a gentle walk** wir wurden immer langsamer, bis wir nur noch gemächlich gingen; **~ to a halt** anhalten; ‹Zug:› zum Stehen kommen; ‹Produktion:› zum Erliegen kommen.

❹ *v.t.* **~ a train/car** die Geschwindigkeit eines Zuges/Wagens verringern; **the accident ~ed traffic to a crawl** der Unfall verlangsamte den Verkehr derart, dass er sich nur noch kriechend vorwärts bewegte

~ **'down** ❶ *v.i.* Ⓐ langsamer werden; seine Geschwindigkeit verringern; (*in working/speaking*) langsamer arbeiten/sprechen; ‹Produktion, Geburten-/Sterbeziffer, Inflations[rate]:› sinken; Ⓑ (*reduce pace of living*) langsamer machen (*ugs.*); **have to ~ down after a heart attack** nach einem Herzanfall kürzer treten müssen. ❷ *v.t.* verlangsamen; **the driver ~ed the car/train down** der Autofahrer/Lokomotivführer fuhr langsamer; **the accident ~ed traffic down to a crawl** der Unfall verlangsamte den Verkehr derart, dass er sich nur noch kriechend vorwärts bewegte; **~ down one's pace of living** kürzer treten; **[You can't help me.] You'd only ~ me down** [Du kannst mir nicht helfen.] Du würdest mich nur aufhalten; **his illness has ~ed him down a lot** durch seine Krankheit ist seine Leistungsfähigkeit stark zurückgegangen. ⇒ *also* **slow-down**

~ **'up** ⇒ ~ **down**

**slow: ~ 'bowler** *n.* (*Cricket*) langsamer Werfer; **~coach** *n.* Trödler, *der*/Trödlerin, *die* (*ugs. abwertend*); **~down** *n.* Ⓐ (*deceleration*) Verlangsamung, *die* (**in** *Gen.*); (*in birth, death, inflation rate, output, production, number*) Sinken, *das* (**in** *Gen.*); **there's been a ~down in the number of ...:** die Zahl der ... ist gesunken; Ⓑ (*go-slow*) Bummelstreik, *der;* **~ 'handclap** *n.* (*Brit.*) müdes Klatschen (*als Ausdruck des Missfallens*)

**slowly** /'sləʊlɪ/ *adv.* langsam; **~ but surely** langsam, aber sicher

**slow: ~ 'march** *n.* (*Mil.*) langsamer Defiliermarsch; **~ match** *n.* Lunte, *die;* **~ 'motion** *n.* (*Cinemat.*) Zeitlupe, *die;* **in ~ motion** in Zeitlupe; **~ motion replay** (*Sport*) Zeitlupenwiederholung, *die;* **~-moving** *adj.* Ⓐ sich langsam fortbewegend; Ⓑ (*Commerc.*) schlecht gehend; **be ~-moving** schlecht gehen

**slowness** /'sləʊnɪs/ *n., no pl.* Ⓐ Langsamkeit, *die;* Ⓑ (*gradualness*) Langsamkeit, *die;* (*of search, work*) Langwierigkeit, *die;* Ⓒ (*slackness*) Zögern, *das;* **his ~ to react** *or* **in reacting** sein zögerndes Reagieren; Ⓓ (*stupidity*) Schwerfälligkeit, *die;* **~ [of comprehension/mind/wit]** Begriffsstutzigkeit, *die* (*abwertend*); Ⓔ (*dullness*) Langweiligkeit, *die*

**slow: ~ 'poison** ⇒ **poison** 1; **~poke** (*Amer.*) ⇒ **slowcoach**; **~ 'puncture** *n.* winziges Loch (*durch das ein Reifen o. ä. nur langsam die Luft verliert*); **~-witted** /sləʊ'wɪtɪd/ *adj.* [geistig] schwerfällig; **~-worm** *n.* (*Zool.*) Blindschleiche, *die*

**SLR** *abbr.* (*Photog.*) **single-lens reflex**

**slub** /slʌb/ *n.* (*Textiles*) Noppe, *die*

**sludge** /slʌdʒ/ *n.* Ⓐ (*mud*) Matsch, *der* (*ugs.*); Schlamm, *der;* Ⓑ (*sediment*) [schlammiger] Bodensatz; Ⓒ (*Motor Veh.*) Ölschlamm, *der;* Ⓓ (*sewage*) Klärschlamm, *der*

**slug¹** /slʌg/ *n.* Ⓐ (*Zool.*) Nacktschnecke, *die;* Ⓑ (*bullet*) [rohe] Gewehrkugel; Flintenlaufgeschoss, *das* (*Waffent.*); Ⓒ (*for airgun*) Luftgewehrkugel, *die;* Ⓓ (*lump of metal*) [rundlicher] Metallklumpen; **a ~ of gold/platinum/silver** *etc.* ein Klumpen Gold/Platin/Silber *usw.;* Ⓔ (*Amer.: tot of liquor*) **a ~ of whisky/rum** *etc.* ein Schluck Whisky/Rum *usw.;* Ⓕ (*Printing*) (*bar*) Reglette, *die;* (*line*) gegossene Zeile

**slug²** (*Amer.: hit*) ❶ *v.t.*, **-gg-** niederschlagen. ❷ *n.* [harter] Schlag; **give sb. a ~:** jmdn. niederschlagen

~ **'out** *v.t.* **~ it out** es [bis zum Ende] austragen; **the boys were ~ging it out to decide who ...:** die Jungen prügelten sich darum, wer ...

**sluggard** /'slʌgəd/ *n.* Faulpelz, *der;* (*lacking in speed*) lahme Ente (*ugs.*)

**sluggish** /'slʌgɪʃ/ *adj.* träge; schleppend ‹Gang, Schritt›; schwerfällig ‹Reaktion, Vorstellungskraft›; (*Commerc.*) flau; schleppend ‹Nachfrage, Geschäftsgang›

**sluggishly** /'slʌgɪʃlɪ/ *adv.* träge; schleppenden Schrittes ‹gehen, sich bewegen›; schwerfällig ‹reagieren›; (*Commerc.*) schleppend ‹sich verkaufen, vorangehen›

**sluice** /slu:s/ ❶ *n.* Ⓐ (*Hydraulic Engin.*) Schütz, *das;* Ⓑ (*water*) *vom Schütz aufgestautes/durch das Schütz fließendes Wasser;* Ⓒ ⇒ **sluiceway**; Ⓓ (*rinsing*) **give sb./sth. a ~ [down]** (*with hose*) jmdn./etw. abspritzen; (*with bucket*) jmdn./etw. [mit Wasser] übergießen. ❷ *v.t.* Ⓐ (*Hydraulic Engin.*) unter Wasser setzen; Ⓑ (*provide with sluices*) mit Schützen versehen; Ⓒ (*Mining*) waschen; Ⓓ **~ [down]** (*douse*) (*with hose*) abspritzen; (*with bucket*) übergießen

~ **a'way** *v.t.* wegspülen; (*with hose*) wegspritzen

~ **'out** *v.t.* ausspülen; (*with hose*) ausspritzen

**sluice: ~ gate** *n.* (*Hydraulic Engin.*) Schütz, *das;* **~ valve** *n.* (*Hydraulic Engin.*) Schieber, *der;* **~way** *n.* Ⓐ (*Hydraulic Engin.: channel for sluice*) Gerinne, *das;* Ⓑ (*Mining*) Waschrinne, *die*

**slum** /slʌm/ ❶ *n.* Slum, *der;* (*single house or apartment*) Elendsquartier, *das.* ❷ *v.i.*, **-mm-: go ~ming** in die Slums gehen; (*fig.*) sich unters [gemeine] Volk mischen. ❸ *v.t.*, **-mm-: ~ it** wie arme Leute leben; (*fig.*) sich unters [gemeine] Volk mischen

**slumber** /'slʌmbə(r)/ (*poet./rhet.*) ❶ *n.* (*lit. or fig.*) **~[s]** Schlummer, *der* (*geh.*); **fall into a light/long ~:** in leichten/tiefen Schlummer sinken; **be in a ~** (*fig.*) schlummern (*geh.*). ❷ *v.i.* (*lit. or fig.*) schlummern (*geh.*); ‹Vulkan:› ruhen

~ **a'way** *v.t.* verschlafen

**slumberous** /'slʌmbərəs/ *adj.* (*poet./rhet.*) Ⓐ (*sleepy*) schläfrig; Ⓑ (*sleep-inducing*) einschläfernd

**'slumberwear** *n.* (*Commerc.*) Nachtwäsche, *die*

**slumbrous** /'slʌmbrəs/ ⇒ **slumberous**

**'slum clearance** *n.* Slumsanierung, *die*

**slummy** /'slʌmɪ/ *adj.* verslumt

**slump** /slʌmp/ ❶ *n.* Sturz, *der* (*fig.*); (*in demand, investment, sales, production*) starker Rückgang (**in** *Gen.*); (*economic depression*) Depression, *die* (*Wirtsch.*); (*in morale, interest, popularity*) Nachlassen, *das* (**in** *Gen.*); **~ in prices** Preissturz, *der.* ❷ *v.i.* Ⓐ (*Commerc.*) stark zurückgehen; ‹Preise, Kurse:› stürzen (*fig.*); **the economy ~ed** die Wirtschaft geriet in eine Depression; Ⓑ (*be diminished*) ‹Popularität, Moral, Unterstützung usw.:› nachlassen; Ⓒ (*collapse*) fallen; **they found him ~ed over the table/in his chair/on the floor** sie fanden ihn über dem Tisch/auf seinem Stuhl/auf dem Boden zusammengesunken

~ **'down** *v.i.* zusammensinken

**slung** ⇒ **sling¹** 2

**slunk** ⇒ **slink**

**slur** /slɜ:(r)/ ❶ *v.t.*, **-rr-: ~ one's words/speech** undeutlich sprechen; **~red speech** undeutliche Aussprache. ❷ *v.i.*, **-rr-: his speech began to ~:** er begann undeutlich zu sprechen. ❸ *n.* Ⓐ (*stigma*) Schande, *die* (**on** für); (*imputation*) Verleumdung, *die;* (*insult*) Beleidigung, *die* (**on** für); **cast a ~ on sb./sth.** jmdn./etw. verunglimpfen (*geh.*); **it's a/no ~ on his reputation** es schmälert seinen Ruf/seinen Ruf nicht; Ⓑ (*Mus.*) [Legato]bogen, *der*

**slurp** /slɜ:p/ ❶ *v.t.* **~ [up]** schlürfen. ❷ *n.* Schlürfen, *das;* **drink one's juice in three big ~s** seinen Saft in drei Zügen ausschlürfen; **drink [one's beer] with a ~:** beim [Bier]trinken schlürfen

**slurry** /'slʌrɪ/ *n.* Ⓐ (*liquid cement*) Zementbrühe, *die;* Ⓑ (*suspension*) Schlamm, *der;* Suspension, *die* (*Chemie*); Ⓒ (*thin mud*) Schlammbrühe, *die;* Ⓓ (*Mining*) Kohlenschlamm, *der;* Ⓔ (*Agric.*) Gülle, *die*

**slush** /slʌʃ/ *n.* Ⓐ (*thawing snow*) Schneematsch, *der;* Ⓑ (*fig. derog.: sentiment*) sentimentaler Kitsch

**'slush fund** *n.* Fonds für Bestechungsgelder

**slushy** /'slʌʃɪ/ *adj.* Ⓐ (*wet*) matschig; Ⓑ (*derog.: sloppy*) sentimental

**slut** /slʌt/ *n.* Schlampe, *die* (*ugs. abwertend*)

**sluttish** /'slʌtɪʃ/ *adj.* schlampig (*ugs. abwertend*)

**sly** /slaɪ/ ❶ *adj.* Ⓐ (*crafty*) schlau; gerissen (*ugs.*) ‹Geschäftsmann, Schachzug, Trick›; verschlagen (*abwertend*) ‹Blick›; **he is a ~ one** *or* **type** *or* **customer** das ist ein ganz Gerissener *od.* Schlauer (*ugs.*); Ⓑ (*secretive*) heimlichtuerisch; verschlagen (*abwertend*) ‹Rivale›; **what a ~ one he is!** so ein Heimlichtuer!; **a ~ dog** (*fig. coll.*) ein Heimlichtuer/eine Heimlichtuerin; Ⓒ (*knowing*) viel sagend ‹Blick, Lächeln›. ❷ *n.* **on the ~:** heimlich; **he is a womanizer on the ~:** er ist ein heimlicher Schürzenjäger

**'slyboots** *n. sing.* (*coll.*) Schlauberger, *der* (*ugs.*); (*secretive person*) Heimlichtuer, *der*/Heimlichtuerin, *die*

**slyly** /'slaɪlɪ/ *adv.* Ⓐ (*craftily*) schlau; arglistig ‹täuschen›; Ⓑ (*secretively*) heimlich; Ⓒ (*knowingly*) viel sagend ‹blicken, lächeln›

**smack¹** /smæk/ ❶ *n.* Ⓐ (*flavour*) Beigeschmack, *der;* (*smell*) Duft, *der;* Ⓑ (*trace*) Spur, *die;* (*fig.*) Anflug, *der.* ❷ *v.i.* **~ of** (*taste of*) schmecken nach; (*smell of*) riechen nach; (*fig.*) riechen nach (*ugs.*)

S

**smack²** ❶ *n.* (A) (*sound*) Klatsch, *der;* (*of lips*) Schmatzen, *das;* (*of hand, stick*) Klatschen, *das;* (B) (*blow*) Schlag, *der;* (*on child's bottom*) Klaps, *der* (*ugs.*); **a ~ in the face** eine Ohrfeige; **a ~ in the eye** *or* **face** (*fig.*) ein Schlag ins Gesicht; (C) (*coll.: attempt*) **have a ~ at sth.** es mit etw. versuchen; **he had a ~ at the world record** er versuchte, den Weltrekord zu verbessern; **have a ~ at doing sth.** versuchen, etw. zu tun; (D) (*loud kiss*) Schmatz, *der* (*ugs.*).
❷ *v.t.* (A) (*slap*) [mit der flachen Hand] schlagen; (*lightly*) einen Klaps (*ugs.*) geben (+ *Dat.*); **~ sb.'s face/bottom/hand** jmdn. ohrfeigen/jmdm. eins hintendrauf geben (*ugs.*)/jmdm. eins auf die Hand geben (*ugs.*); **I'll ~ your bottom!** du kriegst eins hintendrauf! (*ugs.*); (B) **~ one's lips** [mit den Lippen] schmatzen; (C) (*propel*) knallen (*ugs.*).
❸ *v.i.* **~ into the net/wall** ins Netz/gegen die Mauer knallen (*ugs.*); **I ~ed into him** wir knallten zusammen (*ugs.*).
❹ *adv.* (A) (*coll.: with a ~*) **go ~ into a lamp post** gegen einen Laternenpfahl knallen (*ugs.*); (B) (*exactly*) direkt

**smack³** *n.* (*sl.: heroin*) Junk, *der* (*Drogenjargon*)

**smack⁴** *n.* (*Naut.*) Fischkutter, *der*

**smacker** /ˈsmækə(r)/ *n.* (*coll.*) (A) (*loud kiss*) Schmatz, *der* (*ugs.*); (B) (*blow*) [wuchtiger] Schlag; **give** *or* **deal sb. a ~ on the nose** jmdm. voll auf die Nase hauen (*ugs.*); (C) (*Brit.: £1*) Pfund, *das;* ≈ Scheinchen, *das* (*ugs.*); (D) (*Amer.: $1*) Dollar, *der;* ≈ Scheinchen, *das* (*ugs.*)

**small** /smɔːl/ ❶ *adj.* (A) ▶ 1210 (*in size*) klein; gering ‹Wirkung, Appetit, Fähigkeit›; schmal ‹Taille, Handgelenk›; dünn ‹Stimme›; **I'm afraid I've nothing ~er** ich habe es leider nicht kleiner (*ugs.*); **it's a ~ world** die Welt ist klein; **they came in ~ numbers** es kamen nur wenige; **the ~est room** (*fig. coll. euphem.*) das Örtchen (*fam. verhüll.*); ⇒ *also* **hour** B; **still** 1 E; (B) *attrib.* (*~-scale*) klein; Klein‹aktionär, -sparer, -händler, -betrieb, -bauer›; ⇒ *also* **way** 1 K; (C) (*young, not fully grown*) klein; ⇒ *also* **fry²**; (D) (*of the ~er kind*) klein; **~ letter** Kleinbuchstabe, *der;* **spell with a ~ letter** klein schreiben; **feel ~** (*fig.*) sich (*Dat.*) ganz klein vorkommen; **look ~** (*fig.*) [ziemlich] schlecht aussehen (*ugs.*); **make sb. feel/look ~** (*fig.*) jmdn. beschämen/ein schlechtes Licht auf jmdn. werfen; ⇒ *also* **arm²** 1 A; **beer**; **circle** 1 A; **intestine**; **mercy** 1 B; **slam²** A; (E) (*not much*) wenig; **it's ~ comfort** es ist ein geringer Trost; **demand for/interest in the product was ~:** die Nachfrage nach/das Interesse an dem Produkt war gering; **have ~ cause for sth./to do sth.** wenig Grund zu etw. haben/wenig Grund haben, etw. zu tun; **[it's] ~ wonder** [es ist] kein Wunder; **no ~ excitement/feat** einige Aufregung/keine geringe Leistung; (F) (*trifling*) klein; **we have a few ~ matters/points/problems to clear up before ...:** es sind noch ein paar Kleinigkeiten zu klären, bevor ...; (G) (*minor*) unbedeutend; gering ‹Ruhm, Anerkennung›; **great and ~:** hoch und niedrig; (H) (*petty*) kleinlich (*abwertend*); **have a ~ mind** ein Kleinkrämer sein (*abwertend*); (I) (*fine*) fein ‹Kies, Schrot›.
❷ *n.* (*Anat.*) **~ of the back** Kreuz, *das;* ⇒ *also* **smalls**.
❸ *adv.* klein

**small:** **~ 'ad** *n.* (*coll.*) Kleinanzeige, *die;* **the ~ ads section/pages/column** der Teil/die Seiten/die Rubrik mit den Kleinanzeigen; **~-bore** *adj.* (*Arms*) kleinkalibrig; Kleinkaliber-; **~ 'capital** *n.* (*Printing*) Kapitälchen, *das;* **~ 'change** *n., no pl., no indef. art.* (A) (*coins*) Kleingeld, *das;* (B) (*remarks*) Trivialitäten; (*business*) Kleinkram, der (*ugs.*); **~ 'claim** *n.* (*Law*) ≈ Bagatellsache, *die;* **~ 'claims court** *n.* (*Law*) *Gericht für Bagatellsachen;* **~ craft** *n. pl.* (*Naut.*) Boote; **~ goods** *n. pl.* (*Austral.*) feine Fleisch- und Wurstwaren; **~holder** *n.* ▶ 1261 (*Brit. Agric.*) Kleinbauer, *der*/-bäuerin, *die;* **~holding** *n.* (*Brit. Agric.*) landwirtschaftlicher Kleinbetrieb

**smallish** /ˈsmɔːlɪʃ/ *adj.* ziemlich klein/gering; ziemlich schmal ‹Taille›

**small:** **~-'minded** *adj.* kleinlich; engstirnig, kleingeistig ‹Einstellung›; **~mindedness** /smɔːlˈmaɪndɪdnɪs/ *n.* kleinliche Art; Krämergeist, *der* (*abwertend*)

**smallness** /ˈsmɔːlnɪs/ *n., no pl.* (A) Kleinheit, *die;* (*of waist*) Schmalheit, *die;* (*of income, amount, stock*) Bescheidenheit, *die;* (B) (*pettiness*) Kleinlichkeit, *die;* **~ of mind** ⇒ **small-mindedness**

**small:** **~pox** *n.* ▶ 1232 (*Med.*) Pocken *Pl.;* **~ 'print** *n.* (*lit. or fig.*) Kleingedruckte, *das*

**smalls** /smɔːlz/ *n. pl.* (*Brit. coll.*) Unterwäsche, *die*

**small:** **~-scale** *attrib. adj.* in kleinem Maßstab *nachgestellt;* klein ‹Konflikt, Unternehmer›; Klein‹betrieb, -bauer, -gärtner›; **~ 'screen** *n.* (*Telev.*) Bildschirm, *der;* **~-size** ⇒ **-size**; **~ talk** *n.* leichte Unterhaltung; (*at parties*) Smalltalk, *der;* **engage in** *or* **make ~ talk [with sb.]** [mit jmdm.] Konversation machen; **sb. has no ~ talk** leichte Konversation liegt jmdm. einfach nicht; **~-time** *attrib. adj.* (*coll.*) Schmalspur- (*ugs. abwertend*); **~-time crook** kleiner Ganove (*ugs. abwertend*); **~-town** *attrib. adj.* Kleinstadt-; kleinstädtisch

**smarm** /smɑːm/ *v.i.* (*coll.*) schöntun (*ugs.*); **~ to sb.** jmdm. schöntun (*ugs.*); **~ over sb.** sich bei jmdm. anbiedern (*abwertend*)

**~ 'down** *v.t.* **~ down one's hair** sein Haar [mit Frisiercreme/Haarwasser] glätten

**smarmy** /ˈsmɑːmɪ/ *adj.* kriecherisch (*abwertend*); schmeichlerisch ‹Stimme›; **her ~ approaches** ihre Anbiederungsversuche; **he's so ~:** er ist solch ein Kriecher (*abwertend*)

**smart** /smɑːt/ ❶ *adj.* (A) (*clever*) clever; smart; (*ingenious*) raffiniert; (*accomplished*) hervorragend; **get ~** (*Amer. coll.*) zur Vernunft kommen; **act** *or* **get ~ with sb.** (*Amer. coll.*) zu jmdm. *od.* jmdm. gegenüber frech werden; **~ money** (*Finance*) Geld der klugen Geschäftsleute; (B) (*neat*) schick; schön ‹Haus, Garten, Auto›; **keep sth. ~:** etw. gut in Ordnung halten; **he made a ~ job of it** er hat es schön gemacht; (C) *attrib.* (*fashionable*) elegant; smart; **the ~ set** die elegante Welt; die Schickeria; (D) (*vigorous*) hart ‹Schlag, Gefecht›; scharf ‹Zurechtweisung, Schmerz, Schritt›; (E) (*prompt*) flink; **look ~:** sich beeilen; (F) *attrib.* (*dishonest*) nicht ganz reell ‹Geschäft, Handel, Praktiken, Trick›; (G) *attrib.* (*unscrupulous*) clever.
❷ *adv.* ⇒ **smartly**.
❸ *v.i.* schmerzen; **I/my leg ~ed with pain** ich verspürte einen Schmerz/mein Bein schmerzte; **his vanity/pride ~ed** (*fig.*) er fühlte sich in seiner Eitelkeit/seinem Stolz verletzt; **she ~ed from his remarks** seine Bemerkungen verletzten sie; **~ under sth.** (*fig.*) unter etw. (*Dat.*) leiden.
❹ *n.* (*lit. or fig.*) Schmerz, *der;* (*from wound, ointment*) Brennen, *das;* (*from pain*) Stechen, *das*

**smart:** **~ alec[k]**, **~ alick** /smɑːt ˈælɪk/ (*coll. derog.*) ❶ *ns.* Besserwisser, *der* (*abwertend*); ❷ *attrib. adjs.* neunmalklug; besserwisserisch (*abwertend*); **~-arse** (*Amer.*) **~-ass** (*sl.*) ❶ *ns.* Klugscheißer, *der* (*salopp abwertend*); ❷ *attrib. adjs.* klugscheißerisch (*salopp abwertend*); **~ bomb** *n.* intelligente Bombe; **~ card** *n.* Chipkarte, *die;* **~ drug** *n.* Nootropikum *das* (*fachspr.*)

**smarten** /ˈsmɑːtn/ ❶ *v.t.* (A) (*make spruce*) herrichten; **she ~ed her appearance** sie machte sich zurecht; **he ~ed his hair/clothes** er brachte sein Haar/seine Kleidung in Ordnung (*ugs.*); **~ oneself** (*tidy up*) sich zurechtmachen; (*dress up*) sich herrichten; (*improve appearance in general*) auf sein Äußeres achten; (B) (*accelerate*) **~ one's pace** seinen Schritt/seine Schritte beschleunigen.
❷ *v.i.* **the pace ~ed** das Tempo beschleunigte sich

**~ 'up** ❶ *v.t.* (A) ⇒ **~** 1 A; (B) (*fig.*) **~ up one's ideas** sich am Riemen reißen (*ugs.*). ❷ *v.i.* (*tidy up*) sich zurechtmachen; (*dress up*) sich herrichten; (*improve appearance in general*) auf sein Äußeres achten; **the hotel/town has ~ed up a great deal** das Hotel/die Stadt hat sich sehr gemacht (*ugs.*)

**smartish** /ˈsmɑːtɪʃ/ ❶ *adj.* (*fairly neat*) ganz schick; (*fairly prompt*) ziemlich flink. ❷ *adv.* **[pretty] ~:** [ganz] schnell

**smartly** /ˈsmɑːtlɪ/ *adv.* (A) (*cleverly*) clever; (*in a know-all way*) besserwisserisch (*abwertend*); **that was ~ put** das war gut gesagt; (B) (*neatly*) schmuck ‹[an]gestrichen›; smart, flott ‹gekleidet, geschnitten›; (C) (*fashionably*) vornehm; (D) (*vigorously*) hart; (*sharply*) scharf ‹zurechtweisen›; hart ‹anpacken›; **set off ~ down the road** in scharfem Schritt die Straße hinuntergehen; (E) (*promptly*) sofort; auf der Stelle

**smart money** *n.* **the ~ is on ...** Experten setzen auf ...

**smartness** /ˈsmɑːtnɪs/ *n., no pl.* (A) (*cleverness*) Cleverness, *die;* (*attitude of know-all*) Besserwisserei, *die* (*abwertend*); (B) (*neatness*) Gepflegtheit, *die;* **~ [of appearance]** ansprechendes Äußeres; (C) (*vigour*) Härte, *die;* (*sharpness*) Schärfe, *die;* **~ of pace** Tempo, *das;* (D) (*promptness*) Flinkheit, *die*

**smarty**/ˈsmɑːtɪ/: **~-boots**, **~-pants** *ns. sing.* ⇒ **smart aleck** 1

**smash** /smæʃ/ ❶ *v.t.* (A) (*break*) zerschlagen; **~ sth. against the wall/down on the floor** etw. an die Wand/auf den Boden schmettern; **~ one's hand/arm/leg** sich (*Dat.*) die Hand/den Arm/das Bein zerschmettern; **~ sth. to pieces** etw. zerschmettern; (B) (*defeat*) zerschlagen ‹Rebellion, Revolution, Opposition›; zerschmettern ‹Feind›; (*in games*) vernichtend schlagen; klar verbessern ‹Rekord›; (C) (*hit hard*) **~ sb. in the face/mouth** jmdm. [hart] ins Gesicht/auf den Mund schlagen; **I'll ~ your face** (*sl.*) ich polier' dir die Fresse (*derb*); (D) (*Tennis*) schmettern; (E) (*propel forcefully*) schmettern; **he ~ed the car into a wall/his fist down on the table** er knallte (*ugs.*) mit dem Wagen gegen eine Mauer/schlug mit der Faust auf den Tisch; **he ~ed his way into the house with an iron bar** er schlug sich (*Dat.*) seinen Weg in das Haus mit einer Eisenstange frei.
❷ *v.i.* (A) (*shatter*) zerbrechen; (B) (*crash*) krachen; **~ into a wall/lamp post** an *od.* gegen eine Mauer/einen Laternenpfahl krachen; **the cars ~ed into each other** die Wagen krachten zusammen (*salopp*); (C) (*Commerc.*) ⇒ **crash** 3 D.
❸ *n.* (A) (*sound*) Krachen, *das;* (*of glass*) Klirren, *das;* (B) ⇒ **~-up**; (C) (*coll.*) ⇒ **~ hit**; (D) (*Tennis*) Schmetterball, *der;* (E) (*Commerc.*) ⇒ **crash** 1 C.
❹ *adv.* krach

**~ 'down** *v.t.* einschlagen ‹Tür›

**~ 'in** *v.t.* zerschmettern; eindrücken ‹Rippen, Motorhaube, Kotflügel›; einschlagen ‹Fenster, Tür, Schädel›; ‹Explosion:› eindrücken ‹Fenster, Tür›; **~ sb.'s face in** (*coll.*) jmdm. die Fresse polieren (*derb*)

**~ 'up** ❶ *v.t.* zertrümmern. ❷ *v.i.* zerschellen; ‹Auto:› zertrümmert werden; ⇒ *also* **~-up**

**smash-and-'grab [raid]** *n.* (*coll.*) Schaufenstereinbruch, *der*

**smashed** /smæʃt/ *adj.* (*sl.*) (A) (*drunk*) **get ~ on sth.** von etw. besoffen werden (*derb*); (*deliberately*) sich mit etw. voll laufen lassen (*salopp*); **be ~ out of one's head** *or* **mind** *or* **brains** sturzbetrunken (*ugs.*) *od.* (*derb*) sturzbesoffen sein; (B) (*on drugs*) stoned (*Drogenjargon*)

**smasher** /ˈsmæʃə(r)/ *n.* (*coll.*) **be a ~:** [ganz] große Klasse sein (*ugs.*); **what a ~ he/she/it is!** er/sie/es ist ganz große Klasse! (*ugs.*); **a ~ of a girlfriend** eine tolle Freundin

**smash 'hit** *n.* (*coll.*) (*film, play*) Kassenschlager, *der* (*ugs.*); (*song, record*) Riesenhit, *der* (*ugs.*)

**smashing** /ˈsmæʃɪŋ/ *adj.* (*coll.: excellent*) toll (*ugs.*); klasse (*ugs.*); **[how] ~!** toll! (*ugs.*); klasse! (*ugs.*); **he/she is ~** (*physically attractive*) er/sie sieht klasse *od.* ganz toll aus (*ugs.*)

**'smash-up** *n.* schwerer Zusammenstoß; **there has been a ~ between two cars/**

S

**trains** zwei Autos/Züge sind zusammengekracht (*ugs.*); **multiple ~:** Massenkarambolage, *die*

**smatter** /ˈsmætə(r)/, **smattering** /ˈsmætərɪŋ/ *ns.* oberflächliche Kenntnisse; (*feeble*) Halbwissen, *das* (*abwertend*); **have a ~ing of German** ein paar Brocken Deutsch können

**smear** /smɪə(r)/ ❶ *v.t.* A (*daub*) beschmieren; (*put on or over*) schmieren; **~ oneself/one's body/face with a cream/lotion/ointment** sich/seinen Körper/sein Gesicht mit einer Creme/Lotion/Salbe einreiben; **~ cream/ointment over one's body/face/hands** sich (*Dat.*) den Körper/das Gesicht/die Hände mit Creme/Salbe einreiben; **~ed with blood** blutbeschmiert *od.* -verschmiert; **he had paint ~ed on his face** sein Gesicht war mit Farbe beschmiert; **ink was ~ed all over the letter** der ganze Brief war mit Tinte verschmiert; B (*smudge*) verwischen; verschmieren; C (*fig.*: *defame*) in den Schmutz ziehen.
❷ *n.* A (*blotch*) [Schmutz]fleck, *der;* **a ~ of ink/paint/fat** *etc.* ein [verschmierter] Tinten-/Farb-/Fettfleck *usw.;* B (*fig.*: *defamation*) **a ~ on him/his [good] name/his [good] reputation** eine Beschmutzung seiner Person/seines [guten] Namens/seines Ansehens; C (*Med.*) Abstrich, *der;* **blood ~:** Blutausstrich, *der*

**smear: ~ campaign** *n.* Schmutzkampagne, *die;* **~ tactics** *n. pl.* schmutzige Mittel; **~ test** *n.* (*Med.*) Abstrich, *der;* **~ word** *n.* Schmähwort, *das*

**smeary** /ˈsmɪərɪ/ *adj.* A verschmiert ‹Glas, Tischplatte, Kleid›; **make sth. ~:** etw. verschmieren; B (*likely to smear*) schmierend; **be very ~** ‹Farbe, Tinte:› leicht schmieren

**smegma** /ˈsmegmə/ (*Physiol.*) Smegma, *das*

**smell** /smel/ ❶ *n.* A *no pl., no art.* **have a good/bad sense of ~:** einen guten/schlechten Geruchssinn haben; B (*odour*) Geruch, *der* (**of** nach); (*pleasant also*) Duft, *der* (**of** nach); **a ~ of burning/gas** ein Brand-/Gasgeruch; **there was a ~ of coffee** es duftete nach Kaffee; **sth. has a nice/strong** *etc.* **~ [to it]** etw. riecht angenehm/stark *usw.;* C (*stink*) Gestank, *der;* D (*act of inhaling*) **one ~ was enough** einmal riechen genügte; **have** *or* **take a ~ at** *or* **of sth.** an etw. (*Dat.*) riechen.
❷ *v.t.*, **smelt** /smelt/ *or* **~ed** A (*perceive*) riechen; (*fig.*) wittern; **I can ~ burning/gas** es riecht brandig/nach Gas; **I could ~ trouble** (*fig.*) es roch nach Ärger; ⇒ *also* **rat** 1 A; B (*inhale ~ of*) riechen an (+ *Dat.*); **just ~ the sea air!** riech [doch] mal nur die Seeluft!
❸ *v.i.*, **smelt** *or* **~ed** A (*emit ~*) riechen; (*pleasantly also*) duften; B (*recall ~; fig.*: *suggest*) **~ of sth.** nach etw. riechen; C (*stink*) riechen; **his breath ~s** er riecht aus dem Mund; D (*perceive ~*) riechen; **she can't ~ because of her cold** sie riecht nichts wegen ihrer Erkältung; **~ at sth.** an etw. (*Dat.*) riechen

**~ 'out** *v.t.* (*lit. or fig.*) aufspüren

**smelling salts** /ˈsmelɪŋ sɔːlts, ˈsmelɪŋ sɒlts/ *n. pl.* Riechsalz, *das*

**smelly** /ˈsmelɪ/ *adj.* stinkend (*abwertend*); **be ~:** stinken (*abwertend*)

**smelt**[1] /smelt/ *v.t.* (*Metallurgy*) A (*melt*) verhütten ‹Erz›; B (*refine*) erschmelzen ‹Metall›

**smelt**[2] *n., pl.* **~s** *or same* (*Zool.*) Stint, *der*

**smelt**[3] ⇒ **smell** 2, 3

**smelter** /ˈsmeltə(r)/ *n.* (*Metallurgy*) A (*person*) Schmelzer, *der;* B (*smelting works*) Schmelzhütte, *die*

**smidgen, smidgin** /ˈsmɪdʒən/ *n.* (*coll.*) **a ~** ein klein bisschen

**smile** /smaɪl/ ❶ *n.* Lächeln, *das;* **a ~ of joy/satisfaction** ein freudiges/befriedigtes Lächeln; **be all ~s** über das ganze Gesicht strahlen; **break into a ~:** [plötzlich] zu lächeln beginnen; **give a [little] ~:** [schwach] lächeln; **give sb. a ~:** jmdn. anlächeln; **give me a big ~ now!** jetzt mal schön lächeln!; **raise a ~:** ein Lächeln hervorlocken; (*make oneself ~*) sich (*Dat.*) ein Lächeln abringen; **raise a few ~s** zum Lächeln anregen; **take that ~ off your face!** hör auf zu grinsen!; **this'll put a ~ on your face** das wird dich freuen; **with a ~:** mit einem Lächeln [auf den Lippen]; lächelnd.
❷ *v.i.* lächeln; **make sb. ~:** jmdn. zum Lachen bringen; **keep smiling** (*fig.*: *not despair*) das Lachen nicht verlernen (*fig.*); **keep smiling!** Kopf hoch!; keep smiling!; **come up smiling** (*fig. coll.*) sich nicht unterkriegen lassen (*ugs.*); **~ at sb.** jmdn. anlächeln; **~ at sth.** (*lit. or fig.*) über etw. (*Akk.*) lächeln; **~, please!** bitte recht freundlich! **~ with delight/pleasure** vor Freude strahlen; **Fortune ~d on us/our efforts** das Glück lachte uns (*veralt.*).
❸ *v.t.* A **~ encouragement/one's thanks** aufmunternd/dankend lächeln; **~ a welcome** zur Begrüßung [freundlich] lächeln; B **~ a friendly/sad ~:** freundlich/traurig lächeln

**smirch** /smɜːtʃ/ (*literary*) ❶ *v.t.* A besudeln (*geh.*); B (*fig.*: *disgrace*) ⇒ **besmirch.**
❷ *n.* A [Schmutz]fleck, *der;* B (*fig.*: *disgrace*) Schandfleck, *der* (*fig.*); **cast a ~ on sb./sth.** ein Schandfleck für jmdn./etw. sein

**smirk** /smɜːk/ ❶ *v.i.* grinsen. ❷ *n.* Grinsen, *das*

**smite** /smaɪt/ *v.t.*, **smote** /sməʊt/, **smitten** /ˈsmɪtn/ (*arch./literary*) A (*strike*) schlagen (**on** auf, an + *Akk.*); **~ one's breast/forehead** sich (*Dat.*) an die Brust/Stirn schlagen; B (*affect suddenly*) **an idea/his conscience smote him** eine Vorstellung bemächtigte sich seiner (*geh.*)/ihm schlug das Gewissen (*geh.*); **the light smote our eyes** das Licht blendete unsere Augen; C (*afflict*) **be smitten by** *or* **with desire/terror/the plague** von Verlangen/Schrecken ergriffen/mit der Pest geschlagen sein (*geh.*); **be smitten by** *or* **with a** *or* **the desire to do sth.** von dem Verlangen ergriffen sein, etw. zu tun; **be smitten by** *or* **with sb./sb.'s charms** jmdm./jmds. Zauber erlegen sein; D (*defeat*) zerschmettern; erschlagen ‹Person›

**smith** /smɪθ/ *n.* ▶ 1261 Schmied, *der*

**-smith** *n. suf.* A (*metalworker*) -schmied, *der;* B (*fig.*: *creator*) **song~:** versierter Songkomponist; **word~** (*creator of words*) Wortschöpfer, *der;* **the word~ John Updike** der versierte Schriftsteller John Updike

**smithereens** /smɪðəˈriːnz/ *n. pl.* **blow/smash sth. to ~:** etw. in tausend Stücke sprengen/schlagen; **in ~:** in tausend Stücken

**smithy** /ˈsmɪðɪ/ *n.* ▶ 1261 Schmiede, *die*

**smitten** ⇒ **smite**

**smock** /smɒk/ ❶ *n.* A [Arbeits]kittel, *der;* **painter's ~:** Malerkittel, *der;* B ⇒ **smock-frock.** ❷ *v.t.* (*Sewing*) smoken

**'smock-frock** *n.* Bauernkittel, *der* (*veralt.*)

**smocking** /ˈsmɒkɪŋ/ *n.* (*Sewing*) Smokarbeit, *die*

**smog** /smɒg/ *n.* Smog, *der*

**smoke** /sməʊk/ ❶ *n.* A Rauch, *der;* **go up in ~:** in Rauch [und Flammen] aufgehen; (*fig.*) in Rauch aufgehen; **like ~** (*coll.*) wie ein geölter Blitz (*ugs.*) ‹laufen, fahren›; (*without hindrance*) wie geschmiert (*ugs.*) ‹zusammenarbeiten, funktionieren›; **[there is] no ~ without fire** (*prov.*) kein Rauch ohne Flamme (*Spr.*); B (*act of smoking tobacco*) **a ~ would be nice just now** jetzt würde ich gern eine rauchen; **have a [quick] ~:** [schnell eine] rauchen; **I'm dying for a ~:** ich würde schrecklich gern eine rauchen (*ugs.*); C (*coll.*: *cigarette*) **a packet of ~s** ein Päckchen Zigaretten; **have you got a ~?** hast du was (*ugs.*) zu rauchen?.
❷ *v.i.* A (*~ tobacco*) rauchen; **do you mind if I ~?** stört es Sie, wenn ich rauche?; **~ like a chimney** rauchen wie ein Schlot (*ugs.*); B (*emit ~*) rauchen; (*burn imperfectly*) qualmen; (*emit vapour*) dampfen.
❸ *v.t.* A rauchen; ⇒ *also* **pipe** 1 D; B (*darken*) schwärzen ‹Glas›; ‹Petroleumlampe:› verräuchern ‹Wand, Decke›; C räuchern ‹Fleisch, Fisch›

**~ 'out** *v.t.* A (*exterminate, expel*) ausräuchern; B (*fill with ~*) verräuchern; C (*fig.*: *discover*) aufspüren ‹Verbrecher›; auf die Spur kommen (+ *Dat.*) ‹Absicht, Plan›

**smoke: ~ a'batement** *n.* Rauchverringerung, *die;* **~ bomb** *n.* Rauchbombe, *die*

**smoked** /sməʊkt/ *adj.* (*Cookery*) geräuchert; **~ glass** dunkel getöntes Glas; (*for decorative purposes*) Rauchglas, *das*

**'smoke detector** *n.* Rauchmelder, *der*

**'smoke-dried** *adj.* geräuchert

**smokeless** /ˈsməʊklɪs/ *adj.* rauchlos; rauchfrei ‹Zone›

**smoker** /ˈsməʊkə(r)/ *n.* A Raucher, *der*/Raucherin, *die;* **be a heavy ~:** ein starker Raucher/eine starke Raucherin sein; **~'s companion** Raucherbesteck, *das;* **~'s cough/heart/throat** (*Med.*) Raucherhusten, *der*/-herz, *das*/-kehle, *die;* B (*Railw.*) ⇒ **smoking compartment**

**smoke: ~ ring** *n.* Rauchring, *der;* **~ room** *n.* (*Brit.*) Rauchsalon, *der;* Rauchzimmer, *das;* **~screen** *n.* [künstliche] Nebelwand; (*fig.*) Vernebelung, *die* (**for** *Gen.*); **throw up a thick ~screen round a scandal** die Fakten eines Skandals gründlich vernebeln; **~ signal** *n.* Rauchzeichen, *das;* Rauchsignal, *das;* **~stack** ⇒ **stack** 1 F

**smoking** /ˈsməʊkɪŋ/ *n.* A (*act*) Rauchen, *das;* **'no ~'** „Rauchen verboten"; **no-~ compartment** (*Railw.*) Nichtraucherabteil, *das;* B *no art.* (*seating area*) **[do you want to sit in] ~ or non-~?** [möchten Sie für] Raucher oder Nichtraucher?; **the next carriage is ~:** der nächste Wagen ist für Raucher

**smoking: ~ compartment** *n.* (*Railw.*) Raucherabteil, *das;* **~ jacket** *n.* Rauchjacke, *die;* Hausrock, *der;* **~ room** (*Brit.*) ⇒ **smoke room**

**smoky** /ˈsməʊkɪ/ *adj.* (*emitting smoke*) rauchend; qualmend; (*smoke-filled, smoke-stained*) verräuchert; (*coloured or tasting like smoke*) rauchig; **be too ~** ‹Feuer, Kamin, Lampe:› zu stark rauchen *od.* qualmen; **~ quartz/topaz/glass** Rauchquarz, *der*/-topas/-glas, *das;* **~ grey** rauchgrau

**smolder** (*Amer.*) ⇒ **smoulder**

**smooch** /smuːtʃ/ (*coll.*) ❶ *v.i.* [sich] knutschen (*ugs.*). ❷ *n.* Knutschen, *das* (*ugs.*); **have a ~:** [sich] knutschen (*ugs.*)

**smooth** /smuːð/ ❶ *adj.* A (*even*) glatt; eben ‹Straße, Weg›; **as ~ as glass/silk/a baby's bottom** spiegelglatt/glatt wie Seide/wie ein Kinderpopo (*ugs.*); **beat the mixture until ~:** die Mischung glatt rühren; **be ~ to the touch** sich glatt anfühlen; **make sth. ~:** etw. glätten; **be worn ~** ‹Treppenstufe:› abgetreten sein; ‹Reifen:› abgefahren sein; ‹Fels, Stein:› glatt geschliffen sein; **this razor gives a ~ shave** dieser Rasierapparat rasiert glatt; B (*mild*) weich; **as ~ as velvet** (*fig.*) samtweich; C (*fluent*) flüssig; geschliffen ‹Stil, Diktion›; D (*not jerky*) geschmeidig ‹Bewegung›; ruhig ‹Fahrt, Flug, Lauf einer Maschine, Bewegung, Atmung›; weich ‹Start, Landung, Autofahren, Schalten›; **come to a ~ stop** ‹Wagen, Bus, Zug:› weich zum Stehen kommen; E (*without problems*) reibungslos; **the changeover was fairly ~:** der Wechsel ging ziemlich reibungslos vonstatten; F (*equable*) ruhig ‹Art, Wesen›; G (*derog.*: *suave*) glatt; (*~-tongued*) glattzüngig (*geh. abwertend*); **he is a ~ operator** er ist gewieft; H (*coll.*: *elegant*) schick; I (*skilful*) geschickt; souverän.
❷ *adv.* ⇒ **smoothly.**
❸ *v.t.* A glätten; glatt streichen, glätten ‹Stoff, Tuch, Papier›; glatt streichen ‹Haar›; glatt schleifen ‹Stein›; (*with plane*) glatt hobeln ‹Holz›; (*with sandpaper*) glatt schleifen, glätten ‹Holz›; (*fig.*: *soothe*) besänftigen; **he ~ed the creases/wrinkles from the paper/cloth** er strich die Falten aus dem Papier/Stoff; B (*Statistics*) bereinigen; C (*fig.*: *free from impediments*) **~ sb.'s/sth.'s path** jmdm./einer Sache den Weg ebnen *od.* die Wege ebnen; **~ the way for sb./sth.** jmdm./einer Sache den Weg *od.* die Wege ebnen.
❹ *v.i.* (*lit. or fig.*) sich glätten

**~ a'way** *v.t.* glätten, ausstreichen ‹Falten›; (*fig.*) vertreiben ‹Sorgen, Ängste›; ausräumen ‹Differenzen, Schwierigkeiten›

S

~ 'back *v.t.* [glatt] zurückstreichen ‹Haare›; (*with comb*) [glatt] zurückkämmen

~ 'down ❶ *v.t.* glatt streichen ‹Haar›; (*fig.*) schlichten ‹Streit›; besänftigen ‹Person›; ~ **things down a bit** ein wenig die Wogen glätten. ❷ *v.i.* ⇒ **smooth** 4

~ **out** *v.t.* glatt streichen ‹Falte, Tuch›; ausstreichen ‹Farbe, Teig›; (*fig.*) ausräumen ‹Schwierigkeiten, Hindernisse›

~ 'over *v.t.* (*fig.*) beilegen ‹Streit›; ausräumen ‹Schwierigkeiten›; **we ~ed things over** wir bereinigten die Angelegenheit

**'smooth-bore** *n.* (*Arms*) Gewehr mit glattem Lauf

**smoothie** /'smu:ðɪ/ *n.* (*coll. derog.*) aalglatter Typ (*ugs.*)

**smoothly** /'smu:ðlɪ/ *adv.* Ⓐ (*evenly*) glatt; Ⓑ (*fluently*) flüssig; ~ **flowing** eingängig ‹Poesie, Prosa, Musik›; Ⓒ (*not jerkily*) geschmeidig ‹sich bewegen›; reibungslos ‹funktionieren›; ruhig ‹atmen, fließen, fahren›; weich ‹starten, landen, schalten›; **a ~ running engine** (*Motor Veh.*) ein rund laufender Motor; **this pen writes ~:** dieser Füller (*ugs.*) schreibt einwandfrei; Ⓓ (*without problems*) reibungslos; glatt; Ⓔ (*derog.: suavely*) aalglatt (*abwertend*); glattzüngig (*geh. abwertend*) ‹sprechen›; Ⓕ (*coll.: elegantly*) schick; Ⓖ (*skilfully*) geschickt; souverän

**smoothness** /'smu:ðnɪs/ *n., no pl.* Ⓐ (*evenness*) Glätte, *die;* **have the ~ of silk** seidig glatt sein; Ⓑ (*mildness*) Weichheit, *die;* Ⓒ (*fluency*) Flüssigkeit, *die;* Ⓓ (*lack of jerkiness*) (*of movement*) Geschmeidigkeit, *die;* (*of machine operation, breathing*) Gleichmäßigkeit, *die;* **the ~ of his driving** sein gefühlvolles Fahren; Ⓔ (*lack of problems*) Reibungslosigkeit, *die;* Ⓕ (*equability*) Sanftheit, *die;* Ⓖ (*derog.: suavity*) Glätte, *die* (*abwertend*); Ⓗ (*coll.: elegance*) Schick, *der;* Ⓘ (*skill*) Geschicklichkeit, *die;* Souveränität, *die*

**smooth:** ~ **'tongue** *n.* (*fig.: suavity*) Glattzüngigkeit, *die* (*geh. abwertend*); **have a ~:** eine einschmeichelnde Art haben; **~-tongued** *adj.* glattzüngig

**smote** ⇒ **smite**

**smother** /'smʌðə(r)/ ❶ *v.t.* Ⓐ (*stifle*) ersticken; **he was ~ed by the avalanche** er erstickte in der Lawine; Ⓑ (*overwhelm*) überschütten (**with, in** mit); ~ **sb. with kisses** jmdn. mit seinen Küssen [fast] ersticken; Ⓒ (*extinguish*) ersticken; Ⓓ (*fig.: suppress*) unterdrücken ‹Kichern, Gähnen, Schluchzen, Tatsachen, Wahrheit›; ersticken ‹Kritik, Gerücht, Schluchzen, Gelächter, Schreie›; dämpfen ‹Lärm›; Ⓔ (*Amer.: defeat quickly*) erledigen ‹Feind, Gegner›; Ⓕ (*cover entirely*) ~ **sth. in sth.** etw. mit etw. bedecken; **~ed in dust/dirt** voller Staub/Schmutz; **strawberries ~ed in** *or* **with cream** Erdbeeren mit reichlich [flüssiger] Sahne. ❷ *v.i.* ersticken

~ **'up** *v.t.* vertuschen ‹Verbrechen, Skandal›; unterdrücken ‹Gerücht, Wahrheit, Vorschlag›

**smothery** /'smʌðərɪ/ *adj.* stickig; (*overwhelming*) erdrückend

**smoulder** /'sməʊldə(r)/ *v.i.* Ⓐ schwelen; Ⓑ (*fig.*) ‹Hass, Rebellion:› schwelen; ‹Liebe:› glimmen (*geh.*); **she was ~ing with rage** Zorn schwelte in ihr; **she/her eyes ~ed with desire/rage** sie glühte (*geh.*)/ihre Augen glühten vor Verlangen/Zorn; **a ~ing beauty** eine glutvolle Schönheit

**smudge**[1] /smʌdʒ/ ❶ *v.t.* Ⓐ (*blur*) verwischen; Ⓑ (*smear*) schmieren; ~ **sth. on sth.** etw. auf etw. (*Akk.*) schmieren; Ⓒ (*make smear on*) verschmieren; Ⓓ (*fig.: disgrace*) beschmutzen. ❷ *v.i.* ‹Füller, Tinte, Farbe:› schmieren; **my hand slipped and the drawing/ink/paint ~d** meine Hand rutschte aus, und die Zeichnung/Tinte/Farbe war verwischt. ❸ *n.* Ⓐ (*smear*) Fleck, *der;* (*fig.*) Schandfleck, *der;* Ⓑ (*blur*) Schmierage, *die* (*ugs.*); **be a mass of ~s** eine einzige Schmiererei sein (*ugs. abwertend*)

**smudge**[2] *n.* (*Amer.: fire*) Rauchfeuer, *das* (*zum Schutz vor Insekten od. Kälte*)

**'smudge pot** *n.* (*Amer.*) *Kessel mit Brennmaterial für ein Rauchfeuer zur Vertreibung von Insekten od. zum Kälteschutz*

**smudgy** /'smʌdʒɪ/ *adj.* Ⓐ (*dirty*) schmutzig; verschmutzt; Ⓑ (*blurred*) verwischt; Ⓒ (*smudging easily*) schmierend; **be ~** ‹Füller, Tinte:› schmieren

**smug** /smʌg/ *adj.* selbstgefällig (*abwertend*); **she is very ~ about it/her job/her new house** sie ist darauf/auf ihre Stelle/auf ihr neues Haus sehr eingebildet (*abwertend*)

**smuggle** /'smʌgl/ *v.t.* schmuggeln

~ **a'way** *v.t.* wegschaffen; ~ **sb. away through a back door** jmdn. durch eine Hintertür hinausschmuggeln

~ **'in** *v.t.* einschmuggeln; hinein-/hereinschmuggeln ‹Person›

~ **'out** *v.t.* hinaus-/herausschmuggeln

**smuggler** /'smʌglə(r)/ *n.* Schmuggler, *der*/Schmugglerin, *die*

**smuggling** /'smʌglɪŋ/ *n.* Schmuggel, *der;* Schmuggeln, *das;* **the ~ of dogs into Britain** das Einschmuggeln von Hunden nach Großbritannien

**smugly** /'smʌglɪ/ *adv.* selbstgefällig (*abwertend*)

**smugness** /'smʌgnɪs/ *n., no pl.* Selbstgefälligkeit, *die* (*abwertend*)

**smut** /smʌt/ *n.* Ⓐ Rußflocke, *die;* (*smudge*) Rußfleck, *der;* **be covered in ~s** voller Ruß sein; Ⓑ *no art.* (*lewd matter*) Schund, *der* (*abwertend*); **talk ~:** schweinigeln (*ugs. abwertend*); Ⓒ (*Bot.*) (*disease*) Brand, *der;* (*fungus*) Brandpilz, *der*

**smutty** /'smʌtɪ/ *adj.* Ⓐ (*dirty*) verschmutzt; Ⓑ (*lewd*) schmutzig (*abwertend*); **he is ~:** er ist schweinisch (*ugs. abwertend*)

**snack** /snæk/ *n.* Imbiss, *der;* Snack, *der;* **eat many ~s between meals** viel zwischendurch essen; **have a [quick] ~:** [rasch] eine Kleinigkeit essen (*ugs.*)

**'snackbar** *n.* Schnellimbiss, *der;* Snackbar, *die*

**snaffle** /'snæfl/ ❶ *n.* (*Riding*) Trense, *die.* ❷ *v.t.* Ⓐ (*coll.*) mopsen (*fam.*) ‹Schokolade, Zeitung›; klauen (*salopp*) ‹Diamanten, Geheimdokumente, Geld›; Ⓑ (*Riding*) die Trense anlegen (+ *Dat.*)

~ **'up** *v.t.* [sich (*Dat.*)] schnappen (*ugs.*)

**'snaffle bit** *n.* (*Riding*) Trensengebiss, *das*

**snafu** /snæ'fu:/ (*Amer. coll.*) ❶ *pred. adj.* chaotisch. ❷ *n.* Chaos, *das;* **they left us in ~:** sie ließen uns im Schlamassel stecken (*ugs.*)

**snag** /snæg/ ❶ *n.* Ⓐ (*jagged point*) Zacke, *die;* Ⓑ (*problem*) Haken, *der;* **what's the ~?** wo klemmt es [denn]? (*ugs.*); **hit a ~, run up against a ~:** auf ein Problem *od.* eine Schwierigkeit stoßen; **there's a ~ in it** die Sache hat einen Haken; Ⓒ (*tear*) Loch, *das;* (*pulled thread*) gezogener Faden. ❷ *v.t.*, **-gg-** Ⓐ (*catch*) **I've ~ged my coat** mein Mantel hat sich verfangen; ich bin mit dem Mantel hängen geblieben; Ⓑ (*tear*) einreißen; Ⓒ (*Amer.: catch quickly*) ~ **sth.** sich (*Dat.*) etw. schnappen (*ugs.*)

**snail** /sneɪl/ *n.* Schnecke, *die;* **Roman ~:** Weinbergschnecke, *die;* **at [a] ~'s pace** im Schneckentempo (*ugs.*)

**'snail-like** *adj.* schneckenartig; schneckenhaft (*ugs.*)

**'snail mail** *n.* (*coll. joc.*) Schneckenpost, *die;* **send sth. by ~:** etw. mit der Schneckenpost *od.* per Schneckenpost schicken

**snake** /sneɪk/ ❶ *n.* Ⓐ Schlange, *die;* **~s and ladders** *Brettspiel, bei dem je nach Augenzahl beim Würfeln Spielsteine „Leitern" hinauf- und „Schlangen" hinabbewegt werden;* Ⓑ (*derog.*) ~ **[in the grass]** (*woman*) [falsche] Schlange; (*man*) falscher Kerl *od.* (*ugs.*) Hund; Ⓒ (*Econ.*) **the ~:** die Währungsschlange (*Jargon*). ❷ *v.i.* sich schlängeln

**snake:** **~bite** *n.* Ⓐ Schlangenbiss, *der;* Ⓑ (*drink*) *Getränk aus gleichen Teilen Apfelwein und Lagerbier;* ~ **charmer** *n.* Schlangenbeschwörer, *der;* **~skin** *n.* Schlangenleder, *das*

**snaky** /'sneɪkɪ/ *adj.* Ⓐ (*winding*) gewunden; schlangenartig ‹Bewegung›; Ⓑ (*sly*) hinterhältig

**snap** /snæp/ ❶ *v.t.*, **-pp-:** Ⓐ (*break*) zerbrechen; ~ **sth. in two** *or* **in half** etw. in zwei Stücke brechen; Ⓑ ~ **one's fingers** mit den Fingern schnalzen; ~ **one's fingers at sth./sb.** (*fig.*) auf etw./jmdn. pfeifen (*ugs.*); Ⓒ (*move with ~ping sound*) ~ **sth. home** *or* **into place** etw. einrasten *od.* einschnappen lassen; ~ **shut** zuschnappen lassen ‹Portemonnaie, Tür, Schloss›; zuklappen ‹Buch, Zigarettendose, Etui›; ~ **sth. open** etw. aufschnappen lassen; Ⓓ (*take photograph of*) knipsen; Ⓔ (*say in sharp manner*) fauchen; (*speak crisply or curtly*) bellen.

❷ *v.i.*, **-pp-:** Ⓐ (*break*) brechen; Ⓑ (*fig.: give way under strain*) ausrasten (*ugs.*); **my patience has finally ~ped** nun ist mir der Geduldsfaden aber gerissen; **something ~ed in me** (*fig.*) da war bei mir das Maß voll; Ⓒ (*make as if to bite*) [zu]schnappen; Ⓓ (*move smartly*) ~ **into action** loslegen (*ugs.*); ~ **into life** aufschrecken; ~ **to attention** strammstehen; ~ **to it!** (*coll.*) leg/legt los! (*ugs.*); Ⓔ (*move with ~ping sound*) ~ **home** *or* **into place** einrasten; einschnappen; ~ **shut** zuschnappen; ‹Kiefer:› zusammenklappen; ‹Mund:› zuklappen; ~ **together** zusammenklappen; ~ **open** aufschnappen; Ⓕ (*speak sharply*) fauchen; Ⓖ (*take photograph*) knipsen.

❸ *n.* Ⓐ (*sound*) Knacken, *das;* (*of whip*) Knallen, *das;* Ⓑ (*biscuit*) Plätzchen, *das;* ⇒ *also* **brandy-snap**; Ⓒ (*Photog.*) Schnappschuss, *der;* Ⓓ (*Brit. Cards*) Schnippschnapp[schnurr], *das;* Ⓔ **cold ~:** kurze Kälteperiode; Ⓕ (*zest*) Schwung, *der.*

❹ *attrib. adj.* (*spontaneous*) spontan; **call a ~ election/vote** Knall und Fall (*ugs.*) einen Wahltermin festsetzen/eine Abstimmung herbeiführen.

❺ *int.* Ⓐ (*Brit. Cards*) schnapp; Ⓑ (*when two things are seen to match coincidentally*) genau gleich (*ugs.*)

~ **at** *v.t.* Ⓐ (*bite*) ~ **at sb./sth.** nach jmdm./etw. schnappen; ~ **at sb.'s heels** jmdm. auf den Fersen sein; **he ran with a pack of dogs ~ ping at his heels** er rannte, dicht gefolgt von einer Hundemeute; Ⓑ (*speak sharply to*) anfauchen (*ugs.*); Ⓒ (*Amer.: accept eagerly*) ~ **at a chance** eine Gelegenheit beim Schopf[e] ergreifen; ~ **at an invitation/a job** bei einer Einladung/einem Job keinesfalls nein sagen *od.* (*salopp*) gleich zuschlagen

~ **'back** ❶ *v.i.* Ⓐ (*return*) zurückschnellen; Ⓑ (*reply*) ~ **back [at sb.]** jmdn. anfauchen (*ugs.*); Ⓒ (*Amer. fig.: make quick recovery*) sich schnell [wieder] erholen. ❷ *v.t.* (*say as a retort*) zurückgeben

~ **'off** ❶ *v.i.* abbrechen; abknicken ‹Zweig, Antenne›. ❷ *v.t.* Ⓐ (*break*) abbrechen; ~ **sth. off sth.** etw. von etw. abbrechen; Ⓑ (*bite*) abbeißen; ~ **sb.'s head off** (*fig.*) jmdm. den Kopf abreißen (*fig.*); Ⓒ (*Amer.: switch off*) ausknipsen (*ugs.*); ausschalten; Ⓓ aufklappen ‹Deckel, Verschluss›

~ **'on** ❶ *v.i.* zuschnappen; ~ **on to sth.** sich an etw. (*Dat.*) festklemmen. ❷ *v.t.* Ⓐ (*fasten*) festklemmen; zuklappen ‹Deckel›; ~ **sth. on sth.** etw. auf etw. (*Akk.*) klemmen; Ⓑ (*Amer.: switch on*) anknipsen (*ugs.*). ⇒ *also* **snap-on**

~ **'out** *v.t.* bellen ‹Befehl, Anweisung›

~ **'out of** *v.t.* abwerfen; sich befreien von ‹Gefühl, Stimmung, Komplex›; ~ **out of it!** (*coll.*) hör auf damit!; (*wake up*) wach auf!

~ **'up** *v.t.* Ⓐ (*pick up*) [sich (*Dat.*)] schnappen; Ⓑ (*fig. coll.: seize*) [sich (*Dat.*)] schnappen (*ugs.*); ~ **up a bargain/an offer** bei einem Angebot [sofort] zugreifen *od.* (*salopp*) zuschlagen; ~ **sth. up in the sales** etw. beim Ausverkauf ergattern (*ugs.*); **the tickets were ~ped up immediately** die Karten waren sofort weg

**snap:** ~ **bean** *n.* (*Amer.*) Brechbohne, *die;* **~dragon** *n.* (*Bot.*) Löwenmäulchen, *das;* ~ **fastener** *n.* Druckknopf, *der;* **~-on** *attrib. adj.* Klemm-

**snappy** /'snæpɪ/ *adj.* Ⓐ (*lively*) lebhaft; temperamentvoll ‹Tanz, Musik›; Ⓑ (*smart*) schick; **be a ~ dresser** sich flott *od.* schick kleiden; Ⓒ (*coll.*) **look ~!, make it ~!** ein bisschen dalli! (*ugs.*)

**snap:** ~ **'shot** (*gunshot*) ungezielter Schuss; **~shot** (*Photog.*) *n.* Schnappschuss, *der*

**snare** /sneə(r)/ ❶ *n.* Ⓐ (*trap*) Schlinge, *die;* Falle, *die* (*auch fig.*); **set a ~ [for sb.]**

S

[jmdm.] eine Falle stellen; **B** (*temptation*) Fallstrick, *der;* **C** (*Mus.*) Schnarrsaite, *die;* **D** (*Mus.*) ⇒ **snare drum. 2** *v.t.* [mit einer Schlinge] fangen ‹Tier, Vogel›; **~ sb.** jmdn. in eine Falle locken

**'snare drum** *n.* Wirbeltrommel, *die;* kleine Trommel

**snarl¹** /snɑːl/ **1** *v.i.* **A** (*growl*) ‹Hund:› knurren; ‹Tiger:› fauchen; **B** (*speak*) knurren. **2** *v.t.* knurren. **3** *n.* Knurren, *das;* (*of tiger*) Fauchen, *das;* **..., he said to him with a ~:** ..., knurrte er ihn an

**~ at** *v.t.* anknurren; ‹Tiger:› anfauchen

**snarl²** **1** *n.* (*tangle*) Knoten, *der.* **2** *v.t.* verheddern (*ugs.*). **3** *v.i.* sich verheddern (*ugs.*)

**~ 'up 1** *v.t.* (*confuse*) durcheinander bringen; (*bring to a halt*) zum Erliegen bringen; **get ~ed up** ‹Wolle usw.:› sich verheddern (*ugs.*); **get ~ed up in the traffic** im Verkehr stecken bleiben. **2** *v.i.* ‹Verkehr:› stocken; ‹Wolle:› sich verheddern (*ugs.*)

**'snarl-up** *n.* Stau, *der;* Stockung, *die*

**snatch** /snætʃ/ **1** *v.t.* **A** (*grab*) schnappen; **~ a bite to eat** [schnell] einen Bissen zu sich nehmen; **~ a kiss** sich (*Dat.*) einen Kuss stehlen (*scherzh.*); **~ an opportunity** eine Gelegenheit beim Schopf[e] ergreifen; **~ a rest** sich (*Dat.*) eine Ruhepause verschaffen; **~ hold of sb./sth.** jmdn./etw. schnappen; **~ hold of sb. by the collar/ear** jmdn. am Kragen/Ohr packen; **~ some sleep** ein bisschen schlafen; **~ a nap** (*coll.*) ein Nickerchen (*fam.*) halten; **~ the lead** die Führung übernehmen *od.* an sich (*Akk.*) nehmen; **~ sth. from sth.** etw. schnell von etw. nehmen; (*very abruptly*) etw. von etw. reißen; **~ sth. from sb.** jmdm. etw. wegreißen; **~ sth. out of sb.'s hand/pocket** jmdm. etw. aus der Hand reißen/schnell aus der Tasche ziehen; **B** (*steal*) klauen (*ugs.*); (*kidnap*) kidnappen.

**2** *v.i.* einfach zugreifen.

**3** *n.* **A make a ~ at sb./sth.** nach jmdm./etw. greifen; **B** (*Brit. sl.: robbery*) Raub, *der;* **C** (*sl.: kidnap*) Kidnapping, *das;* **D** (*fragment*) **a ~ of a song** ein paar Takte von einem Lied; **~es of talk/conversation** Gesprächsfetzen *od.* -brocken *Pl.;* **E** *in pl.* (*spells*) **do sth. in** *or* **by ~es** etw. mit Unterbrechungen tun; **F** (*weightlifting*) Reißen, *das*

**~ at** *v.t.* **A ~ at sb./sth.** nach jmdm./etw. schnappen; **B** (*fig.*) ⇒ **jump at b**

**~ a'way** *v.t.* [schnell] wegziehen (**from** *Dat.*); **~ sth. away from sb.** jmdm. etw. wegreißen

**~ 'up** *v.t.* [sich (*Dat.*)] schnappen

**snazzy** /'snæzɪ/ *adj.* (*coll.*) [super]schick (*ugs.*)

**sneak** /sniːk/ **1** *v.t.* **A** (*take*) stibitzen (*fam.*); **B** (*fig.*) **~ a look at sb./sth.** nach jmdm./etw. schielen; **C** (*bring*) **~ sth./sb. into a place** etw./jmdn. in einen Ort schmuggeln; **~ sth. into one's bag** etw. heimlich in die Tasche stecken; **D** (*coll.: steal*) klauen (*ugs.*); mitgehen lassen (*ugs.*).

**2** *v.i.* **A** (*Brit. Sch. coll.: tells tales*) petzen (*Schülerspr.*); **~ on sb.** jmdn. verpetzen (*Schülerspr.*); **B** (*move furtively*) schleichen. **3** *attrib. adj.* **A** (*without warning*) **~ attack/raid** Überraschungsangriff, *der;* **B a ~ preview of the film/play/programme** eine inoffizielle Vorpremiere des Films/Stücks/Programms. **4** *n.* **A** (*shifty person*) Fiesling, *der* (*salopp*); **B** (*Brit. Sch. coll.: telltale*) Petze, *die* (*Schülerspr.*)

**~ a'way** *v.i.* [sich] fortschleichen; sich davonmachen

**~ 'in 1** *v.i.* **A** (*enter stealthily*) sich hineinschleichen; (*fig.*) sich einschleichen; **B** (*win narrowly*) knapp siegen. **2** *v.t.* **A** (*bring in*) einschmuggeln (*ugs.*); **B** (*Amer.: include*) **~ in a mention of sth./a word about sth.** etw. [beiläufig] erwähnen/ein Wort über etw. (*Akk.*) einstreuen

**~ 'out** *v.i.* [sich] hinausschleichen

**~ 'out of** (*Amer.: avoid*) **~ out of sth./doing sth.** sich vor etw. (*Dat.*) drücken (*ugs.*)/sich davor drücken (*ugs.*), etw. zu tun

**sneaker** /'sniːkə(r)/ (*Amer.*) Turnschuh, *der*

**sneaking** /'sniːkɪŋ/ *attrib. adj.* heimlich; leise ‹Verdacht›

**'sneak thief** *n.* Einschleichdieb, *der*

**sneaky** /'sniːkɪ/ **A** (*underhand*) hinterhältig; **B have a ~ feeling that ...:** so ein leises Gefühl haben, dass ...

**sneer** /snɪə(r)/ **1** *v.i.* **A** (*smile scornfully*) spöttisch *od.* höhnisch lächeln/grinsen; hohnlächeln; **B** (*speak scornfully*) höhnen (*geh.*); spotten. **2** *v.t.* (*say*) höhnen (*geh.*); spotten. **3** *n.* **A** (*look*) Hohnlächeln, *das;* **B** (*remark*) höhnische *od.* spöttische Bemerkung; **a cynical/sarcastic ~:** eine zynische/sarkastische Bemerkung

**~ at** *v.t.* **A** (*smile scornfully at*) höhnisch anlächeln/angrinsen; **B** (*express scorn for*) verhöhnen (*geh.*); spotten über (+ *Akk.*)

**sneeze** /sniːz/ **1** *v.i.* niesen; **not to be ~d at** (*fig. coll.*) nicht zu verachten (*ugs.*). **2** *n.* Niesen, *das*

**snicker** /'snɪkə(r)/ ⇒ **snigger**

**snide** /snaɪd/ *adj.* **A** (*sneering*) abfällig; **B** *attrib.* (*Amer.: mean, underhand*) mies (*ugs.*)

**sniff** /snɪf/ **1** *n.* **A** Schnüffeln, *das;* Schnuppern, *das;* (*with running nose, while crying*) Schniefen, *das;* (*contemptuous*) Naserümpfen, *das;* **give a disdainful ~:** geringschätzig die Nase rümpfen; **have a ~ at sth.** an etw. (*Dat.*) riechen *od.* schnuppern; **have a ~ at this!** hier, riech *od.* schnupper mal!; **I didn't get a ~ of the food** (*coll.*) ich habe von dem Essen keinen Krümel abbekommen; **not a ~!** leer ausgegangen!; **B** (*quantity ~ed*) **have a [good] ~ of sea air/of perfume** [ausgiebig] die Seeluft/am Parfüm schnuppern.

**2** *v.i.* schniefen; die Nase hochziehen; (*to detect a smell*) schnuppern; (*to express contempt*) die Nase rümpfen.

**3** *v.t.* **A** (*smell*) riechen *od.* schnuppern an (+ *Dat.*) ‹Essen, Getränk, Blume, Parfüm, Wein›; **the dog ~ed the air/the lamp post** der Hund schnupperte/schnupperte am Laternenpfahl [herum]; **~ glue/cocaine** Klebstoff schnüffeln/Kokain sniffen (*Drogenjargon*); **B** (*utter with contempt*) naserümpfend sagen

**~ at** *v.t.* **A** schnuppern *od.* riechen an (+ *Dat.*) ‹Blume, Essen›; **B** (*show contempt for*) die Nase rümpfen über (+ *Akk.*); **not to be ~ed at** = **not to be sneezed at** ⇒ **sneeze 1**

**~ 'out** *v.t.* aufspüren

**sniffer dog** /'snɪfə dɒg/ *n.* Spürhund, *der*

**sniffle** /'snɪfl/ **1** *v.i.* schniefen; schnüffeln (*ugs.*). **2** *n.* (*coll.*) **A** Schniefen, *das;* Schnüffeln, *das* (*ugs.*); **B** *in pl.* **have the ~s** [einen] Schnupfen haben

**sniffy** /'snɪfɪ/ *adj.* (*coll.*) **A** (*contemptuous*) hochnäsig (*ugs.*); **B** (*sniffing*) **sb. is ~:** jmd. schnüffelt; (*has a cold*) schnieft

**snifter** /'snɪftə(r)/ *n.* **A** (*coll.: drink*) Kurze, *der* (*ugs.*); **B** (*Amer.: glass*) [Kognak]schwenker, *der*

**snigger** /'snɪgə(r)/ **1** *v.i.* [boshaft] kichern. **2** *n.* [boshaftes] Kichern

**snip** /snɪp/ **1** *v.t.*, **-pp-** schnippeln (*ugs.*), schneiden ‹Loch›; schnippeln (*ugs.*) *od.* schneiden an (+ *Dat.*) ‹Tuch, Haaren, Hecke›; (*cut off*) abschnippeln (*ugs.*); abschneiden. **2** *v.i.*, **-pp-** schnippeln (*ugs.*); schneiden. **3** *n.* **A** (*Brit. coll: certainty*) **be a ~:** idiotensicher sein (*ugs.*); **B** (*Brit. coll.: good bargain*) Schnäppchen, *das* (*ugs.*); **C** (*cut*) Schnitt, *der;* Schnipser, *der* (*ugs.*); **D** (*piece*) Schnipsel, *der od. das;* **E** *in pl.* (*shears*) [Hand]blechschere, *die*

**snipe** /snaɪp/ **1** *n.*, *pl. same or* **~s** (*Ornith.*) Schnepfe, *die.* **2** *v.i.* (*Mil.*) aus dem Hinterhalt schießen

**~ at** *v.t.* **A** (*Mil.*) aus dem Hinterhalt beschießen; **B** (*fig.: make snide comments about*) anschießen (*ugs.*)

**sniper** /'snaɪpə(r)/ *n.* Heckenschütze, *der; attrib.* **~ fire** Gewehrfeuer von Heckenschützen

**snippet** /'snɪpɪt/ *n.* **A** (*piece*) Schnipsel, *der od. das;* **B** (*of information in newspaper*) Notiz, *die;* (*of knowledge*) Bruchstück, *das;* (*from a book*) Passage, *die;* (*of conversation*) Gesprächsfetzen, *der;* **useful ~s of information** nützliche Hinweise

**snipping** /'snɪpɪŋ/ *n.* Schnipsel, *der od. das*

**snit** /snɪt/ *n.* (*Amer. coll.*) **be in a ~** (*agitated*) am Rotieren sein (*ugs.*); (*annoyed*) auf achtzig sein (*ugs.*)

**snitch** /snɪtʃ/ (*coll.*) **1** *v.t.* klauen (*ugs.*). **2** *v.i.* auspacken (*salopp*); **~ on sb.** jmdn. verpfeifen (*salopp*)

**snivel** /'snɪvl/ *v.i.*, (*Brit.*) **-ll-** **A** (*have runny nose*) **stop ~ling, use a handkerchief** hör auf, dauernd die Nase hochzuziehen — nimm ein Taschentuch; **B** (*sniff, sob*) schniefen; schnüffeln (*ugs.*)

**snivelling** (*Amer.:* **sniveling**) /'snɪvəlɪŋ/ (*fig.*) **1** *attrib. adj.* heulend; greinend (*ugs.*) ‹Opposition›. **2** *n.* Geheule, *das;* Gegreine, *das* (*ugs.*)

**snob** /snɒb/ *n.* Snob, *der* (*abwertend*); *attrib.* **~ appeal** *or* **value** Snob-Appeal, *der;* ⇒ *also* **inverted snob**

**snobbery** /'snɒbərɪ/ *n.* Snobismus, *der*

**snobbish** /'snɒbɪʃ/ *adj.*, **snobbishly** /'snɒbɪʃlɪ/ *adv.* snobistisch

**snog** /snɒg/ (*Brit. coll.*) **1** *v.i.*, **-gg-** knutschen (*ugs.*). **2** *n.* Knutschen, *das* (*ugs.*); **have a ~ [with sb.]** [mit jmdm.] knutschen

**snood** /snuːd/ *n.* Haarnetz, *das*

**snook** /snuːk/ *n.* (*coll.*) **cock a ~ at sb.** jmdm. eine lange Nase drehen (*ugs.*); (*fig. also*) jmdm. eine Nase drehen (*ugs.*)

**snooker** /'snuːkə(r)/ **1** *n.* **A** *no pl.*, *no indef. art.* Snooker [Pool], *das;* Taschenbillard, *das;* **B** (*tactical position*) *Situation beim Billardspiel, in der der Spieler die richtige Kugel nicht direkt spielen kann.* **2** *v.t.* **A** *in eine Lage bringen, in der die richtige Kugel nicht direkt gespielt werden kann;* **be ~ed** *die richtige Kugel nicht direkt spielen können;* **B** (*fig. coll.: thwart*) vereiteln; **he was ~ed** ihm wurde ein Strich durch die Rechnung gemacht

**snoop** /snuːp/ (*coll.*) **1** *v.i.* schnüffeln (*ugs.*); **~ into sth.** in einer Sache [herum]schnüffeln (*ugs.*); **~ about** *or* **around** herumschnüffeln (*ugs.*); **~ around the village** im Dorf herumschnüffeln. **2** *n.* **have a ~ around** sich [ein bisschen] umsehen

**snooper** /'snuːpə(r)/ *n.* (*coll.*) Schnüffler, *der*/Schnüfflerin, *die* (*ugs.*)

**snootily** /'snuːtɪlɪ/ *adv.*, **snooty** /'snuːtɪ/ *adj.* (*coll.*) hochnäsig (*ugs.*)

**snooze** /snuːz/ (*coll.*) **1** *v.i.* dösen (*ugs.*). **2** *n.* Nickerchen, *das* (*fam.*); **have a ~:** ein Nickerchen machen

**'snooze button** *n.* Schlummertaste, *die*

**snore** /snɔː(r)/ **1** *v.i.* schnarchen. **2** *n.* Schnarcher, *der* (*ugs.*); **~s** Schnarchen, *das*

**snorkel** /'snɔːkl/ **1** *n.* Schnorchel, *der.* **2** *v.i.*, (*Brit.*) **-ll-** schnorcheln

**snort** /snɔːt/ **1** *v.i.* schnauben (**with, in** vor + *Dat.*); **~ with laughter** vor Lachen prusten; **~ in disbelief** ungläubig schnauben. **2** *v.t.* **A** schnauben; **~ one's disgust/disbelief/anger** vor Ekel/ungläubig/wütend schnauben; **B** (*sl.: take*) **~ [coke]** [Koks] sniffen (*Drogenjargon*). **3** *n.* **A** Schnauben, *das;* **give a ~ of indignation/rage** vor Missbilligung/Wut schnauben; **with a ~ of rage** wutschnaubend; **~s of laughter** prustendes Gelächter; **B** (*coll.: drink*) Kurze, *der* (*ugs.*); **C** (*sl.: of drug*) Sniff, *der* (*Jargon*)

**snorter** /'snɔːtə(r)/ *n.* (*coll.*) **A** (*gale*) Orkan, *der;* **B** (*difficult task*) **a ~ [of a job]** eine Plackerei (*ugs.*); **the exam was a ~:** die Prüfung war ein Schlauch (*ugs.*)

**snot** /snɒt/ *n.* (*sl.*) Rotz, *der* (*derb*); Schnodder, *der* (*derb*)

**'snot rag** *n.* (*sl.*) Rotzfahne, *die* (*salopp*)

**snotty** /'snɒtɪ/ *adj.* (*sl.*) **A** ⇒ **snooty**; **B** (*running with nasal mucus*) rotznäsig (*salopp*); **~ child** Rotznase, *die* (*salopp*); **~ handkerchief** Rotzfahne, *die* (*salopp*); **~ nose** Rotznase, *die* (*salopp*)

**'snotty-nosed** *adj.* (*sl.*) **A** rotzig; rotznäsig (*salopp*); **B** ⇒ **snooty**

**snout** /snaʊt/ *n.* **A** (*nose*) Schnauze, *die;* (*of pig, anteater*) Rüssel, *der;* (*of wild boar*) Gebrech, *das* (*Jägerspr.*); **B** (*nosepiece*) Nase,

S

*die;* Ⓒ (*derog.: nose*) Rüssel, *der* (*salopp*); Zinken, *der* (*salopp*); Ⓓ (*Brit. coll.*) (*tobacco*) Kraut, *das* (*ugs., oft abwertend*); (*cigarette*) Kippe, *die* (*ugs.*); Lulle, *die* (*ugs.*); Ⓔ (*Brit. sl.: informer*) Schnüffler, *der* (*ugs. abwertend*); Spürhund, *der* (*ugs.*)

**snow** /snəʊ/ ❶ *n., no indef. art.* Ⓐ Schnee, *der;* **be [as] pure as the driven ~** ‹Person:› unschuldig wie ein/die Engel sein; Ⓑ *in pl.* (*areas*) Schnee, *der;* (*falls*) Schneefälle; Ⓒ (*sl.: cocaine*) Schnee, *der* (*Drogenjargon*); Ⓓ (*on TV screen etc.*) Schnee, *der.* ❷ *v.i. impers.* **it ~s** *or* **is ~ing** es schneit; **it starts ~ing** *or* **to ~:** es fängt an zu schneien. ❸ *v.t.* (*Amer. coll.*) **~ sb.** bei jmdm. Eindruck schinden (*ugs.*)

**~ 'in** *v.t.* **they are ~ed in** sie sind eingeschneit

**~ 'under** *v.t.* **be ~ed under** ‹Haus:› eingeschneit sein; ‹Straße:› zugeschneit sein; (*fig.*) (*with work*) erdrückt werden; (*with presents, letters*) überschüttet werden

**~ 'up** ⇒ **~ in**

**snow: ~ball** ❶ *n.* Schneeball, *der;* **~ball fight** Schneeballschlacht, *die;* **have a ~ball effect** eine Kettenreaktion auslösen; **not have** *or* **stand a ~ball's chance in hell** (*coll.*) nicht die geringste Chance haben; ❷ *v.t.* mit Schneebällen bewerfen; ❸ *v.i.* Ⓐ Schneebälle werfen; Ⓑ (*fig.: increase greatly*) lawinenartig zunehmen; **~ blindness** *n.* Schneeblindheit, *die;* **~blower** *n.* Schneefräse, *die;* **~board** ❶ *n.* Snowboard, *das;* ❷ *v.i.* Snowboard fahren; **~boarder** *n.* Snowboarder, *der*/Snowboarderin, *die;* **~boarding** *n.* Snowboardfahren, *das;* Snowboarden, *das;* **~ boot** *n.* Schneestiefel, *der;* **~-bound** *adj.* eingeschneit; **~-capped** *adj.* schneebedeckt; schneegekrönt (*dichter.*); **~ chains** *n. pl.* Schneeketten *Pl.;* **~-covered** *adj.* schneebedeckt; **~drift** *n.* Schneeverwehung, *die;* Schneewehe, *die;* **~drop** *n.* Schneeglöckchen, *das;* **~fall** *n.* Schneefall, *der;* **~flake** *n.* Schneeflocke, *die;* **~ goose** *n.* Schneegans, *die;* **~ job** *n.* (*Amer. coll.*) **do a ~ job on sb.** jmdn. beschwatzen (*ugs.*); **~ leopard** *n.* Schneeleopard, *der;* **~line** *n.* Schneegrenze, *die;* **~man** *n.* Schneemann, *der;* ⇒ *also* **abominable**; **~mobile** /ˈsnəʊməbiːl/ *n.* Schneemobil, *das;* **~plough** *n.* Schneepflug, *der;* **~scape** *n.* Schneelandschaft, *die;* **~shoe** *n.* Schneeschuh, *der;* **~ shovel** *n.* Schneeschaufel, *die;* **~ shower** *n.* Schneeschauer, *der;* **~storm** *n.* Schneesturm, *der;* **~-white** *adj.* schneeweiß; **S~ 'White** *pr. n.* Schneewittchen, *das*

**snowy** /ˈsnəʊɪ/ *adj.* Ⓐ (*having much snow*) schneereich ‹Gegend, Monat›; schneebedeckt ‹Berge›; **~ weather** Schneewetter, *das;* Ⓑ (*white*) schneeweiß

**snowy 'owl** *n.* Schnee-Eule, *die*

**SNP** *abbr.* **Scottish National Party** *Schottische Nationalpartei*

**snub** /snʌb/ ❶ *v.t.*, **-bb-:** Ⓐ (*rebuff*) brüskieren; vor den Kopf stoßen; Ⓑ (*reprove*) zurechtweisen; (*insult*) beleidigen; Ⓒ (*reject*) ablehnen; Ⓓ (*Amer.*) **~ out** ausdrücken. ❷ *n.* Abfuhr, *die;* **get** *or* **receive a ~:** eine Abfuhr erhalten; **give sb. a [proper] ~:** jmdm. eine [gehörige] Abfuhr erteilen

**snub: ~ 'nose** *n.* Stupsnase, *die;* Stupsnäschen, *das* (*fam.*); (*of car, aeroplane*) stumpfe Schnauze (*ugs.*) *od.* Nase; **~-nosed** *adj.* stupsnasig; stumpfnasig ‹Auto, Flugzeug›; mit stumpfer Schnauze (*ugs.*) *nachgestellt*

**snuff¹** /snʌf/ *n.* Ⓐ (*tobacco*) Schnupftabak, *der;* **take a pinch of ~:** eine Prise schnupfen; Ⓑ **be up to ~** (*Brit. coll.: not easily deceived*) mit allen Wassern gewaschen sein (*ugs.*); (*in good health or condition*) auf der Höhe sein (*ugs.*)

**snuff²** *v.t.* beschneiden, putzen ‹Kerze›; **~ it** (*sl.: die*) ins Gras beißen (*salopp*)

**~ 'out** ❶ *v.t.* Ⓐ (*extinguish*) löschen ‹Kerze›; Ⓑ (*fig.: put an end to*) zerstören; zunichte machen ‹Hoffnung›; niederschlagen ‹Revolte›; (*kill*) töten; umbringen. ❷ *v.i.* (*sl.*) ins Gras beißen (*salopp*)

**'snuff-box** *n.* Schnupftabak[s]dose, *die*

**snuffer** /ˈsnʌfə(r)/ *n.* Löschhütchen, *das;* **pair of ~s** Licht[putz]schere, *die*

**snuffle** /ˈsnʌfl/ ❶ *v.i.* Ⓐ (*sniff*) schnüffeln (**at** an + *Dat.*); (*with cold, after crying*) schniefen; Ⓑ (*make sniffing sound*) schnüffeln (**at** an + *Dat.*); Ⓒ (*breathe noisily*) schnaufen. ❷ *n.* Ⓐ (*sniff*) **~[s]** Schnaufen, *das;* (*of horses*) Schnauben, *das;* Ⓑ *in pl.* **have the ~s** [einen] Schnupfen haben

**snug** /snʌg/ ❶ *adj.* Ⓐ (*cosy*) gemütlich, behaglich ‹Haus, Zimmer, Bett›; (*warm*) mollig warm ‹Zimmer, Mantel, Bett›; **in bed sb. is as ~ as a bug in a rug** im Bett hat es jmd. urgemütlich *od.* richtig kuschelig; Ⓑ (*sheltered*) geschützt; Ⓒ (*close-fitting*) **be a ~ fit** genau passen; ‹Kleidung:› wie angegossen sitzen *od.* passen. ❷ *n.* (*Brit.: bar parlour*) *Nebenzimmer in einer Gastwirtschaft, bes. für Stammgäste*

**snuggle** /ˈsnʌgl/ ❶ *v.i.* **~ together** sich aneinander schmiegen *od.* -kuscheln; **~ down in bed** sich ins Bett kuscheln; **~ up with a book** es sich (*Dat.*) mit einem Buch gemütlich machen. ❷ *v.t.* **she ~d the crying child to her body** sie drückte das weinende Kind zärtlich an sich

**snugly** /ˈsnʌglɪ/ *adv.* Ⓐ (*cosily*) gemütlich; behaglich; **be/lie ~ tucked up** behaglich eingemumm[el]t sein/liegen (*fam.*); Ⓑ (*close-fitting*) **fit ~:** genau passen; ‹Kleidung:› wie angegossen sitzen *od.* passen

**so¹** /səʊ/ ❶ *adv.* Ⓐ (*by that amount*) so; **as winter draws near, so it gets darker** je näher der Winter rückt, desto dunkler wird es; **as fast as the water poured in, so we bailed it out** in dem Maße, wie das Wasser eindrang, schöpften wir es heraus; **so … as** so … wie; **there is nothing so fine as …:** es gibt nichts Schöneres als …; nichts ist so schön wie …; **not so [very] difficult/easy** *etc.* nicht so schwer/leicht *usw.;* **it's not so easy/big after all** so einfach/groß ist es nun wieder auch nicht; **so beautiful a present** so ein schönes Geschenk; ein so schönes Geschenk; **so great a general as X** ein so großer General wie X; **[it's] not so bad as …:** [es ist] nicht so schlecht wie …; **so far** bis hierher; (*until now*) bisher; bis jetzt; (*to such a distance*) so weit; **I trust him only so far** ich traue ihm nur bis zu einem gewissen Grad; **and so on [and so forth]** und so weiter und so fort; und so weiter; und so fort; **so long!** bis dann *od.* gleich *od.* nachher *od.* später! (*ugs.*); **so many** so viele; (*unspecified number*) soundso viele; **they looked like so many chimney sweeps** sie sahen alle aus wie die Schornsteinfeger; **so much** so viel; (*unspecified amount*) soundso viel; **[just] so much/many** (*nothing but*) nichts als; **his books are just so much rubbish** seine Bücher taugen alle nichts; **the villages are all so much alike** die Dörfer gleichen sich alle so sehr; **so much for the agenda** so viel zur Tagesordnung; **so much for him/his plans** das wärs, was ihn/seine Pläne angeht; **so much for my hopes** und ich habe mir solche Hoffnungen gemacht; **so much for that** (*after having dealt with a tricky problem*) das wäre geschafft; das hätten wir; **so much the better** umso besser; **if he doesn't want to stay, so much the worse for him** wenn er nicht bleiben will, ist er selber schuld; **not so much … as** weniger … als [eher]; **be not so much angry as disappointed** weniger verärgert als [viel mehr] enttäuscht sein; **not so much as** (*not even*) [noch] nicht einmal; **not so much as glance at sth.** auf etw. (*Akk.*) nicht einmal einen Blick werfen; ⇒ *also* **ever** F; **every** C; **far** 1 D; **long¹** 3 A, B; **more** 3 H; **never** A; Ⓑ (*in that manner*) so; **so be it** einverstanden; so sei es (*geh.*); **this being so** da dem so ist (*geh.*); **it so happened that he was not there** er war [zufällig] gerade nicht da; Ⓒ (*to such a degree*) so; **this answer so provoked him that …:** diese Antwort provozierte ihn so *od.* derart, dass …; **I went straight to bed, I was so tired** ich war so müde, dass ich gleich zu Bett ging; **put it so as not to offend him** sag es so, dass es ihn nicht kränkt; **I am not so big a fool as to believe that** ich bin nicht so dumm, das zu glauben; **I got so I could …** (*Amer.*) ich war so weit, dass ich … konnte; **so much so that …:** so sehr, dass …; das geht/ging so weit, dass …; Ⓓ (*with the intent*) **so as to** um … zu; **run so as not to get wet** rennen, um nicht nass zu werden; **so [that]** damit; Ⓔ (*emphatically*) so; **I'm so glad/tired!** ich bin ja so froh/müde!; **so kind of you!** wirklich nett von Ihnen!; **so sorry!** (*coll.*) Entschuldigung!; Verzeihung!; Ⓕ (*indeed*) **It's a rainbow! — So it is!** Es ist ein Regenbogen! — Ja, wirklich!; **'You suggested this trip. — So I did** Du hast diese Reise vorgeschlagen. — Das stimmt; **you said it was good, and so it was** du sagtest, es sei gut, und so war es auch; **is that so?** so? (*ugs.*); wirklich?; **and so he did** und das machte/tat er [dann] auch; **it 'is so** *expr. certainty* doch!; **it may be so, possibly so** [das ist] möglich; Ⓖ (*likewise*) **so am/have/would/could/will/do I** ich auch; **as a is to b, so is c to d** a verhält sich zu b wie c zu d; **as in the arts, so in politics, it's true that …:** in der Politik wie in der Kunst gilt, dass …; Ⓗ (*thus*) so; **and so it was that …:** und so geschah es, dass …; **not so!** nein, nein! ⇒ *also* **how** 1; **if** 1 A; **just** 2 A; **quite** A; **so so.** Ⓘ (*replacing clause, phrase, word*) **he suggested that I should take the train, and if I had done so, …** er riet mir, den Zug zu nehmen, und wenn ich es getan hätte, …; **we must consider what would be the result of so doing** wir müssen bedenken, was das für Folgen hätte; **I'm afraid so** leider ja; ich fürchte schon; **the teacher said so** der Lehrer hat es gesagt; **it was self-defence — or so the defendant said** es war Selbstverteidigung — so sagte jedenfalls der Angeklagte; **so saying, he departed** mit diesen Worten ging er; **so say all of us** das sagen wir alle; **Why do I have to go to bed? — Because I say so** Warum muss ich ins Bett? — Weil ich es sage; **I suppose so** ich nehme an (*ugs.*); *expr. reluctant agreement* wenn es sein muss; *granting grudging permission* von mir aus; **I told you so** ich habe es dir [doch] gesagt; **so I gathered** ich weiß [es]; **so I gathered from the newspaper** ich weiß es aus der Zeitung *od.* habe es aus der Zeitung erfahren; **he is a man of the world, so to say** *or* **speak** es menschelt sozusagen bei ihm; **it will take a week or so** es wird so (*ugs.*) *od.* etwa eine Woche dauern; **there were twenty or so people** es waren so (*ugs.*) um die zwanzig Leute da; **very much so** in der Tat; allerdings; ⇒ *also* **say** 1 A.

❷ *conj.* (*therefore*) daher; **so 'that's what he meant** das hat er also gemeint; **cigarettes are dangerous, so don't smoke** Zigaretten sind schädlich, also rauch nicht!; **so what is the answer?** wie lautet also die Antwort?; **so you are from Oxford then?** Sie kommen also aus Oxford?; **so 'there you are!** da bist du also!; **so there you 'are!** ich habe also Recht!; **so what are you going to do now?** was machen Sie denn jetzt?; **so what's the joke/problem?** was ist denn daran witzig?/was ist denn das Problem?; **so where have you been?** wo warst du denn?; **so that's 'that** (*coll.*) (*it's done*) [al]so, das wars (*ugs.*); (*it's over*) das wars also (*ugs.*); (*everything has been taken care of*) das wärs dann (*ugs.*); **so there!** [und] fertig!; [und damit] basta! (*ugs.*); **so you see …:** du siehst also …; **so?** na und?

**so²** ⇒ **soh**

**So.** *abbr.* (*Amer.*) **South** S

**soak** /səʊk/ ❶ *v.t.* Ⓐ (*steep*) einweichen ‹Wäsche in Lauge›; eintauchen ‹Brot in Milch, Tapete in Wasser›; **~ oneself in the sun** sich in der Sonne aalen (*ugs.*); Ⓑ (*wet*) nass machen; durchnässen; durchtränken ‹Erde›; **~ sb. from head to foot** jmdn. von Kopf bis Fuß durchnässen *od.* (*ugs.*) patschnass machen; **~ed in sth.** von etw. durchtränkt; mit *od.* von etw. getränkt; **a rag ~ed in petrol** ein mit Benzin getränkter Lappen; **~ed in sweat** schweißgebadet; **~ed with sweat** schweißgetränkt; **this town is ~ed in history** (*fig.*) in dieser Stadt weht der Hauch der Geschichte; Ⓒ (*absorb*) ⇒ **~ up**; Ⓓ (*coll.: obtain money from*) melken (*salopp*); schröpfen (*ugs.*).

❷ *v.i.* Ⓐ (*steep*) **put sth. in sth. to ~:** etw.

S

in etw. (*Dat.*) einweichen; **lie ~ing in the bath** ‹Person:› sich im Bad durchweichen lassen; **the liver was put to ~ in milk** die Leber wurde in Milch eingelegt; **B** (*drain*) ‹Feuchtigkeit, Nässe:› sickern; **~ away** wegsickern.
**3** *n.* **A** **give sth. a [good] ~:** etw. [gründlich] einweichen; **give the garden a [good] ~:** den Garten [gut] wässern; **put in ~:** einweichen; **he leaves his dentures in ~ overnight** er legt sein künstliches Gebiss über Nacht in eine Reinigungsflüssigkeit; **B** (*coll.: drinker*) Säufer, *der*/Säuferin, *die* (*derb, oft abwertend*); Suffkopp, *der* (*ugs.*)

**~ 'in** **1** *v.i.* **A** (*seep in*) einsickern; eindringen; ‹Flecken:› einziehen; **B** (*fig.*) **let the atmosphere ~ in** die Atmosphäre auf sich (*Akk.*) einwirken lassen. **2** *v.t.* ⇒ **~ up**

**~ into** *v.t.* sickern in (+ *Akk.*); ‹Tinte usw.:› einziehen in (+ *Akk.*)

**~ through** **1** *v.t.* **A** /'--/ (*penetrate*) ‹Flüssigkeit, Strahlen:› dringen durch; ‹Regenwasser, Blut:› sickern durch; **B** /-'-/ (*drench*) durchnässen. **2** *v.i.* /-'-/ durchdringen

**~ 'up** *v.t.* **A** (*absorb*) aufsaugen; **~ up the sunshine** in der Sonne baden; **B** (*fig.*) auf sich (*Akk.*) einwirken lassen, aufnehmen ‹Atmosphäre›; aufnehmen, in sich (*Akk.*) aufsaugen ‹Wissen usw.›

**'soakaway** *n.* (*Brit.*) Abflussgrube, *die*

**soaking** /'səʊkɪŋ/ **1** *n.* (*drenching*) **need a [good] ~** ‹Garten:› [gut] gewässert werden müssen; ‹Tuch:› [gründlich] eingeweicht werden müssen; **get a ~:** eine Dusche abbekommen; **give sb./sth. a ~:** jmdn./etw. nass machen. **2** *adv.* **~ wet** völlig durchnässt; klatsch- *od.* patschnass (*ugs.*). **3** *adj.* **A** (*drenched*) nass [bis auf die Haut]; patschnass (*ugs.*); **be ~** ‹Kleidung:› völlig durchnässt sein; ‹Gras:› patschnass sein (*ugs.*); **B** (*saturating*) alles durchnässend ‹Regen, Strom›

**'so-and-so** *n.*, *pl.* **~'s** **A** (*person not named*) [Herr/Frau] Soundso; (*thing not named*) Dings, *das;* **B** (*coll.: contemptible person*) Biest, *das* (*ugs.*); **poor ~:** armes Schwein (*ugs.*)

**soap** /səʊp/ **1** *n.*, *no indef. art.* **A** Seife, *die;* **a bar** *or* **tablet of ~:** ein Stück Seife; **with ~ and water** mit Wasser und Seife; **B** (*coll.*) ⇒ **soap opera**. **2** *v.t.* **~ [down]** einseifen

**soap: ~box** *n.* **A** ⇒ **~ dish** A; **B** (*packing-box*) Seifenschachtel, *die;* **C** (*stand*) ≈ Apfelsinenkiste, *die;* **get on one's ~box** (*fig.*) laut seine Meinung äußern; Volksreden halten; **D** (*cart*) Seifenkiste, *die;* **~box derby** Seifenkistenrennen, *das;* **~ bubble** *n.* Seifenblase, *die;* **~ dish** *n.* **A** (*container*) Seifendose, *die;* **B** (*open dish*) Seifenschale, *die;* **~ flakes** *n. pl.* Seifenflocken *Pl.;* **~ opera** *n.* (*Telev., Radio*) Seifenoper, *die* (*ugs.*); **~ powder** *n.* Seifenpulver, *das;* **~stone** *n.* (*Min.*) Speckstein, *der;* **~suds** *n. pl.* Seifenschaum, *der*

**soapy** /'səʊpɪ/ *adj.* seifig; **~ water** Seifenwasser, *das;* Seifenlauge, *die*

**soar** /sɔ:(r)/ *v.i.* **A** (*fly up*) aufsteigen; (*hover in the air*) segeln; **B** (*extend*) **~ into the sky** in den Himmel ragen; **C** (*fig.: rise rapidly*) steil ansteigen; ‹Preise, Kosten usw.:› in die Höhe schießen (*ugs.*); **my hopes have ~ed again** ich schöpfe wieder große Hoffnung; **~ above sb./sth.** jmdn./etw. überrunden *od.* überragen *od.* hinter sich (*Dat.*) lassen

**soaring** /'sɔ:rɪŋ/ *attrib. adj.* **A** (*flying*) segelnd; [hoch am Himmel] schwebend; **B** (*fig.: rising rapidly*) sprunghaft ansteigend; galoppierend ‹Preise, Inflation, Kosten›; hoch[fliegend, -gesteckt] ‹Ideale›; **C** (*lofty*) hoch aufragend

**sob** /sɒb/ **1** *v.i.*, **-bb-** schluchzen (**with** vor + *Dat.*). **2** *v.t.*, **-bb-** schluchzen. **3** *n.* Schluchzer, *der;* **~s [of anguish/pain]** [schmerzvolles] Schluchzen

**~ 'out** *v.t.* schluchzen; **she ~bed out her story** sie erzählte schluchzend *od.* unter Schluchzen ihre Geschichte; **~ one's heart out** bitterlich weinen

**SOB** /esəʊ'bi:/ *abbr.* (*Amer.*) **son of a bitch**

**sobbing** /'sɒbɪŋ/ **1** *n.* Schluchzen, *das.* **2** *adj.* schluchzend

**sober** /'səʊbə(r)/ *adj.* **A** (*not drunk*) nüchtern; **as ~ as a judge** stocknüchtern; **B** (*moderate*) solide; **C** (*solemn*) ernst; **D** (*subdued*) schlicht; gedeckt ‹Farben›; nüchtern ‹Umgebung›; **be a ~ dresser** sich solide kleiden; **E** (*rational, realistic*) nüchtern; **the ~ truth/fact** die nackte Wahrheit/Tatsache

**~ 'down** *v.i.* ruhig werden; (*after being excited*) sich abkühlen (*ugs.*); **he has ~ed down a lot** er ist wesentlich vernünftiger geworden

**~ 'up** **1** *v.i.* nüchtern werden; ausnüchtern. **2** *v.t.* ausnüchtern

**sobering** /'səʊbərɪŋ/ *adj.* ernüchternd; **he found it a ~ experience** das Erlebnis ernüchterte ihn *od.* brachte ihn zur Vernunft; **it is a ~ thought that ...:** der Gedanke ist ganz schön ernüchternd, dass ...

**soberly** /'səʊbəlɪ/ *adv.* nüchtern; vernünftig; **dress ~:** sich solide kleiden

**sober: ~-minded** *adj.* nüchtern; vernünftig; **~sides** *n.*, *pl. same* Miesepeter, *der* (*ugs. abwertend*)

**sobriety** /sə'braɪətɪ/ *n.*, *no pl.*, *no indef. art.* **A** (*not being drunk*) Nüchternheit, *die;* **B** (*moderation*) Bescheidenheit, *die;* **C** (*seriousness*) Ernsthaftigkeit, *die;* **~ of mind/judgment** Nüchternheit im Denken/Urteilen

**sobriquet** /'səʊbrɪkeɪ/ *n.* (*nickname*) Spitzname, *der*

**sob: ~ sister** *n.* (*Amer. Journ.*) *Schreiberin rührseliger Geschichten;* (*giving advice to readers*) Briefkastentante, *die* (*ugs.*); **~ story** *n.* rührselige Geschichte; **~ stuff** *n.*, *no indef. art.*, *no pl.* (*coll.*) Schmalz, *das* (*ugs.*); (*book, film, etc.*) Schmachtfetzen, *der* (*salopp*)

**'so-called** *adj.* so genannt; (*alleged*) angeblich

**soccer** /'sɒkə(r)/ *n.* Fußball, *der;* **~ ball** Fußball, *der*

**sociability** /səʊʃə'bɪlɪtɪ/ *n.*, *no pl.* Geselligkeit, *die*

**sociable** /'səʊʃəbl/ *adj.* gesellig; **she's not feeling ~ today** ihr ist heute nicht nach Gesellschaft zumute; **he did it just to be ~:** er hat es nur getan, um nicht ungesellig zu sein

**sociably** /'səʊʃəblɪ/ *adv.* gesellig; aufgeschlossen; **they spent the evening ~ together** sie verbrachten den Abend in geselliger Runde

**social** /'səʊʃl/ **1** *adj.* **A** sozial; gesellschaftlich; **~ welfare** Fürsorge, *die;* **B** (*of ~ life*) gesellschaftlich; gesellig ‹Abend, Beisammensein›; **~ behaviour** Benehmen in Gesellschaft; **~ engagement** gesellschaftliche Verpflichtung; **C** (*Zool.*) sozial; gesellig [lebend]. **2** *n.* (*gathering*) geselliges Beisammensein

**social: ~ anthro'pology** *n.* Sozialanthropologie, *die;* **~ 'chapter** *n.* (*Polit.*) Sozialprotokoll, *das;* **~ 'class** *n.* Gesellschaftsschicht, *die;* [Gesellschafts]klasse, *die;* **~ 'climber** *n.* Emporkömmling, *der* (*abwertend*); [sozialer] Aufsteiger (*ugs.*); **~ club** *n.* Klub für geselliges Beisammensein; **~ 'compact**, **~ 'contract** *ns.* (*Polit.*) Gesellschaftsvertrag, *der;* **~ 'conscience** *n.* soziales Gewissen; **S~ 'Democrat** *n.* (*Polit.*) Sozialdemokrat, *der*/-demokratin, *die;* **S~ Demo'cratic Party** *n.* (*Brit. Polit.*) Sozialdemokratische Partei; **~ engi'neering** *n.* Social engineering, *das;* Sozialtechnologie, *die;* **~ 'history** *n.* Sozialgeschichte, *die*

**socialisation**, **socialise** ⇒ **socializ-**

**socialism** /'səʊʃəlɪzm/ *n.* Sozialismus, *der*

**socialist** /'səʊʃəlɪst/ **1** *n.* Sozialist, *der*/Sozialistin, *die.* **2** *adj.* sozialistisch

**socialite** /'səʊʃəlaɪt/ *n. bekannte Persönlichkeit des gesellschaftlichen Lebens*

**socialization** /səʊʃəlaɪ'zeɪʃn/ *n.* Sozialisation, *die*

**socialize** /'səʊʃəlaɪz/ **1** *v.t.* umgänglich machen; **become ~d** umgänglich[er] werden; **~d medicine** (*Amer.*) öffentliche Gesundheitsfürsorge. **2** *v.i.* geselligen Umgang pflegen; **~ with sb.** (*chat*) sich mit jmdm. unterhalten; **he is out socializing** er ist mit Bekannten *od.* (*ugs.*) irgendwelchen Leuten unterwegs

**social life** *n.* gesellschaftliches Leben; **a place with plenty of ~:** ein Ort, wo etwas los ist (*ugs.*); **not have much ~** ‹Person:› nicht viel ausgehen

**socially** /'səʊʃəlɪ/ *adv.* **meet ~:** sich privat treffen; **have a good time ~:** viel unter die Leute kommen; **~ acceptable** aus der richtigen Gesellschaftsschicht; **~ deprived** sozial benachteiligt

**social: ~ 'order** *n.* Gesellschaftsordnung, *die;* **~ 'outcast** *n.* Außenseiter der Gesellschaft; **~ 'policy** *n.* (*Polit.*) Sozialpolitik, *die;* **~ re'form** *n.* Sozialreform, *die;* **fight for ~ reform** für Sozialreformen *od.* gesellschaftliche Reformen kämpfen; **~ 'science** *n.* Sozialwissenschaften *Pl.;* Gesellschaftswissenschaften *Pl.;* **~ 'scientist** *n.* Sozialwissenschaftler, *der*/-wissenschaftlerin, *die;* **~ se'curity** *n.* **A** (*Brit.: benefit*) Sozialhilfe, *die;* **B** (*welfare system*) soziale Sicherheit; **C** (*Amer.: insurance*) Sozialversicherung, *die;* **~ 'service** *n.* **A** (*service to society*) soziales Engagement; **B** (*a service provided by the government*) staatliche Sozialleistung; **~ 'services** *n. pl.* Sozialdienste *Pl.*; **~ 'status** *n.* sozialer Status; **~ structure** *n.* Sozialstruktur, *die;* **~ studies** *n. sing.* (*Educ.*) Gemeinschaftskunde, *die;* **~ system** *n.* Gesellschaftssystem, *das;* **~ work** *n.* Sozialarbeit, *die;* **~ worker** *n.* **▶ 1261** Sozialarbeiter, *der*/-arbeiterin, *die*

**societal** /sə'saɪətl/ *adj.* (*formal*) gesellschaftlich

**society** /sə'saɪətɪ/ **1** *n.* **A** Gesellschaft, *die;* **be embarrassed in ~:** in Gegenwart anderer verlegen sein; **avoid ~:** gesellschaftlichen Umgang meiden; **high ~:** Highsociety, *die;* **B** (*club, association*) Verein, *der;* (*Commerc.*) Gesellschaft, *die;* (*group of persons with common beliefs, aims, interests, etc.*) Gemeinschaft, *die;* ⇒ *also* **friend** C; **Jesus**. **2** *attrib. adj.* **A** (*of high ~*) Gesellschafts-; [High-]Society-; **she is a ~ hostess** sie gibt Feste für die [gehobene] Gesellschaft; **~ people** Leute der High Society; **B** (*of club or association*) Vereins-, Klub‹vorsitzender, -treffen, -ausflug, -sekretär usw.›

**socio-** /səʊsɪəʊ/ *in comb.* sozio-/Sozio-

**sociobi'ology** *n.* Soziobiologie, *die*

**socio'cultural** *adj.* soziokulturell

**socio-eco'nomic** *adj.* sozioökonomisch

**sociolingu'istic** *adj.* soziolinguistisch

**sociolingu'istics** *n. sing.* Soziolinguistik, *die*

**sociological** /səʊsɪə'lɒdʒɪkl/ *adj.* soziologisch

**sociologist** /səʊsɪ'ɒlədʒɪst/ *n.* **▶ 1261** Soziologe, *der*/Soziologin, *die*

**sociology** /səʊsɪ'ɒlədʒɪ/ *n.* Soziologie, *die*

**sock**[1] /sɒk/ *n.* **A** *pl.* **~s** *or* (*Commerc./coll.*) **sox** /sɒks/ Socke, *die;* Socken, *der* (*südd.*, *österr.*, *schweiz.*); (*ankle ~*, *esp. for children also*) Söckchen, *das;* **knee-length ~s** Kniestrümpfe *Pl.;* **pull one's ~s up** (*Brit. fig. coll.*) sich am Riemen reißen (*ugs.*); **put a ~ in it!** (*Brit. sl.*) halt die Klappe! (*salopp*); (*stop doing sth.*) hör auf [damit]!; **B** ⇒ **insole** D; **C** (*of horse*) ⇒ **stocking**[1] B

**sock**[2] (*coll.*) **1** *v.t.* (*hit*) schlagen, hauen (*ugs.*); **~ sb. in the mouth/on the chin/jaw** jmdm. eine reinhauen (*salopp*); jmdn. in die Schnauze hauen (*derb*); **~ it to sb.** (*Amer. coll.*) jmdm. Saures geben (*salopp*); (*fig.: impress sb.*) es jmdm. zeigen (*ugs.*). **2** *n.* **give sb. a ~ on the chin/jaw/in the mouth** jmdm. eine reinhauen (*salopp*)

**socket** /'sɒkɪt/ *n.* **A** (*Anat.*) (*of eye*) Höhle, *die;* (*of joint*) Pfanne, *die;* **~ of a tooth** Zahnfach, *das* (*Anat.*); **B** (*Electr.*) Steckdose, *die;* (*receiving a bulb*) Fassung, *die;* **C** (*for attachment*) Fassung, *die;* (*of pipe*) Muffe, *die;* (*of candle holder*) [Kerzen]tülle, *die*

**socket: ~ spanner**, (*Amer.*) **~ wrench** *ns.* Steckschlüssel, *der*

**sockeye** /'sɒkaɪ/ *n.* (*Zool.*) **~ [salmon]** Blaurückenlachs, *der*

S

**Socrates** /ˈsɒkrətiːz/ *pr. n.* Sokrates (*der*)

**Socratic** /səˈkrætɪk/ *adj.* sokratisch

**sod¹** /sɒd/ *n.* (*turf*) Sode, *die;* **be/lie under the ~:** unter der Erde liegen

**sod²** (*sl.*) ❶ *n.* (*bastard, swine*) Sau, *die* (*derb*); (*fool*) Rindvieh, *das* (*salopp*); **that's ~'s law, ~'s law was proved right** (*coll.*) es musste ja so kommen; **the poor old ~:** das arme Schwein (*salopp*); **not give a ~ = not give a damn ⇒ damn** 2 B. ❷ *v.t.*, **-dd-: ~ that/you!** verdammter Mist/scher dich zum Teufel! (*ugs.*)

**~ 'off** *v.i. imper.* (*sl.*) verpiss dich (*derb*)

**soda** /ˈsəʊdə/ *n.* **A** (*sodium compound*) Soda, *die od. das;* ⇒ *also* **caustic** 1 B; **B** (*drink*) Soda[wasser], *das;* **whisky and ~:** Whisky mit Soda

**soda: ~ bread** *n. mit Backsoda gebackenes Brot;* **~ fountain** *n.* (*Amer.*) **A** (*container*) Mineralwasserbehälter, *der;* **B** (*shop*) *Erfrischungshalle bzw. -bar, in der es vor allem Erfrischungsgetränke und Speiseeis gibt;* **~ siphon** *n.* Siphon, *der;* Siphonflasche, *die;* **~ water** *n.* Soda[wasser], *das*

**sodden** /ˈsɒdn/ *adj.* durchnässt (**with** von)

**sodding** /ˈsɒdɪŋ/ *attrib. adj.* (*sl.*) Scheiß- (*derb*)

**sodium** /ˈsəʊdɪəm/ *n.* (*Chem.*) Natrium, *das*

**sodium: ~ bi'carbonate** *n.* (*Chem.*) doppeltkohlensaures Natrium; Natriumhydrogenkarbonat, *das;* **~ 'carbonate** *n.* (*Chem.*) Natriumkarbonat, *das;* Soda, *die od. das;* **~ 'chloride** *n.* (*Chem.*) Natriumchlorid, *das;* **~ hy'droxide** *n.* (*Chem.*) Ätznatron, *das;* **~ lamp** *n.* Natriumdampflampe, *die;* **~ 'nitrate** *n.* (*Chem.*) Natriumnitrat, *das*

**sodomite** /ˈsɒdəmaɪt/ *n.* Sodomit, *der*

**sodomize** /ˈsɒdəmaɪz/ *v.t.* sodomisieren (*geh.*); anal verkehren mit; Sodomie betreiben mit ‹Tier›

**sodomy** /ˈsɒdəmɪ/ *n.* Analverkehr, *der;* Sodomie, *die* (*veralt.*); (*with animal*) Sodomie, *die*

**soever** ⇒ **howsoever, whatsoever,** *etc.*

**sofa** /ˈsəʊfə/ *n.* Sofa, *das;* **~ bed** Bettcouch, *die*

**soffit** /ˈsɒfɪt/ *n.* (*Archit.*) Windbrett, *das*

**soft** /sɒft/ ❶ *adj.* **A** weich; zart, weich ‹Haut›; **the ground is ~:** der Boden ist aufgeweicht; (*Sport*) der Boden ist schwer; **as ~ as butter** weich wie Butter; butterweich; **~ ice cream** Soft-Eis, *das;* **~ toys** Stofftiere; **~ water area** Gebiet mit weichem Wasser; **B** (*mild*) sanft; mild ‹Klima›; zart ‹Duft›; **C** (*compassionate*) **have a ~ heart** ein weiches Herz haben; weichherzig sein; **have a ~ spot for sb./sth.** eine Vorliebe *od.* Schwäche für jmdn./etw. haben; **you are too ~!** du bist zu weich[herzig]!; **D** (*delicate*) sanft ‹Augen›; weich ‹Farbe, Licht›; **E** (*quiet*) leise; sanft; **F** (*gentle*) sanft; (*amorous*) zärtlich ‹Blicke›; **be ~ on sb.** (*coll.: be in love with*) in jmdn. verknallt sein (*ugs.*); für jmdn. schwärmen; **be ~ on *or* with sb.** (*coll.: be unusually lenient with*) mit jmdm. sanft umgehen; jmdn. [zu] sanft anfassen; ⇒ *also* **nothing** 1 C; **G** (*coll.: easy*) bequem, (*ugs.*) locker ‹Job, Leben›; **have a ~ job** eine ruhige Kugel schieben (*ugs.*); **H** (*compliant*) nachgiebig; ⇒ *also* **touch** 3 I; **I** (*too indulgent*) zu nachsichtig; zu lasch (*ugs.*); **be ~ with sb.** sich (*Dat.*) von jmdm. alles bieten lassen; **J** (*gently curved*) weich ‹Umriss, Linien, Züge›; **K** (*weak*) schlaff ‹Muskeln›; weichlich (*abwertend*) ‹Mann›; verweichlicht ‹Volk›; **L be/go ~ in the head** (*coll.*) nicht alle Tassen im Schrank haben (*ugs.*)/verrückt werden (*ugs.*); **M** (*Scot., Ir.: moist*) feucht ‹Wetter, Tag›; **N** (*Phonet.*) weich.
❷ *adv.* (*quietly*) leise

**soft: ~ball** *n.* Softball, *der* (*Variante des Baseballs mit weicherem Ball*); **~-boiled** *adj.* weich gekocht ‹Ei›; **~-centred** *adj.* ‹Praline usw.› mit weicher Füllung; **~ coal** *n.* Fettkohle, *die;* **~ copy** *n.* (*Computing*) Softcopy, *die;* **~ cover** *n.* **book with a ~ cover** Buch mit einem Softcover (*Verlagsw.*) *od.* mit einem flexiblen Einband; **~ currency** *n.* (*Econ.*) weiche Währung; *attrib.* ‹Markt, Land› mit weicher Währung; **~ detergent** *n.* biologisch abbaubares Waschmittel; **~ drink** *n.* alkoholfreies Getränk; **~ drug** *n.* weiche Droge

**soften** /ˈsɒfn/ ❶ *v.i.* weicher werden; **~ing of the brain** Gehirnerweichung, *die* (*Med.*); (*coll.: stupidity*) Verkalkung, *die* (*ugs.*). ❷ *v.t.* weich klopfen ‹Fleisch›; aufweichen ‹Boden›; dämpfen ‹Beleuchtung›; mildern ‹Farbe, Farbton›; enthärten ‹Wasser›; **~ the blow** (*fig.*) den Schock mildern

**~ 'up** *v.t.* weichklopfen (*ugs.*) ‹Boxgegner›; aufweichen ‹Verteidigungsanlagen›; (*verbally*) milder stimmen

**softener** /ˈsɒfənə(r)/ *n.* **A** (*for water*) [Wasser]enthärter, *der;* **B** (*for fabrics*) Weichspülmittel, *das;* Weichspüler, *der*

**soft: ~ 'focus** *n.* (*Photog.*) Weichzeichnung, *die;* **~ fruit** *n.* Beerenobst, *das;* **~ 'furnishings** *n. pl.* (*Brit.*) Raumtextilien *Pl.;* **~ goods** *n. pl.* (*Brit.*) Textilien *Pl.;* **~'headed** *adj.* dumm; schwachköpfig; **~'hearted** /sɒftˈhɑːtɪd/ *adj.* weichherzig

**softie** ⇒ **softy**

**soft 'landing** *n.* (*Astronaut.*) weiche Landung

**softly** /ˈsɒftlɪ/ *adv.* **A** (*quietly*) leise ‹sprechen, singen, gehen›; **B** (*gently*) sanft; **speak ~:** mit sanfter Stimme sprechen; **C** (*not dazzlingly*) sanft ‹scheinen, leuchten›; **D** (*affectionately*) zärtlich

**softness** /ˈsɒftnɪs/ *n., no pl.* ⇒ **soft** 1: **A** Weichheit, *die;* Zartheit, *die;* **the silky ~ of her hair** ihr seidenweiches Haar; **B** Sanftheit, *die;* Milde, *die;* Zartheit, *die;* **there is a ~ in the air** die Luft ist mild *od.* (*geh.*) lind; **C ~ of heart** Weichherzigkeit, *die;* **D** (*delicacy*) Sanftheit, *die;* Weichheit, *die;* **E** (*of voice, music, etc.*) Gedämpftheit, *die;* **F** (*gentleness*) Sanftheit, *die;* Zärtlichkeit, *die;* **G** (*compliance*) Nachgiebigkeit, *die;* **H** (*leniency*) Nachsichtigkeit, *die;* Laschheit, *die* (*ugs.*); **I** (*of lines, features, outline*) Weichheit, *die;* **J** (*weakness*) Schlaffheit, *die;* Weichlichkeit, *die* (*abwertend*); **K** (*coll.: silliness*) **~ in the head** Gehirnerweichung, *die* (*ugs.*)

**soft: ~ option** *n.* Weg des geringsten Widerstandes; **~ 'palate** *n.* (*Anat.*) weicher Gaumen; Gaumensegel, *das* (*fachspr.*); **~ pedal** ⇒ **pedal** 1 A; **~-'pedal** ❶ *v.i.* **A** (*Mus.*) mit [dem] Pianopedal spielen; **B** (*fig.: go easy*) sich zurückhalten; **~-pedal on sth.** etw. herunterspielen; ❷ *v.t.* **A** (*Mus.*) mit [dem] Pianopedal spielen; **B** (*fig.: tone down*) herunterspielen; **~ 'porn** (*coll.*), **~ por'nography** *ns.* Softpornographie, *die;* **~ roe** *n.* Milch, *die;* **~ 'sell** *n.* **give sb. the ~ sell** jmdn. auf die sanfte Tour (*ugs.*) zum Kauf zu bewegen versuchen; *attrib.* **~ sell salesmanship** sanfte Tour (*ugs.*) beim Verkaufsgespräch; **give sb. the ~ sell treatment** jmdn. auf die sanfte Tour (*ugs.*) zum Kauf zu bewegen versuchen; **~-shell, ~-shelled** *adjs.* **A** (*Zool.*) mit weicher Schale *nachgestellt;* **B** (*fig.*) gemäßigt; lasch (*abwertend*); **~ 'soap** *n.* **A** (*cleanser*) Schmierseife, *die;* **B** (*fig.: flattery*) Schmeichelei, *die;* **use ~ soap** schmeicheln; schöntun (*ugs.*); *attrib.* **~-soap tactics/policy/treatment** gezielte Schmeichelei; gezieltes Schöntun (*ugs.*); **~-'soap** *v.t.* **~-soap sb.** jmdm. Honig um den Bart schmieren (*ugs.*); **~-spoken** *adj.* leise sprechend ‹Person›; leise [gesprochen] ‹Wort›; **be ~-spoken** leise sprechen; **~ 'tissue** *n.* (*Anat.*) weiches Körpergewebe; **~ top** *n.* **A** (*roof*) Stoffverdeck, *das;* **folding ~ top** Faltverdeck, *das;* **B** (*car*) Cabrio, *das;* Kabrio, *das;* **~ 'touch** ⇒ **touch** 3 J; **~ 'toy** *n.* Stoffspielzeug, *das;* (*toy animal*) Stofftier, *das;* **~ verge** *n.* (*Brit.*) Grünstreifen, *der;* **~ware** *n., no pl., no indef. art.* (*Computing*) Software, *die;* **~wood** *n.* Weichholz, *das; attrib.* Weichholz-

**softy** /ˈsɒftɪ/ *n.* **A** (*coll.: weakling*) Weichling, *der;* Waschlappen, *der* (*ugs.*); (*boy/girl who easily cries*) Heulpeter, *der*/Heulsuse, *die* (*ugs.*); **B** (*sentimental person*) **be a ~:** sentimental sein; **you old ~!** du sentimentales Huhn! (*ugs.*)

**soggy** /ˈsɒɡɪ/ *adj.* aufgeweicht ‹Boden›; durchnässt ‹Kleider›; matschig ‹Salat›; nicht durchgebacken, (*landsch.*) glitschig ‹Brot, Kuchen›

**soh** /səʊ/ *n.* (*Mus.*) sol

**soi-disant** /swɑˈdiːzɑ̃/ *adj.* (*calling oneself*) selbst ernannt; (*claimed as such*) so genannt

**soigné** (*fem.:* **soignée**) /ˈswɑnjeɪ/ *adj.* soigniert (*geh.*) ‹Person, Restaurant›; elegant ‹Kleid›

**soil¹** /sɔɪl/ *n.* **A** (*earth*) Erde, *die;* Boden, *der;* **B** (*ground*) Boden, *der;* **on British/foreign ~:** auf britischem Boden/im Ausland *od.* (*geh.*) in der Fremde

**soil²** ❶ *v.t.* (*lit. or fig.*) beschmutzen; **~ one's/sb.'s reputation** (*by scandal, criminal activities*) sein/jmds. Ansehen *od.* seinen/jmds. guten Ruf beflecken (*geh.*); (*by failure*) seinen/jmds. Ruf schmälern; ⇒ *also* **hand** 1 A. ❷ *n.* Schmutz, *der*

**'soil conservation** *n.* Bodenschutz, *der*

**soiled** /sɔɪld/ *adj.* schmutzig ‹Wäsche, Windel›; gebraucht ‹Damenbinde›

**soil: ~ pipe** *n.* senkrechtes Abflussrohr; **~ science** *n.* Bodenkunde, *die*

**soirée** /ˈswɑːreɪ/ *n.* Soiree, *die*

**sojourn** /ˈsɒdʒɜːn, ˈsɒdʒən/ (*literary*) ❶ *v.i.* verweilen (*geh.*); weilen (*geh.*) (**at** in + *Dat.*). ❷ *n.* Aufenthalt, *der*

**sol¹** /sɒl/ *n.* (*Chem.*) Sol, *das*

**sol²** ⇒ **soh**

**solace** /ˈsɒləs/ ❶ *n.* Trost, *der;* **take *or* find ~ in sth.** Trost in etw. (*Dat.*) finden; sich mit etw. trösten; **turn to sb./sth. for ~:** bei jmdm./etw. Trost suchen. ❷ *v.t.* trösten

**solar** /ˈsəʊlə(r)/ *adj.* (*Astron.*) Sonnen-

**solar: ~ battery** *n.* Sonnenbatterie, *die;* Solarbatterie, *die;* **~ cell** *n.* Sonnenzelle, *die;* Solarzelle, *die;* **~ 'day** *n.* (*Astron.*) Sonnentag, *der;* **~ e'clipse** *n.* (*Astron.*) Sonnenfinsternis, *die;* **~ 'energy** *n.* Solarenergie, *die;* Sonnenenergie, *die*

**solarium** /səˈleərɪəm/ *n., pl.* **solaria** /səˈleərɪə/ Solarium, *das*

**solar: ~ 'panel** *n.* Sonnenkollektor, *der;* (*on satellite*) Sonnensegel, *das;* **~ 'plexus** *n.* (*Anat.*) Solarplexus, *der;* Sonnengeflecht, *das;* **~ 'power** *n.* Sonnenenergie, *die;* **~-powered** *adj.* mit Sonnenenergie betrieben; **~ radiation** *n.* Sonnenstrahlung, *die;* **~ system** *n.* (*Astron.*) Sonnensystem, *das*

**sold** ⇒ **sell** 1, 2

**solder** /ˈsɒldə(r), ˈsəʊldə(r)/ ❶ *n.* Lot, *das* (*Technik*). ❷ *v.t.* löten

**soldering iron** /ˈsɒldərɪŋaɪən, ˈsəʊldərɪŋ aɪən/ *n.* Lötkolben, *der*

**soldier** /ˈsəʊldʒə(r)/ ❶ ▶ 1261 *n.* Soldat, *der;* **[common] ~:** einfacher Soldat; **officers and ~s** Offiziere und Mannschaften; **~ of fortune** Glücksritter, *der* (*abwertend*); (*mercenary*) Söldner, *der;* ⇒ *also* **old soldier; private** 2 A; **tin soldier; toy soldier; unknown** 1. ❷ *v.i.* als Soldat dienen

**~ 'on** *v.i.* (*coll.*) weitermachen

**soldierly** /ˈsəʊldʒəlɪ/ ❶ *adj.* soldatisch. ❷ *adv.* wie ein Soldat

**soldiery** /ˈsəʊldʒərɪ/ *n.* **A** *constr. as pl.* (*soldiers*) Militär, *das;* **B** (*troop*) Soldateska, *die* (*abwertend*)

**sole¹** /səʊl/ ❶ *n.* **A** (*Anat.; of shoe*) Sohle, *die;* **inner ~** ⇒ **insole** B; **B** (*of plough*) Pflugsohle, *die;* (*of plane*) Sohle, *die.* ❷ *v.t.* [be]sohlen

**sole²** *n.* (*fish*) Seezunge, *die;* ⇒ *also* **lemon sole**

**sole³** *adj.* einzig; alleinig ‹Verantwortung, Erbe, Recht›; Allein‹erbe, -eigentümer›; **the operation is the surgeon's ~ responsibility** für die Operation ist allein[e] der Chirurg zuständig; **he is the ~ judge of whether ...:** er allein urteilt darüber, ob .../entscheidet, ob ...

**solecism** /ˈsɒlɪsɪzm/ n. **A** (*blunder*) [sprachlicher] Fehler; **B** (*social gaffe*) Fauxpas, *der*

**soled** /səʊld/ *adj.* besohlt; **leather-/thick-~** ‹Schuhe› mit Ledersohlen/dicken Sohlen

**solely** /ˈsəʊllɪ/ *adv.* einzig und allein; ausschließlich; **~ because ...:** nur [deswegen], weil ...; einzig und allein, weil ...

**solemn** /ˈsɒləm/ *adj.* feierlich; ernst ‹Anlass, Gespräch›; **the ~ truth** die reine Wahrheit

**solemnity** /səˈlemnɪtɪ/ *n.* **A** *no pl.* Feierlichkeit, *die;* **B** (*rite*) Feierlichkeit, *die*

**solemnization** /sɒləmnaɪ'zeɪʃn/ *n.* feierlicher Vollzug; (*of mass*) Zelebration, *die;* Feier, *die*

**solemnize** /'sɒləmnaɪz/ *v.t.* [feierlich] vollziehen; zelebrieren, feiern ‹Messe›

**solemnly** /'sɒləmlɪ/ *adv.* feierlich

**solemn 'mass** *n.* Hochamt, *das*

**solenoid** /'səʊlənɔɪd/ *n.* Zylinderspule, *die;* (*converting energy*) Magnetspule, *die*

**sol-fa** /sɒl'fɑː/ (*Mus.*) ❶ *v.t. & i.* solmisieren. ❷ *n.* Solmisation, *die;* ⇒ *also* **tonic sol-fa**

**solicit** /sə'lɪsɪt/ ❶ *v.t.* Ⓐ (*appeal for*) werben um ‹Wählerstimmen, Unterstützung›; Ⓑ (*appeal to*) erregen ‹Interesse›; ~ **sb. for sth.** jmdn. um etw. bitten; Ⓒ (*Commerc.*) ~ **sb. for sth.** bei jmdm. um etw. werben; **he ~ed [interested people for] investment in his enterprise** er warb um Kapitalanleger für sein Unternehmen; Ⓓ (*make sexual offer to*) ~ **sb.** sich jmdm. anbieten. ❷ *v.i.* Ⓐ (*make request*) ~ **for sth.** um etw. bitten *od.* (*geh.*) ersuchen; (*in a petition*) etw. [mit einer Eingabe] fordern; Ⓑ (*Commerc.*) ~ **for sth.** um etw. werben; Ⓒ (*offer illicit sex*) ~ **[for custom]** sich anbieten; **be arrested for ~ing** ‹Prostituierte:› wegen öffentlichen Sichanbietens festgenommen werden

**solicitation** /səlɪsɪ'teɪʃn/ *n.* (*formal: request*) Drängen, *das*

**solicitor** /sə'lɪsɪtə(r)/ *n.* ▶ 1261 Ⓐ (*Brit.: lawyer*) Rechtsanwalt, *der*/-anwältin, *die* (*der/die nicht vor höheren Gerichten auftritt*); Ⓑ (*Amer.: canvasser*) Werber, *der*

**Solicitor-'General** *n., pl.* **Solicitors-General** Ⓐ (*Brit. Law*) *zweiter Kronanwalt;* Ⓑ (*Amer. Law*) *ranghöchster [beamteter] Staatssekretär im Justizministerium*

**solicitous** /sə'lɪsɪtəs/ *adj.* Ⓐ (*eager*) **be ~ of sth.** um etw. bemüht sein; **be ~ to do sth.** [darum] bemüht sein, etw. zu tun; Ⓑ (*anxious*) besorgt; ~ **of** *or* **about** *or* **for sb./sth.** um jmdn./etw. besorgt

**solicitously** /sə'lɪsɪtəslɪ/ *adv.* Ⓐ (*eagerly*) eifrig; Ⓑ (*anxiously*) besorgt

**solicitude** /sə'lɪsɪtjuːd/ *n.* (*anxiety, concern*) Besorgtheit, *die*

**solid** /'sɒlɪd/ ❶ *adj.* Ⓐ (*rigid*) fest; **freeze/be frozen ~:** [fest] gefrieren/gefroren sein; **set ~:** fest werden; Ⓑ (*of the same substance all through*) massiv; ~ **silver** massives Silber; **a ~-silver tea service/watch** *etc.* ein Teeservice/eine Uhr *usw.* aus massivem *od.* reinem Silber; ~ **gold** reines Gold; **a ~-gold watch/crown/bar** eine reingoldene Uhr/Krone/ein Barren reines Gold; ~ **tyre** Vollgummireifen, *der;* **be packed ~** (*coll.*) gerammelt voll sein (*ugs.*); Ⓒ (*well-built*) stabil; solide gebaut ‹Haus, Mauer usw.›; **have a ~ majority** (*Polit.*) eine solide Mehrheit haben; Ⓓ (*reliable*) verlässlich, zuverlässig ‹Freund, Helfer, Verbündeter›; fest ‹Stütze›; Ⓔ (*complete*) ganz; **a good ~ meal** eine kräftige Mahlzeit; **a ~ day/hour/week** ein ganzer Tag/eine ganze *od.* volle Stunde/eine ganze Woche; Ⓕ (*sound*) stichhaltig ‹Argument, Grund›; solide ‹Arbeiter, Finanzlage, Firma›; solide, gediegen ‹Komfort, Grundlage›; Ⓖ (*Geom.: having three dimensions*) dreidimensional; räumlich; Ⓗ (*Geom.: concerned with ~s*) stereometrisch; ~ **geometry** Stereometrie, *die;* Ⓘ (*Printing*) kompress; kompress gesetzt ‹Seite›; Ⓙ (*united*) einig; **a ~ vote for ...:** eine einstimmige Entscheidung für ...; **be ~ with sb.** mit jmdm. einig sein; (*Amer. coll.: friendly*) mit jmdm. auf gutem Fuß stehen; **go** *or* **be ~ for sb./sth.** uneingeschränkt für jmdn./etw. sein; Ⓚ heftig ‹Schlag›.
❷ *n.* Ⓐ (*substance*) fester Körper; Ⓑ *in pl.* (*food*) feste Nahrung; Ⓒ (*Geom.*) Körper, *der*

**solid 'angle** *n.* (*Geom.*) Raumwinkel, *der*

**solidarity** /sɒlɪ'dærɪtɪ/ *n., no pl.* Solidarität, *die;* **show ~ with sb.** sich mit jmdn. solidarisch zeigen

**solid:** ~ **'fuel** *n.* fester Brennstoff; **~-'fuel** *attrib. adj.* Festbrennstoff-; **~-fuel rocket** Feststoffrakete, *die*

**solidification** /səlɪdɪfɪ'keɪʃn/ *n.* Verfestigung, *die;* Verhärtung, *die;* Erstarrung, *die*

**solidify** /sə'lɪdɪfaɪ/ ❶ *v.t.* verfestigen. ❷ *v.i.* (*become solid*) hart *od.* fest werden; erstarren; ‹Flüssigkeit, Lava:› erstarren

**solidity** /sə'lɪdɪtɪ/ *n., no pl.* ⇒ **solid** 1: Ⓐ Festigkeit, *die;* Ⓑ Massivität, *die;* Ⓒ Stabilität, *die;* Ⓓ (*of reasons, argument*) Stichhaltigkeit, *die*

**solidly** /'sɒlɪdlɪ/ *adv.* Ⓐ (*firmly*) stabil; Ⓑ (*compactly*) **a ~ built person** ein kräftig gebauter Mensch; Ⓒ (*ceaselessly*) pausenlos; **he wrote ~ for four hours** er schrieb vier Stunden ohne Pause; Ⓓ (*wholeheartedly*) **be ~ behind sb./sth.** uneingeschränkt hinter jmdm./einer Sache stehen; Ⓔ (*with sound reasons*) stichhaltig; **argue ~ for sth.** stichhaltige Argumente für etw. vorbringen

**solid:** ~ **so'lution** *n.* (*Chem.*) feste Lösung; ~ **'state** *n.* (*Phys.*) fester Zustand; **~-state** *adj.* (*Phys.*) Festkörper‹physik, -geräte, -schaltung›

**soliloquize** /sə'lɪləkwaɪz/ *v.i.* monologisieren; (*to oneself*) Selbstgespräche führen

**soliloquy** /sə'lɪləkwɪ/ *n.* Monolog, *der;* (*talking to oneself*) Selbstgespräch, *das*

**solipsism** /'sɒlɪpsɪzm, 'səʊlɪpsɪzm/ *n.* (*Philos.*) Solipsismus, *der*

**solitaire** /sɒlɪ'teə(r)/ *n.* Ⓐ (*gem*) Solitär, *der;* **a ~ diamond/ring** ein [Diamant]solitär/ein Solitärring; Ⓑ (*ring*) Solitärring, *der;* Ⓒ (*game*) Solitär, *das;* Ⓓ (*Amer. Cards*) Patience, *die;* Ⓔ (*Ornith.*) Einsiedler, *der*

**solitary** /'sɒlɪtərɪ/ ❶ *adj.* Ⓐ einsam; **a ~ existence/life** ein Einsiedlerdasein/-leben; ~ **confinement** Einzelhaft, *die;* Ⓑ (*sole*) einzig; Ⓒ (*Zool.*) solitär; Ⓓ (*Bot.*) ⇒ **single** 1 A. ❷ *n.* (*coll.*) Einzelhaft, *die*

**solitude** /'sɒlɪtjuːd/ *n.* Ⓐ (*loneliness, remoteness*) Einsamkeit, *die;* Ⓑ (*lonely place*) Einöde, *die*

**solmization** /sɒlmɪ'zeɪʃn/ *n.* (*Mus.*) Solmisation, *die*

**solo** /'səʊləʊ/ ❶ *n., pl.* **~s** Ⓐ (*Mus.*) Solo, *das;* Ⓑ (*Cards*) ~ **[whist]** Solo[-whist], *das;* **go ~:** ein Solo spielen; Ⓒ (*Aeronaut.*) Alleinflug, *der.* ❷ *adj.* Ⓐ (*Mus.*) Solo‹spiel, -part, -tanz, -instrument›; Ⓑ (*unaccompanied*) ~ **flight** Alleinflug, *der;* ~ **performance** Solo- *od.* Alleinvorstellung, *die;* ~ **achievement/effort** Einzelleistung, *die;* **a ~ act on the trapeze** eine Solonummer auf dem Trapez; ~ **motorcycle** Motorrad ohne Beiwagen. ❸ *adv.* (*unaccompanied*) solo ‹singen, spielen, tanzen usw.›; **go/fly ~** (*Aeronaut.*) einen Alleinflug machen

**soloist** /'səʊləʊɪst/ *n.* (*Mus.*) Solist, *der*/Solistin, *die*

**Solomon** /'sɒləmən/ *pr. n.* Salomo[n] (*der*); **be as wise as ~:** salomonische Weisheit besitzen; **judgment of ~:** salomonisches Urteil; ⇒ *also* **song**

**Solomon 'Islands** *pr. n. pl.* **the ~:** die Salomoninseln; die Salomonen

**Solomon's 'seal** *n.* (*figure; also Bot.*) Salomonssiegel, *das*

**solstice** /'sɒlstɪs/ *n.* Ⓐ (*time of year*) Sonnenwende, *die;* **summer/winter ~:** Sommer-/Wintersonnenwende, *die;* Ⓑ (*point*) Wendepunkt, *der*

**solubility** /sɒljʊ'bɪlɪtɪ/ *n.* Ⓐ (*capacity to be dissolved*) Löslichkeit, *die;* Ⓑ (*of problem etc.*) Lösbarkeit, *die*

**soluble** /'sɒljʊbl/ *adj.* Ⓐ (*that can be dissolved*) löslich; solubel (*fachspr.*); ~ **in water, water-~:** wasserlöslich; **fat-~:** fettlöslich; Ⓑ (*solvable*) lösbar

**solute** /'sɒljuːt/ *n.* (*Chem.*) gelöster Stoff

**solution** /sə'luːʃn, sə'ljuːʃn/ *n.* Ⓐ (*Phys., Chem.*) Lösung, *die;* Ⓑ ([*result of*] *solving*) Lösung, *die* (**to** *Gen.*); **there is/is no ~ to sth.** etw. kann/kann nicht gelöst werden; **find a ~ to sth.** eine Lösung für etw. finden; etw. lösen

**solvable** /'sɒlvəbl/ *adj.* lösbar

**solve** /sɒlv/ *v.t.* lösen

**solvency** /'sɒlvənsɪ/ *n.* (*Finance*) Solvenz, *die*

**solvent** /'sɒlvənt/ ❶ *adj.* Ⓐ (*Chem.: dissolving*) lösend: ~ **liquid** *or* **fluid** Lösungsmittel, *das;* Ⓑ (*Finance*) solvent. ❷ *n.* (*Chem.*) Lösungsmittel, *das* (**of, for** für); ~ **abuse** Missbrauch von Lösungsmitteln als Rauschmittel

**Somali** /sə'mɑːlɪ/ ▶ 1275, ▶ 1340 ❶ *adj.* somalisch. ❷ *n.* Ⓐ (*person*) Somali, *der/die;* Ⓑ (*language*) Somali, *das*

**Somalia** /sə'mɑːlɪə/ *pr. n.* Somalia (*das*)

**Somalian** /sə'mɑːlɪən/ ❶ *adj.* somalisch. ❷ *n.* Somalier, *der*/Somalierin, *die*

**somatic** /sə'mætɪk/ *adj.* somatisch

**sombre** (*Amer.:* **somber**) /'sɒmbə(r)/ *adj.* dunkel; düster ‹Atmosphäre, Stimmung›; ernst ‹Anlass›

**sombre:** **~-coloured** *adj.* düster; **~looking** *adj.* düster [aussehend]

**sombrely** /'sɒmbəlɪ/ *adv.* düster; dunkel ‹gekleidet›; schwach ‹leuchten›

**sombrero** /sɒm'breərəʊ/ *n., pl.* **~s** Sombrero, *der*

**some** /səm, *stressed* sʌm/ ❶ *adj.* Ⓐ (*one or other*) [irgend]ein; ~ **fool** irgendein Dummkopf (*ugs.*); ~ **day** eines Tages; irgendwann einmal; ~ **[experienced] person** [irgend]jemand[, der Erfahrung hat]; ~ **shop/book or other** irgendein Laden/Buch; ~ **person or other** irgendjemand; irgendwer; Ⓑ (*a considerable quantity of*) einig...; etlich... (*ugs. verstärkend*); **speak at ~ length/wait for ~ time** ziemlich lang[e] sprechen/warten; ~ **time/weeks/days/years ago** vor einiger Zeit/vor einigen Wochen/Tagen/Jahren; ~ **time soon** bald [einmal]; **as ~ small token of** als ein kleines Zeichen (+ *Gen.*); **thirty ~ years** (*coll.*) über dreißig Jahre; ⇒ *also* **few** 1 B; Ⓒ (*a small quantity of*) ein bisschen; **would you like ~ wine?** möchten Sie [etwas] Wein?; **do ~ shopping/reading** einkaufen/lesen; **have ~ sense of decency** ein gewisses Gefühl für Anstand besitzen; **do have ~ sense!** sei doch vernünftig!; Ⓓ (*to a certain extent*) ~ **guide** eine gewisse Orientierungshilfe; **that is ~ proof** das ist [doch] gewissermaßen ein Beweis; **it was ~ help having my sister here** es war mir eine gewisse Hilfe, dass meine Schwester hier war; **you are ~ help!** (*iron.*) du bist [mir] vielleicht eine Hilfe! (*ugs.*); Ⓔ (*coll.: true*) **this is ~ war/poem/car!** das ist vielleicht ein Krieg/Gedicht/Wagen! (*ugs.*); **he's ~ fool!** er ist vielleicht ein Dummkopf!; Ⓕ (*approximately*) etwa; ungefähr.
❷ *pron.* einig...; **Do you want any potatoes? — I have ~ already** Möchtest du Kartoffeln? — Ich habe schon welche; **This chocolate is delicious. — Do have ~ more** Diese Schokolade ist köstlich. — Nimm dir doch noch etwas [davon]; **she only ate ~ of it** sie hat es nur teilweise aufgegessen; **I collect stamps — If I find ~, I'll send them** Ich sammle Briefmarken — Wenn ich welche finde, schicke ich sie dir; ~ **of her ideas are good** sie hat einige gute Ideen; ~ **of the greatest music** einige der größten Werke der Musik; **this country has ~ of the highest mountains in the world** in diesem Land sind mit die höchsten Berge der Welt (*ugs.*); ~ **say ...:** manche sagen ...; ~ **..., others ...:** manche ..., andere ...; die einen ..., andere ...; **... and then ~:** und noch einige/einiges mehr.
❸ *adv.* (*coll.: in ~ degree*) ein bisschen; etwas; ~ **more** noch ein bisschen

**somebody** /'sʌmbədɪ/ *n. & pron.* jemand; ~ **or other** irgendjemand; (*important person*) **be [a] ~:** jemand *od.* etwas sein; etwas vorstellen

**'someday** *adv.* (*Amer.*) eines Tages; irgendwann einmal

**'somehow** *adv.* ~ **[or other]** irgendwie; **we must find money ~ [or other]** wir müssen irgendwie Geld beschaffen

**someone** /'sʌmwən, *stressed* 'sʌmwʌn/ *pron.* ⇒ **somebody**

**'someplace** (*Amer. coll.*) ⇒ **somewhere**

**somersault** /'sʌməsɔːlt, 'sʌməsɒlt/ ❶ *n.* Purzelbaum, *der* (*ugs.*); Salto, *der* (*Sport*); **turn a ~:** einen Purzelbaum schlagen (*ugs.*); einen Salto springen (*Sport*). ❷ *v.i.* einen Purzelbaum schlagen (*ugs.*); einen Salto springen (*Sport*); **the car ~ed [into a tree]** das Auto

S

überschlug sich [und landete an einem Baum]

**'something** *n. & pron.* **A** *(some thing)* etwas; **~ new/old/good/bad** etwas Neues/Altes/Gutes/Schlechtes; **~ told me that .../to do sth.** etwas sagte mir, dass .../befahl mir, etw. zu tun; **B** *(some unspecified thing)* [irgend]-etwas; **~ or other** irgendetwas; **she is a lecturer in ~ or other** sie ist Dozentin für irgendwas *(ugs.)*; **C** *(some quantity of a thing)* etwas; **have ~ before you go** nimm etwas zu dir *od.* iss etwas, bevor du gehst; **will you have a drop of ~?** nimmst du einen Schluck?; **I have seen ~ of his work** ich habe einige seiner Arbeiten *od. (ugs.)* etwas von ihm gesehen; **see ~ of a place/festival** ein bisschen was von einem Ort/Fest sehen *(ugs.)*; **there is ~ in what you say** was du sagst, hat etwas für sich; an dem, was du sagst, ist etwas dran *(ugs.)*; **he has ~ about him** er hat etwas Besonderes an sich *(Dat.)*; **it is ~ to have got so far** es ist schon etwas [Besonderes], so weit gekommen zu sein; **you may have ~ there** *(you have had a good idea)* der Gedanke hat etwas für sich; **D** *(impressive or important thing, person, etc.)* **the party was quite ~:** die Party war spitze *(ugs.)*; **make ~ of oneself** etwas aus sich machen; **to be world champion at that age is quite ~:** in diesem Alter Weltmeister zu sein, das ist schon etwas; **E or ~ ⇒ or**[1] C; **F ~ like** etwa wie; **he left ~ like a million** er hinterließ etwa eine Million; **it looks ~ like a cross** es sieht [etwa] wie ein Kreuz aus; **that's ~ 'like** *(coll.)* lässt sich hören/sehen! *(ugs.)*; **that's ~ like it** das ist schon besser; **G ~ of an expert/a specialist** so etwas wie ein Fachmann/Spezialist; **see ~ of sb.** jmdn. sehen. ⇒ *also* **else** A, B

**'sometime** ❶ *adj.* ehemalig; **he was ~ captain of the team** er war früher Mannschaftskapitän. ❷ *adv.* irgendwann

**'sometimes** *adv.* manchmal; **~ ..., at other times ...:** manchmal ..., manchmal ...

**'somewhat** ❶ *adv. (rather)* irgendwie; ziemlich; **more than ~ surprised/disappointed** *(coll.)* ganz schön *(ugs.) od.* mehr als [nur] überrascht/enttäuscht. ❷ *pron.* **~ of an expert** so etwas wie ein Fachmann

**'somewhere** ❶ *adv.* **A** *(in a place)* irgendwo; **~ about** *or* **around thirty [years old]** [so *(ugs.)*] um die dreißig [Jahre alt]; **~ between five and ten** [so *(ugs.)*] zwischen fünf und zehn; **B** *(to a place)* irgendwohin; **get ~** *(coll.) (in life)* es zu etwas bringen; *(in a task)* weiterkommen. ❷ *n.* **look for ~ to stay** sich nach einer Unterkunft umsehen; **find ~ suitable to do sth.** einen geeigneten Ort finden, [um] etw. zu tun; **she prefers ~ hot for her holidays** in den Ferien fährt sie am liebsten irgendwohin, wo es heiß ist

**somnolence** /'sɒmnələns/ *n.* Schläfrigkeit, *die*

**somnolent** /'sɒmnələnt/ *adj.* **A** *(sleepy)* schläfrig; **B** *(sleep-inducing)* einschläfernd; **C** *(Med.)* somnolent

**son** /sʌn/ *n.* Sohn, *der; (as address)* **[my] ~:** mein Sohn; **adopted ~:** Adoptivsohn, *der;* **~ and heir** Sohn und Erbe; **be a ~ of the soil** mit der Scholle verbunden sein; **the S~ of Man** *(Relig.)* der Menschensohn; **the ~s of men** *(Relig.)* die Menschen; **the S~ [of God]** *(Relig.)* der Sohn [Gottes]; **~ of a bitch** *(derog.)* Scheißkerl, *der (derb)*; *(thing)* Scheißding, *das (derb);* ⇒ *also* **father** 1 A, E; **gun** 1 A; **mother** 1 A

**sonar** /'səʊnɑ:(r)/ *n.* Sonar, *das*

**sonata** /sə'nɑ:tə/ *n. (Mus.)* Sonate, *die;* **~ form** Sonatenform, *die*

**sonde** /sɒnd/ *n. (Meteorol.)* [Raum]sonde, *die*

**song** /sɒŋ/ *n.* **A** Lied, *das; (esp. political ballad)* Song, *der; (pop ~)* [Pop]song, *der;* **S~ of S~s, S~ of Solomon** *(Bibl.)* Hohelied, *das;* Lied der Lieder, *das;* **B** *no pl. (singing)* Gesang, *der;* **on ~** *(fig. coll.)* in Spitzenform; **break** *or* **burst forth into ~:** ein Lied anstimmen; **for a ~:** für einen Apfel und ein Ei *(ugs.)*; **it is nothing to make a ~ about** *(coll.)* es ist nicht der Rede wert; **~ and dance** *(Brit. coll.: fuss; Amer. coll.: rigmarole)* viel *od.* großes Trara *(ugs.)*; **C** *(bird cry)* Gesang, *der; (of cuckoo)* Ruf, *der*

**song: ~bird** *n.* Singvogel, *der;* **~book** *n.* Liederbuch, *das;* **~ cycle** *n. (Mus.)* Liederzyklus, *der*

**songster** /'sɒŋstə(r)/ *n.* **A** *(singer, poet)* Sänger, *der;* **B** *(Amer.: songbook)* Liederbuch, *das*

**songstress** /'sɒŋstrɪs/ *n.* Sängerin, *die*

**'songwriter** *n.* ▶ **1261** Songschreiber, *der*/-schreiberin, *die*

**sonic** /'sɒnɪk/ *attrib. adj.* Schall-; **~ depth finder** Echolot, *das*

**sonic: ~ 'bang** ⇒ **~ boom; ~ barrier** ⇒ **sound barrier; ~ boom** *n.* Überschallknall, *der;* **~ mine** *n.* Geräuschmine, *die*

**'son-in-law** *n., pl.* **sons-in-law** Schwiegersohn, *der*

**sonnet** /'sɒnɪt/ *n.* Sonett, *das;* **~ sequence** Sonettenzyklus, *der*

**sonny** /'sʌnɪ/ *n. (coll.)* Kleiner *(der)*; kleiner Mann *(ugs.)*

**sonority** /sə'nɒrɪtɪ/ *n. (of voice)* Wohlklang, *der;* Sonorität, *die (geh. selten)*; *(of ship's horn, bell, etc.)* voller Klang

**sonorous** /sə'nɔ:rəs, 'sɒnərəs/ *adj.* volltönend; sonor ‹Stimme›; klangvoll ‹Instrument, Sprache›

**soon** /su:n/ *adv.* **A** bald; *(quickly)* schnell; **B** *(early)* früh; **how ~ will it be ready?** wann ist es denn fertig?; **none too ~:** keinen Augenblick zu früh; **no ~er said than done** gesagt, getan; **~er said than done** leichter gesagt als getan; **no ~er had I arrived than ...:** kaum war ich angekommen, da ...; **~ enough** früh genug; **~er or later** früher oder später; **Which train shall I take? — Whichever arrives the ~er** Welchen Zug soll ich nehmen? — Den, der zuerst ankommt; **the car must be serviced every 12 months or every six thousand miles, whichever is the ~er** der Wagen muss alle 12 Monate bzw. alle sechstausend Meilen gewartet werden, je nachdem [, was früher der Fall ist]; **the ~er [...] the better** *(coll.)*, **better ~er than later** je früher *od.* eher [...], desto besser; **C as ~ as his death was known/he heard of it** sobald sein Tod bekannt wurde/er davon gehört hatte; **we'll set off just as ~ as he arrives** sobald er ankommt, machen wir uns auf den Weg; **as ~ as possible** so bald wie möglich; **D** *(willingly)* gern; **just as ~ [as ...]** genauso gern [wie ...]; **she would ~er die than ...:** sie würde lieber sterben, als ...; **which would you ~er/~est do?** was würdest du lieber/am liebsten tun?; **they would kill you as ~ as look at you** *(coll.)* sie würden dich sofort *od.* auf der Stelle umbringen; **~er you than me** lieber du als ich

**soonish** /'su:nɪʃ/ *adv. (coll.)* recht bald

**soot** /sʊt/ ❶ *n.* Ruß, *der.* ❷ *v.t.* verrußen; rußig machen

**soothe** /su:ð/ *v.t.* **A** *(calm)* beruhigen; beschwichtigen ‹Gefühle›; **B** *(make less severe)* mildern; lindern ‹Schmerz›; **~ sb.'s cares away** jmds. Sorgen vertreiben

**soothing** /'su:ðɪŋ/ *adj.* beruhigend; wohltuend ‹Bad, Creme, Massage›

**soothsayer** /'su:θseɪə(r)/ *n. (arch.)* Wahrsager, *der*/Wahrsagerin, *die*

**sooty** /'sʊtɪ/ *adj.* **A** *(soot-covered)* verrußt; rußig; **B** *(black)* schwarz [wie Ruß]

**sop** /sɒp/ ❶ *n.* **A** *(piece of bread)* Stück eingeweichtes Brot; **B** *(fig.)* Beschwichtigungsmittel, *das;* **sth. is intended as a ~ to sb., sth. is a ~ given to sb.** etw. soll jmdn. beschwichtigen. ❷ *v.i.,* **-pp-: be ~ping [wet] [with rain]** [vom Regen] völlig durchnässt sein

**~ 'up** *v.t.* aufnehmen

**sophism** /'sɒfɪzm/ *n.* Sophismus, *der*

**sophist** /'sɒfɪst/ *n.* Sophist, *der*/Sophistin, *die*

**sophistical** /sə'fɪstɪkl/ *adj.* sophistisch

**sophisticate** ❶ /sə'fɪstɪkeɪt/ *v.t.* verbilden. ❷ /sə'fɪstɪkət/ *adj.* ⇒ **sophisticated** A. ❸ *n.* Kultursnob, *der*

**sophisticated** /sə'fɪstɪkeɪtɪd/ *adj.* **A** *(cultured)* kultiviert; gepflegt ‹Restaurant, Küche›; anspruchsvoll ‹Roman, Autor, Unterhaltung, Stil›; **B** *(elaborate)* ausgeklügelt ‹Autozubehör›; differenziert, subtil ‹Argument, System, Ansatz›; hoch entwickelt ‹Technik, Elektronik, Software, Geräte›; *(derog.: over-complex)* spitzfindig ‹Argument›; **~ in style** stilistisch verfeinert

**sophistication** /səfɪstɪ'keɪʃn/ *n.* **A** *(refinement)* Kultiviertheit, *die; (of argument)* Differenziertheit, *die; (derog.)* Spitzfindigkeit, *die; (of style, manner)* Subtilität, *die;* **the ~ of French cooking** die Raffinesse der französischen Küche; **B** *(advanced methods)* hoher Entwicklungsstand [der Technik]; **era of technical ~:** Zeitalter hoch entwickelter Technik

**sophistry** /'sɒfɪstrɪ/ *n.* Sophisterei, *die*

**sophomore** /'sɒfəmɔ:(r)/ *n. (Amer. Sch./Univ.) Student/Studentin einer Highschool bzw. Universität im zweiten Studienjahr*

**soporific** /sɒpə'rɪfɪk/ ❶ *adj.* schläfrig ‹Person›; einschläfernd ‹Wirkung, Rede›; **~ drug/medicine** Schlafmittel, *das.* ❷ *n.* Schlafmittel, *das*

**sopping** ⇒ **sop** 2

**soppy** /'sɒpɪ/ *adj. (Brit. coll.: sentimental)* rührselig; sentimental ‹Person›; **be ~ on sb.** in jmdn. verschossen sein *(ugs.)*

**soprano** /sə'prɑ:nəʊ/ *n., pl.* **~s** *or* **soprani** /sə'prɑ:ni:/ *(Mus.) (voice, singer, part)* Sopran, *der; (female singer also)* Sopranistin, *die;* **~ flute/clarinet** Sopranflöte, *die*/-klarinette, *die;* **~ clef** Sopranschlüssel, *der*

**sorbet** /'sɔ:bɪt, 'sɔ:beɪ/ *n.* Sorbet, *das*

**sorcerer** /'sɔ:sərə(r)/ *n.* Zauberer, *der*

**sorceress** /'sɔ:sərɪs/ *n.* Zauberin, *die*

**sorcery** /'sɔ:sərɪ/ *n.* Zauberei, *die*

**sordid** /'sɔ:dɪd/ *adj.* **A** *(base)* dreckig *(abwertend)*; unehrenhaft, unlauter ‹Motiv›; unerfreulich ‹Detail, Geschichte›; **B** *(greedy)* habgierig ‹Person›; schmutzig ‹Geschäft›; **C** *(squalid)* schmutzig; schäbig ‹Wohnung, Verhältnisse›; heruntergekommen ‹Stadtviertel›

**sore** /sɔ:(r)/ ❶ *adj.* **A** *(painful)* weh; *(inflamed or injured)* wund; **sb. has a ~ back/foot/arm** *etc.* jmdm. tut der Rücken/Fuß/Arm *usw.* weh; **~ point** *or* **spot** *(fig.)* wunder Punkt; **touch on a ~ point, touch a ~ spot** *(fig.)* an einen wunden Punkt rühren; **a ~ subject** ein heikles Thema; **have ~ feelings about sth.** wegen einer Sache verletzt sein; **B** *(irritated)* verärgert; sauer *(ugs.)*; **feel ~:** sich ärgern *od.* aufregen; **C** *(Amer.: vexed)* böse; sauer *(ugs.)*; **be ~ at sb./about** *or* **over sth.** böse *od. (ugs.)* sauer auf jmdn./über etw. *(Akk.)* sein; **D** *(severe)* schwer; groß ‹Not, Schwierigkeiten›; dringlich ‹Problem›.

❷ *n.* **A** *(abrasion)* wunde Stelle; **B** *(fig.: painful thought)* Wunde, *die*

**sorely** /'sɔ:lɪ/ *adv.* sehr; arg *(südd.)*; dringend ‹nötig, benötigt›; **be ~ in need of sth.** etw. dringend brauchen; **~ tempted** stark versucht

**soreness** /'sɔ:nɪs/ *n.* Schmerz, *der; (inflammation)* Wundsein, *das*

**sorghum** /'sɔ:gəm/ *n.* Sorghum, *das*

**sorority** /sə'rɒrɪtɪ/ *n.* **A** *(sisterhood)* Schwesternorden, *der; (Amer.: female section of church congregation)* Frauen der Gemeinde; **B** *(Amer.: society)* Studentinnenvereinigung, *die*

**sorrel**[1] /'sɒrl/ *n. (Bot.)* Sauerampfer, *der*

**sorrel**[2] ❶ *adj.* fuchsrot; rotbraun. ❷ *n. (horse)* Fuchs, *der;* rotbraunes Pferd

**sorrow** /'sɒrəʊ/ ❶ *n.* **A** *(distress)* Kummer, *der;* Leid, *das;* **feel [great] ~ that ...:** es [sehr] bedauern, dass ...; **he felt great ~ at the news** die Nachricht bekümmerte ihn sehr; **cause sb. [great] ~:** jmdm. [großen] Kummer bereiten; **act more in ~ than in anger** mehr aus Kummer *od.* Betrübnis handeln als aus Zorn; **B** *(misfortune)* Sorge, *die;* **he has had many ~s** er hat viel [Schweres] durchgemacht; **all the ~s of the world** alles *od.* das ganze Leid der Welt; **the Man of Sorrows** *(Relig.)* der Schmerzensmann; ⇒ *also* **drown** 2 B.

❷ *v.i.* **A** *(feel ~)* sich grämen *(geh.)* **(at, over, for** über + *Akk.,* um); **B** *(mourn)* trauern **(for, after** um)

**sorrowful** /ˈsɒrəʊfl, ˈsɒrəfl/ *adj.* **A** (*sad*) betrübt ‹Person›; traurig ‹Anlass, Lächeln, Herz›; **with a ~ heart** mit Kummer im Herzen; **feel ~ at sth.** über etw. (*Akk.*) bekümmert sein; **B** (*distressing*) traurig; leidvoll ‹Dasein›

**sorrowing** /ˈsɒrəʊɪŋ/ *attrib. adj.* trauernd

**sorry** /ˈsɒrɪ/ *adj.* **A** ▶ **924** (*regretful*) **sb. is ~ to do sth.** jmdm. tut es Leid, etw. tun zu müssen; **I am ~ to disappoint you** ich muss dich leider enttäuschen; **sb. is ~ that ...:** es tut jmdm. Leid, dass ...; **sb. is ~ about sth.** jmdm. tut etw. Leid; **~ about your accident** es tut mir Leid, dass du einen Unfall hattest; **~, but ...** (*coll.*) tut mir Leid, aber ...; **I'm ~** (*won't change my mind*) tut mir Leid; **~ I'm late** (*coll.*) Entschuldigung, dass ich zu spät komme; **My mother died two months ago. — Oh, I 'am ~!** Meine Mutter ist vor zwei Monaten gestorben. — Herzliches Beileid!; **I'm ~ to say** leider; **I can't say [that] I'm ~!** ich bin nicht gerade traurig darüber; **sb. is** *or* **feels ~ for sb./sth.** jmd. tut jmdm. Leid/jmd. bedauert etw.; **you'll be ~:** das wird dir noch Leid tun; **feel ~ for oneself** sich selbst bemitleiden; sich (*Dat.*) Leid tun; **~!** Entschuldigung!; **~?** wie bitte?; **~ about that!** (*coll.*) tut mir Leid!; **~ to bother you** Entschuldigung, wenn ich störe; ⇒ *also* **safe** 2 B; **B** *attrib.* (*wretched*) traurig; faul, fadenscheinig ‹Entschuldigung›

**sort** /sɔːt/ **1** *n.* **A** Art, *die;* (*type*) Sorte, *die;* **cakes of several ~s** verschiedene Kuchensorten; **a new ~ of bicycle** ein neuartiges Fahrrad; **people of every/that ~:** Menschen jeden/diesen Schlages; **people of every ~ and kind** alle möglichen Leute; **it takes all ~s [to make a world]** (*coll.*) es gibt so'ne und solche (*ugs.*); (*when referring to eccentric behaviour*) jedem Tierchen sein Pläsierchen (*scherzh.*); **all ~s of ...:** alle möglichen ...; **support sb. in all ~s of ways** jmdn. auf vielerlei Art und Weise unterstützen; **there are all ~s of things to do** es gibt alles Mögliche *od.* allerlei zu tun; **she is just/not my ~:** sie ist genau/nicht mein Typ (*ugs.*); **she is not the ~ to do that** es ist nicht ihre Art, das zu tun; **what ~ of [a] person do you think I am?** für wen hältst du mich?; **you'll do nothing of the ~:** das kommt gar nicht infrage; **he's a ~ of stockbroker, I believe** (*coll.*) er ist [so] eine Art [von] Börsenmakler, glaube ich; **~ of** (*coll.*) irgendwie; irgendwo (*salopp*); (*more or less*) mehr oder weniger; (*to some extent*) ziemlich (*ugs.*); **it's ~ of difficult for me to explain** (*coll.*) ich kann es irgendwie nicht so gut *od.* leicht erklären; **Have you finished? — Well, ~ of** (*coll.*) Bist du fertig? — Mehr oder weniger; **I ~ of expected it** (*coll.*) ich habe es irgendwie erwartet; **nothing of the ~:** nichts dergleichen; **or something of the ~:** oder so [etwas Ähnliches] (*ugs.*); **a funny ~ of person/day/car** ein komischer Mensch/Tag/Wagen; **it is music of a ~** (*derog.*) es ist so was Ähnliches wie Musik; **he is a doctor/footballer of a ~** *or* **of ~s** (*derog.*) er nennt sich Arzt/Fußballspieler; **we don't mix with people of that ~:** mit solchen Leuten wollen wir nichts zu tun haben; **he/she is a good ~** (*coll.*) er/sie ist schon in Ordnung (*ugs.*); **he is not a bad ~ at all** (*coll.*) er ist nicht der Schlechteste (*ugs.*); **B be out of ~s** nicht in Form sein; (*be irritable*) schlecht gelaunt sein; **C** (*Printing*) Letter, *die.*
**2** *v.t.* sortieren

**~ 'out** *v.t.* **A** (*arrange*) sortieren; **~ out material for an essay** Material für einen Aufsatz zusammenstellen; **B** (*settle*) klären; schlichten ‹Streit›; beenden ‹Verwirrung›; **it will ~ itself out** es wird schon in Ordnung kommen; **C** (*organize*) durchorganisieren; auf Vordermann bringen (*ugs.*); **~ oneself out** ‹Neuankömmling usw.:› sich einrichten; **things have ~ed themselves out** die Dinge haben sich eingerenkt; **D** (*coll.: punish*) **~ sb. out** jmdm. zeigen, wos langgeht (*ugs.*); **E** (*select*) aussuchen; wählen; **~ out the truth from the lies** die Lügen von der Wahrheit unterscheiden; Lüge und Wahrheit unterscheiden; **~ out the good apples/singers from the bad [ones]** die guten Äpfel/Sänger von den schlechten trennen

**'sort code** *n.* (*Banking*) Bankleitzahl, *die*

**sorter** /ˈsɔːtə(r)/ *n.* **A** (*arranger*) Sortierer, *der*/Sortiererin, *die;* **B** (*for punched cards*) Sorter, *der;* Sortiermaschine, *die*

**sortie** /ˈsɔːtiː, ˈsɔːtɪ/ *n.* (*Mil.; also fig.*) **A** Ausfall, *der;* **B** (*flight*) Einsatz, *der*

**sorting** /ˈsɔːtɪŋ/ *n.* Sortieren, *das*

**sorting: ~-machine** *n.* Sortiermaschine, *die;* **~ office** *n.* Postverteilstelle, *die*

**SOS** /esəʊˈes/ *n.* **A** SOS, *das;* **~ appeal** Hilfeaufruf, *der;* **B** (*Brit.: broadcast*) **~ message** Suchmeldung, *die;* (*to motorists*) Reiseruf, *der*

**'so so, 'so-so** *adj., adv.* so lala (*ugs.*)

**sot** /sɒt/ *n.* Trinker, *der*/Trinkerin, *die;* Säufer, *der*/Säuferin, *die* (*salopp*)

**sottish** /ˈsɒtɪʃ/ *adj.* versoffen (*salopp*)

**sotto voce** /sɒtəʊ ˈvəʊtʃɪ/ *adv.* mit gedämpfter Stimme

**sou** /suː/ *n.* (*Hist./coll.*) Sou, *der;* **not have a ~:** keinen roten Heller haben

**soubrette** /suːˈbret/ *n.* (*Theatre*) Soubrette, *die*

**soufflé** /ˈsuːfleɪ/ *n.* (*Gastr.*) Soufflé, *das;* **~ dish** Souffléform, *die*

**sough** /sʌf, saʊ/ (*literary*) **1** *n.* Rauschen, *das.* **2** *v.i.* rauschen

**sought** ⇒ **seek**

**soul** /səʊl/ *n.* **A** Seele, *die;* **sell one's ~ for sth.** (*fig.*) seine Seele für etw. verkaufen; **upon my ~!** (*dated*) meiner Treu! (*veralt.*); **bare one's ~ to sb.** jmdm. sein Herz ausschütten; ⇒ *also* **heart** 1 B; **life** B; **B** (*intellect*) Geist, *der;* **not be able to call one's ~ one's own** nicht sein eigener Herr sein; **his whole ~ revolted from it** er sträubte sich mit ganzer Seele dagegen; **C** (*person*) Seele, *die;* **not a ~:** keine Menschenseele; **be the ~ of discretion** die Verschwiegenheit selbst *od.* in Person sein; **be a good ~ and fetch me a cup of tea** sei ein Schatz (*ugs.*) und hol mir eine Tasse Tee; **the poor little ~:** das arme kleine Ding; **D** (*Negro Culture*) *die Kultur der schwarzen US-Amerikaner;* (*music*) Soul, *der*

**soul: ~ brother** *n. schwarzer Nordamerikaner (als [bewusster] Teilhaber der schwarzen Kultur);* ≈ Bruder, *der;* **~-destroying** /ˈsəʊldɪstrɔɪɪŋ/ *adj.* **A** (*boring*) nervtötend; geisttötend; **B** (*depressing*) deprimierend

**'soul food** *n. traditionelle Küche der schwarzen Nordamerikaner*

**soulful** /ˈsəʊlfl/ *adj.* gefühlvoll; (*sad*) schwermütig

**soulfully** /ˈsəʊlfəlɪ/ *adv.* mit viel Gefühl; (*sadly*) voll Schwermut

**soulless** /ˈsəʊllɪs/ *adj.* **A** (*ignoble*) seelenlos (*geh.*); gefühllos; **B** (*dull*) öde

**soul: ~mate** *n.* Seelenverwandte, *der/die;* **~ music** *n.* Soul, *der;* Soulmusik, *die;* **~-searching** *n.* Gewissenskampf, *der;* **~ sister** *n. schwarze Nordamerikanerin (als [bewusste] Teilhaberin der schwarzen Kultur);* ≈ Schwester, *die;* **~-stirring** *adj.* aufwühlend; (*inspiring*) mitreißend

**sound**[1] /saʊnd/ **1** *adj.* **A** (*healthy*) gesund; intakt ‹Gebäude, Mauerwerk›; gut ‹Frucht, Obst, Holz, Boden›; **of ~ mind** im Vollbesitz der geistigen Kräfte; **~ in mind and body** gesund an Geist und Seele; **~ in wind and limb** kerngesund; **the building was structurally ~:** das Gebäude hatte eine gesunde Bausubstanz; ⇒ *also* **bell** 1 A; **B** (*well-founded*) vernünftig ‹Argument, Rat›; klug ‹Wahl›; **it makes ~ sense** es ist sehr vernünftig; **make ~ progress** gute Fortschritte machen; **C** (*Finance: secure*) gesund, solide ‹Basis›; klug ‹Investition›; **D** (*competent, reliable*) solide ‹Spieler›; **have a ~ character** charakterfest sein; **E** (*undisturbed*) tief, gesund ‹Schlaf›; **be a ~ sleeper** einen gesunden Schlaf haben; **F** (*thorough*) gehörig (*ugs.*) ‹Niederlage, Tracht Prügel›; gekonnt ‹Leistung›.
**2** *adv.* fest, tief ‹schlafen›; **fall/be ~ asleep** in einen tiefen *od.* festen Schlaf fallen/tief *od.* fest schlafen

**sound**[2] **1** *n.* **A** (*Phys.*) Schall, *der;* **the speed of ~:** die Schallgeschwindigkeit; **B** (*noise*) Laut, *der;* (*of wind, sea, car, footsteps, breaking glass or twigs*) Geräusch, *das;* (*of voices, laughter, bell*) Klang, *der;* **do sth. without a ~:** etw. lautlos tun; **C** (*Radio, Telev., Cinemat.*) Ton, *der;* **loss of ~:** Tonausfall, *der;* **D** (*music*) Klang, *der;* (*jazz, pop, rock*) Sound, *der;* **the king entered to the ~ of trumpets** von Trompetenstößen begleitet, trat der König ein; **the ~ of drums** Trommellaute *Pl.;* **dance to the ~ of a band** zu den Klängen einer Band tanzen; **E** (*Phonet.: articulation*) Laut, *der;* **F** (*fig.: impression*) **I like the ~ of your plan** ich finde, Ihr Plan hört sich gut an; **I like the ~ of him** was du von ihm erzählst, hört sich gut an; **I don't like the ~ of this** das hört sich nicht gut an; **G** *in pl.* (**~** *waves*) Töne; **H** (*meaningless noise*) Wortgeklingel, *das;* Wortschwall, *der;* **I** (*earshot*) **within ~ of sb./sth.** in jmds. Hörweite/in Hörweite einer Sache.
**2** *v.i.* **A** (*seem*) klingen; **it ~s as if .../like ...:** es klingt, als .../wie ...; **it ~s to me as if .../like ...:** es hört sich für mich an, als .../wie ...; **from his lack of enthusiasm it ~s as if he wanted to give up** nach seinem Mangel an Begeisterung zu urteilen, klingt es so, als wolle er aufgeben; **it ~s to me from what you have said that ...:** was du gesagt hast, klingt für mich so, als ob ...; **that ~s a good idea to me** ich finde, die Idee hört sich gut an; **~s good to me!** klingt gut! (*ugs.*); gute Idee! (*ugs.*); **that ~s odd to me** das hört sich seltsam an, finde ich; **B** (*emit ~*) [er]tönen.
**3** *v.t.* **A** (*cause to emit ~*) ertönen lassen; **~ the trumpet** trompeten; in die Trompete blasen; **B** (*utter*) **~ a note of caution** zur Vorsicht mahnen; **his words ~ed a note of alarm in my mind** seine Worte versetzten mich in Alarmstimmung; **C** (*pronounce*) aussprechen; **D** (*cause to be heard*) **~ sb.'s praises** ein Loblied auf jmdn. singen; **~ a fanfare** eine Fanfare erklingen lassen

**~ 'off** *v.i.* (*coll.: talk pompously*) tönen (*ugs.*), schwadronieren (**on, about** von)

**sound**[3] *n.* **A** (*strait*) Sund, *der;* Meerenge, *die;* **B** (*inlet*) Meeresarm, *der;* **Plymouth S~:** die Bucht von Plymouth

**sound**[4] *v.t.* **A** (*Naut.: fathom*) ausloten; sondieren; **B** (*fig.: test*) ⇒ **~ out**; **C** (*Meteorol.*) untersuchen; erforschen; sondieren; **D** (*Med.*) abhorchen

**~ 'out** *v.t.* ausfragen ‹Person›; sondieren (*geh.*), herausbekommen ‹Sache›; **~ sb. out on sth.** bei jmdm. wegen etw. vorfühlen

**sound: ~ barrier** *n.* Schallmauer, *die;* **go through** *or* **break the ~ barrier** die Schallmauer durchbrechen; **~ bite** *n.* kurzes, prägnantes Zitat; **~box** *n.* (*in violin, guitar, etc.*) Resonanzkörper, *der;* **~ broadcasting** *n.* Hörfunk, *der;* **~ card** *n.* (*Computing*) Soundkarte, *die;* **~ check** *n.* Soundcheck, *der;* Tonprobe, *die;* **~ effect** *n.* Geräuscheffekt, *der;* **~ engineer** *n.* ▶ **1261** (*Radio, Telev., Cinemat.*) Toningenieur, *der*/-ingenieurin, *die;* **~hole** *n.* (*Mus.*) Schallloch, *das*

**sounding**[1] /ˈsaʊndɪŋ/ *adj. in comb.* **strange-/clear-/loud-~:** seltsam/klar/laut [klingend]

**sounding**[2] *n.* **A** (*Naut.: measurement*) Lotung, *die;* **take ~s** Lotungen vornehmen; loten; **B** (*fig.*) Sondierung, *die* (*geh.*); **make ~s in a locality** ein Terrain sondieren; **carry out ~s of public opinion/of interested parties** die öffentliche Meinung sondieren/mit den Beteiligten Sondierungsgespräche führen

**sounding: ~ board** *n.* **A** (*canopy*) Schalldeckel, *der;* **B** (*Mus.*) Decke, *die;* **C** (*fig.: means of spreading opinions*) Sprachrohr, *das;* **D** (*fig.: trial audience*) ≈ Testgruppe, *die;* **~ line** *n.* (*Naut.*) Lotleine, *die;* **~ rod** *n.* (*Naut.*) Peilstock, *der*

**soundless** /ˈsaʊndlɪs/ *adj.* lautlos; stumm, tonlos ‹Sprache, Gebet›

**soundly** /ˈsaʊndlɪ/ *adv.* **A** (*solidly*) stabil, solide ‹bauen›; **B** (*well*) vernünftig ‹argumentieren,

S

urteilen, investieren›; [C] (*deeply*) tief, fest ‹schlafen›; [D] (*thoroughly*) anständig, ordentlich (*ugs.*) ‹verhauen›; vernichtend ‹schlagen, besiegen›; **perform ~:** eine gute Leistung zeigen

**soundness** /'saʊndnɪs/ *n., no pl.* [A] (*of mind, body*) Gesundheit, *die;* (*of construction, structure*) Solidität, *die;* [B] (*of argument*) Stichhaltigkeit, *die;* (*of policy, views*) Vernünftigkeit, *die;* [C] (*of sleep*) Tiefe, *die;* [D] (*competence, reliability*) Solidität, *die;* [E] (*solvency*) wirtschaftliche Gesundheit; Solvenz, *die*

**sound: ~ post** *n.* (*Mus.*) Stimmstock, *der;* **~proof** ❶ *adj.* schalldicht; ❷ *v.t.* schalldicht machen; **~proofing** *n.* Schallisolierung, *die;* **~ recorder** *n.* Tonaufnahmegerät, *das;* **~ shift** ⇒ **shift** 3 I; **~ system** *n.* Tonanlage, *die;* **~ technician** ⇒ **sound engineer**; **~track** *n.* (*Cinemat.*) Soundtrack, *der;* **~ truck** *n.* (*Amer.*) Lautsprecherwagen, *der;* **~ wave** *n.* (*Phys.*) Schallwelle, *die*

**soup** /su:p/ *n.* Suppe, *die;* **be/land in the ~** (*fig. coll.*) in der Patsche sitzen/landen (*ugs.*) **~ 'up** *v.t.* (*Motor Veh. coll.*) frisieren (*ugs.*)

**soupçon** /'su:psɔ̃/ *n.* Spur, *die;* (*of anger, irony*) Anflug, *der;* **a ~ of garlic/grey** eine Spur Knoblauch/von Grau

**souped-up** /'su:ptʌp/ *attrib. adj.* (*Motor Veh. coll.*) frisiert (*ugs.*)

**soup: ~ kitchen** *n.* Volksküche, *die;* Suppenküche, *die;* **~ plate** *n.* Suppenteller, *der;* **~ spoon** *n.* Suppenlöffel, *der*

**soupy** /'su:pɪ/ *adj.* [A] (*thick*) sämig ‹Flüssigkeit›; trübe, schlammig ‹Wasser›; [B] (*coll.: sentimental*) rührselig; sentimental

**sour** /'saʊə(r)/ ❶ *adj.* [A] (*having acid taste*) sauer; [B] (*morose*) griesgrämig (*abwertend*); säuerlich ‹Blick›; [C] (*unpleasant*) bitter; **when things go ~:** wenn man *od.* einem alles leid wird; **the place has gone ~ on him** der Ort ist ihm verleidet [worden]; [D] (*rank*) säuerlich ‹Geruch›; [E] (*deficient in lime*) sauer ‹Boden›. ⇒ *also* **grape**. ❷ *v.t.* [A] versauern lassen; sauer machen; [B] (*fig.: spoil*) verbauen ‹Karriere›; trüben ‹Beziehung›; [C] (*fig.: make gloomy*) verbittern. ❸ *v.i.* [A] sauer werden; [B] (*deteriorate*) ‹Beziehungen:› sich trüben. ❹ *n.* (*Amer.: cocktail*) Sour, *der*

**source** /sɔ:s/ *n.* Quelle, *die;* **~ of income/infection** Einkommensquelle, *die*/Infektionsherd, *der;* **the ~ of all woes** die Wurzel allen Übels; **locate the ~ of a leak** (*lit. or fig.*) feststellen, wo eine undichte Stelle ist; **the whole thing is a ~ of some embarrassment to us** das Ganze ist für uns ziemlich unangenehm; **at ~:** an der Quelle; **tax deducted at ~:** Quellensteuer, *die;* **my wages are taxed at ~:** die Steuer wird direkt von meinem Lohn abgezogen

**source: ~ book** *n.* Quellensammlung, *die;* **~ language** *n.* Ausgangssprache, *die*

**sour 'cream** *n.* saure Sahne; Sauerrahm, *der*

**sourly** /'saʊəlɪ/ *adv.* säuerlich

**sour: ~puss** *n.* (*coll.*) (*male*) Miesepeter, der (*ugs.*); (*female*) miesepetrige Ziege (*ugs.*)

**sousaphone** /'su:zəfəʊn/ *n.* (*Mus.*) Sousaphon, *das*

**souse** /saʊs/ *v.t.* [A] (*plunge into liquid*) eintauchen; [B] (*soak*) **get/be ~d** durchnässt werden/sein; [C] (*pickle*) einlegen

**soutane** /su:'tɑ:n/ *n.* (*RC Ch.*) Soutane, *die*

**south** /saʊθ/ ▶ 1024 ❶ *n.* [A] Süden, *der;* **the ~:** Süd (*Met., Seew.*); **in/to[wards]/from the ~:** im/nach *od.* (*geh.*) gen/von Süden; **to the ~ of** südlich von; südlich (+ *Gen.*); [B] *usu.* **S~** (*part lying to the ~*) Süden, *der;* **from the S~:** aus dem Süden; [C] (*Cards*) Süd. ❷ *adj.* südlich; Süd‹küste, -wind, -grenze, -tor›. ❸ *adv.* südwärts; nach Süden; **a ~-facing wall** eine nach Süden gelegene Mauer; **~ of** südlich von; südlich (+ *Gen.*); ⇒ *also* **by¹** 1 D

**South: ~ 'Africa** *pr. n.* Südafrika (*das*); **~ 'African** ▶ 1340 ❶ *adj.* südafrikanisch; ❷ *n.* Südafrikaner, *der*/-afrikanerin, *die;* **~ A'merica** *pr. n.* Südamerika (*das*); **~ A'merican** ▶ 1340 ❶ *adj.* südamerikanisch; ❷ *n.* Südamerikaner, *der*/-amerikanerin, *die*

**south: ~bound** *adj.* ▶ 1024 ‹Zug usw.› in Richtung Süden; **~-'east** ▶ 1024 ❶ *n.* Südosten, *der;* **in/to[wards]/from the ~-east** im/nach *od.* (*geh.*) gen/von Südosten; **to the ~-east of** südöstlich von, südöstlich (+ *Gen.*); ❷ *adj.* südöstlich; Südost‹wind, -fenster, -küste›; ❸ *adv.* südostwärts; nach Südosten; **~-east of** südöstlich von; südöstlich (+ *Gen.*); **~'easter** *n.* Südostwind, *der;* **~-'easterly** ▶ 1024 ❶ *adj.* südöstlich; ❷ *adv.* (*position*) im Südosten; (*direction*) nach Südosten; **~-'eastern** *adj.* ▶ 1024 südöstlich

**southerly** /'sʌðəlɪ/ ▶ 1024 ❶ *adj.* [A] (*in position or direction*) südlich; **in a ~ direction** nach Süden; [B] (*from the south*) ‹Wind› aus südlichen Richtungen; **the wind was ~:** der Wind kam aus südlichen Richtungen. ❷ *adv.* [A] (*in position*) südlich; (*in direction*) südwärts; [B] (*from the south*) aus *od.* von Süd[en]. ❸ *n.* Süd[wind], *der*

**southern** /'sʌðən/ *adj.* ▶ 1024 südlich; Süd‹grenze, -hälfte, -seite, -fenster, -wind›; südländisch ‹Temperament›; **~ Spain** Südspanien; das südliche Spanien; **~ Africa** das südliche Afrika; ⇒ *also* **cross** 1 F; **hemisphere** A

**southerner** /'sʌðənə(r)/ *n.* (*male*) Südengländer/-franzose/-italiener *usw.*, *der;* (*female*) Südengländerin/-französin/-italienerin *usw.*, *die;* (*Amer.*) Südstaatler, *der*/-staatlerin, *die;* **he's a ~:** er kommt aus dem Süden

**Southern: ~ 'Europe** *pr. n.* Südeuropa (*das*); **~ European** ❶ *adj.* südeuropäisch; ❷ *n.* Südeuropäer, *der*/-europäerin, *die;* **~ 'Ireland** *pr. n.* Südirland (*das*); **s~ 'lights** *n. pl.* Südlicht, *das*

**southernmost** /'sʌðənməʊst/ *adj.* ▶ 1024 südlichst ...

**South: ~ 'German** ❶ *adj.* süddeutsch; ❷ *n.* Süddeutsche, *der/die;* **~ 'Germany** *pr. n.* Süddeutschland (*das*); **~ Ko'rea** *pr. n.* Südkorea (*das*); **~ Ko'rean** ❶ *adj.* südkoreanisch; ❷ *n.* Südkoreaner, *der*/-koreanerin, *die*

**South of 'England** *pr. n.* Südengland (*das*); *attrib.* südenglisch

**south: ~paw** (*Boxing coll.*) ❶ *n.* Linkshänder, *der*/Linkshänderin, *die;* ❷ *adj.* linkshändig; **S~ 'Pole** *pr. n.* Südpol, *der;* **S~ Sea** *adj.* Südsee-; **S~ Sea Islander** Südseeinsulaner, *der*/-insulanerin, *die;* **S~ 'Seas** *pr. n. pl.* Südsee, *die;* **~-~-'east** ▶ 1024 ❶ *n.* Südsüdosten, *der;* ❷ *adj.* südsüdöstlich; Südsüdost-; ❸ *adv.* südsüdostwärts; **~-~'west** ▶ 1024 ❶ *n.* Südsüdwesten, *der;* ❷ *adj.* südsüdwestlich; Südsüdwest-; ❸ *adv.* südsüdwestwärts

**southward** /'saʊθwəd/ ▶ 1024 ❶ *adj.* nach Süden gerichtet; (*situated towards the south*) südlich; **in a ~ direction** nach Süden; [in] Richtung Süden. ❷ *adv.* südwärts; **they are ~ bound** sie fahren nach *od.* [in] Richtung Süden. ❸ *n.* Süden, *der*

**southwards** /'saʊθwədz/ ▶ 1024 ⇒ **southward** 2

**south: ~-'west** ▶ 1024 ❶ *n.* Südwesten, *der;* **in/to[wards]/from the ~-west** im/nach *od.* (*geh.*) gen/von Südwesten; **to the ~-west of** südwestlich von; südwestlich (+ *Gen.*). ❷ *adj.* südwestlich; Südwest‹wind, -fenster, -küste›. ❸ *adv.* südwestwärts; nach Südwesten; **~-west of** südwestlich von; südwestlich (+ *Gen.*); **S~-West 'Africa** *pr. n.* Südwestafrika, (*das*); **~wester** /saʊθ'westə(r)/ *n.* Südwestwind, *der;* **~-'westerly** ▶ 1024 ❶ *adj.* südwestlich; ❷ *adv.* (*position*) im Südwesten; (*direction*) nach Südwesten; **~-'western** *adj.* ▶ 1024 südwestlich

**souvenir** /su:və'nɪə(r)/ *n.* (*of holiday*) Andenken, *das;* Souvenir, *das* (**of** aus); (*of wedding day, one's youth, etc.*) Andenken, *das* (*of* an + *Akk.*)

**sou'wester** /saʊ'westə(r)/ *n.* [A] (*hat*) Südwester, *der;* [B] (*coat*) Ölhaut, *die*

**sovereign** /'sɒvrɪn/ ❶ *n.* [A] (*ruler*) Souverän, *der;* [B] (*Brit. Hist.: coin*) Sovereign, *der;* 20-Shilling-Münze, die. ❷ *adj.* [A] (*independent*) souverän ‹Staat, Volk›; [B] (*supreme*) höchst...; [C] (*arch.: royal*) souverän; [D] (*very good*) ausgezeichnet ‹Medikament›

**sovereignty** /'sɒvrɪntɪ/ *n.* [A] (*supreme power*) Souveränität, *die;* Oberhoheit, *die;* [B] (*royal position*) Stellung als Souverän; [C] (*autonomous state*) souveräner Staat

**Soviet** /'səʊvɪət, 'sɒvɪət/ (*Hist.*) ❶ *adj.* sowjetisch; Sowjet‹bürger, -literatur, -kultur, -ideologie›. ❷ *n.* Sowjet, *der;* **Supreme ~:** Oberster Sowjet

**Soviet: ~ 'Russia** *pr. n.* (*Hist.*) Sowjetrussland (*das*); **~ 'Union** *pr. n.* (*Hist.*) Sowjetunion, *die*

**sow¹** /səʊ/ *v.t., p.p.* **sown** /səʊn/ *or* **sowed** /səʊd/ [A] (*plant*) [aus]säen; (*fig.*) legen ‹Minen›; [B] (*plant with seed*) einsäen, besäen ‹Feld, Boden›; [C] (*cover thickly*) spicken (*ugs.*); **meadows ~n with daisies** mit Gänseblümchen bedeckte Wiesen; [D] (*fig.: initiate*) säen. ⇒ *also* **oat** B; **seed** 1 C; **whirlwind** A

**sow²** /saʊ/ *n.* [A] (*female pig*) Sau, *die;* [B] (*Metallurgy*) (*trough*) Kokille, *die;* (*block of iron*) Massel, *die.* ⇒ *also* **silk** 2

**sower** /'səʊə(r)/ *n.* Sämann, *der*/Säerin, *die;* **be a ~ of discord** Zwietracht säen

**sowing** /'səʊɪŋ/ *n.* Säen, *das;* Aussaat, *die*

**sown** ⇒ **sow¹**

**sox** /sɒks/ *n. pl.* (*Commerc./coll.*) ⇒ **sock¹** A

**soya [bean]** /'sɔɪə (bi:n)/, **soy bean** /'sɔɪ bi:n/ *ns.* [A] (*plant*) Soja[bohne], *die;* [B] (*seed*) Sojabohne, *die*

**soy sauce** /'sɔɪ sɔ:s/ *n.* Sojasoße, *die*

**sozzled** /'sɒzld/ *adj.* (*coll.*) voll (*ugs.*); besoffen (*derb*); **get ~:** sich besaufen (*derb*)

**spa** /spɑ:/ *n.* [A] (*place*) Bad, *das;* Badeort, *der;* [B] (*spring*) Mineralquelle, *die*

**space** /speɪs/ ❶ *n.* [A] Raum, *der;* **stare into ~:** in die Luft *od.* ins Leere starren; [B] (*interval between points*) Platz, *der;* **the houses are separated by a ~ of ten feet** die Häuser sind durch einen 10 Fuß breiten Zwischenraum getrennt; **clear a ~:** Platz schaffen; **he needs ~** (*fig.*) er braucht Bewegungsfreiheit; [C] (*area on page*) Platz, *der;* [D] **the wide open ~s** das weite, flache Land; **the vast ~s of the prairie/desert** die weite Fläche *od.* die Weite[n] der Prärie/Wüste; [E] (*Astron.*) Weltraum, *der;* ⇒ *also* **outer space**; [F] (*blank between words*) Zwischenraum, *der;* Spatium, *das* (*Druckw.*); **five ~s from the left margin** fünf Anschläge vom linken Rand [entfernt]; [G] (*interval of time*) Zeitraum, *der;* **in the ~ of a minute/an hour** *etc.* innerhalb einer Minute/Stunde *usw.*; **in a short ~ of time he was back** nach kurzer Zeit war er zurück.
❷ *v.t.* **the line is/the letters are badly ~d** die Zeile ist/die Buchstaben sind schlecht spationiert (*Druckw.*); **the posts are ~d at intervals of one metre** die Pfosten sind im Abstand von einem Meter aufgestellt
**~ 'out** *v.t.* verteilen; **~ the figures out clearly** die Zahlen so weit auseinander schreiben, dass sie deutlich lesbar sind

**space: ~ age** *n.* [Welt]raumzeitalter, *das;* Zeitalter der Raumfahrt, *das;* **~ bar** *n.* Leertaste, *die;* **~craft** *n.* Raumfahrzeug, *das;* (*unmanned*) Raumsonde, *die*

**spaced [out]** /speɪst ('aʊt)/ *adj.* (*coll.: under influence of drug*) high (*Drogenjargon*)

**space: ~ flight** *n.* [A] (*a journey through ~*) [Welt]raumflug, *der;* [B] ⇒ **~ travel**; **~ heater** *n.* Heizgerät, *das;* **~man** ⇒ **~ traveller**; **~ medicine** *n.* Raumfahrtmedizin, *die;* **~ opera** *n.* (*esp. Amer.*) Weltraumoper, *die* (*ugs.*); **~ probe** *n.* Raumsonde, *die;* **~-saving** *adj.* Platz sparend; Raum sparend; **~ship** *n.* Raumschiff, *das;* **~ shuttle** *n.* Raumfähre, *die;* Raumtransporter, *der;* **~ station** *n.* [Welt]raumstation, *die;* **~suit** *n.* Raumanzug, *der;* **~-'time** *n.* (*Phys.*) Raum-Zeit-Welt, *die;* **~ travel** *n.* Raumfahrt, *die;* **~ traveller** *n.* Raumfahrer, *der*/-fahrerin, *die;* **~ vehicle** ⇒ **spacecraft**; **~ walk** *n.* Spaziergang im All

**spacial, spacially** ⇒ **spatial, spatially**

**spacing** /'speɪsɪŋ/ *n.* Zwischenraum, *der;* (*Printing*) Sperrungen; Spationierung, *die* (*Druckw.*); **single/double ~** (*on typewriter*) einfacher/doppelter Zeilenabstand

S

**spacious** /ˈspeɪʃəs/ *adj.* Ⓐ (*vast in area*) weitläufig ‹Garten, Park, Ländereien›; Ⓑ (*roomy*) geräumig ‹Raum›; breit ‹Straße›

**spaciously** /ˈspeɪʃəslɪ/ *adv.* weitläufig

**spade** /speɪd/ *n.* Ⓐ (*for digging*) Spaten, *der;* **call a ~ a ~** *or* (*joc.*) **a bloody shovel** das Kind beim [rechten] Namen nennen (*ugs.*); **she was never afraid to call a ~ a ~:** sie nahm nie ein Blatt vor den Mund (*ugs.*); **in ~s** in höchstem Maße; **have sth. in ~s** etw. in höchstem Maße haben *od.* besitzen; **pay sb. back in ~s** es jmdm. doppelt heimzahlen; Ⓑ (*Cards*) Pik, *das;* ⇒ *also* **club** 1 D; Ⓒ (*Amer. sl. derog.*) Neger, *der*

**spadeful** /ˈspeɪdfʊl/ *n.* **a ~/two ~s of soil** ein/zwei Spaten [voll] Erde

ˈ**spadework** *n.* (*fig.*) Kleinarbeit, *die;* (*preliminary work*) Vorarbeit, *die*

**spadix** /ˈspeɪdɪks/ *n., pl.* **spadices** /ˈspeɪdɪsiːz/ (*Bot.*) Kolben, *der*

**spaghetti** /spəˈgetɪ/ *n.* Ⓐ Spaghetti *Pl.;* Ⓑ (*joc.: cables*) Kabelsalat, *der* (*ugs.*)

**spaghetti** ˈ**Western** *n.* (*Cinemat.*) Italowestern, *der*

**Spain** /speɪn/ *pr. n.* Spanien (*das*)

**spall** /spɔːl/ ❶ *v.t.* Ⓐ (*chip*) absplittern; Ⓑ (*Mining*) mit dem Hammer zerkleinern ‹Erz›. ❷ *v.i.* splittern. ❸ *n.* Splitter, *der*

**Spam** ® /spæm/ *n.* Frühstücksfleisch, *das*

**span**[1] /spæn/ ❶ *n.* Ⓐ (*full extent*) Spanne, *die;* **~ of life/time** Lebens-/Zeitspanne, *die;* **throughout the whole ~ of Roman history** in der gesamten römischen Geschichte; Ⓑ (*of bridge*) Spannweite, *die;* **the bridge crosses the river in a single ~:** die Brücke überspannt den Fluss in einem einzigen Bogen; Ⓒ (*Aeronaut.*) Spannweite, *die;* Ⓓ (*of hand*) Spanne, *die.* ❷ *v.t.*, **-nn-** Ⓐ (*extend across*) überspannen ‹Fluss›; umfassen ‹Zeitraum›; Ⓑ (*measure*) nach Spannen messen

**span**[2] ⇒ **spick**

**spandrel** /ˈspændrl/ *n.* (*Archit.*) [Bogen]zwickel, *der;* Spandrille, *die*

**spang** /spæŋ/ *adv.* (*Amer. coll.*) ganz; **~ in the middle of the night/the road** mitten in der Nacht/auf der Straße

**spangle** /ˈspæŋgl/ ❶ *n.* ⇒ **sequin.** ❷ *v.t.* **~d with stars/buttercups** von glitzernden Sternen/mit leuchtenden Butterblumen übersät; ⇒ *also* **star-spangled**

**Spaniard** /ˈspænjəd/ *n.* ▶ 1340 Spanier, *der*/Spanierin, *die*

**spaniel** /ˈspænjəl/ *n.* Spaniel, *der*

**Spanish** /ˈspænɪʃ/ ▶ 1275, ▶ 1340 ❶ *adj.* spanisch; **sb. is ~:** jmd. ist Spanier/Spanierin; ⇒ *also* **English** 1. ❷ *n.* Ⓐ (*language*) Spanisch, *das;* ⇒ *also* **English** 2 A; Ⓑ *constr. as pl.* (*people*) Spanier

**Spanish: ~ Aˈmerica** *pr. n. die spanischsprachigen Länder Lateinamerikas;* **~ ˈfly** *n.* Spanische Fliege; **~ ˈMain** *pr. n.* (*Hist.*) **the ~ Main** *die Nordostküste Südamerikas zwischen dem Orinoko und Panama sowie der angrenzende Teil der Karibik;* **~ ˈomelette** *n. Omelette mit Zwiebeln, grünem Paprika und Tomaten;* ≈ Omelette andalusische Art (*Kochk.*); **~ ˈonion** *n.* spanische Zwiebel; Bermudazwiebel, *die* (*Kochk.*)

**spank** /spæŋk/ ❶ *n.* ≈ Klaps, *der* (*ugs.*). ❷ *v.t.* **~ sb.** jmdm. den Hintern versohlen (*ugs.*); **get ~ed** den Hintern voll kriegen (*ugs.*). ❸ *v.i.* ‹Pferd:› schnell traben

**spanking** /ˈspæŋkɪŋ/ ❶ *n.* Tracht Prügel, *die* (*ugs.*); (*for sexual gratification*) Hinternversohlen, *das* (*ugs.*). ❷ *adj.* (*coll.*) scharf ‹Trab, Lauf, Galopp, Tempo›. ❸ *adv.* (*coll.*) **~ new** funkelnagelneu (*ugs.*)

**spanner** /ˈspænə(r)/ *n.* (*Brit.*) Schraubenschlüssel, *der;* **put** *or* **throw a ~ in the works** (*fig.*) Sand ins Getriebe streuen

ˈ**span roof** *n.* Satteldach, *das*

**spar**[1] /spɑː(r)/ *v.i.*, **-rr-** Ⓐ (*Boxing*) sparren; Ⓑ (*fig.: argue*) [sich] zanken

**spar**[2] *n.* Ⓐ (*pole*) Rundholz, *das;* Spiere, *die* (*Seemannsspr.*); Ⓑ (*Aeronaut.*) Holm, *der*

**spar**[3] *n.* (*Min.*) Spat, *der*

**spare** /speə(r)/ ❶ *adj.* Ⓐ (*not in use*) übrig; **~ time/moment** Freizeit, *die*/freier Augenblick; **not have ~ cash** kein Bargeld [übrig] haben; **have sth. going ~** (*coll.*) etwas übrig haben; **there is one ~ seat** ein Platz ist noch frei; **are there any ~ tickets for Friday?** gibt es noch Karten für Freitag?; Ⓑ (*for use when needed*) zusätzlich, Extra‹bett, -tasse›; **~ room** Gästezimmer, *das;* **go ~** (*Brit. coll.: be very angry*) durchdrehen (*salopp*); Ⓒ (*frugal*) karg ‹Kost, Mahlzeit›; Ⓓ (*lean*) schlank ‹Wuchs, Gestalt›; Ⓔ schlicht ‹Stil›.
❷ *n.* Ersatzteil, *das*/-reifen, *der usw.;* **I haven't got a pen; have you a ~?** ich hab keinen Stift, hast du einen übrig?
❸ *v.t.* Ⓐ (*do without*) entbehren; **can you ~ me a moment?** hast du einen Augenblick Zeit für mich?; **we arrived with ten minutes to ~:** wir kamen zehn Minuten früher an; als wir ankamen, hatten wir noch zehn Minuten Zeit [übrig]; Ⓑ (*not inflict on*) **~ sb. sth.** jmdm. etw. ersparen; Ⓒ (*not hurt*) [ver]schonen; **if I am ~d** wenn ich so lange lebe; Ⓓ (*not cause*) **~ sb.'s blushes** jmdm. die Verlegenheit *od.* Peinlichkeit ersparen; Ⓔ (*fail to use*) **not ~ any expense/pains** *or* **efforts** keine Kosten/Mühe scheuen; **no expense ~d** an nichts gespart; **not ~ oneself in one's efforts to ...:** keine Mühe scheuen ... ⇒ *also* **enough** 2; **rod** C

**sparely** /ˈspeəlɪ/ *adv.* **~ built** schlank [gebaut]

**spare: ~ ˈpart** *n.* Ersatzteil, *das;* **~ rib** *n.* Ⓐ (*cut of meat*) Kamm, *der;* Ⓑ (*dish*) [Schäl]rippchen, *das;* **~ ˈtyre** *n.* Ⓐ Reserve-, Ersatzreifen, *der;* Ⓑ (*Brit. fig. coll.*) Rettungsring, *der* (*ugs.*); **~ ˈwheel** *n.* Ersatzrad, *das*

**sparing** /ˈspeərɪŋ/ *adj.* sparsam; **be ~ of sth./in the use of sth.** mit etw. sparsam umgehen

**sparingly** /ˈspeərɪŋlɪ/ *adv.* sparsam

**spark** /spɑːk/ ❶ *n.* Ⓐ Funke, *der;* **shower of ~s** Funkenregen, *der;* **the ~s [begin to] fly** (*fig.*) es funkt (*ugs.*); **a ~ of generosity/decency** (*fig.*) ein Funke[n] Großzügigkeit/Anstand; **not a ~ of life remained** (*fig.*) keine Spur von Leben blieb übrig; Ⓑ (*electrical discharge*) Funkenentladung, *die;* Ⓒ (*in ~ing-plug*) Zündfunke[n], *der* (*Kfz-W.*); Ⓓ **a bright ~** (*clever person; also iron.*) ein schlauer Kopf. ❷ *v.t.* ⇒ **spark off.** ❸ *v.i.* Ⓐ Funken sprühen; Ⓑ (*Electr.*) funken

**~ ˈoff** *v.t.* Ⓐ (*cause to explode*) zünden; Ⓑ (*fig.: start*) auslösen

ˈ**spark gap** *n.* (*Electr.*) Funkenstrecke, *die*

**sparking plug** /ˈspɑːkɪŋplʌg/ *n.* (*Brit. Motor Veh.*) Zündkerze, *die*

**sparkle** /ˈspɑːkl/ ❶ *v.i.* Ⓐ (*flash*) ‹Diamant, Tautropfen:› glitzern; ‹Augen:› funkeln, sprühen; Ⓑ (*perform brilliantly*) glänzen; Ⓒ (*be lively*) sprühen (**with** vor + *Dat.*). ❷ *n.* Glitzern, *das;* Funkeln, *das;* **he lost all his ~** (*fig.*) er hat sein sprühendes Temperament verloren

**sparkler** /ˈspɑːklə(r)/ *n.* Ⓐ (*firework*) Wunderkerze, *die;* Ⓑ (*coll.: diamond*) Klunker, *der* (*ugs.*)

**sparkling** /ˈspɑːklɪŋ/ *adj.* Ⓐ (*flashing*) glitzernd ‹Stein, Diamant›; Ⓑ (*bright*) funkelnd ‹Augen›; **~ vivacity** sprühende Lebhaftigkeit; Ⓒ (*brilliant*) glänzend ‹Schauspiel, Aufführung, Rede›

**sparkling** ˈ**wine** *n.* Schaumwein, *der*

ˈ**spark plug** ⇒ **sparking plug**

ˈ**sparring partner** *n.* (*Boxing*) Sparringspartner, *der;* **this is my old ~** (*fig.*) dies ist mein alter Freund, mit dem ich oft die Klingen gekreuzt habe (*geh.*)

**sparrow** /ˈspærəʊ/ *n.* Sperling, *der;* Spatz, *der;* **house ~:** Haussperling, *der;* Hausspatz, *der;* ⇒ *also* **hedge sparrow**

ˈ**sparrowhawk** *n.* Sperber, *der*

**sparse** /spɑːs/ *adj.* spärlich; dünn ‹Besiedlung›

**sparsely** /ˈspɑːslɪ/ *adv.* spärlich; dünn ‹besiedelt›

**sparseness** /ˈspɑːsnɪs/, **sparsity** /ˈspɑːsɪtɪ/ *ns., no pl.* Spärlichkeit, *die*

**Spartan** /ˈspɑːtn/ ❶ *adj.* spartanisch. ❷ *n.* Spartaner, *der*/Spartanerin, *die*

**spasm** /ˈspæzm/ *n.* Ⓐ Krampf, *der;* Spasmus, *der* (*Med.*); Ⓑ (*convulsive movement*) Anfall, *der;* **~ of coughing** Hustenanfall, *der;* Ⓒ (*coll.*) **a ~ of activity** plötzliche fieberhafte Aktivität

**spasmodic** /spæzˈmɒdɪk/ *adj.* Ⓐ (*marked by spasms*) krampfartig; spasmodisch (*Med.*); Ⓑ (*intermittent*) sporadisch ‹Anwachsen, Bemühungen›

**spasmodically** /spæzˈmɒdɪkəlɪ/ *adv.* Ⓐ krampfartig, (*Med.*) spasmodisch ‹zucken›; Ⓑ (*intermittently*) sporadisch

**spastic** /ˈspæstɪk/ (*Med.*) ❶ *n.* Spastiker, *der*/Spastikerin, *die.* ❷ *adj.* spastisch [gelähmt]

**spat**[1] ⇒ **spit**[1] 1, 2

**spat**[2] /spæt/ *n.* (*gaiter*) Gamasche, *die*

**spat**[3] *n.* (*coll.: quarrel*) Krach, *der* (*ugs.*)

**spate** /speɪt/ *n.* Ⓐ ▶ 1480 (*flood*) **the river/waterfall is in [full] ~:** der Fluss/Wasserfall führt Hochwasser; Ⓑ (*fig.: large amount*) **a ~ of sth.** eine Flut von etw.; **a ~ of burglaries** eine Einbruchsserie

**spatial** /ˈspeɪʃl/ *adj.*, **spatially** /ˈspeɪʃəlɪ/ *adv.* räumlich

**spatter** /ˈspætə(r)/ ❶ *v.t.* spritzen ‹Lehm, Wasser›; **~ sb./sth. with sth.** jmdn./etw. mit etw. bespritzen. ❷ *n.* Spritzer, *der*

**spatula** /ˈspætjʊlə/ *n.* Ⓐ Spachtel, *die;* Ⓑ (*Surg.*) Spatel, *der od. die*

**spatulate** /ˈspætjʊlət/ *adj.* spatelförmig

**spawn** /spɔːn/ ❶ *v.t.* Ⓐ (*produce*) ablegen ‹Eier›; (*fig.*) hervorbringen; Ⓑ (*derog.: breed*) produzieren. ❷ *v.i.* laichen. ❸ *n., constr. as sing. or pl.* Ⓐ (*Zool.*) Laich, *der;* Ⓑ (*derog.: offspring*) Brut, *die* (*salopp abwertend*)

**spay** /speɪ/ *v.t.* sterilisieren ‹Katze, Hündin›

**speak** /spiːk/ ❶ *v.i.*, **spoke** /spəʊk/, **spoken** /ˈspəʊkn/ Ⓐ ▶ 1275 sprechen; **we spoke this morning** wir sprachen heute Morgen miteinander; **~ with sb.** mit jmdm. sprechen; **~ [with sb.] on** *or* **about sth.** [mit jmdm.] über etwas (*Akk.*) sprechen; **~ for/against sth.** sich für/gegen etw. aussprechen; **sth. ~s well for sb.** etw. spricht für jmdn.; **~ing as a trade unionist/a European** als Gewerkschafter/Europäer; **the minister rose to ~:** der Minister erhob sich, um das Wort zu ergreifen; Ⓑ (*on telephone*) **Is Mr Grant there? — Speaking!** Ist Mister Grant da? — Am Apparat!; **Mr Grant ~ing** (*when connected to caller*) Grant hier; hier ist Grant; **who is ~ing, please?** wer ist am Apparat, bitte?; mit wem spreche ich, bitte? ⇒ *also* **manner** A; **so**[1] 2.
❷ *v.t.*, **spoke, spoken** Ⓐ (*utter*) sprechen ‹Satz, Wort, Sprache›; Ⓑ (*make known*) sagen ‹Wahrheit›; **~ one's opinion/mind** seine Meinung sagen; sagen, was man denkt; Ⓒ (*convey without words*) **sth. ~s volumes** etw. spricht Bände; **sth. ~s volumes for sth.** etw. spricht sehr für etw.

**~ for** *v.t.* sprechen für; **~ for oneself** für sich selbst sprechen; **~ing for myself, I prefer tea to coffee** ich selber trinke lieber Tee als Kaffee; **~ for yourself!** das ist [nur] deine Meinung!; **~ for itself/themselves** für sich selbst sprechen; **We're all depressed — S~ for yourself!** Wir sind alle deprimiert. — Du vielleicht, ich nicht!; **sth. is spoken for** (*reserved*) etw. ist schon vergeben

**~ of** *v.t.* sprechen von; **~ing of Mary** da wir gerade von Mary sprechen; apropos Mary; **nothing to ~ of** nichts Besonderes *od.* Nennenswertes; **no trees to ~ of** kaum Bäume; **these tyres have no tread to ~ of** bei diesen Reifen kann man kaum noch von Profil sprechen; ⇒ *also* **devil** 1 C

**~ ˈout** *v.i.* seine Meinung sagen; seine Stimme erheben; **~ out against sth.** seine Stimme gegen etw. erheben; sich gegen etw. aussprechen

**~ to** *v.t.* Ⓐ (*address*) sprechen mit; reden mit; **I know him to ~ to** ich kenne ihn [nur] flüchtig; **~ when** *or* **don't ~ until you are spoken to** rede nur, wenn du gefragt wirst; Ⓑ (*request action from*) **~ to sb. about sth.** mit jmdm. wegen einer Sache *od.* über etw. (*Akk.*) sprechen; Ⓒ (*coll.: reprove*) **~ to sb.** sich mit jmdm. unterhalten (*verhüllend*); Ⓓ **~ to a subject** sich zu einem Thema äußern; Ⓔ (**~** *in confirmation of*) **I**

**can ~ to his having been there** ich kann bestätigen *od.* bezeugen, dass er dort war
**~ 'up** *v.i.* **A** (*~ more loudly*) lauter sprechen; **B** ⇒ **~ out**

**'speakeasy** *n.* (*Amer. Hist. coll.*) *Lokal, in dem illegal Alkohol ausgeschenkt wurde*

**speaker** /'spi:kə(r)/ *n.* **A** (*in public*) Redner, *der*/Rednerin, *die;* **be a/the ~ for** *or* **at an event** bei einem Anlass eine/die Rede halten; **B** (*of a language*) Sprecher, *der*/Sprecherin, *die;* **be a French ~, be a ~ of French** Französisch sprechen; **C** **S~** (*Polit.*) Sprecher, *der;* ≈ Parlamentspräsident, *der;* **Mr S~:** Herr Vorsitzender; ⇒ *also* **catch** 1 F; **D** ⇒ **loudspeaker**

**speaking** /'spi:kɪŋ/ ❶ *n.* **A** (*talking*) Sprechen, *das;* **a good ~ voice** eine gute Sprechstimme; **not be on ~ terms with sb.** nicht [mehr] mit jmdm. reden; **B** (*speech-making*) Rede, *die;* ⇒ *also* **public speaking.** ❷ *adv.* **strictly/roughly/generally/legally ~:** genau genommen/grob gesagt/im Allgemeinen/aus juristischer Sicht; **figuratively ~:** bildlich gesprochen

**speaking: ~ acquaintance** *n.* [flüchtige] Bekannte, *der/die;* **~ 'clock** *n.* (*Brit.*) telefonische Zeitansage; **~ tube** *n.* *Sprechverbindung zwischen zwei Räumen, Gebäuden usw. mittels einer Rohrleitung;* Sprachrohr, *das*

**spear** /spɪə(r)/ ❶ *n.* **A** Speer, *der;* **B** (*of plant*) Stange, *die.* ❷ *v.t.* aufspießen

**spear: ~head** ❶ *n.* (*fig.*) Speerspitze, *die;* (*Mil.*) Angriffsspitze, *die;* ❷ *v.t.* (*fig.*) **~head sth.** etw. anführen; die Speerspitze von etw. bilden (*bes. Pol.*); (*Mil.*) bei etw. die Angriffsspitze bilden; **~mint** *n.* Grüne Minze; **~mint sweet/chewing gum** Pfefferminzbonbon/-kaugummi, *der od. das*

**spec**[1] /spek/ *n.* (*coll.: speculation*) Spekulation, *die;* **on ~:** auf gut Glück; auf Verdacht (*ugs.*)

**spec**[2] /spek/ (*coll.*) ⇒ **specification** A

**special** /'speʃl/ ❶ *adj.* speziell; besonder...; Sonder‹korrespondent, -zug, -mission, -behandlung, -ausgabe, -bedeutung, -auftrag›; **nobody ~:** niemand Besonderes; **her own ~ way** ihre eigene Art; **a ~ occasion** ein besonderer Anlass; **a very ~ relationship** eine besonders enge Beziehung; **~ friend** besonders enger Freund/enge Freundin. ❷ *n.* (*newspaper*) Sonderausgabe, *die;* (*train*) Sonderzug, *der*

**special: S~ Branch** *n.* (*Brit. Police*) *Abteilung der britischen Polizei, deren Aufgabe die Wahrung der inneren Sicherheit ist;* ≈ Sicherheitsdienst, *der;* **~ 'case** *n.* Sonderfall, *der;* **~ 'constable** *n.* (*Brit. Police*) Hilfspolizist, *der*/-polizistin, *die;* **~ correspondent** *n.* Sonderkorrespondent, *der*/-korrespondentin, *die;* Sonderberichterstatter, *der*/-berichterstatterin, *die;* **~ de'livery** *n.* (*Post*) Eilzustellung, *die;* **~ 'drawing rights** *n. pl.* (*Finance*) Sonderziehungsrechte *Pl.* [auf den Internationalen Währungsfonds]; **~ e'dition** *n.* Sonderausgabe, *die;* **~ effects** *n. pl.* (*Cinemat.*) Special effects *Pl.* (*fachspr.*); Spezialeffekte **~-'interest** *attrib. adj.* Special-Interest-; **~-interest group** Interessengruppe, *die*

**specialisation, specialise** ⇒ **specializ-**

**specialism** /'speʃəlɪzm/ *n.* **A** ⇒ **specialization;** **B** (*field of study*) Spezialgebiet, *das*

**specialist** /'speʃəlɪst/ *n.* **A** Spezialist, *der*/Spezialistin, *die* (**in** für); Fachmann, *der*/Fachfrau, *die* (**in** für); **an eighteenth-century ~:** ein Spezialist für das achtzehnte Jahrhundert; **~ knowledge** Fachwissen, *das;* **B** (*Med.*) Facharzt, *der*/-ärztin, *die;* **eye/heart/cancer ~:** Augenarzt/Herz-/Krebsspezialist, *der*

**speciality** /speʃɪ'ælɪtɪ/ *n.* **A** (*activity, skill, product*) Spezialität, *die;* (*interest*) Spezialgebiet, *das;* **she makes a ~ of her pies** Pasteten sind ihre Spezialität; **B** (*special feature*) [besonderes] Merkmal *od.* Kennzeichen

**specialization** /speʃəlaɪ'zeɪʃn/ *n.* Spezialisierung, *die*

**specialize** /'speʃəlaɪz/ ❶ *v.i.* sich spezialisieren (**in** auf + *Akk.*). ❷ *v.t.* (*Biol.: modify*) **become ~d** ‹Glied, Organ:› sich gesondert ausbilden

**specialized** /'speʃəlaɪzd/ *adj.* **A** (*requiring detailed knowledge*) speziell; Spezial‹kenntnisse, -gebiet›; **B** (*concentrating on small area*) spezialisiert

**special 'licence** *n.* (*Brit.*) *Sondererlaubnis, die die Heirat ohne Aufgebot oder an einem anderen als dem gewöhnlichen Ort zulässt*

**specially** /'speʃəlɪ/ *adv.* **A** speziell; **make sth. ~:** etw. speziell *od.* extra anfertigen; **~ made/chosen for me** eigens für mich gemacht/ausgewählt; **a ~ made wheelchair/lift** ein spezieller Rollstuhl/Lift; **a ~ adapted bus** ein spezieller Bus; **B** (*especially*) besonders

**special: ~ 'needs** *n.* **children with ~ needs, ~ needs children** Kinder, die besonders betreut werden müssen; **~ 'offer** *n.* Sonderangebot, *das;* **have a ~ offer on sth.** etw. im Sonderangebot haben; **on ~ offer** im Sonderangebot; **~ 'pleading** *n.* **A** (*biased argument*) Rechtsverdrehung, *die* (*abwertend*); **B** (*Law*) *Plädoyer, das die Umstände eines Falles besonders berücksichtigt;* **~ school** *n.* Sonderschule, *die*

**specialty** /'speʃltɪ/ (*esp. Amer.*) ⇒ **speciality** A

**speciation** /spi:sɪ'eɪʃn, spi:ʃɪ'eɪʃn/ *n.* (*Biol.*) Art[en]bildung, *die*

**specie** /'spi:ʃi:, 'spi:ʃɪ/ *n.* Hartgeld, *das*

**species** /'spi:ʃi:z, 'spi:ʃɪz/ *n., pl. same* **A** (*Biol.*) Spezies, *die* (*fachspr.*); Art, *die;* **B** (*sort*) Art, *die;* **a dangerous ~ of criminal** ein gefährlicher Typ [von] Verbrecher

**specific** /spɪ'sɪfɪk/ ❶ *adj.* **A** (*definite*) deutlich, klar ‹Aussage›; bestimmt ‹Ziel, Grund›; **make a ~ request** einen bestimmten Wunsch äußern; **make no ~ preparations** keine besonderen Vorbereitungen treffen; **could you be more ~?** kannst du dich genauer ausdrücken?; **B** (*of a species*) **the ~ name of a plant** der Name einer Pflanzenart; **C** (*individual*) eigen (**to** *Dat.*); typisch (**to** für); ⇒ *also* **gravity** D; **heat** 1 B. ❷ *n.* **A** (*arch. Med.: remedy*) Spezifikum, *das;* **B** *in pl.* (*details*) Einzelheiten *Pl.;* Details *Pl.*

**specifically** /spɪ'sɪfɪkəlɪ/ *adv.* ausdrücklich; eigens; extra (*ugs.*)

**specification** /spesɪfɪ'keɪʃn/ *n.* **A** *often pl.* (*details*) technische Daten; (*instructions*) Konstruktionsplan, *der;* (*for building*) Baubeschreibung, *die;* **B** (*specifying*) Spezifizierung, *die* (*geh.*); **C** **[patent] ~:** Patentschrift, *die*

**specificity** /spesɪ'fɪsɪtɪ/ *n.* Genauigkeit im Detail

**specify** /'spesɪfaɪ/ *v.t.* (*name expressly*) ausdrücklich sagen; ausdrücklich nennen ‹Namen›; (*include in specifications*) [genau] aufführen; **as specified above** wie oben aufgeführt; **unless otherwise specified** wenn nicht anders angegeben; **'other (please ~)'** „andere (bitte genaue Angaben machen)"

**specimen** /'spesɪmən/ *n.* **A** (*example*) Exemplar, *das;* **a ~ of his handwriting** eine Schriftprobe von ihm; **some ~s of her work** ein paar Arbeitsproben von ihr; **~ signature** Unterschriftsprobe, *die;* **B** (*sample*) Probe, *die;* **a ~ of his urine was required** es wurde eine Urinprobe von ihm benötigt; **C** (*coll./derog.: type*) Marke, *die* (*salopp*)

**'specimen page** *n.* Probeseite, *die*

**specious** /'spi:ʃəs/ *adj.* **a ~ argument** ein nur scheinbar treffendes Argument; **a ~ pretence/appearance of honesty** ein Anschein von Ehrlichkeit

**speck** /spek/ *n.* **A** (*spot*) Fleck, *der;* (*of paint also*) Spritzer, *der;* **B** (*particle*) Teilchen, *das;* **~ of soot/dust** Rußflocke, *die*/Staubkörnchen, *das;* **a ~ on the horizon** ein Pünktchen am Horizont; **the ore sparkled with ~s of gold** in dem Erz glitzerten Goldsprenkel; **C** (*blemish*) Fleck, *der;* **have ~s** fleckig sein

**specked** /spekt/ *adj.* fleckig ‹Frucht›; **his coat is ~ with paint/mud** auf seinem Mantel sind Farb-/Schlammspritzer

**speckle** /'spekl/ *n.* Tupfen, *der;* Sprenkel, *der*

**speckled** /'spekld/ *adj.* gesprenkelt

**specs** /speks/ *n. pl.* (*coll.: spectacles*) Brille, *die*

**spectacle** /'spektəkl/ *n.* **A** *in pl.* **[pair of] ~s** Brille, *die;* **B** (*public show*) Spektakel, *das;* **C** (*object of attention*) Anblick, *der;* Schauspiel, *das;* **make a ~ of oneself** sich unmöglich aufführen

**'spectacle case** *n.* Brillenetui, *das*

**spectacled** /'spektəkld/ *adj.* bebrillt

**spectacular** /spek'tækjʊlə(r)/ ❶ *adj.* spektakulär. ❷ *n.* Spektakel, *das*

**spectacularly** /spek'tækjʊləlɪ/ *adv.* außergewöhnlich; **be ~ successful** [einen] spektakulären Erfolg haben

**spectator** /spek'teɪtə(r)/ *n.* Zuschauer, *der*/Zuschauerin, *die*

**spec'tator sport** *n.* Publikumssport, *der*

**specter** (*Amer.*) ⇒ **spectre**

**spectra** *pl. of* **spectrum**

**spectral** /'spektrl/ *adj.* **A** (*ghostly*) geisterhaft; gespenstisch; **B** (*Phys.*) spektral

**spectre** /'spektə(r)/ *n.* (*Brit.*) **A** (*apparition*) Gespenst, *das;* **B** (*disturbing image*) Schreckgespenst, *das*

**spectrogram** /'spektrəgræm/ *n.* (*Phys.*) Spektrogramm, *das*

**spectrograph** /'spektrəgrɑ:f/ *n.* (*Phys.*) Spektrograph, *der*

**spectrometer** /spek'trɒmɪtə(r)/ *n.* (*Phys.*) Spektrometer, *das*

**spectroscope** /'spektrəskəʊp/ *n.* (*Phys.*) Spektroskop, *das*

**spectroscopy** /spek'trɒskəpɪ/ *n.* (*Phys.*) Spektroskopie, *die*

**spectrum** /'spektrəm/ *n., pl.* **spectra** /'spektrə/ (*Phys.; also fig.*) Spektrum, *das;* **~ of opinion** Meinungsspektrum, *das*

**specula** *pl. of* **speculum**

**speculate** /'spekjʊleɪt/ *v.i.* spekulieren (**about, on** über + *Akk.*); Vermutungen *od.* Spekulationen anstellen (**about, on** über + *Akk.*); **~ as to what .../as to the wisdom of doing sth.** darüber spekulieren, was .../ob es klug sei, etw. zu tun; **~ on the Stock Exchange/in the gold market/in rubber** an der Börse/am Goldmarkt/mit *od.* (*Wirtsch. Jargon*) in Gummi spekulieren

**speculation** /spekjʊ'leɪʃn/ *n.* Spekulation, *die* (**over** über + *Akk.*); **~ on the Stock Exchange/in the gold market/in rubber** Spekulation an der Börse/am Goldmarkt/mit *od.* (*Wirtsch. Jargon*) in Gummi; **there has been much ~ that ...:** man hat viel darüber spekuliert, dass ...

**speculative** /'spekjʊlətɪv/ *adj.* spekulativ; **~ transactions** Spekulationsgeschäfte

**speculatively** /'spekjʊlətɪvlɪ/ *adv.* spekulativ

**speculator** /'spekjʊleɪtə(r)/ *n.* Spekulant, *der*/Spekulantin, *die*

**speculum** /'spekjʊləm/ *n., pl.* **specula** /'spekjʊlə/ (*Med.*) Spekulum, *das*

**sped** ⇒ **speed** 2, 3

**speech** /spi:tʃ/ *n.* **A** (*public address*) Rede, *die;* **make** *or* **deliver** *or* **give a ~:** eine Rede halten; **~ for the defence** (*Law*) Plädoyer des Verteidigers; **King's/Queen's S~** (*Parl.*) Thronrede, *die;* **B** (*faculty of speaking*) Sprache, *die;* **lose/recover** *or* **find one's [power of] ~:** die Sprache verlieren/wieder finden; **C** (*act of speaking*) Sprechen, *das;* Sprache, *die;* **D** (*manner of speaking*) Sprache, *die;* Sprechweise, *die;* **his ~ was slurred** er sprach undeutlich; **E** (*Ling.: utterances*) Sprache, *die;* **children's ~:** Kindersprache, *die.* ⇒ *also* **figure** 1 H; **part** 1 J; **set speech**

**speech: ~ act** *n.* (*Ling.*) Sprechakt, *der;* **~ day** *n.* (*Brit. Sch.*) jährliches Schulfest; **~ defect** *n.* Sprachfehler, *der*

**speechify** /'spi:tʃɪfaɪ/ *v.i.* (*coll.*) eine Rede schwingen (*ugs.*)

**speechless** /'spi:tʃlɪs/ *adj.* **A** sprachlos (**with** vor + *Dat.*); **~ with rage** sprachlos vor Wut; **B** (*dumb*) stumm

S

## Speed

In Germany, as in the rest of continental Europe, the speed of road, rail and air traffic is measured in kilometres per hour, for which kph is the usual British abbreviation, and km/h the abbreviation used on the continent and now also found in some English-language publications:

100 kph = 62.14 mph 100 mph ≈ 160 kph
50 mph ≈ 80 kph

***... miles per hour***
= ... Meilen in der *or* pro Stunde

***... kilometres per hour***
= ... Kilometer in der *or* pro Stunde, Stundenkilometer (*coll.*)

***100 miles per hour (mph)***
≈ 160 Kilometer in der *or* pro Stunde (km/h)

***How fast was the car going?, What speed was the car doing?***
= Wie schnell *or* Mit welcher Geschwindigkeit fuhr der Wagen?

***He was driving flat out/at full speed/at 50 miles per hour***
≈ Er fuhr mit Vollgas/mit Höchstgeschwindigkeit/mit 80 Kilometern pro Stunde

***It was going at*** or ***doing 75 [miles per hour]***
≈ Es fuhr mit 120 Stundenkilometern *or* (*coll.*) Sachen

***The car's top speed is 125 [mph]***
≈ Die Höchstgeschwindigkeit des Autos liegt bei 200 km/h, Das Auto fährt 200 Kilometer Spitze (*coll.*)

***You were exceeding the speed limit***
= Sie haben das Tempolimit überschritten

***They were tearing along/going at a crazy speed***
= Sie rasten dahin/fuhren mit rasender Geschwindigkeit *or* in rasendem Tempo

***We had to go at a crawl/were reduced to a crawl***
= Wir mussten im Kriechtempo fahren/kamen nur im Kriechtempo vorwärts

### Speed of light and sound

***The speed of sound is 330 metres per second***
= Die Schallgeschwindigkeit beträgt 330 Meter pro Sekunde (m/s)

***to break the sound barrier***
= die Schallmauer durchbrechen

***The speed of light is 186,300 miles per second***
= Die Lichtgeschwindigkeit beträgt 300 000 Kilometer pro Sekunde (km/s)

***at*** or ***with the speed of light***
= mit Lichtgeschwindigkeit

**speech: ~making** *n., no pl.* **be good at ~making** ein guter Redner/eine gute Rednerin sein; **all the ~making was over** alle Reden waren gehalten; **~ therapy** *n.* Sprachtherapie, *die;* **have ~ therapy** sprachtherapeutisch behandelt werden; **~writer** *n.* ▶ 1261 Redenschreiber, *der*/-schreiberin, *die*

**speed** /spiːd/ **1** *n.* **A** ▶ 1552 Geschwindigkeit, *die;* Schnelligkeit, *die;* (*of typist*) Schreibgeschwindigkeit, *die;* **at full** *or* **top ~:** mit Höchstgeschwindigkeit; mit Vollgas (*ugs.*); **pick up ~:** schneller werden; **top ~:** Spitzengeschwindigkeit, *die;* **with the ~ of light** mit Lichtgeschwindigkeit; (*fig.*) blitzschnell; **drive at a reckless ~:** rücksichtslos schnell fahren; **at a ~ of eighty miles an hour** mit einer Geschwindigkeit von achtzig Meilen in der Stunde; **at ~:** mit hoher Geschwindigkeit; **B** (*gear*) Gang, *der;* **a five-~ gearbox** eine 5-Gang-Schaltung; **C** (*Photog.*) (*of film etc.*) Lichtempfindlichkeit, *die;* (*of lens*) **[shutter] ~:** Belichtungszeit, *die;* **D** (*sl.: drug*) Speed, *das* (*Jargon*). ⇒ *also* **air speed**; **full¹** 1 D; **ground speed**.
**2** *v.i.* **A** *p.t., p.p.* **sped** /sped/ *or* **speeded** (*go fast*) schnell fahren; rasen (*ugs.*); **the hours/days sped by** die Stunden/Tage vergingen wie im Fluge; **B** *p. t., p.p.* **speeded** (*go too fast*) zu schnell fahren; rasen (*ugs.*).
**3** *v.t.*, **sped** *or* **speeded: ~ sb. on his/her way** jmdn. verabschieden; **God ~ you** Gott steh dir/euch bei
**~ 'off** *v.i.* davonbrausen
**~ 'up 1** *v.t.*, **speeded up** beschleunigen; **~ up the work** die Arbeit vorantreiben; (*one's own work*) sich mit der Arbeit beeilen. **2** *v.i.*, **speeded up** sich beeilen. ⇒ *also* **speed-up**

**speed: ~boat** *n.* Rennboot, *das;* **~ bump** *n.* Bodenschwelle, *die;* **~ camera** *n.* Geschwindigkeitsüberwachungskamera, *die;* **be caught by a ~ camera** bei einer Geschwindigkeitskontrolle geblitzt werden; **~ hump** ⇒ **speed bump**

**speedily** /ˈspiːdɪlɪ/ *adv.* **A** (*at speed*) schnell; **B** (*soon*) umgehend

**speeding** /ˈspiːdɪŋ/ *n.* (*going too fast*) zu schnelles Fahren; Rasen, *das* (*ugs. abwertend*); Geschwindigkeitsüberschreitung, *die* (*Verkehrsw.*); **his third ~ offence** seine dritte Geschwindigkeitsüberschreitung

**speed: ~ limit** *n.* ▶ 1552 Tempolimit, *das;* Geschwindigkeitsbeschränkung, *die* (*Verkehrsw.*); **~ merchant** *n.* (*coll.*) Raser, *der* (*ugs. abwertend*)

**speedo** /ˈspiːdəʊ/ *n., pl.* **~s** (*Brit. coll.*) Tacho, *der* (*ugs.*)

**speedometer** /spiːˈdɒmɪtə(r)/ *n.* Tachometer, *der od. das*

**speed: ~ ramp** *n.* Bodenschwelle, *die;* **~ trap** *n.* Geschwindigkeitskontrolle, *die;* (*with radar*) Radarfalle, *die* (*ugs.*); **~-up** *n.* **A** (*acceleration*) Beschleunigung, *die;* **B** (*increase in work rate*) Steigerung der [Arbeits]produktivität; **~way** *n.* **A** (*motorcycle racing*) Speedwayrennen, *das;* **the ~way world champion** der Speedwayweltmeister; **B** (*racetrack*) Speedwaybahn, *die;* **C** (*Amer.: public road*) Schnellstraße, *die*

**speedwell** /ˈspiːdwel/ *n.* (*Bot.*) Ehrenpreis, *der*

**speedy** /ˈspiːdɪ/ *adj.* schnell; umgehend, prompt ‹Antwort›; **the medication is ~ and effective** das Medikament wirkt schnell und gut

**speleology** /speliˈɒlədʒɪ, spiːlɪˈɒlədʒɪ/ *n.* Speläologie, *die;* Höhlenkunde, *die*

**spell¹** /spel/ **1** *v.t.*, **spelled** *or* (*Brit.*) **spelt** [spelt] **A** schreiben; (*aloud*) buchstabieren; **B** (*form*) **what do these letters/what does b-a-t ~?** welches Wort ergeben diese Buchstaben/die Buchstaben b-a-t?; **C** (*fig.: have as result*) bedeuten; **that ~s trouble** das bedeutet nichts Gutes. **2** *v.i.*, **spelled** *or* (*Brit.*) **spelt** (*say*) buchstabieren; (*write*) richtig schreiben; **he can't ~:** er kann keine Rechtschreibung (*ugs.*)
**~ 'out, ~ 'over** *v.t.* **A** (*read letter by letter*) [langsam] buchstabieren; **B** (*fig.: explain precisely*) genau erklären; genau darlegen

**spell²** *n.* **A** (*period*) Weile, *die;* **do a ~ of joinery/in prison** eine Weile *od.* Zeit lang als Tischler arbeiten/im Gefängnis sitzen; **a ~ of overseas service** eine Zeit lang Dienst in Übersee; **on Sunday it will be cloudy with some sunny ~s** am Sonntag wolkig mit sonnigen Abschnitten; **a cold ~:** eine Kälteperiode; **return from a ~ in America** von einem Aufenthalt in Amerika zurückkehren; **a long ~ when ...:** eine lange Zeit, während der ...; **B** (*Austral.: period of rest*) [Ruhe]pause, *die;* **have a ten minutes' ~:** zehn Minuten Pause machen

**spell³** *n.* **A** (*words used as a charm*) Zauberspruch, *der;* **cast a ~ over** *or* **on sb./sth., put a ~ on sb./sth.** jmdn./etw. verzaubern; **B** (*fascination*) Zauber, *der;* **break the ~:** den Bann brechen; **be under a ~:** unter einem Bann stehen

**spell: ~bind** *v.t.* bezaubern; **~bound** *adj.* verzaubert; **he can hold his readers ~bound** er kann seine Leser in seinem Bann halten; **~ checker** ⇒ **spelling checker**

**spelling** /ˈspelɪŋ/ *n.* **A** Rechtschreibung, *die;* **the original Shakespearian ~:** die ursprüngliche Schreibung nach Shakespeare; **B** (*sequence of letters*) Schreibweise, *die*

**spelling: ~ bee** *n.* Rechtschreib[e]wettbewerb, *der;* **~ checker** *n.* Rechtschreibprogramm, *das;* **~ mistake** *n.* Rechtschreibfehler, *der*

**spelt¹** ⇒ **spell¹**

**spelt²** /spelt/ *n.* (*Agric.*) Dinkel, *der*

**spend** /spend/ *v.t.*, **spent** /spent/ **A** (*pay out*) ausgeben; **~ money like water** *or* (*coll.*) **as if it's going out of fashion** sein *od.* das Geld mit beiden Händen ausgeben *od.* hinauswerfen (*ugs.*); **money well spent** sinnvoll ausgegebenes Geld; **it was money well spent** es hat sich ausgezahlt; **~ a penny** (*fig. coll.*) mal verschwinden [müssen] (*ugs.*); **B** (*use*) aufwenden (**on** für); **~ one's time/a day** seine Zeit/einen Tag verbringen; **time well spent** sinnvoll verwendete Zeit; **it was effort/time well spent** es hat sich ausgezahlt; **C ~ itself** (*fig.*) ‹Sturm, Wut:› sich legen

**spendable** /ˈspendəbl/ *adj.* verfügbar

**spender** /ˈspendə(r)/ *n.* **he's a [big] ~:** bei ihm sitzt das Geld locker (*ugs.*)

**'spending money** *n.* **A** (*Amer.*) ⇒ **pocket money**; **B** (*Brit.: sum intended for spending*) verfügbares Geld

**'spendthrift** *n.* Verschwender, *der*/Verschwenderin, *die*

**spent 1** ⇒ **spend**. **2** *adj.* **A** (*used up*) verbraucht; **~ cartridge** leere Geschosshülse; **B** (*drained of energy*) erschöpft; ausgelaugt; hinfällig ‹Kranker, Greis›; **a ~ force** (*fig.*) eine Kraft, die sich erschöpft hat

**sperm** /spɜːm/ *n., pl.* **~s** *or same* (*Biol.*) **A** (*semen*) Sperma, *der;* **B** (*spermatozoon*) Samenfaden, *der*

**spermatic** /spɜːˈmætɪk/ *adj.* Samen-

**spermatic 'cord** *n.* Samenstrang, *der*

**spermatozoon** /spɜːmətəˈzəʊɒn/ *n., pl.* **spermatozoa** /spɜːmətəˈzəʊə/ Spermatozoon, *das;* Spermium, *das*

**sperm: ~ bank** *n.* Samenbank, *die;* **~ count** *n.* Spermienzahl, *die*

S

**spermicidal** /'spɜ:mɪsaɪdl/ *adj.* spermizid

**spermicide** /'spɜ:mɪsaɪd/ *n.* Spermizid, *das*

**'sperm whale** *n.* Pottwal, *der*

**spew** /spju:/ **1** *v.t.* spucken. **2** *v.i.* sich ergießen

**~ 'out 1** *v.t.* erbrechen, [aus]spucken ‹Gegessenes›; ‹Vulkan:› spucken, speien ‹Lava›; **~ out waste products into the rivers** ‹Fabriken:› Abfälle in die Flüsse [aus]speien; **propaganda was ~ed out by the stations** (*fig.*) die Sender spien Propaganda. **2** *v.i.* sich ergießen (**of, from** aus)

**SPF** *abbr.* **sun protection factor** LSF

**sphagnum** /'sfægnəm/ *n., pl.* **sphagna** /'sfægnə/ *n.* Torf, *der;* **~ moss** Torfmoos, *das*

**sphere** /sfɪə(r)/ *n.* **A** (*field of action*) Bereich, *der;* Sphäre, *die* (*geh.*); **be distinguished in many ~s** sich auf vielen Gebieten ausgezeichnet haben; **that's outside my ~:** das gehört nicht zu meinem Tätigkeitsbereich; **~ of life** Lebensbereich, *der;* **~ of influence** Einflussbereich, *der;* **B** (*Geom.*) Kugel, *die;* **C** (*heavenly body*) Sphäre, *die;* **music/harmony of the ~s** Sphärenmusik/-harmonie, *die*

**spherical** /'sferɪkl/ *adj.* **A** (*globular*) kugelförmig; **B** (*Math.*) sphärisch

**sphincter** /'sfɪŋktə(r)/ *n.* (*Anat.*) Sphinkter, *der* (*fachspr.*); Schließmuskel, *der*

**sphinx** /sfɪŋks/ *n.* Sphinx, *die*

**sphinxlike** /'sfɪŋkslaɪk/ *adj.* sphinxhaft; **she gave a ~ smile** sie lächelte wie eine Sphinx

**spica** /'spaɪkə/ *n.* **A** (*Bot.*) Ähre, *die;* **B** (*Med.*) Spica, *die*

**spice** /spaɪs/ **1** *n.* **A** Gewürz, *das;* (*collectively*) Gewürze *Pl.; attrib.* Gewürz-; **dealer in ~s** Gewürzhändler, *der;* **B** (*fig.: excitement*) Würze, *die;* **the ~ of life** die Würze des Lebens. **2** *v.t.* würzen; **a ~d account** (*fig.*) ein ausgeschmückter Bericht; **a book ~d with humour** (*fig.*) ein mit Humor gewürztes Buch

**'spice rack** *n.* Gewürzregal, *das*

**spicily** /'spaɪsɪlɪ/ *adv.* mit Würze

**spiciness** /'spaɪsɪnɪs/ *n., no pl.* Würze, *die*

**spick** /spɪk/ *adj.* **~ and span** blitzblank *od.* -sauber (*ugs.*)

**spicy** /'spaɪsɪ/ *adj.* **A** pikant; würzig; **B** (*racy*) pikant; **~ things** Pikanterien *Pl.*

**spider** /'spaɪdə(r)/ *n.* Spinne, *die;* (**~-like** *creature*) Spinnentier, *das;* **~ and fly** (*fig.*) Raubtier und Beute

**spider: ~ crab** *n.* See- *od.* Meeresspinne, *die;* **~man** *n. Bauarbeiter, der auf Gerüsten in großer Höhe arbeitet;* **~ monkey** *n.* Klammeraffe, *der;* **~ plant** *n.* Grünlilie, *die;* **~'s web** (*Amer.:* **~ web**) Spinnennetz, *das;* (*fig.*) Netz, *das*

**spidery** /'spaɪdərɪ/ *adj.* spinnenförmig; krakelig (*ugs.*) ‹Schrift›; **~ legs** Spinnenbeine

**spiel** /spi:l/ (*coll.*) **1** *n.* Sermon, *der* (*ugs.*); (*excuse*) Story, *die;* **don't give me all that ~:** erzähl mir doch nichts! **2** *v.i.* (*Amer.*) schwadronieren; labern (*salopp*)

**~ 'off** *v.t.* (*Amer. coll.*) **he can ~ off answers to 250 questions** er kann Antworten auf 250 Fragen herunterrasseln (*ugs.*)

**spiffing** /'spɪfɪŋ/ *adj.* (*arch. coll.*) ausgezeichnet; famos (*ugs. veralt.*)

**spigot** /'spɪgət/ *n.* Zapfen, *der*

**spike**[1] /spaɪk/ **1** *n.* **A** Stachel, *der;* (*of running shoe*) Spike, *der;* **B** *in pl.* (*shoes*) Spikes *Pl.;* **C** (*large nail*) großer Nagel; (*Railw.*) Schienennagel, *der;* **D** (*for holding papers*) Zettelspieß, *der.* **2** *v.t.* **A** mit [großen] Nägeln befestigen ‹Schiene›; mit Spikes versehen ‹Schuhe›; **~ sb.'s guns** (*fig.*) jmdm. einen Strich durch die Rechnung machen (*ugs.*); **B** (*coll.: add spirits or drugs to*) **sb. ~d his drink** jmd. hat ihm etwas in seinen Drink getan; **~ coffee with cognac/spirits with LSD** Cognac in den Kaffee/LSD in den Schnaps tun

**spike**[2] *n.* (*Bot.*) Ähre, *die*

**spike 'heel** ⇨ **stiletto** B

**spikelet** /'spaɪklɪt/ *n.* (*Bot.*) Ährchen, *das*

**spiky** /'spaɪkɪ/ *adj.* **A** (*like a spike*) spitz [zulaufend]; stachelig ‹Haare›; **B** (*having spikes*) stach[e]lig; **C** (*coll.: easily offended*) ⇨ **prickly** B

**spill**[1] /spɪl/ **1** *v.t.*, **spilt** /spɪlt/ *or* **~ed A** verschütten ‹Flüssigkeit›; **~ sth. on sth.** etw. auf etw. (*Akk.*) schütten; **~ [sb.'s] blood** [jmds.] Blut vergießen; **B** (*coll.: divulge*) ausquatschen (*salopp*); **~ the beans [to sb.]** [jmdm. gegenüber] aus der Schule plaudern; **not ~ the beans [to sb.]** [jmdm. gegenüber] dichthalten (*ugs.*). ⇨ *also* **milk** 1. **2** *v.i.*, **spilt** *or* **~ed** überlaufen. **3** *n.* (*fall*) Sturz, *der;* **have/take a ~:** stürzen

**~ 'over** *v.i.* überlaufen; (*fig.*) überquellen; ‹Unruhen:› sich ausbreiten; (*develop into something else*) umschlagen

**spill**[2] *n.* (*for lighting*) Fidibus, *der*

**spillage** /'spɪlɪdʒ/ *n.* **A** (*act*) Verschütten, *das;* **~ of oil** (*from tanker*) das Auslaufen von Öl; **B** (*quantity*) Verschüttete, *das;* **there was little ~:** es wurde wenig verschüttet; (*from tanker*) es lief wenig Öl aus

**spillikins** /'spɪlɪkɪnz/ *n. sing.* Mikado, *das*

**'spillway** *n.* Überfall, *der*

**spilt** ⇨ **spill**[1] 1, 2

**spin** /spɪn/ **1** *v.t.*, **-nn-, spun** /spʌn/ **A** spinnen; **~ yarn** Garn spinnen; **~ a yarn** (*fig.*) ein Garn spinnen (*bes. Seemannsspr.*); fabulieren; **B** (*in washing machine etc.*) schleudern; **C** (*cause to whirl round*) [schnell] drehen; wirbeln [lassen]; **~ a top** kreiseln; **~ a coin** eine Münze kreiseln lassen; (*toss*) eine Münze werfen; **D** (*Sport: impart ~ to*) Effet *od.* Spin geben (+ *Dat.*) ‹Ball›.

**2** *v.i.*, **-nn-, spun** sich drehen; **my head is ~ning** (*fig.*) (*from noise*) mir brummt der Schädel (*ugs.*); (*from too much work*) ich weiß nicht [mehr], wo mir der Kopf steht; (*from many impressions*) mir schwirrt der Kopf.

**3** *n.* **A** (*whirl*) **give sth. a ~:** etw. in Drehung versetzen; **give the washing a [short] ~:** die Wäsche [kurz] schleudern; **the decision rested on the ~ of a coin** die Entscheidung sollte durch das Werfen einer Münze herbeigeführt werden; **B** (*Aeronaut.*) Trudeln, *das;* ⇨ *also* **flat spin**; **C** (*Sport: revolving motion*) Effet, *der;* Spin, *der;* **D** (*outing*) **go for a ~:** einen Ausflug machen; **a ~ in the car** eine Spritztour mit dem Auto; **E** (*Phys.*) Spin, *der*

**~ 'out** *v.t.* **A** (*prolong*) in die Länge ziehen; **B** (*use sparingly*) **~ one's money out until pay day** sein Geld bis zum Zahltag strecken; **he spun out his glass of whisky** er trank lange an seinem Glas Whisky

**~ 'round 1** *v.i.* sich drehen; ‹Person:› sich [schnell] umdrehen. **2** *v.t.* [schnell] drehen

**spina bifida** /spaɪnə 'bɪfɪdə/ *n.* ▶ 1232 (*Med.*) Spina bifida, *die* (*fachspr.*); Spaltwirbel, *der*

**spinach** /'spɪnɪdʒ/ *n.* **A** Spinat, *der;* **B** (*Amer. coll.: inessential decoration*) Schnickschnack, *der* (*ugs.*)

**spinal** /'spaɪnl/ *adj.* (*Anat.*) Wirbelsäulen-; Rückgrat[s]-; ⇨ *also* **marrow** B

**spinal: ~ 'column** *n.* Wirbelsäule, *die;* **~ 'cord** *n.* Rückenmark, *das*

**'spin bowler** *n.* (*Cricket*) Werfer, der Spins wirft

**spindle** /'spɪndl/ *n.* **A** Spindel, *die;* **B** (*pin bearing bobbin*) Spulenhalter, *der*

**spindle: ~-shanks** *n. sing.* **be a ~-shanks** spindeldürre Beine haben; **~-shaped** *adj.* spindelförmig

**spindly** /'spɪndlɪ/ *adj.* spindeldürr ‹Person, Beine, Arme›

**spin: ~ doctor** *n.* (*coll.*) Spin-Doktor, *der;* **~ 'drier** *n.* Wäscheschleuder, *die*

**'spindrift** *n.* Gischt, *der od. die*

**spin-'dry** *v.t.* schleudern

**spine** /spaɪn/ *n.* **A** ▶ 966 (*backbone*) Wirbelsäule, *die;* **B** (*Bot., Zool.*) Stachel, *der;* **C** (*fig.: source of strength*) Rückgrat, *das;* **D** (*of book*) Buchrücken, *der;* **E** (*ridge*) [Gebirgs]grat, *der*

**spine: ~-chiller** *n.* Schocker, *der* (*ugs.*); **this film is a ~-chiller** bei diesem Film läuft es einem eiskalt den Rücken herunter (*ugs.*); **~-chilling** *adj.* gruselig

**spineless** /'spaɪnlɪs/ *adj.* **A** (*fig.*) rückgratlos; **B** (*Zool.: without spines*) ‹Fisch› ohne Flossenstrahlen

**spinelessly** /'spaɪnlɪslɪ/ *adv.* **give in/surrender ~:** so rückgratlos sein und nachgeben/sich ergeben

**spinet** /spɪ'net, 'spɪnɪt/ *n.* (*Mus. Hist.*) Spinett, *das*

**spinnaker** /'spɪnəkə(r)/ *n.* (*Naut.*) Spinnaker, *der*

**spinner** /'spɪnə(r)/ *n.* **A** (*Cricket*) Werfer, der Spins wirft; **B** (*spin-drier*) Wäscheschleuder, *die;* **C** (*manufacturer engaged in spinning*) Spinner, *der*/Spinnerin, *die*

**spinneret** /'spɪnəret/ *n.* **A** (*Zool.*) Spinndrüse, *die;* **B** (*Textiles*) Spinndüse, *die*

**spinney** /'spɪnɪ/ *n.* (*Brit.*) Gehölz, *das*

**spinning** /'spɪnɪŋ/ *n.* Spinnen, *das*

**spinning: ~ jenny** *n.* Jenny-[Spinn]maschine, *die;* **~ top** *n.* Kreisel, *der;* **~ wheel** *n.* Spinnrad, *das*

**'spin-off** *n.* Nebenprodukt, *das*

**spinster** /'spɪnstə(r)/ *n.* **A** ledige Frau; Junggesellin, *die;* **remain a ~:** ledig bleiben; **B** (*derog.: old maid*) alte Jungfer (*abwertend*)

**spinsterhood** /'spɪnstəhʊd/ *n., no pl.* Ledigsein, *das*

**spiny** /'spaɪnɪ/ *adj.* dornig; stachelig

**spiny 'lobster** *n.* Languste, *die*

**spiraea** /spaɪə'ri:ə/ *n.* (*Bot.*) Spierstrauch, *der*

**spiral** /'spaɪrl/ **1** *adj.* spiralförmig; spiralig; **~ spring** Spiralfeder, *die.* **2** *n.* Spirale, *die;* **the ~ of rising prices and wages** die Lohn-Preis-Spirale. **3** *v.i.* (*Brit.*) **-ll-** ‹Weg:› sich hochwinden; ‹Kosten, Profite:› in die Höhe klettern; ‹Rauch:› in einer Spirale aufsteigen

**spirally** /'spaɪrəlɪ/ *adv.* spiralig; spiralförmig

**spiral: ~ 'nebula** *n.* (*Astron.*) Spiralnebel, *der;* **~ 'staircase** *n.* Wendeltreppe, *die*

**spirant** /'spaɪrənt/ (*Phonet.*) **1** *adj.* spirantisch. **2** *n.* Spirant, *der* (*fachspr.*); Reibelaut, *der*

**spire** /spaɪə(r)/ *n.* Turmspitze, *die*

**spirit** /'spɪrɪt/ **1** *n.* **A** *in pl.* (*distilled liquor*) Spirituosen *Pl.;* **tax on ~s** Alkoholsteuer, *die;* **B** (*mental attitude*) Geisteshaltung, *die;* **in the right/wrong ~:** mit der richtigen/falschen Einstellung; **take sth. in the wrong ~:** etw. falsch auffassen; etw. in den falschen Hals kriegen (*ugs.*); **take sth. in the ~ in which it is meant** etw. so auffassen, wie es gemeint ist; **as the ~ takes/moves one** wie man gerade Lust hat; **do sth. in a ~ of mischief** etw. in böser Absicht tun ; **enter into the ~ of sth.** innerlich bei einer Sache [beteiligt] sein *od.* dabei sein; **'that's the ~!** das ist die richtige Einstellung!; **C** (*courage*) Mut, *der;* **play with ~:** mit ganzer Seele spielen; **D** (*vital principle, soul, inner qualities*) Geist, *der;* **the ~ is willing but the flesh is weak** der Geist ist willig, aber das Fleisch ist schwach; **give up one's ~:** seinen Geist *od.* seine Seele aushauchen (*geh. verhüll.*); **in [the] ~:** innerlich; im Geiste; **be with sb. in ~:** in Gedanken *od.* im Geist[e] bei jmdm. sein; **the poor in ~** (*arch.*) die Armen im Geiste; **E** (*person supplying energy*) treibende Kraft; Motor, *der* (*fig.*); **F** (*real meaning*) Geist, *der;* Sinn, *der;* **follow the ~ of the instructions** die Anweisungen sinngemäß ausführen; **obey the letter but not the ~ of the law** dem Buchstaben, nicht dem Geist[e] des Gesetzes gehorchen; **G** (*mental tendency*) Geist, *der;* (*mood*) Stimmung, *die;* **the ~ of the age** *or* **times** der Zeitgeist; **H high ~s** gehobene Stimmung; gute Laune; **in high** *or* **great** *or* **good ~s** in gehobener Stimmung; gut gelaunt; **in poor** *or* **low ~s** niedergedrückt; **I** (*liquid got by distillation*) Spiritus, *der;* **J** (*purified alcohol*) reiner Alkohol; **K** (*solution in alcohol*) Geist, *der;* Spiritus, *der;* **~[s] of wine** (*arch.*) Weingeist, *der.*

**2** *v.t.* **~ away, ~ off** verschwinden lassen; **be ~ed away** *or* **off** verschwinden

**spirited** /'spɪrɪtɪd/ *adj.* **A** (*lively*) lebendig ‹Übersetzung, Vortrag›; beherzt ‹Angriff, Versuch, Antwort, Verteidigung›; lebhaft ‹Antwort›; **B low/**

S

**proud-~:** niedergedrückt/stolz; **high-~:** ausgelassen; temperamentvoll ‹Pferd›; **mean-~:** gemein

**spiritedly** /'spɪrɪtɪdlɪ/ *adv.* lebendig ‹schreiben›; vehement ‹ablehnen›

'**spirit lamp** *n.* Spirituslampe, *die*

**spiritless** /'spɪrɪtlɪs/ *adj.* dumpf ‹Person›; stumpfsinnig ‹Apathie›

'**spirit level** *n.* Wasserwaage, *die*

**spiritual** /'spɪrɪtʃʊəl/ ❶ *adj.* Ⓐ spirituell (*geh.*); **a ~ relationship** eine platonische (*geh.*) Beziehung; **his ~ home** seine geistige Heimat; Ⓑ (*concerned with religion*) geistlich; **lords ~** (*Brit. Parl.*) *Bischöfe und Erzbischöfe im britischen Oberhaus.* ❷ *n.* **[Negro] ~:** [Negro] Spiritual, *das*

**spiritualism** /'spɪrɪtʃʊəlɪzm/ *n.* Ⓐ (*belief in contact with spirits*) Spiritismus, *der;* Ⓑ (*system of doctrines*) Spiritualismus, *der*

**spiritualist** /'spɪrɪtʃʊəlɪst/ *n.* Spiritist, *der*/ Spiritistin, *die*

**spirituality** /spɪrɪtʃʊ'ælɪtɪ/ *n., no pl.* Spiritualität, *die* (*geh.*)

**spiritually** /'spɪrɪtʃʊəlɪ/ *adv.* spirituell; **~ minded** vergeistigt ‹Person›

**spirt** ⇒ **spurt**[2]

**spit**[1] /spɪt/ ❶ *v.i.*, **-tt-**, **spat** /spæt/ *or* **spit** Ⓐ spucken; **he spat in his enemy's face** er spuckte seinem Feind ins Gesicht; **it makes you [want to] ~:** es kann einen auf die Palme bringen (*ugs.*); Ⓑ (*make angry noise*) fauchen; **~ at sb.** jmdn. anfauchen; Ⓒ (*rain lightly*) **~ [down]** tröpfeln (*ugs.*); Ⓓ (*throw out sparks*) ‹Feuer:› Funken sprühen; ‹Öl:› spritzen.

❷ *v.t.*, **-tt-**, **spat** *or* **spit** Ⓐ spucken; **~ sth. at sb.** mit etw. nach jmdm. spucken; Ⓑ (*fig.: utter angrily*) **~ defiance at sb.** jmdn. trotzig anfauchen.

❸ *n.* Ⓐ **[dead** *or* **very] ~ [and image]** (*coll.*) ⇒ **spitting image**; Ⓑ (*spittle*) Spucke, *die;* **~ and polish** (*cleaning work*) Putzen und Reinigen; Wienern, *das;* **all that ~ and polish in the army** das ewige Putzen und Wienern in der Armee

**~ 'out** *v.t.* **~ sth. out** etw. ausspucken; **~ out curses at sb.** jmdm. die Flüche nur so ins Gesicht spucken; **she spat out the words** sie spuckte die Worte nur so aus; **~ it out!** (*fig. coll.*) spuck es aus! (*ugs.*)

**spit**[2] ❶ *n.* Ⓐ (*point of land*) Halbinsel, *die;* Ⓑ (*reef*) Riff, *das;* (*shoal*) Untiefe, *die;* (*sandbank*) Sandbank, *die;* Ⓒ (*for roasting meat*) Spieß, *der.* ❷ *v.t.*, **-tt-** (*pierce*) [auf]spießen

**spit**[3] *n.* (*spade-depth*) Spatentiefe, *die*

'**spitball** *n.* (*Amer.: pellet*) [mit Speichel getränktes] Papierkügelchen

**spite** /spaɪt/ ❶ *n.* Ⓐ (*malice*) Boshaftigkeit, *die;* **do sth. from** *or* **out of ~:** etw. aus Boshaftigkeit tun; Ⓑ **in ~ of** trotz; **in ~ of oneself** obwohl man es eigentlich nicht will; wider *od.* gegen seinen [eigenen] Willen. ❷ *v.t.* ärgern; **cut off one's nose to ~ one's face** sich (*Dat. od. Akk.*) ins eigene Fleisch schneiden

**spiteful** /'spaɪtfl/ *adj.*, **spitefully** /'spaɪtfəlɪ/ *adv.* boshaft; gehässig (*abwertend*)

'**spitfire** *n.* Giftspritze, *die* (*ugs. abwertend*)

**spitting 'image** *n.* **be the ~ of sb.** jmdm. wie aus dem Gesicht geschnitten sein

**spittle** /'spɪtl/ *n.* Spucke, *die;* Speichel, *der*

**spittoon** /spɪ'tu:n/ *n.* Spucknapf, *der*

**spiv** /spɪv/ *n.* (*Brit. coll.*) Ⓐ (*person living by his wits*) smarter kleiner Geschäftemacher; Ⓑ (*black-market dealer*) Schwarzhändler, *der;* Schieber, *der* (*ugs.*)

**splash** /splæʃ/ ❶ *v.t.* Ⓐ spritzen; **~ sb./sth. with sth.** jmdn./etw. mit etw. bespritzen; **~ sth. on [to]** *or* **over sb./sth.** jmdn./etw. mit etw. bespritzen; etw. auf jmdn./etw. spritzen; **~ sth. about** etw. herumspritzen (*ugs.*); **sth. gets ~ed on sth.** etw. spritzt auf etw. (*Akk.*); Ⓑ (*Journ.: display prominently*) als Aufmacher bringen ‹Story usw.›; **be ~ed all over the front page** auf der ersten Seite groß aufgemacht sein (*ugs.*); Ⓒ (*with scattered colour*) sprenkeln.

❷ *v.i.* Ⓐ (*fly about in drops*) spritzen; Ⓑ (*cause liquid to fly about*) [umher]spritzen; Ⓒ (*move with ~ing*) platschen (*ugs.*).

❸ *n.* Ⓐ Spritzen, *das;* **hit the water with a ~:** ins Wasser platschen (*ugs.*); **make a [big] ~** (*fig.*) Furore machen; Ⓑ (*liquid*) Spritzer, *der;* Ⓒ (*noise*) Plätschern, *das;* Ⓓ (*prominent display of news etc.*) **get a front-page ~:** der Aufmacher auf der Titelseite sein; Ⓔ (*coll.: dash*) Schuss [Sodawasser]; **whisky and a ~ of ginger ale** Whisky mit einem Schuss Ingwerbier; Ⓕ (*spot of dirt etc.*) Spritzer, *der;* Ⓖ (*patch of colour*) Tupfer, *der*

**~ a'bout** *v.i.* herumspritzen (*ugs.*); [herum]planschen

**~ 'down** *v.i.* wassern; ⇒ *also* **splashdown**

**~ 'out** *v.i.* (*coll.*) **~ out on sth.** für etw. unbekümmert Geld ausgeben

**splash: ~back** *n.* *Wandverkleidung zum Schutz vor Spritzern;* **~down** *n.* Wasserung, *die*

**splatter** /'splætə(r)/ ❶ *v.i.* ‹Bach:› plätschern; ‹Blut:› spritzen. ❷ *v.t.* bespritzen. ❸ *n.* Plätschern, *das*

**splay** /spleɪ/ ❶ *v.t.* Ⓐ (*spread*) **~ [out]** spreizen; Ⓑ (*construct with divergent sides*) ausschrägen. ❷ *v.i.* ‹Linien:› [schräg] auseinander laufen; ‹Tischbeine, Stuhlbeine:› schräg nach außen gehen; ‹Finger, Zehen:› gespreizt sein; ‹Räder:› schräg zueinander stehen. ❸ *n.* Ausschrägung, *die.* ❹ *adj.* gespreizt

**splay: ~-foot** ❶ *n.* Spreizfuß, *der;* ❷ *adj.* ⇒ **~-footed**; **~-footed** *adj.* spreizfüßig

**spleen** /spli:n/ *n.* Ⓐ ▶ **966** (*Anat.*) Milz, *die;* Ⓑ (*bad mood*) schlechte Laune; Übellaunigkeit, *die;* (*anger, rage*) Wut, *die;* **vent one's ~ [on sb.]** seine schlechte Laune/Wut [an jmdm.] abreagieren

**splendid** /'splendɪd/ *adj.* (*excellent, outstanding*) großartig; (*beautiful*) herrlich; (*sumptuous, magnificent*) prächtig; **live in ~ isolation** von der Außenwelt abgeschirmt leben; **cut a ~ figure** imposant aussehen

**splendidly** /'splendɪdlɪ/ *adv.* (*excellently, outstandingly*) großartig; (*sumptuously, magnificently*) prächtig; **live ~:** prunkvoll leben; **get along ~ with sb.** bestens mit jmdm. auskommen; **this flat will suit you ~:** diese Wohnung ist genau das Richtige für Sie

**splendiferous** /splen'dɪfərəs/ *adj.* (*coll.*) prachtvoll

**splendour** (*Brit.;* *Amer.:* **splendor**) /'splendə(r)/ *n.* Ⓐ (*magnificence*) Pracht, *die;* Ⓑ (*brightness*) Glanz, *der*

**splenetic** /splɪ'netɪk/ *adj.* mürrisch; unwirsch

**splice** /splaɪs/ ❶ *v.t.* Ⓐ (*join ends of by interweaving*) verspleißen (*Seemannsspr.*); Ⓑ (*join in overlapping position*) [an den Enden überlappend] zusammenfügen; zusammenkleben ‹Filmstreifen usw.›; **~ a scene into a film** eine Szene in einen Film einschneiden; Ⓒ **get ~d** (*coll.: get married*) sich verehelichen. ⇒ *also* **main brace**. ❷ *n.* Spleiß, *der* (*Seemannsspr.*)

**splint** /splɪnt/ ❶ *n.* Schiene, *die;* **put sb.'s arm in a ~:** jmds. Arm schienen. ❷ *v.t.* schienen

**splinter** /'splɪntə(r)/ ❶ *n.* Splitter, *der.* ❷ *v.i.* Ⓐ (*become split into long pieces*) splittern; **~ away from sth.** von etw. absplittern; Ⓑ (*fig.: split into factions*) sich aufsplittern. ❸ *v.t.* (*also fig.: split into factions*) zersplittern

**splinter: ~ group** *n.* Splittergruppe, *die;* **~ party** *n.* Splitterpartei, *die;* **~-proof** *adj.* splittersicher

**splintery** /'splɪntərɪ/ *adj.* splitterig

**split** /splɪt/ ❶ *n.* Ⓐ (*tear*) Riss, *der;* Ⓑ (*division into parts*) [Auf]teilung, *die;* Ⓒ (*fig.: rift*) Spaltung, *die;* **a ~ between Moscow and her allies** ein Bruch zwischen Moskau und seinen Verbündeten; Ⓓ (*Gymnastics, Skating*) **the ~s** *or* (*Amer.*) **~:** Spagat, *der od. das;* **do the ~s** Spagat machen; in den Spagat gehen. ⇒ *also* **banana split**.

❷ *adj.* gespalten; **~ lip** aufgeplatzte Lippe; **~ decision** (*Boxing*) nicht einstimmige Entscheidung; **be ~ on a question** [sich (*Dat.*)] in einer Frage uneins sein; **be ~ down the middle** in zwei Lager gespalten sein; ⇒ *also* **pin** 1 B.

❸ *v.t.*, **-tt-**, **split** Ⓐ (*tear*) zerreißen; Ⓑ (*divide*) teilen; spalten ‹Holz›; **let's ~ the money between us** lasst uns das Geld unter uns aufteilen; **~ persons/things into groups** Personen/Dinge in Gruppen (*Akk.*) aufteilen *od.* einteilen; **they ~ a bottle of wine** sie teilen/teilten sich (*Dat.*) eine Flasche Wein; **~ the difference** sich in der Mitte treffen; **~ hairs** (*fig.*) Haare spalten; Ⓒ (*divide into disagreeing parties*) spalten; **~ the ticket** *or* **one's vote** (*Amer. Polit.*) splitten; Ⓓ (*remove by breaking*) **~ [off** *or* **away]** abbrechen; Ⓔ (*Phys.*) spalten ‹Atom›. ⇒ *also* **side** 1 D.

❹ *v.i.*, **-tt-**, **split** Ⓐ (*break into parts*) ‹Holz:› splittern; ‹Stoff, Seil:› reißen; Ⓑ (*divide into parts*) sich teilen; ‹Gruppe:› sich spalten; ‹zwei Personen:› sich trennen; Ⓒ (*be removed by breaking*) **~ from** absplittern von; **~ apart** zersplittern; Ⓓ (*coll.: betray secrets*) auspacken (*ugs.*); quatschen (*ugs.*); Ⓔ (*coll.: depart*) abhauen (*ugs.*)

**~ a'way** *v.i.* absplittern; **~ away from** absplittern von; ‹Parteiflügel, Gruppierung:› sich abspalten von

**~ 'off** ❶ *v.t.* abspalten. ❷ *v.i.* ⇒ **~ away**

**~ on** *v.t.* (*coll.*) **~ on sb. [to sb.]** jmdn. [bei jmdm.] verpfeifen (*ugs.*)

**~ 'open** ❶ *v.i.* aufbrechen. ❷ *v.t.* öffnen ‹Nuss, Schote›; **he ~ his head open** er hat sich (*Dat.*) den Kopf aufgeschlagen

**~ 'up** ❶ *v.t.* aufteilen. ❷ *v.i.* (*coll.*) sich trennen; **~ up with sb.** sich von jmdm. trennen; mit jmdm. Schluss machen (*ugs.*)

**~ with** *v.i.* (*coll.*) brechen mit

**split: ~ in'finitive** *n.* (*Ling.*) *Konstruktion im Englischen, bei der zwischen Infinitivkonjunktion und Infinitiv ein Adverb eingeschoben wird;* **~-level** *adj.* mit Zwischengeschoss; auf zwei Ebenen; **a ~-level lounge** ein Wohnraum auf zwei Ebenen; **~-level cooker** *Einbauherd, bei dem Kochplatten und Backofen getrennt sind;* **~ 'pea** *n.* getrocknete [halbe] Erbse; **~ perso'nality** *n.* gespaltene Persönlichkeit (*Psych.*); **~ pin** *n.* Splint, *der;* **~ ring** *n.* Spaltring, *der;* **~ 'second** *n.* **in a ~ second** im Bruchteil einer Sekunde; **a ~ second from now** in einem Augenblick; **~-second timing** [zeitliche] Abstimmung auf die Sekunde genau; **~ 'shift** *n.* Teilschicht, *die;* **~ 'ticket** *n.* (*Amer. Polit.*) *Stimmzettel, auf dem mehrere Kandidaten verschiedener Parteien angekreuzt werden können*

**splitting** /'splɪtɪŋ/ *adj.* **a ~ headache** rasende Kopfschmerzen; **sb.'s head is ~:** jmd. hat rasende Kopfschmerzen

**splodge** /splɒdʒ/ (*Brit.*) ⇒ **splotch**

**splosh** /splɒʃ/ (*coll.*) ❶ *n.* Platschen, *das* (*ugs.*); **there was a great ~:** es platschte (*ugs.*) laut. ❷ *v.i.* platschen (*ugs.*). ❸ *v.t.* ⇒ **splash** 1 A

**splotch** /splɒtʃ/ ❶ *n.* Fleck, *der;* Klecks, *der.* ❷ *v.t.* Ⓐ (*daub*) verschmieren; Ⓑ (*make ~ on*) beklecksen

**splurge** /splɜ:dʒ/ ❶ *n.* Wirbel, *der;* **go on a ~:** ein paar größere Anschaffungen machen; **~ of activity** Aktivitätsschub, *der.* ❷ *v.i.* ⇒ **splash out**

**splutter** /'splʌtə(r)/ ❶ *v.i.* ‹Feuer, Gaslampe:› flackern; ‹Fett:› spritzen; ‹Person:› prusten; ‹Motor:› stottern; **~ with rage/indignation** vor Wut/Entrüstung schnauben. ❷ *v.t.* stottern ‹Worte›

**spoil** /spɔɪl/ ❶ *v.t.*, **spoilt** /spɔɪlt/ *or* **spoiled** Ⓐ (*impair*) verderben; ruinieren ‹Leben›; **he always ~s a joke in the telling** wenn er einen Witz erzählt, verdirbt er immer die Pointe; **the news ~t his dinner/evening** die Nachricht verdarb ihm das Essen/den Abend; **~t ballot papers** ungültige Stimmzettel; ⇒ *also* **tar**[1] 1; Ⓑ (*injure character of*) verderben (*geh.*); verziehen ‹Kind›; **~ sb. for sth.** jmdn. für etw. zu anspruchsvoll machen; ⇒ *also* **rod** C; Ⓒ (*pamper*) verwöhnen; **be ~t for choice** die Qual der Wahl haben.

❷ *v.i.*, **spoilt** *or* **spoiled** Ⓐ (*go bad*) verderben; Ⓑ **be ~ing for a fight/for trouble** Streit/Ärger suchen.

S

❸ *n.* Ⓐ *(plunder)* ~[s] Beute, *die;* ~s **of war** Kriegsbeute, *die;* Ⓑ *(Mining etc.: waste material)* Abraum, *der*

**spoiler** /ˈspɔɪlə(r)/ *n. (of car, aircraft)* Spoiler, *der; (of glider)* Bremsklappe, *die*

**spoil: ~sport** *n.* Spielverderber, *der*/-verderberin, *die;* **~s system** *n.* *(Amer.) vom Gewinner einer Wahl betriebene Ämterpatronage*

**spoilt** ❶ ⇒ **spoil** 1, 2. ❷ *adj.* verzogen ‹Kind›

**spoke¹** /spəʊk/ *n.* Ⓐ *(of wheel)* Speiche, *die;* **put a ~ in sb.'s wheel** *(fig.)* jmdm. einen Knüppel zwischen die Beine werfen; Ⓑ ⇒ **rung¹** A

**spoke²**, **spoken** ⇒ **speak**

ˈ**spokeshave** *n.* Schabhobel, *der*

**spokesman** /ˈspəʊksmən/ *n., pl.* **spokesmen** /ˈspəʊksmən/ Sprecher, *der*

**spokesperson** /ˈspəʊkspɜːsn/ *n.* Sprecher, *der*/Sprecherin, *die*

**spokeswoman** /ˈspəʊkswʊmən/ *n.* Sprecherin, *die*

**spoliation** /spəʊlɪˈeɪʃn/ *n. (plunder)* Plünderung, *die; (of vessel)* Kaperung, *die*

**spondee** /ˈspɒndiː, ˈspɒndɪ/ *n. (Pros.)* Spondeus, *der*

**sponge** /spʌndʒ/ ❶ *n.* Ⓐ Schwamm, *der;* **throw in the ~** *(Boxing)* das Handtuch werfen *od.* schmeißen; *(fig.)* das Handtuch werfen *(ugs.)*; Ⓑ ⇒ **sponge cake; sponge pudding**; Ⓒ *(Surg.)* Tupfer, *der;* Ⓓ *(porous metal)* Schwamm, *der;* Ⓔ **have a ~ down** sich mit dem Schwamm abwaschen; **give the chair a ~ down** den Stuhl [mit dem Schwamm] abwischen. ❷ *v.t.* Ⓐ ⇒ **cadge** 1; Ⓑ *(wipe)* mit einem Schwamm waschen

~ ˈ**down** *v.t.* mit einem Schwamm abwaschen

~ **off** *v.t.* Ⓐ /ˈ-ˈ-/ *(wipe off)* mit einem Schwamm abwischen; *(wash off)* mit einem Schwamm abwaschen; Ⓑ /ˈ--/ ⇒ ~ **on**

~ **on** *v.t. (coll.)* ~ **on sb.** bei *od.* von jmdm. schnorren *(ugs.)*

**sponge: ~ bag** *n. (Brit.)* Kulturbeutel, *der;* **~ biscuit** *n.* ≈ Biskotte, *die (Kochk.)*; **~ cake** *n.* Biskuitkuchen, *der;* ~ ˈ**pudding** *n.* Schwammpudding, *der (Kochk.); leichter, im Wasserbad zubereiteter Pudding*

**sponger** /ˈspʌndʒə(r)/ *n.* Schmarotzer, *der*/Schmarotzerin, *die;* Schnorrer, *der*/Schnorrerin, *die*

**sponge** ˈ**rubber** *n.* Schaumgummi, *der*

**spongy** /ˈspʌndʒɪ/ *adj.* schwammig

**sponsor** /ˈspɒnsə(r)/ ❶ *n.* Ⓐ *(firm paying for event, one donating to charitable event)* Sponsor, *der;* Ⓑ *(of legislative proposal)* **the ~s of this Bill are Labour MPs** hinter dieser Gesetzesvorlage stehen Labour-Abgeordnete; Ⓒ *(group supporting candidate)* **his ~ is a trade union** er wird von einer Gewerkschaft unterstützt; Ⓓ *(godparent)* Pate, *der*/Patin, *die.* ❷ *v.t.* Ⓐ *(pay for)* sponsern ‹Teilnehmer, Programm, Veranstaltung›; Ⓑ *(subscribe to)* finanziell unterstützen, sponsern ‹Wohlfahrtsverband›; Ⓒ *(introduce for legislation)* einbringen ‹Gesetzesvorlage›; Ⓓ *(support in election)* unterstützen ‹Kandidaten›; ~ **sb.** jmds. Kandidatur unterstützen

**sponsored** /ˈspɒnsəd/ *adj.* gesponsert; finanziell gefördert; ~ **run** *als Wohltätigkeitsveranstaltung durchgeführter Dauerlauf mit gesponserten Teilnehmern*

**sponsorship** /ˈspɒnsəʃɪp/ *n.* Ⓐ *(financial support)* Sponsorschaft, *die;* **take over the ~ of sth.** etw. sponsern; **withdraw from the ~ of sth.** etw. nicht mehr sponsern; Ⓑ *(introduction of legislation)* Einbringen, *das;* Ⓒ *(support of candidate)* Unterstützung, *die;* **the party's ~ of sb.** die Unterstützung von jmds. Kandidatur durch die Partei

**spontaneity** /spɒntəˈniːɪtɪ/ *n., no pl.* Spontan[e]ität, *die*

**spontaneous** /spɒnˈteɪnɪəs/ *adj.* spontan; **make a ~ offer of sth.** spontan etw. anbieten

**spontaneous: ~ comˈbustion** *n.* Selbstentzündung, *die;* ~ **geneˈration** *n.* Urzeugung, *die*

**spontaneously** /spɒnˈteɪnɪəslɪ/ spontan; von selbst ‹passieren›

**spoof** /spuːf/ *(coll.)* ❶ *n.* Veralberung, *die* **(of, on** von); Parodie, *die* **(of, on** auf + *Akk.*). ❷ *v.t.* durch den Kakao ziehen *(ugs.)*

**spook** /spuːk/ *n. (joc.)* Geist, *der;* Gespenst, *das; (coll.: spy)* Spion, *der;* **it gives me the ~s** es ist mir richtig unheimlich

**spooky** /ˈspuːkɪ/ *adj.* gespenstisch

**spool** /spuːl/ ❶ *n.* Ⓐ *(reel)* Spule, *die ;* Ⓑ *(Angling)* Trommel, *die.* ❷ *v.t.* spulen

**spoon¹** /spuːn/ ❶ *n.* Ⓐ Löffel, *der;* **fruit ~:** Kompottlöffel, *der;* **be born with a silver ~ in one's mouth** mit einem goldenen *od.* silbernen Löffel im Mund geboren werden; **wooden ~** *(fig.)* Trostpreis *(für den Letzten eines Wettbewerbs, oft in ironischer Weise überreicht)*; Ⓑ *(amount)* ⇒ **spoonful**; Ⓒ *(Angling)* Blinker, *der.* ❷ *v.t.* löffeln

~ ˈ**up** *v.t.* auflöffeln

**spoon²** *v.i. (arch.: be amorous)* schmusen

ˈ**spoonbill** *n. (Ornith.)* Löffler, *der*

**spoonerism** /ˈspuːnərɪzm/ *n. witziges Vertauschen der Anfangsbuchstaben o. Ä. von zwei oder mehr Wörtern (wie bei „Leichenzehrer" für „Zeichenlehrer")*

ˈ**spoon-feed** *v.t.* mit dem Löffel füttern; ~ **sb.** *(fig.)* jmdm. alles vorkauen *(ugs.)*

**spoonful** /ˈspuːnfʊl/ *n.* **a ~ of sugar** ein Löffel [voll] Zucker

**spoor** /spʊə(r)/ *n.* Spur, *die;* Fährte, *die*

**sporadic** /spəˈrædɪk/ *adj.* sporadisch; vereinzelt ‹Schauer, Schüsse, Gebäude›

**sporadically** /spəˈrædɪkəlɪ/ *adv.* hin und wieder

**spore** /spɔː(r)/ *n.* Ⓐ *(Bot.: cell)* Spore, *die;* Ⓑ *(Biol.: bacterium)* Spore, *die*

**sporran** /ˈspɒrən/ *n. (Scot.) mit Fell besetzte Tasche, die von den Bewohnern der Highlands vorne über dem Kilt getragen wird*

**sport** /spɔːt/ ❶ *n.* Ⓐ *(pastime)* Sport, *der;* **~s** Sportarten; **team/winter/water/indoor ~:** Mannschafts-/Winter-/Wasser-/Hallensport, *der;* Ⓑ *no pl., no art. (collectively)* Sport, *der;* **go in for ~, do ~:** Sport treiben; **he likes doing ~ at school** er mag den Sport[unterricht] in der Schule; **have good ~** *(Hunting)* großes Jagdglück haben; Ⓒ *in pl. (Brit.)* **[athletic] ~s** Athletik, *die;* **S~s Day** *(Sch.)* Sportfest, *das;* **the ~s** der sportliche Wettkampf; Ⓓ *no pl., no art. (fun)* Spaß, *der;* **do/say sth. in ~:** etw. im *od.* zum Scherz tun/sagen; **make ~ of sb./sth.** sich über jmdn./etw. lustig machen; Ⓔ *(coll.: good fellow)* netter Kerl *(ugs.)*; *(Austral. as voc.: mate)* Kumpel! *(ugs.)*; Sportsmann! *(ugs.)*; **Aunt Joan is a real ~:** Tante Joan ist echt *(ugs.)* in Ordnung; **be a [good] ~ and help me** sei so nett und hilf mir; **be a good/bad ~** *(in games)* ein guter/schlechter Verlierer sein; Ⓕ *(Amer.: playboy)* Playboy, *der;* Ⓖ *(Zool., Bot.)* Variante, *die.*

❷ *v.t.* stolz tragen ‹Kleidungsstück›; protzen mit ‹Neuerwerbung›.

❸ *v.i.* Ⓐ *(amuse oneself)* sich tummeln; Ⓑ *(Biol.: mutate)* variieren

**sporting** /ˈspɔːtɪŋ/ *adj.* Ⓐ *(interested in sport)* sportlich; Ⓑ *(generous)* großzügig; *(fair)* fair; anständig; **do the ~ thing and do sth.** so anständig sein, etw. zu tun; **give sb. a ~ chance** jmdm. eine [faire] Chance geben; Ⓒ *(relating to sport)* Sport-; ~ **dog/rifle** Jagdhund, *der*/Pirschbüchse, *die;* ~ **giant** *or* **hero** Sportgröße, *die*

ˈ**sporting house** *n. (Amer.)* Bordell, *das*

**sportingly** /ˈspɔːtɪŋlɪ/ *adv.* Ⓐ *(generously)* ~ **do sth.** so großzügig sein, etw. zu tun; Ⓑ *(sportively)* in sportlichem Geist

**sportive** /ˈspɔːtɪv/ *adj.* verspielt ‹junges Tier›; ausgelassen ‹Stimmung, Schar›; **be in a ~ mood** zum Spielen aufgelegt sein

**sports: ~ bra** *n.* Sport-BH, *der;* ~ **car** *n.* Sportwagen, *der;* **~ centre** *n.* Sportzentrum, *das;* **~ channel** *n.* Sportkanal, *der;* **~ commentator** *n. (Radio, Telev.)* Sportberichterstatter, *der*/-berichterstatterin, *die;* **~ complex** *n.* Sportzentrum, *das;* **~ editor** *n.* *(Journ.)* Sportredakteur, *der*/-redakteurin, *die;* **~ field** *n.* Sportplatz, *der;* **~ hall** *n.* Sporthalle, *die;* **~ jacket** *n.* sportlicher Sakko; **~man** /ˈspɔːtsmən/ *n., pl.* **~men** /ˈspɔːtsmən/ Ⓐ Sportler, *der;* Ⓑ *(generous person)* großzügiger Mensch; *(fair-minded person)* anständiger Mensch; Ⓒ *(Hunting)* Jäger, *der*

**sportsmanlike** /ˈspɔːtsmənlaɪk/ ⇒ **sporting** B

**sportsmanship** /ˈspɔːtsmənʃɪp/ *n.* Ⓐ *(fairness)* [sportliche] Fairness; Ⓑ *(skill)* sportliche Leistung

**sports: ~ news** *n. (Radio, Telev.)* Sportnachrichten; ~ **page** *n. (Journ.)* Sportseite, *die;* **~ programme** *n. (Radio, Telev.)* Sportsendung, *die;* **~ section** *n. (Journ.)* Sportteil, *der;* **~wear** *n., no pl.* Sport[be]kleidung, *die;* **~woman** *n.* Sportlerin, *die*

**sporty** /ˈspɔːtɪ/ *adj.* Ⓐ *(coll.: sport-loving)* sportlich; **the whole family is ~:** die ganze Familie ist sportbegeistert; Ⓑ *(jaunty)* sportlich ‹Aussehen›; **wear one's hat at a ~ angle** seinen Hut flott aufgesetzt haben; **be a ~ dresser** sich sportlich kleiden; Ⓒ *(designed for sport)* Sport‹boot, -wagen, -rad›

**spot** /spɒt/ ❶ *n.* Ⓐ *(precise place)* Stelle, *die;* **this is the precise/exact/very ~ where he landed** genau an dieser Stelle *od.* genau hier ist er gelandet; **on this ~:** an dieser Stelle; **the very same ~:** genau die gleiche Stelle; **in ~s** stellenweise; *(fig.: partly)* teilweise; **run on the ~:** auf der Stelle laufen; **on the ~** *(fig.) (instantly)* auf der Stelle; **be on the ~** *(be present)* zur Stelle sein; **and now over to our man on the ~** *(Radio, Telev.)* und nun schalten wir um zu unserem Mann am Ort des Geschehens; **be in/get into/get out of a [tight] ~** *(fig. coll.)* in der Klemme sitzen/in die Klemme geraten/sich aus einer brenzligen Lage befreien *(ugs.)*; **put sb. on the ~** *(fig. coll.: cause difficulties for sb.)* jmdn. in Verlegenheit bringen; *(Amer. sl.: decide to kill sb.)* jmdn. auf die Abschussliste setzen; Ⓑ *(inhabited place)* Ort, *der;* **a nice ~ on the Moselle** ein hübscher Flecken an der Mosel; Ⓒ *(suitable area)* Platz, *der;* **holiday/sun ~:** Ferienort, *der*/Ferienort [mit Sonnengarantie]; **picnic ~:** Picknickplatz, *der;* **a sheltered ~:** ein geschützter Platz; **a nice ~ to live** eine hübsche Wohngegend; **hit the high ~s** *(coll.)* groß ausgehen; Ⓓ *(dot)* Tupfen, *der;* Tupfer, *der;* *(larger)* Flecken, *der;* **change one's ~s** *(fig.)* aus seiner Haut herauskommen *(fig.)*; **knock ~s off sb.** *(fig. coll.)* jmdn. in die Pfanne hauen *(ugs.)*; **see ~s before one's eyes** Sterne sehen *(ugs.)*; Ⓔ *(stain)* **~ [of blood/grease/ink]** [Blut-/Fett-/Tinten]fleck, *der;* Ⓕ *(Brit. coll.: small amount)* **do a ~ of work/sewing** ein bisschen arbeiten/nähen; **how about a ~ of lunch?** wie wärs mit einem Bissen zu Mittag?; **a ~ of whisky** ein Schluck Whisky; **a ~ of culture** ein bisschen Kultur; **have** *or* **be in a ~ of bother** *or* **trouble** etwas Ärger haben; **be in a ~ of trouble with the law** Ärger mit der Polizei haben; Ⓖ *(drop)* **a ~** *or* **a few ~s of rain** ein paar Regentropfen; Ⓗ *(establishment)* **eating/drinking/entertainment ~:** Ess-/Trink-/Vergnügungslokal, *das;* Ⓘ *(area on body)* [Körper]stelle, *die;* **a tender/sore ~** *(lit.)* eine empfindliche/wunde Stelle; **a sore ~ with sb.** *(fig.)* jmds. neuralgischer Punkt; **have a weak ~** *(fig.)* eine Schwachstelle haben; ⇒ *also* **sore** 1 A; Ⓙ *(fig. coll.: job)* Job, *der (ugs.)*; Ⓚ *(Telev. coll.: position in programme)* Sendezeit, *die;* **the 7 o'clock ~:** das Siebenuhrprogramm; Ⓛ *(Med.)* Pickel, *der;* **heat ~:** Hitzebläschen, *das;* **break out in ~s** Ausschlag bekommen; Ⓜ *(on dice, dominoes)* Punkt, *der;* Ⓝ *(spotlight)* Spot, *der;* Ⓞ *(fig.: blemish)* Schandfleck, *der (emotional)*; **remain without a ~ on one's reputation** immer eine weiße Weste behalten *(ugs.)*; Ⓟ *(Sport: dot)* Aufsetzmarke, *die;* **the ~ [ball]** *(Billiards)* der Punktball; **the [penalty] ~:** die Elfmetermarke; der Elfmeterpunkt; Ⓠ *(Commerc.)* **~s, ~ goods** sofort lieferbare Ware; Lokoware, *die (fachspr.)*; **pay ~ cash** [sofort] bar zahlen. ⇒ *also* **blind spot; leopard; soft** 1 C; **tender¹** B.

❷ *v.t.*, **-tt-** Ⓐ *(detect)* entdecken; identifizieren ‹Verbrecher›; erkennen ‹Gefahr›; **it is easy to ~ an American among a group of**

S

tourists man kann leicht feststellen, wer in einer Gruppe von Touristen Amerikaner ist; **B** (*take note of*) erkennen ‹Flugzeugtyp, Vogel, Talent›; **go train-spotting/plane-spotting** Zug-/Flugzeugtypen bestimmen; **C** (*coll.: pick out*) tippen auf (+ *Akk.*) (*ugs.*) ‹Sieger, Gewinner usw.›; **D** (*stain*) beflecken; (*with ink or paint*) beklecksen; (*with mud*) beschmutzen; **E** (*Billiards etc.*) aufstellen; **F** (*Mil.: locate*) orten.

**3** *v.i.*, **-tt-: it is ~ting with rain** es tröpfelt (*ugs.*)

**spot: ~ 'check** *n.* (*test made immediately*) sofortige Überprüfung (**on** *Gen.*); (*test made on randomly selected subject*) Stichprobe, *die;* **make** *or* **carry out a ~ check on sth.** etw. sofort stichprobenweise überprüfen; **~-check** *v.t.* stichprobenweise überprüfen; **~ height** *n.* (*Geog.*) Höhenangabe, *die;* **~ lamp** *n.* Spotlight, *das;* (*Motor Veh.*) Scheinwerfer, *der*

**spotless** /'spɒtlɪs/ *adj.* **A** (*unstained*) fleckenlos; **her house is absolutely ~** (*fig.*) ihr Haus ist makellos sauber; **clean sth. until it is ~:** etw. reinigen, bis man kein Stäubchen mehr findet; **B** (*fig.: blameless*) mustergültig; untadelig ‹Charakter›

**spotlessly** /'spɒtlɪslɪ/ *adv.* **~ clean/white** tadellos sauber/makellos weiß

**spot: ~light 1** *n.* **A** (*Theatre*) [Bühnen]scheinwerfer, *der;* **B** (*Motor Veh.*) Scheinwerfer, *der;* **C** (*fig.: attention*) **the ~light is on sb.** jmd. steht im Rampenlicht [der Öffentlichkeit]; **be in the ~light** im Rampenlicht [der Öffentlichkeit] stehen; **keep out of the ~light** sich von der Öffentlichkeit fernhalten; **2** *v.t.*, **~lighted** *or* **~lit A** (*Theatre*) [mit dem Scheinwerfer] anstrahlen; **B** (*fig.: highlight*) in den Blickpunkt der Öffentlichkeit bringen; **~ market** *n.* (*Commerc.*) Spotmarkt, *der;* **~ 'on** (*coll.*) **1** *adj.* goldrichtig (*ugs.*); **I was ~ on** ich lag genau richtig (*ugs.*); **your estimate was ~ on** mit deiner Schätzung hast du ins Schwarze getroffen; **2** *adv.* haargenau (*ugs.*); **~ remover** *n.* Fleck[en]entferner, *der;* **~ 'survey** *n.* [Blitz]umfrage, *die*

**spotted** /'spɒtɪd/ *adj.* **A** gepunktet; **a blue dress/tie ~ with white** ein blaues Kleid mit weißen Tupfen/eine blaue Krawatte mit weißen Punkten; **B** (*Zool.*) **~ woodpecker/hyena** Buntspecht, *der*/Tüpfelhyäne, *die*

**spotted: ~ 'Dick** *n.* (*Brit.: pudding*) Pudding mit getrockneten Früchten; **~ 'dog** *n.* **A** (*coll.: Dalmatian*) Dalmatiner, *der;* **B** ⇒ **~ Dick**

**spotter** /'spɒtə(r)/ *n.* **~ [plane]** Erkundungsflugzeug, *das*

**spotty** /'spɒtɪ/ *adj.* **A** (*spotted*) gefleckt; (*stained*) fleckig; **B** (*pimply*) picklig; **be ~:** viele Pickel haben; (*have a rash*) einen [starken] Ausschlag haben

**spot: ~-weld 1** *v.t.* punktschweißen; **2** *n.* Punktschweißung, *die;* **~-welding** *n.* Punktschweißen, *das*

**spouse** /spaʊz/ *n.* [Ehe]gatte, *der*/-gattin, *die;* (*joc.*) Angetraute, *der/die;* Gemahl, *der*/Gemahlin, *die*

**spout** /spaʊt/ **1** *n.* **A** (*tube*) Schnabel, *der;* (*of water pump*) [Auslauf]rohr, *das;* (*of overflow*) Überlaufrohr, *das;* (*of tap*) Ausflussrohr, *das;* (*of gargoyle*) Speirohr, *das;* (*of fountain*) Spritzdüse, *die;* **be up the ~** (*coll.: pawned*) im Leihhaus sein; (*coll.: ruined*) im Eimer sein (*ugs.*); (*Brit. coll.: pregnant*) ein Kind kriegen (*ugs.*); **B** (*chute*) Rutsche, *die.* **2** *v.t.* **A** (*discharge*) ausstoßen ‹Wasser, Lava, Öl›; **the wound ~s blood** aus der Wunde strömt Blut; **B** (*declaim*) deklamieren ‹Verse›; (*rattle off*) herunterrasseln (*ugs.*) ‹Zahlen, Fakten usw.›; **~ compliments/remarks** mit Komplimenten/Bemerkungen um sich werfen; **~ nonsense** Unsinn verzapfen (*ugs.*).

**3** *v.i.* **A** (*gush*) schießen (**from** aus); **B** (*declaim*) schwadronieren (*abwertend*); schwafeln (*ugs. abwertend*); **~ at sb.** jmdm. etwas vorpredigen (*ugs.*)

**~ 'out** *v.i.* herausströmen; **~ out of sth.** aus etw. strömen

**sprain** /spreɪn/ ▶ **1232** **1** *v.t.* verstauchen; **~ one's ankle/wrist** sich (*Dat.*) den Knöchel/das Handgelenk verstauchen. **2** *n.* Verstauchung, *die*

**sprang** ⇒ **spring** 2, 3

**sprat** /spræt/ *n.* Sprotte, *die;* **set a ~ to catch a mackerel** *or* **herring** *or* **whale** (*fig.*) mit der Wurst nach dem Schinken *od.* der Speckseite werfen (*ugs.*)

**sprawl** /sprɔːl/ **1** *n.* **A** (*slump*) **lie in a ~:** ausgestreckt [da]liegen; **B** (*straggle*) verstreute Ansammlung; **the city was one huge ~ over the map** die Stadt dehnte sich auf der Landkarte als riesiger Fleck aus; **the ~ of the handwriting across the page** die quer über die ganze Seite gezogene Handschrift; ⇒ *also* **urban**.

**2** *v.i.* **A** (*spread oneself*) sich ausstrecken; **B** (*fall*) der Länge nach hinfallen; **send sb. ~ing** jmdn. zu Boden strecken (*geh.*); **C** (*straggle*) sich ausbreiten.

**3** *v.t.* **A** (*splay out*) ausstrecken; **be** *or* **lie ~ed in/on/over sth.** ausgestreckt in/auf/über etw. (*Dat.*) liegen; **B** (*spread*) verstreuen; **~ words/letters across the page** Wörter/Buchstaben großzügig über die ganze Seite pinseln

**~ a'bout** *v.i.* sich herumflegeln (*ugs. abwertend*)

**~ 'out** *v.i.* **A** (*stretch out*) sich ausstrecken; **B** (*straggle*) sich hinziehen

**sprawled out** /sprɔːld 'aʊt/ *adj.* ausgestreckt [liegend]

**sprawling** /'sprɔːlɪŋ/ *attrib. adj.* **A** (*extended*) ausgestreckt [liegend]; **B** (*falling*) der Länge nach hinfallend; **C** (*straggling*) verstreut liegend ‹Gebäude›; wuchernd ‹Großstadt›; **D** (*spidery*) ausladend, (*scrawled*) krakelig (*ugs.*) ‹Handschrift›

**spray**[1] /spreɪ/ *n.* **A** (*bouquet*) Strauß, *der;* **a ~ of roses** ein Strauß Rosen; **B** (*branch*) Zweig, *der;* (*of palm or fern*) Wedel, *der;* **C** (*brooch*) *Brosche in der Form eines kleinen Straußes od. Zweigs*

**spray**[2] **1** *v.t.* **A** (*in a stream*) spritzen; (*in a mist*) sprühen ‹Parfum, Farbe, Spray›; **they ~ed the general's car with bullets** sie durchsiebten den Wagen des Generals mit Kugeln; **B** (*treat*) besprühen ‹Haar, Haut, Pflanze›; spritzen ‹Nutzpflanzen›; **the vandals ~ed the car with paint** die Rabauken besprühten das Auto mit Farbe. **2** *v.i.* spritzen. **3** *n.* **A** (*drops*) Sprühnebel, *der;* **B** (*liquid*) Spray, *der od. das;* **C** (*container*) Spraydose, *die;* (*in gardening*) Spritze, *die;* **hair/throat ~:** Haar-/Rachenspray, *der od. das;* **perfume ~:** Parfümzerstäuber, *der*

**~ on [to]** *v.t.* **~ sth. on [to] sth.** etw. mit etw. besprühen

**~ 'out** *v.i.* herausspritzen

**'spray can** ⇒ **aerosol** A

**'spray gun** *n.* Spritzpistole, *die*

**sprayer** /'spreɪə(r)/ *n.* **A** (*person*) **[paint] ~:** Spritzlackierer, *der*/-lackiererin, *die;* **B** (*tool*) Sprühgerät, *das;* (*in pest control, gardening*) Spritze, *die*

**spread** /spred/ **1** *v.t.*, **spread A** ausbreiten ‹Tuch, Landkarte› (**on** auf + *Dat.*); streichen ‹Butter, Farbe, Marmelade›; **the peacock ~ its tail** der Pfau schlug ein Rad; **the yacht ~ its sails** die Segel der Jacht blähten sich; **B** (*cover*) **~ a roll with marmalade/butter** ein Brötchen mit Marmelade/Butter bestreichen; **the sofa was ~ with a blanket** auf dem Sofa lag eine Decke [ausgebreitet]; **C** (*fig.: display*) **a magnificent view/meal was ~ before us** uns (*Dat.*) bot sich eine herrliche Aussicht/uns (*Dat.*) wurde ein herrliches Mahl aufgetragen; **D** (*extend range of*) verbreiten; **drought has ~ famine to many areas** durch die Dürre breitete sich in vielen Gebieten eine Hungersnot aus; **E** (*distribute*) verteilen; (*untidily*) verstreuen; streuen ‹Dünger›; verbreiten ‹Zerstörung, Angst, Niedergeschlagenheit›; **F** (*make known*) verbreiten; **~ the word** (*tell news*) es weitersagen; (*coll.: pass on a message*) die Nachricht weitergeben; (*Relig.*) das Wort Gottes verkünden; **G** (*separate*) ausbreiten ‹Arme›; öffnen ‹Lippen›; spreizen ‹Beine›; ⇒ *also* **wing** 1 A.

**2** *v.i.*, **spread A** sich ausbreiten; **a smile/a blush ~ across** *or* **over his face** ein Lächeln breitete sich (*geh.*) über sein Gesicht/er wurde ganz rot im Gesicht; **margarine ~s easily** Margarine lässt sich leicht streichen; **~ing branches/trees** ausladende Äste/Bäume; **~ like wildfire** sich in *od.* mit Windeseile verbreiten; **B** (*scatter, disperse*) sich verteilen; **the odour ~s through the room** der Geruch breitet sich im ganzen Zimmer aus; **C** (*circulate*) ‹Neuigkeiten, Gerücht, Kenntnis usw.:› sich verbreiten.

**3** *n.* **A** (*expanse*) Fläche, *die;* **we could see the whole ~ of the town** wir konnten das ganze Stadtgebiet überblicken; **B** (*span*) (*of tree*) Kronendurchmesser, *der;* (*of wings*) Spann[weite], *die;* **an oak with a magnificent ~ of branches** eine Eiche mit einer prächtigen Baumkrone; **C** (*breadth*) **have a wide ~** ‹Interessen, Ansichten:› breit gefächert sein; **a wide ~ of responsibility** ein großer Verantwortungsbereich; **D** (*extension*) Verbreitung, *die;* (*of city, urbanization, poverty*) Ausbreitung, *die;* **E** (*diffusion*) Ausbreitung, *die;* (*of learning, knowledge*) Verbreitung, *die;* Vermittlung, *die;* **F** (*distribution*) Verteilung, *die;* **G** (*coll.: meal*) Festessen, *das;* Schmaus, *der* (*veralt.*); **H** (*paste*) Brotaufstrich, *der;* ‹Rindfleisch-, Lachs›paste, *die;* ‹Käse-, Erdnuss-, Schokoladen›krem, *die;* **I** (*girth*) ⇒ **middle-aged**; **J** ⇒ **bedspread**; **K** (*Printing*) **the advertisement was a full-page/double-page ~:** die Anzeige war ganzseitig/doppelseitig; **L** (*Amer. coll.: ranch*) Ranch, *die.*

**4** *v. refl.* **A** (*stretch out*) sich ausstrecken; **B** (*talk or write at length*) sich verbreiten

**~ a'bout, ~ a'round** *v.t.* **A** (*convey*) verbreiten ‹Neuigkeiten, Gerücht usw.›; **B** (*strew*) verstreuen; ausstreuen ‹Samen›

**~ 'out 1** *v.t.* **A** (*extend*) ausbreiten ‹Arme›; **B** (*space out*) verteilen ‹Soldaten, Tänzer, Pfosten›; legen ‹Karten›; ausbreiten ‹Papiere›. **2** *v.i.* sich verteilen; ‹Soldaten:› ausschwärmen

**~ 'over 1** *v.t.* **~ sth. over a certain time** etw. über eine bestimmte Zeit ausdehnen; **the mortgage/repayment is ~ over twenty years** die Hypothek hat eine Laufzeit von zwanzig Jahren/die Rückzahlung wird [ratenweise] innerhalb von zwanzig Jahren geleistet. **2** *v.i.* sich erstrecken über (+ *Akk.*); **~ over into** hineinreichen in (+ *Akk.*)

**spread'eagle** *v.t.* **A** (*tie*) an den ausgestreckten Armen und Beinen fesseln; **B** (*flatten*) **the police ~d the suspect against the car** die Polizei ließ den Verdächtigen sich mit ausgestreckten Armen und Beinen gegen das Auto stellen; **lie** *or* **be ~d** ausgestreckt [da]liegen

**spreader** /'spredə(r)/ *n.* Streugerät, *das;* **grit-~:** Splittstreuwagen, *der;* **manure/fertilizer-~:** Stallmist-/Düngerstreuer, *der*

**'spreadsheet** *n.* (*Computing*) Arbeitsblatt, *das*

**spree** /spriː/ *n.* **A** (*spell of spending*) Einkaufsorgie, *die* (*ugs.*); **go on a shopping ~:** ganz groß einkaufen gehen; **have a ~:** viel Geld ausgeben; **B be/go out on the ~** (*coll.*) einen draufmachen (*ugs.*)

**'spree killer** *n.* Amokläufer, *der*

**sprig** /sprɪg/ *n.* **A** (*twig*) Zweig, *der;* **B** (*ornament*) *Schmuck in der Form eines Zweiges;* **C** (*young person*) Spross, *der* (*scherzh.*); **D** (*tack*) Stift, *der*

**sprightly** /'spraɪtlɪ/ *adj.* munter

**spring** /sprɪŋ/ **1** *n.* **A** ▶ **1503** (*season*) Frühling, *der;* **in ~ 1969, in the ~ of 1969** im Frühjahr 1969; **in early/late ~:** zu Anfang/Ende des Frühjahrs; **last/next ~:** letzten/nächsten Frühling; **full of the joys of ~** (*iron.*) aufgekratzt (*ugs.*); fröhlich; **~ weather/fashions/flowers** Frühlingswetter, *das*/Frühlingsmoden/-blumen; **in [the] ~:** im Frühling *od.* Frühjahr; **in the ~ of his/her life** (*literary*) im Frühling seines/ihres Lebens (*dichter.*); **B** (*source, lit. or fig.*) Quelle, *die;* **C** (*Mech.*) Feder, *die;* **~s** (*vehicle suspension*) Federung, *die;* **D** (*jump*) Sprung, *der;* **make a ~ at sb./at an animal** sich auf jmdn./ein Tier stürzen;

**make a ~ at sth.** auf etw. (*Akk.*) zuspringen; Ⓔ (*elasticity*) Elastizität, *die;* **the mattresses have no ~ in them** die Matratzen federn nicht; **walk with a ~ in one's step** mit beschwingten Schritten gehen; **put a ~ in[to] sb.'s step** jmds. Schritt beschwingen; Ⓕ (*recoil*) Zurückschnellen, *das;* **snap back with a ~:** zurückschnellen.
❷ *v.i.*, **sprang** /spræŋ/ *or* (*Amer.*) **sprung** /sprʌŋ/, **sprung** Ⓐ (*jump*) springen; **~ [up] from sth.** von etw. aufspringen; **~ at sb.'s throat** jmdm. an die Kehle springen; **the blood ~s to sb.'s cheeks** jmdm. schießt das Blut ins Gesicht; **~ to one's feet** aufspringen; **~ to sb.'s assistance/defence** jmdm. beispringen; **~ to life** (*fig.*) [plötzlich] zum Leben erwachen; Ⓑ (*arise*) entspringen (**from** *Dat.*); ‹Saat, Hoffnung:› keimen; ‹Bogen:› aufstreben (*geh.*); **~ to fame** über Nacht bekannt werden; **his actions ~ from a false conviction** seine Handlungen entspringen einer falschen Ansicht; **~ to mind** jmdm. einfallen; Ⓒ (*recoil*) **~ back into position** zurückschnellen; **~ to** *or* **shut** ‹Tür, Falle, Deckel:› zuschnappen; Ⓓ (*split*) zerbrechen; (*become warped*) sich verziehen; **~ from sth.** von etw. abbrechen.
❸ *v.t.*, **sprang** *or* (*Amer.*) **sprung**, **sprung** Ⓐ (*make known suddenly*) **~ a new idea/a proposal/a question on sb.** jmdn. mit einer neuen Idee/einem Vorschlag/einer Frage überfallen; **~ a surprise on sb.** jmdn. überraschen; Ⓑ (*cause to operate*) zünden ‹Mine›; aufspringen lassen ‹Schloss›; zuschnappen lassen ‹Falle›; Ⓒ (*coll.: set free*) herausholen (**from** aus); Ⓓ (*Hunting: rouse*) aufscheuchen (**from** aus); Ⓔ (*split*) bersten lassen (*geh.*); **I've sprung my racket** mein Schläger ist gesprungen; Ⓕ (*provide with ~s*) federn; **be well sprung** gut gefedert sein
**~ 'back** *v.i.* zurückschnellen
**~ from** *v.t.* Ⓐ (*appear from*) [plötzlich] herkommen; **where did you ~ from?** wo kommst du so plötzlich her?; Ⓑ (*originate from*) herrühren von; ‹Person:› abstammen von; **he ~s from a country family** er stammt aus einer ländlichen Familie
**~ 'up** *v.i.* ‹Wind, Zweifel:› aufkommen; ‹Gebäude:› aus dem Boden wachsen; ‹Pflanze:› aus dem Boden schießen; ‹Organisation, Freundschaft:› entstehen

**spring: ~ balance** *n.* Federwaage, *die;* **~ bed** ⇒ **bed** 1 A; **~ 'binder** *n.* Klemmmappe, *die;* **~board** *n.* (*Sport; also fig.*) Sprungbrett, *das;* (*in circus*) Schleuderbrett, *das*

**springbok** /ˈsprɪŋbɒk/ *n.* Ⓐ (*Zool.*) Springbock, *der;* Ⓑ *in pl.* **the S~s** (*Rugby*) die Südafrikaner; *Spitzname für Mitglieder südafrikanischer Rugby-/Cricketmannschaften*

**spring: ~ 'cabbage** *n.* Frühkohl, *der;* **~ 'chicken** *n.* Ⓐ (*fowl*) junges Hähnchen; Ⓑ (*fig.: person*) **be no ~ chicken** nicht mehr der/die Jüngste sein (*ugs.*); **~-'clean** ❶ *n.* [großer] Hausputz; (*in spring*) Frühjahrsputz, *der;* ❷ *v.t.* **~-clean [the whole house]** [großen] Hausputz/Frühjahrsputz machen; **~ clip** *n.* Klammer, *die*

**springer** /ˈsprɪŋə(r)/ *n.* **~ [spaniel]** Springerspaniel, *der*

**spring: ~ gun** *n.* (*Hunting*) Legbüchse, *die;* (*Mil.*) Selbstschuss, *der;* **~-loaded** *adj.* mit Sprungfeder *nachgestellt;* **~ 'mattress** *n.* Sprungfedermatratze, *die;* **~ 'onion** *n.* Frühlingszwiebel, *die;* **~ sus'pension** *n.* (*Motor Veh.*) federnde Aufhängung; **~ 'tide** *n.* Springflut, *die;* **~tide** *n.* (*literary*) Frühlingszeit, *die* (*geh.*); **~time** *n.* Frühling, *der;* **~ water** *n.* Quellwasser, *das*

**springy** /ˈsprɪŋɪ/ *adj.* elastisch; federnd ‹Schritt, Brett, Boden›

**sprinkle** /ˈsprɪŋkl/ *v.t.* Ⓐ (*scatter*) streuen; sprengen ‹Flüssigkeit›; **~ sth. over/on sth.** etw. über/auf etw. (*Akk.*) streuen/sprengen; **~ sth. with sth.** etw. mit etw. bestreuen/besprengen; Ⓑ (*fig.: distribute*) verteilen; Ⓒ (*fall on*) spritzen auf (+ *Akk.*)

**sprinkler** /ˈsprɪŋklə(r)/ *n.* Ⓐ (*Hort.: for watering*) Sprinkler, *der;* (*Agric.*) Regner, *der;* Ⓑ (*fire extinguisher*) **~s**, **~ system** Sprinkleranlage, *die*

**sprinkling** /ˈsprɪŋklɪŋ/ *n.* **a ~ of snow/sugar/dust** eine dünne Schneedecke/Zucker-/Staubschicht; **a ~ of gold dust/rain** eine winzige Menge Goldstaub/ein paar Regentropfen; **there was only a ~ of holidaymakers on the beach** nur ein paar vereinzelte Urlauber waren am Strand

**sprint** /sprɪnt/ ❶ *v.t. & i.* rennen; sprinten (*bes. Sport*); spurten (*bes. Sport*); **~ for the line** *or* **tape** den Endspurt anziehen. ❷ *n.* Ⓐ (*race*) Sprint, *der* (*bes. Sport*); **the hundred-metres ~** (*competition*) der Hundertmeterlauf; Ⓑ (*fig.: short burst of speed*) Sprint, *der* (*bes. Sport*); Spurt, *der* (*bes. Sport*); **final ~:** Endspurt, *der*

**sprinter** /ˈsprɪntə(r)/ *n.* Sprinter, *der*/Sprinterin, *die*

**sprit** /sprɪt/ *n.* (*Naut.*) Spriet, *das*

**sprite** /spraɪt/ *n.* [Elementar]geist, *der;* **a ~ of the air** ein Luftgeist

**spritsail** /ˈsprɪtseɪl, ˈsprɪtsl/ *n.* (*Naut.*) Sprietsegel, *das*

**spritzer** /ˈsprɪtsə(r)/ *n.* (*Amer.*) Schorle, *die*

**sprocket** /ˈsprɒkɪt/ *n.* Ⓐ (*projection*) Zahn, *der;* Ⓑ **~ [wheel]** Zahnrad, *das;* (*on bike*) (*front ~*) Kettenblatt, *das;* (*rear ~*) [Ketten]ritzel, *das*

**'sprocket wheel** *n.* (*Mech. Engin.*) [Ketten]zahnrad, *das*

**sprog** /sprɒg/ *n.* (*coll.*) Ⓐ (*child*) Sprössling, *der;* Ⓑ (*trainee*) Stift, *der*

**sprout** /spraʊt/ ❶ *n.* Ⓐ *in pl.* (*coll.*) ⇒ **Brussels sprouts**; Ⓑ (*Bot.*) ⇒ **shoot** 3 A. ❷ *v.i.* Ⓐ (*lit. or fig.*) sprießen (*geh.*); **~ into life** ‹Pflanzen:› sprießen [und blühen]; Ⓑ (*grow*) emporschießen; ‹Bart:› wachsen; Ⓒ (*fig.*) ‹Gebäude:› wie Pilze aus dem Boden schießen; **the garden is ~ing all over with flowers** im Garten schießen überall die Blumen empor. ❸ *v.t.* [aus]treiben ‹Blüten, Knospen›; sich (*Dat.*) wachsen lassen ‹Bart›; (*fig.*) aus dem Boden wachsen lassen ‹Gebäude›; hervorbringen ‹Ideen›; schaffen ‹Arbeitsplätze›; **the young deer was ~ing antlers** dem jungen Rehbock wuchs das Geweih; **my chin is ~ing hairs** auf meinem Kinn wachsen [Bart]haare

**spruce** /spru:s/ ❶ *adj.* gepflegt; **look ~:** adrett aussehen. ❷ *n.* (*Bot.*) Fichte, *die.* ❸ *v.t.* **~ up** verschönern; **~ the house up** das [ganze] Haus aufräumen und putzen; **~ sb./oneself up [for sth.]** jmdn./sich [für etw.] zurechtmachen (*ugs.*); **get ~d up** sich fein machen (*ugs.*)

**sprucely** /ˈspru:slɪ/ *adv.* adrett ‹sich kleiden›; **be ~ kept** sehr gepflegt sein

**sprung** /sprʌŋ/ ❶ ⇒ **spring** 2, 3. ❷ *attrib. adj.* gefedert

**spry** /spraɪ/ *adj.* rege

**spryly** /ˈspraɪlɪ/ *adv.* munter; **walk** *or* **move ~:** munteren Schrittes gehen

**spud** /spʌd/ *n.* Ⓐ (*Brit. coll.: potato*) Kartoffel, *die;* Ⓑ (*spade*) Unkrautstecher, *der*

**spud-bashing** /ˈspʌdbæʃɪŋ/ *n.* (*Brit. Mil. coll.*) Kartoffelschälen, *das*

**spue** ⇒ **spew**

**spume** /spju:m/ ❶ *n.* Gischt, *die.* ❷ *v.i.* aufschäumen; gischten (*geh.*)

**spun** ⇒ **spin** 1, 2

**spunk** /spʌŋk/ *n.* Ⓐ (*coll.: courage*) Mumm, *der* (*ugs.*); Ⓑ (*Brit. coarse: semen*) Samen, *der;* Soße, *die* (*vulg.*)

**spunky** /ˈspʌŋkɪ/ *adj.* mutig; **he is very ~:** er hat viel Mumm in den Knochen (*ugs.*)

**spur** /spɜ:(r)/ ❶ *n.* Ⓐ Sporn, *der;* **put** *or* **set ~s to one's horse** seinem Pferd die Sporen geben; **win one's ~s** (*Hist./fig.*) sich (*Dat.*) die ersten] Sporen verdienen; Ⓑ (*fig.: stimulus*) Ansporn, *der* (**to** für); **act** *or* **serve as a ~ to sb. in sth.** jmdn. bei etw. anspornen; **on the ~ of the moment** ganz spontan; Ⓒ (*branch road*) Nebenstraße, *die;* Ⓓ (*Railw.: branch line*) Nebengleis, *das;* Ⓔ (*climbing iron*) Steigeisen, *das;* Ⓕ (*Bot.: short branch*) Kurztrieb, *der;* kurzer Zweig. ❷ *v.t.*, **-rr-** Ⓐ (*prick*) die Sporen geben (+ *Dat.*); spornen (*veralt.*); Ⓑ (*fig.: incite*) anspornen; **~ sb. [on] to sth./to do sth.** jmdn. zu etw. anspornen/anspornen, etw. zu tun; Ⓒ (*fig.: stimulate*) hervorrufen; in Gang setzen ‹Aktivität›; erregen ‹Interesse›. ❸ *v.i.*, **-rr-** das Pferd/die Pferde antreiben
**~ 'on** *v.t.* anspornen; antreiben ‹Pferd›; ‹Habgier:› treiben; ⇒ *also* **~** 2 B

**spurge** /spɜ:dʒ/ *n.* (*Bot.*) Wolfsmilch, *die*

**'spur gear** *n.* (*Mech.*) Stirnrad, *das*

**spurious** /ˈspjʊərɪəs/ *adj.* unaufrichtig ‹Charakter, Handlung, Verhalten›; gespielt ‹Gefühl, Interesse›; zweifelhaft ‹Anspruch, Vergnügen›; falsch ‹Name, Münze›; **~ coins** Falschgeld, *das;* **be of ~ character/descent** einen unaufrichtigen Charakter haben/illegitimer Abstammung sein

**spuriously** /ˈspjʊərɪəslɪ/ *adv.* fälschlicherweise

**spurn** /spɜ:n/ *v.t.* (*reject*) zurückweisen; abweisen; ausschlagen ‹Angebot, Gelegenheit›; sich entziehen (+ *Dat.*) ‹Realität, Umwelt›; von sich weisen ‹Ansinnen›

**spurt¹** /spɜ:t/ ❶ *n.* Spurt, *der* (*bes. Sport*); **final ~:** Endspurt, *der;* **there was a ~ of activity** es brach kurzzeitig lebhafte Aktivität aus; **in a sudden ~ of energy** in einem plötzlichen Anfall von Energie; **put on a ~:** einen Spurt einlegen. ❷ *v.i.* spurten (*bes. Sport*)

**spurt²** ❶ *v.i.* **~ out [from** *or* **of]** herausspritzen [aus]; **~ from** ‹Rauch:› quellen aus; ‹Flüssigkeit:› spritzen aus. ❷ *v.t.* **the wound ~ed blood** aus der Wunde spritzte Blut. ❸ *n.* Strahl, *der*

**sputnik** /ˈspʊtnɪk, ˈspʌtnɪk/ *n.* Sputnik, *der*

**sputter** /ˈspʌtə(r)/ ❶ *v.t.* (*utter*) heraussprudeln; (*incoherently*) stottern. ❷ *v.i.* Ⓐ (*speak*) (*vehemently*) wettern; (*in hurried fashion*) stammeln; Ⓑ (*crackle*) zischen; Ⓒ ⇒ **splutter** 1

**sputum** /ˈspju:təm/ *n.*, *pl.* **sputa** /ˈspju:tə/ (*Med.*) Ⓐ (*saliva*) Speichel, *der;* Ⓑ (*phlegm*) Sputum, *das*

**spy** /spaɪ/ ❶ *n.* Ⓐ (*secret agent*) Spion, *der*/Spionin, *die;* Ⓑ (*watcher*) Spion, *der*/Spionin, *die;* Schnüffler, *der*/Schnüfflerin, *die* (*abwertend*); **be a ~ for sb./sth.** für jmdn./etw. als Spitzel arbeiten; **~ in the sky/cab** (*coll.*) Spionagesatellit, *der*/Fahrt[en]schreiber, *der.* ❷ *v.t.* (*literary*) ausmachen; **~ a way out of the situation** einen Ausweg aus der Lage finden. ❸ *v.i.* (*watch closely*) [herum]spionieren; (*practise espionage*) Spionage treiben; **~ on sb./a country** jmdn. nachspionieren/gegen ein Land spionieren; **~ on sb.'s movements** jmdm. auf Schritt und Tritt nachspionieren; **~ on each other** sich gegenseitig argwöhnisch beobachten
**~ 'out** *v.t.* aufspüren; ausspionieren ‹Feind, feindliche Stellung›; **~ out the land** (*lit. or fig.*) die Lage erkunden

**spy: ~glass** *n.* Handfernrohr, *das;* Perspektiv, *das;* **~hole** *n.* Spion, *der;* Guckloch, *das;* **~master** *n.* (*coll.*) Chef eines Spionagerings; **~ ring** *n.* Spionagering, *der;* **~ satellite** *n.* Spionagesatellit, *der*

**sq., Sq.** *abbr.* ▶ **928** **square, Square**

**squab** /skwɒb/ *n.* Ⓐ (*Ornith.: fledgeling*) [noch nicht flügger] Jungvogel; (*pigeon*) Jungtaube, *die;* Ⓑ (*cushion*) Kissen, *das;* (*Brit.: of car seat*) Rücken-/Seitenlehne, *die*

**squabble** /ˈskwɒbl/ ❶ *n.* Streit, *der;* **petty ~s** kleine Streitereien; **have a ~ [with sb. about sth.]** [mit jmdm. wegen einer Sache] Streit haben (*ugs.*); sich [mit jmdm. wegen einer Sache] streiten. ❷ *v.i.* sich zanken (**over, about** wegen)

**squad** /skwɒd/ *n.* Ⓐ (*Mil.*) Gruppe, *die;* Trupp, *der;* Ⓑ (*group*) Mannschaft, *die;* ⇒ *also* **firing squad**; Ⓒ (*Police*) **special ~:** Sonder[einsatz]kommando, *das;* **Drug/Fraud S~:** Rauschgift-/Betrugsdezernat, *das;* **~ car** (*Amer.*) Einsatzwagen, *der;* ⇒ *also* **flying squad; vice squad**

**squaddie, squaddy** /ˈskwɒdɪ/ *n.* (*Brit. Mil. coll.*) Gemeine, *der*

**squadron** /ˈskwɒdrən/ *n.* Ⓐ (*Mil.*) (*of tanks*) Bataillon, *das;* (*of cavalry*) Schwadron, *die;* Ⓑ (*Navy*) Geschwader, *das;* Ⓒ ▶ **1617** (*Air Force*) Staffel, *die;* **~ leader** (*Air Force*) Major der Luftwaffe

S

**squalid** /ˈskwɒlɪd/ *adj.* Ⓐ (*dirty*) [abstoßend] schmutzig; **living conditions were ~:** man lebte mitten im Schmutz; Ⓑ (*poor*) schäbig; armselig; Ⓒ (*fig.: sordid*) abstoßend

**squall** /skwɔːl/ ❶ *n.* (*gust*) Bö, *die;* **look out** *or* **be on the look out for ~s** (*fig.*) auf der Hut sein. ❷ *v.i.* brüllen; **~ in pain** brüllen *od.* schreien vor Schmerz

**squally** /ˈskwɔːlɪ/ *adj.* böig

**squalor** /ˈskwɒlə(r)/ *n., no pl.* Ⓐ (*dirtiness*) Schmutz, *der;* **live in ~:** in Schmutz und Elend leben; **a life of ~:** ein Leben in Schmutz und Elend; Ⓑ (*fig.*) Schmutzigkeit, *die*

**squander** /ˈskwɒndə(r)/ *v.t.* vergeuden ‹Talent, Zeit, Geld›; verschleudern ‹Ersparnisse, Vermögen›; nicht nutzen ‹Chance, Gelegenheit›; **~ one's life** sein Leben wegwerfen

**square** /skweə(r)/ ❶ *n.* Ⓐ (*Geom.*) Quadrat, *das;* Ⓑ (*object, arrangement*) Quadrat, *das;* **carpet ~:** Teppichfliese, *die;* **cheese ~:** Scheiblette, *die* Ⓦⓩ; **tile ~:** [quadratische] Kachel; Ⓒ (*on board in game*) Feld, *das;* **be** *or* **go back to ~ one** (*fig. coll.*) wieder von vorn anfangen müssen; Ⓓ (*open area*) Platz, *der;* Ⓔ (*scarf*) [quadratisches] Tuch; **silk ~:** Seidentuch, *das;* Ⓕ (*Mil.: drill area*) **[barrack] ~:** Kasernenhof, *der;* Ⓖ (*Math.: product*) Quadrat, *das;* **a perfect ~:** eine Quadratzahl; Ⓗ (*coll.: old-fashioned person*) Spießer, *der*/Spießerin, *die* (*abwertend*); Ⓘ **on the ~ = on the level** ⇒ **level** 1 A; Ⓙ (*instrument*) Winkel, *der;* **L-/T-~:** L-förmiger Messwinkel/Kreuzwinkel, *der;* ⇒ *also* **set square**; **try-square**; Ⓚ (*Amer.: block of buildings*) Quadrat, *das;* Karree, *das;* Ⓛ (*Cricket: pitch area*) [Haupt]spielfläche, *die.* ⇒ *also* **inverse square law**; **magic square**; **word square**.

❷ *adj.* ▸1352 Ⓐ quadratisch; ⇒ *also* **hole** 1 A; Ⓑ ▸928 **a ~ foot/mile/metre** *etc.* ein Quadratfuß/eine Quadratmeile/ein Quadratmeter *usw.;* **a foot ~:** ein Fuß im Quadrat; **the S~ Mile** die City von London; Ⓒ (*right-angled*) rechtwink[e]lig; **~ with** *or* **to** im rechten Winkel zu; **the wall is not ~ with the ceiling** die Wand ist nicht im Lot mit der Decke; **~ on to sth.** rechtwinklig zu etw.; Ⓓ (*stocky*) gedrungen ‹Statur, Gestalt›; ‹Gegenstand:› von gedrungenem Format; **be ~ in build** gedrungen gebaut sein; Ⓔ (*in outline*) rechteckig; eckig ‹Schultern, Kinn›; **~-shouldered** breitschultrig; Ⓕ (*quits*) quitt (*ugs.*); **be [all] ~:** [völlig] quitt sein (*ugs.*); ‹Spieler:› gleichstehen; ‹Spiel:› unentschieden stehen; **the match finished all ~:** das Spiel ging unentschieden aus; **get ~ with sb.** mit jmdm. quitt werden (*ugs.*); (*get revenge*) es jmdm. heimzahlen; Ⓖ (*coll.: old-fashioned*) spießig (*abwertend*).

❸ *adv.* Ⓐ breit ‹sitzen›; **put sth. ~ in the middle of sth.** etw. mitten auf etw. (*Akk.*) stellen; **hit sb. ~ on the jaw** jmdm. genau auf die Kinnlade schlagen; **the ball hit him ~ on the head** der Ball traf ihn genau am Kopf; **look sb. ~ in the face** *or* **between the eyes** jmdm. fest in die Augen sehen; Ⓑ (*fairly*) ehrlich; fair ‹behandeln›. ⇒ *also* **fair**[2] 2 C.

❹ *v.t.* Ⓐ (*make right-angled*) rechtwinklig machen; vierkantig zuschneiden ‹Holz›; Ⓑ (*place squarely*) **~ one's shoulders** seine Schultern straffen; Ⓒ (*divide into ~s*) in Karos einteilen; **~d paper** kariertes Papier; Ⓓ ▸1352 (*Math.: multiply*) quadrieren; **3 ~d is 9** 3 [im] Quadrat ist 9; 3 hoch 2 ist 9; Ⓔ (*reconcile*) **~ sth. with sth.** etw. mit etw. in Einklang bringen; Ⓕ **~ it with sb.** (*coll.: get sb.'s approval*) es mit jmdm. klären; Ⓖ (*coll.: bribe*) schmieren (*salopp*); Ⓗ (*settle*) begleichen; **~ one's debt[s]** seine Schuld[en] begleichen; **I have a debt to ~ with him** (*fig.*) mit ihm werde ich [noch] abrechnen; ⇒ *also* **account** 2 A; Ⓘ (*draw level in*) **~ [the/one's match** *or* **score]** zum Unentschieden verkürzen; gleichziehen; Ⓙ **~ the circle** (*Geom.*) den Kreis quadrieren.

❺ *v.i.* (*be consistent*) übereinstimmen; **sth. does not ~ with sth.** etw. steht nicht im Einklang mit etw.; **it just does not ~:** hier stimmt doch etwas nicht

**~ 'off** ❶ *v.t.* (*make ~*) ⇒ **~** 4 A. ❷ *v.i.* (*raise fists*) die Fäuste heben

**~ 'up** *v.i.* (*settle up*) abrechnen

**~ 'up to** *v.t.* Ⓐ (*raise fists against*) sich mit erhobenen Fäusten aufbauen (*ugs.*) vor (+ *Dat.*); **they ~d up to each other** sie traten sich kampfbereit gegenüber; Ⓑ (*confront*) **~ up to sb./sth.** jmdm./einer Sache entgegentreten

**square: ~-bashing** /ˈskweəbæʃɪŋ/ *n.* (*Brit. Mil. coll.*) Kasernenhofdrill, *der;* **~ 'brackets** *n. pl.* eckige Klammern; **~-built** *adj.* quadratisch ‹Gebäude›; gedrungen ‹Person›; vierschrötig ‹Mann›; **~ dance** *n.* Squaredance, *der;* **~ 'deal** *n.* faires Geschäft; **get a ~ deal** (*not be swindled*) kein schlechtes Geschäft machen; (*receive adequate compensation*) fair *od.* anständig behandelt werden; **~ 'leg** *n.* (*Cricket*) *Feldspieler, der die Stellung hinter dem Schlagmann innehat*

**squarely** /ˈskweəlɪ/ *adv.* Ⓐ (*directly*) fest ‹ansehen›; genau ‹treffen›; aufrecht ‹sitzen›; **his works place him ~ in the Romantic tradition** mit seinem Werk steht er direkt in der romantischen Tradition; Ⓑ ⇒ **fairly** E

**square: ~ 'meal** *n.* anständige Mahlzeit (*ugs.*); **~ number** *n.* (*Math.*) Quadratzahl, *die;* **~-rigged** /ˈskweərɪgd/ *adj.* (*Naut.*) ‹Schoner› mit Rahsegeln; **a ~-rigged sailing ship** ein voll getakelter Rahsegler; **~ 'root** *n.* ▸1352 (*Math.*) Quadratwurzel, *die;* **~-root sign** [Quadrat]wurzelzeichen, *das;* **~ sail** *n.* (*Naut.*) Rahsegel, *das;* **~-toed** /ˈskweətəʊd/ *adj.* **~-toed shoes/boots** [an den Zehen] breite Schuhe/Stiefel; **~ wave** *n.* (*Phys.*) Rechteckwelle, *die*

**squash**[1] /skwɒʃ/ ❶ *v.t.* Ⓐ (*crush*) zerquetschen; **~ sth. flat** etw. platt drücken; Ⓑ (*compress*) pressen; **~ in/up** eindrücken/zusammendrücken ‹Gegenstand›; **~ sb./sth. into sth.** jmdn./etw. in etw. (*Akk.*) [hinein]zwängen; Ⓒ (*put down*) niederschlagen ‹Aufstand›; zunichte machen ‹Hoffnung, Traum›; Ⓓ (*coll.: dismiss*) ablehnen ‹Vorschlag, Plan›; Ⓔ (*coll.: silence*) zum Schweigen bringen.

❷ *v.i.* sich quetschen; **~ in** sich hineinquetschen; **we ~ed up** wir drängten uns zusammen; **~ into the back seat of a car** sich auf den Rücksitz eines Wagens quetschen.

❸ *n.* Ⓐ (*drink*) Fruchtsaftgetränk, *das;* **orange ~:** Orangensaftgetränk, *das;* (*concentrated*) Orangensaftkonzentrat, *das;* Ⓑ (*Sport*) **~ [rackets]** Squash, *das;* Ⓒ ⇒ **crush** 2 A

**squash**[2] *n.* (*gourd*) [Speise]kürbis, *der*

**squash: ~ ball** *n.* Squashball, *der;* **~ court** *n.* Squashfeld, *das;* **~ racket** *n.* Squashschläger, *der;* **~ rackets** ⇒ **'squash** 3 B

**squashy** /ˈskwɒʃɪ/ *adj.* weich ‹Kuchen, Obst›

**squat** /skwɒt/ ❶ *v.i.,* **-tt-** Ⓐ (*crouch*) hocken; (*crouch down*) sich hocken; Ⓑ (*coll.: sit*) sitzen; (*sit down*) sich setzen; Ⓒ (*coll.: occupy property*) (*house*) eine Hausbesetzung machen; (*land*) eine Landbesetzung machen; **~ in a house/on land** ein Haus besetzen/Land besetzen. ❷ *adj.* rundlich; untersetzt. ❸ *n.* (*coll.*) Ⓐ (*occupation*) (*of house*) Hausbesetzung, *die;* (*of land*) Landbesetzung, *die;* Ⓑ (*house*) besetztes Haus; (*land*) besetztes Land

**~ 'down** *v.i.* sich [nieder]hocken; (*on seat*) sich hinsetzen

**squatter** /ˈskwɒtə(r)/ *n.* (*illegal occupier*) Besetzer, *der*/Besetzerin, *die;* (*of house also*) Hausbesetzer, *der*/-besetzerin, *die*

**squaw** /skwɔː/ *n.* Squaw, *die*

**squawk** /skwɔːk/ ❶ *v.i.* ‹Hahn, Krähe, Rabe:› krähen; ‹Huhn:› kreischen; (*complain*) ‹Person:› keifen (*abwertend*). ❷ *n.* Ⓐ (*bird cry*) **~[s]** (*of crow, cockerel, raven*) Krähen, *das;* (*of hen*) Kreischen, *das;* Ⓑ (*complaint*) Gekeif[e], *das* (*ugs. abwertend*); **utter ~s of complaint** sich keifend beschweren; **~ of anger/indignation** wütendes/entrüstetes Gezeter

**squeak** /skwiːk/ ❶ *n.* Ⓐ (*of animal*) Quieken, *das;* Ⓑ (*of hinge, door, brake, shoe, etc.*) Quietschen, *das;* Ⓒ (*coll.: escape*) **have a narrow ~:** gerade noch [mit dem Leben] davonkommen; **that was a narrow ~!** das war knapp! (*ugs.*). ⇒ *also* **bubble and squeak**. ❷ *v.i.* Ⓐ ‹Tier:› quieken; Ⓑ ‹Scharnier, Tür, Bremse, Schuh usw.:› quietschen; Ⓒ (*coll.: pass*) **~ through/past [sth.]** mit Müh und Not [durch etw.] durchkommen/[an etw. (*Dat.*)] vorbeikommen; Ⓓ (*coll.*) ⇒ **squeal** 1 D

**squeaky** /ˈskwiːkɪ/ *adj.* quietschend; schrill ‹Stimme›; **be ~ clean** blitzsauber sein (*ugs.*); (*fig.*) eine blütenweiße Weste haben (*fig. ugs.*)

**squeal** /skwiːl/ ❶ *v.i.* Ⓐ **~ with pain/in fear** ‹Person:› vor Schmerz/Angst aufschreien; ‹Tier:› vor Schmerz/Angst laut quieken; **~ with laughter/for joy/in excitement** vor Lachen/Freude/Aufregung kreischen; Ⓑ ‹Bremsen, Räder:› kreischen; ‹Reifen:› quietschen; Ⓒ (*coll.: protest*) **~ [in protest]** lauthals protestieren; Ⓓ (*sl.: inform*) singen (*salopp*) (**to** bei); **~ on sb.** jmdn. verpfeifen (*salopp*). ❷ *v.t.* kreischen. ❸ *n.* Kreischen, *das;* (*of tyres*) Quietschen, *das;* (*of animal*) Quieken, *das;* **give a ~ of fear** ‹Person:› vor Angst laut schreien; ‹Tier:› vor Angst laut quieken; **give a ~ of anger** vor Zorn aufschreien; **give a ~ of delight/excitement/joy** vor Vergnügen/Aufregung/Freude kreischen; **with a ~ of delight** kreischend vor Entzücken

**squeamish** /ˈskwiːmɪʃ/ *adj.* Ⓐ (*easily nauseated*) **be ~:** zartbesaitet sein; **this film is not for the ~:** dieser Film ist nichts für zarte Gemüter; Ⓑ (*fastidious*) zimperlich

**squeegee** /skwiːˈdʒiː/ ❶ *n.* Ⓐ (*for floor*) [Boden]wischer, *der;* (*for window*) [Fenster]wischer, *der;* Ⓑ (*Photog.*) (*roller*) Rollenquetscher, *der;* (*stripper*) Abstreifer, *der.* ❷ *v.t.* Ⓐ (*wipe*) mit dem [Boden]wischer putzen ‹Fußboden›; mit dem [Fenster]wischer putzen ‹Fenster›; Ⓑ (*Photog.: roll*) mit dem Rollenquetscher/Abstreifer rollen

**squeeze** /skwiːz/ ❶ *n.* Ⓐ (*pressing*) Druck, *der;* **it only takes a gentle ~:** man braucht nur leicht zu drücken; **give sth. a [small] ~:** etw. [leicht] drücken; **put the ~ on sb.** (*fig. coll.*) jmdm. [die] Daumenschrauben anlegen; jmdn. durch die Mangel drehen (*salopp*); Ⓑ (*small quantity*) **a ~ of juice/washing-up liquid** ein Spritzer Saft/Spülmittel; **a ~ of toothpaste/icing** ganz wenig Zahnpasta/Zuckerguss; Ⓒ (*crush*) Gedränge, *das;* **be in a tight ~** (*fig.*) = **be in a fix** ⇒ **fix** 4 A; Ⓓ (*Econ.: restriction*) Beschränkung, *die* (**on** *Gen.*); Ⓔ (*Brit.: embrace*) **give sb. a [big/final] ~:** jmdn. [fest/ein letztes Mal] an sich drücken.

❷ *v.t.* Ⓐ (*press*) drücken; drücken auf (+ *Akk.*) ‹Tube, Plastikflasche›; kneten ‹Ton, Knetmasse›; ausdrücken ‹Schwamm, Wäsche, Pickel›; (*to get juice*) auspressen ‹Früchte, Obst›; **~ sb.'s hand** jmdm. die Hand drücken; **~ the trigger** auf den Abzug drücken; Ⓑ (*extract*) drücken (**out of** aus); **~ out sth.** etw. herausdrücken; **~ sth. on to sth.** etw. auf etw. (*Akk.*) drücken; Ⓒ (*force*) zwängen; **~ one's way past/into/out of sth.** sich an etw. (*Dat.*) vorbei-/in etw. (*Akk.*) hinein-/aus etw. herauszwängen; Ⓓ (*fig. coll.*) **~ sth. from sb.** etw. aus jmdm. herauspressen; Ⓔ (*emit*) **~ [out]** herauspressen ‹Träne›; herausbringen ‹Laut, Antwort›; sich abringen ‹Lächeln›; Ⓕ (*fig.: constrain*) unter Druck setzen; **~ sb. into doing sth.** jmdn. dazu bringen, etw. zu tun; **~ sb. out of sth./out** (*fig. coll.*) jmdn. aus etw. drängen/hinausdrängen; Ⓖ (*Bridge*) zum Abwerfen zwingen; Ⓗ (*coll.: extort*) **~ money out of sb.** Geld aus jmdm. herauspressen.

❸ *v.i.* **~ past sb./sth.** sich an jmdm./etw. vorbeidrängen; **~ between two persons** sich zwischen zwei Personen (*Dat.*) durchdrängen; **~ under** *or* **underneath sth.** sich unter etw. (*Dat.*) hindurchzwängen; **~ under a bed** sich unter ein Bett zwängen; **~ together** sich zusammendrängen; **~ down a hole** sich in ein Loch zwängen

**~ 'in** ❶ *v.t.* Ⓐ reinquetschen; Ⓑ (*fig.: fit in*) einschieben. ❷ *v.i.* sich hineinzwängen

**~ 'up** *v.i.* sich zusammendrängen; **~ up against sb./sth.** sich [fest] an jmdn./etw. drücken

**squeeze:** ~ **bottle** ⇒ **squeezy bottle**; ~ **box** *n.* (*coll.*) Quetschkommode, *die* (*salopp scherzh.*)

**squeezer** /'skwi:zə(r)/ *n.* (*device*) Presse, *die*

**squeezy bottle** /'skwi:zɪ bɒtl/ *n.* [elastische] Plastikflasche

**squelch** /skweltʃ/ ❶ *v.t.* Ⓐ (*stamp on*) stampfen; Ⓑ (*silence*) zum Schweigen bringen. ❷ *v.i.* Ⓐ (*make sucking sound*) quatschen (*ugs.*); Ⓑ (*go over wet ground*) patschen

**squib** /skwɪb/ *n.* Ⓐ (*firework*) Knallfrosch, *der;* **damp** ~ (*fig.*) Reinfall, *der;* Ⓑ (*lampoon*) [kurze] Satire

**squid** /skwɪd/ *n.* (*Zool., Gastr.*) Kalmar, *der*

**squidgy** /'skwɪdʒɪ/ *adj.* (*Brit. coll.*) durchweicht; matschig (*ugs.*)

**squiggle** /'skwɪgl/ *n.* Schnörkel, *der*

**squiggly** /'skwɪglɪ/ *adj.* schnörk[e]lig; **put a ~ line under sth.** etw. unterschlängeln

**squint** /skwɪnt/ ❶ *n.* Ⓐ (*Med.*) Schielen, *das;* **have a ~:** schielen; Ⓑ (*stealthy look*) Schielen, *das* (*ugs.*); Ⓒ (*coll.: glance*) kurzer Blick; **have** *or* **take a ~ at** einen Blick werfen auf (+ *Akk.*); überfliegen ‹Text, Zeitung›; Ⓓ (*Eccl.: opening*) *schräge Maueröffnung, durch die man den Altar sieht.* ❷ *v.i.* Ⓐ (*Med.*) schielen; Ⓑ (*with half-closed eyes*) blinzeln; die Augen zusammenkneifen; ~ **at sth.** etw. blinzelnd anschauen; Ⓒ (*obliquely*) ~ **through a gap** durch eine Lücke lugen; Ⓓ (*coll.: glance*) ~ **at** einen [kurzen] Blick werfen auf (+ *Akk.*); überfliegen ‹Zeitung, Text›; **I ~ed through his window as I passed** ich schielte im Vorbeigehen durch sein Fenster. ❸ *v.t.* ~ **one's eyes** die Augen zusammenkneifen

**squire** /'skwaɪə(r)/ ❶ *n.* Ⓐ (*country gentleman*) Squire, *der;* ≈ Gutsherr, *der;* Ⓑ (*Brit. coll. voc.: sir*) **want to buy any watches, ~?** möchte der Herr Uhren kaufen? (*veralt.*); wollen Sie Uhren kaufen, Meister? (*ugs.*); Ⓒ (*Hist.: attendant*) Knappe, *der.* ❷ *v.t.* begleiten

**squirm** /skwɜ:m/ *v.i.* Ⓐ ⇒ **wriggle** 1; Ⓑ (*fig.: show unease*) sich winden (**with** vor)

**squirrel** /'skwɪrl/ *n.* Ⓐ (*Zool.*) Eichhörnchen, *das;* ⇒ *also* **grey squirrel**; **ground squirrel**; **red squirrel**; Ⓑ (*fur*) Eichhörnchen[fell], *das;* Feh, *das*

**squirt** /skwɜ:t/ ❶ *v.t.* spritzen; sprühen ‹Spray, Puder›; ~ **sth. at sb.** jmdn. mit etw. bespritzen/besprühen; ~ **sb. in the eye/face [with sth.]** jmdm. [etw.] ins Auge/Gesicht spritzen/sprühen; ~ **oneself with water/deodorant** sich mit Wasser bespritzen/mit Deodorant besprühen. ❷ *v.i.* spritzen. ❸ *n.* Spritzer, *der;* **a ~ of juice** ein Spritzer Saft

**squishy** /'skwɪʃɪ/ *adj.* patschend (*ugs.*)

**Sr.** *abbr.* Ⓐ **Senior** sen.; sr.; Ⓑ **Señor;** Ⓒ (*Relig.*) **Sister** Sr.

**Sri Lanka** /sri: 'læŋkə/ *pr. n.* Sri Lanka (*das*)

**Sri Lankan** /sri: 'læŋkən/ ▶ **1340** ❶ *adj.* srilankisch. ❷ *n.* Sri-Lanker, *der*/Sri-Lankerin, *die;* **sb. is a ~:** jmd. ist aus Sri Lanka

**SRN** *abbr.* **State Registered Nurse** staatl. gepr. Krankenschwester/-pfleger

**SS** *abbr.* Ⓐ /seɪnts/ **Saints** St.; Ⓑ **steamship** D; Ⓒ (*Nazi élite force*) SS, *die*

**SSE** /saʊθsaʊθ'i:st/ *abbr.* ▶ **1024** **south-south-east** SSO

**SSW** /saʊθsaʊθ'west/ *abbr.* ▶ **1024** **south-south-west** SSW

**St** *abbr.* **Saint** St.

**St.** *abbr.* **Street** Str.

**st.** *abbr.* ▶ **1682** (*Brit.: unit of weight*) **stone**

**stab** /stæb/ ❶ *v.t.*, **-bb-** Ⓐ (*pierce*) stechen; ~ **the air** in der Luft herumfuchteln; ~ **sb. in the chest** jmdm. in die Brust stechen; ~ **a piece of meat** in ein Stück Fleisch stechen; **he had been severely ~bed** er hatte gefährliche Stichwunden erhalten; Ⓑ (*fig.*) (*hurt*) ~ **sb.'s heart** jmdm. ins Herz schneiden (*geh.*); ~ **sb.'s conscience** jmds. Gewissen quälen; (*attack*) ~ **sb. in the back** (*fig.*) jmdm. in den Rücken fallen.
❷ *v.i.*, **-bb-** Ⓐ (*pierce*) stechen; Ⓑ (*thrust*) zustechen; ~ **at sb.** nach jmdm. stechen.
❸ *n.* Ⓐ (*act*) Stich, *der;* (*fig.*) **that was a real ~ in the back** ich fühlte mich/er fühlte sich *usw.* wirklich verraten und verkauft; Ⓑ (*coll.: attempt*) **make** *or* **have a ~ [at it]** [es] probieren; Ⓒ (*blow*) Stich, *der;* (*with beak*) Hieb, *der;* Ⓓ (*wound*) Stichwunde, *die;* Ⓔ (*fig.*) (*pang*) ~ **of conscience/guilt** Gewissensbiss, *der*/[quälendes] Schuldbewusstsein

**stabbing** /'stæbɪŋ/ ❶ *n.* Messerstecherei, *die.* ❷ *attrib. adj.* stechend ‹Schmerz›

**stabilisation** *etc.* ⇒ **stabiliz-**

**stability** /stə'bɪlɪtɪ/ *n., no pl.* Stabilität, *die;* **his character lacks ~:** er ist charakterlich nicht gefestigt

**stabilization** /steɪbɪlaɪ'zeɪʃn/ *n.* Stabilisierung, *die*

**stabilize** /'steɪbɪlaɪz/ ❶ *v.t.* stabilisieren. ❷ *v.i.* sich stabilisieren

**stabilizer** /'steɪbɪlaɪzə(r)/ *n.* Ⓐ (*Naut.*) Stabilisator, *der;* Ⓑ (*Aeronaut.*) **vertical ~** ⇒ **tail fin**; **horizontal ~** ⇒ **tailplane**; Ⓒ (*Cycling*) Stützrad, *das*

**stable**[1] /'steɪbl/ *adj.* Ⓐ (*steady*) stabil; **the patient was in a ~ condition** *or* **was ~:** der Zustand des Patienten *od.* der Patient war stabil; **a ~ family background** geordnete Familienverhältnisse; ⇒ *also* **equilibrium**; Ⓑ (*resolute*) gefestigt ‹Person, Charakter›

**stable**[2] ❶ *n.* Ⓐ (*for horses*) Stall, *der;* Ⓑ (*Horseracing: establishment*) [Renn]stall, *der;* **the horses are trained at his ~:** die Pferde werden in seinem Stall trainiert; Ⓒ (*fig.: origin*) Stall, *der* (*ugs.*); **the latest model from the X ~:** das jüngste Modell aus dem Hause X; **from the same ~** ‹Person› aus demselben Stall (*ugs.*); ‹Produkt› aus demselben Haus. ❷ *v.t.* (*put in ~*) in den Stall bringen; (*keep in ~*) **the pony was ~d at a nearby farm** das Pony war im Stall eines nahe gelegenen Bauernhofes untergebracht

**stable:** ~ **boy** ⇒ ~ **lad**; ~ **door** *n.* (*made in two parts*) quer geteilte Tür; ⇒ *also* **lock**[2] 2 A; ~ **lad**, ~**man** *ns.* ▶ **1261** Stallbursche, *der*

**stabling** /'steɪblɪŋ/ *n., no indef. art.* Ställe; Stallungen

**staccato** /stə'kɑ:təʊ/ (*Mus.*) ❶ *adj.* staccato gesetzt; (*fig.*) abgehackt ‹Sprache›; **speak with a ~ delivery** schnell und abgehackt sprechen; ~ **bursts of gunfire** ein Stakkato von Gewehrfeuer. ❷ *adv.* staccato. ❸ *n.* (*also fig.*) Stakkato, *das*

**stac'cato mark** *n.* (*Mus.*) Stakkatozeichen, *das*

**stack** /stæk/ ❶ *n.* Ⓐ (*of hay etc.*) Schober, *der* (*südd., österr.*); Feim, *der* (*nordd., md.*); Ⓑ (*pile*) Stoß, *der;* Stapel, *der;* **place sth. in ~s** etw. [auf]stapeln; Ⓒ (*coll.: large amount*) Haufen, *der* (*ugs.*); **a ~ of work/money** ein Haufen Arbeit/Geld; **have a ~ of things to do** einen Haufen zu tun haben (*ugs.*); **have ~s of money** Geld wie Heu haben (*ugs.*); Ⓓ **[chimney] ~:** Schornstein, *der;* Ⓔ (*factory chimney*) Fabrikschornstein, *der;* **blow one's ~** (*Amer. fig. coll.*) = **blow one's top** ⇒ **blow**[1] 2 H; Ⓕ (*funnel*) **[smoke]~:** Schornstein, *der;* Ⓖ (*Aeronaut.*) *übereinander in Warteschleifen kreisende Flugzeuge;* Ⓗ (*Brit.: rock pillar*) Felssäule, *die;* Ⓘ (*in library*) Magazin, *das.*
❷ *v.t.* Ⓐ (*pile*) ~ **[up]** [auf]stapeln; ~ **logs in a pile** Holz zu einem Stoß aufschichten; **be well ~ed** (*fig. coll.: have large bust*) viel Holz vor der Hütte haben (*ugs. scherzh.*); **~ing** stapelbar ‹Stühle usw.›; Ⓑ (*arrange fraudulently*) ~ **the cards** beim Mischen betrügen; **the odds** *or* **cards** *or* **chips are ~ed against sb.** (*fig.*) jmd. hat schlechte Karten (*fig. ugs.*); Ⓒ (*Aeronaut.*) übereinander Warteschleifen fliegen lassen; **we are ~ed right up to 30,000 feet** der Warteraum ist schon bis in 30 000 Fuß Höhe belegt

~ **'up** ⇒ ~ 2 A

**stadium** /'steɪdɪəm/ *n.* Stadion, *das*

**staff** /stɑ:f/ ❶ *n.* Ⓐ (*stick*) Stock, *der;* Ⓑ *constr. as pl.* (*personnel*) Personal, *das;* **editorial ~:** Redaktion, *die;* **diplomatic ~:** diplomatisches Korps; **the ~ of the firm** die Betriebsangehörigen; die Belegschaft [der Firma]; ~ **meeting** Belegschaftsversammlung, *die;* Ⓒ *constr. as pl.* (*of school*) Lehrerkollegium, *das;* Lehrkörper, *der* (*Amtsspr.*); (*of university or college*) Dozentenschaft, *die;* **~-student ratio** Verhältnis zwischen Lehrenden und Studierenden; ~ **meeting** (*at school*) Lehrerkonferenz, *die;* (*at university or college*) Dozentenkonferenz, *die;* Ⓓ *pl.* **staves** /steɪvz/ (*Mus.*) Liniensystem, *das;* ~ **notation** Notation mithilfe des Liniensystems; Ⓔ (*Mil.: officers*) Stab, *der;* ⇒ *also* **chief** 1 B; Ⓕ (*ceremonial rod*) Stab, *der;* **pastoral ~** (*Eccl.*) Bischofsstab, *der;* Ⓖ (*fig.: support*) Stütze, *die;* **bread/Christ is the ~ of life** Brot ist die Grundlage des Lebens/Christus ist das Brot des Lebens; Ⓗ (*Surv.: rod*) Messlatte, *die.* ⇒ *also* **flagstaff**; **general staff**.
❷ *v.t.* mit Personal ausstatten; **a hospital ~ed by women** ein Krankenhaus, dessen Personal aus Frauen besteht

**'staff college** *n.* (*Brit. Mil.*) Stabsakademie, *die* (*Milit.*)

**staffed** /stɑ:ft/ *adj.* mit Personal ausgestattet

**staffer** /'stɑ:fə(r)/ *n.* (*Amer. Journ.*) Redaktionsmitglied, *das*

**staff:** ~ **meeting** *n.* [Lehrer]konferenz, *die;* ~ **nurse** *n.* (*Brit.*) Zweitschwester, *die*/*Krankenpfleger in der Stellung einer Zweitschwester;* ~ **officer** *n.* (*Mil.*) Stabsoffizier, *der;* **~room** *n.* Lehrerzimmer, *das;* ~ **sergeant** *n.* Ⓐ (*Brit. Mil.*) ≈ Oberfeldwebel, *der;* Ⓑ (*Amer. Mil.*) ≈ Feldwebel, *der*

**stag** /stæg/ *n.* Ⓐ Hirsch, *der;* Ⓑ (*Amer.: lone man*) Herr ohne Damenbegleitung; Ⓒ (*Brit. St. Exch. coll.*) Konzertzeichner, *der*

**'stag beetle** *n.* (*Zool.*) Hirschkäfer, *der*

**stage** /steɪdʒ/ ❶ *n.* Ⓐ (*Theatre*) Bühne, *die;* **down/up ~** (*position*) vorne/hinten auf der Bühne; (*direction*) nach vorn/nach hinten; **[be/appear] on ~:** auf der Bühne [stehen/erscheinen]; **be appearing on ~ at the Royal** am Royal spielen; Ⓑ (*fig.*) **the ~:** das Theater; **write for the ~:** für die Bühne schreiben; **go on the ~:** zur Bühne *od.* zum Theater gehen; Ⓒ (*part of process*) Stadium, *das;* Phase, *die;* **be at a difficult/late/critical ~:** sich in einer schwierigen/späten/kritischen Phase befinden; **negotiations are at an early ~:** die Verhandlungen befinden sich im Anfangsstadium; **at such a late ~:** zu einem so späten Zeitpunkt; **at this ~:** in diesem Stadium; **do sth. in** *or* **by ~s** etw. abschnittsweise *od.* nach und nach tun; **I am past the ~ of caring** das ist mir inzwischen gleich; **in the final ~s** in der Schlussphase; Ⓓ (*raised platform*) Gerüst, *das;* ⇒ *also* **landing stage**; Ⓔ (*of microscope*) Mikroskoptisch, *der;* Ⓕ (*fig.: scene*) Bühne, *die;* **quit the political ~** *or* **the ~ of politics** von der politischen Bühne abtreten; **hold the ~:** die Szene beherrschen; **set the ~ for sb./sth.** jmdm. den Weg ebnen/etw. in die Wege leiten; **the ~ was set for a bitter argument** damit waren die Voraussetzungen für eine erbitterte Auseinandersetzung gegeben; Ⓖ (*stopping place*) Station, *die;* Ⓗ (*distance*) Etappe, *die;* **the ~ from Paris to Marseilles** die Strecke Paris-Marseille; **travel by [easy] ~s** in [kurzen] Etappen reisen; ⇒ *also* **fare stage**; Ⓘ (*Geol., Electr., Astronaut.*) Stufe, *die.*
❷ *v.t.* Ⓐ (*present*) inszenieren; Ⓑ (*arrange*) veranstalten ‹Wettkampf, Ausstellung›; ausrichten ‹Veranstaltung›; organisieren ‹Streik›; bewerkstelligen ‹Rückzug›; ~ **a comeback** ein Comeback schaffen

**stage:** **~coach** *n.* Postkutsche, *die;* **~craft** *n., no pl., no indef. art.* (*Theatre*) Bühnenkunst, *die;* ~ **direction** *n.* (*Theatre*) Bühnenanweisung, *die;* ~ **door** *n.* (*Theatre*) Bühneneingang, *der;* ~ **effect** *n.* (*Theatre*) Bühneneffekt, *der;* ~ **fright** *n.* (*Theatre*) Lampenfieber, *das;* **~hand** *n.* (*Theatre*) Bühnenarbeiter, *der*/-arbeiterin, *die;* ~ **'left** ⇒ **left**[2] 3 C; **~-manage** *v.t.* Ⓐ (*Theatre*) als Inspizient/Inspizientin mitwirken bei ‹Inszenierung›; Ⓑ (*fig.*) veranstalten; inszenieren ‹Revolte usw.›; ~ **manager** *n.* ▶ **1261** (*Theatre*) Inspizient, *der*/Inspizientin, *die;* ~ **name** *n.*

S

(*Theatre*) Künstlername, *der;* ~ **play** *n.* (*Theatre*) Bühnenstück, *das*

**stager** /'steɪdʒə(r)/ ⇒ **old** 1 B

**stage:** ~ **right** ⇒ **right** 3 H; ~ **rights** *n. pl.* Aufführungsrechte; ~**-struck** *adj.* theaterbesessen; ~ **whisper** *n.* Beiseitesprechen, *das;* **in a** ~ **whisper** beiseite

**stagflation** /stæg'fleɪʃn/ *n.* (*Econ.*) Stagflation, *die*

**stagger** /'stægə(r)/ **1** *v.i.* schwanken; torkeln (*ugs.*). **2** *v.t.* **A** (*cause to totter*) zum Schwanken bringen; **B** (*astonish*) die Sprache verschlagen (+ *Dat.*); **I was** ~**ed** es hat mir die Sprache verschlagen; **C** (*position out of line, arrange alternately*) versetzt anordnen; ~**ed junction** versetzt angelegte Kreuzung; ~**ed** (*fig.*) gestaffelt ‹Ferien, Schichten, Essenszeiten›

~ **a'bout,** ~ **a'round** *v.i.* [hin und her] taumeln; [herum]torkeln (*ugs.*)

**staggering** /'stægərɪŋ/ *adj.* erschütternd ‹Schlag, Schock, Verlust›; Schwindel erregend ‹Menge, Höhe›; folgenschwer ‹Auswirkung, Bedeutung›; zutiefst beunruhigend ‹Nachricht›; **the** ~ **fact is that no one really knew who he was** erschütternd ist, dass niemand ihn wirklich kannte

**staggeringly** /'stægərɪŋlɪ/ *adv.* erstaunlich; *as sentence-modifier* erstaunlicherweise

**stagily** /'steɪdʒɪlɪ/ *adv.* betont auffällig ‹sich kleiden›; affektiert ‹sich benehmen›

**staging** /'steɪdʒɪŋ/ *n., no indef. art.* **A** Gerüst, *das;* (*used as stage*) Bühne, *die;* **B** (*Hort.: shelves*) Regale; **C** (*Theatre: production*) Inszenierung, *die*

**staging:** ~ **area** *n.* (*Mil.*) Sammelplatz, *der;* ~ **post** *n.* Zwischenstation, *die*

**stagnant** /'stægnənt/ *adj.* **A** (*motionless*) stehend ‹Gewässer›; **the water is** ~**:** das Wasser steht; **B** (*fig.: lifeless*) abgestumpft ‹Geist, Seele›; stagnierend ‹Wirtschaft›; dumpf ‹Leben›; **the economy is** ~**:** die Wirtschaft stagniert

**stagnate** /stæg'neɪt/ *v.i.* **A** ‹Wasser usw.:› abstehen; **B** (*fig.*) ‹Wirtschaft, Geschäft:› stagnieren; ‹Geist, Künstler:› in Lethargie verfallen; ‹Person:› abstumpfen

**stagnation** /stæg'neɪʃn/ *n., no pl.* **A** (*of water etc.*) Stehen, *das;* **B** (*fig.*) Stagnation, *die*

**stag:** ~ **night** *n. Zechabend des Bräutigams mit seinen Freunden kurz vor seiner Hochzeit;* ~ **party** *n.* Herrenabend, *der;* (*before wedding*) *Trinkgelage des Bräutigams mit seinen Freunden kurz vor seiner Hochzeit*

**stagy** /'steɪdʒɪ/ *adj.* theatralisch; **be a** ~ **dresser** sich betont auffällig kleiden; **they have a** ~ **manner** sie benehmen sich wie die Schauspieler

**staid** /steɪd/ *adj.* **A** (*steady, sedate*) gesetzt; **lead a** ~ **existence** ein gleichförmiges Leben führen; **B** (*serious*) bieder

**staidly** /'steɪdlɪ/ *adv.* **A** (*soberly*) bieder; **B** (*sedately*) ruhig

**stain** /steɪn/ **1** *v.t.* **A** (*discolour*) verfärben; (*make* ~**s** *on*) Flecken hinterlassen auf (+ *Dat.*); **B** (*fig.: besmirch*) beflecken; besudeln (*geh. abwertend*); **C** (*colour*) färben; beizen ‹Holz›; **D** (*Biol.: impregnate*) anfärben. **2** *v.i.* sich verfärben; (*take* ~*s*) Flecken bekommen. **3** *n.* **A** (*discoloration*) Fleck, *der;* **B** (*fig.: blemish*) Schandfleck, *der;* **without a** ~ **on his character** mit einem fleckenlosen Charakter *od.* (*fig.*) einer fleckenlosen Weste; **C** (*colouring-material*) Beize, *die;* **D** (*Biol.*) Farbstoff, *der*

**stained 'glass** *n.* farbiges Glas; Farbglas, *das;* **the** ~ **at the church** die farbigen Glasfenster *od.* die Glasmalereien in der Kirche; **stained-glass window** Fenster mit Glasmalerei

**stainless** /'steɪnlɪs/ *adj.* **A** (*spotless*) fleckenlos; **B** (*non-rusting*) rostfrei

**stainless 'steel** *n.* Edelstahl, *der*

**'stain remover** *n.* Fleck[en]entferner, *der*

**stair** /steə(r)/ *n.* **A** (*set of steps*) ~**s,** (*arch./Scot.*) ~**:** Treppe, *die;* **below** ~**s** in den Wirtschaftsräumen [im Souterrain]; **B** (*step*) [Treppen]stufe, *die;* **C** *in pl.* (*landing stage*) Landungssteg, *der.* ⇒ *also* **downstairs; flight**[1] 1 D; **upstairs**

**stair:** ~ **carpet** ⇒ **carpet** 1 A; ~**carpeting** ⇒ **carpeting** A; ~**case** *n.* Treppenhaus, *das;* (*one flight*) Treppe, *die;* **on the** ~**case** auf der Treppe; ⇒ *also* **spiral staircase; winding staircase;** ~**head** ⇒ **landing** D; ~ **rod** *n.* Läuferstange, *die;* **it's raining** ~ **rods** (*coll.*) es regnet Bindfäden (*ugs.*); ~**way** *n.* **A** (*access via* ~*s*) Treppenaufgang, *der;* **B** (~*case*) Treppe, *die;* ~**well** *n.* Treppenhaus, *das*

**stake** /steɪk/ **1** *n.* **A** (*pointed stick*) Pfahl, *der;* **pull up** ~**s** (*Amer. fig. coll.*) seine Zelte abbrechen; **B** (*wager*) Einsatz, *der;* **be at** ~**:** auf dem Spiel stehen; **at** ~ **is the Gold Medal** es geht um die Goldmedaille; **have a lot of money at** ~ **on a project** viel Geld in ein Projekt gesteckt haben; **have a** ~ **in sth.** in etw. (*Akk.*) investiert haben; **have a 50%** ~ **in a firm** einen fünfzigprozentigen Anteil an einer Firma halten; **C** *in pl.* (*Horseracing*) (*prize money*) Geldpreis, *der;* (*race*) [Wett]rennen um einen Geldpreis; **D** (*for execution*) **be burnt at the** ~**:** auf dem Scheiterhaufen verbrannt werden; **go to the** ~ **for sth.** (*fig.*) sich für etw. kreuzigen lassen.

**2** *v.t.* **A** (*secure*) [an einem Pfahl/an Pfählen] anbinden; ~ **sth. down** etw. einpflocken; ~ **a claim [to sb./sth.]** ⇒ **claim** 3 E; **B** (*wager*) setzen (**on** auf + *Akk.*); **C** (*risk*) aufs Spiel setzen (**on** für); **I'll** ~ **my reputation on his innocence** ich verbürge mich mit meinem guten Namen für seine Unschuld; ~ **one's life on sth.** seinen Kopf auf etw. (*Akk.*) wetten (*ugs.*); **you can** ~ **your life on that** darauf kannst du Gift nehmen (*ugs.*); **D** (*Amer. coll.: finance*) ~ **sb.** jmdm. finanziell unter die Arme greifen; ~ **a business/venture** Geld in ein Geschäft/Unternehmen stecken

~ **'off** *v.t.* [mit Pfählen] abstecken

~ **'out** *v.t.* **A** (*mark out*) mit Pfählen begrenzen; eingrenzen; **B** (*fig.: claim*) beanspruchen; **have** ~**d out a field of study as one's own** ein Fachgebiet für sich alleine gepachtet haben (*ugs.*); **C** (*Amer. coll.: observe*) überwachen; ⇒ *also* **stake-out**

**stake:** ~ **boat** *n.* (*Rowing*) *verankertes Boot, das die Rennstrecke bei einem Bootsrennen markiert;* ~ **net** *n.* Schockernetz, *das;* ~**-out** *n.* (*Amer. coll.*) Überwachung, *die*

**stalactite** /'stæləktaɪt/ *n.* (*Geol.*) Stalaktit, *der*

**stalagmite** /'stæləgmaɪt/ *n.* (*Geol.*) Stalagmit, *der*

**stale** /steɪl/ **1** *adj.* **A** alt; muffig; abgestanden ‹Luft›; alt[backen] ‹Brot›; schal ‹Bier, Wein usw.›; (*fig.*) abgedroschen ‹Witz, Trick›; überholt ‹Nachricht›; **B** (*jaded*) ausgelaugt. **2** *v.t.* alt werden lassen ‹Lebensmittel›; auslaugen ‹Sportler, Schauspieler›

**'stalemate** **1** *n.* (*Chess; also fig.*) Patt, *das;* **end in** *or* **reach** ~**:** mit einem Patt enden. **2** *v.t.* **A** (*Chess*) ~ **sb.** jmdn. in eine Pattsituation bringen; **B** (*fig.: halt*) zum Stillstand bringen; aufhalten ‹Verfahren›; verhindern ‹Fortschritte›

**staleness** /'steɪlnɪs/ *n., no pl.* **A** (*lack of freshness*) Muffigkeit, *die;* (*of air*) Abgestandenheit, *die;* (*of bread*) Altbackenheit, *die;* (*of beer etc.*) Schalheit, *die;* (*fig.: lack of novelty*) Abgedroschenheit, *die;* (*of news*) Überholtheit, *die;* **B** (*jadedness*) Ausgelaugtheit, *die*

**Stalinism** /'stɑ:lɪnɪzm/ *n.* (*Polit.*) Stalinismus, *der*

**Stalinist** /'stɑ:lɪnɪst/ *n.* (*Polit.*) Stalinist, *der*/Stalinistin, *die*

**stalk**[1] /stɔ:k/ **1** *v.i.* **A** stolzieren; ~ **along** einherschreiten/-stolzieren (*geh.*); **B** (*Hunting*) pirschen; **be** ~**ing** auf der Pirsch sein. **2** *v.t.* **A** sich heranpirschen an (+ *Akk.*); **B** (*follow obsessively*) ~ **sb.** jmdm. nachstellen

**stalk**[2] /stɔ:k/ *n.* **A** (*Bot.*) (*main stem*) Stängel, *der;* (*of leaf, flower, fruit*) Stiel, *der;* (*of cabbage*) Strunk, *der;* **B** (*Zool.*) Stiel, *der;* (*of crab etc.*) [Augen]stiel, *der;* **his eyes stood** *or* **were out on** ~**s** (*fig.*) er machte *od.* bekam Stielaugen (*ugs.*)

**stalker** /'stɔ:kə(r)/ *n.* **A** Pirscher, *der;* **B** (*obsessive pursuer*) [lästiger] Verfolger

**stall**[1] /stɔ:l/ **1** *n.* **A** Stand, *der;* **B** (*for horse*) Box, *die;* (*for cow*) Stand, *der;* **C** (*Eccl.: seat*) Stuhl, *der;* **the choir** ~**s** das Chorgestühl; **D** *in pl.* (*Brit. Theatre: seats*) **[front]** ~**s** Parkett, *das;* **in the rear/cheap** ~**s** auf den hinteren/billigen Parkettplätzen; **E** (*Brit. Horseracing*) **the [starting]** ~**s** die Startboxen; **F** (*of engine*) Stehenbleiben, *das;* **G** (*Aeronaut.*) Überziehen, *das;* **go into a** ~**:** durchsacken. **2** *v.t.* abwürgen (*ugs.*) ‹Motor›. **3** *v.i.* **A** ‹Motor:› stehen bleiben; **B** (*Aeronaut.*) durchzusacken beginnen

**stall**[2] **1** *v.i.* ausweichen; ~ **on a promise** (*delay*) die Einlösung eines Versprechens hinauszögern; **quit** ~**ing!** (*Amer. coll.*) hör auf, drum herumzureden! (*ugs.*). **2** *v.t.* blockieren ‹Gesetz, Fortschritt›; aufhalten ‹Feind, Fortschritt›

**'stallholder** *n.* Standinhaber, *der*/-inhaberin, *die*

**stallion** /'stæljən/ *n.* Hengst, *der*

**stalwart** /'stɔ:lwət/ **1** *adj.* **A** (*sturdy*) stämmig; **B** *attrib.* (*fig.: determined*) entschieden; entschlossen ‹Kämpfer›; (*loyal*) treu; getreu (*geh.*). **2** *n.* (*loyal supporter*) treuer Anhänger/treue Anhängerin; **Party** ~**:** treues Parteimitglied

**stamen** /'steɪmen, 'steɪmən/ *n.* (*Bot.*) Staubblatt, *das*

**stamina** /'stæmɪnə/ *n.* **A** (*physical staying power*) Ausdauer, *die;* **B** (*endurance*) Durchhaltevermögen, *das*

**stammer** /'stæmə(r)/ **1** *v.i.* stottern. **2** *v.t.* stammeln; ~ **[out] one's thanks/apologies** stammelnd danken/eine Entschuldigung stammeln. **3** *n.* Stottern, *das;* **have a** ~, **speak with a** ~**:** stottern

**stammerer** /'stæmərə(r)/ *n.* Stotterer, *der*/Stotterin, *die*

**stamp** /stæmp/ **1** *v.t.* **A** (*impress, imprint sth. on*) [ab]stempeln; ~ **sth. on sth.** etw. auf etw. (*Akk.*) [auf]stempeln; ~ **envelopes with sth.** etw. auf Umschläge drucken; **B** ~ **one's foot/feet** mit dem Fuß/den Füßen stampfen; ~ **the snow from one's boots** den Schnee von den Stiefeln stampfen; ~ **the floor** *or* **ground [in anger/with rage]** [ärgerlich/wütend] auf den Boden stampfen; **C** (*put postage* ~ *on*) frankieren; freimachen (*Postw.*); ~**ed addressed envelope** frankierter Rückumschlag; **D** (*mentally*) ~ **oneself/itself** *or* **become** *or* **be** ~**ed on sb.['s memory** *or* **mind]** sich jmdm. fest einprägen; **E** (*crush*) zerstampfen; **F** (*flatten*) ~ **flat** platt stampfen *od.* treten ‹Schachtel, Dose›; ~ **down** feststampfen *od.* -treten ‹Erde, Schnee, Steine›; **G** (*characterize*) kennzeichnen; ~ **sb. [as] a genius** zeigen, dass jmd. ein Genie ist.

**2** *v.i.* aufstampfen; ~ **up and down** auf und ab stampfen.

**3** *n.* **A** Marke, *die;* (*postage* ~) Briefmarke, *die;* ⇒ *also* **first-class** 1 A; **insurance stamp; second-class** 1 B; **trading stamp; B** (*instrument for* ~*ing, mark*) Stempel, *der;* **C** (*fig.: characteristic*) **bear the** ~ **of genius/greatness** Genialität/Größe erkennen lassen; **leave one's** ~ **on sth.** einer Sache seinen Stempel aufdrücken; **D** (*fig.: kind*) [Menschen]schlag, *der;* **men of his** ~**:** Menschen seines Schlages *od.* seiner Prägung

~ **on** *v.t.* **A** (*crush*) zertreten ‹Insekt, Dose›; zertrampeln ‹Blumen›; ~ **on sb.'s foot** jmdm. auf den Fuß treten; **B** (*suppress*) durchgreifen gegen. ⇒ *also* ~ 1 A, D

~ **'out** *v.t.* **A** (*eliminate*) ausmerzen; ersticken ‹Aufstand, Feuer›; niederwalzen ‹Opposition, Widerstand›; **B** (*cut out*) [aus]stanzen

**stamp:** ~ **album** *n.* Briefmarkenalbum, *das;* ~ **book** *n.* Briefmarkenheftchen, *das;* ~ **collecting** *n.* Briefmarkensammeln, *das;* ~ **collection** *n.* Briefmarkensammlung, *die;* ~ **collector** *n.* Briefmarkensammler, *der*/-sammlerin, *die;* ~ **duty** *n.* Stempelsteuer, *die*

**stampede** /stæm'pi:d/ **1** *n.* **A** Stampede, *die;* **B** (*rush of people*) (*due to interest*) Ansturm, *der;* (*due to panic*) wilde Flucht; **C** (*Amer. Polit.*) starker Zulauf. **2** *v.i.* **A** in

Panik fliehen; **B** (*rush*) ‹Personen:› stürmen. ❸ *v.t.* **A** ~ **a herd** bei einer Herde eine Stampede auslösen; **B** ~ **sb. into doing sth.** jmdn. dazu drängen, etw. zu tun

**'stamp hinge** ⇒ hinge 1 C

**stamping-ground** /'stæmpɪŋgraʊnd/ *n.* Revier, *das;* **one's old ~:** der Ort, wo man früher immer zu finden war

**'stamp machine** *n.* Briefmarkenautomat, *der*

**stance** /stæns, stɑːns/ *n.* **A** (*Golf, Cricket: position*) Stellung, *die;* **B** (*posture; fig.: attitude*) Haltung, *die;* **take up a ~ over** *or* **on sth.** (*fig.*) eine Haltung zu etw. einnehmen

**stanch** /stɑːnʃ, stɔːnʃ/ *v.t.* **A** (*stop flow of*) stillen ‹Blut›; **B** (*stop flow from*) abbinden ‹Wunde›

**stanchion** /'stɑːnʃn/ *n.* Stütze, *die;* (*of flat wagon*) Runge, *die;* (*of awning*) Sonnensegelstütze, *die*

**stand** /stænd/ ❶ *v.i.*, **stood** /stʊd/ **A** stehen; **all ~!** aufstehen!; **don't just ~ there [, do something]!** steh nicht so herum[, tu doch etwas!]; **~ for the National Anthem/for a minute's silence** zur Nationalhymne/zu einer Schweigeminute aufstehen; **~ in a line** *or* **row** sich in einer Reihe aufstellen; (*be ~ing*) in einer Reihe stehen; **we stood talking** wir standen da und unterhielten uns; **~ or fall by sth.** (*fig.*) mit etw. stehen und fallen; **~ empty** leer stehen; ⇒ *also* **standstill**; **B** (*have height*) **he ~s six feet tall/the tree ~s 30 feet high** er ist sechs Fuß groß/der Baum ist 30 Fuß hoch; **~ high above sb./sth.** (*fig.*) [rangmäßig] weit über jmdm. stehen/etw. bei weitem übersteigen; **C** (*be at level*) ‹Aktien, Währung, Thermometer:› stehen (**at** auf + *Dat.*); ‹Fonds:› sich belaufen (**at** auf + *Akk.*); ‹Absatz, Export usw.:› liegen (**at** bei); **D** (*hold good*) bestehen bleiben; **my decision still ~s** an meiner Entscheidung hat sich nichts geändert; **my offer/promise still ~s** mein Angebot/Versprechen gilt nach wie vor; **E** (*find oneself, be*) **~ first in line for the throne** in der Thronfolge der Erste sein; **~ convicted of treachery** wegen Verrats verurteilt sein; **as it ~s, as things ~:** wie die Dinge [jetzt] liegen; **the law as it ~s** das bestehende *od.* gültige Recht; **the matter ~s thus** die Sache steht so; **~ prepared to dispute sth.** bereit sein, über etw. (*Akk.*) zu diskutieren; **as a statesman he ~s alone in contemporary politics** (*fig.*) es gibt in der gegenwärtigen Politik keinen, der ihm als Staatsmann das Wasser reichen könnte; **I'd like to know where I ~** (*fig.*) ich möchte wissen, wo ich dran bin; **~ in need** Not leiden; **~ in need of sth.** einer Sache (*Gen.*) dringend bedürfen; **F** (*be candidate*) kandidieren (**for** für); **~ in an election** bei einer Wahl kandidieren; **~ as a candidate/nominee** kandidieren/nominiert sein; **~ as a Liberal/Conservative** für die Liberalen/Konservativen kandidieren; **~ for Parliament** (*Brit.*) für einen Parlamentssitz kandidieren; **~ for office** (*Brit.*) sich um ein Amt bewerben; **G** **~ proxy for sb.** jmdn. vertreten; **H** (*place oneself*) sich stellen; **~ from under sb.** *or* **sb.'s feet** (*Amer.*) jmdm. nicht ständig vor den Füßen herumlaufen; **~ in the way of sth.** (*fig.*) einer Sache (*Dat.*) im Weg stehen; **[not] ~ in sb.'s way** (*fig.*) jmdm. [keine] Steine in den Weg legen; **I** (*be likely*) **~ to win** *or* **gain/lose sth.** etw. gewinnen/verlieren können; **what do I ~ to gain from/by it?** was kann ich dabei gewinnen?; **J** (*Cricket: be umpire*) schiedsrichtern; **K** (*Naut.: hold course*) **~ in for** *or* **towards sth.** Kurs auf etw. (*Akk.*) nehmen; **~ into danger** auf eine Gefahr zusteuern. ⇒ *also* **correct** 1 A; **deliver** D; **ease** 1 F; **easy** 2; **fast**$^{2}$ 2 A; **firm**$^{2}$ 2; **foot** 1 A; **leg** 1 A; **light**$^{1}$ 1 A; **pat**$^{2}$ A.

❷ *v.t.*, **stood** **A** (*set in position*) stellen; **~ sth. on end/upside down** etw. hochkant/auf den Kopf stellen; **B** (*endure*) ertragen; vertragen ‹Klima›; **I can't ~ the heat/noise** ich halte die Hitze/den Lärm nicht aus; **I cannot ~ [the sight of] him/her** ich kann ihn/sie nicht ausstehen; **he can't ~ the pressure/strain/stress** er ist dem Druck/den Strapazen/dem Stress nicht gewachsen; **I can't ~ it any longer!** ich halte es nicht mehr aus; **~ closer examination** einer genaueren [Über]prüfung standhalten; **~ the test of time** sich bewähren; **he can't ~ being told what to do** er kann es nicht leiden *od.* ausstehen, wenn man ihm Vorschriften macht; **C** (*undergo*) ausgesetzt sein (+ *Dat.*); **the play/player has stood much criticism** das Stück/der Spieler stieß auf viel Kritik; **~ trial [for sth.]** [wegen einer Sache] vor Gericht stehen; **D** (*buy*) **~ sb. sth.** jmdm. etw. ausgeben *od.* spendieren (*ugs.*); **can I ~ you a lunch?** Gehen wir zusammen was essen? Ich lade dich ein. ⇒ *also* **chance** 1 C; **ground**$^{1}$ 1 B; **pace**$^{1}$ 1 B; **treat** 1 C.

❸ *n.* **A** (*support*) Ständer, *der;* **B** (*stall; at exhibition*) Stand, *der;* **C** (*raised structure*) Tribüne, *die;* **D** (*resistance*) Widerstand, *der;* **put up a brave ~ against sb./sth.** jmdm./einer Sache tapfer Widerstand leisten; **take** *or* **make a ~** (*fig.*) klar Stellung beziehen (**for/against/on** für/gegen/zu); **E** (*Cricket*) **a ~ of 90 runs** eine gemeinsame Serie von 90 Läufen; **F** (*~ing-place for taxi, bus, etc.*) Stand, *der;* **G** (*performance on tour*) Auftritt, *der;* **H** (*of trees, corn, clover, etc.*) Bestand, *der;* **I** (*position*) **take one's ~:** sich aufstellen; **take one's ~ on the podium** seinen Platz auf der Tribüne einnehmen; **take a [firm] ~ [on sth.]** [in etw. (*Dat.*)] einen festen Standpunkt vertreten; **what's your ~ [on this matter]?** welchen Standpunkt vertrittst du [in dieser Sache]? **J** (*Amer.: witness box*) Zeugenstand, *der;* **take the ~:** in den Zeugenstand treten. ⇒ *also* **grandstand**; **one-night stand**

**~ a'bout, ~ a'round** *v.i.* herumstehen

**~ a'side** *v.i.* **A** (*step aside*) zur Seite treten; Platz machen; **B** (*fig.: withdraw*) abseits stehen; **~ aside from sth.** sich an etw. nicht beteiligen

**~ 'back** *v.i.* **A** **~ [well] back [from sth.]** [ein gutes Stück] [von etw.] entfernt stehen; **B** ⇒ **~ aside** A; **C** (*fig.: distance oneself*) zurücktreten; **sometimes one must ~ back from daily affairs** von Zeit zu Zeit muss man von seinen Alltagsgeschäften Abstand gewinnen; **D** (*fig.: withdraw*) **~ back from sth.** sich aus einer Sache heraushalten

**~ behind** *v.t.* **~ behind sb./sth.** (*lit. or fig.*) hinter jmdm./etw. stehen

**~ between** *v.t.* **sth. ~s between sb. and sth.** (*fig.*) etw. steht jmdm. bei etw. im Wege

**~ by** ❶ /-'-/ *v.i.* **A** (*remain apart*) abseits stehen; **~ [idly] by and watch sth. happen** *or* **while sth. happens** untätig zusehen, wie etw. geschieht; **~ by and do nothing to prevent sth.** sich abseits halten und nicht eingreifen, um etw. zu verhindern; **B** (*be near*) daneben stehen; **C** (*be ready*) sich zur Verfügung halten; **~ by ready to do sth.** Gewehr bei Fuß stehen, um etw. zu tun. ❷ /'--/ *v.t.* **A** (*support*) **~ by sb./one another** jmdm./sich [gegenseitig] *od.* (*geh.*) einander beistehen; **B** (*adhere to*) **~ by sth.** zu etw. stehen; **~ by the terms of a contract** einen Vertrag einhalten; **~ by a promise** ein Versprechen halten; **~ by a resolution** einen Beschluss [in die Tat] umsetzen; **C** (*Naut.: prepare to use*) klarmachen. ⇒ *also* **standby**

**~ 'down** ❶ *v.i.* **A** (*withdraw, retire*) verzichten; **~ down in favour of a person** zugunsten einer Person (*Gen.*) zurücktreten; **B** (*leave witness box*) den Zeugenstand verlassen; **C** (*Brit. Mil.: go off duty*) seinen Posten verlassen; **~ down from guard duty** seinen Wachdienst beenden; **D** (*Mil.: disband*) sich auflösen. ❷ *v.t.* **A** (*Brit. Mil.: relieve from duty*) abziehen; **B** (*Mil.: disband*) auflösen

**~ for** *v.t.* **A** (*signify*) bedeuten; **she hates him and all that he ~s for** sie hasst ihn und alles, was mit ihm zusammenhängt; **B** (*represent*) **~ for sb./sth.** für jmdn./etw. eintreten; sich für jmdn./etw. einsetzen; **C** ⇒ **stand** 1 F; **D** (*coll.: tolerate*) sich bieten lassen; **that's one thing I won't ~ for** das ist etwas, was ich nicht haben kann

**~ 'in** *v.i.* **A** (*deputize*) aushelfen; **~ in for sb.** für jmdn. einspringen; **B** (*share*) **~ in with sb. [for sth.]** mit jmdm. die Kosten [für etw.] teilen; **C** (*Naut.*) ⇒ **stand** 1 K. ⇒ *also* **stand-in**

**~ 'off** ❶ *v.i.* (*move away*) sich entfernen; (*keep away*) sich in einiger Entfernung halten. ❷ *v.t.* ⇒ **lay**$^{2}$ **off** 1 A

**~ 'out** *v.i.* **A** (*persist*) **~ out for/against sth.** hartnäckig für etw. kämpfen/sich hartnäckig gegen etw. wehren; **B** (*be prominent*) herausragen; **the reason for the crisis ~s out** der Grund für die Krise ist augenfällig; **~ out against** *or* **in contrast to sth.** sich gegen etw. abheben; **~ out a mile** nicht zu übersehen sein; ‹Grund, Antwort:› [klar] auf der Hand liegen; **C** (*be outstanding*) herausragen (**from** aus); **D** (*Naut.*) **~ out to sea** in See gehen

**~ over** ❶ *v.t.* **A** /-'--/ ⇒ **hold over**; **B** /'---/ (*watch*) beaufsichtigen. ❷ /-'--/ *v.i.* **sth. can ~ over** etw. kann warten; **any unfinished business ~s over to the next meeting** alle unerledigten Punkte werden bis zum nächsten Treffen zurückgestellt

**~ to** ⇒ **~ by** 1 D; ⇒ *also* **reason** 1 B

**~ to'gether** *v.i.* zusammenstehen; (*for a photograph*) sich [gemeinsam] aufstellen; (*fig.*) zusammenhalten

**~ 'up** ❶ *v.i.* **A** (*rise*) aufstehen; **~ up and be counted** (*fig.*) Farbe bekennen; **B** (*be upright*) stehen; **I have only the clothes I ~ up in** ich besitze nur die Kleider, die ich am Leibe trage; **~ up straight** sich aufrecht hinstellen; **C** (*be valid*) ⇒ **hold**$^{2}$ 2 D; **D** **~ up well [in comparison with sb./sth.]** [im Vergleich zu jmdm./etw.] gut abschneiden; (*maintain worth or position*) ‹Preis, Wert:› sich [im Vergleich zu etw.] gut halten. ❷ *v.t.* **A** (*put upright*) aufstellen; [wieder] hinstellen ‹Fahrrad, Stuhl usw.›; **B** (*coll.: fail to keep date with*) **~ sb. up** jmdn. versetzen (*ugs.*). ⇒ *also* **stand-up**

**~ 'up for** *v.t.* **~ up for sb./sth.** für jmdn./etw. Partei ergreifen; sich für jmdn./etw. stark machen; **why didn't you ~ up for me?** warum hast du mich nicht unterstützt?

**~ 'up to** *v.t.* **A** (*face steadfastly*) **~ up to sb.** sich jmdm. entgegenstellen; jmdm. die Stirn bieten; **~ up to sth.** sich einer Sache (*Dat.*) stellen; **~ up to an ordeal well/badly** eine Tortur tapfer/nicht aushalten; **~ up to criticism** sich von Kritik nicht beirren lassen; **B** (*survive intact under*) **~ up to sth.** einer Sache (*Dat.*) standhalten; **~ up to wear and tear** eine starke Beanspruchung aushalten

**stand-alone** /stændə'ləʊn/ *adj.* (*Computing*) selbstständig

**standard** /'stændəd/ ❶ *n.* **A** (*norm*) Maßstab, *der;* **safety ~s** Sicherheitsnormen; **above/below/up to ~:** überdurchschnittlich [gut]/unter dem Durchschnitt/der Norm entsprechend; **by anybody's ~s** für jeden; **B** (*degree*) Niveau, *das;* **of [a] high/low ~:** von hohem/niedrigem Niveau; **a high ~ of competence** ein hohes Maß an Kompetenz; **set a high/low ~ in** *or* **of sth.** hohe/niedrige Ansprüche an etw. (*Akk.*) stellen; **the first competitor set a high ~:** der erste Bewerber setzte einen hohen Maßstab; **this pupil sets himself too low a ~ in his work** dieser Schüler verlangt zu wenig von sich selbst; **~ of living** Lebensstandard, *der;* **C** *in pl.* (*moral principles*) Prinzipien; **~s of sexual behaviour** Maßstäbe für das Sexualverhalten; **D** (*flag*) Standarte, *die;* (*fig.: cause*) Banner, *das* (*geh.*); **many flocked to the ~** (*fig.*) viele strömten zur Fahne; **E** (*Hort.*) Hochstamm, *der;* **~ rose** Hochstammrose, *die;* **F** (*Bot.*) **~ [shrub]** natürlich gewachsener Strauch; **~ [tree]** Baum mit naturgemäßem Kronenaufbau; **G** **lamp ~** ⇒ **lamp post**; **H** (*in currency*) Feingehalt, *der;* Standard, *der;* **the silver/monetary ~:** der Silberstandard/Münzfuß. ⇒ *also* **double standard**; **gold standard**; **royal standard**.

❷ *adj.* **A** (*conforming to ~, authoritative*) Standard-; (*used as reference*) Normal-; **B** (*widely used*) normal; **what is the ~ thing** to do in such cases? was macht man normalerweise in solchen Fällen?; **be ~ procedure** Vorschrift sein; **have sth.** *or* **include sth.** *or* **be fitted with sth. as ~:** serienmäßig mit etw. ausgerüstet sein; **sth. is a ~ feature** etw. gehört zur Standardausrüstung; **a ~ letter** ein Schemabrief (*Bürow.*); **a ~ model** ein Standardmodell; **be ~ practice** allgemein üblich sein; **it is ~ practice for sb. to do sth.** es ist üblich, dass jmd. etw. tut; **follow the ~ pattern** dem üblichen Muster folgen

**standard: ~-bearer** *n.* Ⓐ (*Mil.: flagbearer*) Standartenträger, *der;* Ⓑ (*fig.: leader*) Bannerträger, *der/-trägerin, die* (*geh.*); Vorkämpfer, *der/-kämpferin, die;* **~-bearer for** *or* **in sth.** Vorkämpfer einer Sache (*Gen.*); **S~bred** *n.* (*Amer.*) Amerikanischer Traber; **S~ 'English** *n.* Standardenglisch, *das*

**standardisation, standardise** ⇒ **standardiz-**

**standardization** /stændədaɪ'zeɪʃn/ *n.* Standardisierung, *die*

**standardize** /'stændədaɪz/ *v.t.* standardisieren

**standard: ~ 'lamp** *n.* (*Brit.*) Stehlampe, *die;* **~ time** *n.* Normalzeit, *die*

**'standby** ❶ *n., pl.* **~s** Ⓐ (*reserve*) **[act] as a ~:** als Ersatz [bereitstehen]; **be on ~** ‹Polizei, Feuerwehr, Truppen:› einsatzbereit sein; ‹Schauspieler:› sich bereithalten; ‹Flugzeug:› startbereit sein; **the army was put on ~:** die Armee wurde in Einsatzbereitschaft versetzt; Ⓑ (*resource*) Rückhalt, *der;* **sth. is a good ~:** auf etw. (*Akk.*) kann man jederzeit zurückgreifen; **drink was his only ~:** das Trinken war seine einzige Zuflucht; **have some tins of food/an emergency pack as a ~:** einige Konserven für Notfälle/einen Notvorrat haben; **the generator is a ~:** der Generator dient als Notaggregat.
❷ *attrib. adj.* Ersatz-; **~ safety equipment** zusätzliche Sicherheitsausrüstung; **~ ticket/passenger** Stand-by-Ticket, *das*/-Passagier, *der*

**standee** /stæn'di:/ *n.* (*Amer. coll.*) stehender Passagier/Zuschauer

**'stand-in** ❶ *n.* Ersatz, *der;* (*in theatre, film*) Ersatzdarsteller, *der/-darstellerin, die;* (*Sport*) Ersatzspieler, *der/-spielerin, die.* ❷ *attrib. adj.* Ersatz-

**standing** /'stændɪŋ/ ❶ *n.* Ⓐ (*repute*) Ansehen, *das;* **have some ~:** recht angesehen sein; **be of** *or* **have [a] high ~:** ein hohes Ansehen genießen; **have no ~:** ein Niemand sein; **what is his ~?** welchen Rang bekleidet er?; **be in good ~ with sb.** sich gut mit jmdm. stehen; ⇒ *also* **equal** 1 A; Ⓑ (*service*) **be an MP of twenty years' ~:** seit zwanzig Jahren [ununterbrochen] dem Parlament angehören; **be a member/judge of long/short ~:** seit langem/kurzem Mitglied/Richter sein; **a girlfriend of long ~:** eine langjährige Freundin; ⇒ *also* **long-standing;** Ⓒ (*duration*) **of long/short ~:** von langer/kurzer Dauer; **a feud of long ~:** ein alter Zwist; Ⓓ **~ place** Standplatz, *der.*
❷ *adj.* Ⓐ (*erect*) stehend; **after the storm there was scarcely a tree still ~:** nach dem Sturm stand kaum mehr ein Baum; **~ corn** stehendes Korn; **~ stone** Menhir, *der;* **leave sb. ~** (*lit. or fig.: progress much faster*) jmdn. weit hinter sich (*Dat.*) lassen; Ⓑ *attrib.* (*established*) fest ‹Regel, Brauch›; **he has a ~ excuse** er bringt immer die gleiche Entschuldigung; ⇒ *also* **joke** 1 B; Ⓒ *attrib.* (*permanent*) stehend ‹Heer›; feststehend ‹Praxis›; **I have a ~ invitation to visit them whenever I want to** sie haben mich eingeladen, sie, wann immer ich will, zu besuchen; Ⓓ *attrib.* (*stationary*) **~ jump** Standsprung, *der;* **~ start** Hochstart, *der*

**standing: ~ com'mittee** *n.* ständiger Ausschuss; **~ 'order** *n.* Ⓐ (*payment instruction*) Dauerauftrag, *der;* (*for regular supply*) Abonnement, *das;* Ⓑ *in pl.* (*rules*) Geschäftsordnung, *die;* **~ o'vation** *n.* stürmischer Beifall; stehende Ovation (*geh.*); **~ room** *n., no pl., no indef. art.* Stehplätze; **~ 'water** *n.* stehendes Gewässer; (*Golf*) Wassergraben, *der;* **~ wave** *n.* (*Phys.*) stehende Welle

**'stand-off** *n.* Ⓐ (*Amer.: deadlock*) verfahrene Situation; **finish/result in a ~:** in einer Sackgasse enden/in eine Sackgasse geraten; Ⓑ **~ [half]** (*Rugby*) ⇒ **fly half**

**stand-offish** /stænd'ɒfɪʃ/ *adj.* reserviert

**stand: ~ 'patter** *n.* (*Amer. Polit.*) strammer Konservativer/stramme Konservative; **~pipe** *n.* (*for water supply*) Standrohr, *das;* **~point** *n.* Ⓐ (*observation point*) Standort, *der;* Ⓑ (*fig.: viewpoint*) Standpunkt, *der;* **~still** *n.* Stillstand, *der;* **be at a ~still** stillstehen; ‹Fahrzeug, Flugzeug:› stehen; ‹Produktion, Verkehr:› zum Erliegen gekommen sein; **come to a ~still** zum Stehen kommen; ‹Verhandlungen:› zum Stillstand kommen; **the traffic/production came to a ~still** der Verkehr/die Produktion kam zum Erliegen; **bring to a ~still** zum Stehen bringen; zum Erliegen bringen ‹Produktion›; **~-up** *adj.* **~-up fight** Schlägerei, *die*

**stank** ⇒ **stink** 1

**stanza** /'stænzə/ *n.* (*Pros.*) Strophe, *die*

**staple**[1] /'steɪpl/ ❶ *n.* (*for fastening paper*) [Heft]klammer, *die;* (*for fastening netting*) Krampe, *die.* ❷ *v.t.* (*with a stapler*) heften (**on to** an + *Akk.*); (*with a hammer*) krampen (**to** an + *Akk.*)

**staple**[2] ❶ *attrib. adj.* Ⓐ (*principal*) Grund-; **a ~ diet** *or* **food** ein Grundnahrungsmittel; Ⓑ (*Commerc.: important*) grundlegend; **~ goods** Haupthandelsartikel; **the ~ export of a country** das Hauptexportgut eines Landes. ❷ *n.* Ⓐ (*Commerc.: major item*) Haupterzeugnis, *das;* Ⓑ (*raw material*) Rohstoff, *der;* Ⓒ (*fig.: fundamental part*) **the ~ of conversation** das zentrale Thema der Unterhaltung; Ⓓ (*Textiles: fibre*) Faser, *die*

**stapler** /'steɪplə(r)/ *n.* [Draht]hefter, *der*

**star** /stɑ:(r)/ ❶ *n.* Ⓐ Stern, *der;* **reach for the ~s** (*fig.*) nach hohen Zielen streben; **three-~ general** (*Amer. Mil.*) Dreisternegeneral, *der;* **three/four ~ hotel** Drei-/Viersternehotel, *das;* **two/four ~ [petrol]** Normal-/Super[benzin], *das;* **the Stars and Stripes** (*Amer.*) das Sternenbanner; **the pupil got a ~ for his work** der Schüler erhielt für seine Arbeit ein Sternchen (*als Auszeichnung*); Ⓑ (*prominent person*) Star, *der;* **be a rising ~ [of the tennis world]** ein aufgehender Stern [am Tennishimmel] sein; Ⓒ (*asterisk*) Stern, *der;* Sternchen, *das;* Ⓓ (*Astrol.*) Stern, *der;* **read one's/the ~s** sein/das Horoskop lesen; **be born under an unlucky ~:** unter einem ungünstigen Stern geboren sein. ⇒ *also* **double star; evening star; morning star; see**[1] 1 A; **shooting star.**
❷ *attrib. adj.* Star-; **~ pupil** bester Schüler/beste Schülerin; **~ turn** *or* **attraction** Hauptattraktion, *die;* **receive ~ billing** als Star/Stars des Abends auftreten.
❸ *v.t.,* **-rr-:** Ⓐ (*decorate*) mit Sternen schmücken; **~red pattern** Sternenmuster, *das;* Ⓑ (*mark with asterisk*) mit einem Stern[chen] versehen; Ⓒ (*feature as ~*) **~ring Humphrey Bogart and Lauren Bacall** mit Humphrey Bogart und Lauren Bacall in den Hauptrollen; **the film ~red Newman and Redford** in dem Film spielten Newman und Redford die Hauptrollen.
❹ *v.i.,* **-rr-: ~ in a film/play/TV series** in einem Film/einem Stück/einer Fernsehserie die Hauptrolle spielen

**starboard** /'stɑ:bəd/ (*Naut., Aeronaut.*) ❶ *n.* Steuerbord, *das;* **land to ~!** Land an Steuerbord!; **turn** *or* **put the helm to ~:** nach Steuerbord drehen. ❷ *adj.* steuerbord-; steuerbordseitig; **on the ~ bow/quarter** Steuerbord voraus/achteraus; ⇒ *also* **tack**[1] 1 C; **watch** 1 C

**starch** /stɑ:tʃ/ ❶ *n.* Ⓐ Stärke, *die;* Ⓑ (*fig.*) Steifheit, *die.* ❷ *v.t.* stärken

**Star 'Chamber** *n.* Ⓐ (*Brit. Hist.*) Sternkammer, *die* (*Gericht zur Verfolgung von Straftaten gegen die Krone*); Ⓑ (*fig.: tribunal*) ≈ Volksgerichtshof, *der* (*fig.*)

**starched** /stɑ:tʃt/ *adj.* gestärkt; (*fig.*) steif

**'starch-reduced** *adj.* stärkearm

**starchy** /'stɑ:tʃɪ/ *adj.* Ⓐ (*containing much starch*) stärkehaltig ‹Nahrungsmittel›; Ⓑ (*fig.: prim*) steif

**'star-crossed** *adj.* **they were ~ lovers** ihre Liebe stand unter einem schlechten Stern

**stardom** /'stɑ:dəm/ *n.* Starruhm, *der*

**stare** /steə(r)/ ❶ *v.i.* Ⓐ (*gaze*) starren; **~ in surprise/amazement** überrascht/erstaunt starren; **~ in horror** erschreckt starren; **~ at sb./sth.** jmdn./etw. anstarren; **it is rude to ~ at people** es ist unhöflich, andere [Leute] anzustarren; Ⓑ (*have fixed gaze*) starr blicken.
❷ *v.t.* **~ sb. into silence** jmdn. durch Anstarren zum Schweigen bringen; **~ sb. in the face** jmdn. [feindselig] fixieren; (*fig.*) jmdm. ins Auge springen; **ruin was staring him in the face** ihm drohte der Ruin; **I looked for my purse for ages and it was staring me in the face all the time** ich suchte eine Ewigkeit mein Portemonnaie, und dabei lag es die ganze Zeit direkt vor meiner Nase (*ugs.*).
❸ *n.* Starren, *das;* **fix sb. with a [curious/malevolent] ~:** jmdn. [neugierig/böse] anstarren

**~ 'down, ~ 'out** *v.t.* **~ sb. down** *or* **out** jmds. Blick niederzwingen (*geh.*); jmdn. so lange anstarren, bis er/sie die Augen abwendet

**star: ~fish** *n.* Seestern, *der;* **~gazer** /'stɑ:geɪzə(r)/ *n.* (*coll.*) Sterngucker, *der* (*ugs. scherzh.*)

**staring** /'steərɪŋ/ *attrib. adj.* starrend ‹Augen›; **with ~ eyes** mit starrem Blick; **be stark ~ mad** (*fig. coll.*) völlig verrückt sein (*ugs.*)

**stark** /stɑ:k/ ❶ *adj.* Ⓐ (*bleak*) öde; spröde ‹Schönheit, Dichtung›; Ⓑ (*obvious*) scharf umrissen; nackt ‹Wahrheit›; scharf ‹Kontrast, Umriss›; krass ‹Unterschied, Gegensatz, Realismus›; **be in ~ contrast [to sb./sth.]** sich stark unterscheiden [von jmdm./etw.]; Ⓒ (*extreme*) schier ‹Entsetzen, Dummheit›; nackt ‹Armut, Angst›. ❷ *adv.* völlig; **~ naked** splitternackt (*ugs.*); ⇒ *also* **staring**

**starkers** /stɑ:kəz/ *pred. adj.* (*Brit. coll.*) splitternackt (*ugs.*)

**starkly** /'stɑ:klɪ/ *adv.* Ⓐ (*clearly*) überdeutlich; Ⓑ (*harshly*) grell ‹erleuchtet›; scharf ‹kontrastieren›; **state a problem in ~ realistic terms** ein Problem krass und realistisch darlegen

**starless** /'stɑ:lɪs/ *adj.* stern[en]los

**starlet** /'stɑ:lɪt/ *n.* (*Cinemat.*) Starlet, *das*

**'starlight** *n., no pl.* Sternenlicht, *das*

**starling** /'stɑ:lɪŋ/ *n.* (*Ornith.*) Ⓐ [Gemeiner] Star; Ⓑ (*of family Sturnidae*) Star, *der;* (*of family Icteridae*) Stärling, *der*

**'starlit** *adj.* sternhell

**Star: ~ of Bethlehem** /stɑ:r əv 'beθlɪhem/ *n.* (*Bot.*) Stern von Bethlehem; Milchstern, *der;* **~ of David** /stɑ:r əv 'deɪvɪd/ *n.* David[s]stern, *der*

**starry** /'stɑ:rɪ/ *adj.* Ⓐ sternklar ‹Himmel, Nacht›; sternenübersät ‹Himmel›; Ⓑ (*shining*) strahlend, leuchtend ‹Augen›

**'starry-eyed** *adj.* blauäugig (*fig.*)

**star: ~ shell** *n.* (*Mil.*) Leuchtgeschoss, *das;* **~ sign** *n.* Sternzeichen, *das;* **~-spangled** *adj.* mit Sternen übersät; sternbesät (*dichter.*); **the S~-Spangled Banner** das Sternenbanner; **~-studded** *adj.* Ⓐ mit Sternen übersät; Ⓑ ‹Show, Film, Besetzung› mit großem Staraufgebot

**start** /stɑ:t/ ❶ *v.i.* Ⓐ (*begin*) anfangen; beginnen (*oft geh.*); **when we first ~ed** ganz zu Anfang; **don't 'you ~!** (*coll.*) nun fang du auch noch [damit] an!; **~ on [at] sb.** (*coll.*) auf jmdn. einhacken (*ugs.*); **don't ~ on at me about that again!** nun fang nicht schon wieder damit an!; **~ on sth.** etw. beginnen; **~ on Latin** mit Latein beginnen; **~ with sth./sb.** bei *od.* mit etw./jmdm. anfangen; **prices ~ at ten dollars** die Preise beginnen bei zehn Dollar; **~ at the beginning** am Anfang beginnen; **to ~ with** zuerst *od.* zunächst einmal; **~ing from next month** ab nächsten Monat; ⇒ *also* **get** 2 B; **scratch** 3 A; Ⓑ (*set out*) aufbrechen; Ⓒ (*make sudden movement*) aufschrecken; **~ with pain/surprise** vor Schmerz/Überraschung auffahren; **~ from one's chair** von seinem Stuhl hochfahren; **~ back** zurückfahren; **~ with**

S

**fright** vor Schreck zurückweichen; **D** (*begin to function*) anlaufen; ‹Auto, Motor usw.:› anspringen; **E** (*burst*) **his eyes ~ed from their sockets/his skull** *or* **head** die Augen traten ihm aus den Höhlen/dem Kopf.
❷ *v.t.* **A** (*begin*) beginnen [mit]; **we ~ed the holiday on Sunday** unser Urlaub begann am Sonntag; **I have just ~ed a book by Böll** ich habe gerade ein Buch von Böll angefangen; **~ life in Australia** (*be born*) seine ersten Lebensjahre in Australien verbringen; **have ~ed life as sth.** (*fig.*) ursprünglich etw. gewesen sein; **~ school** in die Schule kommen; **~ work** mit der Arbeit beginnen (**on** an + *Dat.*); (*after leaving school*) zu arbeiten anfangen; **~ doing** *or* **to do sth.** [damit] anfangen, etw. zu tun; **B** (*cause*) auslösen; anfangen ‹Streit, Schlägerei›; legen ‹Brand›; (*accidentally*) verursachen ‹Brand›; **you've really ~ed something now!** jetzt hast du aber was angerichtet!; **you trying to ~ something?** (*coll.*) willst du 'ne Schlägerei anfangen?; **C** (*set up*) ins Leben rufen ‹Organisation, Projekt›; aufmachen ‹Laden, Geschäft›; herausbringen ‹Zeitung›; gründen ‹Verein, Firma, Zeitung›; **D** (*switch on*) einschalten; starten, anlassen ‹Motor, Auto›; **E ~ sb. doing sth.** jmdn. anfangen lassen, etw. zu tun; **~ sb. working on a project** jmdn. mit der Arbeit an einem Projekt anfangen lassen; **they ~ the children writing at an early age** sie bringen den Kindern schon früh das Schreiben bei; **~ sb. drinking/coughing/laughing** jmdn. zum Trinken/Husten/Lachen bringen; **~ sb. on a diet** jmdn. auf Diät (*Akk.*) setzen; **she ~ed the baby on solid foods** sie gab dem Baby erstmals feste Nahrung; **~ sb. in business/a trade** jmdm. die Gründung eines Geschäfts ermöglichen/jmdn. in ein Handwerk einführen; **F** (*Sport*) **~ a race** ein Rennen starten; **~ a football match** ein Fußballspiel anpfeifen; **G ~ a family** eine Familie gründen; **they have ~ed a baby** sie erwarten ein Kind; **H** (*Hunting: rouse*) aufscheuchen (**from** aus).
❸ *n.* **A** Anfang, *der;* Beginn, *der;* (*of race*) Start, *der;* **from the ~:** von Anfang an; **from ~ to finish** von Anfang bis Ende; **at the ~:** am Anfang; **at the ~ of the war/day** bei Kriegsbeginn/zum Tagesanfang; **be in at** *or* **in on the ~ of sth.** von Anfang an bei etw. dabei sein; **it could be the ~ of something big** (*coll.*) daraus könnte eine größere Sache werden (*ugs.*); **make a ~:** anfangen (**on, with** mit); (*on journey*) aufbrechen; **make an early/late ~ [for town/to one's holiday]** früh/spät [in die Stadt/in die Ferien] aufbrechen; **get off to** *or* **make a good/slow/poor ~:** einen guten/langsamen/schlechten Start haben; **for a ~** (*coll.*) zunächst einmal; **B** (*Sport: ~ing-place*) Start, *der;* **C** (*Sport: advantage*) Vorsprung, *der;* **give sb. 60 metres ~:** jmdm. eine Vorgabe von 60 Metern geben; **have a ~ over** *or* **on sb./sth.** (*fig.*) einen Vorsprung vor jmdm./etw. haben; ⇒ *also* **head start**; **D** (*good beginning*) **[good] ~:** guter Start; **get a good ~ in life** einen guten Start ins Leben haben; **E** (*jump*) **she remembered** *or* **realized with a ~ that ...:** sie schreckte zusammen, als ihr einfiel, dass ...; **give sb. [a] ~:** jmdm. einen Schreck einjagen; **give a ~:** zusammenfahren; **F** *in pl.* (*jerks*) **give several ~s** mehrmals rucken; ⇒ *also* **fit¹** B

**~ for** *v.t.* sich auf den Weg machen nach/zu

**~ 'in** *v.i.* **A** (*coll.: begin to do*) **~ in to do sth.** sich daranmachen (*ugs.*), etw. zu tun; **~ in on sth./on doing sth.** (*Amer. coll.*) sich an etw. (*Akk.*) machen (*ugs.*)/sich daranmachen (*ugs.*), etw. zu tun; **B ~ in on sb. [for sth.]** (*criticize*) jmdn. [wegen etw.] attackieren

**~ 'off** ❶ *v.i.* **A** ⇒ **set off** 1; **B** (*coll.: begin action*) **~ off by showing sth.** zu Beginn etw. zeigen; **C ~ off with** *or* **on sth.** (*begin on*) mit etw. beginnen; **today we ~ed off with Latin** heute hatten wir zuerst Latein. ❷ *v.t.* **A ~ sb. off working** jmdn. mit der Arbeit anfangen lassen; **~ sb. off on a task/job** jmdn. in eine Aufgabe/Arbeit einweisen; **~ sb. off on a craze** jmdm. einen Floh ins Ohr setzen (*ugs.*); **B** ⇒ **set off** 2 B

**~ 'out** *v.i.* **A** ⇒ **set out** 1; **B** ⇒ **set off** 1

**~ 'up** ❶ *v.i.* **A** ⇒ **jump up**; **B** (*be set going*) starten; ‹Motor:› anspringen; **C** (*begin work*) **~ up in engineering/insurance** als Ingenieur/in der Versicherungsbranche anfangen; **~ up in a trade/as a plumber** sich als Handwerker/als Klempner selbstständig machen. ❷ *v.t.* **A** (*form*) beginnen ‹Gespräch›; gründen ‹Geschäft, Firma›; schließen ‹Freundschaft›; **B** (**~** [*engine of*]) starten; anlassen

**starter** /'stɑ:tə(r)/ *n.* **A** (*Sport: signaller*) Starter, *der;* **be under ~'s orders** (*Horseracing*) am Start stehen; **B** (*Sport: entrant*) Starter, *der*/Starterin, *die;* (*horse*) startendes Pferd; **be a ~ in a race** in einem Rennen starten; **C** (*Motor Veh.*) **~ [motor]** Anlasser, *der;* **press the ~:** den Starter- *od.* Anlasserknopf drücken; **D** (*initial action*) Anfang, *der;* **an easy question for a ~:** als Erstes eine leichte Frage; **as a ~:** zuerst; **for ~s** (*coll.*) erstens einmal; **E** (*hors d'œuvre etc.*) Vorspeise, *die;* **for a ~:** als Vorspeise

**starting**/'stɑ:tɪŋ/: **~ block** *n.* (*Athletics*) Startblock, *der;* **~ gate** *n.* (*Horseracing*) Startmaschine, *die;* **~ grid** *n.* (*Motor racing*) Startplatz, *der;* **on the second row of the ~ grid** in der zweiten Startreihe; **~ handle** *n.* (*Brit.*) [Anlasser]kurbel, *die;* **~ line** *n.* Startlinie, *die;* **~ pistol** *n.* (*Sport*) Startpistole, *die;* **~ point** *n.* (*lit. or fig.*) Ausgangspunkt, *der;* (*for solving a problem*) Ansatzpunkt, *der;* **~ post** *n.* (*Sport*) Startpfosten, *der;* **~ price** *n.* (*Horseracing*) endgültige Quote; **~ salary** *n.* Anfangsgehalt, *das;* (*for civil servants also*) Eingangsbesoldung, *die;* **~ stall** ⇒ **stall¹** 1 E; **~ time** *n.* Anfangszeit, *die*

**startle** /'stɑ:tl/ *v.t.* erschrecken; **be ~d by sth.** über etw. (*Akk.*) erschrecken

**startling** /'stɑ:tlɪŋ/ *adj.* erstaunlich; überraschend ‹Nachricht›; (*alarming*) bestürzend ‹Nachricht, Entdeckung›

**startlingly** /'stɑ:tlɪŋlɪ/ *adv.* erstaunlich; (*alarmingly*) bestürzend

**starvation** /stɑ:'veɪʃn/ *n.* Verhungern, *das;* **die of** *or* **from/suffer from ~:** verhungern/hungern *od.* Hunger leiden; **be** *or* **live on a ~ diet** fast am Verhungern sein; **~ wages** Hungerlohn, *der*

**starve** /stɑ:v/ ❶ *v.i.* **A** (*die of hunger*) **~ [to death]** verhungern; **B** (*suffer hunger*) hungern; **C be starving** (*coll.: feel hungry*) am Verhungern sein (*ugs.*); **you must be starving!** (*coll.*) du musst einen Mordshunger haben! (*ugs.*); **D** (*fig.: suffer want*) hungern (*geh.*) (**for** nach); **be spiritually ~d** seelisch ausgehungert sein.
❷ *v.t.* **A** (*kill by starving*) **~ sb. [to death]** jmdn. verhungern lassen; **be ~d [to death]** verhungern; **B** (*deprive of food*) hungern lassen; **feed a cold, ~ a fever** bei Erkältung soll man essen, bei Fieber hungern; **C** (*deprive*) **we were ~d of knowledge** uns (*Dat.*) wurde [viel] Wissen vorenthalten; **feel ~d of affection** unter einem Mangel an Zuneigung leiden; ⇒ *also* **sex-starved**; **D** (*force*) **~ sb. into submission/surrender** jmdn. bis zur Unterwerfung/Kapitulation aushungern

**~ 'out** *v.t.* aushungern

**'star wars** *n. pl.* der Krieg der Sterne

**stash** /stæʃ/ (*coll.*) ❶ *v.t.* **~ [away]** verstecken; **he ~ed the sweets in his pocket** er ließ die Bonbons in seiner Tasche verschwinden; **~ money away** Geld beiseite schaffen. ❷ *n.* [geheimes] Lager

**stasis** /'stæsɪs, 'steɪsɪs/ *n., pl.* **stases** /'stæsi:z, 'steɪsi:z/ **A** (*stagnation*) Stillstand, *der;* (*of economy*) Stagnation, *die;* **B** (*Biol.: stoppage*) Stase, *die*

**state** /steɪt/ ❶ *n.* **A** (*condition*) Zustand, *der;* **~ of the economy** Wirtschaftslage, *die;* **the ~ of play** (*Sport*) der Spielstand; **the ~ of play [at the moment] is that X leads** nach dem gegenwärtigen Spielstand führt X; **the ~ of play in the negotiations/debate** (*fig.*) der [gegenwärtige] Stand der Verhandlungen/Debatte; **the ~ of things** der Stand der Dinge; **the ~ of things in general** die allgemeine Lage; **the ~ of the art** der [gegenwärtige] Stand der Technik; ⇒ *also* **state-of-the-art**; **the ~ of the nation** die Lage der Nation; **be in a ~ of war** sich im Kriegszustand befinden; **a ~ of war exists** es herrscht Kriegszustand; **be in a ~ of excitement/sadness/anxiety** aufgeregt/traurig/ängstlich sein; **B** (*mess*) **what a ~ you're in!** wie siehst du denn aus! **things are in a ~, I can tell you** es herrschen wirklich finstere Zustände, sag ich dir; **C** (*anxiety*) **be in a ~** (*be in a panic*) aufgeregt sein; (*be anxious*) sich (*Dat.*) Sorgen machen; (*be excited*) ganz aus dem Häuschen sein (*ugs.*); **get into a ~** (*coll.*) Zustände kriegen (*ugs.*); **don't get into a ~!** reg dich nicht auf! (*ugs.*); **D** (*nation*) Staat, *der;* **[affairs] of S~:** Staats[geschäfte]; **E** (*federal ~*) (*of Germany, Austria*) Land, *das;* (*of America*) Staat, *der;* **the [United] States** *sing.* die [Vereinigten] Staaten; **the Northern/Southern States** (*Amer.*) die Nord-/Südstaaten; **States' Rights** (*Amer.*) Rechte der einzelnen Bundesstaaten; **F S~** (*civil government*) Staat, *der;* **G** (*pomp*) Prunk, *der;* **in ~:** in vollem Staat; **keep ~:** Hof halten; **lie in ~:** aufgebahrt sein; **H** (*social rank*) soziale Stellung; **I** (*Bibliog.: variant*) Abdruckszustand, *der;* **J** (*Bot.: stage*) Stadium, *das;* **the larval ~** (*Zool.*) das Larvenstadium. ⇒ *also* **affair** B; **evidence** 1 B; **grace** 1 E; **mind** 1 E.
❷ *attrib. adj.* **A** (*of nation or federal ~*) staatlich; Staats‹bank, -sicherheit, -geheimnis, -dienst›; **~ control** staatliche Kontrolle; **~ education** staatliches Erziehungswesen; **S~ university** (*Amer.*) [öffentliche] Universität eines Bundesstaates; **B** (*ceremonial*) Staats-; **the ~ opening of Parliament** (*Brit.*) die feierliche Eröffnung des Parlaments [nach der Sommerpause].
❸ *v.t.* **A** (*express*) erklären; (*fully or clearly*) darlegen; äußern ‹Meinung›; angeben ‹Alter usw.›; **'please ~ full particulars'** „bitte genaue Angaben machen"; **this condition is ~d in the insurance policy** so steht es ausdrücklich in der Versicherungspolice; **~ one's opinion that ...:** die Überzeugung äußern, dass ...; **B** (*specify*) festlegen; **can you ~ the year when ...?** kannst du das Jahr nennen, in dem ...?; **at ~d intervals** in genau festgelegten Abständen; **at** *or* **by the ~d time** zur festgesetzten Zeit; **C** (*Law: set out*) **~ a case** einen Fall vortragen; **D** (*Mus.: introduce*) einführen

**state: ~-aided** *adj.* staatlich gefördert; **~-controlled** *adj.* **A** (*owned*) staatseigen; **B** (*restricted*) staatlich kontrolliert; **~craft** *n.* (*statesmanship*) Kunst der Staatsführung; **S~ Department** *n.* (*Amer. Polit.*) Außenministerium, *das*

**statehood** /'steɪthʊd/ *n.* **A** (*sovereignty*) Eigenstaatlichkeit, *die;* **B** (*Amer.: federation*) **be admitted to ~:** als Bundesstaat aufgenommen werden

**'state house** *n.* (*Amer.: legislature building*) Parlamentsgebäude, *das*

**stateless** /'steɪtlɪs/ *adj.* staatenlos; **~ person** Staatenlose, *der/die*

**stately** /'steɪtlɪ/ *adj.* majestätisch; stattlich ‹Körperbau, Erscheinung, Gebäude›; hochtrabend ‹Stil›; feierlich ‹Prozession›; **at a ~ pace** gemessenen Schrittes

**stately 'home** *n.* (*Brit.*) Herrensitz, *der;* (*grander*) Schloss, *das*

**statement** /'steɪtmənt/ *n.* **A** (*stating, account, thing stated*) Aussage, *die;* (*declaration*) Erklärung, *die;* (*allegation*) Behauptung, *die;* **make a ~** ‹Zeuge:› eine Aussage machen; ‹Politiker:› eine Erklärung abgeben (**on** zu); **B** (*Finance: report*) **~ [of account], [bank] ~:** Kontoauszug, *der*

**state: ~-of-the-'art** *adj.* auf dem neuesten Stand der Technik *nachgestellt;* **~-owned** *adj.* staatlich; in Staatsbesitz *nachgestellt;* **~room** *n.* **A** Prunkzimmer, *das;* **B** (*Naut.*) private [Luxus]kabine; **C** (*Amer. Railw.*) privates [Luxus]abteil; **S~ school** *n.* (*Brit.*) staatliche Schule; **S~side** (*Amer. coll.*) ❶ *adv.* **be/work/travel/head S~side** in

S

den Staaten (*ugs.*) sein/arbeiten/in die Staaten (*ugs.*) reisen/fahren; ❷ *adj.* ‹Szene, Mode› in den Staaten (*ugs.*)

**statesman** /ˈsteɪtsmən/ *n.*, *pl.* **statesmen** /ˈsteɪtsmən/ Staatsmann, *der;* ⇒ *also* **elder statesman**

**statesmanlike** /ˈsteɪtsmənlaɪk/ *adj.* staatsmännisch; diplomatisch ‹Lösung›

**statesmanship** /ˈsteɪtsmənʃɪp/ *n.*, *no pl.* Ⓐ (*Polit.: management*) Staatslenkung, *die;* Ⓑ (*wise leadership*) staatsmännisches Geschick

**ˈState system** *n.*, *no pl.* (*Brit. Educ.*) staatliches Schulwesen

**ˈstatewide** *adj.* landesweit; (*in USA*) im ganzen [Bundes]staat *nachgestellt*

**static** /ˈstætɪk/ ❶ *adj.* Ⓐ (*Phys.*) statisch; Ⓑ (*not moving*) statisch; (*not changing*) konstant ‹Umweltbedingungen›; **be ~:** stagnieren; **remain ~** ‹Zustand:› unverändert bleiben; ‹Preise:› gleich bleiben; Ⓒ (*Electr.*) [elektro]statisch. ❷ *n.* Ⓐ (*atmospherics*) atmosphärische Störungen; Ⓑ ⇒ **static electricity**

**static elecˈtricity** *n.* (*Phys.*) statische Elektrizität

**statics** /ˈstætɪks/ *n.*, *no pl.* (*Mech.*) Statik, *die*

**station** /ˈsteɪʃn/ ❶ *n.* Ⓐ (*position*) Position, *die;* **be assigned a ~:** einen [Stand]ort zugewiesen bekommen; **take up one's ~:** seine Position einnehmen; Ⓑ (*establishment*) Station, *die;* (*Broadcasting*) Sender, *der;* **radar [tracking] ~** (*Mil.*) Radarstation, *die;* Ⓒ ⇒ **railway station**; Ⓓ (*status*) Rang, *der;* **occupy a humble/an exalted ~:** eine niedrige/hohe Position bekleiden; **have ideas above one's ~:** sich für etwas Besseres halten; **marry above/below** *or* **beneath one's ~:** über/unter seinem Stand heiraten; Ⓔ (*Amer.: post office*) Poststelle, *die;* Ⓕ (*post*) (*Mil.*) Posten, *der;* (*Navy, Air Force*) Stützpunkt, *der;* (*Police*) Wache, *die;* Ⓖ (*Austral.: farm*) Farm, *die;* **[sheep] ~:** Schaffarm, *die;* Ⓗ **~ of the Cross** (*Relig.*) Kreuzwegstation, *die* (*kath. Kirche*).
❷ *v.t.* Ⓐ (*assign position to*) stationieren; abstellen ‹Auto›; aufstellen ‹Wache›; Ⓑ (*place*) stellen; (*Sport*) aufstellen; **~ oneself** sich aufstellen

**stationary** /ˈsteɪʃənərɪ/ *adj.* Ⓐ (*not moving*) stehend; **be ~:** stehen; **the traffic was ~:** der Verkehr war zum Erliegen gekommen; Ⓑ (*fixed*) stationär

**ˈstation break** *n.* (*Amer. Radio and Telev.*) Pausenzeichen, *das*

**stationer** /ˈsteɪʃənə(r)/ *n.* ▶ 1261 Schreibwarenhändler, *der*/-händlerin, *die;* **~'s [shop]** Schreibwarengeschäft, *das*

**stationery** /ˈsteɪʃənərɪ/ *n.* Ⓐ (*writing materials*) Schreibwaren *Pl.;* Ⓑ (*writing paper*) Briefpapier, *das;* **a ~ set** [eine Mappe mit] Briefpapier; eine Briefmappe; **office ~:** Bürobedarf, *der;* ⇒ *also* **continuous stationery**

**ˈStationery Office** *n.* (*Brit.*) **[Her/His] Majesty's ~** *britischer Staatsverlag, der auch die staatlichen Stellen mit Bürobedarf versorgt*

**station: ~ house** *n.* (*Amer.: police station*) [Polizei]wache, *die;* **~master** *n.* ▶ 1261 (*Railw.*) Stationsvorsteher, *der*/-vorsteherin, *die;* **~ sergeant** *n.* (*Brit. Police*) *Leiter einer Polizeiwache im Range eines Sergeanten;* **~ wagon** *n.* (*Amer.*) Kombi[wagen], *der*

**statistic** /stəˈtɪstɪk/ *n.* statistische Tatsache; **I disliked being treated as just a ~:** es missfiel mir, nur als Nummer behandelt zu werden

**statistical** /stəˈtɪstɪkl/ *attrib. adj.*, **statistically** /stəˈtɪstɪkəlɪ/ *adv.* statistisch

**statistician** /stætɪˈstɪʃn/ *n.* ▶ 1261 Statistiker, *der*/Statistikerin, *die*

**statistics** /stəˈtɪstɪks/ *n.* Ⓐ *as pl.* (*facts*) Statistik, *die;* **~ of population/crime, population/crime ~:** Bevölkerungs-/Kriminalitätsstatistik, *die;* **according to ~:** nach der Statistik; **~ show that one in three marriages ends in divorce** nach der Statistik endet eine von drei Eheschließungen mit Scheidung; Ⓑ *no pl.* (*science*) Statistik, *die*

**statue** /ˈstætʃuː, ˈstætjuː/ *n.* Statue, *die;* **as still as a ~:** reglos wie eine Statue; ⇒ *also* **liberty**

**statuesque** /stætjʊˈesk, stætʃʊˈesk/ *adj.* statuenhaft; (*imposing*) stattlich

**statuette** /stætʃʊˈet, stætjʊˈet/ *n.* Statuette, *die*

**stature** /ˈstætʃə(r)/ *n.* Ⓐ (*body height*) Statur, *die;* **be of short ~, be short in ~:** von kleiner Statur sein; Ⓑ (*fig.: standing*) Format, *das;* **be of international ~ in one's field** auf seinem Gebiet eine international anerkannte Kapazität sein; **a person of [some] ~:** eine [recht] bedeutende Persönlichkeit; **he was not of the same ~ as Picasso** er hatte nicht das Format *od.* die Größe Picassos

**status** /ˈsteɪtəs/ *n.* Ⓐ (*position*) Rang, *der;* **have no ~ in society** kein angesehenes Mitglied der Gesellschaft sein; **rise in ~:** an Ansehen gewinnen; **social ~:** [gesellschaftlicher] Status; **the ~ of this information is 'secret'** diese Information ist als „geheim" eingestuft; **be a person of high/low ~ in a firm** in einer Firma eine hohe/niedrige Stellung haben; **her ~ among scientists** ihr wissenschaftlicher Rang; **equality of ~ [with sb.]** Gleichstellung [mit jmdm.]; **financial ~:** finanzielle *od.* wirtschaftliche Lage; Ⓑ (*superior position*) Status, *der;* **have [some] ~ in the firm** in der Firma einen [ziemlich] hohen Rang bekleiden; Ⓒ (*Law*) Status, *der;* **have [no] legal ~:** [nicht] rechtsgültig sein; ‹Person:› über keinerlei Rechte verfügen

**status: ~ quo** /steɪtəs ˈkwəʊ/ *n.* Status quo, *der;* **~ symbol** *n.* Statussymbol, *das*

**statute** /ˈstætjuːt/ *n.* Ⓐ (*Law*) Gesetz, *das;* **by ~:** per Gesetz; Ⓑ *in pl.* (*rules*) Statut, *das;* Satzung, *die*

**statute: ~-barred** *adj.* (*Law*) verjährt; **~ book** *n.* (*Law*) Gesetzbuch, *das;* **put an Act** *or* **a law on the ~ book** ein Gesetz durchbringen; **put a measure/provision on the ~ book** einer Maßnahme/Bestimmung Gesetzeskraft (*Dat.*) verleihen; **~ law** *n.* (*Law*) Ⓐ (*statute*) Gesetz, *das;* Ⓑ *no pl.*, *no indef. art.* kodifiziertes *od.* schriftlich niedergelegtes Recht; **~ mile** *n.* englische Meile

**statutory** /ˈstætjʊtərɪ/ *adj.* Ⓐ (*Law*) gesetzlich ‹Feiertag, Bestimmung, Erfordernis, Erbe›; gesetzlich vorgeschrieben ‹Strafe›; gesetzlich festgeschrieben ‹Löhne, Zinssatz›; gesetzlich festgelegt ‹Voraussetzung, Sätze, Zeit›; **~ law** kodifiziertes Recht; **~ rights** [gesetzliche] Rechte; ⇒ *also* **rape**[1] 1; Ⓑ (*relating to the statutes of an institution*) Satzungs‹bestimmungen›; von der Satzung vorgesehen ‹Geldbuße usw.›; **in accordance with the ~ requirements** *or* **conditions** satzungsgemäß

**staunch**[1] /stɔːnʃ, stɑːnʃ/ *adj.* treu ‹Freund, Anhänger›; streitbar ‹Kämpfer, Anhänger›; überzeugt ‹Katholik, Demokrat usw.›; unerschütterlich ‹Mut, Hingabe, Glaube›; standhaft ‹Herz›; **be ~ in one's belief** an seinem Glauben unerschütterlich festhalten; **be ~ in one's support for sb./sth.** jmdn./etw. getreu unterstützen

**staunch**[2] ⇒ **stanch**

**staunchly** /ˈstɔːnʃlɪ, ˈstɑːnʃlɪ/ *adv.* standhaft ‹beistehen›; unerschrocken ‹kämpfen, verteidigen›; treu ‹ergeben sein›; unerschütterlich ‹an etw. (Dat.) festhalten›

**stave** /steɪv/ ❶ *n.* Ⓐ (*Mus.*) ⇒ **staff** 1 D; Ⓑ (*of barrel*) Daube, *die;* Ⓒ (*rung*) Sprosse, *die;* Ⓓ (*lit.: stanza*) Strophe, *die.* ❷ *v.t.*, **~d** *or* **stove** /stəʊv/ ein Loch schlagen in (+ *Akk.*)

**~ ˈin** *v.t.* (*crush*) eindrücken ‹Karosserie, Tür, Fenster, Rippen›; einschlagen ‹Kopf, Kiste›; (*break hole in*) ein Loch schlagen in (+ *Akk.*); **the boat was ~d in** das Boot schlug leck

**~ ˈoff** *v.t.*, **~d off** abwenden; abwehren ‹Angriff›; verhindern ‹Krankheit›; stillen ‹Hunger, Durst›; zurückweisen ‹Forderung›

**stay**[1] /steɪ/ ❶ *n.* Ⓐ Aufenthalt, *der;* (*visit*) Besuch, *der;* **during her ~ with us** während sie bei uns zu Besuch war; **come/go for a short ~ with sb.** jmdn. kurz besuchen; **have a week's ~ in London** eine Woche in London verbringen; Ⓑ (*Law*) **~ [of execution]** Aussetzung [der Vollstreckung]; (*fig.*) Galgenfrist, *die;* Ⓒ (*support*) Stütze, *die;* Ⓓ *in pl.* (*Hist.*) ⇒ **corset** 1 A.
❷ *v.i.* Ⓐ (*remain*) bleiben; **he ~ed in the club/army for five years** er war fünf Jahre Klubmitglied/in der Armee; **~ open till 10 o'clock** ‹Geschäft:› bis 10 Uhr geöffnet sein; **be here to ~, have come to ~:** sich fest eingebürgert haben; ‹Arbeitslosigkeit, Inflation:› zum Dauerzustand geworden sein; ‹Modeartikel:› in Mode bleiben; **~ with the leaders** sich an der Spitze halten *od.* behaupten; **~!** halt!; (*to dog*) bleib hier!; **~ for** *or* **to dinner/for the party** zum Essen/zur Party bleiben; **~ put** (*coll.*) ‹Ball, Haar:› liegen bleiben; ‹Hut:› fest sitzen; ‹Bild:› hängen bleiben; ‹Person:› bleiben[, wo man ist]; **I am ~ing put in this armchair** aus diesem Sessel rühre ich mich so schnell nicht weg; **~ sitting** sitzen bleiben; **~ 'with it!** (*coll.*) bleib dran! (*ugs.*); **~ with me!** bleib bei mir!; **~ around!** bleib in der Nähe!; Ⓑ (*dwell temporarily*) wohnen; **~ abroad** im Ausland leben; **he ~ed [for] two weeks in London before flying to Brussels** er verbrachte zwei Wochen in London, bevor er nach Brüssel flog; (*fig.*) **~ the night in a hotel** die Nacht in einem Hotel verbringen; **~ at sb.'s** *or* **with sb. for the weekend** das Wochenende bei jmdm. verbringen; Ⓒ (*Sport*) durchhalten; **~ well at a fast pace/over any distance** bei schnellem Tempo/über jede Entfernung gut mithalten.
❸ *v.t.* Ⓐ (*arch./literary: stop*) aufhalten; **~ one's hand** (*fig.*) sich bedeckt halten; **~ sb.'s hand** (*fig.*) jmdn. zurückhalten; Ⓑ (*endure*) **~ the course** *or* **distance** die [ganze] Strecke durchhalten; (*fig.*) durchhalten; ⇒ *also* **pace**[1] 1 B; Ⓒ (*satisfy*) stillen ‹Hunger, Durst›; Ⓓ (*Law*) aussetzen; Ⓔ (*literary: support*) stützen

**~ aˈhead** *v.i.* die Führung halten

**~ aˈway** *v.i.* Ⓐ (*not attend*) **~ away [from sth.]** [von etw.] wegbleiben; [einer Sache (*Dat.*)] fernbleiben; **~ away from school/a meeting** nicht zur Schule/zu einem Treffen gehen/kommen; **if the visitors/customers ~ away** wenn die Besucher/Käufer ausbleiben; Ⓑ (*~ distant*) **~ away from the dog!** komm dem Hund nicht zu nahe!; **he ~ed well away from the wall** er hielt sich ein gutes Stück von der Wand entfernt; **~ away from him!** lass ihn in Ruhe!; **~ away from drugs** die Finger von Drogen lassen (*ugs.*)

**~ ˈback** *v.i.* Ⓐ (*not approach*) zurückbleiben; Ⓑ ⇒ **~ behind**; Ⓒ (*remain in place*) **the door won't ~ back** die Tür bleibt nicht offen

**~ beˈhind** *v.i.* zurückbleiben; **have to ~ behind [after school]** nachsitzen müssen; **we ~ed behind after the lecture** wir sind nach der Vorlesung noch dageblieben; **can you ~ behind for a moment?** kannst du einen Augenblick [hier] warten?

**~ ˈdown** *v.i.* Ⓐ (*remain lowered*) unten bleiben; **they ~ed down out of sight** sie blieben unten, sodass man sie nicht sehen konnte; Ⓑ (*not increase*) stabil bleiben; Ⓒ (*Educ.: not go to higher form*) sitzen bleiben (*ugs.*)

**~ ˈin** *v.i.* Ⓐ (*remain in position*) halten; **will these creases ~ in?** bleiben diese Falten [drin (*ugs.*)]?; **this passage [of the book] should ~ in** diese Passage sollte nicht gestrichen werden; Ⓑ (*remain indoors*) im Hause bleiben; (*remain at home*) zu Hause bleiben

**~ ˈoff** ❶ *v.i.* Ⓐ wegbleiben (*ugs.*); Ⓑ (*away from work, school*) **[have to] ~ off** nicht zur Schule/Arbeit gehen [können]. ❷ *v.t.* Ⓐ (*not go on to*) nicht betreten ‹Rasen, Teppich, Beete›; nicht gehen auf (+ *Akk.*) ‹Straße usw.›; **~ off the bottle/off drugs** die Finger vom Alkohol/von Drogen lassen (*ugs.*); Ⓑ (*be absent from*) **~ off school/work** nicht zur Schule/Arbeit gehen

**~ ˈon** *v.i.* Ⓐ (*remain in place*) ‹Hut, Perücke, Kopftuch:› sitzen bleiben; ‹falsche Wimpern, Aufkleber:› haften; ‹Deckel, Rad:› halten; Ⓑ (*remain in operation*) angeschaltet bleiben; anbleiben (*ugs.*); Ⓒ (*remain present*) noch [da]bleiben;

**~ on at school** auf der Schule bleiben; **~ on as chairman** Vorsitzender bleiben
**~ 'out** *v.i.* Ⓐ (*not go home*) wegbleiben (*ugs.*); nicht nach Hause kommen/gehen; **don't ~ out late!** komm nicht zu spät nach Hause!; Ⓑ (*remain outside*) draußen bleiben; Ⓒ (*fig.*) **~ out of sb.'s way** jmdm. aus dem Wege gehen; Ⓓ (*remain on strike*) **~ out [on strike]** im Ausstand bleiben
**~ 'over** *v.i.* (*coll.*) über Nacht bleiben
**~ 'up** *v.i.* Ⓐ (*not go to bed*) aufbleiben; Ⓑ (*remain in position*) ‹Pfosten, Gebäude:› stehen bleiben; ‹Plakat:› hängen bleiben; ‹Flugzeug, Haare:› oben bleiben; **my socks won't ~ up** meine Socken rutschen [ständig]

**stay²** ❶ *n.* Ⓐ (*Naut.*) Stag, *das;* Ⓑ (*guy-rope*) Zeltleine, *die;* (*guy-wire*) Drahtseil, *das;* Ⓒ (*Aeronaut., Archit.*) Strebe, *die.* ❷ *v.t.* (*Naut.*) stagen

**'stay-at-home** ❶ *n.* häuslicher Mensch; **be a real ~:** ein richtiger Stubenhocker (*ugs. abwertend*) sein. ❷ *attrib. adj.* häuslich

**stayer** /'steɪə(r)/ *n.* (*lit. or fig.*) Steher, *der*

**staying power** /'steɪɪŋpaʊə(r)/ *n.* Durchhaltevermögen, *das*

**staysail** /'steɪseɪl, 'steɪsl/ *n.* (*Naut.*) Stagsegel, *das*

**STD** *abbr.* Ⓐ (*Brit. Teleph.*) **subscriber trunk dialling** Selbstwählfernverkehr, *der;* **~ code** Vorwahl[nummer], *die;* Ⓑ (*Med.*) **sexually transmitted disease** ⇒ **sexually** A

**stead** /sted/ *n., no pl., no art.* Ⓐ **in sb.'s ~:** an jmds. Stelle (*Dat.*); **the bishop's deputy went in his ~:** anstelle des Bischofs ging sein Vertreter; Ⓑ **stand sb. in good ~:** jmdm. zustatten kommen; **that car has stood her in good ~:** dieser Wagen hat ihr gute Dienste geleistet

**steadfast** /'stedfəst, 'stedfɑ:st/ *adj.* standhaft; zuverlässig ‹Freund›; fest ‹Entschluss›; unverwandt ‹Blick›; unerschütterlich ‹Glaube›; unverbrüchlich (*geh.*) ‹Freundschaft, Treue›; **be ~ in one's belief that ...:** fest daran glauben, dass ...

**steadfastly** /'stedfəstlɪ, 'stedfɑ:stlɪ/ *adv.* standhaft; fest ‹glauben›; unverwandt ‹[an]blicken›; **adhere ~ to one's principles/faith** fest zu seinen Grundsätzen/seinem Glauben stehen

**steadily** /'stedɪlɪ/ *adv.* Ⓐ (*stably*) fest; festen Schrittes ‹gehen›; sicher ‹Rad fahren›; Ⓑ (*without faltering*) fest ‹[an]blicken›; Ⓒ (*continuously*) stetig; ohne Unterbrechung ‹arbeiten, marschieren›; **it was raining ~:** es hat ununterbrochen geregnet; **progress ~:** stetige Fortschritte machen; **news flowed in ~ all day** den ganzen Tag gingen pausenlos Nachrichten ein; Ⓓ (*firmly*) standhaft ‹sich weigern›; fest ‹glauben›; Ⓔ (*reliably*) zuverlässig

**steady** /'stedɪ/ ❶ *adj.* Ⓐ (*stable*) stabil; (*not wobbling*) standfest; **as ~ as a rock** völlig standfest ‹Leiter, Tisch›; völlig stabil ‹Boot›; ganz ruhig ‹Hand›; **in an emergency he is as ~ as a rock** (*lit. or fig.*) in einer Notsituation lässt er sich durch nichts erschüttern; **be ~ on one's feet** *or* **legs/bicycle** sicher auf den Beinen sein/sicher auf seinem Fahrrad fahren; **hold** *or* **keep one's hand ~:** die Hand ruhig halten; **hold** *or* **keep the ladder ~:** die Leiter festhalten; **~ as she goes!** (*coll.*) immer so weiter!; Ⓑ (*still*) ruhig; **turn a ~ eye** *or* **gaze** *or* **look on sb.** jmdn. fest ansehen; Ⓒ (*regular, constant*) stetig; gleichmäßig ‹Arbeit, Tempo,› stabil ‹Preis, Lohn›; gleich bleibend ‹Temperatur›; beständig ‹Klima, Summen, Lärm›; **we had ~ rain/drizzle** wir hatten Dauerregen/es nieselte [bei uns] ständig; **at a ~ pace** mit gleichmäßiger Geschwindigkeit; **[keep her] ~!** (*Naut.*) Kurs halten!; **prices have remained ~:** die Preise sind stabil geblieben; **~!** Vorsicht!; (*to dog, horse*) ruhig!; **~ on!** langsam! (*ugs.*); **~ on, or you'll knock the vase over/hurt me** Vorsicht, sonst wirfst du die Vase um/verletzt du mich; Ⓓ (*invariable*) unerschütterlich; beständig ‹Wesensart›; standhaft ‹Weigerung›; fest ‹Charakter, Glaube›; **have a ~ character** charakterfest sein; **~ purpose** Zielstrebigkeit, *die;* Ⓔ (*enduring*) **a ~ job** eine feste Stelle; **a ~ boyfriend/girlfriend** ein fester Freund/eine feste Freundin (*ugs.*); Ⓕ (*reliable*) zuverlässig.
❷ *v.t.* festhalten ‹Leiter›; beruhigen ‹Pferd, Nerven›; ruhig halten ‹Boot, Flugzeug›; **~ the table/vase** für einen festen Stand des Tisches/der Vase sorgen; **she steadied herself against the table/with a stick** sie hielt sich am Tisch fest/stützte sich mit einem Stock.
❸ *v.i.* ‹Preise:› sich stabilisieren; ‹Geschwindigkeit:› sich mäßigen; **the boat steadied** das Boot wurde [wieder] ruhiger.
❹ *n.* (*coll.*) fester Freund/feste Freundin (*ugs.*).
❺ *adv.* **go ~ with sth.** mit etw. vorsichtig sein; **go ~ with sb.** (*coll.*) mit jmdm. gehen (*ugs.*); **are you going ~ with anyone?** hast du einen festen Freund/eine feste Freundin? (*ugs.*)

**steak** /steɪk/ *n.* Steak, *das;* (*of ham, bacon, gammon, salmon, etc.*) Scheibe, *die;* **a chicken/turkey/veal ~:** ein Hähnchen-/Puten-/Kalbsschnitzel; **~ and kidney pie/pudding** Rindfleisch-Nieren-Pastete, *die;* **~ au poivre** /steɪk əʊ 'pwɑ:vr/ Pfeffersteak, *das;* **~ tartare** Tatarbeefsteak, *das;* **a [fish] ~:** eine Scheibe [Fisch]; ⇒ *also* **fillet** 1 A; **sirloin** A

**steak: ~house** *n.* Steakhaus, *das;* **~ knife** *n.* Messer mit Sägezahnung

**steal** /sti:l/ ❶ *v.t.*, **stole** /stəʊl/, **stolen** /'stəʊln/ Ⓐ stehlen (**from** *Dat.*); **~ a ride** schwarzfahren; **~ sb.'s boyfriend/girlfriend** jmdm. den Freund/die Freundin ausspannen (*ugs.*); **~ the show** die Hauptattraktion sein; **the newcomer stole the show** ein Newcomer war der Star [des Abends]; **~ the show from sb.** jmdm. die Schau stehlen *od.* den Rang ablaufen; **she was the star of the play, but the little dog stole the show** (*fig.*) sie war der Star des Stückes, aber der kleine Hund stahl ihr die Schau; ⇒ *also* **scene** B; **thunder** 1 C; Ⓑ (*get slyly*) rauben (*geh. scherzh.*) ‹Kuss, Umarmung›; entlocken ‹Worte, Interview›; sich (*Dat.*) genehmigen (*ugs. scherzh.*) ‹Nickerchen›; **~ a glance [at sb./sth.]** jmdm. einen verstohlenen Blick zuwerfen/einen verstohlenen Blick auf etw. (*Akk.*) werfen; Ⓒ (*fig.: win*) **she stole my heart** sie eroberte mein Herz; **~ a march on sb.** jmdm. zuvorkommen.
❷ *v.i.*, **stole, stolen** Ⓐ stehlen; **~ from sb.** jmdn. bestehlen; **~ from the till/supermarket** aus der Kasse/im Supermarkt stehlen; Ⓑ (*move furtively*) sich stehlen; **~ in/out/up** sich hinein-/hinaus-/hinaufstehlen; **mist stole over the valley** beinahe unbemerkt breitete sich Nebel über das Tal aus; **~ up [on sb./sth.]** sich [an jmdn./etw.] heranschleichen; **old age is ~ing up on me** langsam, aber sicher werde ich alt.
❸ *n.* (*Amer. coll.*) Ⓐ (*theft*) Diebstahl, *der;* Ⓑ (*bargain*) **that dress is a ~:** dieses Kleid ist [fast *od.* halb] geschenkt (*ugs.*)
**~ a'bout, ~ a'round** *v.i.* herumschleichen (*ugs.*)
**~ a'way** *v.i.* sich fortstehlen

**stealth** /stelθ/ *n.* Heimlichkeit, *die;* **use ~:** heimlich vorgehen; **by ~:** heimlich

**stealthily** /'stelθɪlɪ/ *adv.* heimlich; verstohlen

**stealthy** /'stelθɪ/ *adj.* heimlich; verstohlen ‹Blick, Bewegung, Tun›

**steam** /sti:m/ ❶ *n., no pl., no indef. art.* Dampf, *der;* **the window was covered with ~:** das Fenster war beschlagen; **all the ~ has gone out of him/the idea** (*coll.*) er hat seinen ganzen Schwung verloren/aus der Idee ist der Dampf raus (*ugs.*); **get up ~:** Dampf aufmachen; (*fig.*) in Fahrt kommen; **get up ~ to do sth.** (*fig.*) den nötigen Dampf aufbringen, um etw. zu tun; **let off ~** (*fig.*) Dampf ablassen (*ugs.*); **run out of ~:** keinen Dampf mehr haben; (*fig.*) den Schwung verlieren; **under its own ~:** mit eigener Kraft; **under one's own ~** (*fig.*) aus eigener Kraft; ⇒ *also* **full¹** 1 D.
❷ *v.t.* Ⓐ (*Cookery*) dämpfen; dünsten; **~ed pudding** gedämpfter Pudding; Ⓑ **~ open an envelope** einen Umschlag mit [heißem] Wasserdampf öffnen.
❸ *v.i.* Ⓐ (*emit ~*) dampfen; **~ing hot** dampfend heiß; **heat the water till ~ing hot** das Wasser erhitzen, bis es dampft; Ⓑ (*move*) dampfen; **he went ~ing after the thief** (*fig. coll.*) er stürmte mit Volldampf (*ugs.*) hinter dem Dieb her
**~ a'head** *v.i.* (*fig. coll.*) rasche Fortschritte machen
**~ 'over** *v.i.* [sich] beschlagen
**~ 'up** ❶ *v.t.* Ⓐ beschlagen lassen; **be ~ed up** beschlagen sein; Ⓑ (*fig. coll.*) **be/get [all] ~ed up** [total] ausrasten (*ugs.*); **don't get ~ed up about it!** reg dich doch darüber nicht so auf! ❷ *v.i.* beschlagen

**steam: ~ bath** *n.* Dampfbad, *das;* **~boat** *n.* Dampfschiff, *das;* (*small*) Dampfboot, *das;* **~ boiler** *n.* Dampfkessel, *der;* **~ coal** *n.* Dampfkesselkohle, *die;* **~driven** *adj.* dampfgetrieben; **a ~-driven boat/train/tractor** ein Dampfboot/eine Dampflok/ein Traktor mit Dampfantrieb; **~ engine** *n.* Ⓐ (*Railw.*) Dampflok[omotive], *die;* Ⓑ (*stationary engine*) Dampf[kraft]maschine, *die*

**steamer** /'sti:mə(r)/ *n.* Ⓐ (*Naut.*) Dampfer, *der;* Ⓑ (*Cookery*) Dämpfer, *der*

**steam: ~ gauge** *n.* Dampfdruckmesser, *der;* **~ hammer** *n.* (*Metallurgy*) Dampfhammer, *der;* **~ iron** *n.* Dampfbügeleisen, *das;* **~ 'radio** *n.* (*coll. joc.*) Dampfradio, *das* (*ugs. scherzh.*); **~roller** ❶ *n.* (*lit. or fig.*) Dampfwalze, *die;* ❷ *v.t.* [mit der Dampfwalze] walzen; (*fig.*) niederwalzen; **~roller a bill through Parliament** ein Gesetz durchpeitschen (*ugs.*); **~ship** *n.* Dampfschiff, *das;* **~ train** *n.* (*Railw.*) Dampfzug, *der;* **~ 'turbine** *n.* Dampfturbine, *die;* **~ whistle** Dampfpfeife, *die*

**steamy** /'sti:mɪ/ *adj.* Ⓐ dunstig; Dunst‹wolke›; feucht ‹Hitze›; beschlagen ‹Glas›; Ⓑ (*coll.: erotic*) heiß

**steed** /sti:d/ *n.* (*literary/joc.*) Ross, *das* (*geh./scherzh.*)

**steel** /sti:l/ ❶ *n.* Ⓐ Stahl, *der;* **have a heart of ~** (*fig.*) stahlhart sein; **a man of ~:** ein stahlharter Mann; **as hard/true as ~:** stahlhart/treu wie Gold; **cold ~:** blanker Stahl; **pressed ~:** Pressstahl, *der;* Ⓑ (*knife sharpener*) Wetzstahl, *der;* Ⓒ (*literary: sword*) Schwert, *das.* ❷ *attrib. adj.* stählern; Stahl‹helm, -block, -platte›. ❸ *v.t.* **~ oneself for/against sth.** sich für/gegen etw. wappnen (*geh.*); **she ~ed her heart/herself against his pleas** sie verschloss ihr Herz/sich seinen Bitten; **~ oneself to do sth.** allen Mut zusammennehmen, um etw. zu tun

**steel: ~ 'band** *n.* (*Mus.*) Steelband, *die;* **~ 'drum** *n.* (*Mus.*) Steeldrum, *die;* **~ grey** *n.* Stahlgrau, *das;* **~-grey** *adj.* stahlgrau; **~ gui'tar** *n.* (*Mus.*) Hawaiigitarre, *die;* **~ industry** *n.* Stahlindustrie, *die;* **~maker** *n.* Stahlproduzent, *der*/-produzentin, *die;* **~ mill** *n.* Stahlwalzwerk, *das;* **~ 'plate** *n.* Stahlplatte, *die;* **~-plated** /'sti:lpleɪtɪd/ *adj.* (*for protection*) mit Stahlplatten gepanzert; (*for durability*) mit Stahl überzogen; **~ 'wool** *n.* Stahlwolle, *die;* **~worker** *n.* ▶ **1261** Stahlarbeiter, *der*/-arbeiterin, *die;* **~works** *n. sing., pl. same* Stahlwerk, *das*

**steely** /'sti:lɪ/ *adj.* Ⓐ (*strong*) stählern; Ⓑ (*resolute*) eisern; Ⓒ (*severe*) steinern

**'steelyard** *n.* Laufgewichtswaage, *die*

**steep¹** /sti:p/ *adj.* Ⓐ steil; Ⓑ (*rapid*) stark ‹Preissenkung›; steil ‹Preisanstieg›; Ⓒ (*coll.: excessive*) happig (*ugs.*); **the bill is [a bit] ~:** die Rechnung ist [ziemlich] gesalzen (*ugs.*); **be a bit ~** = **be a bit much** ⇒ **much** 1 B; **that's pretty ~[, coming from you/him]** das ist ein starkes Stück (*ugs.*) [von dir/ihm]

**steep²** *v.t.* Ⓐ (*soak*) einweichen; Ⓑ (*bathe*) baden

**steeped** /sti:pt/ *adj.* durchdrungen (**in** von); **a place ~ in history/tradition** ein geschichtsträchtiger/von der Tradition durchdrungener Ort

**steepen** /'sti:pn/ ❶ *v.i.* steil[er] werden. ❷ *v.t.* steil[er] machen

**steeple** /'sti:pl/ *n.* Kirchturm, *der*

**steeple: ~chase** *n.* (*Sport*) Ⓐ (*horse race*) Steeplechase, *die;* Hindernisrennen, *das;* Ⓑ (*Athletics*) Hindernislauf, *der;* **~chaser** *n.* (*Sport*) Ⓐ (*rider*) Reiter/Reiterin bei einer

S

Steeplechase; [B] (*runner*) Hindernisläufer, *der*/-läuferin, *die;* [C] (*horse*) Steepler, *der;* **~chasing** /'sti:pltʃeɪsɪŋ/ *n.* (*Sport*) Hindernisrennen, *das;* **~jack** *n.* ▶ 1261 *Arbeiter, der/Arbeiterin, die Reparaturarbeiten an Kaminen, Kirchtürmen usw. ausführt*

**steeply** /'sti:plɪ/ *adv.* steil ‹ansteigen, abfallen›

**'steep-sided** ⇒ **-sided**

**steer¹** /stɪə(r)/ ❶ *v.t.* [A] steuern; lenken; **this car is easy to ~:** dieser Wagen ist leicht lenkbar; [B] (*direct*) **~ a** *or* **one's way through ...:** steuern durch ...; **~ a** *or* **one's course for a place** auf einen Ort zusteuern; (*in ship, plane, etc.*) Kurs auf einen Ort nehmen; **~ a** *or* **one's course for home** Kurs in Richtung Heimat nehmen; **~ a middle course** (*fig.*) einen Mittelweg einschlagen; [C] (*guide movement of*) führen, lotsen ‹Person›; **~ a bill through Parliament** eine Gesetzesvorlage über die parlamentarischen Hürden bringen; **~ sb./the conversation towards/away from a subject** jmdn./das Gespräch auf ein Thema lenken/von einem Thema ablenken.

❷ *v.i.* steuern; **~ in and out of/~ between the obstacles** zwischen den Hindernissen hindurchsteuern; **~ clear of sb./sth.** (*fig. coll.*) jmdm./einer Sache aus dem Weg[e] gehen; **~ clear of opium/politics** die Finger von Opium/der Politik lassen; **~ for sth.** etw. ansteuern; **~ left/right** nach links/rechts steuern; **~ due north** (*Naut.*) direkt nach Norden steuern

**steer²** *n.* (*Zool.*) junger Ochse

**steering** /'stɪərɪŋ/ *n.* [A] (*Motor Veh.*) Lenkung, *die;* [B] (*Naut.*) Ruder, *das;* Steuerung, *die*

**steering: ~ column** *n.* (*Motor Veh.*) Lenksäule, *die;* **~ committee** *n.* Lenkungsausschuss, *der;* **~ gear** *n.* (*Naut.*) Steuervorrichtung, *die;* Ruderanlage, *die;* **~ lock** *n.* (*Motor Veh.*) Lenkradschloss, *das;* **~ wheel** *n.* [A] (*Motor Veh.*) Lenkrad, *das;* [B] (*Naut.*) Steuerrad, *das*

**steersman** /'stɪəzmən/ *n., pl.* **steersmen** /'stɪəzmən/ (*Naut.*) Steuermann, *der*

**stein** /staɪn/ *n.* Bierkrug, *der;* Stein, *der* (*südd.*)

**stellar** /'stelə(r)/ *adj.* stellar

**stem¹** /stem/ ❶ *n.* [A] (*Bot.*) (*of tree, shrub*) Stamm, *der;* (*of flower, leaf, fruit*) Stiel, *der;* (*of corn*) Halm, *der;* [B] (*of glass*) Stiel, *der;* [C] (*Mus.*) Notenhals, *der;* [D] (*of tobacco pipe*) Pfeifenrohr, *das;* [E] (*Ling.*) Stamm, *der;* [F] (*Naut.*) **from ~ to stern** vom Bug bis zum Heck. ❷ *v.i.*, **-mm-: ~ from sth.** auf etw. (*Akk.*) zurückzuführen sein. ❸ *v.t.*, **-mm-** (*make headway against*) standhalten (+ *Dat.*)

**stem²** *v.t.*, **-mm-** (*check, dam up*) aufhalten; eindämmen ‹Flut›; stillen ‹Blutung, Wunde›; (*fig.*) Einhalt gebieten (+ *Dat.*) (*geh.*); stoppen ‹Redefluss›; **~ the tide of criticism** die Welle[n] der Kritik eindämmen

**-stemmed** /stemd/ *adj. in comb.* -stielig ‹Glas, Pfeife, Blume, Frucht›; -stämmig ‹Baum, Strauch›

**'stem turn** *n.* (*Skiing*) Stemmbogen, *der*

**stench** /stentʃ/ *n.* Gestank, *der* (*abwertend*)

**stencil** /'stensl/ ❶ *n.* [A] **~ [ plate]** Schablone, *die;* [B] (*for duplicating*) Matrize, *die;* [C] (*~led pattern/lettering*) schablonierttes Muster/schablonierte Schrift. ❷ *v.t.*, (*Brit.*) **-ll-** [A] (*produce with ~*) mit einer Schablone zeichnen; schablonieren; [B] (*ornament*) [mittels Schablone] mustern

**Sten gun** /'sten gʌn/ *n.* (*Arms*) *Art Maschinenpistole*

**stenographer** /ste'nɒgrəfə(r)/ *n.* ▶ 1261 Stenograf, *der*/Stenografin, *die*

**stentorian** /sten'tɔ:rɪən/ *adj.* laut [hallend]; **a ~ voice** eine Stentorstimme (*geh.*)

**step** /step/ ❶ *n.* [A] (*movement, distance*) Schritt, *der;* **at every ~:** mit jedem Schritt; **watch sb.'s every ~** (*fig.*) jmdn. auf Schritt und Tritt überwachen; **take a ~ towards/away from sb.** einen Schritt auf jmdn. zugehen/von jmdm. wegtreten; **take a ~ back/sideways/forward** einen Schritt zurücktreten/zur Seite treten/nach vorn treten; **a ~ forward/back** (*fig.*) ein Schritt nach vorn/zurück; ein Fortschritt/Rückschritt; **a ~ in the right/wrong direction** (*fig.*) ein Schritt in die richtige/falsche Richtung; **mind** *or* **watch your ~!** (*lit. or fig.*) pass auf!; **I can't walk another ~:** ich kann keinen Schritt mehr gehen; **don't move another ~!** keinen Schritt weiter!; [B] (*stair*) Stufe, *die;* (*on vehicle*) Tritt, *der;* **a flight of ~s** eine Treppe; **mind the ~!** Vorsicht, Stufe!; (*warning by one person to another*) pass auf die Stufe auf!; **[pair of] ~s** (*ladder*) Stehleiter, *die;* (*small*) Trittleiter, *die;* [C] **follow** *or* **walk in sb.'s ~s** (*fig.*) in jmds. Fußstapfen treten; [D] (*short distance*) **it's only a ~ to my house** es sind nur ein paar Schritte bis zu mir; [E] **be in ~:** im Schritt sein; (*with music, in dancing*) im Takt sein; **be in/out of ~ with sth.** (*fig.*) mit etw. Schritt/nicht Schritt halten; **he is rarely in ~ with others** er befindet sich selten in Einklang mit anderen; **be out of ~:** aus dem Schritt geraten sein; (*with music, in dancing*) nicht im Takt sein; **he is out of ~ with his colleagues/the official party line** er ist über Kreuz mit seinen Kollegen/weicht von der offiziellen Parteilinie ab; **break ~:** aus dem Tritt geraten *od.* kommen; **change ~:** den Schritt wechseln; **fall into** *or* **get in ~:** in den Gleichschritt fallen; **fall into** *or* **get in ~ with sb./sth.** mit jmdm./etw. im Gleichschritt [mit]marschieren; (*fig.*) sich jmdm./einer Sache fügen; **prices are out of ~ with wage increases** die Preise stehen in keinem Verhältnis zu den Lohnerhöhungen; **keep in ~:** den Schritt halten; (*with music, in dancing*) im Takt bleiben; **keep in ~ with sth./sb.** (*fig.*) mit etw./jmdm. Schritt halten; [F] (*action*) Schritt, *der;* **take ~s to do sth.** Schritte unternehmen, um etw. zu tun; ⇒ *also* **false ~**; [G] (*stage in process*) Schritt, *der;* **S~ one: ...:** erster Schritt: ...; **keep one ~ ahead [of sb./sth.]** [jmdm./einer Sache] einen Schritt *od.* eine Nasenlänge voraus sein; **~ by ~:** Schritt für Schritt; **the first ~ in sb.'s career** die erste Sprosse auf jmds. Karriereleiter; **what is the next ~?** wie geht es weiter?; [H] (*grade*) Stufe, *die;* [I] (*sound of foot, manner of walking*) Schritt, *der;* **know sb. from his ~, know sb.'s ~:** jmdn. an seinem Schritt erkennen; **walk with a skip in one's ~:** hüpfenden Schrittes gehen; [J] (*Amer. Mus.*) große Sekunde.

❷ *v.i.*, **-pp-** treten; **~ lightly** *or* **softly** leise auftreten; **~ hesitantly/heavily/clumsily** mit zögernden Schritten gehen/einen schweren/unbeholfenen Schritt haben; **~ from the pavement on to the road** vom Bürgersteig auf die Straße treten; **~ across** *or* **over a puddle/gap** einen [großen] Schritt über eine Pfütze/Spalte machen; **don't ~ across the line!** nicht über die Linie treten!; **~ inside** eintreten; **please ~ inside for a moment** kommen Sie bitte auf einen Augenblick herein; **~ into** treten in (+ *Akk.*); steigen in (+ *Akk.*) ‹Fahrzeug, Flugzeug, Wanne›; **~ into sb.'s shoes** (*fig.*) an jmds. Stelle treten; **~ into one's dress/trousers** in sein Kleid/seine Hose steigen (*ugs.*); **~ on sth.** (*on the ground*) auf etw. (*Akk.*) treten; **~ on sb.'s foot/on the dog's tail** jmdm. auf den Fuß/dem Hund auf den Schwanz treten; **~ on a patch of oil/water** in eine Öl-/Wasserpfütze treten; **~ on [to]** steigen auf (+ *Akk.*); steigen in (+ *Akk.*) ‹Fahrzeug, Flugzeug›; **~ on it** (*coll.*) auf die Tube drücken (*ugs.*); **~ on sb.'s toes = tread on sb.'s toes** ⇒ **tread** 2; **~ out of** treten aus; steigen aus ‹Fahrzeug, Bad, Fluss›; **~ out of the room for a few minutes** für ein paar Minuten aus dem Zimmer gehen; **~ out of one's dress/trousers** aus seinem Kleid/seiner Hose steigen (*ugs.*); **~ out of line** (*fig.*) aus der Reihe tanzen (*ugs.*); **I ~ped outside** ich trat hinaus; **Have you been calling my girlfriend names? I think you'd better ~ outside!** Hast du meine Freundin beschimpft? Komm, wir gehen mal zusammen raus (*ugs.*); **~ over sb./sth.** über jmdn./etw. steigen; **~ over the starting line** über die Startlinie treten; **~ this way, please** hier entlang, bitte; **~ through a door/window** durch eine Tür treten/ein Fenster steigen; ⇒ *also* **breach** 1 C; **gas** 1 B

**~ a'side** *v.i.* [A] zur Seite treten; [B] (*fig.: resign*) seine Stellung räumen

**~ 'back** *v.i.* zurücktreten; **~ back in fright/surprise** vor Schreck/Überraschung [einen Schritt] zurückweichen

**~ 'down** ❶ *v.i.* [A] **~ down into the auditorium** ins Publikum herunterkommen *od.* -steigen; **~ down from the train/into the boat** aus dem Zug/in das Boot steigen; [B] (*fig.*) ⇒ **stand down** 1 A. ❷ *v.t.* (*Electr.*) heruntertransformieren (*ugs.*); ⇒ *also* **~-down**

**~ 'forward** *v.i.* [A] [einen Schritt] vortreten; [B] (*fig.: present oneself*) sich melden; **would somebody like to ~ forward and help me with the trick?** würde jemand gern nach vorn kommen und mir bei dem Trick assistieren?; **he has ~ped forward as the new candidate** er präsentierte sich als neuer Kandidat; **several ~ped forward** einige meldeten sich [freiwillig]

**~ 'in** *v.i.* [A] eintreten; (*into vehicle*) einsteigen; (*into pool*) hineinsteigen; **would you mind ~ping in for a moment?** würden Sie bitte einen Augenblick hereinkommen?; [B] (*fig.*) (*take sb.'s place*) einspringen; (*intervene*) eingreifen

**~ 'off** ❶ *v.i.* [A] (*get off*) (*from vehicle*) aussteigen; (*from a height*) hinabspringen; [B] (*Mil.: begin to march*) abmarschieren. ❷ *v.t.* [A] (*get off*) steigen aus ‹Fahrzeug›; treten von ‹Bürgersteig›; springen von ‹Klippe, Brücke›; [B] (*measure by pacing*) abschreiten (*geh.*)

**~ 'out** ❶ *v.i.* [A] (*leave a place*) hinausgehen; **the car/boat stopped and she ~ped out** der Wagen/das Boot hielt an und sie stieg aus; [B] (*lengthen stride*) ausschreiten (*geh.*); [C] (*dated fig.: be active socially*) ausgehen; **he has been ~ping out with this girl for a few months now** er geht jetzt schon seit ein paar Monaten mit diesem Mädchen (*ugs.*). ❷ *v.t.* steigen aus ‹Fahrzeug›

**~ 'up** ❶ *v.i.* [A] (*ascend*) hinaufsteigen; **~ up into** [ein]steigen in (+ *Akk.*) ‹Fahrzeug›; **~ up on to** steigen auf (+ *Akk.*) ‹Podest, Tisch›; [B] (*approach*) **~ up and ask sb.'s name** auf jmdn. zugehen und ihn nach seinem Namen fragen; **~ right up!** treten Sie näher!; **~ up to sb.** zu jmdm. treten; [C] (*increase*) zunehmen. ❷ *v.t.* [A] (*increase*) erhöhen; intensivieren ‹Wahlkampf›; verstärken ‹Anstrengungen›; verschärfen ‹Sicherheitsmaßnahmen, Streik›; [B] (*Electr.*) hinauftransformieren (*ugs.*); ⇒ *also* **~-up** 2

**step: ~ aerobics** *n.* Stepaerobic, *das;* **~brother** *n.* Stiefbruder, *der;* **~child** *n.* Stiefkind, *das;* **~daughter** *n.* Stieftochter, *die;* **~-down** *attrib. adj.* (*Electr.*) **~-down converter** *or* **transformer** Abwärtstransformator, *der;* **~father** *n.* Stiefvater, *der;* **~ladder** *n.* Stehleiter, *die;* **~mother** *n.* Stiefmutter, *die;* **~-parent** *n.* Stiefelternteil, *der;* **~parents** Stiefeltern *Pl.*

**steppe** /step/ *n.* (*Geog.*) Steppe, *die*

**stepped** /stept/ *adj.* gestuft; terrassiert ‹Berg, Hang›; Stufen‹pyramide, -giebel›

**'steppeland** *n.* (*Geog.*) Steppenland, *das*

**stepping stone** /'stepɪŋstəʊn/ *n.* Trittstein, *der;* (*fig.*) Sprungbrett, *das* (**to** für, in)

**step: ~sister** *n.* Stiefschwester, *die;* **~son** *n.* Stiefsohn, *der;* **~-up** ❶ *n.* Erhöhung, *die;* **a ~-up in output/production/security measures** eine Steigerung des Ausstoßes/der Produktion/Verschärfung der Sicherheitsmaßnahmen; ❷ *attrib. adj.* (*Electr.*) **~-up converter** *or* **transformer** Aufwärtstransformator, *der*

**stereo** /'sterɪəʊ, 'stɪərɪəʊ/ ❶ *n., pl.* **~s** [A] (*equipment*) Stereoanlage, *die;* ⇒ *also* **personal** D; [B] (*sound reproduction*) Stereo, *das.* ❷ *adj.* [A] (*sound*) stereo; Stereo‹effekt, -aufnahme, -platte›; [B] (*Optics*) stereoskopisch

**stereophonic** /sterɪə'fɒnɪk, stɪərɪə'fɒnɪk/ *adj.*, **stereophonically** /sterɪə'fɒnɪkəlɪ, stɪərɪə'fɒnɪkəlɪ/ *adv.* stereophon

**stereoscope** /'sterɪəskəʊp, 'stɪərɪəskəʊp/ *n.* Stereoskop, *das*

**stereoscopic** /sterɪə'skɒpɪk, stɪərɪə'skɒpɪk/ *adj.* stereoskopisch

S

**stereotype** /'steriətaip, 'stiəriətaip/ ❶ *n.* A Stereotyp, *das* (*Psych.*); Klischee, *das;* B (*Printing: plate*) Stereotyp[ie]platte, *die;* C *no pl.* (*Printing: process*) (*making of* ~*s*) Stereotypie, *die;* ~ **[printing]** Drucken mit Stereotyp[ie]platten. ❷ *v.t.* in ein Klischee zwängen; ~ **sb. as a villain** jmdn. in das Klischee des Schurken zwängen; ~**d** stereotyp ‹Redensart, Frage, Vorstellung›; klischeehaft ‹Sprache, Denkweise›; **the** ~**d business man** das Klischee des Geschäftsmanns

**sterile** /'sterail/ *adj.* A (*germ-free*) steril; B (*barren, lit. or fig.*) steril; unfruchtbar; (*fig.*) erfolglos ‹Geschäftsjahr, Bemühung›; nutzlos ‹Tätigkeit›; fruchtlos ‹Diskussion, Gespräch›

**sterilisation, sterilise, steriliser** ⇒ **steriliz-**

**sterility** /stə'rilıtı/ *n., no pl.* A (*absence of germs*) Sterilität, *die;* B (*barrenness, lit. or fig.*) Sterilität, *die;* Unfruchtbarkeit, *die;* (*fig.: of discussion*) Fruchtlosigkeit, *die*

**sterilization** /sterılaı'zeıʃn/ *n.* Sterilisation, *die*

**sterilize** /'sterılaız/ *v.t.* A (*make germ-free*) sterilisieren; B (*make barren*) sterilisieren ‹Tier, Mensch›; unfruchtbar machen ‹Land›

**sterilizer** /'sterılaızə(r)/ *n.* Sterilisator, *der*

**sterling** /'stɜ:lıŋ/ ❶ ▶ 1328 *n., no pl., no indef. art.* Sterling, *der;* **do they accept** *or* **take** ~**?** kann man bei ihnen in Pfund [Sterling] bezahlen?; **five pounds** ~**:** fünf Pfund Sterling; **in** ~**:** in Pfund [Sterling]; ~ **area** (*Hist.*) Sterlingblock, *der.* ❷ *attrib. adj.* A ~ **silver** Sterlingsilber, *das;* B (*fig.*) gediegen; **he is a** ~ **chap!** er ist ein zuverlässiger Bursche!; **do** ~ **work** erstklassige Arbeit leisten; **[this is]** ~ **stuff!** (*coll.*) tadellos!; erstklassig!

**stern**[1] /stɜ:n/ *adj.* streng; hart ‹Strafe›; ernst ‹Warnung›; **made of** ~**er stuff** (*fig.*) aus härterem Holz [geschnitzt]; **be** ~ **with sb.** mit jmdm. streng sein; jmdn. hart anpacken (*ugs.*)

**stern**[2] *n.* (*Naut.*) Heck, *das;* ~ **foremost** [mit dem] Heck voraus; ⇒ *also* **stern**[1] 1 F

**sternly** /'stɜ:nlı/ *adv.* streng; ernsthaft ‹warnen›; in strengem Ton ‹sprechen›; mit strenger Hand ‹regieren›

**'sternpost** *n.* (*Naut.*) Achtersteven, *der*

**sternum** /'stɜ:nəm/ *n., pl.* ~**s** *or* **sterna** /'stɜ:nə/ (*Anat.*) Brustbein, *das;* Sternum, *das* (*fachspr.*)

**steroid** /'stıərɔıd, 'sterɔıd/ *n.* (*Chem.*) Steroid, *das*

**stet** /stet/ (*Printing*) *v.i. imper.* bleibt

**stethoscope** /'steθəskəʊp/ *n.* (*Med.*) Stethoskop, *das*

**Stetson** ® /'stetsn/ *n.* Stetson[hut], *der*

**stevedore** /'sti:vədɔ:(r)/ *n.* ▶ 1261 (*Naut.*) Schauermann, *der*

**stew** /stju:/ ❶ *n.* A (*Gastr.*) Eintopf, *der;* **Irish** ~**:** Irishstew, *das;* B (*coll.: state*) **be in/get into a** ~**:** in heller Aufregung sein/völlig aus dem Häuschen geraten (*ugs.*); **be in** *or* **get into a** ~ **about** *or* **over sth.** sich über etw. (*Akk.*) [schrecklich (*ugs.*)] aufregen; **don't get into a** ~ **about nothing!** dreh nicht unnötig durch! (*ugs.*).
❷ *v.t.* (*Cookery*) schmoren [lassen]; ~ **apples/plums** Apfel-/Pflaumenkompott kochen.
❸ *v.i.* A (*Cookery*) schmoren; ‹Obst:› gedünstet werden; ~ **[in one's own juice]** (*fig.*) [im eigenen Saft] schmoren (*ugs.*); B (*fig.: fret*) ~ **over a problem** sich (*Dat.*) über ein Problem den Kopf zerbrechen (*ugs.*); C (*fig.: swelter*) schmoren (*ugs.*)

**steward** /'stju:əd/ ❶ *n.* ▶ 1261 A (*on ship, plane*) Steward, *der;* B (*supervising official*) (*at public meeting, ball, etc.*) Ordner, *der*/Ordnerin, *die;* ~**s** (*of race*) Rennleitung, *die;* ~**s' enquiry** (*Horseracing*) [Untersuchung und] Beratung der Rennleitung; ⇒ *also* **shop steward**; C (*estate manager*) Verwalter, *der*/Verwalterin, *die.* ❷ *v.t.* verwalten; ~ **a meeting** bei einer öffentlichen Veranstaltung Ordner/Ordnerin sein

**stewardess** /'stju:ədıs/ *n.* ▶ 1261 Stewardess, *die*

**stewardship** /'stju:ədʃıp/ *n.* Verwaltung, *die;* **hold the** ~ **of an estate** Verwalter/Verwalterin eines Gutes sein

**stewed** /stju:d/ *adj.* A (*Cookery*) geschmort; ~ **apples/plums** Apfel-/Pflaumenkompott, *das;* B (*over-brewed*) **the tea is** ~**:** der Tee hat zu lange gezogen; C (*coll.: drunk*) blau (*ugs.*); voll (*salopp*)

**stewing steak** /'stju:ıŋ steık/ *n., no pl., no indef. art.* [Rinder]schmorfleisch, *das*

**stew:** ~ **pan** *n.* (*Cookery*) Schmorpfanne, *die;* ~ **pot** *n.* (*Cookery*) Schmortopf, *der*

**stick** /stık/ ❶ *v.t.*, **stuck** /stʌk/ A (*thrust point of*) stecken; ~ **sth. in[to] sth.** mit etw. in etw. (*Akk.*) stechen; **she stuck a needle in[to] her finger** sie stach sich (*Dat.*) mit einer Nadel in den Finger; **get stuck into sb./sth./a meal** (*coll.: begin action*) jmdm. eine Abreibung verpassen/sich in etw. (*Akk.*) reinknien/tüchtig reinhauen (*salopp*); **I stuck a knife in[to] him** ich stieß *od.* (*ugs.*) rammte ihm ein Messer in den Leib; B (*impale*) spießen; ~ **sth. [up]on sth.** etw. auf etw. (*Akk.*) [auf]spießen; **like a stuck pig** ‹bluten› wie ein Schwein; ‹schreien› wie eine gestochene Sau; C (*coll.: put*) stecken; **he stuck a feather in his hat/a rose in his buttonhole** er steckte sich (*Dat.*) eine Feder an den Hut/eine Rose in das Knopfloch; ~ **a picture on the wall/a vase on the shelf** ein Bild an die Wand hängen/eine Vase aufs Regal stellen; ~ **10% on the bill** 10% zusätzlich auf die Rechnung setzen; ~ **one's hat on one's head** sich (*Dat.*) den Hut auf den Kopf stülpen; ~ **one's head out of the window** den Kopf aus dem Fenster strecken; ~ **sth. in the kitchen** etw. in die Küche tun (*ugs.*); ~ **one on sb.** (*sl.: hit*) jmdm. eine langen (*ugs.*); ~ **one's hands in one's pockets** die Hände in den Taschen vergraben; **you know where you can** ~ **that!, [you can]** ~ **it!** (*sl.*) das kannst du dir sonst wohin stecken!; D (*with glue etc.*) kleben; E (*make immobile*) **the car is stuck in the mud** das Auto ist im Schlamm stecken geblieben; **the door is stuck** die Tür klemmt [fest]; **she's been stuck indoors all day** (*fig. coll.*) sie hat den ganzen Tag im Haus hocken müssen (*ugs.*); F (*puzzle*) **be stuck for an answer/for ideas** um eine Antwort/um Ideen verlegen sein; **Can you help me with this problem? I'm stuck** Kannst du mir bei diesem Problem helfen? Ich komme nicht weiter; **be stuck for money** (*coll.*) gerade kein Geld haben; G (*cover*) ~ **sth. with pins/needles** Stecknadeln/Nadeln in etw. (*Akk.*) stecken; H (*stab*) ~ **sb. with a knife** jmdm. einen Messerstich beibringen; I (*Brit.: paste on wall*) kleben; '~ **no bills'** „Plakate ankleben verboten!"; J (*Brit. coll.: tolerate*) ~ **it** durchhalten; **she can't** ~ **him** sie kann ihn nicht riechen (*salopp*); **he can't** ~ **the book/film** er kann das Buch/den Film nicht ausstehen; **she can't** ~ **the heat/such conditions** sie kann die Hitze/solche Bedingungen nicht ertragen; **I can't** ~ **it/my job any longer** das/mein Job steht mir bis oben *od.* hier (*ugs.*); K (*coll.*) **be stuck with sth.** (*have to accept*) sich mit etw. herumschlagen müssen (*ugs.*); **be stuck with sb.** jmdn. am *od.* auf dem Hals haben (*ugs.*); **if we don't sell our car soon we'll be stuck with it** wenn wir unser Auto nicht bald verkaufen, werden wirs überhaupt nicht mehr los (*ugs.*); L (*coll.*) **be stuck on sb./sth.** (*captivated by*) auf jmdn./etw. abfahren (*salopp*); **be stuck on an idea** eine fixe Idee haben.
❷ *v.i.*, **stuck** A (*be fixed by point*) stecken; **there's a splinter** ~**ing in my finger** ich habe einen [Holz]splitter im Finger; B (*adhere*) kleben; **mud** ~**s** (*fig.*) etwas bleibt immer hängen (*fig.*); ~ **to sth.** an etw. (*Dat.*) kleben; **my wet clothes stuck to my body** meine nassen Kleider klebten mir am Körper; ~ **in the/sb.'s mind** (*fig.*) im/jmdm. im Gedächtnis haften bleiben; **she was called the 'iron lady' and the nickname stuck** sie wurde „Eiserne Lady" genannt, und der Spitzname blieb an ihr hängen; C (*become immobile*) ‹Auto, Räder:› stecken bleiben; ‹Schublade, Tür, Griff, Bremse:› klemmen; ‹Schlüssel:› feststecken; ~ **fast** ‹Auto, Rad:› feststecken; ‹Reißverschluss, Tür, Schublade:› festklemmen; **the words stuck in his throat** die Worte blieben ihm in der Kehle stecken; **the record is stuck** die Platte ist hängen geblieben; ⇒ *also* **stick-in-the-mud**; D (*protrude*) **a letter stuck from his pocket** ein Brief schaute ihm aus der Tasche; E (*coll.: remain*) bleiben; **are you going to** ~ **indoors all day?** willst du den ganzen Tag im Haus [herum]hocken? (*ugs.*); F (*coll.: be considered valid*) **the accusations will not** ~**:** die Anschuldigungen ziehen nicht (*ugs.*); **make a charge** ~**:** mit einer Anklage durchkommen (*ugs.*); **be made to** ~**:** hieb- und stichfest gemacht werden; G (*Cards*) **Do you want another card? — No, I'll** ~**:** Willst du noch eine Karte? — Nein, ich behalte mein Blatt.
❸ *n.* A ([*cut*] *shoot of tree, piece of wood*) Stock, *der;* (*staff*) [Holz]stab, *der;* (*walking* ~) Spazierstock, *der;* (*for handicapped person*) Krückstock, *der;* **pick up a large** ~ **from the ground** einen großen Knüppel vom Boden aufheben; **gather dry** ~**s** trockene Äste sammeln; ⇒ *also* **big** 1 A; B ⇒ **rod** C; C (*Hockey etc.*) Schläger, *der;* ~**s!** hoher Stock!; D (*long piece*) **a** ~ **of chalk/shaving soap** ein Stück Kreide/Rasierseife; **a** ~ **of dynamite/sealing wax** eine Stange Dynamit/Siegellack; **a** ~ **of rock/celery/rhubarb** eine Stange Rocks/Sellerie/Rhabarber; **a cinnamon** ~**:** eine Zimtstange; E *no pl., no art.* (*coll.: criticism*) **get** *or* **take [some]** ~**:** viel einstecken müssen; **give sb. [some]** ~**:** jmdn. zusammenstauchen (*ugs.*); F **give sb. the** ~**, take the** ~ **to sb.** (*cane sb.*) jmdn. den Stock spüren lassen; G ~ **of furniture** (*coll.*) Möbelstück, *das;* **up** ~**s** (*coll.*) seine [Sieben]sachen zusammenpacken (*ugs.*); H (*Motor Veh.: gear lever*) ⇒ **gearstick**; I (*Mus.*) ⇒ **baton** C; J (*Printing*) Winkelhaken, *der;* K **the** ~**s** (*Horseracing coll.*) die Hürden; die Hindernisse; **the race is over the** ~**s** das Rennen geht über Hindernisse; L *in pl.* (*coll.: rural area*) **in the** ~**s** in der hintersten Provinz; M (*coll.: person*) **a queer** ~**:** komischer Kauz (*ugs.*); **a funny old** ~**:** ein komischer alter Kauz (*ugs.*); N (*Mil.: of bombs*) Reihenwurf, *der.* ⇒ *also* **cleft**[2] 2; **cross** 4 B; **dirty** 1 H; **wrong** 1 C

~ **a'bout,** ~ **a'round** *v.i.* (*coll.*) dableiben; (*wait*) warten

~ **at** *v.t.* A (*hesitate at*) ~ **at sth./nothing** vor etw. (*Dat.*)/nichts zurückschrecken; B (*keep on with*) ~ **at one's books/studying** fleißig Bücher wälzen/studieren; ~ **'at it** (*coll.*) dranbleiben (*ugs.*)

~ **by** *v.t.* (*fig.*) stehen zu

~ **'down** *v.t.* A (*glue down*) festkleben; zukleben ‹Umschlag›; B (*coll.: put down*) hinknallen (*ugs.*) ‹Tisch, Kiste›; C (*coll.: write down*) schreiben

~ **'in** *v.t.* A (*jab in*) hineinstechen ‹Spritze, Nadel›; anstecken ‹Hutnadel›; **get stuck in** (*coll.*) (*working*) ranklotzen (*salopp*); (*eating*) reinhauen (*salopp*); B (*glue in*) einkleben; C (*coll.: put in*) hineinstecken; ⇒ *also* **nose** 1 A

~ **'on** ❶ *v.t.* A (*glue on*) aufkleben ‹Briefmarke, Etikett›; ankleben ‹Tapete›; B (*attach by pin etc.*) anstecken; C (*coll.: put on*) aufsetzen ‹Hut, Wasserkessel›; auflegen ‹Schallplatte›; ~ **an extra amount on the bill** (*fig.*) einen zusätzlichen Betrag auf die Rechnung setzen. ❷ *v.i.* kleben [bleiben]. ⇒ *also* **stick-on**

~ **'out** ❶ *v.t.* A herausstrecken ‹Brust, Zunge›; ausstrecken ‹Arm, Bein›; ~ **one's tongue out at sb.** jmdm. die Zunge herausstrecken; **would you like to** ~ **your neck out and predict the winner of the race?** (*fig. coll.*) willst du eine Prognose wagen, wer das Rennen gewinnt?; **he is not one to** ~ **his chin out** (*fig. coll.*) er verbrennt sich (*Dat.*) nicht gern die Finger (*ugs.*); B ~ **it out** (*coll.*) = **sweat it out** ⇒ **sweat** 3 D. ❷ *v.i.* A (*project*) ‹Brust, Bauch:› vorstehen; ‹steifes Kleid:› abstehen; ‹Nagel, Ast:› herausstehen; **his ears** ~ **out** er hat abstehende Ohren; **her hair stuck out from under the hat** ihr Haar

S

schaute unter dem Hut hervor; **she lay in bed with her legs/toes ~ing out** sie lag im Bett, und ihre Beine/Zehen schauten heraus; Ⓑ *(fig.: be obvious)* sich abheben; **~ out a mile** *(coll.)* [klar] auf der Hand liegen; **it ~s out a mile that he is only after her money** *(coll.)* dass er nur hinter ihrem Geld her ist, ist klar wie dicke Tinte *(ugs.)*; **~ out like a sore thumb** *(coll.)* ins Auge springen; **if you don't wear the correct clothes you'll ~ out like a sore thumb** *(coll.)* wenn du nicht korrekt gekleidet bist, fällst du unangenehm auf; Ⓒ **~ out for sth.** ⇒ **hold out** 2 C

**~ to** *v.t.* Ⓐ *(be faithful to)* halten zu ‹Person›; halten ‹Versprechen›; bleiben bei ‹Entscheidung, Meinung›; treu bleiben (+ *Dat.*) ‹Idealen, Grundsätzen›; Ⓑ *(not deviate from)* sich halten an (+ *Akk.*) ‹Plan, Text, Original›; bleiben an (+ *Dat.*) ‹Arbeit›; bleiben bei ‹Wahrheit, Thema›; **~ to business** bei der Sache bleiben; **~ to the point** beim Thema bleiben; **~ to what you are good at** bleibe bei dem, was du [gut] kannst; **thanks, but I'll ~ to beer** danke, ich bleibe beim Bier. ⇒ *also* **gun** 1 A; **last**[3]; **stick-to-it-ive**; **story**[1] A

**~ to'gether** ❶ *v.t.* zusammenkleben. ❷ *v.i.* Ⓐ *(adhere together)* zusammenkleben; Ⓑ *(fig.: remain united)* zusammenhalten

**~ 'up** ❶ *v.t.* Ⓐ *(seal)* zukleben; Ⓑ **be stuck up with sth.** *(coll.: sticky)* von etw. klebrig sein; Ⓒ *(coll.: put up, raise)* strecken, recken ‹Kopf, Hals›; anschlagen ‹Bekanntmachung, Poster›; aufschlagen ‹Zelt›; hinbauen, -setzen ‹Häuser›; raufsetzen *(ugs.)* ‹Preise›; anbringen ‹Regal›; **he stuck his nose up [in the air]** er streckte seine Nase in die Luft; **~ up one's hand** die Hand heben; **~ sth. up on a shelf** etw. auf ein Regal tun *(ugs.)*; **~ 'em up!** *(coll.)* Pfoten hoch! *(salopp)*; Ⓓ *(coll.: rob)* ausrauben; ⇒ *also* **stick-up**; Ⓔ **stuck up** *(conceited)* eingebildet; **be stuck up about sth.** sich *(Dat.)* etwas auf etw. *(Akk.)* einbilden. ❷ *v.i.* Ⓐ ‹Haar, Kragen:› hochstehen; ‹Nagel, Pflasterstein:› hervorstehen; Ⓑ **~ up for sb./sth.** für jmdn./etw. eintreten; **~ up for yourself!** setz dich zur Wehr!

**~ with** *v.t.* *(coll.)* Ⓐ *(keep contact with)* **~ with the leaders** sich an der Spitze halten *(bes. Sport)*; **~ 'with it!** bleib dran! *(ugs.)*; Ⓑ *(remain faithful to)* bleiben bei ‹Gruppe, Partei›; halten zu ‹Freund›; die Treue halten (+ *Dat.*) ‹Verein›

**stick de'odorant** *n.* Deo[dorant]stift, *der*

**sticker** /'stɪkə(r)/ *n.* Aufkleber, *der;* ⇒ *also* **billsticker**

**'stick figure** *n.* Strichmännchen, *das*

**sticking**/'stɪkɪŋ/: **~ place** ⇒ **~ point**; **~ plaster** *n.* *(Med.)* Heftpflaster, *das;* **~ point** *n.* *(fig.)* Hürde, *die*

**stick: ~ insect** *n.* Gespenst[heu]schrecke, *die;* **~-in-the-mud** ❶ *n.* *(person lacking initiative)* Trantüte, *die* *(ugs. abwertend)*; *(unprogressive person)* Spießer, *der* *(abwertend)*; ❷ *adj.* *(lacking in initiative)* schlafmützig *(ugs. abwertend)*; *(unprogressive)* spießig *(abwertend)*

**stickleback** /'stɪklbæk/ *n.* *(Zool.)* Stichling, *der*

**stickler** /'stɪklə(r)/ *n.* **be a ~ for tidiness/authority** es mit der Sauberkeit sehr genau nehmen/in puncto Autorität keinen Spaß verstehen

**stick: ~-on** *adj.* selbstklebend; **~pin** *n.* *(Amer.)* Krawattennadel, *die;* **~-to-it-ive** /stɪk'tu:ɪtɪv/ *adj.* *(Amer.)* verbissen; hartnäckig; **~-up** *n.* *(coll.)* bewaffneter Raubüberfall

**sticky** /'stɪkɪ/ ❶ *adj.* Ⓐ klebrig; feucht ‹Farbe, gestrichener/gewaschener Gegenstand›; zäh ‹Teig, Brei, Mischung›; **~ label** Aufkleber, *der;* **~ tape** Klebestreifen, *der;* Ⓑ *(humid)* schwül ‹Klima, Luft›; feucht ‹Haut›; **be all hot and ~:** ganz verschwitzt sein; Ⓒ *(coll.: uncooperative)* unnachgiebig; **be ~ about doing sth.** etw. [nur] widerwillig tun; Ⓓ *(coll.: unpleasant)* vertrackt *(ugs.)*; heikel; **a ~ situation** eine brenzlige Lage; ⇒ *also* **end** 1 H. ❷ *n.* *(coll.)* Post-it, *das* *(ugs.)*

**sticky 'wicket** *n.* *(Cricket) Spielfeld, das nach einem Regen schlecht zu bespielen ist;* **bat** *or* **be on a ~** *(fig.)* sich auf schlüpfrigem Boden befinden

**stiff** /stɪf/ ❶ *adj.* Ⓐ *(rigid)* steif; hart ‹Bürste, Stock›; **be frozen ~:** steif vor Kälte sein; ‹Wäsche, Körper[teile]:› steif gefroren sein; **this brush is ~ with paint** dieser Pinsel ist mit Farbe verklebt; ⇒ *also* **lip** A; Ⓑ *(intense, severe)* hartnäckig; schroff ‹Absage›; kräftig ‹Standpauke›; **~ competition** scharfe Konkurrenz; Ⓒ *(formal)* steif; förmlich ‹Brief, Stil›; Ⓓ *(difficult)* hart ‹Test›; schwer ‹Frage, Prüfung›; steil ‹Abstieg, Anstieg›; **be ~ going** *(fig. coll.)* harte Arbeit sein; Ⓔ stark, *(Seemannsspr.)* steif ‹Wind, Brise›; Ⓕ *(not bending, not working freely, aching)* steif ‹Gelenk, Gliedmaßen, Nacken, Person›; schwergängig ‹Angel, Kolben, Gelenk›; Ⓖ *(coll.: excessive)* saftig *(ugs.)* ‹Preis, Strafe›; Ⓗ *(strong)* steif *(ugs.)* ‹Drink›; stark ‹Dosis, Medizin›; **a ~ shot of rum** ein Schuss steifen Rum; Ⓘ *(thick)* zäh[flüssig]; Ⓙ *(coll.)* **be bored/scared/worried ~:** sich zu Tode langweilen/eine wahnsinnige Angst haben *(ugs.)*/sich *(Dat.)* furchtbare *(ugs.)* Sorgen machen; **bore/scare/worry sb. ~:** jmdn. zu Tode langweilen/jmdm. eine wahnsinnige Angst einjagen *(ugs.)*/jmdm. furchtbare *(ugs.)* Sorgen machen; Ⓚ *pred.* **the road was ~ with police** auf der Straße wimmelte es von Polizisten. ❷ *n.* *(sl.)* Leiche, *die*

**stiffen** /'stɪfn/ ❶ *v.t.* Ⓐ steif machen; stärken ‹Kragen›; versteifen ‹Material›; zäh[flüssig]er machen ‹Paste, Teig›; steif werden lassen ‹Gliedmaße›; Ⓑ *(fig.: bolster)* verstärken ‹Widerstand›; stärken ‹Moral, Entschlossenheit›. ❷ *v.i.* Ⓐ ‹Person:› erstarren; Ⓑ ‹Wind, Brise:› steifer werden *(Seemannsspr.)*, auffrischen; Ⓒ *(become thicker)* ‹Teig:› steifer werden; ‹Mischung:› zäher werden; Ⓓ *(fig.: become more resolute)* sich verstärken; **his resolve ~ed** er wurde in seinem Entschluss bestärkt

**stiffener** /'stɪfnə(r)/ *n.* Ⓐ *(for collar, corset)* Stäbchen, *das;* Ⓑ *(starch)* Stärke, *die;* Ⓒ *(Building)* Queraussteifung, *die;* Ⓓ *(coll.: drink)* kleine Stärkung *(scherzh.)*

**stiffening** /'stɪfnɪŋ/ *n.* Versteifung, *die*

**stiffly** /'stɪflɪ/ *adv.* Ⓐ *(rigidly, formally)* steif; *(fig.)* hartnäckig ‹Widerstand leisten›; Ⓑ *(strongly)* stark, *(Seemannsspr.)* steif ‹wehen›; Ⓒ *(erectly, with restricted movement)* steif ‹sitzen, gehen›; kerzengerade ‹stehen›

**stiff-'necked** *adj.* *(fig.)* starrsinnig

**stiffness** /'stɪfnɪs/ *n., no pl.* Ⓐ *(rigidity, formality)* Steifheit, *die;* *(of letter, language)* Förmlichkeit, *die;* Ⓑ *(intensity)* Härte, *die;* Ⓒ *(difficulty)* Schwierigkeit, *die;* Ⓓ *(of wind)* Stärke, *die;* Steifheit, *die* *(Seemannsspr.)*; Ⓔ *(lack of suppleness)* Steifheit, *die;* *(of hinge, piston)* geringe Beweglichkeit; **have a ~ in one's limbs** steife Glieder haben; *(due to exercise)* Muskelkater haben; Ⓕ *(coll.: excessiveness)* *(of punishment)* Strenge, *die;* *(of demand, price)* Überzogenheit, *die;* Ⓖ *(thick consistency)* Zähheit, *die*

**stifle** /'staɪfl/ ❶ *v.t.* ersticken; *(fig.: suppress)* unterdrücken; ersticken ‹Widerstand, Aufstand, Schrei›; übergehen ‹Einwand›; **we were ~d by the heat** wir erstickten fast vor Hitze. ❷ *v.i.* ersticken; **~ in the bad air/smoke** an der schlechten Luft/vom Rauch fast ersticken

**stifling** /'staɪflɪŋ/ *adj.* stickig; drückend ‹Hitze›; *(fig.)* einengend ‹Atmosphäre›; erdrückend ‹Einfluss, Herrschaft›; **the heat was ~:** es war drückend heiß

**stigma** /'stɪgmə/ *n., pl.* **~s** *or* **~ta** /'stɪgmətə, stɪg'mɑ:tə/ Ⓐ *(mark of shame)* Stigma, *das* *(geh.)*; Makel, *der* *(geh.)*; **the ~ of having been in prison** das Stigma, im Gefängnis gewesen zu sein; Ⓑ *(Bot.)* Stigma, *das;* Narbe, *die;* Ⓒ *in pl.* **~ta** *(Relig.)* Stigmata

**stigmatize (stigmatise)** /'stɪgmətaɪz/ *v.t.* stigmatisieren *(geh.)*; brandmarken

**stile** /staɪl/ *n.* Zauntritt, *der;* Trittleiter, *die;* ⇒ *also* **dog** 1 A

**stiletto** /stɪ'letəʊ/ *n., pl.* **~s** *or* **~es** Ⓐ *(dagger)* Stilett, *das;* Ⓑ **~ [heel]** Stöckelabsatz, *der;* **~[-heeled shoe]** Stöckelschuh, *der*

**still**[1] /stɪl/ ❶ *adj.* Ⓐ *pred.* still; **be ~:** [still] stehen; ‹Fahne:› sich nicht bewegen; ‹Hand:› ruhig sein; **hold** *or* **keep sth. ~:** etw. ruhig halten; **hold** *or* **keep a ladder/horse ~:** eine Leiter/ein Pferd festhalten; **hold ~!** halt still!; **keep** *or* **stay ~:** stillhalten; *(not change posture)* ruhig bleiben; ‹Pferd:› still stehen; ‹Gegenstand:› liegen bleiben; **sit ~:** still sitzen; **stand ~:** stillstehen; ‹Uhr:› stehen; ‹Arbeit:› ruhen; *(stop)* stehen bleiben; **my heart stood ~** *(fig.)* mir blieb das Herz stehen; **the country has just stood ~ for the last 20 years** *(fig.)* das Land hat sich die letzten 20 Jahre einfach nicht weiterentwickelt; **time stood ~:** die Zeit schien stillzustehen; ⇒ *also* **statue**; Ⓑ *(calm)* ruhig; ⇒ *also* **deep** 2; Ⓒ *(without sound)* still; ruhig; Ⓓ *(not sparkling)* nicht moussierend ‹Wein›; still ‹Mineralwasser›; **is this water sparkling or ~?** ist dieses Wasser mit oder ohne Kohlensäure?; Ⓔ *(hushed)* leise; **a** *or* **the ~ small voice [of conscience]** die [leise] Stimme des Gewissens.
❷ *adv.* Ⓐ *(without change)* noch; *expr. surprise or annoyance* immer noch; **drink your tea while it is ~ hot** trink deinen Tee, solange er [noch] heiß ist; Ⓑ *(nevertheless)* trotzdem; **~, we must not forget the opposite standpoint** wir dürfen aber auch den gegensätzlichen Standpunkt nicht außer Acht lassen; **~, what can you do about it?** aber was kann man dagegen tun?; Ⓒ *with comparative (even)* noch; **become fatter ~** *or* **~ fatter** noch *od.* immer dicker werden; **better/worse ~** *as sentence-modifier* besser/schlimmer noch; ⇒ *also* **less** 2.
❸ *n.* Ⓐ *(Photog.)* Fotografie *die;* **~s from the film** Filmbilder; Ⓑ *(silence)* **in the ~ of the night** in der Stille der Nacht.
❹ *v.t.* *(literary)* beruhigen; glätten ‹Wogen›; stillen ‹Hunger, Durst, Schmerz›; beschwichtigen ‹Gefühle›; befriedigen ‹Ehrgeiz›; ausräumen ‹Zweifel›; dämpfen ‹Geräusch›

**still**[2] *n.* Destillierapparat, *der*

**still: ~ birth** *n.* Totgeburt, *die;* **~born** *adj.* Ⓐ tot geboren; **the child was ~born** das Kind war eine Totgeburt *od.* kam tot zur Welt; Ⓑ *(fig.)* ⇒ **abortive**; **~ life** *n., pl.* **~ lifes** *or* **lives** *(Art)* Stillleben, *das*

**stillness** /'stɪlnɪs/ *n., no pl.* Ⓐ *(motionlessness)* Bewegungslosigkeit, *die;* Ⓑ *(quietness)* Stille, *die*

**still: ~ picture** ⇒ **still**[1] 3 A; **~ room** *n.* *(Brit.)* Destillierraum, *der*

**stilt** /stɪlt/ *n.* Ⓐ Stelze, *die;* Ⓑ *(support of building)* Pfahl, *der;* Ⓒ *(Ornith.)* Stelzenläufer, *der*

**stilted** /'stɪltɪd/ *adj.* gestelzt; gespreizt

**Stilton** /'stɪltən/ *n.* Stilton[käse], *der*

**stimulant** /'stɪmjʊlənt/ ❶ *attrib. adj.* *(Med.)* stimulierend. ❷ *n.* *(lit. or fig.)* Stimulans, *das;* Anregungsmittel, *das*

**stimulate** /'stɪmjʊleɪt/ *v.t.* Ⓐ anregen; stimulieren *(geh.)*; beleben ‹Körper›; *(sexually)* erregen; Ⓑ *(fig.)* anregen ‹Geist, Diskussion, Appetit›; hervorrufen ‹Reaktion›; wecken ‹Interesse, Neugier›; beleben ‹Wirtschaft, Wachstum, Markt, Absatz›; **~ sb. to sth./to do sth.** jmdn. zu etw. anregen/dazu anregen, etw. zu tun

**stimulating** /'stɪmjʊleɪtɪŋ/ *adj.* Ⓐ anregend; stimulierend *(geh.)*; belebend ‹Bad›; *(sexually)* erregend; Ⓑ *(fig.)* interessant; inspirierend ‹Prediger, Einfluss, Musik, Buch›

**stimulation** /stɪmjʊ'leɪʃn/ *n.* Ⓐ Anregung, *die;* Stimulierung, *die* *(geh.)*; *(sexual)* Erregung, *die;* Ⓑ *(fig.)* Anregung, *die;* *(of reaction)* Hervorrufen, *das;* *(of interest, curiosity)* Wecken, *das;* *(of economy, market, growth, sales)* Belebung, *die*

**stimulative** /'stɪmjʊlətɪv/ *adj.* anregend; stimulierend *(geh.)*; **the ~ effect of a cold shower** die belebende Wirkung einer kalten Dusche

**stimulus** /'stɪmjʊləs/ *n., pl.* **stimuli** /'stɪmjʊlaɪ/ Ⓐ *(spur)* Ansporn, *der* (**to** zu); **act as a ~ to sb.'s ambition** jmds. Ehrgeiz anspornen; Ⓑ *(rousing effect)* Anregung, *die;* **give a ~ to sales** den Umsatz beleben; Ⓒ *(Physiol.)* Stimulus, *der;* Reiz, *der*

**sting** /stɪŋ/ **1** *n.* **A** (*wounding*) Stich, *der;* (*by jellyfish, nettles*) Verbrennung, *die;* **B** (*pain*) Stechen, *das;* stechender Schmerz; (*from ointment, cane, whip, wind, rash*) Brennen, *das;* **the ~ of his criticism/remark/reproach** der Stachel seiner Kritik/Bemerkung/seines Vorwurfs; **a ~ in the tail** (*fig.*) ein Pferdefuß; **the story/film/letter had a ~ in the tail** am Ende der Geschichte/des Films/Briefs kam es knüppeldick (*ugs.*); **take the ~ out of sth.** (*fig.*) einer Sache (*Dat.*) den Stachel nehmen (*geh.*); **C** (*Zool.*) [Gift]stachel, *der;* (*of jellyfish*) Nesselkapsel, *die;* (*of snake*) Giftzahn, *der;* **D** (*Bot.*) Brennhaar, *das;* **E** (*vigour*) ⇒ **bite** 3 E; **F** (*fraud*) Ding, *das* (*ugs.*); (*police operation*) Operation, *die.*

**2** *v.t.*, **stung** /stʌŋ/ **A** (*wound*) stechen; **a bee stung [him on] his arm** eine Biene stach ihm in den Arm; **a jellyfish stung me/my leg** ich habe mich/mein Bein an einer Qualle verbrannt; **B** (*cause pain to*) **the cane stung the boy's fingers** der Stock brannte dem Jungen auf den Fingern; **the smoke/the wind stung my eyes** der Rauch/der Wind brannte mir in den Augen; **C** (*hurt mentally*) tief treffen; [zutiefst] verletzen; **his conscience stung him** er hatte Gewissensbisse; **~ing** scharf ‹Vorwürfe, Anklagen, Kritik›; **stung by remorse** von Reue gequält; **D** (*incite*) **~ sb. into sth./doing sth.** jmdn. zu etw. anstacheln/dazu anstacheln, etw. zu tun; **he was stung to anger by their insults** ihre Beleidigungen erregten seinen Zorn; **E** (*coll.: swindle*) übers Ohr hauen (*ugs.*); **~ sb. for sth.** jmdn. um etw. neppen (*ugs.*); **how much did they ~ you for [it]?** was haben sie dir [dafür] abgeknöpft? (*salopp*).

**3** *v.i.*, **stung** **A** (*feel pain*) brennen; **smoke makes my eyes ~:** Rauch brennt mir in den Augen; **the antiseptic made the wound/my skin ~:** das Antiseptikum brannte auf der Wunde/auf meiner Haut; **B** (*have ~*) stechen; **not all nettles/sorts of jellyfish ~:** nicht alle Nesseln/Quallenarten brennen

**stingily** /ˈstɪndʒɪlɪ/ *adv.* geizig; **behave ~:** knausern (*ugs.*)

**stinging nettle** /ˈstɪŋɪŋnetl/ *n.* (*Bot.*) Brennnessel, *die*

**ˈstingray** *n.* (*Zool.*) Stechrochen, *der*

**stingy** /ˈstɪndʒɪ/ *adj.* geizig; knaus[e]rig (*ugs.*); kümmerlich ‹Spende, Portion, Mahlzeit›; **be ~ with sth.** mit etw. geizen

**stink** /stɪŋk/ **1** *v.i.*, **stank** /stæŋk/ *or* **stunk** /stʌŋk/, **stunk** **A** stinken (**of** nach); **~ to high heaven** (*coll.*) gottserbärmlich stinken; (*fig.*) ‹Angelegenheit, Korruption:› zum Himmel stinken; **he ~s of money** (*coll.*) er stinkt vor Geld (*ugs.*); **something ~s here** (*coll.: is suspicious*) an dieser Sache stinkt etwas (*ugs.*); **B** (*fig.: be repulsive*) **sth. ~s** an etw. (+ *Dat.*) stinkt etwas (*ugs.*); **the book/film ~s** das Buch/der Film ist widerwärtig.

**2** *n.* **A** (*bad smell*) Gestank, *der;* **B** (*coll.: fuss*) Stunk, *der* (*ugs.*); **the scandal created an almighty ~:** der Skandal führte zu einem Riesenstunk (*ugs.*); **kick up** *or* **raise a ~ about sth.** wegen etw. Stunk machen (*ugs.*); **C** (*coll.*) **like ~:** wie verrückt (*ugs.*); **run like ~:** wie eine gesengte Sau (*derb*) rennen

**ˈstink bomb** *n.* Stinkbombe, *die*

**stinker** /ˈstɪŋkə(r)/ *n.* (*coll.*) **A** (*offensive person*) Stinker, *der* (*salopp*); Stinktier, *das* (*derb*); **B** (*offensive thing*) Widerlichkeit, *die* (*abwertend*); **a ~ [of a letter/reply]** ein stinkiger Brief/eine stinkige Antwort (*salopp*); **a ~ [of a cold]** eine saumäßige Erkältung (*derb*); **C** (*difficult task*) Hammer, *der* (*ugs.*); harte Nuss (*ugs.*)

**stinking** /ˈstɪŋkɪŋ/ **1** *adj.* **A** stinkend; **B** (*coll.: objectionable*) widerlich (*abwertend*); **a ~ cold** eine saumäßige Erkältung (*derb*). **2** *adv.* (*coll.*) **~ rich/drunk** stinkreich (*salopp*)/stinkbesoffen (*derb*)

**stint** /stɪnt/ **1** *v.t.* **A** (*restrict share of*) kurz halten; **~ oneself [of sth.]** sich [mit etw.] einschränken; **~ sb. of sth.** jmdn. mit etw. kurz halten; **B** (*supply stingily*) geizen mit; sparen mit ‹Worten›. **2** *v.i.* **~ on sth.** an etw. (*Dat.*) sparen. **3** *n.* **A** (*allotted amount*) [Arbeits]pensum, *das;* **do** *or* **work** *or* **have a long ~:** ein großes Arbeitspensum erledigen; **each of us did our ~ at the wheel** jeder von uns saß eine Zeit lang am Steuer; **B** (*limitation*) Einschränkung, *die;* **without ~:** uneingeschränkt

**stipend** /ˈstaɪpend/ *n.* Besoldung, *die;* (*Eccl.*) Gehalt, *das*

**stipendiary** /staɪˈpendɪərɪ, stɪˈpendɪərɪ/ **1** *attrib. adj.* besoldet; **~ magistrate** ⇒ **2**. **2** *n.* (*Brit.*) besoldeter Friedensrichter

**stipple** /ˈstɪpl/ *v.t.* **A** (*Art*) punktieren; **B** (*roughen*) [auf]rauen ‹Putz, Farbe›

**stipulate** /ˈstɪpjʊleɪt/ (*demand*) fordern; verlangen; (*lay down*) festlegen; (*insist on*) sich (*Dat.*) ausbedingen

**stipulation** /stɪpjʊˈleɪʃn/ *n.* **A** (*condition*) Bedingung, *die;* **on** *or* **with the ~ that ...:** unter der Bedingung, dass ...; **B** (*act*) ⇒ **stipulate**: Forderung, *die;* Festlegung, *die;* Ausbedingung, *die*

**stipule** /ˈstɪpju:l/ *n.* (*Bot.*) Nebenblatt, *das*

**stir**[1] /stɜ:(r)/ **1** *v.t.*, **-rr-** **A** (*mix*) rühren; umrühren ‹Tee, Kaffee›; **keep ~ring the soup** die Suppe ständig umrühren; **~ sth. into sth.** etw. in etw. (*Akk.*) [ein]rühren; **B** (*move*) bewegen; **~ oneself out of bed** sich aus dem Bett bewegen *od.* (*geh.*) bequemen; **~ one's stumps** (*coll.*) einen Zahn zulegen (*ugs.*); **C** (*fig.: arouse*) bewegen; wecken ‹Neugier, Interesse, Gefühle, Fantasie›; **a story to ~ the heart/blood** eine herzergreifende Geschichte/eine Geschichte, die das Blut in Wallung bringt; **~ sb. to action** jmdn. zum Handeln anstacheln; **~ sb. to greater efforts** jmdn. zu größeren Anstrengungen anspornen.

**2** *v.i.*, **-rr-** **A** (*move*) sich rühren; (*in sleep, breeze*) sich bewegen; **without ~ring** regungslos; **[not] ~ from the spot** sich [nicht] vom Fleck rühren; **B** (*fig.: be aroused*) sich regen (*geh.*); **C** (*rise from bed*) aufstehen; **nobody was ~ring in the house/village** das ganze Haus/Dorf schlief noch.

**3** *n.*, *no pl.* **A** (*commotion*) Aufregung, *die;* (*bustle, activity*) Betriebsamkeit, *die;* **cause** *or* **create** *or* **make a [big** *or* **great] ~:** [großes] Aufsehen erregen; **B** (*act of ~ring sth.*) **give the coffee/paint a ~:** den Kaffee umrühren/die Farbe rühren

**~ ˈin** *v.t.* einrühren

**~ ˈup** *v.t.* **A** (*disturb*) aufrühren; **B** (*fig.: arouse, provoke*) wecken ‹Neugier, Interesse, Leidenschaft›; aufrütteln ‹Anhänger, Gefolgsleute›; entfachen ‹Liebe, Hass, Streit, Zorn, Revolution›; schüren ‹Hass, Feindseligkeit›; **~ up the past/ill feelings** die Vergangenheit aufrühren/ungute Gefühle wecken; **~ up public opinion** die öffentliche Meinung aufbringen; **~ it up** (*coll.*) Unfrieden stiften

**stir**[2] *n.* (*sl.: prison*) Knast, *der* (*ugs.*); **be in ~:** Knast schieben (*salopp*)

**stir: ~-crazy** *adj.* (*sl.*) **be ~-crazy** eine Gefängnispsychose haben; **~-fry** *v.t.* (*Cookery*) unter Rühren schnell braten

**stirrer** /ˈstɜ:rə(r)/ *n.* **A** (*utensil*) Rührer, *der;* **B** (*one who provokes*) Aufwiegler, *der*/Aufwieglerin, *die*

**stirring** /ˈstɜ:rɪŋ/ *adj.* bewegend ‹Musik, Theaterstück, Poesie›; spannend ‹Roman, Geschichte›; mitreißend ‹Auftritt, Rede, Marsch›; bewegt ‹Zeiten›

**stirringly** /ˈstɜ:rɪŋlɪ/ *adv.* bewegend ‹gespielt›; spannend ‹erzählt›; mitreißend ‹gespielter Marsch›

**stirrup** /ˈstɪrəp/ *n.* **A** (*Riding*) Steigbügel, *der;* **B** (*of garment*) Steg, *der;* **C** (*Anat.*) **~ [bone]** Steigbügel, *der*

**stirrup: ~ cup** *n.* Abschiedstrunk, *der* (*geh.*); **~ iron** *n.* (*Riding*) Steigbügel, *der;* **~ pump** *n.* Handpumpe, *die* (*mit Fußstütze*)

**stitch** /stɪtʃ/ **1** *n.* **A** (*Sewing: pass of needle*) Stich, *der;* ⇒ *also* **save** 1 F; **B** (*result of needle movement*) (*Knitting, Crocheting*) Masche, *die;* (*Sewing, Embroidery*) Stich, *der;* **drop a ~** (*Knitting*) eine Masche fallen lassen; **undo the ~es** aufziehen; (*in seam, hem*) die Naht auftrennen; **C** (*kind of ~*) (*Knitting*) Muster, *das;* (*Sewing, Embroidery*) Stich, *der;* **D** (*coll.: piece of clothing*) **not have a ~ on** splitter[faser]nackt (*ugs.*) sein; **the burglars stole every ~ of clothing I had** die Einbrecher stahlen mir sämtliche Klamotten (*salopp*); **E** (*pain*) **[have] a ~ [in the side]** Seitenstechen [haben]; **F** (*coll.*) **be in ~es** sich kugeln vor Lachen (*ugs.*); **he/his jokes had me in ~es** ich wäre [beinahe] vor Lachen über ihn/seine Witze gestorben (*ugs.*); **G** (*Med.: to sew up wound*) Stich, *der;* **~es** Naht, *die;* **he had his ~es taken out** ihm wurden die Fäden gezogen; **need [five] ~es** [mit fünf Stichen] genäht werden müssen; **H** (*Bookbinding*) Heftung, *die.*

**2** *v.t.* nähen; (*Embroidery*) sticken; (*Bookbinding*) heften.

**3** *v.i.* nähen; (*Embroidery*) sticken; (*Bookbinding*) heften

**~ ˈdown** *v.t.* festnähen

**~ ˈon** *v.t.* annähen ‹Knopf›; aufnähen ‹Flicken, Borte›

**~ ˈup** *v.t.* nähen; zusammennähen ‹Stoffteile›; vernähen ‹Loch, Riss, Wunde›

**stitching** /ˈstɪtʃɪŋ/ *n.* **A** (*series of stitches*) Naht, *die;* **B** (*ornamental stitches*) Stickerei, *die;* **C** (*Bookbinding: fastening*) Heftung, *die*

**stoat** /stəʊt/ *n.* Hermelin, *das*

**stochastic** /stəˈkæstɪk/ *adj.* stochastisch; **~ theory** Stochastik, *die*

**stock** /stɒk/ **1** *n.* **A** (*origin, family, breed*) Abstammung, *die;* **a horse of good racing/breeding ~:** ein Renn-/Zuchtpferd mit gutem Stammbaum; **be** *or* **come of farming/French/good ~:** bäuerlicher/französischer Herkunft sein/aus einer guten Familie stammen; **B** (*supply, store*) Vorrat, *der;* (*in shop etc.*) Warenbestand, *der;* **our ~ is high/low** wir haben genug/zu wenig vorrätig; **our ~s of food/sherry** unsere Lebensmittelvorräte/unser Vorrat an Sherry (*Dat.*); **have a good ~ of information/knowledge** umfangreiche Informationen/ein umfangreiches Wissen haben; **be in ~/out of ~** ‹Ware:› vorrätig/nicht vorrätig sein; **sb. is out of ~ of sth.** jmd. hat etw. nicht vorrätig; **get** *or* **lay in a ~ of coal** sich (*Dat.*) einen Kohlevorrat anlegen; **have sth. in ~:** etw. auf *od.* (*Kaufmannsspr.*) am Lager haben; **keep sth. in ~** (*have available as a general policy*) etw. führen; **renew** *or* **replenish one's ~ of sth.** seinen Vorrat an etw. (*Dat.*) auffüllen; **take ~:** Inventur machen; (*fig.*) Bilanz ziehen; **take ~ of sb.** (*fig.*) jmdn. mustern; **take ~ of sth.** (*fig.*) über etw. (*Akk.*) Bilanz ziehen; **take ~ of oneself** (*fig.*) sein Leben Revue passieren lassen; **take ~ of one's position/situation/prospects** seinen Standort/seine Situation/seine Zukunftsaussichten bestimmen; ⇒ *also* **rolling stock**; **C** (*Cookery*) Brühe, *die;* **D** (*Finance*) Wertpapiere; (*shares*) Aktien; **sb.'s ~ is high/low** (*fig.*) jmds. Aktien stehen gut/schlecht (*fig.*); **take** *or* (*Amer.*) **put ~ in sth.** (*fig.*) viel von etw. halten; ⇒ *also* **defer**[1] A; **ordinary** B; **E** (*Hort.*) Stamm, *der;* (*for grafting*) Unterlage, *die;* **F** (*handle*) Griff, *der;* (*of gun*) Schaft, *der;* (*of plough*) Sterz, *der;* ⇒ *also* **lock**[2] 1 E; **G** (*Agric.*) [lebendes und totes] Inventar [eines landwirtschaftlichen Betriebes]; ⇒ *also* **fatstock**; **livestock**; **H** (*raw material*) [Roh]material, *das;* **[film] ~:** Filmmaterial, *das;* **[paper] ~:** Papierstoff, *der;* (*for printing on*) Papier, *das;* **I** (*Bot.*) Levkoje, *die;* ⇒ *also* **night-scented stock**; **Virginia stock**; **J** *in pl.* (*Hist.: punishment-frame*) Stock, *der;* **K** (*Naut.: anchor crossbar*) Stock, *der;* **L** *in pl.* (*Naut.: construction support*) Helling, *die;* Helgen, *der;* **be on the ~s** auf dem Stapel liegen; (*fig.*) in Vorbereitung sein; **have sth. on the ~s** (*fig.*) an etw. (*Dat.*) arbeiten; **M** (*tree stump*) [Baum]stumpf, *der.* ⇒ *also* **laughing stock**.

**2** *v.t.* **A** (*supply with ~*) beliefern; **~ a pond/river/lake with fish** einen Teich/Fluss/See mit Fischen besetzen; **her larder is ~ed with tins** sie hat einen [großen] Vorrat an Konserven in der Speisekammer; **a cellar ~ed with wine/sherry** ein gut mit Wein/Sherry bestückter Keller; **he has a memory ~ed with useless information** sein Gedächtnis ist mit nutzlosem Wissen voll

S

gepfropft (*ugs.*); [B] (*Commerc.: keep in ~*) auf *od.* (*fachspr.*) am Lager haben; führen. ❸ *attrib. adj.* [A] (*Commerc.*) vorrätig; **a ~ size/model** eine Standardgröße/ein Standardmodell; [B] (*fig.: trite, unoriginal*) abgedroschen (*ugs.*); **~ character** Standardrolle, *die*

**~ 'up** ❶ *v.i.* **~ up [with sth.]** sich (*Dat.*) einen Vorrat an etw. (*Dat.*) anlegen; **~ up with coal for the winter** sich für den Winter mit Kohlen eindecken; **~ up on sth.** seine Vorräte an etw. auffüllen. ❷ *v.t.* auffüllen; mit Fischen besetzen ‹Teich, Fluss, See›; **the library needs ~ing up with new books** die Bibliothek muss ihren Bestand um neue Bücher erweitern

**stockade** /stɒˈkeɪd/ ❶ *n.* Palisade, *die.* ❷ *v.t.* mit einer Palisade befestigen

**stock: ~breeder** *n.* Viehzüchter, *der*/-züchterin, *die;* **~breeding** *n.* Viehzucht, *die;* **~broker** *n.* ▶ 1261 (*Finance*) Effektenmakler, *der*/-maklerin, *die;* **~broker belt** *Wohngebiet reicher Geschäftsleute in der Umgebung einer Großstadt;* ≈ Speckgürtel, *der* (*ugs.*); **~broking** /ˈstɒkbrəʊkɪŋ/ *n., no pl.* (*Finance*) Effektenhandel, *der;* **~broking is a lucrative profession** der Handel mit Wertpapieren ist ein einträglicher Beruf; **~ car** *n.* [A] (*Amer. Railw.*) Viehwaggon, *der;* [B] (*racing car*) Stockcar, *der;* **~-car racing** *n.* Stockcarrennen, *das;* **~ cube** *n.* (*Cookery*) Brühwürfel, *der;* **~ exchange** *n.* (*Finance*) Börse, *die;* **the S~ Exchange** (*Brit.*) die [Londoner] Börse; **~fish** *n.* (*Cookery*) Stockfisch, *der;* **~holder** *n.* (*Finance*) Wertpapierbesitzer, *der*/-besitzerin, *die;* (*of shares*) Aktionär, *der*/Aktionärin, *die;* **be a ~holder in the company** Anteile an der Gesellschaft besitzen

**stockily** /ˈstɒkɪlɪ/ *adv.* **~ built** stämmig

**stockinet[te]** /stɒkɪˈnet/ *n.* (*Textiles*) Trikot, *der*

**stocking**[1] /ˈstɒkɪŋ/ *n.* [A] Strumpf, *der;* **in one's ~[ed] feet** in Strümpfen; **hang up one's ~:** den Strumpf für den Weihnachtsmann aufhängen; [B] (*of horse*) Strumpf, *der*

**stocking**[2] *n.* ⇒ **stock** 2: Belieferung, *die;* Besatz, *der;* Lagerhaltung, *die*

**stockinged** /ˈstɒkɪŋd/ *adj.* ⇒ **stocking**[1] A

**stocking: ~ filler** *n.* (*Brit.*) [A] *kleines Geschenk, das in den für den Weihnachtsmann aufgehängten Strumpf gesteckt wird;* [B] zusätzliche Kleinigkeit (*als Weihnachtsgeschenk*); **~ mask** *n.* Strumpfmaske, *die;* **~ stitch** *n.* (*Knitting*) Glattgestrick, *das;* **knit in ~ stitch** glatt rechts stricken; **~ stuffer** (*Amer.*) ⇒ **~ filler**

**stock-in-'trade** *n.* Inventar, *das;* (*workman's tools*) Handwerkszeug, *das;* (*fig.: resource*) [festes] Repertoire; **be the ~ of sb.** zu jmds. festem Repertoire gehören

**stockist** /ˈstɒkɪst/ *n.* (*Brit. Commerc.*) Fachhändler/-händlerin [mit größerem Warenlager]

**stock: ~jobber** *n.* (*Finance*) [A] (*Brit.: dealer*) Jobber, *der;* [B] (*Amer. derog.: broker*) [Börsen]spekulant, *der*/-spekulantin, *die;* **~jobbing** *n.* (*Brit. Finance*) Börsenspekulation, *die;* **~list** *n.* [A] (*Finance*) Kurszettel, *der;* [B] (*Commerc.*) Inventarliste, *die;* **~ market** *n.* (*Finance*) [A] ⇒ **stock exchange;** [B] (*trading*) Börsengeschäft, *das;* **lose money on the ~ market** Geld an der Börse verlieren; **~pile** ❶ *n.* Vorrat, *der;* (*of weapons*) Arsenal, *das;* ❷ *v.t.* horten; anhäufen ‹Waffen›; **~pot** *n.* (*Cookery*) Suppentopf, *der;* **~room** *n.* Lager, *das;* **~-'still** *pred. adj.* bewegungslos; **stand ~-still** regungslos [da]stehen; **~taking** *n.* (*Commerc.*) Inventur, *die;* **closed for ~taking** wegen Inventur geschlossen

**stocky** /ˈstɒkɪ/ *adj.* stämmig; kräftig ‹Pflanze, Trieb›

**'stockyard** *n.* Viehhof, *der*

**stodge** /stɒdʒ/ *n.* (*coll.: food*) Brei, *der*

**stodgy** /ˈstɒdʒɪ/ *adj.* [A] pappig [und schwer verdaulich] ‹Essen›; [B] (*heavy, uninteresting*) langweilig ‹Buch›; schwerfällig ‹Stil, Poesie›; [C] (*dull, drab*) trübselig ‹Person, Leben usw.›

**stoic** /ˈstəʊɪk/ ❶ *n.* [A] **S~** (*Philos.*) Stoiker, *der;* [B] (*impassive person*) Stoiker, *der*/Stoikerin, *die.* ❷ *adj.* [A] **S~** (*Philos.*) stoisch; **the S~ philosophers/school** die Stoiker/die Stoa; [B] stoisch ‹Person, Ablehnung, Antwort usw.›

**stoical** /ˈstəʊɪkl/ *adj.*, **stoically** /ˈstəʊɪkəlɪ/ *adv.* stoisch

**stoicism** /ˈstəʊɪsɪzm/ *n., no pl.* [A] **S~** (*Philos.*) Stoizismus, *der;* [B] (*impassiveness*) Stoizismus, *der* (*geh.*); stoische Ruhe; **do sth. with ~:** etw. mit stoischer Gelassenheit tun

**stoke** /stəʊk/ ❶ *v.t.* heizen ‹Ofen, Kessel›; unterhalten ‹Feuer›; **~ a fire with coal** Kohle nachlegen. ❷ *v.i.* ⇒ **~ up** 2

**~ 'up** ❶ *v.t.* aufheizen ‹Kessel, Ofen, Dampfmaschine›; **~ a fire up** Brennstoff auf ein Feuer legen. ❷ *v.i.* (*coll.: feed oneself*) sich voll stopfen (*ugs.*)

**stoke: ~hold** *n.* (*Naut.*) Heizraum, *der;* **~hole** *n.* Heizerstand, *der*

**stoker** /ˈstəʊkə(r)/ *n.* ▶ 1261 Heizer, *der*/Heizerin, *die* (*Berufsbez.*)

**STOL** /stɒl/ *abbr.* (*Aeronaut.*) **short take off and landing** STOL; Kurzstart

**stole**[1] /stəʊl/ *n.* Stola, *die*

**stole**[2] ⇒ **steal** 1, 2

**stolen** /ˈstəʊln/ ❶ ⇒ **steal** 1, 2. ❷ *attrib. adj.* heimlich ‹Vergnügen, Kuss›; verstohlen ‹Blick›; **~ goods** Diebesgut, *das;* **receiving ~ goods** Hehlerei, *die;* **receiver of ~ goods** Hehler, *der*/Hehlerin, *die*

**stolid** /ˈstɒlɪd/ *adj.* stur (*ugs.*); wacker (*iron.*) ‹Arbeiter›; unbeirrbar ‹Entschlossenheit›; hartnäckig ‹Schweigen, Weigerung, Gleichgültigkeit›

**stolidity** /stəˈlɪdɪtɪ/ *n., no pl.* Sturheit, *die* (*ugs.*); (*of refusal, opposition*) Hartnäckigkeit, *die*

**stolidly** /ˈstɒlɪdlɪ/ *adv.* stur (*ugs.*); wacker (*iron.*) ‹arbeiten›; starrsinnig ‹sich widersetzen, schweigen›; stumpf ‹blicken, marschieren›

**stoma** /ˈstəʊmə/ *n., pl.* **~s** *or* **~ta** /ˈstəʊmətə/ [A] (*Zool.*) Körperöffnung, *die;* [B] (*Bot.*) Spaltöffnung, *die*

**stomach** /ˈstʌmək/ ❶ *n.* [A] ▶ 966 (*Anat., Zool.*) Magen, *der;* **lie heavy on sb.'s ~:** jmdm. schwer im Magen liegen; **on an empty ~:** mit leerem Magen ‹arbeiten, fahren, weggehen›; auf nüchternen Magen ‹Alkohol trinken, Medizin einnehmen›; **on a full ~:** mit vollem Magen; **turn sb.'s ~:** jmdm. den Magen umdrehen (*ugs.*); **the smell/sight of food turned her ~:** bei dem Geruch/beim Anblick des Essens drehte sich ihr der Magen um (*ugs.*); [B] (*abdomen, paunch*) Bauch, *der;* **have a pain in one's ~:** Bauchschmerzen haben; **lie on one's ~:** auf dem Bauch liegen; **develop a ~:** einen Bauch ansetzen; **pull your ~ in!** zieh deinen Bauch ein!; ⇒ *also* **pit**[1] 1 B; [C] **have the/no ~ [for sth.]** (*wish/not wish to eat*) Appetit/keinen Appetit [auf etw. (*Akk.*)] haben; (*fig.: interest*) Lust/keine Lust [auf etw. (*Akk.*)] haben; (*fig.: courage*) Mut/keinen Mut [zu etw.] haben.
❷ *v.t.* [A] (*eat, drink*) herunterbekommen (*ugs.*); (*keep down*) bei sich behalten; [B] (*fig.: tolerate*) ausstehen; hinnehmen ‹Beleidigung›; akzeptieren ‹Vorstellung, Vorgehen, Rat›

**stomach: ~ ache** *n.* ▶ 1232 Magenschmerzen *Pl.;* **have a ~ ache** Magenschmerzen haben; **~ pump** *n.* (*Med.*) Magenpumpe, *die;* **~ upset** *n.* ▶ 1232 Magenverstimmung, *die*

**stomp** /stɒmp/ ❶ *n.* (*dance*) Stomp, *der.* ❷ *v.i.* [A] (*tread heavily*) **~ [about** *or* **around]** [umher]stampfen; [B] (*Amer.: stamp feet*) [mit den Füßen] aufstampfen

**stone** /stəʊn/ ❶ *n.* [A] (*also Med., Bot.*) Stein, *der;* **[as] hard as [a] ~:** steinhart; **his heart is** *or* **he has a heart of** *or* **[as] hard as [a] ~** (*fig.*) sein Herz ist aus Stein; er hat ein Herz aus Stein; **throw ~s/a ~ at sb.** jmdn. mit Steinen bewerfen/einen Stein auf jmdn. werfen; (*fig.*) jmdm. am Zeug flicken (*ugs.*); **cast** *or* **throw the first ~** (*fig.*) den ersten Stein werfen; **only a ~'s throw [away]** (*fig.*) nur einen Steinwurf weit entfernt; **leave no ~ unturned** (*fig.*) Himmel und Hölle in Bewegung setzen; **leave no ~ unturned to achieve sth.** (*fig.*) alles dransetzen, um etw. zu erreichen; **sink like a ~:** wie ein Stein untergehen; **the lift dropped like a ~:** der Aufzug fiel wie ein Stein in die Tiefe; **be written** *or* **carved** *or* **set in ~** (*fig.*) unverrückbar sein; ⇒ *also* **bird** A; **blood** 1 A; **glass** 2; **philosopher's stone; Portland stone; rolling stone;** [B] (*gem*) [Edel]stein, *der;* [C] (*Med., Bot.*) Stein, *der;* [D] ⇒ **hailstone;** [E] ▶ 1682 *pl. same* (*Brit.: weight unit*) *Gewicht von 6,35 kg.*
❷ *adj.* steinern; Stein‹hütte, -kreuz, -mauer, -brücke›; **~ jar/urn** Krug/Urne aus Steingut.
❸ *v.t.* [A] mit Steinen bewerfen; **~ sb. [to death]** jmdn. steinigen; **~ me!, ~ the crows!** (*coll.*) mich laust der Affe! (*ugs.*); [B] entsteinen ‹Obst›

**stone: S~ Age** *n.* (*Archaeol.*) Steinzeit, *die;* *attrib.* Steinzeit-; **~-cold** ❶ *adj.* eiskalt; ❷ *adv.* **~-cold sober** stocknüchtern

**stoned** /stəʊnd/ *adj.* (*sl.*) stoned (*Drogenjargon*); (*drunk*) voll zu (*salopp*); **get ~ [on drugs]** sich anturnen (*ugs.*); **be ~ out of one's head** *or* **mind** völlig stoned *od.* zugekifft sein (*Drogenjargon*); (*drunk*) total zu sein (*ugs.*)

**stone: ~-'dead** *pred. adj.* mausetot (*fam.*); **kill sth. ~-dead** (*fig.*) etw. völlig zunichte machen; **~-'deaf** *adj.* stocktaub (*ugs.*); **~-ground** *adj.* mit Mühlsteinen gemahlen; **~mason** *n.* ▶ 1261 Steinmetz, *der;* **~ pine** *n.* (*Bot.*) Pinie, *die;* Nusskiefer, *die;* **~'wall** (*Brit.*) ❶ *v.i.* mauern (*fig.*); **~wall on an issue** in einer Angelegenheit mauern; ❷ *v.t.* **~wall sth.** bei etw. mauern; **~walling** /ˈstəʊnwɔːlɪŋ/ *n.* (*Brit.*) **~walling [tactics]** Hinhaltetaktik, *die;* **~ware** *n., no pl.* Steingut, *das;* *attrib.* ‹Krug, Vase› aus Steingut; **~washed** *adj.* mit Steinen ausgewaschen; **be ~washed** mit Steinen ausgewaschen *od.* (*fachspr.*) stonewashed sein; **~work** *n.* Mauerwerk, *das*

**stony** /ˈstəʊnɪ/ *adj.* [A] (*full of stones*) steinig; **fall on ~ ground** (*fig.*) auf unfruchtbaren Boden fallen; [B] (*like stone*) steinartig; [C] (*hostile*) steinern (*geh.*) ‹Blick, Miene›; frostig ‹Person, Empfang, Schweigen›; [D] *pred.* (*coll.*) ⇒ **stony-broke**

**stony-'broke** *pred. adj.* (*coll.*) völlig abgebrannt (*ugs.*)

**stood** ⇒ **stand** 1, 2

**stooge** /stuːdʒ/ (*coll.*) ❶ *n.* [A] (*Theatre: comedian*) Stichwortgeber, *der*/-geberin, *die;* [B] (*compliant person*) Marionette, *die* (*fig.*). ❷ *v.i.* **~ for sb.** (*for comedian*) jmdm. die Stichworte liefern; (*as deputy etc.*) jmds. Marionette sein

**stool** /stuːl/ *n.* [A] Hocker, *der;* **fall between two ~s** (*fig.*) sich zwischen zwei Stühle setzen; [B] ⇒ **footstool;** [C] *in sing. or pl.* (*Physiol.: faeces*) Stuhl, *der;* [D] (*Bot.*) (*of tree*) *Baumstumpf mit frisch austreibenden Schösslingen;* (*of dormant plant*) Wurzelstock, *der;* (*of cut plant*) Mutterpflanze, *die*

**'stool pigeon** *n.* [A] (*Hunting*) Locktaube, *die;* [B] (*fig.: decoy*) Lockvogel, *der;* [C] (*police informer*) Polizeispitzel, *der*

**stoop**[1] /stuːp/ ❶ *v.i.* [A] **~ [down]** sich bücken; **~ over sth.** sich über etw. (*Akk.*) beugen; **he'd ~ to anything to get his way** (*fig.*) ihm ist jedes Mittel recht[, um sein Ziel zu erreichen]; **I wouldn't ~ so low!** (*fig.*) ich würde mich nicht so erniedrigen!; **~ to do sth.** (*fig.*) sich dazu erniedrigen, etw. zu tun; **~ to deceit/a lie** sich für Verrat/eine Lüge hergeben; [B] (*have ~*) gebeugt gehen; [C] ⇒ **swoop** 2. ❷ *v.t.* beugen; **~ed with old age** vom Alter gebeugt. ❸ *n.* gebeugte Haltung; **have a/walk with a ~:** einen krummen Rücken haben/gebeugt gehen

**stoop**[2] *n.* (*Amer.*) *nicht überdachte, über Treppen erreichbare Terrasse vor einem Haus*

**stop** /stɒp/ ❶ *v.t.*, **-pp-:** [A] (*not let move further*) anhalten ‹Person, Fahrzeug›; aufhalten ‹Fortschritt, Verkehr, Feind›; verstummen lassen (*geh.*) ‹Gerücht, Geschichte, Lüge›; ‹Tormann:› halten ‹Ball›; **she ~ped her car** sie hielt an; **~ thief!** haltet den Dieb!; **there's no ~ping sb.** jmd. lässt sich nicht aufhalten; **~ a bullet** *or* **one** (*coll.*) (*get killed*) umgelegt werden (*salopp*); (*get wounded*) eine Kugel abkriegen (*ugs.*) ⇒ *also* **track** 1 B; [B] (*not let continue*) unterbrechen ‹Redner, Spiel, Gespräch, Vorstellung›; beenden ‹Krieg, Gespräch, Treffen, Spiel, Versuch, Arbeit›; stillen ‹Blutung›; stoppen ‹Produktion, Uhr, Streik, Inflation›; einstellen ‹Handel, Zahlung, Lieferung, Besuche, Subskriptionen, Bemühungen›; abstellen ‹Strom, Gas, Wasser, Missstände›; beseitigen ‹Schmerz›; **~ that/that nonsense/that noise/your threats!** hör damit/mit diesem Unsinn/diesem Lärm/deinen Drohungen auf!; **he had his grant/holidays ~ped** seine Unterstützung wurde/Ferien wurden gestrichen; **bad light ~ped play** (*Sport*) das Spiel wurde wegen schlechter Lichtverhältnisse abgebrochen; **~ the show** (*fig.*) Furore machen; **just you try and ~ me!** versuch doch, mich daran zu hindern!; **~ working** mit der Arbeit aufhören; **~ smoking/crying** aufhören zu rauchen/weinen; **never ~ doing sth.** etw. unaufhörlich tun; **~ 'saying that!** sag das nicht mehr!; **~ being silly!** hör mit diesem Quatsch auf!; **~ it!** hör auf [damit]!; (*in more peremptory tone*) Schluss damit!; **~ oneself** sich zurückhalten; **I couldn't ~ myself** ich konnte nicht anders; ⇒ *also* **rot** 1 A; **C** (*not let happen*) verhindern ‹Verbrechen, Unfall›; **I managed to ~ myself [from] punching him** ich musste mich sehr zurückhalten, um ihn nicht zu schlagen; **He was determined to do/say it. We couldn't ~ him** Er war entschlossen, es zu tun/sagen. Wir konnten ihn nicht davon abhalten; **she couldn't ~ herself [from] coughing** sie versuchte vergeblich, ihren Husten zu unterdrücken; **you won't ~ me [from] seeing her** du wirst mich nicht daran hindern, sie zu sehen; **he tried to ~ us parking** er versuchte uns am Parken zu hindern; **he phoned his mother to ~ her [from] worrying** er rief seine Mutter an, damit sie sich keine Sorgen machte; **~ sth. [from] happening** verhindern, dass etw. geschieht; **there's nothing to ~ me/you** *etc.* **[doing sth.]** es gibt nichts, was mich/dich *usw.* daran hindern könnte[, etw. zu tun]; **D** (*cause to cease working*) abstellen ‹Maschine usw.›; ‹Streikende:› stilllegen ‹Betrieb›; **his/her face is enough to ~ a clock** (*fig. coll.*) wenn man sein/ihr Gesicht sieht, haut es einen um (*ugs.*); **E** (*block up*) zustopfen ‹Loch, Öffnung, Riss, Ohren›; verschließen ‹Wasserhahn, Rohr, Schlauch, Flasche›; **~ holes in a wall with concrete/filler** Löcher in einer Wand mit Beton/Spachtelmasse füllen; **~ sb.'s mouth** (*fig.*) jmdm. den Mund stopfen (*ugs.*); **F** (*withhold*) streichen; **the cost will be ~ped out of** *or* **from his salary** die Kosten werden von seinem Gehalt abgezogen; **~ payment** (*Finance*) die Zahlungen [wegen Insolvenz] einstellen; **~ [payment of] a cheque** einen Scheck sperren lassen; **G** (*Boxing*) (*parry*) parieren; (*knock out*) k.o. schlagen; **H** (*Mus.*) **~ a string** eine Saite greifen; **a ~ped pipe [of an organ]** eine gedackte [Orgel]pfeife.

❷ *v.i.*, **-pp-**: **A** (*not extend further*) aufhören; ‹Straße, Treppe:› enden; ‹Ton:› verstummen; ‹Ärger:› verfliegen; ‹Schmerz:› abklingen; ‹Zahlungen, Lieferungen:› eingestellt werden; **at this point his knowledge ~s** an diesem Punkt ist sein Wissen erschöpft; **B** (*not move or operate further*) ‹Fahrzeug, Fahrer:› halten; ‹Maschine, Motor:› stillstehen; ‹Uhr, Fußgänger, Herz:› stehen bleiben; **he ~ped in the middle of the sentence** er unterbrach sich mitten im Satz; **he never ~s to think [before he acts]** er denkt nie nach [bevor er handelt]; **~!** halt!; **~ at nothing** vor nichts zurückschrecken; **~ dead** plötzlich stehen bleiben; ‹Redner:› abbrechen; **you never know when to ~:** du weißt einfach nicht, wann du aufhören musst; ⇒ *also* **short** 2 A; **track** 1 B; **C** (*stay*) bleiben; **~ at a hotel/at a friend's house/with sb.** in einem Hotel/im Hause eines Freundes/bei jmdm. wohnen; **~ for** *or* **to dinner** zum Essen bleiben; **~ for coffee afterwards** zum Kaffeetrinken [noch] dableiben; **I'm not ~ping** ich kann nicht lange bleiben.

❸ *n.* **A** (*halt*) Halt, *der;* **there will be two ~s for coffee on the way** es wird unterwegs zweimal zum Kaffeetrinken angehalten; **this train goes to London with only two ~s** dieser Zug fährt mit nur zwei Zwischenhalten nach London; **bring to a ~:** zum Stehen bringen ‹Fahrzeug›; zum Erliegen bringen ‹Verkehr›; unterbrechen ‹Arbeit, Diskussion, Treffen›; **the fire brought the show/performance to a [sudden] ~:** das Feuer setzte der Show/dem Auftritt ein [plötzliches] Ende (*geh.*); **come to a ~:** stehen bleiben; ‹Fahrzeug:› zum Stehen kommen; ‹Gespräch:› abbrechen; ‹Arbeit, Verkehr:› zum Erliegen kommen; ‹Vorlesung:› abgebrochen werden; **make a ~ at** *or* **in a place** in einem Ort Halt machen; **put a ~ to** abstellen ‹Missstände, Unsinn›; unterbinden ‹Versuche›; aus der Welt schaffen ‹Gerücht›; **put a ~ on a cheque** einen Scheck sperren lassen; **without a ~:** ohne Halt ‹fahren, fliegen›; ohne anzuhalten ‹gehen, laufen›; ununterbrochen ‹arbeiten, reden›; **B** (*place*) Haltestelle, *die;* **the ship's first ~ is Cairo** der erste Hafen, den das Schiff anläuft, ist Kairo; **the plane's first ~ is Frankfurt** die erste Zwischenlandung des Flugzeuges ist in Frankfurt; **C** (*Brit.: punctuation mark*) Satzzeichen, *das;* ⇒ *also* **full stop a**; **D** (*in telegram*) stop; **E** (*Mus.*) (*row of organ pipes*) Register, *das;* (*organ knob*) Registerzug, *der;* **pull out all the ~s** (*fig.*) alle Register ziehen; **F** (*to limit movement*) Anschlag, *der;* **G** (*Photog.*) Blende, *die;* **H** (*Phonet.*) Verschlusslaut, *der*

**~ a'way** (*coll.*) ⇒ **stay away** A

**~ be'hind** ⇒ **stay behind**

**~ 'by** (*Amer.*) ❶ *v.i.* vorbeischauen (*ugs.*); **~ by at the store** im Geschäft vorbeigehen (*ugs.*). ❷ *v.t.* **~ by sb.'s house** *or* **place [and have a drink]** bei jmdm. [auf einen Drink] vorbeischauen (*ugs.*); **we'll ~ by the shop and get some apples** wir gehen schnell im Laden vorbei und kaufen [uns] ein paar Äpfel

**~ 'down** *v.t.* (*Photog.*) **~ down to f/16** auf Blende 16 abblenden

**~ 'in** (*coll.*) ⇒ **stay in** B

**~ 'off** *v.i.* einen Zwischenaufenthalt einlegen; **~ off at the pub for a packet of cigarettes** an der Kneipe kurz anhalten, um Zigaretten zu kaufen; ⇒ *also* **stopoff**

**~ 'on** (*coll.*) ⇒ **stay on** C

**~ 'out** *v.i.* **A** draußen bleiben; **B** (*remain on strike*) ‹Arbeiter:› weiterstreiken (*ugs.*)

**~ 'over** *v.i.* einen Zwischenaufenthalt machen; (*remain for the night*) übernachten (**at** bei); ⇒ *also* **stopover**

**~ 'up** ❶ *v.t.* ⇒ **~** 1 E. ❷ *v.i.* ⇒ **stay up** A

**stop: ~ button** *n.* Stopptaste, *die;* **press the ~ button** [auf] die Stopptaste drücken; **~cock** *n.* Abstellhahn, *der;* Absperrhahn, *der* (*Technik*); **~gap** *n.* Notbehelf, *der;* (*scheme, measure, plan, person*) Notlösung, *die; attrib.* behelfsmäßig; **a ~gap measure** eine Behelfsmaßnahme; **~-'go** *n.* (*Brit.*) Hin und Her, *das;* (*boom and recession*) Auf und Ab, *das; attrib.* **~-go strategy/policies** strategisches/politisches Hin und Her; **~ light** *n.* **A** (*red traffic light*) rotes Licht; **if the ~ light shows** wenn die Ampel rot ist; **B** (*Motor Veh.*) Bremslicht, *das;* **~ line** *n.* (*on road*) Haltelinie, *die;* **~off** ⇒ **~over**; **~ order** *n.* **A** (*Finance*) limitierter Börsenauftrag; **B** (*Law*) *gerichtliche Anordnung, dass über bei Gericht hinterlegte Wertpapiere nicht verfügt werden darf;* **~over** *n.* Stopover, *der;* Zwischenaufenthalt, *der;* (*of aircraft*) Zwischenlandung, *die*

**stoppage** /'stɒpɪdʒ/ *n.* **A** (*halt*) Stillstand, *der;* (*strike*) Streik, *der;* (*in traffic*) Stau, *der;* (*Sport*) Unterbrechung, *die;* **B** (*cancellation*) Sperrung, *die;* (*of delivery*) Einstellung, *die;* **C** (*deduction*) Abzug, *der*

**stopper** /'stɒpə(r)/ ❶ *n.* Stöpsel, *der;* Pfropfen, *der;* **put a ~** *or* **the ~s on sth./sb.** (*fig.*) einer Sache (*Dat.*) einen Riegel vorschieben/jmdm. einen Strich durch die Rechnung machen. ❷ *v.t.* zustöpseln

**stopping** /'stɒpɪŋ/ ⇒ **filling** 1 A

**stopping: ~ distance** *n.* Anhalteweg, *der* (*fachspr.*); **~ place, ~ point** *ns.* Station, *die;* (*where train must stop*) Haltepunkt, *der;* (*where one might rest*) Ort zum Rasten; **~ train** *n.* (*Brit. Railw.*) Nahverkehrszug, *der*

**stop: ~ press** *n.* (*Brit. Journ.*) letzte Meldung/Meldungen; *attrib.* **~-press news** letzte Meldungen; **~ sign** *n.* Stoppschild, *das;* **~ signal** *n.* Haltesignal, *das;* **~watch** *n.* Stoppuhr, *die*

**storage** /'stɔːrɪdʒ/ *n.* **A** *no pl., no indef. art.* (*storing*) Lagerung, *die;* (*of furniture*) Einlagerung, *die;* (*of films, books, documents*) Aufbewahrung, *die;* (*of data, water, electricity*) Speicherung, *die;* **my furniture is in ~:** meine Möbel sind [bei einer Spedition] eingelagert; **put in[to] ~:** zur Aufbewahrung geben ‹Möbel›; ⇒ *also* **cold storage**; **B** ⇒ **storage space**; **C** (*cost of warehousing*) Lagergebühr, *die*

**storage: ~ battery** *n.* (*Electr.*) Akkumulator, *der;* **~ capacity** *n.* (*Computing*) Speicherkapazität, *die;* **~ cell** *n.* (*Electr.*) Akkumulator, *der;* **~ device** *n.* (*Computing*) Speichermedium, *das;* Datenträger, *der;* **~ heater** *n.* [Nacht]speicherofen, *der;* **~ space** *n.* Lagerraum, *der;* (*in house*) Platz [zum Aufbewahren]; **I need ~ space for all my books** ich brauche Platz, um alle meine Bücher aufzubewahren; **~ tank** *n.* Sammelbehälter, *der;* Lagertank, *der*

**store** /stɔː(r)/ ❶ *n.* **A** (*Amer.: shop*) Laden, *der;* **B** *in sing. or pl.* (*Brit.: large general shop*) Kaufhaus, *das;* ⇒ *also* **department store**; **C** (*warehouse*) Lager, *das;* (*for grain, hay*) Speicher, *der;* (*for valuables*) Depot, *das;* (*for arms*) Waffenkammer, *die;* (*for books, films, documents*) Magazin, *das;* **put sth. in ~:** etw. [bei einer Spedition] einlagern; **D** (*stock*) Vorrat, *der* (**of** an + *Dat.*); **a great ~ of knowledge** ein großer Wissensschatz; **I don't have an unlimited ~ of patience** meine Geduld ist nicht unerschöpflich; **get in** *or* **lay in a ~ of sth.** einen Vorrat an etw. (*Dat.*) anlegen; **have** *or* **keep coal/food in ~:** einen Kohlenvorrat/einen Vorrat an Lebensmitteln haben; **have enough arms/ammunition in ~:** genug Waffen/Munition in Reserve haben; **be** *or* **lie in ~ for sb.** jmdn. erwarten; **have a surprise in ~ for sb.** eine Überraschung für jmdn. [auf Lager] haben; **there was another surprise in ~ for him** noch eine Überraschung wartete auf ihn; **that's a treat in ~:** das ist eine erfreuliche Aussicht; **there'll be trouble in ~:** es wird Ärger geben; **who knows what the future has in ~?** wer weiß, was die Zukunft mit sich bringt?; **E** *in pl.* (*supplies*) Vorräte; **the ~s** (*place*) das [Vorrats]lager; **F** **lay** *or* **put** *or* **set [great] ~ by** *or* **on sth.** [großen] Wert auf etw. legen; **G** (*Brit. Computing*) Speicher, *der.*

❷ *v.t.* **A** (*put in ~*) einlagern; speichern ‹Getreide, Elektrizität, Wissen›; einspeichern ‹Daten›; ablegen ‹Papiere, Dokumente›; **~ food/nuts/coal/wine** (*collect as reserve*) sich (*Dat.*) einen Vorrat an Lebensmitteln/Nüssen/Kohle/Wein anlegen; **B** (*leave for storage*) unterbringen; **C** (*hold*) aufnehmen; speichern ‹Energie, Daten›.

❸ *attrib. adj.* **A** (*Breeding*) Mast-; **B** (*Amer.: shop-bought*) Konfektions‹kleidung›

**~ a'way** *v.t.* lagern; ablegen ‹Akten›; **~ food away** sich (*Dat.*) einen Lebensmittelvorrat anlegen; **~ things away in a trunk/at a friend's house** Sachen in einer Truhe verstauen/bei einem Freund aufbewahren; **~ away information** Informationen sammeln und aufbewahren

**~ 'up** *v.t.* speichern; **~ up provisions/food/wine/coal/nuts** sich (*Dat.*) Vorräte/Lebensmittel-/Wein-/Kohlenvorräte/einen Vorrat an Nüssen anlegen; **you're only storing up trouble for yourself** du handelst dir nur immer mehr Schwierigkeiten ein

**store: ~ detective** *n.* ▶ 1261 Kaufhausdetektiv, *der;* **~house** *n.* Lager[haus], *das;* **sb. is a ~house of knowledge/information [about angling]** jmd. ist ein wandelndes Lexikon[, was das Angeln betrifft]; **the book is a real ~house of facts [about Germany]** das Buch ist eine wahre Fundgrube [für jeden, der sich über Deutschland orientieren will]; **~keeper** *n.* ▶ 1261 **A** (*one in charge of ~s*) Lagerist, *der*/Lageristin, *die;* (*Mil.*) Verwalter der Materialausgabe; **B** (*Amer.:*

S

*shopkeeper*) Besitzer eines Einzelhandelsgeschäftes; **~man** /ˈstɔːmən/ *n., pl.* **~men** /ˈstɔːmən/ A (*man in charge of ~s*) Lagerist, *der;* (*Mil.*) Verwalter der Materialausgabe; B (*handler of ~d goods*) Lagerarbeiter, *der;* **~room** *n.* Lagerraum, *der;* (*for food on ship*) Proviantraum, *der;* (*in restaurant, canteen*) Speisekammer, *die*

**storey** /ˈstɔːrɪ/ *n.* Stockwerk, *das;* Geschoss, *das;* **a five-~ house** ein fünfgeschossiges Haus; **third-~ window** Fenster im zweiten Stock[werk]

**-storeyed** /ˈstɔːrɪd/ *adj. in comb.* -geschossig; **three-~ house** dreigeschossiges Haus

**storied** /ˈstɔːrɪd/ *adj.* (*literary: legendary*) legendenumwoben

**-storied** (*Amer.*) ⇒ **-storeyed**

**stork** /stɔːk/ *n.* Storch, *der*

**storm** /stɔːm/ ❶ *n.* A Unwetter, *das;* (*thunder~*) Gewitter, *das;* **the night of the ~:** die Sturmnacht; **cross the Channel in a ~:** den Ärmelkanal bei Sturm überqueren; **a ~ in a teacup** (*fig.*) ein Sturm im Wasserglas; B (*fig.: dispute*) Sturm der Entrüstung; **~ and stress** Sturm und Drang; C (*fig.: outburst*) (*of applause, protest, indignation, criticism*) Sturm, *der;* (*of abuse, insults, tears*) Flut, *die;* (*of missiles, shots, arrows, blows*) Hagel, *der;* **a ~ of blows rained down on his head** Schläge hagelten auf seinen Kopf; D (*Mil.: attack*) Sturm, *der;* **take sb./sth. by ~:** jmdn. überrumpeln/etw. im Sturm nehmen; E (*Meteorol.: wind*) [schwerer] Sturm.
❷ *v.i.* A stürmen; **he ~ed in** er kam hereingestürmt; **~ about** *or* **around in a violent temper** voller Wut herumtoben (*ugs.*); B (*talk violently*) toben; **~ at sb.** jmdn. andonnern (*ugs.*); **~ against sth./sb.** gegen etw. wettern (*ugs.*)/gegen jmdn. vom Leder ziehen.
❸ *v.t.* (*Mil.*) stürmen

**storm: ~ centre** *n.* (*Meteorol.*) Auge *od.* Zentrum eines Wirbelsturms; **~ cloud** *n.* A (*Meteorol.*) Gewitterwolke, *die;* B (*fig.*) **the ~ clouds [of war] are gathering** dunkle Wolken ziehen am Horizont auf [und kündigen Krieg an]; **~ damage** *n.* Sturmschaden, *der* (*meist Pl.*); **~ door** *n.* äußere Windfangtür; **~trooper** *n.* (*Hist.*) SA-Mann, *der* (*ns.*); **~ troops** *n. pl.* A (*Mil.*) Sturmtruppen; B (*Hist.*) Sturmabteilung, *die* (*ns.*); SA, *die* (*ns.*)

**stormy** /ˈstɔːmɪ/ *adj.* A stürmisch; wild ‹Beschimpfung›; hitzig ‹Auseinandersetzung›; B (*indicating storms*) auf Sturm hindeutend; **be** *or* **look ~:** nach Sturm aussehen

**story¹** /ˈstɔːrɪ/ *n.* A (*account of events*) Geschichte, *die;* **give the ~ of sth.** etw. schildern *od.* darstellen; **the suspects' stories did not coincide** die Aussagen der Verdächtigen stimmten nicht überein; **[that's] a likely ~** (*iron.*) wers glaubt, wird selig (*ugs. scherzh.*); **it is quite another ~ now** (*fig.*) jetzt sieht alles ganz anders aus; **the [old,] old ~, the same old ~** (*fig.*) das alte Lied (*ugs.*); **tall ~:** unglaubliche Geschichte; **that's [a bit of] a tall ~!** das ist ein bisschen dick aufgetragen! (*ugs.*); **that's a different ~** (*fig.*) das ist etwas ganz anderes; **that's his ~ [and he's sticking to it]** er bleibt bei dem, was er gesagt hat; **that's only ˈhalf the ~:** das ist noch nicht alles; **the bruise told its ˈown ~:** der blaue Fleck sprach für sich selbst; **the ~ goes that ...:** man erzählt sich, dass ...; **or so the ~ goes** so erzählt man sich; **the whole ~ came out** alles kam heraus (*ugs.*); **that's not the whole ~:** das ist noch nicht alles; **to cut** *or* **make a long ~ short, ...:** kurz [gesagt], ...; B (*narrative*) Geschichte, *die;* **but that is another ~:** aber das ist eine andere Geschichte; **that's the ~ of my life!** (*fig.*) das ist mein ewiges Problem!; ⇒ *also* **short story**; C (*news item*) Bericht, *der;* Story, *die* (*ugs.*); D (*past*) ⇒ **history** A; E (*plot*) Story, *die;* F (*set of [interesting] facts*) **the objects in the room have a ~:** die Gegenstände in dem Zimmer haben ihre eigene Geschichte; **there is an interesting ~ behind that sword** um dieses Schwert rankt sich eine interessante Geschichte (*geh.*); G (*coll./child lang.: lie*) Märchen, *das;* **tell stories** Märchen erzählen

**story²** (*Amer.*) ⇒ **storey**

**story: ~ book** ❶ *n.* Geschichtenbuch, *das;* (*with fairy tales*) Märchenbuch, *das;* ❷ *attrib. adj.* Bilderbuch-; **~ book world** Märchenwelt, *die;* **~line** ⇒ **story¹** E; **~teller** *n.* A (*narrator*) [Geschichten]erzähler, *der*/-erzählerin, *die;* B (*writer*) Erzähler, *der*/Erzählerin, *die;* C (*raconteur*) Anekdotenerzähler, *der*/-erzählerin, *die;* **she's a wonderful ~teller** sie kann wundervoll erzählen; D (*coll./child lang.: liar*) Lügenbold, *der;* **~telling** *n.* Geschichtenerzählen, *das;* (*fig.: lying*) Lügengeschichten- *od.* Märchenerzählen, *das*

**stout** /staʊt/ ❶ *adj.* A (*strong*) fest; stabil ‹Boot, Werkzeug, Messer, Zaun›; dick ‹Tür, Mauer, Damm, Stock, Papier›; robust ‹Material, Kleidung›; stark ‹Seil, Abwehr›; kräftig ‹Pflanze, Pferd, Pfeiler›; B (*fat*) beleibt; **of ~ build** von gedrungenem Körperbau; C (*brave, staunch*) unverzagt; heftig ‹Widerstand, Opposition›; entschieden ‹Ablehnung›; stark ‹Gegner›; fest ‹Glaube›; **a ~ heart** ein festes Herz; **be ~ of heart** sehr beherzt sein; **~ fellow** (*arch./coll.*) wackerer Kerl (*veralt.*). ❷ *n.* (*drink*) Stout, *der*

**stout-hearted** /ˈstaʊthɑːtɪd/ *adj.* beherzt; unerschrocken

**stoutly** /ˈstaʊtlɪ/ *adv.* A (*strongly*) stabil ‹gebaut, gezimmert›; **~ made** solide, robust ‹Schuhwerk›; stark ‹Seil›; **~ built** stämmig; kräftig ‹Tier›; stabil ‹Haus, Zaun, Tor›; dick ‹Tür, Mauer›; B (*staunchly*) beherzt; hartnäckig ‹behaupten, ablehnen, widerstehen›; fest ‹glauben›

**stoutness** /ˈstaʊtnɪs/ *n., no pl.* (*fatness*) Beleibtheit, *die*

**stove¹** /stəʊv/ *n.* Ofen, *der;* (*for cooking*) Herd, *der;* **electric ~:** Elektroherd, *der*

**stove²** ⇒ **stave** 2

**ˈstovepipe** *n.* (*also hat*) Ofenrohr, *das*

**stow** /stəʊ/ *v.t.* A (*put into place*) packen (**into** in + *Akk.*); verstauen (**into** in + *Dat.*); (*Naut.*) stauen; **she ~ed the letter out of sight/behind some books** sie steckte den Brief weg (*ugs.*)/hinter ein paar Bücher; B (*fill*) voll packen; voll stopfen (*ugs.*); (*Naut.*) befrachten; C (*coll.: stop*) aufstecken (*ugs.*); **~ it!** hör auf! (*ugs.*); (*stop talking*) [halt die] Klappe! (*salopp*)

**~ aˈway** ❶ *v.t.* verwahren; **he keeps his savings ~ed away in a sock** er hat seine Ersparnisse in einem Strumpf versteckt. ❷ *v.i.* als blinder Passagier reisen; ⇒ *also* **stowaway**

**stowage** /ˈstəʊɪdʒ/ *n.* A (*space for stowing*) Platz, *der;* (*Naut.*) Stauraum, *der;* B (*action of stowing*) Aufbewahrung, *die;* Unterbringung, *die;* (*Naut.*) Stauen, *das;* C (*Naut.: stowed goods*) Ladung, *die*

**ˈstowaway** *n.* blinder Passagier

**straddle** /ˈstrædl/ *v.t.* A (*be positioned across*) **~** *or* **sit straddling a fence/chair** rittlings auf einem Zaun/Stuhl sitzen; **~** *or* **stand straddling a ditch** mit gespreizten Beinen über einem Graben stehen; **his legs ~d the chair/brook** er saß rittlings auf dem Stuhl/stand mit gespreizten Beinen über dem Bach; **their farm ~s the border** ihre Farm liegt beiderseits der Grenze; **the bridge ~s the river/road** die Brücke überspannt den Fluss/die Straße; B (*part widely*) **sit/stand with legs ~d** *or* **~d legs** mit gespreizten Beinen sitzen/stehen; **~ one's legs** die Beine spreizen; C (*Mil.*) eindecken; **the bombs ~d the target** die Bomben schlugen zu beiden Seiten *od.* beiderseits des Ziels ein

**Stradivarius** /strædɪˈveərɪəs/ *n.* (*Mus.*) Stradivari, *die*

**strafe** /strɑːf/ *v.t.* (*Mil.*) beharken (*Soldatenspr.*)

**straggle** /ˈstrægl/ *v.i.* A (*trail*) **~ [along] behind the others** den anderen hinterherzockeln (*ugs.*); **the last few walkers ~d in** die letzten Geher trotteten ins Ziel; **the procession ~d [out] along the road** der Zug zockelte die Straße entlang (*ugs.*); B (*spread in irregular way*) ‹Dorf, Stadt:› sich ausbreiten; ‹Häuser, Bäume:› verstreut stehen; **the brook/fence goes straggling through/over the meadow** der Bach zieht sich mit vielen Windungen/der Zaun verläuft kreuz und quer über die Wiese; C (*grow untidily*) ‹Pflanze:› wuchern; ‹Haar, Bart:› zottig wachsen

**straggler** /ˈstræglə(r)/ *n.* Nachzügler, *der*

**straggling** /ˈstræglɪŋ/ *adj.* A (*trailing*) nachzockelnd (*ugs.*); B (*irregular*) verstreut ‹Häuser›; ungeordnet ‹Reihe›; unregelmäßig ‹Baumreihe, Schrift›; ‹Fluss, Zaun, Straße› mit vielen Krümmungen; weiträumig angelegt ‹Stadt, Gebäude›; **a ~ village** eine Streusiedlung; C (*long and untidy*) wuchernd; zottig ‹Haar, Bart›

**straggly** /ˈstræglɪ/ ⇒ **straggling** C

**straight** /streɪt/ ❶ *adj.* A gerade; aufrecht ‹Haltung›; glatt ‹Haar›; **in a ~ line** in gerader Linie; **the ~ and narrow** der Pfad der Tugend; **keep sb. on/keep to the ~ and narrow** jmdn. im Zaum halten/auf dem Pfad der Tugend wandeln (*geh.*); ⇒ *also* **arrow** 1; B (*not having been bent*) ausgestreckt ‹Arm, Bein›; durchgedrückt ‹Knie›; C (*not misshapen*) gerade ‹Bein›; D (*Fashion*) gerade geschnitten; E (*undiluted, unmodified*) unvermischt; **have** *or* **drink whisky/gin ~:** Whisky/Gin pur trinken; **a ~ choice** eine klare Wahl; **make a ~ bet on a horse** auf ein Pferd auf Sieg setzen; F (*successive*) fortlaufend; **win in ~ sets** (*Tennis*) ohne Satzverlust gewinnen; **the team had ten ~ wins** die Mannschaft hat zehn Spiele hintereinander gewonnen; **~ As** (*Amer.*) lauter Einsen; G (*undeviating*) direkt ‹Blick, Schlag, Schuss, Pass, Ball, Weg›; **sb. has a ~ aim, sb.'s aim is ~:** jmd. zielt genau; **a ~ hit** *or* **blow** (*Boxing*) eine Gerade; **a ~ left/right** (*Boxing*) eine linke/rechte Gerade; **give sb. a ~ look** jmdn. scharf ansehen; H (*candid*) geradlinig ‹Mensch›; ehrlich ‹Antwort›; klar ‹Abfuhr, Weigerung, Verurteilung›; unmissverständlich ‹Rat›; **~ dealings/speaking** direkte Verhandlungen/unverblümte Sprache; **a ~ answer to a ~ question** eine klare Antwort auf eine klare Frage; **he did some ~ talking with her** er sprach sich mit ihr offen aus; **be ~ with sb.** zu jmdm. offen sein; I (*logical*) klar; **her thinking is clear and ~:** ihr Denken ist klar und logisch; J (*Theatre*) ernst; (*not avant-garde*) konventionell; K (*in good order, not askew*) **we/the rooms are ~ now after the move** wir haben uns/die Zimmer nach dem Umzug jetzt eingerichtet; **the accounts are ~:** die Bücher sind in Ordnung; **the picture is ~:** das Bild hängt gerade; **is my hair/tie ~?** sitzt meine Frisur/Krawatte [richtig]?; **is my hat [on] ~?** sitzt mein Hut [richtig]?; **pull sth. ~:** etw. gerade ziehen; **put ~:** gerade ziehen ‹Krawatte›; gerade aufsetzen ‹Hut›; gerade hängen ‹Bild›; aufräumen ‹Zimmer, Sachen›; richtig stellen ‹Fehler, Missverständnis›; **put things ~:** alles in Ordnung bringen; **put things ~ with sb.** mit jmdm. alles klären; **get sth. ~** (*fig.*) etw. genau *od.* richtig verstehen; **let's get it** *or* **the facts** *or* **things ~:** wir sollten alles genau klären; **get this ~!** merk dir das [ein für alle Mal]!; **put sb. ~:** jmdn. aufklären; **put** *or* **set the record ~:** die Sache *od.* das richtig stellen; ⇒ *also* **straight face**; L (*coll.: heterosexual*) hetero (*ugs.*); M (*coll.: conventional*) [spieß]bürgerlich (*abwertend*); (*Mus.*) konventionell.
❷ *adv.* A (*in a ~ line*) gerade; **she came ~ at me** sie kam geradewegs auf mich zu; **~ opposite** genau gegenüber; **head ~ for the wall** genau auf die Mauer zusteuern; **go ~** (*fig.: give up crime*) ein bürgerliches Leben führen; B ▶ 1679 (*directly*) geradewegs; **~ after** sofort nach; **the knife went ~ through his hand** das Messer ging mitten durch seine Hand; **the pianist went ~ into the next piece** der Klavierspieler ging sofort zum nächsten Stück über; **come ~ to the point** direkt *od.* gleich zur Sache kommen; **look sb. ~ in the eye** jmdm. direkt in die Augen blicken; **~ ahead** *or* **on** immer geradeaus; **they went ~ ahead and did it** sie taten es sofort; ⇒ *also* **horse** 1 A; **shoulder** 1 A; C (*honestly, frankly*) aufrichtig; **give it to me ~:** sei ganz offen zu mir!; **he**

came ~ out with it er sagte es ohne Umschweife; **I told him ~ [out] that ...:** ich sagte [es] ihm ins Gesicht, dass ...; **play ~ with sb.** mit jmdm. ein ehrliches Spiel spielen; **D** (*upright*) gerade ‹sitzen, stehen, wachsen›; **E** (*accurately*) zielsicher; **he can't shoot [very] ~:** er ist nicht [sehr] zielsicher; **F** (*clearly*) klar ‹sehen, denken›.
**3** *n.* **A** (~ *condition*) **out of the ~ = out of true** ⇒ **true** 2; **B** (~ *stretch*) gerade Strecke; (*Sport*) Gerade, *die;* **final** *or* **home** *or* **last ~** (*Sport; also fig.*) Zielgerade, *die;* **C** (*Cards*) Straße, *die;* Folge, *die*

**straight: ~ a'way** *adv.* sofort; gleich; **~away** (*Amer.*) *adj.* **A** *attrib.* (~) gerade; **B** (~*forward*) nüchtern; sachlich; **~ 'bat** *n.* (*Cricket*) aufrecht gehaltener Schläger; **keep a ~ bat** (*Brit. fig.*) sich anständig benehmen; **~ edge** *n.* (*for paperhanging*) Tapezierschiene, *die;* (*Metalw.*) Haarlineal, *das*

**straighten** /'streɪtn/ **1** *v.t.* **A** gerade ziehen ‹Kabel, Teppich, Seil›; gerade biegen ‹Draht›; glätten ‹Falte, Kleidung, Haare›; gerade rücken ‹Hut, Krawatte, Brille›; gerade machen ‹Tischkante›; begradigen ‹Fluss, Straße›; gerade halten ‹Rücken›; strecken ‹Beine, Arme›; gerade hängen ‹Bild›; **B** (*put in order*) aufräumen; einrichten ‹neue Wohnung›; in Ordnung bringen ‹Geschäftsbücher, Finanzen›. **2** *v.i.* gerade werden; ‹Haar:› glatt werden

**~ 'out 1** *v.t.* **A** gerade biegen ‹Draht›; gerade ziehen ‹Seil, Kabel›; glätten ‹Decke, Teppich›; begradigen ‹Fluss, Straße›; **B** (*put in order, clear up*) klären; aus der Welt schaffen ‹Missverständnis, Meinungsverschiedenheit›; in Ordnung bringen ‹Angelegenheit›; berichtigen ‹Fehler›; **~ sb. out** jmdn. zur Einsicht bringen; **~ sb. out on sth.** jmdn. über etw. (*Akk.*) aufklären; **things will ~ themselves out** das wird sich von selbst regeln; **C** (*sl.: beat up*) jmdn. vermöbeln (*salopp*); **do you want ~ing out?** soll ich dir eine reinhauen? (*salopp*).
**2** *v.i.* gerade werden; ‹Haar:› glatt werden; **things will ~ out** das wird sich von selbst regeln

**~ 'up 1** *v.t.* ⇒ **tidy up** 2. **2** *v.i.* sich aufrichten

**straight: ~ 'eye** *n.* gute Augen; **~ 'face** *n.* unbewegtes Gesicht; **with a ~ face** ohne eine Miene zu verziehen; **keep a ~ face** keine Miene verziehen; **~-faced** *adj.* mit unbewegter Miene *nachgestellt;* **be ~-faced** keine Miene verziehen; **~ 'fight** *n.* (*Brit. Polit.*) *direkter Kampf zwischen zwei Kandidaten;* **~ 'flush** ⇒ **flush**[4]; **~'forward** *adj.* **A** (*frank*) freimütig; geradlinig ‹Politik›; schlicht ‹Stil, Sprache, Erzählung, Bericht›; klar ‹Anweisung, Vorstellungen›; **have a ~forward approach to a problem** ein Problem direkt angehen; **be ~forward in one's dealings** offen und gerade sein; **B** (*simple*) einfach; eindeutig ‹Lage›; **~'forwardly** *adv.* **A** (*frankly*) ehrlich ‹handeln›; offen ‹sprechen, sagen›; **B** (*simply*) deutlich ‹erklären›; **~ man** *n.* (*Theatre*) *Schauspieler, der einem Komiker die Stichwörter für seine Gags liefert*

**straightness** /'streɪtnɪs/ *n., no pl.* **A** Geradheit, *die;* (*of hair*) Glattheit, *die;* (*Fashion*) gerader Schnitt; **B** (*fig.*) (*candour*) (*of answer*) Offenheit, *die;* (*of purpose*) Geradlinigkeit, *die;* (*of dealings*) Ehrlichkeit, *die*

**straight: ~ 'off** *adv.* (*coll.*) schlankweg (*ugs.*); **~ 'ticket** *n.* (*Amer. Polit.*) **vote the ~ [Republican/Democratic] ticket** die [republikanische/demokratische] Liste unverändert wählen; **~ 'tip** *n.* Insidertipp, *der;* **~ 'up** *adv.* (*coll.: honestly*) echt (*ugs.*); **Do you mean what you say? — S~ up!** Meinst du auch, was du sagst? — Na klar! (*ugs.*); **he offered me a lot of money, ~ up!** er hat mir einen Haufen Geld angeboten, ehrlich! (*ugs.*)

**strain**[1] /streɪn/ **1** *n.* **A** (*pull*) Belastung, *die;* (*on rope*) Spannung, *die;* **put a ~ on sb./sth.** jmdn./etw. belasten; **B** (*extreme physical or mental tension*) Stress, *der;* **feel the ~:** die Anstrengung spüren; **stand** *or* **take the ~:** die Belastung *od.* den Stress aushalten; **he has a lot of ~ at work** die Arbeit nimmt ihn stark in Anspruch; **place sb. under [a] great ~:** jmdn. einer starken Belastung aussetzen; **be under [a great deal of] ~:** unter großem Stress stehen; **C** (*person, thing*) **be a ~ on sb./sth.** jmdn./etw. belasten; eine Belastung für jmdn./etw. sein; **be a ~ on sb.'s nerves** an jmds. Nerven zerren; **find sth. a ~:** etw. als Belastung empfinden; **D** ▶ **1232** (*injury*) (*muscular*) Zerrung, *die;* (*overstrain on heart, back, etc.*) Überanstrengung, *die;* **E** *in sing. or pl.* (*burst of music*) Klänge; (*burst of poetry*) Vers, *der;* Zeile, *die;* **take up the ~** (*lit. or fig.*) einstimmen; einfallen; **F** (*tone*) Ton, *der;* **G** (*Phys.*) Deformation, *die.*
**2** *v.t.* **A** ▶ **1232** (*over-exert*) überanstrengen; zerren ‹Muskel›; überbeanspruchen ‹Geduld, Loyalität usw.›; **~ one's back carrying heavy boxes** sich beim Tragen schwerer Kisten verheben; **~ oneself** (*lit. or fig. iron.*) sich übernehmen; sich überanstrengen; **B** (*stretch tightly*) [fest] spannen; **~ed relations** (*fig.*) gespannte Beziehungen; **C** (*exert to maximum*) **~ oneself/sb./sth.** das Letzte aus sich/jmdm./etw. herausholen; **~ one's ears/eyes/voice** seine Ohren/Augen/Stimme anstrengen; **~ oneself to do sth.** sich nach Kräften bemühen, etw. zu tun; **D** (*use beyond proper limits*) verzerren ‹Wahrheit, Lehre, Tatsachen›; überbeanspruchen ‹Geduld, Wohlwollen›; **E** *in p.p.* (*forced*) gezwungen ‹Lächeln›; künstlich ‹Humor, Witz›; gewagt ‹Interpretation›; **F** (*hug*) **~ sb./sth. to oneself/to sth.** jmdn./etw. an sich/etw. (*Akk.*) drücken; **G** (*filter*) durchseihen; seihen (**through** durch); **~ [the water from] the vegetables** das Gemüse abgießen; **~ sth. from a liquid** etw. aus einer Flüssigkeit herausfiltern.
**3** *v.i.* **A** (*strive intensely*) sich anstrengen; (*resist while being close to breaking point*) ächzen (**under** unter + *Dat.*); **he ~ed to lift the box** er versuchte ächzend *od.* mit aller Kraft, die Kiste hochzuheben; **~ at sth.** an etw. (*Dat.*) zerren; **~ at the leash** an der Leine zerren; (*fig.*) es kaum erwarten können; **~ after sth.** sich mit aller Gewalt um etw. bemühen; **~ after an effect** Effekthascherei betreiben; **B** (*be filtered*) durchlaufen; (*percolate through sand etc.*) durchsickern; **~ at a gnat [and swallow a camel]** Mücken seihen und Kamele verschlucken (*bibl.*)

**~ a'way, ~ 'off** *v.t.* abseihen; abgießen ‹Wasser›

**~ 'out** *v.t.* [her]ausfiltern

**strain**[2] *n.* **A** (*breed*) Rasse, *die;* (*of plants*) Sorte, *die;* (*of virus*) Art, *die;* (*human stock*) Familie, *die;* **B** *no pl.* (*tendency*) Neigung, *die* (**of** zu); Hang, *der* (**of** zu); **a cruel ~:** ein grausamer Zug

**strainer** /'streɪnə(r)/ *n.* Sieb, *das*

**strait** /streɪt/ **1** *n.* **A** *in sing. or pl.* (*Geog.*) [Wasser]straße, *die;* Meerenge, *die;* **the S~s [of Gibraltar/Malacca]** die Straße von Gibraltar/die Malakkastraße; **B** *usu. in pl.* (*distressing situation*) Schwierigkeiten; ⇒ *also* **dire** C. **2** *adj.* (*arch.*) (*narrow*) schmal ‹Weidefläche, Weg›; eng ‹Pforte›

**straitened** /'streɪtnd/ *adj.* beschränkt ‹Verhältnisse›

**strait: ~jacket 1** *n.* (*lit. or fig.*) Zwangsjacke, *die;* **2** *v.t.* (*lit. or fig.*) in eine Zwangsjacke stecken; **~-laced** /streɪt'leɪst/ *adj.* (*fig.*) puritanisch

**Straits of Magellan** /streɪts əv mə'gelən/ *pr. n.* Magellanstraße, *die*

**strake** /streɪk/ *n.* (*Naut.*) Planke, *die*

**strand**[1] /strænd/ *n.* (*thread*) Faden, *der;* (*of wire*) Litze, *die* (*Elektrot.*); (*of rope*) Strang, *der;* (*of beads, pearls, flowers, etc.*) Kette, *die;* (*of hair*) Strähne, *die;* (*Biol., Phys.*) Faser, *die;* (*fig.*) Strang, *der;* **a ~ of beads** eine Perlenkette

**strand**[2] **1** *v.t.* **A** (*leave behind*) trockensetzen; **be [left] ~ed** (*fig.*) seinem Schicksal überlassen sein; (*be stuck*) festsitzen; **leave sb. ~ed** (*fig.*) jmdn. seinem Schicksal überlassen; **the strike left them ~ed in England** wegen des Streiks saßen sie in England fest; **B** (*wash ashore*) an Land spülen ‹Leiche, Wrackteile›; (*run aground*) auf Grund setzen ‹Schiff›. **2** *v.i.* stranden. **3** *n.* (*rhet./poet.: foreshore*) Gestade, *das* (*dichter.*)

**strange** /streɪndʒ/ *adj.* **A** (*peculiar*) seltsam; sonderbar; merkwürdig; **feel [very] ~, come over [very] ~** (*coll.*) sich [ganz] komisch im Kopf *od.* (*ugs. scherzh.*) beduselt fühlen; **it feels ~ to do sth.** es ist ein merkwürdiges *od.* komisches Gefühl, wenn man etw. tut; **~ to say** seltsamerweise; **B** (*alien, unfamiliar*) fremd; **~ to sb.** jmdm. fremd; **C** (*unaccustomed*) **~ to sth.** nicht vertraut mit etw.; **feel ~:** sich nicht zu Hause fühlen; **I feel ~, suddenly having so much power** es ist [für mich] ganz ungewohnt, plötzlich so viel Macht zu haben; **I am [quite] ~ here** ich bin fremd hier; ich kenne mich hier nicht aus

**strangely** /'streɪndʒlɪ/ *adv.* seltsam; merkwürdig; **~ enough, ...:** seltsamerweise ...; so seltsam es klingt, ...

**strangeness** /'streɪndʒnɪs/ *n., no pl.* (*oddness*) Seltsamkeit, *die;* Merkwürdigkeit, *die*

**stranger** /'streɪndʒə(r)/ *n.* **A** (*foreigner, unknown person*) Fremde, *der/die;* **he is a ~ here/to** *or* **in the town** er ist hier/in der Stadt fremd; **she is a /no ~ to the British stage** sie ist auf den britischen Bühnen unbekannt/bekannt; **he is a/no ~ to me** er ist mir nicht bekannt/ist mir bekannt; **you are quite a ~:** man kennt dich ja kaum noch; **hello, ~:** hallo, lange nicht gesehen; **B** (*one lacking certain experience*) **be a ~ in sth.** in etw. (*Dat.*) unerfahren sein; **be a/no ~ to sth.** etw. nicht gewöhnt/etw. gewöhnt sein; **he is no ~ to this sort of work** diese Arbeit ist ihm nicht fremd; **be a/no ~ to Oxford** Oxford gar nicht/[recht gut] kennen; **C** (*Brit. Parl.*) Besucher, *der/*Besucherin, *die;* **S~s' Gallery** Besuchergalerie, *die*

**strangle** /'stræŋgl/ *v.t.* **A** (*throttle*) erdrosseln; erwürgen; **B** (*fig.: suppress*) unterdrücken; **~ at birth** im Keim ersticken

**'stranglehold** *n.* (*lit. or fig.*) Würgegriff, *der;* **have a ~ on sb./sth.** jmdn./etw. im Würgegriff haben

**strangulated** /'stræŋgjʊleɪtɪd/ *adj.* (*Med.*) **~ hernia** eingeklemmter Bruch

**strangulation** /stræŋgjʊ'leɪʃn/ *n.* Erdrosseln, *das;* Erwürgen, *das;* (*fig.*) Unterdrückung, *die;* Strangulierung, *die* (*geh.*)

**strap** /stræp/ **1** *n.* **A** (*leather strip*) Riemen, *der;* (*textile strip*) Band, *das;* (*shoulder ~*) Träger, *der;* (*for watch*) Armband, *das;* **the ~** (*punishment*) die Züchtigung mit dem Riemen; **be given [a lick of] the ~** den Riemen zu schmecken bekommen; **B** (*to grasp in vehicle*) Halteriemen, *der.* **2** *v.t.*, **-pp- A** (*secure with ~*) **~ [into position/down]** festschnallen; **~ oneself in** sich anschnallen; **B** ⇒ **~ up** B; **C be ~ped for cash** (*coll.*) sehr klamm sein (*ugs.*); **D** (*punish with ~*) mit dem Riemen züchtigen

**~ 'up** *v.t.* **A** (*fasten ~s of*) zuschnallen; **B** (*bind with adhesive plaster*) verpflastern

**strap: ~hanger** *n.* stehender Fahrgast; **~ hinge** *n.* Langband, *das* (*Technik*)

**strapless** /'stræplɪs/ *adj.* trägerlos

**strapping** /'stræpɪŋ/ *adj.* stramm

**Strasbourg** /'stræzbɜːg/ *pr. n.* ▶ **1626** Straßburg (*das*)

**strata** *pl. of* **stratum**

**stratagem** /'strætədʒəm/ *n.* (*trick*) [Kriegs]list, *die;* Strategem, *das* (*geh.*)

**strategic** /strə'tiːdʒɪk/, **strategical** /strə'tiːdʒɪkl/ *adj.* **A** strategisch; **a ~ moment** ein strategisch günstiger Zeitpunkt; **B** (*of great military importance*) strategisch wichtig; (*necessary to plan*) bedeutsam ‹Element, Faktor›

**strategically** /strə'tiːdʒɪkəlɪ/ *adv.* strategisch

**strategic 'studies** *n., no pl.* Strategie, *die*

**strategist** /'strætɪdʒɪst/ *n.* Stratege, *der/*Strategin, *die*

**strategy** /'strætɪdʒɪ/ *n.* Strategie, *die;* (*fig. also*) Taktik, *die;* **use ~** (*fig.*) taktisch *od.* strategisch vorgehen; **it was bad ~** (*fig.*) es war taktisch *od.* strategisch unklug

**stratification** /strætɪfɪ'keɪʃn/ *n.* **A** (*Geol., Archaeol.*) Schichtung, *die;* Stratifikation, *die* (*fachspr.*); **B** (*Sociol.*) [soziale] Schichtung

S

**stratify** /ˈstrætɪfaɪ/ *v.t.* [A] (*Geol., Archaeol.*) stratifizieren; **stratified rock** in Schichten gewachsener Fels; [B] (*Sociol.*) in Schichten einteilen; Schichten zuordnen; **a stratified society** eine mehrschichtige Gesellschaft

**stratosphere** /ˈstrætəsfɪə(r)/ *n.* (*Geog.*) Stratosphäre, *die;* (*fig.*) höhere Regionen

**stratospheric** /strætəˈsferɪk/ *adj.* (*Geog.*) stratosphärisch; Stratosphären‹flugzeug, -flug›; (*fig.*) Schwindel erregend ‹Höhe›

**stratum** /ˈstrɑːtəm, ˈstreɪtəm/ *n., pl.* **strata** /ˈstrɑːtə, ˈstreɪtə/ Schicht, *die;* Stratum, *das* (*fachspr.*)

**stratus** /ˈstreɪtəs, ˈstrɑːtəs/ *n., pl.* **strati** /ˈstreɪtaɪ, ˈstrɑːtaɪ/ (*Meteorol.*) Schichtwolke, *die;* Stratus, *der* (*fachspr.*); *attrib.* **~ clouds** Stratuswolken

**straw** /strɔː/ *n.* [A] *no pl.* (*stalks of grain*) Stroh, *das; attrib.* Stroh-; [B] (*single stalk*) Strohhalm, *der;* **catch** *or* **clutch** *or* **grasp at ~s** *or* **a ~** (*fig.*) sich an einen Strohhalm klammern; **be the last ~, be the ~ that broke the camel's back** (*coll.*) das Fass zum Überlaufen bringen; **that's the last** *or* **final ~:** jetzt reichts aber; **draw ~s [for sth.]** Hölzchen [um etw.] ziehen; **draw** *or* **pick the short ~:** das kürzere Hölzchen ziehen; (*fig.*) das schlechtere Los ziehen; **~ in the wind** Vorzeichen, *das;* Vorbote, *der;* [C] **[drinking] ~:** Trinkhalm, *der;* Strohhalm, *der;* [D] (*trifle*) Nichtigkeit, *die;* **it doesn't matter a ~ to me** es kümmert mich keinen Pfifferling (*ugs.*); **I don't give a ~:** ich gebe keinen Pfifferling dafür (*ugs.*); [E] (*hat*) Strohhut, *der.* ⇒ *also* **cheese straw**

**strawberry** /ˈstrɔːbərɪ/ *n.* [A] Erdbeere, *die;* [B] (*colour*) Erdbeerrot, *das;* ⇒ *also* **crush** 1 A

**strawberry: ~ ˈblonde** ❶ *adj.* rotblond; ❷ *n.* Rotblonde, *die;* **~ mark** *n.* [rötliches] Muttermal

**straw: ~board** *n.* Strohpapier, *das;* Strohpappe, *die;* **~ boss** *n.* (*Amer.*) Vorarbeiter, *der;* **~ colour** *n.* Strohgelb, *das;* **~-coloured** *adj.* strohgelb; **~ ˈhat** *n.* Strohhut, *der;* **~ poll, ~ vote** *ns.* Testabstimmung, *die*

**stray** /streɪ/ ❶ *v.i.* [A] (*wander*) streunen; (*fig.: in thought etc.*) abschweifen (**into** in + *Akk.*); **~ [away] from** sich absondern von; **the child had ~ed from his parents** das Kind war seinen Eltern weggelaufen; **~ into enemy territory** sich auf feindliches Gebiet verirren; [B] (*move in meandering course*) ‹Auto:› schlingern; (*move without deliberate control*) **my gaze kept ~ing to the wart on his nose** mein Blick wanderte immer wieder zu der Warze auf seiner Nase; **he could not control his ~ing hands** er konnte seine Hände einfach nicht bei sich behalten; [C] (*deviate*) abweichen (**from** von); **have ~ed** sich verirrt haben; **~ from the path of virtue** vom Pfad der Tugend abweichen (*geh.*); **he had ~ed once** einmal war er vom Wege abgekommen (*fig.*); **~ from the point/from** *or* **off the road** vom Thema/von der Straße abkommen; **somehow I ~ed into acting/the theatre** irgendwie habe ich mich aufs Schauspielern verlegt/bin ich am Theater gelandet.
❷ *n.* (*animal*) streunendes Tier; (*without owner*) herrenloses Tier; (*person*) Streuner, *der*/Streunerin, *die* (*abwertend*); ⇒ *also* **waif.**
❸ *adj.* [A] streunend; (*without owner*) herrenlos; (*out of proper place*) verirrt; [B] (*occasional, isolated*) vereinzelt; [C] (*Phys.*) streuend

**streak** /striːk/ ❶ *n.* [A] (*narrow line*) Streifen, *der;* (*in hair*) Strähne, *die;* **~ of lightning** Blitzstrahl, *der;* **like a ~ [of lightning]** [schnell] wie der Blitz (*ugs.*); wie ein geölter Blitz (*ugs.*); [B] (*fig.: element*) **have a jealous/cruel ~:** zur Eifersucht/Grausamkeit neigen; **have a ~ of meanness/jealousy** eine geizige/eifersüchtige Ader haben; [C] (*fig.: spell*) **~ of good/bad luck, lucky/unlucky ~:** Glücks-/Pechsträhne, *die;* **be on a** *or* **have a winning/losing ~:** eine Glücks-/Pechsträhne haben.
❷ *v.t.* streifen; **~ sth. with green** etw. mit grünen Streifen versehen; **hair ~ed with grey** Haar mit grauen Strähnen; **~ed with paint/mud/tears** farbverschmiert/dreckbeschmiert/tränenverschmiert.
❸ *v.i.* [A] (*move rapidly*) flitzen (*ugs.*); [B] (*coll.: run naked*) blitzen (*ugs.*); flitzen (*ugs.*)

**streaker** /ˈstriːkə(r)/ *n.* (*coll.*) Blitzer, *der*/Blitzerin, *die* (*ugs.*); Flitzer, *der*/Flitzerin, *die* (*ugs.*)

**streaking** /ˈstriːkɪŋ/ *n.* (*coll.: running naked*) Blitzen, *das* (*ugs.*); Flitzen, *das* (*ugs.*)

**streaky** /ˈstriːkɪ/ *adj.* streifig; gestreift ‹Muster, Fell›

**streaky ˈbacon** *n.* durchwachsener Speck

**stream** /striːm/ ❶ *n.* [A] (*of flowing water*) Wasserlauf, *der;* (*brook*) Bach, *der;* [B] (*flow, large quantity*) Strom, *der;* (*of abuse, excuses, words*) Schwall, *der;* **~s** *or* **a ~ of applications** eine Flut von Bewerbungen; **in ~s** in Strömen; **the children rushed in ~s/in a ~ through the school gates** die Kinder strömten durch die Schultore; [C] (*current*) Strömung, *die;* (*fig.*) Trend, *der;* **against/with the ~ of sth.** (*fig.*) gegen den/mit dem Strom einer Sache; **go against/with the ~** ‹Person:› gegen den/mit dem Strom schwimmen; ⇒ *also* **Gulf Stream;** [D] (*Brit. Educ.*) Parallelzug, *der;* [E] **be/go on ~** (*Industry*) in Betrieb sein/den Betrieb aufnehmen.
❷ *v.i.* [A] (*flow*) strömen; ‹Sonnenlicht:› fluten; **tears ~ed down her face** Tränen strömten ihr über das Gesicht; [B] (*run with liquid*) **my eyes ~ed** mir tränten die Augen; **the windows/walls were ~ing with condensation** die Fenster/Wände schwitzten; **his back was ~ing with sweat** sein Rücken war schweißnass *od.* schweißüberströmt; [C] (*wave*) ‹Haare, Fahne:› flattern, wehen.
❸ *v.t.* [A] (*emit*) **his nose was ~ing blood** Blut floss ihm aus der Nase; [B] (*Brit. Educ.*) in Parallelzüge *od.* leistungshomogene Gruppen einteilen

**~ ˈdown** *v.i.* ‹Sonne:› vom Himmel strahlen; **the rain is ~ing down** es regnet in Strömen

**~ ˈin** *v.i.* hereinströmen/hineinströmen

**~ ˈout** *v.i.* [A] (*move out like ~*) herausströmen/hinausströmen; [B] (*float*) flattern; wehen

**~ ˈpast** *v.i.* vorbeiströmen

**~ ˈthrough** *v.i.* hindurchströmen

**streamer** /ˈstriːmə(r)/ *n.* [A] (*ribbon*) Band, *das;* (*of paper*) Luftschlange, *die;* Papierschlange, *die;* [B] (*Journ.: headline*) Schlagzeile, *die;* Aufmacher, *der;* [C] (*pennon*) Wimpel, *der*

**streaming** /ˈstriːmɪŋ/ ❶ *n.* (*Brit. Educ.*) Einteilung in Parallelzüge *od.* leistungshomogene Gruppen; Streaming, *das.* ❷ *adj.* (*flowing*) laufend ‹Nase›; tränend ‹Auge›; schwitzend ‹Wand, Fenster›; **have a ~ cold** Schnupfen haben

**streamlet** /ˈstriːmlɪt/ *n.* Bächlein, *das*

**stream: ~line** ❶ *n.* [A] (*shape*) Stromlinienform, *die* (*Physik, Technik*); [B] (*line of flow*) Stromlinie, *die* (*Physik*); ❷ *v.t.* [A] (*give shape to*) [eine] Stromlinienform geben (+ *Dat.*); **be ~lined** eine Stromlinienform haben; [B] (*simplify*) rationalisieren; (*reduce*) einschränken; **~ of ˈconsciousness** *n.* (*Lit.*) (*flow of thoughts*) Bewusstseinsstrom, *der;* (*literary style*) Stream of Consciousness, *der*

**street** /striːt/ *n.* [A] Straße, *die;* **in** (*Brit.*) *or* **on ... S~:** in der ...straße; **in the ~:** auf der Straße; (*St. Exch.*) nach Börsenschluss; **I wouldn't cross the ~ to do that** (*fig.*) ich würde mir deswegen kein Bein ausreißen (*ugs.*); **be on the ~[s]** (*be published*) ‹Zeitung:› draußen sein; (*have no place to live*) auf der Straße liegen (*ugs.*); (*be available to be bought*) im [Straßen]verkauf sein; **be/go on the ~s** (*be/become a prostitute*) auf die Straße gehen (*ugs.*); **take to the ~s** auf die Straße gehen (*ugs.*); **keep the youngsters off the ~s** dafür sorgen, dass sich die Jugendlichen nicht auf der Straße herumtreiben; **it isn't a very interesting job, but at least it keeps me off the ~s** (*iron.*) der Job ist zwar nicht sehr interessant, aber wenigstens stehe ich nicht mehr auf der Straße (*ugs.*); **not in the same ~ [as sb./sth.]** (*fig. coll.*) nicht zu vergleichen [mit jmdm./etw.]; **~s ahead [of sb./sth.]** (*coll.*) um Längen besser [als jmd./etw.] (*ugs.*); **be [right** *or* **just] up sb.'s ~** (*coll.*) jmds. Fall sein (*ugs.*); **the ~s of San Francisco are paved with gold** (*fig.*) in San Francisco liegt das Geld auf der Straße; [B] (*people in street*) Straße, *die*

**street: ~ball** *n.* Streetball, *der;* **~car** *n.* (*Amer.*) Straßenbahn, *die;* Tram, *die* (*südd., österr., schweiz.*); **~ cred** /ˈstriːt kred/ (*coll.*), **~ credibility** *ns.* [glaubwürdiges] Image; **~ cries** *n. pl.* (*Brit.*) Straßen- *od.* Händlerrufe; **~ crime** *n., no pl., no indef. art.* Straßenkriminalität, *die;* **~ door** *n.* [vordere] Haustür; **~ entertainer** *n.* Straßenkünstler, *der*/-künstlerin, *die;* **~ fight** *n.* Straßenkampf, *der;* (*heavy fighting*) Straßenschlacht, *die;* **~ fighting** *n.* Straßenkampf, *der;* **sporadic ~ fighting broke out** vereinzelt brachen Straßenkämpfe aus; **~ furniture** *n.: Gegenstände wie Straßenlaternen, Abfallkörbe, Telefonzellen, Verkehrszeichen usw.;* **~ lamp, ~ light** *ns.* Straßenlaterne, *die;* Straßenlampe, *die;* **~ lighting** *n.* Straßenbeleuchtung, *die;* **~ map** *n.* Stadtplan, *der;* **~ market** *n.* Markt, *der;* **~ party** *n.* Straßenfest, *das;* **~ plan** ⇒ **~ map;** **~ sweeper** *n.* [A] ▶ **1261** (*person*) Straßenfeger, *der*/-fegerin, *die* (*bes. nordd.*); Straßenkehrer, *der*/-kehrerin, *die* (*bes. südd.*); [B] (*machine*) Kehrmaschine, *die;* (*vehicle*) Straßenkehrmaschine, *die;* **~ theatre** *n.* Straßentheater, *das;* **~ urchin** *n.* Straßenkind, *das;* **~ value** *n.* Straßenverkaufswert, *der;* **~ vendor** *n.* Straßenhändler, *der*/-händlerin, *die;* **~walker** *n.* Nutte, *die* (*ugs.*); **~wise** *adj.* (*coll.*) **be ~wise** wissen, wo es langgeht

**strength** /streŋθ/ *n.* [A] (*power*) Kraft, *die;* (*strong point, force, intensity, amount of ingredient; also Finance*) Stärke, *die;* (*of argument*) [Überzeugungs]kraft, *die;* (*of poison, medicine*) Wirksamkeit, *die;* (*of legal evidence*) [Beweis]kraft, *die;* (*resistance of material, building, etc.*) Stabilität, *die;* (*artistic forcefulness*) [künstlerische/dichterische/musikalische] Kraft; **recover/exhaust one's ~:** seine Kräfte wiedererlangen/erschöpfen; **not know one's own ~:** nicht wissen, wie stark man ist; **give sb. ~:** jmdn. stärken; jmdm. Kraft geben; ⇒ *also* **give** 1 E; **~ of conviction/feeling** Überzeugungskraft, *die*/Stärke der Emotionen; **~ of character/will/purpose** Charakterstärke, *die*/Willensstärke *od.* -kraft, *die*/Zielstrebigkeit, *die;* **from ~:** aus einer Position der Stärke heraus; **go from ~ to ~:** immer erfolgreicher werden; **on the ~ of sth./that** aufgrund einer Sache (*Gen.*)/dessen; **we can have a drink on the ~ of that** darauf können wir einen trinken; [B] (*proportion present*) Stärke, *die;* (*full complement*) **be below ~/up to ~:** weniger als/etwa die volle Stärke haben; **in [full] ~:** in voller Stärke; **the police were there in ~:** ein starkes Polizeiaufgebot war da

**strengthen** /ˈstreŋθən, ˈstreŋkθən/ ❶ *v.t.* (*give power to*) stärken; (*reinforce, intensify, increase in number*) verstärken; erhöhen ‹Anteil›; (*make more effective*) unterstützen; (*increase main ingredient of*) stärker machen ‹Getränk›; kräftiger machen ‹Farbe, Anstrich›; **~ sb.'s resolve** jmdn. in seinem Entschluss bestärken; **~ sb.'s hand** (*fig.*) jmds. Position stärken. ❷ *v.i.* stärker werden

**strenuous** /ˈstrenjʊəs/ *adj.* [A] (*energetic*) energisch; gewaltig ‹Anstrengung›; [B] (*requiring exertion*) anstrengend

**strenuously** /ˈstrenjʊəslɪ/ *adv.* mit aller Kraft ‹sich anstrengen›; angestrengt ‹arbeiten›; heftig ‹bestreiten, bekräftigen›

**strenuousness** /ˈstrenjʊəsnɪs/ *n., no pl.* Schwere, *die*

**streptococcus** /streptəˈkɒkəs/ *n., pl.* **streptococci** /streptəˈkɒkaɪ/ (*Bacteriol.*) Streptokokkus, *der*

**stress** /stres/ ❶ *n.* [A] (*strain*) Stress, *der;* **be [placed] under ~:** unter Stress (*Dat.*) stehen; [B] (*emphasis*) Betonung, *die;* Nachdruck, *der;* **lay** *or* **place** *or* **put [a] ~ on sth.** auf etw. (*Akk.*) Wert *od.* Gewicht legen; [C] (*accentuation*) Betonung, *die;* (*in verse*) Hebung, *die;* **put the/a ~ on sth.** etw.

betonen; **which syllable carries the ~?** welche Silbe trägt den Ton?; Ⓓ (*Mech.*) Belastung, *die;* [elastische] Spannung (*fachspr.*). ⇒ *also* **storm** 1 B.
❷ *v.t.* Ⓐ (*emphasize*) betonen; Wert legen auf (+ *Akk.*) ‹richtige Ernährung, gutes Benehmen, Sport usw.›; **~ [the point] that ...:** darauf hinweisen, dass ...; Ⓑ (*Ling.*) betonen ‹Silbe, Vokal usw.›; Ⓒ (*subject to strain*) überanstrengen; (*Mech.*) belasten; [elastischer] Spannung aussetzen (*fachspr.*)

**ˈstress disease** *n.* Stresskrankheit, *die;* Managerkrankheit, *die* (*volkst.*)

**ˈstressed out** *adj.* (*coll.*) [völlig] gestresst; **be ~ by sb./sth.** von jmdm./etw. [völlig] gestresst sein; **get ~:** [völlig] gestresst werden

**stressful** /ˈstresfl/ *adj.* anstrengend; stressig (*ugs.*)

**ˈstress mark** *n.* Betonungszeichen, *das*

**ˈstress-related** *adj.* stressbedingt

**stretch** /stretʃ/ ❶ *v.t.* Ⓐ (*lengthen, extend*) strecken ‹Arm, Hand›; recken ‹Hals›; dehnen ‹Gummiband›; (*spread*) ausbreiten ‹Decke›; (*tighten*) spannen; **he lay ~ed out on the ground** er lag ausgestreckt auf dem Boden; **~ one's legs** (*by walking*) sich (*Dat.*) die Beine vertreten; Ⓑ (*widen*) dehnen; **~ [out of shape]** ausweiten ‹Schuhe, Jacke›; Ⓒ (*fig.: make the most of*) ausschöpfen ‹Reserve›; fordern ‹Person, Begabung›; Ⓓ (*fig.: extend beyond proper limit*) überschreiten ‹Befugnis, Grenzen des Anstands›; strapazieren (*ugs.*) ‹Geduld›; es nicht so genau nehmen mit ‹Gesetz, Bestimmung, Begriff, Grundsätzen›; **~ a point** großzügig sein; **~ credibility** nicht sehr glaubhaft sein; **~ the truth** ‹Aussage:› nicht ganz der Wahrheit entsprechen; **he's certainly ~ing the truth there** er nimmt es hier mit der Wahrheit nicht so genau; **we're a bit ~ed at the moment** wir sind zurzeit ziemlich überlastet; **~ it/things** den Bogen überspannen; ⇒ *also* **wing** 1 A.
❷ *v.i.* Ⓐ (*extend in length*) sich weiten; sich dehnen; ‹Person, Tier:› sich strecken; Ⓑ (*have specified length*) sich [aus]dehnen; **~ from A to B** sich von A bis B erstrecken; **the traffic jam ~ed all the way back to Junction 9** der Verkehr staute sich bis zur Auffahrt Neun [zurück]; Ⓒ **~ to sth.** (*be sufficient for*) für etw. reichen; **could you ~ to £10?** hast du vielleicht sogar 10 Pfund?
❸ *v. refl.* sich [dehnen und] strecken.
❹ *n.* Ⓐ (*lengthening, drawing out*) **have a ~, give oneself a ~:** sich strecken; **with a ~, I can reach ...:** wenn ich mich strecke, kann ich bis an ... (*Akk.*) reichen; **give sth. a ~:** etw. dehnen *od.* weiter machen; Ⓑ (*exertion*) **by no ~ of the imagination** auch mit viel Fantasie nicht; **at a ~** (*fig.*) wenn es sein muss (⇒ *also* c); **at full ~:** auf Hochtouren; Ⓒ (*expanse, length*) Abschnitt, *der;* **a ~ of road/open country** ein Stück Straße/freies Gelände; (⇒ *also* b); Ⓓ (*period*) **for a ~:** eine Zeit lang; **a four-hour ~:** eine Zeitspanne von vier Stunden; **at a ~:** ohne Unterbrechung; Ⓔ (*Amer. Racing*) Gerade, *die;* Ⓕ (*sl.: length of imprisonment*) **do a [five-year] ~:** [fünf Jahre] im Knast sitzen (*ugs.*); **go down for another ~:** wieder einmal in den Knast wandern (*ugs.*); Ⓖ (*in fabric*) Elastizität, *die;* **there is a lot of ~ in this material** das Material ist sehr dehnbar.
❺ *adj.* dehnbar; Stretch‹hose, -gewebe›

**~ ˈout** ❶ *v.t.* Ⓐ (*extend by straightening*) [aus]strecken ‹Arm, Bein›; ausbreiten ‹Decke›; auseinander ziehen ‹Seil›; **~ oneself out** sich [lang] ausstrecken; Ⓑ (*eke out*) **~ sth. out** mit etw. reichen. ❷ *v.i.* Ⓐ (*~ one's hands out*) (*lit. or fig.*) die Hände ausstrecken (**to** nach); Ⓑ (*extend*) sich ausdehnen; Ⓒ (*last for sufficient time*) reichen

**stretcher** /ˈstretʃə(r)/ ❶ *n.* Ⓐ (*for carrying a person*) [Trag]bahre, *die;* Ⓑ (*between chair legs*) Steg, *der;* Ⓒ (*for canvas*) Rahmen, *der;* Ⓓ (*in boat*) Stemmbrett, *das;* Ⓔ (*Building*) Läufer, *der.* ❷ *v.t.* auf einer Bahre tragen

**ˈstretcher-bearer** *n.* ▶ 1261 [Kranken]träger, *der*

**stretch: ~ marks** *n. pl.* (*after pregnancy*) Schwangerschaftsstreifen; **~ pants** *n. pl.* Stretchhose, *die*

**stretchy** /ˈstretʃɪ/ *adj.* (*coll.*) dehnbar

**strew** /struː/ *v.t.*, *p.p.* **strewed** /struːd/ *or* **strewn** /struːn/ Ⓐ (*scatter*) streuen ‹Blumen, Sand usw.›; **clothes were ~n about the room** Kleider lagen im ganzen Zimmer verstreut herum; Ⓑ (*cover, lit. or fig.*) bestreuen; **the grass was ~n with litter** [überall] auf dem Gras war Abfall verstreut

**stricken** /ˈstrɪkn/ *adj.* Ⓐ (*afflicted*) heimgesucht; havariert ‹Schiff, Flugzeug›; (*showing affliction*) schmerzerfüllt; **be ~ with fever/a disease** von Fieber geschüttelt/einer Krankheit heimgesucht werden; **~ with fear/grief/misfortune** angsterfüllt/gramgebeugt/vom Schicksal geschlagen; **~ in years** (*arch.*) von den Jahren gezeichnet; Ⓑ (*Amer.: deleted*) **~ from sth.** aus etw. gestrichen

**strict** /strɪkt/ *adj.* Ⓐ (*firm*) streng; strenggläubig ‹Katholik, Moslem usw.›; **in ~ confidence** streng vertraulich; **he is ~ about what his children wear** er achtet streng darauf, was seine Kinder anziehen; Ⓑ (*precise*) streng; genau ‹Übersetzung›; **keep a ~ watch** genau *od.* scharf aufpassen; **in the ~ sense [of the word]** im strengen Sinn[e] [des Wortes]

**strictly** /ˈstrɪktlɪ/ *adv.* streng; **there is ~ no smoking here** Rauchen ist hier streng[stens] verboten; **~ between ourselves** ganz im Vertrauen; **this is ~ between ourselves** das muss unter uns bleiben; **~ [speaking]** streng genommen; ⇒ *also* **bird** A

**strictness** /ˈstrɪktnɪs/ *n.*, *no pl.* Ⓐ (*firmness*) Strenge, *die;* Ⓑ (*precision*) Genauigkeit, *die*

**stricture** /ˈstrɪktʃə(r)/ *n.* Ⓐ *usu. in pl.* (*critical remark*) **~[s]** [scharfe *od.* heftige] Kritik; **~[s] [up]on sth.** Kritik an etw. (*Dat.*); **pass ~s [up]on sb.** jmdn. kritisieren; Ⓑ (*Med.*) Verengung, *die;* Striktur, *die*

**stridden** ⇒ **stride** 2, 3

**stride** /straɪd/ ❶ *n.* Ⓐ Schritt, *der;* (*of galloping horse*) [Galopp]sprung, *der;* **make ~s [towards sth.]** (*fig.*) [in Richtung auf etw. (*Akk.*)] Fortschritte machen; **make great ~s** (*fig.*) große Fortschritte machen; **get into one's ~:** seinen Rhythmus finden; (*fig.*) in Fahrt *od.* Schwung kommen; **put sb. off his ~, throw sb. out of his ~** (*fig.*) jmdn. aus dem Konzept bringen; **be thrown out of** *or* **lose one's ~** (*lit. or fig.*) aus dem Tritt kommen; **take sth. in one's ~** (*fig.*) mit etw. gut fertig werden; Ⓑ *in pl.* (*Brit. and Austral. coll.: trousers*) Hose, *die.*
❷ *v.i.*, **strode** /strəʊd/, **stridden** /ˈstrɪdn/ [mit großen Schritten] gehen; (*solemnly*) schreiten (*geh.*); (*take single step*) **~ across sth.** über etw. (*Akk.*) hinwegschreiten (*geh.*).
❸ *v.t.*, **strode, stridden: ~ the streets/moors** durch die Straßen/über die Moore wandern

**~ ˈout** *v.i.* ausschreiten (*geh.*)

**stridency** /ˈstraɪdənsɪ/ *n.*, *no pl.* ⇒ **strident:** Schrillheit, *die;* Grellheit, *die*

**strident** /ˈstraɪdənt/ *adj.* schrill ‹Stimme, Blech[bläser]›; (*fig.*) grell ‹Farbe, Satire›; schrill ‹Protest, Ton›

**stridently** /ˈstraɪdəntlɪ/ *adv.* gellend ‹rufen, laut›; (*fig.*) grell ‹sich kleiden›; aufdringlich ‹vulgär›; in schrillem Ton ‹sich beklagen›

**strife** /straɪf/ *n.*, *no pl.*, *no indef. art.* Streit, *der;* Zwist, *der* (*geh.*); **we live in a world of ~:** wir leben in einer Welt der Zwietracht (*geh.*)

**strike** /straɪk/ ❶ *n.* Ⓐ (*Industry*) Streik, *der;* Ausstand, *der;* **be on/go [out] or come out on ~:** in den Streik getreten sein/in den Streik treten; ⇒ *also* **hunger strike; sit-down** 2; Ⓑ (*Finance, Mining, Oil Industry*) Treffer, *der* (*fig. ugs.*); **make a ~:** sein Glück machen; (*Mining*) fündig werden; **make a gold/an oil ~:** auf Gold/Öl (*Akk.*) stoßen; Ⓒ (*sudden success*) **[lucky] ~:** Glückstreffer, *der;* **make a lucky ~, get one's lucky ~:** Glück haben; Ⓓ (*act of hitting*) Schlag, *der;* (*of snake*) Biss, *der;* Ⓔ (*Mil.*) Angriff, *der* (**at** auf + *Akk.*); **pre-emptive ~:** Präventivschlag, *der;* Ⓕ (*Bowling*) Abräumen, *das;* **get a ~:** abräumen; Ⓖ (*Baseball*) Fehlschlag, *der;* Ⓗ (*Geol.*) Streichen, *das;* **angle of ~:** Streichwinkel, *der.*
❷ *v.t.*, **struck** /strʌk/, **struck** *or* (*arch.*) **stricken** /ˈstrɪkn/ Ⓐ (*hit, send by hitting*) schlagen; ‹Schlag, Geschoss:› treffen ‹Ziel›; ‹Blitz:› [ein]schlagen in (+ *Akk.*), treffen; (*afflict*) treffen; ‹Epidemie, Seuche, Katastrophe usw.:› heimsuchen; ‹Schmerz:› durchzucken; **~ one's head on** *or* **against the wall** mit dem Kopf gegen die Wand schlagen; **his head struck the pavement** er schlug mit dem Kopf auf das Pflaster; **the car struck a pedestrian** das Auto erfasste einen Fußgänger; **the ship struck the rocks** das Schiff lief auf die Felsen; **~ sth. in two** etw. entzweischlagen; etw. spalten; **~ sth. from sb.'s hand** jmdm. etw. aus der Hand schlagen; **~ sb./sth. aside** jmdn. zur Seite stoßen/etw. zur Seite schlagen; Ⓑ (*delete*) streichen (**from, off** aus); Ⓒ (*deliver*) **~ two punches** zweimal zuschlagen; **~ sb. a blow** jmdm. einen Schlag versetzen; **who struck [the] first blow?** wer hat zuerst geschlagen?; **~ a blow against sb./against** *or* **to sth.** (*fig.*) jmdm./einer Sache einen Schlag versetzen; **~ a blow for sth.** (*fig.*) eine Lanze für etw. brechen; Ⓓ (*produce by hitting flint*) schlagen ‹Funken›; (*ignite*) anzünden ‹Streichholz›; **~ a light!** (*dated coll., expr. disgust*) das darf doch nicht wahr sein! (*ugs.*); Ⓔ (*chime*) schlagen; Ⓕ (*Mus.*) anschlagen ‹Töne auf dem Klavier›; anzupfen, anreißen ‹Töne auf der Gitarre›; (*fig.*) anschlagen ‹Ton›; ⇒ *also* **chord**[1] A; Ⓖ (*impress*) beeindrucken; **~ sb.'s notice** jmdm. auffallen; **~ sb. as [being] silly** jmdm. dumm zu sein scheinen *od.* dumm erscheinen; **it ~s sb. that ...:** es scheint jmdm., dass...; **how does it ~ you?** was hältst du davon?; Ⓗ (*occur to*) einfallen (+ *Dat.*); Ⓘ **struck on sb./sth.** (*coll.: infatuated with*) hingerissen von jmdm./etw.; Ⓙ (*cause to become*) **a heart attack struck him dead** er erlag einem Herzanfall; **be struck blind/dumb** erblinden/verstummen; **I was struck speechless by the news** die Nachricht verschlug mir die Sprache; **~ me dead!** (*sl.*) du kannst mich totschlagen (*ugs.*); Ⓚ (*attack*) überfallen; (*Mil.*) angreifen; (*wound with fangs*) ‹Schlange:› ihre Zähne schlagen in (+ *Akk.*); Ⓛ (*encounter*) begegnen (+ *Dat.*); **~ a patch of bad luck** eine Pechsträhne haben; Ⓜ (*Mining*) stoßen auf (+ *Akk.*); **~ gold** auf Gold stoßen; (*fig.*) einen Glückstreffer landen (*ugs.*) (**in** mit); ⇒ *also* **oil** 1 A; Ⓝ (*reach*) stoßen auf (+ *Akk.*) ‹Hauptstraße, Weg, Fluss›; Ⓞ (*achieve*) **~ success** [plötzlich] Erfolg haben; **~ a compromise** einen Kompromiss erreichen; ⇒ *also* **balance** 1 D; **bargain** 1 A; Ⓟ ([*cause to*] *penetrate*) **the cold struck his very marrow** die Kälte ging ihm durch Mark und Bein; **~ sb.'s heart/sb. to the quick** jmdn. ins Herz/Mark treffen; **~ fear into sb.** jmdn. in Angst versetzen; **~ root** Wurzeln treiben *od.* schlagen; Ⓠ (*fill*) **~ sb. with fear/foreboding** jmdn. mit Furcht/Vorahnungen erfüllen; Ⓡ (*Hort.*) setzen; aus Ablegern ziehen ‹Pflanze›; Ⓢ (*adopt*) einnehmen ‹[Geistes]haltung›; Ⓣ (*take down*) einholen ‹Segel, Flagge›; abbrechen ‹Zelt, Lager›; **~ one's flag** (*fig.*) die Flagge streichen; Ⓤ (*mint*) prägen; schlagen (*veralt.*). ⇒ *also* **happy** A; **note** 1 A; **rich** 1 B; **stricken.**
❸ *v.i.*, **struck, struck** *or* (*arch.*) **stricken** Ⓐ (*deliver a blow*) zuschlagen; ‹Pfeil:› treffen; ‹Blitz:› einschlagen; ‹Unheil, Katastrophe, Krise, Leid:› hereinbrechen (*geh.*); (*collide*) zusammenstoßen; (*hit*) schlagen (**against** gegen, **[up]on** auf + *Akk.*); ‹Schiff:› auflaufen (**on** auf + *Akk.*); Ⓑ (*ignite*) zünden; Ⓒ (*chime*) schlagen; **eight o'clock has struck** es hat acht Uhr geschlagen; **hear the hour ~:** den Stundenschlag hören; Ⓓ (*Industry*) streiken; Ⓔ (*attack; also Mil.*) zuschlagen (*fig.*); (*wound with fang*) zubeißen; Ⓕ (*make a find*) (*Mining*) fündig werden; (*Hunting*) die Witterung aufnehmen; **~ lucky** Glück haben; Ⓖ (*penetrate*) **~ through sth.** durch etw. dringen; **the wind ~s cold** der kalte Wind geht durch und durch; **his words struck into my heart** seine Worte trafen mich ins Herz; Ⓗ (*direct course*) **~ south** *etc.* sich nach Süden *usw.*

wenden; ‹Straße:› nach Süden *usw.* verlaufen; ‹Schiff:› Kurs nach Süden *usw.* nehmen; ~ **across the fields/down the hill/through the forest** über die Felder/den Hügel hinunter/durch den Wald gehen; Ⓘ (*launch*) ~ **into sth.** mit etw. beginnen; Ⓙ (*Hort.*) Wurzeln treiben *od.* schlagen; Ⓚ (*Angling*) (*hook fish*) anschlagen; (*seize bait*) anbeißen. ⇒ *also* **iron** 1 A

~ **at** *v.t.* schlagen nach; (*fig.*) einen Schlag versetzen (+ *Dat.*); rütteln an (+ *Dat.*) ‹Grundfesten›; ⇒ *also* **root**[1] 1 A

~ **'back** *v.i.* (*lit. or fig.*) zurückschlagen; ~ **back at sb./sth.** sich gegen jmdn./etw. zur Wehr setzen

~ **'down** *v.t.* niederschlagen; (*fig.*) niederwerfen (*geh.*); (*Amer. Law: reverse*) aufheben

~ **'off** ❶ *v.t.* Ⓐ (*remove*) abschlagen; Ⓑ (*remove from membership*) streichen ‹Namen›; (*from professional body*) die Zulassung/Approbation entziehen (+ *Dat.*); Ⓒ (*produce by copying*) abziehen. ❷ *v.i.* aufbrechen

~ **on** ⇒ ~ **upon**

~ **'out** ❶ *v.t.* Ⓐ (*devise*) ausarbeiten; Ⓑ (*delete*) streichen; Ⓒ (*Baseball*) ausmachen. ❷ *v.i.* Ⓐ (*hit out*) zuschlagen; ~ **out at sb./sth.** nach jmdn./etw. schlagen; (*fig.*) jmdn./etw. scharf angreifen; ~ **out on all sides** um sich schlagen; ~ **out wildly** wild um sich schlagen; Ⓑ (*swim vigorously*) mit kräftigen Zügen schwimmen; (*fig.*) Anstrengungen unternehmen; ~ **out for sth.** (*fig.*) sich mit aller Kraft um etw. bemühen; Ⓒ (*set out*) (*lit. or fig.*) aufbrechen; ~ **out in a new direction** (*fig.*) etwas Neues anfangen; Ⓓ (*Baseball*) aus sein

~ **through** *v.t.* durchstreichen ‹Wort›; (*on list also*) ausstreichen

~ **up** ❶ /'--/ *v.t.* Ⓐ (*start*) beginnen ‹Unterhaltung›; anknüpfen ‹Bekanntschaft›; schließen ‹Freundschaft›; ~ **up a friendship with sb.** sich mit jmdm. anfreunden; Ⓑ (*begin to play*) anstimmen. ❷ /-'-/ *v.i.* beginnen

~ **upon** *v.t.* finden ‹Lösung, Ausweg›; **I have just struck upon an idea** mir ist gerade eine Idee gekommen

**strike:** ~ **action** *n.* Streikaktionen; **take ~ action** Streikmaßnahmen ergreifen; ~ **ballot** *n.* Urabstimmung, *die;* ~ **benefit** ⇒ ~ **pay**; ~**bound** *adj.* bestreikt ‹Fabrik›; vom Streik/von Streiks betroffen ‹Industrie›; durch einen Streik lahm gelegt ‹Zugverkehr, Land›; ~**-breaker** *n.* Streikbrecher, *der*/-brecherin, *die;* ~ **force** ⇒ **striking force**; ~ **pay** *n.* Streikgeld, *das*

**striker** /'straɪkə(r)/ *n.* Ⓐ (*worker on strike*) Streikende, *der/die;* Ⓑ (*Cricket*) Schläger, *der*/Schlägerin, *die;* (*Footb.*) Stürmer, *der*/Stürmerin, *die;* (*Billiards*) Spieler/Spielerin, der/die am Stoß ist; Ⓒ (*Arms*) Schlagbolzen, *der;* Ⓓ (*Horol.*) (*clock*) Schlaguhr, *die;* (*mechanism*) Schlagwerk, *das*

**striking** /'straɪkɪŋ/ *adj.* Ⓐ (*arresting*) auffallend; erstaunlich ‹Ähnlichkeit, Unterschied›; bemerkenswert ‹Idee›; schlagend ‹Beispiel›; Ⓑ (*Horol.*) mit Schlagwerk *nachgestellt;* Schlagwerk-

**striking:** ~ **distance** *n.* Reichweite, *die;* (*of* [*bullet from*] *gun etc.*) Schussweite, *die;* **the troops had advanced to within ~ distance of the capital** die Truppen hatten sich der Hauptstadt auf Reichweite genähert; **within easy ~ distance of a town** (*fig.*) in unmittelbarer Nähe einer Stadt; **I'm now [with]in ~ distance of my own car** (*can almost afford it*) ein eigener Wagen ist inzwischen in Reichweite gekommen; ~ **force** *n.* (*Mil., Police*) Einsatzkommando, *das*

**strikingly** /'straɪkɪŋlɪ/ *adv.* auffallend; umwerfend ‹ähnlich sehen›; **be ~ obvious** ins Auge springen

**Strine** /straɪn/ *n., no pl., no art.* australisches Englisch; *attrib.* australisch ‹Akzent usw.›

**string** /strɪŋ/ ❶ *n.* Ⓐ (*thin cord*) Schnur, *die;* (*to tie up parcels etc. also*) Bindfaden, *der;* (*ribbon*) Band, *das;* **a puppet on ~s/on a ~:** eine Marionette; **how long is a piece of ~?** wie weit ist der Himmel?; **[have/keep sb.] on a ~:** [jmdn.] an der Leine (*ugs.*) *od.* am Gängelband [haben/halten]; **pull the ~s** (*fig.*) die Fäden in der Hand haben; **pull [a few *or* some] ~s** (*fig.*) seine Beziehungen spielen lassen; **there are ~s attached** (*fig.*) es sind Bedingungen/es ist eine Bedingung damit verknüpft; **..., but there are ~s attached ...**, aber nur unter Bedingungen/einer Bedingung; **without ~s, with no ~s attached** ohne Bedingung[en]; Ⓑ (*of bow*) Sehne, *die;* (*of racket, musical instrument*) Saite, *die;* **have another ~ to one's bow** (*fig.*) noch ein Eisen im Feuer haben (*ugs.*); **first/second ~:** erste/zweite Wahl; **as a second ~:** als zweites Eisen im Feuer (*ugs.*); **a racket with nylon ~s** ein Schläger mit Nylonbespannung; **a six-~ guitar** eine sechssaitige Gitarre; Ⓒ *in pl.* (*Mus.*) (*instruments*) Streichinstrumente; (*players*) Streicher; ~ **quartet/orchestra** Streichquartett/-orchester, *das;* **he plays in the ~s** er spielt bei den Streichern; Ⓓ (*series, sequence*) Kette, *die;* (*procession*) Zug, *der;* (*of onions*) Zopf, *der;* (*Computing*) String, *der;* Zeichenfolge, *die;* **he owns a ~ of racehorses** ihm gehören etliche Rennpferde; **he has had a ~ of girlfriends** er hat eine Freundin nach der anderen gehabt; Ⓔ (*in bean*) Faden, *der.* ⇒ *also* **apron** A; **bowstring**; **shoestring**.

❷ *v.t.*, **strung** /strʌŋ/ Ⓐ bespannen ‹Tennisschläger, Bogen, Gitarre usw.›; **be strung to breaking point** (*fig.*) ‹Nerven:› zum Zerreißen gespannt sein; Ⓑ (*thread*) auffädeln; aufziehen; Ⓒ (*arrange in line*) aufreihen; (*stretch out*) spannen; ~ **sth. round one's neck** sich (*Dat.*) etw. um den Hals hängen; Ⓓ (*tie with* ~) verschnüren; Ⓔ die Fäden abziehen von ‹Bohnen›. ⇒ *also* **highly strung**

~ **a'long** (*coll.*) ❶ *v.i.* sich anschließen; ~ **along with sb.** mit jmdm. mitgehen; (*have relationship*) mit jmdm. gehen (*ugs.*). ❷ *v.t.* Ⓐ (*deceive*) an der Nase herumführen (*ugs.*); Ⓑ (*keep dangling*) hinhalten

~ **'out** ❶ *v.t.* verstreuen; ~ **one's meals out at longer intervals** die Abstände zwischen den Mahlzeiten vergrößern. ❷ *v.i.* (*in space*) sich verteilen

~ **to'gether** *v.t.* (*join on a thread*) auffädeln; aufziehen; (*join by tying*) zusammenbinden; (*join coherently*) miteinander verknüpfen; **he can't ~ two sentences together** er kann keine zwei zusammenhängende Sätze hervorbringen

~ **'up** *v.t.* Ⓐ (*tie with* ~) schnüren; (*hang up*) aufhängen ‹Lampions, Papiergirlanden›; Ⓑ (*coll.: kill by hanging*) aufhängen (*ugs.*); Ⓒ (*make tense*) unter Druck setzen; **strung up** angespannt

**string:** ~ **bag** *n.* [Einkaufs]netz, *das;* ~ **band** *n.* (*Mus.*) Streichorchester, *das;* ~ **bass** /strɪŋ 'beɪs/ *n.* (*Mus.*) Kontrabass, *der;* ~ **'bean** *n.* (*Amer.*) grüne Bohne; (*fig. joc.: tall thin person*) Bohnenstange, *die* (*ugs. scherzh.*)

**stringed** /strɪŋd/ *attrib. adj.* (*Mus.*) Saiten-

**-stringed** *adj. in comb.* (*Mus.*) -saitig

**stringency** /'strɪndʒənsɪ/ *n., no pl.* Ⓐ (*strictness*) Strenge, *die;* Ⓑ **financial ~:** Geldknappheit, *die*

**stringent** /'strɪndʒənt/ *adj.* Ⓐ (*strict*) streng ‹Bestimmung, Gesetz, Maßnahme, Test›; schlüssig ‹Argumentation›; überzeugend ‹Plan›; Ⓑ (*tight*) angespannt ‹Finanzlage›

**stringently** /'strɪndʒəntlɪ/ *adv.* Ⓐ (*strictly*) streng; energisch ‹durchsetzen›; stringent ‹logisch›; schlüssig ‹argumentieren›; Ⓑ eisern ‹sparen›

**stringer** /'strɪŋə(r)/ *n.* Ⓐ (*in construction*) Stringer, *der* (*Bauw.*); Ⓑ (*Journ.*) Korrespondent, *der*/Korrespondentin, *die* (*in freier Mitarbeit*)

**string 'vest** *n.* Netzhemd, *das*

**stringy** /'strɪŋɪ/ *adj.* Ⓐ (*fibrous*) faserig; Ⓑ (*resembling string*) dünn ‹Haar›; faserig ‹Gewebe›; Ⓒ (*forming threads*) Fäden ziehend; zäh ‹Konsistenz›; **be ~:** Fäden ziehen; ‹Konsistenz:› zäh sein

**strip**[1] /strɪp/ ❶ *v.t.*, **-pp-** Ⓐ (*denude*) ausziehen ‹Person›; leer räumen, ausräumen ‹Haus, Schrank, Regal›; abziehen ‹Bett›; abtakeln (*Seemannsspr.*) ‹Schiff›; entrinden ‹Baum›; abbeizen ‹Möbel, Türen›; ausschlachten, (*dismantle*) auseinander nehmen ‹Maschine, Auto›; überdrehen ‹Schraube, Mutter›; beschädigen ‹Getriebe›; ~**ped to the waist** mit nacktem Oberkörper; ~ **sb. of sth.** jmdn. einer Sache (*Gen.*) berauben (*geh.*); ~ **sb. of his rank/title/medals/decorations/office** jmdm. seinen Rang/Titel/seine Medaillen/Auszeichnungen aberkennen/jmdn. seines Amtes entkleiden (*geh.*); ~ **sb. of his power** jmdm. die Macht nehmen; ~ **A of B** B von A entfernen; ~ **the garden of [all its] flowers** alle Blumen im Garten abpflücken; ~ **a tree [of fruit]** einen Baum abernten; ~ **the trees [of leaves]** die Bäume entlauben; ~ **the walls** die Tapeten entfernen; Ⓑ (*remove*) entfernen (**from, off** von); abziehen ‹Laken›; abnehmen ‹Vorhang, Bild›; abschälen ‹Rinde, Schale›; abstreifen ‹Hülle›; ~ **the clothes/shirt off sb.'s back** *or* **off sb.** jmdm. die Kleider/das Hemd vom Leibe reißen; ~ **the medals off** *or* **from sb.'s chest** jmdm. die Orden abreißen; ~ **sb.'s property/title from him** (*fig.*) jmdm. seinen Besitz abnehmen/Titel aberkennen.

❷ *v.i.*, **-pp-** sich ausziehen; ~ **to the waist/[down] to one's underwear** den Oberkörper freimachen/sich bis auf die Unterwäsche ausziehen.

❸ *n.* **do a ~:** sich ausziehen; (*erotically*) einen Striptease vorführen; *attrib.* ~ **act** Striptease, *der*

~ **'down** ❶ *v.t.* Ⓐ (*dismantle*) auseinander nehmen; Ⓑ (*undress*) ausziehen; Ⓒ (*reduce*) einschränken. ❷ *v.i.* sich ausziehen

~ **'off** ❶ *v.t.* Ⓐ abreißen; abschälen ‹Rinde›; abziehen ‹Tapete›; ~ **sth. off sth.** etw. von etw. abreißen/abschälen/abziehen; **he ~ped off the soldier's medals** er riss dem Soldaten die Orden ab; Ⓑ ausziehen ‹Kleidung›. ❷ *v.i.* sich ausziehen

**strip**[2] *n.* Ⓐ (*narrow piece*) Streifen, *der;* **the curtains hung in ragged ~s** die Vorhänge hingen in Fetzen; **a ~ of land** ein schmales Stück *od.* Streifen Land; **tear sb. off a ~, tear a ~ off sb.** (*Brit. coll.*) jmdm. den Marsch blasen (*ugs.*); Ⓑ (*Metallurgy*) Band, *das;* Ⓒ ⇒ **strip cartoon**; Ⓓ (*Brit. Sport coll.: clothes*) Trikot, *das*

**strip:** ~ **cartoon** *n.* Comic[strip], *der;* ~ **club** *n.* Stripteaselokal, *das*

**stripe** /straɪp/ *n.* Ⓐ Streifen, *der;* Ⓑ (*Mil.*) [Ärmel]streifen, *der;* **get/lose a ~:** befördert/degradiert werden; Ⓒ (*Amer.: nature*) Schlag, *der.* ⇒ *also* **star** 1 A

**striped** /straɪpt/ *adj.* gestreift; Streifen‹muster, -hyäne›

**strip:** ~ **farming** *n., no pl., no indef. art.* Streifenflurwirtschaft, *die;* ~ **light** *n.* Neonröhre, *die;* (*Theatre*) Lichtwanne, *die;* ~ **lighting** *n.* Neonbeleuchtung, *die;* Neonlicht, *das*

**stripling** /'strɪplɪŋ/ *n.* Jüngelchen, *das*

**'strip mine** *n.* (*Amer. Mining*) Tagebau, *der*

**stripped pine** /strɪpt 'paɪn/ *n.* abgebeizte Kiefer

**stripper** /'strɪpə(r)/ *n.* Ⓐ (*solvent*) Farbentferner, *der;* (*for wallpaper*) Tapetenlöser, *der;* (*tool*) Kratzer, *der;* Ⓑ ▶1261 (*striptease performer*) Stripteasetänzer, *der*/-tänzerin, *die;* Stripper, *der*/Stripperin, *die* (*ugs.*)

**strip:** ~ **'poker** *n.* (*Cards*) Strippoker, *das;* ~**-search** ❶ *n.* *Leibesvisitation, bei der der Durchsuchte sich ausziehen muss;* **do a ~-search on a suspect** *einen Verdächtigen, der sich zuvor ausziehen musste, durchsuchen;* ❷ *v.t.* **we were ~-searched** wir mussten uns zur Durchsuchung ausziehen; ~ **show** *n.* Stripshow, *die;* ~**'tease** ❶ *n.* Striptease, *der;* ❷ *v.i.* strippen (*ugs.*)

**stripy** /'straɪpɪ/ *adj.* gestreift ‹Fell, Blazer›; Streifen‹muster, -stoff›

**strive** /straɪv/ *v.i.*, **strove** /strəʊv/, **striven** /'strɪvn/ Ⓐ (*endeavour*) sich bemühen; ~ **to do sth.** bestrebt sein (*geh.*) *od.* sich bemühen, etw. zu tun; ~ **after** *or* **for sth.** nach etw. streben; ~ **after** *or* **for the right answer** sich bemühen, die richtige Antwort zu finden; Ⓑ (*contend*) kämpfen (**for** um); ~ **together** *or* **with each other [for sth.]** miteinander [um etw.] ringen

**striven** ⇒ **strive**

**strobe** /strəʊb/ (*coll.*), **stroboscope** /'strəʊbəskəʊp/ *ns.* Ⓐ (*instrument*) Stroboskop, *das;* Ⓑ (*lamp*) Stroboskoplicht, *das*

**stroboscopic** /strəʊbə'skɒpɪk/ *adj.* stroboskopisch; ~ **lamp/light** Stroboskoplicht, *das*

**strode** ⇒ **stride** 2, 3

**stroke**[1] /strəʊk/ ❶ *n.* Ⓐ (*act of striking*) Hieb, *der;* Schlag, *der;* (*of sword, axe*) Hieb, *der;* (*of sword also*) Streich, *der* (*geh.*); **finishing** ~ (*lit. or fig.*) Todesstoß, *der* (*see also*, G); Ⓑ (*Med.*) Schlaganfall, *der;* **paralytic/apoplectic** ~: paralytischer/apoplektischer Anfall; Ⓒ (*sudden impact*) ~ **of lightning** Blitzschlag, *der;* **by a** ~ **of fate/fortune** durch eine Fügung des Schicksals/einen [glücklichen] Zufall; ~ **of [good] luck** Glücksfall, *der;* **have a** ~ **of bad/[good] luck** Pech/Glück haben; **by a** ~ **of bad/[good] luck, the door was locked/open** das Unglück/Glück wollte es, dass die Tür verschlossen/offen war; Ⓓ (*single effort*) Streich, *der;* (*skilful effort*) Schachzug, *der;* **at a** *or* **one** ~: auf einen Schlag *od.* Streich; **not do a** ~ **[of work]** keinen [Hand]schlag tun; ~ **of genius** genialer Einfall; Ⓔ (*of pendulum, heart, wings, oar*) Schlag, *der;* (*in swimming*) Zug, *der;* (*of piston*) Hub, *der* (*Technik*); Ⓕ (*Billiards etc.*) Stoß, *der;* (*Tennis, Cricket, Golf, Rowing*) Schlag, *der;* (*Swimming, Rowing: style*) Stil, *der;* **off one's** ~ (*lit. or fig.*) nicht in Form; **put sb. off his/her** ~ (*lit. or fig.*) jmdn. aus dem Takt bringen; Ⓖ (*mark, line*) Strich, *der;* (*of handwriting; also fig.: detail*) Zug, *der;* (*symbol /*) Schrägstrich, *der;* **with a** ~ **of the** *or* **one's pen** mit einem Federstrich; **finishing** ~**s** (*lit. or fig.*) letzte Pinselstriche; (*fig.*) letztes Feilen (*see also* A); Ⓗ (*sound of clock*) Schlag, *der;* **on the** ~ **of nine** Punkt neun [Uhr]; **it was on the** ~ **of nine when ...:** es war Schlag neun [Uhr], als ...; **on the** ~: pünktlich; Ⓘ (*oarsman*) Schlagmann, *der.*
❷ *v.t.* (*Rowing*) als Schlagmann rudern in (+ *Dat.*)

**stroke**[2] ❶ *v.t.* streicheln; ~ **one's chin/beard** sich (*Dat.*) über das Kinn/den Bart streichen; ~ **sth. over/across sth.** mit etw. über etw. (*Akk.*) streichen; ~ **one's hand across one's brow** sich (*Dat.*) mit der Hand über die Stirn streichen; ~ **sth. back** etw. zurückstreichen. ❷ *n.* **give sb./sth. a** ~: jmdn./etw. streicheln; **give the dog's ears a** ~: dem Hund die Ohren streicheln

~ **'down** *v.t.* glatt streichen; (*fig.*) besänftigen

**stroke:** ~ **oar** *n.* (*Rowing*) (*oar*) Schlagriemen, *der;* (*oarsman*) Schlagmann, *der;* ~ **play** *n.* (*Cricket*) *Spiel mit spektakulären, mutigen Schlägen*

**stroll** /strəʊl/ ❶ *v.i.* Ⓐ (*saunter*) spazieren gehen; ~ **into sth.** in etw. (*Akk.*) schlendern; Ⓑ (*go from place to place*) umherziehen; ~ **from town to town** von Ort zu Ort ziehen. ❷ *n.* Spaziergang, *der;* **at a** ~: in gemächlichem Schritt *od.* Tempo; **go for a** ~: einen Spaziergang machen

~ **a'long** ❶ *v.i.* daherspazieren *od.* -schlendern. ❷ *v.t.* ~ **along sth.** an etw. (*Dat.*) entlangspazieren *od.* -schlendern

~ **'on** *v.i.* weiterschlendern

**stroller** /'strəʊlə(r)/ *n.* Ⓐ Spaziergänger, *der;* Ⓑ (*pushchair*) Sportwagen, *der*

**strong** /strɒŋ/ ❶ *adj.*, ~**er** /'strɒŋgə(r)/, ~**est** /'strɒŋgɪst/ Ⓐ (*resistant*) stark; gefestigt ‹Ehe›; stabil ‹Möbel›; solide, fest ‹Fundament, Schuhe›; streng ‹Vorschriften, Vorkehrungen›; robust ‹Konstitution, Magen, Stoff, Porzellan›; (*Econ.*) stark ‹Währung›; **a man of** ~ **will/resolve** ein willensstarker Mann/Mann von großer Entschlusskraft; **you have to have a** ~ **stomach** (*fig.*) man muss einiges vertragen können; **have a** ~ **head [for alcohol]** viel [Alkohol] vertragen können; **be** ~ **[again]** ‹Patient:› [wieder] gesund sein; **the market [in oil] is** ~ (*Commerc.*) die Nachfrage [nach Öl] ist groß; Ⓑ (*powerful*) stark, kräftig ‹Person, Tier›; kräftig ‹Arme, Beine, Muskeln, Tritt, Schlag, Zähne›; stark ‹Linse, Brille, Strom, Magnet›; gut ‹Augen›; **as** ~ **as a horse** *or* **an ox** (*fig.*) bärenstark (*ugs.*); **the** ~ **silent man/type** der starke, schweigsame Mann/Typ; **a man of** ~ **character** ein charakterstarker Mann; Ⓒ (*effective*) stark ‹Regierung, Herrscher, Wille›; streng ‹Disziplin, Lehrer›; gut ‹Gedächtnis, Schüler›; fähig ‹Redner, Mathematiker›; (*formidable*) stark ‹Gegner, Kombination›; aussichtsreich ‹Kandidat›; (*powerful in resources*) reich ‹Nation, Land›; leistungsfähig ‹Wirtschaft›; stark ‹Besetzung›; (*numerous, of specified number*) stark ‹Delegation, Truppe, Kontingent usw.›; (*Cards*) gut ‹Blatt›; (*Games, Sport*) spielstark; stark ‹Mannschaft›; **she is** ~ **in Latin** Latein ist ihre Stärke; sie ist gut in Latein; **Latin is her** ~**est subject** in Latein ist sie am besten; **sb.'s** ~ **point** jmds. Stärke; **the article is not** ~ **on facts** in Bezug auf Tatsachen steht der Artikel auf schwachen Füßen; **the company is a dozen** ~: die Firma hat ein Dutzend Mitarbeiter; **a 10,000-**~ **army** eine 10 000 Mann starke Armee; **fate dealt him a** ~ **hand** (*fig.*) das Schicksal hat es gut mit ihm gemeint; Ⓓ (*convincing*) gut, handfest ‹Grund, Beispiel, Argument›; **there is a** ~ **possibility that ...:** es ist sehr wahrscheinlich, dass ...; Ⓔ (*vigorous, moving forcefully*) stark; voll ‹Unterstützung›; spannend ‹Plot›; fest ‹Überzeugung›; kraftvoll ‹Stil›; (*fervent*) glühend ‹Anhänger, Verfechter einer Sache›; **take** ~ **measures/action** energisch vorgehen; **be a** ~ **believer in sth.** fest an etw. (*Akk.*) glauben; Ⓕ (*affecting the senses*) stark; kräftig, stark ‹Geruch, Geschmack, Stimme›; markant ‹Gesichtszüge›; (*pungent*) streng ‹Geruch, Geschmack›; kräftig ‹Käse›; **the fish is rather** ~: der Fisch riecht schon sehr; Ⓖ (*concentrated*) stark; konzentriert ‹Lösung›; hochprozentig ‹Alkohol›; kräftig ‹Farbe›; **I need a** ~ **drink** ich muss mir erst mal einen genehmigen (*ugs.*); Ⓗ (*emphatic*) stark ‹Ausdruck, Protest›; heftig ‹Worte, Wortwechsel›; (*Phonet., Pros.*) stark betont ‹Silbe›; stark ‹Reim›; Ⓘ (*Ling.*) stark ‹Verb, Deklination usw.›.
❷ *adv.* stark; **the wind was blowing** ~: es wehte ein starker Wind; **come on** ~ (*coll.*) in Fahrt kommen (*ugs.*); **sb. is going** ~: es geht jmdm. gut; **they are still going** ~ (*after years of marriage*) mit ihnen geht es noch immer gut; (*after hours of work*) sie sind noch immer eifrig dabei; **the restaurant is still going** ~: das Restaurant geht immer noch gut; ⇒ *also* **come** O

**strong:** ~ **'arm** *n., no pl.* Muskelkraft, *die; attrib.* ~**-arm methods** brutale Methoden; ~ **box** *n.* Kassette, *die;* ~**hold** *n.* Festung, *die;* (*fig.*) Hochburg, *die;* ~ **'language** *n., no pl., no indef. art.* derbe Ausdrucksweise; **use** ~ **language** sich derb ausdrücken

**strongly** /'strɒŋlɪ/ *adv.* Ⓐ stark; fest ‹etabliert›; solide ‹gearbeitet›; ~ **built** solide gebaut; (*in body*) kräftig gebaut; Ⓑ (*powerfully*) stark; Ⓒ (*convincingly*) überzeugend ‹darlegen›; Ⓓ (*vigorously*) energisch ‹protestieren, bestreiten›; nachdrücklich ‹unterstützen›; dringend ‹raten›; fest ‹glauben›; **I feel** ~ **about it** es ist mir sehr ernst damit; es liegt mir sehr am Herzen; **I** ~ **suspect that ...:** ich habe den starken Verdacht, dass ...

**strong:** ~**man** *n.* Muskelmann, *der* (*ugs.*); (*fig.*) (*capable man*) führender Kopf; (*dictator*) starker Mann; ~ **'meat** *n., no pl., no art.* (*fig.*) starker Tobak (*ugs.*); ~**-'minded** *adj.* [seelisch] robust; (*determined*) willensstark; ~ **point** *n.* (*fortified position*) Stützpunkt, *der;* ⇒ *also* ~ 1 C; ~**room** *n.* Tresorraum, *der;* Stahlkammer, *die;* ~ **'suit** *n.* (*Cards*) lange Farbe; (*fig.*) Stärke, *die;* ~**-'willed** *adj.* willensstark

**strontium** /'strɒntɪəm/ *n.* (*Chem.*) Strontium, *das*

**strop** /strɒp/ ❶ *n.* Streichriemen, *der.* ❷ *v.t.*, **-pp-** [auf dem Streichriemen] schärfen

**stroppy** /'strɒpɪ/ *adj.* (*Brit. coll.*) pampig (*salopp*)

**strove** ⇒ **strive**

**struck** ⇒ **strike** 2, 3

**structural** /'strʌktʃərl/ *adj.* Ⓐ baulich; Bau‹material›; tragend ‹Wand, Säule, Balken›; Konstruktions‹fehler›; statisch ‹Probleme›; Ⓑ (*Biol.*) strukturell; Struktur‹muster, -merkmal›; Ⓒ (*Geol.*) tektonisch; Ⓓ (*Sociol.*) strukturell

**structural:** ~ **engi'neering** *n.* Hochbau, *der;* ~ **formula** *n.* (*Chem.*) Strukturformel, *die*

**structuralism** /'strʌktʃərəlɪzm/ *n.* Strukturalismus, *der*

**structurally** /'strʌktʃərəlɪ/ *adv.* strukturell; (*Geol.*) tektonisch ‹geformt›; **the building is** ~ **sound** das Gebäude hat eine gute Bausubstanz; ~, **the building is ...:** baulich gesehen ist das Gebäude ...

**structural 'steel** *n.* (*Building*) Baustahl, *der*

**structure** /'strʌktʃə(r)/ ❶ *n.* Ⓐ (*manner of construction*) Bauweise, *die;* (*interrelation of parts; also Anat., Biol., Geol., Ling., Lit., Phys.*) Struktur, *die;* Aufbau, *der;* (*Mus.*) Kompositionsweise, *die;* Struktur, *die;* **bone/skeletal** ~: Knochenbau, *der*/Knochengerüst, *das;* **sentence** ~: Satzbau, *der;* **price** ~: Preisverhältnis, *das;* Ⓑ *no pl., no indef. art.* (*formal arrangement of parts*) Strukturierung, *die;* **people must have** ~ **in their daily lives** der Mensch braucht eine gewisse Ordnung in seinem Alltag; Ⓒ (*something constructed*) Konstruktion, *die;* (*building*) Bauwerk, *das;* (*complex whole; also Biol.*) Struktur, *die.*
❷ *v.t.* strukturieren; regeln ‹Leben›; aufbauen ‹literarisches Werk›; (*construct*) konstruieren; bauen

**structured** /'strʌktʃəd/ *adj.* strukturiert; geregelt ‹Leben›

**strudel** /'stru:dl/ *n.* (*Gastr.*) Strudel, *der*

**struggle** /'strʌgl/ ❶ *v.i.* Ⓐ (*try with difficulty*) kämpfen; ~ **to do sth.** sich abmühen, etw. zu tun; ~ **for a place/a better world** um einen Platz/für eine bessere Welt kämpfen; ~ **for breath** nach Atem ringen; ~ **against** *or* **with sb./sth.** mit jmdm./etw. *od.* gegen jmdn./etw. kämpfen; ~ **with sth.** (*try to cope*) sich mit etw. quälen; mit etw. kämpfen; Ⓑ (*proceed with difficulty*) sich quälen; (*into tight dress, through narrow opening*) sich zwängen; **I** ~**d past** ich kämpfte mich vorbei; ~ **to one's feet** unter Schwierigkeiten aufstehen; Ⓒ (*physically*) kämpfen; (*resist*) sich wehren; ~ **free** freikommen; sich befreien; Ⓓ (*be in difficulties, have difficulty in life*) kämpfen (*fig.*); **after three laps I was struggling** nach drei Runden hatte ich zu kämpfen.
❷ *n.* Ⓐ (*exertion*) **with a** ~: mit Mühe; **it was a long** ~: es kostete viel Mühe; **after all our valiant** ~**s** nach all unserem tapferen Bemühen; **have a [hard]** ~ **to do sth.** [große] Mühe haben, etw. zu tun; **a life of hardship and** ~: ein hartes und mühseliges Leben; **the** ~ **for freedom** der Kampf für die Freiheit; Ⓑ (*physical fight*) Kampf, *der;* (*confused wrestle*) Handgemenge, *das;* **legal** ~: Rechtsstreit, *der;* **the** ~ **against** *or* **with sb./sth.** der Kampf gegen *od.* mit jmdm./etw.; **the** ~ **for influence/power** der Kampf um Einfluss/die Macht; **the** ~ **for existence** *or* **life** *or* **survival** der Kampf ums Überleben; **surrender without a** ~: kampflos aufgeben

**struggling** /'strʌglɪŋ/ *adj.* (*in life*) *ums Überleben und um Anerkennung kämpfend*

**strum** /strʌm/ ❶ *v.i.*, **-mm-** klimpern (*ugs.*) (**on** auf + *Dat.*). ❷ *v.t.*, **-mm-** klimpern (*ugs.*) auf (+ *Dat.*). ❸ *n.* Klimpern, *das* (*ugs.*); **have a** ~: klimpern (*ugs.*)

**strumpet** /'strʌmpɪt/ *n.* (*arch./rhet.*) Dirne, *die* (*veralt.*)

**strung** ⇒ **string** 2

**strut**[1] /strʌt/ ❶ *v.i.*, **-tt-** (*walk*) stolzieren. ❷ *n.* stolzierender Gang

**strut**[2] ❶ *n.* (*support*) Strebe, *die.* ❷ *v.t.*, **-tt-** verstreben

**'struth** /stru:θ/ *int.* Himmel! (*ugs.*)

**strychnine** /'strɪkni:n/ *n.* Strychnin, *das*

**Stuart** /'stju:ət/ (*Brit. Hist.*) ❶ *n.* Stuart, *der/die.* ❷ *attrib. adj.* **the** ~ **dynasty** *etc.* die Dynastie *usw.* der Stuarts

**stub** /stʌb/ ❶ *n.* Ⓐ (*short remaining portion*) Stummel, *der;* (*of cigarette*) Kippe, *die;* ~ **of pencil** Bleistiftstummel, *der;* Ⓑ (*counterfoil*) Abschnitt, *der;* (*of ticket*) Abriss, *der;* Ⓒ (*of tree, branch, tooth*) Stumpf, *der;* Ⓓ (*limb, tail, etc.*) Stummel, *der.* ❷ *v.t.*,

S

**-bb-** A **~ one's toe [against** *or* **on sth.]** sich (*Dat.*) den Zeh [an etw. (*Dat.*)] stoßen; B ausdrücken ‹Zigarette usw.›; (*with one's foot*) austreten ‹Zigarette usw.›
**~ 'out** *v.t.* ausdrücken

**'stub axle** *n.* (*Mech.*) Achsschenkel, *der*

**stubble** /'stʌbl/ *n., no pl.* Stoppeln *Pl.*

**stubbly** /'stʌblɪ/ *adj.* stopp[e]lig; **~ field/beard** Stoppelfeld, *das*/-bart, *der* (*ugs.*)

**stubborn** /'stʌbən/ *adj.* A (*obstinate*) starrköpfig (*abwertend*); dickköpfig (*ugs.*); störrisch ‹Tier, Gesicht, Haltung›; hartnäckig ‹Vorurteil, Streit›; **be ~ in insisting on sth.** stur (*ugs. abwertend*) auf etw. (*Dat.*) beharren; **[as] ~ as a mule** störrisch wie ein Maulesel (*ugs.*); B (*resolute*) hartnäckig; fest ‹Mut, Entschlossenheit, Treue›; hart ‹Augen, Kinn›; C (*intractable*) störrisch (*fig.*); vertrackt (*ugs.*) ‹Problem›; hartnäckig ‹Unkraut, Krankheit›

**stubbornly** /'stʌbənlɪ/ *adv.* A (*obstinately*) störrisch; wild ‹entschlossen›; B (*resolutely, intractably*) hartnäckig

**stubbornness** /'stʌbənnis/ *n., no pl.* A (*obstinacy*) Starrköpfigkeit, *die*; B (*resolution, intractability*) Hartnäckigkeit, *die*

**stubby** /'stʌbɪ/ *adj.* kurz [und dick]; gedrungen, untersetzt ‹Person›; **~ tail** Stummelschwanz, *der*

**stucco** /'stʌkəʊ/ **1** *n., pl.* **~es** (*fine plaster*) Stuck, *der*; (*coarse plaster*) Putz, *der*; (*work*) Stuckarbeit, *die*; Stuckatur, *die*; *attrib.* Stuck-. **2** *v.t.* (*coat with coarse plaster*) verputzen; (*decorate with fine plaster*) stuckieren

**stuck** ⇒ **stick** 1, 2

**'stuck up** ⇒ **stick up** 1 E

**stud[1]** /stʌd/ **1** *n.* A (*boss*) Beschlagnagel, *der*; (*on clothes*) Niete, *die*; (*on boot*) Stollen, *der*; (*marker in road*) Nagel, *der* (*Verkehrsw.*); B (*for shirt*) Knebel, *der*; (*cuff link*) Manschettenknopf, *der*; (*for ear*) Ohrstecker, *der*. **2** *v.t.*, **-dd-** (*set with ~s*) beschlagen; (*be scattered over*) verstreut sein über (+ *Akk.*); **~ded** mit Nägeln beschlagen ‹Tür, Möbel›; mit Nieten verziert ‹Jacke, Gürtel›; **~ded with flowers/stars** *etc.* mit Blumen/Sternen *usw.* übersät; **a jewel-~ded crown** eine juwelenbesetzte Krone

**stud[2]** *n.* A (*Breeding*) Gestüt, *das*; **put a horse out to ~:** ein Pferd nur noch zur Zucht verwenden; B (*stallion*) Deckhengst, *der*; Zuchthengst, *der*; Beschäler, *der* (*fachspr.*); C (*sl.: man*) Zuchthengst, *der* (*derb*)

**'stud book** *n.* (*Breeding*) Stutbuch, *das*; Gestütbuch, *das*

**student** /'stju:dənt/ *n.* Student, *der*/Studentin, *die*; (*in school or training establishment*) Schüler, *der*/Schülerin, *die*; **a good ~:** ein eifriger Student/Schüler/eine eifrige Studentin/Schülerin; **be a ~ of sth.** etw. studieren; **~ of medicine** Student/Studentin der Medizin; Medizinstudent, *der*/-studentin, *die*; **eternal ~:** ewiger Student (*ugs.*); *attrib.* **~ days** Studenten-/Schulzeit, *die*; **~ demonstration** Studenten-/Schülerdemonstration, *die*; **~ driver** (*Amer.*) Fahrschüler, *der*/-schülerin, *die*; **~ nurse** Lernschwester, *die*/Pflegeschüler, *der*; **be a ~ doctor/teacher** ein medizinisches Praktikum/Schulpraktikum machen

**studentship** /'stju:dəntʃɪp/ *n.* Stipendium, *das*

**stud: ~ farm** *n.* (*Breeding*) Gestüt, *das*; **~ horse** ⇒ **stud[2]** B

**studied** /'stʌdɪd/ *adj.* A (*thoughtful*) [wohl]überlegt; B (*intentional*) gewollt; gesucht ‹Stil, Ausdrucksweise›; gezielt ‹Beleidigung›; C (*well-read*) belesen

**studiedly** /'stʌdɪdlɪ/ *adv.* A (*thoughtfully*) überlegt; B (*intentionally*) **be ~ casual** sich gewollt lässig geben

**studio** /'stju:dɪəʊ/ *n., pl.* **~s** A (*photographer's or painter's workroom*) Atelier, *das*; (*workshop for the performing arts*) Studio, *das*; B (*Cinemat.*) (*room*) Studio, *das*; (*organization*) Filmgesellschaft, *die*; **~s** (*premises*) Studios; C (*Radio, Telev.*) Studio, *das*

**studio: ~ apartment** (*Amer.*) ⇒ **~ flat**; **~ 'audience** *n.* (*Radio, Telev.*) Publikum im Studio; **~ couch** *n.* Schlafcouch, *die*; Bettcouch, *die*; **~ flat** *n.* (*Brit.*) A Atelier, *das*; B (*one-room flat*) Einzimmerwohnung, *die*

**studious** /'stju:dɪəs/ *adj.* A (*assiduous in study*) lerneifrig; gelehrt ‹Beschäftigung, Buch, Aussehen, Atmosphäre›; **~ life** Gelehrtendasein, *das*; B (*earnest*) ernsthaft ‹Anstrengung›; (*intentional*) bewusst; **~ to do** *or* **in doing sth.** bemüht, etw. zu tun

**studiously** /'stju:dɪəslɪ/ *adv.* A (*with attention to learning*) **be ~ inclined** gern studieren; lernbegierig sein; B (*diligently*) eifrig; (*intentionally*) bewusst ‹rücksichtsvoll, kühl›; geflissentlich ‹aus dem Weg gehen›

**studiousness** /'stju:dɪəsnɪs/ *n., no pl.* A (*application to study*) Lerneifer, *der*; B (*careful attention*) Beflissenheit, *die*

**study** /'stʌdɪ/ **1** *n.* A Studium, *das*; Lernen, *das*; **I enjoy my studies** das Studium macht mir Spaß; **~ does not come naturally to him** das Lernen fällt ihm nicht leicht; **what branch of ~ is he engaged in?** welche Studienrichtung hat er eingeschlagen?; **the ~ of mathematics/law** das Studium der Mathematik/der Rechtswissenschaft; **be still under ~:** noch untersucht *od.* geprüft werden; **[books on] African/Social Studies** (*Educ./Univ.*) [Bücher zur] Afrikanistik/Sozialwissenschaft; **graduate studies** (*Educ./Univ.*) Graduiertenstudium, *das*; B (*piece of work*) **a ~ of** *or* **on sth.** eine Studie über etw. (*Akk.*); **studies are being carried out** zurzeit werden Untersuchungen durchgeführt; **make a ~ of sth.** über etw. (*Akk.*) [wissenschaftliche] Untersuchungen anstellen; C (*object of examination*) Studienobjekt, *das*; **make sth. one's ~:** sich (*Dat.*) etw. zur Aufgabe machen; **a ~ in sth.** ein Musterbeispiel (*fig.*) für etw.; **his face was a ~!** sein Gesicht war sehenswert!; D (*Art*) Studie, *die*; (*Mus.*) Etüde, *die*; Übung, *die*; (*Lit., Theatre*) Studie, *die* (**in, of** über + *Akk.*); **as a ~ in perspective/composition** als perspektivische Studie/Kompositionsstudie; E (*contemplation*) Kontemplation, *die*; ⇒ *also* **brown study**; F (*room*) Arbeitszimmer, *das*.
**2** *v.t.* A (*seek knowledge of*) studieren; (*at school*) lernen; **~ politics all one's life/~ Goethe** sich sein Leben lang mit Politik/sich mit Goethe beschäftigen; B (*scrutinize*) studieren; C (*read attentively*) studieren ‹Fahrplan›; sich (*Dat.*) [sorgfältig] durchlesen ‹Prüfungsfragen, Bericht›; D (*learn by heart*) studieren.
**3** *v.i.* lernen; (*at university*) studieren; **~ under sb.** bei jmdm. studieren; **~ to be a doctor/teach French** Medizin studieren/Französisch für das Lehramt studieren; **~ for the medical profession** Medizin studieren

**'study group** *n.* Arbeitsgruppe, *die*; Arbeitskreis, *der*

**stuff** /stʌf/ **1** *n.* A *no pl., no indef. art.* (*material[s]*) Zeug, *das* (*ugs.*); (*artistic productions*) Sachen *Pl.* (*ugs.*); (*coll.: drugs*) Stoff, *der* (*salopp*); (*coll.: money*) Kohle, *die* (*salopp*); **garden ~:** Grünzeug, *das* (*ugs.*); **have the ~ of a champion** das Zeug zum Champion haben (*ugs.*); **be made of sterner ~:** aus härterem Stoff gemacht sein (*fig.*); **the ~ of fairy stories** der Stoff für Märchen; **the ~ that dreams/heroes are made of** der Stoff, aus dem die Träume sind/Helden gemacht sind (*fig.*); **plastic is useful ~:** Plastik ist eine nützliche Sache; **push [the] ~** (*coll.: deal in drugs*) mit Stoff handeln (*salopp*); **there has been some interesting ~ in the papers/on the radio** es gab ein paar interessante Sachen in den Zeitungen/im Radio (*ugs.*); **that actor has been in some good ~ lately** dieser Schauspieler hat zuletzt ein paar gute Sachen gemacht (*ugs.*); B *no pl., no indef. art.* (*activity, knowledge*) **do painting or drawing, ~ like that** malen oder zeichnen oder so was (*ugs.*); **do one's ~** (*coll.*) seine Sache machen; **get on and do your ~!** (*coll.*) na los, mach schon! (*ugs.*); **know one's ~** (*coll.: be knowledgeable*) sich auskennen; (*know one's job*) seine Sache verstehen; **that's the ~!** (*coll.*) so ists richtig!; **that's the ~ to give the troops** (*fig. coll.*) das ist jetzt genau das richtige; C *no pl.* (*valueless matter*) Zeug, *das* (*ugs. abwertend*); **~ [and nonsense]!** (*coll.*) dummes Zeug! (*ugs. abwertend*); D (*Textiles*) Wolle, *die*; Wollzeug, *das* (*veralt.*); *attrib.* wollen ‹Hemd›. ⇒ *also* **bit[2]** A; **hot stuff**; **kid** 1 C; **rough stuff**.
**2** *v.t.* A stopfen; zustopfen ‹Loch, Ohren›; (*in taxidermy*) ausstopfen; (*Cookery*) füllen; (*make eat to repletion*) stopfen, nudeln ‹Gans›; (*coarse: copulate with*) stoßen (*vulg.*); **~ envelopes [with letters]** Briefe in Umschläge stecken; **~ sth. with** *or* **full of sth.** etw. mit etw. voll stopfen (*ugs.*); **[go and] get ~ed!** (*sl.*) hau ab! (*ugs.*); **~ oneself** (*sl.*) sich voll stopfen (*ugs.*); **~ one's face** (*sl.*) sich (*Dat.*) den Bauch voll stopfen (*ugs.*); **~ ballot boxes** (*Amer.: insert bogus votes*) Stimmen fälschen; **he ~ed a banknote into my hand** er drückte mir einen Geldschein in die Hand; B (*sl.*) **~ him/the family reputation!** zum Teufel mit ihm/der Familienehre!; **~ it!** Scheiß drauf! (*derb*); **he can ~ it!** er kann mich mal! (*derb*).
**3** *v.i.* sich voll stopfen (*ugs.*)
**~ 'up** *v.t.* verstopfen

**stuffed 'shirt** *n.* (*coll. derog.*) Spießer, *der* (*ugs. abwertend*)

**stuffiness** /'stʌfɪnɪs/ *n., no pl.* A (*airlessness*) Stickigkeit, *die*; **the ~ of the room** die stickige Luft im Zimmer; B (*congestion*) **the ~ in his nose/head** seine verstopfte Nase/entzündete Stirnhöhle; C (*coll.: ill humour*) Übellaunigkeit, *die*; D (*coll.: primness*) Spießigkeit, *die* (*abwertend*)

**stuffing** /'stʌfɪŋ/ *n.* A (*material*) Füllmaterial, *das*; **a ~ of horsehair** eine Füllung aus Rosshaar; **knock** *or* **take the ~ out of sb./a theory** (*coll. fig.*) jmdn. umhauen (*ugs.*)/eine Theorie wie ein Kartenhaus in sich zusammenfallen lassen; B (*Cookery*) Füllung, *die*

**stuffy** /'stʌfɪ/ *adj.* A (*stifling*) stickig ‹Zimmer, Atmosphäre›; B (*congested*) verstopft; **my head feels very ~:** meine Stirnhöhle ist ganz zu (*ugs.*); C (*coll.: ill-humoured*) sauertöpfisch (*ugs. abwertend*); **he got very ~ about it** er reagierte sehr sauer (*salopp*) [darauf]; D (*coll.: prim*) spießig (*abwertend*) (**about** gegenüber)

**stultify** /'stʌltɪfaɪ/ *v.t.* A (*reduce to absurdity*) der Lächerlichkeit preisgeben; ins Lächerliche ziehen ‹Entscheidung, Anstrengungen›; B (*neutralize*) zunichte machen; C (*impair*) lähmen; **have a ~ing effect on sth.** sich lähmend auf etw. (*Akk.*) auswirken; **~ing boredom/monotony** lähmende Langeweile/Monotonie

**stumble** /'stʌmbl/ **1** *v.i.* A stolpern (**over** über + *Akk.*); B (*falter*) stocken; **~ over sth./through life** über etw. (*Akk.*)/durchs Leben stolpern; C **~ across** *or* **[up]on sb./sth.** (*find by chance*) über jmdn. stolpern (*fig. ugs.*)/auf etw. (*Akk.*) stoßen. **2** *n.* A (*trip*) Stolpern, *das*; B (*error*) Stocken, *das*

**stumbling block** /'stʌmblɪŋblɒk/ *n.* Stolperstein, *der*

**stump** /stʌmp/ **1** *n.* A (*of tree, branch, tooth*) Stumpf, *der*; (*of cigar, pencil*) Stummel, *der*; **up a ~** (*Amer. coll.*) aufgeschmissen (*salopp*); B (*of limb, tail, etc.*) Stummel, *der*; (*artificial leg*) Stelze, *die*; **~s** (*joc.: legs*) Stelzen (*salopp*); ⇒ *also* **stir[1]** 1 B; C (*Cricket*) Stab, *der*; **draw ~s** das Ende des Spieltages ansagen; D (*improvised platform*) Rednertribüne, *die*; **on the ~** (*coll.*) im Wahlkampf; **go on** *or* **take the ~** (*lit. or fig.*) sich auf die Bühne begeben.
**2** *v.t.* A (*confound*) verwirren; durcheinander bringen; **be ~ed** ratlos sein; **be ~ed for an answer** um eine Antwort verlegen sein; **this problem has got me ~ed** bei diesem Problem weiß ich nicht mehr weiter; B (*Cricket*) ausschalten ‹Schlagmann› (*der außerhalb einer bestimmten Zone steht, durch Umwerfen der Stäbchen*); C (*Amer. Polit.*) als Wahlkämpfer bereisen.
**3** *v.i.* A (*walk stiffly*) stapfen; (*walk noisily*) trampeln; B (*Amer. Polit.: make speeches*)

sich aufs Podium stellen; **~ing tour** Wahlkampfreise, *die*

**~ 'out** ⇒ ~ 2 B

**~ 'up** (*Brit. coll.*) *v.t. & i.* blechen (*ugs.*)

**stumpy** /'stʌmpɪ/ *adj.* gedrungen; **~ tail** Stummelschwanz, *der;* **~ pencil** Bleistiftstummel, *der*

**stun** /stʌn/ *v.t.*, **-nn-** Ⓐ (*knock senseless*) betäuben; **be ~ned** (*unconscious*) bewusstlos sein; (*dazed*) benommen sein; Ⓑ (*fig.*) **be ~ned at** *or* **by sth.** von etw. wie betäubt sein; **a ~ned silence** ein fassungsloses Schweigen; **a superb performance which ~ned the critics and audience alike** eine herausragende Darbietung, die Kritiker und Publikum gleichermaßen in ihren Bann schlug; Ⓒ (*deafen temporarily*) betäuben; **be ~ned by sth.** von etw. wie betäubt sein

**stung** ⇒ **sting** 2, 3

**stunk** ⇒ **stink** 1

**stunner** /'stʌnə(r)/ *n.* (*coll.*) **be a ~:** Spitze sein (*ugs.*)

**stunning** /'stʌnɪŋ/ *adj.* (*coll.*) Ⓐ (*splendid*) hinreißend; umwerfend (*ugs.*); Ⓑ (*causing insensibility*) wuchtig ‹Schlag›; Ⓒ (*shocking*) bestürzend ‹Nachricht›; horrend ‹Preis›; (*amazing*) sensationell; Ⓓ (*deafening*) ohrenbetäubend (*ugs.*)

**stunningly** /'stʌnɪŋlɪ/ *adv.* (*coll.*) umwerfend (*ugs.*); unfassbar ‹langweilig, schrecklich, hässlich›

**stunt¹** /stʌnt/ *v.t.* hemmen, beeinträchtigen ‹Wachstum, Entwicklung›; **~ed trees** verkümmerte Bäume; **emotionally ~ed** seelisch verkümmert

**stunt²** ❶ *n.* halsbrecherisches Kunststück; (*Cinemat.*) Stunt, *der;* (*Advertising*) [Werbe]gag, *der.* ❷ *v.i.* Stunts vollführen

**'stunt man** *n.* Stuntman, *der*

**stupefaction** /stju:pɪ'fækʃn/ *n., no pl.* Ⓐ Benommenheit, *die;* Ⓑ (*astonishment*) Verblüffung, *die*

**stupefy** /'stju:pɪfaɪ/ *v.t.* Ⓐ (*benumb*) ‹Hitze:› benommen machen; ‹Mühsal:› abstumpfen; **be stupefied with** *or* **by** benommen sein von ‹Schlag, Alkohol, Droge›; abgestumpft sein von ‹Armut, Kummer›; Ⓑ (*astound*) die Sprache verschlagen (+ *Dat.*); **be stupefied** wie vor den Kopf geschlagen sein

**stupefying** /'stju:pɪfaɪɪŋ/ *adj.* die Sinne betäubend ‹Hitze›; stumpfsinnig ‹Arbeit›; (*fig.: astonishing*) unfassbar

**stupendous** /stju:'pendəs/ *adj.* gewaltig; außergewöhnlich ‹Schönheit, Intelligenz, Talent›; großartig ‹Urlaub, Schauspieler›

**stupendously** /stju:'pendəslɪ/ *adv.* außergewöhnlich; gewaltig ‹groß›; großartig ‹sich verhalten›

**stupid** /'stju:pɪd/ ❶ *adj.*, **~er** /'stju:pɪdə(r)/, **~est** /'stju:pɪdɪst/ Ⓐ (*slow-witted, unintelligent*) dumm; einfältig ‹Person, Aussehen›; (*ridiculous*) lächerlich; (*pointless*) dumm (*ugs.*) ‹Witz, Geschichte, Gedanke›; *expr. rejection or irritation* blöd (*ugs.*); **where is that ~ key?** wo ist jetzt der blöde (*ugs.*) Schlüssel?; **it would be ~ to do sth.** es wäre töricht, etw. zu tun; **that was a ~ place to leave the car** es war töricht, das Auto dort abzustellen; Ⓑ (*in state of stupor*) benommen (**with** von); teilnahmslos, apathisch ‹Blick›; **be bored ~:** zu Tode gelangweilt sein. ❷ *n.* (*coll.*) Dummkopf, *der* (*ugs.*)

**stupidity** /stju:'pɪdɪtɪ/ *n.* Dummheit, *die;* (*of action also*) Torheit, *die;* (*of facial expression*) Einfältigkeit, *die*

**stupidly** /'stju:pɪdlɪ/ *adv.* dumm; **~ [enough], I have ...:** dummerweise habe ich ...; **he ~ admitted that ...:** törichterweise hat er zugegeben, dass ...

**stupor** /'stju:pə(r)/ *n.* Ⓐ (*torpidity*) Benommenheit, *die;* (*Med.*) Stupor, *der;* **drink oneself into a ~:** sich bis zur Bewusstlosigkeit betrinken; **in a drunken ~:** sinnlos betrunken; Ⓑ (*apathy*) Erstarrung, *die;* Ⓒ (*amazement*) **stand in a ~:** starr vor Staunen stehen

**sturdily** /'stɜ:dɪlɪ/ *adv.* (*robustly*) fest ‹angegeln›; mit festem Schritt ‹gehen›; (*resolutely*) fest ‹überzeugt›; entschlossen ‹sich entgegenstellen›; **~ built** kräftig [gebaut] ‹Person, Pferd›; stabil [gebaut] ‹Stuhl, Fahrrad›

**sturdiness** /'stɜ:dɪnɪs/ *n., no pl.* (*robustness*) Stabilität, *die;* (*of person*) Stämmigkeit, *die;* (*resoluteness*) Stärke, *die;* Festigkeit, *die*

**sturdy** /'stɜ:dɪ/ *adj.* (*robust*) stabil ‹Haus, Stuhl, Schiff›; kräftig ‹Rasse, Pflanze, Pferd, Kind›; kräftig [gebaut] ‹Person›; (*resistant to disease or rough weather*) robust; (*thickset*) stämmig ‹Person›; (*strong*) stämmig ‹Beine, Arme›; (*sound*) solide; (*resolute*) fest ‹Glaube, Grundsätze›; stark ‹Gegner, Verfechter, Widerstand›

**sturgeon** /'stɜ:dʒən/ *n.* (*Zool.*) Stör, *der*

**stutter** /'stʌtə(r)/ ❶ *v.i.* stottern; ‹Gewehr:› tacken. ❷ *v.t.* stottern. ❸ *n.* Stottern, *das;* (*of gun*) Tacken, *das;* (*of flame*) Flackern, *das;* **speak with a ~:** stottern; **have a bad ~:** stark stottern

**~ 'out** *v.t.* stotternd hervorbringen

**stutterer** /'stʌtərə(r)/ *n.* Stotterer, *der*/Stotterin, *die*

**sty¹** /staɪ/ ⇒ **pigsty**

**sty², stye** /staɪ/ *n.* ▶ **1232** (*Med.*) Gerstenkorn, *das*

**Stygian** /'stɪdʒɪən/ *adj.* (*Mythol.; also fig.*) stygisch

**style** /staɪl/ ❶ *n.* Ⓐ (*manner*) Stil, *der;* (*in conversation*) Ton, *der;* (*in performance*) Art, *die;* **~ of swimming/running** Schwimm-/Laufstil, *der;* **that's the ~!** so ist es richtig!; **be bad** *or* **not good ~:** schlechter *od.* kein guter Stil sein; Ⓑ (*collective features*) (*in artistic presentation; also Printing, Publishing*) Stil, *der;* (*of habitual behaviour*) Art, *die;* **it's not my ~ [to do that]** das ist nicht mein Stil; **dress in the latest/modern ~:** sich nach der neuesten/neuen Mode kleiden; **the costumes were in** *or* **of the ~ of the 1940s** es waren Kostüme im Stil der 40er-Jahre; **cook in the French ~:** französisch kochen; ⇒ *also* **cramp** 2 A; **house style**; Ⓒ (*superior way of living, behaving, etc.*) Stil, *der;* **in ~:** stilvoll; (*on a grand scale*) im großen Stil; **in the grand ~:** im großen Stil; **she is a woman of ~:** sie hat Stil; **live a life of ~:** ein luxuriöses Leben führen; **have no ~:** keinen Stil haben; Ⓓ (*sort*) Art, *die;* **~ of music** Musikrichtung, *die;* **she is not his ~:** sie passt nicht zu ihm; **this house is not my ~:** das Haus ist nichts für mich; Ⓔ (*pattern*) Art, *die;* (*of clothes*) Machart, *die;* (*hair~*) Frisur, *die;* **she has had her hair cut in a pageboy ~:** sie hat sich (*Dat.*) einen Pagenkopf schneiden lassen; **have one's hair done in a different ~:** sich (*Dat.*) eine andere Frisur machen lassen; Ⓕ (*descriptive formula*) Titel, *der;* (*of firm*) Firmenbezeichnung, *die;* **~ [of address]** Anrede, *die;* Ⓖ (*Bot.*) Griffel, *der.*
❷ *v.t.* Ⓐ (*design*) entwerfen; stilisieren (*veralt.*); **~ one's own hair** sich (*Dat.*) seine Frisuren selbst machen; **elegantly ~d clothes** elegant geschnittene Kleidung; **clothes ~d for comfort** bequem geschnittene Kleidung; Ⓑ (*designate*) nennen; (*address*) anreden; **~ oneself sth.** sich bezeichnen als etw.

**-style** *in comb.* **a Tudor-~ house** ein Haus im Tudorstil; **a Queen-Anne-~ chair** ein Queen-Anne-Stuhl; **Indian-~ curry** indischer Curry; **French-~ cooking** französische Küche; **peasant-~ skirt** Bauernrock, *der;* **dressed cowboy-~:** wie ein Cowboy gekleidet

**'style book** *n.* Buch mit Modellen; (*of hairdresser*) Frisurenheft, *das;* (*Printing, Publishing*) Buch mit Satzanweisungen

**styling** /'staɪlɪŋ/ *n.* Ⓐ (*imparting of style*) Styling, *das;* **that hairdresser is good at ~:** dieser Friseur kann gut [neue] Frisuren entwerfen; Ⓑ (*Lit., Publishing*) stilistische Überarbeitung; Ⓒ (*ornamentation*) **intricate ~:** komplizierte Verzierungen

**stylise** ⇒ **stylize**

**stylish** /'staɪlɪʃ/ *adj.* stilvoll; elegant ‹Kleidung, Auto, Hotel, Person›

**stylishly** /'staɪlɪʃlɪ/ *adv.* stilvoll; elegant ‹geschnitten, angezogen›; **~ elegant** vornehm und elegant

**stylishness** /'staɪlɪʃnɪs/ *n., no pl.* Stil, *der;* (*of clothes*) Eleganz, *die*

**stylist** /'staɪlɪst/ *n.* ▶ **1261** Ⓐ (*Lit., Sport*) Stilist, *der*/Stilistin, *die;* Ⓑ (*designer*) Designer, *der*/Designerin, *die;* (*hair~*) Haarstilist, *der*/-stilistin, *die*

**stylistic** /staɪ'lɪstɪk/ *adj.* stilistisch; Stil‹mittel, -merkmale›

**stylistically** /staɪ'lɪstɪkəlɪ/ *adv.* stilistisch

**stylistics** /staɪ'lɪstɪks/ *n., no pl.* Stilistik, *die*

**stylize** /'staɪlaɪz/ *v.t.* stilisieren

**stylus** /'staɪləs/ *n., pl.* **styli** /'staɪlaɪ/ *or* **~es** Ⓐ (*gramophone needle*) [Abtast]nadel, *die;* **sapphire/diamond ~:** Saphir, *der*/Diamant, *der;* Ⓑ (*writing tool*) Griffel, *der;* (*engraving-tool*) Grabstichel, *der*

**stymie** /'staɪmɪ/ ❶ *n.* (*difficult situation*) Sackgasse, *die* (*fig.*). ❷ *v.t.* (*thwart*) in die Klemme (*ugs.*) geraten lassen; **be ~d** aufgeschmissen sein (*salopp*); **~ oneself** sich (*Dat.*) selber ein Bein stellen

**styptic** /'stɪptɪk/ ❶ *adj.* blutstillend. ❷ *n.* blutstillendes Mittel; Hämostyptikum, *das* (*Med.*)

**Styria** /'stɪrɪə/ *pr. n.* Steiermark, *die*

**Styx** /stɪks/ *pr. n.* (*Greek Mythol.*) Styx, *der;* **cross the ~** (*fig.*) den Styx überqueren (*geh.*)

**suave** /swɑ:v/ *adj.* Ⓐ (*affable*) verbindlich; Ⓑ (*agreeable*) sanft ‹Farbe, Licht, Musik›; lieblich ‹Wein, Geschmack›

**suavely** /'swɑ:vlɪ/ *adv.* Ⓐ (*affably*) verbindlich; **he was always ~ polite** er war stets verbindlich und höflich; Ⓑ (*agreeably*) sanft

**suavity** /'swɑ:vɪtɪ/ *n.* Ⓐ (*affability*) Verbindlichkeit, *die;* Ⓑ (*agreeableness*) [angenehme] Milde; **suavities** Annehmlichkeiten

**sub** /sʌb/ (*coll.*) ❶ *n.* Ⓐ (*subscription*) Abo, *das* (*ugs.*); Ⓑ (*esp. Sport: substitute*) Ersatz, *der;* Ⓒ (*submarine*) U-Boot, *das;* Ⓓ ⇒ **sub-editor**. ❷ *v.i.*, **-bb-** ⇒ **sub-edit**

**sub-** *pref.* unter-; (*mit Fremdwörtern meist*) sub-

**sub'alpine** *adj.* (*Geog.*) (*of higher mountain slopes*) subalpin (*fachspr.*); (*of lower Alpine slopes*) Voralpen-

**subaltern** /'sʌbltən/ *n.* (*Brit. Mil.*) Subalternoffizier, *der*

**subaqua** /sʌb'ækwə/ *adj.* Tauch‹sport, -klub›

**suba'tomic** *adj.* (*Phys.*) subatomar

**'subcategory** *n.* Subkategorie, *die*

**'subclass** *n.* (*esp. Biol.*) Unterklasse, *die*

**'subcommittee** *n.* Unterausschuss, *der*

**sub'conscious** (*Psych.*) ❶ *adj.* unterbewusst; **~ mind** Unterbewusstsein, *das.* ❷ *n.* Unterbewusstsein, *das*

**sub'consciously** *adv.* (*Psych.*) unterbewusst

**sub'continent** *n.* (*Geog.*) Subkontinent, *der*

**subcontract** ❶ /sʌbkən'trækt/ *v.t.* (*accept under secondary contract*) als Subunternehmer übernehmen; (*offer under secondary contract*) an Subunternehmer/an einen Subunternehmer vergeben; **~ a job to sb.** eine Arbeit an jmdn. [in einem Untervertrag] vergeben. ❷ *v.i.* (*accept secondary contract*) als Subunternehmer arbeiten; (*offer secondary contract*) Aufträge an Subunternehmer/an einen Subunternehmer vergeben. ❸ /sʌb 'kɒntrækt/ *n.* Untervertrag, *der*

**subcon'tractor** *n.* ▶ **1261** Subunternehmer, *der*/-unternehmerin, *die*

**'subculture** *n.* (*Sociol.*) Subkultur, *die*

**subcu'taneous** *adj.* (*Anat.*) subkutan

**'subdirectory** *n.* (*Computing*) Unterverzeichnis, *das*

**subdivide** /'sʌbdɪvaɪd, sʌbdɪ'vaɪd/ ❶ *v.t.* (*further divide*) erneut teilen; (*divide into parts*) unterteilen. ❷ *v.i.* **~ into sth.** sich in etw. (*Akk.*) teilen

**subdivision** /'sʌbdɪvɪʒn, sʌbdɪ'vɪʒn/ *n.* (*subdividing*) erneute Teilung; (*subordinate division*) Unterabteilung, *die;* **~ [of sth.] into sth.** Unterteilung [einer Sache (*Gen.*)] in etw. (*Akk.*)

**sub'dominant** *n.* (*Mus.*) Subdominante, *die*

**subdue** /səb'dju:/ *v.t.* (*conquer*) besiegen; unterwerfen; (*bring under control*) bändigen ‹Kind, Tier›; ruhig stellen ‹Patienten›; unter Kontrolle bringen ‹Demonstranten usw.›; bezähmen

‹Gefühle, zornige Person›; urbar machen ‹Land›; (*reduce in intensity*) dämpfen ‹Zorn, Heftigkeit, gute Laune, Lärm, Licht›; abkühlen (*fig.*) ‹Leidenschaft›; verblassen lassen ‹Farben›

**subdued** /səbˈdjuːd/ *adj.* gedämpft; **he seemed rather ~:** er schien ziemlich gedämpfter Stimmung zu sein

**sub-ˈedit** *v.t.* (*Journ., Publishing*) [A] (*be assistant editor of*) mit herausgeben; [B] (*Brit.: prepare copy for*) redigieren

**subˈeditor** *n.* ▶ **1261** (*Journ., Publishing*) [A] (*assistant editor*) Mitherausgeber, *der*/Mitherausgeberin, *die;* [B] (*Brit.: one who prepares material*) Redaktionsassistent, *der*/-assistentin, *die*

**ˈsubgroup** *n.* Untergruppe, *die*

**ˈsubhead, ˈsubheading** *ns.* [A] (*subordinate division*) Unterabschnitt, *der;* [B] (*subordinate title*) Untertitel, *der*

**subˈhuman** *adj.* unmenschlich; (*Zool.*) menschenähnlich; **treat sb. as ~:** jmdn. wie einen Untermenschen behandeln

**subject** ❶ /ˈsʌbdʒɪkt/ *n.* [A] (*citizen*) Staatsbürger, *der*/-bürgerin, *die;* (*in relation to monarch*) Untertan, *der*/Untertanin, *die;* (*under domination*) Sklave, *der*/Sklavin, *die* (*fig.*); [B] (*topic*) Thema, *das;* (*department of study*) Fach, *das;* (*area of knowledge*) Fach[gebiet], *das;* (*Art*) Motiv, *das;* Sujet, *das* (*geh.*); (*Mus.*) Thema, *das;* **sb. is the ~ of a book** über jmdn. ist ein Buch geschrieben worden; **be the ~ of an investigation** Gegenstand einer Untersuchung sein; **on the ~ of money** über das Thema Geld ‹reden usw.›; beim Thema Geld ‹sein, bleiben›; **change the ~:** das Thema wechseln; [C] **be a ~ for sth.** (*cause sth.*) zu etw. Anlass geben; **she was a ~ for ridicule** man machte sich über sie lustig; [D] (*Ling., Logic, Philos.*) Subjekt, *das;* [E] (*Med.*) Patient, *der;* (*of scientific research*) Versuchsperson, *die*/-tier, *das*/-objekt, *das.* ⇒ *also* **liberty**.
❷ *adj.* [A] (*conditional*) **be ~ to sth.** von etw. abhängig sein *od.* abhängen; **sth. is ~ to alteration** etw. kann geändert werden; **prices/dates/programme details [are] ~ to alteration without further notice** Preis-/Termin-/Programmänderungen [sind] vorbehalten; [B] (*prone*) **be ~ to** anfällig sein für ‹Krankheit›; neigen zu ‹Melancholie›; ausgesetzt sein (+ *Dat.*) ‹Missdeutung, Feuchtigkeit›; [C] (*dependent*) abhängig; **~ to** (*dependent on*) untertan (+ *Dat.*) ‹König usw.›; unterworfen (+ *Dat.*) ‹Verfassung, Gesetz, Krone›; untergeben (+ *Dat.*) ‹Dienstherrn›.
❸ *adv.* **~ to sth.** vorbehaltlich einer Sache (*Gen.*); **~ to the weather['s] being fine** vorausgesetzt, das Wetter ist gut.
❹ /səbˈdʒekt/ *v.t.* [A] (*subjugate, make submissive*) unterwerfen; **~ sb./sth. to sb./sth.** jmdn./etw. jmdm./einer Sache unterwerfen; [B] (*expose*) **~ sb./sth. to sth.** jmdn./etw. einer Sache (*Dat.*) aussetzen; **~ sb. to torture** jmdn. der Folter unterwerfen; **~ sth. to chemical analysis** etw. einer chemischen Analyse unterziehen

**ˈsubject: ~ catalogue** *n.* Schlagwortkatalog, *der;* **~ heading** *n.* Stichwort, *das;* **~ index** *n.* Sachregister, *das*

**subjection** /səbˈdʒekʃn/ *n.* (*subjugation*) Unterwerfung, *die* (**to** unter + *Akk.*); (*condition of being subject*) Abhängigkeit, *die* (**to** von)

**subjective** /səbˈdʒektɪv/ *adj.* [A] subjektiv; [B] (*Ling.*) Subjekt-; **be ~:** Subjekt sein

**subjectively** /səbˈdʒektɪvlɪ/ *adv.* [A] subjektiv; **~ speaking, I like him** ich persönlich mag ihn; [B] (*Ling.*) als Subjekt ‹gebrauchen›

**subjectiveness** /səbˈdʒektɪvnɪs/, **subjectivity** /sʌbdʒɪkˈtɪvɪtɪ/ *ns., no pl.* Subjektivität, *die*

**ˈsubject matter** *n., no pl., no indef. art.* Gegenstand, *der;* **make good ~ for sth.** ein gutes Thema für etw. abgeben

**sub judice** /sʌb ˈdʒuːdɪsɪ, sʊb ˈjuːdɪkeɪ/ *adj.* (*Law*) anhängig; (*not decided*) [noch] nicht entschieden

**subjugate** /ˈsʌbdʒʊgeɪt/ *v.t.* [A] (*conquer*) unterjochen (**to** unter + *Akk.*); [B] (*subdue*) bezwingen; bändigen ‹Kind, Pferd›

**subjugation** /sʌbdʒʊˈgeɪʃn/ *n.* [A] (*conquest*) Unterjochung, *die* (**to** unter + *Akk.*); [B] (*moral subjection*) (*action*) Knechtung, *die* (*geh. abwertend*); (*result*) Knechtschaft, *die;* (*of passions etc.*) Bezwingung, *die;* Unterwerfung, *die* (**to** unter + *Akk.*); (*condition*) sklavische Abhängigkeit (**to** von)

**subjunctive** /səbˈdʒʌŋktɪv/ (*Ling.*) ❶ *adj.* konjunktivisch; Konjunktiv-. ❷ *n.* Konjunktiv, *der;* **past/present ~:** Konjunktiv II *od.* Präteritum/Konjunktiv I *od.* Präsens

**subjunctive ˈmood** *n.* (*Ling.*) Konjunktiv, *der*

**subˈlease** ⇒ **sublet**

**subˈlet** *v.t.*, **-tt-, subˈlet** untervermieten

**sub lieuˈtenant** *n.* (*Brit. Navy*) Oberleutnant zur See

**sublimate** ❶ /ˈsʌblɪmeɪt/ *v.t.* (*Chem., Psych.; also fig.*) sublimieren. ❷ /ˈsʌblɪmət/ *n.* (*sublimated substance*) Sublimat, *das* (*Chemie*)

**sublimation** /sʌblɪˈmeɪʃn/ *n.* [A] (*Chem.*) (*act*) Sublimierung, *die;* (*process*) Sublimation, *die;* (*substance*) Sublimat, *das;* [B] (*elevation; Psych.: diversion*) Sublimierung, *die* (**to** zu, **into** in + *Akk.*); Sublimation, *die*

**sublime** /səˈblaɪm/ ❶ *adj.*, **~r** /səˈblaɪmə(r)/, **~st** /səˈblaɪmɪst/ (*exalted*) erhaben; (*iron.*) vollendet (*fig. iron.*) ‹Chaos›; unglaublich ‹Frechheit›; **sth. goes from the ~ to the ridiculous** (*iron.*) etw. ist ein echter Abstieg [ins Profane]. ❷ *v.t.* (*Chem.*) [A] (*convert*) sublimieren; [B] (*release*) freisetzen. ❸ *v.i.* (*Chem.*) sublimieren

**sublimely** /səˈblaɪmlɪ/ *adv.* schlechthin vollkommen ‹tanzen›; erhaben ‹handeln, edel›; (*iron.*) vollkommen ‹töricht, betrunken›; völlig ‹ohne Ahnung›; **~ beautiful** von erhabener Schönheit *nachgestellt*

**subliminal** /sʌbˈlɪmɪnl/ *adj.* (*Physiol., Psych.*) unterschwellig; subliminal (*fachspr.*); **~ advertising** unterschwellige Werbung

**sublimity** /səˈblɪmɪtɪ/ *n.* (*literary*) Erhabenheit, *die;* (*high degree*) hoher Grad (**of** an + *Dat.*)

**Sub-Lt.** *abbr.* (*Brit. Navy*) **Sub Lieutenant** Olt. zur See

**sub-maˈchinegun** *n.* Maschinenpistole, *die*

**submarine** /sʌbməˈriːn, ˈsʌbməriːn/ ❶ *n.* Unterseeboot, *das;* U-Boot, *das.* ❷ *adj.* Unterwasser-; unterseeisch (*Geol.*); submarin (*fachspr.*); **~ warfare** U-Boot-Krieg, *der*

**submerge** /səbˈmɜːdʒ/ ❶ *v.t.* [A] (*place under water*) **~ sth. [in the water]** etw. eintauchen *od.* ins Wasser tauchen; **be ~d [at high tide]** [bei Flut] unter Wasser stehen; [B] (*inundate*) ‹Wasser:› überschwemmen; **be ~d in water** unter Wasser stehen; [C] (*fig.: obscure, bury*) **be ~d by** *or* **in sth.** unter etw. (*Dat.*) verborgen sein. ❷ *v.i.* abtauchen (*Seemannsspr.*)

**submerged** /səbˈmɜːdʒd/ *adj.* versunken ‹Schiff, Stadt›; überschwemmt ‹Felder›; unter Wasser befindlich ‹Fels, Eisberg›; **~ in work** (*fig.*) mit Arbeit überhäuft; **~ by debts** (*fig.*) bis über die Ohren verschuldet (*ugs.*)

**submersible** /səbˈmɜːsɪbl/ ❶ *adj.* tauchfähig. ❷ *n.* Tauchboot, *das*

**submersion** /səbˈmɜːʃn/ *n.* Eintauchen, *das;* (*in baptism*) Submersion, *die* (*Theol.*); **the watch will not withstand ~:** die Uhr ist nicht wasserfest

**subˈminiature** *adj.* Subminiatur-; (*Photog.*) Kleinstbild-

**submission** /səbˈmɪʃn/ *n.* [A] (*surrender*) Unterwerfung, *die* (**to** unter + *Akk.*); **force/frighten sb. into ~:** jmdn. zwingen, sich zu unterwerfen/jmdm. durch Einschüchterung seinen Willen aufzwingen; [B] *no pl., no art.* (*meekness*) Unterwerfung, *die;* **attitude of ~:** Demutshaltung, *die* (*Verhaltensf.*); [C] (*presentation*) Einreichung, *die* (**to** bei); (*thing put forward*) Einsendung, *die;* (*by witness*) Aussage, *die;* **in my ~:** meiner Meinung nach

**submissive** /səbˈmɪsɪv/ *adj.* gehorsam; unterwürfig (*abwertend*); **be ~ to sb./sth.** sich jmdm./einer Sache unterwerfen

**submissively** /səbˈmɪsɪvlɪ/ *adv.* gehorsam; unterwürfig (*abwertend*)

**submissiveness** /səbˈmɪsɪvnɪs/ *n., no pl.* Gehorsam, *der;* Unterwürfigkeit, *die* (*abwertend*)

**submit** /səbˈmɪt/ ❶ *v.t.*, **-tt-** [A] (*present*) einreichen; vorbringen ‹Vorschlag›; abgeben ‹[Doktor]arbeit usw.›; **~ sth. for sb.'s approval/perusal** jmdm. etw. zur Billigung vorlegen/zu lesen geben; **~ sth. to sb.** jmdm. etw. vorlegen; **~ sth. to scrutiny/investigation** etw. einer Prüfung/Untersuchung unterziehen; **~ sth. to sb.'s examination** jmdm. etw. zur Prüfung vorlegen; **~ one's entry to a competition** seine Teilnehmerkarte *usw.* für ein Preisausschreiben einsenden; **entries must be ~ted by 1 May** Einsendeschluss ist der 1. Mai; **~ that ...** (*urge deferentially*) behaupten, dass ...; [B] (*surrender*) **~ oneself to sb./sth.** sich jmdm./einer Sache unterwerfen; **~ oneself to Fate** sich in sein Schicksal fügen; **~ oneself to ridicule** sich dem Spott aussetzen; [C] (*subject*) **~ sth. to heat** etw. der Hitze (*Dat.*) aussetzen; **~ sb. to a treatment** jmdn. einer Behandlung (*Dat.*) unterziehen; **~ oneself to sth.** sich einer Sache (*Dat.*) unterziehen.
❷ *v.i.*, **-tt-** [A] (*surrender*) aufgeben; sich unterwerfen (**to** *Dat.*); **~ to sb.'s charms** jmds. Zauber (*Dat.*) erliegen; **~ to sb.'s request** jmds. Bitte (*Dat.*) nachkommen; [B] (*defer*) **~ to sb./sth.** sich jmdm./einer Sache beugen; [C] (*agree to undergo*) **~ to sth.** sich einer Sache (*Dat.*) aussetzen

**subˈnormal** *adj.* unterdurchschnittlich; subnormal (*Med.*); (*in intelligence*) minderbegabt

**subordinate** ❶ /səˈbɔːdɪnət/ *adj.* (*inferior*) untergeordnet; (*lower-ranking*) rangniedriger; (*secondary*) zweitrangig; **be ~ to sb./sth.** jmdm./einer Sache untergeordnet sein; **be of ~ importance** von untergeordneter Bedeutung sein; ⇒ *also* **clause** B. ❷ *n.* Untergebene, *der/die.* ❸ /səˈbɔːdɪneɪt/ *v.t.* (*place in lower class*) niedriger einstufen (**to** als); (*render subject; also Ling.*) unterordnen (**to** *Dat.*)

**suborn** /səˈbɔːn/ *v.t.* anstiften; (*by bribery*) bestechen

**ˈsubplot** *n.* Nebenhandlung, *die*

**subpoena** /səbˈpiːnə, səˈpiːnə/ (*Law*) ❶ *n.* Vorladung, *die:* **serve a ~ [up]on sb.** jmdm. eine Vorladung persönlich zustellen. ❷ *v.t.*, **~ed** *or* **~'d** /səbˈpiːnəd, səˈpiːnəd/ vorladen

**sub rosa** /sʌb ˈrəʊzə/ (*literary*) ❶ *adj.* Subrosa- (*geh.*); [streng] geheim. ❷ *adv.* sub rosa (*geh.*); in aller Heimlichkeit

**ˈsubroutine** *n.* (*Computing*) Unterprogramm, *das;* Subroutine, *die*

**subscribe** /səbˈskraɪb/ ❶ *v.t.* [A] (*sign one's name to*) unterzeichnen; [B] ([*promise to*] *contribute*) **~ sth.** zusichern, etw. zu spenden; **be ~d** als Spende zugesichert worden sein; **have ~d half the costs** sich verpflichtet haben, die Hälfte der Kosten zu übernehmen.
❷ *v.i.* [A] (*express adhesion*) **~ to sth.** sich einer Sache (*Dat.*) anschließen; [B] (*sign one's name*) unterzeichnen (**to** *Akk.*); [C] ([*promise to*] *make contribution*) **~ to** *or* **for sth.** eine Spende für etw. zusichern; **~ to [a newspaper]** [eine Zeitung] abonnieren

**subscriber** /səbˈskraɪbə(r)/ *n.* [A] (*one who signs*) Unterzeichner, *der*/Unterzeichnerin, *die* (**of, to** *Gen.*); Unterzeichnete, *der/die* (*Amtsdt.*); [B] (*one who assents*) Befürworter, *der*/Befürworterin, *die* (**to** *Gen.*); [C] (*contributor*) Spender, *der*/Spenderin, *die* (**of, to** für); (*to a newspaper etc.*) Abonnent, *der*/Abonnentin, *die* (**to** *Gen.*); (*of a society etc.*) Mitglied, *das;* [D] (*Teleph.*) Fernsprechkunde, *der*/-kundin, *die*

**subscriber trunk ˈdialling** *n.* (*Brit. Teleph.*) Selbstwählferndienst, *der*

**ˈsubscript** (*Math. etc.*) ❶ *adj.* tiefgestellt. ❷ *n.* [tiefgestellter] Index

**subscription** /səbˈskrɪpʃn/ *n.* [A] (*thing subscribed*) Spendenbeitrag, *der* (**to** für); (*membership fee*) Mitgliedsbeitrag, *der* (**to** für); (*prepayment for newspaper etc.*) Abonnement, *das* (**to** *Gen.*); **[buy] by ~:** im Abonnement [beziehen]; **a year's ~:** ein Jahresabonnement; [B] (*act of subscribing*) (*signing*) Unterzeichnung, *die;* (*subscribing money*) Spende, *die;* **[be built] by ~:** mit Spenden [gebaut werden]; (C) (*Publishing: offer of lower price*) Subskription, *die*

**subscription: ~ concert** *n.* Abonnementskonzert, *das;* **~ library** *n.* (*Mitgliedsbeiträge erhebende*) Leihbücherei

**'subsection** *n.* Unterabschnitt, *der*

**subsequent** /'sʌbsɪkwənt/ *adj.* folgend; nachfolgend ‹Kind›; später ‹Gelegenheit›; **~ events** spätere *od.* die folgenden Ereignisse

**subservient** /səb'sɜːvɪənt/ *adj.* (A) (*merely instrumental*) dienend; **be ~ to sb./sth.** jmdm./einer Sache dienen; (B) (*subordinate*) untergeordnet (**to** *Dat.*); (C) (*obsequious*) unterwürfig; servil (*abwertend*)

**'subset** *n.* (*Math.*) Teilmenge, *die*

**subside** /səb'saɪd/ *v.i.* (A) (*sink to lower level*) ‹Wasser, Flut, Fluss:› sinken; ‹Boden, Haus:› sich senken; ‹Schwellung:› zurückgehen; ‹schwebende Teile:› absinken, sich absetzen; **~ in exhaustion** erschöpft zusammensinken; **~ [on] to one's knees/the ground** auf die Knie/zu Boden sinken; (B) (*abate*) nachlassen; ‹Wellen, Wind, Wut, Lärm, Beifall, Aufregung:› sich legen; ‹Fieber, Delirium, Migräne:› abklingen; (*cease activity*) müde werden; ermatten (*geh.*); **~ into** verfallen in (+ *Akk.*) ‹Untätigkeit, Schweigen usw.›

**subsidence** /səb'saɪdəns, 'sʌbsɪdəns/ *n.* (A) (*sinking*) (*of ground, structure*) Senkung, *die;* (*of liquid*) Sinken, *das;* (*of swelling*) Zurückgehen, *das;* (*of suspended matter*) Sichabsetzen, *das;* (B) (*abatement*) ⇒ **subside** B: Nachlassen, *das;* Sichlegen, *das;* Abklingen, *das;* **~ into sth.** Verfallen in etw. (*Akk.*)

**subsidiary** /səb'sɪdɪərɪ/ **1** *adj.* (A) (*auxiliary*) unterstützend; subsidiär (*fachspr.*); untergeordnet ‹Funktion, Stellung›; Neben‹fach, -fluss, -aspekt›; **~ fund** Hilfsfond, *der;* **~ to sth.** einer Sache (*Dat.*) untergeordnet; (*secondary*) gegenüber einer Sache zweitrangig; (B) (*Commerc.*) **~ company** ⇒ **2**. **2** *n.* (*Commerc.*) Tochtergesellschaft, *die*

**subsidisation, subsidise** ⇒ **subsidiz-**

**subsidization** /sʌbsɪdaɪ'zeɪʃn/ *n.* (*act of subsidizing*) Subventionierung, *die;* (*money given as subsidy*) Subventionen; (*of individual person*) finanzielle Unterstützung

**subsidize** /'sʌbsɪdaɪz/ *v.t.* subventionieren; finanziell unterstützen ‹Person›

**subsidy** /'sʌbsɪdɪ/ *n.* Subvention, *die;* **receive a ~:** subventioniert werden; **grant/pay a ~ to sb./sth.** jmdn./etw. subventionieren; jmdn./etw. mit öffentlichen Mitteln fördern

**subsist** /səb'sɪst/ *v.i.* (A) ([*continue to*] *exist*) existieren; (*remain in force*) bestehen; (B) (*keep oneself alive*) existieren; subsistieren (*veralt.*); **~ on sth.** von etw. leben

**subsistence** /səb'sɪstəns/ *n.* (A) (*subsisting*) [Über]leben, *das;* **be enough for a bare ~:** gerade genug zum [Über]leben sein; ‹Einkommen:› das Existenzminimum sein; **~ is not possible under these conditions** unter diesen Bedingungen kann man nicht leben *od.* existieren; (B) **[means of] ~:** Lebensgrundlage, *die;* **millet is their chief means of ~:** sie leben hauptsächlich von Hirse

**subsistence: ~ allowance** *n.* Außendienstzulage, *die;* (*abroad*) Auslandszulage, *die;* **~ farming** *n.* Subsistenzwirtschaft, *die* (*Soziol., Wirtsch.*); **~ level** *n.* Existenzminimum, *das;* **live at ~ level** gerade genug zum Leben haben; **~ wage** *n.* ≈ Existenzminimum, *das*

**'subsoil** *n.* Untergrund, *der*

**sub'sonic** *adj.* Unterschall-

**'subspecies** *n.*, *pl. same* (*Biol.*) Unterart, *die*

**substance** /'sʌbstəns/ *n.* (A) Stoff, *der;* Substanz, *die;* (B) *no pl.* (*solidity*) Substanz, *die;* **this is an argument of little ~:** dieses Argument ist ziemlich substanzlos; **the food lacks ~:** das Essen ist nicht sehr gehaltvoll; **a man of ~:** ein begüterter Mann; (C) *no pl.* (*content*) (*of book etc.*) Inhalt, *der;* **there is not enough ~ in the plot** die Handlung gibt nicht genug her; **there is no ~ in his claim/the rumour** seine Behauptung/das Gerücht entbehrt jeder Grundlage; (D) *no pl.* (*essence*) Kern, *der;* **in ~:** im Wesentlichen

**'substance abuse** *n.* Drogen- und Genussmittelmissbrauch, *der*

**sub'standard** *adj.* (A) unzulänglich; **the printing/recording was ~:** der Druck/die Aufnahme war nicht zufrieden stellend; (B) (*Ling.*) nicht standardsprachlich

**substantial** /səb'stænʃl/ *adj.* (A) (*considerable*) beträchtlich; erheblich ‹Zugeständnis, Verbesserung›; größer... ‹Darlehen›; **'~ price required'** „namhafte Summe erforderlich"; (B) gehaltvoll ‹Essen, Nahrung›; **you need something more ~ [to eat]** du brauchst etwas Gehaltvolleres *od.* Kräftigeres [zu essen]; (C) (*solid in structure*) solide, stabil ‹Möbel›; solide ‹Haus›; kräftig ‹Körperbau›; wesentlich ‹Unterschied, Argument›; (D) (*having substance*) stofflich; materiell; (E) (*well-to-do*) begütert ‹Person›; zahlungskräftig ‹Firma›; (F) weitgehend ‹Übereinstimmung, Zustimmung›; ziemlich sicher ‹Beweis›; **be in ~ agreement** sich (*Dat.*) so gut wie *od.* praktisch einig sein

**substantially** /səb'stænʃəlɪ/ *adv.* (A) (*considerably*) wesentlich; (B) (*solidly*) **~ built** solide gebaut ‹Haus usw.›; kräftig gebaut ‹Person›; (C) (*essentially*) im Wesentlichen; **~ free from sth.** weitgehend frei von etw.

**substantiate** /səb'stænʃɪeɪt/ *v.t.* erhärten; untermauern

**substantiation** /səbstænʃɪ'eɪʃn/ *n.* Erhärtung, *die;* Untermauerung, *die;* **in ~ of his claim** zur Erhärtung *od.* Untermauerung seines Anspruchs

**substantive 1** /səb'stæntɪv/ *adj.* (A) (*not amended*) in der vorliegenden Form *nachgestellt;* (B) (*Mil.*) **a ~ rank** der Rang eines Berufssoldaten. **2** /'sʌbstəntɪv/ *n.* (*Ling.*) Substantiv, *das*

**'substation** *n.* (*Electr.*) Hochspannungsverteilungsanlage, *die*

**substitutable** /'sʌbstɪtjuːtəbl/ *adj.* substituierbar

**substitute** /'sʌbstɪtjuːt/ **1** *n.* (A) **~[s]** Ersatz, *der;* **~s for rubber** Ersatzstoffe für Gummi; **coffee ~:** Kaffee-Ersatz, *der;* **there is no ~ for real ale/hard work** es geht nichts über das echte englische Bier/über harte Arbeit; (B) (*Sport*) Ersatzspieler, *der*/-spielerin, *die*.

**2** *adj.* Ersatz-; **a ~ teacher/secretary** *etc.* eine Vertretung.

**3** *v.t.* (A) **~ A for B** B durch A ersetzen; **~ oil for butter** statt Butter Öl nehmen; **~ a striker for a midfield player** einen Mittelfeldspieler gegen einen Stürmer auswechseln *od.* austauschen; **he doesn't like potatoes, so we ~d rice** da er keine Kartoffeln mag, gaben wir ihm stattdessen Reis; (B) (*coll.*) **~ A by** *or* **with B** A durch B ersetzen.

**4** *v.i.* **~ for sb.** jmdn. vertreten; für jmdn. einspringen; (*Sport*) für jmdn. ins Spiel kommen; **Thompson ~d for Clark just after half-time** kurz nach der Halbzeit kam Thompson für Clark ins Spiel *od.* wurde Clark gegen Thompson ausgetauscht

**substitution** /sʌbstɪ'tjuːʃn/ *n.* Ersetzung, *die;* Substitution, *die* (*geh., fachspr.*); (*Sport*) Spielerwechsel, *der;* **~ of A for B** Verwendung von A statt B; **make a ~** (*Sport*) [einen Spieler] auswechseln

**sub'stratum** *n.*, *pl.* **substrata** (A) (*Geol.*) **a ~ of rock** ein felsiger Untergrund; (B) (*Ling., Biol., Chem., fig.*) Substrat, *das* (*geh., fachspr.*)

**'substructure** *n.* Unterbau, *der;* (*of oil rig also*) Stützkonstruktion, *die*

**subsume** /səb'sjuːm/ *v.t.* einordnen (**in, into** in + *Akk.*); **~ an item under a category** einen Punkt einer Kategorie (*Dat.*) zuordnen

**'subsystem** *n.* Subsystem, *das* (*geh.*); Teilsystem, *das*

**'subtenancy** *n.* Untervermietung, *die;* (*of land, farm, shop*) Unterverpachtung, *die;* (*relationship*) Untermiete, *die;* (*of land, farm, shop*) Unterpacht, *die*

**'subtenant** *n.* Untermieter, *der*/-mieterin, *die;* (*of land, farm, shop*) Unterpächter, *der*/-pächterin, *die*

**subtend** /sʌb'tend/ *v.t.* (*Geom.*) gegenüberliegen (+ *Dat.*) ‹Winkel›; schneiden ‹Bogen›

**subterfuge** /'sʌbtəfjuːdʒ/ *n.* (A) *no pl., no art.* Täuschungsmanöver *Pl.;* (B) (*trick*) Trick, *der*

**subterranean** /sʌbtə'reɪnɪən/ *adj.* unterirdisch; subterran (*fachspr.*)

**'subtitle 1** *n.* (*for film, of book, etc.*) Untertitel, *der.* **2** *v.t.* untertiteln; **the book is ~d ...:** das Buch hat den Untertitel ...

**subtle** /'sʌtl/ *adj.*, **~r** /'sʌtlə(r)/, **~st** /'sʌtlɪst/ (A) (*delicate*) zart ‹Duft, Dunst, Parfüm›; fein ‹Geschmack, Aroma›; (B) (*elusive*) subtil (*geh.*); fein ‹Unterschied›; unaufdringlich ‹Charme›; (C) (*refined*) fein ‹Ironie, Humor›; zart ‹Hinweis›; subtil (*geh.*) ‹Scherz›; (D) (*perceptive*) feinsinnig ‹Beobachter, Kritiker›; fein ‹Intellekt›; **~ perception** feines Gespür; (E) (*ingenious*) geschickt; raffiniert ‹Plan›; **~ art** hohe Kunst

**subtlety** /'sʌtltɪ/ *n.* (A) *no pl.* ⇒ **subtle**: Zartheit, *die;* Feinheit, *die;* Subtilität, *die* (*geh.*); Unaufdringlichkeit, *die;* Feinsinnigkeit, *die;* Geschicklichkeit, *die;* Raffiniertheit, *die;* (B) **subtleties** Feinheiten

**subtly** /'sʌtlɪ/ *adv.* auf subtile Weise (*geh.*); zart ‹hinweisen auf, andeuten›; geschickt ‹argumentieren›; **~ flavoured/perfumed** von feinem Geschmack *nachgestellt*/zart duftend

**'subtotal** *n.* Zwischensumme, *die*

**subtract** /səb'trækt/ *v.t.* abziehen (**from** von); subtrahieren (**from** von)

**subtraction** /səb'trækʃn/ *n.* Subtraktion, *die;* Abziehen, *das*

**sub'tropical** *adj.* subtropisch

**suburb** /'sʌbɜːb/ *n.* Vorort, *der;* **live in the ~s** am Stadtrand leben

**suburban** /sə'bɜːbən/ *adj.* (A) (*of suburbs*) Vorort-; ‹Leben, Haus› am Stadtrand; **~ spread** *or* **sprawl** eintönige, endlose Vororte; (B) (*derog.: limited in outlook*) spießig (*abwertend*)

**suburbanite** /sə'bɜːbənaɪt/ *n.* Vorstädter, *der*/Vorstädterin, *die*

**suburbia** /sə'bɜːbɪə/ *n.* (*derog.*) die [eintönigen] Vororte

**subvention** /səb'venʃn/ *n.* Subvention, *die* (*Wirtsch.*)

**subversion** /səb'vɜːʃn/ *n.* Subversion, *die;* (*of government, monarchy, etc.*) [Um]sturz, *der*

**subversive** /səb'vɜːsɪv/ **1** *adj.* subversiv; **be ~ of sth.** etw. unterminieren. **2** *n.* Subversive, *der/die*

**subversively** /səb'vɜːsɪvlɪ/ *adv.* subversiv

**subvert** /səb'vɜːt/ *v.t.* stürzen ‹Monarchie, Regierung›; unterminieren ‹Moral, Loyalität›; [zur Illoyalität] aufstacheln ‹Person›

**'subway** *n.* (A) (*passage*) Unterführung, *die;* (B) (*Amer.: railway*) Untergrundbahn, *die;* U-Bahn, *die* (*ugs.*)

**sub-'zero** *adj.* ▶ **1603** **~ temperatures/conditions** Temperaturen unter null

**succeed** /sək'siːd/ **1** *v.i.* (A) (*achieve aim*) Erfolg haben; **sb. ~s in sth.** jmdm. gelingt etw.; jmd. schafft etw.; **sb. ~s in doing sth.** es gelingt jmdm., etw. zu tun; jmd. schafft es, etw. zu tun; **~ in business/college** geschäftlich/im Studium erfolgreich sein; **I did not ~ in doing it** ich habe es nicht geschafft; es ist mir nicht gelungen; **I ~ed in passing the test** ich habe die Prüfung mit Erfolg *od.* erfolgreich abgelegt; **he usually ~s in anything he puts his mind to** ihm gelingt gewöhnlich alles, was er sich (*Dat.*) vornimmt; **~ in one's aims** seine Ziele erreichen; **the plan did not ~:** der Plan ist gescheitert; (B) (*come next*) die Nachfolge antreten; **~ to an office/the throne** die Nachfolge in einem Amt/die Thronfolge antreten; **~ to a title/an estate** einen Titel/ein Gut erben.

**2** *v.t.* (A) (*take place of*) ablösen ‹Monarchen, Beamten›; **~ sb. [in a post]** jmds. Nachfolge [in einem Amt] antreten; (B) (*follow*) **day ~ed day** ein Tag folgte auf den anderen

**succeeding** /sək'siːdɪŋ/ *adj.* [nach]folgend; (*one after another*) aufeinander folgend ‹Generationen, Regierungen›

**success** /sək'ses/ *n.* ▶ **1191** Erfolg, *der;* **meet with ~:** Erfolg haben; erfolgreich sein; **make a ~ of sth.** bei etw. Erfolg haben; **'wishing you every ~'** „ich wünsche/wir wünschen Ihnen viel Erfolg"; **have little/considerable ~ in doing sth.** wenig/beträchtlichen Erfolg dabei haben,

S

etw. zu tun; **I didn't have much ~ with her** ich war bei ihr nicht sonderlich erfolgreich; **~ at last!** endlich hat es geklappt! (*ugs.*); **nothing succeeds like ~** (*prov.*) nichts ist so erfolgreich wie der Erfolg (*Spr.*); **he was a great ~ as headmaster/Hamlet** er war als Schulleiter sehr erfolgreich/als Hamlet ein großer Erfolg

**successful** /sək'sesfl/ *adj.* erfolgreich; **be ~ in sth./doing sth.** Erfolg bei etw. haben/dabei haben, etw. zu tun; **he was ~ in his attempts to ...:** es gelang ihm, ... zu ...; **she made a ~ attempt on the record** der Rekordversuch ist ihr gelungen

**successfully** /sək'sesfəlɪ/ *adv.* erfolgreich; **he ~ avoided the question** es gelang ihm, der Frage auszuweichen

**succession** /sək'seʃn/ *n.* **A** Folge, *die;* **four games/years** *etc.* **in ~:** vier Spiele/Jahre *usw.* hintereinander; **in quick/rapid ~:** in schneller/rascher Folge; **in close ~** (*in space*) dicht hintereinander; (*in time*) kurz hintereinander; **the ~ of the seasons** die Abfolge der Jahreszeiten; **B** (*series*) Serie, *die;* **a ~ of losses/visitors** eine Verlust-/Besucherserie; **C** (*right of succeeding to the throne etc.*) Erbfolge, *die;* **he is second in ~:** er ist Zweiter in der Erbfolge; **in ~ to his uncle** als Nachfolger seines Onkels; **the apostolic ~** (*RC Ch.*) die Apostolische Nachfolge *od.* Sukzession

**successive** /sək'sesɪv/ *adj.* aufeinander folgend; **five ~ games/jobs** fünf Spiele/Stellungen hintereinander

**successively** /sək'sesɪvlɪ/ *adv.* hintereinander

**successor** /sək'sesə(r)/ *n.* Nachfolger, *der*/Nachfolgerin, *die;* **sb.'s ~, the ~ to sb.** jmds. Nachfolger; **the ~ to the throne** der Nachfolger auf dem Thron

**suc'cess story** *n.* Erfolgsstory, *die* (*ugs.*); **he is a typical American ~:** er hat eine typische amerikanische Erfolgskarriere hinter sich (*Dat.*)

**succinct** /sək'sɪŋkt/ *adj.* (*terse*) knapp; (*clear, to the point*) prägnant

**succinctly** /sək'sɪŋktlɪ/ *adv.* (*tersely*) in knappen Worten; (*clearly*) prägnant

**succinctness** /sək'sɪŋktnɪs/ *n., no pl.* (*terseness*) Knappheit, *die;* (*clarity*) Prägnanz, *die*

**succour** (*Amer.:* **succor**) /'sʌkə(r)/ (*literary*) **1** *v.t.* Beistand leisten (+ *Dat.*). **2** *n.* Beistand, *der;* Unterstützung, *die;* **bring ~ to the wounded** die Leiden der Verwundeten lindern

**succulence** /'sʌkjʊləns/ *n., no pl.* Saftigkeit, *die*

**succulent** /'sʌkjʊlənt/ **1** *adj.* **A** saftig ‹Pfirsich, Steak usw.›; **B** (*Bot.*) sukkulent; fleischig; **~ plants** Sukkulenten. **2** *n.* (*Bot.*) Sukkulente, *die;* Fettpflanze, *die*

**succulently** /'sʌkjʊləntlɪ/ *adv.* saftig

**succumb** /sə'kʌm/ *v.i.* **A** (*be forced to give way*) unterliegen; **~ to sth.** einer Sache (*Dat.*) erliegen; **~ to grief/despair** in Kummer/Verzweiflung verfallen; **~ to temptation** der Versuchung erliegen; **~ to pressure** dem Druck nachgeben; **B** (*die*) **~ [to one's illness/wounds** *etc.*] seiner Krankheit/seinen Verletzungen *usw.* erliegen

**such** /sʌtʃ/ **1** *adj., no compar. or superl.* **A** (*of that kind*) solch ...; **~ a person** solch *od.* (*ugs.*) so ein Mensch; ein solcher Mensch; **~ a book** solch *od.* (*ugs.*) so ein Buch; ein solches Buch; **~ people** solche Leute; **~ things** so etwas; **symphonies and other ~ compositions** Sinfonien und andere Kompositionen dieser Art; **shoplifting and ~ crimes** Ladendiebstahl und derartige *od.* ähnliche Vergehen; **there are many ~ cases** so etwas kommt oft vor; **or some ~ thing** oder so etwas; oder etwas in der Art; **some ~ plan** irgend so ein Plan (*ugs.*); **I said no ~ thing** ich habe nichts dergleichen gesagt; **you'll do no ~ thing** das wirst du nicht tun; **there is no ~ bird** solch einen *od.* einen solchen Vogel gibt es nicht; **experiences ~ as these** solche *od.* derartige Erfahrungen; **there is no ~ thing as a unicorn** Einhörner gibt es gar nicht; **there is no ~ thing as honour among thieves** Diebe kennen keine Ehre; **~ writers as Eliot and Fry** Schriftsteller wie Eliot und Fry; **~ grapes as you never saw** Trauben, wie du sie noch nie gesehen hast; **I will take ~ steps as I think necessary** ich werde die Schritte unternehmen, die ich für notwendig halte; **~ money as I have** das bisschen Geld, das ich habe; **at ~ a time** zu einer solchen Zeit; **at ~ a moment as this** in einem Augenblick wie diesem; (*disapproving*) gerade jetzt; **in ~ a case** in einem solchen *od.* (*ugs.*) so einem Fall; **for** *or* **on ~ an occasion** zu einem solchen Anlass; **by all means stay for lunch, ~ as it is** bleib doch zum Mittagessen, aber es gibt nichts Besonderes; **~ a one as he/she is impossible to replace** jemand wie er/sie ist unersetzlich; ⇒ *also* **another** 1 B; **luck** B; **B** (*so great*) solch ...; derartig; **I got ~ a fright that ...:** ich bekam einen derartigen *od.* (*ugs.*) so einen Schrecken, dass ...; **your stupidity is ~ as to fill me with despair** deine Dummheit treibt mich noch zur Verzweiflung; **~ was the force of the explosion that ...:** die Explosion war so stark, dass ...; **to ~ an extent** dermaßen; **C** (*with adj.*) so; **~ a big house** ein so großes Haus; **she has ~ lovely blue eyes** sie hat so schöne blaue Augen; **~ a wonderfully fresh green** so ein herrlich frisches Grün; **~ a long time** so lange.

**2** *pron.* **A as ~:** als solcher/solche/solches; (*strictly speaking*) im Grunde genommen; an sich; **this is not a promotion as ~:** dies ist im Grunde genommen *od.* eigentlich keine Beförderung; **~ is not the case** das ist nicht der Fall; **~ is life** so ist das Leben; **~ as** wie [zum Beispiel]; **~ 'as?** zum Beispiel?; **B** (*people or things of stated kind*) **all ~:** alle seinesgleichen/ihresgleichen; **we do not have any ~:** wir haben nichts dergleichen; **or some ~:** oder so etwas; **I can give you ~ as I have** ich kann dir [das Wenige] geben, was ich habe

**such-and-such** /'sʌtʃənsʌtʃ/ **1** *adj.* **in ~ a place at ~ a time** an dem und dem Ort um die und die Zeit; **Mr ~:** Herr Sowieso. **2** *pron.* der und der/die und die/das und das

**suchlike** /'sʌtʃlaɪk/ (*coll.*) **1** *pron.* derlei. **2** *attrib. adj.* dergleichen

**suck** /sʌk/ **1** *v.t.* saugen (**out of** aus); lutschen ‹Bonbon›; saugen an (+ *Dat.*) ‹Pfeife›; **~ one's thumb** am Daumen lutschen; **~ an orange dry** eine Apfelsine auslutschen; **~ sb. dry** (*extort all sb.'s money*) jmdn. bis aufs Blut aussaugen; (*exhaust sb.*) jmdn. auslaugen. **2** *v.i.* **A** ‹Baby:› saugen; **~ at sth.** an etw. (*Dat.*) saugen; **~ at a lollipop** an einem Lutscher lecken; einen Lolli lutschen; **B sth. ~s** (*esp. Amer. sl.*) etw. ist Scheiße (*derb*). **3** *n.* **have a ~ at an ice lolly/at a straw** an einem Eis lutschen/Strohhalm saugen *od.* ziehen

**~ 'down** *v.t.* hinunterziehen; ‹Strudel:› in die Tiefe ziehen

**~ 'in** *v.t.* einsaugen; ‹Strudel:› in die Tiefe ziehen

**~ 'off** *v.t.* (*coarse*) **~ sb. off** jmdm. einen ablutschen *od.* abkauen (*vulg.*)

**~ 'under** *v.t.* in die Tiefe ziehen

**~ 'up 1** *v.t.* aufsaugen ‹Staub, Feuchtigkeit›; (*with a straw*) einsaugen; (*into a pipette*) ansaugen; (*by dredger, tubes, etc.*) verschlucken. **2** *v.i.* **~ up to sb.** (*coll.*) jmdm. in den Hintern kriechen (*salopp*)

**sucker** /'sʌkə(r)/ *n.* **A** (*suction pad*) Saugfuß, *der;* (*Zool.*) Saugnapf, *der;* (*of leech*) Saugscheibe, *die;* **B** (*one attracted*) **be a ~ for sb./sth.** eine Schwäche für jmdn./etw. haben; **C** (*coll.: dupe*) Dumme, *der/die;* **poor ~:** armer Trottel; **he's always being had for a ~:** er fällt immer auf alles herein; **D** (*Bot.*) unterirdischer Ausläufer; **E** (*fish*) Sauger, *der;* **F** (*Amer.*) ⇒ **lollipop**

**'sucking pig** *n.* Spanferkel, *das*

**suckle** /'sʌkl/ **1** *v.t.* säugen. **2** *v.i.* [an der Brust] trinken

**suckling** /'sʌklɪŋ/ *n.* (*unweaned child*) Säugling, *der;* **these piglets are still ~s** diese Ferkel werden noch gesäugt; ⇒ *also* **mouth** 1 A

**sucrose** /'su:krəʊz, 'sju:krəʊz/ *n.* (*Chem.*) Saccharose, *die*

**suction** /'sʌkʃn/ *n.* **A** (*sucking*) Absaugen, *das;* (*force*) Saugwirkung, *die;* **B** (*of air, currents, etc.*) Sog, *der;* **work by ~:** durch Saugwirkung arbeiten

**suction: ~ pad** *n.* Saugfuß, *der;* **~ pump** *n.* Saugpumpe, *die*

**Sudan** /su:'dɑ:n/ *pr. n.* **[the] ~:** [der] Sudan

**Sudanese** /su:də'ni:z/ **▶ 1340** **1** *adj.* sudanesisch; **sb. is ~:** jmd. ist Sudanese/Sudanesin. **2** *n., pl. same* Sudanese, *der*/Sudanesin, *die*

**sudden** /'sʌdn/ **1** *adj.* **A** (*unexpected*) plötzlich; **I had a ~ thought** auf einmal *od.* plötzlich fiel mir etwas ein; **B** (*abrupt, without warning*) jäh ‹Abgrund, Übergang, Ruck›; **there was a ~ bend in the road** plötzlich machte die Straße eine Biegung. **2** *n.* **all of a ~:** plötzlich

**sudden 'death** *attrib. adj.* (*Sport coll.*) **a ~ playoff** ein Stichentscheid; (*Footb.: using penalties*) ein Elfmeterschießen

**suddenly** /'sʌdnlɪ/ *adv.* plötzlich

**suddenness** /'sʌdnnɪs/ *n., no pl.* Plötzlichkeit, *die*

**suds** /sʌdz/ *n. pl.* **A [soap]~:** [Seifen]lauge, *die;* (*froth*) Schaum, *der;* **B** (*Amer. coll.: beer*) Gerstensaft, *der* (*scherzh.*)

**sudsy** /'sʌdzɪ/ *adj.* (*coll.*) seifig; (*frothy*) schaumig

**sue** /su:, sju:/ **1** *v.t.* (*Law*) verklagen (**for** auf + *Akk.*). **2** *v.i.* **A** (*Law*) klagen (**for** auf + *Akk.*); **B** (*fig.*) **~ for peace/mercy** um Frieden/Gnade bitten

**suede** /sweɪd/ *n.* Wildleder, *das;* (*finer*) Veloursleder, *das*

**suet** /'su:ɪt, 'sju:ɪt/ *n.* Talg, *der*

**suet 'pudding** *n. mit Talg zubereiteter Pudding*

**Suez** /'sʊɪz, 'sju:ɪz/ *pr. n.* Suez (*das*); **~ Canal** Suezkanal, *der*

**suffer** /'sʌfə(r)/ **1** *v.t.* **A** (*undergo*) erleiden ‹Verlust, Unrecht, Schmerz, Niederlage›; durchmachen, erleben ‹Schweres, Kummer›; dulden ‹Unverschämtheit›; **~ disablement** invalide werden; **the dollar ~ed further losses against the yen** der Dollar musste weitere Einbußen gegenüber dem Yen hinnehmen; **~ neglect** vernachlässigt werden; **B** (*tolerate*) dulden; **not ~ fools gladly** mit dummen Leuten keine Geduld haben; **C** (*arch.: allow*) lassen; **~ sth. to be done** (*Bibl.*) etw. geschehen lassen; **~ the little children to come unto me** (*Bibl.*) lasset die Kindlein zu mir kommen; **he ~s no one to contradict him** er duldet *od.* (*veralt.*) leidet keinen Widerspruch.

**2** *v.i.* leiden; **~ for sth.** (*for a cause*) für etw. leiden; (*in expiation*) für etw. büßen; **the engine ~ed severely** der Motor hat sehr gelitten; **if you publish this article, your reputation will ~:** wenn Sie diesen Artikel veröffentlichen, wird das Ihrem Ruf schaden

**~ from** *v.t.* **▶ 1232** leiden unter (+ *Dat.*); leiden an (+ *Dat.*) ‹Krankheit›; **~ from shock** unter Schock[wirkung] stehen; **~ from faulty planning/bad execution** an falscher Planung/schlechter Durchführung kranken; **the trees have ~ed from the frost** die Bäume haben durch den Frost gelitten

**sufferance** /'sʌfərəns/ *n.* Duldung, *die;* **his behaviour is beyond ~:** sein Benehmen ist unerträglich; **he remains here on ~ only** er ist hier bloß geduldet

**sufferer** /'sʌfərə(r)/ *n.* **▶ 1232** Betroffene, *der/die;* (*from disease*) Leidende, *der/die;* **~s from rheumatism/arthritis, rheumatism/arthritis ~s** Rheuma-/Arthritisleidende

**suffering** /'sʌfərɪŋ/ *n.* Leiden, *das;* **he had experienced untold ~ from cancer** als Krebskranker hatte er unsäglich gelitten; **her ~s are now at an end** sie hat jetzt ausgelitten (*geh.*)

**suffice** /sə'faɪs/ **1** *v.i.* genügen; **~ it to say: ...:** nur so viel sei gesagt: ...; **this ~d to infuriate her** das genügte *od.* reichte schon,

S

um sie wütend zu machen. ❷ *v.t.* genügen (+ *Dat.*); reichen für

**sufficiency** /səˈfɪʃənsɪ/ *n.*, *no pl.* Zulänglichkeit, *die;* (*sufficient amount*) ausreichende Menge

**sufficient** /səˈfɪʃənt/ *adj.* genug; **~ money/food** genug Geld/genug zu essen; **be ~:** genügen; **~ reason** Grund genug; **I'm not ~ of an expert** ich bin nicht Fachmann genug; **have you had ~?** (*food, drink*) haben Sie schon genug?; **I think you have drunk quite ~:** ich glaube, du hast schon genug getrunken

**sufficiently** /səˈfɪʃəntlɪ/ *adv.* genug; (*adequately*) ausreichend; **~ large** groß genug; **a ~ large number** eine genügend große Zahl

**suffix** /ˈsʌfɪks/ ❶ *n.* Ⓐ (*Ling.*) Suffix, *das* (*fachspr.*); Nachsilbe, *die;* Ⓑ (*Math.*) ⇒ **subscript** 2. ❷ *v.t.* suffigieren (*fachspr.*); anhängen ‹Nachsilbe›

**suffocate** /ˈsʌfəkeɪt/ ❶ *v.t.* ersticken; **he was ~d by the smoke** der Rauch erstickte ihn; er erstickte an dem Rauch; **suffocating heat** drückende Hitze; **this dreary existence is suffocating me** (*fig.*) dieses eintönige Leben erdrückt mich. ❷ *v.i.* ersticken; **she was suffocating in the hot little kitchen** sie wäre in der heißen kleinen Küche fast erstickt

**suffocation** /sʌfəˈkeɪʃn/ *n.* Erstickung, *die;* **a feeling of ~:** das Gefühl, zu ersticken

**suffragan** /ˈsʌfrəgən/ (*Eccl.*) ❶ *adj.* **~ bishop** Suffraganbischof, *der.* ❷ *n.* **[bishop] ~:** Suffragan, *der*

**suffrage** /ˈsʌfrɪdʒ/ *n.* (*right of voting*) Wahlrecht, *das;* **female** *or* **women's ~:** das Frauenwahlrecht

**suffragette** /sʌfrəˈdʒet/ *n.* (*Hist.*) Frauenrechtlerin, *die;* Suffragette, *die*

**suffuse** /səˈfjuːz/ *v.t.* **a blush ~d her cheeks** Schamröte stieg ihr ins Gesicht; **the evening sky was ~d with crimson** der Abendhimmel war in purpurnes Licht getaucht

**Sufi** /ˈsuːfɪ/ *n.* (*Muslim Relig.*) Sufi, *der*

**sugar** /ˈʃʊgə(r)/ ❶ *n.* Ⓐ Zucker, *der;* **two ~s, please** (*spoonfuls*) zwei Löffel Zucker, bitte; (*lumps*) zwei Stück Zucker, bitte; Ⓑ (*fig.: flattery*) Schöntuerei, *die* (*abwertend*); Ⓒ (*Amer. coll.: money*) Kohle, *die* (*salopp*); Ⓓ (*Amer. coll.: darling*) Süße, *der/die* (*fam.*). ❷ *v.t.* zuckern; (*fig.*) versüßen; verzuckern

**sugar: ~ basin** ⇒ ~ bowl; **~ beet** *n.* Zuckerrübe, *die;* **~ bowl** *n.* Zuckerschale, *die;* (*covered*) Zuckerdose, *die;* **~ cane** *n.* Zuckerrohr, *das;* **~-coated** *adj.* gezuckert; mit Zucker überzogen ‹Dragee usw.›; **~ daddy** *n.* (*coll.*) *spendabler älterer Mann, der ein junges Mädchen aushält;* **~loaf** *n.* Zuckerhut, *der;* **~ lump** *n.* Zuckerstück, *das;* (*when counted*) Stück Zucker, *das;* **~ pea** *n.* Zuckererbse, *die;* **~ refinery** *n.* Zuckerraffinerie, *die;* **~ shaker, ~ sifter** *ns.* Zuckerstreuer, *der;* **~ tongs** *n. pl.* Zuckerzange, *die*

**sugary** /ˈʃʊgərɪ/ *adj.* süß; (*fig.*) süßlich ‹Lächeln, Stimme, Musik›

**suggest** /səˈdʒest/ ❶ *v.t.* Ⓐ (*propose*) vorschlagen; **~ sth. to sb.** jmdm. etw. vorschlagen; **he ~ed going to the cinema** er schlug vor, ins Kino zu gehen; Ⓑ (*assert*) **are you trying to ~ that he is lying?** wollen Sie damit sagen, dass er lügt?; **he ~ed that the calculation was incorrect** er sagte, die Rechnung sei falsch; **I ~ that ...** (*Law*) ich unterstelle, dass ...; Ⓒ (*make one think of*) suggerieren; ‹Symptome, Tatsachen:› schließen lassen auf (+ *Akk.*); **what does this music ~ to you?** woran denken Sie bei dieser Musik? ❷ *v. refl.* **~ itself [to sb.]** ‹Möglichkeiten, Ausweg:› sich [jmdm.] anbieten; ‹Gedanke:› sich [jmdm.] aufdrängen

**suggestible** /səˈdʒestɪbl/ *adj.* beeinflussbar; suggestibel (*geh.*)

**suggestion** /səˈdʒestʃn/ *n.* Ⓐ Vorschlag, *der;* **at** *or* **on sb.'s ~:** auf jmds. Vorschlag (*Akk.*); **I am open to ~s** ich bin Vorschlägen *od.* Anregungen aufgeschlossen; Ⓑ (*insinuation*) Andeutungen *Pl.;* **there is no ~ that he cooperated with the kidnappers** niemand unterstellt, dass er mit den Entführern zusammengearbeitet hat; **what a ~!** wie kann man so etwas nur sagen!; Ⓒ (*fig.: trace*) Spur, *die;* **not a ~ of condescension** nicht die Spur von Herablassung; **she speaks German with a ~ of a Polish accent** sie spricht Deutsch mit einem ganz leichten polnischen Akzent; **there is a ~ of blue in the grey** das Grau hat einen leichten Stich ins Blaue

**sug'gestion[s] box** *n.* Kummerkasten, *der*

**suggestive** /səˈdʒestɪv/ *adj.* Ⓐ suggestiv (*geh.*); **be ~ of sth.** auf etw. (*Akk.*) schließen lassen; **~ power** Suggestion, *die;* Ⓑ (*risqué*) anzüglich; gewagt; zweideutig ‹Scherze, Lieder›

**suggestively** /səˈdʒestɪvlɪ/ *adv.* Ⓐ viel sagend; Ⓑ (*in a risqué manner*) gewagt

**suggestiveness** /səˈdʒestɪvnɪs/ *n.*, *no pl.* Ⓐ Suggestion, *die;* Ⓑ (*sexual undertones*) Anzüglichkeit, *die;* Gewagtheit, *die*

**suicidal** /suːɪˈsaɪdl, sjuːɪˈsaɪdl/ *adj.* Ⓐ (*leading or tending to suicide*) selbstmörderisch ‹Akt, Absicht›; suizidal (*fachspr.*) ‹Verhalten, Patient›; **~ tendencies** eine Neigung zum Selbstmord; **I felt** *or* **was quite ~:** ich hätte mich am liebsten gleich umgebracht; Ⓑ (*dangerous*) selbstmörderisch ‹Fahrweise, Verhalten usw.›

**suicide** /ˈsuːɪsaɪd, ˈsjuːɪsaɪd/ *n.* Ⓐ Selbstmord, *der* (*auch fig.*); Suizid, *der* (*fachspr.*); (*viewed more positively*) Freitod, *der* (*geh.*); **commit ~:** Selbstmord *od.* (*fachspr.*) Suizid begehen; (*viewed more positively*) den Freitod wählen (*geh.*); **attempt ~:** einen Selbstmordversuch unternehmen; Ⓑ (*person*) Selbstmörder, *der*/-mörderin, *die;* Suizidant, *der*/Suizidantin, *die* (*fachspr.*)

**suicide: ~ attempt** *n.* Selbstmordversuch, *der;* **~ pact** *n.* Selbstmordpakt, *der;* **~ squad** *n.* Selbstmordkommando, *das*

**sui generis** /sjuːaɪ ˈdʒenərɪs, suːɪ ˈgenərɪs/ *adj.* einzigartig; **be ~:** einzig in seiner Art sein

**suit** /suːt, sjuːt/ ❶ *n.* Ⓐ (*for men*) Anzug, *der;* (*for women*) Kostüm, *das;* **a three-piece ~:** ein dreiteiliger Anzug; ein Dreiteiler; **~ of armour** Harnisch, *der;* **buy [oneself] a new ~ of clothes** sich neu einkleiden; Ⓑ (*Law*) **~ [at law]** Prozess, *der;* [Gerichts]verfahren, *das;* Ⓒ (*Cards*) Farbe, *die;* **follow ~:** Farbe bedienen; (*fig.*) das Gleiche tun; ⇒ *also* **long¹** 1 M; Ⓓ (*courtship*) Werbung, *die* (*um eine Frau*).
❷ *v.t.* Ⓐ anpassen (**to** *Dat.*); **~ the action to the word** den Worten Taten folgen lassen; Ⓑ **be ~ed [to sth./one another]** [zu etw./zueinander] passen; **he is not at all ~ed to marriage** er eignet sich überhaupt nicht für die Ehe; **they are ill/well ~ed** sie passen schlecht/gut zueinander; Ⓒ (*satisfy needs of*) passen (+ *Dat.*); recht sein (+ *Dat.*); **will Monday ~ you?** ist Montag Ihnen recht?; passt Ihnen Montag?; **he comes when it ~s him** er kommt, wann es ihm gerade passt; **does the climate ~ you/your health?** bekommt Ihnen das Klima?; **dried fruit/asparagus does not ~ me** ich vertrage kein Trockenobst/keinen Spargel; Ⓓ (*go well with*) passen zu; **does this hat ~ me?** steht mir dieser Hut?; **black ~s her** Schwarz steht ihr gut.
❸ *v.i.* Ⓐ (*be convenient*) ‹Termin:› recht sein; Ⓑ (*go well*) **she'll ~:** sie ist genau richtig; **the job ~s with his abilities** die Stelle entspricht seinen Fähigkeiten.
❹ *v. refl.* **~ oneself** tun, was man will; **~ yourself!** [ganz] wie du willst!; **you can ~ yourself whether you come or not** du kannst kommen oder nicht, ganz wie du willst

**suitability** /suːtəˈbɪlɪtɪ, sjuːtəˈbɪlɪtɪ/ *n.*, *no pl.* Eignung, *die* (**for** für); (*of clothing, remark; for an occasion*) Angemessenheit, *die* (**for** für); **his ~ as a teacher** seine Eignung zum *od.* als Lehrer; **we must check the ~ of the date** wir müssen prüfen, ob der Termin passt

**suitable** /ˈsuːtəbl, ˈsjuːtəbl/ *adj.* geeignet; (*for an occasion*) angemessen ‹Kleidung›; angebracht ‹Bemerkung›; (*matching; convenient*) passend; **I did not find anything ~ to go with this dress** ich habe nichts gefunden, was zu diesem Kleid passt; **this girlfriend is not ~ for him** diese Freundin passt nicht zu ihm; **Monday is the most ~ day [for me]** Montag passt [mir] am besten

**suitableness** /ˈsuːtəblnɪs, ˈsjuːtəblnɪs/ ⇒ **suitability**

**suitably** /ˈsuːtəblɪ, ˈsjuːtəblɪ/ *adv.* angemessen; gehörig ‹entrüstet›; gebührend ‹beeindruckt›; entsprechend ‹gekleidet›; **a ~ treated metal** ein in geeigneter Weise bearbeitetes Metall

**'suitcase** *n.* Koffer, *der;* **live out of a ~:** aus dem Koffer leben

**suite** /swiːt/ *n.* Ⓐ (*of furniture*) Garnitur, *die;* **three-piece ~:** Polstergarnitur, *die;* **bedroom ~:** Schlafzimmereinrichtung, *die;* Ⓑ (*of rooms*) Suite, *die;* **executive/bridal ~:** Chef-/Hochzeitssuite, *die;* Ⓒ (*Mus.*) Suite, *die*

**suitor** /ˈsuːtə(r), ˈsjuːtə(r)/ *n.* Freier, *der*

**sulfate, sulfide, sulfite, sulfonamide, sulfur, sulfuric** (*Amer.*) ⇒ **sulph-**

**sulk** /sʌlk/ ❶ *n.*, *usu. in pl.* **have a ~** *or* **the ~s, be in** *or* **have a fit of the ~s** eingeschnappt sein (*ugs.*); schmollen. ❷ *v.i.* schmollen; **he always ~s if he doesn't get his own way** er ist immer gleich eingeschnappt, wenn er seinen Willen nicht kriegt (*ugs.*)

**sulkily** /ˈsʌlkɪlɪ/ *adv.* eingeschnappt (*ugs.*); schmollend

**sulkiness** /ˈsʌlkɪnɪs/ *n.*, *no pl.* Schmollen, *das;* **the ~ of her expression/look** ihr schmollender Gesichtsausdruck/Blick

**sulky** /ˈsʌlkɪ/ ❶ *adj.* schmollend; eingeschnappt (*ugs.*). ❷ *n.* (*Horseracing*) Sulky, *das*

**sullen** /ˈsʌlən/ *adj.* mürrisch; verdrießlich; (*fig.*) düster ‹Himmel›

**sullenly** /ˈsʌlənlɪ/ *adv.* mürrisch; verdrießlich

**sullenness** /ˈsʌlənnɪs/ *n.*, *no pl.* Verdrießlichkeit, *die*

**sully** /ˈsʌlɪ/ *v.t.* (*formal*) besudeln (*geh.*)

**sulphate** /ˈsʌlfeɪt/ *n.* Sulfat, *das*

**sulphide** /ˈsʌlfaɪd/ *n.* Sulfid, *das*

**sulphite** /ˈsʌlfaɪt/ *n.* Sulfit, *das*

**sulphonamide** /sʌlˈfɒnəmaɪd/ *n.* Sulfonamid, *das*

**sulphur** /ˈsʌlfə(r)/ *n.* Schwefel, *der*

**sulphuric** /sʌlˈfjʊərɪk/ *adj.* **~ acid** Schwefelsäure, *die*

**sultan** /ˈsʌltən/ *n.* Sultan, *der*

**sultana** /sʌlˈtɑːnə/ *n.* Ⓐ (*raisin*) Sultanine, *die;* Ⓑ (*wife of sultan*) Sultanin, *die*

**sultriness** /ˈsʌltrɪnɪs/ *n.*, *no pl.* Schwüle, *die;* (*fig.: sensuality*) Sinnlichkeit, *die*

**sultry** /ˈsʌltrɪ/ *adj.* schwül ‹Wetter, Tag, Atmosphäre›; (*fig.: sensual*) sinnlich; schwül ‹Schönheit›

**sum** /sʌm/ ❶ *n.* Ⓐ (*total amount, lit. or fig.*) Summe, *die* (**of** aus); **~ [total]** Ergebnis, *das;* **that was the ~ total of our achievements** *or* **of what we achieved** das war alles, was wir erreicht haben; **in ~:** summa summarum; Ⓑ (*amount of money*) Summe, *die;* **a cheque for this ~:** ein Scheck über diesen Betrag; ⇒ *also* **lump sum**; Ⓒ (*Arithmetic*) Rechenaufgabe, *die;* **do ~s** rechnen; **she is good at ~s** sie kann gut rechnen; sie ist gut im Rechnen. ❷ *v.t.*, **-mm-** addieren

**~ 'up** ❶ *v.t.* Ⓐ zusammenfassen; Ⓑ (*Brit.: assess*) einschätzen; **this ~med him up perfectly** damit war er treffend charakterisiert. ❷ *v.i.* ein Fazit ziehen; ‹Richter:› resümieren; **in ~ming up, I should like to ...:** zusammenfassend möchte ich ...

**sumac[h]** /ˈsuːmæk, ˈʃuːmæk, ˈsjuːmæk/ *n.* Sumach, *der*

**summarily** /ˈsʌmərɪlɪ/ *adv.* Ⓐ (*shortly*) knapp; Ⓑ (*without formalities or delay*) summarisch; **~ dismissed** fristlos entlassen; **~ convicted** (*Law*) im summarischen Verfahren verurteilt

**summarize** /ˈsʌməraɪz/ *v.t.* zusammenfassen

**summary** /ˈsʌmərɪ/ ❶ *adj.* Ⓐ (*short*) knapp; Ⓑ (*without formalities or delay*) summarisch (*geh.*); fristlos ‹Entlassung›; (*Law*) ~ **justice/jurisdiction** Schnelljustiz, *die;* ~ **conviction** Verurteilung im summarischen Verfahren (*Rechtsw.*). ❷ *n.* Zusammenfassung, *die*

**summer** /ˈsʌmə(r)/ ❶ *n.* Ⓐ ▶ 1504 Sommer, *der;* **in [the]** ~: im Sommer; **in early/late** ~: im Früh-/Spätsommer; **last/next** ~: letzten/nächsten Sommer; **a** ~**'s day/night** ein Sommertag/eine Sommernacht; **in the** ~ **of 1983, in** ~ **1983** im Sommer 1983; **two** ~**s ago we went to France** im Sommer vor zwei Jahren waren wir in Frankreich; ⇒ *also* **Indian summer**; **solstice** A; Ⓑ *in pl.* (*literary: years*) Lenze (*geh.*). ❷ *attrib. adj.* Sommer-

**summer:** ~ **house** *n.* [Garten]laube, *die;* ~ **ˈlightning** *n.* Wetterleuchten, *das;* ~ **ˈpudding** *n.* (*Brit.*) *Süßspeise aus Kompott und Weißbrot;* ~ **school** *n.* Sommerkurs, *der;* ~ **term** *n.* Sommerhalbjahr, *das;* **S**~ **Time** *n.* (*Brit.: for daylight saving*) die Sommerzeit; ~**time** *n.* (*season*) Sommer, *der;* ~ **visitor** *n.* Sommergast, *der;* ~ **weight** *adj.* (*Textiles*) [sommerlich] leicht; Sommer-

**summery** /ˈsʌmərɪ/ *adj.* sommerlich

**summing-up** /sʌmɪŋˈʌp/ *n.* Zusammenfassung, *die*

**summit** /ˈsʌmɪt/ *n.* Ⓐ (*peak, lit. or fig.*) Gipfel, *der;* **he was at the** ~ **of his power** er stand auf dem Gipfel[punkt] seiner Macht; Ⓑ (*discussion*) Gipfel, *der;* ~ **conference/meeting** Gipfelkonferenz, *die/* -treffen, *das;* **at** ~ **level** auf höchster Ebene

**summitry** /ˈsʌmɪtrɪ/ *n.* Gipfeldiplomatie, *die*

**summon** /ˈsʌmən/ *v.t.* Ⓐ (*call upon*) rufen (**to** zu); holen ‹Hilfe›; zusammenrufen ‹Aktionäre›; Ⓑ (*call by authority*) zu sich zitieren; einberufen ‹Parlament›; **she was** ~**ed to the presence of the Queen** sie wurde zur Königin befohlen (*veralt.*); Ⓒ (*Law: to court*) vorladen ‹Angeklagten, Zeugen›; Ⓓ ~ **sb. to do sth.** jmdn. auffordern, etw. zu tun

~ **ˈup** *v.t.* aufbringen ‹Mut, Kräfte, Energie, Begeisterung›

**summons** /ˈsʌmənz/ ❶ *n.* Ⓐ Aufforderung, *die;* **receive a** ~ **from sb. to do sth.** von jmdm. aufgefordert werden, etw. zu tun; Ⓑ (*Law*) Vorladung, *die;* **serve a** ~ **on sb.** jmdm. eine Vorladung zustellen. ❷ *v.t.* (*Law*) ~ **sb. to appear in court** jmdn. gerichtlich vorladen *od.* vor Gericht laden

**sumo** /ˈsuːməʊ/ *n., pl.* ~**s:** ~ **[wrestling]** Sumo, *das;* ~ **[wrestler]** Sumokämpfer, *der*

**sump** /sʌmp/ *n.* Ⓐ (*Brit. Motor Veh.*) Ölwanne, *die;* Ⓑ (*Mining*) Sumpf, *der*

**sumptuous** /ˈsʌmptjʊəs/ *adj.* üppig; luxuriös ‹Einband, Möbel, Kleidung›

**sumptuously** /ˈsʌmptjʊəslɪ/ *adv.* üppig; luxuriös ‹eingerichtet›

**sumptuousness** /ˈsʌmptjʊəsnɪs/ *n., no pl.* Üppigkeit, *die;* **the** ~ **of the binding/furnishings** der luxuriöse Einband/die luxuriöse Einrichtung

**sun** /sʌn/ ❶ *n.* Sonne, *die;* **rise with the** ~: in aller Herrgottsfrühe aufstehen; **a place in the** ~ (*fig.*) ein Platz an der Sonne; **catch the** ~ (*be in a sunny position*) viel Sonne abbekommen; (*get* ~*burnt*) einen Sonnenbrand bekommen; **a touch of the** ~: ein leichter Sonnenstich; **under the** ~ (*fig.*) auf der Welt; **chat about everything under the** ~: über alles Mögliche schwatzen; **there is nothing new under the** ~: es gibt nichts Neues unter der Sonne; ⇒ *also* **hay**; **midnight sun**. ❷ *v. refl.*, **-nn-** (*lit. or fig.*) sich sonnen

**Sun.** *abbr.* ▶ 1056 **Sunday** So.

**sun:** ~**baked** *adj.* an der Sonne getrocknet ‹Ziegel›; ausgedörrt ‹Landschaft, Prärie usw.›; ~**bathe** *v.i.* sonnenbaden; ~**bather** *n.* Sonnenbadende, *der/die;* ~**bathing** *n.* Sonnenbaden, *das;* ~**beam** *n.* Sonnenstrahl, *der;* ~**bed** *n.* (*with UV lamp*) Sonnenbank, *die;* (*in garden etc.*) Gartenliege, *die;* ~**belt** *n.* (*Amer.*) Sonnengürtel, *der; die südlichen Staaten der USA;* ~**blind** *n.* Markise, *die;* ~**block** *n.* Sonnenschutzcreme, *die* [mit hohem Lichtschutzfaktor]; Sunblocker, *der;* ~ **bonnet** *n.* Sonnenhäubchen, *das;* ~**burn** ❶ *n.* Sonnenbrand, *der;* ❷ *v.i.* **my skin** ~**burns/I** ~**burn very easily** ich kriege sehr leicht einen Sonnenbrand; ~**burnt** *adj.* Ⓐ (*suffering from* ~*burn*) **be** ~**burnt** einen Sonnenbrand haben; **have a** ~**burnt back/face** einen Sonnenbrand auf dem Rücken/im Gesicht haben; **get badly** ~**burnt** einen schlimmen Sonnenbrand bekommen; Ⓑ (*tanned*) sonnenverbrannt ‹Person, Gesicht usw.›; ~**cream** *n.* Sonnencreme, *die*

**sundae** /ˈsʌndeɪ, ˈsʌndɪ/ *n.* **[ice cream]** ~: Eisbecher, *der*

**Sunday** /ˈsʌndeɪ, ˈsʌndɪ/ ▶ 1056 ❶ *n.* Ⓐ Sonntag, *der;* ~ **opening** die sonntägliche Öffnung (**of** von); ~ **opening is allowed** es darf [auch] sonntags geöffnet werden; ~ **trading** sonntägliche Ladenöffnung; **never in a month of** ~**s** nie im Leben; Ⓑ *in pl.* (*newspapers*) Sonntagszeitungen *Pl.* ❷ *adv.* (*coll.*) **she comes** ~**s** sie kommt sonntags. ⇒ *also* **best** 3 B; **Friday**

**Sunday:** ~ **ˈdriver** *n.* (*derog.*) Sonntagsfahrer, *der/*-fahrerin, *die* (*abwertend*); ~ **painter** *n.* Sonntagsmaler, *der/*-malerin, *die;* ~ **school** *n.* Sonntagsschule, *die;* ≈ Kindergottesdienst, *der*

**ˈsun deck** *n.* Sonnendeck, *das*

**sunder** /ˈsʌndə(r)/ (*arch./literary*) *v.t.* brechen

**sun:** ~**dew** *n.* (*Bot.*) Sonnentau, *der;* ~**dial** *n.* Sonnenuhr, *die;* ~**down** ⇒ **sunset**; ~**downer** /ˈsʌndaʊnə(r)/ *n.* (*Austral.*) Pennbruder, *der* (*ugs.*); ~**-drenched** *adj.* sonnenüberflutet (*geh.*); ~**dress** *n.* Strand- *od.* Sonnenkleid, *das;* ~**-dried** *adj.* an der Sonne getrocknet

**sundry** /ˈsʌndrɪ/ ❶ *adj.* verschieden; ~ **articles** verschiedene *od.* diverse Artikel. ❷ *n. in pl.* Verschiedenes; Diverses; ⇒ *also* **all** 2 A

**sun:** ~**fast** *adj.* (*Amer.*) lichtecht ‹Farben›; ~**fish** *n.* Sonnen-, Mondfisch, *der;* ~**flower** *n.* Sonnenblume, *die;* ~**flower seeds** Sonnenblumenkerne

**sung** ⇒ **sing** 1, 2

**sun:** ~**glasses** *n. pl.* Sonnenbrille, *die;* ~ **god** *n.* Sonnengott, *der;* ~**hat** *n.* Sonnenhut, *der;* ~ **helmet** *n.* Tropenhelm, *der*

**sunk** ⇒ **sink** 2, 3

**sunken** /ˈsʌŋkn/ *adj.* versunken ‹Schatz›; gesunken ‹Schiff›; eingefallen ‹Augen, Wangen›; tiefer liegend ‹Garten, Zimmer›; in den Boden eingelassen ‹Badewanne›

**sunlamp** *n.* Höhensonne, *die*

**sunless** /ˈsʌnlɪs/ *adj.* ‹Ecke, Stelle, Tal› wo die Sonne nie hinkommt; trübe ‹Tag›

**sun:** ~**light** *n.* Sonnenlicht, *das;* **come into the** ~**light!** komm in die Sonne!; ~**lit** *adj.* sonnenbeschienen ‹Landschaft›; sonnig ‹Zimmer, Garten›; ~ **lounge** *n.* Veranda, *die*

**Sunni** /ˈsʌnɪ/ *n.* (*Muslim Relig.*) Sunnit, *der/* Sunnitin, *die; attrib.* sunnitisch

**sunnily** /ˈsʌnɪlɪ/ *adv.* lustig; freundlich

**Sunnite** /ˈsʌnaɪt/ *n.* (*Muslim Relig.*) Sunnit, *der/*Sunnitin, *die*

**sunny** /ˈsʌnɪ/ *adj.* Ⓐ sonnig; ~ **intervals** Aufheiterungen; **the** ~ **side of the house/street** die Sonnenseite des Hauses/der Straße; ~ **side up** ‹Spiegelei› mit dem Gelben nach oben; Ⓑ (*cheery*) fröhlich ‹Wesen, Lächeln›; **have a** ~ **disposition** eine Frohnatur sein

**sun:** ~ **protection factor** *n.* Lichtschutzfaktor, *der;* ~**ray** *n.* Sonnenstrahl, *der;* ~**ray treatment** *n.* Bestrahlung, *die;* ~**rise** *n.* Sonnenaufgang, *der;* **at** ~**rise** bei Sonnenaufgang; *attrib.* ~**rise industry** Zukunftsindustrie, *die;* ~**roof** *n.* Schiebedach, *das;* ~**seeker** *n.* Sonnenhungrige, *der/die;* ~**set** *n.* Sonnenuntergang, *der;* **at** ~**set** bei Sonnenuntergang; ~**shade** *n.* Sonnenschirm, *der;* (*awning*) Markise, *die;* ~**shine** *n.* Ⓐ Sonnenschein, *der;* **sit in the** ~**shine** in der Sonne sitzen; Ⓑ (*joc.: as form of address*) (*to child*) Kleiner/Kleine; (*between men*) Kumpel (*ugs.*); ~**shine roof** ⇒ **sunroof**; ~**spot** *n.* Ⓐ (*Astron.*) Sonnenfleck, *der;* Ⓑ (*place*) Sonnenparadies, *das;* ~**stroke** *n.* Sonnenstich, *der;* **suffer from/get** ~**stroke** einen Sonnenstich haben/bekommen; ~**tan** *n.* [Sonnen]bräune, *die;* **get a** ~**tan** braun werden; ~**tan lotion** *n.* Sonnencreme, *die;* ~**tanned** *adj.* braun [gebrannt]; sonnengebräunt (*geh.*); ~**tan oil** *n.* Sonnenöl, *das;* ~**top** *n.* Sonnentop, *das;* ~**trap** *n.* sonniges Plätzchen; ~**up** (*Amer.*) ⇒ ~**rise**; ~ **visor** *n.* Blendschirm, *der;* ~ **worshipper** *n.* (*lit./joc.*) Sonnenanbeter, *der/*-anbeterin, *die*

**sup** /sʌp/ *v.t.*, **-pp-** Ⓐ (*arch.: have supper*) zu Abend essen; Ⓑ (*Scot., N. Engl.: drink*) süffeln (*ugs.*)

**super** /ˈsuːpə(r)/ (*coll.*) ❶ *n.* Ⓐ (*actor*) Statist, *der/*Statistin, *die;* Ⓑ (*Police*) ⇒ **superintendent** A. ❷ *adj.* (*Brit.*) super (*ugs.*); **you've all been really** ~ **to me** ihr wart wirklich unheimlich nett zu mir

**superabundance** /suːpərəˈbʌndəns/ *n.* Überfluss, *der;* **a** ~ **of wealth** übermäßiger Wohlstand

**superabundant** /suːpərəˈbʌndənt/ *adj.* überreichlich

**superannuate** /suːpəˈrænjʊeɪt/ *v.t.* pensionieren

**superannuated** /suːpəˈrænjʊeɪtɪd/ *adj.* pensioniert; überaltert ‹Ideen›

**superannuation** /suːpərænjʊˈeɪʃn/ *n.* Ⓐ ~ **[contribution/payment]** Beitrag zur Rentenversicherung; ~ **fund** Rentenfonds, *der;* Ⓑ (*pension*) Rente, *die*

**superb** /sʊˈpɜːb, sjuːˈpɜːb/ *adj.* einzigartig; erstklassig ‹Essen, Zustand›; **look** ~: fantastisch aussehen (*ugs.*)

**superbly** /sʊˈpɜːblɪ, sjuːˈpɜːblɪ/ *adv.* erstklassig

**superbug** /ˈsʊːpəbʌg/ *n.* (*resistant strain of bacteria*) multiresistenter Erreger

**supercargo** /ˈsuːpəkɑːgəʊ/ *n., pl.* ~**es** Superkargo, *der*

**supercharge** /ˈsuːpətʃɑːdʒ/ *v.t.* aufladen ‹Motor›; ~**d car/engine** Auto/Motor mit Kompressor

**supercharger** /ˈsuːpətʃɑːdʒə(r)/ *n.* (*Motor Veh.*) Kompressor, *der*

**supercilious** /suːpəˈsɪlɪəs/ *adj.*, **superciliously** /suːpəˈsɪlɪəslɪ/ *adv.* hochnäsig

**superciliousness** /suːpəˈsɪlɪəsnɪs/ *n., no pl.* Hochnäsigkeit, *die*

**supercomputer** /ˈsuːpəkəmpjuːtə(r)/ *n.* Supercomputer, *der*

**superconducting** /suːpəkɒnˈdʌktɪŋ/ *adj.* (*Phys.*) supraleitend

**superconductivity** /suːpəkɒndəkˈtɪvɪtɪ/ *n.* (*Phys.*) Supraleitfähigkeit, *die*

**superconductor** /suːpəkənˈdʌktə(r)/ *n.* (*Phys.*) Supraleiter, *der*

**supercool** /ˈsuːpəkuːl/ *v.t.* (*Phys.*) unterkühlen

**super-duper** /ˈsuːpəduːpə(r)/ *adj.* (*Brit. coll.*) Superklasse- (*ugs.*); **be** ~: Superklasse sein (*ugs.*)

**superego** /suːpərˈiːgəʊ, suːpərˈegəʊ/ *n., pl.* ~**s** (*Psych.*) Über-Ich, *das*

**superficial** /suːpəˈfɪʃl/ *adj.* (*also fig.*) oberflächlich; leicht ‹Änderung, Schaden›; äußerlich ‹Ähnlichkeit›

**superficiality** /suːpəfɪʃɪˈælɪtɪ/ *n.* Oberflächlichkeit, *die*

**superficially** /suːpəˈfɪʃəlɪ/ *adv.* an der Oberfläche; ‹Thema› oberflächlich ‹behandeln›; äußerlich ‹ähnlich sein›

**superfine** /ˈsuːpəfaɪn/ *adj.* Ⓐ (*of extra quality*) hochfein; Ⓑ (*excessively fine*) hauchdünn ‹Unterschied›

**superfluity** /suːpəˈfluːɪtɪ/ *n.* Ⓐ Überflüssigkeit, *die;* Ⓑ (*amount*) Überfluss, *der* (**of** an + *Dat.*)

**superfluous** /sʊˈpɜːflʊəs, sjuːˈpɜːflʊəs/ *adj.* überflüssig

**superfluously** /sʊˈpɜːflʊəslɪ, sjuːˈpɜːflʊəslɪ/ *adv.* überflüssigerweise

**superfluousness** /sʊˈpɜːflʊəsnɪs, sjuːˈpɜːflʊəsnɪs/ *n., no pl.* Überflüssigkeit, *die*

**superglue** /ˈsuːpəgluː/ *n.* Sekundenkleber, *der*

**supergrass** /'su:pəgrɑ:s/ *n.* (*Journ.*) Superspitzel, *der* (*abwertend*)

**superheat** /su:pə'hi:t/ *v.t.* überhitzen

**superhighway** /'su:pəhaɪweɪ/ *n.* Ⓐ (*Amer.*) Autobahn, *die;* Ⓑ (*Computing*) Datenautobahn, *die*

**superhuman** /su:pə'hju:mən/ *adj.* übermenschlich

**superimpose** /su:pərɪm'pəʊz/ *v.t.* aufbringen ‹Schicht usw.›; aufkopieren ‹Bild›; **~ a on b** a auf b legen; (*fig.*) b mit a überlagern; **be ~d on sth.** (*state, lit. or fig.*) etw. überlagern

**superintend** /su:pərɪn'tend/ *v.t.* überwachen; beaufsichtigen

**superintendent** /su:pərɪn'tendənt/ *n.* Ⓐ (*Brit. Police*) Kommissar, *der*/Kommissarin, *die;* (*Amer. Police*) [Polizei]präsident, *der*/-präsidentin, *die;* Ⓑ (*of hostel*) Leiter, *der*/Leiterin, *die;* **~ of schools** ≈ Schulrat, *der*/-rätin, *die;* Ⓒ (*Amer.: caretaker*) Hausverwalter, *der*/-verwalterin, *die*

**superior** /su:'pɪərɪə(r), sju:'pɪərɪə(r), sʊ'pɪərɪə(r)/ ❶ *adj.* Ⓐ (*of higher quality*) besonders gut ‹Restaurant, Qualität, Stoff›; überlegen ‹handwerkliches Können, Technik, Intelligenz›; **he thinks he is ~ to us** er hält sich für besser *od.* etwas Besseres als wir; **this car is ~ in speed to mine** dieser Wagen ist meinem an Geschwindigkeit überlegen; Ⓑ (*having higher rank*) höher… ‹Stellung, Rang, Gericht›; **be ~ to sb.** einen höheren Rang als jmd. haben; Ⓒ (*greater in number*) zahlenmäßig überlegen ‹Truppen›; **the enemy's ~ numbers** die zahlenmäßige Überlegenheit des Feindes; Ⓓ (*supercilious*) überlegen; hochnäsig (*abwertend*); Ⓔ (*not influenced*) **be ~ to sth.** über etw. (*Dat.*) stehen; Ⓕ (*Printing*) hochgestellt ‹Zahl, Buchstabe›.
❷ *n.* Ⓐ (*sb. higher in rank*) Vorgesetzte, *der/die;* Ⓑ (*sb. better*) Überlegene, *der/die;* **he has no ~ in courage** keiner hat mehr Mut als er

**superiority** /su:pɪərɪ'ɒrɪtɪ, sju:pɪərɪ'ɒrɪtɪ, sʊpɪərɪ'ɒrɪtɪ/ *n.* Überlegenheit, *die* (**to** über + *Akk.*); (*of goods*) besondere Qualität; (*haughtiness*) Hochnäsigkeit, *die;* **his ~ in talent** sein größeres Talent

**superlative** /su:'pɜ:lətɪv, sju:'pɜ:lətɪv/ ❶ *adj.* Ⓐ unübertrefflich; einmalig gut; Ⓑ (*Ling.*) superlativisch; **the ~ degree** der Superlativ; die zweite Steigerungsstufe; **a ~ adjective/adverb** ein Adjektiv/Adverb im Superlativ. ❷ *n.* (*Ling.*) Superlativ, *der*

**superlatively** /su:'pɜ:lətɪvlɪ, sju:'pɜ:lətɪvlɪ/ *adv.* einmalig gut

**superman** /'su:pəmæn/ *n., pl.* **supermen** /'su:pəmen/ Supermann, *der;* (*Philos., Lit.*) Übermensch, *der*

**supermarket** /'su:pəmɑ:kɪt/ *n.* Supermarkt, *der*

**supermodel** /'su:pəmɒdl/*n.* Supermodel, *das*

**supernatural** /su:pə'nætʃərl/ *adj.* übernatürlich; **the ~:** das Übernatürliche

**supernaturally** /su:pə'nætʃərəlɪ/ *adv.* auf übernatürliche Weise

**supernova** /su:pə'nəʊvə/ *n., pl.* **~e** /su:pə'nəʊvi:/ *or* **~s** (*Astron.*) Supernova, *die*

**supernumerary** /su:pə'nju:mərərɪ/ ❶ *adj.* überzählig. ❷ *n.* zusätzliche Arbeitskraft; (*actor*) Statist, *der*/Statistin, *die*

**superpose** /su:pə'pəʊz/ ⇒ **superimpose**

**superpower** /'su:pəpaʊə(r)/ *n.* (*Polit.*) Supermacht, *die*

**superscript** /'su:pəskrɪpt/ ❶ *n.* hochgestelltes Zeichen. ❷ *adj.* hochgestellt

**supersede** /su:pə'si:d/ *v.t.* ablösen (**by** durch); **old ~d ideas** alte, überholte Vorstellungen

**supersonic** /su:pə'sɒnɪk/ *adj.* Überschall-; **go ~:** die Schallmauer durchbrechen

**superstar** /'su:pəstɑ:(r)/ *n.* Superstar, *der*

**superstition** /su:pə'stɪʃn/ *n.* (*lit. or fig.*) Aberglaube, *der;* **~s** abergläubische Vorstellungen; (*religious practices*) abergläubische Praktiken

**superstitious** /su:pə'stɪʃəs/ *adj.*, **superstitiously** /su:pə'stɪʃəslɪ/ *adv.* abergläubisch

**superstore** /'su:pəstɔ:(r)/ *n.* Großmarkt, *der*

**superstructure** /'su:pəstrʌktʃə(r)/ *n.* Ⓐ Aufbau, *der;* Ⓑ (*Sociol.*) Überbau, *der*

**supertanker** /'su:pətæŋkə(r)/ *n.* Supertanker, *der*

**supertax** /'su:pətæks/ *n.* Ergänzungsabgabe *od.* -steuer, *die*

**supertonic** /su:pə'tɒnɪk/ *n.* (*Mus.*) zweite Stufe; Subdominantparallele, *die* (*fachspr.*)

**superunleaded** /su:pəʌn'ledɪd/ ❶ *adj.* **~ petrol** Superbleifrei. ❷ *n.* Superbleifrei, *das*

**supervene** /su:pə'vi:n/ *v.i.* dazwischenkommen

**supervise** /'su:pəvaɪz/ *v.t.* beaufsichtigen

**supervision** /su:pə'vɪʒn/ *n.* Aufsicht, *die*

**supervisor** /'su:pəvaɪzə(r)/ *n.* ▶ **1261** Aufseher, *der*/Aufseherin, *die;* (*for Ph. D. thesis*) Doktorvater, *der;* (*Amer.: school officer*) Fachbereichsleiter, *der*/-leiterin, *die;* **works ~:** Vorarbeiter, *der*/-arbeiterin, *die;* **office ~:** Bürovorsteher, *der*/-vorsteherin, *die*

**supervisory** /'su:pəvaɪzərɪ/ *adj.* Aufsichts-

**supine** /'su:paɪn, 'sju:paɪn/ *adj.* **he was** *or* **lay ~:** er lag auf dem Rücken; **assume a ~ position** sich auf den Rücken legen; **~ acceptance** (*fig.*) gleichgültige Hinnahme

**supper** /'sʌpə(r)/ *n.* Abendessen, *das;* (*simpler meal*) Abendbrot, *das;* **have** *or* **eat [one's] ~:** zu Abend essen; **be at** *or* **eating** *or* **having [one's] ~:** beim Abendessen/Abendbrot sein; zu Abend essen; **sing for one's ~** (*fig.*) etwas für sein Geld tun (*ugs.*); **The Last S~:** das [letzte] Abendmahl; ⇒ *also* **Lord** 1 B

**'suppertime** *n.* Abendbrotzeit, *die;* **it's ~:** es ist Zeit zum Abendessen

**supplant** /sə'plɑ:nt/ *v.t.* ablösen, ersetzen (**by** durch); ausstechen ‹Widersacher, Rivalen›

**supple** /'sʌpl/ *adj.* geschmeidig

**supplement** ❶ /'sʌplɪmənt/ *n.* Ⓐ Ergänzung, *die* (**to** + *Gen.*); (*addition*) Zusatz, *der;* **vitamin ~:** Vitaminpräparat, *das;* Ⓑ (*of book*) Nachtrag, *der;* (*separate volume*) Supplement, *das;* Nachtragsband, *der;* (*of newspaper*) Beilage, *die;* Ⓒ (*to fare etc.*) Zuschlag, *der.* ❷ /'sʌplɪmənt, sʌplɪ'ment/ *v.t.* ergänzen

**supplementary** /sʌplɪ'mentərɪ/ *adj.* zusätzlich; Zusatz‹rente, -frage›; **~ fare/charge** Zuschlag, *der;* ⇒ *also* **benefit** 1 B

**suppleness** /'sʌplnɪs/ *n., no pl.* Geschmeidigkeit, *die*

**supplicant** /'sʌplɪkənt/ *n.* Bittsteller, *der*/-stellerin, *die*

**supplicate** /'sʌplɪkeɪt/ ❶ *v.t.* anflehen. ❷ *v.i.* flehen (**for** um)

**supplication** /sʌplɪ'keɪʃn/ *n.* Flehen, *das;* **in ~:** flehentlich

**supplier** /sə'plaɪə(r)/ *n.* (*Commerc.*) Lieferant, *der*/Lieferantin, *die*

**supply** /sə'plaɪ/ ❶ *v.t.* Ⓐ liefern ‹Waren usw.›; sorgen für ‹Unterkunft›; zur Verfügung stellen ‹Lehrmittel, Arbeitskleidung usw.›; beliefern ‹Kunden, Geschäft›; versorgen ‹System›; **~ sth. to sb., ~ sb. with sth.** jmdn. mit etw. versorgen/ (*Commerc.*) beliefern; **could you ~ me with the tools?** könnten Sie mir das Werkzeug zur Verfügung stellen?; Ⓑ (*make good*) erfüllen ‹Nachfrage, Bedarf›; abhelfen (+ *Dat.*) ‹Mangel›.
❷ *n.* Ⓐ (*stock*) Vorräte *Pl.;* **a large ~ of food** große Lebensmittelvorräte; **a good ~ of reading matter** ausreichende Lektüre; **new supplies of shoes** neue Schuhlieferungen; **military/medical supplies** militärischer/medizinischer Nachschub; **~ and demand** (*Econ.*) Angebot und Nachfrage; ⇒ *also* **short** 1 D; Ⓑ (*provision*) Versorgung, *die* (**of** mit); **the wholesaler has cut off our ~:** der Großhändler beliefert uns nicht mehr; **their gas ~ was cut off** ihnen ist das Gas abgestellt worden; **the blood ~ to the brain** die Versorgung des Gehirns mit Blut; Ⓒ (*Brit. Parl.*) Haushalt, *der;* **S~ Day** Tag der Verabschiedung des Parlamentshaushalts; Ⓓ **~ [teacher]** Vertretung, *die;* **be/go on ~:** Vertretung sein/als Vertretung gehen.
❸ *attrib.* Versorgungs‹schiff, -netz, -basis, -lager usw.›; **~ lines** Nachschubwege

**sup'ply-side** *adj.* (*Econ.*) angebotsseitig

**support** /sə'pɔ:t/ ❶ *v.t.* Ⓐ (*hold up*) stützen ‹Mauer, Verletzten›; (*bear weight of*) tragen ‹Dach›; Ⓑ (*give strength to*) stärken; **~ sb. in his struggle** jmdn. in seinem Kampf bestärken; Ⓒ unterstützen ‹Politik, Verein›; (*Footb.*) **~ Spurs** Spurs-Fan sein; Ⓓ (*give money to*) unterstützen; spenden für; Ⓔ (*provide for*) ernähren ‹Familie, sich selbst›; Ⓕ (*Cinemat., Theatre: take secondary part to*) **~ed by …:** mit … in weiteren Rollen; Ⓖ (*bring facts to confirm*) stützen ‹Theorie, Anspruch, Behauptung›; (*speak in favour of*) befürworten ‹Streik, Maßnahme›; Ⓗ (*represent adequately*) verkörpern ‹Rolle›; Ⓘ (*usu. neg.: tolerate*) ertragen; hinnehmen ‹Dreistigkeit usw.›.
❷ *n.* Ⓐ Unterstützung, *die;* **give ~ to sb./sth.** jmdn./etw. unterstützen; **in ~:** zur Unterstützung; **speak in ~ of sb./sth.** jmdn. unterstützen/etw. befürworten; Ⓑ (*money*) Unterhalt, *der;* Ⓒ (*sb./sth. that ~s*) Stütze, *die;* **hold on to sb./sth. for ~:** sich an jmdm./etw. festhalten

**supportable** /sə'pɔ:təbl/ *adj.* vertretbar; erträglich ‹Lärm›

**supporter** /sə'pɔ:tə(r)/ *n.* Ⓐ Anhänger, *der*/Anhängerin, *die;* **a football ~:** ein Fußballfan; **~s of a strike** Befürworter eines Streiks; Ⓑ (*Her.*) Schildhalter, *der*

**sup'porters' club** *n.* (*Sport*) Fanklub, *der*

**supporting** /sə'pɔ:tɪŋ/ *adj.* (*Cinemat., Theatre*) **~ role** Nebenrolle, *die;* **the ~ cast** die Darsteller der Nebenrollen; **~ actor/actress** Schauspieler/-spielerin in einer Nebenrolle; **~ film** Vorfilm, *der;* Beifilm, *der*

**supportive** /sə'pɔ:tɪv/ *adj.* hilfreich; **be very ~ [to sb.]** [jmdm.] eine große Hilfe *od.* Stütze sein

**sup'port price** *n.* (*Finance*) Stützungspreis, *der*

**suppose** /sə'pəʊz/ *v.t.* Ⓐ (*assume*) annehmen; **~** *or* **supposing [that] he …:** angenommen, [dass] er …; **always supposing that …:** immer vorausgesetzt, dass …; **~ we wait until tomorrow/went for a walk** wir könnten eigentlich bis morgen warten/einen Spaziergang machen; **~ we change the subject** reden wir lieber von etwas anderem; Ⓑ (*presume*) vermuten; **I ~d she was in Glasgow** ich vermutete sie in Glasgow; **I ~ she will be here by ten** sie wird wohl bis um zehn kommen; **whom do you ~ he meant by that remark?** wen, glaubst du, hat er mit der Bemerkung gemeint?; **I don't ~ you have an onion to spare?** Sie haben wohl nicht zufällig eine Zwiebel übrig?; **We're not going to manage it, are we? — I ~ not** Wir werden es wohl nicht schaffen — Ich glaube kaum; **I ~ so** ich nehme es an; (*doubtfully*) ja, vermutlich; (*more confidently*) ich glaube schon; **I ~ I shall have to tell you** ich werde es dir wohl sagen müssen; Ⓒ **be ~d to do/be sth.** (*be generally believed to do/be sth.*) etw. tun/sein sollen; **cats are ~d to have nine lives** Katzen sollen angeblich neun Leben haben; **that restaurant is ~d to be quite cheap** das Restaurant soll ziemlich billig sein; Ⓓ (*allow*) **you are not ~d to do that/to kick people** das darfst du nicht/du darfst andere Leute nicht treten!; **I'm not ~d to be here** ich dürfte eigentlich gar nicht hier sein; Ⓔ (*presuppose*) voraussetzen

**supposed** /sə'pəʊzd/ *attrib. adj.* mutmaßlich

**supposedly** /sə'pəʊzɪdlɪ/ *adv.* angeblich

**supposition** /sʌpə'zɪʃn/ *n.* Annahme, *die;* Vermutung, *die;* **be based on ~:** auf Annahmen *od.* Vermutungen beruhen

**suppository** /sə'pɒzɪtərɪ/ *n.* (*Med.*) Zäpfchen, *das;* Suppositorium, *das* (*fachspr.*)

**suppress** /sə'pres/ *v.t.* Ⓐ unterdrücken; (*stop*) zum Stillstand bringen ‹Blutung›; verbieten ‹Zeitung›; Ⓑ (*Electr.*) entstören ‹Zündung, Elektrogerät›; ausschalten ‹Störung›

**suppression** /sə'preʃn/ *n.* Ⓐ Unterdrückung, *die;* Ⓑ (*Electr.*) Entstörung, *die;* (*of interference*) Ausschaltung, *die*

**suppressor** /sə'presə(r)/ *n.* (*Electr.*) Entstörgerät, *das*

**suppurate** /'sʌpjʊreɪt/ *v.i.* (*Med.*) eitern

**suppuration** /sʌpjʊ'reɪʃn/ *n.* (*Med.*) (*formation of pus*) Eiterung, *die;* (*discharge of pus*) Eitern, *das*

**supremacy** /su:'preməsɪ, sju:'preməsɪ/ *n., no pl.* Ⓐ (*supreme authority*) Souveränität, *die;* Ⓑ (*superiority*) Überlegenheit, *die;* **air/naval ~:** Luft-/Seeherrschaft, *die;* **gain ~ over others** Vorherrschaft *od.* eine Vormachtstellung über andere erlangen; ⇒ *also* **white supremacy**

**supreme** /su:'pri:m, sju:'pri:m/ ❶ *adj.* Ⓐ (*highest*) höchst...; **the S~ Being** das Höchste Wesen; **S~ Court** (*Law*) Oberster Gerichtshof; **~ end** *or* **good** höchstes Gut; ⇒ *also* **Soviet** 2; Ⓑ (*ultimate*) **the ~ test** die schwierigste Probe; **make the ~ sacrifice** sein Leben zum Opfer bringen; Ⓒ (*greatest*) höchst...; größt... ‹Stunde›; **a ~ moment** ein unvergleichlicher Augenblick; **he is ~ among musicians** er ist der größte aller Musiker; **a ~ artist** ein unübertroffener Künstler; **reign ~:** souverän herrschen; **confusion reigns ~:** es herrscht große Verwirrung. ❷ *n.* (*Gastr.*) **chicken ~:** Hühnchen in Rahmsoße; **~ of sole** Seezunge in Rahmsoße

**suprême** /su:'prem/ ⇒ **supreme** 2

**supremely** /su:'pri:mlɪ, sju:'pri:mlɪ/ *adv.* äußerst; unvergleichlich ‹schön›

**supremo** /su:'pri:məʊ, sju:'pri:məʊ/ *n., pl.* **~s** (*Brit.*) Boss, *der* (*ugs.*)

**Supt.** *abbr.* **Superintendent**

**sura[h]** /'sʊərə/ *n.* (*Muslim Relig.*) Sure, *die*

**surcharge** /'sɜ:tʃɑ:dʒ/ ❶ *n.* Ⓐ (*extra cost*) Zuschlag, *der;* Ⓑ (*on postage stamp*) [Porto]aufdruck, *der;* Ⓒ (*fine for false tax return*) Steuerzuschlag, *der.* ❷ *v.t.* Ⓐ **~ sb. [10%]** jmdn. mit einem Zuschlag [von 10%] belegen; Ⓑ (*overprint*) überdrucken ‹Briefmarke›

**surcoat** /'sɜ:kəʊt/ *n.* (*arch.*) Überjacke, *die*

**surd** /sɜ:d/ *n.* (*Math.*) Wurzelausdruck, *der*

**sure** /ʃʊə(r)/ ❶ *adj.* Ⓐ (*confident*) sicher; **be ~ of sth.** sich (*Dat.*) einer Sache (*Gen.*) sicher sein; **you may be ~ of his honesty** du kannst dich auf seine Ehrlichkeit verlassen; **~ of oneself** selbstsicher; **he looks very ~ of himself** er macht einen sehr selbstsicheren Eindruck; **I'm not quite ~ why** ich weiß nicht genau, warum; **I can't be ~ about him** ich bin mir über ihn nicht im Klaren; **I'm ~ I didn't mean to insult you** ich wollte dich ganz bestimmt nicht beleidigen; **I'm ~ I don't know** ich weiß es ganz bestimmt nicht; **don't be too ~:** da wäre ich mir nicht so sicher; Ⓑ (*safe*) sicher; **make sth. ~:** etw. sichern; **be on ~r ground** (*lit. or fig.*) sich auf festerem Boden befinden; ⇒ *also* **slow** 1 A; Ⓒ (*certain*) sicher; **you're ~ to be welcome** Sie werden ganz sicher *od.* bestimmt willkommen sein; **it's ~ to rain** es wird bestimmt regnen; **there is ~ to be a garage** es gibt bestimmt eine Tankstelle; **don't worry, it's ~ to turn out well** keine Sorge, es wird schon alles gut gehen; **he is ~ to ask questions about the incident** er wird auf jeden Fall Fragen zu dem Vorfall stellen; Ⓓ (*undoubtedly true*) sicher; **to be ~** *expr. concession* natürlich; *expr. surprise* wirklich!; tatsächlich!; **for ~** (*coll.: without doubt*) auf jeden Fall; Ⓔ **make ~ [of sth.]** sich [einer Sache] vergewissern; (*check*) [etw.] nachprüfen; **you'd better make ~ of a seat** *or* **that you have a seat** du solltest dir einen Platz sichern; **make** *or* **be ~ you do it, be ~ to do it** (*do not fail to do it*) sieh zu, dass du es tust; (*do not forget*) vergiss nicht, es zu tun; **be ~ to write** vergiss nicht zu schreiben; **make ~ you've got everything you need** sieh zu, dass du alles hast, was du brauchst; **make ~ you don't forget to do it** vergiss auf keinen Fall, es zu tun; **be ~ you finish the work by tomorrow** machen Sie die Arbeit auf jeden Fall bis morgen fertig; **be ~ not to be late** sieh zu, dass du nicht zu spät kommst; Ⓕ (*reliable*) sicher ‹Zeichen›; zuverlässig ‹Freund, Bote, Heilmittel›; **a ~ winner** ein todsicherer Tipp (*ugs.*).
❷ *adv.* Ⓐ **as ~ as ~ can be** (*coll.*) so sicher wie das Amen in der Kirche; **as ~ as I'm standing here** so wahr ich hier stehe; **~ as hell** todsicher; **~ enough** tatsächlich; **it's brandy ~ enough!** das ist tatsächlich Weinbrand!; **it's brandy ~ enough, but ...:** es ist wohl Weinbrand, aber ...; ⇒ *also* **egg**[1]; Ⓑ (*Amer. coll.: certainly*) wirklich; echt (*ugs.*); **Can you dance? — I ~ can** Kannst du tanzen? — Und ob!.
❸ *int.* **~!, ~ thing!** (*Amer.*) na klar! (*ugs.*)

**sure:** **~-fire** *attrib. adj.* (*Amer. coll.*) todsicher; **~-footed** *adj.* (*lit. or fig.*) trittsicher

**surely** /'ʃʊəlɪ/ ❶ *adv.* Ⓐ *as sentence-modifier* doch; **there is no truth in it, ~!** das kann doch gar nicht stimmen; **~ we've met before?** wir kennen uns doch, oder?; **~ you are not going out in this snowstorm?** du willst doch wohl in dem Schneesturm nicht rausgehen?; Ⓑ (*steadily*) sicher; **slowly but ~:** langsam, aber sicher; Ⓒ (*certainly*) sicherlich; **the plan will ~ fail** der Plan wird garantiert scheitern. ❷ *int.* (*Amer.*) natürlich; selbstverständlich

**sureness** /'ʃʊənɪs/ *n., no pl.* Sicherheit, *die;* **~ of purpose** Entschlossenheit, *die*

**surety** /'ʃʊərətɪ, 'ʃʊətɪ/ *n.* Bürge, *der*/Bürgin, *die;* **stand ~ for sb.** für jmdn. bürgen

**surf** /sɜ:f/ ❶ *n.* Brandung, *die.* ❷ *v.i.* Ⓐ surfen; Ⓑ (*Computing*) surfen; (*TV*) zappen. ❸ *v.t.* (*Computing, TV*) **~ the Internet** im Internet surfen; **~ the channels** sich durch die Kanäle zappen

**surface** /'sɜ:fɪs/ ❶ *n.* Ⓐ *no pl.* Oberfläche, *die;* **outer ~:** Außenfläche, *die;* **the earth's ~:** die Erdoberfläche; **on the ~ of the table** auf der Tischplatte; **the ~ of the road** die Straßendecke; **the ~ of the lake** die Seeoberfläche; **on the ~:** an der Oberfläche; (*Mining*) über Tage; Ⓑ (*outward appearance*) Oberfläche, *die;* **one never gets below the ~ with him** bei ihm bleibt alles immer oberflächlich; **on the ~:** oberflächlich betrachtet; **she remained calm on the ~:** äußerlich blieb sie ganz ruhig; **come to the ~:** an die Oberfläche kommen; ‹Taucher, Unterseeboot:› auftauchen; (*fig.*) ans Licht kommen (*fig.*); Ⓒ (*Geom.*) Fläche, *die.*
❷ *attrib. adj.* (*lacking depth*) oberflächlich.
❸ *v.i.* Ⓐ auftauchen; (*fig.*) hochkommen; ‹Untergrundbahn:› nach oben kommen; Ⓑ (*coll.: wake up, get up*) hochkommen (*ugs.*).
❹ *v.t.* mit einem Belag versehen ‹Straße›

**surface:** **~ area** *n.* Oberfläche, *die;* **~ mail** *n.* gewöhnliche Post (*die auf dem Land- bzw. Seeweg befördert wird*); **~ noise** *n.* (*on record*) Kratzen, *das;* **~ soil** *n.* oberste Bodenschicht; **~ 'tension** *n.* (*Phys.*) Oberflächenspannung, *die;* **~-to-air** *adj.* **~-to-air missile** Boden-Luft-Rakete, *die;* **~ vessel** *n.* Überwasserfahrzeug, *das;* **~ water** *n.* Oberflächenwasser, *das;* **~ worker** *n.* (*Min.*) Übertagearbeiter, *der*

**'surfboard** *n.* Surfbrett, *das*

**surfeit** /'sɜ:fɪt/ ❶ *n.* Übermaß, *das;* **a ~ of rich food** zu viel schweres Essen. ❷ *v.t.* übersättigen

**surfer** /'sɜ:fə(r)/ *n.* Surfer, *der*/Surferin, *die*

**'surf-riding** *n.* Surfen, *das*

**surge** /sɜ:dʒ/ ❶ *v.i.* ‹Wellen:› branden; ‹Fluten, Menschenmenge:› sich wälzen; ‹elektrischer Strom:› ansteigen; **anger ~d within him** Zorn wallte in ihm auf; **the crowd ~d forward** die Menschenmenge drängte nach vorn. ❷ *n.* Ⓐ (*of the sea*) Branden, *das;* Ⓑ (*of crowd*) Sichwälzen, *das;* (*of electric current*) Anstieg, *der;* Ⓒ (*fig.: of interest, enthusiasm, anger, pity*) Woge, *die*
**~ 'up** *v.i.* aufsteigen; ‹Gefühl:› aufwallen

**surgeon** /'sɜ:dʒən/ *n.* ▶ **1261** Ⓐ Chirurg, *der*/Chirurgin, *die;* Ⓑ (*Mil., Navy: medical officer*) Stabsarzt, *der*/-ärztin, *die*

**surgeon 'general** *n.* Ⓐ (*Amer. Mil.*) Generalstabsarzt, *der*/-ärztin, *die;* Ⓑ (*Amer. Admin.*) ≈ Gesundheitsminister, *der*/-ministerin, *die*

**surgery** /'sɜ:dʒərɪ/ *n.* Ⓐ *no pl., no indef. art.* Chirurgie, *die;* **need ~:** operiert werden müssen; **undergo ~:** sich einer Operation (*Dat.*) unterziehen; **be saved by ~:** durch eine Operation gerettet werden; Ⓑ (*Brit.: place*) Praxis, *die;* **doctor's/dental ~:** Arzt-/Zahnarztpraxis, *die;* Ⓒ (*Brit.: time; session*) Sprechstunde, *die;* **the times of ~:** die Sprechzeiten; **when is his ~?** wann hat er Sprechstunde?; **hold a ~** (*Brit.*) ‹Abgeordneter, Anwalt usw.:› eine Sprechstunde abhalten

**surgical** /'sɜ:dʒɪkl/ *adj.* chirurgisch; **~ treatment** Operation, *die*/Operationen; **~ gauze** Verbandsmull, *der;* **~ boot/stocking** orthopädischer Schuh/Strumpf; **~ spirit** *Methylalkohol [zur Hautdesinfektion vor Operationen];* ≈ Alkohol, *der*

**surgically** /'sɜ:dʒɪkəlɪ/ *adv.* operativ ‹behandeln, entfernen›

**surliness** /'sɜ:lɪnɪs/ *n., no pl.* Verdrießlichkeit, *die;* mürrische Art; **the ~ of his look** sein mürrischer Blick

**surly** /'sɜ:lɪ/ *adj.* mürrisch; verdrießlich

**surmise** /sə'maɪz/ ❶ *n.* Vermutung, *die;* Mutmaßung, *die.* ❷ *v.t.* mutmaßen; **she had ~d as much** das hatte sie schon vermutet. ❸ *v.i.* mutmaßen

**surmount** /sə'maʊnt/ *v.t.* Ⓐ krönen; **a shield ~ed by a crown** ein bekrönter Wappenschild; Ⓑ (*overcome*) überwinden ‹Hindernis, Schwierigkeiten›

**surmountable** /sə'maʊntəbl/ *adj.* überwindbar

**surname** /'sɜ:neɪm/ ❶ *n.* Nachname, *der;* Zuname, *der.* ❷ *v.t.* **be ~d ...** den Zunamen ... tragen

**surpass** /sə'pɑ:s/ *v.t.* übertreffen (**in** an + *Dat.*); **~ oneself** sich selbst übertreffen; **sth. ~es [sb.'s] comprehension** etw. ist [jmdm.] unbegreiflich

**surpassing** /sə'pɑ:sɪŋ/ *adj.* unvergleichlich ‹Schönheit, Leistung›

**surplice** /'sɜ:plɪs/ *n.* (*Eccl.*) Chorhemd, *das*

**surplus** /'sɜ:pləs/ ❶ *n.* Überschuss, *der* (**of** an + *Dat.*); **a ~ of coffee** Kaffeeüberschüsse *Pl.;* **army ~:** Restbestände der Armee; **army ~ store/boots** Laden für Restbestände/Schuhe aus Restbeständen der Armee; ⇒ *also* **government surplus.** ❷ *adj.* überschüssig; **be ~ to sb.'s requirements** von jmdm. nicht benötigt werden; **~ stocks** Überschüsse *Pl.*

**surprise** /sə'praɪz/ ❶ *n.* Ⓐ Überraschung, *die;* **take sb. by ~:** jmdn. überrumpeln; **the fort was taken by ~:** die Festung wurde durch Überrumpelungstaktik eingenommen; **to my great ~, much to my ~:** zu meiner großen Überraschung; sehr zu meiner Überraschung; **look up in ~:** überrascht aufblicken; **it came as a ~ to us** es war für uns eine Überraschung; **~, ~!** (*iron.*) sieh mal einer an! (*spött.*); Ⓑ *attrib.* überraschend, unerwartet ‹Besuch›; **a ~ attack/defeat** ein Überraschungsangriff/eine überraschende Niederlage; **it's to be a ~ party** die Party soll eine Überraschung sein; **~ packet** (*Brit. fig.*) Wundertüte, *die* (*scherzh.*).
❷ *v.t.* überraschen; überrumpeln ‹Feind›; **I shouldn't be ~d if ...:** es würde mich nicht wundern, wenn ...; **be ~d at sb./sth.** sich über jmdn./etw. wundern; **~ sb. into doing sth.** jmdn. dazu überrumpeln, etw. zu tun

**surprising** /sə'praɪzɪŋ/ *adj.* überraschend; **there's nothing ~ about that** daran ist nichts Überraschendes; **it's hardly ~ that ...:** es ist kaum verwunderlich, dass ...; **~ though it may seem** so erstaunlich es auch klingen mag

**surprisingly** /sə'praɪzɪŋlɪ/ *adv.* überraschend; **~ [enough], he was ...:** überraschenderweise war er ...

**surreal** /sə'ri:əl/ *adj.* surrealistisch

**surrealism** /sə'ri:əlɪzm/ *n., no pl.* Surrealismus, *der*

**surrealist** /sə'ri:əlɪst/ ❶ *n.* Surrealist, *der*/Surrealistin, *die.* ❷ *adj.* surrealistisch

**surrealistic** /səri:ə'lɪstɪk/ *adj.* surrealistisch

**surrender** /sə'rendə(r)/ ❶ *n.* Ⓐ (*submitting to enemy*) Kapitulation, *die;* Ⓑ (*giving up possession*) Aufgabe, *die;* (*of insurance policy*) Rückkauf, *der;* (*of firearms*) Abgabe, *die.* ❷ *v.i.* kapitulieren; **~ to sb.** sich jmdm. beugen; **~ to despair/pressure/panic** sich der

Verzweiflung überlassen/sich dem Druck beugen/sich zu Panik hinreißen lassen. ❸ *v.t.* [A] *(give up possession of)* aufgeben; preisgeben ‹Freiheit, Privileg›; niederlegen ‹Amt›; abgeben, aushändigen ‹Wertgegenstände›; [B] zurückkaufen ‹Versicherungspolice›. ❹ *v. refl.* sich hingeben (**to** + *Dat.*)

**sur'render value** *n.* Rückkaufswert, *der*

**surreptitious** /sʌrəp'tɪʃəs/ *adj.* heimlich; verstohlen ‹Blick›

**surreptitiously** /sʌrəp'tɪʃəslɪ/ *adv.* heimlich; verstohlen ‹blicken›

**surrogate** /'sʌrəgət/ *n.* [A] *(deputy)* Stellvertreter, *der*/-vertreterin, *die;* [B] *(substitute)* Ersatz, *der*

**surrogate 'mother** *n.* Leihmutter, *die*

**surround** /sə'raʊnd/ ❶ *v.t.* [A] *(come or be all round)* umringen; ‹Truppen, Heer:› umzingeln ‹Stadt, Feind›; [B] *(enclose, encircle)* umgeben; **be ~ed by** *or* **with sth.** von etw. umgeben sein. ❷ *n.* *(Brit.)* Umrandung, *die*

**surrounding** /sə'raʊndɪŋ/ *adj.* umliegend ‹Dörfer›; **~ area** Umgebung, *die;* **the ~ countryside** die [Landschaft in der] Umgebung

**surroundings** /sə'raʊndɪŋz/ *n. pl.* Umgebung, *die*

**surtax** /'sɜːtæks/ *n.* Ergänzungsabgabe *od.* -steuer, *die*

**surveillance** /sə'veɪləns/ *n.* Überwachung, *die;* **keep sb. under ~:** jmdn. überwachen; **be under ~:** überwacht werden

**survey** ❶ /sə'veɪ/ *v.t.* [A] *(take general view of)* betrachten; *(from high point)* überblicken ‹Landschaft, Umgebung›; [B] *(examine)* inspizieren ‹Gebäude usw.›; [C] *(assess)* bewerten ‹Situation, Problem usw.›; [D] *(Surv.)* vermessen ‹Grundstück, Land usw.›. ❷ /'sɜːveɪ/ *n.* [A] *(general view, critical inspection)* Überblick, *der* (**of** über + *Akk.*); *(of landscape)* Betrachtung, *die;* [B] *(by opinion poll)* Umfrage, *die; (by research)* Untersuchung, *die;* **conduct a ~ into sth.** eine Umfrage zu etw. veranstalten/etw. untersuchen; **a telephone ~:** eine Telefonbefragung; [C] *(Surv.)* Vermessung, *die;* [D] *(building inspection)* Inspektion, *die*

**surveying** /sə'veɪɪŋ/ *n.* [A] Landvermessung, *die;* [B] *(Constr.)* Abstecken, *das;* [C] *(profession)* **go into ~:** Landvermesser/-vermesserin werden

**surveyor** /sə'veɪə(r)/ *n.* ▶ **1261** [A] *(of building)* Gutachter, *der*/Gutachterin, *die;* ⇒ *also* **quantity surveyor;** [B] *(of land)* Landvermesser, *der*/-vermesserin, *die;* Geodät, *der*/Geodätin, *die;* [C] *(official inspector)* **S~ of Weights and Measures** Eichmeister, *der*/-meisterin, *die;* [D] *(Amer.: customs officer)* Zollbeamte, *der*/-beamtin, *die*

**survival** /sə'vaɪvl/ *n.* [A] *no pl.* Überleben, *das; (of tradition)* Fortbestand, *der; (of building)* Erhaltung, *die;* **fight for ~:** Existenzkampf, *der;* **his ~ as Foreign Minister** *(fig.)* sein politisches Überleben als Außenminister; **the ~ of the fittest** *(Biol.)* [das] Überleben der Stärkeren; [B] *(relic)* Überrest, *der*

**sur'vival kit** *n.* Notausrüstung, *die*

**survive** /sə'vaɪv/ ❶ *v.t.* überleben; **she ~d her son by 20 years** sie überlebte ihren Sohn um 20 Jahre. ❷ *v.i.* ‹Person:› überleben; ‹Schriften, Gebäude, Traditionen:› erhalten bleiben; **he'll/you'll** *etc.* **~** *(iron.)* er wirds/du wirsts *usw.* [schon] überleben

**survivor** /sə'vaɪvə(r)/ *n.* Überlebende, *der/die;* **he's a ~:** er ist nicht unterzukriegen

**sus** /sʌs/ *(Brit. coll.)* ❶ *n.* [A] *(suspect)* Verdächtige, *der/die;* [B] *(suspicion)* Verdacht, *der;* **the ~ laws** *die Gesetze, nach denen jmd. festgenommen werden darf, wenn er verdächtigt wird, eine strafbare Handlung begehen zu wollen.* ❷ *v.t.*, **-ss-** spitzkriegen *(ugs.)*; **get sb. ~sed** jmdn. durchschauen

**~ 'out** *v.t.* *(coll.)* checken *(ugs.)*; spannen *(ugs.)*

**susceptibility** /səseptɪ'bɪlɪtɪ/ *n.* [A] *(being susceptible) (to flattery, persuasion, etc.)* Empfänglichkeit, *die* (**to** für); *(to illness, injury, etc.)* Anfälligkeit, *die* (**to** für); **~ to pain** Schmerzempfindlichkeit, *die;* [B] *in pl.* *(feelings)* Feingefühl, *das*

**susceptible** /sə'septɪbl/ *adj.* [A] *(sensitive) (to flattery, persuasion, etc.)* empfänglich (**to** für); *(to illness, injury, etc.)* anfällig (**to** für); [B] *(easily influenced)* empfindsam; beeindruckbar; [C] **be ~ of sth.** etw. zulassen; **your work is ~ of improvement** Ihre Arbeit ließe sich verbessern; **~ of proof** beweisbar

**suspect** ❶ /sə'spekt/ *v.t.* [A] *(imagine to be likely)* vermuten; **~ the worst** das Schlimmste befürchten; **~ sb. to be sth., ~ that sb. is sth.** glauben *od.* vermuten, dass jmd. etw. ist; **I ~ that he doesn't really want to come** ich vermute, dass er eigentlich gar nicht kommen will; **you, I ~, don't care** dir, habe ich das Gefühl, ist das egal; [B] *(mentally accuse)* verdächtigen; **~ sb. of sth./of doing sth.** jmdn. einer Sache verdächtigen/jmdn. verdächtigen, etw. zu tun; **he is ~ed of telling lies** man verdächtigt ihn der Lüge; **~ed of drug-trafficking** des Drogenhandels verdächtig; [C] *(mistrust)* bezweifeln ‹Echtheit›; **~ sb.'s motives** jmds. Beweggründen mit Argwohn gegenüberstehen.

❷ /'sʌspekt/ *adj.* fragwürdig; suspekt *(geh.)*; verdächtig ‹Stoff, Paket, Fahrzeug›.

❸ /'sʌspekt/ *n.* Verdächtige, *der/die;* **political ~s** politisch Verdächtige; **a murder ~:** ein Mordverdächtiger/eine Mordverdächtige

**suspected** /sə'spektɪd/ *adj.* verdächtig; **there is a ~ connection between x and y** man vermutet einen Zusammenhang zwischen x und y; **~ smallpox cases, ~ cases of smallpox** Fälle mit Verdacht auf Pocken

**suspend** /sə'spend/ *v.t.* [A] *(hang up)* [auf]hängen; **be ~ed [from sth.]** [von etw.] [herab]hängen; **be ~ed in mid-air** frei in der Luft schweben; [B] *(stop, defer)* suspendieren ‹Rechte›; **~ hostilities/the publication of the magazine** Kampfhandlungen/das Erscheinen der Zeitschrift [vorübergehend] einstellen; **~ judgement** sich des Urteils enthalten; **~ the proceedings** die Verhandlungen/das Verfahren aussetzen *(Rechtsw.)*; [C] *(remove from post)* ausschließen (**from** von); sperren ‹Sportler›; vom Unterricht ausschließen ‹Schüler›; **~ sb. from duty [pending an inquiry]** jmdn. [während einer schwebenden Untersuchung] vom Dienst suspendieren

**suspended: ~ ani'mation** *n.* vorübergehender Atemstillstand; **wait in a state of ~ animation** *(fig.)* atemlos warten; **~ 'particle** *n.* *(Phys.)* schwebendes Teilchen; **~ 'sentence** *n.* *(Law)* Strafe mit Bewährung; **he was given a two-year ~ sentence** er erhielt zwei Jahre Haft auf Bewährung *(Rechtsw.)*

**suspender belt** /sə'spendə belt/ *n.* *(Brit.)* Strumpfbandgürtel, *der*

**suspenders** /sə'spendəz/ *n. pl.* [A] *(Brit.) (for stockings)* Strumpfbänder *od.* -halter; *(for socks)* Sockenhalter; [B] *(Amer.: for trousers)* Hosenträger

**suspense** /sə'spens/ *n.* Spannung, *die;* **the ~ is killing me** *(joc.)* ich komme um vor Spannung *(scherzh.)*; ich bin gespannt wie ein Regenschirm *(ugs. scherzh.)*; **keep sb. in ~:** jmdn. auf die Folter spannen

**suspension** /sə'spenʃn/ *n.* [A] *(action of debarring)* Ausschluss, *der; (from office)* Suspendierung, *die; (Sport)* Sperrung, *die;* **be under ~** ‹Schüler:› [zeitweilig] vom Unterricht ausgeschlossen sein; ‹Sportler:› [zeitweilig] gesperrt sein; [B] *(temporary cessation)* Suspendierung, *die; (of publication, train service, hostilities)* [vorübergehende] Einstellung; [C] *(hanging)* Aufhängen, *das;* [D] *(Chem.)* Suspension, *die;* [E] *(Motor Veh.)* Federung, *die; (mounting of wheels)* Radaufhängung, *die;* [F] *(Mus.)* Vorhalt, *der*

**su'spension bridge** *n.* Hängebrücke, *die*

**suspicion** /sə'spɪʃn/ *n.* [A] *(uneasy feeling)* Misstrauen, *das* (**of** gegenüber); *(more specific)* Verdacht, *der; (unconfirmed belief)* Ahnung, *die;* Verdacht, *der;* **have a ~ that ...:** den Verdacht haben, dass ...; **I have my ~s about him** er kommt mir verdächtig vor; ich traue ihm nicht ganz; **view** *or* **regard sb./sth. with ~:** jmdm./etw. mit Misstrauen begegnen; [B] *(suspecting)* Verdacht, *der* (**of** auf + *Akk.*); **~ is not enough** ein Verdacht genügt nicht; **protected from ~:** gegen Verdächtigungen geschützt; **on ~ of theft/murder** *etc.* wegen Verdachts auf Diebstahl/Mordverdachts *usw.;* **lay oneself open to ~:** sich verdächtig machen; **be under ~:** verdächtigt werden; [C] *(trace)* **a ~ of salt** eine Spur Salz

**suspicious** /sə'spɪʃəs/ *adj.* [A] *(tending to suspect)* misstrauisch (**of** gegenüber); **be ~ of sb./sth.** jmdm./einer Sache misstrauen; [B] *(arousing suspicion)* verdächtig

**suspiciously** /sə'spɪʃəslɪ/ *adv.* [A] *(as to arouse suspicion)* verdächtig; **look ~ like sth.** verdächtig nach etw. aussehen; [B] *(warily)* misstrauisch

**suspiciousness** /sə'spɪʃəsnɪs/ *n., no pl.* Verdächtigkeit, *die; (disposition to suspect)* Argwohn, *der;* Misstrauen, *das*

**sustain** /sə'steɪn/ *v.t.* [A] *(withstand)* widerstehen (+ *Dat.*) ‹Druck›; standhalten (+ *Dat.*) ‹Angriff›; aushalten ‹Vergleich›; tragen ‹Gewicht›; [B] *(support, uphold)* aufrechterhalten; **too little to ~ life** nicht genug zum Leben; **not enough to ~ a family** nicht genug, um eine Familie zu unterhalten; **~ an objection** einem Einwand stattgeben; [C] *(suffer)* erleiden ‹Niederlage, Verlust, Verletzung›; **~ damage** Schaden nehmen; [D] *(maintain)* bestreiten ‹Unterhaltung›; bewahren ‹Interesse›; wahren ‹Ruf›; [beibe]halten ‹Geschwindigkeit›; durchhalten ‹Rolle›; **~ a note** *(Mus.)* eine Note aushalten; **~ a task** einer Aufgabe gerecht werden

**sustainable** /sʌ'steɪnəbl/ *adj.* *(Ecology)* nachhaltig

**sustained** /sə'steɪnd/ *adj.* [A] *(prolonged)* länger ...; anhaltend ‹Beifall›; ausdauernd ‹Anstrengung›; **~ speed** Dauergeschwindigkeit, *die;* [B] *(Mus.)* ausgehalten

**sustaining** /sə'steɪnɪŋ/ *adj.* stärkend; nahrhaft ‹Essen, Mahlzeit›

**sustaining: ~ 'pedal** *n.* *(Mus.)* Fortepedal, *das;* **~ 'program** *n.* *(Amer. Radio and Telev.)* *nicht von einem Sponsor getragenes Programm*

**sustenance** /'sʌstɪnəns/ *n.* [A] *(nourishment, food)* Nahrung, *die;* **draw** *or* **get one's ~ from sth.** sich von etw. ernähren; [B] *(nourishing quality)* **there is no ~ in it** es hat keinen Nährwert

**suture** /'suːtʃə(r)/ *(Med.)* ❶ *n.* *(stitch)* Naht, *die; (thread)* Faden, *der.* ❷ *v.t.* nähen

**svelte** /svelt/ *adj.* grazil; anmutig ‹Bewegungen›

**SW** *abbr.* [A] /saʊθ'west/ ▶ **1024** **south-west** SW; [B] /saʊθ'westən/ ▶ **1024** **south-western** sw.; [C] *(Radio)* **short wave** KW

**swab** /swɒb/ ❶ *n.* [A] *(Med.: absorbent pad)* Tupfer, *der;* [B] *(Med.: specimen)* Abstrich, *der;* [C] *(pad or mop for cleaning decks)* Dweil, *der (Seemannsspr.).* ❷ *v.t.*, **-bb-** [A] **~ [down]** wischen; schwabbern ‹Deck› *(Seemannsspr.)*; [B] *(Med.)* betupfen ‹Wunde›

**Swabia** /'sweɪbɪə/ *pr. n.* Schwaben *(das)*

**Swabian** /'sweɪbɪən/ ❶ *adj.* schwäbisch; **sb. is ~:** jmd. ist Schwabe/Schwäbin. ❷ *n.* [A] *(person)* Schwabe, *der*/Schwäbin, *die;* [B] *(dialect)* Schwäbisch, *das;* **sb. speaks ~:** jmd. schwäbelt

**swaddle** /'swɒdl/ *v.t.* wickeln ‹Baby›; **swaddling clothes** *(Bibl.)* Windeln

**swag** /swæg/ *n.* [A] *(coll.: stolen goods)* Beute, *die;* Sore, *die (Gaunerspr.)*; [B] *(Austral., NZ: bundle)* Bündel, *das*

**swagger** /'swægə(r)/ ❶ *v.i.* [A] *(walk with a ~)* großspurig stolzieren; [B] *(behave in domineering way)* großspurig auftreten; [C] *(boast)* angeben *(ugs.)*; aufschneiden. ❷ *n.* ⇒ **1:** [A] großspuriges Stolzieren; [B] großspuriges Gehabe; **walk with a ~:** arrogant auftreten; [C] Angeberei, *die (ugs.)*

**'swagger cane** *(Brit.)* ⇒ **swagger stick**

**swaggering** /'swægərɪŋ/ ❶ *n.* [A] *(boasting)* Angeberei, *die (ugs.)*; [B] *(manner)* arrogantes *od.* großspuriges Auftreten. ❷ *adj.* stolzierend ‹Gang›; großspurig ‹Gehabe›

S

**'swagger stick** *n.* Offiziersstöckchen, *das*

**swagman** /'swægmən/ *n., pl.* **swagmen** /'swægmən/ (*Austral., NZ*) Landstreicher, *der*

**Swahili** /swɑ:'hi:lɪ, swə'hi:lɪ/ ▶1275 ❶ *adj.* Swahili-; ⇒ *also* **English** 1. ❷ *n.* Ⓐ *no pl.* (*language*) Swahili, *das;* ⇒ *also* **English** 2 A; Ⓑ *pl. same* (*person*) Swahili, *der/die*

**swain** /sweɪn/ *n.* (*arch./joc.*) Ⓐ (*peasant*) Bauernbursche, *der;* Ⓑ (*lover*) Freier, *der*

**swallow**[1] /'swɒləʊ/ ❶ *v.t.* Ⓐ schlucken; (*by mistake*) verschlucken ‹Fischgräte, fig.: Wort, Silbe›; ~ **the bait** (*fig.*) den Köder schlucken (*ugs.*); Ⓑ (*repress*) hinunterschlucken (*ugs.*) ‹Stolz, Ärger›; ~ **one's words** [demütig] zurücknehmen, was man gesagt hat; Ⓒ (*believe*) schlucken (*ugs.*), glauben ‹Geschichte, Erklärung›; **I find this hard to** ~: das kann ich kaum glauben; Ⓓ (*put up with*) schlucken (*ugs.*) ‹Beleidigung, Unrecht›. ❷ *v.i.* schlucken. ❸ *n.* Schluck, *der*

~ **'up** *v.t.* Ⓐ (*make disappear*) verschlucken; schlucken ‹kleinere Betriebe, Gebiete›; **I wished the earth would** ~ **me up** ich wäre am liebsten vor Scham in den Boden versunken; Ⓑ (*exhaust, consume*) auffressen; verschlingen ‹große Summen›

**swallow**[2] *n.* (*Ornith.*) Schwalbe, *die;* **one** ~ **does not make a summer** (*prov.*) eine Schwalbe macht noch keinen Sommer (*Spr.*)

**swallow:** ~ **dive** *n.* (*Brit.*) *Tauchsprung, bei dem die Arme bis kurz vor dem Eintauchen seitlich ausgestreckt werden;* ~**tail** *n.* Schwalbenschwanz, *der*

**swam** ⇒ **swim** 1, 2

**swamp** /swɒmp/ ❶ *n.* Sumpf, *der.* ❷ *v.t.* Ⓐ (*flood*) überschwemmen; Ⓑ (*overwhelm*) **be** ~**ed with letters/applications/orders/work** mit Briefen/Bewerbungen/Aufträgen überschwemmt werden/bis über den Hals in Arbeit stecken (*ugs.*)

**'swampland** *n.* Sumpfland, *das*

**swampy** /'swɒmpɪ/ *adj.* sumpfig

**swan** /swɒn/ ❶ *n.* Schwan, *der;* **black** ~: Schwarzer Schwan; Trauerschwan, *der.* ❷ *v.i.,* **-nn-** (*coll.*) ziehen; ~ **about** *or* **around** herumziehen (*ugs.*); (*in small area*) rumlaufen (*ugs.*); ~ **off** losziehen (*ugs.*)

**'swan dive** (*Amer.*) ⇒ **swallow dive**

**swank** /swæŋk/ (*coll.*) ❶ *n.* Ⓐ Angeberei, *die* (*ugs.*); Angabe, *die* (*ugs.*); Ⓑ (*person*) Angeber, *der*/Angeberin, *die.* ❷ *v.i.* angeben (*ugs.*) (**about** mit); ~ **around** herumstolzieren (*ugs.*)

**swanky** /'swæŋkɪ/ *adj.* (*coll.*) protzig (*ugs.*); ~ **car** Angeberauto, *das*

**swan:** ~ **neck** *n.* Schwanenhals, *der;* ~**sdown** *n.* Schwanendaunen *Pl.;* ~**song** *n.* (*fig.*) Schwanengesang, *der*

**swap** /swɒp/ ❶ *v.t.,* **-pp-** tauschen (**for** gegen); austauschen ‹Erfahrungen, Erinnerungen›; ~ **jokes** sich (*Dat.*) [gegenseitig] Witze erzählen; ~ **places** [**with sb.**] [mit jmdm.] den Platz *od.* die Plätze tauschen; (*fig.*) [mit jmdm.] tauschen; ⇒ *also* **horse** 1 A. ❷ *v.i.,* **-pp-** tauschen; **will you** ~? tauschst du? ❸ *n.* Tausch, *der;* **do a** ~ [**with sb.**] [mit jmdm.] tauschen

**sward** /swɔ:d/ *n.* (*literary*) Rasen, *der;* Rasenfläche, *die*

**swarf** /swɔ:f/ *n.* feine Metallspäne

**swarm** /swɔ:m/ ❶ *n.* Ⓐ Schwarm, *der;* ~ [**of bees**] Bienenschwarm, *der;* (*settled in a hive*) Bienenvolk, *das;* Ⓑ *in pl.* (*great numbers*) ~**s of tourists/children** Scharen von Touristen/Kindern. ❷ *v.i.* Ⓐ (*move in a* ~) schwärmen; Ⓑ (*teem*) wimmeln (**with** von); **the shops were** ~**ing with tourists** in den Geschäften wimmelte es von Touristen

~ **up** *v.t.* hochklettern

**swarthiness** /'swɔ:ðɪnɪs/ *n., no pl.* (*complexion*) dunkle Gesichtsfarbe; (*of person*) Dunkelhäutigkeit, *die*

**swarthy** /'swɔ:ðɪ/ *adj.* dunkel ‹Gesichtsfarbe›; dunkelhäutig ‹Person›

**swashbuckler** /'swɒʃbʌklə(r)/ *n.* Draufgänger, *der*

**swashbuckling** /'swɒʃbʌklɪŋ/ *adj.* draufgängerisch

**swastika** /'swɒstɪkə/ *n.* (*of Nazis*) Hakenkreuz, *das;* (*ancient symbol*) Swastika, *die*

**swat** /swɒt/ ❶ *v.t.,* **-tt-** Ⓐ (*hit hard*) schlagen; hauen (*ugs.*); Ⓑ (*crush*) totschlagen ‹Fliege, Wespe›. ❷ *n.* Ⓐ (*slap*) Klaps, *der;* **give a fly a** ~, **take a** ~ **at a fly** nach einer Fliege schlagen; Ⓑ (*fly swatter*) Klatsche, *die*

**swatch** /swɒtʃ/ *n.* Ⓐ (*sample*) Muster, *das;* Ⓑ (*collection of samples*) Musterbuch, *das*

**swath** /swɔ:θ/ ⇒ **swathe** 2

**swathe** /sweɪð/ ❶ *v.t.* [ein]hüllen; ~**d in bandages** ganz in Bandagen eingewickelt; ~**d in mist** in Nebel gehüllt. ❷ *n.* (*cut by mower*) gemähte Bahn; (*broad strip*) breiter Streifen; (*in forest*) Schneise, *die;* **cut a** ~ **through the corn/the undergrowth/the forest** eine Bahn durch das Getreide/Unterholz schneiden/eine Schneise durch den Wald schlagen

**swatter** /'swɒtə(r)/ *n.* Klatsche, *die*

**sway** /sweɪ/ ❶ *v.i.* [hin und her] schwanken; (*gently*) sich wiegen; ~ **towards sth.** (*on one's feet*) einer Sache entgegenschwanken; (*lean down to*) sich einer Sache (*Dat.*) zuneigen. ❷ *v.t.* Ⓐ wiegen ‹Kopf, Hüften, Zweig, Wipfel›; hin und her schwanken lassen ‹Baum, Mast, Antenne›; Ⓑ (*have influence over*) beeinflussen; (*persuade*) überreden; **be** ~**ed by sth.** sich von etw. beeinflussen lassen; **she will not be** ~**ed over sanctions** sie bleibt in der Frage der Sanktionen hart. ❸ *n.* Herrschaft, *die;* **have sb. under one's** ~, **hold** ~ **over sb.** über jmdn. herrschen

**swear** /sweə(r)/ ❶ *v.t.,* **swore** /swɔ:(r)/, **sworn** /swɔ:n/ Ⓐ schwören ‹Eid usw.›; **they swore eternal fidelity** sie schworen sich (*Dat.*) ewige Treue; **I could have sworn [that] it was him** ich hätte schwören können, dass er es war; ⇒ *also* **blind** 2 B; Ⓑ (*administer oath to*) vereidigen ‹Zeugen›; ~ **sb. to secrecy** jmdn. auf Geheimhaltung einschwören; ⇒ *also* **sworn.** ❷ *v.i.,* **swore, sworn** Ⓐ (*use* ~ *words*) fluchen; Ⓑ ~ **to sth.** (*be certain of*) etw. beschwören; einen Eid auf etw. (*Akk.*) ablegen; **I wouldn't like to** ~ **to it** (*coll.*) ich will es nicht beschwören; Ⓒ (*take oath*) schwören, einen Eid ablegen (**on** auf + *Akk.*). ❸ *n.* Fluch, *der;* **have a** ~: fluchen

~ **at** *v.t.* beschimpfen

~ **by** *v.t.* (*coll.: have confidence in*) schwören auf (+ *Akk.*)

~ **'in** *v.t.* vereidigen ‹Geschworenen, Zeugen›

~ **'out** *v.t.* (*Amer.*) ~ **a warrant out against sb.** gegen jmdn. durch eine eidliche [Straf]anzeige einen Haftbefehl erwirken

**'swear word** *n.* Kraftausdruck, *der;* Fluch, *der;* **use** ~**s** fluchen

**sweat** /swet/ ❶ *n.* Ⓐ Schweiß, *der;* **in** *or* **by the** ~ **of one's brow** im Schweiße seines Angesichtes; **be in a** ~ [**with fear**] [vor Angst] schwitzen; **be in a** ~ **to do sth.** (*fig.: be anxious*) danach fiebern, etw. zu tun; **I came** *or* **broke out in a** ~: mir brach der [Angst]schweiß aus; **don't get in such a** ~! reg dich nicht so auf!; **be all of a** ~ **at the prospect of the exam** beim Gedanken an die Prüfung ins Schwitzen geraten *od.* kommen; Ⓑ (*spell of* ~*ing*) **have a good** ~: richtig schwitzen; Ⓒ (*drudgery*) Plagerei, *die;* Plackerei, *die* (*ugs.*); **no** ~! (*coll.*) kein Problem! (*ugs.*); Ⓓ (*drops on surface*) Kondenswasser, *das;* (*on cheese*) Fetttröpfchen. ⇒ *also* **cold sweat.**

❷ *v.i.,* ~**ed** *or* (*Amer.*) ~ Ⓐ (*perspire*) schwitzen; ~ **like a pig** (*coll.*) schwitzen wie die Sau (*salopp*); ~ **with fear** vor Angst schwitzen; Ⓑ (*fig.: suffer*) **he made me sit outside** ~**ing** er ließ mich draußen sitzen und schmoren (*ugs.*); Ⓒ (*drudge*) sich placken (*ugs.*); **we had to** ~ **to get the job finished** wir mussten uns anstrengen, um mit der Arbeit fertig zu werden; **make sb.** ~ (*make work in bad conditions*) jmdn. schwitzen *od.* (*ugs.*) schuften lassen; Ⓓ (*produce surface moisture*) schwitzen.

❸ *v.t.* Ⓐ (*employ in bad conditions*) schwitzen *od.* (*ugs.*) schuften lassen; Ⓑ ~ **blood** (*fig.*) Blut und Wasser schwitzen (*ugs.*); Ⓒ (*emit like* ~) ausschwitzen; Ⓓ ~ **it out** (*coll.*) durchhalten; ausharren

**'sweatband** *n.* Schweißband, *das*

**sweated labour** /swetɪd 'leɪbə(r)/ *n.* unterbezahlte [Schwer]arbeit; (*workers*) unterbezahlte Arbeitskräfte

**sweater** /'swetə(r)/ *n.* Pullover, *der*

**sweat:** ~ **gland** *n.* Schweißdrüse, *die;* ~**shirt** *n.* Sweatshirt, *das;* ~**shop** *n.* ausbeuterische [kleine] Klitsche (*ugs.*)

**sweaty** /'swetɪ/ *adj.* (*moist with sweat*) schweißig; schweißnass; schwitzend ‹Käse›

**swede** *n.* Kohlrübe, *die*

**Swede** /swi:d/ *n.* ▶1340 Schwede, *der*/Schwedin, *die*

**Sweden** /'swi:dn/ *pr. n.* Schweden (*das*)

**Swedish** /'swi:dɪʃ/ ▶1275, ▶1340 ❶ *adj.* schwedisch; **sb. is** ~: jmd. ist Schwede/Schwedin; ⇒ *also* **English** 1. ❷ *n.* Schwedisch, *das;* ⇒ *also* **English** 2 A

**sweep** /swi:p/ ❶ *v.t.,* **swept** [swept] Ⓐ fegen (*bes. nordd.*); kehren (*bes. südd.*); ~ **the board,** ~ **all before one** (*fig.: win all awards*) auf der ganzen Linie siegen; Ⓑ (*move with force*) fegen; **the current swept the logs along** die Strömung riss die Hölzer mit; **the wave of protest swept the opposition into office** die Protestwelle katapultierte die Opposition an die Macht; Ⓒ (*traverse swiftly*) ~ **the hillside/plain** ‹Wind:› über die Hügel/Ebene fegen; ~ **the country** ‹Epidemie, Mode:› das Land überrollen; ‹Feuer:› durch das Land fegen; **searchlights swept the sky** Suchscheinwerfer huschten über den Himmel; ~ **an area with fire** (*Mil.*) ein Gebiet mit Feuer bestreichen; Ⓓ (*search*) durchsuchen (**for** nach); ~ **a channel for mines** eine Fahrrinne nach Minen absuchen. ⇒ *also* **carpet** 1 A.

❷ *v.i.,* **swept** Ⓐ (*clean*) fegen (*bes. nordd.*); kehren (*bes. südd.*); Ⓑ (*go fast, in stately manner*) ‹Vogel:› gleiten; ‹Mensch, Auto:› rauschen; ‹Wind usw.:› fegen; Ⓒ (*extend*) sich erstrecken; **the road** ~**s to the left** die Straße macht einen großen Bogen nach links; **his glance swept from left to right** sein Blick glitt von links nach rechts.

❸ *n.* Ⓐ (*cleaning*) **give sth. a** ~: etw. fegen (*bes. nordd.*); etw. kehren (*bes. südd.*); **make a clean** ~ (*fig.*) (*get rid of everything*) gründlich aufräumen; (*win all prizes*) gründlich abräumen (*ugs.*); **make a clean** ~ **of the prizes** alle Preise einheimsen (*ugs.*); Ⓑ ⇒ **chimney sweep;** Ⓒ (*coll.*) ⇒ **sweepstake;** Ⓓ (*motion*) (*of arm*) ausholende Bewegung; **with an impatient** ~ **of his hand** mit einer ungeduldigen Handbewegung; Ⓔ (*stretch*) **a wide/an open** ~ **of country** ein weiter Landstrich; Ⓕ (*curve of road, river*) Bogen, *der;* **the wide** ~ **of the bay** die geschwungene Kurve der Bucht; Ⓖ (*sortie by aircraft*) Einsatz, *der* (*Milit.*)

~ **a'side** *v.t.* Ⓐ (*dismiss*) beiseite schieben ‹Einwand, Zweifel›; überrennen ‹gegnerische Mannschaft›; aus dem Weg scheuchen ‹Reporter›; Ⓑ (*push aside*) wegfegen; beiseite fegen

~ **a'way** *v.t.* fortreißen; (*fig.*) hinwegfegen (*geh.*) ‹Traditionen›; (*abolish*) aufräumen mit ‹Privilegien, Korruption›

~ **'by** *v.i.* vorbeirauschen

~ **'down** *v.i.* Ⓐ ~ **down on sb./sth.** sich auf jmdn./etw. stürzen; Ⓑ **the hills** ~ **down to the sea** die Berge fallen in sanftem Bogen zum Meer hinab

~ **'in** *v.i.* Ⓐ (*enter majestically*) einziehen; Ⓑ (*Polit.*) [mit großer Mehrheit] an die Macht kommen

~ **'off** ❶ *v.i.* abrauschen (*ugs.*). ❷ *v.t.* fortreißen; ⇒ *also* **foot** 1 A

~ **'out** ❶ *v.t.* ausfegen (*bes. nordd.*); auskehren (*bes. südd.*). ❷ *v.i.* abrauschen (*ugs.*)

~ **'up** ❶ *v.t.* zusammenfegen (*bes. nordd.*); zusammenkehren (*bes. südd.*). ❷ *v.i.* angerauscht kommen

**sweeper** /'swi:pə(r)/ *n.* Ⓐ [**road**] ~ (*person*) Straßenfeger, *der* (*bes. nordd.*); Straßenkehrer, *der* (*bes. südd.*); (*machine*) Straßenkehrmaschine, *die;* ⇒ *also* **carpet sweeper; mine-sweeper;** Ⓑ (*Footb.*) Libero, *der*

S

**sweeping** /'swi:pɪŋ/ ❶ *adj.* Ⓐ (*without limitations*) pauschal; Ⓑ (*far-reaching*) weit reichend ‹Einsparung›; umfassend ‹Reform›; durchschlagend ‹Sieg, Erfolg›; umwälzend ‹Veränderung›; Ⓒ (*moving in a wide curve*) ausholend ‹Geste, Bewegung›; schwungvoll ‹Knicks, Verbeugung›; schweifend ‹Blick›. ❷ *n. in pl.* Kehricht, *der*

**sweepingly** /'swi:pɪŋlɪ/ *adv.* pauschal

**sweep: ~ 'second hand** *n.* (*Horol.*) Zentralsekundenzeiger, *der;* **~stake** *n.* Ⓐ (*race, contest*) Sweepstake[rennen], *das;* Ⓑ (*lottery*) *Pferdetoto, bei dem sich die Gewinnsumme aus den Einsätzen zusammensetzt*

**sweet** /swi:t/ ❶ *adj.* Ⓐ (*to taste*) süß; **~ tea** gesüßter Tee; **have a ~ tooth** gern Süßes mögen; **with a ~ tooth like yours ...:** da du so gern *od.* viel Süßes isst ...; Ⓑ (*lovely*) süß; reizend ‹Wesen, Gesicht, Mädchen, Kleid›; **~ dreams!** träum[e]/träumt süß!; **how ~ of you!** wie nett *od.* lieb von dir!; **keep sb. ~:** jmdn. bei [guter] Laune halten; **he's ~ on her** (*dated coll.*) er hat eine Schwäche für sie; **at one's own ~ will, in one's own ~ way** wie es einem [gerade] passt; **go one's own ~ way** machen, was einem passt; Ⓒ (*fragrant*) süß; frisch ‹Atem›; **be ~ with sth.** süß nach etw. duften; **the ~ smell of success** (*fig.*) die Süße des Erfolgs (*geh., scherzh.*); Ⓓ (*musical*) süß (*geh.*); lieblich ‹Stimme, Musik, Klang›. ⇒ *also* **basil**; **chestnut** 1 A; **pepper** 1 B; **sweet potato**; **seventeen** 1; **sixteen** 1; **violet** 1 A.
❷ *n.* Ⓐ (*Brit.: piece of confectionery*) Bonbon, *das od. der;* (*with chocolate, fudge, etc.*) Süßigkeit, *die;* Ⓑ (*Brit.: dessert*) Nachtisch, *der;* Dessert, *das;* **for ~:** zum Nachtisch *od.* Dessert; Ⓒ *in pl.* (*delights*) Freuden; Wonnen (*geh.*); Ⓓ (*darling*) **[my] ~** (*female*) [meine] Liebste; (*male*) [mein] Liebster

**sweet: ~-and-'sour** *attrib. adj.* süßsauer; **~bread** *n.* (*Gastr.*) Bries, *das;* **~ brier** *n.* Weinrose, *die;* **~ corn** *n.* Zuckermais, *der*

**sweeten** /'swi:tn/ *v.t.* Ⓐ (*add sugar etc. to*) süßen; Ⓑ (*add fragrance to*) süß machen; versüßen; (*remove bad smell of*) reinigen ‹Luft, Atem›; Ⓒ (*make agreeable*) versüßen ‹Leben, Abend›; milde stimmen ‹Person›; ⇒ *also* **pill** B

**sweetener** /'swi:tnə(r)/ *n.* Ⓐ Süßstoff, *der;* **use honey as a ~:** Honig zum Süßen verwenden; Ⓑ (*bribe*) kleine Aufmerksamkeit (*iron.*)

**'sweetheart** *n.* Schatz, *der;* Liebling, *der;* **an old ~:** eine alte Liebe (*ugs.*); **how long have they been ~s?** wie lange gehen sie schon miteinander? (*ugs.*)

**sweetie** /'swi:tɪ/ *n.* Ⓐ (*Brit. child lang.*) ⇒ **sweet** 2 A; Ⓑ (*coll.: darling*) Schatz, *der;* **~ [pie]** (*term of endearment*) Liebling, *der;* Schätzchen, *das* (*ugs.*)

**sweetish** /'swi:tɪʃ/ *adj.* süßlich

**sweetly** /'swi:tlɪ/ *adv.* lieb; süß ‹spielen, singen›; **run ~** ‹Motor:› schön rund laufen

**sweet: ~meal** *adj.* **~meal biscuits** süße Vollkornkekse; **~meat** *n.* Süßigkeit, *die*

**sweetness** /'swi:tnɪs/ *n., no pl.* Ⓐ (*in taste*) Süße, *die;* Ⓑ (*fragrance*) süßer Duft; Ⓒ (*melodiousness*) Süße, *die* (*geh.*); Ⓓ **all is ~ and light** es herrscht eitel Freude und Sonnenschein (*meist scherzh.*)

**sweet: ~ 'pea** *n.* (*Bot.*) Wicke, *die;* **~ po'tato** *n.* Batate, *die;* Süßkartoffel, *die;* **~-scented** *adj.* süß [duftend]; wohlriechend; **~shop** *n.* (*Brit.*) Süßwarengeschäft, *das;* **~-smelling** ⇒ **~-scented**; **~ talk** (*Amer.*) *n.* Süßholzgeraspel, *das* (*ugs.*); **~-talk** *v.t.* **~-talk sb. [into doing sth.]** jmdn. beschwatzen[, etw. zu tun]; **~-tempered** /'swi:t tempəd/ *adj.* sanftmütig; **~ 'william** *n.* (*Bot.*) Bartnelke, *die*

**swell** /swel/ ❶ *v.t.,* **~ed, swollen** /'swəʊlən/ *or* **~ed** Ⓐ (*increase in size, height*) anschwellen lassen; aufquellen lassen ‹Holz›; Ⓑ (*increase amount of*) anschwellen lassen; vergrößern; **~ the ranks [of participants]** die Zahl der Teilnehmer vergrößern; Ⓒ blähen ‹Segel›. ❷ *v.i.,* **~ed, swollen** *or* **~ed** Ⓐ (*expand*) ‹Körperteil:› anschwellen; ‹Segel:› sich blähen; ‹Backen:› sich aufblähen; ‹Material:› aufquellen; Ⓑ (*increase in amount*) ‹Anzahl:› zunehmen; ‹Gehalt:› steigen; Ⓒ (*become louder*) anschwellen ([in]to zu); Ⓓ (*fig.*) ‹Herz:› schwellen (*geh.*). ❸ *n.* Ⓐ (*of sea*) Dünung, *die;* Ⓑ (*Mus.*) Schwellwerk, *das;* Ⓒ (*dated coll.*) feiner Herr/feine Dame; **the ~s** die feinen Leute; (*smart set*) die Schickeria (*ugs.*); Ⓓ (*act, condition*) Schwellen, *das.* ❹ *adj.* (*coll.*) Ⓐ (*dated: stylish, socially prominent*) schick; fein; Ⓑ (*Amer.: excellent*) toll (*ugs.*)

**'swell box** *n.* (*Mus.*) Jalousieschweller, *der*

**swelling** /'swelɪŋ/ ❶ *n.* Schwellung, *die* (*Med.*). ❷ *adj.* Ⓐ (*growing larger, louder*) anschwellend; Ⓑ (*increasing*) wachsend; steigend ‹Flut›; Ⓒ (*bulging*) gebläht ‹Segel›

**'swell organ** *n.* (*Mus.*) Schwellwerk, *das*

**swelter** /'sweltə(r)/ *v.i.* [vor Hitze] [fast] vergehen; **~ in the heat** in der Hitze schmoren (*ugs.*); **~ing** glühend heiß ‹Tag, Wetter›; **~ing heat** Bruthitze, *die*

**swept** ⇒ **sweep** 1, 2

**swept: ~-back** *adj.* **~-back wing** positiv gepfeilter Flügel; **~-back hair** zurückgekämmtes Haar; **~-wing** *adj.* ‹Flugzeug› mit Pfeilflügeln

**swerve** /sw3:v/ ❶ *v.i.* (*deviate*) einen Bogen *od.* (*ugs.*) Schlenker machen; **~ to the right/left** nach rechts/links [aus]schwenken; **~ from its path** ‹Fahrzeug:› ausscheren; **~ in the air** ‹Vogel, Ball:› in der Luft abdrehen; **she never ~d from her duty** sie hat ihre Pflicht immer treu erfüllt. ❷ *n.* Ⓐ (*divergence from course*) Bogen, *der;* Schlenker, *der* (*ugs.*); Ⓑ (*swerving motion*) **put a ~ on a ball** einem Ball [einen] Effet geben

**swift** /swɪft/ ❶ *adj.* schnell; flink, schnell ‹Bewegung›; **~ action** rasches Handeln; **~ retribution** prompte Bestrafung; **have a ~ temper, be ~ to anger** jähzornig sein. ❷ *n.* (*Ornith.*) Mauersegler, *der*

**swiftly** /'swɪftlɪ/ *adv.* schnell; (*soon*) bald

**swiftness** /'swɪftnɪs/ *n.* Schnelligkeit, *die;* **~ of action** schnelles *od.* rasches Handeln

**swig** /swɪg/ (*coll.*) ❶ *v.t.,* **-gg-** schlucken (*ugs.*); [herunter]kippen (*ugs.*). ❷ *v.i.,* **-gg-** [hastig] trinken. ❸ *n.* Schluck, *der;* **have/take a ~ [of beer** *etc.*] einen tüchtigen Schluck [Bier *usw.*] trinken/nehmen

**swill** /swɪl/ ❶ *v.t.* Ⓐ (*rinse*) **~ [out]** [aus]spülen; **~ down the floor** den Fußboden abspülen; Ⓑ (*derog.: drink greedily*) hinunterspülen (*ugs.*). ❷ *n.* Ⓐ (*rinsing*) Spülen, *das;* **give sth. a ~ [out]/down** etw. [aus]spülen/abspülen; Ⓑ (*derog.: drink*) Brühe, *die* (*ugs. abwertend*); Ⓒ (*for pigs*) Schweinefutter, *das*

**swim** /swɪm/ ❶ *v.i.,* **-mm-, swam** /swæm/, **swum** /swʌm/ Ⓐ schwimmen; **~ with/against the tide/stream** (*fig.*) mit dem/gegen den Strom schwimmen; Ⓑ (*fig.: be flooded, overflow*) **~ with** *or* **in sth.** in etw. (*Dat.*) schwimmen; **her eyes swam with tears** ihre Augen schwammen; **the deck was ~ming with water** das Deck stand unter Wasser; Ⓒ (*appear to whirl*) **~ [before sb.'s eyes]** [vor jmds. Augen] verschwimmen; Ⓓ (*have dizzy sensation*) **my head was ~ming** mir war schwindelig. ⇒ *also* **sink** 2 A.
❷ *v.t.,* **-mm-, swam, swum** schwimmen ‹Strecke›; durchschwimmen ‹Fluss, See›; **~ [the] breaststroke/crawl** brustschwimmen/kraulen.
❸ *n.* Ⓐ **have a/go for a ~:** schwimmen/schwimmen gehen; **do you fancy a ~?** möchtest du schwimmen gehen?; **a refreshing ~:** ein erfrischendes Bad; **I like an early morning ~:** ich gehe gern frühmorgens schwimmen; Ⓑ **be in the ~ [of things]** mitten im Geschehen sein

**swimmer** /'swɪmə(r)/ *n.* Schwimmer, *der*/Schwimmerin, *die;* **[not] be a ~:** [nicht] schwimmen können; **be a good/poor ~:** gut/schlecht schwimmen können

**swimming** /'swɪmɪŋ/ ❶ *n.* Schwimmen, *das;* **like ~:** gern schwimmen. ❷ *attrib. adj.* schwimmend

**swimming: ~ baths** *n. pl.* Schwimmbad, *das;* **~ costume** *n.* Badeanzug, *der;* **~ lesson** *n.* Schwimmstunde, *die;* **~ lessons** Schwimmunterricht, *der*

**swimmingly** /'swɪmɪŋlɪ/ *adv.* (*coll.*) glänzend; **go ~:** wie am Schnürchen klappen (*ugs.*)

**swimming: ~ pool** *n.* Schwimmbecken, *das;* (*in house or garden*) Swimmingpool, *der;* (*building*) Schwimmbad, *das;* **~ trunks** *n. pl.* Badehose, *die*

**'swimsuit** *n.* Badeanzug, *der*

**swindle** /'swɪndl/ ❶ *v.t.* betrügen; **~ sb. out of sth.** jmdn. um etw. betrügen; (*take by persuasion*) jmdm. etw. abschwindeln. ❷ *n.* Schwindel, *der;* Betrug, *der*

**swindler** /'swɪndlə(r)/ *n.* Schwindler, *der*/Schwindlerin, *die*

**swine** /swaɪn/ *n., pl. same* Ⓐ (*Amer./formal/Zool.*) Schwein, *das;* Ⓑ (*derog.: contemptible person*) Schwein, *das* (*abwertend*); Ⓒ (*coll.: nasty thing*) harter Brocken (*ugs.*); **be a ~ to operate** ‹Maschine:› verteufelt schwer zu bedienen sein (*ugs.*); **a ~ of a job** eine verteufelt (*ugs.*) *od.* (*salopp*) tierisch schwere Arbeit. ⇒ *also* **pearl** B

**swine: ~ fever** *n.* Schweinepest, *die;* **~herd** *n.* Schweinehirt, *der*

**swing** /swɪŋ/ ❶ *n.* Ⓐ (*apparatus*) Schaukel, *die;* Ⓑ (*spell of ~ing*) Schaukeln, *das;* **want/have a ~:** schaukeln wollen/schaukeln; Ⓒ (*Sport: strike, blow*) Schlag, *der;* (*Boxing*) Schwinger, *der;* (*Golf*) Schwung, *der;* **take a ~ at sb./sth.** zum Schlag gegen jmdn./auf etw. (*Akk.*) ausholen; Ⓓ (*of suspended object*) Schwingen, *das;* **in full ~** (*fig.*) in vollem Gang[e]; Ⓔ (*steady movement*) Rhythmus, *der;* **the party went with a ~:** auf der Party herrschte eine tolle Stimmung (*ugs.*); **get into/be in the ~ of things** *or* **it** richtig reinkommen/richtig drin sein (*ugs.*); Ⓕ (*Mus.*) Swing, *der;* Ⓖ (*shift*) Schwankung, *die;* (*of public opinion*) Wende, *die;* (*amount of change in votes*) Abwanderung, *die;* **a ~ to the Left/Right** ein Linksruck/Rechtsruck (*Politik Jargon*). ⇒ *also* **pendulum**; **roundabout** 1 B.
❷ *v.i.,* **swung** /swʌŋ/ Ⓐ (*turn on axis, sway*) schwingen; (*in wind*) schaukeln; **~ open** ‹Tür:› aufgehen; **be ~ing at anchor** schwojen (*Seemannsspr.*); Ⓑ (*go in sweeping curve*) schwenken; **the plane swung low over the field** das Flugzeug schwenkte über dem Feld in den Tiefflug; **~ from sb.'s arm/a tree** an jmds. Arm/einem Baum schwingen (*geh.*) *od.* baumeln; Ⓒ (*go with ~ing gait*) beschwingt gehen; **~ into action** (*fig.*) loslegen (*ugs.*); Ⓓ (*move oneself by ~ing*) sich schwingen; **~ up** sich hinaufschwingen; **the car swung out of the drive** der Wagen schwenkte aus der Einfahrt; Ⓔ (*sl.: be executed by hanging*) baumeln (*salopp*); **he'll ~ for it** dafür wird er baumeln; Ⓕ **be ~ing** (*coll.: be lively*) auf vollen Touren laufen (*ugs.*); Ⓖ (*sl.: be promiscuous*) die Abwechslung lieben (*ugs. verhüll.*); **~ both ways** (*sl.*) es mit Männlein wie Weiblein machen (*ugs. verhüll.*).
❸ *v.t.,* **swung** Ⓐ schwingen; (*rock*) schaukeln; **~ one's legs** mit den Beinen baumeln; die Beine baumeln lassen; **~ a key on a chain** mit einem Schlüssel an einer Kette schlenkern; **~ sth. round and round** etw. kreisen *od.* im Kreise wirbeln lassen; **cranes ~ cargo on to the ship** Kräne befördern schwingende Lasten auf das Schiff; Ⓑ (*cause to face in another direction*) schwenken; **~ sb. round** jmdn. herumwirbeln; **he swung the car off the road/into the road** er schwenkte [mit dem Auto] von der Straße ab/in die Straße ein; Ⓒ (*have influence on*) umschlagen lassen ‹öffentliche Meinung›; **~ the elections** den Ausgang der Wahlen entscheiden; **what swung it for me ...:** was für mich den Ausschlag gab ...; Ⓓ (*suspend by its ends*) aufhängen ‹Hängematte›; Ⓔ (*coll.: arrange*) deichseln (*salopp*). ⇒ *also* **cat** A

**~ at** *v.t.* **~ at sb./sth.** zum Schlag auf jmdn./etw. ausholen

**~ 'round** *v.i.* sich schnell umdrehen (**on** nach); (*in surprise*) herumfahren

S

**swing: ~bin** *n.* Schwingdeckel[müll]eimer, *der;* Mülleimer mit Schwingdeckel; **~bridge** *n.* Drehbrücke, *die;* **~ 'door** *n.* Pendeltür, *die*

**swingeing** /'swɪndʒɪŋ/ *adj.* (*Brit.*) hart ‹Schlag›; (*fig.*) drastisch ‹Kürzung, Maßnahme›; scharf ‹Attacke›

**swinging** /'swɪŋɪŋ/ *adj.* **A** schwingend; **B** (*with strong rhythm*) [stark] rhythmisch; schwungvoll ‹Schritt›; **C** (*coll.: lively*) wild (*ugs.*); swingend (*ugs.*)

**'swing-wing** *n.* Schwenkflügel, *der*

**swipe** /swaɪp/ (*coll.*) **1** *v.i.* **~ at** [wild] schlagen nach; eindreschen auf (+ *Akk.*) (*ugs.*). **2** *v.t.* **A** (*hit hard*) knallen (*ugs.*); **B** (*coll.: steal*) klauen (*ugs.*); **C ~ the card through the swipe reader** die Karte durch das [Karten]lesegerät ziehen. **3** *n.* **A** [wuchtiger] Schlag; **take a wild ~ at sth.** wild auf etw. (*Akk.*) losschlagen; **B** (*device*) **~ [reader]** [Karten]lesegerät, *das*

**'swipe card** *n.* Magnetkarte, *die*

**swirl** /swɜːl/ **1** *v.i.* wirbeln. **2** *v.t.* umherwirbeln. **3** *n.* **A** (*eddying motion*) **with a ~ of the paddle** durch Herumwirbeln des Paddels; **B** (*spiralling shape*) Spirale, *die*

**swish** /swɪʃ/ **1** *v.t.* schlagen mit ‹Schwanz›; sausen lassen ‹Stock›. **2** *v.i.* zischen; **~ past** ‹Auto:› vorbeirauschen. **3** *n.* Zischen, *das.* **4** *adj.* (*coll.*) schick (*ugs.*)

**Swiss** /swɪs/ ▶ **1340** **1** *adj.* Schweizer; schweizerisch; **sb. is ~:** jmd. ist Schweizer/Schweizerin. **2** *n.* Schweizer, *der*/Schweizerin, *die;* **the ~** *pl.* die Schweizer

**Swiss: ~ 'chard** ⇒ **chard**; **~ 'cheese** *n.* Schweizer Käse, *der;* **~ cheese plant** Fensterblatt, *das;* **~ 'French** *adj.* welschschweizerisch; **~ 'German** **1** *adj.* schweizerdeutsch; **2** *n.* Schweizerdeutsch, *das;* **~ 'guards** *n. pl.* (*in Vatican*) Schweizergarde, *die;* **~ 'roll** *n.* Biskuitrolle, *die*

**switch** /swɪtʃ/ **1** *n.* **A** (*esp. Electr.*) Schalter, *der;* **B** (*Amer. Railw.*) Weiche, *die;* **C** (*change with another*) Wechsel, *der;* (*change of procedure*) Umstellung, *die* (**from** von, **to** auf + *Akk.*); **~ of roles** Rollentausch, *der;* **D** (*flexible shoot, whip*) Gerte, *die;* **E** (*tress of hair*) Haarteil, *das.* **2** *v.t.* **A** (*change*) **~ sth. [over] to sth.** etw. auf etw. (*Akk.*) umstellen *od.* (*Electr.*) umschalten; **~ a player to another position** einen Spieler auf eine andere Position stellen; **~ sb. to night duty** jmdn. in den Nachtdienst versetzen; **~ one's vote to another party** seine Stimme einer anderen Partei geben; **~ the conversation to another topic** das Gespräch auf ein anderes Thema lenken; **B** (*exchange*) tauschen; **C** (*Railw.: transfer with ~*) [mittels einer Weiche] umleiten; **D** (*swish*) schlagen mit ‹Schwanz›; sausen lassen ‹Rohrstock›. **3** *v.i.* wechseln; **~ [over] to sth.** auf etw. (*Akk.*) umstellen *od.* (*Electr.*) umschalten

**~ a'round** **1** *v.t.* umstellen ‹Möbel, Dienstplan›. **2** *v.i.* [die Stellung] wechseln

**~ 'off** *v.t.* & *i.* ausschalten; (*also fig. coll.*) abschalten

**~ 'on** **1** *v.t.* einschalten; anschalten; **be ~ed on** (*coll.*) (*high on drugs*) angeturnt sein (*ugs.*); (*up-to-date*) auf Draht sein (*ugs.*); **be ~ed on to jazz/rock** *etc.* auf Jazz/Rock *usw.* stehen (*ugs.*). **2** *v.i.* sich anschalten

**~ 'over** **1** *v.t.* ⇒ **~** 2 A. **2** *v.i.* ⇒ **switch** 3

**~ 'round** ⇒ **~ around**

**~ 'through** *v.t.* durchstellen ‹Telefongespräch, Anrufer›

**switch: ~back** *n.* (*Brit.*) (*road*) [berg]auf und [berg]ab führende Straße; (*roller coaster*) Achterbahn, *die;* **that road is a real ~back** diese Straße ist ein einziges Rauf und Runter (*ugs.*); **~blade** *n.* Springmesser, *das;* **~board** *n.* **A** (*Teleph.*) [Telefon]zentrale, *die;* Vermittlung, *die;* **~board operator** ▶ **1261** Telefonist, *der*/Telefonistin, *die;* **B** (*Electr.*) Schalttafel, *die;* **~ engine** *n.* (*Amer. Railw.*) Rangierlok[omotive], *die;* **~gear** *n.* (*Electr.*) Schaltvorrichtung, *die;* **~-over** ⇒ **changeover**; **~yard** *n.* (*Amer.*) Rangierbahnhof, *der*

**Switzerland** /'swɪtsələnd/ *pr. n.* die Schweiz

**swivel** /'swɪvl/ **1** *n.* Drehgelenk, *das.* **2** *v.i.*, (*Brit.*) **-ll-** sich drehen. **3** *v.t.*, (*Brit.*) **-ll-** drehen

**'swivel chair** *n.* Drehstuhl, *der*

**swiz, swizz** /swɪz/ *n.*, *pl.* **swizzes** (*Brit. coll.*) Beschiss, *der* (*ugs.*); Schwindel, *der*

**'swizzle stick** /'swɪzlstɪk/ *n.* Sektquirl, *der*

**swollen** /'swəʊlən/ **1** ⇒ **swell** 1, 2. **2** *adj.* geschwollen; angeschwollen ‹Fluss›; **eyes ~ with weeping** verweinte Augen; **have a ~ head** (*fig.*) sehr eingebildet *od.* von sich eingenommen sein

**swollen-headed** /'swəʊlənhedɪd/ *adj.* eingebildet

**swoon** /swuːn/ (*literary*) **1** *v.i.* **A** (*faint*) ohnmächtig werden; **B** (*go into ecstasies*) **~ over sb./sth.** von jmdm./etw. schwärmen. **2** *n.* (*literary*) Ohnmacht, *die*

**swoop** /swuːp/ **1** *n.* **A** (*downward plunge*) Sturzflug, *der;* **at a** *or* **one [fell] ~:** auf einen Schlag (*ugs.*); **B** (*coll.: raid*) Razzia, *die;* **make a ~ on a house/an area** eine Razzia in einem Haus/einem Bezirk machen. **2** *v.i.* (*plunge suddenly*) herabstoßen; (*pounce*) **~ on sb.** sich auf jmdn. stürzen; (*to attack*) gegen jmdn. einen Schlag führen; **the police ~ed on several addresses** die Polizei führte in mehreren Wohnungen Razzien durch; **we'll ~ tomorrow** wir schlagen morgen zu

**swoosh** /swuːʃ/ **1** *v.i.* rauschen; **~ by** vorbeirauschen. **2** *n.* (*sound*) Rauschen, *das;* **go past with a ~:** vorbeirauschen

**swop** ⇒ **swap**

**sword** /sɔːd/ *n.* Schwert, *das;* **put sb. to the ~** (*literary*) jmdn. [mit dem Schwert] töten; ⇒ *also* **cross** 2 A; **Damocles**

**sword: ~ dance** *n.* Schwert[er]tanz, *der;* **~fish** *n.* Schwertfisch, *der;* **~play** *n.* (*Fencing*) [Schwert]fechten, *das;* **~sman** /'sɔːdzmən/ *n.*, *pl.* **~smen** /'sɔːdzmən/ [Schwert]fechter, *der;* **~smanship** /'sɔːdzmənʃɪp/ *n.*, *no pl.* Fechtkunst, *die;* **~stick** *n.* Stockdegen, *der;* **~-swallower** /'sɔːdswɒləʊə(r)/ *n.* Schwertschlucker, *der*

**swore** ⇒ **swear** 1, 2

**sworn** /swɔːn/ **1** ⇒ **swear** 1, 2. **2** *attrib. adj.* **A** (*bound by an oath*) verschworen ‹Freund›; **~ enemy** Todfeind, *der;* **B** (*certified by oath*) beeidigt; **~ evidence** Aussage unter Eid; **~ affidavit/statement** eidesstattliche Versicherung/eidliche Erklärung

**swot** /swɒt/ (*Brit. coll.*) **1** *n.* Streber, *der*/Streberin, *die* (*abwertend*). **2** *v.i.*, **-tt-** büffeln (*ugs.*)

**~ 'up** *v.t.* büffeln (*ugs.*)

**swotting** /'swɒtɪŋ/ *n.* (*Brit. coll.*) Büffelei, *die* (*ugs.*)

**swum** ⇒ **swim** 1, 2

**swung** ⇒ **swing** 2, 3

**'swung dash** *n.* Tilde, *die*

**sybarite** /'sɪbəraɪt/ *n.* Sybarit, *der* (*geh.*)

**sycamore** /'sɪkəmɔː(r)/ *n.* Bergahorn, *der;* (*Amer.: plane tree*) Platane, *die*

**sycophancy** /'sɪkəfænsɪ, 'sɪkəfənsɪ/ *n.* Kriecherei, *die;* Speichelleckerei, *die*

**sycophant** /'sɪkəfænt, 'sɪkəfənt/ *n.* Kriecher, *der;* Schranze, *die*

**sycophantic** /sɪkə'fæntɪk/ *adj.* sykophantisch (*bildungsspr.*, *veralt.*); kriecherisch (*abwertend*)

**syllabic** /sɪ'læbɪk/ *adj.* **A** Silben-; **B** (*Pros.*) silbenzählend

**syllable** /'sɪləbl/ *n.* (*lit. or fig.*) Silbe, *die;* **she did not utter a ~ of reproach** mit keiner Silbe äußerte sie einen Vorwurf; **in words of one ~** (*fig.*) mit [sehr] einfachen Worten

**syllabub** /'sɪləbʌb/ *n.* (*Gastr.*) *aromatisierte Süßspeise aus geschlagener Sahne;* (*with wine*) Weinschaumcreme, *die*

**syllabus** /'sɪləbəs/ *n.*, *pl.* **~es** *or* **syllabi** /'sɪləbaɪ/ Lehrplan, *der;* (*for exam*) Studienplan, *der*

**syllogism** /'sɪlədʒɪzm/ *n.* (*Logic*) Syllogismus, *der*

**sylph** /sɪlf/ *n.* (*Mythol.*) (*male*) Sylphe, *der;* (*female; also fig.*) Sylphide, *die*

**'sylphlike** *adj.* sylphidenhaft (*geh.*)

**symbiosis** /sɪmbɪ'əʊsɪs/, *pl.* **symbioses** /sɪmbɪ'əʊsiːz/ *n.* (*Biol.; also fig.*) Symbiose, *die*

**symbiotic** /sɪmbɪ'ɒtɪk/ *adj.* symbiotisch

**symbol** /'sɪmbl/ *n.* Symbol, *das* (**of** für)

**symbolic** /sɪm'bɒlɪk/, **symbolical** /sɪm'bɒlɪkl/ *adj.*, **symbolically** /sɪm'bɒlɪkəlɪ/ *adv.* symbolisch

**symbolise** ⇒ **symbolize**

**symbolism** /'sɪmbəlɪzm/ *n.* **A** Symbolik, *die;* **B** (*Art, Literature*) Symbolismus, *der*

**Symbolist** /'sɪmbəlɪst/ *n.* Symbolist, *der*/Symbolistin, *die; attrib.* symbolistisch

**symbolize** /'sɪmbəlaɪz/ *v.t.* symbolisieren

**symmetric** /sɪ'metrɪk/, **symmetrical** /sɪ'metrɪkl/ *adj.*, **symmetrically** /sɪ'metrɪkəlɪ/ *adv.* symmetrisch

**symmetry** /'sɪmɪtrɪ/ *n.* Symmetrie, *die*

**sympathetic** /sɪmpə'θetɪk/ *adj.* **A** (*showing pity*) mitfühlend; (*understanding*) verständnisvoll; **B** (*favourably inclined*) wohlgesinnt; geneigt ‹Leser›; **be ~ to a cause/to new ideas** einer Sache wohlwollend gegenüberstehen/für neue Ideen empfänglich *od.* zugänglich sein; **give sb. a ~ hearing** ein offenes Ohr für jmdn. haben; **he is not at all ~ to this idea** er ist von dieser Idee ganz und gar nicht angetan; **C** (*to one's taste, likeable*) ansprechend; sympathisch ‹Person, Persönlichkeit›; **I find sb./sth. ~:** ich finde jmdn./etw. sympathisch; jmd./etw. ist mir sympathisch; **D** (*Med.*) sympathetisch ‹Schmerz, Leiden›; (*Anat.*) sympathisch ‹Nervensystem›; **E** (*Mus.*) mitschwingend ‹Saite, Ton›; **F** (*Phys.*) **~ vibration** Mitschwingen, *das*

**sympathetically** /sɪmpə'θetɪkəlɪ/ *adv.* (*with pity*) mitfühlend; (*understandingly*) verständnisvoll; **treat a subject ~:** ein Thema einfühlsam behandeln

**sympathetic: ~ 'nerve** *n.* (*Anat.*) Sympathikus, *der;* **~ 'nervous system** *n.* (*Anat.*) sympathisches *od.* sympathetisches Nervensystem

**sympathise, sympathiser** ⇒ **sympathiz-**

**sympathize** /'sɪmpəθaɪz/ *v.i.* **A** (*feel or express sympathy*) **~ with sb.** mit jmdm. [mit]fühlen *od.* Mitleid haben; (*by speaking*) sein Mitgefühl mit jmdm. äußern; **~ with sb. over the death of a friend** jmds. Trauer beim Tod eines Freundes teilen; **I do ~:** es tut mir wirklich Leid; **B ~ with** (*have understanding for*) Verständnis haben für ‹jmds. Not, Denkweise usw.›; (*Polit.: share ideas of*) sympathisieren mit ‹Partei usw.›

**sympathizer** /'sɪmpəθaɪzə(r)/ *n.* Sympathisant, *der*/Sympathisantin, *die*

**sympathy** /'sɪmpəθɪ/ *n.* **A** (*sharing feelings of another*) Mitgefühl, *das;* **in deepest ~:** mit aufrichtigem Beileid; **my sympathies are with you in your sorrow** ich fühle mit Ihnen in Ihrem Schmerz; **B** (*agreement in opinion or emotion*) Sympathie, *die;* **my sympathies are with Schmidt** ich bin auf Schmidts Seite; **he has radical sympathies/no ~ with the radicals** er sympathisiert/sympathisiert nicht mit den Radikalen; **be in/out of ~ with sth.** mit etw. sympathisieren/nicht sympathisieren; **are you in ~ with what we are trying to do?** stimmst du unseren Zielen zu?; **come out** *or* **strike in ~ with sb.** mit jmdm. in einen Sympathiestreik treten; **vibrate in ~:** mitschwingen

**'sympathy strike** *n.* Sympathiestreik, *der*

**symphonic** /sɪm'fɒnɪk/ *adj.* sinfonisch; symphonisch

**symphony** /'sɪmfənɪ/ *n.* (*Mus.*) **A** Sinfonie, *die;* **B** (*esp. Amer.*) ⇒ **symphony orchestra**

**'symphony orchestra** *n.* Sinfonieorchester, *das*

**symposium** /sɪm'pəʊzɪəm/ *n.*, *pl.* **symposia** /sɪm'pəʊzɪə/ Symposion, *das;* Symposium, *das*

**symptom** /'sɪmptəm/ *n.* (*Med.; also fig.*) Symptom, *das*

**symptomatic** /sɪmptə'mætɪk/ *adj.* (*Med.; also fig.*) symptomatisch (**of** für)

S

**synagogue** (*Amer.:* **synagog**) /'sɪnəgɒg/ *n.* Synagoge, *die*

**sync**, **synch** /sɪŋk/ (*coll.*) *n.* **A** **in/out of ~:** synchron/nicht synchron; **B** (*fig. coll.: in tune*) **be in ~/out of ~:** harmonieren/ nicht harmonieren (**with** mit); **he is out of ~: with the rest** er hat nicht die gleiche Wellenlänge wie die anderen

**synchromesh** /'sɪŋkrəmeʃ/ (*Motor Veh.*) *n.* **~ [gearbox]** Synchrongetriebe, *das;* **there is ~ on all gears** alle Gänge sind synchronisiert

**synchronic** /sɪŋ'krɒnɪk, sɪn'krɒnɪk/ *adj.* (*Ling.*) synchronisch

**synchronisation**, **synchronise** ⇒ **synchroniz-**

**synchronization** /sɪŋkrənaɪ'zeɪʃn/ *n.* Synchronisierung, *die*

**synchronize** /'sɪŋkrənaɪz/ **1** *v.t.* **A** synchronisieren ‹Vorgänge, Maschinen, Bild und Ton›; **B** (*set to same time*) gleichstellen ‹Uhren›; **we'd better ~ [our] watches** wir sollten Uhrenvergleich machen. **2** *v.i.* ‹Bild und Ton:› synchron sein

**synchronized 'swimming** *n.* (*Sport*) Synchronschwimmen, *das*

**synchronous** /'sɪŋkrənəs/ *adj.* synchron; **~ motor** (*Electr.*) Synchronmotor, *der*

**syncopate** /'sɪŋkəpeɪt/ *v.t.* (*Mus., Ling.*) synkopieren

**syncopation** /sɪŋkə'peɪʃn/ *n.* (*Mus., Ling.*) Synkopierung, *die*

**syncope** /'sɪŋkəpɪ/ *n.* (*Ling., Med.*) Synkope, *die*

**syndicalism** /'sɪndɪkəlɪzm/ *n.* Syndikalismus, *der*

**syndicate** **1** /'sɪndɪkət/ *n.* **A** (*for business, in organized crime*) Syndikat, *das;* **B** (*in newspapers*) *Presseagentur, die Beiträge ankauft und an eine od. mehrere Zeitungen vertreibt;* **C** **pools/lottery ~:** Tippgemeinschaft, *die.* **2** /'sɪndɪkeɪt/ *v.t.* in mehreren Zeitungen gleichzeitig veröffentlichen ‹Bericht usw.›

**syndrome** /'sɪndrəʊm/ *n.* (*Med.; also fig.*) Syndrom, *das*

**synod** /'sɪnəd/ *n.* Synode, *die*

**synonym** /'sɪnənɪm/ *n.* Synonym, *das*

**synonymous** /sɪ'nɒnɪməs/ *adj.* **A** (*Ling.*) synonym (**with** mit); **B** **~ with** (*fig.: suggestive of, linked with*) gleichbedeutend mit

**synonymy** /sɪ'nɒnəmɪ/ *n.* (*Ling.*) Synonymie, *die*

**synopsis** /sɪ'nɒpsɪs/, *n.*, *pl.* **synopses** /sɪ'nɒpsi:z/ Inhaltsangabe, *die;* (*overview*) Abriss, *der*

**synoptic** /sɪ'nɒptɪk/ *adj.* synoptisch

**syntactic** /sɪn'tæktɪk/ *adj.*, **syntactically** /sɪn'tæktɪkəlɪ/ *adv.* (*Ling.*) syntaktisch

**syntax** /'sɪntæks/ *n.* (*Ling.*) Syntax, *die*

**synthesis** /'sɪnθɪsɪs/ *n.*, *pl.* **syntheses** /'sɪnθɪsi:z/ Synthese, *die*

**synthesise**, **synthesiser** ⇒ **synthesiz-**

**synthesize** /'sɪnθɪsaɪz/ *v.t.* **A** (*form into a whole*) zur Synthese bringen; **B** (*Chem.*) synthetisieren; **C** (*Electronics*) **~ speech** Sprache elektronisch generieren

**synthesizer** /'sɪnθɪsaɪzə(r)/ *n.* (*Mus.*) Synthesizer, *der*

**synthetic** /sɪn'θetɪk/ **1** *adj.* **A** (*man-made*) synthetisch; **~ fibre** Kunstfaser, *die;* ⇒ *also* **resin** B; **B** (*sham*) unecht. **2** *n.* Kunststoff, *der;* **~s** (*Textiles*) Synthetics

**synthetically** /sɪn'θetɪkəlɪ/ *adv.* synthetisch

**syphilis** /'sɪfɪlɪs/ *n.* ▶ 1232 (*Med.*) Syphilis, *die*

**syphilitic** /sɪfɪ'lɪtɪk/ (*Med.*) **1** *n.* Syphilitiker, *der*/Syphilitikerin, *die.* **2** *adj.* syphilitisch

**Syracuse** /'saɪrəkju:z/ *pr. n.* Syrakus (*das*)

**Syria** /'sɪrɪə/ *pr. n.* Syrien (*das*)

**Syrian** /'sɪrɪən/ ▶ 1340 **1** *adj.* syrisch; **sb. is ~:** jmd. ist Syrer/Syrerin. **2** *n.* Syrer, *der*/ Syrerin, *die*

**syringa** /sɪ'rɪŋgə/ *n.* (*Bot.*) **A** (*mock orange*) Falscher Jasmin; **B** (*lilac*) Flieder, *der*

**syringe** /sɪ'rɪndʒ/ **1** *n.* Spritze, *die;* ⇒ *also* **hypodermic** 1. **2** *v.t.* spritzen; ausspritzen ‹Ohr›

**syrup** /'sɪrəp/ *n.* **A** Sirup, *der;* **cough ~:** Hustensaft, *der;* **B** (*fig.: sickly sentiment*) süßlicher Kitsch (*abwertend*)

**syrupy** /'sɪrəpɪ/ *adj.* **A** (*like syrup*) sirupähnlich; **B** (*fig.: cloyingly sweet*) süßlich

**system** /'sɪstəm/ *n.* **A** (*lit. or fig.*) System, *das;* (*of roads, railways also*) Netz, *das;* **root ~** (*Bot.*) Wurzelgeflecht, *das;* ⇒ *also* **go**[1] 4; **B** (*Anat., Zool.: body*) Körper, *der;* (*part*) **digestive / muscular / nervous / reproductive ~:** Verdauungsapparat, *der*/Muskulatur, *die*/Nervensystem, *das*/Fortpflanzungssystem, *das;* **get sth. out of one's ~** (*fig.*) etw. loswerden; (*by talking*) sich (*Dat.*) etw. von der Seele reden; **C** *no art.* (*methodical procedure*) System *o. Art.;* **D** (*Geol.*) Formation, *die*

**systematic** /sɪstə'mætɪk/ *adj.*, **systematically** /sɪstə'mætɪkəlɪ/ *adv.* systematisch

**systematisation**, **systematise** ⇒ **systematiz-**

**systematization** /sɪstəmətaɪ'zeɪʃn/ *n.* Systematisierung, *die*

**systematize** /'sɪstəmətaɪz/ *v.t.* systematisieren (**into** zu)

**'system disk** *n.* (*Computing*) Systemdiskette, *die;*

**systemic** /sɪ'stemɪk/ *adj.* (*Biol.*) systemisch

**systems: ~ analysis** *n.* Systemanalyse, *die;* **~ analyst** *n.* ▶ 1261 Systemanalytiker, *der*/ -analytikerin, *die*

**'system software** *n.* (*Computing*) Systemsoftware, *die*

**systolic** /sɪs'tɒlɪk/ *adj.* (*Physiol.*) systolisch

S

# Tt

**T, t** /tiː/ *n., pl.* **Ts** *or* **T's** **A** (*letter*) T, t, *das;* **to a T** ganz genau; haargenau; **that's her to a T** das ist sie, wie sie leibt und lebt; **cross the t's** (*fig.*) peinlich genau sein; **B** (*T-shaped object*) T, *das;* **T-junction** Einmündung, *die* (*in eine Vorfahrtsstraße*); **T-bone steak** T-bone-Steak, *das;* **T-shirt** T-shirt, *das;* **T-square** ⇨ **square** 1 J

**t.** *abbr.* ▶1683 **A** **ton[s]** [britische] Tonne[n]; **B** **tonne[s]** t

**TA** *abbr.* (*Brit.*) **Territorial Army**

**ta** /tɑː/ *int.* (*Brit. coll.*) danke

**tab[1]** /tæb/ ❶ *n.* **A** (*projecting flap*) Zunge, *die;* (*label*) Schildchen, *das;* (*on clothing*) Etikett, *das;* (*with name*) Namensschild, *das;* (*on file* [*card*]) Reiter, *der;* **B** (*Amer. coll.: bill*) Rechnung, *die;* **pick up the ~:** die Zeche bezahlen; **C** (*Amer. coll.: price*) Preis, *der;* **D** **keep ~s** *or* **a ~ on sb./sth.** (*watch*) jmdn./etw. [genau] beobachten; **E** (*Brit. Mil.: on collar*) Kragenspiegel, *der;* **F** (*Theatre*) Hängestück, *das;* **G** (*Aeronaut.*) Trimmruder, *das;* Hilfsruder, *das.* ❷ *v.t.*, **-bb-** ⇨ **1** A: mit Zunge/Schildchen/Etikett/Namensschild/Reitern versehen

**tab[2]** ⇨ **tabulator**

**Tabasco** ® /təˈbæskəʊ/ *n.* Tabasco, *der;* Tabascosoße, *die*

**tabby** /ˈtæbɪ/ *n.* **A** ~ **[cat]** Tigerkatze, *die;* **B** (*female cat*) [weibliche] Katze; Kätzin, *die*

**tabernacle** /ˈtæbənækl/ *n.* **A** (*Bibl.*) Stiftshütte, *die;* **B** (*Relig.: meeting house*) Gotteshaus, *das;* **C** (*Eccl.: receptacle*) Tabernakel, *der*

**table** /ˈteɪbl/ ❶ *n.* **A** Tisch, *der;* **at ~:** bei Tisch; **sit down at ~:** sich zu Tisch setzen; **after two whiskies he was under the ~** (*coll.*) nach zwei Whisky lag er unter dem Tisch (*ugs.*); **drink sb. under the ~:** jmdn. unter den Tisch trinken (*ugs.*); **get sb./get round the ~:** jmdn. an einen Tisch bringen/sich an einen Tisch setzen; **turn the ~s [on sb.]** (*fig.*) [jmdm. gegenüber] den Spieß umdrehen *od.* umkehren; ⇨ *also* **lay[2]** 1 E; **B** (*list*) Tabelle, *die;* **~ of contents** Inhaltsverzeichnis, *das;* **~ of logarithms** Logarithmentafel, *die;* **learn one's ~s** das Einmaleins lernen; **say one's nine times ~:** die Neunerreihe aufsagen; **C** (*company at ~*) Runde, *die;* **D** (*food provided*) **keep a good/wretched ~:** eine ausgezeichnete/jämmerliche Küche führen.
❷ *v.t.* **A** (*bring forward*) einbringen, (*ugs.*) auf den Tisch legen ‹Antrag, Resolution›; **B** (*Amer.: shelve*) auf Eis legen (*ugs.*) ‹Plan usw.›

**tableau** /ˈtæbləʊ/ *n., pl.* **~x** /ˈtæbləʊz/ (*lit. or fig.*) Tableau, *das*

**ˈtablecloth** *n.* Tischdecke, *die;* Tischtuch, *das*

**table d'hôte** /tɑːbl ˈdəʊt/ *n.* Table d'hôte, *die* (*geh.*); **~ menu** Tageskarte, *die*

**table: ~ knife** *n.* Messer, *das;* Tischmesser, *das* (*veralt.*); **~ lamp** *n.* Tischlampe, *die;* **~land** *n.* (*Geog.*) Tafelland, *das;* **~ leg** *n.* Tischbein, *das;* **~ linen** *n.* Tischwäsche, *die;* **~ manners** *n. pl.* Tischmanieren *Pl.;* **~ mat** *n.* Set, *das;* **T~ ˈMountain** *pr. n.* Tafelberg, *der;* **~ napkin** *n.* Serviette, *die;* **~ salt** *n.* Tafelsalz, *das;* **~spoon** *n.* Servierlöffel, *der;* **~spoonful** *n.* Servierlöffel [voll], *der*

**tablet** /ˈtæblɪt/ *n.* **A** (*pill*) Tablette, *die;* **B** (*piece*) Stück, *das;* **C** (*stone slab*) Tafel, *die;* **D** (*for writing on*) [Schreib]tafel, *die;* (*Amer.: pad*) Notizblock, *der*

**table: ~ talk** *n., no pl.* Tischgespräch, *das;* **sb.'s ~ talk** jmds. Tischgespräche; **~ tennis** *n.* (*Sport*) Tischtennis, *das;* **~ tennis bat** Tischtennisschläger, *der;* **~ top** *n.* Tischplatte, *die;* **~-top** *adj.* an einer Tischplatte angebracht ‹Dosenöffner usw.›; Tisch‹kühlschrank, -waschmaschine›; **~ware** *n., no pl.* Geschirr, Besteck und Gläser; **~ wine** *n.* Tischwein, *der*

**tabloid** /ˈtæblɔɪd/ *n.* (*kleinformatige, bebilderte*) Boulevardzeitung; **the ~s** (*derog.*) die Boulevardpresse; **~ journalism** Sensationsjournalismus, *der*

**taboo, tabu** /təˈbuː/ ❶ *n.* Tabu, *das;* **be under a ~:** tabu sein. ❷ *adj.* tabuisiert; Tabu‹wort›; **be ~:** tabu sein. ❸ *v.t.* tabuisieren

**tabular** /ˈtæbjʊlə(r)/ *adj.* tabellarisch

**tabulate** /ˈtæbjʊleɪt/ *v.t.* tabellarisch darstellen; tabellarisieren

**tabulation** /tæbjʊˈleɪʃn/ *n.* tabellarische Aufstellung; Tabellarisierung, *die*

**tabulator** /ˈtæbjʊleɪtə(r)/ *n.* Tabulator, *der*

**tachograph** /ˈtækəgrɑːf/ *n.* (*Motor Veh.*) Fahrt[en]schreiber, *der*

**tachometer** /təˈkɒmɪtə(r)/ *n.* Tachometer, *der od. das*

**tacit** /ˈtæsɪt/ *adj.*, **tacitly** /ˈtæsɪtlɪ/ *adv.* stillschweigend

**taciturn** /ˈtæsɪtɜːn/ *adj.* schweigsam; wortkarg

**taciturnity** /tæsɪˈtɜːnɪtɪ/ *n., no pl.* Schweigsamkeit, *die;* Wortkargheit, *die*

**tack[1]** /tæk/ ❶ *n.* **A** (*small nail*) kleiner Nagel; **carpet ~:** Teppichnagel, *der;* **shoe ~:** Täcks, *der;* ⇨ *also* **brass tacks**; **B** (*temporary stitch*) Heftstich, *der;* **C** (*Naut.*) (*direction of vessel; also fig.*) Kurs, *der;* (*in zigzag*) Kreuzen, *das;* **be on the port/starboard ~:** auf Backbord-/Steuerbordhalsen liegen; **on the right/wrong ~** (*fig.*) auf dem richtigen/falschen Weg *od.* Kurs; **change one's ~, try another ~** (*fig.*) einen anderen Kurs einschlagen. ❷ *v.t.* **A** (*stitch loosely*) heften; **B** (*nail*) festnageln. ❸ *v.i.* (*Naut.*) kreuzen

**~ ˈdown** *v.t.* annageln; festnageln

**~ ˈon** *v.t.* anhängen (**to** an + *Akk.*)

**tack[2]** *n.* (*Horse riding*) **[riding] ~:** Sattel- und Zaumzeug, *das*

**tackiness[1]** /ˈtækɪnɪs/ *n., no pl.* Klebrigkeit, *die*

**tackiness[2]** *n., no pl.* (*coll. derog.*) **A** (*tastelessness*) Geschmacklosigkeit, *die;* **B** (*tattiness*) Schäbigkeit, *die*

**tackle** /ˈtækl/ ❶ *v.t.* **A** (*come to grips with*) angehen, in Angriff nehmen ‹Problem usw.›; **~ sb. about/on/over sth.** jmdn. auf etw. (*Akk.*) ansprechen; (*ask for sth.*) jmdn. um etw. angehen; **B** (*Sport*) angreifen ‹Spieler›; (*Amer. Footb.; Rugby*) fassen. ❷ *n.* **A** (*equipment*) Ausrüstung, *die;* **shaving ~:** Rasierzeug, *das;* ⇨ *also* **fishing tackle**; **B** (*Sport*) Angriff, *der;* (*sliding ~*) Tackling, *das;* (*Amer. Footb., Rugby*) Fassen und Halten; **C** ⇨ **block** 1 N

**tackling** /ˈtæklɪŋ/ *n.* (*Sport*) Tackling, *das*

**ˈtack room** *n.* Sattelkammer, *die*

**tacky[1]** /ˈtækɪ/ *adj.* klebrig

**tacky[2]** *adj.* (*coll. derog.*) **A** (*tasteless*) geschmacklos; **B** (*tatty*) schäbig

**tact** /tækt/ *n.* Takt, *der;* **he has no ~:** er hat kein Taktgefühl

**tactful** /ˈtæktfl/ *adj.*, **tactfully** /ˈtæktfəlɪ/ *adv.* taktvoll

**tactfulness** /ˈtæktflnɪs/ *n., no pl.* Taktgefühl, *das*

**tactic** /ˈtæktɪk/ *n.* Taktik, *die;* **delaying ~:** Verzögerungstaktik, *die;* ⇨ *also* **tactics**

**tactical** /ˈtæktɪkl/ *adj.* **A** taktisch ‹Fehler, Manöver, Rückzug›; **~ voting** taktische Stimmabgabe; **B** (*skilled in tactics*) taktisch klug; **have a good ~ sense** taktisch klug *od.* geschickt sein

**tactically** /ˈtæktɪkəlɪ/ *adv.* taktisch

**tactician** /tækˈtɪʃn/ *n.* Taktiker, *der*/Taktikerin, *die*

**tactics** /ˈtæktɪks/ *n. pl.* **A** (*methods*) Taktik, *die;* **dubious ~:** zweifelhafte Methoden; **B** *constr. as sing.* (*Mil.*) Taktik, *die*

**tactile** /ˈtæktaɪl/ *adj.* **A** (*using touch*) Tast‹organ›; taktil (*Med.*); **B** (*tangible*) tastbar

**tactless** /ˈtæktlɪs/ *adj.* taktlos

**tactlessly** /ˈtæktlɪslɪ/ *adv.* taktlos; *as sentence-modifier* taktloserweise

**tactlessness** /ˈtæktlɪsnɪs/ *n., no pl.* Taktlosigkeit, *die*

**tadpole** /ˈtædpəʊl/ *n.* Kaulquappe, *die*

**taffeta** /ˈtæfɪtə/ *n.* (*Textiles*) Taft, *der*

**taffrail** /ˈtæfreɪl/ *n.* (*Naut.*) Heckreling, *die*

**taffy** *n.* (*Amer.*) Karamellbonbon, *das*

**Taffy** /ˈtæfɪ/ *n.* (*coll.: Welshman*) Waliser, *der*

**tag[1]** /tæg/ ❶ *n.* **A** (*label*) Schild, *das;* (*on clothes*) Etikett, *das;* (*on animal's ear*) Ohrmarke, *die;* **B** (*electronic device*) (*on person*) elektronische Fessel; (*on goods*) Sicherungsetikett, *das;* **C** (*loop*) Schlaufe, *die;* **D** (*metal etc. point at end of lace*) Senkelstift, *der;* **E** (*Computing*) Tag, *das;* Markierung, *die;* **F** (*stock phrase*) Zitat, *das;* geflügeltes Wort; **G** (*Amer.: licence plate*) Nummernschild, *das.* ⇨ *also* **price tag**.
❷ *v.t.*, **-gg-:** **A** (*attach*) anhängen (**to** an + *Akk.*); **~ together** aneinander hängen; zusammenheften ‹Blätter, Papier›; (*fig.*) aneinander reihen; **B** (*with electronic device*) **~ sth.** etw. mit einem Sicherungsetikett versehen; **~ sb.** jmdm. eine elektronische Fessel anlegen; **C** (*Computing*) taggen; markieren.
❸ *v.i.*, **-gg-:** **~ behind** [nach]folgen; **~ after sb.** hinter jmdm. hertrotteln (*ugs.*)

**~ aˈlong** *v.i.* mitkommen

**~ ˈon** *v.t.* anhängen (**to** an + *Akk.*)

**tag[2]** *n.* (*game*) Fangen, *das*

**tag: ~ day** (*Amer.*) ⇨ **flag day** B; **~ ˈquestion** *n.* (*Ling.*) (*auf ein bestätigende Antwort zielendes*) Frageanhängsel, *das;* **~ wrestling** *n.* (*Sport*) *Ringkampf zwischen zwei Mannschaften von je zwei Ringern, von denen nur einer im Ring steht und sich von seinem Partner ablösen lassen kann*

**tail** /teɪl/ ❶ *n.* **A** Schwanz, *der;* **tops and ~s** (*of carrots, turnips*) obere und untere Enden; **B** (*fig.*) **have sb./sth. on one's ~:** jmdn./etw. auf den Fersen haben (*ugs.*); **be/keep on sb.'s ~:** jmdm. auf den Fersen sein/bleiben (*ugs.*); **with one's ~ between one's legs** mit eingezogenem Schwanz (*ugs.*); **sb. has his ~ up** jmd. ist übermütig; **turn ~ [and run]** Fersengeld geben (*ugs.*); die Flucht ergreifen; **C** (*of comet*) Schweif, *der;* **D** **[shirt] ~:** Hemdzipfel, *der* (*ugs.*); **E** (*of man's coat*) Schoß, *der;* **F** *in pl.* (*man's evening dress*) Frack, *der;* **G** *in pl.* (*on coin*) **~s [it is]** Zahl; ⇨ **head** 1 E; **H** (*Mus.: stem of note*) [Noten]hals, *der;* **I** (*part of letter below line*) Unterlänge, *die;* **J** (*coll.: person keeping watch*) Schatten, *der;* **have/put a ~ on sb.** jmdn. beschatten lassen.
❷ *v.t.* **A** (*remove stalks of*) **top and ~ gooseberries** Stachelbeeren putzen; **B** (*coll.: follow*) beschatten

**~ aˈway** ⇨ **~ off**

**~ ˈback** *v.i.* sich stauen. ⇨ *also* **tailback**

**~ ˈoff** *v.i.* **A** (*decrease*) zurückgehen; **B** (*fade into silence*) ersterben (*geh.*); verstummen

**tail:** **~back** *n.* (*Brit.*) Rückstau, *der;* **~board** *n.* hintere Bordwand; **~ coat** *n.* Frack, *der;* **~ end** *n.* (*hindmost end*) Schwanz, *der;* (*fig.*) Ende, *das;* **come in at the ~-end** erst am Ende hinzustoßen; **~ fin** *n.* (*Aeronaut.*) Seitenflosse, *die;* **~gate** ❶ *n.* (*Motor Veh.*) Heckklappe, *die;* ❷ *v.i.* zu dicht auffahren

**'tail lamp** (*esp. Amer.*) ⇒ **tail light**

**tailless** /'teɪllɪs/ *adj.* schwanzlos; **the animal was ~:** das Tier hatte keinen Schwanz

**'tail light** *n.* Rück- *od.* Schlusslicht, *das*

**tailor** /'teɪlə(r)/ ❶ *n.* ▶ 1261 Schneider, *der*/Schneiderin, *die;* ⇒ *also* **baker.** ❷ *v.t.* A schneidern; B (*fig.*) **~ed to** *or* **for sb./sth.** für jmdn./etw. maßgeschneidert; **~ed to sb.'s needs** auf jmds. Bedürfnisse zugeschnitten

**tailored** /'teɪləd/ *adj.* maßgeschneidert; **~ suit** Maßanzug, *der;* (*for woman*) Schneiderkostüm, *das*

**tailoring** /'teɪlərɪŋ/ *n., no pl.* Schneiderei, *die;* Schneidern, *das*

**'tailor-made** *adj.* (*lit. or fig.*) maßgeschneidert

**tailor's:** **~ chalk** *n.* Schneiderkreide, *die;* **~ 'dummy** *n.* Schneiderpuppe, *die;* (*fig.*) Geck, *der*/Modepuppe, *die*

**tail:** **~piece** *n.* A (*appendage*) Anhang, *der;* B (*Mus.: for string-ends*) Saitenhalter, *der;* C (*decoration*) [Schluss]vignette, *die;* **~pipe** *n.* Auspuffendstück, *das;* **~plane** *n.* (*Aeronaut.*) Höhenleitwerk, *das;* **~ skid** *n.* (*Aeronaut.*) Sporn, *der;* **~spin** *n.* A (*of aircraft*) Trudeln, *das;* B (*fig.: state of panic*) **send sb./go into a ~spin** jmdn. in Panik versetzen/zu rotieren anfangen (*ugs.*); **~wheel** *n.* (*Aeronaut.*) Spornrad, *das;* **~ wind** *n.* Rückenwind, *der*

**taint** /teɪnt/ ❶ *n.* Makel, *der;* **hereditary ~:** erbliche Belastung. ❷ *v.t.* verderben; beflecken ‹Ruf›; **be ~ed with sth.** mit etw. behaftet sein (*geh.*)

**Taiwan** /taɪ'wɑːn/ *pr. n.* Taiwan (*das*)

**Taiwanese** /taɪwə'niːz/ ▶ 1340 ❶ *adj.* taiwanesisch. ❷ *n.* Taiwanese, *der*/Taiwanesin, *die*

**take** /teɪk/ ❶ *v.t.*, **took** /tʊk/, **~n** /'teɪkn/ A (*get hold of, grasp, seize*) nehmen; **~ sb.'s arm** jmds. Arm nehmen; **~ sb. by the hand/arm** jmdn. bei der Hand/am Arm nehmen; **he took me by the arm/elbow and steered me in the direction of the exit** er fasste mich am Arm/Ellbogen und dirigierte mich zum Ausgang; **~ matters into one's own hands** (*fig.*) die Sache selbst in die Hand nehmen; ⇒ *also* **bit**[1] A; **bull**[1] 1 A; **devil** 1 C; **hold**[2] 3 A; **law** D; **life** A; B (*capture*) einnehmen ‹Stadt, Festung›; machen ‹Gefangenen›; fassen ‹Banditen›; (*chess*) schlagen; nehmen; (*Cards*) stechen; ⇒ *also* **hold**[2] 3 A; **hostage**; **possession** D; **short** 2 C; **storm** 1 D; **surprise** 1; C (*gain, earn*) ‹Laden:› einbringen; ‹Person:› einnehmen; ‹Film, Stück:› einspielen; (*win*) gewinnen ‹Satz, Spiel, Preis, Titel›; erzielen ‹Punkte›; (*Cards*) machen ‹Stich›; **~ a wicket** (*Cricket*) einen Schlagmann zum Ausscheiden bringen; **~ first/second** *etc.* **place** den ersten/zweiten *usw.* Platz belegen; (*fig.*) an erster/zweiter *usw.* Stelle kommen; **~ the biscuit** (*Brit. coll.*) *or* (*coll.*) **cake** (*fig.*) alle/alles übertreffen; D (*assume possession of*) nehmen; (**~ away with one**) mitnehmen; (*steal*) mitnehmen (*verhüll.*); (*obtain by purchase*) besorgen ‹Eintrittskarte, [Logen]platz›; kaufen, (*by rent*) mieten ‹Auto, Wohnung, Haus›; nehmen ‹Klavier-, Deutsch-, Fahrstunden›; mitmachen ‹Tanzkurs›; (*buy regularly*) nehmen; lesen ‹Zeitung, Zeitschrift›; (*subscribe to*) beziehen; (*obtain*) erwerben ‹akademischen Grad›; (*form a relationship with*) sich (*Dat.*) nehmen ‹Frau, Geliebten usw.›; ins Haus nehmen ‹zahlende Gäste›; **that woman took my purse** die Frau hat mir meinen Geldbeutel gestohlen; **he took his degree at Sussex University** er hat sein Examen an der Universität von Sussex gemacht; **~ place** stattfinden; (*spontaneously*) sich ereignen; ‹Wandlung:› sich vollziehen; **I'll ~ this handbag/the curry, please** ich nehme diese Handtasche/das Curry; **who has ~n my pencil?** wer hat meinen Bleistift weggenommen?; **~ [private] pupils** [Privat]stunden geben; **he took her as** *or* **for his wife** er nahm sie zur Frau; ⇒ *also* **order** 1 C, H; **possession** D; **silk** 1 A; E (*avail oneself of, use*) nehmen; machen ‹Pause, Ferien, Nickerchen›; nehmen ‹Beispiel, Zitat usw.› (**from** aus); **~ the opportunity to do/of doing sth.** die Gelegenheit dazu benutzen, etw. zu tun; **~ the car/bus into town** mit dem Auto/Bus in die Stadt fahren; **~ two eggs** *etc.* (*in recipe*) man nehme zwei Eier *usw.;* **~ all the time you want** nimm dir ruhig Zeit; **a story ~n from life** eine Geschichte aus dem Leben; **a quotation ~n from Pope** ein Zitat aus Pope; **[let's] ~ a more recent example/my sister [for example]** nehmen wir ein Beispiel neueren Datums/einmal meine Schwester; **thou shalt not ~ God's name in vain** (*Bibl.*) du sollst den Namen Gott[es] nicht unnütz führen; **do I hear someone taking my name in vain?** (*coll. joc.*) wer lästert denn da gerade über mich?; ⇒ *also* **advantage** A; **advice** A; **cure** 1 C; **leave**[1] C; **liberty**; **time** 1 B; F (*carry, guide, convey*) bringen; **~ sb.'s shoes to the mender['s]/sb.'s coat to the cleaner's** jmds. Schuhe zum Schuster/jmds. Mantel in die Reinigung bringen; **~ a message to sb.** jmdm. eine Nachricht überbringen; **the pipe ~s the water to the tank** das Rohr führt das Wasser zum Tank; **~ sb. to school/hospital** jmdn. zur Schule/ins Krankenhaus bringen; **~ sb. to visit sb.** jmdn. zu Besuch bei jmdm. mitnehmen; **~ sb. to the zoo/cinema/to dinner** mit jmdm. in den Zoo/ins Kino/zum Abendessen gehen; **~ sb. into one's home/house** jmdn. bei sich aufnehmen; **the road ~s you/story ~s us to London** die Straße führt nach/die Erzählung führt uns nach London; **my job has ~n me all over the world** ich bin beruflich in der ganzen Welt gereist; **his ability will ~ him far/to the top** mit seinen Fähigkeiten wird er es weit bringen/wird er ganz nach oben kommen; **~ sb./sth. with one** jmdn./etw. mitnehmen; **~ home** mit nach Hause nehmen; (*earn*) nach Hause bringen ‹Geld›; (*accompany*) nach Hause bringen *od.* begleiten; (*to meet one's parents etc.*) mit nach Hause bringen; ⇒ *also* **~-home**; **~ sb. before sb.** jmdn. jmdm. vorführen; **~ sb. through/over sth.** (*fig.*) mit jmdm. etw. durchgehen; **~ in hand** (*begin*) in Angriff nehmen; (*assume responsibility for*) sich kümmern um; **~ sb. into partnership [with one]/into the business** jmdn. zu seinem Teilhaber machen/in sein Geschäft aufnehmen; **~ an axe to sth.** etw. fällen; (*fig.*) bei etw. den Rotstift ansetzen; **~ a stick** *etc.* **to sb.** den Stock *usw.* bei jmdm. gebrauchen; **~ sth. to pieces** *or* **bits** etw. auseinander nehmen; **you can/can't ~ sb./sth. anywhere** (*fig. coll.*) man kann jmdn./etw. überallhin/nirgendwohin mitnehmen; **you can't ~ it 'with you** (*coll.*) man kann es ja nicht mitnehmen; ⇒ *also* **confidence** E; **court** 1 D; **head** 1 B; G (*remove*) nehmen; (*deduct*) abziehen; **~ sth./sb. from sb.** jmdm. etw./jmdn. wegnehmen; **I took the parcel from her** ich nahm ihr das Paket ab; **death has ~n him from us** (*fig.*) der Tod hat ihn uns genommen; **the children were ~n from their parents by the authorities** die Kinder wurden den Eltern von Amts wegen weggenommen; **be ~n from sb.** (*fig.*) jmdm. genommen werden; **~ all the fun/hard work out of sth.** einem alle Freude an etw. (*Dat.*) nehmen/einem die schwere Arbeit bei etw. ersparen; ⇒ *also* **life** A; **wind**[1] 1 A; H (*conceive, experience*) **sb. ~s courage from sth.** etw. macht jmdm. Mut; **~ courage!** nur Mut!; I **be ~n ill** *or* **sick** krank werden; **be ~n ill with food poisoning** eine Lebensmittelvergiftung bekommen; J (*make*) machen ‹Foto, Kopie›; (*photograph*) aufnehmen; **hate having one's photograph/picture ~n** sich gar nicht gern fotografieren lassen; **the camera ~s good photographs** die Kamera macht gute Bilder *od.* Fotos; **~ sb.'s fingerprints** jmdm. Fingerabdrücke abnehmen; K (*perform, execute*) aufnehmen ‹Brief, Diktat›; machen ‹Prüfung, Sprung, Spaziergang, Reise, Umfrage›; durchführen ‹Befragung, Volkszählung›; ablegen ‹Gelübde, Eid›; übernehmen ‹Rolle, Part›; treffen ‹Entscheidung›; **~ a fall/tumble** stürzen/straucheln; **~ a step forward/backward** einen Schritt vor-/zurücktreten; **~ a turn for the better/worse** eine Wende zum Besseren/Schlechteren nehmen; **~ a scene/movement more slowly** eine Szene/einen Satz langsamer nehmen; ⇒ *also* **action** A; **bow**[2] 3; **effect** 1 D; **vote** 1 A; L (*negotiate*) nehmen ‹Zaun, Mauer, Hürde, Kurve, Hindernis›; **the bus took the corner too fast** der Bus ist zu schnell um die Kurve gefahren; M (*conduct*) halten ‹Gottesdienst, Andacht, Unterricht›; **he ~s the older pupils in Latin** er hat die älteren Schüler in Latein; **Ms X ~s us for maths** in Mathe haben wir Frau X; N (*be taught, be examined in*) **~ Latin at school** in der Schule Latein haben; **~ Latin in an exam** in einem Examen in Latein geprüft werden; **~ an examination/a test** eine Prüfung machen; O (*consume*) trinken ‹Tee, Kaffee, Kognak usw.›; einnehmen (*geh.*) ‹Mahlzeit›; nehmen ‹Zucker, Milch, Überdosis, Tabletten, Medizin›; **~ some food** etwas essen; **~ sugar in one's tea** den Tee mit Zucker trinken; **what can I ~ for a cold?** was kann ich gegen eine Erkältung nehmen?; **to be ~n three times a day** dreimal täglich einzunehmen; **not to be ~n [internally]** nicht zur innerlichen Anwendung; ⇒ *also* **bite** 3 A; **drug** 1 B; **medicine**; **sip** 3; P (*occupy*) einnehmen ‹Sitz im Parlament›; übernehmen, antreten ‹Amt›; **~ sb.'s seat** sich auf jmds. Platz setzen; **is that/this seat ~n?** ist da/hier noch frei?; ⇒ *also* **back seat**; **chair** 1 A, B; **place** 1 F, J; **seat** 1 B; Q (*need, require*) brauchen ‹Platz, Zeit›; haben ‹Kleider-, Schuhgröße usw.›; (*Ling.*) haben ‹Objekt, Plural-s›; gebraucht werden mit ‹Kasus›; **this verb ~s 'sein'** dieses Verb wird mit „sein" konjugiert; **the wound will ~ some time to heal** es braucht einige Zeit, bis die Wunde geheilt ist; **the ticket machine ~s 20p and 50p coins** der Fahrkartenautomat nimmt 20-Pence- und 50-Pence-Stücke; **the work is taking too much of my time** die Arbeit kostet mich zu viel Zeit; **as long as it ~s** so lange wie nötig; **sth. ~s an hour/a year/all day** etw. dauert eine Stunde/ein Jahr/einen ganzen Tag; **it ~s an hour** *etc.* **to do sth.** es dauert eine Stunde *usw.*, [um] etw. zu tun; **the meat ~s three hours to cook** das Fleisch braucht drei Stunden, bis es gar ist; **sb. ~s** *or* **it ~s sb. a long time/an hour** *etc.* **to do sth.** jmd. braucht lange/eine Stunde *usw.*, um etw. zu tun; **what took you so long?** was hast du denn so lange gemacht?; **~ a lot of money/£3,000** viel Geld/3 000 Pfund kosten; **~ a lot of work/effort/courage** viel Arbeit/Mühe/Mut kosten; **it took all my strength/determination** ich brauchte all meine Kraft/Entschlossenheit; **it doesn't ~ much to make him happy** es gehört nicht viel dazu, ihn glücklich zu machen; **have [got] what it ~s** das Zeug dazu haben; **he took a lot of/some convincing** er war schwer/nicht so leicht zu überzeugen; **these windows ~ a lot of cleaning** diese Fenster sind schwer zu putzen; **it will ~ [quite] a lot of explaining** es wird schwer zu erklären sein; **that story of his ~s some believing** die Geschichte, die er da erzählt, ist kaum zu glauben; **it ~s an expert to notice the difference** nur ein Fachmann kann den Unterschied feststellen; **it would ~ a saint to get along with him** man müsste ein Heiliger sein, um mit ihm auszukommen; **it ~s a thief to know a thief** nur ein Dieb kennt einen Dieb; **it ~s all sorts to make a world** es gibt solche und solche; ⇒ *also* **beating** B; **time** 1 B; R (*accommodate, hold*) fassen; (*support*) tragen; **the car will ~ six adults** in dem Auto haben sechs Erwachsene Platz; **that room can't ~ a grand piano** in das Zimmer passt kein Flügel; S (*ascertain and record*) notieren ‹Namen, Adresse, Autonummer usw.›; zu Protokoll nehmen ‹Hergang eines Unfalls usw.›; fühlen ‹Puls›; messen ‹Temperatur, Größe usw.›; **~ sb.'s**

**measurements for a new suit** [bei] jmdm. für einen neuen Anzug Maß nehmen; **~ the minutes of a meeting** bei einer Sitzung [das] Protokoll führen; **~ a reading from the barometer** den Barometerstand ablesen; **T** (*apprehend, grasp*) **~ sb.'s meaning/drift**, (*arch.*) **~ sb.** verstehen, was jmd. meint; **... if you ~ my meaning** ..., Sie verstehen?; **~ sb.'s point** jmds. Standpunkt verstehen; **~ it [that] ...:** annehmen, [dass] ...; **can I ~ it that ...?** kann ich davon ausgehen, dass ...?; **am I to ~ it that ...?** soll ich das so verstehen, dass ...?; **~ sth. to mean sth.** etw. so verstehen, dass ...; **what do you ~ that to mean/signify?** wie verstehen Sie das/was bedeutet das Ihrer Meinung nach?; **~ sth. as settled/as a compliment/refusal** etw. als erledigt betrachten/als eine Ablehnung/ein Kompliment auffassen; **~ sb./sth. for/to be sth.** jmdn./etw. für etw. halten; **what do you ~ me for?** wofür halten Sie mich?; **I ~ him to be in his fifties** ich schätze ihn zwischen fünfzig und sechzig; **not know how to ~ sb.'s reply** nicht wissen, wie man jmds. Antwort verstehen soll; **~ what sb. says the wrong way** jmdn. falsch verstehen; ⇒ *also* **gospel** B; **grant** 1 C; **literally** A; **word** 1 B; **U** (*treat or react to in a specified manner*) aufnehmen; **~ sth. like a man** etw. wie ein Mann nehmen; **~ sth. well/badly/hard** etw. gut/schlecht/nur schwer verkraften; **sb. ~s sth. very badly/hard** etw. trifft jmdn. sehr; **~ sth. calmly** *or* **coolly** etw. gelassen [auf- *od.* hin]nehmen; **~ sth. as read** etw. als bekannt voraussetzen; **you can/may ~ it as read that ...:** du kannst sicher sein, dass ...; **taking it all in all, taking one thing with another** alles in allem; ⇒ *also* **amiss** 2; **easy** 2; **heart** 1 B, C; **kindly** 1 C; **stride** 1 A; **V** (*accept*) annehmen; **~ money** *etc.* **[from sb./for sth.]** Geld *usw.* [von jmdm./für etw.] [an]nehmen; **will you ~ £500 for the car?** wollen Sie den Wagen für 500 Pfund verkaufen?; **[you can] ~ it or leave it** entweder du bist damit einverstanden, oder du lässt es bleiben; **I can ~ it or leave it** (*am indifferent*) ich mache mir nicht besonders viel daraus; **~ the hint** den Wink verstehen; **he can never ~ a hint** er hat kein Feingefühl; **I know how to ~ a hint** ich verstehe schon; **~ sb.'s word for it** sich auf jmdn. *od.* jmds. Wort[e] verlassen; **you can ~ his word for it that ...:** wenn er es sagt, kannst du dich darauf verlassen, dass ...; **you don't have to ~ my word for it** du brauchst es mir nicht zu glauben; **~ things as they come, ~ it as it comes** es nehmen, wie es kommt; ⇒ *also* **advice** A; **chance** 1 E; **consequence** A; **risk** 1 A; **W** (*receive, submit to*) einstecken [müssen] ‹Schlag, Tritt, Stoß›; (*Boxing*) nehmen [müssen] ‹Schlag›; (*endure, tolerate*) aushalten; vertragen ‹Klima, Alkohol, Kaffee, Knoblauch›; verwinden ‹Schock›; (*put up with*) sich (*Dat.*) gefallen lassen [müssen] ‹Kritik, Grobheit›; **~ one's punishment bravely** seine Strafe tapfer ertragen; **the boxer/the car took a lot of punishment** der Boxer musste viel einstecken/das Auto musste eine Menge aushalten; **~ no nonsense** sich (*Dat.*) nichts bieten lassen; **~ 'that!** nimm das!; **~ it** (*coll.*) es verkraften; (*referring to criticism, abuse*) damit fertig werden; **There's a lot of pressure on you. — I can ~ it** Du stehst sehr unter Druck. — Ich werde damit schon fertig; **X** (*adopt, choose*) ergreifen ‹Maßnahmen›; unternehmen ‹Schritte›; einschlagen ‹Weg›; sich entschließen zu ‹Schritt, Handlungsweise›; **~ the wrong road** die falsche Straße nehmen; **~ a firm** *etc.* **stand [with sb./on** *or* **over sth.]** jmdm. gegenüber/hinsichtlich einer Sache nicht nachgeben; **~ the easy way out** die einfachste Lösung wählen; ⇒ *also* **resistance** A; **side** 1 I; **view** 1 D; **Y** (*receive, accommodate*) [an]nehmen ‹Bewerber, Schüler›; aufnehmen ‹Gäste›; annehmen ‹Farbe, Glanz›; **the city ~s its name from its founder** die Stadt ist nach ihrem Gründer benannt; **the rock ~s its colour from the minerals** der Fels hat seine Farbe von den Mineralien; **Z** (*swindle*) **he was ~n for £500 by the conman** (*coll.*) der Schwindler hat ihm 500 Pfund abgeknöpft (*ugs.*); **AA be ~n with sb./sth.** von jmdm./etw. angetan sein; **BB** (*copulate with*) nehmen.

❷ *v.i.*, **took**, **~n A** (*be successful, effective*) ‹Transplantat:› vom Körper angenommen werden; ‹Impfung:› anschlagen; ‹Pfropfreis:› anwachsen; ‹Sämling, Pflanze:› angehen; ‹Feuer:› zu brennen beginnen; ‹trockenes Holz:› Feuer fangen; ‹Farbe:› aufgenommen werden; ‹Anstrich, Leim:› halten; ‹Fisch:› [an]beißen; **B** (*detract*) **~ from sth.** etw. schmälern; **C ~ ill** *or* (*coll.*) **sick** krank werden; **D ~ well/badly** (*Photog.*) sich gut/schlecht fotografieren lassen.

❸ *n.* **A** (*Telev., Cinemat.*) Einstellung, *die;* Take, *der od. das* (*fachspr.*); ⇒ *also* **double ~**; **B** (*takings*) Einnahme, *die;* **our ~ was over £200 for the day** unsere Tageseinnahme betrug über 200 Pfund; **~ [of the loot]** Anteil [an der Beute]; **C** (*catch of fish*) Fang, *der;* (*catch of game*) Jagdbeute, *die*

**~ a'back** ⇒ **aback**

**~ after** *v.t.* **A ~ after sb.** (*resemble*) jmdm. ähnlich sein; (**~** *as one's example*) es jmdm. gleichtun; **B** (*Amer.: chase after*) nachsetzen (+ *Dat.*)

**~ a'long** *v.t.* mitnehmen

**~ a'part** ⇒ **apart** B

**~ a'round** *v.t.* **A** (**~** *with one*) überallhin mitnehmen; **B** (*show around*) herumführen

**~ a'side** ⇒ **aside** 1

**~ a'way** *v.t.* **A** (*remove*) wegnehmen; (*to a distance*) mitnehmen; **~ sth. away from sb.** jmdm. etw. abnehmen; **~ sb.'s licence/passport away** jmdm. den Führerschein/Pass abnehmen; **what the taxman gives with one hand, he ~s away with the other** was der Fiskus mit der einen Hand gibt, das nimmt er mit der anderen wieder; **to ~ away** ‹Pizza, Snack usw.› zum Mitnehmen; **tablets that will ~ away the pain** Tabletten, die einem die Schmerzen nehmen; **~ away sb.'s rights/privileges/freedom/job** jmdm. seine Rechte/Privilegien/die Freiheit/seinen Arbeitsplatz nehmen; **~ away all the flavour of the food** dem Essen jeden Geschmack nehmen; **alcohol ~s away all your worries** Alkohol vertreibt die Sorgen; **it has ~n away all the pleasure in my win** es hat mir die Freude am Sieg verdorben; **no one can ~ that away from you** das kann dir niemand nehmen; **~ sb. away** jmdn. wegbringen; ‹Polizei:› jmdn. abführen; **~ him away!** schafft ihn fort!; hinweg mit ihm! (*geh.*); **~ a child away from its parents/home/from school** ein Kind den Eltern wegnehmen/aus seiner häuslichen Umgebung herausreißen/aus der Schule nehmen; **~ sb. away from his/her work** jmdn. von der Arbeit abhalten; **my job ~s me away from my family/from home a lot** mein Beruf entzieht mich oft der Familie/durch meine Arbeit bin ich oft von zu Hause weg; **death/a cruel fate has ~n our father away from us** der Tod/ein grausames Schicksal hat uns den Vater genommen; **~ sb. away to the cells** jmdn. in seine Zelle bringen; **~ sb. away for a holiday** mit jmdm. in Urlaub fahren; ⇒ *also* **breath** A; **B** (*Math.: deduct*) abziehen. ⇒ *also* **~ away**

**~ a'way from** *v.t.* schmälern

**~ 'back** *v.t.* **A** (*retract, have back*) zurücknehmen; wieder einstellen ‹Arbeitnehmer›; wieder [bei sich] aufnehmen ‹Ehepartner›; (*reclaim*) sich (*Dat.*) wiedergeben lassen; **B** (*return*) zurückbringen; (**~** *somewhere again*) wiederbringen ‹Person›; (*carry or convey back*) wieder mitnehmen; **that ~s me back [to my childhood]** das weckt bei mir [Kindheits]erinnerungen; **C** (*Printing*) hochnehmen; raufziehen (*ugs.*)

**~ 'down** *v.t.* **A** (*carry or lead down*) hinunterbringen; **this path ~s you down to the harbour** auf diesem Weg kommen Sie zum Hafen [hinunter]; **B** (*lower or lift down*) abnehmen ‹Bild, Ankündigung, Weihnachtsschmuck›; einholen ‹Fahne›; umlegen ‹Mast›; herunterziehen, herunterlassen ‹Hose›; tiefer setzen ‹Zeile›; **~ a box down from a shelf** eine Schachtel von einem Regal herunternehmen; **C** (*dismantle*) abreißen; abbauen ‹Gerüst, Zelt›; **D** (*write down*) aufnehmen ‹Brief, Personalien›; aufschreiben ‹Autonummer›; mitschreiben ‹Vortrag›; **E** (*humiliate*) ducken; ⇒ *also* **peg** 1

**~ 'in** *v.t.* **A** (*convey to a place*) hinbringen; (*conduct*) hineinführen ‹Gast›; **~ sb. in a cup of tea** jmdm. eine Tasse Tee [hinein]bringen; **~ the car in for a service** das Auto zur Wartung bringen; **~ sb. in [in the car]** jmdn. [mit dem Auto] reinfahren (*ugs.*); **I took the car in** ich fuhr mit dem Auto rein (*ugs.*); **the police took him in for questioning** die Polizei nahm ihn zum Verhör mit; **B** (*bring indoors*) hereinholen; **~ in parcels for sb.** Pakete für jmdn. annehmen; **~ in the washing from the line** die Wäsche von der Leine [ab]nehmen [und hereinholen]; **C** (*accept for payment*) **~ in washing** für andere Leute waschen; **D** (*receive, admit*) aufnehmen; (*for payment*) vermieten an (+ *Akk.*); [auf]nehmen ‹[Kur]gäste›; **~ in lodgers** ‹Haus-, Wohnungseigentümer:› Zimmer vermieten; ‹Mieter:› untervermieten; **E** (*make narrower*) enger machen ‹Kleidungsstück›; **F** (*include, comprise*) einbeziehen; **G** (*coll.: visit*) mitnehmen (*ugs.*); **our tour took in most of the main sights** auf unserer Rundfahrt haben wir die wichtigsten Sehenswürdigkeiten besichtigt; **H** (*understand, grasp*) begreifen; überblicken, erfassen ‹Lage›; **I cannot ~ in any more of this lecture** ich kann mich auf diese Vorlesung nicht mehr konzentrieren; **I have won — I can't ~ it in yet** ich habe gewonnen — ich kann es noch gar nicht richtig begreifen; **I** (*observe*) erfassen; (*watch, listen to*) mitbekommen; **J** (*deceive*) täuschen; hereinlegen (*ugs.*); **be ~n in [by sb./sth.]** sich [von jmdn./durch etw.] täuschen *od.* (*ugs.*) hereinlegen lassen; ⇒ *also* **~-in**

**~ 'off** ❶ *v.t.* **A** abnehmen ‹Deckel, Hut, Bild, Hörer, Tischtuch, Verband›; abziehen ‹Kissenbezug›; ausziehen ‹Schuhe, Handschuhe›; ablegen ‹Hut, Mantel, Schmuck›; ‹Säure:› wegätzen ‹Farbe›; **~ off sb.'s/one's clothes** jmdm./sich die Kleider ausziehen; **~ sth. off the fire** etw. vom Feuer nehmen; **~ a door off the hinges** eine Tür aus den Angeln heben; **~ the cover off a pillow/bed** ein Kissen abziehen/ein Bett abdecken; **~ a parcel off sb.** jmdm. ein Paket abnehmen; **~ your hands off me!** fass mich nicht an!; **~ your feet off the settee!** nimm die Füße vom Sofa!; **~ off one's make-up** sich abschminken; **the heat has ~n the paint off the door** durch die Hitze ist die Farbe von der Tür abgeblättert; **B** (*transfer from*) übernehmen ‹Passagiere, Besatzung, Fracht›; (*withdraw from a programme*) aus dem Programm nehmen; **~ sb. off sth.** jmdn. von etw. holen; (*withdraw from job, assignment, etc.*) jmdm. etw. entziehen; **he was ~n off the case** er wurde von dem Fall abgezogen; **~ sth. off a list/the menu** etw. von einer Liste streichen/von der Speisekarte nehmen; **~ a train/bus off a route** einen Zug/Bus vom Fahrplan streichen; **~ the weight off one's feet** seine Beine ausruhen; **~ years/ten years off sb.** jmdn. um Jahre jünger machen/jmdn. zehn Jahre jünger machen; ⇒ *also* **edge** 1 A; **eye** 1 A; **gilt** 1 A; **hat** A; **mind** 1 C; **smile** 1; **C** (*cut off*) abtrennen; (*with saw*) absägen; (*with knife, scissors, etc.*) abschneiden; (*amputate*) abnehmen; **she had an inch ~n off her hair** sie ließ sich (*Dat.*) ihr Haar zwei cm kürzer schneiden; **D** (*lead, conduct*) **~ sb. off to hospital/prison** jmdn. ins Krankenhaus/Gefängnis bringen; **~ sb. off on a stretcher/by ambulance** jmdn. auf einer Bahre/im Krankenwagen wegbringen; **~ sb. off to Paris** mit jmdm. nach Paris fahren; **I shall ~ my family off on** *or* **for a holiday** ich werde mit meiner Familie wegfahren *od.* in Urlaub fahren; **~ oneself off home/to bed** nach Hause/ins Bett gehen; **E** (*deduct*) abziehen; **~ sth. off sth.** etw. von etw. abziehen; **~ £10 off the price** den Preis um zehn Pfund reduzieren; **F ~ off weight/a few pounds** (*lose weight*) abnehmen/einige Pfund abnehmen; **the diet has ~n pounds off my weight** die Diät hat mich um Pfunde leichter gemacht; **G** (*have free*) **~ a day** *etc.* **off** sich (*Dat.*) einen Tag *usw.* frei nehmen (*ugs.*); ~ **time off [work** *or* **from work]** sich (*Dat.*) frei nehmen; **H** (*mimic*) nachmachen (*ugs.*).

**2** *v.i.* **A** (*Aeronaut.*) starten; **B** (*Sport*) ‹Springer, Pferd:› abspringen; **C** (*coll.: leave quickly*) losrennen; ~ **off after sb./sth.** hinter jmdm./etw. herrennen; **D** (*become successful*) ‹Wirtschaft:› sich [sprunghaft] aufwärts entwickeln; ‹Verkaufszahlen:› [sprunghaft] steigen; ‹Produkt, Kampagne:› einschlagen; ‹Person:› Karriere machen; **his career is taking off** er macht eine steile Karriere. ⇒ *also* **~-off**

~ **'on 1** *v.t.* **A** (*undertake*) übernehmen; annehmen ‹Herausforderung, Wette usw.›; auf sich (*Akk.*) nehmen ‹Bürde›; (*accept responsibility for*) sich einlassen auf (+ *Akk.*) ‹Person›; sich (*Dat.*) aufbürden *od.* aufladen ‹Sache›; **B** (*enrol, employ*) einstellen; aufnehmen ‹Schüler, Studenten›; annehmen ‹Privatschüler›; **C** (*acquire, assume*) annehmen ‹Farbe, Form, Ausdruck, Ausmaße›; erhalten ‹Bedeutung›; **D** (*accept as opponent*) sich auf eine Auseinandersetzung einlassen mit; es aufnehmen mit; den Kampf aufnehmen mit ‹Regierung, Gesetz›; (*Sport*) antreten gegen; **I'll ~ you on** (*in a contest*) ich nehme es mit dir auf; (*in a bet*) die Wette gilt; **E** (~ *on board*) aufnehmen; **F** (*transport farther*) weiterbringen.

**2** *v.i.* **A** (*coll.: get upset*) sich aufregen; **don't ~ on so!** reg dich nicht so auf!; hab dich nicht so! (*ugs. abwertend*); **B** (*be successful*) einschlagen

~ **'out** *v.t.* **A** (*remove*) herausnehmen; ziehen ‹Zahn›; ~ **sth. out of sth.,** ~ **out sth. from sth.** etw. aus etw. [heraus]nehmen; ~ **out a pizza** *etc.* sich (*Dat.*) eine Pizza *usw.* mitnehmen; **'... to ~ out'** „... zum Mitnehmen"; ~ **out a nail from a piece of wood/a splinter from sb.'s finger** einen Nagel aus einem Stück Holz ziehen/jmdm. einen Splitter aus dem Finger ziehen; ~ **a stain/mark out of a dress** einen Fleck aus einem Kleid entfernen; **the strong sun ~s all the natural moisture out of your skin** die starke Sonnenbestrahlung entzieht der Haut ihre natürliche Feuchtigkeit; ~ **the colour/vitamins out of sth.** etw. ausbleichen/einer Sache (*Dat.*) die Vitamine entziehen; ~ **sb. out of the courtroom** jmdn. aus dem Gerichtssaal führen; **the train took us out of the city** der Zug brachte uns aus der Stadt [heraus]; ~ **it/a lot out of sb.** (*fig.*) jmdn. mitnehmen/sehr mitnehmen; **B** (*destroy*) zerstören; (*fig.*) (*Footb. etc.*) ausschalten; (*kill*) töten; **C** (*withdraw*) abheben ‹Geld›; **D** (*deduct*) abziehen (**of** von); **E** (*go out with*) ~ **sb. out** mit jmdm. ausgehen; ~ **sb. out for a walk/drive** mit jmdm. einen Spaziergang/eine Spazierfahrt machen; ~ **sb. out to** *or* **for lunch/dinner** jmdn. zum Mittagessen/Abendessen einladen; ~ **sb. out to the cinema/the theatre/a restaurant** jmdn. ins Kino/Theater/zum Essen einladen; ~ **the dog out [for a walk]** den Hund ausführen; ~ **sb. out of himself/herself** (*fig.*) jmdn. auf andere Gedanken bringen; **F** (*get issued*) erwerben; erhalten; abschließen ‹Versicherung›; ausleihen ‹Bücher›; aufgeben ‹Anzeige›; ~ **out a subscription to sth.** etw. abonnieren; **G** ~ **it/sth. out on sb./sth.** seine Wut/etw. an jmdm./etw. auslassen. ⇒ *also* **~-out**

~ **'over 1** *v.t.* **A** (*assume control of*) übernehmen; ~ **sth. over from sb.** etw. von jmdm. übernehmen; ~ **over the lead** (*Sport*) in Führung gehen; **let sth. ~ over one's life** (*fig.*) sein Leben von etw. bestimmen lassen; ~ **sb./sth. over** (*fig.*) von jmdm./etw. Besitz ergreifen; ~ **over the world** die Weltherrschaft an sich reißen; **B** (*carry or transport over*) ~ **sb./sth. over to sb./sb.'s flat/Guildford** jmdn./etw. zu jmdm./in jmds. Wohnung/nach Guildford bringen *od.* (*ugs.*) rüberbringen; **I'll ~ you/it over next time** ich werde dich/es nächstes Mal mitnehmen; **C** (*Printing*) rübernehmen (*ugs.*).

**2** *v.i.* übernehmen; ‹Manager, Firmenleiter:› die Geschäfte übernehmen; ‹Regierung, Präsident:› die Amtsgeschäfte übernehmen; ‹Junta:› die Macht übernehmen; ‹Beifahrer:› das Steuer übernehmen; ~ **over from sb.** jmdn. ersetzen; (*temporarily*) jmdn. vertreten; **other organizations will ~ over [from it] and carry out its functions** andere Organisationen werden seine Funktion übernehmen; **the night nurse ~s over at 10 p.m.** um zehn Uhr tritt die Nachtschwester ihren Dienst an. ⇒ *also* **~-over**

~ **'round** *v.t.* **A** (*carry, deliver*) vorbeibringen; **I'll ~ you round one day** ich nehme dich einmal mit hin; **B** (*show around*) [herum]führen; ~ **sb. round the factory** jmdn. durch die Fabrik führen

~ **to** *v.i.* **A** (*get into habit of*) ~ **to doing sth.** anfangen, etw. zu tun; es sich (*Dat.*) angewöhnen, etw. zu tun; ~ **to drugs/gambling/crime** zu Drogen greifen/dem Spiel/der Kriminalität verfallen; **B** (*escape to*) sich flüchten in (+ *Akk.*); ~ **to the [life]boats** sich in die Boote retten; ⇒ *also* **bed** 1 A; **heel**[1] 1 A; **C** (*develop a liking for*) sich hingezogen fühlen zu ‹Person›; sich erwärmen für ‹Sache›; (*adapt oneself to*) sich gewöhnen an (+ *Akk.*); ⇒ *also* **duck**[1] 1 A

~ **'up 1** *v.t.* **A** (*lift up*) hochheben; (*pick up*) aufheben; aufnehmen ‹Staub, Partikel, Laub›; herausnehmen ‹Pflanzen›; herausreißen ‹Schienenstrang, Dielen›; aufreißen ‹Straße›; hochholen, aufnehmen ‹Masche›; **he took up his book again** (*started to read again*) er nahm seine Lektüre wieder auf; ⇒ *also* **arm**[2] 1 A; **cudgel** 1; **gauntlet**[1] D; **glove** A; **B** (*move up*) weiter nach oben rücken; (*shorten*) kürzer machen; **C** (*carry or lead up*) ~ **sb./sth. up** jmdn./etw. hinaufbringen (**to** zu); **I'll ~ you up one day** ich werde dich einmal mit hinaufnehmen; ~ **sth. up to sb.** jmdm. etw. hinaufbringen; **he took the suitcase up to the top floor with him** er nahm den Koffer mit in den obersten Stock; **D** (*absorb*) aufnehmen; **E** (*wind up*) aufwickeln; ⇒ *also* **slack**[1] 2 A; **F** (*occupy, engage*) beanspruchen; brauchen/(*undesirably*) wegnehmen ‹Platz›; **I'm sorry to have ~n up so much of your time** es tut mir Leid, Ihre Zeit so lange in Anspruch genommen zu haben; **most of my time is ~n up with ...:** ich verbringe die meiste Zeit mit ...; **be ~n up with sth./sb.** von etw./jmdm. in Anspruch genommen sein; **G** ergreifen ‹Beruf›; anfangen ‹Jogging, Tennis, Schach, Gitarre›; ~ **up a musical instrument** ein Instrument zu spielen beginnen; ~ **sth. up as a hobby/profession** etw. zu seinem Hobby/Beruf machen; ~ **up German/a hobby** anfangen, Deutsch zu lernen/sich (*Dat.*) ein Hobby zulegen; **H** (*start, adopt*) aufnehmen ‹Arbeit, Kampf›; antreten ‹Stelle›; übernehmen ‹Pflicht, Funktion›; einnehmen ‹Haltung, Position›; eintreten für, sich einsetzen für ‹Sache›; ~ **up a/one's position** ‹Polizeiposten, Politiker:› Position beziehen; **I** (*accept*) annehmen; aufnehmen ‹Idee, Vorschlag, Kredit, Geld›; kaufen ‹Aktien›; ~ **up an option** optieren (*Rechtsw.*); **J** (*raise, pursue further*) aufgreifen; ~ **sth. up with sb.** sich in einer Sache an jmdn. wenden; **K** ~ **sb. up [on sth.]** (*accept*) jmdn. [in Bezug auf etw. (*Akk.*)] beim Wort nehmen; (*challenge*) jmdm. [in Bezug auf etw. (*Akk.*)] widersprechen; **I might ~ you up on that offer/challenge** dein Angebot/deine Herausforderung werde ich vielleicht annehmen; **he took me up on the remark I had made** er hatte gegen meine Bemerkung etwas einzuwenden; **L** (*join in*) einfallen in (+ *Akk.*) ‹Ruf›; sich beteiligen an (+ *Dat.*) ‹Kampf›; **M** (*continue, resume*) [wieder] aufnehmen; weiterführen ‹Geschichte›; ~ **up sth. where one/sb. has left off** mit etw. da fortfahren, wo man/jmd. aufgehört hat; **N be [very] ~n up with sb./sth.** mit jmdm./etw. [sehr] beschäftigt sein.

**2** *v.i.* **A** (*coll.: become friendly*) ~ **up with sb.** sich mit jmdm. einlassen; **B** (*continue*) einsetzen; ~ **up where sb./sth. has left off** da einsetzen, wo jmd./etw. aufgehört hat; **C** (*wind up*) aufwickeln. ⇒ *also* **~-up**

~ **upon** *v.t.* ~ **upon oneself** auf sich (*Akk.*) nehmen ‹Aufgabe, Pflicht, Verantwortung›; ~ **upon oneself the right to do sth.** sich (*Dat.*) [einfach] das Recht nehmen, etw. zu tun; ~ **it upon oneself to do sth.** es auf sich (*Akk.*) nehmen, etw. zu tun; (*unwarrantably*) sich (*Dat.*) herausnehmen (*ugs.*), etw. zu tun

**take: ~away** *n.* (*restaurant*) Restaurant mit Straßenverkauf; (*meal*) Essen zum Mitnehmen; *attrib.* ‹Restaurant› mit Straßenverkauf; ‹Essen, Mahlzeit› zum Mitnehmen; **let's get a Chinese ~away for our supper** lass uns beim Chinesen was zum Abendessen holen (*ugs.*); **~-home** *attrib. adj.* **~-home pay/wages** Nettolohn, *der;* **~-in** *n.* (*coll.*) Schwindel, *der* (*abwertend*)

**taken** ⇒ **take** 1, 2

**take: ~-off** *n.* **A** (*Sport*) Absprung, *der;* (*board*) [Ab]sprungbalken, *der;* **~-off speed** Geschwindigkeit beim Absprung; **B** (*Aeronaut.*) Start, *der;* Take-off, *das* (*fachspr.*); **be cleared/ready for ~-off** Starterlaubnis haben/startklar sein; **~-off speed** Abhebegeschwindigkeit, *die;* **C** (*coll.: caricature*) Parodie, *die;* **do a ~-off of sb.** jmdn. parodieren; **D** (*Econ.*) [rapider] Aufschwung; **~out** (*Amer.*) ⇒ **takeaway; ~over** *n.* (*Commerc.*) Übernahme, *die;* **~over bid** Übernahmeangebot, *das*

**taker** /ˈteɪkə(r)/ *n.* (*of a bet*) Wetter, *der;* (*of shares etc.*) Käufer, *der;* **there were no ~s [for the offer]** niemand hat [das Angebot] angenommen; (*at betting*) keiner nahm die Wette an; **any ~s?** (*at auction*) wer bietet?

**'take-up** *n.* **A** (*response*) **a ~ of over 2,000** über 2 000 Interessenten; **~ has been very poor/low** es gab kaum *od.* sehr wenig Interessenten; **B** (*winding up*) Aufwickeln, *das;* Aufwick[e]lung, *die; attrib.* Aufwickel‹spule, -geschwindigkeit›

**taking** /ˈteɪkɪŋ/ *n.* **A** *in pl.* (*amount taken*) Einnahmen; **B** (*seizure*) Einnahme, *die;* **C they are yours/his** *etc.* **for the ~:** du kannst/er kann *usw.* sie haben; **victory was his for the ~:** sein Sieg war so gut wie sicher

**talc** /tælk/ *n.* **A** Talkum, *das;* **B** (*Min.*) Talk, *der*

**talcum** /ˈtælkəm/ *n.* **~ [powder]** Talkumpuder, *der;* Talkum, *das;* (*as cosmetic*) Körperpuder, *der*

**tale** /teɪl/ *n.* **A** (*story*) Erzählung, *die;* Geschichte, *die* (**of** von, **about** über + *Akk.*); **fisherman's ~[s]** Anglerlatein, *das;* **B** (*piece of gossip*) Geschichte, *die* (*ugs.*). ⇒ *also* **tell** 1 B; **thereby**; **wife**; **woe** A

**talent** /ˈtælənt/ *n.* **A** (*ability*) Talent, *das;* **have [great/no** *etc.***] ~ [for sth.]** [viel/kein *usw.*] Talent [zu *od.* für etw.] haben; **have a ~ for music** musikalisches Talent haben; **have a [great] ~ for doing sth.** das Talent haben, etw. zu tun; **B** (*people with ability*) Talente; Begabungen; **the [local] ~** (*coll.: girls/men*) die interessanten Frauen/(*ugs.*) Typen am Ort; **C** (*arch.: measure, money*) Talent, *das*

**talented** /ˈtæləntɪd/ *adj.* talentiert; **this is a ~ essay** dieser Aufsatz zeugt von Talent

**talent: ~ scout, ~-spotter** *ns.* Talentsucher, *der;* **~-spotting** *n.* Talentsuche, *die*

**tale-teller** *n.* **A** ⇒ **storyteller**; **B** (*sneak/gossip*) jmd., der andere anschwärzt/schlechtmacht

**talisman** /ˈtælɪzmən/ *n.* Talisman, *der*

**talk** /tɔːk/ **1** *n.* **A** (*discussion*) Gespräch, *das;* **have a ~ [with sb.] [about sth.]** [mit jmdm.] [über etw. (*Akk.*)] reden *od.* sprechen; **have a long ~ on the phone** lange miteinander telefonieren; **I've enjoyed our ~:** es war nett, mit Ihnen zu sprechen; **could I have a ~ with you?** könnte ich Sie einmal sprechen?; **have** *or* **hold ~s [with sb.]** [mit jmdm.] Gespräche führen; **B** (*speech, lecture*) Vortrag, *der;* **give a ~/a series of ~s [on sth./sb.]** einen Vortrag/eine Vortragsreihe [über etw./jmdn.] halten; **C** *no pl.* (*form of communication*) Sprache, *die;* **sailors'/men's ~:** Seemanns-/Männersprache, *die;* **D** *no pl.* (*talking*) Gerede, *das* (*abwertend*); **there's too much ~ [of ...]** es wird zu viel [von ...] geredet; **he is all ~ [and no action]** er redet nur [und tut nichts]; **there is [much/some] ~ of ...:** man hört [häufig/öfter] von ...; **be the ~ of**

t

**the town/neighbourhood** *etc.* Stadtgespräch/das Thema in der Nachbarschaft *usw.* sein. ⇨ *also* **big** 1 G; **small talk**.
❷ *v.i.* Ⓐ (*speak*) sprechen, reden (**with, to** mit); (*lecture*) sprechen; (*converse*) sich unterhalten; (*have* ~*s*) Gespräche führen; (*gossip*) reden; **be ~ing in German** deutsch sprechen; **love to hear oneself ~:** sich gern reden hören; **can't** *or* **doesn't she ~!** (*coll.*) die kann vielleicht reden!; **we must ~:** wir müssen miteinander reden; **~ on the phone** telefonieren; **we ~ on the phone every day** wir telefonieren jeden Tag miteinander; **~ to sb. on the phone** mit jmdm. telefonieren; **he sat through the entire meal without ~ing** er hat während des ganzen Essens kein Wort gesagt; **keep sb. ~ing** jmdn. in ein [längeres] Gespräch verwickeln; **she kept me ~ing for an hour** ich musste mich eine Stunde lang mit ihr unterhalten; **now you're ~ing!** (*coll.*) das hört sich schon besser an; **that's no way to ~/~ to your uncle** das darfst du nicht sagen/so darfst du aber nicht mit deinem Onkel reden!; **don't ~ to 'me like that!** mit mir kannst du so nicht reden!; **who do you think you're ~ing to?** was bildest du dir ein, so mit mir zu sprechen?; **it's easy for you/him** *etc.* **to ~:** du hast/er hat *usw.* gut reden; **look who's ~ing** (*iron.*) das musst du gerade sagen; **you can** (*iron.*) *or* **can't ~:** sei du nur ganz still!; **don't ~ daft** (*coll.*) rede doch kein dummes Zeug!; **I'll ~ to that boy when he gets in** (*coll.: scold*) ich werde mal ein ernstes Wort mit dem Jungen reden, wenn er nach Hause kommt; **could I ~ to you for a moment?** könnte ich Sie einen Augenblick sprechen?; **~ to sb. seriously** mit jmdm. ein ernstes Wort reden; **may I ~ with Mr Smith, please?** kann ich bitte Herrn Smith sprechen?; **get ~ing [to sb.]** [mit jmdm.] ins Gespräch kommen; **~ to oneself** mit sich selbst sprechen; Selbstgespräche führen; **ships ~ to each other by radio** Schiffe verständigen sich über Funk; **~ of** *or* **about sb./sth.** über jmdn./etw. reden; **everyone's ~ing about him/his divorce** er/seine Scheidung ist in aller Munde; **everyone is ~ing about his new film** jeder spricht von seinem neuen Film; **~ of** *or* **about doing sth.** davon reden, etw. zu tun; **get oneself ~ed about** sich ins Gespräch bringen; **[not] know what one is ~ing about** [gar nicht] wissen, wovon man redet; **[not] know what sb. is ~ing about** [nicht] wissen, was jmd. meint *od.* wovon jmd. spricht; **~ about trouble** *etc.***!** (*coll.*) da erzähl mir noch einer was von Schwierigkeiten *usw.*!; **What are you ~ing about? Of course he's not going to resign** Was redest du da? Natürlich tritt er nicht zurück; **~ing of holidays** *etc.* da wir [gerade] vom Urlaub *usw.* sprechen; apropos Urlaub *usw.*; Ⓑ (*have power of speech*) sprechen; **animals don't ~:** Tiere können nicht sprechen; Ⓒ (*betray secrets*) reden; **the prisoner refused to ~:** der Gefangene verweigerte jede Aussage; **make sb. ~:** jmdn. zum Reden bringen; **we have ways of making you ~:** wir werden Sie schon noch zum Reden bringen. ⇨ *also* **big** 2; **hat** B; **head** 1 B.
❸ *v.t.* Ⓐ (*utter, express*) **~ [a load of] nonsense** [eine Menge] Unsinn *od.* (*ugs.*) Stuss reden; Ⓑ (*discuss*) **~ politics/music** *etc.* über Politik/Musik *usw.* reden; **~ business** geschäftliche Dinge besprechen; (*get down to business*) zur Sache kommen; ⇨ *also* **shop** 1 B; Ⓒ (*use*) sprechen ‹Sprache, Dialekt usw.›; Ⓓ (*bring into certain condition*) **~ oneself hoarse** sich heiser reden; **~ oneself** *or* **one's way out of trouble** sich aus Schwierigkeiten herausreden; **he ~ed himself into/out of the job** er hat im Gespräch so eine gute/schlechte Figur gemacht, dass er die Stelle bekommen/nicht bekommen hat; **~ sb. into/out of sth.** jmdn. zu etw. überreden/jmdm. etw. ausreden; **~ oneself into believing sth.** sich (*Dat.*) etw. einreden. ⇨ *also* **donkey**

**~ at** *v.t.* einreden auf (+ *Akk.*)

**~ away** ❶ *v.i.* sich [angeregt] unterhalten (**to** mit). ❷ *v.t.* Ⓐ verplaudern ‹Zeit›; Ⓑ **~ sb.'s fears away** jmdm. seine Angst ausreden

**~ 'back** *v.i.* Ⓐ (*reply*) antworten; Ⓑ (*reply defiantly*) widersprechen (**to** *Dat.*)

**~ 'down** ❶ *v.t.* Ⓐ (*silence*) in Grund und Boden reden; Ⓑ (*guide*) Landekommandos geben (+ *Dat.*). ❷ *v.i.* **~ down to sb.** von oben herab *od.* herablassend mit jmdm. reden

**~ 'out** *v.t.* Ⓐ (*discuss*) ausdiskutieren; Ⓑ (*Parl.*) **~ out a bill** die Verabschiedung eines Gesetzes verfahrensmäßig blockieren

**~ 'over** *v.t.* Ⓐ **~ sth. over [with sb.]** etw. [mit jmdm.] besprechen; Ⓑ (*persuade*) **~ sb. over** jmdn. überreden

**~ 'round** *v.t.* Ⓐ (*persuade*) **~ sb. round** jmdn. überreden; Ⓑ (*skirt*) **~ round sth.** um etw. herumreden (*ugs.*)

**~ 'through** *v.t.* **~ sb. through sth.** etw. mit jmdm. durchgehen *od.* durchsprechen; **~ sth. through** etw. durchsprechen

**~ 'up** ❶ *v.t.* loben. ❷ *v.i.* ⇨ **speak up** a

**talkative** /'tɔ:kətɪv/ *adj.* gesprächig; geschwätzig (*abwertend*)

**talkativeness** /'tɔ:kətɪvnɪs/ *n., no pl.* Gesprächigkeit, *die;* Geschwätzigkeit, *die* (*abwertend*)

**talked-about** /'tɔ:ktəbaʊt/ *attrib. adj.* ⇨ **talked-of**

**talked-of** /'tɔ:ktɒv/ *attrib. adj.* **a much ~ book/play/project** ein viel diskutiertes Buch/Stück/Projekt; **a much ~ actor/artist** ein Schauspieler/Künstler, der in aller Munde ist

**talker** /'tɔ:kə(r)/ *n.* Ⓐ Redner, *der*/Rednerin, *die;* **the parrot is an excellent ~:** der Papagei kann ausgezeichnet sprechen; **she is a great ~** (*talks a lot*) sie redet viel; **be a fast ~:** [sehr] schnell sprechen; (*fig. coll.*) verdammt gut reden können (*ugs.*); Ⓑ (*one who talks but does not act*) Schwätzer, *der*/Schwätzerin, *die;* **he's just a ~:** er redet immer nur

**talkie** /'tɔ:kɪ/ *n.* (*coll.*) Tonfilm, *der*

**talking** /'tɔ:kɪŋ/ ❶ *n.* Reden, *das;* **there's been so much ~:** es ist so viel geredet worden; **'no ~'** „bitte nicht sprechen"; **do [all] the ~:** das Gespräch dominieren; **let me do the ~:** überlass lieber mir das Reden. ❷ *adj.* sprechend; **~ doll** Sprechpuppe, *die;* **~ book** Hörbuch, *das;* **~ film** *or* **picture** Tonfilm, *der*

**talking: ~ 'heads** *n. pl.* (*Telev. coll. derog.*) Leute, die man nur reden sieht; **~ point** *n.* Gesprächsthema, *das;* **~ shop** *n.* (*derog.*) Quasselbude, *die* (*ugs. abwertend*); **~-to** /'tɔ:kɪŋtu:/ *n.* (*coll.*) Standpauke, *die* (*ugs.*); **give sb. a good ~-to** jmdm. eine ordentliche Standpauke halten (*ugs.*)

**'talk show** *n.* Talkshow, *die*

**tall** /tɔ:l/ ❶ *adj.* Ⓐ ▶**1210** hoch; groß ‹Person, Tier›; **grow ~:** groß werden; wachsen; **feel ten feet ~** (*fig.*) riesig stolz sein; Ⓑ (*coll.: excessive*) **a ~ tale** eine unglaubwürdige Geschichte; **that is a ~ order** das ist ziemlich viel verlangt; ⇨ *also* **story**[1] A. ❷ *adv.* ▶**1210** **stand six feet** *etc.* **~:** 6 Fuß *usw.* groß sein; **stand ~:** aufrecht stehen; (*be proud*) erhobenen Hauptes stehen/gehen *usw.* (*geh.*); ⇨ *also* **walk** 1 A

**tall: ~boy** *n.* Doppelkommode, *die;* Tallboy, *der;* **~ 'hat** ⇨ **top hat**

**tallish** /'tɔ:lɪʃ/ *adj.* ziemlich hoch; ziemlich groß ‹Person›

**tallness** /'tɔ:lnɪs/ *n., no pl.* Höhe, *die;* (*of person*) Größe, *die*

**tallow** /'tæləʊ/ *n.* Talg, *der*

**'tallow candle** *n.* Talgkerze, *die*

**tall 'ship** *n.* Windjammer, *der*

**tally** /'tælɪ/ ❶ *n.* Ⓐ (*record*) **sb.'s ~ is 18 goals** jmd. kann 18 Tore für sich verbuchen; **a player with a ~ of 18 goals** ein Spieler, der 18 Tore für sich verbuchen kann; **keep a [daily] ~ of sth.** [täglich] über etw. (*Akk.*) Buch führen; Ⓑ (*label, ticket*) Schild, *das.* ❷ *v.i.* übereinstimmen

**tally-'ho** ❶ *int.* ≈ horrido. ❷ *n., pl.* **~s** ≈ Horrido, *das*

**Talmud** /'tælmʊd, 'tælməd/ *n.* Talmud, *der*

**talon** /'tælən/ *n.* Klaue, *die;* **~s** (*fig.: long fingernails*) Krallen (*ugs. abwertend*)

**tamarind** /'tæmərɪnd/ *n.* Tamarinde, *die*

**tamarisk** /'tæmərɪsk/ *n.* (*Bot.*) Tamariske, *die*

**tambourine** /tæmbə'ri:n/ *n.* (*Mus.*) Tamburin, *das*

**tame** /teɪm/ ❶ *adj.* Ⓐ zahm; (*joc.*) hauseigen ‹Anarchist, Genie›; **grow/become ~:** zahm werden; Ⓑ (*spiritless*) lahm (*ugs.*), lustlos ‹Einwilligung, Anerkennung, Kampagne, Versuch›; zahm (*ugs.*) ‹Besprechung, Kritik›; Ⓒ (*dull*) wenig aufregend; lasch ‹Stil›. ❷ *v.t.* (*lit. or fig.*) zähmen

**tameable** /'teɪməbl/ *adj.* (*lit. or fig.*) zähmbar; **be [not] ~:** sich [nicht] zähmen lassen

**tamely** /'teɪmlɪ/ *adv.* Ⓐ (*docilely*) zahm (*ugs.*); Ⓑ (*fig.: unexcitingly*) lahm (*ugs.*); wenig aufregend

**tameness** /'teɪmnɪs/ *n., no pl.* Ⓐ (*docility*) Zahmheit, *die;* Ⓑ ⇨ **tame** 1 B: Lahmheit, *die* (*ugs.*); Lustlosigkeit, *die;* Zahmheit, *die* (*ugs.*); Ⓒ (*dullness*) Langweiligkeit, *die;* (*of style*) Laschheit, *die*

**tamer** /'teɪmə(r)/ *n.* Dompteur, *der*/Dompteuse, *die;* **a ~ of wild animals** ein Tierbändiger

**Tamil** /'tæmɪl/ ▶**1275**, ▶**1340** ❶ *adj.* tamilisch. ❷ *n.* Ⓐ (*person*) Tamile, *der*/Tamilin, *die;* Ⓑ (*language*) Tamil, *das*

**tam-o'-shanter** /tæmə'ʃæntə(r)/ *n.* Tam-o'-Shanter, *der; zur schottischen Tracht gehörende Tellermütze mit Pompon*

**tamper** /'tæmpə(r)/ *v.i.* **~ with** sich (*Dat.*) zu schaffen machen an (+ *Dat.*); (*make unauthorized changes in*) unerlaubte Änderungen vornehmen an (+ *Dat.*) ‹Schriftstück, Text›; (*attempt to bribe*) zu bestechen versuchen ‹Jury, Zeugen›; (*fig.*) ändern wollen ‹Regeln, Tradition›; **the brakes had been ~ed with** jmd. hatte sich an den Bremsen zu schaffen gemacht

**'tamper-proof** *adj.* einbruchsicher ‹Schloss›; verplombt ‹Gasuhr›; aufbruchsicher ‹Münztelefon›

**tampon** /'tæmpɒn/ *n.* Tampon, *der*

**tan**[1] /tæn/ ❶ *v.t.,* **-nn-** Ⓐ gerben ‹Tierhaut, Fell›; Ⓑ (*bronze*) bräunen; ‹Sonne:› bräunen; ‹Person:› braun werden lassen ‹Körperteil›; **the sun had ~ned them dark brown** die Sonne hatte sie dunkelbraun gebrannt; Ⓒ (*coll.: beat*) das Fell gerben (*salopp*) (+ *Dat.*); ⇨ *also* **hide**[2]. ❷ *v.i.,* **-nn-** braun werden. ❸ *n.* Ⓐ (*colour*) Gelbbraun, *das;* Ⓑ (*sun~*) Bräune, *die;* **have/get a ~:** braun sein/werden; Ⓒ (*~ning agent*) Gerbmittel, *das.* ❹ *adj.* gelbbraun

**tan**[2] *abbr.* (*Math.*) **tangent** tan

**tandem** /'tændəm/ ❶ *adv.* hintereinander; **be driven ~** ‹Pferde:› hintereinander im Gespann laufen; **drive/ride ~** ‹Kutscher, Radfahrer:› Tandem fahren. ❷ *n.* (*lit. or fig.*) Tandem, *das;* **~ bicycle** Tandem, *das;* **coupled/harnessed in ~:** hintereinander gekoppelt/gespannt; **work in ~** (*fig.*) zusammenarbeiten

**tandoori** /tæn'dʊərɪ/ *n.* (*Gastr.*) Tandoorigericht, *das; attrib.* Tandoori‹restaurant, -hühnchen›; **~ cooking** Tandooriküche, *die*

**tang** /tæŋ/ *n.* Ⓐ (*taste/smell*) **[sharp] ~:** scharfer Geschmack/Geruch; **[spicy/salty] ~:** würziger/salziger Geschmack/Geruch; **there is a ~ of autumn in the air** es riecht nach Herbst; Ⓑ (*of chisel, knife, sword*) Angel, *die*

**tangent** /'tændʒənt/ (*Math.*) ❶ *n.* Tangente, *die;* (*in triangle*) Tangens, *der;* **run/be drawn at a ~ to a curve/circle** eine Kurve/einen Kreis in einem Punkt berühren; **go** *or* **fly off at a ~** (*fig.*) plötzlich vom Thema abschweifen. ❷ *adj.* Tangenten-; **~ plane** Tangentialebene, *die;* **be ~ to** tangieren (*fachspr.*), in einem Punkt berühren ‹Kurve, Kreis›

**tangential** /tæn'dʒenʃl/ *adj.* (*Math.*) Tangential-; (*fig.: peripheral*) nebensächlich; nicht zur Sache gehörend ‹Kommentar, Information›; **be merely ~ to sth.** (*fig.*) etw. nur am Rande berühren

**tangerine** /tændʒə'ri:n/ ❶ *n.* Ⓐ (*fruit*) **~ [orange]** Tangerine, *die;* Ⓑ (*colour*) Orangerot, *das.* ❷ *adj.* orangerot

**tangible** /'tændʒɪbl/ *adj.* Ⓐ (*perceptible by touch*) fühlbar ‹Schwellung, Verdickung, Verhärtung›; Ⓑ (*fig.: real, definite*) greifbar; spürbar,

t

merklich ‹Unterschied, Verbesserung›; handfest ‹Beweis›; ~ **assets** (*Econ.*) Sachanlagevermögen, *das*

**tangibly** /ˈtændʒɪblɪ/ *adv.* deutlich ‹sichtbar›; **be ~ different** sich merklich unterscheiden (**from** von); **sth. can be ~ proved** es gibt handfeste Beweise für etw.; **you should have been more ~ rewarded** man hätte dir eine handfestere Belohnung geben sollen

**Tangier[s]** /tænˈdʒɪə(z)/ *pr. n.* ▶ **1626** Tanger (*das*)

**tangle** /ˈtæŋgl/ ❶ *n.* Gewirr, *das;* (*in hair*) Verfilzung, *die;* (*fig.: dispute*) Auseinandersetzung, *die;* **be in a ~:** sich verheddert haben (*ugs.*); ‹Haar:› sich verfilzt haben; (*fig.*) ‹Angelegenheiten:› in Unordnung (*Dat.*) sein; ‹Person:› verwirrt sein; **get oneself into a ~** (*fig.*) sich in eine schwierige Lage bringen. ❷ *v.t.* verheddern (*ugs.*); verfilzen ‹Haar›. ❸ *v.i.* sich verheddern (*ugs.*); ‹Haar:› sich verfilzen

~ **ˈup** ❶ *v.t.* verheddern (*ugs.*); verfilzen ‹Haar›; **become** *or* **get ~d up** sich verheddern (*ugs.*); **he's got ~d up in a rather unpleasant affair** (*coll.*) er ist in eine ziemlich unangenehme Sache verstrickt; **get ~d up with sb.** (*fig.*) sich mit jmdm. einlassen. ❷ *v.i.* ⇒ ~ 3

~ **with** *v.t.* (*coll.*) ~ **with sb.** sich mit jmdm. anlegen

**tangled** /ˈtæŋgld/ *adj.* verheddert (*ugs.*); verfilzt ‹Haar›; (*confused, complicated*) verworren; verwickelt ‹Angelegenheit›

**tango** /ˈtæŋgəʊ/ ❶ *n., pl.* **~s** Tango, *der.* ❷ *v.i.* Tango tanzen; **it takes two to ~** (*fig. coll.*) dazu gehören immer noch zwei

**tangy** /ˈtæŋɪ/ *adj.* scharf; (*spicy*) würzig; (*acid*) bitter; (*salty*) salzig

**tank** /tæŋk/ *n.* Ⓐ Tank, *der;* (*Railw.: in tender*) Wasserkasten, *der;* (*for fish etc.*) Aquarium, *das;* (*for catching rainwater*) Auffangbecken, *das;* **fill the ~** (*with petrol*) volltanken; Ⓑ (*Mil.*) Panzer, *der*

~ **ˈup** ❶ *v.i.* (*get fuel*) auftanken. ❷ *v.t.* auftanken; **get ~ed up** (*sl.: drunk*) sich volltanken (*salopp*)

**tankard** /ˈtæŋkəd/ *n.* Krug, *der;* **a ~ of beer** *etc.* ein Krug Bier *usw.*

**ˈtank car** *n.* (*Railw.*) Kesselwagen, *der*

**tanked-up** /tæŋkˈtʌp/ *adj.* (*sl.*) vollgetankt (*salopp*)

**ˈtank engine** *n.* (*Railw.*) Tenderlokomotive, *die*

**tanker** /ˈtæŋkə(r)/ *n.* (*ship*) Tanker, *der;* Tankschiff, *das;* (*aircraft*) Tankflugzeug, *das;* (*vehicle*) Tank[last]wagen, *der*

**tank:** ~ **top** *n.* ≈ Pullunder, *der;* ~ **trap** *n.* (*Mil.*) Panzersperre, *die;* (*ditch*) Panzergraben, *der;* ~ **waggon** *n.* (*Brit. Railw.*) Kesselwagen, *der*

**tanned** /tænd/ *adj.* Ⓐ (*treated by tanning*) gegerbt; Ⓑ (*bronzed*) braun gebrannt

**tanner** /ˈtænə(r)/ *n.* (*person*) Gerber, *der* /Gerberin, *die*

**tannery** /ˈtænərɪ/ *n.* Gerberei, *die*

**tannic** /ˈtænɪk/ *adj.* ~ **acid** (*Chem.*) Tannin, *das*

**tannin** /ˈtænɪn/ *n.* (*Chem.*) Tannin, *das*

**tanning** /ˈtænɪŋ/ *n.* Ⓐ (*of hides*) Gerben, *das;* (*craft also*) Gerberei, *die; attrib.* Gerb-; Ⓑ (*bronzing*) Bräunung, *die; attrib.* Bräunungs-; Ⓒ (*coll.: beating*) Abreibung, *die* (*ugs.*); **give sb. a ~:** jmdm. das Fell gerben (*salopp*)

**Tannoy** ® /ˈtænɔɪ/ *n.* Lautsprecher, *der;* **over** *or* **on the ~:** über Lautsprecher

**tansy** /ˈtænzɪ/ *n.* (*Bot.*) Rainfarn, *der*

**tantalise, tantalising, tantalisingly** ⇒ **tantaliz-**

**tantalize** /ˈtæntəlaɪz/ *v.t.* reizen; (*tease also*) zappeln lassen (*ugs.*); (*with promises*) [falsche] Hoffnungen wecken bei

**tantalizing** /ˈtæntəlaɪzɪŋ/ *adj.* verlockend; **a ~ puzzle** ein Rätsel, das einen nicht loslässt

**tantalizingly** /ˈtæntəlaɪzɪŋlɪ/ *adv.* [falsche] Hoffnungen weckend; verlockend ‹schön, nah, duften, lächeln›

**tantamount** /ˈtæntəmaʊnt/ *pred. adj.* **be ~ to sth.** gleichbedeutend mit etw. sein; einer Sache (*Dat.*) gleichkommen

**tantrum** /ˈtæntrəm/ *n.* Wutanfall, *der;* (*of child*) Trotzanfall, *der;* **be in a ~:** einen Wutanfall/Trotzanfall haben; **get into/throw a ~:** einen Wutanfall/Trotzanfall bekommen

**Tanzania** /tænzəˈniːə/ *pr. n.* Tansania (*das*)

**Tanzanian** /tænzəˈniːən/ ▶ **1340** ❶ *adj.* tansanisch; **sb. is ~:** jmd. ist Tansanier/Tansanierin. ❷ *n.* Tansanier, *der*/Tansanierin, *die*

**Taoiseach** /ˈtiːʃæx/ *n.* (*Ir. Parl.*) Premierminister/-ministerin [der Republik Irland]

**Taoism** /ˈtaʊɪzm/ *n.* (*Relig.*) Taoismus, *der*

**Taoist** /ˈtaʊɪst/ (*Relig.*) ❶ *adj.* taoistisch. ❷ *n.* Taoist, *der*/Taoistin, *die*

**tap**[1] /tæp/ ❶ *n.* Ⓐ Hahn, *der;* (*on barrel, cask*) [Zapf]hahn, *der;* **hot/cold[-water] ~:** Warm-/Kaltwasserhahn, *der;* **leave the ~ running** den Wasserhahn laufen lassen; **on ~:** vom Fass *nachgestellt;* **be on ~** (*fig.*) zur Verfügung stehen; **have on ~** (*fig.*) zur Verfügung haben ‹Geld, Mittel›; an der Hand haben ‹Experten›; Ⓑ (*plug*) Zapfen, *der;* Spund, *der;* Ⓒ **[telephone] ~:** Telefonüberwachung, *die.*
❷ *v.t.,* **-pp-** Ⓐ (*make use of*) erschließen ‹Reserven, Ressourcen, Bezirk, Markt, Land, Einnahmequelle›; anzapfen (*fig. ugs.*) ‹Reserven, Ressourcen›; ~ **sb. for money/information** jmdn. anzapfen (*ugs.*); ~ **sb. for a few pounds** versuchen, bei jmdm. ein paar Pfund lockerzumachen (*ugs.*); Ⓑ (*Teleph.: intercept*) abhören; anzapfen (*ugs.*); Ⓒ (*pierce*) anzapfen ‹Baum, Fass›; anstechen ‹Fass›; (*draw off*) abzapfen ‹Bier›; ~ **a tree for resin** einen Baum zur Harzgewinnung anzapfen; Ⓓ (*Metalw.*) ein Gewinde schneiden in (+ *Akk.*)

~ **ˈoff** *v.t.* abzapfen (**into** in + *Akk.*)

**tap**[2] ❶ *v.t.,* **-pp-** (*strike lightly*) klopfen an (+ *Akk.*); (*on upper surface*) klopfen auf (+ *Akk.*); ~ **one's fingers on the table** (*repeatedly*) mit den Fingern auf den Tisch trommeln; ~ **one's finger against one's forehead** sich (*Dat.*) mit dem Finger an die Stirn tippen; ~ **one's foot** mit dem Fuß auf den Boden klopfen; ~ **one's foot to the music** mit dem Fuß den Takt schlagen; ~ **sb. on the shoulder** jmdm. auf die Schulter klopfen/(*more lightly*) tippen.
❷ *v.i.,* **-pp-:** ~ **at/on sth.** an etw. (*Akk.*) klopfen; (*on upper surface*) auf etw. (*Akk.*) klopfen.
❸ *n.* (*light blow, rap*) Klopfen, *das;* (*given to naughty child*) Klaps, *der* (*ugs.*); **give a nail a little ~:** leicht auf einen Nagel klopfen; **there was a ~ at/on the door** es klopfte an die Tür; **I felt a ~ on my shoulder** jemand klopfte/(*more lightly*) tippte mir auf die Schulter; **~s** (*Amer. Mil.: signal*) Zapfenstreich, *der*

~ **aˈway** *v.i.* ‹Schreibkraft, Funker am Morsegerät:› vor sich hin klappern; ~ **away on the table with one's fingers/a ruler** mit den Fingern/einem Lineal auf dem Tisch trommeln

~ **ˈin** *v.t.* einklopfen ‹Nagel usw.›

~ **ˈout** *v.t.* Ⓐ (*knock out*) ausklopfen ‹Pfeife›; herausklopfen ‹Nagel, Keil›; Ⓑ klopfen ‹Rhythmus, Takt›; (*write*) (*in Morse*) morsen ‹Nachricht›; (*on typewriter*) tippen (*ugs.*)

**tap:** ~ **dance** ❶ *n.* Stepp[tanz], *der;* **do a ~ dance** steppen. ❷ *v.i.* Stepp tanzen; steppen; ~ **dancer** *n.* Stepptänzer, *der*/-tänzerin, *die;* ~ **dancing** *n.* Stepptanz, *der;* Steppen, *das*

**tape** /teɪp/ ❶ *n.* Ⓐ Band, *das;* **adhesive** *or* **sticky ~:** Klebestreifen, *der;* Klebeband, *das;* ⇒ *also* **red tape;** Ⓑ (*Sport*) Zielband, *das;* **breast the ~:** durchs Ziel gehen; Ⓒ (*for recording*) [Ton]band, *das* (**of** mit); **[have sth.] on ~:** [etw.] auf Band (*Dat.*) [haben]; **put/record sth. on ~, make a ~ of sth.** etw. auf Band (*Akk.*) aufnehmen; **blank ~:** unbespieltes Band; Ⓓ **[paper] ~:** Papierstreifen, *der;* (*punched with holes*) Lochstreifen, *der;* **come in on the ~** ‹Nachricht:› über Fernschreiber kommen.
❷ *v.t.* Ⓐ (*record on ~*) [auf Band (*Akk.*)] aufnehmen; **~d music** Tonbandmusik, *die;* Ⓑ (*bind with ~*) [mit Klebeband *od.* Klebstreifen] zukleben ‹Paket›; kleben ‹Einband, eingerissene Seite›; Ⓒ **have got sb./sth. ~d** (*coll.*) jmdn. durchschaut haben/etw. im Griff *od.* unter Kontrolle haben

~ **ˈdown** *v.t.* [mit Klebeband] festkleben

~ **ˈon** *v.t.* [mit Klebeband] ankleben

~ **ˈover** *v.t.* [mit Klebeband] überkleben

~ **toˈgether** *v.t.* [mit Klebeband] zusammenkleben

~ **ˈup** *v.t.* [mit Klebeband] zukleben; [mit Klebeband] zusammenkleben ‹zerrissene Seite, zerbrochene Pfeife usw.›

**tape:** ~ **cassette** *n.* Tonbandkassette, *die;* ~ **deck** *n.* Tapedeck, *das;* ~ **machine** *n.* Fernschreiber, *der;* ~ **measure** *n.* Bandmaß, *das;* (*for measuring garments etc.*) [Zenti]metermaß, *das;* ~ **player** *n.* Tonband[wiedergabe]gerät, *das*

**taper** /ˈteɪpə(r)/ ❶ *v.t.* sich verjüngen lassen; ~ **[to a point]** spitz zulaufen lassen; **be ~ed** sich verjüngen; (*to a point*) spitz zulaufen. ❷ *v.i.* sich verjüngen; ~ **[to a point]** spitz zulaufen. ❸ *n.* Ⓐ **[wax] ~:** Wachsstock, *der;* Ⓑ (*narrowing*) Verjüngung, *die*

~ **away** ⇒ ~ **off** 2

~ **ˈoff** ❶ *v.t.* Ⓐ ⇒ ~ 1; Ⓑ (*fig.: decrease gradually*) drosseln ‹Produktion›. ❷ *v.i.* Ⓐ ⇒ **taper** 2; Ⓑ (*fig.: decrease gradually*) zurückgehen

**tape:** ~**-record** /ˈteɪprɪkɔːd/ *v.t.* [auf Tonband (*Akk.*)] aufnehmen *od.* aufzeichnen; ~ **recorder** *n.* Tonbandgerät, *das;* ~ **recording** *n.* Tonbandaufnahme, *die*

**tapered** /ˈteɪpəd/ *adj.* sich verjüngend; (*to a point*) spitz zulaufend; ~ **trousers** unten eng geschnittene Hose

**tapering** /ˈteɪpərɪŋ/ *adj.* sich verjüngend; (*to a point*) spitz zulaufend; **be ~:** sich verjüngen; (*to a point*) spitz zulaufen

**ˈtape-slide show** *n.* vertonte Diaschau

**tapestry** /ˈtæpɪstrɪ/ *n.* Gobelingewebe, *das;* (*wall hanging*) Bildteppich, *der;* Tapisserie, *die;* (*fig.*) Darstellung, *die;* **Gobelin ~:** Gobelin[teppich], *der;* **the Bayeux ~:** der Bayeuxteppich

**ˈtapeworm** *n.* Bandwurm, *der*

**tapioca** /tæpɪˈəʊkə/ *n.* Tapioka, *die*

**tapir** /ˈteɪpə(r), ˈteɪpɪə(r)/ *n.* (*Zool.*) Tapir, *der*

**tappet** /ˈtæpɪt/ *n.* (*Mech. Engin.*) Mitnehmer, *der*

**tap:** ~**room** *n.* Schankraum, *der;* ~**root** *n.* (*Bot.*) Pfahlwurzel, *die;* ~ **water** *n.* Leitungswasser, *das*

**tar**[1] /tɑː(r)/ ❶ *n.* Teer, *der;* **high-~/low-~ cigarette** Zigarette mit hohem/niedrigem Teergehalt; (*fig.*) **beat** *or* **knock the ~ out of sb.** (*Amer. coll.*) jmdn. fertig machen (*salopp*); **spoil the ship for a ha'p'orth of ~:** am falschen Ende sparen. ❷ *v.t.,* **-rr-** teeren; **~red road** Teerstraße, *die;* ~ **and feather sb.** jmdn. teeren und federn; **they are ~red with the same brush** *or* **stick** (*fig.*) der eine ist nicht besser als der andere

**tar**[2] *n.* **[Jack] ~** (*coll.*) Teerjacke, *die* (*scherzh.*)

**tarantella** /tærənˈtelə/, **tarantelle** /ˈtærənˈtel/ *n.* (*Mus.*) Tarantella, *die*

**tarantula** /təˈræntjʊlə/ *n.* (*Zool.*) Tarantel, *die*

**tardily** /ˈtɑːdɪlɪ/ *adv.* Ⓐ (*slowly*) [zögernd] langsam; Ⓑ (*late*) spät; (*too late*) zu spät

**tardy** /ˈtɑːdɪ/ *adj.* Ⓐ (*slow*) [zögernd] langsam; Ⓑ (*late*) spät; (*too late*) zu spät; **be ~** (*Amer.*) mit Verspätung kommen (**for, to** zu); **be ~ in doing sth.** etw. erst spät tun

**tare** /teə(r)/ *n.* (*Commerc.*) Tara, *die;* (*of lorry, car*) Leergewicht, *das*

**target** /ˈtɑːgɪt/ ❶ *n.* Ⓐ (*lit. or fig.*) Ziel, *das;* **be the ~ of** *or* **a ~ for his mockery/fury** (*fig.*) die Zielscheibe seines Spottes/Zornes sein; **production/export/savings ~:** Produktions-/Export-/Sparziel, *das;* **fixed/moving/towed ~:** feststehendes Ziel/bewegliches Ziel/Schleppscheibe, *die;* **hit/miss the/one's/its ~:** [das Ziel] treffen/das Ziel verfehlen; **set oneself a ~** (*fig.*) sich (*Dat.*) ein Ziel setzen *od.* stecken; **set oneself a ~ of £5,000** sich (*Dat.*) 5 000 Pfund zum Ziel setzen; **set sb. a ~ of six months** jmdm. eine Frist von sechs Monaten setzen; **reach one's ~** (*fig.*) sein Ziel erreichen; **be on/off** *or* **not**

t

on ~ ‹Geschoss, Schuss:› treffen/danebengehen; **be on ~** (*fig.*) ‹Sparer, Sammler:› auf dem Wege dahin sein[, sein Ziel zu erreichen]; **be on ~ for sth.** (*lit. or fig.*) auf etw. (*Akk.*) zusteuern; **be above/below ~** (*fig.*) das Ziel über-/unterschritten haben; **B** (*Sport*) Ziel- *od.* Schießscheibe, *die;* **C** (*Phys.*) Target, *das.* ⇒ *also* **sitting target.**

❷ *v.t.* **A** (*Mil.*) angreifen; **B** (*fig.*) zielen auf ‹Käufergruppe›; **~ benefits at those most in need** Unterstützung auf die Bedürftigsten konzentrieren; **independently ~ed warheads** (*Mil.*) unabhängig voneinander lenkbare Einzelsprengköpfe; **be ~ed on sth.** auf etw. (*Akk.*) gerichtet sein; **be ~ed on** *or* **at sth.** (*fig.*) auf etw. (*Akk.*) abzielen

**target: ~ date** *n.* vorgesehener Termin; **~ figure** *n.* (*esp. Commerc.*) Ziel, *das;* **~ language** *n.* Zielsprache, *die;* **~ practice** *n., no art.* Schießübungen

**tariff** /ˈtærɪf/ *n.* **A** (*tax*) Zoll, *der;* (*table or scale of customs duties*) Zolltarif, *der;* **[import] ~:** Einfuhr- *od.* Importzoll, *der;* **B** (*list of charges*) Tarif, *der;* Preisliste, *die;* **rail way/postal ~:** Eisenbahn-/Posttarif, *der;* **hotel ~:** Hotelpreise

**Tarmac, tarmac** /ˈtɑːmæk/ ❶ *n.* ® **A** Makadam, *der* (*Bauw.*); **B** (*at airport*) Rollbahn, *die.* ❷ *v.t.*, **-ck-** makadamisieren (*Bauw.*)

**tar macadam** /tɑː məˈkædəm/ *n.* Makadam, *der* (*Bauw.*)

**tarn** /tɑːn/ *n.* [kleiner] Bergsee

**tarnish** /ˈtɑːnɪʃ/ ❶ *v.t.* stumpf werden lassen ‹Metall›; (*fig.*) beflecken ‹Ruf, Namen›. ❷ *v.i.* ‹Metall:› stumpf werden, anlaufen. ❸ *n.* **A** (*action*) Anlaufen, *das;* **B** (*discolouring film*) Beschlag, *der;* Überzug, *der*

**tarnished** /ˈtɑːnɪʃt/ *adj.* stumpf ‹Metall›; (*fig.*) befleckt ‹Ruf, Name, Image›

**tarot** /ˈtærəʊ/ *n.* Tarock, *das od. der;* **~ card** Tarockkarte, *die*

**tarpaulin** /tɑːˈpɔːlɪn/ *n.* Plane, *die*

**tarpon** /ˈtɑːpən/ *n.* (*Zool.*) Tarpun, *der*

**tarragon** /ˈtærəgən/ *n.* (*Bot.*) Estragon, *der*

**tarry**[1] /ˈtɑːrɪ/ *adj.* teerig; teerverschmiert ‹Hand, Kleidung›; ‹Strand, Felsen› voller Teer

**tarry**[2] /ˈtærɪ/ *v.i.* (*literary*) verweilen (*geh.*); (*be slow*) säumen (*geh.*); **~ awhile** ein Weilchen bleiben

**tart**[1] /tɑːt/ *adj.* herb; sauer ‹Obst usw.›; (*fig.*) scharfzüngig

**tart**[2] *n.* **A** (*Brit.*) (*filled pie*) ≈ Obstkuchen, *der;* (*small pastry*) Obsttörtchen, *das;* **jam ~:** Marmeladentörtchen, *das;* **B** (*sl.: prostitute*) Nutte, *die* (*salopp*)

**~ ˈup** *v.t.* (*Brit. coll.*) **~ oneself up, get ~ed up** (*dress gaudily*) sich auftakeln (*ugs.*); (*smarten oneself up*) sich fein machen; **~ a pub/restaurant up** (*fig.*) eine Kneipe/ein Lokal aufmotzen (*ugs.*)

**tartan** /ˈtɑːtən/ ❶ *n.* Schotten[stoff], *der;* (*pattern*) **the Stewart ~:** der Stewart (*Textilw.*); *das Schottenmuster des Stewart-Clans.* ❷ *adj.* **A** Schotten‹rock, -jacke›; **~ plaid/rug** Tartan, *der;* **B T~ track** ® Tartanbahn, *die*

**tartar** *n.* **A** (*Chem.*) Tartarus, *der* (*fachspr.*); Weinstein, *der;* ⇒ *also* **cream of tartar**; **B** (*scale on teeth*) Zahnstein, *der*

**Tartar** /ˈtɑːtə(r)/ ▶ **1275**, ▶ **1340** ❶ *adj.* tatarisch; Tataren-. ❷ *n.* **A** (*person*) Tatar, *der*/Tatarin, *die;* **B** (*language*) Tatarisch, das; **C** (*violent-tempered person*) Choleriker, *der*/Cholerikerin, *die*

**tartare** /ˈtɑːtɑː(r)/ *adj.* **~ sauce, sauce ~** ⇒ **tartar sauce; steak tartare** ⇒ **steak**

**tartaric acid** /tɑːtærɪk ˈæsɪd/ *n.* (*Chem.*) Weinsäure, *die*

**tartar sauce** /ˈtɑːtɑː(r)/ *n.* (*Gastr.*) Remoulade[nsoße], *die*

**tartly** /ˈtɑːtlɪ/ *adv.* in scharfem Ton ‹sprechen, antworten›

**tartness** /ˈtɑːtnɪs/ *n., no pl.* ⇒ **tart**[1]: Herbheit, *die;* Säure, *die;* (*fig.*) Scharfzüngigkeit *die*

**tarty** /ˈtɑːtɪ/ *adj.* (*sl.*) nuttig (*ugs. abwertend*)

**Tarzan** /ˈtɑːzən/ *n.* Tarzan, *der* (*fig.*)

**task** /tɑːsk/ *n.* Aufgabe, *die;* **set sb. the ~ of doing sth.** jmdm. auftragen, etw. zu tun; **set oneself the ~ of doing sth.** es sich (*Dat.*) zur Aufgabe machen, etw. zu tun; **undertake the ~ of doing sth.** sich der Aufgabe (*Dat.*) unterziehen, etw. zu tun; **carry out/perform a ~:** eine Aufgabe erfüllen; **take sb. to ~:** jmdm. eine Lektion erteilen

**task: ~ force, ~ group** *ns.* (*sent out*) Sonderkommando, *das;* (*set up*) Sonderkommission, *die;* **~master** *n.* **a hard ~master** ein strenger Vorgesetzter; (*teacher*) ein strenger Lehrmeister

**Tasmania** /tæzˈmeɪnɪə/ *pr. n.* Tasmanien (*das*)

**Tasmanian** /tæzˈmeɪnɪən/ ❶ *adj.* **A** tasmanisch; **B** (*Zool.*) **~ devil/wolf** Beutelteufel/-wolf, *der.* ❷ *n.* Tasmanier, *der*/Tasmanierin, *die*

**tassel** /ˈtæsl/ *n.* Quaste, *die*

**taste** /teɪst/ ❶ *v.t.* **A** schmecken; (*try a little*) probieren; kosten; **she barely ~d her food** sie hat ihr Essen kaum angerührt; **she hadn't ~d food for two days** sie hatte seit zwei Tagen keinen Bissen gegessen; **B** (*recognize flavour of*) [heraus]schmecken; **C** (*fig.: experience*) kosten (*geh.*) ‹Macht, Freiheit, [Miss]erfolg, Glück, Niederlage›.

❷ *v.i.* **A** (*have sense of flavour*) schmecken; **B** (*have certain flavour*) schmecken (**of** nach); **not ~ of anything** nach nichts schmecken.

❸ *n.* **A** (*flavour*) Geschmack, *der;* **to ~:** nach Geschmack ‹verdünnen›; **this dish has no ~:** dieses Gericht schmeckt nach nichts; **there's a ~ of garlic in sth.** etw. schmeckt nach Knoblauch; **leave a nasty/bad** *etc.* **~ in the mouth** (*lit. or fig.*) einen unangenehmen/üblen *usw.* Nachgeschmack hinterlassen; **B** (*sense*) **[sense of] ~:** Geschmack[ssinn], *der;* **C** (*discernment*) Geschmack, *der;* **person of ~:** Person mit Geschmack; **he is a person of ~:** er hat Geschmack; **~ in art/music** Kunst-/Musikgeschmack, *der;* **have good ~ in clothes** sich geschmackvoll kleiden; **it would be bad ~ to do that** es wäre geschmacklos *od.* eine Geschmacklosigkeit, das zu tun; **in good/bad ~:** geschmackvoll/geschmacklos; **in the best/worst of ~:** äußerst geschmackvoll/geschmacklos; **D** (*sample*) (*lit. or fig.*) Kostprobe, *die;* **have a ~ of** probieren ‹Speise, Getränk›; kennen lernen ‹Freiheit, jmds. Jähzorn, Arroganz›; **do you want a ~?** möchtest du mal kosten *od.* probieren?; **first ~ of success/of life in a big city** erstes Erfolgs-/Großstadterlebnis; **give sb. a ~ of sth.** (*lit. or fig.*) jmdm. eine Kostprobe einer Sache (*Gen.*) geben; **give sb. a ~ of the whip** jmdm. die Peitsche zu spüren *od.* (*geh.*) schmecken geben; **a ~ of things to come** ein Vorgeschmack dessen, was noch kommt; ⇒ *also* **medicine**; **E** (*liking*) Geschmack, *der* (**in** für); **have a/no ~ for sth.** an etw. (*Dat.*) Geschmack/keinen Geschmack finden; **have expensive ~s in clothes** *etc.* eine Vorliebe für teure Kleidung *usw.* haben; **be/not be to sb.'s ~:** nach jmds./nicht nach jmds. Geschmack sein; **it's a question** *or* **matter of ~:** das ist eine Frage des Geschmacks; das ist Geschmackssache; **each** *or* **everyone to his ~:** jeder nach seinem Geschmack; **~s differ** die Geschmäcker sind verschieden (*ugs. scherzh.*); **there's no accounting for ~:** über Geschmack lässt sich nicht streiten; ⇒ *also* **acquire B**

**ˈtaste bud** *n.* (*Anat., Zool.*) Geschmacksknospe, *die*

**tasteful** /ˈteɪstfl/ *adj.* geschmackvoll; ‹Person› mit Geschmack

**tastefully** /ˈteɪstfəlɪ/ *adv.* geschmackvoll

**tasteless** /ˈteɪstlɪs/ *adj.* geschmacklos

**tastelessly** /ˈteɪstlɪslɪ/ *adv.* geschmacklos; *as sentence-modifier* geschmackloserweise

**taster** /ˈteɪstə(r)/ *n.* **A** Verkoster, *der*/Verkosterin, *die;* **B** (*sample*) **a ~ for** *or* **of sth.** ein [kleines] Vorgeschmack *od.* eine [kleine] Kostprobe von etw.

**tastily** /ˈteɪstɪlɪ/ *adv.* lecker

**tastiness** /ˈteɪstɪnɪs/ *n., no pl.* leckerer Geschmack

**tasty** /ˈteɪstɪ/ *adj.* lecker; **be a ~ morsel** (*lit. or fig.*) ein Leckerbissen sein

**tat**[1] /tæt/ *n., no pl.* (*coll.*) Schrott, *der* (*ugs.*)

**tat**[2] ⇒ **tit**[2]

**ta-ta** /tæˈtɑː/ *int.* (*child lang.*) ata, ata! (*Kinderspr.*); (*coll.*) tschüs! (*ugs.*)

**tattered** /ˈtætəd/ *adj.* zerlumpt ‹Kleidung, Person›; zerrissen ‹Segel›; zerfleddert ‹Buch, Zeitschrift›; (*fig.*) ramponiert (*ugs.*) ‹Ruf›

**tatters** /ˈtætəz/ *n. pl.* Fetzen; **be in ~:** in Fetzen sein; (*fig.*) ‹Karriere, Leben:› ruiniert sein; ‹Argument, Strategie:› zunichte sein

**tattily** /ˈtætɪlɪ/ *adv.* schäbig (*abwertend*)

**tattiness** /ˈtætɪnɪs/ *n., no pl.* Schäbigkeit, *die* (*abwertend*)

**tatting** /ˈtætɪŋ/ *n.* Schiffchen- *od.* Okkiarbeit, *die;* (*lace*) Schiffchen- *od.* Okkispitze, *die*

**tattle** /ˈtætl/ *v.i.* tratschen (*ugs. abwertend*)

**tattoo**[1] /təˈtuː/ ❶ *v.t.* tätowieren; **~ sth. on sb.'s arm** jmdm. etw. auf den Arm tätowieren. ❷ *n.* Tätowierung, *die*

**tattoo**[2] *n.* **A** (*Mil.: signal*) Zapfenstreich, *der;* **beat** *or* **sound the ~:** den Zapfenstreich schlagen/blasen;(*drumming noise*) Trommeln, *das;* **there was a ~ on the door** jemand trommelte gegen die Tür; **he/his fingers beat a ~ on the table** er trommelte mit den Fingern auf den Tisch; **C** (*military show*) **~:** Großer Zapfenstreich

**tattooed** /təˈtuːd/ *adj.* tätowiert

**tattooer** /təˈtuːə(r)/, **tattooist** /təˈtuːɪst/ *ns.* ▶ **1261** Tätowierer, *der*/Tätowiererin, *die*

**tatty** /ˈtætɪ/ *adj.* (*coll.*) schäbig (*abwertend*); zerfleddert ‹Zeitschrift, Buch›; (*inferior*) mies (*ugs.*) ‹Publikation, Firma›; (*threadbare*) billig ‹Argument, Ausrede›

**taught** ⇒ **teach**

**taunt** /tɔːnt/ ❶ *v.t.* verspotten (**about** wegen); **~ sb. with being a weakling** jmdn. als Schwächling verspotten. ❷ *n.* spöttische Bemerkung; **the ~ of cowardice** *or* **of being a coward hurt him deeply** dass man ihn als Feigling verspottete, traf ihn tief

**taunting** /ˈtɔːntɪŋ/ ❶ *adj.* spöttisch. ❷ *n.* Spott, *der*

**Taurean** /ˈtɔːrɪən/ *n.* (*Astrol.*) Stier, *der*

**Taurus** /ˈtɔːrəs/ *n.* (*Astrol., Astron.*) der Stier; der Taurus; ⇒ *also* **Aries**

**taut** /tɔːt/ *adj.* **A** (*tight*) straff ‹Seil, Kabel, Saite›; gespannt ‹Muskel›; **B** (*fig.: tense*) angespannt ‹Nerven, Ausdruck›; **C** (*fig.: concise*) kurz ‹Geschichte, Erzählung›; knapp ‹Stil›

**tauten** /ˈtɔːtn/ ❶ *v.t.* straffen. ❷ *v.i.* sich straffen; ‹Muskel:› sich spannen

**tautly** /ˈtɔːtlɪ/ *adv.* **A** (*tightly*) straff; **B** (*fig.: tensely*) zum Zerreißen; **C** (*fig.: tersely*) knapp ‹geschrieben›; straff ‹gebaut›

**tautological** /tɔːtəˈlɒdʒɪkl/, **tautologous** /tɔːˈtɒləgəs/ *adjs.* tautologisch; **~ expression/statement** Tautologie, *die;* **it is ~ to talk about ...:** es ist eine Tautologie, von ... zu sprechen

**tautology** /tɔːˈtɒlədʒɪ/ *n.* Tautologie, *die*

**tavern** /ˈtævən/ *n.* (*literary*) Schenke, *die*

**tawdriness** /ˈtɔːdrɪnɪs/ *n., no pl.* Flitter, *der;* **the ~ of sb.'s finery** jmds. Flitterstaat

**tawdry** /ˈtɔːdrɪ/ *adj.* billig und geschmacklos; (*fig.*) zweifelhaft

**tawny** /ˈtɔːnɪ/ *adj.* gelbbraun

**tawny ˈowl** *n.* (*Ornith.*) Waldkauz, *der*

**tax** /tæks/ ❶ *n.* **A** Steuer, *die;* **pay 20% in ~ [on sth.]** 20% Steuern [für etw.] zahlen; **a third of my income will go in ~:** ein Drittel meines Einkommens geht an das Finanzamt; **before/after ~:** vor Steuern/nach Abzug der Steuern; **free of ~:** steuerfrei; (*after ~, ~ paid*) nach Abzug der Steuern; netto; **~ paid, net of ~:** nach Abzug der Steuern; netto; **for ~ reasons** aus steuerlichen Gründen; **for ~ purposes** steuerlich gesehen; fürs Finanzamt (*ugs.*); ⇒ *also* **capital gains tax; corporation B; direct tax; income tax; poll tax; purchase tax; value-added tax**; **B** (*fig.: burden*) Belastung, *die* (**on** für).

❷ *v.t.* **A** (*impose ~ on*) besteuern; (*pay ~ on*) versteuern ‹Einkommen›; **~ sb. on his/her income** jmds. Einkommen besteuern; **I am** *or* **my income is ~ed at 30%** ich bezahle 30% Lohnsteuer/Einkommensteuer; Ⓑ (*make demands on*) strapazieren ‹Mittel, Kräfte, Geduld usw.›; Ⓒ (*accuse*) beschuldigen, bezichtigen (**with** *Gen.*); **~ sb. with doing sth.** jmdn. beschuldigen *od.* bezichtigen, etw. getan zu haben

**taxable** /ˈtæksəbl/ *adj.* steuerpflichtig

**tax: ~ allowance** *n.* Steuerfreibetrag, *der;* **~ assessment** *n.* Steuerbescheid, *der*

**taxation** /tækˈseɪʃn/ *n.* (*imposition of taxes*) Besteuerung, *die;* (*taxes payable*) Steuern; **subject to ~:** steuerpflichtig

**tax: ~ avoidance** *n.* Steuerminderung, *die;* **~ bill** *n.* Steuerbescheid, *der;* (*amount*) Steuerschuld, *die;* **~ bracket** *n.* Stufe im Steuertarif; **move into a higher ~ bracket** nach einem höheren Steuersatz besteuert werden; **~ collector** *n.* Finanzbeamte, *der*/-beamtin, *die;* **~-deductible** *adj.* steuerabzugsfähig; [steuerlich] absetzbar; **~ demand** *n.* Steuerforderung, *die;* **~ disc** *n.* Steuerplakette, *die;* **~ dodge** *n.* Steuertrick, *der;* **~ dodger** *n.* Steuerbetrüger, *der*/-betrügerin, *die;* **~ evasion** *n.* Steuerhinterziehung, *die;* **~-exempt** *adj.* (*Amer.*) steuerbefreit; steuerfrei ‹Einkommen›; **~ exile** *n.* Ⓐ (*person*) Steuerflüchtling, *der;* Ⓑ (*place*) Steueroase, *die* (*ugs.*); **~ form** *n.* Steuerformular, *das;* **~-free** ❶ *adj.* steuerfrei; (*after payment of tax*) Netto-; **~-free allowance** Steuerfreibetrag, *der;* ❷ *adv.* steuerfrei; (*after payment of tax*) netto; **~ haven** *n.* Steueroase, *die* (*ugs.*); Steuerparadies, *das* (*ugs.*)

**taxi** /ˈtæksɪ/ ❶ *n.* Taxi, *das;* **go by ~:** mit dem Taxi fahren. ❷ *v.i.*, **~ing** *or* **taxying** /ˈtæksɪɪŋ/ (*Aeronaut.*) ‹Flugzeug:› rollen; ‹Pilot:› das Flugzeug rollen lassen; **~ to a stop** ‹Flugzeug:› ausrollen. ❸ *v.t.*, **~ing** *or* **taxying** (*Aeronaut.*) rollen lassen

**ˈtaxicab** ⇨ **taxi** 1

**taxidermist** /ˈtæksɪdɜːmɪst/ *n.* ▶ 1261 Taxidermist, *der*/Taxidermistin, *die;* Präparator, *der*/Präparatorin, *die*

**taxidermy** /ˈtæksɪdɜːmɪ/ *n.* Taxidermie, *die*

**ˈtaxi driver** *n.* ▶ 1261 Taxifahrer, *der*/-fahrerin, *die*

**taximeter** /ˈtæksɪmiːtə(r)/ *n.* Taxameter, *das od. der;* Fahrpreisanzeiger, *der*

**ˈtax incentive** *n.* steuerlicher Anreiz

**taxing** /ˈtæksɪŋ/ *adj.* strapaziös, anstrengend ‹Arbeit, Rolle, Reise›; schwierig ‹Problem›

**ˈtax inspector** *n.* ▶ 1261 Steuerinspektor, *der*/-inspektorin, *die*

**taxi: ~ rank** (*Brit.*), (*Amer.*) **~ stand** *ns.* Taxistand, *der;* **~way** *n.* Rollbahn, *die*

**tax: ~man** *n.* (*coll.*) Finanzbeamte, *der*/-beamtin, *die;* **a letter from the ~man** ein Brief vom Finanzamt; **work for the ~man** [nur noch] fürs Finanzamt arbeiten (*fig.*); **~ office** *n.* Finanzamt, *das*

**taxonomy** /tækˈsɒnəmɪ/ *n.* (*Biol.*) Taxonomie, *die*

**tax: ~payer** *n.* Steuerzahler, *der*/-zahlerin, *die;* **~paying** *attrib. adj.* Steuern zahlend…; **~ rebate** *n.* Steuererstattung, *die;* **~ relief** *n.* Steuererleichterung, *die;* **get ~ relief on insurance premiums** Versicherungsprämien von der Steuer absetzen; **~ return** *n.* Steuererklärung, *die;* **~ year** *n.* Steuerjahr, *das*

**TB** *abbr.* ▶ 1232 (*Med.*) **tuberculosis** Tb, *die;* **TB sufferer** Tb-Kranke, *der*/*die*

**T-bone** ⇨ **T** B

**tbsp.** *abbr.*, *pl. same or* **~s: tablespoon** Essl.; EL

**te** /tiː/ *n.* (*Mus.*) si

**tea** /tiː/ *n.* Ⓐ Tee, *der;* **herb/fennel ~:** Kräuter-/Fencheltee, *der;* **early morning ~:** *frühmorgens* [*vor dem Aufstehen*] *getrunkener Tee;* [**not**] **be sb.'s cup of ~** (*fig. coll.*) [nicht] jmds. Fall sein (*ugs.*); **be just** *or* **exactly** *or* **very much sb.'s cup of ~** (*fig. coll.*) genau *od.* ganz jmds. Fall sein (*ugs.*); **not for all the ~ in China** (*coll.*) nicht um alles in der Welt; [**come to sb. for**] **~ and sympathy** (*fig. coll.*) Trost und Rat [bei jmdm. suchen]; Ⓑ (*meal*) [**high**] **~:** Abendessen, *das;* **afternoon ~:** [Nachmittags]tee, *der*

**tea: ~ bag** *n.* Teebeutel, *der;* **~ boy** *n.* ≈ Stift, *der* (*ugs.*); *jüngerer Mann, der in einer Firma, Behörde o. Ä. den Pausentee usw. zubereitet;* **~ break** *n.* (*Brit.*) Teepause, *die;* **~ caddy** *n.* Teebüchse, *die;* **~cake** *n.* Ⓐ (*Brit.: sweet bread bun*) ≈ Rosinenbrötchen, *das;* Ⓑ (*Amer.: biscuit*) Keks, *der;* **~cakes** Teegebäck, *das*

**teach** /tiːtʃ/ ❶ *v.t.*, **taught** /tɔːt/ unterrichten; (*at university*) lehren; **You can't dance? I'll ~ you** Du kannst nicht tanzen? Ich bringe es dir bei *od.* zeige es dir; **~ music** *etc.* **to sb., ~ sb. music** *etc.* jmdn. in Musik *usw.* unterrichten; jmdm. Musikunterricht *usw.* geben; **~ oneself** es sich (*Dat.*) selbst beibringen; **~ sb./oneself/an animal sth.** jmdm./sich/einem Tier etw. beibringen; **~ sb./oneself/an animal to do sth.** jmdm./sich/einem Tier beibringen, etw. zu tun; (*train*) jmdn./sich/ein Tier dazu erziehen, etw. zu tun; **~ sb. to ride/to play the piano** jmdm. das Reiten/Klavierspielen beibringen; **T~ yourself French/car maintenance** (*book title*) Französisch zum Selbststudium/Wie warte ich mein Auto selbst?; **this experience has taught me one thing …:** diese Erfahrung hat mich eins gelehrt …; **I'll/that'll ~ you** *etc.* **to do that!** (*coll. iron.*) ich werde/das wird dich *usw.* lehren, das zu tun! (*iron.*); **that'll ~ him/you** *etc.*! (*coll. iron.*) das hat er/hast du *usw.* nun davon! (*iron.*); **~ sb. how/that …:** jmdm. beibringen, wie/dass …; ‹Bibel, Erfahrung:› jmdn. lehren, wie/dass …; **~ sb. tolerance** *or* **to be tolerant** jmdn. Toleranz lehren; jmdn. lehren, tolerant zu sein; **~ school** (*Amer.*) Lehrer/Lehrerin sein; ⇨ *also* **dog** 1 A; **lesson** C.

❷ *v.i.*, **taught** unterrichten; **he wants to/is going to ~:** er will Lehrer werden/wird Lehrer

**teachable** /ˈtiːtʃəbl/ *adj.* lernfähig ‹Kind, Tier›; erlernbar ‹Eigenschaft›; **a ~ subject** ein Fach, das man gut lehren kann

**teacher** /ˈtiːtʃə(r)/ *n.* ▶ 1261 Lehrer, *der*/Lehrerin, *die;* **she's a university/evening class ~:** sie lehrt an der Universität/unterrichtet an der Abendschule; **kindergarten ~:** ≈ Vorschullehrer, *der*/-lehrerin, *die;* **geography/music ~:** Geographie-/Musiklehrer, *der*/Geographie-/Musiklehrerin, *die*

**teacher: ~ training** *n.* Lehrerausbildung, *die;* **~-training college** *n.* ≈ pädagogische Hochschule

**ˈtea chest** *n.* Teekiste, *die*

**ˈteach-in** *n.* Teach-in, *das*

**teaching** /ˈtiːtʃɪŋ/ *n.* Ⓐ (*act*) Unterrichten, *das* (**of** von); **the ~ of languages, language ~:** der Sprachunterricht; **I enjoy ~ very much** Das Unterrichten macht mir großen Spaß; **all the ~ at this school is in French** an der Schule wird nur in französischer Sprache unterrichtet; Ⓑ *no pl., no art.* (*profession*) Lehrberuf, *der;* **want to go into** *or* **take up** *or* **do ~:** Lehrer/Lehrerin werden wollen; Ⓒ (*doctrine*) Lehre, *die*

**teaching: ~ aid** *n.* Lehr- *od.* Unterrichtsmittel, *das;* **~ hospital** *n.* Ausbildungskrankenhaus, *das;* **~ machine** *n.* Lernmaschine, *die;* **~ method** *n.* Lehr- *od.* Unterrichtsmethode, *die;* **~ practice** *n.* ≈ Schulpraktikum, *das;* **~ profession** *n.* Lehrberuf, *der;* **~ staff** *n.* Lehrerkollegium, *das*

**tea: ~ cloth** *n.* Ⓐ (*for table*) ≈ Kaffeedecke, *die;* Ⓑ (*for drying*) Geschirrtuch, *das;* **~ cosy** *n.* Teewärmer, *der;* **~cup** *n.* Teetasse, *die;* ⇨ *also* **storm** 1 A; **~cupful** *n.* Tasse, *die;* **a ~cupful of sugar** eine Tasse Zucker; **~ dance** *n.* Tanztee, *der;* **~garden** *n.* Ⓐ (*public place*) ≈ Gartencafé, *das;* Ⓑ (*plantation*) Teeplantage, *die;* **~ house** *n.* Teehaus, *das*

**teak** /tiːk/ *n.* Ⓐ (*wood*) Teak[holz], *das; attrib.* Teak[holz]‹öl, -furnier, -möbel›; Ⓑ (*tree*) Teakbaum, *der*

**ˈtea kettle** *n.* Teekessel, *der*

**teal** /tiːl/ *n.*, *pl. same* (*Ornith.*) Krickente, *die*

**tea: ~ lady** *n.* ▶ 1261 *Frau, die in einer Firma, Behörde o. Ä. den Pausentee usw. zubereitet;* **~ leaf** *n.* Teeblatt, *das;* **read the ~ leaves** ≈ aus dem Kaffeesatz lesen

**team** /tiːm/ ❶ *n.* Ⓐ (*group*) Team, *das;* (*Sport also*) Mannschaft, *die;* **a football/cricket ~:** eine Fußball-/Kricketmannschaft; **a ~ of scientists** eine Gruppe *od.* ein Team von Wissenschaftlern; **a research ~:** eine Forschungsgruppe; **make a good ~:** ein gutes Team *od.* Gespann sein; **work as a ~:** im Team zusammenarbeiten; Ⓑ (*draught animals*) Gespann, *das;* **a ~ of oxen/horses** ein Gespann Ochsen/Pferde; **a ~ of four horses** ein Vierergespann [Pferde].

❷ *v.t.* ⇨ **~ up** 1.

❸ *v.i.* ⇨ **~ up** 2

**~ ˈup** ❶ *v.t.* zusammenbringen. ❷ *v.i.* sich zusammentun (*ugs.*)

**ˈtea maker** *n.* Teemaschine, *die*

**team: ~ effort** *n.* Team- *od.* Gemeinschaftsarbeit, *die;* **a great ~ effort** eine großartige Gemeinschaftsleistung; **thanks to good ~ effort** dank guter Teamarbeit; **~ game** *n.* Mannschaftsspiel, *das;* **~ leader** *n.* Gruppenleiter, *der*/-leiterin, *die;* **~mate** *n.* Mannschaftskamerad, *der*/-kameradin, *die;* **~ member** *n.* Mitglied des Teams/der Mannschaft/der Gruppe; **~ ˈspirit** *n.* Teamgeist, *der;* (*Sport also*) Mannschaftsgeist, *der*

**teamster** /ˈtiːmstə(r)/ *n.* (*Amer.*) Lkw-Fahrer, *der*/-Fahrerin, *die*

**ˈteamwork** *n.* Teamarbeit, *die;* **by ~:** in Teamarbeit

**tea: ~ party** *n.* Teegesellschaft, *die;* **~ plantation** *n.* Teeplantage, *die;* **~ planter** *n.* (*proprietor*) Teeplantagenbesitzer, *der*/-besitzerin, *die;* (*cultivator*) Teepflanzer, *der*/-pflanzerin, *die;* **~pot** *n.* Teekanne, *die*

**tear**[1] /teə(r)/ ❶ *n.* Riß, *der;* ⇨ *also* **wear** 1 A.

❷ *v.t.*, **tore** /tɔː(r)/, **torn** /tɔːn/ Ⓐ (*rip; lit. or fig.*) zerreißen; (*pull apart*) auseinander reißen; (*damage*) aufreißen; **~ open** aufreißen ‹Brief, Schachtel, Paket›; **~ one's dress** [**on a nail**] sich (*Dat.*) das Kleid [an einem Nagel (*Dat.*)] aufreißen; **~ one's fingernail** sich (*Dat.*) einen Fingernagel einreißen; **~ a muscle** sich (*Dat.*) einen Muskelriss zuziehen; **a torn muscle** ein Muskel[faser]riss; **~ sb.'s heart** (*fig.*) jmdm. das Herz zerreißen (*geh.*); **~ a hole/gash in sth.** ein Loch/eine klaffende Wunde in etw. (*Akk.*) reißen; **~ sth. in half** *or* **in two** etw. entzweireißen; **~ to shreds** *or* **pieces** (*lit.*) zerfetzen; in Stücke reißen ‹Flagge, Kleidung, Person›; **~ to shreds** (*fig.*) (*destroy*) ruinieren ‹Ruf, Leumund›; zerrütten ‹Nerven›; zunichte machen ‹Argument, Alibi›; auseinander nehmen (*salopp*) ‹Mannschaft›; (*criticize*) verreißen (*ugs.*); **a country torn by war** ein durch Krieg zerrissenes Land; **I was torn by** *or* **with grief** mein Herz war von Kummer zerrissen (*geh.*); **be torn between two things/people/between x and y** zwischen zwei Dingen/Personen/x und y hin- und hergerissen sein; **be torn as to what to do** hin- und hergerissen sein [und nicht wissen, was man tun soll]; **that's torn it** (*Brit. fig. coll.*) das hat alles vermasselt (*salopp*); Ⓑ (*remove with force*) reißen; **~ sth. out of** *or* **from sb.'s hands/a book** jmdm. etw. aus der Hand reißen/etw. aus einem Buch [heraus]reißen; **the wind tore the cap from his head** der Wind riss ihm die Mütze vom Kopf; **~ a child from its parents/home** (*fig.*) ein Kind seinen Eltern entreißen/aus seiner vertrauten Umgebung reißen; **~ oneself from sb./a place** (*fig.*) sich von jmdm./einem Ort losreißen; **~ one's hair** (*fig.*) sich (*Dat.*) die Haare raufen (*ugs.*).

❸ *v.i.*, **tore, torn** Ⓐ (*rip*) [zer]reißen; **it ~s along the perforation** es lässt sich entlang der Perforation abreißen; **~ in half** *or* **in two** entzweireißen; durchreißen; Ⓑ (*move hurriedly*) rasen (*ugs.*); **~ past** vorbeirasen (*ugs.*); **~ along the street** die Straße hinunterrasen (*ugs.*); **~ off** losrasen (*ugs.*); **come**

**~ing out/past** heraus-/vorbeigerast kommen (*ugs.*)
**~ apart** *v.t.* (*lit. or fig.*) auseinander reißen; (*coll.: criticize*) zerreißen (*ugs.*); **they tore the place apart** sie haben den Laden auseinander genommen (*ugs.*)
**~ at** *v.t.* zerren an (+ *Dat.*); **~ at sb.'s heartstrings** (*fig.*) jmdm. sehr zu Herzen gehen
**~ a'way** *v.t.* wegreißen; abreißen ‹Tapete, Verpackung›; **~ away sb.'s mask** (*fig.*) jmds. Maske herunterreißen; **~ sb./oneself away [from sb./sth.]** (*fig.*) jmdn./sich [von jmdm./etw.] loseisen (*ugs.*); **~ oneself away [from a sight/book/game]** (*fig.*) sich [von einem Anblick/Buch/Spiel] losreißen; ⇒ *also* **tearaway**
**~ 'down** *v.t.* herunterreißen; niederreißen ‹Zaun, Mauer›; abreißen ‹Gebäude›; (*fig.*) niederreißen ‹Schranken›
**~ into** *v.t.* ‹Geschoss:› ein Loch reißen in (+ *Akk.*); ‹Säge:› sich [hinein]fressen in (+ *Akk.*); ‹Raubtier:› zerfleischen; (*fig.: tell off, criticize*) heftig angreifen
**~ 'off** *v.t.* abreißen; ⇒ *also* **tear-off**
**~ 'out** *v.t.* herausreißen; ausreißen ‹Baum›; ⇒ *also* ~ 2 B
**~ 'up** *v.t.* **A** (*remove*) aufreißen ‹Straße, Bürgersteig›; herausreißen ‹Zaun, Pflanze›; ausreißen ‹Baum›; **B** (*destroy*) zerreißen; (*fig.*) für null und nichtig erklären ‹Vertrag, Abkommen›

**tear²** /tɪə(r)/ *n.* Träne, *die;* **there were ~s in her eyes** sie hatte *od.* ihr standen Tränen in den Augen; **with ~s in one's eyes** mit Tränen in den Augen; **cry ~s of joy/rage/frustration** Freudentränen/Tränen der Wut/Enttäuschung vergießen; **cry ~s of laughter** Tränen lachen; **burst into ~s** in Tränen ausbrechen; **move sb. to ~s** jmdn. zu Tränen rühren; **bore sb. to ~s** jmdn. zu Tode langweilen; **be in ~s** in Tränen aufgelöst sein; **end in ~s** böse enden *od.* ausgehen; ein böses *od.* schlimmes Ende nehmen; **French/Cooking without ~s** (*book title*) Französisch/Kochen leicht gemacht; **be wet with ~s** tränennass sein; ⇒ *also* **crocodile tears**; **dissolve** 2 A; **reduce** 1 B; **shed¹** B; **vale**

**tearaway** /'teərəweɪ/ **1** *adj.* rabaukenhaft (*ugs.*). **2** *n.* Rabauke, *der* (*ugs.*)

**tear/tɪə(r)/: ~drop** *n.* Träne, *die;* **~ duct** *n.* (*Anat.*) Tränenkanal, *der*

**tearful** /'tɪəfl/ *adj.* (*crying*) weinend; (*wet with tears*) tränenüberströmt; (*accompanied by tears*) tränenreich ‹Versöhnung, Abschied, Anlass›; **say a ~ goodbye** sich unter Tränen verabschieden; **she was looking very ~:** sie sah sehr verweint aus; (*about to cry*) sie schien den Tränen nahe

**tearfully** /'tɪəfəlɪ/ *adv.* unter Tränen

**tear gas** /'tɪəgæs/ *n.* Tränengas, *das*

**tearing** /'teərɪŋ/ *adj.* **A** reißend ‹Geräusch›; **B** (*coll.: violent*) rasend; **be in a ~ hurry** schrecklich in Eile sein

**tear jerker** /'tɪədʒɜ:kə(r)/ *n.* (*coll.*) Schnulze, *die* (*ugs. abwertend*); **this film is a real ~:** in diesem Film wird kräftig auf die Tränendrüsen gedrückt

**tear-off** /'teərɒf/ *attrib. adj.* **~ calendar** Abreißkalender, *der;* **~ slip** Abriss, *der*

**tea: ~room** *n.* Teestube, *die;* ≈ Café, *das;* **~ rose** *n.* Teerose, *die*

**tear sheet** /'teəʃɪ:t/ *n.* Belegseite, *die*

**tear-stained** /'tɪəsteɪnd/ *adj.* tränenüberströmt ‹Gesicht›; ‹Brief, Buchseite› mit Tränenspuren

**tease** /ti:z/ **1** *v.t.* **A** necken; **~ sb. [about sth.]** jmdn. [mit etw.] aufziehen (*ugs.*); jmdn. [wegen etw.] verspotten; **he's only teasing you** er macht nur Spaß (*ugs.*); **stop teasing the dog** hör auf, den Hund zu ärgern; **~ sb. that he has done sth.** jmdn. damit aufziehen (*ugs.*), dass er etw. getan hat; **the children ~d their father for sweets** *or* **to give them sweets** (*Amer.*) die Kinder lagen ihrem Vater damit in den Ohren (*ugs.*), dass er ihnen Süßigkeiten geben sollte; **B** (*Textiles*) (*separate fibres of*) krempeln ‹Flachs, Wolle›; hecheln ‹Flachs›; (*dress with teasels*) [auf]rauen; **C** (*Amer. Hairdressing*) toupieren. **2** *v.i.* seine Späße machen; **I'm only teasing** ich mache nur Spaß. **3** *n.* (*coll.*) **he/she is a great ~:** er/sie muss einen immer aufziehen (*ugs.*)
**~ 'out** *v.t.* **A** (*disentangle*) auskämmen; kämmen, krempeln ‹Wolle, Flachs›; hecheln ‹Flachs›; **B** (*get out, lit. or fig.*) herausholen; **~ out the facts** die Tatsachen herausarbeiten

**teasel** /'ti:zl/ *n.* **A** (*Bot.*) Karde, *die;* **common/fuller's ~:** Wilde Karde/Weberkarde, *die;* **B** (*Textiles*) Karde, *die*

**teaser** /'ti:zə(r)/ *n.* **A** (*coll.: puzzle*) **[brain-]~:** Denk[sport]aufgabe, *die;* **be a [real] ~** (*fig.*) eine harte Nuss sein (*ugs.*); **B** (*one who teases*) **he/she is a great ~:** er/sie muss einen immer aufziehen (*ugs.*)

**tea: ~ service, ~set** *ns.* Tee-Service, *das;* **~ shop** (*Brit.*) ⇒ **tearoom**

**teasing** /'ti:zɪŋ/ *adj.* neckend; **he was in a ~ mood** er war in der Stimmung, andere aufzuziehen (*ugs.*)

**teasingly** /'ti:zɪŋlɪ/ *adv.* neckend; **speak ~:** frotzeln; **ask sb. sth. ~:** jmdn. frotzelnd etw. fragen

**tea: ~spoon** *n.* Teelöffel, *der;* **~spoonful** *n.* Teelöffel, *der;* **a ~spoonful** ein Teelöffel [voll]; **~ strainer** *n.* Teesieb, *das*

**teat** /ti:t/ *n.* **A** (*nipple*) Zitze, *die;* **B** (*of rubber or plastic*) Sauger, *der*

**tea: ~ table** *n.* Teetisch, *der;* **be at the ~ table** beim Tee sitzen; **~ things** *n. pl.* (*coll.*) Teegeschirr, *das;* **~time** *n.* Teezeit, *die;* **~ towel** *n.* Geschirrtuch, *das;* **~ tray** *n.* Teebrett, *das;* **~ trolley** *n.* Teewagen, *der;* **~ urn** *n.* Teebehälter, *der;* **~ wagon** (*Amer.*) ⇒ **~ trolley**

**teazel, teazle** /'ti:zl/ ⇒ **teasel**

**Tech (Tec)** /tek/ *n.* (*dated coll.*) Fachhochschule, *die;* FH, *die*

**'techie** *n.* (*coll.*) Technikfreak, *der;* (*computer expert*) Computerfreak, *der*

**technical** /'teknɪkl/ *adj.* **A** technisch ‹Problem, Detail, Daten, Fortschritt›; (*of particular science, art, etc.*) fachlich; Fach‹kenntnis, -berater, -sprache, -begriff, -wörterbuch›; (*of the execution of a work of art*) technisch ‹Fertigkeit, Schwierigkeit›; **~ expertise/expert** Sachkenntnis, *die*/Fachmann, *der;* **~ college/school** Fachhochschule, *die*/Fachschule, *die;* **[highly] ~ book** [reines] Fachbuch; **the text is very/highly ~:** es ist ein reiner Fachtext; **the text is too ~ for me** der Text ist zu fachsprachlich für mich; **explain sth. without being** *or* **getting too ~:** etw. erklären, ohne sich zu fachsprachlich auszudrücken; **~ hitch** technisches Problem; **~ term** Fachbegriff, *der;* Fachausdruck, *der;* Fachterminus, *der;* **for ~ reasons** aus technischen Gründen; **B** (*strictly interpreted*) (*Law*) formaljuristisch; **~ knockout** (*Boxing*) technischer K.o.

**technical 'drawing** *n.* (*Brit.*) technisches Zeichnen

**technicality** /teknɪ'kælɪtɪ/ *n.* **A** *no pl.* (*technical quality*) technischer Charakter; (*of book, text, style*) fachsprachlicher Charakter; **B** (*technical expression*) Fachausdruck, *der;* **C** (*technical distinction*) technisches Detail; (*technical point*) technische Frage; **legal/financial/military technicalities** rechtliche/finanzielle/militärische [Detail]fragen; **be acquitted on a ~:** aufgrund eines Formfehlers freigesprochen werden

**technically** /'teknɪkəlɪ/ *adv.* **A** technisch; (*in a particular science, art, etc.*) fachlich; **B** (*strictly speaking*) im Prinzip; (*Law*) formaljuristisch

**technician** /tek'nɪʃn/ *n.* ▶ 1261 Techniker, *der*/Technikerin, *die*

**Technicolor**, (*Amer.* ®) /'teknɪkʌlə(r)/ *n.* (*Cinemat.*) Technicolor Ⓦⓩ, *das*

**technique** /tek'ni:k/ *n.* Technik, *die;* (*procedure*) Methode, *die*

**techno** **1** *adj.* Techno-. **2** *n.* Techno, *der od. das*

**technocracy** /tek'nɒkrəsɪ/ *n.* Technokratie, *die*

**technocrat** /'teknəʊkræt/ *n.* Technokrat, *der*/Technokratin, *die*

**technocratic** /teknəʊ'krætɪk/ *adj.* technokratisch

**technological** /teknə'lɒdʒɪkl/ *adj.*, **technologically** /teknə'lɒdʒɪkəlɪ/ *adv.* ⇒ **technology**: technisch; technologisch

**technologist** /tek'nɒlədʒɪst/ *n.* ▶ 1261 Technologe, *der*/Technologin, *die;* ‹Lebensmittel-, Erdöl›techniker, *der*/-technikerin, *die*

**technology** /tek'nɒlədʒɪ/ *n.* Technik, *die;* (*application of science*) Technologie, *die;* **science and ~:** Wissenschaft und Technik; **college of ~:** Fachhochschule für Technik

**technophobe** /'teknəʊfəʊb/ *n.* Mensch mit einer Technikphobie; **be a ~:** eine Technikphobie haben

**technophobia** /teknəʊ'fəʊbɪə/ *n.*, *no pl.* Technikphobie, *die;* **suffer from ~:** eine Technikphobie haben

**techy** ⇒ **tetchy**

**tectonic** /tek'tɒnɪk/ (*Geol.*) **1** *adj.* tektonisch. **2** *n. in pl.* Tektonik, *die;* **plate ~s** Plattentektonik, *die*

**Ted** /ted/ *n.* (*Brit. coll.*) Teddyboy, *der*

**teddy** /'tedɪ/ *n.* **~ [bear]** Teddy[bär], *der*

**Teddy: ~ boy** *n.* (*Brit.*) Teddyboy, *der;* **~ girl** *n.* (*Brit.*) Teddygirl, *das*

**Te Deum** /ti: 'di:əm, teɪ 'deɪəm/ *n.* (*hymn*) Tedeum, *das*

**tedious** /'ti:dɪəs/ *adj.* langwierig ‹Reise, Arbeit›; (*uninteresting*) langweilig

**tediously** /'ti:dɪəslɪ/ *adv.* langatmig ‹reden, schreiben›; (*uninterestingly*) langweilig; **~ familiar** bis zum Überdruss bekannt; **~ repeat sth.** etw. bis zum Überdruss wiederholen; **a ~ long meeting** eine lange, langweilige Besprechung

**tediousness** /'ti:dɪəsnɪs/ *n.*, *no pl.* (*of work, journey*) Langwierigkeit, *die;* (*of book, lecture, wait*) Langweiligkeit, *die*

**tedium** /'ti:dɪəm/ *n.* (*of journey*) Langwierigkeit, *die;* (*of waiting*) Langweiligkeit, *die;* **an hour of unrelieved ~:** eine unendlich langweilige Stunde

**tee** /ti:/ **1** *n.* **A** (*Golf*) Tee, *das;* **B** **to a ~** (*coll.*) = **to a T** ⇒ **T** A. **2** *v.t.* ⇒ **~ up** 1
**~ 'off** *v.i.* (*Golf*) abschlagen
**~ 'up** (*Golf*) **1** *v.t.* auf das Tee legen; aufteen (*fachspr.*). **2** *v.i.* den Ball auf das Tee legen

**tee-hee** /'ti:'hi:/ *int.* hihi

**teem** /ti:m/ *v.i.* **A** (*abound*) wimmeln (**with** von); **B** (*rain heavily*) **~ [with rain]** in Strömen regnen
**~ 'down** *v.i.* **it/the rain was ~ing down** es regnete in Strömen

**teeming** /'ti:mɪŋ/ *adj.* **A** (*pouring*) strömend ‹Regen›; **B** (*abundant*) wimmelnd ‹Menschenmenge›; (*crowded*) von Menschen wimmelnd ‹Straße›

**teen** /ti:n/ *adj.* Teenager-

**teenage** /'ti:neɪdʒ/, **teenaged** /'ti:neɪdʒd/ *attrib. adj.* im Teenageralter *nachgestellt*

**teenager** /'ti:neɪdʒə(r)/ *n.* ▶ 912 Teenager, *der;* (*loosely*) Jugendliche, *der*/*die*

**teens** /ti:nz/ *n. pl.* ▶ 912 Teenagerjahre; **be out of/in one's ~:** aus den Teenagerjahren heraus sein/in den Teenagerjahren sein; **fashions from tots to ~:** Kinder- und Jugendmoden

**teensy-weensy** /'ti:nzɪ wi:nzɪ/, **teeny** /'ti:nɪ/ *adjs.* (*child lang./coll.*) klitzeklein (*ugs.*)

**teeny: ~-bopper** *n.* (*coll.*) *Popfan im Teenageralter;* **~-weeny** ⇒ **teeny**

**teepee** ⇒ **tepee**

**'tee shirt** *n.* T-Shirt, *das*

**teeter** /'ti:tə(r)/ *v.i.* **A** (*waver*) wanken; **~ on the edge** *or* **brink of sth.** schwankend am Rande einer Sache (*Gen.*) stehen; (*fig.*) am Rande einer Sache (*Gen.*) stehen; **B** (*Amer.: see-saw*) wippen; (*fig.*) hin- und herschwanken

**teeth** *pl. of* **tooth**

**teethe** /ti:ð/ *v.i.* zahnen

**teething** /'ti:ðɪŋ/ *n.* Zahnen, *das*

**teething: ~ ring** *n.* Beißring, *der;* **~ troubles** *n. pl.* Beschwerden während des Zahnens; **have ~ troubles** (*fig.*) ‹Person, Vorhaben:› Anfangsschwierigkeiten haben; ‹Maschine usw.:› Kinderkrankheiten haben

t

**teetotal** /tiːˈtəʊtl/ *adj.* abstinent lebend; alkoholfrei ‹Restaurant, Hotel, Feier›; **sb. is ~:** jmd. ist Abstinenzler/Abstinenzlerin

**teetotaler** (*Amer.*) ⇒ **teetotaller**

**teetotalism** /tiːˈtəʊtəlɪzm/ *n.* Abstinenz, *die*

**teetotaller** /tiːˈtəʊtələ(r)/ *n.* Abstinenzler, *der*/Abstinenzlerin, *die*

**TEFL** /ˈtefl/ *abbr.* **teaching of English as a foreign language**

**Teflon** ® /ˈteflɒn/ *n.* Teflon Ⓦⓩ, *das*

**tektite** /ˈtektaɪt/ *n.* (*Min.*) Tektit, *der*

**Tel.**, **tel.** *abbr.* **telephone** Tel.

**telebanking** /ˈtelɪbæŋkɪŋ/ *n.* Telebanking, *das*

**telecast** /ˈtelɪkɑːst/ ❶ *v.t.*, **telecast** [im Fernsehen] senden. ❷ *n.* Fernsehsendung, *die*

**telecommunication** /telɪkəmjuːnɪˈkeɪʃn/ *n.* Ⓐ (*long-distance communication*) Fernmeldeverkehr, *der; attrib.* Fernmelde-; Ⓑ *in pl.* (*science*) Fernmelde- *od.* Nachrichtentechnik, *die; attrib.* Fernmelde- *od.* Nachrichten- ‹techniker, -satellit›

**telecommute** /ˈtelɪkəmjuːt/ *v.i.* Telearbeit verrichten

**telecommuter** /ˈtelɪkəmjuːtə(r)/ *n.* Telearbeiter, *der*/-arbeiterin, *die*

**telecommuting** /ˈtelɪkəmjuːtɪŋ/ *n.* Telearbeit, *die*

**teleconference** /ˈtelɪkɒnfərəns/ *n.* Telekonferenz, *die*

**telecottage** /ˈtelɪkɒtɪdʒ/ *n.: jedermann zugängliche Einrichtung, die bes. Telearbeitern Zugang zu einem ans Internet angeschlossenen Computer bietet*

**telegram** /ˈtelɪgræm/ *n.* Telegramm, *das;* **by ~:** telegrafisch

**telegraph** /ˈtelɪgrɑːf/ ❶ *n.* Ⓐ (*for sending telegrams*) Telegraf, *der; attrib.* Telegrafen-; **ship's ~:** Maschinentelegraf, *der* (*Technik*); ⇒ *also* **bush telegraph**; Ⓑ (*semaphore apparatus*) Semaphor, *der;* Ⓒ (*Sports, Racing: board*) Anzeigetafel, *die.* ❷ *v.t.* Ⓐ telegrafieren; telegrafisch anweisen ‹Geld›; Ⓑ (*Boxing coll.*) telegrafieren ‹Schlag›. ❸ *v.i.* telegrafieren; **~ for sb.** jmdn. telegrafisch rufen lassen

**telegraphese** /telɪgrɑːˈfiːz/ *n.* Telegrammstil, *der*

**telegraphic** /telɪˈgræfɪk/ *adj.* telegrafisch; Telegramm‹adresse, -stil›

**telegraphist** /tɪˈlegrəfɪst/ *n.* ▶ **1261** Telegrafist, *der*/Telegrafistin, *die*

**telegraph: ~ line** *n.* Telegrafenleitung, *die;* **~ pole**, **~ post** *ns.* Telegrafenmast, *der;* **~ wire** *n.* Telegrafendraht, *der*

**telegraphy** /tɪˈlegrəfɪ/ *n.* Telegrafie, *die*

**telemarketing** /ˈtelɪmɑːkɪtɪŋ/ *n., no pl.* Telefonmarketing, *das*

**telemessage** /ˈtelɪmesɪdʒ/ *n.* (*Brit.*) Telegramm, *das*

**telemeter** /ˈtelɪmiːtə(r), tɪˈlemɪtə(r)/ ❶ *n.* Fernmessgerät, *das.* ❷ *v.i.* Messwerte telemetrisch übertragen; **~ing device** Fernmessgerät, *das.* ❸ *v.t.* telemetrisch übertragen

**telemetry** /tɪˈlemɪtrɪ/ *n.* Telemetrie, *die*

**teleological** /telɪəˈlɒdʒɪkl/ *adj.* (*Philos.*) teleologisch

**teleology** /telɪˈɒlədʒɪ/ *n.* (*Philos.*) Teleologie, *die*

**telepathic** /telɪˈpæθɪk/ *adj.* telepathisch; **be ~:** telepathische Fähigkeiten haben

**telepathically** /telɪˈpæθɪkəlɪ/ *adv.* telepathisch

**telepathy** /tɪˈlepəθɪ/ *n.* Telepathie, *die;* **by ~:** telepathisch

**telephone** /ˈtelɪfəʊn/ ❶ *n.* Telefon, *das; attrib.* Telefon-; **~ answering machine** Anrufbeantworter, *der;* **[public] ~:** öffentlicher Fernsprecher (*Amtsspr.*); [öffentliches] Telefon; **answer the ~:** Anrufe entgegennehmen; (*on one occasion*) ans Telefon gehen; (*speak*) sich melden; **by ~:** telefonisch; **over** *or* **on the ~:** am Telefon; **speak** *or* **talk to sb. on the** *or* **by ~:** mit jmdm. telefonieren; **be on the ~** (*be connected to the system*) Telefon haben; (*be speaking*) telefonieren (**to** mit); **it's your sister on the ~:** deine Schwester ist am Apparat; **get on the ~ to sb.** jmdn. anrufen; **get sb. on the ~:** jmdn. telefonisch erreichen; **be wanted on the ~:** am Telefon verlangt werden. ❷ *v.t.* anrufen; telefonisch übermitteln ‹Nachricht, Ergebnis usw.› (**to** *Dat.*); **~ the office/~ home** im Büro/zu Hause anrufen. ❸ *v.i.* anrufen; **~ for a taxi/the doctor** nach einem Taxi/dem Arzt telefonieren; **~ to ask how ...:** telefonisch anfragen, wie ...; **can we ~ from here?** können wir von hier aus telefonieren?

**telephone: ~ ˈanswering machine** *n.* Anrufbeantworter, *der;* **~ ˈbanking** *n.* Telefonbanking, *das;* **~ book** *n.* Telefonbuch, *das;* **~ booth**, (*Brit.*) **~ box** *ns.* Telefonzelle, *die;* **~ call** *n.* Telefonanruf, *der;* Telefongespräch, *das;* **make a ~ call** ein Telefongespräch führen; **have** *or* **receive a ~ call** einen Anruf erhalten; **there was a ~ call for you** es hat jemand für Sie angerufen; **there was a ~ call for you from your brother** Ihr Bruder hat angerufen; **inland ~ call** Inlandsgespräch, *das;* **international ~ call** Auslandsgespräch, *das;* **~ directory** *n.* Telefonverzeichnis, *das;* Telefonbuch, *das;* **~ exchange** *n.* Fernmeldeamt, *das;* **~ kiosk** *n.* Telefonzelle, *die;* **~ line** *n.* Telefonleitung, *die;* **~ message** *n.* telefonische Nachricht; **~ number** *n.* Telefonnummer, *die;* **~ operator** *n.* ▶ **1261** Telefonist, *der*/Telefonistin, *die;* **~ receiver** *n.* Telefonhörer, *der;* **~ subscriber** *n.* Fernsprechteilnehmer, *der*/-teilnehmerin, *die*

**telephonic** /telɪˈfɒnɪk/ *adj.* telefonisch

**telephonist** /tɪˈlefənɪst/ *n.* ▶ **1261** Telefonist, *der*/Telefonistin, *die*

**telephony** /tɪˈlefənɪ/ *n.* Fernsprechwesen, *das*

**telephoto** /telɪˈfəʊtəʊ/ *adj.* (*Photog.*) telefotografisch; **~ lens** Teleobjektiv, *das*

**teleprinter** /ˈtelɪprɪntə(r)/ *n.* Fernschreiber, *der;* **~ network** Fernschreibnetz, *das*

**teleprompter** (*Amer.* ®) /ˈtelɪprɒmptə(r)/ *n.* Teleprompter Ⓦⓩ, *der*

**ˈtelesales** *n. pl.* Telefonverkauf, *der;* Verkauf per Telefon

**telescope** /ˈtelɪskəʊp/ ❶ *n.* Teleskop, *das;* Fernrohr, *das.* ❷ *v.t.* zusammenschieben ‹Antenne, Rohr›; ineinander schieben ‹Abschnitte, Waggons›; (*fig.*) komprimieren (**into** zu). ❸ *v.i.* sich zusammenschieben; ‹Abschnitte, Waggons:› sich ineinander schieben

**telescopic** /telɪˈskɒpɪk/ *adj.* Ⓐ teleskopisch; **~ lens** Teleobjektiv, *das;* Ⓑ (*collapsible*) ausziehbar; Teleskop‹antenne, -mast›; **~ umbrella** Taschenschirm, *der*

**teleshopping** /ˈtelɪʃɒpɪŋ/ *n., no pl.* Teleshopping, *das*

**Teletex** ® /ˈtelɪteks/ *n.* Teletex, *das*

**teletext** /ˈtelɪtekst/ *n.* Teletext, *der*

**telethon** /ˈtelɪθɒn/ *n.* Marathonsendung, *die* (*für einen guten Zweck*)

**Teletype** ® /ˈtelɪtaɪp/, (*Amer.*) **teletypewriter** /telɪˈtaɪpraɪtə(r)/ *n.* Fernschreiber, *der*

**televise** /ˈtelɪvaɪz/ *v.t.* im Fernsehen senden *od.* übertragen; **~d football** Fußballübertragungen im Fernsehen

**television** /ˈtelɪvɪʒn, telɪˈvɪʒn/ *n.* Ⓐ *no pl., no art.* das Fernsehen; **colour/black and white ~:** das Farb-/Schwarzweißfernsehen; **the best-paid jobs are in ~:** die bestbezahlten Stellen gibt es beim Fernsehen; **go into ~:** zum Fernsehen gehen; **we have ten hours of ~ a day** bei uns gibt es täglich 10 Stunden Fernsehprogramm; **make/not make good ~:** sich gut/schlecht für das Fernsehen eignen; **live ~:** Livesendungen [im Fernsehen]; **on ~:** im Fernsehen; **what's on ~?** was läuft *od.* gibts im Fernsehen?; **watch ~:** fernsehen; Ⓑ (**~** *set*) Fernsehapparat, *der;* Fernseher, *der* (*ugs.*); **portable ~:** tragbares Fernsehgerät; Portable, *der od. das.* ⇒ *also* **closed-circuit**; **commercial television**

**television: ~ ˈadvertising** *n.* Fernsehwerbung, *die;* **~ aerial** *n.* Fernsehantenne, *die;* **~ camera** *n.* Fernsehkamera, *die;* **~ channel** *n.* [Fernseh]kanal, *der;* **~ coverage** *n.* Fernsehberichterstattung, *die;* **there will be full ~ coverage of sth.** das Fernsehen wird ausführlich über etw. (*Akk.*) berichten; **~ engineer** *n.* Fernsehtechniker, *der*/-technikerin, *die;* **~ licence** *n.* (*Brit.*) Fernsehgenehmigung, *die* (*die jährlich gegen Zahlen der Gebühren erneuert wird*); *attrib.* **~ licence fee** Fernsehgebühren *Pl.;* **~ lounge** *n.* Fernsehraum, *der;* **~ personality** *n.* Fernsehgröße, *die* (*ugs.*); **~ picture** *n.* Fernsehbild, *das;* **~ programme** *n.* Fernsehsendung, *die;* (*sequence*) Fernsehprogramm, *das;* **my favourite ~ programme** meine Lieblingssendung im Fernsehen; **~ screen** *n.* Bildschirm, *der;* **~ serial** *n.* Fernsehserie, *die;* **~ set** *n.* Fernsehgerät, *das;* **~ studio** *n.* Fernsehstudio, *das;* **~ transmitter** *n.* Fernsehsender, *der;* **~ viewer** *n.* Fernsehzuschauer, *der*/-zuschauerin, *die*

**telework** /ˈtelɪwɜːk/ *v.i.* Telearbeit verrichten

**teleworker** /ˈtelɪwɜːkə(r)/ *n.* Telearbeiter, *der*/-arbeiterin, *die*

**teleworking** /ˈtelɪwɜːkɪŋ/ *n., no pl.* Telearbeit, *die*

**Telex**, **telex** /ˈteleks/ ❶ *n.* Telex, *das;* **by ~** über Telex. ❷ *v.t.* telexen ‹Nachricht›; ein Telex schicken (+ *Dat.*) ‹Person, Firma›

**tell** /tel/ ❶ *v.t.*, **told** /təʊld/ Ⓐ (*make known*) sagen ‹Name, Adresse, Alter›; (*give account of*) erzählen ‹Neuigkeit, Sorgen›; anvertrauen ‹Geheimnis›; **~ sb. sth.** *or* **sth. to sb.** jmdm. etw. sagen/erzählen/anvertrauen; **if he asks, ~ him** sags ihm, wenn er fragt; **~ sb. the way to the station** jmdm. den Weg zum Bahnhof beschreiben; **~ sb. the time** jmdm. sagen, wie spät es ist; jmdm. die Uhrzeit sagen; **~ sb. goodbye/good night** (*Amer.*) jmdm. Auf Wiedersehen/Gute Nacht sagen; **~ all** auspacken (*ugs.*); **~ me another!** (*coll.*) du kannst mir viel erzählen (*ugs.*); **~ sb. [something] about sb./sth.** jmdm. [etwas] von jmdm./etw. erzählen; **~ sb. nothing/all about what happened** jmdm. nichts davon/alles erzählen, was passiert ist; **will you ~ him [that] I will come?** sag ihm bitte, dass ich kommen werde; **they ~ me/us [that] ...** (*according to them*) man sagt, dass ...; **I['ll] ~ you what, ...:** pass mal auf, ...; **I'll ~ you what I'll do** weißt du, was ich machen werde?; **~ everyone/** (*coll.*) **the world [that/how** *etc.*] jedem/(*ugs.*) aller Welt erzählen[, dass/wie *usw.*]; **more than I/words can ~:** mehr, als ich es mit Worten ausdrücken kann/als Worte es ausdrücken können; **I cannot ~ you how ...** (*cannot express how ...*) ich kann dir gar nicht sagen, wie ...; **I couldn't ~ you** (*I don't know*) das kann ich nicht sagen; **I can ~ you, ...** (*I can assure you*) ich kann dir sagen, ...; **..., I can ~ you ...**, das kann ich dir sagen; **you can't ~ me [that] ...** (*it can't be true that ...*) du kannst mir doch nicht erzählen, dass ...; **you can't ~ him anything** (*he won't accept advice*) er lässt sich (*Dat.*) ja nichts sagen; (*he is well-informed*) ihm kannst du nichts erzählen; **words cannot ~ how ..., no words can ~ how ...:** es lässt sich nicht mit Worten ausdrücken, wie ...; **..., let me ~ you** (*let me assure you*) ..., das kann ich dir sagen; **let me ~ you that ...:** ich kann dir versichern, dass ...; **..., I ~ you** *or* **I'm ~ing you ...**, das sage ich dir; **you're ~ing me** *or* **are you ~ing me [that] ...?** du willst mir doch wohl nicht erzählen, dass ...?; **you're ~ing ˈme!** (*coll.*) wem sagst du das! (*ugs.*); **he keeps ~ing me [that] ...:** er erzählt mir ständig, dass ...; **..., or so they keep ~ing us** das erzählen sie uns jedenfalls immer; **I don't need to ~ you [that] ...:** ich brauche dir wohl nicht extra zu sagen, dass ...; **be told sth. by sb.** etw. von jmdm. erfahren; **I was told that ...:** mir wurde gesagt, dass ...; **so I've been told** (*I know that*) [das] habe ich schon gehört; **... or so I've been/I'm told ...**, wie ich gehört habe/höre; **... or so we are told ...**, so heißt es jedenfalls; **but he won't be told** (*won't accept advice*) aber er lässt sich ja nichts sagen; **didn't I ~ you?** (*I told you so*) hab ichs nicht gleich gesagt?; **no, don't ~ me, let me guess** [nein,] sag's nicht, lass mich raten; **don't ~ me [that] ...** (*expressing incredulity, dismay, etc.*) jetzt sag bloß nicht, [dass] ...; **you aren't trying** *or* **don't mean to ~ me [that] ...?** du wirst doch nicht sagen wollen, dass ...?; **B** (*relate, lit. or fig.*) erzählen; **has he ever told you the story of how ...:** hat er dir jemals die Geschichte erzählt, wie ...; **~ one's own story** *or* **tale** (*give one's own account*) selbst erzählen *od.* berichten; **sth. ~s its own story** *or* **tale** (*needs no comment*) etw. spricht für sich selbst; **~ a different story** *or* **tale** (*reveal the truth*) eine andere Sprache sprechen (*fig.*); **every picture ~s a story** das spricht Bände; **live** *or* **survive to ~ the tale** überleben; **~ tales [about sb.]** (*gossip; reveal secret*) [über jmdn.] tratschen (*ugs. abwertend*); **~ tales [to sb.]** (*report*) andere/einen anderen [bei jmdm.] anschwärzen; [bei jmdm.] petzen (*Schülerspr. abwertend*); **~ tales** (*lie*) Lügengeschichten erzählen; **~ tales out of school** (*fig.*) aus der Schule plaudern; **dead men ~ no tales** Tote reden nicht; **the blood stains told their own tale** die Blutflecken sprachen für sich; **now it can be told** jetzt kann man es ja erzählen; **C** (*instruct*) sagen; **~ sb. [not] to do sth.** jmdm. sagen, dass er etw. [nicht] tun soll; jmdm. sagen, er soll[e] etw. [nicht] tun; **I thought I told you to go to bed** ich habe dir doch gesagt, dass du ins Bett gehen sollst; **~ sb. what to do** jmdm. sagen, was er tun soll; **no one ~s 'me what to do** ich lasse mir keine Vorschriften machen; **do as** *or* **what I ~ you** tu, was ich dir sage; **I shan't** *or* **won't ~ you again, don't let me have to ~ you again** ich sags dir nicht noch einmal; **do as you are told** tu, was man dir sagt; **D** (*determine*) feststellen; (*see, recognize*) erkennen (**by** an + *Dat.*); (*with reference to the future*) [vorher]sagen; **~ the time [from the sun]** [am Stand der Sonne] erkennen, wie spät es ist; **the child can't ~ the time yet** das Kind kennt die Uhr noch nicht; **~ the difference [between ...]** den Unterschied [zwischen ...] erkennen *od.* feststellen; **I can't ~ which of the twins ...:** ich kann nicht sagen, welcher der Zwillinge ...; **it's impossible/difficult to ~ [if/what** *etc.*] es ist unmöglich/schwer zu sagen[, ob/was *usw.*]; **it's easy to ~ whether ...:** es lässt sich leicht sagen, ob ...; **you never can ~ how/what** *etc.* man weiß nie, wie/was *usw.*; **how could you ~ he was a policeman?** woran hast du erkannt, dass es ein Polizist war?; **E** (*distinguish*) unterscheiden; **[not] be able to ~ right from wrong** [nicht] zwischen richtig und falsch unterscheiden können; **F** (*utter*) sagen; **~ the truth and shame the devil** die Wahrheit sagen, auch wenn es nicht leicht fällt; ⇒ *also* **fib** 1; **lie**[1] 1 A; **truth** B; **G** (*count*) auszählen ‹Wählerstimmen›; **all told** insgesamt.

**2** *v.i.*, **told A** (*determine*) **how can you ~?** wie kann man das feststellen *od.* wissen?; **it's difficult to ~:** das ist schwer zu sagen; **[it's] hard to ~:** [das ist] schwer zu sagen; **I can ~ he's lying** ich merke ihm an, dass er lügt; **the difference is so slight, even the experts can hardly ~:** der Unterschied ist so gering, dass selbst die Experten ihn kaum erkennen können; **how can one ~?, how can** *or* **do you ~?** woran kann man das erkennen?; **as far as one/I can ~, ...:** wie es aussieht, ...; **you never can ~:** man kann nie wissen; **who can ~?** wer kann das sagen *od.* will das wissen?; **B** (*give information*) erzählen (**of, about** von); (*give evidence*) **~ of sth.** von etw. Zeugnis geben *od.* ablegen; **C** (*reveal secret*) es verraten; **time [alone] will ~:** das wird sich [erst noch] zeigen; **D** (*produce an effect*) sich auswirken; ‹Wort, Fausthieb, Schuss:› sitzen; **quality ~s** *or* **will ~** (*be important*) Qualität ist das, was zählt; **he made every blow ~:** jeder seiner Schläge saß; **make every shot ~:** dafür sorgen, dass jeder Schuss sitzt; **~ in favour of sb.** *or* **in sb.'s favour** sich zu jmds. Gunsten auswirken; **~ against sb./sth.** sich nachteilig für jmdn./auf etw. (*Akk.*) auswirken. ⇒ *also* **fortune** C; **marine** 2 A; **so**[1] 2; **what** 5 A

**~ a'part** *v.t.* auseinander halten

**~ 'off** *v.t.* **A** (*coll.: scold*) **~ sb. off [for sth.]** jmdn. [für *od.* wegen etw.] ausschimpfen; ‹Chef:› jmdn. [für *od.* wegen etw.] rüffeln (*ugs.*); ⇒ *also* **telling-off**; **B** (*assign*) **~ sb. off [for sth.]** jmdn. [zu etw.] abkommandieren

**~ on** *v.t.* **A** (*affect*) **~ on sb./sth.** sich bei jmdm. bemerkbar machen/sich [nachteilig] auf etw. (*Akk.*) auswirken; **B** (*coll.: inform against*) **~ on sb.** jmdn. verpetzen (*Schülerspr. abwertend*)

**~ upon** ⇒ **~ on** A

**teller** /'telə(r)/ *n.* ▶ **1261** **A** (*in bank*) ⇒ **cashier**[1]; **B** (*counter of votes*) Stimmenzähler, *der*/-zählerin, *die*

**telling** /'telɪŋ/ **1** *adj.* (*effective, striking*) schlagend ‹Argument, Antwort›; wirkungsvoll ‹Worte, Phrase, Stil›; (*revealing*) vielsagend ‹Lächeln, Blick›; verräterisch ‹Röte, Reaktion›; **~ blow** (*Boxing*) Wirkungstreffer, *der;* (*fig.*) empfindlicher Schlag; **with ~ effect** mit durchschlagender Wirkung. **2** *n.* Erzählen, *das;* **he did not need any ~, he needed no ~:** dazu brauchte man ihn nicht lange *od.* eigens aufzufordern; **that would be ~:** damit würde ich ein Geheimnis verraten; **there's no ~ what/how ...:** man weiß nie, was/wie ...; **there's no** *or* **never any ~ with her** bei ihr weiß man nie[, woran man ist]; ⇒ *also* **lose** 2 A

**tellingly** /'telɪŋlɪ/ *adv.* wirkungsvoll; **be ~ effective** eine deutlich sichtbare Wirkung zeigen

**telling-'off** *n.* (*coll.*) Standpauke, *die* (*ugs.*); **give sb. a ~:** jmdn. ausschimpfen (**for** wegen); ‹Chef:› jmdn. rüffeln (*ugs.*); **get a ~:** Schimpfe kriegen (*ugs.*); ‹Untergebener:› einen Rüffel kriegen (*ugs.*)

**'telltale** *n.* **A** Klatschmaul, *das* (*ugs. abwertend*); Petzer, *die* (*Schülerspr. abwertend*); *attrib.* vielsagend ‹Blick, Lächeln›; verräterisch ‹Röte, Fleck, Glanz, Zucken, Zeichen›; **B** (*indicator*) Anzeiger, *der;* (*for recording attendance*) Stechuhr, *die*

**tellurium** /te'ljʊərɪəm/ *n.* (*Chem.*) Tellur, *das*

**telly** /'telɪ/ *n.* (*Brit. coll.*) Fernseher, *der* (*ugs.*); Glotze, *die* (*salopp*); **watch ~:** Fernsehen gucken (*ugs.*); **what's on [the] ~?** was kommt im Fernsehen?

**temerity** /tɪ'merɪtɪ/ *n.* Kühnheit, *die;* **have the ~ to do sth.** die Stirn haben, etw. zu tun

**temp** /temp/ (*Brit. coll.*) **1** *n.* Zeitarbeitskraft, *die; attrib.* **~ agency** Zeitarbeitsunternehmen, *das.* **2** *v.i.* Zeitarbeit machen

**temper** /'tempə(r)/ **1** *n.* **A** (*disposition*) Naturell, *das;* **be in a good/bad ~:** gute/schlechte Laune haben; gut/schlecht gelaunt sein; **be in a foul** *or* **filthy ~:** eine miese Laune haben (*ugs.*); **keep/lose one's ~:** sich beherrschen/die Beherrschung verlieren; **lose one's ~ with sb.** die Beherrschung bei jmdm. verlieren; **control one's ~:** sich beherrschen; **B** (*anger*) **fit/outburst of ~:** Wutanfall, *der*/-ausbruch, *der;* **have a ~:** jähzornig sein; **be in/get into a ~:** wütend sein/werden (**over** wegen); **be in a terrible ~:** schrecklich wütend sein; **C** (*degree of hardness of metal*) Härte, *die.* **2** *v.t.* **A** (*moderate*) mäßigen; mildern ‹Trostlosigkeit, Strenge, Kritik›; **~ sb.'s enthusiasm/radical views** jmds. Begeisterung dämpfen/Radikalismus mildern; **~ justice with mercy** bei aller Gerechtigkeit Milde walten lassen (*geh.*); **B** (*Metallurgy*) anlassen; **C** (*Mus.*) temperieren

**tempera** /'tempərə/ *n.* (*Art*) Tempera, *die*

**temperament** /'temprəmənt/ *n.* **A** (*nature*) Veranlagung, *die;* Natur, *die;* (*disposition*) Temperament, *das;* **have an artistic ~:** künstlerisch veranlagt sein; **B** (*passionate disposition*) Temperament, *das*

**temperamental** /temprə'mentl/ *adj.* **A** (*having changeable moods*) launisch (*abwertend*); launenhaft; **be a bit ~** (*fig. coll.*) ‹Auto, Maschine:› seine Mucken haben (*ugs.*); **B** (*caused by, relating to temperament*) anlagebedingt; **suffer from a ~ inability to cope with stress** von Natur aus nicht fähig sein, Stress zu bewältigen

**temperamentally** /temprə'mentəlɪ/ *adv.* **A** (*in a temperamental manner*) launisch (*abwertend*); **the car tends to behave ~** (*fig. coll.*) das Auto hat gelegentlich seine Mucken (*ugs.*); **B** (*by reason of temperament*) der Veranlagung nach

**temperance** /'tempərəns/ *n.* **A** (*moderation*) Mäßigung, *die;* (*in one's eating, drinking*) Mäßigkeit, *die;* **B** (*total abstinence*) Abstinenz, *die*

**temperate** /'tempərət/ *adj.* gemäßigt; **be ~ in one's eating/drinking** maßvoll *od.* mäßig im Essen/Trinken sein; **~ climate** (*Geog.*) gemäßigtes Klima; ⇒ *also* **zone** 1

**temperature** /'temprɪtʃə(r)/ *n.* ▶ **1603** **A** Temperatur, *die;* **what is the ~?** wie viel Grad sind es?; **the ~ is below/above ...:** die Temperatur liegt unter/über ... (*Dat.*); **there are no extremes of ~:** es gibt keine extremen Temperaturen; **the ~ rose during the debate** (*fig.*) die Debatte wurde im Verlauf immer hitziger; **at a ~ of 100°** bei einer Temperatur von 100° ‹kochen›; auf eine Temperatur von 100° ‹einstellen›; **keep the room at a ~ of 10°** die Zimmertemperatur auf 10° (*Dat.*) halten; **at high/low ~s** bei hohen/niedrigen Temperaturen; **B** (*Med.*) Temperatur, *die;* **have** *or* **run a ~** (*coll.*) Temperatur *od.* Fieber haben; **have a slight/high ~:** leichtes/hohes Fieber haben; **take sb.'s ~:** jmds. [Körper]temperatur messen; **a cold accompanied by a ~:** eine fiebrige Erkältung; ⇒ *also* **run** 3 L

**tempered** /'tempəd/ *adj.* **A** (*Metallurgy*) vergütet; **B** (*Mus.*) temperiert

**tempest** /'tempɪst/ *n.* (*lit. or fig.*) Sturm, *der;* **~ in a teapot** (*Amer.*) Sturm im Wasserglas

**tempestuous** /tem'pestjʊəs/ *adj.* (*lit. or fig.*) stürmisch; **be in a ~ rage** vor Wut rasen

**Templar** /'templə(r)/ *n.* (*Hist.*) **[Knight] ~:** Templer, *der;* Tempelritter, *der;* **the [Knights] ~s** der Templerorden

**template** /'templeɪt/ *n.* Schablone, *die*

**temple**[1] /'templ/ *n.* Tempel, *der;* (*Amer.: synagogue*) Synagoge, *die*

**temple**[2] *n.* ▶ **966** (*Anat.*) Schläfe, *die*

**templet** ⇒ **template**

**tempo** /'tempəʊ/ *n., pl.* **~s** *or* **tempi** /'tempi:/ **A** (*fig.: pace*) **the ~ of life in the town** der Rhythmus der Stadt; **the campaign ~ stepped up** der Wahlkampf ging in die heiße Phase über; **B** (*Mus.: speed*) Tempo, *das*

**temporal** /'tempərl/ *adj.* **A** (*of this life*) diesseitig (*geh.*); irdisch; (*secular*) weltlich; **~ power** (*Eccl.*) weltliche Macht; **lords ~** (*Brit. Parl.*) *weltliche Mitglieder des britischen Oberhauses;* **B** (*of time*) zeitlich; **C** (*Anat.*) Schläfen-; **D** (*Ling.*) temporal

**temporally** /'tempərəlɪ/ *adv.* zeitlich

**temporarily** /'tempərərɪlɪ/ *adv.* vorübergehend

**temporary** /'tempərərɪ/ **1** *adj.* vorübergehend; provisorisch ‹Gebäude, Büro›; **~ worker** Aushilfe, *die;* **~ job** Aushilfstätigkeit, *die.* **2** *n.* Aushilfe, *die;* Aushilfskraft, *die*

**temporise, temporiser** ⇒ **temporiz-**

**temporize** /'tempəraɪz/ *v.i.* **A** (*adopt indecisive policy*) sich nicht festlegen; **B** (*act so as to gain time*) sich abwartend verhalten; **~ with sb.** jmdn. hinhalten; **C** (*comply temporarily*) Kompromisse eingehen; sich fügen

**temporizer** /'tempəraɪzə(r)/ *n.* **A** (*one who compromises*) Kompromissler, *der*/Kompromisslerin, *die* (*abwertend*); **B** (*one who acts to gain time*) Hinhaltetaktiker, *der*/-taktikerin, *die*

**tempt** /tempt/ *v.t.* **A** (*attract*) **~ sb. out/into the town** jmdn. hinauslocken/in die Stadt locken; **~ sb. to do sth.** in jmdm. den Wunsch wecken, etw. zu tun; **B** (*cause to have strong urge*) **~ sb. to do sth.** jmdn. geneigt machen, etw. zu tun; **be ~ed to do sth.** versucht sein, etw. zu tun; **I'm ~ed to question this** das möchte ich fast bezweifeln; **be ~ed to resign** an Rücktritt denken;

t

# Temperature

Temperatures in Germany, as in the rest of continental Europe, are always quoted using the centigrade scale only. To convert from Fahrenheit to centigrade (or Celsius which is the term used in Germany), deduct 32 from the number of degrees, divide by 9 and multiply by 5. The table below shows the main equivalents.

| | Fahrenheit (°F) | Celsius (°C) | |
|---|---|---|---|
| Boiling point | 212 | 100 | Siedepunkt |
| | 194 | 90 | |
| | 176 | 80 | |
| | 158 | 70 | |
| | 140 | 60 | |
| | 122 | 50 | |
| | 104 | 40 | |
| Body temperature | 98.4 | 37 | Körpertemperatur |
| | 86 | 30 | |
| | 68 | 20 | |
| | 50 | 10 | |
| Freezing point | 32 | 0 | Gefrierpunkt |
| | 14 | – 10 | |
| | 0 | – 17,8 | |
| Absolute zero | – 459.67 | – 273,15 | absoluter Nullpunkt |

## Weather

***What's the temperature?***
= Wie viel Grad sind es?

***The outside temperature is 20 degrees [centigrade]*** or ***68 degrees Fahrenheit***
= Die Außentemperatur beträgt 20 Grad [Celsius]

***Maximum temperature 27 degrees*** or (esp. Amer.) ***Highs around 80 degrees***
= Höchsttemperaturen um 27 Grad

***Temperatures falling to 10 degrees*** or (esp. Amer.) ***Lows around 50 degrees***
= Tiefsttemperaturen um 10 Grad

***temperatures around freezing***
= Temperaturen um den Gefrierpunkt

***ten degrees below freezing***
= zehn Grad unter null

***– 15°C (minus fifteen degrees centigrade)***
= – 15°[C] (minus fünfzehn Grad [Celsius])

***The temperature is above/below freezing***
= Die Temperatur liegt über/unter dem Gefrierpunkt *or* Nullpunkt

***It's the same temperature in Berlin***
= In Berlin herrscht die gleiche Temperatur

## People

***She has a [slight] temperature, Her temperature is above normal***
= Sie hat [leicht] erhöhte Temperatur

***He has a high temperature/a temperature of 40 [centigrade]*** or ***104 [Fahrenheit]***
= Er hat [hohes] Fieber/40 Grad Fieber

***What is your temperature?***
= Wie hoch ist *or* Was ist Ihre Temperatur?

***My temperature is normal***
= Ich habe kein Fieber

***She took his temperature***
= Sie hat bei ihm Fieber gemessen *or* hat seine Temperatur gemessen

## Things

***What temperature does water boil at?***
= Bei welcher Temperatur kocht Wasser?

***Water boils at 100°C***
= Wasser kocht bei 100°C

***What is the temperature of the wine?***
= Welche Temperatur hat der Wein?

***The wine must be the right temperature***
= Der Wein muss die richtige Temperatur haben

***A is the same temperature as B***
= A hat die gleiche Temperatur wie B

**be strongly ~ed to dismiss sb.** sehr versucht sein, jmdn. zu entlassen; **C** (*entice*) verführen; **be ~ed into doing sth.** sich dazu verleiten lassen, etw. zu tun; **~ sb. away from sth.** jmdn. von etw. weglocken; **don't ~ me!** verleite mich nicht!; **are you sure I can't ~ you to have a whisky?** kann ich dich wirklich nicht zu einem Whisky überreden?; **D** (*provoke*) herausfordern; **~ fate** *or* **providence** das Schicksal herausfordern

**temptation** /temp'teɪʃn/ *n.* **A** *no pl.* (*attracting*) Verlockung, *die;* (*being attracted*) Versuchung, *die;* (*enticing*) Verführung, *die* (**into** zu); (*being enticed*) Versuchung, *die* (*geh.*); **feel a ~ to do sth.** versucht sein, etw. zu tun; **please resist the ~ to make any funny remarks** mach jetzt bitte keine dummen Witze; **give in to [the] ~:** der Versuchung erliegen; **the T~** (*Relig.*) die Versuchung [Jesu]; **B** (*thing*) Verlockung, *die* (**to** zu); **special offers are just a ~ to spend money** Sonderangebote verleiten nur dazu, Geld auszugeben; **C lead us not into ~** (*Bibl.*) führe uns nicht in Versuchung

**tempter** /'temptə(r)/ *n.* Verführer, *der;* **the T~** (*Relig.*) der Versucher

**tempting** /'temptɪŋ/ *adj.* **A** (*inviting*) verlockend; verführerisch; **B** (*enticing*) verführerisch

**temptingly** /'temptɪŋlɪ/ *adv.* **A** (*attractively*) verlockend; verführerisch; **B leave money lying about ~:** Geld [verführerisch] offen herumliegen lassen

**temptress** /'temptrɪs/ *n.* Verführerin, *die*

**ten** /ten/ ▶ **912**, ▶ **1012**, ▶ **1352** **1** *adj.* zehn; **feel ~ feet tall** (*fig.*) sehr stolz auf sich (*Akk.*) sein; ⇒ *also* **eight** 1. **2** *n.* **A** (*number, symbol*) Zehn, *die;* **B** (*set of ~*) Zehnerpackung, *die;* (*of cards*) Zehnerstoß, *der;* **C bet sb. ~ to one that ...** (*fig.*) jede Wette halten, dass ... (*ugs.*). ⇒ *also* **eight** 2 A, C, D

**tenable** /'tenəbl/ *adj.* **A** haltbar; (*fig.*) haltbar ‹Theorie, Annahme›; vertretbar ‹Standpunkt›; **B ~ for five years** auf fünf Jahre befristet ‹Arbeitsverhältnis, Stelle›; **~ at the university of ...:** [anzutreten] an der Universität ...

**tenacious** /tɪ'neɪʃəs/ *adj.* **A** (*holding fast*) hartnäckig haftend ‹Dornen, Samen›; **hold sth. in a ~ grip** etw. hartnäckig *od.* eisern festhalten; **B** (*resolute*) hartnäckig; **be ~:** sich hartnäckig halten; **be ~ of sth.** (*formal*) hartnäckig an etw. (*Dat.*) festhalten; **C** (*retentive*) **~ memory** hervorragendes Gedächtnis; **D** (*strongly cohesive*) fest; **a very ~ link** eine sehr beständige Verbindung

**tenaciously** /tɪ'neɪʃəslɪ/ *adv.* zäh; (*resolutely*) hartnäckig

**tenacity** /tɪ'næsɪtɪ/ *n., no pl.* Hartnäckigkeit, *die;* (*resoluteness*) Beharrlichkeit, *die;* Hartnäckigkeit, *die;* **~ of life** zäher Lebenswille

**tenancy** /'tenənsɪ/ *n.* **A** (*of flat, residential building*) Mietverhältnis, *das;* (*of farm, shop*) Pachtverhältnis, *das;* **have ~ of a flat** eine Wohnung gemietet haben; **~ agreement** Miet-/Pachtvertrag, *der;* **B** (*period*) Mietdauer, *die;* **C** (*occupation of post*) Bekleidung, *die;* **~ of the post will be for 10 years** die Stelle ist auf 10 Jahre befristet

**tenant** /'tenənt/ **1** *n.* **A** (*of flat, residential building*) Mieter, *der*/Mieterin, *die;* (*of farm, shop*) Pächter, *der*/Pächterin, *die;* **B** (*occupant*) Bewohner, *der*/Bewohnerin, *die;* **C** (*Law*) (*possessor*) Besitzer, *der*/Besitzerin, *die;* (*owner*) Eigentümer, *der*/Eigentümerin, *die.* **2** *v.t.* mieten ‹Wohnung, Haus usw.›; pachten ‹Land, Bauernhof, Geschäft›

**'tenant farmer** *n.* ▶ **1261** Pächter, *der*/Pächterin, *die*

**tenantry** /'tenəntrɪ/ *n.* (*formal*) **A** (*people*) Mieter; (*of farm, shop*) Pächter; **B** (*condition*) Mietverhältnis, *das;* (*of farm, shop*) Pachtverhältnis, *das*

**tench** /tentʃ/ *n., pl. same* (*Zool.*) Schleie, *die*

**tend**[1] /tend/ *v.i.* **A** (*be moving or directed*) ‹Strom, Bach:› fließen (**towards** in Richtung); ‹Sterne:› zustreben (**towards** auf + *Akk.*); (*fig.*) sich zubewegen (**towards** auf + *Akk.*); **this ~s to suggest that ...:** dies deutet darauf hin, dass ...; **all opinions ~ to the same conclusion** alle Meinungen führen zur gleichen Schlussfolgerung; **B** (*be apt or inclined*) **~ to do sth.** dazu neigen *od.* tendieren, etw. zu tun; **~ to sth.** zu etw. neigen; **it ~s to get quite cold there at nights** es wird dort nachts oft sehr kalt; **he ~s to get upset if ...:** er regt sich leicht auf, wenn ...

**tend**[2] *v.t.* sich kümmern um; hüten ‹Schafe›; bedienen ‹Maschine›; **the rice has to be ~ed carefully** der Reis erfordert sorgfältige Pflege

**tendency** /'tendənsɪ/ *n.* (*inclination*) Tendenz, *die;* **artistic tendencies** künstlerische Neigungen; **have a ~ to do sth.** dazu neigen, etw. zu tun; **there is a ~ for everyone to get complacent** die Leute neigen dazu, selbstzufrieden zu werden

t

**tendentious** /ten'denʃəs/ *adj.*, **tendentiously** /ten'denʃəslı/ *adv.* (*derog.*) tendenziös

**tendentiousness** /ten'denʃəsnıs/ *n.*, *no pl.* (*derog.*) tendenziöse Färbung

**tender**[1] /'tendə(r)/ *adj.* Ⓐ (*not tough*) zart; Ⓑ (*sensitive*) empfindlich; **~ spot** (*fig.*) wunder Punkt; Ⓒ (*loving*) zärtlich; liebevoll; **~ loving care** liebevolle Zuwendung; Ⓓ (*requiring careful handling*) heikel; Ⓔ (*delicate*) zart ‹Gesundheit, Konstitution›; **be of ~ age** *or* **years** noch sehr jung sein; **at a ~ age** in jungen Jahren; **at the ~ age of twelve** im zarten Alter von zwölf Jahren. ⇒ *also* **mercy** 1 B

**tender**[2] *n.* (*Naut.*, *Railw.*) Tender, *der*

**tender**[3] ❶ *v.t.* Ⓐ (*present*) einreichen ‹Rücktritt›; anbieten ‹Rat›; vorbringen ‹Entschuldigung›; Ⓑ (*offer as payment*) anbieten; **~ a £20 note** mit einer 20-Pfund-Note bezahlen; **please ~ exact fare** bitte den genauen Betrag bereithalten; **the cash register records the amount ~ed** die Registrierkasse zeigt den gezahlten Geldbetrag an. ❷ *v.i.* **~ for sth.** ein Angebot für etw. einreichen. ❸ *n.* Ⓐ Angebot, *das*; **put in a ~:** ein Angebot einreichen; **put sth. out to ~:** etw. ausschreiben; Ⓑ **legal ~:** gesetzliches Zahlungsmittel

**tender: ~foot** *n.*, *pl.* **~foots** *or* **~feet** Greenhorn, *das*; (*in Scouts*) Neuling, *der*; **~-hearted** /'tendəhɑ:tıd/ *adj.* weichherzig

**tenderize** /'tendəraız/ *v.t.* (*Cookery*) zart machen; (*by beating*) weich klopfen

**tenderizer** /'tendəraızə(r)/ *n.* (*Cookery*) Fleischklopfer, *der*

**'tenderloin** *n.* (*Gastr.*) Ⓐ (*Brit.*) Lendenstück, *das*; Ⓑ (*Amer.*) Filet, *das*

**tenderly** /'tendəlı/ *adv.* Ⓐ (*gently*) behutsam ‹behandeln›; Ⓑ (*lovingly*) zärtlich

**tenderness** /'tendənıs/ *n.*, *no pl.* Ⓐ (*of meat etc.*) Zartheit, *die*; Ⓑ (*loving quality*) Zärtlichkeit, *die*; Ⓒ (*delicacy*) Empfindlichkeit, *die*

**tendon** /'tendən/ *n.* (*Anat.*) Sehne, *die*; **Achilles ~:** Achillessehne, *die*

**tendril** /'tendrıl/ *n.* Ranke, *die*

**tenement** /'tenımənt/ *n.* Ⓐ (*Scot.: house containing several dwellings*) Mietshaus, *das*; Mietskaserne, *die* (*abwertend*); Ⓑ (*dwelling place*) Behausung, *die*; Ⓒ (*Amer.: house containing several apartments*) **~ [house]** Mietshaus, *das*; Ⓓ (*Law*) Besitz, *der*

**Tenerife** /tenə'ri:f/ *pr. n.* Teneriffa (*das*)

**tenet** /'tenıt, 'ti:net/ *n.* Grundsatz, *der*

**ten: ~fold** /'tenfəʊld/ *adj.*, *adv.* zehnfach; ⇒ *also* **eightfold**; **~-gallon 'hat** *n.* Cowboyhut, *der*

**tenner** /'tenə(r)/ *n.* (*coll.*) (*Brit.*) Zehnpfundschein, *der*; Zehner, *der* (*ugs.*); (*Amer.*) Zehndollarschein, *der*; Zehner, *der* (*ugs.*)

**tennis** /'tenıs/ *n.*, *no pl.* Tennis, *das*; **real** *or* **royal** *or* (*Amer.*) **court ~:** Real *od.* Royal *od.* Court Tennis, *das*; ⇒ *also* **lawn tennis**; **table tennis**

**tennis: ~ 'arm** *n.* (*Med.*) Tennisarm, *der*; **~ ball** *n.* Tennisball, *der*; **~ club** *n.* Tennisverein, *der*; **~ court** *n.* Ⓐ (*for lawn ~*) Tennisplatz, *der*; (*for indoor ~*) Tennishalle, *die*; Ⓑ (*for real ~*) Tennishalle, *die*; Ballhaus, *das* (*hist.*); **~ 'elbow** *n.*, *no pl.*, *no art.* (*Med.*) Tennisell[en]bogen, *der*; **~ match** *n.* Tennismatch, *das*; Tennisspiel, *das*; **~ player** *n.* Tennisspieler, *der*/-spielerin, *die*; **~ racket** *n.* Tennisschläger, *der*

**tenon** /'tenən/ *n.* (*Woodw.*) Zapfen, *der*

**'tenon saw** *n.* (*Woodw.*) Feinsäge, *die*; feste Zapfensäge (*fachspr.*)

**tenor** /'tenə(r)/ *n.* Ⓐ (*Mus.: voice, singer, part*) Tenor, *der*; **~ voice** Tenorstimme, *die*; Ⓑ (*prevailing course*) Verlauf, *der*; **the general ~ of his life** seine allgemeine Lebensführung; Ⓒ (*of argument, speech*) Tenor, *der*; Ⓓ (*Law*) (*actual wording*) Wortlaut, *der*; Tenor, *der* (*fachspr.*); (*exact copy*) Abschrift, *die*; Ⓔ (*Mus.: instrument with range like ~*) Tenor, *der*; **~ saxophone/recorder** Tenorsaxophon, *das*/-blockflöte, *die*

**tenpenny** /'tenpənı/ *adj.* für zehn Pence *nachgestellt*

**tenpenny 'piece** *n.* (*Brit.*) Zehnpencemünze, *die*

**tenpin bowling** /tenpın 'bəʊlıŋ/ *n.* Bowling, *das*

**tense**[1] /tens/ *n.* (*Ling.*) Zeit, *die*; **in the present/future** *etc.* **~:** im Präsens/Futur *usw.*

**tense**[2] ❶ *adj.* Ⓐ (*taut; showing nervous tension*) gespannt; **her face was ~ with anxiety** ihr Gesicht war vor Sorge angespannt; **his voice was ~ with emotion** seine Stimme bebte vor Erregung; **a ~ silence** eine [an]gespannte Stille; Ⓑ (*causing nervous tension*) spannungsgeladen. ❷ *v.i.* **sb. ~s** jmds. Muskeln spannen sich an; **he ~d with fear** er verkrampfte sich vor Angst. ❸ *v.t.* anspannen

**~ 'up** *v.i.* ‹Muskeln:› sich anspannen; ‹Person:› sich verkrampfen

**tensely** /'tenslı/ *adv.* Ⓐ (*tightly*) straff; Ⓑ (*with nervous tension*) angespannt; **~ gripping** packend ‹Geschichte, Film›

**tenseness** /'tensnıs/ *n.*, *no pl.* (*of person*) Anspannung, *die*; (*of situation etc.*) Angespanntheit, *die*

**tensile** /'tensaıl/ *adj.* Ⓐ Zug‹belastung, -festigkeit›; Ⓑ (*capable of being stretched*) zugfest

**tension** /'tenʃn/ ❶ *n.* Ⓐ (*latent hostility*) Spannung, *die*; **~ between the police and the people is on the increase** die Spannungen zwischen Polizei und Bevölkerung wachsen; **there is a lot of ~ between them** zwischen ihnen herrscht ein gespanntes Verhältnis; **there is a high level of ~ in that area** die Lage in diesem Gebiet ist sehr angespannt; **racial ~:** Rassenspannungen *Pl.*; Ⓑ (*mental strain*) Anspannung, *die*; Ⓒ *no pl.* (*of violin string, tennis racquet*) Spannung, *die*; Ⓓ (*stretching; Mech. Engin.*) Spannung, *die*; Ⓔ (*Knitting*) Festigkeit, *die*; **check the ~:** eine Maschenprobe machen. ⇒ *also* **surface tension**. ❷ *v.t.* spannen

**tent** /tent/ *n.* Zelt, *das*

**tentacle** /'tentəkl/ *n.* Ⓐ (*Zool.*, *Bot.*) Tentakel, *der od. das*; Ⓑ (*fig.*) Fühler, *der*; (*with sinister connotations*) Fangarm, *der*

**tentative** /'tentətıv/ *adj.* Ⓐ (*not definite*) vorläufig; **make a ~ suggestion** einen Vorschlag in den Raum stellen; **say a ~ 'yes'** vorläufig „Ja" sagen; Ⓑ (*hesitant*) zaghaft

**tentatively** /'tentətıvlı/ *adv.* Ⓐ (*not definitely*) vorläufig; Ⓑ (*hesitantly*) zaghaft

**tenterhooks** /'tentəhʊks/ *n. pl.* **be on ~:** [wie] auf glühenden Kohlen sitzen; **keep sb. on ~:** jmdn. auf die Folter spannen

**tenth** /tenθ/ ❶ *adj.* ▶ **1352** zehnt...; ⇒ *also* **eighth** 1. ❷ *n.* Ⓐ (*in sequence, rank*) Zehnte, *der/die/das*; (*fraction*) Zehntel, *das*; Ⓑ ▶ **1055** (*day*) **the ~ of May** der zehnte Mai; **the ~ [of the month]** der Zehnte [des Monats]. ⇒ *also* **eighth** 2

**tent: ~ peg** *n.* Zeltpflock, *der*; Hering, *der*; **~ pole** *n.* Zeltstange, *die*

**tenuity** /te'nju:ıtı/ ⇒ **tenuousness**

**tenuous** /'tenjʊəs/ *adj.* dünn ‹Faden›; zart ‹Spinnwebe›; (*fig.*) dünn ‹Atmosphäre›; dürftig ‹Argument›; unbegründet ‹Anspruch›; **there are only ~ connections** es bestehen kaum Verbindungen; **he had but a ~ hold on life** sein Leben hing nur noch an einem seidenen Faden

**tenuously** /'tenjʊəslı/ *adv.* dünn; (*fig.*) schwach; [nur] locker ‹verbunden sein›; **cling only ~ to life** nur noch einen schwachen Lebenswillen haben

**tenuousness** /'tenjʊəsnıs/ *n.*, *no pl.* Dünne, *die*; (*fig.*) Dürftigkeit, *die*

**tenure** /'tenjə(r)/ *n.* Ⓐ (*right, title*) Besitztitel, *der*; Ⓑ (*possession*) Besitz, *der*; **his ~ of the house is only for a limited period** er kann nur eine begrenzte Zeit über das Haus verfügen; Ⓒ (*period*) **~ [of office]** Amtszeit, *die*; Ⓓ (*permanent appointment*) Dauerstellung, *die*; **have [security of] ~:** eine Dauerstellung haben

**tenuto** /tə'nu:təʊ/ *adj.*, *adv.* (*Mus.*) tenuto

**tepee** /'ti:pi:/ *n.* Tipi, *das*

**tepid** /'tepıd/ *adj.* Ⓐ lauwarm; Ⓑ (*fig.*) halbherzig ‹Interesse, Willkommensgruß›; verhalten ‹Lob, Begeisterung›

**tequila** /te'ki:lə/ *n.* (*drink*) Tequila, *der*

**tercentenary** /tɜ:sen'ti:nərı, tɜ:sen'tenərı/ ❶ *adj.* Dreihundertjahr‹feier, -feierlichkeiten›. ❷ *n.* Dreihundertjahrfeier, *die*

**term** /tɜ:m/ ❶ *n.* Ⓐ (*word expressing definite concept*) [Fach]begriff, *der*; **scientific/legal/medical ~:** wissenschaftlicher/juristischer/medizinischer Fachausdruck; **~ of reproach** Vorwurf, *der*; **in ~s of money/politics** unter finanziellem/politischem Aspekt; **in ~s of financial success** vom finanziellen Erfolg her gesehen; **in set ~s** klipp und klar; ⇒ *also* **contradiction**; Ⓑ *in pl.* (*conditions*) Bedingungen; **he does everything on his own ~s** er tut alles, wie er es für richtig hält; **~s of surrender** Kapitulationsbedingungen; **~s of contract** Vertragsbedingungen; **accept sb. on his own ~s** jmdn. so akzeptieren, wie er ist; **come to** *or* **make ~s [with sb.]** sich [mit jmdm.] einigen; **come to ~s [with each other]** sich einigen; **come to ~s with sth.** (*be able to accept sth.*) mit etw. zurechtkommen; (*resign oneself to sth.*) sich mit etw. abfinden; **come to ~s with oneself** mit sich selbst ins Reine kommen; **~s of reference** (*Brit.*) Aufgabenbereich, *der*; **~s of trade** Austauschverhältnis, *das* (*Wirtsch.*); Ⓒ *in pl.* (*charges*) Konditionen; **their ~s are ...:** sie verlangen ...; **hire purchase on easy ~s** Ratenkauf zu günstigen Bedingungen; ⇒ *also* **inclusive** B; Ⓓ **in the short/long/medium ~:** kurz-/lang-/mittelfristig; Ⓔ (*Sch.*) Halbjahr, *das*; (*Univ.: one of two/three/four divisions per year*) Semester, *das*/Trimester, *das*/Quartal, *das*; **during ~:** während des Halbjahres/Semesters *usw.*; **out of ~:** in den Ferien; **end of ~:** Halbjahres-/Semesterende *usw.*; Ⓕ (*limited period*) Zeitraum, *der*; (*of insurance policy etc.*) Laufzeit, *die*; (*period of tenure*) **~ [of office]** Amtszeit, *die*; Ⓖ (*completion of pregnancy*) **[full] ~:** normale Schwangerschaftszeit; Ⓗ (*period of imprisonment*) Haftzeit, *die*; **be put in prison for a long ~:** für eine längere Haftstrafe ins Gefängnis kommen; Ⓘ *in pl.* (*mode of expression*) Worte; **praise in the highest ~s** in den höchsten Tönen loben; **talk in vague ~s of sth.** sich in vagen Andeutungen über etw. (*Akk.*) ergehen; **in flattering ~s** mit schmeichelnden Worten; ⇒ *also* **uncertain** E; Ⓙ *in pl.* (*relations*) **be on good/poor/friendly ~s with sb.** mit jmdm. auf gutem/schlechtem/freundschaftlichem Fuß stehen; ⇒ *also* **equal** 1 A; **speaking** 1 A; Ⓚ (*Logic, Math.*) Term, *der*. ❷ *v.t.* nennen

**termagant** /'tɜ:məgənt/ *n.* Furie, *die*

**terminal** /'tɜ:mınl/ ❶ *n.* Ⓐ (*Electr.*) Anschluss, *der*; (*of battery*) Pol, *der*; Ⓑ (*for train or bus*) Bahnhof, *der*; (*for airline passengers*) Terminal, *der od. das*; **helicopter ~:** Hubschrauberlandeplatz, *der*; Ⓒ (*Teleph.*, *Computing*) Terminal, *das*. ❷ *adj.* Ⓐ End‹bahnhof, -station›; Ⓑ (*concluding*) abschließend ‹Worte›; End‹reim, -silbe›; **the ~ problem** das letzte große Problem; Ⓒ ▶ **1232** (*Med.*) unheilbar; **have a ~ illness** unheilbar krank sein; **a ~ case** ein hoffnungsloser Fall; Ⓓ (*Bot.*) **~ bud** Terminalknospe, *die*; Ⓔ (*Zool.*, *Anat.*) End‹glied, -lappen›

**terminally** /'tɜ:mınəlı/ *adv.* (*Med.*) **~ ill** unheilbar krank

**terminal ve'locity** *n.* (*Phys.*) Grenzgeschwindigkeit, *die*

**terminate** /'tɜ:mıneıt/ ❶ *v.t.* Ⓐ (*bring to an end*) beenden; **the contract was ~d** der Vertrag wurde gelöst; Ⓑ (*Med.*) unterbrechen ‹Schwangerschaft›. ❷ *v.i.* Ⓐ (*come to an end*) enden; ‹Vertrag:› ablaufen; Ⓑ (*Ling.*) enden; auslauten

**termination** /tɜ:mı'neıʃn/ *n.* Ⓐ *no pl.* (*coming to an end*) Ende, *das*; (*of lease*) Ablauf, *der;* **B** *no pl.* (*bringing to an end*) Beendigung, *die;* (*of a marriage*) Auflösung, *die;* **C** (*Med.*) Schwangerschaftsabbruch, *der*

**terminological** /tɜːmɪnəˈlɒdʒɪkl/ *adj.* terminologisch; (*of science of terminology*) Terminologie-

**terminologically** /tɜːmɪnəˈlɒdʒɪkəlɪ/ *adv.* terminologisch

**terminologist** /tɜːmɪˈnɒlədʒɪst/ *n.* Terminologe, *der*/Terminologin, *die*

**terminology** /tɜːmɪˈnɒlədʒɪ/ *n.* Terminologie, *die*

**terminus** /ˈtɜːmɪnəs/ *n., pl.* **~es** *or* **termini** /ˈtɜːmɪnaɪ/ (*end of route or line*) Ende, *das;* (*of bus, train, etc.*) Endstation, *die*

**termite** /ˈtɜːmaɪt/ *n.* (*Zool.*) Termite, *die*

**tern** /tɜːn/ *n.* (*Ornith.*) Seeschwalbe, *die*

**ternary** /ˈtɜːnərɪ/ *adj.* ternär

**terrace** /ˈterəs, ˈterɪs/ **1** *n.* **A** (*row of houses*) Häuserreihe, *die;* **B** (*adjacent to house; Agric.: on hillside*) Terrasse, *die;* **C** *in pl.* (*Footb.*) Ränge; **D** (*Geol.*) Terrasse, *die;* Stufe, *die.* **2** *v.t.* terrassieren

ˈ**terraced house**, ˈ**terrace house** *ns.* Reihenhaus, *das*

**terracotta** /terəˈkɒtə/ *n., no pl., no indef. art.* Terrakotta, *die*

**terra firma** /terə ˈfɜːmə/ *n., no pl., no art.* fester Boden; **be back on ~:** wieder festen Boden unter den Füßen haben

**terrain** /teˈreɪn/ *n.* Gelände, *das;* Terrain, *das* (*bes. Milit.*)

**terrapin** /ˈterəpɪn/ *n.* (*Zool.*) Sumpfschildkröte, *die*

**terrestrial** /təˈrestrɪəl, tɪˈrestrɪəl/ **1** *adj.* **A** terrestrisch ‹Raumschiff, Fernsehen, Bevölkerung›; Erd‹satellit, -bevölkerung›; (*mundane*) irdisch; weltlich; **the ~ globe** der Erdball; **a ~ globe** ein Erdglobus; ⇒ *also* **magnetism** A; **B** (*of the land*) kontinental; terrestrisch (*Geol.*); **C** (*Biol.*) Land-. **2** *n.* Erdbewohner, *der*/-bewohnerin, *die*

**terrible** /ˈterɪbl/ *adj.* **A** (*coll.: very great or bad*) schrecklich (*ugs.*); fürchterlich (*ugs.*); **I feel ~ about doing it** es tut mir schrecklich Leid, es zu tun; **B** (*coll.: incompetent*) schlecht; **be ~ at maths/tennis/carpentry** in Mathe schlecht sein/schlecht Tennis spielen/ein schlechter Tischler sein; **C** (*causing terror*) furchtbar. ⇒ *also* **enfant terrible**

**terribly** /ˈterɪblɪ/ *adv.* **A** (*coll.: very*) unheimlich (*ugs.*); furchtbar (*ugs.*); **B** (*coll.: appallingly*) furchtbar (*ugs.*); **C** (*coll.: incompetently*) schlecht; **D** (*fearfully*) auf erschreckende Weise

**terrier** /ˈterɪə(r)/ *n.* Terrier, *der*

**terrific** /təˈrɪfɪk/ *adj.* (*coll.*) **A** (*great, intense*) irrsinnig (*ugs.*); Wahnsinns- (*ugs.*); unwahrscheinlich (*ugs.*); **B** (*magnificent*) sagenhaft (*ugs.*); **C** (*highly expert*) klasse (*ugs.*); toll (*ugs.*); **be ~ at sth.** in etw. (*Dat.*) Spitze sein (*ugs.*); **a ~ singer** ein Spitzensänger/eine Spitzensängerin (*ugs.*)

**terrifically** /təˈrɪfɪkəlɪ/ *adv.* (*coll.: extremely*) wahnsinnig (*ugs.*)

**terrify** /ˈterɪfaɪ/ *v.t.* **A** (*fill with terror*) Angst machen (+ *Dat.*); **terrified** verängstigt; **B** (*coll.: make very anxious*) Angst machen (+ *Dat.*); **be terrified that ...:** Angst haben, dass ...; **C** (*scare*) Angst einjagen (+ *Dat.*); **~ sb. into doing sth.** jmdm. eine solche Angst einjagen, dass er etw. tut

**terrifying** /ˈterɪfaɪɪŋ/ *adj.* **A** (*causing terror*) entsetzlich ‹Erlebnis, Film, Buch, Theaterstück›; erschreckend ‹Klarheit, Gedanke›; Furcht erregend ‹Anblick›; beängstigend ‹Geschwindigkeit, Neigungswinkel›; **B** (*formidable*) Furcht erregend; beängstigend ‹Gelehrsamkeit, Förmlichkeit, Intensität›

**terrifyingly** /ˈterɪfaɪɪŋlɪ/ *adv.* beängstigend ‹dicht, knapp›; entsetzlich ‹einsam›

**terrine** /təˈriːn/ *n.* **A** (*dish*) Steinguttopf, *der;* **B** (*Gastr.*) Terrine, *die*

**territorial** /terɪˈtɔːrɪəl/ **1** *adj.* **A** territorial; Gebiets‹anspruch, -hoheit usw.›; Hoheits‹gewässer, -gebiet usw.›; Gelände‹vorteil›; **~ possessions** Territorialbesitz, *der;* **B** (*limited to a district*) regional begrenzt ‹Maßnahme, Regelung›. **2** **T~** *n.* (*Brit. Mil.*) Landwehrsoldat, *der*

**Territorial ˈArmy** *n.* (*Brit. Mil.*) Landwehr, *die;* Territorialarmee, *die*

**territorially** /terɪˈtɔːrɪəlɪ/ *adv.* territorial

**territorial ˈwaters** *n. pl.* Hoheitsgewässer

**territory** /ˈterɪtərɪ/ *n.* **A** (*Polit.*) Staatsgebiet, *das;* Hoheitsgebiet, *das;* **B** (*fig.: area of knowledge or action*) Gebiet, *das;* **C** (*of commercial traveller etc.*) Bezirk, *der;* **D** (*large tract of land*) Region, *die;* Gebiet, *das;* **E** (*Amer.: land not yet a full State*) Territorium, *das;* **F** (*Zool.*) Revier, *das;* **G** (*Sport*) Spielfeldhälfte, *die*

**terror** /ˈterə(r)/ *n.* **A** (*extreme fear*) [panische] Angst; **in ~:** in panischer Angst; **reign of ~:** Schreckensherrschaft, *die;* **the [Red] T~, the Reign of T~** (*Hist.*) die Schreckensherrschaft [der Französischen Revolution]; **B** (*person or thing causing ~*) Schrecken, *der;* **C** **[holy] ~** (*troublesome person*) Plage, *die;* (*formidable person*) Schrecken, *der*

**terrorisation, terrorise** ⇒ **terroriz-**

**terrorism** /ˈterərɪzm/ *n.* Terrorismus, *der;* (*terrorist acts*) Terror, *der;* **acts of ~:** Terrorakte

**terrorist** /ˈterərɪst/ *n.* Terrorist, *der*/Terroristin, *die; attrib.* Terror‹gruppe, -organisation›

**terroristic** /terəˈrɪstɪk/ *adj.* terroristisch

**terrorization** /terəraɪˈzeɪʃn/ *n., no pl.* Terror, *der*

**terrorize** /ˈterəraɪz/ *v.t.* **A** (*frighten*) in [Angst und] Schrecken versetzen; **B** (*coerce by terrorism*) terrorisieren; (*intimidate*) durch Terror[akte] einschüchtern; **~ sb. into submission** jmdn. durch Terror in die Knie zwingen

**terror: ~-stricken, ~-struck** *adjs.* zu Tode erschrocken

**terry** /ˈterɪ/ *adj.* (*Textiles*) **~ towel** Frottier[hand]tuch, *das;* **~ towelling** Frottee, *das od. der*

**terse** /tɜːs/ *adj.* **A** (*concise*) kurz und bündig; **B** (*curt*) knapp

**tersely** /ˈtɜːslɪ/ *adv.* **A** (*concisely*) in kurzen Worten; **B** (*curtly*) kurz angebunden

**terseness** /ˈtɜːsnɪs/ *n., no pl.* **A** (*conciseness*) Bündigkeit, *die;* **B** (*curtness*) Knappheit, *die*

**tertiary** /ˈtɜːʃərɪ/ *adj.* **A** (*of third order or rank*) tertiär; **B** (*next after secondary*) **~ education** der tertiäre Bildungsbereich; **C** **T~** (*Geol.*) tertiär

**Terylene** ® /ˈterɪliːn/ *n.* Terylen, *das* (Wz)

**terza rima** /teətsə ˈriːmə/ *n.* (*Pros.*) Terzine, *die*

**tessellated** /ˈtesəleɪtɪd/ *adj.* mosaikartig; tessellarisch

**tessellation** /tesəˈleɪʃn/ *n.* mosaikartige Musterung

**test** /test/ **1** *n.* **A** (*examination*) (*Sch.*) Klassenarbeit, *die;* (*Univ.*) Klausur, *die;* (*short examination*) Test, *der;* **~ of character** Charakterprüfung, *die;* **put sb./sth. to the ~:** jmdn./etw. erproben; **B** (*critical inspection, analysis*) Test, *der;* **C** (*basis for evaluation*) Prüfstein, *der;* **D** (*Cricket*) Test Match, *das;* **E** (*ground of admission or rejection*) Aufnahmeprüfung, *die;* **F** (*Chem.*) Reagens, *das;* **serve as a ~ for starch** zum Nachweis von Stärke dienen.
**2** *v.t.* **A** (*examine, analyse*) untersuchen ‹Wasser, Gehör, Augen›; testen ‹Gehör, Augen›; prüfen ‹Schüler›; überprüfen ‹Hypothese, Aussage, Leitungen›; **~ a pupil on his/her vocabulary** einem Schüler/einer Schülerin die Vokabeln abfragen; **~ the accuracy of a statement** den Wahrheitsgehalt einer Aussage überprüfen; **~ sb. for AIDS** jmdn. auf Aids untersuchen; **~ the reaction of the workforce** sehen, wie die Belegschaft reagiert; **B** (*try severely*) auf die Probe stellen; **C** (*Chem.*) analysieren; **~ a substance for sth.** eine Substanz auf etw. (*Akk.*) untersuchen; **send sth. for ~ing** etw. zur Analyse schicken
**~ out** *v.t.* ausprobieren ‹neue Produkte› (**on** an + *Dat.*); erproben ‹Theorie, Idee›

**testament** /ˈtestəmənt/ *n.* **A** **Old/New T~** (*Bibl.*) Altes/Neues Testament; **B** ⇒ **will**[2] 1 B

**testamentary** /testəˈmentərɪ/ *adj.* testamentarisch

**testator** /teˈsteɪtə(r)/ *n.* Erblasser, *der* (*Rechtsspr.*)

**testatrix** /teˈsteɪtrɪks/ *n.* Erblasserin, *die* (*Rechtsspr.*)

**test: ~ ban** *n.* Atom[waffen]teststopp, *der;* **~ ban treaty** *n.* [Atom]teststopp-Abkommen, *das;* **~ bed** *n.* (*Aeronaut.*) Prüfstand, *der;* **~ card** *n.* (*Telev.*) Testbild, *das;* **~ ˈcase** *n.* (*Law*) Musterprozess, *der;* **~ drive** *n.* Probefahrt, *die;* **~-drive** *v.t.* Probe fahren

**tester** /ˈtestə(r)/ *n.* Prüfer, *der*/Prüferin, *die;* (*device*) Prüfgerät, *das;* (*sample*) Probe, *die*

**test: ~ flight** *n.* Testflug, *der;* Erprobungsflug, *der;* **first ~ flight** Jungfernflug, *der;* **~-fly** *v.t.* Probe fliegen

**testicle** /ˈtestɪkl/ *n.* ▶ **966** (*Anat., Zool.*) Testikel, *der* (*fachspr.*); Hoden, *der*

**testify** /ˈtestɪfaɪ/ **1** *v.i.* **A** **~ to sth.** etw. bezeugen; **~ to sb.'s high intelligence** jmdm. große Intelligenz bescheinigen; **this testifies to his skills** das zeugt von seinen Fähigkeiten; **B** (*Law*) **~ against sb./before sth.** gegen jmdn./vor etw. (*Dat.*) aussagen. **2** *v.t.* **A** (*declare*) bestätigen; **B** (*be evidence of*) beweisen

**testily** /ˈtestɪlɪ/ *adv.* gereizt

**testimonial** /testɪˈməʊnɪəl/ *n.* **A** (*certificate of character*) Zeugnis, *das;* (*recommendation*) Referenz, *die;* **B** (*gift*) Geschenk [als Ausdruck der Wertschätzung]

**testimony** /ˈtestɪmənɪ/ *n.* **A** (*witness*) Aussage, *die;* **bear ~ to sth., be ~ to** *or* **of sth.** etw. beweisen; von etw. zeugen; **have sb.'s ~ for sth.** jmds. Wort für etw. haben; **~ of his respectability** Zeichen *od.* Beweis seiner Anständigkeit; **B** (*Law*) [Zeugen]aussage, *die;* **C** *no pl.* (*statements*) Angaben

**testiness** /ˈtestɪnɪs/ *n., no pl.* Gereiztheit, *die*

**testis** /ˈtestɪs/ *n., pl.* **testes** /ˈtestiːz/ ⇒ **testicle**

ˈ**test match** *n.* (*Sport*) Testmatch, *das*

**testosterone** /teˈstɒstərəʊn/ *n.* (*Physiol.*) Testosteron, *das*

**test: ~ paper** *n.* **A** (*Educ.*) Übungsarbeit, *die;* (*Univ.*) Übungsklausur, *die;* **B** (*Chem.*) Indikatorpapier, *das;* **~ piece** *n.* Pflicht[übung], *die;* (*Mus.*) Pflichtstück, *das;* **~ pilot** *n.* (*Aeronaut.*) Testpilot, *der*/-pilotin, *die;* **~ run** *n.* Testfahrt, *die;* Probefahrt, *die;* (*of engine*) Testlauf, *der;* Probelauf, *der;* **~ tube** *n.* (*Chem., Biol.*) Reagenzglas, *das; attrib.* **~-tube baby** (*coll.*) Retortenbaby, *das* (*ugs.*)

**testy** /ˈtestɪ/ *adj.* leicht reizbar ‹Person›; gereizt ‹Antwort›

**tetanus** /ˈtetənəs/ *n.* ▶ **1232** (*Med.*) Tetanus, *der* (*fachspr.*); [Wund]starrkrampf, *der*

**tetchy** /ˈtetʃɪ/ *adj.* leicht reizbar; (*on single occasion*) gereizt

**tête-à-tête** /teɪtɑːˈteɪt/ **1** *n.* Tête-à-tête, *das* (*veralt.*); Gespräch unter vier Augen. **2** *adj.* privat; **~ interview/discussion** Gespräch/Diskussion unter vier Augen; **~ conversation** Zwiegespräch, *das.* **3** *adv.* unter vier Augen

**tether** /ˈteðə(r)/ **1** *n.* **A** (*chain*) Kette, *die;* (*rope*) Strick, *der;* **B** (*fig.: limit*) Grenze, *die;* **give sb. a short ~:** jmdn. an der kurzen Leine halten; **be at the end of one's ~:** am Ende [seiner Kraft] sein. **2** *v.t.* anbinden (**to** an)

**tetrahedron** /tetrəˈhiːdrən/ *n., pl.* **~s** *or* **tetrahedra** /tetrəˈhiːdrə/ (*Geom.*) Tetraeder, *das*

**Teuton** /ˈtjuːtən/ *n.* (*Hist.*) Teutone, *der*/Teutonin, *die*

**Teutonic** /tjuːˈtɒnɪk/ *adj.* **A** (*Germanic*) germanisch; **B** (*with Germanic characteristics*) [typisch] deutsch; teutonisch (*abwertend, auch scherzh.*); **C** (*Hist.: of the Teutons*) teutonisch

**Texan** /ˈteksn/ **1** *adj.* texanisch. **2** *n.* Texaner, *der*/Texanerin, *die*

**text** /tekst/ *n.* **A** Text, *der;* **they couldn't agree on the ~ of the agreement** sie konnten sich über den Wortlaut des Vertrages nicht einigen; [B] (*passage of Scripture*) Bibelstelle, *die;* **take as one's ~:** als Predigttext nehmen; predigen über (+ *Akk.*); [C] (*Amer.: book*) ⇒ **textbook**; [D] *in pl.* (*books to be studied*) [Pflicht]lektüre, *die*

**'textbook** *n.* (*Educ.*) Lehrbuch, *das; attrib.* **~ case** Paradefall, *der;* **~ landing** Bilderbuchlandung, *die*

**textile** /'tekstaɪl/ ❶ *n.* Stoff, *der;* **~s** Textilien *Pl.* ❷ *adj.* (*woven*) textil; **~ fabrics** Textilien *Pl.*

**'text processing** *n.* Textverarbeitung, *die*

**textual** /'tekstjʊəl/ *adj.* textlich

**textual 'criticism** *n.* Textkritik, *die*

**textural** /'tekstʃərl/ *adj.* strukturell

**texture** /'tekstʃə(r)/ *n.* [A] Beschaffenheit, *die;* (*of fabric, material*) Struktur, *die;* (*of food*) Konsistenz, *die;* **have a smooth ~:** sich glatt anfühlen; [B] (*of prose, music, etc.*) Textur, *die* (*geh.*); [C] (*Art*) materielle Struktur

**textured** /'tekstʃəd/ *adj.* Struktur‹garn, -farbe›; **~ vegetable protein** Sojafleisch, *das*

**textureless** /'tekstʃəlɪs/ *adj.* gestaltlos ‹Prosa, Gemälde, Darbietung›; formlos ‹Masse›

**Th.** *abbr.* **Thursday** Do.

**Thai** /taɪ/ ▶ **1340** ❶ *adj.* [A] (*of Thailand*) thailändisch; [B] (*Ethnol./Ling.*) Thai-. ❷ *n.* [A] *pl.* **~s** *or same* Thai, *der/die;* Thailänder, *der*/Thailänderin, *die;* [B] (*language*) Thai, *das*

**Thailand** /'taɪlænd/ *pr. n.* Thailand (*das*)

**Thailander** /'taɪlændə(r)/ ⇒ **Thai** 2 A

**thalamus** /'θæləməs/ *n.* (*Anat.*) Thalamus, *der*

**thalidomide** /θə'lɪdəmaɪd/ *n.* (*Med.*) Contergan, *das* Ⓦᶻ; Thalidomid, *das*

**thalidomide: ~ baby, ~ child** *ns.* Contergankind, *das* (*ugs.*)

**Thames** /temz/ *pr. n.* ▶ **1480** Themse, *die;* ⇒ *also* **father** 1 G; **fire** 1 A

**than** /ðən, *stressed* ðæn/ *conj.* [A] (*in comparison*) als; **I know you better ~ [I do] him** ich kenne dich besser als ihn; **I know you better ~ he [does]** ich kenne dich besser als er; **you are taller ~ he [is]** *or* (*coll.*) **him** du bist größer als er; ⇒ *also* **rather**; [B] (*introducing statement of difference*) als; **anywhere else ~ at home** überall außer zu Hause; ⇒ *also* **none** 1; **other** 1 C, 2 B, 3

**thank** /θæŋk/ *v.t.* **~ sb. [for sth.]** jmdm. [für etw.] danken; sich bei jmdm. [für etw.] bedanken; **I don't know how to ~ you** ich weiß gar nicht, wie ich Ihnen danken soll; **I can't ~ you enough** ich kann Ihnen gar nicht genug danken; **have sb./sth. to ~ for sth.** jmdm./einer Sache etw. zu verdanken haben; **have [only] oneself to ~ for sth.** etw. sich (*Dat.*) selbst zuzuschreiben haben; **he won't ~ you for that/for doing that** (*iron.*) er wird dir dafür nicht gerade dankbar sein/er wird dir nicht gerade dankbar sein, dass du das getan hast; **~ God** *or* **goodness** *or* **heaven[s]** Gott sei Dank; **[I] ~ you** danke; (*slightly formal*) vielen Dank; **no, ~ you** nein, danke; **yes, ~ you** ja, bitte; danke, ja; **doing very nicely, ~ you** es läuft alles prima (*auch iron.*); **I can do without language like that, ~ you!** (*iron.*) auf diesen Ton kann ich verzichten, vielen Dank!; **~ you very much [indeed]** vielen herzlichen Dank; **I'll stay in London, ~ you** (*iron.*) vielen Dank, ich bleibe lieber in London; **~ing 'you** (*coll.*) danke; **~ you for nothing!** (*iron.*) danke bestens!; **I will ~ you to do as you are told** (*iron.*) ich wäre dir sehr verbunden, wenn du tätest, was man dir sagt; **~ one's [lucky] stars that ...:** dem Himmel danken, dass ...

**thankful** /'θæŋkfl/ *adj.* dankbar; **I am just ~ that it's all over** ich bin nur froh, dass das jetzt alles vorüber ist

**thankfully** /'θæŋkfəlɪ/ *adv.* [A] (*gratefully*) dankbar; [B] (*as sentence-modifier: fortunately*) glücklicherweise

**thankfulness** /'θæŋkflnɪs/ *n., no pl.* Dankbarkeit, *die*

**thankless** /'θæŋklɪs/ *adj.* undankbar ‹Aufgabe, Person›

**thanks** /θæŋks/ *n. pl.* [A] (*gratitude*) Dank, *der;* **accept sth. with ~:** etw. dankend annehmen; **smile one's ~:** dankend lächeln; **they gave me little ~** *or* (*iron.*) **much ~ they gave me for my troubles** sie haben mir meine Mühen kaum gedankt; **that's all the ~ one gets** das ist nun der Dank dafür!; **give ~ [to God]** dem Herrn danken; das Dankgebet sprechen; **~ to** (*with the help of*) dank; (*on account of the bad influence of*) wegen; **~ to you** dank deiner; (*reproachfully*) deinetwegen; **no ~ to you** (*iron.*) dein Verdienst war es nicht; **it is small** *or* **no ~ to him that we won** ihm haben wir es jedenfalls nicht zu verdanken, dass wir gewonnen haben; **~ to his arriving in time** dank seines rechtzeitigen Erscheinens; ⇒ *also* **return** 2 A; [B] (*as formula expressing gratitude*) danke; **no, ~:** nein, danke; **yes, ~:** ja, bitte; **~ awfully** *or* **a lot** *or* **very much, many ~** (*coll.*) vielen *od.* tausend Dank

**thanksgiving** /'θæŋksgɪvɪŋ/ *n.* [A] (*expression of gratitude*) Dankbarkeit, *die;* **T~ [Day]** (*Amer.*) [amerikanisches] Erntedankfest; Thanksgiving Day, *der;* [B] (*Relig.*) Dankgebet, *das*

**'thank-you** *n.* (*coll.*) Dankeschön, *das;* **a warm** *or* **hearty ~:** ein herzliches Dankeschön; **~ letter** Dankbrief, *der;* **give sb. a ~ present** jmdm. zum Dank etwas schenken

**that** ❶ /ðæt/ *adj., pl.* **those** /ðəʊz/ [A] dieser/diese/dieses; **~ son of yours** Ihr/dein Sohn; [B] *expr. strong feeling* der/die/das; **never will I forget ~ day** den Tag werde ich nie vergessen; [C] (*coupled or contrasted with 'this'*) der/die/das [da].

❷ *pron., pl.* **those** [A] der/die/das; **who is ~ in the garden?** wer ist das [da] im Garten?; **what bird is ~?** was für ein Vogel ist das?; **I know all ~:** ich weiß das alles; **I 'am ~!** das kannst du wohl glauben!; **those below the standard will be rejected** alle, die den Anforderungen nicht genügen, werden abgelehnt; **and [all] ~:** und so weiter; **like ~** (*of the kind or in the way mentioned, of ~ character*) so; **[just] like ~** (*without effort, thought*) einfach so; **don't be like ~!** sei doch nicht so; **if she 'wants to be like ~:** wenn sie sich so anstellen will; **don't talk like ~:** hör auf, so zu reden; **he is 'like ~:** so ist er eben; **~ is [to say]** *introducing explanation* das heißt; *introducing reservation* das heißt; genauer gesagt; **if they'd have me, ~ is** das heißt, wenn sie mich nehmen; **'~'s more like it** (*of suggestion, news*) das hört sich schon besser an; (*of action, work*) das sieht schon besser aus; **~'s right!** *expr. approval* gut *od.* recht so; (*iron.*) nur so weiter!; (*coll.: expr. assent*) jawohl; **~'s a good boy/girl** das ist lieb [von dir, mein Junge/Mädchen]; (*with request*) sei so lieb *usw.;* **~ will do** das reicht; **sb./sth. is not as ... as all '~** (*coll.*) so ... ist jmd./etw. nun auch wieder nicht; **[so] ~'s '~** (*it's finished*) so, das wärs; (*it's settled*) so ist es nun mal; **you are not going to the party, and ~'s '~!** du gehst nicht zu der Party, und damit Schluss!; ⇒ *also* **at** D; **how** 1; **it** G, J; **take** 1 W; **this** 2 E; **with** G; [B] (*Brit.: person spoken to*) **who is ~?** wer ist da?; (*behind wall etc.*) wer ist denn da?; (*on telephone*) wer ist am Apparat?; **who was ~?** wer war das?

❸ /ðət/ *rel. pron., pl. same* der/die/das; **the people ~ you got it from** die Leute, von denen du es bekommen hast; **the box ~ you put the apples in** die Kiste, in die du die Äpfel getan hast; **is he the man ~ you saw last night?** ist das der Mann, den Sie gestern Abend gesehen haben?; **everyone ~ I know** jeder, den ich kenne; **this is all [the money] ~ I have** das ist alles [Geld], was ich habe; **they ~ ...:** diejenigen, die *od.* welche ...; **what is it ~ is making you sad?** was stimmt dich so traurig?.

❹ /ðæt/ *adv.* (*coll.*) so; **he may be daft, but he's not [all] '~ daft** er mag ja blöd sein, aber so blöd [ist er] auch wieder nicht; **a nail about ~ long** ein etwa so langer Nagel.

❺ /ðət/ *rel. adv.* der/die/das; **at the speed ~ he was going** bei der Geschwindigkeit, die er hatte; **tell the way ~ the accident happened** erzählen, wie der Unfall geschah; **the day ~ I first met her** der Tag, an dem ich sie zum ersten Mal sah.

❻ /ðət, *stressed* ðæt/ *conj.* [A] *introducing statement; expr. result, reason or cause* dass; [B] *expr. purpose* **[in order] ~:** damit; **he died ~ others might live** er starb, damit andere [weiter]leben konnten; [C] *expr. wish* **oh ~ I could forget her!** ach, dass ich sie doch vergessen könnte! ⇒ *also* **not** B; **now** 2

**thatch** /θætʃ/ ❶ *n.* [A] (*of straw*) Strohdach, *das;* (*of reeds*) Schilf- *od.* Reetdach, *das;* (*of palm leaves*) Palmblattdach, *das;* (*material*) Stroh, *das*/Schilf, *das*/Palmblätter; (*roofing*) Dachbedeckung, *die;* [B] (*coll.: hair*) Matte, *die* (*salopp*). ❷ *v.t.* mit Stroh/Schilf/Palmblättern decken

**thatched** /θætʃt/ *adj.* strohgedeckt/schilf- *od.* reetgedeckt; gedeckt ‹Dach›; Stroh-/Schilf- *od.* Reet‹dach›

**thatcher** /'θætʃə(r)/ *n.* Dachdecker, *der*/-deckerin, *die*

**Thatcherism** /'θætʃərɪzm/ *n.* (*Polit.*) Thatcherismus, *der*

**thaw** /θɔː/ ❶ *n.* [A] (*warmth*) Tauwetter, *das;* [B] (*act of thawing*) **after the ~:** nachdem es getaut hat/hatte; [C] (*fig.*) Tauwetter, *das;* Tauwetterperiode, *die.* ❷ *v.i.* [A] (*melt*) auftauen; [B] (*become warm enough to melt ice etc.*) tauen; **it looks like ~ing** es sieht nach Tauwetter aus; [C] (*fig.: become less aloof or hostile*) auftauen; [D] (*lose numbness*) [wieder] warm werden. ❸ *v.t.* [A] (*cause to melt*) auftauen; [B] (*fig.: cause to be less aloof or hostile*) auftauen; entspannen ‹Atmosphäre›; [C] (*cause to lose numbness*) aufwärmen

**~ 'out** ⇒ **~** 2, 3

**the** /*before vowel* ðɪ, *before consonant* ðə, *when stressed* ðiː/ ❶ *def. art.* [A] der/die/das; **all ~ doors** alle Türen; **play ~ piano** Klavier spielen; **if you want a quick survey, this is ~ book** für einen raschen Überblick ist dies das richtige Buch; **it's** *or* **there's only ~ one** es ist nur dieser/diese/dieses eine; **he lives in ~ district** er wohnt in dieser Gegend; **he was quite ~ philosopher about his misfortune** er trug sein Unglück wie ein Philosoph; **£5 ~ square metre/~ gallon/~ kilogram** 5 Pfund der Quadratmeter/die Gallone/das Kilogramm; **14 miles to ~ gallon** 14 Meilen auf eine Gallone; ≈ 20 l auf 100 km; **a scale of one mile to ~ inch** ein Maßstab von 1 : 63360; **none but ~ brave deserves ~ fair** allein dem Tapferen gehört die Schöne; [B] (*denoting one best known*) **it is '~ restaurant in this town** das ist das Restaurant in dieser Stadt; **red is '~ colour this year** Rot ist in diesem Jahr die Farbe; **she is no relation to '~ Kipling** mit dem Kipling ist sie nicht verwandt; [C] (*with names of diseases*) **have got ~ toothache/measles** (*coll.*) Zahnschmerzen/die Masern haben; [D] (*Brit. coll.: my, our, etc.*) mein/unser *usw.;* **leave ~ wife and ~ dog at home** Frau und Hund zu Hause lassen; [E] (*Scot., Ir.: with name of clan*) **~ Macnab** das Oberhaupt des Macnab-Klans.

❷ *adv.* **~ more I practise ~ better I play** je mehr ich übe, desto *od.* umso besser spiele ich; **I am not ~ more inclined to help him because he is poor** ich würde ihm genauso gern helfen, wenn er nicht arm wäre; **his car runs ~ faster for having been tuned properly** jetzt, wo es richtig eingestellt ist, fährt sein Auto schneller; **so much ~ worse for sb./sth.** umso schlimmer für jmdn./etw.; ⇒ *also* **all** 3; **more** 1 B, 3 H

**theatre** (*Amer.:* **theater**) /'θɪətə(r)/ *n.* [A] Theater, *das;* **at the ~:** im Theater; **go to the ~:** ins Theater gehen; [B] (*lecture ~*) Hörsaal, *der;* [C] (*Brit. Med.*) ⇒ **operating theatre**; [D] (*dramatic art*) **the ~:** das Theater; **go into the ~:** zum Theater gehen (*ugs.*); [E] *no pl., no art.* **make good ~:** sehr bühnenwirksam sein; sich gut für die Bühne eignen; [F] (*scene of action*) Schauplatz, *der;* (*of war*) Kriegsschauplatz, *der*

**theatre: ~ goer** *n.* Theaterbesucher, *der*/-besucherin, *die;* **~-going** ❶ *n., no pl., no* *indef. art.* Theaterbesuche; **~-going is on the increase** die Zahl der Theaterbesucher steigt; ❷ *adj.* **the ~-going public/type** die Theaterbesucher/der typische Theaterbesucher; **~ sister** *n.* (*Brit. Med.*) OP-Schwester, *die;* **~ weapon** *n.* (*Mil.*) Kurzstreckenrakete, *die*

**theatrical** /θɪ'ætrɪkl/ *adj.* Ⓐ schauspielerisch; **a ~ company** eine Schauspiel- *od.* Theatertruppe; Ⓑ (*showy*) theatralisch ‹Benehmen, Verbeugung, Person›

**theatrically** /θɪ'ætrɪkəlɪ/ *adv.* Ⓐ **~, the play was a disaster** was die Aufführung angeht, war das Stück ein Reinfall; Ⓑ (*showily*) theatralisch

**theatricals** /θɪ'ætrɪklz/ *n. pl.* Ⓐ (*dramatic performances*) Theateraufführungen; **private** *or* **amateur ~:** Amateur- *od.* Laientheater, *das;* Ⓑ (*showy actions*) Theatralik, *die* (*geh.*)

**Thebes** /θi:bz/ *pr. n.* (*Greek/Egyptian Ant.*) Theben (*das*)

**thee** /ði:/ *pron.* (*arch./poet./dial.*) dich; (*as indirect object*) dir; (*Relig.: God*) Dich/Dir; ⇒ *also* **her**[1]

**theft** /θeft/ *n.* Diebstahl, *der;* **~ of cars** Autodiebstahl, *der*

**their** /ðeə(r)/ *poss. pron. attrib.* Ⓐ ihr; ⇒ *also* **her**[2]; **our** A; Ⓑ (*coll.: his or her*) **who has forgotten ~ ticket?** wer hat seine Karte vergessen?

**theirs** /ðeəz/ *poss. pron. pred.* ihrer/ihre/ihres; ⇒ *also* **hers**; **ours**

**theism** /'θi:ɪzm/ *n.* (*Philos.*) Theismus, *der*

**theist** /'θi:ɪst/ *n.* (*Philos.*) Theist, *der*/Theistin, *die*

**them** /ðəm, *stressed* ðem/ *pron.* Ⓐ sie; (*as indirect object*) ihnen; ⇒ *also* **her**[1]; Ⓑ (*coll.: him/her*) ihn/sie

**thematic** /θɪ'mætɪk/ *adj.* thematisch

**thematically** /θɪ'mætɪkəlɪ/ *adv.* (*with regard to topic[s]; also Mus.*) thematisch; **arrange ~:** nach Themen ordnen

**theme** /θi:m/ *n.* Ⓐ (*of speaker, writer, or thinker*) Gegenstand, *der;* Thema, *das;* Ⓑ (*Mus.*) Thema, *das;* **a ~ from 'My Fair Lady'** eine Melodie aus My Fair Lady; Ⓒ (*Amer. Educ.*) Aufsatz, *der*

**theme: ~ music** *n.* Titelmelodie, *die;* **~ park** *n. Freizeitpark, dessen Attraktionen und Einrichtungen auf ein bestimmtes Thema bezogen sind;* **~ song** *n.* Erkennungssong, *der;* **~ tune** *n.* (*Radio, Telev.*) Erkennungsmelodie, *die*

**themselves** /ðəm'selvz/ *pron.* Ⓐ *emphat.* selbst; **they ~ were astonished** sie waren selbst ganz erstaunt; **the results ~ were ...:** die Ergebnisse an sich waren ...; Ⓑ *refl.* sich ‹waschen usw.›; sich selbst ‹die Schuld geben, regieren›. ⇒ *also* **herself**; **ourselves**

**then** /ðen/ ❶ *adv.* Ⓐ (*at that time*) damals; **the ~ existing laws** die damals geltenden *od.* damaligen Gesetze; **~ and there, there and ~:** auf der Stelle; ⇒ *also* **now** 1 A; Ⓑ (*after that*) dann; **~ [again]** (*and also*) außerdem; **the journey will take a long time, and ~ don't forget that it gets dark early** die Fahrt wird lange dauern, und dann dürft ihr auch nicht vergessen, dass es früh dunkel wird; **but ~** (*after all*) aber schließlich; Ⓒ (*in that case*) dann; **~ why didn't you say so?** warum hast du dann nichts gesagt?; **hurry up, ~:** dann beeil dich aber; **but ~ again** aber andererseits; Ⓓ *expr. grudging or impatient concession* dann eben; **well, take it, ~:** dann nimm es eben; Ⓔ (*accordingly*) [dann] also; **the cause of the accident, ~, seems to be established** die Ursache des Unfalls scheint [dann] also festzustehen. ⇒ *also* **well**[2] 1 D, G; **what** 5 A.
❷ *n.* **before ~:** vorher; davor; **by ~:** bis dahin; **from ~ on** von da an; **till ~:** bis dahin; **oh, we should get there long before ~:** ach, bis dahin sind wir längst dort; **since ~:** seitdem.
❸ *adj.* damalig

**thence** /ðens/ *adv.* (*arch./literary*) **[from] ~:** von dort; (*for that reason*) von daher

**thence: ~'forth, ~'forward** *advs.* (*arch./literary*) **[from] ~forth** *or* **~forward** seit dieser Zeit; von da an

**theodolite** /θɪ'ɒdəlaɪt/ *n.* (*Surv.*) Theodolit, *der*

**theologian** /θi:ə'ləʊdʒɪən/ *n.* Theologe, *der*/Theologin, *die*

**theological** /θi:ə'lɒdʒɪkl/ *adj.* theologisch; Theologie‹student, -dozent›

**theology** /θɪ'ɒlədʒɪ/ *n.* Ⓐ *no pl., no indef. art.* Theologie, *die;* Ⓑ (*religious system*) Glaubenslehre, *die*

**theorem** /'θɪərəm/ *n.* (*Math.*) [Lehr]satz, *der;* Theorem, *das* (*fachspr.*)

**theoretic** /θɪə'retɪk/, **theoretical** /θɪə'retɪkl/ *adj.* theoretisch; **your arguments are only ~al** deine Argumentation ist reine Theorie

**theoretically** /θi:ə'retɪkəlɪ/ *adv.* theoretisch

**theoretician** /θɪərɪ'tɪʃn/ *n.* Theoretiker, *der*/Theoretikerin, *die*

**theorise** ⇒ **theorize**

**theorist** /'θɪərɪst/ *n.* Theoretiker, *der*/Theoretikerin, *die*

**theorize** /'θɪəraɪz/ *v.i.* theoretisieren

**theory** /'θɪərɪ/ *n.* (*also Math.*) Theorie, *die;* **~ of evolution/music** Evolutions-/Musiktheorie, *die;* **in ~:** theoretisch; **it's a ~!** das wäre eine Möglichkeit; **I always go on the ~ that ...:** ich gehe immer davon aus, dass ...; **have a ~ that ...:** die Theorie vertreten, dass ...

**theosophic** /θi:ə'sɒfɪk/, **theosophical** /θi:ə'sɒfɪkl/ *adj.* theosophisch

**theosophy** /θɪ'ɒsəfɪ/ *n., no pl., no indef. art.* Theosophie, *die*

**therapeutic** /θerə'pju:tɪk/ *adj.* therapeutisch; (*curative*) therapeutisch wirksam

**therapeutically** /θerə'pju:tɪkəlɪ/ *adv.* therapeutisch

**therapeutics** /θerə'pju:tɪks/ *n., no pl.* (*Med.*) Therapeutik, *die*

**therapist** /'θerəpɪst/ *n.* (*Med.*) Therapeut, *der*/Therapeutin, *die*

**therapy** /'θerəpɪ/ *n.* (*Med., Psych.*) Therapie, *die;* [Heil]behandlung, *die;* **undergo ~:** sich einer Therapie (*Dat.*) unterziehen

**there** /ðeə(r)/ ❶ *adv.* Ⓐ (*in/at that place*) da; dort; (*fairly close*) da; **sb. has been ~ before** (*fig. coll.*) jmd. weiß Bescheid; **~ or ~a'bouts** so ungefähr; **be down/in/up ~:** da unten/drin/oben sein; **~ goes ...:** da geht/fährt *usw.* ...; **are you ~?** (*on telephone*) sind Sie noch da *od.* (*ugs.*) dran?; **~ and then = then and ~** ⇒ **then** 1 A; ⇒ *also* **all** 3; **here** 1 A; Ⓑ (*calling attention*) **hello** *or* **hi ~!** hallo!; **you ~!** Sie da!; **move along ~!** weitergehen!; **~'s a good** *etc.* **boy/girl = that's a good** *etc.* **boy/girl** ⇒ **that** 2 A; ⇒ *also* **for** 1 H; Ⓒ (*in that respect*) da; **so ~:** und damit basta (*ugs.*); **~ you are wrong** da irrst du dich; **~, it is a loose wire** da haben wirs — ein loser Draht; **~ it is** (*nothing can be done about it*) da kann man nichts machen; **~ you are** (*giving sth.*) [da,] bitte schön; **~ you have it** (*fig.*) da ist der Punkt; ⇒ *also* **2** B; **rub** 3; Ⓓ (*to that place*) dahin, dorthin ‹gehen, gelangen, fahren, rücken, stellen›; **we got ~ and back in two hours** wir brauchten für Hin- und Rückweg [nur] zwei Stunden; **down/in/up ~:** dort hinunter/hinein/hinauf; **get ~ first** jmdm./den anderen zuvorkommen; **get ~** (*fig.*) (*achieve*) es [schon] schaffen; (*understand*) es verstehen; Ⓔ /ðə(r), *stressed* ðeə(r)/ (*as introductory function word*) da; **was ~ anything in it?** war da irgendetwas drin? (*ugs.*); **~ is enough food** es gibt genug zu essen; **~ are many kinds of ...:** es gibt viele Arten von ...; **~ were four of them** sie waren zu viert; **~ was once an old woman who ...:** es war einmal eine alte Frau, die ...; **~ was no beer left** es gab kein Bier mehr; **~ appears to be some error** da scheint ein Irrtum unterlaufen zu sein; **~'s no time for that now** dafür haben wir/habe ich jetzt keine Zeit; **~ being no further point in waiting, I left** weil es keinen Zweck mehr hatte, noch länger zu warten, ging ich; **... if ever ~ was one** ... wie er/sie/es im Buche steht; **what is ~ for supper?** was gibts zum Abendessen?; **not a sound was ~ to indicate their presence** kein Laut verriet ihre Anwesenheit; **seldom has ~ been more fuss** selten hat es so viel Aufhebens gegeben; **a fine mess ~ is!** da sieht es vielleicht aus! (*ugs.*).
❷ /ðeə(r)/ *int.* Ⓐ (*to soothe child etc.*) **~, ~:** na, na (*ugs.*); Ⓑ *expr. triumph or dismay* **~ [you are]!** da, siehst du!; **~, you've dropped it!** da, jetzt hast du es doch fallen lassen!; ⇒ *also* **1** C.
❸ *n.* da, dort; **near ~:** da *od.* dort in der Nähe; **the tide comes up to ~:** die Flut kommt bis dahin *od.* da hoch

**there: ~abouts** /'ðeərəbaʊts/ *adv.* Ⓐ (*near that place*) da [in der Nähe]; **the locals ~abouts** die Leute, die dort wohnen; Ⓑ (*near that number*) **two litres or ~abouts** zwei Liter [so] ungefähr; ⇒ *also* **there** 1 A; **~'after** *adv.* danach; **~by** /ðeə'baɪ, 'ðeəbaɪ/ *adv.* dadurch; **~by hangs a tale** dazu gibt es noch etwas zu erzählen; **~fore** *adv.* deshalb; also; **~'from** *adv.* (*arch.*) daraus; **~'in** *adv.* (*formal*) darin; **~'of** *adv.* (*formal*) davon; **the island and all the ports ~of** die Insel und alle ihre Häfen; **~'to** *adv.* (*formal*) dazu; **~u'pon** *adv.* Ⓐ (*soon after that*) kurz darauf; alsbald (*veralt.*); Ⓑ (*in consequence of that*) daraufhin; **~'with** *adv.* (*formal*) damit

**therm** /θɜ:m/ *n.* (*Brit.*) *englische Einheit der Wärmemenge (ca. 1,055 × 10*[8] *J)*

**thermal** /'θɜ:ml/ ❶ *adj.* thermisch ‹Erscheinung, Anforderungen›; Wärme‹dämmung, -strahlung›; **~ underwear** kälteisolierende Unterwäsche.
❷ *n.* (*Aeronaut.*) Thermik, *die*

**thermal imaging** /θɜ:ml'ɪmɪdʒɪŋ/ *n.* Thermographie, *die* (*fachspr.*); Wärmebildtechnik, *die;* **~ camera** Wärmebildkamera, *die;* Thermokamera, *die*

**thermally** /'θɜ:məlɪ/ *adv.* thermisch

**thermal: ~ 'springs** *n. pl.* Thermalquelle, *die;* **~ 'unit** *n.* (*Phys.*) Wärmeeinheit, *die*

**thermionic**/θɜ:mɪ'ɒnɪk/**: ~ 'tube** (*Amer.*), **~ 'valve** (*Brit.*) *ns.* (*Electronics*) Glühkathodenröhre, *die*

**thermocouple** /'θɜ:məkʌpl/ *n.* (*Phys.*) Thermoelement, *das*

**thermodynamic** /θɜ:mədaɪ'næmɪk/ *adj.* thermodynamisch

**thermodynamics** /θɜ:mədaɪ'næmɪks/ *n., no pl.* (*Phys.*) Thermodynamik, *die*

**thermometer** /θə'mɒmɪtə(r)/ *n.* Thermometer, *das;* ⇒ *also* **clinical** A

**thermonuclear** /θɜ:məʊ'nju:klɪə(r)/ *adj.* (*Phys.*) thermonuklear ‹Waffe›; Kern‹fusion, -energie›; Atom‹krieg, -energie›

**thermoplastic** /θɜ:məʊ'plæstɪk/ ❶ *adj.* Ⓐ thermoplastisch; Ⓑ **~ tiles** Kunststofffliesen. ❷ *n.* Thermoplast, *der*

**Thermos, thermos** ® /'θɜ:məs/ *n.* **~ [flask/jug/bottle]** Thermosflasche, *die* (Wz)

**thermostat** /'θɜ:məstæt/ *n.* Thermostat, *der*

**thermostatic** /θɜ:mə'stætɪk/ *adj.* Temperatur‹regler, -schalter›

**thermostatically** /θɜ:mə'stætɪklɪ/ *adv.* durch ein/das Thermostat ‹kontrolliert, reguliert›

**thesaurus** /θɪ'sɔ:rəs/ *n., pl.* **thesauri** /θɪ'sɔ:raɪ/ *or* **~es** Thesaurus, *der*

**these** *pl. of* **this** 1, 2

**thesis** /'θi:sɪs/ *n., pl.* **theses** /'θi:si:z/ Ⓐ (*proposition*) These, *die;* Ⓑ (*dissertation*) Dissertation, *die,* Doktorarbeit, *die* (**on** über + *Akk.*)

**thespian** /'θespɪən/ (*formal*) ❶ *adj.* Theater-.
❷ *n.* Schauspieler, *der*/Schauspielerin, *die*

**they** /ðeɪ/ *pron.* Ⓐ sie; Ⓑ (*people in general*) man; Ⓒ (*coll.: he or she*) **everyone thinks ~ know best** jeder denkt, er weiß es am besten; Ⓓ (*those in authority*) sie; die (*ugs.*). ⇒ *also* **their**; **theirs**; **them**; **themselves**

**they'd** /ðeɪd/ Ⓐ = **they would;** Ⓑ = **they had**

**they'll** /ðeɪl/ ... **they will**

**they're** /ðeə(r)/ = **they are**

**they've** /ðeɪv/ ... **they have**

**thick** /θɪk/ ❶ *adj.* Ⓐ dick; breit, dick ‹Linie›; **that's laying it on [a bit] ~** (*fig. coll.*) das ist ja wohl etwas dick aufgetragen (*ugs.*); **isn't she laying it on a bit ~?** (*fig. coll.*) trägt sie da nicht ein bisschen zu dick auf? (*ugs.*); **that's** *or* **it's a bit ~!** (*Brit. fig. coll.*) das ist ein starkes Stück! (*ugs.*); **get the ~ end of the stick** (*fig.*) den schlechteren Teil erwischen; **have a ~ skin** (*fig.*) ein dickes Fell haben (*ugs.*); **a rope two inches ~, a two-inch ~ rope** ein zwei Zoll starkes *od.* dickes Seil; **B** (*dense*) dicht ‹Haar, Nebel, Wolken, Gestrüpp usw.›; dicht gedrängt ‹Menschenmenge›; **C** (*filled*) **~ with** voll von; **air ~ with fog and smoke** von Nebel und Rauch erfüllte Luft; **the air was ~ with rumours** überall gingen Gerüchte um; **the furniture was ~ with dust** auf den Möbeln lag eine dicke Staubschicht; **D** (*of firm consistency*) steif ‹Gallerte›; dickflüssig ‹Sahne›; (*containing much solid matter*) dick ‹Suppe, Schlamm, Brei, Kleister›; **E** (*stupid*) dumm; **you're just plain ~:** du bist ganz einfach doof (*salopp*); **[as] ~ as two short planks** (*coll.*) dumm wie Bohnenstroh (*ugs.*); **F** (*coll.: intimate*) **be very ~ with sb.** mit jmdm. dick befreundet sein (*ugs.*); **be [as] ~ as thieves** dicke Freunde sein (*ugs.*); **G** tief ‹Dunkelheit›; **H** (*not clear*) trüb ‹Wetter, Morgen, Fluss›; **have a ~ head** einen dicken Kopf haben (*ugs.*); **I** (*Printing*) fett; **J** (*numerous*) dicht; **they are ~/not exactly ~ on the ground** die gibt es wie Sand am Meer/die sind dünn gesät (*ugs.*); **K** (*indistinct*) dumpf; **his speech was ~** (*with drink*) er sprach mit schwerer Zunge (*geh.*); **L** (*marked*) **he has a ~ German accent** er hat einen starken deutschen Akzent.

**2** *n., no pl., no indef. art.* **in the ~ of** mitten in (+ *Dat.*); **in the ~ of it** *or* **things** mitten drin; **in the ~ of the battle** im dichtesten Kampfgetümmel; **she is always in the ~ of things** sie ist bei allem immer voll dabei (*ugs.*); **stay with sb./stick together through ~ and thin** mit jmdm./zusammen durch dick und dünn gehen.

**3** *adv.* **snow was falling ~:** es schneite dicke Flocken; **blows rained on him ~ and fast** die Schläge prasselten nur so auf ihn nieder; **job offers/complaints came in ~ and fast** es kam eine Flut von Stellenangeboten/Beschwerden

**thick 'ear** *n.* (*Brit. coll.*) **give sb. a ~:** jmdm. ein paar hinter die Ohren geben (*ugs.*)

**thicken** /ˈθɪkn/ **1** *v.t.* dicker machen; eindicken ‹Sauce›. **2** *v.i.* **A** dicker werden; **sb.'s waist[line] ~s** jmds. Taille wird umfangreicher; **B** (*become dense*) ‹Nebel:› dichter werden; **C** (*become blurred*) **his speech ~ed** er bekam eine schwere Zunge (*geh.*); **D** (*become complex*) **the plot ~s!** die Sache wird kompliziert!; (*iron.*) die Sache wird langsam interessant!

**thickening** /ˈθɪknɪŋ/ *n.* (*in food*) Bindemittel, *das;* (*in dye*) Verdickungsmittel, *das*

**thicket** /ˈθɪkɪt/ *n.* Dickicht, *das*

**thick: ~ 'head** *n.* dicker Kopf (*ugs.*); **~head** *n.* Dummkopf, *der;* **~'headed** *adj.* dumm

**thickly** /ˈθɪklɪ/ *adv.* **A** (*in a thick layer*) dick; **B** (*densely, abundantly*) dicht; **C** (*in great numbers*) **hailstones fell ~:** die Hagelkörner prasselten nur so herab; **D** (*indistinctly*) mit schwerer Zunge (*geh.*); (*from emotion*) undeutlich ‹sprechen›

**thickness** /ˈθɪknɪs/ *n.* **A** Dicke, *die;* **be two metres in ~:** zwei Meter dick sein; **a plank whose ~ is two centimetres** ein Brett mit einer Dicke *od.* Stärke von 2 Zentimetern; **~ of paper/card** Papier-/Kartonstärke, *die;* **B** *no pl.* (*denseness*) Dichte, *die;* (*of hair*) Fülle, *die;* **C** *no pl.* (*firm consistency*) (*of jelly*) Steifheit, *die;* (*of cream*) Dickflüssigkeit, *die;* (*of soup, mud, porridge, glue*) Dicke, *die;* **D** (*layer*) Lage, *die;* **E** *no pl.* (*stupidity*) Dummheit, *die*

**thicko** /ˈθɪkəʊ/ *n., pl.* **~s** (*coll.*) Schwachkopf, *der* (*ugs.*)

**thick: ~set** *adj.* **A** (*stocky*) gedrungen; **B** (*set close together*) dicht nebeneinander stehend ‹Bäume, Häuser›; **~-skinned** *adj.* (*fig.*) unsensibel; dickfellig (*ugs. abwertend*)

**thief** /θiːf/ *n., pl.* **thieves** /θiːvz/ Dieb, *der*/ Diebin, *die;* **like** *or* **as a ~ in the night** wie ein Dieb in der Nacht (*geh.*); ⇒ *also* **Latin** 2; **take** 1 Q; **thick** 1 F

**thieve** /θiːv/ **1** *v.i.* stehlen; **he makes a living out of petty thieving** er lebt vom Gelegenheitsdiebstahl. **2** *v.t.* stehlen

**thieves** *pl. of* **thief**

**thievish** /ˈθiːvɪʃ/ *adj.* diebisch ‹Wesen, Art›

**thigh** /θaɪ/ *n.* **A** ▶**966** (*Anat.*) Oberschenkel, *der;* **B** (*Zool.*) Schenkel, *der*

**thigh: ~ bone** *n.* (*Anat.*) Oberschenkelknochen, *der;* **~ boot** *n.* Kanonenstiefel, *der;* Schaftstiefel, *der*

**-thighed** /θaɪd/ *adj. in comb.* -schenkelig

**thimble** /ˈθɪmbl/ *n.* Fingerhut, *der*

**thimbleful** /ˈθɪmblfʊl/ *n.* Fingerhut [voll], *der;* **in ~s** in winzigen Mengen

**thin** /θɪn/ **1** *adj.* **A** (*of small thickness or diameter*) dünn; ⇒ *also* **ice** 1 A; **wedge** 1 A; **B** (*not fat*) dünn; **a tall, ~ man** ein großer, hagerer Mann; **as ~ as a rake** *or* **lath** spindeldürr; **C** (*narrow*) schmal ‹Baumreihe›; dünn ‹Linie›; **D** (*sparse*) dünn, schütter ‹Haar›; fein ‹Regen, Dunst›; spärlich ‹Publikum, Besuch›; gering ‹Beteiligung›; dünn ‹Luft›; **the country's population is ~:** das Land ist dünn bevölkert *od.* besiedelt; **he is already ~ on top** *or* **going ~ on top** bei ihm lichtet es sich oben schon; **the attendance at the meeting was ~:** die Versammlung war schwach besucht; **be ~ on the ground** (*fig.*) dünn gesät sein; **vanish** *or* **disappear into ~ air** (*fig.*) sich in Luft auflösen; **it won't appear out of ~ air!** (*fig.*) es fällt nicht einfach vom Himmel!; **produce a delicious meal out of ~ air** (*fig.*) ein köstliches Essen aus dem Nichts zaubern; **E** (*lacking substance or strength*) dünn ‹Bier, Blut, Stimme›; **F** (*fig.: inadequate*) dürftig; fadenscheinig ‹Ausrede›; **sb.'s patience is wearing ~:** jmds. Geduld geht zu Ende; jmdm. reißt allmählich der Geduldsfaden (*ugs.*); **sb.'s credibility begins to wear ~:** jmd. verliert immer mehr an Glaubwürdigkeit; **G** (*coll.: wretched*) enttäuschend, unbefriedigend ‹Zeit›; **he had a pretty ~ time [of it]** er machte eine ziemlich schlimme Zeit durch; **H** (*consisting of ~ lines*) fein ‹Handschrift›; (*Printing*) mager. ⇒ *also* **thick** 2.

**2** *adv.* dünn.

**3** *v.t.*, **-nn-**: **A** (*make less deep or broad*) dünner machen; **B** (*make less dense, dilute*) verdünnen; **C** (*reduce in number*) dezimieren; **D** (*remove young fruit from*) ausbrechen ‹Reben›; ausdünnen ‹Obstbäume›.

**4** *v.i.*, **-nn-** ‹Haar, Nebel:› sich lichten; ‹Menschenmenge:› sich zerstreuen; **~ down to a mere trickle** zu einem kleinen Rinnsal werden

**~ 'out 1** *v.i.* ‹Menschenmenge:› sich verlaufen; ‹Verkehr:› abnehmen; ‹Reihen der Zuschauer:› sich lichten; ‹Häuser:› spärlicher werden. **2** *v.t.* (*Hort., Forestry*) vereinzeln, ausdünnen ‹Pflanzen›; lichten ‹Wald›

**thine** /ðaɪn/ *poss. pron.* (*arch./poet./dial.*) **A** *pred.* deiner/deine/dein[e]s; der/die/das Deinige (*geh.*); ⇒ *also* **hers**; **B** *attrib.* dein

**thing** /θɪŋ/ *n.* **A** (*inanimate object*) Sache, *die;* Ding, *das;* **what's that ~ in your hand?** was hast du da in der Hand?; **be a rare ~:** etwas Seltenes sein; **books are strange** *or* (*coll.*) **funny ~s, aren't they?** Bücher sind schon etwas Seltsames, nicht wahr?; **neither one ~ nor the other** weder das eine noch das andere; **I haven't a '~ to wear** ich habe nichts zum Anziehen; **you haven't a ~ to worry about** du brauchst dir überhaupt keine Sorgen zu machen; **not a ~:** überhaupt *od.* gar nichts; **B** (*action*) **that was a foolish/friendly ~ to do** das war eine große Dummheit/das war sehr freundlich; **that was a mean ~ to do to your brother** das war sehr gemein deinem Bruder gegenüber; **it was the right ~ to do** es war das einzig Richtige; **she is expecting to do great ~s** sie hat große Dinge vor; **the only ~ now is to shout for help** es bleibt uns jetzt nichts anderes mehr übrig, als um Hilfe zu rufen; **we can't do a ~ about it** wir können nichts dagegen tun; **do ~s to sb./sth.** (*fig. coll.*) auf jmdn./etw. eine enorme Wirkung haben (*ugs.*); **she does ~s to me** (*fig. coll.*) sie macht mich total an (*ugs.*); **C** (*fact*) [Tat]sache, *die;* **a ~ which is well known to everybody** eine allgemein bekannte Tatsache; **it's a strange ~ that …:** es ist seltsam, dass …; **for one ~, you don't have enough money[, for another ~ …]** zunächst einmal hast du nicht genügend Geld [, außerdem …]; **and another ~, why were you late this morning?** und noch etwas: Warum bist du heute Morgen so spät gekommen?; **the best/worst ~ about the situation/her** das Beste/Schlimmste an der Situation/an ihr; **know/learn a ~ or two about sth./sb.** sich mit etw./jmdm. auskennen/einiges über etw. (*Akk.*) lernen/über jmdn. erfahren; **I'll teach him a ~ or two!** dem werde ichs [mal] zeigen!; **the [only] ~ is that …:** die Sache ist [nur] die, dass …; ⇒ *also* **another** 1 A, D, 2 C; **D** (*idea*) **say the first ~ that comes into one's head** das sagen, was einem gerade so einfällt; **what a ~ to say!** wie kann man nur so etwas sagen!; **have a ~ about sb./sth.** (*coll.*) (*be obsessed about*) auf jmdn./etw. abfahren (*salopp*); (*be prejudiced about*) etwas gegen jmdn./etw. haben; (*be afraid of or repulsed by*) einen Horror vor jmdm./etw. haben (*ugs.*); **E** (*task*) **she has a reputation for getting ~s done** sie ist für ihre Tatkraft bekannt; **a big ~ to undertake** ein großes Unterfangen; **F** (*affair*) Sache, *die;* Angelegenheit, *die;* **make a mess of ~s** alles vermasseln (*salopp*); **make a [big] ~ of sth.** (*regard as essential*) auf etw. besonderen Wert legen; (*get excited about*) sich über etw. (*Akk.*) aufregen; **you don't have to make such a big ~ of it!** nun mach mal halblang! (*ugs.*); **it's one ~ after another** es kommt eins zum anderen; **G** (*circumstance*) **take ~s too seriously** alles zu ernst nehmen; **how are ~s?** wie gehts [dir]?; **it was a terrible ~:** es war furchtbar; **a strange ~ struck me** mir fiel etwas Seltsames auf; **it was a lucky ~ he didn't do that** es war ein Glück, dass er das nicht tat; **as ~s stand [with me]** so wie die Dinge [bei mir] liegen; **one has to accept these ~s** man muss sich eben damit abfinden; **~s don't work out like that** die Realität sieht anders aus; **it's just one of those ~s** (*coll.*) so was kommt schon mal vor (*ugs.*); ⇒ *also* **close** 1 G; **good** 1 B; **H** (*individual, creature*) Ding, *das;* **she is in hospital, poor ~:** sie ist im Krankenhaus, das arme Ding; **you spiteful ~!** du [gemeines] Biest!; **she's a kind old ~:** sie ist sehr liebenswürdig *od.* (*ugs.*) furchtbar nett; ⇒ *also* **old** 1 C, D; **I** *in pl.* (*personal belongings, outer clothing*) Sachen; **put one's ~s on** sich (*Dat.*) etwas überziehen; **wash up the dinner ~s** das Geschirr vom Abendessen abwaschen; **J** *in pl.* (*matters*) **an expert/authority on ~s historical** ein Fachmann/eine Autorität in geschichtlichen Fragen; **as regards ~s financial I haven't a clue** von finanziellen Dingen habe ich keine Ahnung; **~s feminine** Frauenangelegenheiten; **and ~s** (*coll.*) und so (*ugs.*); **K** (*product of work*) Sache, *die;* **the latest ~ in hats** der letzte Schrei in der Hutmode; **a little ~ of mine** etwas von mir; **L** (*special interest*) **what's your ~?** was machst du gerne?; **do one's own ~** (*coll.*) sich selbst verwirklichen; **we each do our own ~ on holiday** im Urlaub macht jeder von uns, was er will; **M** (*coll.: sth. remarkable*) **now 'there's a ~!** das ist ja ein Ding! (*ugs.*); **N** *in pl.* (*Law*) Sachen; **~s real** unbewegliche Sachen; Immobilien; **~s personal** bewegliche Sachen; Mobilien (*fachspr.*); **O the ~** (*what is proper or needed or important*) das Richtige; **blue jeans are the ~ among teenagers** Bluejeans sind der Hit (*ugs.*) unter den Teenagern; **telling jokes is not the ~ for an occasion such as this one** es ist unpassend, bei einer Gelegenheit wie dieser Witze zu erzählen; **the ~ is to get orders** es geht vor allem darum, Aufträge zu bekommen; **the ~ about him is his complete integrity** sein wesentlicher Vorzug ist seine vollkommene Integrität; **but the ~ is, will she come in fact?** aber die Frage ist, wird sie auch tatsächlich kommen?; **P** (*sl.: penis*) **his**

~: sein Ding (*ugs.*). ⇒ *also* first 1, 2 A; good 1 D; last¹ 1; see¹ 1 A; sure 3

**thingamy** /'θɪŋəmɪ/, **thingumabob** /'θɪŋəməbɒb/, **thingumajig** /'θɪŋəmədʒɪg/, **thingumbob** /'θɪŋəmbɒb/, **thingummy** /'θɪŋəmɪ/, **thingy** /'θɪŋɪ/ *ns.* (*coll.*) Dings, *der/die/das* (*salopp*); Dingsbums, *der/die/das* (*ugs.*); **you know, ~, ...** (*person*) du weißt schon, der/die Dingsda, ...; (*object*) du weißt schon, das Dingsda, ...

**think** /θɪŋk/ **1** *v.t.*, **thought** /θɔ:t/ **A** (*consider*) meinen; **we ~ [that] he will come** wir denken *od.* glauben, dass er kommt; **we do not ~ it probable** wir halten es nicht für wahrscheinlich; **I ~ it a shame that ...:** ich finde, es ist eine Schande, dass ...; **he ~s himself very fine** er meint, er sei etwas Besonderes; **it is not thought proper** es gilt als unschicklich; **he is thought to be a fraud** man hält ihn für einen Betrüger; **what do you ~?** was meinst du?; **what do you ~ of** *or* **about him/it?** was hältst du von ihm/davon?; **I thought to myself ...:** ich dachte mir [im Stillen]...; **that's what 'they ~!** das meinen die!; **..., don't you ~?** ..., findest *od.* meinst du nicht auch?; **where do you ~ you are?** was glaubst du eigentlich, wo du bist?; **who does he/she ~ he/she is?** für wen *od.* wofür hält er/sie sich eigentlich?; **you** *or* **one** *or* **anyone would ~ that ...:** man sollte [doch] eigentlich annehmen, dass ...; **I ~ not** ich glaube nicht; **I should '~ so/~ 'not!** (*indignant*) das will ich meinen/das will ich nicht hoffen; **I thought as much** *or* **so** das habe ich mir schon gedacht; **I ~ so** ich glaube schon; **do you really ~ so?** findest du wirklich?; **I wouldn't ~ so** das glaube ich kaum; **yes, I ~ so too** ja, das finde ich auch (*ugs.*); **I should ~ not!** (*no!*) auf keinen Fall; **you are a model of tact, I 'don't ~!** (*coll. iron.*) du bist mir vielleicht ein Ausbund von Taktgefühl! (*iron.*); **that'll be great fun, I 'don't ~** (*coll. iron.*) das kann ja lustig werden (*ugs. iron.*); **I'll have made my fortune by then, I 'don't ~** (*coll. iron.*) na klar, bis dahin habe ich mein Glück gemacht (*iron.*); **to ~ [that] he should treat me like this!** man sollte es nicht für möglich halten, dass er mich so behandelt!; **this animal was thought to be extinct** dieses Tier galt als ausgestorben; **I wouldn't have thought it possible** ich hätte das nicht für möglich gehalten; **B** (*coll.: remember*) **~ to do sth.** daran denken, etw. zu tun; **C** (*intend*) **he ~s to deceive us** er will uns täuschen; **we thought to return early** wir hatten vor *od.* gedachten, früh zurückzukehren; **that's what 'they ~!** das meinen die [vielleicht]!; **D** (*imagine*) sich (*Dat.*) vorstellen.

**2** *v.i.*, **thought** **A** [nach]denken; **I ~, therefore I am** ich denke, also bin ich; **we want to make the students ~:** wir möchten die Studenten zum Denken bringen; **animals cannot ~:** Tiere können nicht denken; **I need time to ~:** ich muss es mir erst überlegen; **ability to ~:** Denkfähigkeit, *die;* **I've been ~ing** ich habe nachgedacht; **~ in German** *etc.* deutsch *usw.* denken; **it makes you ~:** es macht *od.* stimmt einen nachdenklich; **just ~!** stell dir das mal vor!; **~ for oneself** sich (*Dat.*) seine eigene Meinung bilden; **~ [to oneself] ...:** sich (*Dat.*) im stillen denken ...; bei sich denken ...; **let me ~:** lass [mich] mal nachdenken *od.* überlegen; **I would ~ again** ich würde mir das noch mal überlegen; **there's still time to ~ again** du kannst/wir können das noch einmal überdenken; **you'd better ~ again!** da hast du dich aber geschnitten! (*ugs.*); **~ twice** es sich (*Dat.*) zweimal überlegen; **this made her ~ twice** das gab ihr zu denken; **~ twice about doing sth.** es sich (*Dat.*) zweimal überlegen, ob man etw. tut; **~ on one's feet** (*coll.*) sich (*Dat.*) aus dem Stegreif etwas überlegen; ⇒ *also* big 2; **B** (*have intention*) **I ~ I'll try** ich glaube *od.* denke, ich werde es versuchen; **we ~ we'll enter for the regatta** wir haben vor, an der Regatta teilzunehmen. ⇒ *also* aloud; fit² 1 C.

**3** *n.* (*coll.*) **have a [good] ~:** es sich (*Dat.*) gut überlegen; **have a ~ about that!** denk mal drüber nach! (*ugs.*); **you have [got] another ~ coming!** da irrst du dich aber gewaltig!

**~ about** *v.t.* **A** (*consider*) nachdenken über (+ *Akk.*); **what are you ~ing about?** woran *od.* was denkst du [gerade]?; **give sb. something to ~ about** jmdm. etwas geben, worüber er/sie nachdenken kann; (*to worry about*) jmdm. zu denken geben; **it doesn't bear ~ing about** man darf gar nicht daran denken; **B** (*consider practicability of*) sich (*Dat.*) durch den Kopf gehen lassen; sich (*Dat.*) überlegen; **it's worth ~ing about** es ist überlegenswert

**~ a'head** *v.i.* vorausdenken

**~ 'back to** *v.t.* sich zurückerinnern an (+ *Akk.*); **I thought back to when it had first begun** ich erinnerte mich daran, wie es anfing

**~ of** *v.t.* **A** (*consider*) denken an (+ *Akk.*); **I have many things to ~ of** ich muss an so vieles denken; **... but I can't ~ of everything at once!** ... aber ich habe schließlich auch nur einen Kopf!; **he ~s of everything** er denkt einfach an alles; **he never ~s of anyone but himself** er denkt immer nur an sich; **[just] ~** *or* **to ~ of it!** man stelle sich (*Dat.*) *od.* stell dir das bloß vor!; **[now I] come to ~ of it, ...:** wenn ich es mir recht überlege, ...; **B** (*be aware of in the mind*) denken an (+ *Akk.*); **we ~ of you a lot** wir denken oft an dich; **C** (*consider the possibility of*) denken an (+ *Akk.*); **we must be ~ing of going home soon** wir müssen bald ans Nachhausegehen denken; **be ~ing of getting a new car** mit dem Gedanken spielen, sich (*Dat.*) ein neues Auto anzuschaffen; **be ~ing of resigning** sich mit dem Gedanken tragen, zurückzutreten; **not for a minute would she ~ of helping anybody else** ihr würde es nicht im Traum einfallen, anderen zu helfen; **I couldn't ~ of such a thing** *or* **of doing that** das würde mir nicht im Traum einfallen; **I don't know what she was ~ing of!** ich weiß nicht, was sie sich dabei gedacht hat!; **D** (*choose from what one knows*) **I want you to ~ of a word beginning with B** überlege dir ein Wort, das mit B beginnt; **~ of a number, double it and ...:** denk dir eine Zahl, verdoppele sie und ...; **E** (*have as idea*) **we'll ~ of something** wir werden uns etwas einfallen lassen; **can you ~ of anyone who ...?** fällt dir jemand ein, der ...?; **we're still trying to ~ of a suitable title for the book** wir suchen noch immer einen passenden Titel für das Buch; **he's never yet thought of showing gratitude** bis jetzt ist es ihm noch nie eingefallen, sich dankbar zu zeigen; **I would have telephoned if I had thought of it** ich hätte angerufen, wenn ich daran gedacht hätte; **what 'will they ~ of next?** was werden sie sich (*Dat.*) wohl [sonst] noch alles einfallen lassen?; **F** (*remember*) sich erinnern an (+ *Akk.*); **I just can't ~ of her name** ich komme einfach nicht auf ihren Namen; **G ~ little/nothing of sb./sth.** (*consider contemptible*) wenig/nichts von jmdm./etw. halten; **~ little/nothing of sth.** (*consider insignificant*) wenig/nichts dabei finden, etw. zu tun; **~ much** *or* **a lot** *or* **well** *or* **highly of sb./sth.** viel von jmdm./etw. halten; **not ~ much of sb./sth.** nicht viel von jmdm./etw. halten. ⇒ *also* better 3 A

**~ 'out** *v.t.* **A** (*consider carefully*) durchdenken ‹Plan, Idee›; **~ out what the long-term solution may be** sich (*Dat.*) darüber Gedanken machen, wie eine langfristige Lösung aussehen könnte; **B** (*devise*) sich (*Dat.*) ausdenken ‹Plan, Verfahren›; **the plan had been thought out in a hurry** der Plan entstand unter Zeitdruck

**~ 'over** *v.t.* sich (*Dat.*) überlegen; überdenken; **~ things over** die Lage überdenken; **I will ~ it over** ich lasse es mir durch den Kopf gehen

**~ 'through** *v.t.* [gründlich] durchdenken ‹Problem, Angelegenheit›

**~ 'up** *v.t.* (*coll.*) sich (*Dat.*) ausdenken ‹Plan›; **they thought up ideas of their own** sie entwickelten ihre eigenen Ideen

**thinkable** /'θɪŋkəbl/ *adj.* **A** (*capable of being thought about*) denkbar; **B** (*conceivably possible*) vorstellbar

**thinker** /'θɪŋkə(r)/ *n.* Denker, *der*/Denkerin, *die*

**thinking** /'θɪŋkɪŋ/ **1** *n.* **in modern ~ ...** nach heutiger Auffassung ...; **what is your ~ on this question?** wie ist deine Meinung zu dieser Frage?; **to my [way of] ~:** meiner Meinung nach. **2** *attrib. adj.* [vernünftig] denkend

**'thinking cap** *n.* **put on one's ~:** scharf nachdenken; seinen Geist anstrengen

**think: ~ piece** *n.* Kommentar, *der;* **~ tank** *n.* **A** (*organization*) Beraterstab, *der;* **B** (*Amer. coll.: brain*) [Ge]hirnkasten, *der* (*salopp scherzh.*)

**'thin-lipped** *adj.* dünnlippig ‹Mund, Person›

**thinly** /'θɪnlɪ/ *adv.* **A** dünn; **B** (*sparsely*) spärlich ‹bevölkert, bewaldet›; dünn ‹besiedelt›; schwach ‹besucht›; **C** (*inadequately*) leicht ‹bekleidet›; (*fig.*) dürftig ‹verschleiert, verkleidet›

**thinner** /'θɪnə(r)/ **1** *adj., adv. compar. of* thin 1, 2. **2** *n.* **~[s]** Verdünner, *der;* Verdünnungsmittel, *das*

**thinness** /'θɪnnɪs/ *n., no pl.* **A** (*lack of depth etc.*) Dünne, *die;* geringe Dicke; **B** (*slimness*) Magerkeit, *die;* **C** (*sparseness*) Spärlichkeit, *die;* **D** (*slightness of consistency*) Dünnflüssigkeit, *die;* **E** (*lack of substance or strength*) Dürftigkeit, *die;* **the ~ of her voice** ihre dünne Stimme; **F** (*fig.: inadequacy*) Dürftigkeit, *die*

**'thin-skinned** *adj.* (*fig.*) empfindlich; dünnhäutig (*geh.*)

**third** /θɜ:d/ **1** *adj.* ▶ 1352 dritt...; **the ~ finger** der Ringfinger; **~ largest/highest** *etc.* drittgrößt.../-höchst... *usw.;* **come in/be ~:** Dritter/Dritte sein/als Dritter/Dritte ankommen; **every ~ week** jede dritte Woche; **a ~ part** *or* **share** ein Drittel.
**2** *n.* **A** (*in sequence, rank*) Dritte, *der/die/das;* (*fraction*) Drittel, *das;* **be the ~ to arrive** als Dritter/Dritte ankommen; **B** (*~ form*) dritte [Schul]klasse; Dritte, *die* (*Schuljargon*); **C** (*Motor Veh.*) dritter Gang; **in ~:** im dritten [Gang]; **change into ~:** in den dritten [Gang] schalten; **D** (*Brit. Univ.*) Drei, *die;* **he has a ~ [in History]** er hat eine Drei [in Geschichte]; **get** *or* **take** *or* **be awarded a ~ in one's finals** sein Examen mit [der Note] Drei bestehen; **E** (*Mus.*) Terz, *die;* **F** ▶ 1055 (*day*) **the ~ of May** der dritte Mai; **the ~ [of the month]** der Dritte [des Monats]. ⇒ *also* eighth 2

**third: ~-best 1** /'--/ *adj.* drittbest...; **2** /-'-/ *n., no pl.* Drittbeste, *der/die/das;* **~ 'class** *n.* **A** (*set ranking after second class*) dritte Kategorie; **B** (*Transport*) dritte Klasse; **C** (*Brit. Univ.*) ⇒ third 2 D; **~-class 1** /'--/ *adj.* **A** drittklassig; **he got a ~-class degree** er hat einen Abschluss mit der Note Drei; **B** Dritte[r]-Klasse-‹Wagen, Reisender, Fahrkarte›; ‹Wagen, Fahrkarte› dritter Klasse; ‹Reisender› der dritten Klasse; **2** /-'-/ *adv.* dritter Klasse ‹reisen›; **~ de'gree** ⇒ degree I; **~ 'force** *n.* dritte Kraft; **~ form** ⇒ form 1 D; **~ 'gear** *n., no pl.* (*Motor Veh.*) dritter Gang; ⇒ *also* gear 1 A

**thirdly** /'θɜ:dlɪ/ *adv.* drittens

**third: ~ 'man** *n.* (*Cricket*) [weit zurückstehender] Eckmann; **~ 'party** *n.* Dritte, *der/die;* dritte Person; *attrib.* **~-party insurance** Haftpflichtversicherung, *die;* **be covered by ~-party insurance** haftpflichtversichert sein; **take out ~-party insurance** eine Haftpflichtversicherung abschließen; **~ 'person** *n.* **A** ⇒ **~ party;** **B** ⇒ person D; **~ 'rail** *n.* (*Railw.*) Stromschiene, *die;* **~-rate** *adj.* drittklassig; **~ 'reading** ⇒ reading G; **T~ 'World** *n.* Dritte Welt; **countries of the T~ World, T~ World countries** Länder der Dritten Welt

**thirst** /θɜ:st/ **1** *n.* Durst, *der;* **die of ~:** verdursten; (*fig.: be very thirsty*) vor Durst sterben (*ugs.*); **~ for knowledge** Wissensdurst, *der;* **~ for revenge/after fame** Rachedurst, *der*/Ruhmsucht, *die;* **~ for news** sehnsüchtiges Warten auf Nachricht. **2** *v.i.* **~ for revenge/knowledge** nach Rache/Wissen dürsten (*geh.*)

t

**thirstily** /ˈθɜːstɪlɪ/ *adv.* durstig

ˈ**thirst-quencher** *n.* Durstlöscher, *der*

**thirsty** /ˈθɜːstɪ/ *adj.* Ⓐ durstig; **be ~:** Durst haben; **sb. is ~ for sth.** (*fig.*) jmd. *od.* jmdn. dürstet nach etw. (*dichter.*); **~ after gain/for knowledge/revenge** (*fig.*) gewinnsüchtig/wissbegierig/rachedurstig (*geh.*); Ⓑ (*coll.: causing thirst*) durstig machend; **this is ~ work** diese Arbeit macht durstig

**thirteen** /θɜːˈtiːn/ ▶912, ▶1012, ▶1352 ❶ *adj.* dreizehn; ⇒ *also* **eight** 1. ❷ *n.* Dreizehn, *die;* ⇒ *also* **eight** 2 A, D; **eighteen** 2

**thirteenth** /θɜːˈtɪːnθ/ ▶1055 ❶ *adj.* ▶1352 dreizehnt...; ⇒ *also* **eighth** 1. ❷ *n.* Ⓐ (*fraction*) Dreizehntel, *das;* Ⓑ **Friday the ~:** Freitag, der Dreizehnte. ⇒ *also* **eighth** 2

**thirtieth** /ˈθɜːtɪɪθ/ ▶1055 ❶ *adj.* ▶1352 dreißigst...; ⇒ *also* **eighth** 1. ❷ *n.* (*fraction*) Dreißigstel, *das;* ⇒ *also* **eighth** 2

**thirty** /ˈθɜːtɪ/ ▶912, ▶1012, ▶1352 ❶ *adj.* dreißig; **one-and-~** (*arch.*) ⇒ **thirty-one** 1; ⇒ *also* **eight** 1. ❷ *n.* Dreißig, *die;* **one-and-~** (*arch.*) ⇒ **thirty-one** 2; ⇒ *also* **eight** 2 A; **eighty** 2

**thirty: ~-ˈfirst** *etc. adj.* ▶1055, ▶1352 einunddreißigst... *usw.;* ⇒ *also* **eighth** 1; **~-ˈone** *etc.* ❶ *adj.* einunddreißig *usw.;* ⇒ *also* **eight** 1; ❷ *n.* ▶1352 Einunddreißig *usw., die;* ⇒ *also* **eight** 2 A; **~-ˈsecond-note** *n.* (*Amer. Mus.*) Zweiunddreißigstel[note], *die;* **~-something** ❶ *adj.* **a ~-something woman/man** eine Frau/ein Mann in den Dreißigern; **be ~-something** in den Dreißigern sein; dreißig und noch was [alt] sein; ❷ *n.* Dreißiger, *der*/-in, *die;* Mann/Frau in den Dreißigern; **~-somethings** Leute in den Dreißigern

**this** /ðɪs/ ❶ *adj., pl.* **these** /ðiːz/ Ⓐ dieser/diese/dieses; (*with less emphasis*) der/die/das; **at ~ time** zu dieser Zeit; **before ~ time** vorher; zuvor; **these days** heut[zutag]e; **I'll say ~ much/I can tell you ~ much ...:** so viel kann ich sagen/so viel kann ich dir verraten ...; Ⓑ (*that is the present*) dieser/diese/dieses; **all ~ week** die[se] ganze Woche; **by ~ time** inzwischen; mittlerweile; Ⓒ (*of today*) **~ morning/evening** *etc.* heute Morgen/Abend *usw.;* **where are you going to eat ~ lunchtime?** wo wirst du heute zu Mittag essen?; Ⓓ (*just past*) **these last three weeks** die letzten drei Wochen; **~ day has been a really hard one** der heutige Tag war wirklich anstrengend; Ⓔ (*to come*) **~ Monday** nächsten Montag; **it will not be wanted these eight months** es wird in den nächsten acht Monaten nicht gebraucht werden; Ⓕ (*coll.: previously unspecified*) **they dug ~ great big trench** sie hoben einen riesigen Graben aus; **I was in the pub when ~ fellow came up to me** ich war in der Kneipe, als [so] einer *od.* so'n Typ auf mich zukam (*ugs.*); Ⓖ **he's tried ~ drink and that [drink]** *or* **~ and that drink** er hat schon so manchen Drink *od.* schon allerlei Drinks probiert; **I went to ~ doctor and that** ich ging von einem Arzt zum anderen. ⇒ *also* **that** 1 C; **world** B.

❷ *pron., pl.* **these** Ⓐ **what's ~?** was ist [denn] das?; **what is all ~?** was soll das alles?; **what flower is ~?** was ist das für eine Blume?; **fold it like ~!** falte es so!; **I knew all ~ before** ich wusste dies *od.* das alles schon vorher; **~ is not fair!** das ist nicht fair!; **what's all ~ about Jan and Angela separating?** stimmt das, dass Jan und Angela sich trennen wollen?; **what's ~ about holidays?** was war da mit Ferien?; **John, ~ is Mary** John, das ist Mary; ⇒ *also* **it**[1] J; Ⓑ (*the present*) **before ~:** bis jetzt; Ⓒ (*Brit. Teleph.: person speaking*) **~ is Andy [speaking]** hier [spricht *od.* ist] Andy; Ⓓ (*Amer. Teleph.: person spoken to*) **who did you say ~ was?** wer ist am Apparat?; mit wem spreche ich, bitte?; Ⓔ **~ and that** dies und das; **~, that, and the other** alles Mögliche.

❸ *adv.* (*coll.*) so; **~ much** so viel

**thistle** /ˈθɪsl/ *n.* Distel, *die*

ˈ**thistledown** *n.* Distelwolle, *die;* **[as] light as ~:** leicht wie eine Feder

**thither** /ˈðɪðə(r)/ *adv.* (*arch.*) dorthin; ⇒ *also* **hither**

**tho'** ⇒ **though**

**thong** /θɒŋ/ *n.* [Leder]riemen, *der*

**thoracic** /θɔːˈræsɪk/ *adj.* (*Anat.*) Thorax-; Brust‹höhle, -segment, -wirbel›

**thorax** /ˈθɔːræks/ *n., pl.* **thoraces** /ˈθɔːrəsiːz/ *or* **~es** (*Anat., Zool.*) Thorax, *der*

**thorn** /θɔːn/ *n.* Ⓐ (*part of plant*) Dorn, *der;* **be on ~s** (*fig.*) wie auf Nesseln sitzen (*ugs.*); Ⓑ (*plant*) Dornenstrauch, *der;* Ⓒ **a ~ in the flesh** *or* **side/in sb.'s flesh** *or* **side** ein Pfahl im Fleische/im Fleische für jmdn.

**thorn bush** *n.* Dornbusch, *der*

**thornless** /ˈθɔːnlɪs/ *adj.* dornenlos

**thorny** /ˈθɔːnɪ/ *adj.* Ⓐ dornig; Ⓑ (*fig.: difficult*) heikel; dornenreich ‹Weg›

**thorough** /ˈθʌrə/ *adj.* Ⓐ gründlich; durchgreifend ‹Reform›; genau ‹Beschreibung, Anweisung›; Ⓑ (*downright*) ausgemacht ‹Halunke, Nervensäge›; tief ‹Verachtung›. ⇒ *also* **bass**[3] 2 C

**thorough: ~bred** ❶ *adj.* Ⓐ reinrassig ‹Tier›; vollblütig ‹Pferd›; Ⓑ (*fig.*) rassig ‹Sportwagen›; ❷ *n.* Ⓐ reinrassiges Tier; (*horse*) Rassepferd, *das;* (*Horse Racing*) Vollblut, *das;* Ⓑ (*fig.: car*) Klassewagen, *der* (*ugs.*); **~fare** *n.* Durchfahrtsstraße, *die;* **'no ~fare'** „Durchfahrt verboten"; (*on foot*) „kein Durchgang"; **~going** *adj.* Ⓐ ⇒ **thorough** A; Ⓑ (*extreme*) radikal ‹Konservative, Sozialist›; ausgemacht ‹Halunke›

**thoroughly** /ˈθʌrəlɪ/ *adv.* gründlich ‹untersuchen, prüfen›; gehörig ‹müde, erschöpft›; so richtig ‹genießen›; ausgesprochen ‹langweilig›; zutiefst ‹beschämt›; (*completely*) völlig ‹durchnässt, verzogen›; total ‹verdorben, verwöhnt›; **be ~ fed up with sth.** (*coll.*) von etw. die Nase gestrichen voll haben (*ugs.*); **be ~ delighted with sth.** sich außerordentlich über etw. (*Akk.*) freuen

**thoroughness** /ˈθʌrənɪs/ *n., no pl.* Gründlichkeit, *die*

**those** ⇒ **that** 1, 2

**thou**[1] /ðaʊ/ *pron.* (*arch./poet./dial.*) du; (*Relig.: God*) Du

**thou**[2] /θaʊ/ *n., pl. same* (*coll.*) Ⓐ ⇒ **thousand** 2 A; Ⓑ (*Mech. Engin.*) tausendstel Inch

**though** /ðəʊ/ ❶ *conj.* Ⓐ (*despite the fact that*) obwohl; **late ~ it was** obwohl es so spät war; **the car, ~ powerful, is also economical** der Wagen ist zwar stark, aber [zugleich] auch wirtschaftlich; Ⓑ (*but nevertheless*) aber; **a slow ~ certain method** eine langsame, aber *od.* wenn auch sichere Methode; Ⓒ (*even if*) **[even] ~:** auch wenn; **as ~ = as if** ⇒ **if** 1 A; Ⓓ (*and yet*) **~ you never know** obwohl man nie weiß; **she read on, ~ not to the very end** sie las weiter, wenn auch nicht bis ganz zum Schluss. ❷ *adv.* (*coll.*) trotzdem; **I like him ~:** ich mag ihn aber [trotzdem]; **you don't know him, ~:** aber du kennst ihn nicht

**thought** /θɔːt/ ❶ ⇒ **think** 1, 2. ❷ *n.* Ⓐ *no pl.* Denken, *das;* **[lost] in ~:** in Gedanken [verloren *od.* versunken]; **quick as ~:** blitzschnell; **Greek/Western ~:** das Denken der Griechen/das westliche Denken; Ⓑ *no pl., no art.* (*reflection*) Überlegung, *die;* Nachdenken, *das;* **act without ~:** gedankenlos handeln; **after serious ~:** nach reiflicher Überlegung; Ⓒ (*consideration*) Rücksicht, *die* (**for** auf + *Akk.*); **he has no ~/is full of ~ for others** er nimmt keine Rücksicht auf andere/ist sehr rücksichtsvoll anderen gegenüber; **give [plenty of] ~ to sth., give sth. [plenty of] ~:** [reiflich] über etw. (*Akk.*) nachdenken; **give no ~ to sth.** an etw. (*Akk.*) nicht denken; **he never gave the matter a moment's ~:** er dachte keinen Augenblick daran; **take ~:** überlegen; **she criticized his lack of ~ for his parents** sie kritisierte, dass er zu wenig an seine Eltern dachte; **built with some ~ for the crew** mit Blick auf die Mannschaft gebaut; **with no ~ for her own safety** ohne an ihre eigene Sicherheit zu denken; Ⓓ (*idea, conception*) Gedanke, *der;* **I've just had a ~!** mir ist gerade ein [guter] Gedanke gekommen; **it's the ~ that counts** der gute Wille zählt; **his one ~ is how to get rich** er hat nichts anderes im Sinn, als reich zu werden; **he hasn't a ~ in his head** er ist ein Schussel (*ugs.*); **at the [very] ~ of sth./of doing sth./that ...:** beim [bloßen] Gedanken an etw. (*Akk.*)/daran, etw. zu tun/, dass ...; **that's** *or* **there's a ~!** das ist aber eine [gute] Idee!; **don't give it another ~:** mach dir darüber keine Gedanken; **she is [constantly] in his ~s** er muss ständig an sie denken; ⇒ *also* **penny** C; Ⓔ *in pl.* (*opinion*) Gedanken; **I'll tell you my ~s on the matter** ich sage dir, wie ich darüber denke; Ⓕ (*intention*) **have no ~ of doing sth.** überhaupt nicht daran denken, etw. zu tun; **give up all ~[s] of sth./doing sth.** sich (*Dat.*) etw. aus dem Kopf schlagen/es sich (*Dat.*) aus dem Kopf schlagen, etw. zu tun; **have some ~s of doing sth.** sich mit dem Gedanken tragen *od.* mit dem Gedanken spielen, etw. zu tun; **nothing was further from my ~s** nicht im Traum hätte ich daran gedacht; Ⓖ (*somewhat*) **a ~ arrogant/more considerate** ein wenig arrogant/rücksichtsvoller

**thoughtful** /ˈθɔːtfl/ *adj.* Ⓐ (*meditative*) nachdenklich; Ⓑ (*considerate*) rücksichtsvoll; (*helpful*) aufmerksam; Ⓒ (*showing original thought*) gedankenreich; (*well thought out*) [gut] durchdacht; wohl überlegt ‹Bemerkung›

**thoughtfully** /ˈθɔːtfəlɪ/ *adv.* Ⓐ (*meditatively*) nachdenklich; Ⓑ (*considerately*) rücksichtsvollerweise; **she ~ provided blankets** sie war so umsichtig, Decken bereitzustellen; Ⓒ (*in a well thought out manner*) **a ~ written article** ein gut durchdachter Artikel

**thoughtfulness** /ˈθɔːtflnɪs/ *n., no pl.* ⇒ **thoughtful**: Ⓐ Nachdenklichkeit, *die;* Ⓑ Rücksicht, *die* (**for** auf + *Akk.*); Ⓒ Gedankenreichtum, *der;* Wohlüberlegtheit, *die*

**thoughtless** /ˈθɔːtlɪs/ *adj.* Ⓐ gedankenlos; **~ of the danger, ...:** ohne an die Gefahr zu denken ...; Ⓑ (*inconsiderate*) rücksichtslos; Ⓒ (*due to lack of thought*) leichtfertig ‹Fehler›

**thoughtlessly** /ˈθɔːtlɪslɪ/ *adv.* Ⓐ gedankenlos; **he ~ gave his son a box of matches** in seiner Gedankenlosigkeit gab er seinem Sohn eine Schachtel Streichhölzer; Ⓑ (*inconsiderately*) aus Rücksichtslosigkeit

**thoughtlessness** /ˈθɔːtlɪsnɪs/ *n., no pl.* Ⓐ Gedankenlosigkeit, *die;* Ⓑ (*lack of consideration*) Rücksichtslosigkeit, *die*

**thought: ~ process** *n.* Denkprozess, *der;* **~-provoking** *adj.* nachdenklich stimmend; **be ~-provoking** nachdenklich stimmen; **~-reader** *n.* Gedankenleser, *der*/-leserin, *die;* **you must be/I'm not a ~-reader** du kannst wohl Gedanken lesen/ich bin doch kein Hellseher; **~-reading** *n.* Gedankenlesen, *das;* **~ transference** *n.* Gedankenübertragung, *die*

**thousand** /ˈθaʊznd/ ▶1352 ❶ *adj.* Ⓐ tausend; **a** *or* **one ~:** eintausend; **two/several ~:** zweitausend/mehrere Tausend; **one and a half ~:** [ein]tausendfünfhundert; **a** *or* **one ~ and one** [ein]tausend[und]eins; **a** *or* **one ~ and one people** [ein]tausendundeine Person; **a T~ and one Nights** Tausendundeine Nacht; Ⓑ **a ~ [and one]** (*fig.: innumerable*) tausend (*ugs.*); **a ~ thanks** tausend Dank; **a ~ apologies** ich bitte tausendmal um Entschuldigung. ⇒ *also* **pity** 1 B; **time** 1 F.

❷ *n.* Ⓐ (*number*) tausend; **a** *or* **one/two ~:** ein-/zweitausend; **a ~ and one** [ein]tausend[und]eins; **a ~-to-one chance** eine Chance von tausend zu eins; **she/this chance is one in a ~** (*fig.*) sie ist einmalig/das ist eine einmalige Chance; Ⓑ (*symbol, written figure*) Tausend, *die;* (*in adding numbers by columns*) Tausender, *der* (*Math.*); (*set or group*) Tausend, *das;* Ⓒ (*indefinite amount*) **~s** Tausende; **they came by the ~** *or* **in their ~s** sie kamen zu Tausenden; **~s and ~s of people** Tausend und Abertausend Menschen

ˈ**thousandfold** ❶ *adv.* tausendfach. ❷ *adj.* tausendfach. ❸ *n.* Tausendfache, *das;* ⇒ *also* **hundredfold** 3

**thousandth** /ˈθaʊzndθ/ ❶ *adj.* ▶1352 tausendst...; **a ~ part** ein Tausendstel; ⇒ *also* **eighth** 1. ❷ *n.* Ⓐ (*fraction*) Tausendstel,

t

*das;* Ⓑ *(in sequence, rank)* Tausendste, *der/die/das*

**thraldom** /ˈθrɔːldəm/ *n., no pl. (literary)* Sklaverei, *die*

**thrall** /θrɔːl/ *n. (literary)* Ⓐ *(slave, lit. or fig.)* Sklave, *der*/Sklavin, *die* (**to, of** *Gen.*); *(serf)* Hörige, *der/die;* Ⓑ **have** *or* **hold sb. in ~** *(fig.)* jmdn. in seinen Bann geschlagen haben

**thralldom** *(Amer.)* ⇨ **thraldom**

**thrash** /θræʃ/ ❶ *v.t.* Ⓐ *(beat)* [ver]prügeln; **~ the life out of sb.** jmdm. die Seele aus dem Leib prügeln *(ugs.)*; Ⓑ *(defeat)* vernichtend schlagen; Ⓒ ⇨ **thresh**. ❷ *v.i.* Ⓐ **~ at sth.** auf etw. *(Akk.)* einschlagen; Ⓑ *(Naut.)* **~ to windward** luvwärts gegen die See knüppeln. ❸ *n. (coll.: party)* große Fete

**~ aˈbout, ~ aˈround** *v.i.* sich hin- und herwerfen; ‹Fisch:› zappeln

**~ ˈout** *v.t.* ausdiskutieren ‹Problem, Frage›; ausarbeiten ‹Plan›; **~ out the whole business** Klarheit in die ganze Sache bringen

**thrashing** /ˈθræʃɪŋ/ *n.* Ⓐ *(beating)* Prügel *Pl.;* **give sb. a ~:** jmdm. eine Tracht Prügel verpassen *(ugs.)*; **get a ~:** Prügel bekommen; Ⓑ *(defeat)* Schlappe, *die;* **give sb. a ~:** jmdn. vernichtend schlagen

**thread** /θred/ ❶ *n.* Ⓐ Faden, *der;* **sb. has not a dry ~ on him** jmd. hat keinen trockenen Faden [mehr] am Leib *(ugs.)*; Ⓑ *(fig.)* **hang by a ~** *(be in a precarious state)* an einem [dünnen *od.* seidenen] Faden hängen; *(depend on sth. still in doubt)* auf Messers Schneide stehen; **lose the ~:** den Faden verlieren; **take** *or* **pick up the ~ of the conversation** den Gesprächsfaden wieder aufnehmen; **gather up the ~s of sth.** etw. erläuternd zusammenfassen; Ⓒ *(sth. very thin)* **a ~ of light/water** ein feiner Lichtstrahl/ein Rinnsal *(geh.)*; Ⓓ *(Mech. Engin.: of screw)* Gewinde, *das.*
❷ *v.t.* Ⓐ *(pass ~ through)* einfädeln; auffädeln ‹Perlen›; *(make chain of)* aufreihen; Ⓑ *(place in position)* einfädeln ‹Film, Tonband› (**through** in + *Akk.*); Ⓒ **~ one's way through sth.** *(lit. or fig.)* sich durch etw. schlängeln; Ⓓ *(Mech. Engin.)* mit einem Gewinde versehen

**thread: ~bare** *adj.* Ⓐ *(worn)* abgenutzt; abgetragen ‹Kleidung›; Ⓑ *(fig.)* abgedroschen ‹Argument› *(ugs.)*; **~worm** *n. (Zool., Med.)* Fadenwurm, *der*

**threat** /θret/ *n.* Ⓐ Drohung, *die;* **make a ~ against sb.** jmdm. drohen; **under ~ of** unter Androhung von; **sb./sth. is under ~ of sth.** jmdm./einer Sache droht etw.; **issue ~s to sb.'s life** Morddrohungen gegen jmdn. richten; Ⓑ *(indication of sth. unpleasant)* **at the slightest ~ of sth.** wenn etw. auch nur ganz entfernt droht; **there is a ~ of rain** es kann Regen geben; Ⓒ *(danger)* Bedrohung, *die* (**to** für); **a ~ to our liberty** eine Bedrohung unserer Freiheit

**threaten** /ˈθretn/ *v.t.* Ⓐ *(use threats towards)* bedrohen; **~ sb. with prosecution/a beating** jmdm. Verfolgung/Schläge androhen; **I am ~ed with a visit from my mother** *(joc.)* mir droht ein Besuch meiner Mutter *(scherzh.)*; Ⓑ *(announce one's intention)* **~ to do sth.** damit drohen, etw. zu tun; **the fire ~ed to engulf the whole village** *(fig.)* das Feuer drohte das ganze Dorf einzuschließen; **~ to commit suicide/to resign** mit Selbstmord/dem Rücktritt drohen; Ⓒ drohen mit ‹Gewalt, Repressalien, Rache usw.›; **the sky ~s rain** am Himmel hängen drohende Regenwolken; Ⓓ *abs.* **when danger ~s** wenn [eine] Gefahr droht

**threatening** /ˈθretnɪŋ/ *adj.* drohend; bedrohlich ‹Gegenwart, Verhalten, Situation›; **~ letter** Drohbrief, *der*

**threateningly** /ˈθretnɪŋlɪ/ *adv.* drohend; **~ close** bedrohlich nahe

**three** /θriː/ ▸ **912**, ▸ **1012**, ▸ **1352** ❶ *adj.* drei; **~ parts wine and one part ...:** drei Teile Wein und ein Teil ...; **be ~ parts finished** drei viertel fertig sein; ⇨ *also* **cheer** 1 A; **eight** 1; **R** B. ❷ *n.* Ⓐ *(number, symbol)* Drei, *die;* Ⓑ *(set of ~ people)* Dreiergruppe, *die;* **the ~ [of them]** die drei. ⇨ *also* **eight** 2 A, C, D

**three: ~-cornered** /ˈθriːkɔːnəd/ *adj.* dreieckig; **~-cornered hat** Dreispitz, *der;* **~-cornered contest** Wettkampf mit drei Teilnehmern; **~-diˈmensional** *adj.* dreidimensional; **~fold** *adj., adv.* dreifach; ⇨ *also* **eightfold**; **~-ˈfour time** *n. (Mus.)* Dreivierteltakt, *der;* **~-handed** *adj. (Cards)* ‹Bridge usw.› zu dritt; **~-lane** *adj.* dreispurig; **~-legged** /ˈθriːlegd, ˈθriːlegɪd/ *adj.* dreibeinig; **~-legged race** *n. Wettlauf zwischen Paaren, bei denen jeweils das linke Bein des einen Partners mit dem rechten Bein des anderen zusammengebunden ist;* **~-line ˈwhip** ⇨ **whip** 1 C; **~pence** /ˈθrepəns, ˈθrɪpəns/ *n. (Brit. Hist.)* drei Pence; **~penny** /ˈθrepənɪ, ˈθrɪpənɪ/ *adj. (Brit. Hist.)* Drei-Pence-; ⇨ *also* **bit²** G; **~-phase** *adj.* Dreiphasen-; dreiphasig; **~-phase current** Dreiphasenstrom, *der;* **~-piece** ⇨ **piece** 1 B; **~-pin** ⇨ **pin** 1 C; **~-ply** ❶ *adj.* dreilagig; dreifädig ‹Wolle›; ❷ *n.* Ⓐ *(wool)* dreifädige Wolle; Ⓑ *(wood)* dreischichtiges [Sperr]holz; **~point** *attrib. adj.* **~-point landing** *(Aeronaut.)* Dreipunktlandung, *die;* **~-point turn** *(Brit. Motor Veh.) Wendemanöver auf engem Raum, bei dem vorwärts, rückwärts und wieder vorwärts gefahren wird;* **~-quarter** ❶ *adj.* dreiviertel; **~-quarter portrait** *(down to hips)* Dreiviertelporträt, *das; (of face)* Halbprofilporträt, *das;* **~-quarter length** dreiviertellang; **~-quarter back** ⇨ **2**; ❷ *n. (Rugby)* Dreiviertel, *der;* **~-quarters** ❶ *n.* Ⓐ drei Viertel (**of** *Gen.*); **~-quarters of an hour** eine Dreiviertelstunde; Ⓑ *attrib.* Dreiviertel‹mehrheit usw.›; ❷ *adv.* drei viertel ‹voll›; zu drei Vierteln ‹fertig›; **~score** *adj. (arch.)* sechzig; **~score and ten** siebzig

**threesome** /ˈθriːsəm/ *n.* Dreigespann, *das;* Trio, *das;* **go as a ~:** zu dritt gehen

**three: ~-storey** *adj.* dreistöckig; **~-way** *adj.* Dreiwege-; **~-way adaptor** *(Electr.)* Dreifachstecker, *der;* **~-way intersection** Kreuzung, an der sich drei Straßen treffen; **~-way tie** Unentschieden, bei dem drei Spieler/Mannschaften die gleiche Punktzahl *usw.* haben; **~-way profit split** Dreiteilung des Gewinns; **~-way playoff** Stechen *(Sport)* von drei Teilnehmern; **~-ˈwheeler** *n.* Dreirad, *das (Kfz-W.)*

**thresh** /θreʃ/ *v.t. (Agric.)* dreschen

**thresher** /ˈθreʃə(r)/ *n.* Ⓐ *(Agric.) (person)* Drescher, *der*/Drescherin, *die; (machine)* Dreschmaschine, *die;* Ⓑ *(Zool.: shark)* Fuchshai, *der;* Drescher, *der*

**threshing**/ˈθreʃɪŋ/: **~ floor** *n. (Agric.)* Tenne, *die;* **~ machine** *n. (Agric.)* Dreschmaschine, *die*

**threshold** /ˈθreʃəʊld/ *n.* Ⓐ *(lit. or fig.)* Schwelle, *die;* **be on the ~ of sth.** *(fig.)* an der Schwelle einer Sache *(Gen.)* stehen; **pain ~** *(Physiol., Psych.)* Schmerzschwelle, *die;* Ⓑ *(Phys.)* Schwellenwert, *der*

**threw** ⇨ **throw** 1

**thrice** /θraɪs/ *adv. (arch./literary)* dreimal

**thrift** /θrɪft/ *n.* Ⓐ *no pl.* Sparsamkeit, *die;* Ⓑ *(Bot.)* Grasnelke, *die*

**ˈthrift account** *n. (Amer.)* Sparkonto, *das*

**thriftily** /ˈθrɪftɪlɪ/ *adv.* sparsam

**thriftiness** /ˈθrɪftɪnɪs/ *n., no pl.* Sparsamkeit, *die*

**ˈthrift shop, ˈthrift store** *(Amer.)* ⇨ **charity shop**

**thrifty** /ˈθrɪftɪ/ *adj.* sparsam

**thrill** /θrɪl/ ❶ *v.t. (excite)* faszinieren; *(delight)* begeistern; **be ~ed by/with sth.** von etw. fasziniert/begeistert sein; **we were ~ed to have your letter** wir haben uns wahnsinnig über deinen Brief gefreut *(ugs.)*; ⇨ *also* **bit²** A.
❷ *v.i.* **~ with** zittern *od. (geh.)* beben vor (+ *Dat.*); **~ to** wie elektrisiert sein bei; **~ with horror** vor Entsetzen schaudern; **~ with excitement** ein Prickeln der Erregung verspüren; **~ at the sight of sth./at sb.'s touch** beim Anblick einer Sache *(Gen.)*/bei jmds. Berührung von einem Schauder überlaufen werden.
❸ *n.* Ⓐ *(wave of emotion)* Erregung, *die;* **a ~ of joy/pleasure** freudige Erregung; **a ~ of excitement/hate/horror** prickelnde Erregung/ein starkes Hassgefühl/ein Schauder *(geh.)* des Entsetzens; **a ~ of anticipation** prickelnde Vorfreude; Ⓑ *(exciting experience)* aufregendes Erlebnis; *(titillation)* Nervenkitzel, *der (ugs.)*; **sb. gets a ~ out of sth.** etw. erregt jmdn.; **cheap ~s** anspruchsloser Nervenkitzel *(ugs.)*; **this film will give you the ~ of a lifetime** dieser Film wird das Aufregendste sein, was du je erlebt hast; **~s and spills** Nervenkitzel, *der*

**thriller** /ˈθrɪlə(r)/ *n.* Thriller, *der*

**thrilling** /ˈθrɪlɪŋ/ *adj.* aufregend; spannend ‹Buch, Film, Theaterstück, Geschichte›; packend ‹Ereignis›; mitreißend ‹Musik›; prickelnd ‹Gefühl›

**thrive** /θraɪv/ *v.i.*, **thrived** *or* **throve** /θrəʊv/, **~d** *or* **thriven** /ˈθrɪvn/ Ⓐ *(grow vigorously)* wachsen und gedeihen; **~ on good food/sunlight** bei guter Ernährung/Sonnenschein prächtig gedeihen; Ⓑ *(prosper)* aufblühen (**on** bei); **business is thriving** das Geschäft floriert; **a thriving businessman** ein erfolgreicher Geschäftsmann; Ⓒ *(grow rich)* reich werden; **~ on other people's misfortune** sich am Unglück der anderen bereichern

**thro'** ⇨ **through**

**throat** /θrəʊt/ *n.* Ⓐ ▸ **966** *(outside and inside of neck)* Hals, *der; (esp. inside)* Kehle, *die;* **look down sb.'s ~:** jmdm. in den Hals *od.* Rachen schauen; **pour sth. down one's ~:** etw. hinunterschütten; **cancer of the ~:** Kehlkopfkrebs, *der;* **a [sore] ~:** Halsschmerzen; **cut sb.'s ~:** jmdm. die Kehle durchschneiden; **cut one's own ~** *(fig.)* sich *(Dat.)* ins eigene Fleisch schneiden; **cut one another's ~s** *(fig.)* sich *(Dat.)* gegenseitig das Wasser abgraben; **ram** *or* **cram** *or* **shove** *or* **thrust sth. down sb.'s ~** *(fig.)* jmdm. etw. aufzwingen; **be at each other's ~s** *(fig.)* miteinander im Clinch liegen *(ugs.)*; Ⓑ *(of bottle, vase)* Hals, *der; (of blast furnace)* Gicht, *die (Hüttenw.)*

**-throated** /θrəʊtɪd/ *adj. in comb.* -halsig ‹Mensch, Tier›; **full-~:** aus vollem Halse

**throat: ~ lozenge** *n.* Halspastille, *die;* **~ microphone** *n.* Kehlkopfmikrofon, *das*

**throaty** /ˈθrəʊtɪ/ *adj.* Ⓐ *(produced in throat)* kehlig; Ⓑ *(hoarse)* heiser

**throb** /θrɒb/ ❶ *v.i.*, **-bb-:** Ⓐ *(palpitate, pulsate)* pochen; **his fingers were ~bing [with pain]** er hatte einen pochenden Schmerz in den Fingern; Ⓑ *(vibrate)* ‹Motor, Artillerie:› dröhnen. ❷ *n.* Ⓐ *(palpitation)* Pochen, *das;* **be ~bing with life** voll von pulsierendem Leben sein; **he felt a sudden ~ of pain** ein plötzlicher Schmerz durchfuhr ihn; Ⓑ *(vibration)* Dröhnen, *das; (loud)* Hämmern, *das*

**throes** /θrəʊz/ *n. pl.* Qual, *die;* **~ of childbirth** Geburtswehen *Pl.;* **death ~:** Todesqual[en] *(geh.)*; **be in the ~ of sth.** *(fig.)* mitten in etw. *(Dat.)* stecken *(ugs.)*

**thrombosis** /θrɒmˈbəʊsɪs/ *n., pl.* **thromboses** /θrɒmˈbəʊsiːz/ ▸ **1232** *(Med.)* Thrombose, *die*

**throne** /θrəʊn/ *n.* Thron, *der;* **succeed to the ~:** die Thronfolge antreten; **on the ~** *(coll. joc.)* auf den Thron *od.* Topf *(ugs. scherzh.)*

**ˈthrone room** *n.* Thronsaal, *der*

**throng** /θrɒŋ/ ❶ *n.* [Menschen]menge, *die;* **stand in a ~ around sb.** eine [Menschen]traube um jmdn. bilden; **~s of people** Scharen von Menschen; **join the ~** *(joc.)* sich ins Gewühl stürzen. ❷ *v.i.* strömen (**into** in + *Akk.*); *(press)* sich drängen; **~ round the noticeboard** sich um das schwarze Brett drängen. ❸ *v.t.* sich drängen in (+ *Dat.*)

**throttle** /ˈθrɒtl/ ❶ *n. (Mech. Engin.)* **~ [valve]** Drosselklappe, *die;* **~ [pedal]** *(Motor Veh.)* Gas[pedal], *das;* **~ [lever]** Gashebel, *der;* **at full ~** *(Motor Veh.)* mit Vollgas. ❷ *v.t.* erdrosseln; *(fig.)* ersticken

**~ back, ~ down** ❶ *v.t.* drosseln ‹Motor›. ❷ *v.i.* den Motor drosseln

**through** /θruː/ ❶ *prep.* Ⓐ durch; *(fig.)* **search/read ~ sth.** etw. durchsuchen/durchlesen; **wait ~ ten long years** zehn lange Jahre hindurch warten; **live ~ sth.**

t

(*survive*) etw. überleben; (*experience*) etw. erleben; **sit ~ a long sermon** eine lange Predigt hindurch still sitzen bleiben; Ⓑ (*Amer.: up to and including*) bis [einschließlich]; Ⓒ (*by reason of*) durch; infolge von ‹Vernachlässigung, Einflüssen›; **it was all ~ you that we were late** es war nur deine Schuld, dass wir zu spät gekommen sind; **it all came about ~ his not knowing the way** alles kam so, weil er den Weg nicht wusste; **it happened ~ no fault of yours** es geschah nicht durch deine Schuld; **conceal sth. ~ shame** etw. aus Scham verheimlichen.
❷ *adv.* Ⓐ **let sb. ~:** jmdn. durchlassen; **book your tickets ~ to Vienna** löst eure Fahrkarten durchgehend bis Wien; **be a Communist/be wet ~ and ~:** durch und durch Kommunist/nass sein; **be ~ with a piece of work/with sb.** mit einer Arbeit fertig/mit jmdm. fertig (*ugs.*) sein; **we are ~!** (*have succeeded/finished*) wir haben es geschafft!; (*with each other*) wir sind miteinander fertig!; Ⓑ (*Teleph.*) **be ~:** durch sein (*ugs.*); **be ~ to sb.** mit jmdm. verbunden sein.
❸ *adj.* durchgehend ‹Zug›; **~ coach** *or* **carriage** Kurswagen, *der* (**for** nach); **~ traffic** Durchgangsverkehr, *der;* **'no ~ road'** „keine Durchfahrt[sstraße]"; **~ ticket** [alle Umsteigestationen umfassende] Fahrkarte; **can I buy a ~ ticket to Warsaw?** kann ich bis Warschau durchlösen?

**through: ~-composed** *adj.* (*Mus.*) durchkomponiert; **~'out** ❶ *prep.* **~out the war/period** den ganzen Krieg/die ganze Zeit hindurch; **spread ~out the country** sich im ganzen Land verbreiten; ❷ *adv.* (*entirely*) ganz; (*always*) stets; die ganze Zeit [hindurch]; **lined with fur ~out** ganz mit Pelz gefüttert; **repainted ~out** von oben bis unten neu gestrichen; **~put** *n.* Durchsatz, *der* (*Wirtsch.*); **~way** *n.* (*Amer.: expressway*) Schnellstraße, *die*

**throve** ⇒ **thrive**

**throw** /θrəʊ/ ❶ *v.t.*, **threw** /θruː/, **~n** /θrəʊn/ Ⓐ werfen; **~ sth. to sb.** jmdm. etw. zuwerfen; **~ sth. at sb.** etw. nach jmdm. werfen; **~ me that towel, please** wirf mal bitte das Handtuch rüber (*ugs.*); **the hose ~s a jet of water 50 feet** der Schlauch spritzt das Wasser 50 Fuß weit; **this cannon ~s 50-mm. shells** diese Kanone schießt 50-mm-Geschosse; **~ a punch/punches** zuschlagen; **~ a left/right** eine Linke/Rechte schlagen; **~ oneself on one's knees/to the floor/into a chair** sich auf die Knie/zu Boden/in einen Sessel werfen; **~ oneself down** sich niederwerfen; **~ oneself at sb.** sich auf jmdn. werfen; (*fig.*) sich jmdm. an den Hals werfen (*ugs.*); **~ good money after bad** (*fig.*) [noch mehr] Geld hinauswerfen; ⇒ *also* **glass** 2; Ⓑ (*fig.*) **~ sb. out of work/into prison** jmdn. entlassen *od.* (*ugs.*) hinauswerfen/ins Gefängnis werfen (*geh.*); **be ~n upon one's own resources** selbst für sich aufkommen müssen; **~ sb. into confusion** jmdn. durcheinander bringen; **~ oneself into a task** sich in eine Arbeit (*Akk.*) stürzen; **~ sth. into disarray** *or* **disorder** etw. durcheinander bringen; ⇒ *also* **scent** 1 B; Ⓒ (*project, direct*) werfen; **~ an icy look at sb.** jmdm. einen eisigen Blick zuwerfen; ⇒ *also* **light**[1] 1 H; Ⓓ (*bring to the ground*) zu Boden werfen ‹Ringer, Gegner›; (*unseat*) abwerfen ‹Reiter›; Ⓔ (*coll.: disconcert*) ‹Frage:› aus der Fassung bringen; Ⓕ (*cause to change position*) **~ troops into action** Truppen in den Kampf werfen; **~ a switch/lever** einen Schalter/Hebel betätigen; **~ the car into reverse** den Rückwärtsgang einlegen *od.* (*salopp*) reinhauen; ⇒ *also* **open** 1 A; Ⓖ (*construct*) **~ a bridge across a river** eine Brücke über einen Fluss schlagen; Ⓗ (*Textiles*) **~ silk** Seidenfäden drehen; Ⓘ (*Pottery*) drehen; Ⓙ **~ a fit/tantrum** einen Anfall/Wutanfall bekommen; Ⓚ **~ a party** eine Party schmeißen (*ugs.*); Ⓛ (*Amer.: lose intentionally*) absichtlich verlieren ‹Kampf, Rennen›; Ⓜ (*Cards*) ausspielen; (*discard*) abwerfen; Ⓝ *also abs.* (*Games*) werfen; **~ [the/a dice]** würfeln.
❷ *n.* Ⓐ (*act*) Wurf, *der;* **the first ~ went to the champion** (*Wrestling*) der erste Wurf gelang dem Meister; **$5 a ~** (*coll.: each*) $5 das Stück; ⇒ *also* **stone** 1 A; Ⓑ (*Geol.*) (*fault*) Verwerfung, *die*
**~ a'bout** *v.t.* herumwerfen (*ugs.*); **~ one's arms about** mit den Armen fuchteln (*ugs.*); **~ one's money about** (*fig.*) mit Geld um sich werfen; ⇒ *also* **weight** 1 A
**~ a'round** *v.t.* Ⓐ ⇒ **~ about**; Ⓑ (*surround with*) **~ a cordon around an area** ein Gebiet abriegeln
**~ a'way** *v.t.* Ⓐ (*get rid of, waste*) wegwerfen; (*discard*) abwerfen ‹Spielkarte›; **~ away money on sth.** Geld für etw. wegwerfen; **~ oneself away on sb.** sich an jmdn. wegwerfen; Ⓑ (*lose by neglect*) verschenken ‹Vorteil, Vorsprung, Spiel usw.›; Ⓒ (*Theatr.*) beiläufig fallen lassen ‹Worte›. ⇒ *also* **~away**
**~ 'back** *v.t.* Ⓐ (*return, repulse*) zurückwerfen; **be ~n back on sth.** (*fig.*) auf etw. (*Akk.*) zurückgreifen müssen; Ⓑ (*move back rapidly*) zurückschlagen ‹Bettuch, Vorhang, Teppich›; zurückwerfen ‹Kopf›. ⇒ *also* **~-back**
**~ 'down** *v.t.* **~ down [on the ground]** auf den Boden werfen; **it's ~ing it down** (*coll.*) es gießt [wie aus Eimern] (*ugs.*); ⇒ *also* **gauntlet**[1] D
**~ 'in** *v.t.* Ⓐ (*include as free extra*) [gratis] dazugeben; **with ... ~n in** mit ... als Zugabe; Ⓑ (*interpose*) einstreuen ‹Bemerkung›; Ⓒ (*Footb., Rugby*) einwerfen; ⇒ *also* **~-in**; Ⓓ (*Cricket*) [vom Außenfeld] in das Innenfeld [zurück]werfen; Ⓔ **~ one's hand in** (*Cards*) aussteigen (*ugs.*); (*fig.: withdraw*) aufgeben. ⇒ *also* **lot** G; **towel** 1 A
**~ 'off** *v.t.* Ⓐ (*discard*) ablegen ‹Maske, Verkleidung›; von sich werfen ‹Kleider›; (*get rid of*) loswerden ‹Erkältung, lästige Person›; Ⓑ (*perform or write casually*) [mühelos] hinwerfen ‹Rede, Gedicht usw.›
**~ 'on** ❶ *v.t.* sich werfen in ‹Kleider›. ❷ *v. refl.* **~ oneself [up]on sb.** sich auf jmdn. stürzen; **~ oneself [up]on sb.'s mercy** sich jmdm. auf Gnade oder Ungnade ausliefern
**~ 'out** *v.t.* Ⓐ (*discard*) wegwerfen; Ⓑ (*expel*) **~ sb. out [of sth.]** jmdn. [aus etw.] hinauswerfen (*ugs.*); **~ sb. out of work** jmdn. hinauswerfen (*ugs.*); Ⓒ (*refuse*) verwerfen ‹Plan usw.›; Ⓓ (*put forward tentatively*) in den Raum stellen ‹Vorschläge›; Ⓔ **~ out one's chest** die Brust herausdrücken; Ⓕ (*confuse*) durcheinander bringen; aus dem Konzept bringen ‹Sprecher›; **the mistake threw us out in our calculation/results** der Fehler warf unsere Rechnung um (*ugs.*)/verfälschte unsere Ergebnisse; Ⓖ (*radiate*) ausstrahlen ‹Wärme›. ⇒ *also* **~-out**
**~ 'over** *v.t.* sitzen lassen (*ugs.*) ‹Freund[in] usw.›; den Rücken kehren (+ *Dat.*) ‹Partei, Bekannten, Familie›
**~ to'gether** *v.t.* Ⓐ (*assemble hastily*) zusammenhauen (*ugs.*); zusammenwerfen ‹Zutaten, Ideen›; herzaubern ‹Essen›; zusammenschustern (*ugs. abwertend*) ‹Aufsatz, Artikel›; zusammenschreiben ‹Buch, Artikel, Rede›; Ⓑ (*bring together*) zusammenwürfeln
**~ 'up** ❶ *v.t.* Ⓐ (*lift quickly*) hochwerfen ‹Arme, Hände›; [plötzlich] hochschieben ‹Fenster›; Ⓑ (*erect quickly*) hochziehen (*salopp*) ‹Gebäude›; Ⓒ (*give up*) hinwerfen (*ugs.*) ‹Arbeit›; aufgeben ‹Versuch›; abbrechen ‹Laufbahn, Ausbildung›; Ⓓ (*produce*) hervorbringen ‹Führer, Ideen usw.›; Ⓔ (*coll.: vomit*) ausspucken (*ugs.*). ❷ *v.i.* (*coll.: vomit*) brechen (*ugs.*); **he makes me want to ~ up** ich finde ihn zum Kotzen (*derb*)

**throw: ~away** ❶ *adj.* Ⓐ (*disposable*) Wegwerf-; Einweg-; Ⓑ (*underemphasized*) beiläufig [gesprochen] ‹Bemerkung›; ❷ *n.* Ⓐ (*disposable thing*) Wegwerfartikel, *der;* (*bottle*) Einwegflasche, *die;* Ⓑ (*remark*) beiläufige Bemerkung; **~back** *n.* Rückkehr, *die* (**to** zu); **he/this horse is a ~back** in ihm/diesem Pferd schlägt altes Blut wieder durch

**thrower** /ˈθrəʊə(r)/ *n.* Werfer, *der*/Werferin, *die;* (*Pottery*) Dreher, *der*/Dreherin, *die*

**'throw-in** *n.* (*Footb., Rugby*) Einwurf, *der*

**thrown** ⇒ **throw** 1

**throw: ~-out** *n.* Ⓐ **have a ~-out** ausmisten (*ugs.*); Ⓑ **sb.'s ~-outs** das, was jmd. wegwerfen will; (*clothes*) jmds. abgelegte Kleider; **these are ~-outs** diese sind zum Wegwerfen; **~-rug** *n.* (*Amer.*) Überwurf, *der*

**thru** (*Amer.*) ⇒ **through**

**thrum** /θrʌm/ ❶ *v.t.*, **-mm-** klimpern auf (+ *Dat.*) ‹Gitarre usw.›; trommeln auf (+ *Dat.*) ‹Tisch usw.›; **~ a tune** eine Melodie [herunter]klimpern. ❷ *v.i.*, **-mm-** (*on guitar*) klimpern (**on** auf + *Dat.*); (*on flat surface*) trommeln (**on** auf + *Dat.*)

**thrush**[1] /θrʌʃ/ *n.* (*Ornith.*) Drossel, *die*

**thrush**[2] *n.*, *no pl.*, *no art.* ▶ **1232** (*Med.*) Soor, *der;* Soormykose, *die*

**thrust** /θrʌst/ ❶ *v.t.*, **thrust** Ⓐ (*push suddenly*) stoßen; **he ~ his fist into my face** er stieß mir seine Faust ins Gesicht; **~ a letter into sth.** einen Brief in etw. (*Akk.*) stecken; **~ out one's hand** die Hand ausstrecken; **~ a ten-pound note into sb.'s hand** jmdm. eine Zehnpfundnote in die Hand drücken; (*fig.*) **~ aside** beiseite schieben; in den Wind schlagen ‹Warnungen›; **~ extra work [up]on sb.** jmdm. zusätzliche Arbeit aufbürden; **~ oneself/one's company upon sb.** sich/seine Gesellschaft jmdm. aufdrängen; **fame was ~ upon her** sie wurde unversehens berühmt; Ⓑ **~ one's way through/into/out of sth.** sich durch/in/aus etw. drängen; Ⓒ (*pierce*) **~ sb./sth. through** jmdn./etw. durchbohren.
❷ *v.i.*, **thrust** Ⓐ (*push*) **~ at sb.** nach jmdm. stoßen; Ⓑ (*force one's way*) **~ through the crowd/to the front** sich durch die Menge/nach vorn drängen *od.* kämpfen.
❸ *n.* Ⓐ (*sudden push*) Stoß, *der;* Ⓑ (*fig.: verbal attack*) Seitenhieb, *der* (**at** auf + *Akk.*); Ⓒ (*gist*) Stoßrichtung, *die;* Ⓓ (*Mil.: advance*) Vorstoß, *der;* Ⓔ (*force*) (*of jet engine*) Schub, *der;* (*of arch*) Gewölbeschub, *der*

**'thrust bearing** *n.* (*Mech. Engin.*) Axiallager, *das*

**thruster** /ˈθrʌstə(r)/ *n.* (*Astronaut.*) Korrekturtriebwerk, *das*

**thrustful** /ˈθrʌstfl/ *adj.* energisch

**thrusting** /ˈθrʌstɪŋ/ *adj.* [energisch und] zielstrebig

**thruway** (*Amer.*) ⇒ **throughway**

**thud** /θʌd/ ❶ *v.i.*, **-dd-** dumpf schlagen; **~ to the floor/ground** dumpf [auf den Fußboden/Boden] aufschlagen. ❷ *n.* dumpfer Schlag; **fall with a ~ [to the ground]** dumpf [auf dem Boden] aufschlagen; **the ~ of hoofbeats** dröhnender Hufschlag

**thug** /θʌg/ *n.* Schläger, *der;* **football ~s** Fußballrowdys

**thuggery** /ˈθʌgərɪ/ *n.*, *no pl.* Schlägerunwesen, *das*

**thuggish** /ˈθʌgɪʃ/ *adj.* aggressiv ‹Verhalten, Fußballfan›; **~ lout** Schläger, *der;* **~ youth** jugendlicher Schläger

**thumb** /θʌm/ ❶ *n.* ▶ **966** Daumen, *der;* **give sb. the ~s down on a proposal/idea** jmds. Vorschlag/Idee ablehnen; **get the ~s down** ‹Idee:› verworfen werden; ‹Kandidat:› abgelehnt werden; **give a project the ~s up** für ein Projekt grünes Licht geben; **get the ~s up** ‹Person, Projekt:› akzeptiert werden; **have ten ~s, be all ~s** zwei linke Hände haben (*ugs.*); **have sb. under one's ~:** jmdn. unter der Fuchtel haben (*ugs.*); **be under sb.'s ~:** unter jmds. Fuchtel stehen; ⇒ *also* **rule** 1 A; **stick out** 2 B.
❷ *v.t.* Ⓐ **~ a lift** einem Autofahrer winken, um sich mitnehmen zu lassen; (*hitch-hike*) per Anhalter fahren; Ⓑ (*turn over*) [mit dem Daumen] durchblättern ‹Buch›; [mit dem Daumen] umblättern ‹Seiten›; **well-~ed** abgegriffen ‹Buch›; Ⓒ **~ one's nose [at sb.]** [jmdm.] eine lange Nase machen
**~ through** *v.t.* [mit dem Daumen] durchblättern ‹Buch›

**thumb: ~ index** ❶ *n.* Daumenregister, *das;* ❷ *v.t.* mit Daumenregister ausstatten; **~-indexed edition** Ausgabe mit Daumenregister; **~nail** *n.* Daumennagel, *der; attrib.* **~nail sketch** (*Art*) Miniaturportrait, *das;* (*fig.: brief description*) kurze Beschreibung; **~print** *n.* Daumenabdruck, *der;* **~screw** *n.* (*Hist.*) Daumenschraube, *die;* **~stall** *n.*

t

Däumling, *der;* **~-sucking** /'θʌmsʌkɪŋ/ *n., no pl., no indef. art.* Daumenlutschen, *das;* **~tack** *(Amer.) n.* Reißzwecke, *die*

**thump** /θʌmp/ ❶ *v.t.* Ⓐ *(strike heavily)* [mit Wucht] schlagen; **I'll ~ you if ...:** ich hau dir eine, wenn ... *(ugs.)*; **they ~ed each other** sie prügelten sich; **~ the door with one's fist** mit der Faust an die Tür hämmern; Ⓑ *(play on piano etc.)* **~ [out] a tune** eine Melodie hämmern *(ugs.)*. ❷ *v.i.* Ⓐ hämmern **(at, on** gegen); ‹Herz:› heftig pochen; Ⓑ *(move noisily)* **~ around** herumpoltern; **~ down the stairs** die Treppe hinabpoltern. ❸ *n.* Ⓐ *(blow)* Schlag, *der;* Ⓑ *(dull sound)* Bums, *der (ugs.)*; dumpfer Schlag

**thumping** /'θʌmpɪŋ/ *(coll.)* ❶ *adj. (huge)* gewaltig *(ugs.)*; überwältigend ‹Mehrheit›; faustdick *(ugs.)* ‹Lüge›. ❷ *adv.* **~ great** riesengroß *(ugs.)*; **a ~ big majority** eine überwältigende Mehrheit

**thunder** /'θʌndə(r)/ ❶ *n.* Ⓐ *no pl., no indef. art.* Donner, *der;* **roll/crash of ~:** Donnerrollen, *das*/-schlag, *der;* Ⓑ *(fig.: censure)* Donnerwetter, *das (ugs.)*; Ⓒ **steal sb.'s ~** *(fig.)* jmdm. die Schau stehlen *(ugs.)*. ❷ *v.i.* Ⓐ donnern; Ⓑ *(speak)* **~ against sth.** gegen etw. wettern *(ugs.)*; **~ at sb.** jmdn. andonnern *(ugs.)*. ❸ *v.t.* [mit Donnerstimme] brüllen; **~ [out] orders at sb.** jmdm. Befehle zubrüllen

**thunder: ~bolt** *n.* Ⓐ Blitzschlag [mit Donner]; *(from god)* Blitzstrahl, *der (geh.)*; Ⓑ *(fig.: unexpected event)* **come as something of a ~bolt** wie ein Blitz einschlagen; **~box** *n. (coll.)* Plumpsklo[sett], *das (ugs.)*; **~clap** *n.* Ⓐ Donnerschlag, *der;* Ⓑ *(fig.)* **come** *or* **be like a ~clap** wie der Blitz einschlagen; **~cloud** *n.* Gewitterwolke, *die*

**thundering** /'θʌndərɪŋ/ *(coll.)* ❶ *adj. (huge)* gewaltig *(ugs.)* ‹Erfolg›; faustdick *(ugs.)* ‹Lüge›; **be in a ~ rage** eine Mordswut haben *(ugs.)*. ❷ *adv.* **~ great** gewaltig *(ugs.)*; **we had a ~ good time** wir hatten einen unheimlichen Spaß

**thunderous** /'θʌndərəs/ *adj.* donnernd; **in a ~ voice** mit Donnerstimme

**thunder: ~ shower** *n.* Gewitterschauer, *der;* **~storm** *n.* Gewitter, *das; (very heavy)* Gewittersturm, *der;* **~struck** *adj. (fig.: amazed)* **be ~struck** wie vom Donner gerührt sein

**thundery** /'θʌndərɪ/ *adj.* gewittrig; **it looks ~:** es sieht nach Gewitter aus

**Thuringia** /θʊə'rɪŋgɪə/ *pr. n.* Thüringen *(das)*

**Thuringian** /θʊə'rɪŋgɪən/ ❶ *adj.* thüringisch ‹Stadt›; Thüringer ‹Wald, Dialekt›. ❷ *n.* Thüringer, *der*/Thüringerin, *die*

**Thurs.** *abbr.* ▶1056 **Thursday** Do.

**Thursday** /'θɜːzdeɪ, 'θɜːzdɪ/ ▶1056 ❶ *n.* Donnerstag, *der.* ❷ *adv. (coll.)* **she comes ~s** sie kommt donnerstags. ⇒ *also* **Friday**

**thus** /ðʌs/ *adv.* Ⓐ *(in the way indicated)* so; *(thereby)* dadurch; **I picture the process as happening ~ ...:** ich stelle mir den Ablauf folgendermaßen vor: ...; Ⓑ *(accordingly)* deshalb; daher; Ⓒ *(to this extent)* **~ much/far** so viel/so weit

**thwack** /θwæk/ ⇒ **whack** 1, 2 A

**thwart** /θwɔːt/ ❶ *v.t.* durchkreuzen ‹Pläne, Absichten›; vereiteln ‹Versuch›; **~ sb.** jmdm. einen Strich durch die Rechnung machen; **she was ~ed in her plans** ihre Pläne wurden durchkreuzt. ❷ *n. (Naut.)* Ducht, *die (fachspr.)*; Ruderbank, *die*

**thy** /ðaɪ/ *poss. pron. attrib. (arch./poet./dial.)* dein; ⇒ *also* **her²**

**thyme** /taɪm/ *n. (Bot.)* Thymian, *der;* **wild ~:** Feldthymian, *der;* Quendel, *der*

**thymus** /'θaɪməs/ *n., pl.* **~es** *or* **thymi** /'θaɪmaɪ/ **~ [gland]** *(Anat.)* Thymus, *der;* Thymusdrüse, *die*

**thyroid** /'θaɪrɔɪd/ *n.* **~ [gland]** *(Anat., Zool.)* Schilddrüse, *die*

**thyself** /ðaɪ'self/ *pron. (arch./poet./dial.)* Ⓐ *emphat.* selbst; Ⓑ *refl.* dich/dir; **know ~!** erkenne dich selbst! ⇒ *also* **herself**

**ti** ⇒ **te**

**tiara** /tɪ'ɑːrə/ *n.* Ⓐ *(pope's crown)* Tiara, *die;* Ⓑ *(jewelled band)* Diadem, *das*

**Tibet** /tɪ'bet/ *pr. n.* Tibet *(das)*

**Tibetan** /tɪ'betn/ ▶1275, ▶1340 ❶ *adj.* tibetisch; **sb. is ~:** jmd. ist Tibeter/Tibeterin. ❷ *n.* Ⓐ *(person)* Tibeter, *der*/Tibeterin, *die;* Ⓑ *(language)* Tibetisch, *das*

**tibia** /'tɪbɪə/ *n., pl.* **~e** /'tɪbiː/ *or* **~s** *(Anat.)* Tibia, *die (fachspr.)*; Schienbein, *das*

**tic** /tɪk/ *n.* Tic, *der (Med.)*; nervöse Muskelzuckung

**tich** /tɪtʃ/ ⇒ **titch**

**tichy** ⇒ **titchy**

**Ticino** /tɪ'tʃiːnəʊ/ *pr. n.* das Tessin

**tick¹** /tɪk/ ❶ *v.i.* ticken; **what makes sb. ~** *(fig.)* worauf jmd. anspricht. ❷ *v.t.* Ⓐ mit einem Häkchen versehen; Ⓑ ⇒ **~ off** a. ❸ *n.* Ⓐ *(of clock etc.)* Ticken, *das;* Ⓑ *(Brit. coll.: moment)* Sekunde, *die;* **half a ~!, just a ~!** Momentchen! *(ugs.)*; **I'll be with you in a ~** *or* **two ~s** ich komme gleich; Ⓒ *(mark)* Häkchen, *das;* **put a ~ against your preference** kennzeichnen Sie das, was Sie bevorzugen, mit einem Häkchen

**~ a'way** *v.i.* [weiter]ticken; **the minutes ~ed away** die Minuten verstrichen

**~ 'off** *v.t.* Ⓐ *(cross off)* abhaken; Ⓑ *(coll.: reprimand)* rüffeln *(ugs.)*

**~ 'over** *v.i.* Ⓐ *(Motor Veh.)* im Leerlauf laufen; **~ over noisily/too slowly/too fast** im Leerlauf [zu] laut/zu langsam/zu schnell drehen; Ⓑ *(fig.)* **~ over [nicely]** *(progress satisfactorily)* ganz gut laufen *(ugs.)*; **keep things ~ing over while I'm away** sieh zu, dass alles gemächlich weiterläuft, während ich weg bin. ⇒ *also* **tick-over**

**tick²** *n. (Zool.) (arachnid)* Zecke, *die; (insect)* Lausfliege, *die*

**tick³** *n. (coll.: credit)* **buy on ~:** auf Pump kaufen *(salopp)*; **can I have it on ~?** kann ich das anschreiben lassen?

**ticker** /'tɪkə(r)/ *n. (coll.)* Ⓐ *(watch)* Zwiebel, *die (ugs. scherzh.)*; Ⓑ *(tape machine)* Ticker, *der (ugs.)*; Ⓒ *(heart)* Pumpe, *die (salopp)*

**'ticker tape** *n. (Amer.)* [Papier]streifen, *der (aus dem Fernschreiber)*; **~ welcome** Konfettiparade, *die*

**ticket** /'tɪkɪt/ ❶ *n.* Ⓐ Karte, *die; (for concert, theatre, cinema, exhibition)* [Eintritts]karte, *die; (for public transport)* Fahrschein, *der; (of cardboard)* Fahrkarte, *die; (for aeroplane)* Flugschein, *der;* Ticket, *das; (for ship)* Fahrschein, *der;* Ticket, *das; (of lottery, raffle)* Los, *das; (for library)* Ausweis, *der; (for car park)* Parkschein, *der;* **cloakroom/pawn ~:** Garderobenmarke, *die*/Pfandschein, *der;* **entrance by ~ only** Einlass nur gegen Eintrittskarte; **price ~:** Preisschild, *das;* **[parking]~:** Strafmandat, *das;* Strafzettel, *der (ugs.)*; Ⓑ *(certificate) (Naut.)* Patent, *das; (Aeronaut.)* Pilotenschein, *der;* Ⓒ *(Amer. Polit.) (list of candidates)* [Wahl]liste, *die;* **run on the Democratic/Republican ~:** für die Demokraten/Republikaner kandidieren; **run on a youth ~** *(fig.)* mit einem auf Jungwähler zugeschnittenen Programm antreten; ⇒ *also* **split** 3 C; Ⓓ **be [just] the ~** *(coll.)* genau das Richtige sein. ❷ *v.t.* auszeichnen ‹Waren›

**ticket: ~ agency** *n.* Kartenvorverkaufsstelle, *die;* **~ agent** *n.* ▶1261 Inhaber/Inhaberin einer Kartenvorverkaufsstelle; **~ collector** *n.* ▶1261 *(on train)* Schaffner, *der*/Schaffnerin, *die; (on station)* Fahrkartenkontrolleur, *der*/-kontrolleurin, *die;* **~ holder** *n.* Besitzer/Besitzerin einer Eintrittskarte; **~ inspector** *n.* ▶1261 Fahrkartenkontrolleur, *der*/-kontrolleurin, *die;* **~ office** *n.* Kartenschalter, *der; (for public transport)* Fahrkartenschalter, *der; (for advance booking)* Kartenvorverkaufsstelle, *die*

**ticking** /'tɪkɪŋ/ *n. (Textiles)* Drillich, *der;* Drell, *der (fachspr.)*

**ticking-'off** *n. (coll.)* Rüffel, *der (ugs.)*

**tickle** /'tɪkl/ ❶ *v.t.* Ⓐ *(touch lightly)* kitzeln; **~ sb.'s ribs** *(fig.)* jmdn. zum Lachen bringen; *abs.* **don't ~!** kitzle mich nicht!; **you're tickling!** das kitzelt!; Ⓑ *(amuse)* **be ~d by sth.** sich über etw. *(Akk.)* amüsieren; **be ~d pink about sth.** *(coll.)* sich wahnsinnig über etw. *(Akk.)* freuen *(ugs.)*; **~ sb.'s fancy** jmdn. reizen. ❷ *v.i.* kitzeln. ❸ *n.* Kitzeln, *das;* **give sb. a ~:** jmdn. kitzeln

**ticklish** /'tɪklɪʃ/ *adj. (lit. or fig.)* kitzlig

**tickly** /'tɪklɪ/ *adj. (coll.)* kitzlig

**tick: ~-over** *n. (Motor Veh.)* Leerlauf, *der;* **~-tack-'toe** *(Amer.)* = **noughts and crosses** ⇒ **nought** A; **~-tock** /'tɪktɒk/ *n.* Ⓐ *no pl. (sound)* Ticktack, *das;* Ⓑ *(child lang.: clock)* Ticktack, *die (Kindersp r.)*

**tidal** /'taɪdl/ *adj.* Gezeiten-; **~ river** Tidefluss, *der;* **~ basin/harbour** Tidebecken, *das*/-hafen, *der (Seemannsspr.)*; **~ power station** Gezeitenkraftwerk, *das*

**tidal: ~ flow** *n. (Transport)* dem Verkehrsfluss angepasstes System der Verkehrsführung; **~ wave** *n.* Flutwelle, *die;* **a ~ wave of enthusiasm/protest** *(fig.)* eine gewaltige Welle der Begeisterung/von Protesten

**tidbit** /'tɪdbɪt/ *(Amer.)* ⇒ **titbit**

**tiddledy-wink** /'tɪdldɪwɪŋk/ *(Amer.)* ⇒ **tiddlywink**

**tiddler** /'tɪdlə(r)/ *n. (Brit. coll./child lang.)* Ⓐ *(fish)* Fischchen, *das;* Ⓑ *(child)* Kleine, *das;* **~s** *(things)* Kleinzeug, *das (ugs. abwertend)*

**tiddl[e]y** /'tɪdlɪ/ *adj. (Brit.)* Ⓐ *(coll.: slightly drunk)* angesäuselt *(ugs.)*; Ⓑ **~ [little]** *(coll.: very small)* klitzeklein *(ugs.)*

**tiddlywink** *n.* Ⓐ *(counter)* farbiges Plättchen; Ⓑ **~s** *sing. (game)* Flohhüpfen, *das*

**tide** /taɪd/ ❶ *n.* Ⓐ *(rise or fall of sea)* Tide, *die (nordd., bes. Seemannsspr.)*; **high ~:** Flut, *die;* **low ~:** Ebbe, *die;* **the ~s** die Gezeiten; **sail on the next ~:** mit der nächsten Flut auslaufen; **cut off/washed up by the ~:** von der Flut abgeschnitten/angeschwemmt; **the ~ is in/out** es ist Flut/Ebbe; **when the ~ is in/out** bei Flut/Ebbe; **the rise and fall of the ~s** Ebbe und Flut; der Tidenhub *(Seemannsspr.)*; ⇒ *also* **turn** 1 G; Ⓑ *(fig.: trend)* Trend, *der;* **go with/against the ~:** mit dem/gegen den Strom schwimmen; **the ~ of war was turning** das Kriegsglück wendete sich; **rising ~ of opposition** zunehmende Opposition; ⇒ *also* **turn** 3 C.
❷ *v.t.* **~ sb. over** jmdm. über die Runden helfen *(ugs.)*; **I have enough to ~ me over/over the winter** ich habe genug, um mich über Wasser zu halten/um durch *od.* über den Winter zu kommen; **~ sb. over a difficult period** jmdm. über eine schwierige Zeit hinweghelfen

**'tide gate** *n. (Naut.)* Fluttor, *das*

**tideless** /'taɪdlɪs/ *adj.* gezeitenlos

**tide: ~mark** *n.* Ⓐ Flutmarke, *die;* Ⓑ *(Brit. coll.: line on body, bath, etc.)* Schmutzrand, *der;* **~ table** *n. (Naut.)* Gezeitentafel, *die;* **~way** *n. (of river)* Tidefluss, *der; (channel)* Priel, *der; (current)* Gezeitenströmung, *die*

**tidily** /'taɪdɪlɪ/ *adv.* ordentlich; *(clearly)* übersichtlich ‹präsentieren, gestalten›

**tidiness** /'taɪdɪnɪs/ *n., no pl.* Ordentlichkeit, *die*

**tidings** /'taɪdɪŋz/ *n. pl. (literary)* Kunde, *die (geh.)*

**tidy** /'taɪdɪ/ ❶ *adj.* Ⓐ *(neat)* ordentlich; aufgeräumt ‹Zimmer, Schreibtisch›; **make oneself/a room ~:** sich zurechtmachen/ein Zimmer aufräumen; **have ~ habits** ein ordentlicher Mensch sein; Ⓑ *(coll.: considerable)* ordentlich *(ugs.)*; **a ~ sum** *or* **penny** ein hübsches Sümmchen *(ugs.)*. ❷ *n. (receptacle)* **kitchen/bathroom/desk ~:** Behälter für Küchen-/Badezimmer-/Schreibtischutensilien; **sink ~:** Einsatzkörbchen für die Spüle. ❸ *v.t.* aufräumen ‹Zimmer›; **~ oneself** sich zurechtmachen; **~ one's hair** sich kämmen; *abs.* **be busy ~ing** mit [dem] Aufräumen beschäftigt sein

**~ a'way** *v.t.* wegräumen

**~ 'up** ❶ *v.i.* aufräumen. ❷ *v.t.* aufräumen; in Ordnung bringen ‹Text›

**tie** /taɪ/ ❶ *v.t.*, **tying** /'taɪɪŋ/ Ⓐ binden **(to** an + *Akk.*, **into** zu); **~ the prisoner's legs together** dem Gefangenen die Beine zusammenbinden; **~ an apron round you[r waist]** binde dir eine Schürze um; **can he ~ his own shoes/tie?** kann er sich *(Dat.)* die Schuhe/die Krawatte selbst binden?; **~ a**

**knot** einen Knoten machen; ⇒ *also* **hand** 1 A; Ⓑ (*Sport: gain equal score in*) **~ the match** unentschieden spielen; **they ~d the match at 3 all** es stand unentschieden drei beide; Ⓒ (*restrict*) binden (**to** an + *Akk.*); Ⓓ (*Building*) verbinden ‹Balken›.
❷ *v.i.*, **tying** Ⓐ (*be fastened*) **it won't ~:** es lässt sich nicht binden; **it ~s at the back** es wird hinten gebunden; **where does the sash ~?** wo bindet man die Schärpe?; Ⓑ (*have equal scores, votes, etc.*) **~ for second place in the competition/election** mit gleicher Punktzahl den zweiten Platz im Wettbewerb/mit gleicher Stimmenzahl den zweiten Platz bei der Wahl erreichen; **~ 6 : 6** mit 6 : 6 ein Unentschieden erreichen.
❸ *n.* Ⓐ (*worn round collar*) Krawatte, *die;* ⇒ *also* **old** 1 F; Ⓑ (*cord etc. for fastening*) Band, *das;* **~ fastening** Verschnürung, *die;* Ⓒ (*fig.*) (*bond*) Band, *das;* (*restriction*) Bindung, *die;* **~s of friendship/family ~s** Freundschafts-/Familienbande *Pl.* (*geh.*); **have ~s with a firm** Beziehungen zu einer Firma unterhalten; **find that sth. is a ~:** sich durch etw. gebunden fühlen; **be a ~ for sb.** für jmdn. eine Belastung sein; Ⓓ (*Building*) Binder, *der;* Ⓔ (*Amer. Railw.*) Schwelle, *die;* Ⓕ (*Mus.*) Haltebogen, *der;* Ⓖ (*equality*) (*of scores*) Punktgleichheit, *die;* (*of votes*) Patt, *das;* Stimmengleichheit, *die;* **there was a ~ for third place** zwei Teilnehmer landeten punktgleich auf dem dritten Platz; **end in** *or* **be a ~:** unentschieden *od.* mit einem Unentschieden enden; Ⓗ (*Sport: match*) Begegnung, *die;* **draw an easy ~:** einen leichten Gegner ziehen; Ⓘ (*Amer.: shoe*) Schnürschuh, *der*

**~ 'back** *v.t.* zurückbinden; **~ one's hair back in a ponytail** sein Haar hinten zu einem Pferdeschwanz zusammenbinden

**~ 'down** *v.t.* Ⓐ (*fasten*) festbinden; Ⓑ (*fig.: restrict*) binden; **there are too many things tying me down here** ich bin hier zu sehr gebunden; **be ~d down by sth.** durch etw. gebunden *od.* eingeschränkt sein; **~ sb. down to conditions/a time/a schedule** jmdn. auf Bedingungen/eine Zeit/einen Zeitplan festlegen

**~ 'in** ❶ *v.i.* **~ in with sth.** zu etw. passen. ❷ *v.t.* **~ sth. in with sth.** etw. mit etw. abstimmen; ⇒ *also* **~-in**

**~ 'up** *v.t.* Ⓐ (*bind*) festbinden; festmachen ‹Boot›; **~ up a parcel with string** ein Paket verschnüren; **~ sth. up in[to] bundles** etw. zu Bündeln zusammenbinden; Ⓑ (*complete arrangements for*) abschließen; **~ up a few loose ends** (*fig.*) ein paar letzte Kleinigkeiten erledigen; Ⓒ (*make unavailable*) fest anlegen ‹Geld›; **~ up property** Eigentum einer Verfügungsbeschränkung unterwerfen; Ⓓ ⇒ **~ in** 2; Ⓔ (*keep busy*) beschäftigen; **I am ~d up this evening** ich habe heute Abend zu tun. ⇒ *also* **~-up**

**tie: ~ bar** *n.* (*Building*) Anker, *der;* **~ beam** *n.* (*Building*) Binderbalken, *der;* **~break, ~breaker** *ns.* Tiebreak, *der od. das;* **~ clip** *n.* Krawattenhalter, *der*

**tied** /taɪd/ *adj.* (*Brit.*) Ⓐ **~ cottage** *or* **house** (*of farmworker*) Wohnhaus für Farmarbeiter; (*of caretaker etc.*) Dienstwohnhaus, *das;* Ⓑ **~ house** (*public house supplying one brewer's beers*) Vertragsgaststätte, *die*

**tie: ~-in** *n.: gleichzeitige [Wieder]aufführung eines Films o. Ä. mit der [Neu]veröffentlichung des zugrunde liegenden Buches;* **~-on** *adj.* Anhänge-; **~-on label** Anhänger, *der;* **~pin** *n.* Krawattennadel, *die*

**tier** /tɪə(r)/ *n.* Ⓐ (*row*) Rang, *der;* Ⓑ (*unit*) Stufe, *die*

**tiered** /tɪəd/ *adj.* gestuft ‹Hörsaal, Theater›; **a three-~ wedding cake** eine dreistöckige Hochzeitstorte; **a three-~ shelf [unit]** ein Regal mit drei Fächern

**tie rod** *n.* Ⓐ (*Motor Veh.*) Spurstange, *die;* Ⓑ (*Building*) Querlatte, *die*

**Tierra del Fuego** /tɪerə del 'fweɪgəʊ/ *pr. n.* Feuerland (*das*)

**tie-up** *n.* Verbindung, *die*

**tiff** /tɪf/ *n.* Krach, *der* (*ugs.*); Streit, *der;* **have a ~ with sb. over sth.** mit jmdm. wegen etw. Krach haben

**tiger** /'taɪgə(r)/ *n.* Ⓐ (*Zool.*) Tiger, *der;* **American ~** ⇒ **jaguar**; **paper ~** (*fig.*) Papiertiger, *der;* **ride a ~** (*fig.*) mit dem Feuer spielen; Ⓑ (*fierce or energetic person*) Kämpfernatur, *die*

**tiger: ~ cat** *n.* (*Zool.*) Tigerkatze, *die;* **~ e'conomy** *n.* Tigerstaat, *der;* **~ lily** *n.* (*Bot.*) Tigerlilie, *die;* **~ moth** *n.* (*Zool.*) Bärenspinner, *der;* **~'s eye** *n.* (*Min.*) Tigerauge, *das;* **~ shark** *n.* (*Zool.*) Tigerhai, *der*

**tight** /taɪt/ ❶ *adj.* Ⓐ (*firm*) fest; fest angezogen ‹Schraube, Mutter›; festsitzend ‹Korken, Deckel›; **be very ~:** sehr fest sitzen; **the drawer/window is ~:** die Schublade/das Fenster klemmt; Ⓑ (*close-fitting*) eng ‹Kleid, Hose, Schuh usw.›; **this shoe is rather [too] ~** *or* **a rather ~ fit** dieser Schuh ist etwas zu eng; Ⓒ (*impermeable*) **~ seal/joint** dichter Verschluss/dichte Fuge; Ⓓ (*taut*) straff; **a ~ feeling in one's chest** ein Gefühl der Beklemmung *od.* Enge in der Brust; Ⓔ (*with little space*) knapp; gedrängt ‹Programm›; **it is a ~ space** der Platz ist knapp; es ist [zu] wenig Platz; **it is a ~ squeeze with seven people in the car** es ist sehr eng zu siebt im Wagen; Ⓕ (*strict*) streng ‹Kontrolle, Disziplin›; straff ‹Organisation›; Ⓖ (*Econ.*) knapp ‹Geld›; angespannt ‹Markt›; Ⓗ (*coll.: stingy*) knauserig (*ugs.*); Ⓘ (*difficult to negotiate*) **a ~ corner** eine enge Kurve; **be in/get oneself into a ~ corner** *or* (*coll.*) **spot [over sth.]** (*fig.*) [wegen etw.] in der Klemme sein/in die Klemme geraten (*ugs.*); Ⓙ (*coll.: drunk*) voll (*salopp*); **get ~:** sich voll laufen lassen (*salopp*); **she got ~ on a couple of drinks** nach ein paar Drinks war sie voll (*salopp*); Ⓚ (*Sport: evenly contested*) hart umkämpft; knapp ‹Rennen›.
❷ *adv.* Ⓐ (*firmly*) fest; **hold ~!** halt dich fest!; ⇒ *also* **sit** 1 B; **sleep** 2 A; Ⓑ (*so as to leave no space*) [ganz] voll; **a train packed ~ with commuters** ein mit Pendlern voll gestopfter Zug (*ugs.*).
❸ *n. in pl.* Ⓐ (*Brit.*) **[pair of] ~s** Strumpfhose, *die;* Ⓑ (*of dancer etc.*) Trikothose, *die*

**tighten** /'taɪtn/ ❶ *v.t.* Ⓐ [fest] anziehen ‹Knoten, Schraube, Mutter usw.›; straff ziehen ‹Seil, Schnur›; anspannen ‹Muskeln›; verstärken ‹Griff›; **~ one's belt** (*fig.*) den Gürtel enger schnallen (*ugs.*); Ⓑ (*make stricter*) verschärfen ‹Kontrolle, Gesetz, Vorschrift›. ❷ *v.i.* Ⓐ sich spannen; ‹Knoten:› sich zusammenziehen; **her hands ~ed on the steering wheel** ihre Hände krampften sich um das Steuer; Ⓑ (*become stricter*) ‹Gesetze, Bestimmungen:› verschärft werden

**~ 'up** ❶ *v.t.* Ⓐ anziehen; (*retighten*) nachziehen; Ⓑ (*make stricter*) verschärfen ‹Gesetze, Bestimmungen, Kontrollen›; **~ up security** die Sicherheitsmaßnahmen verschärfen. ❷ *v.i.* härter durchgreifen; **~ up on security/drunken driving** die Sicherheitsmaßnahmen verschärfen/bei Trunkenheit am Steuer schärfer durchgreifen

**tight: ~-'fisted** *adj.* geizig; **a ~-fisted old fellow** ein alter Geizhals; **~-fitting** *adj.* eng anliegend ‹Pullover, Trikot›; **~-lipped** *adj.* Ⓐ (*without emotion*) mit zusammengepressten Lippen *nachgestellt;* Ⓑ (*silent*) verschwiegen

**tightly** /'taɪtlɪ/ *adv.* Ⓐ (*firmly*) fest; **fit ~** ‹Maschinenteil usw.:› fest sitzen; ‹Kleidungsstück:› eng anliegen; **fasten sth. ~:** etw. gut befestigen; **put the cork in ~:** den Korken fest hineindrücken; Ⓑ (*strictly*) streng; Ⓒ (*tautly*) straff; Ⓓ (*closely*) dicht; **~ packed** voll gestopft (*ugs.*) ‹Zug, Koffer›; **a ~ organized schedule** ein gedrängtes Programm; Ⓔ **~ fought** (*evenly contested*) hart umkämpft

**tightness** /'taɪtnɪs/ *n., no pl.* Ⓐ (*lack of leakage*) Dichtheit, *die;* Ⓑ (*firmness*) Festigkeit, *die;* (*closeness of fit*) enger Sitz; Ⓒ (*strictness of control or discipline*) Schärfe, *die;* Strenge, *die;* Ⓓ (*tautness*) Straffheit, *die;* **feel [a] ~ across the chest** ein Gefühl der Beklemmung in der Brust haben; Ⓔ (*of schedule*) Gedrängtheit, *die;* Ⓕ (*Econ.: scarcity*) Knappheit, *die;* (*of market*) Angespanntheit, *die;* Ⓖ (*of bend in road*) Enge, *die;* Ⓗ **~ with money** Knauserigkeit, *die* (*ugs.*); Ⓘ (*Sport: of match*) Ausgeglichenheit, *die*

**'tightrope** *n.* Drahtseil, *das;* **walk a ~** (*fig.*) einen Balanceakt vollführen; *attrib.* **~ walker** Seiltänzer, *der*/-tänzerin, *die*

**tigress** /'taɪgrɪs/ *n.* (*Zool.*) Tigerin, *die*

**tilde** /'tɪldə/ *n.* (*Ling.*) Tilde, *die*

**tile** /taɪl/ ❶ *n.* Ⓐ (*on roof*) Ziegel, *der;* (*on floor, wall*) Fliese, *die;* (*on stove; also esp. designer ~*) Kachel, *die;* **spend the night on the ~s** (*fig. coll.*) die ganze Nacht durchsumpfen (*salopp*); Ⓑ (*Games*) Spielstein, *der.* ❷ *v.t.* [mit Ziegeln] decken ‹Dach›; fliesen ‹Wand, Fußboden, Bad›; kacheln ‹Wand, Bad›; **~d roof** Ziegeldach, *das;* **~d floor** Fliesenboden, *der*

**tiler** /'taɪlə(r)/ *n.* (*of roofs*) Dachdecker, *der*/-deckerin, *die;* (*of floors, walls*) Fliesenleger, *der*/-legerin, *die*

**tiling** /'taɪlɪŋ/ *n., no pl., no indef. art.* ⇒ **tile** 1 A: Ⓐ (*fixing tiles*) (*on roof*) [Dach]decken, *das;* (*on floor*) Fliesen[legen], *das;* (*on wall*) Kacheln, *das;* Fliesen, *das;* Ⓑ (*set of tiles*) Ziegel/Kacheln/Fliesen

**till**[1] /tɪl/ *v.t.* (*Agric.*) bestellen

**till**[2] ❶ *prep.* bis; (*followed by article + noun*) bis zu; **not [...] ~:** erst; **from morning ~ evening** von morgens bis abends; ⇒ *also* **until** 1. ❷ *conj.* bis; ⇒ *also* **until** 2

**till**[3] *n.* Kasse, *die;* **at the ~:** an der Kasse; **have/put one's hand** *or* **fingers in the ~** (*fig.*) in die Kasse greifen

**tillage** /'tɪlɪdʒ/ *n., no pl.* (*Agric.*) (*tilling*) Bestellung, *die;* (*land tilled*) Ackerland, *das*

**tiller** /'tɪlə(r)/ *n.* (*Naut.*) Pinne, *die* (*Seemannsspr.*)

**'till receipt** *n.* Kassenzettel, *der;* Kassenbon, *der*

**tilt** /tɪlt/ ❶ *v.i.* Ⓐ kippen; **the chair ~s back** die Sessellehne kippt nach hinten; **the board ~ed [up] when he stepped on it** das Brett schnellte hoch, als er darauf trat; Ⓑ (*Hist.: joust*) tjostieren; **~ at** mit der Lanze angreifen; (*fig.*) anprangern; ⇒ *also* **windmill** A. ❷ *v.t.* kippen; neigen ‹Kopf›. ❸ *n.* Ⓐ (*sloping position*) Schräglage, *die;* **give sth. a ~:** etw. kippen *od.* schräg stellen; **a 45° ~:** eine Neigung *od.* ein Neigungswinkel von 45°; Ⓑ (*fig.: attack*) Angriff, *der;* **have** *or* **make a ~ at sb./sth.** jmdn./etw. angreifen *od.* attackieren; Ⓒ **[at] full ~:** mit voller Wucht

**tilth** /tɪlθ/ *n.* Ackerkrume, *die;* **rake a seedbed to a good ~:** ein Saatbeet gut [auf]lockern

**timber** /'tɪmbə(r)/ *n.* Ⓐ *no pl.* (*wood for building*) [Bau]holz, *das;* **sawn ~:** Schnittholz, *das;* Ⓑ (*type of wood*) Holzart, *die;* Holz, *das;* Ⓒ *no pl., no indef. art.* (*trees*) Wald, *der;* **cut down** *or* **fell ~:** Holz schlagen; **put land under ~:** Land aufforsten (*Forstw.*); **standing ~:** Baumholz, *das* (*Forstw.*); Ⓓ (*beam, piece of wood*) Balken, *der;* (*Naut.*) Spant, *das;* **floor ~s** [Boden]balken; ⇒ *also* **shiver**[2] 2; Ⓔ **~!** Baum fällt!; Achtung! (*Ausruf bei Holzfällarbeiten*)

**timbered** /'tɪmbəd/ *adj.* Ⓐ (*wooded*) bewaldet; Ⓑ (*built of wood*) hölzern; Holz-; (*covered with planks*) holzverkleidet

**timber: ~-framed** *adj.* Fachwerk‹bau, -haus›; ‹Rathaus, Jagdschloss usw.› in Fachwerkbauweise; **~-framing** *n., no pl., no indef. art.* (*structure*) Fachwerk, *das;* (*method*) Fachwerkbauweise, *die*

**timbering** /'tɪmbərɪŋ/ *n., no pl., no indef. art.* Balkenwerk, *das;* (*of timber-framed house*) Fachwerk, *das*

**timber: ~line** *n.* (*Geog.*) Baumgrenze, *die;* **~ yard** *n.* Holzlager, *das*

**timbre** /'tæmbə(r), 'tæbr/ *n.* (*Mus.*) Timbre, *das*

**Timbuctoo** /tɪmbʌk'tuː/ *pr. n.* ▶ 1626 Timbuktu (*das*)

**time** /taɪm/ ❶ *n.* Ⓐ *no pl., no art.* Zeit, *die;* **the greatest composer of all ~:** der größte Komponist aller Zeiten; **for all ~:** für immer [und ewig]; **past/present/future ~:** Vergangenheit, *die*/Gegenwart, *die*/Zukunft, *die;* **stand the test of ~:** die Zeit überdauern; sich bewähren; **in [the course of] ~, as ~ goes on/went on** mit der Zeit; im

Laufe der Zeit; **as old as ~:** uralt; **~ will tell** *or* **show** die Zukunft wird es zeigen; **~ and tide wait for no man** das Rad der Zeit lässt sich nicht anhalten; **at this point** *or* **moment in ~:** zum gegenwärtigen Zeitpunkt; **~ flies** die Zeit vergeht [wie] im Fluge; **how ~ flies!** wie [schnell] die Zeit vergeht!; **work against ~:** unter Zeitdruck arbeiten; **in ~, with ~** (*sooner or later*) mit der Zeit; ⇒ *also* **healer**; **B** (*interval, available or allotted period*) Zeit, *die;* **in a week's/month's/year's ~:** in einer Woche/in einem Monat/Jahr; **there is ~ for that** dafür ist *od.* haben wir noch Zeit; **it takes me all my ~ to do it** es beansprucht meine ganze Zeit, es zu tun; **it took me all my ~ to persuade him** ich hatte die größte Mühe, ihn zu überreden; **give one's ~ to sth.** einer Sache (*Dat.*) seine Zeit opfern; **waste of ~:** Zeitverschwendung, *die;* **spend [most of one's/a lot of] ~ on sth./[in] doing sth.** [die meiste/viel] Zeit mit etw. zubringen/damit verbringen, etw. zu tun; **I have been waiting for some/a long ~:** ich warte schon seit einiger Zeit/schon lange; **she will be there for [quite] some ~:** sie wird ziemlich lange dort sein; **spend some ~ in a place** sich eine Zeit lang an einem Ort aufhalten; **be pressed for ~:** keine Zeit haben; (*have to finish quickly*) in Zeitnot sein; **pass the ~:** sich (*Dat.*) die Zeit vertreiben; **length of ~:** Zeit[dauer], *die;* **make ~ for sb./sth.** sich (*Dat.*) für jmdn./etw. Zeit nehmen; **a short ~ ago** vor kurzem; **that's a long ~ ago** das ist schon lange her; **in one's own ~:** in seiner Freizeit; (*whenever one wishes*) wann man will; **one's ~ is one's own** man kann über seine Zeit frei verfügen; **take one's ~ [over sth.]** sich (*Dat.*) [für etw.] Zeit lassen; (*be slow*) sich (*Dat.*) Zeit [mit etw.] lassen; **~ is money** (*prov.*) Zeit ist Geld (*Spr.*); **we're out of ~, our ~'s up** unsere Zeit ist um; **on ~** (*Amer.: on hire purchase*) auf Raten; **in [good] ~** (*not late*) rechtzeitig; **all the** *or* **this ~:** die ganze Zeit; (*without ceasing*) ständig; **all the ~ you're standing there arguing things are only getting worse** während du hier herumstehst und argumentierst, wird alles nur immer schlimmer; **since ~ immemorial** *or* **out of mind** seit undenklichen Zeiten; **in [less than** *or* **next to] no ~:** innerhalb kürzester Zeit; im Nu *od.* Handumdrehen; **it was 'no ~ [at all] before she was back** sie war im Nu zurück; **in 'half the ~:** in der Hälfte der Zeit; **'half the ~** (*coll.: as often as not*) die halbe Zeit; **it will take [some] ~:** es wird einige Zeit dauern; **have ~ on one's hands** viel Zeit und Muße haben; (*have nothing to do*) nichts zu tun haben; **have the/no ~:** Zeit/keine Zeit haben; **have no ~ for sb./sth.** für jmdn./etw. ist einem seine Zeit zu schade; **we have no ~ to lose** wir dürfen keine Zeit verlieren; **there is no ~ to lose** *or* **be lost** es ist keine Zeit zu verlieren; **lose no ~ in doing sth.** (*not delay*) etw. unverzüglich tun; **lose no ~ doing sth.** (*not waste ~*) keine Zeit damit vergeuden, etw. zu tun; **do ~** (*coll.*) eine Strafe absitzen (*ugs.*); **he lived out his ~ in peace** er verbrachte den Rest seines Lebens in Ruhe; **in my '~** (*heyday*) zu meiner Zeit (*ugs.*); (*in the course of my life*) im Laufe meines Lebens; **in 'my ~** (*period at a place*) zu meiner Zeit (*ugs.*); **in my father's ~:** zu [Leb]zeiten meines Vaters; **~ off** *or* **out** freie Zeit; **get/take ~ off** frei bekommen/sich (*Dat.*) frei nehmen (*ugs.*); **take ~ out to look at this properly** nimm dir die Zeit, um dir das richtig anzuschauen; **T~!** (*Boxing*) Stop!; Time!; (*Brit.: in pub*) Feierabend!; **~, [ladies and] gentlemen, please!** wir machen Feierabend, meine [Damen und] Herren!; **have a lot of ~ for sb.** (*fig.*) für jmdn. viel übrig haben; ⇒ *also* **gain** 2 A; **hand** 1 C; **serve** 1 D; **C** *no pl.* (*moment or period destined for purpose*) Zeit, *die;* **harvest/Christmas ~:** Ernte-/Weihnachtszeit, *die;* **there is a ~ and place for everything** alles zu seiner Zeit; **now is the ~ to do it** jetzt ist die richtige Zeit, es zu tun; **~ for lunch** Zeit zum Mittagessen; **it is ~ to go** es wird Zeit zu gehen; **it's [about] ~ they were going** es ist [an der] Zeit, dass sie gehen; **his ~ was drawing near** (*~ of death*) seine Zeit nahte (*geh. verhüll.*); **look/get old before one's ~:** vorzeitig altern; **and not before ~:** und es wurde auch Zeit; **when the ~ comes/came** wenn es so weit ist/als es so weit war; **on ~** (*punctually*) pünktlich; **ahead of ~:** zu früh ‹ankommen›; vorzeitig ‹fertig werden›; **all in good ~:** alles zu seiner Zeit; **you'll find out in good ~:** du wirst es früh genug herausfinden; ⇒ *also* **be** 2 A; **behind** 2 E; **D** *in sing. or pl.* (*circumstances*) Zeit, *die;* **~s are good/bad/have changed** die Zeiten sind gut/schlecht/haben sich verändert; **have a good ~:** Spaß haben (*ugs.*); sich amüsieren; **have quite a ~ [of it]** viel durchmachen; **have a hard ~ [of it]** eine schwere Zeit durchmachen; ⇒ *also* **life** E; **E** (*associated with events or person[s]*) Zeit, *die;* **in ~ of peace/war** in Friedens-/Kriegszeiten; **in Tudor/Napoleon's/ancient ~s** zur Zeit der Tudors/Napoleons/der Antike; **in prehistoric ~s** in vorgeschichtlicher Zeit; **in former/modern ~s** früher/heutzutage; **scientists of the ~:** Wissenschaftler jener Zeit; **the good old ~s** die gute alte Zeit; **Queen Victoria and her ~[s]** Königin Viktoria und ihre Zeit; **~ 'was when ...:** es gab eine Zeit, da ...; **ahead of** *or* **before one's/its ~:** seiner Zeit voraus; **at 'one ~** (*previously*) früher; ⇒ *also* **behind** 2 C; **F** (*occasion*) Mal, *das;* **this ~:** diesmal; **for the first ~:** zum ersten Mal; **[the] second ~ [a]round** beim zweiten Mal; **next ~ you come** wenn du das nächste Mal kommst; **ten/a hundred/a thousand ~s** zehn-/hundert-/tausendmal; **~s without number** unzählige Male; **I've told you a hundred ~s ...:** ich habe dir schon hundertmal gesagt, ... (*ugs.*); **many ~s** sehr oft; **many's the ~ [that] ..., many a ~ ...:** viele Male ...; **there are/were ~s when ...:** es gibt Zeiten, wenn .../es gab Zeiten, als ...; **at all ~s** jederzeit; **at ~s** gelegentlich; **from ~ to ~:** von Zeit zu Zeit; **at other ~s** sonst; **at all other ~s** zu allen anderen Zeiten; **at one ~ or another** irgendwann einmal; **this is no ~ to do that** es ist jetzt nicht die Zeit, das zu tun; **at a ~ like this/that** unter diesen/solchen Umständen; **at the** *or* **that ~** (*in the past*) damals; **it depends on which doctor is on duty at the ~:** es hängt davon ab, welcher Arzt gerade Bereitschaftsdienst hat; **at one ~, at [one and] the same ~** (*simultaneously*) gleichzeitig; **at the same ~** (*nevertheless*) gleichwohl; **at the best of ~s** im günstigsten Fall; **a 'fine ~** (*iron.*) genau die richtige Zeit (*iron.*); **between ~s** zwischendurch; **~ and [~] again, ~ after ~:** immer [und immer] wieder; **pay sb. £6 a ~:** jmdm. für jedes Mal 6 Pfund zahlen; **oranges cost 16p a ~:** Orangen kosten 16 Pence das Stück; **one at a ~:** einzeln; **one stone at a ~:** jeweils nur ein Stein; **two at a ~:** jeweils zwei; **hand me the cups two at a ~:** reich mir immer zwei Tassen gleichzeitig; **for hours/weeks at a ~:** stundenlang/wochenlang [ohne Unterbrechung]; **at this ~** (*Amer.*) heute; (*at this moment*) jetzt; ⇒ *also* **be** 2 A; **every** A; **G** ▶ **1012** (*point in day etc.*) [Uhr]zeit, *die;* **at the same ~ every morning** jeden Morgen um dieselbe Zeit; **what ~ is it?, what is the ~?** wie spät ist es?; **have you [got] the ~?** kannst du mir sagen, wie spät es ist?; **tell the ~** (*read a clock*) die Uhr lesen; **~ of day** Tageszeit, *die;* **[at this] ~ of [the] year** [um diese] Jahreszeit; **this ~ of the month** diese Zeit im Monat; **at this ~ of [the] night** zu dieser Nachtstunde; **know the ~ of day** (*fig.*) sich auskennen; **not give sb. the ~ of day** jmdm. nicht einmal Guten Tag sagen; **pass the ~ of day** (*coll.*) ein paar Worte wechseln; **by this/that ~:** inzwischen; **by the ~ [that] we arrived** bis wir hinkamen; **[by] this ~ tomorrow** morgen um diese Zeit; **keep good ~** ‹Uhr:› genau *od.* richtig gehen; **H** (*amount*) Zeit, *die;* **make good ~:** gut vorwärts kommen; **get paid ~ and a half** 50% Zuschlag bekommen; **[your] ~'s up!** deine Zeit ist um (*ugs.*) *od.* abgelaufen; **I** (*multiplication*) mal; **three ~s four** drei mal vier; **four ~s the size of/higher than sth.** viermal so groß wie/höher als etw.; **~s sign** Malzeichen, *das;* **magnified six ~s** auf das Sechsfache vergrößert; **J** (*Mus.*) (*duration of note*) Zeitdauer, *die;* (*measure*) Takt, *der;* **in three-four ~:** im Dreivierteltakt; **keep in ~ with the music** den Takt halten; **out of ~/in ~:** aus dem/im Takt; **keep ~ with sth.** bei etw. den Takt [ein]halten; **K** (*dated: date of childbirth*) **she is near** *or* **nearing her ~:** ihre Zeit rückt näher (*geh. verhüll.*). ❷ *v.t.* **A** (*do at correct ~*) zeitlich abstimmen; **be well/ill ~d** zur richtigen/falschen Zeit kommen; **B** (*set to operate at correct ~*) justieren (*Technik*); einstellen; **~ the bomb to explode at 4 p.m.** den Zeitzünder der Bombe auf 16 Uhr einstellen; **C** (*arrange ~ of arrival/departure of*) **the bus is ~d to connect with the train** der Bus hat einen direkten Anschluss an den Zug; **be ~d to take 90 minutes** fahrplanmäßig 90 Minuten dauern; **D** (*measure ~ taken by*) stoppen; **~ an egg** auf die richtige Kochdauer für ein Ei achten

**time: ~-and-'motion** *adj.* REFA-‹Techniker, Fachmann›; **~-and-motion study** Arbeitsstudie, *die;* **~ bomb** *n.* (*lit. or fig.*) Zeitbombe, *die;* **~ capsule** *n. Behälter mit Zeitdokumenten, der bei der Grundsteinlegung von [öffentlichen] Bauten eingemauert wird;* **~ check** *n.* Zeitvergleich, *der;* (*to verify*) Blick auf die Uhr; **~-consuming** *adj.* **A** (*taking ~*) zeitaufwendig; **B** (*wasteful of ~*) zeitraubend; **~ exposure** *n.* (*Photog.*) Zeitaufnahme, *die;* **~ factor** *n., no pl.* Zeitfaktor, *der;* **~ fault** *n.* (*Show Jumping*) Zeitfehler, *der;* **~ fuse** *n.* Zeitzünder, *der;* **~-honoured** *adj.* altehrwürdig (*geh.*); althergebracht ‹Brauch, Vorstellung›; **~keeper** *n.* **A** (*person*) Zeitnehmer, *der*/-nehmerin, *die;* **B the watch is a good/bad ~keeper** die Uhr geht genau/nicht genau; **~keeping** *n.* **A** (*Sport*) Zeitmessung, *die;* Zeitnahme, *die;* **B** (*at work*) Einhaltung der Arbeitsstunden; **~ lag** *n.* zeitliche Verzögerung; **~-lapse** *attrib. adj.* (*Photog., Cinemat., Telev.*) Zeitraffer-

**timeless** /'taɪmlɪs/ *adj.* (*rhet./poet.*) zeitlos

**'time limit** *n.* Frist, *die;* **put a ~ on sth.** eine Frist für etw. setzen

**timeliness** /'taɪmlɪnɪs/ *n., no pl.* Rechtzeitigkeit, *die*

**'time lock** *n.* Zeitschloss, *das*

**timely** /'taɪmlɪ/ *adj.* rechtzeitig; **be ~:** zur rechten Zeit kommen; **a ~ piece of advice** ein [guter] Rat zur rechten Zeit

**time: ~ machine** *n.* Zeitmaschine, *die;* **~ 'out** *n.* (*Sport*) Spielunterbrechung, *die;* (*called by one team*) Auszeit, *die;* **~piece** *n.* Chronometer, *das*

**timer** /'taɪmə(r)/ *n.* **A** ⇒ **timekeeper** A; **B** (*device*) Kurzzeitmesser, *der;* (*with switch*) Schaltuhr, *die*

**time: ~-saver** *n.* **be a ~-saver** Zeit sparen; **this is a real ~-saver** dies bedeutet eine echte Zeitersparnis; **~scale** *n.* Zeitskala, *die;* **~share** ❶ *attrib. adj.* **~share apartment** *Ferienwohnung, an der man einen Besitzanteil hat, der es einem erlaubt, eine bestimmte Zeit pro Jahr in dieser Wohnung zu verbringen;* ❷ *n.* ⇒ **~-sharing** B; **~-sharing** *n., no pl., no art.* **A** (*Computing*) Timesharing, *das;* **B** (*joint ownership*) *Eigentum an einer Ferienwohnung o. Ä., das für eine festgelegte Zeit des Jahres gilt;* Timesharing, *das* (*Wirtsch.*); **~ sheet** *n.* Stundenzettel, *der;* **~ signal** *n.* Zeitzeichen, *das;* **~ signature** *n.* (*Mus.*) Taktbezeichnung, *die;* **~ switch** *n.* Zeitschalter, *der;* **~table** *n.* **A** (*scheme of work*) Zeitplan, *der;* (*Educ.*) Stundenplan, *der;* **B** (*Transport*) Fahrplan, *der;* **~ travel** *n.* Reise durch die Zeit; **~ trial** *n.* (*Sport*) (*in cycling*) Zeitfahren, *das;* (*in athletics*) Zeitrennen, *das;* **~ warp** *n.* Verwerfung im Raum-Zeit-Kontinuum; **~-worn** *adj.* abgegriffen ‹Witz, Klischee›; verwittert ‹Gebäude›; **~ zone** *n.* Zeitzone, *die*

**timid** /'tɪmɪd/ *adj.* **A** scheu ‹Tier, Vogel›; **B** (*fearful*) ängstlich ‹Person, Miene, Worte›; **C** (*lacking boldness*) zaghaft; (*shy*) schüchtern

t

**timidity** /tɪˈmɪdɪtɪ/ *n., no pl.* ⇒ **timid**: Scheu, *die;* Ängstlichkeit, *die;* Schüchternheit, *die*

**timidly** /ˈtɪmɪdlɪ/ *adv.* ⇒ **timid**: scheu; ängstlich; schüchtern

**timing** /ˈtaɪmɪŋ/ *n., no pl.* Ⓐ zeitliche Abstimmung; Timing, *das;* **that was perfect ~!** (*as sb. arrives*) du kommst gerade im richtigen Augenblick!; **the ~ of the statement was excellent** der Zeitpunkt für die Erklärung war hervorragend [gewählt]; Ⓑ (*Theatre*) Timing, *das;* Ⓒ (*Motor Veh.*) **ignition/valve ~:** Zündeinstellung, *die*/Ventilsteuerzeiten; **adjust the [ignition] ~:** die Zündung einstellen

**timorous** /ˈtɪmərəs/ *adj.* ängstlich; verängstigt ‹Tier›; (*lacking boldness*) zaghaft ‹Stimme, Auftreten›

**timpani** /ˈtɪmpəni:/ *n. pl.* (*Mus.*) Kesselpauken; Timpani (*fachspr.*)

**timpanist** /ˈtɪmpənɪst/ *n.* ▶ 1261 (*Mus.*) Paukist, *der*/Paukistin, *die*

**tin** /tɪn/ ❶ *n.* Ⓐ (*metal*) Zinn, *das;* **~[-plate]** Weißblech, *das;* Ⓑ (*Cookery*) **cooking ~s** Back- und Bratformen; Ⓒ (*Brit.: for preserving*) [Konserven]dose, *die;* **a ~ of peas** eine Dose Erbsen; Ⓓ (*with separate or hinged lid*) Dose, *die;* **bread ~:** Brotkasten, *der.* ❷ *v.t.*, **-nn-** (*Brit.*) zu Konserven verarbeiten. ❸ *attrib. adj.* Zinn-; ⇒ *also* **lid** A

**tincture** /ˈtɪŋktʃə(r)/ *n.* Ⓐ (*solution*) Tinktur, *die;* Ⓑ (*slight flavour*) leichter Geschmack; (*unpleasant*) Beigeschmack, *der;* (*fig.*) Anflug, *der;* **a ~ of green/red** ein Stich ins Grüne/Rote

**tinder** /ˈtɪndə(r)/ *n.* Zunder, *der;* **as dry as ~:** knochentrocken

ˈ**tinder: ~box** *n.* Zunderbüchse, *die* (*veralt.*); (*fig.: person*) Hitzkopf, *der;* (*fig.: thing*) Pulverfass, *das;* **the old houses are like ~boxes** die alten Häuser sind wie Zunder; **~-dry** *adj.* knochentrocken

**tine** /taɪn/ *n.* Ⓐ (*of deer*) Ende, *das* (*Jägerspr.*); Ⓑ (*of rake, fork*) Zinke, *die*

**tin ˈfoil** *n., no pl.* Stanniol, *das;* (*aluminium foil*) Alufolie, *die*

**ting-a-ling** /ˈtɪŋəlɪŋ/ ❶ *n.* Klingeling, *das.* ❷ *adv.* klingeling

**tinge** /tɪndʒ/ ❶ *v.t.*, **~ing** /ˈtɪndʒɪŋ/ tönen; **a white curtain ~d with pink** ein weißer, ins Zartrosa gehender Vorhang; **her black hair was ~d with grey** ihr schwarzes Haar war grau meliert; (*fig.*) **her admiration was ~d with envy** ihre Bewunderung war nicht ganz frei von Neid. ❷ *n.* [leichte] Färbung; (*fig.*) Hauch, *der;* **a ~ of red in the sky** eine leicht rötliche Färbung des Himmels; **white with a ~ of blue** weiß mit einem Stich ins Bläuliche

**tingle** /ˈtɪŋgl/ ❶ *v.i.* Ⓐ (*feel sensation*) kribbeln; Ⓑ (*cause sensation*) **~ in sb.'s ears** jmdm. in den Ohren klingen *od.* tönen. ❷ *n.* Kribbeln, *das;* **feel a ~ of excitement** vor Aufregung ganz kribbelig sein (*ugs.*)

**tin: ~ ˈgod** *n.* Götze, *der* (*geh.*); Abgott, *der;* **~ ˈhat** *n.* (*coll.*) Blechdeckel, *der* (*salopp*); **~horn** (*Amer.*) ❶ *n.* Angeber, *der* (*ugs.*); ❷ *adj.* angeberisch (*ugs.*)

**tinker** /ˈtɪŋkə(r)/ ❶ *n.* Kesselflicker, *der;* **I don't give a ~'s cuss** (*coll.*) es ist mir völlig Wurs[ch]t (*ugs.*). ❷ *v.i.* **~ with sth.** an etw. (*Dat.*) herumbasteln (*ugs.*)/(*incompetently; also fig.*) herumfuschen (*ugs.*)

**tinkle** /ˈtɪŋkl/ ❶ *n.* Klingeln, *das;* (*of coins*) Klimpern, *das;* **give sb. a ~** (*Brit. coll.: telephone call*) bei jmdm. anklingeln (*ugs.*). ❷ *v.t.* klingeln mit; klimpern mit ‹Münzen›. ❸ *v.i.* ‹Glocke:› klingeln; ‹Münzen:› klimpern; **~ on a piano** auf einem Klavier klimpern

ˈ**tin mine** *n.* Zinnbergwerk, *das*

**tinned** /tɪnd/ *adj.* (*Brit.*) Dosen-; **be ~:** aus der Dose sein

**tinny** /ˈtɪnɪ/ *adj.* Ⓐ (*metallic*) Metall‹geschmack›; blechern ‹Klang›; **taste ~:** nach Metall *od.* (*ugs.*) Büchse schmecken; Ⓑ (*of inferior quality*) billig; **be ~:** Tinnef sein (*ugs.*)

**tin: ~-opener** *n.* (*Brit.*) Dosen-, Büchsenöffner, *der;* **~-pan ˈalley** *n.* die Schlagerindustrie; **~ ˈplate** *n.* Weißblech, *das;* **~-plate** *v.t.* verzinnen; **~-plating** *n.* Verzinnung, *die;* **~pot** *adj.* (*derog.*) schäbig; **~pot town** Kaff, *das* (*ugs.*); **~pot little firm** [kleine] Klitsche (*ugs.*); **~pot dictator** Operettendiktator, *der*

**tinsel** /ˈtɪnsl/ *n.* Ⓐ (*thread*) Metallfaden, *der;* (*for decoration*) Lametta, *das;* (*strip*) Lahn, *der* (*Textilw.*); (*sheet*) Metallfolie, *die;* Ⓑ *also attrib.* **~ [glamour]** Talmiglanz, *der*

**tin: ~smith** *n.* Blechschmied, *der;* **~ ˈsoldier** *n.* Zinnsoldat, *der*

**tint** /tɪnt/ ❶ *n.* Farbton, *der;* **flesh ~s** Fleischtöne; **autumn ~s** herbstliche Farbtöne; **red with a blue ~:** Rot mit einem Stich ins Blaue. ❷ *v.t.* tönen; kolorieren ‹Zeichnung, Stich›; **~ with blue** blau tönen/kolorieren

**tin: ~ tack** *n.* [verzinnter] Drahtstift; **~ ˈwhistle** *n.* Blechflöte, *die*

**tiny** /ˈtaɪnɪ/ *adj.* winzig; **a ~ bit better** (*coll.*) ein klein wenig besser; **sb.'s ~ mind** (*derog.*) jmds. Spatzenhirn (*salopp*)

**tip¹** /tɪp/ ❶ *n.* (*end, point*) Spitze, *die;* **the ~ of his nose/finger/toe** seine Nasen-/Finger-/Zehenspitze; **on the ~s of one's toes** auf Zehenspitzen; **from ~ to toe** vom Scheitel bis zur Sohle; **it is on the ~ of my tongue** es liegt mir auf der Zunge; **a cigarette with a [filter] ~:** eine Zigarette mit Filter. ❷ *v.t.*, **-pp- ~ sth. [with stone/brass]** etw. mit einer [Stein-/Messing]spitze versehen; **~ped cigarette** Filterzigarette, *die*

**tip²** ❶ *v.i.*, **-pp-** (*lean, fall*) kippen; **~ over** umkippen; **~ [up]** ‹Sitz:› nach oben klappen. ❷ *v.t.*, **-pp-:** Ⓐ (*make tilt*) kippen; neigen ‹Kopf›; **~ one's hat [to sb.]** (*Amer.*) seinen Hut lüften[, um jmdn. zu grüßen]; **~ the balance** (*fig.*) den Ausschlag geben; ⇒ *also* **scale²** 1 B; Ⓑ (*make overturn*) umkippen; (*Brit.: discharge*) kippen; **'no ~ping', 'no rubbish to be ~ped'** „Müll abladen verboten"; **he was ~ped into the ditch** er wurde in den Graben geworfen; Ⓒ (*mention as likely winner etc.*) voraussagen ‹Sieger›; **~ sb. to win** auf jmds. Sieg tippen; **be ~ped for the Presidency/a post** als Favorit für die Präsidentschaftswahlen/einen Posten genannt werden; Ⓓ (*coll.: give*) geben; **~ sb. the wink** (*fig.*) jmdm. Bescheid sagen; (**~ *sb. off***) jmdm. einen Tipp geben (*ugs.*); Ⓔ (*give money to*) **~ sb. [20p]** jmdm. [20 Pence] Trinkgeld geben. ❸ *n.* Ⓐ (*money*) Trinkgeld, *das;* **as a ~:** als Trinkgeld; Ⓑ (*special information*) Hinweis, *der;* Tipp, *der* (*ugs.*); (*advice*) Rat, *der;* **hot ~:** heißer Tipp; **give sb. a ~ about doing sth.** jmdm. einen Tipp geben, wie man etw. macht; Ⓒ (*Brit.: place for refuse*) Müllkippe, *die;* Ⓓ (*derog.: untidy place*) Schweinestall, *der;* Ⓔ (*Mining*) Halde, *die*

**~ ˈoff** *v.t.* **~ sb. off** jmdm. einen Hinweis *od.* (*ugs.*) Tipp geben; **be ~ped off by sb.** einen Hinweis *od.* (*ugs.*) Tipp von jmdm. erhalten; ⇒ *also* **tip-off**

**~ ˈover** *v.t. & i.* umkippen

**~ ˈup** *v.t.* hochklappen ‹Sitz›

**tip: ~-and-ˈrun raid** *n.* Blitzangriff [mit anschließendem sofortigem Rückzug]; **~-off** *n.* Hinweis, *der*

**tipper** /ˈtɪpə(r)/ *n.* (*Brit. Motor Veh.*) Kipper, *der*

**tipple** /ˈtɪpl/ ❶ *v.i.* trinken. ❷ *n.* (*coll.: drink*) **have a ~:** einen trinken (*ugs.*); **what's your ~?** was trinken Sie?

**tippler** /ˈtɪplə(r)/ *n.* Trinker, *der*/Trinkerin, *die;* **be a ~:** gern einen trinken (*ugs.*)

**tipsily** /ˈtɪpsɪlɪ/ *adv.* (*coll.*) angeheitert; beschwipst (*ugs.*)

**tipster** /ˈtɪpstə(r)/ *n.* Tippgeber, *der*/-geberin, *die*

**tipsy** /ˈtɪpsɪ/ *adj.* (*coll.*) angeheitert; beschwipst (*ugs.*)

**tip: ~toe** ❶ *v.i.* auf Zehenspitzen gehen; (*walk quietly*) sich schleichen *od.* stehlen; ❷ *adv.* auf Zehenspitzen; ❸ *n.* **on ~toe[s]** auf Zehenspitzen; **stand on ~toe** sich auf die Zehenspitzen stellen; **be standing on ~toe** auf den Zehenspitzen stehen; **~top** /ˈtɪptɒp/ (*coll.*) ❶ *adj.* ausgezeichnet; tipptopp (*ugs.*); **it was a ~top hotel** das Hotel war tipptopp; **be in ~top condition** in einem Topzustand/‹Person:› in Topform sein; ❷ *adv.* tipptopp (*ugs.*); ausgezeichnet; **~-up seat** *n.* Klappsitz, *der*

**TIR** *abbr.* (*Brit.*) **Transport International Routier** *Internationaler Straßentransport*

**tirade** /taɪˈreɪd, tɪˈreɪd/ *n.* Tirade, *die* (*geh.*); **a ~ of abuse** eine Schimpfkanonade (*ugs.*)

**tire¹** /ˈtaɪə(r)/ (*Amer.*) ⇒ **tyre**

**tire²** ❶ *v.t.* ermüden. ❷ *v.i.* müde werden; ermüden; **~ of sth./doing sth.** einer Sache (*Gen.*) überdrüssig werden/es müde werden (*geh.*), etw. zu tun

**~ ˈout** *v.t.* erschöpfen; **~ oneself out doing sth.** etw. bis zur Erschöpfung tun

**tired** /ˈtaɪəd/ *adj.* Ⓐ (*weary*) müde; Ⓑ (*fed up*) **be ~ of sth./doing sth.** etw. satt haben/es satt haben *od.* (*geh.*) es müde sein, etw. zu tun; **get** *or* **grow ~ of sb./sth.** jmds./einer Sache überdrüssig werden; Ⓒ (*fig.: hackneyed*) abgegriffen; abgedroschen (*ugs.*)

**tiredness** /ˈtaɪədnɪs/ *n., no pl.* Müdigkeit, *die*

**tireless** /ˈtaɪəlɪs/ *adj.*, **tirelessly** /ˈtaɪəlɪslɪ/ *adv.* unermüdlich

**tiresome** /ˈtaɪəsəm/ *adj.* Ⓐ (*wearisome*) mühsam; Ⓑ (*annoying*) lästig; **how ~!** so ein Ärger!

**tiresomely** /ˈtaɪəsəmlɪ/ *adv.* Ⓐ (*wearisomely*) mühsam; **~ lengthy** mühsam und langwierig; Ⓑ (*annoyingly*) lästigerweise; **~ facetious** auf unangenehme Art albern

**tiring** /ˈtaɪərɪŋ/ *adj.* ermüdend; anstrengend ‹Tag, Person›

**tiro** /ˈtaɪərəʊ/ *n., pl.* **~s** Anfänger, *der*/Anfängerin, *die*

**'tis** /tɪz/ (*arch./poet.*) ... **it is**

**tissue** /ˈtɪʃu:, ˈtɪsju:/ *n.* Ⓐ (*woven fabric; also Biol.*) Gewebe, *das;* Ⓑ (*absorbent paper*) **[paper] ~:** Papiertuch, *das;* (*handkerchief*) Papiertaschentuch, *das;* Ⓒ (*for wrapping*) **~ [paper]** Seidenpapier, *das;* Ⓓ (*fig.: web*) Geflecht, *das;* **~ of lies** Lügengewebe, *das*

**tit¹** /tɪt/ *n.* (*Ornith.*) Meise, *die;* ⇒ *also* **blue tit**; **great tit**

**tit²** *n.* **it's ~ for tat** wie du mir, so ich dir; *attrib.* **~-for-tat killing/assassination** tödlicher Vergeltungsschlag *od.* Racheakt; **give sb. ~ for tat** es jmdm. mit gleicher Münze heimzahlen

**tit³** *n.* (*coarse*) Ⓐ (*nipple*) Zitze, *die* (*derb*); Ⓑ *usu. pl.* (*breast*) Titte, *die* (*derb*)

**tit⁴** *n.* (*coll.: fool*) Trottel, *der* (*ugs.*)

**Titan** /ˈtaɪtən/ *n.* (*fig.*) Titan, *der* (*geh.*)

**titanic** /taɪˈtænɪk/ *adj.* gigantisch

**titanium** /taɪˈteɪnɪəm, tɪˈteɪnɪəm/ *n.* (*Chem.*) Titan, *das*

**titbit** /ˈtɪtbɪt/ *n.* Ⓐ (*food*) Häppchen, *das* (*ugs.*); Ⓑ (*piece of news*) Neuigkeit, *die*

**titch** /tɪtʃ/ *n.* (*coll.*) Knirps, *der* (*ugs.*)

**titchy** /ˈtɪtʃɪ/ *adj.* (*coll.*) klitzeklein (*ugs.*)

**tithe** /taɪð/ *n.* (*Hist.*) Zehnt[e], *der;* **pay ~s** den Zehnten bezahlen; **~ barn** Zehntscheuer, *die*

**Titian** /ˈtɪʃn/ ❶ *pr. n.* Tizian (*der*). ❷ *n.* **~ [red]** Tizianrot, *das.* ❸ *adj.* **~ [red]** tizianrot

**titillate** /ˈtɪtɪleɪt/ *v.t.* erregen; **~ sb.'s palate** jmds. Gaumen kitzeln

**titillation** /tɪtɪˈleɪʃn/ *n.* Kitzel, *der*

**titivate** /ˈtɪtɪveɪt/ *v.t.* (*coll.*) aufmöbeln (*ugs.*); **~ [oneself]** sich zurechtmachen

**title** /ˈtaɪtl/ *n.* Ⓐ (*of book etc.*) Titel, *der;* (*of article, chapter*) Überschrift, *die;* **the flyweight ~** (*Sport*) der Titel im Fliegengewicht; **the ~s** (*Cinemat., Telev.*) der Vorspann; Ⓑ ▶ 1617 (*of person*) Titel, *der;* (*of nobility*) [Adels]titel, *der;* (*of organization*) Name, *der;* **people with ~s** Adlige; Ⓒ (*Law: recognized claim*) Rechtsanspruch, *der* (**to** auf + *Akk.*); **~ [of ownership]** Besitztitel, *der*

**titled** /ˈtaɪtld/ *adj.* adlig

**title: ~ deed** *n.* (*Law*) Eigentumsurkunde, *die;* **~-holder** *n.* (*Sport*) Titelhalter, *der*/-halterin, *die;* **~ page** *n.* Titelseite, *die;* **~ role** *n.* Titelrolle, *die*

# Titles

The equivalent of *Mr* is **Herr**, but remember that an **n** has to be added when writing an address.

····➤ Letter-writing for more details.

**Frau** is the equivalent for both *Mrs* and *Ms*, since it is used for both married women and unmarried women who are old enough to be married. The equivalent for *Miss* is **Fräulein**, but increasingly its use is restricted to young girls of school age.

***Hello, Mr White***
= Guten Tag, Herr White

***Goodbye, Mrs Williams***
= Auf Wiedersehen, Frau Williams

The Germans being more formal than either the British or the Americans, titles and surnames are used far more, and first names are only used between young people and those who know one another really well (and say **du** to one another).

The other important point to remember is that **Herr** and **Frau** are added before other titles, both on letters and when greeting someone:

***Good morning, doctor***
= Guten Morgen, Herr Doktor/(*or to a woman doctor*) Frau Doktor

***Good evening, professor***
= Guten Abend, Herr Professor/(*or to a woman professor*) Frau Professor

In these cases the feminine endings are no longer used (**Frau Doktorin, Frau Professorin**), but they will still be found on other titles such as **Frau Studienrätin** (a secondary school teacher with tenure). The feminine forms of aristocratic titles are used on the other hand (**Fürst→Fürstin, Graf→Gräfin, Baron→Baronin, Freiherr→Freifrau**), but **Herr** and **Frau** are not inserted before the title. Hence you refer to a count as **Graf ...**, and to a countess as **Gräfin ...** .

While the full name is of course given on letters, when speaking to someone with a title the name is usually omitted:

***Good morning, Dr Brown***
= Guten Morgen, Herr/Frau Doktor

***Come in, Professor Evans***
= Kommen Sie herein, Herr/Frau Professor

***How are you, Colonel Weston?***
= Wie geht es Ihnen, Herr Oberst?

An exception is the title **Doktor**, where the name is omitted when addressing a doctor of medicine but not when addressing someone who holds the academic title of **Doktor**.

Even when referring to someone with an academic title in the third person, **Herr** and **Frau** are usually included:

***... as Professor Schmidt explained yesterday***
= wie Herr Professor Schmidt schon gestern erklärt hat

***Tell Dr Wilkenhorst to come here***
= Sagen Sie Herrn/Frau Dr. Wilkenhorst, er/sie soll hierher kommen

Otherwise usage is much as in English, except that titles are used more often (for instance, the director of an institution should be addressed as **Herr Direktor**), and there are many more titles going with particular jobs than in Britain *or* America.

## Forms of address for dignitaries

***Her Majesty***
= Ihre Majestät

***His Highness***
= Seine Hoheit

***Your Grace***
= Euer Gnaden

***Your Eminence***
= Eure Eminenz

***His Holiness***
= Seine Heiligkeit

Note that *Your* with such titles is translated by the form **Euer, Eure**. This can be omitted in some cases, particularly when the reference is in the third person:

***Your Eminence will be pleased about this***
= Eminenz wird sich darüber freuen

**'titmouse** *n.* (*Ornith.*) Meise, *die*

**titter** /'tɪtə(r)/ ❶ *v.i.* kichern. ❷ *n.* **~[s]** Kichern, *das*

**tittle-tattle** /'tɪtltætl/ ❶ *n.* Klatsch, *der* (*ugs. abwertend*). ❷ *v.i.* klatschen (*ugs. abwertend*)

**titular** /'tɪtjʊlə(r)/ *adj.* Ⓐ (*only in name*) nominell (*geh.*) ‹Führer, Staatsoberhaupt›; Ⓑ (*going with title*) Adels‹rang›; mit einem Adelstitel verbunden ‹Besitztümer›; Ⓒ **~ hero** Titelheld, *der*

**tizzy** /'tɪzɪ/ *n.* (*coll.*) **be in a/get into a ~:** durchdrehen (*ugs.*) (**over** wegen); **be all of a ~:** ganz aus dem Häuschen sein (*ugs.*)

**'T-junction** ⇒ T B

**TNT** *abbr.* **trinitrotoluene** TNT, *das*

**to** ❶ /*before vowel* tʊ, *before consonant* tə, *stressed* tu:/ *prep.* ▶ 1618 Ⓐ (*in the direction of and reaching*) zu; (*with name of place*) nach; **go to work/to the theatre** zur Arbeit/ins Theater gehen; **to Paris/France** nach Paris/Frankreich; **go from town to town** von Stadt zu Stadt ziehen; **throw the ball to me** wirf mir den Ball zu; **to bed with you!** ins Bett mit dir/euch!; Ⓑ (*towards a condition or quality*) zu; **appoint sb. to a post** jmdn. auf einen Posten berufen; **be born to a fortune** reich geboren sein; Ⓒ (*as far as*) bis zu; **from London to Edinburgh** von London [bis] nach Edinburgh; **increase from 10% to 20%** von 10% auf 20% steigen; **from green to violet** von Grün bis Violett; Ⓓ (*next to, facing*) **with one's back to the wall** mit dem Rücken zur Wand; Ⓔ (*implying comparison, ratio, etc.*) **[compared] to** verglichen mit; im Vergleich zu; **3 is to 4 as 6 is to 8** 3 verhält sich zu 4 wie 6 zu 8; **it's ten to one he does sth.** die Chancen stehen zehn zu eins, dass er etw. tut; **sing to a guitar** zur Gitarre singen; Ⓕ *introducing relationship or indirect object* **to sb./sth.** jmdm./einer Sache (*Dat.*); **lend/give/write/explain** *etc.* **sth. to sb.** jmdm. etw. leihen/geben/schreiben/erklären *usw.*; **speak to sb.** mit jmdm. sprechen; **relate to sth.** sich auf etw. (*Akk.*) beziehen; **to me** (*in my opinion*) meiner Meinung nach; **be pleasant to the taste** gut schmecken; **secretary to the Minister** Sekretär des Ministers; **be a good father to one's children** seinen Kindern ein guter Vater sein; **a room to oneself** ein eigenes Zimmer; **get four apples to the pound** vier Äpfel je Pfund bekommen; **there is a moral to this tale** diese Geschichte hat eine Moral; **is there a point to all this?** hat das alles einen Sinn?; **that's all there is to it** mehr ist nicht dazu zu sagen; **what's that to you?** was geht das dich an?; **to repair of rear door** (*in bill or account*) Reparatur [der] Hintertür; Ⓖ ▶ 1012 (*until*) bis; **to the end** bis zum Ende; **to this day** bis heute; **five [minutes] to eight** fünf [Minuten] vor acht; **one minute/two minutes to eight** eine Minute/zwei Minuten vor acht; Ⓗ *with infinitive of a verb* zu; (*expressing purpose, or after* **too**) um [...] zu; **want to know** wissen wollen; **do sth. to annoy sb.** etw. tun, um jmdn. zu ärgern; **too young to marry** zu jung, um zu heiraten; zu jung zum Heiraten; **too hot to drink** zu heiß zum Trinken; **to rebel is pointless** es ist sinnlos zu rebellieren; **he woke to find himself in a strange room** er erwachte und fand sich in einem fremden Zimmer wieder; **those days are gone, never to return** diese Zeit ist vorbei und wird nie wiederkehren (*geh.*); **to be honest/precise, ...:** offen/genau[er] gesagt, ...; **to use a technical term** um einen Fachausdruck zu gebrauchen; **to hear him talk ...:** wenn man ihn reden hört, ...; Ⓘ *as substitute for infinitive* **he would have phoned but forgot to** er hätte angerufen, aber er vergaß es; **she didn't want to go there, but she had to** sie wollte nicht hingehen, aber sie musste; **he said he would ring her, but he had no time to** er sagte, er wolle sie anrufen, aber er hatte keine Zeit [dazu]; **you should buy it; you'd be silly not to** du solltest es kaufen; du wärst dumm, wenn du es nicht tätest.
❷ /tu:/ *adv.* Ⓐ (*just not shut*) **be to** ‹Tür, Fenster:› angelehnt sein; **push a door to** eine Tür anlehnen; Ⓑ **to and fro** hin und her

**toad** /təʊd/ *n.* (*Zool.; fig. derog.*) Kröte, *die*

**toad: ~flax** *n.* (*Bot.*) Leinkraut, *das*; **~-in-the-hole** *n.* (*Gastr.*) *Würstchen, in einen Teig eingebacken*; **~stool** *n.* Giftpilz, *der*; (*Bot.*) Schirmpilz, *der*

**toady** /'təʊdɪ/ ❶ *n.* Kriecher, *der*. ❷ *v.i.* **~ [to sb.]** [vor jmdm.] kriechen (*abwertend*)

**toast** /təʊst/ ❶ *n.* Ⓐ *no pl., no indef. art.* Toast, *der*; **a piece of ~:** eine Scheibe Toast; **cheese/egg on ~:** Toast mit Käse/Ei; **as warm as ~** (*fig.*) schön warm (*ugs.*); Ⓑ (*call to drink*) Toast, *der*; **drink/propose a ~ to sb./sth.** auf jmdn./etw. trinken/einen Toast auf jmdn./etw. ausbringen; **be the ~ of the town** von der ganzen Stadt gefeiert werden. ❷ *v.t.* Ⓐ rösten; toasten ‹Brot›; Ⓑ (*fig.: warm*) **~ one's feet** sich (*Dat.*) die Füße wärmen; **~ oneself in the sun** in der Sonne rösten (*scherzh.*); Ⓒ (*drink in honour of*) trinken auf (+ *Akk.*)

**toaster** /'təʊstə(r)/ *n.* Toaster, *der*

**'toasting fork** *n.* Gabel zum Rösten vor dem offenen Feuer

t

# To

## Going places — zu or nach?

There is a simple distinction between the use of **zu** and **nach** to translate *to*:

**nach** is only used with geographical names and points of the compass;

**zu** is used in nearly all other cases. Note that where a noun follows a geographical name in apposition, an article in the dative is needed.

***We are going to Germany***
= Wir fahren nach Deutschland

***They are flying to New York***
= Sie fliegen nach New York

***You are going to Salzburg, Mozart's birthplace***
Sie fahren nach Salzburg, dem Geburtsort Mozarts

***the road to Potsdam/the city centre***
= die Straße nach Potsdam/zum Stadtzentrum

***How do I get to the coast?***
= Wie komme ich zur Küste?

***Go to your mother***
= Geh zu deiner Mutter

***from house to house***
= von Haus zu Haus

But:

***from east to west***
= von Osten nach Westen

Where a distance is given, **bis** is usually inserted before the **zu** or **nach**, or in place of **nach**:

***It's five miles to Exeter/to the next place***
= Es sind noch acht Kilometer bis [nach] Exeter/bis zum nächsten Ort

## Giving

With all verbs expressing giving *to* is translated simply by the dative case:

***She handed the key to me***
= Sie übergab mir den Schlüssel

***The prize was awarded to him***
= Der Preis wurde ihm verliehen

***My father left the estate to my brother***
= Mein Vater hinterließ das Gut meinem Bruder

***They gave a book to Rachel Symons***
= Sie schenkten Rachel Symons ein Buch

From the last example it can be seen that where there is a name which cannot of course show the dative this is simply given without alteration.

Other usages are covered in the entry for *to*.

····➤ The Clock | Measurements | Asking the Way

**toast: ~master** *n. jmd., der bei einem öffentlichen Essen die Toasts ausbringt;* **~ rack** *n.* Toastständer, *der*

**tobacco** /tə'bækəʊ/ *n., pl.* **~s** Tabak, *der*

**tobacco: ~ jar** *n.* Tabak[s]dose, *die;* **~ leaf** *n.* Tabakblatt, *das*

**tobacconist** /tə'bækənɪst/ *n.* ▶ 1261 Tabak[waren]händler, *der*/-händlerin, *die;* ⇒ *also* **baker**

**to'bacco-pouch** *n.* Tabak[s]beutel, *der*

**toboggan** /tə'bɒgən/ ❶ *n.* Schlitten, *der;* Toboggan, *der.* ❷ *v.i.* Schlitten fahren

**toby** /'təʊbɪ/ *n.* **~ [jug]** Figurenkrug, *der;* Tobyjug, *der*

**toccata** /tə'kɑ:tə/ *n.* (*Mus.*) Tokkata, *die*

**Toc H** /tɒk 'eɪtʃ/ *n.* (*Brit.*) *christlich und sozial orientierte Vereinigung [ehemaliger Armeeangehöriger]*

**tod** /tɒd/ *n.* (*Brit. coll.*) **on one's ~:** [ganz] allein

**today** /tə'deɪ/ ▶ 1056 ❶ *n.* heute; **~'s newspaper** die Zeitung von heute; **~'s film industry** die heutige Filmindustrie; **live for ~:** für den Tag leben. ❷ *adv.* heute; **a week/fortnight [from] ~:** heute in einer Woche/in vierzehn Tagen; **a year [ago] ~:** heute vor einem Jahr; **early ~:** heute früh; **later [on] ~:** später [am Tage]; **earlier ~:** heute vor wenigen Stunden

**toddle** /'tɒdl/ *v.i.* Ⓐ (*with tottering steps*) mit wackligen Schritten gehen; wackeln (*ugs.*); Ⓑ (*coll.: leave*) **~ [off]** sich verziehen (*ugs.*); **I must ~ [along** *or* **off] now** ich muss mich jetzt auf die Socken machen (*ugs.*); Ⓒ (*coll.: go*) **~ along** *or* **down to the post** zum Postamt wandern (*ugs.*)

**toddler** /'tɒdlə(r)/ *n.* ≈ Kleinkind, *das;* **he is only a ~:** er hat gerade laufen gelernt

**toddy** /'tɒdɪ/ *n.* Toddy, *der;* **rum ~:** ≈ Grog, *der*

**to-do** /tə'du:/ *n.* Getue, *das* (*ugs.*); **make a great ~ about sth.** viel Theater um etw. machen (*ugs.*); **there was a great ~ when ...:** es gab eine große Aufregung, als ...:

**toe** /təʊ/ ❶ *n.* Ⓐ ▶ 966 (*Anat.*) Zeh, *der;* Zehe, *die;* **be on one's ~s** (*fig.*) auf Zack sein (*ugs.*); **keep sb. on his/her ~s** (*fig.*) jmdn. in Trab halten (*ugs.*); **turn up one's ~s** (*coll. euphem.: die*) ins Gras beißen (*salopp*); Ⓑ (*of footwear*) Spitze, *die;* **at the ~:** an den Zehen; **the ~s of the boots are reinforced** die Stiefel sind an der Spitze verstärkt; Ⓒ (*Zool.*) Zeh, *der.* ❷ *v.t.,* **~ing** (*fig.*) **~ the line** *or* (*Amer.*) **mark** sich einordnen; **refuse to ~ the line** aus der Reihe tanzen (*ugs.*); **~ the party line** linientreu sein

**toe: ~cap** *n.* Vorderkappe, *die;* (*of boot*) Stiefelkappe, *die;* **steel ~cap** Stahlkappe, *die;* **~ clip** *n.* Pedalhaken, *der;* Fußhaken, *der*

**-toed** /təʊd/ *adj. in comb.* -zehig

**toe: ~hold** *n.* Tritt, *der;* (*fig.*) **gain a ~hold:** einen Fuß in die Tür bekommen; **have only a ~hold in Europe** nur ein kleines Gebiet in Europa haben; (*for sales*) in Europa nur schwach vertreten sein; **~nail** *n.* Zeh[en]nagel, *der*

**toff** /tɒf/ *n.* (*Brit. coll. dated*) Lackaffe, *der* (*ugs. abwertend*)

**toffee** /'tɒfɪ/ *n.* Ⓐ Karamell, *der;* Ⓑ (*Brit.: piece*) Toffee, *das;* Sahnebonbon, *das;* Ⓒ **sb. can't do sth. for ~** (*fig. coll.*) jmd. kann etw. nicht für fünf Pfennig tun (*ugs.*)

**toffee: ~ apple** *n.* mit Karamell überzogener Apfel am Stiel; **~-nosed** *adj.* (*Brit. coll.*) hochnäsig

**tofu** /'təʊfu:/ *n., no pl., no indef. art.* Tofu, *der*

**tog** /tɒg/ ❶ *n.* Ⓐ *in pl.* (*coll.: garments*) Klamotten (*ugs.*); Ⓑ (*Textiles*) *Einheit für das Wärmerückhaltevermögen von Textilien.* ❷ *v.t.* **-gg-: ~ [oneself] out** *or* **up** sich in Schale werfen (*ugs.*); **they were ~ged out in their Sunday best** sie waren mit ihrem besten Sonntagsstaat ausstaffiert

**toga** /'təʊgə/ *n.* (*Roman Ant.*) Toga, *die*

**together** /tə'geðə(r)/ *adv.* Ⓐ (*in or into company*) zusammen; **sit down ~:** sich zusammensetzen; **gather ~:** sich [ver]sammeln; **soloist and orchestra were not ~:** Solist und Orchester spielten nicht im Takt; **taken all ~:** alle zusammengenommen; **~ with** zusammen mit; Ⓑ (*simultaneously*) gleichzeitig; **all ~ now!** jetzt alle zusammen *od.* im Chor!; Ⓒ (*one with another*) miteinander; **put them ~ to compare them** halte sie nebeneinander, um sie zu vergleichen; Ⓓ (*without interruption*) **for weeks/days/hours ~:** wochen-/tage-/stundenlang; **for three days ~:** drei Tage hintereinander; Ⓔ (*coll.: organized*) **not ~:** chaotisch (*ugs.*) ‹Person›

**togetherness** /tə'geðənɪs/ *n., no pl.* Zusammengehörigkeit, *die*

**toggle** /'tɒgl/ ❶ *n.* Ⓐ (*button*) Knebelknopf, *der;* Ⓑ (*crosspiece*) Knebel, *der;* Ⓒ (*Computing*) [Kipp]schalter, *der;* Umschalttaste, *die.* ❷ *v.i.* (*Computing*) [hin und her] schalten. ❸ *v.t.* (*Computing*) [um]schalten

**'toggle switch** *n.* (*Electr.*) Kippschalter, *der*

**Togo** /'təʊgəʊ/, **Togoland** /'təʊgəʊlænd/ *pr. ns.* Togo (*das*)

**Togolese** /təʊgəʊ'li:z/ ❶ *adj.* togolesisch. ❷ *n., pl. same* Togolese, *der*/Togolesin, *die*

**toil** /tɔɪl/ ❶ *v.i.* Ⓐ (*work laboriously*) schwer arbeiten; sich abarbeiten; **~ at/over sth.** sich mit etw. abplagen/abmühen; **~ through a book** sich mühsam durch ein Buch arbeiten; **~ [away] on sth.** sich mit etw. abmühen; Ⓑ (*move laboriously*) sich schleppen; **the train ~ed up the incline** der Zug mühte sich die Steigung hinauf; **~ on** sich weiterschleppen. ❷ *n.* [harte] Arbeit; **with much ~:** mit großer Mühe; **the ~s of the day** die Mühen des Tages

**toiler** /'tɔɪlə(r)/ *n.* (*for peace, justice, etc.*) Kämpfer, *der*/Kämpferin, *die*

**toilet** /'tɔɪlɪt/ *n.* Ⓐ Toilette, *die;* **down the ~:** in die Toilette; **go to the ~:** auf die Toilette gehen; **be in the ~:** auf der Toilette sein; **on the ~** (*coll.*) auf dem Klo (*ugs.*); Ⓑ (*washing and dressing*) Toilette, *die;* **be at one's ~** (*dated*) bei der Toilette sein

**toilet: ~ bag** *n.* Kulturbeutel, *der;* **~ bowl** *n.* Toilettenbecken, *das;* Klosettbecken, *das;* **~ brush** *n.* Klosettbürste, *die;* **~ paper** *n.* Toilettenpapier, *das*

**toiletries** /'tɔɪlɪtrɪz/ *n. pl.* Körperpflegemittel; Toilettenartikel

**toilet: ~ roll** *n.* Rolle Toilettenpapier; **~-roll holder** *n.* Toilettenpapierhalter, *der;* **~ seat** *n.* Klosettbrille, *die* (*ugs.*); Toilettensitz, *der;* **~ soap** *n.* Toilettenseife, *die;* **~ tissue** ⇒ **toilet paper**; **~-train** *v.t.* zur Sauberkeit erziehen; an die Toilette gewöhnen; **be ~-trained** sauber sein; auf die Toilette gehen; **~-training** *n.* Sauberkeitserziehung, *die;*

~ **water** *n.* Toilettenwasser, *das;* Eau de Toilette, *das*

**toils** /tɔɪlz/ *n. pl.* (*literary*) Fangnetz, *das;* Fanggarn, *das* (*Jägerspr.*); (*fig.*) Fallstrick, *der*

'**toil-worn** *adj.* abgearbeitet ‹Person›; erschöpft ‹Reisender›; abgehärmt ‹Gesicht›

**toing and froing** /tu:ɪŋ ən 'frəʊɪŋ/ *n.* Hin und Her, *das*

**Tokay** /tə'keɪ/ *n.* Tokaier, *der;* Tokajer, *der*

**token** /'təʊkn/ **1** *n.* **A** (*voucher*) Gutschein, *der;* ⇒ *also* **book token**; **gift token**; **record token**; **B** (*counter, disc*) Marke, *die;* Jeton, *der;* **C** (*sign*) Zeichen, *das;* (*evidence*) Beweis, *der;* **as a** *or* **in ~ of sth.** als Zeichen/zum Beweis einer Sache; **he received a present as a** *or* **in ~ of his 30 years' service with the firm** anlässlich seiner dreißigjährigen Zugehörigkeit zur Firma erhielt er ein Geschenk; **D by the same** *or* **this ~:** ebenso; **if you don't believe me, then by the same ~ you can't believe him** wenn du mir nicht glaubst, dann heißt das, dass du ihm auch nicht glauben kannst; **his wages are low and, by the same ~, not nearly enough to make him stay in this job** seine Bezahlung ist schlecht und daher natürlich auch nicht ausreichend, ihn in diesem Job zu halten; **E** (*keepsake*) Abschiedsgeschenk, *das;* Andenken, *das.*

**2** *attrib. adj.* symbolisch ‹Preis›; nominal (*Wirtsch.*) ‹Lohnerhöhung, Miete›; (*minimal*) geringfügig ‹Schaden›; **a ~ woman/black person on the staff** eine Alibifrau/ein Alibischwarzer als Mitarbeiterin/Mitarbeiter; **his offer of help is only a ~ offer** sein Hilfsangebot ist nur ein Pro-forma-Angebot; **offer** *or* **put up ~ resistance** pro forma Widerstand leisten; **~ strike** Warnstreik, *der*

**tokenism** /'təʊkənɪzm/ *n.* **sth. is just ~:** etw. hat nur Alibifunktion

**Tokyo** /'təʊkjəʊ/ *pr. n.* ▶ **1626** Tokio (*das*)

**told** ⇒ **tell**

**tolerable** /'tɒlərəbl/ *adj.* **A** (*endurable*) erträglich (**to, for** für); **B** (*fairly good*) leidlich; annehmbar; **a very ~ lunch** ein sehr ordentliches Mittagessen; **How are things? — Oh, ~:** Wie gehts? — Oh, es geht

**tolerably** /'tɒlərəblɪ/ *adv.* leidlich; annehmbar; einigermaßen ‹gut, richtig›

**tolerance** /'tɒlərəns/ *n.* **A** Toleranz, *die* (**for, towards,** gegen[über]); **have no ~ for sth.** für etw. kein Verständnis haben; etw. nicht tolerieren [können]; **a mother with three children needs a lot of ~:** eine Mutter mit drei Kindern braucht viel Verständnis; **B** (*Med., Mech. Engin.*) Toleranz, *die*

**tolerant** /'tɒlərənt/ *adj.* **A** tolerant (**of, towards** gegen[über]); **be ~ of criticism** Kritik vertragen; **B** (*Med.*) widerstandsfähig

**tolerate** /'tɒləreɪt/ *v.t.* **A** dulden; tolerieren (*geh.*); **this material will ~ high temperatures/hard wear** dieses Material ist hitzebeständig/strapazierfähig; **B** (*put up with*) **~ sb./sth.** sich mit jmdm./etw. abfinden; **she ~d his moods** sie ließ seine Launen über sich (*Akk.*) ergehen; **~ one another** sich [gegenseitig] akzeptieren; **how can you ~ this awful man?** wie kannst du diesen schrecklichen Mann ertragen?; **I can't ~ football/fanaticism** ich kann Fußball/Fanatismus nicht ausstehen; **C** (*sustain*) ertragen ‹Schmerzen, Hitze, Lärm›; **D** (*Med.*) vertragen

**toleration** /tɒlə'reɪʃn/ *n.* Tolerierung, *die* (*geh.*); **religious/mutual ~:** religiöse/gegenseitige Toleranz

**toll**[1] /təʊl/ *n.* **A** (*tax, duty*) Gebühr, *die;* (*for road*) [Straßen]gebühr, *die;* Maut, *die* (*bes. österr.*); **B** (*damage etc. incurred*) Aufwand, *der;* **take** *or* **exact a /its ~ of sth.** einen Tribut an etw. (*Dat.*) fordern (*fig.*); **the hurricane took a ~ of 5,000 lives** der Hurrikan forderte 5 000 Todesopfer; **the revolution took a heavy ~ of human life** die Revolution forderte viele Menschenleben; **time took its ~ of him** er musste dem Alter Tribut zollen; **C** (*Amer.: Teleph.*) [Gesprächs]gebühr, *die*

**toll**[2] **1** *v.t.* läuten; ‹Turmuhr:› schlagen ‹Stunde›. **2** *v.i.* läuten

**toll: ~ bar** *n.* *Schlagbaum auf gebührenpflichtigen Straßen oder Brücken;* Mautschranke, *die* (*bes. österr.*); **~ bridge** *n.* gebührenpflichtige Brücke; Mautbrücke, *die* (*bes. österr.*); **~ call** *n.* (*Amer. Teleph.*) gebührenpflichtiges Gespräch; **~-free** *adj., adv.* (*Amer. Teleph.*) gebührenfrei; **~ gate** *n.* Absperrung vor einer gebührenpflichtigen Straße/Brücke; **~road** *n.* gebührenpflichtige Straße; Mautstraße, *die* (*bes. österr.*)

**tom** /tɒm/ *n.* **A any** *or* **every T~, Dick, and Harry** Hinz und Kunz (*ugs. abwertend*); **it's me you're talking to, not any T~, Dick, and Harry** du sprichst mit mir, nicht mit irgendjemandem; **every T~, Dick, and Harry is talking about it** alle Welt redet davon; **any T~, Dick, or Harry can open a shop** jeder, der Lust hat, kann einen Laden aufmachen; **B** (*cat*) Kater, *der.* ⇒ *also* **peeping Tom**

**tomahawk** /'tɒməhɔ:k/ *n.* Tomahawk, *der;* ⇒ *also* **bury B**

**tomato** /tə'mɑ:təʊ/ *n., pl.* **~es** Tomate, *die*

**tomato: ~ juice** *n.* Tomatensaft, *der;* **~ 'ketchup** *n.* Tomatenketchup, *der od. das;* **~ 'purée** *n.* Tomatenmark, *das;* **~ 'sauce** *n.* **A** Tomatensoße, *die;* **B** ⇒ **~ ketchup**; **~ 'soup** *n.* Tomatensuppe, *die*

**tomb** /tu:m/ *n.* **A** (*grave*) Grab, *das;* **B** (*monument*) Grabmal, *das;* **C the ~** (*state of death*) das Grab (*geh.*); der Tod; **his ghost came back from the ~:** sein Geist kehrte aus dem Grab zurück; **[as] silent as the ~:** totenstill; **the village/the house is/seems [as] silent as the ~:** im Dorf/Haus herrscht Totenstille; **D** (*vault*) Gruft, *die* (*geh.*)

**tombola** /tɒm'bəʊlə/ *n.* Tombola, *die*

'**tomboy** *n.* Wildfang, *der*

'**tombstone** *n.* Grabstein, *der;* Grabmal, *das*

'**tomcat** *n.* Kater, *der*

**tome** /təʊm/ *n.* dicker Band; Wälzer, *der* (*ugs.*)

**tom: ~fool** *attrib. adj.* blödsinnig; **~'foolery** *n.* Blödsinn, *der* (*ugs.*)

**Tommy** /'tɒmɪ/ *n.* (*coll.: British soldier*) Tommy, *der*

**tommy: ~ gun** *n.* Maschinenpistole, *die;* **~-rot** *n., no pl., no indef. art.* Unfug, *der;* Quatsch, *der* (*ugs.*)

**tomorrow** /tə'mɒrəʊ/ ▶ **1056** **1** *n.* **A** morgen; **~ morning/afternoon/evening/night** morgen früh *od.* Vormittag/Nachmittag/Abend/Nacht; **~ is another day** (*prov.*) morgen ist auch [noch] ein Tag (*Spr.*); **~ never comes** (*prov.*) morgen, morgen, nur nicht heute[, sagen alle faulen Leute] (*Spr.*); **You always say you'll do it some time. But with you, ~ never comes!** Du sagst immer, dass du es einmal tust. Aber bei dir heißt das am Sankt-Nimmerleins-Tag; **~'s edition/newspaper** die morgige Ausgabe/Zeitung; die Ausgabe/Zeitung von morgen; **~'s events will bear me out** morgen wird man sehen, dass ich Recht habe; **~ evening's concert** das Konzert morgen Abend *od.* am morgigen Abend; **B** (*the future*) Morgen, *das;* **who knows what ~ will bring?** wer weiß, was die Zukunft bringt?; **like there's no ~** (*coll.*) als gäbe es kein Morgen; als ginge morgen die Welt unter; **the men and women of ~:** die Männer und Frauen von morgen; **~'s world** die Welt von morgen.

**2** *adv.* **A** morgen; **a week/month [from] ~:** morgen in einer Woche/in einem Monat; **a year [ago] ~:** morgen vor einem Jahr; **[I'll] see you ~!** (*coll.*) bis morgen!; **never put off till ~ what you can do today** (*prov.*) was du heute kannst besorgen, das verschiebe nicht auf morgen (*Spr.*); **the day after ~:** übermorgen; **this time ~:** morgen um diese Zeit; **~ afternoon/morning** morgen Nachmittag/früh; **~ evening** *or* **night** morgen Abend; **B** (*in the future*) morgen; **what will the world be like ~?** wie wird die Welt von morgen aussehen?

**tom: Tom 'Thumb** *n.* **A** (*Lit.*) Däumling, *der;* **B** (*diminutive person*) Knirps, *der* (*ugs.*); **~tit** *n.* (*Ornith.*) Blaumeise, *die;* **~-~** *n.* (*Mus.*) Tomtom, *das*

**ton** /tʌn/ *n.* **A** ▶ **1683** Tonne, *die;* **a five-~ lorry** ein Lastwagen von fünf Tonnen [Leergewicht]; ein Fünftonner (*ugs.*); **[long] ~:** Tonne, *die;* 1 016,05 kg; **metric ~:** metrische Tonne; **[short] ~:** Tonne, *die;* 907,185 kg; **two ~[s] of coal** zwei Tonnen Kohle; ⇒ *also* **brick 1 A**; **B** (*Naut.*) Tonne, *die;* **gross ~:** Bruttoregistertonne, *die;* **net** *or* **register ~:** Registertonne, *die;* **C** (*fig. coll.: a lot*) **it weighs [half] a ~:** es ist zentnerschwer (*fig.*); **I've asked him ~s of times** ich habe ihn x-mal gefragt (*ugs.*); **~s [of food/people/reasons** *etc.*] haufenweise (*ugs.*) [Essen/Leute/Gründe *usw.*]; **D** (*Brit. coll.: 100 m.p.h.*) **do a** *or* **the ~:** mit 160 Sachen fahren; **E** (*Cricket coll.*) ⇒ **century B**

**tonal** /'təʊnl/ *adj.* **A** (*Ling.*) intonatorisch; **~ language** Tonsprache; **~ changes** *or* **variations** Klangvariationen; **B** (*Mus.*) tonal; **C** (*Art*) **~ differences between colours** Unterschiede in den Farbtönen

**tonality** /tə'nælɪtɪ/ *n.* **A** (*Mus.*) Tonalität, *die;* **B** (*Art*) Farbwirkung, *die*

**tonally** /'təʊnəlɪ/ *adv.* (*Mus.*) tonal

**tone** /təʊn/ **1** *n.* **A** (*sound*) Klang, *der;* (*Teleph.*) Ton, *der;* **the clear ~s of the speaker** die klare Stimme des Redners; **the [shrill] ~s of her voice** ihre [schrille] Stimme; **a high-/low-pitched ~:** ein hoher/tiefer Ton; **B** (*style of speaking*) Ton, *der;* **don't speak to me in that ~ [of voice]** sprich mit mir nicht in diesem Ton; **in an angry** *etc.* **~, in angry** *etc.* **~s** in ärgerlichem *usw.* Ton; **in a ~ of reproach/anger** *etc.* in vorwurfsvollem/wütendem *usw.* Ton; **C** (*tint, shade*) [Farb]ton, *der;* **~s of blue** Blautöne; blaue Töne; **grey with a blue ~:** bläulich grau; **D** (*style of writing*) [Grund]stimmung, *die;* (*of letter*) Ton, *der;* **E** (*Mus.*) (*note*) Ton, *der;* (*quality of sound*) Klang, *der;* (*Brit.: interval*) Intervall, *das;* **whole-~ scale** Ganztonleiter, *die;* ⇒ *also* **fundamental 1 B**; **F** (*fig.: character*) Stimmung, *die;* **a ~ of quiet elegance** eine Atmosphäre stiller Eleganz; **the peaceful ~ of the discussions** die friedliche Atmosphäre der Gespräche; **give a serious/flippant ~ to sth.** einer Sache (*Dat.*) eine ernsthafte/frivole Note verleihen; **lower/raise the ~ of sth.** das Niveau einer Sache (*Gen.*) senken/erhöhen; **set the ~:** den Ton angeben; **set the ~ of** *or* **for sth.** für etw. bestimmend sein; **G** (*Art: general effect of colour*) Farbgebung, *die;* Kolorit, *das;* **H** (*degree of brightness*) Schattierung, *die;* Nuancierung, *die;* **bright ~:** Helligkeit, *die;* **I** (*Photog.*) Ton, *der;* **J** (*accent on syllable*) Betonung, *die;* Akzent, *der;* (*way of pronouncing*) Ton, *der;* **K** (*Physiol.: firmness of muscles*) Tonus, *der;* (*of athlete etc.*) Fitness, *die;* **keep oneself** *or* **one's body in ~:** sich fit halten.

**2** *v.t.* **A** (*modify colouring of*) tönen; abtönen ‹Farbe›; **~ paint [with] a darker/lighter shade** Farbe abdunkeln/aufhellen; **B** (*Photog.*) tonen; **~ sth. a reddish-brown** etw. rötlich braun tonen.

**3** *v.i.* ⇒ **~ in**

**~ 'down** *v.t.* **A** (*Art*) [ab]dämpfen ‹Farbe›; **~ a painting down** die Farben eines Bildes abdämpfen; **B** (*fig.: soften*) mäßigen ‹Sprache›; abschwächen ‹Verbalattacke, Forderung›; dämpfen ‹Erregung, Begeisterung›; besänftigen ‹Wut›

**~ 'in** *v.i.* farblich harmonieren

**~ 'up 1** *v.t.* **A** (*Art*) **~ up a picture/colour** die Farben eines Bildes/eine Farbe kräftiger machen; **B** (*Physiol.*) fit machen; straffen ‹Muskeln, Körper›; stärken ‹Nerven›. **2** *v.i.* sich fit machen

**tone: ~ arm** *n.* Tonarm, *der;* **~ control** *n.* (*process*) Klangregelung, *die;* (*device*) Klangregler, *der;* Tonblende, *die;* **~-'deaf** *adj.* ohne musikalisches Gehör; **be ~-deaf** kein musikalisches Gehör haben; **~-deaf people** Leute ohne musikalisches Gehör; **~ dialling** (*Teleph.*) *n.* Tonwahl, *die;* **~ language** *n.* Tonsprache, *die*

t

**toneless** /'təʊnlɪs/ *adj.* **A** tonlos ‹Stimme, Antwort›; **B** (*Mus.*) monoton; **C** (*dull*) stumpf ‹Farbe›

**tone:** ~ **painting** *n.* (*Mus.*) Tonmalerei, *die;* ~ **poem** *n.* **A** (*Mus.*) Tondichtung, *die;* **B** (*Art*) *Gemälde, bei dem die Farbtöne auf poetische Weise harmonisieren*

**toner** /'təʊnə(r)/ *n.* **A** (*Photog.*) Toner, *der;* **B** (*cosmetic*) Tönungsmittel, *das*

**tongs** /tɒŋz/ *n. pl.* **[pair of] ~:** Zange, *die;* ⇨ *also* **curling-tongs**; **fire tongs**; **hammer** 1 A; **sugar tongs**

**tongue** /tʌŋ/ *n.* **A** ▶ 966 Zunge, *die;* **bite one's ~** (*lit. or fig.*) sich auf die Zunge beißen; **put out your ~, please** strecken Sie [bitte] mal Ihre Zunge heraus!; **put** *or* **stick one's ~ out [at sb.]** [jmdm.] die Zunge herausstrecken; **with one's ~ hanging out** mit [heraus]hängender Zunge; **he came into the pub with his ~ hanging out** (*fig.*) ihm hing die Zunge aus dem Hals, als er in das Gasthaus kam; **he made the remark ~ in cheek** (*fig.*) er meinte die Bemerkung nicht ernst; **hold one's ~** (*fig.*) stillschweigen; **watch one's ~** (*fig.*) seine Zunge hüten *od.* zügeln; **watch your ~!** pass auf, was du sagst!; **keep a civil ~ in one's head** seine Zunge hüten; ⇨ *also* **edge** 1 A; **B** (*meat*) Zunge, *die;* **C** (*manner or power of speech*) **find/lose one's ~:** seine Sprache wieder finden/die Sprache verlieren; **have you lost your ~?** hat es dir die Sprache verschlagen?; hast du die Sprache verloren?; **get one's ~ round sth.** etw. aussprechen; **the name is difficult to get one's ~ round** bei dem Namen bricht man sich (*Dat.*) die Zunge ab *od.* verrenkt man sich (*Dat.*) die Zunge (*ugs.*); **have a ready/sharp/wicked** *etc.* **~:** eine flinke/scharfe/böse *usw.* Zunge haben; **the hounds gave ~:** die Hunde gaben Hals (*Jägerspr.*); **give ~:** sprechen; **D** (*language*) Sprache, *die;* Zunge, *die* (*geh.*, *dichter.*); **gift of ~s** (*Bibl.*) Zungenreden, *das;* ⇨ *also* **confusion** A; **mother tongue**; **E** (*of shoe*) Zunge, *die;* **F** (*promontory*) **~ [of land]** Landzunge, *die;* **G** (*of bell*) Klöppel, *der;* **H** (*of buckle*) Dorn, *der;* **I** (*Woodw.*) Feder, *die;* **J** (*pointer of scale etc.*) Zunge, *die;* **K** (*Mus.*) Zunge, *die;* **L** **there were ~s of flame rising from the fire** von der Feuerstelle züngelten Flammen empor. ⇨ *also* **cat** A; **tip**[1] 1; **wag**[1] 2

**tongue:** **~-in-'cheek** *adj.* nicht ernst gemeint; (*ironical*) ironisch; ⇨ *also* **tongue** A; **~-lashing** *n.* Rüffel, *der* (*ugs.*); **give sb. a ~-lashing** jmdm. einen Rüffel geben; jmdn. zusammenstauchen (*ugs.*); **get a ~-lashing [from sb.]** [von jmdm.] einen Rüffel bekommen/zusammengestaucht werden (*ugs.*); **~-tied** *adj.* schüchtern; gehemmt; **the boy sat ~-tied the whole evening** der Junge saß den ganzen Abend da und brachte kein Wort heraus; **be ~-tied [with** *or* **by fear/embarrassment** *etc.*] [vor Angst/Verlegenheit *usw.*] kein Wort herausbringen; **~-twister** *n.* Zungenbrecher, *der* (*ugs.*)

**tonic** /'tɒnɪk/ ❶ *n.* **A** (*Med.*) Tonikum, *das;* **it was as good as a ~:** es hat mir/ihm *usw.* richtig gut getan; **B** (*fig.: invigorating influence*) Wohltat, *die* (*geh.*); **the good news/his visit was a welcome ~:** die gute Nachricht/sein Besuch war eine wahre Wohltat; **C** (~ *water*) Tonic, *das;* **gin** *etc.* **and ~:** Gin *usw.* [mit] Tonic; **D** (*Mus.*) Tonika, *die.* ❷ *adj.* **A** (*Med.*) kräftigend; tonisch (*fachspr.*); (*fig.*) wohltuend ‹Wirkung›; **B** (*Mus.*) tonisch

**tonic:** ~ **'accent** *n.* (*Phonet.: of word*) Betonung, *die;* ~ **sol-'fa** *n.* (*Mus.*) Tonika-Do-System, *das;* ~ **water** *n.* Tonic[wasser], *das*

**tonight** /tə'naɪt/ ❶ *n.* **A** (*this evening*) heute Abend; **~ has been such fun** heute Abend war es so lustig; **after ~:** nach dem heutigen Abend; **I enjoyed ~:** es war ein schöner Abend; **~'s [news]paper** die heutige Abendzeitung; **~'s performance** die heutige [Abend]vorstellung; **~'s the night!** heute Abend ist es soweit!; **~'s weather will be cold** heute Abend wird es kalt; **B** (*this or the coming night*) heute Nacht; **~ will be colder** heute Nacht wird es kälter werden. ❷ *adv.* **A** (*this evening*) heute Abend; **[I'll] see you ~!** bis heute Abend! **B** (*during this or the coming night*) heute Nacht

**tonnage** /'tʌnɪdʒ/ *n.* (*Naut.*) **A** Tonnage, *die;* **B** (*charge on cargo*) Tonnageabgabe, *die*

**tonne** /'tʌn/ *n.* ▶ 1683 [metrische] Tonne

**tonsil** /'tɒnsl/ *n.* (*Anat.*) [Gaumen]mandel, *die;* **have one's ~s out** sich (*Dat.*) die Mandeln herausnehmen lassen

**tonsillectomy** /tɒnsə'lektəmɪ/ *n.* (*Med.*) Mandeloperation, *die;* Tonsillektomie, *die* (*fachspr.*)

**tonsillitis** /tɒnsə'laɪtɪs/ *n.* ▶ 1232 (*Med.*) Mandelentzündung, *die;* Tonsillitis, *die* (*fachspr.*)

**tonsure** /'tɒnʃə(r)/ (*Relig.*) ❶ *n.* Tonsur, *die.* ❷ *v.t.* tonsurieren

**ton-'up** *adj.* (*sl.*) **~ boys** Motorradrocker; **~ machine** Feuerstuhl, *der* (*ugs.*)

**too** /tu:/ *adv.* **A** (*excessively*) zu; **far** *or* **much ~ much** viel zu viel; **~ much** zu viel; **I've had ~ much to eat/drink** ich habe zu viel gegessen/getrunken; **but not ~ much, please** aber bitte nicht allzu viel; **the problem/he was ~ much for her** sie war der Aufgabe/ihm nicht gewachsen; **things are getting ~ much for me** es wird mir allmählich zu viel; es wächst mir allmählich über den Kopf; **this is '~ much!** (*indignantly*) jetzt reichts!; **she's/that's just '~ much** (*intolerable*) sie ist/das ist zu viel! (*ugs.*); (*coll.: wonderful*) sie ist/das ist echt Spitze (*ugs.*); **~ difficult a task** eine zu schwierige Aufgabe; **none ~** *or* **not any ~ easy** nicht allzu leicht; (*less than one had expected*) gar nicht so leicht; **he is none ~** *or* **not any ~ clever/quick** *etc.* er ist nicht der Schlauste/Schnellste *usw.*; **none ~ soon** keinen Augenblick zu früh; **the holidays can come none ~ soon as far as I am concerned** für mich können die Ferien nicht früh genug kommen; ⇨ *also* **all** 3; **good** 1 B, E; **many** 1 A; **much** 1 A, 3 D; **only** 2 D; **B** (*also*) auch; **she can sing, and play the piano, ~:** sie kann singen und auch *od.* außerdem Klavier spielen; **I have been [to Berlin, and] to Cologne, ~:** ich war [in Berlin und] auch *od.* außerdem in Köln; **I, ~, have been to Cologne, 'I have been to Cologne, ~:** ich war auch in Köln; auch ich war in Köln; **C** (*coll.: very*) besonders; **I'm not feeling ~ good** mir geht es nicht besonders [gut]; **I'm not ~ sure** ich bin mir nicht ganz sicher; **not ~ pleased** nicht gerade erfreut; **you're '~ kind!** zu nett von dir!; **the dessert was '~ delicious** die Nachspeise war zu köstlich; **D** (*moreover*) **he lost in twenty moves, and to an amateur ~:** er verlor in zwanzig Zügen, und noch dazu gegen einen Amateur; **there was frost last night, and in May/Spain ~!** es hat letzte Nacht gefroren, und das im Mai/in Spanien!

**toodle-oo** /tu:dl'u:/ *int.* (*Brit. coll.*) tschüs (*ugs.*); ciao (*ugs.*)

**took** ⇨ **take** 1, 2

**tool** /tu:l/ ❶ *n.* **A** Werkzeug, *das;* (*garden ~*) Gerät, *das;* **set of ~s** Werkzeug, *das;* ⇨ *also* **down**[3] 4 D; **B** (*machine*) Werkzeugmaschine, *die;* **electrical ~:** Elektrowerkzeug, *das;* ⇨ *also* **machine tool**; **C** (*Mech. Engin.: lathe ~*) Meißel, *der;* **D** (*Computing*) Tool, *das;* Werkzeug, *das;* **E** (*fig.: means*) [Hilfs]mittel, *das;* **knowledge is a great ~ in the hands of men** [das] Wissen ist für den Menschen ein großartiges Werkzeug; **pen and paper are the writer's basic ~s** Feder und Papier sind das wichtigste Handwerkszeug des Schriftstellers; **the ~s of the trade** das Handwerkszeug; das Rüstzeug; **F** (*fig.: person*) Werkzeug, *das;* **a mere ~ [in the hands] of the dictator** ein bloßes Werkzeug des Diktators; **G** (*sl.: penis*) Apparat, *der* (*ugs.*); Gerät, *das* (*salopp*). ❷ *v.t.* **A** bearbeiten; **B** (*Bookbinding*) prägen

~ **'up** *v.t.* mit Maschinen ausrüsten; **the expense of ~ing-up** die Kosten für die Anschaffung von Maschinen

**tool:** ~ **bag** *n.* Werkzeugtasche, *die;* **~bar** *n.* (*Computing*) Werkzeugleiste, *die;* **~box,** ~ **case** *ns.* Werkzeugkasten, *der;* ~ **chest** *n.* Werkzeugschrank, *der;* ~ **holder** *n.* **A** (*in lathe*) Meißelhalter, *der;* **B** (*handle*) Werkzeuggriff, *der*

**tooling** /'tu:lɪŋ/ *n.* **A** (*Building*) [steinmetzmäßige] Bearbeitung; **B** (*Bookbinding*) Prägen, *das;* (*thing tooled*) Prägung, *die*

**tool:** ~ **kit** *n.* (*Brit.*) Werkzeugsatz, *der;* (*more general*) Werkzeug, *das;* (*for vehicle*) **is there a ~ kit?** gibt es Bordwerkzeug?; ~ **maker** *n.* Werkzeugmacher, *der*/-macherin, *die;* ~ **pusher** *n.* Bohrtechniker, *der;* ~ **set** *n.* Werkzeugsatz, *der;* ~ **shed** *n.* Geräteschuppen, *der*

**toot** /tu:t/ ❶ *v.t.* tuten; **the boy ~ed his toy trumpet** der Junge blies in seine Spielzeugtrompete; **the driver ~ed his horn** der Fahrer hupte. ❷ *v.i.* **A** (*on wind instrument*) blasen; (*on whistle, pipe*) pfeifen; (*on car etc. horn*) hupen; **B** ‹Hupe:› hupen; ‹Lokomotive, Pfeife:› pfeifen; ‹Nebelhorn, Schiff:› tuten. ❸ *n.* Tuten, *das;* (*of pipe, whistle*) Pfeifen, *das;* **give a ~ on one's/its horn** ‹Autofahrer, Auto usw.:› hupen

**tooth** /tu:θ/ *n.*, *pl.* **teeth** /ti:θ/ **A** ▶ 966 Zahn, *der;* **say sth. between one's teeth** etw. mit zusammengebissenen Zähnen hervorstoßen; **draw sb.'s teeth** (*lit.*) jmdm. die Zähne ziehen; (*fig.*) jmdn. kaltstellen; **sth.'s teeth have been drawn** (*fig.*) etw. ist unschädlich gemacht worden; **have a ~ out/filled** sich (*Dat.*) einen Zahn ziehen/füllen lassen; **armed to the teeth** bis an die Zähne bewaffnet; **cast** *or* **fling sth. in sb.'s teeth** (*fig.*) jmdm. etw. [wutentbrannt] unter die Nase reiben (*ugs.*); **~ and nail** verbissen ‹kämpfen, bekämpfen›; **I'm going to fight ~ and nail to keep this house** ich werde dieses Haus mit Zähnen und Klauen verteidigen; **get one's teeth into sth.** (*fig.*) etw. in Angriff nehmen; **sb. would give his back teeth for sth./to do sth.** (*fig.*) jmd. würde alles für etw. geben/alles dafür *od.* darum geben, etw. zu tun; **in the teeth of criticism** ungeachtet der Kritik; **sail in the teeth of the wind** gegen den Wind segeln; **put teeth into a law, give a law some teeth** ein Gesetz zu einem wirksamen Instrument machen; **show one's teeth** ‹Hund:› die Zähne fletschen; (*fig.*) die Zähne zeigen (*ugs.*); ⇨ *also* **edge** 1 A; **false teeth**; **kick** 1 A, 3 A; **lie**[1] 2; **long**[1] 1 A; **set** 1 P; **skin** 1 A; **B** (*of rake, fork, comb*) Zinke, *die;* (*of cogwheel, saw, comb*) Zahn, *der;* **C** (*liking*) **have a ~ for salad** eine Vorliebe für Salat haben; Salat gern essen; ⇨ *also* **sweet** 1 A; **D** (*Bot.*) Zahn, *der;* **have teeth** gezähnt sein

**tooth:** **~ache** *n.* ▶ 1232 Zahnschmerzen *Pl.;* Zahnweh, *das* (*ugs.*); **~brush** *n.* Zahnbürste, *die;* **~brush moustache** Bürste, *die* (*fig.*); ~ **decay** *n.* Zahnverfall, *der;* Zahnfäule, *die*

**toothed** /tu:θt/ *adj.* **A** (*Mech. Engin.*) gezähnt; ~ **wheel** Zahnrad; **B** (*Bot.*) gezähnt; **C** *in comb.* (*having teeth*) **sharp-~** ‹Tier› mit scharfen Zähnen

**'toothglass** *n.* Zahnputzglas, *das*

**toothless** /'tu:θlɪs/ *adj.* zahnlos

**tooth:** ~ **mug** *n.* Zahnputzbecher, *der;* **~paste** *n.* Zahnpasta, *die;* **~pick** *n.* Zahnstocher, *der;* ~ **powder** *n.* Zahnpulver, *das*

**toothsome** /'tu:θsəm/ *adj.* köstlich

**toothy** /'tu:θɪ/ *adj.* **give sb. a ~ smile** jmdn. mit entblößten Zähnen anlächeln; **he is a bit ~:** er hat ein ziemliches Pferdegebiss (*ugs.*)

**toothypeg** /'tu:θɪpeg/ *n.* (*child lang.*) Beißerchen, *das*

**tootle** /'tu:tl/ *v.i.* **A** blasen; dudeln (*ugs. abwertend*); (*on whistle*) pfeifen; (*on flute*) flöten; **~ on sth.** in etw. (*Akk.*) blasen; **B** (*coll.: move casually*) zuckeln (*ugs.*); (*walk casually*) schlendern; (*drive casually*) juckeln (*ugs.*); **I'm just tootling off to the shops/pub** ich gehe nur eben was einkaufen/ich gehe nur eben in die Kneipe (*ugs.*)

**too-too** (*coll.*) ❶ /'tu:tu:/ *pred. adj.* (*marvellous*) himmlisch (*ugs.*); (*la-di-da*) oberfein (*ugs.*). ❷ /tu:'tu:/ *adv.* überaus; über die Maßen (*geh.*); (*too*) übertrieben

**tootsy[-wootsy]** /'tʊtsɪ(wʊtsɪ)/ *n.* (*joc./child lang.*) Füßchen, *das*

**top¹** /tɒp/ ❶ *n.* [A] (*highest part*) Spitze, *die;* (*of table*) Platte, *die;* (*of bench seat*) Sitzfläche, *die;* (~ *floor*) oberstes Stockwerk; (*flat roof, roof garden*) Dach, *das;* (*rim of glass, bottle, etc.*) Rand, *der;* (~ *end*) oberes Ende; (*crest of wave*) Kamm, *der;* (*of tree*) Spitze, *die;* Wipfel, *der;* **the ~ of his head is smooth and shiny** sein Kopf ist oben glatt und glänzend; **a cake with a cherry on ~:** ein Kuchen mit einer Kirsche [oben]drauf; **at the ~:** oben; **at the ~ of the building/hill/pile/stairs** oben im Gebäude/[oben] auf dem Hügel/[oben] auf dem Stapel/oben an der Treppe; **bake at the ~ of the oven** auf der obersten Schiene des Backofens backen; oben im Backofen backen; **be at/get to** *or* **reach the ~ [of the ladder** *or* **tree]** (*fig.*) auf der obersten Sprosse [der Leiter] stehen/die oberste Sprosse [der Leiter] erreichen (*fig.*); oben sein/nach oben kommen (*ugs.*); **be/get on ~ of a situation/subject** eine Situation/eine Materie im Griff haben/in den Griff bekommen; **don't let it get on ~ of you** (*fig.*) lass dich davon nicht unterkriegen! (*ugs.*); **the driver didn't notice me until he was right on ~ of me** (*fig.*) der Fahrer bemerkte mich erst, als er mich schon fast umgefahren hatte; **he put it on [the] ~ of the pile** er legte es [oben] auf den Stapel; **on ~ of one another** *or* **each other** aufeinander; **live on ~ of each other** übereinander wohnen; (*too close*) sehr beengt leben; **on ~ of sth.** (*fig.: in addition*) zusätzlich zu etw.; **on ~ of everything else** zu alledem noch; **come/be on ~ of sth.** (*be additional*) zu etw. [hinzu]kommen; **on ~ of that, this happens!** (*fig.*) zu allem Überfluss passiert auch noch das!; **on ~ of the world** (*fig.*) überglücklich; **be/go thin on ~:** licht auf dem Kopf sein/werden; **be on ~:** ganz oben sein/liegen; **the English team is on ~:** die englische Mannschaft ist [dem Gegner] überlegen; **come out on ~** (*be successful*) Erfolg haben; (*win*) gewinnen; **get to the ~** (*fig.*) eine Spitzenposition erringen; ganz nach oben kommen (*ugs.*); **from ~ to toe** von Kopf bis Fuß; **a Tory from ~ to toe** ein Tory vom Scheitel bis zur Sohle; **be over the ~:** übertrieben *od.* überzogen sein; **go over the ~** (*Mil.*) den Graben verlassen; (*fig.*) (*take decisive step*) eine endgültige Entscheidung treffen; (*be excessive*) über die Stränge schlagen (*ugs.*); es übertreiben (*ugs.*); **he searched the house from ~ to bottom** er durchsuchte das Haus von oben bis unten; **take it from the ~** (*coll.*) noch einmal von vorne anfangen; ⇒ *also* **head** 1 A; [B] (*highest rank*) Spitze, *die;* **the man at the ~:** der [oberste] Chef *od.* (*ugs.*) Boss; **~ of the table** (*Sport*) Tabellenspitze, *die;* **[at the] ~ of the list of things to do/agenda is ...:** ganz oben auf der Liste der Dinge, die getan werden müssen/auf der Tagesordnung steht ...; **be [at the] ~ of the class** der/die Klassenbeste sein; **go to the ~ of the class!** (*fig. coll.*) alle Achtung!; **~ of the bill** (*Theatre*) Zugpferd, *das;* **be ~ of the charts** *or* **pops** an der Spitze der Hitparade stehen; die Hitparade anführen; (*fig.*) die Nummer eins sein; [C] (*of vegetable*) Kraut, *das;* **~s of turnips, turnip-~s** das Kraut von Rüben; [D] (*upper surface*) Oberfläche, *die;* (*of cupboard, wardrobe, chest*) Oberseite, *die;* **on [the] ~ of sth.** [oben] auf etw. (*position: Dat./direction: Akk.*); **don't forget to paint along the ~ of the door** vergiss nicht, die Tür von oben zu streichen; **cut off the ~ [of the apple]** oben ein Stück [vom Apfel] abschneiden; **cut the ~ off an egg** ein Ei köpfen; **they climbed to the ~ of the hill/slope** sie kletterten auf den Hügel/den Hang hinauf; **he laid his hand on the ~ of her head** er legte ihr seine Hand auf den Kopf; [E] (*folding roof*) Verdeck, *das;* [F] (*upper deck of bus, boat*) Oberdeck, *das;* [G] (*cap of pen*) [Verschluss]kappe, *die;* [H] (*cream on milk*) Sahne, *die;* Rahm, *der* (*regional, bes. südd., österr., schweiz.*); [I] (*upper part of page*) oberer Teil; **at the ~ [of the page]** oben [auf der/die Seite]; **be ten lines from the ~:** in der zehnten Zeile [von oben] stehen; [J] (*upper garment*) Oberteil, *das;* (*blouse, T-shirt*) Top, *das* (*Textilw.*); [K] (*turn-down of sock*) Umschlag, *der;* [L] (*head end*) Kopf, *der;* (*of bed*) Kopfende, *das;* (*of street*) oberes Ende; (*of beach*) oberer Teil; [M] (*utmost*) Gipfel, *der;* **shout/talk at the ~ of one's voice** aus vollem Halse schreien/so laut wie möglich sprechen; [N] **be the ~s** (*coll.*) (*the best*) der/die/das Größte sein (*ugs.*); (*marvellous*) Spitze sein (*ugs.*); **he's ~s at squash** er spielt hervorragend Squash; **the ~ of the morning [to you]!** (*Ir.*) einen wunderschönen guten Morgen!; [O] (*surface*) Oberfläche, *die;* [P] (*upper of shoe*) Oberteil, *das;* [Q] (*lid*) Deckel, *der;* (*of bottle, glass jar, etc.*) Deckel, *der;* (*stopper*) Stöpsel, *der;* (*silver foil, crown cork*) Verschluss, *der;* ⇒ *also* **blow¹** 2 H; [R] (*Bookbinding*) Kopfschnitt, *der;* [S] (*upper part of boot*) Stulpe, *die;* [T] (*Naut.: platform*) Saling, *die* (*Seemannsspr.*); [U] (*Brit. Motor Veh.*) größter Gang (*Kfz-W.*); **in ~:** im größten Gang.

❷ *adj.* ▶ 1552 oberst...; höchst... ‹Ton, Preis›; **~ end** oberes Ende; **the/a ~ award** die höchste/eine hohe Auszeichnung; **the/a ~ chess player** der beste Schachspieler/einer der besten Schachspieler *od.* ein Spitzenschachspieler; **~ scientists/actors** *etc.* hochkarätige Wissenschaftler/Schauspieler *usw.;* **~ sportsman/job/politician** Spitzensportler, *der*/Spitzenposition, *die*/Spitzenpolitiker, *der;* **the ~ pupil/school/marks** der beste Schüler/die beste Schule/die besten Noten; **~ score/nation/pop star** höchste Punktzahl/führende Nation/größter Popstar; **a ~ Conservative** ein Spitzenpolitiker der Konservativen Partei; **~ names in industry** Spitzen der Industrie; **~ manager/management** Topmanager/-management; **a ~ speed of 100 m.p.h.** eine Spitzen- *od.* Höchstgeschwindigkeit von 160 k.p.h.; **go at ~ speed** mit Spitzen- *od.* Höchstgeschwindigkeit fahren; **the machine was working at ~ speed** die Maschine lief auf Hochtouren; **I was working at ~ speed** ich arbeitete auf Hochtouren; **read sth. at ~ speed** etw. im Schnellverfahren lesen; **be/come ~ [in a subject]** [in einem Fach] der/die Beste sein/werden; **give sth. ~ priority** einer Sache (*Dat.*) höchste Priorität einräumen; **have a record in the ~ ten** eine Platte in den Top-Ten haben; **in the ~ left/right corner** in der linken/rechten oberen Ecke; **on the ~ floor** im obersten Stockwerk; **the ~ men in the firm** die Spitze der Firma; **they are the ~ men in the firm** sie stehen an der Spitze der Firma; **the ~ people** (*in society*) die Spitzen der Gesellschaft; (*in a particular field*) die besten Leute; ⇒ *also* **form** 1 F; **gear** 1 A.

❸ *v.t.*, **-pp-:** [A] (*cover*) **the hills were ~ped with** *or* **by snow** die Hügelspitzen waren schneebedeckt; **a church ~ped with** *or* **by a dome** eine mit einer Kuppel gekrönte Kirche; **~ a pudding with cream** Sahne auf einen Pudding geben; **a pudding ~ped with cream** ein Pudding mit Sahne obendrauf; [B] (*Hort.: cut ~ off*) stutzen ‹Pflanze›; kappen ‹Baum›; [C] (*be taller than*) überragen; **he ~s six feet** er ist über sechs Fuß groß; [D] (*surpass, excel*) übertreffen; **exports have ~ped [the] £40 million [mark/level]** die Exporte haben die [Grenze von] 40 Millionen Pfund überschritten; **the fish ~ped 2 lb.** der Fisch wog über zwei Pfund; **~ an offer** ein Angebot überbieten; **~ that for a score/story!** überbiete diese Punktzahl/erzähl eine bessere Geschichte!; **to ~ it all** [noch] obendrein; [E] (*head*) anführen; **~ the bill** (*Theatre*) das Zugpferd sein; [F] (*reach ~ of*) **~ the hill/wave** auf die Spitze des Hügels/den Kamm der Welle gelangen

**~ 'off** (*coll.*) ❶ *v.t.* beschließen. ❷ *v.i.* schließen

**~ 'out** *v.t.* (*Building*) richten (*Bauw.*); **~ping-out ceremony** Richtfest, *das*

**~ 'up** (*Brit.*) ❶ *v.t.* auffüllen ‹Batterie, Tank, Flasche, Glas›; **~ up the petrol/oil/water** Benzin/Öl/Wasser nachfüllen; **can I ~ you up?** darf ich dir/Ihnen nachschenken?; **~ up sb.'s drink** jmdm. nachschenken. ❷ *v.i.* (*fill one's tank up*) voll tanken; (*fill one's glass up*) sich nachschenken; **~ up with petrol/oil/water** den Tank mit Benzin/Öl/Wasser auffüllen. ⇒ *also* **top-up**

**top²** *n.* (*toy*) Kreisel, *der;* ⇒ *also* **sleep** 2 A

**top and 'tail** *v.t.* [A] (*start and end*) einleiten und beschließen ‹Vortrag usw.›; [B] **~ gooseberries** *etc.* Stachelbeeren *usw.* putzen (*durch Entfernen des Stiels und des abgestorbenen Blütenteils am anderen Ende*)

**topaz** /'təʊpæz/ *n.* (*Min.*) Topas, *der;* **false ~:** Goldtopas, *der*

**top: ~ 'billing** *n.* (*Theatre*) *prominentester Platz auf einem Plakat/in einer Werbung;* **he vied with her for the ~ billing** er wetteiferte mit ihr um die Rolle des Stars; **give sb. ~ billing** jmdn. groß herausbringen (*ugs.*); **in this film, Richard Burton shares ~ billing with Elizabeth Taylor** in diesem Film sind Richard Burton und Elizabeth Taylor die großen Stars; **~ boot** *n.* langschäftiger Stulpenstiefel; **~ 'brass** ⇒ **brass** 1 G; **~ coat** *n.* [A] (*overcoat*) Überzieher, *der;* Mantel, *der;* [B] (*of paint*) Deckanstrich, *der;* **~ copy** *n.* Original, *das;* **~ 'dog** *n.* (*fig. coll.*) Boss, *der* (*ugs.*); **he/the company came out ~ dog [amongst his/its rivals]** er/die Firma setzte sich [gegen die Konkurrenz] durch; **~ 'drawer** *n.* [A] oberste Schublade; [B] (*fig.: high social status*) **sb. is not out of the ~ drawer** jmd. gehört nicht gerade zur Crème de la Crème; *attrib.* Oberschicht-; **~-dress** *v.t.* (*Agric.*) oberflächlich düngen ‹Land, Acker›; **~ dressing** *n.* [A] (*Agric.*) Oberflächendüngung, *die;* (*substance*) Oberflächendünger, *der;* [B] (*fig.: superficial show*) Kosmetik, *die;* **the whole ceremony is just ~-dressing** die ganze Zeremonie ist nur Fassade

**topee** ⇒ **topi**

**toper** /'təʊpə(r)/ *n.* (*arch./literary*) Zecher, *der*/Zecherin, *die*

**top: ~-flight** *attrib. adj.* erstrangig; Spitzen‹sportler, -politiker›; **~ fruit** *n.* (*Brit. Hort.*) Baumobst, *das;* **~ 'hat** *n.* Zylinder[hut], *der;* **~-heavy** *adj.* oberlastig; kopflastig ‹Baum, Pflanze, Bürokratie›; **don't make your load ~-heavy** sorg dafür, dass der Schwerpunkt der Ladung nicht zu hoch liegt; **she is a bit ~-heavy** sie hat einen ganz schönen Vorbau (*ugs. scherzh.*); **~-'hole** *adj.* (*Brit. dated coll.*) famos (*ugs. veralt.*)

**topi** /'təʊpɪ/ *n.* (*Anglo-Ind.*) Tropenhelm, *der*

**topiary** /'təʊpɪərɪ/ *n.* (*Hort.*) *Kunst des ornamentalen Beschnitts von Bäumen und Sträuchern*

**topic** /'tɒpɪk/ *n.* Thema, *das;* **~ of debate/conversation** Diskussions-/Gesprächsthema, *das*

**topical** /'tɒpɪkl/ *adj.* [A] aktuell; [B] (*with regard to topics*) nach Sachgebieten *nachgestellt;* [C] (*Med.*) lokalisiert

**topicality** /tɒpɪ'kælɪtɪ/ *n., no pl.* Aktualität, *die*

**topically** /'tɒpɪkəlɪ/ *adv.* [A] mit aktuellem Bezug; [B] (*with regard to topics*) nach Sachgebieten

**'topknot** *n.* [A] (*ribbon*) Haarschleife, *die;* [B] (*tuft of hair*) Haarknoten, *der*

**topless** /'tɒplɪs/ *adj.* [A] **a ~ statue/column** eine Statue/Säule mit fehlendem oberem Teil; [B] **a ~ dress/swimsuit** ein busenfreies Kleid/ein Oben-ohne-Badeanzug; [C] (*bare-breasted*) barbusig; **~ girl/waitress** Oben-ohne-Mädchen, *das*/-Bedienung, *die;* **go/bathe ~:** oben ohne gehen/baden

**top: ~-level** *attrib. adj.* Gipfel‹treffen, -konferenz›; Spitzen ‹politiker, -funktionär›; **~-level discussions / negotiations / talks / deals** Diskussionen / Verhandlungen / Gespräche / Vereinbarungen auf höchster Ebene; **~-line** *adj.* (*Commerc.*) **~-line profit** Bruttogewinn, *der;* **~mast** *n.* (*Naut.*) Stenge, *die*

**topmost** /'tɒpməʊst, 'tɒpməst/ *adj.* oberst ... ‹Schicht, Stufe›; höchst... ‹Gipfel, Beamte, Note›

**top-'notch** *adj.* (*coll.*) fantastisch (*ugs.*)

**topographer** /tə'pɒgrəfə(r)/ *n.* Topograph, *der*/-graphin, *die*

**topographic** /tɒpə'græfɪk/, **topographical** /tɒpə'græfɪkl/ *adj.* topographisch

**topography** /tə'pɒgrəfɪ/ *n.* (A) Topographie, *die;* (B) (*features*) örtliche *od.* (*geh.*) topographische Gegebenheiten; Topographie, *die* (*geh.*); **I'm not acquainted with the ~ of the area/town** *etc.* ich kenne mich in der Gegend/Stadt *usw.* nicht aus

**topology** /tə'pɒlədʒɪ/ *n.* (*Math.*) Topologie, *die*

**topper** /'tɒpə(r)/ *n.* (*coll.: hat*) Zylinder, *der;* Angströhre, *die* (*ugs. scherzh.*)

**topping** /'tɒpɪŋ/ **1** *n.* (*Cookery*) Überzug, *der;* **ice cream with a ~ of whipped cream/of raspberry syrup** Eis mit Sahne/Himbeersirup [obendrauf]; **put on a ~ of cream/chopped nuts** das Ganze mit Sahne überziehen/mit gehackten Nüssen bestreuen; **cover sth. with a ~ of mashed potato/sliced potatoes** etw. mit einer Schicht Kartoffelbrei/Kartoffelscheiben bedecken. **2** *adj.* (*Brit. dated coll.: excellent*) famos (*ugs.*); formidabel

**topple** /'tɒpl/ **1** *v.i.* fallen; **the tower/pile ~d to the ground** der Turm/Stapel fiel um *od.* kippte um; **the tower ~d and fell** der Turm wankte und stürzte um; **~ [from power]** (*fig.*) stürzen. **2** *v.t.* stürzen; **~ a pile/wall [to the ground]** einen Stapel/eine Mauer umstürzen *od.* umwerfen; **~ sb./a government [from power]** ‹Gegner:› jmdn./eine Regierung stürzen; ‹Skandal, Abstimmung:› jmdn./eine Regierung zu Fall bringen

**~ 'down** *v.i.* hinab-/herabfallen; ‹Stapel, Turm:› umstürzen, umfallen

**~ 'over 1** *v.i.* ‹Turm, Stapel, Baum, Auto:› umstürzen, umfallen; ‹Vase, Ohnmächtiger:› umfallen; **he lost his balance on the edge of the cliff and ~d over** er verlor am Rand des Kliffs sein Gleichgewicht und stürzte hinunter. **2** *v.t.* umstürzen; umwerfen

**top: ~-quality** *adj.* [qualitativ] hochwertig; **~-ranking** *attrib. adj.* Spitzen‹funktionär, -beamter, -politiker, -sportler, -orchester, -delegierter›; hochrangig ‹Offizier›; erstrangig ‹Autor, Schauspieler›; führend ‹Wissenschaftler›; **~-ranking party member** Mitglied der Parteispitze; **~sail** /'tɒpseɪl, 'tɒpsl/ *n.* (*Naut.*) (*on square-rigger*) Marssegel, *das;* (*on schooner*) Toppsegel, *das;* **~ 'secret** *adj.* streng geheim; **~side** *n.* (A) (*joint of beef*) Oberschale, *die;* (B) (*Naut.*) obere Bordwand; **~soil** *n.* (*Agric.*) Mutterboden, *der;* (*of field*) [Acker]krume, *die;* **~ spin** *n.* (*Sport*) Vorwärtsdrall, *der;* (*tennis, table tennis*) Topspin, *der*

**topsy-turvy** /tɒpsɪ'tɜ:vɪ/ **1** *adv.* verkehrtrum (*ugs.*); auf dem Kopf (*ugs.*) ‹stehen, liegen›; **turn sth. ~** (*lit. or fig.*) etw. auf den Kopf stellen (*ugs.*); **this development turned my plans ~:** diese Entwicklung warf meine Pläne um *od.* (*ugs.*) über den Haufen. **2** *adj.* chaotisch; **the room/house was ~:** das ganze Zimmer/Haus war auf den Kopf gestellt; (*fig.*) **a world where things are all ~:** eine Welt, in der alles auf dem Kopf steht; **a ~ way of reasoning** eine verquere Art zu denken; **it's a ~ world** es ist eine verkehrte Welt; **the whole world has turned ~:** die ganze Welt steht Kopf (*ugs.*)

**top: ~ 'table** *n.* Tisch am Kopf der Tafel; **~-up** *n.* (*Brit.*) Auffüllung, *die;* **sth. needs a ~-up** etw. muss [wieder] aufgefüllt werden; **the oil needs a ~-up** es muss Öl nachgefüllt werden; **give the tank/oil a ~-up** den Tank auffüllen/Öl nachfüllen; **would you like/can I give you a ~-up?** soll/kann ich dir noch mal nachgießen?; **I need a ~-up** ich muss mir noch mal nachgießen/nachgießen lassen

**toque** /təʊk/ *n.* Toque, *die*

**tor** /tɔ:(r)/ *n.* Felsenspitze, *die;* (*hill*) Hügel, *der*

**torch** /tɔ:tʃ/ *n.* (A) **[electric] ~** (*Brit.*) Taschenlampe, *die;* (B) (*blowlamp*) (*for welding*) Schweißbrenner, *der;* (*for soldering*) Lötlampe, *die;* (*for cutting*) Schneidbrenner, *der;* (C) (*flaming stick etc.*) Fackel, *die;* **carry a ~ for sb.** (*fig.*) jmdn. verehren; **hand on the ~** (*fig.*) die Fackel weiterreichen (*geh.*); (D) (*lamp on pole*) Öllampe [an einer Stange]

**torch: ~ battery** *n.* (*Brit.*) Taschenlampenbatterie, *die;* **~light** *n., no pl., no indef. art.* Licht der/einer Taschenlampe; (*of flaming stick*) Fackelschein, *der;* **by ~light** im Schein einer Taschenlampe/Fackel; **~light procession** Fackelzug, *der;* **a ~light ceremony/parade/tattoo** eine Zeremonie/Parade/ein Zapfenstreich im Fackelschein; **~ song** *n.* bluesartiger sentimentaler Song von unerwiderter Liebe

**tore** ⇒ **tear**[1] 2, 3

**toreador** /'tɒrɪədɔ:(r)/ *n.* Toreador, *der*

**torment 1** /'tɔ:ment/ *n.* Qual, *die;* **be in ~:** Qualen ausstehen; **suffer ~s** Qualen erleiden; **be a ~ to sb., be sb.'s ~:** jmdn. quälen *od.* peinigen; **the suspense/uncertainty was a ~:** die Spannung/Ungewissheit war unerträglich. **2** /tɔ:'ment/ *v.t.* (A) quälen; peinigen; **be ~ed by** *or* **with sth.** von etw. gequält werden; (B) (*tease, worry*) quälen; **Don't ~ me so! Tell me ...:** Spann mich nicht auf die Folter! Sag mir doch ...

**tormentor** /tɔ:'mentə(r)/ *n.* Folterer, *der;* (*fig.*) Peiniger, *der*

**torn** ⇒ **tear**[1] 2, 3

**tornado** /tɔ:'neɪdəʊ/ *n., pl.* **~es** Wirbelsturm, *der;* (*in North America*) Tornado, *der;* (*fig.: outburst, volley*) Orkan, *der*

**torpedo** /tɔ:'pi:dəʊ/ **1** *n., pl.* **~es** Torpedo, *der;* **aerial ~:** Lufttorpedo, *der.* **2** *v.t.* (*auch fig.*) torpedieren

**torpedo: ~ boat** *n.* (*Navy*) Torpedoboot, *das;* **~ tube** *n.* Torpedorohr, *das*

**torpid** /'tɔ:pɪd/ *adj.* (A) träge; träge fließend ‹Gewässer›; (B) (*Zool.*) torpid

**torpidity** /tɔ:'pɪdɪtɪ/, **torpor** /'tɔ:pə(r)/ *ns., no pl.* (A) Trägheit, *die;* (*of water*) träges Fließen; (B) (*Zool.*) Torpidität, *die*

**torpor** /'tɔ:pə(r)/ *n.* ⇒ **torpidity**

**torque** /tɔ:k/ *n.* (*Mech.*) Drehmoment, *das*

**torque: ~ converter** *n.* (*Motor Veh.*) Drehmomentwandler, der; **~ wrench** *n.* Drehmomentschlüssel, *der*

**torr** /tɔ:(r)/ *n., pl. same* (*Phys.*) Torr, *das*

**torrent** /'tɒrənt/ *n.* (A) reißender Bach; (*stream having steep course*) Sturzbach, *der;* **mountain ~:** reißender Gebirgsbach; **a brook, sometimes swollen into a ~:** ein Bächlein, das manchmal zu einem reißenden Strom anschwillt; **a ~ of rain** ein Regenguss; **the rain came down in ~s** es regnete in Strömen; (B) (*fig.: violent flow*) Flut, *die;* Schwall, *der*

**torrential** /tə'renʃl/ *adj.* (A) reißend ‹Gebirgsbach, Fluten›; wolkenbruchartig ‹Regen, Schauer›; **the rain was ~:** es regnete in Strömen; **a ~ cloudburst** ein heftiger Wolkenbruch; (B) (*fig.*) überwältigend; gewaltig; **a ~ flow of words/insults/questions** ein Schwall von Worten/Beleidigungen/Fragen

**torrid** /'tɒrɪd/ *adj.* (A) (*intensely hot*) glutheiß; **a ~ land** ein [von der Hitze] versengtes Land; **the ~ heat of the desert** die Gluthitze der Wüste; (B) (*fig.: intense, ardent*) glühend (*geh.*); ‹Liebesszene› voller Leidenschaft

**torsion** /'tɔ:ʃn/ *n.* Verwindung, *die;* Torsion, *die* (*Physik, Technik*); **~ bar** Torsionsstab, *der*

**torso** /'tɔ:səʊ/ *n., pl.* **~s** (A) (*Art*) Torso, *der;* (B) (*human trunk*) Rumpf, *der;* **bare ~:** nackter Oberkörper; (C) (*fig.: incomplete work*) Torso, *der*

**tort** /tɔ:t/ *n.* (*Law*) [zivilrechtliches] Delikt; unerlaubte Handlung

**tortilla** /tɔ:'ti:ljə/ *n.* Tortilla, *die*

**tortoise** /'tɔ:təs/ *n.* Schildkröte, *die*

**tortoiseshell** /'tɔ:təsʃel/ *n.* Schildpatt, *das; attrib.* Schildpatt-

**tortoiseshell: ~ 'butterfly** *n.* Fuchs, *der;* **~ 'cat** *n.* Katze mit Schildpattzeichnung

**tortuous** /'tɔ:tjʊəs/ *adj.* (A) (*full of twists and turns*) verschlungen ‹Weg›; gewunden ‹Flusslauf›; (B) (*fig.: circuitous*) umständlich; verworren ‹Argumentation, Denken, Sprache›; **a ~ speaker/writer** ein Redner/Schriftsteller, der viele Worte macht

**tortuously** /'tɔ:tjʊəslɪ/ *adv.* (A) (*with twists and turns*) verschlungen; **the road/path/river runs ~ through the fields** die Straße/der Weg/Fluss windet sich *od.* schlängelt sich durch die Felder; (B) (*fig.: circuitously*) umständlich; **a ~ reasoned argument** ein verworrenes Argument; **a ~ argued case** eine umständliche Argumentation; **a ~ complex legal document** ein verwirrend komplexer juristischer Schriftsatz

**tortuousness** /'tɔ:tjʊəsnɪs/ *n., no pl.* (A) **the ~ of the road/river** die vielen Windungen der Straße/des Flusses; (B) (*fig.: circuitousness*) Umständlichkeit, *die*

**torture** /'tɔ:tʃə(r)/ **1** *n.* (A) Folter, *die;* **the ~s of the Inquisition** die Folterungen der Inquisition; **the ~ of sb.** jmds. Folterung; **practise ~:** foltern; **instrument of ~:** Folterwerkzeug, *das;* Folterinstrument, *das;* (B) (*fig.: agony*) Qual, *die;* **it was ~:** es war eine Tortur; **the exam was sheer ~:** das Examen war der reinste Horror (*ugs.*) *od.* die Hölle; **suffer the ~s of the damned** Höllenqualen erleiden. **2** *v.t.* foltern; (*fig.*) quälen

**'torture chamber** *n.* Folterkammer, *die*

**torturer** /'tɔ:tʃərə(r)/ *n.* Folterer, *der*/Folterin, *die*

**Tory** /'tɔ:rɪ/ (*Brit. Polit. coll.*) **1** *n.* Tory, *der.* **2** *adj.* Tory-; **he is/they are ~:** er ist ein Tory/sie sind Tories

**Toryism** /'tɔ:rɪɪzm/ *n., no pl.* (*Brit. Polit. coll.*) Toryismus, *der*

**tosh** /tɒʃ/ *n.* (*coll.*) Quark, *der* (*ugs.*)

**toss** /tɒs/ **1** *v.t.* (A) (*throw upwards*) hochwerfen; **~ a ball in one's hand** einen Ball mit der Hand immer wieder hochwerfen und auffangen; **~ a pancake** einen Pfannkuchen [durch Hochwerfen] wenden; **~ sb. in a blanket** jmdn. mit einer Decke in die Höhe schleudern; ⇒ *also* **caber**; (B) (*throw casually*) werfen; schmeißen (*ugs.*); **~ it over!** (*coll.*) schmeiß es/ihn/sie rüber (*ugs.*); **~ sth. to sb.** jmdm. etw. zuwerfen; (C) **~ a coin** eine Münze werfen; **~ sb. for sth.** mit jmdm. durch Hochwerfen einer Münze um etw. losen; (D) **be ~ed by a bull/horse** von einem Stier auf die Hörner genommen werden/von einem Pferd abgeworfen werden; (E) (*move about*) hin und her werfen; ‹Baum/Blume› wiegen ‹Zweige/Köpfe›; (F) (*Cookery: mix gently*) wenden; **~ a salad in oil** einen Salat mit Öl anmachen; (G) **~ one's head** den Kopf zurückwerfen.

**2** *v.i.* (A) (*be restless in bed*) sich hin und her werfen; **~ and turn** sich [schlaflos] im Bett wälzen; (B) ‹Schiff, Boot:› hin und her geworfen werden; ‹Halm, Korn, Äste, Blume:› sich wiegen; ‹Federbusch, Hutfeder, Locken:› wippen; ‹Mähne, Haar› flattern; (C) (**~** *coin*) eine Münze werfen; **~ for sth.** mit einer Münze um etw. losen.

**3** *n.* (A) (*of coin*) **~ of a coin** Hochwerfen einer Münze; **the decision depends on the ~ of a coin** die Entscheidung wird durch Hochwerfen einer Münze gefällt; **the game was decided by the ~ of a coin** das Spiel wurde durch Hochwerfen einer Münze entschieden; **argue the ~** (*fig.*) die Entscheidung nicht akzeptieren wollen; **lose/win the ~:** bei der Auslosung verlieren/gewinnen; (*Footb.*) die Seitenwahl verlieren/gewinnen; (B) **give a contemptuous/proud ~ of the head** den Kopf verächtlich/stolz in den Nacken werfen; (C) (*throw*) Wurf, *der;* **give a pancake a ~:** einen Pfannkuchen [durch Hochwerfen] wenden; (D) (*Brit.: throw from horse*) Abwerfen, *das;* **a bad ~:** ein schlimmer Sturz vom Pferd; **take a ~:** abgeworfen werden; (E) **I couldn't give a ~** (*fig. Brit. sl.*) es ist mir scheißegal (*salopp*)

**~ about, ~ around 1** *v.i.* (A) (*be restless in bed*) sich [schlaflos] im Bett wälzen; (B) ⇒ **~** 2 B. **2** *v.t.* **~ sth. around** *or* **about** etw. herumwerfen; etw. *od.* mit etw. rumschmeißen (*ugs.*); (*fig.*) etw. in die Debatte werfen

**~ a'side** *v.t.* (A) (*throw to one side*) hinwerfen; hinschmeißen (*ugs.*); **the mouldy apples were ~ed aside** die schimmligen Äpfel wurden weggeworfen; (B) (*fig.: reject, abandon*) beiseite schieben; **~ aside all caution** alle Vorsicht außer Acht lassen

**~ a'way** *v.t.* wegwerfen; wegschmeißen (*ugs.*)

t

~ **'back** *v.t.* zurückwerfen ‹Kopf, Haar›; runterkippen (*ugs.*) ‹Getränk›
~ **'down** ⇒ ~ **off** 1 A
~ **'off** ❶ *v.t.* A (*drink off*) runterkippen (*ugs.*); B (*produce casually*) hinwerfen; hinhauen (*ugs. abwertend*); fallen lassen ‹Bemerkung›; **I just ~ed off the first names that came into my head** ich spuckte einfach die ersten besten Namen aus, die mir einfielen; C (*sl.: masturbate*) ~ **sb. off** jmdm. einen runterholen (*salopp*). ❷ *v.i. & refl.* (*sl.*) sich (*Dat.*) einen runterholen (*salopp*)
~ **'out** *v.t.* A (*throw out*) ~ **sb. out** jmdn. rauswerfen *od.* (*ugs.*) -schmeißen; ~ **sth. out** etw. wegwerfen *od.* (*ugs.*) wegschmeißen; B (*fig.: reject*) [kurzerhand] ablehnen
~ **'up** ❶ *v.i.* eine Münze werfen; ~ **up for sth.** mit einer Münze um etw. losen. ❷ *v.t.* A (*throw*) hochwerfen; in die Luft werfen

**'toss-up** *n.* A (*tossing of coin*) Hochwerfen einer Münze; **a ~ decides who ...:** wer ..., wird durch Hochwerfen einer Münze entschieden; **have a ~:** eine Münze werfen; **have a ~ for sth.** mit einer Münze um etw. losen; B (*even chance*) **it is a ~ [whether ...]** es ist noch ganz ungewiss[, ob ...]; **They are both very good. It is a ~ between the two** Sie sind beide sehr gut. Man kann nicht sagen, wer besser ist

**tot**[1] /tɒt/ *n.* (*coll.*) A (*small child*) kleines Kind; Wicht, der (*fam.*); **tiny ~:** kleiner Wicht; B (*dram of liquor*) Gläschen, *das;* **will you have a ~ of rum?** möchtest du ein Gläschen *od.* Schlückchen Rum haben?

**tot**[2] *v.t. & i.*, **-tt-** (*coll.*) ~ **up** ❶ *v.t.* zusammenziehen (*ugs.*). ❷ *v.i.* sich summieren; sich [zusammen]läppern (*ugs.*); **that ~s up to £5** das macht zusammen 5 Pfund (*ugs.*)

**total** /'təʊtl/ ❶ *adj.* A (*comprising the whole*) gesamt; Gesamt‹gewicht, -wert, -bevölkerung usw.›; **what are your ~ debts?** wie viel Schulden hast du insgesamt?; **a ~ increase of £100** eine Steigerung von insgesamt 100 Pfund; ⇒ *also* **sum** 1 A; B (*absolute*) völlig *nicht präd.;* ~ **idiot** (*coll.*) Vollidiot, *der;* **be in ~ ignorance of sth.** von etw. überhaupt *od.* absolut nichts wissen; **a ~ beginner** ein absoluter Anfänger; ~ **nonsense** totaler Unsinn; **have ~ contempt/scorn for sth.** etw. zutiefst verachten; **have a ~ lack of interest in sth.** sich für etw. absolut nicht interessieren; **a ~ success/shock** ein voller Erfolg/totaler *od.* absoluter Schock; **his surrender/refusal was ~:** er gab völlig auf/er weigerte sich strikt; **the silence was ~:** es herrschte völlige Stille; ⇒ *also* **abstinence** A.
❷ *n.* (*number*) Gesamtzahl, *die;* (*amount*) Gesamtbetrag, *der;* (*result of addition*) Summe, *die;* **a ~ of 200/£200** *etc.* insgesamt 200/200 Pfund *usw.;* **in ~:** insgesamt; ⇒ *also* **grand** 1 C; **subtotal**.
❸ *v.t.*, (*Brit.*) **-ll-:** A (*add up*) addieren, zusammenzählen, zusammenrechnen ‹Zahlen, Posten, Beträge›; B (*amount to*) [insgesamt] betragen; **the visitors ~led 131** die Zahl der Besucher betrug [insgesamt] 131; C (*Amer. coll.: wreck*) zusammenfahren (*ugs.*)
~ **'up** ❶ *v.t.* addieren; zusammenrechnen/-zählen. ❷ *v.i.* ~ **up to sth.** sich auf etw. (*Akk.*) belaufen

**total e'clipse** *n.* (*Astron.*) totale Finsternis

**totalitarian** /təʊtælɪ'teərɪən/ *adj.* (*Polit.*) totalitär

**totalitarianism** /təʊtælɪ'teərɪənɪzm/ *n.* (*Polit.*) Totalitarismus, *der*

**totality** /tə'tælɪtɪ/ *n.* A (*completeness*) Gesamtheit, *die;* (*of person*) Ganzheit, *die;* B (*aggregate*) Gesamtheit, *die;* **the ~ of the debt** die Gesamtschuld; C (*Astron.*) Totalität, *die* (*fachspr.*)

**totalizator** /'təʊtəlaɪzeɪtə(r)/ *n.* (*Horseracing*) A (*device*) Totalisatoranzeigetafel, *die;* B (*system*) Totalisator, *der;* Toto, *das*

**totally** /'təʊtəlɪ/ *adv.* völlig

**total:** ~ **re'call** *n.* **have [the power of] ~ recall** ein absolutes Erinnerungsvermögen haben; ~ **'war** *n.* totaler Krieg

**tote**[1] /təʊt/ *v.t.* (*coll.*) schleppen; ~ **a gun** eine Kanone mit sich rumschleppen (*ugs.*)

**tote**[2] *n.* (*Horseracing coll.*) A (*device*) Totoanzeigetafel, *die;* B (*system*) Toto, *das*

**tote:** ~ **bag** *n.* ≈ Reisetasche, *die;* ~ **box** *n.* (*Amer.*) [Transport]kiste, *die*

**totem** /'təʊtəm/ *n.* Totem, *das* (*Völkerk.*)

**totemism** /'təʊtəmɪzm/ *n.* Totemismus, *der* (*Völkerk.*)

**'totem pole** *n.* Totempfahl, *der* (*Völkerk.*)

**t'other, tother** /'tʌðə(r)/ *adj., pron.* = **the other**

**totter** /'tɒtə(r)/ *v.i.* A (*move unsteadily*) wanken; taumeln; (*esp. owing to drunkenness*) torkeln; **the child/blind man went ~ing across the room** das Kind ging mit tapsenden (*ugs.*)/der Blinde ging mit tastenden Schritten durch das Zimmer; B (*be on point of falling*) schwanken; wanken (*geh.*); **make sth. ~:** etw. ins Schwanken bringen; ~ **on the brink of collapse/chaos/bankruptcy/ruin** (*fig.*) am Rande des Zusammenbruchs/Chaos/Bankrotts/Ruins stehen

**tottery** /'tɒtərɪ/ *adj.* wack[e]lig; **a ~ old man** ein alter Mann mit wackligen (*ugs.*) *od.* unsicheren Beinen; **have ~ legs** wacklig (*ugs.*) *od.* unsicher auf den Beinen sein; **feel ~:** sich wacklig (*ugs.*) *od.* unsicher auf den Beinen fühlen

**totting-'up** /tɒtɪŋ'ʌp/ *n.* A Zusammenrechnen, *das;* **the ~ of the votes** die Auszählung der Stimmen; B (*Brit. law*) *Berücksichtigung einschlägiger Vorstrafen, bes. bei der Entscheidung über einen Führerscheinentzug*

**toucan** /'tu:kən/ *n.* (*Ornith.*) Tukan, *der*

**touch** /tʌtʃ/ ❶ *v.t.* A (*lit. or fig.*) berühren; (*inspect by ~ing*) betasten; ~ **one's hat [to sb.]** sich (*Dat.*) [jmdm. zum Gruß] an den Hut tippen; ~ **the sky** (*fig.*) an den Himmel stoßen; ~ **sb. on the shoulder** jmdm. auf die Schulter tippen; ⇒ *also* **bargepole; bottom** 1 D; **wood** B; B (*cause contact between, apply*) ~ **A to B** B mit A berühren; ~ **one's hand to one's hat** mit der Hand an den Hut tippen; ~ **a match to sth.** ein [brennendes] Streichholz an etw. (*Akk.*) halten; **he ~ed the wires together** er hielt die Drähte aneinander; ~ **glasses** anstoßen; C (*harm, interfere with*) anrühren; **the police can't ~ you [for it]** die Polizei kann dich nicht [dafür] belangen; **He can't ~ you here. You are safe** Hier kann er dir nichts tun *od.* anhaben. Du bist sicher; D (*Mus.*) ~ **the keys of a piano/harpsichord** *etc.* in die Tasten eines Klaviers/Spinetts *usw.* greifen; ~ **the strings [of a guitar/lute/harp** *etc.*] in die Saiten [einer Gitarre/Laute/Harfe *usw.*] greifen; E (*fig.: rival*) ~ **sth.** an etw. (*Akk.*) heranreichen; **nobody can ~ her for speed/at tennis/as an actress** niemand kann es mit ihr an Schnelligkeit/im Tennis/als Schauspielerin aufnehmen; **That horse is the fastest. There is none to ~ it** Dieses Pferd ist das schnellste. Keines kommt an es heran; **there is nothing to ~ a glass of whisky before bed** es geht nichts über ein Glas Whisky vor dem Schlafengehen; F (*affect emotionally*) rühren; **it ~ed him to the heart/it ~ed his heart** es rührte ihn ans Herz/es rührte sein Herz; **be ~ed with pity/remorse/sadness** von Mitleid/Reue/Traurigkeit angerührt sein (*geh.*); G (*concern oneself with*) anrühren; **whatever I ~ — I'm a failure at it** was ich auch anfange, es misslingt mir alles; **I would not ~ it** ich würde die Finger davon lassen (*ugs.*); **everything he ~es turns to gold** (*fig.*) er hat bei allem, was er tut, eine glückliche Hand; **I haven't even ~ed the washing up yet** ich habe mit dem Abwasch noch nicht mal angefangen; H (*tinge*) färben; **her hair was chestnut ~ed with blonde streaks** sie hatte kastanienbraunes Haar mit blonden Strähnen; I ~ **sb. for a loan/£5** (*coll.*) jmdn. anpumpen (*salopp*)/um 5 Pfund anpumpen *od.* anhauen (*salopp*); J (*Geom.*) berühren; tangieren (*fachspr.*); K (*reach*) erreichen; L (*anger, wound*) treffen; ~ **sb.'s pride/self-esteem** *etc.* jmdn. in seinem Stolz/in seinem Selbstwertgefühl *usw.* treffen; M (*concern*) berühren; **this does not ~ the point at issue** das hat nichts mit unserem Thema zu tun; N (*injure or damage slightly*) schädigen; ~ **sb.** jmdm. schaden; **he was hardly ~ed by the fall** bei dem Sturz hatte er kaum etwas abbekommen; O (*have effect on*) angreifen.
❷ *v.i.* sich berühren; ‹Grundstücke:› aneinander stoßen; **don't ~!** nicht anfassen!; **'please do not ~'** „bitte nicht berühren".
❸ *n.* A Berührung, *die;* **the rider gave his horse a ~ of the spurs/the whip** der Reiter ließ sein Pferd die Sporen/die Peitsche spüren; **I like the warm ~ of her body** ich spüre gerne ihren warmen Körper [an meiner Haut]; **the surface has a soft/rough/cold/warm** *etc.* **~:** die Oberfläche fühlt sich weich/rau/kalt/warm *usw.* an; **a ~ of the** *or* **one's hand** eine Berührung mit der Hand; **at a ~:** bei bloßer Berührung; **the machine can be stopped at a ~:** die Maschine lässt sich mit einem Fingerdruck abstellen; **be soft/warm** *etc.* **to the ~:** sich weich/warm *usw.* anfühlen; B *no pl., no art.* (*faculty*) **[sense of] ~:** Tastsinn, *der;* **find out sth. by ~:** etw. ertasten; C (*small amount*) **a ~ of salt/pepper** *etc.* eine Spur Salz/Pfeffer *usw.;* **a ~ of irony/sadness** *etc.* ein Anflug von Ironie/Traurigkeit *usw.;* **have a ~ of rheumatism** ein bisschen Rheuma haben; **have a ~ of genius** etwas Geniales haben; **she has a ~ of style/class [about her]** sie hat irgendwie Stil/Klasse; **the palms give a ~ of class/elegance to the restaurant** die Palmen geben dem Restaurant eine stilvolle/elegante Note; **he has a ~ of grey in his hair** er hat ein paar graue Strähnen im Haar; **a ~** (*slightly*) ein [ganz] kleines bisschen; **a ~ higher/too high** eine Idee höher/zu hoch; **a ~ unrealistic** eine Idee zu unrealistisch; ⇒ *also* **sun** 1; D (*game of tag*) Fangen, *das;* E (*Art: stroke*) Strich, *der;* (*fig.*) Detail, *das;* **to mention it in such a way was a clever/subtle ~:** es auf eine solche Weise zu erwähnen, war ein schlauer/raffinierter Einfall; **the book needs a few more humorous ~es** dem Buch fehlen noch ein paar humorvolle Tupfer; **the realistic ~es in the production of the play** die realistischen Elemente in der Inszenierung des Stücks; **add** *or* **put the final ~es to sth.** etw. (*Dat.*) den letzten Schliff geben; letzte Hand an etw. (*Akk.*) legen; **it was now completed except for a few final ~es** es war nun bis auf einige noch fehlende i-Tüpfelchen fertig gestellt; ⇒ *also* **finishing touch**; F (*manner, style*) (*on keyboard instrument, typewriter*) Anschlag, *der;* (*of writer, sculptor*) Stil, *der;* (*of painter*) Pinselführung, *die;* **have the ~ of genius/the professional ~:** genial/professionell gemacht sein; **show the ~ of a genius/professional** die Handschrift eines Genies/Profis verraten; **the play bore/revealed his ~:** das Stück trug/verriet seine Handschrift; **you need to have the right ~:** man muss das richtige Gespür haben; **he just didn't have the ~:** er hatte einfach nicht genug Talent; **this flat needs a woman's ~:** diese Wohnung braucht die Hand einer Frau; **a personal ~:** eine persönliche *od.* individuelle Note; **lose one's ~:** seinen Schwung verlieren; (*Sport*) seine Form verlieren; **I see you haven't lost your ~!** du bist ja noch ganz der/die Alte! (*ugs.*); **he's lost his ~:** er war schon mal besser in Form; **I must be losing my ~:** ich bin wohl auf dem absteigenden Ast (*ugs.*); ⇒ *also* **common** 1 B; G (*communication*) **be in/out of ~ [with sb.]** [mit jmdm.] Kontakt/keinen Kontakt haben; **I shall be in ~ with them** ich werde mit ihnen Kontakt aufnehmen; **they said they would be in ~ with me today** sie haben gesagt, sie würden sich heute bei mir melden; **Goodbye! I'll be in ~:** Auf Wiedersehen! Ich melde mich mal wieder; **they have not been in ~ for a whole week** wir haben/ich habe seit einer ganzen Woche nichts von ihnen gehört; **be in/out of ~ with sth.** über etw. (+ *Akk.*) auf dem Laufenden/nicht auf dem Laufenden sein; **he is out of** *or* **not in ~ with reality/the real world** er ist wirklichkeitsfremd/weltfremd; **get in ~ [with sb.]** mit jmdm. Kontakt/Verbindung aufnehmen; **get in ~ with us by letter/at**

t

**this number** schreiben Sie uns/rufen Sie uns unter dieser Nummer an; **she immediately got in ~ with the doctor/police/her lawyer** sie setzte sich sofort mit dem Arzt/der Polizei/ihrem Anwalt in Verbindung; **keep in ~ [with sb.]** [mit jmdm.] in Verbindung *od.* Kontakt bleiben; **keep in ~!** lass von dir hören!; **I've kept in ~ with him since we were children** meine Verbindung mit ihm ist seit unserer Kindheit nie abgerissen; **keep in ~ with sth.** sich über etw. (*Akk.*) auf dem Laufenden halten; **lose ~ with sb.** den Kontakt zu jmdm. verlieren; **we have lost ~:** wir haben keinen Kontakt mehr [zueinander]; **lose ~ with sth.** etw. aus den Augen verlieren; **have lost ~ with sth.** über etw. (*Akk.*) nicht mehr auf dem Laufenden sein; **put sb. in ~ with sb.** jmdn. mit jmdm. zusammenbringen; **her doctor put her in ~ with a specialist** ihr Arzt hat sie zu einem Spezialisten geschickt; **H** (*Footb., Rugby: part of field*) Aus, *das;* Mark, *die* (*Rugby*); **in ~:** im Aus; **he ran/the ball went into ~:** er rannte/der Ball ging ins Aus; **I** (*coll.*) **be an easy** *or* **a soft ~** (*be a person who gives money readily*) leicht rumzukriegen sein (*ugs.*)

**~ at** *v.t.* (*Naut.*) anlegen in (+ *Dat.*)

**~ 'down** *v.i.* **A** (*Rugby*) den Ball niederlegen; (*Amer. Footb.*) den Ball hinter die Grundlinie bringen; **B** ‹Flugzeug:› aufsetzen; (*land*) landen; ⇨ *also* **touchdown**

**~ 'in** *v.t.* (*Art*) hineinmalen; (*fig.*) ausführen ‹Details›

**~ 'off** *v.t.* **A** (*explode*) zünden ‹Bombe, Sprengladung, Feuerwerkskörper›; auslösen ‹Explosion, Mine›; **B** (*fig.: trigger off*) auslösen

**~ on** *v.t.* **A** (*treat briefly*) ansprechen; **the book ~es on the subject often** in dem Buch wird das Thema immer wieder gestreift; **B** (*verge on*) grenzen an (+ *Akk.*)

**~ 'up** *v.t.* **A** (*improve*) ausbessern; retuschieren ‹Fotografie›; auffrischen ‹Make-up›; in Ordnung bringen ‹Haar›; ausfeilen ‹Text›; **B** (*sl.: fondle*) befummeln (*ugs.*)

**~ upon** ⇨ **touch on** A

**touch: ~-and-'go** *adj.* prekär ‹Situation›; **it is ~-and-go [whether ...]** es steht auf des Messers Schneide[, ob ...]; **~down** *n.* **A** (*Amer. Footb.*) Touchdown, *der;* **B** (*Aeronaut.*) Landung, *die*

**touché** /'tu:ʃeɪ/ *int.* (*Fencing*) Treffer!; (*fig.*) eins zu null für dich!

**touched** /tʌtʃt/ *pred. adj.* **A** (*moved*) gerührt; **B** (*coll.: mad*) meschugge (*salopp*)

**touchiness** /'tʌtʃɪnɪs/ *n., no pl.* (*irritability, oversensitiveness*) [Über]empfindlichkeit, *die;* (*precariousness*) Heikelkeit, *die*

**touching** /'tʌtʃɪŋ/ **1** *adj.* rührend; (*moving*) bewegend; ergreifend. **2** *prep.* (*arch./literary*) **~ sth.** etw. betreffend

**touchingly** /'tʌtʃɪŋlɪ/ *adv.* rührend; (*movingly*) bewegend; ergreifend; **tell/depict sth. ~:** etw. ergreifend erzählen/schildern

**touch: ~ judge** *n.* (*Rugby*) Seitenrichter, *der;* **~line** *n.* (*Footb., Rugby*) Seitenlinie, *die;* Marklinie, *die* (*Rugby*); **~-me-not** *n.* (*Bot.*) Rührmichnichtan, *das;* **~paper** *n.* Zündpapier, *das;* (*on firework*) Papierlunte, *die;* **~stone** *n.* (*fig.*) Prüfstein, *der;* **~-tone** *adj.* **a ~-tone telephone** ein Telefon mit Mehrfrequenzwahl; **~-type** *v.i.* blind schreiben; **~-typing** *n.* Blindschreiben, *das;* **~-up paint** *n.* Ausbesserungslack, *der*

**touchy** /'tʌtʃɪ/ *adj.* empfindlich ‹Person›; heikel ‹Thema, Sache›

**tough** /tʌf/ **1** *adj.* **A** fest ‹Material, Stoff, Leder, Metall, Werkstoff›; zäh ‹Fleisch, fachspr.: Werkstoff, Metall, Kunststoff›; widerstandsfähig ‹Straßenbelag, Bodenbelag, Gummi, Glas, Haut›; strapazierfähig ‹Kleidung, Stoff, Schuhe, Seil›; **be [as] ~ as leather/old boots** zäh wie Leder/wie eine Schuhsohle sein; (*fig.*) hart im Nehmen sein (*ugs.*); **B** (*hardy, unyielding*) zäh ‹Person›; **his parents want him to be ~ when he grows up** seine Eltern wollen, dass aus ihm ein harter Mann wird; **~ guy** (*coll.*) knallharter Bursche; **a ~ customer** (*coll.*) ein harter Brocken (*ugs.*); (*stubborn person*) Dickschädel, *der* (*ugs.*); **C** (*difficult, trying*) schwierig; vertrackt (*ugs.*) ‹Problem›; hart ‹Kampf, Wettkampf›; strapaziös ‹Reise›; schwer ‹Zeit›; **we had a ~ time** wir haben viel durchgemacht; **we had a ~ time convincing her** es hat uns viel Mühe gekostet, sie zu überzeugen; **it's a ~ life being a housewife** als Hausfrau hat man es schwer; **things/life can get ~ if you run out of money** wenn man kein Geld mehr hat, kann das Leben sehr schwer werden; **it was ~ going, the going was ~:** es war ein Schlauch (*ugs.*); **D** (*severe, harsh*) hart; **get ~** (*coll.*) andere Saiten aufziehen; **a get-~ policy** eine Politik des harten Durchgreifens; **get ~ with sb.** (*coll.*) jmdn. hart anfassen; **E** (*coll.: unfortunate, hard*) **~ luck** Pech, *das;* **that's ~ [luck]** so'n Pech (*ugs.*) *od.* (*salopp*) Mist!; **be ~ on sb.** hart für jmdn. sein; **F** (*stiff*) zäh ‹Schlamm, Ton, Brei›; **G** (*Amer.: violent, criminal*) gewalttätig; **a ~ town/neighbourhood** eine Stadt/Gegend, in der das Leben rau ist.

**2** *n.* Schlägertyp, *der* (*abwertend*); **3** *v.t.* (*coll.*) **~ it out** nicht nachgeben; **I've just got to ~ it out** ich darf einfach nicht nachgeben

**toughen** /'tʌfn/ **1** *v.t.* größere Festigkeit geben (+ *Dat.*); zäher machen (*fachspr.*) ‹Werkstoff, Metall, Kunststoff›; abhärten, (*geh.*) stählen ‹Person, Körper›; verschärfen ‹Gesetz, Widerstand›; **his hard life has ~ed him** (*fig.*) sein schweres Leben hat ihn gehärtet *od.* hart gemacht; **he has ~ed his attitude towards lawbreakers** er hat gegenüber Gesetzesbrechern eine härtere Haltung eingenommen; **~ one's policy/stand** einen härteren [politischen] Kurs einschlagen/einen härteren Standpunkt einnehmen; **this setback will only ~ my resolve** dieser Rückschlag wird mich in meiner Entschlossenheit nur noch bestärken.

**2** *v.i.* fester werden; ‹Werkstoff, Metall, Kunststoff:› zäher werden (*fachspr.*); ‹Widerstand:› sich verschärfen; ‹Entschlossenheit:› stärker werden; ‹Standpunkt, Position, politischer Kurs:› sich verhärten

**~ 'up** **1** *v.t.* abhärten; stählen (*geh.*); verschärfen ‹Gesetz, Verbrechensbekämpfung›; **~ up one's attitude/policy** eine härtere Haltung einnehmen/einen härteren [politischen] Kurs einschlagen. **2** *v.i.* sich abhärten; sich stählen (*geh.*); (*fig.*) ‹Politik, Einstellung:› sich verhärten; ‹Widerstand:› sich verschärfen

**toughie** /'tʌfɪ/ *n.* (*coll.*) **A** (*problem*) harte Nuss (*ugs.*); **B** (*person*) Rabauke, *der* (*ugs.*)

**tough-'minded** *adj.* hart

**toughness** /'tʌfnɪs/ *n., no pl.* **A** ⇨ **tough** 1 A: Festigkeit, *die;* Zähheit, *die;* Zähigkeit, *die* (*fachspr.*); Widerstandsfähigkeit, *die;* Strapazierfähigkeit, *die;* **B** ⇨ **tough** 1 B: Zähigkeit, *die;* **C** (*fig.*) (*of problem, job*) Schwierigkeit, *die;* (*of fight, contest, law, policy, attitude, penalty, measure*) Härte, *die;* **the ~ of the exercise** die Schwierigkeit der Übung; **the ~ of life as an unmarried mother** die Schwierigkeiten, mit denen eine ledige Mutter zu kämpfen hat; **D** (*stiffness*) Zähheit, *die;* **E** (*Amer.: violence*) **the ~ of the mining towns** das raue Leben in den Bergarbeiterstädten

**toupee, toupet** /'tu:peɪ/ *n.* Toupet, *das*

**tour** /tʊə(r)/ **1** *n.* **A** [Rund]reise, *die;* Tour, *die* (*ugs.*); **a ~ of** *or* **through Europe** eine Reise durch Europa/eine Europareise; **a world ~/round-the-world ~:** eine Weltreise/Reise um die Welt; **they made a ~ of France** sie machten eine Frankreichreise; **a ~ of the capital cities of Europe/of the overseas branches of the firm** eine Rundreise zu den Hauptstädten Europas/zu den überseeischen Tochtergesellschaften der Firma; **a walking/cycling ~:** eine Wanderung/[Fahr]radtour; **a motoring/bus ~:** eine Auto-/Busreise; **B** (*Theatre, Sport*) Tournee, *die;* Tour, *die* (*Jargon*); **a ~ of the provinces, a provincial ~:** eine Tournee/Tour durch die Provinz; **be/go on ~:** auf Tournee/Tour sein/gehen; **he has gone on ~ to Europe** er ist auf [einer] Europatournee; **take a play on ~:** mit einem Stück auf Tournee/Tour gehen; **C** (*excursion, inspection*) (*of museum, palace, house*) Besichtigung, *die;* **go on/make/do a ~ of** besichtigen ‹Museum, Haus, Schloss usw.›; **a ~ of the countryside/the city/the factory** ein Ausflug in die Umgebung/eine Besichtigungstour durch die Stadt/ein Rundgang durch die Fabrik; **D ~ [of duty]** Dienstzeit, *die;* **between [sb.'s] ~s [of duty]** bevor jmd. einen neuen Posten antritt/antrat. ⇨ *also* **conduct** 2 E; **grand tour**; **guided tour**; **inspection**.

**2** *v.i.* **A ~/go ~ing in** *or* **through a country** eine Reise *od.* (*ugs.*) Tour durch ein Land machen; **be ~ing in a country** auf einer Reise *od.* (*ugs.*) Tour durch ein Land sein; **B** (*Theatre, Sport, exhibition*) eine Tournee *od.* (*Jargon*) Tour machen; (*be on ~*) auf Tournee *od.* (*Jargon*) Tour sein; touren (*Jargon*); (*go on ~*) auf Tournee *od.* (*Jargon*) Tour gehen.

**3** *v.t.* **A** besichtigen ‹Stadt, Gebäude, Museum›; **~ a country/region** eine Reise *od.* (*ugs.*) Tour durch ein Land/Gebiet machen; **~ an area on foot/by bicycle** eine Wanderung/Radtour durch eine Gegend machen; **B** (*Theatre, Sport*) **~ a country/the provinces** eine Tournee *od.* (*Jargon*) Tour durch das Land/die Provinz machen; **~ India/Europe** eine Indien-/Europatournee *od.* (*Jargon*) -tour machen

**tour de force** /tʊə də 'fɔ:s/ *n., pl.* **tours de force** /tʊə də 'fɔ:s/ Glanzleistung, *die*

**tourer** /'tʊərə(r)/ *n.* (*Motor Veh.*) Kabriolimousine, *die*

**'tour guide** *n.* **A** (*Person*) Reiseführer, *der/*Reiseführerin, *die;* **B** (*book*) Reiseführer, *der*

**touring**/'tʊərɪŋ/**: ~ car** ⇨ **tourer**; **~ company** *n.* (*Theatre*) Gastspielensemble, *das;* **~ exhibition** *n.* Wanderausstellung, *die;* **~ holiday** *n.* **have a ~ holiday in a country** in den Ferien/im Urlaub durch ein Land fahren/(*on foot*) durch ein Land wandern; **have a ~ holiday** in den Ferien/im Urlaub eine Reise/(*on foot*) Wanderung machen

**tourism** /'tʊərɪzm/ *n., no pl., no indef. art.* **A** Tourismus, *der;* **~ has increased** der Tourismus hat zugenommen; **B** (*operation of tours*) Touristik, *die;* **work/be involved in ~:** in der Touristikbranche arbeiten/tätig sein

**tourist** /'tʊərɪst/ **1** *n.* Tourist, *der*/Touristin, *die.* **2** *attrib. adj.* Touristen-; **special ~ rates** ermäßigte Preise für Touristen

**tourist: ~ agency** *n.* Reisebüro, *das;* **~ attraction** *n.* Touristenattraktion, *die;* **~ board** *n.* (*Brit.*) Amt für Fremdenverkehrswesen; **~ class** *n.* Touristenklasse, *die;* **~ guide** *n.* **A** (*person*) Touristenführer, *der*/-führerin, *die;* **B** (*book*) Reiseführer, *der* (**to, of** von); **~ hotel** *n.* Touristenhotel, *das;* **~ industry** *n.* **A** (*business*) Tourismusindustrie, *die;* **B** (*firms*) Touristik[branche], *die;* **~ infor'mation centre, ~ office** *ns.* Fremdenverkehrsbüro, *das;* Touristeninformation, *die* (*ugs.*); **~ season** *n.* Touristensaison, *die;* **~ trade** ⇨ **~ industry**; **~ trap** *n.* (*bar, restaurant, etc.*) [auf Touristen spezialisierter] Neppladen (*ugs.*); (*town, place*) Ort, an dem Touristen geneppt werden (*ugs.*)

**touristy** /'tʊərɪstɪ/ *adj.* (*derog.*) auf Tourismus getrimmt (*ugs.*); Touristen‹stadt, -nest, -gegend› (*ugs. abwertend*)

**tourmaline** /'tʊəməlɪn, 'tʊəməli:n/ *n.* (*Min.*) Turmalin, *der*

**tournament** /'tʊənəmənt/ *n.* (*Hist.; Sport*) Turnier, *das*

**tournedos** /'tʊənədəʊ/ *n., pl. same* (*Gastr.*) Tournedos, *das*

**tourney** /'tʊənɪ/ (*Hist.; Sport coll.*) ⇨ **tournament**

**tourniquet** /'tʊənɪkeɪ/ *n.* (*Med.*) Tourniquet, *das*

**'tour operator** *n.* **▶ 1261** Reiseveranstalter, *der*/-veranstalterin, *die*

**tousle** /'taʊzl/ *v.t.* zerzausen

**tout** /taʊt/ **1** *v.i.* **~ [for business/custom/orders]** Kunden anreißen (*ugs.*) *od.* werben; **~ for customers/buyers** Kunden/Käufer anreißen (*ugs.*) *od.* werben; **~ for a hotel**

t

für ein Hotel Gäste werben. ❷ *n.* Anreißer, *der*/Anreißerin, *die* (*ugs.*); Kundenwerber, *der*/-werberin, *die;* **ticket ~:** Kartenschwarzhändler, *der*/-händlerin, *die*

**tow**[1] /təʊ/ ❶ *v.t.* schleppen; ziehen ‹Anhänger, Wasserskiläufer, Handwagen›; **he ~ed my car to get it started** er hat meinen Wagen angeschleppt; **he ~ed his sister [behind him]** (*fig.*) er zog seine Schwester hinter sich (*Dat.*) her; **~ed load** (*Motor Veh.*) Anhängelast, *die.* ❷ *n.* Schleppen, *das;* **My car's broken down. — Do you want a ~?** Mein Wagen ist stehen geblieben. — Soll ich Sie [ab]schleppen?; **give a boat/car a ~:** ein Boot/einen Wagen schleppen; **give a car a ~ [to get it started]** ein Auto anschleppen; **have sth. in** *or* **on ~:** etw. im Schlepp[tau] haben; **have sb. in ~** (*fig.*) jmdn. im Schlepptau haben (*ugs.*); **take sb. in ~** (*fig.*) jmdn. unter seine Fittiche nehmen; **'on ~'** „wird geschleppt"; **take a boat/car in ~:** ein Boot/einen Wagen in Schlepp nehmen

**~ a'way** *v.t.* abschleppen

**tow**[2] *n.* (*Textiles*) Hede, *die;* Werg, *das*

**toward** /tə'wɔ:d/, **towards** /tə'wɔ:dz/ *prep.* [A] (*in direction of*) **~ sb./sth.** auf jmdn./etw. zu; **the ship sailed ~ France/the open sea** das Schiff fuhr in Richtung Frankreich/offenes Meer; **~ [the] town** in Richtung [auf die] Stadt; **point ~ the north** nach Norden zeigen; **march ~ the north** nach Norden *od.* in Richtung Norden *od.* in nördlicher Richtung marschieren; **look ~ the sea** in Richtung Meer blicken; **turn ~ sb.** sich zu jmdm. umdrehen; **the village is farther [to the] south, ~ Dover** das Dorf liegt weiter südlich, in Richtung Dover; **point ~ the horizon** zum Horizont deuten; **sit/stand with one's back [turned] ~ sth.** mit dem Rücken zu etw. sitzen/stehen; **turn one's face/back ~ sb./sth.** jmdm./einer Sache das Gesicht/den Rücken zuwenden; **my back was ~ the door** mein Rücken war der Tür zugewandt; **hold out one's hands ~ sb.** jmdm. die Hände entgegenstrecken; **my house faces ~ the park/sea** die Vorderseite meines Hauses liegt zum Park/Meer hin; **the country was drifting ~ war/economic chaos** das Land trieb dem Krieg/wirtschaftlichem Chaos zu; **he was sliding ~ disaster/financial ruin** er schlitterte in das Verderben/in den finanziellen Ruin; [B] (*in relation to*) gegenüber; **feel sth. ~ sb.** jmdm. gegenüber etw. empfinden; **his attitude ~ death** seine Einstellung zum Tod; **be fair/unfair** *etc.* **~ sb.** jmdm. gegenüber *od.* zu jmdm. fair/unfair *usw.* sein; **his conduct ~ us** sein Verhalten uns gegenüber; **feel angry/sympathetic ~ sb.** böse auf jmdn. sein/Verständnis für jmdn. haben; [C] (*for*) **a contribution ~ sth.** ein Beitrag zu etw.; **save up ~ a car/one's holidays** auf *od.* für einen Wagen/für seine Ferien sparen; **proposals ~ solving a problem** Vorschläge zur Lösung eines Problems; **work together ~ a solution** gemeinsam auf eine Lösung hinarbeiten; **contribute ~ sth.** zu etw. beitragen; **it is/it brings us a step ~ achieving our aim** es bringt uns einen Schritt näher zum Ziel; **efforts are being made ~ reconciliation** man bemüht sich um Versöhnung; [D] (*near*) gegen; **~ the end of May/of the year** *etc.* [gegen] Ende Mai/des Jahres; **it is getting ~ midnight/your bedtime** es geht auf Mitternacht zu/es ist bald Schlafenszeit für dich; **~ the end of his life/of the book** gegen Ende seines Lebens/des Buches; **sit ~ the front/back of the bus** vorne/hinten im Bus sitzen; **~ the bottom of the list** ziemlich weit unten auf der Liste

**'tow bar** *n.* (*Motor Veh.*) Anhängerkupplung, *die;* (*bar fitted between broken-down vehicle and towing vehicle*) Abschleppstange, *die*

**towel** /'taʊəl/ ❶ *n.* Handtuch, *das;* **throw in the ~** (*Boxing; also fig.*) das Handtuch werfen. ❷ *v.t.,* (*Brit.*) **-ll-** abtrocknen; **~ one's/sb.'s face/arms** *etc.* **[dry]** sich/jmdm. das Gesicht/die Arme *usw.* abtrocknen; **~ oneself** sich abtrocknen

**towelling** (*Amer.:* **toweling**) /'taʊəlɪŋ/ *n., no pl., no indef. art.* Frottierware, *die;* Frottee, *das* (*ugs.*)

**'towel rail** *n.* Handtuchhalter, *der*

**tower** /'taʊə(r)/ ❶ *n.* [A] Turm, *der;* (*Aeronaut.*) Tower, *der;* Kontrollturm, *der;* ⇒ *also* **control tower**; **cooling tower**; **water tower**; [B] (*fortress*) Festung, *die;* Wehrturm, *der;* **the T~ [of London]** der Tower [von London]; [C] **be a ~ of strength [to sb.]** (*fig.*) [jmdm.] ein fester Rückhalt sein; [D] ⇒ **tower block**. ⇒ *also* **ivory tower**. ❷ *v.i.* in die Höhe ragen; aufragen; **~ to [a height of] 200 feet** 200 Fuß hoch aufragen

**~ above, ~ over** *v.t.* **~ above** *or* **over sb./sth.** (*lit. or fig.*) jmdn./etw. überragen; **she saw the giant ~ing above her** sie sah die ragende Gestalt des Riesen über sich (*Dat.*) (*geh.*); **the building/mountain ~s above** *or* **over the town/landscape** das Gebäude/der Berg ragt über der Stadt/Landschaft (*geh.*)

**tower: ~ block** *n.* Hochhaus, *das;* **~ crane** *n.* Turmdrehkran, *der*

**towering** /'taʊərɪŋ/ *attrib. adj.* [A] hoch aufragend; riesenhaft ‹Gestalt›; **~ height** schwindelnde Höhe; [B] (*fig.*) herausragend ‹Leistung, Gestalt›; [C] (*fig.: violent, intense*) blind ‹Wut›; maßlos ‹Ehrgeiz, Stolz›; **be in/fly into a ~ passion** *or* **rage** von blinder Wut ergriffen sein/werden

**'towline** *n.* Schleppseil, *das;* (*Naut.*) Schlepptrosse, *die*

**town** /taʊn/ *n.* [A] ▶ **1626** Stadt, *die;* **the ~ of Cambridge** die Stadt Cambridge; **in [the] ~:** in der Stadt; **the ~** (*people*) die Stadt; **be the toast of the ~:** ein gefeierter Star/gefeierte Stars sein; **on the outskirts/in the centre of ~:** in den Randbezirken der Stadt/in der Stadtmitte *od.* Innenstadt; **go [up] to ~:** in die Stadt fahren; **we went [up] to ~ from York** (*to London*) wir sind von York nach London gefahren; **be in/out of ~:** in der Stadt/nicht in der Stadt sein; **head out of ~:** stadtauswärts fahren/gehen/reiten *usw.*; **he is well known about ~:** er ist stadtbekannt; ihn kennt die ganze Stadt; **it's all over ~ [that ...]** die ganze Stadt redet davon[, dass ...]; **the best coffee/tea/cake** *etc.* **in ~:** der beste Kaffee/Tee/Kuchen *usw.* in der Stadt; **go out/have a night on the ~** (*coll.*) [in die Stadt gehen und] einen draufmachen (*ugs.*); **go to ~** (*fig. coll.*) in die Vollen gehen (**on** bei) (*ugs.*); **man about ~** *Mann, der an allen gesellschaftlichen und kulturellen Ereignissen einer Stadt teilnimmt;* ⇒ *also* **gown** B; **paint** 2 A; **talk** 1 D; [B] (*business or shopping centre*) Stadt, *die;* **in ~:** in der Stadt; **go into ~:** in die Stadt gehen/fahren

**town: ~ 'centre** *n.* Stadtmitte, *die;* Stadtzentrum, *das;* **the ~ centres** die Innenstädte; **Brighton still has an old ~ centre** Brighton hat noch einen alten Stadtkern; **~ 'clerk** *n.* ▶ **1261** ≈ [Ober]stadtdirektor, *der*/-direktorin, *die;* **~ 'council** *n.* (*Brit.*) Stadtrat, *der;* **~ 'councillor** *n.* ▶ **1261** (*Brit.*) Stadtrat, *der*/-rätin, *die;* **~ 'crier** *n.* städtischer Ausrufer; **~ gas** *n., no pl., no indef. art.* Stadtgas, *das;* **~ 'hall** *n.* Rathaus, *das;* **~ house** *n.* [A] (*residence in ~*) Stadthaus, *das;* [B] (*terrace house*) Reihenhaus, *das*

**townie** /'taʊni:/ *n.* Stadtmensch, *der*

**town: ~ 'mayor** *n.* ▶ **1261** (*Brit.*) [Stadt]bürgermeister, *der*/-bürgermeisterin, *die;* **~ 'planner** *n.* ▶ **1261** Stadtplaner, *der*/-planerin, *die;* **~ 'planning** *n.* Stadtplanung, *die*

**townscape** /'taʊnskeɪp/ *n.* [A] (*Art, Photog.*) Stadtansicht, *die;* [B] (*town's appearance*) Stadtbild, *das*

**townsfolk** /'taʊnzfəʊk/ *n. pl.* Städter *Pl.;* **the ~** (*inhabitants*) die Stadtbevölkerung; (*citizens*) die Bürger [der Stadt]

**township** /'taʊnʃɪp/ *n.* [A] (*Amer.: division of county*) Township, *die; Verwaltungseinheit unterhalb der County;* [B] (*Amer. Surv.*) Township, *die; 36 Quadratmeilen großes quadratisches Stück Land;* [C] (*Austral., NZ*) (*small town*) Ortschaft, *die;* Siedlung, *die;* (*site*) *Areal für eine neue Siedlung;* [D] (*S. Afr.: non-white urban area*) Township, *die; von Farbigen bewohnte städtische Siedlung*

**town: ~sman** /'taʊnzmən/ *n., pl.* **~smen** /'taʊnzmən/ Stadtbewohner, *der;* Städter, *der;* (*citizen*) [Stadt]bürger, *der;* **[fellow] ~sman** (*fellow citizen*) Mitbürger, *der;* **~speople** /'taʊnzpi:pl/ ⇒ **townsfolk**; **~swoman** /'taʊnzwʊmən/ *n.* Stadtbewohnerin, *die;* Städterin, *die;* (*citizen*) [Stadt]bürgerin, *die*

**tow: ~path** *n.* Leinpfad, *der;* Treidelpfad, *der;* **~ rope** *n.* Abschleppseil, *das;* **~-start** *n.* (*Motor Veh.*) [Start durch] Anschleppen; **give sb. a ~-start** jmdn. anschleppen; **~truck** *n.* (*Amer.*) Abschleppwagen, *der*

**toxaemia** (*Amer.:* **toxemia**) /tɒk'si:mɪə/ *n.* ▶ **1232** (*Med.*) [A] (*blood poisoning*) Toxämie, *die;* [B] (*in pregnancy*) Schwangerschaftstoxikose, *die*

**toxic** /'tɒksɪk/ *adj.* [A] giftig; toxisch (*fachspr.*); [B] (*caused by poison*) toxisch (*fachspr.*); toxigen (*fachspr.*)

**toxicity** /tɒk'sɪsɪtɪ/ *n., no pl.* Giftigkeit, *die;* Toxizität, *die* (*fachspr.*)

**toxicology** /tɒksɪ'kɒlədʒɪ/ *n.* Toxikologie, *die*

**toxic: ~ 'shock syndrome** *n.* (*Med.*) toxisches Schockssyndrom; **~ 'waste** *n.* Giftmüll *der;* **~ wastes** giftige Abfallstoffe; **~ waste tip** *or* **dump** Giftmülldeponie, *die*

**toxin** /'tɒksɪn/ *n.* Toxin, *das*

**toy** /tɔɪ/ ❶ *n.* (*lit. or fig.*) Spielzeug, *das;* **~s** Spielzeug, *das;* Spielwaren *Pl.* (*Wirtsch.*). ❷ *adj.* [A] Spielzeug-; [B] (*Breeding*) Zwerg-. ❸ *v.i.* **~ with the idea of doing sth.** mit dem Gedanken spielen, etw. zu tun; **~ with one's food** mit seinem Essen herumspielen/in seinem Essen herumstochern; **~ with sb.** (*flirt*) mit jmdm. flirten; (*not be serious*) mit jmdm. spielen *od.* sein Spiel treiben

**toy: ~boy** *n.* (*coll.*) Gespiele, *der* (*scherzh.*); **~shop** *n.* Spielwarengeschäft, *das;* **~ 'soldier** *n.* Spielzeugsoldat, *der*

**trace**[1] /treɪs/ ❶ *v.t.* [A] (*copy*) durchpausen; abpausen; **~ sth. on to sth.** etw. auf etw. (*Akk.*) pausen; [B] (*delineate*) zeichnen ‹Form, Linie›; malen ‹Buchstaben, Wort›; (*fig.*) entwerfen; **she ~d our route on the map with her finger/with a pen** sie zeichnete unsere Route mit dem Finger/Stift auf der Landkarte nach; [C] (*follow track of*) folgen (+ *Dat.*); verfolgen; **the leak was ~d to an old cast-iron main** man fand das Leck an einer alten gusseisernen Hauptleitung; **~ a river to its source** einen Fluss [bis] zur Quelle zurückverfolgen; **the doctors ~d the infection to some dirty instruments** die Ärzte fanden heraus, dass die Infektion von verunreinigten Instrumenten herrührte; **he had to resign when the leak was ~d to his office** er musste zurücktreten, als man die undichte Stelle in seiner Behörde ausfindig machte; **the police ~d him to Spain** die Polizei spürte ihn in Spanien auf; [D] (*observe, find*) finden; **~ a connection** einen Zusammenhang sehen; [E] (*Archaeol.*) erkennen; **~ Roman roads** den Verlauf von alten Römerstraßen rekonstruieren.

❷ *n.* [A] (*visible sign*) Spur, *die;* (*of buildings, road*) [Über]rest, *der;* **there is no ~ of your letter in our records** in unseren Aufzeichnungen findet sich kein Hinweis auf Ihr Schreiben; **I can't find any ~ of him/it** (*cannot locate*) ich kann ihn/es nirgends finden; **lose [all] ~ of sb.** jmdn. [völlig] aus den Augen verlieren; **all ~ of the climbers has been lost** von den Bergsteigern fehlt jede Spur; **sink without ~:** sinken, ohne eine Spur zu hinterlassen; (*fig.*) in der Versenkung verschwinden (*ugs.*); ‹bekannte Persönlichkeit:› von der Bildfläche verschwinden (*ugs.*); [B] (*track left behind*) Spur, *die* (*of animal also*) Fährte, *die;* (*of recording instrument*) Kurve, *die;* [C] (*Electronics*) Spur, *die;* [D] (*small amount*) Spur, *die;* **a ~ of a smile/of sarcasm** ein Anflug eines Lächelns/von Sarkasmus; **the product contains a ~ of impurity** das Produkt enthält eine winzige Menge an Fremdstoffen

**~ 'back** *v.t.* zurückverfolgen; **the rumour was ~d back to a journalist** als Quelle des Gerüchts wurde ein Journalist ausfindig gemacht

# Towns and cities

All towns are neuter in German, although this usually only becomes apparent when referring to one as **es**, or when an adjective or article is used:

***Paris is on the Seine; it is the capital of France***
= Paris liegt an der Seine; es ist die Hauptstadt Frankreichs

***We want to create a new Hamburg***
= Wir wollen ein neues Hamburg schaffen

***19th century Berlin***
= das Berlin des 19. Jahrhunderts

## to and from

When it is simply a case of travelling from one town to another, always use **nach** for *to*, and **von** for *from* with the names:

***It is 56 miles from London to Oxford***
= Von London nach Oxford sind es 91 Kilometer

However compare:

***They are coming from Munich***
= Sie kommen von München

***They come from Munich***
= Sie kommen aus München

When referring to someone's place of origin, *from* is translated by **aus**.

## Natives and inhabitants

In English, the words which tell us where someone comes from have many different forms: Londoner, Glaswegian, Lancastrian, Bathonian, New Yorker, Bostonian, Viennese, Roman and so on. But in German it could not be simpler. You just add **-er** to the name of the town, or **-erin** in the case of a woman:

***a Parisian***
= ein Pariser/eine Pariserin

***the Viennese***
= die Wiener

***Viennese women***
= [die] Wienerinnen

Of course in many cases English does not have a specific name for the inhabitants of a particular place, but the formula described above can be used in German for every city, town or village:

***a woman from Madrid***
= eine Madriderin

***the people of Prague***
= die Prager

***an inhabitant of Dinkelsbühl***
= ein Dinkelsbühler/eine Dinkelsbühlerin

In one or two cases the name of the town or city is slightly altered before the ending is added, for instance:

***a Roman***
= ein Römer/eine Römerin

***an inhabitant of Münster***
= ein Münsteraner/eine Münsteranerin

***someone from Hanover, a Hanoverian***
= ein Hannoveraner/eine Hannoveranerin

***a man from Bremen***
= ein Bremer

***the people of Munich***
= die Münchner

With some non-German names adding the **-er** can produce an odd-sounding or barely pronounceable result, so such forms are avoided. It is unlikely for example that a man from Dover would be called "ein Doverer" or a woman from Bath "eine Batherin" ("ein Mann aus Dover" and "eine Frau aus Bath" would be the answers here). The inhabitants of Milwaukee could theoretically be called "die Milwaukeeer" and no doubt have been on occasion, but most Germans would prefer to say "die Bewohner von Milwaukee".

There are also a few exceptions where there is a special term, especially with Italian cities; the Florentines are "die Florentiner", a Venetian is "ein Venezianer" and a woman from Verona "eine Veroneserin". Note also Monegasque = Monegasse.

## Adjectives

To form an adjective from the name of a place is also extremely simple. It has the same form as the noun for a (male) person who comes from the place; you just add **-er**. Unlike other adjectives in German, it retains its capital letter. It is also invariable, so there are no endings to add depending on case or gender. These adjectives can be used as translations where place names in English are used attributively before another noun, or after it with 'of' or 'in'.

***Aachen Cathedral***
= der Aachener Dom

***the New York area***
= die New Yorker Gegend

***Ravensburg Town Council***
= der Ravensburger Stadtrat

***the streets of Paris***
= die Pariser Straßen

***Berlin dialect***
= der Berliner Dialekt

***the traffic in London***
= der Londoner Verkehr

Note that as in the first two examples German always has the definite article where a place name is used attributively before a building or institution. And in the last two cases, one could equally well say "die Straßen von Paris" or "der Verkehr in London". This use of prepositions would also be the only possibility in cases where the addition of **-er** presents problems:

***Amiens Cathedral***
= die Kathedrale von Amiens

***the Portsmouth area***
= die Gegend um Portsmouth

With roads "die Paderborner Straße" may mean "the Paderborn road", i.e."the road to Paderborn", but it will usually be the name of a street in a town, so it is safest to say "die Straße nach Paderborn".

Another group of adjectives formed from place names and ending in **-isch** can be used to express what is typical of a place or its people; these behave like normal adjectives with small initial letters and the usual endings:

***Hamburg humour***
= hamburgischer Humor

***Hanoverian equanimity***
= hannoverischer Gleichmut

**~ 'out** ⇒ **~** 1 B
**~ 'over** ⇒ **~** 1 A

**trace²** *n.* (*strap of harness*) Strang, *der;* (*of horse's headstall*) Zuggurt, *der;* **kick over the ~s** (*fig.*) über die Stränge schlagen (*ugs.*)

**traceable** /'treɪsəbl/ *adj.* **A** **sth. is ~ to sth./through sth.** etw. lässt sich bis zu etw./durch etw. hindurch zurückverfolgen; **this effect is ~ to the following cause** diese Wirkung lässt sich auf folgende Ursache zurückführen; **B** (*discoverable*) auffindbar; **this is a feature ~ in all his novels/paintings** dieses Merkmal lässt sich in allen seinen Romanen/Bildern entdecken

**'trace element** *n.* (*Chem.*) Spurenelement, *das*

**tracer** /'treɪsə(r)/ *n.* **A** (*Mil.*) Leuchtspurgeschoss, *das;* **B** (*radioactive isotope*) Indikator, *der*

**tracery** /'treɪsərɪ/ *n.* **A** (*Archit.*) Maßwerk, *das;* **bar ~:** Maßwerk, *das;* **plate ~:** negatives Maßwerk; **B** (*pattern, network*) Filigranmuster, *das*

**trachea** /trə'ki:ə/ *n., pl.* **~e** /trə'ki:i:/ **A** (*Anat.*) Trachea, *die* (*fachspr.*); Luftröhre, *die;* **B** (*Zool.*) Trachee, *die* (*Zool.*)

**tracheotomy** /treɪkɪ'ɒtəmɪ/ *n.* (*Med.*) Luftröhrenschnitt, *der;* Tracheotomie, *die* (*fachspr.*)

**trachoma** /trə'kəʊmə/ *n.* ▶ **1232** (*Med.*) Trachom, *das* (*Med.*)

**tracing** /'treɪsɪŋ/ *n.* **A** (*action*) [Durch]pausen, *das;* [Ab]pausen, *das;* **do some ~:** einiges durch- *od.* abpausen; **B** (*copy*) Pause, *die;* Kopie, *die*

**'tracing paper** *n.* Pauspapier, *das*

**track** /træk/ **1** *n.* **A** Spur, *die;* (*of wild animal*) Fährte, *die;* **~s** (*footprints*) [Fuß]spuren; (*of animal also*) Fährte, *die;* **cover one's ~s** (*fig.*) seine Spur verwischen; **be on sb.'s ~:** jmdm. auf der Spur sein; (*fig.: in possession of clue to sb.'s plans*) jmdm. auf die Schliche gekommen sein; **they will be on our ~:**

sie kommen uns auf die Spur/(*fig.*) auf die Schliche; **be on the right/wrong ~** (*fig.*) auf der richtigen/falschen Spur sein; **keep ~ of sb./sth.** jmdn./etw. im Auge behalten; **he couldn't keep ~ of her in the crowd** er verlor sie in der Menge aus den Augen; **the police [successfully] kept ~ of him** die Polizei blieb ihm auf der Spur; **they kept ~ of his movements/intentions/plans** sie waren jederzeit über seinen Aufenthaltsort/seine Absichten/Pläne auf dem Laufenden; **The situation is very complicated. I can't keep ~ of it** Die Situation ist sehr verworren. Ich habe den Überblick verloren; **without keeping accounts I can't keep ~ of what I spend** wenn ich nicht Buch führe, verliere ich den Überblick über meine Ausgaben; **lose ~ of sb./sth.** jmdn./etw. aus den Augen verlieren; **the police lost ~ of the gang's movements** die Polizei war über den Aufenthaltsort der Bande nicht mehr auf dem Laufenden; **he has lost ~ of the situation** er ist über die Situation nicht mehr auf dem Laufenden; **she lost ~ of the story** sie hat bei der Geschichte den Überblick verloren; **without keeping accounts you can easily lose ~ of what you spend** wenn man nicht Buch führt, kann man leicht die Übersicht über seine Ausgaben verlieren; **make ~s** (*coll.*) (*depart*) sich auf die Socken machen (*ugs.*); (*run off*) türmen (*ugs.*); **we'd better make ~s for home/the station** (*coll.*) wir sollten uns langsam auf die Socken machen und zusehen, dass wir nach Hause/zum Bahnhof kommen (*ugs.*); **stop [dead] in one's ~s** (*coll.*) auf der Stelle stehen bleiben; **stop sb. [dead] in his ~s** (*coll.*) jmdn. auf der Stelle stehen bleiben lassen; **B** (*path*) [unbefestigter] Weg; (*footpath*) Pfad, *der;* (*fig.*) Weg, *der;* **the road has only a single ~:** die Straße hat nur eine Spur *od.* ist nur einspurig; **they followed in the same ~** (*fig.*) auch sie gingen denselben Weg; ⇒ *also* **beaten** 2 A; **C** (*Sport*) Bahn, *die;* **cycling/greyhound ~:** Radrennbahn, *die*/Windhundrennbahn, *die;* **circuit of the ~:** Bahnrunde, *die;* **D** (*Railw.*) Gleis, *das;* **thousands of miles of ~:** Tausende von Meilen Gleise; **be born/live across the ~s** *or* **on the wrong side of the ~s** (*Amer. fig. coll.*) auf der Schattenseite geboren sein/leben (*fig.*); **'keep off the ~'** „Betreten der Gleise verboten"; **single/double ~:** eingleisige/zweigleisige Strecke; **the train left the ~:** der Zug entgleiste; **E** (*course taken*) Route, *die;* (*of rocket, satellite, comet, missile, hurricane, etc.*) Bahn, *die;* **F** (*of tank, tractor, etc.*) Kette, *die;* **G** (*section of record*) Stück, *das;* Track, *der* (*Jargon*); **H** ⇒ **soundtrack**; **I** (*groove on record*) Rille, *die;* **J** (*section of tape*) Spur, *die;* **two-/four-~ tape recorder** Zwei-/Vierspurtonbandgerät, *das;* **K** (*Motor Veh.: distance between wheels*) Spur[weite], *die;* **L** (*Amer. Educ.*) Kurs, *der.*
**2** *v.t.* **A ~ an animal** die Spur/Fährte eines Tieres verfolgen; **the police ~ed him [to Paris]** die Polizei folgte seiner Spur [bis nach Paris]; **~ a rocket/satellite** die Bahn einer Rakete/eines Satelliten verfolgen; **B** (*Archaeol.*) rekonstruieren; nachvollziehen ‹Entwicklung›; **C** (*Amer.: leave trail of*) **~ dirt over the floor/~ [up] the floor with dirt** Schmutzspuren auf dem Fußboden hinterlassen

**~ 'down** *v.t.* aufspüren; **~ a criminal down to his hideout** einen Verbrecher in seinem Versteck aufspüren

**'trackball** *n.* (*Computing*) Rollball, *der*

**tracker** /'trækə(r)/ *n.* **A** Fährtensucher, *der;* **he is an experienced ~ of animals** er hat viel Erfahrung im Aufspüren von Tieren; **B ~ [dog]** Spürhund, *der*

**'tracker ball** ⇒ **trackball**

**'track events** *n. pl.* (*Athletics*) Laufwettbewerbe

**tracking**/'trækıŋ/**: ~ shot** *n.* (*Cinemat., Telev.*) Fahrt, *die;* **~ station** *n.* (*Astronaut.*) Bahnverfolgungsstation, *die*

**track-laying** *adj.* Raupen-

**trackless** /'træklıs/ *adj.* **A** (*without path*) weglos; **B** (*without footprints etc.*) keinerlei Spuren aufweisend

**track: ~ record** *n.* (*fig.*) **his ~ record is good, he has a good ~ record** er hat gute Leistungen vorzuweisen; **what's his ~ record?** was hat er vorzuweisen?; **this product has a very good ~ record** dieses Produkt hat sich als sehr erfolgreich erwiesen; **~ shoe** *n.* Rennschuh, *der;* **~ suit** *n.* Trainingsanzug, *der;* **~ system** *n.* (*Amer. Educ.*) Kurssystem, *das;* **~way** *n.* **A** (*beaten path*) [Trampel]pfad, *der;* **B** (*ancient roadway*) alte Straße

**tract**[1] /trækt/ *n.* **A** (*area*) Gebiet, *das;* **a narrow/vast ~ [of land]** ein schmaler Streifen [Land]/ein riesiges Gebiet; **B** (*Anat.*) Trakt, *der*

**tract**[2] *n.* (*pamphlet*) [Flug]schrift, *die;* Traktat, *der* (*veralt.*)

**tractable** /'træktəbl/ *adj.* fügsam; leicht formbar ‹Material›

**traction** /'trækʃn/ *n., no pl., no indef. art.* **A** (*drawing along*) Traktion, *die* (*fachspr.*); Ziehen, *das;* **steam/electric ~:** Dampf-/Elektrotraktion, *die;* **B** (*grip of tyre etc.*) Haftung, *die;* **C** (*Med.*) Zug, *der;* **in ~:** im Zug- *od.* Streckverband; **D** (*Amer. Transport*) öffentliche Verkehrsmittel; **~ company** Verkehrsgesellschaft, *die*

**'traction engine** *n.* Zugmaschine, *die;* (*for agricultural use*) Traktor, *der*

**tractor** /'træktə(r)/ *n.* **A** Traktor, *der;* **B** (*Motor Veh.*) (*lorry unit*) Zugwagen, *der;* Zugfahrzeug, *das;* (*of articulated lorry*) Sattelzugmaschine, *die*

**trad** /træd/ (*Mus. coll.*) **1** *adj.* traditional (*Jargon*); **~ jazz** Traditional Jazz, *der.* **2** *n., no pl., no indef. art.* Traditional, *der* (*Jargon*)

**trade** /treıd/ **1** *n.* **A** (*line of business*) Gewerbe, *das;* **the wool/furniture/hotel ~:** die Woll-/Möbel-/Hotelbranche; **the retail/wholesale ~:** der Einzel-/Großhandel; **he's a butcher/lawyer/baker** *etc.* **by ~:** er ist von Beruf Metzger/Rechtsanwalt/Bäcker *usw.;* **trick of the ~:** einschlägiger Trick; **know the tricks of the ~:** die einschlägigen Tricks kennen; **do sth. using every trick of the ~:** etw. nach allen Regeln der Kunst tun; ⇒ *also* **jack of all trades**; **B** *no pl., no indef. art* (*commerce*) Handel, *der;* **be bad/good for ~:** schlecht/gut fürs Geschäft sein; **do ~ with sb.** mit jmdm. Geschäfte machen; **do ~ with a country** mit einem Land Handel treiben; **domestic** *or* **home ~:** Binnenhandel, *der;* **foreign ~:** Außenhandel, *der;* ⇒ *also* **balance** 1 I; **board** 1 I; **free trade**; **term** 1 B; **C** *no pl.* (*business done*) Geschäft, *das;* (*between countries*) Handel, *der;* **a large share of the ~ in wool/leather goods/grain** ein großer Anteil am Geschäft mit Wolle/Lederwaren/Getreide; **an increase in ~:** eine Umsatzsteigerung; **do a good/roaring ~ [in sth.]** ein gutes Geschäft/ein Riesengeschäft [mit etw.] machen; **how's ~?** wie gehen die Geschäfte?; wie geht das Geschäft?; **D** (*craft*) Handwerk, *das;* **learn/study for a ~:** einen Handwerksberuf [er]lernen; **E** *no pl., no indef. art.* (*persons*) **the ~:** die Branche; **sell to the ~:** an Wiederverkäufer verkaufen; **special discounts for [the] ~:** Sonderrabatte für Wiederverkäufer; **F** *in pl.* (*Meteorol.: winds*) Passat, *der;* **G** (*Amer.: a transaction*) Geschäft, *das;* (*exchange*) Tausch, *der.*
**2** *v.i.* **A** (*buy and sell*) Handel treiben; **~ as a wholesale/retail dealer** ein Groß-handels-/Einzelhandelsgeschäft betreiben; **they ~ as Henry Brooks & Co.** sie firmieren als Henry Brooks und Co.; **~ at a store** (*Amer.*) in einem Geschäft einkaufen; **~ in sth.** in *od.* mit etw. (*Dat.*) handeln; **we don't ~ with that firm** wir unterhalten zu dieser Firma keine Geschäftsbeziehungen; **B** (*have an exchange*) tauschen; **~ with sb. for sth.** jmdm. etw. abhandeln; **C** (*carry merchandise*) Handelswaren befördern; **~ to a place** Handelsgüter an einen Ort transportieren.
**3** *v.t.* **A** tauschen; austauschen ‹Waren, Grüße, Informationen, Geheimnisse›; sich (*Dat.*) sagen ‹Beleidigungen›; **B ~ sth. for sth.** etw. gegen etw. tauschen; **~ an old car** *etc.* **for a new one** einen alten Wagen *usw.* für einen neuen in Zahlung geben

**~ 'in** *v.t.* in Zahlung geben; einlösen ‹Gutschein, Kupon usw.›; ⇒ *also* **trade-in**

**~ 'off** *v.t.* **~ sth. off for sth.** etw. gegen etw. tauschen; ⇒ *also* **trade-off**

**~ on** *v.t.* (*fig.*) **~ on sth.** aus etw. Kapital schlagen; sich (*Dat.*) etw. zunutze machen

**~ 'up** *v.i.* sich verbessern

**~ upon** ⇒ **~ on**

**trade: ~ balance** *n.* (*Econ.*) Handelsbilanz, *die;* **~ cycle** *n.* (*Brit. Econ.*) Konjunkturzyklus, *der;* **~ deficit** *n.* (*Econ.*) Handelsbilanzdefizit, *das;* **~ directory** *n.* Branchenadressbuch, *das;* **~ 'discount** *n.* Branchenrabatt, *der;* (*in book ~*) Kollegenrabatt, *der;* **~ fair** *n.* [Fach]messe, *die;* **~ gap** ⇒ **~ deficit**; **~-in** **1** *n.* **A** (*part exchange*) Inzahlungnahme, *die* (**on** *Gen.*); **we offer a ~-in on your old car** wir nehmen Ihren alten Wagen in Zahlung; **can you give me a ~-in on my old car?** nehmen Sie meinen alten Wagen in Zahlung?; **B** (*item*) **we'll accept your old car as a ~-in** wir nehmen Ihren alten Wagen in Zahlung. **2** *attrib. adj.* **the ~-in value of your car is low** der Preis, zu dem Ihr Wagen in Zahlung genommen wird, ist niedrig; **~ journal** *n.* Fachzeitschrift, *die;* **~-last** *n.* (*Amer. coll.*) **swap ~-lasts** Komplimente von Dritten austauschen; **~ mark** *n.* **A** Warenzeichen, *das;* **B** (*fig.*) **leave one's ~ mark on sth.** einer Sache (*Dat.*) seinen Stempel aufdrücken; **it bore all the ~ marks of this director's style** es trug den Stempel *od.* die Handschrift dieses Regisseurs; **honesty/straightforwardness/stubbornness is her ~ mark** sie zeichnet sich durch Ehrlichkeit/Direktheit/Hartnäckigkeit aus; ⇒ *also* **registered**; **~ name** *n.* **A** (*name used in the ~*) Fachbezeichnung, *die;* **B** (*proprietary name*) Markenname, *der;* **C** (*name of business*) Firmenname, *der;* **~-off** *n.* Tauschgeschäft, *das;* (*fig.*) Handel, *der;* **~ paper** ⇒ **~ journal**; **~ plates** *n. pl.* (*Motor Veh.*) ≈ rote Kennzeichen; **~ price** *n.* Einkaufspreis, *der;* **at ~ price** zum Einkaufspreis

**trader** /'treıdə(r)/ *n.* **A** Händler, *der*/Händlerin, *die;* **B** (*Naut.*) Handelsschiff, *das*

**'trade route** *n.* Handelsweg, *der;* Handelsstraße, *die*

**tradescantia** /trædıs'kæntıə/ *n.* (*Bot.*) Tradeskantie, *die*

**trade: ~ 'secret** *n.* Geschäftsgeheimnis, *das;* **~sman** /'treıdzmən/ *n., pl.* **~smen** **A** (*shopkeeper*) [Einzel]händler, *der;* Ladeninhaber, *der;* **~smen's entrance** Lieferanteneingang, *der;* **B** (*craftsman*) Handwerker, *der;* **~speople** /'treıdzpi:pl/ *n. pl.* **A** (*shopkeepers*) [Einzel]händler; Ladeninhaber; **B** (*craft workers*) Handwerker; **~s' 'union** ⇒ **~ union**; **T~s Union 'Congress** *pr. n.* (*Brit.*) Gewerkschaftsbund, *der;* **~ surplus** *n.* (*Econ.*) Handelsbilanzüberschuss, *der;* **~ 'union** *n.* Gewerkschaft, *die; attrib.* Gewerkschafts-; **~ 'unionism** *n., no pl.* Gewerkschaftswesen, *das;* **~ 'unionist** *n.* Gewerkschaft[l]er, *der*/Gewerkschaft[l]erin, *die;* **~ wind** *n.* (*Meteorol.*) Passatwind, *der*

**trading** /'treıdıŋ/ *n.* Handel, *der;* **~ on the Stock Exchange** das Geschäft an der Börse; **the ~ of pounds for dollars** der Verkauf von Pfund gegen Dollar

**trading: ~ estate** *n.* (*Brit.*) Gewerbegebiet, *das;* **~ hours** *n. pl.* Geschäftszeit, *die;* **during/outside ~ hours** während/außerhalb der Geschäftszeit; **'Trading hours: ...'** „Geschäftszeiten: ..."; **~ partner** *n.* Handelspartner, *der;* **~ post** ⇒ **post**[3] 1 E; **~ stamp** *n.* Rabattmarke, *die*

**tradition** /trə'dıʃn/ *n.* Tradition, *die;* (*story*) [mündliche] Überlieferung; **family ~:** Familientradition, *die;* **he is no respecter of ~:** er hält nicht viel von der Tradition; **old universities rich in ~:** alte traditionsreiche Universitäten; **he has no sense of ~** *or* **no feeling for ~:** er hat keinen Sinn für Tradition; **in the best ~[s]** nach bester Tradition; **break with ~:** mit der Tradition brechen;

**by ~:** traditionell[erweise]; **~ has it that ...:** es heißt, dass ...

**traditional** /trəˈdɪʃənl/ *adj.* Ⓐ traditionell; mündlich überliefert ‹Geschichte›; herkömmlich ‹Erziehung, Einrichtung, Methode›; überkommen ‹Brauch, Sitte, Werte, Moral›; **it is ~ to do sth.** es ist Tradition, etw. zu tun; Ⓑ (*Art, Lit.*) konventionell; Ⓒ (*Mus.*) traditionell ‹Jazz›

**traditionalism** /trəˈdɪʃənəlɪzm/ *n., no pl.* Traditionalismus, *der*

**traditionalist** /trəˈdɪʃənəlɪst/ *n.* Traditionalist, *der*/Traditionalistin, *die*

**traditionally** /trəˈdɪʃənəlɪ/ *adv.* (*in a traditional manner*) traditionell; (*by tradition*) traditionell[erweise]; **~, gifts are exchanged at Christmas** an Weihnachten werden traditionell Geschenke ausgetauscht; **the Oxford Union is ~ a good training ground for politicians** die Oxford Union ist seit je eine gute Schule für künftige Politiker; **a ~ designed exterior** ein traditionelles Exterieur

**traduce** /trəˈdjuːs/ *v.t.* (*literary: defame*) verleumden

**traducer** /trəˈdjuːsə(r)/ *n.* (*literary*) Verleumder, *der*/Verleumderin, *die*

**traffic** /ˈtræfɪk/ ❶ *n., no pl.* Ⓐ *no indef. art.* Verkehr, *der;* **~ is heavy/light** es herrscht starker/geringer Verkehr; **~ will increase** der Verkehr wird zunehmen; Ⓑ (*trade*) Handel, *der;* **the ~ in goods/wool/steel between the two countries** der Handelsverkehr mit Gütern/Wolle/Stahl zwischen den beiden Ländern; **there is a brisk ~ in stolen goods/pornography** es wird ein schwunghafter Handel mit Diebesgut/Pornographie getrieben; **~ in drugs/arms** Drogen-/Waffenhandel, *der;* Ⓒ (*amount of business*) Verkehr, *der;* **~ in these goods/in furs/in grain has increased** der Umschlag an diesen Gütern/an Pelzen/Getreide ist gestiegen; Ⓓ (*Teleph., Radio*) **telephone/radio ~:** Fernsprech-/Funkverkehr, *der.*

❷ *v.i.*, **-ck-** Geschäfte machen; **~ in sth.** mit etw. handeln *od.* Handel treiben; (*fig.*) mit etw. schachern (*abwertend*); **~ in drugs** Drogen dealen.

❸ *v.t.*, **-ck-** handeln mit; (*barter, exchange*) Tauschhandel treiben mit

**traffic: ~ calming** *n., no pl.* Verkehrsberuhigung, *die;* **~ circle** *n.* (*Amer.*) Kreisverkehr, *der;* **~ cone** *n.* Pylon, *der;* Leitkegel, *der;* **~ cop** *n.* ▶ **1261** (*Amer. coll.*) Verkehrspolizist, *der*/-polizistin, *die;* **~ hold-up** ⇒ **~ jam**; **~ island** *n.* Verkehrsinsel, *die;* **~ jam** *n.* [Verkehrs]stau, *der*

**trafficker** /ˈtræfɪkə(r)/ *n.* Händler, *der*/Händlerin, *die;* **~ in drugs, drug ~:** Drogenhändler, *der*/-händlerin, *die*

**traffic: ~ lights** *n. pl.* [Verkehrs]ampel, *die;* **~ police** *n.* Verkehrspolizei, *die;* **~ policeman** *n.* ▶ **1261** Verkehrspolizist, *der;* **~ report** *n.* Verkehrsübersicht, *die;* (*on radio*) Verkehrsservice, *der;* **~ sign** *n.* Verkehrszeichen, *das;* **~ signals** ⇒ **~ lights**; **~ warden** *n.* ▶ **1261** (*Brit.*) Hilfspolizist, *der;* (*woman*) Hilfspolizistin, *die;* Politesse, *die*

**tragedian** /trəˈdʒiːdɪən/ *n.* Ⓐ (*Lit.*) Tragödiendichter, *der*/-dichterin, *die;* Ⓑ (*Theatre*) Tragöde, *der*

**tragedy** /ˈtrædʒɪdɪ/ *n.* Ⓐ (*sad event or fact*) Tragödie, *die;* (*sad story*) tragische Geschichte; **the ~ [of it] is that ...:** das Tragische [daran] ist, dass ...; Ⓑ (*accident*) Tragödie, *die;* **earthquake ~/bomb ~:** Erdbebenkatastrophe, *die*/blutiger Bombenanschlag; Ⓒ (*Theatre*) Tragödie, *die;* Trauerspiel, *das*

**tragic** /ˈtrædʒɪk/ *adj.* Ⓐ tragisch; **a ~ waste of talent/money** eine schlimme Vergeudung von Talenten/Geldverschwendung; Ⓑ *attrib.* (*Theatre*) tragisch; **~ actor/actress** Tragöde, *der*/Tragödin, *die;* **~ irony** tragische Ironie

**tragically** /ˈtrædʒɪkəlɪ/ *adv.* tragisch; **their predictions have been ~ fulfilled** ihre Prophezeiungen haben sich auf tragische Weise erfüllt; **~, she had a fatal accident** tragischerweise erlitt sie einen tödlichen Unfall

**tragicomedy** /trædʒɪˈkɒmɪdɪ/ *n.* (*Lit.*) Tragikomödie, *die*

**trail** /treɪl/ ❶ *n.* Ⓐ Spur, *die;* (*of meteor*) Schweif, *der;* **a ~ of blood** eine Blutspur; **~ of smoke/dust** Rauch-/Staubfahne, *die;* **he left a ~ of broken marriages/misery behind him** überall, wo er auftauchte, hinterließ er zerbrochene Ehen/Elend; ⇒ *also* **condensation trail**; **vapour trail**; Ⓑ (*Hunting*) Spur, *die;* Fährte, *die;* **be on the ~ of an animal** der Fährte eines Tieres folgen; **be off the ~** (*lit. or fig.*) nicht auf der richtigen Spur *od.* Fährte sein; **be/get on sb.'s ~** (*lit. or fig.*) jmdm. auf der Spur *od.* Fährte sein/jmdm. auf die Spur *od.* Fährte kommen; **be hard** *or* **hot on the ~ of sb.** (*lit. or fig.*) jmdm. dicht auf den Fersen sein (*ugs.*); **he was hot** *or* **hard on the ~ of the stolen goods** bei der Suche nach dem Diebesgut hatte er eine heiße Spur [gefunden]; Ⓒ (*path*) Pfad, *der;* (*wagon ~*) Weg, *der;* **there was no path or ~ of any kind** es gab keinerlei Weg oder Pfad; ⇒ *also* **blaze²** 2; **nature trail**.

❷ *v.t.* Ⓐ (*pursue*) verfolgen; (*shadow*) beschatten; **~ sb./an animal to a place** jmdm./einem Tier bis zu einem Ort folgen; Ⓑ (*drag*) **~ sth. [after** *or* **behind one]** etw. hinter sich (*Dat.*) herziehen; **~ sth. on the ground** etw. über den Boden schleifen lassen; **he ~ed his hand/fingers in the water as the boat went along** er ließ seine Hand/Finger mit dem fahrenden Boot durchs Wasser gleiten; **a train/car went by, ~ing clouds of smoke/dust** ein Zug/Auto fuhr vorbei und zog eine Rauch-/Staubwolke hinter sich (*Dat.*) her; **~ sb. by 20 points** 20 Punkte hinter jmdm. liegen.

❸ *v.i.* Ⓐ (*be dragged*) schleifen; **the bird's wing/dog's leg was ~ing** der Flügel des Vogels/das Bein des Hundes schleifte am Boden; **a cloud of dust ~ed behind the car** hinter dem Wagen zog sich eine Staubwolke hin; Ⓑ (*hang loosely*) herabhängen; **~ to the ground** auf den Boden hängen; Ⓒ (*walk wearily etc.*) trotten; (*lag*) hinterhertrotten; Ⓓ (*Sport: be losing*) zurückliegen; **the runner was ~ing badly** der Läufer lag weit zurück; **be ~ing by two goals to three** mit zwei zu drei Toren im Rückstand sein; Ⓔ (*creep*) ‹Pflanze:› kriechen

**~ aˈway** ⇒ **~ off**

**~ beˈhind** *v.i.* hinterhertrödeln (*ugs.*); (*Sport*) zurückliegen

**~ ˈoff** *v.i.* Ⓐ (*fade into silence*) **his voice/shout ~ed off into a whisper/into silence** seine Stimme/sein Schreien wurde schwächer, bis er schließlich nur noch flüsterte/bis er schließlich ganz verstummte; **her words/speech ~ed off [into silence]** sie verstummte allmählich; Ⓑ (*move slowly*) lostrotten; abtrotten

**trail: ~ bike** *n. leichtes, geländegängiges Motorrad;* ≈ Enduro, *das;* **~blazer** *n.* (*fig.: pioneer*) Bahnbrecher, *der*/Bahnbrecherin, *die;* Wegbereiter, *der*/Wegbereiterin, *die*

**trailer** /ˈtreɪlə(r)/ *n.* Ⓐ (*Motor Veh.*) Anhänger, *der;* (*boat ~ also*) Trailer, *der;* (*Amer.: caravan*) Wohnanhänger, *der;* Ⓑ (*Cinemat., Telev.*) Trailer, *der;* Ⓒ (*Bot.*) Ranke, *die*

**ˈtrailing edge** *n.* Hinterkante, *die;* (*of sail*) Achterliek, *das*

**train** /treɪn/ ❶ *v.t.* Ⓐ ausbilden (**in** in + *Dat.*); erziehen ‹Kind›; abrichten ‹Hund›; dressieren ‹Tier›; schulen ‹Geist, Auge, Ohr›; bilden ‹Charakter›; **~ sb. as a teacher/soldier/engineer** jmdn. zum Lehrer/Soldaten/Ingenieur ausbilden; **~ sb. for a profession** jmdn. auf einen Beruf vorbereiten *od.* für einen Beruf ausbilden; **~ sb. for a career as an officer** jmdn. zum Offizier ausbilden; **he/she has been well/badly/fully ~ed** er/sie besitzt eine gute/schlechte/umfassende Ausbildung; Ⓑ (*Sport*) trainieren; **~ oneself** trainieren; Ⓒ (*teach and accustom*) **~ an animal to do sth./to sth.** einem Tier beibringen, etw. zu tun/etw. beibringen; **the police dog was ~ed to kill** der Polizeihund war zum Töten abgerichtet; **~ oneself to do sth.** sich dazu erziehen, etw. zu tun; **~ a child to do sth./to sth.** ein Kind dazu erziehen, etw. zu tun/zu etw. erziehen; **~ sb. to use a machine** jmdn. in der Bedienung einer Maschine schulen; **you've got him well ~ed** (*joc.*) du hast ihn dir gut erzogen; Ⓓ (*Hort.*) ziehen; erziehen (*fachspr.*); **the vines are ~ed and supported by poles** die Reben werden an die stützenden Pfosten gezogen *od.* (*fachspr.*) erzogen; **~ a plant up/against a wall/trellis** eine Pflanze an einer Mauer/einem Spalier ziehen *od.* (*fachspr.*) erziehen; Ⓔ (*aim*) richten (**on** auf + *Akk.*).

❷ *v.i.* Ⓐ eine Ausbildung machen; **he is ~ing as** *or* **to be a teacher/doctor/engineer** er macht eine Lehrer-/Arzt-/Ingenieursausbildung; **he is ~ing as a soldier** er lässt sich zum Soldaten ausbilden; **he is ~ing for a responsible position** er bereitet sich auf eine verantwortliche Stellung vor; **he is ~ing for a career as an officer/for the ministry/for the law** er macht eine Offiziers-/Priester-/Rechtsanwaltsausbildung; Ⓑ (*Sport*) trainieren.

❸ *n.* Ⓐ (*Railw.*) Zug, *der;* **go** *or* **travel by ~:** mit dem Zug *od.* der Bahn fahren; **the 2 o'clock ~:** der Zweiuhrzug; **on the ~:** im Zug; **which is the ~ for Oxford?** welcher Zug fährt nach Oxford?; Ⓑ (*of skirt etc.*) Schleppe, *die;* Ⓒ (*Ornith.*) Schwanz, *der;* Ⓓ (*retinue*) Gefolge, *das;* **the king/minister had brought a ~ of advisers/attendants with him** der König/Minister hatte ein großes Gefolge von Beratern/Begleitern mitgebracht; **the long ~ of mourners** der lange Trauerzug; **the tornado brought havoc in its ~:** der Tornado hinterließ Verwüstungen; Ⓔ (*line, series*) Zug, *der;* **a long ~ of causes** eine lange Kette von Ursachen; **an unlucky ~ of events** eine unglückliche [Aufeinander]folge von Ereignissen; **~ of thought** Gedankengang, *der;* **be in ~** (*formal*) im Gange sein; **everything is now in ~ for the party/ceremony/election** alle Vorbereitungen für die Party/Feier/Wahl sind jetzt im Gange

**~ ˈup** *v.t.* heranbilden; **our workers have been ~ed up to a very high standard** unsere Arbeiter sind sehr gut ausgebildet

**trainable** /ˈtreɪnəbl/ *adj.* leicht erziehbar ‹Kind›; ausbildungsfähig ‹Arbeiter›

**train: ~-bearer** *n.* Schleppenträger, *der*/-trägerin, *die;* **~ driver** *n.* Lokomotivführer, *der*/-führerin, *die*

**trained** /treɪnd/ *adj.* ausgebildet ‹Arbeiter, Lehrer, Arzt, Stimme›; abgerichtet ‹Hund›; dressiert ‹Tier›; geschult ‹Geist, Auge, Ohr›

**trainee** /treɪˈniː/ *n.* Auszubildende, *der/die;* (*business management ~*) Trainee, *der/die;* (*in academic, technical professions*) Praktikant, *der*/Praktikantin, *die;* **a ~ manager/nurse/teacher/doctor/cook** *etc.* ein Manager/eine Krankenschwester/ein Lehrer/Arzt/Koch *usw.* in Ausbildung

**trainer** /ˈtreɪnə(r)/ *n.* Ⓐ (*Sport*) [Konditions]trainer, *der*/-trainerin, *die;* Ⓑ (*Aeronaut.*) (*aircraft*) Trainer, *der;* (*simulator*) Flugsimulator, *der;* Ⓒ *in pl.* ⇒ **training shoes**

**train: ~ fare** *n.* Fahrpreis, *der;* **how much is the ~ fare to Oxford?** wie viel kostet die Bahnfahrt nach Oxford?; **we shall reimburse your ~ fare** wir erstatten Ihnen die Kosten der Bahnfahrt; **~ ferry** *n.* Eisenbahnfähre, *die*

**training** /ˈtreɪnɪŋ/ *n., no pl.* Ⓐ Ausbildung, *die;* Ⓑ (*Sport*) Training, *das;* **be in ~** (*train*) trainieren; im Training sein; (*be fit*) in [guter] Form sein; **be out of ~:** außer Form sein; **go into ~:** mit dem Training anfangen; **keep in ~:** sich in Form halten; in Form bleiben

**training: ~ camp** *n.* (*Mil.*) Ausbildungslager, *das;* (*Boxing*) Trainingslager, *das;* **~ college** *n.* berufsbildende Schule; (*Brit. Hist.*) Lehrerseminar, *das;* **~ course** *n.* Lehrgang, *der;* **~ film** *n.* Lehrfilm, *der;* **~ ground** *n.* (*Mil.*) Übungsplatz, *der;* (*fig.*) Schule, *die;* **~ scheme** *n.* Ausbildungsprogramm, *das;* **be on a ~ scheme** an einem Ausbildungsprogramm teilnehmen; **~ ship**

*n.* (*Naut.*) Schulschiff, *das;* ~ **shoes** *n. pl.* Trainingsschuhe

**train:** ~ **journey** *n.* Bahnfahrt, *die;* (*long*) Bahnreise, *die;* ~**load** *n.* ~**loads of coal/livestock/tourists** *etc.* ganze Züge voll Kohle/Vieh/Touristen *usw.;* **football fans arrived in** *or* **by** ~**loads** ganze Züge voll Fußballfans kamen; ~ **service** *n.* Zugverbindung, *die;* [Eisen]bahnverbindung, *die;* (*whole system*) Eisenbahnsystem, *das;* **a better** ~ **service** bessere Zugverbindungen *Pl.;* ~ **set** *n.* [Modell]eisenbahn, *die;* ~**sick** *adj.* **a** ~**sick child/man** ein Kind/Mann, dem vom Zugfahren schlecht geworden ist; **he gets** ~**sick** ihm wird beim Zugfahren schlecht; ~**spotter** *n.: jmd., der als Hobby die Nummern von Lokomotiven aufschreibt;* ~**spotting** *n., no pl., no indef. art.: das Aufschreiben von Lokomotivnummern als Hobby;* ~ **station** *n.* (*Amer.*) Bahnhof, *der;* ~ **surfing** *n.* S-Bahn-Surfen, *das*

**traipse** /treɪps/ *v.i.* (*coll.*) latschen (*salopp*) ~ **about**, ~ **around** *v.i.* rumlatschen (*salopp*)

**trait** /treɪ/ *n.* Eigenschaft, *die;* ~ **of character** Charaktereigenschaft, *die;* **a marked** ~ **in her character** eine ausgeprägte Charaktereigenschaft bei ihr; **it is a national** ~ **[of the British]** es gehört zum [britischen] Nationalcharakter

**traitor** /ˈtreɪtə(r)/ *n.* Verräter, *der*/Verräterin, *die;* **be a** ~ **to one's country/the king/the cause/one's faith** ein Verräter seines Landes/des Königs/der Sache/seines Glaubens sein; **you are a** ~ **to yourself!** du hast deine eigenen Überzeugungen verraten!; **turn** ~**:** zum Verräter/zur Verräterin werden

**traitorous** /ˈtreɪtərəs/ *adj.* verräterisch; **a** ~ **man/woman** ein Verräter/eine Verräterin; **such conduct is** ~**!** solches Verhalten ist Verrat!

**trajectory** /trəˈdʒektərɪ/ *n.* (*Phys.*) [Flug-]bahn, *die*

**tra-la** /trəˈlɑː/ *int.* tralla[la]

**tram** /træm/ *n.* Ⓐ (*Brit.*) Straßenbahn, *die;* **go by** ~**:** mit der Straßenbahn fahren; **on the** ~**:** in der Straßenbahn; Ⓑ (*Mining*) Hund, *der;* Förderwagen, *der*

**tram:** ~**car** *n.* Ⓐ ⇒ **tram** A; Ⓑ (*one car*) Straßenbahnwagen, *der;* ~**lines** *n. pl.* (*Brit.*) Ⓐ Straßenbahnschienen; Ⓑ (*fig.: rigid principles*) starre Vorschriften; Ⓒ (*Tennis coll.*) Korridor, *der*

**trammel** /ˈtræml/ ❶ *v.t.,* (*Brit.*) **-ll-** einengen. ❷ *n. in pl.* Fesseln; **the** ~**s of convention** die Fesseln der Konvention

**tramp** /træmp/ ❶ *n.* Ⓐ (*vagrant*) Landstreicher, *der*/-streicherin, *die;* (*in city*) Stadtstreicher, *der*/-streicherin, *die;* Ⓑ (*sound of steps*) Schritte; (*of horses*) Getrappel, *das;* (*of elephants*) Trampeln, *das;* **the** ~ **of marching feet** Marschschritte; Ⓒ (*walk*) [Fuß]marsch, *der;* Ⓓ (*sl.: dissolute woman*) Flittchen, *das* (*ugs. abwertend*); Nutte, *die* (*derb abwertend*); Ⓔ (*Naut.*) Tramp, *der;* Trampschiff, *das.* ❷ *v.i.* Ⓐ (*tread heavily*) trampeln; Ⓑ (*walk*) marschieren. ❸ *v.t.* Ⓐ ~ **one's way** trotten; Ⓑ (*traverse*) durchwandern; (*with no particular destination*) durchstreifen; Ⓒ (*tread on*) herumtrampeln auf (+ *Dat.*); ~ **the earth** die Erde festtreten

~ **'down** *v.t.* niedertrampeln (*ugs.*); ~ **sth. down [until it is flat]** etw. festtreten

**trample** /ˈtræmpl/ ❶ *v.t.* zertrampeln; ~ **sth. to the ground** etw. zu Boden trampeln; ~ **sth. into the ground** etw. in den Boden treten; **he was** ~**d to death by elephants** er wurde von Elefanten zu Tode getrampelt. ❷ *v.i.* trampeln

~ **'down** *v.t.* niedertrampeln

~ **on** *v.t.* herumtrampeln auf (+ *Dat.*); ~ **on sb./sth./sb.'s feelings** (*fig.*) jmdn./etw./jmds. Gefühle mit Füßen treten

**trampoline** /ˈtræmpəliːn/ ❶ *n.* Trampolin, *das.* ❷ *v.i.* Trampolin springen

**'tramp steamer** *n.* Trampschiff, *das*

**tram:** ~ **ride** *n.* (*Brit.*) Straßenbahnfahrt, *die;* ~**road** *n.* (*Amer.*) ⇒ **tramlines** A; ~ **route** *n.* (*Brit.*) Straßenbahnlinie, *die;* ~ **stop** *n.* Straßenbahnhaltestelle, *die;* ~ **ticket** *n.* (*Brit.*) Straßenbahnfahrschein, *der od.* -fahrkarte, *die;* ~**way** *n.* (*Brit.*) ⇒ **tramlines** A

**trance** /trɑːns/ *n.* Ⓐ Trance, *die;* (*half-conscious state, hypnotic state, ecstasy, etc.*) tranceartiger Zustand; **be** *or* **lie in a** ~**:** in Trance/in einem tranceartigen Zustand sein; **fall** *or* **go into a** ~**:** in Trance/in einen tranceartigen Zustand fallen; **put** *or* **send sb. into a** ~**:** jmdn. in Trance/in einen tranceartigen Zustand versetzen; **she's been walking about in a** ~ **all day** sie ist den ganzen Tag wie in Trance herumgelaufen; Ⓑ (*Med.: catalepsy*) Katalepsie, *die*

**tranche** /trɑːnʃ/ *n.* (*Finance*) Tranche, *die*

**tranny** /ˈtrænɪ/ *n.* (*Brit. coll.*) Transistor, *der* (*ugs.*)

**tranquil** /ˈtræŋkwɪl/ *adj.* ruhig; friedlich ‹Stimmung, Szene›

**tranquilize**, **tranquilizer** (*Amer.*) ⇒ **tranquillize, tranquillizer**

**tranquillise**, **tranquilliser** ⇒ **tranquillize, tranquillizer**

**tranquillity** /træŋˈkwɪlɪtɪ/ *n.* Ruhe, *die;* (*of a scene*) Friedlichkeit, *die;* **live in peace and** ~**:** in Ruhe und Frieden leben

**tranquillize** /ˈtræŋkwɪlaɪz/ *v.t.* beruhigen; **the unruly prisoner was quickly** ~**d** der aufsässige Gefangene wurde schnell ruhig gestellt

**tranquillizer** /ˈtræŋkwɪlaɪzə(r)/ *n.* (*Med.*) Tranquilizer, *der;* Beruhigungsmittel, *das;* ~ **gun** Betäubungsgewehr, *das*

**tranquilly** /ˈtræŋkwɪlɪ/ *adv.* ruhig; friedlich ‹leben›

**transact** /trænˈsækt/ *v.t.* ~ **business [with sb.]** [mit jmdm.] Geschäfte tätigen (*Kaufmannsspr., Papierdt.*); **the two countries have** ~**ed business for a long time** die beiden Länder unterhalten seit langem Handelsbeziehungen; **our company** ~**s business with many foreign firms** unsere Gesellschaft unterhält Geschäftsbeziehungen mit vielen ausländischen Firmen

**transaction** /trænˈsækʃn/ *n.* Ⓐ (*doing of business*) **after the** ~ **of their business** nachdem sie das Geschäftliche erledigt hatten; **most banks close for the** ~ **of business at 3 p.m.** die meisten Banken schließen für den Publikumsverkehr um 15 Uhr; Ⓑ (*piece of business*) Geschäft, *das;* (*financial*) Transaktion, *die;* Ⓒ *in pl.* (*reports of a society*) Sitzungsberichte *Pl.*

**transalpine** /trænsˈælpaɪn/ transalpin

**transatlantic** /trænsətˈlæntɪk/ *adj.* Ⓐ (*Brit.: American*) transatlantisch; amerikanisch; Ⓑ (*Amer.: European*) transatlantisch; europäisch; Ⓒ (*crossing the Atlantic*) transatlantisch; **a** ~ **voyage** eine Reise über den Atlantik; **he is a regular** ~ **traveller** er reist regelmäßig über den Atlantik; ~ **communications** Verbindungen über den Atlantik

**transceiver** /trænˈsiːvə(r)/ *n.* (*Radio*) Sende- und Empfangsgerät, *das*

**transcend** /trænˈsend/ *v.t.* Ⓐ (*be beyond range of*) übersteigen; hinausgehen über ‹Grenzen›; (*Philos.*) transzendieren; Ⓑ (*surpass*) übertreffen; ~ **sb. in beauty** jmdn. an Schönheit übertreffen

**transcendence** /trænˈsendəns/, **transcendency** /trænˈsendənsɪ/ *n., no pl.* (*Philos., Theol.*) Transzendenz, *die*

**transcendent** /trænˈsendənt/ *adj.* (*Philos., Theol.*) transzendent

**transcendental** /trænsenˈdentl/ *adj.* Ⓐ (*Philos.*) transzendental; Ⓑ (*Math.*) transzendent

**transcendentalism** /trænsenˈdentəlɪzm/ *n.* (*Philos.*) Transzendentalismus, *der*

**Transcendental Medi'tation** (*Amer.:* ®) *n.* Transzendentale Meditation

**transcontinental** /trænskɒntɪˈnentl/ *adj.* transkontinental

**transcribe** /trænˈskraɪb/ *v.t.* Ⓐ (*copy in writing*) abschreiben; aufschreiben ‹mündliche Überlieferung›; mitschreiben ‹Rede›; protokollieren ‹Sitzung, Verhandlung usw.›; ~ **a tape/a taped interview** von einem Tonband/von der Tonbandaufzeichnung eines Interviews eine Niederschrift anfertigen; ~ **one's rough notes** aus seinen kurzen Notizen eine Reinschrift herstellen; Ⓑ (*record*) aufzeichnen; ~ **a record on to tape/a tape on to a record** eine Schallplatte auf Tonband überspielen/von einem Tonband eine Schallplattenaufnahme machen; Ⓒ (*Mus.*) transkribieren; Ⓓ (*transliterate*) transkribieren; umschreiben; ~ **some shorthand/sth. from a shorthand version** ein Stenogramm/etw. in Langschrift übertragen

**transcript** /ˈtrænskrɪpt/ *n.* Abschrift, *die;* (*of trial, interview, speech, conference*) Protokoll, *das;* (*of tape, taped material*) Niederschrift, *die*

**transcription** /trænˈskrɪpʃn/ *n.* Ⓐ (*transcribing*) Abschrift, *die;* (*of proceedings, speeches*) Protokollieren, *das;* (*of rough notes*) Reinschrift, *die;* (*of spoken text, tapes, etc.*) Niederschrift, *die;* (*of record on to tape*) Überspielung, *die;* (*of tape on to a record*) Übertragung, *die;* (*Mus.*) Transkription, *die;* (*from shorthand*) Übertragung [in Langschrift]; (*transliteration*) Transkription, *die;* Umschrift, *die;* Ⓑ (*transcribed material*) Abschrift, *die;* (*of proceedings, speech*) Protokoll, *das;* (*of rough notes*) Reinschrift, *die;* (*of text, tape, etc.*) Niederschrift, *die;* (*of record*) [Tonband]aufnahme, *die;* (*Mus.*) Transkription, *die;* (*from shorthand*) Langschriftfassung, *die;* (*transliteration*) Transkription, *die;* Umschrift, *die*

**transducer** /trænsˈdjuːsə(r)/ *n.* (*Electr.*) Wandler, *der*

**transept** /ˈtrænsept/ *n.* (*Eccl. Archit.*) Querschiff, *das;* **north/south** ~**:** nördlicher/südlicher Kreuzarm

**transfer** ❶ /trænsˈfɜː(r)/ *v.t.,* **-rr-** Ⓐ (*move*) verlegen (**to** nach); überweisen ‹Geld› (**to** auf + *Akk.*); transferieren ‹große Geldsumme›; übertragen ‹Befugnis, Macht› (**to** *Dat.*); ~ **a prisoner to a different gaol** einen Gefangenen in ein anderes Gefängnis verlegen *od.* überführen; ~ **one's affections to someone new** seine Gunst jemand anderem schenken; ~ **one's allegiance [from sb.] to sb.** [von jmdm.] zu jmdm. überwechseln; Ⓑ übereignen ‹Gegenstand, Grundbesitz› (**to** *Dat.*); ~ **sth. into new ownership** etw. einem neuen Besitzer *od.* jemand anderem übereignen; Ⓒ versetzen ‹Arbeiter, Angestellte, Schüler›; (*Footb.*) transferieren; Ⓓ übertragen ‹Bedeutung, Sinn›; Ⓔ (*copy*) umdrucken ‹Zeichnung›.

❷ *v.i.,* **-rr-** Ⓐ (*change to continue journey*) umsteigen; ~ **from Heathrow to Gatwick** zum Weiterflug *od.* Umsteigen von Heathrow nach Gatwick fahren; **we had to** ~ **to a special bus** wir mussten in einen Sonderbus umsteigen; Ⓑ (*move to another place or group*) wechseln; ‹Firma:› übersiedeln.

❸ /ˈtrænsfɜː(r)/ *n.* Ⓐ (*moving*) Verlegung, *die;* (*of powers*) Übertragung, *die* (**to** an + *Akk.*); (*of money*) Überweisung, *die;* (*of large sums*) Transfer, *der* (*Wirtsch.*); Ⓑ (*of employee, pupil*) Versetzung, *die;* (*of football player*) Transfer, *der;* Wechsel, *der;* Ⓒ (*Amer.: ticket*) Umsteigefahrkarte, *die;* Ⓓ (*picture*) Abziehbild, *das;* Ⓔ (*conveyance of property*) Übertragung, *die;* Übereignung, *die*

**transferability** /trænsfərəˈbɪlɪtɪ/ *n., no pl.* Übertragbarkeit, *die*

**transferable** /trænsˈfɜːrəbl, ˈtrænsfərəbl/ *adj.* übertragbar; frei transferierbar ‹Devisenkonto›

**transferable 'vote** *n.* übertragbare [Wähler]-stimme

**'transfer company** *n.* (*Amer.*) Transportunternehmen, *das*

**transference** /ˈtrænsfərəns/ *n.* Übertragung, *die*

**'transfer:** ~ **fee** *n.* (*Footb.*) Ablösesumme, *die;* Transfersumme, *die* (*fachspr.*); ~ **list** *n.* (*Footb.*) Transferliste, *die*

**transfiguration** /trænsfɪgəˈreɪʃn/ *n.* Transfiguration, *die* (*fachspr.*); Verklärung Christi, *die;* **the T**~ (*Relig.*) das Fest der Verklärung

**transfigure** /træns'fɪgə(r)/ *v.t.* verklären

**transfix** /træns'fɪks/ *v.t.* **A** (*pierce through*) durchbohren; **B** (*root to the spot*) erstarren lassen, lähmen ‹Person›; **be/stand ~ed** wie gelähmt *od.* angewurzelt sein/dastehen

**transform** ❶ /træns'fɔːm/ *v.t.* **A** verwandeln; **~ heat into energy** Wärme in Energie umwandeln; **the caterpillar is ~ed into a butterfly** die Raupe verwandelt sich zu einem Schmetterling; **I felt ~ed** ich fühlte mich wie umgewandelt; **a new coat of paint would ~ the room** ein neuer Anstrich, und man würde das Zimmer nicht wiedererkennen; **B** (*Electr.*) (*in potential*) transformieren; umspannen; (*in type*) umformen. ❷ /'trænsfɔːm/ *n.* (*Math., Ling.*) Transformation, *die*

**transformation** /trænsfə'meɪʃn/ *n.* **A** Verwandlung, *die;* **B** (*Math., Ling.*) Transformation, *die;* **C** (*Phys.*) Elementumwandlung, *die;* Transmutation, *die;* (*of heat into energy*) Umwandlung, *die*

**transformational** /trænsfə'meɪʃənl/ *adj.* (*esp. Ling.*) Transformations-

**transformational 'grammar** *n.* (*Ling.*) Transformationsgrammatik, *die*

**transfor'mation scene** *n.* (*Theatre*) Verwandlungsszene, *die*

**transformer** /træns'fɔːmə(r)/ *n.* (*Electr.*) Transformator, *der*

**transfuse** /træns'fjuːz/ *v.t.* **A** (*Med.*) transfundieren (*fachspr.*); übertragen; **B** (*permeate, lit. or fig.*) erfüllen; durchdringen

**transfusion** /træns'fjuːʒn/ *n.* (*Med.*) Transfusion, *die;* Übertragung, *die;* ⇒ *also* **blood transfusion**

**transgenic** /træns'dʒenɪk/ *adj.* (*Biol.*) transgen

**transgress** /træns'gres/ *v.t.* übertreten; *abs.* **he was ~ing** er hat sich einer Übertretung (*Gen.*) schuldig gemacht (*geh.*)

**transgression** /træns'greʃn/ *n.* Übertretung, *die*

**transgressor** /træns'gresə(r)/ *n.* Übertreter, *der*/Übertreterin, *die* (**of** *Gen.*); (*sinner*) Sünder, *der*/Sünderin, *die* (**of** gegen)

**transience** /'trænzɪəns/, **transiency** /'trænzɪənsɪ/ *n.* Vergänglichkeit, *die*

**transient** /'trænzɪənt/ ❶ *adj.* **A** kurzlebig; vergänglich; **B** (*Mus.*) durchgehend. ❷ *n.* **A** (*temporary guest*) Durchreisende, *der/die;* **B** (*Electr.*) Ausgleichsvorgang, *der*

**transistor** /træn'sɪstə(r)/ *n.* **A** ~ **[radio]** Transistor, *der;* Transistorradio, *das;* **B** (*Electronics*) Transistor, *der*

**transistorize** /træn'sɪstəraɪz/ *v.t.* (*Electronics*) transistorisieren

**transit** /'trænsɪt/ *n.* **A** Transit, *der;* **passengers in ~:** Transitreisende; Durchreisende; **be in ~:** auf der Durchreise sein; **B** (*conveyance*) Transport, *der;* **goods in ~ from London to Hull** Waren auf dem Transport von London nach Hull; **C** (*Astron.*) Durchgang, *der*

**'transit camp** *n.* Durchgangslager, *das*

**transition** /træn'sɪʒn, træn'zɪʃn/ *n.* **A** Übergang, *der;* (*sudden change*) Wechsel, *der;* **age/period of ~:** Übergangszeit, *die;* **B** (*Mus.*) Ausweichung, *die;* **C** (*Art*) Übergang, *der*

**transitional** /træn'sɪʒənl, træn'zɪʃənl/ *adj.* Übergangs-; **be ~ between a and b** den Übergang von a zu b bilden

**tran'sition: ~ element** *n.* (*Chem.*) Übergangselement, *das;* **~ point** *n.* (*Phys.*) Umwandlungspunkt, *der*

**transitive** /'trænsɪtɪv/ *adj.*, **transitively** /'trænsɪtɪvlɪ/ *adv.* (*Ling.*) transitiv

**'transit lounge** *n.* Transithalle, *die;* Transitlounge, *die*

**transitoriness** /'trænsɪtərɪnɪs/ *n., no pl.* Vergänglichkeit, *die;* (*fleetingness*) Flüchtigkeit, *die*

**transitory** /'trænsɪtərɪ/ *adj.* vergänglich; (*fleeting*) flüchtig

**transit: ~ passenger** *n.* Transitpassagier, *der;* **~ visa** *n.* Transitvisum, *das;* Durchreisevisum, *das*

**translatable** /træns'leɪtəbl/ *adj.* übersetzbar; **some words are not ~ into other languages** manche Wörter lassen sich nicht in andere Sprachen übersetzen

**translate** /træns'leɪt/ ❶ *v.t.* **A** übersetzen; **~ a novel from English into German** einen Roman aus dem Englischen ins Deutsche übersetzen; **~ 'Abgeordneter' as 'Deputy'** „Abgeordneter" mit „Deputy" übersetzen; **B** (*convert*) **~ a vision into reality/words into action[s]** eine Vision Wirklichkeit werden lassen/Worte in die Tat/in Taten umsetzen; **C** (*Relig.*) überführen ‹Reliquien›; **D** (*Eccl.*) versetzen ‹Bischof›. ❷ *v.i.* sich übersetzen lassen

**translation** /træns'leɪʃn/ *n.* **A** ▶ 1275 Übersetzung, *die;* **error in ~:** Übersetzungsfehler, *der;* **his works are available in ~:** seine Werke liegen in Übersetzung *od.* übersetzt vor; **read sth. in ~:** etw. in der Übersetzung lesen; **B** (*conversion*) Umsetzung, *die;* **C** (*Eccl.*) Translation, *die* (*fachspr.*); Versetzung, *die*

**translator** /træns'leɪtə(r)/ *n.* ▶ 1261 Übersetzer, *der*/Übersetzerin, *die*

**transliterate** /træns'lɪtəreɪt/ *v.t.* transliterieren (**into** in + *Akk.*)

**transliteration** /trænslɪtə'reɪʃn/ *n.* Transliteration, *die* (**into** in + *Akk.*)

**translucency** /træns'luːsənsɪ/ *n., no pl.* ⇒ **translucent**: Eigenschaft, durchscheinend zu sein; Durchsichtigkeit, *die*

**translucent** /træns'luːsənt/ *adj.* **A** (*partly transparent*) durchscheinend; **B** (*transparent*) durchsichtig

**transmigrate** /trænsmaɪ'greɪt/ *v.i.* **A** (*pass into different body*) übergehen; **B** (*migrate*) ziehen

**transmigration** /trænsmaɪ'greɪʃn/ *n.* **~ [of souls]** Seelenwanderung, *die;* **the ~ of the soul into another body** der Übergang der Seele in einen anderen Körper

**transmission** /træns'mɪʃn/ *n.* **A** (*passing on*) ⇒ **transmit** A: Übersendung, *die;* Übertragung, *die;* Überlieferung, *die;* [Weiter]vererbung, *die;* **B** (*Radio, Telev.*) Ausstrahlung, *die;* (*via satellite also; by wire*) Übertragung, *die;* **C** (*Motor Veh.*) (*drive*) Antrieb, *der;* (*gearbox*) Getriebe, *das;* **manual/automatic ~:** Schalt-/Automatikgetriebe, *das*

**transmit** /træns'mɪt/ *v.t.*, **-tt-** **A** (*pass on*) übersenden ‹Nachricht›; übertragen ‹Recht, Krankheit›; überliefern ‹Wissen, Kenntnisse›; (*genetically*) [weiter]vererben ‹Eigenschaft›; **B** durchlassen ‹Licht›; übertragen ‹Druck, Schall›; leiten ‹Wärme, Elektrizität›; **C** (*Radio, Telev.*) ausstrahlen; (*via satellite also; by wire*) übertragen

**transmittal** /træns'mɪtl/ ⇒ **transmission** A

**transmitter** /træns'mɪtə(r)/ *n.* Sender, *der*

**transmogrification** /trænsmɒgrɪfɪ'keɪʃn/ *n.* (*joc.*) [wundersame] Verwandlung

**transmogrify** /træns'mɒgrɪfaɪ/ *v.t.* (*joc.*) auf wundersame Weise verwandeln (**into** in + *Akk.*)

**transmutation** /trænsmjuː'teɪʃn/ *n.* **A** Umwandlung, *die* (**into** in + *Akk.*); **B** (*Phys.*) Transmutation, *die;* Elementumwandlung, *die;* **C** (*Biol.*) Umbildung, *die*

**transmute** /træns'mjuːt/ *v.t.* umwandeln

**transnational** /træns'næʃənl/ *adj.* übernational

**transoceanic** /trænsəʊʃɪ'ænɪk, trænsəʊsɪ'ænɪk/ *adj.* transozeanisch; überseeisch

**transom** /'trænsəm/ *n.* (*Archit.*) Quersprosse, *die*

**transom 'window** *n.* Oberlicht, *das*

**transparency** /træns'pærənsɪ/ *n.* **A** Durchsichtigkeit, *die;* (*fig. also*) Durchschaubarkeit, *die;* Fadenscheinigkeit, *die* (*abwertend*); **B** (*Photog.*) Transparent, *das;* (*slide*) Dia, *das*

**transparent** /træns'pærənt/ *adj.* durchsichtig; (*fig.*) (*obvious*) offenkundig; (*easily understood*) klar

**transparently** /træns'pærəntlɪ/ *adv.* offenkundig; **~ lucid** klar und einleuchtend ‹Darstellung›; **~ obvious** ganz offenkundig

**transpiration** /trænspɪ'reɪʃn/ *n.* **A** (*perspiration*) Schwitzen, *das;* Transpiration, *die* (*geh.*); **B** (*Bot.*) Transpiration, *die*

**transpire** /træn'spaɪə(r)/ ❶ *v.i.* **A** (*coll.: happen*) passieren; **B** (*come to be known*) sich herausstellen; **she had not, it ~d, seen the letter** sie hatte, so stellte sich heraus, den Brief nicht gesehen; **C** (*Bot.*) transpirieren; **D** (*be given off as perspiration*) ‹Feuchtigkeit:› ausgedünstet werden. ❷ *v.t.* ausdünsten

**transplant** ❶ /træns'plɑːnt/ *v.t.* **A** (*Med.*) transplantieren (*fachspr.*), verpflanzen ‹Organ, Gewebe›; **B** (*plant in another place*) umpflanzen; **C** (*fig.: move to another place*) umsiedeln; verlegen ‹Institution›. ❷ /'trænsplɑːnt/ *n.* **A** (*Med.*) (*operation*) Transplantation, *die* (*fachspr.*); Verpflanzung, *die;* (*thing transplanted*) Transplantat, *das* (*fachspr.*); **B** (*Hort.*) umgesetzte Pflanze

**transplantation** /trænsplɑːn'teɪʃn/ *n.* (*Med.*) Transplantation, *die* (*fachspr.*); Verpflanzung, *die*

**transponder** /træns'pɒndə(r)/ *n.* (*Electronics*) Transponder, *der*

**transport** ❶ /træn'spɔːt/ *v.t.* **A** (*convey*) transportieren; befördern; **B** (*literary: affect with emotion*) anrühren, anwandeln (*geh.*); **~ed with joy** von Freude überkommen; **C** (*Hist.*) deportieren ‹Sträfling›. ❷ /'trænspɔːt/ *n.* **A** (*conveyance*) Transport, *der;* Beförderung, *die; attrib.* Transport-; Beförderungs-; **B** (*means of conveyance*) Verkehrsmittel, *das;* (*for people also*) Fortbewegungsmittel, *das;* **~ was provided** für die Beförderung wurde gesorgt; **be without ~:** kein [eigenes] Fahrzeug haben; **his only ~ is a battered car** er hat nur ein verbeultes Auto; **Ministry of T~:** Verkehrsministerium, *das;* **the ~ has arrived** der Wagen ist da; **C** (*vehement emotion*) Ausbruch, *der;* **be in/send sb. into ~s of joy** außer sich vor Freude sein/jmdn. in helles Entzücken versetzen; **D** (*Mil.*) [Truppen]transporter, *der*

**transportable** /træn'spɔːtəbl/ *adj.* transportabel

**transportation** /trænspə'teɪʃn/ *n.* **A** (*conveying*) Transport, *der;* Beförderung, *die;* **~ by air/sea/road/rail** Luft-/See-/Straßen-/Bahntransport, *der;* **B** (*Amer.*) ⇒ **transport** 2 B; **C** (*Hist.: of convict*) Deportation, *die*

**'transport café** *n.* (*Brit.*) Fernfahrerlokal, *das*

**transporter** /træn'spɔːtə(r)/ *n.* (*vehicle*) Transporter, *der*

**trans'porter bridge** *n.* Schwebefähre, *die* (*Technik*)

**transpose** /træns'pəʊz/ *v.t.* **A** (*cause to change places*) vertauschen; **B** (*change order of*) umstellen; **C** (*Mus.*) transponieren

**transposition** /trænspə'zɪʃn/ *n.* ⇒ **transpose**: Vertauschung, *die;* Umstellung, *die;* (*Mus.*) Transposition, *die*

**transsexual** /træns'seksjʊəl, træns'sekʃʊəl/ ❶ *adj.* transsexuell. ❷ *n.* Transsexuelle, *der/die*

**trans-ship** /træns'ʃɪp, træn'ʃɪp/ *v.t.*, **-pp-** umladen

**trans-shipment** /træns'ʃɪpmənt, træn'ʃɪpmənt/ *n.* Umschlag, *der*

**transubstantiate** /trænsəb'stænʃɪeɪt/ *v.t.* (*Theol.*) [ver]wandeln

**transubstantiation** /trænsəbstænʃɪ'eɪʃn/ *n.* (*Theol.*) Transubstantiation, *die;* Wandlung, *die*

**transuranic** /trænsjʊ'rænɪk/ *adj.* (*Chem.*) transuranisch

**transverse** /'trænsvɜːs/ *adj.* quer liegend; Quer‹balken, -lage, -streifen, -verstrebung›; **~ flute** Querflöte, *die;* **~ wave** (*Phys.*) Transversalwelle, *die;* **~ section** Querschnitt, *der*

**transversely** /'trænsvɜːslɪ/ *adv.* quer

**transvestism** /træns'vestɪzm/ *n.* (*Psych.*) Transvestismus, *der*

**transvestist** /træns'vestɪst/, **transvestite** /træns'vestaɪt/ *n.* (*Psych.*) Transvestit, *der*

**Transylvania** /trænsɪl'veɪnɪə/ *pr. n.* Transsilvanien (*das*) (*veralt.*); Siebenbürgen (*das*)

**trap** /træp/ ❶ *n.* [A] (*lit. or fig.*) Falle, *die;* **set a ~ for an animal** eine Falle für ein Tier legen *od.* [auf]stellen; **set a ~ for sb.** (*fig.*) jmdm. eine Falle stellen; **fall into a/sb.'s ~** (*fig.*) in die/jmdm. in die Falle gehen; [B] (*sl.: mouth*) Klappe, *die* (*salopp*); Fresse, *die* (*derb*); **shut your ~!, keep your ~ shut!** halt die Klappe (*salopp*) *od.* (*derb*) Fresse!; [C] ⇒ **speed trap**; [D] (*for releasing bird*) Kasten, *der;* (*for throwing ball etc. into the air*) Wurfmaschine, *die;* [E] (*section of pipe*) Geruchsverschluss, *der;* Siphon, *der;* [F] (*carriage*) (*leichter zweirädriger*) Einspänner; [G] (*Golf*) Bunker, *der;* [H] (*Greyhound Racing*) Box, *die;* [I] ⇒ **trapdoor**; [J] *in pl.* (*coll.: percussion instruments*) Schießbude, *die* (*ugs.*).
❷ *v.t.*, **-pp-:** [A] (*catch*) [in *od.* mit einer Falle] fangen ‹Tier›; (*fig.*) in eine Falle locken ‹Person›; **be ~ped** (*fig.*) in eine Falle gehen/in der Falle sitzen; **be ~ped in a cave/by the tide/in the snow** in einer Höhle festsitzen/von der Flut abgeschnitten sein/im Schnee stecken geblieben sein; **she ~ped him into contradicting himself** sie brachte ihn durch eine List dazu, sich zu widersprechen; [B] (*confine*) einschließen; (*immobilize*) einklemmen ‹Person, Körperteil›; **~ one's finger/foot** sich (*Dat.*) den Finger/Fuß einklemmen; [C] (*entangle*) verstricken; [D] stoppen ‹Ball›

**'trapdoor** *n.* Falltür, *die*

**trapeze** /trə'pi:z/ *n.* Trapez, *das*

**tra'peze artist** *n.* Trapezkünstler, *der*/-künstlerin, *die*

**trapezium** /trə'pi:zɪəm/ *n., pl.* **trapezia** /trə'pi:zɪə/ *or* **~s** (*Geom.*) [A] (*Brit.*) Trapez, *das;* [B] (*Amer.*) Trapezoid, *das*

**trapezoid** /'træpɪzɔɪd/ *n.* (*Geom.*) [A] (*Brit.*) Trapezoid, *das;* [B] (*Amer.*) Trapez, *das*

**trapper** /'træpə(r)/ *n.* Fallensteller, *der;* (*in North America*) Trapper, *der*

**trappings** /'træpɪŋz/ *n. pl.* [A] [äußere] Zeichen; (*of power, high office*) Insignien; [B] (*ornamental harness*) ≈ Schabracke, *die*

**Trappist** /'træpɪst/ *n.* Trappist, *der; attrib.* Trappisten-

**trash** /træʃ/ ❶ *n., no pl., no indef. art.* [A] (*rubbish*) Abfall, *der;* [B] (*badly made thing*) Mist, *der* (*ugs. abwertend*); (*bad literature*) Schund, *der* (*ugs. abwertend*); **be [just] ~:** nichts taugen; [C] (*nonsensical talk*) Mist, *der* (*ugs. abwertend*); **what ~ he talks!** was der für 'n Mist redet!; [D] (*worthless person*) Ratte, *die* (*derb*); (*worthless persons*) Gesindel, *das* (*abwertend*); Pack, *das* (*abwertend*); **white ~** (*Amer. derog.*) weißes Gesindel *od.* Pack (*abwertend*). ❷ *v.t.* wegwerfen; wegschmeißen (*ugs.*)

**'trashcan** *n.* (*Amer.*) Mülltonne, *die*

**trashy** /'træʃɪ/ *adj.* minderwertig; Schund‹literatur, -roman›

**trattoria** /trætə'ri:ə/ *n.* Trattoria, *die*

**trauma** /'trɔ:mə/ *n., pl.* **~ta** /'trɔ:mətə/ *or* **~s** Trauma, *das* (*fachspr.*); (*injury also*) Verletzung, *die;* (*shock also*) Schock, *der*

**traumatic** /trɔ:'mætɪk/ *adj.* [A] (*Med.*) traumatisch; [B] (*coll.: devastating*) furchtbar

**traumatize** /'trɔ:mətaɪz/ *v.t.* traumatisieren

**travel** /'trævl/ ❶ *n.* [A] Reisen, *das; attrib.* Reise-; **be off on one's ~s** verreist sein; **if you see him on your ~s, …** (*joc.*) wenn er dir über den Weg läuft, …; [B] (*range of motion*) Weg, *der;* **there's a lot of ~ on the handbrake** der Handbremshebel hat einen sehr langen Weg.
❷ *v.i.*, (*Brit.*) **-ll-;** [A] (*make a journey*) reisen; (*go in vehicle*) fahren; **~ a lot** viel reisen; [B] (*coll.: withstand long journey*) **~ [well]** ‹Ware:› lange Transporte vertragen; **~ badly** ‹Ware:› lange Transporte nicht vertragen; [C] (*work as ~ling sales representative*) reisen; Vertreter/Vertreterin sein; **~ in stationery** in Schreibwaren reisen (*Kaufmannsspr.*); [D] (*move*) sich bewegen; ‹Blick, Schmerz:› wandern; ‹Tier:› sich fortbewegen; ‹Licht, Schall:› sich ausbreiten; [E] (*coll.: move quickly*) kacheln (*ugs.*); **that car can really ~:** das Auto zieht ganz schön ab (*ugs.*); **we were really ~ling** wir hatten einen ganz schönen Zahn drauf (*ugs.*).
❸ *v.t.*, (*Brit.*) **-ll-** zurücklegen ‹Strecke, Entfernung›; bereisen ‹Bezirk›; benutzen, passieren ‹Weg, Straße›; **we had ~led 10 miles** wir waren 10 Meilen gefahren

**~ a'bout, ~ a'round** ❶ *v.i.* umherreisen. ❷ *v.t.* **~ around the country** durchs Land reisen *od.* fahren

**travel: ~ agency** *n.* Reisebüro, *das;* **~ agent** *n.* ▶ 1261 Reisebürokaufmann, *der*/-kauffrau, *die;* **the ~ agent made a mistake** das Reisebüro hat einen Fehler gemacht

**travelator** /'trævəleɪtə(r)/ *n.* Fahr- *od.* Rollsteig, *der*

**travel: ~ brochure** *n.* Reiseprospekt, *der;* **~ bureau** *n.* Reisebüro, *das*

**traveled, traveler, traveling** (*Amer.*) ⇒ **travell-**

**'travel insurance** *n.* Reiseversicherung, *die*

**travelled** /'trævld/ *adj.* (*Brit.*) **be much ~** ‹Person:› weit gereist sein; **be well ~** ‹Weg, Straße:› viel befahren sein

**traveller** /'trævlə(r)/ *n.* (*Brit.*) [A] Reisende, *der/die;* **be a poor ~:** das Reisen nicht [gut] vertragen; [B] (*sales representative*) Vertreter, *der*/Vertreterin, *die;* [C] *in pl.* (*gypsies etc.*) fahrendes Volk

**traveller: ~'s cheque** *n.* ▶ 1328 Reisescheck, *der;* **~'s tale** *n.* fantastischer Reisebericht; **they're just ~'s tales** das sind nur Fantastereien (*abwertend*)

**travelling** /'trævlɪŋ/ *adj.* (*Brit.*) Wander‹zirkus, -ausstellung, -bühne›

**travelling: ~ bag** *n.* Reisetasche, *die;* **~ clock** *n.* Reisewecker, *der;* **~ 'crane** *n.* Laufkran, *der;* **~ expenses** *n. pl.* Reisekosten *Pl.;* **~ 'fellowship** *n.* (*Univ.*) ≈ Auslandsstipendium, *das;* **~ rug** *n.* Reisedecke, *die;* **~ 'salesman** *n.* ▶ 1261 Vertreter, *der;* **~ 'wave** *n.* (*Phys.*) fortschreitende Welle

**travelogue** (*Amer.:* **travelog**) /'trævəlɒg/ *n.* Reisebericht, *der*

**travel: ~-sick** *adj.* reisekrank; **~sickness** *n., no pl.* Reisekrankheit, *die;* **~-sickness pill** *n.* Tablette gegen Reisekrankheit

**traverse** /'trævəs, trə'vɜ:s/ ❶ *v.t.* [A] überqueren ‹Gebirge›; durchqueren ‹Gebäude, Gebiet›; [B] ‹Kanal, Mauer:› durchziehen ‹Gebiet›; [C] (*Mountaineering*) traversieren. ❷ *n.* (*Mountaineering*) Traversierung, *die*

**travesty** /'trævɪstɪ/ ❶ *n.* [A] (*parody*) Karikatur, *die;* **be a ~ [of justice]** ein Hohn [auf die Gerechtigkeit] sein; [B] (*Lit.: burlesque*) Travestie, *die* (*fachspr.*). ❷ *v.t.* ins Lächerliche ziehen

**Travolator** ® /'trævəleɪtə(r)/ ⇒ **travelator**

**trawl** /trɔ:l/ ❶ *v.i.* mit dem Grundnetz fischen. ❷ *n.* [A] Fischen mit dem Grundnetz; [B] **~[-net]** Grund[schlepp]netz, *das;* **~[-line]** (*Amer.*) Langleine, *die*

**trawler** /'trɔ:lə(r)/ *n.* (*vessel*) [Fisch]trawler, *der*

**trawlerman** /'trɔ:ləmən/ *n.* ▶ 1261 ≈ Hochseefischer, *der*

**tray** /treɪ/ *n.* [A] Tablett, *das;* **baking ~:** Backblech, *das;* [B] (*for correspondence*) Ablagekorb, *der*

**'tray cloth** *n.* Deckchen für ein Tablett

**trayful** /'treɪfʊl/ *n.* Tablett voll

**treacherous** /'tretʃərəs/ *adj.* [A] treulos ‹Person›; heimtückisch ‹Intrige, Feind›; [B] (*deceptive*) tückisch; **the ice looks pretty ~:** das Eis sieht nicht sehr vertrauenerweckend aus

**treacherously** /'tretʃərəslɪ/ *adv.* heimtückisch

**treachery** /'tretʃərɪ/ *n.* Verrat, *der;* **act of ~:** Verrat, *der*

**treacle** /'tri:kl/ *n.* (*Brit.*) [A] (*golden syrup*) Sirup, *der;* [B] ⇒ **molasses**

**treacle 'pudding** *n. mit Sirup übergossener Mehlpudding*

**treacly** /'tri:klɪ/ *adj.* sirupartig; (*fig.*) süßlich (*abwertend*)

**tread** /tred/ ❶ *n.* [A] (*of tyre, shoe, boot, etc.*) Lauffläche, *die;* **2 millimetres of ~ on a tyre** 2 Millimeter Profil auf einem Reifen; [B] (*manner of walking*) Gang, *der;* (*sound of walking*) Schritt, *der;* **walk with a springy/catlike ~:** einen federnden/katzenhaften Gang haben; **the ~ of feet** Schritte; [C] (*of staircase*) [Tritt]stufe, *die.*
❷ *v.i.*, **trod** /trɒd/, **trodden** /'trɒdn/ *or* **trod** treten (**in/on** in/auf + *Akk.*); (*walk*) gehen; **~ carefully** *or* **lightly** (*fig.*) behutsam vorgehen; **~ on sb.'s toes** (*lit. or fig.*) jmdm. auf die Füße treten; **~ on the heels of sb./sth.** (*fig.*) jmdm./einer Sache auf den Fersen sein (*ugs.*); **~ dirt into the carpet/all over the house** Schmutz in den Teppich treten/im ganzen Haus herumtreten; ⇒ *also* **foot** 1 A.
❸ *v.t.*, **trod, trodden** *or* **trod** [A] (*walk on*) treten auf (+ *Akk.*); stampfen ‹Weintrauben›; (*fig.*) gehen ‹Weg›; **~ the stage** *or* **boards** (*Theatre*) auf der Bühne *od.* auf den Brettern stehen; **be trodden underfoot** mit Füßen getreten werden; **~ water** (*Swimming*) Wasser treten; [B] (*make by walking or treading*) austreten ‹Weg›

**~ 'down** *v.t.* festtreten ‹Erde›; (*crush, destroy*) zertreten ‹Blume, Beet›

**~ 'in** *v.t.* festtreten

**~ 'out** *v.t.* austreten ‹Feuer, Zigarette›; stampfen ‹Weintrauben›

**treadle** /'tredl/ *n.* Tritt, *der*

**'treadmill** *n.* (*lit. or fig.*) Tretmühle, *die*

**treason** /'tri:zn/ *n.* [A] **[high] ~:** Hochverrat, *der;* [B] (*disloyalty*) Verrat, *der*

**treasonable** /'tri:zənəbl/, **treasonous** /'tri:zənəs/ *adjs.* verräterisch; **a ~ offence** Verrat

**treasure** /'treʒə(r)/ ❶ *n.* [A] Schatz, *der;* Kostbarkeit, *die;* **art ~s** Kunstschätze; [B] *no pl., no indef. art.* (*riches*) Schätze; **buried ~:** ein vergrabener Schatz; **voyage in quest of ~:** Schatzsuche, *die;* [C] (*coll.: valued person*) Schatz, *der* (*ugs.*). ❷ *v.t.* in Ehren halten; die Erinnerung bewahren an (+ *Dat.*); **I'll always ~ this moment/the memory of that day** ich werde diesen Augenblick/Tag niemals vergessen

**~ 'up** *v.t.* wie einen Schatz hüten

**treasure: ~ house** *n.* Schatzkammer, *die;* (*fig.*) [wahre] Fundgrube; **~ hunt** *n.* Schatzsuche, *die*

**treasurer** /'treʒərə(r)/ *n.* [A] (*of club, society*) Kassenwart, *der*/-wartin, *die;* (*of club, party*) Schatzmeister, *der*/-meisterin, *die;* (*of company*) Leiter/Leiterin der Finanzabteilung; [B] (*local government official*) Leiter/Leiterin der Finanzverwaltung

**treasure trove** /'treʒə trəʊv/ *n.* Schatz, *der;* (*fig.: valuable source*) [wahre] Fundgrube

**treasury** /'treʒərɪ/ *n.* [A] (*place where treasure is stored*) Schatzkammer, *die;* [B] (*fig.*) Fundgrube, *die;* (*as book title*) Schatzkästchen, *das;* [C] (*place where public revenues are kept*) Schatzamt, *das;* [D] (*government department*) **the T~:** das Finanzministerium; **the First Lord of the T~** (*Brit.*) der Premierminister/die Premierministerin (*als nomineller Leiter/nominelle Leiterin des „treasury"*)

**treasury: T~ bench** *n.* (*Brit. Parl.*) Regierungsbank, *die;* **~ bill** *n.* (*Finance*) Schatzwechsel, *der;* **~ tag** *n. kurze Kordel mit Metallstiften an den Enden zum Zusammenhalten von [gelochten] Blättern*

**treat** /tri:t/ ❶ *n.* [A] [besonderes] Vergnügen; (*sth. to eat*) [besonderer] Leckerbissen; **what a ~ [it is] to do/not to have to do that!** welch ein Genuss *od.* eine Wohltat, das zu tun/nicht tun zu müssen!; **it was a real ~ to have an entire afternoon at home on my own** es war eine richtige Wohltat, einen ganzen Nachmittag zu Hause für mich allein zu haben; **give sb. a ~:** jmdm. eine besondere Freude machen; **have a ~ in store for sb.** noch eine besondere Freude für jmdn. auf Lager haben; **there was a ~ in store for them** auf sie wartete noch eine besondere Freude; **go down a ~** (*coll.*) ‹Essen, Getränk:› prima schmecken (*ugs.*); **work a ~** (*coll.*) ‹Maschine:› prima arbeiten (*ugs.*); ‹Plan:› prima funktionieren (*ugs.*); [B] (*entertainment*) *Vergnügen, für dessen Kosten jmd. anderes aufkommt;* **lay on a special ~ for sb.** jmdm. etwas Besonderes bieten; **as a Christmas ~ I shall take my sister to the theatre** als

Weihnachtsgeschenk lade ich meine Schwester ins Theater ein; C (*act of* ~*ing*) Einladung, *die;* **it's my** ~: ich lade dich/euch ein; **stand** ~ **for sb.** jmdn. einladen. 2 *v.t.* A (*act towards*) behandeln; ~ **sth. as a joke** etw. als Witz nehmen; ~ **sth. with contempt** für etw. nur Verachtung haben; B ▶1232 (*Med.*) behandeln; ~ **sb. for sth.** jmdn. wegen etw. behandeln; (*before confirmation of diagnosis*) jmdn. auf etw. (*Akk.*) behandeln; C (*apply process to*) behandeln ‹Material, Stoff, Metall, Leder›; klären ‹Abwässer›; D (*handle in literature etc.*) behandeln; ~ **sth. fully** etw. ausführlich behandeln; E (*provide with at own expense*) einladen; ~ **sb. to sth.** jmdm. etw. spendieren; ~ **oneself to a holiday/a new hat** sich (*Dat.*) Urlaub gönnen/sich (*Dat.*) einen neuen Hut leisten. 3 *v.i.* ~ **with sb. [for sth.]** mit jmdm. [über etw. (*Akk.*)] verhandeln

**treatise** /'tri:tɪs, 'tri:tɪz/ *n.* Abhandlung, *die*

**treatment** /'tri:tmənt/ *n.* A Behandlung, *die;* **receive rough** ~ **from sb.** von jmdm. grob behandelt werden; **his** ~ **of the staff/you** die Art, wie er das Personal/dich behandelt; **her** ~ **at the hands of her uncle** die Art, wie ihr Onkel sie behandelt/behandelt hat; **give sb. the [full]** ~ (*coll.*) (*treat cruelly/harshly*) jmdn. in die Mangel nehmen (*salopp*); (*entertain on a lavish scale*) jmdn. verwöhnen; B ▶1232 (*Med.*) Behandlung, *die;* **be having** ~ **for sth.** wegen etw. in Behandlung sein; **need immediate medical** ~: sofort ärztlich behandelt werden müssen; C (*processing*) Behandlung, *die;* (*of sewage*) Klärung, *die*

**treaty** /'tri:tɪ/ *n.* A [Staats]vertrag, *der;* **make** *or* **sign a** ~: einen Vertrag schließen; **the** ~ **of Rome** die Römischen Verträge; **the** ~ **of Versailles** der Versailler Vertrag; B ⇒ **private treaty**

**treble** /'trebl/ 1 *adj.* A dreifach; ~ **row** Dreierreihe, *die;* ~ **the amount compared to ...:** dreimal so viel wie ...; **sell sth. for** ~ **the price** etw. dreimal so teuer verkaufen; B (*Brit. Mus.*) ~ **voice** Sopranstimme, *die.* 2 *n.* A (*Brit. Mus.*) **he is a** ~**/is singing the** ~: er singt Sopran/den Sopran; B (~ *quantity etc.*) Dreifache, *das;* C (*Darts*) dreifach zählender Treffer; D (*Racing*) Dreifachwette, *die.* 3 *v.t.* verdreifachen; **be** ~**d** ‹Wert einer Aktie usw.:› sich verdreifachen. 4 *v.i.* sich verdreifachen

**treble:** ~ **'chance** *n.* *Art des Fußballtotos mit dreifacher Gewinnchance;* ~ **clef** *n.* (*Mus.*) Violinschlüssel, *der;* ~ **re'corder** *n.* (*Mus.*) Altflöte, *die*

**trebly** /'treblɪ/ *adv.* dreifach; **be** ~ **fortunate** in dreifacher Hinsicht Glück haben

**tree** /tri:/ *n.* Baum, *der;* **not grow on** ~**s** (*fig.*) nicht [einfach] vom Himmel fallen; ⇒ *also* **Christmas tree**; **family tree**; **shoe tree**; **top**[1] 1 A

**tree:** ~**creeper** *n.* (*Ornith.*) Baumläufer, *der;* ~ **fern** *n.* (*Bot.*) Baumfarn, *der;* ~ **frog** *n.* Laubfrosch, *der;* ~ **house** *n.* Baumhaus, *das*

**treeless** /'tri:lɪs/ *adj.* baumlos

**tree:** ~**line** ⇒ **timberline**; ~**-lined** *adj.* von Bäumen gesäumt; ~ **ring** *n.* (*Bot.*) Jahresring, *der;* ~**-shaded** *adj.* von Bäumen beschattet (*geh.*); ~ **surgeon** *n.* Baumchirurg, *der;* ~ **surgery** *n.* Baumchirurgie, *die;* ~**top** *n.* [Baum]wipfel, *der;* ~ **trunk** *n.* Baumstamm, *der*

**trefoil** /'trefɔɪl, 'tri:fɔɪl/ *n.* A (*clover*) Klee, *der;* (*plant with similar leaves*) Dreiblatt, *das;* B (*Archit.*) Dreipass, *der*

**trek** /trek/ 1 *v.i.*, **-kk-** A ziehen (**across** durch); B (*travel by ox-wagon*) trecken. 2 *n.* A [schwierige] Reise; B (*journey by ox-wagon, organized migration*) Treck, *der*

**trellis** /'trelɪs/ *n.* Gitter, *das;* (*for plants*) Spalier, *das;* ~**-work** Gitterwerk, *das*

**tremble** /'trembl/ 1 *v.i.* zittern (**with** vor + *Dat.*); ~ **for sb./sth.** (*fig.*) um jmdn./etw. zittern; **I** ~ **to think what .../at the thought** (*fig.*) mir wird bange, wenn ich daran denke, was .../wenn ich daran denke. 2 *n.* Zittern, *das;* **be all of a** ~ (*coll.*) am ganzen Körper zittern; **there was a** ~ **in her voice** ihre Stimme zitterte

**trembling** /'tremblɪŋ/ 1 *adj.* zitternd. 2 *n.* Zittern, *das*

**tremendous** /trɪ'mendəs/ *adj.* A (*immense*) gewaltig; enorm ‹Fähigkeiten›; B (*coll.: wonderful*) großartig

**tremendously** /trɪ'mendəslɪ/ *adv.* wahnsinnig (*ugs.*)

**tremolo** /'tremələʊ/ *n., pl.* ~**s** (*Mus.*) A Tremolo, *das;* B (*in organ*) ~ **[stop]** Tremulant, *der*

**tremor** /'tremə(r)/ *n.* A Zittern, *das;* **feel a** ~ **of delight/fear** freudig erregt sein/vor Angst zittern; **there was a** ~ **of anger in her voice** ihre Stimme zitterte vor Wut; **without a** ~: ohne zu zittern; B **[earth]** ~ (*Geol.*) leichtes Erdbeben

**tremulous** /'tremjʊləs/ *adj.* A (*trembling*) zitternd; **be** ~: zittern; B (*timid*) zaghaft ‹Lächeln›; ängstlich ‹Person›

**tremulously** /'tremjʊləslɪ/ *adv.* A mit zitternder Stimme ‹sprechen›; B (*timidly*) zaghaft

**trench** /trentʃ/ 1 *n.* Graben, *der;* (*Geog.*) [Tiefsee]graben, *der;* (*Mil.*) Schützengraben, *der.* 2 *v.t.* (*dig ditch in*) mit einem Graben durchziehen

**trenchant** /'trentʃənt/ *adj.* deutlich, energisch ‹Kritik, Sprache›; energisch ‹Verteidiger, Kritiker, Politik›; prägnant ‹Stil›; scharf ‹Verstand›

**trenchantly** /'trentʃəntlɪ/ *adv.* energisch ‹verteidigen, argumentieren, unterstützen›

**'trench coat** *n.* (*Mil.*) Wettermantel, *der;* (*coat in this style*) Trenchcoat, *der*

**trencherman** /'trentʃəmən/ *n.* [guter] Esser

**trench:** ~ **mortar** *n.* (*Mil.*) Granatwerfer, *der;* ~ **'warfare** *n.* Grabenkrieg, *der*

**trend** /trend/ 1 *n.* A Trend, *der;* **population** ~**s** die Bevölkerungsentwicklung; **upward** ~: steigende Tendenz; B (*fashion*) Mode, *die;* [Mode]trend, *der;* **set the** ~: den Trend bestimmen; C (*line of direction*) Verlauf, *der.* 2 *v.i.* A (*take a course*) verlaufen; B (*fig.: move*) sich entwickeln; ~ **upward** steigen

**trendily** /'trendɪlɪ/ *adv.* (*Brit. coll.*) modisch

**trendiness** /'trendɪnɪs/ *n., no pl.* (*Brit. coll.*) modische Art

**'trendsetter** *n.* Trendsetter, *der*

**trendy** /'trendɪ/ (*Brit. coll.*) 1 *adj.* modisch; Schickimicki‹kneipe, -wohngegend› (*ugs.*); fortschrittlich-modern ‹Geistlicher, Lehrer›. 2 *n.* Schickimicki, *der* (*ugs.*)

**trepidation** /trepɪ'deɪʃn/ *n.* Beklommenheit, *die;* **with some** ~, **not without** ~: ziemlich beklommen; **wait in** ~: voller Beklommenheit warten; **a look of** ~: ein banger Blick

**trespass** /'trespəs/ 1 *v.i.* A ~ **on** unerlaubt betreten ‹Grundstück›; eingreifen in (+ *Akk.*) ‹jmds. Rechte›; **'no** ~**ing'** „Betreten verboten"; ~ **on sb.'s preserve** (*fig.*) sich in jmds. Angelegenheiten (*Akk.*) einmischen; ~ **on sb.'s time/privacy** (*fig.*) jmds. Zeit über Gebühr in Anspruch nehmen/jmds. Privatsphäre verletzen; B (*literary/arch.: offend*) freveln (*geh. veralt.*) (**against** an + *Dat.*); **as we forgive those who** ~ **against us** (*Relig.*) wie wir vergeben unseren Schuldigern. 2 *n.* A **forgive us our** ~**es** (*Relig.*) vergib uns unsere Schuld; B (*Law*) (*on land*) Hausfriedensbruch, *der;* (*on a person*) ≈ Körperverletzung, *die;* (*on goods*) ≈ Eigentumsdelikt, *das*

**trespasser** /'trespəsə(r)/ *n.* Unbefugte, *der/die;* **'**~**s will be prosecuted'** „Betreten verboten, Zuwiderhandlungen werden verfolgt"; ~ **on sb.'s land** Person, die unerlaubt jmds. Land betritt

**tress** /tres/ *n.* (*literary/arch.*) Haarstrang, *der;* (*curly*) Locke, *die;* **she combed her** ~**es** sie kämmte ihr [langes] Haar

**trestle** /'tresl/ *n.* A [Auflager]bock, *der;* B ~**[ table]** Tapeziertisch, *der*

**trews** /tru:z/ *n. pl.* (*Brit.*) *eng anliegende Hose [im Schottenmuster]*

**triad** /'traɪæd/ *n.* A Triade, *die;* Dreiheit, *die;* B (*Mus.*) Dreiklang, *der*

**trial** /'traɪəl/ *n.* A (*Law*) [Gerichts]verfahren, *das;* **be on** ~ **[for murder]** [wegen Mordes] angeklagt sein; **go on** ~ **[for one's life]** [wegen eines Verbrechens, auf das die Todesstrafe steht,] vor Gericht gestellt werden; **bring sb. to** ~, **put sb. on** ~: jmdm. den Prozess machen (**for** wegen); **the case was brought to** ~: der Fall wurde vor Gericht verhandelt; B (*testing*) Test, *der;* **subject sth. to further** ~: weitere Tests mit etw. durchführen; **be given** ~**s** getestet werden; **sea** ~ (*Naut.*) Probefahrt, *die;* **employ sb. on** ~: jmdn. probeweise einstellen; **be on** ~ ‹Person:› in der Probezeit sein; ‹Maschine:› getestet werden; **give sb. a** ~: es mit jmdm. versuchen; **give sth. a** ~: etw. ausprobieren; **[by]** ~ **and error** [durch] Ausprobieren; ~ **of strength** Kraftprobe, *die;* C (*trouble*) Prüfung, *die* (*geh.*); Problem, *das;* **find sth. a** ~: etw. als lästig empfinden; **be a** ~ **to sb.** jmdm. zu schaffen machen; **that child is a real** ~: das Kind ist eine richtige Plage; D (*Sport*) (*competition*) Prüfung, *die;* (*for selection*) Testspiel, *das.* ⇒ *also* **jury** A; **tribulation** A

**trial:** ~ **'balance** *n.* (*Bookk.*) Probebilanz, *die;* ~ **match** ⇒ **trial** D; ~ **pack** *n.* Probepackung, *die;* ~ **'run** *n.* A (*of car*) Testfahrt, *die;* (*of machine*) Probelauf, *der;* B (*fig.*) Probelauf, *der;* **have a** ~ **run of sth., give sth. a** ~ **run** etw. testen

**triangle** /'traɪæŋgl/ *n.* A Dreieck, *das;* ⇒ *also* **eternal** A; B (*Mus.*) Triangel, *das od. der*

**triangular** /traɪ'æŋgjʊlə(r)/ *adj.* A dreieckig; dreiseitig ‹Pyramide›; B (*between three persons etc.*) Dreier‹beziehung, -wettbewerb›

**triangulate** /traɪ'æŋgjʊleɪt/ *v.t.* (*Surv.*) triangulieren

**triangulation** /traɪæŋgjʊ'leɪʃn/ *n.* (*Surv.*) Triangulation, *die*

**Triassic** /traɪ'æsɪk/ (*Geol.*) 1 *adj.* Trias-. 2 Trias, *die*

**triathlon** /traɪ'æθlɒn/ *n.* Triathlon, *das od. der*

**tribal** /'traɪbl/ *adj.* Stammes-

**tribalism** /'traɪbəlɪzm/ *n.* Tribalismus, *der* (*fachspr.*)

**tribalistic** /traɪbə'lɪstɪk/ *adj.* Stammes-; tribalistisch (*fachspr.*)

**tribe** /traɪb/ *n.* A Stamm, *der;* B (*derog.*) Bande, *die* (*abwertend*); C (*Biol.*) Tribus, *die;* D *in pl.* (*joc.: large numbers*) Horde, *die;* **whole** ~**s of children** ganze Horden von Kindern

**tribesman** /'traɪbzmən/ *n., pl.* **tribesmen** /'traɪbzmən/ Stammesangehörige, *der*

**tribulation** /trɪbjʊ'leɪʃn/ *n.* A (*great affliction*) Kummer, *der;* **bring sb.** ~: jmdm. Kummer bereiten; **trials and** ~**s** Probleme und Sorgen; B (*cause of trouble etc.*) **be a** ~ **to sb.** jmdm. zur Last fallen

**tribunal** /traɪ'bju:nl, trɪ'bju:nl/ *n.* A Schiedsgericht, *das;* (*court of justice*) Gericht, *das;* ⇒ *also* **rent tribunal**; B (*fig.*) Tribunal, *das*

**tribune**[1] /'trɪbju:n/ *n.* (*platform*) [Redner]tribüne, *die*

**tribune**[2] *n.* (*Hist.*) ~ **[of the people]** Volkstribun, *der*

**tributary** /'trɪbjʊtərɪ/ 1 *adj.* A (*paying tribute*) tributpflichtig; B ~ **river** (*of larger river*) Nebenfluss, *der;* (*of lake, stream, etc.*) Zufluss, *der.* 2 *n.* A (*river*) (*flowing into larger river*) Nebenfluss, *der;* (*flowing into lake, stream, etc.*) Zufluss, *der;* B (*State*) tributpflichtiger Staat

**tribute** /'trɪbju:t/ *n.* A (*regard*) Tribut, *der* (**to** an + *Akk.*); **pay** ~ **to sb./sth.** jmdm./einer Sache den schuldigen Tribut zollen (*geh.*); **in silent** ~: in stiller Ehrerbietung; **floral** ~**s** Blumen [als Zeichen der Anerkennung]; (*to deceased person*) Blumen und Kränze; **as a** ~ **to his work** zur Würdigung seiner Arbeit; **she is a** ~ **to her teacher/trainer** sie macht ihrem Lehrer/Trainer alle Ehre; B (*payment*) Tribut, *der*

**trice** /traɪs/ *n.* **in a ~:** im Handumdrehen

**tricentenary** /traɪsen'ti:nərɪ, traɪsen'tenərɪ/ ⇒ **tercentenary**

**trichinosis** /trɪkɪ'nəʊsɪs/ *n.* (*Med.*) Trichinose, *die*

**trichloride** /traɪ'klɔ:raɪd/ *n.* (*Chem.*) Trichlorid, *das*

**trick** /trɪk/ ❶ *n.* Ⓐ Trick, *der;* **I suspect some ~:** es könnte ein Trick sein; **it was all a ~:** das war [alles] nur Bluff; **it was such a shabby ~ [to play on her]** es war [ihr gegenüber] eine derartige Gemeinheit *od.* dermaßen gemein; Ⓑ (*feat of skill etc.*) Kunststück, *das;* **try every ~ in the book** es mit allen Tricks probieren; **he never misses a ~** (*fig.*) ihm entgeht nichts; **that should do the ~** (*coll.*) damit dürfte es klappen (*ugs.*); **know a ~ worth two of that** etwas viel Besseres wissen; Ⓒ (*knack*) **get** *or* **find the ~ [of doing sth.]** den Dreh finden[, wie man etw. tut]; Ⓓ **how's ~s?** (*coll.*) was macht die Kunst? (*ugs.*); Ⓔ (*mannerism*) Eigenart, *die;* **have a ~ of doing sth.** die Eigenart haben, etw. zu tun; Ⓕ (*prank*) Streich, *der;* **play a ~ on sb.** jmdm. einen Streich spielen; **my hearing aid is playing ~s on me again** mein Hörgerät spielt mal wieder verrückt (*ugs.*); **be up to one's [old] ~s again** immer noch auf dieselbe Tour reisen (*ugs.*); **be up to sb.'s ~s** wissen, was jmd. im Schilde führt; **~ or treat** Trick-or-Treat, *das* (*Kinderspiel*); Ⓖ (*illusion*) **~ of vision/lighting/the light** Augentäuschung, *die;* Ⓗ (*Cards*) Stich, *der;* **take a ~:** einen Stich machen; Ⓘ (*prostitute's customer*) Freier, *der.* ⇒ *also* **bag** 1 A; **trade** 1 A.
❷ *v.t.* täuschen; hereinlegen; **~ sb. into doing sth.** jmdn. mit einem Trick *od.* einer List dazu bringen, etw. zu tun; **~ sb. out of/into sth.** jmdm. etw. ablisten.
❸ *adj.* **~ photograph** Trickaufnahme, *die;* **~ photography** Trickfotografie, *die;* **~ question** Fangfrage, *die*

**~ 'out, ~ 'up** *v.t.* schmücken; **~ oneself out** *or* **up** sich herausputzen (**in** mit)

**trick 'cyclist** *n.* Ⓐ Kunstradfahrer, *der*/-fahrerin, *die;* Ⓑ (*joc.: psychiatrist*) Seelendoktor, *der*/-doktorin, *die* (*ugs. scherzh.*)

**trickery** /'trɪkərɪ/ *n.* [Hinter]list, *die;* **piece of ~:** List, *die;* Trick, *der*

**trickiness** /'trɪkɪnɪs/ *n., no pl.* Verzwicktheit, *die* (*ugs.*)

**trickle** /'trɪkl/ ❶ *n.* Rinnsal, *das* (*geh.*) (**of** von); **in a ~:** als Rinnsal; **a ~ of rain ran down the window** Regenwasser rann am Fenster hinunter; **there was a ~ of people leaving the room** (*fig.*) einige wenige Menschen verließen nacheinander den Raum; **the ~ of people leaving the hall swelled to a flood** (*fig.*) erst leerte sich die Halle nur langsam, doch dann strömten die Menschen hinaus; **supplies of food have shrunk to a ~** (*fig.*) die Versorgung mit Nahrungsmitteln ist fast versiegt.
❷ *v.i.* rinnen; (*in drops*) tröpfeln; (*fig.*) ‹Ball:› langsam rollen; **~ out** ‹Zuschauer:› nach und nach [hinaus]gehen; **~ through** *or* **out** ‹Informationen:› durchsickern.
❸ *v.t.* tröpfeln

**'trickle charger** *n.* (*Electr.*) Erhaltungslader, *der*

**trickster** /'trɪkstə(r)/ *n.* Schwindler, *der*/Schwindlerin, *die*

**tricky** /'trɪkɪ/ *adj.* Ⓐ (*full of difficulties*) verzwickt (*ugs.*); **it is ~ doing sth.** es ist gar nicht so einfach, etw. zu tun; Ⓑ (*crafty*) raffiniert; trickreich ‹Spieler›

**tricolour** (*Brit.; Amer.:* **tricolor**) /'trɪkələ(r), 'traɪkʌlə(r)/ *n.* Trikolore, *die*

**tricorne** /'traɪkɔ:n/ *n., adj.* **~ [hat]** Dreispitz, *der*

**tricot** /'trɪkəʊ, 'tri:kəʊ/ *n.* Ⓐ (*hand-knitted woollen fabric*) Wollgestrick, *das;* Ⓑ (*plain-knitted cloth*) Jerseystoff, *der;* Ⓒ (*ribbed woollen cloth*) Trikot[stoff], *der*

**tricycle** /'traɪsɪkl/ ❶ *n.* Dreirad, *das.* ❷ *v.i.* Dreirad fahren

**trident** /'traɪdənt/ *n.* dreizackiger Fischspeer; (*held by Britannia etc.*) Dreizack, *der*

**Tridentine** /trɪ'dentaɪn/ *adj.* tridentinisch

**tried** ⇒ **try** 2, 3

**triennial** /traɪ'enɪəl/ *adj.* Ⓐ (*lasting three years*) dreijährig; Ⓑ (*once every three years*) dreijährlich

**triennially** /traɪ'enɪəlɪ/ *adv.* alle drei Jahre

**trier** /'traɪə(r)/ *n.* **he's a real ~:** er wirft die Flinte nicht so schnell ins Korn; **but at least he's a ~:** aber er gibt sich (*Dat.*) wenigstens Mühe

**Trieste** /tri:'est/ *pr. n.* Triest (*das*)

**trifle** /'traɪfl/ ❶ *n.* Ⓐ (*Brit. Gastron.*) Trifle, *das;* Ⓑ (*thing of slight value*) Kleinigkeit, *die;* **the merest ~:** die geringste Kleinigkeit; **it's only a ~:** es ist nichts Besonderes; Ⓒ (*small amount of money*) Kleinigkeit, *die;* **it only costs a ~:** es kostet so gut wie nichts; Ⓓ **a ~ tired/angry** *etc.* ein bisschen müde/böse *usw.* ❷ *v.i.* tändeln

**~ a'way** *v.t.* vergeuden

**~ with** *v.i.* spielen mit ‹jmds. Gefühlen›; nicht ernst genug nehmen ‹Person›; **he is not a person you can ~ with** er lässt nicht mit sich spaßen

**trifling** /'traɪflɪŋ/ *adj.* unbedeutend ‹Angelegenheit, Irrtum›; lächerlich ‹Gedanke›; gering ‹Gefahr, Wert›; [lächerlich] gering ‹Summe›; **~ objects/gifts** Kleinigkeiten

**trifocal** /traɪ'fəʊkl/ (*Optics*) ❶ *adj.* Trifokal-. ❷ *n. in pl.* Trifokalgläser *Pl.*

**triforium** /traɪ'fɔ:rɪəm/ *n., pl.* **triforia** /traɪ'fɔ:rɪə/ (*Archit.*) Triforium, *das* (*fachspr.*)

**trigger** /'trɪgə(r)/ ❶ *n.* Ⓐ (*of gun*) Abzug, *der;* (*of machine*) Drücker, *der;* **pull the ~:** abdrücken; (*fig.*) den Startschuss geben; **be quick on the ~** (*fig.*) prompt reagieren; Ⓑ (*that sets off reaction*) Auslöser, *der.* ❷ *v.t.* **~ [off]** auslösen

**'trigger-happy** *adj.* schießwütig; (*fig.*) kriegslüstern ‹General, Politiker›

**trigonometric** /trɪgənə'metrɪk/, **trigonometrical** /trɪgənə'metrɪkl/ *adj.* (*Math.*) trigonometrisch

**trigonometry** /trɪgə'nɒmɪtrɪ/ *n.* (*Math.*) Trigonometrie, *die*

**trike** /traɪk/ *n.* (*coll.*) Dreirad, *das*

**trilateral** /traɪ'lætərl/ ❶ *adj.* (*having three sides*) dreiseitig; (*involving three parties also*) trilateral (*geh.*). ❷ *n.* Dreieck, *das*

**trilby** /'trɪlbɪ/ *n.* (*Brit.*) **~ [hat]** Klapprandhut, *der;* Herrenhut, *der*

**trilingual** /traɪ'lɪŋgwəl/ *adj.* dreisprachig

**trill** /trɪl/ ❶ *n.* Ⓐ Trillern, *das;* Ⓑ (*Mus.*) Triller, *der.* ❷ *v.i.* trillern. ❸ *v.t.* rollen ‹r›

**trillion** /'trɪljən/ *n.* ▶ 1352 Ⓐ (*million million*) Billion, *die;* Ⓑ (*Brit. dated: million million million*) Trillion, *die*

**trilobite** /'traɪləbaɪt/ *n.* (*Palaeont.*) Trilobit, *der*

**trilogy** /'trɪlədʒɪ/ *n.* Trilogie, *die*

**trim** /trɪm/ ❶ *v.t.*, **-mm-:** Ⓐ schneiden ‹Hecke›; [nach]schneiden ‹Haar›; beschneiden (*auch fig.*) ‹Papier, Hecke, Docht, Budget›; **~ £100 off** *or* **from a budget** ein Budget um 100 Pfund kürzen; Ⓑ (*ornament*) besetzen (**with** mit); Ⓒ (*adjust balance of*) trimmen ‹Boot, Schiff, Flugzeug›; Ⓓ richtig stellen ‹Segel›; **~ one's sails before the wind** (*fig.*) sich nach der Decke strecken.
❷ *adj.* proper; gepflegt ‹Garten›; **keep sth. ~:** etw. in Ordnung halten.
❸ *n.* Ⓐ (*state of adjustment*) Bereitschaft, *die;* **find sth. in [perfect] ~:** etw. in [bester] Ordnung vorfinden; **everything was in good** *or* **proper ~:** alles war in bester Ordnung; **be in fine physical ~:** in guter körperlicher Verfassung sein; **get/be in ~** (*suitably dressed*) sich angemessen anziehen/angemessen angezogen sein; (*healthy*) sich trimmen/in Form *od.* fit sein; Ⓑ (*proper balance*) (*of ship*) Trimm, *der;* (*of aircraft*) [stabile] Fluglage; **be in/out of ~** ‹Schiff:› in/nicht in Trimm sein; ‹Flugzeug:› in stabiler/unstabiler Fluglage sein; Ⓒ (*cut*) Nachschneiden, *das;* **my hair needs a ~:** ich muss mir die Haare nachschneiden lassen; **give a hedge a ~:** eine Hecke nachschneiden; **just a ~, please** (*said to hairdresser*) nur nachschneiden, bitte; Ⓓ (*adornment*) ⇒ **trimming** A; Ⓔ (*of car*) Innenausstattung, *die;* (*on door panel*) Zierleiste, *die*

**~ a'way** ⇒ **~ off**

**~ 'down** *v.t.* (*fig.*) verringern; **her figure needed ~ming down** sie musste etwas für ihre Figur tun

**~ 'off** *v.t.* abschneiden; (*fig.*) abnehmen

**trimaran** /'traɪməræn/ *n.* (*Naut.*) Trimaran, *der*

**trimmer** /'trɪmə(r)/ *n.* Schneider, *der;* **hedge ~:** Heckenschere, *die*

**trimming** /'trɪmɪŋ/ *n.* Ⓐ (*decorative addition*) Verzierung, *die;* **lace ~s** Spitzenbesatz, *der;* Ⓑ *in pl.* (*coll.: accompaniments*) (*for main dish*) Beilagen; (*extra fittings on car*) Extras; **with all the ~s** mit allem Drum und Dran (*ugs.*); Ⓒ *in pl.* (*pieces cut off*) Abfall, *der* (*vom Zuschneiden*); (*of meat*) abgeschnittene Stücke

**trimness** /'trɪmnɪs/ *n., no pl.* adrettes Aussehen; **the ~ of her figure** ihre gepflegte Figur

**Trinidad** /'trɪnɪdæd/ *pr. n.* Trinidad (*das*)

**Trinidadian** /trɪnɪ'dædɪən/ ▶ 1340 ❶ *adj.* trinidadisch; **sb. is ~:** jmd. ist Trinidader/Trinidaderin. ❷ *n.* Trinidader, *der*/Trinidaderin, *die*

**Trinity** /'trɪnɪtɪ/ *n.* Ⓐ (*Theol.*) **the [Holy] ~:** die [Heilige] Dreifaltigkeit *od.* Dreieinigkeit *od.* Trinität; Ⓑ (*Eccl.*) **~ [Sunday]** Dreifaltigkeitssonntag, *der*

**Trinity 'term** *n.* (*Brit. Univ.*) Sommertrimester, *das*

**trinket** /'trɪŋkɪt/ *n.* Ⓐ (*piece of jewellery*) kleines, billiges Schmuckstück; (*on bracelet*) Anhänger, *der;* Ⓑ (*ornament*) Schmuckgegenstand, *der*

**trio** /'tri:əʊ/ *n., pl.* **~s** Trio, *das;* **string/piano ~** (*Mus.*) Streich-/Klaviertrio, *das*

**trioxide** /traɪ'ɒksaɪd/ *n.* (*Chem.*) Trioxid, *das*

**trip** /trɪp/ ❶ *n.* Ⓐ (*journey*) Reise, *die;* Trip, *der* (*ugs.*); (*shorter*) Ausflug, *der;* Trip, *der* (*ugs.*); **two ~s were necessary to transport everything** zwei Fahrten waren nötig, um alles zu transportieren; **make a ~ to London** nach London fahren; Ⓑ (*coll.: visit for stated purpose*) Gang, *der;* **I must make a ~ to the loo** ich muss mal aufs Klo; **make a ~ to the hairdresser's** zum Friseur gehen; Ⓒ (*coll.: drug-induced hallucinations*) Trip, *der* (*Jargon*); **[good/bad] ~ on LSD** [guter/schlechter] LSD-Trip. ⇒ *also* **round trip.**
❷ *v.i.*, **-pp-:** Ⓐ (*stumble*) stolpern (**on** über + *Akk.*); Ⓑ (*coll.: hallucinate while on drugs*) **~ [on LSD]** auf einem [LSD-]Trip sein; Ⓒ (*walk etc. with light steps*) trippeln; Ⓓ (*fig.: make a mistake*) einen Fehler machen.
❸ *v.t.*, **-pp-:** Ⓐ (*cause to stumble*) ⇒ **~ up** 2 A; Ⓑ (*release*) lichten ‹Anker›; betätigen ‹Schalter›; auslösen ‹Alarm›

**~ over** *v.t.* stolpern über (+ *Akk.*)

**~ 'up** ❶ *v.i.* Ⓐ (*stumble*) stolpern; Ⓑ (*fig.: make a mistake*) einen Fehler machen. ❷ *v.t.* Ⓐ (*cause to stumble*) stolpern lassen; Ⓑ (*cause to make a mistake*) aufs Glatteis führen (*fig.*)

**tripartite** /traɪ'pɑ:taɪt/ *adj.* Ⓐ (*in three parts*) **~ division** Dreiteilung, *die;* Ⓑ (*involving three parties*) trilateral (*geh.*); dreiseitig

**tripe** /traɪp/ *n.* Ⓐ Kaldaunen; (*individual piece*) Kaldaune, *die;* Ⓑ (*coll.: rubbish*) Quatsch, *der* (*ugs. abwertend*)

**triple** /'trɪpl/ ❶ *adj.* Ⓐ (*threefold*) dreifach; Ⓑ (*three times greater than*) **~ the ...:** der/die/das dreifache ...; **at ~ the speed** mit der dreifachen Geschwindigkeit *od.* dreimal so schnell; **~ the number of machines** dreimal so viele Maschinen. ❷ *n.* Dreifache, *das.* ❸ *v.i.* sich verdreifachen. ❹ *v.t.* verdreifachen

**triple: T~ Al'liance** *n.* (*Hist.*) Dreibund, *der;* **~ 'crown** *n.* Ⓐ (*Sport*) Triple Crown, *die;* dreifacher Triumph; Ⓑ (*Pope's tiara*) dreifache Krone; Tiara, *die;* **~ jump** *n.* (*Sport*) Dreisprung, *der*

t

**triplet** /ˈtrɪplɪt/ *n.* Ⓐ Drilling, *der;* Ⓑ (*Pros.*) Dreireim, *der;* Ⓒ (*Mus.*) Triole, *die*

**ˈtriple time** *n.* (*Mus.*) Dreiertakt, *der*

**Triplex** ® /ˈtrɪpleks/ *n.* ~ **[glass]** Verbundglas, *das*

**triplicate** /ˈtrɪplɪkət/ ❶ *adj.* dreifach. ❷ *n.* Drittausfertigung, *die;* Triplikat, *das* (*geh.*); **in ~:** in dreifacher Ausfertigung

**triply** /ˈtrɪplɪ/ *adv.* dreifach

**trip ˈmileage recorder** *n.* (*Motor Veh.*) Tageskilometerzähler, *der*

**tripod** /ˈtraɪpɒd/ *n.* Dreibein, *das;* [dreibeiniges] Stativ

**tripos** /ˈtraɪpɒs/ *n.* (*Brit.*) *Abschlussprüfung für den Honours-Degree an der Universität Cambridge*

**tripper** /ˈtrɪpə(r)/ *n.* (*Brit.*) Ausflügler, *der*/Ausflüglerin, *die*

**triptych** /ˈtrɪptɪk/ *n.* (*Art*) Triptychon, *das*

**ˈtripwire** *n.* Stolperdraht, *der*

**trisect** /traɪˈsekt/ *v.t.* dreiteilen

**trisyllabic** /traɪsɪˈlæbɪk/ *adj.* (*Ling.*) dreisilbig

**trisyllable** /traɪˈsɪləbl/ *n.* (*Ling. Pros.*) dreisilbiges Wort; **be a ~:** dreisilbig sein *od.* drei Silben haben

**trite** /traɪt/ *adj.*, **tritely** /ˈtraɪtlɪ/ *adv.* banal

**triteness** /ˈtraɪtnɪs/ *n., no pl.* Banalität, *die*

**tritium** /ˈtrɪtɪəm/ *n.* (*Chem.*) Tritium, *das*

**triumph** /ˈtraɪəmf, ˈtraɪʌmf/ ❶ *n.* Triumph, *der* (**over** über + *Akk.*); (*Rom. Ant.: procession also*) Triumphzug, *der;* **in ~:** im Triumph; **an expression of ~:** ein triumphierender Ausdruck. ❷ *v.i.* triumphieren (**over** über + *Akk.*)

**triumphal** /traɪˈʌmfl/ *adj.* triumphal ‹Erfolg›; Triumph‹bogen, -zug›

**triumphant** /traɪˈʌmfənt/ *adj.* Ⓐ (*victorious*) siegreich; ⇒ *also* **church** B; Ⓑ (*exulting*) triumphierend ‹Blick›; **~ shouts** Triumphgeschrei, *das;* **the look in her eyes was ~:** sie hatte einen triumphierenden Blick

**triumphantly** /traɪˈʌmfəntlɪ/ *adv.* triumphierend; **be ~ successful** einen triumphalen Erfolg haben

**triumvirate** /traɪˈʌmvərət/ *n.* Triumvirat, *das*

**trivalent** /traɪˈveɪlənt/ *adj.* (*Chem.*) dreiwertig

**trivet** /ˈtrɪvɪt/ *n.* Ⓐ (*in pressure cooker*) Dreifuß, *der;* Ⓑ (*Amer.: used under hot dishes*) [dreifüßiger] Untersetzer

**trivia** /ˈtrɪvɪə/ *n. pl.* Belanglosigkeiten

**trivial** /ˈtrɪvɪəl/ *adj.* Ⓐ belanglos; trivial (*geh.*); Ⓑ (*concerned only with ~ things*) oberflächlich ‹Person›

**triviality** /trɪvɪˈælɪtɪ/ *n.* Belanglosigkeit, *die;* Trivialität, *die* (*geh.*)

**trivialize** /ˈtrɪvɪəlaɪz/ *v.t.* auf eine belanglose Ebene bringen; trivialisieren (*geh.*)

**trivially** /ˈtrɪvɪəlɪ/ *adv.* oberflächlich

**trochaic** /trəˈkeɪɪk/ (*Pros.*) *adj.* trochäisch

**trochee** /ˈtrəʊkiː/ *n.* (*Pros.*) Trochäus, *der*

**trod, trodden** ⇒ **tread** 2, 3

**troglodyte** /ˈtrɒglədaɪt/ *n.* Ⓐ (*cave dweller*) Höhlenbewohner, *der*/-bewohnerin, *die;* Ⓑ (*fig.*) Einsiedler, *der*/Einsiedlerin, *die*

**troika** /ˈtrɔɪkə/ *n.* Troika, *die*

**Trojan** /ˈtrəʊdʒən/ ❶ *n.* Ⓐ (*fig.*) **work like a ~:** arbeiten wie ein Pferd; Ⓑ (*inhabitant of Troy*) Trojaner, *der*/Trojanerin, *die.* ❷ *adj.* trojanisch; **the ~ War** der Trojanische Krieg

**Trojan ˈHorse** *n.* Trojanisches Pferd (*geh.*); (*fig. also*) Danaergeschenk, *das* (*geh.*)

**troll**[1] /trəʊl/ ❶ *v.t.* (*fish*) [mit der Schleppangel] fischen. ❷ *v.i.* (*fish*) [mit der Schleppangel] fischen (**for** *Akk.*)

**troll**[2] *n.* (*Mythol.*) Troll, *der*

**trolley** /ˈtrɒlɪ/ *n.* Ⓐ (*Brit.: on rails*) Draisine, *die;* Ⓑ (*Brit.: for serving food*) Servierwagen, *der;* Ⓒ (*Brit.*) **[supermarket] ~:** Einkaufswagen, *der;* Ⓓ ⇒ **luggage trolley;** Ⓔ (*Amer.*) **~[ car]** Straßenbahn, *die;* Ⓕ **he's off his ~** (*coll.: insane*) bei ihm ist eine Schraube locker (*salopp*)

**ˈtrolley bus** *n.* (*Brit.*) Oberleitungsomnibus, *der*

**trollop** /ˈtrɒləp/ *n.* Ⓐ (*slut*) Schlampe, *die;* Ⓑ (*prostitute*) Dirne, *die*

**trolly** ⇒ **trolley**

**trombone** /trɒmˈbəʊn, ˈtrɒmbəʊn/ *n.* Posaune, *die*

**trombonist** /trɒmˈbəʊnɪst/ *n.* ▸**1261** Posaunist, *der*/Posaunistin, *die*

**trompe-l'œil** /trɒmpˈlɔiː/ (*Art*) ❶ *n.* Trompe-l'œil, *das od. der.* ❷ *adj.* Trompe-l'œil-

**troop** /truːp/ ❶ *n.* Ⓐ *in pl.* Truppen; **our best ~s** unsere besten Soldaten; Ⓑ (*of cavalry*) Schwadron, *die;* (*artillery and armour*) Batterie, *die;* Ⓒ (*assembled company*) Schar, *die;* Ⓓ (*of Scouts*) ≈ Gruppe, *die.* ⇒ *also* **household troops.** ❷ *v.i.* strömen; (*in an orderly fashion*) marschieren; **~ in/out** hinein-/hinausströmen. ❸ *v.t.* **~ing the colour[s]** (*Brit.*) Fahnenparade, *die*

**ˈtroop carrier** *n.* Truppentransporter, *der*

**trooper** /ˈtruːpə(r)/ *n.* Ⓐ (*soldier*) einfacher Soldat; **swear like a ~** (*coll.*) wie ein Fuhrmann fluchen (*ugs.*); Ⓑ (*Amer.: policeman*) Polizist, *der*

**ˈtroopship** *n.* (*Mil.*) Truppentransporter, *der*

**trope** /trəʊp/ *n.* (*Rhet.*) Trope, *die* (*fachspr.*)

**trophy** /ˈtrəʊfɪ/ *n.* Ⓐ Trophäe, *die;* Ⓑ (*competition*) **T~:** ≈ Pokal, *der*

**tropic** /ˈtrɒpɪk/ *n.* **the T~s** (*Geog.*) die Tropen; **the ~ of Cancer/Capricorn** (*Astron., Geog.*) der Wendekreis des Krebses/Steinbocks

**tropical** /ˈtrɒpɪkl/ *adj.* tropisch; Tropen‹krankheit, -kleidung›

**tropical: ~ ˈmedicine** *n.* Tropenmedizin, *die;* **~ ˈrainforest** *n.* tropischer Regenwald

**troposphere** /ˈtrɒpəsfɪə(r), ˈtrəʊpəsfɪə(r)/ *n.* Troposphäre, *die*

**trot** ❶ *n.* Ⓐ (*action of ~ting*) Trab, *der;* **at a ~:** im Trab; Ⓑ (*journey on horseback*) Ausritt, *der;* Ⓒ (*coll.*) **on the ~** (*in succession*) hintereinander; **every weekend for five weeks on the ~:** an fünf Wochenenden hintereinander; **be on the ~:** auf Trab sein (*ugs.*); **keep sb. on the ~** (*continually busy*) jmdn. auf Trab halten (*ugs.*); Ⓓ **have the ~s** (*sl.: diarrhoea*) Dünnpfiff haben (*salopp*). ❷ *v.i.*, **-tt-:** Ⓐ traben; Ⓑ (*coll.: go*) traben (*ugs.*); **~ along now** geh jetzt. ❸ *v.t.*, **-tt-** traben lassen ‹Pferd›

**~ ˈout** *v.t.* (*fig. coll.*) Ⓐ (*produce for approval*) vorführen; Ⓑ (*produce unthinkingly*) kommen mit (*ugs.*)

**Trot** /trɒt/ *n.* (*coll.: Trotskyist*) Trotzkist, *der*/Trotzkistin, *die*

**troth** /trəʊθ/ *n.* (*arch.*) Ⓐ **in ~, by my ~:** bei meiner Ehre!; Ⓑ (*faith*) Treue, *die;* **plight one's ~:** das Eheversprechen geben

**Trotskyism** /ˈtrɒtskɪɪzm/ *n.* Trotzkismus, *der*

**Trotskyist** /ˈtrɒtskɪɪst/, **Trotskyite** /ˈtrɒtskɪaɪt/ *ns.* Trotzkist, *der*/Trotzkistin, *die*

**trotter** /ˈtrɒtə(r)/ *n.* Ⓐ Fuß, *der;* **pigs' ~s** (*Cookery*) Schweinsfüße; Ⓑ (*horse*) Traber, *der*

**trotting** /ˈtrɒtɪŋ/ *n.* Trabrennen, *das*

**ˈtrotting race** *n.* Trabrennen, *das*

**troubadour** /ˈtruːbədʊə(r)/ *n.* Troubadour, *der*

**trouble** /ˈtrʌbl/ ❶ *n.* Ⓐ Ärger, *der;* Schwierigkeiten *Pl.;* **have ~ with sb./sth.** mit jmdm./etw. Ärger haben; **all his ~s** alle seine Probleme; **put one's ~s behind one** seine Probleme vergessen; **be out of ~:** aus den Schwierigkeiten heraus sein; **keep out of ~:** nicht [wieder] in Schwierigkeiten kommen; **in ~:** in Schwierigkeiten; **be in ~ with the police** Ärger mit der Polizei haben; **are you looking for ~?** du willst wohl Ärger [bekommen]?; **be in serious** *or* **real** *or* **a lot of ~ [over sth.]** [wegen einer Sache] in ernsten *od.* großen Schwierigkeiten sein; **get sb. into ~:** jmdn. in Schwierigkeiten bringen; **get a girl into ~** (*coll.*) einem Mädchen ein Kind machen (*ugs.*); **get into ~ [over sth.]** [wegen einer Sache] in Schwierigkeiten geraten; **get into ~ with the bank/law** Ärger *od.* Schwierigkeiten mit der Bank bekommen/mit dem Gesetz in Konflikt geraten; **there'll be ~ [if ...]** es wird Ärger geben[, wenn ...]; **what's** *or* **what seems to be the ~?** was ist denn?; was ist los? (*ugs.*); (*doctor's question to patient*) wo fehlts denn?; **you are asking for ~** (*coll.*) du machst dir nur selber Schwierigkeiten; **that's asking for ~** (*coll.*) das muss ja Ärger geben; **make** *or* **cause ~** (*cause disturbance*) Ärger machen (**about** wegen); (*cause disagreement*) Zwietracht säen; **make ~ for sb.** jmdm. Ärger *od.* Schwierigkeiten machen; **give sb. no ~:** jmdm. keine Schwierigkeiten bereiten *od.* machen; Ⓑ (*faulty operation*) Probleme; **engine/clutch/brake ~:** Probleme mit dem Motor/der Kupplung/der Bremse; **the engine is giving ~:** mit dem Motor stimmt etwas nicht; Ⓒ ▸**1232** (*disease*) **suffer from heart/liver ~:** Probleme mit dem Herz/der Leber haben; es am Herz/an der Leber haben (*ugs.*); **she's got some ~ with her back** ihr Rücken macht ihr zu schaffen; Ⓓ (*cause of vexation etc.*) Problem, *das;* **half the ~** (*fig.*) das größte Problem; **your ~ is that ...:** dein Fehler ist, dass ...; **their daughter is such a terrible ~ to them** ihre Tochter macht ihnen solche Sorgen; Ⓔ (*inconvenience*) Mühe, *die;* **it's more ~ than it's worth** es lohnt sich nicht; **dishwashers are more ~ than they are worth** mit Geschirrspülmaschinen hat man doch nur Ärger; **I don't want to put you to any ~:** ich möchte Ihnen keine Umstände machen; **not worth the ~:** nicht der Mühe wert; **give sb. no ~:** jmdm. keine Mühe machen; **take the ~ to do sth., go to the ~ of doing sth.** sich (*Dat.*) die Mühe machen, etw. zu tun; **go to** *or* **take a lot of/some ~:** sich (*Dat.*) sehr viel/viel Mühe geben; **please don't go to a lot of ~:** bitte machen Sie sich (*Dat.*) nicht allzu viel Umstände; **of course I'll help you — [it's] no ~ at all** natürlich helfe ich dir — das macht keine Umstände *od.* das ist nicht der Rede wert; **nothing was too much ~ for her** nichts war ihr zu viel; Ⓕ (*source of inconvenience*) **be a ~ [to sb.]** jmdm. zur Last fallen; **he won't be any ~:** er wird [Ihnen] keine Schwierigkeiten machen; **the children are no ~:** die Kinder sind keine Last; Ⓖ *in sing. or pl.* (*unrest*) Unruhen; Ⓗ **~ and strife** (*Brit. sl.: wife*) bessere Hälfte (*ugs. scherzh.*).

❷ *v.t.* Ⓐ (*agitate*) beunruhigen; **don't let it ~ you** mach dir deswegen keine Sorgen; **be ~d about money matters** Geldsorgen haben; Ⓑ (*inconvenience*) stören; **[I'm] sorry to ~ you** bitte entschuldigen Sie die Störung; **can I ~ you with one more question?** darf ich Ihnen noch eine letzte Frage stellen?; **my back ~s me sometimes** mein Rücken macht mir manchmal zu schaffen; Ⓒ (*in requests*) **may I ~ you to shut the door?** dürfte ich Sie bitten, die Tür zu schließen?; **may I ~ you to mind your own business?** (*iron.*) kümmern Sie sich gefälligst um Ihre eigenen Angelegenheiten!; **I'll ~ you to wipe your feet** (*iron.*) putz dir gefälligst die Schuhe ab.

❸ *v.i.* Ⓐ (*be disturbed*) sich (*Dat.*) Sorgen machen (**over** um); **don't ~ about it** mach dir deswegen keine Gedanken; Ⓑ (*make an effort*) sich bemühen; **don't ~ to explain/to get up/to see me out** du brauchst mir gar nichts zu erklären/bitte bleiben Sie sitzen/Sie brauchen mich nicht hinauszubringen

**troubled** /ˈtrʌbld/ *adj.* Ⓐ (*worried*) besorgt; **what are you so ~ about?** was macht dir denn solche Sorgen?; Ⓑ (*restless*) unruhig; schlecht ‹Traum›; Ⓒ (*agitated*) aufgewühlt; unruhig ‹Zeit›; bewegt ‹Geschichte›; ⇒ *also* **pour** 1 A

**trouble: ~-free** *adj.* problemlos; harmonisch ‹Ehe›; **~maker** *n.* Unruhestifter, *der*/-stifterin, *die;* **~shooter** *n.: jemand, der Störungen od. Probleme findet und beseitigt;* Troubleshooter, *der;* (*in disputes*) Vermittler, *der*/Vermittlerin, *die;* **~shooting** *n.: das Finden und Beseitigen von Störungen od. Problemen;* (*in disputes*) Vermittlung, *die*

**troublesome** /ˈtrʌblsəm/ *adj.* schwierig; lästig ‹Krankheit›

**ˈtrouble spot** *n.* Ⓐ Unruheherd, *der;* Ⓑ (*in machine*) Schwachstelle, *die*

**trough** /trɒf/ *n.* (A) Trog, *der;* **a drinking ~:** ein Wassertrog; (B) (*between waves*) Wellental, *das;* (C) (*Meteorol.*) Trog, *der;* **a ~ of low pressure** eine Tiefdruckrinne; (D) (*Econ., on graph*) Talsohle, *die*

**trounce** /traʊns/ *v.t.* (A) (*defeat*) vernichtend schlagen; (B) (*beat severely*) durchprügeln (*ugs.*)

**troupe** /tru:p/ *n.* Truppe, *die*

**trouper** /'tru:pə(r)/ *n.* Komödiant, *der*/Komödiantin, *die;* **an old ~** (*fig.*) ein alter Hase; **sb. is a good ~:** jmd. ist ein guter Kollege/eine gute Kollegin

**trouser**/'traʊzə/: **~ leg** *n.* Hosenbein, *das;* **~ pocket** *n.* Hosentasche, *die;* **~ press** *n.* Bügelpresse, *die;* Hosenbügler, *der*

**trousers** /'traʊzəz/ *n. pl.* **[pair of] ~:** Hose, *die;* Hosen *Pl.;* **catch sb. with his ~ down** (*fig. coll.*) jmdn. unvorbereitet treffen; **wear the ~** (*fig.*) die Hosen anhaben (*ugs.*)

**'trouser suit** *n.* (*Brit.*) Hosenanzug, *der*

**trousseau** /'tru:səʊ/ *n., pl.* **~s** *or* **~x** /'tru:səʊz/ Aussteuer, *die*

**trout** /traʊt/ *n., pl. same* Forelle, *die*

**trout: ~ farm** *n.* Forellenzuchtbetrieb, *der;* **~-fishing** *n.* Forellenfang, *der*

**trowel** /'traʊəl/ *n.* (A) Kelle, *die;* **lay it on with a ~** (*fig.*) [es] dick auftragen (*ugs. abwertend*); (B) (*Hort.*) Pflanzkelle, *die*

**troy** *n.* **~ [weight]** Troygewicht, *das*

**Troy** /trɔɪ/ *pr. n.* Troja (*das*)

**truancy** /'tru:ənsɪ/ *n.* [Schule]schwänzen, *das* (*ugs.*); unentschuldigtes Fernbleiben vom Unterricht; **be expelled for ~:** wegen Schwänzerei der Schule verwiesen werden

**truant** /'tru:ənt/ ❶ *n.* [Schul]schwänzer, *der*/-schwänzerin, *die* (*ugs.*); **play ~:** [die Schule] schwänzen (*ugs.*). ❷ *adj.* [schule]schwänzend (*ugs.*). ❸ *v.i.* schwänzen (*ugs.*); unentschuldigt fehlen

**truce** /tru:s/ *n.* Waffenstillstand, *der;* **call a ~:** einen Waffenstillstand schließen; ⇒ *also* **flag**[1] 1

**truck**[1] /trʌk/ ❶ *n.* (A) (*road vehicle*) Last[kraft]wagen, *der;* Lkw, *der;* (B) (*Brit. Railw.: wagon*) offener Güterwagen; (C) (*porter's barrow*) Gepäckkarren, *der;* (D) (*Railw.: bogie*) Drehgestell, *das;* (E) (*wheeled stand*) Hund, *der.* ❷ *v.t.* [per Lastwagen] transportieren. ❸ *v.i.* (*Amer.*) Lastwagen fahren

**truck**[2] *n.* (A) **have no ~ with sb./sth.** (*fig.*) mit jmdm./etw. nichts zu tun haben; (B) (*Amer.: produce*) Gemüse, *das;* **~ farm** Gemüseanbaubetrieb, *der*

**'truck driver** *n.* ▶ 1261 Lastwagenfahrer, *der*/-fahrerin, *die;* (*long-distance*) Fernfahrer, *der*/-fahrerin, *die*

**trucker** /'trʌkə(r)/ *n.* ▶ 1261 (*Amer.*) (A) (*market gardener*) Gemüsegärtner, *der*/-gärtnerin, *die;* (B) ⇒ **truck driver**

**trucking** /'trʌkɪŋ/ *n.* (*Amer.*) Lkw-Fahren, *das;* (*as business*) Lkw-Transport, *der*

**truckle** /'trʌkl/ *v.i.* **~ [to sb.]** [jmdm. gegenüber] klein beigeben; (*fawn*) [vor jmdm.] kriechen

**'truckle bed** *n.* Rollbett, *das*

**truck: ~load** *n.* Wagenladung, *die;* **sand by the ~load** ganze Wagenladungen Sand; **~ stop** (*Amer.*) ⇒ **transport café**

**truculence** /'trʌkjʊləns/, **truculency** /'trʌkjʊlənsɪ/ *n., no pl.* Aufsässigkeit, *die*

**truculent** /'trʌkjʊlənt/ *adj.* aufsässig

**truculently** /'trʌkjʊləntlɪ/ *adv.* aufsässig

**trudge** /trʌdʒ/ ❶ *v.i.* trotten; (*through mud, snow, etc.*) stapfen. ❷ *v.t.* entlangtrotten; (*through mud, snow, etc.*) entlangstapfen. ❸ *n.* [beschwerlicher] Fußmarsch

**true** /tru:/ ❶ *adj.*, **~r** /'tru:ə(r)/, **~st** /'tru:ɪst/ (A) (*in accordance with fact*) wahr; wahrheitsgetreu ‹Bericht, Beschreibung›; **is it ~ that ...?** stimmt es, dass ...?; **[only] too ~:** nur zu wahr; **that is too good to be ~:** das ist zu schön, um wahr zu sein; **sb. is too good to be ~:** jmd. ist einfach zu gut; **[that's] ~ [enough]** [das] stimmt; **..., it is ~: ...,** das stimmt; **you never spoke a ~r word** da hast du wirklich recht; **he is so rude, it isn't ~** (*coll.*) er ist unglaublich unhöflich; **come ~** ‹Traum, Wunsch:› Wirklichkeit werden, wahr werden; ‹Befürchtung, Prophezeihung:› sich bewahrheiten; (B) richtig ‹Vorteil, Einschätzung›; (*rightly so called*) eigentlich; **the frog is not a ~ reptile** der Frosch ist kein echtes Reptil; (C) (*not sham*) wahr; echt, wahr ‹Freund, Freundschaft, Christ›; **that's not a ~ antique** das ist keine echte Antiquität; (D) (*accurately conforming*) getreu ‹Wiedergabe›; **be ~ to sth.** einer Sache (*Dat.*) genau entsprechen; **~ to type** typisch; **~ to life** lebensecht; (E) (*loyal*) treu; **remain ~ to sth.** einer Sache (*Dat.*) treu bleiben; **~ to one's word** *or* **promise** getreu seinem Versprechen; (F) (*in correct position*) gerade ‹Pfosten›; (G) (*Geog.*) **~ north** geographischer Norden. ⇒ *also* **colour** 1 E, H; **form** 1 G.

❷ *n.* **out of [the] ~:** schief ‹Mauer, Pfosten, Räder›.

❸ *adv.* (A) (*truthfully*) aufrichtig ‹lieben›; **speak ~:** die Wahrheit sagen; **tell me ~:** sag mir die Wahrheit; (B) (*accurately*) gerade; genau ‹zielen›; (C) (*without variation*) ohne Veränderung.

❹ *v.t.* **~ [up]** richten; (*alter shape of*) zurichten; (*balance*) auswuchten ‹Rad›

**true: ~-blue** ❶ *adj.* in der Wolle gefärbt; **~-blue Tory** Erzkonservative, *der/die;* ❷ *n.* Hundertfünfzigprozentige, *der/die* (*abwertend*); **~-born** *adj.* echt; rechtmäßig ‹Erbe›; **~-life** *adj.* aus dem Leben gegriffen ‹Geschichte, Drama›; **this is a ~-life story** diese Geschichte hat das Leben geschrieben; **~ love** *n.* Geliebte, *der/die;* Schatz, *der;* **~-love knot** *n.*: *komplizierter Schleifenknoten, der das feste Band der Liebe symbolisiert*

**trueness** /'tru:nɪs/ *n., no pl.* (A) (*loyalty*) Treue, *die;* (B) (*conformity*) genaue Entsprechung; **~ to life** Lebensechtheit, *die;* (C) (*correctness*) Passgenauigkeit, *die;* (*of wheel*) rundes Laufen

**truffle** /'trʌfl/ *n.* Trüffel, *die od.* (*ugs.*) *der*

**truism** /'tru:ɪzm/ *n.* Binsenweisheit, *die*

**truly** /'tru:lɪ/ *adv.* (A) (*genuinely*) wirklich; **be ~ grateful** wirklich sehr *od.* aufrichtig dankbar sein; **he was first, ~ he was!** er war Erster, ganz bestimmt!; **~, I don't think he will make it** ehrlich gesagt, ich glaube nicht, dass er es schafft; (B) (*accurately*) zutreffend, richtig ‹darstellen, sagen›; (C) (*faithfully*) treu; ⇒ *also* **really**; **well**[2] 2 B; **yours** C

**trump**[1] /trʌmp/ ❶ *n.* (*Cards*) Trumpf, *der;* **play a ~** (*lit. or fig.*) einen Trumpf ausspielen; **turn up ~s** (*Brit. coll.*) (*turn out better than expected*) doch noch ein voller Erfolg werden; (*do the right thing*) die Situation retten; **as usual Bertha turned up ~s** wie immer hat Bertha wahre Wunder vollbracht; **hold all the ~s** (*fig.*) alle Trümpfe in der Hand haben *od.* halten. ❷ *v.t.* übertrumpfen. ❸ *v.i.* Trumpf spielen

**~ up** *v.t.* konstruieren; **~ed up charge** falsche Beschuldigung

**trump**[2] *n.* (*arch./poet.: trumpet*) Trompete, *die;* ⇒ *also* **last trump**

**'trump card** *n.* (*lit. or fig.*) Trumpf, *der;* **play one's ~** (*lit. or fig.*) seinen [größten *od.* stärksten] Trumpf ausspielen

**trumpery** /'trʌmpərɪ/ (*dated*) ❶ *n.* (A) (*worthless articles*) Krimskrams, *der* (*ugs.*); (B) (*rubbish*) Unsinn, *der;* **trumperies** Firlefanz, *der;* (C) (*worthless finery*) Tand, *der* (*veralt.*). ❷ *adj.* (*showy but worthless*) billig

**trumpet** /'trʌmpɪt/ ❶ *n.* (*Mus., Bot.*) Trompete, *die;* **~ blast** Trompetenstoß, *der;* ⇒ *also* **blow** 2 D. ❷ *v.t. & i.* trompeten

**'trumpet call** *n.* Trompetensignal, *das;* (*fig.*) Aufruf, *der*

**trumpeter** /'trʌmpɪtə(r)/ *n.* ▶ 1261 Trompeter, *der*/Trompeterin, *die*

**truncate** /trʌŋ'keɪt/ *v.t.* (A) stutzen ‹Baum, Spitze›; **~d cone/pyramid** stumpfer Kegel/stumpfe Pyramide; (B) (*fig.*) kürzen

**truncheon** /'trʌntʃn/ *n.* Schlagstock, *der*

**trundle** /'trʌndl/ *v.t. & i.* rollen

**trunk** /trʌŋk/ *n.* (A) (*of elephant etc.*) Rüssel, *der;* (B) (*large box*) Schrankkoffer, *der;* (C) (*of tree*) Stamm, *der;* (D) (*of human or animal body*) Rumpf, *der;* (E) (*Amer.: of car*) Kofferraum, *der;* (F) *in pl.* (*Brit.: shorts*) Unterhose, *die;* **[swimming] ~s** Badehose, *die;* (G) (*of nerve, artery, etc.*) Stamm, *der*

**trunk: ~ call** *n.* Ferngespräch, *das;* **~ line** *n.* (*Railw.*) Hauptstrecke, *die;* (*Teleph.*) Fernleitung, *die;* **~ road** *n.* (*Brit.*) Fernstraße, *die*

**truss** /trʌs/ ❶ *n.* (A) (*of roof etc.*) Gebälk, *das;* (*of bridge*) Sprengwerk, *das;* **~ joint** Fachwerkknoten, *der;* **~ post** Hängesäule, *die;* (B) (*of flowers etc.*) Büschel, *das;* (*of tomatoes*) Fruchttraube, *die* (*Landw.*); (C) (*Med.: belt*) Bruchband, *das;* (D) (*Brit.: of hay*) Bündel, *das;* Ballen, *der.* ❷ *v.t.* (A) (*tie up before cooking*) dressieren ‹Truthahn, Huhn›; (B) **~ [up]** fesseln

**trust** /trʌst/ ❶ *n.* (A) (*firm belief*) Vertrauen, *das;* **place** *or* **put one's ~ in sb./sth.** sein Vertrauen auf *od.* in jmdn./etw. setzen; **have [every] ~ in sb./sth.** [volles] Vertrauen zu jmdm./etw. haben; **our ~ is in God** wir vertrauen auf Gott; **I don't have any ~ in him** ich vertraue ihm nicht; ich habe kein Vertrauen zu ihm; (B) (*reliance*) **take sth. on ~:** etw. einfach glauben; (C) (*organization managed by trustees*) Treuhandgesellschaft, *die;* **[charitable] ~:** Stiftung, *die;* (D) (*body of trustees*) Treuhänder *Pl.;* (*of charitable ~*) [Stiftungs]beirat, *der;* Kuratorium, *das;* (E) (*organized association of companies*) Trust, *der;* (F) (*commercial credit*) **on ~:** auf Kredit; (G) (*responsibility*) **he failed in his ~:** er hat das in ihn gesetzte Vertrauen enttäuscht; **position of ~:** Vertrauensstellung, *die;* (H) (*obligation*) Verpflichtung, *die;* **public ~:** Verpflichtung der Öffentlichkeit gegenüber; (I) (*Law*) Treuhand[schaft], *die;* (*property*) Treugut, *das;* **hold in ~:** treuhänderisch verwalten. ⇒ *also* **brains trust**; **investment** A; **unit trust**.

❷ *v.t.* (A) (*rely on*) trauen (+ *Dat.*); vertrauen (+ *Dat.*) ‹Person›; **not ~ sb. an inch** jmdm. nicht über den Weg trauen; **you can ~ him to do his best** du kannst dich darauf verlassen, dass er sein Bestes tut; **a ~ed servant/friend** ein getreuer Diener/Freund (*geh.*); **he was widely ~ed by them** er genoss *od.* besaß das Vertrauen der meisten von ihnen; **he/what he says is not to be ~ed** er ist nicht vertrauenswürdig/auf das, was er sagt, kann man sich nicht verlassen; **~ sb. with sth.** jmdm. etw. anvertrauen; **~ 'you/'him!** *etc.* (*coll. iron.*) typisch!; **~ 'him to get it wrong!** er muss natürlich einen Fehler machen!; (B) (*hope*) hoffen; **I ~ he is not hurt?** er ist doch hoffentlich nicht verletzt?; (C) (*entrust*) anvertrauen (**to** *Dat.*).

❸ *v.i.* (A) **~ to** sich verlassen auf (+ *Akk.*); (B) (*believe*) **~ in sb./sth.** auf jmdn./etw. vertrauen

**trust: ~buster** *n.*: *jmd., der [auf der Grundlage der Antitrustgesetze] gegen Trusts vorgeht;* **~ company** *n.* Treuhandgesellschaft, *die;* **~ deed** *n.* Treuhandvertrag, *der*

**trustee** /trʌ'sti:/ *n.* (A) (*person holding property in trust; also fig.*) Treuhänder, *der*/Treuhänderin, *die;* **the Public T~** (*Brit.*) der staatliche Vermögensverwalter; (B) (*one appointed to manage institution*) Verwalter, *der;* Kurator, *der;* **Board of T~s** Vorstand, *der;* Kuratorium, *das;* (C) (*country supervising territory*) Treuhandmacht, *die*

**trusteeship** /trʌ'sti:ʃɪp/ *n.* (A) (*office*) Treuhänderschaft, *die;* (B) (*supervision of trust territory*) Treuhandschaft, *die;* Mandat, *das*

**trustful** /'trʌstfl/ *adj.*, **trustfully** /'trʌstfəlɪ/ *adv.* vertrauensvoll

**'trust fund** *n.* Treuhandvermögen, *das*

**trusting** /'trʌstɪŋ/ *adj.*, **trustingly** /'trʌstɪŋlɪ/ *adv.* vertrauensvoll

**trustworthiness** /'trʌstwɜ:ðɪnɪs/ *n., no pl.* Vertrauenswürdigkeit, *die*

**trustworthy** /'trʌstwɜ:ðɪ/ *adj.* vertrauenswürdig

**trusty** /'trʌstɪ/ ❶ *adj.* (*arch./joc.*) [ge]treu (*dichter.*). ❷ *n.* Kalfaktor, *der*

**truth** /tru:θ/ *n., pl.* **~s** /tru:ðz, tru:θs/ (A) *no pl.* Wahrheit, *die;* **the ~ of that is open to question** es ist fraglich, ob das zutrifft; **there is some/not a word of** *or* **no ~ in**

t

**that** es ist etwas Wahres/kein wahres Wort/ nichts Wahres daran; **in ~** (*literary*), **of a ~** (*arch.*) wahrlich (*geh.*); **B** (*what is true*) Wahrheit, *die;* (*principle*) Grundsatz, *der;* **tell the [whole] ~:** die [ganze] Wahrheit sagen; **the ~ is that I forgot** um ehrlich zu sein, ich habe es vergessen; **to tell the ~, ~ to tell** ehrlich gesagt. ⇒ *also* **moment** A; **out** 1 H

**'truth drug** *n.* Wahrheitsdroge, *die*

**truthful** /'tru:θfl/ *adj.* ehrlich; wahrheitsgetreu ‹Darstellung, Schilderung›; **be ~ about sth.** die Wahrheit über etw. (*Akk.*) sagen

**truthfully** /'tru:θfəlɪ/ *adv.* ehrlich

**truthfulness** /'tru:θflnɪs/ *n., no pl.* Wahrheitstreue, *die*

**try** /traɪ/ ❶ *n.* **A** (*attempt*) Versuch, *der;* **have a ~ at sth./doing sth.** etw. versuchen/versuchen, etw. zu tun; **at least he had a good ~:** er hat sich (*Dat.*) wenigstens Mühe gegeben; **give sb./sth. a ~:** jmdm. eine Chance geben/etw. einmal ausprobieren; **I'll give him another ~** (*ask him again for help, a favour, etc.*) ich versuche es noch einmal bei ihm; (*give him another chance*) ich versuche es noch einmal mit ihm; (*on telephone*) ich versuche noch einmal, ihn zu erreichen; **give it a ~:** es versuchen; **B** (*Rugby*) Versuch, *der;* **score two tries** zwei Versuche erzielen *od.* legen; **C** (*Amer. Footb.*) Versuch, noch einen Punkt zu erzielen.
❷ *v.t.* **A** (*attempt, make effort*) versuchen; **it's ~ing to rain** es tröpfelt ein wenig; **the sun is ~ing to come out** *or* **shine** es sieht so aus, als käme die Sonne bald heraus; **do ~ to be on time** bitte versuche, pünktlich zu sein; **it's no use ~ing to do sth.** es hat keinen Zweck zu versuchen, etw. zu tun; **I've given up ~ing to do sth.** ich versuche schon gar nicht mehr, etw. zu tun; **~ one's best** sein Bestes tun; **don't ~ anything!** keine Tricks!; **don't even ~ to excuse yourself** versuche erst gar nicht, dich zu entschuldigen; **B** (*test usefulness of*) probieren; **if the stain is difficult to remove, ~ soap and water** wenn der Fleck schwer zu entfernen ist, versuche *od.* probiere es doch mal mit Wasser und Seife; **I've tried all the bookshops for this book** ich habe in allen Buchhandlungen versucht, dieses Buch zu bekommen; **you can always ~ the supermarket** du kannst es auf jeden Fall mal im Supermarkt versuchen; **if you can't find it, ~ the top shelf** wenn du es nicht finden kannst, schau mal auf dem obersten Regal nach; **~ one's hand at sth.** sich an etw. (*Dat.*) versuchen; **~ shaking it!** probier es mal mit Schütteln!; **I'll ~ anything once** ich probiere alles einmal aus; **C** (*test*) auf die Probe stellen ‹Fähigkeit, Kraft, Mut, Geduld›; **~ the rope** ausprobieren, ob das Seil auch hält; **~ the door/window [to see if it's locked]** versuchen, die Tür/das Fenster zu öffnen[, um zu sehen, ob sie/es verschlossen ist]; **~ sb. in Sales** jmdn. zur Probe im Verkauf einsetzen; **be tried and found wanting** gewogen und zu leicht befunden werden; **these** *or* **such things are sent to ~ us** das sind die Prüfungen, die uns das Schicksal auferlegt; **D** (*Law.: take to trial*) **~ a case** einen Fall verhandeln; **~ sb. [for sth.]** jmdn. [wegen einer Sache] vor Gericht stellen; jmdm. [wegen einer Sache] den Prozess machen; **he was tried for murder** er stand wegen Mordes vor Gericht; **he was tried before a jury** er wurde vor ein Schwurgericht gestellt. ⇒ *also* **fall** 1 I; **size**[1] 1 A.
❸ *v.i.* es versuchen; **she wasn't even ~ing** sie hat sich (*Dat.*) überhaupt keine Mühe gegeben *od.* es gar nicht erst versucht; **it was not for want of ~ing** es lag nicht daran, dass er/sie *usw.* sich nicht bemüht hätte; **if at first you don't succeed, ~, ~, ~ again** wenn es dir nicht gleich gelingt, musst du es immer wieder versuchen; **you can't say I didn't ~:** du kannst nicht sagen, dass ich es nicht versucht hätte; **~ as he might** sosehr er sich auch bemühte; **~ and do sth.** (*coll.*) versuchen, etw. zu tun; **~ hard/harder** sich (*Dat.*) viel/mehr Mühe geben

**~ for** *v.t.* **A** (*compete for*) sich bemühen um ‹Arbeitsstelle, Stipendium›; kämpfen um ‹Sieg im Sport›; **~ for gold** es auf eine Goldmedaille abgesehen haben; **B** (*seek to reach*) **~ for the summit** den Gipfel in Angriff nehmen; **he had been ~ing so hard for it** er hatte so sehr darum gekämpft

**~ 'on** *v.t.* **A** anprobieren ‹Kleidungsstück›; **B** (*Brit. coll.*) **~ it on** provozieren; **don't ~ anything/it on with me** lege dich nicht mit mir an; ⇒ *also* **try-on**

**~ 'out** *v.t.* **~ sth./sb. out** etw. ausprobieren/ jmdm. eine Chance geben; **let's ~ him out in Sales** setzen wir ihn doch zur Probe im Verkauf ein; ⇒ *also* **try-out**

**trying** /'traɪɪŋ/ *adj.* **A** (*testing*) schwierig; **B** (*difficult to endure*) anstrengend; **be ~ for sb./sth.** jmdm./einer Sache sehr zusetzen (*ugs.*)

**try: ~-on** *n.* (*coll.*) **A** (*Brit. joke*) Scherz, *der;* (*lie*) Lüge, *die;* **it's just a ~-on** (*to discover whether sth. will be tolerated*) er/sie probiert nur aus, wie weit er/sie gehen kann; **B** (*of clothes*) Anprobe, *die;* **~-out** *n.* Erprobung, *die;* **give sth. a ~-out** etw. ausprobieren; **have a ~-out** ‹Maschine usw.:› ausprobiert werden; **would you like [to have] a ~-out?** möchten Sie mal probieren?; (*of vehicle*) möchten Sie eine Probefahrt machen?; **~sail** /'traɪsl/ *n.* (*Naut.*) Gaffelsegel, *das;* **~ square** *n.* Anschlagwinkel, *der*

**tryst** /trɪst/ *n.* (*arch./literary*) Stelldichein, *das* (*veralt.*); **keep/break ~:** zu einem Stelldichein gehen/nicht gehen; **make a ~:** sich zu einem Stelldichein verabreden

**tsar** /zɑ:(r)/ *n.* ▶ 1617 (*Hist.*) Zar, *der*

**tsarina** /zɑ:'ri:nə/ *n.* ▶ 1617 (*Hist.*) (*empress*) Zarin, *die;* (*tsar's wife*) Zariza, *die*

**tsarism** /'zɑ:rɪzm/ *n.* (*Hist.*) Zarentum, *das;* Zarismus, *der*

**tsarist** /'zɑ:rɪst/ (*Hist.*) ❶ *adj.* zaristisch. ❷ *n.* Zarist, *der*/Zaristin, *die*

**tsetse [fly]** /'tsetsɪ (flaɪ)/ *n.* Tsetsefliege, *die*

**T-shirt** *n.* T-Shirt, *das*

**tsp.**, *pl.* **~s** *abbr.* **teaspoon[s]** Teel.

**T-square** ⇒ **square** J

**TT** *abbr.* **A** **teetotal;** **B** **Tourist Trophy** *Motorradrennen auf der Insel Man*

**TU** *abbr.* **Trade Union**

**Tu.** *abbr.* ▶ 1056 **Tuesday** Di.

**tub** /tʌb/ *n.* **A** Kübel, *der;* **B** (*for ice cream etc.*) Becher, *der;* **C** (*Brit. coll.: bath*) Bad, *das;* **D** (*derog./joc.: boat*) Kahn, *der* (*ugs.*)

**tuba** /'tju:bə/ *n.* (*Mus.*) Tuba, *die*

**tubbiness** /'tʌbɪnɪs/ *n.* Rundlichkeit, *die;* (*of child also*) Pummeligkeit, *die* (*ugs.*)

**tubby** /'tʌbɪ/ *adj.* rundlich; pummelig (*ugs.*), rundlich ‹Kind›

**tube** /tju:b/ *n.* **A** (*for conveying liquids etc.*) Rohr, *das;* **be down the ~[s]** (*coll.*) am Ende sein (*ugs.*); **he was down the ~[s] to the tune of £270,000** (*coll.*) er saß mit Schulden in Höhe von 270 000 Pfund in der Tinte (*ugs.*); **go down the ~[s]** (*coll.*) den Bach runter gehen (*ugs.*); **B** (*small cylinder*) Tube, *die;* (*for sweets, tablets*) Röhrchen, *das;* **C** (*Anat., Zool.*) Röhre, *die;* **D** (*cathode-ray ~*) Röhre, *die;* (*coll.: television*) **watch the ~:** vor der Röhre sitzen (*ugs.*); **be on the ~:** im Fernsehen sein; **E** (*Amer.: thermionic valve*) Röhre, *die;* **F** (*Brit. coll.: underground railway*) U-Bahn, *die;* **G** ⇒ **inner ~**

**tubeless** /'tju:blɪs/ *adj.* schlauchlos ‹Reifen›

**tuber** /'tju:bə(r)/ *n.* (*Bot.*) Knolle, *die*

**tubercle** /'tju:bəkl/ *n.* (*Med.*) Tuberkel, *der*

**tubercular** /tju:'bɜ:kjʊlə(r)/ *adj.* (*Med.*) tuberkulös

**tuberculin** /tju:'bɜ:kjʊlɪn/ *n.* Tuberkulin, *das*

**tuberculin-'tested** *adj.* tuberkulingetestet

**tuberculosis** /tju:bɜ:kjʊ'ləʊsɪs/ *n., no pl.* ▶ 1232 (*Med.*) Tuberkulose, *die;* **pulmonary ~:** Lungentuberkulose, *die*

**tuberose** /'tju:bərəʊz/ *n.* (*Bot.*) Tuberose, *die*

**tube: ~ station** *n.* (*Brit. coll.*) U-Bahnhof, *der;* **~ train** *n.* (*Brit. coll.*) U-Bahn-Zug, *der*

**tubful** /'tʌbfʊl/ *n.* Kübel [voll], *der;* **a ~ of water** ein Kübel Wasser

**tubing** /'tju:bɪŋ/ *n.* Rohre *Pl.*

**'tub-thumper** *n.* Demagoge, *der*

**tubular** /'tju:bjʊlə(r)/ *adj.* **A** (*tube-shaped*) röhrenförmig; **B** (*made of ~ pieces*) Stahlrohr‹möbel, -stuhl›

**tubular 'bells** *n. pl.* Glockenspiel, *das*

**TUC** *abbr.* (*Brit.*) **Trades Union Congress**

**tuck** /tʌk/ ❶ *v.t.* **A** stecken; **he ~ed his legs under him** er schlug die Beine unter; **B** (*put ~s in*) Biesen nähen in (+ *Akk.*). ❷ *n.* **A** (*in fabric*) (*for decoration*) Biese, *die;* (*to shorten or tighten*) Abnäher, *der;* **B** *no pl., no indef. art.* (*Brit. Sch. coll.: food*) Erfrischungen [und Süßigkeiten]

**~ a'way** *v.t.* **A** wegstecken; **the house is ~ed away behind the trees** das Haus liegt versteckt hinter den Bäumen; **B** (*coll.: eat*) verputzen (*ugs.*); **she can certainly ~ it away** sie kann ganz schön was verputzen (*ugs.*)

**~ 'in** ❶ *v.t.* hineinstecken; **~ in the blankets** die Decken an den Seiten feststecken; **~ your shirt in!** steck dein Hemd in die Hose! ❷ *v.i.* (*coll.*) zulangen (*ugs.*); ⇒ *also* **tuck-in**

**~ into** *v.i.* (*coll.: eat*) **~ into sth.** sich (*Dat.*) etw. schmecken lassen

**~ 'up** *v.t.* **A** hochkrempeln ‹Ärmel, Hose›; hochnehmen ‹Rock›; **B** (*cover snugly*) zudecken; **be ~ed up [in bed]** zugedeckt [im Bett] sein

**'tuck box** *n.* (*Brit. Sch.*) Kiste [mit Süßigkeiten *usw.*]

**tucker**[1] /'tʌkə(r)/ *n.* (*Austral. coll.: food*) Futter, *das* (*ugs.*); **some ~:** etwas zu futtern (*ugs.*)

**tucker**[2] *v.t.* (*Amer.*) **~ [out]** (*coll.*) fix und fertig machen (*ugs.*); **be ~ed [out]** fix und fertig *od.* total groggy sein (*ugs.*)

**tuck: ~-in** *n.* (*Brit. coll.*) [reichliches] Essen; **they had a really good ~-in** sie hatten ordentlich was zu futtern (*ugs.*); **~ shop** *n.* (*Brit. Sch.*) *Laden für Erfrischungen, Süßigkeiten usw. in einer Schule*

**Tudor** /'tju:də(r)/ (*Brit. Hist.*) ❶ *n.* Tudor, *der/die.* ❷ *attrib. adj.* Tudor-

**Tudor: ~ 'rose** *n.* Tudorrose, *die;* **~ style** *n.* Tudorstil, *der*

**Tue., Tues.** *abbrs.* ▶ 1056 **Tuesday** Di.

**Tuesday** /'tju:zdeɪ, 'tju:zdɪ/ ▶ 1056 ❶ *n.* Dienstag, *der.* ❷ *adv.* (*coll.*) **she comes ~s** sie kommt dienstags. ⇒ *also* **Friday**

**tufa** /'tju:fə/ *n.* (*Geol.*) Sinter, *der*

**tuff** /tʌf/ *n.* (*Geol.*) Tuff, *der*

**tuft** /tʌft/ *n.* Büschel, *das;* **~ of grass/hair** Gras-/Haarbüschel, *das*

**tufted** /'tʌftɪd/ *adj.* **A** (*having tufts*) büschelig; **~ carpet** Tuftingteppich, *der;* **B** (*with tuft of feathers on head*) Hauben-; **~ duck** Reiherente, *die;* **~ puffin** Schopfhund, *der*

**tug** /tʌg/ ❶ *n.* **A** Ruck, *der;* **he felt a ~ on the fishingline** er spürte, wie etwas an der Angel zog; **he gave the rope a ~:** er zerrte am Seil; **~ of love [battle]** (*coll.*) *Streit bei der Ehescheidung, wem das Kind zugesprochen wird;* **~ of war** (*lit. or fig.*) Tauziehen, *das;* **B** **~ [boat]** Schlepper, *der;* **C** (*fig.: emotional pain*) **it was a ~:** es tat weh (*ugs.*); **she felt a big ~ at parting** der Abschied fiel ihr sehr schwer. ❷ *v.t.*, **-gg-** ziehen; schleppen ‹Boot›; **be ~ged this way and that** (*fig.*) hin- und hergerissen sein. ❸ *v.i.*, **-gg-** zerren (**at** an + *Dat.*); **~ at sb.'s heartstrings** (*fig.*) jmdm. das Herz zerreißen

**tuition** /tju:'ɪʃn/ *n.* Unterricht, *der;* **extra ~:** Nachhilfeunterricht, *der;* **~ fees** (*Sch.*) Schulgeld, *das;* (*Univ.*) Studiengebühren *Pl.;* (*for private ~*) Unterrichtshonorar, *das*

**tulip** /'tju:lɪp/ *n.* Tulpe, *die*

**'tulip tree** *n.* Tulpenbaum, *der*

**tulle** /tju:l/ *n.* (*Textiles*) Tüll, *der*

**tum** /tʌm/ *n.* (*joc.*) Bauch, *der*

**tumble** /'tʌmbl/ ❶ *v.i.* **A** (*fall suddenly*) stürzen; fallen; **~ off sth.** von etw. fallen; **B** (*move in headlong fashion*) stürzen; **~ into/out of sth.** in/aus etw. eilen; **~ into bed** ins Bett fallen; **C** ‹Preise usw.:› fallen; (*sharply*) stürzen. ❷ *v.t.* **A** (*fling headlong*)

t

schleudern; **B** (*rumple*) durcheinander bringen, zerzausen ‹Haar›. **3** *n.* Sturz, *der;* **she's taken [a bit of] a ~:** sie ist hingefallen

**~ on** *v.t.* (*chance on*) stolpern über (+ *Akk.*)

**~ 'over** *v.i.* hinfallen; ‹Kartenhaus:› umfallen

**~ to** *v.t.* (*Brit. coll.*) durchschauen

**tumble: ~bug** *n.* Kotkäfer, *der;* **~down** *adj.* verfallen; **~-drier** *n.* Wäschetrockner, *der;* **~-dry** *v.t.* im Automaten trocknen

**tumbler** /'tʌmblə(r)/ *n.* **A** (*glass*) (*short*) Whiskyglas, *das;* (*long*) Wasserglas, *das;* **B** (*in lock*) Zuhaltung, *die;* **C** ⇒ **tumble-drier; D** (*acrobat*) Bodenakrobat, *der*/-akrobatin, *die;* **E** (*pigeon*) Tümmler, *der*

**tumblerful** /'tʌmbləfʊl/ *n.* Glas [voll], *das;* **a ~ of water** ein Glas Wasser

**'tumbler switch** *n.* Kippschalter, *der*

**'tumbleweed** *n.* (*Amer.*) Steppenläufer, *der*

**tumbrel** /'tʌmbrl/, **tumbril** /'tʌmbrɪl/ *n.* (*Hist.*) Karren, *der*

**tumescence** /tjʊ:'mesəns/ *n.* Schwellung, *die*

**tumescent** /tju:'mesənt/ *adj.* anschwellend; **make ~:** anschwellen lassen

**tummy** /'tʌmɪ/ *n.* (*child lang./coll.*) Bäuchlein, *das;* **I've got an upset ~:** ich habe mir den Magen verdorben

**tummy: ~ ache** *n.* (*child lang./coll.*) Bauchweh, *das;* **~ button** *n.* (*child lang./coll.*) Bauchnabel, *der;* **~ upset** *n.* (*child lang./ coll.*) Magenverstimmung, *die*

**tumour** (*Brit.; Amer.:* **tumor**) /'tju:mə(r)/ *n.* Tumor, *der*

**tumult** /'tju:mʌlt/ *n.* **A** (*commotion, uproar*) Tumult, *der;* **be in ~:** sich in Aufruhr befinden; **B** (*confused state of mind*) Verwirrung, *die;* **his mind was in a ~:** er war innerlich in Aufruhr

**tumultuous** /tju:'mʌltjʊəs/ *adj.* **A** stürmisch ‹Empfang, Beifall›; **B** wild ‹Fluss, Sturm, Leidenschaft›

**tumulus** /'tju:mjʊləs/ *n., pl.* **tumuli** /'tju:mjʊlaɪ/ Tumulus, *der*

**tun** /tʌn/ *n.* Fass, *das*

**tuna** /'tju:nə/ *n., pl. same or* **~s A** (*fish*) Thunfisch, *der;* **B** (*as food*) **~[ fish]** Thunfisch, *der; attrib.* Thunfisch-

**tundra** /'tʌndrə/ *n.* (*Geog.*) Tundra, *die*

**tune** /tju:n/ **1** *n.* **A** (*melody*) Melodie, *die;* **change one's ~, sing another** *or* **a different ~** (*fig.*) (*behave differently*) sein Verhalten ändern; (*assume different tone*) einen anderen Ton anschlagen; **call the ~:** den Ton angeben; **B** (*correct pitch*) **sing in/out of ~:** richtig/falsch singen; **be in/out of ~** ‹Instrument:› richtig gestimmt/verstimmt sein; **C** (*fig.: agreement*) **be in/out of ~ with sth.** mit etw. in Einklang/nicht in Einklang stehen; **he doesn't feel in ~ with their attitudes/ideas** ihre Einstellungen/Vorstellungen sind ihm fremd; **D** (*amount*) **to the ~ of [£50,000]** sage und schreibe [50 000 Pfund].

**2** *v.t.* **A** (*Mus.: put in ~*) stimmen; **B** (*Radio, Telev.*) einstellen (**to** auf + *Akk.*); **stay ~d!** bleiben Sie auf dieser Welle!; **C** einstellen ‹Motor, Vergaser›; (*for more power*) frisieren ‹Motor, Auto›

**~ 'in** *v.i.* (*Radio, Telev.*) **~ in to a station** einen Sender einstellen; **~ in at five o'clock to hear the details** schalten Sie [Ihr Radio/Ihren Fernseher] um fünf Uhr ein, wenn Sie die Einzelheiten hören wollen; **~ in to** (*fig.*) sich einstellen auf (+ *Akk.*)

**~ 'up 1** *v.i.* [die Instrumente] stimmen. **2** *v.t.* einstellen

**tuneful** /'tju:nfl/ *adj.*, **tunefully** /'tju:nfəlɪ/ *adv.* melodisch

**tunefulness** /'tju:nflnɪs/ *n., no pl.* Melodik, *die*

**tuneless** /'tju:nlɪs/ *adj.*, **tunelessly** /'tju:nlɪslɪ/ *adv.* unmelodisch

**tunelessness** /'tju:nlɪsnɪs/ *n., no pl.* Mangel an Melodik

**tuner** /'tju:nə(r)/ *n.* **A** ▶ **1261** (*Mus.*) Stimmer, *der*/Stimmerin, *die;* **B** (*knob etc.*) Einstellknopf, *der;* Tuner, *der* (*Technik*); **C** (*radio*) Tuner, *der*

**tungsten** /'tʌŋstən/ *n.* Wolfram, *das*

**tunic** /'tju:nɪk/ *n.* **A** (*of soldier, policeman*) Uniformjacke, *die;* (*of schoolgirl*) Kittel, *der;* **B** (*Fashion*) Kasack, *der;* **C** (*in ancient Greece*) Chiton, *der;* (*in ancient Rome*) Tunika, *die*

**tuning** /'tju:nɪŋ/ *n.* **A** (*Mus.*) Stimmen, *das;* **B** (*Radio*) Einstellen, *das;* **C** (*Motor Veh.*) Einstellen, *das;* (*to increase power*) Frisieren, *das;* Tuning, *das;* **the engine needs ~:** der Motor muss eingestellt werden

**tuning: ~ fork** *n.* (*Mus.*) Stimmgabel, *die;* **~ peg, ~ pin** *ns.* (*Mus.*) Wirbel, *der*

**Tunis** /'tju:nɪs/ *pr. n.* ▶ **1626** Tunis (*das*)

**Tunisia** /tju:'nɪzɪə/ *pr. n.* Tunesien (*das*)

**Tunisian** /tju:'nɪzɪən/ ▶ **1340 1** *adj.* tunesisch; **sb. is ~:** jmd. ist Tunesier/Tunesierin. **2** *n.* Tunesier, *der*/Tunesierin, *die*

**tunnel** /'tʌnl/ **1** *n.* **A** Tunnel, *der;* (*dug by animal*) Gang, *der;* **[the] light at the end of the ~** (*fig.*) [das] Licht am Ende des Tunnels; **B** (*Motor Veh.*) **[transmission] ~:** Kardantunnel, *der;* **C wind ~:** Windkanal, *der.* **2** *v.i.*, (*Brit.*) **-ll-:** einen Tunnel graben; **~ under sth.** etw. untertunneln; **~ through sth.** durch etw. (*Akk.*) einen Tunnel graben. **3** *v.t.*, (*Brit.*) **-ll-: ~ one's way out** sich (*Dat.*) einen Weg nach draußen graben

**'tunnel vision** *n.* Röhrengesichtsfeld, *das* (*Med.*); (*fig.*) enges Blickfeld

**tunny** /'tʌnɪ/ *n.* (*Zool.*) Thunfisch, *der*

**tup** /tʌp/ *n.* (*Brit.*) Widder, *der*

**tuppence** /'tʌpəns/ ⇒ **twopence**

**tuppenny** /'tʌpənɪ/ ⇒ **twopenny**

**turban** /'tɜ:bən/ *n.* Turban, *der*

**turbaned** /'tɜ:bənd/ *adj.* mit einem Turban [auf dem Kopf] *nachgestellt*

**turbid** /'tɜ:bɪd/ *adj.* **A** (*muddy*) trüb[e]; dicht ‹Nebel, Rauchwolke›; **B** (*fig.: confused*) wirr

**turbidity** /tɜ:'bɪdɪtɪ/ *n., no pl.* **A** (*muddiness*) Trübheit, *die;* **B** (*fig.: confusion*) Verworrenheit, *die*

**turbine** /'tɜ:baɪn/ *n.* Turbine, *die*

**turbo** /'tɜ:bəʊ/ *n.* Turbo, *der*

**turbo: ~charged** *adj.* mit Turbolader *nachgestellt;* **~charger** *n.* Turbolader, *der;* **~jet** *n.* Turbojet, *der;* **~jet engine** *n.* Turboluftstrahltriebwerk, *das;* **~prop** *n.* Turbo-Prop-Flugzeug, *das;* **~prop engine** Turbo-Prop-Triebwerk, *das*

**turbot** /'tɜ:bət/ *n.* (*Zool.*) Steinbutt, *der*

**turbulence** /'tɜ:bjʊləns/ *n., no pl.* **A** (*agitation*) Aufgewühltheit, *die;* (*fig.*) Aufruhr, *der;* (*unruliness*) Unruhe, *die;* **B** (*Phys.*) Turbulenz, *die*

**turbulent** /'tɜ:bjʊlənt/ *adj.* **A** aufgewühlt ‹Gedanken, Wellen, Leidenschaften›; turbulent ‹Herrschaft, Kindheit›; ungestüm ‹Menge›; aufrührerisch ‹Stadt, Mob›; **B** (*Phys.*) turbulent

**turd** /tɜ:d/ *n.* (*coarse*) **A** (*lump of excrement*) Scheißhaufen, *der* (*derb*); **B** (*contemptible person*) Scheißkerl, *der* (*derb*)

**tureen** /tjʊə'ri:n/ *n.* Terrine, *die*

**turf** /tɜ:f/ **1** *n., pl.* **~s** *or* **turves** /tɜ:vz/ **A** *no pl.* (*covering of grass etc.*) Rasen, *der;* **B** (*cut patch of grass*) [abgestochenes] Rasenstück; Sode, *die* (*bes. nordd.*); **lay ~:** Fertigrasen verlegen; **C the ~** (*racecourse*) der Turf (*Pferdesport*); die Rennbahn; (*horseracing*) der Pferderennsport. **2** *v.t.* mit Fertigrasen bedecken

**~ 'out** *v.t.* (*coll.*) rausschmeißen (*ugs.*); **~ sb. out of sth.** jmdn. aus etw. [raus]schmeißen

**~ 'over** *v.t.* mit Rasenstücken bedecken

**turf: ~ accountant** *n.* ▶ **1261** Buchmacher, *der;* **~ war** *n.* Revierkampf, *der*

**turgid** /'tɜ:dʒɪd/ *adj.* **A** (*inflated*) [an]geschwollen; **B** (*fig.*) geschwollen; schwülstig (*abwertend*)

**turgidly** /'tɜ:dʒɪdlɪ/ *adv.* geschwollen (*abwertend*)

**Turk** /tɜ:k/ *n.* ▶ **1340** Türke, *der*/Türkin, *die*

**turkey** *n.* **A** (*fowl*) Truthahn, *der*/Truthenne, *die;* (*esp. as food*) Puter, *der*/Pute, *die;* **B** (*coll. derog.: stupid person*) Schwachkopf, *der* (*ugs. abwertend*); **C** (*Amer. coll.: flop*) Reinfall, *der;* **D talk ~** (*Amer. coll.*) Tacheles reden (*ugs.*)

**Turkey** /'tɜ:kɪ/ *pr. n.* die Türkei

**turkey: ~ buzzard** *n.* Truthahngeier, *der;* **~cock** *n.* Truthahn, *der;* (*fig.*) Angeber, *der* (*abwertend*); **red as a ~cock** (*from heat or exertion*) krebsrot; (*with anger or embarrassment*) puterrot; **~ vulture** ⇒ **~ buzzard**

**Turkish** /'tɜ:kɪʃ/ ▶ **1275**, ▶ **1340 1** *adj.* türkisch; **sb. is ~:** jmd. ist Türke/Türkin; ⇒ *also* **English** 1. **2** *n.* Türkisch, *das;* ⇒ *also* **English** 2 A

**Turkish: ~ 'bath** *n.* türkisches Bad; **~ delight** *n. mit Puderzucker bestreutes, gelatinehaltiges Konfekt;* Rachatlukum, *das;* Lokum, *das;* **~ 'towel** *n.* Frotteehandtuch, *das*

**Turk: ~'s cap** *n.* (*Bot.*) Türkenbundlilie, *die;* **~'s 'head** *n.* (*knot*) türkischer Bund

**turmeric** /'tɜ:mərɪk/ *n.* Gelbwurzel, *die;* (*spice*) Kurkuma, *die*

**turmoil** /'tɜ:mɔɪl/ *n.* Aufruhr, *der;* [wildes] Durcheinander; **everything/her mind was in [a] ~:** es herrschte ein wildes Durcheinander/sie war völlig durcheinander

**turn** /tɜ:n/ **1** *n.* **A it is sb.'s ~ to do sth.** jmd. ist an der Reihe, etw. zu tun; **it's your ~ [next]** du bist als Nächster/Nächste dran (*ugs.*) *od.* an der Reihe; **wait one's ~:** warten, bis man an der Reihe ist; **your ~ will come** du kommst auch [noch] an die Reihe; **by ~s** abwechselnd; **each of us in ~ had to give his name** wir mussten nacheinander *od.* der Reihe nach unsere Namen nennen; **he gave it to her, and she in ~ passed it on to me** er gab es ihr, und sie wiederum reichte es an mich weiter; **in one's ~:** wiederum; **out of ~** (*before or after one's ~*) außer der Reihe; (*fig.*) an der falschen Stelle ‹lachen›; **she tried to throw the dice out of ~:** sie wollte würfeln, obwohl sie nicht an der Reihe war; **excuse me if I'm talking out of ~** (*fig.*) entschuldige, wenn ich etwas Unpassendes sage; **your remark was out of ~** (*fig.*) Ihre Bemerkung war fehl am Platz; **take a ~ at the wheel** für eine Weile das Steuer übernehmen; **take [it in] ~s** sich abwechseln; **take ~s at doing sth., take it in ~s to do sth.** etw. abwechselnd tun; **she was unhappy and cheerful, in ~s** sie war abwechselnd unglücklich und fröhlich; ⇒ *also* **about** 1 F, G; **serve** 1 C; **B** (*rotary motion*) Drehung, *die;* **give the handle a ~:** den Griff [herum]drehen; **have/show a good ~ of speed** schnell sein; **put on a ~ of speed** einen Zahn zulegen (*ugs.*); **[done] to a ~:** genau richtig [zubereitet]; **C** ▶ **1679** (*change of direction*) Wende, *die;* **take a ~ to the right/left, do** *or* **make** *or* **take a right/left ~:** nach rechts/links abbiegen; **'no left/right ~'** „links/rechts abbiegen verboten"; **make a ~ to port/starboard** nach Backbord/Steuerbord abdrehen; **the tide was on the ~:** die Flut/Ebbe setzte gerade ein; **the ~ of the year/century** die Jahres-/Jahrhundertwende; **be on the ~** (*be about to change*) sich [zum Besseren/Schlechteren] wenden; (*be about to go sour*) ‹Milch usw.:› einen Stich haben (*ugs.*); **a ~ of fortune** eine Schicksalswende; **take a favourable ~** (*fig.*) sich zum Guten wenden; **take a ~ for the better/worse** ⇒ **take** 1 K; **D** (*deflection*) Biegung, *die;* **E** (*bend*) Kurve, *die;* (*corner*) Ecke, *die;* **at every ~** (*fig.*) (*constantly*) ständig; (*wherever one goes*) überall; **F** (*short performance on stage etc.*) Nummer, *die;* **do one's ~:** auftreten; **G** (*change of tide*) **~ of the tide** Gezeitenwechsel, *der;* **there will be a ~ of the tide** (*fig.*) das Blatt wird sich wenden; **H** (*character*) **be of a mechanical/humorous/speculative ~:** technisch begabt sein/von humorvollem Schlag sein/einen Hang zum Spekulativen haben; **a child with a more enquiring ~ of mind than his brother** ein Kind, das eher Fragen stellt als sein Bruder; **those of a democratic ~ of mind** die demokratisch Eingestellten; **I** (*literary: formation*) Rundung, *die;* **the graceful ~ of her ankle** ihr wohlgeformter Knöchel; **J** (*form of expression*) **an elegant ~ of speech/phrase** eine elegante Ausdrucksweise; **K** (*service*) **do sb. a good/**

t

**bad ~:** jmdm. einen guten/schlechten Dienst erweisen; **do good ~s** Gutes tun; **one good ~ deserves another** (*prov.*) hilfst du mir, so helf ich dir; **L** (*each round in coil of rope etc.*) Umwick[e]llung, *die;* **M** (*coll.: fright*) **give sb. quite a ~:** jmdm. einen gehörigen Schrecken einjagen (*ugs.*); **N** (*coll.: spell of illness etc.*) **have a nasty ~:** einen schlimmen Anfall haben; **I just had a little ~:** ich hatte einen kleinen Schwächeanfall; **O** (*short walk*) **take a ~:** eine Runde drehen *od.* machen; **P** (*short ride*) Runde, *die;* **go out for a ~ on one's bicycle** eine Runde mit dem Fahrrad drehen; **Q** (*Mus.*) Doppelschlag, *der;* **R** (*Brit. St. Exch.: jobber's profit margin*) Gewinnspanne, *die.* ⇒ *also* **about-~; three-point.**

❷ *v.t.* **A** (*make revolve*) drehen; **~ the tap** am Wasserhahn drehen; **~ the key in the lock** den Schlüssel im Schloss herumdrehen; **he ~ed the wheel sharply [to the right]** er riss das Steuer scharf [nach rechts] herum; **B** (*reverse*) umdrehen; wenden ‹Pfannkuchen, Matratze, Auto, Heu, Teppich›; umgraben ‹Erde›; umlegen ‹Kragen›; **~ sth. upside-down** *or* **on its head** (*lit. or fig.*) etw. auf den Kopf stellen; **~ a record** eine Platte umdrehen; **~ sth. back to front** die Vorderseite einer Sache nach hinten drehen; **~ the page** umblättern; **~ sth. inside out** etw. nach außen stülpen *od.* drehen; **C** (*give new direction to*) drehen, wenden ‹Kopf›; **she could still ~ heads** die Leute drehten sich immer noch nach ihr um; **~ a hose/gun on sb./sth.** einen Schlauch/ein Gewehr auf jmdn./etw. richten; **~ one's chair to face the window** seinen Stuhl zum Fenster drehen; **~ one's attention/mind to sth.** sich/seine Gedanken einer Sache (*Dat.*) zuwenden; **~ one's thoughts to a subject** sich [in Gedanken] mit einem Thema beschäftigen; **~ a car into a road** [mit einem Auto] in eine Straße einbiegen; **~ the course of history** dem Gang der Geschichte eine Wende geben; **~ one's eyes on sb.** jmdm. seine Augen zuwenden; **he ~ed his steps homeward** er lenkte seine Schritte heimwärts; **~ the tide [of sth.]** [bei etw.] den Ausschlag geben; **this incident ~ed the tide of opinion in her favour** dieser Vorfall führte einen Meinungsumschwung zu ihren Gunsten herbei; **~ sb. from his purpose** jmdn. von seinem Vorhaben abbringen; **D** (*send*) **~ sb. loose on sb./sth.** jmdn. auf jmdn./etw. loslassen; **~ sb. from one's door/off one's land** jmdn. von seiner Tür/von seinem Land verjagen; **~ a dog on sb.** einen Hund auf jmdn. hetzen; **E** (*put*) leeren ‹Inhalt eines Koffers, einer Büchse›; stürzen ‹Pudding, Kuchen usw.› (**on to** auf + *Akk.*); **F** (*cause to become*) verwandeln; **the cigarette smoke has ~ed the walls yellow** der Zigarettenrauch hat die Wände vergilben lassen; **~ the lights low** das Licht dämpfen; **~ a play/book into a film** ein Theaterstück/Buch verfilmen; **~ water into electricity/a church into a theatre** Wasser in Elektrizität/eine Kirche in ein Theater umwandeln; **the thought ~ed him pale** der Gedanke ließ ihn erbleichen (*geh.*); **G** (*make sour*) sauer werden lassen ‹Milch›; **H** (*translate*) übertragen (**in** in + *Akk.*); **I ~ sb.'s stomach** jmdm. den Magen umdrehen; **J** (*make conceited*) **~ sb.'s head** jmdm. zu Kopf steigen; **~ sb.'s brain** jmds. Sinne *od.* Geist verwirren (*geh.*); **K** (*shape in lathe*) drechseln ‹Holz›; drehen ‹Metall, Ton›; **L** drehen ‹Pirouette›; schlagen ‹Rad, Purzelbaum›; **M** ▶ **912** (*reach the age of*) **~ 40** 40 [Jahre alt] werden; **she has not ~ed 30 yet** sie ist noch keine 30 [Jahre alt]; **N** ▶ **1012** **it's just ~ed 12 o'clock/quarter past 4** es ist gerade 12 Uhr/viertel nach vier vorbei; **it's not yet ~ed 4 o'clock** es ist noch nicht ganz 4 Uhr; **O** (*gain*) **~ a penny/profit** einen Gewinn machen; **~ a quick penny** eine schnelle Mark machen (*ugs.*); **P** wenden ‹Kragen, Jacke usw.›; **Q** (*resist and divert*) abprallen lassen; **the bullet was ~ed by the door** die Kugel prallte an der Tür ab; **R** (*blunt*) stumpf machen; **~ the edge of criticism** (*fig.*) der Kritik die Spitze abbrechen *od.* nehmen; **S** (*go round*) umrunden ‹Kap, Landzunge›; **~ the flank of an army** einer Streitmacht die Flanke aufrollen; **T** (*give elegant form to*) **he knows how to ~ a compliment** er versteht es, Komplimente zu machen; **~ verses** Verse dichten *od.* schmieden. ⇒ *also* **account** 3 H; **back** 1 A; **coat** 1 A; **corner** 1 A; **deaf** 1 B; **evidence** 1 B; **hair** A; **hand** 1 A; **honest** E; **phrase** 2 A; **table** 1 A; **tail** 1 C; **turtle** C.

❸ *v.i.* **A** (*revolve*) sich drehen; ‹Wasserhahn, Schlüssel:› sich drehen lassen; **the earth ~s on its axis** die Erde dreht sich um ihre Achse; **he couldn't get the key to ~:** er konnte den Schlüssel nicht drehen; **B** (*reverse direction*) ‹Person:› sich herumdrehen; ‹Auto:› wenden; **the car ~ed upside down** das Auto überschlug sich; **~ back to front** sich von hinten nach vorne drehen; **C** ▶ **1679** (*take new direction*) sich wenden; (**~ round**) sich umdrehen; **heads ~ed when she ...:** die Leute sahen *od.* drehten sich nach ihr um, als sie ...; **his thoughts/attention ~ed to her** er wandte ihr seine Gedanken/Aufmerksamkeit zu; **left/right ~!** (*Mil.*) links/rechts um!; **he ~ed to the man standing next to him** er wandte sich dem Mann zu, der neben ihm stand; **~ into a road/away from the river** in eine Straße einbiegen/vom Fluss abbiegen; **~ to the left** nach links abbiegen/‹Schiff, Flugzeug:› abdrehen; **~ up/down a street** in eine Straße einbiegen; **~ towards home** den Heimweg einschlagen; **profits are ~ing upward** die Gewinne steigen; **everywhere the eye ~s ...:** wohin sich das Auge wendet ...; **when the tide ~s** wenn die Ebbe/Flut kommt; (*fig.*) wenn sich das Blatt wendet; **not know where** *or* **which way to ~** (*fig.*) keinen Ausweg [mehr] wissen; **my luck has ~ed** (*fig.*) mein Glück hat sich gewendet; **D** (*become*) werden; **~ traitor/statesman/Muslim** zum Verräter/zum Staatsmann/Moslem werden; **~ [in]to sth.** zu etw. werden; (*be transformed*) sich in etw. (*Akk.*) verwandeln; **her face ~ed green** sie wurde [ganz] grün im Gesicht; **E** (*change colour*) ‹Laub:› sich [ver]färben; **F** (*become sour*) ‹Milch:› sauer werden; **G my stomach ~s** mir dreht sich der Magen um (*ugs.*); **H** (*become giddy*) **sb.'s head is ~ing** jmdm. dreht sich alles [im Kopf]. ⇒ *also* **grave**[1]; **heel**[1] 1 B; **toss** 2 A; **worm** 1 A

**~ a'bout** ❶ *v.i.* sich umdrehen; ‹Kompanie:› kehrtmachen; (*fig.*) eine Kehrtwendung machen. ❷ *v.t.* wenden ‹Auto, Boot usw.›. ⇒ *also* **~about**

**~ against** *v.t.* **A ~ against sb.** sich gegen jmdn. wenden; **~ sb. against sb.** jmdn. gegen jmdn. aufbringen; **B they ~ed his own arguments against him** sie verwendeten seine eigenen Argumente gegen ihn

**~ a'round** ⇒ **~ round**

**~ a'way** ❶ *v.i.* sich abwenden; **~ away from sth.** (*fig.*) sich von etw. abwenden. ❷ *v.t.* **A** (*avert*) abwenden; **B** (*send away*) wegschicken; (*refuse admittance also*) abweisen

**~ 'back** ❶ *v.i.* **A** (*retreat, lit. or fig.*) umkehren; kehrtmachen (*ugs.*); **there can be no ~ing back** es gibt kein Zurück *od.* keinen Weg zurück; **B** (*in book etc.*) zurückgehen. ❷ *v.t.* **A** (*cause to retreat*) zurückweisen; zurückschlagen ‹Feind›; **B** (*fold back*) zurückschlagen ‹Bettdecke, Teppich›; herunterschlagen ‹Kragen›; **don't ~ back the corner of the page** bitte mach keine Eselsohren in die Buchseiten (*ugs.*)

**~ 'down** *v.t.* **A** (*fold down*) herunterschlagen ‹Kragen, Hutkrempe›; umknicken ‹Buchseite›; [nach unten] umschlagen ‹Laken›; **B** (*reduce level of*) niedriger stellen ‹Heizung, Kochplatte›; dämpfen ‹Licht›; herunterdrehen ‹Gas, Heizung›; leiser stellen ‹Ton, Radio, Fernseher›; **C** (*reject, refuse*) ablehnen; abweisen ‹Bewerber, Kandidaten usw.›. ⇒ *also* **turndown**

**~ 'in** ❶ *v.t.* **A** (*fold inwards*) nach innen drehen; einschlagen ‹Stoffkante›; einrollen ‹Blatt›; **B** (*hand in*) abgeben; **C** (*surrender*) [der Polizei] übergeben; **~ oneself in** sich stellen; **D** (*register*) hinlegen (*ugs.*) ‹Auftritt, Leistung›; **E** (*coll.: give up*) aufstecken (*ugs.*) ‹Arbeit›; hinschmeißen (*salopp*) ‹Arbeit, Dienstabzeichen›; **F ~ it in!** (*coll.: stop that*) hör auf damit! ❷ *v.i.* **A** (*incline inwards*) nach innen gebogen sein; (*narrow*) sich verjüngen; **B** (*enter*) einbiegen; **C** (*coll.: go to bed*) in die Falle gehen (*salopp*); **D ~ in on oneself** sich in sich selbst zurückziehen

**~ 'off** ❶ *v.t.* **A** abschalten; abstellen ‹Wasser, Gas›; zudrehen ‹Wasserhahn›; **B** (*coll.: cause to lose interest*) anwidern; **~ sb. off sth.** jmdm. etw. vermiesen (*ugs.*). ❷ *v.i.* abbiegen. ⇒ *also* **~-off**

**~ on** ❶ *v.t.* **A** /'-'-/ anschalten; einlassen ‹Badewasser›; aufdrehen ‹Wasserhahn, Gas›; (*fig.: start showing*) aufsetzen ‹Miene›; **B** /'-'-/ (*coll.: cause to take interest*) anmachen (*ugs.*); ‹Droge:› anturnen (*ugs.*); **whatever ~s you on!** jedem das Seine!; ⇒ *also* **~-on**; **C** /'--/ (*be based on*) ‹Argument:› beruhen auf (+ *Dat.*); ‹Gespräch, Diskussion› sich drehen um (*ugs.*); **D** /'--/ (*become hostile towards*) sich wenden gegen; (*attack*) angreifen; **there's no need to ~ on me like that** du brauchst mich nicht so anzufahren.
❷ /'-'-/ *v.i.* (*switch on*) einschalten

**~ 'out** ❶ *v.t.* **A** (*expel*) hinauswerfen (*ugs.*); **~ sb. out of a room/out into the street** jmdn. aus einem Zimmer weisen *od.* (*ugs.*) werfen/auf die Straße werfen *od.* setzen; **~ sb. out of his office** (*temporarily*) jmdn. aus seinem Büro ausquartieren; **B** (*switch off*) ausschalten; abdrehen ‹Gas›; **C** (*incline outwards*) nach außen drehen ‹Füße, Zehen›; **D** (*equip*) ausstaffieren; **E** (*produce*) produzieren; hervorbringen ‹Fachkräfte, Spezialisten›; (*in great quantities*) ausstoßen; **F** (*Brit.*) (*empty*) ausräumen; ausschütten ‹Büchse›; schütten ‹Bohnen usw.›; stürzen ‹Götterspeise usw.›; (*clean*) [gründlich] aufräumen; (*get rid of*) wegwerfen; **~ out one's pockets** seine Taschen umdrehen; **G** (*Mil.*) **~ out [the guard]** [die Wache] antreten lassen; **~ out the guard!** Wache angetreten!
❷ *v.i.* **A** (*prove to be*) **sb./sth. ~s out to be sth.** jmd./etw. stellt sich als jmd./etw. heraus *od.* erweist sich als jmd./etw.; **it ~s out that ...:** es stellt sich heraus, dass ...; **as it ~ed out, as things ~ed out** wie sich [nachher] herausstellte; **B** (*come to be eventually*) **the day ~ed out wet** der Tag wurde regnerisch; **see how things ~ out** sehen, wie sich die Dinge entwickeln; **~ out to be sth.** sich zu etw. entwickeln; **everything ~ed out well/all right in the end** alles endete gut; **she didn't ~ out well** aus ihr ist nichts geworden; **C** (*end*) **the story ~ed out happily** die Geschichte ging gut aus; **the expedition ~ed out well** die Expedition hatte Erfolg; **D** (*appear*) ‹Menge, Fans usw.:› erscheinen; **he ~s out every Saturday to watch his team** er kommt jeden Samstag, um seine Mannschaft zu sehen; **E** (*coll.: get out of bed*) aus den Federn steigen (*ugs.*); **F** (*coll.: go out of doors*) rausgehen (*ugs.*); **G** (*play*) **~ out for a team** für eine Mannschaft spielen *od.* antreten; **H** (*point outwards*) sich nach außen drehen. ⇒ *also* **~-out**

**~ 'over** ❶ *v.t.* **A** (*cause to fall over*) umwerfen; **the car was ~ed over on to its roof** (*by accident*) das Auto überschlug sich und blieb auf dem Dach liegen; **B** (*expose the other side of*) umdrehen; umgraben ‹Erde›; **~ a page over** umblättern; **~ over two pages at once** eine Seite überschlagen; **C** drehen ‹Motor›; **D ~ sth. over [in one's mind]** sich (*Dat.*) etw. hin und her überlegen; **E** (*hand over*) übergeben (**to** *Dat.*) ‹Betrieb, Amt›; **F** (*Commerc.*) umschlagen ‹Waren›; **~ over £150,000 a month** einen Umsatz von 150 000 Pfund im Monat haben.
❷ *v.i.* **A** (*tip over*) umkippen; ‹Boot:› kentern, umschlagen; ‹Auto, Flugzeug:› sich überschlagen; **B** (*from one side to the other*) sich umdrehen; **~ over on to one's back** sich auf den Rücken drehen; **C** ‹Motor:› laufen; **D** (*feel moved by fear, nausea*) **my stomach ~ed over at the thought of it** beim Gedanken daran drehte sich mir der Magen um (*ugs.*); **E** (**~ *a page***) weiterblättern. ⇒ *also* **turnover**

t

~ **'round** ❶ *v.i.* Ⓐ sich umdrehen; **~ round and go back the same way** umkehren und denselben Weg zurückgehen; **[not] have time to ~ round** (*fig.*) [k]eine Minute Zeit haben; Ⓑ (*rotate*) sich drehen; Ⓒ **~ round and do sth.** (*fig.*) plötzlich etw. tun; **they cannot ~ round and blame us** sie können nicht auf einmal uns die Schuld geben; Ⓓ (*change for better*) ‹Geschäfte:› sich erholen. ❷ *v.t.* Ⓐ (*unload and reload*) be- und entladen ‹Frachtschiff›; abfertigen ‹Passagierschiff›; Ⓑ ⇒ **~ about** 2; Ⓒ (*reverse*) umdrehen; auf den Kopf stellen (*ugs.*) ‹Theorie, Argument›; **~ a company round** (*Commerc.*) eine Firma aus der Krise führen. ⇒ *also* **~-round**

**~ to** ❶ /'--/ *v.t.* Ⓐ (*set about*) **~ to work** an die Arbeit gehen; Ⓑ (*go to for help etc.*) **~ to sb./sth.** sich an jmdn. wenden/etw. zu Hilfe nehmen; **~ to God** sich Gott zuwenden; **~ to sb. for money** jmdn. um Geld bitten; **~ to a book** ein Buch zurate ziehen; **~ to sb. for comfort/help/advice** bei jmdm. Trost/Hilfe/Rat suchen; **~ to drugs** zu Drogen greifen; **~ to drink/one's work** (*seeking consolation*) sich in den Alkohol/seine Arbeit flüchten; **make sb. ~ to drink** jmdn. dem Alkohol in die Arme treiben; Ⓒ (*go on to consider next*) **~ to a subject/topic** sich einem Thema zuwenden; ⇒ *also* **~** 2 A, C. ❷ /-'-/ *v.i.* zugreifen

**~ 'up** ❶ *v.i.* Ⓐ (*make one's appearance*) erscheinen; aufkreuzen (*ugs.*); Ⓑ (*happen*) passieren; geschehen; Ⓒ (*present itself*) auftauchen; ‹Gelegenheit:› sich bieten; ‹Lösung:› sich finden; **something is sure to ~ up** irgendetwas wird sich schon finden; Ⓓ (*be found*) sich finden. ❷ *v.t.* Ⓐ (*dig up*) freilegen; (*fig.*) ans Licht bringen; **I ~ed up a lot of interesting information** ich habe viele interessante Informationen aufgetrieben; Ⓑ hochschlagen ‹Kragen, Hutkrempe›; **her nose is ~ed up** sie hat eine Stupsnase; Ⓒ lauter stellen, (*ugs.*) aufdrehen ‹Ton, Fernseher, Radio›; aufdrehen ‹Wasser, Heizung, Gas›; heller machen ‹Licht›; Ⓓ (*Brit.: find and refer to*) heranziehen ‹Artikel, Buch›; Ⓔ **~ it up!** (*Brit. coll.*) hör auf damit!; ⇒ *also* **nose** 1 A; **toe** 1 A

**~ upon** ⇒ **~ on** 1 C, D

**turn: ~about** *n.* (*turning about*) Wende, *die;* (*fig.*) Kehrtwendung, *die;* **a welcome ~about in her fortunes** eine willkommene Wende ihres Geschicks; **~around** *n.* Ⓐ (*change*) [Kehrt]wende, *die;* Ⓑ (*processing, time needed*) Bearbeitungszeit, *die;* Ⓒ (*of aircraft, ship, vehicle*) Abfertigung, *die;* **~coat** *n.* Abtrünnige, *der/die;* **~-down** *attrib. adj.* **~-down collar** Umlegekragen, *der*

**turned-up** /'tɜ:ndʌp/ *adj.* **~ nose** Stupsnase, *die* (*ugs.*)

**turner** /'tɜ:nə(r)/ *n.* Drechsler, *der*/Drechslerin, *die*

**turning** /'tɜ:nɪŋ/ *n.* Ⓐ ▶1679 (*off road*) Abzweigung, *die;* (*fig.*) Kreuzweg, *der* (*geh.*); **take the second ~ to the left** die zweite Abzweigung nach links nehmen; Ⓑ (*use of lathe*) Drechseln, *das;* Ⓒ *in pl.* (*shavings*) Späne

**turning: ~ circle** *n.* (*Motor Veh.*) Wendekreis, *der;* **~ point** *n.* Wendepunkt, *der*

**turnip** /'tɜ:nɪp/ *n.* Kohlrübe, *die;* Steckrübe, *die*

**'turnip top** *n.* Rübenblätter *Pl.*

**turn: ~key** ❶ *n.* (*Hist.*) Kerkermeister, *der.* ❷ *adj.* schlüsselfertig; **a ~key contract** ein Vertrag, der schlüsselfertige Lieferung garantiert; **~-off** *n.* Ⓐ (*~ing*) Abzweigung, *die;* (*off motorway*) Ausfahrt, *die;* **the Leicester ~-off** die Abzweigung nach Leicester/die Ausfahrt Leicester; Ⓑ (*coll.: repellent person or thing*) **be a ~-off** abstoßend sein; **be a ~-off for sb.** jmdn. abstoßen; **~-on** *n.* (*coll.*) **be a ~-on [for sb.]** [jmdn.] anmachen (*ugs.*); **~out** *n.* Ⓐ (*turning out for duty*) Einsatz, *der;* Ausrücken, *das;* Ⓑ (*number voting*) **~out [of voters]** Wahlbeteiligung, *die;* Ⓒ (*number assembled*) Beteiligung, *die* (**for** an + *Dat.*); **there was a large ~out of fans at the airport** eine große Zahl von Fans war zum Flughafen gekommen; Ⓓ ⇒ **output** 1 A; Ⓔ ⇒ **clear-out**; **~over** *n.* Ⓐ (*tart etc.*) **apple/apricot ~over** Apfel-/Aprikosentasche, *die;* **meat ~over** Fleischpastete, *die;* Ⓑ (*Commerc.*) (*of business, money*) Umsatz, *der;* (*of stock*) Umschlag, *der;* Ⓒ (*of staff*) Fluktuation, *die;* (*of patients in hospital*) Zu- und Abgang, *der;* **~pike** *n.* Ⓐ (*Brit. Hist.: toll road*) gebührenpflichtige Straße; Ⓑ (*Amer.: expressway*) gebührenpflichtige Autobahn; **~round** *n.* Ⓐ (*adoption of new policy*) Kehrtwendung, *die;* Ⓑ (*of ship, aircraft, people*) Abfertigung, *die;* (*of material*) Bearbeitung, *die;* **~stile** *n.* Drehkreuz, *das;* **~table** *n.* Ⓐ (*for gramophone record*) Plattenteller, *der;* Ⓑ (*for reversing locomotive etc.*) Drehscheibe, *die;* **~-up** *n.* Ⓐ (*Brit. Fashion*) Aufschlag, *der;* **with ~-ups** ‹Hose› mit Aufschlag; Ⓑ (*Brit. coll.: unexpected event*) **a ~-up [for the book]** eine Riesenüberraschung (*ugs.*)

**turpentine** /'tɜ:pntaɪn/ *n.* Ⓐ (*resin*) Terpentin, *das;* Ⓑ **[oil of] ~:** Terpentin, *das* (*ugs.*); Terpentinöl, *das; attrib.* **~ substitute** Terpentinersatz, *der*

**turpitude** /'tɜ:pɪtju:d/ *n.* Verworfenheit, *die* (*geh.*)

**turps** /tɜ:ps/ *n.* (*coll.*) Terpentin, *das* (*ugs.*)

**turquoise** /'tɜ:kwɔɪz/ ❶ *n.* Ⓐ Türkis, *der;* Ⓑ (*colour*) Türkis, *das.* ❷ *adj.* Ⓐ türkis[farben]; Ⓑ **~ ring** Türkisring, *der*

**turquoise: ~ 'blue** *n.* Türkisblau, *das;* **~ 'green** *n.* Türkisgrün, *das*

**turret** /'tʌrɪt/ *n.* Ⓐ (*Archit.*) Türmchen, *das;* Ⓑ (*of tank etc.*) [Geschütz]turm, *der;* Ⓒ (*Mech. Engin.*) Revolverkopf, *der*

**turreted** /'tʌrɪtɪd/ *adj.* ‹Schloss› mit Mauertürmchen

**'turret lathe** *n.* Revolverdrehmaschine, *die*

**turtle** /tɜ:tl/ *n.* Ⓐ (*marine reptile*) Meeresschildkröte, *die;* Ⓑ (*Amer.: freshwater reptile*) Wasserschildkröte, *die;* Ⓒ **turn ~** ‹Schiff, Boot:› kentern; ‹Auto:› sich überschlagen

**turtle: ~ dove** *n.* Turteltaube, *die;* **~neck** *n.* Stehbundkragen, *der; attrib.* **~neck pullover** Pullover mit Stehbund

**turves** ⇒ **turf** 1 B

**Tuscan** /'tʌskən/ ❶ *adj.* Ⓐ (*of Tuscany*) toskanisch; Ⓑ (*Archit.*) **~ order** toskanische Ordnung. ❷ *n.* Ⓐ (*language*) Toskanisch, *das;* Ⓑ (*person*) Toskaner, *der*/Toskanerin, *die*

**Tuscany** /'tʌskənɪ/ *pr. n.* Toskana, *die*

**tush** /tʌʃ/ *int.* (*arch.*) pah

**tusk** /tʌsk/ *n.* (*of elephant*) Stoßzahn, *der;* (*of boar, walrus*) Hauer, *der*

**tussle** /'tʌsl/ ❶ *n.* Gerangel, *das* (*ugs.*); **they had a ~ over the project** (*fig.*) es gab zwischen ihnen ein Gerangel wegen des Projekts. ❷ *v.i.* sich balgen; (*fig.*) sich auseinander setzen (**about** wegen)

**tussock** /'tʌsək/ *n.* (*clump of grass etc.*) [Gras]büschel, *das*

**tutelage** /'tju:tɪlɪdʒ/ *n.* (*guardianship*) Vormundschaft, *die;* (*of king etc.*) Schutzherrschaft, *die;* (*tuition*) Anleitung, *die;* **a child in ~:** ein unter Vormundschaft stehendes Kind; **be under sb.'s ~:** unter jmds. Obhut stehen (*geh.*)

**tutelar** /'tju:tɪlə(r)/, **tutelary** /'tju:tɪlərɪ/ *adjs.* Ⓐ (*protective*) Schutz‹göttin, -gottheit, -heiliger›; Ⓑ (*of a guardian*) **~y authority** Vormundschaft, *die*

**tutor** /'tju:tə(r)/ ❶ *n.* ▶1261 Ⓐ (*private teacher*) **[private] ~:** [Privat]lehrer, *der*/-lehrerin, *die;* (*for extra help*) Nachhilfelehrer, *der*/-lehrerin, *die;* **piano ~:** Klavierlehrer, *der*/-lehrerin, *die;* (*book*) Klavierschule, *die;* Ⓑ (*Brit. Univ.*) ≈ Tutor, *der;* Ⓒ (*Amer.: college teacher*) Dozent, *der.* ❷ *v.t.* Ⓐ **~ sb.** (*teach privately*) jmdm. Privatstunden geben; (*give extra lessons to*) jmdm. Nachhilfestunden geben; **~ sb. in French/the piano** jmdm. Französisch-/Klavierstunden geben; Ⓑ (*arch./literary*) unterweisen (*geh.*); (*discipline*) erziehen

**tutorial** /tju:'tɔ:rɪəl/ ❶ *adj.* Tutoren-. ❷ *n.* (*Brit. Univ.*) (*for less advanced students*) ≈ Tutorium, *das;* (*for more advanced students*) ≈ Kolloquium, *das*

**tutti-frutti** /tʊtɪ'fru:tɪ/ *n.* (*Gastr.*) Tuttifrutti, *das*

**tut[-tut]** /tʌt('tʌt)/ ❶ *int.* na[, na]. ❷ *v.i.*, **-tt-:** **~ [with disapproval]** [missbilligend] „Na, na!" sagen

**tutu** /'tu:tu:/ *n.* Tutu, *das*

**tu-whit tu-whoo** /tʊwɪt tʊ'wu:/ *int.* [h]uhu

**tux** /tʌks/ *n.* (*Amer. coll.*), **tuxedo** /tʌk'si:dəʊ/ *n., pl.* **~edos** *or* **~edoes** (*Amer.*) Smoking, *der*

**TV** /ti:'vi:/ *n.* Ⓐ (*television*) Fernsehen, *das; attrib.* Fernseh‹star, -magazin, -programm›; **TV dinner** ≈ Fertigmahlzeit, *die;* **on TV** im Fernsehen; Ⓑ (*television set*) Fernseher, *der* (*ugs.*)

**twaddle** /'twɒdl/ *n.* Gewäsch, *das* (*ugs.*); **talk utter ~:** völligen Blödsinn reden (*ugs.*); **don't talk such ~!** hör auf mit dem Gewäsch!

**twain** /tweɪn/ (*arch./poet.*) *n.* **cut/split in ~:** entzweischneiden/in zwei Teile teilen; **never the ~ shall meet** die beiden werden nie zueinander finden

**twang** /twæŋ/ ❶ *v.i.* ‹Bogen:› mit vibrierendem Ton zurückschnellen; **hear the guitar ~ing away** das Klimpern der Gitarre hören (*ugs.*). ❷ *v.t.* zupfen ‹Saite›; **~ a guitar** auf einer Gitarre [herum]klimpern (*ugs.*). ❸ *n.* Ⓐ (*nasal tone of voice*) **[nasal] ~:** Näseln, *das;* **speak with a ~:** näseln; Ⓑ (*of bowstring, string of musical instrument*) vibrierender Ton

**'twas** /twɒz/ (*arch./poet.*) = **it was**

**twat** /twæt, twɒt/ *n.* Ⓐ (*coarse: vagina*) Fotze, *die* (*vulg.*); Ⓑ (*derog. sl.: idiot*) Arschloch, *das* (*derb*)

**tweak** /twi:k/ ❶ *v.t.* **~ sb. in the arm, ~ sb.'s arm** jmdn. in den Arm kneifen; **~ sb.'s ear** jmdn. am Ohr ziehen. ❷ *n.* Kneifen, *das;* **give sb./sth. a ~:** jmdn./etw. kneifen

**twee** /twi:/ *adj.*, **tweer** /'twi:ə(r)/, **tweest** /'twi:ɪst/ (*Brit. derog.*) geziert ‹Wesen, Art, Ausdrucksweise›; kitschig ‹Stil, Bild›; Bilderbuch‹dorf, -landhaus›; niedlich, putzig ‹Kleidung, Dorf›

**tweed** /twi:d/ *n.* Ⓐ (*fabric*) Tweed, *der; attrib.* Tweed-; Ⓑ *in pl.* (*clothes*) Tweedkleidung, *die;* Tweedsachen (*ugs.*)

**tweedy** /'twi:dɪ/ *adj.* Ⓐ (*coll.: dressed in tweeds*) in Tweed gekleidet; Ⓑ (*fig.: heartily informal*) burschikos

**'tween-deck[s]** *n.* (*Naut.*) Zwischendeck, *das*

**tweet** /twi:t/ ❶ *n.* Zwitschern, *das;* **~, ~!** piep, piep! ❷ *v.i.* zwitschern

**tweeter** /'twi:tə(r)/ *n.* Hochtonlautsprecher, *der*

**tweezers** /'twi:zəz/ *n. pl.* **[pair of] ~:** Pinzette, *die*

**twelfth** /twelfθ/ ▶1055 ❶ *adj.* ▶1352 zwölft...; ⇒ *also* **eighth** 1. ❷ *n.* Ⓐ (*fraction*) Zwölftel, *das;* Ⓑ (*Mus.*) Duodezime, *die;* ⇒ *also* **eighth** 2

**Twelfth: ~ Day** *n.* Dreikönigstag, *der;* **t~ 'man** *n.* (*Cricket*) Ersatzspieler, *der;* **~ 'Night** *n.* Vorabend des Dreikönigstages

**twelve** /twelv/ ▶912, ▶1012, ▶1352 ❶ *adj.* zwölf; **~ noon** [zwölf Uhr] Mittag; **~ midnight** [zwölf Uhr] Mitternacht; ⇒ *also* **eight** 1. ❷ *n.* (*number, symbol*) Zwölf, *die;* **the T~:** die Zwölf; die zwölf Apostel; ⇒ *also* **eight** 2 A, D

**twelve: ~month** *n.* (*literary*) **a ~month** zwölf Monate; **~-'note, ~-'tone** *adjs.* (*Mus.*) Zwölfton-

**twentieth** /'twentɪɪθ/ ▶1055 ❶ *adj.* ▶1352 zwanzigst...; ⇒ *also* **eighth** 1. ❷ *n.* (*fraction*) Zwanzigstel, *das;* ⇒ *also* **eighth** 2

**twenty** /'twentɪ/ ▶912, ▶1012, ▶1352 ❶ *adj.* zwanzig; **one-and-~** (*arch.*) ⇒ **twenty-one** 1; ⇒ *also* **eight** 1. ❷ *n.* Zwanzig, *die;* **one-and-~** (*arch.*) ⇒ **twenty-one** 2; ⇒ *also* **eight** 2 A; **eighty** 2

**twenty: ~-first** *etc. adj.* ▶1055, ▶1352 einundzwanzigst... *usw.;* ⇒ *also* **eighth** 1; **~-four-hour** ⇒ **hour** A; **~-one** *etc.* ❶ *adj.* einundzwanzig *usw.;* ⇒ *also* **eight** 1; ❷ *n.* ▶1352 Einundzwanzig *usw., die;* ⇒ *also* **eight** 2 A

t

**'twere** /twə(r), *stressed* twɜː(r)/ (*arch./poet.*) = **it were** 's wäre

**twerp** /twɜːp/ *n.* (*coll.*) (*male*) Blödmann, *der* (*derb*); (*female*) blöde Kuh (*derb*)

**twice** /twaɪs/ *adv.* A (*two times*) zweimal; **she didn't have to be asked ~!** da brauchte man sie nicht zweimal zu fragen!; **~ a year** zweimal im Jahr; **~ weekly** zweimal wöchentlich *nicht attrib.*; **his ~-weekly visit** sein Besuch zweimal in der Woche; B (*doubly*) doppelt; **~ as strong** *etc.* doppelt so stark *usw.*; **he's ~ her age** er ist doppelt so alt wie sie; **have ~ the strength** doppelt so stark sein; **he is ~ the man he was** aus ihm ist ein ganz anderer Mensch geworden; **fly at ~ the speed of sound** mit doppelter Schallgeschwindigkeit fliegen; **sell sth. at ~ the price** (*coll.*) etw. zum doppelten Preis verkaufen; ⇒ *also* **think** 2 A

**twiddle** /'twɪdl/ ❶ *v.t.* herumdrehen an (+ *Dat.*) (*ugs.*); zwirbeln ‹Schnurrbart›; **~ one's cigar** seine Zigarre [zwischen den Fingern] drehen; **~ one's thumbs** (*lit. or fig.*) Däumchen drehen (*ugs.*). ❷ *v.i.* **~ with sth.** mit etw. spielen; an etw. (*Dat.*) herumfummeln (*ugs.*); **~ one's moustache** seinen Schnurrbart zwirbeln. ❸ *n.* Drehung, *die;* **give sth. a ~:** an etw. (*Dat.*) drehen

**twig**[1] /twɪg/ *n.* A (*small branch*) Zweig, *der;* B (*divining rod*) Wünschelrute, *die*

**twig**[2] (*coll.*) ❶ *v.t.* **-gg-:** A (*understand*) kapieren (*ugs.*); B (*notice*) mitkriegen (*ugs.*). ❷ *v.i.* **-gg-:** A (*understand*) es kapieren (*ugs.*); B (*notice*) es mitkriegen (*ugs.*)

**twilight** /'twaɪlaɪt/ *n.* A (*evening light*) Dämmerlicht, *das;* Zwielicht, *das;* B (*period of half-light*) Dämmerung, *die;* **the ~ of the Gods** (*Norse myth.*) die Götterdämmerung; **in the ~ of history** (*fig.*) in grauer Vorzeit; C (*fig.: intermediate state*) Dämmer, *der* (*dichter.*); **his ~ years** sein Lebensabend

**twilight: ~ 'sleep** *n.* (*Med.*) Dämmerschlaf, *der;* **~ zone** *n.* A Niemandsland, *das;* B (*decaying urban area*) heruntergekommene Gegend

**twill** /twɪl/ *n.* (*Textiles*) A (*weave*) Köperbindung, *die;* B (*fabric*) Köper, *der*

**'twill** /twɪl/ (*arch./poet.*) = **it will**

**twin** /twɪn/ ❶ *attrib. adj.* A Zwillings-; **~ brother/sister** Zwillingsbruder, *der*/-schwester, *die;* B (*forming a pair*) Doppel-; doppelt ‹Problem, Verantwortung›; **the ~ threats of war and inflation** die doppelte Bedrohung durch Krieg und Inflation; C (*Bot.*) paarig; D Doppel‹vergaser, -propeller, -schraube usw.›. ❷ *n.* A Zwilling, *der;* **his ~:** sein Zwillingsbruder/seine Zwillingsschwester; B (*Astrol.*) **the T~s** die Zwillinge; ⇒ *also* **Aries**; C (*exact counterpart*) Gegenstück, *das;* Pendant, *das.* ❸ *v.t.*, **-nn-** eng verbinden; **Bottrop is ~ned with Blackpool** Bottrop und Blackpool sind Partnerstädte

**twin: ~ 'bed** *n.* eines von zwei [gleichen] Einzelbetten; **~ beds** zwei Einzelbetten; **~-bedded** *adj.* **a ~-bedded room** ein Zweibettzimmer

**twine** /twaɪn/ ❶ *n.* Bindfaden, *der;* (*thicker*) Kordel, *die;* (*for nets*) Garn, *das.* ❷ *v.t.* A (*form by twisting strands together*) [zusammen]drehen; B (*form by interlacing*) winden (*geh.*) ‹Kranz, Girlande›; C (*coil*) schlingen; **~ sth. round [and round] sth.** etw. [mehrmals] um etw. schlingen; **~ the flowers round the pole** den Mast mit Blumen umwinden. ❸ *v.i.* sich winden (**about, around** um)

**twin-engined** /'twɪnendʒɪnd/ *adj.* zweimotorig

**twinge** /twɪndʒ/ *n.* Stechen, *das;* **a ~ of toothache/rheumatism/pain** ein stechender Zahnschmerz/ziehender rheumatischer Schmerz/stechender Schmerz; **~s** Wehwehchen *Pl.* (*ugs.*); **he suffers from ~s in wet weather** bei feuchtem Wetter zwickt und zwackt es ihn überall; **~[s] of remorse/conscience** (*fig.*) Gewissensbisse

**twinkle** /'twɪŋkl/ ❶ *v.i.* A (*sparkle*) ‹Sterne, Augen:› funkeln, blitzen (**with** vor + *Dat.*); B (*move rapidly*) flink trippeln. ❷ *v.t.* **~ one's eyes** mit den Augen funkeln. ❸ *n.* A **in a ~:** im Handumdrehen; B (*sparkle of the eyes*) Funkeln, *das;* **'...', she said with a ~ in her eye** „...", sagte sie augenzwinkernd; **you were just a ~ in your father's eye then** zu der Zeit wussten deine Eltern noch nicht, dass es dich geben würde; **the project is still only a ~ in his eye** das Projekt ist bis jetzt nur eine ganz vage Idee von ihm; **with a mischievous ~:** mit Schalk in den Augen

**twinkling** /'twɪŋklɪŋ/ *n.* **in a ~, in the ~ of an eye** im Handumdrehen

**twin: ~set** *n.* (*Brit.*) Twinset, *das;* **~ town** *n.* (*Brit.*) Partnerstadt, *die;* **~-tub** *n.* halbautomatische Waschmaschine (*mit separater Schleuder*)

**twirl** /twɜːl/ ❶ *v.t.* A (*spin*) [schnell] drehen; **he ~ed his partner around the dance floor** er wirbelte seine Partnerin über die Tanzfläche; B (*twiddle*) zwirbeln ‹Schnurrbart›; drehen ‹Haar›. ❷ *v.i.* wirbeln (**around** über + *Akk.*); **sb. ~s around** jmd. wirbelt herum. ❸ *n.* A (*~ing*) [Herum]wirbeln, *das;* **give one's moustache a ~:** seinen Schnurrbart zwirbeln; **have a ~ on the dance floor** über die Tanzfläche wirbeln; B (*flourish made in writing*) Schnörkel, *der*

**twirly** /'twɜːlɪ/ *adj.* gewunden; verschnörkelt ‹Schrift›

**twist** /twɪst/ ❶ *v.t.* A (*distort*) verdrehen ‹Worte, Bedeutung›; **~ out of shape** verbiegen; **~ one's ankle** sich (*Dat.*) den Knöchel verrenken; **her face was ~ed with pain** ihr Gesicht war schmerzverzerrt; **~ sb.'s arm** jmdm. den Arm umdrehen; (*fig.*) jmdm. [die] Daumenschrauben anlegen (*scherzh.*); **I didn't have to ~ his arm** ich brauchte ihn nicht lange zu überreden; B (*wind about one another*) flechten ‹Blumen, Haare› (**into** zu); C (*rotate*) drehen; (*back and forth*) hin und her drehen; ⇒ *also* **knife** 1; D (*interweave*) verweben; E (*give spiral form to*) drehen (**into** zu); F (*Brit. coll.: cheat*) beschummeln (*ugs.*); **~ sb. out of sth.** jmdn. um etw. beschummeln (*ugs.*); G (*wrench*) **~ sth. from sb.'s grasp** jmdm. etw. aus der Hand winden. ⇒ *also* **little finger**.
❷ *v.i.* A sich winden; **~ and turn** sich drehen und winden; **~ around sth.** sich um etw. winden; **~ from sb.'s grasp** sich aus jmds. Griff winden; B (*take ~ed position*) sich winden; **he ~ed round in his chair** er verrenkte sich in seinem Sessel; C (*dance*) twisten.
❸ *n.* A (*thread etc.*) Zwirn, *der;* (*loosely twisted*) Twist, *der;* B **~ of lemon/orange** Zitronen-/Orangenscheibe, *die;* C (*~ing*) Drehung, *die;* **give sth. a ~:** an etw. (*Dat.*) drehen; **full of ~s and turns** ‹Straße› voll[er] Biegungen und Kurven; D (*unexpected occurrence*) überraschende Wendung; **~ of fate** Laune des Schicksals; E (*peculiar tendency*) **give a ~ to sth.** etw. verdrehen; **he has an odd ~ to his character** er ist ein bisschen verschroben; **a criminal ~:** eine kriminelle Neigung; F **round the ~** = **round the bend** ⇒ **bend**[1] 1 B; G (*swindle*) Schwindel, *der* (*abwertend*); H (*Amer.: change of procedure*) [überraschender] Wandel; I (*dance*) Twist, *der;* **do the ~:** Twist tanzen; twisten

**~ 'off** ❶ *v.t.* abdrehen. ❷ *v.i.* **the cap ~s off** der Verschluss lässt sich abdrehen

**~ to'gether** *v.t.* zusammendrehen ‹Fäden›

**twisted** /'twɪstɪd/ *adj.* verbogen; (*fig.*) verdreht (*ugs. abwertend*) ‹Geist›; verquer ‹Humor›

**twister** /'twɪstə(r)/ *n.* A Schwindler, *der*/Schwindlerin, *die;* Gauner, *der*/Gaunerin, *die;* B (*Amer.: tornado*) Tornado, *der*

**twisty** /'twɪstɪ/ *adj.* kurvig; kurvenreich

**twit** /twɪt/ ❶ *v.t.*, **-tt-** ⇒ **taunt** 1. ❷ *n.* (*Brit. coll.*) Trottel, *der* (*ugs.*)

**twitch**[1] /twɪtʃ/ ❶ *v.t.* A zupfen; B zucken mit ‹Nase, Schwanz›; wackeln mit ‹Ohr›. ❷ *v.i.* A (*pull sharply*) zupfen (**at** an + *Dat.*); B ‹Mund, Lippen, Hand, Nase:› zucken. ❸ *n.* Zucken, *das*

**twitch [grass]**[2] ⇒ **couch**[2]

**twitchy** /'twɪtʃɪ/ *adj.* (*nervy*) nervös; (*irritable*) reizbar

**twitter** /'twɪtə(r)/ ❶ *n.* A (*coll.: excited state*) **be in a ~, be all of a ~:** [vor Spannung] ganz kribbelig sein (*ugs.*); B (*chirping*) Zwitschern, *das;* Gezwitscher, *das.* ❷ *v.i.* zwitschern; ‹Person:› schnattern (*ugs.*)

**twittish** /'twɪtɪʃ/ *adj.* (*Brit. coll.*) trottelhaft (*ugs.*)

**'twixt** /twɪkst/ *prep.* (*poet./arch.*) zwischen

**two** /tuː/ ▶ **912**, ▶ **1012**, ▶ **1352** ❶ *adj.* zwei; **a box/shirt or ~:** ein, zwei Schachteln/Hemden; ein oder zwei Schachteln/Hemden; ⇒ *also* **eight** 1. ❷ *n.* (*number, symbol*) Zwei, *die;* **the ~:** die beiden; die zwei; **just the ~ of us** nur wir zwei *od.* beiden; **it's as clear as ~ and ~ make four** es ist so klar, wie zwei mal zwei vier sind (*ugs.*); **put ~ and ~ together** (*fig.*) zwei und zwei zusammenzählen; **cut/break in ~:** zweiteilen/entzweibrechen; **~ and ~, ~ by ~** (**~ *at a time***) [zu] zwei und zwei; zu zweien; **that makes ~ of us** (*coll.*) mir gehts/gings genauso (*ugs.*); **~ can play at that game** das kann ich auch. ⇒ *also* **cheer** 1 A; **eight** 2 A, C, D; **game**[1] 1 A; **penny** C

**two: ~-bit** *adj.* (*Amer.*) A (*costing 25 cents*) 25-Cent-; B (*of poor quality*) mies (*ugs.*); **~-by-'four** ❶ *n.* (*piece of wood*) *Holzbalken mit einer Stärke von 2 auf 4 Zoll;* ❷ *adj.* (*Amer. fig.*) Westentaschen-; **~-dimensional** *adj.* zweidimensional; (*fig.*) oberflächlich; **~-door** *attrib. adj.* zweitürig ‹Auto›; **~-edged** *adj.* (*lit. or fig.*) zweischneidig; **~-faced** *adj.* (*fig.*) falsch (*abwertend*); **be ~-faced** ‹Person:› zwei Gesichter haben; **~-'fisted** *adj.* A (*Brit.: clumsy*) ungeschickt; **be ~-fisted** zwei linke Hände haben (*ugs.*); B (*Amer.: vigorous*) kernig; markig

**twofold** /'tuːfəʊld/ *adj., adv.* A zweifach; **be ~:** zweifacher Art *od.* Natur sein; B (*double*) **a ~ increase** ein Anstieg auf das Doppelte; **increase ~:** sich verdoppeln

**two: ~-four time** *n.* (*Mus.*) Zweivierteltakt, *der;* **~-'handed** *adj.* A (*having ~ hands*) zweihändig; B (*requiring both hands*) beidhändig; C (*requiring ~ persons*) **~-handed poker** (*Cards*) Zwei-Mann-Poker, *der;* **~-party system** *n.* Zweiparteiensystem, *das;* **~pence** /'tʌpəns/ *n.* (*Brit.*) zwei Pence; ⇒ *also* **care** 2 C; **~penny** /'tʌpənɪ/ *attrib. adj.* (*Brit.*) Zwei-Pence-; **~penny-halfpenny** /tʌpnɪ'heɪpnɪ/ *attrib. adj.* (*Brit. dated*) unwichtig; lächerlich; (*of poor quality*) mies (*ugs.*); **~pennyhalfpenny novel** Groschenroman, *der* (*abwertend*); **~-piece** ❶ *n.* Zweiteiler, *der;* ❷ *adj.* zweiteilig; **~-pin** ⇒ **pin** 1 C; **~-ply** *adj.* zweifädig ‹Seil, Wolle, Zwirn›; aus zweifädiger Wolle gewebt ‹Teppich›; zweilagig ‹Holz, Papier›; **~-seater** ❶ /-'--/ *n.* Zweisitzer, *der;* ❷ /'---/ *attrib. adj.* zweisitzig

**twosome** /'tuːsəm/ *n.* A Paar, *das;* B (*Golf*) Zweier, *der*

**two: ~-step** *n.* Twostep, *der;* **~-storey** *adj.* zweigeschossig; **~-stroke** *adj.* (*Mech. Engin.*) Zweitakt‹motor, -verfahren›; **~-time** *v.t.* (*coll.*) **~-time sb.** (*be unfaithful*) jmdm. fremdgehen (*ugs.*); (*cheat*) ein falsches Spiel mit jmdm. treiben; **~-timing** *adj.* (*coll.*) falsch; **~-tone** *adj.* A (*in colour*) zweifarbig; **a car in ~-tone green** ein Auto in zwei Grüntönen; B (*in sound*) Zweiklang-

**'twould** /twʊd/ (*arch./poet.*) = **it would**

**two: ~-up ~-down** *n.* kleines [Reihen]haus; **~-way** *adj.* A (*in both directions*) zweibahnig (*Verkehrsw.*); **'~-way traffic ahead'** „Achtung, Gegenverkehr"; B (*involving an exchange between ~ parties*) gegenseitig; **~-way scholarship programme** akademisches Austauschprogramm; **~-way radio** Funksprechgerät, *das;* C (*Electr.*) **~-way switch** Zweiwege[um]schalter, *der;* D **~-way tap** Zweiwegehahn, *der;* E **~-way mirror** Einwegspiegel, *der;* **~-'wheeler** *n.* Zweirad, *das*

**tycoon** /taɪ'kuːn/ *n.* Magnat, *der;* Tycoon, *der*

**tying** ⇒ **tie** 1, 2

**tyke** /taɪk/ *n.* A (*dog*) Köter, *der;* B (*Brit.: churlish person*) Kerl, *der;* C (*Yorkshireman*) **[Yorkshire] ~:** *Mann aus der Grafschaft Yorkshire;* D (*child*) Bengel, *der*

t

**tympani** ⇒ **timpani**

**tympanist** ⇒ **timpanist**

**type** /taɪp/ ❶ *n.* Ⓐ Art, *die;* (*person*) Typ, *der;* **what ~ of car ...?** was für ein Auto ...?; **her beauty is of another ~:** sie verkörpert einen anderen Typ von Schönheit; **she dislikes men of that ~:** sie mag diesen Typ [von] Mann nicht; **she's not my ~:** sie ist nicht mein Typ; **he's not the ~ to let people down** er ist nicht der Typ, der andere im Stich lässt; **he is a different ~ of person** er ist eine andere Art Mensch *od.* ein anderer Typ; **books of this ~:** derartige Bücher; **true to ~:** erwartungsgemäß; Ⓑ (*coll.: character*) Type, *die* (*ugs.*); Ⓒ (*Printing*) Drucktype, *die;* **be in small/italic ~:** klein gedruckt/kursiv gedruckt sein; **in ~:** druckfertig.
❷ *v.t.* Ⓐ (*do typing of*) [mit der Maschine] schreiben; tippen (*ugs.*); **~d letter** maschinegeschriebener Brief; Ⓑ (*classify*) typisieren.
❸ *v.i.* maschineschreiben

**~ 'in** *v.t.* eintippen (*ugs.*); [mit der Schreibmaschine] einfügen

**~ 'out** *v.t.* [mit der Schreibmaschine] abschreiben; abtippen (*ugs.*); (*without original copy*) [in die Maschine] schreiben; tippen (*ugs.*)

**~ 'up** *v.t.* tippen

**-type** /taɪp/ *in comb.* -artig; **ceramic-~ materials** keramikartiges Material; **Cheddar-~ cheese** Käse nach Cheddar-Art

**type: ~cast** *v.t.* [auf eine bestimmte Rolle] festlegen; abstempeln; **be ~cast as the devoted wife** auf die Rolle der treuen Ehefrau festgelegt sein; **~face** *n.* Schriftbild, *das;* **~script** ❶ *n.* maschine[n]geschriebene Fassung; Typoskript, *das;* **in ~script** maschine[n]geschrieben; **be still in ~script** erst als Typoskript vorliegen; ❷ *adj.* ⇒ **typewritten**; **~set** *v.t.* (*Printing*) setzen; **~setter** *n.* (*person*) [Schrift]setzer, *der*/-setzerin, *die;* **~setting** *n.* [Schrift]setzen, *das;* **~setting machine** Setzmaschine, *die;* **~ size** *n.* Schriftgrad, *der;* **~ wheel** ⇒ **daisy-wheel**

**'typewriter** *n.* Schreibmaschine, *die;* **~ ribbon** Farbband, *das*

**'typewritten** *adj.* maschine[n]geschrieben; mit der [Schreib]maschine geschrieben

**typhoid** /'taɪfɔɪd/ *n.* ▶ 1232 (*Med.*) **~ [fever]** Typhus, *der*

**typhoon** /taɪ'fu:n/ *n.* Taifun, *der*

**typhus** /'taɪfəs/ *n.* ▶ 1232 (*Med.*) Fleckfieber, *das*

**typical** /'tɪpɪkl/ *adj.* typisch (**of** für); **that's just ~!** [das ist mal wieder] typisch! (*ugs.*)

**typically** /'tɪpɪklɪ/ *adv.* typischerweise; **~, she turned up late** wie üblich kam sie zu spät

**typify** /'tɪpɪfaɪ/ *v.t.* Ⓐ (*represent*) [symbolhaft] darstellen; Ⓑ (*be an example of*) **~ sth.** als typisches Beispiel für etw. dienen

**typing** /'taɪpɪŋ/ *n.* Maschineschreiben, *das;* **his ~ is excellent** er kann sehr gut Maschine schreiben; **how is your ~?** kannst du [gut] maschineschreiben?; **can you do this piece of ~ for me?** kannst du das für mich [mit der Maschine] schreiben *od.* (*ugs.*) tippen?

**typing: ~ error** *n.* Tippfehler, *der* (*ugs.*); **~ pool** *n.* Schreibzentrale, *die*

**typist** /'taɪpɪst/ *n.* ▶ 1261 Schreibkraft, *die;* **shorthand ~:** Stenotypist, *der*/-typistin, *die;* **she is [not] a good ~:** sie kann [nicht] gut Maschine schreiben

**typo** /'taɪpəʊ/ *n., pl.* **~s** (*coll.*) Druckfehler, *der* (*ugs.*)

**typographer** /taɪ'pɒgrəfə(r)/ *n.* ▶ 1261 Typograph, *der*/Typographin, *die*

**typographic** /taɪpə'græfɪk/, **typographical** /taɪpə'græfɪkl/ *adj.* typographisch; **~ error** Setzfehler, *der*

**typography** /taɪ'pɒgrəfɪ/ *n.* Typographie, *die*

**typology** /taɪ'pɒlədʒɪ/ *n.* Typologie, *die*

**tyrannical** /tɪ'rænɪkl, taɪ'rænɪkl/ *adj.* tyrannisch

**tyrannically** /tɪ'rænɪkəlɪ, taɪ'rænɪkəlɪ/ *adv.* tyrannisch; **behave ~ to sb.** jmdn. tyrannisieren

**tyrannize** (**tyrannise**) /'tɪrənaɪz/ ❶ *v.i.* als Tyrann herrschen; **~ over sb.** jmdn. tyrannisieren. ❷ *v.t.* ‹Chef, Vater, Ehemann:› tyrannisieren; ‹Herrscher:› als Tyrann herrschen über (+ *Akk.*)

**tyrannous** /'tɪrənəs/ *adj.* tyrannisch

**tyranny** /'tɪrənɪ/ *n.* Tyrannei, *die*

**tyrant** /'taɪrənt/ *n.* (*lit. or fig.*) Tyrann, *der*

**tyre** /'taɪə(r)/ *n.* Reifen, *der*

**tyre: ~ chain** *n.* Schneekette, *die;* **~ gauge** *n.* Reifendruckprüfer, *der;* **~ lever** *n.* Reifenheber, *der;* **~ pressure** *n.* Reifendruck, *der*

**tyro** ⇒ **tiro**

**Tyrol** /tɪ'rəʊl/ *pr. n.* Tirol (*das*)

**Tyrolean** /tɪrə'li:ən/ *adj.* Tiroler

**tzar** *etc.* ⇒ **tsar** *etc.*

# Uu

**U**[1], **u** /juː/ *n., pl.* **Us** *or* **U's** U, u, *das*

**U**[2] *adj.* (*Brit. coll.*) für die Oberschicht typisch ‹Benehmen, Ausdruck, Sprache›; **be U** ‹Person:› ein [typischer] Vertreter der Oberschicht sein

**U**[3] *abbr.* Ⓐ (*Brit.*) **universal** jugendfrei ‹Film›; Ⓑ **University** Univ.

**UAE** *abbr.* **United Arab Emirates** VAE

**UB 40** /juːbiː ˈfɔːtɪ/ *n.* (*Brit.*) Ⓐ (*card*) Arbeitslosenausweis, *der;* Ⓑ (*coll.*) Arbeitslose, *der/die*

**ˈU-bend** *n.* U-Rohr, *das;* Knie, *das* (*ugs.*)

**ubiquitous** /juːˈbɪkwɪtəs/ *adj.* allgegenwärtig

**ˈU-boat** *n.* (*Hist.*) [deutsches] U-Boot

**udder** /ˈʌdə(r)/ *n.* Euter, *das*

**UDI** *abbr.* **Unilateral Declaration of Independence** einseitige Unabhängigkeitserklärung

**UDR** *abbr.* **Ulster Defence Regiment** *nordirische paramilitärische Organisation zur Unterstützung der Britischen Armee*

**UEFA** /juːˈeɪfə/ *abbr.* **Union of European Football Associations** UEFA, *die*

**UFO** /ˈjuːfəʊ/ *n., pl.* **~s** Ufo, *das*

**Uganda** /juːˈgændə/ *pr. n.* Uganda (*das*)

**Ugandan** /juːˈgændən/ ▶ 1340 ❶ *adj.* ugandisch; **sb. is ~:** jmd. ist Ugander/Uganderin. ❷ *n.* Ugander, *der*/Uganderin, *die*

**ugh** /ʌh, ʊh, ɜːh/ *int.* bah

**ugli** /ˈʌglɪ/ *n.* **~ [fruit]** Tangelo, *die*

**ugliness** /ˈʌglɪnɪs/ *n., no pl.* Hässlichkeit, *die*

**ugly** /ˈʌglɪ/ *adj.* Ⓐ (*in appearance, morally*) hässlich; **~ duckling** (*fig.*) hässliches Entlein (*ugs. scherzh.*); **as ~ as sin** (*coll.*) potthässlich (*ugs.*); hässlich wie die Nacht; Ⓑ (*nasty*) übel ‹Wunde, Laune, Szene usw.›; **~ customer** (*fig. coll.*) unangenehmer Zeitgenosse/unangenehme Zeitgenossin; **have an ~ temper** übellaunig sein; Ⓒ (*stormy*) übel ‹Wetter, Nacht›; bedrohlich ‹Himmel›

**UHF** *abbr.* **ultra-high frequency** UHF

**UHT** *abbr.* **ultra heat treated** ultrahoch erhitzt; **UHT milk** H-Milch, *die*

**UK** *abbr.* **United Kingdom**

**ukase** /juːˈkeɪz/ *n.* Ukas, *der*

**Ukraine** /juːˈkreɪn/ *pr. n.* Ukraine, *die*

**Ukrainian** /juːˈkreɪnɪən/ ▶ 1275, ▶ 1340 ❶ *adj.* ukrainisch; **sb. is ~:** jmd. ist Ukrainer/Ukrainerin; ⇒ *also* **English** 1. ❷ *n.* Ⓐ (*person*) Ukrainer, *der*/Ukrainerin, *die;* Ⓑ (*language*) Ukrainisch, *das;* ⇒ *also* **English** 2 A

**ukulele** /juːkəˈleɪlɪ/ *n.* (*Mus.*) Ukulele, *die od. das*

**ulcer** /ˈʌlsə(r)/ *n.* ▶ 1232 Geschwür, *das;* (*fig.*) [Krebs]geschwür, *das* (*fig.*); **mouth ~[s]** Aphthe, *die* (*Med.*)

**ulcerate** /ˈʌlsəreɪt/ ❶ *v.i.* (*Med.*) ulzerieren (*fachspr.*); geschwürig werden. ❷ *v.t.* ein Geschwür verursachen in (+ *Dat.*); **an ~d stomach** ein geschwüriger Magen

**ulceration** /ʌlsəˈreɪʃn/ *n.* Ⓐ (*process*) Geschwürbildung, *die;* Ⓑ (*ulcers*) Geschwüre

**ulcerous** /ˈʌlsərəs/ *adj.* (*Med.*) geschwürig; (*fig.*) **racism is an ~ growth in society** der Rassismus ist ein Geschwür am Leibe der Gesellschaft

**ulna** /ˈʌlnə/ *n., pl.* **ulnae** /ˈʌlniː/ (*Anat.*) Elle, *die*

**ulster** *n.* (*coat*) Ulster, *der*

**Ulster** /ˈʌlstə(r)/ *pr. n.* Ulster (*das*)

**Ulster: ~man** /ˈʌlstəmən/ *n., pl.* **~men** /ˈʌlstəmən/ (*inhabitant*) Bewohner von Ulster; (*native*) [geborener] Nordire; **~woman** *n.* (*inhabitant*) Bewohnerin von Ulster; (*native*) [geborene] Nordirin

**ult.** /ʌlt/ *abbr.* (*Commerc.*) **ultimo**

**ulterior** /ʌlˈtɪərɪə(r)/ *adj.* hintergründig; geheim; **~ motive/thought** Hintergedanke, *der*

**ultimate** /ˈʌltɪmət/ ❶ *attrib. adj.* Ⓐ (*final*) letzt...; (*eventual*) endgültig ‹Sieg›; letztendlich ‹Rettung›; größt... ‹Opfer›; **~ result/goal/decision** Endergebnis, *das*/Endziel, *das*/endgültige Entscheidung; **in the ~ analysis** letzten Endes; **he exercises ~ jurisdiction/authority** er hat die höchste richterliche Gewalt/Autorität inne; **the ~ deterrent** das äußerste Abschreckungsmittel; Ⓑ (*fundamental*) tiefst... ‹Grundlage, Wahrheit›; **~ principles** Grundprinzipien; **the ~ particles of matter** die elementaren Teilchen der Materie; **the ~ origin** der eigentliche Ursprung; Ⓒ (*maximum*) maximal; **~ speed** Höchstgeschwindigkeit, *die;* Ⓓ (*best/greatest conceivable*) **the ~ washing machine** die Waschmaschine in Perfektion; **this is the ~ luxury** das ist der Gipfel an Luxus.
❷ *n.* **the ~** (*maximum*) das absolute Maximum; (*minimum*) das absolute Minimum; **the ~ in comfort/luxury/style/fashion** der Gipfel an Bequemlichkeit/Luxus/das Exzellenteste an Stil/in der Mode

**ultimately** /ˈʌltɪmətlɪ/ *adv.* Ⓐ (*in the end*) schließlich; Ⓑ (*in the last analysis*) letzten Endes; (*basically*) im Grunde [genommen]

**ultimatum** /ʌltɪˈmeɪtəm/ *n., pl.* **~s** *or* **ultimata** /ʌltɪˈmeɪtə/ Ultimatum, *das;* **give sb. an ~:** jmdm. ein Ultimatum stellen

**ultimo** /ˈʌltɪməʊ/ *adj.* (*Commerc.*) des vergangenen Monats

**ultra** /ˈʌltrə/ ❶ *n.* Ultra, *der* (*Politikjargon*). ❷ *adj.* extremistisch

**ultra-** /ˈʌltrə/ *in comb.* ultra‹konservativ, -modern›; hyper‹modern, -modisch›

**ultramaˈrine** *n.* Ultramarin, *das*

**ultraˈsonic** *adj.* Ultraschall-

**ultraˈsonically** *adv.* mit Ultraschall

**ultraˈsonics** *n., no pl.* Ⓐ ⇒ **ultrasound;** Ⓑ (*science*) Lehre vom Ultraschall

**ultraˈsound** *n., no pl.* Ultraschall, *der*

**ultraˈviolet** *adj.* (*Phys.*) ultraviolett ‹Strahlen, Licht›; (*using ~ radiation*) UV-‹Lampe, Filter›; **~ treatment** UV-Bestrahlung, *die*

**ululate** /ˈjuːljʊleɪt/ *v.i.* (*literary*) heulen; (*with grief*) wehklagen (*geh.*)

**Ulysses** /ˈjuːlɪsiːz, juːˈlɪsiːz/ *pr. n.* Odysseus (*der*)

**um** /m, əm, ʌm/ ❶ *int.* äh[m]. ❷ /ʌm/ *v.i.*, **-mm-** (*coll.*) **um and ah** herumdrucksen (*ugs.*)

**umbel** /ˈʌmbl/ *n.* (*Bot.*) Dolde, *die*

**umber** /ˈʌmbə(r)/ *n.* **[raw/burnt] ~:** [ungebrannte/gebrannte] Umbra

**umbilical cord** /ʌmˈbɪlɪkl kɔːd/ *n.* Nabelschnur, *die*

**umbra** /ˈʌmbrə/ *n., pl.* **~e** /ˈʌmbriː/ *or* **~s** (*Astron.*) Ⓐ (*in eclipse*) Kernschatten, *der;* Ⓑ (*in sunspot*) Umbra, *die*

**umbrage** /ˈʌmbrɪdʒ/ *n., no pl., no indef. art.* **take ~ [at** *or* **over sth.]** [an etw. (+ *Dat.*)] Anstoß nehmen

**umbrella** /ʌmˈbrelə/ *n.* Ⓐ [Regen]schirm, *der;* **telescopic ~:** Taschenschirm, *der;* **put up an ~:** einen Schirm aufspannen; Ⓑ (*fig.: protection*) Schutz, *der;* (*Mil.*) (*barrage*) Sperrfeuer, *das;* (*air cover*) Jagdschutz, *der;* **the ~ of the Welfare State** das soziale Netz des Wohlfahrtsstaates; Ⓒ (*fig.: unifying agency*) **the company X comes under the ~ of company Y** die Firma X ist eine Tochtergesellschaft der Firma Y; **an ~ organization/group** eine Dachorganisation/eine übergeordnete Gruppe

**umˈbrella stand** *n.* Schirmständer, *der*

**umlaut** /ˈʊmlaʊt/ *n.* Ⓐ (*vowel change*) Umlaut, *der;* Ⓑ (*mark*) Umlautzeichen, *das*

**umpire** /ˈʌmpaɪə(r)/ ❶ *n.* ▶ 1261 Schiedsrichter, *der*/-richterin, *die.* ❷ *v.i.* schiedsrichtern; Schiedsrichter/-richterin sein. ❸ *v.t.* schiedsrichtern bei ‹Spiel, Wettkampf›; pfeifen ‹Fußballspiel usw.›

**umpteen** /ʌmpˈtiːn/ *adj.* (*coll.*) zig (*ugs.*); x (*ugs.*)

**umpteenth** /ʌmpˈtiːnθ/ *adj.* (*coll.*) zigst... (*ugs.*); **for the ~ time** zum zigsten *od.* x-ten Mal (*ugs.*)

**UN** *abbr.* **United Nations** UN[O], *die*

**'un** /ən/ *pron.* (*coll.*) Ⓐ (*person*) Typ, *der;* **he's a tough/bad ~:** er ist ein zäher/übler Bursche (*ugs.*); Ⓑ (*thing*) **a big ~:** ein großer/eine große/ein großes; **big ~s and little ~s** Große und Kleine; ⇒ *also* **wrong 'un**

**unabashed** /ʌnəˈbæʃt/ *adj.* ungeniert; (*without shame*) schamlos; (*undaunted*) unerschrocken ‹Kämpfer›

**unabated** /ʌnəˈbeɪtɪd/ *adj.* unvermindert

**unable** /ʌnˈeɪbl/ *pred. adj.* **be ~ to do sth.** nicht in der Lage sein, etw. zu tun; etw. nicht tun können; **he wanted to attend but was ~ to** er wollte kommen, aber er war dazu nicht in der Lage

**unabridged** /ʌnəˈbrɪdʒd/ *adj.* ungekürzt

**unaccented** /ʌnəkˈsentɪd/ *adj.* unbetont

**unacceptable** /ʌnəkˈseptəbl/ *adj.* unannehmbar; **[be] not ~:** durchaus akzeptabel [sein]; **the ~ face of capitalism** die Kehrseite des Kapitalismus

**unaccommodating** /ʌnəˈkɒmədeɪtɪŋ/ *adj.* ungefällig; (*inflexible*) unnachgiebig

**unaccompanied** /ʌnəˈkʌmpənɪd/ *adj.* ohne Begleitung ‹reisen, singen›; unbegleitet ‹Gepäck, Chor›; (*on aircraft etc.*) **~ minor** allein reisendes Kind; **~ by sth.** nicht begleitet von etw.; **pieces for ~ horn/violin** Solostücke für Horn/Violine

**unaccountable** /ʌnəˈkaʊntəbl/ *adj.* unerklärlich

**unaccountably** /ʌnəˈkaʊntəblɪ/ *adv.* unerklärlicherweise; (*with adj.*) unerklärlich

**unaccounted** /ʌnəˈkaʊntɪd/ *adj.* **~ for** unauffindbar; **several passengers are still ~ for** einige Passagiere werden noch vermisst; **the discrepancy remains ~ for** die Diskrepanz lässt sich nicht erklären

**unaccustomed** /ʌnəˈkʌstəmd/ *adj.* ungewohnt; **be ~ to sth.** etw. (*Akk.*) nicht gewöhnt sein; **~ as I am to public speaking ...:** obwohl ich kein Redner bin ...

**unacquainted** /ʌnəˈkweɪntɪd/ *adj.* **be [completely] ~ with sth.** mit etw. [überhaupt] nicht vertraut sein

**unadopted** /ʌnəˈdɒptɪd/ *adj.* (*Brit.*) von der Gemeinde nicht unterhalten ‹Straße›

**unadorned** /ʌnəˈdɔːnd/ *adj.* schmucklos; ungeschminkt ‹Wahrheit›; schlicht ‹Stil›

**unadulterated** /ʌnəˈdʌltəreɪtɪd/ *adj.* Ⓐ (*pure*) unverfälscht; rein ‹Wasser, Wein›; Ⓑ (*utter*) völlig; **~ rubbish** absoluter Quatsch

**unadventurous** /ʌnədˈventʃərəs/ *adj.* bieder ‹Person›; ereignislos ‹Leben›; (*lacking ideas*) einfallslos ‹Inszenierung, Buch usw.›; **he is an ~ cook** er macht beim Kochen keine Experimente

**unaffected** /ʌnəˈfektɪd/ *adj.* Ⓐ (*not affected*) unberührt; (*Med.*) nicht angegriffen ‹Organ›;

**the area was ~ by the strike** die Gegend war vom Streik nicht betroffen; **she seems to have been ~ by the experience** diese Erfahrung scheint keine Wirkung auf sie gehabt zu haben; **B** (*natural*) natürlich; ungekünstelt; ~ **astonishment** blankes Staunen

**unaffectedly** /ʌnəˈfektɪdlɪ/ *adv.* natürlich; ungekünstelt

**unafraid** /ʌnəˈfreɪd/ *adj.* **be ~ [of sb./sth.]** keine Angst [vor jmdm./etw.] haben

**unaided** /ʌnˈeɪdɪd/ *adj.* ohne fremde Hilfe; **by one's own ~ efforts** ohne jede fremde Hilfe; **walk ~:** ohne Hilfe gehen

**unalike** /ʌnəˈlaɪk/ *pred. adj.* unähnlich; **they are so ~:** sie sind sich (*Dat.*) so unähnlich

**unalloyed** /ʌnˈælɔɪd, ʌnəˈlɔɪd/ *adj.* nicht legiert ‹Metall›; (*fig.*) rein; ungetrübt ‹Freude, Glück›

**unalterable** /ʌnˈɔːltərəbl, ʌnˈɒltərəbl/ *adj.* unabänderlich ‹Gesetz, Schicksal›; unverrückbar ‹Entschluss›

**unaltered** /ʌnˈɔːltəd, ʌnˈɒltəd/ *adj.* unverändert

**unambiguous** /ʌnæmˈbɪgjʊəs/ *adj.* unzweideutig

**unambitious** /ʌnæmˈbɪʃəs/ *adj.* ‹Person› ohne Ergeiz; anspruchslos ‹Buch›; **be ~/a bit ~:** keinen/wenig Ehrgeiz haben

**un-American** /ʌnəˈmerɪkn/ *adj.* **A** (*not typically American*) unamerikanisch; **B** (*contrary to US interests*) antiamerikanisch; ~ **activities** unamerikanische Umtriebe

**unanimity** /juːnəˈnɪmɪtɪ/ *n., no pl.* Einmütigkeit, *die;* **be in perfect ~ over sth.** in etw. (*Dat.*) völlig übereinstimmen

**unanimous** /juːˈnænɪməs/ *adj.* einstimmig; **be ~ in doing sth.** etw. einmütig tun; **be ~ in rejecting** *or* **in their** *etc.* **rejection of sth.** etw. einmütig ablehnen; **the meeting was ~ as to ...:** die Versammlung war einer Meinung über ...

**unanimously** /juːˈnænɪməslɪ/ *adv.* einstimmig

**unannounced** /ʌnəˈnaʊnst/ *adj.* unangemeldet

**unanswerable** /ʌnˈɑːnsərəbl/ *adj.* unbeantwortbar ‹Frage›; unlösbar ‹Rätsel, Problem›; unwiderlegbar ‹Argument›

**unanswered** /ʌnˈɑːnsəd/ *adj.* unbeantwortet; **go ~, be left ~:** unbeantwortet bleiben

**unapologetic** /ʌnəpɒləˈdʒetɪk/ *adj.* **he was quite ~ about it** er machte keinerlei Anstalten, sich zu entschuldigen

**unappealing** /ʌnəˈpiːlɪŋ/ *adj.* unansehnlich ‹Person›; nicht verlockend ‹Aussicht›

**unappetizing** /ʌnˈæpɪtaɪzɪŋ/ *adj.* unappetitlich; unerfreulich ‹Zukunft, Aussicht›

**unappreciative** /ʌnəˈpriːʃɪətɪv, ʌnəˈpriːsɪətɪv/ *adj.* undankbar; **be ~ of sth.** etw. nicht zu würdigen wissen

**unapproachable** /ʌnəˈprəʊtʃəbl/ *adj.* unzugänglich

**unarguable** /ʌnˈɑːgjʊəbl/ *adj.* unhaltbar

**unarm** /ʌnˈɑːm/ ⇒ **disarm** 1

**unarmed** /ʌnˈɑːmd/ *adj.* unbewaffnet; ~ **combat** Kampf ohne Waffen

**unartistic** /ʌnɑːˈtɪstɪk/ *adj.* unkünstlerisch; **be ~:** keinen Sinn für Kunst haben

**unashamed** /ʌnəˈʃeɪmd/ *adj.* schamlos; (*not embarrassed*) ungeniert; unverhohlen ‹Individualist›; **naked and ~:** nackt und ungeniert

**unashamedly** /ʌnəˈʃeɪmɪdlɪ/ *adv.* ungeniert; unverhohlen ‹individualistisch›

**unasked** /ʌnˈɑːskt/ *adj.* **A** (*uninvited*) ungebeten; **B** (*not asked for*) ~ **[for]** ungefragt

**unassailable** /ʌnəˈseɪləbl/ *adj.* **A** (*not open to assault*) uneinnehmbar; **an ~ lead** ein nicht aufzuholender Vorsprung; **B** (*irrefutable*) unwiderlegbar

**unassisted** /ʌnəˈsɪstɪd/ ⇒ **unaided**

**unassuming** /ʌnəˈsjuːmɪŋ/ *adj.* bescheiden; unprätentiös (*geh.*)

**unattached** /ʌnəˈtætʃt/ *adj.* **A** (*not fixed*) nicht befestigt; **B** (*without a partner*) ungebunden

**unattainable** /ʌnəˈteɪnəbl/ *adj.* unerreichbar

**unattempted** /ʌnəˈtemptɪd/ *adj.* **the climb remains ~:** die Ersteigung ist noch nicht versucht worden

**unattended** /ʌnəˈtendɪd/ *adj.* **A** ~ **to** (*not dealt with*) unerledigt, unbearbeitet ‹Post, Angelegenheit›; nicht bedient ‹Kunde›; nicht behandelt ‹Patient, Wunde›; **leave a customer/patient ~ to** einen Kunden nicht bedienen/einen Patienten nicht behandeln; **he left the faults ~ to** er hat sich um die Fehler nicht gekümmert; **B** (*not supervised*) unbeaufsichtigt ‹Kind›; unbewacht ‹Parkplatz, Gepäck›; **leave a patient ~:** einen Patienten allein lassen; **travel ~:** ohne Begleitung reisen

**unattractive** /ʌnəˈtræktɪv/ *adj.* unattraktiv; unschön ‹Ort, Merkmal›; wenig verlockend ‹Angebot, Vorschlag›; **not ~:** nicht ohne Reiz

**unauthorized** /ʌnˈɔːθəraɪzd/ *adj.* unbefugt; nicht autorisiert ‹Biographie›; nicht genehmigt ‹Demonstration›; **no entry for ~ persons** Zutritt für Unbefugte verboten

**unavailable** /ʌnəˈveɪləbl/ *adj.* nicht erhältlich ‹Ware›; **be ~ for comment** zu einer Stellungnahme nicht zur Verfügung stehen; **the manager is ~:** der Manager ist nicht zu sprechen

**unavailing** /ʌnəˈveɪlɪŋ/ *adj.* vergeblich

**unavoidable** /ʌnəˈvɔɪdəbl/ *adj.* unvermeidlich; ~ **delays** unvermeidbare Verzögerungen

**unavoidably** /ʌnəˈvɔɪdəblɪ/ *adv.* **we were ~ delayed** unsere Verspätung ließ sich nicht vermeiden; **he has been ~ detained** er konnte nicht verhindern, dass er aufgehalten wurde

**unaware** /ʌnəˈweə(r)/ *adj.* **be ~ of sth.** sich (*Dat.*) einer Sache (*Gen.*) nicht bewusst sein; **he was not ~ of this fact** diese Tatsache war ihm durchaus bekannt

**unawares** /ʌnəˈweəz/ *adv.* unerwartet; **come upon sb./catch sb. ~:** jmdn. überraschen; **take sb. ~:** für jmdn. unerwartet kommen

**unbalanced** /ʌnˈbælənst/ *adj.* **A** unausgewogen; **B** (*mentally ~*) unausgeglichen

**unbar** /ʌnˈbɑː(r)/ *v.t.*, **-rr-** entriegeln

**unbearable** /ʌnˈbeərəbl/ *adj.*, **unbearably** /ʌnˈbeərəblɪ/ *adv.* unerträglich

**unbeatable** /ʌnˈbiːtəbl/ *adj.* unschlagbar (*ugs.*)

**unbeaten** /ʌnˈbiːtn/ *adj.* **A** (*not defeated*) ungeschlagen; **they lost their ~ record** ihre Siegesserie endete; **B** (*not surpassed*) unerreicht; **this record is still ~:** dieser Rekord ist immer noch ungebrochen

**unbecoming** /ʌnbɪˈkʌmɪŋ/ *adj.* **A** (*improper*) unschicklich (*geh.*); **conduct ~ to a soldier** ein für einen Soldaten ungebührliches Verhalten; **B** (*not attractive*) unvorteilhaft ‹Kleidung, Frisur›; unschön ‹Nase›

**unbeknown** /ʌnbɪˈnəʊn/ *adj.* ~ **to me/her/her boss** ohne mein/ihr Wissen/ohne Wissen ihres Chefs

**unbelievable** /ʌnbɪˈliːvəbl/ *adj.* **A** (*hardly believable*) unglaublich; **B** (*tremendous*) unwahrscheinlich ‹Hunger, Durst›

**unbelievably** /ʌnbɪˈliːvəblɪ/ *adv.* **A** *as intensifier* unglaublich ‹dumm, dick, jung usw.›; **B** *as sentence-modifier* (*not believably*) ~, **the rider managed to stay on the horse** es war kaum zu glauben, aber der Reiter konnte sich auf dem Pferd halten

**unbeliever** /ʌnbɪˈliːvə(r)/ *n.* Ungläubige, *der/die*

**unbelieving** /ʌnbɪˈliːvɪŋ/ *adj.* ungläubig

**unbend** /ʌnˈbend/ **1** *v.t.*, **unbent** /ʌnˈbent/ geradebiegen ‹Draht, Metall, Stoßstange›; auseinander biegen ‹Büroklammer›; ~ **one's body** *or* **oneself** sich aufrichten. **2** *v.i.*, **unbent A** (*sit/stand up*) sich aufrichten; **B** (*become affable*) aus sich (*Dat.*) herausgehen

**unbending** /ʌnˈbendɪŋ/ *adj.* (*inflexible*) unbeugsam

**unbiased, unbiassed** /ʌnˈbaɪəst/ *adj.* unvoreingenommen

**unbidden** /ʌnˈbɪdn/ *adj.* unaufgefordert; (*uninvited*) ungebeten

**unbind** /ʌnˈbaɪnd/ *v.t.*, *forms as* **bind** 1 losbinden ‹Mensch, Tier›; lösen ‹Haare›

**unbirthday** /ʌnˈbɜːθdeɪ/ *adj.* (*Brit. coll.*) ~ **present** Geschenk ohne besonderen Anlass

**unbleached** /ʌnˈbliːtʃt/ *adj.* ungebleicht

**unblemished** /ʌnˈblemɪʃt/ *adj.* makellos ‹Haut, Lack, Ruf›; unbefleckt (*geh.*) ‹Ehre›

**unblinking** /ʌnˈblɪŋkɪŋ/ *adj.* unverwandt ‹Blick›; unbewegt ‹Haltung, Miene›

**unblock** /ʌnˈblɒk/ *v.t.* frei machen *od.* bekommen; **remain ~ed** frei bleiben

**unblushing** /ʌnˈblʌʃɪŋ/ *adj.* (*fig.*) schamlos

**unbolt** /ʌnˈbəʊlt/ *v.t.* aufriegeln

**unborn** /ʌnˈbɔːn, *attrib.* ˈʌnbɔːn/ *adj.* ungeboren; **generations [yet] ~:** künftige Generationen

**unbosom** /ʌnˈbʊzəm/ *v. refl.* ~ **oneself [to sb.]** [jmdm.] sein Herz ausschütten

**unbound** /ʌnˈbaʊnd/ *adj.* **A** (*not tied*) offen ‹Haar›; **Prometheus ~:** der entfesselte Prometheus; **B** ungebunden ‹Buch›

**unbounded** /ʌnˈbaʊndɪd/ *adj.* **A** (*unchecked*) uneingeschränkt ‹Freiheit›; unkontrolliert ‹Gefühl›; **B** (*unlimited*) grenzenlos

**unbowed** /ʌnˈbaʊd/ *adj.* ungebeugt; **bloody but ~:** angeschlagen, aber unbesiegt

**unbreakable** /ʌnˈbreɪkəbl/ *adj.* unzerbrechlich

**unbridled** /ʌnˈbraɪdld/ *adj.* (*fig.*) ungezügelt ‹Machtstreben›; bodenlos (*ugs.*) ‹Unverschämtheit›; grenzenlos ‹Enthusiasmus›

**un-British** /ʌnˈbrɪtɪʃ/ *adj.* unbritisch

**unbroken** /ʌnˈbrəʊkn/ *adj.* **A** (*undamaged*) heil; unbeschädigt; **B** (*not interrupted*) ununterbrochen; ~ **sleep/peace/silence** ungestörter Schlaf/Friede/durch nichts unterbrochene Stille; **have a night's ~ sleep** die Nacht durchschlafen; **C** (*not surpassed*) ungebrochen ‹Rekord›; **D** (*Equit.*) nicht zugeritten ‹Pferd›

**unbuckle** /ʌnˈbʌkl/ *v.t.* aufschnallen

**unbuilt** /ʌnˈbɪlt/ *adj.* ungebaut; ~ **on** (*not occupied by a building*) unbebaut

**unburden** /ʌnˈbɜːdn/ *v.t.* (*literary*) befreien ‹Gewissen›; ~ **oneself/one's heart [to sb.]** [jmdm.] sein Herz ausschütten; ~ **oneself of sth.** sich von etw. befreien; **to her he could ~ himself of all his anxieties** ihr konnte er alle seine Ängste anvertrauen

**unbusinesslike** /ʌnˈbɪznɪslaɪk/ *adj.* **he is ~, he has an ~ approach** er geht nicht wie ein Geschäftsmann an die Dinge heran

**unbutton** /ʌnˈbʌtn/ *v.t.* aufknöpfen

**unbuttoned** /ʌnˈbʌtnd/ *adj.* (*lit. or fig.*) aufgeknöpft; offen

**uncalled-for** /ʌnˈkɔːldfɔː(r)/ *adj.* unangebracht

**uncannily** /ʌnˈkænɪlɪ/ *adv.* unheimlich

**uncanny** /ʌnˈkænɪ/ *adj.* **A** (*seemingly supernatural*) unheimlich; **B** (*mysterious*) verblüffend

**uncap** /ʌnˈkæp/ *v.t.*, **-pp-** öffnen ‹Flasche›

**uncared-for** /ʌnˈkeədfɔː(r)/ *adj.* vernachlässigt

**uncaring** /ʌnˈkeərɪŋ/ *adj.* gleichgültig

**uncarpeted** /ʌnˈkɑːpɪtɪd/ *adj.* teppichlos

**unceasing** /ʌnˈsiːsɪŋ/ *adj.* unaufhörlich; **the rain was ~:** es regnete ununterbrochen

**unceasingly** /ʌnˈsiːsɪŋlɪ/ *adv.* ununterbrochen

**uncensored** /ʌnˈsensəd/ *adj.* unzensiert

**unceremonious** /ʌnserɪˈməʊnɪəs/ *adj.* **A** (*informal*) formlos; **B** (*abrupt*) brüsk

**unceremoniously** /ʌnserɪˈməʊnɪəslɪ/ *adv.* ohne Umschweife

**uncertain** /ʌnˈsɜːtn, ʌnˈsɜːtɪn/ *adj.* **A** (*not sure*) **be ~ [whether ...]** sich (*Dat.*) nicht sicher sein[, ob ...]; **I am ~ of his loyalty** ich bin mir seiner Treue nicht sicher; **B** (*not clear*) ungewiss ‹Ergebnis, Zukunft, Schicksal›; **of ~ age/origin** unbestimmten Alters/unbestimmter Herkunft; **a play of ~ authorship** ein Stück, dessen Verfasser nicht [sicher] bekannt ist; **it is still ~ whether ...:** es ist noch ungewiss, ob ...; **it is ~ who was the inventor** der Erfinder ist nicht [genau] bekannt; **C** (*unsteady*) unsicher

U

‹Schritte›; **D** (*changeable*) unbeständig ‹Charakter, Wetter›; unstet ‹Dasein›; wechselnd ‹Gesundheitszustand›; flackernd ‹Schein›; **E** (*ambiguous*) vage; **in no ~ terms** ganz eindeutig

**uncertainly** /ʌnˈsɜːtnlɪ, ʌnˈsɜːtɪnlɪ/ *adv.* **A** (*without definite aim*) ziellos; **B** (*without confidence*) unsicher

**uncertainty** /ʌnˈsɜːtntɪ, ʌnˈsɜːtɪntɪ/ *n.* **A** *no pl.* (*doubtfulness*) Ungewissheit, *die;* **there is some ~ about it** es ist etwas ungewiss; **any ~ about it was dispelled** jeder Zweifel darüber wurde ausgeräumt; **B** (*doubtful point*) Unklarheit, *die;* **C** *no pl.* (*hesitation*) Unsicherheit, *die;* **the ~ of his touch** seine unsichere Hand

**unˈcertainty principle** *n.* (*Phys.*) Unschärferelation, *die*

**unchallenged** /ʌnˈtʃælɪndʒd/ *adj.* unangefochten; **go ~** ‹Autorität, Position:› nicht infrage gestellt werden; **let a statement go ~:** eine Behauptung unwidersprochen lassen

**unchangeable** /ʌnˈtʃeɪnʒəbl/ *adj.* unabänderlich

**unchanged** /ʌnˈtʃeɪndʒd/ *adj.* unverändert

**unchanging** /ʌnˈtʃeɪndʒɪŋ/ *adj.* unveränderlich; **~ monotony** gleichförmige Eintönigkeit

**uncharacteristic** /ʌnkærɪktəˈrɪstɪk/ *adj.* uncharakteristisch (**of** für); ungewohnt ‹Grobheit, Schärfe›

**uncharged** /ʌnˈtʃɑːdʒd/ *adj.* ungeladen

**uncharitable** /ʌnˈtʃærɪtəbl/ *adj.*, **uncharitably** /ʌnˈtʃærɪtəblɪ/ *adv.* lieblos

**uncharted** /ʌnˈtʃɑːtɪd/ *adj.* auf keiner Landkarte verzeichnet; unerforscht ‹Wildnis›; unbekannt ‹Insel, Gewässer›; (*fig.*) **the ~ regions of the psyche** die unerforschten Bereiche der Psyche

**unchecked** /ʌnˈtʃekt/ *adj.* **A** (*not examined*) ungeprüft; **B** (*unrestrained*) ungehindert; nicht eingedämmt ‹Epidemie, Inflation›; **sth. goes ~:** gegen etw. wird nichts getan

**unchivalrous** /ʌnˈʃɪvlrəs/ *adj.* unritterlich

**unchristian** /ʌnˈkrɪstjən/ *adj.* unchristlich

**uncivil** /ʌnˈsɪvɪl, ʌnˈsɪvl/ *adj.* unhöflich

**uncivilized** /ʌnˈsɪvɪlaɪzd/ *adj.* unzivilisiert; primitiv ‹Zustände›; **an ~ hour** eine unchristliche Tageszeit (*ugs. scherzh.*)

**unclaimed** /ʌnˈkleɪmd/ *adj.* herrenlos; nicht abgeholt ‹Brief, Preis›; **the money is still ~:** bis jetzt hat niemand Anspruch auf das Geld erhoben

**unclassified** /ʌnˈklæsɪfaɪd/ *adj.* nicht klassifiziert; (*not subject to security classification*) nicht geheim

**uncle** /ˈʌŋkl/ *n.* **A** Onkel, *der;* **B** (*arch. coll.: pawnbroker*) Pfandleiher, *der;* **C** **cry ~** (*Amer. coll.: surrender*) sich geschlagen geben

**unclean** /ʌnˈkliːn/ *adj.* unrein

**Uncle: ~ ˈSam** *n.* (*coll.*) Uncle Sam (*der*); **~ ˈTom** *n.* (*Amer.*) *den Weißen gegenüber gefügiger Schwarzer in den USA*

**unclothed** /ʌnˈkləʊðd/ *adj.* unbekleidet

**unclouded** /ʌnˈklaʊdɪd/ *adj.* wolkenlos; (*fig.*) **~ mind/happiness** klarer Verstand/ungetrübtes Glück

**uncluttered** /ʌnˈklʌtəd/ *adj.* ordentlich

**uncoil** /ʌnˈkɔɪl/ **1** *v.t.* abwickeln. **2** *v. refl.* sich abwickeln; ‹Schlange:› sich strecken

**uncoloured** (*Amer.:* **uncolored**) /ʌnˈkʌləd/ *adj.* (*lit. or fig.*) ungefärbt; **~ by prejudice** von keinem Vorurteil gefärbt

**uncomfortable** /ʌnˈkʌmfətəbl/ *adj.* **A** (*causing physical discomfort*) unbequem; **B** (*feeling discomfort*) **be ~:** sich unbehaglich fühlen; **the heat made me ~:** durch die Hitze fühlte ich mich unbehaglich; **C** (*uneasy, disconcerting*) unangenehm; peinlich ‹Stille›; **his gaze made me ~:** sein Blick war mir unangenehm; **if you feel ~ about it** wenn es dir unangenehm ist; **sb. has an ~ awareness of sth.** jmd. ist sich (*Dat.*) einer Sache (*Gen.*) peinlich bewusst

**uncomfortably** /ʌnˈkʌmfətəblɪ/ *adv.* **A** (*with physical discomfort*) unbequem; **~ oppressive** unangenehm [und] drückend; **B** (*uneasily*) unbehaglich; **be** *or* **feel ~ aware of sth.** sich (*Dat.*) einer Sache (*Gen.*) peinlich bewusst sein

**uncommitted** /ʌnkəˈmɪtɪd/ *adj.* unbeteiligt

**uncommon** /ʌnˈkɒmən/ *adj.* ungewöhnlich; **it is not ~ for him to be found there** es ist [ganz und gar] nicht ungewöhnlich, dass man ihn dort findet

**uncommonly** /ʌnˈkɒmənlɪ/ *adv.* ungewöhnlich

**uncommunicative** /ʌnkəˈmjuːnɪkətɪv/ *adj.* verschlossen

**uncompetitive** /ʌnkəmˈpetɪtɪv/ *adj.* wettbewerbsunfähig; **prices were ~:** die Preise waren nicht wettbewerbs- *od.* konkurrenzfähig; **this makes the salaries even more ~:** dadurch nimmt die Wettbewerbsfähigkeit der Gehälter noch weiter ab

**uncomplaining** /ʌnkəmˈpleɪnɪŋ/ *adj.*, **uncomplainingly** /ʌnkəmˈpleɪnɪŋlɪ/ *adv.* klaglos

**uncompleted** /ʌnkəmˈpliːtɪd/ *adj.* unvollendet

**uncomplicated** /ʌnˈkɒmplɪkeɪtɪd/ *adj.* unkompliziert

**uncomplimentary** /ʌnkɒmplɪˈmentərɪ/ *adj.* wenig schmeichelhaft; **be ~ about sb./sth.** sich nicht sehr schmeichelhaft über jmdn./etw. äußern

**uncomprehending** /ʌnkɒmprɪˈhendɪŋ/ *adj.* verständnislos

**uncompromising** /ʌnˈkɒmprəmaɪzɪŋ/ *adj.*, **uncompromisingly** /ʌnˈkɒmprəmaɪzɪŋlɪ/ *adv.* kompromisslos

**unconcealed** /ʌnkənˈsiːld/ *adj.* unverhohlen

**unconcern** /ʌnkənˈsɜːn/ *n.*, *no pl.* Gleichgültigkeit, *die*

**unconcerned** /ʌnkənˈsɜːnd/ *adj.* gleichgültig; (*free from anxiety*) unbekümmert; **sb. is ~ about sb./sth.** jmdm. ist jmd./etw. gleichgültig; **she seemed ~ as to the outcome** das Ergebnis schien ihr gleichgültig zu sein; **he is ~ with** *or* **about style** er kümmert sich nicht um Stil

**unconcernedly** /ʌnkənˈsɜːnɪdlɪ/ *adv.* gleichgültig; (*free from anxiety*) unbekümmert

**unconditional** /ʌnkənˈdɪʃənl/ *adj.* bedingungslos ‹Kapitulation›; kategorisch ‹Ablehnung›; ‹Versprechen› ohne Vorbehalte

**unconditionally** /ʌnkənˈdɪʃənəlɪ/ *adv.* bedingungslos; kategorisch ‹ablehnen›; ohne Vorbehalte ‹versprechen›

**unconfirmed** /ʌnkənˈfɜːmd/ *adj.* unbestätigt

**uncongenial** /ʌnkənˈdʒiːniəl/ *adj.* unsympathisch ‹Person›; **I find him/the work ~:** er ist mir unsympathisch/die Arbeit sagt mir nicht zu *od.* liegt mir nicht; **an ~ atmosphere** ein unangenehmes Klima

**unconnected** /ʌnkəˈnektɪd/ *adj.* **A** nicht verbunden; **~ with any party** nicht parteigebunden; **B** (*disjointed, isolated*) zusammenhanglos

**unconquerable** /ʌnˈkɒŋkərəbl/ *adj.* unbezwingbar; unerschütterlich ‹Entschlossenheit›

**unconquered** /ʌnˈkɒŋkəd/ *adj.* nicht erobert

**unconscionable** /ʌnˈkɒnʃənəbl/ *adj.* übertrieben lang ‹Zeit›; übertrieben hoch ‹Betrag›

**unconscionably** /ʌnˈkɒnʃənəblɪ/ *adv.* übertrieben

**unconscious** /ʌnˈkɒnʃəs/ **1** *adj.* **A** (*Med.: senseless*) bewusstlos; **B** (*unaware*) **be ~ of sth.** sich einer Sache (*Gen.*) nicht bewusst sein; **I was ~ of what was going on around me** ich war mir nicht bewusst *od.* wusste nicht, was um mich herum vorging; **she was ~ of the tragedy** sie wusste nichts von der Tragödie; **he was ~ of the change in her** er merkte *od.* bemerkte nicht, dass sie sich verändert hatte; **C** (*not intended; Psych.*) unbewusst; unfreiwillig ‹Komik›; **an ~ act** eine unbewusst begangene Tat. **2** *n.* Unbewusste, *das*

**unconsciously** /ʌnˈkɒnʃəslɪ/ *adv.* unbewusst; **~, he was falling under her spell** ohne es zu merken, verfiel er ihrem Zauber

**unconsciousness** /ʌnˈkɒnʃəsnɪs/ *n.*, *no pl.* **A** (*loss of consciousness*) Bewusstlosigkeit, *die;* **B** (*unawareness*) fehlende Bewusstheit

**unconsidered** /ʌnkənˈsɪdəd/ *adj.* **A** (*disregarded*) unbedeutend; **B** (*not based on consideration*) unüberlegt, vorschnell ‹Bemerkung›

**unconstitutional** /ʌnkɒnstɪˈtjuːʃənl/ *adj.*, **unconstitutionally** /ʌnkɒnstɪˈtjuːʃənəlɪ/ *adv.* (*in State*) verfassungswidrig; (*in other organization*) satzungswidrig

**unconstrained** /ʌnkənˈstreɪnd/ *adj.* ungezwungen

**uncontaminated** /ʌnkənˈtæmɪneɪtɪd/ *adj.* unverschmutzt, nicht verseucht (**with** von); (*fig.*) unverdorben (**with** durch)

**uncontested** /ʌnkənˈtestɪd/ *adj.* unangefochten; **go ~:** nicht angefochten werden; **it was an ~ election** bei der Wahl gab es keinen Gegenkandidaten

**uncontrollable** /ʌnkənˈtrəʊləbl/ *adj.* unkontrollierbar; **become ~:** außer Kontrolle geraten; **the child is ~:** das Kind ist nicht zu bändigen

**uncontrollably** /ʌnkənˈtrəʊləblɪ/ *adv.* unkontrollierbar; unbeherrscht ‹lachen›; hemmungslos ‹weinen usw.›

**uncontrolled** /ʌnkənˈtrəʊld/ *adj.* unkontrolliert; **leave ~:** nicht kontrollieren; **~ dogs/children** herrenlose Hunde/unbeaufsichtigte Kinder

**uncontroversial** /ʌnkɒntrəˈvɜːʃl/ *adj.* nicht kontrovers; **be ~:** keinerlei Widerspruch hervorrufen; **he is an ~ figure** er gibt keinen Anlass zu Kontroversen

**unconventional** /ʌnkənˈvenʃənl/ *adj.*, **unconventionally** /ʌnkənˈvenʃənəlɪ/ *adv.* unkonventionell

**unconverted** /ʌnkənˈvɜːtɪd/ *adj.* **A** (*not rebuilt*) nicht umgebaut; **B** (*Relig.*) nicht konvertiert; **he is** *or* **remains ~ [to sth.]** er lässt sich nicht [zu etw.] bekehren

**unconvinced** /ʌnkənˈvɪnst/ *adj.* nicht überzeugt; **remain ~:** sich nicht überzeugen lassen; **his arguments left her ~:** seine Argumente überzeugten sie nicht

**unconvincing** /ʌnkənˈvɪnsɪŋ/ *adj.* nicht überzeugend

**unconvincingly** /ʌnkənˈvɪnsɪŋlɪ/ *adv.* nicht überzeugend; **he argues very ~:** seine Argumente überzeugen ganz und gar nicht

**uncooked** /ʌnˈkʊkt/ *adj.* roh; **the cake was still ~ in the centre** der Kuchen war in der Mitte noch nicht durchgebacken

**uncooperative** /ʌnkəʊˈɒpərətɪv/ *adj.* unkooperativ; wenig entgegenkommend; (*unhelpful*) wenig hilfsbereit; **a bit less ~:** ein bisschen hilfsbereiter

**uncoordinated** /ʌnkəʊˈɔːdɪneɪtɪd/ *adj.* unkoordiniert; **very ~:** überhaupt nicht koordiniert

**uncork** /ʌnˈkɔːk/ *v.t.* entkorken

**uncorroborated** /ʌnkəˈrɒbəreɪtɪd/ *adj.* unbestätigt

**uncountable** /ʌnˈkaʊntəbl/ *adj.* (*Ling.*) unzählbar

**uncounted** /ʌnˈkaʊntɪd/ *adj.* nicht gezählt

**uncouple** /ʌnˈkʌpl/ *v.t.* abkoppeln ‹Hunde, Waggon, Lokomotive›

**uncouth** /ʌnˈkuːθ/ *adj.* **A** (*lacking refinement*) ungeschliffen; ungehobelt ‹Person, Benehmen›; grob ‹Bemerkung, Sprache›; **B** (*boorish*) unkultiviert; flegelhaft (*abwertend*)

**uncouthness** /ʌnˈkuːθnɪs/ *n.*, *no pl.* **A** (*lack of refinement*) Ungeschliffenheit, *die;* (*of remark, language*) Grobheit, *die;* **B** (*boorishness*) Unkultiviertheit, *die;* Flegelhaftigkeit, *die* (*abwertend*)

**uncover** /ʌnˈkʌvə(r)/ *v.t.* **A** (*remove cover from*) aufdecken; freilegen ‹Wunde, Begrabenes›; **~ one's head** die Kopfbedeckung abnehmen; **B** (*disclose*) aufdecken ‹Skandal, Verschwörung, Wahrheit›

**uncovered** /ʌnˈkʌvəd/ *adj.* unbedeckt; **[with head] ~:** ohne Kopfbedeckung

**uncritical** /ʌnˈkrɪtɪkl/ *adj.* unkritisch; **be ~ of sth.** etw. nicht kritisieren

**uncritically** /ʌnˈkrɪtɪkəlɪ/ *adv.* unkritisch

**uncross** /ʌnˈkrɒs/ *v.t.* **~ one's legs** seine Beine wieder nebeneinander stellen/nebeneinander legen

**uncrossed** /ʌnˈkrɒst/ *adj.* (*Brit.*) **an ~ cheque/postal order** ein Barscheck/Postbarscheck

**uncrowded** /ʌnˈkraʊdɪd/ *adj.* nicht überlaufen

u

**uncrowned** /ʌnˈkraʊnd/ *adj.* (*lit. or fig.*) ungekrönt

**UNCTAD** /ˈʌŋktæd/ *abbr.* **United Nations Conference on Trade and Development** Welthandels- und Entwicklungskonferenz [der Vereinten Nationen]

**unction** /ˈʌŋkʃn/ ⇨ **extreme** 1 D

**unctuous** /ˈʌŋktjʊəs/ *adj.* salbungsvoll; ölig

**uncultivated** /ʌnˈkʌltɪveɪtɪd/ *adj.* Ⓐ (*Agric.*) nicht bestellt; Ⓑ unkultiviert

**uncultured** /ʌnˈkʌltʃəd/ *adj.* unkultiviert

**uncured** /ʌnˈkjʊəd/ *adj.* Ⓐ (*not made healthy*) ungeheilt; Ⓑ (*not prepared for keeping*) ungepökelt ‹Fleisch›; ungeräuchert ‹Fisch›; nicht getrocknet ‹Häute, Tabak›

**uncurl** /ʌnˈkɜːl/ ❶ *v.t.* auseinander rollen. ❷ *v. refl.* sich strecken. ❸ *v.i.* sich auseinander rollen

**uncurtained** /ʌnˈkɜːtənd/ *adj.* vorhanglos; **be ~:** keine Vorhänge haben

**uncut** /ʌnˈkʌt/ *adj.* Ⓐ (*not cut*) nicht geschnitten ‹Gras, Haare usw.›; nicht gemäht ‹Rasen›; Ⓑ (*with pages not trimmed*) unbeschnitten ‹Buch›; (*not slit open*) nicht aufgeschnitten ‹Seiten›; Ⓒ (*not shaped by cutting*) ungeschliffen ‹Edelstein›; Ⓓ (*not shortened*) ungekürzt ‹Buch, Film›

**undamaged** /ʌnˈdæmɪdʒd/ *adj.* unbeschädigt

**undated** /ʌnˈdeɪtɪd/ *adj.* undatiert

**undaunted** /ʌnˈdɔːntɪd/ *adj.* unverzagt; **~ by threats** durch Drohungen nicht eingeschüchtert

**undecided** /ʌndɪˈsaɪdɪd/ *adj.* Ⓐ (*not settled*) nicht entschieden; Ⓑ (*hesitant*) unentschlossen; **be ~ whether to do sth.** sich (*Dat.*) noch unschlüssig sein, ob man etw. tun soll

**undecipherable** /ʌndɪˈsaɪfərəbl/ *adj.* **be ~:** sich nicht entziffern lassen

**undeclared** /ʌndɪˈkleəd/ *adj.* Ⓐ nicht erklärt ‹Krieg›; Ⓑ nicht deklariert ‹zollpflichtige Waren›; **~ income** (*for tax*) nicht angegebenes Einkommen

**undefeated** /ʌndɪˈfiːtɪd/ *adj.* ungeschlagen ‹Mannschaft›; unbesiegt ‹Heer›

**undefended** /ʌndɪˈfendɪd/ *adj.* Ⓐ unverteidigt; (*not protected*) ungeschützt; Ⓑ (*Law*) unverteidigt; **be ~:** keinen Verteidiger haben; **the case was ~:** der Fall wurde ohne Verteidigung verhandelt

**undefiled** /ʌndɪˈfaɪld/ *adj.* unverdorben; (*not desecrated*) unbefleckt

**undefined** /ʌndɪˈfaɪnd/ *adj.* nicht definiert; (*indefinite*) unbestimmt

**ˈundelete** *v.t.* (*Computing*) wiederherstellen

**undelivered** /ʌndɪˈlɪvəd/ *adj.* nicht zugestellt ‹Postsendung›; nicht überbracht ‹Botschaft, Nachricht›; (*on letter*) **if ~:** wenn unzustellbar

**undemanding** /ʌndɪˈmɑːndɪŋ/ *adj.* anspruchslos

**undemocratic** /ʌndeməˈkrætɪk/ *adj.* undemokratisch

**undemonstrative** /ʌndɪˈmɒnstrətɪv/ *adj.* zurückhaltend

**undeniable** /ʌndɪˈnaɪəbl/ *adj.* unbestreitbar; **it is ~ that ...:** es ist nicht zu leugnen, dass ...; **produce ~ evidence** Beweise vorlegen, deren Echtheit nicht bezweifelt werden kann

**undeniably** /ʌndɪˈnaɪəblɪ/ *adv.* unbestreitbar

**undependable** /ʌndɪˈpendəbl/ *adj.* unzuverlässig

**under** /ˈʌndə(r)/ ❶ *prep.* Ⓐ (*underneath, below*) (*indicating position*) unter (+ *Dat.*); (*indicating motion*) unter (+ *Akk.*); **from ~ the table/bed** unter dem Tisch/Bett hervor; Ⓑ (*undergoing*) **~ treatment** in Behandlung; **~ repair** in Reparatur; **~ construction** im Bau; **be ~ investigation** untersucht werden; **fields ~ cultivation** bebaute Felder; **~ threat of extinction** vom Aussterben bedroht; **~ sentence of death** zum Tode verurteilt; ⇨ *also* **discussion** B; **influence** 1; **pain**; Ⓒ (*in conditions of*) bei ‹Stress, hohen Temperaturen usw.›; Ⓓ (*subject to*) unter (+ *Dat.*); **bring a country ~ one's rule** ein Land unter seine Herrschaft bringen; **~ the doctor, ~ doctor's orders** in ärztlicher Behandlung; ⇨ *also* **delusion**; **illusion** B; **impression** G; **misapprehension**; Ⓔ (*in accordance with*) **~ the circumstances** unter den gegebenen *od.* diesen Umständen; **~ the terms of the will/contract/agreement** nach den Bestimmungen des Testaments/Vertrags/Abkommens; Ⓕ (*with the use of*) unter (+ *Dat.*); **~ an assumed name** *or* **alias/a pen-name** unter falschem Namen/unter einem Pseudonym; Ⓖ (*less than*) unter (+ *Dat.*); (*esp. with time, amount*) weniger als; **no one ~ a bishop** niemand unter Bischofsrang; **the mile was run in ~ four minutes** die Meile wurde in weniger als *od.* unter vier Minuten gelaufen; **for ~ five pounds** für weniger als fünf Pfund; ⇨ *also* **age** 1 A; Ⓗ (*at foot of*) **~ the hill/walls** am Fuße des Berges/der Mauern; Ⓘ (*Naut.: in the lee of*) **close ~ the island** im Schutze der nahen Insel; Ⓙ (*planted with*) **field ~ corn/rice/beans** mit Getreide/Reis/Bohnen bestandenes Feld.

❷ *adv.* Ⓐ (*in or to a lower or subordinate position*) darunter; **stay ~** (**~** *water*) unter Wasser bleiben; ⇨ *also* **go under**; Ⓑ (*in/into a state of unconsciousness*) **be ~/put sb. ~:** in Narkose liegen/jmdn. in Narkose versetzen

**under: ~aˈchieve** *v.i.* unter dem erreichbaren Leistungsniveau bleiben; **~achiever** /ʌndərəˈtʃiːvə(r)/ *n.* Schüler/Schülerin mit enttäuschenden Leistungen; **be an ~ achiever** ⇨ **u~achieve**; **~ˈact** *v.t. & i.* unterspielen (*Theaterjargon*); **~-age** *adj.* minderjährig; **~-age children** Minderjährige; **~-age drinking/smoking** Alkoholgenuss/Rauchen Minderjähriger; **~-age sex** Sex unter Minderjährigen; **~arm** ❶ *adj.* Ⓐ (*Tennis, Cricket, etc.*) ‹Aufschlag, Wurf› von unten; Ⓑ (*in armpit*) Achsel‹haare, -schweiß›; ❷ *adv.* von unten ‹aufschlagen, werfen›; **~belly** *n.* (*Zool.*) Bauch, *der;* (*of aircraft*) Unterseite, *die;* **[soft] ~belly** (*fig.*) verwundbare Stelle; **~body** *n.* Unterseite, *die;* **~brush** *n.* (*Amer.*) Unterholz, *das;* **~carriage** *n.* Fahrwerk, *das;* **~ˈcharge** *v.t.* **~charge sb. [by several pounds]** jmdm. [einige Pfund] zu wenig berechnen; **~clothes** *n. pl.*, **~clothing** ⇨ **underwear**; **~coat** *n.* Ⓐ (*layer of paint*) Grundierung, *die;* Ⓑ (*paint*) Grundierfarbe, *die;* Ⓒ (*of animal*) Unterhaar, *das;* **~ˈcooked** *adj.* zu kurz gekocht/gebraten; noch nicht gar; **~cover** *adj.* (*disguised*) getarnt; (*secret*) verdeckt; (*engaged in international spying*) geheim[dienstlich]; **~cover agent** ▶ **1261** Untergrund-/Geheimagent, *der;* **~croft** *n.* (*Eccl.*) Krypta, *die;* **~current** *n.* Unterströmung, *die;* (*fig.: ~lying feeling*) Unterton, *der;* **he sensed an ~current of resentment** er spürte eine unterschwellige Groll; **~ˈcut** *v.t.*, **~cut** unterbieten; **~deˈveloped** *adj.* unterentwickelt; **~deˈvelopment** *n.*, *no pl.* Unterentwicklung, *die;* **~dog** *n.* Ⓐ (*in fight, match*) Unterlegene, *der/die;* Ⓑ (*fig.: disadvantaged person*) Benachteiligte, *der/die;* **the ~dogs of society** die sozial Unterprivilegierten; **~ˈdone** *adj.* halbgar; **I don't like my steak ~done** ich habe mein Steak gern gut durchgebraten; **~ˈemphasis** *n.* zu schwache Betonung; **there is an ~emphasis on it** es kommt nicht deutlich genug zum Ausdruck; **~ˈemphasize** *v.t.* zu wenig betonen; **~emˈployed** *adj.* unterbeschäftigt; **~emˈployment** *n.* Unterbeschäftigung, *die;* **~estimate** ❶ /ʌndərˈestɪmeɪt/ *v.t.* unterschätzen; ❷ /ʌndərˈestɪmət/ *n.* Unterschätzung, *die;* **that figure is a considerable ~estimate** diese Zahl ist viel zu niedrig geschätzt; **~exˈpose** *v.t.* (*Photog.*) unterbelichten; **~exˈposure** *n.* (*Photog.*) Unterbelichtung, *die;* **~ˈfed** *adj.* unterernährt; **~felt** *n.* Filzunterlage, *die;* **~-ˈfives** *n. pl.* Kinder unter fünf Jahren; **~ˈfloor heating** *n.* [Fuß]bodenheizung, *die;* **~ˈfoot** *adv.* am Boden; **it's rough/muddy ~foot** der Boden ist uneben/matschig; **be trodden/trampled ~foot** mit Füßen getreten/zertrampelt werden; (*fig.: be maltreated*) wie der letzte Dreck behandelt werden (*salopp*); **~garment** *n.* Wäschestück, *das;* **~garments** Unterwäsche, *die;* **~ˈgo** *v.t.*, *forms as* **go**[1] 1 durchmachen ‹schlimme Zeiten›; ertragen ‹Demütigung›; **~go treatment/an operation** sich einer Behandlung/Operation unterziehen; **~go a change** sich verändern; **~go repairs** repariert werden; **~grad** /ˈʌndəɡræd/ (*coll.*), **~ˈgraduate** *ns.* **~graduate [student]** Student/Studentin vor der ersten Prüfung; **~graduate course** Lehrveranstaltung für Studenten vor der ersten Prüfung; **~ground** ❶ /--ˈ-/ *adv.* Ⓐ (*beneath surface of ground*) unter der Erde; (*Mining*) unter Tage; **an explosion ~ground** eine unterirdische Explosion; Ⓑ (*fig.*) (*in hiding*) im Untergrund; (*into hiding*) in den Untergrund; **go ~ground** untertauchen; in den Untergrund gehen; ❷ /ˈ---/ *adj.* Ⓐ unterirdisch ‹Höhle, See›; **~ground railway** Untergrundbahn, *die;* **~ground car park** Tiefgarage, *die;* Ⓑ (*fig.: secret*) **~ground activity** Tätigkeit im Untergrund; **~ground organization/movement/press** Untergrundorganisation/-bewegung/-presse; ❸ *n.* Ⓐ (*railway*) U-Bahn, *die;* Ⓑ (*clandestine movement*) Untergrund, *der;* Untergrundbewegung, *die;* **~growth** *n.* Unterholz, *das;* **~hand, ~handed** ❶ *adjs.* Ⓐ (*secret*) heimlich; Ⓑ (*crafty*) hinterhältig; ❷ *advs.* heimlich; **~hung** *adj.* vorgeschoben ‹Unterkiefer›; **~inˈsured** *adj.* unterversichert; **~ˈlay**[1] ⇨ **~lie**; **~lay**[2] ❶ /--ˈ-/ *v.t.*, *forms as* **lay**[2] 2 unterlegen; ❷ /ˈ---/ *n.* Unterlage, *die;* **~ˈlie** *v.t.*, *forms as* **lie**[2] 2: Ⓐ (*lie ~*) **~lie sth.** unter etw. (*Dat.*) liegen; Ⓑ (*fig.: be [at] the basis of*) **~lie sth.** einer Sache (*Dat.*) zugrunde liegen; **~lying cause of sth.** eigentliche Ursache für etw.; **~line** ❶ /--ˈ-/ *v.t.* (*lit. or fig.*) unterstreichen; ❷ /ˈ---/ *n.* Unterstreichung, *die*

**underling** /ˈʌndəlɪŋ/ *n.* (*derog.*) Untergebene, *der/die*

**under: ~ˈlining** *n.* Unterstreichung, *die;* **there is too much ~lining** es ist zu viel unterstrichen; **~ˈlying** ⇨ **underlie**; **~ˈmanned** *adj.* [personell] unterbesetzt; **~manned industries** Industriezweige, in denen Arbeitskräftemangel herrscht; **~ˈmanning** *n.* [personelle] Unterbesetzung; **~ˈmentioned** *adj.* (*Brit.*) unten genannt; unten erwähnt; **~ˈmine** *v.t.* Ⓐ unterhöhlen; ‹Wasser:› unterspülen; Ⓑ (*fig.*) (*weaken*) untergraben; erschüttern ‹Vertrauen›; unterminieren ‹Autorität›; schwächen ‹Gesundheit›

**underneath** /ʌndəˈniːθ/ ❶ *prep.* (*indicating position*) unter (+ *Dat.*); (*indicating motion*) unter (+ *Akk.*); **from ~ the bed** unter dem Bett hervor. ❷ *adv.* darunter. ❸ *n.* Unterseite, *die*

**under: ~ˈnourished** *adj.* unterernährt; **~ˈpaid** *adj.* unterbezahlt; **~pants** *n. pl.* Unterhose, *die;* Unterhosen *Pl.;* **~part** *n.* Unterseite, *die;* **~pass** *n.* Unterführung, *die;* **~ˈpay** *v.t.*, *forms as* **pay** 2 unterbezahlen; **~ˈpayment** *n.* Unterbezahlung, *die;* **~ˈpin** *v.t.* [ab]stützen; (*fig.*) untermauern; **~pin a social system** die Grundlage eines gesellschaftlichen Systems bilden; **~ˈplay** *v.t.* Ⓐ (*Theatre*) zurückhaltend spielen ‹Rolle, Szene›; Ⓑ (*play down*) herunterspielen; **~ˈprivileged** *adj.* unterprivilegiert; **~proˈduction** *n.*, *no pl.*, *no indef. art.* Unterproduktion, *die;* **~ˈrate** *v.t.* unterschätzen; **be ~rated** [allgemein] unterschätzt werden; **~ripe** *adj.* nicht ausgereift; **~ˈscore** ⇨ **underline** 1; **~score** ⇨ **~line** 2; **~sea** *attrib. adj.* Unterwasser-; **~seal** ❶ *v.t.* mit [einem] Unterbodenschutz versehen; **be ~sealed** Unterbodenschutz haben; ❷ *n.* Unterbodenschutz, *der;* **~secretary** *n.* ▶ **1261** Ⓐ (*esp. Amer.: assistant to secretary*) Unterstaatssekretär, *der;* Ⓑ (*Brit.*) **[Parliamentary] U~secretary** [Parlamentarischer] Staatssekretär; **~ˈsell** *v.t.*, *forms as* **sell** 1 Ⓐ (*sell at lower price than*) [im Preis] unterbieten; Ⓑ (*present inadequately*) nicht genug anpreisen; **~selling actually boosted her business** ihre verhaltene Werbestrategie hat eher zur Geschäftsbelebung geführt; **~ˈsexed** *adj.* sexuell lustlos; **~shirt** *n.* (*Amer.*) Unterhemd, *das;* **~ˈshoot** *v.t.*, *forms as* **shot** 1, 2: **~shoot the runway** vor der Landebahn aufsetzen; **~shorts** *n. pl.* (*Amer.*) Unterhose, *die;* **~shot** ⇨ **underhung**; **~side** *n.* Unterseite, *die;* **~signed** *adj.* (*esp. Law*) **the ~signed** der/die Unterzeichnete/(*pl.*) die Unterzeichneten (*Papierdt.*); **~sized** *adj.* unter Normalgröße

U

*nachgestellt;* [ziemlich] klein geraten ‹Person, Tier›; **~skirt** *n.* Unterrock, *der;* **~slung** *adj.* (*Motor Veh.*) [tiefer als die Achsen] hängend ‹Fahrgestell, Rahmen›; **~'spend** ❶ *v.t., forms as* **spend**: **~spend a budget/an allowance** ein Budget unterschreiten/eine Zuwendung nicht ganz ausgeben; ❷ *v.i., forms as* **spend**: **~spend by £500,000** das Budget um 500 000 Pfund unterschreiten; **~spend on sth.** zu wenig für etw. ausgeben; (*save*) an etw. (*Dat.*) sparen; **~'spent** ⇒ **~spend**; **~'staffed** *adj.* unterbesetzt; **be ~staffed** an Personalmangel leiden

**understand** /ʌndəˈstænd/ ❶ *v.t.,* **understood** /ʌndəˈstʊd/ Ⓐ verstehen; **~ sth. by sth.** etw. unter etw. (*Dat.*) verstehen; **~ mathematics** mathematisches Verständnis haben; **~ carpentry** sich auf das Schreinern verstehen; **I cannot ~ his doing it** ich kann nicht verstehen *od.* begreife nicht, warum er es tut; **is that understood?** ist das klar?; **make oneself understood** sich verständlich machen; Ⓑ (*have heard*) gehört haben; **I ~ that you wish to leave us** wie ich höre, wollen Sie uns verlassen; **I ~ him to be a distant relation** ich glaube, er ist ein entfernter Verwandter; Ⓒ (*take as implied*) **~ sth. from sb.'s words** etw. aus jmds. Worten entnehmen; **I understood [that] we were to be paid expenses** ich dachte, dass wir Spesen bekommen sollten; **it was understood that ...:** es wurde allgemein angenommen, dass ...; **do I ~ that ...?** gehe ich recht in der Annahme, dass ...?; **am I to ~ that you refuse my offer?** wollen Sie damit sagen, dass Sie mein Angebot ablehnen?; **it was understood between them that ...:** es herrschte [stillschweigendes] Einverständnis zwischen ihnen, dass ...; Ⓓ (*supply mentally*) hinzudenken; **be understood** (*Gram.*) ausgelassen werden; **he is seething ('with rage' understood)** er kocht (gemeint ist „vor Wut"). ⇒ *also* **give** 1 E; **make** 1 F.

❷ *v.i.,* **understood** Ⓐ (*have understanding*) verstehen; **~ about sth.** etwas von etw. verstehen; **he doesn't ~ about it [being my job]** er sieht es nicht ein[, dass es meine Aufgabe ist]; **now I ~!** jetzt begreife ich es!; **I quite ~:** ich verstehe schon; Ⓑ (*gather, hear*) **if I ~ correctly** wenn ich mich nicht irre; **your offer is, I ~, still open** Ihr Angebot ist, so nehme ich an, noch offen; **he is, I ~, no longer here** er ist, wie ich höre, nicht mehr hier

**understandable** /ʌndəˈstændəbl/ *adj.* verständlich

**understandably** /ʌndəˈstændəblɪ/ *adv.* verständlicherweise

**understanding** /ʌndəˈstændɪŋ/ ❶ *adj.* (*able to sympathize*) verständnisvoll; **you could be a bit more ~:** du könntest etwas mehr Verständnis zeigen.

❷ *n.* Ⓐ (*agreement*) Verständigung, *die;* **reach an ~ with sb.** sich mit jmdm. verständigen; **the good ~ between them** das gute Einverständnis zwischen ihnen; **have a secret ~ with sb.** eine geheime Vereinbarung mit jmdm. haben; **on the ~ that ...:** unter der Voraussetzung, dass ...; **on the clear** *or* **distinct ~ that ...** (*condition*) unter der ausdrücklichen Bedingung, dass ...; **there has never been much ~ between them** sie haben sich nie besonders gut vertragen; Ⓑ (*intelligence*) Verstand, *der;* Ⓒ (*insight, comprehension*) Verständnis, *das* **(of, for** für); **a person of great ~:** ein sehr verständnisvoller Mensch; **beyond ~:** unbegreiflich; **my ~ of the matter is that she has won** so wie ich es verstehe, hat sie gewonnen

**understandingly** /ʌndəˈstændɪŋlɪ/ *adv.* verständnisvoll

**under: ~'state** *v.t.* Ⓐ herunterspielen; **~state the case** untertreiben; Ⓑ (*represent inadequately*) zu gering veranschlagen; **~'statement** *n.* (*avoidance of emphasis*) Untertreibung, *die;* Understatement, *das;* **~steer** (*Motor Veh.*) ❶ /'-'-/ *v.i.* untersteuern; ❷ /'---/ *n.* Untersteuern, *das;* **~'stocked** *adj.* unterversorgt; **the shops were ~stocked** die Läden hatten zu wenig Ware *od.* Vorräte [auf Lager]; **~'stood** ⇒ **understand**; **~study** ❶ *n.* Ersatzspieler, *der*/-spielerin, *die;* zweite Besetzung; ❷ *v.t.* **~study sb.** jmds. Rolle als Ersatzspieler/-spielerin einstudieren; **~sub'scribed** *adj.* (*St. Exch.*) unterzeichnet; **~surface** *n.* Unterseite, *die;* **~'take** *v.t., forms as* **take** 1 Ⓐ (*set about*) unternehmen; **~take a task** eine Aufgabe übernehmen; **~take to do sth.** sich verpflichten, etw. zu tun; Ⓑ (*guarantee*) **~take sth./that ...:** sich für etw. verbürgen/sich dafür verbürgen, dass ...; **~taker** *n.* ▶ 1261 Leichenbestatter, *der*/-bestatterin, *die;* **[firm of] ~takers** Bestattungsunternehmen, *das;* **~'taking** *n.* Ⓐ *no pl.* (*taking on*) (*of task*) Übernehmen, *das;* (*of journey etc.*) Unternehmen, *das;* Ⓑ (*task*) Aufgabe, *die;* **a dangerous ~taking** ein gefährliches Unterfangen; Ⓒ (*business*) Unternehmen, *das;* Betrieb, *der;* Ⓓ (*pledge*) Versprechen, *das;* **give an ~taking that .../to do sth.** zusichern, dass .../sich verpflichten, etw. zu tun; **I'll need an ~taking from you that ...:** du musst mir [fest] versprechen, dass ...; **~tone** *n.* Ⓐ (*low voice*) **in ~tones** *or* **an ~tone** in gedämpftem Ton; Ⓑ (*~current*) **~tone of criticism** kritischer Unterton; Ⓒ (*subdued colour*) Tönung, *die;* **~tow** *n.* Unterströmung, *die;* **~'used** *adj.* nicht voll genutzt; **~valu'ation** *n.* Unterbewertung, *die;* **~'value** *v.t.* unterbewerten; **~vest** *n.* Unterhemd, *das;* **~water** ❶ /'----/ *attrib. adj.* Unterwasser-; ❷ /-'--/ *adv.* unter Wasser; **~wear** *n., no pl., no indef. art.* Unterwäsche, *die;* **~'weight** *adj.* untergewichtig; **be ~weight** Untergewicht haben; **~whelm** /ʌndəˈwelm/ *v.t.* (*joc.*) nicht gerade überwältigen (*spött.*); **~world** *n.* (*lit. or fig.*) Unterwelt, *die;* **~'write** *v.t., forms as* **write** 1 Ⓐ (*accept liability for*) [als Versicherer] unterzeichnen; **~write a risk** ein Risiko versichern; **~write a share issue** die Übernahme von unverkauften Aktien garantieren; Ⓑ (*finance*) finanzieren; **~writer** *n.* ▶ 1261 (*of insurance policy*) Versicherer, *der;* (*of stock issue*) Garant, *der*/Garantin, *die*

**undeserved** /ʌndɪˈzɜːvd/ *adj.* unverdient

**undeservedly** /ʌndɪˈzɜːvɪdlɪ/ *adv.* unverdientermaßen

**undeserving** /ʌndɪˈzɜːvɪŋ/ *adj.* unwürdig **(of** *Gen.*); **not ~ of attention** schon beachtenswert

**undesigned** /ʌndɪˈzaɪnd/ *adj.* ungeplant

**undesirability** /ʌndɪzaɪərəˈbɪlɪtɪ/ *n., no pl.* Unerwünschtheit, *die*

**undesirable** /ʌndɪˈzaɪərəbl/ ❶ *adj.* unerwünscht; **it is ~ that ...:** es ist nicht wünschenswert, dass ... ❷ *n.* unerwünschte Person

**undesirably** /ʌndɪˈzaɪərəblɪ/ *adv.* unerwünscht

**undesired** /ʌndɪˈzaɪəd/ *adj.* unerwünscht

**undetectable** /ʌndɪˈtektəbl/ *adj.* nicht nachweisbar

**undetected** /ʌndɪˈtektɪd/ *adj.* unentdeckt; **go** *or* **pass ~:** unentdeckt bleiben

**undeterred** /ʌndɪˈtɜːd/ *adj.* nicht entmutigt **(by** durch); **remain ~:** sich nicht abschrecken lassen; **continue ~:** unbeirrt weitermachen

**undeveloped** /ʌndɪˈveləpt/ *adj.* Ⓐ (*immature*) nicht voll ausgebildet; Ⓑ (*Photog.*) nicht entwickelt; Ⓒ (*not built on*) nicht bebaut

**undiagnosed** /ʌndaɪəgˈnəʊzd/ *adj.* nicht diagnostiziert; **die of an ~ brain tumor** an einem nicht erkannten Gehirntumor sterben

**undid** ⇒ **undo**

**undies** /ˈʌndɪz/ *n. pl.* (*coll.*) Unterwäsche, *die*

**undifferentiated** /ʌndɪfəˈrenʃɪeɪtɪd/ *adj.* undifferenziert

**undigested** /ʌndɪˈdʒestɪd, ʌndaɪˈdʒestɪd/ *adj.* (*lit. or fig.*) unverdaut

**undignified** /ʌnˈdɪgnɪfaɪd/ *adj.* würdelos; **consider it ~ to do sth.** es für unter seiner Würde halten, etw. zu tun

**undiluted** /ʌndaɪˈljuːtɪd/ *adj.* unverdünnt; **~ pleasure/nonsense** ungetrübte Freude/barer Unsinn

**undiminished** /ʌndɪˈmɪnɪʃt/ *adj.* unvermindert; **her enthusiasm remained ~:** ihre Begeisterung ließ nicht nach

**undimmed** /ʌnˈdɪmd/ *adj.* nicht gedämpft; ungetrübt ‹Augenlicht›

**undiplomatic** /ʌndɪpləˈmætɪk/ *adj.* undiplomatisch

**undipped** /ʌnˈdɪpt/ *adj.* nicht abgeblendet

**undischarged** /ʌndɪsˈtʃɑːdʒd/ *adj.* Ⓐ (*Finance*) unbeglichen ‹Schuld›; nicht entlastet ‹Schuldner›; Ⓑ (*not unloaded*) nicht entladen; Ⓒ (*not fired off*) nicht abgeschossen

**undisciplined** /ʌnˈdɪsɪplɪnd/ *adj.* undiszipliniert

**undisclosed** /ʌndɪsˈkləʊzd/ *adj.* geheim; **an ~ sum** ein nicht genannter Betrag

**undiscoverable** /ʌndɪˈskʌvərəbl/ *adj.* nicht feststellbar

**undiscovered** /ʌndɪˈskʌvəd/ *adj.* unentdeckt

**undiscriminating** /ʌndɪˈskrɪmɪneɪtɪŋ/ *adj.* unkritisch; (*undemanding*) anspruchslos

**undisguised** /ʌndɪsˈgaɪzd/ *adj.* unverhohlen

**undismayed** /ʌndɪsˈmeɪd/ ⇒ **undeterred**

**undisputed** /ʌndɪˈspjuːtɪd/ *adj.* unbestritten ‹Fertigkeit, Kompetenz›; unangefochten ‹Führer, Autorität›

**undistinguished** /ʌndɪˈstɪŋgwɪʃt/ *adj.* mittelmäßig; (*ordinary*) gewöhnlich

**undisturbed** /ʌndɪˈstɜːbd/ *adj.* Ⓐ (*untouched*) unberührt; Ⓑ (*not interrupted*) ungestört; Ⓒ (*not worried*) ungerührt

**undivided** /ʌndɪˈvaɪdɪd/ *adj.* ungeteilt ‹Sympathie, Aufmerksamkeit›; geschlossen ‹Front›; uneingeschränkt ‹Loyalität›

**undo** /ʌnˈduː/ ❶ *v.t.,* **undoes** /ʌnˈdʌz/, **undoing** /ʌnˈduːɪŋ/, **undid** /ʌnˈdɪd/, **undone** /ʌnˈdʌn/ Ⓐ (*unfasten*) aufmachen; Ⓑ (*cancel*) ungeschehen machen; **his successor undid all his work** sein Nachfolger machte sein ganzes Werk zunichte. ❷ *v.i., forms as* 1 ‹dress etc.:› **~ at the back** hinten aufgemacht werden

**undoing** /ʌnˈduːɪŋ/ *n., no pl., no indef. art.* **be sb.'s ~:** jmds. Verderben sein

**undone** /ʌnˈdʌn/ *adj.* Ⓐ (*not accomplished*) unerledigt; **leave the work** *or* **job ~:** die Arbeit liegen lassen; Ⓑ (*not fastened*) offen; **he went out with his shoelaces ~:** er ging mit offenen Schnürsenkeln aus dem Haus

**undoubted** /ʌnˈdaʊtɪd/ *adj.* unzweifelhaft

**undoubtedly** /ʌnˈdaʊtɪdlɪ/ *adv.* zweifellos

**undraw** /ʌnˈdrɔː/ *v.t., forms as* **draw** 1 aufziehen ‹Vorhang›

**undreamed-of** /ʌnˈdriːmdɒv/, **undreamt-of** /ʌnˈdremtɒv/ *adjs.* (*unheard-of*) unerhört; (*unimaginable*) unvorstellbar; ungeahnt ‹Reichtum›; **such a thing was ~:** an so etwas hätte man nicht im Traum gedacht

**undress** /ʌnˈdres/ ❶ *v.t.* ausziehen; entkleiden (*geh.*); **get ~ed** sich ausziehen; **can he ~ himself?** kann er sich selbst ausziehen? ❷ *v.i.* sich ausziehen. ❸ *n.* Ⓐ **~ [uniform]** Freizeitkleidung, *die;* (*Mil.*) Ausgehuniform, *die;* Ⓑ *no pl., no art.* **in a state of ~:** halb bekleidet

**undressed** /ʌnˈdrest/ *adj.* Ⓐ (*not clothed*) unbekleidet; (*no longer clothed*) ausgezogen; (*not yet clothed*) nicht angezogen; Ⓑ (*unfinished*) unbearbeitet ‹Stein, Holz›; ungegerbt ‹Leder, Haut›; Ⓒ (*not bandaged etc.*) nicht verbunden; **leave a wound ~:** eine Wunde nicht verbinden

**undrinkable** /ʌnˈdrɪŋkəbl/ *adj.* nicht trinkbar; ungenießbar

**undue** /ʌnˈdjuː/ *attrib. adj.* übertrieben; übermäßig; unangemessen hoch ‹Gewinn›; unberechtigt ‹Optimismus›; **~ influence** (*Law*) ungebührliche Beeinflussung; **attract ~ attention** zu viel Aufmerksamkeit auf sich (*Akk.*) lenken; **there is no ~ hurry** es hat keine besondere Eile

**undulate** /ˈʌndjʊleɪt/ *v.i.* Ⓐ (*move with wavelike motion*) wallen (*geh.*); Ⓑ (*have wavelike form*) wogen (*geh.*); **the hills ~ southwards** die Hügel erstrecken sich in sanften Wellen nach Süden

**undulating** /ˈʌndjʊleɪtɪŋ/ *adj.* Wellen‹linie, -bewegung›; ~ **country/hills** sanfte Hügellandschaft; ~ **road** auf- und abführende Straße

**undulation** /ʌndjʊˈleɪʃn/ *n.* A (*wavy motion*) Wellenbewegung, *die;* B (*wavy line*) Wellenlinie, *die*

**unduly** /ʌnˈdjuːlɪ/ *adv.* übermäßig; übertrieben ‹ängstlich›; unangemessen ‹hoch›; **not ~ worried** nicht besonders beunruhigt; **in an ~ hurried manner** in unangebrachter Eile

**undying** /ʌnˈdaɪɪŋ/ *adj.* ewig; unsterblich ‹Ruhm›; unversöhnlich ‹Hass›

**unearned** /ʌnˈɜːnd/ *adj.* unverdient; ~ **income** Kapitalertrag, *der*

**unearth** /ʌnˈɜːθ/ *v.t.* A (*dig up*) ausgraben; B (*fig.: discover*) aufdecken; zutage fördern

**unearthly** /ʌnˈɜːθlɪ/ *adj.* A (*mysterious*) unheimlich; B (*coll.: terrible*) ~ **din** Höllenlärm, *der* (*ugs.*); **at an ~ hour** in aller Herrgottsfrühe

**unease** /ʌnˈiːz/ ⇒ **uneasiness**

**uneasily** /ʌnˈiːzɪlɪ/ *adv.* A (*anxiously*) mit Unbehagen; B (*with embarrassment*) **be ~ aware of sth.** sich (*Dat.*) einer Sache (*Gen.*) peinlich bewusst sein; C (*restlessly*) unruhig ‹schlafen, sitzen›

**uneasiness** /ʌnˈiːzɪnɪs/ *n., no pl.* A (*anxiety*) [ängstliches] Unbehagen; B (*restlessness*) Unruhe, *die*

**uneasy** /ʌnˈiːzɪ/ *adj.* A (*anxious*) besorgt; **be ~ about sth.** sich wegen etw. Sorgen machen; **he felt ~:** ihm war unbehaglich zumute; B (*restless*) unruhig ‹Schlaf›; C (*disturbing*) quälend ‹Zweifel, Verdacht›; ~ **conscience** schlechtes Gewissen

**uneatable** /ʌnˈiːtəbl/ *adj.* ungenießbar

**uneaten** /ʌnˈiːtn/ *adj.* ungegessen

**uneconomic** /ʌniːkəˈnɒmɪk, ʌnekəˈnɒmɪk/ *adj.* unrentabel; **the mine is ~ to run** das Bergwerk ist unwirtschaftlich

**uneconomical** /ʌniːkəˈnɒmɪkl, ʌnekəˈnɒmɪkl/ *adj.* verschwenderisch ‹Person›; ~ **[to run]** unwirtschaftlich

**uneconomically** /ʌniːkəˈnɒmɪkəlɪ, ʌnekəˈnɒmɪkəlɪ/ *adv.* verschwenderisch; unwirtschaftlich

**unedifying** /ʌnˈedɪfaɪɪŋ/ *adj.* A (*uninformative*) unergiebig; B (*not uplifting*) unerquicklich (*geh.*); unerfreulich

**unedited** /ʌnˈedɪtɪd/ *adj.* unredigiert

**uneducated** /ʌnˈedjʊkeɪtɪd/ *adj.* ungebildet

**unemotional** /ʌnɪˈməʊʃənl/ *adj.* emotionslos; nüchtern

**unemphatic** /ʌnɪmˈfætɪk/ *adj.* ausdruckslos

**unemployable** /ʌnɪmˈplɔɪəbl/ *adj.* als Arbeitskraft ungeeignet; **his behaviour makes him ~:** er kann wegen seines Verhaltens nirgends eingestellt werden

**unemployed** /ʌnɪmˈplɔɪd/ ❶ *adj.* A (*out of work*) arbeitslos; B (*with nothing to do*) beschäftigungslos. ❷ *n. pl.* **the ~:** die Arbeitslosen

**unemployment** /ʌnɪmˈplɔɪmənt/ *n., no pl., no indef. art.* Arbeitslosigkeit, *die;* (*number unemployed*) Arbeitslosenzahl, *die*

**unemployment: ~ benefit** *n.* Arbeitslosengeld, *das;* **~ figures** *n. pl.* Arbeitslosenzahl, *die*

**unencumbered** /ʌnɪnˈkʌmbəd/ *adj.* A (*unburdened*) unbelastet; **travel ~ by baggage** ohne viel Gepäck reisen; B (*free from mortgage etc.*) lastenfrei

**unending** /ʌnˈendɪŋ/ *adj.* endlos; ewig ‹Fortschritt›; **her ordeal seemed ~:** ihre Qualen schienen nie enden zu wollen

**unendingly** /ʌnˈendɪŋlɪ/ *adv.* endlos

**unendurable** /ʌnɪnˈdjʊərəbl/ *adj.* unerträglich

**unenforceable** /ʌnɪnˈfɔːsəbl/ *adj.* nicht durchsetzbar

**un-English** /ʌnˈɪŋglɪʃ/ *adj.* unenglisch

**unenlightened** /ʌnɪnˈlaɪtnd/ *adj.* unaufgeklärt ‹Zeit›; rückständig ‹Land, Volk›; **leave sb. ~:** jmdn. im Dunkeln lassen

**unenterprising** /ʌnˈentəpraɪzɪŋ/ *adj.* wenig unternehmungslustig; **an ~ person** eine Person ohne Unternehmungsgeist

**unenthusiastic** /ʌnɪnθjuːzɪˈæstɪk, ʌnɪnθuːzɪˈæstɪk/ *adj.* wenig begeistert (**about** von); distanziert ‹Buchkritik›

**unenviable** /ʌnˈenvɪəbl/ *adj.* wenig beneidenswert

**unequal** /ʌnˈiːkwl/ *adj.* A (*not equal*) unterschiedlich; ungleich ‹Kampf›; B (*inadequate*) **be ~ or show oneself ~ to sth.** einer Sache (*Dat.*) nicht gewachsen sein; **be ~ to the strain** ‹Material:› die Belastung nicht aushalten; C (*of varying quality*) ungleichmäßig

**unequalled** (*Amer.:* **unequaled**) /ʌnˈiːkwld/ *adj.* unerreicht; unübertroffen; (*in negative sense*) beispiellos ‹Dummheit›; **~ for beauty** von unvergleichlicher Schönheit

**unequally** /ʌnˈiːkwəlɪ/ *adv.* ungleichmäßig

**unequivocal** /ʌnɪˈkwɪvəkl/ *adj.*, **unequivocally** /ʌnɪˈkwɪvəkəlɪ/ *adv.* eindeutig

**unerring** /ʌnˈɜːrɪŋ/ *adj.* untrüglich ‹Instinkt, Geschmack›; unbedingt ‹Treffsicherheit›; mathematisch ‹Genauigkeit›; unfehlbar ‹Instinkt›; unerschütterlich ‹Zielstrebigkeit›

**unerringly** /ʌnˈɜːrɪŋlɪ/ *adv.* mit untrüglicher Sicherheit

**UNESCO** /juːˈneskəʊ/ *abbr.* **United Nations Educational, Scientific and Cultural Organization** UNESCO, *die*

**unessential** /ʌnɪˈsenʃl/ ⇒ **inessential**

**unethical** /ʌnˈeθɪkl/ *adj.*, **unethically** /ʌnˈeθɪkəlɪ/ *adv.* unmoralisch

**uneven** /ʌnˈiːvn/ *adj.* A (*not smooth*) uneben; B (*not uniform*) ungleichmäßig; unregelmäßig ‹Pulsschlag›; unausgeglichen ‹Temperament›; **an ~ performance** ein Auftritt mit Höhen und Tiefen; C (*odd*) ungerade ‹Zahl›

**unevenly** /ʌnˈiːvnlɪ/ *adv.* ungleichmäßig

**unevenness** /ʌnˈiːvnnɪs/ *n.* A (*roughness*) Unebenheit, *die;* B (*irregularity*) Ungleichmäßigkeit, *die;* (*of pulse*) Unregelmäßigkeit, *die;* (*of temperament*) Unausgeglichenheit, *die;* **the ~ of the essays** das unterschiedliche Niveau der Aufsätze

**uneventful** /ʌnɪˈventfl/ *adj.* A (*quiet*) ereignislos; ruhig ‹Leben›; B (*normal*) ‹Fahrt, Landung› ohne Zwischenfälle; **be ~** ‹Fahrt usw.:› ohne Zwischenfälle verlaufen

**uneventfully** /ʌnɪˈventfəlɪ/ *adv.* ohne Zwischenfälle

**unexampled** /ʌnɪgˈzɑːmpld/ *adj.* beispiellos

**unexceptionable** /ʌnɪkˈsepʃənəbl/ *adj.* untadelig ‹Charakter›; fehlerlos ‹Arbeit›

**unexceptional** /ʌnɪkˈsepʃənl/ *adj.* alltäglich; (*average*) durchschnittlich

**unexciting** /ʌnɪkˈsaɪtɪŋ/ *adj.* wenig aufregend; (*boring*) langweilig

**unexpected** /ʌnɪkˈspektɪd/ *adj.* unerwartet; **this news was entirely ~:** diese Nachricht kam völlig unerwartet

**unexpectedly** /ʌnɪkˈspektɪdlɪ/ *adv.* unerwartet

**unexpired** /ʌnɪkˈspaɪəd/ *adj.* noch gültig; noch nicht abgelaufen ‹Mandat›

**unexplainable** /ʌnɪkˈspleɪnəbl/ *adj.* unerklärlich

**unexplained** /ʌnɪkˈspleɪnd/ *adj.* ungeklärt; unentschuldigt ‹Abwesenheit›

**unexploded** /ʌnɪkˈspləʊdɪd/ *adj.* nicht explodiert *od.* detoniert

**unexplored** /ʌnɪkˈsplɔːd/ *adj.* unerforscht

**unexposed** /ʌnɪkˈspəʊzd/ *adj.* A (*not brought to light*) unaufgeklärt; nicht entlarvt ‹Verbrecher›; B (*Photog.*) unbelichtet

**unexpressed** /ʌnɪkˈsprest/ *adj.* unausgesprochen

**unexpressive** /ʌnɪkˈspresɪv/ *adj.* ausdruckslos

**unexpurgated** /ʌnˈekspəgeɪtɪd/ *adj.* unzensiert

**unfading** /ʌnˈfeɪdɪŋ/ *adj.* unvergänglich

**unfailing** /ʌnˈfeɪlɪŋ/ *adj.* unerschöpflich; nie versagend ‹gute Laune›; unfehlbar ‹Heilmittel›; **with ~ regularity** (*iron.*) mit schöner Regelmäßigkeit

**unfailingly** /ʌnˈfeɪlɪŋlɪ/ *adv.* stets

**unfair** /ʌnˈfeə(r)/ *adj.* unfair; ungerecht, unfair ‹Kritik, Urteil›; unlauter ‹Wettbewerb›; ungerecht ‹Strafe›; **an ~ share** ein ungerechtfertigt hoher Anteil; **be ~ to sb.** jmdm. gegenüber ungerecht sein

**unfairly** /ʌnˈfeəlɪ/ *adv.* A (*unjustly*) ungerecht; unfair ‹spielen›; B (*unreasonably*) zu Unrecht

**unfairness** /ʌnˈfeənɪs/ *n., no pl.* Ungerechtigkeit, *die;* (*Sport*) Unfairness, *die*

**unfaithful** /ʌnˈfeɪθfl/ *adj.* untreu; ungenau ‹Übersetzung›; **~ to sb./sth.** jmdm./einer Sache untreu

**unfaithfulness** /ʌnˈfeɪθflnɪs/ *n., no pl.* Untreue, *die*

**unfaltering** /ʌnˈfɔːltərɪŋ/ *adj.* unbeirrbar ‹Glaube, Sicherheit›; fest ‹Stimme, Schritt›

**unfamiliar** /ʌnfəˈmɪljə(r)/ *adj.* A (*strange*) unbekannt; fremd ‹Stadt›; ungewohnt ‹Arbeit, Tätigkeit›; B (*not well acquainted*) nicht vertraut; **be ~ with sth.** sich mit etw. nicht auskennen; **workers ~ with this type of machine** Arbeiter, die sich mit diesem Maschinentyp nicht [gut] auskennen; **he is not ~ with German** die deutsche Sprache ist ihm einigermaßen vertraut

**unfamiliarity** /ʌnfəmɪlɪˈærɪtɪ/ *n., no pl.* A (*strangeness*) Fremdheit, *die;* (*of activity*) Ungewohntheit, *die;* B **~ with sth.** (*poor knowledge of*) Unvertrautheit mit etw.; **his ~ with computers** seine fehlende Erfahrung mit Computern

**unfashionable** /ʌnˈfæʃənəbl/ *adj.* unmodern ‹Kleidung›; nicht eben schick ‹Wohngegend›; **become ~:** aus der Mode kommen; **a view now ~:** eine jetzt überholte Ansicht

**unfasten** /ʌnˈfɑːsn/ ❶ *v.t.* A öffnen; B (*detach*) lösen. ❷ *v.i.* **~ at the back** hinten geöffnet werden

**unfastened** /ʌnˈfɑːsnd/ *adj.* nicht verschlossen ‹Tür›; offen ‹Verschluss, Knöpfe›

**unfathomable** /ʌnˈfæðəməbl/ *adj.* A (*incomprehensible*) unergründlich; B (*immeasurable*) unermesslich

**unfathomed** /ʌnˈfæðəmd/ *adj.* unergründet

**unfavorable, unfavorably** (*Amer.*) ⇒ **unfavourable, unfavourably**

**unfavourable** (*Amer.:* **unfavorable**) /ʌnˈfeɪvərəbl/ *adj.* A (*negative*) ungünstig; unfreundlich ‹Kommentar, Reaktion›; negativ ‹Kritik, Antwort›; **my suggestion got an ~ response** die Reaktion auf meinen Vorschlag war ablehnend; **be ~ to a proposal** einen Vorschlag ablehnen; B (*tending to make difficult*) ungünstig (**to, for** für); widrig ‹Wind›; **an atmosphere ~ to calm discussion** eine Atmosphäre, die einer ruhigen Diskussion abträglich ist; **a climate ~ to growth** ein wachstumsfeindliches Klima

**unfavourably** (*Amer.:* **unfavorably**) /ʌnˈfeɪvərəblɪ/ *adv.* ungünstig; **be ~ disposed towards sb./sth.** jmdm./etw. gegenüber ablehnend eingestellt sein; **react ~ to a suggestion** auf einen Vorschlag ablehnend reagieren

**unfeeling** /ʌnˈfiːlɪŋ/ *adj.* (*unsympathetic*) gefühllos

**unfeelingly** /ʌnˈfiːlɪŋlɪ/ *adv.* herzlos

**unfeigned** /ʌnˈfeɪnd/ *adj.* aufrichtig; unverhohlen

**unfenced** /ʌnˈfenst/ *adj.* nicht eingezäunt

**unfettered** /ʌnˈfetəd/ *adj.* ungehindert; **~ by scruples** frei von Skrupeln

**unfilled** /ʌnˈfɪld/ *adj.* frei, offen ‹Stelle›; (*empty*) leer

**unfinished** /ʌnˈfɪnɪʃt/ *adj.* A (*not completed*) unvollendet ‹Gedicht, Werk›; unerledigt ‹Arbeit, Geschäft›; **the U~ [Symphony]** die Unvollendete; B (*in rough state*) unbearbeitet

**unfit** /ʌnˈfɪt/ ❶ *adj.* A (*unsuitable*) ungeeignet; **~ for human consumption** zum Verzehr nicht geeignet; **~ for vehicles** nicht befahrbar; B (*not physically fit*) nicht fit; **she hates to be ~:** sie will unbedingt fit sein; **~ for military service** [wehrdienst]untauglich. ❷ *v.t.*, **-tt-** untauglich machen; ⇒ *also* **unfitted**

U

**unfitness** /ʌnˈfɪtnɪs/ *n., no pl.* Ⓐ (*unsuitability*) fehlende Eignung; Ⓑ (*poor physical condition*) **[state of] ~:** schlechte körperliche Verfassung

**unfitted** /ʌnˈfɪtɪd/ *adj.* (*unsuited*) ungeeignet

**unflagging** /ʌnˈflægɪŋ/ *adj.* unermüdlich

**unflappable** /ʌnˈflæpəbl/ *adj.* (*coll.*) unerschütterlich; **an ~ person** jemand, der sich durch nichts aus der Ruhe bringen lässt

**unflattering** /ʌnˈflætərɪŋ/ *adj.* wenig schmeichelhaft; unvorteilhaft ‹Kleid, Licht›; **very ~:** gar nicht schmeichelhaft

**unfledged** /ʌnˈfledʒd/ *adj.* Ⓐ (*unfeathered*) [noch] ungefiedert; Ⓑ (*fig.: inexperienced*) unerfahren

**unflinching** /ʌnˈflɪntʃɪŋ/ *adj.* unerschrocken; unbeirrbar ‹Entschlossenheit›; **remain ~:** nicht zurückweichen

**unfold** /ʌnˈfəʊld/ ❶ *v.t.* Ⓐ (*open folds of*) entfalten; ausbreiten ‹Zeitung, Landkarte›; **~ one's arms** die Arme ausstrecken; Ⓑ (*fig.: reveal*) **~ sth. to sb.** jmdm. etw. darlegen. ❷ *v.i.* Ⓐ (*open out*) ‹Knospe:› sich öffnen; ‹Flügel:› sich entfalten; **the landscape ~ed before us** (*fig.*) die Landschaft breitete sich vor unseren Augen aus; Ⓑ (*develop*) sich entwickeln; ‹Geheimnis:› sich aufklären; **as the story ~ed** im weiteren Verlauf der Geschichte

**unforeseeable** /ʌnfɔːˈsiːəbl/ *adj.* unvorhersehbar; **be ~:** nicht vorauszusehen sein

**unforeseen** /ʌnfɔːˈsiːn/ *adj.* unvorhergesehen

**unforgettable** /ʌnfəˈgetəbl/ *adj.* unvergesslich

**unforgivable** /ʌnfəˈgɪvəbl/ *adj.* unverzeihlich

**unforgiving** /ʌnfəˈgɪvɪŋ/ *adj.* nachtragend

**unformed** /ʌnˈfɔːmd/ *adj.* unausgereift

**unforthcoming** /ʌnfɔːθˈkʌmɪŋ/ *adj.* zugeknöpft (**about** hinsichtlich)

**unfortified** /ʌnˈfɔːtɪfaɪd/ *adj.* Ⓐ (*without fortification*) unbefestigt; Ⓑ (*not enriched*) nicht gespritet ‹Wein›

**unfortunate** /ʌnˈfɔːtʃʊnət, ʌnˈfɔːtʃənət/ ❶ *adj.* Ⓐ (*unlucky*) unglücklich; (*unfavourable*) ungünstig ‹Tag, Zeit›; **the poor ~ woman** die arme bedauernswerte Frau; **be ~ [enough] to do sth.** das Pech haben, etw. zu tun; Ⓑ (*regrettable*) bedauerlich. ❷ *n.* Unglückliche, *der/die*

**unfortunately** /ʌnˈfɔːtʃʊnətlɪ, ʌnˈfɔːtʃənətlɪ/ *adv.* leider

**unfounded** /ʌnˈfaʊndɪd/ *adj.* (*fig.*) unbegründet; **the rumours are totally ~:** die Gerüchte entbehren jeder Grundlage

**unfreeze** /ʌnˈfriːz/ *v.t. & i.*, **unfroze** /ʌnˈfrəʊz/, **unfrozen** /ʌnˈfrəʊzn/ auftauen

**unfrequented** /ʌnfrɪˈkwentɪd/ *adj.* menschenleer; einsam

**unfriendly** /ʌnˈfrendlɪ/ *adj.* unfreundlich; negativ ‹Kritik›; feindlich ‹Staat›; **the bull looked ~ to him** der Stier schien ihm feindselig [zu sein]

**unfrock** /ʌnˈfrɒk/ *v.t.* **~ sb.** jmdn. des [Priester]amtes entheben

**unfruitful** /ʌnˈfruːtfl/ *adj.* Ⓐ (*sterile*) unfruchtbar; Ⓑ (*unprofitable*) fruchtlos

**unfulfilled** /ʌnfʊlˈfɪld/ *adj.* Ⓐ unerfüllt ‹Person›; Ⓑ (*not carried out*) unerledigt

**unfunny** /ʌnˈfʌnɪ/ *adj.* **[distinctly/decidedly] ~:** [ganz und gar] nicht witzig *od.* komisch

**unfurl** /ʌnˈfɜːl/ ❶ *v.t.* aufrollen; losmachen ‹Segel›. ❷ *v.i.* sich aufrollen

**unfurnished** /ʌnˈfɜːnɪʃt/ *adj.* unmöbliert

**ungainly** /ʌnˈgeɪnlɪ/ *adj.* unbeholfen; ungelenk

**ungallant** /ʌnˈgælənt/ *adj.* unliebenswürdig; ungalant

**ungenerous** /ʌnˈdʒenərəs/ *adj.* Ⓐ (*petty*) kleinlich; Ⓑ (*mean*) wenig großzügig

**ungentlemanly** /ʌnˈdʒentlmənlɪ/ *adj.* unfein; (*impolite*) unhöflich; **it is ~:** es gehört sich nicht für einen Gentleman

**unget-at-able** /ʌngetˈætəbl/ *adj.* unerreichbar; unzugänglich ‹Fonds›

**unglazed** /ʌnˈgleɪzd/ *adj.* Ⓐ nicht glasiert ‹Keramik›; Ⓑ nicht verglast ‹Fenster›

**ungodliness** /ʌnˈgɒdlɪnɪs/ *n., no pl.* Gottlosigkeit, *die*

**ungodly** /ʌnˈgɒdlɪ/ *adj.* Ⓐ (*impious*) gottlos; Ⓑ (*coll.: outrageous*) unchristlich (*ugs.*)

**ungovernable** /ʌnˈgʌvənəbl/ *adj.* unkontrollierbar; unregierbar ‹Volk›

**ungracious** /ʌnˈgreɪʃəs/ *adj.* unhöflich; (*tactless*) taktlos

**ungraciously** /ʌnˈgreɪʃəslɪ/ *adv.* unhöflich; (*tactlessly*) taktlos

**ungrammatical** /ʌngrəˈmætɪkl/ *adj.*, **ungrammatically** /ʌngrəˈmætɪkəlɪ/ *adv.* ungrammatisch

**ungrateful** /ʌnˈgreɪtfl/ *adj.* undankbar

**ungrounded** /ʌnˈgraʊndɪd/ *adj.* Ⓐ ⇒ **unfounded**; Ⓑ (*Amer. Electr.*) ohne Erdung

**ungrudging** /ʌnˈgrʌdʒɪŋ/ *adj.* bereitwillig; (*generous*) großzügig; herzlich ‹Gastfreundschaft›; neidlos ‹Bewunderung›

**unguarded** /ʌnˈgɑːdɪd/ *adj.* Ⓐ (*not guarded*) unbewacht; Ⓑ (*incautious*) unvorsichtig; **in an ~ moment he gave away some vital information** als er einen Moment nicht aufpasste, verriet er einige wichtige Informationen

**unguardedly** /ʌnˈgɑːdɪdlɪ/ *adv.* unvorsichtig

**ungulate** /ˈʌŋgjʊlət/ *n.* (*Zool.*) Huftier, *das*

**unhampered** /ʌnˈhæmpəd/ *adj.* unbehindert; **~ by conscience** nicht von Gewissensbissen geplagt

**unhappily** /ʌnˈhæpɪlɪ/ *adv.* Ⓐ (*unfortunately*) unglücklicherweise; leider; Ⓑ (*without happiness*) unglücklich

**unhappiness** /ʌnˈhæpɪnɪs/ *n., no pl.* Bekümmertheit, *die;* **despite his ~ about the consequences** obwohl er Bedenken über die Folgen hatte; **she spent ten years of ~ with him** sie verbrachte zehn unglückliche Jahre mit ihm; **he has been the cause of much ~ to her** er hat ihr viel Kummer gemacht

**unhappy** /ʌnˈhæpɪ/ *adj.* Ⓐ (*sad, causing misfortune*) unglücklich; (*not content*) unzufrieden (**about** mit); **be** *or* **feel ~ about doing sth.** Bedenken haben, etw. zu tun; Ⓑ (*unfortunate*) unglückselig ‹Zeit, Zufall›; unglücklich ‹Zusammenstellung, Wahl›

**unharmed** /ʌnˈhɑːmd/ *adj.* unbeschädigt; (*uninjured*) unverletzt

**unharness** /ʌnˈhɑːnɪs/ *v.t.* abschirren

**unhealthily** /ʌnˈhelθɪlɪ/ *adv.* krankhaft; ungesund ‹leben›

**unhealthiness** /ʌnˈhelθɪnɪs/ *n., no pl.* Krankhaftigkeit, *die;* (*of place, habit*) Gesundheitsschädlichkeit, *die*

**unhealthy** /ʌnˈhelθɪ/ *adj.* Ⓐ (*not in good health, harmful to health*) ungesund; Ⓑ (*unwholesome*) ungesund, krankhaft ‹Gier›; schädlich ‹Einfluss›; schlecht ‹Angewohnheit›; Ⓒ (*coll.: risky*) gefährlich

**unheard** /ʌnˈhɜːd/ *adj.* Ⓐ **~-of** (*unknown*) [gänzlich] unbekannt; (*unprecedented*) beispiellos; (*outrageous*) unerhört; **that's ~ of** das ist noch nie da gewesen; **this was an ~-of achievement fifty years ago** vor fünfzig Jahren war eine solche Leistung unvorstellbar; Ⓑ (*not heard*) **go ~:** ungehört bleiben

**unheeded** /ʌnˈhiːdɪd/ *adj.* unbeachtet; **go ~:** nicht beachtet werden; ‹Gebet, Wunsch:› nicht erhört werden

**unheedful** /ʌnˈhiːdfʊl/ *adj.* **~ of** ungeachtet (+ *Gen.*)

**unhelpful** /ʌnˈhelpfl/ *adj.* wenig hilfsbereit ‹Person›; ‹Bemerkung, Kritik› die einem nicht weiterhilft

**unhelpfully** /ʌnˈhelpfəlɪ/ *adv.* wenig hilfsbereit

**unhesitating** /ʌnˈhezɪteɪtɪŋ/ *adj.* unverzüglich; **she was ~ in her support for him** sie zögerte keinen Augenblick, ihn zu unterstützen

**unhesitatingly** /ʌnˈhezɪteɪtɪŋlɪ/ *adv.* ohne zu zögern

**unhinged** /ʌnˈhɪndʒd/ *adj.* **his/her mind is ~:** er/sie hat den Verstand verloren

**unhitch** /ʌnˈhɪtʃ/ *v.t.* losmachen; ausspannen ‹Pferd›; abkoppeln ‹Anhänger›

**unholy** /ʌnˈhəʊlɪ/ *adj.* Ⓐ (*wicked*) unheilig ‹Allianz›; Ⓑ (*coll.: dreadful*) fürchterlich (*ugs.*) ‹Krawall, Durcheinander›

**unhook** /ʌnˈhʊk/ *v.t.* Ⓐ (*detach from hook*) vom Haken nehmen; Ⓑ (*unfasten by releasing hook*) aufhaken ‹Kleid›; loshaken ‹Tor›

**unhoped-for** /ʌnˈhəʊptfɔː(r)/ *adj.* unverhofft

**unhurried** /ʌnˈhʌrɪd/ *adj.*, **unhurriedly** /ʌnˈhʌrɪdlɪ/ *adv.* gemächlich

**unhurt** /ʌnˈhɜːt/ *adj.* unverletzt

**unhygienic** /ʌnhaɪˈdʒiːnɪk/ *adj.* unhygienisch

**UNICEF** /ˈjuːnɪsef/ *abbr.* **United Nations Children's Fund** UNICEF, *die*

**unicorn** /ˈjuːnɪkɔːn/ *n.* (*Mythol.*) Einhorn, *das*

**unicycle** /ˈjuːnɪsaɪkl/ *n.* Einrad, *das*

**unidentified** /ʌnaɪˈdentɪfaɪd/ *adj.* nicht identifiziert; **~ flying object** unbekanntes Flugobjekt

**unidiomatic** /ʌnɪdɪəˈmætɪk/ *adj.*, **unidiomatically** /ʌnɪdɪəˈmætɪkəlɪ/ *adv.* nicht idiomatisch

**unification** /juːnɪfɪˈkeɪʃn/ *n.* Einigung, *die;* (*of system*) Vereinheitlichung, *die*

**uniform** /ˈjuːnɪfɔːm/ ❶ *adj.* (*the same for all*) einheitlich; (*unvarying*) gleich bleibend ‹Strömung, Temperatur, Qualität›; gleichmäßig ‹Tempo›; **be of ~ shape/size/appearance, be ~ in shape/size/appearance** die gleiche Form/Größe/das gleiche Aussehen haben; **~ rows of houses** gleichförmige Häuserzeilen. ❷ *n.* Uniform, *die;* **in/out of ~:** in/ohne Uniform; **be in/out of ~:** Uniform/keine Uniform tragen

**uniformed** /ˈjuːnɪfɔːmd/ *adj.* uniformiert

**uniformity** /juːnɪˈfɔːmɪtɪ/ *n.* Einheitlichkeit, *die;* (*constant nature*) Gleichmäßigkeit, *die;* **impose ~ of belief on ...:** jmdm. einen einheitlichen Glauben auferlegen (+ *Dat.*)

**uniformly** /ˈjuːnɪfɔːmlɪ/ *adv.* Ⓐ (*unvaryingly*) einheitlich; Ⓑ (*equally*) gleichmäßig

**unify** /ˈjuːnɪfaɪ/ *v.t.* einigen ‹Volk, Land›; vereinheitlichen ‹System, Wirtschaft›

**unilateral** /juːnɪˈlætərl/ *adj.* einseitig

**unilateralist** /juːnɪˈlætərəlɪst/ *n.* Befürworter der einseitigen Abrüstung

**unilaterally** /juːnɪˈlætərəlɪ/ *adv.* einseitig

**unimaginable** /ʌnɪˈmædʒɪnəbl/ *adj.* unvorstellbar

**unimaginative** /ʌnɪˈmædʒɪnətɪv/ *adj.*, **unimaginatively** /ʌnɪˈmædʒɪnətɪvlɪ/ *adv.* fantasielos

**unimpaired** /ʌnɪmˈpeəd/ *adj.* unbeeinträchtigt; **he emerged from the trial with ~ prestige** er überstand den Prozess ohne Prestigeverlust

**unimpeachable** /ʌnɪmˈpiːtʃəbl/ *adj.* Ⓐ (*blameless*) unanfechtbar; untadelig ‹Ruf›; Ⓑ (*beyond question*) unbezweifelbar; absolut zuverlässig ‹Quelle›

**unimpeded** /ʌnɪmˈpiːdɪd/ *adj.* ungehindert

**unimportance** /ʌnɪmˈpɔːtəns/ *n., no pl.* Unwichtigkeit, *die;* Bedeutungslosigkeit, *die*

**unimportant** /ʌnɪmˈpɔːtənt/ *adj.* unwichtig; bedeutungslos

**unimpressed** /ʌnɪmˈprest/ *adj.* nicht beeindruckt

**unimpressive** /ʌnɪmˈpresɪv/ *adj.* nicht eindrucksvoll; unscheinbar ‹Gebäude›; (*unconvincing*) nicht überzeugend

**uninfluenced** /ʌnˈɪnflʊənst/ *adj.* unbeeinflusst

**uninformative** /ʌnɪmˈfɔːmətɪv/ *adj.* inhaltslos ‹Text›; **he is ~ about his plans** er verrät nichts über seine Pläne

**uninformed** /ʌnɪmˈfɔːmd/ *adj.* Ⓐ (*not informed*) uninformiert; **be [entirely] ~ about the development** [überhaupt] nichts von der Entwicklung wissen; Ⓑ (*based on ignorance*) auf Unkenntnis beruhend ‹Urteil, Ansicht›; **~ guess** reine Vermutung

**uninhabitable** /ʌnɪnˈhæbɪtəbl/ *adj.* unbewohnbar

**uninhabited** /ʌnɪnˈhæbɪtɪd/ *adj.* unbewohnt

**uninhibited** /ʌnɪnˈhɪbɪtɪd/ *adj.* ungehemmt; ohne Hemmungen *nachgestellt*

**uninitiated** /ʌnɪˈnɪʃɪeɪtɪd/ *adj.* uneingeweiht; **~ in the mysteries** nicht in die Geheimnisse eingeweiht; **the ~:** Außenstehende

**uninjured** /ʌnˈɪndʒəd/ *adj.* unverletzt

**uninspired** /ʌnɪnˈspaɪəd/ *adj.* einfallslos; **I am/feel ~:** mir fehlt die Inspiration

**uninspiring** /ʌnɪnˈspaɪərɪŋ/ *adj.* langweilig

**uninsured** /ʌnɪnˈʃʊəd/ *adj.* nicht versichert

**unintelligent** /ʌnɪnˈtelɪdʒənt/ *adj.* nicht intelligent; **pretty ~:** ziemlich dumm

**unintelligible** /ʌnɪnˈtelɪdʒɪbl/ *adj.* unverständlich

**unintended** /ʌnɪnˈtendɪd/ *adj.* unbeabsichtigt

**unintentional** /ʌnɪnˈtenʃənl/ *adj.*, **unintentionally** /ʌnɪnˈtenʃənəlɪ/ *adv.* unabsichtlich; (*Law*) nicht vorsätzlich

**uninterested** /ʌnˈɪntrestɪd, ʌnˈɪntrɪstɪd/ *adj.* desinteressiert (**in** an + *Dat.*)

**uninteresting** /ʌnˈɪntrestɪŋ, ʌnˈɪntrɪstɪŋ/ *adj.* uninteressant

**uninterrupted** /ʌnɪntəˈrʌptɪd/ *adj.* **A** (*continuous*) ununterbrochen; nicht unterbrochen; **B** (*not disturbed*) ungestört

**uninvited** /ʌnɪnˈvaɪtɪd/ *adj.* ungeladen

**uninviting** /ʌnɪnˈvaɪtɪŋ/ *adj.* wenig verlockend; wenig einladend ‹Ort, Wetter›

**uninvolved** /ʌnɪnˈvɒlvd/ *adj.* unbeteiligt (**in** an + *Dat.*); **be** *or* **remain ~:** sich nicht beteiligen

**union** /ˈjuːnɪən, ˈjuːnjən/ *n.* **A** (*trade ~*) Gewerkschaft, *die;* **B** (*political unit*) Union, *die;* **'State of the U~' message** (*Amer. Polit.*) Regierungserklärung zur Lage der Nation; **C** **[Students'] U~:** Studentenvereinigung, *die;* **D** (*marriage*) eheliche Verbindung; **E** (*concord*) Einigkeit, *die;* **they lived together in perfect ~:** sie lebten einträchtig zusammen; **F** (*uniting*) Vereinigung, *die*

**unionism** /ˈjuːnɪənɪzm, ˈjuːnjənɪzm/ *n.* **A** (*of trade unions*) Gewerkschaftswesen, *das;* **B** (*Brit. Polit.*) unionistische Bestrebungen; *Befürwortung der parlamentarischen Einheit von Großbritannien und Nordirland*

**unionist** /ˈjuːnɪənɪst, ˈjuːnjənɪst/ *n.* **A** (*member of trade union*) Gewerkschafter, *der*/Gewerkschafterin, *die;* (*advocate of trade unions*) Gewerkschaftsanhänger, *der*/-anhängerin, *die;* **B** **U~** (*Polit.*) Unionist, *der*/Unionistin, *die*

**unionize** (**unionise**) /ˈjuːnɪənaɪz, ˈjuːnjənaɪz/ *v.t.* **~ a company** in einer Firma eine Gewerkschaftsorganisation aufbauen; **~d labour** gewerkschaftlich organisierte Arbeitskräfte

**Union: ~ 'Jack** *n.* (*Brit.*) Union Jack, *der;* **~ of Soviet Socialist Republics** *pr. n.* (*Hist.*) Union der Sozialistischen Sowjetrepubliken; **u~ suit** *n.* (*Amer.*) Hemdhose, *die* (*veralt.*); Leibchenhose, *die* (*landsch.*)

**unique** /juːˈniːk/ *adj.* **A** (*unparalleled*) einzigartig; (*not repeated*) einmalig ‹Gelegenheit, Angebot›; **this vase is ~:** diese Vase ist ein Einzelstück; **this problem is ~ to our society** dieses Problem gibt es nur in unserer Gesellschaft; **these animals are ~ to Australia** diese Tiere kommen nur in Australien vor; **B** (*coll.: remarkable*) einmalig

**uniquely** /juːˈniːklɪ/ *adv.* **A** (*exclusively*) einzig und allein; **that distinction is ~ his** die Auszeichnung besitzt nur *od.* allein er; **B** (*to a unique degree*) einzigartig; einmalig ‹talentiert, begabt›

**uniqueness** /juːˈniːknɪs/ *n.*, *no pl.* Einzigartigkeit, *die*

**unisex** /ˈjuːnɪseks/ *adj.* Unisex‹mantel, -kleidung›; **~ hairdresser** Damen-und-Herren-Frisör

**unison** /ˈjuːnɪsən/ ❶ *n.* **A** (*Mus.*) Unisono, *das;* **in ~:** unisono; einstimmig; **act in ~** (*fig.*) vereint handeln; **act in ~ with sb.** in Übereinstimmung mit jmdm. handeln; **B** (*concord*) Einmütigkeit, *die.* ❷ *adj.* (*Mus.*) unisono gesungen/gespielt

**unit** /ˈjuːnɪt/ *n.* **A** (*element, group, regarded as complete; also Mil.*) Einheit, *die;* (*in complex mechanism*) Element, *das;* **x-ray ~:** Röntgenabteilung, *die;* **armoured ~** (*Mil.*) Panzereinheit, *die;* **motor ~** (*Railw.*) Triebwagen, *der;* **B** (*in adding numbers by columns*) Einer, *der* (*Math.*); **the ~s column** die Einerspalte; **C** (*quantity chosen as standard*) [Maß]einheit, *die;* (*of gas, electricity*) Einheit, *die;* **~ of length/monetary ~:** Längen-/Währungseinheit, *die;* **D** (*piece of furniture*) Element, *das;* **kitchen ~:** Küchenelement, *das;* **wall ~:** Wandschrank, *der;* **E** (*esp. electrical device*) Gerät, *das;* **F** (*building*) **shop ~:** Ladenlokal, *das;* **residential ~:** Wohneinheit, *die;* **factory ~:** Fabrikgebäude, *das;* **G** (*Brit. Finance*) Anteil[sschein] [an einem Investmentfonds]

**Unitarian** /juːnɪˈteərɪən/ (*Relig.*) ❶ *n.* Unitarier, *der*/Unitarierin, *die.* ❷ *adj.* unitarisch

**unitary** /ˈjuːnɪtərɪ/ *adj.* einheitlich

**unite** /juːˈnaɪt/ ❶ *v.t.* vereinigen; verbinden ‹Einzelteile›; einen, einigen ‹Partei, Mitglieder›. ❷ *v.i.* **A** (*join together*) sich vereinigen; ‹Elemente:› sich verbinden; ‹gebrochene Knochen:› zusammenwachsen; **B** (*join forces*) sich vereinigen; (*form merger*) sich zusammenschließen; **~ in doing sth.** etw. vereint *od.* gemeinsam tun

**united** /juːˈnaɪtɪd/ *adj.* **A** (*harmonious*) einig; **a ~ front** eine geschlossene Front; **~ we stand, divided we fall** gemeinsam siegen wir, getrennt fallen wir; **B** (*combined*) vereint (*geh.*); gemeinsam; **their ~ efforts found the solution** ihre gemeinsamen Anstrengungen führten zur Lösung

**United: ~ Arab 'Emirates** *pr. n. pl.* Vereinigte Arabische Emirate; **~ 'Kingdom** *pr. n.* Vereinigtes Königreich [Großbritannien und Nordirland]; **~ 'Nations** *pr. n. sing.* Vereinte Nationen *Pl.;* **~ Re'formed Church** *n.* Vereinigte Reformierte Kirche; **~ 'States** ⇒ **state** 1 E; **~ States of A'merica** *n. sing.* Vereinigte Staaten von Amerika

**unit: ~ 'furniture** *n.* Anbaumöbel *Pl.;* **~ 'price** *n.* (*Commerc.*) Stückpreis, *der;* **~ 'trust** *n.* (*Brit. Finance*) ≈ Investmentfonds, *der*

**unity** /ˈjuːnɪtɪ/ *n.* **A** (*state of being united*) Einheit, *die;* (*of work of art, idea*) [innere] Geschlossenheit; **their ~ of purpose** die Gemeinsamkeit ihres Wollens; **the dramatic unities** die drei Einheiten (*Literaturw.*); **B** (*Math.*) Einselement, *das;* **C** (*harmony*) Eintracht, *die*

**universal** /juːnɪˈvɜːsl/ *adj.* **A** (*prevailing everywhere*) allgemein; allgemein gültig ‹Regel, Wahrheit›; **less ~:** weniger häufig *od.* verbreitet; **there was ~ terror** überall herrschte große Angst; **become ~:** sich allgemein verbreiten; **B** (*involving or versed in all fields of knowledge*) universal ‹Bildung, Wissen›; universell begabt ‹Person›; **~ genius** Universalgenie, *das;* **C** (*common to all members of a class*) universell; **D** (*meeting varied requirements*) Universal-; **~ remedy** Universalmittel, *das*

**universality** /juːnɪvɜːˈsælɪtɪ/ *n.*, *no pl.* **A** (*universal prevalence*) allgemeine Verbreitung; **B** (*universal comprehensiveness*) Universalität, *die*

**universal: ~ 'joint** *n.* Kardangelenk, *das;* **~ 'language** *n.* Universalsprache, *die*

**universally** /juːnɪˈvɜːsəlɪ/ *adv.* allgemein; **be ~ opposed to these politics/hostile to foreigners** diese Politik einmütig ablehnen/ausnahmslos fremdenfeindlich sein

**universe** /ˈjuːnɪvɜːs/ *n.* **A** Universum, *das;* (*world; fig.: mankind*) Welt, *die;* **B** ⇒ **cosmos** B

**university** /juːnɪˈvɜːsɪtɪ/ *n.* Universität, *die; attrib.* Universitäts-; **go to ~:** auf die *od.* zur Universität gehen; **at ~:** an der Universität

**unjust** /ʌnˈdʒʌst/ *adj.* ungerecht (**to** *Dat.* + gegenüber); **it would be ~ not to refer to X** es ist ein Gebot der Fairness, X zu zitieren

**unjustifiable** /ʌnˈdʒʌstɪfaɪəbl/ *adj.* ungerechtfertigt; **be ~:** nicht zu rechtfertigen sein

**unjustifiably** /ʌnˈdʒʌstɪfaɪəblɪ/ *adv.* ungerechtfertigterweise

**unjustified** /ʌnˈdʒʌstɪfaɪd/ *adj.* ungerechtfertigt; **you are entirely ~ in thinking ...:** du glaubst ganz zu Unrecht, ...

**unjustly** /ʌnˈdʒʌstlɪ/ ungerechterweise; zu Unrecht

**unkempt** /ʌnˈkempt/ *adj.* **A** (*dishevelled*) ungekämmt ‹Haare›; **B** (*untidy*) ungepflegt

**unkind** /ʌnˈkaɪnd/ *adj.* unfreundlich; **be ~ to sb./animals** jmdn./Tiere schlecht behandeln

**unkindly** /ʌnˈkaɪndlɪ/ *adv.* unfreundlich; **fate treated her ~:** das Schicksal meinte es nicht gut mit ihr

**unkindness** /ʌnˈkaɪndnɪs/ *n.* Unfreundlichkeit, *die*

**unknot** /ʌnˈnɒt/ *v.t.*, **-tt-** entknoten

**unknowing** /ʌnˈnəʊɪŋ/ ⇒ **unwitting**

**unknowingly** /ʌnˈnəʊɪŋlɪ/ ⇒ **unwittingly**

**unknown** /ʌnˈnəʊn/ ❶ *adj.* unbekannt; **an ~ number of people died in the accident** die Zahl der Todesopfer bei dem Unfall ist nicht bekannt; **sb./sth. is ~ to sb.** jmd./etw. ist jmdm. nicht bekannt; **a drug ~ to us** ein uns unbekanntes Heilmittel; **it is ~/not ~ for him to do such a thing** es ist nie vorgekommen/ist schon vorgekommen, dass er so etwas getan hat; **~ territory** (*lit. or fig.*) unbekanntes Terrain; **the U~ Soldier** *or* **Warrior** der Unbekannte Soldat; **murder by person** *or* **persons ~:** Mord durch unbekannten Täter; **~ strengths/reserves** (*unsuspected*) ungeahnte Kräfte/Reserven; ⇒ *also* **country** A; **quantity** E.
❷ *adv.* **~ to sb.** ohne dass jmd. davon weiß/wusste.
❸ *n.* **A** **the ~:** das Unbekannte; **fear of the ~:** Angst vor dem Unbekannten; **journey/voyage into the ~** (*lit. or fig.*) Reise in unbekannte Regionen; **B** (*person*) **an ~:** ein Unbekannter/eine Unbekannte; **C** (*Math.: quantity*) Unbekannte, *die;* **an equation with two ~s** eine Gleichung mit zwei Unbekannten; **D** (*factor*) unbekannte Größe

**unlabelled** (*Amer.:* **unlabeled**) /ʌnˈleɪbld/ *adj.* ‹Flasche, Behälter› ohne Etikett *od.* Beschriftung; ‹Gepäck, Koffer, Paket› ohne Aufkleber/Anhänger; unbeschriftet ‹Dokument, Aktenordner, Tonband›

**unlace** /ʌnˈleɪs/ *v.t.* aufschnüren

**unladen** /ʌnˈleɪdn/ *adj.* **~ weight** Leergewicht, *das*

**unladylike** /ʌnˈleɪdɪlaɪk/ *adj.* nicht sehr damenhaft; **very ~:** gar nicht damenhaft

**unlatch** /ʌnˈlætʃ/ ❶ *v.t.* aufklinken. ❷ *v.i.* sich aufklinken lassen

**unlawful** /ʌnˈlɔːfl/ *adj.* ungesetzlich; gesetzwidrig; **~ possession of firearms/drugs** illegaler Waffen-/Drogenbesitz; **~ assembly** verbotene Versammlung

**unlawfully** /ʌnˈlɔːfəlɪ/ *adv.* gesetzwidrig

**unleaded** /ʌnˈledɪd/ *adj.* bleifrei ‹Benzin›

**unlearn** /ʌnˈlɜːn/ *v.t., forms as* **learn** 1 vergessen ‹Idee, Kenntnisse›; ablegen ‹Gewohnheit›

**unleash** /ʌnˈliːʃ/ *v.t.* von der Leine lassen ‹Hund›; (*fig.*) freien Lauf lassen (+ *Dat.*) ‹Gefühlen, Leidenschaften, Kräften›; entfesseln ‹Sturm der Entrüstung›; **~ sth. [up]on sb.** an jmdm. etw. auslassen; **~ violence/[a] war on a country** Gewalt/Krieg über ein Land bringen

**unleavened** /ʌnˈlevnd/ *adj.* ohne Treibmittel *nachgestellt;* ungesäuert ‹Brot›

**unless** /ˈʌnˈles, ənˈles/ *conj.* es sei denn; wenn ... nicht; **I shall not do it ~ I am paid for it** ich werde es nur tun, wenn ich dafür bezahlt werde; **I shall expect you tomorrow ~ I hear from you/hear to the contrary** falls *od.* sofern ich nichts von dir/nichts Gegenteiliges höre, erwarte ich dich morgen; **I might go, but not ~ I'm asked to** vielleicht gehe ich, aber nur, wenn man mich darum bittet; **~ I'm [very much] mistaken** wenn ich mich nicht [sehr] irre *od.* täusche; **~ he comes soon, I shall leave** wenn er nicht bald kommt, dann gehe ich; **~ otherwise indicated** *or* **stated** wenn nicht anders angegeben

**unlettered** /ʌnˈletəd/ *adj.* **A** (*illiterate*) analphabetisch; **B** (*uneducated*) ungebildet

**unliberated** /ʌnˈlɪbəreɪtɪd/ *adj.* nicht emanzipiert ‹Frau›; unfrei ‹Massen, Land›

**unlicensed** /ʌnˈlaɪsənst/ *adj.* ‹Händler, Makler, Buchmacher› ohne Konzession; ‹Pilot› ohne Lizenz; nicht angemeldet ‹Hund, Radio, Fernsehgerät,

Auto›; **~ premises** Gaststättenbetrieb ohne [Schank]konzession

**unlighted** /ʌnˈlaɪtɪd/ ⇒ **unlit**

**unlike** /ʌnˈlaɪk/ ❶ *adj.* nicht ähnlich; unähnlich; (*unequal*) **~ signs** (*Math.*) ungleiche Vorzeichen; **~ poles** (*Phys.*) ungleiche Pole; **they are ~:** sie sind sich (*Dat.*) nicht ähnlich.
❷ *prep.* **be ~ sb./sth.** jmdm./einer Sache nicht ähnlich sein; **those people are ~ us** diese Leute sind nicht wie wir; **be not ~ sb./sth.** jmdm./etw. nicht unähnlich sein *od.* ganz ähnlich sein; **his new novel is ~ his previous ones** sein neuer Roman ist anders als seine früheren; **sth. is ~ sb.** (*not characteristic of*) etw. sieht jmdm. gar nicht ähnlich (*ugs.*); etw. ist für jmdn. nicht typisch; **it is ~ him to be late** es sieht ihm gar nicht ähnlich (*ugs.*) *od.* es ist sonst nicht seine Art, zu spät zu kommen; **~ her brother, she likes walking** im Gegensatz zu ihrem Bruder geht sie gern spazieren; **she sings quite ~ other singers** sie singt ganz anders als andere Sängerinnen

**unlikelihood** /ʌnˈlaɪklɪhʊd/ *n., no pl.* Unwahrscheinlichkeit, *die;* **despite the ~ of the player's being fit** obwohl der Spieler wahrscheinlich nicht fit sein wird

**unlikely** /ʌnˈlaɪklɪ/ *adj.* Ⓐ unwahrscheinlich; unglaubwürdig ‹Geschichte, Erklärung›; **be ~ to do sth.** etw. wahrscheinlich nicht tun; **in the ~ event that ...:** sollte der unwahrscheinliche Fall eintreten, dass ...; **he's ~ to be chosen for the part/post** er wird die Rolle/Stelle kaum bekommen; **it is not ~ that ...:** es ist durchaus wahrscheinlich, dass ...; Ⓑ (*unsuitable*) **an ~ candidate/man for the job** ein Bewerber, der für den Posten kaum geeignet sein dürfte; **she looked in every likely and ~ place to find her key** sie suchte an allen möglichen und unmöglichen Stellen ihren Schlüssel

**unlimited** /ʌnˈlɪmɪtɪd/ *adj.* unbegrenzt; grenzenlos, unendlich ‹Himmel, Meer, Geduld›; **~ drinks** eine unbegrenzte Zahl von Getränken; **~ liability** (*Commerc.*) unbeschränkte Haftung; **~ company** (*Commerc.*) Gesellschaft mit unbeschränkter Haftung; **~ mileage** unbegrenzte Meilenzahl

**unlined**[1] /ʌnˈlaɪnd/ *adj.* (*without lining*) ungefüttert ‹Kleidung, Briefumschlag›

**unlined**[2] *adj.* (*without lines*) unliniert ‹Papier›

**unlisted** /ʌnˈlɪstɪd/ *adj.* nicht eingetragen; **~ stock/securities** (*Finance*) nicht notierte Wertpapiere; **~ [telephone] number** Geheimnummer, *die*

**unlit** /ʌnˈlɪt/ *adj.* unbeleuchtet ‹Straße, Korridor, Zimmer›; nicht angezündet ‹Lampe, Kamin, Kerze›

**unload** /ʌnˈləʊd/ ❶ *v.t.* Ⓐ entladen ‹Lastwagen, Waggon›; löschen ‹Schiff, Schiffsladung›; ausladen ‹Gepäck›; **~ a donkey** einem Esel die Last abnehmen; **the bus/ship ~ed its passengers** die Fahrgäste stiegen aus dem Bus/Schiff; Ⓑ (*dispose of; Commerc.: sell off, dump*) abstoßen ‹Aktien, Wertpapiere›; **~ goods on the market** Waren auf den Markt werfen; **~ sb./sth. on [to] sb.** (*fig.*) jmdn./etw. bei jmdm. abladen ‹Kinder, Hund, Probleme, Sorgen›; **~ one's job/responsibility on[to] sb. else** seine Aufgabe/Verantwortung auf jmd. anders (*Akk.*) abwälzen; Ⓒ entladen ‹Gewehr, Pistole›; **~ [the film from] a camera** den Film aus einer Kamera nehmen.
❷ *v.i.* ‹Schiff:› gelöscht werden; ‹Lastwagen:› entladen werden; **start ~ing** mit dem Entladen anfangen

**unloaded** /ʌnˈləʊdɪd/ *adj.* Ⓐ nicht beladen ‹Schiff, Lastwagen, Waggon›; Ⓑ nicht geladen ‹Gewehr, Pistole›

**unlock** /ʌnˈlɒk/ *v.t.* Ⓐ aufschließen; lösen ‹Rad, Taste›; **~ed** unverschlossen ‹Tür, Tor›; **leave the door ~ed when you go out** schließ die Tür nicht ab, wenn du gehst; **the gate was left ~ed** das Tor war nicht abgeschlossen; (*fig.*) **~ a secret/puzzle** ein Geheimnis/Rätsel entschlüsseln; **this book has ~ed the world of literature for him** dieses Buch hat ihm die Welt der Literatur erschlossen; Ⓑ (*fig.: release*) lösen ‹Hand, Umarmung›

**unlooked-for** /ʌnˈlʊktfɔː(r)/ *adj.* unerwartet; **a virtue perhaps ~ in him** eine Tugend, die man bei ihm vielleicht nicht erwartet hätte

**unloose** /ʌnˈluːs/ ⇒ **loose** 2

**unlovable** /ʌnˈlʌvəbl/ *adj.* wenig liebenswert

**unloved** /ʌnˈlʌvd/ *adj.* ungeliebt

**unlovely** /ʌnˈlʌvlɪ/ *adj.* unschön ‹Anblick, Gegenstand, Haus›; reizlos ‹Person, Gesicht, Stadt›; (*in character*) nicht sehr sympathisch ‹Person›

**unluckily** /ʌnˈlʌkɪlɪ/ *adv.* unglücklich; *as sentence-modifier* unglücklicherweise: **~ for him/her** *etc.* zu seinem/ihrem *usw.* Pech

**unlucky** /ʌnˈlʌkɪ/ *adj.* Ⓐ unglücklich; (*not successful*) glücklos; **be [very/really] ~:** [großes/wirkliches] Pech haben; **lucky at cards, ~ in love** Glück im Spiel, Pech in der Liebe; Ⓑ (*bringing bad luck*) **an ~ date/number** ein Unglückstag/eine Unglückszahl; **an ~ sign/omen** ein schlechtes Zeichen/Omen; **be born under an ~ star** unter keinem glücklichen Stern geboren sein; **be ~:** Unglück bringen; **it was ~ [for him] that he couldn't come** es war Pech [für ihn], dass er nicht kommen konnte

**unmade** /ʌnˈmeɪd/ *adj.* ungemacht ‹Bett›; unbefestigt ‹Straße›

**unmade-up** /ʌnmeɪdˈʌp/ *adj.* ungeschminkt ‹Gesicht, Person›

**unmake** /ʌnˈmeɪk/ *v.t.*, **unmade** /ʌnˈmeɪd/ rückgängig machen ‹Vereinbarung, Entscheidung›; fallen lassen ‹Plan›; ruinieren ‹Laufbahn›

**unman** /ʌnˈmæn/ *v.t.*, **-nn-** Ⓐ **~ sb.** (*deprive of strength*) jmdm. die Kraft nehmen; (*deprive of courage*) jmdn. verzagen lassen; **~ned by grief** von Kummer geschwächt; Ⓑ (*emasculate, castrate*) entmannen

**unmanageable** /ʌnˈmænɪdʒəbl/ *adj.* Ⓐ (*difficult to control*) widerspenstig ‹Kind, Pferd, Haare›; unkontrollierbar ‹Situation›; **the car/boat became ~:** der Wagen/das Boot war nicht mehr zu kontrollieren; Ⓑ (*unwieldy*) sperrig; unhandlich ‹Buch›

**unmanly** /ʌnˈmænlɪ/ *adj.* unmännlich

**unmanned** /ʌnˈmænd/ *adj.* unbemannt ‹Leuchtturm, Raumschiff, Bahnübergang›; (*with nobody in attendance*) nicht besetzt ‹Schalter, Rezeption›; unbewacht ‹Posten, Eingang›

**unmannerly** /ʌnˈmænəlɪ/ *adj.* unmanierlich ‹Person, Benehmen›; ungehörig ‹Benehmen›; **it is ~ to do that** es gehört sich nicht, das zu tun

**unmarked** /ʌnˈmɑːkt/ *adj.* Ⓐ (*without markings*) ‹Schachtel, Kiste› ohne Aufschrift; nicht gezeichnet ‹Wäschestück›; anonym ‹Grab›; **an ~ police car** ein Zivilfahrzeug der Polizei; Ⓑ (*not spoilt by marks*) fleckenlos ‹Fußboden, Oberfläche›; makellos ‹Haut, Pfirsich, Apfel›; unbeschädigt ‹Teller, Buch›; **after ten rounds, the boxer was still ~:** nach zehn Runden war der Boxer immer noch nicht gezeichnet; **his face was ~ by the accident** sein Gesicht zeigte keine Spuren des Unfalls; Ⓒ (*not corrected*) unkorrigiert ‹Klassenarbeit›; Ⓓ (*not noticed*) unbemerkt; Ⓔ (*Sport*) ungedeckt ‹Spieler›; Ⓕ (*Ling.*) nicht markiert ‹Form›

**unmarketable** /ʌnˈmɑːkɪtəbl/ *adj.* unverkäuflich

**unmarriageable** /ʌnˈmærɪdʒəbl/ *adj.* **be ~:** nicht zu verheiraten sein

**unmarried** /ʌnˈmærɪd/ *adj.* unverheiratet; ledig; **~ mother/couple** ledige Mutter/unverheiratetes Paar

**unmask** /ʌnˈmɑːsk/ *v.t.* **~ sb.** jmdm. die Maske entreißen; (*fig.*) jmdn. entlarven (**as** als); **~ a plot/sb.'s intentions** *etc.* eine Verschwörung/jmds. Absichten *usw.* aufdecken

**unmasking** /ʌnˈmɑːskɪŋ/ *n.* Entlarvung, *die*

**unmatched** /ʌnˈmætʃt/ *adj.* **be ~ [for sth.]** [in etw. (*Dat.*)] unübertroffen sein

**unmentionable** /ʌnˈmenʃənəbl/ *adj.* unaussprechlich ‹Sünde, Verbrechen›; **an ~ topic/subject** ein Thema, über das man nicht spricht

**unmerciful** /ʌnˈmɜːsɪfl/ *adj.* erbarmungslos; unbarmherzig

**unmercifully** /ʌnˈmɜːsɪfəlɪ/ *adv.* erbarmungslos; unbarmherzig; **treat sb. ~:** jmdn. unbarmherzig behandeln

**unmerited** /ʌnˈmerɪtɪd/ *adj.* unverdient

**unmetalled** /ʌnˈmetld/ *adj.* (*Brit.*) unbefestigt ‹Straße›

**unmethodical** /ʌnmɪˈθɒdɪkl/ *adj.* unmethodisch

**unmindful** /ʌnˈmaɪndfl/ *adj.* **be ~ of sth.** etw. nicht beachten

**unmistakable** /ʌnmɪˈsteɪkəbl/ *adj.* deutlich; unmissverständlich ‹Drohung, Befehl›; klar ‹Beweis›; unverwechselbar ‹Handschrift, Stimme, Silhouette›; **an ~ sign of sth.** ein sicheres Zeichen für etw.; **there was ~ fear/relief in his voice** in seiner Stimme schwang deutlich Furcht/Erleichterung mit

**unmistakably** /ʌnmɪˈsteɪkəblɪ/ *adv.* unverkennbar

**unmitigated** /ʌnˈmɪtɪgeɪtɪd/ *adj.* vollkommen ‹Unsinn, Schwachkopf›; einzig ‹Übel, Lüge›; **an ~ scoundrel** ein Erzschurke; **be an ~ disaster** (*coll.*) eine einzige Katastrophe sein (*ugs.*)

**unmixed** /ʌnˈmɪkst/ *adj.* unvermischt; (*fig.*) ungetrübt ‹Freude, Vergnügen›; **his joy was not ~ with sadness** in seine Freude mischte sich Traurigkeit

**unmolested** /ʌnmɒˈlestɪd/ *adj.* unbelästigt

**unmoor** /ʌnˈmʊə(r), ʌnˈmɔː(r)/ ❶ *v.t. & i.* [bei einem Boot] die Leinen losmachen. ❷ *v.i.* die Leinen losmachen

**unmotivated** /ʌnˈməʊtɪveɪtɪd/ *adj.* unmotiviert

**unmounted** /ʌnˈmaʊntɪd/ *adj.* nicht gefasst ‹Edelstein›; nicht aufgezogen ‹Bild›

**unmourned** /ʌnˈmɔːnd/ *adj.* unbeweint

**unmoved** /ʌnˈmuːvd/ *adj.* unbewegt; ungerührt; **be/remain ~ by sb.'s pleas** sich von jmds. Bitten nicht rühren *od.* erweichen lassen; **he was ~ by the accusations** er ließ sich von den Anschuldigungen nicht aus der Ruhe bringen; **remain ~ by an argument** von einem Argument nicht beeindruckt sein

**unmusical** /ʌnˈmjuːzɪkl/ *adj.* unmelodisch ‹Gesang, Stimme›; unmusikalisch ‹Person›

**unnameable** /ʌnˈneɪməbl/ *adj.* unbestimmt ‹Angst›; unsagbar ‹Qual›

**unnamed** /ʌnˈneɪmd/ *adj.* Ⓐ (*unidentified*) [namentlich] nicht genannt ‹Ort, Person, Medizin›; ungenannt ‹Wohltäter›; Ⓑ (*having no name*) namenlos ‹Findling›; **an ~ island/lake/mountain** eine Insel/ein See/ein Berg ohne Namen; **a species so far ~:** eine Art, die bisher noch keinen Namen hat

**unnatural** /ʌnˈnætʃrəl/ *adj.* Ⓐ unnatürlich; (*abnormal*) nicht normal; (*perverted*) widernatürlich; (*uncaring*) herzlos ‹Mutter, Kind usw.›; **not ~:** ganz natürlich; **a mother who is cruel to her children is ~:** eine Mutter, die grausam zu ihren Kindern ist, ist widernatürlich *od.* (*ugs.*) nicht normal; Ⓑ (*affected*) unnatürlich; gekünstelt

**unnaturally** /ʌnˈnætʃrəlɪ/ *adv.* Ⓐ unnatürlich; **not ~:** natürlich; wie man sich denken kann; **he expected, not ~, that his father would help him** natürlich rechnete er damit, dass sein Vater ihm helfen werde; Ⓑ (*affectedly*) unnatürlich; gekünstelt

**unnavigable** /ʌnˈnævɪgəbl/ *adj.* nicht schiffbar ‹Fluss›

**unnecessarily** /ʌnˈnesɪsərɪlɪ/ *adv.* Ⓐ unnötig[erweise] ‹sich ärgern, sich aufregen, sich sorgen›; **spend money/time ~** unnötig Geld/Zeit aufwenden; Ⓑ (*excessively*) unnötig ‹streng, kompliziert›; **be ~ high/long** höher/länger als nötig sein

**unnecessary** /ʌnˈnesəsərɪ/ *adj.* unnötig; **it is ~ for sb. to do sth.** es ist unnötig *od.* es muss nicht sein, dass jmd. etw. tut; **no, thank you, that's quite ~:** danke, das ist gar nicht nötig

**unneighbourly** /ʌnˈneɪbəlɪ/ *adj.* nicht gutnachbarlich; **they are ~:** sie sind schlechte Nachbarn

**unnerve** /ʌnˈnɜːv/ *v.t.* entnerven

**unnerving** /ʌnˈnɜːvɪŋ/ *adj.* entnervend; zermürbend ‹Warten›; nervenaufreibend ‹Erlebnis›; **be [too] ~:** [zu viel] Nerven kosten; **an ~ reaction/incident** eine Reaktion, die/ein Vorfall, der an die Nerven geht/ging

**unnoticed** /ʌn'nəʊtɪst/ *adj.* unbemerkt; **~ by her, he came in** er trat ein, ohne dass sie es bemerkte; **pass** *or* **go ~:** unbemerkt bleiben

**unnumbered** /ʌn'nʌmbəd/ *adj.* (*without numbers*) nicht nummeriert; unpaginiert ‹Buchseite›; ‹Haus› ohne Hausnummer

**UNO** /'ju:nəʊ/ *abbr.* **United Nations Organization** UNO, *die*

**unobjectionable** /ʌnəb'dʒekʃənəbl/ *adj.* gefällig; **sth./sb. is ~:** gegen etw./jmdn. gibt es nichts einzuwenden

**unobservant** /ʌnəb'zɜ:vənt/ *adj.* unaufmerksam; **be an ~ person** ein schlechter Beobachter sein

**unobserved** /ʌnəb'zɜ:vd/ *adj.* unbeobachtet

**unobstructed** /ʌnəb'strʌktɪd/ *adj.* frei ‹Weg, Rohr, Ausgang›; ungehindert ‹Vormarsch, Durchfahrt›

**unobtainable** /ʌnəb'teɪnəbl/ *adj.* nicht erhältlich; **number ~** (*Teleph.*) kein Anschluss unter dieser Nummer; **the 'number ~' tone** der Ton für eine Nummer ohne Anschluss

**unobtrusive** /ʌnəb'tru:sɪv/ *adj.* unaufdringlich ‹Geste, Bemerkung, Muster, Farbe›; unauffällig ‹Riss, Bewegung›; **make oneself ~:** sich unauffällig verhalten

**unobtrusively** /ʌnəb'tru:sɪvlɪ/ *adv.* unaufdringlich; unauffällig ‹hinausschleichen, verschwinden›

**unoccupied** /ʌn'ɒkjʊpaɪd/ *adj.* **A** (*empty*) unbesetzt; nicht belegt ‹Bett›; unbewohnt ‹Haus, Wohnung, Raum›; **B** (*not busy*) unbeschäftigt; **~ moments** freie Augenblicke

**unoffending** /ʌnə'fendɪŋ/ *adj.* harmlos; (*innocent*) unschuldig

**unofficial** /ʌnə'fɪʃl/ *adj.* inoffiziell; **an ~ strike** ein wilder Streik; **take ~ action** einen wilden Streik durchführen

**unofficially** /ʌnə'fɪʃəlɪ/ *adv.* inoffiziell

**unopened** /ʌn'əʊpnd/ *adj.* ungeöffnet; noch nicht aufgegangen ‹Knospe, Blüte›

**unopposed** /ʌnə'pəʊzd/ *adj.* unangefochten ‹Kandidat, Wahlsieger›; ungehindert ‹Vormarsch›; **the bill was given an ~ second reading** (*Parl.*) der Gesetzentwurf wurde bei der zweiten Lesung ohne Abstimmung angenommen

**unorganized** /ʌn'ɔ:gənaɪzd/ *adj.* **A** (*untidy*) unsystematisch ‹Arbeitsweise›; konfus ‹Essay, Person›; ungeordnet ‹Struktur, Leben›; **B** (*not belonging to a union*) nicht [gewerkschaftlich] organisiert

**unoriginal** /ʌnə'rɪdʒɪnl/ *adj.* unoriginell

**unoriginality** /ʌnərɪdʒɪ'nælɪtɪ/ *n., no pl.* fehlende Originalität

**unorthodox** /ʌn'ɔ:θədɒks/ *adj.* unorthodox (*geh.*)

**unostentatious** /ʌnɒsten'teɪʃəs/ *adj.* schlicht; unprätentiös (*geh.*)

**unpack** /ʌn'pæk/ *v.t. & i.* auspacken; **do one's ~ing** auspacken

**unpaid** /ʌn'peɪd/ *adj.* **A** (*not yet paid*) unbezahlt; nicht bezahlt; **~ for** nicht bezahlt; **the workmen/troops have been ~ for months** die Arbeiter/Truppen haben monatelang keinen Lohn/Sold erhalten; **B** (*not providing or receiving a salary*) unbezahlt ‹Arbeit, Stelle, Freiwilliger usw.›; (*honorary*) ehrenamtlich; **~ leave** unbezahlter Urlaub

**unpalatable** /ʌn'pælətəbl/ *adj.* ungenießbar; (*fig.*) unverdaulich ‹Tatsache, Wahrheit›

**unparalleled** /ʌn'pærəleld/ *adj.* beispiellos; unvergleichlich ‹Schönheit›

**unpardonable** /ʌn'pɑ:dənəbl/ unverzeihlich; **~ sin** (*Relig.; also fig.*) Todsünde, *die*

**unparliamentary** /ʌnpɑ:lə'mentərɪ/ *adj.* gegen die parlamentarischen Regeln verstoßend; **~ expression** der Würde des Parlaments nicht angemessene Redeweise

**unpatriotic** /ʌnpætrɪ'ɒtɪk, ʌnpeɪtrɪ'ɒtɪk/ *adj.* unpatriotisch

**unpaved** /ʌn'peɪvd/ *adj.* ungepflastert

**unpeeled** /ʌn'pi:ld/ *adj.* ungeschält

**unpeg** /ʌn'peg/ *v.t.*, **-gg-** abnehmen ‹Wäsche›; **~ a tent** bei einem Zelt die Pflöcke herausziehen

**unperceptive** /ʌnpə'septɪv/ *adj.* unaufmerksam; nicht sehr tiefgründig ‹Bemerkung›

**unperfumed** /ʌn'pɜ:fju:md/ *adj.* unparfümiert

**unperson** /'ʌnpɜ:sn/ *n.* Unperson, *die*

**unperturbed** /ʌnpə'tɜ:bd/ *adj.* **he was ~ by the prospect of ...** die Aussicht auf ... beunruhigte ihn nicht; **remain ~:** sich nicht aus der Ruhe bringen lassen; **they were ~ by my presence** sie ließen sich durch meine Gegenwart nicht stören; **the minister seemed ~ by the developments** der Minister schien von den Entwicklungen unbeeindruckt

**unpick** /ʌn'pɪk/ *v.t.* auftrennen

**unpin** /ʌn'pɪn/ *v.t.*, **-nn-** abnehmen ‹Zettel, Brosche›; **~ sb.'s/one's hair** jmdm./sich die Nadeln aus dem Haar nehmen; **~ the seam** die Nadeln aus dem Saum nehmen

**unplaced** /ʌn'pleɪst/ *adj.* (*Sport*) unplatziert

**unplanned** /ʌn'plænd/ *adj.* nicht geplant; ungeplant

**unplayable** /ʌn'pleɪəbl/ *adj.* **A** (*Sport*) unbespielbar ‹Spielfeld›; unspielbar ‹Ball›; unerreichbar ‹Aufschlag, Return›; **B** (*Music*) unspielbar; **C** (*too damaged to be played*) nicht abspielbar ‹Schallplatte, Tonband›

**unpleasant** /ʌn'plezənt/ *adj.* unangenehm; unfreundlich ‹Bemerkung›; böse ‹Lächeln›; **she can be really ~:** sie kann sehr unangenehm werden; **be ~ with sb.** zu jmdm. unfreundlich sein

**unpleasantly** /ʌn'plezəntlɪ/ *adv.* unangenehm; böse ‹lächeln›; unfreundlich ‹antworten›

**unpleasantness** /ʌn'plezəntnɪs/ *n.* **A** *no pl.* (*unpleasant nature*) Unerfreulichkeit, *die;* (*of person*) Unfreundlichkeit, *die;* **the ~ of a taste/smell** das Unangenehme an einem Geschmack/Geruch; **the ~ of the weather/one's neighbour** das unangenehme Wetter/die Unfreundlichkeit seines Nachbarn; **B** (*bad feeling, quarrel*) Verstimmung, *die;* **there has been a lot of ~ between them** zwischen ihnen ist viel Unerfreuliches geschehen *od.* gewesen

**unpleasing** /ʌn'pli:zɪŋ/ *adj.* unschön; **not ~ to the eye** ganz angenehm anzusehen

**unplug** /ʌn'plʌg/ *v.t.*, **-gg-** **A** (*Electr.: disconnect*) **~ a radio/a television set** den Stecker eines Radio-/Fernsehgeräts herausziehen; **always ~ electrical appliances at night** bei Elektrogeräten nachts stets den Stecker aus der Steckdose ziehen; **B** (*take plug out of*) **~ sth.** den Stöpsel aus etw. ziehen

**unplumbed** /ʌn'plʌmd/ *adj.* nicht ausgelotet ‹Gewässer›; (*fig.*) [noch] unergründet ‹Geheimnis, Möglichkeiten›; **~ depths [of the sea/** (*fig.*) **of the human mind]** nicht ausgelotete Tiefen [des Meeres/(*fig. geh.*) des menschlichen Geistes]

**unpolished** /ʌn'pɒlɪʃt/ *adj.* unpoliert ‹Holz, Marmor, Schuhe, Reis›; (*fig.*) ungeschliffen ‹Person, Manieren, Sprache›

**unpolluted** /ʌnpə'lu:tɪd/ sauber ‹Wasser, Fluss, Umwelt›

**unpopular** /ʌn'pɒpjʊlə(r)/ *adj.* unbeliebt ‹Lehrer, Regierung usw.›; unpopulär ‹Maßnahme, Politik›; **be ~ with sb.** (*not liked*) ‹Person:› bei jmdm. unbeliebt sein; ‹Maßnahme, Steuern:› bei jmdm. unpopulär sein; (*out of favour*) **I'm rather ~ with my wife at the moment** meine Frau ist auf mich zurzeit ziemlich schlecht zu sprechen; **if I don't finish it today, I shall be very ~ with my boss** wenn ich heute damit nicht fertig werde, mache ich mich bei meinem Chef ziemlich unbeliebt

**unpopularity** /ʌnpɒpjʊ'lærɪtɪ/ *n., no pl.* ⇒ **unpopular**: Unbeliebtheit, *die* **(with** bei); Unpopularität, *die* **(with** bei)

**unposted** /ʌn'pəʊstɪd/ *adj.* nicht aufgegeben *od.* abgeschickt

**unpractical** /ʌn'præktɪkl/ *adj.* unpraktisch

**unpractised** (*Amer.:* **unpracticed**) /ʌn'præktɪst/ *adj.* **A** (*not skilled*) ungeübt; **be ~ in sth./in doing sth.** in etw. (*Dat.*) ungeübt sein/darin ungeübt sein, etw. zu tun; **B** (*not put into practice*) nicht ausgeübt ‹Handwerk›; ungenutzt ‹Fähigkeit›

**unprecedented** /ʌn'presɪdentɪd/ *adj.* beispiellos; [noch] nie da gewesen; **it is ~ for the Queen to comment publicly** es ist [vorher] noch nie da gewesen, dass die Königin öffentlich Stellung genommen hat

**unprecedentedly** /ʌn'presɪdentɪdlɪ/ *adv.* unerhört; außergewöhnlich

**unpredictable** /ʌnprɪ'dɪktəbl/ *adj.* unberechenbar ‹Person, Charakter, Wetter›; **the outcome of the election is quite ~:** das Wahlergebnis lässt sich kaum voraussagen

**unprejudiced** /ʌn'predʒʊdɪst/ *adj.* unvoreingenommen

**unpremeditated** /ʌnprɪ'medɪteɪtɪd/ *adj.* nicht vorsätzlich ‹Verbrechen›; nicht geplant ‹Angriff, Tat›

**unprepared** /ʌnprɪ'peəd/ *adj.* **A** (*not yet prepared*) nicht vorbereitet ‹Zimmer, Mahlzeit›; **be [not] ~ for sth.** auf etw. (*Akk.*) [nicht] unvorbereitet sein; **B** (*improvised*) Stegreif‹rede, -erklärung›

**unpreparedness** /ʌnprɪ'peərɪdnɪs/ *n., no pl.* ⇒ **unreadiness**

**unprepossessing** /ʌnpri:pə'zesɪŋ/ *adj.* wenig attraktiv; unansehnlich; wenig einnehmend ‹Aussehen, Person›

**unpresentable** /ʌnprɪ'zentəbl/ *adj.* **sb. is ~:** mit jmdm. kann man sich nicht sehen lassen; **your clothes are ~:** in deinen Sachen kannst du dich nicht sehen lassen

**unpretentious** /ʌnprɪ'tenʃəs/ *adj.* unprätentiös (*geh.*); einfach ‹Wein, Mahlzeit, Stil, Haus›; bescheiden ‹Benehmen, Person›

**unpriced** /ʌn'praɪst/ *adj.* ohne Preisangabe *nachgestellt*

**unprincipled** /ʌn'prɪnsɪpld/ *adj.* skrupellos; **be ~:** keine Prinzipien haben

**unprintable** /ʌn'prɪntəbl/ *adj.* (*lit. or fig.*) nicht druckreif

**unproductive** /ʌnprə'dʌktɪv/ *adj.* unfruchtbar ‹Boden, Gegend›; fruchtlos ‹Diskussion, Anstrengung, Nachforschung›; unproduktiv ‹Zeit, Arbeit, Kapital›

**unprofessional** /ʌnprə'feʃənl/ *adj.* **A** (*contrary to standards*) standeswidrig; **B** (*amateurish*) unfachmännisch; stümperhaft

**unprofitable** /ʌn'prɒfɪtəbl/ *adj.* unrentabel ‹Zeche, Investition, Geschäft›; wenig einträglich ‹Arbeit›; (*fig.*) fruchtlos

**unpromising** /ʌn'prɒmɪsɪŋ/ *adj.* nicht sehr vielversprechend

**unprompted** /ʌn'prɒmptɪd/ *adj.* spontan

**unpronounceable** /ʌnprə'naʊnsəbl/ *adj.* unaussprechbar

**unpropitious** /ʌnprə'pɪʃəs/ *adj.* ungünstig

**unprotected** /ʌnprə'tektɪd/ *adj.* ungeschützt (**against** vor + *Dat.*, gegen); nicht geschützt ‹Art, Tier›; **an ~ machine** eine Maschine ohne Schutzvorrichtung[en]; **hands ~ by gloves** Hände, die nicht durch Handschuhe geschützt sind; **employees/buildings ~ by legislation** Angestellte ohne gesetzlichen Schutz/Gebäude, die nicht unter Denkmalschutz stehen; **~ sex** ungeschützter Geschlechtsverkehr

**unproved** /ʌn'pru:vd/, **unproven** /ʌn'pru:vn/ *adj.* **A** (*not proved*) unbewiesen; **B** (*untested*) ungeprüft; **his courage/ability is still unproven** sein Mut/seine Fähigkeit ist noch nicht auf die Probe gestellt worden; **he is unproven as an administrator** er hat seine Fähigkeiten als Verwalter noch nicht unter Beweis gestellt

**unprovided** /ʌnprə'vaɪdɪd/ *pred. adj.* **A ~ for** unversorgt ‹Witwe, Kind usw.›; nicht vorgesehen ‹Ereignis›; **B ~ with sth.** mit etw. nicht versehen

**unprovoked** /ʌnprə'vəʊkt/ *adj.* grundlos; **do sth. ~:** etw. ohne [äußere] Veranlassung tun

**unpublished** /ʌn'pʌblɪʃt/ *adj.* unveröffentlicht

**unpunctual** /ʌn'pʌŋktjʊəl/ *adj.* unpünktlich

**unpunished** /ʌn'pʌnɪʃt/ *adj.* ungesühnt ‹Verbrechen›; unbestraft ‹Verbrecher›; **go ~:** ohne Strafe bleiben; ‹Verbrecher:› straffrei ausgehen

**unpurified** /ʌn'pjʊərɪfaɪd/ *adj.* ungereinigt; nicht gereinigt; (*fig.*) ungeläutert

**unputdownable** /ʌnpʊt'daʊnəbl/ *adj.* (*coll.*) **an ~ book** ein Buch, das man nicht aus der Hand legt; **this novel is ~:** diesen Roman legt man nicht aus der Hand

U

**unqualified** /ʌnˈkwɒlɪfaɪd/ *adj.* **A** (*lacking qualifications*) unqualifiziert; ‹Arzt› ohne Abschluss; **be ~ for sth.** für etw. nicht qualifiziert sein; **be ~ to do sth.** nicht dafür qualifiziert sein, etw. zu tun; **he is ~ to be president** er ist für das Amt des Präsidenten nicht qualifiziert; **B** (*absolute*) uneingeschränkt ‹Zustimmung›; rein ‹Freude, Vergnügen›; voll ‹Erfolg›; **C** (*Ling.: not qualified*) nicht [näher] bestimmt

**unquenchable** /ʌnˈkwentʃəbl/ *adj.* unlöschbar ‹Durst›; unstillbar ‹Verlangen›

**unquestionable** /ʌnˈkwestʃənəbl/ *adj.* unbezweifelbar ‹Tatsache, Beweis›; unbestreitbar ‹Recht, Fähigkeiten, Ehrlichkeit›; unanfechtbar ‹Autorität›; **an ~ decision/ruling/judgement** eine Entscheidung/Verfügung, die/ein Urteil, das nicht angefochten werden kann

**unquestionably** /ʌnˈkwestʃənəblɪ/ *adv.* zweifellos; ohne Frage

**unquestioned** /ʌnˈkwestʃənd/ *adj.* unangefochten ‹Fähigkeit, Macht, Autorität, Recht›; unbestritten ‹Talent›; **his ability/loyalty is ~:** seine Fähigkeit/Loyalität steht außer Frage

**unquestioning** /ʌnˈkwestʃənɪŋ/ *adj.*, **unquestioningly** /ʌnˈkwestʃənɪŋlɪ/ *adv.* bedingungslos; blind

**unquiet** /ʌnˈkwaɪət/ *adj.* unruhig

**unquotable** /ʌnˈkwəʊtəbl/ *adj.* nicht zitierfähig

**unquote** /ʌnˈkwəʊt/ *v.i.* **..., quote, ..., ~:** ..., Zitat, ..., Ende des Zitats

**unquoted** /ʌnˈkwəʊtɪd/ *adj.* (*Commerc.*) unnotiert

**unravel** /ʌnˈrævl/ **1** *v.t.* (*Brit.*) **-ll-** entwirren; (*undo*) aufziehen; (*fig.*) **~ a mystery/the truth/a plot** ein Geheimnis enträtseln/die Wahrheit aufdecken/ein Komplott aufdecken. **2** *v.i.* (*Brit.*) **-ll-** aufgehen; sich aufziehen

**unread** /ʌnˈred/ *adj.* ungelesen

**unreadable** /ʌnˈriːdəbl/ *adj.* **A** (*illegible*) unleserlich; (*fig.: unfathomable*) unergründlich; **B** (*too difficult, boring, etc.*) unlesbar

**unreadiness** /ʌnˈredɪnɪs/ *n.*, *no pl.* **[state of] ~:** mangelnde Vorbereitung; **~ to do sth.** mangelnde Bereitschaft, etwas zu tun

**unready** /ʌnˈredɪ/ *adj.* nicht bereit; **the country is ~ for war** das Land ist für einen Krieg nicht gerüstet; **he is ~ for that position** er ist noch nicht so weit, dass er diese Position übernehmen könnte

**unreal** /ʌnˈrɪəl/ *adj.* unwirklich

**unrealistic** /ʌnrɪəˈlɪstɪk/ *adj.* unrealistisch

**unreality** /ʌnrɪˈælɪtɪ/ *n.*, *no pl.* Unwirklichkeit, *die*

**unrealizable** /ʌnˈrɪəlaɪzəbl/ *adj.* unrealisierbar; nicht verwirklichbar

**unrealized** /ʌnˈrɪəlaɪzd/ *adj.* **A** (*not achieved*) unerfüllt ‹Hoffnung, Ehrgeiz›; nicht erreicht ‹Ziel›; nicht verwirklicht ‹Plan›; ungenutzt ‹Potenzial, Fähigkeiten›; **~ assets/profits** (*Commerc.*) nicht realisierte Vermögenswerte/Gewinne; **B** (*not recognized or known*) ungeahnt ‹Mut, Kraft›; unentdeckt ‹Talent›

**unreasonable** /ʌnˈriːzənəbl/ *adj.* unvernünftig; übertrieben ‹Ansprüche, Forderung›; übertrieben [hoch] ‹Preis, Kosten›; **I am not an ~ man, but ...:** ich erwarte nun wirklich nicht viel, aber ...; **spend an ~ length of time on sth.** sich übertrieben lange mit etw. beschäftigen; **arrive at an ~ hour** zu einer unmöglichen Uhrzeit ankommen; **I'm only asking you to spare me half an hour of your time — is that [so] ~?** ich bitte dich nur um eine halbe Stunde; das ist doch nicht zu viel verlangt, oder?

**unreasonableness** /ʌnˈriːzənəblnɪs/ *n.*, *no pl.* Unvernünftigkeit, *die*; **the ~ of these prices/costs** die übertriebene Höhe dieser Preise/Kosten

**unreasonably** /ʌnˈriːzənəblɪ/ *adv.* unvernünftig ‹sich benehmen›; (*excessively*) übertrieben; **this — not ~ — he refused to do** das lehnte er — nicht ohne Berechtigung — ab

**unreasoning** /ʌnˈriːzənɪŋ/ *adj.* irrational; blind ‹Hass, Wut, Eifersucht, Fanatiker›

**unreceptive** /ʌnrɪˈseptɪv/ *adj.* unempfänglich (**to, for** für)

**unrecognizable** /ʌnˈrekəgnaɪzəbl/ *adj.* **be [absolutely** *or* **quite] ~:** [überhaupt] nicht wiederzuerkennen sein; **the disguise/beard made him ~:** mit der Verkleidung/dem Bart war er nicht wieder zu erkennen

**unrecognized** /ʌnˈrekəgnaɪzd/ *adj.* **A** (*not identified*) unerkannt; **be ~ by sb.** von jmdm. nicht erkannt werden; **B** (*not officially recognized*) nicht anerkannt; **C** (*not appreciated*) nicht [gebührend] gewürdigt ‹Talent, Genie›; nicht [genügend] beachtet ‹Gefahr, Tatsache›

**unrecorded** /ʌnrɪˈkɔːdɪd/ *adj.* **A** (*not documented*) nicht [dokumentarisch] belegt; **B** (*not recorded*) nicht aufgezeichnet; unbespielt, leer ‹Tonband, Kassette›

**unreel** /ʌnˈriːl/ **1** *v.t.* abwickeln; abspulen ‹Film, Tonband›. **2** *v.i.* sich abwickeln; sich abspulen

**unrefined** /ʌnrɪˈfaɪnd/ *adj.* **A** (*not refined*) nicht raffiniert; ungebleicht (*Mehl*); **B** (*fig.*) unkultiviert, ungeschliffen ‹Geschmack, Manieren, Person, Sprache›

**unreflecting** /ʌnrɪˈflektɪŋ/ *adj.* gedankenlos

**unregenerate** /ʌnrɪˈdʒenərət/ *adj.* (*unrepentant, obstinate*) uneinsichtig; (*wicked*) sündig ‹Lebenswandel›

**unregistered** /ʌnˈredʒɪstəd/ *adj.* nicht eingetragen; nicht approbiert ‹Arzt›; nicht zugelassen ‹Rechtsanwalt, Buchmacher, Krankenschwester, Fahrzeug›; nicht eingeschrieben ‹Postsendung›; nicht [gesetzlich] geschützt ‹Warenzeichen›

**unregulated** /ʌnˈregjʊleɪtɪd/ *adj.* unkontrolliert

**unrehearsed** /ʌnrɪˈhɜːst/ *adj.* **A** (*performed without rehearsal*) [vorher] nicht geprobt; **perform a play ~:** ein Stück ohne vorherige Probe[n] spielen; **B** (*not planned*) nicht vorgesehen; **C** (*spontaneous*) spontan

**unrelated** /ʌnrɪˈleɪtɪd/ *adj.* unzusammenhängend; **be ~** (*not connected*) nicht miteinander zusammenhängen; (*not related by family*) nicht [miteinander] verwandt sein; **be ~ to sth.** mit etw. in keinem Zusammenhang stehen; mit etw. nichts zu tun haben

**unrelenting** /ʌnrɪˈlentɪŋ/ *adj.* unvermindert, nicht nachlassend ‹Hitze, Kälte, Regen›; unerbittlich ‹Kampf, Opposition, Verfolgung, Hass›; unnachgiebig ‹Entschlossenheit, Ehrgeiz›; unvermindert ‹Kraft, Stärke›; hartnäckig ‹Kämpfer›; **the heat/pressure/pace is ~:** die Hitze/der Druck/die Geschwindigkeit lässt nicht nach; **be ~ in one's determination to do sth.** unnachgiebig entschlossen sein, etw. zu tun; **be ~ in one's battle** *or* **fight against sth.** etw. unnachgiebig bekämpfen; **remain ~:** unnachgiebig *od.* unerbittlich bleiben

**unreliability** /ʌnrɪlaɪəˈbɪlɪtɪ/ *n.*, *no pl.* Unzuverlässigkeit, *die*

**unreliable** /ʌnrɪˈlaɪəbl/ *adj.* unzuverlässig

**unrelieved** /ʌnrɪˈliːvd/ *adj.* unvermindert ‹Schmerz, Armut, Anstrengung›; unaufhörlich ‹Regen, Lärm›; tödlich ‹Langeweile, Eintönigkeit›; **~ by sth.** nicht durch etw. gemildert; **a forbidding landscape, ~ by vegetation of any kind** eine Landschaft, deren Ödheit auch nicht das kleinste Pflänzchen belebt; **a gloomy film, ~ by even the slightest touch of humour** ein Film, dessen Düsterkeit durch kein Fünkchen von Humor aufgehellt wird

**unremarkable** /ʌnrɪˈmɑːkəbl/ *adj.* nicht weiter bemerkenswert; unauffällig ‹Person, Lebensweise›; **totally/pretty ~:** absolut nicht/kaum bemerkenswert

**unremitting** /ʌnrɪˈmɪtɪŋ/ *adj.* nicht nachlassend; unermüdlich ‹Anstrengung, Versuche, Sorge›; beharrlich ‹Kampf›; **he was ~ in his efforts to help them** er bemühte sich unermüdlich, ihnen zu helfen

**unremittingly** /ʌnrɪˈmɪtɪŋlɪ/ *adv.* unermüdlich ‹kämpfen, arbeiten, sich bemühen›; unnachgiebig ‹Widerstand leisten›

**unremunerative** /ʌnrɪˈmjuːnərətɪv/ *adj.* wenig einträglich *od.* (*geh.*) lukrativ

**unrepeatable** /ʌnrɪˈpiːtəbl/ *adj.* **A** (*unique*) einzigartig; einmalig ‹Angebot, Preis›; **B** (*not fit to be repeated*) **sth. is ~:** etw. ist nicht zitierfähig; **an ~ remark/story/joke** eine Bemerkung/Geschichte, die/ein Witz, der nicht salonfähig ist

**unrepentant** /ʌnrɪˈpentənt/ *adj.* **A** (*impenitent*) reuelos ‹Sünder›; **die ~:** sterben, ohne bereut zu haben; **be ~:** keine Reue zeigen; **be ~ about sth.** etw. nicht bereuen; **B** (*unreformed, obstinate*) halsstarrig; stur

**unreported** /ʌnrɪˈpɔːtɪd/ *adj.* nicht angezeigt ‹Verbrechen›; ‹Fall, Versuch› über den nicht berichtet wurde; **it went ~:** darüber wurde nicht berichtet

**unrepresentative** /ʌnreprɪˈzentətɪv/ *adj.* nicht repräsentativ (**of** für); (*Polit.*) nicht demokratisch gewählt ‹Regierung, Führer›; **be ~ of sth.** etw. nicht repräsentieren

**unrepresented** /ʌnreprɪˈzentɪd/ *adj.* nicht vertreten

**unrequited** /ʌnrɪˈkwaɪtɪd/ *adj.* unerwidert

**unreserved** /ʌnrɪˈzɜːvd/ *adj.* **A** (*not booked*) nicht reserviert; **B** ▸ **924** (*full, without any reservations*) uneingeschränkt ‹Zustimmung, Aufnahme, Entschuldigung usw.›; **he was ~ in his praise** er geizte nicht mit Lob; **C** (*free from reserve*) offen ‹Person, Wesensart›

**unreservedly** /ʌnrɪˈzɜːvɪdlɪ/ *adv.* **A** ▸ **924** (*fully, without any reservations*) uneingeschränkt; **he ~ withdrew the allegation** er nahm die Anschuldigung in vollem Umfang zurück; **B** (*frankly, openly*) offen

**unresolved** /ʌnrɪˈzɒlvd/ *adj.* **A** (*not solved*) ungelöst; nicht gelöst; **B** (*undecided*) **be ~:** sich [noch] nicht entschieden haben; **C** (*Mus.*) nicht aufgelöst

**unresponsive** /ʌnrɪˈspɒnsɪv/ *adj.* **be ~:** nicht reagieren (**to** auf + *Akk.*); **an ~ audience** ein teilnahmsloses Publikum

**unrest** /ʌnˈrest/ *n.* Unruhen *Pl.*; **there is widespread ~ among the population** ein großer Teil der Bevölkerung ist unzufrieden

**unrestrained** /ʌnrɪˈstreɪnd/ *adj.* uneingeschränkt ‹Freude, Begeisterung, Wachstum, Überfluss›; unbeherrscht ‹Gefühlsäußerung, Wut, Gewalt›; unkontrolliert ‹Entwicklung, Wachstum›; ungeniert ‹Sprache, Benehmen›

**unrestricted** /ʌnrɪˈstrɪktɪd/ *adj.* unbeschränkt; uneingeschränkt; frei ‹Sicht›; **have ~ use of sth.** etw. uneingeschränkt nutzen [dürfen]

**unrevealed** /ʌnrɪˈviːld/ *adj.* verborgen

**unrewarded** /ʌnrɪˈwɔːdɪd/ *adj.* **go ~:** keine Belohnung bekommen; ‹Tat, Mühe:› nicht belohnt werden

**unrewarding** /ʌnrɪˈwɔːdɪŋ/ *adj.* unbefriedigend; undankbar ‹Aufgabe›; **financially ~:** wenig einträglich *od.* (*geh.*) lukrativ

**unrighteous** /ʌnˈraɪtʃəs/ *adj.* **A** (*wicked*) schlecht; **B** (*unjust*) ungerecht

**unripe** /ʌnˈraɪp/ *adj.* unreif

**unrivalled** (*Amer.:* **unrivaled**) /ʌnˈraɪvld/ *adj.* unvergleichlich; beispiellos; unübertroffen ‹Ruf, Luxus, Erfahrung, Könnerschaft›; **our goods are ~ in** *or* **for quality** unsere Waren sind in ihrer Qualität konkurrenzlos *od.* unerreicht; **a landscape ~ for beauty** *or* **of ~ beauty** eine Landschaft von unvergleichlicher Schönheit

**unroadworthy** /ʌnˈrəʊdwɜːðɪ/ *adj.* nicht verkehrssicher

**unroll** /ʌnˈrəʊl/ **1** *v.t.* aufrollen. **2** *v.i.* sich aufrollen; (*fig.*) ‹Geschichte, Handlung:› sich entrollen; **he watched the landscape ~ before his eyes** er betrachtete die Landschaft, die sich vor seinen Augen auftat

**unromantic** /ʌnrəˈmæntɪk/ *adj.* unromantisch

**unruffled** /ʌnˈrʌfld/ *adj.* ruhig; glatt ‹Gewässer, Haar, Feder›; **listen with ~ calm/composure** mit unerschütterlicher Ruhe/ruhiger Gefasstheit zuhören; **he was/remained ~ by all the fuss/criticism** er ließ sich von der ganzen Aufregung/Kritik nicht aus der Ruhe bringen

**unruled** /ʌnˈruːld/ *adj.* unliniert ‹Papier›

**unruliness** /ʌnˈruːlɪnɪs/ *n.* Ungebärdigkeit, *die*

**unruly** /ʌnˈruːlɪ/ *adj.* ungebärdig ‹Person, Benehmen›; widerspenstig ‹Haar, Person, Benehmen›

U

**unsaddle** /ʌn'sædl/ *v.t.* Ⓐ absatteln ‹Pferd usw.›; Ⓑ abwerfen ‹Reiter›

**unsafe** /ʌn'seɪf/ *adj.* Ⓐ nicht sicher ‹Leiter, Konstruktion›; baufällig ‹Gebäude›; nicht verkehrssicher ‹Fahrzeug›; gefährlich ‹Maschine, Leitungen, Spielzeug›; **the food is ~ to eat** das Essen ist ungenießbar; **he looked ~ on top of the ladder** es sah gefährlich aus, wie er oben auf der Leiter stand; **feel ~:** sich unsicher fühlen; **it is ~ to do that** es ist gefährlich, das zu tun; Ⓑ (*untenable*) unhaltbar ‹Annahme, Urteil usw.›; **the conviction was ~:** die Verurteilung war juristisch nicht haltbar

**unsaid** /ʌn'sed/ *adj.* ungesagt; unausgesprochen; **leave sth. ~:** etw. ungesagt lassen; **some things are better left ~:** manche Dinge bleiben besser ungesagt

**unsaleable** /ʌn'seɪləbl/ *adj.* unverkäuflich

**unsalted** /ʌn'sɔ:ltɪd, ʌn'sɒltɪd/ *adj.* ungesalzen

**unsanitary** /ʌn'sænɪtərɪ/ *adj.* unhygienisch

**unsatisfactorily** /ʌnsætɪs'fæktərɪlɪ/ *adv.* unbefriedigend; **perform one's tasks ~:** unbefriedigende Leistungen erbringen; **end ~:** zu einem unbefriedigenden Abschluss kommen

**unsatisfactory** /ʌnsætɪs'fæktərɪ/ *adj.* unbefriedigend; nicht befriedigend; schlecht ‹Service, Hotel›; mangelhaft ‹schulische Leistung›

**unsatisfied** /ʌn'sætɪsfaɪd/ *adj.* unzufrieden; unerfüllt ‹Wunsch, Bedürfnis›; nicht befriedigt ‹Wunsch, Bedürfnis, Neugier, Nachfrage›; nicht gestillt ‹Hunger, Neugier, Appetit›; unbeglichen ‹Schuld›; **sexually ~:** sexuell nicht befriedigt; **leave sb. ~:** jmdn. nicht befriedigen

**unsatisfying** /ʌn'sætɪsfaɪɪŋ/ *adj.* unbefriedigend; nicht sättigend ‹Mahlzeit›

**unsaturated** /ʌn'sætʃəreɪtɪd, ʌn'sætjʊreɪtɪd/ *adj.* ungesättigt

**unsavoury** (*Amer.:* **unsavory**) /ʌn'seɪvərɪ/ *adj.* unangenehm ‹Geruch, Geschmack, Mahlzeit›; zwielichtig ‹Charakter, Person›; zweifelhaft ‹Ruf, Geschäfte, Angelegenheit›; unerfreulich ‹Einzelheiten›

**unscalable** /ʌn'skeɪləbl/ *adj.* unbezwinglich ‹Berg, Höhe›

**unscaled** /ʌn'skeɪld/ *adj.* [noch] nicht bezwungen ‹Berg, Höhe›

**unscathed** /ʌn'skeɪðd/ *adj.* unversehrt ‹Person›; unbeschädigt ‹Sache›; (*fig.*) **he emerged from the scandal ~/with his reputation ~:** er überlebte den Skandal ohne einen Flecken auf seiner Weste (*ugs.*)/ohne dass sein Ruf Schaden genommen hätte

**unscented** /ʌn'sentɪd/ *adj.* nicht parfümiert ‹Seife, Shampoo›

**unscheduled** /ʌn'ʃedju:ld/ *adj.* außerplanmäßig

**unscholarly** /ʌn'skɒləlɪ/ *adj.* unwissenschaftlich ‹Buch, Methode›; **be ~** ‹Person:› kein Gelehrter sein

**unschooled** /ʌn'sku:ld/ *adj.* (*without education*) ungebildet; (*without training*) ungeschult

**unscientific** /ʌnsaɪən'tɪfɪk/ *adj.* unwissenschaftlich ‹Methode, Buch, Ansatz usw.›; **be ~** ‹Person:› kein Wissenschaftler sein

**unscientifically** /ʌnsaɪən'tɪfɪkəlɪ/ *adv.* unwissenschaftlich

**unscramble** /ʌn'skræmbl/ *v.t.* (*lit. or fig.*) entwirren; (*Teleph.: decode*) entschlüsseln

**unscratched** /ʌn'skrætʃt/ *adj.* (*unhurt*) unverletzt

**unscrew** /ʌn'skru:/ ❶ *v.t.* ab- *od.* losschrauben ‹Regal, Deckel usw.›; herausdrehen ‹Schraube›. ❷ *v.i.* ‹Brett, Verschluss:› sich abschrauben lassen; ‹Schraube:› sich lösen *od.* abschrauben lassen; **come ~ed** sich lösen

**unscripted** /ʌn'skrɪptɪd/ *adj.* frei vorgetragen ‹Rede›; nicht von einem Skript abgelesen ‹Interview, Rundfunksendung›; **an ~ play** ein Stegreifstück

**unscrupulous** /ʌn'skru:pjʊləs/ *adj.* skrupellos; **be ~ about money** in Geldangelegenheiten skrupellos sein

**unscrupulously** /ʌn'skru:pjʊləslɪ/ *adv.* skrupellos

**unscrupulousness** /ʌn'skru:pjʊləsnɪs/ *n.*, *no pl.* Skrupellosigkeit, *die*

**unseal** /ʌn'si:l/ *v.t.* (*break seal of*) entsiegeln; (*open*) öffnen ‹Brief, Paket, Behälter›

**unsealed** /ʌn'si:ld/ *adj.* offen; unverschlossen; (*without a seal*) nicht versiegelt

**unseasonable** /ʌn'si:zənəbl/ *adj.* nicht der Jahreszeit entsprechend ‹Wetter, Hitze, Schnee›; **the weather is ~:** das Wetter entspricht nicht der Jahreszeit

**unseasonably** /ʌn'si:zənəblɪ/ *adv.* [für die Jahreszeit] ungewöhnlich ‹kalt, warm›

**unseasoned** /ʌn'si:znd/ *adj.* Ⓐ (*not flavoured*) ungewürzt; Ⓑ (*not matured*) nicht abgelagert ‹Holz›; unerfahren ‹Soldat›

**unseat** /ʌn'si:t/ *adj.* Ⓐ (*remove from office*) abwählen; Ⓑ (*throw*) aus dem Sattel werfen; ‹Pferd:› abwerfen

**unseaworthy** /ʌn'si:wɜ:ðɪ/ *adj.* nicht seetüchtig

**unsecured** /ʌnsɪ'kjʊəd/ *adj.* Ⓐ (*not fixed*) nicht gesichert; Ⓑ (*Finance: without security*) ohne Sicherheit[en] *nachgestellt*

**unseeded** /ʌn'si:dɪd/ *adj.* (*Tennis*) nicht gesetzt

**unseeing** /ʌn'si:ɪŋ/ *adj.* blind; leer ‹Blick, Auge›

**unseemly** /ʌn'si:mlɪ/ *adj.* unschicklich; ungehörig ‹Benehmen›; ungebührlich ‹Eile, Benehmen›

**unseen** /ʌn'si:n/ ❶ *adj.* Ⓐ (*not seen*) ungesehen; unbekannt ‹Text›; **~ translation** (*Brit. Sch., Univ.*) Übersetzung eines unbekannten Textes (*aus einer Fremdsprache*); Ⓑ (*invisible*) unsichtbar. ❷ *n.* (*Brit. Sch., Univ.*) **Latin/French ~:** Übersetzung eines unbekannten Textes aus dem Lateinischen/Französischen

**unselfconscious** /ʌnself'kɒnʃəs/ *adj.*, **unselfconsciously** /ʌnself'kɒnʃəslɪ/ *adv.* unbefangen

**unselfconsciousness** /ʌnself'kɒnʃəsnɪs/ *n.* Unbefangenheit, *die*

**unselfish** /ʌn'selfɪʃ/ *adj.*, **unselfishly** /ʌn'selfɪʃlɪ/ *adv.* selbstlos

**unselfishness** /ʌn'selfɪʃnɪs/ *n.*, *no pl.* Selbstlosigkeit, *die*

**unsentimental** /ʌnsentɪ'mentl/ *adj.* unsentimental ‹Person›; **be totally ~ about sth.** einer Sache (*Dat.*) gegenüber keinerlei sentimentale Gefühle haben

**unserviceable** /ʌn'sɜ:vɪsəbl/ *adj.* unbrauchbar

**unsettle** /ʌn'setl/ *v.t.* durcheinander bringen; verwirren ‹menschlichen Geist›; stören ‹Friede›; verstören ‹Kind, Tier›; erschüttern ‹Stabilität, emotionales Gleichgewicht›; aus dem Gleichgewicht bringen ‹Wirtschaft, Markt›

**unsettled** /ʌn'setld/ *adj.* Ⓐ (*changeable*) wechselhaft; (*fig.*) unstet (*geh.*), ruhelos ‹Leben›; unsicher ‹Zukunft›; Ⓑ (*upset*) verstimmt ‹Magen›; gestört ‹Verdauung›; unruhig ‹Zeit, Land›; instabil (*geh.*) ‹Wirtschaft, Markt›; **be/feel ~:** aus dem [gewohnten] Gleis sein; Ⓒ (*open to further discussion*) ungeklärt ‹Angelegenheit, Frage›; Ⓓ (*unpaid*) unbezahlt

**unsettling** /ʌn'setlɪŋ/ *adj.* störend ‹Vorfall, Einfluss›; beunruhigend ‹Nachricht›; unruhig ‹Zeit›; (*Finance*) destabilisierend ‹Einfluss›; **have an ~ effect on sb.** jmdn. aus dem Gleichgewicht bringen; **this constant travelling is ~:** dieses ständige Reisen bringt einen aus dem Gleis

**unshaded** /ʌn'ʃeɪdɪd/ *adj.* schattenlos; nackt ‹Glühbirne, Licht›; **the ~ areas of the design** die nicht schattierten Teile der Zeichnung

**unshak[e]able** /ʌn'ʃeɪkəbl/ *adj.* unerschütterlich

**unshaken** /ʌn'ʃeɪkn/ *adj.* **be ~:** nicht erschüttert sein

**unshaven** /ʌn'ʃeɪvn/ *adj.* unrasiert; **go ~:** sich nicht rasieren

**unsheathe** /ʌn'ʃi:ð/ *v.t.* aus der Scheide ziehen

**unshed** /ʌn'ʃed/ *adj.* ungeweint ‹Tränen›

**unshockable** /ʌn'ʃɒkəbl/ *adj.* **be ~:** durch nichts zu erschüttern sein

**unshrinkable** /ʌn'ʃrɪŋkəbl/ *adj.* (*Textiles*) nicht einlaufend; schrumpffrei; **be ~:** nicht einlaufen

**unsighted** /ʌn'saɪtɪd/ *adj.* **be ~:** in der *od.* seiner Sicht behindert sein

**unsightliness** /ʌn'saɪtlɪnɪs/ *n.*, *no pl.* Hässlichkeit, *die*

**unsightly** /ʌn'saɪtlɪ/ *adj.* unschön

**unsigned** /ʌn'saɪnd/ *adj.* nicht unterzeichnet ‹Brief, Dokument›; unsigniert ‹Gemälde›

**unsinkable** /ʌn'sɪŋkəbl/ *adj.* unsinkbar

**unsized** /ʌn'saɪzd/ *adj.* **~ paper/textiles** ungeleimtes Papier/ungeschlichtete Textilien

**unskilful** /ʌn'skɪlfl/ *adj.* ungeschickt; **be ~ in sth.** bei etw. ungeschickt vorgehen

**unskilled** /ʌn'skɪld/ *adj.* Ⓐ (*lacking skills*) ungeschickt; stümperhaft; Ⓑ (*without special training*) ungelernt ‹Arbeiter›; **~ in sth.** in etw. (*Dat.*) unerfahren; Ⓒ (*done without skill*) schlecht; stümperhaft; Ⓓ keine besonderen Fertigkeiten erfordernd ‹Arbeit›; **~ jobs** Stellen für ungelernte Arbeiter; Hilfsarbeiterstellen; **the work is ~:** die Arbeit erfordert keine besonderen Fertigkeiten

**unskillful** (*Amer.*) ⇒ **unskilful**

**unskimmed** /ʌn'skɪmd/ *adj.* nicht entrahmt; **~ milk** Vollmilch

**unslept-in** /ʌn'sleptɪn/ *adj.* **the bed was ~:** in dem Bett hatte niemand geschlafen

**unsmiling** /ʌn'smaɪlɪŋ/ *adj.* ernst

**unsmoked** /ʌn'sməʊkt/ *adj.* ungeräuchert

**unsnarl** /ʌn'snɑ:l/ *v.t.* entwirren

**unsociability** /ʌnsəʊʃə'bɪlɪtɪ/ *n.* Ungeselligkeit, *die*

**unsociable** /ʌn'səʊʃəbl/ *adj.* ungesellig

**unsocial** /ʌn'səʊʃl/ *adj.* ungesellig; **at this ~ hour** (*joc.*) zu dieser unchristlichen Tageszeit; **work ~ hours** nachts/sonn- und feiertags arbeiten

**unsold** /ʌn'səʊld/ *adj.* unverkauft

**unsolicited** /ʌnsə'lɪsɪtɪd/ *adj.* nicht angefordert *od.* erbeten; nicht bestellt ‹Waren›; unverlangt eingesandt ‹Manuskript›; **~ mail** Wurfsendungen

**unsolved** /ʌn'sɒlvd/ *adj.* ungelöst; unaufgeklärt ‹Verbrechen›

**unsophisticated** /ʌnsə'fɪstɪkeɪtɪd/ *adj.* schlicht, einfach ‹Person, Geschmack, Vergnügen, Spiel›; unkompliziert ‹Maschine, Küche, Methode›; einfach ‹Wein›; **~ food** Hausmannskost, *die*

**unsound** /ʌn'saʊnd/ *adj.* Ⓐ (*diseased*) nicht gesund; krank; **his health is ~:** seine Gesundheit ist angeschlagen *od.* angegriffen; Ⓑ (*defective*) baufällig ‹Gebäude›; morsch ‹Holz›; brüchig ‹Mauerwerk›; **structurally ~:** baufällig; Ⓒ (*ill-founded*) wenig stichhaltig; anfechtbar ‹Gesetz›; nicht vertretbar ‹Ansichten, Methoden›; Ⓓ (*unreliable*) unzuverlässig; **the firm is financially ~:** die Firma steht finanziell auf schwachen Füßen; Ⓔ **of ~ mind** unzurechnungsfähig; **he killed her while of ~ mind** als er sie tötete, war er nicht zurechnungsfähig

**unsoundness** /ʌn'saʊndnɪs/ *n.*, *no pl.* (*of health*) Schwäche, *die;* (*of structure*) Baufälligkeit, *die;* (*of theory, argument, decision*) Zweifelhaftigkeit, *die;* **~ of mind** Unzurechnungsfähigkeit, *die*

**unsparing** /ʌn'speərɪŋ/ *adj.* Ⓐ (*lavish*) großzügig; **work with ~ energy** mit voller Kraft arbeiten; **give sb. one's ~ help/support** jmdm. seine volle Hilfe/Unterstützung geben; **be ~ of** *or* **in sth.** mit etw. nicht geizen; **be ~ in one's efforts** keine Mühe scheuen; Ⓑ (*merciless*) schonungslos

**unsparingly** /ʌn'speərɪŋlɪ/ *adj.* Ⓐ großzügig; Ⓑ (*mercilessly*) schonungslos

**unspeakable** /ʌn'spi:kəbl/ *adj.* unbeschreiblich; (*indescribably bad*) unsäglich

**unspeakably** /ʌn'spi:kəblɪ/ *adv.* unbeschreiblich; unsäglich ‹hässlich›

**unspecified** /ʌn'spesɪfaɪd/ *adj.* nicht näher bezeichnet; nicht genannt ‹Anzahl, Summe›; **the job was for an ~ length of time** die Stelle war nicht befristet

**unspectacular** /ʌnspek'tækjʊlə(r)/ *adj.* wenig eindrucksvoll

**unspent** /ʌn'spent/ *adj.* nicht ausgegeben ‹Geld›; **I still had 30 pence ~ in my pocket** ich hatte noch 30 Pence in der Tasche

**unspoiled** /ʌn'spɔɪld/, **unspoilt** /ʌn'spɔɪlt/ *adj.* unverdorben; unberührt ‹Dorf, Landschaft›; genießbar ‹Lebensmittel›

U

**unspoken** /ʌn'spəʊkn/ *adj.* ungesagt; (*tacit*) unausgesprochen; stillschweigend ‹Übereinkunft›; **be left ~:** ungesagt bleiben

**unsporting** /ʌn'spɔːtɪŋ/, **unsportsmanlike** /ʌn'spɔːtsmənlaɪk/ *adjs.* unsportlich

**unstable** /ʌn'steɪbl/ *adj.* **A** nicht stabil; instabil (*geh.*); labil ‹Wirtschaft, Beziehungen, Verhältnisse›; **the country is ~:** die Lage im Land ist nicht stabil *od.* ist unsicher; **[mentally/emotionally] ~:** [psychisch] labil; **B** (*Phys.*) instabil; ⇒ *also* **equilibrium**

**unstamped** /ʌn'stæmpt/ *adj.* ungestempelt; (*unfranked*) unfrankiert

**unstated** /ʌn'steɪtɪd/ *adj.* nicht genannt

**unstatesmanlike** /ʌn'steɪtsmənlaɪk/ *adj.* wenig staatsmännisch

**unsteadily** /ʌn'stedɪlɪ/ *adv.* unsicher ‹gehen›; unregelmäßig ‹schlagen, brennen›

**unsteadiness** /ʌn'stedɪnɪs/ *n., no pl.* ⇒ **unsteady**: Unsicherheit, *die;* Instabilität, *die;* Wechselhaftigkeit, *die;* Ungleichmäßigkeit, *die;* Wackeligkeit, *die*

**unsteady** /ʌn'stedɪ/ *adj.* unsicher; instabil ‹Wirtschaft, Markt›; wechselhaft ‹Entwicklung›; ungleichmäßig ‹Flamme, Rhythmus›; wackelig ‹Leiter, Stuhl, Tisch, Konstruktion›; **be ~ on one's feet** unsicher auf den Beinen sein

**unstick** /ʌn'stɪk/ *v.t.*, **unstuck** /ʌn'stʌk/ [ab]lösen; ⇒ *also* **unstuck**

**unstinting** /ʌn'stɪntɪŋ/ *adj.* großzügig; **be ~ in sth.** mit etw. nicht geizen; **be ~ in one's efforts** keine Mühe scheuen

**unstitch** /ʌn'stɪtʃ/ *v.t.* auftrennen ‹Naht, Saum›; **the seam has come ~ed** der Saum ist aufgegangen

**unstoppable** /ʌn'stɒpəbl/ *adj.* unhaltbar ‹Schuss aufs Fußballtor›; unerreichbar ‹Aufschlag›; (*fig.*) unaufhaltsam; **she is ~:** sie ist nicht aufzuhalten

**unstrap** /ʌn'stræp/ *v.t.* aufschnallen

**unstreamed** /ʌn'striːmd/ *adj.* (*Sch.*) nicht in Parallelzüge *od.* leistungshomogene Gruppen eingeteilt

**unstressed** /ʌn'strest/ *adj.* **A** (*not subjected to stress*) nicht belastet; **B** (*Phonet.*) unbetont

**unstructured** /ʌn'strʌktʃəd/ unstrukturiert

**unstrung** /ʌn'strʌŋ/ *adj.* **A** **come ~** ‹Perlen usw.:› von der Schnur fallen; **B** entnervt ‹Person›; zerrüttet ‹Nerven›

**unstuck** /ʌn'stʌk/ *adj.* **come ~:** sich lösen; ‹Briefumschlag:› aufgehen; (*fig. coll.: come to grief, fail*) ‹Person:› baden gehen (*ugs.*) (**over** mit); ‹Projekt, Plan, Theorie, Geschäft:› in die Binsen gehen (*ugs.*)

**unstudied** /ʌn'stʌdɪd/ *adj.* ungekünstelt

**unsubsidized** /ʌn'sʌbsɪdaɪzd/ *adj.* nicht subventioniert

**unsubstantial** /ʌnsəb'stænʃl/ *adj.* **A** immateriell; (*ghostly*) körperlos ‹Wesen›; leicht ‹Konstruktion›; **B** (*inadequate*) wenig nahrhaft ‹Essen›

**unsubstantiated** /ʌnsəb'stænʃɪeɪtɪd/ *adj.* unhaltbar; unbegründet

**unsubtle** /ʌn'sʌtl/ *adj.* plump

**unsuccessful** /ʌnsək'sesfl/ *adj.* erfolglos; **be ~:** keinen Erfolg haben; **the operation was ~:** die Operation hatte keinen Erfolg *od.* misslang; **be ~ in an examination/competition** eine Prüfung nicht bestehen/in einem Wettbewerb unterliegen *od.* keinen Erfolg haben; **he has been ~ in his attempt to find a job** es ist ihm nicht gelungen, eine Stelle zu finden

**unsuccessfully** /ʌnsək'sesfəlɪ/ *adv.* erfolglos; vergebens ‹versuchen›

**unsuitability** /ʌnsuːtə'bɪlɪtɪ, ʌnsjuːtə'bɪlɪtɪ/ *n., no pl.* Ungeeignetsein, *das;* (*for job*) mangelnde Eignung

**unsuitable** /ʌn'suːtəbl, ʌn'sjuːtəbl/ *adj.* ungeeignet; **~ clothes** (*for weather, activity*) unzweckmäßige Kleider; (*for occasion, age*) unpassende Kleider; **be ~ for sb./sth.** für jmdn./etw. ungeeignet sein; **this sort of behaviour is ~ for a teacher** ein solches Verhalten gehört sich nicht für einen Lehrer

**unsuitably** /ʌn'suːtəblɪ, ʌn'sjuːtəblɪ/ *adv.* unpassend; **she dresses ~ for her age/figure** sie kleidet sich unpassend für ihr Alter/unvorteilhaft für ihre Figur; **be ~ dressed for a hike** für eine Wanderung unzweckmäßig gekleidet sein

**unsuited** /ʌn'suːtɪd, ʌn'sjuːtɪd/ *adj.* ungeeignet; **be ~ for** *or* **to sb./sth.** für jmdn./etw. ungeeignet sein; ‹Verhalten, Sprache:› für jmdn./etw. unpassend sein; **John and Mary are ~ to each other** John und Mary passen nicht zusammen; **he is ~ to be a teacher** er eignet sich nicht zum Lehrer

**unsullied** /ʌn'sʌlɪd/ *adj.* (*literary*) unbefleckt; unberührt ‹Schnee›; makellos ‹Glanz, Ruf›

**unsung** /ʌn'sʌŋ/ *adj.* unbesungen ‹Held, Tat›

**unsupported** /ʌnsə'pɔːtɪd/ *adj.* **A** nicht abgestützt; **if left ~, the branches will break** wenn man die Äste nicht [ab]stützt, brechen sie; **the old man walked ~:** der alte Mann ging ohne fremde Hilfe; **B** (*Mil.*) ohne Unterstützung *nachgestellt;* (*without cover*) ungedeckt; **an ~ unit** eine ohne Unterstützung operierende Einheit; **C** (*fig.*) durch nichts gestützt ‹Anschuldigung, Forderung, Theorie›; **~ by sb./sth.** nicht gestützt durch jmdn./etw.; **a project ~ by funds** ein finanziell nicht gefördertes Projekt; **we do not accept cheques ~ by cheque cards** wir akzeptieren keine Schecks ohne Scheckkarte

**unsure** /ʌn'ʃʊə(r)/ *adj.* unsicher; **be ~ about sb./sth.** sich (*Dat.*) über jmdn./etw. nicht im Klaren sein; **be ~ whether to do sth.** sich (*Dat.*) nicht sicher sein, ob man etw. tun soll; **be ~ of sb./sth.** sich (*Dat.*) jmds./einer Sache nicht sicher sein; **be ~ of a date/of one's facts** ein Datum nicht genau wissen/seine Fakten nicht genau kennen; **be ~ of oneself** unsicher sein

**unsurpassable** /ʌnsə'pɑːsəbl/ *adj.* unübertrefflich; (*unique*) einzigartig

**unsurpassed** /ʌnsə'pɑːst/ *adj.* unübertroffen; **a landscape ~ in beauty** eine Landschaft von unübertroffener Schönheit; **a novel ~ for suspense** ein Roman von unübertroffener Spannung; **his speeches were ~ for wit** seine Reden waren von unübertroffenem Witz

**unsurprising** /ʌnsə'praɪzɪŋ/ *adj.* wenig überraschend

**unsurprisingly** /ʌnsə'praɪzɪŋlɪ/ *adv.* wie zu erwarten war

**unsuspected** /ʌnsə'spektɪd/ *adj.* **A** (*not known about*) ungeahnt ‹Talent, Kräfte, Stärke, Tiefe, Charme›; unvermutet ‹Defekt, Leck, Ergebnis, Folge›; **he showed an ~ streak of ruthlessness** er zeigte sich überraschend rücksichtslos; **B** (*not under suspicion*) **be ~:** nicht verdächtigt werden; nicht unter Verdacht stehen; **~ by anyone** ohne verdächtigt zu werden

**unsuspecting** /ʌnsə'spektɪŋ/ *adj.*, **unsuspectingly** /ʌnsə'spektɪŋlɪ/ *adv.* nichts ahnend

**unsweetened** /ʌn'swiːtnd/ *adj.* ungesüßt

**unswerving** /ʌn'swɜːvɪŋ/ *adj.* **A** (*not turning aside*) schnurgerade; **follow an ~ course** (*fig.*) seinen Weg unbeirrt fortsetzen; **B** (*steady, constant*) unerschütterlich ‹Glaube, Treue›; unbeirrbar ‹Entschlossenheit, Zuneigung›; **be ~ in sth.** an etw. (*Dat.*) unbeirrbar *od.* unerschütterlich festhalten

**unswervingly** /ʌn'swɜːvɪŋlɪ/ *adv.* unerschütterlich ‹treu›; unbeirrbar ‹unterstützen, festhalten, folgen›

**unsymmetrical** /ʌnsɪ'metrɪkl/ *adj.* unsymmetrisch

**unsympathetic** /ʌnsɪmpə'θetɪk/ *adj.* **A** wenig mitfühlend; **be ~:** kein Mitgefühl zeigen; **be ~ to sth./not ~ to sth.** kein Verständnis/schon Verständnis für etw. haben; **B** (*unlikeable*) unsympathisch

**unsympathetically** /ʌnsɪmpə'θetɪkəlɪ/ *adv.* ohne Mitgefühl

**unsystematic** /ʌnsɪstə'mætɪk/ *adj.*, **unsystematically** /ʌnsɪstə'mætɪkəlɪ/ *adv.* unsystematisch

**untainted** /ʌn'teɪntɪd/ *adj.* unverdorben ‹Lebensmittel›; makellos ‹Ruf›

**untalented** /ʌn'tæləntɪd/ *adj.* untalentiert

**untameable** /ʌn'teɪməbl/ *adj.* unzähmbar; (*fig.*) unbezähmbar; unbezwinglich ‹Wildnis›

**untamed** /ʌn'teɪmd/ *adj.* (*lit. or fig.*) ungezähmt; wild

**untangle** /ʌn'tæŋgl/ *v.t.* entwirren; (*fig.*) entwirren ‹Geschichte, Situation, Handlung›; in Ordnung bringen ‹Finanzen, Angelegenheit›

**untapped** /ʌn'tæpt/ *adj.* nicht angezapft; (*fig.: not used*) ungenutzt ‹Talent›; nicht angebrochen ‹Vorräte›; unerschlossen ‹Bodenschätze, Markt›

**untarnished** /ʌn'tɑːnɪʃt/ *adj.* (*lit. or fig.*) makellos; rein; nicht angelaufen ‹Silber›; **his name is ~ by corruption** sein Name ist nicht durch Korruption befleckt (*geh.*)

**untasted** /ʌn'teɪstɪd/ *adj.* unberührt; **leave one's food ~:** sein Essen nicht anrühren; (*fig.*) **~ pleasures/delights** nie genossene *od.* gekostete Vergnügen/Freuden

**untaught** /ʌn'tɔːt/ *adj.* **A** (*not instructed*) **be [completely] ~ in sth.** in etw. (*Dat.*) [überhaupt] nicht ausgebildet sein; **B** (*not acquired by teaching*) natürlich ‹Begabung›; angeboren ‹Fähigkeit›

**untaxed** /ʌn'tækst/ *adj.* unversteuert ‹Einkommen, Waren›; **an ~ car** ein Auto, für das die [Kraftfahrzeug]steuer nicht bezahlt ist

**unteachable** /ʌn'tiːtʃəbl/ *adj.* nicht bildungsfähig ‹Person, Kind›; nicht lehrbar ‹Fach, Fertigkeit›

**untenable** /ʌn'tenəbl/ *adj.* unhaltbar

**untenanted** /ʌn'tenəntɪd/ *adj.* unbewohnt; leer stehend

**untended** /ʌn'tendɪd/ *adj.* ungepflegt ‹Garten›

**untested** /ʌn'testɪd/ *adj.* nicht erprobt; **a drug ~ on humans** ein an Menschen [noch] nicht erprobtes Medikament

**unthankful** /ʌn'θæŋkfl/ *adj.* undankbar

**unthinkable** /ʌn'θɪŋkəbl/ **1** *adj.* unvorstellbar. **2** *n.* **the ~:** das Unvorstellbare

**unthinkably** /ʌn'θɪŋkəblɪ/ *adv.* unvorstellbar

**unthinking** /ʌn'θɪŋkɪŋ/ *adj.*, **unthinkingly** /ʌn'θɪŋkɪŋlɪ/ *adv.* gedankenlos; **~, I took the key** ganz in Gedanken, nahm ich den Schlüssel

**unthought** /ʌn'θɔːt/ *adj.* **~ of** undenkbar; **hitherto ~-of disadvantages/objections** Nachteile/Einwände, an die bisher noch niemand gedacht hat/hatte

**unthread** /ʌn'θred/ *v.t.* vom Faden abziehen ‹Perlen›

**untidily** /ʌn'taɪdɪlɪ/ *adv.* unordentlich

**untidiness** /ʌn'taɪdɪnɪs/ *n., no pl.* ⇒ **untidy**: Ungepflegtheit, *die;* Unaufgeräumtheit, *die;* Unordentlichkeit, *die;* Unsauberkeit, *die*

**untidy** /ʌn'taɪdɪ/ *adj.* ungepflegt ‹Äußeres, Person, Garten›; unaufgeräumt ‹Bücher, Spielzeug, Zimmer›; unordentlich, unsauber ‹Manuskript›

**untie** /ʌn'taɪ/ *v.t.*, **untying** /ʌn'taɪɪŋ/ aufknüpfen, aufknoten ‹Faden, Seil, Paket›; aufbinden ‹Knoten, Schnürsenkel›; losbinden ‹Pferd, Boot, Seil vom Pfosten›; **~ sb./sb.'s hands** jmdn./jmds. Hände von den Fesseln befreien

**untied** /ʌn'taɪd/ *adj.* offen ‹Schnürsenkel›; ungebunden ‹Krawatte›; **leave sth. ~:** etw. nicht zusammenbinden; **come ~:** sich lösen; ‹Schnürsenkel:› aufgehen

**until** /ən'tɪl/ **1** *prep.* ▶ **1012** bis; (*followed by article + noun*) bis zu; **~ [the] evening/night/the end** bis zum Abend/bis in die Nacht/bis zum Ende; **~ his death/retirement** bis zu seinem Tod/seiner Pensionierung; **~ next week** bis nächste Woche; **~ then** *or* **that time** bis dahin *od.* dann; **~ soon after sth.** bis kurz nach etw.; **not ~:** erst; **not ~ Christmas/the summer/his birthday/this morning** erst zu *od.* (*bes. südd.*) an Weihnachten/im Sommer/an seinem Geburtstag/heute Morgen; **yes, but not ~ [then]** ja, aber nicht vorher. **2** *conj.* bis; **~ you find the key, we shall not be able to get in** solange du den Schlüssel nicht findest, kommen wir nicht hinein; **I am not coming ~ I am asked** ich komme erst, wenn man mich einlädt; solange man mich nicht einlädt, komme ich nicht; **I did not know ~ you told me** ich wusste das nicht, bis du es mir gesagt hast; **not ~ I saw him ...:** erst, als ich ihn sah, ...

**untimely** /ʌn'taɪmlɪ/ **1** *adj.* **A** (*inopportune*) ungelegen; (*inappropriate*) unpassend;

**be ~:** ungelegen kommen/unpassend sein; **an ~ frost** ein nicht der Jahreszeit entsprechender Frost; **an ~ measure/action** eine zur Unzeit getroffene Maßnahme; **his joke was ~:** er machte seinen Witz im unpassenden Moment; **not ~:** zur rechten Zeit; **B** (*premature*) vorzeitig; allzu früh ‹Tod›; **he came to an ~ end** er starb allzu früh. ❷ *adv.* (*inopportunely*) unpassend; (*prematurely*) allzu früh

**untiring** /ʌn'taɪərɪŋ/ *adj.* unermüdlich; **be ~ in one's efforts for sb./to do sth.** sich unermüdlich für jmdn. einsetzen/sich unermüdlich bemühen, etw. zu tun

**untiringly** /ʌn'taɪərɪŋlɪ/ *adv.* unermüdlich

**unto** /'ʌntʊ, 'ʌntə/ *prep.* (*arch./literary*) **A** ⇨ **to** 1; **B** (*Bibl.*) **come ~ me** kommet zu mir (*bibl.*); **~ us a child is born** uns ist ein Kind geboren; **~ this day** bis zum heutigen Tage; **faithful ~ death** getreu bis in den Tod

**untold** /ʌn'təʊld/ *adj.* **A** (*immeasurable*) unbeschreiblich; unsagbar ‹Elend›; unermesslich ‹Reichtümer, Anzahl›; **B** (*countless*) unzählig; **C** (*not related*) nicht erzählt

**untouchable** /ʌn'tʌtʃəbl/ ❶ *adj.* **A** (*beyond reach*) unberührbar; **sth. is ~:** etw. kann nicht berührt werden; ; **B** (*above criticism/reproach*) unantastbar. ❷ *n.* Unberührbare, *der/die*

**untouched** /ʌn'tʌtʃt/ *adj.* **A** (*not handled, untasted*) unberührt; **leave sth. ~:** etw. nicht anrühren; '**~ by human hand**' (*on packaged food*) ≈ „hygienisch verpackt"; **a cup of tea still ~:** eine noch unberührte Tasse Tee; **B** (*not changed*) unverändert; **C** (*not affected*) unberührt; **be ~ by sth.** von etw. unberührt bleiben; **they had left her jewellery ~:** sie hatten ihren Schmuck nicht angerührt; **a town ~ by the war/a people ~ by the pressures of modern times** eine vom Krieg verschont gebliebene Stadt/ein Volk, das von den Zwängen der heutigen Zeit unberührt geblieben ist; **she remained ~ by his tears** seine Tränen ließen sie kalt; **D** (*unequalled*) unerreicht

**untoward** /ʌntə'wɔ:d/ *adj.* **A** (*unfavourable*) ungünstig; unglücklich ‹Unfall›; **in case something ~ were to happen** falls Schwierigkeiten auftauchen/ein Unglück geschieht; **nothing ~ happened** es gab keine Schwierigkeiten/(*more serious*) es passierte kein Unheil; **B** (*unseemly*) ungehörig

**untraceable** /ʌn'treɪsəbl/ *adj.* unauffindbar; **be ~:** nicht aufzuspüren sein

**untraced** /ʌn'treɪst/ *adj.* noch nicht gefunden

**untrained** /ʌn'treɪnd/ *adj.* unausgebildet; ungelernt ‹Arbeitskräfte›; nicht dressiert ‹Tier›; **to the ~ eye/ear** dem ungeschulten Auge/Ohr; **be ~ in sth.** in etw. (*Dat.*) ungeübt sein

**untrammelled** (*Amer.*: **untrammeled**) /ʌn'træmld/ *adj.* (*fig.*) unbeschränkt ‹Freiheit›; **young people ~ by tradition/convention** junge Leute, die sich von Traditionen/Konventionen nicht einengen lassen

**untranslatable** /ʌntræns'leɪtəbl/ *adj.* unübersetzbar

**untravelled** (*Amer.*: **untraveled**) /ʌn'trævld/ *adj.* der/die nicht weit herumgekommen ist; kaum befahren ‹Straße›

**untreated** /ʌn'tri:tɪd/ *adj.* unbehandelt

**untried** /ʌn'traɪd/ *adj.* **A** (*not tested*) unerprobt; **a new treatment, ~ on humans** eine neue, an Menschen noch nicht erprobte Behandlung; **leave nothing ~:** nichts unversucht lassen; **B** (*Law*) nicht vor Gericht gestellt ‹Person›; nicht verhandelt ‹Fall›

**untrodden** /ʌn'trɒdn/ *adj.* unberührt ‹Schnee›; verlassen ‹Weg›

**untroubled** /ʌn'trʌbld/ *adj.* ungestört ‹Schlaf, Ruhe›; sorglos ‹Gesicht, Geist›; ruhig ‹Wasser›; sorgenfrei ‹Zeit, Leben›; **he seemed ~ by the news** die Nachricht schien ihn nicht zu beunruhigen; **we were ~ by doubts/worries** auf uns lasteten keine Zweifel/Sorgen

**untrue** /ʌn'tru:/ *adj.* **A** (*false*) unwahr; **that's ~:** das ist nicht wahr; **B** (*unfaithful*) **~ to sb./sth.** jmdm./etw. untreu; **C** ungenau ‹Ergebnis, Messgerät›

**untrustworthy** /ʌn'trʌstwɜ:ðɪ/ *adj.* unzuverlässig

**untruth** /ʌn'tru:θ/ *n.*, *pl.* **~s** /ʌn'tru:ðz, ʌn'tru:θs/ Unwahrheit, *die*

**untruthful** /ʌn'tru:θfl/ *adj.* verlogen (*abwertend*); **an ~ story** eine Lügengeschichte (*abwertend*); **I am not being ~:** ich lüge nicht

**untruthfully** /ʌn'tru:θfəlɪ/ *adv.* nicht der Wahrheit entsprechend ‹antworten, etw. sagen›

**untruthfulness** /ʌn'tru:θflnɪs/ *n.*, *no pl.* (*of story*) Unwahrheit, *die;* (*of person*) Verlogenheit, *die* (*abwertend*)

**untuneful** /ʌn'tju:nfl/ *adj.* unmelodisch

**unturned** /ʌn'tɜ:nd/ ⇨ **stone** 1 A

**untutored** /ʌn'tju:təd/ *adj.* ungeschult

**untypical** /ʌn'tɪpɪkl/ *adj.* untypisch (**of** für)

**unusable** /ʌn'ju:zəbl/ *adj.* unbrauchbar

**unused**[1] /ʌn'ju:zd/ *adj.* (*new, fresh*) unbenutzt; (*not utilized*) ungenutzt; ungestempelt ‹Briefmarke›; **he still had three days ~ leave** er hatte noch drei Tage Urlaub gut

**unused**[2] /ʌn'ju:st/ *adj.* (*unaccustomed*) **be ~ to sth./to doing sth.** etw. (*Akk.*) nicht gewohnt sein/nicht gewohnt sein, etw. zu tun; **we are not ~ to sudden crises** plötzliche Krisen sind für uns nichts Ungewohntes

**unusual** /ʌn'ju:ʒʊəl/ *adj.* ungewöhnlich; (*exceptional*) außergewöhnlich; **an ~ number of ...:** eine ungewöhnlich große Zahl von ...; **it is ~ for him to do that** er tut das gewöhnlich nicht; **it is not ~ for her to do that** es ist durchaus nicht ungewöhnlich, dass sie das tut

**unusually** /ʌn'ju:ʒʊəlɪ/ *adv.* ungewöhnlich; *as sentence-modifier* **~ [for him], he was late** er kam zu spät, was für ihn ganz ungewöhnlich ist

**unusualness** /ʌn'ju:ʒʊəlnɪs/ *n.*, *no pl.* Ungewöhnlichkeit, *die*

**unutterable** /ʌn'ʌtərəbl/ *adj.*, **unutterably** /ʌn'ʌtərəblɪ/ *adv.* unsäglich

**unvarnished** /ʌn'vɑ:nɪʃt/ *adj.* unlackiert ‹Holz›; unglasiert ‹Keramik›; (*fig.*) ungeschminkt ‹Wahrheit›

**unvarying** /ʌn'veərɪɪŋ/ *adj.* gleich bleibend

**unveil** /ʌn'veɪl/ *v.t.* **A** entschleiern ‹Gesicht›; enthüllen ‹Statue, Gedenktafel›; (*fig.*: *introduce publicly*) vorstellen ‹neues Auto, Produkt, Modell›; **B** (*reveal*) veröffentlichen, (*geh.*) enthüllen ‹Plan, Projekt›

**unveiling** /ʌn'veɪlɪŋ/ *n.* Enthüllung, *die;* (*fig.*) Vorstellung, *die;* **the ~ ceremony** die [feierliche] Enthüllung

**unventilated** /ʌn'ventɪleɪtɪd/ *adj.* ungelüftet; (*having no permanent ventilation system*) unbelüftet

**unverifiable** /ʌn'verɪfaɪəbl/ *adj.* nicht nachprüfbar ‹Tatsache›

**unverified** /ʌn'verɪfaɪd/ *adj.* nicht nachgeprüft

**unversed** /ʌn'vɜ:st/ *adj.* nicht bewandert (**in** in + *Dat.*)

**unvoiced** /ʌn'vɔɪst/ *adj.* **A** unausgesprochen ‹Ansichten, Gefühle, Zweifel›; **B** (*Phonet.*) stimmlos

**unwaged** /ʌn'weɪdʒd/ *adj.* arbeitslos

**unwanted** /ʌn'wɒntɪd/ *adj.* unerwünscht; **one's ~ clothes/books** die Kleider/Bücher, die man nicht mehr [haben] will

**unwarily** /ʌn'weərɪlɪ/ *adv.* unvorsichtig

**unwarrantable** /ʌn'wɒrəntəbl/ *adj.* nicht zu rechtfertigend *nicht präd.;* ungerechtfertigt

**unwarrantably** /ʌn'wɒrəntəblɪ/ *adv.* **be ~ severe with sb.** so streng mit jmdm. sein, dass es nicht zu rechtfertigen ist

**unwarranted** /ʌn'wɒrəntɪd/ *adj.* ungerechtfertigt

**unwary** /ʌn'weərɪ/ *adj.* unvorsichtig; unüberlegt ‹Tat, Schritt›

**unwashed** /ʌn'wɒʃt/ *adj.* ungewaschen ‹Person, Kleidung›; ungespült ‹Geschirr›; **the great ~** (*derog.*) der Pöbel

**unwavering** /ʌn'weɪvərɪŋ/ *adj.* gleichmäßig ‹Flamme, Licht›; fest ‹Blick›; (*fig.*: *firm, resolute*) unerschütterlich

**unwearable** /ʌn'weərəbl/ *adj.* **sth. is ~:** etw. kann man nicht anziehen *od.* tragen

**unwelcome** /ʌn'welkəm/ *adj.* unwillkommen; ungebeten ‹Besucher›; unerwünscht ‹Anwesenheit›

**unwell** /ʌn'wel/ *adj.* unwohl; **look ~:** nicht wohl *od.* gut aussehen; **he feels ~** (*feels poorly*) er fühlt sich nicht wohl; (*feels sick*) ihm ist [es] schlecht *od.* übel; **she is ~:** es geht ihr nicht gut

**unwholesome** /ʌn'həʊlsəm/ *adj.* (*lit. or fig.*) ungesund

**unwieldiness** /ʌn'wi:ldɪnɪs/ *n.*, *no pl.* (*of tool, weapon*) Unhandlichkeit, *die;* (*of box, shape, parcel*) Sperrigkeit, *die;* (*fig.*: *complexity*) Kompliziertheit, *die*

**unwieldy** /ʌn'wi:ldɪ/ *adj.* unhandlich ‹Werkzeug, Waffe›; sperrig ‹Karton, Form, Paket›; (*fig.*) kompliziert ‹Name, Titel, Organisation usw.›

**unwilling** /ʌn'wɪlɪŋ/ *adj.* widerwillig ‹Partner, Unterstützung, Zustimmung›; unfreiwillig ‹Helfer›; **an achievement that commands our ~ admiration/respect** eine Leistung, die wir wider Willen bewundern/respektieren müssen; **be ~ to do sth.** etw. nicht tun wollen; **we are not ~ but unable to help** wir wollen durchaus helfen, können [es] aber nicht; **be ~ for sb. to do sth.** *or* **that sb. should do sth.** nicht wollen, dass jmd. etw. tut; **be ~ for sth. to be done** *or* **that sth. should be done** nicht wollen, dass etw. getan wird

**unwillingly** /ʌn'wɪlɪŋlɪ/ *adv.* widerwillig

**unwillingness** /ʌn'wɪlɪŋnɪs/ *n.*, *no pl.* Widerwille, *der;* **~ to help/listen** mangelnde Bereitschaft zu helfen/zuzuhören

**unwind** /ʌn'waɪnd/ ❶ *v.t.*, **unwound** /ʌn'waʊnd/ abwickeln; abspulen ‹Film›; **the girl unwound her arms from around his neck** das Mädchen löste seine Arme von seinem Hals. ❷ *v.i.*, **unwound** **A** (*unreel*) sich abwickeln; **B** (*fig.*: *unfold*) sich entwickeln; **C** (*coll.*: *relax*) sich entspannen

**unwise** /ʌn'waɪz/ *adj.* unklug; **if you are ~ enough to ignore my advice** wenn du so unklug bist, meinen Rat nicht anzunehmen

**unwisely** /ʌn'waɪzlɪ/ *adv.* unklug; *as sentence-modifier* unklugerweise

**unwitting** /ʌn'wɪtɪŋ/ *adj.* ahnungslos ‹Opfer›; unwissentlich ‹Komplize, Urheber›; (*unintentional*) unbeabsichtigt ‹Fehler, Handlung›; ungewollt ‹Beleidigung›

**unwittingly** /ʌn'wɪtɪŋlɪ/ *adv.* unwissentlich; unabsichtlich ‹beleidigen›

**unwonted** /ʌn'wəʊntɪd/ *adj.* ungewohnt

**unworkable** /ʌn'wɜ:kəbl/ *adj.* unbrauchbar ‹Material›; nicht abbaubar ‹Flöz›; (*fig.*: *impracticable*) unbrauchbar ‹System›; undurchführbar ‹Plan, Projekt›

**unworkmanlike** /ʌn'wɜ:kmənlaɪk/ *adj.* nicht fachmännisch

**unworldly** /ʌn'wɜ:ldlɪ/ *adj.* weltabgewandt; (*naïve, not worldly-wise*) weltfremd

**unworn** /ʌn'wɔ:n/ *adj.* **A** (*new*) ungetragen ‹Kleidung›; **B** (*not damaged*) nicht abgetreten ‹Teppich, Treppe›; nicht abgetragen ‹Kleidungsstück›; nicht abgenutzt ‹Maschinenteil›; nicht abgefahren ‹Reifen›; **completely ~:** überhaupt nicht abgetreten/abgetragen/abgenutzt/abgefahren

**unworried** /ʌn'wʌrɪd/ *adj.* unbekümmert; **she was completely ~ by it** sie machte sich (*Dat.*) keine Sorgen darum

**unworthily** /ʌn'wɜ:ðɪlɪ/ *adv.* unwürdig

**unworthiness** /ʌn'wɜ:ðɪnɪs/ *n.*, *no pl.* Unwürdigkeit, *die*

**unworthy** /ʌn'wɜ:ðɪ/ *adj.* unwürdig; **receive ~ treatment** in einer Weise behandelt werden, die man nicht verdient hat; **be [not] ~ of sth.** einer Sache nicht [un]würdig sein; **an incident ~ of notice/of sb.'s attention** ein Vorfall, der keine Beachtung/der jmds. Beachtung nicht verdient; **be ~ of sb./sth.** ‹Verhalten, Einstellung usw.:› einer Person/Sache (*Gen.*) unwürdig sein

**unwrap** /ʌn'ræp/ *v.t.*, **-pp-** auswickeln; abwickeln ‹Bandage›

**unwritten** /ʌn'rɪtn/ *adj.* ungeschrieben; nicht schriftlich festgehalten ‹Märchen, Lied, Vertrag, Verfassung›; unbeschrieben ‹Papier, Seite›

U

**unyielding** /ʌn'ji:ldɪŋ/ *adj.* hart; (*fig.*) unnachgiebig; unerschütterlich ‹Mut›; unbeirrbar ‹Entschlossenheit›; unerbittlich ‹Widerstand›

**unyoke** /ʌn'jəʊk/ *v.t.* aus dem Joch nehmen; ausspannen ‹Zugtier, Wagen, Pflug›

**unzip** /ʌn'zɪp/ ❶ *v.t.*, **-pp-** öffnen ‹Reißverschluss›; **~ a dress/bag** *etc.* den Reißverschluss eines Kleides/einer Tasche *usw.* öffnen; **can you ~ me, please?** kannst du mir bitte den Reißverschluss öffnen *od.* (*ugs.*) aufmachen?; **her dress had come ~ped** der Reißverschluss ihres Kleides war aufgegangen. ❷ *v.i.*, **-pp-: the dress ~s at the back** das Kleid hat hinten einen Reißverschluss; **this bag/dress won't ~:** der Reißverschluss dieser Tasche/dieses Kleides geht nicht auf (*ugs.*)

**up** /ʌp/ ❶ *adv.* [A] (*to higher place*) nach oben; (*in lift*) aufwärts; **[right] up to sth.** (*lit. or fig.*) [ganz] bis zu etw. hinauf; **the bird flew up to the roof** der Vogel flog aufs Dach [hinauf]; **up into the air** in die Luft [hinauf] …; **climb up on sth./climb up to the top of sth.** auf etw. (*Akk.*) [hinauf]steigen/bis zur Spitze einer Sache hinaufsteigen; **the lift went up to the top of the building** der Lift fuhr bis zur obersten Etage des Gebäudes; **the way up [to sth.]** der Weg hinauf [zu etw.]; **on the way up** (*lit. or fig.*) auf dem Weg nach oben; **up here/there** hier herauf/dort hinauf; **high/higher up** hoch/höher hinauf; **farther up** weiter hinauf; **halfway/a long/little way up** den halben Weg/ein weites/kurzes Stück hinauf; **up and up** immer höher; **up and away** auf und davon; **come on up!** komm [hier/weiter] herauf!; **up it** *etc.* **comes/goes** herauf kommt/hinauf geht es *usw.*; **up you go!** rauf mit dir! (*ugs.*); ⇒ *also* **hand** 1 A; [B] (*to upstairs*) rauf (*bes. ugs.*); herauf/hinauf (*bes. schriftsprachlich*); nach oben; [C] (*to place regarded as higher*) rauf (*bes. ugs.*); herauf/hinauf (*bes. schriftsprachlich*); **go up to the shops/the end of the road** zu den Geschäften/zum Ende der Straße gehen; [D] (*to place regarded as more important*) **go up to Leeds from the country** vom Land in die Stadt Leeds *od.* nach Leeds fahren; [E] (*northwards*) rauf (*bes. ugs.*); herauf/hinauf (*bes. schriftsprachlich*); **come up from London to Edinburgh** von London nach Edinburgh [he]raufkommen; [F] (*Brit.: to capital*) rein (*bes. ugs.*); herein/hinein (*bes. schriftsprachlich*); **go up to town** *or* **London** nach London gehen/fahren; **get up to London from Reading** von Reading nach London [he]reinfahren; [G] (*Brit.: to university*) **up to university/Oxford** auf die Universität/nach Oxford; [H] (*Naut.: with rudder to leeward*) in Luv; **put the helm up** das Ruder in Luv legen; [I] (*in higher place*) oben; **up here/there** hier/da oben; **[right] up at sth.** [ganz] oben auf/an etw. (*Dat.*); **high up** hoch oben; **he is something high up in the Army** (*fig.*) er ist ein hohes *od.* großes Tier in der Armee (*ugs.*); **an order from high up** (*fig.*) ein Befehl von ganz oben (*ugs.*); **higher up in the mountains** weiter oben in den Bergen; **the picture should be higher up** das Bild müsste höher hängen; **farther up** weiter oben; **halfway/a long/little way up** auf halbem Weg nach oben/ein gutes/kurzes Stück weiter oben; **10 metres up** 10 Meter hoch; **live four floors** *or* **storeys up** im vierten Stockwerk wohnen; **his flat is on the next floor up** seine Wohnung ist ein Stockwerk höher; [J] (*erect*) hoch; **keep your head up** halte den Kopf hoch; ⇒ *also* **chin**; [K] (*out of bed*) **be up** auf sein; **up and about** auf den Beinen; [L] (*in place regarded as higher; upstairs*) oben; [M] (*in place regarded as more important; Brit.: in capital*) **up in town** *or* **London/Leeds** in London/Leeds; [N] (*in north*) **up [north]** oben [im Norden] (*ugs.*); [O] (*Brit.: at university*) **up at university/Oxford** an der Universität/in Oxford; [P] (*in price, value, amount*) **prices have gone/are up** die Preise sind gestiegen; **butter is up [by …]** Butter ist […] teurer; **the dollar is/these shares are up** der Dollar ist/diese Aktien sind im Wert gestiegen; (*at high level*) **the temperature was up in the thirties** die Temperatur lag über dreißig Grad; [Q] (*including higher limit*) **up to** bis … hinauf; **up to midday/up to £2** bis zum Mittag/bis zu 2 Pfund; [R] (*in position of gain*) **we're £300 up on last year** wir liegen 300 Pfund über dem letzten Jahr; **the takings were £500 up on the previous month** die Einnahmen lagen 500 Pfund über denen des Vormonats; [S] (*ahead*) **be three points/games/goals up** (*Sport*) mit drei Punkten/Spielen/Toren vorn liegen; **be three points up on sb.** drei Punkte vor jmdm. sein *od.* liegen; [T] (*as far as*) **up to sth.** bis zu etw.; **she is up to Chapter 3** sie ist bis zum dritten Kapitel gekommen *od.* ist beim dritten Kapitel; **where are you/have you got up to [now]?** (*in book*) wie weit bist du?/wie weit bist du jetzt gekommen?; **up to here/there** bis hier[hin]/bis dorthin; **I've had it up to here** (*coll.*) mir steht es bis hier [hin] (*ugs.*); **up to now/then/that time/last week** bis jetzt/damals/zu jener Zeit/zur letzten Woche; ⇒ *also* **ear**[1] A; **eye** 1 A; **neck** 1 A; **point** 1 E; [U] **up to** (*comparable with*) **be up to expectation[s]** den Erwartungen entsprechen; **his last opera is not up to the others he has written** seine neueste Oper reicht an seine früheren nicht heran; [V] **up to** (*capable of*) **[not] be/feel up to sth.** einer Sache (*Dat.*) [nicht] gewachsen sein/sich einer Sache (*Dat.*) [nicht] gewachsen fühlen; **[not] be/feel up to doing sth.** [nicht] in der Lage sein/sich nicht in der Lage fühlen, etw. zu tun; **are you sure you're up to it?** meinst du wirklich, dass du das schaffst?; **not be up to much** nicht viel taugen; **my cooking isn't up to much** ich koche nicht besonders gut; **be up to sb.'s dodges/fiddles** jmds. Schliche kennen; **he is up to all the dodges** er ist mit allen Wassern gewaschen (*ugs.*); [W] **up to** (*derog.: doing*) **be up to sth.** etw. anstellen (*ugs.*); **what is he up to?** was hat er [bloß] vor?; **what do you think you're up to?** was fällt Ihnen [denn *od.* eigentlich] ein?; **I'm sure he's up to something** er führt sicher etwas im Schilde; **I wonder what he's up to with it** ich frage mich, was er damit vorhat; [X] **up to** (*incumbent on*) **it is [not] up to sb. to do sth.** es ist [nicht] jmds. Sache, etw. zu tun; **it is up to us to help them** es ist unsere Pflicht, ihnen zu helfen; **now it's up to him to do something** nun liegt es bei *od.* an ihm, etwas zu tun; **it's not up to me to say** das kann ich nicht sagen; **the decision/choice is [not] up to me** die Entscheidung/Wahl hängt [nicht] von mir ab; **it's/that's up to you** (*is for you to decide*) es/das hängt von dir ab; (*concerns only you*) es/das ist deine Sache; [Y] (*close*) **up against sb./sth.** an jmdm./etw. ‹lehnen›; an jmdn./etw. ‹stellen›; **sit up against the wall** mit dem Rücken zur *od.* an der Wand sitzen; **up near/by sth.** direkt neben etw.; [Z] (*confronted by*) **be up against a problem/difficulty** *etc.* (*coll.*) vor einem Problem/einer Schwierigkeit *usw.* stehen; **find oneself up against the law/the authorities** mit dem Gesetz/mit den Behörden in Konflikt kommen; **be up against a tough opponent** es mit einem harten Gegner zu tun haben; **they don't realize what sort of competition they will be up against** sie wissen nicht, mit welcher Art von Konkurrenz sie es zu tun haben werden; **be up against it** in großen Schwierigkeiten stecken; ⇒ *also* **come up** I; [AA] **up and down** (*upwards and downwards*) hinauf und hinunter; (*to and fro*) auf und ab; **the children are jumping up and down on the settee** die Kinder springen auf dem Sofa herum; **be up and down** (*coll.: variable*) Hochs und Tiefs haben; **How are you? — Oh, up and down** Wie geht es Ihnen? — Ach, mal so, mal so (*ugs.*); ⇒ *also* **up-and-down**; [BB] (*facing upwards*) **'this side/way up'** (*on box etc.*) „[hier] oben“; **turn sth. this/the other side/way up** diese/die andere Seite einer Sache nach oben drehen; **the right/wrong way up** richtig/verkehrt *od.* falsch herum; **which way up is the painting supposed to be?** was soll auf dem Bild oben [und unten] sein?; wie herum ist das Bild denn richtig? (*ugs.*); [CC] (*finished, at an end*) abgelaufen; **time is up** die Zeit ist abgelaufen; **it is all up with him** mit ihm ist es vorbei *od.* aus (*ugs.*); ⇒ *also* **game**[1] 1 B.

❷ *prep.* [A] (*upwards along*) rauf (*bes. ugs.*); herauf/hinauf (*bes. schriftsprachlich*); **walk up sth.** etw. hinaufgehen; **higher up the valley** weiter oben im Tal; **up hill and down dale** bergauf und bergab; **curse sb. up hill and down dale** jmdn. in Grund und Boden verfluchen; [B] (*upwards through*) **force a liquid up a pipe** eine Flüssigkeit durch eine Röhre nach oben pressen; [C] (*upwards over*) **up sth.** etw. (*Akk.*) hinauf; **ivy grew up the wall** Efeu wuchs die Mauer hinauf; **mud was splattered up the back of his coat** sein Mantel war den ganzen Rücken hinauf mit Schlamm bespritzt; [D] (*along*) **go up the road/corridor/track** die Straße/den Korridor/den Weg hinauf- *od.* entlanggehen; **come up the street** die Straße herauf- *od.* entlangkommen; **turn up a side street** in eine Seitenstraße einbiegen; **I'm going up the pub** (*Brit. coll.*) ich gehe in die Kneipe; **walk up and down the platform** auf dem Bahnsteig auf und ab gehen; **up and down the land** landauf, landab; [E] (*at or in higher position in or on*) [weiter] oben; **further up the ladder/coast** weiter oben auf der Leiter/an der Küste; **a house up the mountain** ein Haus oben am Berg; **live/sail up the river** flussaufwärts wohnen/segeln; [F] **up yours/up them!** (*sl.*) du kannst/die können mich [mal]! (*salopp*); [G] (*from bottom to top along*) **up the side of a house** an der Seite eines Hauses hinauf. ⇒ *also* **country** B; **creek** D; **gum tree**; **pole**[1] A; **sleeve** A; **spout** 1 A; **stage** 1 A.

❸ *adj.* [A] (*directed upwards*) aufwärts führend ‹Rohr, Kabel›; ‹Rolltreppe› nach oben; nach oben gerichtet ‹Kolbenhub›; **up train/line/journey** (*Railw.*) Zug/Gleis/Fahrt Richtung Stadt; [B] (*well informed*) **be up in a subject/on the news** in einem Fach auf der Höhe [der Zeit] sein/über alle Neuigkeiten Bescheid wissen *od.* gut informiert sein; [C] **up for** (*in line for*) **be up for a post/for promotion** Kandidat/Kandidatin für eine Stelle/Beförderung sein; [D] (*coll.: ready*) **tea['s]/grub['s] up!** Tee/Essen ist fertig!; [E] (*coll.: amiss*) **what's up?** was ist los? (*ugs.*); **what's up with him** *etc.*? was ist los mit ihm *usw.*? (*ugs.*); **something is up** irgendwas ist los (*ugs.*).

❹ *n. in pl.* **the ups and downs** (*lit. or fig.*) das Auf und Ab; (*fig.*) die Höhen und Tiefen; **life is full of ups and downs** das Leben ist ein dauerndes Auf und Ab; **we've had our ups and downs** wir haben Höhen und Tiefen durchlebt.

❺ *v.i.*, **-pp-** (*coll.*) **up and leave/resign** einfach abhauen (*ugs.*)/kündigen; **he ups and says …:** da sagt er doch [ur]plötzlich …

❻ *v.t.*, **-pp-** (*coll.*) (*increase*) erhöhen; (*raise up*) heben

**'up-and-coming** *adj.* (*coll.*) aufstrebend

**up-and-'down** *attrib. adj.* **~ movement/motion** Aufundabbewegung, *die*; **an ~ life/~ years** (*fig.*) ein Leben/Jahre mit Höhen und Tiefen; **an ~ sort of a year** ein bewegtes Jahr

**up-and-'over door** *n.* Kipptür, *die*

**'up-and-up** *n.* (*coll.*) **be on the ~:** auf dem aufsteigenden Ast sein (*ugs.*)

**'upbeat** ❶ *n.* (*Mus.*) Auftakt, *der.* ❷ *adj.* (*coll.*) (*optimistic*) optimistisch; (*cheerful*) fröhlich; **~ news/export figures** zuversichtlich stimmende Neuigkeiten/Exportraten

**up'braid** *v.t.* **~ sb. with sth./for [doing] sth.** jmdm. wegen etw. Vorwürfe machen/jmdm. vorwerfen, dass er etw. getan hat

**upbringing** /'ʌpbrɪŋɪŋ/ *n.* Erziehung, *die*

**'up-country** *adj.* [A] **an ~ town/region/dialect** eine Stadt/ein Gebiet im Landesinneren/ein Dialekt, wie er im Landesinneren gesprochen wird; [B] (*countrified, unsophisticated*) **a little ~ town/place** ein kleiner Flecken/kleines Fleckchen auf dem Land; **plain ~ folk/people** einfache Leute vom flachen Land

**ˈup current** *n.* (*in air*) Aufwind, *der*

**update** ❶ /ʌpˈdeɪt/ *v.t.* (*bring up to date*) aktualisieren; auf den neuesten *od.* aktuellen Stand bringen; (*modernize*) modernisieren; **an ∼d version/edition** eine aktualisierte Fassung/Ausgabe. ❷ /ˈʌpdeɪt/ *n.* Lagebericht, *der* (**on** zu); (**∼d** *version*) Neuausgabe, *die*

**ˈup draught** *n.* [Luft]zug von unten

**up-ˈend** ❶ *v.t.* (*lit. or fig.*) auf den Kopf stellen; (*knock down*) zu Boden schlagen ‹Gegner›. ❷ *v.i.* ‹Schiff:› sich mit dem Heck nach oben stellen [und sinken]

**ˈupfield** *adv.* (*Sport*) in Richtung des gegnerischen Tores

**up ˈfront** *adv.* (*coll.*) Ⓐ (*at the front*) vorne; Ⓑ (*as down payment*) im Voraus

**upˈgrade¹** *v.t.* Ⓐ (*raise*) befördern ‹Beschäftigte›; aufwerten ‹Stellung›; **∼ fees/salaries/payments in line with inflation** Gebühren/Gehälter/Zahlungen entsprechend der Inflationsrate erhöhen; Ⓑ (*improve*) verbessern; **the stadium will be ∼d to Olympic standards** das Stadion wird den olympischen Normen entsprechend ausgebaut

**ˈupgrade²** *n.* (*Amer.*) Steigung, *die;* **be on the ∼** (*fig.*) ‹Wirtschaft:› im Aufschwung sein; **he was on the ∼:** es ging bergauf mit ihm

**upheaval** /ʌpˈhiːvl/ *n.* Aufruhr, *der;* (*commotion, disturbance*) Durcheinander, *das;* **the ∼ of moving house** das Durcheinander eines Umzugs; **an emotional ∼:** ein Aufruhr der Gefühle; **social/political ∼:** soziale/politische Umwälzung

**upˈhill** ❶ *adj.* bergauf führend ‹Weg, Pfad›; ‹Fahrt, Reise› bergauf; (*fig.*) **an ∼ task/struggle** eine mühselige Aufgabe/ein harter Kampf. ❷ *adv.* bergauf; **it's ∼ all the way** es geht immer bergauf; (*fig.*) es ist ein mühseliges Geschäft; **our task will be ∼ all the way** (*fig.*) unsere Aufgabe wird bis zum Schluss mühselig sein

**upˈhold** *v.t.*, **upheld** /ʌpˈheld/ Ⓐ (*support*) unterstützen; hochhalten, wahren ‹Tradition, Ehre›; schützen ‹Verfassung›; Ⓑ (*confirm*) aufrechterhalten ‹Forderung, Einwand›; einhalten ‹Vertrag›; bestätigen ‹Urteil›; anerkennen ‹Einwand, Beschwerde›

**upˈholder** *n.* Wahrer, *der*/Wahrerin, *die*

**upholster** /ʌpˈhəʊlstə(r)/ *v.t.* polstern; **∼ sth. in** *or* **with sth.** etw. in etw. (*Dat.*) *od.* mit etw. polstern; ⇒ *also* **well-upholstered**

**upholsterer** /ʌpˈhəʊlstərə(r)/ *n.* ▶ 1261 Polsterer, *der*/Polsterin, *die*

**upholstery** /ʌpˈhəʊlstərɪ/ *n.* Ⓐ (*craft*) Polster[er]handwerk, *das; attrib.* Polster-; Ⓑ (*padding*) Polsterung, *die;* (*cover also*) Bezug, *der; attrib.* Polster-; **∼ fabric** Polster- *od.* Möbelstoff, *der*

**ˈupkeep** *n.* Unterhalt, *der*

**upland** /ˈʌplənd/ ❶ *n. in pl.* Hochland, *das.* ❷ *adj.* Hochland-

**uplift** ❶ /-ˈ-/ *v.t.* aufrichten ‹Volk, Seele, Geist›; erheben (*geh.*) ‹Hand, Kopf, Stimme›; **parts of the earth's crust were ∼ed** Teile der Erdkruste hoben sich; **be/feel ∼ed by sth.** (*fig.*) durch etw. erhoben *od.* erbaut werden/sich durch etw. erhoben *od.* erbaut fühlen; **voices ∼ed in song/praise** zum Gesang/Lobpreis erhobene Stimmen. ❷ /ˈ--/ *n.* Erhebung, *die;* Erbauung, *die;* **spiritual ∼:** geistige Erhebung

**upˈlifting** *adj.* (*fig.*) erhebend

**ˈuplighter** *n.* Deckenfluter, *der*

**ˈupmarket** *adj.* exklusiv ‹Waren, Hotel, Geschäft›; Luxus‹güter, -hotel, -restaurant›; anspruchsvoll ‹Kunde›; gehoben ‹Geschmack›; **an ∼ magazine** eine Zeitschrift für den anspruchsvollen Konsumenten ; **go ∼:** exklusiver [und teurer] werden

**upon** /əˈpɒn/ *prep.* Ⓐ (*indicating direction*) auf (+ *Akk.*); (*indicating position*) auf (+ *Dat.*); Ⓑ ⇒ **on** 1 A, B, G; **a house ∼ the river bank** ein Haus am Flussufer

**upper** /ˈʌpə(r)/ ❶ *compar. adj.* Ⓐ ober... ‹Nil, Themse usw., Atmosphäre›; Ober‹grenze, -lippe, -arm usw., -schlesien, -österreich usw., -kreide, -devon usw.›; (*Mus.*) hoch ‹Tonlage, Noten›; **∼ circle** (*Theatre*) oberer Rang; **the temperatures will be in the ∼ twenties** die Temperaturen werden über fünfundzwanzig Grad liegen; **have/get/gain the ∼ hand [of sb./sth.]** die Oberhand [über jmdn./etw.] haben/erhalten/gewinnen; ⇒ *also* **jaw** 1 A; **lip** A; Ⓑ (*in rank*) ober...; **the ∼ ranks/echelons of the civil service/Army** die oberen *od.* höheren Ränge des Beamtentums/der Armee; **∼ class[es]** Oberschicht, *die;* **∼ middle class** obere Mittelschicht; **the ∼ crust** (*coll.*) die oberen Zehntausend.
❷ *n.* Ⓐ (*of footwear*) Oberteil, *das;* **'leather ∼s'** „Obermaterial Leder"; **be [down] on one's ∼s** (*coll.*) auf dem Trockenen sitzen (*ugs.*); Ⓑ (*sl.: drug*) Aufputschmittel, *das;* Speed, *das* (*Jargon*)

**upper: ∼ case** ❶ *n.* Großbuchstaben; **in ∼ case** in Großbuchstaben; ❷ *adj.* groß ‹Buchstabe›; **U∼ Chamber** *n.* (*Parl.*) Oberhaus, *das;* **∼-class** *adj.* Oberschicht-; **∼-class people/family/accent** Leute/Familie aus der Oberschicht/Akzent der Oberschicht; **be very ∼-class** ‹Person:› ein typischer Vertreter der Oberschicht sein; ‹Akzent, Herkunft:› typisch für die Oberschicht sein; **∼-crust** *adj.* (*coll.*) **∼-crust accent/family** Akzent/Familie der oberen Zehntausend; **be very ∼-crust** ‹Person:› ein typischer Vertreter der oberen Zehntausend sein; **∼cut** *n.* (*Boxing*) Uppercut, *der;* Aufwärtshaken, *der;* **∼ ˈdeck** *n.* (*of ship, bus*) Oberdeck, *das;* **U∼ House** *n.* Oberhaus, *das;* **∼most** ❶ *adj.* oberst...; **∼most aim/desire** höchstes Ziel/größter Wunsch; **the questions that are ∼most on the agenda** die Fragen, die auf der Tagesordnung ganz oben stehen; **be ∼most in sb.'s mind** jmdn. am meisten beschäftigen; ❷ *adv.* ganz oben; obenauf; **face ∼most** mit dem Gesicht nach oben; **come ∼most** (*fig.*) an erster Stelle stehen; **U∼ ˈRhine** *pr. n.* Hochrhein [und Oberrhein]; **∼ ˈsixth** *n.* (*Brit.*) ≈ Oberprima, *die*

**uppish** /ˈʌpɪʃ/ *adj.* (*coll.*) hochnäsig (*ugs.*); **be/get ∼ about sth./with sb.** über etw. (*Akk.*) die Nase rümpfen/jmdn. von oben herab behandeln

**uppishness** /ˈʌpɪʃnɪs/ *n., no pl.* (*coll.*) Hochnäsigkeit, *die* (*ugs.*)

**uppity** /ˈʌpɪtɪ/ *adj.* (*coll.*) hochnäsig (*ugs.*); **get ∼:** sich aufblasen (*ugs.*)

**upright** /ˈʌpraɪt/ ❶ *adj.* Ⓐ aufrecht; steil ‹Schrift›; **a chair with an ∼ back** ein Stuhl mit einem geraden Rücken[teil]; **∼ piano** Klavier, *das;* **∼ freezer** Tiefkühlschrank, *der;* **∼ vacuum cleaner** ≈ Handstaubsauger, *der;* **set/stand/hold sth. ∼:** etw. aufrecht hinstellen/halten; **stand ∼:** aufrecht stehen; **sit ∼:** aufrecht sitzen; **hold oneself ∼:** sich gerade halten; **please make sure that your seat is in the ∼ position** bitte stellen Sie Ihre Rückenlehnen senkrecht; ⇒ *also* **bolt¹** 4; Ⓑ (*fig.: honourable*) aufrecht; **be ∼ in sth.** rechtschaffen in etw. (*Dat.*) sein.
❷ *n.* Ⓐ (*of frame*) seitliche Leiste; (*of ladder*) Holm, *der;* (*of scaffolding etc.*) [aufrechter] Stützpfeiler; (*Footb.*) Pfosten, *der;* Ⓑ (*piano*) Klavier, *das*

**uprightly** /ˈʌpraɪtlɪ/ *adv.* aufrecht; (*fig.*) aufrecht; rechtschaffen

**uprightness** /ˈʌpraɪtnɪs/ *n., no pl.* Ⓐ aufrechte Stellung; (*of plant*) aufrechter Wuchs; Ⓑ (*fig.*) Aufrichtigkeit, *die;* Rechtschaffenheit, *die*

**ˈuprising** *n.* Aufstand, *der*

**up-river** ⇒ **upstream**

**ˈuproar** *n.* Aufruhr, *der;* Tumult, *der;* **be in [an] ∼:** in Aufruhr sein

**uproarious** /ʌpˈrɔːrɪəs/ *adj.* lärmend ‹Menge›; überwältigend ‹Begrüßung, Stimmung›; zum Schreien komisch (*ugs.*) ‹Witz, Anblick, Komödie›; schallend ‹Gelächter›

**uproariously** /ʌpˈrɔːrɪəslɪ/ *adv.* lärmend; schallend ‹lachen›; **be ∼ funny** zum Totlachen sein (*ugs.*)

**upˈroot** *v.t.* [her]ausreißen; ‹Sturm:› entwurzeln; (*fig.: eradicate*) ausmerzen ‹Übel›; **∼ sb.** jmdn. aus der gewohnten Umgebung herausreißen; **people were ∼ed by the war** die Menschen wurden durch den Krieg entwurzelt

**upsadaisy** /ˈʌpsədeɪzɪ/ *int.* hoppla

**upset** ❶ /ʌpˈset/ *v.t.*, **-tt-**, **upset** Ⓐ (*overturn*) umkippen; (*accidentally*) umstoßen ‹Tasse, Vase, Milch usw.›; **∼ sth. over sth.** etw. über etw. (*Akk.*) kippen; Ⓑ (*distress*) erschüttern; mitnehmen (*ugs.*); (*disturb the composure or temper of*) aus der Fassung bringen; (*shock, make angry, excite*) aufregen; **it ∼s the children to hear their parents quarrelling** es belastet die Kinder, wenn sie ihre Eltern streiten hören; **the smallest thing ∼s her** jede Kleinigkeit regt sie auf; **don't let it ∼ you** nimm es nicht so schwer; **∼ oneself** sich aufregen; Ⓒ (*make ill*) **sth. ∼s sb.** etw. bekommt jmdm. nicht; **sth. ∼s sb.'s stomach/digestion** etw. schlägt jmdm. auf den Magen/die Verdauung; Ⓓ (*disorganize*) stören; durcheinander bringen ‹Plan, Berechnung, Arrangement›; (*defeat*) ausschalten; **this incident has seriously ∼ our chances** dieser Vorfall hat unsere Chancen erheblich vermindert.
❷ *v.i.*, **-tt-**, **upset** umkippen.
❸ *adj.* Ⓐ (*overturned*) umgekippt; Ⓑ (*distressed*) bestürzt; (*agitated*) aufgeregt; (*unhappy*) unglücklich; (*put out*) aufgebracht; verärgert; (*offended*) gekränkt; **be ∼ [about sth.]** (*be distressed*) [über etw. (*Akk.*)] bestürzt sein; (*be angry*) sich [über etw. (*Akk.*)] ärgern; **we were very ∼ to hear of his illness** die Nachricht von seiner Krankheit ist uns sehr nahe gegangen *od.* hat uns sehr bestürzt; **when they get back they'll be very/so ∼ to have missed you** wenn sie zurückkommen, wird es ihnen sehr Leid tun, dich verpasst zu haben; **get ∼ [about/over sth.]** sich [über etw. (*Akk.*)] aufregen; **there's no point in getting ∼ about it** es hat keinen Sinn, sich darüber aufzuregen; Ⓒ /ˈ--/ (*disordered*) **an ∼ stomach** ein verdorbener Magen; **have an ∼ stomach** sich (*Dat.*) den Magen verdorben haben; Ⓓ (*disorganized*) gestört ‹Routine, Mechanismus, System›; durcheinander gebracht ‹Plan, Berechnung, Mechanismus, System›.
❹ /ˈʌpset/ *n.* Ⓐ (*overturning*) Umkippen, *das;* Ⓑ (*agitation*) Aufregung, *die;* (*shock*) Schock, *der;* (*annoyance*) Verärgerung, *die;* **sth. is a great ∼ for** *or* **to sb.** etw. nimmt jmdn. sehr mit (*ugs.*) *od.* geht jmdm. sehr nahe; **emotional ∼:** seelischer Schock; **have an ∼:** einiges durchmachen [müssen]; Ⓒ (*slight quarrel*) Missstimmung, *die;* Ⓓ (*slight illness*) Unpässlichkeit, *die;* **digestive/stomach ∼:** Verdauungsstörung, *die*/Magenverstimmung, *die;* Ⓔ (*disturbance*) Zwischenfall, *der;* (*confusion, upheaval*) Aufruhr, *der;* Durcheinander, *das;* **an ∼ in his plans/calculations/routine** eine Störung seiner Pläne/Berechnungen/Routine; Ⓕ (*surprising result*) Überraschung, *die;* **a by-election ∼:** eine Überraschung bei der Nachwahl

**upˈsetting** *adj.* erschütternd; (*sad*) traurig; bestürzend; schlimm ‹Zeit›; (*annoying*) ärgerlich; **being mugged/sacked was a very ∼ experience for her** ausgeraubt/entlassen zu werden war ein Erlebnis, das sie ganz schön mitgenommen hat (*ugs.*); **my mother found the obscene language ∼:** meine Mutter fand die obszöne Sprache anstößig; **she missed her train, and what was even more ∼, she was late for the opera** sie verpasste ihren Zug, aber noch ärgerlicher für sie war es, dass sie dadurch zu spät in die Oper kam; **it was/I found it ∼ that X was promoted instead of me** ich ärgerte mich, dass X an meiner Stelle befördert wurde; **the constant changes have been rather ∼ for the children** die laufenden Veränderungen haben die Kinder ziemlich aus dem Gleis gebracht; **these pictures are ∼ to a child** diese Bilder sind für ein Kind [zu] erschütternd

**ˈupshot** *n.* Ergebnis, *das;* **what will be the ∼ of it [all]?** was wird bei der [ganzen] Sache herauskommen? (*ugs.*); **he hummed and hawed a bit and, well, the ∼ of the matter/of it [all] was that ...:** er druckste ein bisschen herum, aber schließlich [und

U

endlich] kam heraus *od.* stellte sich heraus, dass ...; **in the ~:** letztendlich

**upside 'down** ❶ *adv.* verkehrt herum; **turn sth. ~** (*lit. or fig.*) etw. auf den Kopf stellen; **the plane flew ~:** das Flugzeug flog auf dem Kopf (*ugs.*). ❷ *adj.* auf dem Kopf stehend ‹Bild›; **be ~:** auf dem Kopf stehen; **the car came to rest ~:** der Wagen blieb auf dem Dach liegen; **the acrobat hung ~:** der Akrobat hing mit dem Kopf nach unten *od.* kopfüber; (*fig.*) **the whole world seems to be ~:** die ganze Welt scheint Kopfzustehen; **an upside-down world/view of the situation/logic** eine verkehrte Welt/Sicht der Dinge/Logik

**up'stage** ❶ *adv.* (*Theatre*) im Hintergrund [der Bühne]; **move ~:** sich zum Hintergrund der Bühne bewegen. ❷ *adj.* (*Theatre*) **an ~ door/entrance** eine Hintertür/ein Hintereingang zur Bühne. ❸ *v.t.* (*Theatre*) **~ sb.** jmdn. zwingen, sich vom Publikum abzuwenden; (*fig.*) jmdm. die Schau stehlen (*ugs.*)

**upstairs** ❶ /-'-/ *adv.* nach oben ‹gehen, kommen›; oben ‹sein, wohnen›; ⇨ *also* **kick** 3 A. ❷ /'--/ *adj.* im Obergeschoss *nachgestellt.* ❸ /-'-/ *n.* Obergeschoss, *das*

**up'standing** *adj.* **A** (*strong and healthy*) stattlich; **fine ~ children** nette, gesunde und kräftige Kinder; **B** (*honest*) aufrichtig; aufrecht; **C** **be ~** (*stand up*) sich erheben

**'upstart** ❶ *n.* Emporkömmling, *der.* ❷ *adj.* **an ~ landowner** ein emporgekommener Grundbesitzer; **~ ideas/pretensions** Ideen/Angeberei eines Emporkömmlings/von Emporkömmlingen

**'upstate** (*Amer.*) ❶ *adj.* **~ New York** nördlicher Teil des Staates New York; **an ~ town** eine Stadt im nördlichen Teil des Staates. ❷ *adv.* **live ~:** im nördlichen Teil des Staates leben; **go/travel ~:** in den nördlichen Teil des Staates fahren/reisen

**upstream** ▶ 1480 ❶ /-'-/ *adv.* flussaufwärts. ❷ /'--/ *adj.* flussaufwärts gelegen ‹Ort›

**'up-stroke** *n.* **A** (*in writing*) Aufstrich, *der;* **B** (*Mech.: of piston*) Aufwärtshub, *der*

**'upsurge** *n.* Aufwallen, *das* (*geh.*); **she felt an ~ of tenderness** sie fühlte Zärtlichkeit in sich (*Dat.*) aufwallen

**'upswept** *adj.* hochgekämmt ‹Haar›; hochgezogen ‹Linie, Auspuffrohr›

**'upswing** *n.* (*of pendulum, arms*) Aufwärtsschwung, *der;* (*fig., esp. Commerc.*) Aufschwung, *der*

**upsy-daisy** /'ʌpsɪdeɪzɪ/ *int.* hoppla

**'uptake** *n.* **be quick/slow on** *or* **in the ~** (*coll.*) schnell begreifen/schwer von Begriff sein (*ugs.*)

**uptight** /ʌp'taɪt, 'ʌptaɪt/ *adj.* (*coll.*) **A** (*tense*) nervös (**about** wegen); (*touchy, angry*) sauer (*ugs.*) (**about** wegen); **make sb. ~:** jmdm. auf die Nerven gehen *od.* fallen (*ugs.*); **B** (*Amer.: rigidly conventional*) **[very] ~:** stockkonservativ (*ugs.*)

**'uptime** *n.* (*Computing*) Betriebszeit, *die*

**up to 'date** *pred. adj.* **be/keep [very] ~:** auf dem [aller]neusten Stand sein/bleiben; [ganz] up to date sein/bleiben; **keep/bring sth. ~:** etw. auf dem neusten Stand halten/auf den neusten Stand bringen; **bring sb. ~ with all the news** jmdn. auf den neusten Stand der Informationen bringen

**up-to-'date** *attrib. adj.* (*current*) aktuell; (*modern*) modern; aktuell ‹Mode›

**up-to-the-'minute** *adj.* hochaktuell

**'upturn** *n.* Aufschwung, *der* (**in** *Gen.*); **an ~ in prices** ein Anstieg der Preise

**'upturned** *adj.* **A** (*upside-down*) umgedreht; **B** (*turned upwards*) hochgeschlagen ‹Rand, Krempe›; nach oben gerichtet ‹Gesicht, Auge›; **~ nose** Stupsnase, *die*

**upward** /'ʌpwəd/ ❶ *adj.* nach oben *nachgestellt;* nach oben gerichtet; **~ movement/trend** (*lit. or fig.*) Aufwärtsbewegung, *die*/-trend, *der;* **~ gradient** *or* **slope** Steigung, *die;* **move in an ~ direction** sich aufwärts *od.* nach oben bewegen; **~ mobility** (*in social status*) sozialer Aufstieg. ❷ *adv.* aufwärts ‹sich bewegen›; nach oben ‹sehen, gehen›; ⇨ *also* **face up[ward]**

**upwardly** /'ʌpwədlɪ/ *adv.* aufwärts; nach oben; ⇨ *also* **mobile** 1 E

**upwards** /'ʌpwədz/ *adv.* **A** ⇨ **upward** 2; **B** **~ of** mehr als; über; **they cost £200 and ~:** sie kosten 200 Pfund und darüber

**upwind** ❶ *adv.* /ʌp'wɪnd/ gegen den Wind. ❷ /'ʌpwɪnd/ *adj.* **approach from the ~ side** sich mit dem Wind im Rücken nähern

**Urals** /'jʊərlz/ *pr. n. pl.* Ural, *der*

**uranium** /jʊə'reɪnɪəm/ *n.* (*Chem.*) Uran, *das*

**Uranus** /'jʊərənəs, jʊə'reɪnəs/ *pr. n.* (*Astron.*) Uranus, *der*

**urban** /'ɜ:bn/ *adj.* städtisch; Stadt‹gebiet, -bevölkerung, -planung, -sanierung, -guerilla›; **~ life** Leben in der Stadt; **~ sociology** Stadtsoziologie, *die;* **~ decay** Verslumung, *die;* **~ district** (*Brit. Hist.*) *Stadtgebiet bzw. -gebiete unter der Verwaltung eines gewählten Rates;* **~ sprawl** unkontrollierte Ausdehnung städtischer Randgebiete; ⇨ *also* **renewal** B

**urbane** /ɜ:'beɪn/ *adj.*, **urbanely** /ɜ:'beɪnlɪ/ *adv.* weltmännisch

**urbanise** ⇨ **urbanize**

**urbanity** /ɜ:'bænɪtɪ/ *n.* Urbanität, *die;* **urbanities** weltmännische Umgangsform[en]

**urbanize** /'ɜ:bənaɪz/ *v.t.* urbanisieren ‹Land›; verstädtern [lassen] ‹Landbevölkerung›; **become ~d** verstädtern

**urchin** /'ɜ:tʃɪn/ *n.* **A** (*child*) Range, *die;* (*boy*) Strolch, *der;* ⇨ *also* **street urchin**; **B** ⇨ **sea urchin**

**Urdu** /'ʊədu:, 'ɜ:du:/ ▶ 1275 ❶ *adj.* Urdu-; ⇨ *also* **English** 1. ❷ *n.* Urdu, *das;* ⇨ *also* **English** 2 A

**urea** /jʊə'rɪə, 'jʊərɪə/ *n.* (*Chem.*) Harnstoff, *der*

**ureter** /jʊə'ri:tə/ *n.* (*Anat.*) Harnleiter, *der;* Ureter, *der* (*fachspr.*)

**urethra** /jʊə'ri:θrə/ *n., pl.* **~e** /jʊə'ri:θri:/ *or* **~s** (*Anat.*) Harnröhre, *die;* Urethra, *die* (*fachspr.*)

**urge** /ɜ:dʒ/ ❶ *v.t.* **A** **~ sb. to do sth.** jmdn. drängen, etw. zu tun; **~ sb. to sth.** jmdn. zu etw. drängen; **we ~d him to reconsider** wir rieten ihm dringend, es sich (*Dat.*) noch einmal zu überlegen; **~ sth. [on** *or* **upon sb.]** [jmdn.] zu etw. drängen; **~ caution/vigilance/patience [on** *or* **upon sb.]** [jmdn.] zur Vorsicht/Wachsamkeit/Geduld mahnen; **~ on** *or* **upon sb. the need for sth./for doing sth.** jmdm. die Notwendigkeit einer Sache/die Notwendigkeit, etw. zu tun, ans Herz legen; **the leaders ~ acceptance of the offer** die Führer dringen auf Annahme des Angebotes; **~ that sth. [should] be done** darauf dringen, dass etw. getan wird; **B** (*drive on*) [an]treiben; **~ forward/onward** vorwärts treiben; (*fig.*) treiben; **C** (*put forward*) vorbringen; **~ sb.'s youth/inexperience/the difficulty of sth.** jmds. Jugend/Unerfahrenheit/die Schwierigkeit einer Sache zu bedenken geben; **~ sth. on sb.** jmdm. etw. eindringlich nahe legen. ❷ *n.* Trieb, *der;* **have/feel an/the ~ to do sth.** den Drang verspüren, etw. zu tun; **resist the ~ to do sth.** dem [inneren] Drang widerstehen, etw. zu tun

**~ 'on** *v.t.* antreiben; (*hasten*) vorantreiben; (*encourage*) anfeuern; **~d on by hunger/ambition** vom Hunger/Ehrgeiz getrieben

**urgency** /'ɜ:dʒənsɪ/ *n., no pl.* Dringlichkeit, *die;* (*earnestness*) Eindringlichkeit, *die;* **there is no ~:** es eilt nicht *od.* ist nicht dringend; **be of the utmost ~:** äußerst dringend sein; **a matter of great ~:** eine sehr dringende Angelegenheit

**urgent** /'ɜ:dʒənt/ *adj.* **A** (*pressing*) dringend; (*to be dealt with immediately*) eilig; **be in ~ need of sth.** etw. dringend brauchen; **give ~ consideration to sth.** etw. vordringlich in Betracht ziehen; **matters/problems of an ~ nature** dringende Angelegenheiten/drängende Probleme; **on ~ business** in dringenden Geschäften; **at sb.'s ~ request** auf jmds. Drängen; **it is ~:** es eilt; **it is ~ that sb. should do sth.** *or* **does sth.** jmd. muss dringend etw. tun; **if it's ~, call a doctor** in dringenden Fällen den Arzt rufen; **B** (*earnest and persistent*) eindringlich; **be ~ in one's demand/plea for sth.** etw. dringend fordern/eindringlich um etw. bitten

**urgently** /'ɜ:dʒəntlɪ/ *adv.* **A** (*pressingly*) dringend; (*without delay*) eilig; **he had to leave ~ for London on business** er musste in dringenden Geschäften nach London abreisen; **B** (*earnestly*) eindringlich

**uric** /'jʊərɪk/ *adj.* **~ acid** (*Chem.*) Harnsäure, *die*

**urinal** /jʊə'raɪnl, 'jʊərɪnl/ *n.* (*fitting*) Urinal, *das;* **[public] ~:** [öffentliche] Herrentoilette; Pissoir, *das*

**urinary** /'jʊərɪnərɪ/ *adj.* Harn-; **~ diseases** Erkrankungen der Harnwege

**urinate** /'jʊərɪneɪt/ *v.i.* urinieren

**urination** /jʊərɪ'neɪʃn/ *n.* Urinieren, *das*

**urine** /'jʊərɪn/ *n.* Urin, *der;* Harn, *der; attrib.* Urin-; Harn-

**URL** *abbr.* (*Computing*) **uniform resource locator** URL, *der*

**urn** /ɜ:n/ *n.* **A** **tea/coffee ~:** Tee-/Kaffeemaschine, *die;* **B** (*vessel*) Urne, *die*

**urogenital** /jʊərə'dʒenɪtl/ *adj.* (*Anat., Med.*) urogenital; **~ disease/infection** Erkrankung/Infektion des Urogenitaltraktes

**urologist** /jʊər'ɒlədʒɪst/ *n.* ▶ 1261 Urologe, *der*/Urologin, *die*

**urology** /jʊə'rɒlədʒɪ/ *n.* Urologie, *die*

**Ursa** /'ɜ:sə/ *pr. n.* (*Astron.*) **~ Major/Minor** Großer/Kleiner Bär

**Uruguay** /'jʊərəgwaɪ/ *pr. n.* Uruguay (*das*)

**Uruguayan** /jʊərə'gwaɪən/ ▶ 1340 ❶ *adj.* uruguayisch; **sb. is ~:** jmd. ist Uruguayer/Uruguayerin. ❷ *n.* Uruguayer, *der*/Uruguayerin, *die*

**us** /əs, *stressed* ʌs/ *pron.* **A** uns; **it's us** wir sind's (*ugs.*); **one of us** einer von uns; **B** (*coll.: me*) **give us a clue/kiss!** gib mir 'nen Tipp/Kuss! (*ugs.*)

**u/s** *abbr.* **unserviceable** unbrauchbar

**US** *abbr.* **United States** USA; *attrib.* US-

**USA** *abbr.* **United States of America** USA; *attrib.* der USA *nachgestellt*

**usable** /'ju:zəbl/ *adj.* brauchbar; gebräuchlich ‹Wort›; **this nail is no longer ~:** dieser Nagel ist nicht mehr zu gebrauchen

**USAF** *abbr.* **United States Air Force** Luftwaffe der Vereinigten Staaten

**usage** /'ju:zɪdʒ, 'ju:sɪdʒ/ *n.* **A** Brauch, *der;* Gepflogenheit, *die* (*geh.*); **~s and customs** Sitten und Gebräuche; **commercial ~:** Handelsbrauch, *der;* **sanctified by ~:** durch Herkommen Recht geworden; **a custom sanctified by ~:** eine Sitte, die zum Gewohnheitsrecht geworden ist; **be in common ~:** allgemein gebräuchlich sein; **B** (*Ling.: use of language*) Sprachgebrauch, *der;* **~ [of a word]** Verwendung [eines Wortes]; **in American** *etc.* **~:** im amerikanischen *usw.* Sprachgebrauch; **in common ~:** im allgemeinen Sprachgebrauch; allgemein gebräuchlich ‹Wort usw.›; **C** (*treatment*) Behandlung, *die;* **have rough ~:** schlecht behandelt werden

**usance** /'ju:zəns/ *n.* (*Commerc.*) Zahlungsfrist für ausländische Wechsel

**use** ❶ [ju:s] *n.* **A** Gebrauch, *der;* (*of dictionary, calculator, room*) Benutzung, *die;* (*of word, expression; of pesticide, garlic*) Verwendung, *die;* (*of name, title*) Führung, *die;* (*of alcohol, drugs*) Konsum, *der;* **the ~ of brutal means/methods/of trickery** die Anwendung brutaler Mittel/Methoden/von Tricks; **the ~ of troops/tear gas/arms/violence** der Einsatz von Truppen/Tränengas/der Waffengebrauch/die Gewaltanwendung; **achieve sth. by the ~ of deception** etw. durch Täuschung erreichen; **constant/rough ~:** dauernder Gebrauch/schlechte Behandlung; **[not] be in ~:** [nicht] in Gebrauch sein; **be no longer in ~:** nicht mehr verwendet werden; **be in daily** *etc.* **~:** täglich *usw.* in Gebrauch *od.* Benutzung sein; **the word is [not] in everyday ~:** das Wort ist [nicht] allgemein gebräuchlich; **bring into ~:** in Gebrauch nehmen; **come into ~:** in Gebrauch kommen; **[be] out of ~:** außer Betrieb [sein]; **go/fall/pass/drop out of ~:** außer Gebrauch kommen; **instructions/directions for ~:** Gebrauchsanweisung,

u

*die;* **ready for [immediate] ~:** [sofort] gebrauchsfertig; **instruments for ~ by doctors/dentists** Instrumente für den ärztlichen/zahnärztlichen Bedarf; **batteries for ~ in** *or* **with watches** Batterien [speziell] für Armbanduhren; **a course for ~ in schools** ein Kurs für die Schule *od.* zur Verwendung im Schulunterricht; **for the ~ of sb.** für jmdn.; **for personal/private ~:** für den persönlichen Gebrauch/den Privatgebrauch; **these computers are intended for home/office ~:** diese Computer sind Homecomputer/sind für den Einsatz im Büro gedacht; **for external ~ only** nur zur äußerlichen Anwendung; **for ~ in an emergency/only in case of fire** für den Notfall/nur bei Feuer zu benutzen; **with ~:** durch den Gebrauch; **with constant ~:** durch dauernden Gebrauch; **with careful** *etc.* **~:** bei sorgsamer *usw.* Behandlung; **make ~ of sb./sth.** jmdn./etw. gebrauchen/(*exploit*) ausnutzen; **a good cook will make ~ of any leftovers** ein guter Koch/eine gute Köchin verwendet alle Reste; **make ~ of one's connections/friendship with sb.** von seinen Verbindungen/seiner Freundschaft zu jmdm. Gebrauch machen; **make the best ~ of sth./it** das Beste aus etw./daraus machen; **make good ~ of, turn** *or* **put to good ~:** gut nutzen ‹Zeit, Talent, Geld›; **put sth. to ~:** etw. verwenden; **put sth. to effective ~:** etw. wirkungsvoll einsetzen; **B** (*utility, usefulness*) Nutzen, *der;* **these tools/clothes will be of ~ to sb.** dieses Werkzeug wird/diese Kleider werden für jmdn. von Nutzen sein; **is it of [any] ~?** ist das [irgendwie] zu gebrauchen *od.* von Nutzen?; **these addresses might be of ~ to you** diese Adressen könnten für dich von Nutzen sein *od.* kannst du vielleicht gebrauchen; **be of ~ to the enemy/police** für den Feind/die Polizei von Nutzen sein; **can I be of any ~ to you?** kann ich dir irgendwie helfen?; **it is of [great] ~ for this work** man kann es für diese Arbeit [sehr gut] brauchen; **I did not find the book of any practical ~:** das Buch hatte für mich keinen praktischen Nutzen; **be [of] no ~ [to sb.]** [jmdm.] nichts nützen; **I wouldn't be [of] any ~ to you** ich könnte dir kein bisschen helfen; **he is [of] no ~ in a crisis/as a manager** er ist in einer Krise/als Manager zu nichts nütze *od.* (*ugs.*) nicht zu gebrauchen; **it's no ~ [doing that]** es hat keinen Zweck *od.* Sinn[, das zu tun]; **it wouldn't be any ~:** es hätte [überhaupt] keinen Sinn *od.* Zweck; **I have an umbrella at home. — That's no/not much ~ [to us] now** Ich habe einen Schirm zu Hause. — Das nützt [uns] jetzt nichts/nicht viel; **you're/that's a fat lot of ~** (*coll. iron.*) du bist ja eine schöne Hilfe/davon haben wir aber was (*ugs. iron.*); **what's the ~ of that/of doing that?** was nützt das/was nützt es, das zu tun?; **what's the ~?** was nützt es?; **oh well, what's the ~!** ach, was soll's schon! (*ugs.*); **C** (*purpose*) Verwendung, *die;* Verwendungszweck, *der;* **a tool with many ~s** ein vielfältig zu verwendendes Werkzeug; **have its/one's ~s** seinen Nutzen haben; **have/find a ~ for sth./sb.** für etw./jmdn. Verwendung haben/finden; **have no/not much ~ for sth./sb.** etw./jmdn. nicht/kaum brauchen; (*fig.: dislike*) nichts/nicht viel für etw./jmdn. übrig haben; **have no further ~ for sb./sth.** für jmdn. keine Verwendung mehr haben/etw. nicht mehr brauchen; **put sth. to a good/a new ~:** etw. sinnvoll/auf neu[artig]e Weise verwenden; **D** (*right or power of using*) **have the ~ of sth.** etw. benutzen können; **[have the] ~ of kitchen and bathroom** Küchen- und Badbenutzung [haben]; **can I have the ~ of your car while you are away?** kann ich deinen Wagen benutzen, während du weg bist?; **let sb. have** *or* **allow sb.** *or* **give sb. the ~ of sth.** jmdn. etw. benutzen lassen; **he has [the] full/only restricted ~ of his arm** er kann seinen Arm uneingeschränkt/nur eingeschränkt benutzen; **he has lost the ~ of an arm/eye** er kann einen Arm nicht mehr benutzen/er kann auf einem Auge nichts mehr sehen; **E** (*custom, familiarity*) **~s and customs** Sitten und Gebräuche; **long ~ has reconciled me to it** die Gewohnheit hat mich damit versöhnt; **F** (*Eccl.: ritual*) Ritual, *das;* **G** (*Law*) Nießbrauch, *der.*

**2** [ju:z] *v.t.* **A** benutzen; nutzen ‹Gelegenheit›; anwenden ‹Gewalt›; einsetzen ‹Tränengas, Wasserwerfer›; in Anspruch nehmen ‹Firma, Agentur, Agenten, Dienstleistung›; nutzen ‹Zeit, Gelegenheit, Talent, Erfahrung›; führen ‹Namen, Titel›; **do you know how to ~ this tool?** kannst du mit diesem Werkzeug umgehen?; **the swindler/actor ~s the name John Smith** der Betrüger/Schauspieler nennt sich John Smith; **anything you say may be ~d in evidence** was Sie sagen, kann vor Gericht verwendet werden; **~ sb.'s name [as a reference]** sich [als Empfehlung] auf jmdn. berufen; **I could ~ the money/a drink/the door could ~ a coat of paint** (*coll.*) ich könnte das Geld brauchen/einen Drink vertragen (*ugs.*)/die Tür könnte einen Anstrich brauchen *od.* (*ugs.*) vertragen; **~ one's money [to do sth.]** sein Geld verwenden[, um etw. zu tun]; **the money is there to be ~d** das Geld ist da, um ausgegeben zu werden; **~ one's time to do sth.** seine Zeit dazu nutzen, etw. zu tun; **B** (*consume as material*) verwenden; **~ gas/oil for heating** mit Gas/Öl heizen; **the camera ~s 35 mm film** für die Kamera braucht man einen 35-mm-Film; **'~ sparingly'** „sparsam verwenden"; **C** (*finish consuming*) verbrauchen; **she has ~d the last of the milk** sie hat den letzten Rest Milch aufgebraucht; **D** (*take habitually*) **~ drugs/heroin** *etc.* Drogen/Heroin *usw.* nehmen; **~ alcohol** Alkohol trinken *od.* konsumieren; **E** (*employ in speaking or writing*) benutzen; gebrauchen; verwenden; **~ strong language** Kraftausdrücke gebrauchen; **F** (*exercise, apply*) Gebrauch machen von ‹Autorität, Einfluss, Können, Urteilsvermögen, Menschenverstand›; **~ diplomacy/tact [in one's dealings** *etc.* **with sb.]** [bei jmdm.] diplomatisch vorgehen/[zu jmdm.] taktvoll sein; **~ care** vorsichtig sein; **~ care in doing sth.** etw. vorsichtig tun; **he ~d all his strength** er wandte seine ganze Kraft auf; **~ a method/system/tactics** eine Methode anwenden/nach einem [bestimmten] System/einer [bestimmten] Taktik vorgehen; **~ other/stronger methods/tactics** andere/härtere Methoden/eine andere/härtere Taktik anwenden; **~ every means at one's disposal to do sth.** mit allen einem zur Verfügung stehenden Mitteln versuchen, etw. zu tun; **G** (*take advantage of*) **~ sb.** jmdn. ausnutzen; **don't let them ~ you** lass dich nicht [von ihnen] ausnutzen; **H** (*treat*) behandeln; **~ sb./sth. well/badly** jmdn./etw. gut/schlecht behandeln; **I ~d to** /'ju:st tə/ (*formerly*) **I ~d to live in London/work in a factory** früher habe ich in London gelebt/in einer Fabrik gearbeitet; **he ~d to be very shy** er war früher sehr schüchtern; **before I started taking these vitamins, I ~d to be tired all the time** bevor ich anfing, diese Vitamine zu nehmen, war ich immer müde; **my mother always ~d to say ...:** meine Mutter hat immer gesagt *od.* pflegte zu sagen ...; **life ~d to be much more leisurely [than it is now]** früher war das Leben viel beschaulicher [als heute]; **this ~d to be my room** das war [früher] mein Zimmer; **it ~d to be thought ...:** früher glaubte man ...; **things aren't what they ~d to be** es ist nichts mehr so wie früher; **he smokes much more than he ~d to** er raucht viel mehr als früher; **there ~d to be ...:** es gab früher/früher gab es ...; **I ~d not** *or* **I did not ~ to** *or* (*coll.*) **I didn't ~** *or* (*coll.*) **I ~[d]n't to smoke** früher habe ich nicht geraucht; **didn't he ~ to work here?** (*coll.*) hat er nicht früher hier gearbeitet?; **~[d]n't there to be a shop here?** (*dated coll.*) war hier nicht früher ein Laden?; **Does he smoke? He ~d not to** *or* (*coll.*) **He didn't ~ to** Raucht er? Früher hat er das nicht getan; **there never ~d to be all this violence** diese ganze Gewalttätigkeit gab es früher nicht

**~ 'up** *v.t.* aufbrauchen; verwenden ‹[Essens]reste›; verbrauchen, erschöpfen ‹Kraft, Geld, Energie›; **~ up a dozen eggs** ein Dutzend Eier verbrauchen

**'use-by date** *n.* (*esp. Brit.*) [Mindest]haltbarkeitsdatum, *das*

**used** **1** *adj.* **A** [ju:zd] (*no longer new*) gebraucht; benutzt ‹Handtuch, Teller›; gestempelt ‹Briefmarke›; **~ car** Gebrauchtwagen, *der;* **~-car salesman** Gebrauchtwagenhändler, *der;* **B** [ju:st] (*accustomed*) **~ to sth.** [an] etw. (*Akk.*) gewöhnt; etw. gewohnt; **be/get ~ to sb./sth.** [an] jmdn./etw. gewöhnt sein/sich an jmdn./etw. gewöhnen; **I'm not ~ to this kind of treatment** *or* **to being treated in this way** ich bin eine solche Behandlung nicht gewohnt; ich bin es nicht gewohnt, so behandelt zu werden; **you'll soon be ~ to it** du wirst dich bald *od.* schnell daran gewöhnen; **[not] be ~ to sb. doing sth./to having sb. do sth.** [es] [nicht] gewohnt sein, dass jmd. etw. tut; **she was ~ to getting up early** sie war daran gewöhnt, früh aufzustehen; **she is not ~ to drinking alcohol** sie ist es nicht gewöhnt, Alkohol zu trinken.

**2** [ju:st] ⇒ **use** 2 I

**useful** /'ju:sfl/ *adj.* **A** nützlich; praktisch ‹Werkzeug, Gerät, Auto›; brauchbar ‹Rat, Idee, Wörterbuch›; hilfreich ‹Gespräch, Rat, Idee, Wörterbuch›; **~ life** (*of machine etc.*) Lebensdauer, *die;* **~ load** Nutzlast, *die;* **he is a ~ person to know** es ist nützlich, ihn zu kennen; **English is the most ~ language** mit Englisch kommt man am weitesten; **this is ~ to know** das ist gut zu wissen; **this would be ~ to have** es wäre gut *od.* nützlich, wenn man das hätte; **be ~ to sb.** jmdm. *od.* für jmdn. nützlich sein; jmdm. nützen; **the guide was most ~ for finding our way about** der Führer hat uns sehr geholfen, uns zurechtzufinden; **the chest would be very ~ for storing my books** die Truhe würde sich sehr gut zum Lagern meiner Bücher eignen; **it would be ~ to have a tap in the garden** es wäre praktisch, wenn im Garten ein Wasserhahn wäre; **sb. finds sth. ~:** etw. nützt jmdm.; **those screws will come in ~ for my woodwork** diese Schrauben werde ich noch gut zum Schreinern brauchen können; **make oneself ~:** sich nützlich machen; **serve no ~ purpose** zu nichts nütze sein; **B** (*coll.: worthwhile*) ordentlich (*ugs.*); ansehnlich ‹Betrag, Stück, Arbeit›; beachtlich ‹Vorsprung›; wertvoll ‹Mitglied einer Mannschaft›

**usefully** /'ju:sfəlɪ/ *adv.* **a course one might ~ follow** ein Kurs, den zu verfolgen nützlich sein könnte; **a book you could ~ read** ein Buch, von dessen Lektüre du profitieren könntest; **is there anything we can ~ do?** können wir uns irgendwie nützlich machen?; **~ spend an evening doing sth.** einen Abend sinnvoll damit verbringen, etw. zu tun; **everybody should be ~ employed [in some work]** jeder sollte eine nützliche Beschäftigung haben

**usefulness** /'ju:sflnɪs/ *n.*, *no pl.* Nützlichkeit, *die;* Brauchbarkeit, *die;* **limit the ~ of sth.** den Nutzen einer Sache einschränken; **have outlived one's/its ~:** zu nichts mehr nütze *od.* zu gebrauchen sein

**useless** /'ju:slɪs/ *adj.* unbrauchbar ‹Werkzeug, Gerät, Rat, Vorschlag, Idee, Material›; nutzlos ‹Wissen, Information, Fakten, Protest, Anstrengung, Kampf›; vergeblich ‹Anstrengung, Maßnahme, Kampf, Klage›; zwecklos ‹Widerstand, Protest, Argumentieren›; **be ~ to sb.** jmdm. nichts nützen; **credit cards are ~ there** Kreditkarten nützen einem dort nichts; **be ~ at sth.** zu etw. nicht zu gebrauchen sein; **oh, you're ~!** du bist doch zu nichts zu gebrauchen! (*ugs.*); **feel ~:** sich nutzlos fühlen; **it's ~ to do that** *or* **doing that** es hat keinen Zweck *od.* Sinn, das zu tun; **he's worse than ~:** er ist zu gar nichts nütze

**uselessly** /'ju:slɪslɪ/ *adv.* unnütz, sinnlos ‹verschwenden, aufwenden›; vergeblich ‹kämpfen, protestieren›; **throw away one's life ~:** sein Leben sinnlos wegwerfen

**uselessness** /'ju:slɪsnɪs/ *n.*, *no pl.* (*of tool, device, advice, information, suggestion, material*) Unbrauchbarkeit, *die;* (*of protest, effort,*

U

*struggle*) Vergeblichkeit, *die;* (*of action, measure, war*) Sinnlosigkeit, *die;* (*of resistance*) Zwecklosigkeit, *die*

**user** /'ju:zə(r)/ *n.* Benutzer, *der*/Benutzerin, *die;* (*of drugs, alcohol*) Konsument, *der*/Konsumentin, *die;* (*of coal, electricity, gas*) Verbraucher, *der*/Verbraucherin, *die;* (*of telephone*) Kunde, *der*/Kundin, *die*

**user: ~-friendly** *adj.* benutzerfreundlich; **explain sth. in ~-friendly terms** etw. allgemein verständlich erklären; **~ group** *n.* Benutzergruppe, *die;* **~ interface** *n.* (*Computing*) Benutzerschnittstelle, *die;* **~ name** *n.* (*Computing*) Benutzername, *der*

**usher** /'ʌʃə(r)/ ❶ *n.* ▶ **1261** (*in court*) Gerichtsdiener, *der;* (*at cinema, theatre, church*) Platzanweiser, *der*/-anweiserin, *die.* ❷ *v.t.* führen; geleiten (*geh.*); **~ sb. into sb.'s presence** jmdn. vor jmdn. führen *od.* (*geh.*) geleiten; **~ sb. to his seat** jmdn. an seinen Platz führen

**~ 'in** *v.t.* **~ sb. in** jmdn. hineinführen *od.* (*geh.*) -geleiten; **~ sth. in** (*fig.*) etw. einläuten

**~ 'out** *v.t.* hinausführen *od.* (*geh.*) -geleiten

**usherette** /ʌʃə'ret/ *n.* ▶ **1261** Platzanweiserin, *die*

**USN** *abbr.* **United States Navy** Marine der Vereinigten Staaten

**USS** *abbr.* **United States Ship** *Schiff aus den Vereinigten Staaten*

**USSR** *abbr.* (*Hist.*) **Union of Soviet Socialist Republics** UdSSR, *die; attrib.* der UdSSR *nachgestellt*

**usual** /'ju:ʒʊəl/ *adj.* üblich; **be ~ for sb.** bei jmdm. üblich sein; **it is ~ for sb. to do sth.** es ist üblich, dass jmd. etw. tut; **[no] better/bigger/more** *etc.* **than ~:** [nicht] besser/größer/mehr *usw.* als gewöhnlich *od.* üblich; **as [is] ~, (*coll.*) as per ~:** wie üblich; **as is ~ in such cases** wie in solchen Fällen üblich; **the/your ~, sir?** wie immer, der Herr? (*ugs.*); ⇒ *also* **business** B

**usually** /'ju:ʒʊəlɪ/ *adv.* gewöhnlich; normalerweise; **more than ~ tired** *etc.* noch müder *usw.* als üblich; ganz ungewöhnlich müde *usw.;* **this time we were more than ~ careful** diesmal waren wir noch vorsichtiger als sonst

**usufruct** /'ju:zjʊfrʌkt/ *n.* (*Law*) Nutznießung, *die*

**usurer** /'ju:ʒərə(r)/ *n.* Wucherer, *der*/Wucherin, *die*

**usurp** /ju:'zɜ:p/ *v.t.* sich (*Dat.*) widerrechtlich aneignen ‹Titel, Recht, Position›; usurpieren (*geh.*) ‹Macht, Thron›; **~ the leading role in the enterprise** die wichtigste Rolle im Unternehmen an sich (*Akk.*) reißen; **the man who had ~d his place in his wife's affections** der Mann, der jetzt im Herzen seiner Frau seinen Platz erobert hatte

**usurpation** /ju:zə'peɪʃn/ *n.* (*of right, title, position, authority*) widerrechtliche Aneignung; (*of power, the throne*) Usurpation, *die* (*geh.*)

**usurper** /ju:'zɜ:pə(r)/ *n.* Usurpator, *der* (*geh.*)

**usury** /'ju:ʒərɪ/ *n.* Wucher, *der;* **practise ~:** Wucher treiben

**utensil** /ju:'tensɪl/ *n.* Utensil, *das;* **writing ~s** Schreibutensilien

**uterine** /'ju:tərаɪn, 'ju:tərɪn/ *adj.* (*Anat., Med.*) Gebärmutter-; uterin (*fachspr.*)

**uterus** /'ju:tərəs/ *n., pl.* **uteri** /'ju:təraɪ/ (*Anat.*) Gebärmutter, *die;* Uterus, *der* (*fachspr.*)

**utilisable, utilisation, utilise** ⇒ **utiliz-**

**utilitarian** /ju:tɪlɪ'teərɪən/ ❶ *adj.* Ⓐ (*functional*) funktionell; utilitär ‹Ziele›; Ⓑ (*Philos.*) utilitaristisch. ❷ *n.* (*Philos.*) Utilitarist, *der;* Utilitarier, *der*

**utilitarianism** /ju:tɪlɪ'teərɪənɪzm/ *n.* (*Philos.*) Utilitarismus, *der*

**utility** /ju:'tɪlɪtɪ/ ❶ *n.* Ⓐ Nutzen, *der;* **of great ~:** sehr nutzbringend; von großem Nutzen; **total/marginal ~** (*Econ.*) Gesamt-/Grenznutzen, *der;* Ⓑ ⇒ **public utility.** ❷ *adj.* Vielzweck-; (*functional*) funktionell; **~ goods/furniture** Gebrauchsgüter/-möbel

**utility: ~ man** *n.* (*Amer.*) Ⓐ (*Theatre*) Chargenspieler, *der*/-spielerin, *die;* Ⓑ (*Sport*) vielseitig einsetzbarer Spieler; Ⓒ (*odd-job man*) Mädchen für alles (*ugs.*); **~ program** *n.* (*Computing*) Dienstprogramm, *das;* **~ room** *n. Raum, in dem [größere] Haushaltsgeräte (z. B. Waschmaschine) installiert sind;* **~ routine** ⇒ **~ program**

**utilizable** /'ju:tɪlaɪzəbl/ *adj.* nutzbar

**utilization** /ju:tɪlaɪ'zeɪʃn/ *n.* Nutzung, *die*

**utilize** /'ju:tɪlaɪz/ *v.t.* nutzen

**utmost** /'ʌtməʊst/ ❶ *adj.* äußerst...; tiefst... ‹Verachtung›; höchst... ‹Verehrung, Gefahr›; größt... ‹Höflichkeit, Eleganz, Einfachheit, Geschwindigkeit›; **of [the] ~ importance** von äußerster Wichtigkeit; **with the ~ caution** mit größter *od.* äußerster Vorsicht; **with the ~ ease/care/reluctance** mit größter Leichtigkeit/äußerster Sorgfalt/größter Zurückhaltung; **to the ~ degree** bis zum Äußersten. ❷ *n.* Äußerste, *das;* **do** *or* **try one's ~ to do sth.** mit allen Mitteln versuchen, etw. zu tun; **to the ~:** bis zum Äußersten; **to the ~ of one's ability/strength** so gut man eben kann/mit aller Kraft; **try sb.'s patience to the ~:** jmds. Geduld auf das Äußerste strapazieren

**Utopia** /ju:'təʊpɪə/ *n.* (*place*) Utopia (*das*); (*impractical scheme*) Utopie, *die*

**Utopian** /ju:'təʊpɪən/ ❶ *adj.* utopisch. ❷ *n.* Utopist, *der*/Utopistin, *die*

**utter**[1] /'ʌtə(r)/ *attrib. adj.* vollkommen, völlig ‹Chaos, Verwirrung, Fehlschlag, Ablehnung, Friede, Einsamkeit, Unsinn›; ungeheuer ‹Elend, Dummheit, Freude, Glück, Schönheit›; größt... ‹Freude, Vergnügen›; **be in ~ despair/misery** völlig verzweifelt/niedergeschlagen sein; **be an ~ mystery** völlig rätselhaft sein; **be an ~ stranger to sb.** jmdm. völlig fremd sein; **~ fool** Vollidiot, *der* (*ugs.*)

**utter**[2] *v.t.* Ⓐ von sich geben ‹Schrei, Seufzer, Ächzen›; Ⓑ (*say*) sagen ‹Wahrheit, Wort›; schwören ‹Eid›; äußern ‹Drohung›; zum Ausdruck bringen ‹Gefühle›; **the last words he ~ed** die letzten Worte, die er sprach; **she never ~ed a sound** sie gab keinen Ton von sich; **this word/her name must not be ~ed in his presence** dieses Wort/ihr Name darf in seiner Gegenwart nicht gesagt *od.* ausgesprochen werden; Ⓒ **~ a libel** (*Law*) eine Verleumdung verbreiten

**utterance** /'ʌtərəns/ *n.* Ⓐ **~ of a sigh/groan** ein Seufzen/Stöhnen; **give ~ to sth.** etw. zum Ausdruck bringen; einer Sache Ausdruck verleihen; Ⓑ (*spoken words*) Worte *Pl.;* (*Ling.*) [sprachliche] Äußerung; (*sentence*) Satz, *der;* Ⓒ (*power of speech*) Sprache, *die*

**utterly** /'ʌtəlɪ/ *adv.* völlig; vollkommen; restlos ‹elend, deprimiert›; absolut ‹entzückend, bezaubernd›; hinreißend ‹schön›; äußerst ‹dumm, lächerlich›; aus tiefster Seele ‹verabscheuen, ablehnen, bereuen›

**uttermost** /'ʌtəməʊst/ Ⓐ ⇒ **utmost** 1, 2; Ⓑ (*most distant*) entferntest...; **to the ~ ends of the earth** bis ans äußerste Ende der Welt

**'U-turn** *n.* Wende [um 180°]; **the driver/car made a ~:** der Fahrer/Wagen wendete; **'No ~s'** „Wenden verboten"; **make a ~ [on sth.]** (*fig.*) eine Kehrtwendung [bei etw.] vollziehen *od.* machen

**UV** *abbr.* **ultraviolet** UV

**uvula** /'ju:vjʊlə/ *n., pl.* **~e** /'ju:vjʊli:/ (*Anat.*) Zäpfchen, *das;* Uvula, *die* (*fachspr.*)

**uvular** /'ju:vjʊlə(r)/ *adj.* (*Anat., Ling.*) uvular; **the ~ 'r'** das Zäpfchen-R

# V v

**V¹, v¹** /viː/ *n., pl.* **Vs** *or* **V's** Ⓐ *(letter)* V, v, *das;* Ⓑ *(Roman numeral)* V; Ⓒ *(V-shaped thing)* V, *das;* Ⓓ **V1/V2** *(Hist.)* V1/V2, *die.* ⇒ *also* **V-neck**; **V-necked**; **V-sign**

**V², v²** *abbr.* **volt[s]** V

**v.** *abbr.* Ⓐ /ˈvɜːsəs, viː/ **versus** gg.; Ⓑ **very**; Ⓒ **verse**

**vac** /væk/ *n. (Brit. Univ. coll.)* Semesterferien *Pl.;* **the long ~:** die Sommersemesterferien

**vacancy** /ˈveɪkənsɪ/ *n.* Ⓐ *(job)* freie Stelle; **fill a ~:** eine [freie] Stelle besetzen; **have a ~ [on one's staff]** eine freie Stelle *od.* Stelle frei haben; **'vacancies'** *(notice outside factory)* „Stellen frei"; *(in newspaper)* „Stellenangebote"; Ⓑ *(unoccupied room)* freies Zimmer; **have a ~:** ein Zimmer frei haben; **'vacancies'** „Zimmer frei"; **'no vacancies'** „belegt"; Ⓒ *no pl. (of look, mind, etc.)* Leere, *die*

**vacant** /ˈveɪkənt/ *adj.* Ⓐ *(not occupied)* frei; **'~'** *(on door of toilet)* „frei"; **'situations ~'** „Stellenangebote"; **a house with ~ possession** ein bezugsfertiges Haus; Ⓑ *(mentally inactive)* leer

**vacantly** /ˈveɪkəntlɪ/ *adv.* leer; **stare/gaze ~ at sb./into space** jmdn. mit leerem Blick anstarren/abwesend ins Leere starren

**vacate** /vəˈkeɪt/ *v.t.* räumen ‹Gebäude, Büro, Wohnung›; aufgeben ‹Stelle, Amt›; niederlegen ‹Amt›

**vacation** /vəˈkeɪʃn/ ❶ *n.* Ⓐ *(Brit. Law, Univ.: recess)* Ferien *Pl.;* Ⓑ *(Amer.)* ⇒ **holiday** 1 B; Ⓒ *(vacating) (of a room, building)* Räumung, *die; (of a post)* Aufgeben, *das; (of an office)* Niederlegen, *das.* ❷ *v.i. (Amer.)* **~ [at/in a place]** [an einem Ort] Urlaub machen

**vacationer** /vəˈkeɪʃənə(r)/, **vacationist** /vəˈkeɪʃənɪst/ *ns. (Amer.)* Urlauber, *der*/Urlauberin, *die*

**vaccinate** /ˈvæksɪneɪt/ *v.t.* ▶ 1232 *(Med.)* impfen

**vaccination** /væksɪˈneɪʃn/ *n.* ▶ 1232 *(Med.)* Impfung, *die; attrib.* Impf-; **have a ~:** geimpft werden

**vaccine** /ˈvæksiːn, ˈvæksɪn/ *n.* ▶ 1232 Impfstoff, *der*

**vacillate** /ˈvæsɪleɪt/ *v.i. (lit. or fig.)* schwanken; **~ about doing sth.** schwanken, ob man etw. tun soll oder nicht; **~ on sth.** bezüglich einer Sache schwanken

**vacillating** /ˈvæsɪleɪtɪŋ/ *adj.* schwankend

**vacillation** /væsɪˈleɪʃn/ *n.* Schwanken, *das*

**vacua** *pl. of* **vacuum** 1 A

**vacuity** /vəˈkuːətɪ/ *n.* Leere, *die; (of book, play)* Geistlosigkeit, *die*

**vacuous** /ˈvækjʊəs/ *adj.* leer; geistlos, nichts sagend ‹Buch, Theaterstück, Bemerkung›

**vacuously** /ˈvækjʊəslɪ/ *adv.* leer

**vacuum** /ˈvækjʊəm/ ❶ *n.* Ⓐ *pl.* **vacua** /ˈvækjʊə/ *or* **~s** *(Phys.; also fig.)* Vakuum, *das;* **perfect/partial ~:** ideales Vakuum/Unterdruck, *der; (fig.)* **her death has left a ~ in our lives** ihr Tod hat in unserem Leben eine Lücke hinterlassen; **live in a ~** *(lit. or fig.)* im luftleeren Raum leben; Ⓑ *pl.* **~s** *(coll.: ~ cleaner)* Sauger, *der (ugs.).* ❷ *v.t.& i.* [staub]saugen

**vacuum: ~ bottle** *(Amer.)* ⇒ **~ flask**; **~ brake** *n. (Railw.)* Unterdruckbremse, *die;* **~-clean** *v.t. & i.* [staub]saugen; **~ cleaner** *n.* Staubsauger, *der;* **~ flask** *n. (Brit.)* Thermosflasche, *die;* **~ gauge** *n. (Physics)* Vakuummeter, *das;* **~-packed** *adj.* vakuumverpackt; **~ pump** *n.* Vakuumpumpe, *die;* **~ tube** *n. (Electronics)* Vakuumröhre, *die;* Elektronenröhre, *die*

**vade mecum** /veɪdɪˈmiːkəm, vɑːdɪˈmeɪkəm/ *n.* Vademekum, *das (geh.)*

**vagabond** /ˈvægəbɒnd/ ❶ *n.* Landstreicher, *der*/Landstreicherin, *die (oft abwertend);* Vagabund, *der*/Vagabundin, *die (veralt.).* ❷ *adj.* umherziehend, vagabundierend ‹Mensch, Stamm›; **~ life** Vagabundenleben, *das*

**vagaries** /ˈveɪgərɪz/ *n. pl. (lit. or fig.)* Launen *Pl.;* **the ~ of life/politics** die Wechselfälle des Lebens/der Politik

**vagina** /vəˈdʒaɪnə/ *n., pl.* **~e** /vəˈdʒaɪniː/ *or* **~s** ▶ 966 *(Anat.)* Scheide, *die;* Vagina, *die (fachspr.)*

**vaginal** /vəˈdʒaɪnl/ *adj.* Scheiden-; vaginal *(fachspr.)*

**vagrancy** /ˈveɪgrənsɪ/ *n., no indef. art., no pl.* Landstreicherei, *die; (in cities)* Stadtstreicherei, *die*

**vagrant** /ˈveɪgrənt/ ❶ *adj.* vagabundierend; **~ life** Vagabundenleben, *das.* ❷ *n.* Landstreicher, *der*/Landstreicherin, *die (oft abwertend); (in cities)* Stadtstreicher, *der*/Stadtstreicherin, *die*

**vague** /veɪg/ *adj.* vage; verschwommen, undeutlich ‹Form, Umriss›; undefinierbar ‹Farbe›; *(absent-minded)* geistesabwesend; *(inattentive)* unkonzentriert; **describe sth. in ~ terms** etw. vage beschreiben; **not have the ~st idea** *or* **notion** nicht die blasseste *od.* leiseste Ahnung haben; **be ~ about sth.** etw. nur vag[e] andeuten; *(in understanding)* nur eine vage Vorstellung von etw. haben

**vaguely** /ˈveɪglɪ/ *adv.* vage; ungefähr ‹wissen›; entfernt ‹bekannt sein, erinnern an›; schwach ‹sich erinnern›; **he was ~ alarmed/sad/disappointed** er war irgendwie beunruhigt/traurig/enttäuscht; **look/taste ~ like sth.** entfernt aussehen/schmecken wie etw.; **understand sth. ~:** etw. in etwa verstehen; **she looked at me ~** *(uncertainly)* sie sah mich unsicher an; *(absent-mindedly)* sie sah mich zerstreut an

**vagueness** /ˈveɪgnɪs/ *n., no pl.* Vagheit, *die; (of outline, shape)* Verschwommenheit, *die; (of policy)* Unbestimmtheit, *die; (absent-mindedness)* Zerstreutheit, *die; (uncertainty)* Unsicherheit, *die*

**vain** /veɪn/ *adj.* Ⓐ *(conceited)* eitel; **be ~ about sth.** sich *(Dat.)* auf etw. *(Akk.)* viel einbilden; Ⓑ *(useless)* leer ‹Drohung, Versprechen, Worte, Reden›; eitel *(geh.)* ‹Triumph, Vergnügungen›; vergeblich ‹Hoffnung, Erwartung, Versuch›; **in ~:** vergeblich; vergebens; ⇒ *also* **take** 1 E

**vainglorious** /veɪnˈglɔːrɪəs/ *adj. (formal/literary)* prahlerisch ‹Reden, Angebereien›; dünkelhaft ‹Person, Auftreten›

**vainly** /ˈveɪnlɪ/ *adv.* Ⓐ *(uselessly)* vergebens; vergeblich; Ⓑ *(in a conceited way)* eitel; angeberisch

**Valais** /ˈvæleɪ/ *pr. n.* Wallis, *das*

**valance** /ˈvæləns/ *n.* Volant, *der*

**vale** /veɪl/ *n. (arch./poet.)* Tal, *das;* **this ~ of tears** *(fig.)* dies Jammertal

**valediction** /vælɪˈdɪkʃn/ *n. (act)* Abschied, *der; (words)* Abschiedsgruß, *der*

**valedictory** /vælɪˈdɪktərɪ/ *adj.* Abschieds-; **~ remarks** Bemerkungen zum Abschied; **~ speech/address** *(Amer.)* Abschiedsrede/-ansprache, *die*

**valence** /ˈveɪləns/ *(esp. Amer.),* **valency** /ˈveɪlənsɪ/ *ns. (Chem., Phys.) (unit)* Wertigkeit, *die;* Valenz, *die (fachspr.);* **~ bond** kovalente Bindung

**valentine** /ˈvæləntaɪn/ *n.* Ⓐ *jmd., dem man am Valentinstag einen Gruß schickt;* Ⓑ **~ [card]** Grußkarte zum Valentinstag; Ⓒ **St. V~'s Day** Valentinstag, *der*

**valerian** /vəˈlɪərɪən/ *n. (Bot., Pharm.)* Baldrian, *der*

**valet** /ˈvælɪt, ˈvæleɪ/ *n.* ▶ 1261 Ⓐ Kammerdiener, *der;* Ⓑ *(hotel employee) für den Reinigungsservice zuständiger Hotelangestellter;* **~ service** Reinigungs[- und Reparatur]service

**'valet parking** *n.* Parkservice, *der*

**valetudinarian** /vælɪtjuːdɪˈneərɪən/ ❶ *adj.* Ⓐ *(sickly)* kränkelnd; Ⓑ *(anxious about health)* hypochondrisch. ❷ *n.* Ⓐ *(sickly person)* kränklicher Mensch; Ⓑ *(hypochondriac)* Hypochonder, *der*

**Valhalla** /vælˈhælə/ *n. (Mythol.)* Walhall[a], *das*

**valiant** /ˈvæljənt/ *adj.* tapfer; kühn *(geh.);* **he made a ~ effort to disguise his disappointment** er versuchte tapfer, seine Enttäuschung zu verbergen; **it was a ~ try/effort** es war ein tapferer Versuch

**valiantly** /ˈvæljəntlɪ/ *adv.* tapfer; kühn *(geh.)*

**valid** /ˈvælɪd/ *adj.* Ⓐ *(legally acceptable)* gültig; berechtigt ‹Anspruch›; *(legally valid)* rechtsgültig; *(having legal force)* rechtskräftig; bindend ‹Vertrag›; **a ~ claim** ein Rechtsanspruch **(to** auf + *Akk.*); Ⓑ *(justifiable)* stichhaltig ‹Argument, Einwand, Theorie›; triftig ‹Grund›; zuverlässig ‹Methode›; begründet ‹Entschuldigung, Einwand›

**validate** /ˈvælɪdeɪt/ *v.t.* rechtskräftig machen ‹Anspruch, Vertrag, Testament›; bestätigen, beweisen ‹Hypothese, Theorie›; für gültig erklären ‹Wahl›

**validation** /vælɪˈdeɪʃn/ *n. (of claim, contract, etc.)* Gültigkeitserklärung, *die; (of theory, hypothesis)* Bestätigung, *die*

**validity** /vəˈlɪdɪtɪ/ *n., no pl.* Ⓐ *(of ticket, document)* Gültigkeit, *die; (of claim, contract, marriage, etc.)* Rechtsgültigkeit, *die;* **~ check** *(Computing)* Gültigkeitskontrolle, *die;* Ⓑ *(of argument, excuse, objection, theory)* Stichhaltigkeit, *die; (of reason)* Triftigkeit, *die; (of method)* Zuverlässigkeit, *die*

**validly** /ˈvælɪdlɪ/ *adv. (lawfully)* rechtsgültig; *(properly)* überzeugend; mit [vollem] Recht ‹beanspruchen, geltend machen›

**valise** /vəˈliːz/ *n. (esp. Amer.)* Reisetasche, *die*

**Valkyrie** /vælˈkɪərɪ, ˈvælkɪrɪ/ *n. (Mythol.)* Walküre, *die*

**valley** /ˈvælɪ/ *n.* Ⓐ *(lit. or fig.)* Tal, *das;* **~ bottom** Talsohle, *die;* Ⓑ *(of roof)* [Dach]kehle, *die;* **U-shaped/V-shaped ~:** Trogtal, *das*/Kerbtal, *das (Geog.);* ⇒ *also* **hanging valley**; **rift valley**; **river valley**

**valor** *(Amer.)* ⇒ **valour**

**valorous** /ˈvælərəs/ *adj. (literary)* tapfer

**valour** /ˈvælə(r)/ *n.* Tapferkeit, *die;* **fight with ~:** tapfer kämpfen; ⇒ *also* **discretion** A

**valuable** /ˈvæljʊəbl/ ❶ *adj.* wertvoll; **be ~ to sb.** für jmdn. wertvoll sein. ❷ *n., in pl.* Wertgegenstände; Wertsachen

**valuation** /væljʊˈeɪʃn/ *n.* Schätzung, *die;* **make/get a ~ of sth.** etw. schätzen/etw. schätzen lassen; **what is the ~?** wie hoch ist der Schätzwert?; **set a high/low** *etc.* **~ on sth.** den Schätzwert für etw. hoch/niedrig *usw.* ansetzen; **accept sb. at his/her own ~:** jmds. Selbsteinschätzung teilen *od.* akzeptieren

**value** /ˈvæljuː/ ❶ *n.* Ⓐ Wert, *der;* **be of great/little/some/no ~ [to sb.]** [für jmdn.] von großem/geringem/einigem/keinerlei Nutzen sein; **they are taught too few things of real ~ for their future** man lehrt sie zu wenig, was ihnen in der Zukunft wirklich nützen wird; **information that is of great**

~ **to scientists** Informationen, die für Wissenschaftler überaus wertvoll *od.* von großem Wert sind; **this drug has been of some ~ in the treatment of cancer** dieses Medikament hat sich bei der Behandlung von Krebskranken als bedingt wirksam erwiesen; **be of [no] practical ~ to sb.** für jmdn. von [keinerlei] praktischem Nutzen sein; **set** *or* **put a high/low ~ on sth.** etw. hoch/niedrig einschätzen; **attach great ~ to sth.** einer Sache (*Dat.*) große Wichtigkeit beimessen; **B** (*monetary worth*) Wert, *der;* **it has a ~ of one pound** es ist ein Pfund wert; **what would be the ~ of it?** was ist es wohl wert?; **know the ~ of sth.** wissen, was etw. wert ist; **sth./nothing of ~:** etw./nichts Wertvolles; **an object of ~:** ein Wertgegenstand; **items of great/little/no ~:** sehr wertvolle/nicht sonderlich wertvolle/wertlose Gegenstände; **be of great/little/no** *etc.* **~:** viel/wenig/nichts *usw.* wert sein; **increase** *or* **go up in ~:** an Wert gewinnen; wertvoller werden; **decline** *or* **decrease** *or* **fall** *or* **go down in ~:** an Wert verlieren; **an increase/decrease in ~:** ein Wertzuwachs/-verlust; **put a ~ on sth.** den Wert einer Sache schätzen; **sth. to the ~ of ...:** etw. im Werte von ...; **C** (*equivalent*) Wert, *der;* **he offered less than the ~ of the house** er bot weniger, als das Haus wert war; **be good/poor etc. ~ [for money]** seinen Preis wert/nicht wert sein; **customers want [good] ~ for money** Kunden wollen für ihr Geld auch etwas bekommen; **£5 for a tiny steak — do you call that good ~?** 5 Pfund für ein winziges Steak — nennen Sie das reell?; **this handbook is excellent/very good ~ at £10** dieses Handbuch ist die 10 Pfund, die es kostet, unbedingt wert; **get [good]/poor ~ [for money]** etwas/nicht viel für sein Geld bekommen; **give sb. poor ~ for money** jmdm. für sein Geld nicht viel bieten; **D** *in pl.* (*principles*) Werte; Wertvorstellungen; **E** (*rank, significance*) Wert, *der;* **[time] ~** (*Mus.*) Zeitwert, *der;* **~ of a colour, colour ~:** Farbwert, *der;* **F** (*numerical quantity*) (*Math.*) [Zahlen]wert, *der;* (*Phys.*) Größe, *die;* **give x** *or* **let x have the ~ 3** x sei 3.
**2** *v.t.* **A** (*appreciate*) schätzen; **his work has been ~d highly by experts** seine Arbeit hat bei Experten hohe Anerkennung gefunden; **if you ~ your life** wenn dir dein Leben lieb ist; **B** (*put price on*) schätzen, taxieren (**at** auf + *Akk.*)

**value added 'tax** *n.* ▶ **1328** (*Brit.*) Mehrwertsteuer, *die*

**valued** /'vælju:d/ *adj.* geschätzt ‹Freund, Kollege, Kunde›; wertvoll ‹Rat, Hilfe›; **thank you for your ~ order** (*Commerc. dated*) wir bedanken uns für Ihren geschätzten Auftrag (*veralt.*)

**'value judgement** *n.* Werturteil, *das*

**valueless** /'væljʊlɪs/ *adj.* wertlos

**valuer** /'væljʊə(r)/ *n.* ▶ **1261** Schätzer, *der;* Taxator, *der*

**valve** /vælv/ *n.* **A** Ventil, *das;* ⇒ *also* **safety valve**; **B** (*Anat., Zool.*) Klappe, *die;* **C** (*Brit.: thermionic ~*) Röhre, *die*

**vamoose** /və'mu:s/ *v.i.* (*Amer. coll.*) verduften (*ugs.*)

**vamp**[1] /væmp/ **1** *n.* (*of shoe*) Oberleder, *das.* **2** *v.t.* (*Mus.*) improvisieren ‹Begleitung›; improvisierend begleiten ‹Melodie›. **3** *v.i.* (*Mus.*) improvisierend begleiten

~ **'up** *v.t.* (*put together*) zusammenschustern (*ugs. abwertend*); (*renovate*) aufmöbeln (*ugs.*)

**vamp**[2] *n.* (*woman*) Vamp, *der*

**vampire** /'væmpaɪə(r)/ *n.* Vampir, *der*

**'vampire bat** *n.* (*Zool.*) Vampir, *der*

**van**[1] /væn/ *n.* **A [delivery] ~:** Lieferwagen, *der;* **baker's/laundry ~:** Bäckerauto, *das*/Wäschereiauto, *das* (*ugs.*); **B** (*Brit. Railw.*) [geschlossener] Wagen; **C** (*Brit.: caravan*) **[camping] ~:** Wohnwagen, *der*

**van**[2] *n.* (*foremost part*) Vorhut, *die;* (*fig.: leaders of movement, opinion*) Vorkämpfer *Pl.;* **be in the ~ of a movement/the attack** zu den Vorkämpfern einer Bewegung gehören/den Angriff anführen

**van**[3] *n.* (*Tennis*) Vorteil, *der*

**vanadium** /və'neɪdɪəm/ *n.* (*Chem.*) Vanadium, *das*

**vandal** /'vændl/ *n.* **A** Rowdy, *der;* **~-proof** unzerstörbar; **B** (*Hist.*) **V~:** Wandale, *der;* Vandale, *der*

**vandalise** ⇒ **vandalize**

**vandalism** /'vændəlɪzm/ *n.* Wandalismus, *der;* Vandalismus, *der;* **act of ~** (*destruction*) [mutwillige] Zerstörung; (*damaging*) [mutwillige] Beschädigung; **to demolish this beautiful old building would be an act of ~:** dieses schöne alte Gebäude abzureißen wäre Wandalismus

**vandalize** /'vændəlaɪz/ *v.t.* (*destroy*) [mutwillig] zerstören; (*damage*) [mutwillig] beschädigen

**Vandyke**/væn'daɪk/**:** ~ **beard** *n.* Henriquatre, *der;* ~ **brown** *n.* Van-Dyck-Braun, *das*

**vane** /veɪn/ *n.* **A** (*weathercock*) (*in shape of arrow*) Wetterfahne, *die;* (*in shape of cock*) Wetterhahn, *der;* **B** (*blade*) Blatt, *das;* (*of windmill*) Flügel, *der;* (*of watermill, turbine*) Schaufel, *die*

**vanguard** /'vængɑ:d/ *n.* **A** (*Mil., Navy*) Vorhut, *die;* **B** (*fig.: leaders*) Vorreiter; (*of literary, artistic, etc. movement*) Avantgarde, *die;* **in the ~ of [public] opinion** der öffentlichen Meinung stets um eine Nasenlänge voraus; **be in the ~ of progress/a movement** an der Spitze des Fortschritts/einer Bewegung stehen

**vanilla** /və'nɪlə/ **1** *n.* **A** Vanille, *die;* **B** ⇒ **vanilla pod. 2** *adj.* Vanille-

**va'nilla pod** *n.* (*Bot.*) Vanilleschote, *die*

**vanish** /'vænɪʃ/ *v.i.* **A** (*disappear; coll.: leave quickly*) verschwinden; **~ from sight [behind sth.]** [hinter etw. (*Dat.*)] verschwinden; **~ into the distance** in der Ferne verschwinden; **the smile ~ed from his face** das Lächeln verschwand aus seinem Gesicht; **~ off the face of the earth** von der Erde verschwinden; ⇒ *also* **thin** 1 D; **B** (*cease to exist*) ‹Gebäude:› verschwinden; ‹Sitte, Tradition:› untergehen; ‹Art, Gattung:› aussterben; ‹Zweifel, Bedenken:› sich auflösen; ‹Angst:› sich legen; ‹Hoffnung, Chancen:› schwinden; **C** (*Math.*) null werden

**vanishing** /'vænɪʃɪŋ/**:** ~ **act** ⇒ ~ **trick**; ~ **cream** *n.* Feuchtigkeitscreme, *die;* Vanishing-Creme, *die* (*fachspr.*); ~ **point** *n.* (*Art, Math.*) Fluchtpunkt, *der;* (*fig.*) Nullpunkt, *der;* **dwindle to ~-point** auf den Nullpunkt zurückgehen; ~ **trick** *n.* Zaubertrick (*bei dem etwas verschwindet*); **do** *or* **perform a ~ trick with sth.** etw. wegzaubern *od.* verschwinden lassen; **he did his [usual] ~ trick** (*fig. coll.*) er verdrückte sich [wie üblich] (*ugs.*)

**vanity** /'vænɪtɪ/ *n.* **A** (*pride, conceit*) Eitelkeit, *die;* **B** (*worthlessness*) Nichtigkeit, *die;* Eitelkeit, *die* (*geh.*); (*of efforts, hopes, dreams*) Vergeblichkeit, *die;* **all is ~:** alles ist eitel (*geh.*); **C** (*worthless thing*) **these things are vanities** das ist alles bloß Tand (*geh.*); **D** (*Amer.: dressing table*) Frisierkommode, *die*

**vanity:** ~ **bag** *n.* Kosmetiktäschchen, *das;* ~ **case** *n.* Kosmetikkoffer, *der;* **V~ 'Fair** *n.* Jahrmarkt der Eitelkeiten

**vanquish** /'væŋkwɪʃ/ *v.t.* (*literary*) bezwingen

**vantage** /'vɑ:ntɪdʒ/ *n.* **A** (*position of superiority*) Vorteil, *der;* **B** ⇒ **advantage** C

**vantage:** ~ **ground** *n.* (*Mil.*) günstige [Ausgangs]position; ~ **point** *n.* Aussichtspunkt, *der;* (*fig.*) **his ~-point as director** der Überblick, den er als Direktor hat/hatte

**vapid** /'væpɪd/ *adj.* schal ‹Geschmack, Vergnügen›; leer ‹Gerede, Umgangsformen›; geistlos ‹Gerede, Vortrag, Bemerkung, Ergüsse›; unverbindlich ‹Lächeln›; nichts sagend ‹Erscheinung, Person›

**vapidity** /və'pɪdɪtɪ/ *n.* Schalheit, *die;* (*of conversation, remark, book, speech, etc.*) Geistlosigkeit, *die;* **the ~ of his smile/expression** sein unverbindliches Lächeln/sein nichts sagender Gesichtsausdruck

**vapor** (*Amer.*) ⇒ **vapour**

**vaporize (vaporise)** /'veɪpəraɪz/ *v.t.* & *i.* verdampfen

**vaporizer** /'veɪpəraɪzə(r)/ *n.* **A** Verdampfer, *der;* **B** (*atomizer*) Zerstäuber, *der*

**vapour** /'veɪpə(r)/ *n.* (*Brit.*) **A** Dampf, *der;* (*mist*) Dunst, *der;* **~s** (*rising from the ground*) Schwaden; (*arch.: melancholy*) Schwermut, *die;* **B** (*Phys.*) Dampf, *der;* **turn into [a] ~:** zu Dampf werden; **C** (*Med.: inhalant*) Dampf, *der*

**vapour:** ~ **bath** *n.* (*Med.*) Dampfbad, *das;* ~ **trail** *n.* (*Aeronaut.*) Kondensstreifen, *der*

**variability** /veərɪə'bɪlɪtɪ/ *n.* **A** (*ability to be altered*) Variabilität, *die;* **B** (*inconsistency, changeability*) Unbeständigkeit, *die;* (*of health, balance*) Labilität, *die*

**variable** /'veərɪəbl/ **1** *adj.* **A** (*alterable*) veränderbar; **be ~:** verändert werden können; ‹Gerät:› eingestellt werden können; **B** (*inconsistent, changeable*) unbeständig ‹Wetter, Wind, Strömung, Stimmung, Leistung›; wechselhaft ‹Wetter, Launen, Schicksal, Qualität, Erfolg›; labil ‹Gesundheit, Gleichgewicht›; schwankend ‹Kosten›; **How's your health? — Oh, ~:** Wie gehts gesundheitlich? — Mal so, mal so; **with ~ success** mit wechselndem Erfolg; **C** (*Astron., Math.*) veränderlich; variabel.
**2** *n.* **A** (*Math.*) Variable, *die;* Veränderliche, *die;* **B** (*Astron.*) Veränderliche, *der;* **C** (*fig.: varying factor*) veränderliche Größe; Variable, *die*

**'variable star** *n.* (*Astron.*) Veränderliche, *der*

**variably** /'veərɪəblɪ/ *adv.* variabel; beliebig, stufenlos ‹anpassbar, einstellbar›; unterschiedlich ‹stark›

**variance** /'veərɪəns/ *n.* **A** Uneinigkeit, *die;* (*between philosophies, ideologies*) Nichtübereinstimmung, *die;* **be at ~:** [sich (*Dat.*)] uneinig sein (**on** über + *Akk.*); ‹Theorien, Meinungen, Philosophien usw.:› nicht übereinstimmen; **be at ~ with sb./sth.** [sich (*Dat.*)] mit jmdm. uneinig sein/mit etw. nicht übereinstimmen; **this development has set the team at ~:** diese Entwicklung hat zu Meinungsverschiedenheiten im Team geführt; **B** (*Statistics*) Varianz, *die*

**variant** /'veərɪənt/ **1** *attrib. adj.* verschieden; **three ~ spellings/readings** drei [verschiedene] Schreibweisen/Lesarten; **~ type** (*Biol.*) Variante, *die.* **2** *n.* Variante, *die*

**variation** /veərɪ'eɪʃn/ *n.* **A** (*varying*) Veränderung, *die;* (*in style, diet, routine, programme*) Abwechslung, *die;* (*difference*) Unterschied, *der;* **be subject to ~** ‹Preise:› Schwankungen unterworfen sein; ‹Regeln:› Änderungen unterworfen sein; **~s in weather conditions** unbeständiges Wetter; **no ~ of the rules is allowed** die Regeln dürfen nicht geändert werden; **~ in price/colour** Preis-/Farbunterschied, *der;* **the ~s of light and shade** der Wechsel von Licht und Schatten; **~s from earlier editions** Unterschiede im Vergleich zu früheren Ausgaben; **B** (*variant*) Variante, *die* (**of, on** *Gen.*); **C** (*Mus.*) Variation, *die;* **~s on a theme** Variationen über ein Thema; **D** (*Biol., Ballet, Math.*) Variation, *die*

**variational** /veərɪ'eɪʃənl/ *attrib. adj.* (*Mus., Math.*) Variations-

**varicoloured** (*Brit.; Amer.:* **varicolored**) /'veərɪkʌləd/ *adj.* bunt

**varicose vein** /værɪkəʊs 'veɪn/ *n.* (*Med.*) Krampfader, *die*

**varied** /'veərɪd/ *adj.* (*differing*) unterschiedlich; vielfältig ‹Freuden›; (*marked by variation*) abwechslungsreich ‹Land, Diät, Leben›; vielseitig ‹Arbeit, Stil, Sammlung›; vielgestaltig ‹Landschaft›; bunt ‹Mischung›; bunt gemischt ‹Gruppe›

**variegate** /'veərɪgeɪt/ *v.t.* [farblich] auflockern

**variegated** /'veərɪgeɪtɪd/ *adj.* (*Bot.*) mehrfarbig; panaschiert ‹grüne Blätter›

**variegation** /veərɪ'geɪʃn/ *n.* **A** Buntheit, *die;* **B** (*Bot.*) Mehrfarbigkeit, *die;* (*on green leaves*) Panaschierung, *die*

**variety** /və'raɪətɪ/ *n.* **A** (*diversity*) Vielfältigkeit, *die;* (*in style, diet, routine, programme*) Abwechslung, *die;* **add** *or* **give ~ to sth.** etw. abwechslungsreicher gestalten; **for the sake of ~:** zur Abwechslung; **~ is the spice of life** (*prov.*) Abwechslung macht Freude; **B** (*assortment*) Auswahl, *die* (**of** an

V

+ *Dat.*, von); **in a ~ of sizes/ways** in verschiedenen Größen/auf verschiedene Art; **for a ~ of reasons** aus verschiedenen Gründen; **a wide ~ of birds/flowers** viele verschiedene Vogelarten/Blumen; Ⓒ (*Theatre*) Varietee, *das;* (*Telev.*) (*varietéähnliche*) Shows; Ⓓ (*form*) Art, *die;* (*of fruit, vegetable, cigarette*) Sorte, *die;* **rare varieties of butterflies** seltene Exemplare von Schmetterlingen; Ⓔ (*Biol.*) (*subspecies*) Unterart, *die;* Varietät, *die* (*fachspr.*); (*cultivated*) Züchtung, *die;* Rasse, *die*

**variety: ~ act** *n.* Varieteenummer, *die;* **~ artist** *n.* (*Theatre*) Varieteekünstler, *der*/-künstlerin, *die;* (*Telev.*) Showstar, *der;* **~ entertainment** ⇒ **~ show**; **~ meat** *n.* (*Amer.*) Innereien [und essbare Schlachtabfälle]; **~ show** *n.* Ⓐ (*Theatre*) Varietee, *das;* (*single performance*) Varieteevorstellung, *die;* Ⓑ (*Telev.*) (*varietéähnliche*) Show; **~ store** *n.* (*Amer.*) Kramladen, *der;* **~ theatre** *n.* Varietee[theater], *das*

**variola** /vəˈraɪələ/ *n.* (*Med.*) Pocken *Pl.*

**various** /ˈveərɪəs/ *adj.* Ⓐ *pred.* (*different*) verschieden; unterschiedlich; (*manifold*) vielfältig; **the causes of this are many and ~:** es gibt hierfür viele verschiedene Ursachen; Ⓑ *attrib.* (*several*) verschiedene; **at ~ times** mehrere Male

**variously** /ˈveərɪəslɪ/ *adv.* unterschiedlich; **she has been ~ described as a liar and a paragon of virtue** sie ist mal als Lügnerin, mal als Muster an Tugend beschrieben worden

**varlet** /ˈvɑːlɪt/ *n.* (*Hist.: page*) Bursche, *der;* (*arch./joc.: rascal*) Schurke, *der* (*abwertend*)

**varmint** /ˈvɑːmɪnt/ *n.* (*Amer./dial.*) (*animal*) Biest, *das* (*ugs.*); (*person*) Halunke, *der;* (*child*) Racker, *der* (*fam.*)

**varnish** /ˈvɑːnɪʃ/ ❶ *n.* Ⓐ Lack, *der;* (*transparent*) Lasur, *die;* **clear ~:** Klarlack, *der;* ⇒ *also* **nail varnish**; Ⓑ (*Art*) Firnis, *der;* Ⓒ (*Ceramics*) Glasur, *die;* Ⓓ (*glossiness, lit. or fig.*) Glanz, *der;* **high ~:** Hochglanz, *der.* ❷ *v.t.* Ⓐ lackieren; (*with transparent ~*) lasieren; Ⓑ (*Art*) firnissen; Ⓒ (*Ceramics*) glasieren; Ⓓ (*fig.: gloss over*) beschönigen; übertünchen ‹Fehler, Verbrechen, Laster›

**varsity** /ˈvɑːsɪtɪ/ *n.* (*Brit. Univ. coll.*) Uni, *die* (*ugs.*)

**vary** /ˈveərɪ/ ❶ *v.t.* verändern; ändern ‹Bestimmungen, Programm, Methode, Verhalten, Stil, Route, Kurs›; abwandeln ‹Rezept, Muster›; (*add variety to*) abwechslungsreicher gestalten; **~ one's diet** sich abwechslungsreich ernähren; **~ one's tone to suit the situation** seinen Ton der Situation anpassen.
❷ *v.i.* Ⓐ (*become different*) sich ändern; ‹Preis, Nachfrage, Qualität, Temperatur:› schwanken; (*be different*) unterschiedlich sein; (*between extremes*) wechseln; (*deviate*) abweichen; **Are you busy? — Oh, it varies** Hast du viel zu tun? — Ach, ganz unterschiedlich; **~ between A and B** *or* **from A to B** zwischen A (*Dat.*) und B (*Dat.*) schwanken; **~ in weight/size/shape/colour** *etc.* im Gewicht/in der Größe/Form/Farbe variieren (**from ... to ...:** zwischen ... + *Dat.* und ... + *Dat.*); **these items ~ in size/price** diese Artikel gibt es in verschiedenen Größen/Preislagen; **they ~ in their opinions/in character** sie haben unterschiedliche Meinungen/sind charakterlich verschieden; **the two books ~ on this matter** dieser Sachverhalt wird in den beiden Büchern unterschiedlich beurteilt; **opinions ~ on this point** die Meinungen gehen in diesem Punkt auseinander; Ⓑ **~ [directly]/inversely as sth.** sich direkt proportional/umgekehrt proportional zu etw. ändern

**varying** /ˈveərɪɪŋ/ *attrib. adj.* wechselnd; wechselhaft, veränderlich ‹Wetter›; (*different*) unterschiedlich; **in ~ colours** in verschiedenen Farben; **continually ~ prices** ständig schwankende Preise; **at ~ prices** zu unterschiedlichen Preisen

**vascular** /ˈvæskjʊlə(r)/ *adj.* (*Anat., Bot.*) vaskulär; (*Anat., Med.*) Gefäß-; **~ plant** Gefäßpflanze, *die*

**vase** /vɑːz/ *n.* Vase, *die*

**vasectomize** /vəˈsektəmaɪz/ *v.t.* (*Med.*) [durch Vasektomie] sterilisieren

**vasectomy** /vəˈsektəmɪ/ *n.* (*Med.*) Vasektomie, *die*

**Vaseline** ® /ˈvæsəliːn/ *n., no pl., no indef. art.* Vaseline, *die*

**vassal** /ˈvæsl/ *n.* Ⓐ (*Hist.*) Vasall, *der*/Vasallin, *die;* Ⓑ (*rhet.: slave*) Knecht, *der*/Magd, *die* (*fig.*)

**vast** /vɑːst/ *adj.* Ⓐ (*huge*) riesig; weit ‹Fläche, Meer, Kontinent, Welt[raum]›; gewaltig ‹Wolken[massen]›; umfangreich ‹Sammlung›; Ⓑ (*coll.: great*) enorm; Riesen‹menge, -summe, -fehler›; unermesslich ‹Reichtümer›; überwältigend ‹Mehrheit›; **a ~ amount of time/money/a ~ number of things** enorm viel Zeit/viel Geld/viele Dinge; **~ sums of money** enorm hohe Summen; **to a ~ extent** größtenteils; **he has done a ~ amount of work in this field** er hat auf diesem Gebiet enorm viel geleistet

**vastly** /ˈvɑːstlɪ/ *adv.* (*coll.*) enorm; weitaus ‹besser›; weit ‹überlegen, unterlegen›; überaus, äußerst ‹wichtig, dankbar›; in hohem Maße ‹beeinflussen›; gewaltig ‹sich verbessern, irren, überschätzen, unterschätzen›; köstlich ‹sich amüsieren›; **in a ~ different sense** in einem völlig anderen Sinn

**vastness** /ˈvɑːstnɪs/ *n., no pl.* Ⓐ (*hugeness*) [immense *od.* ungeheure] Weite; (*of building, crowd, army*) [immense *od.* ungeheure] Größe; (*of collection etc.*) [riesiger] Umfang; Ⓑ (*greatness*) [immenses] Ausmaß; (*of knowledge*) [immenser] Umfang

**vat** /væt/ *n.* Bottich, *der;* (*in papermaking*) Bütte, *die*

**VAT** /viːeɪˈtiː, væt/ *abbr.* ▶ **1328** **value added tax** MwSt.

**Vatican** /ˈvætɪkən/ *pr. n.* Vatikan, *der*

**Vatican: ~ ˈCity** *pr. n.* ▶ **1626** Vatikanstadt, *die;* **~ ˈCouncil** *n.* (*Hist.*) Vatikanisches Konzil

**Vaud** /vəʊ/ *pr. n.* Waadt, *die*

**vaudeville** /ˈvɔːdəvɪl, ˈvəʊdəvɪl/ *n.* (*Theatre, Mus.*) Varietee, *das;* **appear in ~:** im Varietee auftreten; **a ~ show** eine Varieteevorstellung

**vault¹** /vɔːlt, vɒlt/ ❶ *n.* Ⓐ (*Archit.*) Gewölbe, *das;* **the ~ of heaven** (*poet.*) das Himmelsgewölbe (*dichter.*); Ⓑ (*cellar*) [Gewölbe]keller, *der;* ⇒ *also* **wine vault**; Ⓒ (*in bank*) Tresorraum, *der;* Ⓓ (*tomb*) Gruft, *die.* ❷ *v.t.* (*Archit.*) wölben

**vault²** ❶ *v.i.* (*leap*) sich schwingen; (*Gymnastics*) springen. ❷ *v.t.* sich schwingen über (+ *Akk.*); (*Gymnastics*) springen über (+ *Akk.*). ❸ *n.* Sprung, *der;* **straddle/squat/side ~:** Grätsche, *die*/Hocke, *die*/Flanke, *die*

**vaulted** /ˈvɔːltɪd, ˈvɒltɪd/ *adj.* (*Archit.*) gewölbt

**vaulting** /ˈvɔːltɪŋ, ˈvɒltɪŋ/ *n.* (*Archit.*) Wölbung, *die*

**ˈvaulting horse** *n.* (*Gymnastics*) [Sprung]pferd, *das*

**vaunt** /vɔːnt/ (*literary*) *v.t.* sich brüsten mit; **~ that ...:** sich [damit] brüsten, dass ...; **~ sth. as sth.** etw. als etw. preisen; **much ~ed** viel gepriesen *od.* gerühmt

**VC** *abbr.* **Victoria Cross**

**VD** /viːˈdiː/ *n.* ▶ **1232** Geschlechtskrankheit, *die;* **get** *or* **catch VD** sich (*Dat.*) eine Geschlechtskrankheit zuziehen

**VDU** *abbr.* **visual display unit**

**ˈve** /v/ (*coll.*) ... have

**veal** /viːl/ *n., no pl.* Kalb[fleisch], *das; attrib.* Kalbs-; **roast ~:** Kalbsbraten, *der*

**veal ˈcutlet** *n.* Kalbsschnitzel, *das*

**vector** /ˈvektə(r)/ *n.* (*Math., Aeronaut., Biol.*) Vektor, *der*

**vectorial** /vekˈtɔːrɪəl/ *adj.* (*Math.*) vektoriell

**Veda** /ˈveɪdə, ˈviːdə/ *n.* (*Hindu Relig.*) Weda, *der*

**VE day** /viːˈiː deɪ/ *n.* der 8. Mai 1945; der Tag des Sieges in Europa [im 2. Weltkrieg]

**veer¹** /vɪə(r)/ ❶ *v.i.* Ⓐ ‹Wind:› [sich] im Uhrzeigersinn drehen; ‹Schiff, Flugzeug:› abdrehen; ‹Auto:› ausscheren; **~ to the north** ‹Wind:› auf Nord drehen; ‹Schiff:› nach Norden drehen; **~ off course/off the road** (*unintentionally*) vom Kurs/von der Straße abkommen; (*intentionally*) vom Kurs abdrehen/von der Straße abbiegen; **the driver had to ~ to avoid the sheep** der Fahrer musste das Steuer herumreißen, um dem Schaf auszuweichen; **~ out of control** außer Kontrolle geraten und ins Schleudern kommen; **go ~ing along the road** in Schlangenlinien die Straße entlangfahren; **~ gently/sharply to the right** ‹Straße:› eine leichte/scharfe Rechtskurve machen; Ⓑ (*fig.: change*) schwanken (**from ... to ...:** zwischen ... *Dat.* und ... *Dat.*); **~ from one extreme to the other** ‹Person:› von einem Extrem ins andere fallen; ‹Stimmung:› von einem Extrem ins andere umschlagen; **~ to the left** (*in politics*) auf Linkskurs umschwenken.
❷ *v.t.* Ⓐ **~ the car to the left/right** den Wagen nach links/rechts herumreißen; Ⓑ (*fig.*) abbringen.
❸ *n.* Ausscheren, *das;* **the driver struggled to control the ~:** der Fahrer versuchte, den Wagen noch abzufangen

**~ aˈway, ~ ˈoff** *v.i.* Ⓐ ‹Schiff, Flugzeug:› abdrehen; ‹Auto:› ausscheren; ‹Fahrer, Straße:› abbiegen; Ⓑ (*fig.: change*) **~ away** *or* **off from sth.** von etw. abkommen

**~ ˈround** ❶ *v.i.* drehen; (*through 180°*) wenden; **skid and ~ [right] round** ins Schleudern geraten und sich um die eigene Achse drehen. ❷ *v.t.* wenden

**veer²** *v.i.* (*Naut.*) **~ and haul** fieren und holen

**veg** /vedʒ/ *n., pl. same* (*coll.*) Gemüse, *das;* **meat and two ~:** Fleisch mit Kartoffeln und Gemüse

**vegan** /ˈviːgən/ ❶ *n.* Veganer, *der*/Veganerin, *die;* strenger Vegetarier/strenge Vegetarierin. ❷ *adj.* vegan; streng vegetarisch

**vegetable** /ˈvedʒɪtəbl/ ❶ *n.* Ⓐ Gemüse, *das;* **spring/summer/winter ~:** Frühjahrs-/Sommer-/Wintergemüse, *das;* **fresh ~s** frisches Gemüse; **green ~s** Grüngemüse, *das;* **do you want ~s/a ~ with your steak?** hätten Sie gern Gemüse/eine Portion Gemüse zu Ihrem Steak?; **meat and two ~s** Fleisch mit Kartoffeln und Gemüse; ⇒ *also* **kingdom** D; Ⓑ (*fig.*) **become/be a ~** (*as result of injury or illness*) nur noch [dahin]vegetieren; **you're just a ~/you'll turn into a ~** (*as result of dull routine, lack of ambition, etc.*) du vegetierst nur so vor dich hin/bald wirst du nur noch vor dich hin vegetieren.
❷ *adj.* Gemüse‹suppe, -extrakt›; **~ butter** Pflanzenbutter, *die;* **~ matter** pflanzliche Stoffe

**vegetable: ~ dish** *n.* Ⓐ (*food*) Gemüsegericht, *das;* Ⓑ (*bowl*) Gemüseschüssel, *die;* **~ dye** *n.* Pflanzenfarbe, *die;* **~ garden** *n.* Gemüsegarten, *der;* **~ knife** *n.* Küchenmesser, *das;* **~ ˈmarrow** ⇒ **marrow** A; **~ oil** *n.* (*Cookery*) Pflanzenöl, *das*

**vegetarian** /vedʒɪˈteərɪən/ ❶ *n.* Vegetarier, *der*/Vegetarierin, *die.* ❷ *adj.* vegetarisch; **sb. is ~:** jmd. ist Vegetarier/Vegetarierin

**vegetarianism** /vedʒɪˈteərɪənɪzm/ *n., no pl., no indef. art.* Vegetarismus, *der*

**vegetate** /ˈvedʒɪteɪt/ *v.i.* Ⓐ (*Bot.*) wachsen [und gedeihen]; Ⓑ (*fig.*) (*as result of injury or illness*) nur noch [dahin]vegetieren; (*as result of dull routine, lack of ambition, etc.*) vor sich (*Akk.*) hin vegetieren

**vegetation** /vedʒɪˈteɪʃn/ *n., no pl.* Ⓐ (*plants*) Vegetation, *die;* Ⓑ (*fig.*) (*as result of injury or illness*) Dahinvegetieren, *das;* (*as result of dull routine, lack of ambition, etc.*) Stumpfsinnigkeit, *die*

**vegetative** /ˈvedʒɪtətɪv/ *adj.* (*Biol., Bot.*) vegetativ

**veggie** /ˈvedʒɪ/ (*coll.*) ❶ *adj.* vegetarisch; **~ burger** Bratling, *der.* ❷ *n.* Ⓐ (*vegetarian*) Vegetarier, *der*/Vegetarierin, *die;* Ⓑ (*vegetable*) Gemüse, *das;* **~s** Gemüse, *das*

**vehemence** /ˈviːəməns/ *n., no pl.* Heftigkeit, *die;* Vehemenz, *die;* **with ~:** heftig; vehement (*geh.*)

**vehement** /ˈviːəmənt/ *adj.* heftig; vehement; leidenschaftlich ‹Gefühle, Rede›; stark ‹Wunsch, Abneigung›; hitzig ‹Debatte›

**vehemently** /ˈviːəməntlɪ/ *adv.* heftig; vehement; **hate each other ~:** einander bis aufs Blut hassen; **dislike each other ~:** eine heftige Abneigung gegeneinander empfinden

**vehicle** /ˈviːɪkl/ *n.* **A** Fahrzeug, *das;* **B** (*fig.: medium*) Vehikel, *das;* **the pulpit as a ~ for propaganda** die Kanzel als Bühne für Propaganda; **this newspaper is their ~:** diese Zeitung ist ihr Sprachrohr; **C** (*Art*) Bindemittel, *das;* **D** (*Pharm.*) Vehiculum, *das;* Konstituens, *das*

**vehicular** /vɪˈhɪkjʊlə(r)/ *adj.* Fahrzeug-

**veil** /veɪl/ ❶ *n.* **A** Schleier, *der;* **take the ~** (*Relig.*) den Schleier nehmen (*geh.*); **B** (*Jewish Relig. Hist.*) [Tempel]vorhang, *der;* **beyond the ~** (*fig.*) im Jenseits; **C** (*fig.: obscuring medium*) Schleier, *der;* **~ of mist/clouds** Dunst-/Wolkenschleier, *der;* **under the ~ of patriotism** unter dem Deckmantel des Patriotismus; **draw a ~ over sth.** den Mantel des Schweigens über etw. (*Akk.*) breiten. ❷ *v.t.* **A** verschleiern; **B** (*fig.: cover*) verhüllen; (*conceal*) verbergen ‹Gefühle, Motive› (**with, in** hinter + *Dat.*); verschleiern ‹Fakten, Wahrheit, Bedeutung›; **~ sth. in secrecy** *or* **mystery** etw. mit dem Schleier des Geheimnisses umgeben

**veiled** /veɪld/ *adj.* **A** verschleiert; **B** (*fig.: covert*) versteckt ‹Groll, Drohung›; verhüllt ‹Anspielung›

**vein** /veɪn/ *n.* **A** Vene, *die;* (*in popular use: any blood vessel*) Ader, *die;* **B** (*Geol., Mining, Zool.*) Ader, *die;* **C** (*Bot.*) Blattrippe, *die;* Ader, *die;* **D** (*streak*) Ader, *die;* **~s** (*in wood, marble*) Maserung, *die;* **E** (*fig.: character, tendency*) Zug, *der;* (*of truth*) Spur, *die;* (*of superstition, aggression*) Anflug, *der;* **a ~ of melancholy/humour** ein melancholischer/humorvoller Zug; **have a poetic ~:** eine dichterische Ader haben; **F** (*fig.*) (*mood*) Stimmung, *die;* (*style*) Art, *die;* **be in a happy/sad ~:** froh gelaunt/traurig gestimmt sein; **be in the [right] ~ [for sth./for doing sth.]** in der [richtigen] Stimmung sein [zu etw./, etw. zu tun]; **in a similar ~:** vergleichbarer Art

**veined** /veɪnd/ *adj.* geädert; gemasert ‹Holz›; **red marble ~ with white** roter Marmor, weiß geädert

**velar** /ˈviːlə(r)/ *adj.* (*Phonet.*) velar

**Velcro** ® /ˈvelkrəʊ/ *n., no pl., no indef. art.* Klettverschluss, *der* Ⓦⓩ

**veld, veldt** /velt/ *n.* (*S. Afr.*) Steppe, *die*

**vellum** /ˈveləm/ *n.* **A** (*parchment*) Pergament, *das;* (*manuscript also*) Pergamenthandschrift, *die;* **B** (*writing paper*) Velin[papier], *das*

**velocity** /vɪˈlɒsɪtɪ/ *n.* Geschwindigkeit, *die;* **at** *or* **with a ~ of ...:** mit einer Geschwindigkeit von ...; **~ of the wind, wind ~:** Windgeschwindigkeit, *die;* **~ of light** (*Phys.*) Lichtgeschwindigkeit, *die*

**velour[s]** /vəˈlʊə(r)/ *n.* (*Textiles*) Velours, *der*

**velum** /ˈviːləm/ *n., pl.* **vela** /ˈviːlə/ (*Bot., Zool.*) Velum, *das;* (*Anat.*) Velum, *das;* Gaumensegel, *das*

**velvet** /ˈvelvɪt/ ❶ *n.* **A** Samt, *der;* **[as] smooth as ~:** weich wie Samt; samtweich; **B** (*Zool.*) Bast, *der.* ❷ *adj.* aus Samt *nachgestellt;* Samt-; (*soft as ~*) samten; samtweich; **he operates with an iron hand in a ~ glove** er gibt sich entgegenkommend, in der Sache aber bleibt er unnachgiebig

**velveteen** /velvɪˈtiːn/ ❶ *n.* (*Textiles*) Baumwollsamt, *der;* Velveton, *der* (*fachspr.*). ❷ *adj.* aus Baumwollsamt *nachgestellt;* Velveton-

**velvety** /ˈvelvɪtɪ/ *adj.* (*having the feel of velvet*) samtig; samtweich; (*characteristic of velvet; also fig.*) samtig; samten; **smooth** *or* **soft and ~:** weich und samten

**Ven.** *abbr.* **Venerable** Hochw.

**venal** /ˈviːnl/ *adj.* käuflich, korrupt ‹Person›; korrupt ‹Verhalten, Praktiken›; eigennützig ‹Interessen, Motive, Dienste›

**venality** /viːˈnælɪtɪ/ *n., no pl.* ⇒ **venal**: Käuflichkeit, *die;* Korruptheit, *die;* Eigennützigkeit, *die*

**vend** /vend/ *v.t.* **A** (*Law*) veräußern; (*as a business*) Handel treiben mit; **B** (*offer for sale*) verkaufen

**vendee** /venˈdiː/ *n.* (*Law*) Käufer, *der*/Käuferin, *die*

**vender** /ˈvendə(r)/ ⇒ **vendor A**

**vendetta** /venˈdetə/ *n.* **A** Hetzkampagne, *die;* (*feud*) Fehde, *die;* **conduct a ~ against sb./sth.** eine Hetzkampagne gegen jmdn./etw. führen; **B** (*killings*) Blutrache, *die;* (*in Italy also*) Vendetta, *die*

**ˈvending machine** *n.* [Verkaufs]automat, *der*

**vendor** /ˈvendə(r), ˈvendɔː(r)/ *n.* **A** ▶ **1261** (*esp. Law*) Verkäufer, *der*/Verkäuferin, *die;* **street ~:** Straßenhändler, *der*/-händlerin, *die;* **newspaper ~:** Zeitungsverkäufer, *der*/-verkäuferin, *die;* **B** ⇒ **vending machine**

**veneer** /vɪˈnɪə(r)/ ❶ *n.* **A** (*thin covering of wood*) Furnier, *das;* (*layer in plywood*) Furnierblatt, *das;* **B** (*fig.: disguise*) Tünche, *die;* **beneath a ~ of respectability/civilization** hinter einer Fassade der Wohlanständigkeit/der Zivilisiertheit; **have only a ~ of education** sich (*Dat.*) nur den Anschein von Bildung geben; **it's just a ~:** es ist nur schöner Schein. ❷ *v.t.* furnieren

**venerable** /ˈvenərəbl/ *adj.* **A** ehrwürdig; heilig ‹Reliquien›; **B** (*Eccl.*) **the V~ A. W. Morgan** Hochwürden A. W. Morgan

**venerate** /ˈvenəreɪt/ *v.t.* verehren; hoch achten; ehren ‹Eltern, Wort Gottes›; in Ehren halten ‹jmds. Andenken, Traditionen, heilige Orte›

**veneration** /venəˈreɪʃn/ *n.* **A** (*reverence*) Ehrfurcht, *die* (**of, for** vor + *Dat.*); **in ~ of** zu Ehren (+ *Gen.*); **hold sb./sth. in ~:** jmdn./etw. verehren; **hold sb.'s memory in ~:** jmds. Andenken in Ehren halten; **B** (*venerating, being venerated*) Verehrung, *die* (**of** für); **the community's ~ of its traditions** der tiefe Respekt, den die Gemeinde für ihre Traditionen empfindet/empfand

**venereal** /vɪˈnɪərɪəl/ *adj.* ▶ **1232** (*Med.*) venerisch; **~ clinic** Klinik für Geschlechtskrankheiten; **~ virus** Virus, das eine venerische Krankheit hervorruft

**veˈnereal disease** *n.* (*Med.*) Geschlechtskrankheit, *die;* venerische Krankheit (*fachspr.*)

**Venetian** /vɪˈniːʃn/ ❶ *adj.* venezianisch; **sb. is ~:** jmd. ist Venezianer/Venezianerin; **~ glass** Muranoglas, *das.* ❷ *n.* **A** (*person*) Venezianer, *der*/Venezianerin, *die;* **B** (*dialect*) Venezianisch, *das;* venezianischer Dialekt

**venetian ˈblind** *n.* Jalousie, *die*

**Venezuela** /venɪˈzweɪlə/ *pr. n.* Venezuela (*das*)

**Venezuelan** /venɪˈzweɪlən/ ▶ **1340** ❶ *adj.* venezolanisch; **sb. is ~:** jmd. ist Venezolaner/Venezolanerin. ❷ *n.* Venezolaner, *der*/Venezolanerin, *die*

**vengeance** /ˈvendʒəns/ *n.* **A** Rache, *die;* Vergeltung, *die;* **he wrought a cruel ~ on his enemies** er übte grausame Rache an seinen Feinden; **take ~ [up]on sb. [for sth.]** sich an jmdm. [für etw.] rächen; **B with a ~:** gewaltig (*ugs.*); **go to work with a ~:** sich tüchtig ins Zeug legen (*ugs.*)

**vengeful** /ˈvendʒfl/ *adj.* rachedurstig (*geh.*); rachsüchtig (*geh.*)

**venial** /ˈviːnɪəl/ *adj.* **A** (*pardonable*) verzeihlich; entschuldbar; leichter ‹Vergehen›; **B** (*Theol.*) lässlich ‹Sünde›

**veniality** /viːnɪˈælɪtɪ/ *n., no pl.* **A** Entschuldbarkeit, *die;* **B** (*Theol.*) Lässlichkeit, *die*

**Venice** /ˈvenɪs/ *pr. n.* ▶ **1626** Venedig (*das*)

**venison** /ˈvenɪsn, ˈvenɪzn/ *n., no pl.* Hirsch[fleisch], *das;* (*of roe*) Reh[fleisch], *das;* **roast ~:** Hirsch-/Rehbraten, *der;* **~ steak** Hirsch-/Rehsteak, *das*

**venom** /ˈvenəm/ *n.* **A** (*Zool.*) Gift, *das;* **B** (*fig.*) Boshaftigkeit, *die;* Gehässigkeit, *die;* **unleash one's ~ on sb.** jmdn. angiften (*ugs.*); **the ~ of her hatred** ihr giftiger Hass; **say sth. with great** *or* **real ~:** etw. sehr giftig sagen; **there was much ~ in his criticism** seine Kritik war wirklich giftig

**venomous** /ˈvenəməs/ *adj.* **A** (*Zool.*) giftig; Gift‹schlange, -stachel›; **B** (*fig.*) giftig (*ugs.*); boshaft

**venomously** /ˈvenəməslɪ/ *adv.* (*fig.*) giftig (*ugs.*); boshaft

**venous** /ˈviːnəs/ *adj.* **A** (*Anat., Zool.*) venös; **B** (*Bot.*) geädert

**vent**[1] /vent/ ❶ *n.* **A** (*for gas, liquid to escape*) Öffnung, *die;* **B** (*of gun, cannon, etc.*) Zündloch, *das;* Zündkanal, *der;* **C** (*in barrel*) Spundloch, *das;* **D** (*Mus.*) Griffloch, *das;* **E** (*flue*) [Rauch]abzug, *der;* **F** (*Geol.*) [Vulkan]schlot, *der;* **G** (*fig.: for emotions*) Ventil, *das* (*fig.*); **give ~ to** Luft machen (+ *Dat.*) ‹Ärger, Wut›; freien Lauf lassen (+ *Dat.*) ‹Gefühlen›; Ausdruck verleihen (+ *Dat.*) ‹Freude›; **H** (*Zool.*) Kloake, *die.* ❷ *v.t.* (*fig.*) freien Lauf lassen (+ *Dat.*) ‹Kummer, Schmerz›; Luft machen (+ *Dat.*) ‹Ärger, Wut›; **~ one's anger on sb.** seinen Ärger an jmdm. auslassen *od.* abreagieren; ⇒ *also* **spleen B**

**vent**[2] *n.* (*in garment*) Schlitz, *der;* **a jacket with a ~:** ein Jackett mit Rückenschlitz

**ˈvent hole** ⇒ **vent**[1] **1 A**

**ventilate** /ˈventɪleɪt/ *v.t.* **A** lüften; (*by permanent installation*) belüften; **B** (*fig.*) (*submit to public consideration*) [offen] erörtern; (*voice*) kundtun, äußern ‹Meinung›; vorbringen ‹Beschwerden›; **C** (*Physiol.*) mit Sauerstoff versorgen

**ventilation** /ventɪˈleɪʃn/ *n.* **A** *no pl.* Belüftung, *die;* **the rooms need regular ~:** die Zimmer müssen regelmäßig gelüftet werden; **this room has inadequate ~:** dieses Zimmer ist unzureichend *od.* schlecht belüftet; **B** *no pl.* (*installation*) Lüftung, *die;* **C** (*fig.*) (*open discussion*) [offene] Erörterung; Aussprache, *die* (**of** über + *Akk.*); (*voicing*) (*of opinion*) Äußerung, *die;* (*of grievances*) Vorbringen, *das;* **D** *no pl., no art.* (*Physiol.*) Sauerstoffzufuhr, *die*

**ventiˈlation shaft** *n.* (*Mining*) Wetterschacht, *der*

**ventilator** /ˈventɪleɪtə(r)/ *n.* **A** Lüftung[svorrichtung], *die;* (*fan*) Ventilator, *der;* **B** (*Med.*) Beatmungsgerät, *das;* **be put on a ~:** an ein Beatmungsgerät angeschlossen werden

**ventral** /ˈventrl/ *adj.* **A** (*Anat., Zool.*) ventral (*fachspr.*); Bauch-; **B** (*Bot.*) ventral

**ventricle** /ˈventrɪkl/ *n.* (*Anat.*) Ventrikel, *der*

**ventriloquism** /venˈtrɪləkwɪzm/ *n., no pl.* Bauchreden, *das*

**ventriloquist** /venˈtrɪləkwɪst/ *n.* Bauchredner, *der*/-rednerin, *die*

**venture** /ˈventʃə(r)/ ❶ *n.* **A** Unternehmung, *die;* **their ~ into space/the unknown** ihre Reise in den Weltraum/ins Unbekannte; **a new ~ in sth.** ein neuer Vorstoß in etw. (*Dat.*); **her latest ~ is surfing** neuerdings hat sie sich aufs Surfen verlegt (*ugs.*); **sth. is quite a** *or* **some ~:** etw. ist ein gewagtes *od.* mutiges Unterfangen; **I can't lose much by the ~:** ich kann bei dem Versuch nicht viel verlieren; **B** (*Commerc.*) Unternehmung, *die;* **a successful ~:** ein erfolgreiches Geschäft; **a new publishing ~:** ein neues verlegerisches Vorhaben *od.* Projekt; **join a ~:** sich einem Unternehmen anschließen; ⇒ *also* **joint 2 A.**
❷ *v.i.* **A** (*dare*) wagen; **if I might ~ to suggest ...:** wenn Sie [mir] gestatten, möchte ich vorschlagen ...; **may I ~ to ask ...:** darf ich mir erlauben zu fragen ...; **I would even ~ to say ...:** ich würde sogar so weit gehen zu sagen ...; **B** (*dare to go*) sich wagen; **dare to ~:** sich wagen; **~ further into the cave** sich weiter *od.* tiefer in die Höhle vorwagen; **~ [away] from home** sich von zu Hause fort wagen; **~ abroad/into society** sich ins Ausland/in Gesellschaft wagen; **~ out of doors** sich vor die Tür wagen; **~ into a new area of research** (*fig.*) sich auf ein neues Forschungsgebiet vorwagen; **he would never ~ too far** (*fig.*) er würde sich nie zu weit vorwagen.
❸ *v.t.* **A** wagen ‹Bitte, Bemerkung, Blick, Vermutung›; zu äußern wagen ‹Ansicht›; sich (*Dat.*) erlauben ‹Frage, Scherz, Bemerkung›; **~ an explanation for sth.** etw. zu erklären versuchen; **if I might ~ a suggestion** wenn ich mir einen Vorschlag erlauben darf; **'How about ...?', he ~d** „Wie wärs mit ...?", schlug er

vor; **B** (*risk, stake*) aufs Spiel setzen ‹Leben, Ruf, Vermögen, Glück›; setzen ‹Wettsumme› (**on** auf + *Akk.*); **~ money in** *or* **on sth.** Geld in etw. (*Akk.*) stecken; ⇒ *also* **nothing** 1 A

**~ 'forth** (*literary*) ⇒ **~ out**

**~ on** *v.t.* sich einlassen auf (+ *Akk.*); sich wagen an (+ *Akk.*) ‹Aufgabe›; sich wagen auf (+ *Akk.*) ‹Reise›

**~ 'out** *v.i.* sich hinauswagen; **~ out on to the sea** sich auf das Meer hinauswagen

**~ upon** ⇒ **~ on**

**'venture capital** *n., no pl.* Wagniskapital, *das;* Risikokapital, *das*

**venturer** /'ventʃərə(r)/ *n.* **A** (*Commerc. Hist.*) Unternehmer, *der*/Unternehmerin, *die;* **B** (*adventurer*) Abenteurer, *der*/Abenteu[r]erin, *die*

**'Venture Scout** *n.* (*Brit.*) ≈ Rover, *der; Pfadfinder im Alter von 16 bis 20 Jahren*

**venturesome** /'ventʃəsəm/ *adj.* wagemutig ‹Person, Tat›; (*hazardous*) abenteuerlich ‹Unternehmen, Reise›

**venue** /'venju:/ *n.* (*Sport*) [Austragungs]ort, *der;* (*Mus., Theatre*) [Veranstaltungs]ort, *der;* (*meeting place*) Treffpunkt, *der*

**Venus** /'vi:nəs/ *pr. n.* **A** (*Astron.*) Venus, *die;* **B** (*Roman Mythol.*) Venus (*die*)

**Venusian** /vɪ'nju:zɪən/ **1** *adj.* (*Astron.*) Venus-. **2** *n.* Venusbewohner, der/-bewohnerin, *die*

**Venus['s] 'flytrap** *n.* (*Bot.*) Venusfliegenfalle, *die*

**veracious** /və'reɪʃəs/ *adj.* (*formal*) **A** aufrichtig ‹Person›; **assume sb. to be ~:** davon ausgehen, dass jmd. die Wahrheit sagt; **B** (*true*) wahr; wahrheitsgetreu ‹Schilderung, Bericht›

**veraciously** /və'reɪʃəslɪ/ *adv.* (*formal*) wahrheitsgemäß ‹darstellen›; **speak ~:** die Wahrheit sprechen

**veracity** /və'ræsɪtɪ/ *n., no pl.* **A** (*of person*) Aufrichtigkeit, *die;* **B** (*of statement etc.*) Wahrheitstreue, *die;* **have ~:** wahrheitsgetreu sein

**veranda[h]** /və'rændə/ *n.* Veranda, *die*

**verb** /vɜ:b/ *n.* (*Ling.*) Verb, *das;* Verbum, *das* (*fachspr.*)

**verbal** /'vɜ:bl/ *adj.* **A** (*relating to words*) sprachlich; **~ memory** Gedächtnis für Worte *od.* Sprache; **his skills are ~:** seine Fähigkeiten liegen auf sprachlichem Gebiet; **the distinction is purely ~:** der Unterschied besteht nur in der Wortwahl; **B** (*oral*) mündlich; verbal, mündlich ‹Bekenntnis, Anerkennung, Protest›; **C** (*Ling.*) verbal; **a ~ group** eine Verb[al]gruppe

**verbalize (verbalise)** /'vɜ:bəlaɪz/ *v.t.* **A** (*express*) in Worte fassen, (*geh.*) verbalisieren ‹Gefühle›; **B** (*Ling.: make into verb*) verbalisieren

**verbally** /'vɜ:bəlɪ/ *adv.* **A** (*regarding words*) sprachlich; mit Worten, verbal ‹beschrieben›; **B** (*orally*) mündlich; verbal, mündlich ‹protestieren›; **C** (*Ling.*) verbal

**verbal 'noun** *n.* (*Ling.*) Verbalsubstantiv, *das*

**verbatim** /və'beɪtɪm/ **1** *adv.* im Wortlaut ‹veröffentlichen›; [wort]wörtlich ‹sagen, abschreiben, zitieren›. **2** *adj.* wortgetreu; [wort]wörtlich

**verbena** /və'bi:nə/ *n.* (*Bot.*) **A** Eisenkraut, *das;* Verbene, *die* (*fachspr.*); **B** **[lemon] ~:** Zitronenstrauch, *der*

**verbiage** /'vɜ:bɪɪdʒ/ *n., no pl., no indef. art.* **A** (*wordiness*) Geschwätzigkeit, *die;* **B** (*words*) Geschwätz, *das*

**verbose** /və'bəʊs/ *adj.* geschwätzig; weitschweifig ‹Roman, Vortrag, Autor›; langatmig ‹Rede, Redner, Stil›; **he is too ~:** er macht zu viele Worte

**verbosely** /və'bəʊslɪ/ *adv.* weitschweifig; langatmig

**verboseness** /və'bəʊsnɪs/, **verbosity** /və'bɒsɪtɪ/ *ns.* **A** (*wordiness*) Weitschweifigkeit, die; Langatmigkeit, *die;* **B** (*words*) Geschwafel, *das*

**verdant** /'vɜ:dənt/ *adj.* (*literary*) [saft]grün

**verdict** /'vɜ:dɪkt/ *n.* **A** (*Law*) Urteil, *das;* [Urteils]spruch, *der;* **open ~** *Feststellung eines gewaltsamen Todes ohne Nennung der Ursache (bei einer gerichtlichen Untersuchung);* **~ of guilty/not guilty** Schuld-/Freispruch, *der;* **reach a ~:** zu einem Urteil kommen; ⇒ *also* **bring in d; return** 2 H; **B** (*judgement*) Urteil, *das* (**on** über + *Akk.*); (*decision*) Entscheidung, *die;* **the ~ of the electors** die Entscheidung der Wähler; **what's your ~ on the affair/novel?** wie beurteilst du die Sache/wie ist dein Urteil über den Roman?; **give** *or* **pass a/one's ~ [on sb./sth.]** ein/sein Urteil [über jmdn./etw.] abgeben

**verdigris** /'vɜ:dɪgrɪs/ *n.* **A** (*Chem.*) Grünspan, *der;* **B** (*rust on metal*) Patina, *die*

**verdure** /'vɜ:djə(r)/ *n.* (*literary*) **A** (*greenness*) Grün, *das;* **B** (*green vegetation*) [dichtes] Grün

**verge**[1] /vɜ:dʒ/ *n.* **A** (*grass edging*) Rasensaum, *der;* (*on road*) Bankette, *die;* **'keep off the ~'** „Bankette nicht befahrbar“; ⇒ *also* **soft verge; B** (*brink, border, lit. or fig.*) Rand, *der;* (*fig.: point at which something begins*) Schwelle, *die;* **be on the ~ of economic collapse/of war/of death** am Rand des wirtschaftlichen Zusammenbruchs/an der Schwelle des Krieges/Todes stehen; **be on the ~ of despair/tears/a breakthrough/a breakdown** der Verzweiflung/den Tränen/dem Durchbruch/einem Nervenzusammenbruch nahe sein; **be on the ~ of doing sth.** kurz davor stehen, etw. zu tun; **bring sb./sth. to the ~ of sth.** jmdn./etw. an den Rand von etw. bringen

**verge**[2] *v.i.* ‹Hügel, Land:› abfallen; **~ to[wards] sth.** (*fig.*) einer Sache (*Dat.*) zustreben; **~ towards old age** langsam alt werden

**~ on** *v.t.* [an]grenzen an (+ *Akk.*); **be verging on 70** an die 70 sein; **an estate verging on four acres** (*fig.*) ein Grundstück von fast vier Morgen [Größe]; **be verging on tears/madness** den Tränen/dem Wahnsinn nahe sein; **blue verging on grey** (*fig.*) ein Blau, das schon fast grau wirkt; **be verging on bankruptcy** vor dem Bankrott stehen

**verger** /'vɜ:dʒə(r)/ *n.* (*Eccl.*) Küster, *der*

**Vergil** ⇒ **Virgil**

**verifiable** /'verɪfaɪəbl/ *adj.* nachprüfbar; **this is an easily ~ statement** diese Behauptung lässt sich leicht nachprüfen

**verification** /verɪfɪ'keɪʃn/ *n.* **A** (*check*) Überprüfung, *die;* **~ of the accounts** Prüfung der Bücher; **be open to ~:** sich überprüfen lassen; **B** ⇒ **verify** B: Bestätigung, *die;* Bekräftigung, *die;* Nachweis, *der;* **I'll need some ~ of your identity** ich brauche dann noch einen Ausweis von Ihnen; **C** (*bearing out*) Bestätigung, *die;* **a ~ of their prediction** ein Beweis für die Richtigkeit ihrer Prognose

**verify** /'verɪfaɪ/ *v.t.* **A** (*check*) überprüfen; prüfen ‹Bücher›; **ring sb. up to ~ the news** jmdn. anrufen, um sich (*Dat.*) die [Richtigkeit der] Nachricht bestätigen zu lassen; **B** (*confirm*) bestätigen ‹Vermutung, Diagnose›; bekräftigen ‹Anspruch, Forderung›; nachweisen ‹Identität›; **C** (*bear out*) bestätigen; beweisen ‹Theorie›

**verily** /'verɪlɪ/ *adv.* (*arch.*) wahrlich (*veralt.*); **no** *or* **nay, ~:** nein, fürwahr (*veralt.*)

**verisimilitude** /verɪsɪ'mɪlɪtju:d/ *n., no pl.* Wahrheitsgehalt, *der;* (*in work of art*) Realistik, *die;* **sth. is designed to add** *or* **give ~ to a story** etw. soll eine Geschichte realistischer erscheinen lassen

**veritable** /'verɪtəbl/ *adj.* (*literary*) richtig; wahr, richtig ‹Engel, Genie›; wahr ‹Wunder›

**veritably** /'verɪtəblɪ/ *adv.* (*literary*) wirklich [und wahrhaftig]; **it was ~ miraculous** es war ein wahres Wunder; **a ~ suicidal thing to do** der reinste Selbstmord (*ugs.*); **the place ~ swam with wine** der Wein floss buchstäblich in Strömen

**verity** /'verɪtɪ/ *n.* (*literary*) Wahrheit, *die*

**vermicelli** /vɜ:mɪ'selɪ, vɜ:mɪ'tʃelɪ/ *n.* (*Gastr.*) Vermicelli; Fadennudeln

**vermicide** /'vɜ:mɪsaɪd/ *n.* (*Med.*) Wurmmittel, *das*

**vermiform** /'vɜ:mɪfɔ:m/ *adj.* wurmförmig; ⇒ *also* **appendix** B

**vermifuge** /'vɜ:mɪfju:dʒ/ (*Med.*) *n.* Wurmmittel, *das*

**vermilion** /və'mɪljən/ **1** *n.* (*substance*) Zinnober, *der;* (*colour*) Zinnoberrot, *das.* **2** *adj.* zinnoberrot

**vermin** /'vɜ:mɪn/ *n., no pl., no indef. art.* Ungeziefer, *das;* (*fig. derog.*) Pack, *das* (*abwertend*); Abschaum, *der* (*abwertend*)

**verminous** /'vɜ:mɪnəs/ *adj.* ungezieferverseucht; voller Ungeziefer *nachgestellt;* (*fig. derog.*) übel

**vermouth** /'vɜ:məθ, və'mu:θ/ *n.* Wermut[wein], *der*

**vernacular** /və'nækjʊlə(r)/ **1** *adj.* **A** (*native*) landessprachlich; ‹Predigt, Zeitung› in der Landessprache; (*not learned or technical*) volkstümlich; (*in dialect*) mundartlich; **~ language** Landessprache, *die*/Volkssprache, *die*/Mundart, *die;* **the ~ dialect** der regionale Dialekt; **B** **~ architecture** volkstümliche Baukunst.

**2** *n.* **A** (*native language*) Landessprache, *die;* (*dialect*) Dialekt, *der;* **B** (*jargon*) Sprache, *die;* (*of a profession or group*) Jargon, *der;* **scientific/legal ~:** Wissenschafts-/Juristenjargon, *der;* **thieves' ~:** Gaunersprache, *die;* **~ of youth** Jugendsprache, *die;* **C** (*homely speech*) Umgangssprache, *die;* **if you'll excuse the ~** (*joc.*) wenn ich das mal so sagen darf

**vernal** /'vɜ:nl/ *adj.* Frühlings-; ⇒ *also* **equinox** A

**vernier** /'vɜ:nɪə(r)/ *n.* (*Mech. Engin.*) Nonius, *der*

**veronica** /və'rɒnɪkə/ *n.* (*Bot.*) Ehrenpreis, *das od. der*

**verruca** /ve'ru:kə/ *n., pl.* **~e** /ve'ru:si:/ *or* **~s** (*Med.*) Warze, *die;* Verruca, *die* (*fachspr.*)

**versatile** /'vɜ:sətaɪl/ *adj.* vielseitig; (*mentally*) flexibel; (*having many uses*) vielseitig verwendbar

**versatility** /vɜ:sə'tɪlɪtɪ/ *n., no pl.* Vielseitigkeit, *die;* (*mental*) Flexibilität, *die;* (*variety of uses*) vielseitige Verwendbarkeit

**verse** /vɜ:s/ *n.* **A** (*line*) Vers, *der;* **B** (*stanza*) Strophe, *die;* **of** *or* **in** *or* **with five ~s** fünfstrophig; **C** *no pl., no indef. art.* (*poetry*) Lyrik, *die;* **write some ~:** einige Verse schreiben; **piece of ~:** Gedicht, *das;* **written in ~:** in Versform; **put sth. into ~:** etw. in Verse fassen; **D** (*in Bible*) Vers, *der;* ⇒ *also* **blank verse; chapter** A

**versed** /vɜ:st/ *adj.* **be [well] ~ in sth.** sich in etw. (*Dat.*) [gut] auskennen; **he's [well] ~ in such matters** er ist in diesen Dingen [sehr] versiert

**verse: ~ drama** *n.* (*Lit.*) Versdrama, *das;* **~ translation** *n.* (*Lit.*) Übertragung in Versform

**versification** /vɜ:sɪfɪ'keɪʃn/ *n.* **A** (*composing of verse*) Versedichten, *das;* (*derog.*) Verseschmieden, *das;* **B** (*metrical form*) Versbau, *der;* **C** (*poetical version*) Versfassung, *die*

**versifier** /'vɜ:sɪfaɪə(r)/ *n.* Versdichter, *der*/-dichterin, *die;* (*derog.*) Versemacher, *der*/-macherin, *die*

**versify** /'vɜ:sɪfaɪ/ **1** *v.t.* in Verse fassen. **2** *v.i.* Gedichte schreiben; (*derog.*) Verse schmieden

**version** /'vɜ:ʃn/ *n.* Version, *die;* (*in another language*) Übersetzung, *die;* (*in another form also*) Fassung, *die;* (*of vehicle, machine, tool*) Modell, *das;* ⇒ *also* **authorize** B; **revise** 1 A

**verso** /'vɜ:səʊ/ *n., pl.* **~s** **A** (*Printing, Bibliog.*) (*left-hand page*) linke Seite; (*back of leaf*) Verso, *das* (*fachspr.*); Rückseite, *die;* **B** (*Num.*) Revers, *der* (*fachspr.*); Rückseite, *die*

**versus** /'vɜ:səs/ *prep.* gegen

**vert** /vɜ:t/ (*Her.*) **1** *n.* Grün, *das.* **2** *adj.* grün

**vertebra** /'vɜ:tɪbrə/ *n., pl.* **~e** /'vɜ:tɪbri:/ (*Anat.*) Wirbel, *der;* **~e** (*backbone*) Wirbelsäule, *die*

**vertebral** /'vɜ:tɪbrəl/ *adj.* (*Anat.*) vertebral (*fachspr.*); Wirbel-; **~ column/muscles** Wirbelsäule, *die*/Rückenmuskulatur, *die*

**vertebrate** /'vɜ:tɪbrət, 'vɜ:tɪbreɪt/ (*Zool.*) **1** *adj.* Wirbel‹tier›; Wirbeltier‹skelett, -fossilien, -zoologie›; ‹Stamm› der Wirbeltiere. **2** *n.* Wirbeltier, *das*

**vertex** /'vɜ:teks/ *n., pl.* **vertices** /'vɜ:tɪsi:z/ *or* **~es** **A** (*highest point*) Gipfel, *der;* (*of tower, turret*) Spitze, *die;* (*Archit.: of dome,*

V

*arch*) Scheitel[punkt], *der;* **B** (*Geom.*) (*of curve, surface, angle*) Scheitel[punkt], *der;* (*of triangle, polygon*) Eckpunkt, *der*

**vertical** /ˈvɜːtɪkl/ ❶ *adj.* **A** senkrecht; senkrecht aufragend *od.* abfallend ‹Klippe›; **be ~:** senkrecht stehen; **B** (*esp. Econ., Sociol.: combining levels, stages, etc.*) vertikal; ⇒ *also* **integration** D. ❷ *n.* senkrechte *od.* vertikale Linie; **be out of [the] ~:** nicht im *od.* außer Lot sein

**vertically** /ˈvɜːtɪkəlɪ/ *adv.* **A** senkrecht; vertikal; **B** (*esp. Econ., Sociol.: so as to combine levels, stages, etc.*) vertikal

**vertical: ~ ˈplane** *n.* (*Geom.*) Vertikalebene, *die;* **~ ˈtake-off** *n.* (*Aeronaut.*) Senkrechtstart, *der;* **~ ˈtake-off aircraft** *n.* (*Aeronaut.*) Senkrechtstarter, *der*

**vertices** *pl. of* **vertex**

**vertiginous** /vəˈtɪdʒɪnəs/ *adj.* Schwindel erregend ‹Höhe, Abgrund usw.›

**vertigo** /ˈvɜːtɪgəʊ/ *n., pl.* **~s** Schwindel, *der;* Vertigo, *die* (*Med.*); **give sb. ~:** jmdn. schwindelig machen; **she got ~:** ihr wurde schwindelig; **attack of ~:** Schwindelanfall, *der*

**vervain** /ˈvɜːveɪn/ *n.* (*Bot.*) Eisenkraut, *das*

**verve** /vɜːv/ *n.* Schwung, *der;* (*of artist, orchestra's playing, sports team's play*) Temperament, *das;* (*of music, sb.'s writing*) Ausdruckskraft, die (**of, in** *Gen.*)

**very** /ˈverɪ/ ❶ *attrib. adj.* **A** (*precise, exact*) genau; **you must do it this ~ day** du musst es noch heute tun; **on the ~ day when ...:** genau am [selben] Tag, an dem ...; **you're the ~ person I wanted to see** genau dich wollte ich sehen; **at the ~ moment when ...:** im selben Augenblick, als ...; **just this ~ moment ...:** gerade eben ...; **in the ~ centre** genau in der Mitte; **the ~ opposite** genau das Gegenteil; **the ~ thing** genau das Richtige; **the ~ stones cry out** das schreit ja zum Himmel; **B** (*extreme*) **at the ~ back/front** ganz hinten/vorn; **at the ~ edge of the cliff** ganz am Rand der Klippe; **at the ~ end/beginning** ganz am Ende/Anfang; **from the ~ outset** *or* **beginning** von Anfang an; **go to the ~ end of the street** ganz bis ans Ende der Straße gehen; **climb to the ~ top of the hill** bis auf den Gipfel des Berges steigen; **a ~ little more** ein ganz kleines bisschen mehr; **only a ~ little** nur ein ganz kleines bisschen; **C** (*mere*) bloß ‹Gedanke›; **at the ~ thought** allein schon beim Gedanken; **the ~ fact of his presence** allein schon seine Anwesenheit; **the ~ mention** allein schon die Erwähnung; **D** (*absolute*) absolut ‹Minimum, Maximum›; **do one's ~ best** *or* **utmost** sein Möglichstes tun; **the ~ most I can offer is ...:** ich kann allerhöchstens ... anbieten; **it's the ~ least** das ist das Allermindeste; **£50 at the ~ most** allerhöchstens 50 Pfund; **they should at the ~ least consider the proposal** sie sollten das Angebot zumindest einmal in Erwägung ziehen; **be the ~ first to arrive** als Allererster ankommen; **for the ~ last time** zum allerletzten Mal; **E** (*used as emphatic or intensive*) **his ~ mother** seine eigene Mutter; **before their ~ eyes** vor ihren Augen; **be caught in the ~ act** auf frischer Tat ertappt werden; **be the ~ picture of health** wie die Gesundheit in Person aussehen; **under sb.'s ~ nose** (*fig. coll.*) direkt vor jmds. Augen (*Dat.*); **F** (*arch.: real*) wahr ‹Grund, Seelenfriede, Seele›; richtig ‹Teufel›; rein ‹Wahnsinn›.
❷ *adv.* **A** (*extremely*) sehr; **it's ~ near** es ist ganz in der Nähe; **in the ~ near future** in allernächster Zukunft; **it's ~ possible that ...:** es ist sehr gut möglich, dass ...; **~ probably** höchstwahrscheinlich; **she's ~/so ~ thin** sie ist sehr dünn/so dünn; **how ~ rude [of him]!** das ist aber unhöflich [von ihm]!; **[yes,] ~ much [so]** [ja,] sehr; **~ much prettier/better** [sehr] viel hübscher/besser; **not ~ much** nicht sehr; **~ little** [nur] sehr wenig ‹verstehen, essen›; **there's ~ little reason to do it** es spricht kaum etwas dafür, es zu tun; **thank you [~,] ~ much** [vielen,] vielen Dank; **[yes,] thank you ~ much** o ja, sehr gern; **no, thank you ~ much** nein, danke vielmals; **you are [~,] ~ kind** (*thanking*) das ist [wirklich] sehr freundlich von Ihnen; **not ~ big** (*not extremely big*) nicht sehr groß; (*not at all big*) nicht gerade groß; ⇒ *also* **reverend** 1; **so¹** A, 2; **B** (*absolutely*) aller‹best..., -letzt..., -leichtest...›; **at the ~ latest** allerspätestens; **the ~ last thing I expected** das, womit ich am allerwenigsten gerechnet hatte; **keep sth. for one's ~ own** etw. für sich ganz allein behalten; **have sth. of one's ~ own** etw. haben, das einem ganz allein gehört; **C** (*precisely*) **the ~ same one** genau der-/die-/dasselbe; **that is the ~ word he used** das ist genau das Wort, das er gebrauchte; **meet the ~ next day** sich gleich am nächsten Tag treffen; **in his ~ next sentence/breath** schon im nächsten Satz/Atemzug; **D ~ good** (*accepting*) sehr wohl; (*agreeing*) sehr schön; **~ well** *expr. reluctant consent* also gut; na schön; **that's all ~ well, but ...:** das ist ja alles schön und gut, aber ...

**very high ˈfrequency** *n.* (*Radio*) Ultrakurzwelle, *die*

**Very light** /ˈverɪ laɪt, ˈvɪərɪ laɪt/ *n.* (*Mil.*) Leuchtkugel, *die*

**vesicle** /ˈvesɪkl/ *n.* **A** (*Anat., Geol.*) Blase, *die;* **B** (*Zool., Bot., Med.*) Bläschen, *das*

**vespers** /ˈvespəz/ *n., constr. as sing. or pl.* (*Eccl.*) Vesper, *die*

**vessel** /ˈvesl/ *n.* **A** (*receptacle; also Anat., Bot.*) Gefäß, *das;* **[drinking] ~:** Trinkgefäß, *das;* ⇒ *also* **blood vessel**; **B** (*Naut.*) Schiff, *das;* **C** (*Bibl./joc.: person*) Typ, *der;* **weak ~:** unsicherer Kantonist/unsichere Kantonistin (*ugs.*); **the weaker ~:** das schwache Geschlecht (*ugs.*); (*Bibl.*) das schwächere Gefäß

**vest** /vest/ ❶ *n.* **A** (*Brit.: undergarment*) Unterhemd, *das;* (*woman's*) Hemd, *das;* **B** (*Amer.: waistcoat*) Weste, *die.* ❷ *v.t.* **~ sb. with sth., ~ sth. in sb.** jmdm. etw. verleihen; **be ~ed with the power to do sth.** berechtigt sein, etw. zu tun; **~ sb. with [rights in] sth.** jmdm. Ansprüche auf etw. (*Akk.*) einräumen; **be ~ed in sb.** jmdm. übertragen sein; **by the authority ~ed in me** kraft der mir verliehenen Vollmacht; ⇒ *also* **vested**. ❸ *v.i.* **~ in sb.** jmdm. übertragen werden

**vestal** /ˈvestl/ (*Roman Mythol.*) ❶ *adj.* vestalisch ‹Gesetz, Gelübde›; ‹Schrein, Feuer› der Vesta. ❷ *n.* ⇒ **vestal virgin**

**vestal ˈvirgin** *n.* Vestalin, *die*

**vested** /ˈvestɪd/ *adj.* **~ interest/right** wohlerworbener Anspruch; (*established by law*) gesetzlicher Anspruch; **~ interests** (*groups of persons*) Interessengruppen; **have a ~ interest in sth.** (*fig.*) ein persönliches Interesse an etw. (*Dat.*) haben

**vestibule** /ˈvestɪbjuːl/ *n.* **A** (*indoors*) [Eingangs]halle, *die;* **B** (*external porch*) Vorhalle, *die;* **C** (*Amer. Railw.*) Vorraum, *der;* **D** (*Anat.*) Innenohrvorhof, *der;* Vestibulum, *das* (*fachspr.*)

**vestige** /ˈvestɪdʒ/ *n.* **A** Spur, *die;* **not the slightest** *or* **least ~** *or* **not a single ~ [of sth. remains]** nicht das Geringste *od.* nicht die Spur [ist von etw. übrig]; **not a ~ of truth/honour** kein Fünkchen Wahrheit/Ehre; **B** (*Biol.*) Rudiment, *das*

**vestigial** /veˈstɪdʒɪəl/ *adj.* rudimentär (*geh.; fachspr.*); spärlich ‹Überreste›; verkümmert ‹Tradition, Brauch›

**vestment** /ˈvestmənt/ *n.* [Priester]gewand, *das;* (*worn on special occasions*) Ornat, *das*

**ˈvest-pocket** *attrib. adj.* (*Amer.*) Taschen-; im [Westen]taschenformat *nachgestellt;* (*fig.: very small*) Miniatur‹modell, -ausgabe, -version›

**vestry** /ˈvestrɪ/ *n.* (*Eccl.*) Sakristei, *die*

**Vesuvius** /vɪˈsuːvɪəs/ *pr. n.* der Vesuv

**vet¹** /vet/ ❶ *n.* ▶ **1261** Tierarzt, *der*/-ärztin, *die.* ❷ *v.t.*, **-tt-** überprüfen; **~ an article for errors** einen Artikel auf Fehler [hin] durchsehen

**vet²** (*Amer. coll.*) ⇒ **veteran** 1

**vetch** /vetʃ/ *n.* (*Bot.*) Wicke, *die*

**veteran** /ˈvetərən/ ❶ *n.* Veteran, *der*/Veteranin, *die;* **V~s' Day** *amerikanischer Gedenktag anlässlich des Waffenstillstandes 1918 u. 1945.* ❷ *attrib. adj.* altgedient ‹Offizier, Politiker, Schauspieler›

**veteran ˈcar** *n.* (*Brit.*) Veteran, *der*

**veterinarian** /vetərɪˈneərɪən/ ▶ **1261** (*Amer.*) ⇒ **veterinary surgeon**

**veterinary** /ˈvetərɪnərɪ/ *attrib. adj.* tiermedizinisch; veterinär; **~ science/medicine** Veterinär- *od.* Tiermedizin, *die;* **~ practice** Tierarztpraxis, *die;* **course of ~ training** Ausbildung zum Tierarzt; **~ college** Institut für Tiermedizin

**veterinary ˈsurgeon** *n.* ▶ **1261** (*Brit.*) Tierarzt, *der*/-ärztin, *die*

**veto** /ˈviːtəʊ/ ❶ *n., pl.* **~es** **A** **[power** *or* **right of] ~:** Veto[recht], *das;* ⇒ *also* **pocket veto**; **B** (*rejection, prohibition*) Veto, *das* (**on** gegen, **from** vonseiten); **has there been a ~ of the bill?** hat jemand sein Veto gegen den Gesetzentwurf eingelegt?; **put a** *or* **one's ~ on sth.** sein Veto gegen etw. erheben *od.* einlegen. ❷ *v.t.* sein Veto einlegen gegen

**vex** /veks/ *v.t.* [ver]ärgern; (*cause to worry*) beunruhigen; (*dissatisfy, disappoint*) bekümmern; **[be enough to] ~ a saint** den bravsten Menschen in Harnisch bringen; **be ~ed about** *or* **at sth.** sich über etw. (*Akk.*) ärgern; **be ~ed that ...:** sich darüber ärgern, dass ...; **I am ~ed that ...:** es ärgert mich, dass ...; **be ~ed with sb.** sich über jmdn. ärgern

**vexation** /vekˈseɪʃn/ *n.* **A** (*act of harassing*) Belästigung, *die;* **take pleasure in the ~ of sb.** sich (*Dat.*) ein Vergnügen daraus machen, jmdn. zu ärgern; **B** (*state of irritation*) Verärgerung, *die* (**with, at** über + *Akk.*); (*state of worry*) Beunruhigung, *die;* (*dissatisfaction, disappointment*) Kummer, *der;* **suffer [much] ~:** [viel] Ärger/Kummer haben; **cause sb. ~** (*irritate*) jmdm. Ärger bereiten; (*worry*) jmdn. in Unruhe versetzen; (*disappoint*) jmdm. Kummer machen; **have the ~ of seeing sth. happen** verärgert/bekümmert mit ansehen müssen, wie etw. geschieht; **C** (*annoying thing*) Ärgernis, *das* (**to, for** für); **constant ~s from sb.** ständige Belästigungen durch jmdn.; **D** (*Law*) Schikane, *die*

**vexatious** /vekˈseɪʃəs/ *adj.* **A** ärgerlich; unausstehlich ‹Person›; **it is ~ that .../to ...:** es ist ärgerlich, dass .../zu ...; **B** (*Law*) schikanös

**vexatiously** /vekˈseɪʃəslɪ/ *adv.* **A** ungehörig ‹sich benehmen, sich verhalten›; **he said, rather ~, that ...:** sehr zu meinem Ärger/Kummer sagte er, dass ...; **~ complicated** lästig und kompliziert; **B** (*Law*) aus Schikane; schikanös ‹sich verhalten›

**vexed** /vekst/ *adj.* **A** (*annoyed*) verärgert (**by** über + *Akk.*); (*distressed*) bekümmert (**by** über + *Akk.*); **B ~ question** viel diskutierte Frage

**vexing** /ˈveksɪŋ/ *adj.* lästig ‹Angelegenheit, Problem, Sorgen›; ärgerlich ‹Zwickmühle›

**VFR** *abbr.* (*Aeronaut.*) **visual flight rules** Sichtflugregeln

**VG** *abbr.* **very good**

**VHF** *abbr.* **very high frequency** UKW

**via** /ˈvaɪə/ *prep.* über (+ *Akk.*) ‹Ort, Sender, Telefon›; auf (+ *Dat.*) ‹Weg›; durch ‹Eingang, Schornstein, Person›; per ‹Post›

**viability** /vaɪəˈbɪlɪtɪ/ *n., no pl.* **A** (*of foetus, animal, plant*) Lebensfähigkeit, *die;* (*of seed*) Keimfähigkeit, *die;* **B** (*fig.*) (*of state, company*) Lebensfähigkeit, *die;* (*feasibility*) Realisierbarkeit, *die*

**viable** /ˈvaɪəbl/ *adj.* **A** (*capable of maintaining life*) lebensfähig; keimfähig; **be more ~ than ...:** besser überleben als ...; **B** (*fig.*) lebensfähig ‹Staat, Firma›; (*feasible*) realisierbar

**viaduct** /ˈvaɪədʌkt/ *n.* Viadukt, *das od. der*

**viands** /ˈvaɪəndz/ *n. pl.* (*formal*) Esswaren *Pl.;* (*for journey*) Wegzehrung, *die* (*geh.*)

**vibes** /vaɪbz/ *n. pl.* (*coll.*) **A** (*Mus.*) Vibraphon, *das;* **B** (*vibrations*) Schwingungen; Vibrations (*salopp*); **I get good ~ from him** er törnt *od.* macht mich an (*ugs.*); **give sb. bad ~:** jmdn. abtörnen (*ugs.*); **feel those ~, man!** das törnt echt an! (*ugs.*)

**vibrant** /ˈvaɪbrənt/ *adj.* **A** (*vibrating*) vibrierend; schwingend, vibrierend ‹Saite, Draht›; **B**

V

(*thrilling*) pulsierend ‹Leben›; schwungvoll ‹Vorstellung›; lebensprühend ‹Atmosphäre›; dynamisch ‹Kraft›; lebhaft ‹Farbe, Rot›; **be ~ with activity/life** vor Aktivitäten/Leben (*Dat.*) sprühen; **a painting ~ with colour** ein farbenprächtiges Gemälde; **C** (*resonant*) volltönend ‹Stimme›; voll ‹Ton›

**vibraphone** /'vaɪbrəfəʊn/ *n.* (*Mus.*) Vibraphon, *das*

**vibrate** /vaɪ'breɪt/ ❶ *v.i.* **A** vibrieren; (*under strong impact*) beben; **B** (*resound*) [nach]klingen; **the sound of the anvil ~d in the streets** das Klingen des Ambosses hallte durch die Straßen; **C** (*Phys.*) schwingen; ‹Glocke:› vibrieren; **D** (*thrill*) ‹Stadt, Party, Aufsatz:› sprühen (**with** vor + *Dat.*); ‹Stimme, Körper:› vibrieren (**with** vor + *Dat.*). ❷ *v.t.* vibrieren lassen; zum Schwingen bringen ‹Saite›

**vibration** /vaɪ'breɪʃn/ *n.* **A** (*vibrating*) Vibrationen; (*visible*) Vibrieren, *das;* (*under strong impact*) Beben, *das;* **send ~s** *or* **a ~ through sth.** ‹Erdstoß:› etw. erzittern lassen; **B** (*Phys.*) Schwingung, *die;* **C** *in pl.* (*fig.*) **get some ~s** etwas spüren; **his presence gives me bad ~s** in seiner Gegenwart fühle ich mich [irgendwie] unwohl; **I get good ~s from this place/music** dieser Ort/diese Musik hat eine wohltuende Ausstrahlung

**vibrational** /vaɪ'breɪʃənl/ *adj.* (*Phys.*) Schwingungs-

**vibrato** /vɪ'brɑːtəʊ/ *n., pl.* **~s** (*Mus.*) Vibrato, *das*

**vibrator** /vaɪ'breɪtə(r)/ *n.* **A** Vibrator, *der;* **B** (*Electr.*) Zerhacker, *der*

**viburnum** /vaɪ'bɜːnəm/ *n.* (*Bot.*) Schneeball, *der*

**vicar** /'vɪkə(r)/ *n.* ▶ **1617** Pfarrer, *der;* **lay ~** *Laie, der Teile der Liturgie singt*

**vicarage** /'vɪkərɪdʒ/ *n.* Pfarrhaus, *das*

**vicar apos'tolic** *n.* (*RC Ch.*) Apostolischer Vikar

**vicarious** /vɪ'keərɪəs/ *adj.* **A** (*delegated*) Stellvertreter-; **his authority** *or* **power is ~:** er hat Stellvertreterbefugnisse; **B** (*done for another*) stellvertretend; **perform ~ work/tasks** Arbeit/Aufgaben stellvertretend erledigen; **~ suffering[s]** (*Theol.*) stellvertretendes Leiden; **C** (*experienced through another*) nachempfunden ‹Freude, Erregung usw.›; **~ [sexual] satisfaction** Ersatzbefriedigung, *die;* **take a ~ delight in sb.'s success** sich mit jmdm. *od.* für jmdn. über dessen Erfolg (*Akk.*) freuen

**vicariously** /vɪ'keərɪəslɪ/ *adv.* **A** (*as a substitute for another*) stellvertretend; **B** (*by means of a substitute*) indirekt

**vicariousness** /vɪ'keərɪəsnɪs/ *n., no pl.* stellvertretender Charakter; **the ~ of this experience** die Mittelbarkeit dieses Erlebnisses

**vice**[1] /vaɪs/ *n.* **A** Laster, *das;* **a life/den of ~:** ein Lasterleben/eine Lasterhöhle; **B** (*defect*) Fehler, *der;* **he has no redeeming ~:** er hat aber auch gar kein[e] Laster

**vice**[2] *n.* (*Brit.: tool*) Schraubstock, *der*

**vice**[3] *n.* (*coll.: deputy*) Vize, *der* (*ugs.*)

**vice-** *pref.* Vize-

**vice: ~-'admiral** *n.* (*Navy*) Vizeadmiral, *der;* **~-'chairman** *n.* stellvertretender Vorsitzender; **~-'chairmanship** *n.* Amt des/der stellvertretenden Vorsitzenden; **~-'chancellor** *n.* ▶ **1261** (*Univ.*) Vizekanzler, *der*/Vizekanzlerin, *die*

**'vicelike** *adj.* eisern ‹Griff›; fest ‹Umklammerung, Schwitzkasten›

**vice: ~-'presidency** *n.* Amt des Vizepräsidenten/der Vizepräsidentin; **~-'president** *n.* Vizepräsident, *der*/-präsidentin, *die;* **~-'principal** *n.* (*Educ.*) stellvertretender Leiter/stellvertretende Leiterin; **~'regal** *adj.* eines/des Vizekönigs *nachgestellt*

**viceroy** /'vaɪsrɔɪ/ *n.* Vizekönig, *der*

**viceroyship** /'vaɪsrɔɪʃɪp/ *n.* Amt eines Vizekönigs

**'vice squad** *n.* (*Police*) Sittenpolizei, *die*

**vice versa** /vaɪsɪ 'vɜːsə/ *adv.* umgekehrt

**vicinity** /vɪ'sɪnɪtɪ/ *n.* **A** (*neighbourhood*) Umgebung, *die;* **from London or its ~:** aus London und Umgebung; **in our ~:** nicht weit von uns [entfernt]; **in the immediate ~:** ganz in der Nähe; **in the ~ [of a place]** in der Nähe [eines Ortes]; **in the ~ of 50** (*fig.*) so um die 50; **B** *no pl.* (*nearness*) Nähe, *die;* **in close ~ to the church** ganz in der Nähe der Kirche

**vicious** /'vɪʃəs/ *adj.* **A** (*malicious, spiteful*) böse; boshaft ‹Äußerung›; böswillig ‹Versuch, Kritik›; bösartig ‹Äußerung, Tier›; **B** (*depraved*) übel ‹Benehmen, Charakter›; (*addicted to vice*) verdorben; (*wicked*) skrupellos ‹Tyrann, Verbrecher›; schlecht ‹Person, Menschheit›; **C** (*violent, severe*) brutal; unerträglich ‹Wetter, Schmerz›

**vicious 'circle** *n.* Teufelskreis, *der*

**viciously** /'vɪʃəslɪ/ *adv.* **A** (*maliciously, spitefully*) boshaft; auf gehässige Weise ‹kritisieren›; **B** (*violently, severely*) brutal

**viciousness** /'vɪʃəsnɪs/ *n., no pl.* **A** (*maliciousness, spitefulness*) Boshaftigkeit, *die;* (*of animal*) Bösartigkeit, *die;* **B** (*depravity*) Lasterhaftigkeit, *die;* (*of tyrant, criminal, government*) Skrupellosigkeit, *die;* **C** (*violence, severity*) Brutalität, *die;* (*of weather, pain*) Unerträglichkeit, *die*

**vicious 'spiral** *n.* Teufelskreis, *der;* **the ~ of wage increases and price rises** die Lohn-Preis-Spirale

**vicissitude** /vɪ'sɪsɪtjuːd/ *n.* steter Wandel; **~s** (*fickleness*) Unbeständigkeit, *die;* **the ~s of life** die Wechselfälle des Lebens

**victim** /'vɪktɪm/ *n.* **A** Opfer, *das;* (*of sarcasm, abuse*) Zielscheibe, *die* (*fig.*); **be the ~ of sb.'s anger/envy/policy** unter jmds. Zorn/Neid/Politik (*Dat.*) zu leiden haben; **be one's own ~:** das Opfer seiner selbst sein; **be a ~ of fortune** dem Schicksal ausgeliefert sein; **fall [a] ~ to sth.** das Opfer einer Sache (*Gen.*) werden; **fall ~ to the plague/to drought/famine** der Pest/Trockenheit/Hungersnot (*Dat.*) zum Opfer fallen; **fall a ~ to love/sb.'s charms** sein Herz verlieren/jmds. Charme (*Dat.*) erliegen; **B** (*dupe*) Opfer, *das;* **I refuse to be made his ~:** ich lasse mich von ihm nicht täuschen; **C** (*Relig.*) Opfer, *das;* (*animal*) Opfertier, *das;* **human sacrificial ~s** Menschenopfer

**victimisation, victimise** ⇒ **victimiz-**

**victimization** /vɪktɪmaɪ'zeɪʃn/ *n.* Schikanierung, *die;* (*selective punishment*) gezielte Bestrafung

**victimize** /'vɪktɪmaɪz/ *v.t.* **A** (*make a victim*) schikanieren; **be ~d [by sb.]** unter jmdm. zu leiden haben; **B** (*punish selectively*) gezielt bestrafen

**victor** /'vɪktə(r)/ *n.* Sieger, *der*/Siegerin, *die*

**victoria** *n.* **~ [plum]** Königin-Viktoria-Pflaume, *die*

**Victoria** /vɪk'tɔːrɪə/ *pr. n.* **A** (*Hist., as name of ruler etc.*) Viktoria (*die*); **B** (*Geog.*) Victoria (*das*)

**Victoria: ~ 'Cross** *n.* (*Brit.*) Viktoriakreuz, *das;* **~ 'Falls** *n. pl.* Victoriafälle *Pl.*

**Victorian** /vɪk'tɔːrɪən/ ❶ *adj.* viktorianisch. ❷ *n.* Viktorianer, *der*/Viktorianerin, *die*

**Victoriana** /vɪktɔːrɪ'ɑːnə/ *n. pl.* viktorianische Antiquitäten

**victorious** /vɪk'tɔːrɪəs/ *adj.* **A** siegreich; **be ~ over sb./sth.** über jmdn./etw. siegreich bleiben; **be ~ in one's struggle** aus seinem Kampf siegreich hervorgehen; **B** (*marked by victory*) erfolgreich ‹Verteidigung, Kreuzzug›; siegreich ‹Feldzug, Eroberung, Angriff›; triumphierend ‹Gruß, Lächeln›; **~ procession** Triumphzug, *der*

**victoriously** /vɪk'tɔːrɪəslɪ/ *adv.* erfolgreich; siegreich ‹kämpfen, zurückkehren›; triumphierend ‹rufen, lächeln, marschieren›

**victory** /'vɪktərɪ/ *n.* Sieg, *der* (**over** über + *Akk.*); *attrib.* Sieges-; **achieve ~:** den Sieg erringen; **be sure of ~:** der sichere Sieger sein; **lead one's troops to ~:** seine Truppen zum Sieg führen; **~ will be ours** der Sieg wird unser sein; **gain** *or* **win a ~ over sb./sth.** einen Sieg über jmdn./etw. erringen; ⇒ *also* **moral victory**; **Pyrrhic**

**victual** /'vɪtl/ (*formal*) ❶ *n. in pl.* Esswaren *Pl.;* (*of fort, ship, for journey*) Proviant, *der.* ❷ *v.t.,* (*Brit.*) **-ll-** verproviantieren

**victualler** /'vɪtələ(r)/ *n.* ▶ **1261** **licensed ~** (*Brit.*) Gastwirt, *der*/-wirtin, *die*

**vide** /'vaɪdɪ, 'vɪdeɪ, 'viːdeɪ/ *v.t. imper.* siehe

**video** /'vɪdɪəʊ/ ❶ *adj.* Video‹rekorder, -kassette, -kopf›. ❷ *n., pl.* **~s** **A** (**~ recorder**) Videorekorder, *der;* (**~ film, ~tape, ~ recording**) Video, *das* (*ugs.*); **have sth. on ~:** etw. auf Video haben (*ugs.*); **B** (*visual element of TV broadcasts*) Bild, *das.* ❸ *v.t.* ⇒ **videotape** 2

**video: ~ camera** *n.* Videokamera, *die;* **~ cas'sette** *n.* Videokassette, *die;* **~ cas'sette recorder** *n.* Videokassettenrekorder, *der;* **~ clip** *n.* Videoclip, *der;* **~conference** *n.* Videokonferenz, *die;* **~ disc** *n.* Bild- *od.* Videoplatte, *die;* **~ film** *n.* Videofilm, *der;* **~ frequency** *n.* Videofrequenz, *die;* **~ game** *n.* Videospiel, *das;* **~gram** /'vɪdɪəʊgræm/ *n.: bespielte Videokassette od. -platte, die keine private Kopie und kein Fernsehmitschnitt ist;* **~ library** *n.* Videothek, *die;* **~ 'nasty** *n.* Horrorvideo, *das;* **~-on-demand** *n., no pl.* Video-on-Demand, *das;* **~phone** *n.* Bildtelefon, *das;* **~ recorder** *n.* Videorekorder, *der;* **~ recording** *n.* Videoaufnahme, *die;* **~ signal** *n.* Videosignal, *das;* **~tape** ❶ *n.* Videoband, *das;* ❷ *v.t.* [auf Videoband (*Akk.*)] aufnehmen; **~ telephone** *n.* Bildtelefon, *das;* **~tex** /'vɪdɪəʊteks/, **~text** *n.* Bildschirmtext, *der;* (*teletext*) Videotext, *der*

**vie** /vaɪ/ *v.i.,* **vying** /'vaɪɪŋ/ **~ [with sb.] for sth.** [mit jmdm.] um etw. wetteifern; **~ with sb. in sth.** jmdn. mit etw. zu übertreffen suchen

**Vienna** /vɪ'enə/ ▶ **1626** ❶ *pr. n.* Wien (*das*). ❷ *attrib. adj.* Wiener

**Viennese** /vɪə'niːz/ ▶ **1626** ❶ *adj.* Wiener; **sb. is ~:** jmd. ist Wiener/Wienerin. ❷ *n., pl. same* Wiener, *der*/Wienerin, *die*

**Vietnam** /vjet'næm/ *pr. n.* **A** Vietnam (*das*); **B** **~ [War]** Vietnamkrieg, *der*

**Vietnamese** /vjetnə'miːz/ ▶ **1275**, ▶ **1340** ❶ *adj.* vietnamesisch. ❷ *n., pl. same* **A** (*person*) Vietnamese, *der*/Vietnamesin, *die;* **B** (*language*) Vietnamesisch, *das*

**view** /vjuː/ ❶ *n.* **A** (*range of vision*) Sicht, *die;* **get a good ~ of sth.** etw. gut sehen können; **have** *or* **get one's first ~ of sth.** etw. zum ersten Mal zu sehen bekommen; **have a clear/distant ~ of sth.** etw. deutlich/in der Ferne sehen können; **be out of/in ~:** nicht zu sehen/zu sehen sein; **come into ~:** in Sicht kommen; **be lost to ~:** nicht mehr zu sehen sein; **disappear from ~:** verschwinden; **leave the back exposed to [the] ~** ‹Kleid:› den Rücken freilassen; **our hotel has a good ~ of the sea** von unserem Hotel aus kann man das Meer gut sehen; **in full ~ of everyone in the street** vor den Augen aller Passanten; ⇒ *also* **full**[1] 1 D; **hide**[1] 1 C; **B** (*what is seen*) Aussicht, *die;* **the ~s from here** die Aussicht von hier; **a house with fine ~s** ein Haus mit schöner Aussicht; **a room with a ~:** ein Zimmer mit Aussicht; **just for the ~/~s** nur um die Aussicht zu genießen; **C** (*picture*) Ansicht, *die;* **photographic ~:** Foto, *das;* **take a ~ of sth.** ein Bild von etw. machen; **D** (*opinion*) Ansicht, *die;* **what is your ~** *or* **are your ~s on this?** was meinst du dazu?; **what is your ~ of him?** was hältst du von ihm?; **be grateful for sb.'s ~ of** *or* **~s on sth.** jmdm. für eine Stellungnahme zu etw. dankbar sein; **don't you have any ~[s] about it?** hast du keine Meinung dazu?; **the ~s of the public** die öffentliche Meinung; **the general/majority ~ is that ...:** die Allgemeinheit/Mehrheit ist der Ansicht, dass ...; **take a favourable ~ of sth.** etw. billigen; **have** *or* **hold ~s about** *or* **on sth.** eine Meinung über etw. (*Akk.*) haben; **hold** *or* **take the ~ that ...:** der Ansicht sein, dass ...; **in my ~:** meiner Ansicht nach; **in sb.'s ~:** nach jmds. Ansicht; **I take a different ~:** ich bin anderer Ansicht; **take a critical/grave/optimistic ~ of sth.** etw. kritisch/ernst/optimistisch beurteilen; ⇒ *also* **dim** 1 E; **long**[1] 1 A; **poor** 1 I; **E** **be on ~** ‹Waren, Haus:› besichtigt werden können; ‹Bauplan:› [zur Einsicht] ausliegen; **have sth. in ~** (*fig.*) etw. im Auge haben; **in ~ of sth.** (*fig.*) angesichts einer Sache; **keep sth. in ~** (*fig.*) etw.

V

im Auge behalten; **with a ~ to** *or* **with a** *or* **the ~ of doing sth.** in der Absicht, etw. zu tun; **with a ~ to sth.** (*fig.*) mit etw. im Auge; **with this in ~:** im Hinblick darauf; ⇒ *also* **point** 1 K; **F** (*survey*) Betrachtung, *die;* (*of house, site*) Besichtigung, *die;* **on taking a closer ~:** bei näherer Betrachtung; **if we take a broad** *or* **general ~ of the problem** bei allgemeiner Betrachtung des Problems; **give a ~ of sth.** ‹Buch:› einen Überblick über etw. (*Akk.*) geben; ⇒ *also* **private view[ing]**.

**2** *v.t.* **A** (*look at*) sich (*Dat.*) ansehen; **B** (*consider*) betrachten; beurteilen ‹Situation, Problem›; **~ed in this light ...:** so gesehen ...; **~ed ethically** aus ethischer Sicht; **I ~ the matter differently** ich sehe das anders; **C** (*inspect*) besichtigen; **ask to ~ sth.** darum bitten, etw. besichtigen zu dürfen.

**3** *v.i.* (*Telev.*) fernsehen

**viewdata** /ˈvjuːdeɪtə/ *n.* (*Teleph.*) Bildschirmtextsystem, *das*

**viewer** /ˈvjuːə(r)/ *n.* **A** (*Telev.*) [Fernseh]zuschauer, *der*/-zuschauerin, *die;* **B** (*Photog.*) (*for cine film*) Filmbetrachter, *der;* (*for slides*) Diabetrachter, *der*

**ˈviewfinder** *n.* (*Photog.*) Sucher, *der*

**viewing** /ˈvjuːɪŋ/ *n.* **A** (*Telev.*) Fernsehen, *das;* **~ has decreased** der Fernsehkonsum ist zurückgegangen; **~ figures** Einschaltquoten; **at peak ~ time** zur besten Sendezeit; **B** (*of house, at auction, etc.*) Besichtigung, *die;* ⇒ *also* **private view[ing]**

**viewpoint** /ˈvjuːpɔɪnt/ *n.* Standpunkt, *der;* Sehweise, *die;* **from a general/the political/the social ~ ...:** allgemein/politisch/gesellschaftlich gesehen *od.* betrachtet, ...; **seen from that ~ ...:** so gesehen *od.* betrachtet, ...; **see sth. from sb.'s ~:** etw. aus jmds. Sicht sehen

**vigil** /ˈvɪdʒɪl/ *n.* **A** Wachen, *das;* **nocturnal ~:** Nachtwache, *die;* **keep ~ [over sb.]** [bei jmdm.] wachen; **B** (*Relig.*) Vigil, *die*

**vigilance** /ˈvɪdʒɪləns/ *n., no pl.* Wachsamkeit, *die;* **exercise ~ lest sb. escape** wachsam sein, damit jmd. nicht entkommt; **escape sb.'s ~:** jmds. Wachsamkeit (*Dat.*) entgehen; jmdm. entgehen

**ˈvigilance committee** *n.* (*Amer.*) Bürgerwehr, *die*

**vigilant** /ˈvɪdʒɪlənt/ *adj.* wachsam; **be ~ for sth.** auf etw. (*Akk.*) achten

**vigilante** /vɪdʒɪˈlæntɪ/ *n.* Mitglied einer/der Bürgerwehr; **~ group** Bürgerwehr, *die*

**vigilantly** /ˈvɪdʒɪləntlɪ/ *adv.* wachsam

**vignette** /viːˈnjet/ *n.* **A** (*Lit.*) Skizze, *die;* **B** (*Art, Photog.*) vignettiertes Bild

**vigor** (*Amer.*) ⇒ **vigour**

**vigorous** /ˈvɪgərəs/ *adj.* kraftvoll; kräftig ‹Person, Tier, Stoß, Pflanze, Wachstum, Trieb›; robust ‹Gesundheit›; leidenschaftlich ‹Debattierer, Debatte, Verteidigung, Befürworter›; heftig ‹Nicken, Attacke, Kritik, Protest›; intensiv ‹Gymnastik, Denksport›; energisch ‹Versuch, Anstrengung, Leugnen, Maßnahme›; schwungvoll ‹Rede›; **be too ~ for sb.** ‹Gymnastik:› zu anstrengend für jmdn. sein

**vigorously** /ˈvɪgərəslɪ/ *adv.* heftig; leidenschaftlich ‹musizieren, reden, schreiben›; intensiv ‹Gymnastik treiben›; energisch ‹versuchen, beginnen›; kräftig ‹schrubben, reiben, ziehen, drücken, wachsen›

**vigour** /ˈvɪgə(r)/ *n.* (*Brit.*) **A** (*of person, animal, sexuality*) Vitalität, *die;* (*of limbs, body*) Kraft, *die;* (*of health*) Robustheit, *die;* (*of debate, argument, struggle, protest, denial, attack, criticism*) Heftigkeit, *die;* (*of performance, speech*) Schwung, *der;* (*of words, style, mind, intellect*) Lebendigkeit, *die;* **with ~:** schwungvoll ‹musizieren, reden, singen, schauspielern›; kräftig ‹reiben, schrubben, drücken, ziehen›; **B** (*Bot.*) Wuchskraft, *die*

**Viking** /ˈvaɪkɪŋ/ *n.* (*Hist.*) Wikinger, *der*/Wikingerin, *die; attrib.* Wikinger-

**vile** /vaɪl/ *adj.* **A** (*base*) verwerflich (*geh.*); abscheulich ‹Sünde, Charakter, Verbrechen›; gemein ‹Verleumdung›; vulgär ‹Sprache›; (*repulsive*) widerwärtig; **don't be so ~!** sei nicht so gemein!; **be ~ to sb.** gemein zu jmdm. sein; **B** (*coll.: very unpleasant*) scheußlich (*ugs.*)

**vilely** /ˈvaɪllɪ/ *adv.* **A** in verwerflicher Weise (*geh.*); **act/behave ~:** abscheulich handeln/gemein sein; **speak ~ of sb.** abscheuliche Dinge über jmdn. sagen; **B** (*coll.: very unpleasantly*) scheußlich (*ugs.*)

**vileness** /ˈvaɪlnɪs/ *n., no pl.* ⇒ **vile**: **A** Verwerflichkeit, *die* (*geh.*); Abscheulichkeit, *die;* Gemeinheit, *die;* Vulgarität, *die;* Widerwärtigkeit, *die;* **B** Scheußlichkeit, *die* (*ugs.*)

**vilification** /vɪlɪfɪˈkeɪʃn/ *n.* Verunglimpfung, *die* (*geh.*)

**vilify** /ˈvɪlɪfaɪ/ *v.t.* verunglimpfen (*geh.*)

**villa** /ˈvɪlə/ *n.* **A** (*holiday house*) **[holiday] ~:** Ferienhaus, *das;* **B** (*country house*) **[country] ~:** Landhaus, *das;* **C** (*Brit.: suburban house*) besseres Einfamilienhaus

**village** /ˈvɪlɪdʒ/ *n.* Dorf, *das; attrib.* Dorf‹leben, -kneipe usw.›

**village: ~ ˈgreen** *n.* Dorfwiese, *die;* **~ ˈhall** *n.* Dorfgemeinschaftshaus, *das;* **~ ˈidiot** *n.* Dorftrottel, *der*

**villager** /ˈvɪlɪdʒə(r)/ *n.* Dorfbewohner, *der*/-bewohnerin, *die*

**villain** /ˈvɪlən/ *n.* **A** (*scoundrel*) Verbrecher, *der;* (*arch. derog.*) Schurke, *der;* **B ~ [of the piece]** (*Theatre; also fig.*) Bösewicht, *der;* **C** (*coll.: rascal*) [kleiner] Halunke (*scherzh.*)

**villainous** /ˈvɪlənəs/ *adj.* **A** gemein; abscheulich; **B** (*coll.: very bad*) scheußlich (*ugs.*)

**villainously** /ˈvɪlənəslɪ/ *adv.* gemein; abscheulich; in gemeiner *od.* abscheulicher Weise ‹morden, Verrat üben, sich verschwören›

**villainy** /ˈvɪlənɪ/ *n.* Gemeinheit, *die;* Abscheulichkeit, *die;* **forsake ~:** aller Gemeinheit abschwören

**villein** /ˈvɪlɪn/ *n.* (*Hist.*) Leibeigene, *der/die*

**vim** /vɪm/ *n., no pl.* (*coll.*) Schwung, *der;* **put some [more] ~ into it!** leg dich mal ein bisschen [mehr] ins Zeug! (*ugs.*)

**vinaigrette** /vɪnɪˈgret/ *n.* **A** (*smelling bottle*) Riechfläschchen, *das;* **B ~ [sauce]** (*Cookery*) Vinaigrette, *die*

**vindicate** /ˈvɪndɪkeɪt/ *v.t.* **A** (*justify, establish*) verteidigen, rechtfertigen ‹Person, Meinung, Handeln, Verhalten, Anspruch, Politik›; retten ‹Ruf, Ehre, Stellung›; beweisen ‹Mut, Ehrlichkeit, Integrität, Behauptung›; (*confirm*) bestätigen ‹Recht, Meinung, Urteil, Theorie›; **B** (*exonerate*) rehabilitieren

**vindication** /vɪndɪˈkeɪʃn/ *n.* ⇒ **vindicate**: **A** Verteidigung, *die;* Rechtfertigung, *die;* Rettung, *die;* Beweis, *der* (**of** für); Bestätigung, *die;* **be a ~ of sth.** etw. rechtfertigen/verteidigen/beweisen/bestätigen; **in ~ of his claim/conduct** *etc.* zur Rechtfertigung seines Anspruchs/Benehmens *usw.;* **B** Rehabilitierung, *die;* **be a full ~ of sb.** jmdn. vollständig rehabilitieren

**vindictive** /vɪnˈdɪktɪv/ *adj.* nachtragend ‹Person›; unversöhnlich ‹Stimmung›; **~ act/move/attack** Racheakt, *der* (*geh.*); **feel ~** *or* **be in a ~ mood [towards sb.]** Rachegefühle [gegenüber jmdm.] hegen; **make sb. [feel] ~:** Rachegefühle bei jmdm. wecken; **be purely ~** ‹Tat:› ein reiner Racheakt sein

**vindictively** /vɪnˈdɪktɪvlɪ/ *adv.* aus Rache; **act** *or* **behave ~ [towards sb.]** sich nachtragend [gegenüber jmdm.] verhalten

**vindictiveness** /vɪnˈdɪktɪvnɪs/ *n., no pl.* Rachsucht, *die* (*geh.*); **the ~ of sb.'s nature/mood** jmds. nachtragendes Wesen/jmds. Rachsucht; **feel ~ towards sb.** Rachegefühle gegen jmdn. hegen; **an attitude of ~:** eine nachtragende Haltung

**vine** /vaɪn/ *n.* **A** Weinrebe, *die;* **B** (*stem of trailer or climber*) Ranke, *die;* **C** (*Amer.: trailing or climbing plant*) Rankengewächs, *das*

**vinegar** /ˈvɪnɪgə(r)/ *n.* Essig, *der;* **[as] sour as ~:** sehr sauer; (*fig.*) säuerlich ‹Miene, Lächeln›; sauertöpfisch (*ugs.*) ‹Person›

**vinegary** /ˈvɪnɪgərɪ/ *adj.* sauer; (*fig.*) säuerlich; **have a ~ taste** wie Essig schmecken

**ˈvine leaf** *n.* [Wein]rebenblatt, *das;* **stuffed vine leaves** (*Gastr.*) gefüllte Weinblätter

**vineyard** /ˈvɪnjɑːd, ˈvɪnjəd/ *n.* Weinberg, *der*

**vintage** /ˈvɪntɪdʒ/ **1** *n.* **A** (*season's wine*) Jahrgang, *der;* (*season's grapes*) Traubenernte, *die;* **last/this year's ~:** der letzte/dieser Jahrgang; **the 1981 ~/a 1983 ~:** der 81er/ein 83er; **B** (*fig.: particular period*) Jahrgang, *der;* (*of car, machine*) Baujahr, *das;* **a car of rather ancient ~/1955 ~:** ein Auto ziemlich alten Datums/Baujahr 1955; **music of '60s/1940s ~:** Musik aus den 60ern/40er-Jahren; **of modern ~:** neueren Datums; **C** (*grape harvest; season*) Weinlese, *die;* **D** (*quality wine*) erlesener Wein.

**2** *adj.* erlesen ‹Wein, Sekt, Whisky›; herrlich ‹Komödie, Melodie›; brillant ‹Leistung, Interpretation›; (*old-fashioned*) alt ‹Modell›; altmodisch ‹Stil›; **this year has been a ~ year for port** dieses Jahr war ein gutes Jahr für Portwein; **this play is ~ Pinter** dies ist eines der typischsten und besten Pinter-Stücke

**vintage ˈcar** *n.* (*Brit.*) [zwischen 1917 und 1930 gebauter] Oldtimer

**vintner** /ˈvɪntnə(r)/ *n.* **▶ 1261** Weinhändler, *der*/-händlerin, *die*

**vinyl** /ˈvaɪnɪl/ *n.* **A** Vinyl, *das;* **B** (*polyvinyl chloride*) PVC, *das*

**viol** /ˈvaɪəl/ *n.* (*Mus.*) Viola, *die*

**viola**[1] /vɪˈəʊlə/ *n.* (*Mus.*) Bratsche, *die;* **~ player** Bratschist, *der*/Bratschistin, *die*

**viola**[2] /ˈvaɪələ/ *n.* (*Bot.*) **A** Veilchen, *das;* **B** (*hybrid*) Stiefmütterchen, *das*

**viola da gamba** /vɪəʊlə də ˈgæmbə/ *n.* (*Mus.*) Gambe, *die*

**violate** /ˈvaɪəleɪt/ *v.t.* **A** verletzen; brechen ‹Vertrag, Versprechen, Gesetz›; verstoßen gegen ‹Regel, Vorschrift, Prinzipien, Bestimmungen›; verletzen ‹Vorschrift›; stören ‹Ruhe, Frieden›; verschandeln ‹Wälder, Landschaft›; **B** (*profane*) schänden; entheiligen ‹Sabbat›; **C** (*rape*) vergewaltigen; schänden (*veralt.*)

**violation** /vaɪəˈleɪʃn/ *n.* ⇒ **violate**: **A** Verletzung, *die;* Bruch, *der;* Verstoß, *der* (**of** gegen); Störung, *die;* Verschandelung, *die;* **traffic ~:** Verkehrsdelikt, *das;* **be/act in ~ of** verletzen/brechen/verstoßen gegen; **do sth. in ~ of one's promise/oath** etw. entgegen seinem Versprechen/Eid tun; **they tested nuclear weapons in ~ of the treaty** sie testeten Atomwaffen, obwohl sie damit gegen den Vertrag verstießen; **B** Schändung, *die;* Entheiligung, *die;* **C** Vergewaltigung, *die;* Schändung, *die* (*veralt.*)

**violence** /ˈvaɪələns/ *n., no pl.* **A** (*intensity, force*) Heftigkeit, *die;* (*of blow, waterfall*) Wucht, *die;* (*of temper*) Ungestüm, *das;* (*of contrast*) Krassheit, *die;* **B** (*brutality*) Gewalt, *die;* (*at public event*) Gewalttätigkeiten; **psychological ~:** seelische Grausamkeit; **by** *or* **with ~:** mit Gewalt; **a man of ~:** ein Mann der Gewalt; **resort to** *or* **use ~:** Gewalt anwenden; **commit ~:** Gewalttaten verüben; **do ~ to sth.** (*fig.*) einer Sache (*Dat.*) Gewalt antun; **C** (*Law*) Gewalt, *die;* **threaten sb. with ~:** jmdm. Gewalt androhen; **threat of ~:** Gewaltandrohung, *die;* **act/crime of ~:** Gewalttat, *die*/Gewaltverbrechen, *das;* **robbery with ~:** [bewaffneter] Raubüberfall

**violent** /ˈvaɪələnt/ *adj.* gewalttätig; heftig ‹Schlag, Attacke, Leidenschaft, Auseinandersetzung, Erschütterung, Reaktion, Schmerzen, Wind›; wuchtig ‹Schlag, Stoß›; schwer ‹Schock›; krass ‹Gegensatz, Kontrast›; grell ‹Farbe›; knall‹rot, -grün usw.›; Gewalt‹verbrecher, -tat›; gnadenlos ‹Hitze›; **don't be so ~:** sei nicht so aggressiv; **he has a ~ temper, his character** *or* **temper is ~:** er neigt zum Jähzorn; **by ~ means** gewaltsam ‹öffnen›; unter Gewaltanwendung ‹jmdn. überreden›; **~ death** gewaltsamer *od.* unnatürlicher Tod

**violently** /ˈvaɪələntlɪ/ *adv.* (*by means of violence*) brutal; (*with great vigour, intensity*) heftig; (*to a high degree*) völlig ‹verstört›; äußerst ‹schmerzhaft, verstört, aufgeregt›; absolut ‹gegensätzlich›; **live/die ~:** ein gewalttätiges Leben führen/eines gewaltsamen Todes sterben; **discourage sb. from acting/behaving ~:** jmdn. von Gewalttätigkeiten abhalten; **I dislike him ~:** er ist mir äußerst zuwider; **I was ~ ill** ich musste mich heftig

V

übergeben; **contrast ~:** in eklatantem Widerspruch stehen (**with** zu); **the colours clash ~:** die Farben passen überhaupt nicht zusammen

**violet** /ˈvaɪələt/ ❶ *n.* [A] Veilchen, *das;* **sweet ~:** Märzveilchen, *das;* Wohlriechendes Veilchen (*Bot.*); **shrinking ~** (*fig.*) schüchternes Pflänzchen (*ugs.*); **don't be such a shrinking ~:** sei kein Angsthase; [B] (*colour*) Violett, *das;* **dressed in ~:** violett gekleidet. ❷ *adj.* violett

**violin** /vaɪəˈlɪn/ *n.* (*Mus.*) Violine, *die*

**violin: ~ case** *n.* Geigenkasten, *der;* **~ concerto** *n.* Violinkonzert, *das*

**violinist** /vaɪəˈlɪnɪst/ *n.* ▶ 1261 (*Mus.*) Geiger, *der*/Geigerin, *die*

**violin: ~-maker** *n.* Geigenbauer, *der*/-bauerin, *die;* **~ player** *n.* Geiger, *der*/Geigerin, *die;* **~ sonata** *n.* Violinsonate, *die;* **~ teacher** *n.* Geigenlehrer, *der*/-lehrerin, *die*

**violoncello** /vaɪələnˈtʃeləʊ/ *n., pl.* **~s** (*Mus. formal*) Violoncello, *das*

**VIP** /viːaɪˈpiː/ *n.* Prominente, *der/die;* **the ~s** die Prominenz

**viper** /ˈvaɪpə(r)/ *n.* [A] (*Zool.*) Viper, *die;* **common ~:** Kreuzotter, *die;* [B] (*fig.*) Schlange, *die* (*abwertend*); **nourish** *or* **nurse a ~ in one's bosom** eine Schlange am Busen nähren (*geh.*)

**viperish** /ˈvaɪpərɪʃ/ *adj.* (*fig.*) giftig ‹Blick›; scharf ‹Zunge›; gehässig ‹Mundwerk, Ausdrucksweise›; niederträchtig ‹Angriff, Charakter›; Schmäh‹rede, -wort›

**VIP: ~ lounge** *n.* VIP-Halle, *die;* **~ treatment** *n.* Vorzugsbehandlung, *die;* **give sb. ~ treatment** jmdn. mit allen Ehren behandeln

**virago** /vɪˈrɑːgəʊ/ *n., pl.* **~s** zänkisches Weib (*abwertend*)

**viral** /ˈvaɪərl/ *adj.* (*Med.*) Virus-

**Virgil** /ˈvɜːdʒɪl/ *pr. n.* Vergil (*der*)

**virgin** /ˈvɜːdʒɪn/ ❶ *n.* [A] Jungfrau, *die;* **she/he is still a ~:** sie ist noch Jungfrau/er ist noch unschuldig; [B] **the [Blessed] V~ [Mary]** (*Relig.*) die [Heilige] Jungfrau [Maria]; [C] (*Astrol.*) **the V~:** die Jungfrau; ⇒ *also* **archer** B. ❷ *adj.* [A] (*chaste*) jungfräulich; [B] (*untouched, unspoiled*) unberührt ‹Land, Wälder›; jungfräulich ‹Schnee›; makellos ‹Weiß›; **~ soil** (*esp. fig.*) unberührter Boden; [C] **~ olive oil** natives Olivenöl

**virginal** /ˈvɜːdʒɪnl/ ❶ *adj.* jungfräulich. ❷ *n. in pl.* (*Mus. Hist.*) Spinett, *das*

**virgin ˈbirth** *n.* [A] (*Biol.*) Jungfernzeugung, *die;* [B] (*Relig.*) jungfräuliche Geburt

**Virginia** /vɜːˈdʒɪnɪə/ ❶ *pr. n.* Virginia (*das*). ❷ *n.* **~ [tobacco]** Virginia[tabak], *der;* **~ cigarettes** Virginiazigaretten

**Virginia ˈcreeper** *n.* (*Bot.*) Wilder Wein

**Virginian** /vɜːˈdʒɪnɪən/ ❶ *adj.* virginisch; Virginier-. ❷ *n.* Virginier, *der*/Virginierin, *die*

**Virgin ˈIslands** *pr. n. pl.* Jungferninseln *Pl.*

**virginity** /vɜːˈdʒɪnɪtɪ/ *n.* Unschuld, *die;* (*of girl also*) Jungfräulichkeit, *die*

**Virgo** /ˈvɜːgəʊ/ *n., pl.* **~s** (*Astrol., Astron.*) die Jungfrau; die Virgo; ⇒ *also* **Aries**

**Virgoan** /ˈvɜːgəʊən/ *n.* (*Astrol.*) Jungfrau, *die*

**virile** /ˈvɪraɪl/ *adj.* [A] (*masculine*) männlich; maskulin (*geh.*); [B] (*sexually potent*) viril; [C] (*fig.: forceful, vigorous*) kraftvoll

**virility** /vɪˈrɪlɪtɪ/ *n.* [A] Männlichkeit, *die;* [B] (*sexual potency*) Virilität, *die;* Manneskraft, *die;* [C] (*fig.*) kraftvoller Schwung

**virologist** /vaɪəˈrɒlədʒɪst/ *n.* ▶ 1261 Virologe, *der*/Virologin, *die*

**virology** /vaɪəˈrɒlədʒɪ/ *n.* Virologie, *die*

**virtual** /ˈvɜːtjʊəl/ *adj.* [A] **a ~ ...:** so gut wie ein/eine ...; praktisch ein/eine ... (*ugs.*); **he is the ~ head of the business** er ist quasi der Chef des Geschäfts (*ugs.*); **the whole day was a ~ disaster** der ganze Tag war geradezu eine Katastrophe; **the traffic came to a ~ standstill** der Verkehr kam praktisch zum Stillstand (*ugs.*); [B] (*Optics, Mech.*) virtuell ‹Bild, Verrückung›

**virtually** /ˈvɜːtjʊəlɪ/ *adv.* so gut wie; praktisch (*ugs.*)

**virtual reˈality** *n.* (*Computing*) virtuelle Realität

**virtue** /ˈvɜːtjuː/ *n.* [A] (*moral excellence*) Tugend, *die;* (*chastity*) Tugendhaftigkeit, *die;* **~ is its own reward** (*prov.*) die Tugend trägt ihren Lohn in sich selbst; ⇒ *also* **easy** 1 C; [B] (*advantage*) Vorteil, *der;* Vorzug, *der;* **what is the ~ in that?** welchen Vorteil hat das?; **there's no ~ in doing that** es bringt keinen Vorteil, das zu tun; [C] **by ~ of** aufgrund (+ *Gen.*). ⇒ *also* **necessity** A

**virtuosity** /vɜːtjʊˈɒsɪtɪ/ *n., no pl.* Virtuosität, *die;* **perform with ~:** virtuos spielen

**virtuoso** /vɜːtjʊˈəʊzəʊ/ *n., pl.* **virtuosi** /vɜːtjʊˈəʊziː/ *or* **~s** Virtuose, *der*/Virtuosin, *die; attrib.* virtuos ‹Spiel, Aufführung›; **a ~ performer** ein Virtuose/eine Virtuosin

**virtuous** /ˈvɜːtjʊəs/ *adj.* [A] (*possessing moral rectitude*) rechtschaffen ‹Person›; brav ‹Kind›; tugendhaft ‹Leben›; **if you're feeling ~ you can ...** (*iron.*) wenn du etwas Gutes tun willst, kannst du ...; **that was ~ of you** (*iron.*) das war wirklich löblich (*iron.*); [B] (*chaste*) keusch

**virtuously** /ˈvɜːtjʊəslɪ/ *adv.* löblicherweise; **live ~:** ein rechtschaffenes Leben führen; **we ~ went to bed at ten** (*joc.*) wir sind brav um zehn ins Bett gegangen

**virtuousness** /ˈvɜːtjʊəsnɪs/ *n., no pl.* (*of person*) Rechtschaffenheit, *die;* (*of action, life*) Tugendhaftigkeit, *die*

**virulence** /ˈvɪrʊləns, ˈvɪrjʊləns/ *n., no pl.* [A] (*Med.*) Virulenz, *die;* (*of poison*) starke Wirkung; [B] (*fig.: malignancy*) Bosheit, *die*

**virulent** /ˈvɪrʊlənt, ˈvɪrjʊlənt/ *adj.* [A] (*Med.*) virulent; stark wirkend ‹Gift›; [B] (*fig.: malignant*) heftig; scharf ‹Angriff›

**virulently** /ˈvɪrʊləntlɪ, ˈvɪrjʊləntlɪ/ *adv.* heftig; scharf ‹kritisieren, angreifen›; **be ~ anticommunist** ein erbitterter Gegner/eine erbitterte Gegnerin des Kommunismus sein

**virus** /ˈvaɪərəs/ *n.* [A] ▶ 1232 (*Biol.*) Virus, *das; attrib.* **a ~ infection** eine Virusinfektion; [B] (*Computing*) [Computer]virus, *das od. der*

**visa** /ˈviːzə/ *n.* Visum, *das*

**visage** /ˈvɪzɪdʒ/ *n.* (*literary*) Antlitz, *das* (*geh.*); (*ugly*) Fratze, *die*

**vis-à-vis** /viːzɑːˈviː/ ❶ *prep.* [A] (*in relation to*) bezüglich (+ *Gen.*); [B] (*facing*) gegenüber; [C] (*compared with*) im Vergleich zu. ❷ *adv.* **stand ~:** sich (*Dat.*) gegenüberstehen. ❸ *n., pl. same* [A] (*person facing another*) Gegenüber, *das;* Vis-à-Vis, *das* (*veralt.*); [B] (*Amer.: social partner*) Partner, *der*/Partnerin, *die*

**viscera** /ˈvɪsərə/ *n. pl.* (*Anat.*) Eingeweide

**visceral** /ˈvɪsərl/ *adj.* (*Anat.*) Eingeweide-

**viscid** /ˈvɪsɪd/ *adj.* dickflüssig; sämig

**viscose** /ˈvɪskəʊz, ˈvɪskəʊs/ *n.* Viskose, *die*

**viscosity** /vɪsˈkɒsɪtɪ/ *n.* [A] *no pl.* (*quality*) Dickflüssigkeit, *die;* [B] (*Phys.: of oil etc.*) Viskosität, *die*

**viscount** /ˈvaɪkaʊnt/ *n.* ▶ 1617 Viscount, *der*

**viscountcy** /ˈvaɪkaʊntsɪ/ *n.* Viscountwürde, *die*

**viscountess** /ˈvaɪkaʊntɪs/ *n.* ▶ 1617 Viscountess, *die*

**viscous** /ˈvɪskəs/ *adj.* dickflüssig; (*Phys.*) viskos

**vise** (*Amer.*) ⇒ **vice**[2]

**visibility** /vɪzɪˈbɪlɪtɪ/ *n., no pl.* [A] (*being visible*) Sichtbarkeit, *die;* [B] (*range of vision*) Sicht, *die;* (*Meteorol.*) Sichtweite, *die;* **reduce ~ to ten metres** die Sichtweite auf zehn Meter verringern

**visible** /ˈvɪzɪbl/ *adj.* [A] (*also Econ.*) sichtbar; **be ~ to the naked eye** mit bloßem Auge erkennbar sein; **~ to observers in X** für Beobachter in X zu sehen; **highly ~** (*fig.*) unübersehbar; [B] (*apparent*) erkennbar; **with ~ impatience** mit sichtlicher Ungeduld

**visibly** /ˈvɪzɪblɪ/ *adv.* sichtlich

**Visigoth** /ˈvɪzɪgɒθ/ *n.* (*Hist.*) Westgote, *der*/Westgotin, *die*

**vision** /ˈvɪʒn/ *n.* [A] (*sight*) Sehkraft, *die;* **[range of] ~:** Sichtweite, *die;* **[field of] ~:** Sehfeld, *das;* ⇒ *also* **line**[1] 1 C; [B] (*dream*) Vision, *die;* Gesicht, *das* (*geh.*); (*person seen in dream*) Phantom, *das;* **a ~ in white** (*fig.*) ein Traum in Weiß; **be a [real] ~:** traumhaft schön sein; [C] *usu. pl.* (*imaginings*) Fantasien; Fantasiebilder; **have ~s of sth.** von etw. fantasieren; (*more specific*) sich (*Dat.*) etw. ausmalen; **have ~s of having to do sth.** kommen sehen, dass man etw. tun muss; [D] (*insight, foresight*) Weitblick, *der;* **a man/woman of ~:** ein Mann/eine Frau mit Weitblick; [E] (*Telev.*) Bild, *das;* **in sound and ~:** in Ton und Bild; **the programme will continue in ~ only until sound is restored** wegen vorübergehenden Tonausfalls z.z. nur Bildempfang

**visionary** /ˈvɪʒənərɪ/ ❶ *adj.* [A] (*imaginative*) fantasievoll; (*fanciful*) fantastisch; [B] (*imagined*) eingebildet; imaginär (*geh.*); [C] (*seeing visions*) visionär; **~ power** visionäre *od.* hellseherische Kraft. ❷ *n.* Visionär, *der*/Visionärin, *die;* Hellseher, *der*/Hellseherin, *die* (*auch fig.*)

**visit** /ˈvɪzɪt/ ❶ *v.t.* [A] besuchen; aufsuchen ‹Arzt›; **~ the sick** Krankenbesuche machen; [B] (*dated: afflict*) heimsuchen; **be ~ed with sth.** von etw. heimgesucht werden; [C] (*Bibl.: inflict punishment for*) **~ the iniquity of the fathers upon the children** der Väter Missetat an den Kindern heimsuchen.

❷ *v.i.* [A] einen Besuch/Besuche machen; **be ~ing in a town** als Besucher in einer Stadt sein; **I'm only ~ing** ich bin nur zu Besuch; **spend the afternoon ~ing** nachmittags Besuche machen; **~ at a hotel** (*Amer.*) in einem Hotel absteigen; **be ~ing with sb.** (*Amer.*) bei jmdm. zu Besuch sein; [B] (*Amer.: chat*) plaudern.

❸ *n.* [A] Besuch, *der;* **pay** *or* **make a ~ to sb.** jmdm. einen Besuch abstatten; **pay a ~** (*coll.: go to the toilet*) aufs Klo gehen (*ugs.*); **she was in London on a ~ to some friends** sie war in London bei Freunden zu Besuch; **have** *or* **receive a ~ [from sb.]** [von jmdm.] besucht werden; **we shall be honoured to receive a ~ from you** es wird uns (*Dat.*) eine Ehre sein, Sie als Besucher zu empfangen; **we had a ~ from the police** wir hatten Besuch von der Polizei; **a ~ to a** *or* **the theatre/a museum** ein Theater-/Museumsbesuch; **a ~ to the British Museum** ein Besuch des Britischen Museums; **a ~ to Rome/the USA** ein Besuch *od.* Aufenthalt in Rom/in den USA; **I'm going on a two-day ~ to Athens** ich fahre für zwei Tage nach Athen; **a ~ to the dentist['s]** ein Besuch beim Zahnarzt; **a home ~ by the doctor [to sb.]** ein Hausbesuch des Arztes [bei jmdm.]; [B] (*Amer.: chat*) Plauderei, *die*

**visitation** /vɪzɪˈteɪʃn/ *n.* [A] (*official inspection by bishop etc.*) Visitation, *die;* **a ~ of the sick** eine Krankenvisitation; [B] (*coll. joc.: protracted visit*) Heimsuchung, *die* (*ugs. scherzh.*); **we had a ~ from the director today** der Direktor hat uns heute heimgesucht (*ugs. scherzh.*); [C] (*dated: punishment*) Heimsuchung, *die;* **a ~ of the plague** (*arch.*) eine Heimsuchung durch die Pest

**visiting** /ˈvɪzɪtɪŋ/ *n.* Besuche *Pl.;* Besuchsdienst, *der;* **she does prison ~:** sie macht Gefängnisbesuche

**visiting: ~ card** *n.* Visitenkarte, *die* (*auch fig.*); **~ hours** *n. pl.* Besuchszeiten; **what are the ~ hours in this hospital?** wann ist in diesem Krankenhaus Besuchszeit?; **~ proˈfessor** *n.* Gastprofessor, *der*/-professorin, *die;* **~ team** *n.* (*Sport*) Gastmannschaft, *die*

**visitor** /ˈvɪzɪtə(r)/ *n.* [A] Besucher, *der*/Besucherin, *die;* (*to hotel, beach, etc.*) Gast, *der;* **have ~s/a ~:** Besuch haben; **we've got a ~ staying for a fortnight** wir haben für vierzehn Tage Besuch *od.* einen Gast; **the ~s** (*Sport*) die Gäste; ⇒ *also* **prison visitor;** [B] (*Ornith.*) Zugvogel, *der;* **summer ~s** Sommergäste

**ˈvisitors' book** *n.* Gästebuch, *das;* **sign the ~:** sich ins Gästebuch eintragen

**visor** /ˈvaɪzə(r)/ *n.* [A] (*of helmet*) Visier, *das;* [B] (*eyeshade, peak of cap*) Schirm, *der;* **C** *(Motor Veh.)* **[sun] ~:** Blendschirm, *der*

**vista** /ˈvɪstə/ *n.* **A** *(view)* [Aus]blick, *der* **(of** auf + *Akk.*); *(long, narrow view)* Perspektive, *die;* **B** *(fig.)* **open up new ~s** neue Perspektiven eröffnen

**Vistula** /ˈvɪstjʊlə/ *pr. n.* Weichsel, *die*

**visual** /ˈvɪzjʊəl, ˈvɪʒjʊəl/ *adj.* **A** *(related to vision)* Seh‹nerv, -organ›; **~ sense** Gesichtssinn, *der;* **B** *(attained by sight)* visuell; optisch ‹Eindruck, Darstellung›; bildlich ‹Vorstellungsvermögen›; **the ~ arts** die bildenden und darstellenden Künste; **a ~ landing** eine Sichtlandung; **~ display** *(Computing)* Sichtanzeige, *die*

**visual: ~ aids** *n. pl.* Anschauungsmaterial, *das;* **~ disˈplay unit** *n.* Bildschirmgerät, *das*

**visualisation, visualise** ⇒ **visualiz-**

**visualization** /vɪzjʊəlaɪˈzeɪʃn, vɪʒjʊəlaɪˈzeɪʃn/ *n.* *(making visual)* Veranschaulichung, *die; (imagining)* Sichvorstellen, *das*

**visualize** /ˈvɪzjʊəlaɪz, ˈvɪʒjʊəlaɪz/ *v.t.* **A** *(imagine)* sich *(Dat.)* vorstellen; **I can't ~ myself in retirement** ich als Rentner, das kann ich mir nicht vorstellen; **B** *(envisage, foresee)* voraussehen; **I do not ~ many changes** ich rechne nicht mit großen Veränderungen

**visually** /ˈvɪzjʊəlɪ, ˈvɪʒjʊəlɪ/ *adv.* **A** *(with regard to vision)* optisch; bildnerisch ‹begabt›; **B** *(by visual means)* bildlich; **record sth. ~:** etw. in Bildern festhalten

**vital** /ˈvaɪtl/ ❶ *adj.* **A** *(essential to life)* lebenswichtig; **~ functions** Vitalfunktionen; **~ organs** lebenswichtige Organe; **B** *(essential)* unbedingt notwendig; *(crucial)* entscheidend, ausschlaggebend ‹Frage, Entschluss› **(to** für); **it is of ~ importance** *or* **~ that you ...:** es ist von entscheidender Bedeutung, dass Sie ...; **is it ~ for you to go?** müssen Sie unbedingt gehen?; **your cooperation is ~ to** *or* **for the success of the plan** Ihre Mitarbeit ist unerlässlich für den Erfolg des Plans; **C** *(full of life)* lebendig, kraftvoll ‹Stil›; vital ‹Person›.
❷ *n. pl.* ⇒ **vital parts**

**vitality** /vaɪˈtælɪtɪ/ *n., no pl.* **A** *(ability to sustain life)* Lebenskraft, *die;* **B** *(liveliness)* Vitalität, *die; (of prose, style, language)* Lebendigkeit, *die; (energy)* Energie, *die;* **C** *(fig.: of institution, organization, etc.)* Dauerhaftigkeit, *die*

**vitally** /ˈvaɪtəlɪ/ *adv.* vital; **~ important** von allergrößter Wichtigkeit; *(crucial)* von entscheidender Bedeutung

**vital ˈparts** *n. pl.* **the ~** *(dated or joc.)* die lebenswichtigen Organe; *(genitals)* die edlen Teile *(scherzh.)*

**vital staˈtistics** *n. pl.* **A** *(data)* Bevölkerungsstatistik, *die;* **B** *(coll.: woman's body measurements)* Maße; **her ~ are 34-26-34** sie hat die Maße 34/26/34

**vitamin** /ˈvɪtəmɪn, ˈvaɪtəmɪn/ *n.* Vitamin, *das;* **~ C** Vitamin C

**vitamin: ~ deficiency** *n.* Vitaminmangel, *der;* **~ pill** *n.* Vitamintablette, *die*

**vitiate** /ˈvɪʃɪeɪt/ *v.t.* **A** *(impair quality of, corrupt)* beeinträchtigen; **B** *(invalidate)* zunichte machen; hinfällig machen ‹Vereinbarung, Vertrag›

**viticulture** /ˈvɪtɪkʌltʃə(r)/ *n.* Weinbau, *der*

**vitreous** /ˈvɪtrɪəs/ *adj.* **A** *(glasslike)* glasartig; **~ china** Halbporzellan, *das;* **~ enamel** Glasemail, *das;* **B** *(Anat.)* **~ body** *or* **humour** Glaskörper, *der*

**vitrification** /vɪtrɪfɪˈkeɪʃn/ *n.* Fritten, *das*

**vitrify** /ˈvɪtrɪfaɪ/ *v.t. & i.* fritten

**vitriol** /ˈvɪtrɪəl/ *n.* **A** *(Chem.)* Vitriol, *das;* **B** *(fig.: virulence)* ätzende Schärfe

**vitriolic** /vɪtrɪˈɒlɪk/ *adj.* ätzend; giftig ‹Bemerkung›; geharnischt ‹Attacke, Rede›

**vituperate** /vɪˈtjuːpəreɪt, vaɪˈtjuːpəreɪt/ *v.i.* *(literary)* wettern **(against** gegen)

**vituperation** /vɪtjuːpəˈreɪʃn, vaɪtjuːpəˈreɪʃn/ *n.* *(literary)* Schmähungen *Pl.* *(geh.)*

**vituperative** /vɪˈtjuːpərətɪv, vaɪˈtjuːpərətɪv/ *adj.* *(literary)* schmähend; **~ language** *or* **speech** Schmähreden; **~ attack on sb.** Schmährede/*(written)* Schmähschrift gegen jmdn.

**viva** /ˈvaɪvə/ *(Brit. Univ. coll.)* ❶ *n.* Mündliche, *das (ugs.).* ❷ *v.t.* mündlich prüfen

**vivacious** /vɪˈveɪʃəs/ *adj.* lebhaft; lebendig ‹Stil›; munter ‹Lachen, Lächeln›; bunt ‹Kleider›

**vivaciously** /vɪˈveɪʃəslɪ/ *adv.* lebhaft; munter ‹lächeln, lachen›; bunt ‹angezogen›; lebendig ‹schreiben›

**vivacity** /vɪˈvæsɪtɪ/ *n., no pl.* Lebhaftigkeit, *die; (of smile, laugh)* Munterkeit, *die; (of style)* Lebendigkeit, *die*

**vivarium** /vaɪˈveərɪəm/ *n., pl.* **vivaria** /vaɪˈveərɪə/ Vivarium, *das*

**viva voce** /vaɪvə ˈvəʊtsɪ, vaɪvə ˈvəʊsɪ/ *(Univ.)* ❶ *adv., adj.* mündlich. ❷ *n.* mündliche Prüfung; *(doctoral)* Rigorosum, *das*

**vivid** /ˈvɪvɪd/ *adj.* **A** *(bright)* strahlend ‹Helligkeit›; hell ‹Blitz›; lebhaft ‹Farbe›; **B** *(animated)* lebhaft ‹Person›; **C** *(clear, lifelike)* lebendig ‹Schilderung, Romanfigur›; lebhaft ‹Fantasie, Erinnerung›; **D** *(intense)* heftig ‹Schmerz›; kraftvoll ‹Töne›

**vividly** /ˈvɪvɪdlɪ/ *adv.* **A** *(brightly)* hell; **a ~ coloured dress** ein Kleid in lebhaften Farben; **B** *(clearly)* lebendig ‹beschreiben›; **remember sth. ~:** sich lebhaft an etw. *(Akk.)* erinnern

**vividness** /ˈvɪvɪdnɪs/ *n., no pl.* **A** *(brightness)* Helligkeit, *die;* **B** *(liveliness, realism)* Lebhaftigkeit, *die; (of description)* Lebendigkeit, *die*

**viviparous** /vɪˈvɪpərəs, vaɪˈvɪpərəs/ *adj.* *(Zool.)* vivipar *(fachspr.)*; lebend gebärend

**vivisect** /ˈvɪvɪsekt/ *v.t.* vivisezieren *(fachspr.)*

**vivisection** /vɪvɪˈsekʃn/ *n.* Vivisektion, *die (fachspr.)*

**vivisectionist** /vɪvɪˈsekʃənɪst/ *n.: jmd., der Vivisektionen durchführt/befürwortet*

**vixen** /ˈvɪksn/ *n.* **A** *(Zool.)* Füchsin, *die;* **B** *(fig.: woman)* Drachen, *der (ugs.)*

**viz** /vɪz/ *adv.* d.h.

**vizier** /vɪˈzɪə(r), ˈvɪzɪə(r)/ *n.* Wesir, *der*

**vizor** ⇒ **visor**

**ˈV-neck** *n.* V-Ausschnitt, *der*

**ˈV-necked** *adj.* ‹Pullover, Kleid› mit V-Ausschnitt

**vocabulary** /vəˈkæbjʊlərɪ/ *n.* **A** *(list)* Vokabelverzeichnis, *das;* **learn ~:** Vokabeln lernen; *attrib.* **~ book** Vokabelheft, *das;* **~ test** Vokabeltest, *der;* **B** *(language of particular field)* Vokabular, *das;* **C** *(range of language)* Wortschatz, *der*

**vocal** /ˈvəʊkl/ ❶ *adj.* **A** *(concerned with voice)* stimmlich; **a ~ organ** ein Stimmorgan; **B** *(expressing oneself freely)* gesprächig; lautstark ‹Minderheit, Gruppe, Protest›; **he was very ~ about his rights** er sprach sehr viel von seinen Rechten. ❷ *n. (Mus.)* Vokalpartie, *die;* Vocal, *das (fachspr.)*

**ˈvocal cords** *n. pl.* Stimmbänder

**vocalic** /vəˈkælɪk/ *(Phonet.) adj.* vokalreich

**vocalise** ⇒ **vocalize**

**vocalist** /ˈvəʊkəlɪst/ *n.* Sänger, *der*/Sängerin, *die (bei einer Band od. Combo)*

**vocalize** /ˈvəʊkəlaɪz/ *v.t. & i.* vokalisieren

**vocal: ~ music** *n.* Vokalmusik, *die;* **~ score** *n. (Mus.)* Vokalpartitur, *die*

**vocation** /vəˈkeɪʃn/ *n.* **A** *(call to career; also Relig.)* Berufung, *die;* **he felt no ~ for the ministry** er fühlte sich nicht zum Geistlichen berufen; **teaching is a ~ as well as a profession** Lehrer sein ist Berufung und Beruf zugleich; **B** *(special aptitude)* Begabung, *die* **(for** für); **C** *(profession)* Beruf, *der*

**vocational** /vəˈkeɪʃənl/ *adj.* berufsbezogen

**vocational: ~ college** *n.* Berufsschule, *die;* **~ guidance** *n.* Berufsberatung, *die;* **~ training** *n.* berufliche Bildung

**vocative** /ˈvɒkətɪv/ *(Ling.)* ❶ *adj.* Vokativ-; **~ case** Vokativ, *der.* ❷ *n.* Vokativ, *der*

**vociferate** /vəˈsɪfəreɪt/ ❶ *v.i.* wettern; zetern. ❷ *v.t.* herausschreien ‹Flüche usw.›

**vociferation** /vəsɪfəˈreɪʃn/ *n.* Gezeter, *das; (of opinions etc.)* Herausschreien, *das*

**vociferous** /vəˈsɪfərəs/ *adj.* *(noisy)* laut; krakeelend *(ugs.)* ‹Zwischenrufer usw.›; *(insistent)* lautstark ‹Forderung, Protest›

**vociferously** /vəˈsɪfərəslɪ/ *adv.* laut; lautstark ‹protestieren usw.›

**vociferousness** /vəˈsɪfərəsnɪs/ *n., no pl.* Lautstärke, *die*

**vodka** /ˈvɒdkə/ *n.* Wodka, *der*

**vogue** /vəʊg/ *n.* Mode, *die;* **the ~ for large hats** die Mode mit den großen Hüten; **there is a ~ for holidays on canal boats** Urlaub auf Kanalbooten ist große Mode; **be in/come into ~:** in Mode sein/kommen; **go out of ~:** aus der Mode kommen; **have** *or* **enjoy a ~** ‹Künstler usw.:› gerade sehr populär sein

**ˈvogue word** *n.* Modewort, *das*

**voice** /vɔɪs/ ❶ *n.* **A** *(lit. or fig.)* Stimme, *die;* **in a firm/loud ~:** mit fester/lauter Stimme; **like the sound of one's own ~:** sich selbst gerne reden hören; **lose one's ~:** die Stimme verlieren; **be in [good]/bad ~:** [gut]/nicht [gut] bei Stimme sein; **make one's ~ heard** sich verständlich machen; *(fig.)* sich *(Dat.)* Gehör verschaffen; **B** *(expression)* **give ~ to sth.** einer Sache *(Dat.)* Ausdruck geben; **C** *(expressed opinion)* Stimme, *die;* **with one ~:** einstimmig; **lend one's ~ to sth.** in etw. *(Akk.)* einstimmen; **have a/no ~ in the matter** ein/kein Mitspracherecht bei der Angelegenheit haben; **D** *(Mus.)* Stimme, *die;* **[singing] ~:** Singstimme, *die;* **study ~:** Gesang studieren; **setting for five ~s** fünfstimmige Vertonung; **E** *(Phonet.)* stimmhafter Laut; **F** *(Ling.)* Genus Verbi, *das;* **the active/passive ~:** das Aktiv/Passiv.
❷ *v.t.* **A** *(express)* zum Ausdruck bringen ‹Meinung›; **B** *esp. in p.p. (Phonet.)* stimmhaft aussprechen; **a ~d consonant** ein stimmhafter Konsonant

**ˈvoice box** *n.* Kehlkopf, *der*

**voiceless** /ˈvɔɪslɪs/ *adj.* **A** stumm; sprachlos *(geh.)*; **B** *(Phonet.)* stimmlos

**voice: ~ mail** *n.* Voicemail, *die;* **~-over** *n.* Begleitkommentar, *der;* **~ print** *n.* Sonogramm, *das;* **~ teacher** *n.* Gesang[s]lehrer, *der*/-lehrerin, *die;* **~ vote** *n. (Amer.)* Abstimmung durch Zuruf

**void** /vɔɪd/ ❶ *adj.* **A** *(empty)* leer; öd [und leer] ‹Gelände›; **B** *(invalid)* ungültig; **his efforts were rendered ~:** seine Bemühungen wurden zunichte gemacht; ⇒ *also* **null**; **C** *(Cards)* **my hand was ~ in hearts** ich hatte kein Herz auf der Hand; **D** *(lacking)* **~ of** ohne [jeden/jedes/jede]; **a proposal wholly ~ of sense** ein Vorschlag ohne jeden Sinn.
❷ *n.* **A** *(empty space)* Nichts, *das;* **the vast desert ~s** die endlose Öde der Wüste; **B** *(fig.)* **nobody can fill the ~ left by his death** keiner kann die große Lücke füllen, die sein Tod hinterlassen hat; **there was an aching ~ in her heart** sie spürte im Innern ein schmerzliches Gefühl der Leere; **C** *(Cards)* **have a ~ in spades** kein Pik haben.
❸ *v.t.* **A** *(render invalid)* auflösen ‹Vertrag›; ablösen ‹Rente›; *(Law)* für ungültig erklären ‹Vertrag, Vereinbarung›; **B** *(empty)* entleeren ‹Blase, Darm›

**voile** /vɔɪl, vwɑːl/ *n.* *(Textiles)* Voile, *der*

**vol.** *abbr.* **volume** Bd.

**volatile** /ˈvɒlətaɪl/ *adj.* **A** *(Chem.)* flüchtig; volatil *(fachspr.)*; **~ oil** ⇒ **ethereal oil**; **B** *(fig.)* *(lively)* impulsiv; *(changeable)* unbeständig ‹Person, Laune›; *(likely to erupt)* explosiv ‹Temperament›; brisant ‹Lage›

**volatilise** ⇒ **volatilize**

**volatility** /vɒləˈtɪlɪtɪ/ *n., no pl.* **A** *(Chem.)* Flüchtigkeit, *die;* Volatilität, *die (fachspr.)*; **B** *(fig.)* ⇒ **volatile** B: Impulsivität, *die;* Unbeständigkeit, *die;* Explosivität, *die;* Brisanz, *die*

**volatilize** /vəˈlætɪlaɪz/ ❶ *v.t.* *(Chem.)* verflüchtigen. ❷ *v.i.* sich verflüchtigen

**vol-au-vent** /ˈvɒləʊvɑ̃/ *n.* *(Gastr.)* Pastete, *die;* **chicken ~:** Königinpastete, *die*

**volcanic** /vɒlˈkænɪk/ *adj.* **A** vulkanisch; **~ eruption** Vulkanausbruch, *der;* **~ in origin** vulkanischen Ursprungs; **B** *(fig.: violent)* leidenschaftlich

# Volume

## Cubic measure

| | | | |
|---|---|---|---|
| 1 cubic inch (cu. in.) | = 16,4 $cm^3$ (sechzehn Komma vier Kubikzentimeter) | | |
| 1,728 cubic inches | = 1 cubic foot (cu. ft) | = 0,03 $m^3$ (null Komma null drei Kubikmeter) | |
| 27 cubic feet | = 1 cubic yard (cu. yd) | = 0,76 $m^3$ (null Komma sieben sechs Kubikmeter) | |

## Liquid measure

**BRITISH:**

| | | |
|---|---|---|
| 20 fluid ounces (fl. oz) | = ***1 pint (pt)*** | = 0,57 l (null Komma fünf sieben Liter) |
| 2 pints | = ***1 quart (qt)*** | = 1,14 l (eins Komma eins vier Liter) |
| 4 quarts | = ***1 gallon (gal.)*** | = 4,55 l (vier Komma fünf fünf Liter) |

**AMERICAN:**

| | | |
|---|---|---|
| 16 fluid ounces (fl. oz) | = ***1 pint (pt)*** | = 0,47 l (null Komma vier sieben Liter) |
| 2 pints | = ***1 quart (qt)*** | = 0,94 l (null Komma neun vier Liter) |
| 4 quarts | = ***1 US gallon (gal.)*** | = 3,78 l (drei Komma sieben acht Liter) |

***What is its volume?***
= Wie viel *or* Welches Volumen hat es?
***Its volume is 200 cubic feet***
≈ Es hat ein Volumen von 6 Kubikmetern
***What is the capacity of the tank?, How much does the tank hold?***
= Wie viel fasst der Tank?
***The tank holds 10 UK/US gallons***
≈ Der Tank fasst 45 Liter/38 Liter
***My car does 28 (UK)*** or ***23 (US) miles per gallon (m.p.g.)***
≈ Mein Wagen verbraucht 10 Liter auf 100 Kilometer

In all Continental European countries fuel consumption is quoted in litres per 100 kilometres. To convert m.p.g. to litres per 100 km divide the factor 280 (for British gallons) or 230 (for US gallons) by the m.p.g. figure.

***The two tanks have the same capacity***
= Die beiden Tanks haben das gleiche Fassungsvermögen
***20 litres of petrol***
= 20 Liter Benzin
***It's sold by the litre***
= Es wird literweise verkauft

Note also:

***What is the capacity of the engine?***
= Wie viel Hubraum hat der Motor?
***It's a 1600 cc*** or ***1.6 litre engine*** (Brit.), ***It's a 96 cu. in. motor*** (Amer.)
= Der Motor hat 1 600 $cm^3$ *or* 1,6 Liter Hubraum

**volcano** /vɒl'keɪnəʊ/ *n., pl.* **~es** Vulkan, *der*

**vole** /vəʊl/ *n.* Wühlmaus, *die;* **field ~:** Feldmaus, *die;* **American ~:** Neuweltmaus, *die;* ⇒ *also* **water vole**

**Volga** /'vɒlgə/ *pr. n.* ▶ 1480 Wolga, *die*

**volition** /və'lɪʃn/ *n.* Wille, *der;* **of one's own ~:** aus eigenem Willen; freiwillig

**volley** /'vɒlɪ/ ❶ *n.* [A] (*discharge of missiles*) Salve, *die;* **a ~ of stones/arrows** ein Hagel von Steinen/Pfeilen; ein Stein-/Pfeilhagel; [B] (*fig.*) **a ~ of oaths/curses** eine Schimpfkanonade; **direct a ~ of questions at sb.** jmdn. mit Fragen bombardieren; [C] (*Tennis*) Volley, *der;* (*Football*) Volleyschuss, *der;* **half-~:** Halfvolley, *der.* ❷ *v.t.* (*Tennis, Football*) vollieren

**'volleyball** *n.* Volleyball, *der*

**vols.** *abbr.* **volumes** Bde.

**volt** /vəʊlt/ *n.* (*Electr.*) Volt, *das*

**voltage** /'vəʊltɪdʒ/ *n.* (*Electr.*) Spannung, *die;* **high/low ~:** Hoch-/Niederspannung, *die;* **what's the ~ here?** was für eine Netzspannung hat man hier?

**'voltage regulator** *n.* (*Electr.*) Spannungsregler, *der*

**volte-face** /vɒlt'fæs/ *n.* (*fig.*) Kehrtwendung, *die*

**voltmeter** /'vəʊltmi:tə(r)/ *n.* (*Electr.*) Voltmeter, *das;* Spannungsmesser, *der*

**volubility** /vɒljʊ'bɪlɪtɪ/ *n., no pl.* Redseligkeit, *die* (*abwertend*); (*of speech*) Wortreichtum, *der*

**voluble** /'vɒljʊbl/ *adj.* redselig (*abwertend*); wortreich ‹Rede›; **be ~ in sb.'s defence** jmdn. wortreich verteidigen

**volubly** /'vɒljʊblɪ/ *adv.* wortreich

**volume** /'vɒlju:m/ *n.* [A] (*book, set of periodicals*) Band, *der;* **a two-~ edition** eine zweibändige Ausgabe; (*on periodical*) **V~ II no. 3** Jahrgang II, Nr. 3; ⇒ *also* **speak** 2 C; [B] (*loudness*) Lautstärke, *die;* (*of voice*) Volumen, *das;* **turn the ~ up/down** das Radio *usw.* lauter/leiser stellen; **~ of sound** Klangfülle, *die;* [C] ▶ 1671 (*amount of space*) Rauminhalt, *der;* Volumen, *das;* (*amount of substance*) Teil, *der;* **two ~s of hydrogen to one of oxygen** zwei Teile Wasserstoff auf einen Teil Sauerstoff; [D] (*amount, quantity*) (*of sales etc.*) Volumen, *das;* **~ of traffic/passenger travel** Verkehrs-/Passagieraufkommen, *das;* **he produced a considerable ~ of church music** er hat ein umfangreiches kirchenmusikalisches Werk geschaffen; [E] *in pl.* (*mass*) **~s of black smoke** schwarze Rauchschwaden; **I've got ~s of work to do** ich habe ungeheuer viel Arbeit

**volume: ~ control** *n.* Lautstärkeregelung, *die;* (*device*) Lautstärkeregler, *der;* **~ production** *n.* Serienproduktion, *die;* **~ sales** *n. pl.* verkaufte Stückzahl

**voluminous** /və'lju:mɪnəs, və'lu:mɪnəs/ *adj.* [A] (*great in quantity*) voluminös (*geh.*); sehr umfangreich; (*prolific*) sehr produktiv ‹Autor›; [B] (*bulky, loose*) weit ‹Kleider›; voluminös (*geh.*) ‹Tasche usw.›; voluminös (*scherzh.*), beleibt ‹Person›; **~ garment** wallendes Gewand

**voluntarily** /'vɒləntərɪlɪ/ *adv.* freiwillig

**voluntary** /'vɒləntərɪ/ ❶ *adj.* [A] freiwillig; **~ army** Freiwilligenarmee, *die;* **~ organizations** Freiwilligenverbände; **V~ Service Overseas** (*Brit.*) Freiwilliger Entwicklungsdienst; [B] (*controlled by will*) willkürlich ‹Muskeln, Bewegungen›. ❷ *n.* (*Mus.*) Voluntary, *das*

**volunteer** /vɒlən'tɪə(r)/ ❶ *n.* Freiwillige, *der/die;* **any ~s?** Freiwillige vor!; **as a ~:** als Freiwilliger/Freiwillige; *attrib.* **~ army/force** Freiwilligenheer, *das*/Freiwilligenverband, *der.* ❷ *v.t.* (*offer*) anbieten ‹Hilfe, Dienste›; zur Verfügung stellen ‹Spende›; herausrücken mit (*ugs.*) ‹Informationen, Neuigkeiten›; **~ advice** unerbetene Ratschläge erteilen. ❸ *v.i.* sich [freiwillig] melden; **~ to do** *or* **for the shopping** sich zum Einkaufen bereit erklären

**voluptuary** /və'lʌptjʊərɪ/ *n.* Genussmensch, *der;* Hedonist, *der*/Hedonistin, *die* (*geh.*)

**voluptuous** /və'lʌptjʊəs/ *adj.* [A] (*sexually alluring*) üppig ‹Figur, Kurven, Blondine›; aufreizend ‹Bewegungen›; sinnlich ‹Mund›; [B] (*concerned with pleasures*) ausschweifend; sinnlich, erregend ‹Gefühl›

**voluptuously** /və'lʌptjʊəslɪ/ *adv.* üppig ‹geformt›; sinnlich ‹küssen›; aufreizend ‹sich bewegen›

**voluptuousness** /və'lʌptjʊəsnɪs/ *n.* (*sexual allure*) Üppigkeit, *die;* (*of movements, mouth*) Sinnlichkeit, *die*

**volute** /və'lju:t/ *n.* (*Archit.*) Volute, *die*

**vomit** /'vɒmɪt/ ❶ *v.t.* [A] erbrechen; [B] (*fig.: send out*) **~ [out]** [aus]speien ‹Rauch, Asche, Lava›. ❷ *v.i.* sich übergeben; [sich] erbrechen. ❸ *n.* Erbrochene, *das*

**voodoo** /'vu:du:/ *n.* [A] (*witchcraft*) Wodu, *der;* [B] (*spell*) Woduzauber, *der*

**voracious** /və'reɪʃəs/ *adj.* [A] (*ravenous*) gefräßig ‹Person, Tier›; unbändig ‹Appetit›; [B] (*fig.: insatiable*) unersättlich ‹Lust, Leser›

**voraciously** /və'reɪʃəslɪ/ *adv.* (*lit. or fig.*) gierig ‹verschlingen, lesen›; **be ~ hungry** einen unbändigen Hunger haben

**voracity** /və'ræsɪtɪ/ *n., no pl.* Gefräßigkeit, *die;* (*fig.: insatiability*) Gier, *die*

**vortex** /'vɔ:teks/ *n., pl.* **vortices** /'vɔ:tɪsi:z/ *or* **~es** (*whirlpool, whirlwind*) Wirbel, *der;* (*eddying current; also fig.: whirl*) Strudel, *der*

**Vosges** /vəʊʒ/ *pr. n. pl.* Vogesen *Pl.*

**votary** /'vəʊtərɪ/ *n.* [A] (*Relig.*) Gottesdiener, *der*/-dienerin, *die;* [B] (*literary: ardent follower*) Anhänger, *der*/-hängerin, *die*

**vote** /vəʊt/ ❶ *n.* [A] (*individual ~*) Stimme, *die;* **a majority of ~s** eine Stimmenmehrheit; **my ~ goes to X, X has my ~** (*fig.*) ich stimme *od.* bin für X; [B] (*act of voting*) Abstimmung, *die;* **take a ~ on sth.** über etw. (*Akk.*) abstimmen; ⇒ *also* **put¹** 1 E; [C]

V

(*right to* ~) **have/be given** *or* **get the ~:** das Stimmrecht haben/bekommen; **D** (*collective*) Stimmen; (*result*) Abstimmungsergebnis, *das;* **the ~ in favour of capital punishment** die Stimmenzahl für die Todesstrafe; **the Irish/Black/Labour/Conservative ~:** die Stimmen der Iren/Schwarzen/Labourpartei/Konservativen; **E** (*expression of opinion*) Votum, *das;* **give sb. a ~ of confidence/no confidence** jmdm. sein Vertrauen/Misstrauen aussprechen; **~ of confidence/no confidence** Vertrauens-/Misstrauensvotum, *das;* **propose a ~ of thanks** eine Dankadresse halten; **F** (*Brit. Parl.: money granted*) Etat, *der.*
**2** *v.i.* abstimmen; (*in election*) wählen; **~ for/against** stimmen für/gegen; **~ for Smith** wählen Sie Smith; **~ on a motion** über einen Antrag abstimmen; **~ to do sth.** beschließen, etw. zu tun; **~ by acclamation/ballot/[a] show of hands** durch Akklamation/mit Stimmzetteln/durch Handzeichen abstimmen; **~ with one's feet** (*fig.*) mit den Füßen abstimmen; **~ Conservative/Labour** *etc.* die Konservativen/Labour *usw.* wählen.
**3** *v.t.* **A** (*elect*) **~ sb. Chairman/President** *etc.* jmdn. zum Vorsitzenden/Präsidenten *usw.* wählen; **~ sb. on to a committee** jmdn. in einen Ausschuss wählen; (*approve*) **~ a sum of money for sth.** einen Betrag für etw. bewilligen; **B** (*coll.: pronounce*) bezeichnen; **~ sth. a success/failure** etw. als Erfolg/Misserfolg bezeichnen; **C** (*coll.: suggest*) vorschlagen; **I ~ [that] we go home** ich schlage vor *od.* bin dafür, dass wir nach Hause gehen
**~ 'down** *v.t.* niederstimmen
**~ 'in** *v.t.* wählen ‹Partei, Regierung›
**~ 'out** *v.t.* abwählen
**~ 'through** *v.t.* stimmen für ‹Gesetz›
**'vote-catching** *n.* Stimmenfang, *der;* **~ concessions** Zugeständnisse im Hinblick auf die Wahl
**voter** /'vəʊtə(r)/ *n.* Wähler, *der*/Wählerin, *die;* **the turnout of ~s** die Wahlbeteiligung
**voting** /'vəʊtɪŋ/ *n.* Abstimmen, *das;* (*in election*) Wählen, *das;* **the ~ was 220 for, 165 against** das Ergebnis der Abstimmung war 220 [Stimmen] dafür, 165 dagegen
**voting: ~ age** *n.* Wahlalter, *das;* **~ paper** *n.* Stimmzettel, *der;* **~ slip** *n.* Wahlzettel, *der;* Stimmzettel, *der;* **~ system** *n.* Wahlsystem, *das*
**votive** /'vəʊtɪv/ *adj.* Votiv‹bild, -kerze›
**vouch** /vaʊtʃ/ **1** *v.t.* **~ that ...** sich dafür verbürgen, dass ... **2** *v.i.* **~ for sb./sth.** sich für jmdn./etw. verbürgen
**voucher** /'vaʊtʃə(r)/ *n.* **A** Gutschein, *der;* Voucher, *der* (*Tourismus*); **B** (*proof of payment*) Beleg, *der*
**vouchsafe** /vaʊtʃ'seɪf/ *v.t.* (*dated, formal*) gewähren; zu geben geruhen (*geh.*) ‹Auskünfte›; **~ to do sth.** geruhen, etw. zu tun (*geh.*)
**vow** /vaʊ/ **1** *n.* Gelöbnis, *das;* (*Relig.*) Gelübde, *das;* **make** *or* **take a ~ of loyalty to sb.** jmdm. gegenüber ein Treuegelöbnis ablegen; **lovers' ~s** Treueschwüre; **be under a ~:** an ein Gelübde gebunden sein; **be under a ~ of silence** zu schweigen gelobt haben; (*Relig.*) ein Schweigegelübde abgelegt haben. **2** *v.t.* **~ sth./to do sth.** etw. geloben/geloben, etw. zu tun; **~ to take revenge on sb.** jmdm. Rache schwören
**vowel** /'vaʊəl/ *n.* Vokal, *der;* Selbstlaut, *der;* **~ sound** Vokallaut, *der*
**vox populi** /vɒks 'pɒpjʊli:/ *n.* Vox Populi, *die* (*geh.*); Stimme des Volkes
**voyage** /'vɔɪɪdʒ/ **1** *n.* Reise, *die;* (*sea ~*) Seereise, *die;* **outward/homeward ~, ~ out/home** Hin-/Rückreise, *die;* **a ~ to the moon** ein Mondflug; **he was on a ~ of discovery** (*lit. or fig.*) er war auf einer Entdeckungsreise. **2** *v.i.* (*literary*) reisen. **3** *v.t.* bereisen; befahren ‹Meere›
**voyager** /'vɔɪɪdʒə(r)/ *n.* (*literary*) Reisende, *der/die;* (*sea ~*) Seereisende, *der/die*
**voyeur** /vwɑ:'jɜ:(r)/ *n.* **A** (*sexual*) Voyeur, *der;* **B** (*prying observer*) Gaffer, *der* (*ugs.*)
**voyeurism** /vwɑ:'jɜ:rɪzm/ *n., no pl.* Voyeurismus, *der;* Voyeurtum, *das*
**VP** *abbr.* **Vice-President** VP
**vroom** /vru:m, vrʊm/ *int.* brumm
**vs** *abbr.* **versus** gg.
**'V-shaped** *adj.* v-förmig
**'V-sign** *n.* **A** (*sign for victory*) Siegeszeichen, *das;* **B** (*gesture of abuse, contempt*) *Zeichen, das „Du kannst mich mal!" signalisiert*
**VSO** *abbr.* **Voluntary Service Overseas**
**VTO[L]** /'vi:tɒl/ *abbr.* (*Aeronaut.*) **vertical take-off [and landing]** Senkrechtstart [und -landung]
**vulcanise** ⇨ **vulcanize**
**vulcanite** /'vʌlkənaɪt/ *n.* Hartgummi, *der;* Ebonit, *der* (*fachspr.*)
**vulcanize** /'vʌlkənaɪz/ *v.t.* vulkanisieren
**vulgar** /'vʌlgə(r)/ *adj.* **A** vulgär; ordinär ‹Person, Benehmen, Witz, Film›; geschmacklos ‹Kleidung›; **B** **the ~ tongue** (*dated*) die Volkssprache; **C** (*Math.*) **~ fraction** gemeiner Bruch
**vulgarise** ⇨ **vulgarize**
**vulgarism** /'vʌlgərɪzm/ *n.* (*Ling.*) Vulgarismus, *der*
**vulgarity** /vʌl'gærɪtɪ/ *n., no pl.* Vulgarität, *die;* (*of clothing*) Geschmacklosigkeit, *die;* **her ~ puts me off** ihre ordinäre *od.* gewöhnliche Art stößt mich ab
**vulgarize** /'vʌlgəraɪz/ *v.t.* vulgarisieren; verderben ‹Charakter, Person›
**vulgarly** /'vʌlgəlɪ/ *adv.* vulgär; ordinär; geschmacklos ‹sich kleiden›
**Vulgate** /'vʌlgeɪt, 'vʌlgət/ *n.* (*Bibl.*) Vulgata, *die*
**vulnerability** /vʌlnərə'bɪlɪtɪ/ *n., no pl.* **A** Angreifbarkeit, *die;* (*to criticism, temptation*) Anfälligkeit, *die* (**to** für); **B** (*to injury*) Empfindlichkeit, *die* (**to** gegen); Schutzlosigkeit, *die;* (*emotional*) Verletzlichkeit, *die*
**vulnerable** /'vʌlnərəbl/ *adj.* **A** (*exposed to danger*) angreifbar; **a ~ spot/point** ein schwacher Punkt; **be ~ to sth.** für etw. anfällig sein; **be ~ to attack/in a ~ position** leicht angreifbar sein; **be economically ~:** wirtschaftlich in einer prekären Lage sein; **~ to criticism** leicht zu kritisieren; (*easily hurt*) leicht durch Kritik verletzt; **B** (*susceptible to injury*) empfindlich (**to** gegen); (*without protection*) schutzlos; **~ to infection** anfällig für Infektionen; **look young and ~:** jung und schutzlos aussehen; **emotionally ~:** verletzlich
**vulture** /'vʌltʃə(r)/ *n.* (*lit. or fig.*) Geier, *der*
**vulva** /'vʌlvə/ *n.* (*Anat.*) Vulva, *die*
**vying** ⇨ **vie**

# W w

**W**[1], **w**/'dʌblju:/ *n., pl.* **Ws** *or* **W's** W, w, *das*

**W**[2] *abbr.* **A** **watt[s]** W; **B** ▶ 1024 **west** W.; **C** ▶ 1024 **western** w.

**w.** *abbr.* **with** m.

**WAAF** *abbr.* (*Brit. Hist.*) **A** **Women's Auxiliary Air Force; B** /wæf/ *Mitglied der Women's Auxiliary Air Force*

**WAC** *abbr.* (*Amer.*) **A** **Women's Army Corps; B** /wæk/ *Mitglied des Women's Army Corps*

**wacky** /'wækɪ/ *adj.* (*coll.*) bekloppt (*salopp*); verrückt (*ugs.*) ‹Komödie›

**wad** /wɒd/ **1** *n.* **A** (*material*) Knäuel, *das;* (*smaller*) Pfropfen, *der;* **a ~ of cotton wool** ein Wattebausch; **B** (*of papers*) Bündel, *das;* **~s of money** bündelweise Geld; **he earns ~s of money** (*fig.*) er verdient jede Menge Geld. **2** *v.t.*, **-dd- A** (*form into ~*) zusammenknüllen; **B** (*line*) füttern ‹Kleidungsstück›; (*stuff*) ausstopfen ‹Zwischenräume›; **C** (*protect with cotton wool*) wattieren

**wadding** /'wɒdɪŋ/ *n.* (*lining*) Futter, *das;* (*for packing*) Füllmaterial, *das;* Füllsel *Pl.;* **cotton ~:** Wattierung, *die*

**waddle** /'wɒdl/ **1** *v.i.* watscheln. **2** *n.* watschelnder Gang

**wade** /weɪd/ **1** *v.i.* waten; (*in snow, sand*) stapfen. **2** *v.t.* durchwaten, waten durch ‹Fluss, Bach›

**~ 'in** *v.i.* (*fig. coll.*) [gleich] losgehen; (*tackle task*) sich hineinknien (*ugs.*)

**~ into** *v.t.* (*fig. coll.*) losgehen auf (+ *Akk.*); **~ into the meal** reinhauen (*ugs.*)

**~ through** *v.t.* **A** waten durch; stapfen durch ‹Schnee, Unkraut›; **B** (*fig. coll.*) durchackern (*ugs.*) ‹Manuskript, Buch›

**wader** /'weɪdə(r)/ *n.* **A** (*Ornith.*) Watvogel, *der;* **B** *in pl.* (*boots*) Watstiefel

**wadi** /'wɒdɪ, 'wɑ:dɪ/ *n.* (*Geog.*) Wadi, *das*

**wading bird** /'weɪdɪŋ bɜ:d/ ⇒ **wader** A

**wafer** /'weɪfə(r)/ *n.* **A** Waffel, *die;* (*very thin*) Oblate, *die;* **B** (*Eccl.*) Hostie, *die;* **C** (*Electronics*) Wafer, *der*

**'wafer-thin** *adj.* hauchdünn

**waffle**[1] /'wɒfl/ *n.* (*Gastr.*) Waffel, *die*

**waffle**[2] (*Brit. coll.: talk*) **1** *v.i.* schwafeln (*ugs. abwertend*); faseln (*ugs. abwertend*). **2** *n.* Geschwafel, *das* (*ugs. abwertend*); Faselei, *die* (*ugs. abwertend*)

**'waffle iron** *n.* Waffeleisen, *das*

**waft** /wɒft, wɑ:ft/ **1** *v.t.* wehen. **2** *v.i.* ‹Geruch, Duft:› ziehen, (*with perceptible air movement*) wehen. **3** *n.* Hauch, *der*

**wag**[1] /wæg/ **1** *v.t.*, **-gg-** ‹Hund:› wedeln mit ‹Schwanz›; ‹Vogel:› wippen mit ‹Schwanz›; ‹Person:› schütteln ‹Kopf›; **it was a case of the tail ~ging the dog** (*fig.*) da hat der Schwanz mit dem Hund gewedelt (*ugs.*); **~ one's finger at sb.** jmdm. mit dem Finger drohen. **2** *v.i.*, **-gg-** ‹Schwanz:› wedeln/(*of bird*) wippen; **her tongue never stops ~ging** ihre Zunge steht niemals still; **set people's tongues ~ging** den Leuten etwas zu reden geben. **3** *n.* (*of dog's tail*) Wedeln, *das* (**of** mit); (*of bird's tail*) Wippen, *das* (**of** mit); (*of person's head*) Schütteln, *das* (**of** *Gen.*); **with a ~ of its tail/his head** mit einem Schwanzwedeln/Kopfschütteln

**wag**[2] *n.* (*facetious person*) Witzbold, *der* (*ugs.*)

**wage** /weɪdʒ/ **1** *n. in sing. or pl.* Lohn, *der;* **sb.'s weekly ~[s]** jmds. Wochenlohn; **a job at a reasonable ~/with reasonable ~s** eine anständig bezahlte Arbeit; **~s of sin** (*fig.*) Lohn der Sünde; der Sünde Lohn (*veralt.*). **2** *v.t.* führen ‹Krieg, Feldzug›; **~ war on** *or* **against crime** (*fig.*) gegen das Verbrechen zu Felde ziehen

**wage: ~ claim** *n.* Lohnforderung, *die;* **~ earner** *n.* Lohnempfänger, *der*/-empfängerin, *die;* **be the ~ earner of the family** der Ernährer/die Ernährerin der Familie sein; **~ freeze** *n.* Lohnstopp, *der;* **~ increase** *n.* Lohnerhöhung, *die;* **~ packet** *n.* Lohntüte, *die;* **the size of his ~ packet** wie viel er in der Lohntüte hat

**wager** /'weɪdʒə(r)/ (*dated, formal*) **1** *n.* Wette, *die;* **a ~ of £50** eine Wette um 50 Pfund. **2** *v.t.* wetten; (*on a horse*) setzen; **~ one's life/one's whole fortune on sth.** seinen Kopf/sein ganzes Vermögen auf etw. (*Akk.*) verwetten; **I ~ you £10 that ...:** ich wette mit dir um 10 Pfund, dass ... **3** *v.i.* wetten; **he's there by now, I'll ~:** ich möchte wetten, dass er inzwischen da ist

**wage: ~ rise** *n.* Lohnerhöhung, *die;* **~ scale** *n.* Tarif, *der;* Lohnskala, *die;* **~ slave** *n.* Lohnsklave, *der*

**waggish** /'wægɪʃ/ *adj.* witzig ‹Bemerkung›; **be in a ~ mood** zu Scherzen aufgelegt sein

**waggle** /'wægl/ (*coll.*) **1** *v.t.* **~ its tail** ‹Hund:› mit dem Schwanz wedeln; ‹Vogel:› mit dem Schwanz wippen; **~ a loose tooth** an einem lockeren Zahn wackeln. **2** *v.i.* hin- und herschlagen; **the dog's tail ~d** der Hund wedelte mit dem Schwanz. **3** *n.* Hin- und Herschlagen, *das;* (*of tail*) Wedeln, *das*

**waggon** *etc.* (*Brit.*) ⇒ **wagon** *etc.*

**Wagnerian** /vɑ:g'nɪərɪən/ **1** *n.* Wagnerianer, *der*/Wagnerianerin, *die.* **2** *adj.* wagnerianisch; (*of Wagner*) wagner[i]sch; **~ singer** Wagnersänger, *der*/-sängerin, *die*

**wagon** /'wægən/ *n.* **A** (*horse-drawn*) Wagen, *der;* **covered ~:** Planwagen, *der;* **hitch one's ~ to a star** (*fig.*) sich (*Dat.*) ein hohes Ziel setzen; **B** (*Amer.: motor vehicle*) Wagen, *der;* **C** **[water] ~:** Wasserwagen, *der;* **D** **go/be on the ~** (*go/be teetotal*) keinen Tropfen mehr/keinen Tropfen anrühren; **E** (*trolley*) Wagen, *der;* **F** (*Brit. Railw.*) Wagen, *der;* Waggon, *der* (*volkst.*)

**wagoner** /'wægənə(r)/ *n.* Fuhrmann, *der*

**'wagonload** *n.* [Wagen]ladung, *die*

**'wagtail** *n.* (*Ornith.*) Bachstelze, *die*

**waif** /weɪf/ *n.* Heimatlose, *der/die;* (*child*) verlassenes Kind; (*animal*) herrenloses Tier; **~s and strays** (*children*) obdachlose Kinder; (*animals*) streunende Tiere

**wail** /weɪl/ **1** *v.i.* **A** (*lament*) klagen (*geh.*) (**for** um); jammern (*ugs.*) (**for** um); ‹Kind:› heulen; **stop ~ing!** hör auf zu jammern!; **B** (*fig.*) ‹Wind, Sirene:› heulen. **2** *n.* **A** (*cry*) klagender Schrei; **~s** Geheul, *das;* (*esp. fig.: complaints*) Gejammer, *das;* **~s of protest** Protestgeschrei, *das;* **a ~ of pain** ein Schmerzensschrei; **B** (*fig.: of wind etc.*) Heulen, *das;* Geheul, *das*

**Wailing 'Wall** *n.* Klagemauer, *die*

**wainscot** /'weɪnskət/, **wainscoting** /'weɪnskətɪŋ/ *ns.* Täfelung, *die*

**waist** /weɪst/ *n.* **A** (*part of body or garment*) Taille, *die;* **tight round the ~:** eng in der Taille; ⇒ *also* **strip**[1] 1 A; **B** (*Amer.*) (*blouse*) Bluse, *die;* (*bodice*) Mieder, *das;* **C** (*narrow part*) Einbuchtung, *die;* (*of violin*) Mittelbügel, *der;* (*Naut.: of ship*) Mittelschiff, *das*

**'waistband** *n.* Gürtelbund, *der;* (*of trousers*) [Hosen]bund, *der;* (*of skirt*) [Rock]bund, *der*

**waistcoat** /'weɪskəʊt, 'weɪstkəʊt/ *n.* (*Brit.*) Weste, *die*

**'waist-deep 1** *adj.* bis zur Taille reichend; **be ~:** einem bis zur Taille reichen. **2** *adv.* bis zur Taille

**waisted** /'weɪstɪd/ *adj.* tailliert ‹Kleidungsstück›

**waist: ~-'high** ⇒ **waist-deep; ~line** *n.* Taille, *die;* **be bad for the ~line** schlecht für die schlanke Linie sein

**wait** /weɪt/ **1** *v.i.* **A** warten; **~ [for] an hour** eine Stunde warten; **~ a moment** Moment mal; **keep sb. ~ing, make sb. ~:** jmdn. warten lassen; **how long have you been ~ing?** wie lange wartest du schon?; **~ to see sth. happen** darauf warten, dass etw. passiert; **'repairs [done]/keys cut while you ~'** „Reparatur-/Schlüsselschnelldienst"; **she ~ed to see what would happen if ...:** sie wollte abwarten, was passiert, wenn ...; **sth. is still ~ing to be done** etw. muss noch gemacht werden; **~ and see** abwarten[, was passiert]; **[just] ~ and see!** warte doch ab!; **sth. can/can't** *or* **won't ~:** etw. kann/kann nicht warten; **this bill can't ~:** diese Rechnung muss sofort bezahlt werden; **I can't ~ to do sth.** (*am eager*) ich kann es kaum erwarten, etw. zu tun; **I can hardly ~** (*lit. or iron.*) ich kann es kaum erwarten; **I can't ~** (*for lavatory*) es ist dringend; **[just] you ~!** warte mal ab!; (*as threat*) warte nur!; **B** **~ at** *or* (*Amer.*) **on table** servieren; ‹Ober:› kellnern (*ugs.*).

**2** *v.t.* **A** (*await*) warten auf (+ *Akk.*); **~ one's chance/opportunity** auf eine [günstige] Gelegenheit warten; **~ one's turn** warten, bis man dran ist *od.* drankommt; **~ sb.'s convenience** warten, bis es jmdm. passt; **B** (*delay*) **~ lunch/supper [for sb.]** mit dem Mittag-/Abendessen [auf jmdn.] warten.

**3** *n.* **A** (*act, time*) **after a long/short ~:** nach langer/kurzer Wartezeit; **there is quite a ~ for appointments** auf einen Termin muss man ziemlich lange warten; **have a long/short ~ for sth.** lange/nicht lange auf etw. (*Akk.*) warten müssen; **B** (*watching for enemy*) **lie in ~:** im Hinterhalt liegen; **lie in ~ for sb./sth.** jmdm./einer Sache auflauern; **C** *in pl.* (*Brit.: carol singers*) Sternsinger

**~ a'bout, ~ a'round** *v.i.* herumstehen

**~ be'hind** *v.i.* noch hier-/dableiben; **~ behind for sb.** auf jmdn. warten

**~ for** *v.t.* warten auf (+ *Akk.*); **~ for the rain to stop** warten, bis der Regen aufhört; **we'll ~ for a fine day** wir warten einen schönen Tag ab; **I can hardly ~ for the day when ...:** ich kann den Tag kaum erwarten, an dem ...; **it was worth ~ing for** es hat sich gelohnt, darauf zu warten; **~ for it!** warte/wartet!; (*to create suspense before saying something surprising*) warte ab!

**~ 'in** *v.i.* zu Hause warten (**for** auf + *Akk.*)

**~ on** *v.t.* **A** (*serve*) bedienen; **B** (*await*) warten auf (+ *Akk.*)

**~ 'out** *v.t.* **~ out a storm** *etc.* warten, bis ein Sturm *usw.* vorüber *od.* vorbei ist

**~ 'up** *v.i.* aufbleiben (**for** wegen)

**waiter** /'weɪtə(r)/ *n.* ▶ 1261 Kellner, *der;* **~!** Herr Ober!

**waiting** /'weɪtɪŋ/ *n.* **A** Warten, *das;* **'no ~'** „Halteverbot"; **B** *no pl., no art.* (*working as waiter*) Servieren, *das;* Kellnern, *das* (*ugs.*)

**waiting: ~ game** *n.* Hinhaltetaktik, *die;* **play a ~ game** erst einmal abwarten; sich erst einmal bedeckt halten (*ugs.*); **~ list** *n.* Warteliste, *die;* **a five-year ~ list** eine Wartezeit von fünf Jahren; **~ room** *n.* Wartezimmer, *das;* (*at railway or bus station*) Warteraum, *der;* (*larger*) Wartesaal, *der*

**waitress** /'weɪtrɪs/ *n.* ▶ 1261 Serviererin, *die;* Kellnerin, *die* (*veralt.*); **~!** Fräulein! (*veralt.*); **there is ~ service in the ground**

**floor restaurant** das Restaurant im Erdgeschoss ist mit Bedienung

**waive** /weɪv/ *v.t.* verzichten auf (+ *Akk.*); nicht vollstrecken ‹Strafe›; nicht anwenden ‹Regel›

**waiver** /ˈweɪvə(r)/ *n.* (*Law*) Verzicht, *der* (**of** auf + *Akk.*)

**wake¹** /weɪk/ ❶ *v.i.*, **woke** /wəʊk/ *or* (*arch.*) **waked, woken** /ˈwəʊkn/ *or* (*arch.*) **waked** Ⓐ (*cease sleeping*) aufwachen; (*fig.*) ‹Natur, Gefühle:› erwachen; **we woke to a bright, cold morning** der Morgen war klar und frisch, als wir aufwachten; **I woke to the sound of soft music** beim Aufwachen hörte ich leise Musik; Ⓑ **~ to sth.** (*fig.: realize*) etw. erkennen; sich (*Dat.*) einer Sache (*Gen.*) bewusst werden.
❷ *v.t.* **woke** *or* (*arch.*) **waked, woken** *or* (*arch.*) **waked** Ⓐ wecken; (*fig.*) erwecken (*geh.*) ‹die Natur, Erinnerungen›; wecken ‹Erinnerungen›; **be quiet, you'll ~ your baby brother** sei still, sonst wacht dein Brüderchen auf!; **~ the dead** die Toten erwecken (*geh.*) *od.* aufwecken; **~ the country to the danger of war** (*fig.*) dem Land die Kriegsgefahr bewusst machen; Ⓑ (*cause*) hervorrufen ‹Echo›.
❸ *n.* Ⓐ (*Ir.: watch by corpse*) Totenwache, *die;* Ⓑ *usu. pl.* (*N. Engl.*) **~s week, the ~s** ≈ Kirmes, *die*

**~ ˈup** ❶ *v.i.* (*lit. or fig.*) aufwachen; **~ up!** wach auf!; (*fig.: pay attention*) pass besser auf!; **~ up to sth.** (*fig.: realize*) etw. erkennen; sich (*Dat.*) einer Sache (*Gen.*) bewusst werden. ❷ *v.t.* Ⓐ (*rouse from sleep*) wecken; Ⓑ (*fig.: enliven*) wachrütteln; Leben bringen in (+ *Akk.*) ‹Stadt›; **you need to ~ your ideas up a bit** du müsstest dich ein bisschen zusammenreißen

**wake²** *n.* Ⓐ (*water*) Kielwasser, *das;* Ⓑ (*air*) Turbulenz, *die;* Ⓒ (*fig.*) **in the ~ of sth./sb.** im Gefolge von etw./in jmds. Gefolge; **follow in the ~ of sb./sth.** jmdm./einer Sache folgen; **bring sth. in its ~:** etw. zur Folge haben; **leave a cloud of dust/trail of destruction in its ~:** eine Staubwolke/eine Spur der Verwüstung hinterlassen

**wakeful** /ˈweɪkfl/ *adj.* Ⓐ (*sleepless*) schlaflos ‹Nacht›; **a ~ child** ein Kind, das schlecht schläft; Ⓑ (*vigilant*) wachsam

**wakefulness** /ˈweɪkflnɪs/ *n., no pl.* Ⓐ (*sleeplessness*) Schlaflosigkeit, *die;* Ⓑ (*vigilance*) Wachsamkeit, *die*

**waken** /ˈweɪkn/ ❶ *v.t.* Ⓐ wecken; Ⓑ (*fig.: arouse*) wecken ‹Interesse, Gefühl›; erregen ‹Zorn›. ❷ *v.i.* ⇒ **wake¹** 1

**ˈwake-up call** (*esp. Amer.*) ⇒ **alarm call**

**waking** /ˈweɪkɪŋ/ *adj.* **in one's ~ hours** den ganzen Tag; von früh bis spät; **spend all one's ~ hours [on] doing sth.** etw. von früh bis spät tun; **~ dream** Wachtraum, *der*

**Wales** /weɪlz/ *pr. n.* Wales (*das*); ⇒ *also* **prince** B

**walk** /wɔːk/ ❶ *v.i.* Ⓐ laufen; (*as opposed to running*) gehen; (*as opposed to driving*) zu Fuß gehen; **you can ~ there in five minutes** es sind nur 5 Minuten zu Fuß bis dorthin; **ˈwalk'/ˈdon't ~'** (*Amer.: at pedestrian lights*) „gehen"/„warten"; **~ on crutches/with a stick** an Krücken/am Stock gehen; **learn to ~:** laufen lernen; **can the child ~ yet?** kann das Kind schon laufen?; **be ~ing on air** (*fig.*) sich wie im siebten Himmel fühlen; **~ tall** (*fig.*) erhobenen Hauptes gehen (*fig.*); Ⓑ (*exercise*) gehen; marschieren (*ugs.*); Ⓒ (*appear*) ‹Geist:› erscheinen; Ⓓ (*go with slow gait*) ‹Pferd:› gehen; Ⓔ (*Cricket coll.*) rausgehen; Ⓕ (*coll.: go missing*) Beine bekommen (*fig. ugs.*).
❷ *v.t.* Ⓐ entlanggehen; ablaufen ‹Strecke, Weg›; durchwandern ‹Gebiet›; **~ the course** (*Sport*) die Strecke abgehen; ‹Reiter:› den Parcours abgehen; **~ the** *or* **his beat** ‹Polizist:› seine Runde gehen; **~ the streets** durch die Straßen gehen/(*aimlessly*) laufen; (*as prostitute*) auf den Strich gehen (*ugs.*); **~ the boards** (*be actor*) auf den Brettern stehen; **~ it** (*coll.*) zu Fuß gehen; laufen (*ugs.*); **he ~ed it** (*fig. coll.: won easily*) es war ein Spaziergang für ihn; ⇒ *also* **plank** 1 A; Ⓑ (*cause to ~; lead*) führen; ausführen ‹Hund›; **~ sb. round the room** jmdn. im Zimmer herumführen; **~ sb. off his/her feet** jmdn. [bis zur Erschöpfung] durch die Gegend schleifen (*ugs.*); Ⓒ (*accompany*) bringen; **he ~ed his girlfriend home** er brachte seine Freundin nach Hause; Ⓓ (*push*) schieben ‹Fahrrad, Motorrad›.
❸ *n.* Ⓐ Spaziergang, *der;* **go [out] for** *or* **take** *or* **have a ~:** einen Spaziergang machen; **take sb./the dog for a ~:** jmdn./den Hund spazieren führen; **a ten-mile ~:** eine Wanderung von zehn Meilen; (*distance*) **ten minutes' ~ from here** zehn Minuten zu Fuß von hier; ⇒ *also* **space walk**; Ⓑ (*gait*) Gang, *der;* (*characteristic*) normale Gangart; **I know her by her ~:** ich erkenne sie am Gang; Ⓒ (*~ing speed*) Schritttempo, *das;* **his horse/she slowed to a ~:** sein Pferd ging nur noch im Schritt/sie verfiel in ein normales Schritttempo; Ⓓ (*Sport: race*) Wettbewerb im Gehen; **the 10,000 metres ~:** das 10 000-m-Gehen; Ⓔ (*path, route*) [Spazier]weg, *der;* **a milkman's/postman's ~:** die Tour eines Milchmanns/Briefträgers; Ⓕ **people from all ~s of life** Leute aus den verschiedensten gesellschaftlichen Gruppierungen

**~ aˈbout** *v.i.* herumlaufen; in der Gegend herumlaufen (*ugs.*); ⇒ *also* **walkabout**

**~ aˈway** *v.i.* Ⓐ weggehen; **she was lucky to ~ away from the accident** sie hatte großes Glück, den Unfallort unverletzt verlassen zu können; Ⓑ (*fig.*) **~ away from the opposition** *or* **competition** (*coll.: defeat*) der Konkurrenz weglaufen; **he tried to ~ away from the problem** (*ignore it*) er versuchte, dem Problem aus dem Weg zu gehen; **~ away with sth.** (*coll.*) (*win easily*) etw. spielend leicht gewinnen; (*steal*) sich mit etw. davonmachen (*ugs.*); **~ away with all the prizes** alle Preise einheimsen (*ugs.*)

**~ ˈin** *v.i.* Ⓐ (*enter*) hereinkommen/hineingehen; reinkommen/-gehen (*ugs.*); **'please ~ in'** „[bitte] eintreten, ohne zu klopfen"; Ⓑ (*enter without permission*) hinein-/hereinspazieren; **~ in on sb./sth.** bei jmdm./etw. hereinplatzen (*ugs.*)

**~ into** *v.t.* Ⓐ (*enter*) betreten; treten in (+ *Akk.*) ‹Pfütze›; (*without permission*) eindringen in (+ *Akk.*) ‹Haus›; Ⓑ (*hit by accident*) laufen gegen ‹Pfosten, Laternenpfahl›; **~ into sb.** mit jmdm. zusammenstoßen; **~ into a trap** (*lit. or fig.*) in eine Falle gehen; **the boxer ~ed straight into a right hook** der Boxer lief voll in den rechten Haken [hinein]; **you ~ed straight into that one!** da hast du dich aber reinlegen lassen!; Ⓒ (*coll.: come easily into*) **she ~ed into the top job** ihr ist der Topjob einfach zugefallen

**~ ˈoff** ❶ *v.i.* Ⓐ (*leave*) weggehen; verschwinden; **he has ~ed off with another woman** er ist mit einer anderen Frau durchgebrannt (*ugs.*); Ⓑ **~ off with sth.** (*coll.*) sich mit etw. davonmachen (*ugs.*); **~ off with all the prizes** alle Preise einheimsen (*ugs.*); **he ~ed off with the fight** er hat den Kampf lässig gewonnen. ❷ *v.t.* **I'll have to ~ off some of this fat** ich muss mehr laufen, um ein paar Pfunde loszuwerden (*ugs.*); **~ off a hangover** einen Spaziergang machen, um seinen Kater loszuwerden

**~ ˈon** *v.i.* Ⓐ (*go further*) weitergehen; **~ on!** (*to horse*) hü!; Ⓑ (*go on stage*) auf die Bühne kommen; **~ on as the policeman or the butler** Statistenrollen wie den Polizisten oder Butler spielen

**~ ˈout** *v.i.* Ⓐ (*leave*) hinausgehen; rausgehen (*ugs.*); Ⓑ (*Mil.: leave barracks*) ausgehen; Ⓒ (*leave in protest*) aus Protest den Saal verlassen; (*leave organization*) austreten; Ⓓ (*go on strike*) in den Streik *od.* Ausstand treten; Ⓔ (*Brit. dated: be courting*) miteinander gehen (*ugs.*); **~ out with sb.** mit jmdm. gehen (*ugs.*). ⇒ *also* **walkout**

**~ ˈout of** *v.t.* Ⓐ (*leave*) gehen aus; Ⓑ (*leave in protest*) verlassen ‹Saal, Versammlung›

**~ ˈout on** *v.t.* verlassen; sitzen lassen (*ugs.*) ‹Frau, Mann›; hinschmeißen (*ugs.*) ‹Job›

**~ ˈover** *v.t.* **~ [all] over sb.** jmdn. fertig machen (*ugs.*); ⇒ *also* **walkover**

**~ ˈup** *v.i.* Ⓐ (*approach*) sich nähern; **~ up to sb.** zu jmdm. hingehen; **he ~ed up to me** er kam zu mir [heran]; **~ up to the door** zur Tür gehen; **~ up! ~ up!** (*said by showman*) immer hereinspaziert!; Ⓑ (*ascend*) hochlaufen; nach oben laufen; ⇒ *also* **walk-up**

**ˈwalkabout** *n.* Ⓐ (*through crowds*) Bad in der Menge (*scherzh.*); **go on a ~:** sich unters Volk mischen; Ⓑ (*Austral.: in bush*) Buschwanderung, *die*

**walker** /ˈwɔːkə(r)/ *n.* Ⓐ Spaziergänger, *der*/-gängerin, *die;* (*in race*) Geher, *der*/Geherin, *die;* (*rambler, hiker*) Wanderer, *der*/Wanderin, *die;* **sb. is a good ~:** jmd. ist gut zu Fuß; Ⓑ (*frame*) Laufgestell, *das;* (*baby-~*) Laufstuhl, *der*

**walkies** /ˈwɔːkɪz/ *n. pl.* (*coll.*) **go ~:** Gassi gehen (*ugs.*); **~!** (*said to dog*) komm Gassi! (*ugs.*)

**walkie-talkie** /wɔːkɪˈtɔːkɪ/ *n.* Walkie-Talkie, *das*

**walking** /ˈwɔːkɪŋ/ ❶ *attrib. adj.* **a ~ dictionary/encyclopaedia** (*joc.*) ein wandelndes Wörterbuch/Konversationslexikon; **the ~ wounded** die gehfähigen Verwundeten; ⇒ *also* **disaster area.** ❷ *n., no pl., no art.* [Spazieren]gehen, *das;* Laufen, *das;* **you ought to do more ~:** Sie sollten mehr zu Fuß gehen *od.* spazieren gehen; *attrib.* **at ~ pace** im Schritttempo; **be within ~ distance** zu Fuß zu erreichen sein; **we are within ~ distance [of it]** wir können es zu Fuß erreichen

**walking: ~ frame** *n.* Gehgestell, *das;* **~ holiday** *n.* Wanderurlaub, *der;* **~ shoe** *n.* Wanderschuh, *der;* **~ stick** *n.* Spazierstock, *der;* **she cannot manage now without a ~ stick** sie kommt nicht mehr ohne Stock aus; **~ tour** *n.* Wanderung, *die*

**Walkman** ® /ˈwɔːkmən/ *n., pl.* **Walkmans** Walkman, *der* Ⓦⓩ

**walk: ~-on part** *n.* (*Theatre*) Statistenrolle, *die;* **~out** *n.* Arbeitsniederlegung, *die;* **~over** *n.* (*fig.: easy victory*) Spaziergang, *der* (*ugs.*); **~-up** *n.* (*Amer.*) Haus ohne Aufzug; **~way** *n.* Fußweg, *der;* (*over machinery etc.*) Laufsteg, *der*

**wall** /wɔːl/ ❶ *n.* Ⓐ (*of building, part of structure*) Wand, *die;* (*external, also free-standing*) Mauer, *die;* **town/garden ~:** Stadt-/Gartenmauer, *die;* **the south ~ of the house** die Südwand des Hauses; **a concrete ~:** eine Betonwand/-mauer; **the Great W~ of China** die Chinesische Mauer; **the Berlin W~** (*Hist.*) die [Berliner] Mauer; Ⓑ (*internal*) Wand, *die;* **be hanging on the ~:** an der Wand hängen; **hang a picture on the ~:** ein Bild an die Wand hängen; **within these four ~s** (*fig.*) innerhalb dieser vier Wände; **I'm tired of [staring at] my own four ~s** mir fällt die Decke auf den Kopf (*ugs.*); **~s have ears** die Wände haben Ohren; **drive** *or* **send sb. up the ~** (*fig. coll.*) jmdn. auf die Palme bringen (*ugs.*); **go up the ~** (*fig. coll.*) die Wände hochgehen (*ugs.*); **go to the ~** (*fig.*) an die Wand gedrückt werden; ⇒ *also* **back** 1 A; Ⓒ (*Mount., Min.*) Wand, *die;* (*fig.*) Mauer, *die;* **a ~ of water/fire** eine Wasser-/Feuerwand; **the North W~ of the Eiger** die Eigernordwand; **a ~ of silence/prejudice** (*fig.*) eine Mauer des Schweigens/von Vorurteilen; Ⓓ (*esp. Footb.: protective row*) Mauer, *die;* **a ~ of troops/policemen/tanks** eine Mauer von Soldaten/Polizisten/Panzern; Ⓔ (*Anat., Zool., Bot.: outer layer*) Wand, *die;* **abdominal ~:** Bauchwand, *die.*
❷ *v.t.* **[be] ~ed** von einer Mauer/Mauern umgeben [sein]; **X is a ~ed city/town** X hat eine Stadtmauer

**~ ˈin** *v.t.* mit einer Mauer umgeben; (*fig.*) umzingeln

**~ ˈoff** *v.t.* abteilen

**~ ˈup** *v.t.* zumauern; einmauern ‹Person›

**wallaby** /ˈwɒləbɪ/ *n.* (*Zool.*) Wallaby, *das*

**wallah** /ˈwɒlə/ *n.* (*dated coll.*) **television/advertising ~:** Fernseh-/Werbefritze, *der* (*ugs.*)

**wall: ~ bars** *n. pl.* Sprossenwand, *die;* **~board** *n.* Wandfaserplatte, *die;* **~chart** *n.*

W

Schautafel, *die;* ~ **covering** *n.* (~*paper*) Tapete, *die;* (~ *hanging*) Wandbehang, *der;* ~ **cupboard** *n.* Hängeschrank, *der*

**wallet** /ˈwɒlɪt/ *n.* Brieftasche, *die;* (*for cheque card etc.*) Etui, *das*

**wall:** ~**flower** *n.* Ⓐ (*Bot.*) Goldlack, *der;* Ⓑ (*coll.: person*) Mauerblümchen, *das* (*ugs.*); ~ **hanging** *n.* Wandbehang, *der;* ~ **light** *n.* Wandlampe, *die;* ~ **map** *n.* Wandkarte, *die*

**Wallonia** /wɒˈləʊnɪə/ *pr. n.* Wallonien (*das*)

**Walloon** /wɒˈluːn/ ▶ **1275**, ▶ **1340** ❶ *n.* Ⓐ (*person*) Wallone, *der*/Wallonin, *die;* Ⓑ (*dialect*) Wallonisch, *das;* ⇒ *also* **English** 2 A. ❷ *adj.* wallonisch; ⇒ *also* **English** 1

**wallop** /ˈwɒləp/ (*coll.*) ❶ *v.t.* (*hit*) schlagen; (*with repeated blows*) [ver]prügeln; **he** ~**ed him one over the head** (*coll.*) er hat ihm eins übergebraten (*salopp*). ❷ *n.* Schlag, *der;* **give sb./sth. a** ~: auf jmdn./etw. draufhauen (*ugs.*); **he fell down with a** ~: er fiel mit einem Plumps hin

**walloping** /ˈwɒləpɪŋ/ (*coll.*) ❶ *n.* Ⓐ (*thrashing*) **a** ~: eine Tracht Prügel (*ugs.*); Ⓑ (*defeat*) **get a** ~: eins übergebraten kriegen (*salopp*). ❷ *adj.* gepfeffert (*ugs.*) ‹Niederlage, Rechnung›; faustdick (*ugs.*) ‹Lüge›

**wallow** /ˈwɒləʊ/ ❶ *v.i.* Ⓐ (*roll around*) sich wälzen; ‹Schiff:› schlingern; (*in mud also*) sich suhlen; Ⓑ (*fig.: take delight*) schwelgen (**in** in + *Dat.*); **be** ~**ing in money** (*coll.*) im Geld schwimmen (*ugs.*); ~ **in luxury** im Luxus baden *od.* schwelgen. ❷ *n.* Ⓐ (*mud-bath*) Schlammbad, *das;* **like a good** ~ **in the mud** sich gern im Schlamm wälzen *od.* suhlen; Ⓑ (*fig.: indulgence*) **he likes to have a good** ~ **[in sentiment]** er schwelgt gern in Gefühlen

**wall:** ~ **painting** *n.* Wandgemälde, *das;* ~**paper** ❶ *n.* Tapete, *die;* ❷ *v.t.* tapezieren; ~ **socket** *n.* (*Electr.*) Wandsteckdose, *die;* **W**~ **Street** *n.* [die] Wall Street; die Wallstreet; ~**-to-**~ *adj.* (*covering floor*) ~**-to-**~ **carpeting** Teppichboden, *der;* ~ **unit** *n.* Hängeelement, *das*

**wally** /ˈwɒlɪ/ *n.* (*Brit. coll.*) Blödmann, *der* (*salopp*)

**walnut** /ˈwɔːlnʌt/ *n.* Ⓐ (*nut*) Walnuss, *die;* Ⓑ (*tree*) [Wal]nussbaum, *der;* Ⓒ (*wood*) Nussbaumholz, *das*

**walrus** /ˈwɔːlrəs, ˈwɒlrəs/ *n.* Walross, *das;* ~ **moustache** Walrossbart, *der* (*ugs.*)

**Walter Mitty** /wɒltə ˈmɪtɪ/ ⇒ **Mitty**

**waltz** /wɔːlts, wɔːls, wɒlts, wɒls/ ❶ *n.* Walzer, *der;* **can you dance the** ~**?** können Sie Walzer tanzen? ❷ *v.i.* Walzer tanzen; ~ **round the room** durchs Zimmer tanzen

~ **ˈin** *v.i.* (*fig. coll.*) angetanzt kommen (*ugs.*)

~ **ˈoff**, ~ **ˈout** *v.i.* (*fig. coll.*) abtanzen (*ugs.*)

**wan** /wɒn/ *adj.* fahl (*geh.*); bleich; ~ **smile** mattes Lächeln

**wand** /wɒnd/ *n.* Stab, *der;* (*magician's* ~) Zauberstab, *der*

**wander** /ˈwɒndə(r)/ ❶ *v.i.* Ⓐ (*go aimlessly*) umherirren; (*walk slowly*) bummeln; **she** ~**ed over to me** sie kam zu mir herüber; **I must be** ~**ing** (*coll.*) ich muss mich auf die Socken machen (*ugs.*); Ⓑ (*stray*) ‹Katze:› streunen; ‹Schafe:› sich verlaufen; ~ **from the trail** vom Weg abkommen; ~ **from the path of righteousness**, ~ **from the straight and narrow** (*fig.*) vom Pfad der Tugend abkommen; **the car** ~**s badly** der Wagen hält schlecht Spur; Ⓒ (*fig.: stray from subject*) abschweifen; **his thoughts** ~**ed back to his childhood** seine Gedanken schweiften zurück in die Kindheit.
❷ *v.t.* wandern durch; ~ **the world** durch die Welt ziehen.
❸ *n.* (*coll.: walk*) Spaziergang, *der;* **let's go for a** ~: komm, laufen wir ein bisschen rum (*ugs.*); **I'll go for** *or* **take a** ~ **round** *or* **through the town** ich werd mal einen Bummel durch die Stadt machen

~ **aˈbout** *v.i.* sich herumtreiben

~ **aˈlong** *v.i.* dahintrotten; ‹Fahrzeug:› dahinzockeln (*ugs.*)

~ **ˈin** *v.i.* hineinspazieren; (*towards speaker*) hereinspaziert kommen

~ **ˈoff** *v.i.* Ⓐ (*stray*) weggehen; ‹Kind:› sich selbstständig machen (*scherzh.*); Ⓑ (*coll.: go away*) sich davonmachen (*ugs.*)

**wanderer** /ˈwɒndərə(r)/ *n.* Streuner, *der*/Streunerin, *die;* (*traveller*) Wandervogel, *der* (*veralt. scherzh.*)

**wandering** /ˈwɒndərɪŋ/ ❶ *adj.* Ⓐ (*nomadic*) Wander‹stamm, -volk›; ~ **minstrel** (*Hist.*) fahrender Spielmann; Ⓑ (*meandering*) sich windend ‹Strom›; (*fig.: disjointed*) weitschweifig ‹Rede›; wirr ‹Gedanken›; (*joc.*) vorwitzig (*scherzh.*) ‹Hände›. ❷ *n. in pl.* Ⓐ (*travels*) Wanderschaft, *die;* **in** *or* **on his** ~**s** auf seiner Wanderschaft; Ⓑ (*straying*) **the** ~**s of his mind/thoughts** sein wirres Denken/seine wirren Gedanken

**Wandering ˈJew** *n.* **the** ~: der Ewige Jude; (*fig.*) **a** ~: ein Ahasver (*geh.*)

**wanderlust** /ˈwɒndəlʌst/ *n.* Reiselust, *die;* (*related to distant places*) Fernweh, *das*

**wane** /weɪn/ ❶ *v.i.* ‹Mond:› abnehmen; ‹Kraft, Einfluss, Macht:› schwinden, abnehmen; ‹Ruf, Ruhm:› verblassen; **the light is waning** es wird langsam dunkler. ❷ *n.* **be on the** ~ ‹Mond:› abnehmen; (*fig.*) schwinden; dahinschwinden (*geh.*)

**wangle** /ˈwæŋgl/ (*coll.*) ❶ *v.t.* (*get by devious means*) organisieren (*ugs.*) ‹Karte, Einladung›; ~ **sth. out of sb.** jmdm. etw. abluchsen (*ugs.*); **can you** ~ **it for me?** kannst du das für mich deichseln? (*ugs.*). ❷ *n.* Kniff, *der;* **by a** ~: durch Schiebung (*ugs.*)

**wank** /wæŋk/ (*Brit. coarse*) ❶ *v.i.* wichsen (*derb*). ❷ *v.t.* ~ **sb. off** jmdm. einen abwichsen (*vulg.*). ❸ *n.* **have a** ~: sich (*Dat.*) einen abwichsen (*derb*)

**wanker** /ˈwæŋkə(r)/ *n.* (*Brit. coarse*) Wichser, *der* (*derb*)

**wanly** /ˈwɒnlɪ/ *adv.* schwach ‹beleuchtet›; matt ‹lächeln›

**wanna** /ˈwɒnə/ (*coll.*) = **want to**; **want a**

**wannabe** /ˈwɒnəbɪ/ *n.* (*coll. derog.*) Möchtegern, *der;* (*attrib.*) Möchtegern-; **a** ~ **writer, a writer** ~: ein Möchtegernschriftsteller

**want** /wɒnt/ ❶ *v.t.* Ⓐ (*desire*) wollen; **I** ~ **my mummy** ich will zu meiner Mama; **I** ~ **it done by tonight** ich will, dass es bis heute Abend fertig wird; **I don't** ~ **there to be any misunderstanding** ich will *od.* möchte nicht, dass da ein Missverständnis aufkommt; **I don't** ~ **you to get the idea that I am stingy** ich möchte nicht, dass Sie den Eindruck gewinnen, ich sei geizig; Ⓑ (*require, need*) brauchen; **'Wanted — cook for small family'** „Koch/Köchin für kleine Familie gesucht"; **you're** ~**ed on the phone** du wirst am Telefon verlangt; **feel** ~**ed** das Gefühl haben, gebraucht zu werden; **what you** ~ **is a good holiday** Sie brauchen mal richtigen Urlaub; **the windows** ~ **painting** die Fenster müssten gestrichen werden; **what that naughty girl** ~**s is a good wallop** was dem frechen Gör fehlt, ist eine anständige Tracht Prügel (*ugs.*); **you** ~ **to be [more] careful** (*ought to be*) du solltest vorsichtig[er] sein; **you** ~ **to see a solicitor about that** Sie müssten sich in der Sache an einen Anwalt wenden; Ⓒ ~**ed [by the police]** [polizeilich] gesucht (**for** wegen); **he is a** ~**ed man** er wird [polizeilich] gesucht; Ⓓ (*lack*) **sb./sth.** ~**s sth.** jmdm./einer Sache fehlt es an etw. (*Dat.*); **all the soup** ~**s is some salt** der Suppe fehlt nur noch ein bisschen Salz.
❷ *n.* Ⓐ *no pl.* (*lack*) Mangel, *der* (**of** an + *Dat.*); **there is no** ~ **of ...:** es fehlt nicht an ... (*Dat.*); **for** ~ **of sth.** aus Mangel an etw. (*Dat.*); **for** ~ **of a better word** in Ermangelung eines besseren Ausdrucks; **he took the flat for** ~ **of anything better** er nahm die Wohnung, weil er nichts Besseres finden konnte; Ⓑ *no pl.* (*need*) Not, *die;* **suffer** ~: Not leiden; **be in** ~ **of sth.** (*dated, literary*) einer Sache (*Gen.*) bedürfen (*geh.*); Ⓒ (*desire*) Bedürfnis, *das;* **we can supply all your** ~**s** wir können alles liefern, was Sie brauchen; ~ **ad** (*Amer.*) Kaufgesuch, *das.*
❸ *v.i.* Ⓐ (*arch.: be in want*) Not leiden; Ⓑ (*esp. Amer. coll.*) ~ **in/out** rein-/rauswollen

~ **for** *v.t.* (*dated*) **sb.** ~**s for nothing** *or* **doesn't** ~ **for anything** jmdm. fehlt es an nichts; ~ **for money** an Geldmangel (*Dat.*) leiden

**wanting** /ˈwɒntɪŋ/ *adj.* **be** ~: fehlen; **sb./sth. is** ~ **in sth.** jmdm./einer Sache fehlt es an etw. (*Dat.*); **be found** ~: für unzureichend befunden werden

**wanton** /ˈwɒntən/ ❶ *adj.* Ⓐ (*dated: licentious*) lüstern; wollüstig ‹Person, Gedanken, Benehmen›; Ⓑ (*wilful*) mutwillig ‹Beschädigung, Grausamkeit, Verschwendung›; leichtfertig ‹Vernachlässigung›; Ⓒ (*luxuriant, wild*) üppig ‹Wachstum, Vielfalt›; Ⓓ (*capricious*) übermütig; mutwillig (*veralt.*). ❷ *n.* (*dated*) (*woman*) Kokotte, *die* (*veralt.*); (*man*) Lüstling, *der* (*veralt.*)

**wantonly** /ˈwɒntənlɪ/ *adv.* Ⓐ (*dated: licentiously*) lüstern; wollüstig; Ⓑ (*wilfully*) mutwillig; leichtfertig ‹vernachlässigen›

**wantonness** /ˈwɒntənnɪs/ *n., no pl.* Ⓐ (*dated: licentiousness*) Lüsternheit, *die;* Ⓑ (*wilfulness*) Mutwilligkeit, *die*

**war** /wɔː(r)/ *n.* Ⓐ Krieg, *der;* **between the** ~**s** zwischen den Weltkriegen; **declare** ~: den Krieg erklären (**on** *Dat.*); **an act of** ~: ein kriegerischer Akt; **a** ~ **of conquest/aggression** ein Eroberungs-/Angriffskrieg; **be at** ~: sich im Krieg befinden; **make** ~: Krieg führen (**on** gegen); **go to** ~: in den Krieg ziehen (**against** gegen); **carry the** ~ **into the enemy's camp** (*fig.*) den Spieß umdrehen; **look as though one/it has been in the** ~**s** ziemlich mitgenommen aussehen; Ⓑ (*science*) Kriegführung, *die;* **the art of** ~: die Kriegskunst; **laws of** ~: Kriegsrecht, *das;* **rights of** ~: Kriegsrechte; Ⓒ (*fig.: conflict*) Krieg, *der;* **price** ~: Preiskrieg, *der;* ~ **of nerves** Nervenkrieg, *der;* ~ **of words** Wortgefecht, *das;* Ⓓ (*fig.: fight, campaign*) Kampf, *der* (**on, against** gegen); **declare** ~ **on poverty** der Armut den Kampf ansagen

**ˈwar baby** *n.* [Nach]kriegskind, *das*

**warble** /ˈwɔːbl/ *v.t. & i.* trällern

**warbler** /ˈwɔːblə(r)/ *n.* (*Ornith.*) Grasmücke, *die*

**war:** ~ **bride** *n.* Kriegsbraut, *die;* ~ **correspondent** *n.* Kriegsberichterstatter, *der*/-berichterstatterin, *die;* ~ **crime** *n.* Kriegsverbrechen, *das;* ~ **criminal** *n.* Kriegsverbrecher, *der*/-verbrecherin, *die;* ~ **cry** *n.* Ⓐ (*battle cry*) Kriegsruf, *der;* Ⓑ (*slogan*) Schlachtruf, *der*

**ward** /wɔːd/ *n.* Ⓐ (*in hospital*) Station, *die;* (*single room*) Krankensaal, *der;* **geriatric/maternity** ~: geriatrische Abteilung/Entbindungsstation, *die;* **she's in W**~ **3** sie liegt auf Station 3; Ⓑ (*minor*) Mündel, *das od. die;* ~ **[of court]** (*Law*) Mündel [unter Amtsvormundschaft]; Ⓒ (*electoral division*) Wahlbezirk, *der;* Ⓓ (*Hist.: bailey*) [Burg]hof, *der*

~ **ˈoff** *v.t.* Ⓐ (*prevent*) abwehren; schützen vor (+ *Dat.*) ‹Erkältung, Depressionen›; abwenden ‹Gefahr›; Ⓑ (*keep at distance*) sich (*Dat.*) vom Leibe halten ‹Verehrer›

**war:** ~ **damage** *n.* Kriegsschäden *Pl.;* ~ **dance** *n.* Kriegstanz, *der*

**warden** /ˈwɔːdn/ *n.* ▶ **1261** Ⓐ (*president, governor*) Direktor, *der*/Direktorin, *die;* (*of college, school*) Rektor, *der*/Rektorin, *die;* (*of hostel, sheltered housing*) Heimleiter, *der*/-leiterin, *die;* (*of youth hostel*) Herbergsvater, *der*/-mutter, *die;* Ⓑ (*supervisor*) Aufseher, *der*/Aufseherin, *die;* **[air-raid]** ~: Luftschutzwart, *der;* ⇒ *also* **churchwarden**

**warder** /ˈwɔːdə(r)/ *n.* (*Brit.*) Wärter, *der;* Aufseher, *der*

**wardress** /ˈwɔːdrɪs/ *n.* Wärterin, *die;* Aufseherin, *die*

**wardrobe** /ˈwɔːdrəʊb/ *n.* Ⓐ (*piece of furniture*) Kleiderschrank, *der;* **folding** ~: Kleidersack, *der;* Ⓑ (*stock of clothes*) Garderobe, *die;* (*in theatre*) Kostüme *Pl.*

**wardrobe:** ~ **master/mistress** *ns.* (*Theatre*) Gewandmeister, *der*/-meisterin, *die;* ~ **trunk** *n.* Schrankkoffer, *der*

W

**'wardroom** *n.* (*Navy*) Offiziersmesse, *die*

**-wards** /wədz/ *adv. suff.* -wärts

**wardship** /'wɔːdʃɪp/ *n.* Vormundschaft, *die*

**'ward sister** *n.* Stationsschwester, *die*

**ware** /weə(r)/ *n.* Ⓐ (*pottery*) Steinzeug, *das;* **Delft ~:** Delfter Keramik; Ⓑ *in pl.* (*goods*) Ware, *die*

**warehouse** ❶ /'weəhaʊs/ *n.* (*repository*) Lagerhaus, *das;* (*part of building*) Lager, *das;* (*Brit.: retail or wholesale store*) Großmarkt, *der.* ❷ /'weəhaʊs, 'weəhaʊz/ *v.t.* einlagern ‹Möbel›

**warehouseman** /'weəhaʊsmən/ *n., pl.* **warehousemen** /'weəhaʊsmən/ ▶ **1261** Lagerist, *der*

**warfare** /'wɔːfeə(r)/ *n.* (*lit. or fig.*) Krieg, *der;* **in modern ~:** in der modernen Kriegführung; **economic ~:** Wirtschaftskrieg, *der;* ⇒ *also* **open** 1 H

**war: ~ game** *n.* Kriegsspiel, *das;* **~ gaming** *n.* (*Mil.*) Sandkastenspiele *Pl.;* (*as hobby*) *das Nachstellen historischer Schlachten mit Spielzeugsoldaten;* **~ god** *n.* Kriegsgott, *der;* **~ grave** *n.* Kriegs- *od.* Soldatengrab, *das;* **~head** *n.* Sprengkopf, *der;* **~horse** *n.* (*Hist., fig.*) Schlachtross, *das*

**warily** /'weərɪlɪ/ *adv.* vorsichtig; (*suspiciously*) misstrauisch; **tread ~** (*lit. or fig.*) vorsichtig sein

**wariness** /'weərɪnɪs/ *n., no pl.* Vorsicht, *die* (**of** vor + *Dat.*); **~ of strangers** Misstrauen gegen Fremde

**'warlike** *adj.* Ⓐ (*bellicose*) kriegerisch; Ⓑ (*military*) Kriegs‹vorbereitungen, -gerät›

**'warlord** *n.* Kriegsherr, *der*

**warm** /wɔːm/ ❶ *adj.* Ⓐ warm; **come inside and get ~:** komm rein und wärm dich auf; **I am very ~ from running** mir ist sehr warm vom Rennen; **it's ~ work** bei der Arbeit kommt man ins Schwitzen; **keep sb.'s food ~:** jmdm. das Essen warm halten; **keep a seat/job ~ for sb.** (*fig.*) jmdm. einen Platz/eine Stellung freihalten; Ⓑ (*enthusiastic*) herzlich ‹Grüße, Dank›; eng ‹Freundschaft›; lebhaft ‹Interesse›; begeistert ‹Unterstützung, Applaus›; ⇒ *also* **reception** A; **welcome** 2 B; Ⓒ (*cordial, sympathetic*) warm ‹Herz, Wesen, Gefühl›; herzlich ‹Lächeln›; echt empfunden ‹Hochachtung›; **the thought of her kindness gives me a ~ feeling** wenn ich an ihre Güte denke, wird mir warm ums Herz; Ⓓ (*passionate*) heiß ‹Temperament, Küsse›; Ⓔ (*animated*) hitzig; heftig ‹Entrüstung›; Ⓕ (*unpleasant*) ungemütlich; **he left when things began to get too ~ for him** er ging, als ihm die Sache zu ungemütlich wurde; Ⓖ (*recent*) heiß ‹Spur›; Ⓗ (*in games: close*) **you're getting ~!** warm!

❷ *v.t.* wärmen; warm machen ‹Flüssigkeit›; **~ one's hands** sich (*Dat.*) die Hände wärmen; **the thought [of ...] ~ed [the cockles of] his heart** bei dem Gedanken [an ... (*Akk.*)] wurde ihm warm ums Herz.

❸ *v.i.* Ⓐ **~ to sb./sth.** (*come to like*) sich für jmdn./etw. erwärmen; **my heart ~ed to her** sie wurde mir sympathischer; **the speaker ~ed to his subject** der Redner steigerte sich in sein Thema hinein; Ⓑ (*get ~er*) warm werden.

❹ *n.* Ⓐ (*warming*) **give the food a ~:** das Essen aufwärmen; **have a ~ by the fire** sich am Kamin/Ofen *usw.* aufwärmen; Ⓑ (*warmth*) **the ~:** die Wärme

**~ 'up** ❶ *v.i.* Ⓐ (*get ~*) warm werden; ‹Motor:› warmlaufen; Ⓑ (*prepare*) ‹Sportler:› sich aufwärmen; Ⓒ (*fig.: become animated*) warm werden; ‹Party:› in Schwung kommen; ‹Publikum:› in Stimmung kommen. ❷ *v.t.* aufwärmen ‹Speisen›; erwärmen ‹Raum, Zimmer›; warmlaufen lassen ‹Motor›; (*fig.*) in Stimmung bringen ‹Publikum›. ⇒ *also* **warm-up**

**warm-blooded** /'wɔːmblʌdɪd/ *adj.* Ⓐ warmblütig ‹Tier›; **~-blooded animals** Warmblüter; Ⓑ (*fig.: passionate*) heißblütig; temperamentvoll

**warmed-over** /'wɔːmdəʊvə(r)/ (*Amer.*), **warmed-up** /'wɔːmdʌp/ *adjs.* aufgewärmt

**'war memorial** *n.* Kriegerdenkmal, *das*

**warm 'front** *n.* (*Meteorol.*) Warmfront, *die*

**'warm-hearted** *adj.* herzlich; warmherzig ‹Person›

**'warming pan** *n.* Wärmepfanne, *die*

**warmish** /'wɔːmɪʃ/ *adj.* lau[warm]; warm ‹Wetter›

**warmly** /'wɔːmlɪ/ *adv.* Ⓐ (*to maintain warmth*) warm; Ⓑ (*enthusiastically*) herzlich ‹willkommen heißen, gratulieren, begrüßen, grüßen, danken›; wärmstens ‹empfehlen›; begeistert ‹sprechen von, applaudieren›; Ⓒ (*animatedly*) hitzig

**warmonger** /'wɔːmʌŋgə(r)/ *n.* Kriegshetzer, *der*/-hetzerin, *die*

**warmongering** /'wɔːmʌŋgərɪŋ/ *n.* Kriegshetze, *die*

**warmth** /wɔːmθ/ *n.* Ⓐ (*state of being warm; also of colour*) Wärme, *die;* Ⓑ (*enthusiasm, affection, cordiality*) Herzlichkeit, *die;* Wärme, *die;* **the ~ of her temperament** ihr ungestümes Temperament; Ⓒ (*animation*) Hitzigkeit, *die;* (*indignation*) Schärfe, *die;* **in the ~ of the debate** in der Hitze des Gefechts (*fig.*)

**'warm-up** *n.* **have a ~** (*lit., Sport*) sich aufwärmen; **give a meal a ~:** ein Essen aufwärmen; **~ [lap]** (*Motor Racing*) Aufwärmrunde, *die*

**warn** /wɔːn/ *v.t.* Ⓐ (*inform, give notice*) warnen (**against, of, about** vor + *Dat.*); **~ sb. that ...:** jmdn. darauf hinweisen, dass ...; **you can't say I didn't ~ you** Sie können nicht behaupten, ich hätte Sie nicht gewarnt; **you have been ~ed!** ich habe/wir haben dich gewarnt!; **~ sb. not to do sth.** jmdn. davor warnen, etw. zu tun; **you might have ~ed us you were going to be late** du hättest uns wissen lassen können, dass du später kommen würdest; Ⓑ (*admonish*) ermahnen; (*officially*) abmahnen

**~ 'off** *v.t.* Ⓐ warnen; **~ sb. off doing sth.** jmdn. davor warnen, etw. zu tun; Ⓑ (*Racing*) Platzverbot erteilen (+ *Dat.*)

**warning** /'wɔːnɪŋ/ ❶ *n.* Ⓐ (*advance notice*) Vorwarnung, *die;* **he gave me no ~ of his intentions** er hat mir seine Absichten nicht angekündigt; **we had no ~ of their arrival** sie kamen ohne Vorwarnung; **give sb. plenty of/a few days' ~:** jmdm. rechtzeitig/ein paar Tage vorher Bescheid sagen; Ⓑ (*lesson*) Lehre, *die;* **let that be a ~ to you** lass dir/lasst euch das eine Warnung sein; Ⓒ (*caution*) Verwarnung, *die;* (*less official*) Warnung, *die.* ❷ *attrib. adj.* Warn‹schild, -zeichen, -signal usw.›; **~ light/shot** Warnleuchte, *die*/-schuss, *der;* **~ notice** Warnung, *die;* **a ~ look/gesture** ein warnender Blick/eine warnende Geste

**'War Office** *n.* (*Brit. Hist.*) Kriegsministerium, *das*

**warp** /wɔːp/ ❶ *v.i.* (*become bent*) sich verbiegen; ‹Holz, Schallplatte:› sich verziehen. ❷ *v.t.* Ⓐ (*cause to become bent*) verbiegen; **the sun had ~ed the boards** durch die Sonne hatten sich die Bretter verzogen; Ⓑ (*fig.: pervert*) verformen; verbiegen; **~ed** getrübt ‹Urteilsvermögen›; pervertiert ‹Denken, Gehirn›; **a ~ed sense of humour** ein abartiger Humor. ❸ *n.* Ⓐ (*Weaving*) Kettfaden, *der;* Kette, *die* (*fachspr.*); Ⓑ (*bent state*) Werfen, *das* (*fachspr.*); (*bend in a board etc.*) verzogene Stelle; **there is a ~ in the record** die Platte hat sich verzogen; Ⓒ (*fig.: perversion*) Perversion, *die;* ⇒ *also* **time warp**

**war: ~paint** *n.* (*also fig. coll. joc.*) Kriegsbemalung, *die;* **~path** *n.* Kriegspfad, *der;* **be on the ~path** auf dem Kriegspfad sein; (*fig.*) in Rage sein; **~plane** *n.* Kampfflugzeug, *das;* **~ poet** *n.* Kriegslyriker, *der*

**warrant** /'wɒrənt/ ❶ *n.* Ⓐ (*written order*) (*for sb.'s arrest*) Haftbefehl, *der;* **[search] ~:** Durchsuchungsbefehl, *der;* Ⓑ (*authority*) Befugnis, *die;* (*justification*) Rechtfertigung, *die;* Ⓒ (*dividend voucher*) Dividendenschein, *der;* Ⓓ (*Law*) Vollmacht, *die;* **~ of attorney** anwaltliche Vollmacht. ❷ *v.t.* Ⓐ (*justify*) rechtfertigen; **her small income does not ~ such expenditure** ihr geringes Einkommen erlaubt ihr solche Ausgaben nicht; Ⓑ (*guarantee*) garantieren; garantieren für ‹Produkt, Artikel›; **we ~ [you] the diamond is genuine** wir garantieren [Ihnen], dass der Diamant echt ist; **you'll like it, I** *or* **I'll ~ you** es wird dir gefallen, das garantiere ich dir

**warrantable** /'wɒrəntəbl/ *adj.* vertretbar; **be ~:** zu rechtfertigen sein

**'warrant officer** *n.* Warrant Officer, *der; Dienstgrad zwischen Oberstabsfeldwebel/Oberstabsbootsmann und Leutnant/Leutnant z. S.*

**warranty** /'wɒrəntɪ/ *n.* Ⓐ (*Law*) Garantie, *die;* **it is still under ~:** es steht noch unter *od.* darauf steht noch Garantie; ⇒ *also* **guarantee** 2 A; Ⓑ (*justification*) Rechtfertigung, *die*

**warren** /'wɒrn/ *n.* Ⓐ ⇒ **rabbit warren;** Ⓑ (*fig.: densely populated area*) Ameisenhaufen, *der* (*fig.*); (*maze*) Labyrinth, *das*

**warring** /'wɔːrɪŋ/ *adj.* Krieg führend; (*fig.*) sich bekämpfend *nicht präd.*

**warrior** /'wɒrɪə(r)/ *n.* Ⓐ (*esp. literary*) Krieger, *der* (*geh.*); Ⓑ *attrib.* (*martial*) kriegerisch; **a ~ nation/race** ein Kriegervolk

**Warsaw** /'wɔːsɔː/ ▶ **1626** ❶ *pr. n.* Warschau (*das*). ❷ *attrib. adj.* Warschauer; **~ Pact** (*Hist.*) Warschauer Pakt

**'warship** *n.* Kriegsschiff, *das*

**wart** /wɔːt/ *n.* Warze, *die;* **~s and all** (*fig.*) schonungslos; ungeschminkt [bis ins kleinste Detail]

**'warthog** *n.* Warzenschwein, *das*

**war: ~time** *n.* Ⓐ Kriegszeit, *die;* **in** *or* **during ~time** während des Krieges; im Krieg; Ⓑ *attrib.* Kriegs‹rationierung, -evakuierung usw.›; **~time England** [das] England während des Krieges; **a ~time love affair** eine Kriegsliebe; **~-torn** *adj.* kriegsgeschunden; **~-weary** *adj.* kriegsmüde; **~ widow** *n.* Kriegswitwe, *die;* Kriegerwitwe, *die* (*geh. veralt.*)

**wary** /'weərɪ/ *adj.* vorsichtig; (*suspicious*) misstrauisch (**of** gegenüber); **be ~ of** *or* **about doing sth.** sich davor hüten, etw. zu tun; **be ~ of sb./sth.** sich vor jmdm./etw. in Acht nehmen; **keep a ~ eye on sb.** jmdn. genau beobachten

**'war zone** *n.* Kriegsgebiet, *das*

**was** ⇒ **be**

**wash** /wɒʃ/ ❶ *v.t.* Ⓐ waschen; **~ oneself** sich waschen; **~ one's hands** (*also euphem.*)/**face/hair** sich (*Dat.*) die Hände (*auch verhüll.*)/das Gesicht/die Haare waschen; **~ the clothes** Wäsche waschen; **~ the dishes** abwaschen; [Geschirr] spülen; **~ the floor** den Fußboden aufwischen *od.* feucht wischen; **~ one's hands of sb./sth.** mit jmdm./etw. nichts mehr zu tun haben wollen; **I don't wish to have anything more to do with the whole business. I ~ my hands of it** Ich will mit der ganzen Geschichte nichts mehr zu tun haben. Für mich ist die Sache erledigt; Ⓑ (*remove*) waschen ‹Fleck› (**out of** aus); abwaschen ‹Schmutz› (**off** von); Ⓒ (*by licking*) putzen; **the cat ~ed its face** die Katze putzte sich; **the cat ~ed its fur** die Katze putzte sich (*Dat.*) das Fell; Ⓓ (*carry along*) spülen; **be ~ed overboard/ashore** über Bord/an Land gespült werden; **be ~ed downstream** von der Strömung mitgerissen werden; Ⓔ ‹Wellen, Meer:› bespülen ‹Klippen, Ufer›. ⇒ *also* **linen** 1 B.

❷ *v.i.* Ⓐ sich waschen; Ⓑ (*clean clothes*) waschen; Ⓒ ‹Stoff, Kleidungsstück, Handtuch:› sich waschen lassen; **that won't ~** (*fig. coll.*) das zieht nicht (*ugs.*); **an interesting theory, but it won't ~:** eine interessante Theorie, aber sie lässt sich nicht halten; Ⓓ (*sweep*) ‹Brandung, Wellen:› spülen; **~ over/against sth.** etw. überspülen/gegen etw. spülen.

❸ *n.* Ⓐ **give sb./sth. a [good] ~:** jmdn./etw. [gründlich] waschen; **the baby/car needs a ~** *or* (*coll.*) **could do with a ~:** das Kind/Auto müsste mal gewaschen werden; **I must have a ~ before lunch** ich muss mich vor dem Essen noch waschen; Ⓑ (*laundering*) Wäsche, *die;* **it is in the ~:** es ist in der Wäsche; **it'll all come out in the ~** (*fig. coll.*) das wird sich alles klären; **the** week's ~: die Wäsche von einer Woche; **C** (*of ship, aircraft, etc.*) Sog, *der;* **D** (*lotion*) Waschlotion, *die;* **a ~ for disinfecting the mouth** ein desinfizierendes Mundwasser; ⇒ *also* **eyewash**; **mouthwash**; **E** (*pig food*) Schweinefutter, *das*

~ **a'way** *v.t.* **A** wegspülen; hinwegspülen (*geh.*); **B ~ a stain/the mud away** einen Fleck/den Schmutz auswaschen

~ **'down** *v.t.* **A** (*clean dirt from*) (*with a hose*) abspritzen ‹Auto, Deck, Hof›; (*with soap and water*) abwaschen; aufwaschen ‹Fußboden›; **B** (*help to go down*) runterspülen (*ugs.*); **we lunched on beef ~ed down with beer** wir aßen Roastbeef und tranken Bier dazu

~ **'off** **1** *v.t.* **~ sth. off** etw. abwaschen. **2** *v.i.* abgehen; (*from fabric etc.*) herausgehen

~ **'out** *v.t.* **A** (*clean*) auswaschen ‹Kleidungsstück›; ausscheuern ‹Topf›; ausspülen ‹Mund›; **~ dirt/marks out of clothes** Schmutz/Flecken aus Kleidern [her]auswaschen; **B** (*stop; prevent from taking place*) ins Wasser fallen lassen ‹Sportveranstaltung›; **several matches have been ~ed out** mehrere Spiele sind ins Wasser gefallen; **C** (*damage*) unterspülen ‹Brückenpfeiler, Straße›. ⇒ *also* **washed-out**; **washout**

~ **'over** *v.t.* **A** (*fig. coll.: not affect*) **~ over sb.** ‹Streit, Lärm, Unruhe usw.:› jmdn. gar nicht berühren; **she just sat back and let everything/the criticism ~ over her** sie saß einfach da und ließ alles/die Kritik an sich (*Dat.*) ablaufen (*ugs.*); **B** (*sweep over*) spülen über (+ *Akk.*)

~ **'up** **1** *v.t.* **A** (*Brit.: clean*) **~ up the dishes** das Geschirr abwaschen *od.* spülen; **B** (*carry to shore*) anspülen ‹Leiche, Strandgut, Wrackteile usw.›. **2** *v.i.* **A** abwaschen; spülen; **who's going to help me ~ up?** wer hilft mir beim Abwaschen *od.* Spülen?; **B** (*Amer.*) sich (*Dat.*) [Gesicht und Hände] waschen. ⇒ *also* **washed-up**; **washing-up**

**washable** /'wɒʃəbl/ *adj.* waschbar ‹Stoff›; abwaschbar ‹Tapete, Farbe›

**wash: ~-and-'wear** *adj.* bügelfrei; **~basin** *n.* Waschbecken, *das;* **~board** *n.* Waschbrett, *das;* **~ bowl** ⇒ **~basin**; **~cloth** *n.* **A** (*Brit.: dishcloth*) Abwaschlappen, *der;* Spültuch, *das;* **B** (*Amer.: facecloth*) Waschlappen, *der;* **~day** *n.* Waschtag, *der*

**washed-'out** *adj.* **A** *attrib.* (*faded by washing*) verwaschen ‹Farbe, Kleidungsstück›; **B** (*fig.: exhausted*) abgespannt; mitgenommen; **I was** *or* **felt limp and ~:** ich fühlte mich schlapp und ausgelaugt

**washed-'up** *adj.* (*coll.*) kaputt (*ugs.*)

**washer** /'wɒʃə(r)/ *n.* (*Mech. Engin.*) Unterlegscheibe, *die;* (*of tap*) Dichtungsring, *der;* Dichtungsscheibe, *die*

**'washerwoman** *n.* ▶ 1261 Waschfrau, *die*

**'wash-hand basin** Handwaschbecken, *das*

**washing** /'wɒʃɪŋ/ *n., no pl., no indef. art.* **A** (*clothes to be washed*) Wäsche, *die;* **take in ~:** Wäsche ins Haus nehmen; [zu Hause] für Kunden waschen; **B** (*cleansing*) Waschen, *das;* **do the ~:** waschen; **children often don't like ~:** Kinder waschen sich oft nicht gerne; **the car needs a good ~:** der Wagen muss mal wieder gründlich gewaschen werden

**washing: ~ day** *n.* Waschtag, *der;* **~ machine** *n.* Waschmaschine, *die;* **~ powder** *n.* Waschpulver, *das;* **~ soda** *n.* Bleichsoda, *das* (*veralt.*); Natriumkarbonat, *das;* **~-'up** *n.* (*Brit.*) Abwasch, *der;* **do the ~-up** den Abwasch machen; abwaschen; **there was ~-up everywhere** überall stand schmutziges Geschirr herum; **the ~-up took him hours** er brauchte Stunden für den Abwasch; **~-'up liquid** *n.* Spülmittel, *das;* **~-'up machine** ⇒ **dishwasher A**

**wash: ~ leather** *n.* Fensterleder, *das;* **~out** *n.* **A** (*coll.: failure*) Pleite, *die* (*ugs.*); Reinfall, *der* (*ugs.*); **B** (*coll.: useless person*) Niete, *die* (*salopp abwertend*); **C** (*breach in road etc.*) Unterspülung, *die;* **~room** *n.* (*Amer.*) WC, *das;* Waschraum, *der* (*verhüll.*); **~stand** *n.* Waschtisch, *der;* **~tub** *n.* Waschbottich, *der;* Waschzuber, *der;* **~woman** (*Amer.*) ⇒ **washerwoman**

**washy** /'wɒʃɪ/ *adj.* **A** (*too watery*) wässrig, dünn ‹Tee, Suppe›; **B** (*faded-looking*) verwaschen ‹Farbe›; **C** (*feeble*) verschwommen ‹Ansichten, Meinungen›; schwach, (*ugs.*) saft- und kraftlos ‹Inszenierung, Übersetzung›

**wasn't** /'wɒznt/ (*coll.*) = **was not;** ⇒ **be**

**Wasp** /wɒsp/ *n.* (*Amer. derog.*) Angehöriger des weißen amerikanischen Bürgertums (*angelsächsischer Herkunft und protestantischer Konfession*)

**wasp** *n.* Wespe, *die*

**waspish** /'wɒspɪʃ/ *adj.*, **waspishly** /'wɒspɪʃlɪ/ *adv.* bissig

**waspishness** /'wɒspɪʃnɪs/ *n., no pl.* Bissigkeit, *die*

**'wasp waist** *n.* Wespentaille, *die*

**wassail** /'wɒseɪl, 'wɒsl/ (*arch.*) **1** *n.* **A** (*festivity*) Trinkgelage, *das;* **B** (*liquor*) *Wein/Bier, mit verschiedenen Zutaten gewürzt.* **2** *v.i.* zechen

**wastage** /'weɪstɪdʒ/ *n.* **A** (*loss by wear etc.*) Schwund, *der;* **B** [**natural**] **~** (*Admin.*) ≈ natürliche Fluktuation

**waste** /weɪst/ **1** *n.* **A** (*useless remains*) Abfall, *der;* **disposal of ~:** Abfallbeseitigung, *die;* **kitchen ~, ~ from the kitchen** Küchenabfälle *Pl.;* **B** (*extravagant use*) Verschwendung, *die;* Vergeudung, *die;* **it's a ~ of time/money/energy** das ist Zeit-/Geld-/Energieverschwendung; **it would be a ~ of effort** das wäre vergeudete Mühe; **it's a ~ of your time and mine** wir verschwenden beide nur unsere Zeit; **go** *or* **run to ~:** vergeudet werden; **C** ⇒ **waste pipe**; **D** (*desert*) Wüste, *die.* ⇒ *also* **cotton waste**.

**2** *v.t.* **A** (*squander*) verschwenden; vergeuden (**on** auf + *Akk.*, an + *Akk.*); **he is ~d on an audience like that** für ein solches Publikum ist er zu schade; **all his efforts were ~d** all seine Mühe war umsonst; **don't ~ my time!** stehlen Sie mir nicht die Zeit!; **you didn't ~ much time, did you?** da hast du aber keine Zeit verloren!; **~ one's life** sein Leben vergeuden; **you're wasting your breath** *or* **words!** deine Worte kannst du dir sparen!; **~ not, want not** (*prov.*) spare in der Zeit, so hast du in der Not (*Spr.*); **B be ~d** (*reduced*) ‹Vorräte, Bevölkerung:› abnehmen, schrumpfen; **C** (*cause to shrink*) aufzehren ‹Kräfte›; auszehren ‹Körper›; **a ~d arm** ein geschrumpfter Arm; **D** (*ravage*) verwüsten ‹Land›; **E** (*treat as ~ paper*) makulieren; **F** (*sl.: murder*) umlegen (*salopp*).

**3** *v.i.* dahinschwinden; (*gradually*) im Schwinden begriffen sein.

**4** *adj.* **A** (*not wanted*) **~ material** Abfall, *der;* **~ food** Essensreste *Pl.;* **~ product** Abfallprodukt, *das;* **~ water** Abwasser, *das;* **B** (*uncultivated*) brach; brachliegend *nicht präd.;* **lie ~:** brachliegen; **C lay sth. ~, lay ~ sth.** etw. verwüsten

~ **a'way** *v.i.* immer mehr abmagern

**waste: ~basket** ⇒ **waste-paper basket**; **~ disposal** *n.* Abfallbeseitigung, *die;* Entsorgung, *die* (*Amtsspr.*); **~ di'sposal unit** *n.* Müllzerkleinerer, *der*

**wasteful** /'weɪstfl/ *adj.* **A** (*extravagant*) verschwenderisch; **too much ~ expenditure** zu viel Geldverschwendung; **B** (*causing waste*) unwirtschaftlich; **be ~ of sth.** etw. vergeuden

**wastefully** /'weɪstfəlɪ/ *adv.* verschwenderisch; **sth. is ~ thrown away** etw. wird verschwenderischerweise weggeworfen; **he's ~ extravagant with money** er geht mit dem Geld außerordentlich verschwenderisch um

**wastefulness** /'weɪstflnɪs/ *n., no pl.* **A** (*extravagance*) Verschwendung, *die;* (*character trait*) Verschwendungssucht, *die;* **~ in the use of public funds** Verschwendung öffentlicher Gelder; **B** (*of manufacturing process*) Unwirtschaftlichkeit, *die*

**waste: ~land** *n.* (*not cultivated*) Ödland, *das;* (*not built on*) unbebautes Land; (*fig.*) Einöde, *die;* **~ management** *n.* Abfallmanagement, *das;* Müllmanagement, *das;* **~ 'paper** *n.* Papierabfall, *der;* **~-'paper basket** *n.* Papierkorb, *der;* **~ pipe** *n.* Abflussrohr, *das;* **~ processor** *n.* Müllzerkleinerer, *der*

**waster** /'weɪstə(r)/ *n.* Verschwender, *der*/Verschwenderin, *die*

**wasting** /'weɪstɪŋ/ *adj.* **A** (*diminishing*) schwindend; von Schwund befallen ‹Muskel›; **B** (*reducing vitality, robustness*) **a ~ disease** eine Krankheit, bei der der Patient mehr und mehr verfällt

**wastrel** /'weɪstrl/ *n.* **A** (*good-for-nothing*) Nichtsnutz, *der;* **B** (*wasteful person*) Verschwender, *der*/Verschwenderin, *die*

**watch** /wɒtʃ/ **1** *n.* **A** ▶ 1012 **wristwatch/pocket ~:** [Armband-/Taschen]uhr, *die;* **B** (*constant attention*) Wache, *die;* **keep ~:** Wache halten; **keep [a] ~ for sb./sth.** auf jmdn./etw. achten *od.* aufpassen; **keep a [good** *or* **close] ~ on sb./sth.** [gut] auf jmdn./etw. aufpassen; **keep [a] ~ for enemy aircraft** nach feindlichen Flugzeugen Ausschau halten; **keep a close ~ on the time** genau auf die Zeit achten; **they kept a ~ on all his activities** sie überwachten alle seine Aktivitäten; **the police were on the ~ for car thieves** die Polizei hielt nach Autodieben Ausschau; **C** (*Naut.*) Wache, *die;* **starboard/port ~:** Steuerbord-/Backbordwache, *die;* **the officer of the ~:** der wachhabende Offizier; ⇒ *also* **dogwatch**; **set 1 M**; **D** (*Hist.: street guard*) Wache, *die;* (*one person*) Wachmann, *der;* **E** (*period of wakefulness at night*) Nachtwache, *die*

**2** *v.i.* **A** (*wait*) **~ for sb./sth.** auf jmdn./etw. warten; **~ for signs of improvement** nach Anzeichen einer Verbesserung Ausschau halten; **B** (*keep ~*) Wache stehen.

**3** *v.t.* **A** (*observe*) sich (*Dat.*) ansehen ‹Sportveranstaltung, Fernsehsendung›; **~ [the] television** *or* **TV** fernsehen; Fernsehen gucken (*ugs.*); **~ sth. [on television** *or* **TV]** sich (*Dat.*) etw. [im Fernsehen] ansehen; **~ sb. do** *or* **doing sth.** zusehen, wie jmd. etw. tut; **he just ~ed her drown** er sah einfach zu, wie sie ertrank; **we are being ~ed** wir werden beobachtet; **she had him ~ed** sie ließ ihn beobachten; **the police were ~ing the house** die Polizei beobachtete das Haus; **I want all of you to ~ this closely** ich möchte, dass ihr euch (*Dat.*) dies alle genau anseht; **I shall ~ your career with interest** ich werde Ihre Karriere mit Interesse verfolgen; **~ one's weight** auf sein Gewicht achten; **~ sheep/goats** *etc.* Schafe/Ziegen *usw.* hüten; **just ~ me!** (*coll.*) pass/passt mal auf! (*ugs.*); **~ this space** (*fig.*) man darf gespannt sein; das wird sich zeigen; **a ~ed pot never boils** (*prov.*) wenn man auf etwas wartet, kommt es einem wie eine Ewigkeit vor; ⇒ *also* **clock 1 A**; **B** (*be careful of, look after*) achten auf (+ *Akk.*); **~ your manners!** (*coll.*) benimm dich!; **~ your language!** (*coll.*) drück dich bitte etwas gepflegter *od.* nicht so ordinär aus!; **~ him, he's an awkward customer** (*coll.*) pass/passt auf, er ist mit Vorsicht zu genießen (*ugs.*); **~ how you go/drive** pass auf/fahr vorsichtig!; **~ it** *or* **oneself** sich vorsehen; **[just] ~ it [or you'll be in trouble]!** pass bloß auf[, sonst gibts Ärger]! (*ugs.*); ⇒ *also* **step 1 A**; **C** (*look out for*) warten auf (+ *Akk.*); **~ one's chance** die Gelegenheit abwarten

~ **'out** *v.i.* **A** (*be careful*) sich vorsehen; aufpassen; **~ out! There's a car coming!** Vorsicht! Da kommt ein Auto!; **B** (*look out*) **~ out for sb./sth.** auf jmdn./etw. achten; (*wait*) auf jmdn./etw. warten

~ **'over** *v.t.* sich kümmern um; in Obhut nehmen ‹Wertgegenstand›; ‹Gott, Schutzengel:› wachen über (+ *Akk.*); **she ~ed over the children as they played in the garden** sie passte auf die Kinder auf, die im Garten spielten

**watch: ~ case** *n.* Uhrgehäuse, *das;* **~ chain** *n.* Uhrkette, *die;* **~dog** *n.* Wachhund, *der;* (*fig.*) Wächter, *der;* Aufpasser, *der* (*ugs.*); **the ~dog function of the press** (*fig.*) das Wächteramt der Presse

**watcher** /'wɒtʃə(r)/ *n.* Beobachter, *der*/Beobachterin, *die;* **sky-~** Sterngucker, *der;*

W

television-~s Fernsehzuschauer; royalty-~s Leute, die das Leben der königlichen Familie genau verfolgen

**watchful** /ˈwɒtʃfl/ *adj.* wachsam; be ~ for *or* against sth. vor etw. (*Dat.*) auf der Hut sein; keep ~ guard wachen; spend a ~ night eine Nacht durchwachen; keep a ~ eye on sb./sth. ein wachsames Auge auf jmdn./etw. haben

**watchfully** /ˈwɒtʃfəlɪ/ *adv.* wachsam

**watchfulness** /ˈwɒtʃflnɪs/ *n., no pl.* Wachsamkeit, *die*

**ˈwatch glass** *n.* Uhrglas, *das*

**watching brief** /ˈwɒtʃɪŋ bri:f/ *n.* Kontrollfunktion, *die;* keep *or* hold a ~: Stallwache halten

**watch:** ~maker *n.* ▶ 1261 Uhrmacher, *der*/Uhrmacherin, *die;* ~man /ˈwɒtʃmən/ *n., pl.* ~men /ˈwɒtʃmən/ ▶ 1261 Wachmann, *der;* ~ strap *n.* [Uhr]armband, *das;* ~tower *n.* Wachturm, *der;* ~word *n.* Parole, *die*

**water** /ˈwɔ:tə(r)/ ❶ *n.* Ⓐ Wasser, *das;* this fruit is 80 per cent ~: diese Frucht besteht zu 80 Prozent aus Wasser; be under ~ ‹Straße, Sportplatz usw.:› unter Wasser stehen; the island across *or* over the ~: die Insel drüben; the upper ~s of a river der Oberlauf eines Flusses; send/carry sth. by ~: etw. auf dem Wasserweg versenden/befördern; be in deep ~[s] (*fig.*) in großen Schwierigkeiten sein; get [oneself] into deep ~ (*fig.*) sich in große Schwierigkeiten bringen; make ~ (*urinate*) Wasser lassen; (*Naut.: leak*) Wasser machen; on the ~ (*in boat etc.*) auf dem Wasser; pour *or* throw cold ~ on sth. (*fig.*) einer Sache (*Dat.*) einen Dämpfer aufsetzen; ~ under the bridge *or* over the dam (*fig.*) Schnee von gestern (*fig.*); a lot of ~ has flowed under the bridge since then seitdem ist schon viel Wasser den Rhein hinabgeflossen; ⇒ *also* high water; hold² 1 F; low water; spend A; Ⓑ *in pl.* (*part of the sea etc.*) Gewässer *Pl.;* cross the ~s übers Meer fahren; cast one's bread upon the ~s mit offenen Händen geben; Ⓒ *in pl.* (*mineral ~ at spa etc.*) Heilquelle, *die;* Brunnen, *der;* take *or* drink the ~s eine Brunnenkur machen; Ⓓ (*brilliance of gem*) Wasser, *das;* of the first ~ (*lit. or fig.*) reinsten Wassers; a fool of the first ~: ein Narr erster Güte (*iron.*); a genius of the first ~: ein Genie ersten Ranges.
❷ *v.t.* Ⓐ bewässern ‹Land›; wässern ‹Pflanzen›; ~ the flowers die Blumen [be]gießen; tears ~ed the ground Tränen benetzen den Boden; Ⓑ (*adulterate*) verwässern ‹Wein, Bier usw.›; Ⓒ ‹Fluss:› bewässern ‹Land›; Ⓓ (*give drink of ~ to*) tränken ‹Tier, Vieh›.
❸ *v.i.* Ⓐ ‹Augen:› tränen; her eyes were ~ing from the smoke von dem Rauch tränten ihr die Augen; Ⓑ (*run with saliva*) my mouth was ~ing as ...: mir lief das Wasser im Munde zusammen, als ...; the very thought of it *or* just to think of it made my mouth ~: allein bei dem Gedanken lief mir das Wasser im Munde zusammen; ⇒ *also* mouth-watering; Ⓒ (*take in supply of ~*) Wasser aufnehmen; Ⓓ (*go to drink*) ‹Tier:› saufen; lions ~ing at dusk Löwen in der Dämmerung an der Tränke

~ ˈdown *v.t.* (*lit. or fig.*) verwässern

**water:** ~bed *n.* Wasserbett, *das;* ~bird *n.* Wasservogel, *der;* ~ birth *n.* Unterwassergeburt, *die;* ~ biscuit *n.* Cracker, *der;* Kräcker, *der;* ~ boatman *n.* (*Zool.*) Rückenschwimmer, *der;* ~-borne *adj.* Ⓐ (*transported*) auf dem Wasserweg befördert ‹Güter›; ~-borne traffic Verkehr zu Wasser; Ⓑ (*transmitted*) durch [Trink]wasser übertragen ‹Infektion›; Ⓒ (*afloat*) flott ‹Schiff, Boot›; ~ bottle *n.* Wasserflasche, *die;* ~ buffalo *n.* Wasserbüffel, *der;* ~ bus *n.* Fahrgastschiff, *das;* Linienschiff, *das;* ~ butt *n.* Regentonne, *die;* ~ cannon *n.* Wasserwerfer, *der;* W~ carrier *n.* (*Astrol.*) Wassermann, *der;* ⇒ *also* archer B; ~ cart *n.* Wasserkarren, *der;* (*for sprinkling roads*) Sprengwagen, *der;* ~ closet *n.* Toilette, *die;* WC, *das;* Wasserklosett, *das* (*veralt.*); ~colour *n.* Ⓐ (*paint*) Wasserfarbe, *die;* Ⓑ (*picture*) Aquarell, *das;* Ⓒ *no pl., no indef. art.* (*Art*) Aquarellmalerei, *die;* ~colourist *n.* Aquarellmaler, *der*/-malerin, *die;* ~-cooled *adj.* wassergekühlt ‹Motor usw.›; ~ cooler *n.* Kühltank, *der;* ~course *n.* (*stream etc.*) Wasserlauf, *der;* (*bed*) Flussbett, *das;* ~cress *n.* Brunnenkresse, *die;* ~ diviner *n.* [Wünschel]rutengänger, *der*/-gängerin, *die*

**watered** /ˈwɔ:təd/ *adj.* ~ silk Moiré, *der*

**water:** ~fall *n.* Wasserfall, *der;* ~fowl *n.* Wasservogel, *der;* (*collectively*) Wassergeflügel, *das;* ~front *n.* Ufer, *das;* down on the ~front unten am Wasser; *attrib.* a ~front location/restaurant eine Gegend/ein Restaurant am Wasser; W~gate *n.* (*fig.*) Watergate, *das;* ~ glass *n.* (*Chem.*) Wasserglas, *das;* ~ heater *n.* Heißwassergerät, *das;* ~hole *n.* Wasserloch, *das;* ~ ice *n.* ≈ Sorbet, *das;* ≈ Fruchteis, *das*

**wateriness** /ˈwɔ:tərɪnɪs/ *n., no pl.* Wässrigkeit, *die;* Wässerigkeit, *die*

**watering** /ˈwɔ:tərɪŋ/ *n.* Bewässerung, *die;* (*of flowers, house plants*) Gießen, *das;* give the plants a thorough ~: die Pflanzen gut wässern *od.* gießen

**watering:** ~ can *n.* Gießkanne, *die;* ~ hole *n.* Ⓐ ⇒ waterhole; Ⓑ (*coll.: bar*) Pinte, *die* (*salopp*); Destille, *die* (*salopp*); ~ place *n.* Ⓐ (*for animals*) Wasserstelle, *die;* Tränke, *die;* Ⓑ (*seaside resort*) Seebad, *das;* (*spa*) Kurbad, *das*

**water:** ~ jacket *n.* Kühl[wasser]mantel, *der;* ~ jump *n.* Wassergraben, *der*

**waterless** /ˈwɔ:təlɪs/ *adj.* wasserlos

**water:** ~ level *n.* Ⓐ (*in reservoir etc.*) Wasserstand, *der;* Pegelstand, *der;* Ⓑ (*below which ground is saturated*) Grundwasserspiegel, *der;* Ⓒ (*to determine horizontal*) Wasserwaage, *die;* ~lily *n.* Seerose, *die;* ~line *n.* (*Naut.*) Wasserlinie, *die;* ~logged /ˈwɔ:təlɒgd/ *adj.* voll gesogen ‹Holz›; ‹Boot› voll Wasser; nass, feucht ‹Boden›; aufgeweicht ‹Sportplatz›; a ~logged ship ein Schiff, das voll Wasser gelaufen ist

**Waterloo** /wɔ:təˈlu:/ *n.* the Battle of ~: die Schlacht bei Belle-Alliance *od.* Waterloo; meet one's ~: sein Waterloo erleben

**water:** ~ main *n.* Hauptwasserleitung, *die;* a burst ~ main ein Wasserrohrbruch; ~man /ˈwɔ:təmən/ *n., pl.* ~men /ˈwɔ:təmən/ (*plying for hire*) Fährmann, *der;* (*oarsman*) Ruderer, *der;* ~mark ❶ *n.* Wasserzeichen, *das;* ❷ *v.t.* mit Wasserzeichen versehen; ~marked paper Papier mit Wasserzeichen; ~ meadow *n.* Feuchtwiese, *die;* ~melon *n.* Wassermelone, *die;* ~ meter *n.* Wasseruhr, *die;* ~mill *n.* Wassermühle, *die;* ~ pipe *n.* Ⓐ Wasserrohr, *das;* Ⓑ (*hookah*) Wasserpfeife, *die;* ~ pistol *n.* Wasserpistole, *die;* ~ polo *n.* Wasserball, *der;* Wasserballspiel, *das;* ~ polo ball Wasserball, *der;* ~ power *n.* Wasserkraft, *die;* ~proof ❶ *adj.* wasserdicht; wasserfest ‹Farbe›; ❷ *n.* Regenhaut, *die;* (*raincoat*) Regenmantel, *der;* ❸ *v.t.* wasserdicht machen; imprägnieren ‹Stoff›; wetterfest machen ‹Holzzaun, Gartenmöbel›; ~ rat *n.* Wasserratte, *die;* ~ rate *n.* Wassergeld, *das;* the ~ rates die Wassergebühren; ~-repellent *adj.* Wasser abstoßend; ~-resistant *adj.* wasserundurchlässig; wasserfest ‹Farbe›; ~shed *n.* Ⓐ (*fig.: turning point*) Wendepunkt, *der;* Ⓑ (*Geog.*) Wasserscheide, *die;* ~side *n.* Ufer, *das; attrib.* a ~side restaurant ein Restaurant am Wasser; ~ski ❶ *n.* Wasserski, *der;* ❷ *v.i.* Wasserski laufen; ~skiing *n., no pl., no art.* Wasserskilaufen, *das;* ~ softener *n.* Wasserenthärter, *der;* ~-soluble *adj.* wasserlöslich; ~spout *n.* Ⓐ (*Meteorol.*) Wasserhose, *die;* Ⓑ (*pipe*) Abfluss, *der;* ~ supply *n.* Ⓐ *no pl., no indef. art.* (*providing*) Wasserversorgung, *die;* Ⓑ (*stored drinking ~*) Trinkwasser, *das;* (*amount*) [Trink]wasservorrat, *der;* ~ table *n.* Grundwasserspiegel, *der;* ~ tap *n.* Wasserhahn, *der;* ~tight *adj.* (*lit. or fig.*) wasserdicht; ~tight compartment wasserdichte Abteilung; you can't treat these topics as if they were a series of ~tight compartments man kann diese Dinge nicht völlig isoliert voneinander betrachten; ~ torture *n.* Wasserfolter, *die;* ~ tower *n.* Wasserturm, *der;* ~ vapour *n.* Wasserdampf, *der;* ~ vole *n.* Schermaus, *die;* ~ wagon ⇒ wagon C; ~way *n.* Wasserstraße, *die;* inland ~ways Binnenwasserstraßen; ~weed *n., no pl., no indef. art.* Wasserpflanzen *Pl.;* ~wheel *n.* Wasserrad, *das;* (*used to raise ~*) Schöpfrad, *das;* ~ wings *n. pl.* Schwimmflügel; ~works *n.* Ⓐ *sing., pl. same* (*system*) Wasserversorgungssystem, *das;* (*establishment*) Wasserwerk, *das;* Ⓑ *pl.* (*coll.: tears*) turn on the ~works losheulen (*ugs.*); Ⓒ *pl.* (*coll.: urinary system*) Blase, *die;* he's got something wrong with his ~works er hat was an der Blase (*ugs.*)

**watery** /ˈwɔ:tərɪ/ *adj.* wässrig, wässerig ‹Essen, Suppe›; feucht ‹Augen›; dünn ‹Getränk›; (*fig.: insipid*) [saft- und] kraftlos ‹Stil›; müde, matt ‹Lächeln›; (*fig.: pale*) matt ‹Farbton›; fahl ‹Mond, Himmel›; a ~ grave ein feuchtes *od.* nasses Grab

**watt** /wɒt/ *n.* (*Electr., Phys.*) Watt, *das;* how many ~s is this bulb? wie viel Watt hat diese Birne?

**wattage** /ˈwɒtɪdʒ/ *n.* (*Electr.*) Wattzahl, *die;* what ~ is this bulb? wie viel Watt hat diese Birne?

**ˈwatt-hour** *n.* (*Electr.*) Wattstunde, *die*

**wattle¹** /ˈwɒtl/ *n.* Ⓐ (*material*) Flechtwerk, *das;* a ~ fence ein Flechtzaun; ~ and daub Lehmflechtwerk, *das;* Ⓑ *in sing. or pl.* (*twigs*) Geflecht, *das;* Flechtwerk, *das;* Ⓒ (*Bot.*) Gerberakazie, *die*

**wattle²** *n.* (*Ornith.*) Kehllappen, *der*

**wave** /weɪv/ ❶ *n.* Ⓐ (*lit. or fig.*) Welle, *die;* Woge, *die* (*geh.*); (*in hair, Phys.*) Welle, *die;* rule the ~s die Meere beherrschen; his hair has a natural ~ in it sein Haar ist von Natur aus wellig; a ~ of enthusiasm/prosperity/pain eine Welle der Begeisterung/des Wohlstands/des Schmerzes; a ~ of depression overtook him er versank in tiefe Depression; ~s of immigrants Einwanderungswellen; ~s of attackers Angriffswellen; ⇒ *also* cold wave; heat wave; permanent wave; Ⓑ (*gesture*) give sb. a ~: jmdm. zuwinken; with a ~ of one's hand mit einem Winken.
❷ *v.i.* Ⓐ ‹Fahne, Flagge, Wimpel:› wehen; ‹Baum, Gras, Korn:› sich wiegen; ‹Kornfeld:› wogen; Ⓑ (*gesture with hand*) winken; ~ at *or* to sb. jmdm. winken.
❸ *v.t.* Ⓐ schwenken; (*brandish*) schwingen ‹Schwert, Säbel›; ~ one's hand at *or* to sb. jmdm. winken; ~ one's handkerchief [in the air] mit dem Taschentuch winken; they ~d their arms in exultation sie ruderten vor Begeisterung mit den Armen; she ~d her umbrella angrily at him sie drohte ihm wütend mit dem Regenschirm; stop waving that rifle/those scissors around hör auf, mit dem Gewehr/der Schere herumzufuchteln (*ugs.*); ~ sb. on/over jmdn. weiter-/herüberwinken; ~ sb. to do sth. jmdm. durch Winken zu verstehen geben, dass er etw. tun soll; ~ goodbye to sb. jmdm. zum Abschied zuwinken; she ~d acknowledgement to him sie winkte ihm zu, um [ihm] zu danken; Ⓑ (*make wavy*) wellen

~ aˈside *v.t.* Ⓐ (*refuse to accept*) abtun ‹Zweifel, Einwand›; he refused the dish, waving it aside er wollte das Essen nicht und winkte ab; Ⓑ (*signal to move aside*) I tried to speak but she ~d me aside ich wollte reden, aber sie winkte ab

~ aˈway *v.t.* wegwinken

~ ˈdown *v.t.* [durch Winken] anhalten

~ ˈoff *v.t.* ~ sb. off jmdm. nachwinken

**wave:** ~band *n.* Wellenbereich, *der;* ~ equation *n.* (*Phys.*) Wellengleichung, *die;* ~ form *n.* Wellenform, *die;* ~ front *n.* Wellenfront, *die;* ~length *n.* (*Radio, Telev., Phys.; also fig.*) Wellenlänge, *die;* be on sb.'s ~length (*fig.*) die gleiche Wellenlänge wie jmd. haben; be on the same ~length [as sb.] (*fig.*) die gleiche Wellenlänge [wie jmd.] haben; ~ power *n.* Wellenkraft, *die*

**waver** /ˈweɪvə(r)/ *v.i.* Ⓐ (*begin to give way*) wanken; start *or* begin to ~: ins Wanken geraten; Ⓑ (*be irresolute*) schwanken (between zwischen + *Dat.*); Ⓒ (*flicker*) ‹Kerze,

W

# Asking the way

## The questions

1. ***How do I get to the station?***
= Wie komme ich zum Bahnhof?
2. ***Which is the best way to the museum?***
= Wie kommt man am besten zum Museum?
3. ***Am I right for the Hotel zur Post?***
= Geht es hier zum Hotel zur Post?
4. ***Where is the nearest bank?***
= Wo ist hier die nächste Bank?
5. ***Is there a chemist's near here?***
= Gibt es hier in der Nähe eine Apotheke?
6. ***How far is it to the hospital?***
= Wie weit ist es zum Krankenhaus?
7. ***Can you direct me to a good restaurant?***
= Können Sie mir sagen, wo es hier ein gutes Restaurant gibt?

## Possible replies

1. ***Take the first turning on the right, then the second on the left, then go straight on as far as the junction. Turn right and you will see the station in front of you***
= Gehen Sie die erste Straße rechts, dann die zweite links, dann immer nur geradeaus bis zur Kreuzung. Biegen Sie rechts ein und dann sehen Sie den Bahnhof vor sich
2. ***The best way is to cross over here at the lights and go down the alleyway along the left side of the theatre. You will come out opposite the museum.***
= Am besten, Sie gehen hier an der Ampel über die Straße, dann die Gasse entlang, die links am Theater vorbeiführt. Sie kommen dann gegenüber vom Museum heraus
3. ***No, you've come too far. Go back to the crossroads and turn left, you'll find the hotel about a hundred yards further on the right***
= Nein, Sie sind zu weit gegangen/(*in car*) gefahren. Gehen/Fahren Sie zurück zur Kreuzung und biegen Sie links ab. Das Hotel liegt etwa hundert Meter weiter auf der rechten Seite
4. ***There is a branch of Barclays on the market place, which is a couple of hundred yards along that turning over there on the right***
= Am Marktplatz ist eine Filiale von Barclays. Biegen Sie dort drüben rechts ein, Sie kommen dann nach ein paar Hundert Metern zum Marktplatz
5. ***There's one in the next street on the left, but it's only small. If you want a bigger one you'll have to take the number 11 bus into the centre***
= In der nächsten Straße links ist eine, allerdings nur eine kleine. Falls Sie eine größere brauchen, müssen Sie mit der Linie 11 ins Zentrum fahren
6. ***It's about a mile and a half from here on the main Cardiff road. You'd best take a taxi as the buses aren't very frequent***
= Es liegt etwa zwei Kilometer von hier an der Hauptstraße nach Cardiff. Am besten nehmen Sie ein Taxi, die Busse fahren nämlich nicht sehr oft
7. ***Sorry, I'm a stranger here myself***
= Tut mir Leid, ich bin auch fremd hier

Licht:› flackern; ‹Schatten:› tanzen; **D** (*tremble*) ‹Stimme, Ton:› zittern

**waverer** /ˈweɪvərə(r)/ *n.* Zauderer, *der*/Zauderin, *die*

**wavering** /ˈweɪvərɪŋ/ *adj.* **A** wankend ‹Mut, Entschlossenheit›; schwankend ‹Unterstützung›; **B** (*flickering*) flackernd ‹Kerze, Licht›; tanzend ‹Schatten›; zitternd ‹Stimme, Ton›

**wavy** /ˈweɪvɪ/ *adj.* **A** (*undulating*) wellig; wogend ‹Gras›; **B** (*forming wave-like curves*) geschlängelt; **~ line** Schlangenlinie, *die;* **~ pattern** Wellenmuster, *das*

**wax**[1] /wæks/ **1** *n.* **A** Wachs, *das;* **be [like] ~ in sb.'s hands** [wie] Wachs in jmds. Händen sein; **B** (*in ear*) Schmalz, *das;* **C** ⇒ **sealing wax**. ⇒ *also* **paraffin wax**. **2** *adj.* Wachs-. **3** *v.t.* wachsen; wichsen ‹Schnurrbart›

**wax**[2] *v.i.* **A** (*increase*) ‹Mond:› zunehmen; **~ and wane** (*fig.*) zu- und abnehmen; **the political parties may ~ and wane, but he ...:** die politischen Parteien mögen gewinnen und verlieren, er aber ...; **B** (*become*) werden; **~ enthusiastic about sth.** über etw. (*Akk.*) ins Schwärmen geraten; **she ~ed indignant about the rudeness of the officials** sie empörte sich [immer mehr] über die Unhöflichkeit der Beamten

**wax ˈcrayon** *n.* Wachsmalstift, *der*

**waxed** /wækst/ *adj.* gewachst; gewichst ‹Schnurrbart›; **~ paper** Wachspapier, *das*

**waxen** /ˈwæksn/ *adj.* **A** (*pale, smooth*) wächsern ‹Blässe, Haut›; **B** (*arch.: made of wax*) wächsern; wächsen (*dichter. veralt.*)

**waxing** /ˈwæksɪŋ/ **1** *adj.* (*increasing*) zunehmend; wachsend ‹Begeisterung, Unmut›. **2** *n., no pl.* (*increase*) Zunehmen, *das;* (*of enthusiasm, indignation*) Zunahme, *die;* [An]wachsen, *das*

**wax: ~work** *n.* Wachsfigur, *die;* **~works** *n. sing., pl. same* Wachsfigurenkabinett, *das*

**waxy** /ˈwæksɪ/ *adj.* **A** (*easily moulded*) wachsweich; weich wie Wachs *nicht attr.;* **B** (*pale, smooth*) wächsern ‹Blässe, Glanz, Haut›

**way** /weɪ/ **1** *n.* **A** (*road etc., lit. or fig.*) Weg, *der;* **across** *or* **over the ~:** gegenüber; **go the ~ of all good things** den Weg alles Irdischen gehen; **the W~ of the Cross** der Kreuzweg; ⇒ *also* **flesh** 1 C; **B** ▶ 1679 (*route*) Weg, *der;* **ask the** *or* **one's ~:** nach dem Weg fragen; **ask the ~ to ...:** fragen *od.* sich erkundigen, wo es nach ... geht; **pick one's ~:** sich (*Dat.*) einen Weg suchen; **he picked his ~ through the mud** er bahnte sich mühsam einen Weg durch den Schlamm; **show sb. the ~:** jmdn. den Weg zeigen; **show the ~** (*fig.*) den Weg weisen; **lead the ~:** vorausgehen; (*fig.: show how to do sth.*) es vormachen; **point the ~ to a new solution to the problem** den Weg zu einer neuen Lösung des Problems aufzeigen; **find the** *or* **one's ~ in/out** den Eingang/Ausgang finden; **find a ~ out** (*fig.*) einen Ausweg finden; **I'll take the letter to the post office — it's on my ~:** ich bringe den Brief zur Post — sie liegt auf meinem Weg; **how did your cigarettes find their ~ into my coat pocket?** wie kommen deine Zigaretten in meine Manteltasche?; **'W~ In/Out'** „Ein-/Ausgang"; **go to Italy by ~ of Switzerland** über die Schweiz nach Italien fahren; **there's no ~ out** (*fig.*) es gibt keinen Ausweg; **the ~ back/down/up** der Weg zurück/nach unten/nach oben; **go one's ~:** weggehen; seiner Wege gehen (*veralt.*); **go one's own ~/their separate ~s** (*fig.*) eigene/getrennte Wege gehen; **be going sb.'s ~:** denselben Weg wie jmd. haben; **things are really going my ~ at the moment** (*fig.*) im Moment läuft [bei mir] alles so, wie ich es mir vorgestellt habe; **things could have gone the other ~:** es hätte auch anders ausgehen können; **money came his ~:** er kam zu Geld; **many offers came his ~:** er kriegte viele Angebote; **he worked at any job that came his ~:** er arbeitete in jedem Job, den er kriegen konnte; **I wish some better luck would come my ~:** ich wünschte mir, etwas mehr Glück zu haben; **I feel as though nothing nice has come my ~ for ages** mir ist, als hätte ich schon ewig nichts Schönes mehr erlebt; **when a girl like that comes your ~:** wenn dir so ein Mädchen begegnet *od.* (*ugs.*) über den Weg läuft; **be [a bit] out of sb.'s ~:** ein [kleiner] Umweg [für jmdn.] sein; **go out of one's ~ to collect sth. for sb.** einen Umweg machen, um etw. für jmdn. abzuholen; **go out of one's ~ to be helpful** sich (*Dat.*) besondere Mühe geben, hilfsbereit zu sein; **out of the ~:** abgelegen; **nothing out of the ~** (*fig.*) nichts Un- *od.* Außergewöhnliches; ⇒ *also* **find** 1 I; **go** 1 B, P, Q; **go down** b; **keep out of** b; **lose** 1 C; **out-of-the-way**; **take** 1 T; **way-out**; **C** (*method*) Art und Weise, *die;* **there is a right ~ and a wrong ~ of doing it** es gibt einen richtigen und einen falschen Weg, es zu tun; **that is not the ~ to do it** so macht man das nicht; **do it this ~:** mach es so; **do it my ~:** mach es wie ich; **I did it my ~:** ich habe es auf meine Art gemacht; **it's awful the ~ he swears** es ist fürchterlich, wie er flucht; **I don't like the ~ she smiles** mir gefällt ihr Lächeln nicht; **I don't like the ~ it gets dark so early** mir gefällt nicht, dass es schon so früh dunkel wird; **I object to** *or* **don't like the ~ he looks at me** ich mag nicht, wie er mich ansieht; **that's no ~ to speak to a lady** so spricht man nicht mit einer Dame; **it was his ~ of working** das war seine Art zu arbeiten; **he has a strange ~ of talking** er hat eine seltsame Sprechweise *od.* Art zu sprechen; **from** *or* **by the ~ [that] she looked at me, I knew that there was something wrong** an ihrem Blick konnte ich erkennen, dass etwas nicht stimmte; **she has a strange ~ of behaving** sie hat ein merkwürdiges Benehmen; **what a ~ to behave!** wie kann man sich nur so benehmen!; **she has a very original ~ of saying/seeing things** sie hat eine sehr originelle Art, etwas zu sagen/die Dinge zu sehen; **find a** *or* **some ~ of doing sth.** einen Weg finden, etw. zu tun; **find a ~:** einen Weg finden; **there are no two ~s about it** da gibt es gar keinen Zweifel; **Are you going to give me that money? — No ~!** (*coll.*) Gibst du mir das Geld? — Nichts da! (*ugs.*); **there was no ~ he would change his stand** er würde auf gar keinen Fall seinen Standpunkt ändern; **no ~ is he coming with us** es kommt überhaupt nicht in Frage, dass er mit uns kommt; **one ~ or another** irgendwie; **~s and means [to do sth.** *or* **of doing sth.]** Mittel und Wege, etw. zu tun; **be built** *or* **made that ~** (*fig. coll.*) so gestrickt sein (*fig. ugs.*); **be that ~** (*coll.*)

W

so sein; **better that ~:** besser so; **either ~:** so oder so; **that ~, we can ...:** auf die Weise können wir ...; ⇒ *also* **hard** 1 B; **mend** 1 B; **D** (*desired course of action*) Wille, *der;* **get** *or* **have one's [own] ~, have it one's [own] ~:** seinen Willen kriegen; **all right, have it your own ~[, then]!** na gut *od.* schön, du sollst deinen Willen haben!; **E** ▶ 1079 *in sing. or* (*Amer. coll.*) *pl.* (*distance between two points*) Stück, *das;* **a little ~:** ein kleines Stück[chen]; (*fig.*) ein klein[es] bisschen; **it's a long ~ off** *or* **a long ~ from here** es ist ein ganzes Stück von hier aus; es ist weit weg von hier; **the summer holidays are only a little ~ a~:** bis zu den Sommerferien ist es nicht mehr lange; **we went a little/a long/some ~ with him** wir sind ein kleines/ganzes/ziemliches Stück mit ihm gegangen/gefahren *usw.;* **there's [still] some ~ to go yet** es ist noch ein ganzes Stück; (*fig.*) es dauert noch ein Weilchen; **I went a little/a long/some ~ to meet him** ich bin ihm ein kleines/ganzes/ziemliches Stück entgegengegangen/-gefahren *usw.*, um mich mit ihm zu treffen; (*fig.*) ich bin ihm etwas/sehr/ziemlich entgegengekommen; **it is still a long ~ off perfection** *or* **from being perfect** es ist noch weit davon entfernt, vollkommen zu sein; **India is a long ~ away** *or* **off** Indien ist weit weg; **by a long ~** (*fig.*) bei weitem; **your work isn't good enough yet — not by a long ~:** Ihre Arbeit ist noch nicht gut genug — bei weitem nicht; **have gone/come a long ~** (*fig.*) es weit gebracht haben; **go a long ~ toward sth./doing sth.** viel zu etw. beitragen/viel dazu beitragen, etw. zu tun; **a little kindness/politeness goes a long ~:** ein bisschen Freundlichkeit/Höflichkeit ist viel wert *od.* hilft viel; **all the ~:** den ganzen Weg; **go all the ~ [with sb.]** (*fig.*) [jmdm.] in jeder Hinsicht zustimmen; (*coll.: have full sexual intercourse*) es [mit jmdm.] richtig machen (*salopp*); **F** (*room for progress*) Weg, *der;* **block the ~:** den Weg versperren; **his ~ to promotion was blocked by a jealous rival** seine Karriere wurde durch einen neidischen Rivalen versperrt; **leave the ~ open for sth.** (*fig.*) etw. möglich machen; **clear the ~ [for sth.]** (*lit. or fig.*) [einer Sache (*Dat.*)] den Weg freimachen; **be in sb.'s** *or* **the ~:** [jmdm.] im Weg sein; **you are in my ~:** du bist [mir] im Wege; **get in sb.'s ~** (*lit. or fig.*) jmdm. im Wege stehen; **put difficulties/obstacles in sb.'s ~** (*fig.*) jmdm. Schwierigkeiten bereiten/Hindernisse in den Weg legen; **make ~ for sth.** für etw. Platz schaffen *od.* (*fig.*) machen; **make ~ for sb.** für jmdn. Platz machen; **make ~ for the Mayor!** Platz für den Bürgermeister!; **make ~!** Platz da!; **[get] out of the/my ~!** [geh] aus dem Weg!; **move one's car out of the ~:** seinen Wagen aus dem Weg fahren; **can you get your books out of the ~?** kannst du deine Bücher woanders hinlegen?; **I must put that pile of old newspapers out of the ~:** ich muss den Stapel alte Zeitungen wegräumen; **please get the children out of the ~ while I do this painting** bitte sorge dafür, dass die Kinder nicht im Weg sind, während ich hier streiche; **get sth. out of the ~** (*settle sth.*) etw. erledigen; **let's get the awkward questions out of the ~ first** wir wollen erst einmal die schwierigen Fragen hinter uns bringen; **he'll be out of the ~ for a very long time** (*in prison*) er ist für lange Zeit aus dem Verkehr gezogen; **he wanted this troublesome rival out of the ~ [for good]** er wollte diesen lästigen Rivalen [für immer] aus dem Weg haben; ⇒ *also* **bar**[1] 2 C; **give way; keep out of b; see**[1] 1 A; **stand** 1 H; **G** (*journey*) **on his ~ to the office/London** auf dem Weg ins Büro/nach London; **on the ~ out to Singapore** auf dem Hinweg/der Hinfahrt/dem Hinflug nach Singapur; **on the ~ back from Nigeria** auf dem Rückweg/der Rückfahrt/dem Rückflug von Nigeria; **she is just on the** *or* **her ~ in/out** sie kommt/geht gerade; **be on the ~ in** (*fig. coll.*) ‹Mode, Popstar usw.:› im Kommen sein (*ugs.*); **be on the ~ out** (*fig. coll.*) (*be losing popularity*) passé sein (*ugs.*); (*be reaching end of life*) ‹Hund, Auto, Person:› es nicht mehr lange machen (*ugs.*); **we stopped on the ~ to have lunch** wir hielten unterwegs zum Mittagessen an; **on her ~ home** auf dem Nachhauseweg; **they're on their ~:** sie sind unterwegs; **on the ~ there** auf dem Hinweg; **be well on the ~ to becoming an alcoholic/a top-class player** auf dem besten Weg sein, Alkoholiker/ein Spitzenspieler zu werden; **the book is well on the** *or* **its ~ to completion** das Buch nähert sich dem Abschluss; **be on the ~** (*coll.*) ‹Kind:› unterwegs sein (*ugs.*); **[be] on your ~!** nun geh schon!; **by the ~:** übrigens; **I saw your mother, by the ~:** übrigens, ich habe deine Mutter getroffen; **all this is by the ~:** das alles nur nebenbei; **H** (*specific direction*) Richtung, *die;* **she went this/that/the other ~:** sie ist in diese/die/die andere Richtung gegangen; **look this ~, please** sieh/seht bitte hierher!; **he wouldn't look my ~:** er hat nicht zu mir herübergesehen; **which ~ is he looking/going?** in welche Richtung *od.* wohin sieht/geht er?; **I will call next time I'm [down] your ~:** wenn ich das nächste Mal in deiner Gegend bin, komme ich [bei dir] vorbei; **she lives Brighton ~** (*coll.*) sie wohnt in der Gegend von Brighton; **out Hendon ~** (*coll.*) draußen bei Hendon; **look the other ~** (*lit. or fig.*) weggucken; **the other ~ about** *or* **round** andersherum; **this/which ~ round** so/wie herum; **stand sth. the right/wrong ~ up** etw. richtig/falsch herum stellen; **turn sth. the right ~ round** etw. richtig herum drehen; **'this ~ up'** „hier oben"; ⇒ *also* **look** 1 A; **wrong** 1 C; **I** (*advance*) Weg, *der;* **fight/push** *etc.* **one's ~ through** sich durchkämpfen/-drängen; **be under ~** ‹Person:› aufgebrochen sein; ‹Fahrzeug:› abgefahren sein; (*fig.: be in progress*) ‹Besprechung, Verhandlung, Tagung:› im Gange sein; **get sth. under ~** (*fig.*) etw. in Gang bringen; **get under ~:** wegkommen; **make one's ~ to Oxford/the station** nach Oxford/zum Bahnhof gehen/fahren; **Do you need a lift? — No, I'll make my own ~:** Soll ich dich mitnehmen? — Nein, ich komme alleine; **make one's [own] ~ in the world** seinen Weg gehen (*fig.*); **make** *or* **pay its ~:** ohne Verlust arbeiten; **pay one's ~:** für sich selbst aufkommen; **J** (*respect*) Hinsicht, *die;* **in [exactly] the same ~:** [ganz] genauso; **in some ~s** in gewisser Hinsicht; **in one ~:** auf eine Art; **not in any ~:** in keiner Weise; **in every ~:** in jeder Hinsicht; **in a ~:** auf eine Art; **in more ~s than one** auf mehr als eine Art; **in no ~:** auf keinen Fall; durchaus nicht; **one ~ and** *or* **or another** irgendwie; **K** (*state*) Verfassung, *die;* **in a bad ~:** schlecht; **they are in a very bad ~:** es geht ihnen sehr schlecht; **the ~ things are, we shall never manage to get out of debt** so, wie die Dinge liegen, werden wir nie schuldenfrei sein; **we are all in the same ~ here** wir sind hier alle in der gleichen Lage *od.* Situation; **and she stayed that ~:** und das ist sie auch geblieben; **either ~:** so oder so; **in a small ~:** in bescheidenem Rahmen; **by ~ of** (*as a kind of*) als; (*for the purpose of*) um ... zu; **by ~ of illustration / greeting / apology / introduction** zur Illustration / Begrüßung / Entschuldigung/Einführung; **by ~ of business** geschäftlich; **he is by ~ of being a humorist** er ist eine Art von Humorist; **offer something in the ~ of a concession** eine Art Konzession anbieten; ⇒ *also* **family** A; **L** (*custom*) Art, *die;* **get into/out of the ~ of doing sth.** sich (*Dat.*) etw. an-/abgewöhnen; **he has a ~ of leaving his bills unpaid** es ist so seine Art, seine Rechnungen nicht zu bezahlen; **these bright ideas have a ~ of turning out badly** solche brillanten Ideen haben es an sich (*Dat.*), zu nichts Gutem zu führen; **in its ~:** auf seine/ihre Art; **~ of life** Lebensstil, *der;* **change one's ~s** sich ändern; **~ of thinking** Denkungsart, *die;* **to my ~ of thinking** meiner Meinung nach; **that's just the ~ of the world** das ist ganz natürlich; **that's the ~ it goes** so ist es nun mal; **M** (*normal course of events*) **be the ~:** so *od.* üblich sein; **that is always the ~:** das ist immer so; **N** (*ability to charm sb. or attain one's object*) **he has a ~ with him** er hat so eine Art; **she has a ~ with children/animals** sie kann mit Kindern/Tieren gut umgehen; **O** (*specific manner*) Eigenart, *die;* **I soon got into his ~s** ich hatte mich bald an seine Art gewöhnt; **fall into bad ~s** schlechte [An]gewohnheiten annehmen; **I soon got into the ~ of it** *or* **of things** ich hatte mich bald daran gewöhnt; **it's only his ~:** das ist so seine Art; **P** (*sphere*) Gebiet, *das;* **he is in the grocery ~:** er ist in der Lebensmittelbranche; **a few things in the stationery ~:** ein paar Büroartikel; **Q** (*ordinary course*) Rahmen, *der;* **in the ~ of business** geschäftlich; **in the ordinary ~ [of things] there would be no problem** normalerweise gäbe es keine Schwierigkeiten; **R** (*movement of ship etc.*) Fahrt, *die;* **gather ~:** Fahrt aufnehmen; **lose ~:** die Fahrt verlangsamen; **the vessel has ~ on [her]** das Schiff macht Fahrt; **S** *in pl.* (*parts*) Teile *Pl.;* **split sth. [in] three ~s** etw. in drei Teile teilen; **T** *in pl.* (*down which ship is launched*) Helling, *die;* **U** *as name of road* Weg, *der.*

**2** *adv.* weit; **~ off/ahead/above** weit weg von/weit voraus/weit über; **~ back** (*coll.*) vor langer Zeit; **~ back in the early fifties/before the war** vor langer Zeit, Anfang der Fünfzigerjahre/vor dem Krieg; **~ up in the clouds** hoch oben in den Wolken; **he was ~ out with his guess, his guess was ~ out** er lag mit seiner Schätzung gewaltig daneben; **~ down south/in the valley** tief [unten] im Süden/Tal

**way: ~bill** *n.* Frachtbrief, *der;* **~farer** /ˈweɪfeərə(r)/ *n.* Wandersmann, *der* (*geh. veralt.*); **~faring** /ˈweɪfeərɪŋ/ *adj.* **a ~-faring man/woman** ein Wandersmann/eine Wanderin; **~'lay** *v.t., forms as* **lay**[2] 1 **A** (*ambush*) überfallen; **B** (*stop for conversation*) abfangen; **~mark** *n.* Wegmarke, *die;* Wegzeichen, *das;* **~-'out** *adj.* (*coll.*) verrückt (*ugs.*); irre (*salopp*); **~side** *n.* Wegrand, *der;* **fall by the ~side** (*fig.*) auf der Strecke bleiben (*ugs.*); *attrib.* **~side flowers/inns** Blumen/Gasthöfe am Wegrand; **~station** *n.* (*Amer. Railw.*) Haltepunkt, *der*

**wayward** /ˈweɪwəd/ *adj.* eigenwillig; ungezügelt ‹Talent, Macht›

**waywardly** /ˈweɪwədlɪ/ *adv.* eigenwillig; unberechenbar ‹sich verändern›

**waywardness** /ˈweɪwədnɪs/ *n., no pl.* Eigenwilligkeit, *die*

**WC** *abbr.* **water closet** WC, *das*

**we** /wɪ, *stressed* wiː/ *pl. pron.* wir; **how are we feeling today?** (*coll.*) wie gehts uns denn heute? (*ugs.*); **the royal 'we'** der Pluralis Majestatis; ⇒ *also* **our; ours; ourselves; us**

**weak** /wiːk/ *adj.* **A** (*lit. or fig.*) schwach; matt ‹Lächeln›; schwach ausgeprägt ‹Kinn›; jämmerlich ‹Kapitulation›; (*easily led*) labil ‹Charakter, Person›; **go/feel ~ at the knees** weiche Knie kriegen/haben; **the ~er sex** das schwache Geschlecht; **~ with hunger/excitement** schwach vor Hunger/Aufregung; **~ eyes** *or* **sight** schlechte Augen; **a ~ stomach** ein empfindlicher Magen; **have a ~ chest** schwach auf der Brust sein; **be ~ in the head** schwachsinnig sein; **his French/maths is rather ~, he's rather ~ in French/maths** in Französisch/Mathematik ist er ziemlich schwach; **a ~ hand** (*Cards*) ein schlechtes Blatt; **in a ~ moment** in einem schwachen Moment; **sb.'s ~ side** *or* **point** jmds. schwache Seite *od.* schwacher Punkt *od.* Schwachpunkt; **his logic is a bit ~:** seine Logik steht auf ziemlich schwachen Füßen; **he has only a ~ case** seine Sache steht auf schwachen Füßen; ⇒ *also* **vessel** C; **B** (*watery*) schwach ‹Kaffee, Tee›; wässrig, wässerig ‹Suppe›; dünn ‹Bier, Suppe, Kaffee, Tee›; **C** (*Ling.*) schwach ‹Konjugation, Deklination, Verb›; unbetont ‹Endung, Vokal, Silbe›

**weaken** /ˈwiːkn/ **1** *v.t.* schwächen; beeinträchtigen ‹Augen›; entkräften, schwächen ‹Argument›; lockern ‹Griff›; **be ~ed by stress/too much work** durch Stress/zu viel Arbeit angegriffen werden; **the foundations of the**

W

**house had been ~ed by the earthquake** durch das Erdbeben waren die Fundamente des Hauses in Mitleidenschaft gezogen worden. **2** *v.i.* ‹Kraft, Entschlossenheit:› nachlassen; **the patient was visibly ~ing** der Patient wurde sichtlich schwächer; **the pound ~ed against the dollar** das Pfund wurde gegenüber dem Dollar schwächer; **~ in one's resolve** in seinem Vorsatz schwankend werden; **his hold on power was ~ing** er hielt die Macht nicht mehr so fest in der Hand

**weak-kneed** /ˈwiːkniːd/ *adj.* **A be ~:** weiche Knie haben (**with** vor + *Dat.*); **B** (*fig.*) feige

**weakling** /ˈwiːklɪŋ/ *n.* Schwächling, *der*

**weakly** /ˈwiːklɪ/ **1** *adv.* schwach; matt ‹lächeln›; **be ~ indulgent** schwach und nachgiebig sein. **2** *adj.* schwächlich

**ˈweak-minded** *adj.* **A** (*lacking strength of purpose*) entschlusslos; unentschlossen; **B** (*mentally deficient*) schwachsinnig

**weakness** /ˈwiːknɪs/ *n.* Schwäche, *die;* (*in argument, defence*) schwacher Punkt; **the ~ of her character** ihre Charakterschwäche; **I have a ~ for sweet things** ich habe eine Schwäche für Süßigkeiten

**ˈweak-willed** *adj.* willensschwach

**weal**[1] /wiːl/ *n.* (*literary/archaic: welfare*) Wohl, *das;* **for the public** *or* **common ~:** zum Wohle der Allgemeinheit; **~ and woe, ~ or woe** Wohl und Weh[e] (*geh.*)

**weal**[2] *n.* (*ridge on flesh*) Striemen, *der*

**wealth** /welθ/ *n., no pl.* **A** (*abundance*) Fülle, *die;* **a great ~ of detail** große Detailfülle; **~ of words** Wortreichtum, *der;* **B** (*riches, being rich*) Reichtum, *der*

**ˈwealth tax** *n.* Vermögensteuer, *die*

**wealthy** /ˈwelθɪ/ **1** *adj.* reich. **2** *n. pl.* **the ~:** die Reichen

**wean** /wiːn/ *v.t.* abstillen; entwöhnen ‹Tier›; **~ sb. [away] from sth.** (*fig.*) jmdm. etw. abgewöhnen

**weapon** /ˈwepən/ *n.* (*lit. or fig.*) Waffe, *die;* **use sth. as a ~:** etw. als Waffe benutzen

**weaponry** /ˈwepənrɪ/ *n.* Waffen *Pl.*

**wear** /weə(r)/ **1** *n., no pl., no indef. art.* **A** (*rubbing*) **~ [and tear]** Verschleiß, *der;* Abnutzung, *die;* **show signs of ~:** Verschleiß- *od.* Abnutzungserscheinungen aufweisen; **the ~ and tear on sb.'s nerves** (*fig.*) jmds. Nervenverschleiß; **the worse for ~:** abgetragen ‹Kleider›; abgelaufen ‹Schuhe›; abgenutzt ‹Teppich, Sessel, Möbel›; **feel the worse for ~:** sich angeschlagen fühlen (*ugs.*); **B** (*clothes, use of clothes*) Kleidung, *die;* **clothes for everyday ~:** Alltagskleidung, *die;* **a jacket for casual ~:** ein Freizeit- *od.* (*veralt.*) Sportsakko; **children's/ladies' ~:** Kinder-/Damen[be]kleidung, *die;* **C** (*capacity for enduring rubbing*) **there is a great deal of/no ~ [left] in it** es/das *usw.* hat noch eine große Lebensdauer/keine große Lebensdauer mehr; **there's a great** *or* **good deal of ~ still in those shoes** die Schuhe halten noch lange.

**2** *v.t.*, **wore** /wɔː(r)/, **worn** /wɔːn/ **A** tragen ‹Kleidung, Schmuck, Bart, Brille, Perücke, Abzeichen›; **I haven't a thing to ~:** ich habe überhaupt nichts anzuziehen; **what on earth am I going to ~ tonight?** was soll ich heute Abend bloß anziehen?; **what size shoes do you ~?** welche Schuhgröße haben Sie?; **~ the crown** (*fig.*) die Krone tragen; **~ one's hair long** lange Haare tragen; **always ~ a smile** immer lächeln; **~ a joyful smile** glücklich lächeln; **~ a frown** ein finsteres Gesicht machen; **~ a sour look** eine saure Miene aufsetzen; **~ one's years well** sich gut gehalten haben; ⇒ *also* **heart** 1 B; **trousers**; **B** abtragen ‹Kleidungsstück›; abtreten, abnutzen ‹Teppich›; **be worn [smooth]** ‹Stufen:› ausgetreten sein; ‹Gestein:› ausgewaschen sein; ‹Gesicht:› abgehärmt sein; **the old coat was badly worn** der alte Mantel war ganz abgewetzt; **a [badly] worn tyre** ein [stark] abgefahrener Reifen; **he had worn his trousers into holes** seine Hose hatte überall Löcher; **C** (*make by rubbing*) scheuern; **the water had worn a channel in the rock** das Wasser hatte sich durch den Felsen gefressen; **D** (*exhaust*) erschöpfen; **E** (*coll.: accept*) **I won't ~ that!** das nehme ich dir/ihm *usw.* nicht ab! (*ugs.*).

**3** *v.i.*, **wore, worn A** ‹Kante, Saum, Kleider:› sich durchscheuern; ‹Absätze, Schuhsohlen:› sich ablaufen; ‹Teppich:› sich abnutzen; **~ thin** (*fig.*) ‹Idealismus:› sich langsam legen, nachlassen; ‹Freundschaft, Stil:› verflachen, oberflächlicher werden; ‹Witz, Ausrede:› schon reichlich alt sein; **my patience is ~ing thin** meine Geduld geht allmählich zur Neige *od.* ist langsam erschöpft; **B** (*endure rubbing*) ‹Material, Stoff:› halten; (*fig.*) sich halten; **~ well/badly** sich gut/schlecht tragen

**~ aˈway 1** *v.t.* abschleifen ‹Kanten, Grate›; **be worn away** ‹Stufen:› ausgetreten werden; ‹Inschrift:› verwittern; **she has been worn away to a shadow** sie ist zu einem Schatten ihrer selbst geworden. **2** *v.i.* sich abnutzen; ‹Gestein:› verwittern; ‹Schuhabsätze:› sich ablaufen; (*fig.: weaken, lessen*) dahinschwinden

**~ ˈdown 1** *v.t.* **A be worn down** ‹Stufen:› ausgetreten werden; ‹Absätze:› sich ablaufen; ‹Reifen:› sich abfahren; ‹Berge:› abgetragen werden; **B** (*fig.*) **~ sb. down** jmdn. zermürben; **~ down sb.'s resistance/defence/opposition** jmds. Widerstand/Verteidigung/Opposition zermürben; **worn down with hard work** abgearbeitet; **having to do this for hours at a stretch can ~ one down** es kann einen fertig machen (*ugs.*), wenn man das stundenlang ununterbrochen tun muss. **2** *v.i.* ‹Absätze:› sich ablaufen; ‹Reifen:› sich abfahren; **the stick/tooth had worn down to a stump** der Stock/Zahn war nur noch ein Stummel

**~ ˈoff 1** *v.i.* ‹Auflage, Schicht:› abgehen; ‹Muster:› sich verlieren; (*fig.: pass away gradually*) sich legen; ‹Wirkung, Schmerz:› nachlassen; **the sheen had long since worn off the material** der Stoff hatte schon lange seinen Glanz verloren. **2** *v.t.* **be worn off** ‹Auflage, Schicht:› abgehen

**~ ˈon** *v.i.* ‹Nachmittag, Winter usw.:› voranschreiten; **as the day/evening wore on** im Laufe des Tages/Abends

**~ ˈout 1** *v.t.* **A** (*make useless*) aufbrauchen; ablaufen ‹Schuhe›; auftragen ‹Kleidungsstück›; **B** (*fig.: exhaust*) kaputtmachen (*ugs.*); **his patience was worn out** seine Geduld war erschöpft; **~ oneself out** sich kaputtmachen (*ugs.*); **be worn out** kaputt sein (*ugs.*). **2** *v.i.* (*become unusable*) kaputtgehen; **his patience finally wore out** seine Geduld war schließlich erschöpft

**~ ˈthrough 1** *v.i.* sich durchscheuern; **my trousers have worn through at the knee** meine Hose ist an den Knien durchgescheuert. **2** *v.t.* durchscheuern

**wearable** /ˈweərəbl/ *adj.* **sth. that is still/not ~:** etw., das man noch/nicht anziehen kann

**wearer** /ˈweərə(r)/ *n.* Träger, *der*/Trägerin, *die*

**wearily** /ˈwɪərɪlɪ/ *adv.* müde

**weariness** /ˈwɪərɪnɪs/ *n., no pl.* **A** (*tiredness*) Erschöpfung, *die;* **B** (*boredom*) Überdruss, *der* (**with** an + *Dat.*)

**wearing** /ˈweərɪŋ/ *adj.* **A** (*tiring*) ermüdend; **B** (*boring*) langweilig; ermüdend

**ˈwearing apparel** *n.* (*formal*) Bekleidung, *die*

**wearisome** /ˈwɪərɪsəm/ *adj.*, **wearisomely** /ˈwɪərɪsəmlɪ/ *adv.* (*lit. or fig.*) ermüdend

**weary** /ˈwɪərɪ/ **1** *adj.* **A** (*tired*) müde; **~ to death** sterbensmüde (*geh.*); **B** (*bored, impatient*) **be ~ of sth.** einer Sache (*Gen.*) überdrüssig sein; etw. satt haben (*ugs.*); **C** (*tiring*) ermüdend. **2** *v.t.* **be wearied by sth.** durch etw. erschöpft sein; **a ~ing day** ein anstrengender Tag; **all this bickering was beginning to ~ me** allmählich hatte ich das ganze Gezänk satt (*ugs.*). **3** *v.i.* **~ of sth./sb.** einer Sache/jmds. überdrüssig werden

**weasel** /ˈwiːzl/ **1** *n.* Wiesel, *das.* **2** *v.i.* (*Amer.*) **A** (*quibble*) drumherumreden (*ugs.*); **B** (*default*) sich herauslavieren (*ugs.*); **~ on an obligation** sich aus einer Verpflichtung herausstehlen

**weasel: ~-faced** *adj.* **be ~-faced** ≈ ein Rattengesicht haben; **a ~-faced little man** ≈ ein kleiner Mann mit einem Rattengesicht; **~ word** *n.* vager *od.* unscharfer Begriff

**weather** /ˈweðə(r)/ **1** *n.* Wetter, *das;* **what's the ~ like?** wie ist das Wetter?; **the ~ has turned cooler** es ist kühler geworden; **he goes out in all ~s** er geht bei jedem Wetter hinaus; **he is feeling under the ~** (*fig.*) er ist [zurzeit] nicht ganz auf dem Posten; **make heavy ~ of sth.** (*fig.*) sich mit etw. schwer tun.

**2** *attrib. adj.* **A keep a** *or* **one's ~ eye open [for sth.]** Ausschau [nach etw. (*Dat.*)] halten; **keep a ~ eye on sth.** ein wachsames Auge auf etw. (*Akk.*) haben; **B** (*Naut.*) luvseitig; **the ~ side** die Luvseite; ⇒ *also* **gauge** 1 C.

**3** *v.t.* **A** (*expose to open air*) auswittern ‹Kalk, Holz›; **B be ~ed** ‹Gesicht:› wettergegerbt sein; **C** (*wear away*) verwittern lassen ‹Gestein›; **rocks ~ed by wind and water** Felsen, die durch Wind und Wasser verwittert sind; **D** (*come safely through*) abwettern ‹Sturm›; (*fig.*) durchstehen ‹schwere Zeit›.

**4** *v.i.* **A** (*be discoloured*) ‹Holz, Farbe:› verblassen; (*wear away*) **~ [away]** ‹Gestein:› verwittern; **B** (*survive exposure*) wetterfest sein; **a paint that ~s very well** eine sehr wetterfeste Farbe

**weather: ~-beaten** *adj.* wettergegerbt ‹Gesicht, Haut›; verwittert ‹Felsen, Gebäude›; **~board** *n.* Wetterbrett, *das;* **~boarding** *n., no pl., no indef. art.*, **~boards** *n. pl.* Schindeln *Pl.;* **~ chart** *n.* Wetterkarte, *die;* **~cock** *n.* Wetterhahn, *der;* **~ conditions** *n. pl.* Witterungsverhältnisse; **what are the ~ conditions at the moment?** wie ist das Wetter im Augenblick?; **~ forecast** *n.* Wettervorhersage, *die*

**weathering** /ˈweðərɪŋ/ *n., no pl., no indef. art.* Verwitterung, *die*

**weather: ~man** *n.* ▸ **1261** Meteorologe, *der;* **~ map** *n.* Wetterkarte, *die;* **~proof 1** *adj.* wetterfest; **2** *v.t.* wetterfest machen; **~ report** *n.* Wetterbericht, *der;* **~ satellite** *n.* Wettersatellit, *der;* **~ ship** *n.* Wetterschiff, *das;* **~ station** *n.* Wetterwarte, *die;* **~strip** *n.* Dichtungsstreifen, *der;* **~vane** *n.* Wetterfahne, *die;* **~wise** *adj.* **be ~wise** die Wetterregeln kennen; (*fig.*) die Wetterzeichen am Horizont erkennen

**weave**[1] /wiːv/ **1** *n.* (*Textiles*) Bindung, *die.* **2** *v.t.*, **wove** /wəʊv/, **woven** /ˈwəʊvn/ **A** (*intertwine*) weben ‹[Baum]wolle, Garn, Fäden›; **~ sth. into sth.** etw. zu etw. verweben; **~ threads together** Fäden miteinander verweben; **~ flowers into wreaths** aus Blumen Kränze flechten; **B** (*make by weaving*) weben ‹Textilien›; flechten ‹Girlande, Korb, Kranz›; **C** (*fig.*) einflechten ‹Nebenhandlung, Thema usw.› (**into** in + *Akk.*); **D** (*fig.: contrive*) ausspinnen ‹Geschichte›; **~ a story around an idea** eine Idee zu einer Geschichte ausspinnen. **3** *v.i.*, **wove, woven** (*make fabric by weaving*) weben

**weave**[2] *v.i.* **A** (*move repeatedly from side to side*) torkeln; **B** (*take devious course*) sich schlängeln; **~ between the obstacles** sich zwischen den Hindernissen hindurchschlängeln; **C get weaving** (*coll.*) hinmachen (*ugs.*)

**weaver** /ˈwiːvə(r)/ *n.* **A** ▸ **1261** Weber, *der*/Weberin, *die;* **B** (*Ornith.*) ⇒ **weaver-bird**

**ˈweaver bird** *n.* Webervogel, *der*

**weaving** /ˈwiːvɪŋ/ *n.* Weben, *das;* **an intricate piece of ~:** eine feine Webarbeit

**web** /web/ *n.* **A** Netz, *das;* **spider's ~:** Spinnennetz, *das;* **B** (*woven fabric*) Gewebe, *das;* (*fig.*) Gespinst, *das;* **a ~ of lies/intrigue** ein Gespinst von Lügen/Intrigen; **C** (*membrane*) Interdigitalhaut, *die* (*Anat.*); (*of duck, goose, etc.*) Schwimmhaut, *die;* **D** (*gossamer etc.*) Gespinst, *das;* **E** (*vane of feather*) Federfahne, *die;* **F** (*endless wire mesh*) Drahtgeweberolle, *die;* (*paper roll*) Papierbahn, *die;* **G the Web** (*Computing*) das Web (*fachspr.*); das Netz

**ˈWeb address** *n.* (*Computing*) Webadresse, *die*

**webbed** /webd/ *adj.* **~ feet/toes** Schwimmfüße

W

**webbing** /ˈwebɪŋ/ *n.* Gurtstoff, *der*

**web: Web browser** *n.* (*Computing*) Web-Browser, *der;* **Webcam** *n.* (*Computing*) Webcam, *die;* ~ **foot** *n.* Schwimmfuß, *der;* Ruderfuß, *der* (*Zool.*); ~**-footed** *adj.* schwimmfüßig; **Webmaster** *n.* (*Computing*) Webmaster, *der;* ~ **ˈoffset** *n.* (*Printing*) Rollenoffset[druck], *der;* **Web page** *n.* (*Computing*) Webseite, *die;* **Web site** *n.* (*Computing*) Website, *die;* ~ **toe** ⇒ ~ **foot**; ~**-toed** ⇒ ~**-footed**

**wed** /wed/ ❶ *v.t.*, **-dd-** Ⓐ (*formal: marry*) heiraten; ehelichen (*veralt.*, *scherzh.*); (*perform wedding ceremony for*) trauen ‹Brautpaar›; Ⓑ (*fig.: unite*) vereinen (**to** mit). ❷ *v.i.* (*formal*) heiraten; sich vermählen (*geh.*)

**we'd** /wɪd, *stressed* wiːd/ Ⓐ = **we had;** Ⓑ = **we would**

**Wed.** *abbr.* ▶ 1056 **Wednesday** Mi.

**wedded** /ˈwedɪd/ *adj.* Ⓐ (*married*) angetraut; **a ~ couple** ein getrautes Paar; ⇒ *also* **wife**; Ⓑ (*of marriage*) ~ **life** Eheleben, *das;* ~ **love** eheliche Liebe; Gattenliebe, *die* (*geh.*); ~ **bliss** Eheglück, *das;* Ⓒ (*fig.: devoted*) **be ~ to an idea/a dogma/a party** sich einer Idee/einem Dogma/einer Partei verschrieben haben; **be ~ to the view that ...:** immer noch davon überzeugt sein, dass ...; **he's ~ to his work** er ist mit seiner Arbeit verheiratet; Ⓓ (*fig.: united*) vereint (**to** mit)

**wedding** /ˈwedɪŋ/ *n.* Hochzeit, *die;* **have a registry office/a church ~:** sich standesamtlich/kirchlich trauen lassen; standesamtlich/kirchlich heiraten; ⇒ *also* **diamond wedding**; **golden wedding**; **ruby wedding**; **shotgun**; **silver wedding**

**wedding:** ~ **anniversary** *n.* Hochzeitstag, *der;* ~ **breakfast** *n.* Hochzeitsessen, *das;* ~ **cake** *n.* Hochzeitskuchen, *der;* ~ **day** *n.* Hochzeitstag, *der;* ~ **dress** *n.* Brautkleid, *das;* Hochzeitskleid, *das;* ~ **march** *n.* (*Mus.*) Hochzeitsmarsch, *der;* ~ **night** *n.* Hochzeitsnacht, *die;* ~ **present** *n.* Hochzeitsgeschenk, *das;* ~ **ring** *n.* Ehering, *der;* Trauring, *der*

**wedge** /wedʒ/ ❶ *n.* Ⓐ Keil, *der;* **it's the thin end of the ~** (*fig.*) so fängt es immer an; **be careful that it isn't the thin end of the ~** (*fig.*) pass auf, dass das nicht ausufert *od.* überhand nimmt!; **these disturbances proved to be just the thin end of the ~:** diese Unruhen erwiesen sich bloß als der Anfang; Ⓑ **a ~ of cake** ein Stück Torte; **a ~ of cheese** eine Ecke Käse; **the seats were arranged in ~s** die Sitzreihen waren keilförmig angeordnet; Ⓒ (*heel*) Keilabsatz, *der;* Ⓓ (*shoe*) Schuh mit Keilabsatz; Ⓔ (*Golf*) Keil, *der.*
❷ *v.t.* Ⓐ (*fasten*) verkeilen; **~ a door/window open** eine Tür/ein Fenster festklemmen, damit sie/es offen bleibt; Ⓑ (*pack tightly*) verkeilen; **there were five of them ~d together in the back of the car** sie saßen zu fünft eingezwängt *od.* zusammengepfercht hinten im Wagen; **the book had got ~d in behind the cupboard** das Buch war hinter dem Schrank eingeklemmt

**ˈwedge-shaped** *adj.* keilförmig

**Wedgwood** /ˈwedʒwʊd/ *n.* Ⓐ Wedgwood, *das;* Ⓑ *no pl.* (*colour*) Wedgwoodblau, *das*

**wedlock** /ˈwedlɒk/ *n.* (*literary*) Ehe, *die;* Ehebund, *der* (*geh.*); **born in/out of ~:** ehelich/unehelich geboren

**Wednesday** /ˈwenzdeɪ, ˈwenzdɪ/ ▶ 1056 ❶ *n.* Mittwoch, *der;* ⇒ *also* **Ash Wednesday**. ❷ *adv.* (*coll.*) **she comes ~s** sie kommt mittwochs. ⇒ *also* **Friday**

**wee¹** /wiː/ *adj.* Ⓐ (*child lang./Scot.*) klein; lütt (*nordd.*); Ⓑ (*coll.: extremely small*) **a ~ bit** ein ganz klein bisschen (*ugs.*)

**wee²** ⇒ **wee-wee**

**weed** /wiːd/ ❶ *n.* Ⓐ Unkraut, *das;* **~s** Unkräuter; Unkraut, *das;* **it's only a ~:** das ist bloß Unkraut; **a garden overgrown with ~s** ein von Unkraut überwucherter Garten; Ⓑ (*coll./arch.: tobacco*) **the ~:** das Kraut (*ugs.*); Ⓒ (*sl.: marijuana*) Stoff, *der* (*salopp*); **the ~:** Stoff (*salopp*); Ⓓ (*weakly person*) Kümmerling, *der* (*abwertend*). ⇒ *also* **weeds**. ❷ *v.t.* jäten. ❸ *v.i.* [Unkraut] jäten

~ **ˈout** *v.t.* (*fig.*) aussieben

**weeding** /ˈwiːdɪŋ/ *n.*, *no pl.*, *no indef. art.* [Unkraut]jäten, *das;* **do the/some ~:** Unkraut jäten

**ˈweedkiller** *n.* Unkrautvertilgungsmittel, *das*

**weeds** /wiːdz/ *n. pl.* **widow's ~:** Trauer- *od.* Witwenkleidung, *die*

**weedy** /ˈwiːdɪ/ *adj.* Ⓐ von Unkraut überwachsen; Ⓑ (*coll.: scrawny*) spillerig (*ugs.*); schmächtig

**week** /wiːk/ *n.* ▶ 1056 Woche, *die;* **what day of the ~ is it today?** was für ein Wochentag ist heute?; **can you come to see us for a ~?** kannst du [für] eine Woche zu uns kommen?; **he was away for a ~:** er war [für] eine Woche weg; **I haven't seen you for ~s** ich habe dich seit Wochen nicht gesehen; **~s ago** vor Wochen; **it will be finished in a ~:** es ist in einer Woche fertig; **three times a ~:** dreimal die *od.* in der Woche; **£40 a** *or* **per ~:** 40 Pfund die *od.* in der *od.* pro Woche; **a ~'s leave/rest** eine Woche Urlaub/Pause; **the other ~:** vor ein paar *od.* zwei, drei Wochen; **for several ~s** mehrere Wochen lang; wochenlang; **come every ~:** jede Woche kommen; **once a ~** *or* **every ~:** einmal die Woche *od.* in der Woche; einmal wöchentlich; **~ in ~ out** Woche für Woche; **in a ~['s time]** in einer Woche; **in two ~s[' time]** in zwei Wochen; in vierzehn Tagen; **take a ~'s holiday** [sich (*Dat.*)] eine Woche Urlaub nehmen; **from ~ to ~, ~ by ~:** Woche für *od.* um Woche; **a three-~ period** ein Zeitraum von drei Wochen; **at six-~ intervals** in sechswöchigem Abstand; **a two-~ visit** ein zweiwöchiger Besuch; **a six-~[s]-old baby** ein sechs Wochen altes *od.* sechswöchiges Baby; **a ~ [from] today/from** *or* **on Monday, today/Monday ~:** heute/Montag in einer Woche; **a ~ ago today/Sunday** heute/Sonntag vor einer Woche; **tomorrow ~:** morgen in einer Woche; **in** *or* **during the ~:** während der Woche; **42-hour/five-day ~:** 42-Stunden-Woche, *die*/Fünftagewoche, *die;* ⇒ *also* **knock** 1 C; **next** 1 B, 3 B

**week: ~day** *n.* Werktag, *der;* Wochentag, *der;* **on ~days** werktags; wochentags; *attrib.* **~day opening times** Öffnungszeiten an Werktagen; **~day timetable** Werktagsfahrplan, *der;* **~end** /-ˈ-, ˈ--/ *n.* Wochenende, *das;* **at the ~end** am Wochenende; **at** *or* (*Amer.*) **on ~ends** an Wochenenden; **a long ~end** ein verlängertes Wochenende; **go/be away for the ~end** übers Wochenende wegfahren/weg sein; **~-long** *adj.* einwöchig

**weekly** /ˈwiːklɪ/ ❶ *adj.* wöchentlich; **~ wages** Wochenlohn, *der;* **a ~ season ticket/magazine** eine Wochenkarte/Wochenzeitschrift; **on a ~ basis** wöchentlich; **at ~ intervals** wöchentlich; einmal pro Woche; **three-~:** dreiwöchentlich; **at three-~ intervals** in dreiwöchigen Abständen. ❷ *adv.* wöchentlich; einmal die Woche *od.* in der Woche. ❸ *n.* (*newspaper*) Wochenzeitung, *die;* (*magazine*) Wochenzeitschrift, *die*

**weekly reˈturn** *n.* **~ [ticket]** Wochenrückfahrkarte, *die*

**ˈweek night** *n.* **on a ~:** abends an einem Werktag; **on ~s** werktags abends

**weeny** /ˈwiːnɪ/ *adj.* (*child lang./coll.*) klitzeklein (*ugs.*)

**weeny-bopper** *n.* (*coll.*) *acht- bis zwölfjährige* [*weiblicher*] *Popfan*

**weep** /wiːp/ ❶ *v.i.*, **wept** /wept/ Ⓐ weinen; **~ with** *or* **for joy/rage** vor Freude/Zorn weinen; **~ for sb./sth.** um jmdn./etw. weinen; **the child was ~ing for his mother** das Kind weinte nach seiner Mutter; **it makes you want to ~:** man könnte weinen; Ⓑ ‹Wunde:› nässen. ❷ *v.t.*, **wept** Ⓐ weinen ‹Tränen›; Ⓑ (*lament over*) beweinen; Ⓒ **~ one's eyes** *or* **heart out** sich (*Dat.*) die Augen aus dem Kopf weinen; Ⓓ (*exude*) absondern ‹Eiter›. ❸ *n.* **have a ~:** sich ausweinen; **I had a little ~:** ich habe geweint

**weepie** /ˈwiːpɪ/ *n.* (*coll.*) Schmachtfetzen, *der* (*salopp*)

**weeping ˈwillow** *n.* Trauerweide, *die*

**weepy** /ˈwiːpɪ/ ❶ *adj.* weinerlich. ❷ *n.* ⇒ **weepie**

**weevil** /ˈwiːvɪl/ *n.* Rüsselkäfer, *der*

**ˈwee-wee** (*coll.*) ❶ *n.* Pipi, *das* (*ugs.*); **do a ~:** Pipi machen. ❷ *v.i.* Pipi machen (*ugs.*)

**weft** /weft/ *n.* Ⓐ (*set of threads*) Schuss, *der;* Ⓑ (*yarn*) Schussfaden, *der*

**weigh** /weɪ/ ❶ *v.t.* Ⓐ ▶ 1683 (*find weight of*) wiegen; **the shop assistant was ~ing the fruit for her** die Verkäuferin wog ihr das Obst ab; Ⓑ (*estimate value of*) abwägen; **~ sb. and find him/her wanting** jmdn. wiegen und zu leicht befinden; Ⓒ (*consider*) abwägen; **~ in one's mind whether ...:** sich (*Dat.*) überlegen, ob ...; **~ the consequences of one's actions** sich (*Dat.*) die Folgen seines Handelns klarmachen; **~ the fact that ...:** die Tatsache berücksichtigen, dass ...; **~ one's words** seine Worte abwägen; Ⓓ (*balance in one's hand*) wiegen; Ⓔ (*have the weight of*) wiegen; **it ~s very little** es wiegt sehr wenig; **a steak ~ing two pounds** ein zwei Pfund schweres Steak. ⇒ *also* **anchor** 1; **ton** C.
❷ *v.i.* Ⓐ **~ [very] heavy/light** [sehr] viel/wenig wiegen; Ⓑ (*be important*) **~ with sb.** bei jmdm. Gewicht haben; **~ in sb.'s favour** für jmdn. sprechen.
❸ *n.* **under ~** = **under way** ⇒ **way** 1 I

~ **aˈgainst** *v.t.* (*fig.*) sprechen gegen; **~ heavily against sb.** sehr *od.* stark gegen jmdn. sprechen

~ **ˈdown** *v.t.* Ⓐ (*cause to sag*) **fruit ~ed down the branches of the tree** die Äste des Baumes bogen sich unter der Last der Früchte; **be ~ed down by packages** mit Paketen schwer beladen sein; Ⓑ (*cause to be anxious or depressed*) niederdrücken; **~ed down with cares** bedrückt von Sorgen; **~ed down with sorrow** gramgebeugt

~ **ˈin** *v.i.* Ⓐ (*Sport*) sich wiegen lassen; **~ in at 200 kg** 200 kg auf die Waage bringen; ⇒ *also* **weigh-in**; Ⓑ (*coll.: lend one's support*) sich einschalten

~ **on** *v.t.* lasten auf (+ *Dat.*); **~ [heavily] on sb.'s mind** jmdm. [schwer] auf der Seele liegen

~ **ˈout** *v.t.* abwiegen

~ **ˈup** *v.t.* abwägen; sich (*Dat.*) eine Meinung bilden über (+ *Akk.*) ‹Person›

~ **upon** ⇒ ~ **on**

**weigh: ~bridge** *n.* Brückenwaage, *die;* **~-in** *n.* (*Sport*) Wiegen, *das;* **at the ~-in** beim Wiegen

**ˈweighing machine** *n.* Waage, *die*

**weight** /weɪt/ ❶ *n.* Ⓐ ▶ 1683 (*heaviness*) Gewicht, *das;* **she is twice your ~:** sie wiegt doppelt so viel wie du; **what is your ~?** wie viel wiegen Sie?; **be under/over ~:** zu wenig/zu viel wiegen; Unter-/Übergewicht haben; **throw one's ~ about** *or* **around** (*fig. coll.*) sich wichtig machen; ⇒ *also* **gold** 1 A; Ⓑ (*scale of heaviness*) Gewicht, *das;* **~s and measures** Maße und Gewichte; **avoirdupois/troy ~:** Avoirdupois-/Troygewicht, *das;* Ⓒ (*heavy body*) Gewicht, *das;* **lift ~s** Lasten heben; Ⓓ (*piece of metal used in weighing*) Gewicht, *das;* Ⓔ (*Athletics*) Kugel, *die;* Ⓕ (*load to be supported*) Gewicht, *das;* Ⓖ (*surface density of cloth etc.*) Qualität, *die;* Ⓗ (*fig.: heavy burden*) Last, *die;* **it would be a ~ off my mind if ...:** mir würde ein Stein vom Herzen fallen, wenn ...; Ⓘ (*importance*) Gewicht, *das;* **men of ~:** Leute von Gewicht; bedeutende Leute; **give due ~ to sth.** einer Sache (*Dat.*) die nötige Beachtung schenken; **carry ~:** ins Gewicht fallen; **his opinion carries no ~ with me** seine Meinung ist für mich unbedeutend; Ⓙ (*preponderance*) Übergewicht, *das;* **the ~ of evidence is against him** praktisch alle Beweise sprechen gegen ihn; **~ of numbers** zahlenmäßiges Übergewicht. ⇒ *also* **atomic weight**; **dead weight**; **pull** 1 G.
❷ *v.t.* Ⓐ (*add ~ to*) beschweren; **circumstances are rather ~ed in his favour/against him** (*fig.*) er wird durch die Umstände ziemlich begünstigt/benachteiligt; Ⓑ (*hold with ~*) **~ [down]** beschweren; (*fig.*) belasten; Ⓒ (*Statistics*) gewichten

**weighting** /ˈweɪtɪŋ/ *n.* (*Admin.*) Zulage, *die;* **London ~:** Ortszulage für London

W

# Weight

| | | |
|---|---|---|
| | 1 ounce (oz) | = 28,35 g (achtundzwanzig Komma drei fünf Gramm) |
| 16 ounces | = 1 pound (lb) | = 454 g (vierhundertvierundfünfzig Gramm) |
| 14 pounds | = 1 stone (st.) | = 6,35 kg (sechs Komma drei fünf Kilogramm) |
| 112 pounds | = 1 hundredweight | = 50,8 kg (fünfzig Komma acht Kilogramm) |
| 20 hundredweight | = 1 ton | = 1016 kg (tausendsechzehn Kilogramm) |

Note that in everyday usage **Kilogramm** is shortened to **Kilo**. Also the German pound (**Pfund**) is half a kilogram, i.e. 500 grams as opposed to 454 grams for the British pound.

## People

***What's your weight?, How much do you weigh?***
= Wie viel wiegen Sie?

***I weigh 12 stone*** (Brit.) or ***168 pounds*** (Amer.)
≈ Ich wiege 76,2 Kilo

***He has put on weight***
= Er hat zugenommen

***She has lost a lot of weight***
= Sie hat stark abgenommen

***At over 18 stone*** (Brit.) or ***250 pounds*** (Amer.) ***he is overweight***
≈ Mit mehr als 114 Kilo hat er Übergewicht

## Things

***What's the weight of the parcel?, How much does the parcel weigh?***
= Wie viel wiegt das Paket?

***Is it very heavy?***
= Ist es sehr schwer?

***It weighs about four pounds***
= Es wiegt ungefähr zwei Kilo

***My baggage is ten pounds over weight***
≈ Mein Gepäck hat fünf Kilo Übergewicht

***A is the same weight as B***
= A hat das gleiche Gewicht wie B

***A and B are the same weight***
= A und B sind gleich schwer

***4 oz of liver sausage***
≈ 125 Gramm *or* ein Viertel Leberwurst

***6 lbs of potatoes***
≈ sechs Pfund Kartoffeln

***They are sold by the kilo***
= Sie werden kiloweise verkauft

***a pound box of chocolates***
≈ eine 500-Gramm-Schachtel Pralinen

**weightless** /'weɪtlɪs/ *adj.* schwerelos

**weightlessness** /'weɪtlɪsnɪs/ *n.* Schwerelosigkeit, *die*

**weight: ~lifter** *n.* Gewichtheber, *der*/-heberin, *die;* **~lifting** *n., no pl., no indef. art.* Gewichtheben, *das;* **~-train** *v.i.* mit Hanteln trainieren; **~ training** *n., no pl., no indef. art.* Hanteltraining, *das;* **~-watcher** *n.* Schlankheitsbewusste, *der/die*

**weighty** /'weɪtɪ/ *adj.* Ⓐ (*heavy*) schwer; Ⓑ (*important*) gewichtig

**weir** /wɪə(r)/ *n.* Wehr, *das*

**weird** /wɪəd/ *adj.* Ⓐ (*coll.: odd*) bizarr; verrückt (*ugs.*); Ⓑ (*uncanny*) unheimlich; fantastisch ‹Geschichte›

**weirdie** /'wɪədɪ/ *n.* (*coll.*) Freak, *der* (*ugs.*)

**weirdly** /'wɪədlɪ/ *adv.* ⇒ **weird**: bizarr; verrückt (*ugs.*); unheimlich

**weirdness** /'wɪədnɪs/ *n., no pl.* Ⓐ (*coll.: oddness*) Verrücktheit, *die* (*ugs.*); Ⓑ (*uncanniness*) Unheimlichkeit, *die*

**weirdo** /'wɪədəʊ/ *n., pl.* **~s** ⇒ **weirdie**

**welcome** /'welkəm/ ❶ *int.* willkommen; **~ home/to England!** willkommen zu Hause/in England!; **~ aboard!** willkommen an Bord!
❷ *n.* Ⓐ Willkommen, *das;* **a gesture of ~:** eine Willkommensgeste; **outstay** *or* **overstay one's ~:** zu lange bleiben; **bid sb. ~:** jmdn. willkommen heißen; **give sb. a warm ~:** jmdn. herzlich willkommen heißen; Ⓑ (*reception*) Empfang, *der;* **give a proposal a warm ~:** einen Vorschlag zustimmend aufnehmen; **the committee gave her proposals a rather cool ~:** das Gremium nahm ihre Vorschläge ziemlich kühl auf; **give sb. a warm ~** (*iron.*) jmdn. gebührend empfangen (*iron.*); **we got a really hot ~ from the enemy artillery** (*iron.*) die feindliche Artillerie bereitete uns einen recht heißen Empfang (*iron.*); **receive a rather cool ~:** ziemlich kühl empfangen werden.
❸ *v.t.* Ⓐ (*greet with pleasure*) begrüßen; willkommen heißen (*geh.*); **~ sb. with open arms** jmdn. mit offenen Armen begrüßen *od.* willkommen heißen; Ⓑ (*receive*) empfangen.
❹ *adj.* Ⓐ willkommen; gefällig ‹Anblick›; **make sb. [feel] ~:** jmdm. das Gefühl geben *od.* vermitteln, willkommen zu sein; Ⓑ *pred.* **you are ~ to take it** du kannst es gern nehmen; **you may have it and ~:** du kannst es gerne haben; **no one's ever managed to do it, but you're ~ to have a go** bis jetzt hat es noch keiner geschafft, aber Sie können es ja gern mal versuchen; **you are ~** (*it was no trouble to me*) gern geschehen!; keine Ursache!; **if you want to stay here for the night you are more than ~:** wenn Sie die Nacht über hier bleiben möchten, sind Sie herzlich willkommen

**welcoming** /'welkəmɪŋ/ *adj.* einladend; **a ~ cup of tea awaited us** zur Begrüßung erwartete uns eine Tasse Tee; **the crowd burst into ~ applause** die Menge klatschte zur Begrüßung

**weld** /weld/ ❶ *v.t.* Ⓐ (*unite*) verschweißen; (*repair, make, or attach by ~ing*) schweißen (**[on]to** an + *Akk.*); **~ two pipes together** zwei Rohre zusammenschweißen; Ⓑ (*fig.: unite closely*) zusammenschweißen (**into** zu); **~ two elements together** zwei Elemente zusammenschweißen. ❷ *n.* Schweißnaht, *die*

**welder** /'weldə(r)/ *n.* Ⓐ ▶ **1261** (*person*) Schweißer, *der*/Schweißerin, *die;* Ⓑ (*machine*) Schweißgerät, *das*

**welding** /'weldɪŋ/ *n., no pl., no indef. art.* Schweißen, *das*

**welfare** /'welfeə(r)/ *n.* Ⓐ (*health and prosperity*) Wohl, *das;* Ⓑ (*social work; payments etc.*) Sozialhilfe, *die;* Wohlfahrt, *die* (*veralt.*); **the ~ people** die Leute vom Sozialamt *od.* (*veralt.*) von der Wohlfahrt; **be on ~** (*Amer.*) Sozialhilfe bekommen

**welfare: W~ 'State** *n.* Wohlfahrtsstaat, *der;* **~ work** *n.* Sozialarbeit, *die;* **do ~ work** in der Sozialarbeit *od.* (*veralt.*) bei der Wohlfahrt tätig sein; **~ worker** *n.* ▶ **1261** Sozialarbeiter, *der*/-arbeiterin, *die*

**welkin** /'welkɪn/ *n.* (*poet./literary*) Firmament, *das* (*dichter.*)

**well**[1] /wel/ ❶ *n.* Ⓐ (*water ~, mineral spring*) Brunnen, *der;* Ⓑ ⇒ **oil well**; Ⓒ (*Brit.: of lawcourt*) *Teil des Gerichtssaals, der für die Anwälte bestimmt ist;* Ⓓ (*Archit.*) Schacht, *der;* (*of staircase*) Treppenloch, *das;* Ⓔ (*fig.: source*) Quell, *der* (*dichter.*). ⇒ *also* **artesian**. ❷ *v.i.* (*literary*) sich ergießen
**~ 'up** *v.i.* ‹Tränen, Wasserstrahl:› aufsteigen; ‹Gefühle, Scham, Zorn:› aufwallen (*geh.*)

**well**[2] ❶ *int.* Ⓐ *expr. astonishment* mein Gott; meine Güte; nanu; **~, ~!** sieh mal einer an!; ⇒ *also* **never** C; Ⓑ *expr. relief* mein Gott; Ⓒ *expr. concession* na ja; **~ then, let's say no more about it** schon gut, reden wir nicht mehr davon; Ⓓ *expr. resumption* nun; **~ [then], who was it?** nun, wer wars?; Ⓔ *expr. qualified recognition of point* **~[, but] ...** na ja, aber ...; ja schon, aber ...; Ⓕ *expr. resignation* **[oh] ~:** nun denn; **ah ~:** na ja; Ⓖ *expr. expectation* **~ [then]?** na?
❷ *adv.*, **better** /'betə(r)/, **best** /best/ Ⓐ (*satisfactorily*) gut; **the business is doing ~:** das Geschäft geht gut; **do ~ for oneself** Erfolg haben; **do ~ out of sth.** mit etw. ein gutes Geschäft machen; **the patient is doing ~:** dem Patienten geht es gut; **a ~ situated house** ein günstig gelegenes Haus; **you did ~ to come** gut, dass du gekommen bist; **~ done!** großartig!; **~ begun is half done** (*prov.*) ein guter Anfang ist schon die halbe Arbeit; **didn't he do ~!** hat er sich nicht gut geschlagen?; **you would do ~ to ...:** Sie täten gut daran, zu ...; **come off ~:** gut abschneiden; **you're ~ out of it** es ist gut, dass du damit nichts mehr zu tun hast; **we're ~ rid of them** wir sind froh, dass wir sie los sind; ⇒ *also* **do**[1] 2 D; Ⓑ (*thoroughly*) gründlich ‹trocknen, polieren, schütteln›; tüchtig ‹verprügeln›; genau ‹beobachten›; gewissenhaft ‹urteilen›; **be ~ able to do sth.** durchaus *od.* sehr wohl in der Lage sein, etw. zu tun; **sb. is ~ aware that ...:** jmdm. ist sehr wohl bewusst, dass ...; **I'm ~ aware of what has been going on** mir ist sehr wohl klar *od.* bewusst, was sich abgespielt hat; **let** *or* **leave ~ alone** sich zufrieden geben; **the translator could not leave ~ alone** der Übersetzer hat nur verschlimmbessert; **be ~ worth it/a visit/the effort** es/einen Besuch/die Mühe durchaus wert sein; **he ~ deserved the honour** er hat die Ehre allemal verdient; **be ~ pleased** sehr erfreut sein; **she was not so ~ pleased** sie war nicht sonderlich erfreut; **~ out of sight** (*very far off*) völlig außer Sichtweite (**of** *Gen.*); **make sure you keep the child ~ out of sight** sorg auf jeden Fall dafür, dass keiner das

Kind sieht; ~ past the minimum age längst über dem Mindestalter; we arrived ~ before the performance began wir kamen eine ganze Zeit vor Beginn der Vorstellung; be ~ in with sb. bei jmdm. gut angeschrieben sein; ~ and truly vollkommen; I know only too ~ how/what *etc.* ...: ich weiß nur zu gut, wie/was *usw.* ...; Ⓒ (*considerably*) weit; he is ~ up in the list er steht ziemlich weit oben auf der Liste; she is ~ on in years sie ist nicht mehr die Jüngste; it was ~ on into the afternoon es war schon spät am Nachmittag; he is ~ past *or* over retiring age er hat schon längst das Rentenalter erreicht; he is ~ past *or* over forty er ist weit über vierzig; be ~ away (*lit. or fig.*) einen guten Vorsprung haben; (*coll.: be drunk*) ziemlich benebelt sein (*ugs.*); Ⓓ (*approvingly, kindly*) gut, anständig ‹jmdn. behandeln›; like sb. ~ [enough] jmdn. [sehr] gut leiden können; think ~ of sb./sth. eine gute Meinung von jmdm./etw. haben; speak ~ of sb./sth. sich positiv über jmdn./etw. äußern; wish sb. ~: jmdm. alles Gute wünschen; stand ~ with sb. [sich] gut mit jmdm. stehen; Ⓔ (*in all likelihood*) sehr wohl; Ⓕ (*easily*) ohne weiteres; you cannot very ~ refuse their help du kannst ihre Hilfe nicht ohne weiteres *od.* nicht gut ausschlagen; Ⓖ as ~ (*in addition*) auch; ebenfalls; (*as much, not less truly*) genauso; ebenso; (*with equal reason*) genauso gut; ebenso gut; (*advisable*) ratsam; (*equally ~*) genauso gut; Coming for a drink? — I might as ~: Kommst du mit, einen trinken? — Warum nicht?; you might as ~ go du kannst ruhig gehen; that is [just] as ~ (*not regrettable*) umso besser; it was just as ~ that I had ...: zum Glück hatte ich ...; as ~ as (*in addition to*): A as ~ as B B und auch [noch] A; she can sing as ~ as dance sie kann singen und auch tanzen; as ~ as helping *or* (*coll.*) help me, she continued her own work sie half mir und machte dabei noch mit ihrer eigenen Arbeit weiter. ⇒ *also* best 2; better 2; do[1] 1 U; live[2] 1 A; may A; pretty 2; speak 1 A.
❸ *adj.* Ⓐ ▶ 1191 (*in good health*) gesund; How are you feeling now? — Quite ~, thank you Wie fühlen Sie sich jetzt? — Ganz gut, danke; look ~: gut *od.* gesund aussehen; I am perfectly ~: ich fühle mich bestens; get ~ soon! gute Besserung!; he hasn't been very ~ lately es geht ihm in letzter Zeit nicht sehr gut; feel ~: sich wohl fühlen; she wanted to come, but she isn't ~ enough sie wollte kommen, aber es geht ihr nicht so gut; make sb. ~: jmdn. gesund machen; Ⓑ *pred.* (*satisfactory*) I am very ~ where I am ich bin hier sehr zufrieden; all's ~: es ist alles in Ordnung; all's ~ that ends ~ (*prov.*) Ende gut, alles gut; all is not ~ with sb./sth. mit jmdm./etw. ist etwas nicht in Ordnung; [that's all] ~ and good [das ist alles] gut und schön; all being ~: wenn alles gut geht; Ⓒ *pred.* (*advisable*) ratsam. ⇒ *also* all 2 D; very 2 D

**we'll** /wɪl, *stressed* wiːl/ = we will

**well:** ~-advised ⇒ advised; ~-aimed *adj.* gezielt ‹Schuss, Tritt, Stoß, Schlag›; ~-appointed *adj.* gut ausgestattet; ~-balanced *adj.* Ⓐ (*sensible*) ausgeglichen ‹Person›; ausgewogen ‹Plan›; Ⓑ (*equally matched*) harmonisch ‹Paar›; gleich stark ‹Mannschaften›; ~-behaved ⇒ behave 1 A; ~-being *n.* Wohl, *das;* she felt a sense of ~-being sie fühlte sich wohl; ~-bred *adj.* Ⓐ (*having good manners*) anständig; Ⓑ (*of good stock*) ‹Schwein, Pferd› aus guter Zucht; ~-built *adj.* ‹Person› mit guter Figur; be ~-built eine gute Figur haben; ~-chosen *adj.* wohlgesetzt ‹Worte›; wohl überlegt ‹Bemerkungen›; a few ~-chosen words ein paar wohl überlegte Worte; (*reprimand*) ein paar warme Worte (*iron.*); ~-conducted *adj.* gut geleitet *od.* organisiert; ~-connected *adj.* ‹Person› mit guten Beziehungen; ~-defined *adj.* klar definiert; ~-deserved *adj.* wohlverdient ‹Lob, Ruhe›; verdient ‹Belohnung, Prügel›; ~-disposed ⇒ disposed; ~ done *adj.* (*Cookery*) durchgebraten; durch *nicht attr.;* order a steak ~ done ein durchgebratenes Steak bestellen; ~-dressed *adj.* gut gekleidet ~-earned *adj.* wohlverdient; ~-educated *adj.* gebildet ‹Person, Benehmen›; ~-equipped *adj.* gut ausgestattet ‹Büro, Studio, Krankenwagen›; gut ausgerüstet ‹Polizei, Armee, Expedition, Flugzeug›; ~-established *adj.* bewährt; ~-fed *adj.* wohlgenährt; ~-founded *adj.* [wohl] fundiert; ~-groomed *adj.* gepflegt; ~ 'grounded *adj.* Ⓐ (*trained*) be ~ grounded in a subject gute Grundkenntnisse in einem Fach haben; Ⓑ ⇒ ~-founded; ~-heeled *adj.* (*coll.*) gut betucht (*ugs.*)

**wellies** /ˈwelɪz/ *n. pl.* (*Brit. coll.*) Gummistiefel

**'well-informed** *adj.* Ⓐ she is one of the most ~ people I have ever met von allen, die ich kenne, weiß sie am besten Bescheid; Ⓑ (*having access to reliable information*) gut unterrichtet

**wellington** /ˈwelɪŋtən/ *n.* ~ [boot] Gummistiefel, *der*

**well:** ~-intentioned /ˈwelɪntenʃənd/ *adj.* gut gemeint; ~-judged *adj.* gut gezielt; ~-kept *adj.* gepflegt; in gutem Zustand *nachgestellt;* wohlgehütet ‹Geheimnis›; ~-knit *adj.* gut gebaut ‹Körper, Figur, Sportler›; ~-known *adj.* Ⓐ (*known to many*) bekannt; Ⓑ (*known thoroughly*) vertraut; ~-loved *adj.* beliebt; ~ made *adj.* Ⓐ (*skilfully manufactured*) gut [gearbeitet]; Ⓑ (*having good build*) gut gebaut; ~-mannered ⇒ mannered B; ~ marked *adj.* gut gekennzeichnet ‹Strecke, Wanderung›; ~-matched *adj.* einander ebenbürtig ‹Gegner, Mannschaften›; they are a ~-matched couple sie passen gut zueinander; ~-meaning *adj.* wohlmeinend; be ~-meaning es gut meinen; ~-meant *adj.* gut gemeint; ~-nigh *adv.* (*literary/arch.*) nahezu; ~ off *adj.* Ⓐ (*rich*) wohlhabend; sb. is ~ off jmdm. geht es [finanziell] gut; Ⓑ be ~ off for sth. (*provided with*) mit etw. gut versorgt sein; Ⓒ (*favourably situated*) she is perfectly ~ off es geht ihr ausgezeichnet; ~ oiled *adj.* (*fig. coll.: drunk*) abgefüllt (*salopp*); ~ paid *adj.* gut bezahlt; he's ~ paid enough er kriegt genug bezahlt; ~-preserved *adj.* gut erhalten ‹Holz, Mumie, (scherzh.) Achtzigjährige usw.›; ~-read /ˈwelred/ *adj.* belesen; ~-rounded *adj.* Ⓐ (*complete and symmetrical*) abgerundet; Ⓑ (*complete and ~ expressed*) ausgewogen; ~-spent *adj.* sinnvoll verbracht ‹Zeit›; vernünftig ausgegeben ‹Geld›; ~-spoken *adj.* sprachlich gewandt; mit angenehmer Sprechweise *nachgestellt;* ~-stocked *adj.* gut gefüllt ‹Kühlschrank, Vorratskammer, Hausbar›; ‹Geschäft› mit reichem Sortiment; their shop is ~-stocked ihr Geschäft hat ein reiches Sortiment; ~-thought-out *adj.* gut durchdacht; ~-thumbed *adj.* zerlesen ‹Buch›; ~-timed *adj.* zeitlich gut gewählt; ~-to-do *adj.* wohlhabend; ~-tried *adj.* bewährt; ~-trodden *adj.* (*lit. or fig.*) ausgetreten; ~-turned *adj.* wohlgesetzt; ~-upholstered *adj.* (*fig. joc.*) gut gepolstert; ~-wisher *n.* Sympathisant, *der*/Sympathisantin, *die;* cards and gifts from ~-wishers Kartengrüße und Geschenke; ~-worn *adj.* abgetragen ‹Kleidungsstück›; abgenutzt ‹Teppich›; abgegriffen ‹Einband, Buch, Zeitschrift›; ausgetreten ‹Pfad›; abgedroschen ‹Redensart, Ausdruck›

**welsh** *v.i.* (*leave without paying*) sich davonmachen, ohne zu bezahlen; sich auf Französisch verabschieden (*ugs.*)
~ on *v.t.* (*coll.*) ~ on sb./sth. jmdn. sitzen lassen/sich um etw. herumdrücken (*ugs.*)

**Welsh** /welʃ/ ▶ 1275, ▶ 1340 ❶ *adj.* walisisch; sb. is ~: jmd. ist Waliser/Waliserin; ⇒ *also* corgi; English 1. ❷ *n.* Ⓐ (*language*) Walisisch, *das;* ⇒ *also* English 2 A; Ⓑ *pl.* the ~: die Waliser

**Welsh:** ~man /ˈwelʃmən/ *n., pl.* ~men /ˈwelʃmən/ Waliser, *der;* ~ 'rabbit, ~ 'rarebit *ns.* Käsetoast, *der;* ~woman *n.* Waliserin, *die*

**welt** /welt/ *n.* Ⓐ (*of shoe*) Rahmen, *der;* Ⓑ (*heavy blow*) Hieb, *der;* Ⓒ (*trimming*) Bündchen, *das;* Ⓓ ⇒ weal[2]

**Weltanschauung** /veltanˈʃaʊʊŋ/ *n.* Ⓐ (*philosophy of life*) Weltanschauung, *die;* Ⓑ (*conception of the world*) Weltbild, *das*

**welter** /ˈweltə(r)/ ❶ *v.i.* sich wälzen. ❷ *n.* Chaos, *das;* a ~ of foam eine schäumende Flut; a ~ of emotions ein Sturm von Gefühlen

**'welterweight** *n.* (*Boxing etc.*) Weltergewicht, *das;* (*person also*) Weltergewichtler, *der*

**Wenceslas** /ˈwensɪsləs/ *pr. n.* (*Hist.*) Wenzel (*der*)

**wench** /wentʃ/ *n.* (*arch./joc.*) Mädel, *das;* (*arch.: maid-servant*) Magd, *die* (*veralt.*)

**wend** *v.t.* (*literary/arch.*) ~ one's way homewards sich auf den Heimweg machen; they ~ed their way back towards the village sie machten sich auf den Weg zurück ins Dorf

**Wend** /wend/ *n.* Wende, *der*/Wendin, *die*

**Wendy house** /ˈwendɪ haʊs/ *n.* Spielhaus, *das*

**went** ⇒ go[1] 1, 2

**wept** ⇒ weep 1, 2

**were** ⇒ be

**we're** /wɪə(r)/ = we are

**weren't** (*coll.*) = were not; ⇒ be

**werewolf** /ˈwɪəwʊlf, ˈweəwʊlf/ *n., pl.* werewolves /ˈwɪəwʊlvz, ˈweəwʊlvz/, werwolf /ˈwɜːwʊlf/ *n., pl.* werwolves /ˈwɜːwʊlvz/ (*Mythol.*) Werwolf, *der*

**west** /west/ ▶ 1024 ❶ *n.* Ⓐ Westen, *der;* the ~: West (*Met., Seew.*); (*Amer.: western part of US*) der Westen; in/to[wards]/from the ~: im/nach *od.* (*geh.*) gen/von Westen; to the ~ of westlich von; westlich (+ *Gen.*); Ⓑ (*European civilization*) Westen, *der;* Abendland, *das;* Ⓒ (*Cards*) West. ⇒ *also* east 1; Far West; Middle West; Wild West. ❷ *adj.* westlich; West‹küste, -wind, -grenze, -tor›. ❸ *adv.* westwärts; nach Westen; ~ of westlich von; westlich (+ *Gen.*); go ~ (*fig. coll.: be killed or wrecked or lost*) hopsgehen (*salopp*); ~ by north/south ⇒ by[1] 1 D; ⇒ *also* east 3

**West:** ~ 'Africa *pr. n.* Westafrika (*das*); ~ 'Bank *pr. n.* the ~ Bank (*of the Jordan*) das Westjordanland; ~ Ber'lin *pr. n.* (*Hist.*) West-Berlin (*das*); Berlin (West) (*Amtsspr.*); w~bound *adj.* ▶ 1024 ‹Zug usw.› in Richtung Westen; ~ Country *n.* (*Brit.*) Westengland, *das;* ~ 'End *n.* (*Brit.*) Westend, *das;* the ~ End theatres die Theater des Londoner Westends

**westering** /ˈwestərɪŋ/ *attrib. adj.* im Westen stehend

**westerly** /ˈwestəlɪ/ ▶ 1024 ❶ *adj.* Ⓐ (*in position or direction*) westlich; in a ~ direction nach Westen; Ⓑ (*from the west*) ‹Wind› aus westlichen Richtungen; the wind was ~: der Wind kam aus Westen. ❷ *adv.* Ⓐ (*in position*) westlich; (*in direction*) nach West[en]; Ⓑ (*from the west*) aus *od.* von Westen. ❸ *n.* West[wind], *der*

**western** /ˈwestən/ ❶ ▶ 1024 *adj.* westlich; West‹grenze, -hälfte, -seite, -fenster, -wind›; ~ Germany Westdeutschland, *das;* ⇒ *also* bloc; Middle Western. ❷ *n.* Western, *der*

**westerner** /ˈwestənə(r)/ *n.* Abendländer, *der*/Abendländerin, *die*

**Western:** ~ 'Europe *pr. n.* Westeuropa (*das*); ~ Euro'pean ❶ *adj.* westeuropäisch; ❷ *n.* Westeuropäer, *der*/-europäerin, *die*

**westernization** /westənaɪˈzeɪʃn/ *n.* Verwestlichung, *die*

**westernize** /ˈwestənaɪz/ *v.t.* verwestlichen

**westernmost** /ˈwestənməʊst/ *adj.* ▶ 1024 westlichst...

**West:** ~ 'German (*Hist.*) ❶ *adj.* westdeutsch; ❷ *n.* Westdeutsche, *der/die;* ~ 'Germany *pr. n.* (*Hist.*) Westdeutschland (*das*); ~ 'Indian ▶ 1340 ❶ *adj.* westindisch; ❷ *n.* Westinder, *der*/-inderin, *die;* ~ 'Indies ⇒ Indies B

**Westminster** /ˈwestmɪnstə(r)/ *n.* (*Brit.: Parliament*) Westminster (*das*); London (*das*) (*ugs.*)

**west:** ~-north-'~ ▶ 1024 ❶ *n.* Westnordwest[en], *der;* ❷ *adj.* westnordwestlich; ❸ *adv.* nach Westnordwest[en]; W~ of 'England *pr. n.* Westengland (*das*)

**Westphalia** /west'feɪlɪə/ *pr. n.* Westfalen (*das*)

**Westphalian** /west'feɪlɪən/ ❶ *adj.* westfälisch. ❷ *n.* Westfale, *der*/Westfalin, *die*

**West:** ~ **Side** *n.* (*Amer.*) West Side, *die;* **w~-south-'w~** ▶ 1024 ❶ *n.* Westsüdwest[en], *der;* ❷ *adj.* westsüdwestlich; ❸ *adv.* nach Westsüdwest[en]

**westward** /'westwəd/ ▶ 1024 ❶ *adj.* nach Westen gerichtet; (*situated towards the west*) westlich; **in a ~ direction** nach Westen; [in] Richtung Westen. ❷ *adv.* westwärts; **they are ~ bound** sie fahren nach *od.* [in] Richtung Westen. ❸ *n.* Westen, *der*

**westwards** /'westwədz/ ▶ 1024 ⇨ **westward 2**

**wet** /wet/ ❶ *adj.* Ⓐ nass; **~ with tears** tränenfeucht; **~ behind the ears** (*fig.*) feucht hinter den Ohren (*ugs.*); **~ to the skin, ~ through** nass bis auf die Haut; Ⓑ (*rainy*) regnerisch; feucht ‹Klima›; Ⓒ (*recently applied*) frisch ‹Farbe›; '**~ paint**' „frisch gestrichen"; Ⓓ (*coll.: feeble*) schlapp (*ugs.*); schlappschwänzig (*salopp*); Ⓔ (*Brit. Polit. coll.*) pflaumenweich (*ugs. abwertend*); schlappschwänzig (*salopp abwertend*). ⇨ *also* **blanket** 1 A; **rag**[1] A.
❷ *v.t.*, **-tt-**, **wet** *or* **wetted** Ⓐ befeuchten; ⇨ *also* **whistle** 3 C; Ⓑ (*urinate on*) **~ one's bed/pants** das Bett/sich (*Dat.*) die Hosen nass machen.
❸ *n.* Ⓐ (*moisture*) Feuchtigkeit, *die;* Ⓑ (*rainy weather*) Regenwetter, *das;* (*rainy conditions*) Nässe, *die;* **in the ~:** im Regen; Ⓒ (*coll.: feeble person*) Flasche, *die* (*salopp abwertend*); Ⓓ (*Brit. Polit. coll.*) Schlappschwanz, *der* (*salopp abwertend*)

**wet:** **~back** *n.* (*Amer. coll.*) illegaler mexikanischer Einwanderer; **~ 'dream** *n.* feuchter Traum

**wether** /'weðə(r)/ *n.* (*Zool.*) Hammel, *der*

**wet:** **~lands** *n. pl.* Feuchtgebiete; **~ look** *n.* Hochglanz, *der;* (*of hair*) Wet Look, *der*

**wetness** /'wetnɪs/ *n., no pl.* Ⓐ (*being wet*) Nässe, *die;* **a patch of ~:** ein nasser Fleck; Ⓑ (*being rainy*) Feuchtigkeit, *die*

**wet:** **~ nurse** ❶ *n.* Amme, *die;* ❷ *v.t.* (*fig. derog.*) bemuttern; **~suit** *n.* Tauchanzug, *der*

**wetting** /'wetɪŋ/ *n.* **get a ~:** nass werden; **give sb. a ~:** jmdn. nass machen

**'wetting agent** *n.* Netzmittel, *das*

**we've** /wɪv, *stressed* wi:v/ = **we have**

**WFTU** *abbr.* **World Federation of Trade Unions** WGB

**whack** /wæk/ ❶ *v.t.* (*coll.: strike heavily*) hauen (*ugs.*). ❷ *n.* Ⓐ (*coll.: heavy blow*) Schlag, *der;* **give sb. a ~ on the bottom** jmdm. eins auf den Hintern geben (*ugs.*); Ⓑ (*coll.: share*) Anteil, *der;* Ⓒ (*coll.: attempt*) **have a ~ at sth./at doing sth.** etw. probieren/probieren, etw. zu tun; Ⓓ **out of ~** (*Amer.*) aus dem Leim (*ugs.*); Ⓔ **top ~** (*coll.*) Spitzentarif, *der*

**whacked** /wækt/ *adj.* (*Brit. coll.: tired out*) erledigt (*ugs.*); kaputt (*ugs.*)

**whacking** /'wækɪŋ/ ❶ *adj.* (*coll.*) satt (*salopp*). ❷ *adv.* (*coll.*) wahnsinnig (*salopp*); **~ great lies** faustdicke Lügen. ❸ *n.* (*coll.*) Tracht Prügel, *die*

**whacko** /'wækəʊ/ *int.* (*Brit. dated coll.*) juchhe; juchhu

**whale** /weɪl/ *n., pl.* **~s** *or same* Ⓐ (*Zool.*) Wal, *der;* Walfisch, *der* (*volkst.*); **right ~:** Glattwal, *der;* Ⓑ *no pl.* (*coll.*) **we had a ~ of a [good] time** wir haben uns bombig (*ugs.*) *od.* toll (*ugs.*) amüsiert; **it made a ~ of a difference** es machte ungeheuer viel aus (*ugs.*)

**'whalebone** *n.* Fischbein, *das*

**whaler** /'weɪlə(r)/ *n.* ▶ 1261 Walfänger, *der*

**whaling** /'weɪlɪŋ/ *n., no pl., no indef. art.* Walfang, *der; attrib.* Walfang-

**wham** /wæm/ ❶ *int.* wumm. ❷ *n.* Knall, *der.* ❸ *v.t.*, **-mm-:** **~ sb.** jmdm. einen Schlag versetzen. ❹ *v.i.*, **-mm-** knallen

**whammy** ⇨ **double whammy**

**wharf** /wɔ:f/ *n., pl.* **wharves** /wɔ:vz/ *or* **~s** Kai, *der;* Kaje, *die* (*nordd.*)

**what** /wɒt/ ❶ *interrog. adj.* Ⓐ *asking for selection* welch...; **~ book did you choose?** welches Buch hast du ausgesucht?; Ⓑ *asking for statement of amount* wieviel; *with pl. n.* wie viele; **~ men/money has he?** wie viele Leute/wie viel Geld hat er?; **I know ~ time it starts** ich weiß, um wie viel Uhr es anfängt; **~ more can I do/say?** was kann ich sonst noch tun/sagen?; **~ more do you want?** was willst du [noch] mehr?; Ⓒ *asking for statement of kind* was für; **~ kind of man is he?** was für ein Mensch ist er?; **~ good** *or* **use is it?** wozu soll das gut sein? ⇨ *also* **price** 1 D.
❷ *excl. adj.* Ⓐ (*how great*) was für; **~ a fool you are!** was für ein Dummkopf du doch bist!; **~ impudence** *or* **cheek/luck!** was für eine Unverschämtheit *od.* Frechheit/was für ein Glück!; Ⓑ *before adj. and n.* (*to ~ extent*) was für.
❸ *rel. adj.* **we can dispose of ~ difficulties there are remaining** wir können die verbleibenden Schwierigkeiten ausräumen; **lend me ~ money you can** leih mir so viel Geld, wie du kannst; **I will give you ~ help I can** ich werde dir helfen, so gut ich kann.
❹ *adv.* Ⓐ (*to what extent*) **~ do I care?** was kümmerts mich?; **~ does it matter?** was machts?; Ⓑ **~ with ...:** wenn man an ... denkt; **~ with changing jobs and moving house I haven't had time to do any studying** da ich eine neue Stellung angetreten habe und umgezogen bin, hatte ich keine Zeit zum Lernen; **~ with one thing and another** wie das so ist *od.* geht.
❺ *interrog. pron.* Ⓐ (**~** *thing*) was; **~ is your name?** wie heißt du/heißen Sie?; **~ about ...?** (*is there any news of ...?, ~ will become of ...?*) was ist mit ...?; **~ about a game of chess?** wie wärs mit einer Partie Schach?; **~ to do?** was tun?; **~-d'you-[ma-] call-him/-her/-it, ~'s-his/-her/-its-name** wie heißt er/sie/es noch; **~ for?** wozu?; **~ do you want the money for?** wozu *od.* wofür willst du das Geld?; **and/or ~ 'have you** und/oder was sonst noch [alles]; **~ if ...?** was ist, wenn ...?; **~ is he?** was ist er für einer?; **~ is it** *etc.* **like?** wie ist es *usw.*?; **I've lost a pen here somewhere — Well, ~ is it like?** Ich habe hier irgendwo einen Stift verloren. — Was ist es denn für einer?; **~ next?** (*fig.*) sonst noch was?; **~ not** wer weiß was alles; **~ 'of him/her?** was ist mit ihm/ihr?; **~ 'of it?** was ist dabei?; was soll [schon] dabei sein?; **~ do you say** *or* (*Amer.*) **~ say we have a rest?** was hältst du davon, wenn wir mal Pause machen?; wie wärs mit einer Pause?; **~ will people say?** was werden die Leute sagen?; **all she ever thinks about is ~ people will say** sie denkt immer nur daran, was die Leute sagen; **[I'll] tell you ~:** weißt du, was; pass mal auf; **[and] ~ then?** [na] und?; **or ~?** oder was?; **so ~?** na und?; Ⓑ *asking for confirmation* **~?** wie?; was? (*ugs.*); **you did ~?** was hast du gemacht?; **nice day, ~?** (*Brit. coll.*) schöner Tag, was? (*ugs.*); Ⓒ *in rhet. questions equivalent to neg. statement* **~ is the use in trying/the point of going on?** wozu [groß] versuchen/weitermachen? ⇨ *also* **give** 2 C; **know** 1 C.
❻ *rel. pron.* Ⓐ (*that which*) was; **do ~ I tell you** tu, was ich dir sage; **~ little I know/remember** das bisschen, das ich weiß/an das ich mich erinnere; **this is ~ I mean: ...:** ich meine Folgendes: ...; **give me ~ you can** gib mir, so viel du kannst; **I disagree with ~ you are saying** ich stimme dem nicht zu, was du sagst; **tell sb. ~ to do** *or* **~ he can do with sth.** (*coll. iron.*) jmdm. sagen, wo er sich (*Dat.*) etw. hinstecken kann (*salopp*); **~ is more** außerdem; zusätzlich; **the weather being ~ it is ...:** so, wie es mit dem Wetter aussieht, ...; **for ~ it is** in seiner Art; Ⓑ (*uneducated: who, which*) wo (*salopp*); **it's the poor ~ gets the blame** die Armen müssen immer alles ausbaden. ⇨ *also* **but** 1 B; **come** M.
❼ *excl. pron.* was; **~ she must have suffered!** wie sie gelitten haben muss!

**whate'er** /wɒt'eə(r)/ (*poet.*), **whatever** /wɒt'evə(r)/ ❶ *adj.* Ⓐ *rel. adj.* **whatever measures we take** welche Maßnahmen wir auch immer ergreifen; **whatever materials you will need** alle Materialien, die du vielleicht brauchst; Ⓑ (*notwithstanding which*) was für ... auch immer; **whatever problems you encounter** auf welche Probleme Sie auch stoßen [mögen]; Ⓒ (*at all*) überhaupt; **I can't see anyone whatever** ich kann überhaupt niemanden sehen.
❷ *pron.* Ⓐ *rel. pron.* was für ... [auch immer]; **whatever you do to complain, they will still take no notice** man kann sich beschweren, wie man will, sie beachten es doch nicht; **do whatever you like** mach, was du willst; Ⓑ (*notwithstanding anything*) was auch [immer]; **whatever happens, ...:** was auch geschieht, ...; Ⓒ **or whatever** oder was auch immer; oder sonst was (*ugs.*); Ⓓ (*coll.*) = **what ever** ⇨ **ever** E

**'whatnot** *n.* Ⓐ (*coll.: indefinite thing*) Dingsbums, *das* (*ugs.*); Ⓑ (*stand with shelves*) Etagere, *die*

**whatsit** /'wɒtsɪt/ *n.* (*coll.*) (*thing*) Dingsbums, *das* (*ugs.*); (*person*) Dingsda, *der* (*ugs.*)

**whatsoe'er** /wɒtsəʊ'eə(r)/ (*poet.*), **whatsoever** /wɒtsəʊ'evə(r)/ ⇨ **whatever**

**wheat** /wi:t/ *n., no pl., no indef. art.* Weizen, *der;* **sort out** *or* **separate the ~ from the chaff** (*fig.*) die Spreu vom Weizen trennen

**'wheat belt** *n.* (*Geog.*) Weizengürtel, *der*

**wheaten** /'wi:tn/ *adj.* Weizen-

**wheat:** **~ germ** ⇨ **germ**; **~meal** *n.* (*Brit.*) Weizen[vollkorn]mehl, *das*

**whee** /wi:/ *int.* juchhe

**wheedle** /'wi:dl/ *v.t.* Ⓐ (*coax*) **~ sb.** jmdm. gut zureden; **~ sb. into doing sth.** jmdm. so lange gut zureden, bis er etw. tut; Ⓑ (*get by cajoling*) sich (*Dat.*) etw. verschaffen; **~ sth. out of sb.** jmdm. etw. abschwatzen (*ugs.*)

**wheel** /wi:l/ ❶ *n.* Ⓐ Rad, *das;* (*of roller skate*) Rolle, *die;* **[potter's] ~:** Töpferscheibe, *die;* **[roulette] ~:** Roulett, *das;* **re-invent the ~** (*fig.*) sich mit Problemen aufhalten, die längst gelöst sind; **get oneself some ~s** (*coll.*) sich (*Dat.*) einen fahrbaren Untersatz zulegen (*ugs.*); **put** *or* **set the ~s in motion** (*fig.*) die Sache in Gang setzen; **the ~s of bureaucracy turn slowly** (*fig.*) die Mühlen der Bürokratie mahlen langsam; **there are ~s within ~s** (*fig.*) es spielen Dinge eine Rolle, von denen man gar nichts ahnt; **break sb. on the ~** (*Hist.*) jmdn. rädern; ⇨ *also* **butterfly** A; **oil** 2 A; **shoulder** 1 A; **spoke**[1] A; Ⓑ (*for steering*) (*Motor Veh.*) Lenkrad, *das;* (*Naut.*) Steuerrad, *das;* **at** *or* **behind the ~** (*of car*) am *od.* hinterm Steuer; (*of ship; also fig.*) am Ruder; Ⓒ (*movement in a circle*) Kreisbewegung, *die;* **the ~[s] of the vultures** das Kreisen der Geier; Ⓓ (*Mil.: drill movement*) Schwenkung, *die;* **left/right ~:** Links-/Rechtsschwenkung, *die.*
❷ *v.t.* Ⓐ (*turn round*) wenden; Ⓑ (*Mil.*) schwenken lassen; Ⓒ (*push*) schieben; **~ oneself** (*in a wheelchair*) fahren.
❸ *v.i.* Ⓐ (*turn round*) kehrtmachen; Ⓑ (*circle*) kreisen; Ⓒ (*Mil.*) schwenken; **left/right ~!** links/rechts schwenkt!

**~ a'bout**, **~ a'round** ❶ *v.t.* herumdrehen; wenden ‹Pferd›. ❷ *v.i.* kehrtmachen; (*face the other way*) sich umdrehen; (*fig.*) kreisen; ‹Tänzer:› sich im Kreise drehen

**~ 'in** *v.t.* hinein-/hereinschieben

**~ 'out** *v.t.* hinaus-/herausschieben; **~ sb. out** (*fig. derog.*) jmdn. vorführen

**~ 'round** ⇨ **~ about**

**wheel:** **~ and 'deal** *v.i.* mauscheln; **~barrow** *n.* Schubkarre, *die;* Schubkarren, *der;* **~barrow race** *n.* Schubkarrenrennen, *das;* **~base** *n.* (*Motor Veh., Railw.*) Radstand, *der;* **~ brace** *n.* Radschlüssel, *der;* (*cross-shaped*) Kreuzschlüssel, *der;* **~chair** *n.* Rollstuhl, *der;* **~ clamp** *n.* Parkkralle, *die*

**wheeled** /wi:ld/ *adj.* mit Rädern *nachgestellt;* ‹Möbel, Kulisse usw.› auf *od.* mit Rollen; **~ vehicle** Räderfahrzeug, *das*

**-wheeled** *adj. in comb.* ‹vier-, sechs-, acht›räd[e]rig

**wheeler-dealer** /wi:lə'di:lə(r)/ *n.* Mauschler, *der*/Mauschlerin, *die;* (*financial*) Geschäftemacher, *der*/-macherin, *die*

# When

## als or wenn?

There is a simple distinction between these two translations for *when*:

**als** is used for happenings in the past

**wenn** is used for happenings in the present or future

***When I saw him I smiled***
= Als ich ihn sah, lächelte ich

***When I see him I always feel sorry for him***
= Wenn ich ihn sehe, tut er mir immer Leid

***When I see him I'll tell him***
= Wenn ich ihn sehe, werde ich es ihm sagen *or* sage ich es ihm

As can be seen, **wenn** translates two uses of *when* in English: in the sense of *whenever* (present tense in both clauses) and referring to the future (present tense in the *when* clause, future tense in the main clause). German does the same, except that the present is often also used in this last case.

Occasionally *when* is used with a verb in the past in the sense of *whenever*, and here too it should be translated by **wenn**:

***When(ever) I saw him, I always felt sorry for him***
= Wenn ich ihn sah, tat er mir immer Leid

**wenn** is also used to translate *when* where it occurs with the English present participle (the *-ing* form), a normal subject and verb being used. The subject and the tense of the verb will be that of the English main clause; if this is impersonal, **man** can be used.

***When speaking German I often get embarrassed***
= Wenn ich deutsch spreche, werde ich oft verlegen

***When speaking German it is important to enunciate clearly***
= Wenn man deutsch spricht, ist es wichtig, deutlich zu artikulieren

Often the sense of *when* in this construction is *while*, and the appropriate translation is **als**, but **bei** plus the verbal noun can also be used and is often neater.

***He was killed when crossing the road***
= Er kam beim Überqueren der Straße ums Leben
Er kam ums Leben, als er die Straße überquerte

***Be careful when cleaning the gun***
= Sei vorsichtig beim Putzen des Gewehrs

## In questions (direct and indirect)

Here the translation is always **wann**:

***When is she coming?***
= Wann kommt sie?

***I don't know when she's coming***
= Ich weiß nicht, wann sie kommt

***When do you want to eat?***
= Wann willst du essen?

***Tell me when you want to eat***
= Sag mir, wann du essen willst

***From when is the licence valid?***
= Ab wann gilt der Schein?

***Since when do you give the orders?***
= Seit wann gibst du die Befehle?

Other usages are covered in the entry for **when**.

**'wheelhouse** *n.* (*Naut.*) Steuerhaus, *das*

**wheelie** /'wi:lɪ/ *n.* (*coll.*) *Fahren auf dem Hinterrad;* Wheelie, *das;* **do a ~/do ~s** auf dem Hinterrad fahren; ein Wheelie/Wheelies fahren

**'wheelie bin** *n.* (*Brit. coll.*) Müllcontainer auf Rollen; Rollcontainer für Müll

**wheeling** /'wi:lɪŋ/ *n., no pl., no indef. art.* Kreisen, *das*

**wheeling and 'dealing** *n.* Mauschelei, *die;* (*shady deals*) undurchsichtige Geschäfte; **there is a lot of ~ going on** es wird eifrig gemauschelt

**wheel: ~ of 'fortune** *n.* Glücksrad, *das;* **~ of 'life** *n.* (*Buddhism*) Rad des Lebens *od.* Werdens; **~ reflector** *n.* Speichenreflektor, *der;* **~spin** *n.* (*Motor Veh., Railw.*) Durchdrehen der Räder; **because of ~spin** wegen durchdrehender Räder; **~wright** /'wi:lraɪt/ *n.* Stellmacher, *der*

**wheeze** /wi:z/ ❶ *v.i.* schnaufen; keuchen. ❷ *n.* Ⓐ Schnaufen, *das;* Keuchen, *das;* **give a [loud] ~:** [laut] schnaufen *od.* keuchen; Ⓑ (*coll.*) (*trick*) Trick, *der;* (*plan*) Idee, *die;* **think up a ~:** einen Dreh finden (*ugs.*); **a good ~ for making money** eine gute Masche, zu Geld zu kommen
**~ 'out** *v.t.* keuchen

**wheezy** /'wi:zɪ/ *adj.* (*coll.*) pfeifend, keuchend ‹Atem, Stimme›; asthmatisch ‹Husten›; schnaufend ‹Orgel›; **be ~** ‹Atem:› pfeifend gehen, pfeifen; ‹Person:› pfeifend atmen

**whelk** /welk/ *n.* (*Zool.*) Wellhornschnecke, *die*

**whelp** /welp/ ❶ *n.* Welpe, *der.* ❷ *v.i.* (*also derog.*) werfen

**when** /wen/ ▶ 1686 ❶ *adv.* Ⓐ (*at what time*) wann; **say ~** (*coll.: pouring drink*) sag halt; **that was ~ I intervened** das war der Moment, wo ich eingriff; **the best part of the film was ~ the car exploded** das Beste in dem Film war die Szene, als das Auto explodierte; Ⓑ (*at which*) **the time ~ ...:** die Zeit, zu der *od.* (*ugs.*) wo/(*with past tense*) als ...; **the day ~ ...:** der Tag, an dem *od.* (*ugs.*) wo/(*with past tense*) als ...; **do you remember [the time] ~ we ...:** erinnerst du dich daran, wie wir ...
❷ *conj.* Ⓐ (*at the time that*) als; (*with present or future tense*) wenn; **~ [I was] young** als ich jung war; in meiner Jugend; **~ in doubt** im Zweifelsfall; (*with gerund*) **~ cleaning the gun** beim Putzen des Gewehrs; **~ speaking French** wenn ich/sie *usw.* Französisch spreche/spricht *usw.;* Ⓑ (*whereas*) **why do you go abroad ~ it's cheaper here?** warum fährst du ins Ausland, wo es doch hier billiger ist?; **I received only £5 ~ I should have got £10** ich bekam nur 5 Pfund, hätte aber 10 Pfund bekommen sollen; Ⓒ (*considering that*) wenn; **how can I finish it ~ you won't help?** wie soll ich es fertig machen, wenn du nicht hilfst?; Ⓓ (*and at that moment*) als.
❸ *pron.* **by/till ~ ...?;** bis wann ...?; **from/since ~ ...?** ab/seit wann ...?; **~ are we invited for?** für wann sind wir eingeladen?; **but that was yesterday, since ~ things have changed** aber das war gestern, und inzwischen hat sich manches geändert.
❹ *n.* Wann, *das;* ⇒ *also* **where** 4

**whence** /wens/ (*arch./literary*) ❶ *adv.* woher; **~ did you learn this news?** wo[her] hast du das erfahren?; **the village ~ comes the famous cheese** das Dorf, aus dem der berühmte Käse kommt; **the source ~ these evils spring** die Quelle dieser Übel; **these are the facts, ~ we can conclude that ...:** das sind die Tatsachen, aus denen wir schließen können, dass ...; **~ my doubts about his abilities** daher meine Zweifel über seine Fähigkeiten. ❷ *conj.* (*to the place from which*) dorthin, woher; **he returned it ~ it came** er brachte es dorthin zurück, wo es herkam. ❸ *pron.* **from ~** ⇒ **1**

**whene'er** /wen'eə(r)/ (*poet.*), **whenever** /wen'evə(r)/ ❶ *adv.* Ⓐ wann immer; **or whenever** oder wann immer; Ⓑ (*coll.*) = **when ever** ⇒ **ever** E. ❷ *conj.* jedes Mal wenn

**whensoe'er** /wensəʊ'eə(r)/ (*poet.*), **whensoever** /wensəʊ'evə(r)/ *adv.* wann auch immer

**where** /weə(r)/ ❶ *adv.* Ⓐ (*in or at what place*) wo; **~ shall we sit?** wo wollen wir sitzen *od.* uns hinsetzen?; wohin wollen wir uns setzen?; **~ was I?** (*fig.*) wo war ich stehen geblieben?; **~ did Orwell say/write that?** wo *od.* an welcher Stelle sagt/schreibt Orwell das? **~ is the harm in it/the sense of it?** (*rhet.*) was macht das schon/welchen *od.* was für einen Sinn hat das?; **this is ~ I was born** hier bin ich geboren; Ⓑ (*from what place*) woher; **~ did you get that information?** wo hast du das erfahren?; Ⓒ (*to what place, to which*) wohin; **she's going ~ she's wanted** sie geht dahin, wo sie gebraucht wird; **~ shall I put it?** wohin soll ich es legen?; wo soll ich es hinlegen?; **the town ~ they were going** die Stadt, wohin sie fuhren; **~ do we go from here?** (*fig.*) was tun wir jetzt *od.* als nächstes?; **I know ~ I'm going** (*fig.*) ich weiß, was ich erreichen will; Ⓓ (*in what respect*) inwiefern; **I don't know ~ they differ/I've gone wrong** ich weiß nicht, worin sie sich unterscheiden/wo ich den Fehler gemacht habe; **~ he is weakest is in maths** am schwächsten ist er in Mathematik; **that is ~ you are wrong** in diesem Punkt irrst du dich; Ⓔ (*in which*) wo; **in the box ~ I keep my tools** in der Kiste, worin *od.* in der ich mein Werkzeug habe; Ⓕ (*in what situation*) wo; **~ will/would they be if ...?** was wird/würde aus ihnen, wenn ...?; **~ would I be without you?** was täte ich ohne dich?; **~ will it all end?** wo wird das noch enden?
❷ *conj.* wo; **~ uncertain, leave blank** bei Unsicherheit [bitte] freilassen; **delete ~ inapplicable** Nichtzutreffendes [bitte] streichen.
❸ *pron.* **near/not far from ~ it happened** nahe der Stelle/nicht weit von der *od.* unweit der Stelle, wo es passiert ist; **from ~ I'm standing** von meinem Standort [aus]; **they continued from ~ they left off** sie machten da weiter, wo sie aufgehört hatten; **to Oxford, from ~ we took a train to London** nach Oxford, wo wir den Zug nach London nahmen; **within ten metres of ~**

W

**we stood** keine zehn Meter von der Stelle, wo wir standen; **we drove out to ~ the air was fresh and clean** wir fuhren dorthin, wo die Luft frisch und sauber war; **~ [...] from?** woher [...]?; von wo [...]?; **~ do/have you come from?** woher kommst du?; wo kommst du her?; **he is never sure ~ his next meal is coming from** er weiß nie, woher er seine nächste Mahlzeit kriegt; **~ [...] to?** wohin [...]?; **~ are you going to?** wohin gehst du?; wo gehst du hin?; **~ have you got to [in the book]?** wie weit bist du [in dem Buch]?
❹ *n.* Wo, *das;* **I can't recall the ~ and when [of it]** ich weiß nicht mehr, wo und wann [es war]

**whereabouts** ❶ /weərə'baʊts/ *adv.* (*in what place*) wo; (*to what place*) wohin. ❷ /weərə 'baʊts/ *pron.* **~ are you from?** woher kommst du? ❸ /'weərəbaʊts/ *n., constr. as sing. or pl.* (*of thing*) Verbleib, *der;* (*of person*) Aufenthalt[sort], *der;* **her/its present ~ is** *or* **are unknown** wo sie sich zurzeit aufhält/ wo es sich zurzeit befindet, ist unbekannt

**where: ~'as** *conj.* A während; **he is very quiet, ~as she is an extrovert** er ist sehr ruhig, sie dagegen ist eher extravertiert; B (*Law: considering that*) in Anbetracht dessen, dass; da; **~'by** *adv.* A (*by which*) mit dem/ der/denen; mit dessen/deren Hilfe; B (*dated/ literary: by what means?*) wie; **~ by shall I know this?** woran erkenne ich das?

**where'er** /weər'eə(r)/ (*poet.*) ⇒ **wherever**

**wherefore** /'weəfɔ:(r)/ ❶ *adv.* (*arch./literary*) weshalb. ❷ *n.* **the whys and ~s** ⇒ **why** 3

**where: ~'in** *adv.* (*formal*) A (*in which*) worin; in dem/der/denen; B (*in what respect*) inwiefern; worin ‹sich unterscheiden, sich finden›; womit ‹dienen›; **~'of** *adv.* (*formal*) (*of which*) von dem/der/denen; woraus ‹gemacht sein›; **the house ~ he is the owner** das Haus, dessen Eigentümer er ist

**wheresoe'er** /weəsəʊ'eə(r)/ (*poet.*), **wheresoever** /weəsəʊ'evə(r)/ *adv., conj.* wo auch immer

**whereupon** /weərə'pɒn/ *adv.* worauf

**wherever** /weər'evə(r)/ ❶ *adv.* A (*in whatever place*) wo immer; **sit ~ you like** setz dich, wohin du magst; **I'll find him, ~ he lives** ich werde ihn finden, wo er auch wohnt *od.* wohnen mag; **or ~:** oder wo immer; oder sonstwo (*ugs.*); B (*to whatever place*) wohin immer; **I shall go ~ I like** ich gehe, wohin ich will; **I shall go ~ there is work** ich gehe dahin, wo es Arbeit gibt; **or ~:** oder wohin immer; oder sonstwohin (*ugs.*); C (*coll.*) = **where ever** ⇒ **ever** E.
❷ *conj.* A (*in every place that*) überall [da], wo; **~ security is involved** wann immer es um die Sicherheit geht; **do it ~ possible** tun Sie es, wo *od.* wenn [irgend] möglich; B (*to every place that*) wohin auch; **~ he went** wohin er auch ging; wo er auch hinging.
❸ *pron.* wo ... auch; **~ you're going to** wo du auch hingehst; wohin du auch gehst; **~ it/ he comes from** wo es/er auch herkommt; woher es/er auch kommt; **carry on reading from ~ you've got to** lies da weiter, bis wohin du gekommen bist

**wherewithal** /'weəwɪðɔ:l/ *n.* (*coll.*) **the ~:** das nötige Kleingeld (*ugs.*)

**wherry** /'werɪ/ *n.* A (*rowing boat*) [Ruder]-kahn, *der;* B (*Brit.: barge*) [Last]kahn, *der*

**whet** /wet/ *v.t.*, **-tt-** A (*sharpen*) wetzen; B (*fig.: stimulate*) anregen ‹Appetit›; erregen ‹Interesse›; reizen ‹Neugier›

**whether** /'weðə(r)/ *conj.* ob; **I don't know ~ to go [or not]** ich weiß nicht, ob ich gehen soll [oder nicht]; **the question [of] ~ to do it [or not]** die Frage, ob man es tun soll [oder nicht]; **~ you like it or not, I'm going** ob es dir passt oder nicht, ich gehe; ⇒ *also* **doubt** 1 A, 3; **no** 2 C

**'whetstone** *n.* (*lit. or fig.*) Wetzstein, *der*

**whew** /hwju:/ *int. expr. surprise* oh; *expr. consternation etc.* puh; *expr. relief* ah

**whey** /weɪ/ *n., no pl., no indef. art.* Molke, *die*

**which** /wɪtʃ/ ❶ *adj.* A *interrog.* welch...; **~ one** welcher/welche/welches; **~ ones** welche; **~ one of you did it?** wer von euch hat es getan?; **~ way** (*how*) wie; (*in ~ direction*) wohin; B *rel.* welch... (*geh.*); **I told him to go to the doctor, ~ advice he took** ich habe ihm geraten, zum Arzt zu gehen, was er auch getan hat; **he usually comes at one o'clock, at ~ time I'm having lunch/by ~ time I've finished** er kommt immer um ein Uhr; dann esse ich gerade zu Mittag/bis dahin bin ich schon fertig; **a 5 × 4 camera (~ size I prefer)** eine 5 × 4-Kamera (das Format, das ich vorziehe).
❷ *pron.* A *interrog.* welcher/welche/welches; **~ of you?** wer von euch?; **~ is ~?** welcher/welche/welches ist welcher/welche/ welches?; **I can't tell ~ is ~:** ich kann sie nicht auseinander halten *od.* unterscheiden; B *rel.* der/die/das; welcher/welche/welches (*veralt.*); *referring to a clause* was; **of ~:** dessen/deren; **everything ~ I predicted** alles, was ich vorausgesagt habe; **the crime of ~ you accuse him** das Verbrechen, dessen Sie ihn anklagen; **the house of ~ I am speaking** das Haus, von dem *od.* wovon ich rede; **the bed on ~ she lay** das Bett, auf dem *od.* worauf sie lag; **he grinned, from ~ I gathered he wasn't serious** er grinste, woraus ich schloss, dass es nicht sein Ernst war; **the shop opposite/near ~ we parked** der Laden, gegenüber dem/in dessen Nähe wir parkten; **I have received your kind gift, for ~ many thanks** ich habe dein nettes Geschenk bekommen. Vielen Dank dafür; **I intervened, after ~ they calmed down** ich griff ein, worauf[hin] sie sich beruhigten; **Our Father, ~ art in Heaven** (*Rel.*) Vater unser, der du bist im Himmel

**whichever** /wɪtʃ'evə(r)/ ❶ *adj.* A (*any ... that*) der *od.* derjenige, der/die *od.* diejenige, die/das *od.* dasjenige, das/die *od.* diejenigen, die; **go ~ way you want** es ist egal, welchen Weg du nimmst; **take ~ apple/apples you wish** nimm den Apfel, den du willst/die Äpfel, die du willst; **..., ~ period is the longer** ..., je nachdem, welches der längere Zeitraum ist; B (*no matter which/who/ whom*) welcher/welche/welches ... auch; **~ way you go** welchen Weg du auch nimmst; C (*coll.*) = **which ever** ⇒ **ever** E.
❷ *pron.* A (*any one[s] that*) der *od.* derjenige, der/die *od.* diejenige, die/das *od.* dasjenige, das/die *od.* diejenigen, die; **~ of you/ the children wins will get a prize** wer von euch gewinnt/das Kind, das gewinnt, bekommt einen Preis; **a list of ~ of the children want to come** eine Liste aller Kinder, die kommen wollen; **at a walk, trot, or gallop, ~ you please** gehend, im Trab oder im Galopp, [ganz] wie du magst; **to dinner — or supper, ~ it ought to be called** zum Diner — oder Abendessen, wie immer man es nennen soll; B (*no matter which one[s]*) welcher/welche/welches ... auch; **~ of them comes/come** wer von ihnen auch kommt; C (*coll.*) = **which ever** ⇒ **ever** E

**whichsoever** /wɪtʃsəʊ'evə(r)/ (*arch.*) ⇒ **whichever** 1 A, B, 2 A, B

**whiff** /wɪf/ *n.* A (*smell*) [leichter] Geruch; (*puff, breath*) Hauch, *der;* **~s of smoke** Rauchwölkchen; **a ~ of honeysuckle** ein leichter Geißblattduft; **the ~ from his smelly feet** der Geruch seiner Schweißfüße; **give her another ~ of chloroform** gib ihr noch mal etwas Chloroform; **catch a ~ of sth.** den Geruch von etw. wahrnehmen; B (*fig.: trace*) Hauch, *der;* **the faintest ~ of sentiment** der leiseste Anflug von Sentimentalität

**Whig** /wɪg/ (*Hist.*) ❶ *n.* Whig, *der.* ❷ *attrib. adj.* Whig-

**while** /waɪl/ ❶ *n.* Weile, *die;* **quite a** *or* **quite some ~, a good ~:** eine ganze Weile; ziemlich lange; **it takes a ~:** es dauert eine Weile *od.* Zeit lang; **[for] a ~:** eine Weile; **where have you been all the** *or* **this ~?** wo warst du die ganze Zeit?; **[only] a little** *or* **short ~ ago** [erst] kürzlich *od.* vor kurzem; **all the ~ we were there** die ganze Zeit, als wir da waren; **a long ~:** lange; **a long ~ ago** *or* **back** vor langer Zeit; **between ~s** zwischendurch; **for a little** *or* **short ~:** eine kleine Weile; **stay a little ~ [longer]** bleib noch ein Weilchen; **I haven't seen him for a long ~:** ich habe ihn lange nicht [mehr] gesehen; **in a little** *or* **short ~:** gleich; **in a long ~:** lange; seit langem; **be worth [sb.'s] ~:** sich [für jmdn.] lohnen; **make sth. worth sb.'s ~:** jmdn. für etw. entsprechend belohnen; **I'll make it worth your ~:** es soll dein Schaden nicht sein; **once in a ~:** von Zeit zu Zeit [mal]; hin und wieder [mal]; **he read the newspaper smoking a cigar the ~** (*dated/literary*) er las die Zeitung und rauchte dabei eine Zigarre.
❷ *conj.* A während; (*as long as*) solange; **~ in London he took piano lessons** als er in London war, nahm er Klavierstunden; **don't smoke ~ in bed** rauchen Sie nicht im Bett; **could you get me a paper as well ~ you are about it?** könntest du mir auch eine Zeitung mitbringen, wenn du schon dabei bist?; B (*although*) obgleich; C (*whereas*) während.
❸ *v.t.* **~ away the time** sich (*Dat.*) die Zeit vertreiben (**by, with** mit); **~ away the evening/an hour** sich (*Dat.*) den Abend über/eine Stunde lang die Zeit vertreiben

**whilst** /waɪlst/ (*Brit.*) ⇒ **while** 2

**whim** /wɪm/ *n.* (*mood*) Laune, *die;* (*idea*) Spleen, *der;* **he acts as the ~ takes him** er handelt je nach Laune

**whimper** /'wɪmpə(r)/ ❶ *n.* **~[s]** Wimmern, *das;* (*of dog etc.*) Winseln, *das;* **with a ~:** wimmernd/winselnd; **he gave a ~ of pain** er wimmerte vor Schmerz; **not with a bang but a ~** (*fig.*) sang- und klanglos. ❷ *v.i.* wimmern; ‹Hund:› winseln. ❸ *v.t.* in weinerlichem Ton vorbringen ‹Klage›; **'...', he ~ed** „...", wimmerte er

**whimsical** /'wɪmzɪkl/ *adj.* A (*frivolous*) launenhaft; (*odd, fanciful*) spleenig; (*tinged with humour*) launig; humorig; (*teasing*) neckisch ‹Blick, Lächeln›; B (*odd-looking*) kurios; ulkig (*ugs.*)

**whimsicality** /wɪmzɪ'kælɪtɪ/ *n., no pl.* ⇒ **whimsical**: A Launenhaftigkeit, *die;* Spleenigkeit, *die;* Launigkeit, *die;* Humorigkeit, *die;* B Kuriosität, *die;* Ulkigkeit, *die* (*ugs.*)

**whimsically** /'wɪmzɪkəlɪ/ *adv.* launenhaft; (*teasingly*) neckisch ‹ansehen, lächeln›; **he said ~ that ...:** er machte die launige Bemerkung, dass ...

**whimsy** /'wɪmzɪ/ *n.* A *no pl.* ⇒ **whimsicality** A; B (*idea*) Spleen, *der*

**whine** /waɪn/ ❶ *v.i.* A (*make moaning sound*) heulen; ‹Hund:› jaulen; ‹Baby:› quengeln (*ugs.*); **~ for mercy/alms** um Gnade/Almosen winseln (*abwertend*); B (*complain*) jammern; **he's been whining to the boss about it** er hat dem Chef darüber etwas vorgejammert. ❷ *n.* A (*sound*) Heulen, *das;* (*esp. of dog*) Jaulen, *das;* **the ~ in his voice** der winselnde Ton in seiner Stimme; **the baby's ~s** das Gequengel des Babys (*ugs.*); B (*complaint*) **~[s]** Gejammer, *das*

**whiner** /'waɪnə(r)/ *n.* Jammerer, *der;* **be a ~:** immer was zu jammern haben

**whinge** /wɪndʒ/ (*coll.*) ❶ *v.i.*, **~ing** ⇒ **whine** 1 B. ❷ *n.* ⇒ **whine** 2 B

**whinny** /'wɪnɪ/ ❶ *v.i.* wiehern. ❷ *n.* Wiehern, *das;* **whinnies** Gewieher, *das*

**whip** /wɪp/ ❶ *n.* A Peitsche, *die;* **use one's ~ on** *or* **take one's ~ to sb./a horse** jmdm./einem Pferd die Peitsche geben; ⇒ *also* **crack** 1 A, 3 C; B (*Brit. Parl.: official*) Einpeitscher, *der*/Einpeitscherin, *die* (*Jargon*); **chief ~:** Haupteinpeitscher, *der*/ -einpeitscherin, *die* (*Jargon*); Fraktionsgeschäftsführer, *der*/-führerin, *die* (*Amtsspr.*); C (*Brit. Parl.: notice*) **[three-line] ~** [*verbindliche*] *Aufforderung zur Teilnahme an einer Plenarsitzung* [*wegen einer wichtigen Abstimmung*]; **issue a three-line ~:** Fraktionszwang verhängen; **take/be deprived of/resign the ~:** in die Fraktion eintreten/aus der Fraktion ausgeschlossen werden/aus der Fraktion austreten; D (*Hunting: whipper-in*) Pikör, *der;* E (*Cookery*) Schaumspeise, *die.*
❷ *v.t.*, **-pp-:** A (*lash*) peitschen; **the rider ~ped his horse** der Reiter gab seinem Pferd die Peitsche; **he was ~ped in public** er

W

wurde öffentlich ausgepeitscht; **the rain ~ped the window panes** der Regen peitschte [gegen] die Fensterscheiben; **B** (*Cookery*) schlagen; **~ sth. until stiff/to a froth** etw. steif/schaumig schlagen; **C** (*move quickly*) reißen ‹Gegenstand›; **she ~ped it out of my hand** sie riss es mir aus der Hand; **he quickly ~ped it out of sight** er ließ es schnell verschwinden; **~ sth. from one's pocket** etw. blitzschnell aus der Tasche ziehen; **~ sb. into hospital** jmdn. schleunigst ins Krankenhaus bringen; **she was ~ped through customs** sie wurde am Zoll blitzschnell abgefertigt; **D** (*coll.: defeat*) auseinander nehmen (*salopp bes. Sport*); **E** (*coll.: steal*) klauen (*ugs.*); **F** (*bind*) umwickeln; [be]takeln (*Seemannsspr.*); (*Sewing: overcast*) umnähen; **G** (*fig.: reprove, criticize*) **~ sb./sth.** jmdm. die Leviten lesen/etw. geißeln; **H** **~ a top** kreiseln; einen Kreisel treiben.

**3** *v.i.*, **-pp-**: **A** (*move quickly*) flitzen (*ugs.*); **he ~ped down the stairs** er sauste *od.* flitzte die Treppe hinunter; **~ through a book in no time** ein Buch in null Komma nichts durchlesen (*ugs.*); **B** (*lash*) peitschen

**~ a'way** *v.t.* wegreißen (**from** *Dat.*)

**~ 'back** *v.i.* **A** (*spring back*) zurückschnellen; **B** (*return quickly*) zurückflitzen (*ugs.*)

**~ 'in** **1** *v.i.* reinwitschen (*ugs.*); **the wind came ~ping in** der Wind kam reingefegt (*ugs.*). **2** *v.t.* (*Hunting*) [mit der Peitsche] wieder zur Meute treiben ‹Hunde›

**~ 'off** *v.t.* **A** (*snatch off*) herunterreißen; ‹Wind:› herunterfegen; **~ one's clothes off** seine Kleider von sich werfen; **~ off one's hat** [sich (*Dat.*)] den Hut vom Kopf reißen; **~ sb. off to hospital/France** jmdn. schleunigst ins Krankenhaus/nach Frankreich bringen; **B** (*Hunting*) [mit der Peitsche] zurücktreiben ‹Hunde›

**~ 'on** *v.t.* **A** (*put on quickly*) draufwerfen; **~ one's coat/clothes on** sich in seinen Mantel/seine Kleider werfen; **~ one's hat on** schnell seinen Hut aufsetzen; **B** (*urge on*) mit der Peitsche antreiben; (*fig.*) antreiben; anspornen

**~ 'out** **1** *v.t.* [blitzschnell] herausziehen; **~ sb.'s appendix/tonsils out** jmds. Blinddarm/Mandeln schleunigst herausnehmen. **2** *v.i.* rauswitschen (*ugs.*)

**~ 'round** *v.i.* **A** (*turn quickly*) herumschnellen; **B** (*go quickly*) **~ round to see sb.** *or* **to sb.'s place** schnell bei jmdn. vorbeischauen; **I'm just ~ping round to my neighbour's/to the shops** ich gehe nur schnell zum Nachbarn/einkaufen; ⇒ *also* **whip-round**

**~ 'up** *v.t.* **A** (*snatch up*) [blitz]schnell aufheben; **B** (*Cookery*) [kräftig] schlagen; **C** (*arouse*) aufpeitschen ‹Wellen›; (*fig.*) anheizen (*ugs.*), anfachen (*geh.*) ‹Emotionen, Interesse›; schüren ‹Hass, Unzufriedenheit›; **he knows how to ~ up enthusiasm in his pupils** er versteht es, seine Schüler zu begeistern; **~ up trouble/a riot** die Leute zu Unruhen/zum Aufruhr aufstacheln; **D** (*coll.: make quickly*) schnell hinzaubern ‹Gericht, Essen›

**whip: ~cord** *n.* **A** (*cord*) Peitschenschnur, *die;* **B** (*fabric*) Whipcord, *der;* **~ hand** *n.* **have** *or* **hold the ~ hand [of** *or* **over sb.]** (*fig.*) die Oberhand [über jmdn.] haben; **~lash** *n.* **A** Peitschenriemen, *der;* **B** (*Med.*) **~lash [injury]** Peitschenschlagverletzung, *die;* Schleudertrauma, *das*

**whipped 'cream** *n.* Schlagsahne, *die*

**whipper-in** /wɪpər'ɪn/ (*Hunting*) Pikör, *der*

**whippersnapper** /'wɪpəsnæpə(r)/ *n.* (*dated*) [junger] Dachs; (*cheeky*) Frechdachs, *der*

**whippet** /'wɪpɪt/ *n.* Whippet, *der*

**whipping** /'wɪpɪŋ/ *n.* **A** (*flogging*) Schlagen [mit der Peitsche]; (*as form of punishment*) Prügelstrafe, *die;* (*flagellation*) Geißelung, *die;* **give sb. a ~:** jmdn. auspeitschen; (*with stick etc.*) jmdm. eine Tracht Prügel verpassen (*ugs.*); (*coll.: defeat*) jmdm. eins überbraten (*salopp*); **get** *or* **take** *or* **be given a ~:** ausgepeitscht werden; (*coll.: be defeated*) eins übergebraten kriegen (*salopp*); **B** (*cord*) Umwicklung, *die;* Takling, *der* (*Seemannsspr.*)

**whipping: ~ boy** *n.* (*Hist.; also fig.*) Prügelknabe, *der;* **~ cream** *n.* [flüssige] Schlagsahne; **~ top** *n.* [Treib]kreisel, *der*

**whippoorwill** /'wɪpʊəwɪl/ *n.* (*Ornith.*) Whip-Poor-Will, *der*

**whippy** /'wɪpɪ/ *adj.* biegsam; elastisch

**whip: ~-round** *n.* (*Brit. coll.*) Sammlung, *die;* **have** *or* **hold a ~-round [for sb./sth.]** [für jmdn./etw.] den Hut herumgehen lassen (*ugs.*); **~-saw** *v.t.* (*Amer. fig.*) *beim Poker betrügen, indem man zusammen mit dem Partner den Einsatz erhöht;* **~stock** *n.* Peitschenstiel, *der*

**whir** /wɜ:(r)/ **1** *v.i.*, **-rr-** ⇒ **whirr** 1. **2** *n.* ⇒ **whirr** 2

**whirl** /wɜ:l/ **1** *v.t.* **A** (*rotate*) [im Kreis] herumwirbeln; **B** (*fling*) schleudern; (*with circling motion*) wirbeln ‹Blätter, Schneeflocken usw.›; **C** (*convey rapidly*) in Windeseile fahren; **the train ~ed us to our destination** der Zug brachte uns in Windeseile ans Ziel. **2** *v.i.* **A** (*rotate*) wirbeln; **the ice skaters ~ed at a tremendous speed** die Eisläufer wirbelten in ungeheurer Geschwindigkeit [im Kreis herum]; **~ing dervish** tanzender Derwisch; **B** (*move swiftly*) sausen; (*with circling motion*) wirbeln; **I could see the leaves ~ing in the wind** ich sah, wie die Blätter vom Wind herumgewirbelt wurden; **C** (*fig.: reel*) **everything/the room ~ed about me** mir drehte sich alles/das Zimmer drehte sich vor meinen Augen; **the excitements of the city made her head ~:** von den aufregenden Eindrücken der Stadt wirbelte ihr der Kopf. **3** *n.* **A** Wirbeln, *das;* **the wind threw up a ~ of leaves/sand** der Wind wirbelte Blätter/Sand auf; **she was** *or* **her thoughts were** *or* **her head was in a ~** (*fig.*) ihr schwirrte der Kopf; **B** (*bustle*) Trubel, *der;* **her dull life suddenly became a ~ of activity** ihr eintöniges Leben war plötzlich voller Trubel und Betriebsamkeit; **the social ~:** der Trubel des gesellschaftlichen Lebens; **C** (*coll.: attempt*) **give sb./sth. a ~:** jmdn./etw. mal probieren

**~ a'bout** **1** *v.t.* herumwirbeln. **2** *v.i.* herumwirbeln; ‹Vögel:› sich tummeln

**~ a'long** **1** *v.t.* ‹Fluss:› mitreißen; **~ sb. along** mit jmdm. dahinsausen. **2** *v.i.* dahinsausen

**~ a'round** ⇒ **~ about**

**~ a'way, ~ 'off** **1** *v.t.* in Windeseile wegfahren; **~ sb. off** *or* **away somewhere** jmdn. in Windeseile irgendwohin bringen. **2** *v.i.* lossausen

**~ 'round** **1** *v.t.* [im Kreis] herumwirbeln. **2** *v.i.* [im Kreis] herumwirbeln; ‹Rad, Rotor, Strudel:› wirbeln; **the leaf ~ed round as it fell** das Blatt drehte sich im Fall in einem Wirbel

**~ 'up** *v.t.* aufwirbeln; hochwirbeln

**whirligig** /'wɜ:lɪgɪg/ *n.* **A** (*top*) Kreisel, *der;* (*toy windmill*) Windrädchen, *das;* **B** (*Zool.*) Taumelkäfer, *der;* Kreiselkäfer, *der*

**whirl: ~pool** *n.* Strudel, *der;* (*bathing pool*) Whirlpool, *der;* **~wind** *n.* **A** Wirbelwind, *der;* (*stronger*) Wirbelsturm, *der;* **sow the wind and reap the ~wind** (*prov.*) Wind säen und Sturm ernten; **B** (*fig.: tumult*) Wirbel, *der;* Trubel, *der;* **I've been caught up all week in a ~wind of activity** für mich war die ganze Woche über ständig Trubel; *attrib.* **~wind romance** heftige Romanze

**whirlybird** /'wɜ:lɪbɜ:d/ *n.* (*coll.: helicopter*) Hubschrauber, *der*

**whirr** /wɜ:(r)/ **1** *v.i.* surren; ‹Heuschrecke, Grille usw.:› zirpen; ‹Flügel eines Vogels, Propeller:› schwirren. **2** *n.* ⇒ **1**: Surren, *das;* Zirpen, *das;* Schwirren, *das*

**whisk** /wɪsk/ **1** *n.* **A** Wedel, *der;* **B** (*Cookery*) Schneebesen, *der;* (*part of mixer*) Rührbesen, *der;* **C** (*movement*) wischende Bewegung; **a few ~s of the broom** ein paar Besenstriche *od.* Striche mit dem Besen; **the horse gave a ~ of its tail** das Pferd schlug mit dem Schwanz. **2** *v.t.* **A** (*Cookery*) [mit dem Schnee-/Rührbesen] schlagen; **B** (*convey rapidly*) in Windeseile bringen; **the taxi will ~ you to town in no time** das Taxi bringt dich im Nu in die Stadt; **C** (*flip*) schlagen mit ‹Schwanz›. **3** *v.i.* sausen; schießen (*ugs.*)

**~ a'way** *v.t.* **A** (*flap away*) wegscheuchen; **B** (*remove suddenly*) **~ sth. away [from sb.]** [jmdm.] etw. [plötzlich] wegreißen; **C** (*convey rapidly*) in Windeseile wegbringen; **~ sb. away to the station** jmdn. in Windeseile zum Bahnhof bringen

**~ 'off** *v.t.* **A** (*flap off*) ⇒ **~ away** A; **B** (*remove suddenly*) [plötzlich] wegreißen; **~ one's coat off** seinen Mantel von sich werfen; **~ off one's hat** rasch den Hut abnehmen; **C** ⇒ **~ away** C

**~ 'up** ⇒ **~** 2 A

**whisker** /'wɪskə(r)/ *n.* **A** *in pl.* (*hair on man's cheek*) Backenbart, *der;* **B** (*Zool.*) (*of cat, mouse, rat*) Schnurrhaar, *das;* (*of walrus*) Bartborste, *die;* **a walrus's ~s** der Bart eines Walrosses; ⇒ *also* **cat's whiskers**; **C** (*fig. coll.: small distance*) **be within a ~ of sth./doing sth.** kurz vor etw. (*Dat.*) stehen/kurz davor stehen, etw. zu tun; **win by a ~:** ganz knapp gewinnen

**whiskered** /'wɪskəd/ *adj.* backenbärtig; ‹Tier› mit Schnurrhaaren

**whiskery** /'wɪskərɪ/ *adj.* backenbärtig; **be ~:** einen [mächtigen] Backenbart haben

**whiskey** (*Amer., Ir.*), **whisky** /'wɪskɪ/ *n.* Whisky, *der;* (*Irish or American ~*) Whiskey, *der*

**whisper** /'wɪspə(r)/ **1** *v.i.* **A** flüstern; **~ to sb.** jmdm. etwas zuflüstern; **~ to me so that no one else will hear** flüster es mir ins Ohr, damit es niemand [anders] hört; **~ to each other** miteinander flüstern; **B** (*speak secretly*) tuscheln; **~ against sb.** über jmdn. tuscheln; **C** (*rustle*) [leise] rauschen; säuseln (*geh.*); flüstern (*poet.*).

**2** *v.t.* **A** flüstern; **~ sth. to sb./in sb.'s ear** jmdm. etw. zuflüstern/ins Ohr flüstern; **~ it to me so that no one else will hear** flüster es mir ins Ohr, damit es niemand [anders] hört; **~ sb. to do sth./that ...:** jmdm. zuflüstern, er solle etw. tun/dass ...; **B** (*rumour*) [hinter vorgehaltener Hand] erzählen; **the story is being ~ed about the village that ...:** im Dorf macht die Geschichte die Runde, dass ...; **it is ~ed that ...:** man munkelt, dass ... (*ugs.*).

**3** *n.* **A** (*~ed speech*) Flüstern, *das;* **in a ~, in ~s** im Flüsterton; **B** (*~ed remark*) **their ~s** ihr Geflüster; ⇒ *also* **stage whisper**; **C** (*rumour*) Gerücht, *das;* **there were ~s that ...:** es gab Gerüchte, dass ...; man munkelte, dass ... (*ugs.*); **D** (*rustle*) [leises] Rauschen; Säuseln, *das* (*geh.*); Flüstern, *das* (*poet.*)

**whispering: ~ campaign** *n.* Verleumdungskampagne, *die;* **~ gallery** *n.* Flüstergalerie, *die*

**whist** /wɪst/ *n.* (*Cards*) Whist, *das;* ⇒ *also* **drive** 1 K

**whistle** /'wɪsl/ **1** *v.i.* pfeifen; **~ at a girl** hinter einem Mädchen herpfeifen; **the spectators ~d at the referee** die Zuschauer pfiffen den Schiedsrichter aus; **he ~d loudly when he heard how valuable it was** er ließ ein lautes Pfeifen vernehmen, als er hörte, wie wertvoll es war; **~ to sb.** jmdm. pfeifen; **~ for sth.** nach etw. pfeifen; **the policeman ~d for help/reinforcement** der Polizist pfiff, um Hilfe/Verstärkung herbeizurufen; **the referee ~d for half-time** der Schiedsrichter pfiff Halbzeit; **~ in the dark** (*fig.*) seine Angst verdrängen; **you can ~ for it!** (*fig. coll.*) da kannst du lange warten!

**2** *v.t.* **A** pfeifen; **B** (*summon*) her[bei]pfeifen; **he ~d his dog and it came running** er pfiff seinem Hund, und er kam angelaufen.

**3** *n.* **A** (*sound*) Pfiff, *der;* (*whistling*) Pfeifen, *das;* **the joyful ~s of the birds** das fröhliche Zwitschern der Vögel *od.* Vogelgezwitscher; **give a [brief] ~:** [kurz] pfeifen; **he gave a ~ of surprise** er ließ ein überraschtes Pfeifen vernehmen; **B** (*instrument*) Pfeife, *die;* **penny** *or* **tin ~:** Blechflöte, *die;* **the referee blew his ~:** der Schiedsrichter pfiff; **[as] clean/clear as a ~** (*fig.*) blitzsauber/absolut frei; **get away [as] clean as a ~:** ganz unbehelligt davonkommen; **blow**

**the ~ on sb./sth.** (*fig.*) jmdn./etw. auffliegen lassen (*ugs.*); **C** (*coll.: throat*) **wet one's ~** (*coll.*) sich (*Dat.*) die Kehle anfeuchten (*ugs.*)
**~ 'back** *v.t.* zurückpfeifen
**~ 'up** *v.t.* [he]ranpfeifen

**whistle: ~-blower** *n.* (*fig.*) *jmd., der etw. auffliegen lässt;* **~-stop** *n.* (*Amer.*) **A** (*Railw.*) (*small town*) kleines Nest (*ugs.*) (*an einer Bahnlinie*); (*station*) Bedarfshaltepunkt, *der;* **B** (*Polit.*) *kurzer Auftritt eines Politikers während einer Wahlkampfreise;* (*rapid visit*) Stippvisite, *die; attrib.* **~-stop tour/campaign** Reise mit vielen Kurzaufenthalten/Wahlkampf[reise] mit vielen kurzen Auftritten *od.* Terminen

**whistling: ~ buoy** *n.* (*Naut.*) Heulboje, *die;* **~ 'kettle** *n.* Pfeifkessel, *der*

**whit** /wɪt/ *n., no pl., no def. art.* (*dated*) **no ~, not a ~:** kein bisschen; **it matters not a ~:** es macht überhaupt nichts; **not a ~ of sense** nicht ein Funke [von] Verstand

**white** /waɪt/ **1** *adj.* **A** weiß; **[as] ~ as snow** schneeweiß; **he prefers his coffee ~** (*Brit.*) er trinkt seinen Kaffee am liebsten mit Milch; **B** (*pale*) weiß; (*through illness*) blass; bleich; (*through fear or rage*) bleich; weiß; **[as] ~ as chalk** *or* **a sheet** kreidebleich; **go** *or* **turn ~:** weiß *od.* bleich werden; erbleichen (*geh.*); **he was ~ with rage** er war weiß *od.* bleich vor Wut; ⇒ *also* **bleed** 2 A; **C ~r than ~** (*fig.: morally pure*) engelrein (*geh.*); **D** (*light-skinned*) weiß; **~ people** Weiße *Pl.;* **~ oppression** Unterdrückung durch die Weißen.
**2** *n.* **A** (*colour*) Weiß, *das;* **B** (*of egg*) Eiweiß, *das;* **C** (*of eye*) Weiße, *das;* **the ~s of their eyes** das Weiße in ihren Augen; **D W~** (*person*) Weiße, *der/die;* **E** (*~ clothes*) **dressed in ~:** weiß gekleidet; **~s** weißer Dress; (*laundry*) Weißwäsche, *die;* **F** (*Printing*) Zwischenraum, *der;* **G** (*butterfly*) Weißling, *der;* **H** (*Snooker*) weiße Kugel

**white: ~ 'ant** *n.* Termite, *die;* **~bait** *n., pl. same: junger Hering/junge Sprotte o. Ä.;* **~beam** *n.* (*Bot.*) Mehlbeere, *die;* **~ 'bread** *n.* Weißbrot, *das;* **~ cell** *n.* (*Anat., Zool.*) weißes Blutkörperchen; **~ 'Christmas** *n.* weiße Weihnachten; **~ 'coffee** *n.* (*Brit.*) Kaffee mit Milch; **~-'collar** *adj.* **~-collar worker** Angestellte, *der/die;* **~-collar union** Angestelltengewerkschaft, *die;* **~ corpuscle** ⇒ **~ cell;** **~ 'currant** *n.* weiße Johannisbeere; **~ 'dwarf** *n.* (*Astron.*) weißer Zwerg; **~ 'elephant** ⇒ **elephant;** **~-faced** *adj.* [kreide]bleich; **~ fish** *n.* **A** (*light-coloured fish*) [*Speise*]*fisch mit weißlicher od. silbriger Färbung;* Weißfisch, *der;* **B** (*lake fish*) Weißfisch, *der;* Renke, *die;* **~ 'flag** *n.* weiße Fahne; **W~ 'Friar** *n.* Karmeliter, *der;* **~ 'frost** *n.* Reif, *der;* **~ 'gold** *n.* Weißgold, *das;* **~ goods** *n. pl.* (*Commerc.*) **A** (*fabrics*) Weißwaren *Pl.;* **B** (*appliances*) weiße Ware; **W~hall** *pr. n.* (*Brit. Polit.: Government*) Whitehall (*das*); **~ heat** *n.* **A** (*Phys.*) Weißglut, *die;* **to a ~ heat** bis zum Weißglühen; **at [a] ~ heat** in weiß glühendem Zustand; **B** (*fig.*) Glut, *die;* **work at ~ heat** auf Hochtouren arbeiten; **~ 'hope** *n.* Hoffnungsträger, *der*/Hoffnungsträgerin, *die;* **~ 'horse** *n.* **A** Schimmel, *der;* **B** *in pl.* (*on waves*) Schaumkronen; **~-'hot** *adj.* **A** (*Phys.*) weiß glühend; **B** (*fig.*) glühend; **W~ House** *pr. n.* (*Amer. Polit.*) **the W~ House** das Weiße Haus; **~ 'knight** *n.* (*fig.*) Retter in der Not; **~ 'lead** *n.* Bleiweiß, *das;* **~ 'lie** ⇒ **lie**[1] 1 A; **~ 'light** *n.* (*Phys.*) weißes Licht; **~ 'line** *n.* (*in middle of road*) Mittellinie, *die;* (*at side of road*) Randlinie, *die;* **~-lipped** /'waɪtlɪpt/ *adj.* mit kreidebleichen Lippen *nachgestellt;* **~ 'magic** *n.* weiße Magie; **~ man** *n.* (*Anthrop.*) Weiße, *der;* **the ~ man** (*~ people*) der weiße Mann; **~ 'meat** *n.* weißes Fleisch [und Geflügel]; **~ 'metal** *n.* Weißmetall, *das;* **W~ 'Monk** *n.* Zisterzienser, *der*

**whiten** /'waɪtn/ **1** *v.t.* weiß machen; weißen ‹Wand, Schuhe›. **2** *v.i.* **A** (*become white*) weiß werden; **B** (*turn pale*) [kreide]weiß werden

**whitener** /'waɪtənə(r)/ *n.* (*for shoes*) Schuhweiß, *das;* (*bleaching agent*) Bleichmittel, *das;* (*for coffee*) Kaffeeweißer, *der*

**whiteness** /'waɪtnɪs/ *n., no pl.* **A** Weiß, *das;* **B** (*paleness*) Blässe, *die*

**white: ~ 'night** *n.* schlaflose Nacht; **~ 'noise** *n.* (*Phys.*) weißes Rauschen; **~-out** *n.* (*Meteorol.*) Whiteout, *der;* **W~ 'Paper** *n.* (*Brit.*) *öffentliches Diskussionspapier über Vorhaben der Regierung;* **W~ 'Russia** *pr. n.* Weißrussland (*das*); **W~ 'Russian 1** *adj.* weißrussisch; **sb. is W~ Russian** jmd. ist Weißrusse/-russin; **2** *n.* Weißrusse, *der*/-russin, *die;* **~ 'sale** *n.* (*Commerc.*) ≈ Weiße Woche/Wochen; Weißwarenausverkauf, *der;* **~ 'sauce** *n.* weiße *od.* helle Soße; **W~ 'Sea** *pr. n.* Weiße Meer, *das;* **~ 'slave** *n.* weiße Sklavin; *Opfer des Mädchenhandels; attrib.* **~ slave trade** *or* **traffic** Mädchenhandel, *der;* **~ 'spirit** *n.* (*Chem.*) Terpentin[öl]ersatz, *der;* **~ 'stick** *n.* Blindenstock, *der;* **~ 'sugar** *n.* weißer Zucker; **~ su'premacy** *n.* Überlegenheit der weißen Rasse; **~thorn** *n.* (*Bot.*) Weißdorn, *der;* **~throat** *n.* (*Ornith.*) **A** (*warbler*) Grasmücke, *die;* **B** (*Amer.: sparrow*) Weißkehlammerfink, *der;* **~ 'tie** *n.* **A** (*bow tie*) weiße Fliege *od.* Schleife(, *die zum Cutaway getragen wird*); **B** (*evening dress*) Frack, *der;* **is it dinner jacket or ~ tie?** soll man im Smoking oder im Frack erscheinen?; **~ 'trash** ⇒ **trash** 1 D; **~wall 'tyre** *n.* Weißwandreifen, *der;* **~wash 1** *n.* **A** [weiße] Tünche; (*fig.*) Schönfärberei, *die;* **the report is a ~wash of the Government** der Bericht versucht, die Regierung reinzuwaschen; **B** (*defeat*) Zu-null-Niederlage, *die;* **2** *v.t.* **A** [weiß] tünchen; **the report ~washes the Government** (*fig.*) der Bericht zielt darauf ab, die Regierung reinzuwaschen; **be ~washed** (*Finance*) [als Gemeinschuldner] entlastet werden; **B** (*defeat*) zu Null schlagen; **~ 'water** *n.* (*foamy*) weiß schäumendes Wasser; (*shallow*) Flachwasser, *das;* **~-water canoeing** Wildwassersport, *der;* **~ 'wedding** *n.* Hochzeit in Weiß; **have a ~ wedding** in Weiß heiraten; **~ 'whale** *n.* (*Zool.*) Weißwal, *der;* **~ 'wine** *n.* Weißwein, *der;* **~ woman** *n.* (*Anthrop.*) Weiße, *die;* **~wood** *n.* Weißholz, *das*

**Whitey** /'waɪtɪ/ *n.* (*coll. derog.*) weißes Schwein (*derb*)

**whither** /'wɪðə(r)/ (*arch./rhet.*) **1** *adv.* wohin; **~ democracy/Ulster?** (*fig. rhet.*) wohin *od.* (*geh.*) quo vadis, Demokratie/Ulster?; **the town ~ he was sent** die Stadt, in die er geschickt wurde. **2** *conj.* dorthin *od.* dahin, wohin; (*to wherever*) wohin auch; **I shall go ~ she goes** ich werde gehen, wo immer sie hingeht

**whiting** /'waɪtɪŋ/ *n., pl. same* (*Zool.*) Wittling, *der*

**whitish** /'waɪtɪʃ/ *adj.* weißlich

**Whit Monday** /wɪt 'mʌndeɪ, wɪt 'mʌndɪ/ *n.* Pfingstmontag, *der*

**Whitsun** /'wɪtsn/ *n.* Pfingsten, *das od. Pl.;* **at ~:** zu *od.* an Pfingsten; **next/last ~:** nächste/letzte Pfingsten

**Whitsunday, Whit Sunday** /wɪt'sʌndeɪ, wɪt'sʌndɪ/ *n.* Pfingstsonntag, *der*

**Whitsuntide** /'wɪtsntaɪd/ *n.* Pfingstzeit, *die*

**whittle** /'wɪtl/ **1** *v.t.* schnitzen an (+ *Dat.*); **~ a stick to a point** einen Stock anspitzen. **2** *v.i.* **~ at sth.** an etw. (*Dat.*) [herum]schnitzen

**~ a'way, ~ 'down** *v.t.* (*fig.*) **A** (*completely*) auffressen ‹Gewinn, Geldmittel usw.›; **~ away sb.'s rights/power** jmdm. nach und nach alle Rechte/alle Macht nehmen; **B** (*partly*) allmählich reduzieren ‹Anzahl, Team, Gewinn, Verlust›; verkürzen ‹Liste›

**Whit**/wɪt/**: ~ week** *n.* Pfingstwoche, *die;* **~ week'end** *n.* Pfingstwochenende, *das*

**whiz, whizz** /wɪz/ **1** *v.i.,* **-zz-** zischen; **we could hear the arrows/shells whizzing above our heads** wir hörten das Zischen der über uns hinwegfliegenden Pfeile/Granaten. **2** *n.* Zischen, *das;* **with a ~** zischend

**~ 'past, whizz 'past** *v.i.* vorbeizischen; ‹Vogel:› vorbeischießen

**'whiz[z]-kid** *n.* (*coll.*) Senkrechtstarter, *der;* **he is a financial ~:** er macht eine steile Karriere als Finanzmann; **a mathematical ~:** ein mathematisches Wunderkind (*ugs. scherzh.*)

**who** /hʊ, *stressed* hu:/ *pron.* **A** *interrog.* wer; (*coll.: whom*) wen; (*coll.: to whom*) wem; **~ are you talking about?** (*coll.*) von wem *od.* über wen sprichst du?; **~ did you give it to?** (*coll.*) wem hast du es gegeben?; **it was John — ~ else?** es war John — wer [denn] sonst?; **it was Mr ~?** es war Herr wie?; **I don't know ~'s ~ in the firm yet** ich kenne die Leute in der Firma noch nicht richtig; **he knows ~'s ~ in the publishing world** er weiß, wer in der Verlagsbranche welche Rolle spielt; **~ am I to object/argue** *etc.***?** wie könnte ich Einwände erheben/etwas dagegen sagen *usw.*?; **~ would have thought it?** (*rhet.*) wer hätte das gedacht!; **B** *rel.* der/die/das; *pl.* die; (*coll.: whom*) den/die/das; (*coll.: to whom*) dem/der/denen; **any person/he/those ~ ...:** wer ...; **they ~ ...:** diejenigen, die *od.* welche ...; **everybody ~ ...:** jeder, der ...; **I/you ~ ...:** ich, der ich/du, der du ...; **the man ~ I met last week/~ you were speaking to** der Mann, den ich letzte Woche getroffen habe/mit dem du gesprochen hast; **C** (*arch.: whoever*) wer

**WHO** *abbr.* **World Health Organization** WHO, *die*

**whoa** /wəʊ/ *int.* brr

**who'd** /hʊd, *stressed* hu:d/ **A** = **who had; B** = **who would**

**whodun[n]it** /hu:'dʌnɪt/ *n.* (*coll.*) Krimi, *der* (*ugs.*)

**whoe'er** /hu:'eə(r)/ (*poet.*), **whoever** /hu:'evə(r)/ *pron.* **A** wer [immer]; **whoever comes will be welcome** jeder, der kommt, ist willkommen; **marry/give it to whoever you like** heirate, wen/gib es, wem du willst; **B** (*no matter who*) wer ... auch; **whoever you may be** wer Sie auch sind; **whoever you saw, it was not John** wen du auch gesehen hast, es war nicht John; **C** (*coll.*) = **who ever** ⇒ **ever** E

**whole** /həʊl/ **1** *adj.* **A** ganz; **give me your ~ attention, please** ich bitte um Ihre ganze Aufmerksamkeit; **that's the ~ point [of the exercise]** das ist der ganze Zweck der Übung (*ugs.*); **the ~ lot [of them]** [sie] alle; **a ~ lot of people** eine ganze Menge Leute; ⇒ *also* **hog** 1 A; **B** (*intact*) ganz; **roast sth. ~:** etw. im Ganzen braten; **C** (*undiminished*) ganz; **three ~ hours** drei volle Stunden.
**2** *n.* **A the ~:** das Ganze; **the ~ of my money/the village/London** mein ganzes *od.* gesamtes Geld/das ganze Dorf/ganz London; **he spent the ~ of that year/of Easter abroad** er war jenes Jahr/zu Ostern die ganze Zeit im Ausland; **the ~ of Shakespeare** *or* **of Shakespeare's works** Shakespeares gesamte Werke; **until he had completed the ~ of it** bis er es ganz fertig hatte; **B** (*total of parts*) Ganze, *das;* **as a ~:** als Ganzes; **sell sth. as a ~:** etw. im Ganzen verkaufen; **on the ~:** im Großen und Ganzen; **on the ~ I am against it** alles in allem bin ich dagegen

**whole: ~ 'cloth** *n.* Tuchbahn, *die;* **[made up] out of ~ cloth** (*Amer. fig.*) von vorne bis hinten erfunden; **~food** *n.* Vollwertkost, *die;* **~hearted** /həʊl'hɑ:tɪd/ *adj.* herzlich ‹Dank, Dankbarkeit, Glückwünsche›; tief empfunden ‹Dankbarkeit, Reue›; rückhaltlos ‹Unterstützung, Hingabe, Ergebenheit›; leidenschaftlich ‹Anhänger, Verfechter usw.›; **with ~hearted devotion/dedication** mit äußerster Hingabe; **~heartedly** /həʊl'hɑ:tɪdlɪ/ *adv.* von ganzem Herzen ‹gratulieren, danken, zustimmen›; rückhaltlos ‹unterstützen›; **~ 'holiday** *n.* ganzer freier Tag; **~-length** ⇒ **full-length;** **~ 'life insurance** *n.* Todesfallversicherung, *die;* **~ meal** *n.* Vollkornmehl, *das;* **~meal** *adj.* Vollkorn-; **~ 'milk** *n.* Vollmilch, *die*

**wholeness** /'həʊlnɪs/ *n., no pl.* Ganzheit, *die;* (*completeness*) Vollständigkeit, *die*

**whole: ~ note** *n.* (*Amer. Mus.*) ganze Note; **~ 'number** *n.* (*Math.*) ganze Zahl; **~sale 1** *adj.* **A** (*Commerc.*) Großhandels-; **~sale dealer** *or* **merchant** Großhändler, *der*/

-händlerin, *die;* **~sale grocer** Lebensmittelgroßhändler, *der*/-großhändlerin, *die;* **the ~sale trade** der Großhandel; **our business is ~sale only** wir sind ein reines Großhandelsgeschäft; **these prices are ~sale** das sind Großhandelspreise; **B** (*fig.: on a large scale*) massenhaft; Massen-; **in a ~sale way** massenweise; **C** (*fig.: indiscriminate*) pauschal; **2** *adv.* **A** (*Commerc.*) en gros ‹[ein]kaufen, verkaufen›; im Großhandel ‹[ein]kaufen›; (*at wholesale price*) zum Einkaufs- *od.* Großhandelspreis; **B** (*fig.: on a large scale*) massenweise; **C** (*fig.: indiscriminately*) pauschal; **he punished them ~sale** er bestrafte sie samt und sonders; **3** *n.* (*Commerc.*) Großhandel, *der;* **4** *v.t.* (*Commerc.*) en gros *od.* als Großhändler/-händlerin verkaufen

**wholesaler** /ˈhəʊlseɪlə(r)/ *n.* (*Commerc.*) Grossist, *der*/Grossistin, *die* (*fachspr.*); Großhändler, *der*/-händlerin, *die*

**wholesome** /ˈhəʊlsəm/ *adj.* gesund; bekömmlich ‹Essen, Getränk›; erbaulich ‹Lektüre, Thema, Anblick›; positiv ‹Einfluss›

**wholesomely** /ˈhəʊlsəmlɪ/ *adv.* **~ cooked food** auf gesunde Art zubereitetes Essen

**wholesomeness** /ˈhəʊlsəmnɪs/ *n., no pl.* Bekömmlichkeit, *die;* (*fig.: of reading, subject, etc.*) Erbaulichkeit, *die*

**whole: ~-time** ⇒ **full-time**; **~ tone** *n.* (*Mus.*) Ganzton, *der;* **~ ˈwheat** *n.* Vollweizen, *der*

**who'll** /hʊl, *stressed* huːl/ ... **who will**

**wholly** /ˈhəʊllɪ/ *adv.* völlig; durch und durch ‹böse›; **a ~ bad example** ein in jeder Hinsicht schlechtes Beispiel

**ˈwholly-owned** *adj.* (*Commerc.*) **~ subsidiary** hundertprozentige Tochter

**whom** /huːm/ *pron.* **A** *interrog.* wen; *as indirect object* wem; **to ~/of ~ did you speak?** mit wem/von wem haben Sie gesprochen?; **B** *rel.* den/die/das; *pl.* die; *as indirect object* dem/der/dem; *pl.* denen; **the children, the mother of ~ ...:** die Kinder, deren Mutter ...; **five children, all of ~ are coming** fünf Kinder, die alle mitkommen; **ten candidates, only the best of ~ ...:** zehn Kandidaten, von denen nur die besten ...; **C** (*arch.: whomever*) wen/wem

**whomever** /huːmˈevə(r)/, **whomsoever** /huːmsəʊˈevə(r)/ *pron.* **A** wen [immer]; *as indirect object* wem [immer]; **B** (*no matter whom*) wen ... auch; *as indirect object* wem ... auch

**whoop** /wuːp/ **1** *v.i.* [aufgeregt] schreien; (*with joy, excitement*) juchzen (*ugs.*); jauchzen. **2** *v.t.* **~ it up** (*coll.*) die Sau rauslassen (*salopp*); (*Amer.: stir up enthusiasm*) Stimmung machen. **3** *n.* [aufgeregter] Schrei; (*of joy, excitement*) Juchzer, *der* (*ugs.*); Jauchzer, *der;* **with loud ~s** mit lautem Geschrei; **~ of joy** Freudenschrei, *der*

**whoopee** **1** /wʊˈpiː/ *int.* juhu. **2** /ˈwʊpiː/ *n.* **make ~** (*coll.*) die Sau rauslassen (*ugs.*)

**whooping**/ˈhuːpɪŋ/**: ~ cough** *n.* ▶ **1232** (*Med.*) Keuchhusten, *der;* **~ swan** *n.* (*Ornith.*) Singschwan, *der*

**whoops** /wʊps/ *int.* hoppla

**whoosh** /wʊʃ/ **1** *v.i.* brausen; ‹Rakete, Geschoss:› zischen; **a train ~ed past** ein Zug brauste vorbei. **2** *n.* Brausen, *das;* (*of rocket, projectile*) Zischen, *das;* **with a [loud] ~:** [laut] brausend/zischend

**whop** /wɒp/ *v.t.*, **-pp-** (*coll.*) vermöbeln (*salopp*); (*fig.: defeat*) bügeln (*salopp*)

**whopper** /ˈwɒpə(r)/ *n.* (*coll.*) **A** Riese, *der;* **a ~ of a marrow/fish** ein Riesending von einem Kürbis/Fisch (*ugs.*); **B** (*lie*) faustdicke Lüge; **tell a ~:** faustdick lügen

**whopping** /ˈwɒpɪŋ/ (*coll.*) **1** *adj.* riesig; Riesen- (*ugs.*); gepfeffert (*ugs.*) ‹Rechnung›; faustdick ‹Lüge›. **2** *adv.* **~ big** *or* **great** ⇒ **1**

**whore** /hɔː(r)/ (*derog.*) **1** *n.* **A** (*prostitute*) Hure, *die;* **B** (*loose woman*) Flittchen, *das.* **2** *v.i.* **~ [around]** [herum]huren

**ˈwhorehouse** *n.* (*derog.*) Hurenhaus, *das* (*abwertend*)

**whorl** /wɔːl/ *n.* **A** (*Bot.*) Wirtel, *der;* Quirl, *der;* **B** (*circle in fingerprint*) Wirbel, *der;* **C** (*turn of spiral*) Windung, *die*

**whortleberry** /ˈwɜːtlbərɪ/ ⇒ **bilberry**

**who's** /huːz/ **A** = **who is**; **B** = **who has**

**whose** /huːz/ *pron.* **A** *interrog.* wessen; **B** *rel.* dessen/deren/dessen; *pl.* deren; **the people ~ house this is** die Leute, denen dieses Haus gehört

**whosesoever** /huːzsəʊˈevə(r)/, **whosever** /huːzˈevə(r)/ *pron.* wessen ... auch; **~ it is, ...:** wem er/sie/es auch gehört, ...

**whosoe'er** /huːsəʊˈeə(r)/ (*poet.*), **whosoever** /huːsəʊˈevə(r)/ wer auch immer

**Who's Who** /huːz ˈhuː/ *n.* biografisches Lexikon; Who's who, *das*

**who've** /hʊv, *stressed* huːv/ (*coll.*) ... **who have**

**why** /waɪ/ **1** *adv.* **A** (*for what reason*) warum; (*for what purpose*) wozu; **~ is that?** warum das?; **and this/that is ~ I believe ...:** und darum glaube ich ...; **~ not buy it, if you like it?** kauf es dir doch, wenn es dir gefällt; **~ do we need another car?** wozu brauchen wir noch ein Auto?; **B** (*on account of which*) **the reason ~ he did it** der Grund, aus dem *od.* warum er es tat; **I can see no reason ~ not** ich wüsste nicht, warum nicht. **2** *int.* **~, certainly/of course!** aber sicher!; **~, if it isn't Jack!** na, das ist doch Jack!; aber das ist ja Jack!; **What should I do? — W~, pay up** Was soll ich machen? — Na *od.* Nun, zahlen!; **~, yes, I think so** jaja, ich glaube schon. **3** *n.* **the ~s and wherefores** das Warum und Weshalb

**WI** *abbr.* **A West Indies; B** (*Brit.*) **Women's Institute**

**wick** /wɪk/ *n.* Docht, *der;* **get on sb.'s ~** (*fig. sl.*) jmdm. auf den Keks gehen (*salopp*)

**wicked** /ˈwɪkɪd/ **1** *adj.* **A** (*evil*) böse; schlecht ‹Charakter, Person, Welt›; niederträchtig ‹Gedanken, Plan, Verhalten›; schändlich ‹Gesetz, Buch›; **the ~ villain** der Schurke; der Bösewicht (*veralt.*); **it was ~ of you to torment the poor cat** es war gemein von dir, die arme Katze zu quälen; **torture is ~:** die Folter ist etwas Böses; **B** (*vicious*) boshaft ‹Zunge›; übel ‹Schlag, Wetter, Wind, Frost, Geruch›; **have a ~ temper** furchtbar jähzornig sein; **C** (*coll.: scandalous*) himmelschreiend; sündhaft (*ugs.*) ‹Preis›; **it's ~ how he's been treated** wie man ihn behandelt hat, das schreit zum Himmel; **it's a ~ shame** es ist eine wahre Schande; **D** (*mischievous*) schalkhaft (*geh.*); **a ~ little fellow** ein kleiner Schlingel (*scherzh.*); **there was a ~ gleam in his eye** ihm sah der Schalk aus den Augen; **suddenly a ~ idea came to him** plötzlich fiel ihm etwas ganz Tückisches ein.
**2** *n. pl.* **the ~:** die Bösen

**wickedly** /ˈwɪkɪdlɪ/ *adv.* **A** (*evilly*) niederträchtig; *as sentence-modifier* niederträchtigerweise; **~ acquired gains** auf niederträchtige Weise erzielte Gewinne; **B** (*viciously*) fürchterlich ‹kalt, schmerzend›; **~ accurate** ätzend ‹Satire, Kritik, Karikatur›; **C** (*coll.: scandalously*) himmelschreiend; sündhaft (*ugs.*) ‹teuer›; **D** (*mischievously*) schalkhaft; **a ~ playful look** ein verschmitzter Blick

**wickedness** /ˈwɪkɪdnɪs/ *n.* **A** *no pl.* ⇒ **wicked** A: Bosheit, *die;* Schlechtigkeit, *die;* Niederträchtigkeit, *die;* Schändlichkeit, *die;* **B** (*evil act*) Niederträchtigkeit, *die;* **the greatest ~ that anyone can commit** die schlimmste Bosheit, die ein Mensch begehen kann; **C** *no pl.* (*viciousness*) Boshaftigkeit, *die;* **D** *no pl.* (*coll.: scandalousness*) Schändlichkeit, *die;* **the ~ of this waste** so eine himmelschreiende Verschwendung; **the ~ of the prices** die sündhaft hohen Preise; **E** *no pl.* (*mischievousness*) Schalkhaftigkeit, *die;* **the ~ in her sense of humour** das Schalkhafte an ihrer Art Humor

**wicker** /ˈwɪkə(r)/ *n.* Korbgeflecht, *das; attrib.* Korb‹waren, -möbel, -stuhl›; geflochten ‹Korb, Matte›; **~ fence** Flechtzaun, *der*

**ˈwickerwork** *n.* **A** (*material*) Korbgeflecht, *das;* **B** (*articles*) Korbwaren

**wicket** /ˈwɪkɪt/ *n.* **A** (*Cricket*) (*stumps*) Tor, *das;* Wicket, *das;* (*part of innings*) *Spielabschnitt, der mit dem Ausscheiden eines Schlagmannes endet;* (*central area of pitch*) Wurfbahn, *die;* **another ~ has fallen** *or* **is down** noch ein Schlagmann ist aus; **at the ~:** [als Schlagmann] auf dem Spielfeld; **keep ~:** als Torwächter spielen; **lose one's ~** ‹Schlagmann:› ausscheiden; **they lost four ~s** vier Schlagmänner ihrer Mannschaft sind ausgeschieden; **take a ~:** einen Schlagmann zum Ausscheiden bringen; **third** *etc.* **~:** *Spielabschnitt zwischen zweitem und drittem usw. Schlagmannwechsel;* **win by two ~s** mit acht ausgeschiedenen Schlagmännern gewinnen; ⇒ *also* **sticky wicket**; **B** (*gate*) Tor, *das;* **C** (*Amer.: window-like opening*) Fenster, *das;* **D** (*Amer.: croquet hoop*) Tor, *das*

**wicket: ~ gate** *n.* Tor, *das;* **~keeper** *n.* (*Cricket*) Torwächter, *der*/-wächterin, *die;* Wicketkeeper, *der*

**widdle** /ˈwɪdl/ (*coll./child lang.*) ⇒ **pee**

**wide** /waɪd/ **1** *adj.* **A** ▶ **1284** (*broad*) breit; groß ‹Unterschied, Abstand, Winkel, Loch›; weit ‹Kleidung›; **allow** *or* **leave a ~ margin** (*fig.*) viel Spielraum lassen; **three feet ~:** drei Fuß breit; **B** (*extensive*) weit; umfassend ‹Lektüre, Wissen, Kenntnisse›; weit reichend ‹Einfluss›; vielseitig ‹Interessen›; groß ‹Vielfalt, Bekanntheit, Berühmtheit›; reichhaltig ‹Auswahl, Sortiment›; breit ‹Publizität›; weit verzweigt ‹Netz›; **have ~ appeal** weite Kreise ansprechen; **it has now achieved ~ acceptance** es wird jetzt weithin akzeptiert; **a species of ~ distribution** eine weitverbreitete Art; **the ~ world** die weite Welt; **I'll search the ~ world over** ich werde auf der ganzen weiten Welt suchen; **C** (*liberal*) großzügig; **D** (*fully open*) weit geöffnet; **E** (*off target*) **be ~ of sth.** etw. verfehlen; **be ~ of the mark** (*fig.*) ‹Annahme, Bemerkung:› nicht zutreffen; **you're ~ of the mark** (*fig.*) du liegst falsch (*ugs.*); ⇒ *also* **berth** 1 A; **F** (*Brit. coll.*) **~ boy** gerissener Kerl (*ugs.*).
**2** *adv.* **A** (*fully*) weit; **open ~!** ganz [weit] aufmachen!; **~ awake** hellwach; (*fig. coll.*) gewitzt; **I'm ~ awake to your tricks** ich durchschaue deine Tricks; ⇒ *also* **wide open**; **B** (*off target*) **shoot ~:** danebenschießen; **fall ~ of the target, go ~:** das Ziel verfehlen; **aim ~/~ of sth.** daneben/neben etw. (*Akk.*) zielen; **C** (*~ly*) weit; ⇒ *also* **far** 1 D.
**3** *n.* **A** (*Cricket*) Weitball, *der;* **B** **dead to the ~:** fix und fertig (*ugs.*)

**-wide** *in comb.* **city-/county-~:** in der ganzen Stadt/Grafschaft *nachgestellt;* **Europe-~:** europaweit; ⇒ *also* **countrywide**; **worldwide** *etc.*

**wide: ~-angle ˈlens** *n.* (*Photog.*) Weitwinkelobjektiv, *das;* **~-eyed** *adj.* (*surprised*) mit großen Augen *nachgestellt;* **gaze with ~-eyed innocence** mit großen, unschuldigen [Kinder]augen gucken

**widely** /ˈwaɪdlɪ/ *adv.* **A** (*over a wide area*) weit ‹verbreitet, gestreut›; locker, in großen Abständen ‹verteilt›; **a ~ distributed species** eine weit verbreitete Art; **he has travelled ~ in Europe** er ist in Europa viel gereist; **advertise a product ~:** für ein Produkt in großem Stil werben; **a ~ travelled man** ein weit gereister Mann; **a ~ read man** ein [sehr] belesener Mann; **B** (*by many people*) weithin ‹bekannt, akzeptiert›; **a ~ held view** eine weit verbreitete Ansicht; **it is ~ rumoured that ...:** allgemein wird gemunkelt (*ugs.*), dass ...; **it is not ~ understood why ...:** es wird vielfach nicht verstanden *od.* viele verstehen nicht, warum ...; **C** (*in a wide sense*) im weiten Sinne ‹gebraucht›; weit ‹interpretiert›; **D** (*greatly*) stark, erheblich ‹sich unterscheiden›; sehr ‹verschieden, unterschiedlich›

**widen** /ˈwaɪdn/ **1** *v.t.* verbreitern; (*fig.*) erweitern; vergrößern ‹Unterschied, Gegensatz›; **let's ~ our campaign to include young people** wir wollen unsere Kampagne auch auf die jungen Leute ausdehnen. **2** *v.i.* sich verbreitern; breiter werden; (*fig.*) sich erweitern; ‹Interessen:› vielfältiger werden; ‹Unterschied, Gegensatz:› größer werden; **the valley ~s into a plain** das Tal erweitert sich zu einer Ebene

**~ ˈout** *v.i.* sich verbreitern; breiter werden; **~ out into sth.** sich zu etw. erweitern

**wide: ~-open** *attrib. adj.*, **~ ˈopen** *pred. adj.* weit aufstehend *od.* geöffnet ‹Fenster, Tür›;

weit aufgerissen ‹Mund, Augen›; weit ‹Landschaft, Fläche›; **the ~-open spaces of North America** die Weite der nordamerikanischen Landschaft; **be ~ open** ‹Fenster, Tür:› weit offen stehen; ‹Mund, Augen:› weit aufgerissen sein; **be ~ open to attack/criticism/immoral influences** Angriffen/der Kritik/moralisch verderblichen Einflüssen ausgesetzt sein; **be ~ open to exploitation** der Ausbeutung schutzlos preisgegeben sein; **lay** *or* **leave oneself/sb. ~ open to sth.** sich/jmdn. einer Sache (*Dat.*) schutzlos preisgeben; **the contest is still ~ open** der Wettbewerb *od.* der Ausgang des Wettbewerbs ist noch völlig offen; **a ~-open town** (*Amer.*) eine Stadt, in der jeder macht, was er will; **~-ranging** /'waɪdreɪndʒɪŋ/ *adj.* weit gehend ‹Maßnahme, Veränderung›; weit reichend ‹Auswirkungen›; ausführlich ‹Diskussion, Gespräch›; universal ‹Geist›; **~ 'screen** *n.* (*Cinemat.*) Breitwand, *die;* **~screen television, ~screen TV** *ns.* Breitwandfernsehen, *das;* **~spread** *adj.* weit verbreitet ‹Art, Ansicht›; groß ‹Nachfrage, Beliebtheit›; von vielen geteilt ‹Sympathie›; **become ~spread** sich [weit] ausbreiten; **there was a ~spread demand for reform** Reformen wurden allgemein *od.* allerseits gefordert

**widgeon** /'wɪdʒən/ *n.* (*Ornith.*) Pfeifente, *die*

**widow** /'wɪdəʊ/ ❶ *n.* A Witwe, *die;* **be left/made a ~:** zur Witwe werden; **golf ~** (*joc.*) Golfwitwe, *die;* ⇒ *also* **black widow; grass widow;** B (*Cards*) zusätzliches Blatt; C (*Printing*) Hurenkind, *das.* ❷ *v.t.* zur Witwe machen ‹Frau›; zum Witwer machen ‹Mann›; **be ~ed** zur Witwe/zum Witwer werden (**by** durch)

**widowed** /'wɪdəʊd/ *adj.* verwitwet

**widower** /'wɪdəʊə(r)/ *n.* Witwer, *der*

**widowhood** /'wɪdəʊhʊd/ *n.* Witwenschaft, *die;* **[the state of] ~:** der Witwenstand; **during her ~:** als sie Witwe war

**widow's: ~ 'peak** *n. in der Stirnmitte spitz zulaufender Haaransatz;* **~ 'pension** *n.* Witwenrente, *die;* **~ 'weeds** ⇒ **weeds**

**width** /wɪdθ/ *n.* A ▶ **1284** (*measurement*) Breite, *die;* (*of garment*) Weite, *die;* **what is the ~ of ...?** wie breit/weit ist ...?; **be half a metre in ~:** einen halben Meter breit/weit sein; B (*large scope*) großer Umfang; (*of definition*) Weite, *die;* (*of interests*) Vielseitigkeit, *die;* C (*piece of material*) Bahn, *die*

**widthways** /'wɪdθweɪz/, **widthwise** /'wɪdθwaɪz/ *adv.* in der Breite; **insert the card ~ into the machine** die Karte quer in den Automaten stecken

**wield** /wiːld/ *v.t.* (*literary*) führen (*geh.*); (*fig.*) ausüben ‹Macht, Einfluss usw.›; **~ a stick/sword** einen Stock/ein Schwert schwingen

**wiener** /'viːnə(r)/ *n.* (*Amer.*) Würstchen, *das*

**wife** /waɪf/ *n., pl.* **wives** /waɪvz/ Frau, *die;* **give my regards to your** *or* (*coll.*) **the ~:** grüßen Sie Ihre Frau *od.* (*geh.*) Gattin von mir; **make sb. one's ~:** jmdn. zur Frau nehmen; **lawful wedded ~** (*Eccl.*) rechtmäßig angetraute Frau; **old wives' tale** Ammenmärchen, *das*

**wife-swapping** /'waɪfswɒpɪŋ/ *n.* (*coll.*) Partnertausch, *der*

**wig** /wɪɡ/ *n.* Perücke, *die*

**wigging** /'wɪɡɪŋ/ *n.* Rüffel, *der* (*ugs.*)

**wiggle** /'wɪɡl/ (*coll.*) ❶ *v.t.* hin und her bewegen; **~ one's ears/bottom** mit den Ohren/dem Hintern wackeln (*ugs.*). ❷ *v.i.* wackeln; (*move*) sich schlängeln; **make one's ears ~:** mit den Ohren wackeln; **~ into sth.** sich in etw. (*Akk.*) zwängen; **~ out of sth.** sich aus etw. winden/(*fig.*) herauswinden. ❸ *n.* Wackeln, *das;* **get a ~ on** (*Amer. coll.*) sich ranhalten (*ugs.*)

**wiggly** /'wɪɡlɪ/ *adj.* schlangenlinienförmig ‹Naht, Saum›; Schlangenlinien‹muster, -form›; **~ line** Schlangenlinie, *die*

**wigwam** /'wɪɡwæm/ *n.* Wigwam, *der*

**wild** /waɪld/ ❶ *adj.* A (*undomesticated*) wild lebend ‹Tier›; (*uncultivated*) wild wachsend ‹Pflanze›; **an animal in its ~ state** ein Tier in freier Wildbahn *od.* in Freiheit; **grow ~:** wild wachsen; **~ beast** wildes Tier; B (*rough*) unzivilisiert; (*bleak*) wild ‹Landschaft, Gegend›; C (*unrestrained*) wild; ungezügelt; wild, wüst ‹Bursche, Unordnung, Durcheinander›; wütend ‹Mob›; **he was a little ~:** er führte ein etwas ungestümes Leben; **~ and woolly** (*coll.*) wüst ‹Aussehen, Kerl›; verrückt ‹Ideen›; **run ~** ‹Pferd, Hund:› frei herumlaufen; ‹Kind:› herumtoben; ‹Pflanzen:› wuchern; (*derog.*) ‹Hund:› herumstreunen; **let one's imagination run ~:** seiner Fantasie freien Lauf lassen; D (*stormy*) stürmisch; tobend ‹Wellen›; E (*excited*) rasend ‹Wut, Zorn, Eifersucht, Beifall›; unbändig ‹Freude, Wut, Zorn, Schmerz›; wild ‹Erregung, Zorn, Geschrei›; erregt ‹Diskussion›; panisch ‹Angst›; irr ‹Blick›; **be/become ~ [with sth.]** [vor etw. (*Dat.*)] außer sich (*Dat.*) sein/außer sich (*Akk.*) geraten; **send** *or* **drive sb. ~:** jmdn. rasend vor Erregung machen; F (*coll.: very keen*) **be ~ about sb./sth.** wild auf jmdn./etw. sein; **be ~ to do sth.** wild darauf sein, etw. zu tun; **I'm not ~ about it** ich bin nicht wild darauf (*ugs.*); G (*coll.: angry*) wütend; **be ~ with** *or* **at sb.** eine Wut auf jmdn. haben; **make** *or* **drive sb. ~:** jmdn. in Rage bringen (*ugs.*); **I was ~ when I heard ...:** ich sah rot (*ugs.*) *od.* wurde wild (*ugs.*), als ich hörte, ...; H (*reckless*) ungezielt ‹Schuss, Schlag›; unbedacht ‹Verhalten, Versprechen, Gerede›; aus der Luft gegriffen ‹Anschuldigungen, Behauptungen›; abwegig ‹Geschichte›; maßlos ‹Übertreibung›; irrwitzig ‹Plan, Idee, Versuch, Hoffnung›; **he made a ~ guess** er hat aufs Geratewohl *od.* (*ugs.*) ins Blaue hinein geschätzt; ⇒ *also* **dream 1 C.**
❷ *n.* **the ~[s]** die Wildnis; **see an animal in the ~:** ein Tier in freier Wildbahn sehen; **in the ~s** (*coll.*) in der Pampa (*ugs.*); **[out] in the ~s of Yorkshire** (*coll.*) im tiefsten Yorkshire (*ugs.*); **the call of the ~:** der Ruf der Wildnis.
❸ *adv.* wild; **shoot ~** (*randomly*) wild in die Gegend ballern (*ugs.*)

**wild: ~ 'boar** *n.* (*Zool.*) Wildschwein, *das;* **~ card** *n.* A (*Cards*) wilde Karte; B (*Tennis*) Wildcard (*ugs.*); **~ 'cat** *n.* (*Zool.*) Wildkatze, *die;* **~cat** *attrib. adj.* fragwürdig; **~cat strike** wilder Streik; **~cat well** Aufschlussbohrung, *die;* Wildcatbohrung, *die*

**wilderness** /'wɪldənɪs/ *n.* Wildnis, *die;* (*desert*) Wüste, *die;* **cry in the ~** (*fig.*) tauben Ohren predigen; **a voice [crying] in the ~** (*fig.*) ein Rufer in der Wüste; **be in the ~** (*Polit.*) alle Bedeutung verloren haben

**wild: ~-eyed** *adj.* mit irrem Blick *nachgestellt;* **~fire** *n.* (*Mil. Hist.*) griechisches Feuer; ⇒ *also* **spread 2 A; ~fowl** *n., pl. same* Federwild, *das;* (*Cookery*) Wildgeflügel, *das;* **~ 'goose chase** *n.* (*fig.: hopeless quest*) aussichtslose Suche; **send sb. on a ~ goose chase** jmdn. einem Phantom nachjagen lassen; **~ 'horse** *n.* Wildpferd, *das;* **~ horses would not drag it from me** (*fig.*) eher beiße ich mir die Zunge ab[, als dass ich es erzähle]; **~ horses would not make me leave here** keine zehn Pferde kriegen mich von hier weg (*ugs.*); **~life** *n., no pl., no indef. art.* die Tier- und Pflanzenwelt; die Natur; *attrib.* **~life park/reserve/sanctuary** Naturpark, *der*/-reservat, *das*/-schutzgebiet, *das*

**wildly** /'waɪldlɪ/ *adv.* A (*unrestrainedly*) wild; **run ~ all over the house** ‹Kinder:› wie wild im ganzen Haus herumtoben; B (*stormily*) wild; **the wind blew ~:** der Wind blies heftig; C (*excitedly*) rasend ‹eifersüchtig›; unbändig ‹verliebt, sich freuen, sich verlieben›; wild ‹schreien, applaudieren›; erregt ‹diskutieren›; **I'm not ~ interested in it** (*iron.*) ich interessiere mich nicht übermäßig dafür; **be ~ excited about sth.** über etw. (*Akk.*) ganz aus dem Häuschen sein (*ugs.*); **he looked ~ about him** er blickte irr um sich; D (*recklessly*) aufs Geratewohl; maßlos ‹übertreiben›; wirr ‹daherreden, denken›; **hit out ~:** [wie] wild um sich schlagen; **~ inaccurate** völlig ungenau

**'wild man** *n.* A (*Anthrop.*) Wilde, *der;* B (*Polit.*) Scharfmacher, *der*

**wildness** /'waɪldnɪs/ *n., no pl.* A (*bleakness*) Wildheit, *die;* B (*lack of restraint*) Wildheit, *die;* **I was frightened by the ~ of the mob** der wütende Mob machte mir Angst; **after the ~ of his youth** nach seiner wilden *od.* stürmischen Jugend; C (*storminess*) **the ~ of the weather/sea** das stürmische Wetter/die stürmische See; **the ~ of the waves/storm** die Gewalt der Wellen/des Sturms; D (*excitement*) **the ~ of her joy** die Unbändigkeit, mit der sie sich freute; **the ~ of her jealousy** ihre rasende Eifersucht; **the ~ of their cheers/applause** die Begeisterung, mit der sie jubelten/applaudierten; E (*of blow, shot*) Ungezieltheit, *die;* (*of promise, words*) Unbedachtheit, *die;* (*of scheme, attempt, idea, hope, quest*) Irrwitzigkeit, *die;* F (*distractedness*) **the ~ of his look/eyes** sein irrer Blick; **there was a dangerous ~ in his eyes** seine Augen hatten etwas gefährlich Irres

**wild: ~ 'oat** ⇒ **oat B; ~ 'rice** *n.* (*Bot.*) Wasserreis, *der;* **~ 'silk** *n.* Wildseide, *die;* **~ 'thyme** ⇒ **thyme; W~ 'West** *pr. n.* Wilder Westen

**wile** /waɪl/ *n.* List, *die;* Schlich, *der*

**wilful** /'wɪlfl/ *adj.* A (*deliberate*) vorsätzlich; bewusst ‹Täuschung›; B (*obstinate*) starrsinnig

**wilfully** /'wɪlfəlɪ/ *adv.* A (*deliberately*) vorsätzlich; bewusst ‹täuschen›; B (*obstinately*) starrsinnig

**wilfulness** /'wɪlflnɪs/ *n., no pl.* A (*deliberateness*) Vorsätzlichkeit, *die;* B (*obstinacy*) Starrsinnigkeit, *die;* **out of ~:** aus Starrsinn

**wiliness** /'waɪlɪnɪs/ *n., no pl.* ⇒ **wily**: Gewieftheit, *die;* Raffiniertheit, *die;* **the ~ of a fox** die Schläue eines Fuchses

**will**[1] /wɪl/ ❶ *v.t., only in pres.* **~,** *neg.* (*coll.*) **won't** /wəʊnt/, *past* **would** /wʊd/, *neg.* (*coll.*) **wouldn't** /'wʊdnt/ A (*consent to*) wollen; **They won't help me. W~/Would you?** Sie wollen mir nicht helfen. Bist du bereit?; **you ~ help her, won't you?** du hilfst ihr doch *od.* du wirst ihr doch helfen, nicht wahr?; **the car won't start** das Auto will nicht anspringen *od.* springt nicht an; **if you ~:** wenn Sie wollen; (*in request*) bitte; **~/would you pass the salt, please?** gibst du bitte mal das Salz rüber?/würdest du bitte mal das Salz rübergeben?; **~/would you come in?** kommen Sie doch herein; **now just listen, ~ you!** jetzt hör/hört gefälligst zu!; **~ you be quiet!** willst du/wollt ihr wohl ruhig sein!; **well, if you '~ go rock climbing, ...:** bitte, wenn du unbedingt klettern gehen musst, ...; B (*be accustomed to*) pflegen; **the car ~ occasionally break down** das Auto hat ab und zu mal eine Panne; **he ~ sit there hour after hour** er pflegt dort stundenlang zu sitzen; (*emphatic*) **children '~ make a noise** Kinder machen [eben] Lärm; **..., as young people '~:** ..., wie alle jungen Leute [es tun]; **he '~ insist on doing it** er besteht unbedingt darauf, es zu tun; **it 'would have to rain** natürlich musste es regnen; C (*wish*) wollen; **~ you have some more cake?** möchtest *od.* willst du noch etwas Kuchen?; **it shall be as you ~:** ganz wie Sie wünschen (*geh.*) *od.* wollen; **do as/what you ~:** mach, was du willst; **call it what [ever] you ~:** nenn es, wie du willst; **would to God that ...:** wollte Gott, dass ...; D (*be able to*) **the box ~ hold 5 lb. of tea** in die Kiste gehen 5 Pfund Tee; **the theatre ~ seat 800** das Theater hat 800 Sitzplätze.
❷ *v. aux., forms as* **1** A *expr. simple future* werden; **this time tomorrow he ~ be in Oxford** morgen um diese Zeit ist er in Oxford; **tomorrow he ~ have been here a month** morgen ist er einen Monat hier; **one more cherry, and I ~ have eaten a pound** noch eine Kirsche und ich habe ein Pfund gegessen; **if today is Monday, tomorrow ~ be Tuesday** wenn heute Montag ist, ist morgen Dienstag; B *expr. intention* **I promise I won't do it again** ich verspreche, ich machs nicht noch mal; **You won't do that, ~ you? — Oh yes, I ~!** Du machst es doch nicht, oder? — Doch[, ich machs]!; **~ do** (*coll.*) wird gemacht; mach ich (*ugs.*); C *in conditional clause* **if he tried, he would succeed** wenn er es versuchen würde, würde er es erreichen; **he would**

**like/would have liked to see her** er würde sie gerne sehen/er hätte sie gerne gesehen; Ⓓ (*request*) **∼ you please tidy up** würdest du bitte aufräumen?

**will²** ❶ *n.* Ⓐ (*faculty*) Wille, *der;* **freedom of the ∼:** Willensfreiheit, *die;* **have a ∼ of one's own** [s]einen eigenen Willen haben; **an iron ∼, a ∼ of iron** ein eiserner Wille; **strength of ∼:** Willensstärke, *die;* Ⓑ (*Law: testament*) Testament, *das;* **under his father's ∼:** aufgrund des Testaments seines Vaters; ⇒ *also* **remember** D; Ⓒ (*desire*) **at ∼:** nach Belieben; **∼ to live** Lebenswille, *der;* **you must have the ∼ to win** du musst gewinnen wollen; **∼ to** *or* **for peace** Friedenswille, *der;* Wille zum Frieden; **he has the power to do it, but lacks the ∼:** er könnte es zwar, aber er will es nicht; **against one's/sb.'s ∼:** gegen seinen/jmds. Willen; **of one's own [free] ∼:** aus freien Stücken; **clash of ∼s** ≈ Kollision der Interessen; **do sth. with a ∼:** etw. mit großem Eifer *od.* Elan tun; **where there's a ∼ there's a way** (*prov.*) wo ein Wille ist, ist auch ein Weg; **Thy ∼ be done** (*Bibl.*) Dein Wille geschehe; ⇒ *also* **free will**; Ⓓ (*disposition*) **with the best ∼ in the world** bei allem Wohlwollen; *in neg. clause* beim besten Willen; ⇒ *also* **good will**; **ill will**.

❷ *v.t.* Ⓐ (*intend*) wollen; **God has ∼ed it so** Gott hat es so gewollt; Ⓑ (*compel by ∼*) durch Willenskraft erzwingen; **∼ oneself to do sth.** sich zwingen, etw. zu tun; **∼ sb. to do sth.** ‹Hypnotiseur, Therapeut:› jmdm. suggerieren, etw. zu tun; **∼ sb. to win** jmds. Sieg mit aller Kraft herbeiwünschen.

❸ *v.i.* wollen; **if God so ∼s, God ∼ing** so Gott will

**-willed** /wɪld/ *adj. in comb.* **strong-/weak-∼:** willensstark/-schwach; **be iron-∼:** einen eisernen Willen haben

**willful** *etc.* (*Amer.*) ⇒ **wilful** *etc.*

**William** /ˈwɪljəm/ *pr. n.* (*Hist., as name of ruler etc.*) Wilhelm (*der*)

**willies** /ˈwɪlɪz/ *n. pl.* (*coll.*) **sb. gets the ∼:** jmdm. wird ganz anders (*ugs.*); **it gives me the ∼:** dabei wird mir ganz anders (*ugs.*)

**willing** /ˈwɪlɪŋ/ ❶ *adj.* Ⓐ (*ready*) willig; **ready and ∼:** bereit; **be ∼ to do sth.** bereit sein, etw. zu tun; **I'm ∼ to believe you're right** ich will gerne glauben, dass du Recht hast; **she'd be more ∼ to do it/to help if ...:** sie wäre eher dazu bereit/eher bereit zu helfen, wenn ...; **he was ∼ to be converted** er ließ sich bereitwillig bekehren; **if my daughter is ∼, then you may marry her** wenn meine Tochter es will, dürfen Sie sie heiraten; Ⓑ *attrib.* (*readily offered*) willig; **she gave ∼ assistance/help** sie half bereitwillig; **lend a ∼ hand** bereitwillig helfen.

❷ *n.* **show ∼:** guten Willen zeigen

**willingly** /ˈwɪlɪŋlɪ/ *adv.* Ⓐ (*with pleasure*) gern[e]; **their ∼ offered services** ihre bereitwillig angebotenen Dienste; Ⓑ (*voluntarily*) freiwillig; **they did not come ∼:** sie kamen nur widerstrebend

**willingness** /ˈwɪlɪŋnɪs/ *n., no pl.* Bereitschaft, *die;* **eager ∼:** Beflissenheit, *die;* **he always shows a ∼ to help** er ist immer bereit zu helfen

**will-o'-the-wisp** /wɪləðəˈwɪsp/ *n.* Ⓐ Irrlicht, *das;* Ⓑ (*fig.*) Schimäre, *die*

**willow** /ˈwɪləʊ/ *n.* Weide, *die*

**willow: ∼herb** *n.* (*Bot.*) Weidenröschen, *das;* **∼ pattern** *n.* Weidenmuster, *das;* **∼ warbler** *n.* (*Ornith.*) Laubsänger, *der*

**willowy** /ˈwɪləʊɪ/ *adj.* gertenschlank

**ˈwill power** *n.* Willenskraft, *die;* **her ∼ has cracked** ihr Wille ist gebrochen

**willy** /ˈwɪlɪ/ *n.* (*coll./child lang.*) Pimmel, *der* (*salopp, fam.*)

**willy-nilly** /wɪlɪˈnɪlɪ/ *adv.* wohl oder übel ‹etw. tun müssen›; **it will happen ∼:** es wird so oder so passieren

**wilt** /wɪlt/ ❶ *v.i.* Ⓐ (*Bot.: wither*) welk werden; welken; Ⓑ (*fig.: lose vigour*) ‹Person:› schlapp werden, (*ugs.*) abschlaffen; ‹Interesse, Begeisterung:› abflauen; ‹Hoffnung, Energie, Kraft› dahinschwinden. ❷ *v.t.* (*Bot.*) welken lassen; **the drought has ∼ed the plants** durch die Trockenheit sind die Pflanzen welk geworden

**Wilton** /ˈwɪltən/ *n.* Wiltonteppich, *der*

**wily** /ˈwaɪlɪ/ *adj.* listig; gewieft ‹Person›; raffiniert ‹Trick, Argumentation, Plan usw.›

**wimp** /wɪmp/ *n.* (*coll. derog.*) Schlappschwanz, *der* (*ugs.*)

**wimpish** /ˈwɪmpɪʃ/ *adj.* (*coll. derog.*) lahm (*ugs. abwertend*)

**win** /wɪn/ ❶ *v.t.*, **-nn-, won** /wʌn/ Ⓐ gewinnen; bekommen ‹Stipendium, Auftrag, Vertrag, Recht›; ernten ‹Beifall, Dank›; **∼ the long jump** im Weitsprung gewinnen; **∼ an argument/debate** aus einem Streit/einer Debatte als Sieger hervorgehen; **∼ promotion** befördert werden; **∼ sb. sth.** jmdm. etw. einbringen; **∼ sb. sb.'s friendship** jmdm. jmds. Freundschaft gewinnen; **her sad story won his sympathy** ihre traurige Geschichte fand sein Mitgefühl; **∼ a reputation [for oneself]** sich (*Dat.*) einen Ruf erwerben *od.* einen Namen machen; **∼ sth. from** *or* **off sb.** jmdm. etw. abnehmen; **you can't ∼ them all** (*coll.*), **you ∼ some, you lose some** (*coll.*) man kann nicht immer Glück haben; ⇒ *also* **spur** 1 A; **toss** 3 A; Ⓑ (*coll.: steal*) organisieren (*ugs.*); Ⓒ **∼ one's way to the top** (*fig.*) sich an die Spitze hocharbeiten; **∼ one's way to a scholarship** sich (*Dat.*) ein Stipendium verdienen; **∼ oneself a place in the history books** sich (*Dat.*) einen Platz in den Geschichtsbüchern sichern; **∼ one's way into sb.'s heart/affections** jmds. Herz/Zuneigung gewinnen; Ⓓ (*Mining*) gewinnen.

❷ *v.i.*, **-nn-, won** Ⓐ gewinnen; (*in battle*) siegen; **you ∼** (*have defeated me*) du hast gewonnen (*ugs.*); **those who ∼:** die Gewinner/Sieger; **∼ or lose** wie es auch ausgeht/ausgehen würde; **you can't ∼** (*lit. or fig.*) (*coll.*) da hat man keine Chance (*ugs.*); (*you can't satisfy everyone*) man kann es nicht allen recht machen; ⇒ *also* **canter** 1; **hand** 1 G; **head** 1 A; Ⓑ **∼ clear/free** sich befreien.

❸ *n.* Sieg, *der;* **have a ∼:** gewinnen

**∼ ˈback** *v.t.* zurückgewinnen

**∼ ˈout** *v.i.* **∼ out [over sb./sth.]** sich [gegen jmdn./etw.] durchsetzen

**∼ ˈover, ∼ ˈround** *v.t.* bekehren; (*to one's side*) auf seine Seite bringen; (*convince*) überzeugen; **∼ sb. over** *or* **round to a plan/to a faith/to one's point of view** jmdn. für einen Plan gewinnen/zu einem Glauben bekehren/zu seiner Ansicht bekehren *od.* von seiner Ansicht überzeugen

**∼ ˈthrough** *v.i.* Erfolg haben; **∼ through to the next round** die nächste Runde erreichen

**wince** /wɪns/ ❶ *v.i.* zusammenzucken (**at** bei); **she did not ∼ when the dentist started drilling** sie verzog keine Miene, als der Zahnarzt anfing zu bohren; **he ∼d under the pain/the insult** der Schmerz/die Beleidigung ließ ihn zusammenzucken. ❷ *n.* Zusammenzucken, *das;* **give a ∼ [of pain]** [vor Schmerz] zusammenzucken; **without a ∼:** ohne eine Miene zu verziehen; ohne mit der Wimper zu zucken

**winceyette** /wɪnsɪˈet/ *n.* (*Brit. Textiles*) Flanell, *der*

**winch** /wɪntʃ/ ❶ *n.* Ⓐ (*crank*) Kurbel, *die;* Ⓑ (*Brit. Fishing*) Rolle, *die;* Haspel, *die;* Ⓒ (*windlass*) Winde, *die.* ❷ *v.t.* winden; mit einer Winde ziehen; **∼ up** hochwinden

**wind¹** /wɪnd/ ❶ *n.* Ⓐ Wind, *der;* **before the ∼** (*Naut.*) vor dem Wind; **be in the ∼** (*fig.*) in der Luft liegen; **down the ∼:** mit dem Wind; in der Richtung des Windes; **see how** *or* **which way the ∼ blows** *or* **lies** (*fig.*) sehen, woher der Wind weht; **into the ∼** (*Naut.*) in den Wind; **off the ∼** (*Naut.*) aus dem Wind; **like the ∼:** wie der Wind ‹laufen, fahren usw.›; **sail close to** *or* **near the ∼:** hart am Wind segeln; (*fig.*) sich hart an der Grenze des Erlaubten bewegen; **sail too close to** *or* **near the ∼** (*fig.*) den Bogen überspannen; **take the ∼ out of sb.'s sails** (*fig.*) jmdm. den Wind aus den Segeln nehmen; **throw sb.'s advice to the ∼s** jmds. Rat in den Wind schlagen; **throw caution/discretion/one's principles to the ∼s** alle Vorsicht/alle Diskretion/seine Grundsätze über Bord werfen; **to the [four] ∼s** in alle [vier] Winde; **the ∼[s] of change** ein frischer Wind (*fig.*); ⇒ *also* **whirlwind** A; Ⓑ *no pl.* (*Mus.*) (*stream of air*) (*in organ*) Wind, *der;* (*in other instruments*) Luftstrom, *der;* (*instruments*) Bläser; Ⓒ *no pl.* (*blast of air*) Luftstrom, *der;* (*of missile*) Druckwelle, *die;* Ⓓ (*Hunting*) Witterung, *die;* **get ∼ of sth.** (*fig.*) Wind von etw. bekommen; Ⓔ *no pl., no indef. art.* (*flatulence*) Blähungen; **break ∼:** eine Blähung abgehen lassen; **get/have the ∼ up** (*coll.*) Manschetten (*ugs.*) *od.* Schiss (*salopp*) kriegen/haben; **put the ∼ up sb.** (*coll.*) jmdm. Schiss machen (*salopp*); Ⓕ (*breath*) **lose/have lost one's ∼:** außer Atem kommen/sein; **recover** *or* **get one's ∼:** wieder zu Atem kommen; **you need a lot of ∼ to run such a long distance** der Atem darf einem nicht so schnell ausgehen, wenn man so eine lange Strecke laufen will; **get one's second ∼** (*lit. or fig.*) sich wieder steigern; **pause to get one's second ∼** (*fig.*) eine Pause machen, um einen neuen Anlauf zu nehmen; Ⓖ *no pl., no art.* (*empty words*) [leeres] Geschwätz.

❷ *v.t.* Ⓐ (*make breathless*) außer Atem bringen; **the blow ∼ed him** der Schlag nahm ihm den Atem; **be ∼ed** außer Atem sein; **he was ∼ed by the blow to his stomach** nach dem Schlag in die Magengrube schnappte er nach Luft; Ⓑ (*burp*) ein Bäuerchen machen lassen (*fam.*) ‹Baby›

**wind²** /waɪnd/ ❶ *v.i.*, **wound** /waʊnd/ Ⓐ (*curve*) sich winden; (*move*) sich schlängeln; **the road wound through/among the hills** die Straße wand *od.* schlängelte sich zwischen den Hügeln hindurch; Ⓑ (*coil*) sich wickeln. ❷ *v.t.*, **wound** Ⓐ (*coil*) wickeln; (*on to reel*) spulen; **∼ wool into a ball** Wolle zu einem Knäuel aufwickeln; **∼ sth. off sth./on [to] sth.** etw. von etw. [ab]wickeln/auf etw. (*Akk.*) [auf]wickeln; **∼ sb. round one's finger** jmdn. um den Finger wickeln (*ugs.*); Ⓑ (*with key etc.*) aufziehen ‹Uhr›; Ⓒ **∼ one's/its way** sich winden; sich schlängeln; **a road ∼ing its way among the mountains** eine Straße, die sich zwischen den Bergen hindurchwindet *od.* -schlängelt; Ⓓ (*coil into ball*) zu einem Knäuel/zu Knäueln aufwickeln; Ⓔ (*surround*) wickeln; (*cover with coil*) umwickeln; bewickeln ‹Spule›; **he wound the injured arm in a piece of cloth** er umwickelte den verletzten Arm mit einem Tuch; Ⓕ (*winch*) winden; **∼ sth. with a winch** etw. mit einer Winde ziehen. ❸ *n.* Ⓐ (*curve*) Windung, *die;* Ⓑ (*turn*) Umdrehung, *die;* **give sth. a ∼:** etw. aufziehen; **give the clock one more ∼:** die Uhr noch [um] eine Umdrehung weiter aufziehen

**∼ ˈback** *v.t. & i.* zurückspulen

**∼ ˈdown** ❶ *v.t.* Ⓐ (*lower*) mit einer Winde herunter-/hinunterlassen; herunterdrehen ‹Autofenster›; Ⓑ (*fig.: reduce gradually*) einschränken; drosseln ‹Produktion›; (*and cease*) allmählich einstellen; auslaufen lassen ‹Produktion›. ❷ *v.i.* (*lose momentum*) ablaufen; (*fig.*) ‹Produktion:› zurückgehen; (*cease*) auslaufen

**∼ ˈforward** ⇒ **∼ on**

**∼ ˈin** *v.t.* einrollen ‹Angelschnur›; einholen ‹Fisch, Tau›; (*on to sth.*) aufwickeln

**∼ ˈon** *v.t. & i.* weiterspulen

**∼ ˈup** ❶ *v.t.* Ⓐ (*raise*) hochwinden; (*winch up*) [mit einer Winde] hochziehen; hochdrehen ‹Autofenster›; Ⓑ (*coil*) aufwickeln; Ⓒ (*with key etc.*) aufziehen ‹Uhr›; Ⓓ (*make tense*) aufregen; erregen; **get wound up** sich aufregen; sich erregen; **she was wound up to a fury** sie kochte vor Wut; Ⓔ (*coll.: annoy deliberately*) auf die Palme bringen (*ugs.*); Ⓕ (*conclude*) beschließen ‹Debatte, Rede›; Ⓖ (*Finance, Law*) auflösen; einstellen ‹Aktivitäten›; **∼ up one's affairs** seine Angelegenheiten in Ordnung bringen.

❷ *v.i.* Ⓐ (*conclude*) schließen; **he wound up for the Government** er sprach als letzter Redner aus dem Regierungslager; **..., he said, ∼ing up** ... sagte er abschließend; Ⓑ **up with ice cream** mit Eis abschließen; Ⓒ (*Commerc.*) ‹Firma:› aufgelöst werden; Ⓒ

W

(*coll.: end up*) ~ **up in prison/hospital** [zum Schluss] im Gefängnis/Krankenhaus landen (*ugs.*); ~ **up with a broken leg** sich (*Dat.*) am Ende noch ein gebrochenes Bein einhandeln. ⇒ *also* **wind-up**

**wind**/wɪnd/: ~**bag** *n.* (*derog.*) Schwätzer, *der*/Schwätzerin, *die;* ~ **band** *n.* (*Mus.*) Blaskapelle, *die;* (*section of orchestra*) Bläsergruppe, *die;* ~**-blown** *adj.* vom Wind zerzaust ‹Haar›; ~**break** *n.* Windschutz, *der;* ~**breaker** (*Amer.*), ~**cheater** (*Brit.*) *ns.* Windjacke, *die;* ~**chest** *n.* (*Mus.*) Windlade, *die;* ~ **chill** *n.* (*Meteorol.*) ~ **chill [factor** *or* **index]** Windchill-Index, *der;* ~ **cone** ⇒ **windsock**

**winded** /ˈwɪndɪd/ *adj.* nach Luft schnappend *nicht präd.*; **be** ~**:** außer Atem sein

**winder** /ˈwaɪndə(r)/ *n.* (*of watch*) Krone, *die;* (*of clock, toy*) Aufziehschraube, *die;* (*key*) Schlüssel, *der*

**wind** /wɪnd/: ~**fall** *n.* Ⓐ Stück Fallobst; (*apple*) Fallapfel, *der;* ~**s** Fallobst, *das;* Ⓑ (*fig.*) warmer Regen (*ugs.*); **repeated** ~**falls** ein warmer Regen nach dem anderen; *attrib.* ~**fall tax** (*einmalige*) *Sondersteuer auf Privatisierungsgewinne;* ~ **farm** *n.* Windpark, *der;* Windfarm, *die;* ~**flower** *n.* (*Bot.*) Windröschen, *das;* ~ **force** *n.* (*Meteorol.*) Windstärke, *die;* ~ **gauge** *n.* (*Meteorol.*) Windmesser, *der;* ~**hover** *n.* (*Ornith.*) Rüttelfalke, *der*

**winding** /ˈwaɪndɪŋ/ ❶ *attrib. adj.* gewunden; **the** ~ **procession** der sich dahinschlängelnde Zug. ❷ *n.* Ⓐ *in pl.* (*of road, river*) Windungen; Ⓑ (*Electr.*) Wicklung, *die*

**winding:** ~ **sheet** *n.* Leichentuch, *das;* ~ **ˈstaircase** *n.* Wendeltreppe, *die*

**wind**/wɪnd/: ~ **instrument** *n.* (*Mus.*) Blasinstrument, *das;* ~**jammer** /ˈwɪnddʒæmə(r)/ *n.* (*Naut.*) Windjammer, *der*

**windlass** /ˈwɪndləs/ *n.* Winde, *die*

**windless** /ˈwɪndlɪs/ *adj.* windstill

**windmill** /ˈwɪndmɪl/ *n.* Ⓐ Windmühle, *die;* (*to drive generator, water pump, etc.*) Windrad, *das;* **tilt at** *or* **fight** ~**s** (*fig.*) gegen Windmühlen kämpfen; Ⓑ (*toy*) Windrädchen, *das*

**window** /ˈwɪndəʊ/ *n.* Ⓐ Fenster, *das;* **break a** ~**:** eine Fensterscheibe zerbrechen; ‹Einbrecher:› eine Fensterscheibe einschlagen; **go out of the** ~ (*fig. coll.*) den Bach runtergehen (*ugs.*); Ⓑ (*fig.: means of observation*) **a** ~ **on the West/world** ein Fenster zum Westen/zur Welt; **a** ~ **on life** ein Spiegel des Lebens; Ⓒ (*for display of goods*) [Schau]fenster, *das;* Ⓓ (*for issue of tickets etc.*) Schalter, *der;* Ⓔ (*Astronaut.: time when launch is possible*) Startfenster, *das;* Ⓕ (*Computing*) Fenster, *das*

**window:** ~ **box** *n.* Blumenkasten, *der;* ~ **cleaner** *n.* ▸1261 Fensterputzer, *der*/-putzerin, *die;* ~ **cleaning** *n.* Fensterputzen, *das;* ~ **display** *n.* Schaufensterauslage, *die;* ~ **dresser** *n.* ▸1261 Schaufensterdekorateur, *der*/-dekorateurin, *die;* ~ **dressing** *n.* Schaufensterdekoration, *die;* (*fig.*) Schönfärberei, *die;* ~ **envelope** *n.* Fenster[brief]umschlag, *der;* ~ **frame** *n.* Fensterrahmen, *der;* ~ **ledge** *n.* (*inside*) Fensterbank, *die;* (*outside*) Fenstersims, *der od. das;* ~ **pane** *n.* Fensterscheibe, *die;* ~ **seat** *n.* (*in building*) Fensterbank, *die;* (*in train etc.*) Fensterplatz, *der;* ~**shopper** *n.* Schaufensterbummler, *der*/-bummlerin, *die;* ~ **shopping** *n.* Schaufensterbummeln, *das;* **go** ~ **shopping** einen Schaufensterbummel machen; ~ **sill** ⇒ ~ **ledge**

**wind**/wɪnd/: ~**pipe** *n.* (*Anat.*) Luftröhre, *die;* ~ **power** *n.* Windkraft, *die;* ~ **proof** *adj.* windabweisend; ~**proof jacket** Windjacke, *die;* ~ **pump** *n.* Windpumpe, *die;* ~ **rose** *n.* (*Meteorol.*) Windrose, *die;* ~**screen**, (*Amer.*) ~**shield** *ns.* (*Motor Veh.*) Windschutzscheibe, *die;* ~**screen**/~**shield wiper** Scheibenwischer, *der;* ~ **sleeve**, ~**sock** *ns.* (*Aeronaut.*) Windsack, *der;* ~**surfer** *n.* Windsurfer, *der;* ~**surfing** *n.* (*Sport*) Windsurfen, *das;* ~**swept** *adj.* windgepeitscht; vom Wind zerzaust ‹Person, Haare›; **the** ~**swept lake** der vom Wind bewegte See; ~ **tunnel** *n.* (*Aeronaut.*) Windkanal, *der*

**wind-up** /ˈwaɪndʌp/ *n.* Ⓐ (*end*) [Ab]schluss, *der;* Ⓑ (*coll.: attempt to annoy*) **is this a** ~? willst du mich auf die Palme bringen? (*ugs.*)

**windward** /ˈwɪndwəd/ ❶ *adj.* ~ **side** Windseite, *die;* Luvseite, *die* (*bes. Seemannsspr.*); **in a** ~ **direction** gegen den Wind; luvwärts (*Seemannsspr.*); **W**~ **Islands** *pr. n. pl.* Inseln über dem Winde. ❷ *adv.* gegen den Wind. ❸ *n.* Windseite, *die;* Luv, *die* (*Seemannsspr.*); **sail to** ~**:** gegen den Wind segeln; **get to** ~ **of sth.** auf die Windseite einer Sache (*Gen.*) gehen/fahren *usw.*

**windy** /ˈwɪndɪ/ *adj.* Ⓐ windig ‹Tag, Ort, Wetter›; Ⓑ (*wordy, empty*) phrasenhaft; Phrasen dreschend (*abwertend*) ‹Person›; **he is** ~ **and ineffectual** er drischt nur Phrasen und tut nichts; Ⓒ (*coll.: frightened*) **be/get** ~**:** Manschetten (*ugs.*) *od.* (*salopp*) Schiss haben/kriegen

**wine** /waɪn/ *n.* Ⓐ Wein, *der;* ~, **women, and song** Wein, Weib und Gesang; **put new** ~ **in old bottles** (*fig.*) neuen Wein in alte Schläuche füllen; ⇒ *also* **spirit** 1 K; Ⓑ (*colour*) Weinrot, *das*

**wine:** ~ **and ˈdine** *v.t.* in großem Stil *od.* (*ugs.*) groß bewirten; **be** ~**d and dined at sb.'s expense** auf jmds. Kosten schlemmen; ~ **bar** *n.* Weinstube, *die;* ~ **bottle** *n.* Weinflasche, *die;* ~ **cellar** *n.* [Wein]keller, *der;* ~ **cooler** *n.* Weinkühler, *der;* ~**glass** *n.* Weinglas, *das;* ~**grower** *n.* ▸1261 Winzer, *der;* ~**growing** ❶ *n.* Weinbau, *der;* ❷ *adj.* ~**-growing area** Weingegend, *die;* ~ **list** *n.* Weinkarte, *die;* ~**making** *n. Herstellung von Wein zu Hause in kleineren Mengen;* ~ **merchant** *n.* ▸1261 Weinhändler, *der*/-händlerin, *die;* ~ **merchants** (*business*) Weinhandlung, *die;* ~**-ˈred** *adj.* weinrot

**winery** /ˈwaɪnərɪ/ *n.* Weinkellerei, *die*

**wine:** ~ **taster** *n.* ▸1261 Weinverkoster, *der*/-verkosterin, *die;* ~ **tasting** /ˈwaɪnteɪstɪŋ/ *n.* Weinprobe, *die;* ~ **vault** *n.* Weinkeller, *der;* ~ **ˈvinegar** *n.* Weinessig, *der;* ~ **waiter** *n.* ▸1261 Weinkellner, *der*

**wing** /wɪŋ/ ❶ *n.* Ⓐ (*Ornith., Archit., Sport*) Flügel, *der;* **take** ~**:** auffliegen; **on the** ~**:** im Fluge; **spread** *or* **stretch one's** ~**s** (*fig.*) sich auf eigene Füße stellen; **take sb. under one's** ~**:** jmdn. unter seine Fittiche nehmen; **lend sb.** ~**s/lend** ~**s to sb.'s feet** jmdn./jmds. Schritte beflügeln; **on a** ~ **and a prayer** (*fig.*) mit minimalen Erfolgsaussichten; Ⓑ (*Aeronaut.*) [Trag]flügel, *der;* Tragfläche, *die;* ~**s** (*badge*) Pilotenabzeichen, *das;* Fliegerabzeichen, *das;* **get/have [got] one's** ~**s** seinen Pilotenschein kriegen/haben; Ⓒ *in pl.* (*Theatre*) Kulissen; **wait in the** ~**s** (*fig.*) auf seine Chance warten; Ⓓ (*Brit. Motor Veh.*) Kotflügel, *der;* Ⓔ (*Air Force*) Geschwader, *das.*
❷ *v.t.* Ⓐ (*wound*) am Flügel treffen, (*Jägerspr.*) flügeln ‹Vogel›; am Arm treffen ‹Person›; Ⓑ (*fig.: speed*) beflügeln (*geh.*); Ⓒ (*fly*) ~ **one's way** fliegen.
❸ *v.i.* fliegen

**wing:** ~ **case** *n.* (*Zool.*) Deckflügel, *der;* ~ **chair** *n.* Ohrensessel, *der;* ~ **ˈcollar** *n.* Ecken- *od.* Klappenkragen, *der;* ~ **commander** *n.* (*Brit. Air Force*) Geschwaderkommandeur, *der*

**wingding** /ˈwɪŋdɪŋ/ *n.* (*Amer. coll.*) Ⓐ (*party*) Sause, *die* (*salopp*); Ⓑ (*seizure*) [simulierter] Krampfanfall; **throw a** ~**:** einen Krampfanfall simulieren

**winged** /wɪŋd/ *adj.* Ⓐ (*having wings*) geflügelt; Ⓑ (*wounded*) flügellahm geschossen; geflügelt (*Jägerspr.*)

**-winged** *adj. in comb.* mit ... Flügeln *nachgestellt;* **white-/black-/short-/long-**~**:** weiß-/schwarz-/kurz-/langflügelig

**winger** /ˈwɪŋə(r)/ *n.* (*Sport*) Außenstürmer, *der*/-stürmerin, *die;* Flügel, *der*

**wing:** ~ **mirror** *n.* (*Brit. Motor Veh.*) Außenspiegel, *der;* ~ **nut** *n.* Flügelmutter, *die;* ~**span**, ~**spread** *ns.* [Flügel]spannweite, *die;* ~ **tip** *n.* Flügelspitze, *die*

**wink** /wɪŋk/ ❶ *v.i.* Ⓐ (*blink*) blinzeln; (*as signal*) zwinkern; ~ **at sb.** jmdm. zuzwinkern; **be as easy as** ~**ing** kinderleicht *od.* ein Kinderspiel sein; **do sth. as easy as** ~**ing** (*coll.*) etw. mit Leichtigkeit tun; Ⓑ (*twinkle, flash*) blinken; Ⓒ ~ **at sth.** (*fig.: ignore*) über etw. (*Akk.*) hinwegsehen.
❷ *v.t.* Ⓐ ~ **one's eye/eyes** blinzeln; (*as signal*) zwinkern; ~ **one's eye at sb.** jmdm. zuzwinkern; Ⓑ (*flash*) blinken ‹Signal, Nachricht usw.›.
❸ *n.* Ⓐ Blinzeln, *das;* (*signal*) Zwinkern, *das;* **give sb. a [secret/sly/knowing** *etc.*] ~**:** jmdm. [heimlich/verschmitzt/wissend *usw.*] zuzwinkern; ⇒ *also* **tip²** 2 D; **in the** ~ **of an eye** (*fig.*) in null Komma nichts (*ugs.*); Ⓑ **not get a** ~ **of sleep, not sleep a** ~**:** kein Auge zutun; ⇒ *also* **forty** 1

**winker** /ˈwɪŋkə(r)/ *n.* (*Motor Veh.*) Blinker, *der*

**winkle** /ˈwɪŋkl/ ❶ *n.* Strandschnecke, *die.* ❷ *v.t.* ~ **out** herausholen, (*ugs.*) rauspfriemeln ‹Gegenstand, Substanz›; herausholen ‹Person, Tier›; ~ **sth. out of sb.** (*fig.*) etw. aus jmdm. rauskriegen (*ugs.*)

**ˈwinkle-picker** *n.* (*coll. dated*) *spitzer Schuh*

**winner** /ˈwɪnə(r)/ *n.* Ⓐ Sieger, *der*/Siegerin, *die;* (*of competition or prize*) Gewinner, *der*/Gewinnerin, *die;* (*winning shot*) Siegestreffer, *der;* (*winning goal*) Siegestor, *das;* **who is the** ~ **in this deal?** wer profitiert bei diesem Geschäft mehr?; Ⓑ (*successful thing*) Erfolg, *der;* (*successful play, product*) Renner, *der* (*ugs.*); Hit, *der* (*ugs.*); **you're on [to] a** ~ **with this idea/book** (*coll.*) diese Idee/dieses Buch wird garantiert ein Renner *od.* Hit (*ugs.*)

**winning** /ˈwɪnɪŋ/ *adj.* Ⓐ *attrib.* siegreich; ~ **team** siegreiche Mannschaft; Siegermannschaft, *die;* **the** ~ **captain** der Kapitän der Siegermannschaft; Ⓑ *attrib.* (*bringing victory*) den Sieg bringend; ~ **number** Gewinnzahl, *die;* **the** ~ **entry** die preisgekrönte Einsendung; Ⓒ (*charming*) einnehmend; gewinnend ‹Lächeln›

**winningly** /ˈwɪnɪŋlɪ/ *adv.* einnehmend; gewinnend ‹lächeln›

**ˈwinning post** *n.* (*Sport*) Zielpfosten, *der*

**winnings** /ˈwɪnɪŋz/ *n. pl.* Gewinn, *der*

**winnow** /ˈwɪnəʊ/ *v.t.* (*Agric.*) worfeln; (*fig.*) scheiden; trennen

~ **ˈout** *v.t.* (*Agric.*) ausscheiden ‹Spreu›

**wino** /ˈwaɪnəʊ/ *n., pl.* ~**s** (*coll.*) Wermutpenner, *der*/-pennerin, *die* (*salopp*)

**winsome** /ˈwɪnsəm/ *adj.* einnehmend; gewinnend ‹Lächeln›; **a** ~ **couple** ein reizendes Paar; **look** ~**:** reizend aussehen

**winter** /ˈwɪntə(r)/ ❶ *n.* ▸1504 Winter, *der;* **in [the]** ~**:** im Winter; **last/next** ~**:** letzten/nächsten Winter; **the** ~ **of 1947-8** *or* **of 1947** der Winter 1947-48 *od.* [des Jahres] 1947; ~**'s day** Wintertag, *der.* ❷ *attrib. adj.* Winter-. ❸ *v.i.* den Winter verbringen; ‹Truppe, Tier:› überwintern

**winter:** ~ **garden** *n.* Wintergarten, *der;* ~**green** *n.* (*Bot.*) (*Pyrola*) Wintergrün, *das;* (*Gaultheria*) Gaultheria, *die*

**winterize (winterise)** /ˈwɪntəraɪz/ *v.t.* winterfest machen

**winter:** ~ **ˈjasmine** ⇒ **jasmin[e]**; **W**~ **Oˈlympics** ⇒ **Olympics**; ~ **ˈquarters** *n. pl.* (*Mil.*) Winterquartier, *das;* Winterlager, *das;* ~ **ˈsleep** *n.* Winterschlaf, *der;* ~ **ˈsolstice** ⇒ **solstice** A; ~ **ˈsport** *n.* Ⓐ *usu. in pl.* Wintersport, *der;* Ⓑ (*particular sport*) Wintersportart, *die;* ~**time** *n.* Winter[s]zeit, *die;* **in [the]** ~**time** im Winter; ~**-weight** *adj.* (*Textiles*) Winter-; **the coat is** ~**-weight** dies ist ein Wintermantel

**wintry** /ˈwɪntrɪ/ *adj.* Ⓐ winterlich; rau ‹Klima›; kalt ‹Wind›; ~ **shower** Schneegestöber, *das;* **cold and** ~**:** winterlich kalt; Ⓑ (*fig.*) frostig ‹Lächeln›

**wipe** /waɪp/ ❶ *v.t.* Ⓐ abwischen; [auf]wischen ‹Fußboden›; (*dry*) abtrocknen; ~ **one's mouth** sich (*Dat.*) den Mund abwischen; ~ **one's brow/eyes/nose** sich (*Dat.*) die Stirn wischen/die Tränen abwischen/die Nase abwischen; ~ **one's feet/shoes** [sich (*Dat.*)] die Füße/Schuhe abtreten; ~ **sb./sth. clean/dry** jmdn./etw. abwischen/abtrocknen; ⇒ *also* **floor** 1 A; Ⓑ (*get rid of*) [ab]wischen; löschen ‹Bandaufnahme›; ~ **one's/sb.'s**

W

**tears/the tears from one's/sb.'s eyes** sich/jmdm. die Tränen abwischen/aus den Augen wischen; **~ sb./sth. off the face of the earth** jmdn./etw. vollständig *od.* restlos austilgen; **~ that smile off your face!** hör auf, so unverschämt zu grinsen!; **I'll soon ~ the smile off your face** dir wird das Grinsen gleich vergehen; ⇒ *also* **map** 1 B.
❷ *n.* [A] Wisch, *der* (*ugs.*); **give sth. a ~:** etw. abwischen; (*dry sth.*) etw. abtrocknen; **this glass/your face needs a ~:** dieses Glas/dein Gesicht müsste einmal abgewischt werden; [B] (*tissue*) Reinigungstuch, *das* (*aus Papier*)

**~ a'way** *v.t.* wegwischen; **~ away a tear/one's tears** sich (*Dat.*) eine Träne/die Tränen abwischen

**~ 'down** *v.t.* abwischen; (*dry*) abtrocknen

**~ 'off** *v.t.* [A] (*remove*) wegwischen; löschen ‹Bandaufnahme›; [B] (*pay off*) zurückzahlen ‹Schulden›; ablösen ‹Hypothek›

**~ 'out** *v.t.* [A] (*clean*) auswischen; [B] (*remove*) wegwischen; (*erase*) auslöschen; [C] (*cancel*) tilgen; zunichte machen ‹Vorteil, Gewinn usw.›; [D] (*destroy, abolish*) ausrotten ‹Rasse, Tierart, Feinde›; ersticken ‹Widerstand›; ausmerzen ‹Seuche, Korruption, Terrorismus›; [E] (*coll.: murder*) aus dem Weg räumen

**~ 'over** *v.t.* wischen über (+ *Akk.*)

**~ 'up** ❶ *v.t.* [A] aufwischen; [B] (*dry*) abtrocknen. ❷ *v.i.* abtrocknen

**wiper** /'waɪpə(r)/ *n.* [A] (*Motor Veh.*) Wischer, *der;* [B] (*Electr.*) Kontaktarm, *der*

**'wiper blade** *n.* (*Motor Veh.*) Wischerblatt, *das*

**wire** /'waɪə(r)/ ❶ *n.* [A] Draht, *der;* **go down to the ~** (*fig.*) ‹Wettkampf, Rennen usw.:› bis zuletzt offen sein; **this test of nerves will go down to the ~:** dies wird eine Nervenzerreißprobe bis zum Äußersten; **pull ~s** (*fig.*) = **pull strings** ⇒ **string** 1 A; [B] (*barrier*) Drahtverhau, *der od. das;* (*fence*) Drahtzaun, *der;* ⇒ *also* **mesh** 1 B; [C] (*Electr., Teleph.*) Leitung, *die;* **a piece** *or* **length of ~:** ein Stück [Leitungs]draht; **telephone/telegraph ~:** Telefon-/Telegrafenleitung, *die;* **the ~s were humming** die Drähte summten; **get one's** *or* **the ~s crossed** (*fig.*) auf der Leitung stehen (*ugs.*); ⇒ *also* **live wire**; [D] (*coll.: telegram*) Telegramm, *das.*
❷ *v.t.* [A] (*fasten with ~*) mit Draht zusammenbinden; (*stiffen with ~*) mit Draht versteifen; **~ sth. together** etw. mit Draht verbinden; [B] (*Electr.*) **~ sth. to sth.** etw. an etw. (*Akk.*) anschließen; **~ a house** (*lay wiring circuits*) in einem Haus die Stromleitungen legen; **is the house ~d for a telephone?** hat das Haus einen Telefonanschluss?; **~ a studio for sound** in einem Studio Tonleitungen [ver]legen; [C] (*coll.: telegraph*) **~ sb.** jmdm. *od.* an jmdn. telegrafieren; **~ money** Geld telegrafisch überweisen.
❸ *v.i.* (*coll.*) telegrafieren; **she ~d for him to come** sie telegrafierte ihm, er solle kommen

**~ 'up** *v.t.* (*Electr.*) anschließen (**to** an + *Akk.*)

**wire: ~ 'brush** *n.* Drahtbürste, *die;* **~ cutters** *n. pl.* Drahtschneider, *der;* **~ gauge** *n.* [A] (*instrument*) Drahtlehre, *die;* [B] (*series of sizes*) *Standardstärken für Drähte/Bleche;* **~-haired** *adj.* (*Zool.*) drahthaarig; Drahthaar‹terrier, -fox›

**wireless** /'waɪəlɪs/ ❶ *adj.* (*Brit.*) ⇒ **radio** 2 A. ❷ *n.* [A] (*Brit.*) Radio, *das;* [B] (*telegraphy*) Funk, *der;* **by ~:** über Funk (*Akk.*)

**wireless: ~ set** *n.* (*Brit. dated*) Radioapparat, *der* (*veralt.*); **~ te'legraphy** *n.* drahtlose Telegrafie



**wire: ~ 'netting** ⇒ **netting** B; **~ 'rope** *n.* Drahtseil, *das;* **~ strippers** *n. pl.* Abisolierzange, *die;* **~tapping** ⇒ **phonetapping**; **~ 'wheel** *n.* (*Motor Veh.*) [Draht]speichenrad, *das;* **~ 'wool** *n.* Stahlwolle, *die;* **~worm** *n.* (*Zool.*) Drahtwurm, *der*

**wiring** /'waɪərɪŋ/ *n., no pl., no indef. art.* (*Electr.*) [elektrische] Leitungen

**'wiring diagram** *n.* (*Electr.*) Schaltplan, *der;* Schaltbild, *das*

**wiry** /'waɪərɪ/ *adj.* drahtig; drahtartig ‹Stängel›

**wisdom** /'wɪzdəm/ *n., no pl.* [A] Weisheit, *die;* **worldly ~:** Weltklugheit, *die;* [B] (*prudence*) Klugheit, *die;* **where is the ~ of such a move/in doing that?** was für einen Sinn hat solch ein Schritt/hat es, das zu tun?; **her words are always full of ~:** was sie sagt, ist immer sehr klug; **words of ~:** weise Worte; (*advice*) weise Ratschläge

**'wisdom tooth** *n.* Weisheitszahn, *der*

**wise**[1] /waɪz/ *adj.* [A] weise; vernünftig ‹Meinung›; **be ~ after the event** so tun, als hätte man es immer schon gewusst; [B] (*prudent*) klug ‹Vorgehensweise›; vernünftig ‹Lebensweise, Praktik›; **the ~ thing to do would be to …:** am klügsten wäre es, … zu …; **you'd be ~ to ignore it** du tätest gut daran, es zu ignorieren; [C] (*informed*) **be none the** *or* **no/not much ~r** kein bisschen *od.* nicht/nicht viel klüger als vorher sein; **without anyone's being [any] the ~r** ohne dass es jemand merkt; [D] (*coll.: aware*) **be ~ to sb./sth.** jmdn./etw. kennen; **be ~ to what's going on** wissen, was läuft (*ugs.*); **she was ~ to the fact that …:** ihr war klar, dass …; **get ~ to sb./sb.'s tricks** jmdm. auf die Schliche kommen; **get ~ to sth.** etw. spitzkriegen (*ugs.*); **get ~ to sb.'s plans** dahinter kommen (*ugs.*), was jmd. vorhat; **put sb. ~:** jmdm. die Augen öffnen; **put sb. ~ to sth.** jmdn. über etw. (*Akk.*) aufklären; **put sb. ~ to sb.** jmdm., was jmdn. betrifft, die Augen öffnen

**~ 'up** (*Amer. coll.*) ❶ *v.t.* **~ sb. up [to sth.]** jmdn. [über etw.] aufklären; **I'd like to ~ you up to him** ich möchte dir über ihn die Augen öffnen. ❷ *v.i.* **~ up to sth.** sich (*Dat.*) über etw. klar werden; **~ up to sb./sb.'s tricks** jmdm. auf die Schliche kommen

**wise**[2] *n.* (*arch.: manner*) Weise, *die*

**-wise** *adv. in comb.* [A] (*in the direction of*) **length~:** der Länge nach; **clock~:** im Uhrzeigersinn; [B] (*coll.: as regards*) -mäßig; was … betrifft; **weather~:** wettermäßig; was das Wetter betrifft; **health~:** in puncto Gesundheit; gesundheitlich

**wise: ~acre** *n.* Klugschwätzer, *der*/-schwätzerin, *die* (*ugs. abwertend*); **~crack** (*coll.*) ❶ *n.* witzige Bemerkung; **make a ~crack** witzeln (**about** über + *Akk.*); ❷ *v.i.* witzeln; **~ guy** *n.* (*coll.*) Klugscheißer, *der* (*salopp abwertend*)

**wisely** /'waɪzlɪ/ *adv.* [A] weise; **live ~:** das Leben eines Weisen führen; [B] (*prudently*) klug; *as sentence-modifier* klugerweise

**wise 'man** *n.* Weise, *der;* (*arch.: magician*) Magier, *der;* **the Three Wise Men** (*Bibl.*) die drei Weisen [aus dem Morgenland]

**wish** /wɪʃ/ ❶ *v.t.* [A] ▶1191 (*desire, hope*) wünschen; **I ~ I was** *or* **were rich** ich wollte *od.* (*geh.*) wünschte, ich wäre reich; **I do ~ he would come** wenn er nur kommen würde; **I ~ you would shut up** es wäre mir lieb, wenn du den Mund hieltest; **it is to be ~ed that …** (*formal*) es ist zu hoffen *od.* man muss hoffen, dass …; '**~ you were here**' (*on postcard*) ≈ „schade, dass du nicht hier bist"; ≈ „das hättest du alles sehen sollen!"; [B] *with inf.* (*want*) wünschen (*geh.*); **do you really ~ me to go?** ist es wirklich dein Wunsch *od.* möchtest du wirklich, dass ich gehe?; **I ~ to go** ich möchte *od.* will gehen; **I ~ you to stay** ich möchte *od.* will, dass du bleibst; **I ~ it [to be] done** ich wünsche (*geh.*) *od.* möchte *od.* will, dass es getan wird; [C] ▶1191 (*say that one hopes sb. will have sth.*) wünschen; **~ sb. luck/success** *etc.* jmdm. Glück/Erfolg *usw.* wünschen; **~ sb. good morning/a happy birthday** jmdm. guten Morgen sagen/zum Geburtstag gratulieren; **~ sb. ill/well** jmdm. [etwas] Schlechtes/alles Gute wünschen; **I ~ him no harm** ich wünsche ihm nichts Schlechtes; [D] (*coll.: foist*) **~ sb./sth. on sb.** (*coll.*) jmdm. jmdn./etw. aufhalsen (*ugs.*).
❷ *v.i.* wünschen; **come on, ~!** nun, wünsch dir was!; **~ for sth.** sich (*Dat.*) etw. wünschen; **or is that too much to ~ for?** (*iron.*) oder ist das [vielleicht] zu viel verlangt?; **what more could one ~ for?** was will man mehr?; **they have everything they could possibly ~ for** sie haben alles, was sie sich (*Dat.*) nur wünschen können; **she ~ed for something to happen** sie wünschte, dass etwas passierte.
❸ *n.* [A] ▶1286 Wunsch, *der;* **her ~ is that …:** es ist ihr Wunsch *od.* sie wünscht, dass …; **I have no [great/particular] ~ to go** ich habe keine [große/besondere] Lust zu gehen; **I have no ~ for fame/anything** mir ist an Ruhm (*Dat.*) nicht gelegen/ich habe keine Wünsche; **make a ~:** sich (*Dat.*) etwas wünschen; **the ~ is father to the thought** (*prov.*) der Wunsch ist der Vater des Gedankens; **your ~ is my command** (*joc.*) dein Wunsch ist mir Befehl (*scherzh.*); **send sb. one's best ~es for a speedy recovery** jmdm. die besten Wünsche für eine schnelle Genesung schicken; **she sends you her good/best ~es** sie lässt dich herzlich grüßen; **with best/[all] good ~es, with every good ~:** mit den besten/allen guten Wünschen (**on, for** zu); [B] (*thing desired*) **get** *or* **have one's ~:** seinen Wunsch erfüllt bekommen; **at last he has [got] his ~:** endlich ist sein Wunsch in Erfüllung gegangen

**~ a'way** *v.t.* wegwünschen

**'wishbone** *n.* (*Ornith.*) Gabelbein, *das*

**wishful** /'wɪʃfl/ *adj.* sehnsuchtsvoll (*geh.*) ‹Blick, Verlangen›; **~ thinking** Wunschdenken, *das*

**'wish-fulfilment** *n.* (*Psych.*) Wunscherfüllung, *die*

**'wishing well** *n.* Wunschbrunnen, *der*

**wishy-washy** /'wɪʃɪwɒʃɪ/ *adj.* labberig (*ugs.*); (*fig.*) lasch

**wisp** /wɪsp/ *n.* (*of straw*) Büschel, *das;* **~ of hair** Haarsträhne, *die;* **~ of cloud/smoke** Wolkenfetzen, *der*/Rauchfahne, *die;* **she is just a ~ of a girl** sie ist nur ein Strich

**wispy** /'wɪspɪ/ *adj.* dünn ‹Gras, Haar›; schmächtig ‹Person, Figur›; **~ clouds/smoke** Wolkenfetzen/Rauchfähnchen

**wistaria** /wɪ'steərɪə/, **wisteria** /wɪ'stɪərɪə/ *n.* (*Bot.*) Glyzine, *die;* Glyzinie, *die*

**wistful** /'wɪstfl/ *adj.* wehmütig; melancholisch ‹Person, Typ›; traurig ‹Augen›

**wistfully** /'wɪstfəlɪ/ *adv.* wehmütig

**wistfulness** /'wɪstflnɪs/ *n., no pl.* Wehmütigkeit, *die;* Wehmut, *die* (*geh.*); (*of eyes*) Traurigkeit, *die;* **a look/an expression full of ~:** ein wehmutsvoller Blick/Ausdruck (*geh.*)

**wit**[1] /wɪt/ *n.* [A] (*humour*) Witz, *der;* **have a ready ~:** schlagfertig sein; [B] (*intelligence*) Geist, *der;* **battle of ~s** intellektueller Schlagabtausch; **be at one's ~'s** *or* **~s' end** sich (*Dat.*) keinen Rat mehr wissen; **he was at his ~'s** *or* **~s' end to know what to do next** er wusste nicht mehr weiter; **collect** *or* **gather one's ~s** zu sich kommen; **drive sb. out of his/her ~s** jmdn. um den Verstand bringen; **frighten** *or* **scare sb. out of his/her ~s** jmdm. Todesangst einjagen; **be frightened** *or* **scared out of one's ~s** Todesangst haben; **have/keep one's ~s about one** auf Draht sein (*ugs.*)/nicht den Kopf verlieren; **live by one's ~s** sich irgendwie durchschlagen *od.* durchs Leben schlagen; [C] (*person*) geistreicher Mensch

**wit**[2] *v.i.* **to ~:** nämlich

**witch** /wɪtʃ/ *n.* (*lit. or fig.*) Hexe, *die;* ⇒ *also* **sabbath** C

**witch: ~craft** *n., no pl.* Hexerei, *die;* **~ doctor** *n.* Medizinmann, *der;* **~ hazel** ⇒ **wych hazel**; **~-hunt** *n.* (*lit. or fig.*) Hexenjagd, *die* (**for** auf + *Akk.*)

**witching** /'wɪtʃɪŋ/ *adj.* **the ~ hour** die Geisterstunde

**with** /wɪð/ *prep.* [A] mit; **put sth. ~ sth.** etw. zu etw. stellen/legen; **have no pen to write ~:** nichts zum Schreiben haben; **I'll be ~ you in a minute** ich komme gleich; **a frontier ~ a country** eine Grenze zu einem Land; **be ~ it** (*coll.*) up to date sein; **not be ~ sb.** (*coll.: fail to understand*) jmdm. nicht folgen können; **I'm not ~ you** (*coll.*) ich komme nicht mit; **he that is not ~ me is against me** wer nicht mit mir ist, der ist wider mich (*bibl.*); **be one ~ sb./sth.** mit jmdm./etw. eins sein; [B] (*in the care or possession of*) bei; **I have no money ~ me** ich habe kein Geld dabei *od.* bei mir; [C] (*owing to*) vor (+ *Dat.*); **tremble ~ fear** vor Angst zittern; [D] (*displaying*) mit; **~ courage**

mutig; **handle ~ care** vorsichtig behandeln; **E** (*while having*) bei; **sleep ~ the window open** bei offenem Fenster schlafen; **speak ~ one's mouth full** mit vollem Mund sprechen; **F** (*in regard to*) **be patient ~ sb.** mit jmdm. geduldig sein; **have influence ~ sb.** auf jmdn. Einfluss haben; **what do you want ~ me?** was wollen Sie von mir?; **how are things ~ you?** wie geht es dir?; **what can he want ~ it?** was mag er damit vorhaben?; **G** (*at the same time as, in the same way as*) mit; **~ that** damit; **H** (*employed by*) bei; **I** (*despite*) trotz; ⇒ *also* **will**[2] 1 D

**withal** /wɪ'ðɔːl/ (*arch.*) *adv.* obendrein

**with'draw** ❶ *v.t., forms as* **draw** 1: **A** (*pull back, retract*) zurückziehen; **B** (*remove*) nehmen (*fig.*) (**from** aus); abziehen ‹Truppen› (**from** aus); **~ sth. from circulation/an account** etw. aus dem Verkehr ziehen/von einem Konto abheben. ❷ *v.i., forms as* **draw** 1, 2 sich zurückziehen

**withdrawal** /wɪð'drɔːəl/ *n.* **A** Zurücknahme, *die;* **B** (*removal*) (*of privilege*) Entzug, *der;* (*of troops*) Abzug, *der;* (*of money*) Abhebung, *die;* **make a ~ from the bank** Geld von der Bank abheben; **C** (*from drugs*) Entzug, *der;* **~ symptoms** Entzugserscheinungen

**with'drawal slip** *n.* Auszahlungsschein, *der*

**with'drawn** *adj.* (*unsociable*) verschlossen

**withe** /wɪθ, wɪð, waɪð/ *n.* Weidenrute, *die*

**wither** /'wɪðə(r)/ ❶ *v.t.* **A** (*shrivel*) verdorren lassen; **the plants had been ~ed by the heat** die Pflanzen waren durch die Hitze verdorrt; **age cannot ~ her** (*literary*) ihre Schönheit welkt nicht mit dem Alter; **B** (*overwhelm with scorn*) mit Verachtung strafen. ❷ *v.i.* [ver]welken

**~ a'way** *v.i.* (*lit. or fig.*) dahinwelken (*geh.*)

**~ 'up** ⇒ ~ 2

**withered** /'wɪðəd/ *adj.* verwelkt ‹Gras, Pflanze›; verkrüppelt ‹Gliedmaße›

**withering** /'wɪðərɪŋ/ *adj.* vernichtend ‹Blick, Bemerkung›; sengend ‹Hitze›

**witheringly** /'wɪðərɪŋlɪ/ *adv.* voller Verachtung

**withers** /'wɪðəz/ *n. pl.* Widerrist, *der*

**with'hold** *v.t., forms as* **hold**[2] **A** (*refuse to grant*) verweigern; versagen (*geh.*); **B** (*hold back*) verschweigen ‹Wahrheit›; **~ sth. from sb.** jmdm. etw. vorenthalten

**with'holding tax** *n.* (*Amer.*) Abzug[s]steuer, *die*

**within** /wɪ'ðɪn/ ❶ *prep.* **A** (*on the inside of*) innerhalb; **~ myself/yourself** *etc.* in meinem/deinem *usw.* Inneren; **~ doors** drinnen; im Haus; **her heart sank ~ her** (*literary*) aller Mut verließ sie; ⇒ *also* **wheel** 1 A; **B** (*not beyond*) im Rahmen (+ *Gen.*); **~ the meaning of the Act** *etc.* im Sinne des Gesetzes *usw.;* **stay/be ~ the law** den Boden des Gesetzes nicht verlassen; **~ oneself** ohne sich zu verausgaben; ⇒ *also* **bound**[1] 1 A; **means** B; **reason** 1 B; **C** (*not farther off than*) **~ eight miles of sth.** acht Meilen im Umkreis von etw.; **we were ~ eight miles of our destination when …:** wir waren kaum noch acht Meilen von unserem Ziel entfernt, als …; ⇒ *also* **sight** 1 F; **D** (*subject to*) innerhalb; **work ~ certain conditions** unter bestimmten Bedingungen arbeiten; **E** (*in a time no longer than*) innerhalb; binnen; **~ an/the hour** innerhalb einer Stunde.
❷ *adv.* (*arch./literary*) **A** (*inside*) innen; **B** (*in spirit*) im Innern

**without** /wɪ'ðaʊt/ ❶ *prep.* **A** ohne; **~ doing sth.** ohne etw. zu tun; **can you do it ~ his knowing?** kannst du das machen, ohne dass er davon weiß?; **~ end** ohne Ende; **B** (*arch.: outside*) außerhalb. ❷ *adv.* (*arch./literary*) **A** (*outside*) außen; **B** (*in outward appearance*) nach außen hin. ❸ *conj.* (*arch./coll.*) **you're not coming in here ~ you've been invited** du kommst hier nicht herein, ohne dass du eingeladen wärest (*geh.*)

**with'stand** *v.t., forms as* **stand** 1, 2: standhalten (+ *Dat.*); aushalten ‹Beanspruchung, hohe Temperaturen›

**withy** /'wɪðɪ/ ⇒ **withe**

**witless** /'wɪtlɪs/ *adj.* **A** (*foolish*) töricht; **B** (*insane*) geistesgestört; **C** (*dull-witted*) beschränkt (*abwertend*)

**witness** /'wɪtnɪs/ ❶ *n.* **A** Zeuge, *der*/Zeugin, *die* (**of, to** *Gen.*); **be a ~ against oneself** gegen sich selbst zeugen; **as God is my ~** (*fig.*) Gott ist mein Zeuge! (*geh.*); **B** ⇒ **eyewitness**; **C** *no pl.* (*evidence*) Zeugnis, *das* (*geh.*); **bear ~ to** *or* **of sth.** ‹Person:› etw. bezeugen; (*fig.*) von etw. zeugen; **D** *no pl.* (*confirmation*) **in ~ of sth.** zum Zeugnis (*geh.*) einer Sache; **call sb. to ~:** jmdn. zum Zeugen aufrufen; **E** *no pl.* (*proof*) **~ to** *or* **of sth.** Zeugnis für etw. (*geh.*).
❷ *v.t.* **A** (*see*) **~ sth.** Zeuge/Zeugin einer Sache (*Gen.*) sein; **sth. is ~ed by sb.** jmd. ist Zeuge/Zeugin einer Sache (*Gen.*); **~ scenes of brutality** brutale Szenen mitansehen müssen; **they have ~ed many changes** sie haben viele Veränderungen erlebt; **B** (*attest genuineness of*) bestätigen ‹Unterschrift, Echtheit eines Dokuments›; ⇒ *also* **hand** 1 L.
❸ *v.i.* **~ against/to sth.** Zeugnis gegen/für etw. ablegen (*geh.*); **[as] ~ …:** wie … bezeugt

**witness: ~ box** (*Brit.*), **~ stand** (*Amer.*) *ns.* Zeugenstand, *der*

**witter** /'wɪtə(r)/ *v.i.* (*Brit. coll.*) **~ [on]** quatschen (*ugs. abwertend*)

**witticism** /'wɪtɪsɪzm/ *n.* Witzelei, *die*

**wittily** /'wɪtɪlɪ/ *adv.* geistreich

**wittiness** /'wɪtɪnɪs/ *n., no pl.* Witz, *der*

**witting** /'wɪtɪŋ/ *adj.* bewusst

**wittingly** /'wɪtɪŋlɪ/ *adv.* wissentlich

**witty** /'wɪtɪ/ *adj.* **A** witzig; **B** (*possessing wit*) geistreich ‹Person›

**wives** *pl. of* **wife**

**wizard** /'wɪzəd/ ❶ *n.* **A** (*sorcerer*) Zauberer, *der;* **B** (*very skilled person*) Genie, *das* (**at** in + *Dat.*); **she's a ~ with a computer** sie vollbringt wahre Wunder mit einem Computer. ❷ *adj.* (*dated coll.*) zauberhaft

**wizardry** /'wɪzədrɪ/ *n.* **A** (*sorcery*) Zauberei, *die;* **B** (*seemingly magical technique*) Zauberkunst, *die* (*meist Pl.*); **footballing ~:** [Fuß]ballartistik, *die*

**wizened** /'wɪzənd/ *adj.* runz[e]lig

**wk.** *abbr.* **week** Wo.

**WNW** /westnɔːθ'west/ *abbr.* ▶ **1024** **west-north-west** WNW

**woad** /wəʊd/ *n.* Färberwaid, *der*

**wobble** /'wɒbl/ ❶ *v.i.* **A** (*rock*) wackeln; ‹Kompassnadel:› zittern; **I was wobbling like a jelly** ich zitterte wie Espenlaub; **B** (*go unsteadily*) wackeln (*ugs.*); **C** (*fig.: waver*) schwanken; **D** (*quaver*) vibrieren; ‹Stimme:› zittern. ❷ *n.* **A** (*unequal motion*) Flattern, *das* (*ugs.*); **walk with a ~:** schwankend gehen; **the front wheel has developed a ~:** das Vorderrad eiert (*ugs.*); **B** (*change of direction, piece of vacillation*) Schwankung, *die;* **C** (*quaver*) Vibrieren, *das;* (*in voice*) Zittern, *das*

**wobbly** /'wɒblɪ/ *adj.* wack[e]lig; zitt[e]rig ‹Schrift, Hand, Stimme›; zitternd ‹Pudding›; holp[e]rig ‹Fahrt›; eiernd (*ugs.*) ‹Rad›

**Woden** /'wəʊdn/ *pr. n.* (*Mythol.*) Wotan (*der*)

**wodge** /wɒdʒ/ *n.* (*Brit. coll.*) **a ~ of press cuttings** ein Packen Zeitungsausschnitte; **a great ~ of cake/butter** ein mächtiges Stück Kuchen/Butter

**woe** /wəʊ/ *n.* (*arch./literary/joc.*) **A** (*distress*) Jammer, *der;* **a scene of ~ greeted her** ein jammervoller Anblick bot sich ihr; **a tale of ~:** eine jammervolle Geschichte; **~ is me!** weh[e] mir!; **~ betide you!** wehe dir!; **B** *in pl.* (*troubles*) Jammer, *der;* **pour out one's ~s [to sb.]** [jmdm.] sein Leid klagen

**woebegone** /'wəʊbɪgɒn/ *adj.* jammervoll

**woeful** /'wəʊfl/ *adj.* **A** (*deplorable*) beklagenswert; **B** (*distressed*) jammervoll

**woefully** /'wəʊfəlɪ/ *adv.* **A** (*deplorably*) beklagenswert; **B** (*in a distressed manner*) jammervoll

**wog** /wɒg/ *n.* (*sl. derog.*) Kanake, *der* (*ugs. abwertend*)

**wok** /wɒk/ *n.* (*Cookery*) Wok, *der*

**woke, woken** ⇒ **wake**[1] 1, 2

**wold** /wəʊld/ *n.* (*Geog.*) Hochebene, *die;* **the Yorkshire W~s** die York Wolds

**wolf** /wʊlf/ ❶ *n., pl.* **wolves** /wʊlvz/ **A** (*Zool.*) Wolf, *der;* **cry ~ [too often]** (*fig.*) [zu oft] Zetermordio schreien (*ugs.*); **keep the ~ from the door** (*fig.*) den größten Hunger stillen; **be a ~ in sheep's clothing** (*fig.*) ein Wolf im Schafspelz sein; **throw sb. to the wolves** (*fig.*) jmdn. fallen lassen; **B** (*coll.: sexually aggressive man*) Aufreißer, *der* (*salopp*); ⇒ *also* **lone wolf**. ❷ *v.t.* **~ [down]** verschlingen

**wolf: ~ cub** *n.* **A** (*Zool.*) Wolfsjunge, *das;* **B** (*Brit. Hist.: Cub Scout*) Wölfling, *der;* **~ hound** *n.* Wolfshund, *der* (*volkst.*)

**wolfish** /'wʊlfɪʃ/ *adj.* wölfisch; **a ~ hunger/appetite** ein Wolfshunger (*ugs.*)

**'wolf pack** *n.* (*Navy, Air Force*) in Rudeltaktik operierende Einheit

**wolfsbane** /'wʊlfsbeɪn/ *n.* (*Bot.*) Eisenhut, *der*

**'wolf-whistle** ❶ *n.* anerkennender Pfiff. ❷ *v.i.* anerkennend pfeifen

**wolverine** (**wolverene**) /'wʊlvəriːn/ *n.* (*Zool.*) Vielfraß, *der*

**wolves** *pl. of* **wolf** 1

**woman** /'wʊmən/ *n., pl.* **women** /'wɪmɪn/ **A** Frau, *die;* **women and children first** Frauen und Kinder zuerst; **shut up, ~!** (*derog.*) halts Maul, Alte! (*derb*); **a ~'s work is never done** eine Frau hat immer etwas zu tun; **that's ~'s work** das ist Frauenarbeit; **women's page** Frauenseite, *die;* **women's [toilet]** Damen[toilette], *die;* **the shop sells women's clothing** in dem Geschäft wird Damenkleidung verkauft; **he wears women's clothing** er trägt Frauenkleider; **the other ~:** die Geliebte; **~ of the streets** Straßenmädchen, *das;* ⇒ *also* **honest** D; **house** 1 A; **little** 1 A; **old woman**; **past** 2 B; **world** A; **B** *attrib.* (*female*) weiblich; **~ friend** Freundin, *die;* **~ doctor** Ärztin, *die;* **a ~ driver** eine Frau am Steuer; **C** *no pl.* **[the] ~** (*an average ~*) die Frau; **D** (*coll.: char~*) Putzfrau, *die;* **E** (*arch.: female attendant*) Zofe, *die;* **F** (*feminine emotions*) **the ~ in her** die Frau in ihr

**'woman-hater** *n.* Frauenhasser, *der;* Weiberfeind, *der*

**womanhood** /'wʊmənhʊd/ *n., no pl.* Weiblichkeit, *die;* **reach ~:** zur Frau werden

**womanise, womaniser** ⇒ **womanize, womanizer**

**womanish** /'wʊmənɪʃ/ *adj.* (*derog.*) weibisch (*abwertend*)

**womanize** /'wʊmənaɪz/ *v.i.* den Frauen nachstellen; **with all his womanizing** mit all seiner Schürzenjägerei (*ugs.*)

**womanizer** /'wʊmənaɪzə(r)/ *n.* Schürzenjäger, *der*

**woman: ~kind** *n., no pl., no indef. art.* das weibliche Geschlecht; **the whole of ~kind** alle Frauen; **~like** *adj.* fraulich

**womanliness** /'wʊmənlɪnɪs/ *n., no pl.* Fraulichkeit, *die*

**womanly** /'wʊmənlɪ/ *adj.* fraulich; weiblich

**woman's rights** ⇒ **women's rights**

**womb** /wuːm/ *n.* **A** (*Anat.*) Gebärmutter, *die;* **the child in the ~:** das Kind im Mutterleib; **in her ~:** in ihrem Leib (*geh.*); ⇒ *also* **fruit** 1 D; **B** (*fig.: place of development*) Schoß, *der* (*geh. fig.*)

**wombat** /'wɒmbæt/ *n.* (*Zool.*) Wombat, *der*

**women** *pl. of* **woman**

**Women: w~folk** *n. pl.* Frauen *Pl.* Frauensleute, *Pl.* (*veralt.*); **w~kind** ⇒ **womankind**; **~'s 'Institute** *n.* (*Brit.*) *britischer Frauenverband;* **~'s 'Lib** (*coll.*) ⇒ **~'s Liberation**; **~'s Libber** /wɪmɪnz 'lɪbə(r)/ *n.* (*coll.*) Emanze, *die* (*ugs. abwertend*); Frauenrechtlerin, *die;* **~'s Libe'ration** *n.* die Frauenbewegung; **~'s movement** *n.* Frauenbewegung, *die;* **~'s 'refuge** *n.* Frauenhaus, *das;* **~'s 'rights** *n. pl.* die Rechte der Frau

**won** ⇒ **win** 1, 2

**wonder** /'wʌndə(r)/ ❶ *n.* **A** (*extraordinary thing*) Wunder, *das;* **do** *or* **work ~s** Wunder

W

tun *od.* wirken; (*fig.*) Wunder wirken; **~s will never cease** (*iron.*) Wunder über Wunder!; **small** *or* **what** *or* **[it is] no ~ [that] ...:** [es ist] kein Wunder, dass ...; **the ~ is, ...:** das Erstaunliche ist, ...; [B] (*marvellously successful person*) Wunderkind, *das;* (*marvellously successful thing*) Wunderding, *das;* **boy/girl ~:** Wunderkind, *das;* **the seven ~s of the world** die Sieben Weltwunder; [C] *no pl.* (*feeling*) Staunen, *das;* **a feeling of ~:** ein Staunen; **be lost in ~:** in Staunen versunken sein; **look at sb. in open-mouthed ~:** jmdn. mit offenem Mund anstaunen; ⇒ *also* **nine** 1.
❷ *adj.* Wunder-.
❸ *v.i.* sich wundern; staunen (**at** über + *Akk.*); **that's not to be ~ed at** darüber braucht man sich nicht zu wundern; **I shouldn't ~ [if ...]** (*coll.*) es würde mich nicht wundern[, wenn ...]; **Why do you ask? — Oh, I was just ~ing** Warum fragst du? — Ach, nur so; **I ~** *expr. agreement with another's doubts* das frage ich mich auch; *expr. disagreement with another's assertion* es sollte mich wundern; **I don't think we'll see him again. — I ~:** Den sehen wir nie wieder. — Da wäre ich nicht so sicher.
❹ *v.t.* [A] sich fragen; **I ~ what the time is** wie viel Uhr mag es wohl sein?; **I was ~ing what to do** ich habe mir überlegt, was ich tun soll; **I ~ whether I might open the window** dürfte ich vielleicht das Fenster öffnen?; **she ~ed if ...** (*enquired*) sie fragte, ob ...; **I ~ if you'd mind if ...?** würde es Ihnen etwas ausmachen, wenn ...?; [B] (*be surprised to find*) **~ [that] ...:** sich wundern, dass ...

**wonderful** /ˈwʌndəfl/ *adj.* wunderbar; wundervoll

**wonderfully** /ˈwʌndəfəlɪ/ *adv.* wunderbar; **~ beautiful** wunderschön; **~ charming** einfach bezaubernd

**wondering** /ˈwʌndərɪŋ/ *adj.*, **wonderingly** /ˈwʌndərɪŋlɪ/ *adv.* staunend

ˈ**wonderland** *n.* [A] (*wonderful place*) Paradies, *das;* [B] (*fairyland*) Wunderland, *das*

**wonderment** /ˈwʌndəmənt/ *n.*, *no pl.* Verwunderung, *die;* **say sth. in ~:** etw. voll Verwunderung sagen; **in ~ at** voll Verwunderung über (+ *Akk.*); **her mouth was open in ~:** ihr stand vor Staunen der Mund offen

ˈ**wonder-worker** *n.* Wundertäter, *der*/-täterin, *die*

**wondrous** /ˈwʌndrəs/ *adj.*, **wondrously** /ˈwʌndrəslɪ/ *adv.* (*poet.*) wundersam (*geh.*)

**wonky** /ˈwɒŋkɪ/ *adj.* (*Brit. coll.*) wack[e]lig; (*crooked*) schief; **a bit ~ [on one's legs]** etwas wack[e]lig [auf den Beinen] (*ugs.*)

**wont** /wəʊnt/ ❶ *pred. adj.* (*dated/literary*) gewohnt; **as he was ~ to say** wie er zu sagen pflegte. ❷ *n.* (*literary/joc.*) Gepflogenheit, *die* (*geh.*); **as was her ~:** wie sie zu tun pflegte

**won't** /wəʊnt/ (*coll.*) = **will not;** ⇒ **will¹**

**wonted** /ˈwəʊntɪd/ *attrib. adj.* (*literary*) gewohnt; **with one's ~ courtesy** mit gewohnter Höflichkeit

**woo** /wuː/ *v.t.* [A] (*literary: court*) **~ sb.** um jmdn. werben (*geh.*); [B] (*seek to win*) umwerben ‹Kunden, Wähler›; **~ away** abwerben ‹Arbeitskräfte›; [C] (*coax*) umwerben

**wood** /wʊd/ *n.* [A] *in sing. or pl.* (*area with trees*) Wald, *der;* **sb. cannot see the ~ for the trees** (*fig.*) jmd. sieht den Wald vor [lauter] Bäumen nicht (*scherzh.*); **be out of the ~** (*Brit.*) *or* (*Amer.*) **~s** (*fig.*) über den Berg sein (*ugs.*); [B] (*substance, material*) Holz, *das;* **touch ~** (*Brit.*), **knock [on] ~** (*Amer.*) unberufen!; **you'd better touch ~ when you say that** wenn du das sagst, klopfst du besser dreimal auf Holz; [C] (*cask for beer, wine, etc.*) **from the ~:** vom Fass; **matured in the ~:** in Holzfässern gereift; [D] (*Bowls*) Kugel, *die;* [E] (*Golf*) Holzschläger, *der;* Holz, *das*

**wood: ~ anemone** *n.* (*Bot.*) Buschwindröschen, *das;* Anemone, *die;* **~bind** /ˈwʊdbaɪnd/, **~bine** /ˈwʊdbaɪn/ *n.* (*Bot.*) [A] (*wild honeysuckle*) Waldgeißblatt, *das;* [B] (*Amer.: Virginia creeper*) Jungfernrebe, *die*

ˈ**wood-burning** *attrib. adj.* holzbefeuert

**wood~ carving** *n.* (*craft, object*) Holzschnitzerei, *die;* **~chuck** *n.* (*Zool.*) Waldmurmeltier, *das;* **~cock** *n.*, *pl. same* (*Ornith.*) Waldschnepfe, *die;* **~craft** *n.*, *no pl.* [A] (*knowledge of forest conditions*) Kenntnis des Waldes; [B] (*skill in ~work*) Holzschnitzerei, *die;* **~cut** *n.* (*Art*) Holzschnitt, *der;* **~cutter** *n.* ▶ **1261** [A] Holzfäller, *der;* [B] (*Art*) Holzschnitzer, *der*

**wooded** /ˈwʊdɪd/ *adj.* bewaldet

**wooden** /ˈwʊdn/ *adj.* [A] hölzern ‹Brücke, Spielzeug›; Holz‹haus, -brücke, -bein, -griff, -spielzeug›; [B] (*fig.: stiff*) hölzern

**wooden: ~head** *n.* (*derog.*) Holzkopf, *der* (*salopp abwertend*); **~headed** *adj.* (*derog.*) dumm; **~ ˈhorse** *n.* (*fig.*) Trojanisches Pferd

**woodenly** /ˈwʊdnlɪ/ *adv.* ausdruckslos ‹blicken, starren›; tonlos ‹sagen›

**woodenness** /ˈwʊdnnɪs/ *n.*, *no pl.* Hölzernheit, *die*

**wooden ˈspoon** ⇒ **spoon¹** 1 A

**wood: ~ hyacinth** ⇒ **hyacinth** A; **~land** /ˈwʊdlənd/ *n.* Waldland, *das;* Wald, *der; attrib.* Wald-; **~louse** *n.* (*Zool.*) Kellerassel, *die;* **~man** /ˈwʊdmən/ *n.*, *pl.* **~men** /ˈwʊdmən/ ▶ **1261** Waldarbeiter, *der;* **~pecker** *n.* Specht, *der;* **~ pigeon** *n.* Ringeltaube, *die;* **~pile** *n.* Holzstapel, *der;* Holzstoß, *der;* ⇒ *also* **nigger**; **~ pulp** *n.* Holzschliff, *der;* **~ruff** *n.* (*Bot.*) **[sweet] ~ruff** Waldmeister, *der;* **~ screw** *n.* Holzschraube, *die;* **~shed** *n.* Holzschuppen, *der;* **~ sorrel** *n.* (*Bot.*) Waldsauerklee, *der*

**woodsy** /ˈwʊdzɪ/ *adj.* (*Amer.*) waldig

**wood: ~wind** *n.* (*Mus.*) Holzblasinstrument, *das;* **the ~wind [section]** die Holzbläser; **~wind instrument** Holzblasinstrument, *das;* **~work** *n.*, *no pl.* [A] (*making things out of ~*) Arbeiten mit Holz; **~work and metalwork** (*Sch.*) Werkunterricht, *der;* [B] (*things made of ~*) Holzarbeit[en]; **crawl out of the ~work** (*coll.*) [aus dem Nichts] auftauchen (*ugs.*); **~worm** *n.*, *no pl.*, *no art.* Holzwurm; **it's got ~worm** da ist der Holzwurm drin (*ugs.*)

**woody** /ˈwʊdɪ/ *adj.* [A] (*well-wooded*) waldreich; [B] (*consisting of wood*) holzig ‹Pflanze[nteil], Wurzel›; Holz‹stamm›; [C] (*resembling wood*) holzig; ⇒ *also* **nightshade**

**wooer** /ˈwuːə(r)/ *n.* Verehrer, *der* (*veralt.*)

**woof¹** /wuːf/ ⇒ **weft**

**woof²** /wʊf/ ❶ *n.* [dumpfes] Bellen; **at the sound of the dog's ~:** als der Hund aufbellte; **give a short ~:** kurz aufbellen; **~ ~! went the dog** wau, wau!, bellte der Hund. ❷ *v.i.* [dumpf] bellen; **~ at sb.** jmdn. anbellen

**woofer** /ˈwʊfə(r)/ *n.* Bass[lautsprecher], *der*

**wool** /wʊl/ *n.* [A] Wolle, *die; attrib.* Woll-; **pull the ~ over sb.'s eyes** jmdm. etwas vormachen (*ugs.*); [B] (*garments*) Wolle, *die.* ⇒ *also* **cotton wool**; **dye** 2; **glass wool**; **steel wool**; **wire wool**

**woolen** (*Amer.*) ⇒ **woollen**

ˈ**wool-gathering** ❶ *n.*, *no pl.* Hirngespinste (*abwertend*). ❷ *adj.* zerstreut; **she's ~ again** sie träumt schon wieder

**woollen** /ˈwʊlən/ ❶ *adj.* wollen; **~ goods** Wollwaren *Pl.* ❷ *n.* [A] *in pl.* (*garments*) Wollsachen *Pl.;* [B] (*fabric*) Wollgewebe, *das;* Wollstoff, *der*

**woolliness** /ˈwʊlɪnɪs/ *n.*, *no pl.* Verschwommenheit, *die*

**woolly** /ˈwʊlɪ/ ❶ *adj.* [A] wollig; Woll‹pullover, -mütze›; [B] (*confused*) verschwommen; [C] (*indistinct*) unklar; undeutlich ‹Klang, Geräusch›. ⇒ *also* **wild** 1 C. ❷ *n.* (*coll.*) [A] (*Brit.: knitted garment*) **[winter] woollies** [Winter]wollsachen *Pl.* (*ugs.*); **a ~:** ein Wollpullover/eine Wolljacke; [B] *in pl.* (*Amer.: undergarments*) wollene Unterwäsche

**wool: ~pack** *n.* Schäfchenwolken *Pl.;* **W~sack** *n.* (*Brit. Parl.*) *großes, mit Wolle gefülltes Sitzkissen des Lord Chancellors im britischen Oberhaus*

**woozy** /ˈwuːzɪ/ *adj.* (*coll.*) [A] (*dizzy*) duselig (*ugs.*); [B] (*slightly drunk*) angeduselt (*salopp*)

**wop** /wɒp/ *n.* (*sl. derog.*) Spaghettifresser, *der* (*salopp abwertend*)

**Worcester[shire] sauce** /wʊstə(ʃɪə) ˈsɔːs, wʊstə(ʃə) ˈsɔːs/ *n.* Worcestersoße, *die*

**word** /wɜːd/ ❶ *n.* [A] Wort, *das;* **have no ~s for sth.** für etw. keine Worte finden; **be beyond ~s** sich mit Worten nicht ausdrücken lassen; **~s cannot describe it** mit Worten lässt sich das nicht beschreiben; **in a** *or* **one ~** (*fig.*) mit einem Wort; **[not] in so many ~s** [nicht] ausdrücklich; **in other ~s** mit anderen Worten; **not a ~ of sth.** kein Wort von etw.; **bad luck/drunk is not the ~ for it** Pech/betrunken ist gar kein Ausdruck dafür (*ugs.*); **that's not the ~ I would have used** das ist gar kein Ausdruck (*ugs.*); **put sth. into ~s** etw. in Worte fassen; **'rude' would be a better ~ for it** „unverschämt" wäre ein treffenderes Wort dafür; **~ for ~:** Wort für Wort; **without a** *or* **one/another ~:** ohne ein/ein weiteres Wort; **too funny** *etc.* **for ~s** unsagbar komisch *usw.;* **the written ~:** das geschriebene Wort; ⇒ *also* **fail** 2 E; **play** 1 B, 2 A; [B] (*thing said*) Wort, *das;* **hard ~s** harte Worte; **exchange** *or* **have ~s** einen Wortwechsel haben; **a man of few ~s** ein Mann von wenig Worten; **have a ~ [with sb.] about sth.** [mit jmdm.] über etw. (*Akk.*) sprechen; **could I have a ~ [with you]?** kann ich dich mal sprechen?; **have ~s with sb.** sich mit jmdm. streiten; **say a few ~s** ein paar Worte sprechen; **suit the action to the ~:** seinen Worten Taten folgen lassen; **it's his ~ against mine** sein Wort steht gegen meins; **take sb. at his/her ~:** jmdn. beim Wort nehmen; **~ of command/advice** Kommando, *das*/Rat, *der;* **don't say** *or* **breathe a ~ to anyone** sag niemandem auch nur ein Sterbenswort; **at a ~ of command** auf Befehl; **the W~ [of God]** (*Bible*) das Wort [Gottes]; **in the ~s of Shakespeare ...:** mit Shakespeares Worten: ...; **put in a good ~ for sb. [with sb.]** [bei jmdm.] ein [gutes] Wort für jmdn. einlegen; **never have a good ~ to say about anybody** nie etwas Gutes über andere zu sagen haben; **never say a bad ~ about anybody** nie etwas Schlechtes über andere sagen; **[it's] all ~s** [das sind] nichts als leere Worte; [C] (*promise*) Wort, *das;* **doubt sb.'s ~:** jmds. Wort in Zweifel ziehen; **give [sb.] one's ~:** jmdm. sein Wort geben; **keep/break one's ~:** sein Wort halten/brechen; **I give you my ~ for it** ich gebe Ihnen mein Wort darauf; **upon my ~** (*dated*) auf mein Wort; **upon my ~!** (*dated*) meiner Treu! (*veralt.*); **my ~!** meine Güte!; **my** *etc.* **~ of honour** mein *usw.* Ehrenwort; **a man of his ~:** ein Mann von Wort; **be as good as/better than one's ~:** sein Wort halten/mehr als halten; **sb.'s ~ is [as good as] his/her bond** man kann auf jmds. Wort (*Akk.*) bauen; ⇒ *also* **take** 1 V; [D] *no pl.* (*speaking*) Wort, *das;* **by ~ of mouth** durch mündliche Mitteilung; [E] *in pl.* (*text of song, spoken by actor*) Text, *der;* [F] *no pl.*, *no indef. art.* (*news*) Nachricht, *die;* **~ had just reached them** die Nachricht hatte sie gerade erreicht; **~ has it** *or* **the ~ is [that] ...:** es geht das Gerücht, dass ...; **~ went round that ...:** es ging das Gerücht, dass ...; **send/leave ~ that/of when ...:** Nachricht geben/eine Nachricht hinterlassen, dass/wenn ...; **is there any ~ from her?** hat sie schon von sich hören lassen?; [G] (*command*) Kommando, *das;* **just say the ~:** sag nur ein Wort; **at the ~ 'run', you run!** bei dem Wort „rennen" rennst du!; [H] (*pass~*) Parole, *die* (*Milit.*); **give the ~:** die Parole sagen; ⇒ *also* **sharp** 1 F; [I] (*Computing*) Wort, *das.*
❷ *v.t.* formulieren

**wordage** /ˈwɜːdɪdʒ/ *n.* die Anzahl der Wörter

**word: ~ association** *n.* assoziative Verknüpfung von Wörtern; **~-blind** *adj.* (*Med.*) wortblind; **~ break** *n.* Trennung, *die;* **~-deaf** *adj.* worttaub (*Med.*); **~ division** *n.* Silbentrennung, *die;* **~ formation** *n.* (*Ling.*) Wortbildung, *die;* **~ game** *n.* Buchstabenspiel, *das*

**wordiness** /ˈwɜːdɪnɪs/ *n.*, *no pl.* Weitschweifigkeit, *die*

W

**wording** /ˈwɜːdɪŋ/ *n.* Formulierung, *die;* Wortwahl, *die;* **the exact ~ of the contract** der genaue Wortlaut des Vertrages

**wordless** /ˈwɜːdlɪs/ *adj.* **A** (*not expressed in words*) wortlos; stumm ‹Schmerz, Trauer›; **B** (*not accompanied by words*) ohne Worte *nachgestellt*

**word: ~ list** *n.* Wortliste, *die;* **~ order** *n.* (*Ling.*) Wortstellung, *die;* **~-ˈperfect** *adj.* **be ~-perfect** seinen Text beherrschen; ‹Rede:› perfekt vorgetragen sein; **~ picture** *n.* anschauliche Schilderung; Wortgemälde, *das;* **~play** *n., no pl., no indef. art.* Wortspiel, *das;* **~ processing** *n.* Textverarbeitung, *die;* **~ processor** *n.* Textverarbeitungssystem, *das*

**wordy** /ˈwɜːdɪ/ *adj.* weitschweifig

**wore** ⇒ **wear** 2, 3

**work** /wɜːk/ ❶ *n.* **A** *no pl., no indef. art.* Arbeit, *die;* **at ~** (*engaged in working*) bei der Arbeit; (*fig.: operating*) am Werk (⇒ *also* E); **be at ~ on sth.** an etw. (*Dat.*) arbeiten; (*fig.*) auf etw. (*Akk.*) wirken; **set to ~** ‹Person:› sich an die Arbeit machen; **set sb. to ~:** jmdn. an die Arbeit schicken; **get to ~ on sb./sth.** jmdn. bearbeiten (*ugs.*)/mit [der Arbeit an] etw. (*Dat.*) anfangen; **all ~ and no play** immer nur arbeiten; **have one's ~ cut out** viel zu tun haben; sich ranhalten müssen (*ugs.*); **the ~ of a moment** *etc.* das Werk eines Augenblicks *usw.;* **that's too much like hard ~:** das könnte ja in Arbeit ausarten; **make light ~ of sth.** mit etw. leicht fertig werden; ⇒ *also* **day** A; **short** 1 A; **thirsty** B; **B** (*thing made or achieved*) Werk, *das;* **a good day's ~:** eine gute Tagesleistung; **do a good day's ~:** ein tüchtiges Stück Arbeit hinter sich bringen; **is that all your own ~?** hast du das alles selbst gemacht?; **~ of art** Kunstwerk, *das;* ⇒ *also* **good** 1 G; **C** (*book, piece of music*) Werk, *das;* **a ~ of reference/literature/art** ein Nachschlagewerk/literarisches Werk/Kunstwerk; **D** *in pl.* (*all compositions of author or composer*) Werke; **E** (*employment*) Arbeit, *die;* **out of ~:** arbeitslos; ohne Arbeit; **be in ~:** eine Stelle haben; **go out to ~:** arbeiten gehen; **put people out of ~:** Leute um ihren Arbeitsplatz bringen; **at ~** (*place of employment*) auf der Arbeit; **from ~:** von der Arbeit; **the conditions at ~:** die Arbeitsbedingungen; **F** *in pl., usu. constr. as sing.* (*factory*) Werk, *das;* **G** *in pl.* (*Mil.*) Werke; Befestigungen; **H** *in pl.* (*operations of building etc.*) Arbeiten; ⇒ *also* **clerk** C; **public works;** **I** *in pl.* (*machine's operative parts*) Werk, *das;* **J** *in pl.* (*coll.: all that can be included*) **the [whole/full] ~s** der ganze Kram (*ugs.*); **give sb. the ~s** (*fig.*) (*give sb. the best possible treatment*) jmdn. richtig verwöhnen (*ugs.*); (*tell sb. everything*) jmdm. alles erzählen; (*give sb. the worst possible treatment*) jmdn. fertig machen (*salopp*); **K** *no pl.* (*ornamentation*) Verzierung, *die;* (*ornamented or ornamental article*[*s*]) Arbeit, *die;* **L** *no pl., no indef. art.* (*knitting, needle~*) Handarbeit, *die;* **M** (*Phys.*) Arbeit, *die.* ⇒ *also* **nasty** 1 A; **piece** 1 D.

❷ *v.i.,* **~ed** *or* (*arch./literary*) **wrought** /rɔːt/ **A** arbeiten; **be ~ing all morning over a hot oven** den ganzen Morgen am Herd stehen (*ugs.*); **~ with sb.** mit jmdm. zusammenarbeiten; **~ to rule** Dienst nach Vorschrift machen; **~ for a cause** *etc.* für eine Sache *usw.* arbeiten; **~ against sth.** (*impede*) einer Sache (*Dat.*) entgegenstehen; ⇒ *also* **work-to-rule**; **B** (*function effectively, have intended effect*) funktionieren; ‹Charme:› wirken (**on** auf + *Akk.*); **make the washing machine/television ~:** die Waschmaschine/den Fernsehapparat in Ordnung bringen; **make a relationship/an arrangement ~:** dafür sorgen, dass eine Beziehung klappt (*ugs.*)/eine Regelung funktioniert; **it doesn't ~ like that** (*fig.*) so geht das nicht; **C** ‹Rad, Getriebe, Kette:› laufen; **D** (*be craftsman*) **~ in a material** mit *od.* (*fachspr.*) in einem Material arbeiten; **E** ‹Faktoren, Einflüsse:› wirken (**on** auf + *Akk.*); **~ to do sth.** darauf hinwirken, etw. zu tun; **~ against** arbeiten gegen; ⇒ *also* **work on**; **F** (*make its/one's way*) sich schieben; **~ loose** sich lockern; **~ round** ‹Kleidung:› herumrutschen; ‹Wind:› sich drehen; **be ~ing upstream** ‹Angler:› sich stromaufwärts arbeiten; **~ round to a question** (*fig.*) sich zu einer Frage vorarbeiten; **start at the end and ~ back** fang hinten an und arbeite dich nach vorne; **G** (*be agitated*) ‹Gesichtszüge:› arbeiten; **H** (*Naut.: sail*) sich arbeiten; **I** (*ferment, lit. or fig.*) arbeiten.

❸ *v.t.,* **~ed** *or* (*arch./literary*) **wrought** **A** (*operate*) bedienen ‹Maschine›; fahren ‹Schiff›; betätigen ‹Bremse›; **a pump that is ~ed by hand/by a wind wheel** eine Pumpe, die von Hand betätigt/von einem Windrad angetrieben wird; **~ed by electricity** elektrisch betrieben; ⇒ *also* **oracle** D; **B** (*get labour from*) arbeiten lassen; **~ horses/oxen to death** Pferde/Ochsen zu Tode schinden; **he ~s his employees hard** er nimmt seine Angestellten hart heran; ⇒ *also* **bone** 1 A; **death** A; **C** (*get material from*) ausbeuten ‹Steinbruch, Grube›; **D** (*operate in or on*) ‹Vertreter:› bereisen; **beggars ~ing the main street** Bettler, die auf der Hauptstraße arbeiten/arbeiteten; **E** (*control*) steuern; **F** (*effect*) bewirken ‹Änderung›; wirken ‹Wunder›; **~ one's mischief** Unheil anrichten; **~ one's will [upon sb./sth.]** Einfluss [auf jmdn./etw.] ausüben; **I'll ~ it if I can** (*coll.*) ich werde das schon irgendwie deichseln (*ugs.*); **~ it** *or* **things so that …** (*coll.*) es deichseln, dass … (*ugs.*); **G** (*cause to go gradually*) führen; **~ a key/rod into sth.** einen Schlüssel/eine Stange [vorsichtig] in etw. (*Akk.*) einführen; **~ one's way up/into sth.** sich hocharbeiten/in etw. (*Akk.*) hineinarbeiten; **H** (*get gradually*) bringen; **~ oneself out of sth./into a position** sich von etw. befreien/sich in eine Position hocharbeiten; **I** (*knead, stir*) **~ sth. into sth.** etw. zu etw. verarbeiten; (*mix in*) etw. unter etw. (*Akk.*) rühren; **J** (*gradually excite*) **~ oneself into a state/a rage** sich aufregen/in einen Wutanfall hineinsteigern; **~ sb. into a state** jmdn. aufregen; **K** (*make by needle~ etc.*) arbeiten; aufsticken ‹Muster› (**on** auf + *Akk.*); **L** (*purchase, obtain with labour*) abarbeiten; (*fig.*) **~ one's keep** für sein Geld etwas leisten; **she ~ed her way through college** sie hat sich (*Dat.*) ihr Studium selbst verdient; **he ~ed his way up from office boy to company chairman** er hat sich vom Bürogehilfen zum Generaldirektor hochgearbeitet; ⇒ *also* **passage** F; **M** (*Math.*) lösen ‹Rechenaufgabe, Problem›

**~ aˈway** *v.i.* **~ away [at sth.]** [an etw. (*Dat.*)] arbeiten

**~ ˈin** *v.t.* (*include*) hineinbringen; (*mix in*) hineinrühren; (*rub in*) einreiben; ⇒ *also* **work-in**

**~ ˈoff** *v.t.* **A** (*get rid of*) loswerden; abreagieren ‹Wut›; **~ sth. off on sb./sth.** etw. an jmdm./etw. auslassen; **~ off some excess energy** überschüssige Energie loswerden; **B** (*pay off*) abtragen ‹Schuld›

**~ on** ❶ /ˈ--/ *v.t.* **A** (*expend effort on*) **~ on sth.** an etw. (*Dat.*) arbeiten; **B** (*use as basis*) **~ on sth.** von etw. ausgehen; **C** (*try to persuade*) **~ on sb.** jmdn. bearbeiten (*ugs.*). ❷ /-ˈ-/ *v.i.* weiterarbeiten

**~ ˈout** ❶ *v.t.* **A** (*find by calculation*) ausrechnen; **B** (*solve*) lösen ‹Problem, Rechenaufgabe›; **C** (*resolve*) **~ things out with sb./for oneself** die Angelegenheit mit jmdm./sich selbst ausmachen; **things ~ themselves out** es erledigt sich alles von selbst; **D** (*devise*) ausarbeiten ‹Plan, Strategie›; **E** (*make out*) herausfinden; (*understand*) verstehen; **I can't ~ him out** ich werde aus ihm nicht klug; **F** (*Mining: exhaust*) ausbeuten. ❷ *v.i.* **A** (*be calculated*) **sth. ~s out at £250/[an increase of] 22%** etw. ergibt 250 Pfund/bedeutet [eine Steigerung von] 22%; **it will ~ out more expensive to buy the car on h.p.** es wird mehr kosten, das Auto auf Kredit zu kaufen; **B** (*give definite result*) ‹Gleichung, Rechnung:› aufgehen; **C** (*have result*) laufen; **things ~ed out [well] in the end** es ist schließlich doch alles gut gegangen; **things didn't ~ out the way we planned** es kam ganz anders, als wir geplant hatten; **how are the new arrangements ~ing out?** wie klappt es mit der neuen Regelung? (*ugs.*); **D** (*train*) trainieren; ⇒ *also* **workout**

**~ ˈover** *v.t.* **A** (*examine thoroughly*) durcharbeiten; **B** (*coll.: beat up*) in die Mache nehmen (*salopp*)

**~ through** *v.t.* durcharbeiten

**~ towards** *v.t.* (*lit. or fig.*) hinarbeiten auf (+ *Akk.*)

**~ ˈup** ❶ *v.t.* **A** (*develop*) verarbeiten (**into** zu); (*create*) erarbeiten; **B** (*excite by degrees*) aufpeitschen ‹Menge›; **get ~ed up** sich aufregen; **~ oneself up into a rage/fury** sich in einen Wutanfall/in Raserei hineinsteigern; **C** (*acquire familiarity with*) **~ up one's French/maths/history** seine Französisch-/Mathematik-/Geschichtskenntnisse vertiefen; **D** (*mix*) verarbeiten (**into** zu). ❷ *v.i.* **A** (*advance gradually*) **~ up to sth.** ‹Musik:› sich zu etw. steigern; ‹Geschichte, Film:› auf etw. (*Akk.*) zusteuern; **I'll have to ~ up to it** ich muss darauf hinarbeiten; **B** ‹Rock usw.:› sich hochschieben

**workable** /ˈwɜːkəbl/ *adj.* **A** (*capable of being worked*) bebaubar ‹Land›; abbauwürdig ‹Mine›; **be ~** ‹Mörtel:› sich verarbeiten lassen; ‹Stahl:› sich bearbeiten lassen; ‹Mine:› sich ausbeuten lassen; **B** (*feasible*) durchführbar

**workaday** /ˈwɜːkədeɪ/ *adj.* alltäglich

**workaholic** /wɜːkəˈhɒlɪk/ *n.* (*coll.*) arbeitswütiger Mensch; Workaholic, *der* (*Psych.*); *attrib.* arbeitswütig

**work: ~bag** *n.* [Hand]arbeitsbeutel, *der;* **~basket** *n.* Handarbeitskorb, *der;* **~bench** *n.* Werkbank, *die;* (*of tailor, glazier*) Arbeitstisch, *der;* **~box** *n.* Nähkasten, *der;* **~ camp** *n.:* *Lager freiwilliger Helfer;* (*labour camp*) Arbeitslager, *das;* **~day** *n.* Werktag, *der*

**worker** /ˈwɜːkə(r)/ *n.* **A** Arbeiter, *der*/Arbeiterin, *die;* **he is not one of the world's ~s** (*coll.*) er hat die Arbeit nicht gerade erfunden (*ugs.*); **~ of miracles** Wundertäter, *der;* **B** (*Zool.*) Arbeiterin, *die*

**worker: ~ bee** *n.* (*Zool.*) Arbeiterbiene, *die;* **~ ˈpriest** *n.* (*Eccl.*) Arbeiterpriester, *der*

**work: ~ ethic** *n., no pl.* Arbeitsethos, *das;* **~ experience** *n.* Arbeitserfahrung, *die;* **~force** *n.* Belegschaft, *die;* **~horse** *n.* (*lit. or fig.*) Arbeitspferd, *das;* **~house** *n.* (*Brit. Hist., Amer.*) Arbeitshaus, *das;* **~-in** *n.* Betriebsbesetzung, *die* (*mit Weiterführung der Arbeit bei drohender Aussperrung*)

**working** /ˈwɜːkɪŋ/ ❶ *n.* **A** Arbeiten, *das;* **forbid sb.'s ~:** verbieten, dass jmd. arbeitet; **B** (*way sth. works*) Arbeitsweise, *die;* **I cannot follow the ~s of his mind** ich kann seinen Gedankengängen nicht folgen; **the ~s of fate** die Wege des Schicksals; **C** (*Mining*) Stollen, *der.* ❷ *adj.* **A** handlungsfähig ‹Mehrheit›; ‹Entwurf, Vereinbarung› als Ausgangspunkt; **B** (*in employment*) arbeitend; werktätig; **~ man** (*labourer*) Arbeiter, *der*

**working: ~ ˈbreakfast** *n.* Arbeitsfrühstück, *das;* **~ ˈcapital** *n.* (*Commerc.*) Betriebskapital, *das;* **~ ˈclass** *n.* Arbeiterklasse, *die;* **~-class** *adj.* der Arbeiterklasse *nachgestellt;* **sb. is ~-class** jmd. gehört zur Arbeiterklasse; **~ clothes** *n. pl.* Arbeitskleidung, *die;* **~ ˈday** *n.* **A** (*portion of the day*) Arbeitstag, *der;* **B** (*day when work is done*) ⇒ **workday;** **~ ˈdrawing** *n.* Konstruktionszeichnung, *die;* (*for building*) Bauplan, *der;* **~ girl** *n.* berufstätige junge Frau; **she's a ~ girl** (*coll. euphem.*) sie ist im horizontalen Gewerbe tätig (*ugs. scherzh.*); **~ ˈhours** *n. pl.* Arbeitszeit, *die;* **~ hyˈpothesis** *n.* Arbeitshypothese, *die;* **~ ˈknowledge** *n.* ausreichende Kenntnisse (**of** in + *Dat.*); **sb. with a ~ knowledge of these machines** jmd., der im Umgang mit diesen Maschinen erfahren ist; **~ ˈlunch** *n.* Arbeitsessen, *das;* **~ ˈmodel** *n.* funktionsfähiges Modell; **~ ˈmother** *n.* berufstätige Mutter; **~ ˈorder** *n.* betriebsfähiger Zustand; **be in good ~ order** betriebsbereit sein; **~-ˈout** *n.* **A** (*calculation of results*) Berechnung, *die;* **B** (*elaboration of details*) Ausarbeitung, *die;* **~-ˈover** *n.* (*sl.*) Abreibung, *die* (*ugs.*); **~ party** *n.* (*Brit.*) Arbeitsgruppe, *die;* **~ ˈtitle** *n.* Arbeitstitel, *der;* **~ ˈweek** *n.* Arbeitswoche, *die;*

W

a **35-hour ~ week** eine 35-Stunden-Woche; **~ 'wife** *n.* berufstätige Ehefrau; **~ 'woman** *n.* berufstätige Frau

**work: ~load** *n.* Arbeitslast, *die;* **increase sb.'s ~load** jmds. Arbeitspensum erhöhen; **~man** /'wɜ:kmən/ *n., pl.* **~men** /'wɜ:kmən/ Arbeiter, *der;* **council ~man** städtischer Arbeiter; **a bad ~man quarrels with** *or* **blames his tools** (*prov.*) ein schlechter Handwerker schimpft über sein Werkzeug; **~manlike** /'wɜ:kmənlaɪk/ *adj.* fachmännisch; **do a ~manlike job** fachmännisch arbeiten; **~manship** /'wɜ:kmənʃɪp/ *n., no pl.* **A** (*person's skill*) handwerkliches Können; **B** (*quality of execution*) Kunstfertigkeit, *die;* **C** *no indef. art.* (*thing made*) Werk, *das;* **~mate** *n.* (*Brit.*) Arbeitskollege, *der*/-kollegin, *die;* **~out** *n.* [Fitness]training, *das;* **have a good ~out** hart trainieren; **go for a ~out** zum [Fitness]training gehen; **~people** *n. pl.* Arbeiter; **~ permit** *n.* Arbeitserlaubnis, *die;* **~piece** *n.* Werkstück, *das;* **~place** *n.* Arbeitsplatz, *der;* **~room** *n.* Arbeitsraum, *der;* **~-sharing** *n.* Jobsharing, *das;* **~sheet** *n.* **A** (*recording ~ done etc.*) Arbeitszettel, *der;* **B** (*for student*) Formular mit Prüfungsfragen; **~shop** *n.* **A** (*place*) (*room*) Werkstatt, *die;* (*building*) Werk, *das;* **B** (*meeting*) Workshop, *der;* Arbeitstreffen, *das;* **drama ~shop** Theaterworkshop, *der;* **~-shy** *adj.* arbeitsscheu; **~space** *n.* Arbeitsraum, *der;* **~station** *n.* **A** (*in manufacturing*) Fertigungsstation, *die;* **B** (*Computing*) Workstation, *die;* **~ study** *n.* Arbeitsstudien; (*case*) Arbeitsstudie, *die;* **~ surface** ⇒ **~top**; **~ table** *n.* Arbeitstisch, *der;* **~top** *n.* Arbeitsplatte, *die;* **~-to-'rule** *n.* Dienst nach Vorschrift

**world** /wɜ:ld/ *n.* **A** Welt, *die; attrib.* Welt-; **the ~'s worst novel** der schlechteste Roman der Welt; **the biggest aspidistra in the ~:** die größte Schusterpalme der Welt; **go/sail round the ~:** eine Weltreise machen/die Welt umsegeln; **money makes the ~ go round** Geld regiert die Welt; **that's what/it's love that makes the ~ go round** darum/um die Liebe dreht sich letztlich alles; **it's the same the ~ over** es ist doch überall das Gleiche; **the eyes of the ~ are on them** die Welt blickt auf sie; **all the ~** *or* **the whole ~ knows** alle Welt (*ugs.*) weiß; **[all] the ~ over, all over the ~:** in *od.* auf der ganzen Welt; **it's the same the whole ~ over** es ist überall das Gleiche; **people from all over the ~ wrote to him** er bekam Post aus aller Welt; **give sth. to the ~:** etw. der Welt übergeben (*fig.*); **lead the ~ [in sth.]** [in etw. (*Dat.*)] führend in der Welt sein; **the Old/New W~:** die Alte/Neue Welt; **the Roman ~:** die römische Welt; **she had the ~ at her feet** die ganze Welt lag ihr zu Füßen; **who/what in the ~ was it?** wer/was in aller Welt war es? (*ugs.*); **how in the ~ was it that ...?** wie in aller Welt (*ugs.*) war es möglich, dass ...?; **nothing in the ~ would persuade me** um nichts in der Welt ließe ich mich überreden; **not for anything in the ~:** um nichts in der Welt; **look for all the ~ as if ...:** geradezu aussehen, als ob ...; **in a ~ of one's own** in einer anderen Welt (*fig.*); **the external ~:** die Außenwelt *od.* äußere Welt; **the ~ of dreams** die Welt der Träume; **not do sth. for the** *or* **to gain the whole ~:** etw. um alles in der Welt nicht tun; **be all the ~ to sb.** jmdm. das Wichtigste/Liebste auf der Welt sein; **think the ~ of sb.** große Stücke auf jmdn. halten (*ugs.*); **I would give the ~ to know why ...:** ich gäbe alles darum, zu wissen, warum ...; **all alone in the ~:** ganz allein auf der Welt; **the Napoleons of this ~:** die Napoleons dieser Erde; **sb. is not long for this ~:** jmds. Tage sind gezählt; **out of this ~** (*fig. coll.*) fantastisch (*ugs.*); **the other** *or* **next ~, the ~ to come** das Jenseits; die zukünftige Welt; **bring into the ~** (*possess at one's birth*) in die Welt bringen; (*deliver at birth*) auf die Welt holen; (*beget*) in die Welt setzen (*ugs.*); (*give birth to*) zur Welt bringen; **come into the ~:** auf die Welt kommen; **the best of all possible ~s** die beste aller Welten; **get the best of both ~s** am meisten profitieren; **the ~'s end, the end of the ~:** das Ende der Welt; **it's not the end of the ~** (*iron.*) davon geht die Welt nicht unter (*ugs.*); **~ without end** in alle Ewigkeit; **know/have seen a lot of the ~:** die Welt kennen/viel von der Welt gesehen haben; **see the ~:** die Welt kennen lernen; **a man/woman of the ~:** ein Mann/eine Frau mit Welterfahrung; **think that all's right with the ~:** glauben, dass die Welt in Ordnung ist; **take the ~ as it is** *or* **as one finds it** alles nehmen, wie es kommt; **what 'is the ~ coming to?** wo soll das noch hinführen? (*ugs.*); **how goes the ~ with you?** wie gehts[, wie stehts]?; **all the ~ and his wife** alle Welt (*ugs.*); **go up/come down in the ~:** [gesellschaftlich] aufsteigen/absteigen; *attrib.* **~ politics** Weltpolitik, *die;* ⇒ *also* **oyster**; **B** (*domain*) **the literary/scientific/ancient/sporting/animal ~:** die literarische/wissenschaftliche/antike Welt (*geh.*)/die Welt (*geh.*) des Sports/die Tierwelt; **the ~ of letters/art/sport** die Welt (*geh.*) der Literatur/Kunst/des Sports; **C** (*vast amount*) **a ~ of meaning/trouble** eine unendliche Bedeutungsfülle/Fülle von Schwierigkeiten; **it will do him a** *or* **the ~ of good** es wird ihm unendlich gut tun; **a ~ of difference** ein weltweiter Unterschied; **a ~ away from sth.** Welten von etw. entfernt; **they are ~s apart in their views** ihre Ansichten sind Welten voneinander entfernt

**world: W~ 'Bank** *n.* Weltbank, *die;* **~-beater** *n.* **be a ~-beater** zur Spitzenklasse gehören; **~ 'champion** *n.* Weltmeister, *der*/-meisterin, *die;* **W~ 'Cup** *n.* (*Sport*) Worldcup, *der;* **~-famous** *adj.* weltberühmt; **~ 'language** *n.* Weltsprache, *die*

**worldliness** /'wɜ:ldlɪnɪs/ *n., no pl.* Weltlichkeit, *die*

**worldly** /'wɜ:ldlɪ/ *adj.* weltlich; weltlich eingestellt ‹Person›

**worldly: ~ 'goods** *n. pl.* weltliche Güter; **~ 'wisdom** *n.* Weltklugheit, *die;* **~ 'wise** *adj.* weltklug

**world: ~ 'power** *n.* Weltmacht, *die;* **~ 'record** *n.* Weltrekord, *der; attrib.* **~-record holder** Weltrekordhalter, *der*/-halterin, *die;* **W~ Series** *n.* (*Amer. Sport*) *Baseball-Ausscheidungen zwischen den Gewinnern der bedeutendsten Ligen der USA;* **~-shaking** *adj.* welterschütternd; **~ view** *n.* Weltsicht, *die;* **~ 'war** *n.* Weltkrieg, *der;* **the First/Second W~ War, W~ War I/II** der Erste/Zweite Weltkrieg; der 1./2. Weltkrieg; **~-weary** *adj.* lebensüberdrüssig; **~wide** ❶ /'--/ *adj.* weltweit *nicht präd.;* ❷ /-'-/ *adv.* weltweit; **W~ Wide 'Web** *n.* (*Computing*) World Wide Web, *das*

**worm** /wɜ:m/ ❶ *n.* **A** Wurm, *der;* **[even] a ~ will turn** (*prov.*) auch der Wurm krümmt sich, wenn er getreten wird (*Spr.*); **B** *in pl.* (*intestinal parasites*) Würmer; **C** (*fig.: contemptible person*) Wurm, *der;* **feel like a ~:** sich (*Dat.*) klein und hässlich vorkommen; **he's a real ~:** er ist ein richtiger Widerling. ❷ *v.t.* **A he ~ed his hand into his trouser pocket** er zwängte seine Hand in die Hosentasche; **~ one's way through sth.** sich durch etw. winden (*geh.*) *od.* zwängen; **~ oneself** *or* **one's way into sth.** (*fig.*) sich in etw. (*Akk.*) hineindrängen; **~ oneself into sb.'s favour** sich in jmds. Gunst (*Akk.*) schleichen; **B** (*draw by crafty persistence*) **~ sth. out of sb.** etw. aus jmdm. herausbringen (*ugs.*); **C** (*rid of ~s*) entwurmen. ❸ *v.i.* sich winden

**worm: ~ cast** *n.* Kothäufchen des Regenwurms; **~-eaten** *adj.* wurmstichig; (*fig.*) vom Zahn der Zeit angenagt; **~ gear** *n.* Schneckengetriebe, *das* (*Technik*); **~hole** *n.* Wurmloch, *das;* **~ powder** *n.* Wurmpulver, *das;* **~'s-eye 'view** *n.* Froschperspektive, *die* (*auch fig.*)

**'wormwood** *n.* Wermut, *der*

**wormy** /'wɜ:mɪ/ *adj.* wurmig ‹Apfel›; von Würmern befallen ‹Tier›; wurmreich ‹Boden, Erde›

**worn** ⇒ **wear** 2, 3

**'worn-out** *attrib. adj.* abgetragen ‹Kleidungsstück›; abgenutzt ‹Teppich›; abgedroschen ‹Redensart, Ausdruck›; erschöpft, (*ugs.*) erledigt ‹Person›

**worried** /'wʌrɪd/ *adj.* besorgt; **give sb. a ~ look** jmdn. besorgt ansehen; **you had me ~:** ich habe mir [deinetwegen] Sorgen gemacht; **don't look so ~!** schau nicht so bekümmert drein!; **~ sick** krank vor Sorge; **be much** *or* **very ~:** sich (*Dat.*) große Sorgen machen

**worrier** /'wʌrɪə(r)/ *n.* **be too much of a ~:** sich (*Dat.*) immer [zu viel] Sorgen machen; **he's a [real] ~:** er macht sich (*Dat.*) um alles Sorgen

**worrisome** /'wʌrɪsəm/ *adj.* besorgniserregend

**worry** /'wʌrɪ/ ❶ *v.t.* **A** beunruhigen; **it worries me to death to think that ...:** ich sorge mich zu Tode, wenn ich [daran] denke, dass ...; **~ oneself [about sth.]** sich (*Dat.*) um etw. Sorgen machen; **~ oneself sick [about sb./sth.]** krank vor Sorge [um jmdn./etw.] werden; **B** (*bother*) stören; **C ~ a bone** ‹Hund usw.:› an einem Knochen [herum]nagen; **D** (*attack*) ‹Hund usw.:› reißen ‹Schaf›. ❷ *v.i.* sich (*Dat.*) Sorgen machen; sich sorgen; **~ about sth.** sich (*Dat.*) um etw. Sorgen machen; **don't ~ about it** mach dir deswegen keine Sorgen!; **'I should ~** (*coll. iron.*) was kümmert mich das?; **not to ~** (*coll.*) kein Problem (*ugs.*). ❸ *n.* Sorge, *die;* **sth. is the least of sb.'s worries** etw. ist jmds. geringste Sorge; **it must be a great ~ to you** es muss dir große Sorgen bereiten

**'worry beads** *n. pl. Perlenschnur zur Beschäftigung für nervöse Hände*

**worrying** /'wʌrɪɪŋ/ ❶ *adj.* **A** (*causing worry*) beunruhigend; **sth. is very ~ for sb.** etw. macht jmdm. große Sorgen; **B** (*full of worry*) sorgenvoll ‹Zeit, Woche usw.›; **it is a ~ time for her** sie hat zurzeit große Sorgen. ❷ *n.* **~ only makes everything worse** sich (*Dat.*) Sorgen zu machen macht alles nur noch schlimmer

**worse** /wɜ:s/ ❶ *adj. compar. of* **bad** 1 schlechter; schlimmer ‹Schmerz, Krankheit, Benehmen›; **things could not/could be ~:** es kann nicht mehr schlimmer kommen/es könnte schlimmer sein; **the food is bad, and the service ~:** das Essen ist schlecht und die Bedienung noch schlechter; **his manners are ~ than a pig's** er benimmt sich schlimmer als ein Schwein; **he's getting ~:** mit ihm wird es schlimmer; (*his health*) ihm geht es schlechter; **be ~ than useless** ‹Sache:› mehr als unbrauchbar sein; ‹Person:› ein hoffnungsloser Fall sein; **be [none] the ~ for sth.** ‹Sache:› in [k]einem schlechteren Zustand wegen etw. sein; **sb. is [none] the ~ for sth.** jmdm. geht es wegen etw. [nicht] schlechter; **~ and ~:** immer schlechter/schlimmer; **to make matters ~, ...:** zu allem Übel ...; **it could have been ~:** es hätte schlimmer sein *od.* kommen können; **~ luck!** so ein Pech!; ⇒ *also* **drink** 1 D; **liquor** A; **wear** 1 A. ❷ *adv. compar. of* **badly** schlechter; schlimmer, schlechter ‹sich benehmen›; **~ and ~:** immer schlechter/schlimmer; ⇒ *also* **better** 3 A; **off** 1 I. ❸ *n.* Schlimmeres; **she might do ~ than settle for that job** es wäre bestimmt kein Fehler, wenn sie sich für die Stelle entschiede; **go from bad to ~:** immer schlimmer werden; **or ~:** oder noch Schlimmeres; **~ still** schlimmer noch; **a change for the ~:** eine Wende zum Schlechteren; **take a turn for the ~:** sich verschlechtern; ‹Krankheit:› sich verschlimmern; **nobody will think any the ~ of you** niemand wird deswegen schlechter von dir denken; **there is ~ to come** es kommt noch schlimmer; ⇒ *also* **worst** 3

**worsen** /'wɜ:sn/ ❶ *v.t.* verschlechtern; verschlimmern ‹Knappheit›. ❷ *v.i.* sich verschlechtern; ‹Hungersnot, Sturm, Problem:› sich verschlimmern; **she ~ed in the night** ihr Zustand hat sich über Nacht verschlimmert

W

**worship** /ˈwɜːʃɪp/ ❶ *v.t.*, (*Brit.*) **-pp-:** Ⓐ verehren ‹Gott, Götter, Kaiser›; anbeten ‹Gott, Götter›; Ⓑ (*idolize*) abgöttisch verehren; **he ~s the ground she walks on** er küsst den Boden unter ihren Füßen.
❷ *v.i.*, (*Brit.*) **-pp-:** Ⓐ am Gottesdienst teilnehmen; Ⓑ (*be full of adoration*) tiefe Verehrung empfinden.
❸ *n.* Ⓐ Anbetung, *die;* (*service*) Gottesdienst, *der;* **public ~:** [öffentlicher] Gottesdienst; **dedicated as a place of ~:** dem Gottesdienst geweiht; **gather for ~:** sich zum Gottesdienst versammeln; **freedom of ~:** Glaubensfreiheit, *die;* Ⓑ (*adoration*) Verehrung, *die;* **an object of ~:** ein Gegenstand der Verehrung; **the ~ of wealth/intellect** die Anbetung des Wohlstands/Intellekts; Ⓒ ▶ **1617** (*form of address*) **Your/His W~** *Anrede für Richter, Bürgermeister;* ≈ Euer/Seine Ehren

**worshiper** (*Amer.*) ⇒ **worshipper**

**worshipful** /ˈwɜːʃɪpfl/ *adj.* (*Brit.*) *Titulierung von Friedensrichtern, Zünften, Freimaurerlogen usw.*

**worshipper** /ˈwɜːʃɪpə(r)/ *n.* Ⓐ (*in church etc.*) Gottesdienstbesucher, *der*/-besucherin, *die;* Ⓑ (*of deity*) Anbeter, *der*/Anbeterin, *die;* Ⓒ (*of person, money, etc.*) Verehrer, *der*/Verehrerin, *die;* **be a ~ of sth.** etw. anbeten (*fig.*)

**worst** /wɜːst/ ❶ *adj. superl. of* **bad** 1 Ⓐ ⇒ **worse** 1: schlechtest.../schlimmst...; **be ~:** am schlechtesten/schlimmsten sein; **the ~ thing about it was ...:** das Schlimmste daran war ...; **the ~ thing you could do** das Schlechteste, was du machen könntest; Ⓑ (*least efficient, of poorest quality*) schlechtest...
❷ *adv. superl. of* **badly** am schlimmsten; am schlechtesten ‹gekleidet›.
❸ *n.* Ⓐ **[the] ~:** der/die/das Schlimmste; **you saw him at his ~:** du hast ihn in seinem schlimmsten Zustand erlebt; **prepare for the ~:** sich auf das Schlimmste gefasst machen; **at ~, at the [very] ~:** schlimmstenfalls; im [aller]schlimmsten Fall[e]; **get** *or* **have the ~ of it** (*be defeated*) [vernichtend] geschlagen werden; (*suffer the most*) am meisten zu leiden haben; **if the ~** *or* **it comes to the ~** (*Brit.*), **if worse comes to ~** (*Amer.*) wenn es zum Schlimmsten kommt; **do your ~:** mach, was du willst!; **let him do his ~:** er soll machen, was er will; Ⓑ (*what is of poorest quality*) Schlechteste, *der/die/das.*
❹ *v.t.* [vernichtend] schlagen; **be ~ed in argument** sich geschlagen geben müssen

**worsted** /ˈwʊstɪd/ *n.* (*Textiles*) Kammgarn, *das*

**wort** /wɜːt/ *n.* [Bier]würze, *die*

**worth** /wɜːθ/ ❶ *adj.* Ⓐ ▶ **1328** (*of value equivalent to*) wert; **it's ~/not ~ £80** es ist 80 Pfund wert/80 Pfund ist es nicht wert; **it is not ~ much** *or* **a lot [to sb.]** es ist [jmdm.] nicht viel wert; **be ~ the money** das Geld wert sein; **not ~ a penny** keinen Pfennig wert (*ugs.*); **it's ~ a lot to me that ...:** es bedeutet mir viel, dass ...; **he's ~ the lot of you put together** er ist so viel wert wie ihr alle zusammen; **for what it is ~:** was immer auch davon zu halten ist; ⇒ *also* **gold** 1 A; Ⓑ (*worthy of*) **is it ~ hearing/the effort?** ist es hörenswert/der Mühe wert?; **is it ~ doing?** lohnt es sich?; **if it's ~ doing, it's ~ doing well** wenn schon, denn schon; **it isn't ~ it** es lohnt sich nicht; **an experience ~ having** eine lohnenswerte Erfahrung; **it's ~ a try** es ist einen Versuch wert; **it would be [well] ~ it** (*coll.*) es würde sich [sehr] lohnen; **be well ~ sth.** durchaus *od.* sehr wohl etw. wert sein; **you can have my opinion for what it's ~:** ich kann dir sagen, was meine bescheidene Meinung ist; **it's more than my job's ~:** es könnte mich meine Stelle kosten; Ⓒ **be ~ sth.** (*possess*) etw. wert sein (*ugs.*); **run/cycle for all one is ~** (*coll.*) rennen/fahren, was man kann. ⇒ *also* **salt** 1 A; **while** 1.
❷ *n.* Ⓐ ▶ **1328** (*equivalent of money etc. in commodity*) **ten pounds' ~ of petrol** Benzin für zehn Pfund; (*more formal*) Benzin im Wert von zehn Pfund; Ⓑ (*value, excellence*) Wert, *der;* **of great/little/no ~:** von hohem/geringem Wert/ohne Wert. ⇒ *also* **money's-worth**; **pennyworth**

**worthily** /ˈwɜːðɪlɪ/ *adv.* ehrenhaft; zu Recht ‹verdienen›

**worthiness** /ˈwɜːðɪnɪs/ *n., no pl.* Ehrenhaftigkeit, *die;* (*of cause, charity*) Wert, *der*

**worthless** /ˈwɜːθlɪs/ *adj.* Ⓐ (*valueless*) wertlos; Ⓑ (*despicable*) nichtswürdig

ˈ**worthwhile** *attrib. adj.* lohnend; ⇒ *also* **while** 1

**worthy** /ˈwɜːðɪ/ ❶ *adj.* Ⓐ (*adequate, estimable*) würdig; verdienstvoll ‹Tat›; angemessen ‹Belohnung›; **~ of the occasion** dem Anlass angemessen; Ⓑ (*deserving*) würdig; verdienstvoll ‹Sache, Organisation›; **be ~ of the name** den Namen verdienen; **~ of note/mention** erwähnenswert; **is he ~ of her?** ist er ihrer würdig? ❷ *n.* Ⓐ (*person of distinction*) Würdenträger, *der;* Ⓑ **local worthies** (*joc.*) örtliche Honoratioren

**wotcher** /ˈwɒtʃə(r)/ *int.* (*Brit. coll.*) hallo (*ugs.*)

**would** ⇒ **will**[1]

**would-be** /ˈwʊdbiː/ *attrib. adj.* **a ~ philosopher** ein Möchtegernphilosoph; **a ~ aggressor** ein möglicher Aggressor

**wouldn't** /ˈwʊdnt/ (*coll.*) = **would not;** ⇒ **will**[1]

**wound**[1] /wuːnd/ ❶ *n.* (*lit. or fig.*) Wunde, *die;* **a war ~:** eine Kriegsverletzung; **receive a ~ in the chest/leg** an der Brust/am Bein verwundet werden; **a knife-~ across the palm** eine Schnittwunde quer über die Handfläche; **this was a great ~ to her pride** (*fig.*) das verletzte ihren Stolz zutiefst. ❷ *v.t.* verwunden; (*fig.*) verletzen; **be ~ed in the thigh/arm** am Oberschenkel/Arm verwundet werden

**wound**[2] ⇒ **wind**[2] 1, 2

**wove, woven** ⇒ **weave**[1] 2, 3

**wow**[1] /waʊ/ ❶ *int.* hoi. ❷ *n.* (*coll.*) **be a ~:** eine Wucht sein (*salopp*). ❸ *v.t.* (*coll.*) umhauen (*ugs.*)

**wow**[2] *n.* (*Electronics*) Jaulen, *das* (*fig.*)

**WP** *abbr.* **word processor**

**w. p. b.** *abbr.* **waste-paper basket**

**WPC** *abbr.* **woman police constable** Wachtmeisterin, *die*

**w. p. m.** *abbr.* **words per minute** WpM

**wraith** /reɪθ/ *n.* Gespenst, *das*

ˈ**wraithlike** *adj.* gespenstisch

**wrangle** /ˈræŋgl/ ❶ *v.i.* [sich] streiten. ❷ *n.* Streit, *der;* **what are those two having such a ~ about?** worüber streiten die beiden sich denn so?

**wrap** /ræp/ ❶ *v.t.*, **-pp-** Ⓐ einwickeln; (*fig.*) hüllen; **~ped** abgepackt ‹Brot usw.›; **~ sth. in paper/cotton wool** etw. in Papier/Watte [ein]wickeln; **~ sth. [a]round sth.** (*lit. or fig.*) etw. um etw. wickeln; **~ one's arms around sb.** die Arme um jmdn. schlingen; Ⓑ (*arrange*) schlingen ‹Schal, Handtuch usw.› (**about, round** um); **she ~ped her motorcycle round a tree** (*coll.*) sie hat ihr Motorrad um einen Baum gewickelt (*ugs.*). ❷ *n.* Umschlag[e]tuch, *das;* **take the ~s off sth.** (*fig.*) etw. der Öffentlichkeit vorstellen; **under ~s** (*fig.*) unter Verschluss; **keep sth. under ~s** etw. geheim halten

~ ˈ**up** ❶ *v.t.* Ⓐ ⇒ **wrap** 1; **wrapped up;** Ⓑ (*fig.: conclude*) abschließen; **that just about ~s it up for today** damit sind wir für heute fertig. ❷ *v.i.* Ⓐ (*put on warm clothing*) sich warm einpacken (*ugs.*); **mind you ~ up well** du musst dich gut einpacken (*ugs.*); Ⓑ (*sl.: be quiet*) den Rand halten (*salopp*)

ˈ**wraparound** ❶ *adj.* Ⓐ Wickel‹kleid, -rock›; Ⓑ Panorama‹windschutzscheibe, -sonnenbrille›. ❷ *n.* Wickelrock, *der*

**wrapped up** /ræpt ˈʌp/ *adj.* **be ~ in one's work** in seine Arbeit völlig versunken sein; **she is very ~ in her family** sie geht ganz in ihrer Familie auf; **be too ~ in one's problems** zu sehr mit seinen [eigenen] Problemen beschäftigt sein; **a country whose prosperity is ~ in its shipping** ein Land, dessen Reichtum eng mit seiner Schifffahrt verknüpft ist

**wrapper** /ˈræpə(r)/ *n.* Ⓐ (*around newspaper etc.*) Streifband, *das* (*Postw.*); Ⓑ (*around sweet etc.*) **sweet/toffee ~[s]** Bonbonpapier, *das;* Ⓒ (*of book*) ⇒ **jacket** C

**wrapping** /ˈræpɪŋ/ *n.* Verpackung, *die;* **~s** Verpackung, *die;* (*fig.*) Hülle, *die* (*dichter.*)

ˈ**wrapping paper** *n.* (*strong paper*) Packpapier, *das;* (*decorative paper*) Geschenkpapier, *das*

**wrasse** /ræs/ *n.* (*Zool.*) Lippfisch, *der*

**wrath** /rɒθ/ *n.* (*poet./rhet.*) Zorn, *der*

**wrathful** /ˈrɒθfl/ *adj.* (*poet./rhet.*) zornig

**wreak** /riːk/ *v.t.* Ⓐ (*inflict*) **~ vengeance on sb.** an jmdm. Rache nehmen; Ⓑ (*vent*) auslassen ‹Wut, Ärger› (**on** an + *Dat.*); Ⓒ (*cause*) anrichten ‹Verwüstung, Unheil›

**wreath** /riːθ/ *n., pl.* **wreaths** /riːðz, riːθs/ Kranz, *der;* **a ~ of smoke** ein Ring aus Rauch

**wreathe** /riːð/ ❶ *v.t.* Ⓐ (*encircle*) umkränzen; **her face was ~d in smiles** ein Lächeln umspielte ihre Lippen; Ⓑ (*form into wreath*) zu einem Kranz flechten *od.* (*geh.*) winden; Ⓒ (*make by interweaving*) flechten; winden (*geh.*). ❷ *v.i.* sich winden; ‹Rauch:› sich ringeln *od.* kräuseln (**from** aus)

**wreck** /rek/ ❶ *n.* Ⓐ (*destruction*) Schiffbruch, *der;* (*fig.*) Zerstörung, *die;* Ⓑ (*ship*) Wrack, *das;* Ⓒ (*broken remains, lit. or fig.*) Wrack, *das;* **she was a physical/mental ~:** sie war körperlich/geistig ein Wrack; **I feel/you look a ~** (*coll.*) ich fühle mich kaputt (*ugs.*)/du siehst kaputt aus (*ugs.*). ❷ *v.t.* Ⓐ (*destroy*) ruinieren; zu Schrott fahren ‹Auto›; **be ~ed** (*shipwrecked*) ‹Schiff, Person:› Schiffbruch erleiden; **a ~ed ship/aircraft** ein wrackes *od.* (*fachspr.*) havariertes Schiff/Flugzeug; Ⓑ (*fig.: ruin*) zerstören; ruinieren ‹Gesundheit, Urlaub›; verderben ‹Party, Urlaub›; zunichte machen ‹Hoffnung, Plan›; zerrütten ‹Ehe›

**wreckage** /ˈrekɪdʒ/ *n.* Wrackteile; (*fig.*) Trümmer *Pl.*

**wrecker** /ˈrekə(r)/ *n.* Ⓐ (*who disrupts deliberately*) Umstürzler, *der*/Umstürzlerin, *die;* Ⓑ (*who brings about shipwreck for profit*) Strandräuber, *der;* Ⓒ (*employed in demolition*) Abwracker, *der;* Ⓓ (*who recovers wrecked ships*) Bergungsarbeiter, *der;* Ⓔ (*Amer.: breakdown vehicle*) Bergungsfahrzeug, *das;* Abschleppfahrzeug, *das;* Ⓕ (*Amer.: train*) Hilfszug, *der*

ˈ**wrecking bar** *n.* Brechstange, *die*

**Wren** /ren/ *n.* (*Brit. Hist.*) *Angehörige des weiblichen Marinedienstes;* **join the ~s** in den weiblichen Marinedienst eintreten

**wren** *n.* Zaunkönig, *der*

**wrench** /rentʃ/ ❶ *n.* Ⓐ (*tool*) verstellbarer Schraubenschlüssel; **pipe ~:** Rohrzange, *die;* **screw ~:** Franzose, *der;* Ⓑ (*esp. Amer.*) ⇒ **spanner**; Ⓒ (*violent twist*) Verrenkung, *die;* **give one's ankle/shoulder a ~:** sich (*Dat.*) den Knöchel/die Schulter verrenken; **give a ~ at the door handle** an der Türklinke reißen; Ⓓ (*fig.*) **be a great ~ [for sb.]** sehr schmerzhaft für jmdn. sein; **what a ~ it must have been for her** wie schmerzlich muss es für sie gewesen sein.
❷ *v.t.* Ⓐ (*tug violently*) reißen; **~ at sth.** an etw. (*Dat.*) reißen; **~ sth. round/off/open** etw. herum-/ab-/aufreißen; **~ sth. from sb.** jmdm. etw. entreißen; Ⓑ (*injure by twisting*) **~ one's ankle** *etc.* sich (*Dat.*) den Knöchel *usw.* verrenken

**wrest** /rest/ *v.t.* **~ sth. from sb./sb.'s grasp** (*lit. or fig.*) jmdm./jmds. Griff etw. entreißen *od.* (*geh.*) entwinden; **~ a confession from sb.** jmdm. ein Geständnis abnötigen (*geh.*); **~ sth. from sth.** einer Sache (*Dat.*) etw. abringen

**wrestle** /ˈresl/ ❶ *n.* Ⓐ (*hard struggle*) Ringen, *das;* Ⓑ (*wrestling match*) Ringkampf, *der;* **have a ~:** einen Ringkampf austragen. ❷ *v.i.* Ⓐ ringen; Ⓑ (*fig.: grapple*) sich abmühen; **~ with one's conscience** mit seinem Gewissen ringen; **~ with the controls of the aircraft** mit der Steuerung des Flugzeugs kämpfen. ❸ *v.t.* **~ sth. from sth.** etw. mühsam von etw. entfernen

**wrestler** /ˈreslə(r)/ *n.* Ringer, *der*/Ringerin, *die*

W

**wrestling** /ˈreslɪŋ/ *n., no pl., no indef. art.* Ringen, *das;* **~ match** Ringkampf, *der*

**wretch** /retʃ/ *n.* Kreatur, *die;* (*joc.: child*) Gör, *das*

**wretched** /ˈretʃɪd/ *adj.* A (*miserable*) unglücklich; **feel ~ about sb./sth.** (*be embarrassed*) über jmdn./etw. todunglücklich sein; **feel ~** (*be very unwell*) sich elend fühlen; B (*coll.: damned*) elend (*abwertend*); **I wish he would control that ~ dog of his!** wenn er nur besser auf seinen elenden Köter aufpassen würde!; C (*very bad*) erbärmlich; miserabel ‹Wetter›; **she's had a bout of ~ health** es ging ihr gesundheitlich sehr schlecht; D (*causing discomfort*) schrecklich ‹Reise, Erfahrung, Zeit›

**wretchedly** /ˈretʃɪdlɪ/ *adv.* A (*in misery*) jämmerlich ‹weinen›; jammervoll ‹anblicken›; B (*very badly*) erbärmlich

**wretchedness** /ˈretʃɪdnɪs/ *n., no pl.* A (*misery*) Elend, *das;* B (*badness*) Erbärmlichkeit, *die*

**wrick** ⇒ **rick²**

**wriggle** /ˈrɪgl/ ❶ *v.i.* A zappeln; **~ [about] on one's chair** auf dem Stuhl herumrutschen (*ugs.*); B (*make one's/its way by wriggling*) sich winden; **a worm ~d across the lawn** ein Wurm schlängelte sich über den Rasen; **~ free of the ropes** sich aus den Stricken winden; **~ out of a difficulty** *etc.* (*fig.*) sich aus einer schwierigen Situation *usw.* herauswinden. ❷ *v.t.* A **~ one's way** (*lit. or fig.*) sich schlängeln; **~ one's way out of a difficulty** *etc.* sich aus einer schwierigen Situation *usw.* herauswinden; B (*move*) **~ one's hips** die Hüften kreisen lassen. ❸ *n.* Windung, *die*

**wriggly** /ˈrɪglɪ/ *adj.* sich windend ‹Wurm, Aal›; zappelnd ‹Fisch, Kind›

**wring** /rɪŋ/ *v.t.*, **wrung** /rʌŋ/ A wringen; **~ out** auswringen; **~ the water out of the towels** das Wasser aus den Handtüchern wringen; B (*squeeze forcibly*) **~ sb.'s hand** jmdm. fest die Hand drücken; (*twist forcibly*) **~ one's hands** die Hände ringen (*geh.*); **~ the neck of an animal** einem Tier den Hals umdrehen; **I could have wrung his neck** (*fig.*) ich hätte ihm den Hals umdrehen können; C (*extract*) wringen; **~ sth. from** *or* **out of sb.** (*fig.*) jmdm. etw. abpressen; D (*distress*) **~ the heart** einem das Herz abdrücken

**wringer** /ˈrɪŋə(r)/ *n.* Wringmaschine, *die*

**wringing wet** /rɪŋɪŋ ˈwet/ *adj.* tropfnass; **our clothes were ~:** unsere Kleider waren zum Auswringen

**wrinkle** /ˈrɪŋkl/ ❶ *n.* Falte, *die;* (*in paper*) Knick, *der.* ❷ *v.t.* falten; in Falten legen ‹Stirn›; kräuseln ‹Nase›. ❸ *v.i.* sich in Falten legen

**wrinkled** /ˈrɪŋkld/ *adj.* runz[e]lig; **~ with age** runzlig vom Alter

**wrinklie** /ˈrɪŋklɪ/ ⇒ **wrinkly** 2

**wrinkly** /ˈrɪŋklɪ/ ❶ *adj.* runz[e]lig. ❷ *n.* (*coll.*) Grufti, *der* (*ugs.*)

**wrist** /rɪst/ *n.* ▶ **966** Handgelenk, *das;* **slash one's ~s** sich (*Dat.*) die Pulsadern aufschneiden; **the glove was too tight at the ~:** der Handschuh war zu eng am Handgelenk

**wrist: ~band** *n.* A (*cuff*) Manschette, *die;* B ⇒ **sweatband**; **~watch** *n.* Armbanduhr, *die*

**writ¹** /rɪt/ *n.* (*Law*) A Verfügung, *die;* **serve a ~ on sb.** jmdm. eine Verfügung zustellen; **sb.'s ~ runs in ...** (*fig.*) jmds. Macht reicht bis nach ...; B (*Crown document*) *königlicher Erlass, mit dem ein Peer ins Parlament gerufen wird/mit dem Parlamentswahlen ausgerufen werden;* C (*Relig.*) **Holy W~:** die Heilige Schrift

**writ²** ⇒ **write** 2 A

**write** /raɪt/ ❶ *v.i.*, **wrote** /rəʊt/, **written** /ˈrɪtn/ schreiben; **~ to sb./a firm** jmdm./an eine Firma schreiben; **~ for a fresh supply** schriftlich eine neue Lieferung anfordern; **she ~s for a living** sie ist Schriftstellerin; ⇒ *also* **home.**
❷ *v.t.*, **wrote, written** A schreiben; ausschreiben ‹Scheck›; **the written language** die Schriftsprache; **~ it, don't print it** schreibe es nicht in Druckschrift, sondern in Schreibschrift; **written applications** schriftliche Anträge; **the paper had been written all over** das Papier war ganz voll geschrieben; **it is written that ...:** es steht geschrieben, dass ...; **be written into the contract** [ausdrücklich] im Vertrag stehen; **~ sb. into/out of a serial** für jmdn. eine Rolle in einer Serie schreiben/jmdm. einen Abgang aus einer Serie verschaffen; **writ large** (*fig.*) im Großformat (*fig.*); B (*Amer./Commerc./coll.: ~ letter to*) anschreiben; C *in pass.* (*fig.: be apparent*) **sb. has sth. written in his face** jmdm. steht etw. im Gesicht geschrieben; **guilt was written all over her face** die Schuld stand ihr ins Gesicht geschrieben; **she had 'career woman' written all over her** man sah ihr die Karrierefrau schon von weitem an; D (*Computing*) schreiben; **~ in** *or* **into** *or* **on** *or* **to a disk** auf eine Diskette schreiben; E ⇒ **underwrite**

**~ a'way** *v.i.* **~ away for sth.** etw. [schriftlich] anfordern

**~ 'back** *v.i.* zurückschreiben

**~ 'down** *v.t.* A (*record*) aufschreiben; B (*Commerc.: reduce nominal value of*) abschreiben (*Wirtsch.*)

**~ 'in** ❶ *v.i.* hinschreiben (*ugs.*); (*include*) hineinschreiben; **~ in for sth.** etw. [schriftlich] anfordern; **~ in to sb.** an jmdn. schreiben. ❷ *v.t.* (*Amer. Polit.*) eintragen; ⇒ *also* **write-in**

**~ 'off** ❶ *v.t.* A (*compose with ease*) herunterschreiben (*ugs.*); B (*cancel*) abschreiben ‹Schulden, Verlust›; (*fig.*) **~ sb. off [as a failure** *etc.*] jmdn. [als Versager] abschreiben (*ugs.*); C (*destroy*) zu Schrott fahren. ❷ *v.i.* ⇒ **~ away.** ⇒ *also* **write-off**

**~ 'out** *v.t.* A ausschreiben ‹Scheck›; schreiben ‹Rezept›; B (**~** *in final form*) ausarbeiten; (**~** *in full*) ausschreiben; C (*from serial*) verschwinden lassen

**~ 'up** *v.t.* A (*praise*) eine gute Kritik schreiben über (+ *Akk.*); B (**~** *account of*) einen Bericht schreiben über (+ *Akk.*); (**~** *in full*) aufarbeiten; C (*bring up to date*) auf den neuesten Stand bringen. ⇒ *also* **write-up**

**write: ~-in** *n.* (*Amer.*) *Kandidat, der nicht auf dem offiziellen Stimmzettel steht, sondern vom Wähler selbst eingetragen wird;* **he received 10,000 ~-in votes** sein Name wurde auf zehntausend Stimmzettel geschrieben; **~-off** *n.* (*person*) Versager, *der*/Versagerin, *die;* (*event*) Reinfall, *der;* (*vehicle*) Totalschaden, *der*

**writer** /ˈraɪtə(r)/ *n.* A ▶ **1261** (*author*) Schriftsteller, *der*/Schriftstellerin, *die;* (*of letter, article*) Schreiber, *der*/Schreiberin, *die;* Verfasser, *der*/Verfasserin, *die;* (*of lyrics, advertisements*) Texter, *der*/Texterin, *die;* (*of music*) Komponist, *der*/Komponistin, *die;* **be a ~:** Schriftsteller/Schriftstellerin sein; **the present ~:** der Autor/die Autorin des vorliegenden Textes; **a ~ of historical fiction** ein Verfasser/eine Verfasserin historischer Romane; B **be a good/bad ~** (*as to handwriting*) eine gute/schlechte Schrift haben

**writer's 'cramp** *n.* (*Med.*) Schreibkrampf, *der*

**'write-up** *n.* Bericht, *der;* (*by critic*) Kritik, *die;* **get a good ~:** gut besprochen werden

**writhe** /raɪð/ *v.i.* (*lit. or fig.*) sich winden; **he/it makes me ~** (*with embarrassment*) er/es bringt mich in ziemliche Verlegenheit; (*with disgust*) er/es ist mir zuwider

**writing** /ˈraɪtɪŋ/ *n.* A Schreiben, *das;* **at the time of ~:** als dies geschrieben wurde; **put sth. in ~:** etw. schriftlich machen (*ugs.*); ⇒ *also* **commit** D; B (*handwriting*) Schrift, *die;* C (*composing*) Schreiben, *das;* **creative-~ course** Kurs für kreatives Schreiben; **earn sth. from one's ~:** mit Schreiben etw. verdienen; **this poem is a lovely piece of ~:** dieses Gedicht ist herrlich geschrieben; D (*something written*) Schrift, *die;* **the ~s of Plato** die platonischen Schriften; **the ~ on the wall** (*fig.*) das Menetekel an der Wand; **she's seen the ~ on the wall** sie hat die Zeichen erkannt; **the ~ is on the wall for this department** diese Abteilung hat keine Zukunft

**writing: ~ case** *n.* Schreibmappe, *die;* **~ desk** *n.* Schreibpult, *das;* Sekretär, *der;* **~ pad** *n.* Schreibblock, *der;* **~ paper** *n.* Schreibpapier, *das;* Briefpapier, *das*

**written** ⇒ **write**

**wrong** /rɒŋ/ ❶ *adj.* A (*morally bad*) unrecht (*geh.*); (*unfair*) ungerecht; **you were ~ to be so angry** es war nicht richtig von dir, so ärgerlich zu sein; **what's ~ with sth./that?** was ist gegen etw./dagegen einzuwenden?; **what's ~ with having a drink?** warum sollte man nicht mal ein Glas trinken?; B (*mistaken*) falsch; **be ~** ‹Person:› sich irren; **I was ~ about you** ich habe mich in dir geirrt; **the clock is ~:** die Uhr geht falsch; **the clock is ~ by ten minutes** die Uhr geht 10 Minuten vor/nach; **how ~ can you be** *or* **get!** wie man sich irren kann!; C (*not suitable*) falsch; **give the ~ answer** eine falsche Antwort geben; **that was the ~ move to make** das war genau das Falsche; **say/do the ~ thing** das Falsche sagen/tun; **you've come to the ~ person** Sie sind bei mir an der falschen Adresse; **be the ~ person for the job** für die Stelle ungeeignet sein; **take the ~ turning** falsch abbiegen; **get hold of the ~ end of the stick** (*fig.*) alles völlig falsch verstehen; **[the] ~ way round** verkehrt herum; ⇒ *also* **go down b**; **number** 1 A; D (*out of order*) nicht in Ordnung; **there's something ~ here/with him** hier/mit ihm stimmt etwas nicht; **there's nothing ~:** es ist alles in Ordnung; **what's ~?** was ist los? ⇒ *also* **wrong side**.
❷ *adv.* falsch; **get it ~:** es falsch *od.* verkehrt machen; (*misunderstand*) sich irren; **I got the answer ~ again** meine Antwort war wieder falsch; **get sb. ~:** jmdn. falsch verstehen; **go ~** (*take ~ path*) sich verlaufen; (*fig.*) ‹Person:› vom rechten Weg abkommen (*fig. geh.*); ‹Maschine, Mechanismus:› kaputtgehen (*ugs.*); ‹Angelegenheit:› danebengehen (*ugs.*); **you can't go ~ if you study engineering** wenn du auf die Ingenieurschule gehst, bist du immer gut daran; **the television/dishwasher has gone ~:** der Fernseher/die Spülmaschine ist kaputt (*ugs.*).
❸ *n.* A (*what is morally bad*) Unrecht, *das;* **know the difference between right and ~:** zwischen Recht und Unrecht unterscheiden können; **two ~s don't make a right** das gibt nur ein Unrecht mehr; **do ~:** unrecht tun; **she can do no ~:** sie kann überhaupt nichts Unrechtes tun; **be in the ~:** im Unrecht sein; **put sb. in the ~:** jmdn. ins Unrecht setzen; B (*injustice*) Unrecht, *das* **(towards** gegenüber); **suffer a ~/many ~s** Unrecht/viel Unrecht erleiden; **do ~ to sb., do sb. a ~:** jmdm. ein Unrecht zufügen; **do sb. ~:** jmdm. unrecht tun.
❹ *v.t.* **~ sb.** (*treat unjustly*) jmdn. ungerecht behandeln; (*mistakenly discredit*) jmdm. unrecht tun

**wrong: ~doer** *n.* Übeltäter, *der*/-täterin, *die;* Missetäter, *der*/-täterin, *die* (*geh.*); **~doing** *n.* A *no pl., no indef. art.* Missetaten (*geh.*); B (*instance*) Missetat, *die* (*geh.*); **~-'foot** *v.t.* A (*Sport*) **~-foot sb.** jmdn. auf dem falschen Fuß erwischen (*Sportjargon*); B (*fig. coll.*) unvorbereitet treffen; **he was ~-footed by that** darauf war er überhaupt nicht vorbereitet

**wrongful** /ˈrɒŋfl/ *adj.* A (*unfair*) unrecht (*geh.*); B (*unlawful*) rechtswidrig

**wrongfully** /ˈrɒŋfəlɪ/ *adv.* A (*unfairly*) unrecht (*geh.*) ‹handeln›; zu Unrecht ‹beschuldigen›; B (*unlawfully*) rechtswidrig

**'wrong-headed** *adj.* starrköpfig (*abwertend*) **(about** in + *Dat.*)

**wrongly** /ˈrɒŋlɪ/ *adv.* A (*inappropriately, incorrectly*) falsch; B (*mistakenly*) zu Unrecht; **I believed, ~, that ...:** ich habe fälschlicherweise geglaubt, dass ...; C ⇒ **wrongfully** A

**wrongness** /ˈrɒŋnɪs/ *n., no pl.* A (*moral ~*) Unrecht, *das;* B (*inappropriateness, mistakenness*) Unrichtigkeit, *die*

**wrong:** ~ **side** *n.* Ⓐ (*of fabric*) linke Seite; **[the] ~ side out/up** verkehrt herum; Ⓑ **be on the ~ side of thirty** die dreißig überschritten haben; **get on the ~ side of sb./the law** (*fig.*) jmdn. falsch anfassen/mit dem Gesetz in Konflikt geraten; ⇒ *also* **bed** 1 A; **blanket** 1 A; ~ **'un** *n.* (*coll.: person*) falscher Fuffziger (*salopp*)

**wrote** ⇒ **write**

**wrought** ⇒ **work** 2

**wrought 'iron** *n.* Schmiedeeisen, *das; attrib.* schmiedeeisern ‹Tor, Zaun›

**wrung** ⇒ **wring**

**WRVS** *abbr.* (*Brit.*) **Women's Royal Voluntary Service** *britischer Hilfsdienst für Menschen in Not*

**wry** /raɪ/ *adj.*, **~er** *or* **wrier** /'raɪə(r)/, **~est** *or* **wriest** /'raɪɪst/ ironisch ‹Blick›; fein ‹Humor, Witz›; **a ~ smile** ein schiefes Lächeln; **make** *or* **pull a ~ face** das Gesicht verziehen

**wryly** /'raɪlɪ/ *adv.* ironisch ‹blicken, sagen›; schief ‹lächeln›

**WSW** /westsaʊθ'west/ *abbr.* ▶ 1024 **west-south-west** WSW

**wt.** *abbr.* **weight** Gew.

**WW** *abbr.* (*Amer.*) **World War** WK

**WWW** *abbr.* **World Wide Web** WWW

**wych hazel** /'wɪtʃheɪzl/ *n.* Ⓐ (*shrub*) Virginische Zaubernuss; Ⓑ (*lotion*) Hamameliswasser, *das*

W

**X**[1], **x** /eks/ *n.*, *pl.* **Xs** *or* **X's** /'eksɪz/ A (*letter*) X, x, *das;* B (*Math.*) x; C (*unknown person or number*) **Mr X** Herr X; **x tons of cement** soundso viel Tonnen Zement; **x number of ...** (*coll.*) x ... (*ugs.*); D (*Roman numeral*) X; E (*cross-shaped symbol*) Kreuz, *das;* **x marks the spot** die Stelle ist durch ein Kreuz markiert

**X**[2] *symb.* (*Brit. Hist.*) nicht jugendfrei

**xenon** /'zenɒn/ *n.* (*Chem.*) Xenon, *das*

**xenophobe** /'zenəfəʊb/ *n.* Fremdenfeindliche, *der/die;* Xenophobe, *der/die*

**xenophobia** /zenə'fəʊbɪə/ *n.* Fremdenfeindlichkeit, *die;* Xenophobie, *die*

**xerography** /zɪə'rɒgrəfɪ, ze'rɒgrəfɪ/ *n.* Xerographie, *die* (*Druckw.*)

**Xerox** ®, **xerox** /'zɪərɒks, 'zerɒks/ **1** *n.* A (*process*) Xerographie, *die* (*Druckw.*); B (*copy*) Xerokopie, *die.* **2** **xerox** *v.t.* xerokopieren

**Xmas** /'krɪsməs, 'eksməs/ *n.* (*coll.*) Weihnachten, *das*

**X-rated** /'eksreɪtɪd/ *adj.* (*Brit. Hist.*) nicht jugendfrei ‹Film›

'**X-ray** **1** *n.* A *in pl.* Röntgenstrahlen *Pl.;* X-Strahlen *Pl.;* B (*picture*) Röntgenaufnahme, *die;* C *attrib.* Röntgen-. **2** *v.t.* röntgen; durchleuchten ‹Gepäck›

**xylophone** /'zaɪləfəʊn/ *n.* (*Mus.*) Xylophon, *das*

# Y y

**Y**[1], **y** /waɪ/ *n.*, *pl.* **Ys** *or* **Y's** Ⓐ (*letter*) Y, y, *das;* Ⓑ (*Math.*) y

**Y**[2] *abbr.* Ⓐ (*Amer.*) **YMCA/YWCA** CVJM/ CVJF; Ⓑ **yen**

**y.** *abbr.* **year[s]** J.

**yacht** /jɒt/ ❶ *n.* Ⓐ (*for racing*) Segelboot, *das;* Segeljacht, *die;* Ⓑ (*for pleasure travel etc.*) Jacht, *die.* ❷ *v.i.* segeln

**'yacht club** *n.* Jachtklub, *der*

**yachting** /'jɒtɪŋ/ *n.*, *no pl.*, *no art.* Segeln, *das; attrib.* Segel-

**yachtsman** /'jɒtsmən/ *n.*, *pl.* **yachtsmen** /'jɒtsmən/ Segler, *der*

**yack** /jæk/, **yackety-yack** /jækətɪ'jæk/ (*coll. derog.*) ❶ *ns.* Gequassel, *das* (*ugs. abwertend*). ❷ *v.i.* quasseln (*ugs. abwertend*)

**yah** /jɑː/ *int.* ~ **[boo sucks]** bäh

**yahoo** /jə'huː/ *n.* Untier, *das* (*fig.*)

**yak** /jæk/ *n.* (*Zool.*) Jak, *der*

**Yale**/jeɪl/**:** ~ **key** ® *n.* Yaleschlüssel, *der* Ⓦⓩ (*Technik*); ≈ Sicherheitsschlüssel, *der;* ~ **lock** ® *n.* Yaleschloss, *das* Ⓦⓩ (*Technik*); ≈ [Zylinder]sicherheitsschloss, *das*

**Yalta** /'jæltə/ *pr. n.* Jalta (*das*)

**yam** /jæm/ *n.* Ⓐ (*plant, tuber*) Jamswurzel, *die;* Ⓑ (*Amer.*) ⇒ **sweet potato**

**yammer** /'jæmə(r)/ (*coll./dial.*) ❶ *v.i.* maulen (*ugs.*); **he's always ~ing on about sth.** dauernd muss er über etw. (*Akk.*) maulen. ❷ *n.* Gemaule, *das* (*ugs. abwertend*)

**yang** /jæŋ/ *n.*, *no pl.*, *no indef. art.* (*Chinese Philos.*) Yang, *das*

**yank** (*coll.*) ❶ *v.t.* reißen an (+ *Dat.*); ~ **sth. off/out** etw. ab-/ausreißen. ❷ *n.* Reißen, *das;* **give a ~ at sth.** an etw. (*Dat.*) reißen; **give the rope a good ~:** kräftig am Seil ziehen

**Yank** /jæŋk/ ❶ *n.* Ⓐ (*Brit. coll.: American*) Yankee, *der;* Ami, *der* (*ugs.*); Ⓑ (*Amer.: inhabitant of New England or northern States*) Yankee, *der.* ❷ *adj.* Ⓐ (*Brit. coll.: American*) Ami- (*ugs.*); Ⓑ (*Amer.: of New England or northern States*) Yankee-

**Yankee** /'jæŋkɪ/ ⇒ **Yank**

**yap** /jæp/ ❶ *v.i.*, **-pp-** Ⓐ (*bark shrilly*) kläffen; Ⓑ (*coll.: talk*) quatschen (*salopp abwertend*); (*complainingly*) lamentieren (*ugs. abwertend*). ❷ *n.* Kläffen, *das;* **give a ~:** kläffen

**yarborough** /'jɑːbərə/ *n.* (*Cards*) Blatt (*bei Whist und Bridge*), *bei dem keine Karte höher als 9 ist*

**yard**[1] /jɑːd/ *n.* Ⓐ ▶ 928, ▶ 1079, ▶ 1284 Yard, *das;* **by the ~:** ≈ meterweise; (*fig.*) am laufenden Band (*ugs.*); **sell books by the ~** (*fig.*) Bücher meterweise verkaufen; **have a face a ~ long** ein Gesicht wie drei Tage Regenwetter machen; Ⓑ *in pl.* (*coll.: great amount*) **have/get** *etc.* **~s of sth.** etw. massenweise haben/bekommen *usw.;* **~s of toilet paper** meterweise Toilettenpapier; Ⓒ (*Naut.*) Rah[e], *die;* Ⓓ ~ **of ale** (*Brit.*) [Stangen]glas, *das;* Stange, *die* (*bes. westd.*); Ⓔ ⇒ **square** 2 B; Ⓕ ⇒ **cubic** B

**yard**[2] *n.* Ⓐ (*attached to building*) Hof, *der;* **in the ~:** auf dem Hof; Ⓑ (*for manufacture*) Werkstatt, *die;* (*for storage*) Lager, *das;* (*ship~*) Werft, *die;* **builder's ~:** Bauhof, *der;* Ⓒ (*Amer.: garden*) Garten, *der;* Ⓓ **the Y~** (*Brit. coll.*) ⇒ **Scotland Yard**. ⇒ *also* **back yard**; **goods yard**

**yard: ~arm** *n.* (*Naut.*) Rahnock, *das od. die;* **~stick** *n.* Ⓐ Messstab, *der;* Maßstab, *der* (*veralt.*); Ⓑ (*fig.: standard*) Maßstab, *der*

**yarn** /jɑːn/ ❶ *n.* Ⓐ (*thread*) Garn, *das;* Ⓑ (*coll.: story*) Geschichte, *die;* (*of sailor*) [Seemanns]garn, *das;* **have a ~ with sb.** (*chat*) mit jmdm. plauschen (*bes. südd.*) *od.* klönen (*nordd.*); ⇒ *also* **spin** 1 A. ❷ *v.i.* (*coll.*) Geschichten erzählen; ‹Seemann:› [s]ein Garn spinnen

**yarrow** /'jærəʊ/ *n.* (*Bot.*) Schafgarbe, *die*

**yashmak** /'jæʃmæk/ *n.* Jaschmak, *der*

**yaw** /jɔː/ (*Naut.*, *Aeronaut.*) ❶ *v.i.* gieren. ❷ *n.* Gieren, *das*

**yawl** /jɔːl/ *n.* (*Naut.*) Yawl, *die;* Heckmaster, *der*

**yawn** /jɔːn/ ❶ *n.* Ⓐ Gähnen, *das;* **give a [long] ~:** [herzhaft] gähnen; **there were a few ~s** es wurde ein paarmal gegähnt; Ⓑ **be a ~** (*coll.: be boring*) zum Gähnen langweilig sein. ❷ *v.i.* Ⓐ gähnen; **~ with exhaustion** vor Müdigkeit gähnen; Ⓑ (*fig.*) ‹Abgrund, Kluft, Spalte:› gähnen (*geh.*)

**yawning** /'jɔːnɪŋ/ *adj.* gähnend (*auch fig. geh.*)

**yawp** /jɔːp/ (*Amer.*) ❶ *v.i.* Ⓐ (*squawk*) kreischen; Ⓑ (*talk foolishly*) faseln (*ugs. abwertend*). ❷ *n.* Ⓐ (*squawk*) Gekreisch[e], *das;* Ⓑ (*foolish talk*) Gefasel, *das* (*ugs. abwertend*)

**yaws** /jɔːz/ *n. sing.* (*Med.*) Himbeerpocken *Pl.;* Frambösie, *die* (*fachspr.*)

**yd[s].** *abbr.* ▶ 928, ▶ 1079, ▶ 1284 **yard[s]** Yd[s].

**ye**[1] /jiː/ *pron.* (*arch./poet./dial./joc.*) Ihr (*veralt.*); (*as direct or indirect object*) Euch (*veralt.*)

**ye**[2] *adj.* (*pseudo-arch.*) = **the**

**yea** /jeɪ/ (*arch.*) ❶ *adv.* ja. ❷ *n.* Ja, *das;* **~s and nays** Ja- und Neinstimmen; **~ and nay** Ja und Nein

**yeah** /jeə/ *adv.* (*coll.*) ja; **[oh] ~?** [ach] ja?

**year** /jɪə(r)/ *n.* Ⓐ ▶ 912, ▶ 1055 Jahr, *das;* **solar ~:** Sonnenjahr, *das;* **sidereal ~:** siderisches Jahr; Sternjahr, *das;* **she gets £10,000 a ~:** sie verdient 10 000 Pfund im Jahr; **~ in ~ out** jahrein, jahraus; **~ after ~:** Jahr für *od.* um Jahr; **all [the] ~ round** das ganze Jahr hindurch; **in a ~['s time]** in einem Jahr; **once a ~, once every ~:** einmal im Jahr; **Christian** *or* **Church** *or* **ecclesiastical ~** (*Eccl.*) Kirchenjahr, *das;* liturgisches Jahr (*kath. Kirche*); **a ten-~-old** ein Zehnjähriger/eine Zehnjährige; **a ten-~[s]-old child/animal/thing** ein zehn Jahre altes Kind/Tier/Ding; **in her thirtieth ~:** in ihrem 30. Lebensjahr; **financial** *or* **fiscal** *or* **tax ~:** Finanz- *od.* Rechnungsjahr, *das;* **calendar** *or* **civil ~:** Kalenderjahr, *das;* **school ~:** Schuljahr, *das;* **for a ~ and a day** ein Jahr und einen Tag [lang]; **a ~ [from] today** *etc.* heute *usw.* in einem Jahr; **a ~ [ago] today** *etc.* heute *usw.* vor einem Jahr; **... of the ~** (*best*) ... des Jahres; ⇒ *also* **by**[1] 1 M; **dot** 1 C; **from** B; **grace** 1 E; **leap year**; **lord** 1 B; **sabbatical** 1; Ⓑ (*group of students*) Jahrgang, *der;* **first-~ student** Student/Studentin im ersten Jahr; Ⓒ *in pl.* (*age*) **he doesn't look his ~s** man sieht ihm seine Jahre nicht an; **be old for** *or* **beyond one's ~s** (*unexpectedly mature*) für sein Alter schon sehr reif sein; (*looking older than one is*) älter wirken, als man ist; **be young for one's ~s** jünger wirken, als man ist; **be getting on/be well on in ~s** in die Jahre kommen/in vorgerücktem Alter sein (*geh.*); Ⓓ *in pl.* (*very long time*) Jahre; **she looks ~s older** sie sieht um Jahre älter aus; **sth. has put ~s on sb.** etw. hat jmdn. um Jahre altern lassen; **take ~s off sb./sb.'s life** jmdn. um Jahre jünger/älter machen

**'yearbook** *n.* Jahrbuch, *das*

**yearling** /'jɪəlɪŋ/ ❶ *n.* (*Zool.*, *Agric.*) Jährling, *der.* ❷ *adj.* (*a year old*) einjährig

**'year-long** *adj.* (*lasting a year*) einjährig; (*lasting the whole year*) ganzjährig

**yearly** /'jɪəlɪ/ ❶ *adj.* Ⓐ (*annual*) jährlich; **ten-~:** zehnjährig; **at twice-~ intervals** zweimal im Jahr; Ⓑ (*lasting a year*) Einjahres‹vertrag, -abonnement›. ❷ *adv.* jährlich

**yearn** /jɜːn/ *v.i.* **~ for** *or* **after sth./for sb./to do sth.** sich nach etw./jmdm. sehnen/sich danach sehnen, etw. zu tun

**yearning** /'jɜːnɪŋ/ ❶ *n.* Sehnsucht, *die.* ❷ *adj.* sehnsüchtig ‹Blick, Liebe›; sehnlich ‹Wunsch, Gebet›

**'year-round** *adj.* ganzjährig

**yeast** /jiːst/ *n.* Hefe, *die*

**yeast: ~ cake** *n.* Ⓐ (*mass of ~*) Hefewürfel, *der;* Ⓑ (*cake made with ~*) Hefekuchen, *der;* **~ pastry** *n.* Hefeteig, *der*

**yeasty** /'jiːstɪ/ *adj.* hefig

**yell** /jel/ ❶ *n.* Ⓐ gellender Schrei; **let out a ~:** einen Schrei ausstoßen; **when supper's ready, I'll give you a ~** (*coll.*) wenn das Abendessen fertig ist, rufe ich dich; Ⓑ (*Amer.: students' cry*) Anfeuerungsruf, *der.* ❷ *v.i.* [gellend] schreien; **~ with rage/laughter** wütend schreien/vor Lachen brüllen; **~ at each other** einander anschreien. ❸ *v.t.* [gellend] schreien

**yellow** /'jeləʊ/ ❶ *adj.* Ⓐ gelb; flachsblond ‹Haar›; golden ‹Getreide›; vergilbt ‹Papier›; Ⓑ (*fig. coll.: cowardly*) feige; **have got/show a ~ streak** feige *od.* ein Feigling sein. ⇒ *also* **flag**[1] 1. ❷ *n.* Ⓐ (*colour*) Gelb, *das;* Ⓑ (*pigment*) Gelbton, *der;* Ⓒ (*~ clothes*) **dressed in ~:** gelb gekleidet; Ⓓ (*Snooker*) gelbe Kugel; Ⓔ (*butterfly*) Gelbling, *der;* (*brimstone*) Zitronenfalter, *der;* **clouded ~:** Postillon, *der.* ❸ *v.t. & i.* vergilben

**yellow: ~-belly** *n.* (*sl. derog.*) Feigling, *der* (*ugs.*); **~ 'card** *n.* (*Footb.*) gelbe Karte; **be shown a ~ 'card:** Gelb sehen (*Jargon*); eine gelbe Karte bekommen; **~ 'fever** *n.* ▶ 1232 (*Med.*) Gelbfieber, *das;* **~hammer** *n.* (*Ornith.*) Goldammer, *die*

**yellowish** /'jeləʊɪʃ/ *adj.* gelblich

**yellow 'line** *n.* (*Brit.*) gelbe [Markierungs]linie; **I'm on double ~s** ich stehe im Parkverbot

**yellowness** /'jeləʊnɪs/ *n.*, *no pl.* gelbe Farbe

**Yellow 'Pages** ® *n. pl.* gelbe Seiten; Branchenverzeichnis, *das*

**yelp** /jelp/ ❶ *v.i.* aufheulen (*ugs.*); ‹Hund:› jaulen. ❷ *n.* Heulen, *das;* (*of dog*) Jaulen, *das;* **the child/dog gave a ~:** das Kind heulte auf/der Hund jaulte

**yelping** /'jelpɪŋ/ *n.* Geheule, *das* (*ugs.*); (*of dog*) Gejaule, *das*

**Yemen** /'jemən/ *pr. n.* **[the] ~:** [der] Jemen

**Yemeni** /'jemənɪ/ ▶ 1340 ❶ *adj.* jemenitisch. ❷ *n.* Jemenit, *der*/Jemenitin, *die*

**Yemenite** /'jemənaɪt/ *n.* ⇒ **Yemeni** 2

**yen**[1] /jen/ *n.*, *pl. same* ▶ 1328 (*Japanese currency*) Yen, *der*

**yen**[2] *n.* (*coll.: longing*) Drang, *der* (**for** nach); **sb. has a ~ to do sth.** es drängt jmdn. danach, etw. zu tun

**yeoman** /'jəʊmən/ *n.*, *pl.* **yeomen** /'jəʊmən/ Ⓐ (*with small estate*) Kleinbauer, *der;* Ⓑ (*Hist.: freeholder*) Freisasse, *der;* Ⓒ (*Brit. Mil. Hist.*) Angehöriger der Yeomanry; Ⓓ **~ [of signals]** (*Brit. Navy*) Signalmaat, *der;* Ⓔ (*Amer. Navy*) *Marineunteroffizier, der mit Verwaltungsarbeiten betraut ist*

**Yeoman of the 'Guard** *n.* (*Brit. Mil.*) königlicher Leibgardist; (*in popular use: warder in Tower of London*) Wärter im Tower von London

y

**yeomanry** /ˈjəʊmənrɪ/ *n., no pl.* Yeomanry, *die (hist.); berittene Freiwilligentruppe*

ˈ**yeoman['s] service** *n.* **give sb. ~:** jmdm. gute Dienste tun; **do ~:** gute Dienste leisten

**yep** /jep/ *int. (Amer. coll.)* ja

**yes** /jes/ ❶ *adv.* ja; *(in contradiction)* doch; **~, sir** jawohl!; **I didn't do it! — Oh ~ you did!** Ich war es nicht! — Doch warst du es!; **~?** *(indeed?)* ach ja?; *(what do you want?)* ja?; *(to customer)* ja, bitte?; **say '~'** Ja sagen; **say ~ to a proposal** einem Vorschlag zustimmen; **she'll say ~ to anything** sie sagt zu allem Ja und Amen; **~ and no** ja und nein; jein *(scherzh.)*; ⇒ *also* **oh**[1]. ❷ *n., pl.* **~es** Ja, *das*

ˈ**yes-man** *n. (coll. derog.)* Jasager, *der (abwertend)*

**yesterday** /ˈjestədeɪ, ˈjestədɪ/ ▶1056 ❶ *n.* Ⓐ gestern; **the day before ~:** vorgestern; **~'s paper** die gestrige Zeitung; die Zeitung von gestern; **~ morning/afternoon/evening/night** gestern Vormittag/Nachmittag/Abend/Nacht; **a week [from] ~:** gestern in einer Woche; **a year [ago] ~:** gestern vor einem Jahr; **~ evening's concert** das Konzert gestern Abend *od.* am gestrigen Abend; Ⓑ *(recent time)* **of ~:** von gestern; **all our ~s** unsere Vergangenheit; **be ~'s men** passé sein. ❷ *adv.* Ⓐ gestern; **the day before ~:** vorgestern; **~ morning/afternoon/evening/night** gestern Vormittag/Nachmittag/Abend/Nacht; Ⓑ *(in the recent past)* gestern; ⇒ *also* **born** 1

**yet** /jet/ ❶ *adv.* Ⓐ *(still)* noch; **have ~ to reach sth.** etw. erst noch erreichen müssen; **have a few days free ~:** noch ein paar Tage frei haben; **much ~ remains to be done** noch bleibt viel zu tun; ⇒ *also* **as** 4; Ⓑ *(hitherto)* bisher; **the play is his best ~:** das Stück ist sein bisher bestes; Ⓒ *neg. or interrog. (so soon as now/then)* **not [just] ~:** [jetzt] noch nicht; **never ~:** noch nie; **need you go just ~?** musst du [jetzt] schon gehen?; **is he dead ~?** ist er schon gestorben?; **you haven't seen anything** *or (coll.)* **ain't seen nothing ~:** das ist noch gar nichts; Ⓓ *(before all is over)* doch noch; **he could win ~:** er könnte noch gewinnen; Ⓔ *with compar. (even)* noch; Ⓕ *(nevertheless)* doch; Ⓖ *(again)* noch; **~ again** *or* **once more** noch einmal; **nor ~:** noch [...] jemals; **she has never voted for that party, nor ~ intends to** sie hat nie für diese Partei gestimmt und sie hat es auch nicht vor. ❷ *conj.* doch; **a faint ~ unmistakable smell** ein schwacher, aber unverkennbarer Geruch

**yeti** /ˈjetɪ/ *n.* Yeti, *der;* Schneemensch, *der*

**yew** /juː/ *n.* Ⓐ *(tree)* Eibe, *die;* Ⓑ *(wood)* Eibenholz, *das*

ˈ**yew tree** ⇒ **yew** A

ˈ**Y-fronts** ® *n. pl. Herrenunterhose mit y-förmiger Vorderseite*

**YHA** *abbr. (Brit.)* **Youth Hostels Association** Jugendherbergsverband, *der*

**Yid** /jɪd/ *n. (sl. derog.)* Itzig, *der (ugs. abwertend)*

**Yiddish** /ˈjɪdɪʃ/ ▶1275 ❶ *adj.* jiddisch; ⇒ *also* **English** 1. ❷ *n.* Jiddisch, *das;* ⇒ *also* **English** 2 A

**yield** /jiːld/ ❶ *v.t.* Ⓐ *(give)* bringen; hervorbringen ‹Ernte›; tragen ‹Obst›; abwerfen ‹Gewinn›; ergeben ‹Resultat, Informationen›; Ⓑ *(surrender)* übergeben ‹Festung›; lassen ‹Vortritt›; abtreten ‹Besitz› **(to** an + *Akk.*); **~ the point** [in diesem Punkt] nachgeben; **~ a point to sb.** jmdm. in einem Punkt nachgeben; **~ ground to the enemy** vor dem Feind zurückweichen; **~ right of way** Vorfahrt gewähren. ❷ *v.i.* Ⓐ *(surrender)* sich unterwerfen; **~ to threats/temptation** Drohungen *(Dat.)* nachgeben/der Versuchung *(Dat.)* erliegen; **~ to persuasion/sb.'s entreaties** sich überreden lassen/jmds. Bitten *(Dat.)* nachgeben; **the girl had ~ed to the wily seducer** das Mädchen war dem raffinierten Verführer erlegen; Ⓑ *(be or feel inferior)* **~ to none in sth.** niemandem in etw. *(Dat.)* nachstehen; Ⓒ *(give right of way)* Vorfahrt gewähren; Ⓓ *(Amer.: allow another the right to speak)* **~ to sb.** jmdm. das Wort überlassen. ❸ *n.* Ⓐ Ertrag, *der;* Ⓑ *(revenue from tax etc.)* Aufkommen, *das;* Ⓒ *(return on investment)* Zins[ertrag], *der;* **a 10% ~:** 10% Zinsen; **the ~ on this bond** die Zinsen für dieses Wertpapier

**~ ˈup** *v.t.* Ⓐ *(surrender)* übergeben ‹Stadt, Festung›; ausliefern ‹Gefangenen, sich selbst›; Ⓑ *(reveal)* enthüllen ‹Geheimnis›; hervorbringen ‹Reichtum, Ertrag, Ernte›

ˈ**yield point** *n. (Phys.)* Fließgrenze, *die*

**yin** /jɪn/ *n., no pl., no indef. art. (Chinese Philos.)* Yin, *das*

**yip** /jɪp/ *(Amer.)* ❶ *v.i.,* **-pp-** ⇒ **yelp** 1. ❷ *n.* ⇒ **yelp** 2

**yippee** /ˈjɪpiː, jɪˈpiː/ *int.* hurra

**YMCA** *abbr.* **Young Men's Christian Association** CVJM

**yob** /jɒb/, *n. (Brit. coll.)* Rowdy, *der (abwertend)*

**yobbish** /ˈjɒbɪʃ/ *adj. (Brit. coll.)* rowdyhaft

**yobbo** /ˈjɒbəʊ/ *n. pl.* **~s** ⇒ **yob**

**yodel** /ˈjəʊdl/ ❶ *v.i. & t., (Brit.)* **-ll-** jodeln. ❷ *n.* Jodeln, *das*

**Yoga** /ˈjəʊgə/ *n.* Yoga, *der od. das*

**yoghurt** /ˈjɒgət/ *n.* Joghurt, *der od. das*

**yogi** /ˈjəʊgɪ/ *n. (Hindu Philos.)* Yogi[n], *der*

**yogurt** ⇒ **yoghurt**

**yo-heave-ho** /ˈjəʊhiːvhəʊ/ = **heave ho** ⇒ **heave** 2 B

**yo[-ho]-ho** /jəʊ(həʊ)ˈhəʊ/ *int.* Ⓐ *(to attract attention)* he *(ugs.)*; Ⓑ = **heave ho** ⇒ **heave** 2 B

**yoke** /jəʊk/ ❶ *n.* Ⓐ *(for animal)* Joch, *das;* Ⓑ *(for person)* [Trag]joch, *das;* Ⓒ *(of garment)* Sattel, *der (Textilw.)*; Ⓓ *(fig.: bond, oppressive control)* Joch, *das (geh.)*; Ⓔ *(pair of oxen etc.)* Joch, *das.* ❷ *v.t.* Ⓐ ins Joch spannen ‹Tier›; **~ an animal to sth.** ein Tier vor etw. *(Akk.)* spannen; Ⓑ *(fig.: couple)* verbinden

**yokel** /ˈjəʊkl/ *n. (derog.)* [Bauern]tölpel, *der*

**yolk** /jəʊk/ *n.* Dotter, *der od. das;* Eigelb, *das*

ˈ**yolk sac** *n. (Zool.)* Dottersack, *der*

**Yom Kippur** /jɒm ˈkɪpə(r)/ = **Day of Atonement** ⇒ **atonement** B

**yomp** /jɒmp/ *(coll.) v.i. & t.* stapfen

**yon** /jɒn/ *(arch./poet./dial.)* ❶ *adj.* **~ mountain/field** jener Berg/jenes Feld dort *(geh.)*. ❷ *adv.* dort drüben; ⇒ *also* **hither**

**yonder** /ˈjɒndə(r)/ *(literary)* ❶ *adj.* **~ tree/peasant** jener Baum/Bauer dort *(geh.)*. ❷ *adv.* dort drüben

**yoo-hoo** /ˈjuːhuː/ *int.* juhu

**yore** /jɔː(r)/ *n. (literary)* **of ~:** von früher [her] ‹kennen›; **customs of ~:** Bräuche von einst; **in days of ~:** in früheren Tagen

**yorker** /ˈjɔːkə(r)/ *n. (Cricket) Ball, der so geworfen wird, dass er direkt vor dem Schlagmann auftrifft*

**Yorkist** /ˈjɔːkɪst/ *(Hist.)* ❶ *adj.* zum Hause York gehörig; des Hauses York *nachgestellt.* ❷ *n.* Mitglied/Anhänger des Hauses York

**Yorkshire**/ˈjɔːkʃɪə(r), ˈjɔːkʃə(r)/: **~man** /ˈjɔːkʃɪəmən, jɔːkʃəmən/ *n., pl.* **~men** /ˈjɔːkʃɪəmən, jɔːkʃəmən/ Mann aus Yorkshire; **~ ˈpudding** *n. (Gastr.)* Yorkshirepudding, *der;* **~ ˈterrier** *n.* Yorkshireterrier, *der;* **~ tyke** ⇒ **tyke** C; **~woman** *n.* Frau aus Yorkshire

**you** /jʊ, *stressed* ˈjuː/ *pron.* Ⓐ *sing./pl.* du/ihr; *as polite address sing. or pl.* Sie; *as direct object* dich/euch/Sie; *as indirect object* dir/euch/Ihnen; *refl.* dich/dir/euch/sich; **it was ~:** du warst/ihr wart/Sie waren es; **~'re another** *(coll.)* du bist selber einer/eine/eins *(ugs.)*; **~-know-what/-who** du weißt/ihr wisst/Sie wissen schon, was/wer/wen/wem; **that hat is not quite ~:** dieser Hut passt nicht ganz zu dir/Ihnen; Ⓑ *(one)* man; **smoking is bad for ~:** Rauchen ist ungesund. ⇒ *also* **he**[1]; **her**[1]; **your**; **yours**; **yourself**; **yourselves**

ˈ**you-all** *pron. (Amer. coll.)* ihr/Sie [alle]

**you'd** /jʊd, *stressed* juːd/ Ⓐ = **you had;** Ⓑ = **you would**

**you'll** /jʊl, *stressed* juːl/ Ⓐ = **you will;** Ⓑ = **you shall**

**young** /jʌŋ/ ❶ *adj.,* **~er** /ˈjʌŋgə(r)/, **~est** /ˈjʌŋgɪst/ Ⓐ ▶912 *(lit. or fig.)* jung; neu, jung ‹Wein›; **a very ~ child** ein ganz kleines Kind; **the ~ boys** die [kleinen] Jungen; **~ at heart** im Herzen jung geblieben; **sb. is not getting any ~er** jmd. wird auch nicht jünger; **you ~ rascal** du [kleiner] Racker *(fam.)*; **you're only ~ once** man ist nur einmal jung; **she's a ~ sixty** sie ist eine jung gebliebene Sechzigerin; **the night is still ~:** die Nacht ist jung; **~ Jones** der junge Jones *(ugs.)*; **at a ~ age** in jungen Jahren; **he's not as ~ as he used to be** er ist nicht mehr der Jüngste; Ⓑ ▶912 *in compar. (of two namesakes)* jünger; *(Scot.: heir)* Erbe, *der;* **Teniers the Y~er** Teniers der Jüngere; Ⓒ *(characteristic of youth)* jugendlich; **~ love/fashion** junge Liebe/Mode; Ⓓ *(Polit.)* **Y~ Conservatives/Liberals** *etc.* Junge Konservative/Liberale *usw.* ⇒ *also* **hopeful** 2; **married** 2; **shoulder** 1 B; **year** C. ❷ *n. pl. (of animals)* Junge; *(of humans)* Kinder; **with ~:** trächtig; **the ~** (**~ people**) die jungen Leute; **~ and old** Jung und Alt

**young: ~ ˈblood** ⇒ **blood** 1 C; **~ day[s]** *n.* [*pl.*] Jugendjahre *Pl.;* **in my ~ days** in meiner Jugend[zeit]; **~ ˈfamily** *n.* junge Familie; **have a ~ family** kleine Kinder haben; **~ ˈfogey** *n. junger angepasster und erzkonservativer Mann*

**youngish** /ˈjʌŋgɪʃ/ *adj.* ziemlich jung

**young: ~ ˈlady** *n.* Ⓐ junge Dame; Ⓑ *(girlfriend)* Freundin, *die;* **~ ˈman** *n.* Ⓐ junger Mann; Ⓑ *(boyfriend)* Freund, *der;* **Y~ Pretender** ⇒ **pretender**

**youngster** /ˈjʌŋstə(r)/ *n.* Ⓐ *(child)* Kleine, *der/die/das;* Ⓑ *(young person)* Jugendliche, *der/die;* **you're just a ~ compared with me** im Vergleich zu mir bist du noch jung; **come on, you ~s!** kommt, ihr jungen Hüpfer! *(ugs.)*

**young: ~ thing** *n.* junges Ding *(ugs.)*; **~ 'un** *n. (coll.)* **he's only a ~ 'un** er ist noch jung; **all the ~ 'uns** das ganze junge Gemüse *(ugs.)*; **~ ˈwoman** *n.* Ⓐ junge Frau; Ⓑ *(girlfriend)* Freundin, *die*

**your** /jə(r), *stressed* jʊə(r), jɔː(r)/ *poss. pron. attrib.* Ⓐ *(of you, sing./pl.)* dein/euer; *in polite address* Ihr; **~ average TV viewer** *(coll.)* der durchschnittliche Fernsehzuschauer; Ⓑ *(one's)* **it's bad for ~ health/eyesight** es ist schlecht für die Gesundheit/Augen. ⇒ *also* **her**[2]; **our** A

**you're** /jə(r), *stressed* jʊə(r), jɔː(r)/ = **you are**

**yours** /jʊəz, jɔːz/ *poss. pron. pred.* Ⓐ *(to or of you, sing.)* deiner/deine/dein[e]s; *(to or of you, pl.)* eurer/eure/eures; *in polite address* Ihrer/Ihre/Ihr[e]s; **you and ~:** du und die Deinen/das Deine; **what's ~?** *(coll.)* was nimmst du/nehmen Sie?; ⇒ *also* **hers**; **ours**; Ⓑ *(your letter)* Ihr Brief; *(Commerc.)* Ihr Schreiben; Ⓒ ▶1286 *(ending letter)* **~ [obediently]** Ihr [sehr ergebener *(geh.)*]; **~ truly** in alter Verbundenheit dein/deine; *(in business letter)* mit freundlichen Grüßen; *(joc.: I)* meine Wenigkeit *(scherzh.)*; ⇒ *also* **ever** A; **faithfully**; **sincerely** C; **up** 2 F

**yourself** /jəˈself, jʊəˈself, jɔːˈself/ *pron.* Ⓐ *emphat.* selbst; **for ~:** für dich/Sie selbst; **you must do sth. for ~:** du musst selbst etw. tun; **how's ~?** *(coll.)* wie gehts? *(ugs.)*; *(as reply)* und selbst? *(ugs.)*; **relax and be ~:** entspann dich und gib dich ganz natürlich; Ⓑ *refl.* dich/dir/sich. ⇒ *also* **herself**; **myself**

**yourselves** /jəˈselvz, jʊəˈselvz, jɔːˈselvz/ *pron.* Ⓐ *emphat.* selbst; **for ~:** für euch/Sie selbst; Ⓑ *refl.* euch/sich. ⇒ *also* **herself**; **ourselves**

**youth** /juːθ/ *n.* Ⓐ *no pl., no art.* Jugend, *die;* **she has kept her ~:** sie hat sich *(Dat.)* ihr jugendliches Aussehen bewahrt; Ⓑ *pl.* **~s** /juːðz/ *(young man)* Jugendliche, *der;* Ⓒ *constr. as pl. (young people)* Jugend, *die;* Ⓓ *no pl., no art. (fig.: early stage of development*

Y

*etc.*) Anfangsstadium, *das;* **in its [early] ~:** in den [ersten] Anfängen

**youth: ~ centre** *n.* Jugendzentrum, *das;* **~ club** *n.* Jugendklub, *der;* **~ 'custody** *n.* (*Brit.*) Jugendstrafe, *die;* **~ 'custody centre** *n.* (*Brit.*) Jugendstrafanstalt, *die*

**youthful** /'ju:θfl/ *adj.* jugendlich

**youthfulness** /'ju:θflnɪs/ *n., no pl.* A (*being young*) Jugend, *die;* B (*having freshness of youth*) Jugendlichkeit, *die*

**youth: ~ hostel** *n.* Jugendherberge, *die;* **~ hosteller** *n.* Herbergsgast, *der*

**you've** /jʊv, *stressed* ju:v/ = **you have**

**yowl** /jaʊl/ ❶ *n.* **~[s]** Jaulen, *das;* (*of cat*) Maunzen, *das;* (*of wolf*) Heulen, *das;* **give a ~:** jaulen/maunzen/heulen. ❷ *v.i.* jaulen; ‹Katze:› maunzen; ‹Wolf:› heulen

**yo-yo** ® /'jəʊjəʊ/ *n., pl.* **~s** Jo-Jo, *das*

**yr.** *abbr.* A **year[s]** J.; B **your**

**yrs.** *abbr.* A **years** J.; B **yours**

**'Y-shaped** *adj.* y-förmig

**yucca** /'jʌkə/ *n.* (*Bot.*) Yucca, *die;* Palmlilie, *die*

**yuck** ⇨ **yuk**

**yucky** ⇨ **yukky**

**Yugoslav** /'ju:gəslɑ:v/ ▶ 1340 ⇨ **Yugoslavian**

**Yugoslavia** /ju:gə'slɑ:vɪə/ *pr. n.* Jugoslawien (*das*)

**Yugoslavian** /ju:gə'slɑ:vɪən/ ▶ 1340 ❶ *adj.* A jugoslawisch; **sb. is ~:** jmd. ist Jugoslawe/Jugoslawin; B (*Ling.*) ⇨ **Serbo-Croat** 2. ❷ *n.* A (*person*) Jugoslawe, *der*/Jugoslawin, *die;* B (*Ling.*) ⇨ **Serbo-Croat** 1

**yuk** /jʌk/ *int.* (*coll.*) bäh; äks

**yukky** /'jʌkɪ/ *adj.* (*coll.*) eklig

**yule** /ju:l/ ⇨ **Yuletide**

**yule: ~ log** *n.* Weihnachtsblock, *der* (*Volksk.*); (*in Scandinavia*) Julblock, *der* (*Volksk.*); **Y~tide** *n.* (*arch.*) Weihnachtszeit, *die*

**yummy** /'jʌmɪ/ (*coll.*) ❶ *adj.* lecker. ❷ *int.* (*child lang.*) lecker, lecker; (*not referring to food*) au fein

**yum-yum** /jʌm'jʌm/ *int.* lecker, lecker

**yuppie** /'jʌpɪ/ *n.* (*coll.*) Yuppie, *der*

**yuppie 'flu** *n.* ▶ 1232 (*coll.*) Yuppiegrippe, *die*

**YWCA** *abbr.* **Young Women's Christian Association** CVJF

# Z z

**Z, z** /zed/ *n.*, *pl.* **Zs** *or* **Z's** **A** (*letter*) Z, z, *das;* **B** (*Math.*) z

**zabaglione** /zabɑˈljəʊneɪ/ *n.* (*Gastr.*) Zabaglione, *die;* Zabaione, *die*

**Zaire** /zɑːˈɪə(r)/ *pr. n.* Zaire (*das*)

**Zambezi** /zæmˈbiːzɪ/ *pr. n.* ▶ **1480** Sambesi, *der*

**Zambia** /ˈzæmbɪə/ *pr. n.* Sambia (*das*)

**Zambian** /ˈzæmbɪən/ ▶ **1340** **1** *adj.* sambisch. **2** *n.* Sambier, *der*/Sambierin, *die*

**zany** /ˈzeɪnɪ/ *adj.* irre komisch (*ugs.*); Wahnsinns‹humor, -komiker›

**Zanzibar** /zænzɪˈbɑː(r)/ *pr. n.* Sansibar (*das*)

**Zanzibari** /zænzɪˈbɑːrɪ/ **1** *adj.* sansibarisch. **2** *n.* Sansibarer, *der*/Sansibarerin, *die*

**zap** /zæp/ (*coll.*) **1** *int.* zack. **2** *v.t.*, **-pp-: A** ~ **sb. [one]** jmdm. eine knallen (*ugs.*); **B** (*do away with, kill*) erledigen (*salopp*). **3** *v.i.* **-pp-** (*Telev. coll.*) zappen (*ugs.*)

**zapper** /ˈzæpə(r)/ *n.* (*Telev. coll.*) Drücker, *der* (*ugs.*); Fernbedienung, *die*

**zeal** /ziːl/ *n.*, *no pl.* **A** (*fervour*) Eifer, *der;* **B** (*hearty endeavour*) Hingabe, *die*

**zealot** /ˈzelət/ *n.* **A** (*zealous person*) Besessene, *der/die;* **B** (*fanatic*) Eiferer, *der*/Eiferin, *die;* Zelot, *der*/Zelotin, *die* (*geh.*)

**zealous** /ˈzeləs/ *adj.* **A** (*fervent*) glühend (*geh.*) ‹Verehrer›; begeistert ‹Fan›; **B** (*eager*) eifrig

**zealously** /ˈzeləslɪ/ *adv.* **A** (*fervently*) mit glühendem Eifer (*geh.*); begeistert ‹anfeuern›; **B** (*eagerly*) eifrig ‹suchen, arbeiten›

**zebra** /ˈzebrə, ˈziːbrə/ *n.* Zebra, *das*

**zebra:** ~ **ˈcrossing** *n.* (*Brit.*) Zebrastreifen, *der;* ~ **finch** (*Ornith.*) *n.* Zebrafink, *der*

**zebu** /ˈziːbjuː/ *n.* (*Zool.*) Zebu, *der od. das*

**zed** /zed/ (*Brit.*), **zee** /ziː/ (*Amer.*) *ns.* Zett, *das*

**Zen** /zen/ *n.*, *no pl.*, *no art.* (*Relig.*) Zen, *das*

**zenith** /ˈzenɪθ/ *n.* (*lit. or fig.*) Zenit, *der*

**zephyr** /ˈzefə(r)/ *n.* (*literary*) Zephir, *der* (*dichter. veralt.*)

**Zeppelin** /ˈzepəlɪn/ *n.* Zeppelin, *der*

**zero** /ˈzɪərəʊ/ **1** *n.*, *pl.* ~**s** ▶ **1352** **A** (*nought*) Null, *die;* **B** (*fig.: nil*) null; **her chances are** ~**:** ihre Aussichten sind gleich null (*ugs.*); **C** ▶ **1603** (*starting point of scale; of temperature*) Null, *die;* **in** ~ **gravity** im Zustand der Schwerelosigkeit; **absolute** ~ (*Phys.*) absoluter Nullpunkt; **D** ~ **[hour]** die Stunde X. ⇒ *also* **ground zero**. **2** *v.i.* ~ **in on sth.** (*take aim at sth.*) sich auf etw. (*Akk.*) einschießen; (*focus one's attention on sth.*) sich auf etw. (*Akk.*) konzentrieren

**zero:** ~ **option** *n.* (*Polit.*) Nulllösung, *die;* ~-**ˈrated** *adj.* ~**-rated goods** nicht mehrwertsteuerpflichtige Güter; ~ **ˈtolerance** *n.* Nulltoleranz, *die* (**for, to, of** gegenüber); *attrib.* ‹Politik, Konzept› der Nulltoleranz

**zest** /zest/ *n.* **A** (*lit. or fig.*) Würze, *die;* **add a** ~ **to the dish** das Gericht würzig machen; **add** ~ **and life to sth.** etw. beleben; **B** (*gusto*) Begeisterung, *die;* ~ **for living** Lebenslust, *die;* **C** (*peel*) Schale, *die*

**zestful** /ˈzestfl/ *adj.* freudig; ‹Person› voller Begeisterung

**zeugma** /ˈzjuːgmə/ *n.* (*Ling.*, *Lit.*) Zeugma, *das* (*Sprachw.*)

**Zeus** /zjuːs/ *pr. n.* (*Greek Mythol.*) Zeus (*der*)

**zigzag** /ˈzɪgzæg/ **1** *adj.* zickzackförmig; Zickzack‹muster, -anordnung›; ~ **line** Zickzacklinie, *die;* **steer a** ~ **course** im Zickzack fahren/laufen *usw.* **2** *adv.* zickzack. **3** *n.* Zickzacklinie, *die.* **4** *v.i.*, **-gg-** im Zickzack verlaufen/‹Person:› laufen

**zilch** /zɪltʃ/ *n.*, *no pl.*, *no art.* (*Amer. coll.*) rein *od.* reineweg gar nichts (*ugs.*); **be** ~**:** gleich null sein (*ugs.*)

**zillion** /ˈzɪljən/ *n.* (*coll.*) **a** ~ **mosquitoes** Myriaden von Stechmücken; ~**s of dollars** zig (*ugs.*) Millionen Dollar

**Zimbabwe** /zɪmˈbɑːbwɪ/ *pr. n.* Simbabwe (*das*)

**Zimbabwean** /zɪmˈbɑːbwɪən/ ▶ **1340** **1** *adj.* simbabwisch. **2** *n.* Simbabwer, *der*/Simbabwerin, *die*

**zinc** /zɪŋk/ *n.* Zink, *das*

**zing** /zɪŋ/ (*coll.*) **1** *n.* Schwung, *der.* **2** *v.i.* ‹Geschoss:› sirren

**zinnia** /ˈzɪnɪə/ *n.* (*Bot.*) Zinnie, *die*

**Zion** /ˈzaɪən/ *n.*, *no pl.* Zion, *der*

**Zionism** /ˈzaɪənɪzm/ *n.*, *no pl.* Zionismus, *der*

**Zionist** /ˈzaɪənɪst/ *n.* Zionist, *der*/Zionistin, *die*

**zip** /zɪp/ **1** *n.* **A** Reißverschluss, *der;* **B** (*fig.: energy, vigour*) Schwung, *der;* **C** (*sound*) Zischen, *das.* **2** *v.t.*, **-pp-: A** (*close*) ~ **[up] sth.** den Reißverschluss an etw. (*Dat.*) zuziehen; **I put on the jacket and** ~**ped it up** ich zog die Jacke an und machte den Reißverschluss zu; ~ **sb. up** jmdm. den Reißverschluss zumachen; **B** ~ **[up]** (*enclose*) [durch Schließen des Reißverschlusses] einpacken (*ugs.*); **he was** ~**ped [up] into his sleeping bag** er wurde in seinen Schlafsack gepackt (*ugs.*). **3** *v.i.*, **-pp-: A** (*fasten*) ~ **[up]** mit Reißverschluss geschlossen werden; **the dress** ~**s up [at the back/side]** das Kleid hat [hinten/seitlich] einen Reißverschluss; **the lining** ~**s in easily** das [Ausreiß]futter lässt sich leicht einziehen; **it won't** ~ **up** der Reißverschluss lässt sich nicht zuziehen; **B** (*move fast*) sausen

**ˈzip bag** *n.* Tasche mit Reißverschluss

**ˈZip code** *n.* (*Amer.*) Postleitzahl, *die*

**zip:** ~ **fastener** ⇒ **zip** 1 A; ~ **gun** *n.* (*Amer.*) selbst gebastelte Pistole

**zipper** /ˈzɪpə(r)/ ⇒ **zip** 1 A

**zippy** /ˈzɪpɪ/ *adj.* (*coll.*) spritzig

**zirconium** /zɜːˈkəʊnɪəm/ *n.* (*Chem.*) Zirkonium, *das;* Zirconium, *das* (*fachspr.*)

**zit** /zɪt/ *n.* (*coll.*) Pickel, *der*

**zither** /ˈzɪðə(r)/ *n.* (*Mus.*) Zither, *die*

**zodiac** /ˈzəʊdɪæk/ *n.* (*Astron.*) Tierkreis, *der;* Zodiakus, *der* (*fachspr.*); **sign of the** ~ (*Astrol.*) Tierkreiszeichen, *das;* Sternzeichen, *das*

**zodiacal** /zəˈdaɪəkl/ *adj.* (*Astron.*, *Astrol.*) Tierkreis-; zodiakal (*fachspr.*)

**zodiacal ˈlight** *n.* (*Astron.*) Zodiakallicht, *das*

**zombie** (*Amer.:* **zombi**) /ˈzɒmbɪ/ *n.* (*lit. or fig.*) Zombie, *der*

**zonal** /ˈzəʊnl/ *adj.* zonal; ~ **tariff** Zonentarif, *der*

**zone** /zəʊn/ **1** *n.* Zone, *die;* **[time]** ~**:** Zeitzone, *die;* **Temperate Z**~**:** gemäßigte Zone. **2** *v.t.* [in Zonen] einteilen

**zoning** /ˈzəʊnɪŋ/ *n.* Zoneneinteilung, *die*

**zonked** /zɒŋkt/ *adj.* (*coll.*) **be** ~ (*by drugs*) stoned sein (*Drogenjargon*); (*by alcohol*) zu sein (*salopp*); (*be tired*) erschlagen sein (*ugs.*)

**zoo** /zuː/ *n.* Zoo, *der*

**ˈzookeeper** *n.* ▶ **1261** Zoowärter, *der*/-wärterin, *die*

**zoological** /zuːəˈlɒdʒɪkl/ *adj.* zoologisch

**zoological ˈgarden[s]** *n.* zoologischer Garten

**zoologist** /zuːˈɒlədʒɪst/ *n.* ▶ **1261** Zoologe, *der*/Zoologin, *die*

**zoology** /zuːˈɒlədʒɪ/ *n.* Zoologie, *die*

**zoom** /zuːm/ **1** *v.i.* **A** (*move quickly*) rauschen; **we** ~**ed along on our bicycles** wir sausten auf unseren Fahrrädern daher; ~ **through a script** ein Manuskript überfliegen; **B** (*Aeronaut.*) das Flugzeug steil hochziehen; **C** (*Photog.*) ‹Kamera, Objektiv:› die Brennweite stufenlos verändern; ‹Bild:› herangeholt werden. **2** *n.* ⇒ **zoom lens**

~ **ˈin** *v.i.* **A** (*Cinemat.*, *Telev.*) zoomen (*fachspr.*); nahe heranfahren; ~ **in on sth.** auf etw. (*Akk.*) zoomen (*fachspr.*); etw. nahe heranholen; **B** ~ **in on sth.** (*fig.*) sich auf etw. (*Akk.*) konzentrieren

**ˈzoom lens** *n.* (*Photog.*) Zoomobjektiv, *das;* Gummilinse, *die* (*ugs.*)

**Zoroastrianism** /zɒrəʊˈæstrɪənɪzm/ *n.* (*Relig.*) Zoroastrismus, *der*

**zucchini** /zʊˈkiːnɪ/ *n.*, *pl. same or* ~**s** (*esp. Amer.*) Zucchino, *der*

**zugzwang** /ˈtsuːktsvɑːŋ/ *n.* (*Chess*) Zugzwang, *der*

**Zulu** /ˈzuːluː/ ▶ **1275** **1** *n.* **A** (*person*) Zulu, *der/die;* **B** (*language*) Zulu, *das.* **2** *adj.* Zulu-

**Zurich** /ˈzjʊərɪk/ ▶ **1626** **1** *pr. n.* Zürich (*das*). **2** *attrib. adj.* **A** (*of canton*) des Kantons Zürich *nachgestellt;* **B** (*of city*) Züricher; Zürcher (*schweiz.*)

**zygomatic bone** /zaɪgəˈmætɪk bəʊn/ *n.* (*Anat.*) Jochbein, *das*

**zygote** /ˈzaɪgəʊt/ *n.* (*Biol.*) Zygote, *die*

# The revision of German spellings / Die neue Regelung der deutschen Rechtschreibung

German spellings in this dictionary are in accordance with the reforms ratified by the governments of Germany, Austria, and Switzerland in July 1996 and in force since August 1998. Key points of the reforms are summarized below. In cases of doubt the editors have followed *Duden—Rechtschreibung der deutschen Sprache*, twenty-first edition, 1996.

To help the user who may not yet be familiar with the reforms, the German-English section of the dictionary gives both the new spellings and the old versions which will become 'invalid' in 2005 after a transition period during which both spellings are 'valid'. The old spellings are marked with an asterisk and are cross-referred where necessary to the new. For example, the translations of the compound verb *wiedererkennen* will no longer be found at this headword, since under the new spelling rules the word will vanish from the language. Instead they are covered by two phrases at the entry for *wieder: jemanden/etwas wieder erkennen* (in the form *jmdn./etw. ~ erkennen*) and *er war kaum wieder zu erkennen* (in the form *er war kaum ~ zu erkennen*). Similarly, the translations of the adjective previously written *belemmert* will be found at the new entry for the headword *belämmert*.

In a number of cases, however, implementing the new spelling rules has meant that just some, but not all, uses of a word have had to be transferred from one entry to another. In these cases the headword is not marked with an asterisk, but the entry is provided with a cross reference to where the transferred information is now to be found. So, for example, the user who consults the entry for *leid* looking for a translation of the phrase previously written *jemandem leid tun* will find a cross reference to the entry for *Leid*[2], since according to the new spelling rules the word is written with a capital L in this expression. The headword *leid* itself is not marked with an asterisk, since it continues to exist in its own right as an adjective.

## The following summary lists the most important changes:

### 1. The ß character

The ß character, which is generally replaced in Switzerland by a double s, will be retained in Germany and Austria, but will only be written after a long vowel (as in Fuß, Füße) and after a diphthong (as in Strauß, Sträuße).

*Fluß, Baß, keß, läßt, Nußknacker* become in future:
*Fluss, Bass, kess, lässt, Nussknacker*

### 2. Nominalized adjectives

Nominalized adjectives will be written with a capital even in set phrases.

*sein Schäfchen ins trockene bringen, im trüben fischen, im allgemeinen* become in future:
*sein Schäfchen ins Trockene bringen, im Trüben fischen, im Allgemeinen*

### 3. Words from the same word family

In certain cases the spelling of words belonging to the same family will be made uniform.

*numerieren, überschwenglich* become in future:
*nummerieren* (like Nummer), *überschwänglich* (being related to Überschwang)

### 4. The same consonant repeated three times

When the same consonant repeated three times occurs in compounds, all three will be written even when a vowel follows.

*Brennessel, Schiffahrt* become in future:
*Brennnessel, Schifffahrt* (exceptions are dennoch, Drittel, Mittag)

### 5. Verb, adjective and participle compounds

Verb, adjective and participle compounds will be written more frequently than previously in two words.

*spazierengehen, radfahren, ernstgemeint, erdölexportierend* become in future: *spazieren gehen, Rad fahren, ernst gemeint, Erdöl exportierend*

### 6. Compounds containing numbers in figures

Compounds containing numbers in figures will in future be written with a hyphen.

*24karätig, 8pfünder* become in future:
*24-karätig, 8-Pfünder*

### 7. The division of words containing *st*

*st* will be treated like a normal combination of consonants and no longer be indivisible.

*Ha-stig, Ki-ste* become in future: *has-tig, Kis-te*

## 8. The division of words containing *ck*

The combination *ck* will not be divided and will go on to the next line.

*Bäk-ker, schik-ken* become in future:
*Bä-cker, schi-cken*

## 9. The division of foreign words

Compound foreign words which are hardly recognized as such today may be divided by syllables, without regard to their original components.

*He-li-ko-pter* (from the Greek helix and pteron) may also become in future: *He-li-kop-ter*

## 10. The comma before *und*

Where two complete clauses are connected by *und* a comma will not be obligatory.

*Karl war in Schwierigkeiten, und niemand konnte ihm helfen.* may also in future be written: *Karl war in Schwierigkeiten und niemand konnte ihm helfen.*

## 11. The comma with infinitives and participles

Even longer clauses containing an infinitive or participle will not have to be divided off with a comma.

*Er begann sofort, das neue Buch zu lesen. Ungläubig den Kopf schüttelnd, verließ er das Zimmer.* may also in future be written: *Er begann sofort das neue Buch zu lesen. Ungläubig den Kopf schüttelnd verließ er das Zimmer.*

# Outline of German grammatical forms

The following outline is intended to be used in conjunction with the grammatical information included in the Dictionary, which it complements and explains. It does not attempt to cover all forms.

## Verbs

### General Notes

a) Verbs with prefixes, such as *ab-*, *auf-*, *er-*, *mit-*, and *zer-*, are conjugated like the corresponding simple verbs, e.g. *absagen* like *sagen*, but see the section on past participles below.

b) *ß* is used, and not *ss*, after a long vowel or diphthong:

| | |
|---|---|
| essen | heißen |
| ich aß | ich hieß |
| gegessen | geheißen |

c) To discover the stem of a verb, take away the *-en* (or just the *-n* if the penultimate letter is not *-e-*) from the end of the infinitive (the form given as a headword in the German-English section of the Dictionary):

| | |
|---|---|
| machen | handeln |
| mach- | handel- |

## Regular verbs

### Participles

#### Present

Add *-d* to the infinitive:

lachen
lachend

#### Past

Add *ge-* and *-t* to the stem:

machen
gemacht

If the stem ends with *-d*, *-t*, or a consonant + *m* or *n*, add *ge-* and *-et* to the stem:

| | |
|---|---|
| reden | trocknen |
| geredet | getrocknet |

If the infinitive ends with *-ieren* or *-eien*, add *-t* to the stem:

| | |
|---|---|
| diskutieren | prophezeien |
| diskutiert | prophezeit |

Verbs with a separable prefix (marked with | in the German-English section of the Dictionary) that is not followed by another prefix add *-ge-* between the prefix and the stem and *-[e]t* to the end of the stem:

| | |
|---|---|
| an\|klagen | zu\|leiten |
| angeklagt | zugeleitet |

Verbs with

a) any of the inseparable prefixes *be-*, *ent-*, *er-*, *ge-*, *ver-*, and *zer-*

b) an inseparable prefix (marked by · in the German-English section of the Dictionary)

c) a separable prefix (marked by | in the German-English section of the Dictionary) that is followed by an inseparable prefix

add *-[e]t* to the stem:

| | | |
|---|---|---|
| a) | beneiden | gehören |
| | beneidet | gehört |
| b) | durch·leuchten | über·blicken |
| | durchleuchtet | überblickt |
| c) | zu\|bereiten | aus\|erwählen |
| | zubereitet | auserwählt |

### Active

#### a) Indicative

#### Present

| | |
|---|---|
| | machen |
| ich | mache |
| du | machst |
| er/sie/es | macht |
| wir | machen |
| ihr | macht |
| sie/Sie | machen |

If the stem ends with *-l* or *-r*, the 1st person singular may omit the preceding *-e-*:

| | |
|---|---|
| | lächeln |
| ich | lächele *or* lächle |

If the stem ends with *-s*, *-ß*, *-x*, or *-z*, the 2nd person singular adds only *-t*:

| | | | |
|---|---|---|---|
| | rasen | | boxen |
| du | rast | du | boxt |

If the stem ends with *-d*, *-t*, or a consonant + *m* or *n*, the 2nd person singular adds *-est*, and the 2nd person plural adds *-et*:

| | reden |
|---|---|
| du | redest |
| ihr | redet |

**Preterite** (or past or imperfect)

| | machen |
|---|---|
| ich | machte |
| du | machtest |
| er/sie/es | machte |
| wir | machten |
| ihr | machtet |
| sie/Sie | machten |

If the stem ends with *-d*, *-t*, or a consonant + *m* or *n*, add *-e-* to the stem first:

| | reden |
|---|---|
| ich | redete |
| du | redetest |
| er/sie/es | redete |
| wir | redeten |
| ihr | redetet |
| sie/Sie | redeten |

**Future**

Present indicative of *werden* + infinitive:

| | reden |
|---|---|
| ich werde | reden *etc.* |

**Perfect**

Present indicative of *sein* or *haben* + past participle:

| reisen | machen |
|---|---|
| ich bin gereist *etc.* | ich habe gemacht *etc.* |

Verbs which take *sein* are labelled accordingly in the German-English section of the Dictionary.

**Pluperfect**

Preterite indicative of *sein* or *haben* (see note at **Perfect**) + past participle:

| reisen | machen |
|---|---|
| ich war gereist *etc.* | ich hatte gemacht *etc.* |

**Future perfect**

Future indicative of *sein* or *haben* (see note at **Perfect**) + past participle:

| reisen | machen |
|---|---|
| ich werde gereist sein *etc.* | ich werde gemacht haben *etc.* |

### b) Subjunctive

**Present**

| | machen |
|---|---|
| ich | mache |
| du | machest |
| er/sie/es | mache |
| wir | machen |
| ihr | machet |
| sie/Sie | machen |

If the stem ends with *-l* or *-r*, the preceding *-e-* may be omitted:

| | lächeln |
|---|---|
| ich | lächele *or* lächle *etc.* |

**Preterite**

Identical with preterite indicative.

### c) Conditional

**Present**

Preterite subjunctive of *werden* + infinitive:

ich würde reden *etc.*

**Perfect**

Preterite subjunctive of *sein* or *haben* + past participle:

| reisen | machen |
|---|---|
| ich wäre gereist *etc.* | ich hätte gemacht *etc.* |

or present conditional of *sein* or *haben* + past participle:

| reisen | machen |
|---|---|
| ich würde gereist sein *etc.* | ich würde gemacht haben *etc.* |

Verbs which take *sein* are labelled accordingly in the German-English section of the Dictionary.

### d) Imperative

| | |
|---|---|
| 2nd person singular | red[e]! |
| 2nd person plural | redet! |
| 2nd person (polite) | reden Sie! |

## Passive

**General note**

Passive tenses are formed from the corresponding active tense of *werden* + past participle.

### a) Infinitives

| | |
|---|---|
| Present | geliebt [zu] werden |
| Perfect | geliebt worden [zu] sein |

### b) Indicative

| | |
|---|---|
| Present | ich werde geliebt *etc.* |
| Preterite | ich wurde geliebt *etc.* |
| Future | ich werde geliebt werden *etc.* |
| Perfect | ich bin geliebt worden *etc.* |
| Pluperfect | ich war geliebt worden *etc.* |
| Future perfect | ich werde geliebt worden sein *etc.* |

### c) Subjunctive

| | |
|---|---|
| Present | ich werde*) geliebt *etc.* |
| Preterite | ich würde geliebt *etc.* |
| Future | ich werde*) geliebt werden *etc.* |
| Perfect | ich sei geliebt worden *etc.* |
| Pluperfect | ich wäre geliebt worden *etc.* |
| Future perfect | ich werde*) geliebt worden sein *etc.* |

*) NB du werdest ...; er/sie/es werde ...

### d) Conditional

| | |
|---|---|
| Present | ich würde geliebt [werden] |
| Perfect | ich wäre geliebt worden |

### e) Imperative

| | |
|---|---|
| 2nd person singular | sei *or* werde gegrüßt! |
| 2nd person plural | seid *or* werdet gegrüßt! |
| 2nd person (polite) | seien *or* werden Sie gegrüßt! |

# Irregular verbs

These are conjugated as regular verbs except for the forms given in the table (pp. 1723–1726) and the preterite indicative:

### a) Preterite indicative

If the form given in the table ends with *-te*, the tense is conjugated as for a regular verb; otherwise as follows:

| | singen |
|---|---|
| ich | sang |
| du | sangst |
| er/sie/es | sang |
| wir | sangen |
| ihr | sangt |
| sie/Sie | sangen |

If the form given ends with *-s* or *-ß*, the 2nd person singular adds only *-t*:

| | blasen | | heißen |
|---|---|---|---|
| | blies | | hieß |
| du | bliest | du | hießt |

### b) Compound tenses of modal verbs

The past participle forms shown in the table are not used with an infinitive, but only where the verb functions as a full verb (usually with a direct object or an indication of direction):

Er hat es gedurft. Ich habe damals kein Englisch gekonnt. Sie hat nach Frankfurt gemusst.

Where the verb is used with an infinitive, i.e. modally, the infinitive form is used instead:

Sie hat kommen müssen. Wir hatten zusehen dürfen.

# Nouns

## Singular

The first or only ending given in the entry for a noun in the German-English section of the Dictionary is the genitive singular. Shown here are examples of each, together with the corresponding other cases.

| | **Stadt** ... ~ ... | **Manna ...** ~[s] ... | **Feuer ...** ~s ... | **Buch ...** ~[e]s ... |
|---|---|---|---|---|
| Nom. | die Stadt | das Manna | das Feuer | das Buch |
| Acc. | die Stadt | das Manna | das Feuer | das Buch |
| Gen. | der Stadt | des Manna[s] | des Feuers | des Buch[e]s |
| Dat. | der Stadt | dem Manna | dem Feuer | dem Buch[e] |

| | **Löwe** ... ~n ... | **Name** ... ~ns ... | **Bär** ... ~en ... | **Herz** ... ~ens ... |
|---|---|---|---|---|
| Nom. | der Löwe | der Name | der Bär | das Herz |
| Acc. | den Löwen | den Namen | den Bären | das Herz |
| Gen. | des Löwen | des Namens | des Bären | des Herzens |
| Dat. | dem Löwen | dem Namen | dem Bären | dem Herzen |

## Plural

The second ending (if any) given in the entry for a noun in the German-English section of the Dictionary is used for each plural case, except that, if it does not end with *-n* or *-s*, the dative plural adds *-n*:

| | **Fahrer** ... ~s, ~ | **Frau** ... ~, ~en | **Streik** ... ~[e]s, ~s |
|---|---|---|---|
| Nom. | die Fahrer | die Frauen | die Streiks |
| Acc. | die Fahrer | die Frauen | die Streiks |
| Gen. | der Fahrer | der Frauen | der Streiks |
| Dat. | den Fahrern | den Frauen | den Streiks |

| | **Nacht** ... ~, **Nächte** | **Brettel** ... ~s, ~[n] | **Bild** ... ~[e]s, ~er |
|---|---|---|---|
| Nom. | die Nächte | die Brettel[n] | die Bilder |
| Acc. | die Nächte | die Brettel[n] | die Bilder |
| Gen. | der Nächte | der Brettel[n] | der Bilder |
| Dat. | den Nächten | den Bretteln | den Bildern |

The genitive singular or the plural form is given in full in the German-English section of the Dictionary if it involves changes to the stem:

**Wald** ... ~**es**, **Wälder**

### Adjectival declension

If a noun entry gives no endings but instead states '*adj. Dekl.*', noun and adjective endings are as follows:

| | *Masc.* | *Fem.* | *Neut.* | *Pl. (all genders)* |
|---|---|---|---|---|
| | **[1]Alte** *der; adj. Dekl.* | **[2]Alte** *die; adj. Dekl.* | **[3]Alte** *das; adj. Dekl.* | **[4]Alte** *Pl.; adj. Dekl.* |
| Nom. | der gute Alte | die gute Alte | das gute Alte | die guten Alten |
| Acc. | den guten Alten | die gute Alte | das gute Alte | die guten Alten |
| Gen. | des guten Alten | der guten Alten | des guten Alten | der guten Alten |
| Dat. | dem guten Alten | der guten Alten | dem guten Alten | den guten Alten |
| Nom. | ein guter Alter | eine gute Alte | ein gutes Altes | gute Alte |
| Acc. | einen guten Alten | eine gute Alte | ein gutes Altes | gute Alte |
| Gen. | eines guten Alten | einer guten Alten | eines guten Alten | guter Alter |
| Dat. | einem guten Alten | einer guten Alten | einem guten Alten | guten Alten |

### Endings for personal names

The genitive singular ending of personal names is *-s*, or, if the name ends with *-s*, *-ß*, *-x*, or *-z*, it is simply an apostrophe or sometimes *-ens*:

Barbaras Buch
Hans' Auto or Hansens Auto

If a title (other than *Herr*) or more than one name is given, only the last element has an ending:

Frau Brauns Hut
König Ottokars Glück und Ende
eine Symphonie Ludwig van Beethovens

Following words in apposition are declined as well as the name:

| | | |
|---|---|---|
| Nom. | Wilhelm der Erste | Heinrich der Vogler |
| Acc. | Wilhelm den Ersten | Heinrich den Vogler |
| Gen. | Wilhelms des Ersten | Heinrichs des Voglers |
| Dat. | Wilhelm dem Ersten | Heinrich dem Vogler |

When used as names, the words for family members take *-s* in the genitive singular:

Vaters/Mutters Aktentasche

The genitive singular of a name does not take an ending if preceded by an article or other inflected word other than *Herrn*:

eine Ausgabe des „Grünen Heinrich"
*but*: Herrn Dr. Baiers Praxis

Surnames often have an *-s* in the plural, especially when denoting a family:

[die] Remanns wohnen nebenan

If the name ends with *-s*, *-ß*, *-x*, or *-z*, the ending is *-ens*:

[die] Schwarzens

# Adjectives and adverbs

## Article and adjective endings

### a) Weak declension

The qualifying words *der/die/das*, *dieser/diese/dieses*, *jener/jene/jenes*, *all...*, *welch...*, *solch...*, *beide*, *sämtliche*, etc. and any following adjectives are declined as follows:

| | *Masc.* | *Fem.* | *Neut.* | *Pl. (all genders)* |
|---|---|---|---|---|
| Nom. | der gute Tag | die gute Frau | das gute Buch | die guten Dinge |
| Acc. | den guten Tag | die gute Frau | das gute Buch | die guten Dinge |
| Gen. | des guten Tag[e]s | der guten Frau | des guten Buch[e]s | der guten Dinge |
| Dat. | dem guten Tag[e] | der guten Frau | dem guten Buch[e] | den guten Dingen |

### b) Mixed declension

The qualifying words *ein* and *kein*, possessive adjectives, and any following adjectives are declined as follows:

| | *Masc* | *Fem* | *Neut.* | *Pl. (all genders)* |
|---|---|---|---|---|
| Nom. | ein guter Tag | eine gute Frau | ein gutes Buch | keine guten Bücher |
| Acc. | einen guten Tag | eine gute Frau | ein gutes Buch | keine guten Bücher |
| Gen. | eines guten Tag[e]s | einer guten Frau | eines guten Buch[e]s | keiner guten Bücher |
| Dat. | einem guten Tag[e] | einer guten Frau | einem guten Buch[e] | keinen guten Büchern |

### c) Strong declension

Adjectives are declined as follows when preceded either by no qualifying word or by an indeclinable one, e.g. *viel, mehr, wenig, weniger, manch, solch*, or *welch*, or by *dessen, deren, ander..., einig..., etlich..., folgend...*, or *mehrer...*:

| | *Masc* | *Fem* | *Neut.* | *Pl. (all genders)* |
|---|---|---|---|---|
| Nom. | guter Wein | gute Milch | gutes Bier | gute Dinge |
| Acc. | guten Wein | gute Milch | gutes Bier | gute Dinge |
| Gen. | guten Wein[e]s | guter Milch | guten Biers | guter Dinge |
| Dat. | gutem Wein[e] | guter Milch | gutem Bier[e] | guten Dingen |

### d) Exceptions

Adjectives which are marked *'indekl. Adj.'* or which end with *-er* and are derived from place names do not inflect at all:

klasse — Berliner
ein klasse Wagen — die Berliner Philharmoniker

Adjectives which end with *-el* drop the *-e-* when inflected and in their comparative forms:

übel
ein übler Mensch

and adjectives which end with *-en* and *-er* sometimes drop the *-e-*:

trocken — finster
trock[e]nes Holz — die finst[e]re Nacht

but *clever* does not:

clever
ein cleverer Trick

and the *-e-* is always dropped in:

integer — makaber
eine integre Persönlichkeit — eine makabre Geschichte

and when *-er* is preceded by *-au-* or *-eu-*:

teuer — sauer
ein teures Haus — saure Gurken

Adjectives which end with a vowel, other than those marked *'indekl. Adj.'*, drop the vowel:

müde
die müden Arbeiter

The adjective *hoch* drops its *-c-* when inflected:

eine hohe Stirn

### Comparison of adjectives and adverbs

The regular endings are *-er, -st...*:

| | |
|---|---|
| positive | schön |
| comparative | schöner |
| superlative attributive adjective | schönst... |
| superlative predicative adjective | am schönsten |
| superlative adverb | am schönsten |

Irregular forms are given in the German-English section of the Dictionary:

**arm** ... **ärmer** ... **ärmst** ...

See also above for adjectives ending with *-el, -en*, and *-er*.

If an adjective or adverb ends with *-d, -t, -sch, -s, -ß, -x, -z*, a long vowel, or a diphthong and has only one syllable or is stressed on its last syllable, the superlative ending is *-est...*:

laut — zäh — genau
lautest... — zähest... — genauest...

# Pronouns

## Personal pronouns

| *Nom.* | *Acc.* | *Gen.* | *Dat.* |
|---|---|---|---|
| ich | mich | meiner | mir |
| du | dich | deiner | dir |
| er | ihn | seiner | ihm |
| sie | sie | ihrer | ihr |
| es | es | seiner | ihm |
| wir | uns | unser | uns |
| ihr | euch | euer | euch |
| sie | sie | ihrer | ihnen |
| Sie | Sie | Ihrer | Ihnen |

Reflexive and reciprocal pronouns are the same as personal pronouns, except that the accusative and dative forms of *er, sie, es, sie*, and *Sie* are *sich*.

## Possessive pronouns (*mein, dein, sein, ihr, unser, euer*, and *Ihr*)

| | *Masc.* | *Fem.* | *Neut.* | *Pl. (all genders)* |
|---|---|---|---|---|
| Nom. | mein | meine | mein | meine |
| Acc. | meinen | meine | mein | meine |
| Gen. | meines | meiner | meines | meiner |
| Dat. | meinem | meiner | meinem | meinen |

*euer* is usually contracted in all inflected forms, e.g. *eure*.

When used other than attributively, i.e. as independent pronouns, these forms differ:

| | |
|---|---|
| Nom. masc.: | meiner *etc.*, uns[e]rer, eurer |
| Nom. and acc. neut.: | mein[e]s *etc.*, uns[e]res, eures |

## Demonstrative pronouns (*dieser*, *jener*, *der*, *derjenige*, and *derselbe*)

*dieser* and *jener*:

| | *Masc.* | *Fem.* | *Neut.* | *Pl. (all genders)* |
|---|---|---|---|---|
| Nom. | dieser | diese | dieses | diese |
| Acc. | diesen | diese | dieses | diese |
| Gen. | dieses | dieser | dieses | dieser |
| Dat. | diesem | dieser | diesem | diesen |

*der* is the same as when a definite article, except for:

| | *Masc.* | *Fem.* | *Neut.* | *Pl. (all genders)* |
|---|---|---|---|---|
| Gen. | dessen | deren | dessen | derer *or* deren |
| Dat. | | | | denen |

*derjenige* and *derselbe* are declined as if two separate words:

| | *Masc.* | *Fem.* | *Neut.* | *Pl. (all genders)* |
|---|---|---|---|---|
| Nom. | derjenige | diejenige | dasjenige | diejenigen |
| Acc. | denjenigen | diejenige | dasjenige | diejenigen |
| Gen. | desjenigen | derjenigen | desjenigen | derjenigen |
| Dat. | demjenigen | derjenigen | demjenigen | denjenigen |

## Relative pronouns

| | *Masc.* | *Fem.* | *Neut.* | *Pl. (all genders)* |
|---|---|---|---|---|
| Nom. | der *or* welcher | die *or* welche | das *or* welches | die *or* welche |
| Acc. | den *or* welchen | die *or* welche | das *or* welches | die *or* welche |
| Gen. | dessen | deren | dessen | deren |
| Dat. | dem *or* welchem | der *or* welcher | dem *or* welchem | denen *or* welchen |

## Interrogative pronouns

*welch* follows the strong adjective declension (see p. 1713). The declensions of *was* and *wer* are given at their entries in the Dictionary.

## Indefinite pronouns

*etwas*, *was*, and *nichts* are invariable. Other indefinite pronouns are declined as follows:

| | | | |
|---|---|---|---|
| Nom. | man | jemand | niemand |
| Acc. | einen | jemand[en] | niemand[en] |
| Gen. | eines | jemandes | niemandes |
| Dat. | einem | jemand[em] | niemand[em] |

# Key points of German orthography and punctuation

## Use of capital and small initial letters

The use of capital and small initial letters in German is governed by the following guidelines.

a) The first word of a sentence has a capital initial letter.

b) All true nouns have capital initial letters:

Himmel, Kindheit, Reichtum, Verständnis

c) All types of word have capital initial letters when they are used as nouns:

das Gute, der Abgeordnete, allerlei Schönes, etwas Wichtiges, die Deinigen, ein Achtel, das Auf und Nieder, das Entweder-oder, das Lesen, das Zustandekommen, das In-den-Tag-hinein-Leben

d) The polite form *Sie* and the accompanying possessive pronoun *Ihr* always have capital initials, but the reflexive pronoun *sich* always has a small initial:

Würden *Sie* mir bitte *Ihr* Programmheft leihen?
Setzen *Sie sich*.

e) Words which are derived from geographical names and which end in *-er* have capital initial letters:

die Schweizer Industrie, eine Kölner Firma

f) Adjectives ending in *-isch* which are derived from geographical names have small initials unless they form part of a proper name:

chinesische Seide, westfälischer Schinken
*but*: Holsteinische Schweiz

g) When nouns function other than as nouns they have small initial letters:

anfangs, abends, sonntags, ein bisschen, schuld sein

## One word or two?

The continuing development of the conventions governing spelling and punctuation in German means that it is impossible to say for certain when words are written together (as one word) and when separately (as two words). The following examples are designed to serve as a general guide only. In cases of doubt write as two words.

a) Words are written together if they combine to form a new meaning:

Er wird mir die Summe gutschreiben.

Words are written separately if they retain their original meanings:

Der Schüler kann gut schreiben.

b) Compounds formed with a noun are written as one word if the noun no longer embodies a separate concept:

wetterleuchten, infolge, zugunsten

Words are written separately if the noun retains its independent meaning:

Sorge tragen, Posten stehen, unter Bezugnahme auf

The continuing development of the language means that some words are found in both forms:

Dank sagen *and* danksagen, auf Grund *and* aufgrund, in Frage *and* infrage

## The comma

The role of the comma is to divide the sentence and indicate the pauses occurring in speech.

a) In lists, the comma is placed between words of the same type or between similar groups of words if they are not linked by *und* or *oder*:

Feuer, Wasser, Luft und Erde.
Wir gingen bei gutem, warmem Wetter spazieren.
Das Autorennen findet am Montag, dem 5. Mai statt.
(Here, the comma divides two statements of time; compare b.)

b) The comma separates following qualifying phrases from the rest of the sentence:

In Frankfurt, der bekannten Handelsstadt, befindet sich ein großes Messegelände.
Das Schiff kommt wöchentlich einmal, und zwar sonntags.
Das Autorennen findet am Montag, dem 5. Mai, statt.
(Here, an embedded phrase is enclosed by commas; compare a.)

c) An infinitive phrase is usually divided from the rest of the sentence by a comma; *zu* + infinitive alone is not divided off.

Wir hatten keine Gelegenheit, uns zu sehen.
*but*: Wir hatten keine Gelegenheit zu baden.

d) The comma separates main clauses but may also be omitted if the clauses are linked by *und* or *oder*. However the comma is never used between main clauses linked by *und* or *oder* if one part of the sentence is common to both clauses:

Ich kam, ich sah, ich siegte.
Wir trinken noch ein Bier [,] und dann gehe ich nach Hause.

*but*: sie bestiegen den Wagen und fuhren davon. (*sie* is common to both clauses)
Er geht ins Kino und sein Bruder ins Konzert. (*geht* is common to both clauses)

e) The comma separates the subordinate clause from the main clause:

Dass du zuverlässig bist, freut mich.
Alle Kinder, die fleißig sind, erhalten ein Buch.

## Syllable division in German

Polysyllabic words are divided in accordance with the phonetic syllables which can be identified by pronouncing the word slowly:

Freun-de, Män-ner, for-dern, wei-ter, Or-gel, kal-kig, Bes-se-rung, Bal-kon, Fis-kus, Ho-tel, Pla-net, Kon-ti-nent, Fas-zi-kel, Re-mi-nis-zenz, El-lip-se, Ber-lin, El-ba, Tür-kei, las-ten, Diens-tes

In such cases, a single consonant goes on to the following line; if there is a series of consonants, the last of these goes on to the following line:

tre-ten, nä-hen, Ru-der, rei-ßen, bo-xen, Ko-kon, Kre-ta, Chi-na, An-ker, Fin-ger, war-ten, Fül-lun-gen, Rit-ter, Was-ser, Knos-pen, kämp-fen, Ach-sel, steck-ten, Kat-zen, Städ-ter, Drechs-ler, dunk-le, gest-rig, an-de-re, neh-men, Ar-sen, Hip-pie, Kas-ko, Pek-tin, Un-garn, Hes-sen, At-lan-tik (For exceptions see below.)

Suffixes which begin with a vowel take the preceding consonant when divided:

Freun-din, Bäcke-rei, Lüf-tung

The consonant groups *ch* and *sch* – as well as *ph*, *rh*, *sh*, and *th* in foreign words – represent single sounds and are not divided:

Bü-cher, Fla-sche, Ma-chete, Pro-phet, Myr-rhe, Ca-shew-nuß, ka-tho-lisch
Grü-sse (*for*: Grü-ße), hei-ssen (*for*: hei-ßen)

*ck* is regarded as a single consonant and is placed on the following line:

Zu-cker, ba-cken
Sen-ckenberg, Fran-cke, bismar-ckisch

Words are not divided before the 'lengthening' letters *e* and *i*:

Wie-se
Coes-feld (*pronounced*: kos...)

Compound words and words with a prefix are divided in accordance with their constituent word elements:

ein-armig, be-inhalten

The same applies to foreign words:

Des-interesse, in-adäquat

Many foreign words, however, may be divided according to phonetic syllables, as the constituent elements of a foreign word are not always generally known:

Epi-sode (*instead of*: Epis-ode)
ab-strakt (*instead of*: abs-trakt)

Word divisions which obey the rules but disrupt the flow of reading should be avoided:

Spar-gelder, *not*: Spargel-der
be-inhalten, *not*: bein-halten

# Kleine Formenlehre des Englischen

## Das Verb

### Die Stammformen

Die regelmäßigen Verben bilden das Präteritum und das gleichlautende 2. Partizip mit Hilfe der Endung *-ed*:

call – called – called

Hierbei sind die folgenden Besonderheiten zu beachten:

Ein auslautender Konsonant wird häufig verdoppelt, und *-c* wird zu *-ck-*:

dub – dubbed
pod – podded
hug – hugged
focus – focused *od.* focussed
panic – panicked

Ein auslautendes *-e* fällt aus:

love – loved
tie – tied
dye – dyed
guarantee – guaranteed

Ein auslautendes, auf einen Konsonanten folgendes *-y* wird zu *-i-*:

worry – worried
satisfy – satisfied

Die Stammformen der unregelmäßigen Verben sind im englisch-deutschen Wörterverzeichnis bei dem jeweiligen Stichwort angegeben (vgl. S. 19). Außerdem sind sie in der Liste auf S. 1727f. verzeichnet. (Zu den Hilfsverben und den Modalverben s.u., S. 1718f).

### Das Präsens

Die 3. Person Singular Präsens der Vollverben (außer *have* und *be*) wird durch die Endung *-s*, nach *s*, *sh*, *ch*, *x*, *o* zu *-es* erweitert, gebildet:

read – reads
see – sees
miss – misses
fish – fishes
reach – reaches
mix – mixes
echo – echoes
do – does

Hierbei wird ein auslautendes, auf einen Konsonanten folgendes *-y* zu *-ie-*:

cry – cries
worry – worries

Alle übrigen Präsensformen haben keine Personalendungen. Sie lauten wie der Infinitiv.

### Das Präteritum

Das Präteritum hat keine Personalendungen und lautet (außer im Falle von *be*) in allen Personen gleich.

### Das Futur

Das Futur wird gewöhnlich aus *will*, in der 1. Person Singular und Plural auch aus *shall* und dem Infinitiv gebildet:

you/he/she/it/they will win
I/we will *oder* shall win

### Das Konditional Präsens

Das Konditional Präsens wird gewöhnlich aus *would*, in der 1. Person Singular und Plural auch aus *should* und dem Infinitiv gebildet:

you/he/she/it/they would win
I/we would *oder* should win

### Das Perfekt

Das Perfekt wird aus dem Präsens von *have* und dem 2. Partizip gebildet:

I have seen/gone/been *usw.*

### Das Plusquamperfekt

Das Plusquamperfekt wird aus dem Präteritum von *have* und dem 2. Partizip gebildet:

I had seen/gone/been *usw.*

### Das Futur II

Das Futur II wird aus dem Futur I von *have* und dem 2. Partizip gebildet:

I will/shall have seen/gone/been *usw.*

### Das Konditional Perfekt

Das Konditional Perfekt wird aus dem Konditional Präsens von *have* und dem 2. Partizip gebildet:

I would/should have seen/gone/been *usw.*

### Das Passiv

Das Passiv wird aus den Formen des Hilfsverbs *be* und dem 2. Partizip gebildet:

I am/was/have been *usw.* stopped

### Die Verlaufsform

Neben den vom Deutschen her vertrauten einfachen Verbformen gibt es im Englischen die so genannten

Verlaufsformen (continuous tenses). Diese werden aus den Formen von *be* und dem 1. Partizip gebildet:

I am/you were/they had been *usw.* reading

Die Verlaufsform wird vor allem verwendet, um auszudrücken, dass ein Vorgang noch nicht beendet ist bzw. ein Zustand noch andauert:

They were having supper.
The old house is still standing there.

Die Verlaufsform des Präsens kann daneben aber auch in futurischem Sinne, etwa zum Ausdruck einer Absicht verwendet werden:

I'm travelling to London next week.

## Die *going to*-Form

Zum Ausdruck des Zukünftigen hat das Englische neben der mit *will/shall* gebildeten Futurform noch eine weitere Form. Sie ist zusammengesetzt aus der Verlaufsform von *go* und dem Infinitiv mit *to* des betreffenden Verbs.

Durch diese *going to*-Form wird, wenn sie im Präsens steht, ausgedrückt, dass etwas geschehen wird, weil es geplant oder beabsichtigt ist, oder dass etwas mit großer Gewissheit geschehen wird:

I'm going to stay with friends.
I'm not going to accept that.
It's going to rain

Durch die *going to*-Form im Präteritum kann ausgedrückt werden, dass etwas geplant oder beabsichtigt war, jedoch nicht geschehen ist:

I was going to phone you yesterday, but I forgot.

## Mit dem Hilfsverb *do* gebildete Verbformen

In Fragesätzen, die nicht ein Fragewort als Subjekt haben, und in mit *not* verneinten Sätzen werden die einfachen Präsens- und Präteritumformen der Vollverben mit dem Hilfsverb *do* gebildet:

Does he like it? – He does not like it.
*aber*: Who likes it? – No one likes it.

Dies gilt außer im verneinten Imperativ nicht für das Kopulaverb *be*:

Is he a doctor? – No, he is not a doctor.
*aber*: Do not be so noisy.

Das Vollverb *have* kommt in Verneinung und Frage mit und ohne *do* vor:

Do they have a car? – No, they do not have a car.
Have you any idea? – No, I haven't a clue.

Ebenfalls mit *do* gebildet werden emphatische Formen in nicht verneinten Aussage- und Aufforderungssätzen:

But I 'did see him.
'Do listen to me.
'Do be quiet.

## Die *ing*-Form

Die mit der Endung *-ing* gebildete Verbform ist je nach Gebrauch entweder 1. Partizip oder Gerundium. Ein auslautender Konsonant wird häufig verdoppelt; *-c* wird zu *-ck-*:

dub – dubbing
pod – podding
hug – hugging
focus – focusing *od.* focussing
panic – panicking

Ein auf einen Konsonanten folgendes auslautendes *-e* fällt aus:

live – living

Ein auslautendes *-ie* wird zu *-y-*:

die – dying

## Die Formen der Hilfsverben *have, be, do*

(In Klammern sind – soweit vorhanden – jeweils die zugehörigen Kurzformen und die Kurzformen der verneinten Formen angegeben.)

### have

| | | |
|---|---|---|
| Präsens: | 3. Person Singular | has ('s; hasn't) |
| | alle übrigen Personen | have ('ve; haven't) |
| Präteritum: | alle Personen | had ('d; hadn't) |

(Das 2. Partizip *had* spielt nur beim Vollverb *have* eine Rolle.)

### be

| | | |
|---|---|---|
| Präsens: | 1. Person Singular | am ('m; *nur in Fragesätzen*: aren't) |
| | 3. Person Singular | is ('s; isn't) |
| | alle übrigen Personen | are ('re; aren't) |
| Präteritum: | 1. und 3. Person Singular | was (wasn't) |
| | alle übrigen Personen | were (weren't) |
| 2. Partizip: | | been |

### do

| | | |
|---|---|---|
| Präsens: | 3. Person Singular | does (doesn't) |
| | alle übrigen Personen | do (don't) |
| Präteritum: | alle Personen | did (didn't) |

(Das 2. Partizip *done* spielt nur beim Vollverb *do* eine Rolle.)

## Die Formen der Modalverben *can, may, must, shall, will*

Diese Verben, von denen *shall* und *will* auch als nicht modale Hilfsverben verwendet werden (vgl. **Futur** und **Konditional**), haben keine infiniten, sondern nur die folgenden, jeweils in allen Personen gleichlautenden, finiten Formen:

| *Vollform* | *Kurzform* | *Kurzform verneint* |
|---|---|---|
| Präsens | | |
| can; *verneint*: cannot | | can't |
| may | | mayn't |
| must | | mustn't |
| shall | 'll | shan't |
| will | 'll | won't |

| *Vollform* | *Kurzform* | *Kurzform verneint* |
|---|---|---|
| Präteritum | | |
| could | | couldn't |
| might | | mightn't |
| must | | mustn't |
| should | 'd | shouldn't |
| would | 'd | wouldn't |

Für die fehlenden Formen werden, je nach Bedeutung, verschiedene Ersatzformen verwendet: so z.B. für die fehlenden Formen von *can* im Sinne von „fähig sein zu" die entsprechenden Formen der Fügung *be able to* (z.B. *I shall be able to come*).

# Das Substantiv

## Das Genus

Im Englischen ist, anders als im Deutschen, das Genus der Substantive praktisch nur für den richtigen Gebrauch des Personal- und des Possessivpronomens von Bedeutung.

Es stimmt in der Regel mit dem natürlichen Geschlecht überein; Substantive, die männliche Personen bezeichnen, sind Maskulina, solche, die weibliche Personen bezeichnen, sind Feminina, alle übrigen sind in der Regel Neutra.

Zu beachten sind jedoch die folgenden Besonderheiten:

Substantive, die Personen beiderlei Geschlechts bezeichnen können (z.B. *friend, teacher*) sind je nach vorliegender Bedeutung Maskulina oder Feminina.

Substantive wie *child* und *baby* sowie Substantive, die Tiere beiderlei Geschlechts bezeichnen können (z.B. *elephant, cat*) sind je nach vorliegender Bedeutung Maskulina oder Feminina. Wenn das Geschlecht jedoch dem Sprecher unbekannt ist, dann werden sie als Neutra behandelt.

Geschlechtsspezifische Tierbezeichnungen haben dagegen meist das dem natürlichen Geschlecht entsprechende Genus (z.B. *tomcat, lioness, ewe, he-goat, she-bear*).

Bezeichnungen für Schiffe (z.B. *ship, boat, steamer*), Schiffsnamen, manchmal auch Bezeichnungen für andere Fahrzeuge (z.B. *car, train, aeroplane*) sowie, besonders in literarischem Stil, Länder- und Städtenamen (z.B. *Britain, Europe, Paris*) können als Feminina verwendet werden.

Fluss- und Bergnamen, das Substantiv *sun* sowie bestimmte Abstrakta (z.B. *death, love*) werden in literarischem Stil oft als Maskulina verwendet.

Die Substantive *moon, earth, sea* und bestimmte Abstrakta (z.B. *fortune, nature, liberty*) können in poetischem Stil als Feminina verwendet werden.

## Der Plural

Der Plural der Substantive wird in der Regel durch Anhängen der Endung *-s*, nach *s, sh, ch, x, z* und in einigen Fällen nach *o* zu *-es* erweitert, gebildet:

cat – cats
bus – buses
bush – bushes
beach – beaches
box – boxes
fez – fezes
tomato – tomatoes
*aber*: dynamo – dynamos

Hierbei sind die folgenden Besonderheiten zu beachten:

Ein auslautendes, auf einen Konsonanten folgendes *-y* wird in der Regel zu *-ie-*:

lady – ladies
fly – flies

Einige auf *-f* oder *-fe* endende Substantive lauten im Plural auf *-ves*:

leaf – leaves
life – lives

Einige Substantive haben eine unregelmäßige, manche auch eine mit dem Singular übereinstimmende Pluralform (z.B. *man – men, child – children, sheep – sheep*). Solche Pluralformen wie auch diejenigen auf *-ves* sind im englisch-deutschen Wörterverzeichnis jeweils beim entsprechenden Stichwort angeführt.

## Der Genitiv

Der Genitiv Singular aller Substantive und der Genitiv Plural der Substantive mit unregelmäßigem (nicht auf *-s* lautendem) Plural wird durch Anhängen von 's gebildet:

man's
men's
James's

Ebenso bei nicht auf *-s* endenden pluralischen Substantiven:

people – people's

Der Genitiv Plural der Substantive, die im Plural die Endung *-s* bzw. *-es* haben, wird durch einen hinter dem Plural -s stehenden Apostroph gekennzeichnet:

fathers'
Joneses'

Der Genitiv Singular eines auf *-s* ausgehenden Eigennamens wird oft nur durch einen Apostroph gekennzeichnet:

Dickens' *neben* Dickens's
James' *neben* James's

Griechische und lateinische Eigennamen auf *-s* haben im Genitiv stets nur einen Apostroph:

Socrates'
Augustus'

Dies gilt auch für auf *-s* endende Substantive in Verbindung mit *for … sake*:

for goodness' sake

## Die Steigerung der Adjektive und Adverbien

Einsilbige Adjektive werden – mit Ausnahme solcher, die aus Partizipien entstanden sind (z.B. *pleased*) und soweit sie keine unregelmäßigen Steigerungsformen haben (s.u.) – stets mithilfe der Suffixe *-er* (für den Komparativ) und *-est* (für den Superlativ) gesteigert:

clean – cleaner – cleanest
short – shorter – shortest

Ein auslautendes *-b, -d, -g, -m, -n, -p* oder *-t* nach kurzem Vokal wird verdoppelt:

big – bigger – biggest
hot – hotter – hottest

Ein auslautendes *-e* fällt aus:

large – larger – largest
wide – wider – widest
free – freer – freest

Ein auf einen Konsonanten folgendes auslautendes *-y* wird meist zu *-i-*:

dry – drier – driest
*aber*: shy – shyer *oder* shier – shyest *oder* shiest

Von den zweisilbigen Adjektiven werden solche auf *-y*, solche mit Endbetonung und einige weitere ebenfalls meist auf diese Art gesteigert, wobei ein auf einen Konsonanten folgendes auslautendes *-y* zu *-i-* wird und ein auslautendes *-e* ausfällt:

narrow – narrower – narrowest
easy – easier – easiest
polite – politer – politest

Alle zweisilbigen Adjektive können aber auch durch ein vorangestelltes *more* (für den Komparativ) bzw. *most* (für den Superlativ) gesteigert werden.

Stets mit *more* und *most* werden alle übrigen Adjektive (insbesondere auch diejenigen, die aus Partizipien entstanden sind, wie z.B. *bored, lasting, delighted*) gesteigert.

Von Adjektiven abgeleitete Adverbien auf *-ly* werden mit vorangestelltem *more* und *most* gesteigert:

carefully – more/most carefully
easily – more/most easily

Die übrigen Adverbien werden soweit sie keine unregelmäßigen Steigerungsformen haben (wie z.B. *much, well*) mit Hilfe der Suffixe *-er* und *-est* gesteigert:

fast – faster – fastest
soon – sooner – soonest
hard – harder – hardest

Hierbei gelten auch die oben für die mit *-er* und *-est* steigernden Adjektive genannten, den Stammauslaut betreffenden Besonderheiten.

Einige wenige Adjektive und Adverbien haben unregelmäßige Steigerungsformen.

Diese sind im englisch-deutschen Wörterverzeichnis sowohl beim zugehörigen Positiv als auch an ihrer alphabetischen Stelle angeführt.

# Pronomen

In der folgenden Übersicht sind die Formen der wichtigsten Pronomen aufgeführt.

## Personalpronomen

| | *Subjektsform* | *Objektsform* |
|---|---|---|
| 1. Pers. Sing. | I | me |
| 2. Pers. Sing. | you | you |
| 3. Pers. Sing. | he/she/it | him/her/it |
| 1. Pers. Pl. | we | us |
| 2. Pers. Pl. | you | you |
| 3. Pers. Pl. | they | them |

## Reflexivpronomen

| | *Sing.* | *Pl.* |
|---|---|---|
| 1. Pers. | myself | ourselves |
| 2. Pers. | yourself | yourselves |
| 3. Pers. | himself/ herself/itself | themselves |

## Possessivpronomen

attributiv gebraucht:

| | *Sing.* | *Pl.* |
|---|---|---|
| 1. Pers. | my | our |
| 2. Pers. | your | your |
| 3. Pers. | his/her/its | their |

alleinstehend gebraucht:

| | *Sing.* | *Pl.* |
|---|---|---|
| 1. Pers. | mine | ours |
| 2. Pers. | yours | yours |
| 3. Pers. | his/hers/– | theirs |

## Demonstrativpronomen

Die Demonstrativpronomen *this* und *that* haben außer diesen Singularformen nur noch je eine weitere Form: *these* (Plural zu *this*) und *those* (Plural zu *that*).

## Relativpronomen

**who**

| | | |
|---|---|---|
| Subjektsform | Sing. u. Pl.: | who |
| Objektsform | Sing. u. Pl.: | whom, who |
| Genitiv | Sing. u. Pl.: | whose |

**which**

(keine weiteren Formen)

**that**

(keine weiteren Formen)

## Interrogativpronomen

**who**

| | |
|---|---|
| Subjektsform: | who |
| Objektsform: | whom, who |
| Genitiv: | whose |

**which**

(keine weiteren Formen)

**what**

(keine weiteren Formen)

# Die Zeichensetzung im Englischen

## Apostroph

a) Der Apostroph steht als Auslassungszeichen:

I'm (= I am)
he's (= he is/has)
thro' (= through)
they'd (= they had/would)
the summer of '68 (= 1968)

Gelegentlich wird er – jedoch unnötigerweise – auch bei einigen Kurzformen wie *bus, cello, flu, phone, plane* gesetzt (*'bus* usw.).

b) Der Apostroph steht zur Kennzeichnung des Genitivs. Näheres hierzu findet sich unter „Kleine Formenlehre des Englischen" auf S. 1719.

c) Manchmal steht der Apostroph mit einem s zur Bildung des Plurals von Buchstaben, Zahlen oder Abkürzungen, z.B.:

pronounce the r's more clearly;
during the 1960's;
all the MP's

## Doppelpunkt

a) Der Doppelpunkt steht zur Markierung des Beginns einer Aufzählung nach einem Gattungsnamen oder einem die Aufzählung ankündigenden Ausdruck wie z.B. *as follows, in the following manner*:

His library consists of two books: the Bible and Shakespeare.
Proceed as follows: switch on the computer, insert a disk, and press any key.

b) Der Doppelpunkt steht vor Sätzen oder Ausdrücken, die den vorausgehenden Satz erläutern oder erklären:

The garden had been neglected for a long time: it was overgrown and full of weeds.

(Statt des Doppelpunkts kann hier auch ein Punkt, jedoch kein Komma stehen.)

## Komma

a) Das Komma steht zwischen Adjektiven, die ein Substantiv in gleicher Weise attribuieren:

a cautious, eloquent man

Wenn mehrere Adjektive ein Substantiv in unterschiedlicher Weise attribuieren oder wenn ein Adjektiv das andere attribuiert, steht dagegen kein Komma:

a distinguished foreign author; a bright red tie

b) Das Komma steht zwischen den Gliedern einer Aufzählung. Wenn vorletztes und letztes Aufzählungsglied durch eine Konjunktion verbunden sind, steht das Komma vor dieser Konjunktion:

potatoes, peas, and carrots; potatoes, peas, or carrots; potatoes, peas, etc.; red, white, and blue

c) Das Komma steht zwischen nebengeordneten Hauptsätzen, die nicht durch ein anderes Satzzeichen voneinander getrennt sind:

Cars turn here, and coaches go straight on.

Es steht jedoch nicht, wenn es sich um eng zusammengehörige Sätze handelt:

Do as I tell you and you'll never regret it.

d) Das Komma steht vor und hinter aus einem oder mehreren Wörtern bestehenden Einschüben sowie vor und hinter Zwischensätzen:

I am sure, however, that it will not happen.
Fred, who is bald, complained of the cold.

Es steht jedoch nicht vor und hinter notwendigen Relativsätzen:

Men who are bald should wear hats.

e) Das Komma steht nach am Satzanfang stehenden Infinitiv- und Partizipalgruppen und gleichwertigen verblosen Teilen:

To be sure of arriving on time, she left an hour early.
Worn out by their journey, the children soon fell asleep.

f) Das Komma steht zwischen einer adverbialen Bestimmung und dem übrigen Satz sowie zwischen Haupt- und Nebensatz, wenn ohne Komma ein Missverständnis möglich wäre:

In the valley below, the villages looked very small.
He did not go to church, because he was playing golf.
In 1980, 2000 seemed a long time off.

g) Das Komma steht nach Wörtern, die eine direkte Rede einleiten:

They answered, 'Here we are'.

h) Das Komma steht in Briefen nach der Anrede (*Dear Sir, Dear John* usw.) und nach der Grußformel (*Yours sincerely* usw.)

Nicht notwendig ist ein Komma zwischen Monat und Jahr in Datumsangaben (z.B. *in December 1999*) oder zwischen Hausnummer und Straßenname in Adressen (z.B. *12 Acacia Avenue*).

## Semikolon

Das Semikolon steht zwischen Teilsätzen oder Satzstücken, wo ein Komma eine zu schwache, ein Punkt jedoch eine zu starke Zäsur bedeuten würde. D.h., es steht typischerweise zwischen Sätzen, die inhaltlich etwa gleiches Gewicht und grammatisch eine ähnliche Struktur haben:

To err is human; to forgive, divine.

## Punkt

a) Der Punkt steht am Satzende, sofern kein Frage- oder Ausrufezeichen steht; das folgende Wort beginnt in der Regel mit einem Großbuchstaben.

b) Der Punkt steht nach Abkürzungen. Wenn ein Abkürzungspunkt ans Satzende zu stehen kommt, dient er gleichzeitig als Schlusspunkt:

She also kept dogs, cats, birds, etc.
*aber*: She also kept pets (dogs, cats, birds, etc.).

c) Wenn ein Satz mit einer Anführung schließt, die ihrerseits mit einem Punkt, Fragezeichen oder Ausrufezeichen endet, entfällt der Schlusspunkt:

He cried, 'Be off!' But the child would not move.

Wenn die Anführung jedoch kurz ist und der übrige Satz deutlich größeres Gewicht hat, steht der Punkt außerhalb der Anführungszeichen:

Over the entrance to the temple at Delphi were written the words 'Know thyself'.

## Anführungszeichen

a) Anführungszeichen haben gewöhnlich die Form '...' („halbe Anführungszeichen"); Anführungszeichen der Form "..." stehen bei einer Anführung innerhalb einer Anführung; bei einer Anführung innerhalb einer angeführten Anführung stehen wiederum halbe Anführungszeichen:

'I said, "He used the word 'murder' although no one had told him how Smith died".'

b) Schließende Anführungszeichen stehen vor allen weiteren Satzzeichen, es sei denn, diese sind Bestandteil der Anführung:

Did Nelson really say, 'Kiss me, Hardy'?
aber: Then she asked, 'What is your name?'.

Das Komma am Schluss einer Anführung, auf die Ausdrücke wie *he said* folgen, ersetzt den Schlusspunkt des angeführten Satzes und steht innerhalb der Anführungszeichen:

'That is nonsense,' he said.

Die Kommas, durch die *he said* usw. eingeschlossen wird, wenn es die Anführung unterbricht, stehen gewöhnlich außerhalb der Anführungszeichen:

'That', he said, 'is nonsense.'

Das erste Komma steht jedoch innerhalb der Anführungszeichen, wenn es auch ohne die Unterbrechung stehen müsste:

'That, my dear fellow,' he said, 'is nonsense.'

# German Irregular Verbs

Irregular and partly irregular verbs are listed alphabetically by infinitive. 1st, 2nd, and 3rd person present and imperative forms are given after the infinitive, and preterite subjunctive forms after the preterite indicative, where they take an umlaut, change *e* to *i*, etc. Verbs with a raised number in the German–English section of the Dictionary have the same number in this list. Compound verbs (including verbs with prefixes) are only given if a) they do not take the same forms as the corresponding simple verb, e.g. *befehlen*, or b) there is no corresponding simple verb, e.g. *bewegen*. An asterisk (*) indicates a verb which is also conjugated regularly.

| **Infinitive**<br>***Infinitiv*** | Preterite<br>*Präteritum* | Past Participle<br>*2. Partizip* |
|---|---|---|
| **abwägen** | wog (wöge) ab | abgewogen |
| **backen[1] (du bäckst, er bäckt; *auch*: du backst, er backt)** | backte, *älter* : buk (büke) | gebacken |
| **befehlen (du befiehlst, er befiehlt; befiehl!)** | befahl (beföhle, befähle) | befohlen |
| **beginnen** | begann (begänne, *seltener* : begönne) | begonnen |
| **beißen** | biss | gebissen |
| **bergen (du birgst, er birgt; birg!)** | barg (bärge) | geborgen |
| **bersten (du birst, er birst; birst!)** | barst (bärste) | geborsten |
| **bewegen[2]** | bewog (bewöge) | bewogen |
| **biegen** | bog (böge) | gebogen |
| **bieten** | bot (böte) | geboten |
| **binden** | band (bände) | gebunden |
| **bitten** | bat (bäte) | gebeten |
| **blasen (du bläst, er bläst)** | blies | geblasen |
| **bleiben** | blieb | geblieben |
| **bleichen*** | blich | geblichen |
| **braten (du brätst, er brät)** | briet | gebraten |
| **brechen (du brichst, er bricht; brich!)** | brach (bräche) | gebrochen |
| **brennen** | brannte (brennte) | gebrannt |
| **bringen** | brachte (brächte) | gebracht |
| **denken** | dachte (dächte) | gedacht |
| **dingen*** | dang (dänge) | gedungen |
| **dreschen (du drischst, er drischt; drisch!)** | drosch (drösche) | gedroschen |
| **dringen** | drang (dränge) | gedrungen |
| **dünken* (es dünkt, *auch*: deucht)** | deuchte | gedeucht |
| **dürfen (ich darf, du darfst, er darf)** | durfte (dürfte) | gedurft / dürfen |
| **empfehlen (du empfiehlst, er empfiehlt, empfiehl!)** | empfahl (empföhle, *seltener* : empfähle) | empfohlen |
| **erlöschen (du erlischst, er erlischt, erlisch!)** | erlosch (erlösche) | erloschen |
| **erschallen*** | erscholl (erschölle) | erschollen |
| **erschrecken[1, 3] (du erschrickst, er erschrickt, erschrick!)** | erschrak (erschräke) | erschrocken |
| **essen (du isst, er isst, iss!)** | aß (äße) | gegessen |
| **fahren (du fährst, er fährt)** | fuhr (führe) | gefahren |
| **fallen (du fällst, er fällt)** | fiel | gefallen |
| **fangen (du fängst, er fängt)** | fing | gefangen |
| **fechten (du fichtst, er ficht; ficht!)** | focht (föchte) | gefochten |
| **finden** | fand (fände) | gefunden |
| **flechten (du flichtst, er flicht; flicht!)** | flocht (flöchte) | geflochten |
| **fliegen** | flog (flöge) | geflogen |
| **fliehen** | floh (flöhe) | geflohen |

| **Infinitive**<br>***Infinitiv*** | Preterite<br>*Präteritum* | Past Participle<br>*2. Partizip* |
|---|---|---|
| **fließen** | floss (flösse) | geflossen |
| **fressen (du frisst, er frisst; friss!)** | fraß (fräße) | gefressen |
| **frieren** | fror (fröre) | gefroren |
| **gären*** | gor (göre) | gegoren |
| **gebären (du gebärst, sie gebärt, gebäre!; *geh.*: du gebierst, sie gebiert; gebier!)** | gebar (gebäre) | geboren |
| **geben (du gibst, er gibt; gib!)** | gab (gäbe) | gegeben |
| **gedeihen** | gedieh | gediehen |
| **gehen** | ging | gegangen |
| **gelingen** | gelang (gelänge) | gelungen |
| **gelten (du giltst, er gilt; gilt!)** | galt (gölte, gälte) | gegolten |
| **genesen** | genas (genäse) | genesen |
| **genießen** | genoss (genösse) | genossen |
| **geschehen (geschieht)** | geschah (geschähe) | geschehen |
| **gewinnen** | gewann (gewönne, gewänne) | gewonnen |
| **gießen** | goss (gösse) | gegossen |
| **gleichen** | glich | geglichen |
| **gleiten** | glitt | geglitten |
| **glimmen** | glomm (glömme) | geglommen |
| **graben (du gräbst, er gräbt)** | grub (grübe) | gegraben |
| **greifen** | griff | gegriffen |
| **haben (du hast, er hat)** | hatte (hätte) | gehabt |
| **halten (du hältst, er hält)** | hielt | gehalten |
| **hängen[1]** | hing | gehangen |
| **hauen** | haute, *geh.*: hieb | gehauen |
| **heben** | hob (höbe) | gehoben |
| **heißen** | hieß | geheißen/heißen |
| **helfen (du hilfst, er hilft; hilf!)** | half (hülfe, *selten*: hälfe) | geholfen/helfen |
| **kennen** | kannte (kennte) | gekannt |
| **kiesen*** | kor (köre) | gekoren |
| **klimmen*** | klomm (klömme) | geklommen |
| **klingen** | klang (klänge) | geklungen |
| **kneifen** | kniff | gekniffen |
| **kommen** | kam (käme) | gekommen |
| **können (ich kann, du kannst, er kann)** | konnte (könnte) | gekonnt/können |
| **kreischen*** | krisch | gekrischen |
| **kriechen** | kroch (kröche) | gekrochen |
| **küren*** | kor (köre) | gekoren |
| **laden[1, 2] (du lädst, er lädt; *veralt.*, *landsch.*: du ladest, er ladet)** | lud (lüde) | geladen |
| **lassen (du lässt, er lässt)** | ließ | gelassen/lassen |
| **laufen (du läufst, er läuft)** | lief | gelaufen |
| **leiden** | litt | gelitten |
| **leihen** | lieh | geliehen |
| **lesen[1, 2] (du liest, er liest; lies!)** | las (läse) | gelesen |
| **liegen** | lag (läge) | gelegen |
| **lügen** | log (löge) | gelogen |
| **mahlen** | mahlte | gemahlen |
| **meiden** | mied | gemieden |
| **melken* (du milkst, er milkt; milk!** | molk (mölke) | gemolken |
| **messen (du misst, er misst; miss!)** | maß (mäße) | gemessen |
| **misslingen** | misslang (misslänge) | misslungen |
| **mögen (ich mag, du magst, er mag)** | mochte (möchte) | gemocht |
| **müssen (ich muss, du musst, er muss)** | musste (müsste) | gemusst/müssen |
| **nehmen (du nimmst, er nimmt; nimm!)** | nahm (nähme) | genommen |
| **nennen** | nannte (nennte) | genannt |
| **pfeifen** | pfiff | gepfiffen |
| **pflegen*** | pflog (pflöge) | gepflogen |
| **preisen** | pries | gepriesen |

| **Infinitive** *Infinitiv* | Preterite *Präteritum* | Past Participle *2. Partizip* |
|---|---|---|
| **quellen[1] (du quillst, er quillt; quill!)** | quoll (quölle) | gequollen |
| **raten (du rätst, er rät)** | riet | geraten |
| **reiben** | rieb | gerieben |
| **reißen** | riss | gerissen |
| **reiten** | ritt | geritten |
| **rennen** | rannte (rennte) | gerannt |
| **riechen** | roch (röche) | gerochen |
| **ringen** | rang (ränge) | gerungen |
| **rinnen** | rann (ränne, *seltener* : rönne) | geronnen |
| **rufen** | rief | gerufen |
| **salzen*** | salzte | gesalzen |
| **saufen (du säufst, er säuft)** | soff (söffe) | gesoffen |
| **saugen*** | sog (söge) | gesogen |
| **schaffen*** | schuf (schüfe) | geschaffen |
| **schallen*** | scholl (schölle) | geschallt |
| **scheiden** | schied | geschieden |
| **scheinen** | schien | geschienen |
| **scheißen** | schiss | geschissen |
| **schelten (du schiltst, er schilt; schilt!)** | schalt (schölte) | gescholten |
| **scheren[1]** | schor (schöre) | geschoren |
| **schieben** | schob (schöbe) | geschoben |
| **schießen** | schoss (schösse) | geschossen |
| **schinden** | schindete | geschunden |
| **schlafen (du schläfst, er schläft)** | schlief | geschlafen |
| **schlagen (du schlägst, er schlägt)** | schlug (schlüge) | geschlagen |
| **schleichen** | schlich | geschlichen |
| **schleifen[1]** | schliff | geschliffen |
| **schleißen*** | schliss | geschlissen |
| **schließen** | schloss (schlösse) | geschlossen |
| **schlingen** | schlang (schlänge) | geschlungen |
| **schmeißen** | schmiss | geschmissen |
| **schmelzen (du schmilzt, er schmilzt; schmilz!)** | schmolz | geschmolzen |
| **schnauben*** | schnob (schnöbe) | geschnoben |
| **schneiden** | schnitt | geschnitten |
| **schrecken* (du schrickst, er schrickt; schrick!)** | schrak (schräke) | geschreckt |
| **schreiben** | schrieb | geschrieben |
| **schreien** | schrie | geschrien |
| **schreiten** | schritt | geschritten |
| **schweigen** | schwieg | geschwiegen |
| **schwellen[1] (du schwillst, er schwillt; schwill!)** | schwoll (schwölle) | geschwollen |
| **schwimmen** | schwamm (schwömme, *seltener* : schwämme) | geschwommen |
| **schwinden** | schwand (schwände) | geschwunden |
| **schwingen** | schwang (schwänge) | geschwungen |
| **schwören** | schwor (schwüre) | geschworen |
| **sehen (du siehst, er sieht; sieh[e]!)** | sah (sähe) | gesehen/sehen |
| **sein (ich bin, du bist, er ist, wir sind, ihr seid, sie sind; sei!)** | war (wäre) | gewesen |
| **senden*** | sandte | gesandt |
| **sieden*** | sott (sötte) | gesotten |
| **singen** | sang (sänge) | gesungen |
| **sinken** | sank (sänke) | gesunken |
| **sinnen** | sann (sänne, sönne) | gesonnen |
| **sitzen** | saß (säße) | gesessen |
| **sollen (ich soll, du sollst, er soll)** | sollte | gesollt/sollen |
| **spalten*** | spaltete | gespalten |
| **speien** | spie | gespien |
| **spinnen** | spann (spönne, spänne) | gesponnen |

| **Infinitive**<br>***Infinitiv*** | Preterite<br>*Präteritum* | Past Participle<br>*2. Partizip* |
|---|---|---|
| **spleißen*** | spliss | gesplissen |
| **sprechen (du sprichst, er spricht; sprich!)** | sprach (spräche) | gesprochen |
| **sprießen** | spross (sprösse) | gesprossen |
| **springen** | sprang (spränge) | gesprungen |
| **stechen (du stichst, er sticht; stich!)** | stach (stäche) | gestochen |
| **stecken*** | stak (stäke) | gesteckt |
| **stehen** | stand (stünde, *auch*: stände) | gestanden |
| **stehlen (du stiehlst, er stiehlt; stiehl!)** | stahl (stähle, *seltener* : stöhle) | gestohlen |
| **steigen** | stieg | gestiegen |
| **sterben (du stirbst, er stirbt; stirb!)** | starb (stürbe) | gestorben |
| **stieben** | stob (stöbe) | gestoben |
| **stinken** | stank (stänke) | gestunken |
| **stoßen (du stößt, er stößt)** | stieß | gestoßen |
| **streichen** | strich | gestrichen |
| **streiten** | stritt | gestritten |
| **tragen (du trägst, er trägt)** | trug (trüge) | getragen |
| **treffen (du triffst; er trifft; triff!)** | traf (träfe) | getroffen |
| **treiben** | trieb | getrieben |
| **treten (du trittst, er tritt; tritt!)** | trat (träte) | getreten |
| **triefen*** | troff (tröffe) | getroffen |
| **trinken** | trank (tränke) | getrunken |
| **trügen** | trog (tröge) | getrogen |
| **tun** | tat (täte) | getan |
| **verderben (du verdirbst, er verdirbt; verdirb!)** | verdarb (verdürbe) | verdorben |
| **verdrießen** | verdross (verdrösse) | verdrossen |
| **vergessen (du vergisst, er vergisst, vergiss!)** | vergaß (vergäße) | vergessen |
| **verlieren** | verlor (verlöre) | verloren |
| **verlöschen (du verlischst, er verlischt; verlisch!)** | verlosch (verlösche) | verloschen |
| **verschleißen*** | verschliss | verschlissen |
| **wachsen[1] (du wächst, er wächst)** | wuchs (wüchse) | gewachsen |
| **wägen** | wog (wöge) | gewogen |
| **waschen (du wäschst, er wäscht)** | wusch (wüsche) | gewaschen |
| **weben*** | wob (wöbe) | gewoben |
| **weichen** | wich | gewichen |
| **weisen** | wies | gewiesen |
| **wenden[2]*** | wandte | gewandt |
| **werben (du wirbst, er wirbt; wirb!)** | warb (würbe) | geworben |
| **werden (du wirst, er wird; werde!)** | wurde, *dichter*.: ward (würde) | geworden/worden |
| **werfen (du wirfst, er wirft; wirf!)** | warf (würfe) | geworfen |
| **wiegen[1]** | wog (wöge) | gewogen |
| **winden[1]** | wand (wände) | gewunden |
| **wissen (ich weiß, du weißt, er weiß)** | wusste (wüsste) | gewusst |
| **wollen (ich will, du willst, er will)** | wollte | gewollt/wollen |
| **wringen** | wrang (wränge) | gewrungen |
| **zeihen** | zieh | geziehen |
| **ziehen** | zog (zöge) | gezogen |
| **zwingen** | zwang (zwänge) | gezwungen |

# Englische unregelmäßige Verben

Die im englisch–deutschen Wörterverzeichnis mit einer hochgestellten Ziffer versehenen unregelmäßigen Verben haben diese Ziffer auch in dieser Liste. Ein Sternchen* weist darauf hin, dass die korrekte Form von der jeweiligen Bedeutung abhängt.

| Infinitive *Infinitiv* | Past Tense *Präteritum* | Past Participle *2. Partizip* |
|---|---|---|
| **abide** | abided, abode | abided, abode |
| **arise** | arose | arisen |
| **awake** | awoke | awoken |
| **be** | was *sing.*, were *pl.* | been |
| **bear** | bore | borne |
| **beat** | beat | beaten |
| **beget** | begot, (*arch.*) begat | begotten |
| **begin** | began | begun |
| **behold** | beheld | beheld |
| **bend** | bent | bent |
| **beseech** | besought, beseeched | besought, beseeched |
| **bet** | bet, betted | bet, betted |
| **bid** | *bade, bid | *bidden, bid |
| **bind** | bound | bound |
| **bite** | bit | bitten |
| **bleed** | bled | bled |
| **bless** | blessed, blest | blessed, blest |
| **blow** | *blew, blowed | *blown, blowed |
| **break** | broke | broken |
| **breed** | bred | bred |
| **bring** | brought | brought |
| **broadcast** | broadcast, broadcasted | broadcast, broadcasted |
| **build** | built | built |
| **burn** | burnt, burned | burnt, burned |
| **burst** | burst | burst |
| **bust** | bust, busted | bust, busted |
| **buy** | bought | bought |
| **cast** | cast | cast |
| **catch** | caught | caught |
| **chide** | chided, chid | chided, chid, chidden |
| **choose** | chose | chosen |
| **cleave**[1] | cleaved, clove, cleft | cleaved, cloven, cleft |
| **cling** | clung | clung |
| **come** | came | come |
| **cost** | *cost, costed | *cost, costed |
| **countersink** | countersunk | countersunk |
| **creep** | crept | crept |
| **cut** | cut | cut |
| **deal** | dealt | dealt |
| **dig** | dug | dug |
| **dive** | dived, *(Amer.)* dove | dived |
| **do**[1] | did | done |
| **draw** | drew | drawn |
| **dream** | dreamt, dreamed | dreamt, dreamed |
| **drink** | drank | drunk |
| **drive** | drove | driven |
| **dwell** | dwelt | dwelt |
| **eat** | ate | eaten |
| **fall** | fell | fallen |
| **feed** | fed | fed |
| **feel** | felt | felt |
| **fight** | fought | fought |
| **find** | found | found |
| **flee** | fled | fled |
| **fling** | flung | flung |
| **floodlight** | floodlit | floodlit |
| **fly** | flew | flown |
| **forbear** | forbore | forborne |
| **forbid** | forbade, forbad | forbidden |
| **forecast** | forecast, forecasted | forecast, forecasted |
| **foretell** | foretold | foretold |
| **forget** | forgot | forgotten |
| **forgive** | forgave | forgiven |
| **forsake** | forsook | forsaken |
| **freeze** | froze | frozen |
| **gainsay** | gainsaid | gainsaid |
| **get** | got | *got, *(Amer.)* gotten |
| **gird** | girded, girt | girded, girt |
| **give** | gave | given |
| **go** | went | gone |
| **grind** | ground | ground |
| **grow** | grew | grown |
| **hamstring** | hamstrung, hamstringed | hamstrung, hamstringed |
| **hang** | *hung, hanged | *hung, hanged |
| **have** | had | had |
| **hear** | heard | heard |
| **heave** | *heaved, hove | *heaved, hove |
| **hew** | hewed | hewn, hewed |
| **hide** | hid | hidden |
| **hit** | hit | hit |
| **hold** | held | held |
| **hurt** | hurt | hurt |
| **inlay** | inlaid | inlaid |
| **input** | input, inputted | input, inputted |
| **inset** | inset, insetted | inset, insetted |
| **interweave** | interwove | interwoven |
| **keep** | kept | kept |
| **ken** | kenned, kent | kenned, kent |
| **kneel** | knelt, *(esp. Amer.)* kneeled | knelt, *(esp. Amer.)* kneeled |

| **Infinitive** ***Infinitiv*** | Past Tense *Präteritum* | Past Participle *2. Partizip* |
|---|---|---|
| **knit** | *knitted, knit | *knitted, knit |
| **know** | knew | known |
| **lay** | laid | laid |
| **lead** | led | led |
| **lean** | leaned, *(Brit.)* leant | leaned, *(Brit.)* leant |
| **leap** | leapt, leaped | leapt, leaped |
| **learn** | learnt, learned | learnt, learned |
| **leave** | left | left |
| **lend** | lent | lent |
| **let** | let | let |
| **lie**[2] | lay | lain |
| **light** | lit, lighted | lit, lighted |
| **lose** | lost | lost |
| **make** | made | made |
| **mean** | meant | meant |
| **meet** | met | met |
| **mow** | mowed | mown, mowed |
| **output** | output, outputted | output, outputted |
| **outshine** | outshone | outshone |
| **overhang** | overhung | overhung |
| **pay** | paid | paid |
| **plead** | pleaded, *(esp. Amer., Scot., dial.)* pled | pleaded, *(esp. Amer., Scot., dial.)* pled |
| **prove** | proved | *proved, *(esp. Amer., Scot., dial.)* proven |
| **put** | put | put |
| **quit** | quitted, *(Amer.)* quit | quitted, *(Amer.)* quit |
| **read [ri:d]** | read [red] | read [red] |
| **reeve** | rove, reeved | rove, reeved |
| **rend** | rent | rent |
| **rid** | rid | rid |
| **ride** | rode | ridden |
| **ring**[2] | rang | rung |
| **rise** | rose | risen |
| **run** | ran | run |
| **saw** | sawed | sawn, sawed |
| **say** | said | said |
| **see** | saw | seen |
| **seek** | sought | sought |
| **sell** | sold | sold |
| **send** | sent | sent |
| **set** | set | set |
| **sew** | sewed | sewn, sewed |
| **shake** | shook | shaken, *(arch./ coll.)* shook |
| **shear** | sheared | shorn, sheared |
| **shed** | shed | shed |
| **shine** | *shone, shined | *shone, shined |
| **shit** | shitted, shit, shat | shitted, shit, shat |
| **shoe** | shod | shod |
| **shoot** | shot | shot |
| **show** | showed | shown, showed |
| **shrink** | shrank | shrunk |
| **shrive** | shrove | shriven |
| **shut** | shut | shut |
| **sing** | sang | sung |
| **sink** | sank, sunk | sunk |
| **sit** | sat | sat |
| **slay** | *slew, slayed | *slain, slayed |
| **sleep** | slept | slept |
| **slide** | slid | slid |
| **sling** | slung | slung |
| **slink** | slunk | slunk |
| **slit** | slit | slit |
| **smell** | smelt, smelled | smelt, smelled |
| **smite** | smote | smitten |
| **sow** | sowed | sown, sowed |
| **speak** | spoke | spoken |
| **speed** | *sped, speeded | *sped, speeded |
| **spell** | spelled, *(Brit.)* spelt | spelled, *(Brit.)* spelt |
| **spend** | spent | spent |
| **spill** | spilt, spilled | spilt, spilled |
| **spin** | spun | spun |
| **spit** | spat, spit | spat, spit |
| **split** | split | split |
| **spoil** | spoilt, spoiled | spoilt, spoiled |
| **spread** | spread | spread |
| **spring** | sprang, *(Amer.)* sprung | sprung |
| **stand** | stood | stood |
| **stave** | *staved, stove | *staved, stove |
| **steal** | stole | stolen |
| **stick** | stuck | stuck |
| **sting** | stung | stung |
| **stink** | stank, stunk | stunk |
| **strew** | strewed | strewed, strewn |
| **stride** | strode | stridden |
| **strike** | struck | struck, *(arch.)* stricken |
| **string** | strung | strung |
| **strive** | strove | striven |
| **sublet** | sublet | sublet |
| **swear** | swore | sworn |
| **sweep** | swept | swept |
| **swell** | swelled | swollen, swelled |
| **swim** | swam | swum |
| **swing** | swung | swung |
| **take** | took | taken |
| **teach** | taught | taught |
| **tear** | tore | torn |
| **tell** | told | told |
| **think** | thought | thought |
| **thrive** | thrived, throve | thrived, thriven |
| **throw** | threw | thrown |
| **thrust** | thrust | thrust |
| **tread** | trod | trodden, trod |
| **unbend** | unbent | unbent |
| **understand** | understood | understood |
| **undo** | undid | undone |
| **wake** | woke, *(arch.)* waked | woken, *(arch.)* waked |
| **wear** | wore | worn |
| **weave**[1] | wove | woven |
| **weep** | wept | wept |
| **wet** | wet, wetted | wet, wetted |
| **win** | won | won |
| **wind**[2] [waɪnd] | wound [waʊnd] | wound [waʊnd] |
| **work** | worked, *(arch., literary)* wrought | worked, *(arch., literary)* wrought |
| **wring** | wrung | wrung |
| **write** | wrote | written |